Deutschsprachige Kunden

An **Bucher & Co., Publikationen**

☐ **Informations-Dienst**
Ich/Wir möchte(n) gerne über
BUCH*air* (*jp airline-fleets* int
lagen unverbindlich informiert

☐ ***jp airline-fleets* auf CD-ROM!**
Ich/Wir möchte(n) gerne mehr über das ***jp airline-fleets* international
99/2000** auf CD-ROM informiert werden (siehe Werbung im Farbteil).

☐ ***jp airline-fleets* als BUCHairDATABASE!**
Ich/Wir möchte(n) gerne mehr über die verschiedenen Versionen der
BUCHairDATABASE informiert werden (siehe Werbung in Section 2).

Telefon: Fax:

Ort und Datum: Unterschrift:

_____   _____

Name und Adresse in Druckbuchstaben auf Vorderseite notieren!

Je schneller Sie uns die Karte zuschicken, desto schneller erhalten Sie unsere Informationen!

All other customers

To **Bucher & Co., Publikationen:**

☐ **Information Service**
I/We would like to be informed, without any obligation, about new publications of Messrs. **Bucher & Co.**/BUCH*air* and other publishers, including the ***jp airline-fleets* international 2000/2001.**

☐ ***jp airline-fleets* on CD-ROM!**
I/We would like to receive more detailed information about the ***jp airline-fleets* international 99/2000** on **CD-ROM** (see advert in photo-section).

☐ ***jp airline-fleets* as BUCHairDATABASE!**
I/We would like to receive more detailed information about the different versions of the **BUCHairDATABASE** (see advert in Section 2).

Phone: Fax:

Place and date: Signature:

_____   _____

Name and address to be printed clearly on reverse side!

The sooner you return this card, the sooner our information service will start!

North American customers

To **Bucher & Co., Publikationen:**

☐ **Information Service**
I/We would like to be informed, without any obligation, about new publications of Messrs. **Bucher & Co.**/BUCH*air* and other publishers, including the ***jp airline-fleets* international 2000/2001.**

☐ ***jp airline-fleets* on CD-ROM!**
I/We would like to receive more detailed information about the ***jp airline-fleets* international 99/2000** on **CD-ROM** (see advert in photo-section).

☐ ***jp airline-fleets* as BUCHairDATABASE!**
I/We would like to receive more detailed information about the different versions of the **BUCHairDATABASE** (see advert in Section 2).

Phone: Fax:

Place and date: Signature:

_____   _____

Name and address to be printed clearly on reverse side!

The sooner you return this card, the sooner our information service will start!

jp airline-fleets international 99/2000

By Ulrich Klee
(Chief Editor)

Frank E. Bucher (Production Editor) and Ernst Sommer (Research Editor)

Antonio Härry and Werner Wyder (Contributing Editors)

33rd edition

ISBN 3 85758 133 6

78 color photos

Compiled, Produced, Published and Distributed by:

Bucher & Co., Publikationen
P. O. Box 44
CH-8058 Zurich-Airport/Switzerland

Phone:	**+41 (01) 8741 747**
Fax:	**+41 (01) 8741 757**
E-Mail:	**jp@buchair.ch**
Internet:	**http://www.buchairnet.com**

Correct through March 1999

Printed in Switzerland

Headquarters:

Bucher & Co., Publikationen
Kanalstrasse 17
CH-8152 Glattbrugg/Switzerland

We wish to thank the people who helped us, as well as the magazines who contributed to this issue. Not everybody who sent us useful information is listed, but those who are, did tremendous jobs. Some sent us news regularly and others mailed pages of amendments:

Aebersold-Takeuchi Daniel
Air Britain News and Monographs
Airclaims Blue Print
Airnieuws Nederland
Altherr Jean-Luc
AMCAR Quarterly (Runway Six Nine)
Aviation Letter
Aviation Week & Space Technology
Ballantine Ai Hua & Colin
Becker Andreas
BN Historians

Bucher-Grendelmeier Edith
Constant Olivier
Fischdick Werner
Flight International
Gonzalo Fischer Daniel
Härry-Schönenberger Astrid
Helicopters (Canada)
Japan Aviation News
Jetstream Zurich
Jonard Alain

Jost Peter («Joggi»)
Köhler Thomas
Litaudon Frank
Lloyd William M.
Luftfahrt-Journal (COINCAT)
Petit Pierre-Alain
Propliner
Roosens Dominique
Santaner Bosch José Manuel
Scramble (Dutch Aviation Society)

Siegrist E. Martin
Soviet Transports (TAHS)
Sulista Edi D.S.
Tröndle Françoise
Ward Jeffrey D.
Wings (Canada)
World Airline Fleets News

Special thanks go to co-editors who supplied us with entire fleetlists of their regions:

Enrique M. Argento & Jorge Felix Nunez Padin (Argentina)
James L. Bell (Australia & New Zealand)
Thierry Flagothier (Belgium)
Michal Beran (C.I.S.)
Milan Cvrkal (Czechia)
Flemming Lovenvig & Tavs Aas Mortensen (Denmark & SAS)
Hugo Klopfstein-Keller (Ecuador)
Jeremy W. Parkin (Helicopters, Great Britain)
Jimmy J. Wadia (India)
Eamon C. Power (Ireland)
Noam Hartoch (Israel)

Colasanto Gianfilippo (Helicopters, Italy)
Willem F. Wendt (Netherlands)
Kjell Oskar Granlund (Norway)
Javier Goto (Peru)
Capt. Miguel Santos (Portugal)
Oto Chudy (Slovakia)
Javier Ortega Figueral (Spain)
Kelvin Hung (Taiwan)
Gökhan Sarigöl (Turkey)
Tony De Bruyn (Zaïre)

We would also like to say thank you to all airlines and civil aviation authorities who answered our questions or questionnaires.

Please be kind enough to note, that the next jp airline-fleets international will be published in May 2000. Make sure you will not miss it!

Where to get the products of Bucher & Co., Publikationen & BUCHair (UK), Ltd?

If you cannot get your jp airline-fleets international or any of our other products at your local bookstore or if you need information about publication dates or prices, please contact the following organizations in, or nearest to, your country:

Australia:
Mr. James L. Bell
Bucher Publications
P.O. Box 232
Riddell, Victoria 3431

Phone: (03) 54 28 63 12
Telefax: (03) 93 79 07 67

Canada:
Aviation World
195 Carlingview Drive
Rexdale, Ontario M9W 5E8

Phone: (416) 674-5959
Telefax: (416) 674-5915
website: http://www.interlog.com/~avworld
e-mail: avworld@interlog.com

Danmark:
Nyboder Boghandel, ApS
114 Store Kongensgade
1264 Copenhagen K

Phone: 33 32 33 20
Telefax: 33 32 33 62
e-mail: nyboder@bogpost.dk

Deutschland: (Bestellungen)
Bucher & Co., Publikationen
Postfach 44
CH-8058 Zürich-Flughafen
Schweiz

Postbankkonto für Zahlungen in DM und Euro:
Ffm 3010 21-604 (Bankleitzahl: 500 100 60)

Kreditkarten: American Express, Diners,
EuroCard/Mastercharge and VISA

Telefon: +41 1 874 1 747
Telefax: +41 1 874 1 757
website: http://www.buchair.com
e-mail: jp@buchair.ch

Finland:
Aviation Shop
Kajanuksenkatu 12
00250 Helsinki

Phone: (09) 44 98 01
Telefax: (09) 149 6163
website: http://www.aviationshop.fi
e-mail: kai@aviationshop.fi

France:
La Maison du Livre Aviation, Sarl.
75, Boulevard Malesherbes
75008 Paris

Phone: (01) 1 45 22 74 16
Telefax: (01) 1 42 93 81 23

Great Britain:
BUCHair (U.K.), Ltd.
P.O. Box 89
Reigate, Surrey RH2 7FG

Phone: (01737) 224 747
Telefax: (01737) 226 777
website: http://www.buchair.rotor.com
e-mail: buchair_uk@compuserve.com

Japan:
Nishiyama Yosho, Co. Ltd
Naritaya Bldg. 7–13
Ginza, 3-Chome, Chuo-ku
Tokyo 104-0061

Phone: (03) 3562-0820
Telefax: (03) 3562-0828

Netherlands:
Boekhandel Venstra, B.V.
Binnenhof 50
Postbus 77
1180 AB Amstelveen

Phone: (020) 641 98 80
Telefax: (020) 640 02 52
e-mail: venstra.boeken@wxs.nl

Österreich: (Bestellungen)
Bucher & Co., Publikationen
Postfach 44
CH-8058 Zürich-Flughafen
Schweiz

Postkonto International für Zahlungen in Euro:
91-13445-6

Kreditkarten: American Express, Diners,
EuroCard/Mastercharge and VISA

Telefon: 050 1 8741 747
Telefax: 050 1 8741 757
website: http://www.buchairnet.com
e-mail: jp@buchair.ch

Schweiz: (Bestellungen)
Bucher & Co., Publikationen
Postfach 44
8058 Zürich-Flughafen
Schweiz

Postcheckkonto für Zahlungen in CHF:
80-30353-6

Kreditkarten: American Express, Diners,
EuroCard/Mastercharge and VISA

Telefon: +41 1 8741 747
Telefax: +41 1 8741 757
website: http://www.buchairnet.com
e-mail: jp@buchair.ch

Schweiz: (Laden – Glattbrugg)
BUCHairSHOP (1)
Bucher & Co., Publikationen
Schaffhauserstr. 76
8152 Glattbrugg

Kreditkarten: American Express, Diners,
EuroCard/Mastercharge and VISA

Telefon: +41 1 8741 747
Telefax: +41 1 8741 757
website: http://www.buchairnet.com
e-mail: jp@buchair.ch

Schweiz: (Laden – Flughafen)
BUCHairSHOP (2)
Bucher & Co., Publikationen
Terrasse, Terminal B
8058 Zürich-Flughafen

Kreditkarten: American Express, Diners,
EuroCard/Mastercharge and VISA

Telefon: +41 1 8741 747
Telefax: +41 1 8741 757
website: http://www.buchair.com
e-mail: jp@buchair.ch

South Africa:
Mr. Karel Zaayman
Sky Needs
P.O. Box 316
Melville 2109

Phone: (011) 792 8318
Telefax: (011) 325 4146
e-mail: moport@icon.co.z

Spain:
La Aeroteca
Libreria Miguel Creus
C/ Congost, 11
E-08024 Barcelona

Phone: (93) 210 54 07
Telefax: (93) 210 59 92
website: http://www.aeroteca.com
e-mail: info@aeroteca.com

United States of America:
BUCHair (USA), Inc.
Mr. Kivanç N. Hurturk
P.O. Box 750515
Forest Hills, NY 11375-0515

Phone: (718) 263-8748
Telefax: (718) 275 6190
website: http://www.buchair.com
e-mail: buchair@mail.idt.net

United States and Central America:
Bucher Publications
PO Box 300053
JFK International Airport
Jamaica, NY 11430-0053

(Transfer of mail
to headquarter in Switzerland only)

Realization: Werner Keller, Industriestrasse 11, CH-6343 Rotkreuz/Switzerland

Dear Reader

jp airline-fleets international **99/2000** is the 33rd edition of the ORIGINAL annual fleetlist directory.

Today, **jp airline-fleets** international is the standard yearbook for the industry and aviation enthusiasts worldwide. Ulrich Klee and his research team have developped a unique system to provide the best quality and most up-to-date information. News are gathered from several different sources and updated daily. **This is our guarantee for accuracy!**

The yearbook is fundamental for the group of "BUCHair" companies. People all over the world ensure the accuracy of the most renown fleetlist yearbook on paper, on CD-ROM and as a database along with self-developped software are being offered to you at fair market prices.

New computer software, which allows us to do more production work in-house, is one of the reasons of the lower price of the **jp airline-fleets** international **99/2000,** even its quality and contents have again increased. Many things have been fine-tuned and the coloursection in the middle of the books has been enhanced.

It is still our goal to increase the number of direct sales drastically in order to allow us to further lower the price. Please help us to reach that aim, it will be also to your benefit! Buy all our products directly from us. Only we are able to offer you the best deals and the fastest delivery! Please fill in the coloured card, which you find in the front section of this book, and mail it to us. The first 1999 applicants will be honoured with a millennium-voucher in the value of Swiss Cents 2000 (CHF 20.–), which you can use as credit toward your purchase of the **jp airline-fleets** international **2000/2001.** Your name and address will be stored in our address database. Whenever available, we will send you special offers for our products. Never are you obliged to buy anything from us. Your name and address will not be released to anybody else!

The layout of the **jp airline-fleets** international **99/2000** is described on page 6 in front of section 1. Please read it, in order to understand our system and criteria.

As every year, we would like to remind you: the **jp airline-fleets** international is used by a great number of people. It has to meet different needs. Some data which is of no use to you, may be required by someone else. Information about fleets is our business. **We do it professionally!** We hope, the **jp airline-fleets** international **99/2000** provides you with the details you need; if not, please let us know.

Please show the **jp airline-fleets** international **99/2000** to your friends!

We thank you in advance for every single recommendation. To make ordering easy for you and your friends, we accept the four major creditcards as well as Eurocheques and we operate several bank- and postal giro accounts (even in EURO) for direct orders. We are also able to accept our orders on e-mail or, even better, if you browse through our website on Internet. We make your life easy by offering the use of BUCHairNET for electronic shopping!

jp airline-fleets international **99/2000** was realized by the employees of our company and the team mentioned below. But without the help of many readers and a lot of very good friends, we would not have been able to publish such a high quality product. Thank you very much to all of you who ever helped us!

The next issue – **jp airline-fleets** international **2000/2001** – will be published in **May 2000**, and we hope, that you will again be among our readers.

April 1999

Bucher & Co., Publikationen
F. E. Bucher   Ulrich Klee
Antonio Härry, Ernst Sommer, Werner Wyder

Lieber Leser

Die 33. Ausgabe des ORIGINAL-Fluggesellschaften-Flottenverzeichnisses liegt vor Ihnen.

Heute ist das Jahrbuch **jp airline-fleets** international **das** Standardwerk für Industrie und Flugzeugenthusiasten weltweit. Ulrich Klee hat mit seinem Redaktionsteam ein einzigartiges System entwickelt. Daten werden täglich von verschiedenen Quellen gesammelt und überarbeitet. **Das ist unsere Garantie für Qualität!** Wir setzten internationale Standards, welche zwischenzeitlich auch von anderen Institutionen übernommen worden sind.

Das Jahrbuch bildet das Fundament für die Gruppe um unsere Firma. Leute auf der ganzen Welt sichern Qualität, Konstanz und Pünktlichkeit des inhaltlich stärksten und genauesten Flottenjahrbuchs auf Papier, auf CD-ROM und als Datenbank mit selbst entwickelter Software, zu marktgerechten Preisen!

Dank Anschaffung neuer Software, mit welcher wir weitere Arbeiten selbst machen können, ist es uns möglich, den Preis des **jp airline-fleets** international **99/2000** zu senken, obwohl wir beim Inhalt qualitatives und quantitatives Wachstum vorweisen. Nebst vielen Kleinigkeiten haben wir zum Beispiel den Farbteil in der Mitte des Buchs vergrössert.

Kaufen Sie das **jp airline-fleets** international **immer bei uns direkt!** Wir offerieren Ihnen den besten Preis und den schnellsten Lieferservice. Ihr direkter Kauf ermöglicht uns, die Preise so tief als möglich zu halten, was wiederum Ihr Vorteil ist. Bitte senden Sie die farbige Postkarte (ganz vorne im Buch) mit Ihren Adressangaben schnellstmöglich an uns. Dieses Jahr erhalten die ersten 1999 Einsender solcher Karten einen Millennium-Voucher im Wert von 2000 Schweizer Rappen (CHF 20.–), welchen Sie beim Kauf des **jp airline-fleets** international **2000/2001** anrechnen können. Ihre Angaben behandeln wir vertraulich. Sollten Sie unsere Mitteilungen nicht mehr wollen, löschen wir Ihre Daten sofort. Es besteht keine Kaufverpflichtung und die Daten werden nicht weitergegeben.

Die Beschreibung des Hauptteils von **jp airline-fleets** international finden Sie auf Seite 6. Bitte lesen Sie diese, damit Sie unser System und unsere Kriterien verstehen.

Wie jedes Jahr möchten wir Sie daran erinnern, dass das **jp airline-fleets** international **99/2000** für verschiedene Benützer gedacht ist und deshalb auch ganz unterschiedlichen Ansprüchen genügen muss. So werden Daten, die Sie persönlich vielleicht nicht gebrauchen können, von jemand anderem unbedingt benötigt. Unser Ziel ist ein Universaljahrbuch, welches einem möglichst grossen Kreis von Interessenten Information über die Fluggesellschaften in der ganzen Welt vermittelt. Ihre Wünsche und Anregungen zur Verbesserung nehmen wir gerne entgegen.

Zeigen Sie das **jp airline-fleets** international **99/2000** Ihren Freunden oder Geschäftspartnern. Wir sind Ihnen für jede Empfehlung dankbar. Bestellen bei uns direkt ist ganz einfach. Wir akzeptieren die vier gängigsten Kreditkarten sowie Euroschecks. Verschiedene Bank- und Postgirokonten (selbst in EURO) stehen Ihnen zur Verfügung. Benützen Sie unseren E-Mail-Anschluss oder unseren elektronischen Shop im Internet. Bitte denken Sie daran, wenn immer möglich sollten Sie direkt bei uns bestellen. Sie helfen damit, die Preise tief zu halten.

jp airline-fleets international **99/2000** wurde durch das unten aufgeführte Team und die Angestellten unserer Firma realisiert. Jedoch geht es nicht ohne Mithilfe von vielen Lesern und guten Freunden. Diesen danken wir ganz herzlich. Ohne Ihre Hilfe wären wir nicht in der Lage, ein so gutes Buch zu publizieren.

Die nächste Ausgabe – **jp airline-fleets** international **2000/2001** – erscheint Anfang **Mai 2000** und wir möchten Sie weiterhin zu unseren Kunden zählen.

Im April 1999

Die Redaktion
Bucher & Co., Publikationen
F. E. Bucher   Ulrich Klee
Antonio Härry, Ernst Sommer, Werner Wyder

ABBREVIATIONS and their meaning in different languages / ABKÜRZUNGEN und ihre Übersetzungen

SHORT	English	Dansk	Deutsch	Español	Français	Italiano	Português	日本語
Ap	airport	Lufthavn	Flughafen	aeropuerto	aéroport	aeroporto	aéroporto	空 港
bsd	based	baseret, stationeret	stationiert	basado	basé	basato	baseado	定置場
Calib	Calibration	Calibrere	Vermessung	calibración	mesuration	calibrazione	calibre	飛行検査機
cn	construction number serial number	Konstruktionsnummer	Werknummer/ Produktionsnummer	número de construcción	numéro de construction	numero di fabbricazione	número de construção/ número de série	製造番号
config	configuration	configuration/version	Ausrüstung	configuración	configuration	configurazione	configuração	仕 様
cs	call sign	Kalde signal	Rufzeichen	señal de llamada	indicatif d'appel	segnale di chiamata	sinal de chamada	呼出符号
cvtd	converted	ombygget	umgebaut	convertido	converti	ricostruito	convertido	仕様変更
dba	doing business as	gør forretning som	arbeitet unter dem Namen:	trasmitemos como	faisant affaire comme	fare affari come	fazendo negócio como	
Dept	Department	Afdeling	Abteilung	departamento	département	dipartimento	departamento	省 庁
ex	previous identity	Tidligere registrering	früher	anteriormente	précédemment	precedentemente	identade prévia	旧登録記号
fln	fleet number	Flåde nummer	Flottennummer	número de flota	numéro de la flotte	numero di flotta	número da frota	所有機番号
Frtr	Freighter	Fragter	Frachter	avion de cargo	affrêter	aereo adibito al trasporto merci	cargueiro	貨物機
Gvmt	Government	Regering	Regierung	gobierno	gouvernement	governo	governo	政 府
HO	Head Office	Hovedkontor	Hauptsitz	sede principal	siège principal	sede principale	sede	本 社
jty	jointly	i samarbejde	zusammen	conjuntamente	associé à	aggiunto	junto	共同使用
lsd	leased	lejet	ge-/vermietet	alquilado	loué	dato a nolo	alugado	リース
lsf	leased from	lejet fra	gemietet von	alquilado de	loué par	dato a nolo da	alugado por	…からリース中
lst	leased to	lejet til	vermietet an	alquilado a	loué à	dato a nolo a	alugado a	…へリース中
mfd	manufactured in (year)	bygget i (år)	gebaut im (Jahr)	construido en el (año)	année de construction	costruito nel (anno)	manufacturado em (ano)	製造年月
mtow	maximum takeoff weight	maximum startvægt	Höchstabfluggewicht	carga máxima al despene	poids maximum au départ	peso massimo decollo	peso máximo de decolagem	最大離陸重量
ntu	not taken up	aldrig benyttet eller aldrig modtaget	nicht übernommen	no recebido	non repris	non ripreso	não recebido	割当未使用
occ	occasionally	af og til	von Zeit zu Zeit	ocasionalmente	occasionellement	occasionalmente	ocasionalmente	一時的
oo	on order	på ordre/på bestilling	bestellt	pedido	commandé	ordinato	encomendado	発注済
oopt	on option	Forudbestilling	vorbestellt/reserviert	reservado	réservé	prenotato	em opção de compra	仮発注
op	operated	opereres/benyttes	betrieben	ejecutado	en opération	operato	operado	運航者
opb	operated by	opereres af/benyttes af	betrieben durch	ejecutado por	exploité par	operato da	operado por	…により運航
opf	operated for	flyver for	betrieben für	ejecutado para	en service pour	operato per	operado para	…のために運航
opw	operated with	beflyves med	betrieben mit	ejecutado con	en service avec	operato con	operado com	…と共同運航
reg	registration	Rogistroring	Immatrikulation	registro	immatriculation	registrazione	registo	登録記号
(SCD)	Side Cargo Door	Fragtdør i siden (af kroppen)	Seiten-Frachttor	Cargo puerta lateral	porte latérale de cargo	porta di carico laterale	porta lateral da carga	サイドカーゴドア
std	stored	Langtidsparkeret	abgestellt	parado	en dépôt	in riserva	armazenado	放 置
temp	temporary	midlertidigt	vorübergehend	temporalmente	temporaire	temporaneamente	temporário	一時的
VIP	Very Important Person	VIP (meget vigtig person)	VIP – sehr wichtige Person	persona muy importante	personne très importante	persona molto importante	pessoa muito importante	要 人
wfu	withdrawn from use	taget ud af drift	aus dem Verkehr gezogen	retirado	mis hors service	ritirato	retirado do uso	退 役
wo	written off	styrtet ned (Afskrevet)	aus dem Register gestrichen (Unfall)	borrado del registro	rayé du registre	radiato dal registro	desusado	抹 消

International Air Carrier Association (Charter airlines)
Bldg. 28, P.O. Box 36, Brussels-National-Airport
B-1930 Zaventem, Belgium
Phone: (2) 720 58 80 ext. 238
Fax: (2) 721 22 88

International Air Transport Association
IATA Bldg., 200 Peel Street
Montreal, Québec H3A 2R4, Canada
Phone: (514) 844-6311
Fax: (514) 844-5286

International Civil Aviation Organization
1000 Sherbrooke Street West, Suite 400
Montreal, Québec H3A 2R2, Canada
Phone: (514) 285-8219
Fax: (514) 288-4722

DESCRIPTION / KEY

Country prefix according to ICAO system (coding and decoding see at the end)

▼ Name of country
▼ Official name in English
▼ Official name in national language(s)

OE = AUSTRIA (Republic of Austria) (Republik Oesterreich)
Capital: Vienna   Official Language: German   Population: 8,5 million   Square Km: 83856   Dialling code: +43   Acting political head: Viktor Klima (Federal Chancellor)

Name of airline (alphabetical listing see section 2) ▼

IATA two-letter-abbreviation of the airline (for decoding see section 2)✦
ICAO three-letter-abbreviation of the airline (for decoding see section 2)✦

Base ▼
Logo ▼

TYROLEAN AIRWAYS Tiroler Luftfahrt AG = VO / TYR

Innsbruck

✦tyrolean

Postfach 58, A-6026 Innsbruck, Austria   ☎ (0512) 22 22   Tx: none   Fax: (0512) 22 22 90 05   SITA: INNDMVO
F: 1958   ♦♦♦ 880   Head/Chief: Fritz A. Feitl   IATA: 734   ICAO: TYROLEAN   Net: http://www.telecom.at/tyrolean

☐ OE-LLS	De Havilland DHC-7-102 Dash 7	022	OE-HLS	0080 0480	4 PWC PT6A-50	19958	Y48	LQ-AJ	Stadt Innsbruck
000 registration	type of aircraft	cn/fn	ex/ex*	mfd del	powered by	mtow kg	configuration	selcal	name/fln/specialities/remarks

▲ page number ▲

registration	= registration (tail number)
type of aircraft	= exact type of aircraft
cn/fn	= construction number (manufacturers serial number)/manufacturers fuselage number
ex/ex*	= previous identity (condensed registrations* indicate previous manufacturers identity)
mfd	= month and year of manufacture
del	= month and year of delivery or registration
powered by	= number, manufacturer and exact type of engine
mtow kg	= official maximum take-off weight in kgs (multiply by 2,205 for conversion to pounds)
configuration	= configuration (indicates other use then for passenger service or exact seat configuration where available)
selcal	= SelCal code (selected call code for HF communication)
name	= christened name
fln	= fleet number (call sign)
specialities	= remarks if aircraft is not operated on wheels
remarks	= remarks regarding operating status, such as leased, sold, stored or withdrawn from use

✦(four-letter-abbreviations in brackets for leasing companies are not official!)

jp airline-fleets international 99/2000

Section 1

FLEET-LISTS

The Original annual fleet-list reference book since 1966,

including 6000 airlines, airtaxi, relief speciality
and large non-commercial government and corporate operators,

plus 78 color photos of airliners.

Fleet-lists

Section No. 1 of the *jp airline-fleets* international **99/2000** is the main part of the best-known and most comprehensive book about airlines, their fleets, facts and figures and transport-aircraft.
The research and updating is being done throughout the year by a team of specialists with the help of several individuals and institutions all over the world and gathered to a new edition every April.

Following is a guide to how this part of the book is to be read and description of columns and abbreviations used:

- **Country**
  - countries are listed alphabetically according to the prefixes given by ICAO
  - short name of country
  - full name in conjunction with the political status of the country in brackets (for coding and decoding and page-index see section 2)

- **Government / VIP / Executive** *(where applicable)*
  - alphabetical listing of aircraft used by governments and official agencies (aircraft with a mtow of 5000 kgs [11 000 lbs] or more are listed)
  - large airliner built aircraft used by individuals or companies as corporate transports (aircraft with a mtow of 5000 kgs [11 000 lbs] or more are listed)

- **Airline**
  - bold type: airline name, IATA two- and ICAO three-letter-abbreviations (for decoding see section 2)
  - small type: additional information regarding legal name and status of company (decoding of abbreviations is on page 4)
  - bold type right margin: base or bases of the fleet (any particular deviation will be mentioned in the remarks-column)
  - small type: full address of the headoffice, ☎ (phone-number), Tx: (telex-number), Fax: (telefax-number), SITA-code
  - small type: F: (year of foundation), ⋔⋔⋔ (number of employees), Head of company, IATA: (IATA accounting-number), ICAO: (ICAO call sign), Net: (Internet-address)
  - far right margin: logo

- **first line** *(where applicable)*
  - small type: additional information regarding activities of special organizations, aircraft on options, small aircraft listing or aircraft used for training purposes only

- **(start of) the fleet**
  - all commercial airlines, speciality, non-commercial government & relief operators known to have at least one aircraft with mtow of 1361 kgs (3000 lbs) or more for aerial work, charter or scheduled flights are included
  - commercial operators performing aerial spraying or training only need to have an aircraft with a mtow of 5000 kgs (11 000 lbs) or more, to be listed
  - leasing companies involved in leasing & financing of commuter & airliner transport aircraft are listed with types offered

- **description of columns:**

  - **square:** to be used to mark a particular aircraft in view of your own criteria

  - **registration** (tailnumber) (entry)
    in section 2 you will find a list of coding and decoding of all International Civil Aircraft Markings

  - **type of aircraft**
    exact name of the aircraft type for each entry
    (names of manufacturer in brackets are indicating the original manufacturer if the company has merged or been taken over by another company, which now carries on the responsibility for the products)

  - **cn/fn** (manufacturers' construction- and/or serial-number / manufacturers fuselage linenumber)
    manufacturers' individual construction number for each aircraft
    (Boeing and Douglas aircraft have two numbers divided by a slash, the first number is the total-number of the orders received by all customers, the second number is the real fuselage-number of the particular aircraft-type)
    (Several manufacturers use the construction-number to indicate production location, batch, date, type of aircraft or other informations)

  - **ex/ex*** (previous identity)
    normal type of letters or numbers indicate previous identity; condensed registrations* indicate previous registrations used by the manufacturer for certification- or test-flights
    (ntu = not taken up = allocated officially by the authorities and reserved by the airline, but not used for various reasons)

  - **mfd** (month and year of manufacture)
    here we list the month and year combination when the aircraft officially has been manufactured

  - **del** (month and year of delivery)
    here we list the month and year combination when the aircraft officially has been delivered or the titles have been transferred to this airline

  - **powered by**
    number of engines   manufacturer   exact type of engine(s)

  - **mtow** (maximum take-off weight)
    figure given in kilograms (multiply by 2.205 for conversion into pounds)

  - **configuration**
    for passenger aircraft we try to list the exact seating-configuration (list of abbreviations see section 2)

  - **selcal** (High Frequency communication code)
    SelCal code used by this particular aircraft (if applicable)

  - **name**
    name of aircraft (if applicable)

  - **fln**
    fleet number or call sign (if applicable)

  - **specialities**
    deviations of normal landing equipment (wheels)
    (the expression «Floats/Wheel-Skis» means that the aircraft is equipped with floats in summer and Wheel-Skis in winter)

  - **remarks**
    conversions (if applicable)
    indication of special status of aircraft, such as:
    lsf   =   leased from
    lst   =   leased to   for decoding of further abbreviations and translation in foreign languages use our list on page 4
    wfu   =   withdrawn from use

At the bottom of each page you will find a reference line regarding the columns and the page-number.

AP = PAKISTAN (Islamic Republic of Pakistan) (Islami Jamhuriya-e-Pakistan)

Capital: Islamabad Official Language: Urdu, English Population: 144,0 million Square Km: 796095 Dialling code: +92 Year established: 1947 Acting political head: Mohammad Rafiq Tarar (President)

Government / Corporate / Executive / VIP Aircraft

☐ AP-BBR	De Havilland DHC-6 Twin Otter 300	782	C-GEVP*	0080	1083	2 PWC PT6A-27	5670	Corporate		Oil & Gas Development Corp.
☐ AP-BEK	Learjet 31A	31A-062	N25997*	0093	0393	2 GA TFE731-2-3B	7484	VIP		Gvmt of Balochistan
☐ AP-BEX	Beech Beechjet 400A	RK-80	N8180Q	0094	1295	2 PWC JT15D-5	7303	VIP		Gvmt of Punjab
☐ AP-CAA	Beech King Air 200	BB-278	AP-CAD	0077		2 PWC PT6A-41	5670	Liaison		CAA
☐ J 468	Dassault Falcon 20F	468	F-WMKG*	0084		2 GE CF700-2D2	13000	VIP		Lohdi / Pakistan Air Force
☐ J 469	Dassault Falcon 20F	469	F-WMKI*	0084		2 GE CF700-2D2	13000	VIP		Iqbal / Pakistan Air Force
☐ J 752	Fokker F27 Friendship 200 (F27 Mk200)	10281	AP-ATW	0065	0082	2 RR Dart 532-7	19731	VIP		Pakistan Air Force
☐ J 753	Dassault Falcon 20E	277	F-WPXD*	0072		2 GE CF700-2D	13000	VIP		AP-TVC / Pakistan Air Force
☐ 68-19635	Boeing 707-351B	19635 / 706	AP-BAA	0068	0489	4 PW JT3D-3B	150410	VIP	BK-FJ	Pakistan 1 / Pakistan Air Force
☐ 68-19866	Boeing 707-340C	19866 / 738	AP-AWY	0068	0986	4 PW JT3D-3B	150410	Freighter	AK-EH	Pakistan Air Force

AERO ASIA International (Pvt), Ltd = E4 / RSO (Member of Tabani Group) Karachi

47-E/1, Block 6, Pechs, Karachi 75400, Pakistan ☎ (21) 454 49 46 Tx: 20811 arsia pk Fax: (21) 454 49 40 SITA: KHIDDE4
F: 1993 ⁂ 1250 Head: Rauf Tabani IATA: 532 ICAO: AERO ASIA Net: n/a

☐ AP-BFC	RomBac One-Eleven 561RC	401	YR-BRA	0982	0593	2 RR Spey 512-14DW	47400	Y109		
☐ AP-BFD	RomBac One-Eleven 561RC	404	YR-BRD	0485	0493	2 RR Spey 512-14DW	47400	Y109		
☐ AP-BFE	RomBac One-Eleven 561RC	406	YR-BRF	1286	0793	2 RR Spey 512-14DW	47400	Y109		
☐ AP-BFF	RomBac One-Eleven 561RC	407	YR-BRG	1087	0194	2 RR Spey 512-14DW	47400	Y109		
☐ YR-BRI	RomBac One-Eleven 561RC	409		0989	1194	2 RR Spey 512-14DW	47400	Y109	CD-AB	lsf RMV
☐ 9M-PMW	Boeing 737-209 (A)	24197 / 1581	B-1878	0788	0798	2 PW JT8D-9A	52390	Y123		Tabani / lsf TSE
☐ 9M-PMZ	Boeing 737-209 (A)	23796 / 1420	PK-RIV	0787	1298	2 PW JT8D-9A	52390	Y117		lsf TSE
☐ RA-42360	Yakovlev 42D	4520423811421	CCCP-42360	0088	0098	3 LO D-36	57500	Y108		lsf VLA / cvtd 42

AIRCRAFT SALES & SERVICES, (Private) Ltd (formerly Agricultural Aviation, (Private) Ltd) Karachi

Kassam Building, 1st Floor, 1/29 Randal Road, Karachi, Pakistan ☎ (21) 772 80 46 Tx: 23656 spray pk Fax: (21) 772 49 08 SITA: n/a
F: 1972 ⁂ 50 Head: Yusuf E.H. Jaffer Net: n/a Aircraft below MTOW 1361 kg: Piper PA-28.

☐ AP-BAU	Piper PA-34-200T Seneca II	34-7970476		0079		2 CO TSIO-360-EB	2073			
☐ AP-BBU	Piper PA-34-220T Seneca III	34-8433032		0084		2 CO TSIO-360-KB	2155			
☐ AP-BCK	Piper PA-34-220T Seneca III	34-8533018		0085		2 CO TSIO-360-KB	2155			
☐ AP-BFK	Reims/Cessna F406 Caravan II	F406-0059	N3122E	0091	1196	2 PWC PT6A-112	4468			

BHOJA AIRLINES, (Pvt) Ltd = B4 / BHO (Member of Bhoja Group) Karachi

Bhoja Terrace, Shahrah-E-Liaquat, Karachi 74200, Pakistan ☎ (21) 45 79 11 18 Tx: 21394 bhoja pk Fax: (21) 45 79 10 48 SITA: KHIHOB4
F: 1993 ⁂ 400 Head: Farouk Bhoja IATA: 896 ICAO: BHOJA Net: http://www.jamals.com/bhoja

☐ LY-AAU	Yakovlev 42D	4520424711397	CCCP-42354	0087	0098	3 LO D-36	56500	Y108		lsf LIL
☐ LY-AAV	Yakovlev 42D	4520424711399	CCCP-42355	0087	0095	3 LO D-36	56500	Y108		lsf LIL

PAKISTAN AVIATORS & AVIATION, (Pvt) Ltd (Member of Bhoja Group) Lahore

PO Box 6300, Lahore, Pakistan ☎ (42) 667 50 65 Tx: 27272 bhoja pk Fax: (42) 667 50 64 SITA: KHIHOBU
F: 1993 ⁂ 23 Head: Capt. Nadir Iqbal Mirza Net: n/a Aircraft below MTOW 1361kg: Cessna 152 & 172

☐ AP-BEM	Britten-Norman BN-2A-26 Islander	915	N661J	0077	0893	2 LY O-540-E4C5	2812			

PIA – Pakistan International Airlines, Corp. = PK / PIA Karachi

PIA Building, Quaid-e-Azam Int'l Airport, Karachi 75200, Pakistan ☎ (21) 457 20 11 Tx: 23296 piac Fax: (21) 772 77 27 SITA: n/a
F: 1954 ⁂ 20800 Head: Shahid Khaqan Abbasi IATA: 214 ICAO: PAKISTAN Net: http://www.piac.com/index.htm

☐ AP-BCG	De Havilland DHC-6 Twin Otter 300	726	C-GCVZ	0080	0285	2 PWC PT6A-27	5670	Y19		
☐ AP-BCH	De Havilland DHC-6 Twin Otter 300	768	C-GFJC	0081	0285	2 PWC PT6A-27	5670	Y19		
☐ UK-27089	Mil Mi-8MTV-1	95925	CCCP-27089	1092	0096	2 IS TV3-117VM	13000	Y24		lsf SAR
☐ AP-ALW	Fokker F27 Friendship 400 (F27 Mk400)	10187	PH-FDB*	0061	1061	2 RR Dart 532-7	19051	Y38		
☐ AP-ATU	Fokker F27 Friendship 200 (F27 Mk200)	10278	PH-FGV*	0065	0765	2 RR Dart 532-7	19051	Y40		
☐ AP-AUR	Fokker F27 Friendship 200 (F27 Mk200)	10307	PH-FKB*	0066	0966	2 RR Dart 532-7	19731	Y40		
☐ AP-AXB	Fokker F27 Friendship 200 (F27 Mk200)	10288	I-ATIG	0065	0473	2 RR Dart 532-7	19051	Y40		
☐ AP-BAL	Fokker F27 Friendship 200 (F27 Mk200)	10243	F-BUFE	0064	0179	2 RR Dart 532-7	19051	Y40		
☐ AP-BAO	Fokker F27 Friendship 200 (F27 Mk200)	10230	F-BVTE	0063	0679	2 RR Dart 532-7	19051	Y40		
☐ AP-BCT	Fokker F27 Friendship 200 (F27 Mk200)	10289	G-BDDH	0065	0688	2 RR Dart 532-7	19051	Y40		
☐ AP-BCZ	Fokker F27 Friendship 200 (F27 Mk200)	10305	VH-FNP	0066	0987	2 RR Dart 532-7	19731	Y40		
☐ AP-BDB	Fokker F27 Friendship 200 (F27 Mk200)	10292	VH-FNM	0066	0188	2 RR Dart 532-7	19731	Y40		
☐ AP-BDP	Fokker F27 Friendship 200 (F27 Mk200)	10170	PT-LCY	0061	1189	2 RR Dart 532-7	19731	Y40		
☐ AP-BDQ	Fokker F27 Friendship 200 (F27 Mk200)	10253	PT-LDJ	0064	1289	2 RR Dart 532-7	19731	Y40		
☐ AP-BDR	Fokker F27 Friendship 200 (F27 Mk200)	10134	PT-LGH	0059	0590	2 RR Dart 532-7	19731	Y40		
☐ AP-BDS	Fokker F27 Friendship 200 (F27 Mk200)	10133	PT-LCX	0059	0390	2 RR Dart 532-7	19731	Y40		
☐ AP-BCA	Boeing 737-340	23294 / 1114		0085	0585	2 CFMI CFM56-3B2	61235	C30Y88	GL-FM	
☐ AP-BCB	Boeing 737-340	23295 / 1116		0085	0685	2 CFMI CFM56-3B2	61235	C30Y88	GL-HJ	
☐ AP-BCC	Boeing 737-340	23296 / 1121		0085	0685	2 CFMI CFM56-3B2	61235	C30Y88	GL-HK	
☐ AP-BCD	Boeing 737-340	23297 / 1122		0085	0685	2 CFMI CFM56-3B2	61235	C30Y88	GL-HM	
☐ AP-BCE	Boeing 737-340	23298 / 1123		0085	0685	2 CFMI CFM56-3B2	61235	C30Y88	GL-JM	
☐ AP-BCF	Boeing 737-340	23299 / 1235		0086	0686	2 CFMI CFM56-3B2	61235	C30Y88	GL-KM	
☐ AP-BEH	Boeing 737-33A	25504 / 2341		0092	0992	2 CFMI CFM56-3B2	61235	VIP 49 Pax	CF-GS	Pakistan 2 / opf Gvmt in Gvmt-colors
☐ AP-AXG	Boeing 707-340C	20488 / 849	G-AZRO	0070	1270	4 PW JT3D-3B (HK2/COM)	150410	Freighter	DK-AE	std KHI / for sale
☐ AP-BBK	Boeing 707-323C	19576 / 719	N8413	0068	1282	4 PW JT3D-3B	150410	Freighter	DG-AK	std KHI / for sale
☐ AP-BDZ	Airbus Industrie A310-308	585	F-WWCH*	0091	0691	2 GE CF6-80C2A8	157000	C12Y169	AS-BL	
☐ AP-BEB	Airbus Industrie A310-308	587	F-WWCT*	0091	0791	2 GE CF6-80C2A8	157000	C12Y169	AS-GJ	
☐ AP-BEC	Airbus Industrie A310-308	590	F-WWCX*	0091	0991	2 GE CF6-80C2A8	157000	C12Y169	AS-GP	
☐ AP-BEG	Airbus Industrie A310-308	653	F-WWCZ*	0092	0992	2 GE CF6-80C2A8	157000	C12Y169	BQ-DK	
☐ AP-BEQ	Airbus Industrie A310-308	656	F-WWCB*	0093	1293	2 GE CF6-80C2A8	157000	C12Y169	FR-BP	
☐ AP-BEU	Airbus Industrie A310-308	691	F-WWCD*	0094	0594	2 GE CF6-80C2A8	157000	C12Y169	BC-EP	
☐ AP-BAX	Airbus Industrie A300B4-203	096	F-WZEP*	0079	0380	2 GE CF6-50C2	165000	C24Y214	AG-EH	
☐ AP-BAY	Airbus Industrie A300B4-203	098	F-WZER*	0079	0380	2 GE CF6-50C2	165000	C24Y214	AG-EK	
☐ AP-BAZ	Airbus Industrie A300B4-203	099	F-WZET*	0080	0480	2 GE CF6-50C2	165000	C24Y214	AG-EL	City of Rawalpindi
☐ AP-BBA	Airbus Industrie A300B4-203	114	F-WZEN*	0080	0880	2 GE CF6-50C2	165000	C24Y214	AG-EM	
☐ AP-BBM	Airbus Industrie A300B4-203	064	D-AHLA	0079	0883	2 GE CF6-50C2	165000	C24Y214	AE-FH	cvtd B4-103
☐ AP-BBV	Airbus Industrie A300B4-203	144	G-BIMC	0081	0684	2 GE CF6-50C2	165000	C24Y214	FL-BH	
☐ AP-BCJ	Airbus Industrie A300B4-203	268	9V-STG	0083	0585	2 GE CF6-50C2	165000	C24Y214	AG-FM	
☐ AP-BEL	Airbus Industrie A300B4-203	269	EI-CBW	0083	0493	2 GE CF6-50C2	165000	C24Y214	CM-BD	lsf GPAG
☐ AP-BEY	Airbus Industrie A300B4-203	146	F-BVGQ	0081	0593	2 GE CF6-50C2	165000	C24Y214	EK-CM	
☐ AP-BFL	Airbus Industrie A300B4-203	204	SX-BFI	0782	0197	2 GE CF6-50C2	165000	C24Y214		lsf INGL
☐ AP-AYV	Boeing 747-282B	20928 / 239	CS-TJC	0074	0476	4 PW JT9D-7A	351534	C30Y368	AK-FM	
☐ AP-AYW	Boeing 747-282B	21035 / 256	CS-TJD	0075	0476	4 PW JT9D-7A	351534	C30Y368	AK-FL	
☐ AP-BAK	Boeing 747-240B (M)	21825 / 383		0079	0779	4 GE CF6-50E2	362873	C30Y238/Plts	DK-CE	
☐ AP-BAT	Boeing 747-240B (M)	22077 / 429		0080	0380	4 GE CF6-50E2	362873	C30Y238/Plts	DK-EG	
☐ AP-BCL	Boeing 747-217B	20929 / 247	C-FCRE	0074	1285	4 PW JT9D-7A	351534	C30Y368	FL-AH	
☐ AP-BCM	Boeing 747-217B	20802 / 226	C-FCRB	0073	0586	4 PW JT9D-7A	351534	C30Y368	GL-CH	
☐ AP-BCN	Boeing 747-217B	20801 / 225	C-FCRA	0073	0986	4 PW JT9D-7A	351534	C30Y368	GM-BF	
☐ AP-BCO	Boeing 747-217B	20927 / 244	C-FCRD	0074	1186	4 PW JT9D-7A	351534	C30Y368	DL-FK	
☐ AP-	Boeing 747-367	23392 / 634	B-HIJ	0286		4 RR RB211-524C2	362873	C40Y400		to be lsf CPA 0099
☐ AP-	Boeing 747-367	23534 / 659	B-HIK	1086		4 RR RB211-524C2	362873	C40Y400		to be lsf CPA 0099
☐ AP-	Boeing 747-367	23709 / 671	B-HOL	0287		4 RR RB211-524C2	362873	C40Y400		to be lsf CPA 0099
☐ AP-	Boeing 747-367	23920 / 690	B-HOM	1087		4 RR RB211-524C2	362873	C40Y400		to be lsf CPA 0099
☐ AP-	Boeing 747-367	24215 / 709	B-HON	0788		4 RR RB211-524C2	362873	C40Y400		to be lsf CPA 0099

SCHOEN AIR, (Pvt) Ltd Karachi

Schön Centre, I.I Chundrigar Road, Karachi 74200, Pakistan ☎ (21) 263 60 00 Tx: 21386 schon pk Fax: (21) 263 08 54 SITA: n/a
F: 1986 ⁂ 56 Head: Capt. Saiyid Ather Husain Net: n/a Aircraft below MTOW 1361kg: Cessna 152 & 172.

☐ AP-BDT	Piper PA-34-220T Seneca III	34-8133238	N508MB	0081	1189	2 CO TSIO-360-KB	2155			
☐ AP-BCV	Cessna 402C II	402C0254	N2749U	0080	1186	2 CO TSIO-520-VB	3107			
☐ AP-BFH	Cessna 402C II	402C0048	5Y-MIM	0078	0895	2 CO TSIO-520-VB	3107			
☐ AP-BCX	Cessna 421C Golden Eagle III	421C0432	G-BREF	0078		2 CO GTSIO-520-L	3379			

SHAHEEN AIR CARGO (Private), Ltd = SEE (Associated with Shaheen Foundation) Lahore

PO Box 6389, Lahore, Pakistan ☎ (42) 666 57 86 Tx: 47459 saint pk Fax: (42) 666 32 29 SITA: n/a
F: 1995 ⁂ n/a Head: Mirza Ilyas Balg IATA: 587 ICAO: SHAHEEN CARGO Net: n/a Operates cargo flights with Boeing 707C leased from Pakistan Air Force & other companies when required.

SHAHEEN AIR INTERNATIONAL = NL / SAI (Associated with Shaheen Foundation) Karachi

PO Box 6389, Lahore, Pakistan ☎ (42) 666 57 86 Tx: 47459 saint pk Fax: (42) 666 32 29 SITA: n/a
F: 1993 ⁂ n/a Head: ACM Abbas Khattak IATA: 740 ICAO: SHAHEEN AIR Net: n/a Beside aircraft listed, also leases Boeing 707B aircraft from Mahfooz Aviation (C5-) when required.

☐ 9M-MQK	Boeing 737-4H6	27384 / 2673		0094	0498	2 CFMI CFM56-3C1	62822	F16Y128	DK-GS	lsf MAS

7 registration type of aircraft cn/fn ex/ex* mfd del powered by mtow kg configuration selcal name/fln/specialitites/remarks

A2 = BOTSWANA (Republic of Botswana)

Capital: Gaborone Official Language: English, Tswana Population: 1,5 million Square Km: 581730 Dialling code: +267 Year established: 1966 Acting political head: Sir Quett Ketumile Joni Masire (President)

Government / Corporate / Executive / VIP Aircraft

☐ OK1	GAC G-IV Gulfstream IV	1173	N17587*	0091	0692	2 RR Tay 611-8	33203	VIP		Gvmt

AERIAL SURVEYS BOTSWANA, (Pty) Ltd (Affiliated with AOC Surveys, South Africa) — Gaborone

Box 73, Gaborone, Botswana ☎ 35 35 17 Tx: 2424 bd Fax: 37 55 67 SITA: n/a
F: n/a ✈ n/a Head: n/a Net: n/a

☐ A2-AGN	Cessna 404 Titan II	404-0031	PT-OPY	0077		2 CO GTSIO-520-M	3810	Surveyer		

AIR BOTSWANA, Corp. = BP / BOT (Southern Links) — Gaborone

PO Box 92, Gaborone, Botswana ☎ 37 39 51 Tx: 2413 airhq bd Fax: 30 98 63 SITA: n/a
F: 1972 ✈ 420 Head: A.V. Leonjanga IATA: 636 ICAO: BOTSWANA Net: n/a
SOUTHERN LINKS is the marketing name of the internal charter division which manages its own and other surplus aircraft on behalf of several regional airlines.

☐ A2-ABB	ATR 42-320	101	F-WWEY*	0088	0788	2 PWC PW121	16700	Y42		
☐ A2-ABC	ATR 42-320	111	F-WWEH*	0088	1088	2 PWC PW121	16700	Y42		Kgalagadi
☐ A2-AJD	ATR 42-320	084	F-OIET	0088	0397	2 PWC PW121	16700	Y42		cvtd -300
☐ A2-ABD	BAe 146-100	E1101	G-5-101*	0089	1189	4 LY ALF502R-5	38102	CY77		lst AZW

AIR CHOBE (Chobe Explorations, (Pty) Ltd dba / Affiliated with Chobe Game Lodge Botswana) — Kasane

PO Box 32, Kasana, Botswana ☎ 65 03 40 Tx: 2765 bd Fax: 65 02 80 SITA: n/a
F: 1985 ✈ 7 Head: Jonathan M. Gibson Net: n/a Aircraft below MTOW 1361kg: Cessna 182

☐ A2-CEX	Cessna 207 Skywagon	20700154	ZS-IDG	0070		1 CO IO-550-F	1724			cvtd Cessna T207

DELTA AIR, (Pty) Ltd — Maun

PO Box 39, Maun, Botswana ☎ 66 00 44 Tx: 2484 bd Fax: 66 17 03 SITA: n/a
F: 1989 ✈ n/a Head: Peter Landenbergh Net: n/a

☐ A2-AGR	Cessna U206F Stationair	U20601837	ZS-OCC	0072		1 CO IO-520-F	1633			
☐ A2-AHN	Cessna U206G Stationair 6 II	U20606432	ZS-LKX	0082		1 CO IO-520-F	1633			
☐ A2-AID	Cessna U206G Stationair 6 II	U20605755	N9353Z	0080		1 CO IO-520-F	1724			
☐ A2-AIW	Cessna 210N Centurion II	21064163	ZS-MYC	0080		1 CO IO-520-L	1724			
☐ A2-AJB	Piper PA-31-350 Navajo Chieftain	31-8152047	N6261N	0080	0696	2 LY TIO-540-J2BD	3349			
☐ A2-AJA	Britten-Norman BN-2A-21 Islander	271	ZS-LKE	0076	0096	2 LY IO-540-K1B5	2994			

EXECUTIVE CHARTER, (Pty) Ltd — Gaborone

Private Bag SK6, Gaborone, Botswana ☎ 37 52 57 Tx: n/a Fax: 37 52 58 SITA: n/a
F: 1990 ✈ 8 Head: M. Sampson Net: n/a

☐ A2-AIH	Twin (Aero) Turbo Commander 690A	11105	ZS-MXE	0073	0893	2 GA TPE331-5-251K	4649			lsf Motor Centre
☐ A2-AGM	Cessna 501 Citation I/SP	501-0245	ZS-LDO	0082		2 PWC JT15D-1A	5375			lsf Motor Centre

FLYING MISSION (Go Preach Heal) — Gaborone

PO Box 1022, Gaborone, Botswana ☎ 30 02 97 Tx: none Fax: 31 29 81 SITA: n/a
F: 1980 ✈ 12 Head: Malcolm J. McArthur Net: n/a Private organisation conducting flights for missionaries and medical workers & commercial charters.

☐ A2-ABG	Cessna U206G Stationair	U20604049	ZS-JOJ	0077		1 CO IO-520-F	1633			
☐ A2-AEP	Cessna U206G Stationair 6 II	U20606756	ZS-LIB	0083		1 CO IO-550-F	1633			
☐ A2-AFU	Cessna U206F Stationair II	U20602922	ZS-JDV	0075		1 CO IO-520-F	1633			lsf Dewet Drilling P/L
☐ A2-AHX	Cessna U206D Super Skywagon	U206-1316	ZS-MXO	0069		1 CO IO-520-F	1633			
☐ A2-AGG	Cessna 210N Centurion II	21064078	ZS-LAP	0080		1 CO IO-550-L	1724			
☐ A2-OCB	Cessna 421B Golden Eagle	421B0250	ZS-OCB	0072	1197	2 CO GTSIO-520-H	3379			

KALAHARI AIR SERVICES & CHARTER (Air Charter Botswana, (Pty) Ltd dba) — Gaborone

PO Box 41278, Gaborone, Botswana ☎ 35 18 04 Tx: none Fax: 31 20 15 SITA: n/a
F: 1968 ✈ 35 Head: N.M. Fitz Gerald Net: n/a Aircraft below MTOW 1361kg: Cessna 172

☐ A2-AFK	Cessna 210N Centurion II	21064203	N5427Y	0080		1 CO IO-520-L	1724	5 Pax		
☐ A2-ACP	Beech Baron 58	TH-171	9J-ADA	0071		2 CO IO-520-C	2449	5 Pax		rebuilt 1996
☐ A2-ACS	Beech Baron 58	TH-614	9J-ADX	0075		2 CO IO-520-C	2449	5 Pax		
☐ A2-ACT	Beech Baron 58	TH-87	9J-ACA	0070		2 CO IO-520-C	2449	5 Pax		
☐ A2-ACR	Piper PA-31-350 Navajo Chieftain	31-7404256	ZS-ISZ	0074		2 LY TIO-540-J2BD	3175	9 Pax		
☐ A2-CAM	Piper PA-31-310 Navajo	31-569	G-AZBG	0070		2 LY TIO-540-A1A	2948	7 Pax		
☐ A2-AEZ	Beech King Air 200	BB-421	N4488L	0079		2 PWC PT6A-41	5670	11 Pax		
☐ A2-AHZ	Beech King Air 200	BB-95	ZS-JPD	0076	0096	2 PWC PT6A-41	5670	11 Pax		

MACK AIR, (Pty) Ltd — Maun

Private Bag 329, Maun, Botswana ☎ 66 06 75 Tx: none Fax: 66 06 75 SITA: n/a
F: 1995 ✈ n/a Head: Stuart Mackay Net: n/a Aircraft below MTOW 1361kg: Cessna 182

☐ A2-AEI	Cessna U206F Stationair	U20602470	ZS-LDJ	0074	0098	1 CO IO-520-F	1633			
☐ A2-AIC	Cessna U206G Stationair 6 II	U20606419	N9353Z	0081	0098	1 CO IO-550-F	1633			
☐ A2-AKB	Cessna U206F Stationair	U20601889	A2-ZHJ	0073	0095	1 CO IO-520-F	1633			
☐ A2-FMD	Cessna U206G Stationair 6 II	U20606005	ZS-KSM	0081	0098	1 CO IO-550-F	1633			
☐ A2-ZFF	Cessna U206D Super Skywagon	U206-1263	ZS-FPD	0069	0098	1 CO IO-520-F	1633			
☐ A2-MAC	Cessna 210N Centurion II	21063337		0079	0098	1 CO IO-520-L	1724			

MOREMI AIR SERVICES — Maun

Private Bag 187, Maun, Botswana ☎ 66 20 78 Tx: none Fax: 66 20 78 SITA: n/a
F: n/a ✈ n/a Head: Mike Smith Net: n/a Aircraft below MTOW 1361kg: Cessna 172

☐ A2-APE	Cessna U206F Stationair	U20602452	A2-AFE	0074		1 CO IO-520-F	1633			
☐ A2-FUN	Cessna U206F Stationair	U20602396		0074		1 CO IO-520-F	1633			
☐ A2-AIY	Cessna 210L Centurion II	21061141	ZS-MXA	0076		1 CO IO-520-L	1724			

NAC EXECUTIVE CHARTER, (Pty) Ltd — Gaborone

Private Bag SK6, Gaborone, Botswana ☎ 37 52 57 Tx: none Fax: 37 52 58 SITA: n/a
F: n/a ✈ n/a Head: Les Trotter Net: n/a

☐ A2-AJJ	Cessna 210L Centurion II	21061533	ZS-KPV	0076	0798	1 CO IO-520-L	1724			
☐ A2-LBD	Beech King Air 200	BB-837	ZS-LBD	0081	0198	2 PWC PT6A-41	5670			

NORTHERN AIR, (Pty) Ltd (Subsidiary of Safari South, (Pty) Ltd) — Maun

PO Box 27, Maun, Botswana ☎ 66 03 85 Tx: 2485 safso bd Fax: 66 03 79 SITA: n/a
F: 1976 ✈ 12 Head: n/a Net: n/a

☐ A2-ADK	Cessna U206G Stationair 6 II	U20606056	ZS-KUO	0081		1 CO IO-520-F	1633			
☐ A2-AER	Cessna U206G Stationair 6 II	U20606324	ZS-KXE	0081		1 CO IO-520-F	1633			
☐ A2-NAB	Cessna U206G Stationair 6 II	U20605439	ZS-KDA	0080		1 CO IO-520-F	1633			

SEFOFANE AIR CHARTERS (Sefofane Air, (Pty) Ltd dba) — Maun

Private Bag 159, Maun, Botswana ☎ 66 07 78 Tx: none Fax: 66 16 49 SITA: n/a
F: 1991 ✈ 18 Head: Neil Lumsden Net: n/a Aircraft below MTOW 1361kg: Cessna 177

☐ A2-AIB	Cessna U206G Stationair 6 II	U20605026	N4647U	0079		1 CO IO-520-F	1633			
☐ A2-AIF	Cessna U206G Stationair 6 II	U20605627	N5308X	0080	0793	1 CO IO-520-F	1633			
☐ A2-AIV	Cessna U206G Stationair 6 II	U20606410	ZS-LUA	0081	1294	1 CO IO-520-F	1633			
☐ A2-BEE	Cessna U206G Stationair 6 II	U20605665	ZS-KUL	0080	0897	1 CO IO-520-F	1633			
☐ A2-OWL	Cessna U206G Stationair 6 II	U20606978	ZS-NXR	0086	0598	1 CO IO-520-F	1633			
☐ A2-AIM	Cessna 210L Centurion II	21060795	ZS-MJY	0075	0694	1 CO IO-520-L	1724			
☐ A2-TAU	Britten-Norman BN-2B-20 Islander	2173	N999BR	0088	0196	2 LY IO-540-K1B5	2994			
☐ A2-ZOO	Britten-Norman BN-2B-20 Islander	2203	N628RC	0088	0196	2 LY IO-540-K1B5	2994			

SKYE AFRICA, (Pty) Ltd — Gaborone

Private Bag SK 11, Gaborone, Botswana ☎ 30 97 75 Tx: none Fax: 30 97 76 SITA: n/a
F: 1992 ✈ n/a Head: Deon Goubert Net: n/a

☐ A2-AHM	Cessna 210L Centurion II	21061481	ZS-LOT	0076		1 CO IO-520-L	1724			
☐ A2-AIT	Twin (Aero) Commander 500U	500U-1649-8	ZS-NEU	0066		2 LY IO-540-E1A5	3062			

SWAMP AIR CHARTERS, (Pty) Ltd — Maun

Private Bag 33, Maun, Botswana ☎ 66 05 69 Tx: 2612 bd Fax: 66 00 40 SITA: n/a
F: 1991 ✈ 4 Head: Mike Gunn Net: n/a

☐ A2-AIE	Cessna U206F Stationair II	U20602931	ZS-LZX	0075		1 CO IO-520-F	1633			
☐ A2-MJG	Cessna U206G Stationair	U20604061		0077		1 CO IO-520-F	1633			

8 registration type of aircraft cn/fn ex/ex* mfd del powered by mtow kg configuration selcal name/fln/specialitites/remarks

TRANS AIR, (Pty) Ltd — Maun

Box 147, Maun, Botswana ☎ 66 09 07 Tx: none Fax: 66 09 07 SITA: n/a
F: 1993 ⚲ 4 Head: Stephen A. Mckissock Net: n/a

☐ A2-AFO	Cessna U206E Stationair	U20601591	ZS-LSR	0071	0097	1 CO IO-520-F	1633			
☐ A2-AHB	Cessna U206F Stationair	U20601940	ZS-IVE	0073		1 CO IO-550-F	1633			
☐ A2-AJE	Cessna U206F Stationair II	U20603168	ZS-NXJ	0076	0097	1 CO IO-520-F	1633			

WILDLIFE HELICOPTERS, (Pty) Ltd — Maun

Private Bag 161, Maun, Botswana ☎ 66 06 64 Tx: 2612 bd Fax: 66 06 64 SITA: n/a
F: 1988 ⚲ n/a Head: Peter Perlstein Net: n/a Aircraft below MTOW 1361kg: Hughes 269C (300C)

☐ A2-HAL	Bell 206B JetRanger III	4190	ZS-RBX	0091		1 AN 250-C20J	1451			

WORLD GEOSCIENCE BOTSWANA, (Pty) Ltd (formerly Aerodata Botswana) — Gaborone

PO Box 10072, Gaborone, Botswana ☎ 31 24 97 Tx: none Fax: 37 35 98 SITA: n/a
F: 1988 ⚲ n/a Head: Paul Larkin Net: n/a

☐ A2-AIU	Cessna 404 Titan II	404-0082	5Y-ZBA	0077		2 CO GTSIO-520-M	3810	GeophysicSurvey		

XUGANA AIR, (Pty) Ltd (formerly Okavango Exploration) — Maun

Private Bag 198, Maun, Botswana ☎ 66 00 22 Tx: 2962 bd Fax: 66 00 37 SITA: n/a
F: 1986 ⚲ 10 Head: Derek Flatt Net: n/a

☐ A2-AGW	Cessna U206F Stationair	U20602393	ZS-LLZ	0074		1 CO IO-520-F	1633			
☐ A2-AIX	Cessna U206F Stationair	U20601944	ZS-MAD	0073		1 CO IO-520-F	1633			
☐ A2-AJI	Cessna U206G Stationair 6 II	U20606842	ZS-NSS	0084	0598	1 CO IO-520-F	1633			
☐ A2-ZIB	Cessna U206G Stationair 6 II	U20606845	ZS-OBE	0084	0698	1 CO IO-520-F	1633			
☐ A2-AJC	Cessna 210L Centurion II	21060321		0074	0096	1 CO IO-520-L	1724			

A3 = TONGA FRIENDLY ISLANDS (Kingdom of Tonga) (Pule'anga Tonga)

Capital: Nuku'alofa Official Language: Polynesian, English Population: 0,2 million Square Km: 2831 Dialling code: +676 Year established: 1970 Acting political head: Baron Vaea Houma (Prime Minister)

PACIFIC ISLAND SEAPLANES — Tongatapu-SPB

PO Box 1675, Nuku'alofa, Tonga ☎ 25 177 Tx: none Fax: 25 165 SITA: n/a
F: 1996 ⚲ n/a Head: Larry Simon Net: n/a

☐ A3-GQW	De Havilland DHC-2 Beaver I	124	C-FGQW	0051	1196	1 PW R-985	2313			Floats

ROYAL TONGAN AIRLINES = WR / HRH (Friendly Islands Airways, Ltd dba) — Tongatapu-Fua'amotu Int'l

Private Bag 9, Nuku'alofa, Tonga ☎ 23 414 Tx: 66282 fiair ts Fax: 24 056 SITA: TBUZQWR
F: 1984 ⚲ 140 Head: Jim Bradfield IATA: 971 ICAO: TONGA ROYAL Net: n/a

☐ A3-FQL	De Havilland DHC-6 Twin Otter 300	685	ZK-FQL	0080	0588	2 PWC PT6A-27	5670	Y20		
☐ A3-MCA	BAe (HS) 748-242 Srs 2A	1712 / 188	ZK-MCA	0072	1195	2 RR Dart 534-2	20183	Y44		
☐ DQ-FJD	Boeing 737-33A	27285 / 2608	N102AN	0094	0195	2 CFMI CFM56-3C1	62822	C8Y118	CQ-DR	lsf/jtly opw FJI

TONGA DEFENCE SERVICES - Air Wing (Air Wing division of Tonga Defence Services) — Tongatapu-Fua'amotu Int'l

PO Box 72, Nuku'alofa, Tonga ☎ 32 149 Tx: none Fax: 23 934 SITA: n/a
F: n/a ⚲ n/a Head: Col. F. Tupou Net: n/a Government organisation conducting non-commercial maritime surveillance, search/rescue & PADS life raft and Storpedo drop missions.

☐ AW-01	Beech G18S	BA-483	N9644R	0059	0596	2 PW R-985-AN14B	4600	Maritime Survey		

A4O = OMAN (Sultanate of Oman) (Saltanat Uman)

Capital: Muscat Official Language: Arabic Population: 2,5 million Square Km: 212457 Dialling code: +968 Year established: 900 Acting political head: Qabûs bin Saïd ibn Taimur as-Saïd (Sultan)

Government / Corporate / Executive / VIP Aircraft

ROYAL AIR FORCE OF OMAN (Air Transport) uses the ICAO three letter code: MJN and call sign MAJAN.

☐ 551	BAe (BAC) One-Eleven 485GD (F)	247	1001	0074	1274	2 RR Spey 512-14DW	41730	mil trans		Sultan of Oman's Air Force
☐ 552	BAe (BAC) One-Eleven 485GD (F)	249	1002	0074	0175	2 RR Spey 512-14DW	41730	mil trans		Sultan of Oman's Air Force
☐ 553	BAe (BAC) One-Eleven 485GD (F)	251	1003	0075	1175	2 RR Spey 512-14DW	41730	mil trans		Sultan of Oman's Air Force

GULF AIR Company, GSC = GF / GFA (formerly Gulf Aviation, Co. Ltd) — Bahrain

PO Box 138, Manama, Bahrain ☎ 32 22 00 Tx: 8255 gulf hq bn Fax: 33 04 66 SITA: n/a
F: 1950 ⚲ 6345 Head: Sheikh Ahmed Bin Saif Al Nahyan IATA: 072 ICAO: GULF AIR Net: http://www.gulfairco.com/
Multinational airline of the following states: Bahrain, Oman, Qatar, and United Arab Emirates (Abu Dhabi).

☐ A4O-EA	Airbus Industrie A320-212	313	F-WWIZ*	0092	0592	2 CFMI CFM56-5A3	75500	F16C12Y96	CG-BS	801
☐ A4O-EB	Airbus Industrie A320-212	325	F-WWDI*	0092	0692	2 CFMI CFM56-5A3	75500	F16C12Y96	CG-DR	802
☐ A4O-EC	Airbus Industrie A320-212	345	F-WWDU*	0092	0992	2 CFMI CFM56-5A3	75500	F16C12Y96	CG-DS	803 / Al Ruwais
☐ A4O-ED	Airbus Industrie A320-212	375	F-WWDT*	0092	1292	2 CFMI CFM56-5A3	75500	F12C15Y96	CG-ER	804 / Sitra
☐ A4O-EE	Airbus Industrie A320-212	419	F-WWDP*	0093	0593	2 CFMI CFM56-5A3	75500	F16C12Y96	BR-HP	805 / Al-Rumaitha
☐ A4O-EF	Airbus Industrie A320-212	421	F-WWIO*	0093	0693	2 CFMI CFM56-5A3	75500	F16C12Y96	BR-HS	806
☐ A4O-EG	Airbus Industrie A320-212	438	F-WWDT*	0093	0993	2 CFMI CFM56-5A3	75500	F16C12Y96	CE-HS	807
☐ A4O-EH	Airbus Industrie A320-212	445	F-WWBZ*	0093	1093	2 CFMI CFM56-5A3	75500	F12C15Y96	CE-JP	808
☐ A4O-EI	Airbus Industrie A320-212	459	F-WWDK*	0094	0594	2 CFMI CFM56-5A3	75500	F16C12Y96	EJ-KR	809
☐ A4O-EJ	Airbus Industrie A320-212	466	F-WWBB*	0094	0694	2 CFMI CFM56-5A3	75500	F16C12Y96	EJ-HS	810
☐ A4O-EK	Airbus Industrie A320-212	481	F-WWIE*	0094	0994	2 CFMI CFM56-5A3	75500	F12C15Y96	EJ-KP	811
☐ A4O-EL	Airbus Industrie A320-212	497	F-WWDF*	0094	1294	2 CFMI CFM56-5A3	75500	F16C12Y96	EJ-KQ	812
☐ A4O-EN	Airbus Industrie A320-212	537	F-WWBX*	0095	0695	2 CFMI CFM56-5A3	75500	F16C12Y96	FP-DS	814
☐ A4O-GH	Boeing 767-3P6 (ER)	24484 / 260		0089	0489	2 GE CF6-80C2B4	175540	F10C22Y186	CQ-BL	603
☐ A4O-GI	Boeing 767-3P6 (ER)	24485 / 264		0089	0589	2 GE CF6-80C2B4	175540	F10C22Y186	CQ-BM	604 / Alkhor
☐ A4O-GJ	Boeing 767-3P6 (ER)	24495 / 267		0089	0689	2 GE CF6-80C2B4	175540	F10C22Y186	CQ-BP	605
☐ A4O-GK	Boeing 767-3P6 (ER)	24496 / 270		0089	0689	2 GE CF6-80C2B4	175540	F10C22Y186	CQ-DE	606 / Al Burami
☐ A4O-GS	Boeing 767-3P6 (ER)	26236 / 436		0092	0692	2 GE CF6-80C2B4	175540	F10C22Y186	CQ-ES	613
☐ A4O-GT	Boeing 767-3P6 (ER)	26238 / 440		0092	0692	2 GE CF6-80C2B4	175540	F10C22Y186	CG-FR	614 / Auwakrah
☐ A4O-GU	Boeing 767-3P6 (ER)	26233 / 501		0093	0693	2 GE CF6-80C2B4	175540	F10C22Y186	CS-FR	615
☐ A4O-GV	Boeing 767-3P6 (ER)	26235 / 502		0093	0693	2 GE CF6-80C2B4	175540	F10C22Y186	CS-GH	616 / Dukhan
☐ A4O-GY	Boeing 767-3P6 (ER)	26234 / 538		0094	0594	2 GE CF6-80C2B4	175540	F10C22Y186	EP-MR	619
☐ A4O-GZ	Boeing 767-3P6 (ER)	26237 / 544		0094	0694	2 GE CF6-80C2B4	175540	F10C22Y186	EP-MS	620
☐ A4O-KA	Airbus Industrie A330-243	276				2 RR Trent 772B-60	230000	F12C24Y207	JM-BR	501 / oo-delivery 0599
☐ A4O-KB	Airbus Industrie A330-243	281				2 RR Trent 772B-60	230000	F12C24Y207	JM-BS	502 / oo-delivery 0599
☐ A4O-KC	Airbus Industrie A330-243	286				2 RR Trent 772B-60	230000	F12C24Y207	JM-CP	503 / oo-delivery 0699
☐ A4O-KD	Airbus Industrie A330-243	287				2 RR Trent 772B-60	230000	F12C24Y207	JM-CQ	504 / oo-delivery 0699
☐ A4O-KE	Airbus Industrie A330-243	343				2 RR Trent 772B-60	230000	F12C24Y207	JM-CR	505 / oo-delivery 0600
☐ A4O-KF	Airbus Industrie A330-243	344				2 RR Trent 772B-60	230000	F12C24Y207	JM-FP	506 / oo-delivery 0600
☐ A4O-LB	Airbus Industrie A340-312	039	F-WWJZ*	0094	0794	4 CFMI CFM56-5C3	260000	F18C36Y209	EJ-HQ	Al Fateh
☐ A4O-LC	Airbus Industrie A340-312	040	F-WWJA*	0094	0794	4 CFMI CFM56-5C3	260000	F18C36Y209	EJ-HR	Doha
☐ A4O-LD	Airbus Industrie A340-312	097	F-WWJT*	0095	0695	4 CFMI CFM56-5C3	260000	F18C36Y209	AP-GM	Abu Dhabi
☐ A4O-LE	Airbus Industrie A340-312	103	F-WWJG*	0095	1095	4 CFMI CFM56-5C3	260000	F18C18Y241	FQ-JR	
☐ A4O-LF	Airbus Industrie A340-312	133	F-WWJP*	0096	1296	4 CFMI CFM56-5C3	260000	F18C18Y241	FQ-JS	

OMAN AIR = WY / OMA (Oman Aviation Services, Company (S.A.O.G.) dba) — Muscat-Seeb Int'l

PO Box 58, CPO, Seeb International Airport, 111, Oman ☎ 51 92 37 Tx: 5424 oas seeb on Fax: 51 08 05 SITA: MCTCZWY
F: 1981 ⚲ 2270 Head: H.E. Salin bin Abdulla Al Ghazali IATA: 910 ICAO: OMAN AIR Net: n/a

☐ A4O-DB	De Havilland DHC-6 Twin Otter 300	813	C-GDKL*	0084	0884	2 PWC PT6A-27	5670	Y20		
☐ A4O-AS	ATR 42-500	574	F-WWEO*	0098	1298	2 PWC PW127E	18600	Y46		
☐ A4O-AT	ATR 42-500	576	F-WWEP*	0098	1298	2 PWC PW127E	18600	Y46		
☐ A4O-FB	Fokker F27 Friendship 500RF (F27 Mk500RF)	10630	PH-EXH*	0082	0582	2 RR Dart 536-7	20412	Y52		
☐ A4O-FC	Fokker F27 Friendship 500RF (F27 Mk500RF)	10631	PH-EXM*	0082	0682	2 RR Dart 536-7	20412	Y52		
☐ A4O-FE	Fokker F27 Friendship 500RF (F27 Mk500RF)	10641	PH-SFI	0082	0183	2 RR Dart 536-7	20412	Y52		
☐ A4O-FG	Fokker F27 Friendship 500RF (F27 Mk500RF)	10642	PH-EXJ*	0082	1182	2 RR Dart 536-7	20412	Y52		
☐ A4O-OA	Airbus Industrie A310-322 (ET)	409	HB-IPH	0085	0499	2 PW JT9D-7R4E1	150000			lsf ILFC
☐ A4O-OB	Airbus Industrie A310-322 (ET)	410	HB-IPI	0085		2 PW JT9D-7R4E1	150000			lsf ILFC

OMAN ROYAL FLIGHT = RS / ORF — Muscat-Seeb Int'l

PO Box 43, Seeb International Airport, 111, Oman ☎ 51 01 11 Tx: 5381 royalair on Fax: 51 01 79 SITA: MCTOPRS
F: 1973 ⚲ n/a Head: n/a ICAO: OMAN Net: n/a Non-commercial state organisation conducting VIP passenger & cargo flights for the government.

☐ A4O-AG	Eurocopter (Aerosp.) SA330J Puma	1603		0079		2 TU Turmo IVC	7400	VIP		
☐ A4O-AH	Eurocopter (Aerosp.) SA330J Puma	1605		0079		2 TU Turmo IVC	7400	VIP		
☐ A4O-AV	Eurocopter (Aerosp.) SA330J Puma	1629		0080		2 TU Turmo IVC	7400	VIP		
☐ A4O-HB	Eurocopter (Aerosp.) AS332C Super Puma	2027		0082		2 TU Makila 1A	8600	VIP		
☐ A4O-HC	Eurocopter (Aerosp.) AS332C Super Puma	2037		0082		2 TU Makila 1A	8600	VIP		
☐ A4O-HM	Eurocopter (Aerosp.) AS332L1 Super Puma	2315		0090		2 TU Makila 1A1	8600	VIP		
☐ A4O-AB	GAC G-IV Gulfstream IV	1168	N462GA*	0091	0292	2 RR Tay 611-8	33203	VIP	CL-GK	
☐ A4O-AC	GAC G-IV Gulfstream IV	1196	N420GA*	0092	1292	2 RR Tay 611-8	33203	VIP		
☐ A4O-SO	Boeing 747SP-27	21785 / 405	N351AS	0079	0784	4 PW JT9D-7J	318422	VIP	FG-JM	
☐ A4O-SP	Boeing 747SP-27	21992 / 447	N150UA	0080	0193	4 PW JT9D-7A	318422	VIP	CL-EH	

9 registration type of aircraft cn/fn ex/ex* mfd del powered by mtow kg configuration selcal name/fln/specialitites/remarks

ROYAL OMAN POLICE - Flight Operations = ROP (Division of the Royal Oman Police) — Muscat-Seeb Int'l

PO Box 41, Seeb International Airport, 111, Oman ☎ 51 11 11 Tx: 5263 polair on Fax: 51 04 63 SITA: n/a
F: n/a staff n/a Head: Kamil al-Hassani Net: n/a Non-commercial state organisation conducting police transport, overland & coast surveyer flights.

registration	type of aircraft	cn/fn	ex/ex*	mfd	del	powered by	mtow kg	configuration	selcal	remarks
☐ A4O-CT	Britten-Norman BN-2T Turbine Islander	2201	G-51-2201*	0089	0989	2 AN 250-B17C	3175			cvtd BN-2A-26
☐ A4O-AO	Bell 205A-1	30175		0075		1 LY T5313B	4309			
☐ A4O-AP	Bell 205A-1	30176		0075		1 LY T5313B	4309			
☐ A4O-AQ	Bell 205A-1	30177		0075		1 LY T5313B	4309			
☐ A4O-CJ	Bell 214ST	28118		0083		2 GE CT7-2A	7938			
☐ A4O-CL	Bell 214ST	28120	N31803	0083		2 GE CT7-2A	7938			
☐ A4O-CM	Bell 214ST	28122		0083		2 GE CT7-2A	7938			
☐ A4O-CO	Bell 214ST	28138		0084		2 GE CT7-2A	7938			
☐ A4O-CQ	Dornier 228-100	7028	D-IBLN*	0084	0584	2 GA TPE331-5-252D	5700			
☐ A4O-CU	CASA (IPTN) CN-235M-100	C062		0093	0193	2 GE CT7-9C	16500			
☐ A4O-CV	CASA (IPTN) CN-235M-100	C063		0093	0193	2 GE CT7-9C	16500			

A5 = BHUTAN (Kingdom of Bhutan) (Druk Gyal Khab)

Capital: Thimbu Official Language: Dzongkha Population: 2,0 million Square Km: 47000 Dialling code: +975 Year established: 1947 Acting political head: Jigme Singye Wangchuk (King)

DRUK-AIR - Royal Bhutan Airlines = DRK (Druk Air, Corp. Ltd dba) — Paro

PO Box 209, Thimphu 700019, Bhutan ☎ 22 825 Tx: 0890-219 druair tpu Fax: 22 775 SITA: n/a
F: 1981 staff 110 Head: Dasho Leki Dorji ICAO: ROYAL BHUTAN Net: n/a

registration	type of aircraft	cn/fn	ex/ex*	mfd	del	powered by	mtow kg	configuration	selcal	remarks
☐ A5-RGD	BAe 146-100	E1095	G-BOEA*	0088	1188	4 LY ALF502R-5	38102	C10Y62		
☐ A5-RGE	BAe 146-100	E1199	G-RJET*	0091	1292	4 LY ALF502R-5	38102	C10Y61		

A6 = UNITED ARAB EMIRATES (Al Imarat al-Arabiya al-Muttahida)

(Member states: Abu Dhabi, Ajman, Dubai, Fujairah, Ras-al-Khaimah, Sharjah, Umm-al-Qiwain)
Capital: Abu Dhabi Official Language: Arabic Population: 3,2 million Square Km: 83600 Dialling code: +971 Year established: 1971 Acting political head: Sheikh Zayid bin Sultan al-Nahayan (President)

ABU DHABI AVIATION — Abu Dhabi-Bateen

PO Box 2723, Abu Dhabi, United Arab Emirates ☎ (2) 44 91 00 Tx: 22656 adaco em Fax: (2) 44 90 81 SITA: n/a
F: 1975 staff 415 Head: H.E. Hamdan Bin Mubarek Al-Nahyan Net: n/a

registration	type of aircraft	cn/fn	ex/ex*	mfd	del	powered by	mtow kg	configuration	selcal	remarks
☐ A6-BCE	Bell 206B JetRanger II	2185		0477		1 AN 250-C20	1451			Hi Skids
☐ A6-BCF	Bell 206B JetRanger III	2423		0078		1 AN 250-C20B	1451			Hi Skids
☐ A6-BCK	Bell 206B JetRanger III	2426		0078		1 AN 250-C20B	1451			Hi Skids
☐ A6-BCL	Bell 206B JetRanger III	2720		0079		1 AN 250-C20B	1451			Hi Skids
☐ A6-BAB	Bell 212	31227		0083		2 PWC PT6T-3B TwinPac	5080			Offshore
☐ A6-BAC	Bell 212	31231		0083		2 PWC PT6T-3B TwinPac	5080			Offshore
☐ A6-BBA	Bell 212	30773	N9997K	0076		2 PWC PT6T-3 TwinPac	5080			Offshore
☐ A6-BBC	Bell 212	30777		0076		2 PWC PT6T-3 TwinPac	5080			Offshore
☐ A6-BBE	Bell 212	30783	N9937K	0076		2 PWC PT6T-3 TwinPac	5080			Offshore
☐ A6-BBK	Bell 212	30802		0076		2 PWC PT6T-3 TwinPac	5080			Offshore
☐ A6-BBL	Bell 212	30822		0077		2 PWC PT6T-3 TwinPac	5080			Offshore
☐ A6-BBO	Bell 212	30903		0078		2 PWC PT6T-3 TwinPac	5080			Offshore
☐ A6-BBP	Bell 212	30917		0079		2 PWC PT6T-3 TwinPac	5080			Offshore
☐ A6-BBQ	Bell 212	30942		0079		2 PWC PT6T-3 TwinPac	5080			Offshore
☐ A6-BBR	Bell 212	30976		0079		2 PWC PT6T-3 TwinPac	5080			Offshore
☐ A6-BBS	Bell 212	30977		0079		2 PWC PT6T-3 TwinPac	5080			Offshore
☐ A6-BBU	Bell 212	31183		0081		2 PWC PT6T-3B TwinPac	5080			Offshore
☐ A6-BBV	Bell 212	31189		0081		2 PWC PT6T-3B TwinPac	5080			Offshore
☐ A6-BBW	Bell 212	32123		0081		2 PWC PT6T-3 TwinPac	5080			Offshore
☐ A6-BBY	Bell 212	32125		0081		2 PWC PT6T-3 TwinPac	5080			Offshore
☐ A6-BBZ	Bell 212	32141		0081		2 PWC PT6T-3 TwinPac	5080			Offshore
☐ A6-BAE	Bell 412HP	36072		0094	0194	2 PWC PT6T-3BE TwinPac	5400			Offshore
☐ A6-BAF	Bell 412HP	36082		0094	0394	2 PWC PT6T-3BE TwinPac	5400			Offshore
☐ A6-BAG	Bell 412HP	36061	N6173M	0093	0395	2 PWC PT6T-3BE TwinPac	5400			Offshore
☐ A6-BAH	Bell 412EP	36119	C-GBUP*	0095	1295	2 PWC PT6T-3D TwinPac	5400			Offshore
☐ A6-BAI	Bell 412EP	36122		0196	0296	2 PWC PT6T-3D TwinPac	5400			Offshore
☐ A6-BAK	Bell 412EP	36123		0696	0896	2 PWC PT6T-3D TwinPac	5400			Offshore
☐ A6-BAL	Bell 412EP	36150		1296	0197	2 PWC PT6T-3D TwinPac	5400			Offshore
☐ A6-BAO	Bell 412EP	36152		0097	0097	2 PWC PT6T-3D TwinPac	5400			Offshore
☐ A6-BAP	Bell 412EP	36189		0098	0098	2 PWC PT6T-3D TwinPac	5400			Offshore
☐ A6-BAQ	Bell 412EP	36190		0098	0098	2 PWC PT6T-3D TwinPac	5400			Offshore
☐ A6-BAS	Bell 412EP	36215		0098	1198	2 PWC PT6T-3D TwinPac	5400			Offshore
☐ A6-BAT	Bell 412EP	36216		0098	1198	2 PWC PT6T-3D TwinPac	5400			Offshore
☐ A6-MRM	De Havilland DHC-6 Twin Otter 300	674		0080	1094	2 PWC PT6A-27	5670			
☐ A6-ADA	De Havilland DHC-8-202 Dash 8Q	471	C-GLOT*	0097	0597	2 PWC PW123D	16465			
☐ A6-ADC	De Havilland DHC-8-202 Dash 8Q	473	C-GFRP*	0097	0697	2 PWC PW123D	16465			

AEROGULF SERVICES, Co. — Dubai

شركة الخليج للخدمات الجوية AEROGULF SERVICES CO

PO Box 10566, Dubai, United Arab Emirates ☎ (4) 82 31 57 Tx: 46674 aero em Fax: (4) 82 30 28 SITA: n/a
F: 1976 staff 80 Head: Capt. J.H. Kirk ICAO: AEROGULF Net: n/a On order (Letter of intent): 4 Bell 427 for delivery 1999/2000 & 2 Bell Boeing 609 (tilt-rotor) for delivery 2001.

registration	type of aircraft	cn/fn	ex/ex*	mfd	del	powered by	mtow kg	configuration	selcal	remarks
☐ A6-ALB	Bell 206B JetRanger	709	N72131	0072		1 AN 250-C20	1451			cvtd 206A
☐ A6-ALF	Bell 206B JetRanger III	1361	N59507	0074		1 AN 250-C20B	1451			cvtd JetRanger
☐ A6-ALP	Bell 206B JetRanger III	2495		0078		1 AN 250-C20B	1451			
☐ A6-ALG	Eurocopter (MBB) BO105CB	S-94		0074		2 AN 250-C20B	2300			
☐ A6-ALQ	Eurocopter (MBB) BO105CB	S-100	RP-C1667	0073		2 AN 250-C20B	2300			
☐ A6-ALS	Eurocopter (MBB) BO105CB	S-66	VR-BFU	0073		2 AN 250-C20B	2300			
☐ A6-ALA	Bell 212	30664	N71AL	0074		2 PWC PT6T-3 TwinPac	5080			
☐ A6-ALC	Bell 212	30790	N2781A	0076		2 PWC PT6T-3 TwinPac	5080			
☐ A6-ALD	Bell 212	30809	N143AL	0076		2 PWC PT6T-3 TwinPac	5080			
☐ A6-ALU	Bell 212	30729	C-GBKC	0075	1297	2 PWC PT6T-3 TwinPac	5080			
☐ A6-ALV	Bell 212	30703	A6-HMR	0075	0098	2 PWC PT6T-3 TwinPac	5080			

DESERT AIR TOURS, Llc — Dubai

PO Box 60794, Dubai, United Arab Emirates ☎ (4) 299 44 11 Tx: none Fax: (4) 299 44 22 SITA: n/a
F: 1998 staff 7 Head: Richard Seed Net: n/a

registration	type of aircraft	cn/fn	ex/ex*	mfd	del	powered by	mtow kg	configuration	selcal	remarks
☐ A6-DAT	Cessna 207 Skywagon	20700153		0070	0098	1 CO IO-520-F	1724			
☐ A6-DES	Cessna 207A Stationair 8 II	20700588	N779EA	0080	0299	1 CO IO-520-F	1724			

EMIRATES = EK / UAE — Dubai

Emirates

PO Box 686, Dubai, United Arab Emirates ☎ (4) 22 81 51 Tx: 49262 ekeng em Fax: (4) 23 91 87 SITA: DXBCAEK
F: 1985 staff 4000 Head: H.H. Sheikh Ahmed Bin Saeed Al-Maktoum IATA: 176 ICAO: EMIRATES Net: http://www.ekgroup.com/

registration	type of aircraft	cn/fn	ex/ex*	mfd	del	powered by	mtow kg	configuration	selcal	remarks
☐ A6-EKB	Airbus Industrie A310-304	436	F-WWCV*	0087	0787	2 GE CF6-80C2A2	153000	F18C32Y131	FQ-GL	
☐ A6-EKG	Airbus Industrie A310-308	545	F-WWCY*	0091	0192	2 GE CF6-80C2A8	157000	F28C32Y131	BM-RS	cvtd -304
☐ A6-EKH	Airbus Industrie A310-308	600	F-WWCB*	0092	0292	2 GE CF6-80C2A8	157000	F18C25Y131	BP-AR	
☐ A6-EKI	Airbus Industrie A310-308	588	F-WWCM*	0091	0792	2 GE CF6-80C2A8	157000	F18C32Y131	BP-AS	lsf Athimar Leasing Ltd
☐ A6-EKJ	Airbus Industrie A310-308	597	F-WWCU*	0091	0892	2 GE CF6-80C2A8	164000	F18C32Y131	BP-CR	lsf Athimar Leasing Ltd
☐ A6-EKK	Airbus Industrie A310-308	658	F-WWCY*	0092	1192	2 GE CF6-80C2A8	157000	F18Y177	GH-AF	
☐ A6-EKL	Airbus Industrie A310-308	667	F-WWCZ*	0092	0393	2 GE CF6-80C2A8	164000	F18C32Y131	GH-AK	lsf Shir Ltd
☐ A6-EKN	Airbus Industrie A310-308	573	S7-RGA	0091	0294	2 GE CF6-80C2A8	157000	F18C32Y131	GK-JS	lsf GATX / cvtd -304
☐ A6-EKP	Airbus Industrie A310-308	695	F-WWCO*	0094	0595	2 GE CF6-80C2A8	164000	F18C32Y131	GL-AS	lsf ILFC
☐ A6-EKC	Airbus Industrie A300-605R (A300B4-605R)	505	F-WWAO*	0089	0589	2 GE CF6-80C2A5	171700	C28Y235	FQ-GM	
☐ A6-EKD	Airbus Industrie A300-605R (A300B4-605R)	558	F-WWAR*	0090	0690	2 GE CF6-80C2A5	171700	F18C42Y163	CJ-KQ	
☐ A6-EKE	Airbus Industrie A300-605R (A300B4-605R)	563	F-WWAA*	0090	0990	2 GE CF6-80C2A5	171700	C28Y235	CJ-LQ	
☐ A6-EKF	Airbus Industrie A300-605R (A300B4-605R)	608	F-WWAD*	0091	0691	2 GE CF6-80C2A5	171700	F18C42Y163	CJ-MQ	
☐ A6-EKM	Airbus Industrie A300-605R (A300B4-605R)	701	F-WWAN*	0093	0893	2 GE CF6-80C2A5	171700	F18C42Y163	EH-GK	
☐ A6-EKO	Airbus Industrie A300-605R (A300B4-605R)	747	F-WWAT*	0095	0395	2 GE CF6-80C2A5	171700	F18C42Y163	GL-AR	lsf ILFC
☐ A6-EMD	Boeing 777-21H	27247 / 30		0096	0696	2 RR Trent 871	247208	C49Y290	HM-BP	
☐ A6-EME	Boeing 777-21H	27248 / 33		0096	0796	2 RR Trent 871	247208	C49Y290	HM-BR	
☐ A6-EMF	Boeing 777-21H	27249 / 42		0096	1096	2 RR Trent 871	247208	C49Y290	HM-BS	
☐ A6-EMG	Boeing 777-21H (ER)	27252 / 63	N5020K*	0097	0497	2 RR Trent 890	286978	F18C49Y236	HM-CR	
☐ A6-EMH	Boeing 777-21H (ER)	27251 / 54		0097	0597	2 RR Trent 890	286978	F18C49Y236	HM-CS	
☐ A6-EMI	Boeing 777-21H (ER)	27250 / 47	N5028Y*	1196	0797	2 RR Trent 890	263086	F18C49Y236	HM-DR	
☐ A6-EMJ	Boeing 777-21H (ER)	27253 / 91		0097	0997	2 RR Trent 890	286978	F18C49Y236	HM-DS	
☐ A6-EMK	Boeing 777-21H (ER)	29324 / 171		1098	1098	2 RR Trent 892	267700	F18C49Y236		
☐ A6-EML	Boeing 777-21H (ER)	29325 / 176		1198	1198	2 RR Trent 892	267700	F18C49Y236		
☐ A6-EKQ	Airbus Industrie A330-243	248	F-WWKL*	0098	0399	2 RR Trent 772B-60	230000	FCY243orCY285		
☐ A6-EKR	Airbus Industrie A330-243	251	F-WWKO*	0099	0399	2 RR Trent 772B-60	230000	FCY243orCY285		

☐ A6-EKS	Airbus Industrie A330-243	283				2 RR Trent 772B-60	230000	FCY243orCY285		oo-delivery 0699
☐ A6-EKT	Airbus Industrie A330-243	293				2 RR Trent 772B-60	230000	FCY243orCY285		oo-delivery 0799
☐ A6-EKU	Airbus Industrie A330-243	295				2 RR Trent 772B-60	230000	FCY243orCY285		oo-delivery 0999
☐ A6-EKV	Airbus Industrie A330-243	313				2 RR Trent 772B-60	230000	FCY243orCY285		oo-delivery 1299
☐ A6-EKW	Airbus Industrie A330-243	316				2 RR Trent 772B-60	230000	FCY243orCY285		oo-delivery 0100
☐ A6-EKX	Airbus Industrie A330-243	324				2 RR Trent 772B-60	230000	FCY243orCY285		oo-delivery 0200
☐ A6-EKY	Airbus Industrie A330-243	326				2 RR Trent 772B-60	230000	FCY243orCY285		oo-delivery 0300
☐ A6-EKZ	Airbus Industrie A330-243	375				2 RR Trent 772B-60	230000	FCY243orCY285		oo-delivery 1200
☐ A6-	Airbus Industrie A330-243	379				2 RR Trent 772B-60	230000	FCY243orCY285		oo-delivery 0101
☐ A6-	Airbus Industrie A330-243	388				2 RR Trent 772B-60	230000	FCY243orCY285		oo-delivery 0201
☐ A6-	Airbus Industrie A330-243	390				2 RR Trent 772B-60	230000	FCY243orCY285		oo-delivery 0201
☐ A6-	Airbus Industrie A330-243					2 RR Trent 772B-60	230000	FCY243orCY285		oo-delivery 0002
☐ A6-	Airbus Industrie A330-243					2 RR Trent 772B-60	230000	FCY243orCY285		oo-delivery 0002
☐ A6-	Airbus Industrie A330-243					2 RR Trent 772B-60	230000	FCY243orCY285		oo-delivery 0002
☐ A6-	Airbus Industrie A330-243					2 RR Trent 772B-60	230000	FCY243orCY285		oo-delivery 0002
☐ A6-	Boeing 777-31H					2 RR Trent 892	299371			to be lsf SALE 1199
☐ A6-	Boeing 777-31H					2 RR Trent 892	299371			to be lsf SALE 1299
☐ A6-	Airbus Industrie A340-541					4 RR Trent 553	365000			oo-delivery 0002
☐ A6-	Airbus Industrie A340-541					4 RR Trent 553	365000			oo-delivery 0002
☐ A6-	Airbus Industrie A340-541					4 RR Trent 553	365000			oo-delivery 0003
☐ A6-	Airbus Industrie A340-541					4 RR Trent 553	365000			oo-delivery 0003
☐ A6-	Airbus Industrie A340-541					4 RR Trent 553	365000			oo-delivery 0004
☐ A6-	Airbus Industrie A340-541					4 RR Trent 553	365000			oo-delivery 0004

FALCON EXPRESS CARGO AIRLINES, Ltd = FC (Associated with FEDEX-Federal Express Corporation) — Dubai & Bahrain

PO Box 9372, Dubai, United Arab Emirates ☎ (4) 82 68 86 Tx: n/a Fax: (4) 82 31 25 SITA: n/a
F: 1995 ⁂ n/a Head: n/a IATA: 553 Net: n/a

☐ A6-FCA	Beech 1900C-1 Airliner	UC-57	OY-GED	0089	1095	2 PWC PT6A-65B	7550	Freighter		
☐ A6-FCB	Beech 1900C-1 Airliner	UC-66	OY-GEI	0089	1095	2 PWC PT6A-65B	7550	Freighter		
☐ A6-FCC	Beech 1900C-1 Airliner	UC-68	OY-GEJ	0089	1095	2 PWC PT6A-65B	7550	Freighter		
☐ A6-FCD	Beech 1900C-1 Airliner	UC-71	OY-GEK	0089	1095	2 PWC PT6A-65B	7550	Freighter		

FUJAIRAH AVIATION CENTRE = FUJ — Fujairah

PO Box 777, Fujairah, United Arab Emirates ☎ (9) 22 47 47 Tx: none Fax: (9) 22 63 18 SITA: n/a
F: 1986 ⁂ 8 Head: Capt. David Hopkins ICAO: FUJAIRAH Net: n/a Trainer-aircraft below MTOW 5000kg: Cessna 172 & Piper PA-34

☐ A6-SMS	Learjet 60	60-094	N60LR*	0097	0697	2 PWC PW305A	10660	VIP		

GULF AIR = multinational state airline – see under A4O- markings

UNITED ARAB EMIRATES/Abu Dhabi Amiri Flight = MO / AUH — Abu Dhabi-Int'l

PO Box 689, Abu Dhabi, United Arab Emirates ☎ (2) 75 78 00 Tx: none Fax: (2) 75 77 99 SITA: n/a
F: n/a ⁂ n/a Head: Patrick King ICAO: SULTAN Net: n/a Non-commercial state organisation conducting VIP passenger & cargo flights for the government.

☐ A6-KHZ	Beech King Air 350 (B300)	FL-132	N3263Y*	0096	1096	2 PWC PT6A-60A	6804	VIP 8 Pax		
☐ A6-MHH	Beech King Air 350 (B300)	FL-131	N3251S*	0096	0996	2 PWC PT6A-60A	6804	VIP 8 Pax		
☐ A6-AUH	Dassault Falcon 900	84	F-WWFD*	0090	1090	3 GA TFE731-5A-1C	20640	VIP	BQ-EF	
☐ A6-UAE	Dassault Falcon 900	86	F-WWFE*	0090	1090	3 GA TFE731-5A-1C	20640	VIP	PQ-EG	
☐ A6-ZKM	Dassault Falcon 900	47	F-WWFA*	0088	0189	3 GA TFE731-5A-1C	21092	VIP	HM-CQ	
☐ A6-SHK	BAe 146-100	E1091	G-BOMA*	0088	1288	4 LY ALF502R-5	38302	VIP	BQ-EL	
☐ A6-PFD	Airbus Industrie A300C-620 (A300C4-620)	374	F-WWAJ*	0085	1285	2 PW JT9D-7R4H1	165000	VIP / Combi	BJ-MP	
☐ A6-SHZ	Airbus Industrie A300-620 (A300B4-620)	354	F-ODRM*	0084	0985	2 PW JT9D-7R4H1	165000	VIP	AL-BG	
☐ A6-ZSN	Boeing 747SP-Z5	23610 / 676	N60697*	0089	1289	4 RR RB211-524	319328	VIP	AM-HP	

UNITED ARAB EMIRATES/Dubai Air Wing = DUB — Dubai

PO Box 11097, Dubai, United Arab Emirates ☎ (4) 24 51 51 Tx: n/a Fax: (4) 24 44 10 SITA: n/a
F: n/a ⁂ n/a Head: n/a ICAO: DUBAI Net: http://www.westpac.com/ Non-commercial state organisation conducting VIP passenger & cargo flights for the government.

☐ A6-HHH	GAC G-IV Gulfstream IV	1011	N17581*	0087	1287	2 RR Tay 610-8	33203	VIP	GJ-AM	
☐ A6-HRS	Boeing 737-7E0 (BBJ)	29251 / 150		0098	1298	2 CFMI CFM56-7B26	77565	VIP		
☐ A6-	Airbus Industrie A319-133 (CJ)	910	D-AVYB*			2 IAE V2527-A5	70000	VIP		oo-delivery 0799
☐ A6-SMM	Boeing 747SP-31	21963 / 441	N602AA	0580	0494	4 PW JT9D-7AH	318743	VIP	FK-CG	
☐ A6-SMR	Boeing 747SP-31	21961 / 415	N58201	0079	0285	4 PW JT9D-7A	315800	VIP	GH-JM	

UNITED ARAB EMIRATES/Sharjah Ruler's Flight = SHJ — Sharjah

PO Box 8, Sharjah, United Arab Emirates ☎ (6) 58 12 14 Tx: n/a Fax: (6) 58 10 88 SITA: n/a
F: 1985 ⁂ 10 Head: Robert Tabet ICAO: SHARJAH Net: n/a Non-commercial state organisation conducting VIP passenger flights for the government.

☐ A6-ESH	Boeing 737-2W8 (A)	22628 / 820	N180RN	0081	0585	2 PW JT8D-17	58105	VIP	DG-BE	

A7 = QATAR (State of Qatar) (Dawlat al Qatar)

Capital: Doha Official Language: Arabic Population: 0,6 million Square Km: 11437 Dialling code: +974 Year established: 1971 Acting political head: Hamad bin Khalifa bin Hamad al-Thani (Emir)

GULF AIR = multinational state airline – see under A4O- markings

GULF HELICOPTERS Company (Subsidiary of Gulf Air Company , GSC) — Doha-Heliport

PO Box 811, Doha, Qatar ☎ 33 38 88 Tx: 4353 glfhel dh Fax: 41 10 04 SITA: n/a
F: 1973 ⁂ 60 Head: Abdulla Bin Hamad Al Attiyah Net: n/a

☐ A7-HAO	Agusta-Bell 206B JetRanger	8044	A4O-DC	0068		1 AN 250-C20	1451	4 Pax		cvtd 206A
☐ A7-HAP	Bell 206B JetRanger III	2943	G-BSGW	0080	1090	1 AN 250-C20B	1451	4 Pax		
☐ A7-HAH	Bell 212	30861		0077		2 PWC PT6T-3B TwinPac	5080	13 Pax		
☐ A7-HAJ	Bell 212	30902		0079		2 PWC PT6T-3B TwinPac	5080	13 Pax		lst GESCO as VT-HGA
☐ A7-HAL	Bell 212	30918		0078		2 PWC PT6T-3B TwinPac	5080	13 Pax		lst GESCO as VT-HGD
☐ A7-HAM	Bell 212	30911		0079		2 PWC PT6T-3B TwinPac	5080	13 Pax		
☐ A7-HAN	Bell 212	31124		0080		2 PWC PT6T-3B TwinPac	5080	13 Pax		lst GESCO as VT-HGB
☐ A7-HAS	Bell 212	31130	C-GLZG	0080	0991	2 PWC PT6T-3B TwinPac	5080	13 Pax		
☐ A7-HAT	Bell 212	31149	C-GMUJ	0080	0991	2 PWC PT6T-3B TwinPac	5080	13 Pax		lst GESCO as VT-HGC
☐ A7-HAQ	Bell 412SP	36017	N66104*	0090	1290	2 PWC PT6T-3B TwinPac	5262	13 Pax		
☐ A7-HAR	Bell 412SP	36016	N6611A*	0090	1290	2 PWC PT6T-3B TwinPac	5262	13 Pax		
☐ A7-HAU	Bell 412SP	33116	VH-EEH	0085	0794	2 PWC PT6T-3B TwinPac	5398	13 Pax		
☐ A7-HAV	Bell 412SP	33205	D-HHNN	0090	1095	2 PWC PT6T-3B TwinPac	5398	13 Pax		
☐ A7-HAW	Bell 412HP	36046	N9124N	0092	0296	2 PWC PT6T-3B TwinPac	5398	13 Pax		
☐ A7-HAY	Bell 412EP	36126	N2045S*	0096	0996	2 PWC PT6T-3F TwinPac	5398	13 Pax		
☐ A7-HAZ	Bell 412HP	36041	N92801	0091	0597	2 PWC PT6T-3B TwinPac	5398	13 Pax		

QATAR AIR CARGO = QAC (Subsidiary of United Tours & Travels) — Doha

PO Box 3286, Doha, Qatar ☎ 86 77 00 Tx: none Fax: 86 98 04 SITA: n/a
F: 1993 ⁂ n/a Head: Essa Al Khulaifi ICAO: QATAR CARGO Net: n/a Operates cargo flights with Antonov 12 & Ilyushin 18 aircraft leased from other companies when required.

QATAR AIRWAYS, (W.L.L.) = QR / QTR — Doha

PO Box 22550, Doha, Qatar ☎ 62 17 17 Tx: 4444 qatair dh Fax: 62 15 33 SITA: DOHAZQR
F: 1993 ⁂ 470 Head: Akbar Al-Baker IATA: 157 ICAO: QATARI Net: http://www.qatarairways.com On order (Letter of Intent): 6 Airbus Industrie A320-232 for delivery 2001-3.

☐ A7-ABR	Airbus Industrie A320-232	928	F-WWIK*	0098	0199	2 IAE V2527-A5	75500	F12Y132		lsf SALE
☐ A7-ABS	Airbus Industrie A320-232	932	F-WWIG*	0099	0299	2 IAE V2527-A5	75500	F12Y132		lsf SALE
☐ A7-ABT	Airbus Industrie A320-232	943	F-WWIV*	0099	0399	2 IAE V2527-A5	75500	F12Y132		lsf SALE
☐ A7-ABU	Airbus Industrie A320-232	977				2 IAE V2527-A5	75500	F12Y132		to be lsf SALE 0499
☐ A7-ABC	Boeing 727-2M7 (A)	21951 / 1680	A6-EMA	1180	0595	3 PW JT8D-17R	88360	F16Y119		for sale
☐ A7-ABD	Boeing 727-264 (A)	22982 / 1802	A6-EMB	0782	1095	3 PW JT8D-17R	86409	F16Y119		for sale
☐ A7-ABE	Boeing 727-294 (A)	22044 / 1561	N221AL	0079	0695	3 PW JT8D-17	86409	F16Y119		for sale
☐ A7-ABG	Boeing 727-294 (A)	22043 / 1559	N921TS	0079	0397	3 PW JT8D-17	86409	F16Y119		for sale
☐ A7-ABN	Airbus Industrie A300-622R (A300B4-622R)	664	VH-PWD	0092	0497	2 PW PW4158	171700	F12C18Y201	MS-EP	lsf AWAS
☐ A7-ABO	Airbus Industrie A300-622R (A300B4-622R)	668	VH-OPW	0092	0497	2 PW PW4158	171700	F12C18Y201	MS-EQ	lsf AWAS
☐ A7-ABP	Airbus Industrie A300-622R (A300B4-622R)	630	VH-EFW	0092	1097	2 PW PW4158	171700	F18C32Y201		lsf AWAS
☐ A7-AHM	Boeing 747SP-27	21786 / 413	A7-ABM	0080	0398	4 PW JT9D-7J	318421	VIP		Musheireb / lsf Varma Int'l / opf Gvmt

QATAR AMIRI FLIGHT = QAF — Doha

PO Box 3320, Doha, Qatar ☎ 86 41 61 Tx: n/a Fax: 82 12 90 SITA: DOHAFBA
F: n/a ⁂ n/a Head: n/a ICAO: AMIRI Net: n/a Non-commercial state organisation conducting VIP passenger & cargo flights for the government.

☐ A7-AAD	Dassault Falcon 900	91	F-WWFH*	0091	0291	3 GA TFE731-5A-1C	20639	VIP	QR-AM	
☐ A7-AAE	Dassault Falcon 900	94	F-WWFC*	0091	0491	3 GA TFE731-5A-1C	20639	VIP	QR-BH	
☐ A7-	Airbus Industrie A320-232	927	F-WWBA*			2 IAE V2527-A5	77000	VIP		oo-delivery 0499
☐ A7-AAA	Boeing 707-3P1C	21334 / 923		0077	0777	4 PW JT3D-3B (HK2/COM)	146200	VIP	BE-HL	

11 registration type of aircraft cn/fn ex/ex* mfd del powered by mtow kg configuration selcal name/fln/specialitites/remarks

☐ A7-AAF	Airbus Industrie A310-304	473	F-ODSV	0089	0298	2 GE CF6-80C2A2	153000	VIP		
☐ A7-HHK	Airbus Industrie A340-211	026	F-WWJQ*	0093	0593	4 CFMI CFM56-5C2	257000	VIP	QR-HK	

A9C = BAHRAIN (State of Bahrain) (Dawlat al Bahrain)

Capital: Manama Official Language: Arabic Population: 0,6 million Square Km: 695 Dialling code: +973 Year established: 1783 Acting political head: Hamad bin Isa bin Salman al-Khalifa(Emir)

BAHRAIN AMIRI FLIGHT = BAH — Bahrain

PO Box 245, Manama, Bahrain ☎ 62 33 77 Tx: n/a Fax: 62 20 44 SITA: n/a
F: n/a ⁂ n/a Head: n/a ICAO: BAHRAIN ONE Net: n/a Non-commercial state organisation conducting VIP flights for the government.

☐ A9C-HA	Bell 430	49020	N11753*	0097	0898	2 AN 250-C40	4082	VIP		
☐ A9C-BG	GAC (Grumman) G-1159 Gulfstream II (TT)	202	N17586	0077		2 RR Spey 511-8	29710	VIP	CF-JK	
☐ A9C-BB	GAC G-1159A Gulfstream III	393	N17587*	0083		2 RR Spey 511-8	30935	VIP	DG-HL	
☐ A9C-BA	Boeing 727-2M7 (A/RE) (Super 27/winglets)	21824 / 1595	N740RW	0080	0781	2/1 PW JT8D-217C/17R(BFG)	88360	VIP	FM-DJ	Al Bahrain / cvtd -2M7
☐ A9C-ISA	Boeing 747SP-21	21649 / 373	V8-AC1	0079	1298	4 PW JT9D-7A	318422	VIP		

DHL AVIATION = ES / DHX (Division of DHL International, E.C. / Associated with SNAS Aviation Ltd, Saudi Arabia) — Bahrain

PO Box 5741, Manama, Bahrain ☎ 32 26 40 Tx: 9531 dhlavi bn Fax: 33 45 08 SITA: n/a
F: 1979 ⁂ 70 Head: George Semak IATA: 155 ICAO: DILMUN Net: http://www.dhl.com

☐ HZ-SN8	Fairchild (Swearingen) SA227AT Merlin IVC	AT-434B	N3110F	0082	0488	2 GA TPE331-11U-611G	7257	Freighter		lsf / joint opw SNAS Aviation
☐ A9C-DHL1	Fairchild (Swearingen) SA227AC Metro III	AC-788B	N3003M	0091	1092	2 GA TPE331-11U-612G	7257	Freighter		
☐ HZ-SN10	Fairchild (Swearingen) SA227AC Metro III	AC-769B	HZ-SN1	0091	0391	2 GA TPE331-11U-612G	7257	Freighter		lsf / joint opw SNAS Aviation
☐ HZ-SN7	Fairchild (Swearingen) SA227AC Metro III	AC-565B	N3113G*	0083	0284	2 GA TPE331-11U-612G	7257	Freighter		lsf / joint opw SNAS Aviation
☐ HZ-SN11	Convair 580 (F) (SCD)	385	C-FKFA	0056	0791	2 AN 501-D13H	26379	Freighter		lsf / joint opw SNAS Avn / cvtd 440-32
☐ HZ-SN14	Convair 580 (F) (SCD)	361	OO-DHJ	0056	1095	2 AN 501-D13H	26379	Freighter		lsf / joint opw SNAS Avn / cvtd 440-12
☐ VH-AWE	Boeing 757-23APF	24635 / 258	9J-AFO	0090	0496	2 RR RB211-535E4	113398	Freighter	FR-BD	City of Al Manama / lsf AWAS

GULF AIR = multinational state airline – see under A4O- markings

B = CHINA (People's Republic of China) (Zhonghua Renmin Gongheguo)

(Hongkong became a semi-autonomous territory within Mainland-China on 1st July 97, but while loosing its VR-H ICAO nationality-mark could retain its 3-letter- registrations instead of 4-digit-numbers, therefore is not included here)
Capital: Beijing Official Language: Chinese Population: 1250,0 million Square Km: 9560980 Dialling code: +86 Year established: 1949 Acting political head: Jiang Zemin (President)

AIRBORNE REMOTE SENSING SERVICES (Division of China Institute of Remote Sensing) — Beijing & Xian

c/o Poly Technologies Inc., 17th Floor, CITIC Bldg, 19 Jianguomenwai Street, 100600 Beijing, People's Republic of China ☎ (1)65003334 EXT.627 Tx: none Fax: (1) 65 00 44 84 SITA: n/a
F: n/a ⁂ n/a Head: Tong Qingxi Net: n/a Non-commercial state organisation conducting aerial survey & remote sensing flights for the government.

☐ B-4101	Cessna S550 Citation S/II	S550-0049	N1270K*	0085	0686	2 PWC JT15D-4B	6849	Survey/RemoteSen		
☐ B-4102	Cessna S550 Citation S/II	S550-0050	N1270S*	0085	0686	2 PWC JT15D-4B	6849	Survey/RemoteSen		
☐ HY984	Learjet 36A	36A-053	N39418*	0085	0085	2 GA TFE731-2-2B	8301	Survey/RemoteSen		
☐ HY985	Learjet 36A	36A-034	N763R*	0078	0085	2 GA TFE731-2-2B	8301	Survey/RemoteSen		
☐ HY986	Learjet 35A	35A-601		0085	0086	2 GA TFE731-2-2B	8301	Survey/RemoteSen		
☐ HY987	Learjet 35A	35A-602		0085	0086	2 GA TFE731-2-2B	8301	Survey/RemoteSen		
☐ HY988	Learjet 35A	35A-603		0085	0086	2 GA TFE731-2-2B	8301	Survey/RemoteSen		

AIR CHANGAN AIRLINES - ACA = 2Z / CGN — Xian-Xianyang

長安航空公司

PO Box 2, 710077 Xian, (Shaanxi), People's Republic of China ☎ (29) 425 76 62 Tx: none Fax: (29) 426 34 32 SITA: n/a
F: 1992 ⁂ 280 Head: She Yining ICAO: CHANGAN Net: n/a

☐ B-3444	Xian Yunshuji Y7-100C	09701		0090	0095	2 WJ 5A-1	21800	Y52		
☐ B-3445	Xian Yunshuji Y7-100C	09705		0090	0095	2 WJ 5A-1	21800	Y52		
☐ B-3475	Xian Yunshuji Y7-100C	06703		0087	0094	2 WJ 5A-1	21800	Y52		
☐ B-3707	Xian Yunshuji Y7-100C	12701		0092	0092	2 WJ 5A-1	21800	Y50		
☐ B-3708	Xian Yunshuji Y7-100C	11705		0092	0092	2 WJ 5A-1	21800	Y50		
☐ B-3720	Xian Yunshuji Y7-200A	0001		0099	0399	2 PWC PW127C	21800	Y60		
☐ B-3721	Xian Yunshuji Y7-200A	0003		0099	0399	2 PWC PW127C	21800	Y60		

AIR CHINA International, Corp. = CA / CCA (Assoc.with CAAC-Civil Aviation Adm.of China/Member of Air China Group) — Beijing-Capital, Hohhot & Tianjin

AIR CHINA

Capital International Airport, 100621 Beijing, (Beijing), People's Republic of China ☎ (10) 64 56 32 20 Tx: 210327 bjklh cn Fax: (10) 64 56 38 31 SITA: n/a
F: 1988 ⁂ 12660 Head: Wang Li An IATA: 999 ICAO: AIR CHINA Net: http://www.airchina.com Fleet includes division at Dalian, Inner Mongolia (Hohhot), Shanghai & Tianjin.

☐ B-8032	Shijiazhuang Yunshuji Y5	316405		0076	0788	1 HS 5	5500	Y12 / Sprayer		
☐ B-8033	Shijiazhuang Yunshuji Y5	316410		0076	0788	1 HS 5	5500	Y12 / Sprayer		
☐ B-8037	Shijiazhuang Yunshuji Y5	4705516		0076	0788	1 HS 5	5500	Y12 / Sprayer		
☐ B-8038	Shijiazhuang Yunshuji Y5	4705517		0076	0788	1 HS 5	5500	Y12 / Sprayer		
☐ B-8040	Shijiazhuang Yunshuji Y5	5705507		0076	0788	1 HS 5	5500	Y12 / Sprayer		
☐ B-8041	Shijiazhuang Yunshuji Y5	5705509		0076	0788	1 HS 5	5500	Y12 / Sprayer		
☐ B-8221	Nanchang Yunshuji Y5	432007		0060	0788	1 HS 5	5500	Y12 / Sprayer		
☐ B-8382	Nanchang Yunshuji Y5	932028		0063	0788	1 HS 5	5500	Y12 / Sprayer		
☐ B-8419	Nanchang Yunshuji Y5	1132006		0064	0788	1 HS 5	5500	Y12 / Sprayer		
☐ B-3450	Xian Yunshuji Y7-100C	08710		0090	0090	2 WJ 5A-1	21800	Y52		
☐ B-3462	Xian Yunshuji Y7-100C	04704		0085	0788	2 WJ 5A-1	21800	Y52		cvtd Y7
☐ B-3463	Xian Yunshuji Y7-100C	04705		0085	0788	2 WJ 5A-1	21800	Y52		cvtd Y7
☐ B-3492	Xian Yunshuji Y7-100C	08703		0089	0089	2 WJ 5A-1	21800	Y52		
☐ B-2707	BAe 146-100	E1076	G-5-076*	0087	0788	4 LY ALF502R-5	38102	Y82	EM-AG	
☐ B-2708	BAe 146-100	E1081	G-5-081*	0087	0788	4 LY ALF502R-5	38102	Y82	EM-AH	
☐ B-2709	BAe 146-100	E1083	G-5-083*	0087	0788	4 LY ALF502R-5	38102	Y82	EM-AJ	
☐ B-2710	BAe 146-100	E1085	G-5-085*	0087	0788	4 LY ALF502R-5	38102	Y82	EM-AK	
☐ B-2531	Boeing 737-3J6	23302 / 1224	N1792B*	0086	0788	2 CFMI CFM56-3B1	61235	F8Y116		
☐ B-2532	Boeing 737-3J6	23303 / 1237	N5573B*	0086	0788	2 CFMI CFM56-3B1	61235	F8Y116		
☐ B-2535	Boeing 737-3J6	25078 / 2002		0091	0391	2 CFMI CFM56-3B1	61235	F8Y116		
☐ B-2536	Boeing 737-3J6	25079 / 2016		0091	0391	2 CFMI CFM56-3B1	61235	F8Y116		
☐ B-2580	Boeing 737-3J6	25080 / 2254		0092	0492	2 CFMI CFM56-3B1	61235	F8Y116		
☐ B-2581	Boeing 737-3J6	25081 / 2263		0092	0492	2 CFMI CFM56-3B1	61235	F8Y116		
☐ B-2584	Boeing 737-3J6	25891 / 2385		0092	1292	2 CFMI CFM56-3B1	61235	F8Y116		
☐ B-2585	Boeing 737-3J6	27045 / 2384		0092	1292	2 CFMI CFM56-3B1	61235	F8Y116		
☐ B-2587	Boeing 737-3J6	25892 / 2396		0092	0193	2 CFMI CFM56-3B1	61235	F8Y116		
☐ B-2588	Boeing 737-3J6	25893 / 2489		0093	0693	2 CFMI CFM56-3B1	61235	F8Y116		
☐ B-2598	Boeing 737-3J6	27128 / 2493		0093	0693	2 CFMI CFM56-3B1	61235	F8Y116		
☐ B-2905	Boeing 737-33A	25506 / 2360	N403AW	0092	0493	2 CFMI CFM56-3B2	61235	F8Y116		
☐ B-2906	Boeing 737-33A	25507 / 2373	N404AW	0092	0493	2 CFMI CFM56-3B2	61235	F8Y116		
☐ B-2907	Boeing 737-33A	25508 / 2414	N405AW	0093	0693	2 CFMI CFM56-3B2	61235	F8Y116		
☐ B-2947	Boeing 737-33A	25511 / 2599		0094	0494	2 CFMI CFM56-3B2	61235	F8Y116		
☐ B-2948	Boeing 737-3J6	27361 / 2631		0094	0794	2 CFMI CFM56-3B1	61235	F8Y116		
☐ B-2949	Boeing 737-3J6	27372 / 2650		0094	1094	2 CFMI CFM56-3B1	61235	F8Y116		
☐ B-2953	Boeing 737-3J6	27523 / 2710		0095	0495	2 CFMI CFM56-3B1	61235	F8Y116		
☐ B-2954	Boeing 737-3J6	27518 / 2768		0096	0196	2 CFMI CFM56-3B1	61235	F8Y116		
☐ B-3002	Lockheed L-382G (L-100-30) Hercules	69C-5025	N4276M*	0087	1092	4 AN 501-D22A	70307	Freighter		
☐ B-3004	Lockheed L-382G (L-100-30) Hercules	69C-5027	N4278M*	0087	1092	4 AN 501-D22A	70307	Freighter		
☐ B-2641	Boeing 737-89L	29876				2 CFMI CFM56-7B26	78245			oo-delivery 0499
☐ B-2642	Boeing 737-89L	29877				2 CFMI CFM56-7B26	78245			oo-delivery 0599
☐ B-2643	Boeing 737-89L	29878				2 CFMI CFM56-7B26	78245			oo-delivery 0699
☐ B-2645	Boeing 737-89L	29879				2 CFMI CFM56-7B26	78245			oo-delivery 1099
☐ B-	Boeing 737-89L					2 CFMI CFM56-7B26	78245			oo-delivery 0400
☐ B-2551	Boeing 767-2J6 (ER)	23307 / 126	N6065Y*	0085	0788	2 PW JT9D-7R4E4	159211	F10C13Y188	HL-FG	
☐ B-2552	Boeing 767-2J6 (ER)	23308 / 127	N60659*	0085	0788	2 PW JT9D-7R4E4	159211	F10C13Y188	HL-FM	
☐ B-2553	Boeing 767-2J6 (ER)	23744 / 155	N60659*	0087	0788	2 PW JT9D-7R4E4	159211	F10C13Y188		
☐ B-2554	Boeing 767-2J6 (ER)	23745 / 156	N6009F*	0087	0788	2 PW JT9D-7R4E4	159211	F10C13Y188		
☐ B-2555	Boeing 767-2J6 (ER)	24007 / 204		0088	0788	2 PW PW4052	159211	F10C13Y188	JM-DE	
☐ B-2556	Boeing 767-2J6 (ER)	24157 / 253	N6018N*	0089	0289	2 PW PW4052	159211	F10C13Y188	HM-AF	
☐ B-2557	Boeing 767-3J6	25875 / 429		0092	0592	2 PW PW4056	159211	F10C21Y189		
☐ B-2558	Boeing 767-3J6	25876 / 478		0093	0393	2 PW PW4056	159211	F10C21Y189		
☐ B-2559	Boeing 767-3J6	25877 / 530		0094	0394	2 PW PW4056	159211	F10C21Y189	BK-QR	
☐ B-2560	Boeing 767-3J6	25878 / 569		0095	0395	2 PW PW4056	159211	F10C21Y189		
☐ B-2059	Boeing 777-2J6	29153 / 168		1098	1098	2 PW PW4077	233600	C47Y296		
☐ B-2060	Boeing 777-2J6	29154 / 173		1098	1098	2 PW PW4077	233600	C47Y296		
☐ B-2061	Boeing 777-2J6	29155 / 179		1198	1198	2 PW PW4077	233600	C47Y296		
☐ B-2063	Boeing 777-2J6	29156				2 PW PW4077	233600	C47Y296		oo-delivery 0499
☐ B-2064	Boeing 777-2J6	29157				2 PW PW4077	233600	C47Y296		oo-delivery 0899
☐ B-2385	Airbus Industrie A340-313	192	F-WWJJ*	0097	1097	4 CFMI CFM56-5C4	275000	F12C30Y259	EF-AD	
☐ B-2386	Airbus Industrie A340-313	199	F-WWJN*	0097	1197	4 CFMI CFM56-5C4	275000	F12C30Y259	EF-AG	
☐ B-2387	Airbus Industrie A340-313	201	F-WWJQ*	0097	1197	4 CFMI CFM56-5C4	275000	F12C30Y259	EF-AH	

12 registration type of aircraft cn/fn ex/ex* mfd del powered by mtow kg configuration selcal name/fln/specialitites/remarks

☐	B-2438	Boeing 747SP-J6	21933 / 455	B-2444	0080	0788	4 PW JT9D-7J	315700	F18C27Y231	DF-CJ	
☐	B-2442	Boeing 747SP-J6	21932 / 433		0080	0788	4 PW JT9D-7J	315700	F18C27Y231	DF-CH	
☐	B-2452	Boeing 747SP-J6	21934 / 467	N1304E	0080	0788	4 PW JT9D-7J	315700	F18C27Y231	DF-EG	
☐	B-2454	Boeing 747SP-27	22302 / 473	N1301E	0080	0788	4 PW JT9D-7J	315700	F16C34Y226	FL-BE	
☐	B-2446	Boeing 747-2J6B (SF)	23071 / 591	N1781B*	0083	0788	4 PW JT9D-7R4G2	377842	Freighter	HK-BD	cvtd -2J6B (M)
☐	B-2448	Boeing 747-2J6B (SF)	23461 / 628	N60668*	0085	0788	4 PW JT9D-7R4G2	377842	Freighter	JL-AC	cvtd -2J6B (M)
☐	B-2450	Boeing 747-2J6B (M)	23746 / 670	N6018N*	0087	0788	4 PW JT9D-7R4G2	377842	F18C30Y222 / Plt	HL-JM	
☐	B-2462	Boeing 747-2J6F (SCD)	24960 / 814		0090	1090	4 PW JT9D-7R4G2	377842	Freighter	FP-GH	
☐	B-2443	Boeing 747-4J6	25881 / 957		0093	0293	4 PW PW4056	385554	F18C35Y347	BK-AP	
☐	B-2445	Boeing 747-4J6	25882 / 1021		0094	0294	4 PW PW4056	385554	F18C35Y347	BK-AR	
☐	B-2447	Boeing 747-4J6	25883 / 1054		0095	0295	4 PW PW4056	385554	F18C35Y347	BK-AS	
☐	B-2456	Boeing 747-4J6 (M)	24346 / 743		0089	1089	4 PW PW4056	385554	F18C35Y243 / Plt	HM-AE	
☐	B-2458	Boeing 747-4J6 (M)	24347 / 775		0090	0290	4 PW PW4056	385554	F18C35Y243 / Plt	JM-DH	
☐	B-2460	Boeing 747-4J6 (M)	24348 / 792		0090	0690	4 PW PW4056	385554	F18C35Y243 / Plt	JM-DK	
☐	B-2464	Boeing 747-4J6	25879 / 904		0092	0392	4 PW PW4056	385554	F18C35Y347		
☐	B-2466	Boeing 747-4J6	25880 / 926		0092	0892	4 PW PW4056	385554	F18C35Y347	BE-PR	
☐	B-2467	Boeing 747-4J6 (M)	28754 / 1119		0697	0697	4 PW PW4056	385554	F18C35Y243 / Plt	GS-DM	
☐	B-2468	Boeing 747-4J6 (M)	28755 / 1128		0997	0997	4 PW PW4056	385554	F18C35Y243 / Plt	GS-DP	
☐	B-2469	Boeing 747-4J6 (M)	28756 / 1175		0998	0998	4 PW PW4056	385554	F18C35Y243 / Plt		
☐	B-2470	Boeing 747-4J6 (M)	29070 / 1181		1098	1098	4 PW PW4056	385554	F18C35Y243 / Plt		
☐	B-2471	Boeing 747-4J6 (M)	29071				4 PW PW4056	385554	F18C35Y243 / Plt		oo-delivery 0599
☐	B-	Boeing 747-4J6					4 PW PW4056	385554	F18C35Y347		oo-delivery 0000

AIR GREAT WALL = CGW (Subsidiary of CAAC Flying College) **Ningbo**

長城航空公司

32 Nanliu Road, Taigucheng, 315040 Ningbo, (Zhejiang), People's Republic of China ☎ (574) 772 42 60 Tx: none Fax: (574) 772 41 81 SITA: n/a

F: 1992 ✱✱✱ 300 Head: Zhang Jia Biao ICAO: CHANGCHENG Net: n/a

☐	B-2506	Boeing 737-2T4 (A)	23272 / 1093		0085	0495	2 PW JT8D-17A	56472	Y128		
☐	B-2507	Boeing 737-2T4 (A)	23273 / 1097	N5375S*	0085	0495	2 PW JT8D-17A	56472	Y128		
☐	B-2508	Boeing 737-2T4 (A)	23274 / 1099	N6067U*	0085	0495	2 PW JT8D-17A	56472	Y128		

AIR GUIZHOU - Guizhou Airlines, Co. Ltd = CGH (Member of China Southern Group) **Guiyang**

貴州省航空公司 Guizhou Airlines

No. 110 Yanan Zhonglu, 550001 Guiyang, (Guizhou), People's Republic of China ☎ (851) 584 76 41 Tx: none Fax: (851) 584 76 72 SITA: n/a

F: 1991 ✱✱✱ 300 Head: Duan Yanchen ICAO: GUIZHOU Net: n/a

☐	B-3809	Harbin Yunshuji Y12 II	012B		0087	0991	2 PWC PT6A-27	5300	Y17		
☐	B-3448	Xian Yunshuji Y7-100C	09706		0090	0991	2 WJ 5A-1	21800	Y52		
☐	B-3449	Xian Yunshuji Y7-100C	08708		0090	0991	2 WJ 5A-1	21800	Y52		
☐	B-3458	Xian Yunshuji Y7-100C	03705		0085	0096	2 WJ 5A-1	21800	Y52		cvtd Y7
☐	B-3464	Xian Yunshuji Y7-100C	04706		0085	0991	2 WJ 5A-1	21800	Y52		cvtd Y7
☐	B-3465	Xian Yunshuji Y7-100C	05702		0086	0094	2 WJ 5A-1	21800	Y52		cvtd Y7
☐	B-3494	Xian Yunshuji Y7-100C	08705		0089	0096	2 WJ 5A-1	21800	Y52		
☐	B-2582	Boeing 737-31B	25895 / 2499		0093	0698	2 CFMI CFM56-3B1	61235	Y140		lsf CSN in China Southern-colors

CAAC Flying College (Division of CAAC - Civil Aviation Administration of China) **Guanghan, Changzhi, Luoyang & Xinjing**

CAAC

The Airport, 618307 Guanghan, (Sichuan), People's Republic of China ☎ (8233) 22 36 01 Tx: 610526 ghcfc cn Fax: (8233) 22 30 97 SITA: n/a

F: n/a ✱✱✱ n/a Head: Bian Shao Bin Net: n/a Trainer-aircraft below MTOW 5000kg: Bell 206B JetRanger III, Shijazhuang Yunshuji Y5, Socata TB20 & TB200. Non-commercial state org conducting flight training activities.

☐	B-3621	Piper PA-42-720 Cheyenne IIIA	42-5501051	N9240Q*	0090	0090	2 PWC PT6A-61	5080	Trainer		
☐	B-3622	Piper PA-42-720 Cheyenne IIIA	42-5501052	N92402*	0090	0090	2 PWC PT6A-61	5080	Trainer		
☐	B-3623	Piper PA-42-720 Cheyenne IIIA	42-5501054	N92409*	0090	0090	2 PWC PT6A-61	5080	Trainer		
☐	B-3625	Piper PA-42-720 Cheyenne IIIA	42-5501059	N9094U*	0092	0992	2 PWC PT6A-61	5080	Trainer		
☐	B-3626	Piper PA-42-720 Cheyenne IIIA	42-5501060	N9115*	0093	0094	2 PWC PT6A-61	5080	Trainer		
☐	B-3435	Xian Yunshuji Y7-100	10702		0091	0096	2 WJ 5A-1	21800	Trainer		
☐	B-3436	Xian Yunshuji Y7-100	10701		0091	0096	2 WJ 5A-1	21800	Trainer		
☐	B-3469	Xian Yunshuji Y7-100	05704		0087	0087	2 WJ 5A-1	21800	Trainer		opb Luoyang Flying College
☐	B-3470	Xian Yunshuji Y7-100	05705		0087	0087	2 WJ 5A-1	21800	Trainer		opb Luoyang Flying College
☐	B-3480	Xian Yunshuji Y7-100	06709		0088	0087	2 WJ 5A-1	21800	Trainer		opb Luoyang Flying College
☐	B-3487	Xian Yunshuji Y7-100	07706		0089	0096	2 WJ 5A-1	21800	Trainer		
☐	B-82700	Xian Yunshuji Y7-100C	12709		0095	0095	2 WJ 5A-1	21800	Trainer		opb Changzhi Flying College
☐	B-82701	Xian Yunshuji Y7-100C	12710		0095	0095	2 WJ 5A-1	21800	Trainer		opb Changzhi Flying College
☐	B-89050	Xian Yunshuji Y7-100C	13704		0096	0096	2 WJ 5A-1	21800	Trainer		opb Changzhi Flying College
☐	B-89060	Xian Yunshuji Y7-100C	13705		0096	0096	2 WJ 5A-1	21800	Trainer		opb Changzhi Flying College

CAAC Special Services Division (Division of CAAC - Civil Aviation Administration of China) **Beijing-Capital & -Xijiao**

No. 155 Dongsi Xidajie, 100710 Beijing, (Beijing), People's Republic of China ☎ (10) 64 01 22 33 Tx: 22101 caxt cn Fax: (10) 64 01 41 04 SITA: n/a

F: n/a ✱✱✱ n/a Head: n/a Net: n/a Non-commercial state organisation conducting calibration, surveyer & VIP flights for the Government.

☐	B-3551	Beech King Air B200	BB-1204	N6927C*	0086	0086	2 PWC PT6A-42	5670	Calibrator		
☐	B-3552	Beech King Air B200	BB-1205	N6927D*	0086	0086	2 PWC PT6A-42	5670	Calibrator		
☐	B-3553	Beech King Air B200	BB-1206	N6927G*	0086	0086	2 PWC PT6A-42	5670	Calibrator		
☐	B-3581	Beech King Air 350 (B300)	FL-111	N8139K*	0094	0995	2 PWC PT6A-60A	6804	Calibrator		
☐	B-3582	Beech King Air 350 (B300)	FL-113	N8291Y*	0094	1095	2 PWC PT6A-60A	6804	Calibrator		
☐	B-4106	Cessna 650 Citation VI	650-0220	N6830T*	0092	0893	2 GA TFE731-3B-100S	9979	Calibrator		
☐	B-4107	Cessna 650 Citation VI	650-0221	N1301A*	0092	1293	2 GA TFE731-3B-100S	9979	Calibrator		
☐	B-4005	Canadair 200ER JetLiner (CL-600-2B19)	7138	C-FZAT*	0097	0797	2 GE CF34-3B1	23133	VIP F25-32		
☐	B-4006	Canadair 200ER JetLiner (CL-600-2B19)	7149	C-FZIS*	0097	0797	2 GE CF34-3B1	23133	VIP F25-32		
☐	B-4007	Canadair 200ER JetLiner (CL-600-2B19)	7180	C-GATM*	0098	0298	2 GE CF34-3B1	23133	VIP F25-32		
☐	B-4010	Canadair 200ER JetLiner (CL-600-2B19)	7189	C-GATY*	0098	0498	2 GE CF34-3B1	23133	VIP F25-32		
☐	B-4011	Canadair 200ER JetLiner (CL-600-2B19)	7193	C-GBFR*	0098	0698	2 GE CF34-3B1	23133	VIP F25-32		
☐	B-4008	Boeing 737-3T0	23839 / 1507	N19357	0088	0688	2 CFMI CFM56-3B1	61235	VIP		
☐	B-4009	Boeing 737-3T0	23840 / 1516	N27358	0088	0688	2 CFMI CFM56-3B1	61235	VIP		
☐	B-4020	Boeing 737-34N	28081 / 2746		0095	0995	2 CFMI CFM56-3B1	61235	VIP		
☐	B-4021	Boeing 737-34N	28082 / 2747		0095	0995	2 CFMI CFM56-3B1	61235	VIP		
☐	B-4027	Tupolev 154M	943		0093	0693	3 SO D-30KU-154-II	100000	VIP		
☐	B-4029	Tupolev 154M	950		0093	0093	3 SO D-30KU-154-II	100000	VIP		

CHINA CARGO AIRLINES, Co. Ltd (Subsidary of China Eastern Airlines & China Ocean Shipping Group) **Shanghai**

No. 6 Road, Hongqiao Airport, 200335 Shanghai, (Shanghai), People's Republic of China ☎ (21)62686268ex37608 Tx: none Fax: (21) 62 68 65 05 SITA: n/a

F: 1998 ✱✱✱ n/a Head: Li Zhong Ming Net: n/a Operates cargo flights with aircraft leased from other companies when required. Expects to add 2 Boeing (Douglas) MD-11F (cvtd MD-11) from China Eastern early 2000.

CHINA EASTERN AIRLINES, Co. Ltd = MU / CES (Assoc.with CAAC-Civil Aviation Adm.of China/Member of China Eastern Group) **Shanghai/Nanchang/Hefei**

中國東方航 China Eastern

2550 Hongqiao Road, Hongqiao Int'l Airport, 200335 Shanghai, (Shanghai), People's Republic of China ☎ (21) 62 68 62 68 Tx: 33189 shamu cn Fax: (21) 62 68 60 39 SITA: n/a

F: 1988 ✱✱✱ 10700 Head: Li Zhongming IATA: 781 ICAO: CHINA EASTERN Net: http://www.chinaeasternair.com Fleet includes divisions at Anhui, Jinagxi, Jiangsu & Shandong.

☐	B-7701	Bell 212	30946	B-721	0079	0198	2 PWC PT6T-3 TwinPac	5080	Utility		
☐	B-7702	Bell 212	30948	B-722	0079	0198	2 PWC PT6T-3 TwinPac	5080	Utility		
☐	B-7703	Bell 212	30957	B-723	0079	0198	2 PWC PT6T-3 TwinPac	5080	Utility		
☐	B-7704	Bell 212	30951	B-724	0079	0198	2 PWC PT6T-3 TwinPac	5080	Utility		
☐	B-7705	Bell 212	30962	B-725	0079	0198	2 PWC PT6T-3 TwinPac	5080	Utility		
☐	B-7706	Bell 212	30956	B-726	0079	0198	2 PWC PT6T-3 TwinPac	5080	Utility		
☐	B-7707	Bell 212	30966	B-727	0079	0198	2 PWC PT6T-3 TwinPac	5080	Utility		
☐	B-7708	Bell 212	30960	B-728	0079	0198	2 PWC PT6T-3 TwinPac	5080	Utility		
☐	B-7709	Bell 212	31161	B-729	0080	0198	2 PWC PT6T-3 TwinPac	5080	Utility		
☐	B-8062	Shijiazhuang Yunshuji Y5	0621		0082	0688	1 HS 5	5500	Sprayer		
☐	B-8063	Shijiazhuang Yunshuji Y5	0622		0082	0688	1 HS 5	5500	Sprayer		
☐	B-8073	Nanchang Yunshuji Y5	382027		0062	0688	1 HS 5	5500	Sprayer		
☐	B-8075	Nanchang Yunshuji Y5	382037		0062	0688	1 HS 5	5500	Sprayer		
☐	B-8076	Nanchang Yunshuji Y5	834026		0062	0688	1 HS 5	5500	Sprayer		
☐	B-8080	Nanchang Yunshuji Y5	1032044		0064	0688	1 HS 5	5500	Sprayer		
☐	B-8081	Nanchang Yunshuji Y5	232006		0058	0688	1 HS 5	5500	Sprayer		
☐	B-8085	Nanchang Yunshuji Y5	932003		0063	0688	1 HS 5	5500	Sprayer		
☐	B-8092	Nanchang Yunshuji Y5	832018		0062	0688	1 HS 5	5500	Sprayer		
☐	B-8094	Nanchang Yunshuji Y5	1132008		0064	0688	1 HS 5	5500	Sprayer		
☐	B-8095	Nanchang Yunshuji Y5	1032011		0063	0688	1 HS 5	5500	Sprayer		
☐	B-8100	Nanchang Yunshuji Y5	292008		0058	0688	1 HS 5	5500	Sprayer		
☐	B-8102	Nanchang Yunshuji Y5	532023		0060	0688	1 HS 5	5500	Sprayer		
☐	B-8109	Shijiazhuang Yunshuji Y5	1009		0083	0688	1 HS 5	5500	Sprayer		
☐	B-8111	Shijiazhuang Yunshuji Y5	116405		0072	0688	1 HS 5	5500	Sprayer		
☐	B-8112	Shijiazhuang Yunshuji Y5	1018		0083	0688	1 HS 5	5500	Sprayer		
☐	B-8113	Shijiazhuang Yunshuji Y5	1019		0083	0688	1 HS 5	5500	Sprayer		
☐	B-8452	Nanchang Yunshuji Y5	1732006		0066	0688	1 HS 5	5500	Sprayer		

13 registration type of aircraft cn/fn ex/ex* mfd del powered by mtow kg configuration selcal name/fln/specialitites/remarks

☐ B-8453	Nanchang Yunshuji Y5	1732008		0066	0688	1 HS 5	5500	Sprayer		
☐ B-8454	Nanchang Yunshuji Y5	1832038		0068	0688	1 HS 5	5500	Sprayer		
☐ B-3453	Xian Yunshuji Y7-100C	02704		0084	0688	2 WJ 5A-1	21800	Y52		cvtd Y7
☐ B-3460	Xian Yunshuji Y7-100C	04702		0085	0688	2 WJ 5A-1	21800	Y52		cvtd Y7
☐ B-3473	Xian Yunshuji Y7-100C	05708		0087	0198	2 WJ 5A-1	21800	Y52		op in ex China General Aviation-colors
☐ B-3474	Xian Yunshuji Y7-100C	06701		0087	0198	2 WJ 5A-1	21800	Y52		op in ex China General Aviation-colors
☐ B-3481	Xian Yunshuji Y7-100C	06710		0088	0198	2 WJ 5A-1	21800	Y52		op in ex China General Aviation-colors
☐ B-3482	Xian Yunshuji Y7-100C	07701		0089	0089	2 WJ 5A-1	21800	Y52		
☐ B-3493	Xian Yunshuji Y7-100C	08704		0089	0089	2 WJ 5A-1	21800	Y52		
☐ B-2235	Fokker 100 (F28 Mk0100)	11409	PH-KXP*	0093	0293	2 RR Tay 650-15	44452	Y108		for TAM, 0099
☐ B-2236	Fokker 100 (F28 Mk0100)	11430	PH-LXB*	0093	0793	2 RR Tay 650-15	44452	Y108		for TAM, 0099
☐ B-2237	Fokker 100 (F28 Mk0100)	11421	PH-LXH*	0093	0793	2 RR Tay 650-15	44452	Y108		for TAM, 0099
☐ B-2238	Fokker 100 (F28 Mk0100)	11423	PH-KXZ*	0093	0893	2 RR Tay 650-15	44452	Y108		for TAM, 0099
☐ B-2239	Fokker 100 (F28 Mk0100)	11429	PH-LXA*	0093	0893	2 RR Tay 650-15	44452	Y108		for TAM, 0099
☐ B-2240	Fokker 100 (F28 Mk0100)	11431	PH-LXC*	0093	1093	2 RR Tay 650-15	44452	Y108		for TAM, 0099
☐ B-2751	Yakovlev 42D	4520423116650		0092	0198	3 LO D-36	56500	Y120		fn 0314/opin ex China General Avn-cs/FS
☐ B-2752	Yakovlev 42D	4520424116664		0092	0198	3 LO D-36	56500	Y120		fn 0414/std TYN in China General-cs/FS
☐ B-2753	Yakovlev 42D	4520424116677		0092	0198	3 LO D-36	56500	Y120		fn 0614/std TYN in China General-cs/FS
☐ B-2754	Yakovlev 42D	4520423116579		0091	0198	3 LO D-36	56500	Y120		fn 0613/opin ex China General Avn-cs/FS
☐ B-2756	Yakovlev 42D	4520424116669		0091	0198	3 LO D-36	56500	Y120		fn 0514/opin ex China General Avn-cs/FS
☐ B-2757	Yakovlev 42D	4520423403018		0094	0198	3 LO D-36	56500	Y120		op in ex China General Aviation-cs / FS
☐ B-2758	Yakovlev 42D	4520424404018		0094	0198	3 LO D-36	56500	Y120		op in ex China General Aviation-cs / FS
☐ B-2571	Boeing 737-39P	29410 / 3053		0098	0798	2 CFMI CFM56-3C1	61235	Y148		
☐ B-2572	Boeing 737-39P	29411 / 3071		0098	0998	2 CFMI CFM56-3C1	61235	Y148		
☐ B-2573	Boeing 737-39P	29412 / 3080	N1786B*	0098	1198	2 CFMI CFM56-3C1	61235	Y148		
☐ B-2977	Boeing 737-36N	28560 / 2888		0597	0198	2 CFMI CFM56-3B1	61235	Y148		lsf GECA
☐ B-2978	Boeing 737-36N	28561 / 2896		0697	0198	2 CFMI CFM56-3B1	61235	Y148		lsf GECA
☐ B-2979	Boeing 737-36N	28562 / 2908	N1786B*	0797	0198	2 CFMI CFM56-3B1	61235	Y148		lsf GECA
☐ B-2101	Boeing (Douglas) MD-82 (DC-9-82)	49140 / 1092	N1004S*	0082	0688	2 PW JT8D-217A	67812	F12Y135		
☐ B-2102	Boeing (Douglas) MD-82 (DC-9-82)	49141 / 1093	N10046*	0082	0688	2 PW JT8D-217A	67812	F12Y135		
☐ B-2107	Boeing (Douglas/SAIC) MD-82 (DC-9-82)	49501 / 1292		0087	0688	2 PW JT8D-217A	67812	F12Y135		SAIC No.2
☐ B-2109	Boeing (Douglas/SAIC) MD-82 (DC-9-82)	49503 / 134		0088	0788	2 PW JT8D-217A	67812	F12Y135		SAIC No.4
☐ B-2120	Boeing (Douglas/SAIC) MD-82 (DC-9-82)	49504 / 1363		0088	1188	2 PW JT8D-217A	67812	F12Y135		SAIC No.5
☐ B-2123	Boeing (Douglas/SAIC) MD-82 (DC-9-82)	49507 / 1425		0089	0589	2 PW JT8D-217A	67812	F12Y135		SAIC No.8
☐ B-2125	Boeing (Douglas/SAIC) MD-82 (DC-9-82)	49509 / 1482		0089	1189	2 PW JT8D-217A	67812	F12Y135		SAIC No.10
☐ B-2127	Boeing (Douglas/SAIC) MD-82 (DC-9-82)	49511 / 1537		0089	0490	2 PW JT8D-217A	67812	F12Y135		SAIC No.12
☐ B-2129	Boeing (Douglas/SAIC) MD-82 (DC-9-82)	49513 / 1568		0090	0490	2 PW JT8D-217A	67812	F12Y135		SAIC No.14
☐ B-2131	Boeing (Douglas/SAIC) MD-82 (DC-9-82)	49515 / 1609		0090	1090	2 PW JT8D-217A	67812	F12Y135		SAIC No.16
☐ B-2133	Boeing (Douglas/SAIC) MD-82 (DC-9-82)	49517 / 1633		0090	1090	2 PW JT8D-217A	67812	F12Y135		SAIC No.18
☐ B-2135	Boeing (Douglas/SAIC) MD-82 (DC-9-82)	49519 / 1658		0090	1290	2 PW JT8D-217A	67812	F12Y135		SAIC No.20
☐ B-2137	Boeing (Douglas/SAIC) MD-82 (DC-9-82)	49521 / 1690		0091	0491	2 PW JT8D-217A	67812	F12Y135		SAIC No.22
☐ B-2256	Boeing (Douglas) MD-90-30	53582 / 2198		0097	1097	2 IAE V2525-D5	70760	F12Y145		
☐ B-2257	Boeing (Douglas) MD-90-30	53583 / 2200		0097	1097	2 IAE V2525-D5	70760	F12Y145		
☐ B-2258	Boeing (Douglas) MD-90-30	53584 / 2203		1097	1297	2 IAE V2525-D5	70760	F12Y145		
☐ B-2262	Boeing (Douglas) MD-90-30	53585 / 2224		0098	0398	2 IAE V2525-D5	70760	F12Y145		
☐ B-2263	Boeing (Douglas) MD-90-30	53586 / 2233		0098	0698	2 IAE V2525-D5	70760	F12Y145		
☐ B-2265	Boeing (Douglas) MD-90-30	53587 / 2240		0098	0998	2 IAE V2525-D5	70760	F12Y145		
☐ B-2268	Boeing (Douglas) MD-90-30	53588 / 2248		0098	1298	2 IAE V2525-D5	70760	F12Y145		
☐ B-	Boeing (Douglas) MD-90-30	53589				2 IAE V2525-D5	70760	F12Y145		oo-delivery 0499
☐ B-	Boeing (Douglas) MD-90-30	53590				2 IAE V2525-D5	70760	F12Y145		oo-delivery 0699
☐ B-2201	Airbus Industrie A320-214	914	F-WWDV*	0098	1298	2 CFMI CFM56-5B4/P	73500	F8Y150		lsf GECA
☐ B-2202	Airbus Industrie A320-214	925	F-WWID*	0098	0199	2 CFMI CFM56-5B4/P	73500	F8Y150		lsf GECA
☐ B-2360	Airbus Industrie A320-214	772	F-WWDK*	0098	0298	2 CFMI CFM56-5B4/P	73500	F8Y150		lsf GECA
☐ B-2361	Airbus Industrie A320-214	799	F-WWDI*	0098	0498	2 CFMI CFM56-5B4/P	73500	F8Y150	BF-GP	lsf GECA
☐ B-2362	Airbus Industrie A320-214	828	F-WWIM*	0098	0698	2 CFMI CFM56-5B4/P	73500	F8Y150		lsf GECA
☐ B-2363	Airbus Industrie A320-214	883	F-WWDC*	0098	1098	2 CFMI CFM56-5B4/P	73500	F8Y150		lsf GECA
☐ B-	Airbus Industrie A320-214	1028				2 CFMI CFM56-5B4/P	73500	F8Y150		to be lsf GECA 0799
☐ B-	Airbus Industrie A320-214	1030				2 CFMI CFM56-5B4/P	73500	F8Y150		to be lsf GECA 0799
☐ B-	Airbus Industrie A320-214	1052				2 CFMI CFM56-5B4/P	73500	F8Y150		to be lsf GECA 0799
☐ B-	Airbus Industrie A320-214	1067				2 CFMI CFM56-5B4/P	73500	F8Y150		to be lsf GECA 0999
☐ B-2306	Airbus Industrie A300-605R (A300B4-605R)	521	F-WWAF*	0089	1189	2 GE CF6-80C2A5	170500	F24Y250	JL-CP	
☐ B-2307	Airbus Industrie A300-605R (A300B4-605R)	525	F-WWAJ*	0089	1289	2 GE CF6-80C2A5	170500	F24Y250	JL-DP	
☐ B-2308	Airbus Industrie A300-605R (A300B4-605R)	532	F-WWAH*	0089	1289	2 GE CF6-80C2A5	170500	F24Y250		
☐ B-2318	Airbus Industrie A300-605R (A300B4-605R)	707	F-WWAU*	0093	1093	2 GE CF6-80C2A5	170500	F24Y250		
☐ B-2319	Airbus Industrie A300-605R (A300B4-605R)	732	F-WWAT*	0094	0694	2 GE CF6-80C2A5	170500	F24Y250		
☐ B-2320	Airbus Industrie A300-605R (A300B4-605R)	709	N190PL	0093	0594	2 GE CF6-80C2A5	170500	F24Y250	DJ-ER	lsf POLA
☐ B-2321	Airbus Industrie A300-605R (A300B4-605R)	713	N191PL	0093	0594	2 GE CF6-80C2A5	170500	F24Y250	DJ-ES	lsf POLA
☐ B-2322	Airbus Industrie A300-605R (A300B4-605R)	715	N192PL	0093	0594	2 GE CF6-80C2A5	170500	F24Y250	DJ-FR	lsf POLA
☐ B-2325	Airbus Industrie A300-605R (A300B4-605R)	746	F-WWAA*	0095	0395	2 GE CF6-80C2A5	170500	F24Y250		
☐ B-2326	Airbus Industrie A300-605R (A300B4-605R)	754	F-WWAY*	0095	0795	2 GE CF6-80C2A5	170500	F24Y250		
☐ B-2380	Airbus Industrie A340-313	129	F-WWJQ*	0096	0596	4 CFMI CFM56-5C4	275000	C24Y251	GS-HJ	
☐ B-2381	Airbus Industrie A340-313	131	F-WWJO*	0096	0596	4 CFMI CFM56-5C4	275000	C24Y251	GS-HK	
☐ B-2382	Airbus Industrie A340-313	141	F-WWJC*	0096	0796	4 CFMI CFM56-5C4	275000	C24Y251	GS-HL	
☐ B-2383	Airbus Industrie A340-313	161	F-WWJQ*	0097	0397	4 CFMI CFM56-5C4	275000	C24Y251	EM-CF	
☐ B-2384	Airbus Industrie A340-313	182	F-WWJM*	0097	0697	4 CFMI CFM56-5C4	275000	C24Y251	FP-EK	
☐ B-2170	Boeing (Douglas) MD-11F	48461 / 475		0091	1091	3 PW PW4460	280320	Freighter	FG-CQ	
☐ B-2171	Boeing (Douglas) MD-11	48495 / 461		0091	0591	3 PW PW4460	280320	C46Y294	FG-DQ	
☐ B-2172	Boeing (Douglas) MD-11	48496 / 496		0092	0592	3 PW PW4460	280320	C46Y294	FG-EQ	
☐ B-2173	Boeing (Douglas) MD-11	48497 / 512		0092	1092	3 PW PW4460	280320	C46Y294	FG-HQ	to be cvtd to MD-11F -1299
☐ B-2174	Boeing (Douglas) MD-11	48498 / 522		0092	1292	3 PW PW4460	280320	C46Y294	FG-JQ	to be cvtd to MD-11F -1299
☐ B-2175	Boeing (Douglas) MD-11	48520 / 541	N9134D*	0093	1293	3 PW PW4460	280320	C46Y294	FG-KQ	

CHINA FLYING DRAGON AVIATION Company = CFA (China Feilong Airlines) (Subsidiary of Harbin Aircraft Manufacturing Co.) **Harbin-Ping Fang**

中國飛龍專業航空公司

PO Box 201-95, 150066 Harbin, (Heilongjiang), People's Republic of China ☎ (451) 650 25 41 Tx: none Fax: (451) 650 25 41 SITA: n/a

F: 1981 ⁂ 610 Head: Lin Zhaoren ICAO: FEILONG Net: n/a CHINA FEILONG AIRLINES is the company short name called in Chinese.

☐ B-7420	Eurocopter (Aerosp.) AS350B2 Ecureuil	2522	F-WYMH*	0091	0592	1 TU Arriel 1D1	2250	Utility		opf Ministry of Forestry
☐ B-7421	Eurocopter (Aerosp.) AS350B2 Ecureuil	2523	F-WYMG*	0091	0592	1 TU Arriel 1D1	2250	Utility		opf Ministry of Forestry
☐ B-7422	Eurocopter (Aerosp.) AS350B2 Ecureuil	2534	F-WYMB*	0091	0592	1 TU Arriel 1D1	2250	Utility		opf Ministry of Forestry
☐ B-7423	Eurocopter (Aerosp.) AS350B2 Ecureuil	2538	F-WYMF*	0091	0592	1 TU Arriel 1D1	2250	Utility		opf Ministry of Forestry
☐ B-7424	Eurocopter (Aerosp.) AS350B2 Ecureuil	2547	F-WYME*	0091	0592	1 TU Arriel 1D1	2250	Utility		opf Ministry of Forestry
☐ B-7425	Eurocopter (Aerosp.) AS350B2 Ecureuil	2554	F-WYMF*	0091	0592	1 TU Arriel 1D1	2250	Utility		opf Ministry of Forestry
☐ B-7427	Eurocopter (Aerosp.) AS350B2 Ecureuil	2566		0091	0592	1 TU Arriel 1D1	2250	Utility		opf Ministry of Forestry
☐ B-3201	Harbin Yunshuji Y11B	003		0090	0494	2 CO TSIO-550-B	3500	Sprayer / Frtr		
☐ B-3862	Harbin Yunshuji Y11	0407		0089	1089	2 HS 6D	3500	Sprayer / Frtr		
☐ B-3863	Harbin Yunshuji Y11	0408		0089	1089	2 HS 6D	3500	Sprayer / Frtr		
☐ B-3864	Harbin Yunshuji Y11	0409		0089	1189	2 HS 6D	3500	Sprayer / Frtr		
☐ B-3874	Harbin Yunshuji Y11	0102		0077	0085	2 HS 6D	3500	Sprayer / Frtr		
☐ B-3875	Harbin Yunshuji Y11	0105		0077	0085	2 HS 6D	3500	Sprayer / Frtr		
☐ B-3876	Harbin Yunshuji Y11	0106		0077	0085	2 HS 6D	3500	Sprayer / Frtr		
☐ B-3877	Harbin Yunshuji Y11	0107		0078	0085	2 HS 6D	3500	Sprayer / Frtr		
☐ B-3878	Harbin Yunshuji Y11	0110		0078	0085	2 HS 6D	3500	Sprayer / Frtr		
☐ B-3879	Harbin Yunshuji Y11	0201		0080	0085	2 HS 6D	3500	Sprayer / Frtr		
☐ B-3880	Harbin Yunshuji Y11	0202		0080	0085	2 HS 6D	3500	Sprayer / Frtr		
☐ B-3881	Harbin Yunshuji Y11	0203		0080	0085	2 HS 6D	3500	Sprayer / Frtr		
☐ B-3882	Harbin Yunshuji Y11	0204		0080	0480	2 HS 6D	3500	Sprayer / Frtr		
☐ B-3883	Harbin Yunshuji Y11	0205		0080	0085	2 HS 6D	3500	Sprayer / Frtr		
☐ B-3884	Harbin Yunshuji Y11	0210		0081	0085	2 HS 6D	3500	Sprayer / Frtr		
☐ B-7107	Eurocopter (Aerosp.) SA365N Dauphin 2	6027	B-734	0082	0082	2 TU Arriel 1C	4000	Utility		
☐ B-7109	Harbin Z-9A Haitun (Euro./Aerosp.SA365N1)	045		0091	0592	2 WZ 8 (TU Arriel 1C1)	4100	Utility		opf Ministry of Forestry
☐ B-7110	Harbin Z-9A Haitun (Euro./Aerosp.SA365N1)	047		0091	0592	2 WZ 8 (TU Arriel 1C1)	4100	Utility		opf Ministry of Forestry
☐ B-3801	Harbin Yunshuji Y12 II	0006		0086	0286	2 PWC PT6A-27	5300	Y17 / Freighter		
☐ B-3803	Harbin Yunshuji Y12 II	0003		0084	0185	2 PWC PT6A-27	5300	Surveyer		
☐ B-3804	Harbin Yunshuji Y12 II	0011		0085	0985	2 PWC PT6A-27	5300	Surveyer		tail sensor
☐ B-3805	Harbin Yunshuji Y12 II	0005		0086	1086	2 PWC PT6A-27	5300	Surveyer		
☐ B-3806	Harbin Yunshuji Y12 II	0008		0086	1086	2 PWC PT6A-27	5300	Y17 / Freighter		
☐ B-3807	Harbin Yunshuji Y12 II	0016		0087	0587	2 PWC PT6A-27	5300	CMS MaritimeSurv		opf CMS China Maritime Services
☐ B-3808	Harbin Yunshuji Y12 II	0017		0087	0787	2 PWC PT6A-27	5300	CMS MaritimeSurv		opf CMS China Maritime Services
☐ B-3819	Harbin Yunshuji Y12 II	0004		0084	0890	2 PWC PT6A-27	5300	Y17 / Freighter		
☐ B-3501	De Havilland DHC-6 Twin Otter 300	563	512	0078	0081	2 PWC PT6A-27	5670	Y19/Frtr/Survey		
☐ B-3502	De Havilland DHC-6 Twin Otter 300	565	514	0078	0081	2 PWC PT6A-27	5670	Y19/Frtr/Survey		

14 registration type of aircraft cn/fn ex/ex* mfd del powered by mtow kg configuration selcal name/fln/specialitites/remarks

☐ B-3503	De Havilland DHC-6 Twin Otter 300	602	516	0079	0081	2 PWC PT6A-27	5670	Y19/Frtr/Survey		
☐ B-3504	De Havilland DHC-6 Twin Otter 300	564	510	0078	0081	2 PWC PT6A-27	5670	Y19/Frtr/Survey		

CHINA NORTHERN AIRLINES = CJ / CBF (Assoc. with CAAC-Civil Aviation Administration of China)

Shenyang-Taoxian & Changchun

中國北方航空公司

Taoxian International Airport, 110043 Shenyang, (Liaoning), People's Republic of China ☎ (24) 88 29 44 32 Tx: 804136 cnaia cn Fax: (24) 88 29 40 37 SITA: n/a

F: 1990 ✝✝✝ 8200 Head: Jiang Lianying IATA: 782 ICAO: CHINA NORTHERN Net: n/a Fleet includes Dalian & Jilin division & joint-venture (with local goverments) companies:

Beiya Airlines (Sanya) & Swan Airlines (Harbin). Both joint-venture companies are reservation and code-sharing (no own operations) companies. All flights are in China Northern colors and operates under CJ flight numbers.

☐ B-3446	Xian Yunshuji Y7-100C	09703		0090	0690	2 WJ 5A-1	21800	Y52		
☐ B-3466	Xian Yunshuji Y7-100	04707		0087	0690	2 WJ 5A-1	21800	Y52		
☐ B-3467	Xian Yunshuji Y7-100	05701		0087	0690	2 WJ 5A-1	21800	Y52		
☐ B-3468	Xian Yunshuji Y7-100	05703		0087	0690	2 WJ 5A-1	21800	Y52		
☐ B-3477	Xian Yunshuji Y7-100C	06705		0087	0690	2 WJ 5A-1	21800	Y52		
☐ B-3478	Xian Yunshuji Y7-100	06707		0088	0690	2 WJ 5A-1	21800	Y52		
☐ B-3484	Xian Yunshuji Y7-100C	07703		0089	0690	2 WJ 5A-1	21800	Y52		
☐ B-3486	Xian Yunshuji Y7-100	07705		0088	0690	2 WJ 5A-1	21800	Y52		
☐ B-3488	Xian Yunshuji Y7-100	07707		0089	0690	2 WJ 5A-1	21800	Y52		
☐ B-3490	Xian Yunshuji Y7-100C	07709		0089	0690	2 WJ 5A-1	21800	Y52		
☐ B-3495	Xian Yunshuji Y7-100C	08706		0089	0690	2 WJ 5A-1	21800	Y52		
☐ B-2104	Boeing (Douglas) MD-82 (DC-9-82)	49425 / 1240	N1005T*	0085	0690	2 PW JT8D-217A	67812	F12Y133		
☐ B-2105	Boeing (Douglas) MD-82 (DC-9-82)	49428 / 1241	N1005U*	0085	0690	2 PW JT8D-217A	67812	F12Y133		
☐ B-2106	Boeing (Douglas/SAIC) MD-82 (DC-9-82)	49415 / 1260		0087	0690	2 PW JT8D-217A	67812	F12Y133		SAIC No.1
☐ B-2108	Boeing (Douglas/SAIC) MD-82 (DC-9-82)	49502 / 1300		0088	0690	2 PW JT8D-217A	67812	F12Y133		SAIC No.3
☐ B-2121	Boeing (Douglas/SAIC) MD-82 (DC-9-82)	49505 / 1381		0088	0690	2 PW JT8D-217A	67812	F12Y133		SAIC No.6
☐ B-2122	Boeing (Douglas/SAIC) MD-82 (DC-9-82)	49506 / 1400		0089	0690	2 PW JT8D-217A	67812	F12Y133		SAIC No.7
☐ B-2124	Boeing (Douglas/SAIC) MD-82 (DC-9-82)	49508 / 1449		0089	0690	2 PW JT8D-217A	67812	F12Y133		SAIC No.9
☐ B-2126	Boeing (Douglas/SAIC) MD-82 (DC-9-82)	49510 / 1514		0089	0690	2 PW JT8D-217A	67812	F12Y133		SAIC No.11
☐ B-2128	Boeing (Douglas/SAIC) MD-82 (DC-9-82)	49512 / 1548		0089	0690	2 PW JT8D-217A	67812	F12Y133		SAIC No.13
☐ B-2130	Boeing (Douglas/SAIC) MD-82 (DC-9-82)	49514 / 1589		0090	0690	2 PW JT8D-217A	67812	F12Y133		SAIC No.15
☐ B-2132	Boeing (Douglas/SAIC) MD-82 (DC-9-82)	49516 / 1622		0090	0990	2 PW JT8D-217A	67812	F12Y133		SAIC No.17
☐ B-2134	Boeing (Douglas/SAIC) MD-82 (DC-9-82)	49518 / 1647		0090	1290	2 PW JT8D-217A	67812	F12Y133		SAIC No.19
☐ B-2136	Boeing (Douglas/SAIC) MD-82 (DC-9-82)	49520 / 1671		0091	0391	2 PW JT8D-217A	67812	F12Y133		SAIC No.21
☐ B-2138	Boeing (Douglas/SAIC) MD-82 (DC-9-82)	49522 / 1702		0091	0791	2 PW JT8D-217A	67812	F12Y133		SAIC No.23
☐ B-2139	Boeing (Douglas/SAIC) MD-82 (DC-9-82)	49523 / 1724		0091	1091	2 PW JT8D-217A	67812	F12Y133		SAIC No.24
☐ B-2140	Boeing (Douglas/SAIC) MD-82 (DC-9-82)	49524 / 1746		0091	1091	2 PW JT8D-217A	67812	F12Y133		SAIC No.25
☐ B-2142	Boeing (Douglas/SAIC) MD-82 (DC-9-82)	49850 / 1798		0092	0292	2 PW JT8D-217A	67812	F12Y133		SAIC No.27
☐ B-2143	Boeing (Douglas/SAIC) MD-82 (DC-9-82)	49851 / 1807		0092	0392	2 PW JT8D-217A	67812	F12Y133		SAIC No.28
☐ B-2145	Boeing (Douglas/SAIC) MD-82 (DC-9-82)	49853 / 1981		0094	1094	2 PW JT8D-217A	67812	F12Y133		SAIC No.35
☐ B-2146	Boeing (Douglas) MD-82 (DC-9-82)	53162 / 2010	N831US	0092	0992	2 PW JT8D-217C	66678	F12Y133		
☐ B-2147	Boeing (Douglas) MD-82 (DC-9-82)	53163 / 2025	N832AU	0092	1092	2 PW JT8D-217C	66678	F12Y133		
☐ B-2148	Boeing (Douglas) MD-82 (DC-9-82)	53169 / 2063	N838AU	0093	0993	2 PW JT8D-217C	66678	F12Y133		
☐ B-2149	Boeing (Douglas) MD-82 (DC-9-82)	53170 / 2065	N839AU	0093	0993	2 PW JT8D-217C	66678	F12Y133		
☐ B-2150	Boeing (Douglas) MD-82 (DC-9-82)	53171 / 2067	N840AU	0093	1093	2 PW JT8D-217C	66678	F12Y133		
☐ B-2151	Boeing (Douglas/SAIC) MD-82 (DC-9-82)	49852 / 1959		0093	1293	2 PW JT8D-217A	67812	F12Y133		SAIC No.34
☐ B-2152	Boeing (Douglas) MD-82 (DC-9-82)	53164 / 2041	N833AU	0092	0595	2 PW JT8D-217C	66678	F12Y133		lsf POLA
☐ B-2250	Boeing (Douglas) MD-90-30	53523 / 2143		0096	0796	2 IAE V2525-D5	70760	F12Y145		
☐ B-2251	Boeing (Douglas) MD-90-30	53524 / 2146		0096	0896	2 IAE V2525-D5	70760	F12Y145		
☐ B-2252	Boeing (Douglas) MD-90-30	53525 / 2150		0096	0996	2 IAE V2525-D5	70760	F12Y145		
☐ B-2253	Boeing (Douglas) MD-90-30	53526 / 2170		0097	0297	2 IAE V2525-D5	70760	F12Y145		
☐ B-2254	Boeing (Douglas) MD-90-30	53527 / 2175		0097	0397	2 IAE V2525-D5	70760	F12Y145		
☐ B-2255	Boeing (Douglas) MD-90-30	53528 / 2177		0097	0497	2 IAE V2525-D5	70760	F12Y145		
☐ B-2259	Boeing (Douglas) MD-90-30	53529 / 2220		0098	0298	2 IAE V2525-D5	70760	F12Y145		
☐ B-2260	Boeing (Douglas) MD-90-30	53530 / 2222		0098	0398	2 IAE V2525-D5	70760	F12Y145		
☐ B-2261	Boeing (Douglas) MD-90-30	53531 / 2228		0098	0498	2 IAE V2525-D5	70760	F12Y145		
☐ B-2266	Boeing (Douglas) MD-90-30	53532 / 2253		0099	0299	2 IAE V2525-D5	70760	F12Y145		
☐ B-	Boeing (Douglas) MD-90-30	53533				2 IAE V2525-D5	70760	F12Y145		oo-delivery 0499
☐ B-2311	Airbus Industrie A300-622R (A300B4-622R)	688	F-WWAH*	0093	0593	2 PW PW4158	171700	F24Y250		lsf AWAS
☐ B-2312	Airbus Industrie A300-622R (A300B4-622R)	690	F-WWAP*	0093	0693	2 PW PW4158	171700	F24Y250		lsf AWAS
☐ B-2315	Airbus Industrie A300-622R (A300B4-622R)	733	F-WWAU*	0094	0794	2 PW PW4158	171700	F24Y250		
☐ B-2316	Airbus Industrie A300-622R (A300B4-622R)	734	F-WWAE*	0094	0794	2 PW PW4158	171700	F24Y250		
☐ B-2323	Airbus Industrie A300-622R (A300B4-622R)	739	F-WWAB*	0094	1094	2 PW PW4158	171700	F24Y250		
☐ B-2327	Airbus Industrie A300-622R (A300B4-622R)	750	HL7583	0095	0595	2 PW PW4158	171700	F24Y250		
☐ HL7580	Airbus Industrie A300-622R (A300B4-622R)	756	F-WWAB*	0095	1195	2 PW PW4158	171700	F24Y250		lst KAL
☐ HL7581	Airbus Industrie A300-622R (A300B4-622R)	762	F-WWAZ*	0095	0196	2 PW PW4158	171700	F24Y250		lst KAL

CHINA NORTHWEST AIRLINES - CNWA = WH / CNW (Associated with CAAC – Civil Aviation Administration of China)

Xian-Xiguan & -Xianyang / Lanzhou

中國西北航空公司
China Northwest Airlines

Xiguan Airport, Laodong Nanlu, 710082 Xian, (Shaanxi), People's Republic of China ☎ (29) 870 20 21 Tx: 700224 siaca cn Fax: (29) 870 20 27 SITA: n/a

F: 1989 ✝✝✝ 5600 Head: Nie Shengli IATA: 783 ICAO: CHINA NORTHWEST Net: n/a

☐ B-8210	Nanchang Yunshuji Y5	832022		0092	1289	1 HS 5	5500	Y12 / Sprayer		
☐ B-8215	Nanchang Yunshuji Y5	1032030		0064	1289	1 HS 5	5500	Y12 / Sprayer		
☐ B-8218	Nanchang Yunshuji Y5	832046		0062	1289	1 HS 5	5500	Y12 / Sprayer		
☐ B-8228	Shijiazhuang Yunshuji Y5	316409		0076	1289	1 HS 5	5500	Y12 / Sprayer		
☐ B-8239	Shijiazhuang Yunshuji Y5	4705514		0076	1289	1 HS 5	5500	Y12 / Sprayer		
☐ B-8241	Shijiazhuang Yunshuji Y5	4705506		0076	1289	1 HS 5	5500	Y12 / Sprayer		
☐ B-8242	Shijiazhuang Yunshuji Y5	5705513		0076	1289	1 HS 5	5500	Y12 / Sprayer		
☐ B-8245	Shijiazhuang Yunshuji Y5	0623		0082	1289	1 HS 5	5500	Y12 / Sprayer		
☐ B-8463	Nanchang Yunshuji Y5	1132036		0064	1289	1 HS 5	5500	Y12 / Sprayer		
☐ B-8464	Nanchang Yunshuji Y5	1232023		0065	1289	1 HS 5	5500	Y12 / Sprayer		
☐ B-8465	Shijiazhuang Yunshuji Y5	1332020		0065	1289	1 HS 5	5500	Y12 / Sprayer		
☐ B-8466	Nanchang Yunshuji Y5	1432032		0066	1289	1 HS 5	5500	Y12 / Sprayer		
☐ B-8467	Nanchang Yunshuji Y5	1532006		0066	1289	1 HS 5	5500	Y12 / Sprayer		
☐ B-2701	BAe 146-100	E1019	G-XIAN*	0086	1289	4 LY ALF502R-5	38102	Y82		
☐ B-2702	BAe 146-100	E1026	G-5-026*	0086	1289	4 LY ALF502R-5	38102	Y82		
☐ B-2703	BAe 146-100	E1032	G-5-032*	0086	1289	4 LY ALF502R-5	38102	Y82		
☐ B-2711	BAe 146-300	E3207	G-BUHV*	0092	1192	4 LY LF507-1H	44225	Y112		
☐ B-2712	BAe 146-300	E3212	G-6-212*	0092	1292	4 LY LF507-1H	44225	Y112		
☐ B-2715	BAe 146-300	E3214	G-6-214*	0092	1292	4 LY LF507-1H	44225	Y112		lst CNJ
☐ B-2717	BAe 146-300	E3216	G-6-216*	0093	0393	4 LY LF507-1H	44225	Y112	DH-QR	
☐ B-2718	BAe 146-300	E3222	G-6-222*	0093	0194	4 LY LF507-1H	44225	Y112		
☐ B-2719	BAe 146-300	E3218	G-6-218*	0093	0493	4 LY LF507-1H	44225	Y112		
☐ B-2720	BAe 146-300	E3219	G-6-219*	0093	0893	4 LY LF507-1H	44225	Y112		
☐ B-2356	Airbus Industrie A320-214	665	F-WWBB*	0097	1197	2 CFMI CFM56-5B4	73500	F8Y150		
☐ B-2357	Airbus Industrie A320-214	754	F-WWIY*	0097	1297	2 CFMI CFM56-5B4	73500	F8Y150		
☐ B-2358	Airbus Industrie A320-214	838	F-WWBB*	0098	0698	2 CFMI CFM56-5B4	73500	F8Y150		
☐ B-2359	Airbus Industrie A320-214	854	F-WWBK*	0098	0798	2 CFMI CFM56-5B4	73500	F8Y150		
☐ B-2372	Airbus Industrie A320-214	897	F-WWDK*	0098	1198	2 CFMI CFM56-5B4	73500	F8Y150		
☐ B-2375	Airbus Industrie A320-214	909	F-WWDS*	0098	1198	2 CFMI CFM56-5B4	73500	F8Y150		
☐ B-2378	Airbus Industrie A320-214	939	F-WWIQ*	0099	0299	2 CFMI CFM56-5B4	73500	F8Y150		
☐ B-	Airbus Industrie A320-214	967	F-WWBN*			2 CFMI CFM56-5B4	73500	F8Y150		oo-delivery 0499
☐ B-	Airbus Industrie A320-214	986				2 CFMI CFM56-5B4	73500	F8Y150		oo-delivery 0499
☐ B-	Airbus Industrie A320-214	984				2 CFMI CFM56-5B4	73500	F8Y150		oo-delivery 0499
☐ B-	Airbus Industrie A320-214	1041				2 CFMI CFM56-5B4	73500	F8Y150		oo-delivery 0899
☐ B-	Airbus Industrie A320-214					2 CFMI CFM56-5B4	73500	F8Y150		oo-delivery 0600
☐ B-	Airbus Industrie A320-214					2 CFMI CFM56-5B4	73500	F8Y150		oo-delivery 0800
☐ B-2608	Tupolev 154M	734		0086	1289	3 SO D-30KU-154-II	100000	Y160		
☐ B-2609	Tupolev 154M	735		0086	1289	3 SO D-30KU-154-II	100000	Y160		
☐ B-2619	Tupolev 154M	814		0089	1289	3 SO D-30KU-154-II	100000	Y160		
☐ B-2620	Tupolev 154M	815		0089	1289	3 SO D-30KU-154-II	100000	Y160		
☐ B-2623	Tupolev 154M	855		0090	0090	3 SO D-30KU-154-II	100000	Y160		
☐ B-2301	Airbus Industrie A310-222	311	F-WZEJ*	0084	0492	2 PW JT9D-7R4E1	138600	F18Y210		lsf Pratt & Whitney
☐ B-2302	Airbus Industrie A310-222	320	F-WZER*	0084	0492	2 PW JT9D-7R4E1	138600	F18Y210		lsf Pratt & Whitney
☐ B-2303	Airbus Industrie A310-222 (winglets)	419	LZ-JXB	0086	1093	2 PW JT9D-7R4E1	138600	F18Y210	JL-AF	lsf Pratt & Whitney
☐ B-2309	Airbus Industrie A300-605R (A300B4-605R)	584	N165PL	0091	1092	2 GE CF6-80C2A5	171700	F24Y250		lsf POLA
☐ B-2310	Airbus Industrie A300-605R (A300B4-605R)	603	N166PL	0091	1092	2 GE CF6-80C2A5	171700	F24Y250	PQ-BG	lsf POLA
☐ B-2317	Airbus Industrie A300-605R (A300B4-605R)	741	F-WWAY*	0094	1194	2 GE CF6-80C2A5	171700	F24Y244		
☐ B-2324	Airbus Industrie A300-605R (A300B4-605R)	725	F-WWAR*	0094	1094	2 GE CF6-80C2A5	171700	F24Y244		
☐ B-2330	Airbus Industrie A300-605R (A300B4-605R)	763	F-WWAH*	0096	0296	2 GE CF6-80C2A5	171700	F24Y244		

15 registration type of aircraft cn/fn ex/ex* mfd del powered by mtow kg configuration selcal name/fln/specialitites/remarks

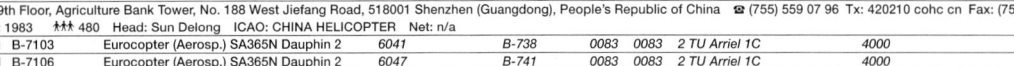

CHINA OCEAN HELICOPTER Corp. - COHC = CHC — Nantou Heliport & Zhanjiang Heliport

中國海洋直升飛機專業公司 (廣東深圳) CHINA OCEAN HELICOPTER CORPORATION

19th Floor, Agriculture Bank Tower, No. 188 West Jiefang Road, 518001 Shenzhen (Guangdong), People's Republic of China ☎ (755) 559 07 96 Tx: 420210 cohc cn Fax: (755) 559 07 57 SITA: n/a

F: 1983 ✈ 480 Head: Sun Delong ICAO: CHINA HELICOPTER Net: n/a

☐ B-7103	Eurocopter (Aerosp.) SA365N Dauphin 2	6041	B-738	0083	0083	2 TU Arriel 1C	4000			
☐ B-7106	Eurocopter (Aerosp.) SA365N Dauphin 2	6047	B-741	0083	0083	2 TU Arriel 1C	4000			
☐ B-7951	Eurocopter (Aerosp.) AS332L Super Puma	2165	F-WYMI*	0085	0085	2 TU Makila 1A	8600			

CHINA POSTAL AIRLINES, Ltd = CYZ (Subsidiary of The Ministry of Posts & Telecommunications) — Tianjin

Binhai International Airfield, 300030 Tianjin, People's Republic of China ☎ (22) 24 95 74 01 Tx: none Fax: (86) 74 95 74 00 SITA: n/a

F: 1994 ✈ 330 Head: Shi Shuming ICAO: CHINA POSTAIR Net: n/a

☐ B-3101	Yunshuji Y8F-100	1001		0096	0297	4 WJ 6A	61000	Freighter 16t		
☐ B-3102	Yunshuji Y8F-100	1002		0096	0297	4 WJ 6A	61000	Freighter 16t		
☐ B-3103	Yunshuji Y8F-100	1003		0097	0097	4 WJ 6A	61000	Freighter 16t		

CHINA SOUTHERN AIRLINES, Co. Ltd = CZ / CSN (Assoc.with CAAC-Civil Aviation Adm.of China/Member of China Southern Group) — Guangzhou, Wuhan & Zhuhai Heliport

中國南方航空(集團)公司 China Southern

Baiyun Int'l Airport, 510405 Guangzhou, (Guangdong), People's Republic of China ☎ (20) 86 68 18 18 Tx: 44218 canca cn Fax: (20) 86 66 54 36 SITA: n/a

F: 1991 ✈ 12800 Head: Yu Yanen IATA: 784 ICAO: CHINA SOUTHERN Net: http://www.chinasouthernair.com Aircraft below MTOW 1361kg: Mooney MSE.

Fleet includes divisions at Guilin, Henan, Hunan, Shenzhen, Shantou, Xiamen & Zhuhai.

☐ B-2541	Boeing 737-5Y0	24696 / 1960		0091	0291	2 CFMI CFM56-3B1	60555	Y133		lsf Citicorp
☐ B-2542	Boeing 737-5Y0	24897 / 2003		0091	0291	2 CFMI CFM56-3B1	60555	Y133		lsf GECA
☐ B-2543	Boeing 737-5Y0	24898 / 2079		0091	0791	2 CFMI CFM56-3B1	60555	Y133		lsf BBAM
☐ B-2544	Boeing 737-5Y0	24899 / 2093		0091	0891	2 CFMI CFM56-3B1	60555	Y133		lsf GECA
☐ B-2545	Boeing 737-5Y0	24900 / 2095		0091	0891	2 CFMI CFM56-3B1	60555	Y133		lsf GECA
☐ B-2546	Boeing 737-5Y0	25175 / 2150		0091	1091	2 CFMI CFM56-3B1	60555	Y133		lsf GECA
☐ B-2547	Boeing 737-5Y0	25176 / 2155		0091	1191	2 CFMI CFM56-3B1	60555	Y133		lsf GECA
☐ B-2548	Boeing 737-5Y0	25182 / 2211		0092	0292	2 CFMI CFM56-3B1	60555	Y133		lsf GECA
☐ B-2549	Boeing 737-5Y0	25183 / 2218		0092	0292	2 CFMI CFM56-3B1	60555	Y133		lsf GECA
☐ B-2550	Boeing 737-5Y0	25188 / 2238		0092	0392	2 CFMI CFM56-3B1	60555	Y133		lsf GECA
☐ B-2912	Boeing 737-5Y0	26100 / 2538	N35108*	0093	0394	2 CFMI CFM56-3B1	60555	Y133		lsf GECA
☐ B-2915	Boeing 737-5Y0	26101 / 2544		0093	0394	2 CFMI CFM56-3B1	60555	Y133		lsf GECA
☐ B-2525	Boeing 737-3Y0	24918 / 2087		0091	0791	2 CFMI CFM56-3B1	61235	Y140		lsf GECA
☐ B-2526	Boeing 737-3Y0	25172 / 2089		0091	0791	2 CFMI CFM56-3B1	61235	Y140		lsf GECA
☐ B-2527	Boeing 737-3Y0	25173 / 2097		0091	0891	2 CFMI CFM56-3B1	61235	Y140		lsf GECA
☐ B-2528	Boeing 737-3Y0	25174 / 2168		0091	1191	2 CFMI CFM56-3B1	61235	Y140		lsf GECA
☐ B-2582	Boeing 737-31B	25895 / 2499		0093	0893	2 CFMI CFM56-3B1	61235	Y140		lst CGH in China Southern-colors
☐ B-2583	Boeing 737-31B	25897 / 2554		0093	1293	2 CFMI CFM56-3B1	61235	Y140		
☐ B-2596	Boeing 737-31B	27151 / 2437		0093	0393	2 CFMI CFM56-3B1	61235	Y140		
☐ B-2909	Boeing 737-3Y0	26082 / 2456		0093	0493	2 CFMI CFM56-3B1	61235	Y140		lsf GECA
☐ B-2910	Boeing 737-3Y0	26083 / 2459		0093	0493	2 CFMI CFM56-3B1	61235	Y140		lsf GECA
☐ B-2911	Boeing 737-3Y0	26084 / 2460		0093	0493	2 CFMI CFM56-3B1	61235	Y140		lsf GECA
☐ B-2920	Boeing 737-3Q8	27271 / 2523		0093	0993	2 CFMI CFM56-3B1	61235	Y140		
☐ B-2921	Boeing 737-3Q8	27286 / 2528		0093	0993	2 CFMI CFM56-3B1	61235	Y140		
☐ B-2922	Boeing 737-31B	27272 / 2555		0093	1293	2 CFMI CFM56-3B1	61235	Y140		
☐ B-2923	Boeing 737-31B	27275 / 2565		0093	0194	2 CFMI CFM56-3B1	61235	Y140		
☐ B-2924	Boeing 737-31B	27287 / 2575		0094	0294	2 CFMI CFM56-3B1	61235	Y140		
☐ B-2926	Boeing 737-31B	27289 / 2593		0094	0394	2 CFMI CFM56-3B1	61235	Y140		
☐ B-2927	Boeing 737-31B	27290 / 2595		0094	0394	2 CFMI CFM56-3B1	61235	Y140		
☐ B-2929	Boeing 737-31B	27343 / 2619		0094	0694	2 CFMI CFM56-3B1	61235	Y140		
☐ B-2941	Boeing 737-31B	27344 / 2622		0094	0694	2 CFMI CFM56-3B1	61235	Y140		
☐ B-2952	Boeing 737-31B	27519 / 2678		0094	1294	2 CFMI CFM56-3B1	61235	Y140		
☐ B-2959	Boeing 737-31B	27520 / 2775		0096	0396	2 CFMI CFM56-3B1	61235	Y140		
☐ N999CZ	Boeing 737-3Y9	25604 / 2405	N1784B*	0092	0193	2 CFMI CFM56-3C1	61235	Y140		lsf ITOH
☐ B-2343	Airbus Industrie A320-232	696	F-WWII*	0097	0697	2 IAE V2527-A5	73500	F8Y150		
☐ B-2345	Airbus Industrie A320-232	698	F-WWBT*	0097	0697	2 IAE V2527-A5	73500	F8Y150		
☐ B-2346	Airbus Industrie A320-232	704	F-WWDY*	0097	0797	2 IAE V2527-A5	73500	F8Y150		
☐ B-2347	Airbus Industrie A320-232	705	F-WWIL*	0097	0797	2 IAE V2527-A5	73500	F8Y150		
☐ B-2348	Airbus Industrie A320-232	709	F-WWIP*	0097	0897	2 IAE V2527-A5	73500	F8Y150		
☐ B-2349	Airbus Industrie A320-232	710	F-WWIT*	0097	0897	2 IAE V2527-A5	73500	F8Y150		
☐ B-2350	Airbus Industrie A320-232	712	F-WWDI*	0097	0997	2 IAE V2527-A5	73500	F8Y150		
☐ B-2351	Airbus Industrie A320-232	718	F-WWBI*	0097	0997	2 IAE V2527-A5	73500	F8Y150		
☐ B-2352	Airbus Industrie A320-232	720	F-WWBU*	0097	1097	2 IAE V2527-A5	73500	F8Y150		
☐ B-2353	Airbus Industrie A320-232	722	F-WWBM*	0097	1097	2 IAE V2527-A5	73500	F8Y150		
☐ B-2365	Airbus Industrie A320-232	849	F-WWBI*	0098	0898	2 IAE V2527-A5	73500	F8Y150		
☐ B-2366	Airbus Industrie A320-232	859	F-WWBO*	0098	0898	2 IAE V2527-A5	73500	F8Y150		
☐ B-2367	Airbus Industrie A320-232	881	F-WWDB*	0098	1098	2 IAE V2527-A5	73500	F8Y150		
☐ B-2368	Airbus Industrie A320-232	895	F-WWDJ*	0098	1098	2 IAE V2527-A5	73500	F8Y150		
☐ B-2369	Airbus Industrie A320-232	900	F-WWDM*	0098	1198	2 IAE V2527-A5	73500	F8Y150		
☐ B-2391	Airbus Industrie A320-232	950	F-WWIZ*	0099	0299	2 IAE V2527-A5	73500	F8Y150		
☐ B-	Airbus Industrie A320-232	966	F-WWBK*			2 IAE V2527-A5	73500	F8Y150		oo-delivery 0499
☐ B-	Airbus Industrie A320-232	1035				2 IAE V2527-A5	73500	F8Y150		oo-delivery 0799
☐ B-	Airbus Industrie A320-232	1039				2 IAE V2527-A5	73500	F8Y150		oo-delivery 0799
☐ B-	Airbus Industrie A320-232	1057				2 IAE V2527-A5	73500	F8Y150		oo-delivery 0899
☐ B-2801	Boeing 757-21B	24014 / 144	N1792B*	0087	0291	2 RR RB211-535E4	108862	F8Y192		
☐ B-2802	Boeing 757-21B	24015 / 148	N5573B*	0087	0291	2 RR RB211-535E4	108862	F8Y192		
☐ B-2803	Boeing 757-21B	24016 / 150	N5573K*	0087	0291	2 RR RB211-535E4	108862	F8Y192		
☐ B-2804	Boeing 757-21B	24330 / 200		0088	0291	2 RR RB211-535E4	108862	F8Y192		lsf TOMB
☐ B-2805	Boeing 757-21B	24331 / 203		0088	0291	2 RR RB211-535E4	108862	F8Y192		lsf TOMB
☐ B-2806	Boeing 757-21B	24401 / 232	N6067B*	0089	0291	2 RR RB211-535E4	108862	F8Y192		
☐ B-2807	Boeing 757-21B	24402 / 233	N6069D*	0089	0291	2 RR RB211-535E4	108862	F8Y192		
☐ B-2811	Boeing 757-21B	24714 / 262		0090	0291	2 RR RB211-535E4	108862	F8Y192		
☐ B-2815	Boeing 757-21B	24774 / 288		0090	0291	2 RR RB211-535E4	108862	F8Y192		
☐ B-2816	Boeing 757-21B	25083 / 359		0091	0491	2 RR RB211-535E4	108862	F8Y192		
☐ B-2817	Boeing 757-21B	25258 / 389		0091	0891	2 RR RB211-535E4	108862	F8Y192		
☐ B-2818	Boeing 757-21B	25259 / 392		0091	0991	2 RR RB211-535E4	108862	F8Y192		
☐ B-2822	Boeing 757-21B	25884 / 461		0092	0692	2 RR RB211-535E4	108862	F8Y192		
☐ B-2823	Boeing 757-21B	25888 / 575		0093	0993	2 RR RB211-535E4	108862	F8Y192		
☐ B-2824	Boeing 757-21B	25889 / 583		0093	1193	2 RR RB211-535E4	108862	F8Y192		
☐ B-2825	Boeing 757-21B	25890 / 585		0093	1193	2 RR RB211-535E4	108862	F8Y192		
☐ B-2835	Boeing 757-236	25598 / 445	N5573P*	0092	0693	2 RR RB211-535E4	108862	F8Y192		
☐ B-2838	Boeing 757-2Z0	27260 / 613		0094	0594	2 RR RB211-535E4	108862	F8Y192		
☐ B-2051	Boeing 777-21B	27357 / 20		0095	1295	2 GE GE90-85B	233600	C24Y356		
☐ B-2052	Boeing 777-21B	27358 / 24	N5017V*	0096	0296	2 GE GE90-85B	233600	C24Y356		
☐ B-2053	Boeing 777-21B	27359 / 46		0096	1196	2 GE GE90-85B	233600	C24Y356		
☐ B-2054	Boeing 777-21B	27360 / 48		0096	1296	2 GE GE90-85B	233600	C24Y356		
☐ B-2055	Boeing 777-21B (ER)	27524 / 55		0097	0397	2 GE GE90-92B	286897		FL-ES	
☐ B-2056	Boeing 777-21B (ER)	27525 / 66		0097	0497	2 GE GE90-92B	286897	F18C67Y207		
☐ B-2057	Boeing 777-21B (ER)	27604 / 106	N5022E*	0097	0198	2 GE GE90-92B	286897	F18C67Y207		
☐ B-2058	Boeing 777-21B (ER)	27605 / 110	N5028Y*	0097	0198	2 GE GE90-92B	286897	F18C67Y207	GM-AJ	
☐ B-	Boeing 777-21B (ER)					2 GE GE90-92B	286897			to be lsf ILFC 0100
☐ B-	Boeing 777-21B (ER)					2 GE GE90-92B	286897			to be lsf ILFC 0700
☐ B-	Boeing 777-21B (ER)					2 GE GE90-92B	286897			to be lsf ILFC 0900
☐ N688CZ	Boeing 777-21B (ER)	27606 / 121	B-2062	0098	0298	2 GE GE90-92B	286897	F18C67Y207	BJ-RS	lsf ILFC

CHINA SOUTHWEST AIRLINES = SZ / CXN (Associated with CAAC – Civil Aviation Administration of China) — Chengdu-Shuangliu & Chongqing-Jiangbei

中國西南航空公司 China Southwest

Shuangliu Airport, 610202 Chengdu, (Sichuan), People's Republic of China ☎ (28) 570 33 61 Tx: 600049 cswa cn Fax: (28) 570 43 73 SITA: n/a

F: 1987 ✈ 8500 Head: Wang Rucen IATA: 785 ICAO: CHINA SOUTHWEST Net: http://www.cswa.com

☐ B-3811	Harbin Yunshuji Y12 II	0012		0087	1087	2 PWC PT6A-27	5300	Y17 / Freighter		
☐ B-3812	Harbin Yunshuji Y12 II	0024		0087	0388	2 PWC PT6A-27	5300	Y17 / Sprayer		
☐ B-3813	Harbin Yunshuji Y12 II	0025		0087	0388	2 PWC PT6A-27	5300	Y17 / Sprayer		
☐ B-3814	Harbin Yunshuji Y12 II	0026		0087	0388	2 PWC PT6A-27	5300	Y17 / Sprayer		
☐ B-2519	Boeing 737-3Z0	23448 / 1168	N5573P*	0085	1087	2 CFMI CFM56-3B1	61235	Y140		
☐ B-2520	Boeing 737-3Z0	23449 / 1184	N1789B*	0086	1087	2 CFMI CFM56-3B1	61235	Y140		
☐ B-2521	Boeing 737-3Z0	23450 / 1196	N1790B*	0086	1087	2 CFMI CFM56-3B1	61235	Y140		
☐ B-2522	Boeing 737-3Z0	23451 / 1240	N5573K*	0086	1087	2 CFMI CFM56-3B1	61235	Y140		
☐ B-2530	Boeing 737-3Z0	27046 / 2252		0092	0492	2 CFMI CFM56-3B1	61235	Y140		
☐ B-2533	Boeing 737-3Z0	27138 / 2436		0093	0393	2 CFMI CFM56-3B1	61235	Y140		
☐ B-2534	Boeing 737-3Y0	26070 / 2349		0092	0992	2 CFMI CFM56-3B1	61235	Y140		lsf GECA
☐ B-2537	Boeing 737-3Z0	25089 / 2027		0091	0491	2 CFMI CFM56-3B1	61235	Y140		

registration	type of aircraft	cn/fn	ex/ex*	mfd	del	powered by	mtow kg	configuration	selcal	name/fln/specialitites/remarks
☐ B-2586	Boeing 737-3Z0	27047 / 2357		0092	0992	2 CFMI CFM56-3B1	61235	Y140		
☐ B-2590	Boeing 737-3Z0	27126 / 2370		0092	0992	2 CFMI CFM56-3B1	61235	Y140		
☐ B-2595	Boeing 737-3Y0	26072 / 2369		0092	1092	2 CFMI CFM56-3B1	61235	Y140		lsf GECA
☐ B-2597	Boeing 737-3Z0	27176 / 2495		0093	0693	2 CFMI CFM56-3B1	61235	Y140		
☐ B-2599	Boeing 737-3Z0	25896 / 2558		0093	1293	2 CFMI CFM56-3B1	61235	Y140		
☐ B-2901	Boeing 737-3Q8	26284 / 2418	N571LF	0093	0293	2 CFMI CFM56-3B2	61235	Y140		lsf ILFC
☐ B-2902	Boeing 737-3Q8	24988 / 2466	N481LF	0093	0593	2 CFMI CFM56-3B2	61235	Y140		lsf ILFC
☐ B-2903	Boeing 737-3Q8	26292 / 2519		0093	0993	2 CFMI CFM56-3B2	61235	Y140		lsf ILFC
☐ B-2904	Boeing 737-3Q8	26288 / 2480	N471LF	0093	0693	2 CFMI CFM56-3B2	61235	Y140		lsf ILFC
☐ B-2950	Boeing 737-3Z0	27374 / 2647		0094	0994	2 CFMI CFM56-3B1	61235	Y140		
☐ B-2951	Boeing 737-3Z0	27373 / 2658		0094	1194	2 CFMI CFM56-3B1	61235	Y140		
☐ B-2957	Boeing 737-3Z0	27521 / 2738		0095	0795	2 CFMI CFM56-3B1	61235	Y140		
☐ B-	Boeing 737-8Z0					2 CFMI CFM56-7B26	78245			oo-delivery 1099
☐ B-	Boeing 737-8Z0					2 CFMI CFM56-7B26	78245			oo-delivery 1199
☐ B-	Boeing 737-8Z0					2 CFMI CFM56-7B26	78245			oo-delivery 1299
☐ B-2615	Tupolev 154M	783		0088	0088	3 SO D-30KU-154-II	100000	Y160		
☐ B-2616	Tupolev 154M	790		0088	0088	3 SO D-30KU-154-II	100000	Y160		
☐ B-2617	Tupolev 154M	791		0088	0088	3 SO D-30KU-154-II	100000	Y160		
☐ B-2618	Tupolev 154M	797		0089	0089	3 SO D-30KU-154-II	100000	Y160		
☐ B-2820	Boeing 757-2Z0	25885 / 476		0092	0892	2 RR RB211-535E4	108862	F8Y192		
☐ B-2821	Boeing 757-2Z0	25886 / 480		0092	0892	2 RR RB211-535E4	108862	F8Y192		
☐ B-2826	Boeing 757-2Y0	26155 / 495		0092	1092	2 RR RB211-535E4	108862	F8Y192		lsf GECA
☐ B-2827	Boeing 757-2Y0	26156 / 503		0092	1192	2 RR RB211-535E4	108862	F8Y192		lsf GECA
☐ B-2831	Boeing 757-2Y0	26153 / 482		0092	0892	2 RR RB211-535E4	108862	F8Y192		lsf GECA
☐ B-2832	Boeing 757-2Z0	25887 / 554		0093	0693	2 RR RB211-535E4	108862	F8Y192		
☐ B-2836	Boeing 757-2Z0	27258 / 595		0094	0294	2 RR RB211-535E4	108862	F8Y192		
☐ B-2837	Boeing 757-2Z0	27259 / 609		0094	0894	2 RR RB211-535E4	108862	F8Y192		
☐ B-2839	Boeing 757-2Z0	27269 / 615		0094	0894	2 RR RB211-535E4	108862	F8Y192		
☐ B-2840	Boeing 757-2Z0	27270 / 622		0094	0894	2 RR RB211-535E4	108862	F8Y192		
☐ B-2841	Boeing 757-2Z0	27367 / 624		0094	0894	2 RR RB211-535E4	108862	F8Y192		
☐ B-2844	Boeing 757-2Z0	27511 / 669		0095	0595	2 RR RB211-535E4	108862	F8Y192		
☐ B-2845	Boeing 757-2Z0	27512 / 674		0095	0695	2 RR RB211-535E4	108862	F8Y192		
☐ B-2855	Boeing 757-2Z0	29792 / 822		0998	0998	2 RR RB211-535E4	108862	F8Y192		
☐ B-2856	Boeing 757-2Z0	29793 / 833		1198	1198	2 RR RB211-535E4	108862	F8Y192		
☐ B-2388	Airbus Industrie A340-313	242	F-WWJD*	0098	1298	4 CFMI CFM56-5C4	275000			
☐ B-2389	Airbus Industrie A340-313	243	F-WWJE*	0098	1198	4 CFMI CFM56-5C4	275000			
☐ B-	Airbus Industrie A340-313	264				4 CFMI CFM56-5C4	275000			oo-delivery 0499

CHINA UNITED AIRLINES = CUA (Commercial div. of Chinese Air Force) **Beijing-Nanyuan, -Fo Shan Air Base, -Xijiao & Wuhan-CUA**

中國聯合航空公司 China United Airlines

No. 14 Xisanhuan Nanlu, 100073 Beijing, (Beijing), People's Republic of China ☎ (10) 63 40 25 90 Tx: 210404 cua cn Fax: (10) 63 26 72 85 SITA: n/a
F: 1986 ⁂ 960 Head: Lan Dingshou ICAO: LIANHANG Net: n/a

registration	type of aircraft	cn/fn	ex/ex*	mfd	del	powered by	mtow kg	configuration	selcal	name/fln/specialitites/remarks
☐ B-4061	Antonov 24RV				1286	2 IV AI-24VT	21800	Y40		
☐ B-4062	Antonov 24RV				1286	2 IV AI-24VT	21800	Y40		
☐ B-4063	Antonov 24RV				1286	2 IV AI-24VT	21800	Y40		
☐ B-4064	Antonov 24RV				1286	2 IV AI-24VT	21800	Y40		
☐ B-4065	Antonov 24RV				1286	2 IV AI-24VT	21800	Y40		
☐ B-4018	Boeing 737-33A	25502 / 2310		0092	0692	2 CFMI CFM56-3B1	61235	Y140		
☐ B-4019	Boeing 737-33A	25503 / 2313		0092	0692	2 CFMI CFM56-3B1	61235	Y140		
☐ B-4001	Tupolev 154M	711		0085	1286	3 SO D-30KU-154-II	100000	Y160		std NAY
☐ B-4003	Tupolev 154M	713		0085	1286	3 SO D-30KU-154-II	100000	Y160		std NAY
☐ B-4004	Tupolev 154M	714		0085	1286	3 SO D-30KU-154-II	100000	Y160		std NAY
☐ B-4014	Tupolev 154M	847		0090	0090	3 SO D-30KU-154-II	100000	Y160		
☐ B-4015	Tupolev 154M	856		0090	0090	3 SO D-30KU-154-II	100000	Y160		
☐ B-4016	Tupolev 154M	872		0091	0091	3 SO D-30KU-154-II	100000	Y160		
☐ B-4022	Tupolev 154M	765	OK-SCA	0087	0992	3 SO D-30KU-154-II	100000	Y160		
☐ B-4023	Tupolev 154M	770	OK-TCB	0088	0992	3 SO D-30KU-154-II	100000	Y160		
☐ B-4024	Tupolev 154M	789	OK-TCC	1188	0992	3 SO D-30KU-154-II	100000	Y160		
☐ B-4050	Tupolev 154M		B-	0086	1286	3 SO D-30KU-154-II	100000	Y160		
☐ B-4051	Tupolev 154M		B-	0086	1286	3 SO D-30KU-154-II	100000	Y160		
☐ B-4052	Tupolev 154M		B-	0086	1286	3 SO D-30KU-154-II	100000	Y160		
☐ B-4138	Tupolev 154M	712	B-4002	0085	1286	3 SO D-30KU-154-II	100000	Y160		std NAY
☐ B-4030	Ilyushin 76MD	1013407233		0091	0091	4 SO D-30KP	190000	Freighter		
☐ B-4031	Ilyushin 76MD	1013408254		0091	0091	4 SO D-30KP	190000	Freighter		
☐ B-4032	Ilyushin 76MD	1013409289		0091	0091	4 SO D-30KP	190000	Freighter		
☐ B-4033	Ilyushin 76MD	1033416512		0093	0093	4 SO D-30KP	190000	Freighter		
☐ B-4034	Ilyushin 76MD	1033416524		0093	0093	4 SO D-30KP	190000	Freighter		
☐ B-4035	Ilyushin 76MD	1033416529		0093	0093	4 SO D-30KP	190000	Freighter		
☐ B-4036	Ilyushin 76MD	1033417550		0093	0093	4 SO D-30KP	190000	Freighter		
☐ B-4037	Ilyushin 76MD	1033417557		0094	0094	4 SO D-30KP	190000	Freighter		
☐ B-4038	Ilyushin 76MD	1033417567		0094	0094	4 SO D-30KP	190000	Freighter		
☐ B-4039	Ilyushin 76MD	1043418576		0094	0094	4 SO D-30KP	190000	Freighter		
☐ B-4040	Ilyushin 76MD	1053419656		0095	0095	4 SO D-30KP	190000	Freighter		
☐ B-4041	Ilyushin 76MD	1053420663		0095	0095	4 SO D-30KP	190000	Freighter		
☐ B-4042	Ilyushin 76MD	1063418587		0096	0096	4 SO D-30KP	190000	Freighter		
☐ B-4043	Ilyushin 76MD	1063420671		0096	0096	4 SO D-30KP	190000	Freighter		

CHINA XINHUA AIRLINES = CXH **Beijing-Capital & Tianjin**

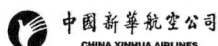

中國新華航空公司 CHINA XINHUA AIRLINES

No. 1, South Jingsong Road, Chaoyang District, 100021 Beijing, People's Republic of China ☎ (10) 67 74 01 18 Tx: none Fax: (10) 67 74 01 26 SITA: n/a
F: 1992 ⁂ 700 Head: Jiang Boyue ICAO: XINHUA Net: n/a

registration	type of aircraft	cn/fn	ex/ex*	mfd	del	powered by	mtow kg	configuration	selcal	name/fln/specialitites/remarks
☐ B-2908	Boeing 737-341	26854 / 2303		0092	0493	2 CFMI CFM56-3B2	61235	Y138		
☐ B-2934	Boeing 737-39K	27274 / 2559		0093	1293	2 CFMI CFM56-3B1	61235	Y144		
☐ B-2942	Boeing 737-332	25997 / 2506	N304DE	0093	1193	2 CFMI CFM56-3B1	61235	Y144		
☐ B-2943	Boeing 737-332	25998 / 2510	N305DE	0093	1193	2 CFMI CFM56-3B1	61235	Y144		
☐ B-2945	Boeing 737-39K	27362 / 2639		0094	0894	2 CFMI CFM56-3B1	61235	Y138		
☐ B-2982	Boeing 737-36Q	28657 / 2859		0097	0397	2 CFMI CFM56-3C1	61235	Y138		lsf BOUL
☐ B-2987	Boeing 737-46Q	28663 / 2922		0897	0897	2 CFMI CFM56-3C1	68040			lsf BOUL
☐ B-2989	Boeing 737-46Q	28758 / 2939		0097	1097	2 CFMI CFM56-3C1	68040			lsf BOUL
☐ B-2993	Boeing 737-46Q	28759 / 2981		0097	0198	2 CFMI CFM56-3C1	68040			lsf BOUL

CHINA XINJIANG AIRLINES = XO / CXJ (Associated with CAAC – Civil Aviation Administration of China) **Urumqi-Diwobao & Changzhou**

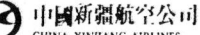

中国新疆航空公司 CHINA XINJIANG AIRLINES

Diwobao Airport, 830016 Urumqi, (Xinjiang Uygur Autonomous Region), People's Republic of China ☎ (991) 380 17 03 Tx: 79067 urcxt cn Fax: (991) 371 10 84 SITA: n/a
F: 1985 ⁂ 6000 Head: Zhang Ruifu IATA: 651 ICAO: XINJIANG Net: n/a

registration	type of aircraft	cn/fn	ex/ex*	mfd	del	powered by	mtow kg	configuration	selcal	name/fln/specialitites/remarks
☐ B-3022	ATR 72-500 (72-212A)	521	F-WWED*	0097	0897	2 PWC PW127F	22500	Y70		
☐ B-3023	ATR 72-500 (72-212A)	531	F-WWLK*	0097	1197	2 PWC PW127F	22500	Y70		
☐ B-3025	ATR 72-500 (72-212A)	547	F-WWLO*	0098	0398	2 PWC PW127F	22500	Y70		
☐ B-3026	ATR 72-500 (72-212A)	552	F-WWLP*	0098	0598	2 PWC PW127F	22500	Y70		
☐ B-3027	ATR 72-500 (72-212A)	555	F-WWLL*	0098	0698	2 PWC PW127F	22500	Y70		
☐ B-2930	Boeing 737-31L	27273 / 2556		0093	1293	2 CFMI CFM56-3B1	61235	Y140		
☐ B-2931	Boeing 737-31L	27276 / 2567		0093	0194	2 CFMI CFM56-3B1	61235	Y140		
☐ B-2939	Boeing 737-31L	27345 / 2625		0094	0794	2 CFMI CFM56-3B1	61235	Y140		lst CSZ
☐ B-2940	Boeing 737-31L	27346 / 2636		0094	0794	2 CFMI CFM56-3B1	61235	Y140		lst CSZ
☐ B-	Boeing 737-78S					2 CFMI CFM56-7B24	63276			oo-delivery 0301
☐ B-	Boeing 737-78S					2 CFMI CFM56-7B24	63276			oo-delivery 0401
☐ B-	Boeing 737-78S					2 CFMI CFM56-7B24	63276			oo-delivery 0501
☐ B-2603	Tupolev 154M	718		0085	0085	3 SO D-30KU-154-II	100000	Y160		
☐ B-2606	Tupolev 154M	728		0086	0086	3 SO D-30KU-154-II	100000	Y160		
☐ B-2607	Tupolev 154M	729		0086	0086	3 SO D-30KU-154-II	100000	Y160		
☐ B-2611	Tupolev 154M	726		0086	0086	3 SO D-30KU-154-II	100000	Y160		
☐ B-2621	Tupolev 154M	823		0089	1289	3 SO D-30KU-154-II	100000	Y160		
☐ B-2630	Tupolev 154M	954	RA-85772	0093	0497	3 SO D-30KU-154-II	100000	Y164		
☐ RA-85716	Tupolev 154M	892	CCCP-85716	0091	0096	3 SO D-30KU-154-II	100000	Y166		lsf VOG
☐ RA-85739	Tupolev 154M	925	CCCP-85739	0092	0096	3 SO D-30KU-154-II	100000	Y164		lsf VOG
☐ B-2851	Boeing 757-28S	29215 / 797		0098	0498	2 RR RB211-535E4	113398			
☐ B-2852	Boeing 757-28A	28833 / 782	N711LF	0097	1297	2 RR RB211-535E4	113398			lsf ILFC
☐ B-2853	Boeing 757-28S	29216 / 811		0098	0798	2 RR RB211-535E4	113398			
☐ B-2854	Boeing 757-28S	29217				2 RR RB211-535E4	113398			oo-delivery 0499
☐ B-2016	Ilyushin 86	51483210097		0093	0093	4 KU NK-86	215000	Y350		
☐ B-2018	Ilyushin 86	51483210099		0093	0093	4 KU NK-86	215000	Y350		
☐ B-2019	Ilyushin 86	51483210100		0093	0093	4 KU NK-86	215000	Y350		

CHINA YUNNAN AIRLINES = 3Q / CYH (Associated with CAAC – Civil Aviation Administation of China) **Kunming**

Wujiabao Airport, 650200 Kunming, (Yunnan), People's Republic of China ☎ (871) 711 61 14 Tx: none Fax: (871) 717 59 77 SITA: n/a
F: 1992 ⁂ 4100 Head: Xue Xiaoming IATA: 592 ICAO: YUNNAN Net: n/a

☐ B-2517	Boeing 737-3W0	23396 / 1166	N5573K*	0085	0792	2 CFMI CFM56-3B1	58967	Y140		
☐ B-2518	Boeing 737-3W0	23397 / 1193	N1791B*	0086	0792	2 CFMI CFM56-3B1	58967	Y140		
☐ B-2538	Boeing 737-3W0	25090 / 2040		0091	0792	2 CFMI CFM56-3B1	58967	Y140		
☐ B-2539	Boeing 737-3Y0	26068 / 2306		0092	0792	2 CFMI CFM56-3C1	61235	Y148		lsf GPAG
☐ B-2589	Boeing 737-3W0	27127 / 2377		0092	1192	2 CFMI CFM56-3C1	58967	Y140		
☐ B-2594	Boeing 737-341	26853 / 2275		0092	0892	2 CFMI CFM56-3C1	58967	Y144		
☐ B-2955	Boeing 737-33A	27453 / 2687		0095	0295	2 CFMI CFM56-3C1	61235	Y148		lsf AWAS
☐ B-2956	Boeing 737-33A	27907 / 2690		0095	0295	2 CFMI CFM56-3C1	61235	Y148		lsf AWAS
☐ B-2958	Boeing 737-3W0	27522 / 2727		0095	0695	2 CFMI CFM56-3B1	61235	Y148		
☐ B-2966	Boeing 737-33A	27462 / 2765		0096	0196	2 CFMI CFM56-3C1	61235	Y148		lsf AWAS
☐ B-2981	Boeing 737-3W0	28972 / 2919		0897	0897	2 CFMI CFM56-3C1	61235	Y148		
☐ B-2983	Boeing 737-3W0	28973 / 2941		1097	1097	2 CFMI CFM56-3C1	61235	Y148		
☐ B-2985	Boeing 737-3W0	29068 / 2945		0097	1197	2 CFMI CFM56-3C1	61235	Y148		
☐ B-2986	Boeing 737-3W0	29069 / 2951		0097	1297	2 CFMI CFM56-3C1	61235	Y148		
☐ B-2639	Boeing 737-7W0	29912 / 140	N1787B*	0098	1298	2 CFMI CFM56-7B24	63276			
☐ B-2640	Boeing 737-7W0	29913 / 148		0098	1298	2 CFMI CFM56-7B24	63276			
☐ B-	Boeing 737-7W0					2 CFMI CFM56-7B24	63276			oo-delivery 1200
☐ B-	Boeing 737-7W0					2 CFMI CFM56-7B24	63276			oo-delivery 0201
☐ B-2568	Boeing 767-3W0 (ER)	28148 / 620		0096	0796	2 RR RB211-524H	181436	FY263		
☐ B-2569	Boeing 767-3W0 (ER)	28149 / 627		0096	0996	2 RR RB211-524H	181436	FY263		
☐ B-5001	Boeing 767-3W0 (ER)	28264 / 644		0097	0197	2 RR RB211-524H	181436	FY263		

CNAC-ZHEJIANG AIRLINES = F6 / CAG (Subsidiary of China National Aviation Corp./formerly Zhejiang Airlines) **Hangzhou**

Jianqiao Airport, 310021 Hangzhou, (Zhejiang), People's Republic of China ☎ (571) 640 08 88 Tx: 351006 cnezh cn Fax: (571) 640 07 77 SITA: n/a
F: 1986 ⁂ 200 Head: Luo Qiang IATA: 619 ICAO: CHINA NATIONAL Net: n/a

☐ B-3351	De Havilland DHC-8-301 Dash 8	116	C-GDNG*	0089	0789	2 PWC PW123	18643	Y54		
☐ B-3352	De Havilland DHC-8-301 Dash 8	194	C-GFCF*	0090	0390	2 PWC PW123	18643	Y54		
☐ B-3353	De Havilland DHC-8-301 Dash 8	108	N108CL	0088	0792	2 PWC PW123	18643	Y54		
☐ B-2354	Airbus Industrie A320-214	707	F-WWIN*	0097	0897	2 CFMI CFM56-5B4	73500	F8Y150		lsf GECA
☐ B-2355	Airbus Industrie A320-214	724	F-WWBN*	0097	1097	2 CFMI CFM56-5B4	73500	F8Y150		lsf GECA
☐ B-2376	Airbus Industrie A320-214	876	F-WWIF*	0098	1098	2 CFMI CFM56-5B4	73500	F8Y150		
☐ B-2377	Airbus Industrie A320-214	921	F-WWDY*	0098	1298	2 CFMI CFM56-5B4	73500	F8Y150		
☐ B-	Airbus Industrie A320-214	1054				2 CFMI CFM56-5B4	73500	F8Y150		oo-delivery 0899
☐ B-	Airbus Industrie A320-214					2 CFMI CFM56-5B4	73500	F8Y150		oo-delivery 1099
☐ B-	Airbus Industrie A320-214					2 CFMI CFM56-5B4	73500	F8Y150		oo-delivery 1199
☐ B-	Airbus Industrie A320-214					2 CFMI CFM56-5B4	73500	F8Y150		oo-delivery 1299

DEERJET, Co. Ltd **Beijing-Capital**

Capital International Airport, 570206 Beijing, (Beijing), People's Republic of China ☎ (10) 65 03 83 00 Tx: none Fax: (10) 65 06 82 21 SITA: n/a
F: 1998 ⁂ n/a Head: Tu Zhizheng Net: http://www.hphs.com

☐ B-3989	Beech Beechjet 400A	RK-203	N2359W*	0098	1098	2 PWC JT15D-5	7303	Executive		
☐ B-3981	Learjet 60	60-053	N5053Y*	0096	0198	2 PWC PW305	10319	Executive		

FUJIAN AIRLINES = IV / CFJ (Subsidiary of Xiamen Airlines) **Fuzhou**

Tiedao Bldg, Wuyi Central Road (5.1) Zhong Lu, 350005 Fuzhou, (Fujian), People's Republic of China ☎ (591) 801 35 50 Tx: none Fax: (591) 367 43 04 SITA: n/a
F: 1993 ⁂ 500 Head: Yu Kaizhi IATA: 791 ICAO: FUJIAN Net: n/a Beside aircraft listed, also uses 2 Boeing 737-500, leased from XIAMEN AIRLINES, when required.

☐ B-3447	Xian Yunshuji Y7-100C	09702		0090	0096	2 WJ 5A-1	21800	Y52		
☐ B-3476	Xian Yunshuji Y7-100C	06704		0087	0096	2 WJ 5A-1	21800	Y52		
☐ B-3715	Xian Yunshuji Y7-100C	08707	6071	0089	0893	2 WJ 5A-1	21800	Y52		
☐ B-3716	Xian Yunshuji Y7-100C	09707	6081	0091	0893	2 WJ 5A-1	21800	Y52		

GUANGDONG PROVINCE GENERAL AVIATION (Subsidiary of China Southern Airlines / Member of China Southern Group) **Guangzhou & Zhuhai**

c/o China Southern Airlines, Baiyun Int'l Airport, 510405 Guangzhou (Guangdong), People's Republic of China ☎ (20) 86 68 18 18 Tx: 44218 canca cn Fax: (20) 86 66 54 36 SITA: n/a
F: 1998 ⁂ n/a Head: Yu Yanen Net: n/a Aircraft below MTOW 1361kg: Mooney MSE

☐ B-3610	Cessna 208 Caravan I	20800244	N1286A*	0096	0098	1 PWC PT6A-114	3629	Utility		
☐ B-7101	Eurocopter (Aerosp.) SA365N Dauphin 2	6012	B-730	0082	0098	2 TU Arriel 1C	4000	Utility		
☐ B-7102	Eurocopter (Aerosp.) SA365N Dauphin 2	6013	B-731	0082	0098	2 TU Arriel 1C	4000	Utility		
☐ B-7303	Sikorsky S-76A	760289		0084	0098	2 AN 250-C30	4672	Utility		
☐ B-7304	Sikorsky S-76A	760293		0084	0098	2 AN 250-C30	4672	Utility		
☐ B-8009	Nanchang Yunshuji Y5	732025		0061	0098	1 HS 5	5500	Utility		
☐ B-8011	Nanchang Yunshuji Y5	932033		0063	0098	1 HS 5	5500	Utility		
☐ B-8012	Nanchang Yunshuji Y5	1032017		0063	0098	1 HS 5	5500	Utility		
☐ B-8014	Nanchang Yunshuji Y5	1132001		0064	0098	1 HS 5	5500	Utility		
☐ B-8015	Nanchang Yunshuji Y5	1132003		0064	0098	1 HS 5	5500	Utility		
☐ B-8017	Nanchang Yunshuji Y5	532011		0060	0098	1 HS 5	5500	Utility		
☐ B-8145	Nanchang Yunshuji Y5	932004		0063	0098	1 HS 5	5500	Utility		
☐ B-8148	Nanchang Yunshuji Y5	1032042		0064	0098	1 HS 5	5500	Utility		
☐ B-8171	Nanchang Yunshuji Y5	1032047		0064	0098	1 HS 5	5500	Utility		
☐ B-8172	Nanchang Yunshuji Y5	1032018		0063	0098	1 HS 5	5500	Utility		
☐ B-8176	Nanchang Yunshuji Y5	732034		0062	0098	1 HS 5	5500	Utility		
☐ B-8177	Shijiazhuang Yunshuji Y5	016402		0072	0098	1 HS 5	5500	Utility		
☐ B-8178	Shijiazhuang Yunshuji Y5	116401		0072	0098	1 HS 5	5500	Utility		
☐ B-8179	Shijiazhuang Yunshuji Y5	1011		0083	0098	1 HS 5	5500	Utility		
☐ B-8180	Shijiazhuang Yunshuji Y5	1010		0083	0098	1 HS 5	5500	Utility		
☐ B-8181	Shijiazhuang Yunshuji Y5	316402		0076	0098	1 HS 5	5500	Utility		
☐ B-8182	Shijiazhuang Yunshuji Y5	0618		0082	0098	1 HS 5	5500	Utility		
☐ B-8183	Shijiazhuang Yunshuji Y5	0620		0082	0098	1 HS 5	5500	Utility		
☐ B-8449	Nanchang Yunshuji Y5	1832035		0068	0098	1 HS 5	5500	Utility		
☐ B-8450	Nanchang Yunshuji Y5	1732037		0068	0098	1 HS 5	5500	Utility		
☐ B-8451	Nanchang Yunshuji Y5	1732005		0066	0098	1 HS 5	5500	Utility		
☐ B-8787	Shijiazhuang Yunshuji Y5B			0097	0098	1 HS 5	5500	Utility		
☐ B-8788	Shijiazhuang Yunshuji Y5B			0097	0098	1 HS 5	5500	Utility		

HAINAN AIRLINES, Co. Ltd = H4 / CHH **Haikou & Sanya**

Haihang Development Bldg, 29 Haixiu Dadao, 570206 Haikou, (Hainan), People's Republic of China ☎ (898) 679 88 29 Tx: none Fax: (898) 679 89 76 SITA: n/a
F: 1993 ⁂ 1600 Head: Chen Feng ICAO: HAINAN Net: http://www.hphs.com

☐ B-3950	Fairchild (Swearingen) SA227DC Metro 23	DC-864B	N3028U*	0094	0994	2 GA TPE331-12U-701G	7484	Y19		
☐ B-3951	Fairchild (Swearingen) SA227DC Metro 23	DC-866B	N3029F*	0094	1094	2 GA TPE331-12U-701G	7484	Y19		
☐ B-3952	Fairchild (Swearingen) SA227DC Metro 23	DC-868B	N30296*	0097	0897	2 GA TPE331-12U-701G	7484	Y19		
☐ B-3953	Fairchild (Swearingen) SA227DC Metro 23	DC-882B	N3004X*	0097	0897	2 GA TPE331-12U-701G	7484	Y19		
☐ B-3955	Fairchild (Swearingen) SA227DC Metro 23	DC-888B	N3007H*	0097	1097	2 GA TPE331-12U-701G	7484	Y19		
☐ B-3956	Fairchild (Swearingen) SA227DC Metro 23	DC-891B	N3018T*	0097	1297	2 GA TPE331-12U-701G	7484	Y19		
☐ B-3957	Fairchild (Swearingen) SA227DC Metro 23	DC-889B	N3007R*	0097	1097	2 GA TPE331-12U-701G	7484	Y19		
☐ B-3958	Fairchild (Swearingen) SA227DC Metro 23	DC-892B	N3031Z*	0097	1297	2 GA TPE331-12U-701G	7484	Y19		
☐ B-3959	Fairchild (Swearingen) SA227DC Metro 23	DC-890B	N30135*	0097	1097	2 GA TPE331-12U-701G	7484	Y19		
☐ B-2578	Boeing 737-33A	25603 / 2333	N401AW	0092	0493	2 CFMI CFM56-3B2	61235	F8Y118		
☐ B-2579	Boeing 737-33A	25505 / 2342	N402AW	0092	0493	2 CFMI CFM56-3B2	61235	F8Y118		
☐ B-2937	Boeing 737-3Q8	26295 / 2557		0093	1293	2 CFMI CFM56-3B2	61235	F8Y118		lsf ILFC
☐ B-2938	Boeing 737-3Q8	26296 / 2581		0094	0294	2 CFMI CFM56-3B2	61235	F8Y118		lsf ILFC
☐ B-2963	Boeing 737-3Q8	26325 / 2772		0096	0296	2 CFMI CFM56-3B2	61235	F8Y118		lsf ILFC
☐ B-2501	Boeing 737-44P	29914 / 3067	N1786B*	0098	0998	2 CFMI CFM56-3C1	68030			
☐ B-2576	Boeing 737-44P	29915				2 CFMI CFM56-3C1	68030			oo-delivery 0699
☐ B-2960	Boeing 737-4Q8	24332 / 1866	N191LF	0090	0795	2 CFMI CFM56-3C1	68030			lsf ILFC
☐ B-2965	Boeing 737-4Q8	26334 / 2782		0096	0496	2 CFMI CFM56-3C1	68030			lsf ILFC
☐ B-2967	Boeing 737-4Q8	26335 / 2793		0096	0596	2 CFMI CFM56-3C1	68030			lsf ILFC
☐ B-2970	Boeing 737-4Q8	26337 / 2811		0096	0896	2 CFMI CFM56-3C1	68030			lsf ILFC
☐ B-2990	Boeing 737-48E	25766 / 2543	HL7231	0094	0398	2 CFMI CFM56-3C1	64637			lsf SUNR
☐ B-2636	Boeing 737-86N	28574 / 67	N574GE	0098	0898	2 CFMI CFM56-7B26	78245			lsf GECA
☐ B-2637	Boeing 737-86N	28576 / 103	N1786B*	0998	1098	2 CFMI CFM56-7B26	78245			lsf GECA
☐ B-2638	Boeing 737-8Q8	28220 / 212	N361LF	0299	0299	2 CFMI CFM56-7B26	78245			lsf ILFC
☐ B-2646	Boeing 737-8Q8	28056				2 CFMI CFM56-7B26	78245			to be lsf ILFC 0200
☐ B-	Boeing 737-84P					2 CFMI CFM56-7B26	78245			oo-delivery 0899

18 registration type of aircraft cn/fn ex/ex* mfd del powered by mtow kg configuration selcal name/fln/specialitites/remarks

JIANGNAN UNIVERSAL AVIATION, Corp. (Subs.of Changzhou Aircraft Factory/Assoc.with Chinese Civil Aircraft Developing, Corp.) — Changzhou-West Suburbs 常州江南通用航空公司

23 Airport Road, West Suburbs Airport, 213016 Changzhou, (Jiangsu), People's Republic of China ☎ (519) 60 46 40 Tx: none Fax: (519) 60 20 37 SITA: n/a
F: 1989 ♣♣♣ 50 Head: Gu Qun Net: n/a

registration	type of aircraft	cn/fn	ex/ex*	mfd	del	powered by	mtow kg	configuration	selcal	name/fln/specialitites/remarks
☐ B-3865	Harbin Yunshuji Y11	0410		0089	0590	2 HS 6D	3500	Photo / Survey		
☐ B-3866	Harbin Yunshuji Y11	0104		0077	0590	2 HS 6D	3500	Photo / Survey		
☐ B-3867	Harbin Yunshuji Y11	0206		0080	0590	2 HS 6D	3500	Photo / Survey		
☐ B-3868	Harbin Yunshuji Y11	0109		0078	0590	2 HS 6D	3500	Photo / Survey		
☐ B-8479	Shijiazhuang Yunshuji Y5B	0107		0090	0090	1 HS 5	5500	Y12		
☐ B-8481	Shijiazhuang Yunshuji Y5B	0109		0090	0090	1 HS 5	5500	Y12		

JIHUA AIRLINES (Subsidiary of Shijiazhuang Aircraft Plant) — Shijiazhuang

Hepingxi Road, PO Box 164, 050071 Shijiazhuang, (Hebei), People's Republic of China ☎ (311) 704 15 03 Tx: 26236 hbjxc cn Fax: none SITA: n/a
F: 1987 ♣♣♣ 85 Head: Zhang Bingsheng Net: n/a

registration	type of aircraft	cn/fn	ex/ex*	mfd	del	powered by	mtow kg	configuration	selcal	name/fln/specialitites/remarks
☐ B-8447	Shijiazhuang Yunshuji Y5			0083	0487	1 HS 5	5500	Utility		
☐ B-8448	Shijiazhuang Yunshuji Y5	1105		0083	0487	1 HS 5	5500	Utility		
☐ B-8460	Nanchang Yunshuji Y5	1232029		0065	0487	1 HS 5	5500	Utility		
☐ B-8461	Nanchang Yunshuji Y5	1232047		0065	0487	1 HS 5	5500	Utility		
☐ B-8462	Shijiazhuang Yunshuji Y5	1110		0083	0487	1 HS 5	5500	Utility		

JINGMEN UNITED GENERAL AVIATION, Corp. (Joint venture company of Hongtu Aircraft Factory, China National Civil Aircraft Corp & Goverment of Jingmen City) — Jingmen

No. 25 Baiyun Road, 448000 Jingmen, (Hubei), People's Republic of China ☎ (724) 888 90 49 Tx: none Fax: (724) 888 90 49 SITA: n/a
F: 1989 ♣♣♣ n/a Head: Ma Zhongpei Net: n/a

registration	type of aircraft	cn/fn	ex/ex*	mfd	del	powered by	mtow kg	configuration	selcal	name/fln/specialitites/remarks
☐ B-8473	Shijiazhuang Yunshuji Y5B	0101		0089	0089	1 HS 5	5500	Utility		
☐ B-8474	Shijiazhuang Yunshuji Y5B	0102		0090	0090	1 HS 5	5500	Utility		
☐ B-8480	Shijiazhuang Yunshuji Y5B	0108		0090	0090	1 HS 5	5500	Utility		

NANJING AIRLINES, Ltd = CNJ (Nanjing Aviation, Co. Ltd dba / Joint venture of China Northwest Airlines & Nanjing Government) — Nanjing

Dajiao Chang Airport, 210000 Nanjing, People's Republic of China ☎ (25) 460 26 29 Tx: none Fax: (25) 449 44 61 SITA: n/a
F: 1994 ♣♣♣ n/a Head: Jiang Heping ICAO: NINGHANG Net: n/a

registration	type of aircraft	cn/fn	ex/ex*	mfd	del	powered by	mtow kg	configuration	selcal	name/fln/specialitites/remarks
☐ B-3491	Xian Yunshuji Y7-100C	07710		0089	0096	2 WJ 5A-1	21800	Y52		
☐ B-3717	Xian Yunshuji Y7-100C	07702	6051	0088	0096	2 WJ 5A-1	21800	Y52		
☐ B-3718	Xian Yunshuji Y7-100C	07704	6061	0088	0096	2 WJ 5A-1	21800	Y52		
☐ B-2715	BAe 146-300	E3214	G-6-214*	0092	0096	4 LY LF507-1H	44225	Y112		lsf CNW

NORTHEAST GENERAL AVIATION, Co. Ltd (Subsidiary of China Northern Airlines) — Shenyang-Dongta

Shenyang Air Force Signal Regiment Hostel, 100043 Dongta Airport, (Liaoning), People's Republic of China ☎ (24) 23 21 59 57 Tx: none Fax: none SITA: n/a
F: n/a ♣♣♣ n/a Head: n/a Net: n/a

registration	type of aircraft	cn/fn	ex/ex*	mfd	del	powered by	mtow kg	configuration	selcal	name/fln/specialitites/remarks
☐ B-8005	Shijiazhuang Yunshuji Y5	317405		0076		1 HS 5	5500	Utility		
☐ B-8306	Nanchang Yunshuji Y5	732018		0061		1 HS 5	5500	Utility		
☐ B-8307	Nanchang Yunshuji Y5	732019		0061		1 HS 5	5500	Utility		
☐ B-8308	Nanchang Yunshuji Y5	732028		0062		1 HS 5	5500	Utility		
☐ B-8309	Nanchang Yunshuji Y5	732029		0062		1 HS 5	5500	Utility		
☐ B-8310	Nanchang Yunshuji Y5	832032		0062		1 HS 5	5500	Utility		
☐ B-8311	Nanchang Yunshuji Y5	832045		0062		1 HS 5	5500	Utility		
☐ B-8313	Nanchang Yunshuji Y5	1032021		0063		1 HS 5	5500	Utility		
☐ B-8314	Nanchang Yunshuji Y5	332002		0059		1 HS 5	5500	Utility		
☐ B-8317	Nanchang Yunshuji Y5	732020		0061		1 HS 5	5500	Utility		
☐ B-8318	Nanchang Yunshuji Y5	732003		0061		1 HS 5	5500	Utility		
☐ B-8319	Nanchang Yunshuji Y5	932029		0063		1 HS 5	5500	Utility		
☐ B-8321	Nanchang Yunshuji Y5	432006		0060		1 HS 5	5500	Utility		
☐ B-8324	Nanchang Yunshuji Y5	732026		0062		1 HS 5	5500	Utility		
☐ B-8325	Nanchang Yunshuji Y5	732027		0062		1 HS 5	5500	Utility		
☐ B-8326	Nanchang Yunshuji Y5	832038		0062		1 HS 5	5500	Utility		
☐ B-8332	Nanchang Yunshuji Y5	1032024		0063		1 HS 5	5500	Utility		
☐ B-8333	Nanchang Yunshuji Y5	532020		0060		1 HS 5	5500	Utility		
☐ B-8336	Nanchang Yunshuji Y5	532025		0060		1 HS 5	5500	Utility		
☐ B-8337	Nanchang Yunshuji Y5	432012		0060		1 HS 5	5500	Utility		
☐ B-8340	Nanchang Yunshuji Y5	532009		0060		1 HS 5	5500	Utility		
☐ B-8341	Nanchang Yunshuji Y5	1032043		0064		1 HS 5	5500	Utility		
☐ B-8343	Nanchang Yunshuji Y5	932021		0063		1 HS 5	5500	Utility		
☐ B-8345	Nanchang Yunshuji Y5	732038		0062		1 HS 5	5500	Utility		
☐ B-8346	Nanchang Yunshuji Y5	532022		0060		1 HS 5	5500	Utility		
☐ B-8348	Shijiazhuang Yunshuji Y5	316415		0076		1 HS 5	5500	Utility		
☐ B-8349	Shijiazhuang Yunshuji Y5	4705501		0076		1 HS 5	5500	Utility		
☐ B-8350	Shijiazhuang Yunshuji Y5	4705508		0076		1 HS 5	5500	Utility		
☐ B-8351	Shijiazhuang Yunshuji Y5	4605510		0076		1 HS 5	5500	Utility		
☐ B-8352	Shijiazhuang Yunshuji Y5	4705511		0076		1 HS 5	5500	Utility		
☐ B-8353	Shijiazhuang Yunshuji Y5	0615		0082		1 HS 5	5500	Utility		
☐ B-8354	Shijiazhuang Yunshuji Y5	0602		0082		1 HS 5	5500	Utility		
☐ B-8355	Shijiazhuang Yunshuji Y5	1006		0083		1 HS 5	5500	Utility		
☐ B-8356	Shijiazhuang Yunshuji Y5	1007		0083		1 HS 5	5500	Utility		
☐ B-8440	Shijiazhuang Yunshuji Y5	1116		0083		1 HS 5	5500	Utility		
☐ B-8441	Shijiazhuang Yunshuji Y5	1115		0083		1 HS 5	5500	Utility		
☐ B-8468	Nanchang Yunshuji Y5	1632044		0066		1 HS 5	5500	Utility		
☐ B-8469	Nanchang Yunshuji Y5	1732013		0066		1 HS 5	5500	Utility		
☐ B-8470	Nanchang Yunshuji Y5	1732034		0067		1 HS 5	5500	Utility		
☐ B-8471	Nanchang Yunshuji Y5	1732057		0067		1 HS 5	5500	Utility		
☐ B-8472	Nanchang Yunshuji Y5	1732063		0067		1 HS 5	5500	Utility		
☐ B-7805	Mil Mi-8	20215		0072		2 IS TV2-117A	12000	Utility		
☐ B-7806	Mil Mi-8	20216		0072		2 IS TV2-117A	12000	Utility		
☐ B-7811	Mil Mi-8	20246		0084		2 IS TV2-117A	12000	Utility		
☐ B-7812	Mil Mi-8	20247		0084		2 IS TV2-117A	12000	Utility		
☐ B-7813	Mil Mi-8	20248		0084		2 IS TV2-117A	12000	Utility		
☐ B-7814	Mil Mi-8	20249		0084		2 IS TV2-117A	12000	Utility		
☐ B-7815	Mil Mi-8	20278		0085		2 IS TV2-117A	12000	Utility		
☐ B-7816	Mil Mi-8	20279		0085		2 IS TV2-117A	12000	Utility		
☐ B-7818	Mil Mi-8	20281		0085		2 IS TV2-117A	12000	Utility		

SHANDONG AIRLINES – SDA = SC / CDG — Jinan

Jinan Yaoqianq Airport, 250107 Jinan, (Shandong), People's Republic of China ☎ (531) 873 46 25 Tx: none Fax: (531) 873 46 16 SITA: n/a
F: 1994 ♣♣♣ 740 Head: Sun Dehan ICAO: SHANDONG Net: n/a

registration	type of aircraft	cn/fn	ex/ex*	mfd	del	powered by	mtow kg	configuration	selcal	name/fln/specialitites/remarks
☐ B-3651	Saab 340B	340B-289	SE-G89*	0092	1096	2 GE CT7-9B	13155	Y36		
☐ B-3652	Saab 340B	340B-292	SE-G92*	0092	0196	2 GE CT7-9B	13155	Y36		
☐ B-3653	Saab 340B	340B-296	SE-G96*	0092	0196	2 GE CT7-9B	13155	Y36		
☐ B-3654	Saab 340B	340B-302	SE-C02*	0092	1096	2 GE CT7-9B	13155	Y36		
☐ B-	Saab 340B	340B-336	B-12233	0093	1298	2 GE CT7-9B	13155	Y36		lsf Sean-Ho Aircraft Leasing
☐ B-	Saab 340B	340B-351	B-12261	0093	1298	2 GE CT7-9B	13155	Y36		lsf Sean-Ho Aircraft Leasing
☐ B-	Saab 340B	340B-357	B-12262	0093	1298	2 GE CT7-9B	13155	Y36		lsf Sean-Ho Aircraft Leasing
☐ B-	Saab 340B	340B-360	B-12263	0094	1298	2 GE CT7-9B	13155	Y36		lsf Sean-Ho Aircraft Leasing
☐ B-2961	Boeing 737-35N	28156 / 2774		0096	0396	2 CFMI CFM56-3B1	61235	Y141		
☐ B-2962	Boeing 737-35N	28157 / 2778		0096	0396	2 CFMI CFM56-3B1	61235	Y141		
☐ B-2968	Boeing 737-35N	28158 / 2818		0096	1096	2 CFMI CFM56-3B1	61235	Y141		
☐ B-2995	Boeing 737-35N	29315 / 3054		0098	0798	2 CFMI CFM56-3C1	61235	Y141		
☐ B-2996	Boeing 737-35N	29316 / 3065	N1786B*	0098	0998	2 CFMI CFM56-3C1	61235	Y141		

SHANGHAI AIRLINES = FM / CSH — Shanghai-Hongqiao 上海航空公司 SHANGHAI AIRLINES

Hongqiao International Airport, 200335 Shanghai, (Shanghai), People's Republic of China ☎ (21) 62 68 85 55 Tx: 33536 sal cn Fax: (21) 62 68 81 07 SITA: n/a
F: 1985 ♣♣♣ 1400 Head: Zhou Chi IATA: 774 ICAO: SHANGHAI AIR Net: http://www.china-on-web.com/sh-air/index.htm

registration	type of aircraft	cn/fn	ex/ex*	mfd	del	powered by	mtow kg	configuration	selcal	name/fln/specialitites/remarks
☐ B-2980	Boeing 737-3Q8	24300 / 1666	G-OBML	0089	0597	2 CFMI CFM56-3B1	54849			lsf ILFC
☐ B-2631	Boeing 737-7Q8	28212 / 35	N301LF	0098	0498	2 CFMI CFM56-7B24	63276			lsf ILFC
☐ B-2632	Boeing 737-7Q8	28216 / 122	N1795B*	0098	1098	2 CFMI CFM56-7B24	63276			lsf ILFC
☐ B-2997	Boeing 737-7Q8	28223				2 CFMI CFM56-7B24	63276			to be lsf ILFC 0499
☐ B-	Boeing 737-76D					2 CFMI CFM56-7B24	63276			oo-delivery 0701
☐ B-	Boeing 737-76D					2 CFMI CFM56-7B24	63276			oo-delivery 0801
☐ B-2808	Boeing 757-26D	24471 / 231	N1792B*	0089	0889	2 PW PW2037	108862	F8Y192		
☐ B-2809	Boeing 757-26D	24472 / 235	N5573B*	0089	0889	2 PW PW2037	108862	F8Y192		
☐ B-2810	Boeing 757-26D	24473 / 301		0090	0890	2 PW PW2037	108862	F8Y192		

19 registration type of aircraft   cn/fn   ex/ex*   mfd   del   powered by   mtow kg   configuration   selcal   name/fln/specialitites/remarks

registration	type of aircraft	cn/fn	ex/ex*	mfd	del	powered by	mtow kg	configuration	selcal	name/fln/specialitites/remarks
☐ B-2833	Boeing 757-26D	27152 / 560		0093	0693	2 PW PW2037	108862	F12Y188	DH-LS	
☐ B-2834	Boeing 757-26D	27183 / 576		0093	0993	2 PW PW2037	108862	F12Y188		
☐ B-2842	Boeing 757-26D	27342 / 626		0094	0894	2 PW PW2037	108862	F12Y188		
☐ B-2843	Boeing 757-26D	27681 / 684		0095	0795	2 PW PW2037	108862	F12Y188		
☐ B-2563	Boeing 767-36D	27309 / 546		0094	0794	2 PW PW4056	159211	F18C31Y214		
☐ B-2567	Boeing 767-36D	27685 / 686		0198	0198	2 PW PW4056	159211	F18C31Y214		
☐ B-	Boeing 767-36D					2 PW PW4056	159211	F18C31Y214		oo-delivery 0699

SHANXI AVIATION, Corp. = 8C / CXI — Taiyuan-Wusu

Wusu Airport, 030031 Taiyuan, (Shanxi), People's Republic of China ☎ (351) 442 00 47 Tx: none Fax: (351) 442 95 95 SITA: n/a
F: 1988 ✝✝✝ 150 Head: Qin Jianming ICAO: SHANXI Net: n/a

☐ B-3701	Xian Yunshuji Y7-100	12705		0093	1293	2 WJ 5A-1	21800	Y50		
☐ B-3702	Xian Yunshuji Y7-100C	12707		0093	0993	2 WJ 5A-1	21800	Y52		
☐ B-3703	Xian Yunshuji Y7-100	12708		0093	1193	2 WJ 5A-1	21800	Y50		

SHENZHEN AIRLINES = 4G / CSZ — Shenzhen-Huangtian

Lingtian Bldg, Lingxiao Garden, Airport, 518128 Shenzhen, (Guangdong), People's Republic of China ☎ (755) 777 19 99 Tx: none Fax: (755) 777 72 42 SITA: n/a
F: 1993 ✝✝✝ 400 Head: Gao Junyue ICAO: SHENZHEN AIR Net: n/a

☐ B-2932	Boeing 737-3K9	25787 / 2302	N41069	0092	0893	2 CFMI CFM56-3B2	60950	Y140		lsf BAVA
☐ B-2933	Boeing 737-3K9	25788 / 2331	N4113D	0092	0893	2 CFMI CFM56-3B2	60950	Y140		lsf BAVA
☐ B-2939	Boeing 737-31L	27345 / 2625		0094	0794	2 CFMI CFM56-3B1	61235	Y140		lsf CXJ
☐ B-2940	Boeing 737-31L	27346 / 2636		0094	0794	2 CFMI CFM56-3B1	61235	Y140		lsf CXJ
☐ B-2971	Boeing 737-3Q8	25373 / 2290	CC-CYJ	0092	0696	2 CFMI CFM56-3B2	62142	Y140		lsf ILFC
☐ B-2972	Boeing 737-33A	27463 / 2831		0096	1196	2 CFMI CFM56-3C1	62142	Y140		lsf AWAS
☐ B-2633	Boeing 737-79K	29190 / 110	N1786B*	0998	0998	2 CFMI CFM56-7B24	63276			
☐ B-2635	Boeing 737-79K	29191 / 127	N1786B*	0098	1098	2 CFMI CFM56-7B24	63276			

SHUANGYANG GENERAL AVIATION, Corp. = CSY (Subsidiary of Shuangyang Aircraft Factory) — Anshun

PO Box 8, 561018 Anshun, (Guizhou), People's Republic of China ☎ (853) 339 68 93 Tx: 66018 aimga cn Fax: (853) 339 69 88 SITA: n/a
F: 1991 ✝✝✝ 40 Head: Fan Yuemin ICAO: SHUANGYANG Net: n/a

☐ B-3895	Harbin Yunshuji Y11	0401		0088	0991	2 HS 6D	3500	Sprayer / Frtr		
☐ B-3896	Harbin Yunshuji Y11	0402		0088	0991	2 HS 6D	3500	Sprayer / Frtr		
☐ B-3897	Harbin Yunshuji Y11	0403		0088	0991	2 HS 6D	3500	Sprayer / Frtr		
☐ B-3898	Harbin Yunshuji Y11	0404		0088	0991	2 HS 6D	3500	Sprayer / Frtr		

SICHUAN AIRLINES = 3U / CSC — Chengdu

9 Nanshan Duan, Yihuan Road, 610041 Chengdu, (Sichuan), People's Republic of China ☎ (28) 555 11 61 Tx: 600070 scal cn Fax: (28) 558 26 41 SITA: n/a
F: 1986 ✝✝✝ 1200 Head: Lan Xinguo Net: n/a

☐ B-3437	Xian Yunshuji Y7-100C	09710		0391	0391	2 WJ 5A-1	21800	Y52		
☐ B-3441	Xian Yunshuji Y7-100C	08709		1289	1289	2 WJ 5A-1	21800	Y52		
☐ B-3496	Xian Yunshuji Y7-100C	05709		0888	0888	2 WJ 5A-1	21800	Y52		
☐ B-3497	Xian Yunshuji Y7-100C	06702		1287	1287	2 WJ 5A-1	21800	Y52		
☐ B-3498	Xian Yunshuji Y7-100C	06706		1287	1287	2 WJ 5A-1	21800	Y52		
☐ B-2340	Airbus Industrie A320-232	540	F-WWDK*	0095	1295	2 IAE V2527-A5	73500	CY150		lsf ILFC
☐ B-2341	Airbus Industrie A320-232	551	F-WWBI*	0095	0196	2 IAE V2527-A5	73500	CY150		lsf ILFC
☐ B-2342	Airbus Industrie A320-232	556	F-WWIL*	0095	0296	2 IAE V2527-A5	73500	CY150		lsf ILFC
☐ B-2373	Airbus Industrie A320-232	919	F-WWIC*	0098	1298	2 IAE V2527-A5	73500	CY150	GJ-AS	
☐ B-	Airbus Industrie A320-232	1013				2 IAE V2527-A5	73500	CY150		oo-delivery 0699
☐ B-2370	Airbus Industrie A321-231	878	D-AVZF*	0098	0998	2 IAE V2533-A5	89000	CY194		
☐ B-2371	Airbus Industrie A321-231	915	D-AVZM*	0098	1298	2 IAE V2533-A5	89000	CY194		
☐ B-2624	Tupolev 154M	886		0091	1191	3 SO D-30KU-154-II	100000	Y164		
☐ B-2625	Tupolev 154M	893		0091	1291	3 SO D-30KU-154-II	100000	Y164		
☐ B-2626	Tupolev 154M	894		0091	0292	3 SO D-30KU-154-II	100000	Y164		
☐ B-2629	Tupolev 154M	919		0092	0992	3 SO D-30KU-154-II	100000	Y164		

WUHAN AIRLINES – WAL = CWU (Air Wuhan) — Wuhan-Wangjiadun

435 Jianshe Dadao, 430030 Wuhan, (Hubei), People's Republic of China ☎ (27) 83 62 46 00 Tx: none Fax: (27) 83 62 56 93 SITA: n/a
F: 1986 ✝✝✝ 500 Head: Cheng Yaoshen ICAO: WUHAN AIR Net: n/a

☐ B-3442	Xian Yunshuji Y7-100C	08701		0090	0090	2 WJ 5A-1	21800	Y52		
☐ B-3443	Xian Yunshuji Y7-100C	08702		0090	0090	2 WJ 5A-1	21800	Y52		
☐ B-3471	Xian Yunshuji Y7-100C	05706		0087	0093	2 WJ 5A-1	21800	Y52		
☐ B-3472	Xian Yunshuji Y7-100C	05707		0087	0096	2 WJ 5A-1	21800	Y52		
☐ B-3479	Xian Yunshuji Y7-100C	06708		0088	0093	2 WJ 5A-1	21800	Y52		
☐ B-2918	Boeing 737-3Q8	24986 / 2192	N551LF	0092	0893	2 CFMI CFM56-3B2	62823	Y149		lsf ILFC
☐ B-2919	Boeing 737-3Q8	24987 / 2268	N561LF	0092	1293	2 CFMI CFM56-3B2	62823	Y148		lsf ILFC
☐ B-2928	Boeing 737-3Q8	26294 / 2550	N261LF	0093	1293	2 CFMI CFM56-3B2	62823	Y148		lsf ILFC
☐ B-2976	Boeing 737-3S3	29244 / 3059	N244SR	0098	0898	2 CFMI CFM56-3C1	62823	Y148		lsf SUNR
☐ B-2988	Boeing 737-36R	29087 / 2970		0097	1297	2 CFMI CFM56-3C1	62823	Y148		
☐ B-	Boeing 737-36R					2 CFMI CFM56-3C1	62823	Y148		oo-delivery 0200

XIAMEN AIRLINES, Ltd = MF / CXA (Member of China Southern Group) — Xiamen

Gaoqi Int'l Airport, 361009 Xiamen, (Fujian), People's Republic of China ☎ (592) 573 98 88 Tx: 93071 cxacl cn Fax: (592) 573 97 77 SITA: XMNXMMF
F: 1984 ✝✝✝ 2400 Head: Wu Rongnan IATA: 731 ICAO: XIAMEN AIR Net: n/a

☐ B-2505	Boeing 737-2T4C (A)	23066 / 992	N676MA	0083	1295	2 PW JT8D-17A	56472	Y128		lsf GECA
☐ B-2512	Boeing 737-2T4 (A)	23444 / 1154	N1790B*	0085	1194	2 PW JT8D-17A	56472	Y128		
☐ B-2515	Boeing 737-2T4 (A)	23446 / 1165	N1792B*	0085	0994	2 PW JT8D-17A	56472	Y128		lsf GECA
☐ B-2516	Boeing 737-2T4 (A)	23447 / 1167	N5573B*	0085	0091	2 PW JT8D-17A	56472	Y128		
☐ B-2524	Boeing 737-25C (A)	24236 / 1585	N5573B*	0088	0888	2 PW JT8D-17A	56472	Y128		
☐ B-2529	Boeing 737-505	26297 / 2578	LN-BUA	0094	0394	2 CFMI CFM56-3C1	60555	Y131		lsf BRA
☐ B-2591	Boeing 737-505	25792 / 2353	LN-BRW	0092	0992	2 CFMI CFM56-3C1	60555	Y131		lsf BRA
☐ B-2592	Boeing 737-505	27153 / 2516	LN-BRZ	0093	0993	2 CFMI CFM56-3C1	60555	Y131		lsf BRA
☐ B-2593	Boeing 737-505	27155 / 2449	LN-BRY	0093	0493	2 CFMI CFM56-3C1	60555	Y131		lsf BRA
☐ B-2973	Boeing 737-505	26336 / 2805		0096	0796	2 CFMI CFM56-3B1	60555	Y133		lsf ILFC
☐ B-2975	Boeing 737-505	26338 / 2822		0096	1096	2 CFMI CFM56-3B1	60555	Y133		lsf ILFC
☐ B-2991	Boeing 737-75C	29085 / 90		0098	0998	2 CFMI CFM56-7B24	63276	F8Y120		
☐ B-2992	Boeing 737-75C	29086 / 108	N1786B*	0998	0998	2 CFMI CFM56-7B24	63276	F8Y120		
☐ B-2998	Boeing 737-75C	29042 / 73	N1786B*	0098	0898	2 CFMI CFM56-7B24	63276	F8Y120		
☐ B-2999	Boeing 737-75C	29084 / 86	N1796B*	0898	0898	2 CFMI CFM56-7B24	63276	F8Y120		
☐ B-2819	Boeing 757-25C	25898 / 475		0092	0892	2 RR RB211-535E4	108862	F8Y192		
☐ B-2828	Boeing 757-25C	25899 / 565		0093	0793	2 RR RB211-535E4	108862	F8Y192		
☐ B-2829	Boeing 757-25C	25900 / 574		0093	0893	2 RR RB211-535E4	108862	F8Y192		
☐ B-2848	Boeing 757-25C	27513 / 685		0095	0895	2 RR RB211-535E4	108862	F8Y192		
☐ B-2849	Boeing 757-25C	27517 / 698		0196	0296	2 RR RB211-535E4	108862	F8Y192		

XINJIANG GENERAL AVIATION, Company (Subs. of China Xinjiang Airlines & Aviation Team of Xinjiang Productive Army Corps/formerly Aviation Team) — Shihezi

14 District, 832000 Shihezi, (Xinjiang), People's Republic of China ☎ (993) 26 710 Tx: none Fax: none SITA: n/a
F: 1983 ✝✝✝ n/a Head: Wang Yijie Net: n/a

☐ B-3869	Harbin Yunshuji Y11	0501		0090	0090	2 HS 6D	3500	Sprayer / Frtr		
☐ B-3870	Harbin Yunshuji Y11	0502		0090	0090	2 HS 6D	3500	Sprayer / Frtr		
☐ B-3885	Harbin Yunshuji Y11	0301		0084	0084	2 HS 6D	3500	Sprayer / Frtr		
☐ B-3886	Harbin Yunshuji Y11	0302		0084	0084	2 HS 6D	3500	Sprayer / Frtr		
☐ B-3887	Harbin Yunshuji Y11	0303		0084	0084	2 HS 6D	3500	Sprayer / Frtr		
☐ B-3888	Harbin Yunshuji Y11	0304		0084	0084	2 HS 6D	3500	Sprayer / Frtr		
☐ B-3889	Harbin Yunshuji Y11	0305		0084	0084	2 HS 6D	3500	Sprayer / Frtr		
☐ B-3890	Harbin Yunshuji Y11	0306		0084	0084	2 HS 6D	3500	Sprayer / Frtr		
☐ B-3891	Harbin Yunshuji Y11	0307		0084	0084	2 HS 6D	3500	Sprayer / Frtr		
☐ B-3892	Harbin Yunshuji Y11	0308		0084	0084	2 HS 6D	3500	Sprayer / Frtr		
☐ B-3893	Harbin Yunshuji Y11	0309		0084	0084	2 HS 6D	3500	Sprayer / Frtr		
☐ B-3894	Harbin Yunshuji Y11	0310		0084	0084	2 HS 6D	3500	Sprayer / Frtr		
☐ B-3810	Harbin Yunshuji Y12 II	0009		0087	0096	2 PWC PT6A-27	5300	Surveyer		
☐ B-3815	Harbin Yunshuji Y12 II	0023		0087	0096	2 PWC PT6A-27	5300	Surveyer		
☐ B-3816	Harbin Yunshuji Y12 II	0028		0089	0096	2 PWC PT6A-27	5300	Photo / Survey		
☐ B-3817	Harbin Yunshuji Y12 II	0029		0089	0096	2 PWC PT6A-27	5300	Photo / Survey		
☐ B-3818	Harbin Yunshuji Y12 II	0030		0089	0096	2 PWC PT6A-27	5300	Photo / Survey		
☐ B-8222	Nanchang Yunshuji Y5	632032		0061	0083	1 HS 5	5500	Y12 / Sprayer		
☐ B-8224	Nanchang Yunshuji Y5	932022		0063	0083	1 HS 5	5500	Y12 / Sprayer		
☐ B-8229	Nanchang Yunshuji Y5	732047		0062	0083	1 HS 5	5500	Y12 / Sprayer		

	registration	type of aircraft	cn/fn	ex/ex*	mfd	del	powered by	mtow kg	configuration	selcal	name/fln/specialitites/remarks
☐	B-8230	Nanchang Yunshuji Y5	532018		0060	0083	1 HS 5	5500	Y12 / Sprayer		
☐	B-8231	Nanchang Yunshuji Y5	732050		0062	0083	1 HS 5	5500	Y12 / Sprayer		
☐	B-8232	Nanchang Yunshuji Y5	632015		0061	0083	1 HS 5	5500	Y12 / Sprayer		
☐	B-8243	Shijiazhuang Yunshuji Y5	5705515		0076	0083	1 HS 5	5500	Y12 / Sprayer		
☐	B-8475	Shijiazhuang Yunshuji Y5	0103		0090	0090	1 HS 5	5500	Y12 / Sprayer		
☐	B-8476	Shijiazhuang Yunshuji Y5	0104		0090	0090	1 HS 5	5500	Y12 / Sprayer		
☐	B-8477	Shijiazhuang Yunshuji Y5	0105		0090	0090	1 HS 5	5500	Y12 / Sprayer		
☐	B-8478	Shijiazhuang Yunshuji Y5	0106		0090	0090	1 HS 5	5500	Y12 / Sprayer		

ZHONGFEI AIRLINES = CFZ (CFGAC-China Zhongfei General Aviation Co. dba / Subsidiary of Chinese Flight Test Establishment)

Xian-Yanliang

CFGAC 中飛通用航空公司

PO Box 73-90, 710089 Xian, (Shaanxi), People's Republic of China ☎ (29) 620 21 06 Tx: none Fax: (29) 620 20 94 SITA: n/a

F: 1995 ✈✈✈ 75 Head: Cheng Dunbin ICAO: ZHONGFEI Net: n/a

	registration	type of aircraft	cn/fn	ex/ex*	mfd	del	powered by	mtow kg	configuration	selcal	name/fln/specialitites/remarks
☐	B-3820	Harbin Yunshuji Y12 II	0031		0089	0495	2 PWC PT6A-27	5300	calibr./survey		
☐	B-8482	Shijiazhuang Yunshuji Y5	0608		0082	0495	1 HS 5	5500	calibr./survey		
☐	B-4103	Cessna 550 Citation II	550-0301	091	0081	0495	2 PWC JT15D-4	6033	calibr./survey		
☐	B-4104	Cessna 550 Citation II	550-0297	092	0081	0495	2 PWC JT15D-4	6033	calibr./survey		
☐	B-4105	Cessna 550 Citation II	550-0305	090	0081	0495	2 PWC JT15D-4	6033	calibr./survey		

ZHONGYUAN AIRLINES, Corp. = CYN

Zhengzhou

中原航空公司

No. 106 Jinshua Road, 450003 Zhengzhou, (Henan), People's Republic of China ☎ (371) 622 25 42 Tx: none Fax: (371) 622 25 42 SITA: n/a

F: 1986 ✈✈✈ 300 Head: Xu Jianguo ICAO: ZHONGYUAN Net: n/a

	registration	type of aircraft	cn/fn	ex/ex*	mfd	del	powered by	mtow kg	configuration	selcal	name/fln/specialitites/remarks
☐	B-3438	Xian Yunshuji Y7-100C	09709		0091	0091	2 WJ 5A-1	21800	Y52		
☐	B-3439	Xian Yunshuji Y7-100C	09708		0091	0091	2 WJ 5A-1	21800	Y52		
☐	B-2574	Boeing 737-37K	29407				2 CFMI CFM56-3C1	61235	Y140		oo-delivery 0499
☐	B-2575	Boeing 737-37K	29408				2 CFMI CFM56-3C1	61235	Y140		oo-delivery 0499
☐	B-2935	Boeing 737-37K	27283 / 2547		0094	0294	2 CFMI CFM56-3C1	61235	Y140		
☐	B-2936	Boeing 737-37K	27335 / 2609		0094	1194	2 CFMI CFM56-3C1	61235	Y140		
☐	B-2946	Boeing 737-37K	27375 / 2655		0094	1194	2 CFMI CFM56-3C1	61235	Y140		

B-H = HONGKONG

(Hongkong on 1st July 1997 became a semi-autonomous territory within Mainland-China, while loosing its VR-H ICAO-nationality-mark retains its three-letter-registrations (instead of the 4-digit-numbers, used generally in China)
Official Language: Chinese, English Population: 6,5 million Square Km: 1071 Dialling code: +852

AIRHONG KONG = LD / AHK (AHK Air Hong Kong, Ltd dba / Member of Swire Group)

Hong Kong-Int'l

2nd Floor, Block 2, Tien Chu Centre, 1E Mok Cheong Street, Kowloon, Hong Kong ☎ 27 61 85 88 Tx: 37625 ahk hx Fax: 27 61 85 86 SITA: HKGHQLD

F: 1986 ✈✈✈ 179 Head: Dr. Stanley Ho IATA: 288 ICAO: AIR HONG KONG Net: n/a

	registration	type of aircraft	cn/fn	ex/ex*	mfd	del	powered by	mtow kg	configuration	selcal	name/fln/specialitites/remarks
☐	B-HMD	Boeing 747-2L5B (SF)	22105 / 435	VR-HMD	0080	0696	4 GE CF6-50E2	377842	Freighter	EH-AF	lsf CPA / cvtd -2L5B
☐	B-HME	Boeing 747-2L5B (SF)	22106 / 443	VR-HME	0080	0596	4 GE CF6-50E2	377842	Freighter	EH-AG	lsf CPA / cvtd -2L5B
☐	B-HMF	Boeing 747-2L5B (SF)	22107 / 469	VR-HMF	0080	0896	4 GE CF6-50E2	377842	Freighter	FK-DJ	lsf CPA / cvtd -2L5B

CATHAY PACIFIC = CX / CPA (Cathay Pacific Airways, Ltd dba / Member of Swire Group & Oneworld Alliance)

Hong Kong-Int'l

CATHAY PACIFIC

Cathay City, 8 Scenic Roadoad, Hong Kong-Int'l Airport, Lantan, Hong Kong ☎ 27 47 50 00 Tx: 82345 cxair hx Fax: 28 10 65 63 SITA: n/a

F: 1946 ✈✈✈ 13900 Head: Peter Sutch IATA: 160 ICAO: CATHAY Net: http://www.cathaypacific.com

	registration	type of aircraft	cn/fn	ex/ex*	mfd	del	powered by	mtow kg	configuration	selcal	name/fln/specialitites/remarks
☐	B-HLA	Airbus Industrie A330-342	071	VR-HLA	0095	0395	2 RR Trent 772-60	212000	C44Y270	FR-EG	
☐	B-HLB	Airbus Industrie A330-342	083	VR-HLB	0095	0295	2 RR Trent 772-60	212000	C44Y270	FR-EH	
☐	B-HLC	Airbus Industrie A330-342	099	VR-HLC	0095	0595	2 RR Trent 772-60	212000	C44Y270	FR-EJ	
☐	B-HLD	Airbus Industrie A330-342	102	VR-HLD	0095	0695	2 RR Trent 772-60	212000	C44Y270	FR-EK	
☐	B-HLE	Airbus Industrie A330-342	109	VR-HLE	0095	0895	2 RR Trent 772-60	212000	C44Y270	FR-EL	
☐	B-HLF	Airbus Industrie A330-342	113	VR-HLF	0095	1195	2 RR Trent 772-60	217000	C44Y270	FR-EM	
☐	B-HLG	Airbus Industrie A330-342	118	VR-HLG	0095	1295	2 RR Trent 772-60	217000	C44Y270	FR-EP	
☐	B-HLH	Airbus Industrie A330-342	121	VR-HLH	0095	0196	2 RR Trent 772-60	217000	C44Y270	FR-EQ	
☐	B-HLI	Airbus Industrie A330-342	155	VR-HLI	0096	1196	2 RR Trent 772-60	217000	C44Y270	FR-ES	
☐	B-HLJ	Airbus Industrie A330-342	012	VR-HLJ	1192	1096	2 RR Trent 772-60	217000	C44Y270	FR-GQ	cvtd -341
☐	B-HLK	Airbus Industrie A330-342	017	VR-HLK	1292	0197	2 RR Trent 772-60	217000	C44Y270	FR-GS	cvtd -322
☐	B-HLL	Airbus Industrie A330-342	244	F-WWKG*	0098	1198	2 RR Trent 772-60	217000	C44Y270	HM-FL	
☐	B-HNA	Boeing 777-267	27265 / 14	VR-HNA	0095	0896	2 RR Trent 877	247207	C45Y291	BQ-AK	
☐	B-HNB	Boeing 777-267	27266 / 18	VR-HNB	0096	1096	2 RR Trent 877	247207	C45Y291	BQ-CJ	
☐	B-HNC	Boeing 777-267	27263 / 28	VR-HNC	0096	0596	2 RR Trent 877	247207	C45Y291	BQ-CK	
☐	B-HND	Boeing 777-267	27264 / 31	VR-HND	0096	0696	2 RR Trent 877	247207	C45Y291	BQ-DK	
☐	B-HNE	Boeing 777-367	27507 / 94	N5014K*	1097	1098	2 RR Trent 890	286897	C80Y287	BQ-DP	
☐	B-HNF	Boeing 777-367	27506 / 102	N5016R*	0097	0898	2 RR Trent 890	286897	C80Y287	BQ-EF	
☐	B-HNG	Boeing 777-367	27505 / 118	N5017V*	0098	0698	2 RR Trent 890	286897	C80Y287	BQ-FG	
☐	B-HNH	Boeing 777-367	27504 / 136		0098	0598	2 RR Trent 890	286897	C80Y287	BQ-FH	
☐	B-HNI	Boeing 777-367	27508				2 RR Trent 890	286897	C80Y287	AG-DH	oo-delivery 0499
☐	B-HNJ	Boeing 777-367					2 RR Trent 890	286897	C80Y287	AG-DK	oo-delivery 0599
☐	B-HNK	Boeing 777-367					2 RR Trent 890	286897	C80Y287	CJ-AK	oo-delivery 0699
☐	B-HXA	Airbus Industrie A340-313	136	VR-HXA	0096	0696	4 CFMI CFM56-5C4	275000	F12C40Y197	FR-GH	
☐	B-HXB	Airbus Industrie A340-313	137	VR-HXB	0096	0696	4 CFMI CFM56-5C4	275000	F12C40Y197	FR-GJ	
☐	B-HXC	Airbus Industrie A340-313	142	VR-HXC	0096	0896	4 CFMI CFM56-5C4	275000	F12C40Y197	FR-GK	
☐	B-HXD	Airbus Industrie A340-313	147	VR-HXD	0096	0996	4 CFMI CFM56-5C4	275000	F12C40Y197	FR-GL	
☐	B-HXE	Airbus Industrie A340-313	157	VR-HXE	0096	1296	4 CFMI CFM56-5C4	275000	F12C40Y197	FR-GM	
☐	B-HXF	Airbus Industrie A340-313	160	VR-HXF	0097	0197	4 CFMI CFM56-5C4	275000	F12C49Y197	FR-GP	
☐	B-HXG	Airbus Industrie A340-313	208	F-WWJC*	0098	0298	4 CFMI CFM56-5C4	275000	F12C40Y197	FR-HJ	
☐	B-HXH	Airbus Industrie A340-313	218	F-WWJT*	0098	0398	4 CFMI CFM56-5C4	275000	F12C40Y197	FR-HK	
☐	B-HXI	Airbus Industrie A340-313	220	F-WWJO*	0098	0698	4 CFMI CFM56-5C4	275000	F12C40Y197	GH-DL	
☐	B-HXJ	Airbus Industrie A340-313	227	F-WWJL*	0098	0798	4 CFMI CFM56-5C4	275000	F12C40Y197	GJ-BF	
☐	B-HXK	Airbus Industrie A340-313	228	F-WWJI*	0098	0898	4 CFMI CFM56-5C4	275000	F12C40Y197	GJ-CD	
☐	B-HIA	Boeing 747-267B	21966 / 446	VR-HIA	0480	0580	4 RR RB211-524C2	362873	C69Y336	DJ-CG	std VCV / for sale or lease
☐	B-HIB	Boeing 747-267B	22149 / 466	VR-HIB	0780	0780	4 RR RB211-524C2	362873	C69Y336	BJ-CD	special Spirit of Hong Kong 97-colors
☐	B-HIH	Boeing 747-267B (SF)	23120 / 596	VR-HIH	0484	0484	4 RR RB211-524D4	377842	Freighter	KL-CG	cvtd -267B
☐	B-HKG	Boeing 747-267B	21746 / 385	VR-HKG	0779	0779	4 RR RB211-524C2	362873	C69Y336	BE-AM	std VCV / for sale or lease
☐	B-HMD	Boeing 747-2L5B (SF)	22105 / 435	VR-HMD	0080	0696	4 GE CF6-50E2	377842	Freighter	EH-AF	lst AHK / cvtd -2L5B
☐	B-HME	Boeing 747-2L5B (SF)	22106 / 443	VR-HME	0080	0596	4 GE CF6-50E2	377842	Freighter	EH-AG	lst AHK / cvtd -2L5B
☐	B-HMF	Boeing 747-2L5B (SF)	22107 / 469	VR-HMF	0080	0896	4 GE CF6-50E2	377842	Freighter	FK-DJ	lst AHK / cvtd -2L5B
☐	B-HVX	Boeing 747-267F (SCD)	24568 / 776	VR-HVX	0290	0290	4 RR RB211-524D4	377842	Freighter	FK-DL	
☐	B-HVY	Boeing 747-236F (SCD)	22306 / 480	VR-HVY	0980	0382	4 RR RB211-524D4	371945	Freighter	GH-DJ	
☐	B-HVZ	Boeing 747-267F (SCD)	23864 / 687	VR-HVZ	0987	0987	4 RR RB211-524D4	371945	Freighter	DL-EK	
☐	B-HII	Boeing 747-367	23221 / 615	VR-HII	0685	0685	4 RR RB211-524C2	362873	C90Y328	KL-CJ	to be wfu/for sale or lease eff. 1099
☐	B-HIJ	Boeing 747-367	23392 / 634	VR-HIJ	0286	0286	4 RR RB211-524C2	362873	C90Y328	CJ-GH	to be lst PIA 0099
☐	B-HIK	Boeing 747-367	23534 / 659	VR-HIK	1086	1086	4 RR RB211-524C2	362873	C90Y328	CK-DH	to be lst PIA 0099
☐	B-HOL	Boeing 747-367	23709 / 671	VR-HOL	0287	0287	4 RR RB211-524C2	362873	C90Y328	DL-EJ	to be lst PIA 0099
☐	B-HOM	Boeing 747-367	23920 / 690	VR-HOM	1087	1187	4 RR RB211-524C2	362873	C90Y328	DL-EM	to be lst PIA 0099
☐	B-HON	Boeing 747-367	24215 / 709	VR-HON	0788	0788	4 RR RB211-524C2	362873	C90Y328	EG-CK	to be lst PIA 0099
☐	B-HOO	Boeing 747-467	23814 / 705	VR-HOO	0889	0989	4 RR RB211-524G/H	394625	F18C56Y313	HJ-CG	
☐	B-HOP	Boeing 747-467	23815 / 728	VR-HOP	0589	0689	4 RR RB211-524G/H	394625	F18C56Y313	HJ-CK	
☐	B-HOR	Boeing 747-467	24631 / 771	VR-HOR	0090	0290	4 RR RB211-524G/H	394625	F18C56Y313	HJ-CL	
☐	B-HOS	Boeing 747-467	24850 / 788	VR-HOS	0590	0590	4 RR RB211-524G/H	394625	F18C56Y313	HJ-CM	
☐	B-HOT	Boeing 747-467	24851 / 813	VR-HOT	0990	0990	4 RR RB211-524G/H	394625	F18C56Y313	AD-HJ	
☐	B-HOU	Boeing 747-467	24925 / 834	VR-HOU	0191	0191	4 RR RB211-524G/H	394625	F18C56Y313	AD-HK	
☐	B-HOV	Boeing 747-467	25082 / 849	VR-HOV	0091	0491	4 RR RB211-524G/H	394625	F18C56Y313	AD-HL	lsf Whirlpool Financial Corp.
☐	B-HOW	Boeing 747-467	25211 / 873	VR-HOW	0091	0891	4 RR RB211-524G/H	394625	F18C56Y313	AD-JK	
☐	B-HOX	Boeing 747-467	24955 / 877	VR-HOX	0091	0991	4 RR RB211-524G/H	394625	F18C56Y313	AD-JL	lsf ILFC
☐	B-HOY	Boeing 747-467	25351 / 887	VR-HOY	0091	1191	4 RR RB211-524G/H	394625	F18C56Y313	AD-JM	
☐	B-HOZ	Boeing 747-467	25871 / 925	VR-HOZ	0092	0692	4 RR RB211-524G/H	394625	F18C56Y313	AD-LM	
☐	B-HUA	Boeing 747-467	25872 / 930	VR-HUA	0092	0792	4 RR RB211-524G/H	394625	F18C56Y313	AF-BE	
☐	B-HUB	Boeing 747-467	25873 / 937	VR-HUB	0092	1092	4 RR RB211-524G/H	394625	F18C56Y313	AF-BJ	
☐	B-HUD	Boeing 747-467	25874 / 949	VR-HUD	0092	1292	4 RR RB211-524G/H	394625	F18C56Y313	AF-BK	
☐	B-HUE	Boeing 747-467	27117 / 970	VR-HUE	0093	0593	4 RR RB211-524G/H	394625	F18C56Y313	AF-CE	
☐	B-HUF	Boeing 747-467	25869 / 993	VR-HUF	0093	0893	4 RR RB211-524G/H	394625	F18C56Y313	AF-CG	
☐	B-HUG	Boeing 747-467	25870 / 1007	VR-HUG	0093	1293	4 RR RB211-524G/H	394625	F18C56Y313	AG-DL	
☐	B-HUH	Boeing 747-467F (SCD)	27175 / 1020	VR-HUH	0094	0594	4 RR RB211-524G/H	394625	Freighter	AF-CL	
☐	B-HUI	Boeing 747-467	27230 / 1033	VR-HUI	0094	0694	4 RR RB211-524G/H	394625	F18C56Y313	AF-EK	
☐	B-HUJ	Boeing 747-467	27595 / 1061	VR-HUJ	0095	0595	4 RR RB211-524G/H	394625	F18C56Y313	AF-EL	lsf ILFC
☐	B-HUK	Boeing 747-467F (SCD)	27503 / 1065	VR-HUK	0095	0795	4 RR RB211-524G/H	394625	Freighter	AF-EM	

DRAGONAIR Hong Kong = KA / HDA (Hong Kong Dragon Airlines, Ltd dba/Assoc.with CNAC/CITIC/Cathay Pacific & Swire Pacific)

Hong Kong-Int'l — 港龍航空 DRAGONAIR

22nd Floor, Devon House, Taikoo Place, 979 Kings Road, Quarry Bay, Hong Kong ☎ 25 90 13 28 Tx: 45936 dragh hx Fax: 25 90 13 33 SITA: HKGSMKA
F: 1985 ⚲ 1100 Head: Wang Guixiang IATA: 043 ICAO: DRAGONAIR Net: http://www.dragonair.com

☐ B-HSD	Airbus Industrie A320-232	756	F-WWBC*	0098	0298	2 IAE V2527-A5	75500	C12Y144		lsf ILFC
☐ B-HSE	Airbus Industrie A320-232	784	F-WWDL*	0098	0398	2 IAE V2527-A5	75500	C12Y144		lsf ILFC
☐ B-HSF	Airbus Industrie A320-232	816	F-WWIT*	0098	0598	2 IAE V2527-A5	75500	C12Y144		lsf ILFC
☐ B-HSG	Airbus Industrie A320-232	812	F-WWIG*	0098	0698	2 IAE V2527-A5	75500	C12Y144		
☐ B-HSH	Airbus Industrie A320-232	877	F-WWIH*	0098	1098	2 IAE V2527-A5	75500	C12Y144		lsf ILFC
☐ B-HSI	Airbus Industrie A320-232	930	F-WWIE*	0098	0199	2 IAE V2527-A5	75500	C12Y144		lsf ILFC
☐ B-HYU	Airbus Industrie A320-231	447	VR-HYU	0093	1293	2 IAE V2500-A1	75500	Y168	EL-FR	lsf ILFC -0599
☐ B-HYV	Airbus Industrie A320-231	415	VR-HYV	0094	0394	2 IAE V2500-A1	75500	Y168	FH-DR	lsf ILFC -0599
☐ B-HTD	Airbus Industrie A321-231	993		0099	0399	2 IAE V2533-A5	89000	C12Y178		lsf ILFC
☐ B-HTE	Airbus Industrie A321-231					2 IAE V2533-A5	89000	C12Y178		to be lsf ILFC 0599
☐ B-HYA	Airbus Industrie A330-342	098	VR-HYA	0095	0595	2 RR Trent 772-60	212000	F36Y286	HR-GK	lsf ILFC
☐ B-HYB	Airbus Industrie A330-342	106	VR-HYB	0095	0795	2 RR Trent 772-60	212000	F36Y286	HR-GL	
☐ B-HYC	Airbus Industrie A330-342	111	VR-HYC	0095	0995	2 RR Trent 772-60	212000	F36Y286	HR-GM	lsf ILFC
☐ B-HYD	Airbus Industrie A330-342	132	VR-HYD	0096	0496	2 RR Trent 772-60	212000	F36Y286		lsf ILFC
☐ B-HYE	Airbus Industrie A330-342	177	VR-HYE	0097	0697	2 RR Trent 772-60	212000	F36Y286		lsf ILFC
☐ B-HYF	Airbus Industrie A330-342	234	F-WWKF*	0098	1098	2 RR Trent 772-60	212000	F36Y286		

GOVERNMENT FLYING SERVICE – GFS

Hong Kong-Int'l

1 Cheung Yip Street, Kowloon Bay, Kowloon, Hong Kong ☎ 23 05 83 01 Tx: none Fax: 27 53 84 38 SITA: n/a
F: 1993 ⚲ 240 Head: Brian Butt Net: n/a Non-commercial government organisation conducting government VIP transport, police trooping, fire-fighting, rescue and medevac missions.

☐ B-HRS	BAe 4124 Jetstream 41	41102	G-BXWM*	0098	1298	2 GA TPE331-14HR-805H	10886	Patrol survey		
☐ B-HRT	BAe 4124 Jetstream 41	41104	G-BXWN*	0098	0199	2 GA TPE331-14HR-805H	10886	Patrol survey		
☐ B-HZA	Sikorsky S-76A++	760296	VR-HZA	0085	0493	2 TU Arriel 1S1	4899			cvtd S-76A
☐ B-HZD	Sikorsky S-76A++	760295	VR-HZD	0085	0493	2 TU Arriel 1S1	4899			cvtd S-76A
☐ B-HZE	Sikorsky S-76A++	760300	VR-HZE	0085	0493	2 TU Arriel 1S1	4899			cvtd S-76A
☐ B-HZF	Sikorsky S-76A++	760301	VR-HZF	0085	0493	2 TU Arriel 1S1	4899			cvtd S-76A
☐ B-HZG	Sikorsky S-76C	760375	VR-HZG	0091	0493	2 TU Arriel 1S1	5307			
☐ B-HZH	Sikorsky S-76C	760376	VR-HZH	0091	0493	2 TU Arriel 1S1	5307			
☐ B-HZI	Sikorsky S-70A	701825	VR-HZI	0092	0493	2 GE T700-GE-701A	9979			
☐ B-HZJ	Sikorsky S-70A	701835	VR-HZJ	0092	0493	2 GE T700-GE-701A	9979			
☐ B-HZK	Sikorsky S-70A	702127	VR-HZK	0095	0095	2 GE T700-GE-701A	9979			
☐ B-HZM	Beech King Air B200C	BL-128	VR-HZM	0087	0493	2 PWC PT6A-42	5670			for sale
☐ B-HZN	Beech King Air B200C	BL-130	VR-HZN	0088	0493	2 PWC PT6A-42	5670			for sale

HELICOPTERS HONG KONG, Ltd

Lamma Island-Private Heliport

Lot 64, DD6, Sok Kwu Wan, Lamma Island, Hong Kong ☎ 28 93 55 27 Tx: none Fax: 25 73 38 78 SITA: n/a
F: 1996 ⚲ n/a Head: n/a Net: n/a

☐ B-HJJ	Bell 206B JetRanger III	3018	VR-HJJ	0080	0096	1 AN 250-C20B	1451			

HELISERVICES (Hong Kong), Ltd

Hong Kong-Sek Kong Airfield

22nd Floor, St. George's Bldg., Ice House Street, Central, Hong Kong ☎ 25 23 64 07 Tx: none Fax: 25 96 03 59 SITA: n/a
F: 1978 ⚲ 20 Head: Hon. Michael D. Kadoorie Net: n/a

☐ B-HJH	Eurocopter (Aerosp.) SA315B Lama	2611	VR-HJH	0081	0892	1 TU Artouste IIIB	1950			
☐ B-HJL	Eurocopter (Aerosp.) SA315B Lama	2618	VR-HJL	0081	0095	1 TU Artouste IIIB	1950			
☐ B-HJK	Eurocopter (Aerosp.) AS355N Ecureuil 2	5579	VR-HJK	0094	1194	2 TU Arrius 1A	2540			

METROJET, Ltd = MTJ

Hong Kong-Int'l

20/F St. George's Building, 2 Ice House Street, Central, Hong Kong ☎ 25 25 47 47 Tx: none Fax: 25 25 43 42 SITA: n/a
F: 1997 ⚲ n/a Head: John Leigh ICAO: METROJET Net: n/a

☐ B-HSS	Hawker 700B (HS 125-700B)	257169	VH-HSS	0082	0697	2 GA TFE731-3-1H	11567	Executive		

ROTAIR, Ltd

Hong Kong-Heliport

24 St. George's Street, ICI House, Central, Hong Kong ☎ 25 24 92 21 Tx: none Fax: 28 45 91 33 SITA: n/a
F: 1981 ⚲ 2 Head: The Hon. Michael D. Kadoorie Net: n/a

☐ B-HHM	MD Helicopters MD 500D (Hughes 369D)	711019D	VR-HHM	0081	0082	1 AN 250-C20B	1361			
☐ B-HMK	MD Helicopters MD 520N (Hughes 500N)	LN061	VR-HMK	0095	0096	1 AN 250-C20R	1520			

TRINITY AVIATION, Ltd = (TRIN)

Hong Kong

13/A Wyndham Place, Central, Hong Kong ☎ 25 24 55 25 Tx: none Fax: 28 69 13 13 SITA: n/a
F: 1986 ⚲ n/a Head: Stephen H. Miller Net: n/a New and used aircraft leasing, sales and financing company.
Owner / lessor of following (main) aircraft types: Boeing 757. Aircraft leased from TRIN are listed and mentioned as such under the leasing carriers.

B = CHINA - TAIWAN (Republic of China) (Ta Chung-Hwa Min-Kuo)

Capital: Taipei Official Language: Chinese Population: 21,5 million Square Km: 36179 Dialling code: +886 Year established: 1949 Acting political head: Lee Teng-hui (President)

Government / Corporate / Executive / VIP Aircraft

☐ B-	Boeing 737-809					2 CFMI CFM56-7B26	78245	VIP		Gvmt-Presidential Flight / oo-del. 0000
☐ B-10001	Boeing 737-43Q	28492 / 2837	B-18675	0096	0998	2 CFMI CFM56-3C1	62822	VIP		Gvmt-Presidential Flight / lsf BOUL
☐ B-13105	Sikorsky S-76B	760334		0086		2 PWC PT6B-36	5171	VIP		Provincial Gvmt
☐ B-13106	Sikorsky S-76B	760393		0091	1291	2 PWC PT6B-36	5171	VIP		Provincial Gvmt
☐ B-13152	Beech King Air 200	BB-449	N2068L	0079		2 PWC PT6A-41	5670	VIP		Provincial Gvmt
☐ B-135	Beech King Air 350 (B300)	FL-52	N81664*	0091	0091	2 PWC PT6A-60A	7031	Liaison		CAA
☐ 1901	Beech 1900C-1 Airliner	UC-23	N3188K*	0088	0388	2 PWC PT6A-65B	7530	VIP / mil trans		Republic of China Air Force
☐ 1902	Beech 1900C-1 Airliner	UC-25	N3189F*	0088	0788	2 PWC PT6A-65B	7530	VIP / mil trans		Republic of China Air Force
☐ 1903	Beech 1900C-1 Airliner	UC-27	N31904*	0088	0888	2 PWC PT6A-65B	7530	VIP / mil trans		Republic of China Air Force
☐ 1904	Beech 1900C-1 Airliner	UC-29	N3192E*	0088	1188	2 PWC PT6A-65B	7530	VIP / mil trans		Republic of China Air Force
☐ 1906	Beech 1900C-1 Airliner	UC-6	N72423*	0088	0388	2 PWC PT6A-65B	7530	VIP / mil trans		Republic of China Air Force
☐ 1907	Beech 1900C-1 Airliner	UC-7	N72424*	0088	0888	2 PWC PT6A-65B	7530	VIP / mil trans		Republic of China Air Force
☐ 1908	Beech 1900C-1 Airliner	UC-8	N3179U*	0088	0588	2 PWC PT6A-65B	7530	VIP / mil trans		Republic of China Air Force
☐ 1909	Beech 1900C-1 Airliner	UC-34	N3206K*	0088	1088	2 PWC PT6A-65B	7530	VIP / mil trans		Republic of China Air Force
☐ 1910	Beech 1900C-1 Airliner	UC-35	N3214Z*	0088	1288	2 PWC PT6A-65B	7530	VIP / mil trans		Republic of China Air Force
☐ 1911	Beech 1900C-1 Airliner	UC-30	N3199H*	0088	0588	2 PWC PT6A-65B	7530	VIP / mil trans		Republic of China Air Force
☐ 1912	Beech 1900C-1 Airliner	UC-32	N3206C*	0088	0688	2 PWC PT6A-65B	7530	VIP / mil trans		Republic of China Air Force
☐ 5001	Fokker 50 (F27 Mk050)	20229	PH-JXE*	0091	0392	2 PWC PW125B	20820	VIP / mil trans		Republic of China Air Force
☐ 5002	Fokker 50 (F27 Mk050)	20238	PH-JXH*	0092	0392	2 PWC PW125B	20820	VIP / mil trans		Republic of China Air Force
☐ 5003	Fokker 50 (F27 Mk050)	20242	PH-JXI*	0092	0492	2 PWC PW125B	20820	VIP / mil trans		Republic of China Air Force

ASIA PACIFIC AIRLINES – APA (formerly Fortune Air Systems)

Taipei-Sung Shan

8F, 108 Sec. 5, Nanking East Road, Taipei, Taiwan ☎ (2) 27 62 24 48 Tx: none Fax: (2) 27 62 20 48 SITA: n/a
F: 1988 ⚲ 46 Head: Chai Tung Hai Net: http://www.caa_motc.gov.tw/airline/e_ap.html

☐ B-66062	Bell 206B JetRanger III	4325	N644H	0094	0597	1 AN 250-C20J	1451			
☐ B-66121	Bell 412HP	36023	N887H	0491	0595	2 PWC PT6T-3B TwinPac	5398			
☐ B-6616	Bell 412SP	33185		1288		2 PWC PT6T-3B TwinPac	5398			

CHINA AIRLINES, Ltd = CI / CAL (Subsidiary of China Aviation Development Foundation)

Taipei-Sung Shan & Chiang Kai Shek Int'l

131 Nanking East Road, 3rd Section, Taipei 104, Taiwan ☎ (2) 27 15 22 33 Tx: 11346 chinair Fax: (2) 27 17 51 20 SITA: n/a
F: 1959 ⚲ 8200 Head: Chiang Hung-I IATA: 297 Net: http://www.china-airlines.com
Beside aircraft listed, also uses up to 6 Boeing 747-200F lsf/opb ATLAS AIR (N, some in full China-colors) for all cargo services, when required. For details –see under Atlas Air.

☐ B-18601	Boeing 737-809	28402 / 113	N1787B*	0098	1098	2 CFMI CFM56-7B26	78245	C8Y148	EP-BK	
☐ B-18602	Boeing 737-809	28403 / 117	N1786B*	0098	1098	2 CFMI CFM56-7B26	78245	C8Y148	EP-BL	
☐ B-18603	Boeing 737-809	29103 / 129	N1784B*	0098	1198	2 CFMI CFM56-7B26	78245	C8Y148	EP-BM	
☐ B-18605	Boeing 737-809	28404 / 130	N1784B*	0098	1198	2 CFMI CFM56-7B26	78245	C8Y148	EP-CD	
☐ B-18606	Boeing 737-809	28405 / 132	N1786B*	0098	1198	2 CFMI CFM56-7B26	78245	C8Y148	EP-CF	
☐ B-18607	Boeing 737-809	29104 / 139		0098	1298	2 CFMI CFM56-7B26	78245	C8Y148	EP-CG	
☐ B-18608	Boeing 737-809	28406 / 141	N1786B*	0098	1298	2 CFMI CFM56-7B26	78245	C8Y148	EP-CH	
☐ B-18609	Boeing 737-809	28407 / 161	N1786B*	1298	1298	2 CFMI CFM56-7B26	78245	C8Y148	EP-CJ	
☐ B-18610	Boeing 737-809	29105				2 CFMI CFM56-7B26	78245	C8Y148	EP-CK	oo-delivery 1299
☐ B-18611	Boeing 737-809	29106				2 CFMI CFM56-7B26	78245	C8Y148	EP-CL	oo-delivery 0200
☐ B-	Boeing 737-809					2 CFMI CFM56-7B26	78245	C8Y148		oo-delivery 0500
☐ B-	Boeing 737-809					2 CFMI CFM56-7B26	78245	C8Y148		oo-delivery 0500
☐ B-	Boeing 737-809					2 CFMI CFM56-7B26	78245	C8Y148		oo-delivery 0600
☐ B-	Boeing 737-809					2 CFMI CFM56-7B26	78245	C8Y148		oo-delivery 0600
☐ B-	Boeing 737-809					2 CFMI CFM56-7B26	78245	C8Y148		oo-delivery 0700

22 registration type of aircraft cn/fn ex/ex* mfd del powered by mtow kg configuration selcal name/fln/specialitites/remarks

☐ B-1810	Airbus Industrie A300B4-220	179	F-WZMW*	0682	0785	2 PW JT9D-59A	165000	C24Y221	KM-AE	cvtd B4-120
☐ B-1812	Airbus Industrie A300B4-220	171	F-WZMR*	0482	0687	2 PW JT9D-59A	165000	C24Y221	KM-AB	cvtd B4-120
☐ B-190	Airbus Industrie A300B4-220	193	F-WZMM*	0682	0682	2 PW JT9D-59A	165000	C24Y221	FG-DH	lsf CCAA
☐ B-192	Airbus Industrie A300B4-220	197	F-WZEP*	0782	0782	2 PW JT9D-59A	165000	C24Y221	FG-DJ	lsf CCAA
☐ B-194	Airbus Industrie A300B4-220	221	F-WZMX*	1282	1282	2 PW JT9D-59A	165000	C24Y221	FG-DK	lsf CCAA
☐ B-196	Airbus Industrie A300B4-220	232	F-WZMD*	0783	0783	2 PW JT9D-59A	165000	C24Y221	AL-GK	lsf CCAA
☐ B-1800	Airbus Industrie A300-622R (A300B4-622R)	529	F-WWAK*	0989	0989	2 PW PW4158	170500	C26Y237	KM-CF	lsf Fuyo Leasing
☐ B-1802	Airbus Industrie A300-622R (A300B4-622R)	533	F-WWAM*	1189	1189	2 PW PW4158	170500	C26Y237	DQ-KL	lsf Fuyo Leasing
☐ B-1804	Airbus Industrie A300-622R (A300B4-622R)	536	F-WWAB*	1289	1289	2 PW PW4158	170500	C26Y237	DQ-KM	lsf Fuyo Leasing
☐ B-1806	Airbus Industrie A300-622R (A300B4-622R)	666	F-WWAY*	0092	1292	2 PW PW4158	170500	C26Y237	JM-AG	
☐ B-18501	Airbus Industrie A300-622R (A300B4-622R)	767	F-WWAL*	0096	1296	2 PW PW4158	170500	C20Y245	LR-AD	
☐ B-18502	Airbus Industrie A300-622R (A300B4-622R)	775	F-WWAT*	0097	1297	2 PW PW4158	170500	C20Y245	LR-AE	
☐ B-18503	Airbus Industrie A300-622R (A300B4-622R)	788	F-WWAE*	0098	0998	2 PW PW4158	170500	C20Y245	JQ-DS	
☐ B-18505	Airbus Industrie A300-622R (A300B4-622R)	559	F-GHEG	0090	0898	2 PW PW4158	171700	C26Y237	FR-DQ	lsf ILFC
☐ N88881	Airbus Industrie A300-622R (A300B4-622R)	743	F-WWAH*	0094	0195	2 PW PW4158	170500	C26Y237	HS-BE	lsf ILFC
☐ N88887	Airbus Industrie A300-622R (A300B4-622R)	625	PK-GAM	0092	0896	2 PW PW4158	171700	C26Y237	CR-QS	lsf ILFC
☐ N8888B	Airbus Industrie A300-622R (A300B4-622R)	677	PK-GAT	0092	0697	2 PW PW4158	171700	C26Y237	JQ-DL	lsf ILFC
☐ N8888P	Airbus Industrie A300-622R (A300B4-622R)	555	F-WQGP	0090	0398	2 PW PW4158	171700	C20Y245	JP-CG	lsf ILFC
☐ B-150	Boeing (Douglas) MD-11	48468 / 518		0092	1092	3 PW PW4460	280320	C34Y270	BC-RS	lsf CCAA/sub-lst/opb MDA in Mandarin-cs
☐ B-151	Boeing (Douglas) MD-11	48469 / 519		0092	1192	3 PW PW4460	280320	C34Y270	BD-AR	lsf CCAA/sub-lst/opb MDA in Mandarin-cs
☐ B-18151	Boeing (Douglas) MD-11	48470 / 546	B-152	0093	0693	3 PW PW4460	280320	C34Y270	BD-AS	lst / opb MDA in Mandarin-colors
☐ B-18152	Boeing (Douglas) MD-11	48471 / 558	B-153	0093	1293	3 PW PW4460	280320	C34Y270	BD-CR	
☐ N489GX	Boeing (Douglas) MD-11	48458 / 449	N280WA	0090	1097	3 PW PW4460	280320	C34Y270	LP-DF	lsf GATX/sub-lst/opb MDA in Mandarin-cs
☐ B-1862	Boeing 747SP-09	21300 / 304		0477	0477	4 PW JT9D-7A	315700	C42Y261	AL-EF	for sale
☐ B-1880	Boeing 747SP-09	22298 / 445		0480	0480	4 PW JT9D-7A	317741	C42Y261	CL-BJ	for sale
☐ B-160	Boeing 747-209F (SCD)	24308 / 752		0889	0889	4 PW JT9D-7R4G2	377842	Freighter	DQ-KP	lsf CCAA
☐ B-18255	Boeing 747-209B	21843 / 386	B-1866	0779	0779	4 PW JT9D-7AW	356070	C48Y328	KM-AD	
☐ B-18751	Boeing 747-209B (SF)	21454 / 322	B-1864	0378	0478	4 PW JT9D-7AW	356070	Freighter	CK-HL	cvtd -209B (SCD)
☐ B-18752	Boeing 747-209F (SCD)	22299 / 462	B-1894	0780	0780	4 PW JT9D-7R4G2	371946	Freighter	JM-AH	Dynasty Cargo
☐ B-18753	Boeing 747-209B	22446 / 519	B-1886	0481	0481	4 PW JT9D-7Q	371946	C48Y328	JL-EF	to be cvtd to (SF) mid 99
☐ B-18755	Boeing 747-209B (SF)	22447 / 556	B-1888	0382	0382	4 PW JT9D-7Q	371946	Freighter	AB-FL	cvtd -209B
☐ B-161	Boeing 747-409	24309 / 766		0090	0290	4 PW PW4056	394625	C93Y300	CK-JL	lsf CCAA
☐ B-162	Boeing 747-409	24310 / 778		0090	0390	4 PW PW4056	394625	C93Y300	KM-AC	lsf CCAA
☐ B-163	Boeing 747-409	24311 / 869		0091	0891	4 PW PW4056	394625	C93Y300	AB-CR	lsf CCAA
☐ B-164	Boeing 747-409	24312 / 954		0092	0193	4 PW PW4056	394625	C93Y300	CE-LR	lsf CCAA
☐ B-16801	Boeing 747-409	27965 / 1063		0095	0695	4 PW PW4056	394625	C93Y300	CE-LS	lsf / opb MDA in Mandarin-colors
☐ B-18201	Boeing 747-409	28709 / 1114		0597	0597	4 PW PW4056	394625	C93Y300	AS-JR	
☐ B-18202	Boeing 747-409	28710 / 1132		1097	1097	4 PW PW4056	394625	C93Y300	BC-FP	
☐ B-18203	Boeing 747-409	28711 / 1136		0097	1297	4 PW PW4056	394625	C93Y300	BC-KR	
☐ B-18205	Boeing 747-409	28712 / 1137		1297	1297	4 PW PW4056	394625	C93Y300	BC-MP	
☐ B-18206	Boeing 747-409	29030 / 1145		0298	0298	4 PW PW4056	394625	C93Y300	LP-AK	
☐ B-18207	Boeing 747-409	29219 / 1176		0998	0998	4 PW PW4056	394625	C93Y300	LP-AM	
☐ B-18208	Boeing 747-409	29031 / 1186		1198	1198	4 PW PW4056	394625	C93Y300	LP-DE	
☐ B-18209	Boeing 747-409	29906				4 PW PW4056	394625	C93Y300		oo-delivery 0099

DAILY AIR Corporation (Subsidiary of D'Urban Group) — Taipei-Sung Shan — 達信航空 DAILY AIR

170 Ming Chung East Road, Sec. 3, 10F-1, Taipei, Taiwan ☎ (2) 25 46 68 35 Tx: none Fax: (2) 25 45 31 90 SITA: n/a
F: 1993 120 Head: Larry Lin Net: n/a

☐ B-55501	Kawasaki (Eurocopter/MBB) BK117B-1	1057	ZK-HIC	0090	0794	2 LY LTS101-750B.1	3200	8 Pax / EMS		
☐ B-55502	Kawasaki (Eurocopter/MBB) BK117B-1	1033	B-99117	1189	0399	2 LY LTS101-750B.1	3200	8 Pax / EMS		
☐ B-55503	Kawasaki (Eurocopter/MBB) BK117B-1	1093	B-99999	0691	0399	2 LY LTS101-750B.1	3200	8 Pax / EMS		
☐ B-55505	Kawasaki (Eurocopter/MBB) BK117B-1	1056	B-99168	0790	0399	2 LY LTS101-750B.1	3200	8 Pax / EMS		
☐ B-55531	Bell 430	49015		0096	1296	2 AN 250-C40	4082	VIP 5 Pax		
☐ B-55532	Bell 430	49016	N6845C	0096	1296	2 AN 250-C40	4082	VIP 5 Pax		
☐ B-55521	Bell 412SP	33179	N7078S	0088	0795	2 PWC PT6T-3B TwinPac	5398	13 Pax		
☐ B-55523	Bell 412EP	36140		0096	1196	2 PWC PT6T-3D TwinPac	5398	13 Pax		
☐ B-55525	Bell 412EP	36206	N4438D*	0098	0098	2 PWC PT6T-3D TwinPac	5398	13 Pax		
☐ B-	Mil Mi-171TP					2 IS TV3-117MT-3	13000	28 Pax		oo-delivery 1099
☐ B-	Mil Mi-171TP					2 IS TV3-117MT	13000	28 Pax		oo-delivery 1099
☐ B-	Mil Mi-171TP					2 IS TV3-117MT	13000	Freighter		oo-delivery 0000
☐ B-	Mil Mi-171TP					2 IS TV3-117MT-3	13000	Freighter		oo-delivery 0000
☐ B-	Mil Mi-171TP					2 IS TV3-117MT-3	13000	28 Pax		oo-delivery 0000
☐ B-	Mil Mi-171TP					2 IS TV3-117MT-3	13000	28 Pax		oo-delivery 0000
☐ B-	Mil Mi-171TP					2 IS TV3-117MT-3	13000	28 Pax		oo-delivery 0000
☐ B-	Mil Mi-171TP					2 IS TV3-117MT-3	13000	28 Pax		oo-delivery 0000
☐ B-	Mil Mi-171TP					2 IS TV3-117MT-3	13000	28 Pax		oo-delivery 0000
☐ B-	Mil Mi-171TP					2 IS TV3-117MT-3	13000	28 Pax		oo-delivery 0000

EMERALD PACIFIC AIRLINES — Taichung

3F, No. 81, Section 4, Wen-Hsin Road, Taichung, Taiwan ☎ (4) 293 55 38 Tx: none Fax: (4) 293 54 01 SITA: n/a
F: 1994 n/a Head: Vincent Lee Net: n/a Aircraft below MTOW 1361kg: Hiller UH-12E

☐ B-31135	Bell 206B JetRanger III	3644	N202FC	0082	0895	1 AN 250-C20J	1451			

EVA AIR = BR / EVA (EVA Airways Corp. dba / Member of Evergreen Group of Companies) — Taipei-Chiang Kai Shek-Int'l — EVA AIR 長榮航空

EVA Air Bldg, 376 Hsin-nan Road, Section 1, Luchu, Taoyuan Hsien 338, Taiwan ☎ (3) 351 26 97 Tx: 11476 evermarine Fax: (3) 335 22 46 SITA: TPEWBBR
F: 1989 5660 Head: Frank Hsu IATA: 695 Net: http://www.evaair.com.tw

☐ B-16621	Boeing 767-25E	27192 / 524		0093	0194	2 GE CF6-80C2B2	136078	C12Y200	AR-DG	
☐ B-16622	Boeing 767-25E	27193 / 527		0093	0294	2 GE CF6-80C2B2	136078	C12Y200	EF-HS	
☐ B-16623	Boeing 767-25E	27194 / 532		0094	0394	2 GE CF6-80C2B2	136078	C12Y200	EF-JR	
☐ B-16625	Boeing 767-25E	27195 / 535		0094	0494	2 GE CF6-80C2B2	136078	C12Y200	EF-MS	
☐ B-16603	Boeing 767-35E (ER)	26063 / 434		0092	0692	2 GE CF6-80C2B6F	184612	C18Y217	BP-CS	lsf HHL Lease
☐ B-16605	Boeing 767-35E (ER)	26064 / 438		0092	0692	2 GE CF6-80C2B6F	184612	C18Y217	BP-DR	lsf HHL Lease
☐ N601EV	Boeing 767-3T7 (ER)	25076 / 366	B-16601	0091	0591	2 GE CF6-80C2B6F	184612	C18Y220	KM-AP	lsf SALE
☐ N602EV	Boeing 767-3T7 (ER)	25117 / 370	B-16602	0091	0591	2 GE CF6-80C2B6F	184612	C18Y220	KM-AQ	lsf SALE
☐ B-16101	Boeing (Douglas) MD-11	48542 / 570		0094	0894	3 GE CF6-80C2D1F	280320	C24Y83K168	FK-PR	
☐ B-16102	Boeing (Douglas) MD-11	48543 / 572		0094	0994	3 GE CF6-80C2D1F	280320	C24Y83K168	FK-PS	
☐ B-16106	Boeing (Douglas) MD-11F	48545 / 587		0095	0695	3 GE CF6-80C2D1F	280320	Freighter	BC-PR	
☐ B-16107	Boeing (Douglas) MD-11F	48546 / 589		0095	0895	3 GE CF6-80C2D1F	280320	Freighter	BC-PS	
☐ B-16108	Boeing (Douglas) MD-11F	48778 / 619		0097	1197	3 GE CF6-80C2D1F	285990	Freighter	PR-AE	
☐ B-16109	Boeing (Douglas) MD-11F	48779 / 620		0097	1297	3 GE CF6-80C2D1F	285990	Freighter	PR-AF	
☐ B-16110	Boeing (Douglas) MD-11F	48786 / 630		0098	1098	3 GE CF6-80C2D1F	285990	Freighter		
☐ B-16111	Boeing (Douglas) MD-11F	48787 / 631		0098	1198	3 GE CF6-80C2D1F	285990	Freighter		
☐ B-16112	Boeing (Douglas) MD-11F					3 GE CF6-80C2D1F	285990	Freighter		oo-delivery 0799
☐ B-16113	Boeing (Douglas) MD-11F					3 GE CF6-80C2D1F	285990	Freighter		oo-delivery 0899
☐ N103EV	Boeing (Douglas) MD-11	48415 / 576		0094	1194	3 GE CF6-80C2D1F	280320	C24Y83K168	AR-KS	lsf FSBU Trustee
☐ N105EV	Boeing (Douglas) MD-11F	48544 / 580		0095	0395	3 GE CF6-80C2D1F	280320	Freighter	BC-MS	lsf FSBU Trustee
☐ B-16401	Boeing 747-45E	27062 / 942		0092	1192	4 GE CF6-80C2B1F	394625	F8C16Y142K220	CE-GS	lsf Chailease Finance Co. Ltd
☐ B-16402	Boeing 747-45E	27063 / 947		0092	1192	4 GE CF6-80C2B1F	394625	F8C16Y142K220	CE-HR	lsf Chailease Finance Co. Ltd
☐ B-16410	Boeing 747-45E	29061 / 1140		0198	0198	4 GE CF6-80C2B1F	394625	F8C16Y142K220	LS-DM	
☐ B-16411	Boeing 747-45E	29111 / 1151		0098	0498	4 GE CF6-80C2B1F	394625	F8C16Y142K220	PR-AG	lsf Chailease Finance Co. Ltd
☐ B-16412	Boeing 747-45E	29112 / 1159		0598	0598	4 GE CF6-80C2B1F	394625	F8C16Y142K220		
☐ B-16461	Boeing 747-45E (M)	27154 / 994		0093	0993	4 GE CF6-80C2B1F	394625	F8C16Y86K156/Plt	DH-GR	lsf HHL Lease
☐ B-16462	Boeing 747-45E (M)	27173 / 998		0093	1093	4 GE CF6-80C2B1F	394625	F8C16Y86K156/Plt	DH-GS	
☐ B-16463	Boeing 747-45E (M)	27174 / 1004		0093	1193	4 GE CF6-80C2B1F	394625	F8C16Y86K156/Plt	AC-LP	
☐ B-16465	Boeing 747-45E (M)	26062 / 1016		0094	0194	4 GE CF6-80C2B1F	394625	F8C16Y86K156/Plt	AE-DR	lsf Chailease Finance Co. Ltd
☐ N403EV	Boeing 747-45E (M)	27141 / 976		0093	0593	4 GE CF6-80C2B1F	394625	F8C16Y86K156/Plt	AJ-ER	lsf FSBU Trustee / cvtd -45E
☐ N405EV	Boeing 747-45E (M)	27142 / 982		0093	0693	4 GE CF6-80C2B1F	394625	F8C16Y86K156/Plt	AJ-ES	lsf FSBU Trustee / cvtd -45E
☐ N406EV	Boeing 747-45E (M)	27898 / 1051		0094	0195	4 GE CF6-80C2B1F	394625	F8C16Y86K156/Plt	BJ-GQ	lsf FSBU Trustee
☐ N407EV	Boeing 747-45E (M)	27899 / 1053	N6018N*	0095	0295	4 GE CF6-80C2B1F	394625	F8C16Y86K156/Plt	BJ-HR	lsf FSBU Trustee
☐ N408EV	Boeing 747-45E (M)	28092 / 1076		0096	0496	4 GE CF6-80C2B1F	394625	F8C16Y86K156/Plt	JR-FM	lsf FSBU Trustee
☐ N409EV	Boeing 747-45E (M)	28093 / 1077		0096	0596	4 GE CF6-80C2B1F	394625	F8C16Y86K156/Plt	JR-FP	lsf FSBU Trustee

FAR EASTERN AIR TRANSPORT, Corp. – FAT = EF / FEA (Associated with China Airlines) — Taipei-Sung Shan — FAT 遠東航空公司 FAR EASTERN AIR TRANSPORT

No. 5, Alley 123, Lane 405, Tun Hwa N Road, FAT Bldg, Taipei 10592, Taiwan ☎ (2) 27 12 15 55 Tx: 11639 fatc Fax: (2) 27 12 24 28 SITA: n/a
F: 1957 1700 Head: Capt. Y.L. Lee IATA: 265 Net: http://www.fat.com.tw

☐ B-2615	Boeing 737-2Q8 (A)	21687 / 554	N821L	0079	0279	2 PW JT8D-9A	52163	Y120		
☐ B-2625	Boeing 737-27A (A)	23794 / 1424		0087	0887	2 PW JT8D-9A	52163	Y120		
☐ B-28007	Boeing (Douglas) MD-83 (DC-9-83)	49807 / 1829	N6200N*	0091	1292	2 PW JT8D-219	72575	Y165		lsf Sino Pac

23 registration type of aircraft cn/fn ex/ex* mfd del powered by mtow kg configuration selcal name/fln/specialitites/remarks

☐ B-28011	Boeing (Douglas) MD-82 (DC-9-82)	53118 / 1954	N6202S*	0092	0693	2 PW JT8D-219	67812	F10Y144		lsf Sino Pac / cvtd MD-83 (DC-9-83)
☐ B-28017	Boeing (Douglas) MD-82 (DC-9-82)	53166 / 2052	N835AU	0093	0595	2 PW JT8D-217C	66678	F10Y144		lsf POLA
☐ B-28021	Boeing (Douglas) MD-82 (DC-9-82)	53167 / 2056	N836AU	0093	0695	2 PW JT8D-217C	66678	F10Y144		lsf POLA
☐ B-28023	Boeing (Douglas) MD-83 (DC-9-83)	49952 / 1934	G-TONW	1091	1295	2 PW JT8D-219	72575	Y172		lsf GECA
☐ B-28025	Boeing (Douglas) MD-83 (DC-9-83)	53602 / 2214		0097	0198	2 PW JT8D-219	72575	F8Y137		
☐ B-28027	Boeing (Douglas) MD-83 (DC-9-83)	53603 / 2218		0098	0298	2 PW JT8D-219	72575	F8Y137		
☐ B-28031	Boeing (Douglas) MD-83 (DC-9-83)	49950 / 1913	P4-MDE	0091	0498	2 PW JT8D-219	72575	F8Y137		lsf GECA
☐ B-27001	Boeing 757-2Q8	25044 / 369	CC-CYG	0091	0696	2 PW PW2037	113398	Y207		lsf ILFC
☐ B-27005	Boeing 757-29J	27203 / 588	N1792B*	0093	1194	2 PW PW2037	113398	Y207		
☐ B-27007	Boeing 757-29J	27204 / 591		0094	1194	2 PW PW2037	113398	Y207		
☐ B-27011	Boeing 757-27A	29607 / 832		0098	1298	2 PW PW2037	113398	Y207		
☐ B-27013	Boeing 757-27A	29608 / 835		0098	1298	2 PW PW2037	113398	Y207		
☐ B-27015	Boeing 757-27A	29609				2 PW PW2037	113398	Y207		oo-delivery 0799
☐ B-27017	Boeing 757-27A	27017				2 PW PW2037	113398	Y207		oo-delivery 1299
☐ B-27021	Boeing 757-27A	29611				2 PW PW2037	113398	Y207		oo-delivery 0200

FORMOSA AIRLINES, Corp. = VY / FOS (Subsidiary of China Airlines / formerly Yung Shing Airlines) — Taipei-Sung Shan

永興航空股份有限公司 FORMOSA AIRLINES

12F, No. 1 Nanking East Road, Sec. 4, Taipei 102, Taiwan ☎ (2) 25 14 98 11 Tx: none Fax: (2) 25 14 98 17 SITA: n/a
F: 1966 ⁂ 600 Head: Huang-Hsiang Sun IATA: 986 Net: http://www.formosa-airlines.com.tw Aircraft below MTOW 1361kg: Hiller UH-12E. Company is expected to be merged into MANDARIN AIRLINES in mid 1999.

☐ B-12232	Britten-Norman BN-2B-26 Islander	2039	G-BNMJ*	0087		2 LY O-540-E4C5	2994	Y9		
☐ B-12252	Dornier 228-202	8158		0091	0591	2 GA TPE331-5-252D	6200	Y19		
☐ B-12253	Dornier 228-212	8215		0092	1292	2 GA TPE331-5A-252D	6400	Y19		
☐ B-12259	Dornier 228-212	8224		0094	0194	2 GA TPE331-5A-252D	6400	Y19		
☐ B-12265	Saab 340B	340B-364	SE-C64*	0094	0195	2 GE CT7-9B	13155	Y36		
☐ B-12266	Saab SF340A	340A-154	SE-F54*	0089	0889	2 GE CT7-5A2	12372	Y34		
☐ B-12271	Fokker 50 (F27 Mk050)	20284	PH-MXG*	0095	0195	2 PWC PW125B	20820	Y56		
☐ B-12272	Fokker 50 (F27 Mk050)	20286	PH-MXH*	0095	0195	2 PWC PW125B	20820	Y56		
☐ B-12273	Fokker 50 (F27 Mk050)	20303	PH-JCF*	0095	1095	2 PWC PW125B	20820	Y56		
☐ B-12275	Fokker 50 (F27 Mk050)	20306	PH-JPB*	0095	0995	2 PWC PW125B	20820	Y56		
☐ B-12276	Fokker 50 (F27 Mk050)	20312	PH-JCR*	0096	1096	2 PWC PW125B	20820	Y56		
☐ B-12291	Fokker 100 (F28 Mk0100)	11500	PH-JCO*	0095	1295	2 RR Tay 650-15	44452	Y109		
☐ B-12292	Fokker 100 (F28 Mk0100)	11496	PH-JCP*	0096	0496	2 RR Tay 650-15	44452	Y109		

GOLDEN EAGLE AIR TRANSPORT, Co. Ltd — Taipei-Sung Shan

340 Tun Hwa North Road, Taipei 10592, Taiwan ☎ (2) 25 46 04 52 Tx: none Fax: (2) 25 14 70 96 SITA: n/a
F: 1992 ⁂ 14 Head: Yung Shen Net: n/a

☐ B-98183	Learjet 35A	35A-654	ZS-NSB	0090	0495	2 GA TFE731-2-2B	8301	C8		

MANDARIN AIRLINES, Ltd = AE / MDA (Subsidiary of China Airlines) — Taipei-Chiang Kai Shek Int'l

華信航空公司 MANDARIN AIRLINES

13F, No. 134 Min Sheng East Road, Sec.3, Taipei, Taiwan ☎ (2) 27 17 11 88 Tx: n/a Fax: (2) 27 17 07 16 SITA: TPEBDAE
F: 1991 ⁂ 230 Head: Chiang Hung-I IATA: 803 ICAO: MANDARIN AIR Net: http://www.mandarin-airlines.com

☐ B-150	Boeing (Douglas) MD-11	48468 / 518		0092	0793	3 PW PW4460	280320	C34Y270	BC-RS	lsf / opf CAL in Mandarin-colors
☐ B-151	Boeing (Douglas) MD-11	48469 / 519		0092	1195	3 PW PW4460	280320	C34Y270	BD-AR	lsf / opf CAL in Mandarin-colors
☐ B-18151	Boeing (Douglas) MD-11	48470 / 546	B-152	0093	0693	3 PW PW4460	280320	C34Y270	BD-AS	lsf / opf CAL in Mandarin-colors
☐ N489GX	Boeing (Douglas) MD-11	48458 / 449	N280WA	0090	1097	3 PW PW4460	280320	C34Y270	LP-DF	lsf / opf CAL in Mandarin-colors
☐ B-16801	Boeing 747-409	27965 / 1063		0095	0695	4 PW PW4056	394625	C93Y300	CE-LS	lst / opf CAL in Mandarin-colors

ROC AVIATION, Co. Ltd — Taipei-Sung Shan

340 Run Hwa North Road, Sung Shan Airport Terminal, Taipei 10592, Taiwan ☎ (2) 27 18 41 75 Tx: n/a Fax: (2) 27 18 41 74 SITA: n/a
F: 1992 ⁂ 15 Head: Yung-Lung Chou Net: n/a

☐ B-66801	Britten-Norman BN-2B-26 Islander	2255	G-BTVI*	0091	0692	2 LY O-540-E4C5	2994			

SUNRISE AIRLINES, Co. Ltd (Subsidiary of Tseng-Chow Group) — Chai-Yi Hsien-Chu Chee Heliport

340 Tun-Hwa North Road, Sung Shan Airport, Taipei 10592, Taiwan ☎ (2) 25 14 28 77 Tx: none Fax: (2) 27 19 64 94 SITA: n/a
F: 1992 ⁂ 37 Head: Weng-Teng Lin Net: n/a

☐ B-77008	Kawasaki (Eurocopter/MBB) BK117B-1	1032	ZK-HKA	0089	0994	2 LY LTS101-750B.1	3200	8 Pax		
☐ B-77009	Kawasaki (Eurocopter/MBB) BK117B-2	1059	ZK-HKL	0090	0195	2 LY LTS101-750B.1	3350	8 Pax		
☐ B-77088	Kawasaki (Eurocopter/MBB) BK117B-1	1082	ZK-HTK	0091	0698	2 LY LTS101-750B.1	3200			

TRANSASIA AIRWAYS, Corp. = GE / TNA (Member of Gold Sun Group) — Taipei-Sung Shan

TransAsia Airways

9F, 139 Cheng Chou Road, Taipei, Taiwan ☎ (2) 25 57 57 67 Tx: 17172 foshing Fax: (2) 25 57 06 31 SITA: TPESPGE
F: 1951 ⁂ 1730 Head: Charles C. Lin IATA: 170 ICAO: TRANSASIA Net: http://www.tna.com.tw

☐ B-22712	ATR 72-202	364	F-WWEA*	0093	1293	2 PWC PW124B	21500	Y72		for sale
☐ B-22715	ATR 72-201	381	F-WWEG*	0093	0194	2 PWC PW124B	21500	Y74		for sale
☐ B-22716	ATR 72-201	389	F-WWEH*	0094	0194	2 PWC PW124B	21500	Y74		for sale
☐ B-22801	ATR 72-500 (72-212A)	517	F-WWLK*	0997	0797	2 PWC PW127F	22500	Y72		
☐ B-22802	ATR 72-500 (72-212A)	525	F-WWLB*	0097	0897	2 PWC PW127F	22500	Y72		
☐ B-22803	ATR 72-500 (72-212A)	527	F-WWLC*	0097	0897	2 PWC PW127F	22500	Y72		
☐ B-22805	ATR 72-500 (72-212A)	558	F-WWLN*	0098	1198	2 PWC PW127F	22500	Y72		
☐ B-22806	ATR 72-500 (72-212A)	560	F-WQIY*	0098	1298	2 PWC PW127F	22500	Y72		
☐ B-22807	ATR 72-500 (72-212A)	567	F-WWEF*	0099	0199	2 PWC PW127F	22500	Y72		
☐ B-22301	Airbus Industrie A320-231	332	F-WWIC*	0092	0892	2 IAE V2500-A1	73500	C12Y138		lsf Goldsun Leasing Co. Ltd
☐ B-22302	Airbus Industrie A320-231	369	F-WWIL*	0092	1292	2 IAE V2500-A1	73500	C12Y138		
☐ B-22310	Airbus Industrie A320-232	791	F-WWDR*	0098	0698	2 IAE V2527-A5	73500	Y162		
☐ B-22311	Airbus Industrie A320-232	822	F-WWBY*	0098	0798	2 IAE V2527-A5	73500	Y162		
☐ B-22601	Airbus Industrie A321-131	538	F-WGYZ*	0095	0795	2 IAE V2530-A5	83000	Y194		
☐ B-22602	Airbus Industrie A321-131	555	F-WGYZ*	0095	1095	2 IAE V2530-A5	83000	Y194		
☐ B-22603	Airbus Industrie A321-131	602	F-WGYZ*	0096	0696	2 IAE V2530-A5	83000	Y194	HM-FS	
☐ B-22605	Airbus Industrie A321-131	606	F-WGYY*	0096	0796	2 IAE V2530-A5	83000	Y194		
☐ B-22606	Airbus Industrie A321-131	731	F-WQGL*	0097	0198	2 IAE V2530-A5	83000	Y194		
☐ B-22607	Airbus Industrie A321-131	746	F-WQGM*	0097	0198	2 IAE V2530-A5	83000	Y194		

U-LAND AIRLINES = WI (Member of U-Land Enterprise Group) — Taipei-Sung Shan & Kaoshiung

340 Tun Hwa North Road, Sung Shan Airport, Taipei 10592, Taiwan ☎ (2) 27 13 41 66 Tx: none Fax: (2) 27 13 29 35 SITA: n/a
F: 1987 ⁂ 370 Head: K.G. Wang Net: n/a

☐ B-8811	Shorts 360-300 (SD3-60)	SH3760	G-BPXN*	0089	0095	2 PWC PT6A-67R	12292	Y36		std TSA
☐ B-88888	Boeing (Douglas) MD-82 (DC-9-82)	53479 / 2124	N9012S*	0095	1195	2 PW JT8D-217C	67812	Y165		lst/opf GAP
☐ B-88889	Boeing (Douglas) MD-82 (DC-9-82)	53480 / 2127		0095	1295	2 PW JT8D-217C	67812	Y165		lst/opf PIC
☐ B-88898	Boeing (Douglas) MD-82 (DC-9-82)	53481 / 2145		0096	0896	2 PW JT8D-217C	67812	Y165		lsf Centrel Leasing/sub-lst/opf GAP
☐ B-88899	Boeing (Douglas) MD-82 (DC-9-82)	53542 / 2152		0096	1096	2 PW JT8D-217C	67812	Y165		lst/opf GAP
☐ B-88988	Boeing (Douglas) MD-82 (DC-9-82)	53577 / 2189		0097	1097	2 PW JT8D-217C	67812	Y165		lsf Centrel Leasing
☐ B-88989	Boeing (Douglas) MD-82 (DC-9-82)	53581 / 2204	N6203D*	0097	1197	2 PW JT8D-217C	67812	Y165		lsf Centrel Leasing

UNI AIR = B7 / UIA (Uni Airways Corp. dba/Associated with EVA Air/formerly Makung Int'l Airlines Co. Ltd & Makung Airlines, Co. Ltd) — Kaoshiung

No. 2-6 Chung-Shan 4th Road, Kaoshiung, Taiwan ☎ (7) 791 76 11 Tx: none Fax: (7) 791 75 11 SITA: HDQWBB7
F: 1988 ⁂ 2000 Head: Frank Hsu IATA: 525 Net: http://www.uniair.com.tw

☐ B-11110	Britten-Norman BN-2A-26 Islander	575	G-BEIY*	0077	0798	2 LY O-540-E4C5	2994	Y9		
☐ B-11123	Britten-Norman BN-2A-26 Islander	2032	G-BNAE*	0086	0798	2 LY O-540-E4C5	2994	Y9		
☐ B-11126	Britten-Norman BN-2B-26 Islander	2193	G-BLNS*	0086	0798	2 LY O-540-E4C5	2994	Y9		
☐ B-11150	Dornier 228-212	8177	D-CPDD*	0089	0798	2 GA TPE331-5A-252D	6400	Y19		for sale
☐ B-11156	Dornier 228-212	8235	D-CBDP*	0096	0798	2 GA TPE331-5A-252D	6400	Y19		for sale
☐ B-	De Havilland DHC-8-202 Dash 8Q					2 PWC PW123D	16500	Y37		oo-delivery 0899
☐ B-	De Havilland DHC-8-202 Dash 8Q					2 PWC PW123D	16500	Y37		oo-delivery 1099
☐ B-15215	De Havilland DHC-8-311 Dash 8	320	C-FDHD*	0092	0798	2 PWC PW123	18643	Y56		
☐ B-15217	De Havilland DHC-8-311 Dash 8	379	C-GEOA*	0094	0798	2 PWC PW123	18643	Y56		
☐ B-15219	De Havilland DHC-8-311 Dash 8	381	C-FDHD*	0094	0798	2 PWC PW123	18643	Y56		
☐ B-15221	De Havilland DHC-8-311 Dash 8	325	C-FNJD*	0092	0798	2 PWC PW123	18643	Y56		
☐ B-15223	De Havilland DHC-8-311 Dash 8	404	C-GDKL*	0095	0798	2 PWC PW123	18643	Y56		lsf Hwa-Hsia Leasing Ltd
☐ B-15225	De Havilland DHC-8-311 Dash 8	405	C-GFHZ*	0095	0798	2 PWC PW123	18643	Y56		lsf Hwa-Hsia Leasing Ltd
☐ B-15227	De Havilland DHC-8-311 Dash 8	406	C-FDHD*	0095	0798	2 PWC PW123	18643	Y56		lsf Hwa-Hsia Leasing Ltd
☐ B-15229	De Havilland DHC-8-311 Dash 8	407	C-GFEN*	0095	0798	2 PWC PW123	18643	Y56		lsf Hwa-Hsia Leasing Ltd
☐ B-15231	De Havilland DHC-8-311 Dash 8	414	C-GFBW*	0095	0798	2 PWC PW123	18643	Y56		
☐ B-15233	De Havilland DHC-8-311 Dash 8	402	C-GDFT*	0095	0798	2 PWC PW123	18643	Y56		
☐ B-15235	De Havilland DHC-8-311 Dash 8Q	443	C-FWBB*	0096	0798	2 PWC PW123	18643	Y56		lsf Hwa-Hsia Leasing Ltd
☐ B-15237	De Havilland DHC-8-311 Dash 8Q	467	C-GELN*	0097	0798	2 PWC PW123	18643	Y56		lsf Hwa-Hsia Leasing Ltd
☐ B-17401	De Havilland DHC-8-401 Dash 8Q					2 PWC PW150A	26989	Y78		oo-delivery 0099

registration	type of aircraft	cn/fn	ex/ex*	mfd	del	powered by	mtow kg	configuration	selcal	name/fln/specialitites/remarks
☐ B-17402	De Havilland DHC-8-401 Dash 8Q					2 PWC PW150A	26989	Y78		oo-delivery 0099
☐ B-17403	De Havilland DHC-8-401 Dash 8Q					2 PWC PW150A	26989	Y78		oo-delivery 0000
☐ B-17405	De Havilland DHC-8-401 Dash 8Q					2 PWC PW150A	26989	Y78		oo-delivery 0000
☐ B-17406	De Havilland DHC-8-401 Dash 8Q					2 PWC PW150A	26989	Y78		oo-delivery 0000
☐ B-17407	De Havilland DHC-8-401 Dash 8Q					2 PWC PW150A	26989	Y78		oo-delivery 0000
☐ B-1775	BAe 146-300	E3161	G-BSOC*	0090	0890	4 LY ALF502R-5	39995	C8Y104		for sale
☐ B-1776	BAe 146-300	E3174	G-BSXZ*	0090	0191	4 LY ALF502R-5	39995	C8Y104		for sale
☐ B-1777	BAe 146-300	E3205	G-BTVO*	0091	1192	4 LY ALF502R-5	39995	C8Y104		for sale
☐ B-1778	BAe 146-300	E3209	G-BVCE*	0092	0594	4 LY ALF502R-5	39995	C8Y104		for sale
☐ B-17811	BAe 146-300	E3202	G-BTUY*	0091	0195	4 LY ALF502R-5	39995	C8Y104		lsf Hwa-Hsia Leasing Ltd
☐ B-15301	Boeing (Douglas) MD-90-30	53547 / 2169		0097	0798	2 IAE V2525-D5	70760	C12Y140		
☐ B-17911	Boeing (Douglas) MD-90-30	53535 / 2158		0096	1196	2 IAE V2525-D5	63957	C12Y143		lsf Hwa-Hsia Leasing Ltd
☐ B-17912	Boeing (Douglas) MD-90-30	53536 / 2160		0096	1196	2 IAE V2525-D5	63957	C12Y143		lsf Hwa-Hsia Leasing Ltd
☐ B-17913	Boeing (Douglas) MD-90-30	53537 / 2162		0096	1296	2 IAE V2525-D5	63957	C12Y143		
☐ B-17915	Boeing (Douglas) MD-90-30	53538 / 2168		0097	0197	2 IAE V2525-D5	63957	C12Y143		lsf Chailease Finance Co. Ltd
☐ B-17916	Boeing (Douglas) MD-90-30	53539 / 2171		0097	0397	2 IAE V2525-D5	63957	C12Y143		
☐ B-17917	Boeing (Douglas) MD-90-30	53572 / 2217		0098	0198	2 IAE V2525-D5	63957	C12Y143		
☐ B-17918	Boeing (Douglas) MD-90-30	53571 / 2193		0097	1297	2 IAE V2525-D5	63957	C12Y143		lsf Chailease Finance Co. Ltd
☐ B-17919	Boeing (Douglas) MD-90-30	53569 / 2173		0098	1098	2 IAE V2525-D5	63957	C12Y143		
☐ B-17920	Boeing (Douglas) MD-90-30	53574 / 2186		0098	1198	2 IAE V2528-D5	63957	C12Y143		
☐ B-17921	Boeing (Douglas) MD-90-30	53554 / 2166	N6204C*	0098	1198	2 IAE V2528-D5	63957	Y166		
☐ B-17922	Boeing (Douglas) MD-90-30	53601 / 2243		0098	1298	2 IAE V2528-D5	63957	Y170		
☐ B-17923	Boeing (Douglas) MD-90-30	53534 / 2153	B-16901	0096	1298	2 IAE V2525-D5	63957	C12Y140		lsf FCB Leasing Ltd
☐ B-17925	Boeing (Douglas) MD-90-30	53568 / 2171	B-16902	0097	0497	2 IAE V2525-D5	63957	C12Y143		lsf FCB Leasing Ltd

C = CANADA

Until 1st January 1974, Canada had "CF" as ICAO-nationality-mark, but then changed to "C" . Whenever many aircraft with CF-reg's were re-registered to "C", others retained their CF-reg's. In case of aircraft which were previously CF-registered and are now C-registered we do not regard the CF-reg. as previous reg. but take the earlier one.
Capital: Ottawa   Official Language: English, French   Population: 30,0 million   Square Km: 9976139   Dialling code: +1   Year established: 1867   Acting political head: Jean Chrétien (Prime Minister)

Government / Corporate / Executive / VIP Aircraft

registration	type of aircraft	cn/fn	ex/ex*	mfd	del	powered by	mtow kg	configuration	selcal	name/fln/specialitites/remarks
☐ C-FETB	Boeing 720-023B	18024 / 177	OD-AFQ	0061	0186	4 PW JT3D-1	106142	CorporateTestbed		Pratt & Whitney Canada
☐ C-FJJA	De Havilland DHC-8-401 Dash 8Q	4001			0097	2 PWC PW150A	28690	Testbed		Bombardier Inc. / Prototype
☐ C-FNRJ	Canadair Regional Jet 100LR (CL-600-2B19)	7002		0090	0791	2 GE CF34-3A1	24041	CorporateTestbed		2nd Prototype / Bombardier Inc.
☐ C-FPAW	Embraer 120RT Brasilia (EMB-120RT)	120018	N516P	0086	0290	2 PWC PW118	11500	CorporateTestbed		Pratt & Whitney Canada
☐ 144601	Canadair CL-600S (CC-144) Challenger	1040	C-GLYM*	0082		2 LY ALF502L-2	18711	VIP / mil trans	GH-DE	CAF Air Transport Group
☐ 144602	Canadair CL-600S (CC-144) Challenger	1065	C-GBVE*	0082		2 LY ALF502L-2	18711	VIP / mil trans	FM-GK	CAF Air Transport Group
☐ 144603	Canadair CL-600S (CC-144) Challenger	1006	C-GCSN*	0080	0085	2 LY ALF502L-2	18711	VIP / mil trans	KM-CH	CAF Air Transport Group
☐ 144604	Canadair CL-600S (CC-144) Challenger	1007	C-GBKC*	0080		2 LY ALF502L-2	18711	VIP / mil trans	CK-LM	CAF Air Transport Group
☐ 144605	Canadair CL-600S (CC-144) Challenger	1008	C-GBEY*	0080		2 LY ALF502L-2	18711	VIP / mil trans	GM-BL	CAF Air Transport Group
☐ 144606	Canadair CL-600S (CC-144) Challenger	1009	C-GCVQ*	0080		2 LY ALF502L-2	18711	VIP / mil trans	KM-DH	CAF Air Transport Group
☐ 144607	Canadair CL-600S (CC-144) Challenger	1014	C-GBLL*	0080	0085	2 LY ALF502L-2	18711	VIP / mil trans	KM-DE	CAF Air Transport Group
☐ 144608	Canadair CL-600S (CC-144) Challenger	1015	C-GBLN*	0080		2 LY ALF502L-2	18711	VIP / mil trans	FM-EL	CAF Air Transport Group
☐ 144609	Canadair CL-600S (CC-144) Challenger	1017	C-GBPX*	0081		2 LY ALF502L-2	18711	VIP / mil trans	GH-CM	CAF Air Transport Group
☐ 144610	Canadair CL-600S (CC-144) Challenger	1022	C-GOGO*	0081		2 LY ALF502L-2	18711	VIP / mil trans	KM-CJ	CAF Air Transport Group
☐ 144611	Canadair CL-600S (CC-144) Challenger	1030	C-GCZU*	0081	0086	2 LY ALF502L-2	18711	VIP / mil trans	KM-CG	CAF Air Transport Group
☐ 144612	Canadair CL-600S (CC-144) Challenger	1002	C-GCGS-X*	0079	0088	2 LY ALF502L-2	18711	VIP / mil trans		CAF Air Transport Group
☐ 144614	Canadair CL-601-1A (CC-144) Challenger	3036	C-GCUP*	0084		2 GE CF34-1A	19550	VIP / mil trans	AG-KP	CAF Air Transport Group
☐ 144615	Canadair CL-601-1A (CC-144) Challenger	3037	C-GCUR*	0084		2 GE CF34-1A	19550	VIP / mil trans	AG-LP	CAF Air Transport Group
☐ 144616	Canadair CL-601-1A (CC-144) Challenger	3038	C-GCUT*	0084		2 GE CF34-1A	19550	VIP / mil trans	AG-MP	CAF Air Transport Group
☐ 15001	Airbus Ind. A310-304 (F) (CC-150) Polaris	446	F-WQCQ	1287	0393	2 GE CF6-80C2A2	157000	VIP C106 miltr	AS-CQ	216 / CAF Air Transport Group / cvtd -304
☐ 15002	Airbus Ind. A310-304 (F) (CC-150) Polaris	482	C-GLWD	0193	0193	2 GE CF6-80C2A2	157000	Combi miltrans	AS-CP	212 / CAF Air Transport Group / cvtd -304
☐ 15003	Airbus Ind. A310-304 (F) (CC-150) Polaris	425	C-FWDX	1286	1292	2 GE CF6-80C2A2	157000	Combi miltrans	AS-CM	202 / CAF Air Transport Group / cvtd -304
☐ 15004	Airbus Ind. A310-304 (F) (CC-150) Polaris	444	C-FNWD	1087	0293	2 GE CF6-80C2A2	157000	Combi miltrans	AS-CR	205 / CAF Air Transport Group / cvtd -304
☐ 15005	Airbus Ind. A310-304 (F) (CC-150) Polaris	441	F-ZJEP	0087	0993	2 GE CF6-80C2A2	157000	Combi miltrans	AS-DE	201 / CAF Air Transport Group / cvtd -304

ABERDEEN HELICOPTERS, Ltd

Prince George, B.C.

6150 Tasa Court, Prince George, British Columbia V2K 4J3, Canada   ☎ (250) 962-5566   Tx: none   Fax: (250) 962-2556   SITA: n/a
F: 1993   ♦♦♦ 3   Head: Peter McGill   Net: n/a

registration	type of aircraft	cn/fn	ex/ex*	mfd	del	powered by	mtow kg	configuration	selcal	name/fln/specialitites/remarks
☐ C-FHTT	Bell 206B JetRanger	1042		0073	0496	1 AN 250-C20	1451			
☐ C-GIWE	Bell 206B JetRanger II	2129		0076	0698	1 AN 250-C20	1451			

ABITIBI Helicopters, Ltd   (Les Hélicoptères Abitibi, Ltée)

La Sarre, Qué.

CP188, 341 Route 111 Ouest, La Sarre, Québec J9Z 2X5, Canada   ☎ (819) 333-4047   Tx: none   Fax: (819) 333-9894   SITA: n/a
F: 1976   ♦♦♦ 90   Head: Bertrand Perron   Net: n/a

registration	type of aircraft	cn/fn	ex/ex*	mfd	del	powered by	mtow kg	configuration	selcal	name/fln/specialitites/remarks
☐ C-GNBS	Bell 206B JetRanger	1138		0073	0693	1 AN 250-C20	1451			
☐ C-GNMD	Bell 206L LongRanger	45080		0077		1 AN 250-C20B	1814			
☐ C-FHAD	Eurocopter (Aérosp.) AS350B2 AStar	2767		0094	0494	1 TU Arriel 1D1	2250			Hi-skids
☐ C-FHAF	Eurocopter (Aérosp.) AS350BA AStar	1543	N516WW	0082	0192	1 TU Arriel 1B	2100			Hi-skids / cvtd AS350D
☐ C-FHAU	Eurocopter (Aérosp.) AS350BA AStar	2778		0094	0494	1 TU Arriel 1B	2100			Hi-skids
☐ C-FHBG	Eurocopter (Aérosp.) AS350BA AStar	1440	N513HC	0081	0898	1 TU Arriel 1B	2100			cvtd AS350B
☐ C-FLHA	Eurocopter (Aérosp.) AS350B2 AStar	2480	N6040Y	0091	0496	1 TU Arriel 1D1	2250			cvtd AS350B
☐ C-FNJY	Eurocopter (Aérosp.) AS350BA AStar	2546		0091	1194	1 TU Arriel 1B	2100			cvtd AS350B
☐ C-FSPE	Eurocopter (Aérosp.) AS350BA AStar	2787		0094	0798	1 TU Arriel 1B	2100			
☐ C-GHAQ	Eurocopter (Aérosp.) AS350D AStar	1542	N515WW	0082	0292	1 LY LTS101-600A.3	1950			Hi-skids
☐ C-GHAV	Eurocopter (Aérosp.) AS350BA AStar	2758		0094	0494	1 TU Arriel 1B	2100			Hi-skids
☐ C-GHSL	Eurocopter (Aérosp.) AS350D AStar	1484	N510WW	0081	0192	1 LY LTS101-600A.3	1950			Hi-skids
☐ C-GHSM	Eurocopter (Aérosp.) AS350D AStar	1468	N700WW	0082	0991	1 LY LTS101-600A.3	1950			Hi-skids

ACCENT AVIATION SERVICES, Ltd

Calgary & Edmonton, Alta.

5414-11th Street NE, Calgary, Alberta T2E 7E9, Canada   ☎ (403) 291-2131   Tx: none   Fax: (403) 274-1547   SITA: n/a
F: 1987   ♦♦♦ 9   Head: Shane Lepage   Net: n/a

registration	type of aircraft	cn/fn	ex/ex*	mfd	del	powered by	mtow kg	configuration	selcal	name/fln/specialitites/remarks
☐ C-FZNM	Cessna A185E Skywagon	18501829		0070	0694	1 CO IO-520-D	1520			
☐ C-GWWO	Cessna 310I	310I0161	N8161M	0064	0889	2 CO IO-470-U	2313			
☐ C-FTEC	Cessna 414A Chancellor II	414A0298	N2620C	0079	1291	2 CO TSIO-520-NB	3223			
☐ C-GVZE	Cessna 414A Chancellor III	414A0219	N414WB	0079	0397	2 CO TSIO-520-NB	3062			
☐ C-FWWF	Cessna 402C II	402C0280	N189B	0080	1095	2 CO TSIO-520-VB	3107			
☐ C-FOBF	Cessna 421B Golden Eagle	421B0934	N22FX	0075	0299	2 CO GTSIO-520-H	3379			
☐ C-GPAT	Cessna 421B Golden Eagle	421B0263		0072	0897	2 CO GTSIO-520-H	3379			
☐ C-GWWQ	Beech King Air 100	B-76	N300DA	0071	0696	2 PWC PT6A-28	4808			

ACTION AVIATION   (Ross River Flying Services, Ltd dba)

Whitehorse, Y.T.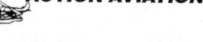

PO Bo 5898, Whitehorse, Yukon Territories Y1A 5L6, Canada   ☎ (867) 633-3343   Tx: none   Fax: (867) 667-4765   SITA: n/a
F: 1986   ♦♦♦ n/a   Head: Ray Harbats   Net: n/a   Aircraft below MTOW 1361 kg: Cessna 150 / 172 & Piper PA-18

registration	type of aircraft	cn/fn	ex/ex*	mfd	del	powered by	mtow kg	configuration	selcal	name/fln/specialitites/remarks
☐ C-GCRR	Cessna TU206G Turbo Stationair 6 II	U20605672		0080	0595	1 CO TSIO-520-M	1633			Floats / Wheel-Skis
☐ C-GIBG	Cessna TU206G Turbo Stationair 6 II	U20605949		0081	0190	1 CO TSIO-520-M	1633			Floats / Wheel-Skis
☐ C-GGOL	Cessna T207A Turbo Stationair 8 II	T20700636		0080	0490	1 CO TSIO-520-M	1724			

ADLAIR AVIATION (1983), Ltd

Cambridge Bay & Yellowknife, N.W.T.

PO Box 111, Cambridge Bay, Northwest Territories X0E 0C0, Canada   ☎ (867) 983-2569   Tx: none   Fax: (867) 983-2847   SITA: n/a
F: 1983   ♦♦♦ 27   Head: Paul W. Laserich   Net: n/a

registration	type of aircraft	cn/fn	ex/ex*	mfd	del	powered by	mtow kg	configuration	selcal	name/fln/specialitites/remarks
☐ C-FGYN	De Havilland DHC-2 Beaver I	134			0051	1 PW R-985	2313			Floats / Wheel-Skis
☐ C-GSYN	Beech King Air 100	B-61	N418LA	0070		2 PWC PT6A-28	4808			
☐ C-GFYN	De Havilland DHC-6 Twin Otter 200	209	N915SA	0069	0888	2 PWC PT6A-20	5252			
☐ C-GBFP	Learjet 25B	25B-167	N664CL	0074	0992	2 GE CJ610-6	6804	EMS		Ernie Lyall

ADLER AVIATION, Ltd

Waterloo-Regional, Ont.

Box 360, Breslau, Ontario N0B 1M0, Canada   ☎ (519) 648-3886   Tx: none   Fax: (519) 648-3264   SITA: n/a
F: 1995   ♦♦♦ 5   Head: Capt. Steven A. Hause   Net: n/a   Aircraft below MTOW 1361kg: Aeronca 50C, Cessna 150 & Piper PA-28

registration	type of aircraft	cn/fn	ex/ex*	mfd	del	powered by	mtow kg	configuration	selcal	name/fln/specialitites/remarks
☐ C-GHOL	Piper PA-31-310 Navajo B	31-7401238	N56V	0074	0696	2 LY TIO-540-A2C	2948			
☐ C-GTGR	Cessna 421C Golden Eagle II	421C0061	N15LW	0076	0698	2 CO GTSIO-520-L	3379			

ADVANCE AIR CHARTER SERVICE   (Advance Flight Training Centre, Inc. dba)

Oro-Lake Simcoe Regional, Ont.

Box 23024, Barrie, Ontario L4N 7W8, Canada   ☎ (705) 487-6910   Tx: none   Fax: (705) 487-7176   SITA: n/a
F: 1996   ♦♦♦ n/a   Net: n/a   Aircraft below MTOW 1361kg: Piper PA-28

registration	type of aircraft	cn/fn	ex/ex*	mfd	del	powered by	mtow kg	configuration	selcal	name/fln/specialitites/remarks
☐ C-FHLI	Piper PA-23-250 Aztec C	27-2774	N5657Y	0065	0698	2 LY IO-540-C4B5	2359			
☐ C-FXWT	Cessna 421	421-0177		0068	0598	2 CO GTSIO-520-D	3103			

ADVENTURE AIR, Corp. — Gander, Nfld.

Box 10, Gander, Newfoundland A1V 1W5, Canada ☎ (709) 256-4620 Tx: none Fax: (709) 256-2358 SITA: n/a
F: 1993 ⁂ n/a Head: Gerald B. Pritchett Net: n/a

☐ C-FSDE	De Havilland DHC-2 Beaver I	1593		0064	0594	1 PW R-985	2313			Floats / Wheel-Skis

AERIAL RECON SURVEYS, Ltd — Whitecourt, Alta.

PO Box 1229, Whitecourt, Alberta T7S 1P1, Canada ☎ (780) 778-3080 Tx: none Fax: (780) 778-2064 SITA: n/a
F: 1985 ⁂ n/a Head: Eric Gould Net: http://www.agt.net/public/aerial/ Aircraft below MTOW 1361 kg: Cessna 177 & Robinson R22, R44.

☐ C-GCKH	MD Helicopters MD 500D (Hughes 369D)	500716D	N3115Y	0080	0597	1 AN 250-C20B	1361			
☐ C-GSHE	MD Helicopters MD 500D (Hughes 369D)	1280431D	N8639F	0078	0197	1 AN 250-C20B	1361			
☐ C-FARJ	Bell 206B JetRanger	741	N700BH	0071	0688	1 AN 250-C20	1451			cvtd 206A
☐ C-FBKH	Bell 206B JetRanger	575		0070	0689	1 AN 250-C20	1451			cvtd 206A
☐ C-FMAD	Bell 206B JetRanger	408	N725BB	0069	1095	1 AN 250-C20	1451			cvtd 206A
☐ C-GAHP	Bell 206B JetRanger	805	N2959W	0072	1197	1 AN 250-C20	1451			
☐ C-GJEL	Bell 206B JetRanger	116	N855NR	0067	0998	1 AN 250-C20	1451			cvtd 206A
☐ C-GTEZ	Bell 206B JetRanger	746		0071	0797	1 AN 250-C20	1451			
☐ C-GXAG	Bell 206B JetRanger	150	N6283N	0068	0998	1 AN 250-C20	1451			cvtd 206A
☐ C-GXBY	Bell 206B JetRanger	477	N72HP	0069	0692	1 AN 250-C20	1451			cvtd 206A
☐ C-FARA	Cessna U206C Super Skywagon	U206-1009	N29011	0068	0798	1 CO IO-520-F	1633			
☐ C-FVGV	Cessna U206G Stationair 6 II	U20604500	N1029M	0078	0595	1 CO IO-520-F	1633			
☐ C-FPKM	Eurocopter (Aerosp.) AS350B AStar	2426	JA6045	0090	0199	1 TU Arriel 1B	1950			
☐ C-FKMN	Bell 407	53110		0097	0297	1 AN 250-C47B	2268			
☐ C-FAMO	BAe (HS) 748-258 Srs 2A	1669 / 144		0069	0697	2 RR Dart 534-2	20183	Y41		

AERO ACADEMY, Inc. (Affiliated with Air London, Ltd) — London, Ont.

2410 Aviation Lane, London, Ontario N5V 3Z9, Canada ☎ (519) 453-8611 Tx: none Fax: (519) 451-1981 SITA: n/a
F: 1978 ⁂ n/a Head: Sharon Moon Net: n/a Aircraft below MTOW 1361 kg: Cessna 152 & 172.

☐ C-GNFD	Piper PA-34-200 Seneca	34-7450178	N43056	0074		2 LY IO-360-C1E6	1905			

AERO ARCTIC, Ltd — Yellowknife & -Aero Arctic Heliport N.W.T.

PO Box 1496, Yellowknife, Northwest Territories X1A 2P1, Canada ☎ (867) 873-5230 Tx: none Fax: (867) 920-4488 SITA: n/a
F: 1969 ⁂ 9 Head: Bob O'Connor Net: n/a

☐ C-GQAA	Bell 206B JetRanger	1278	N59465	0074		1 AN 250-C20	1451			
☐ C-GTAA	Cessna A185F Skywagon II	18503559	N4815Q	0078	0281	1 CO IO-520-D	1520			
☐ C-FJAL	Bell 206L-1 LongRanger II	45295	N91465	0079	0497	1 AN 250-C28B	1882			
☐ C-GEAP	Bell 204B	2063	Thai 917	0067		1 LY T5311A	3856			

AERO CHARTER OF OTTAWA (154279 Canada, Inc. dba) — Ottawa-Int'l, Ont.

39 Amberwood Crescent, Nepean, Ontario K2E 7C1, Canada ☎ (613) 723-8092 Tx: none Fax: none SITA: n/a
F: 1987 ⁂ 2 Head: Donald S. Cameron Net: n/a

☐ C-FKWE	Cessna 310Q	310Q0822		0073	0594	2 CO IO-470-VO	2404			

AERO GOLFE, Ltée — Havre St. Pierre, Qué.

1511 Boreale, CP 998, Havre St. Pierre, Québec G0G 1P0, Canada ☎ (418) 538-3866 Tx: none Fax: (418) 538-3805 SITA: n/a
F: 1988 ⁂ n/a Head: n/a Net: n/a

☐ C-FTBC	Cessna U206F Stationair	U20602047		0073	0189	1 CO IO-520-F	1633			Floats / Wheel-Skis
☐ C-FKLC	De Havilland DHC-3 Otter	255		0058	0698	1 PW R-1340	3629			Floats / Wheel-Skis

AERO LINK (Ains Express Cargo dba) — Toronto-Int'l, Ont.

7035 Fir Tree Drive, Unit 33, 2nd Floor, Mississauga, Ontario L5S 1V6, Canada ☎ (905) 677-5362 Tx: none Fax: (905) 677-4189 SITA: n/a
F: 1997 ⁂ 12 Head: Ainsworth Whyte Net: http://www.aerolink.ca

☐ C-FCDi	Piper PA-30-160 Twin Comanche B	30-1027	N7936Y	0066	0797	2 LY IO-320-B1A	1633			
☐ C-FAAL	Embraer 120RT Brasilia (EMB-120RT)	120063	N7215U	0087	0499	2 PWC PW118	11500	Freighter		
☐ C-	Embraer 120RT Brasilia (EMB-120RT)	120023	N227AS	0086	0499	2 PWC PW118	11500	Freighter		

AERO-NOR (Av-Gaz Plus, Inc. dba / Seasonal May-November ops only) — Montreal-Commodore SPB, Qué.

3178 Boul. Le Corbusier, Laval, Québec H7L 4S8, Canada ☎ (514) 336-2296 Tx: none Fax: (514) 687-3900 SITA: n/a
F: 1973 ⁂ n/a Head: n/a Net: n/a

☐ C-GYXE	Cessna U206G Stationair	U20603801		0077		1 CO IO-520-F	1633			Floats

AERO NORD-EST, Inc. — Sept-Iles, Qué.

909 Dequen, Sept-Iles, Québec G4R 2S4, Canada ☎ (418) 962-2404 Tx: none Fax: none SITA: n/a
F: 1985 ⁂ n/a Head: Jules Blouin Net: n/a

☐ C-FEGE	De Havilland DHC-2 Beaver I	1539	VH-IDK	0064	1290	1 PW R-985	2313			Ist Air Outaouais
☐ C-FGCW	De Havilland DHC-2 Beaver I	198		0052		1 PW R-985	2309			Floats / Wheel-Skis
☐ C-FMPR	De Havilland DHC-2 Beaver I	971		0056	1296	1 PW R-985	2313			Ist Brassard Air Service
☐ C-FZKU	De Havilland DHC-2 Beaver I	382	N7942C	0052	0993	1 PW R-985	2313			Ist Air Bellevue
☐ C-GUHN	De Havilland DHC-2 Beaver I	1325	58-1999	0059	0691	1 PW R-985	2313			Floats / Wheel-Skis

AEROPAC SERVICES (547962 Alberta, Ltd dba) — Fort Smith, N.W.T.

Box 3, Fort Smith, Northwest Territories X0E 0P0, Canada ☎ (867) 872-4004 Tx: none Fax: (867) 872-4002 SITA: n/a
F: 1993 ⁂ n/a Head: Melvin Walker Net: n/a Aircraft below MTOW 1361kg: Cessna 180 (on Floats / Wheel-Skis)

☐ C-GSJR	Cessna U206C Super Skywagon	U206-1091	N29121	0068	0598	1 CO IO-520-F	1633			Floats / Wheel-Skis

AERO PENINSULE, Ltée — Pokemouche, N.B.

CP 3601, Tracadie-Sheila, New Brunswick E1X 1G5, Canada ☎ (506) 395-6361 Tx: none Fax: (506) 395-5663 SITA: n/a
F: n/a ⁂ n/a Head: Ron Legault Net: n/a Aircraft below MTOW 1361kg: Cessna 172

☐ C-FIML	Cessna 310Q	310Q0758		0073	0697	2 CO IO-470-VO	2404			
☐ C-GABL	Cessna 310R II	310R0927	N3840G	0077	0797	2 CO IO-520-M	2495			
☐ C-FAPL	Piper PA-31-310 Navajo B	31-7401249	N13TL	0074	1198	2 LY TIO-540-A2C	2948			

AERO PHOTO (1961), Inc. — Québec, Qué. & Conakry (Guinea)

1564 rue Notre-Dame, Ancienne Lorette, Québec G2E 3B3, Canada ☎ (418) 872-6633 Tx: none Fax: (418) 872-9810 SITA: n/a
F: 1961 ⁂ 10 Head: Claude Guérard Net: n/a

☐ C-GQKP	Piper PA-23-250 Aztec E	27-4747	N14183	0072	0694	2 LY IO-540-C4B5	2359	Photo / Survey		
☐ C-FPED	Twin (Aero) Super Commander 680	680-408-84		0056		2 LY GSO-480-B1A6	3175	Photo / Survey		
☐ C-FSRG	Twin (Aero) Commander 680F	680F-1163-86		0062		2 LY IGSO-540-B1A	3629	Photo / Survey		
☐ C-GLMC	Twin (Aero) Hawk Commander 681	681-6044	N4798M	0071	0195	2 GA TPE331-1-151K	4264	Photo / Survey		
☐ C-GUIZ	Twin (Aero) Commander 680F	680F-1161-85	N6278X	0062		2 LY IGSO-540-B1A	3629	Photo / Survey		

AEROPRO = APO (2553-4330 Québec, Inc. dba) — Québec, Qué.

714-7e Ave, Aéroport Int'l Jean Lesage, Sainte-Foy, Québec G2E 5W1, Canada ☎ (418) 877-2808 Tx: none Fax: (418) 871-9483 SITA: n/a
F: 1988 ⁂ 30 Head: Aurèle Labbé ICAO: AEROPRO Net: n/a Aircraft below MTOW 1361 kg: Cessna 180

☐ C-GAWT	Cessna 310R II	310R1600	N36846	0079	0597	2 CO IO-520-M	2495			
☐ C-GMCR	Cessna 310R II	310R1424	N5149C	0078	0494	2 CO IO-520-M	2495			
☐ C-GSVI	Cessna 310R II	310R0833	N58JB	0077	0496	2 CO IO-520-M	2495			
☐ C-GYOT	Cessna 310R II	310R0912		0077	0194	2 CO IO-520-M	2495			
☐ C-GAKM	Piper PA-31-310 Navajo	31-577	N800CM	0070	0299	2 LY TIO-540-A1A	2948			
☐ C-GBYL	Piper PA-31-350 Navajo Chieftain	31-7752144	N456JB	0077	0489	2 LY TIO-540-J2BD	3175			
☐ C-GHRL	Piper PA-31-350 Navajo Chieftain	31-8052014	N3547A	0080	0698	2 LY TIO-540-J2BD	3175			
☐ C-GNIE	Piper PA-31-350 Navajo Chieftain	31-7552047		0075	0590	2 LY TIO-540-J2BD	3175			
☐ C-GQAM	Piper PA-31-310 Navajo C	31-7912093		0079	0890	2 LY TIO-540-A1A	2948			
☐ C-GQZE	Piper PA-31-310 Navajo C	31-7912065	N3520E	0079	0997	2 LY TIO-540-A2C	2948			
☐ C-GRFJ	Piper PA-31-310 Navajo C	31-7812031	N27485	0078	1291	2 LY TIO-540-A2C	2948			
☐ C-GDLG	Cessna 425 Conquest I	425-0063	N425TY	0081	0298	2 PWC PT6A-112	3719			
☐ C-FGIN	Beech King Air A100	B-164	N164RA	0073	0593	2 PWC PT6A-28	5216			
☐ C-FXNB	Beech King Air A90 (65-A90)	LJ-257	N711VP	0067	0896	2 PWC PT6A-20	4218			
☐ C-GLPG	Beech King Air A100	B-159	N110KF	0073	1296	2 PWC PT6A-28	5216			
☐ C-GRSL	Beech King Air C90	LJ-609	N38BA	0074	0197	2 PWC PT6A-20	4377			
☐ C-GTCL	Beech King Air B100	BE-130	N6241P	0082	0199	2 GA TPE331-6-252B	5352			
☐ C-GCVE	Beech King Air B200	BB-1368	N981GA	0090	0898	2 PWC PT6A-42	5670			
☐ C-FLPD	Cessna 550 Citation II	550-0234	N511WC	0080	0697	2 PWC JT15D-4	6033			

AERO QUEBEC, Inc. — Québec, Qué.

230-2ième Ave, Aéroport Int'l J. Lesage, Ste-Foy, Québec G2E 5W1, Canada ☎ (418) 872-0206 Tx: none Fax: (418) 872-0207 SITA: n/a
F: 1995 ⁂ n/a Head: n/a Net: n/a

☐ C-FNNM	Cessna TR182 Turbo Skylane RG II	R18200946	N738NR	0079	0497	1 LY O-540-L3C5D	1406			
☐ C-FQTA	Cessna R182 Skylane RG II	R18200324	N4107C	0078	0497	1 LY O-540-J3C5D	1406			

26 registration type of aircraft cn/fn ex/ex* mfd del powered by mtow kg configuration selcal name/fln/specialitites/remarks

☐ C-FQTC	Cessna R182 Skylane RG II	R18201717	N4608T	0081	0497	1 LY O-540-J3C5D	1406			
☐ C-FRGN	Cessna R182 Skylane RG II	R18200394	N9083C	0078	0497	1 LY O-540-J3C5D	1406			
☐ C-FRYF	Cessna R182 Skylane RG II	R18201001	N65ET	0079	0597	1 LY O-540-J3C5D	1406			
☐ C-FRYP	Cessna R182 Skylane RG II	R18200479	N9879C	0078	0597	1 LY O-540-J3C5D	1406			
☐ C-FRZE	Cessna R182 Skylane RG II	R18200197	N2657C	0078	0497	1 LY O-540-J3C5D	1406			
☐ C-GCJA	Cessna R182 Skylane RG II	R18201219		0079	0597	1 LY O-540-J3C5D	1406			
☐ C-GDKZ	Cessna R182 Skylane RG II	R18201491	N4854S	0080	0897	1 LY O-540-J3C5D	1406			
☐ C-GHVC	Cessna R182 Skylane RG II	R18201886	N5532T	0082	0497	1 LY O-540-J3C5D	1406			
☐ C-GOAL	Cessna TR182 Turbo Skylane RG II	R18201127		0079	0497	1 LY O-540-L3C5D	1406			
☐ C-GRUA	Cessna R182 Skylane RG II	R18200077	N7325X	0078	0598	1 LY O-540-J3C5D	1406			
☐ C-GSCF	Cessna R182 Skylane RG II	R18201257	N757QM	0079	0597	1 LY O-540-J3C5D	1406			
☐ C-GVCV	Cessna R182 Skylane RG II	R18200030	N7343T	0078	0697	1 LY O-540-J3C5D	1406			
☐ C-GWRJ	Cessna TR182 Turbo Skylane RG II	R18200740	N736MG	0078	0597	1 LY O-540-L3C5D	1406			
☐ C-GPKR	Cessna 210L Centurion II	21061447	N732EA	0076	0597	1 CO IO-520-L	1724			
☐ C-GPZK	Cessna 210L Centurion II	21061393		0076	0597	1 CO IO-520-L	1724			
☐ C-GADG	Piper PA-34-200T Seneca II	34-7870051	N6094H	0078	0897	2 CO TSIO-360-E	2073			
☐ C-GAWN	Cessna 310R II	310R0957	N37211	0077	0696	2 CO IO-520-M	2495			
☐ C-GAWZ	Cessna 310R II	310R0580	OO-AUO	0076	0696	2 CO IO-520-M	2495			
☐ C-GCYB	Cessna 310R II	310R0013		0075	0597	2 CO IO-520-M	2495			
☐ C-FTIW	Piper PA-31-350 Navajo Chieftain	31-7752123	N39CA	0074	0398	2 LY TIO-540-J2BD	3175			

AEROSMITH, Inc. — Gander, Nfld.

PO Box 122, Gander, Newfoundland A1V 1W5, Canada ☎ (709) 651-3222 Tx: none Fax: (709) 256-8271 SITA: n/a
F: 1996 ⅏ n/a Head: Kenneth Smith Net: n/a Aircraft below MTOW 1361kg: Cessna 180 & Piper PA-28

☐ C-GAAZ	Cessna A185F Skywagon	18502735		0075	1097	1 CO IO-520-D	1520			
☐ C-GGBC	Piper PA-32-260B Cherokee SIX	32-1161	N4721S	0069	0796	1 LY O-540-E4B5	1542			

AEROTAXI = QAT (Air Quasar, Ltée/Ltd dba) — Montreal-St. Hubert, Qué.

6050 Rte de l'Aéroport, St. Hubert, Québec J3Y 8Y9, Canada ☎ (450) 445-4034 Tx: none Fax: (450) 445-2634 SITA: n/a
F: 1987 ⅏ 45 Head: Sylvain Michaud ICAO: AEROTAXI Net: n/a Aircraft below MTOW 1361 kg: Cessna 152/172, Katana DA 20 & Robin R2160

☐ C-GBVW	Piper PA-44-180 Seminole	4495004	N192ND	0089	0298	2 LY O-360-A1H6	1724			
☐ C-GEAD	Piper PA-44-180 Seminole	44-7995098	N62RA	0079	1198	2 LY O-360-E1A6D	1724			
☐ C-GNEL	Cessna 210L Centurion II	21060004	N35636	0073	0691	1 CO IO-520-L	1724			
☐ C-GYYP	Cessna T210L Turbo Centurion II	21060612	N8124L	0075	1292	1 CO TSIO-520-H	1724			

AERO 3000 (Parachutisme Aventure, Inc. dba) — Montreal-St. Hubert, Qué.

6200 Route de l'Aéroport, St-Hubert, Québec J3Y 8Y9, Canada ☎ (514) 893-6609 Tx: none Fax: (450) 443-3444 SITA: n/a
F: 1993 ⅏ 13 Head: Mario Noel Net: n/a

☐ C-FSJA	Piper PA-31P Pressurized Navajo	31P-7300161	N161JA	0073	0398	2 LY TIGO-541-E1A	3538			
☐ C-GAFG	Piper PA-31P Pressurized Navajo	31P-76	N52MC	0072	0298	2 LY TIGO-541-E1A	3538			

AG AIR, Ltd — Dawson Creek, B.C.

Box 1022, Dawson Creek, British Columbia V1G 4H9, Canada ☎ (250) 782-8952 Tx: none Fax: (250) 782-3733 SITA: n/a
F: 1969 ⅏ 6 Head: Donald A. Lumsden Net: n/a Ag-Aircraft below MTOW 5000 kg: Ayres S2R, Cessna A188 & Grumman G-164.

☐ C-FBQT	Grumman TBM-3 Avenger	91171		0045		1 WR R-2600-20	7983	Sprayer/Tanker		

A.G. AVIATION, Ltd — Charlo, N.B.

PO Box 1001, Charlo, New Brunswick E0B 1M0, Canada ☎ (506) 684-5808 Tx: none Fax: (506) 684-5509 SITA: n/a
F: 1992 ⅏ n/a Head: Brian D. Stote Net: n/a Aircraft below MTOW 1361kg: Cessna 172

☐ C-GQTJ	Piper PA-23-250 Aztec E	27-7405327	N100TE	0074	0796	2 LY IO-540-C4B5	2359			

AHLSTROM CONSTRUCTION – Heli division (Heli division of Ahlstrom Construction, Ltd) — Alhambra, Alta.

General Delivery, Alhambra, Alberta T0M 0C0, Canada ☎ (780) 729-3958 Tx: none Fax: (780) 729-2880 SITA: n/a
F: 1997 ⅏ n/a Head: Graeme Meyer Net: n/a

☐ C-FZWK	Eurocopter (Aerosp.) AS350B1 AStar	2133	HB-XSE	0088	0397	1 TU Arriel 1D	2200			

AIR ALBERTA, Inc. (Affiliated with Okotoks Flight Centre) — Calgary-Okotoks Air Park, Alta.

Box 670, Okotoks, Alberta T0L 1T0, Canada ☎ (780) 938-5252 Tx: none Fax: (780) 938-2940 SITA: n/a
F: 1988 ⅏ n/a Head: Mrs. Debbie McLean Net: n/a

☐ C-GJVB	Beech Travel Air D95A	TD-554		0063	1292	2 LY IO-360-B1B	1905			

AIR ALMA, Inc. = AAJ (Partenaire CANADIEN / CANADIAN Partner) — Alma, Qué.

CP 577, Alma, Québec G8B 5W1, Canada ☎ (418) 668-5566 Tx: 05136173 air alma al Fax: (418) 668-7711 SITA: n/a
F: 1959 ⅏ 42 Head: Roland Simard ICAO: AIR ALMA Net: n/a
Scheduled services with Embraer Bandeirante aircraft are operated in conjunction with Canadian / Canadien as a Partenaire CANADIEN / CANADIAN Partner (in own cs) using CP flt no's.

☐ C-GLBA	Bell 206L LongRanger	45017		0075	0085	1 AN 250-C20B	1814	6 Pax		
☐ C-GUKO	Piper PA-31-310 Navajo	31-170	N878BB	0068		2 LY TIO-540-A1A	2948	6 Pax		
☐ C-GFSI	Bell 222UT	47504		0083	0895	2 LY LTS101-750C.1	3742	7 Pax		
☐ C-GDJG	Cessna 404 Titan Courier II	404-0620		0080		2 CO GTSIO-520-M	3810	9 Pax		
☐ C-GUAY	Bell 412	33065	N412PA	0082	0397	2 PWC PT6T-3B TwinPac	5262	13 Pax		
☐ C-FOYJ	Embraer 110P2 Bandeirante (EMB-110P2)	110197	N212GA	0078	0693	2 PWC PT6A-34	5670	15 Pax		
☐ C-GDBF	Embraer 110P1 Bandeirante (EMB-110P1)	110290	PT-SBZ*	0080	1087	2 PWC PT6A-34	5670	15 Pax		
☐ C-GPDI	Embraer 110P1 Bandeirante (EMB-110P1)	110207	G-BGCS	0079	1286	2 PWC PT6A-34	5670	15 Pax		

AIR AVENTURE COTE-NORD (9017-6546 Québec, Inc. dba) — Aguanish-SPB, Qué.

235 Jacques-Cartier, Aguanish, Québec G0G 1A0, Canada ☎ (418) 533-2316 Tx: none Fax: (418) 533-2357 SITA: n/a
F: 1994 ⅏ n/a Head: Alain Deraps Net: n/a

☐ C-FSZU	Cessna 185E Skywagon	185-0996		0066	0898	1 CO IO-520-D	1520			Floats / Wheel-Skis
☐ C-FJKH	De Havilland DHC-2 Beaver I	988		0056	0796	1 PW R-985	2309			Floats / Wheel-Skis

AIRBC = ZX / ABL (Liaison AIR CANADA Connector) (Air BC, Ltd dba / Subsidiary of Air Canada) — Vancouver-Int'l, B.C.

5520 Miller Road, Richmond, British Columbia V7B 1L9, Canada ☎ (604) 273-2464 Tx: 04355612 air bc vcr Fax: (604) 273-1016 SITA: n/a
F: 1980 ⅏ 1200 Head: Mel Cooper IATA: 742 ICAO: AIRCOACH Net: n/a
Scheduled commuter services are operated by AirBC on behalf of Air Canada as a Liaison AIR CANADA Connector (in such colours & both titles), using AC flight designators.

☐ C-FABA	De Havilland DHC-8-102 Dash 8	092		0088	0288	2 PWC PW120A	15649	Y37		805 / Regina
☐ C-FABG	De Havilland DHC-8-102 Dash 8	147		0089	0489	2 PWC PW120A	15649	Y37		807 / Penticton / Isf ARN
☐ C-FABN	De Havilland DHC-8-102 Dash 8	044		0086	0886	2 PWC PW120A	15649	Y37		803 / Dawson Creek
☐ C-FABT	De Havilland DHC-8-102 Dash 8	049		0086	1086	2 PWC PW120A	15649	Y37		804 / Calgary / Isf ARN
☐ C-FABW	De Havilland DHC-8-102 Dash 8	097		0088	0488	2 PWC PW120A	15649	Y37		806 / Vancouver
☐ C-FACD	De Havilland DHC-8-102 Dash 8	150		0089	0489	2 PWC PW120A	15649	Y37		808 / Grand Prairie
☐ C-FADJ	De Havilland DHC-8-102 Dash 8	322		0092	0492	2 PWC PW120A	15649	Y37		811 / Kelowna
☐ C-FADK	De Havilland DHC-8-102 Dash 8	324		0092	0592	2 PWC PW120A	15649	Y37		812 / Castlegar
☐ C-GABF	De Havilland DHC-8-102 Dash 8	025		0086	0386	2 PWC PW120A	15649	Y37		802 / Spokane / Isf ARN
☐ C-GABH	De Havilland DHC-8-102 Dash 8	211		0090	0590	2 PWC PW120A	15649	Y37	BC-GM	810 / Nanaimo
☐ C-GABI	De Havilland DHC-8-102 Dash 8	205		0090	0390	2 PWC PW120A	15649	Y37		809 / Manitoba
☐ C-GGOM	De Havilland DHC-8-102 Dash 8	003		0083	1285	2 PWC PW120A	15649	Y37		801 / Alberta
☐ C-FACF	De Havilland DHC-8-311 Dash 8	259		0091	0291	2 PWC PW123	18643	Y50		852 / Williams Lake
☐ C-FACT	De Havilland DHC-8-311 Dash 8	262		0091	0391	2 PWC PW123	18643	Y50		853
☐ C-FACV	De Havilland DHC-8-311 Dash 8	278		0091	0591	2 PWC PW123	18643	Y50		855 / Campbell River
☐ C-FADF	De Havilland DHC-8-311 Dash 8	272	C-FACU	0091	0591	2 PWC PW123	18643	Y50		854 / Comox
☐ C-GABO	De Havilland DHC-8-311 Dash 8	248		0090	0191	2 PWC PW123	18643	Y50		856 / Quesnel
☐ C-GABP	De Havilland DHC-8-311 Dash 8	257		0091	0291	2 PWC PW123	18643	Y50		851 / Victoria
☐ C-FBAB	BAe 146-200A	E2090	G-5-090*	0088	0588	4 LY ALF502R-5	42184	C8Y68		401 / British Columbia
☐ C-FBAE	BAe 146-200A	E2092	G-5-092*	0088	0688	4 LY ALF502R-5	42184	C8Y68		402 / Prince George
☐ C-FBAF	BAe 146-200A	E2096	G-5-096*	0088	0688	4 LY ALF502R-5	42184	C8Y68		403 / Prince Rupert
☐ C-FBAO	BAe 146-200A	E2111	G-5-111*	0089	0189	4 LY ALF502R-5	42184	C8Y68		404 / Edmonton
☐ C-FBAV	BAe 146-200A	E2121	G-11-121*	0089	0289	4 LY ALF502R-5	42184	C8Y68		405 / Vancouver

AIR BELLEVUE, Inc. (formerly Bellevue Air Service, Inc.) — Bellevue-SPB & Dolbeau, Qué.

875 Bellevue Sud, St. Felicien, Québec G8K 1H6, Canada ☎ (418) 679-3722 Tx: none Fax: (418) 679-3778 SITA: n/a
F: 1970 ⅏ 4 Head: Yves Brassard Net: n/a

☐ C-GIIU	Cessna U206G Stationair 6 II	U20605961		0080	1097	1 CO IO-520-F	1633			Floats
☐ C-FZKU	De Havilland DHC-2 Beaver I	382	N7942C	0052	0798	1 PW R-985	2313			Isf Aero Nord-Est / Floats
☐ C-GATO	De Havilland DHC-2 Beaver I	330	N212NY	0051		1 PW R-985	2313			Floats
☐ C-GDXY	De Havilland DHC-2 Beaver I	1159	56-0410	0057	0698	1 PW R-985	2313			Floats

27 registration type of aircraft cn/fn ex/ex* mfd del powered by mtow kg configuration selcal name/fln/specialitites/remarks

registration	type of aircraft	cn/fn	ex/ex*	mfd	del	powered by	mtow kg	configuration	selcal	name/fln/specialitites/remarks
☐ C-GDFC	Britten-Norman BN-2A-6 Islander	239	N66HA	0071	0199	2 LY O-540-E4C5	2858			
☐ C-GVNL	De Havilland DHC-3 Otter	105	N5341G	0056	0798	1 PW R-1340	3629			Floats

AIR BGM, Inc. (Member of Groupe Gamac) La Tuque, Qué.

CP 715, La Tuque, Québec G9X 3P5, Canada ☎ (819) 523-9952 Tx: none Fax: (819) 523-5156 SITA: n/a

F: 1980 ✈✈✈ 9 Head: Yvon Pelletier Net: n/a

registration	type of aircraft	cn/fn	ex/ex*	mfd	del	powered by	mtow kg	configuration	selcal	name/fln/specialitites/remarks
☐ C-FBYV	Piper PA-34-200T Seneca II	34-7570229	N1173X	0075	0198	2 CO TSIO-360-EB	2073			

AIRBORNE SENSING (The Airborne Sensing, Corp. dba) Toronto-City Centre, Ont.

Suite 110, Hangar 6, Toronto City Centre Airport, Toronto, Ontario M5V 1A1, Canada ☎ (416) 203-9858 Tx: none Fax: (416) 203-9843 SITA: n/a

F: 1982 ✈✈✈ n/a Head: Alexander Gianelia Net: n/a

registration	type of aircraft	cn/fn	ex/ex*	mfd	del	powered by	mtow kg	configuration	selcal	name/fln/specialitites/remarks
☐ C-FIDS	Piper PA-23-250 Aztec F	27-7654028	N44LG	0076	0898	2 LY IO-540-C4B5	2359	Surveyer		
☐ C-GIQC	Piper PA-23-250 Aztec F	27-7654177	N102AE	0076		2 LY IO-540-C4B5	2359	Surveyer		

AIR CAB (CBE Construction, Ltd dba) Coal Harbour, B.C.

Box 40, Coal Harbour, British Columbia V0N 1K0, Canada ☎ (250) 949-6371 Tx: none Fax: (250) 949-7582 SITA: n/a

F: 1987 ✈✈✈ n/a Head: Joel M. Eilertsen Net: n/a

registration	type of aircraft	cn/fn	ex/ex*	mfd	del	powered by	mtow kg	configuration	selcal	name/fln/specialitites/remarks
☐ C-FBMO	Cessna A185E Skywagon	18501627		0070	0188	1 CO IO-520-D	1520			Floats
☐ C-GHAO	Cessna A185F Skywagon	18502370	N53088	0074	0598	1 CO IO-520-D	1520			Floats
☐ CF-QGZ	Cessna A185E Skywagon	18501691		0070	1087	1 CO IO-520-D	1520			Floats
☐ C-FRJG	De Havilland DHC-2 Beaver I	1550		0064	0698	1 PW R-985	2309			Floats
☐ C-GJZE	De Havilland DHC-2 Beaver I	1276	N87780	0058	0293	1 PW R-985	2309			Floats

AIR CANADA = AC / ACA (Member of Star Alliance / formerly Trans-Canada Air Lines, Ltd – TCA) Montreal, Qué. & Toronto, Ont.

AIR CANADA

PO Box 14000, Montréal, Québec H4Y 1H4, Canada ☎ (514) 422-5000 Tx: n/a Fax: (514) 422-7741 SITA: YMQHHAC

F: 1937 ✈✈✈ 21200 Head: Lamar Durrett IATA: 014 ICAO: AIR CANADA Net: http://www.aircanada.ca/

Scheduled Liaison AIR CANADA Connector (commuter) services are operated on behalf of AIR CANADA by AIRBC, AIR NOVA, AIR ONTARIO, ALBERTA CITYLINK, AVIATION QUEBEC LABRADOR & CENTRAL MOUNTAIN AIR – for details see under each company. On order (subject to re-confirmation): further 6 Airbus Industrie A320-200, 4 A330-300 & 4 A340-300.

registration	type of aircraft	cn/fn	ex/ex*	mfd	del	powered by	mtow kg	configuration	selcal	name/fln/specialitites/remarks
☐ C-FRIA	Canadair Regional Jet 100ER (CL-600-2B19)	7045	C-FMLQ*	0094	0994	2 GE CF34-3A1	23100	CY50	NONE	101
☐ C-FRIB	Canadair Regional Jet 100ER (CL-600-2B19)	7047	C-FMLT*	0094	1094	2 GE CF34-3A1	23100	CY50	NONE	102
☐ C-FRID	Canadair Regional Jet 100ER (CL-600-2B19)	7049	C-FMLV*	0094	1194	2 GE CF34-3A1	23100	CY50	NONE	103
☐ C-FRIL	Canadair Regional Jet 100ER (CL-600-2B19)	7051	C-FMML*	0094	1294	2 GE CF34-3A1	23100	CY50	NONE	104
☐ C-FSJF	Canadair Regional Jet 100ER (CL-600-2B19)	7054	C-FMMT*	0094	0195	2 GE CF34-3A1	23100	CY50	NONE	105
☐ C-FSJJ	Canadair Regional Jet 100ER (CL-600-2B19)	7058	C-FMNB*	0094	0195	2 GE CF34-3A1	23100	CY50	NONE	106
☐ C-FSJU	Canadair Regional Jet 100ER (CL-600-2B19)	7060	C-FMNH*	0095	0395	2 GE CF34-3A1	23100	CY50	NONE	107
☐ C-FSKE	Canadair Regional Jet 100ER (CL-600-2B19)	7065	C-FMOI*	0095	0495	2 GE CF34-3A1	23100	CY50	NONE	108
☐ C-FSKM	Canadair Regional Jet 100ER (CL-600-2B19)	7071	C-FMKZ*	0095	0695	2 GE CF34-3A1	23100	CY50	NONE	110
☐ C-FVKM	Canadair Regional Jet 100ER (CL-600-2B19)	7074	C-FMLI*	0095	0795	2 GE CF34-3A1	23100	CY50	NONE	111
☐ C-FVKN	Canadair Regional Jet 100ER (CL-600-2B19)	7078	C-FMLU*	0095	0895	2 GE CF34-3A1	23100	CY50	NONE	112
☐ C-FVKR	Canadair Regional Jet 100ER (CL-600-2B19)	7083	C-FMNQ*	0095	1095	2 GE CF34-3A1	23100	CY50	NONE	114
☐ C-FVMD	Canadair Regional Jet 100ER (CL-600-2B19)	7082		0095	0995	2 GE CF34-3A1	23100	CY50	NONE	113
☐ C-FWJB	Canadair Regional Jet 100ER (CL-600-2B19)	7087		0095	1195	2 GE CF34-3A1	23100	CY50	NONE	115
☐ C-FWJF	Canadair Regional Jet 100ER (CL-600-2B19)	7095		0095	1295	2 GE CF34-3A1	23100	CY50	NONE	116
☐ C-FWJI	Canadair Regional Jet 100ER (CL-600-2B19)	7096		0095	0196	2 GE CF34-3A1	23100	CY50	NONE	117
☐ C-FWJS	Canadair Regional Jet 100ER (CL-600-2B19)	7097		0095	0196	2 GE CF34-3A1	23100	CY50	NONE	118
☐ C-FWJT	Canadair Regional Jet 100ER (CL-600-2B19)	7098		0095	0296	2 GE CF34-3A1	23100	CY50	NONE	119
☐ C-FWRR	Canadair Regional Jet 100ER (CL-600-2B19)	7107		0096	0496	2 GE CF34-3A1	23100	CY50	NONE	120
☐ C-FWRS	Canadair Regional Jet 100ER (CL-600-2B19)	7112		0096	0496	2 GE CF34-3A1	23100	CY50	NONE	121
☐ C-FWRT	Canadair Regional Jet 100ER (CL-600-2B19)	7118		0096	0696	2 GE CF34-3A1	23100	CY50	NONE	122
☐ C-FWSC	Canadair Regional Jet 100ER (CL-600-2B19)	7120		0096	0696	2 GE CF34-3A1	23100	CY50	NONE	123
☐ C-FXMY	Canadair Regional Jet 100ER (CL-600-2B19)	7124		0096	0796	2 GE CF34-3A1	23100	CY50	NONE	124
☐ C-FZAQ	Canadair Regional Jet 100ER (CL-600-2B19)	7155		0097	0297	2 GE CF34-3B1	23100	CY50	NONE	151
☐ C-FZSI	Canadair Regional Jet 100ER (CL-600-2B19)	7160	LV-WZU	0097	0297	2 GE CF34-3B1	23100	Y50	NONE	152
☐ C-FTLH	Boeing (Douglas) DC-9-32	45845 / 91		0067	0367	2 PW JT8D-7A	48988	C16Y70	NONE	707
☐ C-FTLJ	Boeing (Douglas) DC-9-32	47019 / 113		0067	0567	2 PW JT8D-7A	48988	C16Y70	NONE	709
☐ C-FTLL	Boeing (Douglas) DC-9-32	47021 / 133		0067	0767	2 PW JT8D-7A	48988	C16Y70	NONE	711
☐ C-FTLM	Boeing (Douglas) DC-9-32	47022 / 144		0067	0767	2 PW JT8D-7A (HK3/ABS)	48988	C16Y70	NONE	712 / std MZJ
☐ C-FTLO	Boeing (Douglas) DC-9-32	47024 / 159		0067	0867	2 PW JT8D-7A (HK3/ABS)	48988	C16Y70	NONE	714 / std MZJ
☐ C-FTLT	Boeing (Douglas) DC-9-32	47195 / 278		0068	0368	2 PW JT8D-7A (HK3/ABS)	48988	C16Y70	NONE	719
☐ C-FTLW	Boeing (Douglas) DC-9-32	47198 / 302		0068	0468	2 PW JT8D-7A (HK3/ABS)	48988	C16Y70	NONE	722 / std MZJ
☐ C-FTLX	Boeing (Douglas) DC-9-32	47199 / 321		0068	0568	2 PW JT8D-7A (HK3/ABS)	48988	C16Y70	NONE	723
☐ C-FTLZ	Boeing (Douglas) DC-9-32	47265 / 339		0068	0768	2 PW JT8D-7A (HK3/ABS)	48988	C16Y70	NONE	725 / std MZJ
☐ C-FTMB	Boeing (Douglas) DC-9-32	47289 / 353		0068	0768	2 PW JT8D-7A (HK3/ABS)	48988	C16Y70	NONE	727
☐ C-FTMC	Boeing (Douglas) DC-9-32	47290 / 367		0068	0868	2 PW JT8D-7A	48988	C16Y70	NONE	728
☐ C-FTMD	Boeing (Douglas) DC-9-32	47292 / 383		0068	0968	2 PW JT8D-7A	48988	C16Y70	NONE	729
☐ C-FTME	Boeing (Douglas) DC-9-32	47293 / 384		0068	0968	2 PW JT8D-7A	48988	C16Y70	NONE	730
☐ C-FTMF	Boeing (Douglas) DC-9-32	47294 / 402		0068	1168	2 PW JT8D-7A	48988	C16Y70	NONE	731
☐ C-FTMM	Boeing (Douglas) DC-9-32	47611 / 726		0074	0474	2 PW JT8D-7A	48988	C16Y70	NONE	752
☐ C-FTMP	Boeing (Douglas) DC-9-32	47354 / 483		0069	0469	2 PW JT8D-7A	48988	C16Y70	NONE	741 / std MZJ
☐ C-FTMQ	Boeing (Douglas) DC-9-32	47422 / 576		0069	0270	2 PW JT8D-7A	48988	C16Y70	NONE	742 / std MZJ
☐ C-FTMT	Boeing (Douglas) DC-9-32	47546 / 655		0072	0372	2 PW JT8D-7A	48988	C16Y70	NONE	745
☐ C-FTMU	Boeing (Douglas) DC-9-32	47554 / 658		0072	0472	2 PW JT8D-7A	48988	C16Y70	NONE	746
☐ C-FTMV	Boeing (Douglas) DC-9-32	47557 / 661		0072	0572	2 PW JT8D-7A	48988	C16Y70	NONE	747
☐ C-FTMW	Boeing (Douglas) DC-9-32	47560 / 664		0072	0672	2 PW JT8D-7A	48988	C16Y70	NONE	748
☐ C-FTMX	Boeing (Douglas) DC-9-32	47485 / 666		0072	0772	2 PW JT8D-7A	48988	C16Y70	NONE	749 / std MZJ
☐ C-FTMY	Boeing (Douglas) DC-9-32	47592 / 712		0073	1273	2 PW JT8D-7A	48988	C16Y70	NONE	750
☐ C-FTMZ	Boeing (Douglas) DC-9-32	47598 / 719		0073	0274	2 PW JT8D-7A	48988	C16Y70	NONE	751
☐ C-FYIY	Airbus Industrie A319-114	634	D-AVYP*	0096	1296	2 CFMI CFM56-5A5	70000	C16Y96	PR-FM	252
☐ C-FYJB	Airbus Industrie A319-114	639	D-AVYU*	0096	0197	2 CFMI CFM56-5A5	70000	C16Y96	PR-FQ	253
☐ C-FYJD	Airbus Industrie A319-114	649	D-AVYW*	0097	0297	2 CFMI CFM56-5A5	70000	C16Y96	PR-FS	254
☐ C-FYJE	Airbus Industrie A319-114	656	D-AVYZ*	0097	0397	2 CFMI CFM56-5A5	70000	C16Y96	PR-GH	255
☐ C-FYJG	Airbus Industrie A319-114	670	D-AVYE*	0097	0497	2 CFMI CFM56-5A5	70000	C16Y96	PR-GJ	256
☐ C-FYJH	Airbus Industrie A319-114	672	D-AVYF*	0097	0497	2 CFMI CFM56-5A5	70000	C16Y96	PR-GK	257
☐ C-FYJI	Airbus Industrie A319-114	682	D-AVYH*	0097	0597	2 CFMI CFM56-5A5	70000	C16Y96	PR-GL	258
☐ C-FYJP	Airbus Industrie A319-114	688	D-AVYJ*	0097	0697	2 CFMI CFM56-5A5	70000	C16Y96	PR-GM	259
☐ C-FYKC	Airbus Industrie A319-114	691	D-AVYP*	0697	0697	2 CFMI CFM56-5A5	70000	C16Y96	PR-GQ	260
☐ C-FYKR	Airbus Industrie A319-114	693	D-AVYQ*	0097	0797	2 CFMI CFM56-5A5	70000	C16Y96	PR-GS	261
☐ C-FYKW	Airbus Industrie A319-114	695	D-AVYS*	0097	0797	2 CFMI CFM56-5A5	70000	C16Y96	FQ-AB	262
☐ C-FYNS	Airbus Industrie A319-114	572	D-AVYK*	1095	0797	2 CFMI CFM56-5A5	70000	C16Y96	PQ-FL	251 / cvtd A319-131
☐ C-FZUG	Airbus Industrie A319-114	697	D-AVYT*	0097	0897	2 CFMI CFM56-5A5	70000	C16Y96	FQ-AC	263
☐ C-FZUH	Airbus Industrie A319-114	711	D-AVYV*	0097	0897	2 CFMI CFM56-5A5	70000	C16Y96	FQ-AD	264 / spec. orig. Trans Canada Airl. cs
☐ C-FZUJ	Airbus Industrie A319-114	719	D-AVYW*	0097	0997	2 CFMI CFM56-5A5	70000	C16Y96	FQ-AR	265
☐ C-FZUL	Airbus Industrie A319-114	721	D-AVYY*	0097	0997	2 CFMI CFM56-5A5	70000	C16Y96	FQ-AS	266
☐ C-GAPY	Airbus Industrie A319-114	728	D-AVYE*	0097	1097	2 CFMI CFM56-5A5	70000	C16Y96	RS-AQ	267
☐ C-GAQL	Airbus Industrie A319-114	732	D-AVYX*	0097	1097	2 CFMI CFM56-5A5	70000	C16Y96	RS-BC	268
☐ C-GAQX	Airbus Industrie A319-114	736	D-AVYG*	0097	1097	2 CFMI CFM56-5A5	70000	C16Y96	RS-BD	269
☐ C-GAQZ	Airbus Industrie A319-114	740	D-AVYH*	0097	1197	2 CFMI CFM56-5A5	70000	C16Y96	RS-BE	270
☐ C-GARG	Airbus Industrie A319-114	742	D-AVYM*	0097	1197	2 CFMI CFM56-5A5	70000	C16Y96	RS-BF	271
☐ C-GARJ	Airbus Industrie A319-114	752	D-AVYP*	0097	1297	2 CFMI CFM56-5A5	70000	C16Y96	RS-BG	272
☐ C-GARO	Airbus Industrie A319-114	757	D-AVYQ*	0097	1297	2 CFMI CFM56-5A5	70000	C16Y96	RS-BH	273
☐ C-GBHM	Airbus Industrie A319-114	769	D-AVYB*	0097	0198	2 CFMI CFM56-5A5	70000	C16Y96	FP-EH	274
☐ C-GBHN	Airbus Industrie A319-114	773	D-AVYK*	0098	0198	2 CFMI CFM56-5A5	70000	C16Y96	FP-EJ	275
☐ C-GBHO	Airbus Industrie A319-114	779	D-AVYT*	0098	0298	2 CFMI CFM56-5A5	70000	C16Y96	FP-EK	276
☐ C-GBHR	Airbus Industrie A319-114	785	D-AVYU*	0098	0298	2 CFMI CFM56-5A5	70000	C16Y96	FP-EL	277
☐ C-GBHY	Airbus Industrie A319-114	800	D-AVYE*	0098	0398	2 CFMI CFM56-5A5	70000	C16Y96	FP-EM	278
☐ C-GBHZ	Airbus Industrie A319-114	813	D-AVYG*	0098	0498	2 CFMI CFM56-5A5	70000	C16Y96	FP-GH	279
☐ C-GBIA	Airbus Industrie A319-114	817	D-AVYM*	0098	0498	2 CFMI CFM56-5A5	70000	C16Y96	FP-GJ	280
☐ C-GBIJ	Airbus Industrie A319-114	829	D-AVYH*	0598	0598	2 CFMI CFM56-5A5	70000	C16Y96	FP-GK	281
☐ C-GBIK	Airbus Industrie A319-114	831	D-AVYI*	0598	0598	2 CFMI CFM56-5A5	70000	C16Y96	FP-GL	282
☐ C-GBIM	Airbus Industrie A319-114	840	D-AVYQ*	0098	0698	2 CFMI CFM56-5A5	70000	C16Y96	FP-GM	283
☐ C-GBIN	Airbus Industrie A319-114	845	D-AVYA*	0098	0698	2 CFMI CFM56-5A5	70000	C16Y96	FP-HJ	284
☐ C-GBIP	Airbus Industrie A319-114	546	D-AVYV*	0895	0498	2 CFMI CFM56-5A5	70000	C16Y96	FP-HK	285 / cvtd -112
☐ C-FDQQ	Airbus Industrie A320-211	059	F-WWDI*	0090	0190	2 CFMI CFM56-5A1	75500	C24Y108	FQ-BG	201 / lsf GECA
☐ C-FDQV	Airbus Industrie A320-211	068	F-WWDO*	0090	0290	2 CFMI CFM56-5A1	75500	C24Y108	FQ-BH	202
☐ C-FDRH	Airbus Industrie A320-211	073	F-WWDC*	0090	0290	2 CFMI CFM56-5A1	75500	C24Y108	FQ-BJ	203
☐ C-FDRK	Airbus Industrie A320-211	084	F-WWDP*	0090	0390	2 CFMI CFM56-5A1	75500	C24Y108	FQ-BK	204
☐ C-FDRP	Airbus Industrie A320-211	122	F-WWIP*	0090	1090	2 CFMI CFM56-5A1	75500	C24Y108	FQ-BL	205 / lsf GECA
☐ C-FDSN	Airbus Industrie A320-211	126	F-WWIU*	0090	1190	2 CFMI CFM56-5A1	75500	C24Y108	FQ-BM	206 / special Toronto Raptors colors

	registration	type of aircraft	cn/fn	ex/ex*	mfd	del	powered by	mtow kg	configuration	selcal	name/fln/specialitites/remarks
☐	C-FDST	Airbus Industrie A320-211	127	F-WWIV*	0090	1190	2 CFMI CFM56-5A1	75500	C24Y108	FQ-BP	207
☐	C-FDSU	Airbus Industrie A320-211	141	F-WWDH*	0090	0191	2 CFMI CFM56-5A1	75500	C24Y108	FQ-CD	208 / lsf GECA
☐	C-FFWI	Airbus Industrie A320-211	149	F-WWDP*	0090	0291	2 CFMI CFM56-5A1	75500	C24Y108	FQ-CE	209
☐	C-FFWJ	Airbus Industrie A320-211	150	F-WWDQ*	0090	0291	2 CFMI CFM56-5A1	75500	C24Y108	FQ-CG	210
☐	C-FFWM	Airbus Industrie A320-211	154	F-WWDY*	0091	0391	2 CFMI CFM56-5A1	75500	C24Y108	FQ-CH	211 / lsf GECA
☐	C-FFWN	Airbus Industrie A320-211	159	F-WWIG*	0091	0391	2 CFMI CFM56-5A1	75500	C24Y108	FQ-CJ	212 / lsf GECA
☐	C-FGYL	Airbus Industrie A320-211	254	F-WWBF*	0091	1291	2 CFMI CFM56-5A1	75500	C24Y108	AR-GK	218
☐	C-FGYS	Airbus Industrie A320-211	255	F-WWBG*	0091	1291	2 CFMI CFM56-5A1	75500	C24Y108	AR-GL	219
☐	C-FKAJ	Airbus Industrie A320-211	333	F-WWBJ*	0092	0792	2 CFMI CFM56-5A1	75500	C24Y108	AR-HM	227
☐	C-FKCK	Airbus Industrie A320-211	265	F-WWDR*	0091	0192	2 CFMI CFM56-5A1	75500	C24Y108	AR-GM	220
☐	C-FKCO	Airbus Industrie A320-211	277	F-WWDX*	0092	0292	2 CFMI CFM56-5A1	75500	C24Y108	AR-GP	221
☐	C-FKCR	Airbus Industrie A320-211	290	F-WWBY*	0091	0392	2 CFMI CFM56-5A1	75500	C24Y108	AR-GQ	222
☐	C-FKOJ	Airbus Industrie A320-211	330	F-WWIB*	0092	0792	2 CFMI CFM56-5A1	75500	C24Y108	AR-HL	226
☐	C-FKPO	Airbus Industrie A320-211	311	F-WWIL*	0092	0592	2 CFMI CFM56-5A1	75500	C24Y108	AR-HJ	224
☐	C-FKPS	Airbus Industrie A320-211	310	F-WWIK*	0092	0592	2 CFMI CFM56-5A1	75500	C24Y108	AR-GS	223
☐	C-FKPT	Airbus Industrie A320-211	324	F-WWDC*	0092	0692	2 CFMI CFM56-5A1	75500	C24Y108	AR-HK	225
☐	C-FMJK	Airbus Industrie A320-211	342	F-WWDB*	0092	0992	2 CFMI CFM56-5A1	75500	C24Y108	AR-HQ	229
☐	C-FMST	Airbus Industrie A320-211	350	F-WWDF*	0092	1092	2 CFMI CFM56-5A1	75500	C24Y108	AR-HS	230
☐	C-FMSV	Airbus Industrie A320-211	359	F-WWIT*	0092	1192	2 CFMI CFM56-5A1	75500	C24Y108	AR-JK	231
☐	C-FMSX	Airbus Industrie A320-211	378	F-WWIY*	0092	0293	2 CFMI CFM56-5A1	75500	C24Y108	AR-JL	232
☐	C-FMSY	Airbus Industrie A320-211	384	F-WWBG*	0092	0293	2 CFMI CFM56-5A1	75500	C24Y108	AR-JM	233
☐	C-FNNA	Airbus Industrie A320-211	426	F-WWBU*	0093	0693	2 CFMI CFM56-5A1	75500	C24Y108	AR-JP	234
☐	C-FPDN	Airbus Industrie A320-211	341	F-WWBR*	0092	0992	2 CFMI CFM56-5A1	75500	C24Y108	AR-HP	228
☐	C-FTJO	Airbus Industrie A320-211	183	F-WWIX*	0091	0591	2 CFMI CFM56-5A1	75500	C24Y108	FQ-CK	213 / lsf GECA
☐	C-FTJP	Airbus Industrie A320-211	233	F-WWIQ*	0091	1091	2 CFMI CFM56-5A1	75500	C24Y108	FQ-CL	214
☐	C-FTJQ	Airbus Industrie A320-211	242	F-WWDJ*	0091	1091	2 CFMI CFM56-5A1	75500	C24Y108	FQ-CM	215
☐	C-FTJR	Airbus Industrie A320-211	248	F-WWDT*	0091	1191	2 CFMI CFM56-5A1	75500	C24Y108	FQ-CP	216
☐	C-FTJS	Airbus Industrie A320-211	253	F-WWBE*	0091	1191	2 CFMI CFM56-5A1	75500	C24Y108	FQ-DE	217
☐	C-FBEF	Boeing 767-233 (ER)	24323 / 250	N6009F*	0088	1288	2 PW JT9D-7R4D	159200	C25Y152	HP-DL	617
☐	C-FBEG	Boeing 767-233 (ER)	24324 / 252	N6009F*	0089	0289	2 PW JT9D-7R4D	159200	C25Y152	HP-DM	618
☐	C-FBEM	Boeing 767-233 (ER)	24325 / 254	N6038E*	0089	0389	2 PW JT9D-7R4D	159200	C25Y152	HP-EF	619
☐	C-FUCL	Boeing 767-209 (ER)	22682 / 60	N682SH	0083	0495	2 PW JT9D-7R4D	152000	C36Y159	JM-DR	622 / lsf BOUL / cvtd -209
☐	C-FVNM	Boeing 767-209 (ER)	22681 / 18	N681SH	0082	0695	2 PW JT9D-7R4D	152000	C36Y159	JM-CS	621 / lsf Aerospace Finance / cvtd -209
☐	C-GAUB	Boeing 767-233	22517 / 16		0082	1082	2 PW JT9D-7R4D	140600	C36Y159	DE-FH	601
☐	C-GAUE	Boeing 767-233	22518 / 22		0082	1282	2 PW JT9D-7R4D	140600	C36Y159	DE-FJ	602
☐	C-GAUH	Boeing 767-233	22519 / 40		0083	0283	2 PW JT9D-7R4D	140600	C36Y159	DE-GM	603
☐	C-GAUN	Boeing 767-233	22520 / 47		0083	0383	2 PW JT9D-7R4D	140600	C36Y159	DE-HJ	604
☐	C-GAUP	Boeing 767-233	22521 / 66	N1791B*	0083	0983	2 PW JT9D-7R4D	140600	C36Y159	DE-HK	605
☐	C-GAUS	Boeing 767-233	22522 / 75	N60659*	0083	1283	2 PW JT9D-7R4D	140600	C36Y159	DE-HL	606
☐	C-GAUU	Boeing 767-233	22523 / 87	N1784B*	0084	0484	2 PW JT9D-7R4D	140600	C36Y159	AK-BF	607
☐	C-GAUW	Boeing 767-233	22524 / 88	N6038E*	0084	0484	2 PW JT9D-7R4D	140600	C36Y159	AK-CD	608
☐	C-GAUY	Boeing 767-233	22525 / 91	N6055X*	0084	0584	2 PW JT9D-7R4D	140600	C36Y159	AK-CG	609
☐	C-GAVA	Boeing 767-233	22526 / 92		0084	0684	2 PW JT9D-7R4D	140600	C36Y159	BJ-CG	610
☐	C-GAVC	Boeing 767-233 (ER)	22527 / 102	N1783B*	0084	1084	2 PW JT9D-7R4D	152000	C36Y159	FJ-AE	611
☐	C-GAVF	Boeing 767-233 (ER)	22528 / 105	N6066U*	0084	1184	2 PW JT9D-7R4D	152000	C36Y159	FJ-AG	612
☐	C-GDSP	Boeing 767-233 (ER)	24142 / 229	N6009F*	0088	0788	2 PW JT9D-7R4D	159200	C25Y152	HP-EJ	613
☐	C-GDSS	Boeing 767-233 (ER)	24143 / 233	N6005C*	0088	0888	2 PW JT9D-7R4D	159200	C25Y152	HP-EK	614
☐	C-GDSU	Boeing 767-233 (ER)	24144 / 234	N6018N*	0088	0888	2 PW JT9D-7R4D	159200	C25Y152	HP-EL	615
☐	C-GDSY	Boeing 767-233 (ER)	24145 / 236	N6005C*	0088	0988	2 PW JT9D-7R4D	159200	C25Y152	HP-EM	616
☐	C-GPWA	Boeing 767-275	22683 / 36		0082	0585	2 PW JT9D-7R4D	142900	C36Y159	DE-JK	671
☐	C-GPWB	Boeing 767-275	22684 / 52	N1791B*	0083	0585	2 PW JT9D-7R4D	142900	C36Y159	DE-JL	672
☐	C-FMWP	Boeing 767-333 (ER)	25583 / 508		0093	0893	2 PW PW4060	184600	C35Y168	CQ-JR	631
☐	C-FMWQ	Boeing 767-333 (ER)	25584 / 596		0095	1095	2 PW PW4060	184600	C35Y168	CQ-JS	632
☐	C-FMWU	Boeing 767-333 (ER)	25585 / 597		0095	1195	2 PW PW4060	184600	C35Y168	CQ-KR	633
☐	C-FMWV	Boeing 767-333 (ER)	25586 / 599		0095	1295	2 PW PW4060	184600	C35Y168	CQ-KS	634
☐	C-FMWY	Boeing 767-333 (ER)	25587 / 604		0096	0296	2 PW PW4060	184600	C35Y168	CQ-LR	635
☐	C-FMXC	Boeing 767-333 (ER)	25588 / 606		0096	0396	2 PW PW4060	184600	C35Y168	CQ-LS	636
☐	C-	Airbus Industrie A330-343	279				2 RR Trent 772B-60	230000	C44Y228		931 / oo-delivery 1099
☐	C-	Airbus Industrie A330-343	284				2 RR Trent 772B-60	230000	C44Y228		932 / oo-delivery 1199
☐	C-	Airbus Industrie A330-343	277				2 RR Trent 772B-60	230000	C44Y228		933 / oo-delivery 0100
☐	C-	Airbus Industrie A330-343	337				2 RR Trent 772B-60	230000	C44Y228		934 / oo-delivery 0500
☐	C-	Airbus Industrie A330-343					2 RR Trent 772B-60	230000	C44Y228		935 / oo-delivery 1001
☐	C-	Airbus Industrie A330-343					2 RR Trent 772B-60	230000	C44Y228		936 / oo-delivery 0002
☐	C-FTNP	Airbus Industrie A340-313	093	F-WWJD*	0095	0695	4 CFMI CFM56-5C4	257000	C44Y220	HM-GR	982 / lsf ILFC
☐	C-FTNQ	Airbus Industrie A340-313	088	F-WWJV*	0095	0695	4 CFMI CFM56-5C4	257000	C44Y220	HM-GQ	981 / lsf ILFC
☐	C-FYKX	Airbus Industrie A340-313	150	F-WWJT*	0096	1196	4 CFMI CFM56-5C4	275000	C44Y220	PR-HJ	901
☐	C-FYKZ	Airbus Industrie A340-313	154	F-WWJI*	0096	1296	4 CFMI CFM56-5C4	275000	C44Y220	PR-HK	902
☐	C-FYLC	Airbus Industrie A340-313	167	F-WWJZ*	0096	0397	4 CFMI CFM56-5C4	275000	C44Y220	PR-HL	903
☐	C-FYLD	Airbus Industrie A340-313	170	F-WWJF*	0097	0497	4 CFMI CFM56-5C4	275000	C44Y220	PR-HM	904 / Star Alliance-colors
☐	C-FYLG	Airbus Industrie A340-313	175	F-WWJE*	0097	0597	4 CFMI CFM56-5C4	275000	C44Y220	PR-HQ	905
☐	C-FYLU	Airbus Industrie A340-313	179	F-WWJY*	0097	0597	4 CFMI CFM56-5C4	275000	C44Y220	PR-HS	906
☐	C-GBQM	Airbus Industrie A340-313	216	F-WWJK*	0098	0598	4 CFMI CFM56-5C4	275000	C44Y220		907 / lsf ILFC
☐	C-GDVV	Airbus Industrie A340-313	257	F-WWJS*	0099	0299	4 CFMI CFM56-5C4	275000	C44Y220		908 / lsf ILFC
☐	C-GDVW	Airbus Industrie A340-313	273				4 CFMI CFM56-5C4	275000	C44Y220		909 / oo-delivery 0599
☐	C-GDVZ	Airbus Industrie A340-313	278				4 CFMI CFM56-5C4	275000	C44Y220		910 / oo-delivery 0699
☐	C-	Airbus Industrie A340-313					4 CFMI CFM56-5C4	275000	C44Y220		to be lsf ILFC 0002
☐	C-GAGA	Boeing 747-233B (M)	20977 / 250	N8287V*	0074	0375	4 PW JT9D-7J	362880	C39Y377	EH-FK	306 / std MZJ
☐	C-GAGB	Boeing 747-233B (M)	21627 / 355		0079	0179	4 PW JT9D-7J	362880	C39Y377	CG-JM	307 / std MZJ
☐	C-GAGC	Boeing 747-238B (M)	21354 / 314	VH-ECA	0077	0188	4 PW JT9D-7J	362880	C39Y241 / Plt	AK-GM	308 / std MZJ
☐	C-	Airbus Industrie A340-642	391				4 RR Trent 556	365000	CY360		oo-delivery 0002
☐	C-	Airbus Industrie A340-642					4 RR Trent 556	365000	CY360		oo-delivery 0002
☐	C-	Airbus Industrie A340-642					4 RR Trent 556	365000	CY360		oo-delivery 0002
☐	C-	Airbus Industrie A340-541					4 RR Trent 553	365000	CY308		oo-delivery 0002
☐	C-	Airbus Industrie A340-541					4 RR Trent 553	365000	CY308		oo-delivery 0002
☐	C-GAGL	Boeing 747-433 (M)	24998 / 840	N6018N*	0091	0691	4 PW PW4056	394600	C63Y199 / Plt	DP-JQ	341 / lsf GECA
☐	C-GAGM	Boeing 747-433 (M)	25074 / 862	N6009F*	0091	0791	4 PW PW4056	394600	C63Y199 / Plt	DP-KQ	342
☐	C-GAGN	Boeing 747-433 (M)	25075 / 868	N6009F*	0091	0891	4 PW PW4056	394600	C63Y199 / Plt	DP-LQ	343 / lsf GECA

AIR CHARTERS, Inc. = ACX (Agence d'Affrètement Aérien Inc.dba/Subs. of Air Holdings Inc./Sister co. of Air Montreal)   Montreal-Dorval, Qué.

AIR CHARTERS

10105 Ryan Avenue, Dorval, Québec H9P 1A2, Canada   ☎ (514) 631-2111   Tx: none   Fax: (514) 631-8335   SITA: n/a
F: 1982   ✦✦✦ 15   Head: Reginald Overing   ICAO: PARAIR   Net: n/a

☐	C-FGAT	Cessna 550 Citation II	550-0229	N50FC	0081	0497	2 PWC JT15D-4	6033	Executive	
☐	C-FPEL	Cessna 550 Citation II	550-0042	N66ATH	0079	0596	2 PWC JT15D-4	6033	Executive	

AIRCO AIRCRAFT CHARTERS, Ltd   Edmonton, Alta.

Building No.6, 11930-109 Street, Edmonton, Alberta T5G 2T8, Canada   ☎ (780) 471-4771   Tx: none   Fax: (780) 479-4579   SITA: n/a
F: 1987   ✦✦✦ 13   Head: Ed Schlemko   Net: n/a

☐	C-FRKZ	Piper PA-34-220T Seneca III	34-8233048	N8473T	0082	0294	2 CO TSIO-360-KB	2155		
☐	C-GBMI	Piper PA-31-350 Navajo Chieftain	31-8352007	N23NP	0083	1097	2 LY TIO-540-J2BD	3175		
☐	C-GCJH	Piper PA-31-350 Navajo Chieftain	31-7952109	N42FL	0079	0398	2 LY TIO-540-J2BD	3175		
☐	C-GNSO	Piper PA-31-350 Navajo Chieftain	31-7852128	N174E	1298		2 LY TIO-540-J2BD	3175		
☐	C-GZNB	Piper PA-31-350 Navajo Chieftain	31-7752079	N6654B	0077	0891	2 LY TIO-540-J2BD	3175		
☐	C-FWYO	Beech King Air 100	B-28	N27JJ	0070	1195	2 PWC PT6A-28	4808		

AIR CONQUEST (Armbuster Industries, Inc. dba)   Ottawa, Ont.

Box 5747, Station F, Ottawa, Ontario K2C 3M1, Canada   ☎ (613) 745-6747   Tx: none   Fax: (613) 745-5506   SITA: n/a
F: 1987   ✦✦✦ n/a   Head: Patrick Dunn   Net: n/a

☐	C-FPPC	Piper PA-23-250 Aztec C	27-2485		0063		2 LY IO-540-C4B5	2359	Photo / Survey	
☐	C-GWAG	Piper PA-23-250 Aztec C	27-2699	N5592Y	0065		2 LY IO-540-C4B5	2359	Photo / Survey	

AIR CREEBEC, Inc. = YN / CRQ (formerly Air Creebec, (1994) Inc.)   Val d'Or, Qué. & Timmins, Ont.

PO Box 430, Val d'Or, Québec J9P 4P4, Canada   ☎ (819) 825-8355   Tx: none   Fax: (819) 825-0208   SITA: n/a
F: 1982   ✦✦✦ 175   Head: Albert Diamond   IATA: 219   ICAO: CREE   Net: http://www.aircrebec.ca

☐	C-FYRH	Embraer 110P1 Bandeirante (EMB-110P1)	110259	N91PB	0080	0796	2 PWC PT6A-34	5670	Y19	
☐	C-FZAU	Embraer 110P1 Bandeirante (EMB-110P1)	110228	OH-EBB	0079	1096	2 PWC PT6A-34	5670	Y19	
☐	C-FTOW	Beech 1900D Airliner	UE-130		1294	0295	2 PWC PT6A-67D	7688	Y19	
☐	C-FTQR	Beech 1900D Airliner	UE-129		1294	0295	2 PWC PT6A-67D	7688	Y19	
☐	C-FCSK	De Havilland DHC-8-102 Dash 8	122		0088	1188	2 PWC PW120A	15649	Y37	

registration	type of aircraft	cn/fn	ex/ex*	mfd	del	powered by	mtow kg	configuration	selcal	name/fln/specialitites/remarks
☐ C-GGNZ	BAe (HS) 748-272 Srs 2A	1690 / 172	ZS-SBU	0070	1288	2 RR Dart 534-2	21092	Y32 / Combi		
☐ C-GMAA	BAe (HS) 748-214 Srs 2A (SCD)	1576 / 14	TR-LQY	0065	0389	2 RR Dart 534-2	21092	Freighter		
☐ C-GQTG	BAe (HS) 748-234 Srs 2A	1619 / 132	CC-CEH	0068	0886	2 RR Dart 534-2	21092	Y32 / Combi		
☐ C-GQWO	BAe (HS) 748-221 Srs 2A	1597 / 75	T-03	0066	1288	2 RR Dart 534-2	21092	Y32 / Combi		

AIR-DALE FLYING SERVICE, Ltd (Seasonal May-November ops only) — Sault Ste Marie & Wawa-Hawk Junction, Ont.

235 River Road, Sault Ste Marie, Ontario P6A 6C3, Canada ☎ (705) 759-1300 Tx: none Fax: (705) 759-2466 SITA: n/a
F: 1986 ✱✱✱ n/a Head: Robert Dale Net: n/a Aircraft below MTOW 1361kg: Cessna 180 (on Floats)

registration	type of aircraft	cn/fn	ex/ex*	mfd	del	powered by	mtow kg	configuration	selcal	name/fln/specialitites/remarks
☐ C-FGYT	De Havilland DHC-2 Beaver I	182		0052		1 PW R-985	2313			Floats
☐ C-GELP	De Havilland DHC-2 Beaver I	780	N5318G	0053		1 PW R-985	2313			Floats
☐ C-GQXI	De Havilland DHC-2 Beaver I	427	N1059	0053		1 PW R-985	2313			Floats
☐ C-FBEP	De Havilland DHC-3 Otter	118	55-3272	0056		1 PW R-1340	3629			Floats

AIR DIRECT (Division of First Nations Air Services, Ltd) — Deseronto-Tyendinaga Mohawk, Ont.

RR 1, Deseronto, Ontario K0K 1X0, Canada ☎ (613) 396-1081 Tx: none Fax: (613) 396-1083 SITA: n/a
F: 1990 ✱✱✱ 12 Head: Ken Maclennan Net: n/a

registration	type of aircraft	cn/fn	ex/ex*	mfd	del	powered by	mtow kg	configuration	selcal	name/fln/specialitites/remarks
☐ C-GPFP	Piper PA-23-250 Aztec E	27-7405295		0074	0992	2 LY IO-540-C4B5	2359			
☐ C-FSUN	Piper PA-31-310 Navajo	31-750	N7228L	0071	0191	2 LY TIO-540-A1A	2948			

AIR EXPRESS ONTARIO (Canadian Flight Academy, Ltd dba) — Oshawa, Ont.

1200 Airport Blvd., Oshawa, Ontario L1J 8P5, Canada ☎ (905) 579-4777 Tx: none Fax: (905) 404-1803 SITA: n/a
F: 1994 ✱✱✱ n/a Head: Brian Holden Net: n/a Aircraft below MTOW 1361kg: Cessna 152 & Piper PA-28

registration	type of aircraft	cn/fn	ex/ex*	mfd	del	powered by	mtow kg	configuration	selcal	name/fln/specialitites/remarks
☐ C-FXKN	Piper PA-44-180 Seminole	44-7995312	N8517D	0079	0696	2 LY O-360-E1A6D	1724			
☐ C-GRWN	Piper PA-31-350 Navajo Chieftain	31-8152044	N4076J	0080	1297	2 LY TIO-540-J2BD	3175			

AIR 500, Ltd = BRM (Member of Innotech Execair Aviation Group) — Toronto-Int'l, Ont.

2450 Derry Road East, Hangar 7A, Mississauga, Ontario L5S 1B2, Canada ☎ (905) 673-1500 Tx: none Fax: (905) 673-5186 SITA: n/a
F: 1986 ✱✱✱ 20 Head: Dennis Chadala ICAO: BOOMERANG Net: n/a

registration	type of aircraft	cn/fn	ex/ex*	mfd	del	powered by	mtow kg	configuration	selcal	name/fln/specialitites/remarks
☐ C-FFSS	Mitsubishi MU-2B-60 Marquise	783SA	N81604	0080	0889	2 GA TPE331-10-501M	5250			
☐ C-GFFH	Mitsubishi MU-2B-60 Marquise	1522SA	N902M	0081	1293	2 GA TPE331-10-511M	5250			
☐ C-GGDC	Mitsubishi MU-2B-60 Marquise	796SA	N700MA	0080	1092	2 GA TPE331-10-501M	5250			
☐ C-GCLQ	Cessna 500 Citation I	500-0348	N301HC	0077	1295	2 PWC JT15D-1A	5375			
☐ C-GDMF	Cessna 550 Citation II	550-0113	N227PC	0079	1094	2 PWC JT15D-4	6033			

AIR FOLEYET, Ltd (Affiliated with Gosenda Lodge, Ltd / Seasonal May-November ops only) — Timmins, Ont.

562 Laminen Ave., Timmins, Ontario P4N 4R3, Canada ☎ (705) 268-2476 Tx: n/a Fax: (705) 268-2476 SITA: n/a
F: 1993 ✱✱✱ n/a Head: Richard Glazier Net: n/a

registration	type of aircraft	cn/fn	ex/ex*	mfd	del	powered by	mtow kg	configuration	selcal	name/fln/specialitites/remarks
☐ C-FMRN	De Havilland DHC-2 Beaver I	480	N5844N	0053	0693	1 PW R-985	2313			Floats

AIR GEORGIAN, Ltd – Ontario Regional Airline = GGN (Partenaire CANADIEN / CANADIAN Partner) — Toronto-Int'l, Ont.

2450 Derry Road East, Shell Aerocentre, Mississauga, Ontario L5S 1B2, Canada ☎ (905) 676-1221 Tx: none Fax: (905) 676-1151 SITA: n/a
F: 1994 ✱✱✱ n/a Head: Paul Mulrooney ICAO: GEORGIAN Net: n/a
Scheduled services are operated on behalf of Canadian Airlines Int'l (with Beech 1900D aircraft) as Partenaire CANADIEN / CANADIAN Partner using the marketing name ONTARIO REGIONAL.
Expects to use the marketing name WESTERN REGIONAL AIRLINES for a new base at Calgary, Alta for flights with additional Beech 1900D as Partnaire CANADIEN/CANADIAN Partner.

registration	type of aircraft	cn/fn	ex/ex*	mfd	del	powered by	mtow kg	configuration	selcal	name/fln/specialitites/remarks
☐ C-GCGA	Cessna 208 Caravan I	20800242		0095	0795	1 PWC PT6A-114	3629	Y9 / Freighter		Amphibian
☐ C-FAGA	Cessna 208B Grand Caravan	208B0658		0098	0298	1 PWC PT6A-114A	3969	Y9 / Freighter		
☐ C-FESA	Cessna 208B Caravan I Super Cargomaster	208B0049	N7565B	0088	1294	1 PWC PT6A-114	3969	Freighter		
☐ C-FESH	Cessna 208B Caravan I Super Cargomaster	208B0047	N7393B	0088	1294	1 PWC PT6A-114	3969	Freighter		
☐ C-FFGA	Cessna 208B Grand Caravan	208B0662		0098	0398	1 PWC PT6A-114A	3969	Y9 / Freighter		
☐ C-GEGA	Cessna 208B Grand Caravan	208B0379	N1119A	0093	0496	1 PWC PT6A-114A	3969	Y9 / Freighter		
☐ C-GLGA	Cessna 208B Grand Caravan	208B0350	N64AP	0093	0196	1 PWC PT6A-114A	3969	Y9 / Freighter		
☐ C-GQGA	Beech King Air F90	LA-106	N19112	0081	0497	2 PWC PT6A-135	4967	Y9		
☐ C-GKGA	Beech 1900C-1 Airliner	UC-117	N117ZR	0790	1196	2 PWC PT6A-65B	7530	Y19		lst / opf Executive Air Link
☐ C-GGGA	Beech 1900D Airliner	UE-291	N20704*	0097	1197	2 PWC PT6A-67D	7688	Y19		051 / Ontario Regional-Canad.Partner-cs
☐ C-GHGA	Beech 1900D Airliner	UE-293	N21063*	0097	1297	2 PWC PT6A-67D	7688	Y19		053 / Ontario Regional-Canad.Partner-cs
☐ C-GMGA	Beech 1900D Airliner	UE-315	N22890*	0098	0698	2 PWC PT6A-67D	7688	Y19		056 / Ontario Regional-Canad.Partner-cs
☐ C-GORA	Beech 1900D Airliner	UE-326	N23164*	0098	1098	2 PWC PT6A-67D	7688	Y19		057 / Ontario Regional-Canad.Partner-cs
☐ C-GORC	Beech 1900D Airliner	UE-320	N22976*	0098	1198	2 PWC PT6A-67D	7688	Y19		059 / Ontario Regional-Canad.Partner-cs
☐ C-GORF	Beech 1900D Airliner	UE-330	N23222*	0098	1098	2 PWC PT6A-67D	7688	Y19		058 / Ontario Regional-Canad.Partner-cs
☐ C-GORI	Beech 1900D Airliner	UE-346		0098	1298	2 PWC PT6A-67D	7688	Y19		060 / Ontario Regional-Canad.Partner-cs
☐ C-GVGA	Beech 1900D Airliner	UE-292	N20707*	0097	1297	2 PWC PT6A-67D	7688	Y19		052 / Ontario Regional-Canad.Partner-cs
☐ C-GWGA	Beech 1900D Airliner	UE-309	N22874*	0098	0498	2 PWC PT6A-67D	7688	Y19		055 / Ontario Regional-Canad.Partner-cs
☐ C-GZGA	Beech 1900D Airliner	UE-306	N22700*	0098	0398	2 PWC PT6A-67D	7688	Y19		054 / Ontario Regional-Canad.Partner-cs

AIR HART AVIATION (Canadian Institute of Aviation Technology, Inc. dba) — Kelowna, B.C.

6095 Airport Road, Kelowna, British Columbia V1V 1S1, Canada ☎ (250) 765-6699 Tx: none Fax: (250) 765-6651 SITA: n/a
F: 1994 ✱✱✱ n/a Head: Trevor Erhart Net: n/a Aircraft below MTOW 1361kg: Bellanca 8GCBC, Champion 7GC, Cessna 140 & 172

registration	type of aircraft	cn/fn	ex/ex*	mfd	del	powered by	mtow kg	configuration	selcal	name/fln/specialitites/remarks
☐ C-FQRT	Cessna TU206A Turbo Skywagon	U206-0515	N4815F	0066	0198	1 CO TSIO-520-C	1633			
☐ C-GZOR	Piper PA-34-200T Seneca II	34-7970173	N2080X	0079	0198	2 CO TSIO-360-EB	2073			

AIR INUIT (1985), Ltd = 3H / AIE (Owned by Makivik, Corp.) — Kuujjuaq, Qué.

547 Meloche, Dorval, Québec H9P 2W2, Canada ☎ (514) 636-9445 Tx: none Fax: (514) 636-8916 SITA: n/a
F: 1978 ✱✱✱ 200 Head: Mark T. Gordon IATA: 875 ICAO: AIR INUIT Net: n/a

registration	type of aircraft	cn/fn	ex/ex*	mfd	del	powered by	mtow kg	configuration	selcal	name/fln/specialitites/remarks
☐ C-FJFR	De Havilland DHC-6 Twin Otter 300	784	HK-2762	0082	1290	2 PWC PT6A-27	5670	Y18 / Frtr		
☐ C-GKCJ	De Havilland DHC-6 Twin Otter 300	698	A6-AMM	0080	0197	2 PWC PT6A-27	5670	Y18 / Frtr		
☐ C-GMDC	De Havilland DHC-6 Twin Otter 300	763		0081	0581	2 PWC PT6A-27	5670	Y18 / Frtr		
☐ C-GTYX	De Havilland DHC-6 Twin Otter 300	631		0079	0688	2 PWC PT6A-27	5670	Y18 / Frtr		
☐ C-FDAO	De Havilland DHC-8-102 Dash 8	123		0088	0395	2 PWC PW120A	15649	Y37		
☐ C-FDOX	BAe (HS) 748-310 Srs 2A (SCD)	1749 / 231	TJ-CCD	0077	0189	2 RR Dart 534-2	21092	Y40 / Frtr		
☐ C-FGET	BAe (HS) 748-244 Srs 2A	1724 / 218	D-AFSG	0075	0789	2 RR Dart 534-2	21092	Y40 / Frtr		cvtd Srs 2
☐ C-GCUK	BAe (HS) 748-343 Srs 2A (SCD)	1762 / 245	V2-LAZ	0078	0185	2 RR Dart 534-2	20183	Y40 / Frtr		
☐ C-GEGJ	BAe (HS) 748-244 Srs 2A	1711 / 209	TF-GMB	0073	1286	2 RR Dart 534-2	20183	Y40 / Frtr		cvtd Srs 2
☐ C-GFHB	Convair 580	38	N4802C	0052	0591	2 AN 501-D13	24766	Corporate 49Pax		opf APZ in Hydro-Québec cs/cvtd 340-38
☐ C-GFHF	Convair 580	176	N4634C	0054	0591	2 AN 501-D13	24766	Corporate 49Pax		opf APZ in Hydro-Québec cs/cvtd 340-54
☐ C-GFHH	Convair 580	109	N3429	0053	0591	2 AN 501-D13	24766	Corporate 49Pax		opf APZ in Hydro-Québec cs/cvtd 340-32
☐ C-GQBP	Convair 580	137	N7528U	0053	0293	2 AN 501-D13	26379	Corporate 49Pax		opf APZ in Hydro-Québec cs/cvtd 340-54
☐ C-GTTA	Convair 580	501	N5122	0058	0498	2 AN 501-D13	24766	Corporate 36Pax		opf APZ in Corporate cs / cvtd 440-62

AIR IVANHOE, Ltd — Foleyet, Ont.

PO Box 99, Foleyet, Ontario P0M 1T0, Canada ☎ (705) 899-2155 Tx: n/a Fax: none SITA: n/a
F: 1980 ✱✱✱ 10 Head: George H. Theriault Net: http://www.virtualnorth.com/ivanhoe/ Aircraft below MTOW 1361kg: Cessna 180.

registration	type of aircraft	cn/fn	ex/ex*	mfd	del	powered by	mtow kg	configuration	selcal	name/fln/specialitites/remarks
☐ C-GERE	De Havilland DHC-2 Beaver I	352	N62874	0051		1 PW R-985	2313			Floats

AIR JASPER, Inc. — Jasper-Hinton, Alta.

Box 1959, Jasper, Alberta T0E 1E0, Canada ☎ (780) 865-3616 Tx: none Fax: (780) 865-5530 SITA: n/a
F: 1997 ✱✱✱ n/a Head: n/a Net: n/a

registration	type of aircraft	cn/fn	ex/ex*	mfd	del	powered by	mtow kg	configuration	selcal	name/fln/specialitites/remarks
☐ C-GMST	Cessna T210N Turbo Centurion II	21063929		0080	0797	1 CO TSIO-520-R	1814			

AIR KENDA (William R. Bennett dba / Seasonal May-October ops only) — Gogama, Ont.

Box 340, Gogama, Ontario P0M 1W0, Canada ☎ (705) 894-2096 Tx: n/a Fax: none SITA: n/a
F: 1991 ✱✱✱ n/a Head: William R. Bennett Net: n/a

registration	type of aircraft	cn/fn	ex/ex*	mfd	del	powered by	mtow kg	configuration	selcal	name/fln/specialitites/remarks
☐ C-FVKH	De Havilland DHC-2 Beaver I	844	N1599V	0056	0591	1 PW R-985	2313			Floats

AIR KILLARNEY, Ltd (Affiliated with Killarney Mountain Lodge) — Killarney, Ont.

3 Commissioner Street, Killarney, Ontario P0M 2A0, Canada ☎ (705) 287-2242 Tx: none Fax: (705) 287-2691 SITA: n/a
F: 1993 ✱✱✱ 3 Head: Maurice East Net: n/a

registration	type of aircraft	cn/fn	ex/ex*	mfd	del	powered by	mtow kg	configuration	selcal	name/fln/specialitites/remarks
☐ C-GJII	Piper PA-32-300 Cherokee SIX	32-40236	N300DP	0067	0693	1 LY IO-540-K1A5	1542			

AIR KIPAWA, Inc. (Associated with Air North Bay, Inc.) — Kipawa, Qué. & North Bay, Ont.

550 Chemin Kipawa, Kipawa, Québec J0Z 2H0, Canada ☎ (819) 627-3471 Tx: none Fax: (819) 627-9256 SITA: n/a
F: 1962 ✱✱✱ 15 Head: Gilbert Vaillancourt Net: n/a

registration	type of aircraft	cn/fn	ex/ex*	mfd	del	powered by	mtow kg	configuration	selcal	name/fln/specialitites/remarks
☐ C-FWXJ	Cessna A185E Skywagon	185-1331		0068	0696	1 CO IO-520-D	1520			Floats / Wheel-Skis
☐ C-FDNK	De Havilland DHC-3 Otter	385	N80945	0060	0890	1 PW R-1340	3629			Floats / Wheel-Skis

AIR LABRADOR – Wings of the North = WJ / LAL (Labrador Airways, Ltd dba) — Goose Bay, Stephenville & St. John's, Nfld

PO Box 310, Station A, Goose Bay, (Labrador), Newfoundland A0P 1S0, Canada ☎ (709) 896-8113 Tx: none Fax: (709) 896-0644 SITA: n/a
F: 1970 ✱✱✱ 120 Head: Roger W. Pike IATA: 927 ICAO: LAB AIR Net: http://www.airlabrador.com

registration	type of aircraft	cn/fn	ex/ex*	mfd	del	powered by	mtow kg	configuration	selcal	name/fln/specialitites/remarks
☐ C-FQOS	De Havilland DHC-3 Turbo Otter	398	CAF9418	0060	0698	1 PWC PT6A-135A	3629	Y9 / Freighter		cvtd Otter / Floats / Wheel-Skis
☐ C-FPEX	Cessna 208B Caravan I Super Cargomaster	208B0118	N986FE ntu	0088	1088	1 PWC PT6A-114	3969	Freighter		

☐ C-FGON	De Havilland DHC-6 Twin Otter 300	369		0073	0285	2 PWC PT6A-27	5670	Y19		
☐ C-GDQY	De Havilland DHC-6 Twin Otter 100	77	YA-GAS	0067	0678	2 PWC PT6A-20	5252	Y19		Floats / Wheels
☐ C-GLAI	De Havilland DHC-6 Twin Otter 300	296	N5377G	0071	0588	2 PWC PT6A-27	5670	Y19		
☐ C-GNQY	De Havilland DHC-6 Twin Otter 300	450		0075	0085	2 PWC PT6A-27	5670	Y19		
☐ C-GLHO	Beech 1900D Airliner	UE-266	N10950*	0097	0597	2 PWC PT6A-67D	7688	Y19		Capt. Harold Oake
☐ C-GLAP	Shorts 330 (SD3-30 Variant 300)	SH3033	N996HA	0079	0693	2 PWC PT6A-45R	10387	Y30		
☐ C-GAAN	De Havilland DHC-8-102 Dash 8	051		0086	0696	2 PWC PW120A	15649	Y37		

AIR LIMO CANADA, Inc. — Montreal-St. Hubert, Qué.

4800 Route de l'Aéroport, St. Hubert, Québec J3Y 8Y9, Canada ☎ (450) 656-5688 Tx: none Fax: (450) 656-7490 SITA: n/a

F: 1985 ⁂ n/a Head: n/a Net: n/a Aircraft below MTOW 1361kg: Cessna 172

☐ C-FDLW	Cessna T210L Turbo Centurion II	21059911	N30319	0072	0395	1 CO TSIO-520-H	1724			
☐ C-GJAX	Cessna 310R II	310R0210		0075	1198	2 CO IO-520-M	2495			

AIR MELANCON, Inc. — Ste-Anne-du-Lac, Qué.

2 Chemin Tour-du-Lac, Ste-Anne-du-Lac, Québec J0W 1V0, Canada ☎ (819) 586-2220 Tx: none Fax: (819) 586-2388 SITA: n/a

F: 1957 ⁂ 15 Head: Francine Melançon-Milot Net: n/a

☐ C-FBPB	De Havilland DHC-2 Beaver I	1434	VH-IDF	0060		1 PW R-985	2313			Floats / Wheel-Skis
☐ C-FQQD	De Havilland DHC-2 Beaver I	1580	64-374	0065		1 PW R-985	2313			Floats / Wheel-Skis
☐ C-FZVP	De Havilland DHC-2 Beaver I	1033	N564	0056		1 PW R-985	2313			Floats / Wheel-Skis
☐ C-GQXH	De Havilland DHC-2 Beaver I	536	N1579	0052		1 PW R-985	2313			Floats / Wheel-Skis

AIR MONT-LAURIER (1985), Inc. — Mont-Laurier-Lac-des-Barges & Ste. Véronique-Lac Tibériade

CP 58, Sainte-Véronique, Québec J0W 1X0, Canada ☎ (819) 275-2794 Tx: none Fax: (819) 275-3991 SITA: n/a

F: 1985 ⁂ 8 Head: Norman Ouellette Net: n/a

☐ C-GVLK	Cessna U206G Stationair 6 II	U20604329	N756SW	0078	0894	1 CO IO-520-F	1633			Floats
☐ C-FTUR	De Havilland DHC-2 Beaver I	1529		0063	0396	1 PW R-985	2313			Floats
☐ C-GUML	De Havilland DHC-2 Beaver I	307	N1402Z	0051		1 PW R-985	2313			Floats
☐ C-GGSC	De Havilland DHC-3 Otter	366	N5072F	0060		1 PW R-1340	3629			Floats

AIR MONTMAGNY (Montmagny Air Service, Inc. dba) — Montmagny, Qué.

640 Boulevard Taché Est, Montmagny, Québec G5V 4G9, Canada ☎ (418) 248-3545 Tx: none Fax: (418) 248-5817 SITA: n/a

F: 1980 ⁂ 2 Head: Gaston Gosselin Net: n/a

☐ C-GCTM	Cessna U206G Stationair	U20603794	N8920G	0077		1 CO IO-520-F	1633			
☐ C-GBFU	Britten-Norman BN-2A-27 Islander	535	N70JA	0076		2 LY O-540-E4C5	2994			

AIR MONTREAL, Inc. = F8 / AMO (Subsidiary of Air Holdings Inc./Sister company of Air Charters Inc.) — Montreal-Dorval, Qué.

10105 Ryan Avenue, Dorval, Québec H9P 1A2, Canada ☎ (514) 631-2111 Tx: none Fax: (514) 631-8335 SITA: n/a

F: 1990 ⁂ 50 Head: Reginald Overing ICAO: AIR MONTREAL Net: n/a

☐ C-GIQI	Fairchild (Swearingen) SA226TC Metro II	TC-349	N100ED	0080	0494	2 GA TPE331-3UW-303G	5670	Y19		
☐ C-FAMC	Fairchild (Swearingen) SA227AC Metro III	AC-719B	N436MA	0088	0398	2 GA TPE331-11U-612G	7257	Y19		
☐ C-FAMH	Fairchild (Swearingen) SA227AC Metro III	AC-588	N3115M	0084	0597	2 GA TPE331-11U-611G	6577	Y19		
☐ C-GAMI	Fairchild (Swearingen) SA227AC Metro III	AC-587	N3115T	0084	0596	2 GA TPE331-11U-611G	6577	Y19		
☐ C-GIQN	Fairchild (Swearingen) SA227AC Metro III	AC-485	N3049D	0081	1294	2 GA TPE331-11U-611G	6577	Y19		

AIR MUSKOKA = AMS (744185 Ontario, Inc. dba) — Muskoka, Ont.

Muskoka Airport, RR 1, Gravenhurst, Ontario P1P 1R1, Canada ☎ (705) 687-6696 Tx: none Fax: (705) 687-4045 SITA: n/a

F: 1975 ⁂ 17 Head: Dave Gronfors ICAO: AIR MUSKOKA Net: n/a Aircraft below MTOW 1361 kg: Cessna 182.

☐ C-GFOB	Piper PA-23-250 Aztec D	27-4000	N6680Y	0069	1296	2 LY IO-540-C4B5	2359			
☐ C-FNSJ	Twin (Aero) Commander 700	70013	N9903S	0078	0792	2 LY TIO-540-R2AD	3151			
☐ C-FNTJ	Twin (Aero) Commander 700	70023	N702SA	0079	0692	2 LY TIO-540-R2AD	3151			

AIR NOOTKA, Ltd — Gold River, B.C.

Box 19, Gold River, British Columbia V0P 1G0, Canada ☎ (250) 283-2255 Tx: n/a Fax: (250) 283-2256 SITA: n/a

F: 1981 ⁂ 5 Head: Grant C. Howatt Net: n/a Aircraft below MTOW 1361 kg: Cessna 180 (Floats).

☐ C-FOXD	De Havilland DHC-2 Beaver I	807	N90723	0055	0294	1 PW R-985	2309			Floats
☐ C-FSCM	De Havilland DHC-2 Beaver I	1583		0065	0898	1 PW R-985	2309			Floats

AIR NORD OUEST (Guy Bilodeau dba / Affiliated with Pourvoiries G.R.B. / Seasonal April-November ops only) — Senneterre-SPB, Qué.

CP 785, Senneterre, Québec J0Y 2M0, Canada ☎ (819) 753-2302 Tx: none Fax: (819) 737-8442 SITA: n/a

F: 1970 ⁂ n/a Head: Guy Bilodeau Net: http://daisy.lino.com

☐ CF-GRB	Cessna A185F Skywagon	18502212		0073		1 CO IO-520-D	1520			Floats

AIR NORTH = 4N / ANT (Air North Charter & Training, Ltd dba) — Whitehorse, Y.T.

PO Box 4998, Whitehorse, Yukon Territory Y1A 4S2, Canada ☎ (867) 668-2228 Tx: none Fax: (867) 668-6224 SITA: n/a

F: 1977 ⁂ 20 Head: Joseph T. Sparling IATA: 287 ICAO: AIR NORTH Net: http://www.airnorth.yk.net

☐ C-FRQI	Beech 99 Airliner	U-124	TF-ELB	0069	1198	2 PWC PT6A-20	4717	Y14		
☐ C-FAGI	BAe (HS) 748-276 Srs 2A	1699 / 175	G-11-6*	0071	0898	2 RR Dart 534-2	20183	Y44		
☐ C-FYDU	BAe (HS) 748-273 Srs 2A	1694 / 171	ZK-MCP	0070	0896	2 RR Dart 534-2	21092	Y44		
☐ C-FYDY	BAe (HS) 748-233 Srs 2A	1661 / 140	ZK-MCJ	0068	0896	2 RR Dart 534-2	21092	Y44		

AIR NORTHLAND (Hunt River Camps, Ltd dba / Seasonal summer ops only) — Goose Bay, Nfld.

PO Box 1015, Station C, Goose Bay, (Labrador), Newfoundland A0P 1C0, Canada ☎ (709) 896-8049 Tx: none Fax: (709) 896-2563 SITA: n/a

F: 1986 ⁂ n/a Head: Clyde House Net: n/a

☐ C-GANW	Partenavia P.68C	274	N3832Q	0083	0792	2 LY IO-360-A1B6	1990			

AIR NOUVEAU-QUEBEC, Inc. (Les Pourvoiries Fortier, Inc. dba / Affiliated with Auberge Wedge Hills Lodge) — Schefferville, Qué.

CP 280, Schefferville, Québec G0G 1T0, Canada ☎ (418) 585-2605 Tx: none Fax: (418) 585-3555 SITA: n/a

F: n/a ⁂ 4 Head: Lina Fortier Net: n/a

☐ C-FFYK	Cessna A185F Skywagon	18502174		0073		1 CO IO-520-D	1520			Floats / Wheel-Skis

AIR NOVA, Inc. = QK / ARN (Liaison AIR CANADA Connector) (Subsidiary of Air Canada) — Halifax, N.S. & Québec, Qué.

310 Goudey Drive, Halifax Int'l Airport, Enfield, Nova Scotia B2T 1E4, Canada ☎ (902) 873-5000 Tx: none Fax: (902) 873-4901 SITA: n/a

F: 1986 ⁂ 900 Head: Dr. Angus Bruneau IATA: 983 ICAO: NOVA Net: http://www.airnova.com

Scheduled commuter services are operated on behalf of Air Canada as a Liaison AIR CANADA Connector (in such colours & both titles) using AC flight designators.

☐ C-GAAR	Beech 1900D Airliner	UE-207	N10625*	0096	0499	2 PWC PT6A-67D	7688	Y18		901 / Bas St-Laurent
☐ C-GAAS	Beech 1900D Airliner	UE-209	N10659*	0096	0499	2 PWC PT6A-67D	7688	Y18		902 / Iles de la Madelaine
☐ C-GAAT	Beech 1900D Airliner	UE-217	N1564J*	0096	0499	2 PWC PT6A-67D	7688	Y18		903 / Gaspé
☐ C-GAAU	Beech 1900D Airliner	UE-232	N10705*	0096	0499	2 PWC PT6A-67D	7688	Y18		904 / Baie Comeau
☐ C-GAAV	Beech 1900D Airliner	UE-235	N10708*	0096	0499	2 PWC PT6A-67D	7688	Y18		905 / Saguenay Lac St. Jean
☐ C-FABG	De Havilland DHC-8-102 Dash 8	147		0089	1097	2 PWC PW120A	15649	Y37		899 / City of Halifax / *lsf ABN*
☐ C-FABT	De Havilland DHC-8-102 Dash 8	049		0086	0499	2 PWC PW120A	15649	Y37		817 / *lsf ABL*
☐ C-FCTA	De Havilland DHC-8-102 Dash 8	039		0086	0786	2 PWC PW120A	15649	Y37		801 / Town of Yarmouth
☐ C-FDOJ	De Havilland DHC-8-102 Dash 8	128		1288	0299	2 PWC PW120A	15649	Y37		895 / *lsf Air Manitoba Leasing*
☐ C-FGRY	De Havilland DHC-8-102 Dash 8	212		0590	1294	2 PWC PW120A	15649	Y37		812 / Greater Moncton Area
☐ C-FHRA	De Havilland DHC-8-102 Dash 8	206		0390	0499	2 PWC PW120A	15649	Y37		810 / Montreal / *lsf GECA*
☐ C-FHRC	De Havilland DHC-8-102 Dash 8	209	TJ-AIA	0490	0499	2 PWC PW120A	15649	Y37		811 / Québec / *lsf GECA*
☐ C-FJMG	De Havilland DHC-8-102 Dash 8	255		0091	0792	2 PWC PW120A	15649	Y37		824 / Town of Gander
☐ C-FPON	De Havilland DHC-8-102 Dash 8	171		0089	0989	2 PWC PW120A	15649	Y37		808 / Town of St. Leonard
☐ C-FTON	De Havilland DHC-8-102 Dash 8	178		0089	1189	2 PWC PW120A	15649	Y37		809 / City of Charlottetown
☐ C-GABF	De Havilland DHC-8-102 Dash 8	025		0086	0499	2 PWC PW120A	15649	Y37		816 / Rouyn-Noranda / *lsf ABL*
☐ C-GANF	De Havilland DHC-8-102 Dash 8	042		0086	0786	2 PWC PW120A	15649	Y37		802 / Cities of Wabush/Labrador
☐ C-GANI	De Havilland DHC-8-102 Dash 8	064		0087	0287	2 PWC PW120A	15649	Y37		804/Cities of Deer Lake/Cornerbrook
☐ C-GANK	De Havilland DHC-8-102 Dash 8	087		0087	0887	2 PWC PW120A	15649	Y37		805 / City of Fredericton
☐ C-GANQ	De Havilland DHC-8-102 Dash 8	096		0088	0388	2 PWC PW120A	15649	Y37		806
☐ C-GANS	De Havilland DHC-8-102 Dash 8	057		0086	1286	2 PWC PW120A	15649	Y37		803 / City of Sydney
☐ C-GCTC	De Havilland DHC-8-102 Dash 8	065	V2-LEE	0187	0696	2 PWC PW120A	15649	Y37		815
☐ C-GCWZ	De Havilland DHC-8-102 Dash 8	362	N861MA	0093	0498	2 PWC PW120A	15649	Combi Y21		896 / *lsf De Havilland Corp.*
☐ C-GJSV	De Havilland DHC-8-102 Dash 8	085		0087	0499	2 PWC PW120A	15649	Y37		805 / Val d'Or / *lsf Wing-Co Leasing*
☐ C-GOND	De Havilland DHC-8-102 Dash 8	090		0288	1294	2 PWC PW120A	15649	Y37		810 / City of Saint John
☐ C-GONH	De Havilland DHC-8-102 Dash 8	093		0288	0499	2 PWC PW120A	15649	Y37		804 / Sept-Iles / *lsf Wing-Co Leasing*
☐ C-GONN	De Havilland DHC-8-102 Dash 8	101		0088	0694	2 PWC PW120A	15649	Y37		898 / Happy Valley/Goose Bay
☐ C-GONO	De Havilland DHC-8-102 Dash 8	102		0088	0688	2 PWC PW120A	15649	Y37		807 / City of Bathurst
☐ C-GRNT	BAe 146-200A	E2140	G-11-140*	0089	1289	4 LY ALF502R-5	42184	C10Y67		206 / City of Halifax
☐ C-GRNU	BAe 146-200A	E2139	G-5-139*	0089	0190	4 LY ALF502R-5	42184	C10Y67		205

31 registration type of aircraft cn/fn ex/ex* mfd del powered by mtow kg configuration selcal name/fln/specialitites/remarks

☐ C-GRNV	BAe 146-200A	E2133	G-5-133*	0089	1089	4 LY ALF502R-5	42184	C10Y67		204
☐ C-GRNX	BAe 146-200A	E2130	G-5-130*	0089	0789	4 LY ALF502R-5	42184	C10Y67		203 / City of St. John's
☐ C-GRNZ	BAe 146-200A	E2106	G-5-106*	0088	0189	4 LY ALF502R-5	42184	C10Y67		201

AIR NUNAVUT, Ltd = BFF (formerly Air Baffin, Ltd) — Iqaluit, Nun.

PO Box 1239, Iqaluit, Nunavut X0A 0H0, Canada ☎ (867) 979-4018 Tx: none Fax: (867) 979-4318 SITA: n/a
F: 1987 ⁂ 14 Head: Jeff Mahoney Net: n/a

☐ C-GYRS	Piper PA-31-310 Navajo B	31-7300937	N90AB	0073	1289	2 LY TIO-540-A2C	2948			
☐ C-FCGW	Beech Catpass 200	BB-207	N111WH	0076	0795	2 PWC PT6A-41	5670			cvtd King Air 200

AIR ONTARIO, Inc. = GX / ONT (Liaison AIR CANADA Connector) (Subsidiary of Air Canada) — London & Thunder Bay, Ont.

1000 Air Ontario Drive, London, Ontario N5V 3S4, Canada ☎ (519) 453-8440 Tx: 0647571 airontario I Fax: (519) 453-0063 SITA: n/a
F: 1987 ⁂ 740 Head: David R. McCamus IATA: 368 ICAO: ONTARIO Net: n/a
Scheduled commuter services are operated on behalf of Air Canada as a Liaison AIR CANADA Connector (in such colours & both titles) using AC flight designators.

☐ C-FCON	De Havilland DHC-8-102 Dash 8	179		0089	1189	2 PWC PW120A	15649	Y37		817 / City of/Ville de Colombus
☐ C-FGQI	De Havilland DHC-8-102 Dash 8	185		0089	0190	2 PWC PW120A	15649	Y37		818 / City of/Ville de Toronto
☐ C-FGQK	De Havilland DHC-8-102 Dash 8	193		0089	0290	2 PWC PW120A	15649	Y37		819 / City of/Ville de Timmins
☐ C-FGRC	De Havilland DHC-8-102 Dash 8	195		0089	0390	2 PWC PW120A	15649	Y37		821
☐ C-FGRM	De Havilland DHC-8-102 Dash 8	199		0090	0390	2 PWC PW120A	15649	Y37		820 / City of/Ville de Thunder Bay
☐ C-FGRP	De Havilland DHC-8-102 Dash 8	207		0090	0490	2 PWC PW120A	15649	Y37		822 / Metro Ottawa
☐ C-FVON	De Havilland DHC-8-102 Dash 8	181		1189	1189	2 PWC PW120A	15649	Y37		808 / City of/Ville de North Bay
☐ C-FXON	De Havilland DHC-8-102 Dash 8	183	V2-LDZ	1189	1289	2 PWC PW120A	15649	Y37		814 / City of/Ville de Richmond
☐ C-GION	De Havilland DHC-8-102 Dash 8	127		0088	1288	2 PWC PW120A	15649	Y37		805 / City of/Ville de Windsor
☐ C-GJIG	De Havilland DHC-8-102 Dash 8	068		0087	0487	2 PWC PW120A	15649	Y37		801 / City of/Ville de Harrisburg
☐ C-GJMI	De Havilland DHC-8-102 Dash 8	077		0587	0687	2 PWC PW120A	15649	Y37		825 / City of/Ville de Montreal
☐ C-GJMK	De Havilland DHC-8-102 Dash 8	081		0087	0687	2 PWC PW120A	15649	Y37		804 / City of/Ville de Sault Ste.Marie
☐ C-GJMO	De Havilland DHC-8-102 Dash 8	079		0487	0687	2 PWC PW120A	15649	Y37		806 / City of/Ville de Providence
☐ C-GJSX	De Havilland DHC-8-102 Dash 8	088		1187	1187	2 PWC PW120A	15649	Y37		807 / City of/Ville de Kingston
☐ C-GKON	De Havilland DHC-8-102 Dash 8	130		0088	0189	2 PWC PW120A	15649	Y37		815 / City of/Ville de Baltimore
☐ C-GLON	De Havilland DHC-8-102 Dash 8	133		0088	0189	2 PWC PW120A	15649	Y37		816 / The Lehigh Valley
☐ C-GONJ	De Havilland DHC-8-102 Dash 8	095		0088	0388	2 PWC PW120A	15649	Y37		809 / City of/Ville de Sarnia
☐ C-GONR	De Havilland DHC-8-102 Dash 8	109		0088	0788	2 PWC PW120A	15649	Y37		811 / City of/Ville de London
☐ C-GONW	De Havilland DHC-8-102 Dash 8	112		0088	0888	2 PWC PW120A	15649	Y37		812 / City of/Ville de Hartford
☐ C-GONX	De Havilland DHC-8-102 Dash 8	118		0088	1088	2 PWC PW120A	15649	Y37		803 / City of/Ville de Mississauga
☐ C-GONY	De Havilland DHC-8-102 Dash 8	115		0088	0988	2 PWC PW120A	15649	Y37		802 / City of/Ville de Sudbury
☐ C-FJVV	De Havilland DHC-8-311 Dash 8	271		0091	0491	2 PWC PW123	18643	Y52		306 / City of/Ville de Windsor
☐ C-FMDW	De Havilland DHC-8-311 Dash 8	269		0091	0491	2 PWC PW123	18643	Y52		305 / City of/Ville de Sault Ste.Marie
☐ C-GMON	De Havilland DHC-8-301 Dash 8	131		0089	0689	2 PWC PW123	18643	Y52		301 / City of/Ville de Sudbury
☐ C-GNON	De Havilland DHC-8-301 Dash 8	137		0089	0789	2 PWC PW123	18643	Y52		302 / City of/Ville de Timmins
☐ C-GUON	De Havilland DHC-8-301 Dash 8	143		0089	0989	2 PWC PW123	18643	Y52		303 / City of/Ville de London
☐ C-GVON	De Havilland DHC-8-301 Dash 8	149		0089	1089	2 PWC PW123	18643	Y52		304 / City of/Ville de Cleveland

AIR OUTAOUAIS (2819651 Canada, Inc. dba/formerly Air Calumet/Seasonal April-October ops only) — Ottawa-Gatineau, Qué.

Box 442, Aylmer, Québec J9H 5E7, Canada ☎ (819) 568-2359 Tx: none Fax: (819) 243-7934 SITA: n/a
F: n/a ⁂ n/a Head: Robert Burns Net: n/a

☐ C-GHTX	Cessna U206C Super Skywagon	U206-0940	N3940G	0068	0793	1 CO IO-520-F	1633			Floats
☐ C-FEGE	De Havilland DHC-2 Beaver I	1539	VH-IDK	0064	0697	1 PW R-985	2313			lsf Aero Nord-Est / Floats

AIR PROVIDENCE, Ltd — Fort Providence, N.W.T.

Hangar 1, Fort Providence, Northwest Territories X0E 0L0, Canada ☎ (867) 699-3551 Tx: n/a Fax: (867) 699-3526 SITA: n/a
F: 1969 ⁂ 4 Head: K.T. Malewski Net: n/a Aircraft below MTOW 1361kg: Cessna 150.

☐ C-GMTK	Cessna A185F Skywagon	18503149		0076		1 CO IO-520-D	1520			Floats / Wheel-Skis
☐ C-FFCM	Piper PA-32RT-300T Turbo Lance II	32R-7887161	N39757	0078		1 LY TIO-540-S1AD	1633			
☐ C-GSNC	Piper PA-32R-300 Lance	32R-7680359		0076		1 LY IO-540-K1G5D	1633			

AIR RAINBOW MID-COAST (444316 B.C., Ltd dba) — Port McNeill-SPB, B.C.

Box 520, Port McNeill, British Columbia V0N 2R0, Canada ☎ (250) 956-2020 Tx: none Fax: (250) 956-2025 SITA: n/a
F: 1993 ⁂ 10 Head: Mark Alexander Net: n/a Aircraft below MTOW 1361kg: Cessna 180 (on Floats)

☐ C-GPEO	Cessna A185E Skywagon	18501808	N5839J	0070	0698	1 CO IO-520-D	1520			Floats
☐ C-FHRT	De Havilland DHC-2 Beaver I	1203	N64390	0057	1094	1 PW R-985	2309			Floats
☐ C-FIUY	De Havilland DHC-2 Beaver I	921		0056	1293	1 PW R-985	2309			Floats
☐ C-FOCQ	De Havilland DHC-2 Beaver I	52		0050	0595	1 PW R-985	2309			Floats
☐ C-FUVQ	De Havilland DHC-2 Beaver I	696	N34M	0054	0698	1 PW R-985	2309			Floats
☐ C-GACK	De Havilland DHC-2 Beaver I	711	53-7903	0053	0497	1 PW R-985	2309			Floats
☐ C-GCYN	De Havilland DHC-2 Beaver I	1158	N67681	0057	0698	1 PW R-985	2309			lsf Northwest Seaplanes / Floats
☐ C-GCYX	De Havilland DHC-2 Beaver I	1242	N67689	0058	0698	1 PW R-985	2309			lsf Northwest Seaplanes / Floats
☐ C-GCZA	De Havilland DHC-2 Beaver I	1667	N67684	0067	0698	1 PW R-985	2309			lsf Northwest Seaplanes / Floats
☐ C-GCZC	De Havilland DHC-2 Beaver I	1250	N67685	0058	0698	1 PW R-985	2309			lsf Northwest Seaplanes / Floats
☐ C-GMJU	De Havilland DHC-2 Beaver I	237	5T-CAA	0051	1293	1 PW R-985	2309			Floats

AIR ROBERVAL, Ltée = RBV (Member of Groupe Gamac) — Roberval & Lac St-Jean, Qué.

RR 1, Aéroport de Roberval, Roberval, Québec G8H 2M9, Canada ☎ (418) 275-2344 Tx: none Fax: (418) 275-1597 SITA: n/a
F: 1962 ⁂ 12 Head: Jacques Cleary ICAO: AIR ROBERVAL Net: n/a

☐ C-GABM	Piper PA-23-250 Aztec F	27-7754081	N63770	0077		2 LY IO-540-C4B5	2359			
☐ C-GUGQ	De Havilland DHC-2 Beaver I	400	51-16845	0051		1 PW R-985	2313			Floats / Wheel-Skis
☐ C-FQQB	Piper PA-31-310 Navajo	31-310	N9239Y	0069	1298	2 LY TIO-540-A1A	2948			
☐ C-GDBK	Piper PA-31-310 Navajo	31-8012074	N35865	0080		2 LY TIO-540-A2C	2948			
☐ C-FIUZ	De Havilland DHC-3 Otter	135		0056		1 PW R-1340	3629			Floats / Wheel-Skis
☐ C-GLAB	De Havilland DHC-3 Otter	348	59-2210	0059	0299	1 PW R-1340	3629			Floats / Wheel-Skis

AIR SAGUENAY (1980), Inc. — Lac St-Sébastien, Qué.

CP 1102, Chicoutimi, Québec G7H 5G4, Canada ☎ (418) 548-5505 Tx: n/a Fax: (418) 548-2037 SITA: n/a
F: 1980 ⁂ 50 Head: Jean-Claude Tremblay Net: n/a

☐ C-GUJQ	Cessna A185F Skywagon	18503048		0076	1283	1 CO IO-520-D	1520			Floats / Wheel-Skis
☐ C-FGYK	De Havilland DHC-2 Beaver I	123	N4773C	0051	0498	1 PW R-985	2313			Floats / Wheel-Skis
☐ C-FJAC	De Havilland DHC-2 Beaver I	937		0055	1189	1 PW R-985	2313			Floats / Wheel-Skis
☐ C-FJKI	De Havilland DHC-2 Beaver I	992		0056	0580	1 PW R-985	2313			Floats / Wheel-Skis
☐ C-FKRJ	De Havilland DHC-2 Beaver I	1210		0057	0580	1 PW R-985	2313			Floats / Wheel-Skis
☐ C-FUWJ	De Havilland DHC-2 Beaver I	453	N7691	0053	0997	1 PW R-985	2313			Floats / Wheel-Skis
☐ C-GAEF	De Havilland DHC-2 Beaver I	372	51-16830	0051	0987	1 PW R-985	2313			Floats / Wheel-Skis
☐ C-GAXL	De Havilland DHC-2 Beaver I	1032	N4739S	0056	0693	1 PW R-985	2313			Floats / Wheel-Skis
☐ C-GUJI	De Havilland DHC-2 Beaver I	1141	N9821F	0056	0580	1 PW R-985	2313			Floats / Wheel-Skis
☐ C-GLFL	De Havilland DHC-3 Otter	329	58-1712	0059	0484	1 PZL ASh-62IR-M18	3629			Floats / Wheel-Skis / cvtd DHC-3 PW
☐ C-GLMT	De Havilland DHC-3 Otter	216	IM 1716	0057	0596	1 PW R-1340	3629			Floats / Wheel-Skis
☐ C-GQDU	De Havilland DHC-3 Otter	43	N94472	0054	0388	1 PZL ASh-62IR-M18	3629			Floats / Wheel-Skis / cvtd DHC-3 PW
☐ C-GUTQ	De Havilland DHC-3 Otter	402	HK-3049X	0060	0987	1 PW R-1340	3629			Floats / Wheel-Skis

AIR SAINT-MAURICE, Inc. — Lac-à-Beauce, Qué.

30 Ch. Contour du Lac, La Tuque, Québec G9X 3N8, Canada ☎ (819) 523-2655 Tx: none Fax: (819) 523-4280 SITA: n/a
F: 1989 ⁂ n/a Head: Marc Leclerc Net: n/a Aircraft below MTOW 1361kg: Cessna 180 (on Floats / Wheel-Skis)

☐ C-FDFF	Cessna A185F Skywagon	18502095		0072	0791	1 CO IO-520-D	1520			Floats / Wheel-Skis
☐ C-FIAV	Cessna A185F Skywagon	18502186		0073	0796	1 CO IO-520-D	1520			Floats / Wheel-Skis
☐ C-GVND	Cessna A185F Skywagon II	18503599		0078	1195	1 CO IO-520-D	1520			Floats / Wheel-Skis
☐ C-FASO	Cessna U206F Stationair	U20602081	N70558	0073	0696	1 CO IO-520-F	1633			Floats / Wheel-Skis
☐ C-GRJI	Cessna U206F Stationair II	U20603225	N5367U	0076	0299	1 CO IO-520-F	1633			Floats / Wheel-Skis
☐ C-GAZJ	De Havilland DHC-2 Beaver I	748	53-7934	0054	0299	1 PW R-985	2313			Floats / Wheel-Skis
☐ C-GPUO	De Havilland DHC-2 Beaver I	810	54-1677	0054	0290	1 PW R-985	2313			Floats / Wheel-Skis

AIR SASK = 7W / ASK (Air Sask Aviation (1991) & La Ronge Aviation Services, Ltd dba) — La Ronge, Sask. & Yellowknife, N.W.T.

PO Box 320, La Ronge, Saskatchewan S0J 1L0, Canada ☎ (306) 425-2382 Tx: 074-29225 Fax: (306) 425-2960 SITA: n/a
F: 1958 ⁂ 45 Head: Pat Campling, Sr. IATA: 094 ICAO: AIR SASK Net: n/a

☐ C-GALM	Cessna A185F Skywagon II	18503711	N783A	0077	0597	1 CO IO-520-D	1520	Y3		Floats / Wheel-Skis
☐ C-GMAO	Cessna A185F Skywagon	18502714	N1058F	0075		1 CO IO-520-D	1520	Y3		Floats / Wheel-Skis
☐ C-GZVF	Cessna A185F Skywagon	18503202	N93256	0077	0592	1 CO IO-520-D	1520	Y3		Floats / Wheel-Skis
☐ C-FGHY	De Havilland DHC-2 Beaver I	1344	58-2015	0059	1093	1 PW R-985	2313	Y4		Floats / Wheel-Skis
☐ C-GMAQ	De Havilland DHC-2 Beaver I	234	51-16784	0052		1 PW R-985	2313	Y4		Floats / Wheel-Skis
☐ C-GBGP	Beech Baron E55	TE-924	N1897W	0073	0795	2 CO IO-520-C	2404	Y5		

32 registration type of aircraft cn/fn ex/ex* mfd del powered by mtow kg configuration selcal name/fln/specialitites/remarks

☐ C-GSYC	Beech Baron 58	TH-872	N40DS	0077		2 CO IO-520-C	2449	Y5		
☐ C-FQWP	Piper PA-31-325 Navajo C/R	31-7400990	N7082Y	0074	1193	2 LY TIO-540-F2BD	2948	Y7		
☐ C-FZPJ	Piper PA-31-350 Navajo Chieftain	31-7752185	N27359	0077	0197	2 LY TIO-540-J2BD	3175	Y9		
☐ C-GAYY	Piper PA-31-310 Navajo	31-8012006		0079	0890	2 LY TIO-540-A2C	2948	Y7		
☐ C-GCTG	Piper PA-31-350 Navajo Chieftain	31-7552087	N72ET	0075	1093	2 LY TIO-540-J2BD	3175	Y9		
☐ C-GNOV	Piper PA-31-310 Navajo C	31-7812087		0078	0989	2 LY TIO-540-A2C	2948	Y7		
☐ C-FQEI	De Havilland DHC-3 Otter	397	LN-TSC	0060	0697	1 PW R-1340	3629	Y8		Floats / Wheel-Skis
☐ C-FKIO	Mitsubishi MU-2N (MU-2B-36A)	725SA	N888RH	0078	1097	2 GA TPE331-5-252M	5250	Y9		
☐ C-FDYF	Beech 99A Airliner	U-110	N396HA	0069	0593	2 PWC PT6A-27	4944	Y14		lsf OASL
☐ C-FCCE	De Havilland DHC-6 Twin Otter 100	8	VH-TGS	0066	0972	2 PWC PT6A-20	5252	Y14		Floats / Wheel-Skis
☐ C-FVOG	De Havilland DHC-6 Twin Otter 100	35		0067	0568	2 PWC PT6A-20	5252	Y14		Floats / Wheel-Skis
☐ C-FBID	BAe 3112 Jetstream 31	802	G-31-802*	0088	1195	2 GA TPE331-10UG-513H	6950	Y19		301
☐ C-FBIP	BAe 3112 Jetstream 31	820	G-31-820*	0088	1195	2 GA TPE331-10UG-513H	6950	Y19		305
☐ C-FSEW	BAe 3112 Jetstream 31	764	N223JL	0087	1097	2 GA TPE331-10UR-513H	6900	Y19		
☐ C-GPDC	BAe 3112 Jetstream 31	766	N222JF	0087	1097	2 GA TPE331-10UR-513H	6900	Y19		

AIR SATELLITE, Inc. = ASJ — Baie-Comeau, Qué.

Aéroport de Baie-Comeau, Pointe Lebel, Québec G5C 2S6, Canada ☎ (418) 589-8923 Tx: none Fax: (418) 589-7416 SITA: n/a
F: 1968 ⁂ 35 Head: Jean Fournier ICAO: SATELLITE Net: http://www.air-satellite.com Aircraft below MTOW 1361 kg: Cessna 152 & 172

☐ C-FCRX	Cessna P337H Press. Skymaster II	P3370293	N2QT	0078		2 CO TSIO-360-C	2132			
☐ C-FFJL	Cessna 310R II	310R1616	N2631A	0079	0889	2 CO IO-520-MB	2495			
☐ C-GGTF	Cessna 310R II	310R0550	N84709	0076		2 CO IO-520-M	2495			
☐ C-GBOE	Cessna 335	3350020	N27066	0079		2 CO TSIO-520-EB	2717			
☐ C-FQAS	Cessna 402B II	402B1045	TF-GTI	0076	1094	2 CO TSIO-520-E	2858			
☐ C-GIAS	Cessna 402B	402B0545	N678CM	0073	0595	2 CO TSIO-520-E	2858			
☐ C-GURS	Cessna 402	402-0214	N26309	0068	0296	2 CO TSIO-520-E	2858			
☐ C-GZAS	Cessna 402B	402B0626	N2083K	0074	0494	2 CO TSIO-520-E	2858			
☐ C-GOXZ	Britten-Norman BN-2A Mk.III Trislander	361	G-BBWP	0074	0790	3 LY O-540-E4C5	4726			
☐ C-FEAS	Embraer 110P1 Bandeirante (EMB-110P1)	110260	HR-IAE	0080	0996	2 PWC PT6A-34	5670			

AIR SCHEFFERVILLE = ASF (3113990 Canada, Inc. dba) — Schefferville & Squaw Lake-SPB, Qué.

Bldg T-39, Lindbergh Place, Ottawa, Québec K1V 1H7, Canada ☎ (613) 738-2454 Tx: none Fax: (613) 738-9184 SITA: n/a
F: 1981 ⁂ n/a Head: Iain Bogie ICAO: SCHEFF Net: n/a

☐ C-FEJL	Beech 99 Airliner	U-75	SE-IRE	0069	1089	2 PWC PT6A-27	4944			

AIR SENNETERRE, Inc. (Seasonal April-November ops only) — Senneterre-SPB, Qué.

CP 220, Senneterre, Québec J0Y 2M0, Canada ☎ (819) 737-2262 Tx: none Fax: (819) 737-2129 SITA: n/a
F: 1994 ⁂ n/a Head: René Lupien Net: n/a

☐ C-GAHU	Cessna U206F Stationair II	U20602839		0075	0796	1 CO IO-550-F	1633			Floats / lsf 9034-5109 Québec Inc.

AIR SOUTHWEST, Ltd = ASW — Chilliwack, B.C.

1-46244 Airport Road, Chilliwack, British Columbia V2P 1A5, Canada ☎ (604) 792-1123 Tx: none Fax: (604) 792-3114 SITA: n/a
F: 1984 ⁂ 4 Head: Bob Hasell ICAO: AIRSOUTHWEST Net: n/a Aircraft below MTOW 1361 kg: Cessna 182

☐ C-FQMO	Cessna U206F Stationair II	U20603456	N8606Q	0076	0893	1 CO IO-520-F	1633			
☐ C-GYTJ	Cessna U206G Stationair	U20603703		0077		1 CO IO-520-D	1633			

AIRSPAN HELICOPTERS, Ltd. — Sechelt, B.C.

Box 1009, Sechelt, British Columbia V0N 3A0, Canada ☎ (604) 885-7474 Tx: none Fax: (604) 885-7617 SITA: n/a
F: 1982 ⁂ 5 Head: Steve Rogers Net: n/a

☐ C-FBVY	MD Helicopters MD 500D (Hughes 369D)	570143D	N8513Q	0077	1198	1 AN 250-C20B	1361			
☐ C-FOUA	MD Helicopters MD 500D (Hughes 369D)	310904D	N1100A	0081	0695	1 AN 250-C20B	1361			
☐ C-FPMK	Bell 206B JetRanger III	3611	N8BG	0082		1 AN 250-C20J	1451			
☐ C-GOKA	Bell 206B JetRanger	156	N4052G	0068	0398	1 AN 250-C20	1451			cvtd 206A
☐ C-GVRM	Bell 206B JetRanger III	2980	N5741S	0080		1 AN 250-C20B	1451			

AIRSPEED AVIATION, Inc. = SPD — Abbotsford, B.C.

Abbotsford Airport, RR7, Abbotsford, British Columbia V2S 5W6, Canada ☎ (604) 852-9245 Tx: n/a Fax: (604) 850-2756 SITA: n/a
F: 1979 ⁂ 2 Head: John Giesbrecht ICAO: SPEEDLINE Net: n/a

☐ C-GZOI	Cessna 414 II	414-0844	N3814C	0075		2 CO TSIO-520-N	2880			

AIR SPRAY (1967), Ltd = ASB — Edmonton-Industrial & Red Deer, Alta.

63 Airport Road, Suite 201, Edmonton, Alberta T5G 0W6, Canada ☎ (780) 453-1737 Tx: none Fax: (780) 454-4384 SITA: n/a
F: 1967 ⁂ 60 Head: Don T. Hamilton ICAO: AIR SPRAY Net: http://www.airspray.com

☐ C-FGWE	Cessna 310Q II	310Q0920		0074		2 CO IO-470-VO	2404	Birddog		302
☐ C-GVKY	Cessna 310P	310P0074		0069		2 CO IO-470-VO	2359	Birddog		301
☐ C-GXJP	Cessna 310P	310P0073	N101QC	0069		2 CO IO-470-VO	2359	Birddog		305
☐ C-GXXN	Cessna T310P	310P0002	N5702M	0069		2 CO TSIO-520-B	2449	Birddog		306
☐ C-FEHK	AAC (Ted Smith) Aerostar 600A	60-0400-140	N17LH	0077	0389	2 LY IO-540-K1F5	2495	Birddog		397
☐ C-FJCF	AAC (Ted Smith) Aerostar 600A	60-0153-067	N37HA	0074	1190	2 LY IO-540-K1F5	2495	Birddog		308
☐ C-FTUE	AAC (Ted Smith) Aerostar 601	61-0145-076	N601RD	0073	0295	2 LY IO-540-S1A5	2585	Birddog		311
☐ C-GFGT	Cessna 340A II	340A0081		0076		2 CO TSIO-520-N	2717	Birddog		66
☐ C-FZRQ	Twin (Aero) Turbo Commander 690	11025	N100LS	0072	0497	2 GA TPE331-5-251K	4649	Birddog		51
☐ C-GNSA	Cessna 500 Citation	500-0160	N59TS	0074	0395	2 PWC JT15D-1	5216	Birddog		50
☐ C-GBUI	Canadair F-86E Sabre 6	1710	N89FS	0058	0398	1 AV Orenda 14	7938	Target Towing		opf Canadian Forces
☐ C-FKBM	Boeing (Douglas) B-26B-45-DL Invader	27415	N8017E	0044		2 PW R-2800	15876	Tanker		20
☐ C-FOVC	Boeing (Douglas) B-26C-35-DT Invader	28776	N3426G	0044	0193	2 PW R-2800	15876	Tanker		56
☐ C-FPGF	Boeing (Douglas) B-26C-50-DT Invader	29154	44-35875	0044		2 PW R-2800	15876	Tanker		1
☐ C-FPGP	Boeing (Douglas) B-26C-50-DT Invader	29177	N3328G	0044		2 PW R-2800	15876	Tanker		2
☐ C-FTFB	Boeing (Douglas) B-26C-35-DT Invader	28723	N7656C	0044		2 PW R-2800	15876	Tanker		4
☐ C-GHCC	Boeing (Douglas) B-26C-50-DT Invader	29179	N4812E	0044		2 PW R-2800	15876	Tanker		31
☐ C-GHLX	Boeing (Douglas) B-26C-55-DT Invader	29227	N161H	0044		2 PW R-2800	15876	Tanker		32
☐ C-GPTW	Boeing (Douglas) B-26C-25-DT Invader	18800	N9402Z	0043		2 PW R-2800	15876	Tanker		26
☐ C-GPUC	Boeing (Douglas) B-26C-50-DT Invader	29089	N9403Z	0044		2 PW R-2800	15876	Tanker		27
☐ C-GTOX	Boeing (Douglas) B-26B-61-DL Invader	27802	N9174Z	0043		2 PW R-2800	15876	Tanker		14
☐ C-GWLT	Boeing (Douglas) B-26B Invader	28057	N67943	0044		2 PW R-2800	15876	Tanker		98
☐ C-GWLU	Boeing (Douglas) B-26B-66-DL Invader	28017	N600D	0044		2 PW R-2800	15876	Tanker		8 / Old Yeller
☐ C-GXGY	Boeing (Douglas) B-26C-45-DT Invader	28987	N5530V	0044		2 PW R-2800	15876	Tanker		10
☐ CF-AGO	Boeing (Douglas) B-26C-35-DT Invader	28735	N330WC	0044		2 PW R-2800	15876	Tanker		36 / Dragon Lady
☐ CF-CBK	Boeing (Douglas) B-26C-45-DT Invader	28940	N9996Z	0044		2 PW R-2800	15876	Tanker		11
☐ CF-CUI	Boeing (Douglas) B-26C-35-DT Invader	28803	N9401Z	0044		2 PW R-2800	15876	Tanker		12
☐ CF-EZX	Boeing (Douglas) B-26C-25-DT Invader	18807	N3711G	0043		2 PW R-2800	15876	Tanker		3
☐ CF-ZTC	Boeing (Douglas) B-26C-50-DT Invader	29136	N9300R	0044		2 PW R-2800	15876	Tanker		13 / Lucky Jack
☐ C-FTUU	Canadair CL-215 (CL-215-1A10)	1011		0069	1198	2 PW R-2800-CA3	19731	Tanker		205 / lst/opf Prov.of Alberta/Amphibian
☐ C-FTUW	Canadair CL-215 (CL-215-1A10)	1030		0070	1198	2 PW R-2800-CA3	19731	Tanker		206 / lst/opf Prov.of Alberta/Amphibian
☐ C-GFSK	Canadair CL-215 (CL-215-1A10)	1085	C-GKDN*	0086		2 PW R-2800-CA3	19731	Tanker		201 / lsf/opf Prov.of Alberta/Amphibian
☐ C-GFSL	Canadair CL-215 (CL-215-1A10)	1086	C-GKDP*	0086		2 PW R-2800-CA3	19731	Tanker		202 / lsf/opf Prov.of Alberta/Amphibian
☐ C-GFSM	Canadair CL-215 (CL-215-1A10)	1098	C-GKDP*	0088		2 PW R-2800-CA3	19731	Tanker		203 / lsf/opf Prov.of Alberta/Amphibian
☐ C-GFSN	Canadair CL-215 (CL-215-1A10)	1099	C-GKDY*	0088		2 PW R-2800-CA3	19731	Tanker		204 / lsf/opf Prov.of Alberta/Amphibian
☐ C-FQYB	Lockheed L-188A Electra (LongLiner)	1063	PP-VLX	0059	0494	4 AN 501-D13	51256	Tanker		88
☐ C-FVFH	Lockheed L-188C Electra (LongLiner)	1006	PK-RLF	0058	0695	4 AN 501-D13	52617	Tanker		89 / cvtd L-188A

AIR SUPERIOR (Wayne D. & Karen Roberts dba) — Wawa, Ont.

PO Box 300, Wawa, Ontario P0S 1K0, Canada ☎ (705) 856-2780 Tx: n/a Fax: none SITA: n/a
F: 1990 ⁂ n/a Head: Wayne D. & Karen Roberts Net: n/a

☐ C-GCWO	Cessna A185F Skywagon	18503207	N93275	0077	0490	1 CO IO-520-D	1520			Floats / Wheel-Skis

AIR TAXI ROHNAIR, Ltd — Elk Point, Alta.

5321-51st Avenue, St. Paul, Alberta T0A 3A1, Canada ☎ (780) 645-1690 Tx: none Fax: none SITA: n/a
F: 1997 ⁂ n/a Head: Heinz Rohner Net: n/a

☐ CF-WUX	Cessna 210C	21058098	N9798X	0063	0198	1 CO IO-470-S	1361			

AIR THELON, Ltd (Seasonal April-October ops only) — Yellowknife, N.W.T.

Box 2481, Yellowknife, Northwest Territories X1A 2P8, Canada ☎ (867) 920-7110 Tx: none Fax: (867) 920-7180 SITA: n/a
F: 1998 ⁂ n/a Head: Tom Faess Net: n/a

☐ C-FZVR	De Havilland DHC-2 Beaver I	639	N563	0054	0598	1 PW R-985	2313			Floats

33 registration type of aircraft cn/fn ex/ex* mfd del powered by mtow kg configuration selcal name/fln/specialitites/remarks

AIR TINDI, Ltd = 8T

Yellowknife, N.W.T.

PO Box 1693, Yellowknife, Northwest Territories X1A 2P3, Canada ☎ (867) 669-8200 Tx: none Fax: (867) 669-8210 SITA: n/a
F: 1988 ✈✈✈ 109 Head: Peter Arychuk IATA: 744 Net: http://www.airtindi.com Aircraft below MTOW 1361 kg: Aviat Husky A-1

☐ C-GPHO	Cessna A185F Skywagon	18503099		0076	0692	1 CO IO-520-D	1520			Floats / Wheel-Skis
☐ C-GWXI	Cessna A185F Skywagon	18502818		0075	0598	1 CO IO-520-D	1520			Floats / Wheel-Skis
☐ C-GZIX	Cessna A185F Skywagon II	18504182	N302CH	0081	0896	1 CO IO-520-D	1520			Floats / Wheel-Skis
☐ C-GMXS	De Havilland DHC-2 Beaver I	1213	N5382G	0057	0891	1 PW R-985	2313			Floats / Wheel-Skis
☐ C-FXUY	De Havilland DHC-3 Turbo Otter	142	N214L	0056	0493	1 PWC PT6A-135A	3629			cvtd Otter / Floats / Wheel-Skis
☐ C-FKAY	Cessna 208B Grand Caravan	208B0470	N1294N	0095	0997	1 PWC PT6A-114A	3969			
☐ C-GATV	Cessna 208B Grand Caravan	208B0308		0092	0792	1 PWC PT6A-114A	3969			
☐ C-FATW	Beech King Air C90	LJ-685	N110SE	0076	0697	2 PWC PT6A-20	4377			
☐ C-FATM	De Havilland DHC-6 Twin Otter 300	265	N304PC	0069	0398	2 PWC PT6A-27	5670			Floats / Wheel-Skis
☐ C-FGOG	De Havilland DHC-6 Twin Otter 300	348		0072	0492	2 PWC PT6A-27	5670			Floats / Wheel-Skis
☐ C-GATU	De Havilland DHC-6 Twin Otter 300	525	G-BEJP	0077	0694	2 PWC PT6A-27	5670			Floats / Wheel-Skis
☐ C-GMAS	De Havilland DHC-6 Twin Otter 300	438	N546N	0074	0590	2 PWC PT6A-27	5670			Floats / Wheel-Skis
☐ C-GNPS	De Havilland DHC-6 Twin Otter 300	558		0078	1091	2 PWC PT6A-27	5670			
☐ C-GDPB	Beech King Air B200C	BL-44	N18379	0082	0192	2 PWC PT6A-42	5670			
☐ C-FASC	De Havilland DHC-7-103 Dash 7	072	N722A	0082	0496	4 PWC PT6A-50	19958	Y48		lsf AGES

AIR TRANSAT = TS / TSC (Air Transat A T, Inc. dba / Subsidiary of Transat AT, Inc.)

Montreal-Mirabel, Qué.

11600 Cargo Road A1, Mirabel Int'l Airport, Mirabel, Québec J7N 1G9, Canada ☎ (450) 476-1011 Tx: none Fax: (450) 476-1038 SITA: YMXOCTS
F: 1986 ✈✈✈ 900 Head: Philippe Sureau IATA: 649 ICAO: TRANSAT Net: http://www.transat.com

☐ C-GBIW	Boeing 737-46M	28549 / 2844	OO-VEC	0097	1298	2 CFMI CFM56-3C1	64636	Y170	LQ-CP	lsf VEX in winter
☐ C-GBIX	Boeing 737-46M	28550 / 2847	OO-VED	0097	1298	2 CFMI CFM56-3C1	64636	Y170	LQ-DK	lsf VEX in winter
☐ C-GTSE	Boeing 757-23A	25488 / 471	N1792B*	0092	1192	2 RR RB211-535E4	113398	Y228	DS-AG	TSE / lsf Finova Capital Ltd
☐ C-GTSF	Boeing 757-23A (ET)	25491 / 511		0092	1292	2 RR RB211-535E4	108862	Y228	DS-AH	TSF / lsf AWAS
☐ C-GTSJ	Boeing 757-236	24772 / 271	C-GNXB	0090	0493	2 RR RB211-535E4	113398	Y228	EG-JM	TSJ / lsf ILFC
☐ C-GTSN	Boeing 757-28A	24543 / 268	C-GNXU	0090	0493	2 RR RB211-535E4	113398	Y228	EG-KM	TSN / lsf ILFC
☐ C-GTSV	Boeing 757-28A	25622 / 530	S7-AAX	0093	1296	2 RR RB211-535E4	104554	Y228	DE-CQ	622 / lsf ILFC
☐ C-FTNA	Lockheed L-1011-385-1-14 TriStar 150	193M-1019	N312EA	0072	0588	3 RR RB211-22B	215003	C19Y343	FK-BM	501 / cvtd TriStar 1
☐ C-FTNB	Lockheed L-1011-385-1-14 TriStar 150	193A-1010	N309EA	0072	0589	3 RR RB211-22B	215003	C19Y343	FL-EG	549 / cvtd TriStar 1
☐ C-FTNC	Lockheed L-1011-385-1-14 TriStar 150	193M-1023	N315EA	0072	1187	3 RR RB211-22B	215003	C19Y343	EL-AJ	503 / cvtd TriStar 1
☐ C-FTNG	Lockheed L-1011-385-1-14 TriStar 150	193E-1048		0073	0797	3 RR RB211-22B	215003	C19Y343	DL-BH	507 / cvtd TriStar 1
☐ C-FTNH	Lockheed L-1011-385-1-14 TriStar 150	193E-1049		0073	0593	3 RR RB211-22B	215003	C19Y343	HM-EG	508 / cvtd TriStar 1
☐ C-FTNL	Lockheed L-1011-385-1-15 TriStar 100	193E-1073	4R-TNL	0074	0496	3 RR RB211-22B	215003	C19Y343	FK-BL	512 / cvtd TriStar 1
☐ C-GTSB	Lockheed L-1011-385-1-15 TriStar 100	193T-1122	V2-LEN	0975	1296	3 RR RB211-22B	204117	C19Y343	EL-JM	122
☐ C-GTSK	Lockheed L-1011-385-1 TriStar 1	193E-1021	VR-HOE	0172	1196	3 RR RB211-22B	195045	C19Y343	AG-FH	502
☐ C-GTSX	Lockheed L-1011-385-1 TriStar 1	193N-1094	VR-HMW	0074	1095	3 RR RB211-22B	195045	C19Y343	HK-DM	547
☐ C-GTSZ	Lockheed L-1011-385-1-14 TriStar 100	193P-1103	N703TT	0475	1289	3 RR RB211-22B	215003	C19Y343	EK-JM	548 / lsf FACE/cvtd TriStar 1
☐ C-FTSW	Lockheed L-1011-385-3 TriStar 500	293A-1246	V2-LEJ	0083	0199	3 RR RB211-524B4-02	231332	C19Y290	FK-EL	246
☐ C-GTSP	Lockheed L-1011-385-3 TriStar 500	293B-1242	CS-TED	0083	1296	3 RR RB211-524B4-02	231332	C19Y290	FG-HM	242
☐ C-GTSQ	Lockheed L-1011-385-3 TriStar 500	293B-1243	CS-TEE	0083	1296	3 RR RB211-524B4-02	231332	C19Y290	HJ-BE	243
☐ C-GTSR	Lockheed L-1011-385-3 TriStar 500	293B-1239	CS-TEA	0082	1197	3 RR RB211-524B4-02	231332	C19Y290	HJ-CM	239 / lst SEU
☐ C-GGTS	Airbus Industrie A330-243	250	F-WWKK*	0099	0299	2 RR Trent 772B-60	230000	C20Y343	CS-TK	lsf ILFC
☐ C-GITS	Airbus Industrie A330-243	271		0099	0399	2 RR Trent 772B-60	230000	C20Y343	CS-GJ	lsf ILFC

AIR UNGAVA, Inc.

Chibougamau-Lac Caché SPB, Qué.

1158 Principale, CP 69, Tourville, Québec G0R 4M0, Canada ☎ (418) 745-2656 Tx: none Fax: (418) 745-2656 SITA: n/a
F: 1998 ✈✈✈ n/a Head: n/a Net: n/a

☐ C-FZEM	Cessna A185E Skywagon	18502083		0072	0898	1 CO IO-520-D	1520			Floats / Wheel-Skis

AIR WAPUS, Enr. (2740-2726 Québec, Inc. dba)

Lac McArthur, Qué.

CP 1020, Mont Tremblant, Québec J0T 1Z0, Canada ☎ (819) 686-1440 Tx: none Fax: none SITA: n/a
F: 1989 ✈✈✈ 2 Head: Alain Lussier Net: n/a

☐ C-FPDU	De Havilland DHC-2 Beaver I	1515		0063		1 PW R-985	2313			Floats

AIRWAVE TRANSPORT = AWV (812971 Ontario, Inc. dba)

Toronto-Int'l, Ont.

2450 Derry Road East, Hangar 9, Box 29, Mississauga, Ontario L5S 1B2, Canada ☎ (905) 405-8622 Tx: none Fax: (905) 405-9228 SITA: n/a
F: 1989 ✈✈✈ 5 Head: Chris Dunn ICAO: AIRWAVE Net: n/a

☐ C-FAWT	Piper PA-31-350 Navajo Chieftain	31-8052034	N3549X	0079	0691	2 LY TIO-540-J2BD	3175			
☐ C-FYZE	Piper PA-31-350 Navajo Chieftain	31-7952160	N222KB	0079	1191	2 LY TIO-540-J2BD	3175			
☐ C-FAWG	GAC (Grumman) G-159 Gulfstream I	106	N64CG	0063	1095	2 RR Dart 529-8X	16329			
☐ C-GPTG	GAC (Grumman) G-159 Gulfstream I	189	N776G	0068	0197	2 RR Dart 529-8X	16329			
☐ C-FAWV	Convair 580 (F) (SCD)	154	C-FMGB	0254	0797	2 AN 501-D13	24766	Freighter		cvtd CV 340-31

AIR WEMINDJI, Inc.

La Grande Rivière, Qué.

CP 907, Radisson, Québec J0Y 2X0, Canada ☎ (819) 638-3392 Tx: none Fax: (819) 638-3746 SITA: n/a
F: 1987 ✈✈✈ n/a Head: Louis-Paul Cyr Net: n/a

☐ C-GAWJ	Cessna 208 Caravan I	20800175		0090	0290	1 PWC PT6A-114A	3629			Amphibian / Wheel-Skis
☐ C-GAWM	Cessna 208 Caravan I	20800196		0090	0990	1 PWC PT6A-114	3629			Amphibian / Wheel-Skis
☐ C-GJDP	Cessna 208 Caravan I	20800255		0096	0997	1 PWC PT6A-114	3629			Amphibian / Wheel-Skis
☐ C-GAWP	Pilatus PC-12/45	187		0097	1297	1 PWC PT6A-67B	4500			

AIR WEST = AWT (3379354 Manitoba, Ltd dba)

Winnipeg-Int'l, Man.

Box 303, Sanford, Manitoba R0G 2J0, Canada ☎ (204) 888-2220 Tx: none Fax: (204) 736-4748 SITA: n/a
F: 1982 ✈✈✈ 4 Head: Paul McCulloch ICAO: AIR WEST Net: http://www.avisit.to/airwest

☐ C-FTNZ	Cessna 402C II	402C0021	N2643W	0079	1194	2 CO TSIO-520-VB	3107			

AKLAK AIR, Inc. = 6L / AKK (Subsidiary of Inuvialuit Development Corporation / formerly Aklak Air, Ltd)

Inuvik, N.W.T.

Box 1190, Inuvik, Northwest Territories X0E 0T0, Canada ☎ (867) 979-3555 Tx: none Fax: (867) 979-3388 SITA: n/a
F: 1977 ✈✈✈ n/a Head: Dennie Lennie IATA: 709 ICAO: AKLAK Net: n/a Operates scheduled flights with Beechcraft 99 & De Havilland DHC-6 Twin Otter aircraft, leased from KENN BOREK AIR as required.

ALBERTA CENTRAL AIRWAYS, Ltd

Lac La Biche, Alta.

PO Box 518, Lac La Biche, Alberta T0A 2C0, Canada ☎ (780) 623-4122 Tx: none Fax: (780) 623-2232 SITA: n/a
F: 1972 ✈✈✈ 10 Head: Wendell Umble Net: n/a

☐ C-GGBZ	Cessna U206G Stationair 6 II	U20605637		0080		1 CO IO-520-F	1633			
☐ C-GYUW	Cessna U206G Stationair 6	U20603738		0077	0493	1 CO IO-520-F	1633			
☐ C-FOKF	Cessna T210N Turbo Centurion II	21063574	N135JM	0079	0892	2 CO TSIO-520-R	1814			
☐ C-GUWO	Piper PA-31-310 Navajo	31-203	N9154Y	0068		2 LY TIO-540-A1A	2948			
☐ C-GWFF	Piper PA-31-310 Navajo C	31-7512063	N61390	0075		2 LY TIO-540-A2C	2948			
☐ C-FNED	Beech King Air C90	LJ-680	N928RD	0076	0394	2 PWC PT6A-20	4377			
☐ C-FWPG	Beech King Air 100	B-67	N26KW	0071	0697	2 PWC PT6A-28	4808			
☐ C-FWPN	Beech King Air 100	B-51	N16SW	0070	0995	2 PWC PT6A-28	4808			

ALBERTA CITYLINK = ABK (Palliser Air dba / Division of 650584 Alberta, Inc. / Affiliated with Bar XH Air, Ltd)

Calgary & Medicine Hat, Alta.

PO Box 161, Medicine Hat, Alberta T1A 7E8, Canada ☎ (780) 527-3328 Tx: none Fax: (780) 527-4721 SITA: n/a
F: 1996 ✈✈✈ n/a Head: Les N. Little ICAO: ALBERTA CITYLINK Net: n/a Operates scheduled flights in conjunction with AIR CANADA as an Liaison AIR CANADA Connector (in own colors), using AC-flight numbers.

☐ C-FBIJ	BAe 3112 Jetstream 31	817	G-31-817*	0088	0896	2 GA TPE331-10UR-513H	6950	Y19		038 / lsf BAMT
☐ C-FCPF	BAe 3112 Jetstream 31	827	G-31-827*	0088	0796	2 GA TPE331-10UR-513H	6950	Y19		039 / lsf BAMT
☐ C-FZYB	BAe 3212 Jetstream 32	837	C-FYWY	0089	0397	2 GA TPE331-12UAR-705H	7350	Y19		033 / lsf BAMT
☐ C-GEAZ	BAe 3212 Jetstream 32	843	C-GQRO	0089	1098	2 GA TPE331-12UAR-705H	7350	Y19		034 / lsf BAMT

ALEXANDAIR (1994), Inc. = JMR (formerly Alexandair, Inc. & Air Brousse (1983), Inc.)

Sept-Iles & Sept-Iles Lac des Rapides, Qué.

BG 2009, 18 Rte de l'Aviation, Sept-Iles, Québec G4R 4K2, Canada ☎ (418) 968-2545 Tx: none Fax: (418) 962-0378 SITA: n/a
F: 1987 ✈✈✈ 30 Head: Capt. Jean-Marc Roy ICAO: ALEXANDAIR Net: n/a

☐ C-FJGV	De Havilland DHC-2 Beaver I	977		0056		1 PW R-985	2313			Floats / Wheel-Skis
☐ C-FJZN	De Havilland DHC-3 Otter	205		0057		1 PW R-1340	3629			Floats / Wheel-Skis

ALGONQUIN FLIGHT CENTRE, Inc.

North Bay, Ont.

RR 1, North Bay, Ontario P1B 8G2, Canada ☎ (705) 495-6450 Tx: none Fax: (705) 495-4832 SITA: n/a
F: 1991 ✈✈✈ 8 Head: Tom Fraser Net: http://www.venturenorth.com/algon/ Aircraft below MTOW 1361kg: Cessna 152/172 & Citabrica 7GCBC

☐ C-FUGJ	Piper PA-30-160 Twin Comanche C	30-1925	N8HR	0069	0595	2 LY IO-320-B1A	1633			

34 registration type of aircraft cn/fn ex/ex* mfd del powered by mtow kg configuration selcal name/fln/specialitites/remarks

ALKAN-AIR, Ltd = AKN

Whitehorse, Y.T.

PO Box 4008, Whitehorse, Yukon Territory Y1A 3S9, Canada ☎ (867) 668-2107 Tx: none Fax: (867) 667-6117 SITA: n/a
F: 1977 ⭢ 16 Head: Barry Watson ICAO: ALKAN AIR Net: http://www.yukonweb.wis.net/tourism/alkanair/

registration	type of aircraft	cn/fn	ex/ex*	mfd	del	powered by	mtow kg	configuration	name/fln/specialtites/remarks
C-GYTB	Cessna U206G Stationair	U20603685		0077		1 CO IO-520-F	1633		
C-GHQF	Piper PA-31-350 Navajo Chieftain	31-8052050	N3554F	0080		2 LY TIO-540-J2BD	3175		
C-GSDT	Piper PA-31-350 Navajo Chieftain	31-8152102	N120FL	0081		2 LY TIO-540-J2BD	3175		
C-GMOC	Beech King Air 200	BB-513		0079	0297	2 PWC PT6A-41	5670		
C-GWUY	Beech King Air 200	BB-77	N300CP	0073	1294	2 PWC PT6A-41	5670		

ALL CANADA EXPRESS, Ltd = CNX

Toronto-Int'l, Ont.

50 Burnhamthorpe Road West, Suite 603, Mississauga, Ontario L5B 3C2, Canada ☎ (905) 896-7175 Tx: none Fax: (905) 896-4443 SITA: n/a
F: 1992 ⭢ n/a Head: John MacKenzie ICAO: CANEX Net: n/a

registration	type of aircraft	cn/fn	ex/ex*	mfd	del	powered by	mtow kg	configuration	name/fln/specialtites/remarks
C-FACW	Boeing 727-82 (F)	19405 / 398	N357NE	0067	0298	3 PW JT8D-7B (HK3/FDX)	72802	Freighter	cvtd -82
C-FACX	Boeing 727-27 (F)	19500 / 448	N727EV	0067	1294	3 PW JT8D-7B	72575	Freighter	cvtd -27
C-FACJ	Boeing 727-260 (F) (A)	21979 / 1534	N979AL	0079	1096	3 PW JT8D-17R (HK3/FDX)	89448	Freighter	cvtd -260
C-FACM	Boeing 727-260 (F) (A)	22759 / 1789	N980AL	0081	1096	3 PW JT8D-17R (HK3/FDX)	89448	Freighter	cvtd -260
C-FACN	Boeing 727-221 (F) (A)	22540 / 1796	N368PA	0082	1297	3 PW JT8D-17 (HK3/FDX)	89448	Freighter	cvtd -221
C-FACR	Boeing 727-217 (F) (A)	21055 / 1117	C-GRYC	0075	0898	3 PW JT8D-15 / -17	89356	Freighter	cvtd -217
C-GACC	Boeing 727-277 (F) (A)	20550 / 1030	C-GRYZ	0074	0897	3 PW JT8D-15	90719	Freighter	cvtd -277

ALLEN AIRWAYS, Ltd

Sioux Lookout, Ont.

Box 148, Sioux Lookout, Ontario P8T 1A1, Canada ☎ (807) 737-2668 Tx: none Fax: (807) 737-1227 SITA: n/a
F: 1977 ⭢ n/a Head: G.A. Allen Net: n/a Aircraft below MTOW 1361kg: Cessna 180 (on Floats / Wheel-Skis)

registration	type of aircraft	cn/fn	ex/ex*	mfd	del	powered by	mtow kg	configuration	name/fln/specialtites/remarks
C-GEXS	Cessna A185F Skywagon	18502955		0076	1192	1 CO IO-520-D	1520		Floats / Wheel-Skis
C-GQDO	Cessna A185F Skywagon II	18503745		0079		1 CO IO-520-D	1520		Floats / Wheel-Skis
C-GYEB	Cessna A185F Skywagon	18503017	N5186R	0076	0897	1 CO IO-520-D	1520		Floats / Wheel-Skis
C-GVHS	De Havilland DHC-2 Beaver I	733	53-7922	0053		1 PW R-985	2313		Floats / Wheel-Skis
CF-HWK	Beech D18S	A-280	N118J	0046	0893	2 PW R-985	3969		Floats / Wheel-Skis

ALL-WEST AIR SERVICES, Ltd

Calgary, Alta.

5438-11 Street N.E., Room 250, Calgary, Alberta T2E 7E9, Canada ☎ (403) 295-7700 Tx: none Fax: (403) 295-1704 SITA: n/a
F: n/a ⭢ n/a Head: n/a Net: http://www.allwestair.com Aircraft below MTOW 1361kg: Cessna 172 & Piper PA-28

registration	type of aircraft	cn/fn	ex/ex*	mfd	del	powered by	mtow kg	configuration	name/fln/specialtites/remarks
C-GQIU	Piper PA-34-200 Seneca	34-7350012	N15076	0073	0598	2 LY IO-360-C1E6	1905		
C-GJEF	Piper PA-31-350 Navajo Chieftain	31-8152020	N797RC	0081	0199	2 LY TIO-540-J2BD	3349		

AL MCDONALD AIRMAC ENTERPRISES, Inc.

Port Hawkesbury, N.S.

PO Box 510, D'Escousse, Nova Scotia B0E 1K0, Canada ☎ (902) 625-5053 Tx: none Fax: (902) 625-5053 SITA: n/a
F: 1998 ⭢ n/a Head: Al McDonald Net: n/a Aircraft below MTOW 1361kg: Cessna 150 & 172

registration	type of aircraft	cn/fn	ex/ex*	mfd	del	powered by	mtow kg	configuration	name/fln/specialtites/remarks
C-FIUK	Piper PA-23-150 Apache	23-540		0056	0398	2 LY O-320-A1A	1588		

ALMON LANDAIR, Ltd (Seasonal May-October ops only)

Whitehorse, Y.T.

200-307 Jarvis Street, Whitehorse, Yukon Territory Y1A 1H3, Canada ☎ (867) 668-6132 Tx: n/a Fax: (867) 668-6132 SITA: n/a
F: 1992 ⭢ n/a Head: Alexander Landolt Net: n/a

registration	type of aircraft	cn/fn	ex/ex*	mfd	del	powered by	mtow kg	configuration	name/fln/specialtites/remarks
C-GDAO	Grumman G-21A Goose	1153	N848HP	0042	0598	2 PW R-985	3629		Amphibian

ALPENGLOW AVIATION, Inc.

Golden, B.C.

Box 4031, Golden, British Columbia V0A 1H0, Canada ☎ (250) 344-7117 Tx: none Fax: (250) 344-5115 SITA: n/a
F: 1997 ⭢ n/a Head: Steve Neill Net: http://www.rockiesairtours.com Aircraft below MTOW 1361kg: Cessna 180

registration	type of aircraft	cn/fn	ex/ex*	mfd	del	powered by	mtow kg	configuration	name/fln/specialtites/remarks
C-FZEN	Cessna A185F Skywagon	18502070		0072	0198	1 CO IO-520-D	1520		Wheel-Skis
C-GZGS	Cessna U206F Stationair II	U20602799	N35919	0075	0597	1 CO IO-520-F	1633		

ALPEN HELICOPTERS, Ltd

Langley & Prince Rupert, B.C.

215-5333-216 Street, Langley, British Columbia V3A 4R1, Canada ☎ (604) 644-1274 Tx: none Fax: (604) 532-8719 SITA: n/a
F: 1980 ⭢ 4 Head: Robert Owens Net: n/a

registration	type of aircraft	cn/fn	ex/ex*	mfd	del	powered by	mtow kg	configuration	name/fln/specialtites/remarks
C-GAHL	Bell 206B JetRanger III	2600	N8264U	0079	0496	1 AN 250-C20B	1451		
C-GLHL	Bell 206B JetRanger	1645		0075	0495	1 AN 250-C20	1451		
C-GRBO	Cessna A185F Skywagon	18503414	N9037H	0077	0592	1 CO IO-520-D	1520		

ALPINE AVIATION (Yukon), Ltd

Whitehorse, Y.T.

Box 6, CSC, Whitehorse, Yukon Territory Y1A 2B0, Canada ☎ (867) 668-7725 Tx: none Fax: (867) 668-2973 SITA: n/a
F: 1997 ⭢ n/a Head: n/a Net: n/a Aircraft below MTOW 1361kg: Piper PA-18

registration	type of aircraft	cn/fn	ex/ex*	mfd	del	powered by	mtow kg	configuration	name/fln/specialtites/remarks
C-FGSI	Cessna U206F Stationair	U20602165	N71849	0073	0597	1 CO IO-520-F	1633		

ALPINE HELICOPTERS, Ltd

Calgary, Alta. & Kelowna, B.C.

1295 Industrial Road, Kelowna, British Columbia V1Z 1G4, Canada ☎ (250) 769-4111 Tx: none Fax: (250) 769-2040 SITA: n/a
F: 1961 ⭢ 75 Head: Pat Aldous Net: n/a Aircraft below MTOW 1361 kg: Bell 47 Soloy.

registration	type of aircraft	cn/fn	ex/ex*	mfd	del	powered by	mtow kg	configuration	name/fln/specialtites/remarks
C-FALE	Bell 206B JetRanger III	1074	N83160	0073		1 AN 250-C20B	1451		cvtd JetRanger
C-FALU	Bell 206B JetRanger III	1072		0073		1 AN 250-C20B	1451		cvtd JetRanger
C-FTED	Bell 206B JetRanger III	3556		0081		1 AN 250-C20B	1451		
C-GALR	Bell 206B JetRanger III	1892	N100YB	0076		1 AN 250-C20B	1451		cvtd JetRanger II
C-GALX	Bell 206B JetRanger	1046	N58096	0073		1 AN 250-C20	1451		
C-GALZ	Bell 206B JetRanger III	1563	N59640	0074		1 AN 250-C20B	1451		cvtd JetRanger
C-GJSL	Bell 206B JetRanger III	3557		0081		1 AN 250-C20B	1451		
C-GALJ	Bell 206L-3 LongRanger III	51010	N22654	0082		1 AN 250-C30P	1882		
C-GALL	Bell 206L-3 LongRanger III	51015	N22660	0082		1 AN 250-C30P	1882		
C-GRLK	Bell 206L-3 LongRanger III	51028	N42814	0083	0198	1 AN 250-C30P	1882		
C-FAHE	Eurocopter (Aerosp.) AS350B2 AStar	2651	D-HWPD	0092	0394	1 TU Arriel 1D1	2250		
C-FAHS	Eurocopter (Aerosp.) AS350B2 AStar	2358	HB-XVE	0090	0494	1 TU Arriel 1D1	2250		
C-FALA	Bell 407	53115		0097	0397	1 AN 250-C47B	2268		
C-FAHB	Bell 212	30794	A6-BBH	0076	0798	2 PWC PT6T-3 TwinPac	5080		
C-FAHC	Bell 212	30827	A6-BBM	0077	0898	2 PWC PT6T-3 TwinPac	5080		
C-FAHG	Bell 212	30940	N8530F	0079	0393	2 PWC PT6T-3 TwinPac	5080		
C-FAHI	Bell 212	30776	A6-BBB	0076	0898	2 PWC PT6T-3 TwinPac	5080		
C-FAHP	Bell 212	30933	D-HELL	0079	0693	2 PWC PT6T-3 TwinPac	5080		
C-FAHR	Bell 212	30789	A6-BBI	0076	1298	2 PWC PT6T-3 TwinPac	5080		
C-FAHZ	Bell 212	30651	A6-BBN	0075	0299	2 PWC PT6T-3 TwinPac	5080		
C-FALK	Bell 212	30982	N212EL	0080	0697	2 PWC PT6T-3 TwinPac	5080		
C-FALV	Bell 212	30816	N74AL	0076		2 PWC PT6T-3 TwinPac	5080		
C-FHDY	Bell 212	30594	N83263	0073	0589	2 PWC PT6T-3 TwinPac	5080		
C-FNOB	Bell 212	31172	N3897D	0081	0192	2 PWC PT6T-3 TwinPac	5080		
C-GAHO	Bell 212	30937		0079		2 PWC PT6T-3 TwinPac	5080		
C-GAHV	Bell 212	30699	N90221	0075		2 PWC PT6T-3 TwinPac	5080		
C-GALI	Bell 212	30525	JA9510	0071	0590	2 PWC PT6T-3 TwinPac	5080		
C-GIRZ	Bell 212	30622	RP-C1677	0074		2 PWC PT6T-3 TwinPac	5080		
C-GRNR	Bell 212	30999		0079	0580	2 PWC PT6T-3 TwinPac	5080		

ALPINE LAKES AIR, Ltd – ALA (Associated with Saltwater West Enterprises, Ltd / Seasonal May-October ops only)

Smithers-Tyhee Lake, B.C.

RR2, Glover Road, Smithers, British Columbia V0J 2N0, Canada ☎ (250) 847-9385 Tx: none Fax: (250) 847-9385 SITA: n/a
F: 1996 ⭢ 2 Head: Wendel Imhof Net: n/a

registration	type of aircraft	cn/fn	ex/ex*	mfd	del	powered by	mtow kg	configuration	name/fln/specialtites/remarks
C-GYLX	Cessna A185F Skywagon	18503354		0077	0597	1 CO IO-520-D	1520		Floats / Wheel-Skis
CF-WYR	Beech 3N (18)	CA-49	RCAF 1474	0051	0696	2 PW R-985	3969		Floats

ALTA FLIGHTS (Charters), Inc. = ALZ

Edmonton-Int'l & Calgary-Int'l, Alta.

PO Box 9831, Edmonton Int'l Airport, Edmonton, Alberta T5J 2T2, Canada ☎ (780) 890-7676 Tx: none Fax: (780) 890-7042 SITA: n/a
F: 1986 ⭢ 60 Head: Christine Robertson Net: n/a

registration	type of aircraft	cn/fn	ex/ex*	mfd	del	powered by	mtow kg	configuration	name/fln/specialtites/remarks
C-FAFC	Cessna 414A Chancellor III	414A0615	N414AB	0080	0796	2 CO TSIO-520-NB	3062		
C-FAFB	Cessna 402C II	402C0266	N150PB	0080	0290	2 CO TSIO-520-VB	3107		
C-FAFF	Cessna 402C II	402C0074	N2611Z	0079	0192	2 CO TSIO-520-VB	3107		
C-FKQM	Cessna 404 Titan II	404-0108	N37102	0077	0193	2 CO GTSIO-520-M	3810		
C-FAFG	Cessna 208B Grand Caravan	208B0724	N997Q	0098	0299	1 PWC PT6A-114A	3969		
C-FAFJ	Cessna 208B Grand Caravan	208B0641		0097	1297	1 PWC PT6A-114A	3969		
C-FAFV	Cessna 208B Grand Caravan	208B0528	N9510W	0096	1097	1 PWC PT6A-114A	3969		
C-FAFT	Beech Catpass 200	BB-57	N121DA	0075	0197	2 PWC PT6A-41	5670		cvtd King Air 200
C-FAFW	Fairchild (Swearingen) SA227AC Metro III	AC-756	N27330	0090	0597	2 GA TPE331-11U-611G	6577		
N585MA	Fairchild (Swearingen) SA227AC Metro III	AC-684	C-FAFR	0087	0797	2 GA TPE331-11U-611G	6577		

35 registration   type of aircraft   cn/fn   ex/ex*   mfd   del   powered by   mtow kg   configuration   selcal   name/fln/specialtites/remarks

ANDERSON AIR, Ltd — Vancouver-Int'l, B.C.

4360 Agar Drive, Richmond, British Columbia V7B 1A3, Canada ☎ (604) 270-1588 Tx: none Fax: (604) 270-2489 SITA: n/a
F: 1981 ☧ 20 Head: John T. Anderson Net: n/a

☐ C-FMSP	Cessna 441 Conquest II	441-0072	N441PL	0079	0190	2 GA TPE331-8-401S	4468			
☐ C-GMSL	Cessna 441 Conquest II	441-0283	N925WS	0083	0396	2 GA TPE331-8-403S	4468			

ANDERSON AVIATION, Ltd — Kindersley, Sask.

Box 621, Kindersley, Saskatchewan S0L 1S0, Canada ☎ (306) 463-2835 Tx: none Fax: (306) 463-6833 SITA: n/a
F: n/a ☧ n/a Head: n/a Net: n/a

☐ C-FXPS	Piper PA-23-250 Aztec D	27-4476	N13834	0070	0498	2 LY IO-540-C4B5	2359			

ANDREW LAKE LODGE & Air Services (Dancal Holding, Ltd dba / Seasonal June-September ops only) — Fort Smith, N.W.T.

Box 5846, Station L, Edmonton, Alberta T6C 0Y0, Canada ☎ (780) 464-7537 Tx: none Fax: none SITA: n/a
F: 1981 ☧ n/a Head: Carl G. Wettlaufer Net: n/a

☐ C-GTPU	Cessna U206G Stationair 6 II	U20604749	N733BH	0079	0398	1 CO IO-520-F	1633			Floats

ANIK AIR DRC, Inc. — Montreal-Dorval, Qué.

10225 Ryan Ave., Dorval Int'l Airport, Dorval, Québec H9P 1A2, Canada ☎ (514) 233-3092 Tx: none Fax: (514) 739-9147 SITA: n/a
F: 1994 ☧ 4 Head: n/a Net: n/a

☐ C-FJWG	Piper PA-23-250 Aztec C	27-3617		0067	1194	2 LY IO-540-C4B5	2359			

ANS ALLIANCE NORD SUD, Inc. — Montreal-Dorval & Sept-Iles, Qué.

900 Chemin de l'Aéroport, RR 4, Canton Eaton, Québec J0B 1M0, Canada ☎ (819) 832-1117 Tx: none Fax: (819) 832-1118 SITA: n/a
F: 1995 ☧ n/a Head: Richard Lambrelle Net: n/a

☐ C-GFEE	Cessna 501 Citation I/SP	501-0169	D-IBWG	0080	0797	2 PWC JT15D-1A	5375			

APEX AIR CHARTERS, Ltd — Atlin, B.C.

Box 356, Atlin, British Columbia V0W 1A0, Canada ☎ (604) 651-7784 Tx: none Fax: (604) 651-7664 SITA: n/a
F: 1996 ☧ n/a Head: n/a Net: n/a Aircraft below MTOW 1361kg: Piper PA-14 (on Floats / Wheel-Skis)

☐ C-GIYQ	Cessna A185F Skywagon II	18503618		0078	0697	1 CO IO-520-D	1520			Floats / Wheel-Skis
☐ C-FYEX	De Havilland DHC-2 Beaver I	302	N9762Z	0052	0696	1 PW R-985	2313			Floats / Wheel-Skis

ARCOT AVIATION, Ltd — Airdrie, Alta.

RR 2, Airdrie Airport, Airdrie, Alberta T4B 2A4, Canada ☎ (780) 948-2399 Tx: none Fax: none SITA: n/a
F: 1985 ☧ 5 Head: Thomas P. Conroy Net: n/a

☐ C-FXEX	CCF Harvard 4 (N.A. T-6J)	CCF4-265	RCAF 20474	0052	0392	1 PW R-1340	2608	Pleasure rides		Aerial combat/Aerobatic rides

ARCTIC EXCURSIONS, Ltd — Yellowknife, N.W.T.

3503 Macdonald Drive, Yellowknife, Northwest Territories X1A 2H2, Canada ☎ (867) 669-7216 Tx: none Fax: (867) 669-7322 SITA: n/a
F: 1997 ☧ n/a Head: Michael Wood Net: http://www.arcticx.yk.com

☐ C-GIVW	Cessna A185F Skywagon II	18503753	N8629Q	0079	0198	1 CO IO-520-D	1520			Floats / Wheel-Skis
☐ C-FFLN	De Havilland DHC-2 Beaver I	150	N4791C	0051	0498	1 PW R-985	2313			Floats

ARCTIC SUNWEST (171817 Canada, Inc. dba) — Yellowknife, N.W.T.

Box 1807, Yellowknife, Northwest Territories X1A 2P4, Canada ☎ (867) 873-4464 Tx: none Fax: (867) 873-9334 SITA: n/a
F: 1993 ☧ n/a Head: Marvin Robinson Net: n/a

☐ C-GVSW	MD Helicopters MD 500E (Hughes 369E)	0011E	N5195Y	0093	0798	1 AN 250-C20B	1361			
☐ C-GSDJ	Cessna A185F Skywagon II	18504212	N31079	0081	0393	1 CO IO-520-D	1520			Floats / Wheel-Skis
☐ C-GRTL	Eurocopter (Aerosp.) AS350BA AStar	1377	N5770L	0080	0598	1 TU Arriel 1B	2100			cvtd AS350B
☐ C-GRTM	Eurocopter (Aerosp.) AS350BA AStar	1402	C-GAHE	0080	0598	1 TU Arriel 1B	2100			cvtd AS350B
☐ C-FOEV	De Havilland DHC-2 Turbo Beaver III	1680TB48		0067	0596	1 PWC PT6A-20	2436			Floats / Wheel-Skis
☐ C-FOPE	De Havilland DHC-2 Turbo Beaver III	1691TB59		0068	0596	1 PWC PT6A-27	2436			Amphibian / Wheel-Skis
☐ C-FSWN	Piper PA-31-350 Navajo Chieftain	31-7952182	C-GREP	0079	0598	2 LY TIO-540-J2BD	3175			
☐ C-GXTC	Piper PA-31T Cheyenne II	31T-7720052	N82165	0077	0199	2 PWC PT6A-28	4082			
☐ C-FASN	Beech King Air B100	BE-17	N178NC	0076	1198	2 GA TPE331-6-252B	5352			

ARCTIC WINGS & ROTORS, Ltd = AWR — Inuvik, N.W.T.

Box 1159, Inuvik, Northwest Territories X0E 0T0, Canada ☎ (867) 979-2220 Tx: none Fax: (867) 979-3440 SITA: n/a
F: 1991 ☧ 10 Head: Frank D. Carmichael ICAO: ARCTIC WINGS Net: n/a Aircraft below MTOW 1361kg: Cessna 180 & Piper PA-28

☐ C-GMKU	Cessna A185F Skywagon	18502808		0075	0796	1 CO IO-520-D	1520			Floats / Wheel-Skis
☐ C-GWVT	Cessna U206F Stationair II	U20602918		0075	0796	1 CO IO-520-F	1633			Floats / Wheel-Skis
☐ C-GALF	Cessna 207A Stationair 8 II	20700674	N9118M	0080	0391	1 CO IO-520-F	1724			
☐ C-GMOK	Cessna 207A Stationair 8 II	20700673	N6373D	0080	0598	1 CO IO-520-F	1724			

ARDUINI HELICOPTERS, Ltd — Williams Lake, B.C.

741-9 Avenue North, Williams Lake, British Columbia V2G 2K7, Canada ☎ (250) 398-5551 Tx: none Fax: (250) 392-5885 SITA: n/a
F: 1998 ☧ n/a Head: n/a Net: n/a

☐ C-GIWB	Bell 206B JetRanger II	2125		0076	0698	1 AN 250-C20	1451			

ARIES AVIATION SERVICES, Corp. — Calgary, Alta.

5420-11th Street N.E., Calgary, Alberta T2E 7E9, Canada ☎ (403) 274-3930 Tx: none Fax: (403) 274-3951 SITA: n/a
F: 1995 ☧ n/a Head: Ken Grandia Net: n/a

☐ C-GTGS	Piper PA-23-250 Aztec F	27-8054002		0080	0198	2 LY IO-540-C4B5	2359	Photo / Survey		
☐ C-FFRY	Piper PA-31-310 Navajo	31-521		0069	0595	2 LY TIO-540-A1A	2948	Photo / Survey		Tail gradiometer
☐ C-GKMW	Piper PA-31-310 Navajo	31-725	N231CD	0071	0796	2 LY TIO-540-A1A	2948	Photo / Survey		
☐ C-GKMV	Piper PA-31T Cheyenne II	31T-7820003	N444ER	0078	1097	2 PWC PT6A-28	4082	Photo / Survey		
☐ C-GKMX	Piper PA-31T Cheyenne II	31T-7720058	N7WS	0077	1196	2 PWC PT6A-28	4082	Photo / Survey		

ARROW LAKES HELICOPTERS, Ltd — Nakusp, B.C.

PO Box 430, Nakusp, British Columbia V0G 1R0, Canada ☎ (250) 265-4855 Tx: none Fax: (250) 265-3183 SITA: n/a
F: 1997 ☧ n/a Head: n/a Net: n/a

☐ C-GCHK	Bell 206B JetRanger II	2067		0076	0797	1 AN 250-C20	1451			

ART LATTO AIR SERVICE, Ltd (Seasonal May-October ops only) — Savant Lake, Ont.

General Delivery, Savant Lake, Ontario P0V 2S0, Canada ☎ (807) 584-2970 Tx: n/a Fax: (807) 584-2222 SITA: n/a
F: 1987 ☧ n/a Head: Art J. Latto Net: n/a Aircraft below MTOW 1361kg: Cessna 180 (on Floats).

☐ C-FBHZ	Noorduyn Norseman V	N29-13		0046		1 PW R-1340	3420			Floats

A.S.F. - Avion sans Frontières (Division of Terre sans Frontières) — Africa

399 rue des Conseillers, Porte 23, La Prairie, Québec J5R 4H6, Canada ☎ (450) 659-7717 Tx: none Fax: (450) 659-2276 SITA: n/a
F: 1984 ☧ n/a Head: Robert Gonneville Net: http://www.terresansfrontieres.ca Non-commercial organisation conducting flights for relief & development agencies & missions in remote areas of third world countries.

☐ 9Q-CPQ	Cessna U206F Stationair	U20601995	N51301	0073	0485	1 CO IO-520-F	1633			

ASHUANIPI AVIATION, Ltd — Jonquiere-SPB, Qué.

2730 rue de la Salle, Jonquiere, Québec G7S 2A7, Canada ☎ (418) 548-5505 Tx: none Fax: (418) 548-2037 SITA: n/a
F: 1975 ☧ n/a Head: Michel Cayouette Net: n/a

☐ C-FYAO	Cessna A185E Skywagon	18501472		0069	0498	1 CO IO-520-D	1520			Floats / Wheel-Skis
☐ C-GLCO	De Havilland DHC-3 Otter	420	N17681	0061	0498	1 PW R-1340	3629			Floats / Wheel-Skis

ATAI AIR CHARTERS, Ltd (Vols Nolises ATAI, Ltée) — Kuujjuaq, Qué.

CP 606, Kuujjuaq, Québec J0M 1C0, Canada ☎ (819) 964-2998 Tx: n/a Fax: (819) 964-2159 SITA: n/a
F: 1993 ☧ n/a Head: Johnny Adams Net: n/a

☐ C-GARI	Piper PA-23-250 Aztec E	27-7305169	N40455	0073	0793	2 LY IO-540-C4B5	2359			
☐ C-FTIV	Piper PA-31-350 Navajo Chieftain	31-7405415	N103KH	0074	0695	2 LY TIO-540-J2BD	3175			

ATHABASKA AIRWAYS, Ltd = 9T / ABS — Prince Albert & La Ronge & Stony Rapids & Saskatoon, Sask.

Box 100, Prince Albert, Saskatchewan S6V 5R4, Canada ☎ (306) 764-1404 Tx: none Fax: (306) 763-1313 SITA: n/a
F: 1955 ☧ 130 Head: Floyd R. Glass IATA: 909 ICAO: ATHABASKA Net: n/a Aircraft below MTOW 1361 kg: Cessna 172.

☐ C-GCNC	Bell 206B JetRanger	1142	N58152	0073		1 AN 250-C20	1451			
☐ C-GELT	Bell 206B JetRanger III	2994		0080		1 AN 250-C20B	1451			
☐ C-GYHY	Bell 206B JetRanger III	2317		0078		1 AN 250-C20B	1451			
☐ C-GCJF	Cessna A185F Skywagon II	18503960		0080		1 CO IO-520-D	1520			Floats / Wheel-Skis
☐ C-GCJM	Cessna A185F Skywagon II	18503955		0079		1 CO IO-520-D	1520			Floats / Wheel-Skis

36 registration type of aircraft cn/fn ex/ex* mfd del powered by mtow kg configuration selcal name/fln/specialitites/remarks

registration	type of aircraft	cn/fn	ex/ex*	mfd	del	powered by	mtow kg	configuration	selcal	name/fln/specialitites/remarks
☐ C-GCVJ	Cessna A185F Skywagon II	18503964		0080		1 CO IO-520-D	1520			Floats / Wheel-Skis
☐ C-GAEB	De Havilland DHC-2 Beaver I	703	53-7895	0054		1 PW R-985	2313			Floats / Wheel-Skis
☐ C-GAON	Cessna 310 R II	310R1627		0079		2 CO IO-520-M	2495			
☐ C-GZYJ	Cessna 310 R II	310R1311		0078		2 CO IO-520-M	2495			
☐ C-FAWP	Cessna 402C II	402C0051	N125ST	0079		2 CO TSIO-520-VB	3107			
☐ C-FFCH	Cessna 402C II	402C0496	N402HD	0081	0689	2 CO TSIO-520-VB	3107			
☐ C-FAAF	Piper PA-31-350 Navajo Chieftain	31-7752096	N27229	0077	1091	2 LY TIO-540-J2BD	3175			
☐ C-FATS	Piper PA-31-350 Navajo Chieftain	31-7952072	N27964	0079	1289	2 LY TIO-540-J2BD	3175			
☐ C-GUNP	Piper PA-31-350 Navajo Chieftain	31-8052048	N3554D	0080	1097	2 LY TIO-540-J2BD	3175			
☐ C-FJTB	Sikorsky S-55BT	55792		0054		1 GA TPE331-3U-303N	3266			cvtd S-55B
☐ C-FUNT	Sikorsky S-55BT	55325		0052		1 GA TPE331-3U-303N	3266			cvtd S-55B
☐ C-GHKR	Sikorsky S-55BT	55750	53-4414	0054	0590	1 GA TPE331-3U-303N	3266			cvtd S-55B
☐ CF-BVP	Sikorsky S-55BT	55188		0052		1 GA TPE331-3U-303N	3266			cvtd S-55B / rebuilt
☐ C-FSGD	De Havilland DHC-3 Otter	316	N521BK	0059	0594	1 PW R-1340	3629			
☐ C-FHPE	De Havilland DHC-3 Turbo Otter	273	4651	0058	0590	1 PWC PT6A-135A	3629			Floats / Wheel-Skis / cvtd Otter
☐ C-GCTA	Cessna 441 Conquest II	441-0140		0080		2 GA TPE331-8-401S	4468			
☐ C-FDTJ	De Havilland DHC-6 Twin Otter 100	37	VP-LIT	0067	0596	2 PWC PT6A-20	5252			
☐ C-FPGE	De Havilland DHC-6 Twin Otter 200	197	N790M	0069	0792	2 PWC PT6A-20	5252			
☐ C-FSCA	De Havilland DHC-6 Twin Otter 100	17		0066	0678	2 PWC PT6A-20	5252			Floats / Wheel-Skis
☐ C-GAAF	Beech 1900C-1 Airliner	UC-136		0090	0191	2 PWC PT6A-65B	7530			
☐ N1568W	Beech 1900C-1 Airliner	UC-64		0089	0998	2 PWC PT6A-65B	7530		Y19	203 / lsf Raytheon Aircraft Credit Corp
☐ C-FVJU	Beech 1900D Airliner	UE-156	N3214J*	0095	0895	2 PWC PT6A-67D	7688			
☐ C-FVKC	Beech 1900D Airliner	UE-160		0095	0895	2 PWC PT6A-67D	7688			
☐ C-GDHE	Beech 1900D Airliner	UE-336	N23320*	0098	1298	2 PWC PT6A-67D	7688			
☐ C-GDHF	Beech 1900D Airliner	UE-339	N23340*	0098	0199	2 PWC PT6A-67D	7688			

ATIKOKAN AERO SERVICE, Ltd
Atikokan, Ont.

Box 716, Atikokan, Ontario P0T 1C0, Canada ☎ (807) 597-6086 Tx: n/a Fax: (807) 597-2862 SITA: n/a
F: 1976 ♦♦♦ 5 Head: Sandy Dickson Net: n/a Aircraft below MTOW 1361 kg: Cessna 180 (on Floats / Wheel-Skis).

☐ C-GDZH	De Havilland DHC-2 Beaver I	356	51-16555	0055		1 PW R-985	2313			Floats / Wheel-Skis
☐ CF-IPL	De Havilland DHC-2 Beaver I	132		0051		1 PW R-985	2313			Floats / Wheel-Skis

ATLANTIC CHARTERS (Manan Air Services, Inc. dba / formerly Seagull Aviation)
Grand Manan Island, N.B.

Box 61, Grand Harbour, New Brunswick E0G 1Y0, Canada ☎ (506) 662-8720 Tx: none Fax: none SITA: n/a
F: 1980 ♦♦♦ n/a Head: Klaus Sonnenberg Net: n/a Aircraft below MTOW 1361kg: Cessna 172.

☐ C-FREZ	Piper PA-34-200T Seneca II	34-7970016	HB-LII	0079	1198	2 CO TSIO-360-EB	2073			
☐ C-GLLH	Piper PA-34-200 Seneca	34-7450063		0074	0297	2 LY IO-360-C1E6	1905			

ATR (A.T.R. Seminars Inc. – Airline Training Resources dba)
Toronto-City Centre, Ont.

Toronto City Centre Airport, Aerocentre East, Toronto, Ontario M5V 1A1, Canada ☎ (416) 203-1199 Tx: none Fax: (416) 203-1140 SITA: n/a
F: 1988 ♦♦♦ 25 Head: Capt. Carlos M. Monsalvé Net: http://www.fly-atr.com Aircraft below MTOW 1361kg: Cessna 150, 172 & Dimona DA20

☐ C-GISY	Partenavia P.68C	370		0086	0291	2 LY IO-360-A1B6	1990			

AVIATION BATISCAN, Inc. (Seasonal June-October ops only)
Sept-Iles, Qué.

5773-I, Lac Sept-Iles, St-Raymond, Québec G0A 4G0, Canada ☎ (418) 337-2099 Tx: n/a Fax: (418) 337-3099 SITA: n/a
F: 1989 ♦♦♦ n/a Head: Pierre Ginac Net: n/a

☐ C-FEYR	De Havilland DHC-2 Beaver I	497		0053	0998	1 PW R-985	2309			Floats
☐ C-GOER	De Havilland DHC-2 Beaver I	514	N99830	0054	0490	1 PW R-985	2309			Floats

AVIATION BOREAL (1988), Inc. (formerly Transport Nord-Ouest, Inc.)
Val d'Or & La Grande, Qué.

CP 1390, Val d'Or, Québec J9P 4P8, Canada ☎ (819) 825-0405 Tx: none Fax: (819) 825-1260 SITA: n/a
F: 1989 ♦♦♦ n/a Head: Jean-Marie Arseneault Net: n/a

☐ C-GDDX	Piper PA-31-310 Navajo B	31-770	N7245L	0071	1296	2 LY TIO-540-A2C	2948			
☐ C-FQBC	Boeing (Douglas) DC-3C (C-47B-20-DK)	27026	N94598	0044	0889	2 PW R-1830	12202	Freighter		
☐ C-GCXD	Boeing (Douglas) DC-3C (C-47B-1-DK)	25612	CAF 12948	0043	0190	2 PW R-1830	12202	Freighter		

AVIATION COMMERCIAL AVIATION = CMS (160878 Canada, Ltd dba)
Hearst, Ont.

PO Box 460, Hearst, Ontario P0L 1N0, Canada ☎ (705) 362-8505 Tx: none Fax: (705) 362-7437 SITA: n/a
F: 1984 ♦♦♦ 32 Head: Michel L. Boucher ICAO: ACCESS Net: n/a Aircraft below MTOW 1361 kg: Cessna 172.

☐ C-GIKA	Piper PA-31-350 Navajo Chieftain	31-7952161	LN-TEL	0079	0596	2 LY TIO-540-J2BD	3175			
☐ C-GPAK	Piper PA-31-350 Navajo Chieftain	31-8052070	N3558S	0080	0593	2 LY TIO-540-J2BD	3175			
☐ C-FGSX	Piper PA-31T2 Cheyenne II XL	31T-8166048	N600XL	0282	1291	2 PWC PT6A-135	4297			
☐ C-GBFO	Piper PA-31T2 Cheyenne II XL	31T-8166069	N511SC	0081	0398	2 PWC PT6A-135	4297			

AVIATION INTERNATIONAL (Canada), Inc. (formerly Neiltown Air, Ltd)
Guelph, Ont.

RR 2, Skyway Drive, Guelph, Ontario N1H 6H8, Canada ☎ (519) 824-2660 Tx: none Fax: (519) 824-0190 SITA: n/a
F: 1989 ♦♦♦ n/a Head: Adele Fogle Net: n/a Aircraft below MTOW 1361 kg: Cessna 150, 152, 172 & Piper PA-28

☐ C-GBNU	Piper PA-44-180 Seminole	44-7995272		0079		2 LY O-360-E1A6D	1724			
☐ C-GAWS	Piper PA-31-310 Navajo	31-184	N9137Y	0068	0396	2 LY TIO-540-A1A	2948			

AVIATION JUSTAIR (1992), Inc.
Fermont-Lac d'Aigle, Qué.

CP 509, Fermont, Quebec G0G 1J0, Canada ☎ (418) 287-3300 Tx: n/a Fax: (418) 287-5668 SITA: n/a
F: 1988 ♦♦♦ 2 Head: François Jinchereau Net: n/a Aircraft below MTOW 1361kg: Piper PA-12 (on Floats / Wheel-Skis)

☐ C-FYNX	Cessna A185E Skywagon	185-1544		0069	0888	1 CO IO-520-D	1520			Floats / Wheel-Skis

AVIATION LES ILES, Ltée
Ste-Anne-de-Sorel, Qué.

2790 Chenal du Moine, Ste-Anne-de-Sorel, Québec J3P 5N3, Canada ☎ (450) 743-4380 Tx: none Fax: (450) 743-4380 SITA: n/a
F: 1995 ♦♦♦ n/a Head: Robert Ethier Net: n/a

☐ C-FPTD	Piper PA-23-250 Aztec C	27-2483	N5408Y	0063	0595	2 LY IO-540-C4B5	2359			

AVIATION QUEBEC LABRADOR, Ltée = QLA (Member of Groupe Gamac)
Sept-Iles, Qué.

CP 575, Sept-Iles, Québec G4R 4K7, Canada ☎ (418) 962-7901 Tx: none Fax: (418) 962-9202 SITA: n/a
F: 1983 ♦♦♦ 15 Head: Jacques Cleary ICAO: QUEBEC LABRADOR Net: n/a Aircraft below MTOW 1361kg: Cessna 180
Operates scheduled flights (with Bandeirante aircraft) in conjunction with AIR CANADA as an Liaison AIR CANADA Connector (in own colors), using AC-flight numbers.

☐ C-FPDK	Piper PA-31-350 Navajo Chieftain	31-7405131	N202RC	0074	0594	2 LY TIO-540-J2BD	3175			
☐ C-GRLP	Piper PA-31-350 Navajo Chieftain	31-7305020	N7ZG	0073		2 LY TIO-540-J2BD	3175			
☐ C-FMUS	De Havilland DHC-6 Twin Otter 300	573	ZK-TFS	0078	0898	2 PWC PT6A-27	5670			
☐ C-FGCL	Embraer 110P1 Bandeirante (EMB-110P1)	110339	N696RA	0081	0692	2 PWC PT6A-34	5670			
☐ C-FSXR	Embraer 110P1 Bandeirante (EMB-110P1)	110372	N880AC	0081	0794	2 PWC PT6A-34	5670			
☐ C-GDCQ	Embraer 110P1 Bandeirante (EMB-110P1)	110451	N218EB	0084	1094	2 PWC PT6A-34	5670			

AVIATION ROGER FORGUES, Inc.
Québec & -Lac Saint-Augustin SPB, Qué.

2029-15e Avenue, St-Augustin de des Maures, Québec G3A 1W7, Canada ☎ (418) 871-4455 Tx: none Fax: SUMMER(418)871-8010 SITA: n/a
F: 1982 ♦♦♦ 5 Head: Roger Forgues Net: http://www.aviation-rforgues.com FAX number in winter: (418) 622-2792

☐ C-GMJF	Cessna U206G Stationair 6 II	U20606241		0081		1 CO IO-520-F	1633	4 Pax / Frtr		Floats / Wheel-Skis
☐ C-FARF	De Havilland DHC-2 Beaver I	1216	N1356Y	0058	0396	1 PW R-985	2313	6 Pax / Frtr		Floats / Wheel-Skis
☐ C-FOQW	De Havilland DHC-2 Beaver I	1601	G-JAFE	0065	0793	1 PW R-985	2313	6 Pax / Frtr		Floats / Wheel-Skis
☐ C-GBZS	De Havilland DHC-2 Beaver I	1595	HZ-ZAI	0065	0793	1 PW R-985	2313	6 Pax / Frtr		Floats / Wheel-Skis

AVIATION WHEEL AIR (3112390 Canada Inc. dba)
Mont Tremblant-Lac Ouimet, Qué.

310 des Pignons, CP 1454, St-Jovite, Québec J0T 2H0, Canada ☎ (819) 425-5662 Tx: none Fax: (819) 425-2862 SITA: n/a
F: 1995 ♦♦♦ 4 Head: Pierre Routhier Net: n/a

☐ C-FCTF	Cessna A185E Skywagon	18501949		0071	1295	1 CO IO-520-D	1520			Floats / Wheel-Skis
☐ C-FYZC	Cessna A185E Skywagon	185-1540		0069	0396	1 CO IO-520-D	1520			Floats / Wheel-Skis

AVIONAIR, Inc. = ANU
Montreal-Dorval, Qué.

Aéroport Int'l de Montreal, 9025 Ave Ryan, Dorval, Québec H9P 1A2, Canada ☎ (514) 631-7696 Tx: 058-26852 Fax: (514) 631-7501 SITA: n/a
F: 1981 ♦♦♦ 12 Head: Gilles Bruneau ICAO: AVIONAIR Net: n/a

☐ C-GBXX	Fairchild (Swearingen) SA226TC Metro II	TC-293	N161SW	0079	0290	2 GA TPE331-10UA-511G	5670			
☐ C-GQAJ	Fairchild (Swearingen) SA226TC Metro II	TC-295	C-FUIF	0079	1197	2 GA TPE331-10UA-511G	5670			
☐ C-GWSP	Fairchild (Swearingen) SA226AT Merlin IV	AT-010	N603L	0073		2 GA TPE331-3U-303G	5670			
☐ C-GQJG	Beech King Air 200	BB-249		0077		2 PWC PT6A-41	5670			

AVNORTH AVIATION, Ltd (formerly Springhouse Aviation, Ltd)
Nimpo Lake, B.C.

Box 5, Nimpo Lake, British Columbia V0L 1R0, Canada ☎ (250) 742-3285 Tx: n/a Fax: (250) 742-3769 SITA: n/a
F: 1975 ♦♦♦ 5 Head: n/a Net: n/a Aircraft below MTOW 1361 kg: Cessna 172 & 180 (on Floats / Wheel-Skis)

☐ C-FGPL	Cessna A185E Skywagon	185-1591	N1920U	0069	0695	1 CO IO-520-D	1520			Floats

37 registration type of aircraft   cn/fn   ex/ex*   mfd   del   powered by   mtow kg   configuration   selcal   name/fln/specialitites/remarks

registration	type of aircraft	cn/fn	ex/ex*	mfd	del	powered by	mtow kg	configuration	selcal	name/fln/specialitites/remarks
☐ C-FGCU	De Havilland DHC-2 Beaver I	503		0053	0798	1 PW R-985	2313			Floats
☐ C-GAXE	De Havilland DHC-2 Beaver I	841	54-1698	0055	0493	1 PW R-985	2313			Floats

AVWEST CHARTERS (Avwest Aviation, Inc. dba / formerly Laughing Sky Air Charters)
Victoria, B.C.

Box 102, Victoria, British Columbia V8W 2M1, Canada ☎ (250) 655-3620 Tx: none Fax: (250) 655-0466 SITA: n/a
F: 1992 ✦✦✦ 3 Head: Raymond Rosenkranz Net: http://www.avcharters.com

☐ C-GXPZ	Cessna 401A	401A0104	N6192Q	0069	1292	2 CO TSIO-520-E	2858			
☐ C-GXPT	Cessna 421B Golden Eagle	421B0418	N421NP	0073	0998	2 CO GTSIO-520-H	3379			

BABIN AIR, Ltd (formerly Horizon Air)
Invermere & Fairmont, B.C.

Athalmer Highway, Invermere, British Columbia V0A 1K0, Canada ☎ (250) 342-3565 Tx: none Fax: (250) 342-0086 SITA: n/a
F: 1978 ✦✦✦ 5 Head: Norm Babin Net: http://www.discoveryweb.com/babinair Aircraft below MTOW 1361kg: Cessna 172 & 182

☐ C-FRVM	Cessna 206 Super Skywagon	206-0100		0064	0889	1 CO IO-520-F	1588			

BAILEY HELICOPTERS, Ltd (formerly Wayne G. Bailey Holdings, Ltd)
Delta, B.C.

46-4400-72 Street, Boundary Bay Airport, Delta, British Columbia V4K 5B3, Canada ☎ (604) 940-2799 Tx: none Fax: (604) 940-2744 SITA: n/a
F: 1989 ✦✦✦ n/a Head: Wayne G. Bailey Net: n/a Aircraft below MTOW 1361kg: Robinson R22 & R44

☐ C-FBYD	Bell 206B JetRanger III	2519	N5008L	0078	0395	1 AN 250-C20B	1451			
☐ C-FCQD	Bell 206B JetRanger III	534		0070	0394	1 AN 250-C20B	1451			
☐ C-FVSP	Bell 206B JetRanger	899	N83070	0072	0598	1 AN 250-C20	1451			cvtd 206A
☐ C-GAXB	Bell 206B JetRanger III	3527	N226EC	0081	0697	1 AN 250-C20B	1451			
☐ C-GIFR	Bell 206B JetRanger	681	N124NC	0071	1290	1 AN 250-C20	1451			cvtd 206A
☐ C-GTEK	Bell 206B JetRanger III	1684	N222ML	0075	0593	1 AN 250-C20B	1451			cvtd JetRanger
☐ C-GAVK	Eurocopter (Aerosp.) AS350BA AStar	1538	N57955	0082	1198	1 TU Arriel 1B	2100			cvtd AS350B

BAJO REEF HELICOPTERS, Ltd
Langley, B.C.

21735-48th Avenue NE, Langley, British Columbia V3A 3N1, Canada ☎ (604) 533-0139 Tx: none Fax: none SITA: n/a
F: 1989 ✦✦✦ 2 Head: Michel Lamarche Net: n/a Aircraft below MTOW 1361kg: Hughes 369HS (500C)

☐ C-GHTG	Hiller UH-12E	970		0058	0293	1 LY VO-540-B1A	1406			

BALDWIN AIR (Baldwin Aerial Imagery dba)
Carvel, Alta.

Box 10, Site 7, RR 2, Carvel, Alberta T0E 0H0, Canada ☎ (780) 963-7152 Tx: none Fax: (780) 963-7152 SITA: n/a
F: 1990 ✦✦✦ n/a Head: Craig Baldwin Net: n/a

☐ C-GBLA	Beech Travel Air 95	TD-180	N2013C	0058	0995	2 LY O-360-A1A	1814	Photo / Survey		

B. ALLISON FLYING SERVICES (593897 Alberta, Ltd dba)
Edmonton-Municipal, Alta.

400, 10339-124 Street, Edmonton, Alberta T5N 3W1, Canada ☎ (780) 448-7442 Tx: none Fax: (780) 452-9060 SITA: n/a
F: 1997 ✦✦✦ n/a Head: Brock Allison Net: n/a Aircraft below MTOW 1361kg: Piper PA-18

☐ C-FYCP	Cessna T210J Turbo Centurion	T2100407		0069	0498	1 CO TSIO-520-H	1542			
☐ C-GPZO	Piper PA-34-200T Seneca II	34-7670236		0076	1098	2 CO TSIO-360-E	2073			

BAR XH AIR, Ltd = BXH
Medicine Hat & Calgary, Alta. XH BAR XH AIR INC.

PO Box 161, Medicine Hat, Alberta T1A 7E8, Canada ☎ (780) 527-3328 Tx: none Fax: (780) 527-4721 SITA: n/a
F: 1975 ✦✦✦ 10 Head: Les N. Little ICAO: PALLISER Net: n/a Aircraft below MTOW 1361 kg: Cessna 150, 172, & Piper PA-28

☐ C-GXHK	Piper PA-31-350 Navajo Chieftain	31-7752108	N115SC	0077		2 LY TIO-540-J2BD	3175			
☐ C-GXHP	Beech King Air A100	B-132	XB-SLG	0072	0994	2 PWC PT6A-28	5216			
☐ C-FCGB	Beech Catpass 200	BB-24	N183MC	0074	0195	2 PWC PT6A-41	5670			035 / cvtd King Air 200, conv. No.6
☐ N252AF	Beech 1300 Airliner	BB-1339	N339YV	0089	0095	2 PWC PT6A-42	5670			036/Ruth / lsf Raytheon/cvtd S.K.A.B200
☐ N256AF	Beech 1300 Airliner	BB-1340	N340YV	0089	0095	2 PWC PT6A-42	5670			034/Tex / lsf Raytheon/cvtd S.K.A.B200

BATCHAWANA BAY AIR SERVICES, Ltd
Batchawan, Bay Ont.

PO Box 129, Batchawana Bay, Ontario P0S 1A0, Canada ☎ (705) 882-2361 Tx: none Fax: none SITA: n/a
F: 1970 ✦✦✦ 3 Head: D. Pipoli Net: n/a Aircraft below MTOW 1361kg: Cessna 180 (on Floats/Wheels). Phone winter: (616) 868-0042.

☐ C-GOUX	De Havilland DHC-2 Beaver I	314	51-16813	0052		1 PW R-985	2313			Floats / Wheel-Skis

BATES AIR, Ltd
Powell River, B.C.

Box 277, Powell River, British Columbia V8A 4Z6, Canada ☎ (604) 485-2551 Tx: none Fax: (604) 485-7218 SITA: n/a
F: 1998 ✦✦✦ n/a Head: Bob Bates Net: n/a

☐ C-GSKY	De Havilland DHC-2 Beaver I	1358	58-2027	0058	0199	1 PW R-985	2313			Floats

BAXTER AVIATION, Ltd = 6B
Nanaimo-SPB, B.C. Baxter AVIATION

PO Box 1110, Nanaimo, British Columbia V9R 6E7, Canada ☎ (250) 683-6525 Tx: none Fax: (250) 754-1075 SITA: n/a
F: 1988 ✦✦✦ 16 Head: Tom Baxter Net: n/a

☐ C-GBTJ	Cessna A185F Skywagon II	18503950		0079	0493	1 CO IO-520-D	1520			Floats
☐ C-GMFG	Cessna A185F Skywagon II	18503773	N8786Q	0079	0789	1 CO IO-520-D	1520			Floats
☐ C-FAWA	De Havilland DHC-2 Beaver I	1430	VH-IDR	0060	0390	1 PW R-985	2313			Floats
☐ C-FEBE	De Havilland DHC-2 Beaver I	792	N99838	0054	0691	1 PW R-985	2313			Floats
☐ C-FJBP	De Havilland DHC-2 Beaver I	942		0056	0194	1 PW R-985	2313			Floats
☐ C-FWAC	De Havilland DHC-2 Beaver I	1356	N68089	0059	0694	1 PW R-985	2313			Floats
☐ C-GEZS	De Havilland DHC-2 Beaver I	1277	57-6170	0057	1090	1 PW R-985	2313			Floats
☐ C-GFDI	De Havilland DHC-2 Beaver I	606	53-2810	0053	1296	1 PW R-985	2313			Floats
☐ C-GOLC	De Havilland DHC-2 Beaver I	1392	N62354	0059	1094	1 PW R-985	2313			Floats
☐ C-GTBQ	De Havilland DHC-2 Beaver I	1316	N9036	0059	1194	1 PW R-985	2313			Floats
☐ C-GWCT	De Havilland DHC-2 Beaver I	1227	N67665	0057	0296	1 PW R-985	2313			Floats

BEARSKIN AIRLINES = JV / BLS (Bearskin Lake Air Service, Ltd dba)
Sioux Lookout & Thunder Bay, Ont. Bearskin Airlines

PO Box 1447, Sioux Lookout, Ontario P8T 1C1, Canada ☎ (807) 474-2635 Tx: none Fax: (807) 737-4360 SITA: n/a
F: 1963 ✦✦✦ 375 Head: Harvey Friesen IATA: 632 ICAO: BEARSKIN Net: http://www.bearskin-airlines.com Aircraft below MTOW 1361kg: Cessna 150.

☐ C-FWGL	Piper PA-23-250 Aztec C	27-3707		0067	0691	2 LY IO-540-C4B5	2359	Y5		
☐ C-GEHY	Piper PA-23-250 Aztec C	27-3843	N6548Y	0068		2 LY IO-540-C4B5	2359	Y5		
☐ C-FAJV	Pilatus PC-12/45	234	HB-FRE*	0098	1298	1 PWC PT6A-67B	4500	Y9		
☐ C-FCJV	Pilatus PC-12/45	240	N240PD	0098	0399	1 PWC PT6A-67B	4500	Y9		
☐ C-FKAE	Pilatus PC-12/45	195	HB-FQD*	0097	0898	1 PWC PT6A-67B	4500	Y9		
☐ C-GBJV	Pilatus PC-12/45	237	HB-FRH*	0098	1298	1 PWC PT6A-67B	4500	Y9		
☐ C-GDFX	Beech 99 Airliner	U-123	N18RA	0069	0189	2 PWC PT6A-28	4944	Y14		
☐ C-GDSL	Beech 99 Airliner	U-92	N112PA	0069	0481	2 PWC PT6A-28	4944	Y14		
☐ C-GFQC	Beech 99 Airliner	U-120	HS-SKF	0069	1188	2 PWC PT6A-28	4944	Y14		
☐ C-GHVI	Beech B99 Airliner	U-153	N17RX	0074	0589	2 PWC PT6A-28	4944	Y14		
☐ C-GPEM	Beech 99 Airliner	U-98	N991GP	0069	0081	2 PWC PT6A-28	4944	Y14		
☐ C-GQAH	Beech B99 Airliner	U-58	N7801R	0068		2 PWC PT6A-28	4944	Y14		Spirit of Muskrat Dam
☐ C-GKAJ	Beech King Air A100	B-232	N91295	0077	0690	2 PWC PT6A-28	5216	Y12		Spirit of Marathon
☐ C-GNEX	Beech King Air A100	B-211	N9194F	0074	0893	2 PWC PT6A-28	5216	Y12		
☐ C-GUPP	Beech King Air A100	B-157	N123CS	0073		2 PWC PT6A-28	5216	Y12		Spirit of Sioux Lookout
☐ C-GYQK	Beech King Air A100	B-153	N120AS	0073		2 PWC PT6A-28	5216	Y12		Spirit of Kenora
☐ C-FFZN	Fairchild (Swearingen) SA227AC Metro III	AC-785B	N30019*	0091	0492	2 GA TPE331-11U-612G	7257	Y19		Spirit of Service
☐ C-FXUS	Fairchild (Swearingen) SA227CC Metro 23	CC-841B	N456LA	0093	0496	2 GA TPE331-11U-612G	7484	Y19		
☐ C-FYAG	Fairchild (Swearingen) SA227AC Metro III	AC-670B	N670VG	0087	0695	2 GA TPE331-11U-612G	7257	Y19		
☐ C-FYWG	Fairchild (Swearingen) SA227AC Metro III	AC-782B	N300DS*	0091	0894	2 GA TPE331-11U-612G	7257	Y19		Spirit of Winnipeg
☐ C-GYHD	Fairchild (Swearingen) SA227AC Metro III	AC-739B	N227JH	0089	0894	2 GA TPE331-11U-612G	7257	Y19		Spirit of Dryden
☐ C-GYQT	Fairchild (Swearingen) SA227AC Metro III	AC-644B	N644VG	0086	0695	2 GA TPE331-11U-612G	7257	Y19		
☐ C-GYTL	Fairchild (Swearingen) SA227CC Metro 23	CC-829B		0093	0693	2 GA TPE331-11U-612G	7484	Y19		Spirit of Big Trout Lake

BEAU DEL AIR, Ltd (Subsidiary of Beau del Leasing, Inc.)
Inuvik, N.W.T.

PO Box 2040, Inuvik, Northwest Territories X0E 0T0, Canada ☎ (867) 777-2333 Tx: none Fax: (867) 777-3758 SITA: n/a
F: 1990 ✦✦✦ n/a Head: Gay Walker Net: n/a

☐ C-FQXR	Cessna A185E Skywagon	18501894		0071	0696	1 CO IO-520-D	1520			Floats / Wheel-Skis
☐ C-FTTJ	Cessna A185E Skywagon	185-1085		0066	0491	1 CO IO-520-D	1520			Floats / Wheel-Skis
☐ C-GLJC	Cessna A185F Skywagon	18502996		0076	0594	1 CO IO-520-D	1520			Floats / Wheel-Skis
☐ C-GAAP	Pilatus PC-6/B1-H2 Turbo Porter	569	N2851T	0065	0697	1 PWC PT6A-20	2200			Floats / Wheel-Skis
☐ C-FBRN	Piper PA-31-310 Navajo C	31-508	N6582L	0079	0898	2 LY TIO-540-A2C	2948			

BEAVER AIR SERVICES, Ltd
The Pas-Grace Lake Air Base, Man.

Box 2557, The Pas, Manitoba R9A 1M3, Canada ☎ (204) 623-7160 Tx: none Fax: (204) 623-3635 SITA: n/a
F: 1981 ✦✦✦ 10 Head: Ralph Caribou Net: n/a Aircraft below MTOW 1361 kg: Cessna 182.

☐ C-GTTZ	Cessna A185F Skywagon II	18503694	N8423Q	0079		1 CO IO-520-D	1520			Floats / Wheel-Skis

registration type of aircraft   cn/fn   ex/ex*   mfd   del   powered by   mtow kg configuration   selcal   name/fln/specialitites/remarks

☐ C-FSGX	Cessna U206 Super Skywagon	U206-0375		0065	0594	1 CO IO-520-A	1497			Floats / Wheel-Skis
☐ C-GADW	Piper PA-31-350 Navajo Chieftain	31-7752078	N27191	0077	0192	2 LY TIO-540-J2BD	3175			
☐ C-GYQD	Piper PA-31-350 Navajo Chieftain	31-8152039	N4075T	0081	0497	2 LY TIO-540-J2BD	3175			
☐ C-GEBA	Piper PA-31T Cheyenne II	31T-7620029	N177JE	0076	0495	2 PWC PT6A-28	4082			

BELLA COOLA AIR, Ltd — Bella Coola, B.C.

Box 180, Hagensborg, British Columbia V0T 1H0, Canada ☎ (250) 982-2545 Tx: none Fax: (250) 982-2957 SITA: n/a
F: 1995 n/a Head: n/a Net: n/a Aircraft below MTOW 1361kg: Cessna 172

☐ C-FYUW	Cessna A185E Skywagon	185-1541		0069	1095	1 CO IO-520-D	1520			Floats / Wheels

BERRY AIR, Ltd — Prince George, B.C.

1031 Heritage Crescent, Prince George, British Columbia V2M 6X2, Canada ☎ (604) 563-0877 Tx: none Fax: (604) 240-2700 SITA: n/a
F: 1995 n/a Head: Doug Berry Net: n/a

☐ C-FAVP	Cessna 210G Centurion	21058920	N5920F	0068	0795	1 CO IO-520-A	1542			
☐ C-GTTB	Cessna 210L Centurion II	21060848		0075	0995	1 CO IO-520-L	1724			

BIGHORN HELICOPTERS, Inc. (formerly Bighorn Aviation, Inc.) — Cranbrook, B.C.

Bighorn Aviation

PO Box 220, Cranbrook, British Columbia V1C 4H7, Canada ☎ (250) 489-2517 Tx: none Fax: (250) 489-6139 SITA: n/a
F: 1981 10 Head: Clay Wilson Net: http://www.bighorn.ca Aircraft below MTOW 1361kg: Robinson R22

☐ C-FYIP	MD Helicopters MD 500D (Hughes 369D)	1260061D	N346BB	0076	0197	1 AN 250-C20B	1361			
☐ C-FEHT	Bell 206B JetRanger III	3141	N5758G	0080	0195	1 AN 250-C20B	1451			
☐ C-GCHE	Bell 206B JetRanger	1249		0074	0195	1 AN 250-C20	1451			
☐ C-FBHI	Eurocopter (Aerosp.) AS350D AStar	1096	C-FWWW	0079	0598	1 LY LTS101-600A.3	1950			

BIG RIVER AIR, Ltd (formerly dba Loon Air) — Fort Smith & Four Mile Lake-SPB, N.W.T.

Loon·Air

PO Box 688, Fort Smith, Northwest Territories X0E 0P0, Canada ☎ (867) 872-3030 Tx: none Fax: (867) 872-5202 SITA: n/a
F: 1980 10 Head: Richard Funk Net: http://www.auroranet.nt.ca/bigriver Aircraft below MTOW 1361kg: Cessna 172 (on Wheels) & Cessna 180 (on Floats / Wheel-Skis)

☐ C-GAIX	Cessna A185F Skywagon II	18503890		0079		1 CO IO-520-D	1520			Floats / Wheel-Skis
☐ C-GVYE	Cessna A185F Skywagon II	18503778		0079	0998	1 CO IO-520-D	1520			Floats / Wheel-Skis
☐ C-GFZT	Cessna U206F Stationair II	U20603406		0076	0395	1 CO IO-520-F	1724			Floats / Wheels
☐ C-GIJL	Cessna 210L Centurion II	21061226		0076		1 CO IO-520-L	1724			
☐ C-GPMC	Cessna 210L Centurion II	21060888	N5272V	0075	0397	1 CO IO-520-L	1724			
☐ C-GTOI	De Havilland DHC-2 Beaver I	712	N6084	0053	0694	1 PW R-985	2313			Floats / Wheel-Skis
☐ C-GKYG	De Havilland DHC-3 Otter	261	N2750	0058	1094	1 PZL ASh-62IR-M18	3818			cvtd DHC-3 PW / Floats

BIG ROCK HELICOPTERS, Inc. — High Level, Alta.

Box 3597, High Level, Alberta T0H 1Z0, Canada ☎ (780) 926-5558 Tx: none Fax: (780) 926-5518 SITA: n/a
F: 1998 n/a Head: Roch Dellare Net: n/a

☐ C-GLQI	Bell 206B JetRanger II	1964	N49694	0076	0298	1 AN 250-C20	1451			

BIG SALMON AIR, Ltd — Whitehorse, Y.T.

PO Box 6001, Whitehorse, Yukon Territory Y1A 5L7, Canada ☎ (867) 668-4608 Tx: n/a Fax: none SITA: n/a
F: 1988 n/a Head: David George Young Net: n/a

☐ C-FZNL	Cessna A185E Skywagon	18501826		0070	0798	1 CO IO-520-D	1520			Floats / Wheel-Skis
☐ C-GJSR	Cessna U206C Super Skywagon	U206-1106	N29136	0068	1292	1 CO IO-520-F	1633			Floats / Wheel-Skis
☐ C-GMEK	Cessna U206F Stationair II	U20603083	N3755C	0076	1198	1 CO IO-520-F	1633			Floats / Wheel-Skis

BIRCH LAKE LODGE & Air Service (1010648 Ontario, Inc. dba / Seasonal May-October ops only) — Red Lake, Ont.

Box 408, 14 Mill Road, Red Lake, Ontario P0V 2M0, Canada ☎ (807) 727-2158 Tx: n/a Fax: (807) 727-3073 SITA: n/a
F: 1991 n/a Head: n/a Net: n/a

☐ C-GQVL	Cessna U206G Stationair 6 II	U20605168		0079	0991	1 CO IO-520-F	1633			Floats
☐ C-FFUU	Noorduyn Norseman IV	74	RCAF 3530	0040	1094	1 PW R-1340	3089			Floats

BLACKCOMB HELICOPTERS, Ltd — Whistler, B.C.

8621 Fissile Lane, Whistler, British Columbia V0N 1B8, Canada ☎ (604) 938-1700 Tx: n/a Fax: (604) 932-3776 SITA: n/a
F: 1989 n/a Head: n/a Net: n/a

☐ C-FYYA	Eurocopter (Aerosp.) AS350BA AStar	2295	ZK-HOU	0089	0896	1 TU Arriel 1B	2100			
☐ C-GSKI	Eurocopter (Aerosp.) AS350BA AStar	1650	ZK-HRK	0082	0697	1 TU Arriel 1B	2100			cvtd AS350B
☐ C-GYYR	Eurocopter (Aerosp.) AS350B AStar	1675	ZK-HBT	0083	0198	1 TU Arriel 1B	1950			

BLACK SHEEP AVIATION & Cattle, Co. Ltd — Whitehorse, Y.T.

Box 4087, Whitehorse, Yukon Territory Y1A 3S9, Canada ☎ (867) 668-7761 Tx: none Fax: (867) 668-6922 SITA: n/a
F: 1993 n/a Head: n/a Net: n/a Aircraft below MTOW 1361kg: Piper PA-18.

☐ C-GJZO	Cessna TU206G Turbo Stationair 6 II	U20606149		0081	0597	1 CO TSIO-520-M	1633			Floats / Wheel-Skis
☐ C-GMCW	De Havilland DHC-3 Otter	108	N5339G	0056	0897	1 PW R-1340	3629			Floats / Wheel-Skis
☐ C-GSUV	De Havilland DHC-3 Otter	376	N445FD	0060	0495	1 PZL ASh-62IR-M18	3629			cvtd DHC-3 PW / Floats / Wheel-Skis

BLACK TUSK HELICOPTER, Inc. — Squamish, B.C.

PO Box 1469, Squamish, British Columbia V0N 3G0, Canada ☎ (604) 898-4800 Tx: none Fax: (604) 898-9688 SITA: n/a
F: 1994 n/a Head: Mike Saindon Net: n/a

☐ C-GSEE	Bell 206B JetRanger	451	N95SB	0069	0594	1 AN 250-C20	1451			cvtd 206A
☐ C-FWQU	Bell 214B-1 BigLifter	28029	N3999N	0078	1095	1 LY T5508D	5670			
☐ C-FZVT	Bell 214B-1 BigLifter	28016	LN-OSG	0077	0597	1 LY T5508D	5670			

BLADES AVIATION, Ltd — Pitt Meadows, B.C.

5-11465 Baynes Road South, Pitt Meadows, British Columbia V3Y 2B4, Canada ☎ (604) 465-1662 Tx: none Fax: (604) 465-1663 SITA: n/a
F: 1996 n/a Head: Allan Kaake Net: n/a

☐ C-FNBA	Eurocopter (Aerosp.) AS350BA AStar	1495	9M-BMV	0081	0199	1 TU Arriel 1B	2100			cvtd AS350B
☐ C-GVYI	Eurocopter (Aerosp.) AS350D AStar	1041		0079	0296	1 LY LTS101-600A.2	1950			

BLOK AIR, Ltd (Seasonal May-October ops only) — Thompson-SPB, Man.

BLOK AIR

Box 385, Thompson, Manitoba R8N 1N2, Canada ☎ (204) 778-8225 Tx: none Fax: (204) 778-8243 SITA: n/a
F: 1995 n/a Head: Mark Blok Net: n/a

☐ C-FSSZ	Cessna A185E Skywagon	185-0993		0066	0795	1 CO IO-520-D	1520			Floats
☐ C-FXFO	De Havilland DHC-3 Otter	48	55-2975	0055	0497	1 PW R-1340	3629			Floats

BLUE SKY AVIATION (Control Power, Ltd dba) — Edmonton, Alta.

52327 Range Road 214, Sherwood Park, Alberta T8E 1A5, Canada ☎ (780) 922-6797 Tx: none Fax: (780) 922-6798 SITA: n/a
F: 1997 n/a Head: n/a Net: n/a

☐ C-FHMY	Cessna A185F Skywagon	18502349		0074	0597	1 CO IO-520-D	1520			

BLUE WATER AVIATION SERVICES, Ltd — Silver Falls, Man.

Box 20, Pine Falls, Manitoba R0E 1M0, Canada ☎ (204) 367-2762 Tx: none Fax: (204) 367-2157 SITA: n/a
F: 1995 n/a Head: Ed Gaffray Net: n/a

☐ C-GFVZ	Cessna A185F Skywagon	18503058		0076	0596	1 CO IO-520-D	1520			Floats / Wheel-Skis
☐ C-GGRJ	Cessna A185F Skywagon	18502745		0075	1095	1 CO IO-520-D	1520			Floats / Wheel-Skis
☐ C-FCUW	Cessna 337 Super Skymaster	337-0009		0065	1095	2 CO IO-360-C/D	1905			
☐ C-FIFP	De Havilland DHC-3 Otter	73		0055	1095	1 PZL ASh-62IR-M18	3629			Floats / Wheel Skis / cvtd DHC-3 PW
☐ C-FVQD	De Havilland DHC-3 Otter	466		0067	0498	1 PW R-1340	3629			Floats / Wheel-Skis
☐ C-GBTU	De Havilland DHC-3 Otter	209	IM-1711	0057	0998	1 PW R-1340	3629			Floats / Wheel-Skis

BOLTON LAKE AIR SERVICES, Inc. (Affiliated with Bolton Lake Lodge, Inc. / Seasonal May-October ops only) — Winnipeg-St. Andrews, Man.

505 Airline Road, St. Andrews, Manitoba R1A 3P4, Canada ☎ (204) 339-4010 Tx: none Fax: (204) 339-4224 SITA: n/a
F: 1995 n/a Head: n/a Net: n/a

☐ C-GYWE	Piper PA-32-260 Cherokee SIX	32-141	N3305W	0065	0596	1 LY O-540-E4B5	1542			
☐ C-GMOW	Britten-Norman BN-2A-27 Islander	179	TF-REJ	0070	0595	2 LY O-540-E4C5	2994			
☐ C-GTZK	Piper PA-31-310 Navajo	31-381	N9SG	0069	0698	2 LY TIO-540-A1A	2948			
☐ CF-BSB	Noorduyn Norseman V	N29-15		0046	0595	1 PW R-1340	3420			Floats

BOMBARDIER – Amphibious Flight Operations (Bombardier, Inc. dba / Member of Bombardier Aerospace) — Montreal-Dorval, Qué.

Box 6087, Station Centre-Ville, Montreal, Québec H3C 3G9, Canada ☎ (514) 855-6246 Tx: none Fax: (514) 855-7315 SITA: n/a
F: 1997 n/a Head: Ralph Hanson Net: n/a Operates the CL-215 on commercial Tanker/Water Bombing-missions as required but offers all its aircraft also for sale or lease.

☐ C-FTXB	Canadair CL-215 (CL-215-1A10)	1007		0069	0697	2 PW R-2800-CA3	19731	Tanker		225 / Amphibian

39 registration type of aircraft cn/fn ex/ex* mfd del powered by mtow kg configuration selcal name/fln/specialitites/remarks

registration	type of aircraft	cn/fn	ex/ex*	mfd	del	powered by	mtow kg	configuration	selcal	name/fln/specialitites/remarks
☐ C-GBXQ	Canadair CL-215 (CL-215-1A10)	1076		0083	0998	2 PW R-2800-CA3	19731	Tanker		261 / Amphibian
☐ C-GOFM	Canadair CL-215 (CL-215-1A10)	1090		0086	0998	2 PW R-2800-CA3	19731	Tanker		264 / Amphibian
☐ C-GOFN	Canadair CL-215 (CL-215-1A10)	1097	C-GKDN	0087	1098	2 PW R-2800-CA3	19731	Tanker		265 / Amphibian
☐ C-GOFO	Canadair CL-215 (CL-215-1A10)	1102	C-GBPU	0087	1298	2 PW R-2800-CA3	19731	Tanker		266 / Amphibian
☐ C-GOFP	Canadair CL-215 (CL-215-1A10)	1103	C-GKDN	0087	1298	2 PW R-2800-CA3	19731	Tanker		267 / Amphibian
☐ C-GOFR	Canadair CL-215 (CL-215-1A10)	1104		0087	0898	2 PW R-2800-CA3	19731	Tanker		268 / Amphibian
☐ C-GUKM	Canadair CL-215 (CL-215-1A10)	1049		0076	1298	2 PW R-2800-CA3	19731	Tanker		260 / Amphibian

BONANZA AIR (3349209 Canada, Inc. dba / formerly Bonanza Aviation, Ltd)
Dawson City, Y.T.

Box 284, Dawson City, Yukon Territory Y0B 1G0, Canada ☎ (867) 993-6904 Tx: none Fax: (867) 993-5815 SITA: n/a
F: 1987 ⋌⋌⋌ 3 Head: Marco Giovanoli Net: n/a Aircraft below MTOW 1361kg: Beech Bonanza F35

| ☐ C-GGVU | Cessna U206G Stationair 6 II | U20605050 | N5013H | 0079 | 0293 | 1 CO IO-520-F | 1633 | | | |

BONNYVILLE AIR SERVICES (1980), Ltd
Bonnyville, Alta.

Box 7599, Bonnyville, Alberta T9N 2H9, Canada ☎ (780) 826-6885 Tx: none Fax: (780) 826-7195 SITA: n/a
F: 1980 ⋌⋌⋌ n/a Head: Terry Spence Net: n/a Aircraft / Ag-aircraft below MTOW 1361 / 5000 kg: Cessna A188B

| ☐ C-GWQW | Cessna U206E Super Skywagon | U20601573 | N9173M | 0070 | 1193 | 1 CO IO-520-F | 1633 | | | |

BORDER CITY AVIATION, Ltd
Lloydminster, Alta.

Box 963, Lloydminster, Alberta S9V 0Y9, Canada ☎ (403) 875-5834 Tx: none Fax: (403) 875-5834 SITA: n/a
F: 1985 ⋌⋌⋌ n/a Head: Richard Bell Net: n/a Aircraft below MTOW 1361kg: Cessna 150 / 152 / 182 & Piper PA-28

| ☐ C-FOOO | Piper PA-31-310 Navajo | 31-167 | | 0068 | 0299 | 2 LY TIO-540-A1A | 2948 | | | |

BRANTFORD FLIGHT CENTRE (Division of Brantford Flying Club)
Brantford, Ont.

Box 903, Brantford, Ontario N3T 5S1, Canada ☎ (519) 753-1241 Tx: none Fax: (519) 753-3617 SITA: n/a
F: n/a ⋌⋌⋌ n/a Head: Phil Quinlan Net: n/a Aircraft below MTOW 1361kg: Cessna 152 & 172

| ☐ C-GBWM | Piper PA-23-250 Aztec E | 27-4721 | N14157 | 0071 | | 2 LY IO-540-C4B5 | 2359 | | | |

BRASSARD AIR SERVICE, Enr. (2541-8377 Québec, Inc. dba)
Sept-Iles, Qué.

40 Ungava, Sept-Iles, Québec G4R 4E3, Canada ☎ (418) 962-5944 Tx: none Fax: none SITA: n/a
F: 1987 ⋌⋌⋌ 3 Head: Marc Brassard Net: n/a

| ☐ C-GCCT | Cessna A185F Skywagon | 18502432 | | 0074 | 0389 | 1 CO IO-520-D | 1520 | | | Floats |
| ☐ C-FMPR | De Havilland DHC-2 Beaver I | 971 | | 0056 | 0797 | 1 PW R-985 | 2313 | | | lsf Aero Nord-Est / Floats |

BROCK AIR SERVICES, Ltd = BRD
Brockville & Kingston, Ont.

BROCK

4620 Airport Road, RR4, Brockville, Ontario K6V 5T4, Canada ☎ (613) 342-4511 Tx: n/a Fax: (613) 342-4588 SITA: n/a
F: 1978 ⋌⋌⋌ 8 Head: Francis D. Glover ICAO: BROCK AIR Net: http://www.plan-net.com/brockair Aircraft below MTOW 1361 kg: Cessna 172.

| ☐ C-GJGJ | Cessna 421B Golden Eagle | 421B0905 | | 0075 | 1091 | 2 CO GTSIO-520-H | 3379 | | | |

BROUGHAM GEOQUEST, Ltd
Calgary, Alta.

3100-205 5th Avenue SW, Calgary, Alberta T2P 2V7, Canada ☎ (403) 262-1838 Tx: n/a Fax: none SITA: n/a
F: 1981 ⋌⋌⋌ 2 Head: Douglas J. Rowe Net: n/a

| ☐ C-GORP | Twin (Aero) Grand Commander 680FL | 680FL-1663-12 | N4528E | 0067 | 0990 | 2 LY IGSO-540-B1A | 3856 | Photo / Survey | | |

BRUCELANDAIR INTERNATIONAL (138883 Canada, Inc. dba)
Wiarton, Ont.

BRUCELANDAIR

RR 2, Wiarton, Ontario N0H 2T0, Canada ☎ (519) 534-3737 Tx: none Fax: (519) 534-4848 SITA: n/a
F: 1985 ⋌⋌⋌ 12 Head: Mervyn D. Cowen Net: n/a Aircraft below MTOW 1361kg: Cessna 172.

☐ C-GNNN	Cessna U206F Stationair II	U20602728		0075	0398	1 CO IO-520-F	1633	Pax		
☐ C-GGNA	Piper PA-23-250 Aztec C	27-3757	N6463Y	0067	1195	2 LY IO-540-C4B5	2359	Pax		
☐ C-GPVN	Piper PA-31-310 Navajo B	31-7400979	TF-EGT	0074	1195	2 LY TIO-540-A2C	2948	Surveyer		
☐ C-GISS	Twin (Aero) RPM Commander 800L	680FLP-1497-15	N77WD	0065		2 LY IO-720-B1BD	3856	Surveyer		cvtd Grand 680FLP

BUFFALO AIRWAYS, Ltd = J4 / BFL
Hay River, N.W.T.

Buffalo AIRWAYS

1000 Buffalo Drive, Hay River Airport, Hay River, Northwest Territories X0E 0R9, Canada ☎ (867) 874-3333 Tx: none Fax: (867) 874-3572 SITA: n/a
F: 1970 ⋌⋌⋌ 62 Head: Joe W.C. McBryan ICAO: BUFFALO Net: n/a

☐ C-FUPT	Cessna A185E Skywagon	185-1075		0066	0792	1 CO IO-520-D	1520			141
☐ C-FYFJ	Cessna A185F Skywagon II	18503797	N9913Q	0079	0696	1 CO IO-520-D	1520			142
☐ C-GIWJ	Beech Travel Air 95	TD-32	N2707Y	0058	0199	2 LY O-360-A1A	1814			
☐ C-GWCB	Beech Travel Air B95	TD-369	N9914R	0060	0792	2 LY O-360-A1A	1860			
☐ C-GYFM	Beech Travel Air 95	TD-202		0059	0199	2 LY O-360-A1A	1814			
☐ CF-SAN	Noorduyn Norseman V	N29-29		0047	0395	1 PW R-1340	3357			
☐ C-FCUE	Boeing (Douglas) DC-3C (C-47A-10-DK)	12983	NC41407	0042	1292	2 PW R-1830	12202	Freighter		Mel Bryan / ex Transport Canada colors
☐ C-FDTB	Boeing (Douglas) DC-3C (C-47A-15-DK)	12597	CF-TEC	0042	1292	2 PW R-1830	11884	Freighter		std Red Deer in ex Transport Canada cs
☐ C-FDTH	Boeing (Douglas) DC-3C (C-47A-15-DK)	12591	CF-TEB	0042	0596	2 PW R-1830	11884	Freighter		std Red Deer in ex Transport Canada cs
☐ C-FFAY	Boeing (Douglas) DC-3C (C-47-DL)	4785	N47218	0042	0993	2 PW R-1830	12202	Freighter		
☐ C-FLFR	Boeing (Douglas) DC-3C (C-47A-20-DK)	13155	KG563	0044	0193	2 PW R-1830	12202	Freighter		
☐ C-FROD	Boeing (Douglas) DC-3C (C-47A-20-DK)	13028	C-GPNW	0044	1080	2 PW R-1830	11430	Freighter		std Red Deer in ex CAF colors
☐ C-GJKM	Boeing (Douglas) DC-3C (C-47A-25-DK)	13580	CAF 12946	0042	1080	2 PW R-1830	12202	Freighter		
☐ C-GPNR	Boeing (Douglas) DC-3C (C-47A-25-DK)	13333	CAF 12932	0042	1080	2 PW R-1830	12202	Freighter		
☐ C-GWIR	Boeing (Douglas) DC-3C (C-47A-20-DL)	9371	N18262	0042	0191	2 PW R-1830	12202	Y29		Y29
☐ C-GWZS	Boeing (Douglas) DC-3C (C-47A-5-DK)	12327	CAF 12913	0042	0688	2 PW R-1830	12202	Y29		Y29
☐ C-FNJE	Consolidated PBY-5A Canso	CV-437	RCAF 11094	0044	0696	2 PW R-1830-92S	13835	Tanker		702 / Amphibian
☐ C-FOFI	Consolidated PBY-5A Canso	CV-343	RCAF 11047	0043	0696	2 PW R-1830-92S	13835	Tanker		703 / Amphibian
☐ C-FPQM	Consolidated PBY-5A Canso	CV-425		0040	0696	2 PW R-1830-92S	13835	Tanker		714 / Amphibian
☐ C-FUAW	Consolidated PBY-5A Canso	CV-201	RCAF 11024	0040	0597	2 PW R-1830-92	13835	Tanker		708 / Amphibian
☐ C-GBPD	Canadair CL-215 (CL-215-1A10)	1084		0086	0495	2 PW R-2800-CA3	19731	Tanker		291 / lsf/opf N.W.T. Gvmt / Amphibian
☐ C-GBYU	Canadair CL-215 (CL-215-1A10)	1083	C-GKEA*	0086	0495	2 PW R-2800-CA3	19731	Tanker		290 / lsf/opf N.W.T. Gvmt / Amphibian
☐ C-GCSX	Canadair CL-215 (CL-215-1A10)	1088	C-GKEA*	0086	0495	2 PW R-2800-CA3	19731	Tanker		295 / lsf/opf N.W.T. Gvmt / Amphibian
☐ C-GDHN	Canadair CL-215 (CL-215-1A10)	1089	C-GKEE*	0086	0495	2 PW R-2800-CA3	19731	Tanker		296 / lsf/opf N.W.T. Gvmt / Amphibian
☐ C-FAVO	Curtiss C-46D-10-CU Commando	33242	N9891Z	0045	0295	2 PW R-2800	21772	Freighter		Arctic Thunder
☐ C-GTPO	Curtiss C-46F-1-CU Commando	22556	N519AC	0044	0693	2 PW R-2800	21772	Freighter		
☐ C-FIQM	Boeing (Douglas) DC-4 (C-54G-15-DO)	36088 / DO 482	N4218S	0045	0292	4 PW R-2000	33113	Tanker/Freighter		457 / Arctic Trader
☐ C-GBNV	Boeing (Douglas) DC-4 (C-54G-5-DO)	35988 / DO 382	N3303F	0045	0395	4 PW R-2000	30241	Tanker/Freighter		456
☐ C-GCTF	Boeing (Douglas) DC-4 (C-54E-5-DO)	27281 / DO 227	N51819	0045	0995	4 PW R-2000	33475	Tanker/Freighter		58
☐ C-GPSH	Boeing (Douglas) DC-4 (C-54A-1-DO)	7458 / DO 66	N7171H	0044	0291	4 PW R-2000	33112	Freighter		Arctic Distributor

BUSH LAND AIRWAYS, Ltd (formerly Northern Missionary Fellowship, Inc. dba)
Baie-du-Poste, Qué. & Moosonee, Ont.

Box 267, Moosonee, Ontario P0L 1Y0, Canada ☎ (705) 336-2966 Tx: n/a Fax: (705) 336-2460 SITA: n/a
F: 1979 ⋌⋌⋌ 2 Head: n/a Net: n/a

☐ C-FYJR	Cessna A185E Skywagon	185-1520		0069		1 CO IO-520-D	1520			Floats / Wheel-Skis
☐ C-FBGB	Cessna U206E Super Skywagon	U20601514		0070	0689	1 CO IO-520-F	1633			Floats / Wheel-Skis
☐ C-GGSV	Cessna U206G Stationair 6 II	U20605861		0080		1 CO IO-520-F	1633			Floats / Wheel-Skis
☐ C-GSNU	Cessna 207A Stationair 7 II	20700491	N6351H	0079		1 CO IO-520-F	1724			

BUSINESS FLIGHTS (414660 Alberta, Ltd / Subsidiary of North American Airlines, Ltd)
Calgary, Alta.

Business Flights

Box 630, 1441 Aviation Park NE, Calgary, Alberta T2E 8M7, Canada ☎ (403) 275-7700 Tx: none Fax: (403) 275-5947 SITA: n/a
F: 1946 ⋌⋌⋌ 7 Head: Don G. Hollier Net: n/a

| ☐ C-GVCA | Learjet 35 | 35-043 | | 0076 | 0376 | 2 GA TFE731-2-2B | 7711 | | | |

CALGARY POLICE SERVICE – Air Services Unit (Division of The City of Calgary)
Calgary, Alta.

133 6th Avenue SE, Calgary, Alberta T2G 4Z1, Canada ☎ (403) 250-5735 Tx: none Fax: (403) 291-0086 SITA: n/a
F: 1995 ⋌⋌⋌ n/a Head: Insp. Bill Webb Net: www.gov.calgary.ab.ca/police/ Non commercial provincial government organisation conducting police mission flights.

| ☐ C-FCPS | MD Helicopters MD 520N (Hughes 500N) | LN024 | N599DB | 0092 | 0595 | 1 AN 250-C20R | 1520 | | | HAWC 1 |

CALM AIR = MO / CAV (Partenaire CANADIEN / CANADIAN Partner) (Calm Air International Ltd dba/Associated with Canadian Airlines International Ltd)
Thompson, Man.

CalmAir
Canadian Partner

90 Thompson Drive, Thompson, Manitoba R8N 1Y8, Canada ☎ (204) 778-6471 Tx: none Fax: (204) 778-6954 SITA: YTHMOHQ
F: 1960 ⋌⋌⋌ 230 Head: Carl A. Morberg IATA: 622 ICAO: CALM AIR Net: http://www.calmair.com
Scheduled commuter services are operated on behalf of Canadian / Canadien as a Partenaire CANADIEN / CANADIAN Partner (in such colours & both titles) using CP flight designators.

☐ C-GALP	Piper PA-31-350 Navajo Chieftain	31-7405441	N54317	0074		2 LY TIO-540-J2BD	3175	Y9		
☐ C-FQBV	De Havilland DHC-6 Twin Otter 100	103		0068	0377	2 PWC PT6A-20	5252	Y19		
☐ C-FQXW	De Havilland DHC-6 Twin Otter 200	121	N1372T	0068	1171	2 PWC PT6A-20	5252	Y19		
☐ C-FTJV	Saab 340B (Plus)	340B-366	SE-C66*	0094	1294	2 GE CT7-9B	13155	Y34		
☐ C-FTJW	Saab 340B (Plus)	340B-377	SE-C77*	0095	1294	2 GE CT7-9B	13155	Y34		
☐ N587MA	Saab 340B	340B-166	SE-F66*	0089	0597	2 GE CT7-9B	13155	Y34		lsf Saab
☐ C-FMAK	BAe (HS) 748-257 Srs 2A	1668 / 142		0069	1279	2 RR Dart 534-2	20183	Y36		

☐ C-GDOP	BAe (HS) 748-283 Srs 2A	1745 / 226	F-ODQQ	0076	0188	2 RR Dart 534-2	20183	Y36		
☐ C-GEPB	BAe (HS) 748-254 Srs 2A	1686 / 156	9G-ABX	0070	0687	2 RR Dart 534-2	20183	Y36		
☐ C-GHSC	BAe (HS) 748-372 Srs 2B	1790 / 271	G-BJTL	0081	0597	2 RR Dart 536-2	21092	Y36		
☐ C-GSBF	BAe (HS) 748-210 Srs 2A	1662 / 143	G-11-3*	0069	1084	2 RR Dart 534-2	20183	Y36		cvtd 748-227

CAMERON AIR SERVICE, Inc. Toronto-City Centre, Ont.

107 Ballacaine Drive, Etobicoke, Ontario M8Y 4B9, Canada ☎ (416) 233-7663 Tx: none Fax: (416) 203-2037 SITA: n/a
F: 1992 ✱✱✱ 2 Head: Graham Wishart Net: n/a

☐ C-FXWH	Cessna U206C Super Skywagon	U206-1170		0068	0492	1 CO IO-550-F	1633			Amphibian / Wheels
☐ C-GGSG	Cessna TU206G Turbo Stationair 6 II	U20605852		0080	0597	1 CO TSIO-520-M	1724			Amphibian / Wheels

CAMPBELL HELICOPTERS, Ltd (formerly Pender Holdings, Ltd – Flight Operations) Abbotsford, B.C.

Box 2008, Clearbrook Postal Stn., Abbotsford, British Columbia V2T 3T8, Canada ☎ (604) 852-1122 Tx: none Fax: (604) 852-4982 SITA: n/a
F: 1987 ✱✱✱ 50 Head: Bruce H. Campbell Net: n/a

☐ C-FBWR	Bell 204B	2015 / 2		0064	0491	1 LY T5311A	3856			
☐ C-FFJY	Bell 205A-1	30002	VH-NGM	0068	0889	1 LY T5313B	4309			
☐ C-FJTG	Bell 205A-1	30104	N8138J	0072	0592	1 LY T5313B	4309			
☐ C-FMQN	Bell 205A-1	30082		0070		1 LY T5313B	4309			
☐ C-FNTR	Bell 205A-1	30297	N1067S	0078	0790	1 LY T5313B	4309			
☐ C-GPET	Bell 205A-1	30209	N205KA	0075		1 LY T5313B	4309			
☐ C-FMPZ	Bell 212	30528	HC-BOI	0071	1195	2 PWC PT6T-3 TwinPac	5080			
☐ C-GLOG	Sikorsky S-58ET	58-827	N17FT	0368	0195	1 PWC PT6T-3 TwinPac	5897			rebuilt/cvtd S-58E

CANADA JET CHARTERS, Ltd (formerly Canada Learjet, Ltd) Vancouver-Int'l, B.C.

4380 Agar Drive, Vancouver Airport South, Richmond, British Columbia V7B 1A3, Canada ☎ (604) 273-1166 Tx: none Fax: (604) 273-9332 SITA: n/a
F: 1975 ✱✱✱ 30 Head: Kenneth Jens Net: http://www.canadajet.com

☐ C-GCJN	Cessna 550 Citation II	550-0371	N551MC	0079	0798	2 PWC JT15D-4	6033			
☐ C-GYCJ	Cessna 550 Citation II	550-0561	PT-OYP	0087	1098	2 PWC JT15D-4	6033			
☐ C-FBFP	Learjet 35	35-038	VH-ELJ	0075	0686	2 GA TFE731-2-2B	7711			
☐ C-GDJH	Learjet 35A	35A-353		0080	1280	2 GA TFE731-2-2B	8165			
☐ C-GRMJ	Learjet 35A	35A-664	N117RJ	0090	0995	2 GA TFE731-2-2B	8165			
☐ C-FCLJ	Learjet 55	55-118		0085	0485	2 GA TFE731-3AR-2B	9525			

CANADA 3000 Airlines, Ltd = 2T / CMM (formerly Air 2000 Airlines, Ltd) Toronto-Int'l, Ont.

27 Fasken Drive, Toronto, Ontario M9W 1K6, Canada ☎ (416) 674-0257 Tx: none Fax: (416) 674-0256 SITA: n/a
F: 1988 ✱✱✱ 1800 Head: John M.S. Lecky IATA: 570 ICAO: ELITE Net: http://www.canada3000.com/

☐ C-GVXA	Airbus Industrie A320-212	397	N541LF	0092	0593	2 CFMI CFM56-5A3	75500	Y168	EF-RS	lsf ILFC / cvtd -211
☐ C-GVXB	Airbus Industrie A320-212	409	F-WWDU*	0093	0693	2 CFMI CFM56-5A3	77000	Y168	EQ-AR	lsf ILFC / sub-lst RYN / cvtd -231
☐ C-GVXC	Airbus Industrie A320-212	427	F-WWIH*	0094	0494	2 CFMI CFM56-5A3	77000	Y168		lsf ILFC / cvtd -211
☐ C-GVXD	Airbus Industrie A320-212	579	C-WWDU*	0096	0396	2 CFMI CFM56-5A3	77000	Y168	LS-GK	lsf ILFC
☐ C-GVXE	Airbus Industrie A320-212	645	F-WWDL*	0097	0197	2 CFMI CFM56-5A3	77000	Y168		lsf ILFC
☐ C-GVXF	Airbus Industrie A320-212	671	F-WWDE*	0097	0497	2 CFMI CFM56-5A3	77000	Y168	KR-FJ	lsf ILFC
☐ C-FOOE	Boeing 757-28A	24369 / 226		0089	0589	2 RR RB211-535E4	113398	Y226	JL-MP	lsf BBAM/tbsublst FCL in summer,05-1099
☐ C-FOOH	Boeing 757-23A (ET)	24293 / 220	N989AN	0489	0595	2 RR RB211-535E4	113398	Y226	HS-MQ	lsf AWAS
☐ C-FOON	Boeing 757-28A	28161 / 723		0096	0996	2 RR RB211-535E4	113398	Y226	PR-JM	lsf ILFC
☐ C-FXOF	Boeing 757-28A	24544 / 280		0090	0490	2 RR RB211-535E4	113398	Y226	JQ-HK	lsf ILFC
☐ C-FXOK	Boeing 757-23A (ET)	24924 / 333	5Y-BHG	0090	0391	2 RR RB211-535E4	113398	Y226	AR-BJ	lsf AWAS
☐ C-FXOO	Boeing 757-2Q8	25621 / 457		0092	0592	2 RR RB211-535E4	113398	Y226	BS-AF	lsf ILFC
☐ C-GGWA	Airbus Industrie A330-202	205	F-WWKK*	0098	0598	2 GE CF6-80E1A4	230000	Y340	LP-HS	lsf ILFC
☐ C-GGWB	Airbus Industrie A330-202	211	F-WWKL*	0098	0598	2 GE CF6-80E1A4	230000	Y340	LP-HR	lsf ILFC
☐ C-GGWC	Airbus Industrie A330-202					2 GE CF6-80E1A4	230000	Y340		to be lsf ILFC 0599

CANADIAN AIR-CRANE, Ltd (formerly Erickson Air Crane (Canada), Ltd) Delta, B.C.

7293 Wilson Ave, Delta, British Columbia V4G 1E5, Canada ☎ (604) 940-1715 Tx: none Fax: (604) 940-1735 SITA: n/a
F: 1986 ✱✱✱ 12 Head: Ron Brooks Net: http://www.air-crane.com/

☐ C-FCRN	Sikorsky S-64E Skycrane	64061	N172AC	0068	0695	2 PW JFTD12-4A	19051			lsf Erickson Air Crane
☐ C-GESG	Sikorsky S-64E Skycrane	64065	N157AC	0068	0297	2 PW JFTD12-4A	19051			lsf Erickson Air Crane

CANADIAN AIRWAYS, Ltd (Seasonal April-November ops only) Chapleau, Ont.

PO Box 1448, Chapleau, Ontario P0M 1K0, Canada ☎ (705) 864-0765 Tx: none Fax: (705) 864-1292 SITA: n/a
F: 1996 ✱✱✱ n/a Head: n/a Net: n/a

☐ C-GUBS	De Havilland DHC-2 Beaver I	1124	N9751F	0057	1296	1 PW R-985	2313			Floats

CANADIAN – CANADIEN = CP / CDN (Canadian Airl.Ltd/Lignes Aériennes Canadien Ltée dba/Subs.of Canadian Airl. Corp./Member of Oneworld Alliance) Calgary, Alta.

Scotia Centre 2800, 700-2nd Street S.W., Calgary, Alberta T2P 2W2, Canada ☎ (403) 294-2000 Tx: 03821124 pwa exec cg Fax: (403) 294-2066 SITA: n/a
F: 1987 ✱✱✱ 15500 Head: Harry Steele IATA: 018 ICAO: CANADIAN Net: http://www.cdnair.ca
Scheduled Partenaire CANADIEN/CANADIAN Partner services are operated on behalf of CP/in conjuntion with: AIR ALMA, AIR GEORGIAN-Ontario Ontario Regional, AIR ST-PIERRE, CALM AIR, CANADIAN REGIONAL, INTER-CANADIAN & PACIFIC COASTAL AIRLINES – under each company. On order (subject to re-confirmation): further 10 Airbus Industrie A320-200.

☐ C-FACP	Boeing 737-2L9 (A)	22072 / 623	C2-RN9	0079	0487	2 PW JT8D-17 (HK3/AVA)	58105	C12Y88	JK-DM	728
☐ C-FCPM	Boeing 737-2T7 (A)	22761 / 850	G-DWHH	0082	0487	2 PW JT8D-17	58105	C12Y88	DL-BF	730
☐ C-FCPN	Boeing 737-2T7 (A)	22762 / 856	G-DGDP	0082	0487	2 PW JT8D-17	58105	C12Y88	EF-DH	731
☐ C-FHCP	Boeing 737-2T5 (A)	22024 / 641	EI-BPV	0080	0487	2 PW JT8D-17	53070	C12Y88	JK-EG	729
☐ C-GAPW	Boeing 737-275 (A)	20922 / 370	N127AW	0074	1187	2 PW JT8D-9A (HK3/AVA)	53070	C12Y88	NONE	739
☐ C-GBPW	Boeing 737-275 (A)	20958 / 391	N128AW	0075	0487	2 PW JT8D-9A (HK3/AVA)	53070	C12Y88	NONE	740
☐ C-GCPM	Boeing 737-217 (A)	21716 / 560	N1262E*	0079	0487	2 PW JT8D-17 (HK3/AVA)	56472	C12Y88	BE-GK	708
☐ C-GCPN	Boeing 737-217 (A)	21717 / 581		0079	0487	2 PW JT8D-17 (HK3/AVA)	56472	C12Y88	BE-HJ	709
☐ C-GCPO	Boeing 737-217 (A)	21718 / 584		0079	0487	2 PW JT8D-17 (HK3/AVA)	56472	C12Y88	BE-HK	710
☐ C-GCPP	Boeing 737-217 (A)	22255 / 666		0080	0487	2 PW JT8D-17	56472	C12Y88	DK-EG	711
☐ C-GCPQ	Boeing 737-217 (A)	22256 / 672		0080	0487	2 PW JT8D-17 (HK3/AVA)	56472	C12Y88	DK-EH	712
☐ C-GCPS	Boeing 737-217 (A)	22257 / 756		0081	0487	2 PW JT8D-17	56472	C12Y88	DK-GM	714
☐ C-GCPT	Boeing 737-217 (A)	22258 / 770		0081	0487	2 PW JT8D-17	56472	C12Y88	DL-AC	715 / lsf Arkia Leasing
☐ C-GCPU	Boeing 737-217 (A)	22259 / 771		0081	0487	2 PW JT8D-17 (HK3/AVA)	56472	C12Y88	BF-CM	716 / lsf TRIT
☐ C-GCPV	Boeing 737-217 (A)	22260 / 784		0081	0487	2 PW JT8D-17 (HK3/AVA)	58105	C12Y88	BF-DE	717 / lsf TRIT
☐ C-GCPW	Boeing 737-275 (A)	20959 / 395	N126AW	0075	1187	2 PW JT8D-9A (HK3/AVA)	53070	C12Y88	NONE	741
☐ C-GCPX	Boeing 737-217 (A)	22341 / 786		0081	0487	2 PW JT8D-17	58105	C12Y88	BF-DG	718 / lsf TRIT
☐ C-GCPY	Boeing 737-217 (A)	22342 / 810		0081	0487	2 PW JT8D-17 (HK3/AVA)	56472	C12Y88	BF-DH	719 / lsf TRIT
☐ C-GCPZ	Boeing 737-217 (A)	22658 / 861		0082	0487	2 PW JT8D-17	58105	C12Y88	DJ-BH	720
☐ C-GDPA	Boeing 737-2T2C (A)	22056 / 655		0080	0487	2 PW JT8D-17	58105	Y112/Combi	NONE	784/Yellowknife / opf Canadian North
☐ C-GEPW	Boeing 737-275 (A)	21115 / 425	N129AW	0075	0487	2 PW JT8D-9A (HK3/AVA)	53070	C12Y88	NONE	743
☐ C-GFCP	Boeing 737-217 (A)	22659 / 874		0082	0487	2 PW JT8D-17	56472	C12Y88	DJ-BK	721
☐ C-GFPW	Boeing 737-275C (A)	21294 / 481		0076	0487	2 PW JT8D-9A (HK3/AVA)	53070	C12Y88	NONE	752
☐ C-GGPW	Boeing 737-275 (A)	21639 / 539		0078	0487	2 PW JT8D-9A (HK3/AVA)	53070	C12Y88	NONE	744
☐ C-GIPW	Boeing 737-275 (A)	21712 / 556		0079	0487	2 PW JT8D-9A (HK3/AVA)	53070	C12Y88	NONE	745
☐ C-GJCP	Boeing 737-217 (A)	22728 / 911	N178EE*	0082	0487	2 PW JT8D-17A	56472	C12Y88	DJ-BL	722
☐ C-GJPW	Boeing 737-275 (A)	21713 / 598		0079	0487	2 PW JT8D-9A (HK3/AVA)	53070	C12Y88	NONE	746 / lsf TRIT
☐ C-GKCP	Boeing 737-217 (A)	22729 / 915		0082	0487	2 PW JT8D-17A (HK3/AVA)	56472	C12Y88	DL-BM	723 / lsf Arkia Leasing
☐ C-GKPW	Boeing 737-275 (A)	21819 / 627		0079	0487	2 PW JT8D-9A (HK3/AVA)	53070	C12Y88	NONE	748
☐ C-GMCP	Boeing 737-217 (A)	22864 / 945		0083	0487	2 PW JT8D-17A	56472	C12Y88	EJ-FH	724 / lsf Arkia Leasing
☐ C-GNDC	Boeing 737-242C (A)	21728 / 580		0079	0487	2 PW JT8D-9A (HK3/AVA)	53070	C12Y88	NONE	761
☐ C-GNDU	Boeing 737-242C (A)	22877 / 880		0082	0487	2 PW JT8D-9A	53070	C12Y88	NONE	762
☐ C-GNPW	Boeing 737-275 (A)	22159 / 684		0080	0487	2 PW JT8D-9A (HK3/AVA)	53070	C12Y88	NONE	751 / lsf TRIT
☐ C-GOPW	Boeing 737-275C (A)	22160 / 688	N8288V*	0080	0487	2 PW JT8D-17A	53070	Y112/Combi	NONE	782/Norman Wells / opf Canadian North
☐ C-GPPW	Boeing 737-275 (A)	22264 / 753		0081	0487	2 PW JT8D-9A	53070	C12Y88	NONE	753
☐ C-GQBB	Boeing 737-296 (A)	22276 / 665	N387PA	0080	0487	2 PW JT8D-9A	54204	C12Y88	BC-GJ	732
☐ C-GQBH	Boeing 737-296 (A)	22516 / 759	N389PA	0081	0487	2 PW JT8D-9A	54204	C12Y88	BC-GM	734
☐ C-GQCP	Boeing 737-217 (A)	22865 / 960		0083	0487	2 PW JT8D-17A (HK3/AVA)	56472	C12Y88	EJ-FK	725
☐ C-GRPW	Boeing 737-275 (A)	22266 / 765		0081	0487	2 PW JT8D-9A (HK3/AVA)	53070	C12Y88	NONE	755 / lsf TRIT
☐ C-GSPW	Boeing 737-275C (A)	22618 / 813		0081	0487	2 PW JT8D-17	53070	C12Y88	NONE	783 / lsf Arkia Leasing
☐ C-GTPW	Boeing 737-275 (A)	22807 / 824		0081	0487	2 PW JT8D-9A (HK3/AVA)	53070	C12Y88	NONE	756 / lsf TRIT
☐ C-GUPW	Boeing 737-275 (A)	22873 / 898		0082	0487	2 PW JT8D-9A (HK3/AVA)	53070	C12Y88	NONE	758 / lsf GECA
☐ C-GVPW	Boeing 737-275 (A)	22874 / 904		0082	0487	2 PW JT8D-9A (HK3/AVA)	53070	C12Y88	NONE	759
☐ C-GWPW	Boeing 737-275 (A)	23283 / 1109		0085	0487	2 PW JT8D-17A (HK3/AVA)	53070	C12Y88	HM-AL	760
☐ C-FDCA	Airbus Industrie A320-211	232	F-WWIY*	0091	1091	2 CFMI CFM56-5A1	75500	C24Y108	BJ-AQ	405 / lsf GECA
☐ C-FLSI	Airbus Industrie A320-211	283	F-WWBT*	0092	0392	2 CFMI CFM56-5A1	75500	C24Y108	BR-GP	407 / lsf GECA
☐ C-FLSS	Airbus Industrie A320-211	284	F-WWBU*	0092	0392	2 CFMI CFM56-5A1	75500	C24Y108	BR-GQ	408 / lsf GECA
☐ C-FLSU	Airbus Industrie A320-211	309	F-WWIJ*	0092	0592	2 CFMI CFM56-5A1	75500	C24Y108	BR-HK	411 / lsf GECA
☐ C-FMEQ	Airbus Industrie A320-211	302	F-WWIY*	0092	0592	2 CFMI CFM56-5A1	75500	C24Y108	BR-HJ	409

41 registration type of aircraft cn/fn ex/ex* mfd del powered by mtow kg configuration selcal name/fln/specialitites/remarks

registration	type of aircraft	cn/fn	ex/ex*	mfd	del	powered by	mtow kg	configuration	selcal	name/fln/specialitites/remarks
☐ C-FMES	Airbus Industrie A320-211	305	F-WWDE*	0092	0592	2 CFMI CFM56-5A1	75500	C24Y108	BR-GS	410
☐ C-FNVU	Airbus Industrie A320-211	403	F-WWBO*	0393	0194	2 CFMI CFM56-5A1	75500	C24Y108	DR-CH	415 / lsf GECA
☐ C-FNVV	Airbus Industrie A320-211	404	F-WWDF*	0393	0194	2 CFMI CFM56-5A1	75500	C24Y108	DR-CJ	416 / lsf GECA
☐ C-FPWD	Airbus Industrie A320-211	231	F-WWDV*	0091	0891	2 CFMI CFM56-5A1	75500	C24Y108	BH-PQ	404 / lsf GECA
☐ C-FPWE	Airbus Industrie A320-211	175	F-WWIN*	0091	0491	2 CFMI CFM56-5A1	75500	C24Y108	BH-LQ	402 / lsf GECA
☐ C-GPWG	Airbus Industrie A320-211	174	F-WWIM*	0091	0491	2 CFMI CFM56-5A1	75500	C24Y108	BH-KQ	401 / lsf GECA
☐ C-GQCA	Airbus Industrie A320-211	210	F-WWIC*	0091	0791	2 CFMI CFM56-5A1	75500	C24Y108	BH-MQ	403 / lsf GECA
☐ C-	Airbus Industrie A320-212	279	G-MONY	0092		2 CFMI CFM56-5A3	75500	C24Y108		406 / to be lsf ILFC 0699 / cvtd -211
☐ C-FCAB	Boeing 767-375 (ER)	24082 / 213	N6055X*	0088	0488	2 GE CF6-80C2B6	181437	C30Y180	EJ-CM	631
☐ C-FCAE	Boeing 767-375 (ER)	24083 / 215	N6046P*	0088	0588	2 GE CF6-80C2B6	181437	C30Y180	DL-FG	632
☐ C-FCAF	Boeing 767-375 (ER)	24084 / 219	N6038E*	0088	0588	2 GE CF6-80C2B6	181437	C30Y180	HJ-AL	633
☐ C-FCAG	Boeing 767-375 (ER)	24085 / 220	N6009F*	0088	0588	2 GE CF6-80C2B6	181437	C30Y180	HJ-BC	634
☐ C-FOCA	Boeing 767-375 (ER)	24575 / 311		0090	0690	2 GE CF6-80C2B6F	184612	C30Y180	CQ-AM	640
☐ C-FPCA	Boeing 767-375 (ER)	24306 / 258		0089	0489	2 GE CF6-80C2B6F	184612	C30Y180	DQ-CM	637
☐ C-FTCA	Boeing 767-375 (ER)	24307 / 259		0089	0489	2 GE CF6-80C2B6F	184612	C30Y180	DQ-CP	638
☐ C-FXCA	Boeing 767-375 (ER)	24574 / 302		0090	0490	2 GE CF6-80C2B6F	184612	C30Y180	CQ-AL	639
☐ C-GBZR	Boeing 767-38E (ER)	25404 / 411	HL7267	0092	0998	2 GE CF6-80C2B4F	184612	C30Y180	DR-CG	645 / lsf ILFC
☐ C-GDUZ	Boeing 767-38E (ER)	25347 / 399	HL7266	0091	1298	2 GE CF6-80C2B4F	184612	C30Y180	DR-CQ	646 / lsf ILFC
☐ C-GLCA	Boeing 767-375 (ER)	25120 / 361		0091	0491	2 GE CF6-80C2B6F	184612	C30Y180	KL-JQ	641
☐ C-GSCA	Boeing 767-375 (ER)	25121 / 372	B-2564	0491	0598	2 GE CF6-80C2B6F	184612	C30Y180	KL-MQ	642 / lsf TOMB
☐ C-	Boeing 767-375 (ER)					2 GE CF6-80C2B6F	184612	C30Y180		647 / to be lsf GECA 1099
☐ C-	Boeing 767-375 (ER)					2 GE CF6-80C2B6F	184612	C30Y180		648 / to be lsf GECA 1199
☐ C-FCRD	Boeing (Douglas) DC-10-30	47889 / 229	N6150Z	0076	0395	3 GE CF6-50C2	256280	C28Y236	DL-FK	912 / Pride of Canadian / lsf POTO
☐ C-FCRE	Boeing (Douglas) DC-10-30	47868 / 200	N42783	0075	0395	3 GE CF6-50C2	256280	C28Y236	DL-FM	911 / Spirit of Canadian / lsf POTO
☐ C-GBQQ	Boeing (Douglas) DC-10-30	46916 / 202	PP-VMD	0675	0398	3 GE CF6-50C2	256280	C28Y236	DL-GH	915 / lsf BBAM
☐ C-GCPC	Boeing (Douglas) DC-10-30	46540 / 268	PP-VMO	0078	0487	3 GE CF6-50C2	259455	C28Y236	DL-AB	901
☐ C-GCPD	Boeing (Douglas) DC-10-30	46541 / 281	PP-VMP	0079	0487	3 GE CF6-50C2	259455	C28Y236	HJ-BD	902
☐ C-GCPE	Boeing (Douglas) DC-10-30 (ER)	46542 / 295		0079	0487	3 GE CF6-50C2B	267619	C28Y228	HJ-AG	903 / cvtd -30
☐ C-GCPF	Boeing (Douglas) DC-10-30 (ER)	46543 / 341		0080	0487	3 GE CF6-50C2B	267619	C28Y228	DM-EH	904 / cvtd -30
☐ C-GCPG	Boeing (Douglas) DC-10-30 (ER)	48285 / 352		0081	0487	3 GE CF6-50C2B	267619	C28Y228	DM-EJ	905 / cvtd -30
☐ C-GCPH	Boeing (Douglas) DC-10-30 (ER)	48288 / 364		0081	0587	3 GE CF6-50C2B	267619	C28Y228	DM-EK	906 / cvtd -30
☐ C-GCPI	Boeing (Douglas) DC-10-30 (ER)	48296 / 370		0082	0487	3 GE CF6-50C2B	267619	C28Y228	DL-FJ	907 / cvtd -30
☐ C-FBCA	Boeing 747-475	25422 / 912		0092	0492	4 GE CF6-80C2B1F	394625	C48Y379	AB-HQ	884 / Grant McConachie
☐ C-FCRA	Boeing 747-475	24895 / 837		1290	0291	4 GE CF6-80C2B1F	394625	C48Y379	AB-GQ	882 / T. Russ Baker
☐ C-FGHZ	Boeing 747-4F6	27827 / 1038	N6055X*	0094	0595	4 GE CF6-80C2B1F	394625	C48Y383	CD-GR	885 / Rhys T. Eyton / lsf GECA
☐ C-GMWW	Boeing 747-475	24883 / 823	N6018N*	1190	1290	4 GE CF6-80C2B1F	394625	C48Y379	AB-EQ	881 / Maxwell W. Ward

CANADIAN HELICOPTERS, Ltd = WSR (Subs.of CHC Helicopter Corp. / formerly Okanagan,Sealand & Toronto Helic.Ltd) **Edmonton / Montreal-Les Cèdres & Vancouver-Int'l**

Canadian Helicopters

PO Box 5188, St. John's, Newfoundland A1C 5V5, Canada ☎ (709) 570-0700 Tx: 0163159 sealand snf Fax: (709) 570-0748 SITA: n/a
F: 1947 ⁂ 970 Head: Craig L. Dobbin ICAO: WHISTLER Net: http://www.chc.ca Aircraft below MTOW 1361kg: Robinson R22
WSR consists of 4 operating divisions: Eastern/Est at Cèdres/Qué.(formerly Viking Helicopters), Int'l & ACRO at Richmond/B.C. & Western at Edmonton/Alta. On order (LoI): 2 Bell Boeing 609 (tilt-rotor) for delivery 2001.

registration	type of aircraft	cn/fn	ex/ex*	mfd	del	powered by	mtow kg	configuration	selcal	name/fln/specialitites/remarks
☐ C-GLHK	MD Helicopters MD 500D (Hughes 369D)	300659D		0080	0692	1 AN 250-C20B	1361			
☐ C-GLHU	MD Helicopters MD 500D (Hughes 369D)	1200857D		0080	1096	1 AN 250-C20B	1361			
☐ C-GOPC	MD Helicopters MD 500D (Hughes 369D)	1280405D	N58253	0078	1295	1 AN 250-C20B	1361			
☐ C-GSZM	MD Helicopters MD 500D (Hughes 369D)	1170237D		0077	0693	1 AN 250-C20B	1361			
☐ C-GTZP	MD Helicopters MD 500D (Hughes 369D)	590519D		0079	0794	1 AN 250-C20B	1361			
☐ C-GTZQ	MD Helicopters MD 500D (Hughes 369D)	590521D		0079	0693	1 AN 250-C20B	1361			
☐ C-FAHT	Bell 206B JetRanger	631		0071		1 AN 250-C20	1451			cvtd 206A
☐ C-FAHU	Bell 206B JetRanger III	624		0071	0889	1 AN 250-C20B	1451			cvtd 206A
☐ C-FAHV	Bell 206B JetRanger	767		0072		1 AN 250-C20	1451			
☐ C-FAHW	Bell 206B JetRanger	785		0072		1 AN 250-C20	1451			
☐ C-FAJR	Bell 206B JetRanger	123		0068		1 AN 250-C20	1451			cvtd 206A
☐ C-FBQH	Bell 206B JetRanger	745		0071		1 AN 250-C20	1451			cvtd 206A
☐ C-FCJC	Bell 206B JetRanger	832		0072		1 AN 250-C20	1451			
☐ C-FCQE	Bell 206B JetRanger	535		0070		1 AN 250-C20	1451			cvtd 206A
☐ C-FDYD	Bell 206B JetRanger	936		0073		1 AN 250-C20	1451			
☐ C-FFVC	Bell 206B JetRanger	934		0073	0896	1 AN 250-C20	1451			
☐ C-FHTM	Bell 206B JetRanger	1017		0073		1 AN 250-C20	1451			
☐ C-FHTP	Bell 206B JetRanger	1024		0073		1 AN 250-C20	1451			
☐ C-FHTR	Bell 206B JetRanger	1036		0073		1 AN 250-C20	1451			
☐ C-FHTS	Bell 206B JetRanger	1037		0073		1 AN 250-C20	1451			
☐ C-FKNX	Bell 206B JetRanger III	2440	N5003X	0078	0891	1 AN 250-C20B	1451			
☐ C-FOAH	Bell 206B JetRanger	627		0071		1 AN 250-C20	1451			cvtd 206A
☐ C-FOAN	Bell 206B JetRanger	791		0072		1 AN 250-C20	1451			
☐ C-FPOD	Bell 206B JetRanger	696		0071		1 AN 250-C20	1451			cvtd 206A
☐ C-FPOM	Bell 206B JetRanger	703		0072		1 AN 250-C20	1451			cvtd 206A
☐ C-FPZK	Bell 206B JetRanger	1281	N654AA	0074		1 AN 250-C20	1451			
☐ C-FWTX	Bell 206B JetRanger	343		0069		1 AN 250-C20	1451			cvtd 206A
☐ C-GAHC	Bell 206B JetRanger	468	N2268W	0069		1 AN 250-C20	1451			cvtd 206A
☐ C-GAHR	Bell 206B JetRanger	873	N1488B	0072		1 AN 250-C20	1451			
☐ C-GBHE	Bell 206B JetRanger	1335		0074		1 AN 250-C20	1451			
☐ C-GBHI	Bell 206B JetRanger III	1758	N49584	0075	0889	1 AN 250-C20B	1451			cvtd JetRanger
☐ C-GCIR	Bell 206B JetRanger III	3029		0080		1 AN 250-C20B	1451			
☐ C-GDBA	Bell 206B JetRanger III	2232	N16821	0077	0889	1 AN 250-C20B	1451			
☐ C-GETF	Bell 206B JetRanger III	3036		0080		1 AN 250-C20B	1451			
☐ C-GFQH	Bell 206B JetRanger	1090	N100JG	0073		1 AN 250-C20	1451			
☐ C-GGNC	Bell 206B JetRanger II	2123		0076		1 AN 250-C20	1451			
☐ C-GHUQ	Bell 206B JetRanger	1721	N3199G	0075		1 AN 250-C20	1451			
☐ C-GIFY	Bell 206B JetRanger II	2008		0076		1 AN 250-C20	1451			
☐ C-GIXS	Bell 206B JetRanger III	2304	N272RM	0077		1 AN 250-C20B	1451			
☐ C-GLAH	Bell 206B JetRanger	912	N200JJ	0072	0889	1 AN 250-C20	1451			
☐ C-GLRA	Bell 206B JetRanger	1753	N300SE	0075	0896	1 AN 250-C20	1451			
☐ C-GNLD	Bell 206B JetRanger III	2357	N57PH	0078	0490	1 AN 250-C20B	1451			
☐ C-GNLE	Bell 206B JetRanger III	2358	N56PH	0078	0590	1 AN 250-C20B	1451			
☐ C-GNLG	Bell 206B JetRanger III	2360		0078		1 AN 250-C20B	1451			
☐ C-GNPH	Bell 206B JetRanger III	2352		0078		1 AN 250-C20B	1451			
☐ C-GOKE	Bell 206B JetRanger III	1830	N49655	0075		1 AN 250-C20B	1451			cvtd JetRanger
☐ C-GOKJ	Bell 206B JetRanger	499	N2298W	0070		1 AN 250-C20	1451			cvtd 206A
☐ C-GRGN	Bell 206B JetRanger	1824		0075		1 AN 250-C20	1451			
☐ C-GSRX	Bell 206B JetRanger	1823	N999PA	0075	0390	1 AN 250-C20	1451			
☐ C-GUMO	Bell 206B JetRanger II	1943	N49721	0076	0896	1 AN 250-C20	1451			
☐ C-GVTK	Bell 206B JetRanger	104	N6200N	0067		1 AN 250-C20	1451			cvtd 206A
☐ C-GXHC	Bell 206B JetRanger	395	N28956	0069		1 AN 250-C20B	1451			cvtd 206A
☐ C-GYQH	Bell 206B JetRanger III	1394	N111BH	0074		1 AN 250-C20B	1451			cvtd JetRanger
☐ C-GZQH	Bell 206B JetRanger	1055	N58148	0073		1 AN 250-C20	1451			
☐ C-FNYQ	Bell 206L LongRanger	45047	N20LT	0076	0692	1 AN 250-C20B	1814			
☐ C-GGZQ	Bell 206L LongRanger	45006	N49637	0075		1 AN 250-C20B	1814			
☐ C-GLMX	Bell 206L-1 LongRanger II	45439	N92ZT	0080	0592	1 AN 250-C28B	1882			
☐ C-GLQY	Bell 206L LongRanger	45146		0077		1 AN 250-C20B	1814			
☐ C-GMHS	Bell 206L LongRanger	45120		0077		1 AN 250-C20B	1814			
☐ C-GMHT	Bell 206L LongRanger	45127	N16847	0077	0996	1 AN 250-C20B	1814			
☐ C-GNLC	Bell 206L LongRanger	45055	N9978K	0076	0896	1 AN 250-C20B	1814			
☐ C-GNLK	Bell 206L LongRanger	46601	N16939	0078		1 AN 250-C20B	1814			
☐ C-GNMC	Bell 206L LongRanger	45067		0076		1 AN 250-C20B	1814			
☐ C-GNZR	Bell 206L LongRanger	45118	N16809	0077		1 AN 250-C20B	1814			
☐ C-GPCX	Bell 206L-1 LongRanger II	45554		0080	0592	1 AN 250-C28B	1882			
☐ C-GQEZ	Bell 206L LongRanger	45038	N9942K	0076		1 AN 250-C20B	1814			
☐ C-GSVH	Bell 206L LongRanger	45072	N206U	0076	0896	1 AN 250-C20B	1814			
☐ C-GTLB	Bell 206L LongRanger	45031	N9927K	0075		1 AN 250-C20B	1814			
☐ C-GTOM	Bell 206L LongRanger	45010		0075		1 AN 250-C20B	1814			
☐ C-GVHX	Bell 206L LongRanger	45138	N90AC	0077	0996	1 AN 250-C20B	1814			
☐ C-GVII	Bell 206L-1 LongRanger II	45158		0078	0696	1 AN 250-C28B	1882			
☐ C-FCCA	Eurocopter (Aerosp.) AS350BA AStar	2900		0095	0696	1 TU Arriel 1B	2100			
☐ C-FCHN	Eurocopter (Aerosp.) AS350BA AStar	2921		0096	0696	1 TU Arriel 1B	2100			
☐ C-FETA	Eurocopter (Aerosp.) AS350D AStar	1085	N137BH	0079	0996	1 LY LTS101-600A.2	1950			
☐ C-FETD	Eurocopter (Aerosp.) AS350D AStar	1025	N135BH	0078	0996	1 LY LTS101-600A.2	1950			
☐ C-FFBU	Eurocopter (Aerosp.) AS350BA AStar	1215	N3605B	0080	0290	1 TU Arriel 1B	1950			
☐ C-FHVH	Eurocopter (Aerosp.) AS350BA AStar	1256	N36075	0080	0996	1 TU Arriel 1B	2100			cvtd AS350D
☐ C-FPBA	Eurocopter (Aerosp.) AS350B2 AStar	2492	JA6091	0091	0696	1 TU Arriel 1D1	2250			
☐ C-FPER	Eurocopter (Aerosp.) AS350BA AStar	2552		0092	0193	1 TU Arriel 1B	2100			

☐ C-FPLJ	Eurocopter (Aerosp.) AS350D AStar	1060		0079	0896	1 LY LTS101-600A.2	1950			
☐ C-FQNS	Eurocopter (Aerosp.) AS350D AStar	1423	N5783Y	0081	0896	1 LY LTS101-600A.2	1950			
☐ C-FSHV	Eurocopter (Aerosp.) AS350B AStar	1287	N5143R	0080	0594	1 TU Arriel 1B	1950			
☐ C-FSLB	Eurocopter (Aerosp.) AS350B AStar	2142	JA9786	0088	0894	1 TU Arriel 1B	1950			
☐ C-FVVH	Eurocopter (Aerosp.) AS350BA AStar	2612		0092	0594	1 TU Arriel 1B	2100			
☐ C-FYCO	Eurocopter (Aerosp.) AS350BA AStar	2899		0095	0796	1 TU Arriel 1B	2100			
☐ C-GAHH	Eurocopter (Aerosp.) AS350B AStar	1036		0079	0896	1 TU Arriel 1B	1950			cvtd AS350D
☐ C-GAHI	Eurocopter (Aerosp.) AS350D AStar	1086		0079	0696	1 LY LTS101-600A.2	1950			
☐ C-GALD	Eurocopter (Aerosp.) AS350BA AStar	1146		0079		1 TU Arriel 1B	2100			cvtd AS350D
☐ C-GALE	Eurocopter (Aerosp.) AS350B AStar	1350		0081		1 TU Arriel 1B	1950			cvtd AS350D
☐ C-GATX	Eurocopter (Aerosp.) AS350B AStar	1221		0080		1 TU Arriel 1B	1950			cvtd AS350D
☐ C-GAYX	Eurocopter (Aerosp.) AS350B AStar	1179		0079		1 TU Arriel 1B	1950			cvtd AS350D
☐ C-GBBX	Eurocopter (Aerosp.) AS350B AStar	1180		0079		1 TU Arriel 1B	1950			cvtd AS350D
☐ C-GBCZ	Eurocopter (Aerosp.) AS350D AStar	1159	N3600W	0079	0696	1 LY LTS101-600A.2	1950			
☐ C-GBPS	Eurocopter (Aerosp.) AS350BA AStar	1277		0080	0493	1 TU Arriel 1B	2100			cvtd AS350D
☐ C-GCDN	Eurocopter (Aerosp.) AS350D AStar	1029	N9002G	0078	0996	1 LY LTS101-600A.2	1950			
☐ C-GCEC	Eurocopter (Aerosp.) AS350BA AStar	1431	N666JK	0081	0390	1 TU Arriel 1B	2100			cvtd AS350B
☐ C-GCKP	Eurocopter (Aerosp.) AS350D AStar	1138	N3598Y	0079	0996	1 LY LTS101-600A.2	1950			
☐ C-GCWD	Eurocopter (Aerosp.) AS350BA AStar	2047	N844BP	0087	0494	1 TU Arriel 1B	2100			cvtd AS350B
☐ C-GCWW	Eurocopter (Aerosp.) AS350D AStar	1435	N340DF	0081	0996	1 LY LTS101-600A.2	1950			
☐ C-GDSX	Eurocopter (Aerosp.) AS350BA AStar	1134	N35972	0079	0896	1 TU Arriel 1B	2100			cvtd AS350B
☐ C-GDUF	Eurocopter (Aerosp.) AS350B AStar	1309		0080		1 TU Arriel 1B	1950			cvtd AS350D
☐ C-GELC	Eurocopter (Aerosp.) AS350B AStar	1162		0079	0993	1 TU Arriel 1B	1950			cvtd AS350D
☐ C-GEPH	Eurocopter (Aerosp.) AS350BA AStar	1193	ZK-HET	0079	0993	1 TU Arriel 1B	2100			cvtd AS350B
☐ C-GEVH	Eurocopter (Aerosp.) AS350BA AStar	2620	F-WYMN*	0092	0896	1 TU Arriel 1B	2100			
☐ C-GFHS	Eurocopter (Aerosp.) AS350B AStar	1401		0081		1 TU Arriel 1B	1950			
☐ C-GHCT	Eurocopter (Aerosp.) AS350D AStar	1271		0080	0996	1 LY LTS101-600A.2	1950			
☐ C-GHVD	Eurocopter (Aerosp.) AS350D AStar	1236	N3606Y	0080	0490	1 LY LTS101-600A.2	1950			
☐ C-GLMH	Eurocopter (Aerosp.) AS350BA AStar	1012		0078	0896	1 TU Arriel 1B	2100			cvtd AS350D
☐ C-GLNE	Eurocopter (Aerosp.) AS350BA AStar	1128		0079	0696	1 TU Arriel 1B	2100			cvtd AS350D
☐ C-GLNK	Eurocopter (Aerosp.) AS350D AStar	1261	N3608C	0081	0896	1 LY LTS101-600A.2	1950			
☐ C-GLNM	Eurocopter (Aerosp.) AS350D AStar	1262	N3608R	0081	0896	1 LY LTS101-600A.2	1950			
☐ C-GLNO	Eurocopter (Aerosp.) AS350D AStar	1264		0081	0896	1 LY LTS101-600A.2	1950			
☐ C-GMEY	Eurocopter (Aerosp.) AS350B AStar	1004	N350AS	0079	0492	1 TU Arriel 1B	1950			cvtd AS350D
☐ C-GMIZ	Eurocopter (Aerosp.) AS350D AStar	1170		0079	0896	1 LY LTS101-600A.2	1950			
☐ C-GNMN	Eurocopter (Aerosp.) AS350BA AStar	1315		0081	0298	1 TU Arriel 1B	2100			cvtd AS350D
☐ C-GOVH	Eurocopter (Aerosp.) AS350BA AStar	1286	N224GA	0080	0896	1 TU Arriel 1B	2100			cvtd AS350D
☐ C-GRBT	Eurocopter (Aerosp.) AS350D AStar	1246	N877JM	0080	0896	1 LY LTS101-600A.2	1950			
☐ C-GRGJ	Eurocopter (Aerosp.) AS350B AStar	1171		0079		1 TU Arriel 1B	1950			cvtd AS350D
☐ C-GRGU	Eurocopter (Aerosp.) AS350BA AStar	1213	N7172H	0080		1 TU Arriel 1B	2100			cvtd AS350D
☐ C-GSDF	Eurocopter (Aerosp.) AS350D AStar	1292	N149BH	0080		1 LY LTS101-600A.2	1950			
☐ C-GSLF	Eurocopter (Aerosp.) AS350D AStar	1310		0081		1 LY LTS101-600A.2	1950			
☐ C-GTPF	Eurocopter (Aerosp.) AS350BA AStar	2932		0095	0696	1 TU Arriel 1B	2100			
☐ C-GTVH	Eurocopter (Aerosp.) AS350BA AStar	2611	N600CH	0092	0993	1 TU Arriel 1B	2100			
☐ C-GVHB	Eurocopter (Aerosp.) AS350D AStar	1297	N352EH	0081	0291	1 LY LTS101-600A.2	1950			
☐ C-GVYK	Eurocopter (Aerosp.) AS350D AStar	1094		0079	0896	1 LY LTS101-600A.2	1950			
☐ C-GTLC	Eurocopter (Aerosp.) AS355F1 TwinStar	5097	N911BR	0081	0698	2 AN 250-C20F	2400			
☐ C-GVHC	Eurocopter (Aerosp.) AS355F1 TwinStar	5195	N5801T	0082	0690	2 AN 250-C20F	2400			
☐ C-GVHK	Eurocopter (Aerosp.) AS355F1 TwinStar	5098	N60031	0081	0796	2 AN 250-C20F	2400			
☐ C-FCHG	Sikorsky S-76A++	760187	N62WW	0081	1296	2 TU Arriel 1S1	4763			lst Thai Aviation as HS-HTG/cvtd S-76A
☐ C-FTGD	Sikorsky S-76A+	760165	G-BVRX	0081	0795	2 TU Arriel 1S	4763			cvtd S-76A
☐ C-GIMA	Sikorsky S-76A	760018	G-BZAC	0079	1092	2 AN 250-C30	4763			
☐ C-GIMB	Sikorsky S-76A	760111	G-BIAW	0080	1092	2 AN 250-C30	4763			
☐ C-GIME	Sikorsky S-76A	760004		0079		2 AN 250-C30	4763			
☐ C-GIMJ	Sikorsky S-76A	760009	N333AA	0079		2 AN 250-C30	4763			
☐ C-GIMK	Sikorsky S-76A	760016	ZS-REI	0079		2 AN 250-C30	4763			
☐ C-GIML	Sikorsky S-76A++	760017	HS-HTL	0079		2 TU Arriel 1S1	4763			cvtd S-76A
☐ C-GIMM	Sikorsky S-76A	760044		0080		2 AN 250-C30	4763			lst Thai Aviation Services as HS-HTM
☐ C-GIMN	Sikorsky S-76A	760110	G-BIAV	0080	1092	2 AN 250-C30	4763			
☐ C-GIMQ	Sikorsky S-76A	760102	HS-HTQ	0080		2 AN 250-C30	4763			
☐ C-GIMR	Sikorsky S-76A	760079	G-BHYB	0080	0993	2 AN 250-C30	4763			
☐ C-GIMT	Sikorsky S-76A	760130	N1548S	0081		2 AN 250-C30	4763			
☐ C-GIMU	Sikorsky S-76A	760131	N1548T	0081		2 AN 250-C30	4763			
☐ C-GIMV	Sikorsky S-76A	760005	VH-WXE	0079		2 AN 250-C30	4763			
☐ C-GIMX	Sikorsky S-76A+	760213	G-BVNX	0081	1096	2 TU Arriel 1S	4763			lst Thai Aviation as HS-HTX/cvtd S-76A
☐ C-GIMZ	Sikorsky S-76A	760169	N399PK	0081	0994	2 AN 250-C30	4763			
☐ C-GKWS	Sikorsky S-76A++	760297	VR-HZB	0085	1295	2 TU Arriel 1S1	4763			cvtd S-76A
☐ C-FAOC	Bell 212	35103		0098	0998	2 PWC PT6T-3B TwinPac	5080			
☐ C-FBHF	Bell 212	30509		0071		2 PWC PT6T-3 TwinPac	5080			
☐ C-FNJJ	Bell 212	30944	N2093S	0079	0594	2 PWC PT6T-3 TwinPac	5080			
☐ C-FOKV	Bell 212	30819	N16787	0077		2 PWC PT6T-3 TwinPac	5080			
☐ C-FPKW	Bell 212	30893	C-FARC	0078	1292	2 PWC PT6T-3 TwinPac	5080			
☐ C-FPMR	Bell 212	31115	N48ZP	0080	1293	2 PWC PT6T-3 TwinPac	5080			lst Helisur, Peru
☐ C-FRUT	Bell 212	30891	ZK-HID	0078	0394	2 PWC PT6T-3 TwinPac	5080			
☐ C-FRWI	Bell 212	30672	N72AL	0074	0394	2 PWC PT6T-3 TwinPac	5080			
☐ C-FRWL	Bell 212	30829	N93AL	0077	0394	2 PWC PT6T-3 TwinPac	5080			
☐ C-FTAG	Bell 212	30739	C-FNMP	0075	0498	2 PWC PT6T-3 TwinPac	5080			
☐ C-FXDS	Bell 212	30806	BH-806	0077	1295	2 PWC PT6T-3 TwinPac	5080			
☐ C-GAHD	Bell 212	30570	N7034J	0073		2 PWC PT6T-3 TwinPac	5080			
☐ C-GBPH	Bell 212	30630	N947AA	0074	0690	2 PWC PT6T-3 TwinPac	5080			lst Helisur, Peru
☐ C-GDVG	Bell 212	30762		0076		2 PWC PT6T-3 TwinPac	5080			
☐ C-GFQP	Bell 212	30578	N58120	0073	0690	2 PWC PT6T-3 TwinPac	5080			
☐ C-GHVH	Bell 212	30877	N8555V	0078		2 PWC PT6T-3 TwinPac	5080			
☐ C-GMOH	Bell 212	31133		0080		2 PWC PT6T-3 TwinPac	5080			
☐ C-GOKL	Bell 212	30597	N2990W	0073		2 PWC PT6T-3 TwinPac	5080			
☐ C-GSQM	Bell 212	31160	N9725N	0080	0996	2 PWC PT6T-3 TwinPac	5080			
☐ C-FIBN	Sikorsky S-61N	61811	PT-HPV	0078		2 GE CT58-140-1	9318			
☐ C-FOKB	Sikorsky S-61L	61266	N266HL	0065		2 GE CT58-140-1	9318			
☐ C-FOKP	Sikorsky S-61N	61297	HS-HTP	0065		2 GE CT58-140-1	9318			
☐ C-FPZR	Sikorsky S-61L	61362	N305V	0067	0693	2 GE CT58-140-1	9318			
☐ C-GARC	Sikorsky S-61N	61722	N225BF	0074	0590	2 GE CT58-140-1	9318			lst Thai Aviation Services as HS-HTC
☐ C-GJDK	Sikorsky S-61L Helipro Short	61425	N425HL	0068		2 GE CT58-140-1	9318			cvtd S-61L
☐ C-GOLH	Sikorsky S-61N	61815	G-BIMV	0078		2 GE CT58-140-1	9318			lst Thai Aviation Services as HS-HTH
☐ C-GSAB	Sikorsky S-61N	61823	ZS-RFU	0080	0898	2 GE CT58-140-1	9318			
☐ C-GSBL	Sikorsky S-61N	61754	G-BEDI	0076	0798	2 GE CT58-140-1	9318			

CANADIAN NORTH (NorTerra, Inc. dba/Subs. of Inuvialuit Development Corp. & Nunsasi Corp.) Yellowknife, N.W.T.

3300-5201 50th Avenue, Yellowknife, Northwest Territories X1A 3F9, Canada ☎ (867) 669-4000 Tx: none Fax: (867) 920-7433 SITA: n/a

F: 1998 ✈✈✈ n/a Head: Mrs Carmen Loburgh Net: n/a Flights are contracted out/operated on behalf of Canadian North by CANADIAN-CANADIEN using their IATA/ICAO-codes CP/CDN.

☐ C-GDPA	Boeing 737-2T2C (A)	22056 / 655		0080	1098	2 PW JT8D-17	58105	Y112/Combi	NONE	784/Yellowknife / lsf Arkia Lsg/opb CDN
☐ C-GOPW	Boeing 737-275C (A)	22160 / 688	N8288V*	0080	1098	2 PW JT8D-17A	53070	Y112/Combi	NONE	782/Norman Wells / lsf ArkiaLsg/opb CDN

CANADIAN REGIONAL AIRLINES (1998), Ltd = KI / CDR (Partenaire CANADIEN / CANADIAN Partner) (formerly Time Air, Inc.) Calgary, Alta. & Toronto-Int'l, Ont.

Hangar 101, 8050-22nd Street NE, Calgary, Alberta T2E 7H6, Canada ☎ (403) 974-2300 Tx: none Fax: (403) 974-7760 SITA: YYCTTKI

F: 1993 ✈✈✈ 2220 Head: Robert Reding ICAO: CANADIAN REGIONAL Net: n/a

Scheduled commuter services are operated on behalf of Canadian / Canadien as a Partenaire CANADIEN / CANADIAN Partner (in such colours & both titles) using CP flight numbers.

☐ C-FCIZ	De Havilland DHC-8-102 Dash 8	138		0089	1294	2 PWC PW120A	15649	Y37		169
☐ C-FDND	De Havilland DHC-8-102 Dash 8	129		0088	0695	2 PWC PW120A	15649	Y37		170
☐ C-GAAC	De Havilland DHC-8-102 Dash 8	047		0086	0295	2 PWC PW120A	15649	Y37		166 / Spirit of Peace River
☐ C-GAAM	De Havilland DHC-8-102 Dash 8	059		0086	0495	2 PWC PW120A	15649	Y37		168 / Spirit of Rainbow Lake
☐ C-GTAE	De Havilland DHC-8-102 Dash 8	073		0087	0393	2 PWC PW120A	15649	Y37		172
☐ C-GTAF	De Havilland DHC-8-102 Dash 8	083		0087	0393	2 PWC PW120A	15649	Y37		174 / Spirit of Portland
☐ C-GTAI	De Havilland DHC-8-102 Dash 8	078		0087	0393	2 PWC PW120A	15649	Y37		173
☐ C-GTBP	De Havilland DHC-8-102 Dash 8	066		0087	0393	2 PWC PW120A	15649	Y37		175 / Spirit of Peace Country
☐ C-GTCO	De Havilland DHC-8-102 Dash 8	119		0088	1295	2 PWC PW120A	15649	Y37		167 / Spirit of High Level
☐ C-GWRR	De Havilland DHC-8-102 Dash 8	070		0087	0393	2 PWC PW120A	15649	Y37		171 / Spirit of Nanaimo
☐ C-FJFM	De Havilland DHC-8-311 Dash 8	240		0090	0393	2 PWC PW123	18643	Y50		191 / Spirit of Grande Prairie
☐ C-FJXZ	De Havilland DHC-8-311 Dash 8	264	C-FTAQ	0091	0393	2 PWC PW123	18643	Y50		193 / Spirit of Penticton / lsf AVII
☐ C-FTAK	De Havilland DHC-8-311 Dash 8	246		0090	0393	2 PWC PW123	18643	Y50		190 / Spirit of Kamloops
☐ C-GETA	De Havilland DHC-8-301 Dash 8	186		0089	0393	2 PWC PW123	18643	Y50		188 / Spirit of Fort Nelson

43 registration type of aircraft cn/fn ex/ex* mfd del powered by mtow kg configuration selcal name/fln/specialitites/remarks

☐ C-GEWQ	De Havilland DHC-8-311 Dash 8	202		0090	0393	2 PWC PW123	19505	Y50		192 / Spirit of Comox Valley
☐ C-GHTA	De Havilland DHC-8-301 Dash 8	198		0089	0393	2 PWC PW123	18643	Y50		179 / Spirit of Castlegar
☐ C-GKTA	De Havilland DHC-8-301 Dash 8	124		0089	0393	2 PWC PW123	18643	Y50		184 / Spirit of Lethbridge
☐ C-GLTA	De Havilland DHC-8-301 Dash 8	154		0089	0393	2 PWC PW123	18643	Y50		185 / Spirit of Thunder Bay
☐ C-GMTA	De Havilland DHC-8-301 Dash 8	174		0089	0393	2 PWC PW123	18643	Y50		186 / Spirit of Victoria
☐ C-GSTA	De Havilland DHC-8-301 Dash 8	182		0089	0393	2 PWC PW123	18643	Y50		187 / Spirit of Seattle
☐ C-GTAG	De Havilland DHC-8-301 Dash 8	200		0090	0393	2 PWC PW123	18643	Y50		178 / Spirit of Cranbrook
☐ C-GTAQ	De Havilland DHC-8-301 Dash 8	180	C-FGVK	0089	0393	2 PWC PW123	18643	Y50		176 / Spirit of Campbell River
☐ C-GTAT	De Havilland DHC-8-301 Dash 8	188	C-FGVT	0089	0393	2 PWC PW123	18643	Y50		177 / Spirit of Smithers
☐ C-GVTA	De Havilland DHC-8-301 Dash 8	190		0089	0393	2 PWC PW123	18643	Y50		189
☐ C-FANA	Fokker F28 Fellowship 1000 (F28 Mk1000)	11075	N466US	0073	0498	2 RR Spey 555-15N	29484	C10Y45		159 / *lsf USAL*
☐ C-FCRB	Fokker F28 Fellowship 1000 (F28 Mk1000)	11107	N454US	0076	1097	2 RR Spey 555-15N	28576	C10Y45		150/Spirit of Raleigh Durham / *lsf USAL*
☐ C-FCRC	Fokker F28 Fellowship 1000 (F28 Mk1000)	11044	N460AU	0071	0196	2 RR Spey 555-15N	30164	C10Y45		144 / *lsf USAL*
☐ C-FCRI	Fokker F28 Fellowship 1000 (F28 Mk1000)	11043	N459US	0071	0993	2 RR Spey 555-15N	28576	C10Y45		139 / Spirit of Montréal / *lsf USAL*
☐ C-FCRK	Fokker F28 Fellowship 1000 (F28 Mk1000)	11087	N467US	0074	1194	2 RR Spey 555-15N	29484	C10Y45		136 / *lsf USAL*
☐ C-FCRM	Fokker F28 Fellowship 1000 (F28 Mk1000)	11035	N456US	0071	1194	2 RR Spey 555-15N	29484	C10Y45		138 / Spirit of Ottawa / *lsf USAL*
☐ C-FCRP	Fokker F28 Fellowship 1000 (F28 Mk1000)	11037	N458US	0071	0995	2 RR Spey 555-15N	29484	C10Y45		141 / Spirit of Edmonton / *lsf USAL*
☐ C-FCRU	Fokker F28 Fellowship 1000 (F28 Mk1000)	11032	C-FAIF	0071	0295	2 RR Spey 555-15N	29484	C10Y45		140 / Spirit of Calgary / *lsf USAL*
☐ C-FCRW	Fokker F28 Fellowship 1000 (F28 Mk1000)	11029	PK-PJU	0071	0995	2 RR Spey 555-15	30164	C10Y45		142 / Spirit of Kelowna
☐ C-FCRZ	Fokker F28 Fellowship 1000 (F28 Mk1000)	11061	N463AU	0072	1195	2 RR Spey 555-15N	30164	C10Y45		143 / Spirit of Québec City / *lsf USAL*
☐ C-FFCR	Fokker F28 Fellowship 1000 (F28 Mk1000)	11095	N468US	0075	0596	2 RR Spey 555-15N	29484	C10Y45		146 / *lsf USAL*
☐ C-FJRI	Fokker F28 Fellowship 1000 (F28 Mk1000)	11103	N451US	0075	0393	2 RR Spey 555-15	29484	C10Y45		133 / Spirit of Thunder Bay
☐ C-FOCR	Fokker F28 Fellowship 1000 (F28 Mk1000)	11063	N464US	0073	0996	2 RR Spey 555-15N	30164	C10Y45		147 / *lsf USAL*
☐ C-FPCR	Fokker F28 Fellowship 1000 (F28 Mk1000)	11096	N469US	0075	0398	2 RR Spey 555-15N	28576	C10Y45		152 / Spirit of San Jose CA / *lsf USAL*
☐ C-FQCR	Fokker F28 Fellowship 1000 (F28 Mk1000)	11036	N457US	0071	0897	2 RR Spey 555-15N	28576	C10Y45		148 / *lsf USAL*
☐ C-FTAR	Fokker F28 Fellowship 1000 (F28 Mk1000)	11047	VH-ATD	0072	0498	2 RR Spey 555-15	28576	C10Y45		157 / Spirit of New York
☐ C-FTAS	Fokker F28 Fellowship 1000 (F28 Mk1000)	11098	N470US	0075	0393	2 RR Spey 555-15	29484	C10Y45		135 / Spirit of Regina
☐ C-FTAV	Fokker F28 Fellowship 1000 (F28 Mk1000)	11106	N453US	0076	0393	2 RR Spey 555-15	29484	C10Y45		134 / Spirit of Saskatoon
☐ C-FTAY	Fokker F28 Fellowship 1000 (F28 Mk1000)	11084	VH-ATG	0074	0498	2 RR Spey 555-15	28576	C10Y45		158 / Spirit of Terrace
☐ C-FXTA	Fokker F28 Fellowship 1000 (F28 Mk1000)	11064	N465AU	0073	0393	2 RR Spey 555-15N	29484	C10Y45		137/Spirit of Fort McMurray / *lsf USAL*
☐ C-FZCR	Fokker F28 Fellowship 1000 (F28 Mk1000)	11054	N462AU	0072	1197	2 RR Spey 555-15N	30164	C10Y45		149 / *lsf USAL*
☐ C-GCRD	Fokker F28 Fellowship 1000 (F28 Mk1000)	11097	N801PH	0075	0496	2 RR Spey 555-15	29484	C10Y45		145 / Spirit of The Pas
☐ C-GCRN	Fokker F28 Fellowship 1000 (F28 Mk1000)	11051	F-GBBR	0072	0798	2 RR Spey 555-15	30164	C10Y45		155 / Spirit of Las Vegas
☐ C-GKCR	Fokker F28 Fellowship 1000 (F28 Mk1000)	11101	N450US	0075	1297	2 RR Spey 555-15N	30164	C10Y45		151 / *lsf USAL*
☐ C-GLCR	Fokker F28 Fellowship 1000 (F28 Mk1000)	11105	N452US	0076	0498	2 RR Spey 555-15N	28576	C10Y45		153 / *lsf USAL*
☐ C-GNCR	Fokker F28 Fellowship 1000 (F28 Mk1000)	11034	F-BUTI	0071	0398	2 RR Spey 555-15	28576	C10Y45		156
☐ C-GTAH	Fokker F28 Fellowship 1000 (F28 Mk1000)	11082	VH-ATE	0074	0393	2 RR Spey 555-15	28576	C10Y45		130 / Spirit of Winnipeg
☐ C-GTAN	Fokker F28 Fellowship 3000 (F28 Mk3000)	11163	PK-YPT	0080	0998	2 RR Spey 555-15H	32205	C10Y45		301
☐ C-GTEO	Fokker F28 Fellowship 1000 (F28 Mk1000)	11991	I-TIDI	0070	0393	2 RR Spey 555-15	29484	C10Y45		131 / Spirit of Fort St. John
☐ C-GTUU	Fokker F28 Fellowship 1000 (F28 Mk1000)	11006	I-TIDB	0069	0393	2 RR Spey 555-15	29484	C10Y45		132 / Spirit of Hay River
☐ C-GYCR	Fokker F28 Fellowship 1000 (F28 Mk1000)	11050	F-GDBC	0072	0598	2 RR Spey 555-15	28576	C10Y45		154 / Spirit of Prince George

CANADIAN TERRITORIAL HELICOPTERS, Inc. — **The Pas, Man.**

Box 2948, The Pas, Manitoba R9A 1R6, Canada ☎ (204) 624-5721 Tx: none Fax: (204) 624-5761 SITA: n/a
F: 1988 ⁂ 14 Head: Joe Barr Net: n/a

☐ C-FIAN	Bell 206B JetRanger	32		0067	0798	1 AN 250-C20	1451			cvtd 206A
☐ C-FCTH	Bell 206L-1 LongRanger II	45437	N70Q	0080		1 AN 250-C28B	1882			
☐ C-FKHB	Bell 206L-1 LongRanger II	45180	N73MM	0078	0496	1 AN 250-C28B	1882			
☐ C-FNEG	Bell 206L-1 LongRanger II	45579	N660CC	0080	0597	1 AN 250-C28B	1882			
☐ C-GCTQ	Bell 206L-1 LongRanger II	45786	N3183F	0083	0492	1 AN 250-C28B	1882			
☐ C-FRSR	Bell 204B	2020		0065	0590	1 LY T5311A	3856			
☐ C-GSHB	Bell 204B	2038		0065	0691	1 LY T5311A	3856			

CANAGRAD SURVEYS, Ltd — **Calgary, Alta.**

1715-27 Avenue NE, No 2, Calgary, Alberta T2E 7E1, Canada ☎ (403) 250-8705 Tx: n/a Fax: (403) 250-6857 SITA: n/a
F: 1986 ⁂ n/a Head: n/a Net: n/a Aircraft below MTOW 1361kg: Cessna 172

☐ C-GEMA	Cessna T310R II	310R0538	N310SH	0076	0590	2 CO TSIO-520-B	2495	Photo / Survey		

CANUCK-AIR SERVICE, Ltd — **Cranbrook, B.C.**

19-21st Ave SO, Cranbrook, British Columbia V1C 3H2, Canada ☎ (250) 489-4000 Tx: none Fax: (250) 489-4449 SITA: n/a
F: 1998 ⁂ n/a Head: n/a Net: n/a

☐ C-FPWM	Cessna U206F Stationair	U20602191	N7398Q	0073	0498	1 CO IO-520-F	1633			

CAPITAL HELICOPTERS (1995), Inc. (formerly Capital Helicopters, Inc. & Keystone Helicopters, Ltd) — **Whitehorse, Y.T.**

PO Box 4387, Whitehorse, Yukton Territory Y1A 3T5, Canada ☎ (867) 668-6200 Tx: none Fax: (867) 668-6201 SITA: n/a
F: 1982 ⁂ 3 Head: Delmar Washington Net: n/a

☐ C-FCHQ	Bell 206B JetRanger	1212	N59433	0073	0891	1 AN 250-C20	1451			

CARAVAN AVIATION (Les Chantiers de Chibougamau, Ltée. dba) — **Chibougamau, Qué.**

521 Chemin Merrill, Chibougamau, Québec G8P 2K7, Canada ☎ (418) 748-6481 Tx: none Fax: (418) 748-2469 SITA: n/a
F: 1997 ⁂ 3 Head: Jean Filiow Net: n/a

☐ C-GFLN	Cessna 208 Caravan I	20800261		0097	0297	1 PWC PT6A-114	3629			Floats / Wheel-Skis

CARGAIR, Ltée — **St-Michel-des-Saints-Kaiagamac Lake, Qué.**

CARGAIR

CP 370, St.-Michel-des-Saints, Québec J0K 3B0, Canada ☎ (514) 833-6836 Tx: none Fax: (514) 833-5761 SITA: n/a
F: 1961 ⁂ 60 Head: Guy Prudhomme Net: n/a Aircraft below MTOW 1361kg: Cessna 150 & 172

☐ C-FDMP	Piper PA-23-250 Aztec C	27-3560		0066	0197	2 LY IO-540-C4B5	2359			
☐ C-FTSJ	Piper PA-23-250 Aztec D	27-4387		0069		2 LY IO-540-C4B5	2359			
☐ C-FZAA	Piper PA-23-250 Aztec E	27-4710		0071		2 LY IO-540-C4B5	2359			
☐ C-FGQA	De Havilland DHC-2 Beaver I	72		0051		1 PW R-985	2313			Floats
☐ C-FIVA	De Havilland DHC-2 Beaver I	515	HK-453	0052		1 PW R-985	2313			Floats
☐ C-FODG	De Havilland DHC-2 Beaver I	205		0051		1 PW R-985	2313			Floats
☐ C-FQQC	De Havilland DHC-2 Beaver I	56		0051		1 PW R-985	2313			Floats
☐ C-GATD	Piper PA-31-350 Navajo Chieftain	31-7405143	N74986	0074	0698	2 LY TIO-540-J2BD	3175			
☐ C-GBLT	Piper PA-31-310 Navajo	31-102	N123TR	1167	0695	2 LY TIO-540-A1A	2948			
☐ C-GITW	Piper PA-31-350 Navajo Chieftain	31-7652114	N59891	0076	0598	2 LY TIO-540-J2BD	3175			
☐ C-GMRG	Piper PA-31-310 Navajo C	31-7812051	N27563	0078	0695	2 LY TIO-540-A2C	2948			
☐ C-FSUB	De Havilland DHC-3 Otter	8	RCAF3662	0053		1 PW R-1340	3629			Floats
☐ C-FSIK	Beech King Air B100	BE-39	N129CP	0078	0197	2 GA TPE331-6-252B	5352			
☐ C-GWSL	Fairchild (Swearingen) SA226AT Merlin IVA	AT-028	N5341M	0074	0197	2 GA TPE331-3U-303G	5670			

CARIBOO CHILCOTIN HELICOPTERS, Ltd — **Lillooet, B.C.**

CARIBOO CHILCOTIN

Box 1345, Lillooet, British Columbia V0K 1V0, Canada ☎ (250) 256-4888 Tx: none Fax: none SITA: n/a
F: 1985 ⁂ 10 Head: Faye Holt Net: n/a

☐ C-FGYQ	Bell 206B JetRanger	1357		0074	0981	1 AN 250-C20	1451			
☐ C-FHTQ	Bell 206B JetRanger III	1030		0073	0691	1 AN 250-C20B	1451			cvtd JetRanger
☐ C-FKOD	Bell 206B JetRanger	1228		0074	0890	1 AN 250-C20	1451			
☐ C-GPOS	Bell 206B JetRanger	845	N2987W	0072	0586	1 AN 250-C20	1451			
☐ C-FSMI	Bell 205A-1	30263	YV-O-KWH-2	0078	0794	1 LY T5313B	4309			
☐ C-FXFT	Kaman K-1200 K-Max	A94-0007	N135KA	0094	0496	1 LY T5317A-1	2722			

CARSON AIR, Ltd — **Kelowna & Williams Lake, B.C.**

6191 Kelowna Airport, Kelowna, British Columbia V1V 1S1, Canada ☎ (250) 765-7776 Tx: none Fax: (250) 765-9248 SITA: n/a
F: 1987 ⁂ n/a Head: Kevin Carson Net: http://www.carsonair.com Aircraft below MTOW 1361kg: Cessna 172 & 182.

☐ C-FRSC	Beech Baron B55 (95-B55)	TC-1538		0073	0495	2 CO IO-470-L	2313			
☐ C-GBNF	Beech Baron C55 (95-C55)	TE-197		0066	1195	2 CO IO-520-C	2404			
☐ C-FCAR	Piper PA-31-350 Navajo Chieftain	31-7405483	D-IMAR	0074	0997	2 LY TIO-540-J2BD	3175			
☐ C-FDME	Piper PA-310 Navajo C	31-7812107	N21PJ	0078	1294	2 LY TIO-540-A2C	2948			
☐ C-FCAW	Fairchild (Swearingen) SA26AT Merlin IIB	T26-172E	N135SR	0069	0893	2 GA TPE331-1-151G	4536			
☐ C-FCAV	Piper PA-42 Cheyenne III	42-8001006	N131RC	0080	0692	2 PWC PT6A-41	5080			
☐ C-GIDC	Piper PA-42 Cheyenne III	42-8001002	N61QR	0080	0297	2 PWC PT6A-41	5080			
☐ C-FBWQ	Fairchild (Swearingen) SA226TC Metro II	TC-379	N1011U	0080	0199	2 GA TPE331-10UA-511G	5670			
☐ C-GCAW	Fairchild (Swearingen) SA226TC Metro II	TC-358	N1009R	0080	1298	2 GA TPE331-10UA-511G	5670			
☐ C-GRET	Fairchild (Swearingen) SA226TC Metro IIA	TC-418	N58EA	0081	0597	2 GA TPE331-10UA-511G	5670			cvtd II
☐ C-FTIL	Cessna 550 Citation II	550-0289	N22HP	0081	0199	2 PWC JT15D-4	6033			

44 registration type of aircraft cn/fn ex/ex* mfd del powered by mtow kg configuration selcal name/fln/specialitites/remarks

CARTER AIR SERVICES, Ltd
Hay River, N.W.T.

9-103 Street, Hay River, Northwest Territories X0E 0R9, Canada ☎ (867) 874-2281 Tx: none Fax: (867) 874-2282 SITA: n/a
F: 1963 ⁂ 5 Head: Merlyn Carter Net: n/a Aircraft below MTOW 1361kg: Cessna 180 (Floats / Wheel-Skis)

☐ C-GJEM	Cessna 208 Caravan I	20800152	N9728F	0089	0797	1 PWC PT6A-114	3629			Amphibian

CAT AIR SERVICES (1170879 Ontario, Ltd dba)
Sioux Lookout, Ont.

Box 337, Sioux Lookout, Ontario P8T 1A5, Canada ☎ (807) 474-2635 Tx: none Fax: (807) 474-2645 SITA: n/a
F: 1997 ⁂ n/a Head: n/a Net: n/a

☐ C-GFVY	Cessna A185F Skywagon	18503056		0076	0698	1 CO IO-520-D	1520			Floats

CEC FLIGHTEXEC = FEX (Division of The Craig Evan Corporation / formerly Flightexec)
London, Ont.

2530 Blair Blvd, London, Ontario N5V 3Z9, Canada ☎ (519) 455-6760 Tx: none Fax: (519) 451-8946 SITA: n/a
F: 1988 ⁂ 43 Head: Charles Buchanan ICAO: FLIGHTEXEC Net: http://www.flightexec.com

☐ C-GJLR	Piper PA-31-350 Navajo Chieftain	31-8052107	N170PA	0080	0199	2 LY TIO-540-J2BD	3175			
☐ C-FCEC	Piper PA-31T2 Cheyenne II XL	31T-8166030	N76TW	0081	0989	2 PWC PT6A-135	4297			
☐ C-FCED	Piper PA-31T2 Cheyenne II XL	31T-8166013	N2501Y	0081	0497	2 PWC PT6A-135	4297			
☐ C-FCEF	Piper PA-31T Cheyenne II	31T-7920069	N250KA	0079	1297	2 PWC PT6A-28	4082			
☐ C-FGWA	Piper PA-31T Cheyenne II	31T-7920045	N52LS	0079	0596	2 PWC PT6A-28	4082			
☐ C-GVKK	Piper PA-31T Cheyenne II	31T-7820038	N679MM	0078	0698	2 PWC PT6A-28	4082			

CENTAERO AVIATION, Ltd
Windsor, Ont.

2450 Central Avenue, Windsor, Ontario N8W 4J3, Canada ☎ (519) 948-2300 Tx: none Fax: (519) 945-7281 SITA: n/a
F: 1990 ⁂ n/a Head: Victor A. Dominato Net: n/a

☐ C-FYQC	Piper PA-32R-301 Saratoga IIHP	3246037	N963DA	0096	1096	1 LY IO-540-K1G5	1633			

CENTENNIAL FLIGHT Centre, Ltd = CNS
Edmonton-Municipal, Alta.

Bldg 15, 25 Airport Road, Edmonton, Alberta T5G 0W6, Canada ☎ (780) 451-4951 Tx: none Fax: (780) 452-3575 SITA: n/a
F: 1984 ⁂ 21 Head: Bob Lamoureux ICAO: CENTENNIAL Net: http://www.centennial.ca Aircraft below MTOW 1361 kg: Cessna 152, 172, 182 & Piper PA-28.

☐ C-GLIL	Cessna 182R Skylane II	18267949	N9446H	0081	0294	1 CO O-470-U	1406			
☐ C-GBFG	Piper PA-34-200T Seneca II	34-8070006		0080		2 CO TSIO-360-EB	2073			
☐ C-GNJX	Piper PA-34-200 Seneca	34-7450212	N44574	0074		2 LY IO-360-C1E6	1814			
☐ C-FTNY	Piper PA-31-350 Navajo Chieftain	31-7952245	N2169X	0079	1194	2 LY TIO-540-J2BD	3175			
☐ C-FVVS	Piper PA-31-350 Navajo Chieftain	31-7952199	N35347	0079	0795	2 LY TIO-540-J2BD	3175			
☐ C-GFSF	Piper PA-31-310 Navajo	31-8112043		0081	1290	2 LY TIO-540-A2C	2948			
☐ C-GBVX	Beech King Air B100	BE-99	N524BA	0080	0198	2 GA TPE331-6-252B	5352			

CENTRAL AVIATION, Inc. (Seasonal May-October ops only)
Wetaskiwin, Alta.

5821-47 Avenue, Wetaskiwin, Alberta T9A 2G6, Canada ☎ (780) 352-3443 Tx: none Fax: (780) 352-4666 SITA: n/a
F: 1994 ⁂ n/a Head: John P. Cummings Net: n/a Aircraft below MTOW 1361kg: Boeing A75N1 & Piper PA-12

☐ C-GMTW	Piper PA-30-160 Twin Comanche	30-23	N7022Y	0063	1194	2 LY IO-320-B1A	1633			

CENTRAL MOUNTAIN AIR, Ltd = 9M / GLR
Smithers, B.C.

PO Box 998, Smithers, British Columbia V0J 2N0, Canada ☎ (250) 847-4780 Tx: none Fax: (250) 847-3744 SITA: n/a
F: 1987 ⁂ 185 Head: Neil Blackwell IATA: 634 ICAO: GLACIER Net: n/a Operates scheduled flights in conjunction with AIR CANADA as a Liaison AIR CANADA Connector (in own colors), using AC-flight numbers.

☐ C-FCGX	Beech Catpass 200	BB-250	N1008J	0077	0691	2 PWC PT6A-41	5670			cvtd King Air 200
☐ C-GCMJ	Beech 1900C-1 Airliner	UC-49	N80198	0089	1295	2 PWC PT6A-65B	7530	Y19		216
☐ C-GCMT	Beech 1900C-1 Airliner	UC-120	N15683*	0090	1290	2 PWC PT6A-65B	7530			214
☐ C-GCMZ	Beech 1900C-1 Airliner	UC-61	N1568L	0089	0890	2 PWC PT6A-65B	7530			215
☐ C-FCMB	Beech 1900D Airliner	UE-278		0097	0797	2 PWC PT6A-67D	7688	Y19		206
☐ C-FCME	Beech 1900D Airliner	UE-277		0097	0697	2 PWC PT6A-67D	7688	Y19		205
☐ C-FCMN	Beech 1900D Airliner	UE-276		0097	0697	2 PWC PT6A-67D	7688	Y19		204
☐ C-FCMO	Beech 1900D Airliner	UE-281		0097	0897	2 PWC PT6A-67D	7688	Y19		207
☐ C-FCMP	Beech 1900D Airliner	UE-271	N11037*	0097	0497	2 PWC PT6A-67D	7688	Y19		202
☐ C-FCMR	Beech 1900D Airliner	UE-283	N21872*	0097	0997	2 PWC PT6A-67D	7688	Y19		
☐ C-FCMU	Beech 1900D Airliner	UE-285		0097	0997	2 PWC PT6A-67D	7688	Y19		
☐ C-FCMV	Beech 1900D Airliner	UE-272	N11079*	0097	0497	2 PWC PT6A-67D	7688	Y19		203
☐ C-GCMA	Beech 1900D Airliner	UE-289		0097	1097	2 PWC PT6A-67D	7688	Y19		
☐ C-GCML	Beech 1900D Airliner	UE-243	N10879*	0096	1296	2 PWC PT6A-67D	7688	Y19		201
☐ C-GCMY	Beech 1900D Airliner	UE-287		0097	1097	2 PWC PT6A-67D	7688	Y19		

CEP ATMOSPHAIR (3453448 Canada, Inc./Centre Ecole de Parachutisme Atmosphair, Inc. dba)
St. Jean-Chrysostome, Qué.

1600G Route de l'Aéroport, St. Jean-Chrysostome, Québec 6GZ 2L2, Canada ☎ (418) 834-7272 Tx: none Fax: (418) 839-5751 SITA: n/a
F: 1996 ⁂ n/a Head: Eric Vignault Net: n/a Aircraft below MTOW 1361kg: Cessna 182

☐ C-FUZE	Beech Twin Bonanza E50	EH-43	N80EC	0057	0796	2 LY GSO-480-B1B6	3175	Para		

C.F. AVIATION, Inc.
Victoriaville, Qué.

408 Route de l'Aéroport, Victoriaville, Québec G6P 6R9, Canada ☎ (819) 752-4297 Tx: none Fax: (819) 752-4302 SITA: n/a
F: 1988 ⁂ n/a Head: n/a Net: n/a Aircraft below MTOW 1361kg: Cessna 182

☐ C-GDCT	Cessna 205A (210-5A)	205-0494	N8494Z	0063	0292	1 CO IO-470-S	1497	Para		

CFC Canadian Flight Centre (a division of Canadian I.F.R. Rating, Inc.)
Delta, B.C.

4400-72 Street, Unit 94, Delta, British Columbia V4K 5B3, Canada ☎ (604) 946-7744 Tx: none Fax: (604) 946-8753 SITA: n/a
F: 1979 ⁂ 7 Head: Ron Harcus Net: n/a Aircraft below MTOW 1361 kg: Cessna 172 & Piper PA-28.

☐ C-FCFS	Piper PA-44-180 Seminole	44-7995260		0079	0994	2 LY O-360-E1A6D	1724			

CFF AIR SERVICE, Ltd (Affiliated with Canadian Fly-In Fishing, Ltd / Seasonal May-October ops only)
Red Lake, Ont.

Box 184, Red Lake, Ontario P0V 2M0, Canada ☎ (807) 727-8214 Tx: none Fax: (807) 727-2881 SITA: n/a
F: 1996 ⁂ n/a Head: n/a Net: n/a

☐ C-FWNV	Cessna A185E Skywagon	185-1334		0068	0596	1 CO IO-520-D	1520			Floats

CHAMPLAIN AIR SURVEYS, Ltd
Pembroke, Ont.

Pembroke & Area Municipal Airport, RR 6, Pembroke, Ontario K8A 6W7, Canada ☎ (613) 687-5553 Tx: none Fax: (613) 687-8558 SITA: n/a
F: 1982 ⁂ 5 Head: Robert Duncan Net: n/a

☐ C-FLHW	Piper PA-23-180 Apache	23-1664		0059		2 LY O-360-A1A	1724	Photo / Survey		
☐ C-FMTD	Piper PA-23-160 Apache	23-1892		0060		2 LY O-320-B3B	1724	Photo / Survey		
☐ C-FYLR	Piper PA-31-310 Navajo	31-345	N9262Y	0069	0992	2 LY TIO-540-A1A	3102	Photo / Survey		

CHAPLEAU AIR SERVICES, Ltd (Seasonal May-November ops only)
Chapleau, Ont.

Box 1090, Chapleau, Ontario P0M 1K0, Canada ☎ (705) 864-1115 Tx: n/a Fax: none SITA: n/a
F: 1974 ⁂ 14 Head: n/a Net: n/a Aircraft below MTOW 1361 kg: Cessna 180.

☐ C-FJFE	De Havilland DHC-2 Beaver I	986		0055		1 PW R-985	2313			Floats

CHARTRIGHT AIR, Inc.
Toronto-Int'l, Ont.

2450 Derry Road East, Hangar 9, Mississauga, Ontario L5S 1B2, Canada ☎ (905) 671-4674 Tx: none Fax: (905) 671-3962 SITA: n/a
F: 1989 ⁂ 33 Head: George Rependa Net: n/a

☐ C-FWWW	Cessna 550 Citation II	550-0175	N10JK	0080	1098	2 PWC JT15D-4	6577			
☐ C-FGGH	IAI 1124 Westwind I	431	N431AM	0087	1289	2 GA TFE731-3-1G	10659			
☐ C-GAAA	Hawker 700A (HS 125-700A)	257179 / NA0327	N810SC	0082	1097	2 GA TFE731-3R-1H	11567			
☐ C-FDDD	Hawker 800A (BAe 125-800A)	258038	C-GTNT	0085	0298	2 GA TFE731-5R-1H	12428			
☐ C-GRGE	Hawker 800A (BAe 125-800A)	258124 / NA0417	C-GCRP	0088	1297	2 GA TFE731-5R-1H	12428			
☐ C-GSSS	Dassault Falcon 900	78	N332MC	0088	1197	3 GA TFE731-5AR-1C	20638			

CHIMO AIR SERVICE (Peter Hagedorn Investments, Ltd dba / Seasonal May-November ops only)
Red Lake-SPB, Ont.

Box 860, Red Lake, Ontario P0V 2M0, Canada ☎ (807) 727-3245 Tx: none Fax: (807) 727-3697 SITA: n/a
F: 1994 ⁂ n/a Head: Dave Robertson Net: n/a Aircraft below MTOW 1361kg: Cessna 180 (on Floats)

☐ CF-JIN	Noorduyn Norseman V	N29-55	CF-LFR	0059	1295	1 PW R-1340	3420			Floats
☐ CF-KAO	Noorduyn Norseman VI (UC-64A)	636	44-70371	0044	1194	2 PW R-1340	3420			Floats
☐ C-FODQ	De Havilland DHC-3 Otter	111		0056	0797	1 PW R-1340	3629			Floats

CLARM-AIRE, Ltd
Sault Ste Marie, Ont.

RR 1, Box 11, Airport, Sault Ste Marie, Ontario P6A 5K6, Canada ☎ (705) 779-2100 Tx: none Fax: (705) 779-2177 SITA: n/a
F: 1969 ⁂ 5 Head: Donald J. Currie Net: n/a Aircraft below MTOW 1361 kg: Cessna 152 & PA-12

☐ C-FWHQ	Piper PA-30-160 Twin Comanche B	30-1628		0067		2 LY IO-320-B1A	1633			
☐ C-GCTL	Piper PA-30-160 Twin Comanche	30-156	N7134Y	0064		2 LY IO-320-B1A	1633			
☐ C-GGHE	Piper PA-30-160 Twin Comanche B	30-1614	N19EH	0067		2 LY IO-320-B1A	1633			

45 registration type of aircraft cn/fn ex/ex* mfd del powered by mtow kg configuration selcal name/fln/specialitites/remarks

CLUB CESAR, Inc. – Air Services (Seasonal May-October ops only) — **Lac César, Qué.**

10 rue Charbonneau, St-Hilaire, Québec J3H 3P3, Canada ☎ (514) 446-5914 Tx: n/a Fax: (514) 446-1950 SITA: n/a
F: 1969 ♟♟♟ n/a Head: n/a Net: n/a Aircraft below MTOW 1361kg: Piper PA-12

☐ C-GZBM	Cessna A185F Skywagon II	18503764		0079	0994	1 CO IO-520-D	1520			Floats
☐ C-GFRD	De Havilland DHC-2 Beaver I	654	N5151G	0053		1 PW R-985	2313			Floats

COASTAL MOUNTAIN AIRWAYS, Ltd — **Pemberton, B.C.**

Box 105, Pemberton, British Columbia V0N 2L0, Canada ☎ (604) 894-5850 Tx: none Fax: (604) 894-6531 SITA: n/a
F: 1996 ♟♟♟ n/a Head: n/a Net: n/a Aircraft below MTOW 1361kg: Cessna 172

☐ C-GJPF	Cessna U206G Stationair 6 II	U20605250	N5369U	0079	0897	1 CO IO-520-F	1633			

COASTAL PACIFIC AVIATION, Ltd (formerly Coastal Pacific Flight Centre, Ltd) — **Abbotsford, B.C.**

30575 Approach Drive, Abbotsford, British Columbia V2T 6H5, Canada ☎ (604) 855-1112 Tx: none Fax: (604) 855-1088 SITA: n/a
F: 1973 ♟♟♟ n/a Head: Cole Shelby Net: http://www.coastalpacific.com Aircraft below MTOW 1361kg: Cessna 170 & 172

☐ C-FADS	Piper PA-30-160 Twin Comanche	30-613		0065	0380	2 LY IO-320-B1A	1633			
☐ C-GIFB	Piper PA-30-160 Twin Comanche	30-64	N7054Y	0064	1185	2 LY IO-320-B1A	1633			
☐ C-GRCG	Piper PA-30-160 Twin Comanche B	30-1299	N8182Y	0067	0291	2 LY IO-320-B1A	1633			

COAST WESTERN AIRLINES, Ltd — **Sechelt, B.C.**

Box 1827, Sechelt, British Columbia V0N 3A0, Canada ☎ (604) 885-4711 Tx: none Fax: (604) 885-1083 SITA: n/a
F: 1988 ♟♟♟ n/a Head: n/a Net: n/a Aircraft below MTOW 1361kg: Cessna 180 (on Floats)

☐ C-FMPD	De Havilland DHC-2 Beaver I	1510		0062	0695	1 PW R-985	2309			Floats
☐ CF-FAQ	De Havilland DHC-2 Beaver I	94		0049	0489	1 PW R-985	2309			Floats

COCHRANE AIR SERVICES, Ltd (Seasonal May-November ops only) — **Cochrane-Lillabelle Lake, Ont.**

PO Box 1893, Cochrane, Ontario P0L 1C0, Canada ☎ (705) 272-5570 Tx: none Fax: (705) 272-4388 SITA: n/a
F: 1978 ♟♟♟ 6 Head: Jerry J. Krahenbuhl Net: http://onlink1.onlink.net/puc/cair.htm Aircraft below MTOW 1361kg: Cessna 180 (on Floats)

☐ C-FGBF	De Havilland DHC-2 Beaver I	168		0051		1 PW R-985	2309			Floats
☐ C-FGYP	De Havilland DHC-2 Beaver I	145		0051		1 PW R-985	2309			Floats
☐ C-FITS	De Havilland DHC-3 Otter	90		0056	0197	1 PW R-1340	3629			Floats

COMMANDO AIR TRANSPORT, Inc. — **Winnipeg-Int'l, Man.**

1 Allen Dyne Road, Winnipeg, Manitoba R3H 0Z9, Canada ☎ (204) 783-8933 Tx: none Fax: (204) 783-9058 SITA: n/a
F: 1996 ♟♟♟ n/a Head: Jeff Schroeder Net: n/a

☐ C-GIBX	Curtiss C-46F-1-CU Commando	22472	5Y-IBX	0045	1096	2 PW R-2800	21772	Freighter		
☐ C-GTXW	Curtiss C-46A-45-CU Commando	30386	5Y-TXW	0044	1096	2 PW R-2800	21772	Freighter		

CONAIR AVIATION = CRC (Conair Aviation, Ltd dba) — **Abbotsford, B.C.**

Box 220, Abbotsford, British Columbia V2S 4N9, Canada ☎ (604) 855-1171 Tx: none Fax: (604) 855-1017 SITA: n/a
F: 1969 ♟♟♟ 300 Head: K. Barry Marsden ICAO: CONAIR CANADA Net: http://www.conair.ca

☐ C-FFIF	AAC (Piper) Aerostar 600A	60-0702-7961218	N6073K	0079	0689	2 LY IO-540-K1J5	2495	Birddog		122
☐ C-GBBP	AAC (Ted Smith) Aerostar 600A	60-0142-062	N17HA	0073		2 LY IO-540-G1B5	2495	Birddog		120
☐ C-GHUR	AAC (Ted Smith) Aerostar 601	61-0174-085	N75438	0074		2 LY IO-540-S1A5	2585	Birddog		114
☐ C-GLVG	AAC (Piper) Aerostar 600A	60-0695-7961217	N6072U	0079		2 LY IO-540-K1J5	2495	Birddog		111
☐ C-GMGZ	AAC (Piper) Aerostar 600A	60-0708-7961220	N6075C	0079		2 LY IO-540-K1J5	2495	Birddog		112
☐ C-GOSX	AAC (Piper) Aerostar 600A	60-0863-8161246		0081		2 LY IO-540-K1J5	2495	Birddog		110
☐ C-GRIK	AAC (Piper) Aerostar 600A	60-0563-7961183	N8040J	0079		2 LY IO-540-K1J5	2495	Birddog		108
☐ C-GRSQ	AAC (Piper) Aerostar 600A	60-0896-8161254	N6893S	0081		2 LY IO-540-K1J5	2495	Birddog		116
☐ C-GSXX	AAC (Ted Smith) Aerostar 600A	60-0430-146	N9795Q	0077		2 LY IO-540-K1F5	2495	Birddog		109
☐ C-GUHK	AAC (Piper) Aerostar 600A	60-0761-8061230	N8EA	0080		2 LY IO-540-K1J5	2495	Birddog		119
☐ C-GUSZ	AAC (Piper) Aerostar 600A	60-0894-8161253	N6893Q	0081		2 LY IO-540-K1J5	2495	Birddog		118
☐ C-GUTV	AAC (Piper) Aerostar 600A	60-0722-8061224	N8NF	0080		2 LY IO-540-K1J5	2495	Birddog		121
☐ C-GAAL	Twin (Aero) Turbo Commander 690A	11104	N690DA	0073	0597	2 GA TPE331-5-251K	4649	Liaison		131
☐ C-GTUC	Beech King Air 200	BB-268	N565RA	0077		2 PWC PT6A-41	5670	Liaison		115
☐ C-FXVF	Air Tractor AT-802	802-0033		0096	0596	1 PWC PT6A-67R	7257	Tanker		678
☐ C-FXVL	Air Tractor AT-802	802-0034		0096	0596	1 PWC PT6A-67R	7257	Tanker		679
☐ C-FEFK	Conair Firecat	014	F-ZBEH	0057	0389	2 PW R-982-C9HE2	11793	Tanker		574 / cvtd Grumman S2 Tracker cn 360
☐ C-FEFX	Conair Firecat	031	N425DF	0058	0489	2 PW R-982-C9HE2	11793	Tanker		575 / cvtd Grumman S2 Tracker cn 527
☐ C-FJOH	Conair Firecat	034	N424DF	0057	0191	2 PW R-982-C9HE2	11793	Tanker		576 / cvtd Grumman S2 Tracker cn 254
☐ C-FOPU	Conair Firecat	007	RCAF3680	0058		2 PW R-982-C9HE2	11793	Tanker		564 / cvtd DHC CS2F-1 Tracker cn DHC-38
☐ C-FOPV	Conair Firecat	006	RCAF3676	0058		2 PW R-982-C9HE2	11793	Tanker		566 / cvtd DHC CS2F-1 Tracker cn DHC-34
☐ C-FOPY	Conair Firecat	019	CF-IOF	0057		2 PW R-982-C9HE2	11793	Tanker		569 / cvtd DHC CS2F-1 Tracker cn DHC-24
☐ C-GABC	Conair Firecat	011	CAF12189	0060		2 PW R-982-C9HE2	11793	Tanker		567 / cvtd DHC CS2F-2 Tracker cn DHC-90
☐ C-GHDY	Conair Firecat	029	USN136465	0057		2 PW R-982-C9HE2	11793	Tanker		573 / cvtd Grumman S2 Tracker cn 374
☐ C-GHPJ	Conair Firecat	022	USN136600	0058		2 PW R-982-C9HE2	11793	Tanker		571 / cvtd Grumman S2 Tracker cn 509
☐ C-GWUO	Conair Firecat	003	CAF12140	0058		2 PW R-982-C9HE2	11793	Tanker		563 / cvtd DHC CS2F-1 Tracker cn DHC-39
☐ C-GWUP	Conair Firecat	012	RCN1520	0057		2 PW R-982-C9HE2	11793	Tanker		568 / cvtd DHC CS2F-1 Tracker cn DHC-19
☐ C-GYQI	Conair Firecat	030	USN136515	0057		2 PW R-982-C9HE2	11793	Tanker		570 / cvtd Grumman S2 Tracker cn 424
☐ C-FWYU	De Havilland DHC-7-103 Dash 7	012	N678MA	0079	1195	4 PWC PT6A-50	19958	Y50/Combi/Frtr		170
☐ C-FCZZ	Boeing (Douglas) DC-6A/B	45498 / 1005	F-ZBAP	0058	0588	4 PW R-2800-CB16	47174	Tanker		452
☐ C-GHCB	Boeing (Douglas) DC-6B	44893 / 647	N62876	0056	1273	4 PW R-2800-CB16	47083	Tanker		443
☐ C-GHLY	Boeing (Douglas) DC-6B	45501 / 953	OO-VGE	0058	0175	4 PW R-2800-CB16	47083	Tanker		446
☐ C-GIBS	Boeing (Douglas) DC-6A/C	45531 / 1015	HB-IBS	0058	0982	4 PW R-2800-CB16	47083	Tanker		451
☐ C-GIOY	Boeing (Douglas) DC-6B	45506 / 1002	OO-VGK	0058	1076	4 PW R-2800-CB16	47083	Tanker		448
☐ C-GJKT	Boeing (Douglas) DC-6A	45179 / 865	N864TA	0057	0482	4 PW R-2800-CB16	47083	Tanker		449 / cvtd DC-6B
☐ C-GKUG	Boeing (Douglas) DC-6A	45177 / 859	N863TA	0057	0482	4 PW R-2800-CB16	47083	Tanker		450 / cvtd DC-6B
☐ C-FZCS	Lockheed L-188A (F) Electra	1060	HR-SHN	0059	0397	4 AN 501-D13	51256	Frtr / Tanker		453 / cvtd L-188A

CONCORDE EXECUTIVE AIR (Lid Brokerage & Reality, Co (1977), Ltd dba) — **Saskatoon, Sask.**

1171-8th Street East, Saskatoon, Saskatchewan S7H 0S3, Canada ☎ (306) 668-3000 Tx: none Fax: (306) 668-3096 SITA: n/a
F: 1995 ♟♟♟ n/a Head: Les Dubé Net: n/a

☐ C-GUUU	Cessna 550 Citation II	550-0423	N45MC	0082	1295	2 PWC JT15D-4	6033			

CONFORTAIR, Inc. = COF — **Sept-Iles**

CP 1622, Sept-Iles, Québec G4R 5C7, Canada ☎ (418) 968-4660 Tx: none Fax: (418) 962-0190 SITA: n/a
F: 1991 ♟♟♟ 15 Head: Yvan Tremblay ICAO: CONFORT Net: n/a Aircraft below MTOW 1361kg: Cessna 152 & 172

☐ C-FOPF	Piper PA-23-250 Aztec C	27-3400		0066	1193	2 LY IO-540-C4B5	2359			
☐ C-FVTQ	Piper PA-31-350 Navajo Chieftain	31-7852034	N300DT	0078	1198	2 LY TIO-540-J2BD	3175			
☐ C-GAVY	Piper PA-31-350 Navajo Chieftain	31-7752165	N27409	0077	0992	2 LY TIO-540-J2BD	3175			

CONTACT AIR = V8 (Air Mikisew, Ltd dba / Subsidiary of Mikisew Cree First Nation / formerly Contact Airways, Ltd) — **Fort McMurray, Alta.**

PO Box 5175, Fort McMurray, Alberta T9H 3G3, Canada ☎ (780) 743-8218 Tx: none Fax: (780) 743-8225 SITA: n/a
F: 1961 ♟♟♟ 28 Head: Ray McKenzie Net: n/a Aircraft below MTOW 1361 kg: Cessna 172 & 177.

☐ C-GVQU	Cessna A185F Skywagon	18503648	N8206Q	0078	0595	1 CO IO-520-D	1520			Floats / Wheels
☐ C-GVAM	Cessna U206G Stationair 6 II	U20606177	N918WJ	0081	0997	1 CO IO-520-F	1633			Floats / Wheel-Skis
☐ C-FBAM	Cessna T207A Turbo Stationair 7 II	20700455	N98DF	0078	1198	1 CO TSIO-520-M	1724			
☐ C-GFJN	Cessna 207A Stationair 8 II	20700592		0080	0695	1 CO IO-520-F	1724			
☐ C-GUJV	De Havilland DHC-2 Beaver I	1643	Oman303	0066	0598	1 PW R-985	2313			Floats / Wheels
☐ CF-FHC	De Havilland DHC-2 Beaver I	12		0049	0794	1 PW R-985	2313			Floats / Wheels
☐ C-FVGT	Piper PA-31-350 Navajo Chieftain	31-7405133	N74981	0074	0595	2 LY TIO-540-J2BD	3175			
☐ C-GURM	Piper PA-31-350 Navajo Chieftain	31-7752184	N273RH	0077	0492	2 LY TIO-540-J2BD	3175			
☐ C-GZAM	Beech 99A Airliner	U-116	N17AL	0069	0297	2 PWC PT6A-27	4944			
☐ C-FXAJ	Beech King Air A100	B-122	N8181Z	0072	1295	2 PWC PT6A-28	5216			
☐ C-FKAM	BAe 3112 Jetstream 31	724	N852JS	0086	0498	2 GA TPE331-10UG-513H	6900			

CONTINENTAL HELICOPTERS (2822636 Canada, Inc. dba) — **Inuvik, N.W.T.**

Box 2020, Inuvik, Northwest Territories X0E 0T0, Canada ☎ (867) 777-2323 Tx: none Fax: (867) 777-2444 SITA: n/a
F: 1993 ♟♟♟ 9 Head: Brian Morrison Net: n/a

☐ C-GABE	Bell 206B JetRanger II	2070		0076	0393	1 AN 250-C20	1451			
☐ C-GSHC	Bell 206B JetRanger	1282	N65031	0074	0498	1 AN 250-C20	1451			
☐ C-GUCX	Bell 206B JetRanger	1781		0075	0693	1 AN 250-C20	1451			
☐ C-GRGY	Bell 204B	2022	CF-OKZ	0064	0395	1 LY T5311A	3856			

COOPER AIR, Inc. — **Victoria, B.C.**

Box 2082, Sidney, British Columbia V8L 3S3, Canada ☎ (250) 656-3968 Tx: none Fax: (250) 656-3968 SITA: n/a
F: 1987 ♟♟♟ 3 Head: Richard G. Cooper Net: http://www.cooperair.com

☐ C-GHZP	Cessna A185F Skywagon	18502878		0076	0893	1 CO IO-520-D	1520			Floats
☐ C-GSAI	Cessna U206G Stationair 6 II	U20604745		0079	0489	1 CO IO-520-F	1633			Floats

46 registration type of aircraft cn/fn ex/ex* mfd del powered by mtow kg configuration selcal name/fln/specialitites/remarks

☐ C-GCYM	De Havilland DHC-2 Beaver I	354	N63PS	0051	0598	1 PW R-985	2309		Floats
☐ C-GYOK	De Havilland DHC-2 Beaver I	677	N5152G	0053	0892	1 PW R-985	2309		Floats

CORILAIR CHARTERS, Ltd
Box 350, Whaletown, British Columbia V0P 1Z0, Canada ☎ (250) 935-6981 Tx: n/a Fax: (250) 935-6981 SITA: n/a
F: 1991   ♦♦♦ n/a Head: n/a Net: n/a

Whaletown, B.C.

☐ C-GTNE	Cessna A185E Skywagon	18501889		0071		1 CO IO-520-D	1520		Floats

CORNWALL AVIATION (1979), Ltd (Affiliated with Professional Flight Centre of Canada)
RR 1, Summerstown, Ontario K0C 2E0, Canada ☎ (613) 931-3311 Tx: none Fax: (613) 931-3349 SITA: n/a
F: 1979   ♦♦♦ 14 Head: Gordon Small Net: http://www.pro-flight.on.ca./cornav/   Aircraft below MTOW 1361 kg: Cessna 150, 172 & Piper PA-28

Cornwall-Summerstown, Ont.

☐ C-FGKD	Piper PA-44-180 Seminole	44-7995035	N20943	0078	1089	2 LY O-360-E1A6D	1724		
☐ C-FZLJ	Piper PA-44-180 Seminole	44-7995244	N2095S	0079	0297	2 LY O-360-E1A6D	1724		

CORP AIR, Inc. (Subsidiary of Echo Bay Mines)
9818 International Airport, Edmonton, Alberta T5J 2T2, Canada ☎ (780) 890-7200 Tx: none Fax: (780) 890-7060 SITA: n/a
F: 1991   ♦♦♦ 30 Head: Bill Wheeler Net: n/a   Private, non-commercial company conducting corporate flights for Echo Bay Mines exclusively.

Edmonton, Alta.

☐ C-FPXD	Boeing 727-171C	19859 / 559	N1727T	0468	1091	3 PW JT8D-7A	76657	Corp./Combi/Frtr	Billie Dean

CORPORATE AIR CHARTER, Ltd
55 Holly Street NW, Calgary, Alberta T2K 2C9, Canada ☎ (403) 250-3243 Tx: none Fax: (403) 250-9198 SITA: n/a
F: 1991   ♦♦♦ n/a Head: Peter Lubig Net: n/a

Calgary, Alta.

☐ C-GKFM	Cessna 310N	310N0043	N4143Q	0068	1293	2 CO IO-470-V	2359		

CORPORATE AIRLINK, Ltd
240-2450 Derry Road East, Hangar 9, Mississauga, Ontario L5S 1BL, Canada ☎ (905) 405-0001 Tx: none Fax: (905) 405-0888 SITA: n/a
F: n/a   ♦♦♦ n/a Head: Chuck Montgomery Net: n/a

Toronto-Int'l

☐ C-GLIM	Cessna 560 Citation V Ultra	560-0430	N433CV	0097	0399	2 PWC JT15D-5D	7394		

CORPORATE EXPRESS = CPB (Corpac Canada, Ltd dba / Affiliated with Peariso Aviation, Inc.)
575 Palmer Road NE, Calgary, Alberta T2E 7G4, Canada ☎ (403) 216-4050 Tx: none Fax: (403) 216-4055 SITA: n/a
F: 1975   ♦♦♦ 21 Head: Gordon Peariso ICAO: PENTA Net: http://www.corpxair.com

Calgary, Alta.

☐ C-FMIP	BAe 3112 Jetstream 31	778	N778JX	0087	0897	2 GA TPE331-10UGR-513H	6950	Y19	lsf BAMT
☐ C-GKGM	BAe 3112 Jetstream 31	727	G-SWAC	0087	1196	2 GA TPE331-10UGR-514H	6950	Y19	lsf BAMT
☐ C-GMDJ	BAe 3112 Jetstream 31	829	G-BSIW	0088	0197	2 GA TPE331-10UGR-514H	6950	Y19	lsf BAMT
☐ C-GNRG	BAe 3112 Jetstream 31	791	N791JX	0087	1098	2 GA TPE331-10UG-513H	6900	Y19	lsf BAMT

COUGAR HELICOPTERS, Inc. = CHI
PO Box 248, Waverley, Nova Scotia B0N 2S0, Canada ☎ (902) 873-3611 Tx: none Fax: (902) 873-3972 SITA: n/a
F: 1984   ♦♦♦ 45 Head: James Johnston ICAO: COUGAR Net: n/a

Halifax, N.S.

☐ C-FDCX	Bell 206B JetRanger	652	N7935J	0571	0595	1 AN 250-C20	1451	4 Pax	Floats / Skids / cvtd 206A
☐ C-GXCH	Bell 206B JetRanger II	2000	N49735	0076		1 AN 250-C20	1451	4 Pax	Floats / Skids
☐ C-GCHA	Bell 206LR+ LongRanger	45121	N102MM	0077		1 AN 250-C20R	1814	6 Pax	Pop-out-Floats / cvtd 206L
☐ C-FBCH	Eurocopter (Aerosp.) AS355F1 TwinStar	5124	N220	0082	0498	2 AN 250-C20F	2400		
☐ C-GKCH	Sikorsky S-76A	760228	N117BG	0083	0790	2 AN 250-C30S	4763	12 Pax / EMS	Offshore
☐ C-GSCH	Sikorsky S-76A	760147	N32HA	0081		2 AN 250-C30S	4763	12 Pax / EMS	Offshore
☐ C-GYCH	Sikorsky S-61N	61762	PH-NZI	0077	0191	2 GE CT58-140-1	9318	19 Pax	Offshore
☐ C-GQCH	Eurocopter (Aerosp.) AS332L Super Puma	2139	LN-OLF	0085	0597	2 TU Makila 1A	8600		lsf HKS / Offshore
☐ C-GTCH	Eurocopter (Aerosp.) AS332L Super Puma	2048	LN-OMD	0082	0497	2 TU Makila 1A	8600		lsf HKS / Offshore
☐ C-GVCH	Eurocopter (Aerosp.) AS332L Super Puma	2074	LN-OLA	0083	0497	2 TU Makila 1A	8600		lsf HKS / Offshore

COULSON AIRCRANE, Ltd (Affiliated with Coulson Forest Products, Ltd & Coulson Aircrane USA, Inc. / formerly Coulson Helicopters, Ltd)
RR3, Site 360, Comp. 8, Port Alberni, British Columbia V9Y 7L7, Canada ☎ (250) 723-8100 Tx: none Fax: (250) 723-0608 SITA: n/a
F: 1985   ♦♦♦ 30 Head: Wayne C. Coulson Net: n/a

Port Alberni, B.C.

☐ C-FBQI	Bell 206B JetRanger	747		0071	1297	1 AN 250-C20	1451		cvtd 206A
☐ C-FDYK	Bell 206B JetRanger	972		0073	0695	1 AN 250-C20	1451		
☐ C-GXOH	Bell 206B JetRanger	865	N14844	0072	0585	1 AN 250-C20	1451		
☐ C-FMHR	De Havilland DHC-6 Twin Otter 100	51	N51FW	0067	0397	2 PWC PT6A-20	5252		Floats
☐ C-FCLM	Sikorsky S-61N	61492	N226BF	0072	0390	2 GE CT58-140-1	9979		
☐ C-FMAG	Sikorsky S-61N	61821	N611RM	0078	0994	2 GE CT58-140-1	9979		
☐ C-FMAY	Sikorsky S-61N	61363	N306V	0067	0287	2 GE CT58-140-1	9979		

COUNTRY AIRLINES, Ltd
Box 49, Cassidy, British Columbia V0R 1H0, Canada ☎ (250) 245-4647 Tx: none Fax: (250) 245-4647 SITA: n/a
F: 1993   ♦♦♦ n/a Head: Donald F. McGillivary Net: n/a

Nanaimo, B.C.

☐ C-FZGO	Cessna 337F Super Skymaster	33701348	N1748M	0071	0197	2 CO IO-360-C/D	2100		
☐ C-FVEY	Cessna 320C SkyKnight	320C0048	N4449	0065	0998	2 CO TSIO-470-D	2359		

COURTESY AIR (Buffalo Narrows Airways, Ltd dba)
PO Box 176, Buffalo Narrows, Saskatchewan S0M 0J0, Canada ☎ (306) 235-4373 Tx: none Fax: (306) 235-4622 SITA: n/a
F: 1977   ♦♦♦ 7 Head: Karen O'Brien Net: n/a Aircraft below MTOW 1361kg: Piper PA-18.

Buffalo Narrows, Sask.

☐ C-GOZP	Cessna A185F Skywagon	18503258		0077		1 CO IO-520-D	1520		Floats / Wheel-Skis
☐ C-GDOB	De Havilland DHC-2 Beaver I	774	C-GEZR	0055		1 PW R-985	2313		Floats / Wheel-Skis
☐ C-GDVD	Beech Baron 58	TH-668	N4557S	0075		2 CO IO-520-C	2449		
☐ C-GKLO	Piper PA-31-350 Navajo Chieftain	31-8152118	N4505N	0081	1095	2 LY TIO-540-J2BD	3175		
☐ C-GKNL	Piper PA-31-350 Navajo Chieftain	31-7852083		0078		2 LY TIO-540-J2BD	3175		
☐ C-GNRM	Piper PA-31-350 Navajo Chieftain	31-7752145	G-BMIN	0077	1096	2 LY TIO-540-J2BD	3175		
☐ C-GBNA	De Havilland DHC-3 Otter	125	N5368G	0056		1 PW R-1340	3629		Floats / Wheel-Skis

COYOTE AIR SERVICE, Ltd
Fox Point Bay, Teslin, Yukon Territory Y0A 1B0, Canada ☎ (867) 390-2605 Tx: n/a Fax: (867) 390-2207 SITA: n/a
F: 1979   ♦♦♦ n/a Head: Denny Denison Net: n/a Aircraft below MTOW 1361 kg: Maule M-7-235.

Teslin, Y.T.

☐ C-FBGL	Pilatus PC-6/350-H2 Porter	540	N17077	0062	0693	1 LY GO-540-A1A	2200		Floats / Wheel-Skis

CRANBERRY AIR (3122999 Manitoba, Ltd dba)
Box 2976, The Pas, Manitoba R9A 1R7, Canada ☎ (204) 623-5489 Tx: none Fax: (204) 623-6264 SITA: n/a
F: 1994   ♦♦♦ n/a Head: Bob Gladstone Net: n/a Aircraft below MTOW 1361kg: Cessna 180 (on Floats / Wheel-Skis)

The Pas, Man.

☐ C-FOPB	Cessna A185F Skywagon	18502404	N1681R	0074	0895	1 CO IO-520-D	1520		Floats / Wheel-Skis

CREE LAKE AIR, Inc. (Seasonal May-October ops only)
315 Bayview Crescent, Saskatoon, Saskatchewan S7V 1B5, Canada ☎ (306) 249-1617 Tx: none Fax: (306) 955-7732 SITA: n/a
F: 1998   ♦♦♦ n/a Head: Gary Lynchuk Net: n/a Aircraft below MTOW 1361kg: Cessna 180

Cree Lake, Sask.

☐ C-FWLE	Piper PA-32-300 Cherokee SIX	32-40256		0067	0598	1 LY IO-540-K1A5	1542		
☐ C-FRGH	Piper PA-23-250 Aztec C	27-2577		0064	0598	2 LY IO-540-C4B5	2359		

CROSS LAKE AIR SERVICE, Ltd - C.L.A.S.
Box 100, Waboweden, Manitoba R0B 1S0, Canada ☎ (204) 689-2166 Tx: none Fax: none SITA: n/a
F: 1960   ♦♦♦ 5 Head: George Dram Net: n/a

Wabowden, Man.

☐ C-GYBQ	Cessna A185F Skywagon II	18503568		0078		1 CO IO-520-D	1520		Floats / Wheel-Skis
☐ C-FBQY	De Havilland DHC-2 Beaver I	1496	N147Q	0061		1 PW R-985	2313		Floats
☐ C-FLLL	De Havilland DHC-3 Otter	292		0059		1 PW R-1340	3629		Floats

CROWN CHARTER SERVICES (Div. of Crown Mail & Delivery Services, Ltd / Sister co. of Gateway Airlines)
PO Box 1434, Brantford, Ontario N3T 5T6, Canada ☎ (519) 758-8287 Tx: none Fax: (519) 758-9753 SITA: n/a
F: 1992   ♦♦♦ n/a Head: Blaine Field Net: n/a

Branford, Ont.

☐ C-FESC	Piper.PA-31-350 Navajo Chieftain	31-7952207	N3536J	0079	1297	2 LY TIO-540-J2BD	3288		
☐ C-GIXE	Piper PA-31-310 Navajo B	31-7401208	N20RL	0073	0297	2 LY TIO-540-A2C	2948		
☐ C-GJET	Piper PA-31-350 Navajo Chieftain	31-7752134	N27304	0077	0196	2 LY TIO-540-J2BD	3175		
☐ C-GPTB	Piper PA-31-310 Navajo B	31-836	N7444L	0072	0298	2 LY TIO-540-A2C	2948		
☐ C-GEGH	Cessna 421B Golden Eagle	421B0208	N5965M	0072	1298	2 CO GTSIO-520-H	3379		
☐ C-FYAU	Cessna 404 Titan II	404-0431	N408EX	0079	1194	2 CO GTSIO-520-M	3810		
☐ C-GHRM	Piper PA-31T Cheyenne II	31T-7620053	N16HA	0076	1097	2 PWC PT6A-28	4082		
☐ C-GBTS	Beech King Air B100	BE-73	N54CK	0079	0498	2 GA TPE331-6-252B	5352		
☐ C-GKNP	Beech King Air B100	BE-89	N737MG	0077	1297	2 GA TPE331-6-252B	5352		
☐ C-GDRG	Shorts Skyvan 3 Variant 200 (SC-7)	SH1847	PT-WYA	0068	0198	2 GA TPE331-2-201A	5670	Surveyer	

CSI AVIATION, Inc.
Hamilton, Ont.

332 Jones Road North, Stoney Creek, Ontario L8E 5N2, Canada ☎ (519) 740-7798 Tx: none Fax: (519) 740-7798 SITA: n/a
F: 1996   ✦✦✦ 3   Head: Edward (Ted) Tofflemire   Net: n/a

registration	type of aircraft	cn/fn	ex/ex*	mfd	del	powered by	mtow kg	configuration	name/fin/remarks
☐ C-FZEI	IAI 1124 Westwind I	441	HK-3893X	0087	1196	2 GA TFE731-3-1G	10365		

CUSTOM HELICOPTERS, Ltd
Winnipeg-St. Andrews / Gillam / Island Lake & The Pas, Man.

401 Helicopter Drive, St. Andrews Airport, St. Andrews, Manitoba R1A 3P7, Canada ☎ (204) 338-7953 Tx: none Fax: (204) 663-5037 SITA: n/a
F: 1977   ✦✦✦ 31   Head: James Hawes   Net: n/a   Aircraft below MTOW 1361 kg: Hughes 269C (300C).

registration	type of aircraft	cn/fn	ex/ex*	mfd	del	powered by	mtow kg	name/fin/remarks
☐ C-FDUV	Bell 206B JetRanger	70	N7883S	0067	0995	1 AN 250-C20	1451	cvtd 206A
☐ C-FKBV	Bell 206B JetRanger	364	N465CC	0069	1092	1 AN 250-C20	1451	cvtd 206A
☐ C-FSVG	Bell 206B JetRanger III	2865	N1074G	0079	0992	1 AN 250-C20B	1451	
☐ C-FZSJ	Bell 206B JetRanger	648	N7108J	0070		1 AN 250-C20	1451	cvtd 206A
☐ C-GAHX	Bell 206B JetRanger	187	N4014G	0068	0793	1 AN 250-C20	1451	cvtd 206A
☐ C-GBWN	Bell 206B JetRanger II	2204		0077		1 AN 250-C20	1451	
☐ C-GFIV	Bell 206B JetRanger	424	N1481W	0069		1 AN 250-C20	1451	cvtd 206A
☐ C-GGZS	Bell 206B JetRanger	1885		0075		1 AN 250-C20	1451	
☐ C-GIOC	Bell 206B JetRanger	212	N209E	0068	1295	1 AN 250-C20	1451	cvtd 206A
☐ C-GKBU	Bell 206B JetRanger	386	N1448W	0069	1092	1 AN 250-C20	1451	cvtd 206A
☐ C-GQQO	Bell 206B JetRanger	1096	N83182	0073		1 AN 250-C20	1451	
☐ C-GQQT	Bell 206B JetRanger	1657	N90218	0075		1 AN 250-C20	1451	
☐ C-GSHJ	Bell 206B JetRanger	114	N125GW	0067	1092	1 AN 250-C20	1451	cvtd 206A
☐ C-GAVH	Bell 206L-1 LongRanger III	45740	N385FP	0081	0196	1 AN 250-C30P	1882	cvtd LongRanger II
☐ C-GCHI	Bell 206L-1 LongRanger II	45516	N141VG	0080	0395	1 AN 250-C28B	1882	
☐ C-GCHZ	Bell 206L-1 LongRanger III	45314	N210AH	0079	0496	1 AN 250-C30P	1882	cvtd LongRanger II
☐ C-GIPG	Bell 206L-1 LongRanger II	45592	N3895K	0080	1295	1 AN 250-C28B	1882	
☐ C-FCHD	Bell 205A-1	30014	N5598M	0068	0589	1 LY T5313B	4309	
☐ C-GRWK	Bell 205A-1	30005	N3764U	0068	0696	1 LY T5313B	4309	

CYPRESS HELICOPTERS, Ltd
Bow Island, Alta.

Box 716, Bow Island, Alberta T0K 0G0, Canada ☎ (780) 545-6453 Tx: none Fax: (780) 545-6453 SITA: n/a
F: 1981   ✦✦✦ 3   Head: Al Strom   Net: n/a

registration	type of aircraft	cn/fn	ex/ex*	mfd	del	powered by	mtow kg
☐ C-GIMO	Sikorsky S-58E	58-067		0055	0181	1 WR R-1820	5897

DAL AVIATION   (Associated with High Arctic Sportfishing, Ltd / Commercial ops in summers (sportfishing support) only)
Cambridge Bay, N.W.T.

Box 280, Penticton, British Columbia V2A 6K4, Canada ☎ (250) 497-2000 Tx: none Fax: (250) 497-2001 SITA: n/a
F: 1974   ✦✦✦ 1   Head: Fred Hamilton   Net: http://www.higharctic.com

registration	type of aircraft	cn/fn	ex/ex*	mfd	del	powered by	mtow kg	remarks
☐ C-GBIY	Cessna U206G Stationair 6 II	U20605275		0079	0789	1 CO IO-520-F	1633	Amphibian
☐ C-GUCE	Cessna U206F Stationair II	U20602887	N70503	0075	0594	1 CO IO-520-F	1633	Amphibian

DALZIEL HUNTING, Ltd – Airservices
Watson Lake, Y.T.

PO Box 44, Dease Lake, British Columbia V0C 1L0, Canada ☎ (604) 771-3055 Tx: n/a Fax: (604) 771-3056 SITA: n/a
F: 1943   ✦✦✦ n/a   Head: n/a   Net: n/a   Aircraft below MTOW 1361 kg: Piper PA-18 (on floats / wheel-skis).

registration	type of aircraft	cn/fn	ex/ex*	mfd	del	powered by	mtow kg	remarks
☐ CF-DLL	De Havilland DHC-2 Beaver I	98	N4790C	0051		1 PW R-985	2313	Floats / Wheel-Skis

DANIEL'S HARBOUR AVIATION, Ltd   (Seasonal May-October ops only)
Daniel's Harbour, Nfld.

PO Box 33, Daniel's Harbour, Newfoundland A0K 2C0, Canada ☎ (709) 898-2557 Tx: none Fax: (709) 898-2249 SITA: n/a
F: 1994   ✦✦✦ n/a   Head: n/a   Net: n/a

registration	type of aircraft	cn/fn	ex/ex*	mfd	del	powered by	mtow kg	remarks
☐ C-GUWA	Cessna A185F Skywagon	18503302		0077	0994	1 CO IO-520-D	1520	Floats

DAUPHIN AIR SERVICE   (Dauphin Air Service, Ltd dba)
Dauphin, Man.

PO Box 830, Dauphin, Manitoba R7N 3B3, Canada ☎ (204) 638-63 83 Tx: n/a Fax: (204) 638-8299 SITA: n/a
F: 1978   ✦✦✦ 6   Head: Robert & Pat Simpson   Net: n/a   Aircraft below MTOW 1361 kg: Bellanca 7ECA & Cessna 172.

registration	type of aircraft	cn/fn	ex/ex*	mfd	del	powered by	mtow kg	remarks
☐ C-GRRU	Helio H-250 Courier	2509	N5452E	0065		1 LY O-540-A1A5	1542	Wheel-Skis
☐ C-GEXT	Cessna U206F Stationair II	U20603249		0076		1 CO IO-520-F	1633	

DAY AIRWAYS, Ltd
Haliburton, Ont.

Box 965, Haliburton, Ontario K0M 1S0, Canada ☎ (705) 457-3068 Tx: none Fax: (705) 457-1520 SITA: n/a
F: 1988   ✦✦✦ 1   Head: Barry Day   Net: n/a

registration	type of aircraft	cn/fn	ex/ex*	mfd	del	powered by	mtow kg	remarks
☐ C-FIDG	De Havilland DHC-2 Beaver I	718	N99872	0054		1 PW R-985	2313	Floats

D.B. AIR   (D.B. Aviation Ltd dba)
Toronto-Int'l, Ont.

25 Waterford Crescent, Stoney Creek, Ontario L8E 4Z8, Canada ☎ (905) 643-7268 Tx: none Fax: (905) 643-7267 SITA: n/a
F: 1997   ✦✦✦ 6   Head: Dave Babiak   Net: n/a

registration	type of aircraft	cn/fn	ex/ex*	mfd	del	powered by	mtow kg
☐ C-FNAG	Piper PA-31-350 Navajo Chieftain	31-8152077	N975CG	0081	0198	2 LY TIO-540-J2BD	3175

DEH CHO AIR, Ltd   (Subsidiary of Liard Valley Development, Corp.)
Fort Liard, N.W.T.

Box 78, Fort Liard, Northwest Territories X0G 0A0, Canada ☎ (867) 770-4103 Tx: 036-73133 govt nwt f Fax: (867) 770-4102 SITA: n/a
F: 1985   ✦✦✦ 6   Head: Ray Harbats   Net: http://www.dehchoair.com

registration	type of aircraft	cn/fn	ex/ex*	mfd	del	powered by	mtow kg	remarks
☐ C-GZXU	Cessna A185F Skywagon II	18503527	N2726Q	0078	0292	1 CO IO-520-D	1520	Floats / Wheel-Skis
☐ C-FILO	Cessna U206F Stationair	U20602076		0073		1 CO IO-520-F	1633	Floats / Wheel-Skis
☐ C-GIHF	Britten-Norman BN-2A-26 Islander	475	G-BDJU	0075	0494	2 LY O-540-E4C5	2858	

DEH CHO HELICOPTERS, Ltd   (Sister company of Deh Cho Air, Ltd)
Fort Liard, N.W.T.

Box 78, Fort Liard, Northwest Territories X0G 0A0, Canada ☎ (867) 770-4103 Tx: 036-73133 govt nwt f Fax: (867) 770-3555 SITA: n/a
F: 1996   ✦✦✦ n/a   Head: Harry Deneron   Net: n/a

registration	type of aircraft	cn/fn	ex/ex*	mfd	del	powered by	mtow kg	remarks
☐ C-FWDV	Bell 212	30973	N2768N	0079	0796	2 PWC PT6T-3 TwinPac	5080	lsf Northern Mountain Helicopters

DEL AIR, Ltd   (Seasonal May-October ops only)
Kenora-SPB, Ont.

Box 619, Kenora, Ontario P0N 3X6, Canada ☎ (807) 468-7954 Tx: none Fax: none SITA: n/a
F: 1995   ✦✦✦ n/a   Head: n/a   Net: n/a

registration	type of aircraft	cn/fn	ex/ex*	mfd	del	powered by	mtow kg	remarks
☐ C-FWMM	Cessna A185F Skywagon	18502238	N4361Q	0073	0597	1 CO IO-520-D	1520	Floats
☐ C-GYJY	Cessna A185F Skywagon	18502468	N1748R	0074	0797	1 CO IO-520-D	1506	Floats

DELCO AVIATION, Ltée
Montreal-Commodore SPB & Montreal-St-Hubert, Qué.

CP 261, Laval-des-Rapides, Québec H7N 4Z9, Canada ☎ (514) 663-4311 Tx: n/a Fax: (514) 663-7247 SITA: n/a
F: 1975   ✦✦✦ 8   Head: Jean Heppell   Net: n/a

registration	type of aircraft	cn/fn	ex/ex*	mfd	del	powered by	mtow kg	remarks
☐ C-FSSA	Cessna U206F Stationair	U20602068		0073		1 CO IO-520-F	1633	Jésus est le Chemin / Floats/Wheel-Skis
☐ C-GMJH	Cessna U206F Stationair II	U20602787	N35895	0075	0591	1 CO IO-520-F	1633	Jésus est le Chemin / Floats/Wheel-Skis
☐ CF-GYJ	De Havilland DHC-2 Beaver I	133		0051	0595	1 PW R-985	2313	Floats/Wheel-Skis

DELTA HELICOPTERS, Ltd
High Level & Lac La Biche, Alta.

Site 6, Box 1, RR1, St. Albert, Alberta T8N 1M8, Canada ☎ (780) 458-3564 Tx: none Fax: (780) 458-3591 SITA: n/a
F: 1972   ✦✦✦ 20   Head: Donald G. Stubbs   Net: n/a   Aircraft below MTOW 1361 kg: Bell 47G, Hughes 269C (300C) / 369HS (500C) & Robinson R44

registration	type of aircraft	cn/fn	ex/ex*	mfd	del	powered by	mtow kg	remarks
☐ C-FCQJ	Bell 206B JetRanger	540		0070	0297	1 AN 250-C20	1451	cvtd 206A
☐ C-FDYO	Bell 206B JetRanger	994		0073		1 AN 250-C20	1451	
☐ C-GDBN	Bell 206B JetRanger III	2467	C-GDEN	0078		1 AN 250-C20B	1451	
☐ C-GDJW	Bell 206B JetRanger III	2909	N353E	0080		1 AN 250-C20B	1451	
☐ C-GGOZ	Bell 206B JetRanger	443	N2162L	0069	0297	1 AN 250-C20	1451	cvtd 206A
☐ C-GPEZ	Bell 206B JetRanger	1130	N9JJ	0073		1 AN 250-C20	1451	
☐ C-GSHN	Bell 206B JetRanger	616		0071		1 AN 250-C20	1451	cvtd 206A
☐ C-GTIS	Bell 206B JetRanger	827	N3YE	0072		1 AN 250-C20	1451	
☐ C-GERI	Bell 206L-1 LongRanger II	45668		0082	0598	1 AN 250-C28B	1882	
☐ C-GPGO	Bell 206L-1 LongRanger II	45475	N57416	0080	0197	1 AN 250-C28B	1882	
☐ C-FAHO	Bell 204B	2060		0067		1 LY T5311A	3856	
☐ C-GDUK	Bell 204B	2034	N636	0065		1 LY T5311A	3856	
☐ C-GJLV	Bell 204B	2064	Thai918	0067		1 LY T5311B	3856	
☐ C-GTNP	Bell 204B	2028	OY-HBS	0065		1 LY T5311B	3856	
☐ C-GVEX	Bell 204B	2031	OY-HBV	0066	0391	1 LY T5311A	3856	

DENENDEH HELICOPTERS, Ltd   (Affiliated with Frontier Helicopters & Evergreen Forestry Management)
Hay River, N.W.T.

Box 3070, Hay River Dene Reserve, Northwest Territories X0E 1G4, Canada ☎ (867) 874-3399 Tx: none Fax: (867) 874-3229 SITA: n/a
F: 1993   ✦✦✦ n/a   Head: Chief Pat Martel   Net: n/a

registration	type of aircraft	cn/fn	ex/ex*	mfd	del	powered by	mtow kg	remarks
☐ C-GMJS	Bell 206L LongRanger	46608	N120RM	0078	0797	1 AN 250-C20B	1814	lsf Frontier Helicopters

DERAPS AVIATION, Inc.
Natashquan, Qué.

CP 53, Natashquan, Québec G0G 2E0, Canada ☎ (418) 726-3657 Tx: n/a Fax: (418) 726-3755 SITA: n/a
F: 1986   ✦✦✦ 5   Head: Leonard Deraps   Net: n/a

registration	type of aircraft	cn/fn	ex/ex*	mfd	del	powered by	mtow kg	remarks
☐ C-GUBN	Cessna U206F Stationair II	U20602860		0075		1 CO IO-520-F	1633	Floats / Wheel-Skis

☐ C-GUJU	De Havilland DHC-2 Beaver I	1639		0063	0891	1 PW R-985	2313		Floats / Wheel-Skis
☐ C-FLGA	De Havilland DHC-3 Otter	279		0059	0997	1 PW R-1340	3629		Floats / Wheel-Skis

DIAMOND AVIATION, Ltd (Associated with Diamond Construction Equipment, Ltd) — Fredericton, N.B.

Box 2100, Fredericton, New Brunswick E3B 4Y6, Canada ☎ (506) 446-6060 Tx: n/a Fax: (506) 446-6062 SITA: n/a
F: 1988 ✈ n/a Head: Ian Smith Net: n/a

☐ C-GDCL	Twin (Aero) Turbo Commander 690A	11192		0074	0792	2 GA TPE331-5-251K	4649		

DISCOVERY HELICOPTERS, Ltd — Atlin, B.C.

Box 178, Atlin, British Columbia V0W 1A0, Canada ☎ (250) 651-7569 Tx: none Fax: (250) 651-7667 SITA: n/a
F: 1990 ✈ 4 Head: Norman D. Graham Net: n/a

☐ C-GFSD	Bell 206B JetRanger III	2658		0079	0494	1 AN 250-C20B	1451		
☐ C-GOMO	Bell 206B JetRanger	1295		0074	0491	1 AN 250-C20	1451		

D.K. HELI-CROPPER INTERNATIONAL, Ltd — Mt Lehman-Private Heliport, B.C.

29325 Marsh McCormick Road, Mt Lehman, British Columbia V4X 2B4, Canada ☎ (604) 857-2250 Tx: none Fax: (604) 857-2260 SITA: n/a
F: 1968 ✈ 30 Head: Gene Drader Net: n/a

☐ C-GHCA	Hiller UH-12ET	2095	N62PH	0061	0898	1 AN 250-C20B	1406		cvtd UH-12E

DWAYNE AIR, Ltd — Calgary, Alta.

Box 163, Longview, Alberta T0L 1H0, Canada ☎ (780) 938-1429 Tx: none Fax: (780) 938-1431 SITA: n/a
F: 1982 ✈ 4 Head: Bernard (Wayne) Bell Net: n/a

☐ C-GXYM	Eurocopter (Aerosp.) SA315B Lama	2634	N220US	0082	1096	1 TU Artouste IIIB1	1950		
☐ C-GZXX	Eurocopter (Aerosp.) SA315B Lama	2401	N62339	0074	1197	1 TU Artouste IIIB	1950		
☐ C-GANA	Eurocopter (Aerosp.) AS350D AStar	1458	N350GT	0081	0898	1 LY LTS101-600A.2	1950		

DYMOND LAKE AIR SERVICES, Ltd (Affiliated with Dymond Lake Outfitters, Ltd) — Churchill, Man.

PO Box 304, Churchill, Manitoba R0B 0E0, Canada ☎ (204) 675-2583 Tx: none Fax: (204) 675-2386 SITA: n/a
F: 1976 ✈ 1 Head: D.A. Webber Net: n/a Aircraft below MTOW 1361 kg: Cessna 180.

☐ C-FYMV	De Havilland DHC-2 Beaver I	1589	N2118	0065	0693	1 PW R-985	2313		

DYNAMAIR AVIATION, Inc. = DNR — St. Jean, Qué.

5 Chemin de l'Aéroport, St. Jean-sur-Richelieu, Québec J3B 7B5, Canada ☎ (450) 347-7050 Tx: none Fax: (450) 347-4669 SITA: n/a
F: 1984 ✈ 10 Head: Marie-Héline Simard ICAO: DYNAMAIR Net: http://www.odysee.net/dynamair Aircraft below MTOW 1361 kg: Cessna 152 & 172

☐ C-FDNR	Piper PA-34-200 Seneca	34-7250298	N1580X	0072	0691	2 LY IO-360-C1E6	1814		
☐ C-FDYA	Piper PA-34-200 Seneca	34-7350058	N15399	0073	0299	2 LY IO-360-C1E6	1905		
☐ C-GQET	Piper PA-34-200T Seneca II	34-7770030		0076	0299	2 CO TSIO-360-E	2073		

DYNAMIC FLIGHT SERVICES, Inc. — Calgary, Alta

Hangar 5, 620 McTavish Road NE, Calgary, Alberta T2E 7G6, Canada ☎ (403) 735-3290 Tx: none Fax: (403) 735-3291 SITA: n/a
F: 1994 ✈ n/a Head: Arnie W. Toews Net: n/a Aircraft below MTOW 1361kg: Cessna 172

☐ C-GXNL	Cessna 210L Centurion II	21060909	N5327V	0075	0594	1 CO IO-520-L	1724		
☐ C-GTFG	Piper PA-34-200T Seneca II	34-7770021	N5443F	0076	0595	2 CO TSIO-360-E	2073		
☐ C-GDFK	Piper PA-31-350 Navajo Chieftain	31-8052106	N741T	0080	0297	2 LY TIO-540-J2BD	3349		
☐ C-GDFR	Piper PA-31-325 Navajo C/R	31-7812085	N51DW	0078	0498	2 LY TIO-540-F2BD	2948		

E & B HELICOPTERS, Ltd — Campbell River, B.C.

PO Box 1000, Campbell River, British Columbia V9W 6Y4, Canada ☎ (250) 287-4421 Tx: none Fax: (250) 287-4352 SITA: n/a
F: 1990 ✈ n/a Head: Ed Wilcock Net: http://www.vquest.com/ebhelicopter Aircraft below MTOW 1361kg: Robinson R22 & R44

☐ C-FMGS	Bell 206B JetRanger	988	N98VV	0073	0497	1 AN 250-C20	1451		
☐ C-GMGS	Bell 206B JetRanger	450	N96SB	0069	0197	1 AN 250-C20	1451		cvtd 206A
☐ C-GBVD	Bell 206L-3 LongRanger III	51027	D-HHMS	0082	0198	1 AN 250-C30P	1882		

EAST-WEST TRANSPORTATION, Corp. — Salmon Arm, B.C.

Box 160, Salmon Arm, British Columbia V1E 4N4, Canada ☎ (250) 832-8128 Tx: none Fax: (250) 832-9848 SITA: n/a
F: 1996 ✈ n/a Head: n/a Net: n/a

☐ C-FXNI	Bell 214B-1 BigLifter	28022	N214GL	0077	0596	1 LY T5508D	5670		
☐ C-GEWT	Bell 214B BigLifter	28025	JA9201	0078	0898	1 LY T5508D	6123		

ECLIPSE HELICOPTERS, Ltd — Penticton, B.C.

176 Ponderosa Road, Penticton, British Columbia V2A 7Y3, Canada ☎ (250) 492-5221 Tx: none Fax: (250) 492-4813 SITA: n/a
F: 1993 ✈ 2 Head: Eric Stoof Net: n/a

☐ C-FPMW	Eurocopter (Aerosp.) AS350B AStar	2323	JA9879	0090	0993	1 TU Arriel 1B	1950		

E.J. AVIATION, Ltd (Seasonal (summer) operations only. — River of Ponds, Nfld.

River of Ponds, (St. Barbe Dist.), Newfoundland A0K 4M0, Canada ☎ (709) 225-3221 Tx: none Fax: (709) 225-5591 SITA: n/a
F: 1991 ✈ n/a Head: Eric Patey Net: n/a

☐ C-FDSB	De Havilland DHC-2 Beaver I	1154	56-4423	0056	0794	1 PW R-985	2313		Floats

ELLIOT LAKE AVIATION, Ltd (Affiliated with Fishland Camps, Ltd) — Mount Lake, Ont.

PO Box 425, Elliot Lake, Ontario P5A 2J8, Canada ☎ (705) 848-7501 Tx: n/a Fax: (705) 848-8313 SITA: n/a
F: 1972 ✈ 3 Head: Bruno Rapp Net: n/a Aircraft below MTOW 1361 kg: Piper J3C & PA-18.

☐ C-GNXG	De Havilland DHC-2 Beaver I	650	N5148G	0053		1 PW R-985	2313	5 Pax	Floats / Wheel-Skis
☐ C-GTYE	De Havilland DHC-2 Beaver I	990	N202NY	0057		1 PW R-985	2313	5 Pax	Floats / Wheel-Skis

ELMHIRST VACATION AIR, Ltd – Free Spirit Air Adventures (Affiliated with Elmhirst's Resort) — Keene-Rice Lake, Ont.

RR 1, Keene, Ontario K0L 1G0, Canada ☎ (705) 295-4591 Tx: none Fax: (705) 295-4596 SITA: n/a
F: 1978 ✈ 3 Head: Peter Elmhirst Net: http://www.elmhirst.com Aircraft below MTOW 1361 kg: Cessna 172 & Piper PA-12.

☐ C-GCBY	Cessna A185F Skywagon R/STOL	18502378	N1655R	0074		1 CO IO-520-D	1520	4 Pax	Floats / Wheels
☐ C-GCMK	Cessna U206F Stationair	U20602390	N1005V	0074	0394	1 CO IO-520-F	1633	5 Pax	Floats / Wheels

ENTERPRISE AIR, Inc. — Oshawa, Ont.

1000 Stevenson Road North, Hangar 3, Oshawa, Ontario L1J 5P5, Canada ☎ (905) 721-0054 Tx: none Fax: (905) 721-0349 SITA: n/a
F: 1993 ✈ 20 Head: Walter L. Clow Net: n/a

☐ C-FRYZ	Cessna 310J	310J0036	G-BPNS	0065	0798	2 CO IO-470-U	2313	Pax/Freighter	
☐ C-FVRK	Cessna 310L	310L0105		0067	1095	2 CO IO-470-V	2359	Frtr/Pax/Photo	
☐ C-GJMT	Piper PA-31-310 Navajo B	31-7400992	N614C	0074	0198	2 LY TIO-540-A2C	2948	Pax/Freighter	
☐ C-FCLO	Beech E18S	BA-143	N31M	0056	0196	2 PW R-985-AN14B	4581	Freighter	
☐ C-FAMF	Fairchild (Swearingen) SA226T Merlin IIIA	T-274	I-SWAA	0076	1098	2 GA TPE331-3UW-304G	5670	Pax/Freighter	
☐ C-FOOW	Boeing (Douglas) DC-3C (C-47A-25-DK)	13342	8P-OOW	0044	0296	2 PW R-1830-92	12202	Freighter	
☐ C-FCRR	Consolidated 28-5ACF Canso	21996	RCAF 9767	0040	1095	2 PW R-1830-92S	13835	Photo/FilmStudio	Amphibian

ENVIRONMENT CANADA – Flight Dept. (Flight Dept. of Environment Canada-Emergencies Science div., a Government of Canada organisation) — Ottawa, Ont.

Emergencies Science division, 3439 River Road, Ottawa, Ontario K1A 0H3, Canada ☎ (613) 991-1118 Tx: none Fax: (613) 991-9485 SITA: n/a
F: 1997 ✈ n/a Head: Dr. Carl Brown Net: n/a Government organisation conducting remote sensing & surveying flights.

☐ C-GRSB	Boeing (Douglas) DC-3C (C-47A-5-DK)	12295	N91GA	0042	0297	2 PW R-1830	12202	Remote Sensing	
☐ C-GRSC	Convair 580	72	N8EG	0053	0297	2 AN 501-D13	24766	Remote Sensing	cvtd 340-31

EPHESUS TWO TWENTY, Ltd — Winnipeg-St. Andrews, Man.

7 Argate Drive, Winnipeg, Manitoba R2P 1V3, Canada ☎ (204) 231-2992 Tx: none Fax: (204) 632-6251 SITA: n/a
F: 1997 ✈ n/a Head: Michael Graham Net: n/a

☐ C-FSHA	Piper PA-31-350 Navajo Chieftain	31-7752062	PH-NTB	0077	0597	2 LY TIO-540-J2BD	3175		
☐ C-GPYJ	Piper PA-31-350 Navajo Chieftain	31-7405430	N54298	0074	1298	2 LY TIO-540-J2BD	3175		
☐ C-GSHO	Piper PA-31-350 Navajo Chieftain	31-7852079	N93EE	0078	0697	2 LY TIO-540-J2BD	3175		

ESSOR-HELICOPTERES, Inc. — Québec, Qué.

705-7e Ave, Aéroport de Québec, Sainte-Foy, Québec G2E 5W1, Canada ☎ (418) 872-2222 Tx: none Fax: (418) 872-2224 SITA: n/a
F: 1986 ✈ 11 Head: Pierre Fiset Net: n/a

☐ C-GIFV	Bell 206B JetRanger II	2004		0076	0491	1 AN 250-C20	1451		
☐ C-FXZU	Bell 206L-4 LongRanger IV	52164		0096	0596	1 AN 250-C30P	2018		
☐ C-FESS	Bell 407	53129		0097	0497	1 AN 250-C47B	2268		

EXACT AIR, Inc. — Chicoutimi-St. Honoré, Qué.

850 Chemin du Volair, St-Honoré, Québec G0V 1L0, Canada ☎ (418) 673-3522 Tx: none Fax: (418) 673-6156 SITA: n/a
F: 1983 ✈ 14 Head: André Perron Net: n/a Aircraft below MTOW 1361 kg: Cessna 152 & 172

☐ C-GABJ	Piper PA-34-200T Seneca II	34-7870152	N6352C	0078	1293	2 CO TSIO-360-E	2073		
☐ C-GPTU	Piper PA-31-310 Navajo B	31-7401218	N7116A	0074		2 LY TIO-540-A2C	2948		

49 registration type of aircraft cn/fn ex/ex* mfd del powered by mtow kg configuration selcal name/fln/specialitites/remarks

EXECAIRE, Inc. = MB / EXA (Member of Innotech Execaire Aviation Group) — Montreal-Dorval, Qué. & YYZ & YYC

10225 Ryan Avenue, Dorval, Québec H9P 1A2, Canada ☎ (514) 636-7070 Tx: 05821838 execaire mt Fax: (514) 636-8520 SITA: n/a
F: 1960 ☨ 189 Head: Richard Gage ICAO: CANADIAN EXECAIRE Net: n/a

☐ C-FJBO	Cessna 550 Citation Bravo	550-0812	N5223P	0097	0597	2 PWC PW530A	6713			
☐ C-FABR	Beech King Air 350 (B300)	FL-100	N350AM	0093	0199	2 PWC PT6A-60A	6804			
☐ C-GIWO	Learjet 35A	35A-407	C-GIWD	0081	0398	2 GA TFE731-2-2B	7711			
☐ C-GQBR	Learjet 55	55-105	N274	0084	0196	2 GA TFE731-3AR-2B	9752			
☐ C-GABX	Hawker 700A (HS 125-700A)	257047 / NA0233	G-BFZI	0078		2 GA TFE731-3R-1H	11567			
☐ C-GAWH	Hawker 800A (BAe 125-800A)	258087	N800TR	0087		2 GA TFE731-5R-1H	12428		CP-KM	
☐ C-FBEL	Canadair CL-601-1A (CL-600-2A12) Challen.	3028		0084		2 GE CF34-1A	19550		AK-BP	
☐ C-FUND	Canadair CL-601-3R (CL-600-2B16) Challen.	5172	N601FS	0095	0898	2 GE CF34-3A1	20457			
☐ C-GQPA	Canadair CL-604 (CL-600-2B16) Challen.	5379	N604CA	0097	0299	2 GE CF34-3B	21591			
☐ C-GRIO	Canadair CL-604 (CL-600-2B16) Challen.	5353	C-GLXH	0097	0498	2 GE CF34-3B	21591			
☐ C-GSQI	Canadair CL-601-3R (CL-600-2B16) Challen.	5096	HB-IKW	0091	0296	2 GE CF34-3A1	20457		BD-AP	

EXECUTIVE AIR LINK = C7 (Air Direct, Inc. dba) — Oshawa, Ont.

1200 Airport Road, Suite 201, Oshawa, Ontario L1J 8P5, Canada ☎ (905) 721-9696 Tx: none Fax: (905) 721-0672 SITA: n/a
F: 1996 ☨ n/a Head: Mrs. Carol Graham Net: n/a

☐ C-GKGA	Beech 1900C-1 Airliner	UC-117	N117ZR	0790	0097	2 PWC PT6A-65B	7530	Y19		lsf / opb GGN

EXECUTIVE EDGE AIR CHARTER, Inc. — Toronto-Buttonville Municipal, Ont.

2833, 16th Avenue, Box 115, Suite 204, Markham, Ontario L3R 0P8, Canada ☎ (905) 479-3512 Tx: none Fax: (905) 513-8986 SITA: n/a
F: 1994 ☨ n/a Head: n/a Net: n/a

☐ C-GJHF	Cessna 425 Conquest I	425-0080	N880EA	0081	1297	2 PWC PT6A-112	3901			

EXECUTIVE HELICOPTERS (Donfield Industries, Inc. dba / formerly Executive Helicopter Services, Inc.) — Toronto-Int'l, Ont.

400 Brunel Road, Mississauga, Ontario L4Z 2C2, Canada ☎ (905) 507-4613 Tx: none Fax: (905) 507-4177 SITA: n/a
F: 1989 ☨ 7 Head: Richard H. Cooper Net: n/a

☐ C-FFUN	Bell 222U	47508	N3183U	0083	0798	2 LY LTS101-750C.1	3742			

EXPEDITAIR (1989), Inc. — Alma, Qué.

CP 696, Alma, Québec G8B 5W1, Canada ☎ (418) 662-3620 Tx: n/a Fax: (418) 668-8775 SITA: n/a
F: 1989 ☨ 4 Head: n/a Net: n/a

☐ C-FRZL	De Havilland DHC-2 Beaver I	1283	N5554V	0058	0689	1 PW R-985	2313			Floats / Wheel-Skis
☐ CF-GIB	De Havilland DHC-2 Beaver I	6		0047	0689	1 PW R-985	2313			Floats / Wheel-Skis
☐ C-FODT	De Havilland DHC-3 Otter	218		0057	0694	1 PW R-1340	3629			Floats / Wheel-Skis

EXPLOITS VALLEY AIR SERVICES, Ltd — Gander, Nfld.

PO Box 355, Gander, Newfoundland A1V 1W7, Canada ☎ (709) 256-7464 Tx: none Fax: (709) 256-7953 SITA: n/a
F: 1992 ☨ n/a Head: Patrick White Net: n/a Aircraft below MTOW 1361kg: Cessna 150, 152 & 172

☐ C-GYOB	Cessna 337G Super Skymaster II	33701780		0077	0996	2 CO IO-360-G	2100			
☐ C-FYSU	PZL Mielec M-18A Dromader	1Z017-24	N22549	0087	0497	2 PZL Kalisz ASz-621R	4690	Sprayer/Tanker		

EXPRESSAIR (102662 Canada, Inc. dba) — Ottawa-Gatineau, Qué.

900 Bl. St-Joseph, Hull, Québec J8Z 1S9, Canada ☎ (819) 778-2112 Tx: none Fax: (819) 778-2432 SITA: n/a
F: 1994 ☨ 6 Head: Roger Lachapelle Net: n/a

☐ C-GCHL	Bell 206B JetRanger II	2082		0076	1095	1 AN 250-C20	1451			
☐ C-FTIN	Cessna A185F Skywagon	18503362	N7325H	0077	1294	1 CO IO-520-D	1520			
☐ C-FKAZ	Cessna 208 Caravan I	20800236		0094	0494	1 PWC PT6A-114	3629			
☐ C-GPOP	Cessna 650 Citation III	650-0042	M342AS	0085	0797	2 GA TFE731-3C-100S	9752			

E-Z AIR, Inc. — Edmonton-Municipal, Alta.

Bldg 38, 11941-121 Street, Edmonton, Alberta T5L 4H7, Canada ☎ (780) 453-2085 Tx: none Fax: (780) 453-2085 SITA: n/a
F: 1994 ☨ n/a Head: Ezra Bavly Net: n/a Aircraft below MTOW 1361kg: Robinson R22

☐ C-FHUY	Bell 206B JetRanger	1682	N3776D	0075	0497	1 AN 250-C20	1451			

FAR WEST HELICOPTERS, Ltd — Terrace, B.C.

RR 4, Terrace, British Columbia V8G 4V2, Canada ☎ (250) 638-8441 Tx: none Fax: (250) 638-0059 SITA: n/a
F: 1987 ☨ n/a Head: n/a Net: n/a

☐ C-FJSL	Bell 206B JetRanger III	1154	N59384	0073	0490	1 AN 250-C20B	1451			cvtd JetRanger
☐ C-GFKD	Bell 206B JetRanger III	2869	N1072N	0080	0898	1 AN 250-C20B	1451			
☐ C-GVTM	Bell 206B JetRanger II	194	N4038G	0070	0996	1 AN 250-C20	1451			cvtd 206A

FAST AIR, Ltd — Winnipeg-Int'l, Man.

Unit 105, 1 Allen Dyne Road, Winnipeg, Manitoba R3H 0Z9, Canada ☎ (204) 772-1476 Tx: none Fax: (204) 783-2483 SITA: n/a
F: 1986 ☨ 10 Head: Dylan Fast Net: n/a Aircraft below MTOW 1361kg: Piper PA-18

☐ C-GMDL	Piper PA-31-325 Navajo C/R	31-7512033	N775WM	0075	0895	2 LY TIO-540-F2BD	2948			
☐ C-GMOB	Piper PA-31-350 Navajo Chieftain	31-7852072	N27596	0078	0298	2 LY TIO-540-J2BD	3175			
☐ C-GWTT	Piper PA-31-350 Navajo Chieftain	31-7852024	N27496	0078	1196	2 LY TIO-540-J2BD	3175			
☐ C-GNDI	Piper PA-31T Cheyenne II	31T-7620036	N73TB	0076	0795	2 PWC PT6A-28	4082			
☐ C-GFSB	Beech King Air 200	BB-84		0075	0598	2 PWC PT6A-41	5670			

FAWNIE MOUNTAIN OUTFITTERS, Ltd – Air Services — Moose Lake, B.C.

Box 3310, Anahim Lake, British Columbia V0L 1C0, Canada ☎ (250) 742-3463 Tx: n/a Fax: none SITA: n/a
F: 1985 ☨ n/a Head: n/a Net: n/a

☐ C-FSOO	Found FBA-2C	19		0065	0789	1 LY GO-480-B1D	1361			Floats
☐ CF-RXI	Found FBA-2C	13		0065	0890	1 LY GO-480-B1D	1361			Floats

FIREWEED HELICOPTERS, Ltd — Whitehorse, Y.T.

Box 5450, Whitehorse, Yukon Territory Y1A 5H4, Canada ☎ (867) 668-5888 Tx: none Fax: (867) 668-7875 SITA: n/a
F: 1992 ☨ n/a Head: Bruno Meili Net: n/a

☐ C-FZWC	Bell 206B JetRanger II	2064	N16706	0076	0597	1 AN 250-C20	1451			
☐ C-GBJZ	Bell 206B JetRanger II	1900	N12DY	0076	0398	1 AN 250-C20	1451			

FIRST AIR = 7F / FAB (Bradley Air Services Ltd dba/Subs.of Makivik Development Corp.) — Carp & Ottawa, Ont. / Iqaluit & Yellowknife, N.W.T.

3257 Carp Road, Carp Airport, Carp, Ontario K0A 1L0, Canada ☎ (613) 839-3340 Tx: none Fax: (613) 839-5690 SITA: n/a
F: 1946 ☨ 700 Head: Robert Davis IATA: 245 Net: http://www.firstair.com

☐ C-FJXO	De Havilland DHC-2 Beaver I	1036		0056		1 PW R-985	2313	Y6		Floats / Wheel-Skis
☐ C-FODA	De Havilland DHC-2 Beaver I	112		0051		1 PW R-985	2313	Y6		Floats / Wheel-Skis
☐ C-FQCN	Beech 99 Airliner	U-126	N4302J	0069	0598	2 PWC PT6A-27	4944	Y15		
☐ C-GJHW	Beech King Air A100	B-175	N92DL	0073	0992	2 PWC PT6A-28	5216	Y9		
☐ C-FASG	De Havilland DHC-6 Twin Otter 300	373		0073	1173	2 PWC PT6A-27	5670	Y19		
☐ C-FASS	De Havilland DHC-6 Twin Otter 300	362	N304EH	0073	0282	2 PWC PT6A-27	5670	Y19		
☐ C-FIZD	De Havilland DHC-6 Twin Otter 300	461	PK-NUX	0075	1196	2 PWC PT6A-27	5670	Y19		
☐ C-FNAN	De Havilland DHC-6 Twin Otter 300	242		0069	0078	2 PWC PT6A-27	5670	Y19		
☐ C-FTFX	De Havilland DHC-6 Twin Otter 300	340		0072	1179	2 PWC PT6A-27	5670	Y19		
☐ C-FTXQ	De Havilland DHC-6 Twin Otter 300	308	N776A	0071	1196	2 PWC PT6A-27	5670	Y19		
☐ C-FUGT	De Havilland DHC-6 Twin Otter 300	382	N677A	0073	0595	2 PWC PT6A-27	5670	Y19		
☐ C-GARW	De Havilland DHC-6 Twin Otter 300	367	N200DA	0073	1196	2 PWC PT6A-27	5670	Y19		
☐ C-GNDO	De Havilland DHC-6 Twin Otter 300	430		0074	1078	2 PWC PT6A-27	5670	Y19		
☐ C-GPTN	GAC (Grumman) G-159C Gulfstream IC	088	N857H	0062	1196	2 RR Dart 529-8X	15238	Y33		cvtd G-159
☐ C-GBFA	BAe (HS) 748-FAA Srs 2B	1781 / 262	N117CA	0081	0488	2 RR Dart 535-2	21092	Y43 / Combi		
☐ C-GDUL	BAe (HS) 748-215 Srs 2A	1578 / 40	YV-05C	0065	0987	2 RR Dart 534-2	21092	Y43 / Combi		
☐ C-GDUN	BAe (HS) 748-215 Srs 2A	1581 / 59	YV-07C	0066	1084	2 RR Dart 534-2	21092	Y43 / Combi		
☐ C-GFNW	BAe (HS) 748-335 Srs 2A (SCD)	1758 / 234	9Y-TFX	0078	0987	2 RR Dart 535-2	21092	Y43 / Combi		
☐ C-GJVN	BAe (HS) 748-209 Srs 2A	1640 / 104	RP-C1018	0067	1079	2 RR Dart 534-2	21092	Y43 / Combi		
☐ C-GTLD	BAe (HS) 748-216 Srs 2A	1722 / 200	PK-IHR	0073	1278	2 RR Dart 534-2	21092	Y43 / Combi		
☐ C-GYMX	BAe (HS) 748-233 Srs 2A	1665 / 150	DQ-FBK	0069	1280	2 RR Dart 534-2	21092	Y43 / Combi		
☐ C-GCFR	De Havilland DHC-7-150 Dash 7	102		0085	0586	4 PWC PT6A-50	21319	Survey/Ice recon		lsf Transport Canada
☐ C-FNVT	Boeing 737-248C (A)	21011 / 411	F-GKTK	0075	1197	2 PW JT8D-9A (HK3/AVA)	52390	Combi		
☐ C-GNWI	Boeing 737-210C (A)	21066 / 413	N4951W	0075	0698	2 PW JT8D-9A	53070	Combi		
☐ C-GNWN	Boeing 737-210C (A)	21067 / 414	N4952W	0075	0698	2 PW JT8D-9A	53070	Combi	GK-LM	
☐ C-GHPW	Lockheed L-382G (L-100-30) Hercules	42C-4799		0078	0698	4 AN 501-D22A	70307	Freighter	BE-CF	
☐ C-FRST	Boeing 727-90C	19169 / 320	N797AS	0066	1285	3 PW JT8D-7B	76657	Y125 / Combi		Spirit of Iqaluit
☐ C-GFRB	Boeing 727-27C	19120 / 396	5N-AWH	0067	1286	3 PW JT8D-7B (HK3/FDX)	76657	Y125 / Combi	DG-AB	

50 registration type of aircraft cn/fn ex/ex* mfd del powered by mtow kg configuration selcal name/fln/specialitites/remarks

☐ C-GVFA	Boeing 727-44C	20475 / 854	N26879	0071	0688	3 PW JT8D-7B (HK3/FDX)	76657	Y125 / Combi		
☐ C-FIFA	Boeing 727-225 (F)	20381 / 823	N8838E	0070	0593	3 PW JT8D-7B (HK3/FDX)	83008	Freighter	FL-BC	cvtd -225
☐ C-FUFA	Boeing 727-233 (F) (A)	20941 / 1128	N727LS	0075	0794	3 PW JT8D-15 (HK3/FDX)	89358	Freighter	NONE	cvtd -233
☐ C-GXFA	Boeing 727-233 (F) (A)	20938 / 1105	C-GAAG	0075	1194	3 PW JT8D-15	89358	Y180 / Combi	HK-CM	cvtd -233

FIVE MILE LAKE LODGE & Air Service (1277962 Ontario, Ltd dba / formerly dba Northwoods Air Services / Seasonal May-October ops only) — Five Mile Lake, Ont.

PO Box 516, Chapleau, Ontario P0M 1K0, Canada ☎ (705) 864-0201 Tx: none Fax: (705) 864-2975 SITA: n/a
F: 1995 ⁂ n/a Head: Frank C. Yuhas Net: n/a

☐ C-FODN	De Havilland DHC-2 Beaver I	615		0054	0488	1 PW R-985	2313			Floats

FLANAGAN ENTERPRISES, Inc. — Pitt Meadows, B.C.

1400-1166 Alberni Street, Vancouver, British Columbia V6E 3Z3, Canada ☎ (604) 669-0886 Tx: none Fax: (604) 669-0860 SITA: n/a
F: 1996 ⁂ n/a Head: Ian Flanagan Net: n/a Aircraft below MTOW 1361kg: Cessna 182

☐ C-FQRW	Cessna 205 (210-5)	205-0168	N8186Z	0063	1096	1 CO IO-520-F	1497			
☐ C-FCML	Beech D18S	A-240	N428B	0046	1096	2 PW R-985	3969			

FLIGHT INTERNATIONAL AIR SERVICES, Ltd — Calgary, Alta.

Suite 100-640 Palmer Road NE, Calgary, Alberta T2E 7R3, Canada ☎ (403) 219-1040 Tx: none Fax: (403) 250-1016 SITA: n/a
F: 1997 ⁂ 6 Head: Scott Forester Net: n/a

☐ C-GAVV	Beech 99A Airliner	U-142	FAC 305	0070	0198	2 PWC PT6A-27	4717			lsf Ashe Aircraft Enterprises Ltd

FLOWERS AVIATION, Inc. (Seasonal April-November ops only) — Rivière-des-Prairies, Qué.

6324, 3e Ave, Montreal, Québec H1Y 2X5, Canada ☎ (514) 727-6486 Tx: none Fax: (514) 845-4140 SITA: n/a
F: 1995 ⁂ 1 Head: Robert Flowers Net: n/a

☐ C-GACI	Cessna U206F Stationair	U20602352		0074	0695	1 CO IO-520-F	1633			Floats

FORDE LAKE AIR SERVICES, Ltd (Seasonal May-October ops only) — Hearst-Nassau Lake, Ont.

PO Box 2365, Hearst, Ontario P0L 1N0, Canada ☎ (705) 463-4551 Tx: none Fax: (705) 946-5659 SITA: n/a
F: 1968 ⁂ 4 Head: George E. Martin Net: n/a

☐ C-GGNM	Cessna A185F Skywagon	18502807		0075		1 CO IO-520-D	1520			Floats
☐ C-GRAP	De Havilland DHC-2 Beaver I	829	54-1690	0054		1 PW R-985	2313			Floats

FOREST HELICOPTERS, Inc. — Kenora, Ont.

RR 1, Anderson Road, Kenora, Ontario P9N 3W7, Canada ☎ (807) 548-5647 Tx: none Fax: (807) 548-8362 SITA: n/a
F: 1997 ⁂ 5 Head: Bart Stevenson Net: n/a

☐ C-GCDM	Bell 206B JetRanger	1285		0074	1097	1 AN 250-C20	1451			
☐ C-GGSX	Bell 206B JetRanger III	3964	N43BL	0087	1297	1 AN 250-C20J	1451			

FOREST INDUSTRIES FLYING TANKERS, Ltd - FIFT — Port Alberni-Sproat Lake, B.C.

R.R. No 3, Port Alberni, British Columbia V9Y 7L7, Canada ☎ (250) 723-6225 Tx: 04-51471 mb vcr Fax: (250) 723-6200 SITA: n/a
F: 1959 ⁂ 38 Head: W. Cafferata Net: n/a

☐ C-GVFT	Bell 206L-1 LongRanger II	45698	N62EA	0081	0695	1 AN 250-C28B	1882			
☐ C-GWFH	Bell 206L-1 LongRanger II	45304		0079		1 AN 250-C28B	1882			
☐ C-GWFW	Bell 206L-1 LongRanger II	45248		0079		1 AN 250-C28B	1882			
☐ C-GZFT	Bell 206L-1 LongRanger II	45628		0081		1 AN 250-C28B	1882			
☐ C-FVFU	Grumman G-21A Goose	B-101		0044		2 PW R-985	4173	Birddog		Amphibian
☐ C-FLYK	Martin JRM-3 Mars (Waterbomber Seaplane)	76820	Bu76820	0046	0059	4 WR R-3350-24	73482	Tanker		Philippine Mars / cvtd JRM-1
☐ C-FLYL	Martin JRM-3 Mars (Waterbomber Seaplane)	76823	Bu76823	0048	0059	4 WR R-3350-24	73482	Tanker		Hawaii Mars / cvtd JRM-1

FOREST PROTECTION, Ltd - FPL — Fredericton, N.B.

Fredericton Airport, 2502 Route 102 Hwy, Lincoln, New Brunswick E3B 7E6, Canada ☎ (506) 446-6930 Tx: none Fax: (506) 446-6934 SITA: n/a
F: 1952 ⁂ 10 Head: David Ch. Davies Net: n/a Aircraft below MTOW 1361kg: Cessna 172 & 182 Non-profit (New Brunswick) Government organisation conducting seasonal Sprayer & Tanker flights.

☐ C-GXJI	Cessna 210J Centurion	21059155	N3355S	0069	0591	1 CO IO-520-J	1542	Liaison		
☐ C-FIMY	Cessna A188B AgTruck	18801247T	N8144G	0073	0496	1 CO IO-550-D	2086	Sprayer		
☐ C-GLFA	Cessna A188B AgTruck	18802222T		0075	0496	1 CO IO-550-D	2086	Sprayer		
☐ C-GJDF	Cessna 337G Super Skymaster	33701516	N72488	0073	0592	2 CO IO-360-G	2100	Liasion		
☐ C-GXMA	Cessna 337G Super Skymaster	33701644	N53468	0075	0692	2 CO IO-360-G	2100	Liasion		
☐ C-GMVQ	PZL Mielec M-18 Dromader	1Z003-03		0080	0496	1 SH ASh-62IR	5670	Sprayer		
☐ C-FIMR	Grumman TBM-3 Avenger	53610	RCN303	0043	0076	1 WR R-2600-20	7983	Tanker	23	
☐ C-GFPL	Grumman TBM-3 Avenger	86020	N7157C	0045	0076	1 WR R-2600-20	7983	Tanker	22	
☐ C-GFPM	Grumman TBM-3 Avenger	53857	N7017C	0045	0075	1 WR R-2600-20	7983	Tanker	21	
☐ C-GFPN	Grumman TBM-3 Avenger	91289	N7833C	0045	0076	1 WR R-2600-20	7983	Sprayer	17	
☐ C-GFPR	Grumman TBM-3 Avenger	53858	N3357G	0045	0076	1 WR R-2600-20	7983	Sprayer	4	
☐ C-GFPS	Grumman TBM-3 Avenger	85460	N7032C	0045	0076	1 WR R-2600-20	7983	Tanker	3	
☐ C-GFPT	Grumman TBM-3 Avenger	53787	N3969A	0045	0076	1 WR R-2600-20	7983	Sprayer	10	
☐ C-GLEJ	Grumman TBM-3 Avenger	69323	N7961C	0045	0074	1 WR R-2600-20	7983	Tanker	24	
☐ C-GLEL	Grumman TBM-3 Avenger	53200	N9010C	0043	0074	1 WR R-2600-20	7983	Tanker	13	
☐ CF-MUD	Grumman TBM-3 Avenger	86180	RCN324	0045	0077	1 WR R-2600-20	7983	Sprayer	12	
☐ CF-MUE	Grumman TBM-3 Avenger	91426		0045	0077	1 WR R-2600-20	7983	Sprayer	18	

FORESTVILLE HELICOPTERES, Inc. — Forestville, Qué.

128 Route 385, CP 1718, Forestville, Québec G0T 1E0, Canada ☎ (418) 587-4712 Tx: none Fax: (418) 587-2020 SITA: n/a
F: 1984 ⁂ 13 Head: Guy Tremblay Net: n/a Aircraft below MTOW 1361kg: Hughes 269B/C (300B/C) & 369HS (500C)

☐ C-GHNF	MD Helicopters MD 500D (Hughes 369D)	770165D	N912EG	0077	0591	1 AN 250-C20B	1361			
☐ C-GBNP	Bell 206B JetRanger	798		0072	0492	1 AN 250-C20	1451			

FORT FRANCES AIR (427112 Ontario, Ltd dba) — Fort Frances, Ont.

RMB 19, RR 1, Fort Frances, Ontario P9A 3M2, Canada ☎ (807) 274-9763 Tx: n/a Fax: (807) 274-8387 SITA: n/a
F: 1988 ⁂ 5 Head: Tom Ivey Net: n/a

☐ C-GBTI	Beech King Air E90	LW-111	N11GE	0074	1191	2 PWC PT6A-28	4581			

FORT FRANCES SPORTSMEN AIRWAYS, Ltd (Associated with Northern Wilderness Outfitters, Ltd) — Fort Frances-Lake Land Bay, Ont.

Box 637, Fort Frances, Ontario P9A 1S5, Canada ☎ (807) 274-3666 Tx: n/a Fax: (807) 274-4229 SITA: n/a
F: 1972 ⁂ 6 Head: Bruce Lavigne Net: n/a Aircraft below MTOW 1361 kg: Cessna 180 & Piper PA-18.

☐ C-GBQC	De Havilland DHC-3 Otter	401	CAF 9420	0060		1 PW R-1340	3629			Floats / Wheel-Skis
☐ C-GMDG	De Havilland DHC-3 Otter	302	N90575	0058		1 PW R-1340	3629			Amphibian / Wheel-Skis

FOTO FLIGHT SURVEYS, Ltd — Calgary, Alta.

8, 3610-32 Street NE, Calgary, Alberta T1Y 6G7, Canada ☎ (403) 291-2299 Tx: none Fax: (403) 291-0608 SITA: n/a
F: 1980 ⁂ 6 Head: David J. Skelton Net: http://www.fotoflight.com

☐ C-FEAC	Piper PA-31-310 Navajo	31-60		0067	0798	2 LY TIO-540-A1A	2948	Photo / Survey		
☐ C-FFSL	Piper PA-31-310 Navajo	31-586		0070		2 LY TIO-540-A1A	2948	Photo / Survey		

FOUR SEASONS AIR CHARTERS, Ltd — Edmonton-Cooking Lake, Alta.

503 Alder Avenue, Sherwood Park, Alberta T8A 3K6, Canada ☎ (780) 464-5167 Tx: none Fax: (780) 464-5167 SITA: n/a
F: 1996 ⁂ n/a Head: n/a Net: n/a

☐ C-GXSM	Cessna A185F Skywagon	18503430		0077	0596	1 CO IO-520-D	1520			Floats / Wheel-Skis

FOUR SEASONS AVIATION, Ltd — Toronto-Int'l, Ont.

170 Elmpine Trail, King City, Ontario L7B 1K4, Canada ☎ (905) 671-9644 Tx: none Fax: (905) 671-9536 SITA: n/a
F: 1988 ⁂ 4 Head: David Tommasini Net: http://www.hype.com/fsa.helitoronto

☐ C-FHKJ	Bell 206L LongRanger	45116	N222CD	0077	0196	1 AN 250-C20B	1814			
☐ C-FHNB	Eurocopter (Aerosp.) AS355F1 TwinStar	5174	N5798B	0082	0697	2 AN 250-C20F	2400			

FRASER AVIATION (Division of Fraser Paper, Inc. / Member of Nexfor Group / formerly Fraser Helicopter Services) — Edmundston, N.B.

27 Rice Street, Edmundston, New Brunswick E3V 1S9, Canada ☎ (506) 737-2520 Tx: none Fax: (506) 737-2102 SITA: n/a
F: 1969 ⁂ 6 Head: John Harrigan Net: n/a

☐ C-GMNW	Bell 206L-1 LongRanger II	45512		0080	1180	1 AN 250-C28B	1882	Exec / Charter		
☐ C-GTVO	Dassault Falcon 10	137	N837F	0079	0487	2 GA TFE731-2-1C	8700	Corporate		

FRONTIER AVIATION, Inc. — Toronto-Int'l, Ont.

2450 Derry Road East, Hangar 8A, Mississauga, Ontario L5S 1B2, Canada ☎ (905) 676-8822 Tx: none Fax: (905) 676-9153 SITA: n/a
F: 1996 ⁂ 3 Head: David Mander Net: n/a

☐ C-GFRN	Piper PA-34-200T Seneca II	34-7970239	N98PB	0079	0397	2 CO TSIO-360-E	2073			

51 registration type of aircraft cn/fn ex/ex* mfd del powered by mtow kg configuration selcal name/fln/specialitites/remarks

FRONTIER HELICOPTERS (Division of Conair Aviation, Ltd)   Abbotsford, B.C. / Watson Lake, Y.T.

PO Box 220, Abbotsford, British Columbia V2S 4N9, Canada   ☎ (604) 855-1190   Tx: 04363529 conairav ab   Fax: (604) 855-1189   SITA: n/a
F: 1968   ♠♠♠ 49   Head: K.B. Marsden   Net: n/a

		cn/fn	ex/ex*	mfd	del	powered by	mtow kg	configuration	name/fln/specialitites/remarks
☐ C-FDMO	Bell 206B JetRanger II	317	N1414W	0069	0590	1 AN 250-C20	1451		cvtd 206A
☐ C-FFHK	Bell 206B JetRanger	1065		0073		1 AN 250-C20	1451		
☐ C-FZXI	Bell 206B JetRanger	660		0071	1195	1 AN 250-C20	1451		cvtd 206A
☐ C-GFHY	Bell 206B JetRanger	367	N297BC	0069		1 AN 250-C20	1451		cvtd 206A
☐ C-GXGA	Bell 206B JetRanger II	2009	N9970K	0076		1 AN 250-C20	1451		
☐ C-GXMH	Bell 206B JetRanger	671	N2900W	0071	0691	1 AN 250-C20	1451		cvtd 206A
☐ C-GMJS	Bell 206L LongRanger	46608	N120RM	0078	0995	1 AN 250-C20B	1814		lst Denendeh Helicopters
☐ C-FFHB	Bell 205A-1	30294	VH-HHW	0079	0489	1 LY T5313B	4309		lst Heli-Union Peru
☐ C-GFHA	Bell 205A-1	30086	VH-NHA	0071	0489	1 LY T5313B	4309		
☐ C-GFHC	Bell 205A-1	30038	VH-HHC	0069	0489	1 LY T5313B	4309		
☐ C-GFHD	Bell 205A-1	30017	VH-HHD	0068	0489	1 LY T5313B	4309		
☐ C-GFHM	Bell 205A-1	30289	VH-HHM	0079	0489	1 LY T5313B	4309		lst Heli-Union Peru
☐ C-GFHW	Bell 205A-1	30115	VH-NGI	0072	0190	1 LY T5313B	4309		
☐ C-GFRE	Bell 205A-1	30185	EC-FYZ	0075	0596	1 LY T5313B	4309		
☐ C-GXLF	Bell 205A-1	30142	N26AL	0073		1 LY T5317A	4309		
☐ C-GXNE	Bell 205A-1	30127	N58056	0073		1 LY T5317A	4309		
☐ C-FNSA	Bell 212	30524	VH-NSC	0071	0595	2 PWC PT6T-3 TwinPac	5080		
☐ C-GFRS	Bell 212	30716	I-ZCMA	0075	0394	2 PWC PT6T-3 TwinPac	5080		

GARDINER OUTFITTERS & Airservices (Ronald W. & Shirley R. Barron dba/formerly Gardiner Lake Air Service, Ltd/ Seasonal May-November ops only)   Cochrane, Ont.

PO Box 1029, Cochrane, Ontario P0L 1C0, Canada   ☎ (705) 272-6698   Tx: n/a   Fax: none   SITA: n/a
F: 1991   ♠♠♠ n/a   Head: Ronald W. & Shirley R. Barron   Net: n/a

☐ C-FYYV	De Havilland DHC-2 Beaver I	1576	VH-IMC	0064	1090	1 PW R-985	2313		Floats

GATEWAY AIRLINES (Div. of Crown Mail & Delivery Services, Ltd / Sister co. of Crown Charter Services)   Branford, Ont.

9655 8th Lane, Georgetown, Ontario 07G 4S5, Canada   ☎ (905) 873-6416   Tx: none   Fax: (905) 873-6420   SITA: n/a
F: 1998   ♠♠♠ n/a   Head: Blaine Field   Net: n/a

☐ C-GDIK	Boeing (Douglas) Super DC-3S (C-117D)	43369	N8538F	0042	1198	2 WR R-1820-80	13301	Freighter	cvtd R4D-5 cn 11948
☐ C-GDOG	Boeing (Douglas) Super DC-3S (C-117D)	43374	N1334K	0044	1198	2 WR R-1820-80	13301	Freighter	cvtd R4D-5 cn 25446
☐ C-GGKE	Boeing (Douglas) Super DC-3S (C-117D)	43366	N2577G	0043	0299	2 WR R-1820-80	13301	Freighter	cvtd R4D-6 cn 26403

GATEWAY HELICOPTERS, Ltd   North Bay, Ont.

PO Box 21028, North Bay, Ontario P1B 9N8, Canada   ☎ (705) 474-4214   Tx: none   Fax: (705) 474-1813   SITA: n/a
F: 1994   ♠♠♠ n/a   Head: David Lauzon   Net: n/a   Aircraft below MTOW 1361kg: Enstrom 280

☐ C-GENL	Bell 206B JetRanger III	2505	N5008F	0078	0399	1 AN 250-C20B	1451		
☐ C-GINF	Bell 206B JetRanger III	3294	N39108	0081	0697	1 AN 250-C20B	1451		
☐ C-GUIK	Bell 206B JetRanger II	1908		0076	0295	1 AN 250-C20	1451		
☐ C-GRYS	Bell 206L LongRanger	45097	N16783	0077	0497	1 AN 250-C20B	1814		
☐ C-GPOI	Eurocopter (Aerosp.) AS350BA AStar	1210		0080	0698	1 TU Ariel 1B	2100		cvtd AS350D

GEFFAIR Canada, Inc.   Montreal-Dorval, Qué.

9501 Ryan Avenue, Dorval, Québec H9P 1A2, Canada   ☎ (514) 636-6830   Tx: none   Fax: (514) 636-0185   SITA: n/a
F: 1989   ♠♠♠ 7   Head: Guy Geoffrion   Net: n/a

☐ C-GCYL	Piper PA-31-310 Navajo	31-688	G-BOIS	0070	0199	2 LY TIO-540-A2B	2948		
☐ C-GIPV	Piper PA-31-310 Navajo B	31-7300963	N7569L	0073	0390	2 LY TIO-540-A2B	2948		
☐ C-GMHZ	Piper PA-31-310 Navajo	31-434	N712NT	0069	1093	2 LY TIO-540-A2C	2948		

GEODESY REMOTE SENSING, Inc.   Calgary, Alta.

820 McTavish Road N.E., Calgary, Alberta T2E 7G6, Canada   ☎ (403) 291-9655   Tx: none   Fax: (403) 291-4988   SITA: n/a
F: 1987   ♠♠♠ 6   Head: Patrick Gropp   Net: n/a

☐ C-GJMZ	Partenavia P.68 Observer	369-27-OB		0087	0498	2 LY IO-360-A1B6	1960	Survey/remote se	lsf North West Construction Ltd
☐ C-GBLB	Cessna T310R II	310R0249	N5129J	0075		2 CO TSIO-520-B	2495	Survey/remote se	

GEOGRAPHIC AIR SURVEY, Ltd = GSL   Edmonton, Alta.

59 Airport Road, Edmonton, Alberta T5G 0W6, Canada   ☎ (780) 451-1406   Tx: none   Fax: (780) 452-4361   SITA: n/a
F: 1975   ♠♠♠ 14   Head: Paul Hagedorn   ICAO: SURVEY-CANADA   Net: n/a

☐ C-GEOG	Twin (Aero) Commander 680F	1120-73	N444UB	0062		2 LY IGSO-540-B1A	3629	Surveyer	
☐ C-GEOS	Twin (Aero) Turbo Commander 690A	11279	N57180	0076		2 GA TPE331-5-251K	4649	Surveyer	

GILLAM AIR SERVICES (1985), Ltd   Gillam, Man.

PO Box 56, Gillam, Manitoba R0B 0L0, Canada   ☎ (204) 652-2109   Tx: n/a   Fax: (204) 652-2980   SITA: n/a
F: 1985   ♠♠♠ 4   Head: Harvey J. Young   Net: n/a

☐ C-GFZX	Cessna A185F Skywagon	18503108		0076		1 CO IO-520-D	1520		
☐ C-FFEA	Piper PA-34-200 Seneca	34-7350345		0073	0595	2 LY IO-360-C1E6	1905		
☐ C-GSAD	Britten-Norman BN-2A-26 Islander	7	N32JC	0067	0390	2 LY O-540-E4C5	2858		

GLACIER AIR (A.A.L. AIR ALPS, Ltd dba)   Squamish, B.C.

PO Box 2014, Squamish, British Columbia V0N 3G0, Canada   ☎ (604) 898-9016   Tx: none   Fax: (604) 898-1553   SITA: n/a
F: 1978   ♠♠♠ 5   Head: Ron Banner   Net: http://www.netbistro.com/glacier/   Aircraft below MTOW 1361 kg: Cessna 150.

☐ C-FXDA	Cessna A185E Skywagon	185-1353		0068	0594	1 CO IO-520-D	1520		Wheel-Skis
☐ C-GAWR	Cessna P206D Super Skylane	P206-0560	N8760Z	0069	0784	1 CO IO-520-A	1633		

GLACIER AIR, Ltd   Prince George, B.C.

2502 Laurentian Drive, Prince George, British Columbia V2N 1Z3, Canada   ☎ (250) 964-9690   Tx: none   Fax: (250) 964-9691   SITA: n/a
F: 1989   ♠♠♠ 3   Head: Brian Marynonich   Net: n/a

☐ C-FHRX	Cessna A185F Skywagon	18502185		0073	0692	1 CO IO-520-D	1520		Floats / Wheel-Skis

GLEN AIR SERVICES, Ltd   Fort Nelson, B.C.

PO Box 502, Fort Nelson, British Columbia V0C 1R0, Canada   ☎ (250) 774-2055   Tx: n/a   Fax: none   SITA: n/a
F: 1977   ♠♠♠ n/a   Head: n/a   Net: n/a

☐ C-GYOP	Cessna A185F Skywagon	18503277		0077		1 CO IO-520-D	1520		

GLOBAL REMOTE SENSING, Inc.   Edmonton, Alta.

203-10008-109 Street, Edmonton, Alberta T5J 1M4, Canada   ☎ (780) 428-8063   Tx: n/a   Fax: (780) 426-7043   SITA: n/a
F: 1979   ♠♠♠ 8   Head: Daniel G. Newnham   Net: n/a

☐ C-GQSX	Piper PA-23-235 Apache	27-600	N4318Y	0064	0694	2 LY O-540-B1A5	2177	Photo / Survey	
☐ C-GQHL	Cessna T310P	310P0034	N310WM	0069	0492	2 CO TSIO-520-B	2449	Photo / Survey	
☐ C-FGRS	Cessna 414	414-0388	N414CF	0073	0694	2 CO TSIO-520-J	2880	Photo / Survey	

GOGAL AIR SERVICE, Ltd (formerly Gogal Air Service)   Snow Lake, Man.

PO Box 599, Snow Lake, Manitoba R0B 1M0, Canada   ☎ (204) 358-2259   Tx: none   Fax: (204) 358-7114   SITA: n/a
F: 1983   ♠♠♠ 2   Head: Larry B. Gogal   Net: n/a

☐ C-GBAO	Piper PA-31-350 Navajo Chieftain	31-7405234	N54309	0074	0597	2 LY TIO-540-J2BD	3175		
☐ CF-ECG	Noorduyn Norseman V	N29-43		0048		1 PW R-1340	3420		Floats / Wheel-Skis
☐ CF-GLI	Noorduyn Norseman VI (UC-64A)	365	N88719	0044	0694	1 PW R-1340	3420		Floats / Wheel-Skis

GOLDAK EXPLORATION TECHNOLOGY, Ltd   Saskatoon, Sask.

Box 54, Langham, Saskatchewan S0K 2L0, Canada   ☎ (306) 283-4242   Tx: none   Fax: (306) 283-4242   SITA: n/a
F: 1970   ♠♠♠ n/a   Head: Ben Goldak   Net: n/a

☐ C-GJBA	Piper PA-31-310 Navajo	31-159	N9119Y	0068	0697	2 LY TIO-540-A1A	2948	Surveyer	

GOLD BELT AIR TRANSPORT, Inc. = GBT (formerly Central Air Transport, Ltd)   Sioux Lookout & Pickle Lake, Ont.

Box 89, Pickle Lake, Ontario P0V 3A0, Canada   ☎ (807) 928-2251   Tx: none   Fax: (807) 928-2663   SITA: n/a
F: 1987   ♠♠♠ 25   Head: Genevieve A. Swartman   ICAO: GOLDBELT   Net: n/a   Aircraft below MTOW 1361kg: Cessna 180.

☐ C-GJOW	Cessna A185F Skywagon II	18504214		0081	0592	1 CO IO-520-D	1520		Floats / Wheel-Skis
☐ C-FFHO	De Havilland DHC-2 Beaver I	50		0049		1 PW R-985	2313		Floats / Wheel-Skis
☐ C-FCZO	De Havilland DHC-3 Otter	71		0055		1 PW R-1340	3629		Floats / Wheel-Skis
☐ C-FMQS	Beech E18S	BA-3	N3606B	0054	1093	2 PW R-985	4218	Freighter	
☐ C-FXKG	Beech E18S	BA-192	N125X	0056	0396	2 PW R-985	4218	Freighter	
☐ C-GJKA	Beech G18S	BA-466	N788MW	0059	0697	2 PW R-985	4581		

GOLDEN FALCON AVIATION, Inc.
Golden, B.C.

Box 1589, Golden, British Columbia V0A 1H0, Canada ☎ (250) 344-2534 Tx: n/a Fax: (250) 344-5808 SITA: n/a
F: 1992 ♁♁♁ 4 Head: Michael Klinzmann Net: n/a Aircraft below MTOW 1361 kg: Cessna 172.

registration	type of aircraft	cn/fn	ex/ex*	mfd	del	powered by	mtow kg	configuration	selcal	name/fln/specialitites/remarks
☐ C-FATY	Cessna A185F Skywagon	18503323	C-GYUU	0077	0395	1 CO IO-520-D	1520			Wheel-Skis
☐ C-FATZ	Cessna A185E Skywagon	185-1424	C-FTCL	0068	0896	1 CO IO-520-D	1520			Wheel-Skis
☐ C-GAQN	Cessna U206F Stationair II	U20602687		0075	0198	1 CO IO-520-F	1633			
☐ C-GGFA	Cessna 337E Super Skymaster	33701263	N1263M	0070	0493	2 CO IO-360-C/D	1996			

GOLDWING HELICOPTERS (Goldwing Flyte, Inc. dba)
Sechelt, B.C.

RR1, C7, Southwood Site, Halfmoon Bay, British Columbia V0N 1Y0, Canada ☎ (604) 740-0880 Tx: none Fax: (604) 740-0811 SITA: n/a
F: 1996 ♁♁♁ n/a Head: Robin MacGregor Net: n/a

registration	type of aircraft	cn/fn	ex/ex*	mfd	del	powered by	mtow kg	configuration	selcal	name/fln/specialitites/remarks
☐ C-FKKM	Bell 206B JetRanger	883	N14854	0072	0397	1 AN 250-C20	1451			

GOOSE BAY OUTFITTERS, Ltd & Air Service (Seasonal May-October ops only)
Goose Bay-SPB, Nfld.

Box 70, Glovertown, Newfoundland A0G 2M0, Canada ☎ (709) 533-9121 Tx: none Fax: (709) 533-9121 SITA: n/a
F: 1977 ♁♁♁ Head: n/a Net: n/a

registration	type of aircraft	cn/fn	ex/ex*	mfd	del	powered by	mtow kg	configuration	selcal	name/fln/specialitites/remarks
☐ C-GGSS	Cessna A185F Skywagon II	18504084	C-GCSS	0080	0596	1 CO IO-520-D	1520			Floats

GOUVERNEMENT DU QUEBEC – Service aérien gouvernemental = QUE (Division of Ministère du Conseil du Tresor)
Québec, Qué.

Service aérien gouvernemental, 700-7e Rue, Sainte-Foy, Québec G2E 5W1, Canada ☎ (418) 528-8686 Tx: none Fax: (418) 872-6567 SITA: n/a
F: 1960 ♁♁♁ 200 Head: Michel Gagnon ICAO: QUEBEC Net: http://www.restor.gouv.qc.ca/services/serv.3a Non-commercial provincial government organisation conducting fire fighting, ambulance & transport missions.

registration	type of aircraft	cn/fn	ex/ex*	mfd	del	powered by	mtow kg	configuration	selcal	name/fln/specialitites/remarks
☐ C-FPQR	Bell 206B JetRanger	1263	N59159	0074		1 AN 250-C20	1451			
☐ C-FPQU	Bell 206B JetRanger	1000	N83131	0073		1 AN 250-C20	1451			
☐ C-GBPQ	Bell 206B JetRanger III	2897		0079		1 AN 250-C20B	1451			
☐ C-GPQS	Bell 206B JetRanger III	2382		0078		1 AN 250-C20B	1451			
☐ C-GPQY	Bell 206B JetRanger	1638		0075		1 AN 250-C20	1451			
☐ C-GSQA	Bell 206LT TwinRanger	52060		0094	0594	2 AN 250-C20R	2018			
☐ C-FURG	Canadair CL-601-1A (CL-600-2A12) Challen.	3063	C-GLYH*	0086		2 GE CF34-1A	19550	Ambulance		
☐ C-FPQH	Fairchild Ind. F-27F	84	N1410	0061	0371	2 RR Dart 529-7E	19051	Y20		
☐ C-FPQI	Fairchild Ind. F-27F	66	N42Q	0059	0473	2 RR Dart 529-7E	19051	Y31		cvtd F-27A
☐ C-FASE	Canadair CL-215T (CL-215-6B11)	1114		0087	1089	2 PWC PW123AF	19731	Tanker		238 / cvtd CL-215/Amphibian
☐ C-FAWQ	Canadair CL-215T (CL-215-6B11)	1115		0087	1089	2 PWC PW123AF	19731	Tanker		239 / cvtd CL-215/Amphibian
☐ C-FTXG	Canadair CL-215 (CL-215-1A10)	1014		0069		2 PW R-2800-CA3	19731	Tanker		228 / Amphibian
☐ C-FTXJ	Canadair CL-215 (CL-215-1A10)	1017		0069		2 PW R-2800-CA3	19731	Tanker		230 / Amphibian
☐ C-FTXK	Canadair CL-215 (CL-215-1A10)	1018		0069		2 PW R-2800-CA3	19731	Tanker		231 / Amphibian
☐ C-GFQB	Canadair CL-215 (CL-215-1A10)	1092	C-GKDP*	0086	1286	2 PW R-2800-CA3	19731	Tanker		237 / Amphibian
☐ C-GQBA	Canadair CL-415 (CL-215-6B11)	2005		0095	0796	2 PWC PW123AF	19890	Tanker		240 / Amphibian
☐ C-GQBC	Canadair CL-415 (CL-215-6B11)	2012		0095	0995	2 PWC PW123AF	19890	Tanker		241 / Amphibian
☐ C-GQBD	Canadair CL-415 (CL-215-6B11)	2016		0095	0296	2 PWC PW123AF	19890	Tanker		242 / Amphibian
☐ C-GQBE	Canadair CL-415 (CL-215-6B11)	2017		0095	0296	2 PWC PW123AF	19890	Tanker		243 / Amphibian
☐ C-GQBF	Canadair CL-415 (CL-215-6B11)	2019		0096	0596	2 PWC PW123AF	19890	Tanker		244 / Amphibian
☐ C-GQBG	Canadair CL-415 (CL-215-6B11)	2022		0096	0796	2 PWC PW123AF	19890	Tanker		245 / Amphibian
☐ C-GQBI	Canadair CL-415 (CL-215-6B11)	2023		0096	1196	2 PWC PW123AF	19890	Tanker		246 / Amphibian
☐ C-GQBK	Canadair CL-415 (CL-215-6B11)	2026		0096	0197	2 PWC PW123AF	19890	Tanker		247 / Amphibian

GRAHAM AIR, Ltd
Merritt, B.C.

Box 339, Merritt, British Columbia V1K 1B8, Canada ☎ (250) 378-9444 Tx: none Fax: (250) 378-6366 SITA: n/a
F: 1996 ♁♁♁ n/a Head: n/a Net: n/a

registration	type of aircraft	cn/fn	ex/ex*	mfd	del	powered by	mtow kg	configuration	selcal	name/fln/specialitites/remarks
☐ C-FHSM	Cessna A185F Skywagon	18502183	N70469	0073	1296	1 CO IO-520-D	1520			

GRAND BEND SPORT PARACHUTING CENTER, Inc.
Grand Bend, Ont.

Box 777, Grand Bend, Ontario N0M 1T0, Canada ☎ (519) 238-8610 Tx: none Fax: none SITA: n/a
F: 1982 ♁♁♁ 2 Head: Bob Wright Net: http://www.skydivegrandbend.com Aircraft below MTOW 1361kg: Cessna 182 (Para)

registration	type of aircraft	cn/fn	ex/ex*	mfd	del	powered by	mtow kg	configuration	selcal	name/fln/specialitites/remarks
☐ C-GVZY	Britten-Norman BN-2A-21 Islander	513	N63JA	0076	0798	2 LY IO-540-K1B5	2994	Para		

GRAND FALLS AVIATION SERVICE, Ltd
Grand Falls, N.B.

Box 829, Grand Falls, New Brunswick E3Z 1C3, Canada ☎ (506) 473-2566 Tx: none Fax: (506) 473-6132 SITA: n/a
F: 1995 ♁♁♁ n/a Head: Claude Ouillette Net: n/a Aircraft below MTOW 1361kg: Cessna 150/152/172/180 & Schweizer G-164B

registration	type of aircraft	cn/fn	ex/ex*	mfd	del	powered by	mtow kg	configuration	selcal	name/fln/specialitites/remarks
☐ C-FWYY	Piper PA-23-150 Apache	23-993	N3075P	0057	0798	2 LY O-320-A1A	1588			

GRAND ISLAND AVIATION, Ltd
Wabush-SPB, Nfld.

Box 151, Labrador City, Newfoundland A2V 2J4, Canada ☎ (709) 944-1049 Tx: none Fax: (709) 944-2943 SITA: n/a
F: 1994 ♁♁♁ n/a Head: n/a Net: n/a

registration	type of aircraft	cn/fn	ex/ex*	mfd	del	powered by	mtow kg	configuration	selcal	name/fln/specialitites/remarks
☐ C-FOCU	De Havilland DHC-2 Beaver I	73		0050	0796	1 PW R-985	2313			Floats / Wheel-Skis

GREAT BEAR AVIATION (Spur Aviation, Ltd dba)
Yellowknife, N.W.T.

Box 2635, Yellowknife, Northwest Territories X1A 2P9, Canada ☎ (867) 873-3626 Tx: n/a Fax: (867) 873-6195 SITA: n/a
F: 1971 ♁♁♁ 6 Head: Robert O. Jensen Net: n/a Aircraft below MTOW 1361 kg: Cessna 150 & 172.

registration	type of aircraft	cn/fn	ex/ex*	mfd	del	powered by	mtow kg	configuration	selcal	name/fln/specialitites/remarks
☐ C-GKOG	Piper PA-23-250 Aztec C	27-3385	N6166Y	0066	0690	2 LY IO-540-C4B5	2359			
☐ C-GNTE	Piper PA-23-250 Aztec D	27-4494	N13854	0070	0193	2 LY IO-540-C4B5	2359			
☐ C-GREX	Piper PA-23-250 Aztec C	27-3907	N6603Y	0068		2 LY IO-540-C4B5	2359			
☐ C-GXSC	Piper PA-23-250 Aztec E	27-7554121	N54824	0075	0892	2 LY IO-540-C4B5	2359			
☐ C-GZOM	Piper PA-23-250 Aztec F	27-7754046	N62814	0077	1190	2 LY IO-540-C4B5	2359			

GREAT SLAVE HELICOPTERS, Ltd
Yellowknife, N.W.T.

Bag 7500, Yellowknife, Northwest Territories X1A 2R3, Canada ☎ (867) 873-2081 Tx: none Fax: (867) 873-6087 SITA: n/a
F: 1984 ♁♁♁ 40 Head: Adam Bembridge Net: n/a Aircraft below MTOW 1361kg: Hughes 269C (300C)

registration	type of aircraft	cn/fn	ex/ex*	mfd	del	powered by	mtow kg	configuration	selcal	name/fln/specialitites/remarks
☐ C-FERA	MD Helicopters MD 500D (Hughes 369D)	980346D	N22BB	0078	0595	1 AN 250-C20B	1361			
☐ C-FLGK	MD Helicopters MD 500D (Hughes 369D)	890579D	P2-HCF	0079	0598	1 AN 250-C20B	1361			
☐ C-GGSI	MD Helicopters MD 500D (Hughes 369D)	370101D	N108TB	0077	0394	1 AN 250-C20B	1361			
☐ C-GIFZ	MD Helicopters MD 500D (Hughes 369D)	490505D	N58311	0079	0493	1 AN 250-C20B	1361			
☐ C-GMNU	MD Helicopters MD 500D (Hughes 369D)	380271D		0078	0198	1 AN 250-C20B	1361			
☐ C-GMTB	MD Helicopters MD 500D (Hughes 369D)	310918D		0081	0298	1 AN 250-C20B	1361			
☐ C-GRYW	MD Helicopters MD 500D (Hughes 369D)	190451D		0079	0793	1 AN 250-C20B	1361			
☐ C-GTNM	MD Helicopters MD 500D (Hughes 369D)	490485D		0079	0794	1 AN 250-C20B	1361			
☐ C-GVZD	MD Helicopters MD 500D (Hughes 369D)	1070209D	N58165	0077	1293	1 AN 250-C20B	1361			
☐ C-GWPK	MD Helicopters MD 500D (Hughes 369D)	300676D		0080	0494	1 AN 250-C20B	1361			
☐ C-GXQI	MD Helicopters MD 500D (Hughes 369D)	370104D		0077	0898	1 AN 250-C20B	1361			
☐ C-FAFL	Bell 206B JetRanger	1256		0074	0494	1 AN 250-C20	1451			
☐ C-FGSD	Bell 206B JetRanger	427	N83TA	0069	0195	1 AN 250-C20	1451			cvtd 206A
☐ C-FHZP	Bell 206B JetRanger	1238		0073	0790	1 AN 250-C20	1451			
☐ C-FJAD	Bell 206A JetRanger	18		0067		1 AN 250-C18A	1361			
☐ C-FPQS	Bell 206B JetRanger III	3231	N333EA	0081	0693	1 AN 250-C20B	1451			
☐ C-FPRB	Bell 206B JetRanger III	3232	N20EA	0081	0693	1 AN 250-C20B	1451			
☐ C-GHPO	Bell 206B JetRanger II	2151		0077	0793	1 AN 250-C20	1451			
☐ C-GJVZ	Bell 206B JetRanger III	2780	N2724N	0079	0491	1 AN 250-C20B	1451			
☐ C-GOMK	Bell 206B JetRanger	1889		0075	0193	1 AN 250-C20	1451			
☐ C-GPGF	Bell 206B JetRanger	1836		0075		1 AN 250-C20	1451			
☐ C-GTYU	Bell 206B JetRanger II	2144		0077	0493	1 AN 250-C20	1451			
☐ C-FBFH	Bell 206L-1 LongRanger II	45178	N5005G	0078	0294	1 AN 250-C28B	1882			
☐ C-FYID	Bell 206L-1 LongRanger II	45206	N78CF	0078	0596	1 AN 250-C28B	1882			
☐ C-GFEG	Bell 206L LongRanger	45150	N71JH	0078	0989	1 AN 250-C28B	1814			
☐ C-GRFZ	Bell 206L-1 LongRanger II	45610		0081		1 AN 250-C28B	1882			
☐ C-GSHL	Bell 206L LongRanger	45092	N16751	0077	0597	1 AN 250-C20B	1814			
☐ C-FGSC	Eurocopter (Aerospat.) AS350BA AStar	3067		0098	0698	1 TU Arriel 1B	2100			
☐ C-GAVO	Eurocopter (Aerospat.) AS350B3 AStar	3139		0098	0199	1 TU Arriel 2B	2250			
☐ C-GGSW	Eurocopter (Aerospat.) AS350B2 AStar	2675		0092	0293	1 TU Arriel 1D1	2250			
☐ C-GHMZ	Eurocopter (Aerospat.) AS350BA AStar	2325		0090	0693	1 TU Arriel 1B	2100			cvtd AS350B
☐ C-GVEL	Bell 204B	2197	OY-HCA	0066	1289	1 LY T5311A	3856			
☐ C-GVVI	Bell 204B	2196	N1304X	0066		1 LY T5311A	3856			
☐ C-GKTL	Bell 212	32124		0080	0395	2 PWC PT6T-3 TwinPac	5080			

GREEN AIRWAYS, Ltd
Red Lake, Ont.

PO Box 331, Red Lake, Ontario P0V 2M0, Canada ☎ (807) 727-2848 Tx: none Fax: (807) 727-2282 SITA: n/a
F: 1950 ♁♁♁ 15 Head: John A. Green Net: n/a Aircraft below MTOW 1361 kg: Cessna 180 (Floats / Wheel-Skis).

registration	type of aircraft	cn/fn	ex/ex*	mfd	del	powered by	mtow kg	configuration	selcal	name/fln/specialitites/remarks
☐ C-GYUY	Cessna A185F Skywagon II	18503731		0079		1 CO IO-520-D	1520			Floats / Wheel-Skis
☐ C-FVIA	De Havilland DHC-2 Beaver I	714	N9047U	0053	1197	1 PW R-985	2313			Floats / Wheel-Skis

registration   type of aircraft   cn/fn   ex/ex*   mfd   del   powered by   mtow kg   configuration   selcal   name/fln/specialitites/remarks

registration	type of aircraft	cn/fn	ex/ex*	mfd	del	powered by	mtow kg	configuration	name/fln/specialities/remarks
☐ C-GEZU	De Havilland DHC-2 Beaver I	647	53-8159	0053		1 PW R-985	2313		Floats / Wheel-Skis
☐ C-GEZW	De Havilland DHC-2 Beaver I	1217	57-6138	0057		1 PW R-985	2313		Floats / Wheel-Skis
☐ C-FOBE	Noorduyn Norseman VI (UC-64A)	480	43-35406	0044		1 PW R-1340	3420		Floats / Wheel-Skis
☐ C-FLEA	De Havilland DHC-3 Otter	286		0058		1 PZL ASh-62IR-M18	3629		Floats / Wheel-Skis / cvtd DHC-3 PW
☐ C-FODJ	De Havilland DHC-3 Otter	14		0053		1 PW R-1340	3629		Floats / Wheel-Skis

GRENFELL REGIONAL HEALTH SERVICES – GRHS
St. Anthony, Nfld.

Air Operations, St. Anthony, Newfoundland A0K 4S0, Canada ☎ (709) 454-3333 Tx: none Fax: (709) 454-2464 SITA: n/a
F: 1981 ✻✻✻ 13 Head: Thomas C. Green Net: n/a Non-profit medical organization conducting EMS flights/health services to the people of Northern Newfoundland & Labrador.

registration	type of aircraft	cn/fn	ex/ex*	mfd	del	powered by	mtow kg	configuration	name/fln/specialities/remarks
☐ C-FGWT	Twin (Aero) Jetprop Commander 900 (690D)	15042	N71GA	0085	1285	2 GA TPE331-5-254K	4853	EMS	SMA-version

GRIMSBY AVIATION (869311 Ontario, Inc. dba)
Grimsby Airpark, Ont.

General Delivery, Grassie, Ontario L0R 1M0, Canada ☎ (905) 945-6161 Tx: none Fax: (905) 945-6262 SITA: n/a
F: 1990 ✻✻✻ 2 Head: Ralph H. Meyer Net: n/a Aircraft below MTOW 1361kg: Bellanca Citabria, Cessna 150 & 172.

registration	type of aircraft	cn/fn	ex/ex*	mfd	del	powered by	mtow kg	configuration	name/fln/specialities/remarks
☐ C-FCFC	Piper PA-23-150 Apache	23-312		0055	1091	2 LY O-320-A1A	1588		

GRONDAIR (Division of Grondin Transport, Inc.)
St-Frédéric, Qué. **GRONDAIR** ⇒

32, Route 112, St-Frédéric, Québec G0N 1P0, Canada ☎ (418) 426-2313 Tx: none Fax: (418) 426-2319 SITA: n/a
F: 1965 ✻✻✻ 10 Head: Gaston Grondin Net: n/a Aircraft below MTOW 1361 kg: Cessna 172

registration	type of aircraft	cn/fn	ex/ex*	mfd	del	powered by	mtow kg	configuration	name/fln/specialities/remarks
☐ C-GIFF	Piper PA-31-310 Navajo	31-256		0068	0997	2 LY TIO-540-A1A	2948		
☐ C-GSRW	Piper PA-31-310 Navajo	31-262		0068	0894	2 LY TIO-540-A1A	2948		
☐ C-GUMQ	Piper PA-31-310 Navajo	31-84	N777GS	0068	1297	2 LY TIO-540-A1A	2948		
☐ C-FHWI	Beech King Air A90 (65-A90)	LJ-309	N329H	0067	0597	2 PWC PT6A-20	4218		

HARBOUR AIR SEAPLANES = H3 (Harbour Air, Ltd dba / formerly Windoak Air Services)
Vancouver-Int'l SPB, B.C. **HA HARBOUR AIR**

4760 Inglis Drive, Richmond, British Columbia V7B 1W4, Canada ☎ (604) 278-3478 Tx: none Fax: (604) 278-9897 SITA: n/a
F: 1979 ✻✻✻ 100 Head: Greg McDougall IATA: 458 Net: http://www.harbour-air.com Aircraft below MTOW 1361kg: Cessna 180 (on Floats).
Additional aircraft (DHC-6 Twin Otter on floats) are lsf/opb KENN BOREK AIR when required.

registration	type of aircraft	cn/fn	ex/ex*	mfd	del	powered by	mtow kg	configuration	name/fln/specialities/remarks
☐ C-GQDS	Cessna A185F Skywagon II	18503754		0079		1 CO IO-520-D	1520		Floats
☐ C-GZSH	Cessna A185F Skywagon II	18503482		0078		1 CO IO-520-D	1520		Floats
☐ C-FAOP	De Havilland DHC-2 Beaver I	1249		0058	0396	1 PW R-985	2313		Floats
☐ C-FAXI	De Havilland DHC-2 Beaver I	1514	N6535D	0063		1 PW R-985	2313		Floats
☐ C-FCQP	De Havilland DHC-2 Beaver I	370	N11257	0052	1295	1 PW R-985	2313		Floats
☐ C-FFHQ	De Havilland DHC-2 Beaver I	42		0049	0594	1 PW R-985	2313		Floats
☐ C-FHGZ	De Havilland DHC-2 Beaver I	759		1154	0694	1 PW R-985	2313		Floats
☐ C-FIFQ	De Havilland DHC-2 Beaver I	825		0055	0593	1 PW R-985	2313		Floats
☐ C-FJFQ	De Havilland DHC-2 Beaver I	963		0055	0595	1 PW R-985	2313		Floats
☐ C-FJOS	De Havilland DHC-2 Beaver I	1030		0056	0593	1 PW R-985	2313		Floats
☐ C-FKDC	De Havilland DHC-2 Beaver I	1080		0056	0593	1 PW R-985	2313		Floats
☐ C-FMXS	De Havilland DHC-2 Beaver I	1010	N43882	0055	0693	1 PW R-985	2313		Floats
☐ C-FOCN	De Havilland DHC-2 Beaver I	44		0050		1 PW R-985	2313		Floats
☐ C-FOCY	De Havilland DHC-2 Beaver I	79		0051		1 PW R-985	2313		Floats
☐ C-FOCZ	De Havilland DHC-2 Beaver I	100	N254BD	0051		1 PW R-985	2313		Floats
☐ C-FOSP	De Havilland DHC-2 Beaver I	1501		0062		1 PW R-985	2313		Floats
☐ C-FTCW	De Havilland DHC-2 Beaver I	646	VH-SMH	0053	0593	1 PW R-985	2313		Floats
☐ C-GMKP	De Havilland DHC-2 Beaver I	1374	N87775	0059	0592	1 PW R-985	2313		Floats
☐ C-GQHT	De Havilland DHC-2 Beaver I	682	53-3725	0053	0797	1 PW R-985	2313		Floats
☐ C-GOPP	De Havilland DHC-3 Turbo Otter	355	N53KA	0059	0397	1 PWC PT6A-135A	3629		Floats / cvtd Otter
☐ C-GUTW	De Havilland DHC-3 Turbo Otter	405	CAF 9423	0060	0691	1 PWC PT6A-135A	3629		Floats / cvtd Otter
☐ C-FRNO	De Havilland DHC-3 Otter	21	N128F	0054	0593	1 PW R-1340	3629		Floats

HARBOUR CITY HELICOPTERS, Ltd (formerly Southern Mountain Helicopters, Ltd)
Langley, B.C.

Unit 104, 5225-216th Street, Langley, British Columbia V2Y 2N3, Canada ☎ (604) 534-7918 Tx: none Fax: (604) 532-3946 SITA: n/a
F: 1992 ✻✻✻ 8 Head: John Louis Net: n/a Aircraft below MTOW 1361kg: Hughes 369HS (500C) & Robinson R22

registration	type of aircraft	cn/fn	ex/ex*	mfd	del	powered by	mtow kg	configuration	name/fln/specialities/remarks
☐ C-FJTC	Eurocopter (Aerosp.) AS350B2 AStar	3068		0098	0898	1 TU Arriel 1D1	2250		
☐ C-GQLL	Bell 205A-1	30018	A7-HAG	0068	0698	1 LY T5313B	4309		

HARV'S AIR SERVICE, Ltd
Steinbach, Man.

Box 1056, Steinbach, Manitoba R0A 2A0, Canada ☎ (204) 326-2434 Tx: n/a Fax: (204) 326-4182 SITA: n/a
F: 1977 ✻✻✻ n/a Head: Harvey Penner Net: http://www.cavok.com/has/ Aircraft below MTOW 1361 kg: Cessna 150, 152, 172 & Pitts S-2B

registration	type of aircraft	cn/fn	ex/ex*	mfd	del	powered by	mtow kg	configuration	name/fln/specialities/remarks
☐ C-FVJC	Beech Travel Air D95A	TD-618		0065		2 LY IO-360-B1B	1905		
☐ C-FQLC	Piper PA-31-310 Navajo B	31-7300929	F-WIQJ	0073	0993	2 LY TIO-540-A2C	2948		

HAUTS-MONTS, Inc.
Québec, Qué. **hauts-monts**

1924 Ave du Cheminot, Beauport, Québec G1E 4M1, Canada ☎ (418) 667-1913 Tx: none Fax: (418) 667-8340 SITA: n/a
F: 1960 ✻✻✻ 73 Head: Paul Grenier Net: n/a

registration	type of aircraft	cn/fn	ex/ex*	mfd	del	powered by	mtow kg	configuration	name/fln/specialities/remarks
☐ C-FROG	Piper PA-23-235 Apache	27-603		0066		2 LY O-540-B1A5	2177	Photo / Survey	
☐ C-FZAZ	Piper PA-23-250 Turbo Aztec E	27-7305132		0073		2 LY TIO-540-C1A	2359	Photo / Survey	
☐ C-GARX	Piper PA-23-250 Turbo Aztec E	27-4789	N14231	0072		2 LY TIO-540-C1A	2359	Photo / Survey	
☐ C-GDEB	Piper PA-23-250 Aztec E	27-4685	N14082	0071	0391	2 LY TIO-540-C1A	2359	Photo / Survey	
☐ C-GHMN	Piper PA-23-250 Aztec C	27-3893	N6590Y	0068	0496	2 LY IO-540-C4B5	2359	Photo / Survey	
☐ C-GNZQ	Piper PA-23-250 Turbo Aztec E	27-7554067	N54755	0075		2 LY TIO-540-C1A	2359	Photo / Survey	
☐ C-GMAP	Cessna 414 II Riley Rocket	414-0962		0077		2 LY IO-720-B1BD	3096	Photo / Survey	cvtd Cessna 414 II
☐ C-GPSP	Cessna 441 Conquest II	441-0058	OY-BHM	0078	0693	2 GA TPE331-8-403S	4468	Photo / Survey	

HAWK AIR (formerly Hawk Airways, Ltd / 705833 Ontario, Ltd dba / Seasonal May-October ops only)
Wawa-Hawk Junction, Ont. **HAWK AIR**

Box 186, Wawa, Ontario P0S 1K0, Canada ☎ (705) 889-2250 Tx: n/a Fax: (705) 856-2024 SITA: n/a
F: 1987 ✻✻✻ 5 Head: Mary F. Haight Net: n/a Aircraft below MTOW 1361kg: Cessna 180.

registration	type of aircraft	cn/fn	ex/ex*	mfd	del	powered by	mtow kg	configuration	name/fln/specialities/remarks
☐ C-FBBG	De Havilland DHC-2 Beaver I	358	N2848D	0055	0889	1 PW R-985	2313		Floats
☐ C-FQMN	De Havilland DHC-3 Otter	184	N2959W	0056	0692	1 PW R-1340	3629		Floats

HAWKAIR AVIATION SERVICES, Ltd
Terrace, B.C.

RR 4, Site 166, Comp. 5, Bristol Road, Terrace, British Columbia V8G 4V2, Canada ☎ (250) 635-4295 Tx: none Fax: (250) 635-4295 SITA: n/a
F: 1994 ✻✻✻ 14 Head: Paul Hawkins Net: n/a

registration	type of aircraft	cn/fn	ex/ex*	mfd	del	powered by	mtow kg	configuration	name/fln/specialities/remarks
☐ C-GYQS	BAe (Bristol) 170 Mk. 31 Freighter	13060	ZK-EPD	0052	0894	2 BR Hercules 734	19958	Freighter	
☐ C-GAAH	ATL-98 Carvair	42994 / D4 55	N5459X	0046	0597	4 PW R-2000	33475	Freighter	cvtd Douglas DC-4-1009 / convers.no.20

HAYES HELI-LOG SERVICES, Ltd (Member of Hayes Forest Services Group)
Cobble Hill, B.C.

Box 100, Cobble Hill, British Columbia V0R 1L0, Canada ☎ (250) 743-5501 Tx: none Fax: (250) 743-6328 SITA: n/a
F: n/a ✻✻✻ n/a Head: Donald Hayes Net: n/a

registration	type of aircraft	cn/fn	ex/ex*	mfd	del	powered by	mtow kg	configuration	name/fln/specialities/remarks
☐ C-FBHG	Bell 206B JetRanger	713		0072	0896	1 AN 250-C20	1451		cvtd 206A
☐ C-GPCT	Bell 206B JetRanger III	3085		0080	0395	1 AN 250-C20B	1451		
☐ C-FHFS	Sikorsky S-61N Helipro Short	61702	ZS-HHN	0072	0696	2 GE CT58-140-1	9318		cvtd S-61N
☐ C-FHHD	Sikorsky S-61N	61490	ZS-HDK	0071	0497	2 GE CT58-140-1	9318		

HEARST AIR SERVICE, Ltd
Hearst-Carey Lake, Ont. **HEARST AIR**

PO Box 2650, Hearst, Ontario P0L 1N0, Canada ☎ (705) 362-5700 Tx: none Fax: (705) 362-8004 SITA: n/a
F: 1974 ✻✻✻ 3 Head: Georges M. Veilleux Net: n/a

registration	type of aircraft	cn/fn	ex/ex*	mfd	del	powered by	mtow kg	configuration	name/fln/specialities/remarks
☐ C-FBTU	De Havilland DHC-2 Beaver I	1564		0064		1 PW R-985	2313		Floats / Wheel-Skis
☐ C-FDPM	De Havilland DHC-2 Beaver I	1247	N87878	0058	0390	1 PW R-985	2313		Floats

HELIBEC, Inc. (Seasonal May-October ops only)
La Tuque

CP 421, La Tuque, Québec G9X 3P3, Canada ☎ (819) 523-9616 Tx: none Fax: (819) 523-9671 SITA: n/a
F: 1993 ✻✻✻ n/a Head: n/a Net: n/a

registration	type of aircraft	cn/fn	ex/ex*	mfd	del	powered by	mtow kg	configuration	name/fln/specialities/remarks
☐ C-GZTS	Cessna A185F Skywagon II	18503496		0077	0494	1 CO IO-520-D	1520		Floats
☐ C-GSJO	Cessna U206G Stationair 6 II	U20606827		0084	0498	1 CO IO-520-F	1633		Floats
☐ C-FMPT	De Havilland DHC-2 Beaver I	1260		0058	0595	1 PW R-985	2313		Floats
☐ C-GNKR	De Havilland DHC-2 Beaver I	331	N5698	0052	0196	1 PW R-985	2313		Floats

HELICO AIR SERVICES, Ltd
Trenton, N.S.

PO Box 1425, Trenton, Nova Scotia B0K 1X0, Canada ☎ (902) 928-2200 Tx: none Fax: (902) 928-2203 SITA: n/a
F: 1993 ✻✻✻ n/a Head: Peter Skinner Net: n/a Aircraft below MTOW 1361kg: Bell 47G-2 & Hughes 269C (300C).

registration	type of aircraft	cn/fn	ex/ex*	mfd	del	powered by	mtow kg	configuration	name/fln/specialities/remarks
☐ C-GOPL	Bell 206B JetRanger	315	N816JH	0068	0698	1 AN 250-C20	1451		cvtd 206A

HELICOPTER COMPANY (The Helicopter Company, Inc. dba)
Toronto-City Centre, Ont.

212-Aerocentre West, Toronto City Centre Airport, Ontario M5V 1A1, Canada ☎ (416) 203-3280 Tx: none Fax: (416) 203-3282 SITA: n/a
F: 1997 ✻✻✻ 5 Head: Kevin Smith Net: http://www.thehelicoptercompany.com

registration	type of aircraft	cn/fn	ex/ex*	mfd	del	powered by	mtow kg	configuration	name/fln/specialities/remarks
☐ C-GCXO	Bell 206B JetRanger	248	N4723R	0068	0698	1 AN 250-C20	1451		cvtd 206A

HELICOPTERES GILLES LEGER, Enr. (Placements Giller Leger, Inc. dba)
Lachute, Qué.

430 Boulevard Aeroparc, Lachute, Québec J8H 3R8, Canada ☎ (514) 562-2408 Tx: none Fax: (514) 562-2336 SITA: n/a
F: 1993 ♦♦♦ 5 Head: Gilles Léger Net: n/a Aircraft below MTOW 1361kg: Robinson R22

registration	type of aircraft	cn/fn	ex/ex*	mfd	del	powered by	mtow kg	configuration	selcal	name/fln/remarks
☐ C-GGUB	Bell 206B JetRanger	1802		0075	0898	1 AN 250-C20	1451			

HELICOPTER TRANSPORT SERVICES (Canada), Inc. – HTSC (Heli-Transport) (formerly Huisson Aviation, Ltd)
Carp/Timmins/Moosonee, Ont. & Sept-Iles, Qué.

PO Box 250, Carp, Ontario K0A 1L0, Canada ☎ (613) 839-5868 Tx: none Fax: (613) 839-2976 SITA: n/a
F: 1969 ♦♦♦ 40 Head: Luc Pilon Net: n/a Aircraft below MTOW 1361kg: Robinson R22 & R44
Helicopter training is done by subsidiary HELICOPTER TRAINING Corp., Sept-Iles, Québec base operations by subsidiary HELI-TRANSPORT, Inc. Both same headquarters & fleet.

registration	type of aircraft	cn/fn	ex/ex*	mfd	del	powered by	mtow kg	configuration	selcal	name/fln/remarks
☐ C-FCTV	Bell 206B JetRanger	690	C-FQCL	0071	0797	1 AN 250-C20	1451			cvtd 206A
☐ C-FMUO	Bell 206B JetRanger III	3265	N39082	0081	0392	1 AN 250-C20B	1451			
☐ C-GJWL	Bell 206B JetRanger III	3660	N3171N	0082	1087	1 AN 250-C20J	1451			
☐ C-GQMR	Bell 206B JetRanger II	2207		0077	0391	1 AN 250-C20	1451			
☐ C-FLRU	Bell 206L-1 LongRanger II	45402	G-CINE	0080	1091	1 AN 250-C28B	1882			
☐ C-FLTX	Bell 206LR+ LongRanger	45043	N96AT	0076	0992	1 AN 250-C20B	1814			cvtd 206L
☐ C-FWGN	Bell 206L-4 LongRanger IV	52010	N2292Z	0093	0895	1 AN 250-C30P	2018			
☐ C-GJOL	Bell 206L LongRanger	45065	N9998K	0076	0587	1 AN 250-C20B	1814			
☐ C-GOVB	Bell 206L-1 LongRanger II	45162		0079		1 AN 250-C28B	1882			
☐ C-FPXN	Eurocopter (Aerosp.) AS350B1 AStar	2205	N6080C	0089	0693	1 TU Arriel 1D	2200			
☐ C-FJSM	Bell 222	47065	N824D	0081	0891	2 LY LTS101-650C.3	3561			
☐ C-GINA	Bell 222	47072	N905X	0081		2 LY LTS101-650C.3	3674			
☐ C-FPAZ	Bell 205A-1	30016	N1347N	0068	0595	1 LY T5313B	4309			
☐ C-GFFY	Bell 205A-1	30123	N1084C	0073	0391	1 LY T5313B	4309			
☐ C-GSIT	Bell 205A-1	30120		0072	0391	1 LY T5313B	4309			
☐ C-FIWE	Sikorsky S-76A	760095	N330DP	0080	1090	2 AN 250-C30	4763			
☐ C-GAHZ	Bell 212	30758	N5306T	0076	0490	2 PWC PT6T-3 TwinPac	5080			

HELICRAFT, Ltd / Ltée
St. Hubert, Qué.

6500 Chemin de la Savane, St. Hubert, Québec J3Y 5K2, Canada ☎ (514) 468-3431 Tx: none Fax: (514) 468-5497 SITA: n/a
F: 1969 ♦♦♦ 10 Head: Sylvain Séguin Net: n/a Aircraft below MTOW 1361 kg: Hughes 269B (300B), 269C (300C) & 269D (300D)

registration	type of aircraft	cn/fn	ex/ex*	mfd	del	powered by	mtow kg	configuration	selcal	name/fln/remarks
☐ C-GARE	Bell 206B JetRanger	1852		0075		1 AN 250-C20	1451			

HELI DYNAMICS, Ltd
Whitehorse, Y.T.

PO Box 4280, Whitehorse, Yukon Y1A 3T3, Canada ☎ (867) 668-3536 Tx: none Fax: (867) 668-5637 SITA: n/a
F: 1987 ♦♦♦ 5 Head: Karl Ziehe Net: n/a

registration	type of aircraft	cn/fn	ex/ex*	mfd	del	powered by	mtow kg	configuration	selcal	name/fln/remarks
☐ C-FKOX	Bell 206B JetRanger	1261		0074	0692	1 AN 250-C20	1451			
☐ C-GHDD	Bell 206B JetRanger	1810	N49636	0075	0691	1 AN 250-C20	1451			

HELI-EXCEL, Inc.
Sept-Iles, Qué.

C.P. 188, Sept-Iles, Québec G4R 4K5, Canada ☎ (418) 962-7126 Tx: none Fax: (418) 962-9809 SITA: n/a
F: 1989 ♦♦♦ 10 Head: Carol Soucy Net: n/a

registration	type of aircraft	cn/fn	ex/ex*	mfd	del	powered by	mtow kg	configuration	selcal	name/fln/remarks
☐ C-GHQW	Bell 206B JetRanger	1708		0075	0697	1 AN 250-C20	1451			
☐ C-FHEI	Eurocopter (Aerosp.) AS350BA AStar	2969		0097	0597	1 TU Arriel 1B	2100			
☐ C-FJYL	Eurocopter (Aerosp.) AS350BA AStar	2959		0096	0497	1 TU Arriel 1B	2100			
☐ C-FSPF	Eurocopter (Aerosp.) AS350B2 AStar	2787		0094	0694	1 TU Arriel 1D1	2250			
☐ C-FTII	Eurocopter (Aerosp.) AS350BA AStar	2806		0094	0595	1 TU Arriel 1B	2100			
☐ C-FVRT	Eurocopter (Aerosp.) AS350B2 AStar	2849		0095	0595	1 TU Arriel 1D1	2250			

HELI-EXPRESS, Inc.
Québec, Qué.

222-2e Avenue, Aéroport du Québec, Sainte-Foy, Québec G2E 5W1, Canada ☎ (418) 877-5890 Tx: none Fax: (418) 877-5891 SITA: n/a
F: 1990 ♦♦♦ 20 Head: Paul Dubois Net: n/a

registration	type of aircraft	cn/fn	ex/ex*	mfd	del	powered by	mtow kg	configuration	selcal	name/fln/remarks
☐ C-FCCI	Eurocopter (Aerosp.) AS350BA AStar	1303	N5768Y	0080	0591	1 TU Arriel 1B	2100			cvtd AS350D
☐ C-FWAU	Eurocopter (Aerosp.) AS350B2 AStar	2866		0095	1195	1 TU Arriel 1D1	2250			
☐ C-GDEH	Eurocopter (Aerosp.) AS350BA AStar	1348	N805DB	0086	0595	1 TU Arriel 1B	2100			cvtd AS350D
☐ C-GHEX	Eurocopter (Aerosp.) AS350B2 AStar	2867	C-FWAV	0095	0396	1 TU Arriel 1D1	2250			

HELI-EXPRESS AVIATION, Inc.
Weston, Ont.

130 Toryork Drive, Weston, Ontario M9L 1X9, Canada ☎ (416) 740-3279 Tx: none Fax: (416) 740-1953 SITA: n/a
F: 1998 ♦♦♦ n/a Head: n/a Net: n/a

registration	type of aircraft	cn/fn	ex/ex*	mfd	del	powered by	mtow kg	configuration	selcal	name/fln/remarks
☐ C-GTDA	Bell 206B JetRanger III	3130		0080	0398	1 AN 250-C20B	1451			

HELI FOREX (Forexport, Inc. dba / Member of Le Groupe Forex, Inc.)
Val d'Or, Qué.

CP 296, Val d'Or, Québec J9P 4P3, Canada ☎ (819) 825-4844 Tx: none Fax: (819) 825-5995 SITA: n/a
F: 1990 ♦♦♦ 8 Head: Jean-Pierre Fuchs Net: n/a

registration	type of aircraft	cn/fn	ex/ex*	mfd	del	powered by	mtow kg	configuration	selcal	name/fln/remarks
☐ C-FHVO	Bell 206B JetRanger	1421	N379EH	0074	0890	1 AN 250-C20	1451			
☐ C-GKCW	Bell 206L LongRanger	45122	N6139U	0077	0890	1 AN 250-C20B	1814			

HELIFOR Industries, Ltd (Division of INTERFOR Int'l Forest Products, Ltd)
Campbell River, B.C.

Box 49114, Bentall Postal Station, Vancouver, British Columbia V7X 1H7, Canada ☎ (604) 681-3221 Tx: none Fax: (604) 681-2924 SITA: n/a
F: 1978 ♦♦♦ 80 Head: Gary McDermid Net: n/a

registration	type of aircraft	cn/fn	ex/ex*	mfd	del	powered by	mtow kg	configuration	selcal	name/fln/remarks
☐ C-GHFA	MD Helicopters MD 500D (Hughes 369D)	290459D	N58291	0079	0493	1 AN 250-C20B	1361			
☐ C-GHFL	MD Helicopters MD 500D (Hughes 369D)	1143D	N305CK	0082	0290	1 AN 250-C20B	1361			
☐ C-GHFP	MD Helicopters MD 500D (Hughes 369D)	1270245D	C-GSZP	0078	0197	1 AN 250-C20B	1361			
☐ C-GTZR	MD Helicopters MD 500D (Hughes 369D)	790554D		0079		1 AN 250-C20B	1361			
☐ C-FHFW	Boeing Vertol 107-II	107	N188CH	0064	0198	2 GE CT58-140-2	9977			lsf Columbia Helicopters
☐ C-GHFF	Boeing Vertol 107-II (HKP-4A)	406	N195CH	0062	0199	2 GE CT58-140-2	9977			lsf Columbia Helicopters
☐ C-GHFT	Boeing Vertol 107-II (HKP-4A)	402	N193CH	0062	0494	2 GE CT58-140-2	9977			lsf Columbia Helicopters

HELI-INTER, Inc.
Chicoutimi-St. Honoré, Qué.

108 rue No. 1, Aéroport St. Honoré, St. Honoré, Québec G0V 1L0, Canada ☎ (418) 673-6442 Tx: none Fax: (418) 673-6472 SITA: n/a
F: 1998 ♦♦♦ n/a Head: Benoit Allard Net: n/a

registration	type of aircraft	cn/fn	ex/ex*	mfd	del	powered by	mtow kg	configuration	selcal	name/fln/remarks
☐ C-GAWV	Eurocopter (Aerosp.) AS350B2 AStar	2998		0097	0498	1 TU Arriel 1D1	2250			
☐ C-GPHN	Eurocopter (Aerosp.) AS350D AStar	1251	N81RJ	0080	0498	1 LY LTS101-600A.2	1950			

HELIJET AIRWAYS, Inc. = JB / JBA
Vancouver-Int'l, B.C.

5911 Airport Road South, Richmond, British Columbia V7B 1B5, Canada ☎ (604) 273-4688 Tx: none Fax: (604) 273-5301 SITA: n/a
F: 1986 ♦♦♦ 90 Head: Alistair MacLennan IATA: 613 ICAO: HELIJET Net: n/a Aircraft below MTOW 1361kg: Robinson R22

registration	type of aircraft	cn/fn	ex/ex*	mfd	del	powered by	mtow kg	configuration	selcal	name/fln/remarks
☐ C-GZPM	Bell 206B JetRanger	880	N2NU	0072	0796	1 AN 250-C20	1451			
☐ C-GRMH	Bell 206L-3 LongRanger III	51003	N2123X	0082	0796	1 AN 250-C30P	1882			
☐ C-GDWH	Eurocopter (Aerosp.) AS350B AStar	1123	VH-HBA	0079	0299	1 TU Arriel 1B	1950			
☐ C-FHJJ	Eurocopter (Aerosp.) AS355F1 TwinStar	5053	N442PT	0081	0297	2 AN 250-C20F	2400			
☐ C-GHJG	Sikorsky S-76A+	760015	N90459	0079	0892	2 TU Arriel 1S	4763			cvtd S-76A
☐ C-GHJL	Sikorsky S-76A	760214	N101PB	0081	0987	2 AN 250-C30S	4763	EMS		opf B.C. Ambulance Service
☐ C-GHJP	Sikorsky S-76A	760065	N176EH	0080	0390	2 AN 250-C30S	4763			
☐ C-GHJT	Sikorsky S-76A	760166	VH-HRQ	0081	1098	2 AN 250-C30S	4763			
☐ C-GHJV	Sikorsky S-76A	760271	N884	0085	0290	2 AN 250-C30S	4763			
☐ C-GHJW	Sikorsky S-76A	760074	N586C	0080	1289	2 AN 250-C30S	4763			

HELI-LIFT INTERNATIONAL, Inc.
Yorkton, Sask.

Box 1971, Yorkton, Saskatchewan S3N 3X3, Canada ☎ (306) 783-5438 Tx: n/a Fax: (306) 782-3590 SITA: n/a
F: 1994 ♦♦♦ Head: Bob Parker Net: n/a

registration	type of aircraft	cn/fn	ex/ex*	mfd	del	powered by	mtow kg	configuration	selcal	name/fln/remarks
☐ C-GQCE	Bell 206B JetRanger	645		0071	0697	1 AN 250-C20	1451			cvtd 206A
☐ C-GQCW	Eurocopter (Aerosp.) AS350D AStar	1255	N3607T	0080	0594	1 LY LTS101-600A.2	1950			

HELI-MANICOUAGAN, Inc.
Baie-Comeau, Qué.

1575 Pagé, Baie-Comeau, Québec G5C 3V5, Canada ☎ (418) 589-4847 Tx: none Fax: (418) 589-4147 SITA: n/a
F: 1988 ♦♦♦ 8 Head: Ginette & Francis Otis Net: n/a

registration	type of aircraft	cn/fn	ex/ex*	mfd	del	powered by	mtow kg	configuration	selcal	name/fln/remarks
☐ C-GIVV	Bell 206B JetRanger III	2823	N2757C	0079	0689	1 AN 250-C20B	1451			
☐ C-GVHD	Bell 206LR+ LongRanger	45141		0077	0697	1 AN 250-C20R	1814			cvtd 206L
☐ C-FGYM	Eurocopter (Aerosp.) AS350BA AStar	2531		0091	1291	1 TU Arriel 1B	2100			cvtd AS350B
☐ C-FHVV	Eurocopter (Aerosp.) AS350D AStar	1225	N215EH	0080	0290	1 LY LTS101-600A.2	1950			
☐ C-FPHY	Eurocopter (Aerosp.) AS350BA AStar	1496	N5805B	0081	0593	1 TU Arriel 1B	2100			cvtd AS350D
☐ C-GMAN	Eurocopter (Aerosp.) AS350B2 AStar	3073		0098	0498	1 TU Arriel 1D1	2250			
☐ C-GMYG	Eurocopter (Aerosp.) AS350D AStar	1201	N3604X	0079	1294	1 LY LTS101-600A.3	1950			

HELI-MAX, Ltée / Ltd
Trois-Rivières & Maniwaki & Québec, Qué.

🚁 HELI·MAX

3650 Boul. de l'Aéroport, Trois-Rivières, Québec G9A 5E1, Canada ☎ (819) 377-3344 Tx: none Fax: (819) 377-5858 SITA: n/a
F: 1976 ♦♦♦ 30 Head: Wilfrid Hamel Net: n/a

registration	type of aircraft	cn/fn	ex/ex*	mfd	del	powered by	mtow kg	name/fln/specialitites/remarks
☐ C-FHMF	MD Helicopters MD 500E (Hughes 369E)	0370E		0089	0190	1 AN 250-C20R	1361	
☐ C-FHMJ	MD Helicopters MD 500E (Hughes 369E)	0378E		0089	0190	1 AN 250-C20R	1361	
☐ C-FMHM	MD Helicopters MD 500E (Hughes 369E)	0380E		0090	0690	1 AN 250-C20R	1361	
☐ C-FXQH	MD Helicopters MD 500E (Hughes 369E)	0248E	N132KC	0087	0696	1 AN 250-C20B	1361	
☐ C-GYTY	MD Helicopters MD 500D (Hughes 369D)	270078D		0077	0498	1 AN 250-C20B	1361	
☐ C-FMYW	MD Helicopters MD 520N (Hughes 500N)	LN016		0092	0492	1 AN 250-C20R	1520	
☐ C-FMYX	MD Helicopters MD 520N (Hughes 500N)	LN019		0092	0692	1 AN 250-C20R	1520	
☐ C-FPRX	MD Helicopters MD 520N (Hughes 500N)	LN046	N5219F*	0093	0493	1 AN 250-C20R	1520	
☐ C-FPRZ	MD Helicopters MD 520N (Hughes 500N)	LN047	N5219V*	0093	0493	1 AN 250-C20R	1520	
☐ C-FOZT	Eurocopter (Aerosp.) AS350BA AStar	2644		0092	1192	1 TU Arriel 1B	2100	
☐ C-FQHC	Eurocopter (Aerosp.) AS350D AStar	1011	N49561	0078	0298	1 LY LTS101-600A.2	1950	cvtd AS350C
☐ C-GCYE	Eurocopter (Aerosp.) AS350BA AStar	1507	F-GEDP	0082	0598	1 TU Arriel 1B	2100	cvtd AS350B
☐ C-GQHK	Eurocopter (Aerosp.) AS350D AStar	1198	N360SP	0079	1098	1 LY LTS101-600A.2	1950	
☐ C-GAHM	Bell 205A-1	30215	N59607	0075	0197	1 LY T5313B	4309	

HELIMAX NUNAVUT (3349209 Canada, Inc. dba / Subsidiary of Heli-Max, Ltée/Ltd)
Arviat-Eskimo Point, N.W.T.

3650 Boul. de l'Aéroport, Trois-Rivières, Québec G9A 5E1, Canada ☎ (819) 377-3344 Tx: none Fax: (819) 377-5858 SITA: n/a
F: 1997 ♦♦♦ n/a Head: Nancy Karetak-Lindell Net: n/a

registration	type of aircraft	cn/fn	ex/ex*	mfd	del	powered by	mtow kg
☐ C-FYTZ	MD Helicopters MD 500E (Hughes 369E)	0259E	N535JP	0088	0997	1 AN 250-C20B	1361
☐ C-FPSG	MD Helicopters MD 520N (Hughes 500N)	LN049	N52042*	0093	1297	1 AN 250-C20R	1520

HELI-NORTH AVIATION, Inc. (Heli-Nord Aviation, Inc.)
Garson-Skead, Ont.

HELI-NORTH / HELI-NORD

Box 3007, Garson, Ontario P3L 1V4, Canada ☎ (705) 693-0856 Tx: none Fax: (705) 693-0858 SITA: n/a
F: 1990 ♦♦♦ 24 Head: Sylvain Seguin Net: http://www.isys.ca/heli-north Aircraft below MTOW 1361kg: Schweizer 269B (300B) & 269C (300C & 330)

registration	type of aircraft	cn/fn	ex/ex*	mfd	del	powered by	mtow kg	name/fln/specialitites/remarks
☐ C-FEEN	Bell 206B JetRanger	236		0068	0690	1 AN 250-C20	1451	cvtd 206A
☐ C-GBSP	Bell 206B JetRanger	1153		0073	0493	1 AN 250-C20	1451	
☐ C-FDDS	Bell 206L-1 LongRanger II	45773	C-FSUE	0083	0398	1 AN 250-C28B	1882	
☐ C-FHNN	Bell 206L-1 LongRanger II	45172	N20LN	0078	0696	1 AN 250-C28B	1882	
☐ C-FVEU	Bell 206L-1 LongRanger II	45611	N3908N	0081	0595	1 AN 250-C28B	1882	
☐ C-FAHA	Bell 204B	2037		0065	0898	1 LY T5311A	3856	
☐ C-GAPJ	Bell 204B	2012 / 2	THAI 912	0064	0696	1 LY T5311A	3856	
☐ C-GEAW	Bell 204B	2010	N588P	0063	0199	1 LY T5313B	3856	

HELIQWEST AVIATION, Inc.
Edmonton-Municipal, Alta.

PO Box 34058, Kingsway Mall P.O., Edmonton, Alberta T5G 3G4, Canada ☎ (780) 940-4561 Tx: none Fax: (780) 447-5998 SITA: n/a
F: 1994 ♦♦♦ 10 Head: Robert Chalifoux Net: n/a

registration	type of aircraft	cn/fn	ex/ex*	mfd	del	powered by	mtow kg
☐ C-GEAG	Bell 205A-1	30262	XC-CIC	0078	0198	1 LY T5313B	4309
☐ C-GEAK	Bell 205A-1	30183	N393EH	0075	0296	1 LY T5313B	4309
☐ C-GEAT	Bell 205A-1	30088	G-BKGH	0070	0196	1 LY T5313B	4309
☐ C-GBVU	Bell 212	30646	N64730	0074	0297	2 PWC PT6T-3 TwinPac	5080

HELI-STAR, Inc. (formerly Hélicoptère La Tuque, Inc.)
La Tuque, Qué.

3142 Boul. Ducharme, La Tuque, Québec G9X 4T2, Canada ☎ (819) 523-6133 Tx: none Fax: (819) 523-7500 SITA: n/a
F: 1995 ♦♦♦ n/a Head: Richard Veillette Net: n/a

registration	type of aircraft	cn/fn	ex/ex*	mfd	del	powered by	mtow kg
☐ C-GEAQ	Bell 206B JetRanger	1653	N383EH	0075	0697	1 AN 250-C20	1451

HELI-UNGAVA (1997), Inc.
Matagami, Qué.

CP 1420, Matagami, Québec J0Y 2P0, Canada ☎ (819) 739-5293 Tx: none Fax: (819) 739-5297 SITA: n/a
F: 1997 ♦♦♦ n/a Head: n/a Net: n/a

registration	type of aircraft	cn/fn	ex/ex*	mfd	del	powered by	mtow kg	name/fln/specialitites/remarks
☐ C-FGKP	Eurocopter (Aerosp.) AS350B AStar	1032	N8107V	0078	0698	1 TU Arriel 1B	1950	cvtd AS350D
☐ C-FOZC	Eurocopter (Aerosp.) AS350BA AStar	2631		0092	0897	1 TU Arriel 1B	2100	
☐ C-FOZE	Eurocopter (Aerosp.) AS350BA AStar	2623		0092	0897	1 TU Arriel 1B	2100	

HELI-WASK (3416992 Canada, Inc. dba / Member of Le Groupe Forex, Inc.)
Val d'Or, Qué.

CP 296, Val d'Or, Québec J9P 4P3, Canada ☎ (819) 825-8424 Tx: none Fax: (819) 874-3361 SITA: n/a
F: 1998 ♦♦♦ n/a Head: Albert Diamond Net: n/a

registration	type of aircraft	cn/fn	ex/ex*	mfd	del	powered by	mtow kg	name/fln/specialitites/remarks
☐ C-FHVG	Bell 206B JetRanger	1677	N38653	0075	1298	1 AN 250-C20	1451	
☐ C-FHAJ	Eurocopter (Aerosp.) AS350D AStar	1493	N511WW	0082	0299	1 LY LTS101-600A.3	1950	
☐ C-FHAK	Eurocopter (Aerosp.) AS350BA AStar	1545	N517WW	0082	0299	1 TU Arriel 1B	2100	cvtd AS350D

HEMISPH-AIR (Hemisph-Air Services, Ltd / Services Hemisph-Air, Ltée dba)
Montreal-Dorval, Qué.

9501 Avenue Rue, Dorval, Québec H9P 1A2, Canada ☎ (514) 633-9752 Tx: none Fax: (514) 633-8581 SITA: n/a
F: 1993 ♦♦♦ 12 Head: Hugues Acker & Marc Moullard Net: http://www.hemisph-air.com Aircraft below MTOW 1361kg: Cessna 150, 152 & 172

registration	type of aircraft	cn/fn	ex/ex*	mfd	del	powered by	mtow kg
☐ C-GKPR	Piper PA-34-200T Seneca II	34-7970148	N3071T	0079	0698	2 CO TSIO-360-EB	2073

HICKS & LAWRENCE, Ltd
St. Thomas, Ont.

PO Box 519, St. Thomas, Ontario N5P 3V6, Canada ☎ (519) 633-1884 Tx: none Fax: (519) 631-8289 SITA: n/a
F: 1982 ♦♦♦ n/a Head: Duane Hicks Net: n/a Ag-aircraft below MTOW 5000kg: Ayres S-2R, Cessna A188B, PZL M-18 & Piper PA-36

registration	type of aircraft	cn/fn	ex/ex*	mfd	del	powered by	mtow kg	configuration	name/fln/specialitites/remarks
☐ C-FIXO	Cessna 337G Super Skymaster II	33701820	N1328L	0078		2 CO IO-360-G	2100		
☐ C-GEOR	Cessna 337G Super Skymaster II	33701730		0076		2 CO IO-360-G	2100		
☐ C-GFSC	Cessna 337G Super Skymaster II	33701793	N53699	0077		2 CO IO-360-G	2100		
☐ C-GIGB	Cessna 337G Super Skymaster	33701599	N72478	0074		2 CO IO-360-G	2100		
☐ C-GIOG	Cessna 337G Super Skymaster II	33701746		0076		2 CO IO-360-G	2100		
☐ C-FEGW	Piper PA-23-250 Aztec A	27-361		0061	0296	2 LY O-540-A1B5	2177		
☐ C-FMUM	Twin (Aero) Shrike Commander 500S	3103	N37GW	0071		2 LY IO-540-E1B5	3062		
☐ C-GAYR	Twin (Aero) Shrike Commander 500S	3118		0072	0596	2 LY IO-540-E1B5	3062		
☐ C-GJMA	Twin (Aero) Commander 500B	500B-1319-128	N330U	0063		2 LY IO-540-B1A5	3062		
☐ C-FNJB	Consolidated PBY-5A Canso	CV-249	RCAF 9815	0041	0997	2 PW R-1830-92	13835	Tanker	Amphibian
☐ C-FNJF	Consolidated PBY-5A Canso	CV-283	RCAF 11005	0041	0997	2 PW R-1830-92	13835	Tanker	Amphibian

HIGHLAND HELICOPTERS, Ltd
Vancouver-Int'l, B.C. **HIGHLAND** HELICOPTERS

4240 Agar Drive, Vancouver Airport South, Richmond, British Columbia V7B 1A3, Canada ☎ (604) 273-6161 Tx: none Fax: (604) 273-6088 SITA: n/a
F: 1959 ♦♦♦ 60 Head: Terry Churcott Net: n/a

registration	type of aircraft	cn/fn	ex/ex*	mfd	del	powered by	mtow kg	name/fln/specialitites/remarks
☐ C-FCDL	Bell 206B JetRanger III	3852	JA9748	0085	0798	1 AN 250-C20J	1451	
☐ C-FCOY	Bell 206B JetRanger III	3280	N7023J	0081	0297	1 AN 250-C20B	1451	
☐ C-FHHB	Bell 206B JetRanger	519		0070		1 AN 250-C20	1451	cvtd 206A
☐ C-FHHI	Bell 206B JetRanger III	2310	N101CD	0077	0498	1 AN 250-C20B	1451	
☐ C-GHHD	Bell 206B JetRanger	1566	N90003	0074		1 AN 250-C20	1451	
☐ C-GHHG	Bell 206B JetRanger	1396	N918TR	0074		1 AN 250-C20	1451	
☐ C-GHHM	Bell 206B JetRanger III	2712		0079		1 AN 250-C20B	1451	
☐ C-GHHO	Bell 206B JetRanger	1690		0075		1 AN 250-C20	1451	
☐ C-GHHR	Bell 206B JetRanger II	1963		0076		1 AN 250-C20	1451	
☐ C-GHHX	Bell 206B JetRanger III	2714		0079		1 AN 250-C20B	1451	
☐ C-GHXJ	Bell 206B JetRanger	1832		0075		1 AN 250-C20	1451	
☐ C-GIZO	Bell 206B JetRanger III	2715		0079		1 AN 250-C20B	1451	
☐ C-GJJA	Bell 206B JetRanger II	2032	N9958K	0076		1 AN 250-C20	1451	
☐ C-GKDG	Bell 206B JetRanger III	2969		0080		1 AN 250-C20B	1451	
☐ C-GKGI	Bell 206B JetRanger	1790	N49629	0075		1 AN 250-C20	1451	
☐ C-GKJL	Bell 206B JetRanger III	3005		0080		1 AN 250-C20B	1451	
☐ C-GMDQ	Bell 206B JetRanger III	3045		0080		1 AN 250-C20B	1451	
☐ C-GMDX	Bell 206B JetRanger III	3032		0080		1 AN 250-C20B	1451	
☐ C-GMXE	Bell 206B JetRanger	1109	N58144	0073		1 AN 250-C20	1451	
☐ C-GMZH	Bell 206B JetRanger III	3203		0080		1 AN 250-C20B	1451	
☐ C-GNLT	Bell 206B JetRanger III	2973		0080		1 AN 250-C20B	1451	
☐ C-GNSQ	Bell 206B JetRanger III	3274		0081		1 AN 250-C20B	1451	
☐ C-GOPF	Bell 206B JetRanger III	3227		0081		1 AN 250-C20B	1451	
☐ C-GOPK	Bell 206B JetRanger III	3247		0081		1 AN 250-C20B	1451	
☐ C-FHHJ	Bell 206L-3 LongRanger III	51382		0090	0890	1 AN 250-C30P	1882	
☐ C-FTHH	Bell 206L-3 LongRanger III	51369		0090	0790	1 AN 250-C30P	1882	
☐ C-GHHF	Bell 206L-3 LongRanger III	51510	N9146H	0091	0596	1 AN 250-C30P	1882	
☐ C-GHHY	Bell 206L-3 LongRanger III	51349		0090	0590	1 AN 250-C30P	1882	
☐ C-GLHH	Bell 206L-3 LongRanger III	51517		0091	1191	1 AN 250-C30P	1882	
☐ C-GMCJ	Bell 206L-3 LongRanger III	51459		0091	0591	1 AN 250-C30P	1882	

registration   type of aircraft   cn/fn   ex/ex*   mfd   del   powered by   mtow kg   configuration   selcal   name/fln/specialitites/remarks

☐ C-FHHC	Eurocopter (Aerosp.) AS350B2 AStar	2569	N2PW	0091	1293	1 TU Arriel 1D1	2250			
☐ C-FKHH	Eurocopter (Aerosp.) AS350B2 AStar	2736		0094	0294	1 TU Arriel 1D1	2250			
☐ C-GHHW	Eurocopter (Aerosp.) AS350B2 AStar	3039		0097	0298	1 TU Arriel 1D1	2250			
☐ C-GHHZ	Eurocopter (Aerosp.) AS350B2 AStar	3054		0097	0298	1 TU Arriel 1D1	2250			
☐ C-GNHH	Eurocopter (Aerosp.) AS350B2 AStar	2737		0094	0294	1 TU Arriel 1D1	2250			
☐ C-GEAI	Bell 204B	2070	N7879S	0067		1 LY T5311A	3856			
☐ C-GEAV	Bell 204B	2024	N1189W	0065		1 LY T5311A	3856			

HIGH RIVER FLIGHT CENTRE, Ltd
High River, Alta.

Box 5337, High River, Alberta T1V 1M5, Canada ☎ (780) 652-3444 Tx: none Fax: (780) 652-3444 SITA: n/a
F: 1987 ⋔⋔⋔ 5 Head: Alex Bahlsen Net: n/a Aircraft below MTOW 1361kg: Cessna 172, 182, Piper PA-18, PA-38 & Zlin Z142C

☐ C-GRPL	Piper PA-23-250 Aztec C	27-3842	N6547Y	0068	1296	2 LY IO-540-C4B5	2359			
☐ C-FQYW	AAC (Piper) Aerostar 601P	61P-0585-7963258	N49BL	0079	1193	2 LY IO-540-S1A5	2722			

HIGH TERRAIN HELICOPTERS, Ltd
Nelson, B.C.

407, 622 Front Street, Nelson, British Columbia V1L 4B7, Canada ☎ (250) 354-8445 Tx: none Fax: (250) 352-2211 SITA: n/a
F: 1992 ⋔⋔⋔ n/a Head: Steve Benwell Net: n/a Aircraft below MTOW 1361kg: Hiller UH-12E.

☐ C-GGSZ	Bell 206B JetRanger	1571	N12SM	0075	0795	1 AN 250-C20	1451			

HI-WOOD HELICOPTERS, Ltd
Calgary, Alta. *Hi-WOOD HELICOPTERS*

71 Sienna Park Terrace SW, Calgary, Alberta T3H 3L4, Canada ☎ (403) 217-2278 Tx: none Fax: (403) 217-2275 SITA: n/a
F: 1979 ⋔⋔⋔ 6 Head: Hermann Lorenz Net: n/a

☐ C-FSQY	Eurocopter (Aerosp.) AS350B2 AStar	2790		0094	0894	1 TU Arriel 1D1	2250			

HOME AVIATION (Division of Toma Jetprop, Ltd)
Calgary, Alta.

100-445 Palmer Road NE, Calgary, Alberta T2E 7G4, Canada ☎ (403) 291-4566 Tx: none Fax: (403) 291-4911 SITA: n/a
F: 1991 ⋔⋔⋔ 20 Head: Richard Hotchkiss Net: http://www.homeaviation.com

☐ C-GBDX	Piper PA-31-350 Navajo Chieftain	31-8152136	N36RS	0081	1097	2 LY TIO-540-J2BD	3175			
☐ C-GHOP	Beech King Air 200	BB-120	N6773S	0076	0192	2 PWC PT6A-41	5670			
☐ C-GDLR	Cessna 550 Citation II	550-0062		0079	0192	2 PWC JT15D-4	6033			
☐ C-GMTV	Cessna S550 Citation S/II	S550-0015		0085	1196	2 PWC JT15D-4B	6668			
☐ C-GTJL	Learjet 35A	35A-124	N8LA	0077	0596	2 GA TFE731-2-2B	8301			
☐ C-GMTR	Hawker 800A (BAe 125-800A)	258157 / NA0435	N800BA	0089	1196	2 GA TFE731-5R-1H	12428			

HORIZON AEROSPORT (1982), Ltd
Abbotsford, B.C.

PO Box 198, Matsqui, British Columbia V4X 3R2, Canada ☎ (604) 854-3255 Tx: none Fax: (604) 864-0224 SITA: n/a
F: 1982 ⋔⋔⋔ n/a Head: n/a Net: n/a Aircraft below MTOW 1361kg: Cessna 170, 180 & 182

☐ C-FVUO	Cessna U206B Super Skywagon	U206-0868	N81337	0067	0597	1 CO IO-520-F	1633			

HORNE AIR, Ltd (Subsidiary of Maurice Olivier Colts / Seasonal May-October ops only)
Hornepayne, Ont.

Box 510, Hornepayne, Ontario P0M 1Z0, Canada ☎ (807) 868-2337 Tx: n/a Fax: (807) 868-3230 SITA: n/a
F: 1962 ⋔⋔⋔ n/a Head: n/a Net: n/a

☐ C-FFHP	De Havilland DHC-2 Beaver I	57		0049		1 PW R-985	2313			Floats
☐ C-FIDM	De Havilland DHC-2 Beaver I	1323	N99871	0058		1 PW R-985	2313			Floats
☐ C-GEWG	De Havilland DHC-2 Beaver I	842	N87572	0054		1 PW R-985	2313			Floats

HOT WINGS AVIATION, Inc.
Vancouver-Int'l, B.C.

1501-1188 Quebec Street, Vancouver, British Columbia V6A 4B3, Canada ☎ (604) 683-1415 Tx: none Fax: (604) 602-0884 SITA: n/a
F: 1996 ⋔⋔⋔ n/a Head: Brian Harton Net: http://www.hot-wings.com

☐ C-FWNG	Piper PA-31-310 Navajo B	31-7300917	N7492L	0073	0597	2 LY TIO-540-A2C	2948	8 Pax		

HUDSON BAY HELICOPTERS, Ltd
Churchill, Man.

Box 337, Churchill, Manitoba R0B 0E0, Canada ☎ (204) 675-2576 Tx: none Fax: (204) 675-2331 SITA: n/a
F: 1997 ⋔⋔⋔ n/a Head: n/a Net: n/a

☐ C-FHBH	Bell 206B JetRanger III	3258	N904R	0081	0498	1 AN 250-C20B	1451			
☐ C-FTWM	Bell 206B JetRanger	712		0072	0398	1 AN 250-C20	1451			cvtd 206A

HUGHES AIR, Corp.
Calgary & Red Deer, Alta.

575 Palmer Road NE, Calgary, Alberta T2E 7G4, Canada ☎ (403) 291-3911 Tx: none Fax: (403) 250-5920 SITA: n/a
F: 1987 ⋔⋔⋔ 1 Head: Robert E. Pilling Net: n/a

☐ C-GBNR	Bell 206B JetRanger III	4400	N62760	0096	1296	1 AN 250-C20J	1451			
☐ C-FHRV	Piper PA-42-1000 Cheyenne 400LS	42-5527010	N100AK	0084	0195	2 GA TPE331-14-801A/B	5466			
☐ C-GPDQ	Learjet 35A	35A-170	N354RZ	0078	0299	2 GA TFE731-2-2B	8301			

HURON AIR & OUTFITTERS, Inc.
Armstrong-McKenzie Lake, Ont.

PO Box 122, Armstrong, Ontario P0T 1A0, Canada ☎ (807) 583-2051 Tx: none Fax: (807) 583-2812 SITA: n/a
F: 1981 ⋔⋔⋔ 8 Head: Ernest & Donna Nicholl Net: n/a Aircraft below MTOW 1361kg: Piper PA-18 (on Floats / Wheel-Skis).

☐ C-FDPW	De Havilland DHC-2 Beaver I	1339	58-2011	0059	1088	1 PW R-985	2313			Floats / Wheel-Skis
☐ C-GKEN	De Havilland DHC-2 Beaver I	1072	56-371	0056	0891	1 PW R-985	2313			Floats / Wheel-Skis
☐ C-FGBG	Twin (Aero) Commander 520	520-32		0052	0296	2 LY GO-435-C2B	2585			
☐ C-FGSR	Noorduyn Norseman V	N29-47		0050	0997	1 PW R-1340	3420			Floats
☐ C-GOFF	De Havilland DHC-3 Otter	65	CAF 3698	0054	1198	1 PW R-1340	3629			Floats

HYDRO-QUEBEC – Service Transport Aérien = APZ (Transport Avion division of Hydro-Québec / formerly James Bay Energy Corp.)
Montreal-Dorval, Qué.

651 Bl. Stuart Graham, Hangar 6B, Dorval, Québec H4Y 1E4, Canada ☎ (514) 633-6807 Tx: none Fax: (514) 633-6809 SITA: n/a
F: 1988 ⋔⋔⋔ n/a Head: Guy Arsenault ICAO: AMPERE Net: n/a
Avn Dept conducting non-commercial flights (flight operations contracted out to AIR INUIT) related to the energy supply business & seasonally to transport deer hunters to Anticosti Island under contract to the Province of Québec.

☐ C-GFHB	Convair 580	38	N4802C	0052	1076	2 AN 501-D13	24766	Corporate 49Pax		opb AIE in Hydro-Québec cs/cvtd 340-38
☐ C-GFHF	Convair 580	176	N4634C	0054	0477	2 AN 501-D13	24766	Corporate 49Pax		opb AIE in Hydro-Québec cs/cvtd 340-54
☐ C-GFHH	Convair 580	109	N3429	0053	0591	2 AN 501-D13	24766	Corporate 49Pax		opb AIE in Hydro-Québec cs/cvtd 340-32
☐ C-GQBP	Convair 580	137	N7528U	0053	0293	2 AN 501-D13	26379	Corporate 49Pax		opb AIE in Hydro-Québec cs/cvtd 340-54
☐ C-GTTA	Convair 580	501	N5122	0058	0498	2 AN 501-D13	24766	Corporate 36Pax		opb AIE in Corporate cs / cvtd 440-62

HY-RIDGE HELICOPTERS, Ltd
Fairmont Hot Springs, B.C.

Box 1171, Fairmont Hot Springs, British Columbia V0B 1L0, Canada ☎ (250) 345-0068 Tx: none Fax: (250) 345-0011 SITA: n/a
F: 1986 ⋔⋔⋔ 3 Head: Kim Hyllestad Net: n/a

☐ C-GNIX	Eurocopter (Aerosp.) AS350B2 AStar	2467	N822SA	0091	0697	1 TU Arriel 1D1	2250			

ICARUS FLYING SERVICE, Inc. (Les Services Aériens Icare, Inc.)
Iles de la Madeleine-Havre aux Maisons, Qué.

CP 181, Havre aux Maisons (Iles de la Madeleine), Québec G0B 1K0, Canada ☎ (418) 986-6067 Tx: n/a Fax: (418) 969-2139 SITA: n/a
F: 1977 ⋔⋔⋔ n/a Head: David Craig Quinn Net: n/a Aircraft below MTOW 1361 kg: Maule M-4-220C.

☐ C-GFBF	Britten-Norman BN-2B-27 Islander	2125	VP-FBF	0082	0490	2 LY O-540-E4C5	2994			

ICC Air Cargo Canada = CIC (ICC-International Cargo Charter Canada, Ltd / formerly ACS of Canada)
Calgary, Alta.

780 Magenta Blvd, Farnham, Québec J2N 1B8, Canada ☎ (450) 293-3656 Tx: none Fax: (450) 293-5169 SITA: n/a
F: 1986 ⋔⋔⋔ 75 Head: Edward CC Peagram ICAO: AIR TRADER Net: n/a

☐ C-FICA	Airbus Industrie A300B4-203 (F)	023	N741SC	0076	1098	2 GE CF6-50C2	165000	Freighter		Kimberley Joe / lsf CSAV / cvtd -203
☐ C-FICB	Airbus Industrie A300B4-203 (F)	078	N828SC	0079	0299	2 GE CF6-50C2	165000	Freighter		lsf CSAV / cvtd -203

IGNACE AIRWAYS (1996), Ltd (formerly Ignace Airways, Ltd / Seasonal May-November ops only)
Ignace & Thunder Bay, Ont. **IGNACE AIRWAYS LTD.**

Box 244, Ignace, Ontario P0T 1T0, Canada ☎ (807) 934-2273 Tx: none Fax: (807) 934-6647 SITA: n/a
F: 1960 ⋔⋔⋔ n/a Head: David Sutton Net: n/a Aircraft below MTOW 1361kg: Cessna 180 (on Floats)

☐ CF-TTL	Cessna U206C Super Skywagon	U206-1062		0068		1 CO IO-520-F	1633			Floats
☐ C-FOBV	De Havilland DHC-2 Beaver I	5		0049		1 PW R-985	2313			Floats
☐ C-FOCC	De Havilland DHC-2 Beaver I	23		0048	0896	1 PW R-985	2313			Floats
☐ C-FOCV	De Havilland DHC-2 Beaver I	74		0051		1 PW R-985	2313			Floats
☐ C-GKBW	De Havilland DHC-2 Beaver I	310	N1441Z	0051	0896	1 PW R-985	2313			Floats
☐ C-GZBR	De Havilland DHC-2 Beaver I	1272	N434GR	0058		1 PW R-985	2313			Floats
☐ C-FAPR	De Havilland DHC-3 Otter	31	LN-LMM	0053		1 PW R-1340	3629			Floats

INLAND AIR CHARTERS, Ltd
Prince Rupert, B.C.

PO Box 592, Prince Rupert, British Columbia V8J 3R5, Canada ☎ (250) 624-2577 Tx: none Fax: (250) 627-1356 SITA: n/a
F: 1981 ⋔⋔⋔ 14 Head: Trevor Pearce Net: http://www.inlandair.bc.ca

☐ C-GYJX	Cessna A185F Skywagon	18503187		0077		1 CO IO-520-D	1520			Floats
☐ C-FGQC	De Havilland DHC-2 Beaver I	75		0051	0195	1 PW R-985	2309			Floats

registration   type of aircraft   *cn/fn*   *ex/ex**   *mfd*   *del*   powered by   *mtow kg*   configuration   selcal   name/fln/specialitites/remarks

☐ C-FIAX	De Havilland DHC-2 Beaver I	*140*	*CF-XGH*	*0051*	*0398*	*1 PW R-985*	*2309*			*Floats*
☐ C-FJPX	De Havilland DHC-2 Beaver I	*1076*		*0057*		*1 PW R-985*	*2309*			*Floats*
☐ C-GPVB	De Havilland DHC-2 Beaver I	*871*	*N9253Z*	*0055*	*0896*	*1 PW R-985*	*2309*			*Floats*
☐ C-FRHW	De Havilland DHC-3 Otter	*445*	*5N-ABN*	*0063*	*1295*	*1 PW R-1340*	*3629*			*Floats*

INSTITUT AERONAUTIQUE DE LA CAPITALE (3009408 Canada, Inc. dba) **Québec, Qué.**

603, 6e Ave, Aéroport Int'l Jean Lesage, Ste-Foy, Québec G2E 5W1, Canada ☎ (418)872-0045 Tx: none Fax: (418) 872-1998 SITA: n/a
F: 1993 ✈ n/a Head: Michel Boulanger Net: n/a Aircraft below MTOW 1361kg: Cessna 152 & Piper PA-28

☐ C-GTCG	Piper PA-34-200T Seneca II	*34-7670335*		*0076*	*0396*	*2 CO TSIO-360-E*	*2073*			

INTEGRA AIR INTERNATIONAL (783269 Alberta, Ltd dba) **Lethbridge, Alta.**

113 Mount Blakiston Place West, Lethbridge, Alberta T1K 6M4, Canada ☎ (403) 381-1939 Tx: none Fax: (403) 320-9993 SITA: n/a
F: 1998 ✈ n/a Head: Brent Gateman Net: n/a

☐ C-FHGG	Beech King Air A100	*B-207*	*N727LE*	*0075*	*0299*	*2 PWC PT6A-28*	*5216*			

INTER AIR CHARTER SERVICE (317184 B.C. Ltd dba / Affiliated with Elkin Creek Guest Ranch / Seasonal May-November ops only) **Vancouver, B.C.**

4462 Marion Road, North Vancouver, British Columbia V7K 2V2, Canada ☎ (604) 984-4666 Tx: none Fax: (604) 984-4686 SITA: n/a
F: 1996 ✈ 2 Head: Paul Zoeller Net: n/a

☐ C-GHQI	Cessna U206F Stationair II	*U20602854*		*0075*	*0696*	*1 CO IO-520-F*	*1633*			*Floats*

INTER-CANADIAN/CANADIEN (1991), Inc. = ICN (Partenaire CANADIEN / CANADIAN Partner) (form.L.A.Inter-Québec/Subs.of Can. Investors) **Montreal-Dorval, Qué.**

795 Stuart Graham Boulevard North, Dorval, Québec H4Y 1E4, Canada ☎ (514) 631-9802 Tx: none Fax: (514) 631-2699 SITA: n/a
F: 1985 ✈ 400 Head: Robert Myhill ICAO: INTER-CANADIAN Net: n/a
Scheduled commuter services are operated on behalf of Canadian / Canadien as a Partenaire CANADIEN / CANADIAN Partner (in such colours both titles) using CP flight designators. Beside aircraft listed, also uses 3 Fokker F28 leased from Canadian Regional Airlines (registration varies), when required.

☐ C-FICG	ATR 42-300	*129*	*N4209G*	*0089*	*1098*	*2 PWC PW120*	*16700*	*Y44*		549
☐ C-FICO	ATR 42-320	*061*	*N4204G*	*0087*	*1198*	*2 PWC PW121*	*16700*	*Y44*		542 / *cvtd -300*
☐ C-FICP	ATR 42-300	*086*	*F-WQHK*	*0088*	*1098*	*2 PWC PW120*	*16700*	*Y44*		554
☐ C-FICW	ATR 42-300	*081*	*N4206G**	*0088*	*1298*	*2 PWC PW120*	*16700*	*Y44*		543
☐ C-FIQR	ATR 42-300	*133*	*F-WWEE**	*0089*	*0489*	*2 PWC PW120*	*16700*	*Y44*		544 / Spirit of Sept Iles/Cote Nord
☐ C-FIQU	ATR 42-300	*138*	*F-WWEK**	*0089*	*0589*	*2 PWC PW120*	*16700*	*Y44*		545 / Spirit of Quebec City
☐ C-FLCP	ATR 42-300	*085*	*F-WWEK**	*0088*	*0591*	*2 PWC PW120*	*16700*	*Y44*		540 / Spirit of Kingston / *lsf GECA*
☐ C-FNCP	ATR 42-300	*088*	*F-WWEN**	*0088*	*0591*	*2 PWC PW120*	*16700*	*Y44*		541 / *lsf GECA*
☐ C-FQCP	ATR 42-300	*116*	*F-WWEM**	*0088*	*0592*	*2 PWC PW120*	*16700*	*Y44*		552 / Spirit of Windsor
☐ C-FTCP	ATR 42-300	*143*	*F-WWEO**	*0089*	*0791*	*2 PWC PW120*	*16700*	*Y44*		547
☐ C-GHCP	ATR 42-300	*123*	*F-WWET**	*0089*	*0892*	*2 PWC PW120*	*16700*	*Y44*		553 / Spirit of Sudbury
☐ C-GICB	ATR 42-300	*050*	*N4202G*	*0087*	*1198*	*2 PWC PW120*	*16700*	*Y44*		550
☐ C-GICX	ATR 42-300	*178*	*N4211G*	*0090*	*1298*	*2 PWC PW120*	*16700*	*Y44*		555
☐ C-GIQD	ATR 42-300	*148*	*F-WWEQ**	*0089*	*0789*	*2 PWC PW120*	*16700*	*Y44*		548 / Spirit of Mont Joli
☐ C-GIQV	ATR 42-300	*203*	*F-WWEQ**	*0090*	*0990*	*2 PWC PW120*	*16700*	*Y44*		551 / Spirit of Bas St. Laurent
☐ C-GXCP	ATR 42-300	*139*	*F-WWEL**	*0089*	*0691*	*2 PWC PW120*	*16700*	*Y44*		546 / Spirit of London

INTERIOR HELICOPTERS, Ltd **Fort St. James, B.C.**

Box 1478, Fort St. James, British Columbia V0J 1P0, Canada ☎ (250) 996-8644 Tx: none Fax: (250) 996-8655 SITA: n/a
F: 1996 ✈ n/a Head: Grant Luck Net: n/a

☐ C-FJOR	Bell 206B JetRanger III	*3015*		*0080*	*0697*	*1 AN 250-C20B*	*1451*			
☐ C-FPOC	Bell 206B JetRanger	*695*		*0072*	*0397*	*1 AN 250-C20*	*1451*			*cvtd 206A*
☐ C-GENT	Bell 206L LongRanger	*45041*	*ZK-HYV*	*0076*	*0299*	*1 AN 250-C20B*	*1814*			

ISLAND AERO HELICOPTERS, Ltd **Victoria, B.C.**

9548 Canora Road, Sidney, British Columbia V8L 4R1, Canada ☎ (250) 658-1595 Tx: none Fax: (250) 658-1595 SITA: n/a
F: n/a ✈ n/a Head: n/a Net: n/a

☐ C-FNHL	Bell 206B JetRanger III	*3311*		*0081*	*1095*	*1 AN 250-C20B*	*1451*			
☐ C-GIJN	Cessna A185F Skywagon	*18502961*		*0076*	*0299*	*1 CO IO-520-D*	*1520*			

ISLAND AERO SERVICES (Division of Island Aeromotive, Inc.) **Victoria, B.C.**

108-9800 McDonald Park Road, Sidney, British Columbia V8L 5W5, Canada ☎ (250) 656-7627 Tx: none Fax: (250) 656-7627 SITA: n/a
F: n/a ✈ n/a Head: Jim McLaren Net: n/a Aircraft below MTOW 1361kg: Cessna 150

☐ C-FVEG	Cessna T210L Turbo Centurion II	*21060762*	*N1741X*	*0075*	*0595*	*1 CO TSIO-520-H*	*1724*			

ISLAND AIR (Island Air Flight School & Charters, Inc. dba) **Toronto-City Centre, Ont.**

Shell Aerocentre, Hangar 5, Suite 151, Toronto, Ontario M5V 1A1, Canada ☎ (416) 203-6242 Tx: none Fax: (416) 203-6581 SITA: n/a
F: 1994 ✈ 18 Head: Joseph Suarez Net: http://www.ica.net/islandair Aircraft below MTOW 1361kg: Cessna 150 & 172

☐ C-FBIL	Piper PA-23-250 Aztec D	*27-3975*		*0068*	*0596*	*2 LY IO-540-C4B5*	*2359*			

ISLAND AIR CHARTERS (Division of Island Airlink Corporation) **Toronto-City Centre, Ont.**

201-Hangar 6, Toronto City Centre Airport, Toronto, Ontario M5V 1A1, Canada ☎ (416) 203-2036 Tx: none Fax: (416) 203-2037 SITA: n/a
F: n/a ✈ n/a Head: David McDevitt Net: http://www.the-wire.com/eagle/ Aircraft below MTOW 1361kg: AA-1B & Mooney M20C

☐ C-FORR	Piper PA-30-160 Twin Comanche C	*30-1820*	*N44278*	*0069*	*0698*	*2 LY IO-320-B1A*	*1633*			
☐ C-FXLO	Piper PA-31-350 Navajo Chieftain	*31-8052022*	*N3547N*	*0080*	*1096*	*2 LY TIO-540-J2BD*	*3175*			

ISLAND AVIATION, Ltd **Springdale, Nfld.**

PO Box 428, Springdale, Newfoundland A0J 1T0, Canada ☎ (705) 856-2841 Tx: none Fax: (705) 856-7492 SITA: n/a
F: 1997 ✈ n/a Head: n/a Net: n/a

☐ C-GYLB	Cessna A185F Skywagon	*18503211*	*N93286*	*0076*	*0997*	*1 CO IO-520-D*	*1520*			*Floats / Wheel-Skis*

ISLAND VALLEY AIRWAYS, Ltd **Langley, B.C.**

Unit 105-5225-216th Street, Langley, British Columbia V2V 3N3, Canada ☎ (604) 533-7555 Tx: none Fax: (604) 533-5688 SITA: n/a
F: 1998 ✈ n/a Head: Carry Welsh Net: http://www.flyiva.com

☐ C-GASV	De Havilland DHC-6 Twin Otter 300	*587*	*A6-FAM*	*0078*	*0498*	*2 PWC PT6A-27*	*5670*			

ISLAND WEST AIR, Inc. **Courtenay, B.C.**

Site 299, RR2, Comp.13, Courtenay, British Columbia V9N 5M9, Canada ☎ (250) 339-3507 Tx: none Fax: (250) 339-3507 SITA: n/a
F: 1998 ✈ n/a Head: n/a Net: n/a

☐ C-GYMW	Britten-Norman BN-2A-26 Islander	*88*	*D-IFDS*	*0069*	*0398*	*2 LY O-540-E4C5*	*2858*			

JACKSON AIR SERVICES, Ltd = JCK **Sandy Bay, Sask. & Flin Flon-Channing, Man.**

Box 1000, Flin Flon, Manitoba R8A 1N7, Canada ☎ (204) 687-8247 Tx: none Fax: (204) 687-7694 SITA: n/a
F: 1976 ✈ 11 Head: Bill Jackson ICAO: JACKSON Net: n/a Aircraft below MTOW 1361kg: Cessna 172

☐ C-FWXV	Cessna A185E Skywagon	*185-1355*		*0068*		*1 CO IO-520-D*	*1520*			*Floats / Wheel-Skis*
☐ C-GISX	Cessna A185F Skywagon II	*18503836*		*0079*		*1 CO IO-520-D*	*1520*			*Floats / Wheel-Skis*
☐ C-GVOQ	Cessna A185F Skywagon II	*18503790*		*0079*	*0489*	*1 CO IO-520-D*	*1520*			*Floats / Wheel-Skis*
☐ C-GGGT	Cessna TU206G Turbo Stationair 6 II	*U20604170*		*0078*		*1 CO TSIO-520-M*	*1633*			
☐ C-FAXC	De Havilland DHC-2 Beaver I	*1048*	*ZK-CMV*	*0057*		*1 PW R-985*	*2313*			*Floats / Wheel-Skis*
☐ C-GADE	De Havilland DHC-2 Beaver I	*730*	*53-7919*	*0055*		*1 PW R-985*	*2313*			*Floats / Wheel-Skis*
☐ C-GWHW	Piper PA-31-350 Navajo Chieftain	*31-8052060*	*N223CH*	*0080*	*1191*	*2 LY TIO-540-J2BD*	*3175*			
☐ C-FFVZ	De Havilland DHC-3 Otter	*145*	*N80944*	*0056*	*0199*	*1 PW R-1340*	*3629*			*Floats / Wheel-Skis*
☐ C-FMAJ	De Havilland DHC-3 Otter	*383*	*Burma 4655*	*0060*	*0290*	*1 PW R-1340*	*3629*			*Floats / Wheel-Skis*
☐ C-FWEJ	De Havilland DHC-3 Otter	*208*	*IM 1710*	*0058*	*0396*	*1 PW R-1340*	*3629*			*Floats / Wheel-Skis*

JETPORT, Ltd = THD (611897 Alberta, Ltd dba / Subsidiary of Tim Horton Donuts) **Hamilton, Ont.**

520-9300 Airport Road, Mount Hope, Ontario L0R 1W0, Canada ☎ (905) 679-2400 Tx: none Fax: (905) 679-2810 SITA: n/a
F: 1996 ✈ n/a Head: Emil Nashburgh ICAO: DONUT Net: http://www.jetport.com

☐ C-FHRB	Cessna 208 Caravan I	*20800291*		*0098*	*1098*	*1 PWC PT6A-114*	*3629*			
☐ C-GBIT	Cessna 208 Caravan I	*20800135*	*N9706F*	*0088*	*0296*	*1 PWC PT6A-114*	*3629*			
☐ C-GRVJ	Learjet 31A	*31A-111*	*N50114**	*0095*	*0196*	*2 GA TFE731-2-3B*	*7484*			
☐ C-FRJZ	IAI 1125A Astra SPX	*087*	*4X-CUU**	*0097*	*0497*	*2 GA TFE731-40R-200G*	*11181*			

JOHNNY MAY'S AIR CHARTER, Ltd – JMAC (Subsidiary of Air Inuit (1985), Ltd) **Kuujjuaq, Qué.**

547 Meloche, Dorval, Québec H9P 2W2, Canada ☎ (514) 636-9445 Tx: none Fax: (514) 636-8916 SITA: n/a
F: 1974 ✈ 5 Head: Bob Davis Net: n/a

☐ C-GMAY	De Havilland DHC-2 Beaver I	*1123*	*56-0393*	*0056*		*1 PW R-985*	*2313*			Pengo Pallee / *Floats / Wheel-Skis*
☐ C-FLAP	De Havilland DHC-3 Otter	*289*		*0059*	*0689*	*1 PW R-1340*	*3629*			*Floats / Wheel-Skis*
☐ C-FMPX	De Havilland DHC-3 Otter	*280*		*0058*	*0490*	*1 PW R-1340*	*3629*			*Floats / Wheel-Skis*

58 registration type of aircraft *cn/fn* *ex/ex** *mfd* *del* *powered by* *mtow kg* *configuration* *selcal* *name/fln/specialitites/remarks*

JOHN THERIAULT AIR, Ltd (Seasonal April-November ops only) — Chapleau, Ont.

PO Box 269, Chapleau, Ontario P0M 1K0, Canada ☎ (705) 864-0321 Tx: n/a Fax: none SITA: n/a
F: 1986 ♟♟♟ 3 Head: John Theriault Net: n/a Aircraft below MTOW 1361kg: Cessna 180 (on Floats)

☐ C-GPUQ	De Havilland DHC-2 Beaver I	1341	58-2013	0058	1090	1 PW R-985	2313			Floats

JUAN AIR (1979), Ltd = WON — Victoria, B.C.

PO Box 2182, Sidney, British Columbia V8L 3S8, Canada ☎ (250) 656-4312 Tx: none Fax: (250) 656-4355 SITA: n/a
F: 1979 ♟♟♟ n/a Head: Bruce Gorle ICAO: JUAN AIR Net: n/a Aircraft below MTOW 1361 kg: Cessna 150, 152, 172 & 180.

☐ C-GXPC	Piper PA-34-200T Seneca II	34-7970234	N29076	0079		2 CO TSIO-360-EB	2073			
☐ C-GRJA	Piper PA-31-350 Navajo Chieftain	31-7952154	N35282	0079		2 LY TIO-540-J2BD	3175			

KABEELO AIRWAYS, Limited (Kabeelo Lodge dba) — Confederation Lake, Ont.

PO Box 670, Ear Falls, Ontario P0V 1T0, Canada ☎ (807) 222-3246 Tx: none Fax: (807) 222-3791 SITA: n/a
F: 1977 ♟♟♟ 3 Head: H.L. Lohn Net: n/a

☐ C-FLUA	De Havilland DHC-2 Beaver I	1318		0058	0698	1 PW R-985	2313			Floats / Wheel-Skis
☐ C-GDYT	De Havilland DHC-2 Beaver I	1109	56-4403	0056		1 PW R-985	2313			Floats / Wheel-Skis
☐ C-GLSA	De Havilland DHC-2 Beaver I	1389	N94471	0059	1091	1 PW R-985	2313			Floats / Wheel-Skis
☐ C-FSRE	Beech 3N (18)	CA-61	RCAF 1486	0051		2 PW R-985	3969			Floats / Wheel-Skis

KAKABEKA AIR SERVICE (988578 Ontario, Inc. dba / Affiliated with Holinshead Lake Resort) — Holinshead Lake, Ont.

Box 300, Kakabeka Falls, Ontario P0T 1W0, Canada ☎ (807) 768-1924 Tx: none Fax: (807) 768-1935 SITA: n/a
F: 1982 ♟♟♟ n/a Head: Mitch Hagen Net: http://www.virtualnorth.com/holinshead Aircraft below MTOW 1361kg: Piper PA-11 (on Floats)

☐ C-GUNE	De Havilland DHC-2 Beaver I	1403	N31339	0058	0889	1 PW R-985	2313			Floats / Wheel-Skis

KALUM AIR, Ltd — Terrace, B.C.

1 Ave, RR 4, Site 9, Comp 2, Terrace, British Columbia V8G 4V2, Canada ☎ (604) 798-2210 Tx: n/a Fax: (604) 798-2210 SITA: n/a
F: 1993 ♟♟♟ 2 Head: Syd Munson Net: n/a

☐ C-FWEE	Cessna A185E Skywagon	185-1255		0067	0793	1 CO IO-520-D	1520			Floats / Wheel-Skis

KASBA AIR SERVICE (Kasba Lake Lodge, Ltd dba / Seasonal summer ops only) — Kasba Lake, N.W.T.

PO Box 96, Parksville, British Columbia V9P 2G3, Canada ☎ (250) 248-3572 Tx: none Fax: (250) 248-4576 SITA: n/a
F: 1983 ♟♟♟ 2 Head: Mike Hill Net: http://www.kasba.com

☐ CF-MAS	De Havilland DHC-2 Beaver I	38		0048		1 PW R-985	2313			Floats

KAYAIR SERVICE, Inc. — Ear Falls, Ont.

Box 284, Ear Falls, Ontario P0V 1T0, Canada ☎ (807) 222-2434 Tx: none Fax: (807) 222-2322 SITA: n/a
F: n/a ♟♟♟ 1 Head: Peter A. Kay Net: n/a Aircraft below MTOW 1361kg: Cessna 180 (on Floats / Wheel-Skis).

☐ CF-TBH	Beech 3T (18)	6226	43-35671	0041	1294	2 PW R-985	3969			Floats

KD AIR Corporation = XC / KDC — Port Alberni, B.C.

RR2, Site 225, C11, Port Alberni, British Columbia V9Y 7L6, Canada ☎ (250) 752-5884 Tx: none Fax: (250) 752-5750 SITA: n/a
F: 1991 ♟♟♟ 8 Head: Mrs Ketty Banke ICAO: KAY DEE Net: n/a Aircraft below MTOW 1361kg: Cessna 172.

☐ C-GPCA	Piper PA-31-310 Navajo	31-42	N333DG	0069	0492	2 LY TIO-540-A2B	2948			
☐ C-GXEY	Piper PA-31-350 Navajo Chieftain	31-7305044	N74910	0073	0594	2 LY TIO-540-J2BD	3175			

KECHIKA VALLEY AIR, Ltd — Dawson Creek, B.C.

Box 1, Dawson Creek, British Columbia V1G 4E9, Canada ☎ (250) 782-2908 Tx: none Fax: (250) 782-6244 SITA: n/a
F: 1990 ♟♟♟ n/a Head: n/a Net: n/a Aircraft below MTOW 1361kg: Piper PA-18

☐ C-GOSC	Cessna U206G Stationair	U20603757		0077	0894	1 CO IO-520-D	1633			

KEEWATIN AIR, Ltd — Churchill & Thompson, Man. / Rankin Inlet, N.W.T.

15-20 Hangar Line Road, Winnipeg, Manitoba R3J 3Y8, Canada ☎ (204) 888-0100 Tx: none Fax: (204) 888-3300 SITA: n/a
F: 1970 ♟♟♟ 25 Head: F. Robert May Net: n/a

☐ C-FYZS	Pilatus PC-12/45	227	N227PB	0098	1298	1 PWC PT6A-67B	4500			
☐ C-FSVC	Fairchild (Swearingen) SA26T Merlin IIA	T26-19	N2JE	0068	0794	2 PWC PT6A-28	4445			
☐ C-GLKA	Fairchild (Swearingen) SA26T Merlin IIA	T26-20	N59TC	0068	0790	2 PWC PT6A-20	4445			
☐ C-FZPW	Beech King Air B200	BB-940	N519SA	0081	0197	2 PWC PT6A-42	5670			
☐ C-FICU	Learjet 35A	35A-249	N300DA	0079	0797	2 GA TFE731-2-2B	8301			

KELOWNA FLIGHTCRAFT Air Charter, Ltd = KFA — Kelowna, B.C. — Flightcraft

1-5655 Kelowna Airport, Kelowna, British Columbia V1V 7S1, Canada ☎ (250) 491-5500 Tx: none Fax: (250) 491-5504 SITA: n/a
F: 1970 ♟♟♟ 600 Head: Barry Lapointe ICAO: FLIGHTCRAFT Net: n/a

☐ C-GJRH	Cessna 340	340-0058	N340BD	0072	0598	2 CO TSIO-520-K	2710	Pax		
☐ C-GKFX	Beech Duke A60	P-235	N60GF	0073		2 LY TIO-541-E1B4	3073	Corporate		
☐ C-GIHM	Cessna 402B	402B0203	N7875Q	0072	1289	2 CO TSIO-520-E	2858	Freighter		opf Purolator Courier
☐ C-GKFK	Cessna 402B	402B0213	N7885Q	0072		2 CO TSIO-520-E	2858	Freighter		opf Purolator Courier
☐ C-FCJP	Piper PA-42 Cheyenne III	42-8001045	N181CC	0081	0597	2 PWC PT6A-41	5080	Executive / EMS		
☐ C-GWKF	IAI 1124 Westwind I	271	N218SC	0079	0195	2 GA TFE731-3-1G	10365	Executive		
☐ C-FKFA	Convair 580	100	N5807	0053	0991	2 AN 501-D13	26379	Freighter		507 / cvtd CV340-38
☐ C-FKFL	Convair 580	465	ZK-JDQ	0057	0197	2 AN 501-D13	26379	Freighter		517 / cvtd CV440-97
☐ C-FKFM	Convair 580	70	N73133	0053	1291	2 AN 501-D13	26379	Freighter		503 / cvtd CV340-31
☐ C-FKFY	Convair Super 580	129	N5814	0053	1291	2 AN 501-D22G	24766	Freighter		509 / cvtd CV340-47/580
☐ C-FKFZ	Convair 580	151	N5823	0054	1291	2 AN 501-D13	24766	Y52		510 / cvtd CV340-54
☐ C-GKFF	Convair 580	160	N9067R	0054	1188	2 AN 501-D13	26379	Freighter		511 / cvtd CV340-54
☐ C-GKFG	Convair 580	22	N32KA	0052	0597	2 AN 501-D13	24766	Y52		516 / cvtd CV340-35
☐ C-GKFJ	Convair 580 (F) (SCD)	114	CS-TMG	0053	0691	2 AN 501-D13	26379	Freighter		508 / cvtd CV340-48
☐ C-GKFO	Convair 580	78	N5815	0053	1291	2 AN 501-D13	26379	Freighter		504 / cvtd CV340-32
☐ C-GKFP	Convair 580	446	N589PL	0057	0890	2 AN 501-D13	26379	Y52		514 / cvtd CV440-62
☐ C-GKFQ	Convair 580 (F) (SCD)	86	N73136	0053	0789	2 AN 501-D13	26379	Freighter		505 / opf Purolator Courier/cvtd 340-31
☐ C-GKFU	Convair 580	82	N90857	0053	0196	2 AN 501-D13	26379	Freighter		516 / cvtd 340-35 / std YLW
☐ C-GKFY	Convair 580	91	N400AB	0053	0681	2 AN 501-D13	26379	Freighter		503 / std YLW / cvtd YC-131C
☐ C-FKFO	Boeing 727-25 (F)	18971 / 230	N280NE	0066	0797	3 PW JT8D-7B	72802	Freighter		700 / cvtd -25
☐ C-FKFP	Boeing 727-22C	19205 / 438	N109FE	0867	0294	3 PW JT8D-7B (HK3/FDX)	76884	Freighter		703 / opf Purolator Courier
☐ C-GKFA	Boeing 727-22C	19806 / 547	N110FE	0368	0294	3 PW JT8D-7B (HK3/FDX)	76884	Freighter	AH-CE	704 / opf Purolator Courier
☐ C-GKFB	Boeing 727-25C	19358 / 367	N122FE	0367	0294	3 PW JT8D-7B (HK3/FDX)	72575	Freighter		705 / opf Purolator Courier
☐ C-GKFC	Boeing 727-51C (QWS / winglets)	18897 / 211	OB-R-1115	0065	0987	3 PW JT8D-7B (HK3/DUG)	76884	Freighter		701 / opf Purolator Courier
☐ C-GKFN	Boeing 727-25C (QWS / winglets)	19359 / 368	N123FE	0267	0294	3 PW JT8D-7B (HK3/DUG)	72575	Freighter		707 / opf Purolator Courier
☐ C-GKFT	Boeing 727-172C	19807 / 575	N722JE	0068	0887	3 PW JT8D-7B	76884	Freighter		702 / opf Purolator Courier
☐ C-GKFV	Boeing 727-92C	19173 / 308	N18476	0066	0694	3 PW JT8D-9	76658	Freighter	CM-JL	708 / std YLW
☐ C-GKFW	Boeing 727-22C	19805 / 543	N111FE	0368	1094	3 PW JT8D-7B (HK3/FDX)	76884	Freighter	AH-CD	709 / opf Purolator Courier
☐ C-GKFZ	Boeing 727-22C	19204 / 436	N108FE	0767	0394	3 PW JT8D-7B (HK3/FDX)	72575	Freighter		706 / opf Purolator Courier
☐ C-GACU	Boeing 727-225 (F)	20152 / 775	N8833E	0069	0895	3 PW JT8D-7B	78245	Freighter	BM-CF	710 / opf Purolator Courier / cvtd -225
☐ C-GIKF	Boeing 727-227 (A)	20772 / 982	N99763	0073	0396	3 PW JT8D-7B (HK3/FDX)	79606	Y170	EH-DK	721 / lst RYN
☐ C-GJKF	Boeing 727-227 (F) (A)	21042 / 1106	N10756	0075	0496	3 PW JT8D-9A (HK3/FDX)	79606	Freighter	EJ-DF	722 / opf Purolator Courier / cvtd -227
☐ C-GKFH	Boeing 727-225 (F)	20153 / 779	N8834E	0069	0496	3 PW JT8D-7B	80559	Freighter	BM-CH	711 / cvtd -225
☐ C-GKKF	Boeing 727-227 (A)	21043 / 1113	N16758	0075	0496	3 PW JT8D-9A (HK3/FDX)	79606	Y170	CG-EH	723 / lst Panagra Airways
☐ C-GLKF	Boeing 727-227 (F) (A)	21118 / 1167	N14760	0075	0496	3 PW JT8D-9A (HK3/FDX)	79606	Freighter	GM-AH	724 / opf Purolator Courier / cvtd -227
☐ C-GMKF	Boeing 727-227 (A)	21119 / 1175	N16761	0075	0496	3 PW JT8D-9A (HK3/FDX)	79606	Y170	DG-BF	725 / lst RYN
☐ C-GNKF	Boeing 727-227 (A)	20839 / 1031	N88770	0074	0396	3 PW JT8D-9A (HK3/FDX)	79605	Y170	AH-FL	726 / lst GRO
☐ C-GOKF	Boeing 727-214	20162 / 715	N409BN	0069	0696	3 PW JT8D-9A (HK3/FDX)	80650	Y170		729 / lst SNP

KENN BOREK AIR, Ltd = 4K / KBA — Calgary, Alta. & Inuvik & Norman Wells & Resolute Bay, N.W.T

290 McTavish Road N.E., Hangar 4, Int'l Airport, Calgary, Alberta T2E 7G5, Canada ☎ (403) 291-3300 Tx: 038-25870 borekair c Fax: (403) 250-6908 SITA: n/a
F: 1971 ♟♟♟ 70 Head: Kenn Borek ICAO: BOREK AIR Net: n/a Aircraft below MTOW 1361 kg: Cessna 150, 152 & 172.

☐ C-FCXQ	Cessna A185F Skywagon	18502235		0073	0595	1 CO IO-520-D	1520			
☐ C-FEXA	Beech Baron B55 (95-B55)	TC-566		0064		2 CO IO-470-L	2313			
☐ C-FKBK	Beech 99 Airliner	U-18	HP-1233AP	0068	0880	2 PWC PT6A-20	4717			
☐ C-GKBA	Beech B99 Airliner	U-164	SE-GRB	0074		2 PWC PT6A-27	4944			
☐ C-GKKB	Beech B99 Airliner	U-149	HP-1230AP	0072	0293	2 PWC PT6A-27	4944			
☐ C-FAFD	Beech King Air 100	B-42	LN-VIP	0070		2 PWC PT6A-28	4808			
☐ C-GAVI	Beech King Air A100	B-201	G-BBVM	0074	1196	2 PWC PT6A-28	5216			
☐ C-GHOC	Beech King Air A100	B-194	N57237	0074	0890	2 PWC PT6A-28	5216			
☐ C-GKBB	Beech King Air C90	LJ-607	N48DA	0073		2 PWC PT6A-20	4377			
☐ C-GKBQ	Beech King Air 100	B-62	LN-NLB	0070	0493	2 PWC PT6A-28	4808			
☐ C-GKBZ	Beech King Air 100	B-85	LN-PAJ	0071	0891	2 PWC PT6A-28	4808			

59 registration type of aircraft cn/fn ex/ex* mfd del powered by mtow kg configuration selcal name/fln/specialitites/remarks

registration	type of aircraft	cn/fn	ex/ex*	mfd	del	powered by	mtow kg	configuration	selcal	name/fln/specialitites/remarks
☐ C-GSFM	Beech King Air B90	LJ-422	N513SC	0068	0691	2 PWC PT6A-20	4377			
☐ C-FLKB	Embraer 110P1 Bandeirante (EMB-110P1)	110397	N903LE	0082	0496	2 PWC PT6A-34	5900			
☐ C-GFKB	Embraer 110P1 Bandeirante (EMB-110P1)	110400	N900LE	0082	0496	2 PWC PT6A-34	5670			
☐ C-FBCN	Beech King Air 200	BB-7		0074	0690	2 PWC PT6A-41	5670			
☐ C-GKBN	Beech King Air 200	BB-29	LN-ASG	0075	1191	2 PWC PT6A-41	5670			
☐ C-GKBP	Beech King Air 200	BB-505	N110KA	0079	0291	2 PWC PT6A-41	5670			
☐ C-FDHB	De Havilland DHC-6 Twin Otter 300	338		0071	0972	2 PWC PT6A-27	5670			
☐ C-FKBI	De Havilland DHC-6 Twin Otter 300	259	HP-1197AP	0069		2 PWC PT6A-27	5670			
☐ C-FPAT	De Havilland DHC-6 Twin Otter 100	2	N856AC	0066	1078	2 PWC PT6A-6	4990			
☐ C-FSJB	De Havilland DHC-6 Twin Otter 300	377	N4901D	0073	0973	2 PWC PT6A-27	5670			
☐ C-FWUL	De Havilland DHC-6 Twin Otter 300	360	LN-BNY	0073	1196	2 PWC PT6A-27	5670			
☐ C-GDHC	De Havilland DHC-6 Twin Otter 300	494		0076	0794	2 PWC PT6A-27	5670			
☐ C-GKBC	De Havilland DHC-6 Twin Otter 300	650	N55921	0079	1179	2 PWC PT6A-27	5670			
☐ C-GKBG	De Havilland DHC-6 Twin Otter 300	733		0081	0588	2 PWC PT6A-27	5670			
☐ C-GKBH	De Havilland DHC-6 Twin Otter 300	732	G-BIEM	0081	0590	2 PWC PT6A-27	5670			
☐ C-GKBO	De Havilland DHC-6 Twin Otter 300	725	HP-1273APP	0080	0595	2 PWC PT6A-27	5670			
☐ C-GKBR	De Havilland DHC-6 Twin Otter 300	617	HP-1167APP	0079	0290	2 PWC PT6A-27	5670			
☐ C-GKBX	De Havilland DHC-6 Twin Otter 300	571	VP-LVT	0078	0391	2 PWC PT6A-27	5670			
☐ C-GOKB	De Havilland DHC-6 Twin Otter 300	339	N916MA	0072	0195	2 PWC PT6A-27	5670			
☐ C-GPAO	De Havilland DHC-6 Twin Otter 300	447	N5356A	0075	1098	2 PWC PT6A-27	5670			
☐ C-GXXB	De Havilland DHC-6 Twin Otter 300	426		0075	0974	2 PWC PT6A-27	5670			
☐ 8Q-CSL	De Havilland DHC-6 Twin Otter 100	64	C-FCSL	0067		2 PWC PT6A-20	5252			Ist Maldivian Air Taxi
☐ 8Q-MAA	De Havilland DHC-6 Twin Otter 300	693	C-GKBE	0080	0580	2 PWC PT6A-27	5670			Ist Maldivian Air Taxi
☐ 8Q-MAB	De Havilland DHC-6 Twin Otter 300	287	C-GKBV	0070	0295	2 PWC PT6A-27	5670			Ist Maldivian Air Taxi
☐ 8Q-MAC	De Havilland DHC-6 Twin Otter 100	60	C-GTKB	0067	0588	2 PWC PT6A-20	5252			Ist Maldivian Air Taxi
☐ 8Q-MAD	De Havilland DHC-6 Twin Otter 300	273	C-FIOK	0069	0593	2 PWC PT6A-27	5670			Ist Maldivian Air Taxi
☐ 8Q-MAE	De Havilland DHC-6 Twin Otter 300	464	C-FPOO	0075	0393	2 PWC PT6A-27	5670			Ist Maldivian Air Taxi
☐ 8Q-MAF	De Havilland DHC-6 Twin Otter 100	106	C-FGQH	0068	0997	2 PWC PT6A-20	5252			Ist Maldivian Air Taxi
☐ 8Q-MAG	De Havilland DHC-6 Twin Otter 200	224	C-GENT	0069	0589	2 PWC PT6A-20	5252			Ist Maldivian Air Taxi
☐ 8Q-MAH	De Havilland DHC-6 Twin Otter 300	374	C-FMYV	0073	0691	2 PWC PT6A-27	5670			Ist Maldivian Air Taxi
☐ 8Q-MAI	De Havilland DHC-6 Twin Otter 300	279	C-GKBM	0070	0195	2 PWC PT6A-27	5670			Ist Maldivian Air Taxi
☐ 8Q-MAJ	De Havilland DHC-6 Twin Otter 300	325	C-FTJJ	0072	0199	2 PWC PT6A-27	5670			Ist Maldivian Air Taxi
☐ 8Q-NTA	De Havilland DHC-6 Twin Otter 200	146	C-GNTA	0068	0483	2 PWC PT6A-20	5252			Ist Maldivian Air Taxi
☐ 8Q-OEQ	De Havilland DHC-6 Twin Otter 100	44	C-FOEQ	0067	0488	2 PWC PT6A-6	5252			Ist Maldivian Air Taxi
☐ 8Q-QBU	De Havilland DHC-6 Twin Otter 100	99	C-FQBU	0068	0693	2 PWC PT6A-20	5252			Ist Maldivian Air Taxi
☐ 8Q-QHC	De Havilland DHC-6 Twin Otter 100	21	C-FQHC	0067	0881	2 PWC PT6A-20	5252			Ist Maldivian Air Taxi
☐ J6-AAL	De Havilland DHC-6 Twin Otter 300	532	C-GQKZ	0077	0997	2 PWC PT6A-27	5670			Ist HCL
☐ C-GGKG	Boeing (Douglas) Super DC-3S (C-117D)	43354	N2071X	0042	0994	2 WR R-1820	13301	Freighter		cvtd R4D-5 cn 10207

KENORA AIR SERVICE, Ltd (Seasonal May-October ops only)

Kenora-SPB, Ont.

Box 1120, Kenora, Ontario V2P 1A5, Canada ☎ (807) 468-9818 Tx: n/a Fax: (807) 468-5591 SITA: n/a
F: 1977 ↟↟↟ n/a Head: Frank Kuby Net: n/a

☐ C-FWDB	Cessna A185E Skywagon	185-1250		0067		1 CO IO-520-D	1520			Floats
☐ CF-JEI	De Havilland DHC-2 Beaver I	1020		0056		1 PW R-985	2313			Floats
☐ C-FCBA	De Havilland DHC-3 Otter	230	N80941	0057		1 PW R-1340	3629			Floats
☐ CF-TBX	Beech D18S	A-479	N481B	0048		2 PW R-985	3969			Floats

KEYAMAWUN LODGE, Ltd & Airservices (Seasonal May-October ops only)

Deer Lake, Ont.

Box 939, Ear Falls, Ontario P0V 1T0, Canada ☎ (807) 222-3734 Tx: n/a Fax: (807) 222-3734 SITA: n/a
F: 1980 ↟↟↟ n/a Head: n/a Net: n/a

☐ C-GUME	De Havilland DHC-2 Beaver I	1095	56-0382	0055	0783	1 PW R-985	2313			Floats

KEYSTONE AIR SERVICE, Ltd = BZ / KEE (formerly Gabrielle Air Service)

Swan River, Man.

PO Box 2140, Swan River, Manitoba R0L 1Z0, Canada ☎ (204) 734-9351 Tx: none Fax: (204) 734-9181 SITA: n/a
F: 1984 ↟↟↟ 6 Head: Clifford W. Arlt ICAO: KEYSTONE Net: n/a Aircraft below MTOW 1361kg: Piper PA-28

☐ C-GRUH	Piper PA-34-200 Seneca	34-7350118	N16254	0073		2 LY IO-360-C1E6	1905			
☐ C-GBDN	Piper PA-31-350 Navajo Chieftain	31-7652035	N59763	0076	0595	2 LY TIO-540-J2BD	3349			
☐ C-GGQU	Piper PA-31-310 Navajo	31-155	N9116Y	0068		2 LY TIO-540-A1A	2948			
☐ C-GPOW	Piper PA-31-350 Navajo Chieftain	31-7305093	N74947	0073	1090	2 LY TIO-540-J2BD	3349			
☐ C-FPCD	Beech B99 Airliner	U-151	C-FBRO	0072	1197	2 PWC PT6A-27	4944			

KISTIGAN – Ministic Air, Ltd = MNS (formerly Big Hook Air Lines, Ltd)

Sandy Lake, Ont. & Island Lake & Winnipeg, Man.

Box 42008, Winnipeg, Manitoba R3J 3X7, Canada ☎ (204) 832-8550 Tx: none Fax: (204) 889-4731 SITA: n/a
F: 1981 ↟↟↟ 70 Head: John Briggs ICAO: MINISTIC Net: n/a KISTIGAN is the indigenous language (translated Ministic) of the region and appears as titles on the aircraft.

☐ C-FCUL	Cessna U206C Super Skywagon	U206-1054		0068		1 CO IO-520-F	1633	Y5 / Freighter		Floats / Wheel-Skis
☐ C-FDCY	Piper PA-31-310 Navajo C	31-7912007	N27768	0079		2 LY TIO-540-A1A	2948	Y7		
☐ C-FJQI	Piper PA-31-350 Navajo Chieftain	31-7552065	N59972	0075	0291	2 LY TIO-540-J2BD	3175	Y8		
☐ C-FNVH	Piper PA-31-350 Navajo Chieftain	31-7305098	N98BJ	0073	0692	2 LY TIO-540-J2BD	3175	Y8		
☐ C-GYPF	Piper PA-31-350 Navajo Chieftain	31-7552063	N899WS	0075	0698	2 LY TIO-540-J2BD	3175	Y8		
☐ C-FMWM	Beech King Air 100	B-59	N702JL	0070	1292	2 PWC PT6A-28	4808	EMS		
☐ C-GAPK	Beech King Air A100	B-198	N712AS	0074	0697	2 PWC PT6A-28	5216	EMS		
☐ C-FPSH	Dornier 228-202	8071	N253MC	0085	0493	2 GA TPE331-5-252D	6200	Y19		Isf Dornier Aviation
☐ C-FYEV	Dornier 228-202	8133	N261MC	0087	1195	2 GA TPE331-5-252D	6200	Y19		Isf Dornier Aviation / cvtd -201
☐ C-GEFA	Beech 1900C-1 Airliner	UC-94	N80346	0090	1298	2 PWC PT6A-65B	7530	Y19		
☐ C-FYSJ	Beech 1900D Airliner	UE-223	N1123J*	0096	0996	2 PWC PT6A-67D	7688	Y19		
☐ C-GBPY	Beech 1900D Airliner	UE-302	N11197*	0097	0198	2 PWC PT6A-67D	7688	Y19		

KLAHANIE AIR, Ltd

Mission, B.C.

33344 Harbour Avenue, Mission, British Columbia V2V 2W4, Canada ☎ (604) 826-4222 Tx: n/a Fax: (604) 856-2087 SITA: n/a
F: 1976 ↟↟↟ 2 Head: Christopher H. Marshall Net: n/a

☐ C-FJFL	De Havilland DHC-2 Beaver I	898		0056	0798	1 PW R-985	2309			Floats

KLITSA AIR, Ltd

Port Alberni, B.C.

4855 Johnston Road, Port Alberni, British Columbia V9Y 5M2, Canada ☎ (250) 723-2375 Tx: n/a Fax: (250) 724-7188 SITA: n/a
F: 1991 ↟↟↟ n/a Head: Jack McKay Net: n/a

☐ C-GZVI	Cessna A185F Skywagon	18503419	N9149H	0077	0392	1 CO IO-520-D	1520			Floats

KLUANE AIRWAYS, Ltd

Burwash Landing, Y.T.

PO Box 4730, Whitehorse, Yukon Territory Y1A 4N6, Canada ☎ (250) 764-2885 Tx: none Fax: (250) 764-2885 SITA: n/a
F: 1980 ↟↟↟ 4 Head: Warren LaFave Net: n/a

☐ C-FMPS	De Havilland DHC-2 Beaver I (DBS/STOL)	1114		0056		1 PW R-985	2313			Floats / Wheel-Skis

KLUANE HELICOPTERS (528470 Alberta, Ltd dba)

Haines Junction, Y.T.

PO Box 2128, Haines Junction, Yukon Territory Y0B 1L0, Canada ☎ (867) 634-2224 Tx: none Fax: (867) 634-2226 SITA: n/a
F: 1991 ↟↟↟ 5 Head: Bill & Shirley Karman Net: n/a

☐ C-GKHS	Eurocopter (Aerosp.) AS350B1 AStar	2009	N128TM	0087	0197	1 TU Arriel 1D	2200			

KNEE LAKE AIR SERVICE, Inc. (Seasonal April-October ops only)

Knee Lake, Man.

814-1661 Portage Avenue, Winnipeg, Manitoba R3J 3T7, Canada ☎ (204) 775-4073 Tx: none Fax: (204) 775-7773 SITA: n/a
F: 1988 ↟↟↟ n/a Head: Al Reed Net: n/a Aircraft below MTOW 1361kg: Cessna 172

☐ C-FCIP	Cessna U206G Stationair 6 II	U20605815	N5538X	0080	0695	1 CO IO-520-F	1633			Floats
☐ C-FPMQ	De Havilland DHC-3 Otter	197		0057	0694	1 PW R-1340	3629			Floats

KNIGHTHAWK AIR EXPRESS = KNX (2734141 Canada, Inc. dba)

Ottawa, Ont. *KnightHawk* AIR EXPRESS

55 York Street, Suite 1601, Toronto, Ontario M5J 1R7, Canada ☎ (416) 214-4880 Tx: none Fax: (416) 214-4883 SITA: n/a
F: 1991 ↟↟↟ 45 Head: Hugh MacMillan ICAO: KNIGHT FLITE Net: n/a

☐ C-GKHB	Beech 1900C Airliner	UB-52	N817BE	0086	0696	2 PWC PT6A-65B	7530	Freighter		
☐ C-FONX	Dassault Falcon 20D	225	N102AD	0070	1191	2 GE CF700-2D2	13000	Freighter		
☐ C-GKHA	Dassault Falcon 20C	19	N41PC	0066	0896	2 GE CF700-2D2	13000	Freighter		
☐ C-GRSD	Dassault Falcon 20C	157	CAF 117508	0068	0994	2 GE CF700-2D2	13000	Freighter		
☐ C-GTAK	Dassault Falcon 20D	197	N399SW	0069	1191	2 GE CF700-2D2	13000	Freighter		

KOBILSKI AIR, Ltd

Nelson House, Man.

Box 286, Nelson House, Manitoba R0B 1A0, Canada ☎ (204) 484-2225 Tx: none Fax: (204) 484-2377 SITA: n/a
F: 1996 ↟↟↟ n/a Head: n/a Net: n/a

☐ C-GXQV	Cessna A185F Skywagon	18503375		0077	0297	1 CO IO-520-D	1520			Floats

KOKANEE HELICOPTERS (Kelowna Helicopters Charters, Corp. dba) — Kelowna, B.C.

106-1449 Saint Paul Street, Kelowna, British Columbia V1Y 2E4, Canada ☎ (250) 762-2659 Tx: none Fax: (250) 762-2659 SITA: n/a
F: 1995 ⁂ n/a Head: Michael Culos Net: n/a

☐ C-FLMN	Bell 206B JetRanger	*158*	*C-GRWR*	*0068*	*0395*	*1 AN 250-C20*	*1451*	*cvtd 206A*
☐ C-FKHG	Eurocopter (Aerosp.) AS350B AStar	*1399*	*N14MW*	*0080*	*0896*	*1 TU Arriel 1B*	*1950*	

KONOPELKY AIR SERVICE (Affiliated with Polar Bear Sports Camps & Outfitters / Seasonal May-October ops only) — Cochrane-Lillabelle Lake, Ont.

PO Box 396, Cochrane, Ontario P0L 1C0, Canada ☎ (705) 272-5680 Tx: n/a Fax: (705) 272-4619 SITA: n/a
F: 1975 ⁂ 4 Head: Steve Konopelky Net: n/a Aircraft below MTOW 1361 kg: Cessna 180 (Floats).

☐ C-GHEP	Cessna A185F Skywagon	*1850652*	*N2652Z*	*0063*	*0990*	*1 CO IO-520-D*	*1520*	*cvtd 185B/Floats / opf Polar Bear Camp*

KOOTENAY AIRWAYS, Ltd (formerly R.M. Horizon Air (1986), Ltd) — Cranbrook & Castlegar, B.C.

PO Box 118, Cranbrook, British Columbia V1C 4H6, Canada ☎ (250) 426-3762 Tx: none Fax: (250) 426-4050 SITA: n/a
F: 1986 ⁂ n/a Head: Bill Gillespie Net: n/a Aircraft below MTOW 1361 kg: Cessna 150, 152, 172, 180, 182 & Piper PA-18.

☐ C-GXHY	Piper PA-34-200T Seneca II	*34-7670330*	*N4307F*	*0076*	*0194*	*2 CO TSIO-360-E*	*2073*	
☐ C-FGWH	Cessna 337G Super Skymaster	*33701555*		*0074*		*2 CO IO-360-G*	*2100*	
☐ CF-ZPL	Cessna 337F Super Skymaster	*33701336*		*0071*	*0492*	*2 CO IO-360-C/D*	*2100*	
☐ C-GYEA	Cessna 414 II	*414-0843*		*0076*	*0695*	*2 CO TSIO-520-N*	*2880*	

LABRADOR AIR SAFARI (1984), Inc. — Manicouagan-Lac Louise SPB, Qué.

CP 1312, Chicoutimi, Québec G7H 5G7, Canada ☎ (418) 589-9511 Tx: none Fax: (418) 548-2037 SITA: n/a
F: 1970 ⁂ 20 Head: Richard Tremblay Net: http://www.labrador-airsafari.com

☐ C-GVYR	Cessna A185F Skywagon II	*18503783*		*0078*		*1 CO IO-520-D*	*1520*	*Floats / Wheel-Skis*
☐ C-FIUS	De Havilland DHC-2 Beaver I	*901*		*0056*	*0199*	*1 PW R-985*	*2313*	*Floats / Wheels-Skis*
☐ C-FPQC	De Havilland DHC-2 Beaver I	*873*		*0054*		*1 PW R-985*	*2313*	*Floats / Wheel-Skis*
☐ C-FYYT	De Havilland DHC-2 Beaver I	*1569*		*0065*		*1 PW R-985*	*2313*	*Floats / Wheel-Skis*
☐ C-GWAE	De Havilland DHC-2 Beaver I	*1094*	*56-0381*	*0058*		*1 PW R-985*	*2313*	*Floats / Wheel-Skis*
☐ C-FBEU	De Havilland DHC-3 Otter	*119*	*55-3273*	*0056*		*1 PW R-1340*	*3629*	*Floats / Wheel-Skis*
☐ C-GLJI	De Havilland DHC-3 Otter	*150*	*55-3297*	*0056*		*1 PW R-1340*	*3629*	*Floats / Wheel-Skis*
☐ C-GVNX	De Havilland DHC-3 Otter	*353*	*N5335G*	*0060*		*1 PW R-1340*	*3629*	*Floats / Wheel-Skis*

LABRADOR TRAVEL AIR, Ltd — Charlottetown, Nfld

PO Box 160, Charlottetown, (Labrador), Newfoundland A0K 5Y0, Canada ☎ (709) 949-0273 Tx: n/a Fax: (709) 949-0293 SITA: n/a
F: 1987 ⁂ 5 Head: Tony F. Powell Net: n/a

☐ C-GJSH	Partenavia P.68C	*376*		*0087*	*0492*	*2 LY IO-360-A1B6*	*1990*	

LAC LA CROIX QUETICO AIR SERVICES, Ltd (Div. of Campbell's Cabins & Trading Post / Seasonal May-November ops only) — Lac la Croix, Ont. & Crane Lake, MN

General Delivery, Fort Frances, Ontario P9A 3M4, Canada ☎ (807) 485-2441 Tx: none Fax: (807) 485-2579 SITA: n/a
F: 1951 ⁂ 9 Head: Robert J. Handberg Net: n/a Aircraft below MTOW 1361kg: Aeronca 7CCM.

☐ C-GUEC	Cessna A185F Skywagon II	*18503986*	*N5513E*	*0080*		*1 CO IO-520-D*	*1520*	*Floats*
☐ CF-VSF	Cessna A185E Skywagon	*185-1223*		*0067*		*1 CO IO-520-D*	*1497*	*Floats*
☐ C-FHAN	De Havilland DHC-2 Beaver I	*316*	*N11255*	*0052*		*1 PW R-985*	*2313*	*Floats*
☐ C-GDZD	De Havilland DHC-2 Beaver I	*496*	*52-6116*	*0052*		*1 PW R-985*	*2313*	*Floats*
☐ C-FNFI	De Havilland DHC-3 Otter	*379*		*0060*		*1 PW R-1340*	*3629*	*Floats*

LAC SEUL AIRWAYS, Ltd (Seasonal May-October ops only) — Ear Falls, Ont.

Box 39, Ear Falls, Ontario P0V 1T0, Canada ☎ (807) 222-3067 Tx: none Fax: (807) 222-3499 SITA: n/a
F: 1960 ⁂ 6 Head: Bruce La Vigne Net: n/a Aircraft below MTOW 1361kg: Piper PA-18 (on floats).

☐ C-FDUW	De Havilland DHC-2 Beaver I	*736*	*53-7925*	*0052*		*1 PW R-985*	*2309*	*Floats*
☐ C-FPEN	De Havilland DHC-3 Otter	*439*		*0063*		*1 PW R-1340*	*3629*	*Floats*
☐ CF-HXY	De Havilland DHC-3 Otter	*67*		*0053*		*1 PW R-1340*	*3629*	*Floats*

LAFRENI-AIR, Ltd — Chapleau, Ont.

Box 39, Chapleau, Ontario P0M 1K0, Canada ☎ (705) 864-2942 Tx: none Fax: (705) 864-2943 SITA: n/a
F: n/a ⁂ 5 Head: Jacques Lafrenière Net: n/a Aircraft below MTOW 1361kg: Cessna 172 / 182, Piper PA-28 & Hughes 369HS (500C)

☐ C-FFBV	Bell 206B JetRanger	*1016*	*N90819*	*0073*	*0493*	*1 AN 250-C20*	*1451*	

LAKE CENTRAL AIRWAYS (126700 Aircraft Canada, Inc. dba) — Toronto, Ont.

PO Box 6036, Toronto AMF, Ontario L5P 1B2, Canada ☎ (416) 617-6223 Tx: none Fax: (416) 769-0394 SITA: n/a
F: 1983 ⁂ 4 Head: Gregory B. Street Net: n/a

☐ C-GAGE	Cessna 441 Conquest II	*441-0086*	*N20BF*	*0079*	*0494*	*2 GA TPE331-10N-534S*	*4468*	

LAKELAND AIRWAYS, Ltd (Affiliated with Three Buoys Houseboat Vacations) — Temagami, Ont.

PO Box 249, Temagami, Ontario P0H 2H0, Canada ☎ (705) 569-3455 Tx: none Fax: (705) 569-3687 SITA: n/a
F: 1948 ⁂ 8 Head: Judy Gareh Net: n/a Aircraft below MTOW 1361 kg: Cessna 180.

☐ C-GDIV	Cessna A185F Skywagon II	*18503977*		*0080*		*1 CO IO-520-D*	*1520*	*Floats / Wheel-Skis*
☐ C-FJKT	De Havilland DHC-2 Beaver I	*1023*		*0056*		*1 PW R-985*	*2313*	*Floats / Wheel-Skis*

LAKELSE AIR, Ltd — Terrace, B.C.

3752 Highway 16E, Terrace, British Columbia V8G 5J3, Canada ☎ (250) 635-3407 Tx: none Fax: (250) 635-6129 SITA: n/a
F: 1978 ⁂ n/a Head: George Munson Net: n/a Aircraft below MTOW 1361kg: Robinson R22 & R44

☐ C-GRJR	MD Helicopters MD 500D (Hughes 369D)	*300678D*	*N68GS*	*0080*	*0697*	*1 AN 250-C20B*	*1361*	
☐ C-FCDT	De Havilland DHC-2 Beaver I	*390*	*N9758Z*	*0052*	*1094*	*1 PW R-985*	*2313*	*Floats*

LAKES DISTRICT AIR SERVICES, Ltd — Burns Lake, B.C.

PO Box 128, Burns Lake, British Columbia V0J 1E0, Canada ☎ (250) 692-3229 Tx: none Fax: (250) 692-7563 SITA: n/a
F: 1976 ⁂ 3 Head: Lou P. Dubuc Net: n/a

☐ C-FVXQ	Cessna A185E Skywagon	*185-1198*		*0067*		*1 CO IO-520-D*	*1520*	*Floats / Wheel-Skis*
☐ C-FFHS	De Havilland DHC-2 Beaver I	*51*		*0050*		*1 PW R-985*	*2313*	*Floats / Wheel-Skis*

LA LOCHE AIRWAYS, Ltd (formerly C and M Airways) — La Loche, Sask.

Box 10, La Loche, Saskatchewan S0M 1G0, Canada ☎ (306) 822-2022 Tx: none Fax: (306) 822-2026 SITA: n/a
F: 1988 ⁂ 4 Head: Craig Schnell Net: n/a Aircraft below MTOW 1361kg: Cessna 172 & 180

☐ C-GMFV	Cessna U206G Stationair 6 II	*U20604714*		*0079*	*0989*	*1 CO IO-520-F*	*1633*	
☐ C-GUWL	De Havilland DHC-2 Beaver I	*1223*	*57-6140*	*0058*	*0593*	*1 PW R-985*	*2313*	
☐ C-GEUA	Piper PA-31-310 Navajo	*31-187*	*N64JK*	*0068*	*0989*	*2 LY TIO-540-A1A*	*2948*	
☐ C-GNAA	Beech King Air 100	*B-24*	*N382WC*	*0069*	*0798*	*2 PWC PT6A-28*	*4808*	

L'AMI AVIATION, Inc. (Seasonal summer ops only) — Ste-Rose (Marina Venise), Qué.

27 Brunet, St-Joseph du Lac, Québec J0N 1M0, Canada ☎ (514) 984-2150 Tx: n/a Fax: (514) 984-2150 SITA: n/a
F: 1984 ⁂ 3 Head: J.P. Blanchard Net: n/a

☐ C-GUXH	Cessna U206G Stationair	*U20603814*		*0077*		*1 CO IO-520-F*	*1633*	*Floats*

LANDA AVIATION (L & A Aviation, Ltd dba) — Hay River, N.W.T.

100 Whitlock Road, Hay River, Northwest Territories X0E 0R9, Canada ☎ (867) 874-3500 Tx: none Fax: (867) 874-2927 SITA: n/a
F: 1978 ⁂ 10 Head: Larry Buckmaster Net: n/a

☐ C-GJHM	Cessna A185F Skywagon II	*18504203*		*0081*	*0587*	*1 CO IO-550-D*	*1520*	*Amphibian / Wheel-Skis*
☐ CF-ZEB	Cessna 337F Super Skymaster	*33701428*		*0072*	*0483*	*2 CO IO-360-C*	*2100*	
☐ C-GERO	AAC (Ted Smith) Aerostar 600	*60-0039*	*N452D*	*0069*	*0595*	*2 LY IO-540-G1B5*	*2495*	
☐ C-GYFG	Cessna 402B II	*402B1015*	*N87186*	*0076*	*0582*	*2 CO TSIO-520-EB*	*2858*	

LAURENTIDE AVIATION, Ltd (2737-5633 Québec, Inc. dba) — Montreal-Cedres, Qué.

Aéroport les Cèdres, 870 Ch. St. Féréol, Les Cèdres, Québec J7T 1N3, Canada ☎ (514) 875-6669 Tx: none Fax: (514) 452-4405 SITA: n/a
F: 1946 ⁂ 20 Head: John Scholefield Net: http://www.sympatico.ca/laurentide Aircraft below MTOW 1361 kg: Cessna 152, 172 & Piper PA-28.

☐ C-FLPB	Piper PA-32-300E Cherokee SIX	*32-7240124*	*N1458T*	*0072*	*0397*	*1 LY IO-540-K1A5*	*1542*	
☐ C-FHTA	Piper PA-34-200 Seneca	*34-7350157*		*0073*		*2 LY IO-360-C1E6*	*1905*	
☐ C-GYKL	Piper PA-34-200 Seneca	*34-7250084*	*N1081U*	*0072*	*0291*	*2 LY IO-360-C1E6*	*1905*	

LAUZON AVIATION, Co. Ltd — Algoma Mills-Elliot Lake, Ont.

PO Box 1750, Blind River, Ontario P0R 1B0, Canada ☎ (705) 849-2389 Tx: none Fax: (705) 849-2758 SITA: n/a
F: 1961 ⁂ 5 Head: Reino M. Makela Net: n/a Aircraft below MTOW 1361 kg: Cessna 180 (Floats / Wheel-Skis).

☐ C-FRUY	De Havilland DHC-2 Beaver I	*687*	*N74157*	*0054*	*0694*	*1 PW R-985*	*2313*	*Floats / Wheel-Skis*

61 registration type of aircraft *cn/fn* *ex/ex** *mfd* *del* *powered by* *mtow kg* *configuration* *selcal* name/fln/specialitites/remarks

LAWRENCE AVIATION (Larry L. Chambers dba) — Springhouse Airpark, B.C.

Box 4418, Williams Lake, British Columbia V2G 2V4, Canada ☎ (250) 392-3195 Tx: none Fax: (250) 392-3222 SITA: n/a
F: 1992 ⁂ n/a Head: Larry L. Chambers Net: n/a Aircraft -& Ag-aircraft below MTOW 1361/5000kg: Cessna 172 / 182 & G164A AgCat

☐ C-FEDE	Cessna 205 (210-5)	205-0012		0062	0795	1 CO IO-470-S	1497			

LAWRENCE BAY AIRWAYS, Ltd (Affiliated with Lawrence Bay Lodge, Ltd / Summer ops only) — Southend-Reindeer Lake, Sask.

PO Box 583, La Ronge, Saskatchewan S0J 1L0, Canada ☎ (306) 758-2060 Tx: none Fax: none SITA: n/a
F: 1985 ⁂ n/a Head: Randy Engen Net: n/a Aircraft below MTOW 1361kg: Cessna 180 (on Floats) Winter-address: POB 243, Tolna, ND 58380, USA. Phone: (701) 262-4560.

☐ C-GUJX	De Havilland DHC-2 Beaver I	1132	56-4412	0055	0397	1 PW R-985	2313			Floats

LEDAIR, Inc. — Montreal-Dorval, Qué.

161 Leech, Les Cedres (Comte de Soulanges), Québec J0P 1L0, Canada ☎ (514) 452-4298 Tx: none Fax: (514) 455-0232 SITA: n/a
F: 1965 ⁂ n/a Head: n/a Net: n/a

☐ C-GKPM	Hawker 700A (HS 125-700A)	257049 / NA0239	N33BK	0078	1296	2 GA TFE731-3R-1H	11249	Executive		

LES AILES DE GASPE, Inc. — Gaspé, Qué.

CP 1928, Gaspé, Québec G0C 1R0, Canada ☎ (418) 368-1995 Tx: none Fax: (418) 368-2966 SITA: n/a
F: 1980 ⁂ n/a Head: Marc Bouchard Net: n/a

☐ C-FARL	Piper PA-31-310 Navajo	31-306		0068	0489	2 LY TIO-540-A1A	2948			

LES LEVES AEROSCAN, Inc. — Québec, Qué.

714-7e Ave, Aéroport Int'l Jean Lesage, Ste-Foy, Québec G2E 5W1, Canada ☎ (418) 849-5701 Tx: none Fax: (418) 849-2603 SITA: n/a
F: 1993 ⁂ n/a Head: n/a Net: n/a

☐ C-GOVX	Piper PA-31-310 Navajo	31-625	N401CA	0070	0196	2 LY TIO-540-A1A	2948	Photo		

LEUENBERGER AIR SERVICE, Ltd (Seasonal May-October ops only) — Nakina, Ont.

Box 60, Nakina, Ontario P0T 2H0, Canada ☎ (807) 329-5940 Tx: none Fax: (807) 329-5267 SITA: n/a
F: 1971 ⁂ 15 Head: Ernie Leuenberger Net: n/a

☐ C-GNPQ	De Havilland DHC-2 Beaver I	1168	N9281Z	0056		1 PW R-985	2313			Floats
☐ C-FSOX	De Havilland DHC-3 Otter	437	UNO308	0063		1 PW R-1340	3629			Floats
☐ C-GLCS	De Havilland DHC-3 Otter	428	N17685	0061	0789	1 PW R-1340	3629			Floats
☐ C-GLCW	De Havilland DHC-3 Otter	172	55-3310	0056		1 PW R-1340	3629			Floats

LIARD AIR, Ltd (Affiliated with Liard Tours, Ltd & Highland Glen Lodge, Ltd) — Muncho Lake & Fort Nelson, B.C.

Box 8, Muncho Lake, British Columbia V0C 1Z0, Canada ☎ (250) 776-3481 Tx: none Fax: (250) 776-3482 SITA: n/a
F: 1981 ⁂ 3 Head: Urs Schildknecht Net: n/a

☐ C-GUGE	Cessna A185F Skywagon	18502904		0075	0590	1 CO IO-520-D	1520			Floats / Wheel-Skis
☐ C-GUDK	De Havilland DHC-2 Beaver I	708	53-7900	0054		1 PW R-985	2313			Floats / Wheel-Skis

LIB-AIR-T AVIATION (M.C.M.), Inc. (Seasonal May-November ops only) — Montreal-Marina Venise SPB, Qué.

4101 Rue Radisson, Montréal, Québec H1M 1X7, Canada ☎ (514) 254-6345 Tx: none Fax: (514) 254-6159 SITA: n/a
F: 1996 ⁂ 2 Head: Guy Handfield Net: n/a

☐ C-GYDK	Cessna U206F Stationair II	U20603442		0076	0396	1 CO IO-520-F	1633			Floats

LINVIC FLYING CLUB — Lindsay & Oro-Lake Simcoe Regional, Ont.

Box 863, Lindsay, Ontario K9V 5N3, Canada ☎ (705) 324-8921 Tx: none Fax: (705) 324-9804 SITA: n/a
F: 1986 ⁂ 11 Head: Dr. Kerstin Kelly Net: http://www.linvic.com Aircraft below MTOW 1361kg: Cessna 150, 152 & 172 Beside Flying Club-activities also conducting commerical passenger & cargo & sightseeing-flights.

☐ C-GAEQ	Cessna 310Q	310Q0044	N7544Q	0070	0197	2 CO IO-470-VO	2404			

LITTLE RED AIR SERVICE, Ltd = LRA (Division of Little Red River Tribe) — Fort Vermilion, Alta.

Box 584, Fort Vermilion, Alberta T0H 1N0, Canada ☎ (780) 927-4630 Tx: none Fax: (780) 927-3667 SITA: n/a
F: 1986 ⁂ 33 Head: Henry Grandjambe ICAO: LITTLE RED Net: n/a Aircraft below MTOW 1361kg: Cessna 172 & 180.

☐ C-GHLU	Cessna A185F Skywagon	18502655		0075	0695	1 CO IO-520-D	1520			
☐ C-GICJ	Cessna U206F Stationair II	U20603044	N4318Q	0076	0998	1 CO IO-520-F	1633			
☐ C-GVBC	Cessna U206F Stationair II	U20603158		0076	0797	1 CO IO-520-F	1633			
☐ C-GXAJ	Cessna U206F Stationair II	U20602810	N35935	0075	0186	1 CO IO-520-F	1633			
☐ C-GMIC	De Havilland DHC-2 Beaver I	791	N5218G	0055	0797	1 PW R-985	2309			
☐ C-FLRA	Piper PA-31-350 Navajo Chieftain	31-7952091	N52MS	0079	1095	2 LY TIO-540-J2BD	3175			
☐ C-FGAQ	Britten-Norman BN-2A-27 Islander	212	G-51-212*	0070	0896	2 LY O-540-E4C5	2994			
☐ C-FLRB	Britten-Norman BN-2B-26 Islander	2038	9M-WKC	0087	0798	2 LY O-540-E4C5	2994			
☐ C-FIDN	Beech King Air 100	B-3	N128RC	0069	0996	2 PWC PT6A-28	4808			
☐ C-FQOV	Beech King Air 100	B-38	N931M	0070	1093	2 PWC PT6A-28	4808			

LOCKHART AIR SERVICES, Ltd — Pickle Lake, Ont.

Box 985, Sioux Lookout, Ontario P8T 1B3, Canada ☎ (807) 737-2268 Tx: none Fax: (807) 737-2277 SITA: n/a
F: 1988 ⁂ 10 Head: Howard B. Lockhart Net: n/a Aircraft below MTOW 1361 kg: Cessna 180 (Floats / Wheel-Skis).

☐ C-GQDP	Cessna A185F Skywagon II	18503747		0079	0691	1 CO IO-520-D	1520			Floats / Wheel-Skis
☐ C-GFIT	Cessna 310R II	310R1865		0080	1196	2 CO IO-520-M	2495			
☐ C-GMLN	Cessna 310R II	310R1884	N316U	0080	0798	2 CO IO-520-M	2495			

LONG BEACH HELICOPTERS, Ltd — Nanaimo, B.C.

2363 Cienar Drive, Nanaimo, British Columbia V9T 3L6, Canada ☎ (250) 758-0024 Tx: none Fax: (250) 758-2531 SITA: n/a
F: 1967 ⁂ 7 Head: Peter Oehlenschlaeger Net: n/a Aircraft below MTOW 1361kg: Hughes 500C (369HS).

☐ C-FNTA	Eurocopter (Aerosp.) AS350B AStar	1356	N511FP	0080	0692	1 TU Arriel 1B	1950			
☐ C-FQCD	Eurocopter (Aerosp.) AS350B AStar	1854	JA9412	0086	0793	1 TU Arriel 1B	1950			
☐ C-FSUL	Eurocopter (Aerosp.) AS350B AStar	1696	JA9346	0083	0794	1 TU Arriel 1B	1950			
☐ C-FSWH	Eurocopter (Aerosp.) AS350B AStar	1990	N6007S	0087	0297	1 TU Arriel 1B	1950			

LONG POINT AIRWAYS (Thomas E. Wilson dba / Seasonal May-November ops only) — Gowganda-Longpoint Lake SPB, Ont.

General Delivery, Gowganda, Ontario P0J 1J0, Canada ☎ (705) 624-3512 Tx: none Fax: (805) 624-2418 SITA: n/a
F: 1960 ⁂ n/a Head: Thomas E. Wilson Net: n/a

☐ C-GLEV	Cessna A185F Skywagon	18502649	C-GEFA	0075	0498	1 CO IO-520-D	1520			Floats / Wheel-Skis

LOON HAUNT AIR SERVICE (Loon Haunt Enterprises, Inc. dba / Seasonal May-October ops only) — Goose Lake, Ont.

Box 127, Red Lake, Ontario POV 2M0, Canada ☎ (807) 735-2400 Tx: n/a Fax: (807) 735-2400 SITA: n/a
F: 1987 ⁂ n/a Head: n/a Net: n/a

☐ C-GGRL	Cessna A185E Skywagon	185-1200	N4746Q	0067	0591	1 CO IO-520-D	1520			Floats

LOYAL-AIR, Ltd — Belleville, Ont.

PO Box 322, Belleville, Ontario K8N 5A5, Canada ☎ (613) 962-0124 Tx: none Fax: (613) 962-4881 SITA: n/a
F: 1972 ⁂ 3 Head: James E. Marker Net: n/a Aircraft below MTOW 1361 kg: Cessna 172 & Piper PA-28.

☐ C-GBLW	Piper PA-32-300 Cherokee SIX	32-7340124		0073		1 LY IO-540-K1A5	1542			
☐ C-FLAL	Piper PA-23-150 Apache	23-701		0056		2 LY O-320-A1A	1588			
☐ C-GSMD	Piper PA-34-200 Seneca	34-7450204		0074		2 LY IO-360-C1E6	1905			
☐ C-GQKQ	Piper PA-23-250 Aztec E	27-7305141	N40377	0073		2 LY IO-540-C4B5	2359			

MAF Canada – Mission Aviation Fellowship — Africa

264 Woodlawn Road West, Box 368, Guelph, Ontario N1H 6K5, Canada ☎ (519) 821-3914 Tx: none Fax: (519) 823-1650 SITA: n/a
F: 1973 ⁂ 50 Head: Eugene Parkins & John Polonenko Net: n/a Non-commercial multinational ecclesiastical consortium conducting flights for relief&development agencies&missions in remote areas of 3rd world countries.

☐ C-GWOH	Cessna 208 Caravan I	20800018	N9346F	0085	1192	1 PWC PT6A-114	3629			
☐ C-FWOL	Beech King Air 100	B-84	N401TJ	0071	0192	2 PWC PT6A-28	4808			

MANDAIR (Walsten Aircraft Parts & Leasing, Inc. dba / Seasonal May-October ops only) — Kenora, Ont.

Box 706, Kenora, Ontario P9N 3X6, Canada ☎ (807) 468-5970 Tx: none Fax: (807) 468-3922 SITA: n/a
F: 1992 ⁂ 2 Head: Neil Walsten Net: n/a

☐ C-GQOF	Cessna U206G Stationair 6 II	U20605023		0079		1 CO IO-520-F	1633			Floats

MAQUAYAN AIRWAYS, Ltd — Bearskin Lake, Ont.

Box 55, Bearskin Lake, Ontario P0V 1E0, Canada ☎ (807) 363-2527 Tx: none Fax: (807) 363-1095 SITA: n/a
F: 1989 ⁂ 2 Head: Tom Kam Net: n/a Winter phone: (807) 363-1046

☐ C-FYCK	Cessna A185E Skywagon	185-1478		0069	0191	1 CO IO-520-D	1520			Floats

62 registration type of aircraft cn/fn ex/ex* mfd del powered by mtow kg configuration selcal name/fln/specialitites/remarks

MARITIME AIR CHARTER, Ltd
Halifax, N.S.

693 Barnes Road, Suite 343, Enfield, Nova Scotia B2T 1K3, Canada ☎ (902) 873-3330 Tx: none Fax: (902) 468-8443 SITA: n/a
F: 1996 ✦✦✦ n/a Head: Ted Brekleman Net: n/a

	registration	type of aircraft	cn/fn	ex/ex*	mfd	del	powered by	mtow kg	configuration	selcal	name/fln/remarks
☐	C-FYKQ	Piper PA-31-310 Navajo	31-399		0069	1096	2 LY TIO-540-A1A	2948			

MARLIN HELICOPTERS, Inc.
Lac La Biche, Alta.

Box 5, Clairmont, Alberta T0H 0W0, Canada ☎ (780) 532-8233 Tx: none Fax: (780) 532-2516 SITA: n/a
F: 1986 ✦✦✦ n/a Head: Merle Morrison Net: n/a

☐	C-GMHL	Bell 206B JetRanger	1784	N49609	0075	0493	1 AN 250-C20	1451			

MATT'S AIR SERVICE, Ltd
Sioux Lookout, Ont.

Box 1267, Sioux Lookout, Ontario P8T 1B8, Canada ☎ (807) 737-1020 Tx: none Fax: (807) 737-1040 SITA: n/a
F: 1990 ✦✦✦ 4 Head: Matthias J. Mitchell Net: n/a Aircraft below MTOW 1361kg: Cessna 180 (on Floats / Wheel-Skis).

☐	C-FFXQ	Cessna A185E Skywagon	18501913		0071	0798	1 CO IO-520-D	1520			Floats / Wheel-Skis
☐	C-GBKA	Cessna A185F Skywagon	18502375	N53099	0074	0299	1 CO IO-520-D	1520			Floats / Wheel-Skis
☐	C-FODL	De Havilland DHC-3 Otter	15		0053	0593	1 PW R-1340	3629			Floats / Wheel-Skis

MAXWELL AVIATION, Inc.
Squamish, B.C.

Box 577, 40363 Tantalus Way, Garibaldi Highlands, British Columbia V0N 3T0, Canada ☎ (604) 892-9135 Tx: none Fax: (604) 892-9217 SITA: n/a
F: 1997 ✦✦✦ n/a Head: Wayne Podlasly Net: n/a

☐	C-GJTJ	Cessna A185F Skywagon	18503368		0077	0697	1 CO IO-520-D	1520			Floats

MCGAVOCK LAKE AIR SERVICE, Inc. (Affil. with Laurie River Lodge/formerly Laurie Air Services, Inc./Seasonal May-September ops only)
McGavock Lake, Man.

PO Box 550, Lynn Lake, Manitoba R0B 0W0, USA ☎ (800) 426-2533 Tx: none Fax: winter(541)247-2033 SITA: n/a
F: 1980 ✦✦✦ 3 Head: Brent & Erin Fleck Net: n/a Winter-address: PO Box 1046, Gold Beach, OR 97444, USA.

☐	C-FIDF	De Havilland DHC-2 Beaver I	1321	N99870	0058	0797	1 PW R-985	2309			Floats

MCLEAN & MCLEAN AIR SERVICES (Chris S. McLean dba)
Delta, B.C.

13518-56 Ave, Surrey, British Columbia V3X 2Z6, Canada ☎ (604) 594-7363 Tx: none Fax: (604) 594-7358 SITA: n/a
F: 1996 ✦✦✦ 2 Head: Chris S. & Kathy McLean Net: n/a

☐	C-GMMJ	De Havilland DHC-2 Beaver I	226	N2748	0051	0896	1 PW R-985	2313	6 Pax		

MCMURRAY AVIATION (WMK Holdings, Ltd dba)
Fort McMurray, Alta. McMurray Aviation

Site 1, Box 5, RR1, Fort McMurray, Alberta T9H 3B4, Canada ☎ (780) 791-2182 Tx: none Fax: (780) 790-2364 SITA: n/a
F: 1984 ✦✦✦ 5 Head: Wade Komarnisky Net: n/a Aircraft below MTOW 1361 kg: Cessna 172.

☐	CF-IHR	Piper PA-32-300 Cherokee SIX	32-7340027		0073	0397	1 LY IO-540-K1A5	1542			
☐	C-GHJB	Cessna U206E Stationair	U20601677	N9477G	0071	1098	1 CO IO-520-F	1633			
☐	C-GZZD	Cessna U206F Stationair	U20601957	N50946	0073	0397	1 CO IO-520-F	1633			
☐	C-GBSM	Cessna T210L Turbo Centurion II	21061337	N2603S	0076	0592	1 CO TSIO-520-H	1724			
☐	C-GPRL	Piper PA-34-200T Seneca II	34-7570090	N33120	0075	0491	2 CO TSIO-360-E	2073			
☐	C-FIAZ	Britten-Norman BN-2A Islander	65	N25DA	0069	0694	2 LY O-540-E4C5	2858			
☐	C-GVSO	Piper PA-31-310 Navajo	31-393	N4WR	0069	0397	2 LY TIO-540-A1A	2948			

MICMAC AIR SERVICES (Taqamkuk Development Corporation dba)
River Pond Park, Nfld.

PO Box 10, Conne River, Newfoundland A0H 1J0, Canada ☎ (709) 882-2470 Tx: none Fax: (709) 882-2292 SITA: n/a
F: 1998 ✦✦✦ 1 Head: David McDonald Net: n/a

☐	C-GQDT	Cessna A185F Skywagon II	18503756		0079	0798	1 CO IO-520-D	1520			Floats

MID COAST AIR SERVICES, Ltd
Port McNeill-SPB, B.C.

Box 425, Gibsons, British Columbia V0N 1V0, Canada ☎ (604) 886-3488 Tx: none Fax: (604) 886-9988 SITA: n/a
F: 1995 ✦✦✦ n/a Head: n/a Net: n/a

☐	C-FJIM	De Havilland DHC-2 Beaver I	462	ZK-CPZ	0052	0595	1 PW R-985	2309			Floats
☐	C-GFLT	De Havilland DHC-2 Beaver I	279	N5149G	0052	0695	1 PW R-985	2309			Floats
☐	C-GLCP	De Havilland DHC-3 Otter	422	N17682	0061	0897	1 PW R-1340	3629			Floats

MIDWEST HELICOPTERS (Midwest Helicopters, Ltd dba)
Winnipeg-Int'l, Man. MIDWEST HELICOPTERS

3025 Portage Ave, Suite 250, Winnipeg, Manitoba R3K 2E2, Canada ☎ (204) 885-6212 Tx: none Fax: (204) 831-0879 SITA: n/a
F: 1978 ✦✦✦ 42 Head: Wayne McAulay Net: n/a

☐	C-GMHJ	Kaman K-1200 K-Max	A94-0011		0095	0695	1 LY T5317A-1	2722			
☐	C-GMHO	Kaman K-1200 K-Max	A94-0015	N165KA	0095	0396	1 LY T5317A-1	2722			

MIKE DENIS AVIATION, Inc.
Maniwaki, Qué.

140 Ch. Rivière Gatineau, Maniwaki, Québec J9E 3A6, Canada ☎ (819) 465-2735 Tx: n/a Fax: (819) 465-2735 SITA: n/a
F: 1983 ✦✦✦ n/a Head: n/a Net: n/a

☐	C-FMPM	De Havilland DHC-2 Beaver I	62		0054	0792	1 PW R-985	2313			Floats / Wheel-Skis

MITCHINSON FLYING SERVICE, Ltd
Saskatoon, Sasks.

PO Box 1521, Saskatoon, Saskatchewan S7K 3R3, Canada ☎ (306) 244-6714 Tx: none Fax: (306) 244-6741 SITA: n/a
F: 1946 ✦✦✦ 10 Head: Janet Keim Net: n/a Aircraft below MTOW 1361 kg: Cessna 152 & 172.

☐	C-GEUM	Cessna 310R II	310R0508	N87305	0076	0198	2 CO IO-520-M	2495			
☐	C-GFXA	Cessna 310R II	310R0711		0076	1097	2 CO IO-520-M	2495			

MOBIL OIL AVIATION = MBO (Division of Mobil Oil Canada, Ltd / Subsidiary of Mobil Oil, Corp.)
Rainbow Lake, Alta.

Box 90, Rainbow Lake, Alberta T0H 2Y0, Canada ☎ (780) 956-3133 Tx: none Fax: (780) 956-3183 SITA: n/a
F: 1968 ✦✦✦ n/a Head: n/a ICAO: MOBIL Net: n/a Non-commercial company conducting corporate flights for the oil production activities of its parent company only.

☐	C-FMOL	De Havilland DHC-6 Twin Otter 300	303	C-FUGP	0071	0695	2 PWC PT6A-27	5670	Corporate		

MONTAIR AVIATION, Inc.
Boundary Bay, B.C.

7673 Garfield Drive, Delta, British Columbia V4C 4E6, Canada ☎ (604) 946-6688 Tx: none Fax: (604) 946-6508 SITA: n/a
F: 1995 ✦✦✦ n/a Head: //www.montair.com Net: n/a Aircraft below MTOW 1361kg: Cessna 140, 152 & 172

☐	C-GYPD	Piper PA-34-200T Seneca II	34-7870025	N47991	0078	0595	2 CO TSIO-360-E	2073			
☐	C-GMWO	Piper PA-31-310 Navajo	31-8112042	N4086Y	0081	0398	2 LY TIO-540-A2C	2948			

MORGAN AIR SERVICES, Co. Ltd
Calgary, Alta. MORGAN AIR

840 McTavish Road NE, Calgary, Alberta T2E 7G6, Canada ☎ (403) 291-3644 Tx: none Fax: (403) 250-6596 SITA: n/a
F: 1983 ✦✦✦ 12 Head: Tim Morgan Net: n/a Aircraft below MTOW 1361kg: Cessna 150 / 172 & Piper PA-28

☐	C-FCCM	Piper PA-30-160 Twin Comanche B	30-1632		0068		2 LY IO-320-B1A	1633			
☐	C-GINN	Piper PA-30-160 Twin Comanche C	30-1828	D-GINN	0069	0994	2 LY IO-320-B1A	1633			
☐	C-GQHV	Piper PA-31-350 Navajo Chieftain	31-7405230	N54298	0074	0898	2 LY TIO-540-J2BD	3175			

MORNINGSTAR AIR EXPRESS, Inc. = MAL (formerly Brooker-Wheaton Aviation, Ltd)
Edmonton, Alta. MORNINGSTAR AIR EXPRESS

Box 14, 29 Airport Road, Edmonton, Alberta T5G 0W6, Canada ☎ (780) 453-3022 Tx: none Fax: (780) 453-6057 SITA: n/a
F: 1970 ✦✦✦ 70 Head: Kim Ward & Donald Wheaton Net: n/a

☐	C-FEXE	Cessna 208B Caravan I Super Cargomaster	208B0244		0090	1290	1 PWC PT6A-114A	3969	Freighter		lsf/opf FDX in FedEx-colors
☐	C-FEXX	Cessna 208B Caravan I Super Cargomaster	208B0209		0090	0390	1 PWC PT6A-114	3969	Freighter		lsf/opf FDX in FedEx-colors
☐	C-GOGM	Hawker 700A (HS 125-700A)	257143 / NA0325	N26H	0081	0695	2 GA TFE731-3R-1H	11567			
☐	C-FBWX	Boeing 727-25 (F)	18286 / 182	N153FE	0865	0591	3 PW JT8D-7B (HK3/FDX)	72802	Freighter	FM-DH	lsf/opf FDX in FedEx-colors / cvtd -25
☐	C-FBWY	Boeing 727-22 (F)	19085 / 349	N192FE	1066	0691	3 PW JT8D-7B	72802	Freighter	AJ-FM	Shane Christopher / lsf/opf FDX/cvtd-22
☐	C-GBWH	Boeing 727-116C	19814 / 600	N115FE	0768	0497	3 PW JT8D-7B (HK/FDX)	76884	Freighter		lsf/opf FDX in FedEx-colors
☐	C-GBWS	Boeing 727-22 (F)	18867 / 247	N180FE	0266	0691	3 PW JT8D-7B (HK3/FDX)	72802	Freighter	AK-DH	lsf/opf FDX in FedEx-colors / cvtd -22

MOUNT LAKE AIR SERVICES (749563 Ontario, Ltd dba / Affiliated with Blake's Wilderness Outpost Camps)
Mount Lake, Ont

Box 681, Elliot Lake, Ontario P5A 2R5, Canada ☎ (705) 848-8535 Tx: n/a Fax: (705) 848-8535 SITA: n/a
F: 1988 ✦✦✦ 5 Head: John Blake Net: n/a

☐	C-GLDU	Cessna A185E Skywagon	185-1281	N3348L	0067		1 CO IO-520-D	1520			Floats / Wheel-Skis
☐	C-GCWS	De Havilland DHC-2 Beaver I	1459	VH-IMG	0061	0598	1 PW R-985	2313			Floats / Wheel-Skis

MUSKWA SAFARIS, Ltd – Airservices (Seasonal summer ops only)
Muskwa River, B.C.

Box 6488, Fort St. John, British Columbia V1J 4H9, Canada ☎ (250) 785-4681 Tx: n/a Fax: (250) 785-1594 SITA: n/a
F: 1962 ✦✦✦ n/a Head: Gary Bince Net: n/a Aircraft below MTOW 1361kg: Piper PA-18.

☐	C-GKSJ	Cessna A185F Skywagon II	18504078		0080	0980	1 CO IO-520-D	1520			

MYRAND AVIATION, Inc.
Québec City, Qué.

218-2ème Avenue, Aéroport Int'l Jean-Lesage, Sainte-Foy, Québec G2E 5W1, Canada ☎ (418) 871-8225 Tx: none Fax: (418) 681-1324 SITA: n/a
F: 1981 ♠♠♠ 10 Head: André Cloutier Net: n/a

	registration	type of aircraft	cn/fn	ex/ex*	mfd	del	powered by	mtow kg	configuration	selcal	name/fln/specialitites/remarks
☐	C-GMZV	Cessna 335	3350029	N2708B	0080		2 CO TSIO-520-EB	2717			
☐	CF-UCA	Cessna 401	401-0290		0068		2 CO TSIO-520-E	2858			
☐	C-FMAI	Beech King Air A100	B-145	N380W	0073	0893	2 PWC PT6A-28	5216			
☐	C-GMAJ	Cessna 500 Citation	500-0247	XA-JUA	0075	1195	2 PWC JT15D-1A	5216			

NAKINA OUTPOST CAMPS & AIRSERVICE, Ltd
Nakina, Ont.

PO Box 126, Nakina, Ontario P0T 2H0, Canada ☎ (807) 329-5341 Tx: none Fax: (807) 329-5876 SITA: n/a
F: 1973 ♠♠♠ 4 Head: Don & Millie Bourdignon Net: n/a

☐	C-GZBS	De Havilland DHC-2 Beaver I	975	N4703Z	0057		1 PW R-985	2313	4 Pax		Floats
☐	CF-MIQ	De Havilland DHC-3 Turbo Otter	336		0060		1 PWC PT6A-135A	3629	8 Pax		cvtd Otter / Floats / Wheel-Skis
☐	C-FZRJ	Cessna 208B Grand Caravan	208B0597		0097	0397	1 PWC PT6A-114A	3969	9 Pax		
☐	C-GMVB	Cessna 208B Grand Caravan	208B0317		0092	1292	1 PWC PT6A-114A	3969	9 Pax		
☐	C-FDGV	De Havilland DHC-6 Twin Otter 200	154	TF-JMD	0068	1188	2 PWC PT6A-20	5252	18 Pax		

NALAIR = NLT (Newfoundland Labrador Air Transport, Ltd dba)
South Brook / Deer Lake, Nfld

PO Box 3, Corner Brook, Newfoundland A2H 6C3, Canada ☎ (709) 635-3574 Tx: none Fax: (709) 635-3901 SITA: n/a
F: 1977 ♠♠♠ 14 Head: Pierre Meagher ICAO: NALAIR Net: n/a

☐	C-FOEX	De Havilland DHC-2 Turbo Beaver III	1684TB52		0067	0694	1 PWC PT6A-27	2436			Floats / Wheel-Skis
☐	C-FPMA	De Havilland DHC-2 Turbo Beaver III	1625TB15	N1454T	0066	0691	1 PWC PT6A-27	2436			Floats / Wheel-Skis
☐	C-GVKA	Piper PA-31T Cheyenne II	31T-7920008		0079	0293	2 PWC PT6A-28	4082			

NATIONAL AVIATION CENTRE (5H Management Co.Ltd dba/Affiliated with National Aviation Collect/formerly P.A.Aviation Services Inc.)
Prince Albert, Sask.

PO Box 66, Prince Albert, Saskatchewan S6V 5R4, Canada ☎ (306) 764-4077 Tx: 074-29223 Fax: (306) 763-6532 SITA: n/a
F: 1976 ♠♠♠ 16 Head: Arthur Hauser Net: http://www.citylightsnews.com/nac.htm Aircraft below MTOW 1361 kg: Cessna 150 & 172.

☐	C-GPFK	Piper PA-34-200 Seneca	34-7250220	N5204T	0072		2 LY IO-360-C1E6	1905			
☐	C-GRXC	Cessna 310R II	310R1286	N6118C	0078	0689	2 CO IO-520-M	2495			
☐	C-FSAC	Piper PA-31-310 Navajo	31-85		0067	0789	2 LY TIO-540-A1A	2948			
☐	C-GJXP	Piper PA-31-310 Navajo	31-280	N9216Y	0068		2 LY TIO-540-A1A	2948			
☐	C-GVCD	Piper PA-31-350 Navajo Chieftain	31-7405457	N61418	0074		2 LY TIO-540-J2BD	3175			

NATIONAL HELICOPTERS, Inc. (Associated with Muscillo Transport, Ltd)
Toronto, Ont.

RR1, Kleinburg, Ontario L0J 1C0, Canada ☎ (905) 893-2727 Tx: none Fax: (905) 893-2699 SITA: n/a
F: 1985 ♠♠♠ 5 Head: Dan Munro Net: n/a Aircraft below MTOW 1361kg: Robinson R22

☐	C-FFUJ	Bell 206B JetRanger III	2982	N525W	0080	1092	1 AN 250-C20B	1451			rebuilt 1991
☐	C-GIGS	Bell 206B JetRanger	1434	N59474	0074		1 AN 250-C20	1451			
☐	C-GSZZ	Bell 206B JetRanger III	2319	XA-TCU	0078	0296	1 AN 250-C20B	1451			
☐	C-FLYC	Bell 206L-1 LongRanger II	45478	XA-SPN	0080	0495	1 AN 250-C28B	1882			
☐	C-FNHG	Bell 206L-1 LongRanger II	45784	N220HC	0083	0589	1 AN 250-C28B	1882			
☐	C-GNHX	Bell 222	47046	N19FH	0080	0291	2 LY LTS101-650C.2	3561			

NAV AIR CHARTER, Inc. = FCV (formerly F.C.V. Aircraft Charter Service)
Victoria, B.C.

9556 Hampden Road, Sidney, British Columbia V8L 5V5, Canada ☎ (250) 656-3937 Tx: n/a Fax: (250) 656-3936 SITA: n/a
F: 1979 ♠♠♠ 14 Head: Bernie L'Hirondelle ICAO: NAVAIR Net: n/a

☐	C-GXJD	Piper PA-32-300 Cherokee SIX	32-7340094	N16571	0073		1 LY IO-540-K1A5	1542			
☐	C-FBDT	Piper PA-31-310 Navajo	31-77	N9054Y	0067		2 LY TIO-540-A1A	2948			
☐	C-FCAI	Piper PA-31-310 Navajo	31-475	N22DC	0069	0589	2 LY TIO-540-A1A	2948			
☐	C-GJNV	Piper PA-31-310 Navajo	31-389	N9294Y	0069		2 LY TIO-540-A1A	2948			
☐	C-GSIO	Piper PA-31-310 Navajo	31-186	N823PC	0068	0793	2 LY TIO-540-A1A	2948			
☐	C-GVCP	Piper PA-31-350 Navajo Chieftain	31-7652080	N96SC	0076		2 LY TIO-540-J2BD	3175			
☐	C-GXHM	Piper PA-31-310 Navajo B	31-752	N7230L	0072	0790	2 LY TIO-540-A2C	2948			
☐	C-GILS	Britten-Norman BN-2A-21 Islander	416	N92JA	0074		2 LY IO-540-K1B5	2994			
☐	C-FIFE	Mitsubishi MU-2L (MU-2B-36) Cargoliner	683	OY-CEF	0074	0793	2 GA TPE331-6-251M	5250	Freighter		Cavenaugh SCD conversion
☐	C-FROM	Mitsubishi MU-2J (MU-2B-35)	601	N308MA	0073		2 GA TPE331-6-251M	4899			
☐	C-FROW	Mitsubishi MU-2J (MU-2B-35) Cargoliner	628	N4202M	0074	0593	2 GA TPE331-6-251M	4899	Freighter		Cavenaugh SCD conversion
☐	C-FTOO	Mitsubishi MU-2J (MU-2B-35) Cargoliner	549	N65198	0072	1290	2 GA TPE331-6-251M	4899	Freighter		Cavenaugh SCD conversion
☐	C-FTWO	Mitsubishi MU-2L (MU-2B-36) Cargoliner	672	N709US	0075		2 GA TPE331-6-251M	5250	Freighter		Cavenaugh SCD conversion
☐	C-GMET	Fairchild (Swearingen) SA226TC Metro II	TC-380	I-FSAG	0080	0595	2 GA TPE331-10UA-511G	5670			

NAV CANADA = NVC
Ottawa, Ont.

NAV CANADA

77 Metcalfe Street, Ottawa, Ontario K1P 5L6, Canada ☎ (613) 563-7838 Tx: none Fax: (613) 563-7319 SITA: n/a
F: 1996 ♠♠♠ 6300 Head: Louis R. Comeau ICAO: NAV CAN Net: n/a

☐	C-GCFK	De Havilland DHC-8-102 Dash 8	028		0086	1196	2 PWC PW120A	15649	Calibrator		
☐	C-GCFG	Canadair CL-601-1A (CL-600-2A12) Challen.	3022		0084	1296	2 GE CF34-1A	19550	Calibrator		
☐	C-GCFI	Canadair CL-601-1A (CL-600-2A12) Challen.	3020		0084	1196	2 GE CF34-1A	19550	Calibrator		

NELSON MOUNTAIN AIR, Inc.
Nelson, B.C.

Lakeside GP Box 9, Nelson, British Columbia V1L 6B9, Canada ☎ (250) 354-1456 Tx: none Fax: (250) 354-1455 SITA: n/a
F: 1993 ♠♠♠ 5 Head: Christopher W. Royals Net: http://www.netidea.com/nmtair Aircraft below MTOW 1361kg: Cessna 172 & 180 (on Floats).

☐	C-GBZI	Piper PA-34-200T Seneca II	34-7770416	N47537	0077	0598	2 CO TSIO-360-E	2073			
☐	C-GWQG	Cessna 337A Super Skymaster	337-0371	N6371F	0066	0793	2 CO IO-360-C/D	1905			
☐	CF-SHY	Cessna 337A Super Skymaster	337-0404	N5304S	0066	0698	2 CO IO-360-C/D	1905			

NESTOR FALLS FLY-IN Outposts, Ltd (formerly Nestor Falls Bait & Tackle, Ltd / Seasonal May-October ops only)
Nestor Falls-SPB, Ont.

PO Box 35, Nestor Falls, Ontario P0X 1K0, Canada ☎ (807) 484-2345 Tx: none Fax: (807) 484-2657 SITA: n/a
F: 1979 ♠♠♠ 7 Head: Dave Beauchene Net: n/a

☐	C-GYGL	Cessna A185F Skywagon	18503298		0077	0593	1 CO IO-520-D	1520			Floats
☐	C-FMDB	De Havilland DHC-2 Beaver I	268	N2104X	0052	0304	1 PW R-985	2313			Floats
☐	C-FSOR	De Havilland DHC-3 Otter	239	IM 1725	0057	0596	1 PW R-1340	3629			Floats
☐	C-FWWV	Beech 3N (18)	CA-18	RCAF 1443	0051	0596	2 PW R-985	3969			Floats

NEWFOUNDLAND HELICOPTERS, Ltd
Appleton & Clarenville, Nfld.

PO Box 1028, Clarenville, Newfoundland A0E 1J0, Canada ☎ (709) 466-2841 Tx: none Fax: (709) 466-3968 SITA: n/a
F: 1996 ♠♠♠ n/a Head: David Brown Net: n/a

☐	C-GGJP	Bell 206B JetRanger	1113	N37EA	0073	0496	1 AN 250-C20	1451			
☐	C-GNLB	Bell 206B JetRanger III	2356		0078	0396	1 AN 250-C20B	1451			

NIAGARA AIR TOURS, Ltd
St. Catharines-Niagara District, Ont.

Niagara District Airport, Niagara-on-the-Lake, Ontario L0S 1J0, Canada ☎ (905) 688-9000 Tx: none Fax: (905) 688-9100 SITA: n/a
F: 1995 ♠♠♠ n/a Head: Anthony E. Easton Net: n/a Aircraft below MTOW 1361kg: Cessna 172

☐	C-GDIL	Cessna U206D Super Skywagon	U206-1405		0069	0596	1 CO IO-520-F	1633			
☐	C-GMXZ	Cessna U206F Stationair II	U20603303	N8445Q	0076	0695	1 CO IO-520-F	1633			
☐	C-GRNC	Cessna U206F Stationair	U20601933	N50518	0073	0695	1 CO IO-520-F	1633			
☐	C-GCNU	Cessna T207A Turbo Stationair 8 II	20700646	N75841	0080	0498	1 CO TSIO-520-M	1724			

NIAGARA HELICOPTERS, Ltd
Niagara Falls, Ont.

PO Box 636, Niagara Falls, Ontario L2E 6V5, Canada ☎ (905) 357-5672 Tx: none Fax: (905) 374-2856 SITA: n/a
F: 1985 ♠♠♠ 37 Head: Ruedi H. Hafen Net: http://www.niagara-helicopters.com

☐	C-FLRH	Bell 407	53010		0096	0696	1 AN 250-C47B	2268			
☐	C-FLYD	Bell 407	53014		0096	0696	1 AN 250-C47B	2268			
☐	C-FLYF	Bell 407	53024		0096	0796	1 AN 250-C47B	2268			
☐	C-FLYG	Bell 407	53033		0096	0696	1 AN 250-C47B	2268			
☐	C-GOTU	Bell 407	53005		0096	0596	1 AN 250-C47B	2268			

NOLINOR AVIATION (Les Investissements Nolinor, Inc. dba)
Montreal-Dorval, Qué.

10105 Avenue Ryan, Dorval, Québec H9P 1A2, Canada ☎ (514) 631-0018 Tx: none Fax: (514) 631-0027 SITA: n/a
F: 1997 ♠♠♠ n/a Head: Daniel Paquet Net: n/a

☐	C-FTAP	Convair 580	334	N580N	0056	0298	2 AN 501-D13	26379	Y40 / Combi		cvtd CV440-47
☐	C-GDBX	Convair 580	312	N73157	0055	0598	2 AN 501-D13	26379	Y50		cvtd CV440-77
☐	C-GQHB	Convair 580	376	ZS-KRX	0056	0298	2 AN 501-D13	26379	Y55		cvtd CV440-32
☐	C-GHLQ	Convair 580	347	N580TA	0056	0298	2 AN 501-D13	26379	Y52		cvtd CV440-47

registration   type of aircraft   cn/fn   ex/ex*   mfd   del   powered by   mtow kg   configuration   selcal   name/fln/specialitites/remarks

NORANDA Flight Operations (Flight Operations division of Noranda, Inc.) — Toronto-Int'l, Ont.

2450 Derry Road East, Hangar 1, Mississauga, Ontario L5S 1B2, Canada ☎ (905) 677-2991 Tx: none Fax: (905) 677-0010 SITA: n/a
F: 1956 n/a Head: Dave Newland Net: n/a Operates non-commercial corporate flights for itself only.

registration	type of aircraft	cn/fn	ex/EX*	mfd	del	powered by	mtow kg	configuration	selcal	name/fln/specialitites/remarks
☐ C-FTEN	Dassault Falcon 10	45	N110CG	0075	0988	2 GA TFE731-2-1C	8500	Corporate		
☐ C-GJLN	Boeing 737-210C	19594 / 102	TF-ABJ	0068	0597	2 PW JT8D-9A	54204	Corporate Combi		

NORDPLUS (1998), Ltée (Seasonal May-October ops only) — Schefferville-Squaw Lake SPB, Qué.

CP 127, Cap Rouge, Québec G1Y 3C6, Canada ☎ (418) 871-4202 Tx: none Fax: (418) 877-4652 SITA: n/a
F: 1998 n/a Head: Jean Paquet Net: n/a

registration	type of aircraft	cn/fn	ex/EX*	mfd	del	powered by	mtow kg	configuration	selcal	name/fln/specialitites/remarks
☐ C-GFUT	De Havilland DHC-3 Otter	404	CAF9422	0060	0898	1 PW R-1340	3629			Floats

NOR-ROSE AIR (Charter) Services, Ltd — Fort Chipewyan, Alta.

Box 18, Fort Chipewyan, Alberta T0P 1B0, Canada ☎ (780) 697-3774 Tx: n/a Fax: (780) 697-3930 SITA: n/a
F: 1987 n/a Head: Mike Chadi Net: n/a Aircraft below MTOW 1361kg: Cessna 180.

registration	type of aircraft	cn/fn	ex/EX*	mfd	del	powered by	mtow kg	configuration	selcal	name/fln/specialitites/remarks
☐ C-GHGT	Cessna U206G Stationair 6 II	U20605874		0080		1 CO IO-520-F	1633			

NORTH AMERICAN AIRLINES, Ltd = NTM — Calgary, Alta

Box 630, 1441 Aviation Park NE, Calgary, Alberta T2E 8M7, Canada ☎ (403) 275-7700 Tx: none Fax: (403) 275-5947 SITA: n/a
F: 1978 40 Head: Don G. Hollier ICAO: NORTHAM Net: http://www.northamericanairlines.com

registration	type of aircraft	cn/fn	ex/EX*	mfd	del	powered by	mtow kg	configuration	selcal	name/fln/specialitites/remarks
☐ C-FTCE	Piper PA-31-310 Navajo	31-398	N9295Y	0069	0297	2 LY TIO-540-A2C	2948			
☐ C-FWAG	Piper PA-31-350 Navajo Chieftain	31-7652165	N62913	0076	1195	2 LY TIO-540-J2BD	3175			
☐ C-GLYG	Piper PA-31-350 Navajo Chieftain	31-7952036	N27901	0079	1195	2 LY TIO-540-J2BD	3175			
☐ C-GPAY	Piper PA-31-310 Navajo	31-8012090		0080	1195	2 LY TIO-540-A2C	2948			
☐ C-FNAL	Fairchild (Swearingen) SA227AC Metro III	AC-604	N3117V	0085	0695	2 GA TPE331-11U-611G	6577			
☐ C-GJTB	Fairchild (Swearingen) SA227AC Metro III	AC-552	N31113	0083	0496	2 GA TPE331-11U-611G	6577			
☐ C-GNAV	Fairchild (Swearingen) SA227AC Metro III	AC-586	N3115K	0084	0595	2 GA TPE331-11U-611G	6577			
☐ C-GNAZ	Hawker 700A (HS 125-700A)	257030 / NA0222	HB-VLJ	0078	0497	2 GA TFE731-3R-1H	11567		EG-BF	
☐ C-FTUT	Dassault Falcon 20C	21	N20LT	0066	0598	2 GE CF700-2D2	12000			
☐ C-GNAK	GAC (Grumman) G-159 Gulfstream I	154	G-BNKO	0065	0595	2 RR Dart 529-8X	16329			

NORTH CARIBOO AIR = NCB (North Cariboo Flying Service, Ltd dba) — Fort St. John, B.C. & Edmonton, Alta.

North Cariboo

PO Box 6789, Fort St. John, British Columbia V1J 4J2, Canada ☎ (250) 787-0311 Tx: n/a Fax: (250) 787-6086 SITA: n/a
F: 1957 26 Head: Dan Wuthrich ICAO: NORTH CARIBOO Net: n/a Aircraft below MTOW 1361kg: Cessna 172 & Piper PA-28.

registration	type of aircraft	cn/fn	ex/EX*	mfd	del	powered by	mtow kg	configuration	selcal	name/fln/specialitites/remarks
☐ C-GHXR	Cessna U206F Stationair II	U20603064		0076		1 CO IO-520-F	1633			
☐ C-GMJO	Cessna U206G Stationair 6 II	U20605536		0080	1298	1 CO IO-520-F	1633			
☐ C-GTST	Cessna TU206G Turbo Stationair 6 II	U20605619	N5300X	0080	0898	1 CO TSIO-520-M	1633			
☐ C-GLAC	Beech Baron 58	TH-339	N162JC	0073		2 CO IO-520-C	2449			
☐ C-GELD	Piper PA-31-310 Navajo	31-555	N6621L	0070	0797	2 LY TIO-540-A1A	2948			
☐ C-FMKD	Beech King Air B90	LJ-376	N300RV	0068	0392	2 PWC PT6A-20	4377			
☐ C-FMXY	Beech King Air 100	B-40	N923K	0070	0893	2 PWC PT6A-28	4808			
☐ C-FAWC	De Havilland DHC-6 Twin Otter 100	108	N204E	0068	0393	2 PWC PT6A-20	5252			
☐ C-FSXF	De Havilland DHC-6 Twin Otter 300	521	YV-528C	0077	1194	2 PWC PT6A-27	5670			
☐ C-GNPG	Beech 1900C Airliner	UB-71	N3069K	0087	1197	2 PWC PT6A-65B	7530			

NORTH CENTRAL HELICOPTERS, Ltd — La Ronge, Sask.

PO Box 1440, La Ronge, Saskatchewan S0J 1L0, Canada ☎ (306) 425-3100 Tx: none Fax: (306) 425-4116 SITA: n/a
F: 1985 8 Head: Brooke Ede Net: n/a Aircraft below MTOW 1361kg: Hughes 269C (300C)

registration	type of aircraft	cn/fn	ex/EX*	mfd	del	powered by	mtow kg	configuration	selcal	name/fln/specialitites/remarks
☐ C-FMAO	Bell 206B JetRanger	407		0069	0697	1 AN 250-C20	1451			cvtd 206A
☐ C-FARV	Bell 206L LongRanger	45117	N111WR	0077	0697	1 AN 250-C20B	1814			
☐ C-FJRG	Bell 206L-1 LongRanger II	45669	N48EA	0081	0591	1 AN 250-C28B	1882			
☐ C-FKEP	Bell 206L LongRanger	45024	N111AL	0075	0697	1 AN 250-C20B	1814			
☐ C-FVVR	Eurocopter (Aerosp.) AS350B AStar	1353	N9101N	0080	1095	1 TU Arriel 1B	1950			
☐ C-FCYW	Bell 204B	2004	N8589F	0063	0790	1 LY T5311A	3856			
☐ C-FDZE	Bell 204B	2055		0067	0494	1 LY T5311A	3856			
☐ C-GMHE	Bell 205A-1	30212	PT-HHZ	0075	0498	1 LY T5313B	4309			

NORTH COAST AVIATION, Ltd (Seasonal June-November ops only) — Goose Bay, Nfld.

PO Box 1036, Station C, Goose Bay, (Labrador), Newfoundland A0P 1C0, Canada ☎ (709) 896-5376 Tx: none Fax: (709) 896-5386 SITA: n/a
F: 1997 n/a Head: n/a Net: n/a

registration	type of aircraft	cn/fn	ex/EX*	mfd	del	powered by	mtow kg	configuration	selcal	name/fln/specialitites/remarks
☐ C-GANM	Cessna U206G Stationair	U20603886	N7347C	0077	0798	1 CO IO-520-F	1633			Floats
☐ C-GDWT	De Havilland DHC-2 Beaver I	1136	N4414W	0057	0798	1 PW R-985	2313			Floats
☐ C-GLQX	De Havilland DHC-3 Otter	362	N5321G	0060	0698	1 PW R-1340	3629			Floats

NORTHERN AIR CHARTER (P.R.), Inc. — Peace River, Alta.

Box 677, Grimshaw, Alberta T0H 1W0, Canada ☎ (780) 624-1911 Tx: none Fax: (780) 624-1155 SITA: n/a
F: 1980 n/a Head: Robert T. King Net: n/a Aircraft below MTOW 1361 kg: Cessna 150 & 172

registration	type of aircraft	cn/fn	ex/EX*	mfd	del	powered by	mtow kg	configuration	selcal	name/fln/specialitites/remarks
☐ C-GIRG	Cessna A185F Skywagon II	18504181		0081		1 CO IO-520-D	1520			
☐ C-GNAS	Cessna T210N Turbo Centurion II	21063233	N888BD	0079	1092	2 CO TSIO-520-R	1814			
☐ C-GNAC	Piper PA-310 Navajo C	31-7812106	N27707	0078		2 LY TIO-540-A2C	2948			
☐ C-GNAJ	Beech King Air A100	B-107	LN-AAH	0072	0596	2 PWC PT6A-28	5216			
☐ C-GNAR	Beech King Air A100	B-190	LN-AAG	0074	1195	2 PWC PT6A-28	5216	EMS		
☐ C-GNAX	Beech King Air 100	B-47	XB-CIP	0070	0894	2 PWC PT6A-28	4808	EMS		

NORTHERN AIR SUPPORT, Ltd — Kelowna, B.C.

6285 Kelowna Airport, Kelowna, British Columbia V1V 1S1, Canada ☎ (250) 765-0100 Tx: none Fax: (250) 765-0077 SITA: n/a
F: 1993 n/a Head: Louis Trottier Net: n/a

registration	type of aircraft	cn/fn	ex/EX*	mfd	del	powered by	mtow kg	configuration	selcal	name/fln/specialitites/remarks
☐ C-GCOM	Bell 206B JetRanger III	2767	N98RJ	0079	0398	1 AN 250-C20B	1451			
☐ C-GIHP	Bell 206B JetRanger	871	N144CB	0072	0696	1 AN 250-C20	1451			
☐ C-GCKX	Eurocopter (Aerosp.) AS350B AStar	1078	SE-JDD	0079	0698	1 TU Arriel 1B	1950			
☐ C-GDMM	Eurocopter (Aerosp.) AS350B2 AStar	2980		0097	0597	1 TU Arriel 1D1	2250			

NORTHERN DENE AIRWAYS, Ltd (formerly Fond du Lac Air, Ltd) — Fond du Lac, Sask.

Box 2106, Prince Albert, Saskatchewan S6V 6K1, Canada ☎ (306) 953-0070 Tx: none Fax: (306) 764-0550 SITA: n/a
F: 1989 25 Head: David J. Webster Net: n/a Aircraft below MTOW 1361kg: Cessna 180 (on Floats / Wheel-Skis)

registration	type of aircraft	cn/fn	ex/EX*	mfd	del	powered by	mtow kg	configuration	selcal	name/fln/specialitites/remarks
☐ C-FFNK	Cessna A185F Skywagon	18502126		0073	0797	1 CO IO-520-D	1520			Floats / Wheel-Skis
☐ C-GXZA	Cessna A185F Skywagon	18503019	N5211R	0076	0598	1 CO IO-520-D	1520			Floats / Wheel-Skis
☐ C-FGQD	De Havilland DHC-2 Beaver I	76		0050	0698	1 PW R-985	2313			Floats / Wheel-Skis
☐ C-FIFJ	De Havilland DHC-2 Beaver I	831		0054	0794	1 PW R-985	2313			Floats / Wheel-Skis
☐ C-GICM	Beech Baron C55 (95-C55)	TE-64	N171M	0066	1191	2 CO IO-520-C	2404			
☐ C-GPNO	Beech Baron B55 (95-B55)	TC-734	N174E	0064	1090	2 CO IO-470-L	2313			
☐ C-FWAK	Piper PA-31-310 Navajo	31-255	N407CA	0068	0495	2 LY TIO-540-A1A	2948			
☐ C-FZOW	Piper PA-31-310 Navajo	31-743	N7223L	0071	0798	2 LY TIO-540-A2C	2948			
☐ C-GGIQ	Piper PA-31-350 Navajo Chieftain	31-7552082	N59989	0075	1091	2 LY TIO-540-J2BD	3175			
☐ C-GQXX	Piper PA-31-350 Navajo Chieftain	31-7852009		0078	0396	2 LY TIO-540-J2BD	3175			
☐ C-GWUM	Piper PA-31-350 Navajo Chieftain	31-7405404	N66878	0074	0792	2 LY TIO-540-J2BD	3175			

NORTHERN LIGHTS AIR, Ltd — Smithers/Dease Lake/Tyhee Lake & Watson Lake, B.C.

Box 909, Smithers, British Columbia V0J 2N0, Canada ☎ (250) 847-4400 Tx: none Fax: (250) 847-4453 SITA: n/a
F: 1995 15 Head: Dan Young Net: n/a Aircraft below MTOW 1361kg: Cessna 172

registration	type of aircraft	cn/fn	ex/EX*	mfd	del	powered by	mtow kg	configuration	selcal	name/fln/specialitites/remarks
☐ C-GYIS	Cessna A185F Skywagon	18502895	N8679Z	0076	1095	1 CO IO-520-D	1520			Floats / Wheel-Skis
☐ C-GZXV	Cessna A185F Skywagon II	18503537		0078	0697	1 CO IO-520-D	1520			Floats
☐ C-GJNC	Cessna TU206G Turbo Stationair	U20603600	N7280N	0076	0895	1 CO TSIO-520-M	1633			
☐ CF-GWM	Cessna U206F Stationair	U20601802		0072	0995	1 CO IO-520-F	1633			
☐ C-FOED	De Havilland DHC-2 Turbo Beaver III	1591TB9		0065	0298	1 PWC PT6A-20	2436			Floats / Wheel-Skis
☐ C-FMPY	De Havilland DHC-3 Otter	324		0059	1095	1 PW R-1340	3629			Floats / Wheel-Skis
☐ C-GQXF	Beech King Air 200	BB-285		0077	0197	2 PWC PT6A-41	5670			

NORTHERN LIGHTS AIR SERVICE, Ltd — Goose Bay, Nfld

PO Box 1035, Stn A, Goose Bay, (Labrador), Newfoundland A0P 1S0, Canada ☎ (709) 896-2002 Tx: none Fax: (709) 896-2274 SITA: n/a
F: 1988 7 Head: George Hudson Net: n/a Aircraft below MTOW 1361kg: Piper PA-28

registration	type of aircraft	cn/fn	ex/EX*	mfd	del	powered by	mtow kg	configuration	selcal	name/fln/specialitites/remarks
☐ C-GBOL	Cessna A185E Skywagon	185-1099		0066	0797	1 CO IO-520-D	1520			
☐ C-FSVP	De Havilland DHC-3 Turbo Otter	28	N252KA	0053	1295	1 PWC PT6A-135A	3629			cvtd Otter

NORTHERN MOUNTAIN HELICOPTERS, Inc.

Prince George, B.C.

PO Box 368, Prince George, British Columbia V2L 4S2, Canada ☎ (250) 963-1200 Tx: 047-8027 n m h inc p Fax: (250) 963-9015 SITA: n/a
F: 1959 ✈✈✈ 300 Head: Walter Palubiski Net: http://www.forestindustry.com/nmh/ Aircraft below MTOW 1361 kg: Bell 47, Cessna 182 & Robinson R44 On order (Letter of Intent): 2 Bell Boeing 609 (tilt-rotor) for delivery 2003.

registration	type of aircraft	cn/fn	ex/ex*	mfd	del	powered by	mtow kg	configuration	selcal	name/fln/specialitites/remarks
☐ C-FLDW	MD Helicopters MD 500D (Hughes 369D)	280258D	N58185	0078	0595	1 AN 250-C20B	1361			
☐ C-FRZP	MD Helicopters MD 500D (Hughes 369D)	290455D	N58288	0079	0697	1 AN 250-C20B	1361			
☐ C-GDCM	MD Helicopters MD 500D (Hughes 369D)	310916D		0081	0489	1 AN 250-C20B	1361			
☐ C-GFOI	MD Helicopters MD 500D (Hughes 369D)	790542D	HB-XLP	0079	0990	1 AN 250-C20B	1361			
☐ C-GLHS	MD Helicopters MD 500D (Hughes 369D)	1100853D		0080		1 AN 250-C20B	1361			
☐ C-GLHW	MD Helicopters MD 500D (Hughes 369D)	110888D		0080		1 AN 250-C20B	1361			
☐ C-GNMG	MD Helicopters MD 500D (Hughes 369D)	300693D	N5065T	0080		1 AN 250-C20B	1361			
☐ C-GRYT	MD Helicopters MD 500D (Hughes 369D)	190448D		0079	1094	1 AN 250-C20B	1361			
☐ HP-1223CC	MD Helicopters MD 500D (Hughes 369D)	1100842D	C-GPDH	0080		1 AN 250-C20B	1361			lst Coclesana de Aviacion
☐ HP-1240CC	MD Helicopters MD 500D (Hughes 369D)	1270249D	C-GSZT	0078		1 AN 250-C20B	1361			lst Coclesana de Aviacion
☐ HP-1253CC	MD Helicopters MD 500D (Hughes 369D)	711031D	C-GESC	0081		1 AN 250-C20B	1361			lst Coclesana de Aviacion
☐ HP-1278CC	MD Helicopters MD 500D (Hughes 369D)	280260D	C-GRLC	0078		1 AN 250-C20B	1361			lst Coclesana de Aviacion
☐ C-FBQG	Bell 206B JetRanger	737		0071	0597	1 AN 250-C20	1451			cvtd 206A
☐ C-FGYD	Bell 206B JetRanger	1139	N59432	0073	1189	1 AN 250-C20	1451			
☐ C-FHMO	Bell 206B JetRanger	1078	N83165	0073	0894	1 AN 250-C20	1451			
☐ C-FJRH	Bell 206B JetRanger	456		0069	0795	1 AN 250-C20	1451			cvtd 206A
☐ C-FNMK	Bell 206B JetRanger	965		0073		1 AN 250-C20	1451			
☐ C-FNMW	Bell 206B JetRanger	665		0071		1 AN 250-C20	1451			cvtd 206A
☐ C-FOAI	Bell 206B JetRanger	773		0071	0493	1 AN 250-C20	1451			
☐ C-GAHF	Bell 206B JetRanger	1217	N83108	0073	0298	1 AN 250-C20	1451			
☐ C-GBSH	Bell 206B JetRanger	470	N22JC	0069		1 AN 250-C20	1451			cvtd 206A
☐ C-GCQT	Bell 206B JetRanger	492		0069	0795	1 AN 250-C20	1451			cvtd 206A
☐ C-GGRG	Bell 206B JetRanger III	1951		0076		1 AN 250-C20B	1451			cvtd JetRanger II
☐ C-GHGG	Bell 206B JetRanger	1342		0074		1 AN 250-C20	1451			
☐ C-GHHA	Bell 206B JetRanger	1577	N90076	0075		1 AN 250-C20	1451			
☐ C-GHHE	Bell 206B JetRanger II	1979	N9906K	0076	0797	1 AN 250-C20	1451			
☐ C-GHHN	Bell 206B JetRanger	1712		0075	0989	1 AN 250-C20	1451			
☐ C-GHHU	Bell 206B JetRanger II	2196		0077	1089	1 AN 250-C20	1451			
☐ C-GJVU	Bell 206B JetRanger	1731	N90304	0075	0689	1 AN 250-C20	1451			
☐ C-GLCD	Bell 206B JetRanger	1284		0074		1 AN 250-C20	1451			lst Peace Helicopters
☐ C-GNMB	Bell 206B JetRanger	1631		0075		1 AN 250-C20	1451			
☐ C-GNMH	Bell 206B JetRanger	1872		0072		1 AN 250-C20	1451			
☐ C-GNMT	Bell 206B JetRanger III	2295	N722CH	0077		1 AN 250-C20B	1451			
☐ C-GNMU	Bell 206B JetRanger III	2283	N88AM	0077	0294	1 AN 250-C20B	1451			
☐ C-GNMY	Bell 206B JetRanger	132	N6261N	0068	0391	1 AN 250-C20	1451			cvtd 206A
☐ C-GNNH	Bell 206B JetRanger	1632		0075	0697	1 AN 250-C20	1451			
☐ C-GNNK	Bell 206B JetRanger	1639		0075	0692	1 AN 250-C20	1451			
☐ C-GORO	Bell 206B JetRanger II	2086	N16668	0076		1 AN 250-C20	1451			
☐ C-GPFR	Bell 206B JetRanger	483		0069	0794	1 AN 250-C20	1451			cvtd 206A
☐ C-GTVL	Bell 206B JetRanger II	2166		0077	0994	1 AN 250-C20	1451			
☐ C-GUYI	Bell 206B JetRanger III	2543	N15SJ	0078	0297	1 AN 250-C20B	1451			
☐ C-GUYM	Bell 206B JetRanger	1687	N90191	0075	0297	1 AN 250-C20	1451			
☐ C-GVIF	Bell 206B JetRanger	782		0072		1 AN 250-C20	1451			
☐ C-GWML	Bell 206B JetRanger	269	N30AL	0068	0593	1 AN 250-C20	1451			cvtd 206A
☐ C-GXBX	Bell 206B JetRanger	476	N71HP	0069	0493	1 AN 250-C20	1451			cvtd 206A
☐ HP-1268CC	Bell 206B JetRanger III	2387	C-GNME	0078		1 AN 250-C20B	1451			lst Coclesana de Aviacion
☐ HP-1351CC	Bell 206B JetRanger	291	C-GTQD	0068	0598	1 AN 250-C20	1451			lst Coclesana de Aviacion / cvtd 206A
☐ C-FJCH	Bell 206L-1 LongRanger III	45737	N144JD	0081	0496	1 AN 250-C30P	1882			cvtd LongRanger II
☐ C-GVIW	Bell 206L-1 LongRanger II	45410		0080	0597	1 AN 250-C28B	1882			
☐ C-FSPR	Eurocopter (Aerosp.) AS350B AStar	1814	ZK-HHY	0085	1095	1 TU Arriel 1B	1950			
☐ C-FXHS	Eurocopter (Aerosp.) AS350B1 AStar	2248		0089	0196	1 TU Arriel 1D	2200			
☐ C-GNME	Eurocopter (Aerosp.) AS350BA AStar	2826		0094	0195	1 TU Arriel 1B	2100			
☐ C-GNMJ	Eurocopter (Aerosp.) AS350BA AStar	2829		0094	0195	1 TU Arriel 1B	2100			
☐ C-GNMP	Eurocopter (Aerosp.) AS350B AStar	1040	C-GSKI	0078	0996	1 TU Arriel 1B	1950			
☐ C-GOLV	Eurocopter (Aerosp.) AS350BA AStar	1108		0079		1 TU Arriel 1B	2100			lst Peace Helicopters / cvtd AS350B
☐ C-GPHM	Eurocopter (Aerosp.) AS350B2 AStar	2488		0091		1 TU Arriel 1D1	2250			lst Peace Helicopters
☐ C-GPHQ	Eurocopter (Aerosp.) AS350B1 AStar	2017	N855NM	0087		1 TU Arriel 1D	2200			lst Peace Helicopters
☐ C-GPHR	Eurocopter (Aerosp.) AS350B1 AStar	2268		0089		1 TU Arriel 1D	2200			lst Peace Helicopters
☐ C-GPTC	Eurocopter (Aerosp.) AS350B1 AStar	2092	OY-HDY	0088	0593	1 TU Arriel 1D	2200			
☐ C-GPTL	Eurocopter (Aerosp.) AS350B2 AStar	2103	OY-HEH	0088	0593	1 TU Arriel 1D1	2250			cvtd AS350B1
☐ C-GPTY	Eurocopter (Aerosp.) AS350B2 AStar	2360	D-HFSA	0090	0797	1 TU Arriel 1D1	2250			
☐ C-GREV	Eurocopter (Aerosp.) AS350B AStar	1039	N98TV	0078	0298	1 TU Arriel 1B	1950			
☐ C-GTPK	Eurocopter (Aerosp.) AS350B1 AStar	2177	ZK-HTL	0089	1298	1 TU Arriel 1D	2200			
☐ C-GYHT	Eurocopter (Aerosp.) AS350B AStar	1340	VH-HBD	0080		1 TU Arriel 1B	1950			lst Peace Helicopters / cvtd AS350D
☐ C-GZPY	Eurocopter (Aerosp.) AS350B AStar	1321	N5769V	0080	0596	1 TU Arriel 1B	1950			
☐ HP-1349CC	Eurocopter (Aerosp.) AS350B AStar	1317	C-FPTR	0080	0498	1 TU Arriel 1B	1950			lst Coclesana de Aviacion
☐ C-FBWB	Piper PA-31-310 Navajo C	31-7912094	N35368	0079	0698	2 LY TIO-540-A2C	2948			
☐ C-FLIN	Piper PA-31-350 Navajo Chieftain	31-8152013	N81TT	0081	0597	2 LY TIO-540-J2BD	3175			
☐ C-GAHN	Bell 204B	2044	N1308X	0066		1 LY T5313B	3856			lst Peace Helicopters
☐ C-GSHK	Bell 204B	2067	Thai 920	0067		1 LY T5311A	3856			lst Peace Helicopters
☐ C-FKHQ	Bell 205A-1	30030		0068		1 LY T5313B	4309			
☐ C-FNMO	Bell 205A-1	30128	N58057	0073	0490	1 LY T5313B	4309			
☐ C-FNMQ	Bell 205A-1	30058	N1483W	0069	0490	1 LY T5313B	4309			
☐ C-GAYB	Bell 205A-1	30295		0079		1 LY T5313B	4309			
☐ C-FCAP	Bell 212	30923	XA-ECQ	0079	0597	2 PWC PT6T-3 TwinPac	5080			
☐ C-FNIL	Bell 212	30798	N8224V	0075	0593	2 PWC PT6T-3 TwinPac	5080			
☐ C-FNMD	Bell 212	30730	PT-HRK	0075	0593	2 PWC PT6T-3 TwinPac	5080			
☐ C-FWDV	Bell 212	30973	N2768N	0079	0895	2 PWC PT6T-3 TwinPac	5080			lst Deh Cho Helicopters
☐ C-GERH	Bell 212	30768	N42434	0076	0394	2 PWC PT6T-3 TwinPac	5080			
☐ C-GGAT	Bell 212	30846	XA-HIW	0077	1293	2 PWC PT6T-3 TwinPac	5080			
☐ C-GOKX	Bell 212	30680	VH-OHC	0075		2 PWC PT6T-3 TwinPac	5080			
☐ C-FZLS	Sikorsky S-61N	61033	N4721S	0061	0597	2 GE CT58-140-1	9318			
☐ C-FZLU	Sikorsky S-61N	61468	N6968R	0069	0197	2 GE CT58-140-1	9318			

NORTHERN SKY AVIATION (477470 Alberta, Ltd dba)

High Level, Alta.

PO Box 205, High Level, Alberta T0H 1Z0, Canada ☎ (780) 926-3672 Tx: none Fax: (780) 926-4460 SITA: n/a
F: 1992 ✈✈✈ n/a Head: n/a Net: n/a Operates charter flights with Piper PA-31 aircraft, currently leased from private when required.

NORTH OF SIXTY FLYING SERVICES, Inc.

Minneapolis-St. Paul Int'l, MN (USA)

14375 23 rd Avenue North, Plymouth, MN 55447, USA ☎ (612) 745-7888 Tx: none Fax: (612) 745-7979 SITA: n/a
F: 1993 ✈✈✈ n/a Head: Clark Jenny Net: n/a

registration	type of aircraft	cn/fn	ex/ex*	mfd	del	powered by	mtow kg	configuration	selcal	name/fln/specialitites/remarks
☐ C-FMBY	Cessna 206 Super Skywagon	206-0064		0064	0693	1 CO IO-520-A	1588			Amphibian
☐ C-FAYR	De Havilland DHC-3 Otter	436	N9744F	0062	0793	1 PW R-1340	3629			Amphibian
☐ C-FTOK	De Havilland DHC-3 Otter	207	IM 1709	0057	0696	1 PW R-1340	3629			Amphibian

NORTH SHORE AIR (Subsidiary of Hicks & Lawrence, Ltd / Division of 504934 Ontario, Inc.)

St. Thomas, Ont.

PO Box 519, St. Thomas, Ontario N5P 3V6, Canada ☎ (519) 633-1884 Tx: none Fax: (519) 631-8289 SITA: n/a
F: 1982 ✈✈✈ n/a Head: Twain Hicks Net: http://www.hickslawrence.com.

registration	type of aircraft	cn/fn	ex/ex*	mfd	del	powered by	mtow kg	configuration	selcal	name/fln/specialitites/remarks
☐ C-FBME	Cessna 337G Super Skymaster II	33701734	N146HA	0076		2 CO IO-360-G	2100			
☐ C-FBNX	Cessna 337G Super Skymaster II	33701738	N53614	0076		2 CO IO-360-G	2100			
☐ C-FBRG	Cessna 337G Super Skymaster II	33701695	N26286	0076		2 CO IO-360-G	2100			
☐ C-FBRH	Cessna 337G Super Skymaster II	33701662	N53496	0075		2 CO IO-360-G	2100			
☐ C-FBRK	Cessna 337H Super Skymaster II	33701884	N75BP	0079		2 CO IO-360-GB	2100			
☐ C-FIGS	Cessna 337G Super Skymaster II	33701728	N714GP	0076	0590	2 CO IO-360-G	2100			
☐ C-FIKM	Cessna 337G Super Skymaster	33701588	N72448	0074	0796	2 CO IO-360-G	2100			
☐ C-FSIW	Cessna 337G Super Skymaster	33701571	N72377	0074	0796	2 CO IO-360-G	2100			
☐ C-FSIY	Cessna 337H Super Skymaster II	33701949	N959CC	0080	0796	2 CO IO-360-GB	2100			
☐ C-FSIZ	Cessna 337G Super Skymaster II	33701632	N53450	0075	0796	2 CO IO-360-GB	2100			
☐ C-GDQU	Cessna 337G Super Skymaster II	33701607	N53413	0075		2 CO IO-360-G	2100			
☐ C-GNRO	Cessna 337D Super Skymaster	337-1101	N86169	0069	0796	2 CO IO-360-C/D	1996			
☐ C-GWDU	Cessna 337B Super Skymaster	337-0665	N2365S	0067	0692	2 CO IO-360-C/D	1950			
☐ CF-JIP	Cessna 337G Super Skymaster	33701534		0073	0796	2 CO IO-360-G	2100			
☐ C-FBPA	Piper PA-23-250 Aztec D	27-4434	N13783	0060	0790	2 LY IO-540-C4B5	2359			
☐ C-GJLO	Twin (Aero) Shrike Commander 500S	500S-1796-11	N5009E	0068		2 LY IO-540-E1B5	3062			

NORTH STAR AIR, Ltd
Pickle Lake, Ont.

PO Box 38, Pickle Lake, Ontario P0V 3A0, Canada ☎ (807) 928-2346 Tx: none Fax: (807) 928-9918 SITA: n/a
F: 1998 ☨☨☨ n/a Head: n/a Net: n/a Aircraft below MTOW 1361kg: Cessna 182 (on Floats / Wheel-Skis)

registration	type of aircraft	cn/fn	ex/ex*	mfd	del	powered by	mtow kg	configuration	selcal	name/fln/specialitites/remarks
☐ C-GMGD	De Havilland DHC-2 Beaver I	519	N67091	0054	0598	1 PW R-985	2313			Floats / Wheel-Skis
☐ C-GZBQ	De Havilland DHC-2 Beaver I	919	55-0697	0056	1298	1 PW R-985	2313			Floats / Wheel-Skis
☐ C-GCQA	De Havilland DHC-3 Otter	77	N129JH	0055	0398	1 PW R-1340	3629			Floats / Wheel-Skis

NORTH VANCOUVER AIRLINES, Ltd = VL / NRV
Vancouver-Int'l, B.C.

5360 Airport Road South, Richmond, British Columbia V7B 1B4, Canada ☎ (604) 278-1608 Tx: none Fax: (604) 278-2608 SITA: n/a
F: 1994 ☨☨☨ 10 Head: Zoltan Kuun ICAO: NORVAN Net: n/a

registration	type of aircraft	cn/fn	ex/ex*	mfd	del	powered by	mtow kg	configuration	selcal	name/fln/specialitites/remarks
☐ C-GTXF	Cessna U206G Stationair	U20603647	N7390N	0077	0797	1 CO IO-520-F	1633			
☐ C-FLGW	Piper PA-31-310 Navajo	31-557	N6622L	0070	0794	2 LY TIO-540-A2B	2948			
☐ C-GDJR	Piper PA-31-310 Navajo	31-289	N9223Y	0068	0894	2 LY TIO-540-A2B	2948			
☐ C-GRNK	Piper PA-31-350 Navajo Chieftain	31-7652112	N59888	0076	0797	2 LY TIO-540-J2BD	3175			
☐ C-GZFK	Piper PA-31-350 Navajo Chieftain	31-7752107	N303CH	0077	1194	2 LY TIO-540-J2BD	3175			
☐ C-GNVB	Beech King Air A100	B-143	N151U	0072	1096	2 PWC PT6A-28	5216			
☐ C-GPCB	Beech King Air 100	B-45	N704S	0069	0496	2 PWC PT6A-28	4808			
☐ C-	BAe 3101 Jetstream 31	799	N423UE	0288		2 GA TPE331-10UG-513H	6900	Y19		to be lsf BAMT 0599
☐ C-	BAe 3101 Jetstream 31	782	N422UE	1187		2 GA TPE331-10UG-513H	6900	Y19		to be lsf BAMT 0599
☐ C-	BAe 3101 Jetstream 31	804	N421UE	0388		2 GA TPE331-10UG-513H	6900	Y19		to be lsf BAMT 0599

NORTHWARD AIR, Ltd
Dawson Creek, B.C.

Box 506, Dawson Creek, British Columbia V1G 4H4, Canada ☎ (250) 786-5548 Tx: none Fax: (250) 782-8108 SITA: n/a
F: 1988 ☨☨☨ 4 Head: Larry Moody Net: n/a Aircraft below MTOW 1361 kg: Cessna 172.

registration	type of aircraft	cn/fn	ex/ex*	mfd	del	powered by	mtow kg	configuration	selcal	name/fln/specialitites/remarks
☐ C-GLKM	Helio H-391B Courier	034	N74037	0056		1 LY GO-435-C2B2	1361			
☐ C-FOMF	Cessna 185A Skywagon	185-0423		0062	0790	1 CO IO-520-D	1492			
☐ CF-SLV	Cessna U206A Super Skywagon	U206-0412		0065	0693	1 CO IO-520-A	1633			

NORTHWAY AVIATION, Ltd = NAL
Arnes & Pine Dock, Man.

PO Box 70, Arnes, Manitoba R0C 0C0, Canada ☎ (204) 642-5631 Tx: none Fax: (204) 642-8160 SITA: n/a
F: 1972 ☨☨☨ 20 Head: Jim Johnson ICAO: NORTHWAY Net: n/a Aircraft below MTOW 1361 kg: Cessna 180

registration	type of aircraft	cn/fn	ex/ex*	mfd	del	powered by	mtow kg	configuration	selcal	name/fln/specialitites/remarks
☐ CF-ZZP	Cessna A185E Skywagon	18501843		0071		1 CO IO-520-D	1520			Floats / Wheel-Skis
☐ C-GWAZ	Cessna U206F Stationair	U20602400		0074		1 CO IO-520-F	1633			Floats / Wheel-Skis
☐ C-FBHP	Cessna 207A Stationair 8 II	20700647	N75857	0080	1290	1 CO IO-520-F	1724			
☐ C-FQQG	De Havilland DHC-2 Beaver I	1675	FAP 383	0067		1 PW R-985	2313			Floats / Wheel-Skis
☐ C-FBKK	Piper PA-31-310 Navajo	31-734		0071	0593	2 LY TIO-540-A2C	2948			
☐ C-GYYK	Piper PA-31-350 Navajo Chieftain	31-7752029	N63680	0077	0795	2 LY TIO-540-J2BD	3175			
☐ C-GVCJ	Britten-Norman BN-2A Islander	90	N871JA	0069		2 LY O-540-E4C5	2722			
☐ C-GJJM	Cessna 208 Caravan I	20800029	N9370F	0085	0792	1 PWC PT6A-114	3311			Viking Express
☐ CF-UKN	De Havilland DHC-3 Otter	456		0065		1 PW R-1340	3629			Floats / Wheel-Skis

NORTHWESTERN AIR = J3 / PLR (Northwestern Air Lease, Ltd dba)
Fort Smith, N.W.T.

Box 23, Fort Smith, Northwest Territories X0E 0P0, Canada ☎ (867) 872-2216 Tx: none Fax: (867) 872-2214 SITA: n/a
F: 1965 ☨☨☨ 25 Head: Terry Harrold IATA: 325 ICAO: POLARIS Net: n/a

registration	type of aircraft	cn/fn	ex/ex*	mfd	del	powered by	mtow kg	configuration	selcal	name/fln/specialitites/remarks
☐ C-GPZL	Cessna 337G Super Skymaster II	33701742		0076	0695	2 CO IO-360-G	2100			
☐ C-GNAE	AAC (Ted Smith) Aerostar 600	60-0044-99	N614SG	0070	0595	2 LY IO-540-G1B5	2495			
☐ C-GRHV	Cessna 401	401-0228	N8083F	0068	1188	2 CO TSIO-520-E	2858			
☐ C-FWXE	Cessna 402	402-0162		0068	0696	2 CO TSIO-520-E	2858			
☐ C-GNAH	Beech 99 Airliner	U-107	N207BH	0069	0194	2 PWC PT6A-20	4717	Y15		
☐ C-GNAL	Beech 99 Airliner	U-57	TF-ELD	0068	0193	2 PWC PT6A-20	4717	Y15		
☐ C-FCPE	BAe 3112 Jetstream 31	825	G-31-825*	0088	0195	2 GA TPE331-10UGR-516H	6950	Y19		
☐ C-FNAM	BAe 3112 Jetstream 31	767	N767JX	0087	0897	2 GA TPE331-10UGR-513H	6950	Y19		

NORTHWESTERN HELICOPTERS, Ltd
Big River, Sask.

Box 670, Big River, Saskatchewan S0J 0E0, Canada ☎ (306) 469-4816 Tx: none Fax: (306) 469-4599 SITA: n/a
F: 1987 ☨☨☨ n/a Head: Linda Peterson Net: n/a

registration	type of aircraft	cn/fn	ex/ex*	mfd	del	powered by	mtow kg	configuration	selcal	name/fln/specialitites/remarks
☐ C-GCKV	MD Helicopters MD 500D (Hughes 369D)	570141D	N505SH	0077	0398	1 AN 250-C20B	1361			
☐ C-GJMP	MD Helicopters MD 500D (Hughes 369D)	310915D	N47861	0081	0698	1 AN 250-C20B	1361			
☐ C-GREP	MD Helicopters MD 500E (Hughes 369E)	0242E	N536BH	0087	0898	1 AN 250-C20B	1361			
☐ C-FWGS	Bell 206B JetRanger	755	N505TV	0072	0596	1 AN 250-C20	1451			
☐ C-FFZM	Sikorsky S-58E	58-202		0055		1 WR R-1820	5897			

NORTHWEST FLYING, Inc. (formerly Northwestern Flying Services, Ltd / Seasonal May-October ops only)
Nestor Falls-SPB, Ont.

PO Box 6, Nestor Falls, Ontario P0X 1K0, Canada ☎ (807) 484-2126 Tx: none Fax: (807) 484-2275 SITA: n/a
F: 1987 ☨☨☨ 8 Head: Jack Pope Net: n/a Aircraft below MTOW 1361kg: Cessna 180 (on Floats)

registration	type of aircraft	cn/fn	ex/ex*	mfd	del	powered by	mtow kg	configuration	selcal	name/fln/specialitites/remarks
☐ C-FNFO	De Havilland DHC-2 Beaver I	819	N80LC	0054	0591	1 PW R-985	2313			Floats
☐ C-GEBL	De Havilland DHC-2 Beaver I	1068	N33466	0056		1 PW R-985	2313			Floats
☐ C-GYYS	De Havilland DHC-3 Otter	276	N1UW	0058		1 PW R-1340	3629			Floats
☐ CF-NKL	Beech C-45H (18)	AF-378		0053		2 PW R-985	3969			Floats

NORTH WEST GEOMATICS, Ltd = PTO (Sister co. of North West Group Inc., Denver/USA/formerly North West Survey Corp. (Yukon) Ltd)
Edmonton, Alta. & Denver, CO (USA)

11941-121 Street, Bldg 38, Municipal Airport, Edmonton, Alberta T5L 4H7, Canada ☎ (780) 453-6751 Tx: none Fax: (780) 455-3500 SITA: n/a
F: 1988 ☨☨☨ 12 Head: John F. Welter ICAO: PHOTO Net: n/a

registration	type of aircraft	cn/fn	ex/ex*	mfd	del	powered by	mtow kg	configuration	selcal	name/fln/specialitites/remarks
☐ N15NW	Cessna 340A II	340A0533	C-GNWS	0078		2 CO TSIO-520-NB	2717	Photo/Survey		single camera
☐ C-GNWC	Cessna 335 II	335-0001	N14NW	0080		2 CO TSIO-520-EB	2717	Photo/Survey		single camera
☐ C-GNWL	Cessna 414A Chancellor III	414A0223	N5692C	0079	0593	2 CO TSIO-520-NB	3062	Photo/Survey		single camera
☐ N13NW	Cessna 441 Conquest II	441-0090	C-GNWM	0079		2 GA TPE331-10-401S	4468	Photo/Survey		dual camera
☐ N14NW	Cessna 441 Conquest II	441-0171	C-GKMA	0080	0996	2 GA TPE331-8-401S	4468	Photo/Survey		dual camera

NORTHWEST INTERNATIONAL JET (Northwest International Airways, Ltd dba)
Vancouver-Int'l, B.C. & Yellowknife, N.W.T.

125-5360 Airport Road South, Richmond, British Columbia V7B 1B4, Canada ☎ (604) 273-5573 Tx: none Fax: (604) 273-4009 SITA: n/a
F: 1980 ☨☨☨ n/a Head: Robert Engle Net: n/a

registration	type of aircraft	cn/fn	ex/ex*	mfd	del	powered by	mtow kg	configuration	selcal	name/fln/specialitites/remarks
☐ C-GLMK	Cessna 550 Citation II	550-0100	N140DA	0079	0390	2 PWC JT15D-4	6033			cvtd 551 cn 551-0143
☐ C-GNWM	Cessna 550 Citation II	550-0410	N46MF	0082	0795	2 PWC JT15D-4	6033			

NORTHWOODS FLYING SERVICE (Gary K. Shelton dba)
Hudson's Hope, B.C.

Box 119, Hudson's Hope, British Columbia V0C 1V0, Canada ☎ (604) 783-9121 Tx: n/a Fax: (604) 783-9247 SITA: n/a
F: 1992 ☨☨☨ 1 Head: Gary K. Shelton Net: n/a Aircraft below MTOW 1361kg: Taylorcraft BL-65.

registration	type of aircraft	cn/fn	ex/ex*	mfd	del	powered by	mtow kg	configuration	selcal	name/fln/specialitites/remarks
☐ C-FISB	Cessna 210K Centurion II	21059415	N8155G	0071	1292	1 CO IO-520-L	1724			

NORTH WRIGHT AIRWAYS, Ltd = HW / NWL (formerly Nort Wright Air, Ltd & Nahanni Air Services, Ltd)
Norman Wells, Good Hope & Deline, N.W.T.

Bag Service 2200, Norman Wells, Northwest Territories X0E 0V0, Canada ☎ (867) 587-2288 Tx: none Fax: (867) 587-2962 SITA: n/a
F: 1986 ☨☨☨ 30 Head: Warren Wright ICAO: NORTHWRIGHT Net: n/a Aircraft below MTOW 1361kg: Cessna 172.

registration	type of aircraft	cn/fn	ex/ex*	mfd	del	powered by	mtow kg	configuration	selcal	name/fln/specialitites/remarks
☐ C-GHDT	Helio H-295 Super Courier	1401	N6327V	0067		1 LY GO-480-G1D6	1542			
☐ CF-DMA	Cessna U206F Stationair	U20602017		0073	0696	1 CO IO-520-F	1588			Floats / Wheel-Skis
☐ C-FBAX	Cessna 207 Skywagon	20700355	N1755U	0076	0595	1 CO IO-520-F	1724			
☐ CF-WHP	Cessna 337C Super Skymaster	337-0895		0068		2 CO IO-360-C/D	1996			
☐ CF-ZIZ	Fairchild (Pilatus) PC-6/B1-H2 Porter	2009	N353FH	0066		1 PWC PT6A-20	2200			Floats / Wheel-Skis
☐ C-GZGO	Britten-Norman BN-2A-26 Islander	2017	N59360	0078		2 LY O-540-E4C5	2994			
☐ C-GJNH	Piper PA-31-350 Navajo Chieftain	31-7952240	N35429	0079	1192	2 LY TIO-540-J2BD	3175			
☐ C-GZIZ	Cessna 208B Grand Caravan	208B0546		0096	0696	1 PWC PT6A-114A	3969			
☐ C-FKHD	Beech 99 Airliner	U-11	F-BRUN	0068	0393	2 PWC PT6A-20	4717			
☐ C-GAWW	Beech 99A Airliner	U-137	FAC 300	0070	1298	2 PWC PT6A-27	4717			
☐ C-GXVX	Beech King Air 100	B-18	N7007N	0070	0398	2 PWC PT6A-28	4808			
☐ C-GRDD	De Havilland DHC-6 Twin Otter 100	54	N8081N	0067	0889	2 PWC PT6A-20	5252			Floats / Wheel-Skis

NOSTALGIC FLIGHTS, Ltd
Wetaskiwin, Alta.

PO Box 6151, Wetaskiwin, Alberta T9A 2E9, Canada ☎ (780) 352-9978 Tx: n/a Fax: (780) 352-8507 SITA: n/a
F: 1994 ☨☨☨ n/a Head: Francis B. Davis Net: n/a Aircraft below MTOW 1361kg: De Havilland DH.82C.

registration	type of aircraft	cn/fn	ex/ex*	mfd	del	powered by	mtow kg	configuration	selcal	name/fln/specialitites/remarks
☐ CF-FBD	CCF Harvard 4 (N.A. T-6J)	CCF4-98	RCAF 20307	0052	0394	1 PW R-1340	2608	1 Pax		Scenic flights

NRC Flight Research Laboratory (Division of National Research Council Canada / Conseil National de Recherches Canada)
Ottawa, Ont.

Montreal Road, Ottawa, Ontario K1A 0R6, Canada ☎ (613) 998-3071 Tx: 0533145 nrc admin ot Fax: (613) 952-1704 SITA: n/a
F: 1946 ☨☨☨ 55 Head: Dr. Barrie Leach Net: n/a Non-commercial state organisation conducting experimental/research aerial missions.

registration	type of aircraft	cn/fn	ex/ex*	mfd	del	powered by	mtow kg	configuration	selcal	name/fln/specialitites/remarks
☐ C-FZUQ	Bell 206B JetRanger	629		0071		1 AN 250-C20	1451	Research		cvtd 206A

☐ C-FPTP	CCF Harvard 4 (N.A. T-6J)	CCF4-1	RCAF 20210	0051		1 PW R-1340	2608	Research		
☐ C-FYZV	Bell 205A-1	30055		0069		1 LY T5313B	4309	Research		
☐ C-FPGV	Bell 412	36034	N3101P	0092	0593	2 PWC PT6T-3B TwinPac	5398	Research		
☐ C-FPOK	De Havilland DHC-6 Twin Otter 200	116	N594MA	0068	0372	2 PWC PT6A-20	5252	Research		
☐ C-FSKH	Canadair T-33AN Silver Star	379	RCAF 21379	0055		1 RR Nene 10	7620	Research		
☐ C-FWIS	Canadair T-33AN Silver Star	590	RCAF 21590	0055		1 RR Nene 10	7620	Research		
☐ C-FIGD	Dassault Falcon 20C	109	CAF 117506	0067	0790	2 GE CF700-2D2	12400	Research		
☐ C-FNRC	Convair 580	473	N916R	0057	0873	2 AN 501-D13D	24766	Research		cvtd CV440-3

NT AIR = 4R / NTA (Northern Thunderbird Air, Ltd dba) — Prince George, Fort St.James & Mackenzie, B.C.

4245 Hangar Road, RR8, Site 10, Comp. 29, Prince George, British Columbia V2N 4M6, Canada ☎ (250) 963-9611 Tx: none Fax: (250) 963-1314 SITA: n/a
F: 1971 ⁂ 43 Head: Vernon Martin ICAO: THUNDERBIRD Net: http://www.netbistro.com/ntair/index.html

☐ C-GIPB	Piper PA-31-350 Navajo Chieftain	31-7852170		0078	0192	2 LY TIO-540-J2BD	3175			
☐ C-FCGC	Beech Catpass 200	BB-236	N48KA	0077	0396	2 PWC PT6A-41	5670			cvtd King Air 200, cvn 7

NUELTIN LAKE AIR SERVICE, Ltd (Affiliated with Nueltin Flying Lodge, Ltd / Seasonal June-August ops only) — Nueltin Lake, Man.

Box 500, Alonsa, Manitoba R0H 0A0, Canada ☎ (204) 767-2330 Tx: none Fax: (204) 767-2331 SITA: n/a
F: 1986 ⁂ 3 Head: Garry & Lois Gurke Net: n/a Aircraft below MTOW 1361kg: Cessna 180 (on Floats)

☐ C-FDCL	Cessna U206G Stationair	U20603542	N8790Q	0077	0291	1 CO IO-520-F	1633			Floats
☐ C-FSAP	Noorduyn Norseman VI (UC-64A)	231	43-5240	0043		1 PW R-1340	3357			Floats
☐ C-FYLZ	De Havilland DHC-3 Otter	257	VH-SBR	0058	0998	1 PW R-1340	3629			Floats

NUNASI HELICOPTERS, Inc. — Yellowknife, N.W.T.

9 Yellowknife Airport, Yellowknife, Northwest Territories X1A 3T2, Canada ☎ (867) 873-3306 Tx: none Fax: (867) 873-3307 SITA: n/a
F: 1996 ⁂ n/a Head: Barry Wilson Net: n/a

☐ C-GSRH	Bell 212	30618	N208DS	0074	0297	2 PWC PT6T-3 TwinPac	5080			

OAKHILLS AVIATION, Ltd — Stirling, Ont.

RR 3, Trenton, Ontario K8V 5P6, Canada ☎ (613) 394-5966 Tx: none Fax: (613) 394-0887 SITA: n/a
F: 1993 ⁂ 5 Head: William R. MacKenzie Net: n/a Aircraft below MTOW 1361kg: Cessna 150, 172 & Piper PA-28

☐ C-GQWF	Piper PA-23-150 Apache	23-367	N1324P	0054	0797	2 LY O-320-A1A	1588			

OCEANVIEW HELICOPTERS, Ltd — Powell River, B.C.

7490 Duncan Street, Powell River, British Columbia V8A 1W7, Canada ☎ (604) 485-7490 Tx: none Fax: (604) 485-7460 SITA: n/a
F: 1989 ⁂ n/a Head: Marv Deans Net: n/a

☐ C-FOHE	MD Helicopters MD 500D (Hughes 369D)	410942D	N500DW	0081	0198	1 AN 250-C20B	1361			
☐ C-GPGE	MD Helicopters MD 500D (Hughes 369D)	1160022D		0076	1294	1 AN 250-C20B	1361			
☐ C-FOHL	Bell 206B JetRanger II	2078	C-GMDK	0070	0195	1 AN 250-C20	1451			
☐ C-GNRH	Bell 206L-1 LongRanger II	45218	N2777B	0079	1295	1 AN 250-C28B	1882			

ODESSEY AVIATION, Ltd — Toronto-Int'l, Ont.

2450 Derry Road East, Hangar 2, Mississauga, Ontario L5S 1B2, Canada ☎ (905) 672-0880 Tx: none Fax: (905) 672-2790 SITA: n/a
F: 1982 ⁂ 31 Head: Nigel Argent Net: http://www.cwings.com

☐ C-GXXD	Socata TBM 700	75	F-OHBJ	0092	0194	1 PWC PT6A-64	2984			
☐ C-GQCC	Piper PA-31T Cheyenne II	31T-7620033	LV-LZO	0076	0597	2 PWC PT6A-28	4082			
☐ C-FLTL	Cessna 650 Citation III	650-0007	N929DS	0083	0690	2 GA TFE731-3C-100S	9526			

OKANAGAN AVIATION SERVICES, Ltd (formerly Tri-Lake Flight Centre, Ltd) — Vernon, B.C.

6200 Trensen Road, Vernon, British Columbia V1H 1N5, Canada ☎ (250) 549-5221 Tx: none Fax: (250) 549-5268 SITA: n/a
F: 1982 ⁂ n/a Head: Stephen Drinkwater Net: n/a Aircraft below MTOW 1361kg: Cessna 152 & 172

☐ C-FRLL	Piper PA-30-160 Twin Comanche	30-72	N7060Y	0064	0197	2 LY IO-320-B1A	1633			

OMEGA AIR, Corp. — Vancouver-Int'l, B.C.

4360 Agar Drive, Richmond, British Columbia V7B 1A3, Canada ☎ (604) 273-5311 Tx: none Fax: (604) 273-8991 SITA: n/a
F: 1997 ⁂ n/a Head: John Morras Net: n/a

☐ C-GBFH	Bell 206B JetRanger II	2171		0077	0697	1 AN 250-C20	1451			
☐ C-GOMH	Bell 206B JetRanger III	3992	N188ND	0087	0998	1 AN 250-C20J	1451			
☐ C-GFCC	Bell 407	53031		0096	0697	1 AN 250-C47B	2268			

ONTARIO AIRCRAFT SALES & LEASING, Inc. = (OASL) — Peterborough, Ont.

RR 5, Peterborough, Ontario K9J 6X6, Canada ☎ (705) 742-9631 Tx: n/a Fax: (705) 742-7233 SITA: n/a
F: n/a ⁂ n/a Head: John Gillespie Net: n/a
Used turboprop-aircraft leasing & sales company. Owner / lessor of following (main) aircraft types: Beechcraft 99, Beechcraft 1900, Beechcraft King Air, & Convair 580.
Aircraft leased form OASL are listed & mentioned as such under the leasing carriers.

ONTARIO BOREAL AIR SERVICES, Ltd — Dryden, Ont.

Box 239, Dryden, Ontario P8N 2Y8, Canada ☎ (807) 755-2307 Tx: none Fax: (807) 755-2351 SITA: n/a
F: 1997 ⁂ n/a Head: n/a Net: n/a

☐ C-FODO	De Havilland DHC-2 Beaver I	822		0055	0697	1 PW R-985	2313			Floats

ONTARIO FUN FLYERS, Inc. — Kingston, Ont.

Hangar 4, Norman Rogers Airport, Kingston, Ontario K7M 4M1, Canada ☎ (613) 547-5255 Tx: none Fax: (613) 389-2926 SITA: n/a
F: 1992 ⁂ 8 Head: Barry Smith Net: n/a Aircraft below MTOW 1361kg: Cessna 150 & Piper PA-28

☐ C-GOMY	Piper PA-23-250 Aztec E	27-4837	N60DB	0072	0695	2 LY IO-540-C4B5	2359			

ONTARIO HYDRO – Helicopter Section — Toronto, Ont.

70 Baywood Road, Etiobicoke, Ontario M9V 3Z3, Canada ☎ (416) 744-2272 Tx: 06-217662 ont hydro Fax: (416) 744-7298 SITA: n/a
F: 1949 ⁂ 18 Head: Barry G. Williams Net: http://www.hydro.on.ca/ Commercial corporation of the provincial government of Ontario, conducting helicopter aerial work for utility (electrical) business.

☐ C-GPQW	Bell 206B JetRanger III	2439		0078		1 AN 250-C20B	1451			
☐ C-FANV	Bell 206L-1 LongRanger II	45665	N26EA	0081		1 AN 250-C28B	1882			
☐ C-GIKX	Bell 206L-1 LongRanger II	45672	N3913Y	0081		1 AN 250-C28B	1882			
☐ C-GOHH	Eurocopter (Aerosp.) AS350B2 AStar	2568		0091	0192	1 TU Arriel 1D1	2250			
☐ C-GOHY	Eurocopter (Aerosp.) AS350B2 AStar	2589		0091	0592	1 TU Arriel 1D1	2250			

ONTARIO SUNSET FLY-INS (Richard L. & Judy A. Edwardson dba/Affiliated with Pickerel Arm Camps/ Seasonal May-October ops only) — Pickerel Arm-Minnitaki Lake, Ont.

Box 458, Sioux Lookout, Ontario P8T 1A8, Canada ☎ (807) 737-2499 Tx: n/a Fax: (608) 752-3564 SITA: n/a
F: 1983 ⁂ n/a Head: Richard L. & Judy A. Edwardson Net: n/a Aircraft below MTOW 1361 kg: Cessna 180 (on Floats). Winter phone no: (705) 842-2108.

☐ C-FNFE	De Havilland DHC-2 Beaver I	546	N2715A	0056	0684	1 PW R-985	2313			Floats

OPERATION FIRE FLY, Ltd (Affiliated with General Air Care, Ltd) — Souris, Man.

Box 970, Souris, Manitoba R0K 2C0, Canada ☎ (204) 483-3935 Tx: none Fax: (204) 483-3456 SITA: n/a
F: 1994 ⁂ n/a Head: n/a Net: n/a

☐ C-GKGE	North American SNJ-5 (AT-6D) Texan	88-16563	N7982C	0044	0395	1 PW R-1340	2404	Pleasure rides		
☐ C-FVCJ	CCF Harvard 4 (N.A. T-6J)	CCF4-206	RCAF 20415	0052	0395	1 PW R-1340	2608	Pleasure rides		

OPP Helicopter Unit (Division of Ontario Provincial Police) — Brampton, Kenora & Sudbury, Ont.

777 Memorial Avenue, Orillia, Ontario L3V 7V3, Canada ☎ (705) 329-7525 Tx: none Fax: (705) 329-7523 SITA: n/a
F: 1974 ⁂ n/a Head: Doug Thurlbeck Net: n/a Non-commercial provincial government organisation conducting ambulance, aerial police & transport missions.

☐ C-FOPP	Eurocopter (Aerosp.) AS355F2 TwinStar	5459		0090	0391	2 AN 250-C20R	2540			
☐ C-FOPS	Eurocopter (Aerosp.) AS355F2 TwinStar	5460		0090	0391	2 AN 250-C20R	2540			
☐ C-GOGP	Cessna 402C II	402C0516	N401SA	0081	0496	2 CO TSIO-520-VB	3107			

ORCUTT AIR CHARTERS, Ltd — Warner, Alta.

Box 279, Warner, Alberta T0K 2L0, Canada ☎ (780) 642-2209 Tx: none Fax: (780) 642-2209 SITA: n/a
F: 1991 ⁂ n/a Head: Rick Orcutt Net: n/a Ag-aircraft below MTOW 5000kg: Piper PA-36

☐ C-GYGY	Piper PA-32R-300 Lance	32R-7680182	N8872E	0076	0492	1 LY IO-540-K1G5D	1633			

OSIMAS HELICOPTERS, Ltd — Meadow Lake, Man.

Box 547, Meadow Lake, Manitoba S0M 1V0, Canada ☎ (306) 236-3427 Tx: none Fax: (306) 236-3286 SITA: n/a
F: 1988 ⁂ n/a Head: Cecile Mistickokat Net: n/a

☐ C-GRCT	Bell 206B JetRanger	280	N37738	0068	0494	1 AN 250-C20	1451			cvtd 206A
☐ C-GTQU	Bell 206B JetRanger	766	N8199J	0072	0697	1 AN 250-C20	1451			

68 registration type of aircraft cn/fn ex/8x* mfd del powered by mtow kg configuration selcal name/fln/specialitites/remarks

OSNABURGH AIRWAYS, Ltd

Rat Rapids, Ont.

PO Box 220, Pickle Lake, Ontario P0V 3A0, Canada ☎ (807) 928-2547 Tx: n/a Fax: (807) 928-2908 SITA: n/a
F: 1978 7 Head: Peter R. Johnson Net: n/a Aircraft below MTOW 1361 kg: Cessna 180.

☐ C-GIRN	Cessna A185F Skywagon II	18504187		0081		1 CO IO-520-D	1520			Floats / Wheel-Skis
☐ C-GYBJ	Cessna A185F Skywagon II	18503623		0078	0898	1 CO IO-520-D	1520			Floats / Wheel-Skis
☐ C-GMAU	De Havilland DHC-2 Beaver I	1134	N775E	0056		1 PW R-985	2313			Floats / Wheel-Skis
☐ C-FFQX	Noorduyn Norseman VI (UC-64A)	625	N51131	0044	0190	1 PW R-1340	3420			Floats / Wheel-Skis

OSPREY WINGS, Ltd (formerly Nipawin Air Services, Ltd)

Missinipe, Sask.

PO Box 419, La Ronge, Saskatchewan S0J 1L0, Canada ☎ (306) 635-2112 Tx: none Fax: (306) 635-2134 SITA: n/a
F: 1961 10 Head: Garry Thompson Net: n/a

☐ C-GCIM	Cessna A185F Skywagon II	18503953		0079	0691	1 CO IO-520-D	1520			Floats / Wheel-Skis
☐ C-FZCO	De Havilland DHC-2 Beaver I	1027	N8034J	0056	0598	1 PW R-985	2313			Floats / Wheel-Skis
☐ C-GAIJ	De Havilland DHC-2 Beaver I	1373	N5334G	0058		1 PW R-985	2313			Floats / Wheel-Skis
☐ C-FTCL	De Havilland DHC-2 Turbo Beaver III	1605TB11	C-FOEF	0065	0598	1 PWC PT6A-20	2436			Floats / Wheel-Skis
☐ C-FXRI	De Havilland DHC-3 Otter	258	VH-SBT	0058		1 PW R-1340	3629			Floats / Wheel-Skis
☐ C-GQOQ	De Havilland DHC-6 Twin Otter 200	155	EC-BPE	0068		2 PWC PT6A-20	5252			Floats / Wheel-Skis

OUTLAW HELICOPTERS, Inc.

Fort Nelson, B.C.

Box 3317, Fort Nelson, British Columbia V0C 1R0, Canada ☎ (250) 774-2445 Tx: none Fax: (250) 774-3104 SITA: n/a
F: 1995 n/a Head: Graydon Kowal Net: n/a

☐ C-GBZL	Bell 206B JetRanger III	2534	N5007G	0078	0698	1 AN 250-C20B	1451			
☐ C-GKGK	Bell 206B JetRanger	807	ZK-HWU	0072	0698	1 AN 250-C20	1451			
☐ C-FRGK	Eurocopter (Aerosp.) AS350B AStar	1164	N55AK	0080	1196	1 TU Arriel 1B	1950			

PACIFIC COASTAL AIRLINES - PCA = 8P / PCO (Partenaire CANADIEN / CANADIAN Partner)

Vancouver-Int'l/Bella Bella/Nanaimo/Pt Hardy/Powell River,BC

Suite 117-4440 Cowley Crescent, Vancouver, British Columbia V7B 1B8, Canada ☎ (604) 273-8666 Tx: none Fax: (604) 273-6864 SITA: YVRRR8P
F: 1979 n/a Head: Daryl Smith IATA: 905 ICAO: PASCO Net: http://www.pacific-coastal.com/
Some scheduled services with Shorts 360 aircraft are operated in conjunction with Canadian / Canadien as a Partenaire CANADIEN / CANADIAN (in special cs) using CP flt no's.

☐ C-FJNQ	Cessna A185F Skywagon	18502233		0073	1298	1 CO IO-520-D	1520	Y5		Floats
☐ C-GMRX	Cessna U206F Stationair II	U20602909	N1543X	0074	1298	1 CO IO-520-F	1633	Y5		Floats
☐ C-FDSG	De Havilland DHC-2 Beaver I	892	54-1737	0054		1 PW R-985	2313	Y5		Floats
☐ C-FMAZ	De Havilland DHC-2 Beaver I	1413		0058		1 PW R-985	2313	Y5		Floats
☐ C-GASF	De Havilland DHC-2 Beaver I	1202	57-2561	0057		1 PW R-985	2313	Y5		Floats
☐ C-GEVX	Britten-Norman BN-2A-20 Islander	464	TI-AKI	0075	1298	2 LY IO-540-K1B5	2994	Y9		
☐ C-FHUZ	Grumman G-21A Goose	B-83		0044	1194	2 PW R-985	4173	Y9		Amphibian
☐ C-FIOL	Grumman G-21A Goose	B-107		0044	1194	2 PW R-985	4173	Y9		Amphibian
☐ C-FPCK	Grumman G-21A Goose	1187	N8229	0042	0796	2 PW R-985	3629	Y9		Amphibian
☐ C-FUAZ	Grumman G-21A Goose	1077	N95400	0040		2 PW R-985	3629	Y9		Amphibian
☐ C-FPCM	Embraer 110P1 Bandeirante (EMB-110P1)	110340	LN-TDI	0081	0697	2 PWC PT6A-34	5670	Y15		501
☐ C-FPCO	Embraer 110P1 Bandeirante (EMB-110P1)	110405	LN-TED	0082	1197	2 PWC PT6A-34	5670	Y15		503
☐ C-FPCU	Embraer 110P1 Bandeirante (EMB-110P1)	110445	LN-TDA	0084	0698	2 PWC PT6A-34	5670	Y15		504
☐ C-GPCQ	Embraer 110P1 Bandeirante (EMB-110P1)	110342	N486FS	0081	0597	2 PWC PT6A-34	5670	Y15		502
☐ C-GPCP	Beech King Air 200	BB-140		0076	1298	2 PWC PT6A-41	5670	Y9		
☐ C-GPCY	Beech 1900C Airliner	UB-45	C-FYZD	0085	1198	2 PWC PT6A-65B	7530	Y19		
☐ C-GPCG	Shorts 360 (SD3-60 Variant 300)	SH3619	N364MQ	0083	0595	2 PWC PT6A-65AR	11999	Y30		701
☐ C-GPCN	Shorts 360 (SD3-60 Variant 300)	SH3621	N365MQ	0083	0595	2 PWC PT6A-65AR	11999	Y30		702
☐ C-GPCW	Shorts 360 (SD3-60 Variant 300)	SH3622	N622FB	0083	0697	2 PWC PT6A-65R	11999	Y30		703

PACIFIC EAGLE AVIATION, Ltd

Port McNeill-SPB, B.C.

PO Box 1487, Port McNeill, British Columbia V0N 2R0, Canada ☎ (250) 974-3002 Tx: none Fax: (250) 974-3009 SITA: n/a
F: 1998 n/a Head: Jim O'Donnell Net: n/a

☐ C-GIDE	Republic RC-3 Seabee	355	N6167K	0047	0398	1 LY GO-480-G1A6	1429			Amphibian

PACIFIC SPIRIT AIR, Ltd (formerly Hanna's Air Saltspring)

Ganges-Harbour, B.C.

300-235, 15th Street, West Vancouver, British Columbia V7T 2X1, Canada ☎ (250) 247-9992 Tx: none Fax: (250) 247-9992 SITA: n/a
F: 1985 7 Head: Chris Holmes Net: n/a Aircraft below MTOW 1361kg: Cessna 180 (on Floats)

☐ C-FICK	De Havilland DHC-2 Beaver I	796		0054	0698	1 PW R-985	2309			Floats

PACIFIC WESTERN HELICOPTERS, Ltd - PWH

Prince George, Dease Lake, Fort St. James & Mackenzie, B.C.

4214 Cowart Road, Prince George, British Columbia V2N 6H9, Canada ☎ (250) 562-7911 Tx: none Fax: (250) 561-2697 SITA: n/a
F: 1990 9 Head: Robert Shaw Net: n/a

☐ C-GIZE	Bell 206B JetRanger	1385	N59545	0075	0291	1 AN 250-C20	1451			
☐ C-GPGM	Bell 206B JetRanger III	3178	N38902	0080	0591	1 AN 250-C20B	1451			
☐ C-GPWD	Bell 206B JetRanger	1124	N41AJ	0073	0995	1 AN 250-C20	1451			
☐ C-GPWH	Bell 206B JetRanger III	3131	N81AJ	0080	1291	1 AN 250-C20B	1451			
☐ C-GPWI	Bell 206B JetRanger III	2234	N347BB	0077	0593	1 AN 250-C20B	1451			
☐ C-GPWJ	Bell 206B JetRanger III	2240	C-GNMM	0081	0591	1 AN 250-C20B	1451			
☐ C-GRGT	Bell 206B JetRanger	1688	N90022	0075	0291	1 AN 250-C20	1451			
☐ C-GRWG	Bell 206B JetRanger III	3318		0081	0591	1 AN 250-C20B	1451			
☐ C-GTES	Bell 206B JetRanger III	2292	N16877	0077	0393	1 AN 250-C20B	1451			
☐ C-GTVE	Bell 206B JetRanger III	2163		0077	0893	1 AN 250-C20B	1451			cvtd JetRanger II
☐ C-GHHI	Bell 206L-3 LongRanger III	51037	N30EA	0082	0594	1 AN 250-C30P	1882			
☐ C-GPWP	Eurocopter (Aerosp.) AS350B AStar	2294	N7722A	0089	0496	1 TU Arriel 1B	1950			

PANTHER HELICOPTERS, Ltd

Powell River, B.C.

3821 Ontario Ave., Powell River, British Columbia V8A 5C7, Canada ☎ (604) 485-6634 Tx: none Fax: (604) 485-6656 SITA: n/a
F: 1989 n/a Head: Michael Salisbury Net: n/a

☐ C-GPHE	MD Helicopters MD 500E (Hughes 369E)	0082E	N765KV	0084	1198	1 AN 250-C20B	1361			
☐ C-GOKW	Bell 212	30855	N16865	0077	0196	2 PWC PT6T-3 TwinPac	5080			

PARA AEROSERVICE (Para Aerosvc, Inc. / Associated with Clagry Skydive Centre (1995), Inc.)

Beiseker, Alta.

Suite 203, 3112-11 Street NE, Calgary, Alberta T2E 7J1, Canada ☎ (403) 285-5867 Tx: none Fax: (403) 291-0334 SITA: n/a
F: 1997 n/a Head: n/a Net: n/a

☐ C-FSGW	Cessna P206 Super Skylane	P206-0126	N2626X	0065	0497	1 CO IO-520-A	1497	Para		
☐ C-FYCQ	Cessna P206D Super Skylane	P206-0549		0068	0497	1 CO IO-520-A	1633	Para		

PARACHUTISME NOUVEL AIR, Inc. (Seasonal May-October ops only)

St-Jean, Qué.

200 Chemin Lebeau, Farnham, Québec J2N 2P9, Canada ☎ (514) 293-8118 Tx: none Fax: (514) 293-2700 SITA: n/a
F: 1990 n/a Head: Michel Lamey Net: n/a Aircraft below MTOW 1361kg: Cessna 182

☐ C-FZNH	Beech 3NM (18)	CA-275	RCAF5198	0052	0494	2 PW R-985	3969	Para		

PARA VISION (2859-2228 Québec, Inc. dba)

St-Jerome, Qué.

CP 95, St. Jeromé, Québec J7Z 5T7, Canada ☎ (514) 438-0855 Tx: none Fax: (514) 432-1420 SITA: n/a
F: 1982 n/a Head: Alain Clousiaur Net: n/a Aircraft below MTOW 1361kg: Cessna 182

☐ CF-SEB	Beech 3NM (18)	CA-185	2312	0052	0598	2 PW R-985-AN14B	3969	Para		

PARRY SOUND AIR SERVICES, Inc. (Seasonal May-October ops only)

McKellar-SPB, Ont.

PO Box 25, McKellar, Ontario P0G 1C0, Canada ☎ (705) 389-3793 Tx: none Fax: (705) 389-1136 SITA: n/a
F: 1990 2 Head: Dietmar Zschogner Net: http://www.parrysoundair.com Aircraft below MTOW 1361kg: Cessna 172/180 (on Floats)

☐ C-FODB	De Havilland DHC-2 Beaver I	113		0052	0793	1 PW R-985	2313			Floats

PARTNER JET, Inc.

Toronto-Int'l, Ont.

2450 Derry Road East, Hangar 9, Mississauga, Ontario L5S 1B2, Canada ☎ (905) 676-0092 Tx: none Fax: (905) 676-0192 SITA: n/a
F: 1996 n/a Head: Don Henderson Net: n/a

☐ C-GTOR	Hawker 700A (HS 125-700A)	257029 / NA0221	N705JH	0078	0398	2 GA TFE731-3R-1H	11249	Executive / EMS		

PATROUILLE AERIENNE DU QUEBEC PAQ, Inc. (formerly Transport Air)

Québec, Qué.

230-2ieme, Aéroport Int'l J. Lesage, Sainte-Foy, Québec G2E 5W1, Canada ☎ (418) 872-0366 Tx: none Fax: (418) 828-2488 SITA: n/a
F: 1980 25 Head: Jean-Pierre Duchesne Net: n/a

☐ C-FBKJ	Cessna R182 Skylane RG II	R18200149	N2306C	0078	0294	1 LY O-540-J3C5D	1406	Patrol		
☐ C-FDSC	Cessna R182 Skylane RG II	R18200395	N9088C	0078	0494	1 LY O-540-J3C5D	1406	Patrol		
☐ C-FMUB	Cessna R182 Skylane RG II	R18200752	N736QE	0079	0497	1 LY O-540-J3C5D	1406	Patrol		
☐ C-FPLO	Cessna R182 Skylane RG II	R18200301	N3669C	0078	0493	1 LY O-540-J3C5D	1406	Patrol		

69 registration type of aircraft cn/fn ex/EX* mfd del powered by mtow kg configuration selcal name/fln/specialitites/remarks

☐ C-FPLP	Cessna R182 Skylane RG II	R18200082	N7346X	0078	0493	1 LY O-540-J3C5D	1406	Patrol		
☐ C-FPQN	Cessna R182 Skylane RG II	R18200044		0078	0493	1 LY O-540-J3C5D	1406	Patrol		
☐ C-FSCE	Cessna R182 Skylane RG II	R18201244	N757LH	0079	0294	1 LY O-540-J3C5D	1406	Patrol		
☐ C-FSCK	Cessna R182 Skylane RG II	R18200490	N9950C	0078	0294	1 LY O-540-J3C5D	1406	Patrol		
☐ C-FSCR	Cessna R182 Skylane RG II	R18200349	N6008C	0078	0394	1 LY O-540-J3C5D	1406	Patrol		
☐ C-FSCX	Cessna R182 Skylane RG II	R18200421	N9148C	0078	0294	1 LY O-540-J3C5D	1406	Patrol		
☐ C-FXDH	Cessna R182 Skylane RG II	R18200879	N737ST	0079	0196	1 LY O-540-J3C5D	1406	Patrol		
☐ C-GBSC	Cessna R182 Skylane RG II	R18201448	N4908S	0080	0394	1 LY O-540-J3C5D	1406	Patrol		
☐ C-GHVJ	Cessna R182 Skylane RG II	R18200423		0078	0394	1 LY O-540-J3C5D	1406	Patrol		
☐ C-GIXN	Cessna R182 Skylane RG II	R18200078		0077	0294	1 LY O-540-J3C5D	1406	Patrol		
☐ C-GJQU	Cessna R182 Skylane RG II	R18200206		0078	0394	1 LY O-540-J3C5D	1406	Patrol		
☐ C-GSCC	Cessna R182 Skylane RG II	R18200240	N3139C	0078	0394	1 LY O-540-J3C5D	1406	Patrol		
☐ C-GSCD	Cessna R182 Skylane RG II	R18200420	N9146C	0078	0294	1 LY O-540-J3C5D	1406	Patrol		
☐ C-GSCG	Cessna R182 Skylane RG II	R18201573	N5452S	0080	0394	1 LY O-540-J3C5D	1406	Patrol		
☐ C-GSCI	Cessna R182 Skylane RG II	R18200108	N785LR	0078	0394	1 LY O-540-J3C5D	1406	Patrol		

PAVILLON DU LAC BERTHELOT, Inc. – Service Aériens (Berthelot Lake Lodge, Inc. – Air Services) — Berthelot Lake, Qué.

CP 297, Senneterre, Québec J0Y 2M0, Canada ☎ (819) 737-4684 Tx: n/a Fax: none SITA: n/a
F: 1984 ☨☨☨ 12 Head: Gary Koch Net: n/a

☐ C-FJBM	De Havilland DHC-2 Beaver I	931		0056	0396	1 PW R-985	2313			Floats / Wheel-Skis
☐ C-GEXK	De Havilland DHC-2 Beaver I	699	N5230G	0054	0688	1 PW R-985	2313			Floats / Wheel-Skis
☐ C-GSZA	De Havilland DHC-2 Beaver I	610	53-2813	0056	1298	1 PW R-985	2313			Floats / Wheel-Skis

PEACE AIR, Ltd — Peace River, Alta.

PO Box 6036, Peace River, Alberta T8S 1S1, Canada ☎ (780) 624-3060 Tx: none Fax: (780) 624-3063 SITA: n/a
F: 1966 ☨☨☨ 13 Head: Albert G. Cooper Net: n/a Aircraft below MTOW 1361kg: Cessna 172

☐ C-GRAC	Cessna 210L Centurion II	21060605	N2560L	0075	0689	1 CO IO-520-L	1724			
☐ C-GPAC	Piper PA-34-220T Seneca III	34-8133190	N32JP	0081	0293	2 CO TSIO-360-KB	2155			
☐ C-GAEN	Piper PA-31-350 Navajo Chieftain	31-8052196	N3528X	0080	0592	2 LY TIO-540-J2BD	3288			
☐ C-GRBF	Fairchild (Swearingen) SA26AT Merlin IIB	T26-171E	N50AK	0069	0395	2 GA TPE331-1-151G	4536			

PEACE HELICOPTERS, Ltd — Peace River, Alta.

Box 6, Bldg 6, 11930-109 Street, Edmonton, Alberta T5G 2T8, Canada ☎ (780) 477-1100 Tx: none Fax: (780) 471-5305 SITA: n/a
F: 1977 ☨☨☨ 40 Head: Steve Matthews Net: n/a

☐ C-GLCD	Bell 206B JetRanger	1284		0074	0592	1 AN 250-C20	1451			lsf Northern Mountain Helicopters
☐ C-GOLV	Eurocopter (Aerosp.) AS350BA AStar	1108		0079		1 TU Arriel 1B	2100			lsf Northern Mountain Heli./cvtd AS350B
☐ C-GPHM	Eurocopter (Aerosp.) AS350B2 AStar	2488		0091	0791	1 TU Arriel 1D1	2250			lsf Northern Mountain Helicopters
☐ C-GPHQ	Eurocopter (Aerosp.) AS350B1 AStar	2017	N855NM	0087	1095	1 TU Arriel 1D	2200			lsf Northern Mountain Helicopters
☐ C-GPHR	Eurocopter (Aerosp.) AS350B1 AStar	2268		0089	0290	1 TU Arriel 1D	2200			lsf Northern Mountain Helicopters
☐ C-GUPH	Eurocopter (Aerosp.) AS350B AStar	1368	N99PS	0080		1 TU Arriel 1B	1950			cvtd AS350D
☐ C-GYHT	Eurocopter (Aerosp.) AS350B AStar	1340	VH-HBD	0080	0995	1 TU Arriel 1B	1950			lsf Northern Mountain Heli./cvtd AS350D
☐ C-GAHN	Bell 204B	2044	N1308X	0066	0997	1 LY T5313B	3856			lsf Northern Mountain Helicopters
☐ C-GSHK	Bell 204B	2067	Thai 920	0067	0696	1 LY T5311A	3856			lsf Northern Mountain Helicopters

PEACOCK AIR (Peacock's Yukon Camps, Ltd dba) — Whitehorse, Y.T.

77 Alsek Road, Whitehore, Yukon Territory Y1A 3K5, Canada ☎ (867) 667-2846 Tx: none Fax: (867) 667-6076 SITA: n/a
F: 1986 ☨☨☨ 2 Head: John E. Peacock Net: n/a

☐ C-GORH	Cessna A185F Skywagon II	18504332		0082	1292	1 CO IO-550-D	1520			Floats / Wheel-Skis

PELICAN NARROWS AIR SERVICES, Ltd — Pelican Narrows, Sask.

Box 39, Pelican Narrows, Saskatchewan S0P 0E0, Canada ☎ (306) 632-2020 Tx: none Fax: (306) 632-2122 SITA: n/a
F: 1988 ☨☨☨ n/a Head: Kelly Stevenson Net: n/a

☐ C-GFZA	Cessna A185F Skywagon	18503084		0076	0690	1 CO IO-520-D	1520			Floats / Wheel-Skis
☐ C-GTBC	De Havilland DHC-2 Beaver I	1364	58-2032	0058	0690	1 PW R-985	2313			Floats / Wheel-Skis

PEM-AIR, Ltd = PD / PEM — Pembroke, Ont.

Pembroke & Area Municipal Airport, RR 6, Pembroke, Ontario K8A 6W7, Canada ☎ (613) 687-8139 Tx: none Fax: (613) 687-5166 SITA: n/a
F: 1970 ☨☨☨ 22 Head: Delbert A. O'Brien IATA: 329 ICAO: PEM AIR Net: n/a Aircraft below MTOW 1361 kg: Cessna 150, 152 & 172.

☐ C-GILJ	Piper PA-31-350 Navajo Chieftain	31-7552010	N374SA	0075	0596	2 LY TIO-540-J2BD	3175			
☐ C-GRYE	Piper PA-31-350 Navajo Chieftain	31-7852155		0078	0297	2 LY TIO-540-J2BD	3175			
☐ C-FATX	Beech King Air E90	LW-147	N4RG	0075	0497	2 PWC PT6A-28	4581			
☐ C-FDAM	Beech King Air 100	B-8	N59T	0069		2 PWC PT6A-28	4808			
☐ C-FKIJ	Beech King Air 100	B-52	N8NP	0070	0691	2 PWC PT6A-28	4808			

PEMBERTON HELICOPTERS, Inc. (formerly Pemberton Helicopter Services, Ltd) — Pemberton, B.C.

PO Box 579, Pemberton, British Columbia V0N 2L0, Canada ☎ (604) 894-6919 Tx: none Fax: (604) 894-6987 SITA: n/a
F: 1976 ☨☨☨ 2 Head: John Goats Net: n/a Aircraft below MTOW 1361kg: Enstrom 280.

☐ C-FJPH	Bell 206B JetRanger III	2769	N2775R	0079	0593	1 AN 250-C20B	1451			
☐ C-FJPL	Bell 206L-1 LongRanger II	45747	N70EA	0082	0594	1 AN 250-C28B	1882			
☐ C-GJPA	Eurocopter (Aerosp.) AS350D AStar	1075	C-FHAH	0079	1298	1 LY LTS101-600A.3	1950			

PENINSULAIR, Ltd — Hamilton, Ont.

PO Box 100, Mount Hope, Ontario L0R 1W0, Canada ☎ (905) 679-4165 Tx: none Fax: (905) 679-4626 SITA: n/a
F: 1946 ☨☨☨ 50 Head: Rick White Net: n/a Aircraft below MTOW 1361 kg: Piper PA-28 & 38.

☐ C-GBGG	Piper PA-44-180 Seminole	44-8095007		0080		2 LY O-360-E1AD	1724			
☐ C-GTJF	Piper PA-31-350 Navajo Chieftain	31-7952170		0079		2 LY TIO-540-J2BD	3175			

PERIMETER AIRLINES (Inland), Ltd (Sister company of Perimeter Aviation, Ltd) — Winnipeg-Int'l, Man.

626 Ferry Road, Winnipeg, Manitoba R3H 0T7, Canada ☎ (204) 786-7031 Tx: none Fax: (204) 783-7911 SITA: n/a
F: 1960 ☨☨☨ n/a Head: William J. Wehrle IATA: 711 Net: n/a

☐ C-FIHB	Fairchild (Swearingen) SA226TC Metro II	TC-361	N166SW	0080	0590	2 GA TPE331-10UA-511G	5670	Y18		
☐ C-FIHE	Fairchild (Swearingen) SA226TC Metro II	TC-373	N1010Z	0079	0990	2 GA TPE331-10UA-511G	5670	Y18		
☐ C-FIIA	Fairchild (Swearingen) SA226TC Metro II	TC-329	N236AM	0080	0590	2 GA TPE331-10UA-511G	5670	Y18		
☐ C-FJNW	Fairchild (Swearingen) SA226TC Metro II	TC-352	N167MA	0081	0191	2 GA TPE331-10UA-511G	5670	Y18		
☐ C-FKEX	Fairchild (Swearingen) SA226TC Metro II	TC-332	N237AM	0080	0991	2 GA TPE331-10UA-511G	5670	Y18		
☐ C-FSLZ	Fairchild (Swearingen) SA226TC Metro II	TC-222EE	N104GS	0076	0694	2 GA TPE331-10UA-511G	5670	Y18		
☐ C-FTNV	Fairchild (Swearingen) SA226TC Metro II	TC-239E	N227AM	0078	1194	2 GA TPE331-10UA-511G	5670	Y18		
☐ C-GIQF	Fairchild (Swearingen) SA226TC Metro II	TC-279	F-GFGE	0078	0798	2 GA TPE331-10UA-511G	5670	Y18		
☐ C-GIQG	Fairchild (Swearingen) SA226TC Metro II	TC-285	F-GFGD	0079	1296	2 GA TPE331-10UA-511G	5670	Y18		
☐ C-GIQK	Fairchild (Swearingen) SA226TC Metro II	TC-288	F-GFGF	0079	0197	2 GA TPE331-10UA-511G	5670	Y18		
☐ C-GPCL	Fairchild (Swearingen) SA226AT Merlin IV	AT-017	N511M	0074	1293	2 GA TPE331-10UA-511G	5670	Y18		
☐ C-GQAP	Fairchild (Swearingen) SA226TC Metro II	TC-263	N103UR	0078	0194	2 GA TPE331-10UA-511G	5670	Y18		
☐ C-GYPA	Fairchild (Swearingen) SA226TC Metro II	TC-250	N5452M*	0078	0778	2 GA TPE331-3UW-303G	5670	Y18		
☐ C-GYRD	Fairchild (Swearingen) SA226TC Metro II	TC-278	N5493M*	0078	1178	2 GA TPE331-10UA-511G	5670	Y18		
☐ C-GAJS	Learjet 35A	35A-380	N903WJ	0079	1094	2 GA TFE731-2-2B	8165	Executive		
☐ C-GCGS	Hawker 800A (BAe 125-800A)	258123 / NA0416	N353WC	0088	1296	2 GA TFE731-5R-1H	12428	Executive		

PERIMETER AVIATION, Ltd = PAG (Sister company of Perimeter Airlines (Inland), Ltd) — Winnipeg-Int'l, Man.

626 Ferry Road, Winnipeg, Manitoba R3H 0T7, Canada ☎ (204) 786-7031 Tx: none Fax: (204) 783-7911 SITA: n/a
F: 1960 ☨☨☨ n/a Head: William J. Wehrle ICAO: PERIMETER Net: n/a

☐ C-FCNU	Beech Travel Air D95A	TD-668	N7957M	0066	0698	2 LY IO-360-B1B	1905			
☐ C-FDMX	Beech Travel Air D95A	TD-587	N5663K	0064		2 LY IO-360-B1B	1905			
☐ C-FKMZ	Beech Travel Air E95	TD-708		0068		2 LY IO-360-B1B	1905			
☐ C-GQQC	Beech Travel Air D95A	TD-676	N7874L	0067		2 LY IO-360-B1B	1905			
☐ C-FEQK	Beech Baron B55 (95-B55)	TC-1374		0070	1297	2 CO IO-470-L	2313			
☐ C-GEFX	Beech Baron B55 (95-B55)	TC-1332	N4263A	0070		2 CO IO-470-L	2313			
☐ C-GEUJ	Beech Duke B60	P-498	N36RR	0079	0794	2 LY TIO-541-E1C4	3073			

PHOENIX HELI-FLIGHT (506795 Alberta, Ltd dba) — Fort McMurray, Alta.

RR 1, Site 1, Box 6, Fort McMurray, Alberta T9H 5B4, Canada ☎ (780) 799-0141 Tx: none Fax: (780) 791-0355 SITA: n/a
F: 1992 ☨☨☨ 2 Head: Paul Spring Net: n/a

☐ C-FHLF	Eurocopter (Aerosp.) AS350BA AStar	1074	N35934	0079	0594	1 TU Arriel 1B	2100			cvtd AS350B & 350D

PIMICHIKAMAC AIR, Ltd = MKS — Cross Lake, Man.

Box 130, Cross Lake, Manitoba R0B 0J0, Canada ☎ (204) 676-2121 Tx: none Fax: (204) 676-2183 SITA: n/a
F: 1990 ☨☨☨ n/a Head: Eric Sinclair ICAO: MIKISEW Net: n/a

☐ C-GPPZ	Cessna U206G Stationair 6 II	U20606568		0082	0895	1 CO IO-520-F	1633			Floats / Wheel-Skis
☐ C-GMSF	Piper PA-34-200T Seneca II	34-7870332	N36465	0078	0997	2 CO TSIO-360-E	2073			

70 registration type of aircraft cn/fn ex/ex* mfd del powered by mtow kg configuration selcal name/fln/specialitites/remarks

registration	type of aircraft	cn/fn	ex/ex*	mfd	del	powered by	mtow kg	configuration	selcal	name/fln/specialitites/remarks
☐ C-FEYQ	De Havilland DHC-2 Beaver I	465		0053	0893	1 PW R-985	2313			Floats / Wheel-Skis
☐ C-GEUY	Cessna 414 II	414-0821		0076	0894	2 CO TSIO-520-N	2880			
☐ C-GMOM	Cessna 414	414-0409	N1629T	0073	0694	2 CO TSIO-520-J	2880			
☐ C-GTRK	Cessna 414	414-0604	N936DC	0075	0198	2 CO TSIO-520-J	2880			
☐ C-GROJ	Piper PA-31-350 Navajo Chieftain	31-7405249	N555AN	0074	0798	2 LY TIO-540-J2BD	3175			
☐ C-GTQR	Piper PA-31-310 Navajo	31-551	N1AL	0070	0492	2 LY TIO-540-A1A	2948			
☐ C-GNAM	Piper PA-31T Cheyenne II	31T-8020065	N118EL	0080	1196	2 PWC PT6A-28	4082			

PINE AIR, Inc. (Seasonal May-October ops only)
Sioux Lookout, Ont.

Box 248, Sioux Lookout, Ontario P8T 1A3, Canada ☎ (807) 737-1349 Tx: none Fax: (807) 737-3716 SITA: n/a
F: 1970 ♦♦♦ n/a Head: n/a Net: n/a Winter phone: (847) 428-2900

| ☐ C-GAJU | De Havilland DHC-2 Beaver I | 1169 | 56-0415 | 0056 | | 1 PW R-985 | 2313 | | | Floats |

PIONEER HELICOPTERS, Ltd
Abbotsford, B.C.

38910 Campbell Road, Abbotsford, British Columbia V3G 2G8, Canada ☎ (604) 807-1934 Tx: none Fax: (604) 852-4783 SITA: n/a
F: 1997 ♦♦♦ 3 Head: Chad Davis Net: n/a

☐ C-GDPE	Bell 206B JetRanger	630	N213EL	0070	0798	1 AN 250-C20	1451			cvtd 206A
☐ C-GJBW	Bell 206B JetRanger	612	N71SP	0071	0598	1 AN 250-C20	1451			cvtd 206A
☐ C-GZPG	Bell 206B JetRanger	867	N28EE	0072	0299	1 AN 250-C20	1451			

PLUMMER'S LODGES – Sioux Narrows Airways, Ltd (Seasonal April-October ops only)
Great Bear Lake, N.W.T.

950 Bradford Street, Winnipeg, Manitoba R3H 0N5, Canada ☎ (204) 774-5775 Tx: none Fax: (204) 783-2320 SITA: n/a
F: 1955 ♦♦♦ 5 Head: Chummy Plummer

☐ C-GBDW	De Havilland DHC-2 Beaver I	954	C9-AGS	0056	0798	1 PW R-985	2309	6 Pax		Floats
☐ C-GSMG	De Havilland DHC-3 Otter	363	CAF 9405	0060		1 PZL ASh-62IR-M18	3629	10 Pax		cvtd DHC-3 PW-engine / Floats
☐ CF-KOA	De Havilland DHC-3 Otter	130	N88753	0056	0290	1 PZL ASh-62I-M18	3629	10 Pax		cvtd DHC-3 PW-engine / Floats
☐ CF-QHY	Boeing (Douglas) DC-3C (C-47B-5-DK)	26005	CAF 12958	0042	0279	2 PW R-1830	12202	24 Pax		

PLUMRIDGE AIR (Donald R. Plumridge dba)
Mattice-Armstrong Lake, Ont.

RR 14, Thunder Bay, Ontario P7B 5E5, Canada ☎ (807) 767-5586 Tx: none Fax: (807) 767-1563 SITA: n/a
F: 1993 ♦♦♦ n/a Head: Donald R. Plumridge Net: n/a

| ☐ C-FLPL | De Havilland DHC-2 Beaver I | 1313 | | 0059 | 1298 | 1 PW R-985 | 2313 | | | Floats / Wheel-Skis |

POINTS NORTH AIR (Points North Air Services, Inc. dba)
Points North Landing, Sask.

Bag 7000, La Ronge, Saskatchewan S0J 1L0, Canada ☎ (306) 633-2137 Tx: none Fax: (306) 633-2152 SITA: n/a
F: 1988 ♦♦♦ 17 Head: George Eikel Net: n/a

☐ C-GZWR	Cessna A185F Skywagon II	18503509		0078	0394	1 CO IO-520-D	1520			Floats / Wheel-Skis
☐ C-GQKS	De Havilland DHC-2 Beaver I	1096	56-4399	0058	0694	1 PW R-985	2313			Floats / Wheel-Skis
☐ C-FASD	Cessna 402B II	402B1354	N6395X	0078	0697	2 CO TSIO-520-E	2858			
☐ C-GCGQ	Cessna 402C II	402C0249		0080	0491	2 CO TSIO-520-VB	3107			
☐ C-FASV	De Havilland DHC-3 Otter	23	N2631U	0053	1290	1 PW R-1340	3629			Floats / Wheel-Skis
☐ C-FASZ	De Havilland DHC-3 Otter	463	IM 672	0066	0595	1 PW R-1340	3629			Floats
☐ C-FODW	De Havilland DHC-3 Otter	403		0061	0596	1 PW R-1340	3629			Floats / Wheel-Skis
☐ C-FPNG	Cessna 208B Grand Caravan	208B0667		0098	0498	1 PWC PT6A-114A	3969			
☐ C-FNTF	Boeing (Douglas) DC-3C (C-47A-10-DK)	12344	CAF 12914	0044		2 PW R-1830	12202	Freighter		Wheel-Skis

PRECISION HELICOPTERS, Inc.
Grande Prairie, Alta.

Box 22132, Grande Prairie, Alberta T8V 6X1, Canada ☎ (780) 538-1155 Tx: none Fax: (780) 532-3377 SITA: n/a
F: 1980 ♦♦♦ 5 Head: Catherine Carlton Net: n/a

☐ C-GPGA	Bell 206B JetRanger	1442	N310PC	0074	0495	1 AN 250-C20	1451			
☐ C-GPGX	Bell 206B JetRanger	1362	N59529	0074	1289	1 AN 250-C20	1451			
☐ C-GTDQ	Bell 206B JetRanger	1503	C-GOXX	0074	0597	1 AN 250-C20	1451			

PRECISION HELI-LIFT, Inc.
Powell River, B.C.

RR2, Comp. 32, Southview Road, Powell River, British Columbia V8A 4Z3, Canada ☎ (604) 483-9114 Tx: none Fax: (604) 483-9134 SITA: n/a
F: 1997 ♦♦♦ n/a Head: Deryk Whitson Net: n/a

| ☐ C-GVOU | MD Helicopters MD 500D (Hughes 369D) | 490486D | | 0079 | 1297 | 1 AN 250-C20B | 1361 | | | |

PRESIDENT AIR CHARTER (926724 Ontario, Ltd dba)
Peterborough, Ont.

PO Box 778, Peterborough, Ontario K9J 7A2, Canada ☎ (705) 745-5763 Tx: none Fax: (705) 745-0220 SITA: n/a
F: 1994 ♦♦♦ 2 Head: Anthony Ambler Net: n/a

| ☐ C-GZBU | Cessna 414A Chancellor III | 414A0253 | | 0079 | 0594 | 2 CO TSIO-52O-N | 3062 | Executive | | |

PRINCE EDWARD AIR, Ltd = CME
Charlottetown, P.E.I.

250 Brackley Point Road, Box 3, Charlottetown, Prince Edward Island C1A 6YA, Canada ☎ (902) 566-4488 Tx: none Fax: (902) 368-3573 SITA: n/a
F: 1990 ♦♦♦ 24 Head: Robert M. Bateman ICAO: COMET Net: http://www.cyor.ca/peiair/

☐ C-FFFH	Piper PA-31-350 Navajo Chieftain	31-7552130	N54CG	0075	1297	2 LY TIO-540-J2BD	3175	Y8		
☐ C-GIIZ	Piper PA-31-350 Navajo Chieftain	31-7552099	N29TW	0075	0192	2 LY TIO-540-J2BD	3175	Y8		
☐ C-GRFA	Piper PA-31-350 Navajo Chieftain	31-7405228	N54292	0074	0290	2 LY TIO-540-J2BD	3175	Y8		
☐ C-GYYJ	Piper PA-31-350 Navajo Chieftain	31-7652086	N59833	0076	1292	2 LY TIO-540-J2BD	3175	Y8		
☐ N9514F	Cessna 208 Caravan I	20800079		0086	0396	1 PWC PT6A-114	3629	Freighter		lsf Avion Capital Corp.
☐ C-FJCC	Beech B99 Airliner	U-150	N999CA	0072	0199	2 PWC PT6A-28	4944	Freighter		
☐ C-FKCG	Beech 99 Airliner	U-23	N218BH	0068	1296	2 PWC PT6A-27	4944	Freighter		
☐ C-FKAX	Beech 1900C Airliner	UB-67	N3067X	0087	0698	2 PWC PT6A-65B	7530	Y19		

PRISM HELICOPTERS, Ltd
Pitt Meadows, B.C.

12-11465 Baynes Road North, Pitt Meadows, British Columbia V3Y 2B3, Canada ☎ (604) 465-7979 Tx: none Fax: (604) 465-7970 SITA: n/a
F: 1985 ♦♦♦ 33 Head: Dave Zall Net: http://www.prism-helicopters.com

☐ C-FASX	MD Helicopters MD 500D (Hughes 369D)	1150D	N51720	0082	0291	1 AN 250-C20B	1361			
☐ C-FMAL	MD Helicopters MD 500D (Hughes 369D)	611010D	N1109W	0082	1192	1 AN 250-C20B	1361			
☐ C-GBUY	MD Helicopters MD 500D (Hughes 369D)	610958D	N1102B	0081	0692	1 AN 250-C20B	1361			
☐ C-GHVO	MD Helicopters MD 500D (Hughes 369D)	1100833D		0081	1092	1 AN 250-C20B	1361			
☐ C-GKHV	MD Helicopters MD 500D (Hughes 369D)	200655D	C-GLHH	0080	0898	1 AN 250-C20B	1361			
☐ C-GLCB	MD Helicopters MD 500D (Hughes 369D)	280259D		0078	0896	1 AN 250-C20B	1361			
☐ C-GLHQ	MD Helicopters MD 500D (Hughes 369D)	200662D		0080	0695	1 AN 250-C20B	1361			
☐ C-GPHC	MD Helicopters MD 500D (Hughes 369D)	180257D	N8648F	0078	0398	1 AN 250-C20B	1361			
☐ C-GSZQ	MD Helicopters MD 500D (Hughes 369D)	1270246D		0077	1296	1 AN 250-C20B	1361			
☐ C-GUMA	MD Helicopters MD 500D (Hughes 369D)	890556D	N11121	0079	0998	1 AN 250-C20B	1361			
☐ C-GVEB	MD Helicopters MD 500D (Hughes 369D)	611006D	N5028E	0081		1 AN 250-C20B	1361			
☐ C-GVHG	MD Helicopters MD 500D (Hughes 369D)	570132D		0077	1095	1 AN 250-C20B	1361			
☐ C-GXON	MD Helicopters MD 500D (Hughes 369D)	370093D		0077	0395	1 AN 250-C20B	1361			
☐ C-GLNH	Eurocopter (Aerosp.) AS350D AStar	1230		0080	0996	1 LY LTS101-600A.3	1950			

PRO AIR Aviation International (2638-8421 Québec, Inc. dba)
Bromont, Qué.

939 Route 220, Bonsecours, Québec J0E 1H0, Canada ☎ (514) 532-5380 Tx: none Fax: (514) 532-5494 SITA: n/a
F: 1989 ♦♦♦ n/a Head: Gaétan Belanger Net: n/a

| ☐ C-FPQO | Consolidated PBY-5A Canso | CV-427 | | 0040 | 0394 | 2 PW R-1830-92S | 13835 | Tanker | | 15 / Amphibian |

PRO-FLIGHT, Ltd (Affiliated with RLW Engineering, Ltd)
Regina, Sask.

203-4040 Gordon Road, Regina, Saskatchewan S4S 6W2, Canada ☎ (306) 585-1855 Tx: n/a Fax: (306) 585-1842 SITA: n/a
F: 1985 ♦♦♦ n/a Head: R.L. Wilde Net: n/a Aircraft below MTOW 1361kg: Piper PA-28 & Mooney M20.

☐ C-FSPX	Piper PA-31-310 Navajo	31-342		0068	0593	2 LY TIO-540-A1A	2948			
☐ C-GPJT	Piper PA-31-310 Navajo	31-7712008		0077	0898	2 LY TIO-540-A2C	2948			
☐ C-GORW	Piper PA-31P Pressurized Navajo	31P-7400179	N123GZ	0074	0696	2 LY TIGO-541-E1A	3538			

PROPAIR, Inc. = PRO
La Sarre & Rouyn & La Grande & Chibougamau & Matagami, Qué.

BG GR20, RR 1, Rouyn, Québec J9X 5B7, Canada ☎ (819) 762-0811 Tx: none Fax: (819) 762-1852 SITA: n/a
F: 1981 ♦♦♦ 75 Head: Jean Pronovost ICAO: PROPAIR Net: n/a Aircraft below MTOW 1361 kg: Cessna 180 (on Floats / Wheel-Skis).

☐ C-GQAB	Cessna A185F Skywagon	18502766		0075		1 CO IO-520-D	1520			Floats / Wheel-Skis
☐ C-FJAB	De Havilland DHC-2 Beaver I	934		0056		1 PW R-985	2313			Floats / Wheel-Skis
☐ C-FLEO	De Havilland DHC-2 Beaver I	1270		0058		1 PW R-985	2313			Floats / Wheel-Skis
☐ C-FJUH	De Havilland DHC-3 Otter	214		0057		1 PW R-1340	3629			Floats / Wheel-Skis
☐ C-FODH	De Havilland DHC-3 Otter	3		0052		1 PW R-1340	3629			Floats / Wheel-Skis
☐ C-FVVY	De Havilland DHC-3 Otter	410	RCAF9427	0060		1 PW R-1340	3629			Floats / Wheel-Skis
☐ C-FPAJ	Beech King Air A100	B-151	N324B	0073	0595	2 PWC PT6A-28	5216			

registration	type of aircraft	cn/fn	ex/ex*	mfd	del	powered by	mtow kg	configuration	selcal	name/fln/specialities/remarks
☐ C-FWRM	Beech King Air A100	B-125	N89JM	0072	0689	2 PWC PT6A-28	5216			
☐ C-GJLJ	Beech King Air A100	B-235	N23517	0077		2 PWC PT6A-28	5216			
☐ C-GJLP	Beech King Air A100	B-148	N67V	0073		2 PWC PT6A-28	5216			
☐ C-GDEF	Fairchild (Swearingen) SA226AT Merlin IVA	AT-069	N311RV	0078	0696	2 GA TPE331-3U-303G	5670			
☐ C-FOGY	Beech King Air 200	BB-168	N10VW	0076	0596	2 PWC PT6A-41	5670			
☐ C-FAWE	GAC (Grumman) G-159 Gulfstream I	188	HB-LDT	0068	1197	2 RR Dart 529-8X	15422			

PROVINCE OF ALBERTA – Air Transportation Services = GOA (Department of Public Works Supply & Services) **Edmonton, Alta.**

11940-109 St., Edmonton, Alberta T5G 2T8, Canada ☎ (780) 427-7341 Tx: none Fax: (780) 422-1232 SITA: n/a
F: 1905 ⁂ 35 Head: John Dillon ICAO: ALBERTA Net: n/a Non-commercial provincial government organisation conducting fire fighting Tanker, aerial & transport missions.

registration	type of aircraft	cn/fn	ex/ex*	mfd	del	powered by	mtow kg	configuration	selcal	name/fln/specialities/remarks
☐ C-GFSG	Beech King Air 200	BB-671		0080		2 PWC PT6A-41	5670	Pax		
☐ C-GFSH	Beech King Air 200	BB-912		0081		2 PWC PT6A-41	5670	Pax		
☐ C-GFSA	Beech King Air 350 (B300)	FL-174		0097	0997	2 PWC PT6A-60A	6804	Pax		
☐ C-GFSJ	De Havilland DHC-8-103 Dash 8	017		0085	1285	2 PWC PW121	15649	Pax		cvtd -101
☐ C-FTUU	Canadair CL-215 (CL-215-1A10)	1011		0069	0599	2 PW R-2800-CA3	19731	Tanker		205 / lsf / opb ASB / Amphibian
☐ C-FTUW	Canadair CL-215 (CL-215-1A10)	1030		0070	0599	2 PW R-2800-CA3	19731	Tanker		206 / lsf / opb ASB / Amphibian
☐ C-GFSK	Canadair CL-215 (CL-215-1A10)	1085	C-GKDN*	0086	0386	2 PW R-2800-CA3	19731	Tanker		201 / lst / opb ASB / Amphibian
☐ C-GFSL	Canadair CL-215 (CL-215-1A10)	1086	C-GKDP*	0086	0586	2 PW R-2800-CA3	19731	Tanker		202 / lst / opb ASB / Amphibian
☐ C-GFSM	Canadair CL-215 (CL-215-1A10)	1098	C-GKDP*	0088		2 PW R-2800-CA3	19731	Tanker		203 / lst / opb ASB / Amphibian
☐ C-GFSN	Canadair CL-215 (CL-215-1A10)	1099	C-GKDY*	0088		2 PW R-2800-CA3	19731	Tanker		204 / lst / opb ASB / Amphibian

PROVINCE OF MANITOBA – Air Services (Department of Government Services) **Winnipeg-Int'l & Thompson, Man.**

Hangar T-5, 900 Ferry Road, Winnipeg, Manitoba R3H 0Y8, Canada ☎ (204) 945-8990 Tx: none Fax: (204) 945-5148 SITA: n/a
F: 1932 ⁂ 72 Head: Ken Giesbrecht Net: n/a Non-commercial provincial government organisation conducting fire fighting Tanker, ambulance and transport missions.

registration	type of aircraft	cn/fn	ex/ex*	mfd	del	powered by	mtow kg	configuration	selcal	name/fln/specialities/remarks
☐ C-GDAT	Cessna 310R II	310R1883	N315U	0080	0698	2 CO IO-520-M	2495			
☐ C-GKCE	Cessna 310R II	310R0649		0076	0494	2 CO IO-520-M	2495			
☐ C-GRNE	Piper PA-31-350 Navajo Chieftain	31-7952224	N91834	0079		2 LY TIO-540-J2BD	3175			
☐ C-FMAU	De Havilland DHC-3 Otter	74		0055		1 PW R-1340	3629			Floats / Wheel-Skis
☐ C-FMAX	De Havilland DHC-3 Otter	267		0058		1 PW R-1340	3629			Floats / Wheel-Skis
☐ C-FODY	De Havilland DHC-3 Otter	429		0062	0589	1 PW R-1340	3629			Floats / Wheel-Skis
☐ C-GBNE	Cessna 500 Citation I	500-0378	N3156M*	0078		2 PWC JT15D-1A	5375			
☐ C-FEMA	Cessna S550 Citation S/II	S550-0040		0085		2 PWC JT15D-4B	6668	Ambulance		
☐ C-FTUV	Canadair CL-215 (CL-215-1A10)	1020		0069	0298	2 PW R-2800-CA3	19731	Tanker		256 / Amphibian
☐ C-FTXI	Canadair CL-215 (CL-215-1A10)	1016		0069	0298	2 PW R-2800-CA3	19731	Tanker		255 / Amphibian
☐ C-GBOW	Canadair CL-215 (CL-215-1A10)	1087	C-GKDY*	0086	0786	2 PW R-2800-CA3	19731	Tanker		253 / Amphibian
☐ C-GMAF	Canadair CL-215 (CL-215-1A10)	1044		0074		2 PW R-2800-CA3	19731	Tanker		250 / Amphibian
☐ C-GMAK	Canadair CL-215 (CL-215-1A10)	1107	C-GKEA*	0088		2 PW R-2800-CA3	19731	Tanker		254 / Amphibian
☐ C-GUMW	Canadair CL-215 (CL-215-1A10)	1065		0078		2 PW R-2800-CA3	19731	Tanker		251 / Amphibian
☐ C-GYJB	Canadair CL-215 (CL-215-1A10)	1068		0082		2 PW R-2800-CA3	19731	Tanker		252 / Amphibian

PROVINCE OF NEW BRUNSWICK – Executive Flight Service (Div. of New Brunswick Department of Transportation) **Fredericton, N.B.**

PO Box 6000, Fredericton, New Brunswick E3B 5H1, Canada ☎ (506) 357-4072 Tx: 014-46230 nb gov frn Fax: (506) 357-4073 SITA: n/a
F: 1970 ⁂ 7 Head: Glyn Morgan Net: n/a Non-commercial provincial government organisation conducting executive flights.

registration	type of aircraft	cn/fn	ex/ex*	mfd	del	powered by	mtow kg	configuration	selcal	name/fln/specialities/remarks
☐ C-GXBF	Piper PA-31T Cheyenne II	31T-7620010	N54988	0076	1193	2 PWC PT6A-28	4082			

PROVINCE OF NEWFOUNDLAND – Air Services Division **St. John's, Nfld.**

PO Box 8700, St. John's, Newfoundland A1B 4J6, Canada ☎ (709) 729-4610 Tx: none Fax: (709) 729-3491 SITA: n/a
F: 1973 ⁂ 63 Head: Henry Hillier Net: n/a Non-commercial provincial government organization conducting fire fighting Tanker, ambulance and surveillance missions.

registration	type of aircraft	cn/fn	ex/ex*	mfd	del	powered by	mtow kg	configuration	selcal	name/fln/specialities/remarks
☐ C-GLFY	Cessna 337G Super Skymaster II	33701700		0076	0477	2 CO IO-360-G	2100	Surveyer		
☐ C-FGNL	Beech King Air A100	B-184		0073	1173	2 PWC PT6A-28	5216	EMS		
☐ C-FIZU	Consolidated PBY-5A Catalina	2019	N10014	0045	0573	2 PW R-1830-92	13835	Tanker		704 / Amphibian
☐ C-FNJC	Consolidated PBY-5A Canso	CV-430	44-33929	0043	0573	2 PW R-1830-92	13835	Tanker		701 / Amphibian
☐ C-FAYN	Canadair CL-215 (CL-215-1A10)	1105	C-GKET*	0087	0388	2 PW R-2800-CA3	19731	Tanker		282 / Amphibian
☐ C-FAYU	Canadair CL-215 (CL-215-1A10)	1106		0088	0388	2 PW R-2800-CA3	19731	Tanker		283 / Amphibian
☐ C-FTXA	Canadair CL-215 (CL-215-1A10)	1006		0069	1095	2 PW R-2800-CA3	19731	Tanker		284 / Amphibian
☐ C-FYWP	Canadair CL-215 (CL-215-1A10)	1002		0068	1095	2 PW R-2800-CA3	19731	Tanker		285 / Amphibian
☐ C-GDKW	Canadair CL-215 (CL-215-1A10)	1095		0087	0587	2 PW R-2800-CA3	19731	Tanker		280 / Amphibian
☐ C-GDKY	Canadair CL-215 (CL-215-1A10)	1096		0087	0587	2 PW R-2800-CA3	19731	Tanker		281 / Amphibian

PROVINCE OF NOVA-SCOTIA – Aviation Services = PTR (Division of Department of Natural Resources) **Halifax, N.S.**

PO Box 130, Shubenacadie, Nova Scotia B0N 2H0, Canada ☎ (902) 758-3438 Tx: none Fax: (902) 758-3355 SITA: n/a
F: 1963 ⁂ 16 Head: Ross Wickwire ICAO: PATROL Net: n/a Non-commercial provincial government organisation conducting aerial and transport missions.

registration	type of aircraft	cn/fn	ex/ex*	mfd	del	powered by	mtow kg	configuration	selcal	name/fln/specialities/remarks
☐ C-FDML	MD Helicopters MD 500E (Hughes 369E)	0318E		0088		1 AN 250-C20R	1361			
☐ C-FGJK	MD Helicopters MD 500E (Hughes 369E)	0262E	C-FPNS	0087		1 AN 250-C20B	1361			
☐ C-GLAF	MD Helicopters MD 500E (Hughes 369E)	0379E		0089	0390	1 AN 250-C20B	1361			
☐ C-GRVV	MD Helicopters MD 500E (Hughes 369E)	0086E		0084	1294	1 AN 250-C20R	1361			
☐ C-GRTO	Piper PA-23-250 Aztec E	27-7554076	N54767	0075	0489	2 LY IO-540-C4B5	2359			
☐ C-GPNS	Bell 212	31148		0080		2 PWC PT6T-3 TwinPac	5080			Skids

PROVINCE OF ONTARIO – MNR Aviation Section = TRI (Division of Ministry of Natural Resources) **Sault St. Marie, Ont.**

RR 1, Box 2, Sault Ste. Marie, Ontario P6A 5K6, Canada ☎ (705) 779-2149 Tx: none Fax: (705) 945-6893 SITA: n/a
F: 1924 ⁂ 80 Head: Lou Lingenfelter ICAO: TRILLIUM Net: n/a Aircraft below MTOW 1361kg: Maule M-7-235 Non-commercial provincial government organisation conducting fire fighting Tanker, executive, ambulance and transport missions. On Air Ambulance Service-flights for Ministry of Health, the 3-letter ICAO code MED and callsign MEDICAL are used.

registration	type of aircraft	cn/fn	ex/ex*	mfd	del	powered by	mtow kg	configuration	selcal	name/fln/specialities/remarks
☐ C-FCHZ	Bell 206L-1 LongRanger II	45567	N313HL	0080	0192	1 AN 250-C28C	1882			Skids
☐ C-GEOM	Bell 206L-1 LongRanger II	45625		0081		1 AN 250-C28B	1882			Skids
☐ C-GOFH	Bell 206L-1 LongRanger II	45359	N100U	0080		1 AN 250-C28B	1882			Skids
☐ C-GOFI	Bell 206L-1 LongRanger II	45342	N167CP	0079		1 AN 250-C28B	1882			Skids
☐ C-GOGJ	Eurocopter (Aerosp.) AS350B2 AStar	2749		0093	1093	1 TU Arriel 1D1	2250			
☐ C-GOGL	Eurocopter (Aerosp.) AS350B2 AStar	2738		0093	1093	1 TU Arriel 1D1	2250			
☐ C-GOGN	Eurocopter (Aerosp.) AS350B2 AStar	2834		0094	0495	1 TU Arriel 1D1	2250			
☐ CF-OBS	De Havilland DHC-2 Beaver I	2		0048		1 PW R-985	2313			Floats / Wheel-Skis
☐ C-FOEH	De Havilland DHC-2 Turbo Beaver III	1644TB24		0066		1 PWC PT6A-27	2436			Floats / Wheel-Skis
☐ C-FOEK	De Havilland DHC-2 Turbo Beaver III	1650TB28		0066	1298	1 PWC PT6A-20	2436			Floats / Wheel-Skis
☐ C-FOER	De Havilland DHC-2 Turbo Beaver III	1671TB41		0067		1 PWC PT6A-27	2436			Amphibian / Wheel-Skis
☐ C-FOEU	De Havilland DHC-2 Turbo Beaver III	1678TB46		0067		1 PWC PT6A-20	2436			Floats / Wheel-Skis
☐ C-FOEW	De Havilland DHC-2 Turbo Beaver III	1682TB50		0067		1 PWC PT6A-27	2436			Floats / Wheel-Skis
☐ C-FOPA	De Havilland DHC-2 Turbo Beaver III	1688TB56		0068		1 PWC PT6A-27	2436			Amphibian / Wheel-Skis
☐ C-GCJX	Piper PA-31-350 Navajo Chieftain	31-7552064	N4WE	0075		2 LY TIO-540-J2BD	3175	Aerial Photo		
☐ C-FODU	De Havilland DHC-3 Otter	369		0060		1 PW R-1340	3629			Floats / Wheel-Skis
☐ C-GOGT	Beech King Air 200	BB-535		0079		2 PWC PT6A-41	5670	Executive		
☐ C-GQNJ	Beech King Air 200	BB-275		0077		2 PWC PT6A-41	5670	Executive		
☐ C-FOPG	De Havilland DHC-6 Twin Otter 300	232		0069	0569	2 PWC PT6A-27	5670			Amphibian / Wheel-Skis
☐ C-FOPI	De Havilland DHC-6 Twin Otter 300	243		0069	0869	2 PWC PT6A-27	5670			Amphibian / Wheel-Skis
☐ C-FOPJ	De Havilland DHC-6 Twin Otter 300	344		0072	0772	2 PWC PT6A-27	5670			Amphibian / Wheel-Skis
☐ C-FTVO	De Havilland DHC-6 Twin Otter 300	334		0071		2 PWC PT6A-27	5670			Amphibian / Wheel-Skis
☐ C-GOGA	De Havilland DHC-6 Twin Otter 300	739		0081	0281	2 PWC PT6A-27	5670			Amphibian / Wheel-Skis
☐ C-GOGB	De Havilland DHC-6 Twin Otter 300	761		0081	0581	2 PWC PT6A-27	5670			Amphibian / Wheel-Skis
☐ C-GOGC	De Havilland DHC-6 Twin Otter 300	750		0081	0381	2 PWC PT6A-27	5670			Amphibian / Wheel-Skis
☐ C-GDRS	Canadair CL-215 (CL-215-1A10)	1081	C-GKDN	0085	1085	2 PW R-2800-CA3	19731	Tanker		262 / Amphibian
☐ C-GENU	Canadair CL-215 (CL-215-1A10)	1082	C-GKDP	0085	1285	2 PW R-2800-CA3	19731	Tanker		263 / Amphibian
☐ C-GOGD	Canadair CL-415 (CL-215-6B11)	2028	C-GAOI	0097	0498	2 PWC PW123AF	19890	Tanker		270 / Amphibian
☐ C-GOGE	Canadair CL-415 (CL-215-6B11)	2031	C-GAUR	0097	0598	2 PWC PW123AF	19890	Tanker		271 / Amphibian
☐ C-GOGF	Canadair CL-415 (CL-215-6B11)	2032	C-GBGE	0097	0498	2 PWC PW123AF	19890	Tanker		272 / Amphibian
☐ C-GOGG	Canadair CL-415 (CL-215-6B11)	2033	C-GBFY	0097	0498	2 PWC PW123AF	19890	Tanker		273 / Amphibian
☐ C-GOGH	Canadair CL-415 (CL-215-6B11)	2034	C-GCNO	0098	0598	2 PWC PW123AF	19890	Tanker		274 / Amphibian
☐ C-GOGW	Canadair CL-415 (CL-215-6B11)	2037		0098	1298	2 PWC PW123AF	19890	Tanker		275 / Amphibian
☐ C-GOGX	Canadair CL-415 (CL-215-6B11)	2038		0098	1298	2 PWC PW123AF	19890	Tanker		276 / Amphibian

PROVINCE OF SASKATCHEWAN – Air Transportation Services = SGS (Executive Air Svc. & Air Ambulance Svc.) **Regina & Saskatoon & La Ronge, Sask.**

Hangar 4, 2710 Airport Road, Regina, Saskatchewan S4W 1A3, Canada ☎ (306) 787-2013 Tx: 071-2490 sask purch Fax: (306) 787-1424 SITA: n/a
F: 1946 ⁂ 39 Head: Rick Sinotte ICAO: SASKATCHEWAN Net: n/a Non-commercial provincial government organisation conducting fire fighting Tanker, executive, ambulance & transport missions. On Air Ambulance Service-flights, the 3-letter ICAO code SLG and callsign LIFEGUARD are used.

registration	type of aircraft	cn/fn	ex/ex*	mfd	del	powered by	mtow kg	configuration	selcal	name/fln/specialities/remarks
☐ C-FCOD	Beech Baron B55 (95-B55)	TC-1325		0070		2 CO IO-470-L	2313			
☐ C-FSPM	Beech Baron B55 (95-B55)	TC-1008		0066		2 CO IO-470-L	2313			
☐ C-GNBA	Beech Baron B55 (95-B55)	TC-1787		0075		2 CO IO-470-L	2313			
☐ C-GPVD	Beech Baron B55 (95-B55)	TC-1966		0076		2 CO IO-470-L	2313			
☐ C-FNAO	AAC (Piper) Aerostar 600A	60-0737-8001227	N6079U	0080	0895	2 LY IO-540-K1J5	2495			

registration	type of aircraft	cn/fn	ex/ex*	mfd	del	powered by	mtow kg	configuration	selcal	name/fln/specialitites/remarks
☐ C-GZJR	AAC (Piper) Aerostar 600A	60-0764-8061231	N6082Y	0080	0895	2 LY IO-540-K1J5	2495			
☐ C-GGPS	Piper PA-31T Cheyenne II	31T-7820023		0078		2 PWC PT6A-28	4082			
☐ C-GJPT	Piper PA-31T Cheyenne II	31T-7520039	N531PT	0075		2 PWC PT6A-28	4082			
☐ C-GNKP	Piper PA-31T Cheyenne II	31T-7520008		0075		2 PWC PT6A-28	4082			
☐ C-GSAA	Piper PA-42-720 Cheyenne IIIA	42-5501057	OE-FAA	0091	1096	2 PWC PT6A-61	5080			
☐ C-GEAS	Beech King Air 350 (B300)	FL-17	N56872	0090	0997	2 PWC PT6A-60A	6804			
☐ C-GEHP	Grumman CS2F-2 Tracker	DHC-97	CAF12198	0060		2 PW R-982-C9HE2	11793	Tanker		1
☐ C-GEHR	Grumman CS2F-2 Tracker	DHC-51	CAF12185	0051		2 PW R-982-C9HE2	11793	Tanker		3
☐ C-GEQC	Grumman CS2F-2 Tracker	DHC-53	CAF12187	0059		2 PW R-982-C9HE2	11793	Tanker		4
☐ C-GEQD	Grumman CS2F-2 Tracker	DHC-98	CAF12199	0060		2 PW R-982-C9HE2	11793	Tanker		5
☐ C-GEQE	Grumman CS2F-2 Tracker	DHC-92	CAF12193	0060		2 PW R-982-C9HE2	11793	Tanker		6
☐ C-GWHK	Grumman CS2F-1 Firecat	DHC-37	RCN1538	0058		2 PW R-982-C9HE2	11793	Tanker		2 / cvtd Tracker
☐ C-FAFN	Canadair CL-215 (CL-215-1A10)	1093	C-GKDY*	0087	0387	2 PW R-2800-CA3	19731	Tanker		216 / Amphibian
☐ C-FAFO	Canadair CL-215 (CL-215-1A10)	1094	C-GKEO*	0087	0387	2 PW R-2800-CA3	19731	Tanker		217 / Amphibian
☐ C-FAFP	Canadair CL-215 (CL-215-1A10)	1100	C-GKEA*	0087		2 PW R-2800-CA3	19731	Tanker		218 / Amphibian
☐ C-FAFQ	Canadair CL-215 (CL-215-1A10)	1101	C-GKEE*	0087		2 PW R-2800-CA3	19731	Tanker		219 / Amphibian
☐ C-FYWO	Canadair CL-215 (CL-215-1A10)	1003		0068	0497	2 PW R-2800-CA3	19731	Tanker		214 / Amphibian
☐ C-FYXG	Canadair CL-215 (CL-215-1A10)	1009		0069	0497	2 PW R-2800-CA3	19731	Tanker		215 / Amphibian

PROVINCIAL AIRLINES, Ltd - PAL = AG (Interprovincial Airlines) — St. John's, Nfld. & Halifax, N.S.

PO Box 29030, St. John's, Newfoundland A1A 5B5, Canada ☎ (709) 576-1800 Tx: none Fax: (709) 576-1802 SITA: n/a
F: 1972 ⁂ 300 Head: Thomas W. Collingwood IATA: 967 Net: n/a
Scheduled services in conjunction with AIR NOVA (with Fairchild SA227AC aircraft) are operated under the marketing name INTERPROVINCIAL AIRLINES.

registration	type of aircraft	cn/fn	ex/ex*	mfd	del	powered by	mtow kg	configuration	selcal	name/fln/specialitites/remarks
☐ C-FPKA	Piper PA-23-250 Aztec B	27-2404		0063	0680	2 LY O-540-A1D5	2177			
☐ C-FMPV	De Havilland DHC-2 Beaver I	1304		0058	0685	1 PW R-985	2313			Floats / Wheel-Skis
☐ C-FAOU	Britten-Norman BN-2A-21 Islander	4	N43MJ	0067	1290	2 LY IO-540-K1B5	2994			
☐ C-GETT	Piper PA-31-310 Navajo	31-602	N110BC	0070	1290	2 LY TIO-540-A1A	2948			
☐ C-GLEW	Piper PA-31-310 Navajo	31-685	N6775L	0070	1290	2 LY TIO-540-A1A	2948			
☐ C-GMHX	Piper PA-31-310 Navajo	31-75	N9052Y	0067	1290	2 LY TIO-540-A1A	2948			
☐ C-GMNX	Piper PA-31-310 Navajo	31-528	N6601L	0069	1290	2 LY TIO-540-A1A	2948			
☐ C-GRTG	Piper PA-31-350 Navajo Chieftain	31-7652004	N180RM	0076	1290	2 LY TIO-540-J2BD	3175			
☐ C-GTWY	Piper PA-31-310 Navajo	31-124	N9089Y	0068	1290	2 LY TIO-540-A1A	2948			
☐ C-GWLW	Piper PA-31-350 Navajo Chieftain	31-7405221	N54277	0074	0088	2 LY TIO-540-J2BD	3175			
☐ C-FGPW	Fairchild (Swearingen) SA226TC Metro II	TC-404	N1013B	0081	0290	2 GA TPE331-10UA-511G	5670			
☐ C-FLNG	Fairchild (Swearingen) SA226TC Metro II	TC-409	N1013G	0081	1290	2 GA TPE331-10UA-511G	5670			
☐ C-GTMW	Fairchild (Swearingen) SA226AT Merlin IV	AT-002	N39RD	0070	0693	2 GA TPE331-3UW-303G	5670			
☐ C-FWLG	De Havilland DHC-6 Twin Otter 300	731	N915MA	0080	0995	2 PWC PT6A-27	5670			
☐ C-FWLQ	De Havilland DHC-6 Twin Otter 300	724	N914MA	0080	1095	2 PWC PT6A-27	5670			
☐ C-FGFZ	Beech King Air 200	BB-403	N147K	0078	0989	2 PWC PT6A-41	5670			
☐ C-FIFO	Beech King Air 200	BB-527	N662L	0079	0590	2 PWC PT6A-41	6350	Maritime Patrol		Survey Canada-colors
☐ C-GMWR	Beech King Air 200	BB-68	N844N	0075	1288	2 PWC PT6A-41	6350	Maritime Patrol		Survey Canada-colors
☐ C-GPCD	Beech King Air 200	BB-76	N500DR	0075	0783	2 PWC PT6A-41	6350	Maritime Patrol		Special Missions colors
☐ C-FIPW	Fairchild (Swearingen) SA227AC Metro III	AC-524	N4442F	0082	0395	2 GA TPE331-11U-611G	6577			
☐ C-FITW	Fairchild (Swearingen) SA227AC Metro III	AC-638	N353AE	0086	0395	2 GA TPE331-11U-611G	6577			
☐ C-GERW	Fairchild (Swearingen) SA227AC Metro III	AC-479	N479NE	0081	0593	2 GA TPE331-11U-601G	6577			

PROVINCIAL HELICOPTERS, Ltd (formerly Rotor-Ways, Ltd & TJ Helicopter Charter Services) — Lac du Bonnet, Man.

Box 579, Lac du Bonnet, Manitoba R0E 1A0, Canada ☎ (204) 345-8332 Tx: none Fax: (204) 345-8679 SITA: n/a
F: 1981 ⁂ 8 Head: John M. Gibson Net: n/a

registration	type of aircraft	cn/fn	ex/ex*	mfd	del	powered by	mtow kg	configuration	selcal	name/fln/specialitites/remarks
☐ C-FPHB	Bell 206B JetRanger	1213	N62SH	0073	1198	1 AN 250-C20	1451			
☐ C-GCHB	Bell 206B JetRanger	1226		0073	0697	1 AN 250-C20	1451			
☐ C-GEKM	Bell 206B JetRanger	1786		0075	0697	1 AN 250-C20	1451			
☐ C-FBHM	Bell 206L LongRanger	45066	N16698	0076	1198	1 AN 250-C20B	1814			
☐ C-FYUN	Eurocopter (Aerosp.) AS350B AStar	1384	N666MP	0081	1196	1 TU Arriel 1B	1950			cvtd AS350D
☐ C-FOKY	Bell 204B	2043		0066	0598	1 LY T5313A	3856			

Q.N.S. & L. AVIATION (Aviation division of Québec North Shore & Labrador Railway, Co.) — Sept-Iles, Qué.

Box 1000, Sept-Iles, Québec G4R 4L5, Canada ☎ (418) 968-7515 Tx: none Fax: (418) 968-7896 SITA: n/a
F: 1948 ⁂ 7 Head: James Court Net: n/a Non-commercial company conducting corporate & club-charter flights for its parent company only.

registration	type of aircraft	cn/fn	ex/ex*	mfd	del	powered by	mtow kg	configuration	selcal	name/fln/specialitites/remarks
☐ C-FQYP	Fairchild Ind. F-27F	95	N270E	0062	0772	2 RR Dart 529-7E	19051	Corporate 30Pax		

QUANTUM HELICOPTERS, Ltd — Terrace, B.C.

RR4, Site 16, Comp. 2, Terrace, British Columbia V8G 4V2, Canada ☎ (250) 615-0168 Tx: none Fax: (250) 615-0169 SITA: n/a
F: 1998 ⁂ n/a Head: n/a Net: n/a

registration	type of aircraft	cn/fn	ex/ex*	mfd	del	powered by	mtow kg	configuration	selcal	name/fln/specialitites/remarks
☐ C-GSLV	Bell 206B JetRanger III	4199	N3202G	0091	1198	1 AN 250-C20B	1451			
☐ C-GTNX	Bell 206B JetRanger III	3583	N2300Z	0082	1198	1 AN 250-C20B	1451			

QUEBEC AVENTURE B.L., Inc. — Montebello-SPB, Qué.

533 Route 315, Montpellier, Québec J0V 1M0, Canada ☎ (819) 428-2700 Tx: none Fax: (819) 428-1354 SITA: n/a
F: 1993 ⁂ n/a Head: Gilles Belisle Net: http://www.quebec-aventure.com Aircraft below MTOW 1361kg: Cessna 172 (on Floats / Wheels)

registration	type of aircraft	cn/fn	ex/ex*	mfd	del	powered by	mtow kg	configuration	selcal	name/fln/specialitites/remarks
☐ C-GHSA	Cessna U206G Stationair 6 II	U20605858		0080	0793	1 CO IO-520-F	1633			Québec Hydravion / Floats

QUEBEC CARTIER MINING - Aviation Dept. (Aviation division of Québec Cartier Mining, Co.) — Sept-Iles, Qué.

Box, Port Cartier, Québec G0G 2J0, Canada ☎ (418) 968-5333 Tx: none Fax: (418) 968-1413 SITA: n/a
F: 1962 ⁂ n/a Head: Lloyd Carp Net: n/a Non-commercial company conducting corporate flights for its parent company only.

registration	type of aircraft	cn/fn	ex/ex*	mfd	del	powered by	mtow kg	configuration	selcal	name/fln/specialitites/remarks
☐ C-GQCM	Fairchild Ind. F-27F	110	N966P	0065	0674	2 RR Dart 529-7E	19051	Corporate 22Pax		

QUEBEC HELICOPTERS, Inc. (Québec Hélicopteres, Inc.) — Beloeil, Qué.

2343 Chemin de l'Aéroport, St-Mathieu de Beloeil, Québec J3G 4S5, Canada ☎ (514) 464-5290 Tx: none Fax: (514) 464-9462 SITA: n/a
F: 1989 ⁂ 10 Head: Steve Jaksi Net: n/a Aircraft below MTOW 1361kg: Robinson R22.

registration	type of aircraft	cn/fn	ex/ex*	mfd	del	powered by	mtow kg	configuration	selcal	name/fln/specialitites/remarks
☐ C-GVNB	Bell 206B JetRanger	1629	N90176	0075	1293	1 AN 250-C20	1451			
☐ C-GDQH	Bell 206L LongRanger	45046	N663JB	0076	0398	1 AN 250-C20B	1814			

QUESTRAL HELICOPTERS, Ltd — Kingston, Ont.

RR 1, Bath, Ontario K0H 1G0, Canada ☎ (613) 352-3692 Tx: none Fax: (613) 352-7587 SITA: n/a
F: 1987 ⁂ 10 Head: Roger Morrow Net: n/a

registration	type of aircraft	cn/fn	ex/ex*	mfd	del	powered by	mtow kg	configuration	selcal	name/fln/specialitites/remarks
☐ C-FZTA	Eurocopter (Aerosp.) AS350B2 AStar	2604	HB-XYV	0092	0397	1 TU Arriel 1D1	2250			
☐ C-GBKV	Eurocopter (Aerosp.) AS350B2 AStar	3027		0097	1197	1 TU Arriel 1D1	2250			
☐ C-GECL	Eurocopter (Aerosp.) AS350B3 AStar	3132		0098	1198	1 TU Arriel 2B	2250			
☐ C-GJIX	Eurocopter (Aerosp.) AS350BA AStar	1084	N350AA	0078		1 TU Arriel 1B	2100			cvtd AS350B

QUIKWAY AIR SERVICES, Ltd (formerly Quikway Aviation, Ltd & Brooks Aviation, Ltd) — Brooks, Alta.

Box 1780, Brooks, Alberta T1R 1C5, Canada ☎ (780) 362-5400 Tx: none Fax: (780) 362-5543 SITA: n/a
F: 1973 ⁂ 9 Head: Pat Stinnissen Net: n/a Aircraft / Ag-Aircraft below MTOW 1361 / 5000 kg: Air Tractor AT-401B, Ayres S-2R & Cessna 172

registration	type of aircraft	cn/fn	ex/ex*	mfd	del	powered by	mtow kg	configuration	selcal	name/fln/specialitites/remarks
☐ C-GITJ	Piper PA-31-310 Navajo	31-287	N9222Y	0068	1197	2 LY TIO-540-A1A	2948			
☐ C-GPTE	Piper PA-31-325 Navajo C/R	31-7712059	N111RC	0077		2 LY TIO-540-F2BD	2948			
☐ C-GQWX	Piper PA-31-350 Navajo Chieftain	31-8152095	N4083L	0081	1296	2 LY TIO-540-J2BD	3175			

RAINBOW AIRWAYS, Inc. (Seasonal Ice break-up to freeze-up ops only) — Ardbeg, Ont.

15 Confederation Street, Halton Hills (Georgetown), Ontario L7G 3R4, Canada ☎ (905) 873-2740 Tx: n/a Fax: (905) 873-2775 SITA: n/a
F: 1984 ⁂ n/a Head: David Williamson Net: n/a Aircraft below MTOW 1361kg: Cessna 172 & 180 (on Floats)

registration	type of aircraft	cn/fn	ex/ex*	mfd	del	powered by	mtow kg	configuration	selcal	name/fln/specialitites/remarks
☐ C-FOCB	De Havilland DHC-2 Beaver I	21		0049		1 PW R-985	2309			Floats
☐ C-GRYG	De Havilland DHC-2 Beaver I	1335	N5345G	0059	0598	1 PW R-985	2309			Floats

RANGER AIR CHARTER (Tincup Enterprises, Ltd dba / Seasonal May-October ops only) — Whitehorse, Y.T.

PO Box 5275, Whitehorse, Yukon Territory Y1A 4Z2, Canada ☎ (867) 633-4368 Tx: none Fax: (867) 633-4368 SITA: n/a
F: 1993 ⁂ n/a Head: n/a Net: n/a Aircraft below MTOW 1361kg: Cessna 180 (on Floats)

registration	type of aircraft	cn/fn	ex/ex*	mfd	del	powered by	mtow kg	configuration	selcal	name/fln/specialitites/remarks
☐ CF-JRO	De Havilland DHC-2 Beaver I	1108	56-387	0055	0593	1 PW R-985	2313			Floats

RCMP - GRC Air Services (Division of Royal Canadian Mounted Police / Gendarmarie royale du Canada) — Ottawa, Ont.

1200 Vanier Parkway, Ottawa, Ontario K1A 0R2, Canada ☎ (613) 998-3360 Tx: 053-3305 rcmp 10 ott Fax: (613) 998-0365 SITA: n/a
F: 1937 ⁂ 114 Head: Supt. Dave Sperry Net: http://www.rcmp-grc.gc.ca Aircraft below MTOW 1361kg: Cessna 182Q. Non-commercial federal government organisation conducting aerial police missions.

registration	type of aircraft	cn/fn	ex/ex*	mfd	del	powered by	mtow kg	configuration	selcal	name/fln/specialitites/remarks
☐ C-FMPQ	Bell 206B JetRanger III	3512	N2178F	0081		1 AN 250-C20B	1451			Skids
☐ C-FDGM	Cessna U206G Turbine Stationair 6 II	U20606864	N9450R	0085	0993	1 AN 250-C20S	1633			cvtd Stationair 6B
☐ C-FMPK	Bell 206L-4 LongRanger IV	52036		0093	0793	1 AN 250-C30P	2018			

registration	type of aircraft	cn/fn	ex/ex*	mfd	del	powered by	mtow kg	configuration	selcal	name/fln/specialitites/remarks
☐ C-GMPA	Bell 206L-4 LongRanger IV	52017		0093	0493	1 AN 250-C30P	2018			
☐ C-GMPM	Bell 206L LongRanger	45086		0077		1 AN 250-C20B	1814			Skids / Pop-out Floats
☐ C-GMPT	Bell 206L LongRanger	45149		0078		1 AN 250-C20B	1814			Skids / Pop-out Floats
☐ C-GMPV	Bell 206L-1 LongRanger II	45414		0080		1 AN 250-C28B	1882			Skids / Pop-out Floats
☐ C-FMPG	Eurocopter (Aerosp.) AS350B3 AStar	3082		0098	0798	1 TU Arriel 2B	2250			
☐ C-GMPN	Eurocopter (Aerosp.) AS350B3 AStar	3072		0098	0798	1 TU Arriel 2B	2250			
☐ C-GMPB	Cessna 208 Caravan I	20800082		0086		1 PWC PT6A-114	3629			Amphibian
☐ C-GMPR	Cessna 208 Caravan I	20800116	N9663F*	0087		1 PWC PT6A-114	3629			
☐ C-FRPH	Cessna 208B Grand Caravan	208B0377	N1118B*	0094	0394	1 PWC PT6A-114A	3969			
☐ C-FSUJ	Cessna 208B Grand Caravan	208B0373	N973CC*	0094	0994	1 PWC PT6A-114A	3969			
☐ C-FMPA	Pilatus PC-12/45	164	HB-FRZ*	0096	0397	1 PWC PT6A-67B	4500			
☐ C-GMPE	Pilatus PC-12/45	184	HB-FSS*	0098	0798	1 PWC PT6A-67B	4500			
☐ C-FMPH	Beech King Air 200	BB-757	N72GA	0080	0192	2 PWC PT6A-41	5670			
☐ C-GMPO	Beech King Air 200	BB-667	N183DW	0080	0493	2 PWC PT6A-41	5670			
☐ C-FMPB	De Havilland DHC-6 Twin Otter 300	276		0070	0270	2 PWC PT6A-27	5670			
☐ C-FMPC	De Havilland DHC-6 Twin Otter 300	311		0071	0671	2 PWC PT6A-27	5670			
☐ C-FMPF	De Havilland DHC-6 Twin Otter 300	312		0071	0771	2 PWC PT6A-27	5670			
☐ C-FMPL	De Havilland DHC-6 Twin Otter 300	320		0071	0771	2 PWC PT6A-27	5670			
☐ C-FMPN	De Havilland DHC-6 Twin Otter 300	321		0071	0771	2 PWC PT6A-27	5670			
☐ C-FMPW	De Havilland DHC-6 Twin Otter 300	828		0085	0985	2 PWC PT6A-27	5670			
☐ C-GMPJ	De Havilland DHC-6 Twin Otter 300	534		0077	0377	2 PWC PT6A-27	5670			
☐ C-GMPK	De Havilland DHC-6 Twin Otter 300	471		0076	0376	2 PWC PT6A-27	5670			
☐ C-GMPX	De Havilland DHC-6 Twin Otter 300	588		0078	1278	2 PWC PT6A-27	5670			
☐ C-GMPY	De Havilland DHC-6 Twin Otter 300	796		0082	0782	2 PWC PT6A-27	5670			
☐ C-FMPP	Cessna 550 Citation II	550-0411	N200YM	0082		2 PWC JT15D-4	6033			
☐ C-GMPQ	Cessna 550 Citation II	550-0456	N20RF	0083	0695	2 PWC JT15D-4	6033			
☐ C-GMPF	IAI 1124A Westwind II	391	N24VH	0083	0693	2 GA TFE731-3-1G	10365			

RED DEER AVIATION, Ltd — Red Deer, Alta.

47 Donnelly Crescent, Red Deer, Alberta T4R 2K4, Canada ☎ (780) 342-6893 Tx: none Fax: (780) 340-8053 SITA: n/a
F: 1997 n/a Head: Bruce J. Walton Net: n/a

☐ C-GGHM	Cessna TR182 Skylane RG II	R18201547		0080	0397	1 LY O-540-L3C5D	1406			

RED LAKE AIRWAYS (1987), Ltd (Seasonal May-October ops only) — Red Lake, Ont.

Box 214, Red Lake, Ontario P0V 2M0, Canada ☎ (807) 735-3335 Tx: none Fax: (807) 735-3338 SITA: n/a
F: 1987 n/a Head: Lynn Poulton Net: n/a Aircraft below MTOW 1361kg: Cessna 180 (on Floats)

☐ C-GAQJ	De Havilland DHC-2 Beaver I	1130	56-4411	0056		1 PW R-985	2313			Floats
☐ C-FTBD	Beech 3N (18)	CA-89	RCAF 2291	0052	0694	2 PW R-985	3969			Floats
☐ C-GEHX	Beech 3NM (18)	CA-112	CAF 5181	0052		2 PW R-985	3969			Floats

RED SUCKER LAKE AIR SERVICES, Ltd (Associated with Gods Narrows Airlines) — Red Sucker Lake, Man.

381 Lindenwood Drive W, Winnipeg, Manitoba R3P 2J7, Canada ☎ (204) 469-5388 Tx: none Fax: (204) 487-2824 SITA: n/a
F: 1981 2 Head: Eddie & Stella Cull Net: n/a

☐ C-GMAM	De Havilland DHC-2 Beaver I	1558	G-AZLU	0064	0795	1 PW R-985	2313			Floats / Wheel-Skis
☐ C-FTHE	Piper PA-31-310 Navajo C	31-7512005	N121L	0075	0296	2 LY TIO-540-A2C	2948			

REGENCY AIR CHARTER (International Express Air Charter, Ltd dba/affiliated with Regency Flying School/formerly Astra Air, Ltd) — Boundary Bay, B.C.

4400-72 Street, Unit 100, Delta, British Columbia V4K 5B3, Canada ☎ (604) 940-8841 Tx: none Fax: (604) 940-8499 SITA: n/a
F: 1982 n/a Head: Gill Ranjit Net: n/a Aircraft below MTOW 1361kg: Cessna 172, Piper PA-28 & PA-38

☐ C-FBFL	Piper PA-34-200 Seneca	34-7250082		0072	0395	2 LY IO-360-C1E6	1814			
☐ C-FDEB	Britten-Norman BN-2A Islander	58	N592JA	0069	0995	2 LY O-540-E4C5	2722			
☐ C-GRXX	Piper PA-31-350 Navajo Chieftain	31-7405244	N79423	0074	1197	2 LY TIO-540-J2BD	3175			
☐ C-GWFZ	Piper PA-31-350 Navajo Chieftain	31-7405162	N74003	0074	1195	2 LY TIO-540-J2BD	3175			
☐ N9529G	Cessna 208B Caravan I Super Cargomaster	208B0091		0088	0398	1 PWC PT6A-114	3969	Freighter		Isf Avon Capital Corp.

REGIONNAIR, Inc. = RH / GIO — St-Augustin, Qué.

CP 29, Chevery, Québec G0G 1G0, Canada ☎ (418) 787-2001 Tx: n/a Fax: (418) 787-2004 SITA: n/a
F: 1992 n/a Head: Guy Marcoux IATA: 256 ICAO: GIONNAIR Net: n/a

☐ C-GOVZ	Piper PA-31-310 Navajo C	31-7912003		0079	0398	2 LY TIO-540-A2C	2948	Y7		
☐ C-GDWY	Cessna 208B Grand Caravan	208B0705		0098	1098	1 PWC PT6A-114A	3969	Y9		
☐ C-GGGL	Beech King Air 90 (65-90)	LJ-38	N1128B	0065	0895	2 PWC PT6A-20	4218	Y7		
☐ C-FJCL	De Havilland DHC-6 Twin Otter 200	151	N141FS	0068	0794	2 PWC PT6A-20	5252	Y19		
☐ C-FGOI	Beech 1900C-1 Airliner	UC-85	N85YV	0089	0497	2 PWC PT6A-65B	7530	Y19		
☐ C-FUCB	Beech 1900C Airliner	UB-63	N63MK	0086	0595	2 PWC PT6A-65B	7530	Y19		
☐ C-GURG	Beech 1900D Airliner	UE-337	N23159*	0098	1298	2 PWC PT6A-67D	7688	Y19		

REMOTE HELICOPTERS (NWT), Ltd (formerly Remote Helicopters, Ltd) — Slave Lake, Alta. & Hay River, N.W.T.

Box 1340, Slave Lake, Alberta T0G 2A0, Canada ☎ (780) 849-2222 Tx: none Fax: (780) 849-2288 SITA: n/a
F: 1984 8 Head: William K. Lukan Net: n/a

☐ C-GBHG	Bell 206B JetRanger	802	N2954W	0072	1291	1 AN 250-C20	1451			
☐ C-GJID	Bell 206B JetRanger	756	N2942W	0072	0598	1 AN 250-C20	1451			
☐ C-GRHI	Eurocopter (Aerosp.) AS350B AStar	1901	F-GEDA	0086	1097	1 TU Arriel 1B	1950			
☐ C-GRHJ	Eurocopter (Aerosp.) AS350BA AStar	2149		0088	0489	1 TU Arriel 1B	2100			cvtd AS350B
☐ C-GRHK	Eurocopter (Aerosp.) AS350B Ecureuil	2305	F-GGPE	0089	1097	1 TU Arriel 1B	1950			
☐ C-GRHL	Eurocopter (Aerosp.) AS350B AStar	1960	N5806D	0086		1 TU Arriel 1B	1950			
☐ C-GTAM	Eurocopter (Aerosp.) AS350B AStar	1232	G-MAGI	0080		1 TU Arriel 1B	1950			
☐ C-GRHW	Bell 204B	2056	N204FB	0067	0290	1 LY T5313B	3856			
☐ C-GRHA	Bell 212	30791	N82283	0076	0591	2 PWC PT6T-3 TwinPac	5080			
☐ C-GRHS	Bell 212	30785	N8228R	0076	0591	2 PWC PT6T-3 TwinPac	5080			

RICHMOND HELICOPTERS, Ltd — Vancouver-Int'l, B.C.

4380 Agar Drive, Richmond, British Columbia V7B 1A3, Canada ☎ (604) 821-1077 Tx: none Fax: (604) 732-4959 SITA: n/a
F: 1990 3 Head: Don Broeder Net: n/a

☐ C-FPCL	Bell 206L-3 LongRanger III	51362		0090	0790	1 AN 250-C30P	1882			

RIVER AIR, Ltd — Minaki & Caribou Falls, Ont.

PO Box 189, Kenora, Ontario P9N 3X3, Canada ☎ (807) 224-6531 Tx: none Fax: (807) 224-1060 SITA: n/a
F: 1978 4 Head: George H. Halley Net: n/a Aircraft below MTOW 1361 kg: Cessna 180, Piper J3C & PA-18.

☐ C-GNNO	Cessna A185F Skywagon	18502685		0075	0597	1 CO IO-520-D	1520			Floats
☐ C-FAYM	Cessna U206E Super Skywagon	U20601541		0070		1 CO IO-520-F	1633			Floats
☐ C-GPDS	De Havilland DHC-2 Beaver I	1349	N62352	0059		1 PW R-985	2313			Floats
☐ C-GYKO	De Havilland DHC-3 Otter	287	N22UT	0058	0696	1 PW R-1340	3629			Floats

RND AVIATION, Ltd — Leaf Rapids, Man.

PO Box 609, Leaf Rapids, Manitoba R0B 1W0, Canada ☎ (204) 473-2963 Tx: none Fax: (204) 473-8123 SITA: n/a
F: 1978 6 Head: Donna Hohle Net: n/a

☐ C-GBFT	Cessna A185F Skywagon	18503228		0077		1 CO IO-520-D	1520			Floats / Wheel-Skis
☐ C-GIAL	Cessna A185F Skywagon II	18504138		0080	0592	1 CO IO-520-D	1520			Floats / Wheel-Skis
☐ C-FIKP	De Havilland DHC-2 Beaver I	890		0056		1 PW R-985	2313			Floats / Wheel-Skis

ROAERO, Ltd — Oshawa, Ont.

1748 Baseline Road West, Courtice, Ontario L1E 2T1, Canada ☎ (905) 436-2600 Tx: none Fax: (905) 436-9605 SITA: n/a
F: 1990 n/a Head: Hannu T. Halminen Net: n/a Aircraft below MTOW 1361kg: De Havilland DH-82C & Waco YMF-5

☐ C-FGUY	CCF Harvard 4 (N.A. T-6J)	CCF4-27	RCAF 20236	0052	0491	1 PW R-1340	2608	Pleasure rides		Aerial combat/Aerobatic rides
☐ CF-ROA	CCF Harvard 4 (N.A. T-6J)	CCF4-242	RCAF 20451	0052	0794	1 PW R-1340	2608	Pleasure rides		Aerial combat/Aerobatic rides

ROCKY WEST AVIATION SERVICES, Ltd — Rocky Mountain House, Alta.

Box 488, Rocky Mountain House, Alberta T0M 1T0, Canada ☎ (780) 845-2664 Tx: none Fax: (780) 845-2399 SITA: n/a
F: 1997 n/a Head: Ray Williams Net: n/a

☐ C-GRWD	Beech Baron A55 (95-A55)	TC-481	N177AM	0063	1298	2 CO IO-470-L	2214			

ROSS AIR (Emo Investments, Ltd dba / Affiliated with True North Outfitters) — Burditt Lake, Ont.

Box 454, Emo, Ontario P0W 1E0, Canada ☎ (807) 482-2362 Tx: none Fax: (807) 482-2351 SITA: n/a
F: 1979 5 Head: Chuck & Cathy Mosbeck Net: n/a

☐ C-GCIZ	Cessna A185F Skywagon	18503316	N1614H	0077	0398	1 CO IO-520-D	1520			Floats / Wheel-Skis
☐ C-GDCN	De Havilland DHC-2 Turbo Beaver III	1661TB35	N8PE	0066	0497	1 PWC PT6A-20	2436			Floats / Wheel-Skis
☐ CF-HZA	Beech D18S	A-111		0048	1090	2 PW R-985	3969			Floats

ROYAL AVIATION, Inc. = QN / ROY (formerly Royal Airlines-Transport Aérien Royal) — Montreal-Dorval, Qué.

685 Blvd Stuart Graham North, Dorval, Québec H4Y 1E4, Canada ☎ (514) 828-9000 Tx: none Fax: (514) 828-9090 SITA: n/a
F: 1991 👥 600 Head: Michel LeBlanc IATA: 498 ICAO: ROY Net: n/a

☐ C-FJLT	Boeing 737-2A9C	20206 / 249	N803AL	0070	0897	2 PW JT8D-9A	53070	Freighter		lsf Integrated Leasing
☐ C-FNAP	Boeing 737-242C	20496 / 268	N1788B*	0070	0897	2 PW JT8D-9A (HK3/AVA)	53070	Y122 or Frtr		Spirit of Max Galiger / lsf POLA
☐ C-FNAQ	Boeing 737-242C	20455 / 254	EI-BOC	0070	0897	2 PW JT8D-9A (HK3/AVA)	53070	Y122 or Frtr		lsf POLA
☐ C-GCDG	Boeing 737-2E1 (F) (A)	20776 / 328	N212PL	0073	0897	2 PW JT8D-9A	54204	Freighter		lsf POLA / cvtd -2E1
☐ C-GDCC	Boeing 737-2E1 (F) (A)	20681 / 319	N211PL	0073	0897	2 PW JT8D-9A	54204	Freighter		lsf POLA / cvtd -2E1
☐ C-GDPW	Boeing 737-275C (A)	21116 / 427		0075	0897	2 PW JT8D-9A	53070	Freighter		lsf POLA
☐ C-FRYS	Boeing 727-212 (A) (Valsan/winglets)	21349 / 1289	G-BHVT	0077	1192	3 PW JT8D-17	90039	Y187	HM-CK	lsf CLA Canada
☐ C-GRYR	Boeing 727-217 (A)	21056 / 1122	G-NROA	0075	1092	3 PW JT8D-17 (HK3/FDX)	89356	Y187	FJ-HM	lsf CLA Canada
☐ C-FRYH	Boeing 757-28A	23822 / 130	G-OOOB	0487	1298	2 RR RB211-535E4	108862	Y233		lsf AMM in winter
☐ C-FRYL	Boeing 757-28A	24017 / 162	G-OOOC	0388	1298	2 RR RB211-535E4	104554	Y233		lsf AMM in winter
☐ C-GRYK	Boeing 757-236	25593 / 466	N593KA	0092	0398	2 RR RB211-535E4	113398	Y228	AB-CJ	lsf BBAM
☐ C-GRYO	Boeing 757-236	24118 / 163	N769BE	0088	1098	2 RR RB211-535E4	108862	Y228		lsf BBAM
☐ C-GRYU	Boeing 757-28A	24235 / 180	G-OOOD	0588	1298	2 RR RB211-535E4	104554	Y233		lsf AMM in winter
☐ C-GRYY	Boeing 757-23A (ER)	24292 / 219	G-OOOG	0389	1298	2 RR RB211-535E4	113398	Y233		lsf AMM in winter
☐ C-GRYZ	Boeing 757-236	24119 / 167	N770BE	0088	1198	2 RR RB211-535E4	108862	Y228		lsf BBAM
☐ C-GRYA	Airbus Industrie A310-304	448	D-APOM	0088	0598	2 GE CF6-80C2A2	157000	Y264	FJ-DK	lsf GECA
☐ C-GRYD	Airbus Industrie A310-304	435	TU-TAU	0086	0597	2 GE CF6-80C2A2	153000	Y264	FG-JK	lsf GECA
☐ C-GRYI	Airbus Industrie A310-304	432	F-WGYW	0086	0797	2 GE CF6-80C2A2	153000	Y264	RS-BK	lsf Airbus Industrie Financial Services
☐ C-GRYV	Airbus Industrie A310-304	440	EC-311	0087	0497	2 GE CF6-80C2A2	153000	Y264	FS-CH	lsf GECA
☐ C-FTNI	Lockheed L-1011-385-1-15 TriStar 100	193E-1058	N64854*	0074	0693	3 RR RB211-22B	215003	Y362	FJ-DK	lst Chile Inter, CC-CZF/cvtd TriStar 1
☐ C-FTNK	Lockheed L-1011-385-1-15 TriStar 100	193E-1069	4R-TNK	0074	0993	3 RR RB211-22B	215003	Y362	FK-BJ	lst Chile Inter, CC-CZR / cvtd 1

ROYAL EXPRESS = RXP (Royal Aviation Express, Inc. dba / Subsidiary of Royal Aviation, Inc.) — Montreal-Dorval, Qué.

685 Blvd Stuart Graham North, Dorval, Québec H4Y 1E4, Canada ☎ (514) 828-9000 Tx: none Fax: (514) 828-9090 SITA: n/a
F: 1998 👥 n/a Head: Michel LeBlanc ICAO: ROY EXPRESS Net: n/a Operates scheduled services with Airbus Industrie A310 & Boeing 757 leased from parent company ROYAL AVIATION when required.

RUPERT'S LAND OPERATIONS, Inc. — La Ronge, Sask.

Box 6099, Bonnyville, Alberta T9N 2G7, Canada ☎ (780) 826-7777 Tx: none Fax: (780) 826-7713 SITA: n/a
F: 1988 👥 5 Head: Donald Nykiforuk Net: n/a

☐ C-FBVH	MD Helicopters MD 500D (Hughes 369D)	800779D	N1095W	0080	1290	1 AN 250-C20B	1361			
☐ C-GSSN	MD Helicopters MD 500D (Hughes 369D)	590506D	N113RS	0079	0597	1 AN 250-C20B	1361			
☐ C-GTNB	MD Helicopters MD 500D (Hughes 369D)	1160011D	N27385	0076	0689	1 AN 250-C20B	1361			
☐ C-GDEN	MD Helicopters MD 600N (Hughes 600N)	RN014	N9214Q	0097	1297	1 AN 250-C47M	1860			

RUSH AIR, Ltd — Campbell River, B.C.

PO Box 704, Campbell River, British Columbia V9W 6J3, Canada ☎ (250) 287-7555 Tx: n/a Fax: (250) 287-7760 SITA: n/a
F: 1986 👥 3 Head: Mark Murphy Net: n/a

☐ C-FDTV	De Havilland DHC-2 Beaver I	34	C-FDTC	0049	0394	1 PW R-985	2313			Floats
☐ C-FEYN	De Havilland DHC-2 Beaver I	508	N28365	0053	0296	1 PW R-985	2313			Floats
☐ C-GMKG	De Havilland DHC-2 Beaver I	1248	N8772Z	0057		1 PW R-985	2313			Floats

RUSTY MYERS Flying Service (1986), Ltd (formerly Rusty Myers Flying Service, Ltd) — Fort Frances, Ont.

PO Box 668, Fort Frances, Ontario P9A 3M9, Canada ☎ (807) 274-5335 Tx: none Fax: (807) 274-4278 SITA: n/a
F: 1956 👥 10 Head: A. Korzinski Net: n/a

☐ C-GGNL	Cessna A185F Skywagon	18502804		0075		1 CO IO-520-D	1520			Floats
☐ C-FOBT	De Havilland DHC-2 Beaver I	3		0048	0591	1 PW R-985	2313			Floats
☐ C-FOBY	De Havilland DHC-2 Beaver I	13		0049		1 PW R-985	2313			Floats
☐ C-FBGO	Beech 3NM (18)	CA-215	RCAF2336	0052		2 PW R-985	3969			Floats
☐ C-FERM	Beech 3N (18)	CA-62	RCAF1487	0051		2 PW R-985	3969			Floats
☐ C-FRPL	Beech 3NM (18)	CA-225	RCAF2346	0052		2 PW R-985	3969			Floats
☐ C-FRVL	Beech 3T (18)	7835	RCAF1396	0044		2 PW R-985	3969			Floats
☐ CF-ZRI	Beech D18S	A-940	N164U	0053		2 PW R-985	3969			Floats

SABOURIN LAKE LODGE, Ltd – Flying Services (Seasonal May-October ops only) — Sabourin Lake, Man.

2 Aldershot Blvd, Winnipeg, Manitoba R3P 0C8, Canada ☎ (204) 888-8045 Tx: none Fax: (204) 889-3047 SITA: n/a
F: 1962 👥 32 Head: Shirley Williams Net: n/a

☐ C-GYER	Cessna U206F Stationair II	U20603503	N8750Q	0076	0082	1 CO IO-520-F	1633			Floats
☐ C-FSJX	De Havilland DHC-2 Beaver I	1592		0065	0084	1 PW R-985	2313			Floats

SAINT THERESA POINT AIR SERVICES, Ltd — St. Theresa Point-Island Lake, Man.

n/a, St. Theresa Point, Manitoba R0B 1J0, Canada ☎ (204) 462-2071 Tx: none Fax: (204) 462-2645 SITA: n/a
F: 1986 👥 3 Head: Morris Manoakeesik Net: n/a

☐ C-GORJ	Cessna A185F Skywagon	18502486	N1766R	0074		1 CO IO-520-D	1520			Floats / Wheel-Skis

SAMARITAN AIR SERVICE, Ltd = HLO (Keeshig Airlines) — Toronto-Int'l, Ont.

2450 Derry Road East, Hangar 9, Box 9, Mississauga, Ontario L5S 1B2, Canada ☎ (905) 672-2226 Tx: none Fax: (905) 672-2229 SITA: n/a
F: 1987 👥 25 Head: Adam Keller ICAO: HALO Net: n/a KEESHIG AIRLINES is a marketing name used for some Passenger-Charter & scheduled-flights (same fleet/headquarters).

☐ C-GBTL	Pilatus PC-12/45	159	N159PB	0096	0198	1 PWC PT6A-67B	4500	EMS/Pax/Frtr		
☐ C-GBXW	Pilatus PC-12/45	170	N170PD	0097	1298	1 PWC PT6A-67B	4500	EMS/Pax/Frtr		
☐ C-FFFG	Mitsubishi MU-2L (MU-2B-36)	662	N5191B	0074	1098	2 GA TPE331-6-251M	5250	EMS/Pax/Frtr		
☐ C-FJEL	Mitsubishi MU-2N (MU-2B-36A)	706SA	N866MA	0078	1098	2 GA TPE331-5-252M	5250	EMS/Pax/Frtr		
☐ C-FRWK	Mitsubishi MU-2B-60 Marquise	1521SA	N437MA	0081	0593	2 GA TPE331-10-501M	5250	EMS/Pax/Frtr		
☐ C-GAMC	Mitsubishi MU-2B-60 Marquise	785SA	N273MA	0080	1098	2 GA TPE331-10-501M	5250	EMS/Pax/Frtr		
☐ C-GJEO	Beech E18S	BA-405	N651Q	0059	0396	2 PW R-985	4581	Freighter		
☐ C-FZHT	Learjet 24B	24B-217	N217AT	0070	1196	2 GE CJ610-6	6123	EMS/Pax/Frtr		
☐ C-FZHU	Learjet 25C	25C-070	N32SM	0070	1196	2 GE CJ610-6	6804	EMS/Pax/Frtr		
☐ C-GBOT	Learjet 25B	25B-090	N112ME	0072	1297	2 GE CJ610-6	6804	EMS/Pax/Frtr		
☐ C-FBII	BAe 3112 Jetstream 31	816	G-31-816*	0088	1195	2 GA TPE331-10UG-513H	6950	EMS/Y12/Frtr		
☐ C-FSAS	BAe 3112 Jetstream 31	779	N419UE	1087	0299	2 GA TPE331-10UG-513H	6950	EMS/Y12/Frtr		lsf BAMT
☐ C-FZVY	BAe 3212 Jetstream 32	833	N833JX	0089	1197	2 GA TPE331-12UAR-705H	7350	EMS/Y12/Frtr		lsf BAMT
☐ C-GEMQ	BAe 3112 Jetstream 31	747	N103XV	0387	0299	2 GA TPE331-10UG-513H	6950	EMS/Y12/Frtr		lsf BAMT

SANDER GEOPHYSICS, Ltd — Ottawa, Ont.

260 Hunt Club Road, Ottawa, Ontario K1V 1C1, Canada ☎ (613) 521-9626 Tx: none Fax: (613) 521-2262 SITA: n/a
F: 1956 👥 60 Head: Dr. George W. Sander Net: n/a

☐ C-GSGX	Britten-Norman BN-2B-21 Islander	596	N331MS	0079	0795	2 LY IO-540-K1B5	2994	Geophys.Survey		
☐ C-GCKB	Cessna 402B	402B0865	CC-CKB	0075		2 CO TSIO-520-E	2858	Geophys.Survey		
☐ C-FWZG	Beech Queen Air B80 (65-B80)	LD-386		0068		2 LY IGSO-540-A1D	3992	Geophys.Survey		
☐ C-GBWE	Cessna 404 Titan II	404-0624	N5277J	0080		2 CO GTSIO-520-M	3810	Geophys.Survey		
☐ C-GSGW	Cessna 208B Grand Caravan	208B0646		0097	1297	1 PWC PT6A-114A	3969	Geophys.Survey		
☐ C-GSGY	Cessna 208B Grand Caravan	208B0600		0097	0497	1 PWC PT6A-114A	3969	Geophys.Survey		
☐ C-GSGZ	Cessna 208B Grand Caravan	208B0493		0096	0896	1 PWC PT6A-114A	3969	Geophys.Survey		

SANDY LAKE SEAPLANE SERVICE, Ltd — Sandy Lake, Man.

Box 245, Sandy Lake, Manitoba P0V 1V0, Canada ☎ (807) 774-1219 Tx: none Fax: (807) 774-1281 SITA: n/a
F: 1998 👥 n/a Head: n/a Net: n/a

☐ C-FZQV	Cessna A185E Skywagon	18501853		0071	0998	1 CO IO-520-D	1520			Floats / Wheel-Skis
☐ C-GBBZ	Cessna U206G Stationair 6 II	U20605712		0080	0998	1 CO IO-520-F	1633			Floats / Wheel-Skis
☐ C-GYPX	Cessna U206G Stationair	U20603584		0077	0998	1 CO IO-520-F	1633			Floats / Wheel-Skis

SASAIR, Inc. - Service Aérien du Saint-Laurent = SSB — Rimouski, Qué.

599-3e rue, Rimouski-Est, Québec G5L 7M9, Canada ☎ (418) 724-0704 Tx: none Fax: (418) 724-0705 SITA: n/a
F: 1995 👥 5 Head: Gérard Ducarme ICAO: SASAIR Net: n/a

☐ C-GBDM	Piper PA-23-250 Aztec E	27-7405381	N54071	0074	1296	2 LY IO-540-C4B5	2359			
☐ C-GGLT	Piper PA-23-250 Aztec C	27-3424	F-OCIF	0066	0897	2 LY IO-540-C4B5	2359			
☐ C-FYFF	Piper PA-31-310 Navajo	31-363		0069	0895	2 LY TIO-540-A1A	2948			
☐ C-GPXW	Piper PA-31-350 Navajo Chieftain	31-7652134		0076	0196	2 LY TIO-540-J2BD	3175			

SCOOP LAKE AIR, Ltd (Affiliated with Scoop Lake Outfitters, Ltd / Seasonal May-November ops only) — Scoop Lake, B.C.

5615 Deadpine Drive, Kelowna, British Columbia V1P 1A3, Canada ☎ (250) 491-1885 Tx: none Fax: (250) 491-1885 SITA: n/a
F: 1980 👥 n/a Head: n/a Net: n/a

☐ C-FPKJ	Cessna 185B Skywagon	185-0601		0063	0192	1 CO IO-470-F	1492			Floats

75 registration type of aircraft cn/fn ex/ex* mfd del powered by mtow kg configuration selcal name/fln/specialitites/remarks

SCOTIA FLIGHT CENTRE (1994), Inc. (formerly Scotia Flight Centre, Inc.)   Cambridge Station, N.S.

PO Box 44, Cambridge Station, Nova Scotia B0P 1G0, Canada   ☎ (902) 538-8057 Tx: none Fax: (902) 538-7353 SITA: n/a
F: 1990   ♦♦♦ 8 Head: William Young Net: n/a Aircraft below MTOW 1361 kg: Cessna 152, 172 & Piper PA-28.

registration	type of aircraft	cn/fn	ex/ex*	mfd	del	powered by	mtow kg	configuration	selcal	name/fln/specialitites/remarks
☐ C-GXGD	Piper PA-23-250 Aztec D	27-4137	N6800Y	0069	0594	2 LY IO-540-C4B5	2359			

SCOTIA WEST AVIATION, Ltd   Waterville, N.S.

PO Box 50, Falmouth, Nova Scotia B0P 1L0, Canada   ☎ (902) 538-1207 Tx: none Fax: (902) 538-7220 SITA: n/a
F: 1996   ♦♦♦ n/a Head: n/a Net: n/a Aircraft below MTOW 1361kg: Cessna 150 & 172

registration	type of aircraft	cn/fn	ex/ex*	mfd	del	powered by	mtow kg	configuration	selcal	name/fln/specialitites/remarks
☐ C-GHSE	Piper PA-34-200 Seneca	34-7450189		0074	0197	2 LY IO-360-C1E6	1814			

SEAIR SERVICES (1990), Ltd   Vancouver-Int'l SPB, B.C.

4640 Inglis Drive, Richmond, British Columbia V7B 1W4, Canada   ☎ (604) 273-8900 Tx: none Fax: (604) 273-7351 SITA: n/a
F: 1990   ♦♦♦ n/a Head: Peter Clarke Net: n/a

registration	type of aircraft	cn/fn	ex/ex*	mfd	del	powered by	mtow kg	configuration	selcal	name/fln/specialitites/remarks
☐ C-FFFC	Cessna A185F Skywagon	18502906	N8740Z	0076	0392	1 CO IO-520-D	1520			Floats
☐ C-GYIX	Cessna A185F Skywagon	18503162		0077	0790	1 CO IO-520-D	1520			Floats
☐ C-FPCG	De Havilland DHC-2 Beaver I	1000	N188JM	0056	0790	1 PW R-985	2309			Floats
☐ C-GTMC	De Havilland DHC-2 Beaver I	1171	N100HF	0057	0198	1 PW R-985	2309			Floats
☐ C-FDHC	De Havilland DHC-2 Turbo Beaver III	1677TB45	N164WC	0067	0893	1 PWC PT6A-20	2436			Floats
☐ C-FOES	De Havilland DHC-2 Turbo Beaver III	1673TB43		0067	0694	1 PWC PT6A-20	2436			Floats

SELKIRK AIR (Enterlake Air Services, Ltd dba)   Selkirk, Man.

Group 214, Box 2, RR No. 2, Selkirk, Manitoba R1A 2A7, Canada   ☎ (204) 482-3270 Tx: none Fax: (204) 482-3438 SITA: n/a
F: 1954   ♦♦♦ 8 Head: Robert (Bob) W. Polinuk Net: n/a Aircraft below MTOW 1361 kg: Bellanca 7GCBC.

registration	type of aircraft	cn/fn	ex/ex*	mfd	del	powered by	mtow kg	configuration	selcal	name/fln/specialitites/remarks
☐ C-FHXA	Cessna A185E Skywagon	185-1391		0069	0390	1 CO IO-520-D	1520			Floats / Wheel-Skis
☐ C-FXZK	Cessna A185E Skywagon	185-1440		0068	0596	1 CO IO-520-D	1520			Floats / Wheel-Skis
☐ C-GCKZ	Cessna A185F Skywagon	18502665		0075		1 CO IO-520-D	1520			Floats / Wheel-Skis
☐ C-FYNW	Cessna U206D Super Skywagon	U206-1370		0069		1 CO IO-520-F	1633			Floats / Wheel-Skis
☐ C-GFIQ	De Havilland DHC-2 Beaver I	632	N90525	0054		1 PW R-985	2313			Floats / Wheel-Skis
☐ C-GPVC	De Havilland DHC-2 Beaver I	290	N9257Z	0051		1 PW R-985	2313			Floats / Wheel-Skis
☐ C-GCDX	De Havilland DHC-3 Otter	314	58-1700	0058	0796	1 PZL ASh-62IR-M18	3629			Floats / Wheel-Skis / cvtd DHC-3 PW-eng
☐ C-GGSL	De Havilland DHC-3 Otter	166	N5248G	0056		1 PZL ASh-62IR-M18	3629			Floats / Wheel-Skis / cvtd DHC-3 PW-eng

SELKIRK MOUNTAIN HELICOPTER, Ltd – SMH   Revelstoke, B.C.

Box 2968, Revelstoke, British Columbia V0E 2S0, Canada   ☎ (250) 837-2455 Tx: none Fax: (250) 837-4066 SITA: n/a
F: 1991   ♦♦♦ 5 Head: Gerald Richard Net: n/a

registration	type of aircraft	cn/fn	ex/ex*	mfd	del	powered by	mtow kg	configuration	selcal	name/fln/specialitites/remarks
☐ C-GDGH	Bell 206B JetRanger III	2476	N352E	0078	0893	1 AN 250-C20J	1451			
☐ C-FRCL	Bell 206L+ LongRanger	45019	SE-HUD	0075	0398	1 AN 250-C20R	1814			cvtd 206L
☐ C-	Bell 206L+ LongRanger	45056	ZK-HRA	0076	0499	1 AN 250-C20P	1814			cvtd 206L

SELKIRK REMOTE SENSING, Ltd = SRS   Vancouver-Int'l, B.C.

4380 Agar Drive, Richmond, British Columbia V7B 1A3, Canada   ☎ (604) 276-8111 Tx: none Fax: (604) 276-8061 SITA: n/a
F: 1983   ♦♦♦ 4 Head: Parker G. Williams ICAO: PHOTO CHARLIE Net: http://www.selkirk.com

registration	type of aircraft	cn/fn	ex/ex*	mfd	del	powered by	mtow kg	configuration	selcal	name/fln/specialitites/remarks
☐ C-GVSC	Cessna TU206F Turbo Stationair	U20601955	N357DP	0073	1085	1 CO TSIO-520-F	1633	Photo		
☐ C-GVSG	Piper PA-31-310 Navajo	31-418	N2119V	0069	1289	2 LY TIO-540-A2B	2948	Photo		

SEPT-ILES AVIATION, Enr. (2431-9154 Québec Inc. dba / formerly Les Entreprises Jacques Levesque Enr.)   Sept-Iles, Qué.

769 de la Rive, RR2, BG3515, Sept-Iles, Québec P7E 3N9, Canada   ☎ (418) 968-8775 Tx: n/a Fax: (418) 927-2166 SITA: n/a
F: 1980   ♦♦♦ 1 Head: Jacques Lévesque Net: n/a Aircraft below MTOW 1361kg: Cessna 172.

registration	type of aircraft	cn/fn	ex/ex*	mfd	del	powered by	mtow kg	configuration	selcal	name/fln/specialitites/remarks
☐ C-GCXF	Cessna 402C II	402C0069	N410GA	0079		2 CO TSIO-520-VB	3107			

SERVICE AERIEN LAC-DES-ILES, Enr. (André S. Lépine dba / Seasonal May through October ops only)   Lac-des-Iles, Qué.

39, Ch. Kiamika, Lac-des-Iles, Québec J0W 1J0, Canada   ☎ (819) 597-2656 Tx: none Fax: none SITA: n/a
F: 1985   ♦♦♦ 1 Head: André S. Lépine Net: n/a

registration	type of aircraft	cn/fn	ex/ex*	mfd	del	powered by	mtow kg	configuration	selcal	name/fln/specialitites/remarks
☐ C-FDCF	Cessna 185A Skywagon	185-0358		0062		1 CO IO-470-F	1451	4 Pax		Floats

SERVICE AIR (Service Air Group, Inc. dba)   Vancouver-Int'l SPB, B.C.

1415-54th Street, Delta, British Columbia V4M 3H6, Canada   ☎ (604) 948-2105 Tx: none Fax: (604) 948-2106 SITA: n/a
F: 1997   ♦♦♦ n/a Head: Jack Dhillon Net: n/a Aircraft below MTOW 1361kg: Cessna 180 (on Floats)

registration	type of aircraft	cn/fn	ex/ex*	mfd	del	powered by	mtow kg	configuration	selcal	name/fln/specialitites/remarks
☐ C-FGQZ	De Havilland DHC-2 Beaver I	118		0051	1297	1 PW R-985	2313			Floats

SHARP WINGS, Ltd (Seasonal May-November ops only)   Williams Lake, B.C.

PO Box 4659, Williams Lake, British Columbia V2G 2V6, Canada   ☎ (250) 989-4334 Tx: none Fax: (250) 989-0112 SITA: n/a
F: 1965   ♦♦♦ 8 Head: Rolf S. Schuetze Net: n/a Aircraft below MTOW 1361kg: Cessna 150 & 172

registration	type of aircraft	cn/fn	ex/ex*	mfd	del	powered by	mtow kg	configuration	selcal	name/fln/specialitites/remarks
☐ C-GWDW	De Havilland DHC-2 Beaver I	306	N311N	0051		1 PW R-985	2313			Floats

SHOWALTER'S FLY-IN SERVICE (1987), Ltd (Affiliated with Showalter's Fly-In Camps, Ltd / Seasonal May-October ops only)   Ear Falls-SPB, Ont.

Box 880, Ear Falls, Ontario P0V 1T0, Canada   ☎ (807) 222-2332 Tx: none Fax: (807) 484-2295 SITA: n/a
F: 1987   ♦♦♦ 6 Head: Edwin L. Showalter Net: n/a Aircraft below MTOW 1361kg: Cessna 180 (on Floats).

registration	type of aircraft	cn/fn	ex/ex*	mfd	del	powered by	mtow kg	configuration	selcal	name/fln/specialitites/remarks
☐ C-FXUO	Beech 3NM (18)	CA-208	RCAF 2329	0052	0590	2 PW R-985	3969			Floats
☐ C-FZNG	Beech 3NM (18)	CA-182	RCAF 2309	0052		2 PW R-985	3969			Floats

SHUNDA HELICOPTER SERVICE, Ltd   Rocky Mountain House, Alta.

Box 463, Rocky Mountain, Alberta T0M 1T0, Canada   ☎ (780) 845-2534 Tx: none Fax: (780) 845-4620 SITA: n/a
F: 1982   ♦♦♦ 6 Head: Jochen Rübeling Net: n/a

registration	type of aircraft	cn/fn	ex/ex*	mfd	del	powered by	mtow kg	configuration	selcal	name/fln/specialitites/remarks
☐ C-GLVJ	Bell 206B JetRanger	19	N504EH	0067		1 AN 250-C20	1451	5 Pax		cvtd 206A
☐ C-GQRQ	Bell 206B JetRanger	582	N98SF	0070		1 AN 250-C20	1451	5 Pax		cvtd 206A

SHUSWAP AIR = 3S / SFC (Shuswap Flight Center, Ltd dba)   Salmon Arm, B.C.

PO Box 1887, Salmon Arm, British Columbia V1E 4P9, Canada   ☎ (250) 832-8830 Tx: none Fax: (250) 832-2825 SITA: YSNHQ3S
F: 1980   ♦♦♦ 6 Head: Stephen W. Raffel ICAO: SHUSWAP Net: http://www.shuswapair.com Aircraft below MTOW 1361 kg: Cessna 172 & 182.

registration	type of aircraft	cn/fn	ex/ex*	mfd	del	powered by	mtow kg	configuration	selcal	name/fln/specialitites/remarks
☐ C-GTNO	Piper PA-31-350 Navajo Chieftain	31-8152146	N4090T	0081	0498	2 LY TIO-540-J2BD	3175			
☐ C-GXRX	Beech King Air 100	B-36	N600CB	0072	0695	2 PWC PT6A-28	4808			

SIFTON AIR (Kazar Construction, Ltd / Seasonal May-November ops only)   Haines Junction-Pine Lake SPB, Y.T.

Box 5419, Haines Junction, Yukon Territory Y0B 1L0, Canada   ☎ (867) 634-2916 Tx: none Fax: (867) 634-2034 SITA: n/a
F: 1991   ♦♦♦ n/a Head: Eric Oles Net: n/a Aircraft below MTOW 1361kg: Cessna 180

registration	type of aircraft	cn/fn	ex/ex*	mfd	del	powered by	mtow kg	configuration	selcal	name/fln/specialitites/remarks
☐ C-GVKJ	Cessna 205 (210-5)	205-0092		0063	0993	1 CO IO-470-S	1497			Floats
☐ C-GNHN	Cessna A185F Skywagon	18503245		0077	0596	1 CO IO-520-D	1520			Floats

SIGNATURE AIRWAYS, Ltd   Red Deer, Alta.

Box 21047, Red Deer, Alberta T4R 2M1, Canada   ☎ (780) 357-4152 Tx: none Fax: (780) 347-0068 SITA: n/a
F: 1998   ♦♦♦ n/a Head: n/a Net: n/a

registration	type of aircraft	cn/fn	ex/ex*	mfd	del	powered by	mtow kg	configuration	selcal	name/fln/specialitites/remarks
☐ C-FBBC	Piper PA-31-310 Navajo	31-48	N9035Y	0068	0998	2 LY TIO-540-A1A	2948			
☐ C-GSGA	Piper PA-31-310 Navajo	31-426	N1XK	0069	0598	2 LY TIO-540-A1A	2948			

SIGURDSON & MARTIN, Ltd   Churchill, Man.

Box 247, Churchill, Manitoba R0B 0E0, Canada   ☎ (204) 675-2846 Tx: none Fax: (204) 675-8814 SITA: n/a
F: 1993   ♦♦♦ n/a Head: Bruce Martin Net: n/a

registration	type of aircraft	cn/fn	ex/ex*	mfd	del	powered by	mtow kg	configuration	selcal	name/fln/specialitites/remarks
☐ C-GWNU	Cessna A185F Skywagon	18502726		0075	0294	1 CO IO-520-D	1520			

SILVER HELICOPTERS, Ltd   Prince George, B.C.

Box 2034, Prince George, British Columbia V2N 2J6, Canada   ☎ (604) 963-9808 Tx: none Fax: (604) 963-9808 SITA: n/a
F: 1979   ♦♦♦ n/a Head: Doug Baragar Net: n/a Aircraft below MTOW 1361kg: Hughes 369HS (500C).

registration	type of aircraft	cn/fn	ex/ex*	mfd	del	powered by	mtow kg	configuration	selcal	name/fln/specialitites/remarks
☐ C-GDDE	MD Helicopters MD 500D (Hughes 369D)	911084D	N5110N	0081	0393	1 AN 250-C20B	1361			

SILVERSTAR HELICOPTERS, Ltd   Vancouver, B.C.

5280 Ranger Ave, North Vancouver, British Columbia V7R 3M6, Canada   ☎ (604) 986-2100 Tx: none Fax: (604) 987-4531 SITA: n/a
F: 1996   ♦♦♦ n/a Head: Wilson Southam Net: n/a

registration	type of aircraft	cn/fn	ex/ex*	mfd	del	powered by	mtow kg	configuration	selcal	name/fln/specialitites/remarks
☐ C-FFVI	Bell 206B JetRanger	964		0073	0796	1 AN 250-C20	1451			

SILVERTIP AVIATION, Ltd   Revelstoke, B.C.

SS1, Site 13, Comp.1, Revelstoke, British Columbia V0E 2S0, Canada   ☎ (250) 837-4414 Tx: none Fax: (250) 837-6793 SITA: n/a
F: 1986   ♦♦♦ 2 Head: Dave Mair Net: http://www.alaskan.com/vendors/silvertip.html

registration	type of aircraft	cn/fn	ex/ex*	mfd	del	powered by	mtow kg	configuration	selcal	name/fln/specialitites/remarks
☐ C-FBEW	Cessna 337G Super Skymaster	33701528	N337DX	0073		2 CO IO-360-G	2100			
☐ CF-KWX	Cessna 336 Skymaster	336-0112		0063	0296	2 CO IO-360-A	1769			

SIMPSON AIR (Simpson Air (1981), Ltd dba)

Fort Simpson, N.W.T.

PO Box 260, Fort Simpson, Northwest Territories X0E 0N0, Canada ☎ (867) 695-2505 Tx: none Fax: (867) 695-2925 SITA: n/a
F: 1981 ☨☨☨ 4 Head: Edward (Ted) J. Grant Net: n/a

☐ C-GGHU	Cessna U206G Stationair 6 II	U20605723		0080	0990	1 CO IO-520-F	1633			
☐ C-GPMS	Cessna U206G Stationair 6 II	U20604207		0077	0597	1 CO IO-520-F	1633			

SIOUX AIR, Ltd (Affiliated with Knobbys Flying Camps, Ltd)

Sioux Lookout, Ont.

Box 382, Sioux Lookout, Ontario P8T 1A5, Canada ☎ (807) 737-3291 Tx: none Fax: (807) 737-1040 SITA: n/a
F: 1966 ☨☨☨ n/a Head: Glen Clark Net: n/a Aircraft below MTOW 1361kg: Cessna 182 (on Floats)

☐ C-GGRU	Cessna U206G Stationair 6 II	U20605838		0080	0792	1 CO IO-520-F	1633			Floats / Wheel-Skis
☐ C-GGRW	Cessna U206G Stationair 6 II	U20605689		0080	0694	1 CO IO-520-F	1633			Floats / Wheel-Skis
☐ C-FHEP	De Havilland DHC-2 Beaver I	69	CF-IOB	0050	0589	1 PW R-985	2313			Floats / Wheel-Skis
☐ C-GFDS	De Havilland DHC-2 Beaver I	1269	N31343	0063	0589	1 PW R-985	2313			Floats / Wheel-Skis

SKEENA AIR, Ltd (Seasonal May-October ops only)

Topley Landing-SPB, B.C.

Box 1, SS 1, Topley Landing, Granisle, British Columbia V0J 1W0, Canada ☎ (250) 697-2380 Tx: none Fax: (250) 697-2390 SITA: n/a
F: 1985 ☨☨☨ 1 Head: William Domonkos Net: n/a

☐ C-GWKX	Cessna A185E Skywagon	18502032	N70167	0072	0897	1 CO IO-520-D	1520			Floats

SKYCHARTER, Ltd = SKL

Toronto-Int'l, Ont.

2450 Derry Road East, Hangar 8, Mississauga, Ontario L5S 1B2, Canada ☎ (905) 677-6901 Tx: 069-68881 skychart m Fax: (905) 676-0264 SITA: n/a
F: 1968 ☨☨☨ 65 Head: Irving O. Shoichet ICAO: SKYCHARTER Net: http://www.skycharter.com

☐ C-GSKL	Learjet 25B	25B-179	N659HX	0074		2 GE CJ610-8A	6804	Executive		252
☐ C-GRIS	Dassault Falcon 10	2	N103JM	0073		2 GA TFE731-2-2C	8500	Executive		101

SKYJET AVIATION, Inc.

Halifax, NS

PO Box 83, Hubbards, Nova Scotia B0J 1T0, Canada ☎ (902) 835-6330 Tx: none Fax: (902) 835-7133 SITA: n/a
F: 1994 ☨☨☨ 5 Head: Gary Hamblen Net: n/a

☐ C-GMEV	Beech King Air B200	BB-1433	C-GMEH	0092	1194	2 PWC PT6A-42	5670			

SKYLINE HELICOPTERS, Ltd

Kelowna, B.C.

6095 Airport Road, Kelowna, British Columbia V1V 1S1, Canada ☎ (250) 765-1910 Tx: none Fax: (250) 765-1972 SITA: n/a
F: 1996 ☨☨☨ 8 Head: Grant Louden Net: n/a

☐ C-GSLH	Bell 212	30565	N94W	0073	1196	2 PWC PT6T-3B TwinPac	5080			
☐ C-GSLT	Bell 212	30851	JA9527	0077	0298	2 PWC PT6T-3 TwinPac	5080			

SKYLINK AVIATION, Inc. = SKK (Sister company of SkyLink Express, Inc.)

Toronto, Ont. & Africa

1027 Yonge Street, Suite 300, Toronto, Ontario M4W 2K9, Canada ☎ (416) 924-9000 Tx: 06218100 Fax: (416) 924-9006 SITA: YTONSCR
F: 1976 ☨☨☨ 250 Head: Surjit Babra ICAO: SKYLINK Net: n/a Beside ac listed, leases Antonov 12 & 26, Ilyushin 76MD/TD, Mil Mi-8 & Mi-26 on a contract basis, with aircraft rotated frequently during maintenance inspections.
Most aircraft are operated for Relief Agencies & commercial customers abroad. Kenya base is operated by assoc.co. SKYLINK Aeromanagement. For details see under 5Y- markings.

☐ C-GARB	Bell 206B JetRanger	1086	4X-BJS	0073	0793	1 AN 250-C20	1451			
☐ C-GFQN	Bell 212	30571	N554CR	0073	0595	2 PWC PT6T-3 TwinPac	5080			
☐ C-GZRC	Bell 212	30746	N50932	0075	0496	2 PWC PT6T-3 TwinPac	5080			lst Chim-Nir Aviation as 4X-BJN
☐ C-FSKQ	Beech King Air 200	BB-99	N274T	0076	0293	2 PWC PT6A-41	5670			lst Skylink Aeromanagement as 5Y-SEL

SKYLINK EXPRESS, Inc. (Sister company of SkyLink Aviation, Inc.)

Toronto-Int'l, Ont.

1027 Yonge Street, Suite 300, Toronto, Ontario M4W 2K9, Canada ☎ (416) 925-4530 Tx: 06218100 Fax: (416) 925-2975 SITA: YTONSCR
F: 1996 ☨☨☨ n/a Head: Dan Rocheleau Net: n/a

☐ C-GSKR	Cessna 208B Caravan I Super Cargomaster	208B0436	N677SC	0095	0596	1 PWC PT6A-114	3969	Freighter		
☐ N1117G	Cessna 208B Grand Caravan	208B0370		0094	1197	1 PWC PT6A-114A	3969	Freighter		lsf Cessna Finance Corp.
☐ C-GSKA	Beech 1900C Airliner	UB-32	N317BH	0085	0198	2 PWC PT6A-65B	7530	Freighter		
☐ C-GSKC	Beech 1900C Airliner	UB-27	N6929M	0084	0298	2 PWC PT6A-65B	7530	Freighter		
☐ C-GSKG	Beech 1900C-1 Airliner	UC-22	N19016	0088	1098	2 PWC PT6A-65B	7530	Freighter		
☐ C-GSKM	Beech 1900C Airliner	UB-21	N61MK	0084	0598	2 PWC PT6A-65B	7530	Freighter		
☐ C-GSKN	Beech 1900C-1 Airliner	UC-54	N31729	0089	0397	2 PWC PT6A-65B	7530	Freighter		
☐ C-GSKU	Beech 1900C Airliner	UB-35	N735GL	0085	0496	2 PWC PT6A-65B	7530	Freighter		
☐ C-GSKW	Beech 1900C Airliner	UB-33	N318BH	0085	0797	2 PWC PT6A-65B	7530	Freighter		

SKYSERVICE = SSV (Skyservice Airlines, Inc. / Lignes Aériennes Skyservice, Inc. dba)

Montreal-Dorval, Qué. & Toronto-Int'l, Ont.

9785 Ryan Avenue, Dorval, Québec H9P 1A2, Canada ☎ (514) 636-1626 Tx: none Fax: (514) 636-3300 SITA: n/a
F: 1986 ☨☨☨ n/a Head: Russel L. Payson IATA: 884 ICAO: SKYTOUR Net: http://www.skyservice.com

☐ C-GSSA	Beech King Air F90	LA-6	N7PB	0079	0198	2 PWC PT6A-135	4967	Executive		
☐ C-GJPX	BAe 3112 Jetstream 31	756	N2275S	0087	0397	2 GA TPE331-10UGR-514H	6950	Y19		
☐ C-FZQP	Learjet 35A	35A-168	C-GPDO	0078	0197	2 GA TFE731-2-2B	8301	EMS		
☐ C-GIRE	Learjet 35	35-004	N74MJ	0074	1092	2 GA TFE731-2-2B	7711	EMS		
☐ C-GRFO	Learjet 35A	35A-100	N558E	0077	1293	2 GA TFE731-2-2B	8301	EMS		
☐ C-GTDE	Learjet 35	35-057	N35MR	0077	1194	2 GA TFE731-2-2B	7711	EMS		
☐ C-FJJC	Cessna 650 Citation III	650-0116	N788BA	0086	0797	2 GA TFE731-3B-100S	9979	Executive		
☐ C-GWFM	Hawker 800A (BAe 125-800A)	258015	C-FTLA	0084	0396	2 GA TFE731-5R-1H	12428	Executive		
☐ C-FNNT	Canadair CL-601-3A (CL-600-2B16) Challen.	5068	N113WA	0090	0997	2 GE CF34-3A	19550	Executive	CR-KL	
☐ C-GESR	Canadair CL-601-1A (CL-600-2A12) Challen.	3003	N500TD	0083	0398	2 GE CF34-1A	20457	Executive		
☐ C-GSAP	Canadair CL-601-1A (CL-600-2A12) Challen.	3034	N120MP	0084	0498	2 GE CF34-1A	20457	Executive		
☐ C-FTDA	Airbus Industrie A320-212	795	F-WWDX*	0098	0498	2 CFMI CFM56-5A3	73500	Y179	BJ-FP	lsf ILFC
☐ C-FTDI	Airbus Industrie A320-212	446	G-MONZ	0093	1198	2 CFMI CFM56-5A3	73500	Y180	FH-LR	lsf MON in winter
☐ C-FTDW	Airbus Industrie A320-212	389	G-OZBB	0094	1198	2 CFMI CFM56-5A3	77000	Y180	AE-GQ	lsf MON in winter
☐ C-GTDB	Airbus Industrie A320-212	525	F-GJVV	0095	1097	2 CFMI CFM56-5A3	73500	Y179		lsf ILFC / cvtd -211
☐ C-GTDC	Airbus Industrie A320-232	496	F-WWBV*	0094	0195	2 IAE V2527-A5	73500	Y179	HS-CP	lsf ILFC
☐ C-GSHI	Boeing 727-231	20055 / 719	N64322	0069	0298	3 PW JT8D-9A	78019	C50-70orF20Y102		lsf / opf Sport Hawk Int'l Airlines
☐ C-FBUS	Airbus Industrie A330-322	095	D-AERJ	0495	0597	2 PW PW4168	212000	C32Y331	HS-FQ	lsf ILFC

SKYTECH CHARTERS, Inc.

Ottawa, Ont.

2161 Thurston Drive, Ottawa, Ontario K1G 6C9, Canada ☎ (613) 860-0068 Tx: none Fax: (613) 739-8349 SITA: n/a
F: 1997 ☨☨☨ 6 Head: Perry Pezoucas Net: http://www.skytechcharters.com

☐ C-GJTC	Piper PA-34-220T Seneca III	34-8533008	N69152	0085	0997	2 CO TSIO-360-KB	2155			

SKYWARD AVIATION, Ltd = K9 / SGK (formerly Len's Flying Service, Ltd)

Thompson, Man.

PO Box 1207, Thompson, Manitoba R8N 1P1, Canada ☎ (204) 778-7088 Tx: none Fax: (204) 677-5945 SITA: n/a
F: 1986 ☨☨☨ 45 Head: Frank P. Behrendt IATA: 470 ICAO: SKYWARD Net: http://www.skyward.mb.ca Aircraft below MTOW 1361 kg: Cessna 172.

☐ C-GEIF	Cessna U206F Stationair II	U20602938		0075	1094	1 CO IO-520-F	1633			
☐ C-GYWQ	Cessna U206G Stationair 6 II	U20604439		0078		1 CO IO-520-F	1633			
☐ C-GGRB	Cessna 207A Stationair 8 II	20700611	N73643	0080		1 CO IO-520-F	1724			
☐ C-GKBL	Cessna 310R II	310R0951	N37200	0077		2 CO IO-520-M	2495			
☐ C-GSJP	Cessna 310R II	310R0816		0077	0592	2 CO IO-520-M	2495			
☐ C-GLHP	Cessna 414	414-0099	N8199Q	0070	0995	2 CO TSIO-520-J	2880			
☐ C-GINR	Cessna 402C II	402C0242	N2721B	0080		2 CO TSIO-520-VB	3107			
☐ C-GSRL	Cessna 402B	402B0027	N5427M	0070		2 CO TSIO-520-E	2858			
☐ C-FZUT	Britten-Norman BN-2A-27 Islander	183	G-AYGT	0071	0797	2 LY O-540-E4C5	2994			
☐ C-FGMO	Cessna 421C Golden Eagle II	421C0124	N421GT	0076	1189	2 CO GTSIO-520-L	3379			
☐ C-FSKF	Cessna 208B Grand Caravan	208B0673		0098	0598	1 PWC PT6A-114A	3969			
☐ C-FSKS	Cessna 208B Grand Caravan	208B0722	N5268M*	0098	1298	1 PWC PT6A-114A	3969			
☐ C-FSKA	Beech King Air A100	B-239	N154TC	0078	0498	2 PWC PT6A-28	5216			
☐ C-FSKJ	Embraer 110P1 Bandeirante (EMB-110P1)	110272	N272GA	0080	0595	2 PWC PT6A-34	5670			
☐ C-FSKL	Embraer 110P1 Bandeirante (EMB-110P1)	110353	N623KC	0081	0893	2 PWC PT6A-34	5670			
☐ C-FSKR	Embraer 110P1 Bandeirante (EMB-110P1)	110331	N331GA	0080	0695	2 PWC PT6A-34	5670			
☐ C-GSKD	Embraer 110P1 Bandeirante (EMB-110P1)	110329	N850AC	0081	0193	2 PWC PT6A-34	5670			
☐ C-FCGL	Beech Catpass 200	BB-190	N190MD	0076	1298	2 PWC PT6A-41	5670			cvtd King Air 200

SKYWAYS (565176 Ontario, Ltd dba)

Waterloo-Guelph, Ont.

PO Box 358, Breslau, Ontario N0B 1M0, Canada ☎ (519) 648-2202 Tx: none Fax: (519) 648-2786 SITA: n/a
F: 1986 ☨☨☨ 6 Head: Mervin "Bud" Witter Net: n/a Aircraft below MTOW 1361 kg: Cessna 152, 172 & 177

☐ C-GTGN	Cessna A185E Skywagon	18501876	N1690M	0071	1197	1 CO IO-520-D	1520			Floats / Wheel-Skis
☐ C-FBHH	Cessna 421C Golden Eagle II	421C0295	N300RT	0077		2 CO GTSIO-520-L	3379			
☐ C-FWRL	Cessna 441 Conquest II	441-0079	N441KR	0079	0397	2 GA TPE331-8-403S	4468			

77 registration type of aircraft cn/fn ex/ex* mfd del powered by mtow kg configuration selcal name/fln/specialitites/remarks

SKY WINGS AVIATION Academy, Ltd
Red Deer, Alta.

PO Box 190, Penhold, Alberta T0M 1R0, Canada ☎ (780) 886-5191 Tx: none Fax: (780) 886-4279 SITA: n/a
F: 1983 ⁂ 8 Head: Jim Vomastic Net: n/a Aircraft below MTOW 1361 kg: Cessna 152 & 172.

registration	type of aircraft	cn/fn	ex/ex*	mfd	del	powered by	mtow kg	configuration	selcal	name/fin/specialities/remarks
☐ C-FFEE	Piper PA-34-200 Seneca	34-7450022		0074		2 LY IO-360-C1E6	1905			

SLATE FALLS AIRWAYS (1987), Ltd = SYJ
Sioux Lookout, Ont.

PO Box 188, Sioux Lookout, Ontario P8T 1A3, Canada ☎ (807) 737-3640 Tx: none Fax: (807) 737-1097 SITA: n/a
F: 1987 ⁂ 8 Head: Verne Hollett Net: n/a Aircraft below MTOW 1361 kg: Cessna 180 (on Floats / Wheel-Skis)

registration	type of aircraft	cn/fn	ex/ex*	mfd	del	powered by	mtow kg	configuration	selcal	name/fin/specialities/remarks
☐ C-GPCR	Cessna U206G Stationair 6 II	U20605082	N206JW	0079		1 CO IO-520-F	1633			Floats / Wheel-Skis
☐ CF-DIN	De Havilland DHC-2 Beaver I	68		0050		1 PW R-985	2313			Floats
☐ C-GSFA	Cessna 208 Caravan I	20800212	8Q-MAT	0091	0896	1 PWC PT6A-114	3629			Floats / Wheels
☐ C-FNWX	De Havilland DHC-3 Otter	412		0061	0592	1 PW R-1340	3629			Floats

SLAVE AIR (1988) Ltd
Slave Lake, Alta.

Box 40, Slave Lake, Alberta T0G 2A0, Canada ☎ (780) 849-5353 Tx: none Fax: (780) 849-4552 SITA: n/a
F: 1988 ⁂ 11 Head: Arthur F. Schooley Net: n/a

registration	type of aircraft	cn/fn	ex/ex*	mfd	del	powered by	mtow kg	configuration	selcal	name/fin/specialities/remarks
☐ C-GAYZ	Cessna A185F Skywagon II	18504040		0080		1 CO IO-520-D	1520			
☐ C-GMLP	Cessna A185F Skywagon II	18504275		0081		1 CO IO-520-D	1520			
☐ C-GYDD	Cessna A185F Skywagon	18503124		0076		1 CO IO-520-D	1520			
☐ C-FOOS	Cessna U206E Stationair	U20601698		0071	0596	1 CO IO-520-F	1633			
☐ C-GLGD	Cessna U206G Stationair 6 II	U20606261		0081		1 CO IO-520-F	1633			
☐ C-GSAZ	Piper PA-31-310 Navajo	31-8112063	N4094Y	0081	0490	2 LY TIO-540-A2C	2948			
☐ C-GSAX	Beech King Air C90	LJ-697	N90AW	0076	0397	2 PWC PT6A-20	4377			

SLAVE LAKE HELICOPTERS, Ltd
Slave Lake, Alta.

PO Box 1160, Slave Lake, Alberta T0G 2A0, Canada ☎ (780) 849-6666 Tx: none Fax: (780) 849-6007 SITA: n/a
F: 1997 ⁂ n/a Head: George Kelham Net: n/a

registration	type of aircraft	cn/fn	ex/ex*	mfd	del	powered by	mtow kg	configuration	selcal	name/fin/specialities/remarks
☐ C-FGSL	Bell 206L-1 LongRanger II	45759	N3174L	0082	0198	1 AN 250-C28B	1882			

SMART FLIGHTS
Thunder Bay, Ont.

c/o V. Kelner Pilatus Center, 2380 Whitehall Drive, Site 3, Comp. 30, Thunder Bay, Ontario P7C 4T9 ☎ (807) 475-5353 Tx: none Fax: (807) 475-5405 SITA: n/a
F: 1999 ⁂ n/a Head: n/a Net: n/a

Presently being set-up. Intends to start up during 1999 with 10 Pilatus PC-12 aircraft. Aircraft will be operated in conjunction with other operators in different markets under a partnership/franchise-agreement & under the banner & colors of Smart Flights.

SNAKE FALLS AIRWAYS (Robert A. & Nancy A. Rowe dba / Affiliated with Snake Falls Camp / formerly Snake Falls Flying Service)
Snake Falls (Pakwash Lake), Ont.

PO Box 327, Red Lake, Ontario P0V 2M0, Canada ☎ (807) 222-3337 Tx: none Fax: (807) 222-3337 SITA: n/a
F: 1974 ⁂ 3 Head: Robert A. & Nancy A. Rowe Net: n/a

registration	type of aircraft	cn/fn	ex/ex*	mfd	del	powered by	mtow kg	configuration	selcal	name/fin/specialities/remarks
☐ C-FAWY	De Havilland DHC-2 Beaver I	1458	N9066P	0061		1 PW R-985	2313			Floats / Wheel-Skis

SONTAIR, Ltd
Chatham, Ont.

PO Box 175, Chatham, Ontario N7M 5K3, Canada ☎ (519) 676-3455 Tx: none Fax: (519) 676-8433 SITA: n/a
F: 1969 ⁂ 5 Head: Murray Ward Net: n/a Aircraft below MTOW 1361 kg: Cessna 150 & 172

registration	type of aircraft	cn/fn	ex/ex*	mfd	del	powered by	mtow kg	configuration	selcal	name/fin/specialities/remarks
☐ C-GSTU	Piper PA-23-250 Aztec E	27-7304937	N14353	0072		2 LY IO-540-C4B5	2359			
☐ C-FWGT	Cessna T303 Crusader	T30300296	N5432V	0084	0195	2 CO TSIO-520-AE	2336			
☐ C-FWLR	Piper PA-31-350 Navajo Chieftain	31-8152168	N4092Z	0081	0795	2 LY TIO-540-J2BD	3175			

SOUTHERN AVIATION, Ltd – SAL
Regina, Sask.

PO Box 812, Regina, Saskatchewan S4P 3A8, Canada ☎ (306) 352-5252 Tx: none Fax: (306) 525-0440 SITA: n/a
F: 1973 ⁂ 9 Head: Albert D. Morrice Net: n/a Ag-aircraft below MTOW 5000kg: Ayres S-2R

registration	type of aircraft	cn/fn	ex/ex*	mfd	del	powered by	mtow kg	configuration	selcal	name/fin/specialities/remarks
☐ C-FSAL	Cessna 414	414-0497	N8055Q	0074		2 CO TSIO-520-J	2880			
☐ C-GKKL	Cessna 414A Chancellor III	414A0301	N579CD	0079		2 CO TSIO-520-NB	3062			
☐ C-GPRO	Fairchild (Swearingen) SA226T Merlin III	T-239	N833S	0073	0290	2 GA TPE331-3U-303G	5670			

SOUTH MORESBY AIR CHARTERS, Ltd
Queen Charlotte City, B.C.

Box 969, Queen Charlotte City, British Columbia V0T 1S0, Canada ☎ (250) 559-4222 Tx: none Fax: (250) 559-4222 SITA: n/a
F: 1986 ⁂ 3 Head: Marvin Boyd Net: n/a

registration	type of aircraft	cn/fn	ex/ex*	mfd	del	powered by	mtow kg	configuration	selcal	name/fin/specialities/remarks
☐ C-GEHH	Cessna A185E Skywagon	185-1067	N4560F	0067	0594	1 CO IO-520-D	1520			Floats
☐ C-GHWA	Cessna A185F Skywagon	18502800		0075	0193	1 CO IO-520-D	1520			Floats

SOUTH NAHANNI AIRWAYS (3119378 Canada, Inc. dba)
Fort Simpson, N.W.T.

PO Box 407, Fort Simpson, Northwest Territories X0E 0N0, Canada ☎ (867) 695-2007 Tx: none Fax: (867) 695-2943 SITA: n/a
F: 1995 ⁂ 5 Head: Jacques J. Harvey Net: n/a

registration	type of aircraft	cn/fn	ex/ex*	mfd	del	powered by	mtow kg	configuration	selcal	name/fin/specialities/remarks
☐ C-FAKM	De Havilland DHC-6 Twin Otter 100	78	N242GW	0067	0796	2 PWC PT6A-20	5252			Floats / Wheel-Skis

SOWIND AIR, Ltd = SOW
Winnipeg-St. Andrews & Little Grand Rapids-SPB, Man.

501 Airline Road, Unit 101, St.Andrews, Manitoba R1A 3P4, Canada ☎ (204) 338-5429 Tx: none Fax: (204) 338-5431 SITA: n/a
F: 1991 ⁂ 30 Head: Oliver Owen ICAO: SOWIND Net: n/a

registration	type of aircraft	cn/fn	ex/ex*	mfd	del	powered by	mtow kg	configuration	selcal	name/fin/specialities/remarks
☐ C-FKGL	Cessna A185F Skywagon	18502151		0073	0597	1 CO IO-520-D	1520			Floats
☐ C-GYXY	Cessna A185F Skywagon	18503370		0077	1194	1 CO IO-520-D	1520			Floats
☐ C-GPHI	De Havilland DHC-2 Beaver I	838	N67687	0054	0493	1 PW R-985	2313			Floats
☐ C-FXOQ	Piper PA-31-310 Navajo	31-440	N6478L	0069	0497	2 LY TIO-540-A1A	2948			
☐ C-GHMK	Piper PA-31-350 Navajo Chieftain	31-7752080	N27194	0077	0492	2 LY TIO-540-J2BD	3175			
☐ C-GKNX	Piper PA-31-350 Navajo Chieftain	31-7852120		0078	0299	2 LY TIO-540-J2BD	3175			
☐ C-GQAI	Piper PA-31-350 Navajo Chieftain	31-7952120	N44WP	0079	0194	2 LY TIO-540-J2BD	3175			
☐ C-GLJH	De Havilland DHC-3 Otter	310	N5324G	0058	0597	1 PW R-1340	3629			Floats
☐ C-GDOX	Cessna 208B Grand Caravan	208B0541	N621BB	0096	0898	1 PWC PT6A-114A	3969			
☐ C-GSOW	Cessna 208B Grand Caravan	208B0664	N5264U	0098	0498	1 PWC PT6A-114A	3969			

SPECTRA AVIATION SERVICES, Corp.
Calgary-Springbank, Alta.

Suite 2610, 520 5th Avenue SW, Calgary, Alberta T2P 3R7, Canada ☎ (403) 777-9280 Tx: none Fax: (403) 777-9289 SITA: n/a
F: 1997 ⁂ 12 Head: James A. Genereux Net: n/a

registration	type of aircraft	cn/fn	ex/ex*	mfd	del	powered by	mtow kg	configuration	selcal	name/fin/specialities/remarks
☐ C-FYTT	Piper PA-31-310 Navajo C	31-7512058	N700KA	0075	1097	2 LY TIO-540-A2C	2948			
☐ C-FZHG	Piper PA-31-310 Navajo	31-753	N103DE	0071	1097	2 LY TIO-540-A1A	2948			

SPECTRUM AIRWAYS (514744 Ontario, Ltd dba)
Burlington, Ont.

RR 6, 5336 Bell School Line, Milton, Ontario L9T 2Y1, Canada ☎ (905) 336-4010 Tx: none Fax: (905) 336-6676 SITA: n/a
F: 1982 ⁂ n/a Head: Paul Kovachik Net: n/a Aircraft below MTOW 1361 kg: Cessna 152/172 & Piper PA-28.

registration	type of aircraft	cn/fn	ex/ex*	mfd	del	powered by	mtow kg	configuration	selcal	name/fin/specialities/remarks
☐ C-FDIS	Piper PA-34-200 Seneca	34-7250321		0072	1197	2 LY IO-360-C1E6	1814			
☐ C-GMQR	Piper PA-34-200 Seneca	34-7250092	N4419T	0072	0990	2 LY IO-360-C1E6	1905			

SPORT HAWK INTERNATIONAL AIRLINES
Toronto-Int'l, Ont.

6520 Gottardo Court, Mississauga, Ontario L5T 2T8, Canada ☎ (905) 670-8806 Tx: none Fax: (905) 670-0336 SITA: n/a
F: 1995 ⁂ n/a Head: Mike Simmons Net: n/a

registration	type of aircraft	cn/fn	ex/ex*	mfd	del	powered by	mtow kg	configuration	selcal	name/fin/specialities/remarks
☐ C-GSHI	Boeing 727-231	20055 / 719	N64322	0069	0298	3 PW JT8D-9A	78019	C50-70orF20Y102		lst / opb SSV

SPORTSMAN'S LANDING (1163921 Ontario, Inc. Clearwater Airways dba / Seasonal May-October ops only)
Burditt Lake, Ont.

RR 2, Emo, Ontario P0W 1E0, Canada ☎ (807) 482-1048 Tx: none Fax: (807) 482-1263 SITA: n/a
F: 1995 ⁂ n/a Head: n/a Net: n/a Aircraft below MTOW 1361kg: Cessna 182

registration	type of aircraft	cn/fn	ex/ex*	mfd	del	powered by	mtow kg	configuration	selcal	name/fin/specialities/remarks
☐ C-GMGV	De Havilland DHC-2 Beaver I	432	N62278	0054	0596	1 PW R-985	2313			Floats

SPRINGDALE AVIATION, Ltd
Springdale, Nfld.

PO Box 346, Springdale, Newfoundland A0J 1T0, Canada ☎ (709) 673-3272 Tx: n/a Fax: none SITA: n/a
F: 1981 ⁂ 4 Head: Rick Adams Net: n/a Aircraft below MTOW 1361 kg: Cessna 150, 172 & Piper PA-18.

registration	type of aircraft	cn/fn	ex/ex*	mfd	del	powered by	mtow kg	configuration	selcal	name/fin/specialities/remarks
☐ C-GDGJ	Cessna A185F Skywagon II	18503967		0079	0894	1 CO IO-520-D	1520			Floats / Wheel-Skis
☐ C-GGBX	Cessna A185F Skywagon II	18504031		0080		1 CO IO-520-D	1520			Floats / Wheel-Skis
☐ C-GMIR	Cessna A185F Skywagon II	18504072		0080	0790	1 CO IO-520-D	1520			Floats / Wheel-Skis
☐ C-GGWZ	Piper PA-34-200 Seneca	34-7250259	N5487T	0072	0299	2 LY IO-360-C1E6	1905			
☐ C-GOOO	Piper PA-34-200 Seneca	34-7250181	N2890T	0072	0194	2 LY IO-360-C1E6	1905			

STAGE AIR, Ltd
Penticton, B.C.

RR2, S-30, C-20 Airport Road, Penticton, British Columbia V2A 6J7, Canada ☎ (250) 492-0074 Tx: none Fax: (250) 493-7733 SITA: n/a
F: 1986 ⁂ 6 Head: Brian Spence Net: n/a Aircraft below MTOW 1361kg: Aeronca 7GC, Cessna 172 & 180

registration	type of aircraft	cn/fn	ex/ex*	mfd	del	powered by	mtow kg	configuration	selcal	name/fin/specialities/remarks
☐ C-GRKK	Cessna 205 (210-5)	205-0203	N82033	0063	0594	1 CO IO-470-S	1497			
☐ C-GCJO	Piper PA-44-180T Turbo Seminole	44-8107062	D-GIKA	0081	0498	2 LY TO-360-E1A6D	1700			
☐ C-FWBJ	Beech Duke 60	P-23	N23DU	0069	1095	2 LY TIO-541-E1B4	3050			

STANDARD Ag. Helicopter, Inc. — Chatham, Ont.

RR 1, Chatham, Ontario N7M 5J1, Canada ☎ (519) 436-6900 Tx: none Fax: (519) 436-6901 SITA: n/a
F: 1986 👥 4 Head: James M. Standard Net: n/a

☐ C-GMLS	Bell 206B JetRanger	378	N1442W	0069	0590	1 AN 250-C20	1451			cvtd 206A
☐ C-GMMS	Bell 206B JetRanger	715	N97RR	0071		1 AN 250-C20	1451			cvtd 206A
☐ C-GSEB	Bell 206B JetRanger	1602		0075	0798	1 AN 250-C20	1451			
☐ C-GMHK	Bell 206L-1 LongRanger II	45286	N29EA	0079	0696	1 AN 250-C28B	1882			

STAN REYNOLDS OUTFITTING & Airservice (Stan L. Reynolds dba) — Dawson, Y.T.

Box 108, Dawson, Yukon Territory Y0B 1G0, Canada ☎ (867) 667-1046 Tx: none Fax: (867) 667-1046 SITA: n/a
F: n/a 👥 n/a Head: Stan L. Reynolds Net: n/a Aircraft below MTOW 1361kg: Piper PA-18.

☐ C-GVBL	Cessna A185F Skywagon	18502916		0076		1 CO IO-520-D	1520			

STANTON AIRWAYS (Division of Stanton Mackenzie Flying Services, Inc.) — Sparrow Lake SPB, Ont.

RR 1, Severn Bridge, Ontario P0E 1N0, Canada ☎ (705) 689-2249 Tx: none Fax: (705) 689-2249 SITA: n/a
F: 1977 👥 2 Head: John A. Stanton Net: http://www.inter-pc.com/user/stantonairways Aircraft below MTOW 1361 kg: Stinson 108-3.

☐ C-GAXK	Cessna A185F Skywagon	18502673		0075	0995	1 CO IO-520-D	1520			Floats / Wheel-Skis
☐ C-GDIZ	Cessna U206G Stationair 6 II	U20605438		0080		1 CO IO-520-F	1633			Floats / Wheel-Skis

STAR HELICOPTERS, Ltd — Buffalo Narrows, Sask.

Box 201, Pierceland, Saskatchewan S0M 2K0, Canada ☎ (306) 839-2253 Tx: none Fax: (306) 839-2199 SITA: n/a
F: 1980 👥 n/a Head: Mel Troniak Net: n/a

☐ C-GSKX	Bell 206B JetRanger III	2691		0079	0490	1 AN 250-C20B	1451			

STARS AVIATION CANADA, Inc. (formerly ALC Airlift Canada, Inc.) — Calgary, Alta.

Box 570, 1441 Aviation Park NE, Calgary, Alberta T2E 8M7, Canada ☎ (403) 295-1811 Tx: none Fax: (403) 275-4242 SITA: n/a
F: 1979 👥 20 Head: Bob Toews Net: n/a

☐ C-FIOM	Eurocopter (MBB) BK117A-4D	7106	SE-JBK	0086	0693	2 LY LTS101-650B.1	3200			
☐ C-GDGP	Eurocopter (MBB) BK117B-1D	7218A		0090	0191	2 LY LTS101-750B.1	3200	EMS		1 / opf Alberta-Shock Trauma Air Rescue

STARWEST AVIATION = FSR (598142 Alberta, Ltd dba / formerly Air Link Express & Air Link Charters) — Vancouver-Int'l, B.C.

315-5360 Airport Road S, Richmond, British Columbia V7B 1B4, Canada ☎ (604) 214-6622 Tx: none Fax: (604) 214-6660 SITA: n/a
F: 1993 👥 15 Head: Pat Cowman ICAO: FLIGHT STAR Net: n/a Aircraft below MTOW 1361kg: Cessna 172 & Piper PA-38

☐ C-GKAW	Britten-Norman BN-2A-8 Islander	128	N158MA	0069	0394	2 LY O-540-E4C5	2994			
☐ C-GZOC	Piper PA-31-325 Navajo C/R	31-7512018	N59934	0075	0596	2 LY TIO-540-F2BD	2948			

STERLING PACIFIC AIR, Ltd — Vernon, B.C.

8146 Silver Star Road, Vernon, British Columbia V1B 3N1, Canada ☎ (250) 558-1948 Tx: none Fax: (250) 558-1948 SITA: n/a
F: 1985 👥 n/a Head: Dave Crerar Net: n/a Aircraft below MTOW 1361kg: Cessna 182

☐ C-GBWT	Cessna 337A Super Skymaster	337-0305	N6305F	0066	0196	2 CO IO-360-C/D	1905			
☐ C-GPMA	Cessna 337H Super Skymaster II	33701946	N704GZ	0080	0196	2 CO IO-360-GB	2100			
☐ C-FJOM	De Havilland DHC-2 Beaver I	1024		0056	0196	1 PW R-985	2313			Floats

SUDBURY AVIATION, Ltd — Whitewater Lake-Azilda, Ont.

PO Box 340, Azilda, Ontario P0M 1B0, Canada ☎ (705) 983-4255 Tx: none Fax: (705) 983-4255 SITA: n/a
F: 1956 👥 5 Head: Margaret Watson Net: n/a Aircraft below MTOW 1361 kg: Cessna 172.

☐ C-GQVG	Cessna A185F Skywagon II	18503818	N4619E	0079	0693	1 CO IO-520-D	1520			Floats / Wheel-Skis
☐ C-FHVT	De Havilland DHC-2 Beaver I	1098	VP-PAT	0056	0890	1 PW R-985	2313			Floats / Wheel-Skis
☐ C-FIUU	De Havilland DHC-2 Beaver I	945		0056		1 PW R-985	2313			Floats / Wheel-Skis

SUMMIT AIR CHARTERS, Ltd — Whithorse, Y.T. & Atlin, B.C.

Box 5299, Whitehorse, Yukon Territory Y1Y 4Z2, Canada ☎ (867) 667-7327 Tx: none Fax: (867) 667-4510 SITA: n/a
F: 1987 👥 3 Head: James B. Tait Net: n/a Aircraft below MTOW 1361kg: Cessna 172

☐ C-GNYD	Cessna 207 Skywagon	20700254	N1654U	0074	0491	1 CO IO-520-F	1724			
☐ C-FSDZ	Shorts Skyvan 3 Variant 100 (SC-7)	SH1951	N52NS	0077	0594	2 GA TPE331-2-201A	5670	9 Pax/Freighter		

SUNSHINE COAST AIR SERVICES, Ltd — Powell River, B.C.

7494 Duncan Street, Powell River, British Columbia V8A 1W7, Canada ☎ (604) 485-2915 Tx: none Fax: (604) 485-7460 SITA: n/a
F: 1983 👥 n/a Head: n/a Net: n/a Aircraft below MTOW 1361kg: Piper PA-28

☐ C-FAAP	Piper PA-32-260 Cherokee SIX	32-528	N3627W	0066	1297	1 LY O-540-E4B5	1542			
☐ C-FVDM	Piper PA-32-300 Cherokee SIX	32-40063	N4047W	0066	0495	1 LY IO-540-K1A5	1542			

SUNWEST HELICOPTERS, Ltd — Qualicum Beach, B.C.

582 Panorama Place, Parksville, British Columbia V9P 1A4, Canada ☎ (250) 752-0707 Tx: n/a Fax: (250) 752-0909 SITA: n/a
F: 1995 👥 n/a Head: Brian Sallows Net: n/a

☐ C-GEAX	Bell 206B JetRanger III	2746	N2766N	0079	1198	1 AN 250-C20B	1451			
☐ C-GMUV	Eurocopter (Aerosp.) SA341G Gazelle	1200		0074	1198	1 TU Astazou IIIA	1800			
☐ C-GHSW	Eurocopter (Aerosp.) AS350D AStar	1082	N4268V	0079	0796	1 LY LTS101-600A.2	1950			

SUNWEST INTERNATIONAL AVIATION SERVICES, Ltd = CNK (formerly Sunwest Charters, Ltd & Skocdopole Brothers Aviation, Ltd) — Calgary, Alta.

230 Aviation Place N.E., Calgary, Alberta T2E 7G1, Canada ☎ (403) 275-8121 Tx: none Fax: (403) 275-4637 SITA: n/a
F: 1986 👥 45 Head: Gordon Laing ICAO: CHINOOK Net: http://www.sunwest.ab.ca Aircraft below MTOW 1361kg: Boeing B75N1 & Cessna 182

☐ C-GSWC	Cessna A185F Skywagon	18503433	C-GZJP	0077	0797	1 CO IO-520-D	1520			
☐ C-FRDI	Piper PA-31-310 Navajo B	31-7401205		0073	0991	2 LY TIO-540-A2C	2948			
☐ C-GOSU	Piper PA-31-350 Navajo Chieftain	31-7752148	N27327	0077		2 LY TIO-540-J2BD	3175			
☐ C-GPAE	Piper PA-31-310 Navajo	31-8012086		0080	0493	2 LY TIO-540-A2C	2948			
☐ C-GSWY	Piper PA-31-310 Navajo	31-595	C-GPOP	0070	0798	2 LY TIO-540-A1A	2948			
☐ C-GVAG	Piper PA-31-350 Navajo Chieftain	31-7752166	N27411	0077	0597	2 LY TIO-540-J2BD	3175			
☐ C-GSWF	Beech King Air B100	BE-129	LV-VCU	0082	0696	2 GA TPE331-6-252B	5352			
☐ C-GSWG	Beech King Air B100	BE-131	N6354H	0082	1297	2 GA TPE331-6-252B	5352			
☐ C-FGEW	Fairchild (Swearingen) SA226TC Metro II	TC-347	N330BA	0080	0295	2 GA TPE331-10UA-511G	5670			
☐ C-FSWC	Fairchild (Swearingen) SA226TC Metro II	TC-274	N5499M	0078	0687	2 GA TPE331-10UA-511G	5670			
☐ C-FSWT	Fairchild (Swearingen) SA226TC Metro II	TC-382	N1011N	0080	1294	2 GA TPE331-10UA-511G	5670			196 / Spirit of Medicine Hat
☐ C-GSWK	Fairchild (Swearingen) SA226TC Metro II	TC-368	F-GEBU	0080	1293	2 GA TPE331-10UA-511G	5670			
☐ C-GAPV	Cessna 550 Citation II	550-0691	C-GAPD	0091	0498	2 PWC JT15D-4	6396			
☐ C-FAFE	Fairchild (Swearingen) SA227AC Metro III	AC-581	N3115H	0084	1198	2 GA TPE331-11U-611G	6577			
☐ N227FA	Fairchild (Swearingen) SA227AC Metro III	AC-406	N379PH	0081	0098	2 GA TPE331-11U-611G	6577			lsf Air Metro Lsng/cvtd 226TC cn TC-406
☐ C-GVVA	Learjet 35	35-002	N35SC	0075	0192	2 GA TFE731-2-2B	7711			
☐ C-GSWP	Learjet 55	55-019	N141SM	0082	1297	2 GA TFE731-3AR-2B	9525			

SUPERIOR HELICOPTERS Canada, Inc. — Longlac, Ont.

Box 464, Longlac, Ontario P0T 2A0, Canada ☎ (807) 876-4364 Tx: none Fax: (807) 876-4510 SITA: n/a
F: 1992 👥 3 Head: John Leslie Net: n/a

☐ C-GKCA	Bell 206L-3 LongRanger III	51341		0090	0594	1 AN 250-C30P	1882			

SWAN AERO, Inc. — Grande Prairie, Alta.

RR 2, Grande Prairie Airport, Grande Prairie, Alberta T8V 2Z9, Canada ☎ (780) 532-3607 Tx: none Fax: (780) 814-7387 SITA: n/a
F: 1997 👥 n/a Head: n/a Net: n/a

☐ C-GLRE	Cessna TR182 Turbo Skylane RG II	R18200763	N736RL	0079	1297	1 LY O-540-L3C5D	1406			
☐ C-FSEP	Piper PA-34-220T Seneca III	34-8133089	N83828	0081	0498	2 CO TSIO-360-KB	2155			
☐ C-GPMV	Piper PA-31-310 Navajo C	31-7712081	N273PE	0077	1098	2 LY TIO-540-A2C	2948			

SWANN-AIR SERVICES — Unionville, Ont.

11 Hedgewood Drive, Unionville, Ontario L3R 6J2, Canada ☎ (905) 475-2058 Tx: none Fax: (905) 475-2058 SITA: n/a
F: 1990 👥 2 Head: Lawrence J. & Christina M. Swanton Net: n/a

☐ C-GXXL	De Havilland DHC-2 Beaver I	1607	AF405	0065	0491	1 PW R-985	2309			Floats

TAGISH AIR SERVICE, Ltd — Whitehorse, Y.T.

Site 15, Comp 75, Whitehorse, Yukon Territory Y1A 5W7, Canada ☎ (867) 668-7268 Tx: none Fax: (867) 663-6541 SITA: n/a
F: 1988 👥 2 Head: Thomas R. Pasetka Net: http://www.yukonweb.wis.net/tourism/tagishair/

☐ C-GTRP	Cessna A185F Skywagon II	18503991	N5551E	0080		1 CO IO-520-D	1520			Floats / Wheel-Skis

TAIGA AIR (Taiga Educational Associates, Inc./Les Associes en Education Taiga, Inc. dba) — Waskaganish, Qué.

CP 180, Waskaganish, Québec J0M 1R0, Canada ☎ (819) 895-8634 Tx: none Fax: (819) 895-8748 SITA: n/a
F: 1992 👥 n/a Head: Capt. John Murdoch Net: n/a

☐ C-GNOR	Cessna P206 Super Skylane	P206-0095	N2595X	0065	1097	1 CO IO-520-A	1633			

79 registration type of aircraft cn/fn ex/ex* mfd del powered by mtow kg configuration selcal name/fln/specialitites/remarks

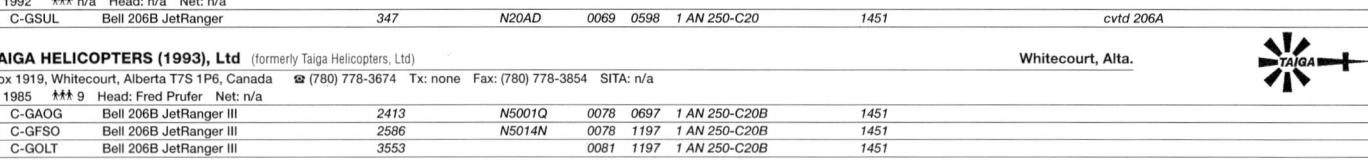

TAIGA AIR SERVICES, Ltd — Winnipeg-St. Andrews, Man.

Suite 200, 70 Arthur Street, Winnipeg, Manitoba R3B 1G7, Canada ☎ (204) 943-3645 Tx: n/a Fax: (204) 943-3657 SITA: n/a
F: 1992 👥 n/a Head: n/a Net: n/a

☐ C-GSUL	Bell 206B JetRanger	347	N20AD	0069	0598	1 AN 250-C20	1451			cvtd 206A

TAIGA HELICOPTERS (1993), Ltd (formerly Taiga Helicopters, Ltd) — Whitecourt, Alta.

Box 1919, Whitecourt, Alberta T7S 1P6, Canada ☎ (780) 778-3674 Tx: none Fax: (780) 778-3854 SITA: n/a
F: 1985 👥 9 Head: Fred Prufer Net: n/a

☐ C-GAOG	Bell 206B JetRanger III	2413	N5001Q	0078	0697	1 AN 250-C20B	1451			
☐ C-GFSO	Bell 206B JetRanger III	2586	N5014N	0078	1197	1 AN 250-C20B	1451			
☐ C-GOLT	Bell 206B JetRanger III	3553		0081	1197	1 AN 250-C20B	1451			
☐ C-GTTY	Bell 206B JetRanger	878	N14851	0072	0791	1 AN 250-C20	1451			

TAL AIR CHARTERS (Division of Sky Freight Express, Ltd) — Toronto-Int'l, Ont.

P.I.A., PO Box 229, Toronto AMF, Ontario L5P 1B1, Canada ☎ (905) 673-8100 Tx: none Fax: (905) 677-2828 SITA: n/a
F: 1994 👥 14 Head: Michael Talker Net: n/a

☐ C-GVIV	Piper PA-31 Navajo C	31-7712043	N6374Z	0077	0795	2 LY TIO-540-A2C	2948			

TALON HELICOPTERS, Ltd — Vancouver-Int'l, B.C.

4380 Agar Drive, Richmond, British Columbia V7B 1A3, Canada ☎ (604) 214-3585 Tx: none Fax: (604) 214-3586 SITA: n/a
F: 1997 👥 n/a Head: Peter Murray & Grant Hislop Net: n/a

☐ C-GUYY	Bell 206B JetRanger III	2367		0078	1097	1 AN 250-C20B	1451			
☐ C-FTHZ	Eurocopter (Aerosp.) AS350B AStar	2362	N85GA	0090	1297	1 TU Arriel 1B	1950			

TAMARAC AIR SERVICE (9006-7745 Québec, Inc. dba / formerly Tamarac Air Service, Ltée / Seasonal May-October ops only) — Clova-Lac Duchamp, Qué

3955 Laurier, St-Hyacinthe, Québec J2S 3T8, Canada ☎ (514) 771-9294 Tx: none Fax: (514) 773-9795 SITA: n/a
F: n/a 👥 n/a Head: n/a Net: n/a

☐ C-FDCW	Cessna A185E Skywagon	18501935		0072	0495	1 CO IO-520-D	1497			Floats
☐ C-FMMO	De Havilland DHC-2 Beaver I	1431		0060	0598	1 PW R-985	2313			Floats

TASMAN HELICOPTERS, Ltd — Vancouver-Int'l, B.C.

5455 Airport Road South, Richmond, British Columbia V7B 1B5, Canada ☎ (604) 276-0031 Tx: none Fax: (604) 279-0341 SITA: n/a
F: 1990 👥 12 Head: James C. Jones Net: n/a

☐ C-GHMH	Bell 206B JetRanger	1582	N116PC	0075	0696	1 AN 250-C20	1451			
☐ C-FKGT	Bell 212	30901	N16989	0078	1191	2 PWC PT6T-3 TwinPac	5080			
☐ C-FTVL	Bell 212	30551	XC-UHE	0072	0798	2 PWC PT6T-3 TwinPac	5080			
☐ C-FVTS	Bell 212	30546	N2164Z	0072	0594	2 PWC PT6T-3 TwinPac	5080			
☐ C-GSGT	Bell 212	30771	C-FSAT	0076	1298	2 PWC PT6T-3 TwinPac	5080			

TERRAQUEST, Ltd — Toronto-Buttonville Municipal, Ont.

100-1373 Queen Victoria Avenue, Mississauga, Ontario L5H 3H2, Canada ☎ (905) 274-1795 Tx: none Fax: (905) 274-3936 SITA: n/a
F: 1984 👥 15 Head: Howard A. Barrie Net: n/a

☐ C-GGLS	Cessna U206 Super Skywagon	U206-0371	N2TQ	0065		1 CO IO-520-A	1497	Surveyer		
☐ C-GXKS	Piper PA-31-325 Navajo C/R	31-7512038	N59969	0075	0696	2 LY TIO-540-F2BD	2948	Surveyer		

TERRA SURVEYS, Ltd — Ottawa, Ont.

2060 Walkley Road, Ottawa, Ontario K1G 3P5, Canada ☎ (613) 731-9571 Tx: none Fax: (613) 731-0453 SITA: n/a
F: 1966 👥 170 Head: Michael Carson Net: n/a

☐ C-GGTA	Cessna 404 Titan II	404-0234	D-IAAW	0078		2 CO GTSIO-520-M	3810	Surveyer		lsf Geoterrex Ltd / tail magnetometer
☐ C-GMEL	Cessna 404 Titan II	404-0092	D-IBFL	0077	0495	2 CO GTSIO-520-M	3810	Surveyer		lsf Geoterrex Ltd
☐ C-FZLK	Cessna 208B Grand Caravan	208B0569		0096	1197	1 PWC PT6A-114A	3969	Surveyer		
☐ C-GDPP	CASA 212-CC50 Aviocar Srs 200	265	N430CA	0082	0596	2 GA TPE331-10-501C	7700	Surveyer		lsf Geoterrex Ltd
☐ VH-TEM	CASA 212 Aviocar Srs 200	138	P2-CNP	0078	0888	2 GA TPE331-10-501C	7450	Surveyer		opb Geocommander P/L, Australia

TERRY AIR (TGH Holdings, Ltd dba) — Mackenzie, B.C.

Box 555, Mackenzie, British Columbia V0J 2C0, Canada ☎ (604) 997-3374 Tx: n/a Fax: (604) 997-3779 SITA: n/a
F: 1994 👥 4 Head: Darryl Langen Net: n/a

☐ C-FWTW	Piper PA-34-220T Seneca III	34-8133059	N8371G	0081	0694	2 CO TSIO-360-KB	2155			
☐ C-GBFZ	Piper PA-31-350 Navajo Chieftain	31-7752151	N701LS	0077	0399	2 LY TIO-540-J2BD	3175			

THEBACHA HELICOPTERS, Ltd — Fort Smith, N.W.T.

Box 161, Fort Smith, Northwest Territories X0E 0P0, Canada ☎ (867) 872-4354 Tx: none Fax: (867) 872-4355 SITA: n/a
F: 1995 👥 3 Head: Kim Hornsby Net: n/a

☐ C-FGKO	Eurocopter (Aerosp.) AS350B AStar	1095	N138BH	0079	0597	1 TU Arriel 1B	1950			cvtd AS350D
☐ C-GXLE	Eurocopter (Aerosp.) AS350B AStar	1337	N2069B	0080	0495	1 TU Arriel 1B	1950			

THERIAULT AIR SERVICES, Ltd (Seasonal April-November ops only) — Chapleau, Ont.

PO Box 269, Chapleau, Ontario P0M 1K0, Canada ☎ (705) 864-0321 Tx: n/a Fax: none SITA: n/a
F: 1947 👥 3 Head: George L. Theriault Net: n/a

☐ C-GPUS	De Havilland DHC-2 Beaver I	624	53-2824	0053		1 PW R-985	2313			Floats

THETIS AIR, Ltd — Thetis Island, B.C.

Box 9-11, Lot 145 Pilkey Pt Road, Thetis Island, British Columbia V0R 2Y0, Canada ☎ (250) 246-2500 Tx: none Fax: (250) 246-2377 SITA: n/a
F: 1995 👥 n/a Head: n/a Net: n/a Aircraft below MTOW 1361kg: Cessna 172 & 180 (on Floats)

☐ C-FMXR	De Havilland DHC-2 Beaver I	374	N7160C	0052	0598	1 PW R-985	2313			Floats

THE WINNIPEG FLYING CLUB — Winnipeg-St. Andrews, Man.

601 Club Road, Unit 100, St. Andrews, Manitoba R1A 3P6, Canada ☎ (204) 338-7927 Tx: none Fax: (204) 338-7920 SITA: n/a
F: 1972 👥 n/a Head: Dorothy Daly Net: http://www.wfc.mb.ca Aircraft below MTOW 1361kg: Bellanca 7GCBC & Cessna 152/172/177/182 Beside Flying Club-activities conducting commercial pax & cargo & sightseeing-flights.

☐ C-FEES	Piper PA-34-200 Seneca	34-7250021		0071	1298	2 LY IO-360-C1E6	1905			

THORBURN AVIATION, Limited — Thorburn Lake (Clarenville), Nfld.

PO Box 213, Shoal Harbour, (Trinity Bay), Newfoundland A0C 2L0, Canada ☎ (709) 466-7823 Tx: none Fax: (709) 466-7046 SITA: n/a
F: 1980 👥 3 Head: Gene E. Ploughman Net: http://www.telework.nf.ca/tu/thorburn

☐ C-GFCJ	Cessna A185F Skywagon II	18503987		0080		1 CO IO-520-D	1520			Floats / Wheel-Skis
☐ C-FXPD	De Havilland DHC-2 Beaver I	1507	HK-1012X	0063		1 PW R-985	2313			Floats / Wheel-Skis

THORSONS PROJECTS CANADA, Inc. — Toronto-Int'l, Ont.

71 Bulvuleum Street, Etobicoke, Ontario M9W 1L4, Canada ☎ (416) 242-7226 Tx: none Fax: (416) 242-7652 SITA: n/a
F: 1998 👥 n/a Head: Andy Thorndyke Net: n/a

☐ C-GJIE	Percival P.57 Sea Prince T.1	P57 / 1	N57AW	0052	0199	2 ALV Leonides 504/5	5375	Pleasure rides		Prince Rudolph / Royal Navy-colors

THOUSAND LAKES AIRWAYS, Ltd (Affiliated with Gibson's Thousand Lakes Resort) — Upsala, Ont.

Box 1000, Upsala, Ontario P0T 2Y0, Canada ☎ (807) 986-2318 Tx: n/a Fax: (807) 986-2267 SITA: n/a
F: 1971 👥 7 Head: Ronald A. Gibson Net: n/a Aircraft below MTOW 1361 kg: Cessna 180.

☐ C-FJAY	Cessna U206F Stationair	U20601992		0073	0790	1 CO IO-520-F	1633			Floats / Wheel-Skis

3 RIV AIR AVIATION, Inc. — Trois-Rivières, Qué.

3500 Boul. de l'Aéroport, Trois-Rivières, Québec G9A 5E1, Canada ☎ (819) 377-0365 Tx: none Fax: (819) 377-4615 SITA: n/a
F: 1994 👥 3 Head: Sylvain Demontigny Net: n/a

☐ C-GJMM	Piper PA-31-310 Navajo Panther	31-806	N7421L	0072	0197	2 LY TIO-540-J2BD	2948			cvtd Navajo

30000 ISLAND AIR (645604 Alberta, Ltd dba / formerly Blackwell Air Service / Seasonal May-November ops only) — Parry Sound & Gananoque, Ont.

11A Bay Street, Parry Sound, Ontario P2A 1S4, Canada ☎ (705) 746-2161 Tx: none Fax: (705) 746-4668 SITA: n/a
F: 1991 👥 12 Head: Thomas Blackwell Net: n/a Aircraft below MTOW 1361kg: Cessna 172 & 180 (on Floats)

☐ C-GBZH	De Havilland DHC-2 Beaver I	1518	HZ-ZAB	0063	0798	1 PW R-985	2313			Floats

THUNDER AIRLINES, Ltd = THU — Thunder Bay & Pickle Lake, Ont.

310 Hector Dougall Way, Thunder Bay, Ontario P7E 6M6, Canada ☎ (807) 475-4211 Tx: none Fax: (807) 475-5841 SITA: n/a
F: 1994 👥 45 Head: Ken Bittle ICAO: AIR THUNDER Net: n/a

☐ C-FWVR	Cessna 208B Grand Caravan	208B0483		0095	1295	1 PWC PT6A-114A	3969	9 Pax		for sale
☐ C-FKEN	Pilatus PC-12/45	222	HB-FQN*	0098	0998	1 PWC PT6A-67B	4500	9 Pax		
☐ C-FKRB	Pilatus PC-12/45	233	HB-FRD*	0098	1298	1 PWC PT6A-67B	4500	9 Pax		

80 registration type of aircraft cn/fn ex/ex* mfd del powered by mtow kg configuration selcal name/fln/specialitites/remarks

☐ C-FASB	Beech King Air A100	B-163	SE-ING	0073	0495	2 PWC PT6A-28	5216	12 Pax		
☐ C-GASI	Beech King Air A100	B-126	N23BW	0072	1295	2 PWC PT6A-28	5216	12 Pax		
☐ C-GASW	Beech King Air A100	B-108	N1101J	0072	0495	2 PWC PT6A-28	5216	12 Pax		
☐ C-FYBO	Shorts 330 (SD3-30 Variant 300)	SH3026	N330L	0082	0696	2 PWC PT6A-45R	10387	Freighter		

THUNDERBIRD AVIATION (590730 Alberta, Ltd dba / formerly Aero-North Aviation Services / Seasonal May-October ops only) — Stony Rapids, Sask.

Box 7800, Saskatoon, Saskatchewan S7K 4R5, Canada ☎ (306) 653-5490 Tx: n/a Fax: (306) 653-5525 SITA: n/a
F: 1982 ⁂ n/a Head: n/a Net: n/a

☐ CF-PEM	De Havilland DHC-3 Otter	438		0063	0594	1 PW R-1340	3629			Floats

TIMBERLAND HELICOPTERS, Inc. — Courtenay, B.C.

Box 3623, Courtenay, British Columbia V9N 6Z8, Canada ☎ (250) 703-0234 Tx: none Fax: (250) 703-0235 SITA: n/a
F: 1997 ⁂ n/a Head: Brian Dunn Net: n/a

☐ C-GOCA	Eurocopter (Aerosp.) SA341G Gazelle	1072	N88918	0074	0697	1 TU Astazou IIIA	1800			
☐ C-GTHJ	Eurocopter (Aerosp.) AS350B AStar	1540	N4454Y	0082	0698	1 TU Arriel 1B	1950			

TIMBERLINE AIR, Ltd — Chilliwack, B.C.

46190-A Airport Road, Chilliwack, British Columbia V2P 1A5, Canada ☎ (604) 792-4614 Tx: none Fax: (604) 792-0822 SITA: n/a
F: 1975 ⁂ 8 Head: Walter Weigelmann Net: http://www.timberlineair.com

☐ C-FLTS	Beech King Air A100	B-149	N883CA	0073	0797	2 PWC PT6A-28	5216			
☐ C-GTLF	Beech King Air 100	B-72	N5476R	0070	0393	2 PWC PT6A-28	4808			
☐ C-GTLA	Beech King Air B200	BB-1224	N94LC	0085	1098	2 PWC PT6A-42	5670			
☐ C-GTLT	Beech King Air B200	BB-1126	N175BC	0083	1098	2 PWC PT6A-42	5670			

TIMBER WOLF AIR (1267932 Ontario, Inc. dba / Seasonal April-October ops only) — Lake of The Mountains, Ont.

Lot 8, Conc. 6, Granary Lake Road, Box 444, Blind River, Ontario P0R 1B0, Canada ☎ (705) 356-1887 Tx: none Fax: (705) 687-4045 SITA: n/a
F: 1998 ⁂ n/a Head: n/a Net: n/a

☐ C-FQKW	Cessna U206F Stationair	U20601728		0072	0598	1 CO IO-520-F	1633			Floats

TINKER'S PLACES, Ltd – Air Services (Seasonal May-October ops only) — Nestor Falls-Sabaskong SPB, Ont.

PO Box 266, Nestor Falls, Ontario P0X 1K0, Canada ☎ (807) 484-2664 Tx: n/a Fax: none SITA: n/a
F: 1982 ⁂ n/a Head: n/a Net: n/a

☐ C-FRXJ	Found FBA-2C	14		0065	0788	1 LY GO-480-B1D	1361			Floats

TK AIR CHARTERS, Ltd — Terrace, B.C.

3098 Thornhill Street, Terrace, British Columbia V8G 4Z7, Canada ☎ (250) 635-7355 Tx: none Fax: (250) 635-7355 SITA: n/a
F: 1995 ⁂ n/a Head: Grant Bowker Net: n/a

☐ C-FVAS	Cessna 337G Skymaster II	33701733	N99681	0076	0296	2 CO IO-360-G	2100			
☐ C-GQRM	Piper PA-31-310 Navajo	31-158	N1024P	0068	0298	2 LY TIO-540-A1A	2948			

TOFINO AIR LINES, Ltd — Tofino, B.C.

Box 99, Tofino, British Columbia V0R 2Z0, Canada ☎ (250) 725-4454 Tx: n/a Fax: (250) 725-4421 SITA: n/a
F: 1975 ⁂ 13 Head: W.G. Richards Net: n/a Aircraft below MTOW 1361 kg: Cessna 180 (on Floats)

☐ C-FGCY	De Havilland DHC-2 Beaver I	216		0051		1 PW R-985	2313			Floats

TORONTAIR = TOR (Toronto Airways, Ltd dba) — Toronto-Buttonville Municipal, Ont.

Toronto-Buttonville Municipal Airport, 2833-16th Ave, Box 100, Markham, Ontario L3R 0P8, Canada ☎ (905) 477-8100 Tx: none Fax: (905) 477-8053 SITA: n/a
F: 1961 ⁂ 95 Head: Heather A. Sifton ICAO: TORONTAIR Net: http://www.toronto-airways.ca Aircraft below MTOW 1361kg: Cessna 150 / 172, Dimona DV20, Piper PA-28 & Zlin Z142C

☐ C-GGSY	Piper PA-44-180 Seminole	44-7995031	N39929	0079	0584	2 LY O-360-E1A6D	1724			
☐ C-GPFG	Piper PA-44-180 Seminole	44-7995282	N2206X	0079	0496	2 LY O-360-E1A6D	1724			
☐ C-GWGD	Piper PA-44-180 Seminole	44-7995060		0079	1193	2 LY O-360-E1A6D	1724			
☐ C-GZYO	Cessna 337H Super Skymaster II	33701846		0078	0697	2 CO IO-360-GB	2100			

TRANSCANADA PIPELINE – Aviation Department (Division of TransCanada Pipeline, Ltd) — Calgary, Alta.

600 Palmer Road NE, Calgary, Alberta T2E 7R3, Canada ☎ (403) 267-8876 Tx: none Fax: (403) 250-7877 SITA: n/a
F: n/a ⁂ n/a Head: Gregory Montgomery Net: n/a Operates commercial patrol, external cargo flights, photography & corporate transport flights for the main company only.

☐ C-FTCH	Bell 206B JetRanger	860	N809JA	0072		1 AN 250-C20	1451			
☐ C-GGAS	Bell 206B JetRanger	1489		0074		1 AN 250-C20	1451			
☐ C-GGAZ	Bell 206B JetRanger II	2156		0077		1 AN 250-C20	1451			
☐ C-GTCE	Bell 206B JetRanger III	3418	N2270B	0081		1 AN 250-C20B	1451			
☐ C-GTZB	Bell 206B JetRanger III	2656		0079		1 AN 250-C20B	1451			
☐ C-GTCP	Dassault Falcon 900	29	N421FJ	0087		3 GA TFE731-5BR-1C2	20638	Corporate		

TRANS CAPITAL (Trans Capital Air, Ltd/Ltée dba) — Toronto-City Centre, Ont.

Hangar 1, Toronto City Centre Airport, Toronto, Ontario M5V 1A1, Canada ☎ (416) 203-1144 Tx: none Fax: (416) 203-1120 SITA: n/a
F: 1994 ⁂ n/a Head: Victor Pappalardo Net: n/a

☐ C-GGXS	De Havilland DHC-7-102 Dash 7	064	4X-AHB	0081	0994	4 PWC PT6A-50	19958	Y50		lsf A.L.S. Aero Leasing & Sales Ltd
☐ C-GLPP	De Havilland DHC-7-102 Dash 7	067	N939HA	0081	0997	4 PWC PT6A-50	19958	Y50		lsf Stolcraft Inc.

TRANS FAIR, Inc. (formerly Transport Aerien Sept-Iles, Inc.) — Longue-Pointe-de-Mingan, Qué.

CP 9, Longue-Pointe-de-Mingan, Québec G0G 1V0, Canada ☎ (418) 949-2261 Tx: none Fax: (418) 949-2304 SITA: n/a
F: 1972 ⁂ 9 Head: Jean-Paul Fafard Net: n/a

☐ C-GTFC	Convair 240-27 (T-29B)	279	N152PA	0052	0389	2 PW R-2800	18956	Freighter		

TRANSIT HELICOPTERS, Ltd (Helicoptères Transit, Ltée) — Val d'Or, Qué.

CP 322, Val d'Or, Qué. J9P 4P4, Canada ☎ (819) 825-5915 Tx: none Fax: (819) 825-7720 SITA: n/a
F: 1988 ⁂ 3 Head: Claude Richard Net: n/a Aircraft below MTOW 1361kg: Enstrom F28C

☐ C-GMAH	Bell 206B JetRanger II	2135	N90522	0077	0593	1 AN 250-C20	1451			
☐ C-FLIZ	Eurocopter (Aerosp.) AS350BA AStar	2484	F-GHRD	0091	0598	1 TU Arriel 1B	2100	EMS		cvtd AS350B

TRANS NORTH AIR = TNT (Trans North Turbo Air, Limited dba) — Whitehorse, Y.T.

20 Norseman Road, Airport Hangar C, Whitehorse, Yukon Territory Y1A 6E6, Canada ☎ (867) 668-2177 Tx: none Fax: (867) 668-3420 SITA: n/a
F: 1967 ⁂ 25 Head: Ronald. F. Connelly ICAO: TRANS NORTH Net: n/a

☐ C-FCHU	Bell 206B JetRanger III	2213	N70TT	0077	0191	1 AN 250-C20B	1451			
☐ C-FDRZ	Bell 206B JetRanger	764		0072		1 AN 250-C20	1451			
☐ C-FMBT	Bell 206B JetRanger	667		0071		1 AN 250-C20	1451			cvtd 206A
☐ C-GMIG	Bell 206B JetRanger II	2186		0077		1 AN 250-C20	1451			
☐ C-GMYQ	Bell 206B JetRanger III	2628		0079	0191	1 AN 250-C20B	1451			
☐ C-GTNY	Bell 206B JetRanger	990	CF-KNY	0073	0395	1 AN 250-C20	1451			

TRANSPORT CANADA – TRANSPORTS CANADA = TGO (Division of Dept of Transport / Ministère des Transports) — Ottawa, Ont.

Aircraft Services / Services des Aéronefs, 58 Service Road, Macdonald-Cartier Int'l Airport, Gloucester, Ontario K1V 9B2, Canada ☎ (613) 998-3036 Tx: none Fax: (613) 991-0365 SITA: n/a
F: 1946 ⁂ 450 Head: Manzur Huq ICAO: TRANSPORT Net: n/a Non-commercial federal government organisation conducting calibration, surveillance, aerial & transport missions from 18 bases.
Several helicopters are operated on behalf of Canadian Coast Guard/Department of Fisheries & Oceans (ICAO 3-letter code CTG, call sign Canadian Coast Guard.

☐ C-GCFE	Cessna 182Q Skylane II	18266328		0078	0378	1 CO O-470-U	1338			959 / based Ottawa, Ont.
☐ C-FCGK	Bell 206B JetRanger	24		0067		1 AN 250-C20	1451			861 / based Winnipeg, Man. / cvtd 206A
☐ C-FCGO	Bell 206B JetRanger	140		0068		1 AN 250-C20	1451			866 / based Ottawa, Ont.
☐ C-FCGQ	Bell 206B JetRanger	182		0068		1 AN 250-C20	1451			863 / based Vancouver, BC
☐ C-FCGR	Bell 206B JetRanger	189		0068		1 AN 250-C20	1451			867 / based Hamilton, Ont.
☐ C-FDOC	Bell 206B JetRanger	349		0069		1 AN 250-C20	1451			869 / based Ottawa, Ont. / cvtd 206A
☐ C-FDOD	Bell 206B JetRanger	379		0069		1 AN 250-C20	1451			868 / based Montreal, Qué. / cvtd 206A x
☐ C-FDOE	Bell 206B JetRanger	381		0069		1 AN 250-C20	1451			864 / based Edmonton, Alta / cvtd 206A
☐ C-GCFH	Cessna U206G Stationair 6 II	U20606179		0081	0481	1 CO IO-520-F	1633			973 / based Vancouver, BC
☐ C-GCHM	Bell 206L LongRanger	45083		0077		1 AN 250-C20B	1814	Coast Guard		124 / based Québec, Qué.
☐ C-GCHO	Bell 206L LongRanger	46606		0078		1 AN 250-C20B	1814	Coast Guard		126 / based Québec, Qué.
☐ C-GCHP	Bell 206L LongRanger	46607		0078		1 AN 250-C20B	1814	Coast Guard		127 / based Saint John, NB
☐ C-GCHQ	Bell 206L LongRanger	46611		0078		1 AN 250-C20B	1814	Coast Guard		128 / based Québec, Qué.
☐ C-GCHR	Bell 206L-1 LongRanger II	45220		0079		1 AN 250-C28B	1882	Coast Guard		129 / based Parry Sound, Ont.
☐ C-GCHS	Bell 206L-1 LongRanger II	45221		0079		1 AN 250-C28B	1882	Coast Guard		130 / based Prescott, Ont.
☐ C-FDTY	De Havilland DHC-2 Beaver I	26		0048	1148	1 PW R-985	2313			981 / Amph./Wheel-Skis/based Moncton,NB
☐ C-FDTZ	De Havilland DHC-2 Beaver I	33		0049	0549	1 PW R-985	2313			976 / Amph./Wheel-Skis/bsd Montreal,Qué
☐ C-GCFN	Eurocopter (MBB) BO105S CDN-BS-4	S-682	D-HDUX	0085		2 AN 250-C20B	2500	Coast Guard		359 / based Yarmouth, NS
☐ C-GCFO	Eurocopter (MBB) BO105S CDN-BS-4	S-715	N715XY	0085		2 AN 250-C20B	2500	Coast Guard		360 / based St. John's, Nfld
☐ C-GCFQ	Eurocopter (MBB) BO105S CDN-BS-4	S-716	N716XY	0085		2 AN 250-C20B	2500	Coast Guard		361 / based Dartmouth, NS

81 registration type of aircraft cn/fn ex/ex* mfd del powered by mtow kg configuration selcal name/fln/specialitites/remarks

☐ C-GCFS	Eurocopter (MBB) BO105S CDN-BS-4	S-725	N959MB	0085		2 AN 250-C20B	2500	Coast Guard		362 / based Charlottetown, PEI
☐ C-GCFT	Eurocopter (MBB) BO105S CDN-BS-4	S-726	N726S	0085		2 AN 250-C20B	2500	Coast Guard		363 / based Dartmouth, NS
☐ C-GCFU	Eurocopter (MBB) BO105S CDN-BS-4	S-727	N963MB	0085		2 AN 250-C20B	2500	Coast Guard		364 / based Québec, Qué.
☐ C-GCFV	Eurocopter (MBB) BO105S CDN-BS-4	S-728	N966MB	0085		2 AN 250-C20B	2500	Coast Guard		365 / based Québec, Qué.
☐ C-GCFX	Eurocopter (MBB) BO105S CDN-BS-4	S-730	N956MB	0085		2 AN 250-C20B	2500	Coast Guard		366 / based Québec, Qué.
☐ C-GCFY	Eurocopter (MBB) BO105S CDN-BS-4	S-733	N900MB	0085		2 AN 250-C20B	2500	Coast Guard		367 / based Stephenville, Nfld
☐ C-GCHU	Eurocopter (MBB) BO105S CDN-BS-4	S-696	N696CB	0085		2 AN 250-C20B	2500	Coast Guard		358 / based Prince Rupert, BC
☐ C-GCHV	Eurocopter (MBB) BO105S CDN-BS-4	S-641		0085		2 AN 250-C20B	2500	Coast Guard		354 / based Victoria, BC
☐ C-GCHW	Eurocopter (MBB) BO105S CDN-BS-4	S-681		0085		2 AN 250-C20B	2500	Coast Guard		355 / based Victoria, BC
☐ C-GCHX	Eurocopter (MBB) BO105S CDN-BS-4	S-695	N695ME	0085		2 AN 250-C20B	2500	Coast Guard		357 / based Victoria, BC
☐ C-GCHY	Eurocopter (MBB) BO105S CDN-BS-4	S-729	N969MB	0085		2 AN 250-C20B	2500	Coast Guard		356 / based Québec, Qué.
☐ C-GGGC	Eurocopter (MBB) BO105S CDN-BS-4	S-617	D-HDSM*	0083		2 AN 250-C20B	2400	Coast Guard		352 / based St. John's, Nfld
☐ C-GGGM	Eurocopter (MBB) BO105S CDN-BS-4	S-618	D-HDSN*	0083		2 AN 250-C20B	2400	Coast Guard		353 / based Dartmouth, NS
☐ C-FCGE	Beech King Air A90 (65-A90)	LJ-118		0066	0366	2 PWC PT6A-20	4218			993 / based Ottawa, Ont.
☐ C-FCGH	Beech King Air A90 (65-A90)	LJ-203		0067	0367	2 PWC PT6A-20	4218			983 / based Winnipeg, Man.
☐ C-FCGI	Beech King Air A90 (65-A90)	LJ-220		0067	0367	2 PWC PT6A-20	4218			957 / based Ottawa, Ont.
☐ C-FCGN	Beech King Air A90 (65-A90)	LJ-313		0068	0368	2 PWC PT6A-20	4377			975 / based Winnipeg, Man.
☐ C-FDOR	Beech King Air A100	B-103		0072	0372	2 PWC PT6A-28	5216			963 / based Ottawa, Ont.
☐ C-FDOS	Beech King Air A100	B-106		0072	0472	2 PWC PT6A-28	5216			964 / based Montreal, Qué.
☐ C-FDOU	Beech King Air A100	B-112		0072	0672	2 PWC PT6A-28	5216			967 / based Edmonton, Alta
☐ C-FDOV	Beech King Air A100	B-117		0072	0872	2 PWC PT6A-28	5216			965 / based Edmonton, Alta
☐ C-FDOY	Beech King Air A100	B-120		0072	1072	2 PWC PT6A-28	5216			966 / based Montreal, Qué.
☐ C-GCFB	Beech King Air C90	LJ-929	N81DD	0080	1187	2 PWC PT6A-21	4377			992 / based Vancouver, BC
☐ C-GCFD	Beech King Air A100	B-104	N72K	0072	0378	2 PWC PT6A-28	5216			962 / based Ottawa, Ont.
☐ C-GCFL	Beech King Air B90	LJ-500	N20WC	0070	0186	2 PWC PT6A-20	4377			994 / based Hamilton, Ont.
☐ C-GCFM	Beech King Air C90	LJ-886	N15SL	0080	0887	2 PWC PT6A-21	4377			960 / based Vancouver, BC
☐ C-GCFZ	Beech King Air C90	LJ-849	N6647P	0079	1187	2 PWC PT6A-21	4377			969 / based Vancouver, BC
☐ C-GHVR	Beech King Air B90	LJ-337	N69J	0068	0382	2 PWC PT6A-20	4377			968 / based Hamilton, Ont.
☐ C-FDOF	Bell 212	30536		0071		2 PWC PT6T-3 TwinPac	5080	Coast Guard		302 / based Québec, Qué.
☐ C-FDOP	Bell 212	30567		0072		2 PWC PT6T-3 TwinPac	5080	Coast Guard		303 / based Dartmouth, NS
☐ C-GCHF	Bell 212	30617		0074		2 PWC PT6T-3 TwinPac	5080	Coast Guard		304 / based Victoria, BC
☐ C-GCHG	Bell 212	30625		0074		2 PWC PT6T-3 TwinPac	5080	Coast Guard		305 / based St. John's, Nfld
☐ C-GCHT	Bell 212	30910		0079		2 PWC PT6T-3 TwinPac	5080	Coast Guard		306 / based Parry Sound, Ont.
☐ C-FCST	De Havilland DHC-6 Twin Otter 300	351		0073	0776	2 PWC PT6A-27	5670			970 / based Moncton, NB
☐ C-FCSU	De Havilland DHC-6 Twin Otter 300	352		0073	0876	2 PWC PT6A-27	5670			979 / based Vancouver, BC
☐ C-FCSW	De Havilland DHC-6 Twin Otter 300	355		0073	0776	2 PWC PT6A-27	5670			980 / based Edmonton, Alta
☐ C-FCSX	De Havilland DHC-6 Twin Otter 300	357		0073	0676	2 PWC PT6A-27	5670			985 / based Edmonton, Alta
☐ C-FCSY	De Havilland DHC-6 Twin Otter 300	358		0073	0676	2 PWC PT6A-27	5670			990 / based Vancouver, BC
☐ C-FCVY	De Havilland DHC-6 Twin Otter 300	840		0088	0489	2 PWC PT6A-27	5670			952 / based Winnipeg, Man.
☐ C-GCFF	Beech King Air 200	BB-474		0079	0379	2 PWC PT6A-41	5670			961 / based Moncton, NB
☐ C-FJCZ	Cessna 550 Citation II	550-0700		0092	0592	2 PWC JT15D-4	6033			858 / based Montreal, Qué.
☐ C-FJWZ	Cessna 550 Citation II	550-0685		0091	1091	2 PWC JT15D-4	6033			853 / based Ottawa, Ont.
☐ C-FJXN	Cessna 550 Citation II	550-0684		0091	1091	2 PWC JT15D-4	6033			852 / based Ottawa, Ont.
☐ C-FKCE	Cessna 550 Citation II	550-0686		0091	0991	2 PWC JT15D-4	6396			854 / based Edmonton, Alta
☐ C-FKDX	Cessna 550 Citation II	550-0687		0091	1091	2 PWC JT15D-4	6033			855 / based Hamilton, Ont.
☐ C-FKEB	Cessna 550 Citation II	550-0688		0091	1091	2 PWC JT15D-4	6396			858 / based Ottawa, Ont.
☐ C-FKLB	Cessna 550 Citation II	550-0699		0091	0492	2 PWC JT15D-4	6033			857 / based Hamilton, Ont.
☐ C-FLZA	Cessna 550 Citation II	550-0701		0092	0692	2 PWC JT15D-4	6033			859 / based Moncton, NB
☐ C-FMFM	Cessna 550 Citation II	550-0702		0092	0692	2 PWC JT15D-4	6033			860 / based Montreal, Qué.
☐ C-FDOH	Sikorsky S-61N	61704		0072		2 GE CT58-140-1	9318	Coast Guard		253 / Amphibian/based Prince Rupert, BC
☐ C-GCFJ	De Havilland DHC-8-102 Dash 8	020		0086	0586	2 PWC PW120A	15649	Fisheries&Oceans		300 / based Ottawa, Ont.
☐ C-GCFR	De Havilland DHC-7-150 Dash 7	102		0085	0586	4 PWC PT6A-50	21319	Survey/Ice recon		Ist First Air
☐ C-GBPD	Canadair CL-215 (CL-215-1A10)	1084		0086	0386	2 PW R-2800-CA3	19731	Tanker		895 / Ist NWT Gvmt/opb BFL / Amphibian
☐ C-GBYU	Canadair CL-215 (CL-215-1A10)	1083	C-GKEA*	0086	0286	2 PW R-2800-CA3	19731	Tanker		894 / Ist NWT Gvmt/opb BFL / Amphibian
☐ C-GCSX	Canadair CL-215 (CL-215-1A10)	1088	C-GKEA*	0086	0786	2 PW R-2800-CA3	19731	Tanker		899 / Ist NWT Gvmt/opb BFL / Amphibian
☐ C-GDHN	Canadair CL-215 (CL-215-1A10)	1089	C-GKEE*	0086	0287	2 PW R-2800-CA3	19731	Tanker		900 / Ist NWT Gvmt/opb BFL / Amphibian

TRANSWEST HELICOPTERS Ltd — **Chilliwack, B.C.**

PO Box 160, Chilliwack, British Columbia V2P 6H7, Canada ☎ (604) 792-5992 Tx: none Fax: (604) 792-6959 SITA: n/a
F: 1990 n/a Head: Tim McEvoy Net: n/a

☐ C-GTWF	Bell 214B-1 BigLifter	28014	C-FQTJ	0076	1093	1 LY T5508D	5670			
☐ C-GTWH	Bell 214B-1 BigLifter	28017	N214MV	0076	0695	1 LY T5508D	5670			
☐ C-GTWI	Bell 214B-1 BigLifter	28011	LN-OSW	0476	1196	1 LY T5508D	5670			

TRIPPIER AIR (Edward G. Trippier dba) — **Ear Falls, Ont.**

Box 11, Ear Falls, Ontario P0V 1T0, Canada ☎ (807) 222-3356 Tx: n/a Fax: none SITA: n/a
F: 1984 n/a Head: Edward G. Trippier Net: n/a

☐ C-GXAO	Cessna A185F Skywagon	18502959		0076		1 CO IO-520-D	1520			Floats / Wheel-Skis

TROUT LAKE AIRWAYS (Booi's Wilderness Lodge & Outposts, Ltd dba / Seasonal May-October ops only) — **Red Lake, Ont.**

33 Howey Bay Road, Box 301, Red Lake, Ontario P0V 2M0, Canada ☎ (807) 727-2489 Tx: n/a Fax: none SITA: n/a
F: 1993 n/a Head: n/a Net: n/a Phone number in winter: (807) 727-2324

☐ C-FNNR	Cessna 185 Skywagon	185-0097		0061	0893	1 CO IO-470-F	1492			Floats

TSAYTA AVIATION, Ltd — **Fort St. James & Tsayta Lake, B.C.**

PO Box 1178, Fort St. James, British Columbia V0J 1P0, Canada ☎ (250) 996-8540 Tx: none Fax: (250) 996-8655 SITA: n/a
F: 1989 n/a Head: Clarence L. Hogan Net: n/a

☐ C-GLKK	Cessna A185F Skywagon	18502244	N2525S	0073	0894	1 CO IO-520-D	1520			Floats

TUDHOPE AIRWAYS, Ltd — **Hudson, Ont.**

Box 296, Hudson, Ontario P0V 1X0, Canada ☎ (807) 582-3206 Tx: none Fax: none SITA: n/a
F: 1984 n/a Head: Glen Tudhope Net: n/a Aircraft below MTOW 1361 kg: Cessna 180 (on Floats / Wheel-Skis).

☐ C-FSDC	Found FBA-2C	17		0064		1 LY GO-480-B1D	1361			Floats / Wheel-Skis
☐ C-FOCP	De Havilland DHC-2 Beaver I	49		0050		1 PW R-985	2313			Floats / Wheel-Skis

TUNDRA HELICOPTERS, Ltd — **Langley, B.C.**

5225-216 Street, Langley, British Columbia V2Y 2N3, Canada ☎ (604) 533-6535 Tx: none Fax: (604) 534-7674 SITA: n/a
F: 1973 25 Head: Steve Harrison Net: n/a

☐ C-FMTF	MD Helicopters MD 530F (Hughes 369FF)	0075FF	N382F	0088	0593	1 AN 250-C30	1406			
☐ C-FTHT	Hiller UH-12ET	2198	ZK-HCE	0062	0291	1 AN 250-C20B	1406			Skids / cvtd UH-12E
☐ C-GTHK	Bell 212	30641	N708H	0073	0596	2 PWC PT6T-3 TwinPac	5080			
☐ C-GHOG	Sikorsky S-58ET	58-1662	N58BH	0063	0196	1 PWC PT6T-3 TwinPac	5897			cvtd S-58E
☐ C-GHOS	Sikorsky S-58ET	58-1537	N85HA	0062	0195	1 PWC PT6T-3 TwinPac	5897			cvtd S-58E

TURBOWEST HELICOPTERS, Ltd (formerly Darvill Helicopters, Ltd) — **Calgary, Alta.**

10-575 Palmer Road NE, Calgary, Alberta T2E 7G4, Canada ☎ (403) 291-3855 Tx: none Fax: (403) 291-1525 SITA: n/a
F: 1979 8 Head: A. Lang Net: n/a

☐ C-GWPQ	MD Helicopters MD 500D (Hughes 369D)	700755D		0080	0197	1 AN 250-C20B	1361			
☐ C-FIHL	Bell 206B JetRanger II	2077	8R-GEX	0076	0697	1 AN 250-C20	1451			
☐ C-GJIJ	Bell 206B JetRanger	758		0072	0698	1 AN 250-C20	1451			
☐ C-FJJW	Eurocopter (Aerosp.) SA315B Lama	2658	N15DY	0083	0191	1 TU Artouste IIIB1	1950			
☐ C-FTLK	Eurocopter (Aerosp.) SA315B Lama	2549	XC-CUF	0079	1094	1 TU Artouste IIIB	1950			
☐ C-FPHN	Eurocopter (Aerosp.) AS350D AStar	1444	N35SV	0081	0595	1 LY LTS101-600A.3	1950			

TWEEDSMUIR AIR SERVICES, Ltd (Seasonal May-October ops only) — **Nimpo Lake, B.C**

Box 19, Nimpo Lake, British Columbia V0L 1R0, Canada ☎ (250) 742-3388 Tx: none Fax: (250) 742-3383 SITA: n/a
F: 1987 2 Head: Duncan Stewart Net: http://www.on-the-fly.com.

☐ C-GFRJ	Cessna A185F Skywagon II	18504011		0080	0793	1 CO IO-520-D	1520			Floats
☐ CF-BUO	Cessna A185F Skywagon	18502201		0073		1 CO IO-520-D	1520			Floats
☐ C-FFHT	De Havilland DHC-2 Beaver I	55		0049		1 PW R-985	2313			Floats
☐ C-GNPO	De Havilland DHC-2 Beaver I	773	C-GMOJ	0053	0695	1 PW R-985	2313			Floats

TWIN LAKE OUTFITTERS - Air Services (Twin Lake Outfitters & Wilderness Camps Inc., dba) — **Lower Twin Lake, Ont.**

PO Box 188, Nakina, Ontario P0T 2H0, Canada ☎ (807) 329-5771 Tx: none Fax: none SITA: n/a
F: 1982 8 Head: Bill Pocock Net: n/a Winter (November-April) phone/fax number: (519) 537-3656

☐ C-GDQJ	Cessna A185F Skywagon	18502930		0076	0391	1 CO IO-520-D	1520			Floats / Wheels
☐ C-FNOT	De Havilland DHC-2 Beaver I	1067	N4193A	0057	0887	1 PW R-985	2313			Floats / Wheels
☐ C-GCQK	De Havilland DHC-3 Otter	141	N80939	0056	0394	1 PW R-1340	3629			Floats / Wheels

82 registration type of aircraft cn/fn ex/ex* mfd del powered by mtow kg configuration selcal name/fln/specialitites/remarks

TWIN OTTER INTERNATIONAL, Ltd = (TWIN)

Calgary, Alta.

Box 27, Site 16, RR2, Calgary, Alberta T2P 2G5, Canada ☎ (403) 288-3305 Tx: none Fax: (403) 247-6846 SITA: n/a
F: 1967 ♦♦♦ n/a Head: George Stephenson Net: n/a Used aircraft leasing company.
Owner / Lessor of following (main) aircraft types: De Havilland DHC-6 Twin Otter. Aircraft leased from Twin Otter Int'l are listed and mentioned as lsf TWIN under the leasing carriers.

TYAX AIR SERVICES, Ltd (Affiliated with Tyax Mountain Lake Resort)

Gold Bridge, B.C.

Tyaughton Lake Road, Gold Bridge, British Columbia V0K 1P0, Canada ☎ (250) 238-2221 Tx: none Fax: (250) 238-2528 SITA: n/a
F: 1990 ♦♦♦ 2 Head: Gus Abel Net: http://www.tyax.bc.ca

registration	type of aircraft	cn/fn	ex/ex*	mfd	del	powered by	mtow kg	configuration	selcal	name/fln/specialtites/remarks
☐ C-GIYV	De Havilland DHC-2 Beaver I	1488	XP823	0061	0691	1 PW R-985	2313			Floats / Wheel-Skis

ULTRA HELICOPTERS, Ltd

Grimshaw, Alta.

PO Box 1188, Grimshaw, Alberta T0H 1W0, Canada ☎ (780) 332-2995 Tx: none Fax: (780) 332-1851 SITA: n/a
F: 1993 ♦♦♦ n/a Head: Rene Brule Net: n/a

registration	type of aircraft	cn/fn	ex/ex*	mfd	del	powered by	mtow kg	configuration	selcal	name/fln/specialtites/remarks
☐ C-GBPB	Bell 206B JetRanger	321		0068	0598	1 AN 250-C20	1451			cvtd 206A
☐ C-GHHK	Bell 206B JetRanger	1588		0075	0398	1 AN 250-C20	1451			
☐ C-GMXU	Bell 206B JetRanger	1520	N15DW	0074	0199	1 AN 250-C20	1451			
☐ C-GQKU	Bell 206B JetRanger II	2173		0077	0493	1 AN 250-C20	1451			

UNIVERSAL HELICOPTERS (Nfld), Ltd – UHNL

St. John's, Nfld.

PO Box 21208, St. John's, Newfoundland A1A 5B2, Canada ☎ (709) 576-4611 Tx: none Fax: (709) 576-0083 SITA: n/a
F: 1963 ♦♦♦ 35 Head: Paul W.S. Williams Net: n/a Aircraft below MTOW 1361kg: Enstrom 480.

registration	type of aircraft	cn/fn	ex/ex*	mfd	del	powered by	mtow kg	configuration	selcal	name/fln/specialtites/remarks
☐ C-FKOV	Bell 206LR+ LongRanger	45144	ZK-HXL	0077	0891	1 AN 250-C20R	1814			cvtd 206L
☐ C-FVEF	Bell 206L-4 LongRanger IV	52071	N21379	0094	0495	1 AN 250-C30P	2018			
☐ C-GAHS	Bell 206LR+ LongRanger	45048	D-HMHS	0076		1 AN 250-C20R	1814			cvtd 206L
☐ C-GDCA	Bell 206LR+ LongRanger	45021		0075	0893	1 AN 250-C20R	1814			cvtd 206L
☐ C-GIZY	Bell 206LR+ LongRanger	45027	N176KH	0076		1 AN 250-C20R	1814			cvtd 206L
☐ C-GLSH	Bell 206LR+ LongRanger	45018		0075		1 AN 250-C20R	1814			cvtd 206L
☐ C-GQIX	Bell 206L LongRanger	45008	N8EL	0075	0795	1 AN 250-C20B	1814			
☐ C-GQNS	Bell 206LR+ LongRanger	45134		0077		1 AN 250-C20R	1814			cvtd 206L
☐ C-GTHE	Bell 206L-4 LongRanger IV	52035		0093	0497	1 AN 250-C30P	2018			
☐ C-GVYM	Bell 206LR+ LongRanger	45143	N16922	0077		1 AN 250-C20R	1814			cvtd 206L
☐ C-GVYO	Bell 206LR+ LongRanger	46609	N16950	0078		1 AN 250-C20R	1814			cvtd 206L
☐ C-FHHH	Eurocopter (Aerosp.) AS350BA AStar	1421	N5782X	0081	0598	1 TU Arriel 1B	2100			cvtd AS350D
☐ C-FXAL	Eurocopter (Aerosp.) AS350B AStar	1816	SE-HNP	0085	0598	1 TU Arriel 1B	1950			
☐ C-FXYF	Bell 407	53022		0096	0596	1 AN 250-C47B	2268			
☐ C-GOFL	Bell 407	53130		0097	0497	1 AN 250-C47B	2268			

URSUS AVIATION (102643 Aviation, Ltd dba)

Fort Norman, N.W.T.

General Delivery, Fort Norman, Northwest Territories X0E 0K0, Canada ☎ (867) 588-4141 Tx: n/a Fax: (867) 588-4131 SITA: n/a
F: 1980 ♦♦♦ 2 Head: Blair W. Jensen Net: n/a Aircraft below MTOW 1361kg: Cessna 172 & Maule M-5-210C.

registration	type of aircraft	cn/fn	ex/ex*	mfd	del	powered by	mtow kg	configuration	selcal	name/fln/specialtites/remarks
☐ C-FBMA	Piper PA-23-150 Apache	23-1013		0057	1191	2 LY O-320-A1A	1588			
☐ C-FKFV	Piper PA-23-160 Apache	23-1285		0058	0395	2 LY O-320-B3B	1724			
☐ C-FWHV	Cessna T207A Turbo Stationair 7 II	20700505	N6385H	0079	0698	1 CO TSIO-520-M	1724			
☐ C-GJTE	Piper PA-31-310 Navajo	31-464	N11AW	0069	0196	2 LY TIO-540-A2C	2948			

VALLEY HELICOPTERS, Ltd

Hope & Merritt, B.C.

RR 2, 63235 Flood Hope Road, Hope, British Columbia V0X 1L0, Canada ☎ (250) 869-2131 Tx: none Fax: (250) 869-2598 SITA: n/a
F: 1985 ♦♦♦ 7 Head: Fred Fandrich Net: n/a

registration	type of aircraft	cn/fn	ex/ex*	mfd	del	powered by	mtow kg	configuration	selcal	name/fln/specialtites/remarks
☐ C-FCHV	Bell 206B JetRanger	1541	N59620	0074	0394	1 AN 250-C20	1451			
☐ C-GTYV	Bell 206B JetRanger II	1976		0076		1 AN 250-C20	1451			
☐ C-GXVS	Bell 206B JetRanger II	1893		0076		1 AN 250-C20	1451			

VALUE AIR, Ltd

Chatham, N.B.

325 Radio Street, Miramichi, New Brunswick E1V 2W6, Canada ☎ (506) 778-0088 Tx: none Fax: (506) 778-0088 SITA: n/a
F: 1992 ♦♦♦ 3 Head: Ronald J. Knowles Net: n/a

registration	type of aircraft	cn/fn	ex/ex*	mfd	del	powered by	mtow kg	configuration	selcal	name/fln/specialtites/remarks
☐ C-FPWL	Piper PA-23-250 Aztec B	27-2116	N5093Y	0063	0498	2 LY O-540-A1D5	2177			

VANCOUVER ISLAND AIR, Ltd – VIA

Campbell River, B.C

Box 727, Campbell River, British Columbia V9W 6J3, Canada ☎ (250) 287-2433 Tx: none Fax: (250) 286-3269 SITA: n/a
F: 1985 ♦♦♦ 15 Head: Larry Langford Net: n/a Aircraft below MTOW 1361 kg: Cessna 180 (on Floats)

registration	type of aircraft	cn/fn	ex/ex*	mfd	del	powered by	mtow kg	configuration	selcal	name/fln/specialtites/remarks
☐ C-FIGF	De Havilland DHC-2 Beaver I	834		0054		1 PW R-985	2313	6 Pax		Floats
☐ C-FCSN	Beech 3N (18)	CA-16	RCAF 1441	0052	0390	2 PW R-985	3969	9 Pax		Floats
☐ C-GAIV	Beech TC-45G (18)	AF-80	N158L	0054	1097	2 PW R-985	3969	9 Pax		Floats
☐ C-GVIB	Beech D18S VIA Seawind	A-480	N483B	0049	0691	2 PW R-985	3969	9 Pax		Floats / cvtd D18S
☐ CF-GNR	Beech 3NM (18)	CA-191	RCAF 2318	0052	1197	2 PW R-985	3969	9 Pax		Floats

VANCOUVER ISLAND HELICOPTERS, Ltd – VIH

Victoria, B.C.

1-9600 Canora Road, Sidney, British Columbia V8L 5V5, Canada ☎ (250) 656-3987 Tx: none Fax: (250) 655-1180 SITA: n/a
F: 1955 ♦♦♦ 25 Head: Frank Norie Net: n/a Aircraft below MTOW 1361 kg: Bell 47G & Robinson R22.

registration	type of aircraft	cn/fn	ex/ex*	mfd	del	powered by	mtow kg	configuration	selcal	name/fln/specialtites/remarks
☐ C-FFYO	MD Helicopters MD 500D (Hughes 369D)	580315D	C-GVXT	0078	0297	1 AN 250-C20B	1361			
☐ C-FQHB	MD Helicopters MD 500D (Hughes 369D)	980334D	N811CA	0078	0793	1 AN 250-C20B	1361			
☐ C-FYED	MD Helicopters MD 500D (Hughes 369D)	490487D	N4571V	0079	0696	1 AN 250-C20B	1361			
☐ C-GBCW	MD Helicopters MD 500D (Hughes 369D)	1260057D		0076	0593	1 AN 250-C20B	1361			
☐ C-GLWE	MD Helicopters MD 500D (Hughes 369D)	370103D	N8394F	0077	0790	1 AN 250-C20B	1361			
☐ C-GRYH	MD Helicopters MD 500D (Hughes 369D)	190442D		0079	0791	1 AN 250-C20B	1361			
☐ C-GVIJ	MD Helicopters MD 500D (Hughes 369D)	390482D	N58338	0079	0594	1 AN 250-C20B	1361			
☐ C-FANC	Bell 206B JetRanger	1283		0074		1 AN 250-C20	1451			
☐ C-FBER	Bell 206B JetRanger III	2648	N5018L	0079		1 AN 250-C20B	1451			
☐ C-FBHQ	Bell 206B JetRanger	970		0074		1 AN 250-C20	1451			
☐ C-FEBU	Bell 206B JetRanger	1642	N90178	0075	0689	1 AN 250-C20	1451			
☐ C-FGGC	Bell 206B JetRanger	1080	N58113	0073	1195	1 AN 250-C20	1451			
☐ C-FIQF	Bell 206B JetRanger	1110	N58143	0073		1 AN 250-C20	1451			
☐ C-FMCH	Bell 206B JetRanger II	2132	N306CK	0077	0794	1 AN 250-C20	1451			
☐ C-FMPI	Bell 206B JetRanger	978		0073		1 AN 250-C20	1451			
☐ C-FPCH	Bell 206B JetRanger III	3030	C-GMCJ	0080	0894	1 AN 250-C20B	1451			
☐ C-FPZI	Bell 206B JetRanger	1280		0074	0595	1 AN 250-C20	1451			
☐ C-GBNS	Bell 206B JetRanger	1805	N49634	0075		1 AN 250-C20	1451			
☐ C-GCXT	Bell 206B JetRanger	1551		0074		1 AN 250-C20	1451			
☐ C-GGQL	Bell 206B JetRanger II	2117	N16723	0076		1 AN 250-C20	1451			
☐ C-GHCQ	Bell 206B JetRanger	1302		0074		1 AN 250-C20	1451			
☐ C-GISE	Bell 206B JetRanger	839	N300FH	0072	0595	1 AN 250-C20	1451			
☐ C-GJSG	Bell 206B JetRanger	326		0068	0895	1 AN 250-C20	1451			cvtd 206A
☐ C-GJTV	Bell 206B JetRanger	352	N1428W	0069		1 AN 250-C20	1451			cvtd 206A
☐ C-GMGN	Bell 206B JetRanger III	2867		0079		1 AN 250-C20B	1451			
☐ C-GNMI	Bell 206B JetRanger III	2602		0079	0693	1 AN 250-C20B	1451			
☐ C-GRFD	Bell 206B JetRanger III	2332	N16887	0078	0689	1 AN 250-C20B	1451			
☐ C-GTPH	Bell 206B JetRanger	1531	N59629	0074		1 AN 250-C20	1451			
☐ C-GTWP	Bell 206B JetRanger	946	N29979	0073	0690	1 AN 250-C20	1451			
☐ C-GVIH	Bell 206B JetRanger	1689		0075		1 AN 250-C20	1451			
☐ C-GWUF	Bell 206B JetRanger	1182		0073		1 AN 250-C20	1451			
☐ C-FCTD	Bell 206L-1 LongRanger II	45159	HC-BUC	0078	0497	1 AN 250-C28B	1882			
☐ C-FJTO	Bell 206L LongRanger	45085	SE-HOP	0077	0894	1 AN 250-C20B	1814			
☐ C-FVIX	Bell 206L LongRanger	45139	SE-HTL	0077	0894	1 AN 250-C20B	1814			
☐ C-FTDE	Eurocopter (Aerosp.) AS350B2 AStar	2796		0094	0298	1 TU Arriel 1D1	2250			
☐ C-GPWO	Eurocopter (Aerosp.) AS350BA AStar	2236	N2BQ	0089	0598	1 TU Arriel 1B	2100			cvtd AS350B
☐ C-GVIA	Eurocopter (Aerosp.) AS350B1 AStar	2297	N4428V	0089	0698	1 TU Arriel 1D	2200			
☐ C-GZPT	Eurocopter (Aerosp.) AS350BA AStar	2643		0092	0398	1 TU Arriel 1B	2100			
☐ C-FUHF	Eurocopter (Aerosp.) AS355F1 TwinStar	5255	VH-HRT	0084	0396	2 AN 250-C20F	2400			
☐ C-GEBM	Bell 222U	47524	VH-ZHJ	0084	1298	2 LY LTS101-750C.1	3742			
☐ C-GFCB	Bell 222	47026	N299CK	0080	0494	2 LY LTS101-650C.3	3561			
☐ C-GVIM	Bell 222U	47571	JA9912	0088	0692	2 LY LTS101-750C.1	3742			
☐ C-GVIY	Bell 222U	47562	JA9665	0087	0993	2 LY LTS101-750C.1	3742			
☐ C-FVIH	Bell 205A-1	30164	N809KA	0074		1 LY T5313B	4309			
☐ C-GPWS	Bell 205A-1	30217	N183AH	0075	0398	1 LY T5313B	4309			
☐ C-GPWT	Bell 205A-1	30231	N57954	0075	0398	1 LY T5313B	4309			
☐ C-FVIK	Bell 212	30990	YV-O-CVG-8	0079	0299	2 PWC PT6T-3 TwinPac	5080			
☐ C-GZMQ	Bell 212	30820	N5595U	0077	0598	2 PWC PT6T-3 TwinPac	5080			

VANDERHOOF FLYING SERVICE, Ltd
Vanderhoof, B.C.

Box 955, Vanderhoof, British Columbia V0J 3A0, Canada ☎ (250) 567-4114 Tx: none Fax: (250) 567-4115 SITA: n/a
F: 1970 ♠♠♠ 6 Head: Brent Miskuski Net: n/a Aircraft below MTOW 1361kg: Cessna 172 & 182.

	registration	type of aircraft	cn/fn	ex/ex*	mfd	del	powered by	mtow kg	configuration	name/fln/specialitites/remarks
☐	C-FUEO	Cessna 337A Super Skymaster	337-0360		0066	0598	2 CO IO-360-C/D	1905		
☐	C-FVGI	Cessna 337B Super Skymaster	337-0650		0067	0798	2 CO IO-360-C/D	1950		
☐	CF-YUJ	Cessna 337B Super Skymaster	337-0694		0067	0498	2 CO IO-360-C/D	1950		
☐	C-GXHN	Beech Baron B55 (95-B55)	TC-952	N8934U	0065	0694	2 CO IO-520	2313		
☐	C-GZEB	Piper PA-31-350 Navajo Chieftain	31-7952124		0079	1298	2 LY TIO-540-J2BD	3175		

VENTURE AIR, Ltd
Meadow Lake, Sask.

Box 398, Meadow Lake, Saskatchewan S0M 1V0, Canada ☎ (306) 236-3161 Tx: none Fax: (306) 236-3772 SITA: n/a
F: 1986 ♠♠♠ n/a Head: George L. Jones Net: n/a Aircraft below MTOW 1361kg: Cessna 182

	registration	type of aircraft	cn/fn	ex/ex*	mfd	del	powered by	mtow kg	configuration	name/fln/specialitites/remarks
☐	C-GYLT	Cessna A185F Skywagon	18503338		0077		1 CO IO-520-D	1520		

VENTURE HELICOPTERS (M.K.C.), Inc.
Calgary, Alta.

1060 McTavish Road NE, Calgary, Alberta T2E 7G6, Canada ☎ (403) 291-3069 Tx: none Fax: (403) 291-3071 SITA: n/a
F: 1992 ♠♠♠ 10 Head: Harry Chernetz Net: n/a

	registration	type of aircraft	cn/fn	ex/ex*	mfd	del	powered by	mtow kg	configuration	name/fln/specialitites/remarks
☐	C-FETK	Bell 205A-1	30299	OE-EXH	0079	0592	1 LY T5313B	4309		
☐	C-GQLG	Bell 205A-1	30008	A7-HAF	0068	0696	1 LY T5313B	4309		
☐	C-GRVQ	Bell 205A-1	30034	N1439W	0069	0598	1 LY T5313B	4309		

VIH LOGGING, Ltd (Related to Vancouver Island Helicopters, Ltd)
Victoria, B.C.

21-9600 Canora Road, Sidney, British Columbia V8L 4R1, Canada ☎ (250) 656-1220 Tx: none Fax: (250) 656-2598 SITA: n/a
F: 1999 ♠♠♠ 50 Head: Ken Norie Net: n/a

	registration	type of aircraft	cn/fn	ex/ex*	mfd	del	powered by	mtow kg	configuration	name/fln/specialitites/remarks
☐	C-GLJJ	Cessna U206G Stationair 6 II	U20606205	N6257Z	0081	0895	1 CO IO-520-F	1633	Corporate	Amphibian
☐	C-FQNG	Sikorsky S-61N Helipro Short	61032	N301Y	0060	0993	2 GE CT58-140-1	9318		cvtd S-61N
☐	C-FTIG	Sikorsky S-61N	61491	N613RM	0072	0994	2 GE CT58-140-1	9318		cvtd S-61N / std Victoria
☐	C-FIGR	Kamov Ka-32A-IIBC	8707	RA-31585	0091	0097	2 IS TV3-117V	12600		
☐	C-GKHL	Kamov Ka-32A-IIBC	8801	RA-31594	0092	0097	2 IS TV3-117V	12600		

VIKING OUTPOST AIR (Viking Outpost Cabins, Ltd dba / Seasonal May-October ops only)
Red Lake, Ont.

Box 320, Red Lake, Ontario P0V 2M0, Canada ☎ (807) 727-2262 Tx: none Fax: (807) 727-3462 SITA: n/a
F: 1993 ♠♠♠ 4 Head: Hugh Carlson Net: n/a Aircraft below MTOW 1361kg: Cessna 180 (on Floats).

	registration	type of aircraft	cn/fn	ex/ex*	mfd	del	powered by	mtow kg	configuration	name/fln/specialitites/remarks
☐	C-GGMB	De Havilland DHC-2 Beaver I	1263	N1440Z	0058	0697	1 PW R-985	2313		Floats
☐	CF-FQI	Noorduyn Norseman VI (UC-64A)	364	43-5373	0044	0593	1 PW R-1340	3420		Floats

VILLERS AIR SERVICES, Ltd
Fort Nelson, B.C.

PO Box 328, Fort Nelson, British Columbia V0C 1R0, Canada ☎ (250) 774-2072 Tx: none Fax: (250) 774-6182 SITA: n/a
F: 1977 ♠♠♠ 4 Head: Peter Villers Net: n/a

	registration	type of aircraft	cn/fn	ex/ex*	mfd	del	powered by	mtow kg	configuration	name/fln/specialitites/remarks
☐	C-GZNG	Piper PA-32-300 Cherokee SIX	32-7440158	N44529	0074	0297	1 LY IO-540-K1A5	1542		
☐	C-GEBH	Cessna U206E Stationair	U20601697	N8232Q	0071	1098	1 CO IO-520-F	1633		
☐	C-FJBD	Beech Baron 58	TH-260	N518SW	0072	1190	2 CO IO-520-C	2449		
☐	C-FTUP	Piper PA-31-350 Navajo Chieftain	31-7652101	N76DE	0076	1294	2 LY TIO-540-J2BD	3175		
☐	C-GPPP	Britten-Norman BN-2A-27 Islander	423	G-BCSH	0075		2 LY O-540-E4C5	2885		

VISION AIR, Inc.
Vancouver-Int'l, B.C.

Suite 118, 5360 Airport Road South, Richmond, British Columbia V7B 1B4, Canada ☎ (604) 303-9336 Tx: none Fax: (604) 303-9337 SITA: n/a
F: 1996 ♠♠♠ 5 Head: Peter Morgan ICAO: JAGUAR Net: n/a

	registration	type of aircraft	cn/fn	ex/ex*	mfd	del	powered by	mtow kg	configuration	name/fln/specialitites/remarks
☐	C-FGES	Cessna 401	401-0213	N7898F	0068	1096	2 CO TSIO-520-E	2858		
☐	C-FZJE	Cessna 401B	401B0032		0070	1298	2 CO TSIO-520-E	2858		

VISION AIR AVIATION (9048-9741 Québec, Inc. dba / Seasonal May-October ops only)
Delisle-Lac St-Jean, Qué.

3145 Rang St-Michel, Delisle, Québec G0W 1L0, Canada ☎ (418) 662-5199 Tx: none Fax: none SITA: n/a
F: 1997 ♠♠♠ 1 Head: Pierre Gagnon Net: n/a

	registration	type of aircraft	cn/fn	ex/ex*	mfd	del	powered by	mtow kg	configuration	name/fln/specialitites/remarks
☐	C-FTZV	Cessna 185A Skywagon	185-0319		0062	0697	1 CO IO-520-D	1451		Floats

VOYAGE AIR (634643 Alberta, Ltd dba)
Fort McMurray, Alta. & Buffalo Narrows, Sask.

Box 5838, Fort McMurray, Alberta T9H 4V9, Canada ☎ (780) 743-0255 Tx: none Fax: (780) 743-4625 SITA: n/a
F: 1997 ♠♠♠ 5 Head: Barry J. O'Brien Net: n/a

	registration	type of aircraft	cn/fn	ex/ex*	mfd	del	powered by	mtow kg	configuration	name/fln/specialitites/remarks
☐	C-GOLB	Cessna A185F Skywagon	18503188	N93173	0077	0997	1 CO IO-520-D	1520		Floats / Wheel-Skis
☐	C-GQQJ	De Havilland DHC-2 Beaver I	719	N202PS	0054	0997	1 PW R-985	2313		Floats / Wheel-Skis
☐	C-GUJW	De Havilland DHC-2 Beaver I	1657	Oman305	0066	0997	1 PW R-985	2313		Floats / Wheel-Skis
☐	C-GZSI	De Havilland DHC-2 Beaver I	1003	N5327G	0056	0997	1 PW R-985	2313		Floats / Wheel-Skis

VOYAGEUR AIRWAYS, Ltd = 4V / VAL
Sudbury & North Bay, Ont.

1500 Airport Road, Norh Bay, Ontario P0H 1P0, Canada ☎ (705) 476-1750 Tx: none Fax: (705) 474-6773 SITA: n/a
F: 1968 ♠♠♠ 100 Head: Max Shapiro IATA: 908 ICAO: VOYAGEUR Net: http://www.voyageurairways.com
EMS/Ambulance flights are operated in conjunction with the Air Ambulance Section of the Ontarios Ministry of Health's Emergency Health Services Branch.
Expects to start flights in conjunction with AIR CANADA as AIR CONNEXION & using AC-flight numbers during 1999 or 2000. 12 Beech 1900D are on option for this planned unit.

	registration	type of aircraft	cn/fn	ex/ex*	mfd	del	powered by	mtow kg	configuration	name/fln/specialitites/remarks
☐	C-FAMU	Beech King Air A100	B-166	N221SS	0073		2 PWC PT6A-28	5216	EMS / Y9	
☐	C-FAPP	Beech King Air A100	B-169	N305TZ	0073		2 PWC PT6A-28	5216	EMS / Y9	
☐	C-FBGS	Beech King Air A100	B-204	N108JL	0074		2 PWC PT6A-28	5216	EMS / Y9	
☐	C-FCSD	Beech King Air 100	B-75	N24MK	0071		2 PWC PT6A-28	4808	EMS / Y9	
☐	C-GDPI	Beech King Air A100	B-156	N21RX	0073		2 PWC PT6A-28	5216	EMS / Y9	
☐	C-GISH	Beech King Air A100	B-152	N67LC	0073		2 PWC PT6A-28	5216	EMS / Y9	
☐	C-GJBV	Beech King Air A100	B-100	N100S	0071		2 PWC PT6A-28	5216	EMS / Y9	
☐	C-GJJF	Beech King Air A100	B-123	N741EB	0072		2 PWC PT6A-28	5216	EMS / Y9	
☐	C-FZVW	Beech King Air 200	BB-787	N26G	0080	0497	2 PWC PT6A-41	5670	EMS / Y9	
☐	C-FZVX	Beech King Air 200	BB-231	N200FH	0077	0697	2 PWC PT6A-41	5670	EMS / Y9	
☐	C-GIND	Beech King Air B200C	BL-42	N819CD	0081		2 PWC PT6A-42	5670	EMS / Y9	
☐	C-FWZV	De Havilland DHC-7-103 Dash 7	081	P2-ANP	0082	0299	4 PWC PT6A-50	19958	Y48	
☐	C-FZKM	De Havilland DHC-7-102 Dash 7	061	N903HA	0081	0698	4 PWC PT6A-50	19958	Y48	
☐	C-GCEV	De Havilland DHC-7-103 Dash 7	063	P2-ANN	0081	0299	4 PWC PT6A-50	19958	Y48	
☐	C-GELW	De Havilland DHC-7-102 Dash 7	090	S5-ACA	0082	0299	4 PWC PT6A-50	19958	Y48	
☐	C-GELY	De Havilland DHC-7-102 Dash 7	092	S5-ACB	0082	0299	4 PWC PT6A-50	19958	Y48	
☐	C-GFOF	De Havilland DHC-7-102 Dash 7	037	N67RM	0081	0196	4 PWC PT6A-50	19958	Y48	
☐	C-GJPI	De Havilland DHC-7-102 Dash 7	036	N702GW	0080	1092	4 PWC PT6A-50	19958	Y48	
☐	C-GLOL	De Havilland DHC-7-102 Dash 7	039	N87RM	0081	0695	4 PWC PT6A-50	19958	Y48	

WAASHESHKUN AIRWAYS, Ltd (Compagnie d'Aviation Waasheskun, Ltée)
Baie-du-Poste (Mistassini Lake), Qué.

Mistassini Lake, Baie-du-Poste, Québec G0W 1C0, Canada ☎ (418) 923-3236 Tx: n/a Fax: (418) 923-3377 SITA: n/a
F: 1982 ♠♠♠ 5 Head: Paul Petawabano Net: n/a

	registration	type of aircraft	cn/fn	ex/ex*	mfd	del	powered by	mtow kg	configuration	name/fln/specialitites/remarks
☐	C-FDIO	De Havilland DHC-3 Otter	452	TAF 9102	0066		1 PW R-1340	3629		Floats / Wheel-Skis

WABAKIMI AIR, Ltd (Affiliated with Mattice Lake Outfitters)
Armstrong, Ont.

Box 157, Armstrong, Ontario P0T 1A0, Canada ☎ (807) 583-2483 Tx: none Fax: (807) 583-2114 SITA: n/a
F: 1978 ♠♠♠ n/a Head: Donald R. Elliot Net: n/a

	registration	type of aircraft	cn/fn	ex/ex*	mfd	del	powered by	mtow kg	configuration	name/fln/specialitites/remarks
☐	C-FBPC	De Havilland DHC-2 Beaver I	144	VH-AAS	0051	1292	1 PW R-985	2313		Floats / Wheel-Skis
☐	C-FLLX	De Havilland DHC-2 Beaver I	1293		0057	0997	1 PW R-985	2313		Floats / Wheel-Skis
☐	CF-BJY	De Havilland DHC-2 Beaver I	173	N4792C	0051	0592	1 PW R-985	2313		Floats / Wheel-Skis

WABUSK AIR, Inc.
Moosonee, Ont.

62 Revillion Road, Moosonee, Ontario P0L 1Y0, Canada ☎ (705) 336-3935 Tx: none Fax: (705) 336-2795 SITA: n/a
F: 1997 ♠♠♠ n/a Head: Paul Cox Net: n/a

	registration	type of aircraft	cn/fn	ex/ex*	mfd	del	powered by	mtow kg	configuration	name/fln/specialitites/remarks
☐	C-FQNP	Piper PA-23-250 Aztec C	27-3236		0066	0998	2 LY IO-540-C4B5	2359		

WALSTEN AIR SERVICE (1986), Ltd = WAS
Kenora, Ont.

PO Box 2430, Kenora, Ontario P9N 3X8, Canada ☎ (807) 468-8951 Tx: 07592544 tilden ken Fax: (807) 468-4656 SITA: n/a
F: 1986 ♠♠♠ 90 Head: Tom Ivey ICAO: WALSTEN Net: n/a Aircraft below MTOW 1361 kg: Cessna 180 & Piper PA-18.

	registration	type of aircraft	cn/fn	ex/ex*	mfd	del	powered by	mtow kg	configuration	name/fln/specialitites/remarks
☐	C-GFZQ	Cessna U206E Super Skywagon	U20601543	N9143M	0070		1 CO IO-520-F	1633		Floats
☐	C-FMAQ	De Havilland DHC-2 Beaver I	14		0048		1 PW R-985	2313		Floats / Wheel-Skis
☐	C-GHMW	Cessna 402C II	402C0469	N68379	0081		2 CO TSIO-520-VB	3107		
☐	C-GPAL	Cessna 402B	402B0320	N2959Q	0073		2 CO TSIO-520-E	2858		
☐	C-FCZP	De Havilland DHC-3 Otter	69		0055	0798	1 PW R-1340	3629		Floats / Wheel-Skis

registration   type of aircraft   cn/fn   ex/ex*   mfd   del   powered by   mtow kg   configuration   selcal   name/fln/specialitites/remarks

☐ C-GTWW	Beech King Air C90	LJ-657	N9030R	0075		2 PWC PT6A-28	4377			
☐ C-FWTE	De Havilland DHC-6 Twin Otter 100	96		0068	1268	2 PWC PT6A-20	5252			Floats / Wheel-Skis
☐ C-FKJI	Beech King Air 200	BB-105	N71TZ	0076	0591	2 PWC PT6A-41	5670			

WAMAIR SERVICE & OUTFITTING, Inc. — Matheson Island, Man.

General Delivery, Matheson Island, Manitoba R0C 2A0, Canada ☎ (204) 276-2330 Tx: none Fax: (204) 276-2410 SITA: n/a
F: 1993 ⁂ 3 Head: William Mowat Net: n/a Aircraft below MTOW 1361kg: Cessna 180 (on Floats / Wheel-Skis).

☐ C-GWAB	Cessna A185F Skywagon	18502399		0074	0396	1 CO IO-520-D	1520			Floats / Wheel-Skis
☐ C-GKCK	Cessna U206E Super Skywagon	U20601487	N1487M	0070	0898	1 CO IO-520-F	1633			Floats / Wheel-Skis
☐ C-GMJP	Cessna U206C Super Skywagon	U206-1122		0068	1193	1 CO IO-520-F	1633			Floats / Wheel-Skis
☐ C-GXSK	Cessna U206G Stationair	U20603635	N7365N	0077	0896	1 CO IO-520-F	1633			Floats / Wheel-Skis
☐ C-GDCJ	De Havilland DHC-2 Beaver I	1055	N4411F	0057	0595	1 PW R-985	2313			Floats / Wheel-Skis

WASAGAMACK AIR, Ltd — Waasagomach Bay, Man.

PO Box 163, Waasagomach Bay, Manitoba R0B 1Z0, Canada ☎ (204) 457-2451 Tx: none Fax: (204) 457-2255 SITA: n/a
F: 1992 ⁂ n/a Head: n/a Net: n/a

☐ C-GGGD	Cessna TU206G Turbo Stationair 6 II	U20605664		0080	0792	1 CO TSIO-520-M	1633			Floats

WASAYA AIRWAYS, Ltd = WG / WSG (formerly Kelner Airways) — Pickle Lake & Thunder Bay, Ont.

RR 1, 1485 Rosslyn Road, Thunder Bay, Ontario P7C 4T9, Canada ☎ (807) 473-1200 Tx: none Fax: (807) 475-9181 SITA: n/a
F: 1986 ⁂ 180 Head: Tom Kam IATA: 093 ICAO: WASAYA Net: http://www.wasaya.com

☐ C-FKAB	Cessna 208B Grand Caravan	208B0305		0092	0692	1 PWC PT6A-114A	3969	Y9 / Freighter		
☐ C-FKAD	Cessna 208B Grand Caravan	208B0327		0092	1292	1 PWC PT6A-114A	3969	Y9 / Freighter		
☐ C-FKDL	Cessna 208B Grand Caravan	208B0240		0090	1194	1 PWC PT6A-114A	3969	Y9 / Freighter		
☐ C-FKSL	Cessna 208B Caravan I Super Cargomaster	208B0129		0088		1 PWC PT6A-114	3969	Freighter		
☐ C-FSDK	Cessna 208B Grand Caravan	208B0524		0096	1296	1 PWC PT6A-114A	3969	Y9 / Freighter		
☐ C-GSDG	Cessna 208B Grand Caravan	208B0376	N1118P	0093	1296	1 PWC PT6A-114A	3969	Y9 / Freighter		
☐ C-FCGT	Beech Catpass 200	BB-159	N47FH	0076	0695	2 PWC PT6A-41	5670	Y11 / Freighter		cvtd King Air 200
☐ C-FCGU	Beech Catpass 200	BB-301	N611SW	0078	0595	2 PWC PT6A-41	5670	Y11 / Freighter		cvtd King Air 200
☐ C-FWAX	Beech 1900D Airliner	UE-297	N21679*	0097	0298	2 PWC PT6A-67D	7688	Y19 / Freighter		
☐ C-FFFS	BAe (HS) 748-209 Srs 2A (SCD)	1663 / 141	G-BHCJ	0069	1296	2 RR Dart 534-2	21092	Freighter		cvtd Srs 2A
☐ C-FTTW	BAe (HS) 748-264 Srs 2A	1681 / 154	G-AYIR	0070	0197	2 RR Dart 534-2	21092	Y40 / Freighter		
☐ C-GDTD	BAe (HS) 748-398 Srs 2B	1779 / 260	5U-BAR	0081	1191	2 RR Dart 536-2	21092	Y40 / Freighter		803
☐ C-GLTC	BAe (HS) 748-244 Srs 2A	1656 / 146	N57910	0069	0490	2 RR Dart 550-2	20183	Y40 / Freighter		cvtd Srs 2

WATSON'S SKYWAYS (Watson's Algoma Vacations, Ltd dba) — Wawa, Ont.

Box 1129, Wawa, Ontario P0S 1K0, Canada ☎ (705) 856-2223 Tx: none Fax: (705) 856-1049 SITA: n/a
F: 1961 ⁂ 10 Head: Richard A. Watson Net: n/a

☐ C-FAZQ	Cessna U206 Super Skywagon	U206-0337		0065		1 CO IO-520-A	1588			Floats / Wheels
☐ C-GOFB	De Havilland DHC-3 Otter	39	RCAF 3681	0054	0592	1 PW R-1340	3629			Floats
☐ C-GPPL	De Havilland DHC-3 Otter	7	BM-1004	0053	0495	1 PW R-1340	3629			Floats

WEAGAMOW AIR (Weagamow Corp. dba) — Weagamow-Round Lake, Ont.

General Delivery, Weagamow Lake, Ontario P0V 2Y0, Canada ☎ (807) 469-1269 Tx: n/a Fax: (807) 469-1328 SITA: n/a
F: 1975 ⁂ n/a Head: n/a Net: n/a

☐ C-GEHJ	Cessna A185F Skywagon	18502788		0075		1 CO IO-520-D	1520			Floats / Wheel-Skis
☐ C-FOCD	De Havilland DHC-2 Beaver I	24		0048	0494	1 PW R-985	2313			Floats / Wheel-Skis

WELLAND AERO CENTER (Falls Aviation, Ltd dba) — Welland, Ont.

PO Box 244, Welland, Ontario L3B 5P4, Canada ☎ (905) 735-9511 Tx: none Fax: (905) 735-7773 SITA: n/a
F: 1972 ⁂ 7 Head: Bruce H. MacRitchie Net: n/a Aircraft below MTOW 1361 kg: Cessna 150, 172 & Piper PA-28

☐ C-FZIT	Piper PA-30-160 Twin Comanche B	30-1294		0066	0496	2 LY IO-320-B1A	1633			

WENTAIR (Rental Sales & Leasing, Ltd dba / Seasonal May-November ops only) — Corner Brook, Nfld.

PO Box 9, Corner Brook, Newfoundland A2H 6C3, Canada ☎ (709) 634-2347 Tx: none Fax: (709) 634-2347 SITA: n/a
F: 1992 ⁂ n/a Head: n/a Net: n/a

☐ C-GBWZ	Cessna A185F Skywagon II	18503751		0079	0892	1 CO IO-520-D	1520			Floats / Wheel-Skis

WESTAIR Aviation (Mylight Aircraft, Inc. dba) — Carp, Ont.

Box 358, Carp, Ontario K0A 1L0, Canada ☎ (613) 839-5431 Tx: none Fax: (613) 839-5449 SITA: n/a
F: 1984 ⁂ 10 Head: Tony Taylor Net: n/a Aircraft below MTOW 1361 kg: Cessna 150, 152 & 172

☐ C-FNNC	Dassault Falcon 50	176	VR-CFI	0087	0996	2 GA TFE731-3-1C	18500			

WESTAIR AVIATION, Inc. — Kamloops, B.C.

2810 Aviation Way, Kamloops, British Columbia V2B 7W1, Canada ☎ (250) 554-4202 Tx: none Fax: (250) 376-1119 SITA: n/a
F: 1980 ⁂ n/a Head: Ralph Emsland Net: n/a Aircraft below MTOW 1361kg: Cessna 182

☐ C-FRJE	Piper PA-31T Cheyenne II	31T-7820002	C-GCUL	0078	0797	2 PWC PT6A-28	4082			

WEST CARIBOU AIR SERVICE, Ltd — Savant Lake, Ont.

RR 2, Site 214, Box 22, Dryden, Ontario P8N 2Y5, Canada ☎ (807) 937-5815 Tx: none Fax: (807) 937-6644 SITA: n/a
F: 1996 ⁂ n/a Head: n/a Net: n/a

☐ C-FBWP	Cessna 185A Skywagon	185-0430	N169E	0062	0798	1 CO IO-470-F	1451			Floats
☐ C-GSAE	Cessna A185E Skywagon	18502089	HR-AAD	0072	0397	1 CO IO-520-D	1520			Floats
☐ C-FKAS	Noorduyn Norseman VI (UC-64A)	267	43-5376	0043	0597	1 PW R-1340	3357			Floats

WEST COAST AIR, Ltd = 8O — Vancouver-Harbour SPB, B.C.

PO Box 48197, Bentall Centre, Vancouver, British Columbia V7X 1N8, Canada ☎ (604) 606-6800 Tx: none Fax: (604) 606-6820 SITA: CXHRR8O
F: 1995 ⁂ 35 Head: Allan Baydala Net: n/a

☐ C-GSUE	De Havilland DHC-2 Beaver I	1199	N37AT	0058	0898	1 PW R-985	2309	Y6		Floats
☐ C-FGQE	De Havilland DHC-6 Twin Otter 100	40	5H-MNK	0067	0196	2 PWC PT6A-20	5252	Y18		Floats
☐ C-GGAW	De Havilland DHC-6 Twin Otter 100	86	N2228H	0067	0196	2 PWC PT6A-20	5252	Y18		Floats
☐ C-GJAW	De Havilland DHC-6 Twin Otter 200	176	N2261L	0068	0296	2 PWC PT6A-20	5252	Y18		Floats
☐ C-GQKN	De Havilland DHC-6 Twin Otter 100	94	PZ-TAV	0068	0296	2 PWC PT6A-20	5252	Y18		Floats

WEST COAST ENERGY - Flight Dept. = BLK (Flight Dept. of West Coast Energy, Inc.) — Vancouver-Int'l, B.C.

1333 West Georgia Street, Vancouver, British Columbia V6E 3K9, Canada ☎ (604) 278-8112 Tx: none Fax: (604) 278-6538 SITA: n/a
F: 1995 ⁂ n/a Head: Don Osterhout ICAO: BLUE FLAME Net: n/a The Flight Dept. operates non-commerical corporate flights for the main company only.

☐ C-FWCE	Hawker 800A (BAe 125-800A)	258163 / NA0443	C-GMOL	0089	1095	2 GA TFE731-5R-1H	12428	Corporate		

WEST COAST HELICOPTERS (West Coast Helicopters Maintenance & Contracting, Ltd dba) — Port McNeill, B.C.

West Coast Helicopters

Box 1030, Port McNeill, British Columbia V0N 2R0, Canada ☎ (250) 956-2244 Tx: none Fax: (250) 956-2070 SITA: n/a
F: 1992 ⁂ 10 Head: Peter Barratt Net: n/a

☐ C-GPWR	Bell 206B JetRanger III	2989	N577AH	0080	0498	1 AN 250-C20BIII	1451			
☐ C-FWCH	Eurocopter (Aerosp.) AS350B2 AStar	2850		0096	0696	1 TU Arriel 1D1	2250			
☐ C-FWCL	Eurocopter (Aerosp.) AS350BA AStar	2869	C-FWAW	0095	0296	1 TU Arriel 1B	2100			
☐ C-FWCO	Eurocopter (Aerosp.) AS350BA AStar	2868	C-FVTM	0095	0695	1 TU Arriel 1B	2100			

WESTERN AERIAL APPLICATIONS, Ltd — Delta, B.C.

Hangar 3, 6455-64th Street, Delta, British Columbia V4K 4E2, Canada ☎ (604) 940-9220 Tx: none Fax: (604) 940-9244 SITA: n/a
F: 1989 ⁂ n/a Head: Jim Cooper Net: n/a

☐ C-FBVZ	Hiller UH-12ET	985	N101EH	0058	1189	1 AN 250-C20B	1406			cvtd UH-12E
☐ C-FPWK	Hiller UH-12ET	5182	C-FTHA	0082	0593	1 AN 250-C20B	1406			
☐ C-FWAA	Hiller UH-12E	5080	N4027S	0079	0794	1 LY VO-540-C2A	1406			
☐ C-GFVV	Hiller UH-12ET	HA3011	N111HA	0074	1189	1 AN 250-C20B	1406			cvtd UH-12E
☐ C-GHTE	Hiller UH-12E	944	57-2987	0058	1189	1 LY VO-540-B1A	1406			
☐ C-GJQQ	Hiller UH-12E	2045	CF-MHF	0060	0493	1 LY VO-540-B1A	1406			
☐ C-FFHL	Bell 206B JetRanger	199		0068	0897	1 AN 250-C20	1451			
☐ C-FBMI	Cessna T337B Turbo Skymaster	337-0592	N5492S	0067	1194	2 CO TSIO-360-A/B	1950			

WESTERN AIR SERVICES (Clinton Aviation, Ltd dba) — Goderich, Ont.

Box 307, Goderich, Ontario N7A 4C6, Canada ☎ (519) 524-8304 Tx: none Fax: (519) 524-7090 SITA: n/a
F: 1980 ⁂ 2 Head: James E. Kirk Net: n/a Aircraft below MTOW 1361 kg: Cessna 150 & 172

☐ C-GPAA	Beech Baron 58	TH-866	N877D	0077		2 CO IO-520-C	2449			

85 registration type of aircraft cn/fn ex/EX* mfd del powered by mtow kg configuration selcal name/fln/specialitites/remarks

WESTERN WATERS AIR SERVICES, Ltd Vancouver-Harbour SPB, B.C.

Suite 204, 814 West 15th Street, North Vancouver, British Columbia V7P 1M6, Canada ☎ (604) 988-7011 Tx: none Fax: (604) 988-7092 SITA: n/a
F: 1995 ⁂ n/a Head: Mike Deering Net: n/a

☐ C-FFRL	De Havilland DHC-2 Beaver I	482	N4798C	0054	0595	1 PW R-985	2309			Floats

WESTEX AIRLINES = WES (Western Express Air Lines, Inc. dba) Vancouver-Int'l, B.C.

Box 24259, Vancouver APO, Richmond, British Columbia V7B 1Y4, Canada ☎ (604) 273-1500 Tx: none Fax: (604) 273-3863 SITA: n/a
F: 1995 ⁂ 25 Head: David Oliver ICAO: WESTEX Net: http://www.westex.ca

☐ C-FTIX	Fairchild (Swearingen) SA226AT Merlin IVA	AT-066	N5455M	0078	0595	2 GA TPE331-10UA-511G	5670	Freighter		for sale
☐ N2734X	Fairchild (Swearingen) SA227AC Metro III	AC-738		0089	0698	2 GA TPE331-11U-611G	6577	Freighter		lsf Finova Capital Corp.
☐ C-FVQE	Fairchild Ind. F-27F	89	N4425B	0061	1195	2 RR Dart 529-7E	19051	Freighter		opf DHL
☐ C-GWXD	Fokker F27 Troopship 300M (F27 Mk300M)	10156	C-6	0060	0897	2 RR Dart 514-7	19051	Freighter		opf Purolator Courier

WESTJET AIRLINES, Ltd = M3 Calgary, Alta

35 McTavish Place NE, Calgary, Alberta T2E 7J7, Canada ☎ (403) 735-2600 Tx: none Fax: (403) 735-2601 SITA: n/a
F: 1995 ⁂ 700 Head: Clive Beddoe ICAO: WESTJET Net: http://www.westjet.com

☐ C-FGWJ	Boeing 737-217	20196 / 143	F-GTCA	0369	0298	2 PW JT8D-9A (HK3/AVA)	52390	Y125		706
☐ C-GCWJ	Boeing 737-297 (A)	21739 / 561	N70723	0079	0598	2 PW JT8D-9A (HK3/AVA)	52390	Y125		
☐ C-GGWJ	Boeing 737-284 (A)	21500 / 491	N311VA	0077	1297	2 PW JT8D-9A (HK3/AVA)	52390	Y125		738 / lsf POLA
☐ C-GMWJ	Boeing 737-281 (A)	21771 / 594	JA8457	0079	0998	2 PW JT8D-17	52390	Y125		739
☐ C-GQWJ	Boeing 737-281 (A)	21769 / 587	JA8455	0079	1198	2 PW JT8D-17 (HK3/AVA)	52390	Y125		740
☐ C-GUWJ	Boeing 737-204 (A)	20807 / 341	N107TR	0074	0399	2 PW JT8D-15	54204	Y125		lsf TRIT
☐ C-GVWJ	Boeing 737-281 (A)	20563 / 296	JA8417	0072	0199	2 PW JT8D-17 (HK3/NOR)	52390	Y125		
☐ C-GWJE	Boeing 737-275 (A)	20588 / 300	N861SY	0072	1195	2 PW JT8D-9A (HK3/AVA)	54432	Y125		735
☐ C-GWJG	Boeing 737-275 (A)	20670 / 315	N862SY	0072	1195	2 PW JT8D-9A (HK3/AVA)	54432	Y125		736
☐ C-GWJK	Boeing 737-275C	19743 / 139	N331XV	0369	0396	2 PW JT8D-9A	54432	Y120		732
☐ C-GWJO	Boeing 737-2A3	20299 / 158	HR-SHO	0070	0696	2 PW JT8D-9A (HK3/AVA)	52390	Y125		730
☐ C-GWJT	Boeing 737-2H4 (A)	21262 / 470	N27SW	0076	1296	2 PW JT8D-9A (HK3/AVA)	52390	Y125		731
☐ C-GWJU	Boeing 737-2H4 (A)	21117 / 423	N26SW	0075	0997	2 PW JT8D-9A (HK3/AVA)	52390	Y125		733
☐ C-GWWJ	Boeing 737-204 (A)	21694 / 542	N109TR	0078	0399	2 PW JT8D-15	54204	Y125		lsf TRIT
☐ C-GXWJ	Boeing 737-281 (A)	21766 / 583	JA8452	0079	0399	2 PW JT8D-17 (HK3/AVA)	52390	Y125		

WESTLAND HELICOPTERS, Inc. Delta, B.C.

13027-19A Ave, Surrey, British Columbia V4A 8A8, Canada ☎ (604) 230-4422 Tx: none Fax: (604) 538-8143 SITA: n/a
F: 1984 ⁂ 3 Head: Norman Rafuse Net: n/a

☐ C-FMQT	Bell 206B JetRanger II	1950	N950PC	0076	0694	1 AN 250-C20	1451			
☐ C-GDRH	Bell 206B JetRanger III	2452	N37EA	0078	0795	1 AN 250-C20B	1451			
☐ C-GQKT	Bell 206B JetRanger II	2148		0077	0896	1 AN 250-C20	1451			
☐ C-GRJH	Bell 206B JetRanger	1543	N59552	0074		1 AN 250-C20	1451			

WESTPOINT AVIATION (WestPoint School of Aviation, Inc. dba / formerly WestPoint Air Services) Calgary-Int'l & -Springbank, Alta.

783 McTavish Road NE, Calgary, Alberta T2E 7G4, Canada ☎ (403) 250-3321 Tx: none Fax: (403) 250-3851 SITA: n/a
F: 1991 ⁂ 15 Head: Michael Dupuis Net: n/a Aircraft below MTOW 1361kg: AA5A, Bellanca 7ECA/8GCBC, Cessna 140/170/172/182, Piper PA-28 & Zlin Z242L

☐ C-FMFB	Piper PA-34-200T Seneca II	34-7670303		0076	0892	2 CO TSIO-360-E	2073			

WEST WIND AVIATION, Inc. = WEW Saskatoon & Regina, Sask. & Winnipeg, Man.

Hangar 10, John G. Diefenbaker Airport, Saskatoon, Saskatchewan S7L 6S1, Canada ☎ (306) 652-9121 Tx: none Fax: (306) 652-3958 SITA: n/a
F: 1983 ⁂ 60 Head: Dennis Goll ICAO: WESTWIND Net: n/a

☐ C-FDAD	Cessna 401A	401A0058	N50MR	0069	0694	2 CO TSIO-520-E	2858			
☐ C-GAXR	Cessna 401B	401B0050	N1250C	0070	0694	2 CO TSIO-520-E	2858			
☐ C-GRSY	Cessna 401	401-0248	N8400F	0068	0694	2 CO TSIO-520-E	2858			
☐ C-GSQD	Cessna 401	401-0300		0068	0694	2 CO TSIO-520-E	2858			
☐ C-GGPX	Cessna 402C II	402C0260	YV-1073P	0080	0694	2 CO TSIO-520-VB	3107			
☐ C-GWWB	Cessna 414	414-0514	N414DM	0074	0598	2 CO TSIO-520-J	2880			
☐ C-GWWA	Beech King Air 100	B-27	N5377C	0069		2 PWC PT6A-28	4808			
☐ C-GVER	Cessna 500 Citation I	500-0369	N3132M	0077		2 PWC JT15D-1A	5375			
☐ C-FPQQ	Beech King Air B200	BB-1304	N3173K	0088	0493	2 PWC PT6A-42	6350			
☐ C-GWWN	Beech King Air 200	BB-14	N418CS	0074	0595	2 PWC PT6A-41	5670			
☐ C-FFCL	Cessna 550 Citation II	550-0069	N550AB	0079	0797	2 PWC JT15D-4	6033			
☐ C-FCPD	BAe 3112 Jetstream 31	822	G-31-822*	0088	0195	2 GA TPE331-10UGR-514H	6950			
☐ C-FCSE	BAe (HS) 748-269 Srs 2A	1679 / 164	G-AYFL*	0070	0993	3 RR Dart 534-2	20183			
☐ C-FQVE	BAe (HS) 748-378 Srs 2B	1792 / 273	G-SSFS	0084	1293	2 RR Dart 536-2	21092			

WHAPCHIWEM HELICOPTERS, Ltd (Les Hélicoptères Whapchiwem, Ltée) La Grande-Rivière, Qué.

CP 699, Aéroport la Grande, Radisson, Québec J0Y 2X0, Canada ☎ (819) 638-3392 Tx: none Fax: (819) 638-3746 SITA: n/a
F: 1998 ⁂ n/a Head: n/a Net: n/a

☐ C-GMHY	Bell 206L LongRanger	45145	N16924	0077	0798	1 AN 250-C20B	1814			
☐ C-GDKD	Eurocopter (Aerosp.) AS350BA AStar	1432	N5785H	0081	0299	1 TU Arriel 1B	2100			cvtd AS350D
☐ C-GDLY	Eurocopter (Aerosp.) AS350BA AStar	1318		0080	0998	1 TU Arriel 1B	2100			cvtd AS350D

WHISTLER AIR SERVICES, Ltd Whistler, B.C.

Box 834, Whistler, British Columbia V0N 1B0, Canada ☎ (604) 932-6615 Tx: none Fax: (604) 932-6100 SITA: n/a
F: 1985 ⁂ 4 Head: Michael J. Quinn Net: http://www.whisair.com Aircraft below MTOW 1361kg: Bell 47G-3B-1.

☐ C-GEJC	Cessna A185F Skywagon	18502823		0075		1 CO IO-520-D	1520			Floats
☐ C-FSKZ	De Havilland DHC-2 Beaver I	1594		0065	0494	1 PW R-985	2309			Floats
☐ C-GDBJ	De Havilland DHC-2 Beaver I	1511	JA3176	0064	0598	1 PW R-985	2309			Floats

WHITE RIVER AIR (612372 Ontario, Ltd dba / Seasonal May-October ops only) White River-SPB, Ont.

PO Box 220, White River, Ontario P0M 3G0, Canada ☎ (807) 822-2222 Tx: n/a Fax: (807) 822-2223 SITA: n/a
F: 1979 ⁂ 10 Head: Don MacLachlan Net: n/a

☐ C-GIAY	Cessna A185F Skywagon II	18504143		0081	0692	1 CO IO-520-D	1520			Floats
☐ CF-FHR	De Havilland DHC-2 Beaver I	46		0050		1 PW R-985	2313			Floats
☐ C-FWRA	De Havilland DHC-3 Otter	213	IM-1714	0057	0797	1 PW R-1340	3629			Floats

WHITE RIVER HELICOPTERS, Inc. Terrace, B.C.

5115 Jolliette Ave., Terrace, British Columbia V8G 5P5, Canada ☎ (604) 635-1310 Tx: n/a Fax: (604) 635-1303 SITA: n/a
F: 1993 ⁂ n/a Head: Tom Bond Net: n/a

☐ C-FOXJ	Hiller UH-12E	2258		0063	0795	1 LY VO-540-B1A	1406			
☐ C-GWRL	Hiller UH-12E	2163	N9737C	0062	0594	1 LY VO-540-B1A	1406			
☐ C-FLES	Bell 206B JetRanger	103	N696MR	0067	1198	1 AN 250-C20	1451			cvtd 206A
☐ C-GTMH	Bell 206B JetRanger	175	N352ET	0068	0997	1 AN 250-C20	1451			cvtd 206A

WHITE SADDLE AIR SERVICES, Ltd Bluff Lake, B.C.

PO Box 44, Tatla Lake, British Columbia V0L 1V0, Canada ☎ (250) 476-1182 Tx: none Fax: (250) 476-1189 SITA: n/a
F: 1961 ⁂ 4 Head: Mrs. Jen G. King Net: n/a Aircraft below MTOW 1361 kg: Cessna 180.

☐ C-FKPM	Bell 206B JetRanger III	4031		0088		1 AN 250-C20J	1451			

WHITESHELL AIR SERVICE, Ltd Lac du Bonnet, Man.

Box 975, Lac du Bonnet, Manitoba R0E 1A0, Canada ☎ (204) 345-8339 Tx: none Fax: (204) 345-2553 SITA: n/a
F: 1968 ⁂ 9 Head: Thomas A. Johnston Net: n/a Aircraft below MTOW 1361 kg: Cessna 180 (on Floats / Wheel-Skis)

☐ C-FASH	Cessna A185E Skywagon	185-1489		0069	0398	1 CO IO-520-D	1520			Floats / Wheel-Skis
☐ C-GEHD	Cessna A185F Skywagon	18502787		0075		1 CO IO-520-D	1520			Floats / Wheel-Skis
☐ CF-JFA	De Havilland DHC-2 Beaver I	1581	N5563	0065		1 PW R-985	2313			Floats / Wheel-Skis
☐ C-FQZH	Piper PA-31-350 Navajo Chieftain	31-7952070	N105TT	0079	1293	2 LY TIO-540-J2BD	3175			
☐ C-GUEH	Piper PA-31-310 Navajo C	31-7712057	N27255	0077		2 LY TIO-540-A2C	2948			
☐ C-GGON	De Havilland DHC-3 Otter	225	TI-SPG	0057		1 PW R-1340	3629			Floats / Wheel-Skis
☐ C-GGOR	De Havilland DHC-3 Otter	97	TI-SPE	0056		1 PW R-1340	3629			Floats / Wheel-Skis

WILDCOUNTRY AIRWAYS, Ltd Red Lake, Ont.

Box 1134, Red Lake, Ontario P0V 2M0, Canada ☎ (807) 662-2078 Tx: n/a Fax: (807) 662-2465 SITA: n/a
F: n/a ⁂ n/a Head: William Roy Cousineau Net: n/a

☐ C-GTCC	Cessna U206F Stationair	U20602167	N7303Q	0073	0892	1 CO IO-520-F	1633			Floats / Wheel-Skis
☐ C-FPIO	Piper PA-31-350 T1020	31-8353007	N4112U	0083	0393	2 LY TIO-540-J2B	3175			
☐ C-GZIS	Piper PA-31-310 Navajo	31-316	N9243Y	0068	0594	2 LY TIO-540-A1A	2948			
☐ C-FITF	De Havilland DHC-3 Otter	89		0055	0693	1 PW R-1340	3629			Floats / Wheel-Skis
☐ C-GPHD	De Havilland DHC-3 Otter	113	55-3267	0056	0597	1 PW R-1340	3629			Floats / Wheel-Skis
☐ C-FKEL	Beech G18S	BA-565	N9374Y	0060	0493	2 PW R-985	4397			

86 registration type of aircraft cn/fn ex/ex* mfd del powered by mtow kg configuration selcal name/fln/specialitites/remarks

WILDERNESS AIR, Ltd (formerly Wilderness Air (Vermilion Bay (1982), Ltd)
Vermilion Bay, Ont.

Box 83, Vermilion Bay, Ontario P0V 2V0, Canada ☎ (807) 227-5473 Tx: none Fax: (807) 227-5475 SITA: n/a
F: 1981 ⋀⋀⋀ 8 Head: Robert Huitikka Net: n/a Aircraft below MTOW 1361kg: Cessna 180 (on Floats / Wheel-Skis) Winter phone numer: (807) 484-2512

registration	type of aircraft	cn/fn	ex/ex*	mfd	del	powered by	mtow kg	configuration	selcal	name/fln/remarks
☐ C-GFZF	Cessna A185E Skywagon	18502002	N70118	0072	0590	1 CO IO-520-D	1520			Floats / Wheel-Skis
☐ C-FGMK	De Havilland DHC-2 Beaver I	1329	58-2003	0058		1 PW R-985	2313			Floats / Wheel-Skis
☐ C-FJOF	De Havilland DHC-2 Beaver I	1053		0057		1 PW R-985	2313			Floats / Wheel-Skis
☐ C-FZYE	De Havilland DHC-2 Beaver I	192		0052	0496	1 PW R-985	2313			Floats / Wheel-Skis
☐ C-FODV	De Havilland DHC-3 Otter	411		0061		1 PW R-1340	3629			Floats / Wheel-Skis
☐ C-FCUK	Beech 3NM (18)	CA-181	N7813	0052	0598	2 PW R-985-AN14B	3969			Floats

WILDERNESS HELICOPTERS, Ltd
Wawa, Ont.

36 Montreal Avenue, Box 1400, Wawa, Ontario P0S 1K0, Canada ☎ (705) 856-2799 Tx: none Fax: (705) 856-1365 SITA: n/a
F: 1995 ⋀⋀⋀ n/a Head: Peter Moore Net: http://www.wilderness.on.ca Aircraft below MTOW 1361kg: Hiller UH-12C

☐ C-FQCK	Bell 206B JetRanger	692		0071	0295	1 AN 250-C20	1451			cvtd 206A
☐ C-FALS	Bell 206L LongRanger	45061	N56DE	0076	0697	1 AN 250-C20B	1814			

WILDERNESS NORTH AIR, Ltd (Seasonal May-October ops only)
Armstrong-Waweig Lake, Ont.

704 East Leighton Avenue, Milwaukee, WI 53207, USA ☎ (807) 623-3633 Tx: none Fax: (414) 486-0565 SITA: n/a
F: 1995 ⋀⋀⋀ n/a Head: Jack Mark Net: n/a

☐ C-GNZO	De Havilland DHC-2 Beaver I	399	51-16844	0051	0795	1 PW R-985	2313			Floats
☐ C-FQND	De Havilland DHC-3 Otter	233	N5325G	0057	0795	1 PW R-1340	3629			Floats
☐ C-FYCX	De Havilland DHC-3 Otter	44	N44NB	0054	0596	1 PW R-1340	3629			Floats
☐ C-GMLB	De Havilland DHC-3 Otter	359	N3125H	0060	0695	1 PW R-1340	3629			Floats

WILDLIFE OBERSERVATION SERVICES, Inc.
Calgary-Springbank, Alta.

Box 15, Site 16, RR2, Calgary, Alberta T2P 2G5, Canada ☎ (403) 247-2799 Tx: none Fax: (403) 247-2753 SITA: n/a
F: 1998 ⋀⋀⋀ n/a Head: Michael Dupuis Net: http://www.aviation.ca/bearpatrol/

☐ C-GGDW	Cessna 337 Super Skymaster	337-0153	N2253X	0065	1098	2 CO IO-360-C/D	1905	Patrol		

WILLISTON LAKE AIR SERVICES, Ltd
Mackenzie, B.C.

Box 490, Mackenzie, British Columbia V0J 2C0, Canada ☎ (250) 997-5557 Tx: none Fax: (250) 997-5595 SITA: n/a
F: 1986 ⋀⋀⋀ 6 Head: Dwight Manguson Net: n/a

☐ C-GAKJ	Piper PA-34-220T Seneca III	34-8233032	N8464Z	0082	1092	2 CO TSIO-360-KB	2155			
☐ C-FBAD	Piper PA-31-350 Navajo Chieftain	31-7752101	N6196C	0077	0493	2 LY TIO-540-J2BD	3349			
☐ C-GRQG	Piper PA-31-350 Navajo Chieftain	31-7952073		0079	0598	2 LY TIO-540-J2BD	3175			
☐ C-GRWP	Piper PA-31-350 Navajo Chieftain	31-7952095		0079	0196	2 LY TIO-540-J2BD	3349			

WINDSOCK LODGE, Inc. – Air Services (Seasonal May-November ops only)
Long Lake, Man.

General Delivery, Bissett, Manitoba R0E 0J0, Canada ☎ (204) 254-0901 Tx: none Fax: (204) 256-2432 SITA: n/a
F: 1997 ⋀⋀⋀ n/a Head: Timothy J. Hastings Net: n/a

☐ C-FOFX	Cessna 185A Skywagon	185-0473		0062	1197	1 CO IO-470-F	1451			Floats

WINNPORT AIR CARGO = KN / WNT (Kelowna Flightcraft Int'l Air Cargo Ltd dba/Subs. of Kelowna Flightcraft Air Charter Ltd)
Winnipeg-Int'l, Man.

204-2000 Wellington Avenue, Winnipeg, Manitoba R3H 1C1, Canada ☎ (204) 784-5411 Tx: none Fax: (204) 784-5414 SITA: n/a
F: 1998 ⋀⋀⋀ n/a Head: Barry Lapointe IATA: 489 ICAO: WINNPORT Net: n/a Operates cargo flights with Boeing 747F freighter aircraft, leased from EVERGREEN INTERNATIONAL (N), when required.

WOLVERINE AIR (1988), Ltd
Fort Simpson, N.W.T.

PO Box 316, Fort Simpson, Northwest Territories X0E 0N0, Canada ☎ (867) 695-2263 Tx: none Fax: (867) 695-3400 SITA: n/a
F: 1973 ⋀⋀⋀ 5 Head: Chris Pinckard Net: http://www.netminder.com/wal-sna

☐ C-GHWO	Cessna A185F Skywagon	18502835		0075		1 CO IO-520-D	1520			
☐ C-GQOA	Cessna U206G Stationair 6 II	U20604993		0079		1 CO IO-520-F	1633			
☐ C-GTUG	Cessna U206G Stationair 6 II	U20606214		0081		1 CO IO-520-F	1633			
☐ C-GHKB	Cessna 207 Skywagon	20700228	N1628U	0073	0394	1 CO IO-550-F	1724			

WRONG LAKE AIRWAYS, Ltd (Affiliated with Thunderbird Lodge & Outposts / Seasonal May-October ops only)
Wrong Lake, Man.

PO Box 23087, RPO McGillivray, Winnipeg, Manitoba R3T 5S3, Canada ☎ (204) 475-7818 Tx: none Fax: (204) 478-1799 SITA: n/a
F: 1993 ⋀⋀⋀ 3 Head: Scott Compton Net: n/a

☐ C-GZEV	Cessna A185F Skywagon II	18504413		0083	0593	1 CO IO-520-D	1520			Floats
☐ C-FLZO	Noorduyn Norseman VI (UC-64A)	535	N50646	0044	0495	1 PW R-1340	3311			Floats
☐ C-FOBR	Noorduyn Norseman V	N29-35		0046	0493	1 PW R-1340	3420			Floats

YELLOWHEAD HELICOPTERS, Ltd
Valemount, B.C.

Box 190, Valemount, British Columbia V0E 2Z0, Canada ☎ (250) 566-4401 Tx: none Fax: (250) 566-4333 SITA: n/a
F: 1975 ⋀⋀⋀ 10 Head: Gary Foreman Net: http://www.yellowheadheli.com

☐ C-FPQX	Bell 206B JetRanger	1330		0074	0498	1 AN 250-C20	1451			
☐ C-FYHB	Bell 206B JetRanger	1655	C-GCHH	0075	0597	1 AN 250-C20	1451			
☐ C-FYHJ	Bell 206B JetRanger III	2900	N344P	0080	0590	1 AN 250-C20B	1451			
☐ C-GXYH	Bell 206B JetRanger III	2267	N130VG	0077		1 AN 250-C20B	1451			
☐ C-GYHL	Bell 206B JetRanger III	1702		0075		1 AN 250-C20B	1451			cvtd JetRanger
☐ C-GYHR	Bell 206B JetRanger III	2571	N5015A	0078		1 AN 250-C20J	1451			
☐ C-GJWC	Cessna T210L Turbo Centurion II	21060438	N93858	0074	0598	1 CO TSIO-520-H	1724	Corp./Liaison		
☐ C-FYHN	Bell 206L LongRanger	45050	N600FB	0076	0798	1 AN 250-C20B	1814			
☐ C-GYHZ	Bell 206L LongRanger	45126	N16840	0077	0198	1 AN 250-C20B	1814			
☐ C-GVEG	Bell 204C	2199	OY-HCB	0066		1 LY T5313B	3856			cvtd 204B
☐ C-GYHU	Bell 204C	2053	N120LA	0067	0190	1 LY T5313B	3856			cvtd 204B

YUKON HELICOPTERS, Ltd
Winnipeg-St. Andrews, Man.

411 Helicopter Drive, St. Andrews, Manitoba R1A 3P7, Canada ☎ (204) 339-1163 Tx: none Fax: (204) 339-1163 SITA: n/a
F: 1978 ⋀⋀⋀ n/a Head: Brian E. Robertson Net: n/a Aircraft below MTOW 1361kg: Bell 47G & Hughes 369HE/HS (500C)

☐ C-FWTP	Bell 206LR+ LongRanger	45053	N2617	0076	0497	1 AN 250-C20R	1814			cvtd 206L

ZATKO CONTRACTING, Ltd
Keg River, Alta.

Box 44, Keg River, Alberta T0H 2G0, Canada ☎ (780) 981-2273 Tx: none Fax: (780) 981-2055 SITA: n/a
F: 1980 ⋀⋀⋀ n/a Head: n/a Aircraft below MTOW 1361kg: Robinson R22 & R44

☐ C-GCHD	Bell 206B JetRanger	1248		0073	0897	1 AN 250-C20	1451			

ZIMMER AIR SERVICES, Inc.
Blenheim, Ont.

RR 7, Burke Line, Blenheim, Ontario N0P 1A0, Canada ☎ (519) 676-9550 Tx: none Fax: (519) 676-9552 SITA: n/a
F: 1975 ⋀⋀⋀ n/a Head: Paul Zimmer Net: n/a Aircraft below MTOW 1361kg: Bell 47G-3B

☐ C-GBCL	Bell 206B JetRanger III	3458	N2145R	0081	0797	1 AN 250-C20B	1451			
☐ C-GFEC	Bell 206B JetRanger	1611		0075	0697	1 AN 250-C20	1451			
☐ C-GMLO	Bell 206B JetRanger	957	N809JA	0073	0497	1 AN 250-C20	1451			

CC = CHILE (Republic of Chile) (Republica de Chile)
Capital: Santiago de Chile Official Language: Spanish Population: 15,0 million Square Km: 756945 Dialling code: +56 Year established: 1818 Acting political head: Eduardo Frei (President)

Government / Corporate / Executive / VIP Aircraft

☐ CC-DAC	Cessna 650 Citation VI	650-0233	N1303H	0093	0893	2 GA TFE731-3B-100S	9979	Liaison		Direccion General de Aeronautica Civil
☐ CC-DGA	Cessna 550 Citation II	550-0657	N3986G	0091	0991	2 PWC JT15D-4	6577	Liaison		Direccion General de Aeronautica Civil
☐ CC-DIV	Beech King Air B200CT	BN-1	CC-EAA	0080		2 PWC PT6A-42	6350	Liaison		Direccion General de Aeronautica Civil
☐ CC-DSS	Beech King Air B200T	BT-33	CC-EAG	0088		2 PWC PT6A-42	6350	Liaison		cvtd B200 cn BB-1301 / DGAC
☐ 901	Boeing 707-321B	19374 / 658	904	0067	0291	4 PW JT3D-3B (HK2/COM)	150850	VIP / mil trans	HJ-EF	Fuerza Aérea de Chile
☐ 902	Boeing 707-351C	19443 / 611	CC-CCK	0067	1182	4 PW JT3D-3B	150850	Freighter	CJ-BM	Fuerza Aérea de Chile
☐ 905	Boeing 707-385C	19000 / 447	CC-CEB	0065	0191	4 PW JT3D-3B (HK2/COM)	150850	Freighter	CJ-BG	Fuerza Aérea de Chile
☐ 911	GAC G-1159A Gulfstream III	465	N465GA	0087	0596	2 RR Spey 511-8	31615	VIP		Fuerza Aérea del Chile
☐ 921	Boeing 737-58N	28866 / 2929		0097	0997	2 CFMI CFM56-3C1	60555	VIP / mil trans		Fuerza Aérea del Chile

AEROCARDAL = CDA (Subsidiary of Cardal AG)
Santiago-Tobalaba

Casilla 9630, La Reina, Chile ☎ (2) 279 35 35 Tx: 340320 benz ck Fax: (2) 279 42 72 SITA: n/a
F: 1989 ⋀⋀⋀ 25 Head: Alex E. Casasempere ICAO: CARDAL Net: n/a

☐ CC-CWB	Bell 206L-3 LongRanger III	51023		0082		1 AN 250-C30P	1882			
☐ CC-CWY	Piper PA-34-200T Seneca II	34-8170031	CC-PLW	0081		2 CO TSIO-360-EB	2073			lsf pvt
☐ CC-CWA	Eurocopter (MBB) BO105LS-A3	2006		0087		2 AN 250-C28C	2600			
☐ CC-CWZ	Cessna 441 Conquest II (Super 8)	441-0315	N1208A	0084	0894	2 GA TPE331-8-511S	4468			cvtd Conquest II
☐ CC-CWX	Dornier 228-100	7027	CC-CSA	0084	1191	2 GA TPE331-5-252D	5700			
☐ CC-CWW	Cessna S550 Citation S/II	S550-0002	N211VP	0084		2 PWC JT15D-4B	6849			

AEROCHAITEN, Ltda
Puerto Montt

Quillota 127, Puerto Montt, Chile ☎ (65) 25 32 19 Tx: none Fax: (65) 25 32 19 SITA: n/a
F: 1994 n/a Head: Alfonso Cuadrado Kaiser Net: n/a

☐ CC-CHW	Cessna 402	402-0321	LV-JJZ	0068	0097	2 CO TSIO-520-E	2858	8 Pax		

AERO LLOYD, Ltda
Antofagasta

Casilla 1040, Antofagasta, Chile ☎ (83) 22 20 20 Tx: n/a Fax: n/a SITA: n/a
F: n/a n/a Head: Francisco Baltolu Net: n/a

☐ CC-CFQ	Piper PA-31-310 Navajo C	31-7712052		0077		2 LY TIO-540-A2C	2948			
☐ CC-CFT	Piper PA-31-310 Navajo C	31-7712099		0077		2 LY TIO-540-A2C	2948			
☐ CC-CIO	Piper PA-31-350 Navajo Chieftain	31-7752188	CC-PIB	0077		2 LY TIO-540-J2BD	3175			
☐ CC-CRV	Piper PA-31-310 Navajo B	31-733		0071	1191	2 LY TIO-540-A2C	2948			lsf Geocen Integral Ltda
☐ CC-CRE	Twin (Aero) Turbo Commander 690A	11155	N536	0074	0796	2 GA TPE331-5-251K	4649			

AEROMET – Transportes Aéreos Metalurgicos, Ltda
Santiago-Los Cerrillos

Casilla 11, Correo Los Cerrillos, Santiago de Chile, Chile ☎ (2) 557 47 56 Tx: none Fax: (2) 557 05 45 SITA: n/a
F: 1986 27 Head: José Pedro Cifuentes C. Net: n/a Aircraft below MTOW 1361 kg: Cessna 152 & 172.

☐ CC-CDR	Piper PA-31-350 Navajo Chieftain	31-8052169		0080		2 LY TIO-540-J2BD	3175			

AEROPESCA – Servicios Aéreos Aeropesca, Ltda
Iquique & Santiago-Tobalaba

Aeropuerto Diego Aracena, Casilla 29-D, Iquique, Chile ☎ (51) 41 16 64 Tx: none Fax: (51) 41 16 64 SITA: n/a
F: 1980 50 Head: Raúl Zárate Moreno Net: n/a

☐ CC-CAJ	Cessna 337H Super Skymaster II	33701860	N1368L	0078		2 CO IO-360-GB	2100			
☐ CC-CAZ	Cessna 337G Super Skymaster II	33701673	N53515	0076		2 CO IO-360-GB	2100			
☐ CC-CGB	Cessna 337H Super Skymaster II	33701941	N123YM	0080		2 CO IO-360-GB	2100			
☐ CC-CGC	Cessna 337G Super Skymaster II	33701771	N53672	0077		2 CO IO-360-GB	2100			
☐ CC-CGJ	Cessna 337H Super Skymaster II	33701914	N1396S	0079		2 CO IO-360-GB	2100			
☐ CC-CGR	Cessna 337G Super Skymaster II	33701638	N53457	0075		2 CO IO-360-GB	2100			
☐ CC-CAE	Twin (Aero) Shrike Commander 500S	3148	N768WC	0073		2 LY IO-540-E1B5	3062			
☐ CC-CGX	Twin (Aero) Shrike Commander 500S	3306	N10PP	0078		2 LY IO-540-E1B5	3062			
☐ CC-CHG	Twin (Aero) Shrike Commander 500S	3293	N916AC	0077		2 LY IO-540-E1B5	3062			

AEROVIAS DAP, S.A. = DAP (Associated with Maquinarias Pivcevic e Hijos, Ltda)
Punta Arenas

Casilla 406, Punta Arenas, Chile ☎ (61) 22 33 40 Tx: 380053 Fax: (61) 22 16 93 SITA: n/a
F: 1980 40 Head: Alex R. Pivcevic ICAO: DAP Net: n/a

☐ CC-CIB	Eurocopter (Aerosp.) AS355F2 Ecureuil 2	5371	XA-MDE	0088		2 AN 250-C20F	2540			lsf Banestado Leasing SA
☐ CC-CIM	Eurocopter (Aerosp.) AS355F2 Ecureuil 2	5370	G-BSLL	0088		2 AN 250-C20F	2540			lsf Banestado Leasing SA
☐ CC-CIN	Eurocopter (Aerosp.) AS355F1 Ecureuil 2	5147	N22TS	0081		2 AN 250-C20F	2400			lsf Banestado Leasing SA
☐ CC-CLV	Cessna 402C II	402C0073	CC-CDU	0079		2 CO TSIO-520-VB	3107			lsf Banestado Leasing SA
☐ CC-COV	Cessna 402C II	402C0282	CC-CDS	0080		2 CO TSIO-520-VB	3107			
☐ CC-CLY	Beech King Air 100	B-79	CC-PIE	0071	1091	2 PWC PT6A-28	4808			
☐ CC-COT	Beech King Air A90 (65-A90)	LJ-227	CC-PIR	0067		2 PWC PT6A-20	4218			
☐ CC-CHV	De Havilland DHC-6 Twin Otter 300	709		0080	0980	2 PWC PT6A-27	5670			

ALFA HELICOPTEROS
Santiago-Tobalaba

Avda Larrain 7941, Aérodromo Eulogio Sanchez-Tobalaba, Santiago de Chile, Chile ☎ (2) 273 99 99 Tx: none Fax: (2) 273 19 37 SITA: n/a
F: 1982 14 Head: Mauricio Gutierrez Manzi Net: n/a

☐ CC-CMG	Eurocopter (Aerosp.) SA316B Alouette III	1166	N608RM	0064		1 TU Artouste IIIB	2200			lsf Inversiones Cirrus SA
☐ CC-CRO	Eurocopter (Aerosp.) SA316B Alouette III	2239	N223E	0076		1 TU Artouste IIIB	2200			lsf Inversiones Cirrus SA
☐ CC-CMJ	Bell 204 (UH-1B)	412	CC-PMS	0062		1 LY T53-L-11	3856			lsf Inversiones Cirrus SA
☐ CC-CMK	Bell 204 (UH-1B)	711	FAP024	0062		1 LY T53-L-11	3856			lsf Banedwards Sogelasing SA

AQUELARRE – Linea Aérea Aquelarre, Ltda = AQE
Santiago-Tobalaba & Puerto Montt

Arturo Prat 998, Santiago de Chile, Chile ☎ (2) 665 31 10 Tx: none Fax: (2) 665 31 24 SITA: n/a
F: 1995 32 Head: Nicolas Vidal Hamilton-Toovey Net: n/a

☐ CC-CVO	Piper PA-31-350 Navajo Chieftain	31-8052142	N35896	0080	0096	2 LY TIO-540-J2BD	3175	Y9		
☐ CC-CET	Beech 1900C-1 Airliner	UC-140	N140YV	1290	1198	2 PWC PT6A-65B	7530	Y19		lsf Raytheon Aircraft Credit Corp.

ASPAR – Aeroservicio Parrague, Ltda = PRG
Santiago-Los Cerrillos

Casilla 86, Correo Los Cerrillos, Santiago de Chile, Chile ☎ (2) 557 29 04 Tx: none Fax: (2) 557 29 04 SITA: n/a
F: 1960 12 Head: Roberto Parragué Opazo ICAO: ASPAR Net: n/a Aircraft below MTOW 1361 kg: Boelkow 208C, Cessna 150 & 182.

☐ CC-CCS	Consolidated PBY-6A Catalina	2043	CC-CNF	0046		2 PW R-1830-92	15000	Tanker		34 / lst ARD / rebuilt 1988
☐ CC-CDT	Consolidated 28-5ACF Catalina	CV-332	F-YCHB	0045		2 PW R-1830-92	15000	Tanker		32 / lst ARD
☐ CC-CNP	Consolidated PBY-6A Catalina	2029	EC-FXN	0046		2 PW R-1830-92	15000	Tanker		35 / lst ARD

AVANT AIRLINES Chile = OT / VAT (Lineas Aéreas Chilenas, S.A. dba / Subsidiary of Tur Bus)
Santiago-A. Merino Benitez

Av. Bernardo O'Higgins No. 107, Santiago de Chile, Chile ☎ (2) 337 08 00 Tx: none Fax: (2) 290 51 41 SITA: n/a
F: 1996 700 Head: Fernando Fernandez IATA: 246 ICAO: AVANT AIRLINES Net: n/a

☐ CC-CSD	Boeing 737-204	20417 / 255	TF-ABD	0070	1198	2 PW JT8D-9A	53070	Y130		lsf Buluca Aviation N.V.
☐ CC-CSF	Boeing 737-222	19945 / 185	CC-CAS	0069	1198	2 PW JT8D-9A	49442	Y130		lsf Fortitude Investments Ltd / pink-cs
☐ CC-CSH	Boeing 737-204 (A)	20632 / 316	G-BADP	0072	0498	2 PW JT8D-15	53750	Y130		lsf TNH Leasing AG / blue-colors
☐ CC-CSI	Boeing 737-204 (A)	20633 / 318	G-BADR	0072	1198	2 PW JT8D-15	53750	Y130		lsf TNH Leasing AG / yellow-colors
☐ CC-CSL	Boeing 737-248	20223 / 252	EI-ASH	0070	1198	2 PW JT8D-9A	49000	Y130		lsf Eurojet Leasing N.V./yellow-colors
☐ CC-CSP	Boeing 737-204 (A)	20808 / 342	9Q-COW	0074	1198	2 PW JT8D-15	53070	Y130		lsf Clipper Leasing / pink-colors
☐ CC-CVC	Boeing 737-229 (A)	21596 / 529	OO-SBQ	0078	1097	2 PW JT8D-15A	54200	Y135		lsf Glendale Services / yellow-colors
☐ CC-CVD	Boeing 737-229 (A)	21840 / 617	OO-SBT	0079	1097	2 PW JT8D-15A	54200	Y135		lsf Glendale Services / pink-colors
☐ CC-CSW	Boeing 727-2M7 (A)	21655 / 1452	VP-CDL	0079	0199	3 PW JT8D-17R	88360	Y172		lsf Inversiones Aeronauticas/sublst SCX

CEPRISER
Santiago-Los Cerrillos

Av. Francisco Bilbao 3771, Of. 308, Santiago de Chile, Chile ☎ (2) 274 69 05 Tx: n/a Fax: n/a SITA: n/a
F: n/a n/a Head: Raul Espinosa Pizarro Net: n/a Aircraft below MTOW 1361kg: Cessna 150 & 172.

☐ CC-CKZ	Beech Baron 56TC	TG-61	DGAC A-2	0067		2 LY TIO-541-E1B4	2717			

CHILE INTER, S.A. = CLE (Subsidiary of STAF, Argentina)
Santiago-A. Merino Benitez

Maciver 440, Piso 7, Santiago de Chile, Chile ☎ (2) 632 29 05 Tx: none Fax: (2) 638 59 88 SITA: n/a
F: 1997 n/a Head: Fernando Leiva ICAO: CHILE INTER Net: n/a

☐ CC-CZF	Lockheed L-1011-385-1-15 TriStar 100	193E-1058	C-FTNI*	0074	0198	3 RR RB211-22B	215003	C19Y343	FJ-DK	lsf ROY / cvtd TriStar 1
☐ CC-CZR	Lockheed L-1011-385-1-15 TriStar 100	193E-1069	C-FTNK	0074	0198	3 RR RB211-22B	215003	C19Y343	FK-BJ	lsf ROY / cvtd TriStar 1

COPTERS – Servicios Aéreos Copters, Ltda
Rancagua

Las Condes 10373, Oficina 30, Santiago de Chile, Chile ☎ 269 80 42 Tx: none Fax: 269 81 46 SITA: n/a
F: 1997 15 Head: Carlos Lopez van del Valk Net: n/a

☐ CC-CLE	Bell UH-1H (205)	8535	N46666	0067		1 LY T53-L-13	4309			
☐ CC-CLF	Bell AH-1P (209) Cobra Lifter	22060	N82277	0076	0697	1 LY T53-L-703	4763			

FAST AIR CARRIER, S.A. = FST (Subsidiary of LAN Chile / Member of Cueto Group)
Santiago-A. Merino Benitez

Estado 10, Piso 21, Casilla 147-D, Santiago de Chile, Chile ☎ (2) 639 44 11 Tx: 441062 lascl cz Fax: (2) 638 38 84 SITA: n/a
F: 1978 56 Head: Juan Cueto-Sierra ICAO: FASTER Net: n/a Beside aircraft listed, also uses a Boeing 747-200F, lsf/opb ATLAS AIR (N), when required.

☐ CC-CAR	Boeing (Douglas) DC-8-71F	45976 / 372	EI-CGY	0068	0393	4 CFMI CFM56-2C	147418	Freighter	AL-CF	lsf GECA / cvtd DC-8-61/-71
☐ CC-CAX	Boeing (Douglas) DC-8-71F	45970 / 343	N8080U	0068	1192	4 CFMI CFM56-2C	147418	Freighter	AJ-HL	lsf GECA/sub-lst MAA/cvtd DC-8-61/-71
☐ CC-CYQ	Boeing (Douglas) DC-8-71F	45810 / 252	N8070U	0066	1194	4 CFMI CFM56-2C	147418	Freighter	AJ-EL	lsf GECA/sub-lst TUS, PP-ABS/cvtd 8-61
☐ N872SJ	Boeing (Douglas) DC-8-71F	46040 / 449	N8096U	0069	1198	4 CFMI CFM56-2C	147418	Freighter		lsf Aircraft Int'l Lsng / cvtd -61/-71

HALCON Centro Aéreo (Didier Rousset Buy dba)
Concepcion

Sanders 200 Alto, Concepcion, Chile ☎ (41) 33 19 19 Tx: n/a Fax: (41) 33 19 16 SITA: n/a
F: 1980 8 Head: Didier Rousset Buy Net: n/a Aircraft below MTOW 1361kg: Cessna 172, 177, 182 & Piper PA-25.

☐ CC-CGQ	Cessna 337H Super Skymaster II	33701903	N1318S	0079		2 CO IO-360-GB	2100			
☐ CC-CKE	Cessna 337H Super Skymaster II	33701916		0079	0096	2 CO IO-360-G	2100			

HELISERVICIOS, SA (Sister company of Transporte Aéreo y Maritimo, SA / Affiliated with Rio Claro SA)
Santiago-Tobalaba

Agustinas 972, Of. 709, Santiago de Chile, Chile ☎ (2) 698 35 80 Tx: none Fax: (2) 242 28 55 SITA: n/a
F: 1991 2 Head: José Miguel Infante Net: n/a

☐ CC-CGL	Eurocopter (MBB) BO105LS-A3	2002	C-GTGJ	0087	0193	2 AN 250-C28C	2600	VIP 4 Pax		

88 registration type of aircraft cn/fn ex/ex* mfd del powered by mtow kg configuration selcal name/fln/specialitites/remarks

LAASA – Linea de Aeroservicios, S.A. — Santiago-Tobalaba

Aerodromo Tobalaba, Larrain 7941, Santiago de Chile, Chile ☎ (2) 273 43 09 Tx: n/a Fax: (2) 273 43 09 SITA: n/a
F: n/a ✈✈✈ n/a Head: Juan Griffin Net: n/a Ag-aircraft below MTOW 5000kg: Cessna A188B.

☐ CC-CNN	Bell 206B JetRanger III	3597	N22675	0082	0894	1 AN 250-C20J	1451			
☐ CC-CJG	Eurocopter (Aerosp.) SA315B Lama	2556	N3835Q	0079		1 TU Artouste IIIB	1950			
☐ CC-CFY	Piper PA-31-310 Navajo	31-600	EJERC.E-203	0070		2 LY TIO-540-A1A	2948			
☐ CC-CIZ	Bell UH-1B (204)	1124	EC-EOH	0064		1 LY T53-L-11	3856			
☐ CC-CNK	Garlick-Bell UH-1B (204)	755	LV-WGS	0063	0096	1 LY T53-L-13	3856			cvtd Bell UH-1B
☐ CC-CNL	Garlick-Bell UH-1B (204)	318	LV-WNR	0061	0096	1 LY T53-L-13	3856			cvtd Bell UH-1B
☐ CC-CNH	Piper PA-31T Cheyenne II	31T-8020069	OB-1193	0080		2 PWC PT6A-28	4082			
☐ CC-CNI	Bell UH-1H (205)	5119	N6743X	0065	0096	1 LY T53-L-13	4309			cvtd UH-1D
☐ CC-CNJ	Bell UH-1H (205)	5146	N8154G	0065	0096	1 LY T53-L-13	4309			cvtd UH-1D

LADECO Airlines = UC / LCO (Linea Aérea del Cobre, SA dba / Subsidiary of LAN Chile / Member of Cueto Group) — Santiago-A. Merino Benitez

Estado 10, Piso 21, Casilla 147-D, Santiago de Chile, Chile ☎ (2) 639 44 11 Tx: 441061 lascl cz Fax: (2) 638 38 84 SITA: n/a
F: 1958 ✈✈✈ 1800 Head: Jose L. Ibanez IATA: 145 ICAO: LADECO Net: n/a

☐ CC-CYC	Boeing 737-219 (A)	21131 / 428	G-BGNW	0075	0690	2 PW JT8D-15	53070	C18Y96		
☐ CC-CYD	Boeing 737-205 (A)	21219 / 460	N7031A	0076	0393	2 PW JT8D-9A	53070	C18Y96	BE-AK	lsf AIG Leasing
☐ CC-CYK	Boeing 737-205 (A)	21445 / 506	N7031F	0077	1093	2 PW JT8D-9A	53070	C18Y97	BE-GL	lsf Integrated Resources
☐ CC-CYN	Boeing 737-2M8 (A)	21231 / 462	9M-MBN	0076	1191	2 PW JT8D-15	54204	C18Y96	CE-BH	lsf ILFC
☐ CC-CYR	Boeing 737-2A6	20195 / 205	N909LH	0069	1292	2 PW JT8D-9A	53070	C18Y96		lsf CORS
☐ CC-CYT	Boeing 737-2E1 (A)	21112 / 424	EI-BDY	0075	0395	2 PW JT8D-9A	53070	C18Y97	BL-AC	lsf ACG Acquisition Corp.
☐ CC-CYV	Boeing 737-2Q8 (A)	23148 / 1059	N137AW	0084	0795	2 PW JT8D-15A	53070	C18Y97	AC-FK	lsf PEGA
☐ CC-CYW	Boeing 737-2M6 (A)	20913 / 399	ZK-NAZ	0075	1095	2 PW JT8D-15	53070	C18Y97	GJ-HK	lsf ACG Aquisition Corp.
☐ CC-CZK	Boeing 737-236 (A)	21804 / 686	G-BGDP	0080	1197	2 PW JT8D-15A	54204	Y114		lsf GECA
☐ CC-CZO	Boeing 737-236 (A)	22030 / 693	G-BGJI	0080	1197	2 PW JT8D-15A	54204	Y114		lsf GECA

LAN Chile – Linea Aérea Nacional de Chile, SA = LA / LAN (Member of Cueto Group) — Santiago-A. Merino Benitez

Estado 10, Piso 21, Casilla 147-D, Santiago de Chile, Chile ☎ (2) 639 44 11 Tx: 441061 lascl cz Fax: (2) 638 38 84 SITA: n/a
F: 1929 ✈✈✈ 2700 Head: Enrique P. Cueto IATA: 045 ICAO: LAN Net: http://www.lanchile.cl

☐ CC-CDE	Boeing 737-291 (A)	22744 / 923	EI-BWY	0082	0894	2 PW JT8D-17A	53070	Y124	CJ-BH	lsf PLMI
☐ CC-CDG	Boeing 737-291 (A)	23024 / 965	CS-TIS	0083	1092	2 PW JT8D-17A	53000	Y124	CJ-BG	lsf GECA
☐ CC-CEA	Boeing 737-291 (A)	22743 / 909	EI-BXW	0082	1188	2 PW JT8D-17A	53070	Y124	BC-AH	lsf GECA
☐ CC-CEE	Boeing 737-2L9 (A)	22407 / 698	EC-DXV	0080	1288	2 PW JT8D-17	56472	Y124	CJ-DE	lsf GECA
☐ CC-CEI	Boeing 737-248C	20219 / 208	EI-ASD	0069	1195	2 PW JT8D-9A	50349	Freighter	CD-EF	lsf Eurojet Leasing N.V.
☐ CC-CHR	Boeing 737-236 (A)	21792 / 628	G-BGDC	0079	0595	2 PW JT8D-15A	52752	Y124	CD-AK	lsf BOUL
☐ CC-CHS	Boeing 737-236 (A)	21802 / 670	G-BGDN	0080	0695	2 PW JT8D-15A	52752	Y124	CD-BJ	lsf BOUL
☐ CC-CJW	Boeing 737-2T5 (A)	22397 / 737	G-BHVI	0081	0487	2 PW JT8D-15	53070	Y124	CJ-BE	lsf GECA
☐ CC-CLD	Boeing 737-2Q8 (A)	21960 / 642	G-IBTW	0080	0596	2 PW JT8D-15A	54204	Y124	DH-JL	lsf GECA
☐ CC-CRP	Boeing 737-230 (A)	22134 / 777	D-ABHF	0081	1196	2 PW JT8D-15	50900	Y124	BJ-KQ	lsf JETZ
☐ CC-CRQ	Boeing 737-230 (A)	22135 / 781	D-ABHH	0081	1296	2 PW JT8D-15	50900	Y124	CJ-BK	lsf JETZ
☐ CC-CRR	Boeing 737-230 (A)	22114 / 657	D-ABFA	0080	1196	2 PW JT8D-15	50900	Y124	AL-BE	lsf JETZ
☐ CC-CRS	Boeing 737-230 (A)	22139 / 791	D-ABHN	0081	0197	2 PW JT8D-15	50900	Y124	AL-FH	lsf JETZ
☐ CC-CYP	Boeing 737-2T5 (A)	22632 / 847	CN-RMH	0082	0596	2 PW JT8D-15	54204	Y124	DK-FH	lsf GECA
☐ CC-CZL	Boeing 737-236 (A)	21808 / 712	G-BGDU	0080	0498	2 PW JT8D-15A	54204	Y124		lsf GECA
☐ CC-CZM	Boeing 737-236 (A)	22027 / 654	G-BGJF	0080		2 PW JT8D-15A	54204	Y124		to be lsf GECA 0699
☐ CC-CZN	Boeing 737-236 (A)	22029 / 662	G-BGJH	0080		2 PW JT8D-15A	54204	Y124		to be lsf GECA 0599
☐ CC-CZP	Boeing 737-236 (A)	22031 / 722	G-BGJJ	0080	0698	2 PW JT8D-15A	54204	Y124		lsf GECA
☐ CC-	Airbus Industrie A319-132					2 IAE V2524-A5	64000			oo-delivery 1100
☐ CC-	Airbus Industrie A319-132					2 IAE V2524-A5	64000			oo-delivery 0201
☐ CC-	Airbus Industrie A319-132					2 IAE V2524-A5	64000			oo-delivery 0601
☐ CC-	Airbus Industrie A319-132					2 IAE V2524-A5	64000			oo-delivery 1001
☐ CC-	Airbus Industrie A319-132					2 IAE V2524-A5	64000			oo-delivery 0002
☐ CC-	Airbus Industrie A319-132					2 IAE V2524-A5	64000			oo-delivery 0002
☐ CC-	Airbus Industrie A319-132					2 IAE V2524-A5	64000			oo-delivery 0002
☐ CC-	Airbus Industrie A319-132					2 IAE V2524-A5	64000			oo-delivery 0003
☐ CC-	Airbus Industrie A319-132					2 IAE V2524-A5	64000			oo-delivery 0003
☐ CC-	Airbus Industrie A319-132					2 IAE V2524-A5	64000			oo-delivery 0003
☐ CC-	Airbus Industrie A319-132					2 IAE V2524-A5	64000			oo-delivery 0003
☐ CC-	Airbus Industrie A320-232					2 IAE V2527-A5	73500			oo-delivery 1000
☐ CC-	Airbus Industrie A320-232					2 IAE V2527-A5	73500			oo-delivery 0101
☐ CC-	Airbus Industrie A320-232					2 IAE V2527-A5	73500			oo-delivery 0701
☐ CC-	Airbus Industrie A320-232					2 IAE V2527-A5	73500			oo-delivery 0002
☐ CC-	Airbus Industrie A320-232					2 IAE V2527-A5	73500			oo-delivery 0002
☐ CC-	Airbus Industrie A320-232					2 IAE V2527-A5	73500			oo-delivery 0003
☐ CC-	Airbus Industrie A320-232					2 IAE V2527-A5	73500			oo-delivery 0003
☐ CC-	Airbus Industrie A320-232					2 IAE V2527-A5	73500			oo-delivery 0004
☐ CC-	Airbus Industrie A320-232					2 IAE V2527-A5	73500			oo-delivery 0004
☐ CC-CDS	Boeing (Douglas) DC-8-71F	45996 / 397	N8092U	0068	1192	4 CFMI CFM56-2C	147418	Freighter	DE-BG	lsf GECA / cvtd DC-8-61/-71
☐ CC-CDU	Boeing (Douglas) DC-8-71F	45997 / 398	N8093U	0068	1292	4 CFMI CFM56-2C	147418	Freighter	DE-CH	lsf GECA / cvtd DC-8-61/-71
☐ CC-CBJ	Boeing 767-316 (ER)	27613 / 652		0097	0397	2 GE CF6-80C2B6F	184612	F10C28Y181		lsf ILFC
☐ CC-CDM	Boeing 767-352 (ER)	26261 / 575	N181LF	0095	0595	2 PW PW4062	184612	F10C28Y181	AB-PR	lsf ILFC
☐ CC-CDP	Boeing 767-316 (ER)	27597 / 602		0096	0296	2 GE CF6-80C2B6F	184612	F10C28Y181		lsf ILFC
☐ CC-CEB	Boeing 767-316 (ER)	26327 / 621		0096	0796	2 GE CF6-80C2B6F	184612	F10C28Y181	AB-PS	lsf ILFC
☐ CC-CEK	Boeing 767-316 (ER)	26329 / 641		0096	1296	2 GE CF6-80C2B6F	184612	F10C28Y181	CJ-BM	lsf ILFC
☐ CC-CEL	Boeing 767-3Y0 (ER)	26204 / 464	XA-RKJ	0092	0696	2 PW PW4060	184612	F10C28Y181	BC-JR	lsf GECA
☐ CC-CEY	Boeing 767-3Y0 (ER)	24947 / 351	PT-TAD	0091	0393	2 PW PW4060	184612	F10C28Y181	AH-BS	lsf GECA
☐ CC-CRG	Boeing 767-375 (ER)	25865 / 430	B-2561	0092	0197	2 GE CF6-80C2B6F	184612	F10C28Y181	BC-HM	lsf GECA
☐ CC-CRH	Boeing 767-375 (ER)	25864 / 426	B-2562	0092	0197	2 GE CF6-80C2B6F	184612	F10C28Y181	BJ-HQ	lsf GECA
☐ CC-CRT	Boeing 767-316 (ER)	27615 / 681		1297	1297	2 GE CF6-80C2B7F	186880	F10C28Y181		lsf ILFC
☐ CC-CZT	Boeing 767-316 (ER)	29228 / 699		0498	0498	2 GE CF6-80C2B7F	186880	F10C28Y181		
☐ CC-CZU	Boeing 767-316 (ER)	29229 / 729		0098	1298	2 GE CF6-80C2B7F	186880	F10C28Y181		
☐ CC-CZW	Boeing 767-316 (ER)	29227 / 698		0098	0498	2 GE CF6-80C2B7F	186880	F10C28Y181		
☐ CC-CZX	Boeing 767-316 (ER)	29881				2 GE CF6-80C2B7F	186880	F10C28Y181		oo-delivery 0899
☐ CC-CZZ	Boeing 767-316F (ER)	25756 / 712		0998	0998	2 GE CF6-80C2B7F	186880	Freighter		

LINEA AEREA COSTA NORTE, SA — Santiago-Tobalaba & Iquique

Providencia 2653, Piso 14, Casillo 134, Correo 35, Santiago de Chile, Chile ☎ (2) 232-3435 Tx: 240284 colso cl Fax: (2) 232-6726 SITA: n/a
F: n/a ✈✈✈ n/a Head: Sergio Lecaros Net: n/a

☐ CC-CKD	Cessna 337H Super Skymaster II	33701889	N1397L	0079		2 CO IO-360-G	2100			
☐ CC-CFW	Twin (Aero) Shrike Commander 500S	3230		0075		2 LY IO-540-E1B5	3062			
☐ CC-CKI	Twin (Aero) Shrike Commander 500S	3291	N12RZ	0077		2 LY IO-540-E1B5	3062			
☐ CC-CKK	Twin (Aero) Shrike Commander 500S	3134	N345RJ	0073		2 LY IO-540-E1B5	3062			

NSW – New South Ways, Llc — Santiago-A. Merino Benitez & Miami-FL (USA)

US Operations Office: PO Box 520827, Miami, FL 33152, USA ☎ (305) 871-1250 Tx: none Fax: (305) 871-4152 SITA: n/a
F: 1998 ✈✈✈ n/a Head: Francisco Rodriguez Net: n/a

☐ XA-TDC	Boeing (Douglas) DC-10-30F (CF)	46891 / 127	N105WA	0973	0998	3 GE CF6-50C2	256280	Freighter		lsf / opb TEJ

PULLMAN EXPRESS, Ltda — Santiago-Los Cerrillos

Avda Pedro Aguirre Cerva 6100, Los Cerrillos, Hangar Pullman, Santiago de Chile, Chile ☎ (2) 557 21 10 Tx: none Fax: (2) 533 00 95 SITA: n/a
F: 1997 ✈✈✈ n/a Head: Joaquin Delarosa Net: n/a Suspended operations (with Convair 580 Freighter) 1198. Intends to restart during 1999 with Aero Commander & Turbo Commander 680.

SAE – Servicio Aéreo Ejecutivo S.A.E., Ltda — Santiago-Los Cerrillos

Av. Apoquindo 7850, Torro 3, L4, Las Condes, Santiago de Chile, Chile ☎ (2) 211 24 43 Tx: n/a Fax: (2) 229 34 19 SITA: n/a
F: 1995 ✈✈✈ 5 Head: Luis Bochetti Net: n/a

☐ CC-CBX	Cessna 401A	401A0121		0069		2 CO TSIO-520-E	2858	7 Pax		

SOCIEDAD DE AERONAVEGACION PESQUERA, Ltda – S.A.P. (Affiliated with Sociedad Pesquera Guahaye, Ltda) — Iquique

Barrio Industrial Sitio 5, Casilla 52-D, Iquique, Chile ☎ (57) 41 34 00 Tx: none Fax: (57) 42 17 19 SITA: n/a
F: 1979 ✈✈✈ 16 Head: Antonio Walker Z. Net: n/a

☐ CC-CGE	Britten-Norman BN-2B-27 Islander	2166	G-BKOC*	0083		2 LY O-540-E4C5	2885			
☐ CC-CGG	Britten-Norman BN-2B-27 Islander	2168	G-BKOE	0083		2 LY O-540-E4C5	2885			
☐ CC-CGH	Britten-Norman BN-2B-27 Islander	2169	G-BKOF*	0083		2 LY O-540-E4C5	2885			
☐ CC-CFU	Twin (Aero) Shrike Commander 500S	3320	N348TT	0079		2 LY IO-540-E1B5	3062			

89 registration type of aircraft cn/fn ex/ex* mfd del powered by mtow kg configuration selcal name/fln/specialitites/remarks

TRANSPORTES AEREOS DON CARLOS, Ltda (Associated with Soc. Comercial e Ind. Triple)

Coyhaique-Teniente Vidal

Casilla 514, Coyhaique, Chile   ☎ (67) 23 19 81   Tx: none   Fax: (67) 23 13 79   SITA: n/a
F: 1978   ♦♦♦ 23   Head: Carlos Martinez Villegas   Net: n/a

☐ CC-CCI	Beech Baron E55	TE-1008			0075	2 CO IO-520-C	2404	5 Pax		
☐ CC-CCM	Beech Twin Bonanza C50	CH-358	FAC		0056	2 LY GO-480-F1A6	2722	7 Pax		
☐ CC-CCB	Cessna 402B II	402B1089	N82930		0076	2 CO TSIO-520-E	2858	9 Pax		
☐ CC-CFS	Beech Excalibur Queenaire 8800	LD-220	N12JQ		0065	2 LY IO-720-A1B	3992	10 Pax		cvtd Queen Air 65-A80

TRANSPORTES AEREOS ISLA ROBINSON CRUSOE, Ltda – ROC

Santiago-Los Cerrillos

Monumento 2570 Maipu, Santiago de Chile, Chile   ☎ (2) 531 37 72   Tx: n/a   Fax: (2) 531 37 72   SITA: n/a
F: 1984   ♦♦♦ 7   Head: Santiago Figueroa Navarrete   Net: n/a

☐ CC-CEZ	Piper PA-31-310 Navajo C	31-7612035		0076	0096	2 LY TIO-540-A2C	2948			
☐ CC-CBV	GAF N22B Nomad	N22B-57	VH-FAI	0077		2 AN 250-B17B	3856			Isf Gen Air S.A.

TRANSPORTES AEREOS SAN RAFAEL

Coyhaique

18 de Septiembre 469, Coyhaique, Chile   ☎ (67) 22 34 08   Tx: n/a   Fax: n/a   SITA: n/a
F: n/a   ♦♦♦ n/a   Head: Heinz Meyer   Net: n/a

☐ CC-CHE	Piper PA-34-200 Seneca	34-7350294	CC-KIH	0073	0291	2 LY IO-360-C1E6	1905			
☐ CC-CSE	Piper PA-31-310 Navajo	31-731	CC-KKW	0071		2 LY TIO-540-A2C	2948			

CN = MOROCCO   (Kingdom of Morocco)   (al Mamlakah al-Maghrebiya)
Capital: Rabat   Official Language: Arabic   Population: 32,0 million   Square Km: 446550   Dialling code: +212   Year established: 1956   Acting political head: Hassan II (King)

Government / Corporate / Executive / VIP Aircraft

☐ CN-ANL	GAC (Grumman) G-1159 Gulfstream II (TT)	182	N17589*	0076	0477	2 RR Spey 511-8	29710	VIP / mil trans		Gvmt / opb Royal Moroccan Air Force
☐ CN-ANO	Dassault Falcon 50	12	F-WZHC*	0080	0580	3 GA TFE731-3-1C	17600	VIP / mil trans		Gvmt / opb Royal Moroccan Air Force
☐ CN-ANU	GAC G-1159A Gulfstream III	365	HZ-AFO	0083	0189	2 RR Spey 511-8	30935	VIP / mil trans		Gvmt / opb Royal Moroccan Air Force
☐ CN-ANV	Cessna 560 Citation V	560-0025		0089	0889	2 PWC JT15D-5A	7212	VIP / mil trans		Gvmt / opb Royal Moroccan Air Force
☐ CN-ANW	Cessna 560 Citation V	560-0039		0089	1289	2 PWC JT15D-5A	7212	VIP / mil trans		Gvmt / opb Royal Moroccan Air Force
☐ CN-TNA	Dassault Falcon 10	212	F-WZGU*	0088	0888	2 GA TFE731-2-1C	8755	VIP		Gvmt
☐ CN-TNC	Beech King Air 300	FA-107	I-ADLA	0086	1091	2 PWC PT6A-60A	6350	VIP		Gvmt

CASA AIR SERVICES   (Division of Agricolair Maghreb)

Casablanca-Anfa

c/o Agricolair Maghreb, Aéroport Casablanca-Anfa, Casablanca, Morocco   ☎ (2) 90 30 36   Tx: 23007 agroair m   Fax: (2) 90 45 28   SITA: n/a
F: n/a   ♦♦♦ n/a   Head: Hassan Lyoussi   Net: n/a

☐ CN-TCS	Aerospatiale SN601 Corvette	34	F-GKGD	0078	0898	2 PWC JT15D-4	7000			
☐ CN-TDE	Aerospatiale SN601 Corvette	5	F-BVPA	0074	0595	2 PWC JT15D-4	7000			

LES TRAVAUX AERIENS, S.A.

Rabat

22 rue Moulay Rachid, Rabat, Morocco   ☎ (7) 73 24 23   Tx: none   Fax: (7) 72 54 18   SITA: n/a
F: n/a   ♦♦♦ n/a   Head: n/a   Net: n/a

☐ CN-TKS	Beech Queen Air B80 (65-B80)	LD-410			0069	2 LY IGSO-540-A1D	3992			

MAGHREB AERO SERVICE

Casablanca-Anfa

6 Rue Capitaine Thiriat, Casablanca, Morocco   ☎ (2) 33 29 27   Tx: none   Fax: 2(9 33 29 27   SITA: n/a
F: n/a   ♦♦♦ n/a   Head: n/a   Net: n/a   Aircraft below MTOW 1361kg: Cessna 150

☐ CN-TAY	Piper PA-34-200 Seneca	34-7350196			0073	2 LY IO-360-C1E6	1905			
☐ CN-TCC	Britten-Norman BN-2A-3 Islander	673	F-BUFV		0073	2 LY IO-540-K1B5	2858			

MAINTAERO

Marrakech

Avenue Allal El Fassi, Résidence N'Fiss 1, Immeuble 15, Ap. 4, Marrakech, Morocco   ☎ (4) 30 06 58   Tx: none   Fax: (4) 30 64 48   SITA: n/a
F: 1994   ♦♦♦ n/a   Head: Patrick Simon & Vincent Ducrocq   Net: n/a

☐ CN-TEA	Cessna 207A Stationair 8 II	20700684			0081	1 CO IO-520-F	1724			

PRIVAIR, S.A.

Casablanca-Anfa

Hangar 775, Aéroport de Casablanca-Anfa, Casablanca, Morocco   ☎ (2) 91 57 03   Tx: none   Fax: (2) 90 69 89   SITA: n/a
F: n/a   ♦♦♦ n/a   Head: n/a   Net: n/a   Aircraft below MTOW 1361kg: Cessna 150/172 & Socata TB9

☐ CN-TEQ	Cessna 414	414-0369	N9889F		0072	2 CO TSIO-520-J	2883			

REGIONAL AIR LINES = FN / RGL

Casablanca-Mohamed V

BP 12518, Aeroport Mohamed V, Casablanca 20050, Morocco   ☎ (2) 53 80 20   Tx: none   Fax: (2) 53 84 11   SITA: CMNDGFN
F: 1996   ♦♦♦ 100   Head: Mehdi Alaoui   IATA: 259   ICAO: MAROC REGIONAL   Net: n/a

☐ CN-RLE	Beech King Air 350 (B300)	FL-170	N2015G*	0097	1097	2 PWC PT6A-60A	6804	Y9		
☐ CN-RLA	Beech 1900D Airliner	UE-259	N10863*	0097	0397	2 PWC PT6A-67D	7688	Y19		
☐ CN-RLB	Beech 1900D Airliner	UE-263	N10963*	0097	0497	2 PWC PT6A-67D	7688	Y19		
☐ CN-RLC	Beech 1900D Airliner	UE-265	N10969*	0097	0597	2 PWC PT6A-67D	7688	Y19		
☐ CN-RLD	Beech 1900D Airliner	UE-267	N10999*	0097	0597	2 PWC PT6A-67D	7688	Y19		

ROYAL AIR MAROC = AT / RAM

Casablanca-Anfa & -Mohamed V   royal air maroc   الخطوط الملكية المغربية

Aéroport Anfa, Casablanca, Morocco   ☎ (3) 91 20 00   Tx: 21880 marocair   Fax: ((3) 91 24 97   SITA: n/a
F: 1953   ♦♦♦ 4800   Head: Mohammed Hassad   IATA: 147   ICAO: ROYAL AIR MAROC   Net: http://www.xbrcom.qc.ca/RAM/RAM_home.html
Trainer-aircraft below MTOW 5000kg: FFA AS.202/18A, SIAI Marchetti SF260 & Socata TB20 Trinidad.

☐ CN-CDH	Beech Baron B55 (95-B55)	TC-2424		0082	0183	2 CO IO-470-L	2313	3 Pax/Trainer		
☐ CN-CDI	Beech Baron B55 (95-B55)	TC-2430		0082	0183	2 CO IO-470-L	2313	3 Pax/Trainer		
☐ CN-CDF	Beech King Air 200	BB-577		0079	0588	2 PWC PT6A-41	5670	6 Pax/Trainer		
☐ CN-CDN	Beech King Air 200	BB-713	N36741	0080	0787	2 PWC PT6A-41	5670	6 Pax/Trainer		
☐ CN-CDU	ATR 42-300	134	F-WWEF*	0089	0489	2 PWC PW120	16700	Y46		Isf Int'l Leasing (Vanuatu) Ltd
☐ CN-CDV	ATR 42-300	137	F-WWEI*	0089	0589	2 PWC PW120	16700	Y46		Isf Int'l Leasing (Vanuatu) Ltd
☐ CN-RMI	Boeing 737-2B6 (A)	21214 / 449		0076	0276	2 PW JT8D-15 (HK3/NOR)	54204	Y125	AC-DF	El Ayounne
☐ CN-RMJ	Boeing 737-2B6 (A)	21215 / 452		0076	0376	2 PW JT8D-15 (HK3/NOR)	54204	Y125	AC-DG	Oujda
☐ CN-RMK	Boeing 737-2B6 (A)	21216 / 456		0076	0476	2 PW JT8D-15 (HK3/NOR)	54204	Y125	AC-DH	Smara
☐ CN-RML	Boeing 737-2B6 (A)	22767 / 851		0082	0382	2 PW JT8D-15 (HK3/NOR)	54204	Y125	BH-AG	
☐ CN-RMM	Boeing 737-2B6C (A)	23049 / 951		0083	0383	2 PW JT8D-15A (HK3/NOR)	54204	Y127 or Frtr	BM-EG	
☐ CN-RMN	Boeing 737-2B6C (A)	23050 / 975		0083	0683	2 PW JT8D-15A (HK3/NOR)	54204	Y127 or Frtr	BM-EH	
☐ CN-RMV	Boeing 737-5B6	25317 / 2157		0091	1191	2 CFMI CFM56-3C1	56472	F16Y93orY129	AM-BS	
☐ CN-RMW	Boeing 737-5B6	25364 / 2166		0091	1191	2 CFMI CFM56-3C1	56472	F16Y93orY129	AM-CR	Isf RAM2 Leasing Ltd
☐ CN-RMY	Boeing 737-5B6	26525 / 2209		0092	0392	2 CFMI CFM56-3C1	56472	F16Y93orY129	AS-CD	
☐ CN-RNB	Boeing 737-5B6	26527 / 2472		0093	0593	2 CFMI CFM56-3C1	58740	F16Y93orY129		
☐ CN-RNG	Boeing 737-5B6	27679 / 2734		0095	0795	2 CFMI CFM56-3C1	58740	F16Y93orY129	HQ-PS	
☐ CN-RNH	Boeing 737-5B6	27680 / 2855		0097	0297	2 CFMI CFM56-3C1	58740	F16Y93orY129		
☐ CN-RNL	Boeing 737-7B6	28982				2 CFMI CFM56-7B24	69400			oo-delivery 0499
☐ CN-RNM	Boeing 737-7B6	28984				2 CFMI CFM56-7B24	69400			oo-delivery 0699
☐ CN-RMF	Boeing 737-4B6	24807 / 1880		0090	0790	2 CFMI CFM56-3C1	68038	C24Y114orY168	GP-HM	Isf CLS Garnet Leasing Ltd
☐ CN-RMG	Boeing 737-4B6	24808 / 1888		0090	0790	2 CFMI CFM56-3C1	68038	C24Y114orY168	GP-HQ	Isf CLS Garnet Leasing Ltd
☐ CN-RMX	Boeing 737-4B6	26526 / 2219		0092	0392	2 CFMI CFM56-3C1	68038	C24Y114orY168	AS-BR	
☐ CN-RNA	Boeing 737-4B6	26531 / 2453		0093	0493	2 CFMI CFM56-3C1	68038	C24Y114orY168	DH-AS	Isf RAM3 Leasing Ltd
☐ CN-RNC	Boeing 737-4B6	26529 / 2584		0094	0594	2 CFMI CFM56-3C1	68038	C24Y114orY168	EQ-HS	
☐ CN-RND	Boeing 737-4B6	26530 / 2588		0094	0594	2 CFMI CFM56-3C1	68038	C24Y114orY168	EQ-JK	
☐ CN-RNF	Boeing 737-4B6	27678 / 2733		0095	0795	2 CFMI CFM56-3C1	68038	C24Y114orY168		
☐ CN-RNJ	Boeing 737-8B6	28980 / 55		0098	0798	2 CFMI CFM56-7B26	78245	C16Y141orY189	AB-KS	
☐ CN-RNK	Boeing 737-8B6	28981 / 60		0098	0798	2 CFMI CFM56-7B26	78245	C16Y141orY189	AB-LS	
☐ CN-	Boeing 737-8B6					2 CFMI CFM56-7B26	78245	C16Y141orY189		oo-delivery 0899
☐ CN-	Boeing 737-8B6					2 CFMI CFM56-7B26	78245	C16Y141orY189		oo-delivery 1099
☐ CN-	Boeing 737-8B6					2 CFMI CFM56-7B26	78245	C16Y141orY189		oo-delivery 0500
☐ CN-	Boeing 737-8B6					2 CFMI CFM56-7B26	78245	C16Y141orY189		oo-delivery 1100
☐ CN-	Boeing 737-8B6					2 CFMI CFM56-7B26	78245	C16Y141orY189		oo-delivery 0301
☐ CN-RMT	Boeing 757-2B6	23686 / 103	N32831*	0086	0786	2 PW PW2037	108862	F20Y159	AE-BP	Isf Chemco Equipment Finance Ltd
☐ CN-RMZ	Boeing 757-2B6	23687 / 106		0086	0886	2 PW PW2037	108862	F20Y159	AE-CP	Isf Chemco Equipment Finance Ltd
☐ CN-RME	Boeing 747-2B6B (M)	21615 / 330		0080	0978	4 PW JT9D-7F	351534	F12C24Y368	BG-JK	
☐ CN-RGA	Boeing 747-428	25629 / 956	F-OGTG	0093	1093	4 GE CF6-80C2B1F	371900	F16C38Y393	FJ-GR	Isf Tangerine Aircraft Ltd

registration   type of aircraft   cn/fn   ex/ex*   mfd   del   powered by   mtow kg   configuration   selcal   name/fin/specialitites/remarks

Government / Corporate / Executive / VIP Aircraft

registration	type of aircraft	cn/fn	ex/ex*	mfd	del	powered by	mtow kg	configuration	selcal	name/fln/specialitites/remarks
☐ FAB001	Sabreliner 60 (Rockwell NA265-60)	306-115	N2118J	0076		2 PW JT12A-8	9150	VIP		Fuerza Aérea Bolivana

AERODINOS, Ltda   *Santa Cruz-El Trompillo*

Casilla Correo 2308, Santa Cruz de la Sierra, Bolivia   ☎ (3) 53 14 28   Tx: none   Fax: (3) 53 14 28   SITA: n/a
F: 1978   ♠♠♠ n/a   Head: Javier Marquez Ostria   Net: n/a

☐ CP-2270	PZL Mielec (Antonov) An-2R	1G192-43	N20579	0080	0495	1 SH ASh-62IR	5500			

AEROSUR = 5L (Compania Boliviana de Transporte Aéreo Privado Aerosur, S.A. dba)   *Santa Cruz-Viru Viru Internacional*

Casilla Correo 3104, Santa Cruz de la Sierra, Bolivia   ☎ (3) 36 44 46   Tx: 4209 aerosur bv   Fax: (3) 34 17 32   SITA: n/a
F: 1992   ♠♠♠ 550   Head: Frankling Teandler   IATA: 275   Net: n/a

☐ OB-1653	Yakovlev 40	9041860	OB-1606	0080	0098	3 IV AI-25	16800	Y34		lsf TEA
☐ CP-2370	Boeing 727-23	18449 / 132	N801MJ	0465	0998	3 PW JT8D-7B	72847	F10Y99		lsf Miami Jet Lease Inc.
☐ CP-2365	Boeing 727-221 (A)	22538 / 1782	N366PA	0081	0998	3 PW JT8D-17R	88360	Y170		lsf ARON

AIR BENI   *La Paz*

Lado Aeropuerto Internacional El Alto, La Paz, Bolivia   ☎ (2) 81 28 73   Tx: n/a   Fax: (2) 81 28 73   SITA: n/a
F: n/a   ♠♠♠ n/a   Head: Capt. Victor Hugo Liberia   Net: n/a

☐ CP-2290	Boeing (Douglas) DC-3C (C-47B-28-DK)	32626	TAM25	0045	0095	2 PW R-1830	11431	Freighter		
☐ CP-987	Curtiss C-46A-45-CU Commando	27079	N91365	0044		2 PW R-2800	21772	Freighter		std LPB / being restored
☐ CP-2292	Boeing (Douglas) DC-4 (C-54G-5-DO)	36004 / DO 398	TAM51	0045	1094	4 PW R-2000	33112	Freighter		rebuilt 1997
☐ CP-2291	Boeing (Douglas) DC-6B	43272 / 190	CP-740	0751	1094	4 PW R-2800	45359	Freighter		rebuilt 1997

CAMBA Transportes Aéreos (Comericalizadora Aérea Mixta Boliviana, Ltda dba)   *La Paz*

Lado Aeropuerto Internacional El Alto, La Paz, Bolivia   ☎ (2) 82 17 45   Tx: none   Fax: (2) 82 17 45   SITA: n/a
F: n/a   ♠♠♠ n/a   Head: Luis Gusman Serrir   Net: n/a

☐ CP-1319	Curtiss C-46F-1-CU Commando	22428	N600SE	0045		2 PW R-2800	21772	Freighter		

FRIGORIFICO SANTA RITA – FSR   *La Paz*

Lado Aeropuerto Internacional El Alto, La Paz, Bolivia   ☎ (2) 81 14 06   Tx: n/a   Fax: (2) 35 62 47   SITA: n/a
F: n/a   ♠♠♠ n/a   Head: n/a   Net: n/a

☐ CP-1080	Curtiss C-46A-35-CU Commando	26771	TAM61	0044		2 PW R-2800	21772	Freighter		std LPB / to be restored
☐ CP-973	Curtiss Super C-46C Commando	32941	N32227	0044		2 PW R-2800	21772	Freighter		cvtd C-46D-10-CU

FRI REYES – Frigorifico Reyes   *La Paz*

Av. Juan Pablo II No. 505, El Alto, La Paz, Bolivia   ☎ (2) 38 95 38   Tx: none   Fax: (2) 33 44 50   SITA: n/a
F: n/a   ♠♠♠ n/a   Head: Oscar Bowles S.   Net: n/a

☐ CP-1207	Boeing (Douglas) DC-4 (C-54D-10-DC)	10790 / DC 521	N62441	0045	0175	4 PW R-2000	33112	Freighter		lstSAS-Servicio Aéreo Santiago/for sale
☐ CP-1651	Boeing (Douglas) DC-6B	44433 / 516	OB-R-827	0054	0481	4 PW R-2800	45359	Freighter		for sale

HELIMAR – Servicios Petrolero Helimar, Srl.   *Santa Cruz-El Trompillo*

Casilla Correo 491, Santa Cruz de la Sierra, Bolivia   ☎ (3) 52 60 30   Tx: n/a   Fax: (3) 53 13 94   SITA: n/a
F: n/a   ♠♠♠ n/a   Head: n/a   Net: n/a

☐ CP-2047	Euroc.(Helibras/Aerosp.)HB350B Esquilo	1497 / HB1023	PT-HLN	0081		1 TU Arriel 1B	1950			
☐ CP-2093	Euroc.(Helibras/Aerosp.)HB350B Esquilo	1405 / HB1018	PT-HLJ	0081		1 TU Arriel 1B	1950			

LAB – Lloyd Aéreo Boliviano, S.A.M. = LB / LLB (LAB Airlines) (Associated with VASP, Brazil)   *Cochabamba*

Casilla Correo 132, Cochabamba, Bolivia   ☎ (42) 50 738   Tx: 6290 lb bv   Fax: (42) 50 766   SITA: CBBDDLB
F: 1925   ♠♠♠ 1530   Head: Ulisses C. Azevedo   IATA: 051   ICAO: LLOYDAEREO   Net: n/a

☐ CP-2013	Fokker F27 Friendship 200 (F27 Mk200)	10138	PH-FBF	0059	0885	2 RR Dart 536-7P	20412	Y40		Reina Beatrix
☐ CP-2313	Boeing 737-3A1	28389 / 2836		0096	1296	2 CFMI CFM56-3C1	63276	C12Y114		Paititi
☐ CP-1070	Boeing 727-171C	19860 / 599	N1728T	0068	0974	3 PW JT8D-9A	76657	C12Y99		City of Puerto Suarez
☐ CP-1223	Boeing 727-78	18795 / 104	N306BN	0065	0375	3 PW JT8D-9A	76657	C12Y99		City of Trinidad
☐ CP-861	Boeing 727-1A0	20279 / 748		0069	0270	3 PW JT8D-9A	76657	C12Y99		City of Sucre
☐ CP-1276	Boeing 727-2K3 (A)	21082 / 1124	N48054*	0075	1075	3 PW JT8D-17R	94801	C12Y134		City of Cochabamba
☐ CP-1366	Boeing 727-2K3 (A)	21494 / 1373		0078	0878	3 PW JT8D-17R	94801	C12Y134		City of La Paz
☐ CP-1367	Boeing 727-2K3 (A)	21495 / 1403		0078	1078	3 PW JT8D-17R	94801	C12Y134		City of Santa Cruz
☐ CP-2323	Boeing 727-287 (A)	22605 / 1787	N917PG	0082	0797	3 PW JT8D-17	86411	C12Y134		City of Oruro / lsf PACA
☐ CP-2324	Boeing 727-2M7 (A)	21823 / 1591	N918PG	0080	0897	3 PW JT8D-17	87997	C12Y134		lsf PACA/Virgen de Urkupina
☐ CP-1698	Boeing 707-323C	19586 / 670	N8406	0068	0681	4 PW JT3D-3B (HK2/COM)	146510	Freighter	DF-AL	Bolivia
☐ CP-2232	Airbus Industrie A310-304	562	F-GKTE	1290	1191	2 GE CF6-80C2A2	157000	C18Y191	LQ-CK	lsf ILFC
☐ CP-2307	Airbus Industrie A310-304	661	HC-BSF	0093	0996	2 GE CF6-80C2A2	157000	C18Y191		lsf ILFC/Villa de Oropeza

LINEAS AEREAS CANEDO – LAC   *Santa Cruz-El Trompillo & Cochabamba*

Aeropuerto El Trompillo, Oficina 19, Santa Cruz de la Sierra, Bolivia   ☎ (3) 54 83 00   Tx: none   Fax: (3) 54 83 00   SITA: n/a
F: 1979   ♠♠♠ 6   Head: Capt. Rolando Canedo Lopez   Net: n/a   Aircraft below MTOW 1361kg: Cessna 182.

☐ CP-744	Twin (Aero) Super Commander 680	341-34	OB-M-573	0056		2 LY GSO-480-B1A6	3175	Y6		Juan Salvador Gaviota
☐ CP-2255	Boeing (Douglas) DC-3C (C-47B-5-DK)	25951	N259DC	0044	0593	2 PW R-1830-94	11431	Y28		lst Caribbean Flights as YV-912C
☐ CP-2236	Convair 440 Metropolitan	215	YV-913C	0054	0792	2 PW R-2800-CB16	21772	F8Y24		Queen of Hearts / cvtd 340-79 (C-131D)
☐ CP-2237	Convair 440 Metropolitan	228	YV-914C	0054	0792	2 PW R-2800-CB16	21772	F20Y20		Ace of Spades / cvtd 340-67 (VC-131D)

NACIF Transportes Aéreos (formerly SASA-Servicios Aéreos Santa Ana)   *La Paz*

Casilla Correo 275, La Paz, Bolivia   ☎ (2) 81 01 27   Tx: none   Fax: (2) 81 01 27   SITA: n/a
F: 1982   ♠♠♠ n/a   Head: Elias Nacif Landivar   Net: n/a

☐ CP-2026	Convair 340 (C-131B)	249	53-7797	0055	0194	2 PW R-2800	21772	Freighter		Gianfranco

NEBA – North East Bolivian Airways, Ltda = NBA   *Cochabamba*

Casilla 1740, Cochabamba, Bolivia   ☎ (42) 29 595   Tx: n/a   Fax: (42) 29 595   SITA: n/a
F: 1970   ♠♠♠ n/a   Head: Edgar Rios Caero   ICAO: NEBA   Net: n/a

☐ CP-1616	Curtiss Super C-46C Commando	22501	N8875	0045	0980	2 PW R-2800	21772	Freighter		cvtd C-46F-1-CU
☐ CP-1040	Convair 440-86 Metropolitan	422	N9308	0057	0076	2 PW R-2800	21772	Freighter		lstearn / std CBB

SAO – Servicios Aéreos del Oriente, Ltda (formerly UNIVERSAL – Transportes Aéreos Universal, Ltda)   *La Paz*

Lado Aeropuerto Internacional El Alto, La Paz, Bolivia   ☎ (2) 81 00 81   Tx: n/a   Fax: none   SITA: n/a
F: 1977   ♠♠♠ n/a   Head: Capt. Estefan Acha   Net: n/a

☐ CP-1655	Curtiss C-46D-10-CU Commando	33294	PP-BUB	0045		2 PW R-2800	21772	Freighter		rebuilt 1992
☐ CP-746	Curtiss C-46A-5-CU Commando	26417	N91295	0043		2 PW R-2800	21772	Freighter		rebuilt 1990

SAPSA – Servicios Aéreos Petroleros, S.A. (formerly YPFB Transportes Aéreos)   *Santa Cruz-El Trompillo*

Hangar 48, Casilla 960, Aeropuerto El Trompillo, Santa Cruz de la Sierra, Bolivia   ☎ (3) 52 63 17   Tx: none   Fax: (3) 55 59 00   SITA: n/a
F: 1953   ♠♠♠ 20   Head: Lic. René Anez Hurtado   Net: n/a

☐ CP-1106	Twin (Aero) Turbo Commander 690A	11193	N9149N	0074		2 GA TPE331-5-251K	4649			
☐ CP-1019	De Havilland DHC-6 Twin Otter 300	368		0073	0673	2 PWC PT6A-27	5670			
☐ CP-2176	Dornier 228-202	8163	D-CIKI*	0088	1288	2 GA TPE331-5-252D	6200			

SAS – Servicio Aéreo Santiago, Ltda   *La Paz*

Casilla Correo 1673, La Paz, Bolivia   ☎ (2) 84 05 38   Tx: none   Fax: none   SITA: n/a
F: n/a   ♠♠♠ n/a   Head: n/a   Net: n/a

☐ CP-1207	Boeing (Douglas) DC-4 (C-54D-10-DC)	10790 / DC 521	N62441	0045	0094	4 PW R-2000	33112	Freighter		lsf Fri Reyes

SAVCO – Servicios Aéreos Virgen de Copacabana   *Cochabamba*

Casilla Correo 2604, Cochabamba, Bolivia   ☎ (42) 54 506   Tx: n/a   Fax: none   SITA: n/a
F: 1970   ♠♠♠ 8   Head: Capt. Edgar Tardio   Net: n/a

☐ CP-1128	Boeing (Douglas) DC-3-201	1998	N15M	0037		2 WR R-1830-92	11431	Freighter		

SAVE – Servicio Aéreo Vargas Espana   *Santa Cruz-El Trompillo*

Barr Aeronautico, Santa Cruz de la Sierra, Bolivia   ☎ (3) 52 12 47   Tx: none   Fax: (3) 53 38 34   SITA: n/a
F: 1974   ♠♠♠ 6   Head: Hugo Vargas Espana   Net: n/a

☐ CP-1804	Beech C99 Airliner	U-180		0082	0096	2 PWC PT6A-36	5126	Y15		
☐ CP-2350	Beech 1900C-1 Airliner	UC-12	N76013	0087	0398	2 PWC PT6A-65B	7530	Y19		

STAP - Servicios y Transportes Aéreos Petroleros, SA — Santa Cruz-El Trompillo

Casilla Correo 3730, Santa Cruz de la Sierra, Bolivia ☎ (3) 34 47 36 Tx: n/a Fax: (3) 52 32 51 SITA: n/a
F: n/a ✈✈✈ n/a Head: n/a Net: n/a

☐ CP-1758	Piper PA-31-350 Navajo Chieftain	31-7405492		0074		2 LY TIO-540-J2BD	3175			

TASA - Transportes Aéreos San Antonio, Ltda — Cochabamba

Aeropuerto Jorge Wilsterman, Rampa Este, Cochabamba, Bolivia ☎ (14) 91 565 Tx: none Fax: none SITA: n/a
F: 1984 ✈✈✈ 6 Head: Capt. Max Guzman Net: n/a

☐ CP-1940	Boeing (Douglas) DC-3A	2120	N222TS	0040		2 PW R-1830-92	11431	Freighter		

TAVIC - Transportes Aéreos Virgen de Carmen — Cochabamba

Contorejo Industrial Frigorifico, Cochabamba, Bolivia ☎ (42) 51 592 Tx: n/a Fax: (42) 22 138 SITA: n/a
F: n/a ✈✈✈ n/a Head: n/a Net: n/a

☐ CP-607	Boeing (Douglas) DC-3C (C-47A-15-DK)	12570	CP-534	0044		2 PW R-1830	11431	Freighter		

TRANSPORTE AEREO MILITAR - TAM (Division of FAB-Fuerza Aérea Boliviana) — La Paz

Avenida Montes, Edificio Fuerza Aérea Boliviana, La Paz, Bolivia ☎ (2) 37 90 66 Tx: none Fax: none SITA: n/a
F: n/a ✈✈✈ n/a Head: Jaime Iroga Net: n/a Transport-branch of FAB-Fuerza Aérea Boliviana which beside non-commercial military flights also operates non-profit, scheduled passenger/cargo flts to remote parts in Bolivia.

☐ TAM85	CASA 212 Aviocar Series 100	90	FAS221	0077		2 GA TPE331-5-251C	6500			
☐ FAB76	IAI 201 Arava	24	TAM76	0075	1075	2 PWC PT6A-36	6867			
☐ FAB90	Fokker F27 Troopship 400M (F27 Mk400M)	10578	TAM90	0078	0579	2 RR Dart 536-7P	19731			
☐ FAB91	Fokker F27 Troopship 400M (F27 Mk400M)	10580	TAM91	0078	0579	2 RR Dart 536-7P	19731			
☐ FAB92	Fokker F27 Troopship 400M (F27 Mk400M)	10584	TAM92	0079	0479	2 RR Dart 536-7P	19731			
☐ TAM93	Fokker F27 Troopship 400M (F27 Mk400M)	10599	PH-EXC	0080	0580	2 RR Dart 536-7P	19731			std LPB
☐ FAB94	Fokker F27 Troopship 400M (F27 Mk400M)	10600	CP-2282	0080	0281	2 RR Dart 536-7P	19731			
☐ TAM95	Fokker F27 Troopship 400M (F27 Mk400M)	10601	PH-FTW*	0080	0281	2 RR Dart 536-7P	19731			std LPB
☐ FAB71	Convair 580	370	TAM71	0056	1174	2 AN 501-D13H	24766			cvtd CV440-47 / std LPB
☐ FAB72	Convair 580	132	TAM72	0053	0991	2 AN 501-D13	24766			cvtd CV340-31
☐ FAB73	Convair 580	170	TAM73	0054	0991	2 AN 501-D13	24766			cvtd CV340-31
☐ TAM70	Convair 580	94	N73140	0053	0991	2 AN 501-D13	24766			cvtd CV340-31 / std LPB
☐ TAM74	Convair 580	367	N73164	0056	0991	2 AN 501-D13	24766			cvtd CV440-12 / std LPB
☐ TAM01	Lockheed L-188A Electra	1125	TAM69	0060	0575	4 AN 501-D13A	51256			std LPB
☐ TAM60	Lockheed L-282 (C-130B) Hercules	1B-3559	58-0758	0059	0093	4 AN T56-A-9D	56245			
☐ TAM61	Lockheed L-182 (C-130A) Hercules	1A-3181	57-0474	0058	0888	4 AN T56-A-9D	56245			std LPB
☐ TAM63	Lockheed L-182 (C-130A) Hercules	1A-3188	57-0481	0058	0888	4 AN T56-A-9D	56245			std LPB
☐ TAM64	Lockheed L-182 (C-130A) Hercules	1A-3023	54-1636	0057	1088	4 AN T56-A-9D	56245			std LPB
☐ TAM65	Lockheed L-182 (C-130A) Hercules	1A-3034	55-0007	0057	1088	4 AN T56-A-9D	56245			std LPB
☐ TAM66	Lockheed L-282 (C-130B) Hercules	1B-3560	59-1524	0060	0090	4 AN T56-A-9D	56245			
☐ TAM68	Lockheed L-282 (C-130B) Hercules	1B-3655	61-0968	0062	0092	4 AN T56-A-9D	56245			std LPB
☐ TAM69	Lockheed L-182 (C-130A) Hercules	2A-3228	CP-2184	0059	1088	4 AN T56-A-9D	56245			std LPB

CS = PORTUGAL (Portuguese Republic) (Republica Portuguesa)

(including territory of Macao/Macau)
Capital: Lisbon Official Language: Portuguese Population: 10,6 million Square Km: 92389 Dialling code: +351 Year established: 1143 Acting political head: Antonio Guterres (Prime Minister)

MACAO/MACAU
Capital: Macao/Macau Official Language: Portuguese, English, Chinese Population: 0,4 million Square Km: 18 Dialling code: +853

AEROMUNDO - Comércio e Industria de Aeronautica, Lda (Associated with Aeropiloto / formerly Aerodelta) — Cascais-Tires

Aérodromo Municipal de Cascais-Tires, P-2775 S. Domingos de Rana, Portugal ☎ (1) 444 36 84 Tx: none Fax: (1) 445 61 66 SITA: n/a
F: 1985 ✈✈✈ 14 Head: Justino Joaquim Cardoso Borralho Net: n/a Aircraft below MTOW 1361 kg: Cessna 172

☐ CS-AJE	Helio H-295 Super Courier	1404		0068		1 LY GO-480-G1D6	1542	5 Pax		lsf Aviometa Lda/jtly opw Aeropiloto
☐ CS-APC	Piper PA-34-200 Seneca	34-7450080	N56539	0073		2 LY IO-360-C1E6	1905	6 Pax		lsf Aviometa Lda / jtly opw Aeropiloto
☐ CS-ARL	Cessna 402B	402B0318	PJ-SAB	0072		2 CO TSIO-520-E	2858	6 Pax		opf Traço-Constroi/jtly opw Aeropiloto
☐ CS-AJD	Cessna 421B Golden Eagle	421B0270	N3395Q	0072		2 CO GTSIO-520-H	3379	6 Pax		lsf Admitur-Ad. Apart.Turisticos Lda

AERONORTE - Transportes Aereos, Lda = RTE — Braga

CP 102, Aerodromo Municipal de Palmeira, P-4700 Braga, Portugal ☎ (53) 62 69 67 Tx: none Fax: (53) 62 69 68 SITA: n/a
F: 1989 ✈✈✈ 8 Head: Cmdte. Pedro Inverno ICAO: LUZAVIA Net: n/a Aircraft/Ag-aircraft below MTOW 1361/5000kg: Ayres S-2R Trush Commander, Bell 47G & Cessna 172

☐ CS-HDO	Agusta-Bell 206B JetRanger III	8559	3A-MMM	0078	0196	1 AN 250-C20B	1451	4 Pax		
☐ G-BXUF	Agusta-Bell 206B JetRanger III	8633	EC-DUS	0081	0299	1 AN 250-C20B	1450	4 Pax		lsf SJ Contracting Services

AEROPILOTO - Soc. Expl. de Serviços Aéreos Comercio e Industria, Lda = AOP — Cascais-Tires & Faro

Hangar 5, Aérodromo Municipal de Cascais-Tires, P-2775 S. Domingos de Rana, Portugal ☎ (1) 444 22 44 Tx: 65236 p Fax: (1) 444 01 27 SITA: n/a
F: 1977 ✈✈✈ 19 Head: Justino Joaquim Cardoso Borralho ICAO: AEROPILOTO Net: n/a Aircraft / Ag-aircraft below MTOW 1361/5000 kg: Ayres S-2R Trush Commander & Cessna 172

☐ CS-AJE	Helio H-295 Super Courier	1404		0068		1 LY GO-480-G1D6	1542	5 Pax		lsf Aviometa Lda / jtly opw Aeromundo
☐ CS-DGL	Beech Bonanza P35	D-7230	N8605M	0063		1 CO IO-470-N	1417	3 Pax		lsf Aviometa Lda / based Faro
☐ CS-APC	Piper PA-34-200 Seneca	34-7450080	N56539	0073		2 LY IO-360-C1E6	1905	6 Pax		lsf Aviometa Lda / jtly opw Aeromundo
☐ CS-ARL	Cessna 402B	402B0318	PJ-SAB	0072		2 CO TSIO-520-E	2858	6 Pax / Corp.		opf Traço-Constroi/jtly opw Aeromundo

AGROAR - Trabalhos Aéreos/Carga Aérea, Lda = GRR — Evora & Lisbon

Hangar 2, Aerodromo de Evora, Apartado 385, P-7002-505 Evora, Portugal ☎ (66) 28 335 Tx: none Fax: (66) 74 20 60 SITA: n/a
F: 1992 ✈✈✈ 26 Head: Antonio Galinha Dias ICAO: AGROAR Net: n/a Ag-aircraft below MTOW 5000kg: Grumman G-164A/B

☐ CS-DBO	Britten-Norman BN-2A-20 Islander	352	LN-FSK	0073	0296	2 LY IO-540-K1B5	2994	Airtaxi/Frtr		
☐ CS-TML	Convair 440-0 (F) (SCD)	484	N357SA	0057	0597	2 PW R-2800-CB16	21772	Freighter		cvtd 440-0
☐ CS-TMM	Convair 580 (F) (SCD)	375	C-FHEN	0056	0498	2 AN 501-D13D	24766	Freighter		cvtd 440-32

AIR GLOBAL, Transportes Aéreos, S.A. (Member of Euroclub Travel Agent) — Lisbon

Rua Augusto Santos 2-2, P-1050 Lisboa, Portugal ☎ (1) 354 36 97 Tx: none Fax: (1) 354 36 97 SITA: n/a
F: 1998 ✈✈✈ n/a Head: Cmdte. Nasi Pereira Net: n/a Operates charter flights with Boeing 737-300 leased from other companies when required but intends to acquire an own 737-300 during 1999.

AIR LUXOR, Lda = LXR — Lisbon, Macau, Paris-LBG & London-Luton

Aeroporto Int'l de Lisboa, Hangar 7, P-1700 Lisboa, Portugal ☎ (1) 847 35 07 Tx: none Fax: (1) 847 13 28 SITA: n/a
F: 1988 ✈✈✈ 60 Head: Dr. Paulo Mirpuri ICAO: AIRLUXOR Net: n/a Some aircraft are opf NETJETS EUROPE Ltd, a shared-ownership (QS=Quarter-Share) joint-venture program in conjunction with Executive Jet Aviation (N).

☐ CS-DCA	Cessna 500 Citation	500-0157	N190AB	0074	0897	2 PWC JT15D-1	5375	7 Pax		
☐ CS-DCE	Cessna S550 Citation S/II	S550-0007	N30CX	0084	0498	2 PWC JT15D-4B	6849	8 Pax		based Paris-LBG
☐ CS-DNA	Cessna S550 Citation S/II	S550-0032	N232QS	0084	1096	2 PWC JT15D-4B	6849	7 Pax		lsf EJA / opf NetJets Europe
☐ CS-DNB	Cessna S550 Citation S/II	S550-0051	N251QS	0085	1096	2 PWC JT15D-4B	6849	7 Pax		lsf EJA / opf NetJets Europe
☐ CS-DNC	Cessna S550 Citation S/II	S550-0077	N277QS	0085	1096	2 PWC JT15D-4B	6849	7 Pax		lsf EJA / opf NetJets Europe
☐ CS-	Cessna 550 Citation II	550-0071	N404BF	0079	0499	2 PWC JT15D-4	6668	8 Pax		
☐ CS-DND	Cessna 650 Citation III	650-0093	N222GT	0085	0997	2 GA TFE731-3B-100S	9979	7 Pax		lsf EJA / opf NetJets Europe
☐ CS-DNF	Cessna 650 Citation VII	650-7080	N780QS	0097	0198	2 GA TFE731-4R-2S	10180	7 Pax		lsf EJA / opf NetJets Europe
☐ CS-DNG	Cessna 650 Citation VII	650-7081	N781QS	0097	0198	2 GA TFE731-4R-2S	10180	7 Pax		lsf EJA / opf NetJets Europe
☐ CS-DBY	Shorts 330-100 (SD3-30 Variant 100)	SH3030	5N-OJU	0080	0497	2 PWC PT6A-45R	10387	30 Pax / Frtr		lsf BACL
☐ CS-DNH	Hawker 800A (BAe 125-800A)	258193 / NA0457	N699EC	0091		2 GA TFE731-5R-1H	12428	8 Pax		tblsf EJA 0499/to be opf NetJets Europe
☐ CS-DNI	Hawker 800A (BAe 125-800A)	258183 / NA0451	N599EC	0090	0499	2 GA TFE731-5R-1H	12428	8 Pax		tblsf EJA 0499/to be opf NetJets Europe
☐ CS-DNJ	Hawker 800XP	258399	N899QS	0099		2 GA TFE731-5BR-1H	12701	8 Pax		tblsf EJA 0599/to be opf NetJets Europe
☐ CS-DNK	Hawker 800XP					2 GA TFE731-5BR-1H	12701	8 Pax		tblsf EJA 0999/to be opf NetJets Europe
☐ CS-DNL	Hawker 800XP					2 GA TFE731-5BR-1H	12701	8 Pax		tblsf EJA 1199/to be opf NetJets Europe
☐ CS-	Hawker 800XP					2 GA TFE731-5BR-1H	12701	8 Pax		tblsf EJA 0000/to be opf NetJets Europe
☐ CS-	Hawker 800XP					2 GA TFE731-5BR-1H	12701	8 Pax		tblsf EJA 0000/to be opf NetJets Europe
☐ CS-	Hawker 800XP					2 GA TFE731-5BR-1H	12701	8 Pax		tblsf EJA 0001/to be opf NetJets Europe
☐ CS-	Hawker 800XP					2 GA TFE731-5BR-1H	12701	8 Pax		tblsf EJA 0001/to be opf NetJets Europe
☐ CS-	Hawker 800XP					2 GA TFE731-5BR-1H	12701	8 Pax		tblsf EJA 0002/to be opf NetJets Europe
☐ CS-	Hawker 800XP					2 GA TFE731-5BR-1H	12701	8 Pax		tblsf EJA 0002/to be opf NetJets Europe
☐ CS-	Hawker 800XP					2 GA TFE731-5BR-1H	12701	8 Pax		tblsf EJA 0003/to be opf NetJets Europe
☐ CS-	Dassault Falcon 2000					2 CFE CFE738-1-1B	16238	10 Pax		tblsf EJA 0099/to be opf NetJets Europe
☐ CS-	Dassault Falcon 2000					2 CFE CFE738-1-1B	16238	10 Pax		tblsf EJA 0099/to be opf NetJets Europe
☐ CS-	Dassault Falcon 2000					2 CFE CFE738-1-1B	16238	10 Pax		tblsf EJA 0099/to be opf NetJets Europe
☐ CS-	Dassault Falcon 2000					2 CFE CFE738-1-1B	16238	10 Pax		tblsf EJA 0000/to be opf NetJets Europe
☐ CS-	Dassault Falcon 2000					2 CFE CFE738-1-1B	16238	10 Pax		tblsf EJA 0000/to be opf NetJets Europe
☐ CS-	Dassault Falcon 2000					2 CFE CFE738-1-1B	16238	10 Pax		tblsf EJA 0000/to be opf NetJets Europe
☐ CS-	Dassault Falcon 2000					2 CFE CFE738-1-1B	16238	10 Pax		tblsf EJA 0001/to be opf NetJets Europe
☐ CS-	Dassault Falcon 2000					2 CFE CFE738-1-1B	16238	10 Pax		tblsf EJA 0001/to be opf NetJets Europe
☐ CS-	Dassault Falcon 2000					2 CFE CFE738-1-1B	16238	10 Pax		tblsf EJA 0001/to be opf NetJets Europe
☐ CS-	Dassault Falcon 2000					2 CFE CFE738-1-1B	16238	10 Pax		tblsf EJA 0002/to be opf NetJets Europe
☐ CS-	Dassault Falcon 2000					2 CFE CFE738-1-1B	16238	10 Pax		tblsf EJA 0002/to be opf NetJets Europe
☐ CS-	Dassault Falcon 2000					2 CFE CFE738-1-1B	16238	10 Pax		tblsf EJA 0002/to be opf NetJets Europe
☐ CS-TEB	Lockheed L-1011-385-3 TriStar 500	293B-1240	V2-LEO	0083	0697	3 RR RB211-524B4-02	231000	Y271		lsf / opf Air Madeira

92 registration type of aircraft cn/fn ex/ex* mfd del powered by mtow kg configuration selcal name/fln/specialitites/remarks

AIR MACAU, Co. Ltd = NX / AMU (Associated with MASC Macau Aviation Services Co. & SEAP Serviços, Administraçao e Participaçoes) — **Macau-Int'l**

PO Box 1910, Macau, Macau ☎ 396 68 88 Tx: n/a Fax: 396 68 66 SITA: n/a
F: 1994 ⁂ 270 Head: Dr. Lionel Miranda IATA: 675 ICAO: AIR MACAU Net: http://www.unitel.net/airmacau

☐ CS-MAD	Airbus Industrie A320-232	573	F-WWDJ*	0096	0296	2 IAE V2527-A5	73500	C12Y138		Algarve / lsf ILFC/sublst TRZ as N573DC
☐ CS-MAE	Airbus Industrie A320-232	582	F-WWDX*	0096	0496	2 IAE V2527-A5	73500	C12Y138	KQ-DJ	Cidade de Coimbra / lsf ILFC
☐ CS-MAH	Airbus Industrie A320-232	805	F-WWID*	0098	0498	2 IAE V2527-A5	73500	C12Y138	JP-CF	Ilha de Madeira / lsf ILFC/sub-lst TAP
☐ CS-MAA	Airbus Industrie A321-131	550	D-AVZG*	0095	1195	2 IAE V2530-A5	85000	C16Y162	KQ-BS	Cidade de Macau / lsf ILFC
☐ CS-MAB	Airbus Industrie A321-131	557	D-AVZJ*	0095	1295	2 IAE V2530-A5	85000	C16Y162	KQ-CR	Ilha da Taipa / lsf ILFC
☐ CS-MAF	Airbus Industrie A321-131	620	D-AVZE*	0097	0297	2 IAE V2530-A5	85000	C16Y162	CF-JS	lsf ILFC
☐ CS-MAG	Airbus Industrie A321-131	631	D-AVZF*	0097	0497	2 IAE V2530-A5	85000	C16Y162	CF-KR	Ilha de Coloane / lsf ILFC
☐ CS-MAJ	Airbus Industrie A321-231	908	F-WWDT*	0098	0299	2 IAE V2533-A5	89000	C16Y162		

AIR MADEIRA, S.A. = MM — **Lisbon**

Hotel Atlantic Gardens, Guia, P-2750 Cascais, Portugal ☎ (1) 483 24 03 Tx: none Fax: (1) 483 51 37 SITA: n/a
F: 1993 ⁂ 120 Head: Tomaz Metello Net: n/a

☐ CS-TEB	Lockheed L-1011-385-3 TriStar 500	293B-1240	V2-LEO	0083	0697	3 RR RB211-524B4-02	231000	Y271		Naughton Simao / lst / opb LXR

AIRVIP – Companhia de Transportes e Serviços Aéreos, Lda = RVP (Associated with Airvip, Jersey & Sao Paulo) — **Portimao & Cascais-Tires**

Aerodromo Municipal de Portimao, Hangar 3, Montes de Alvor, P-8500-059 Alvor, Portugal ☎ (82) 49 59 26 Tx: none Fax: (82) 49 59 51 SITA: n/a
F: 1990 ⁂ 8 Head: Cmdt Joao Pedro Calhamar ICAO: AEROVIP Net: http://www.airvip.com Aircraft below MTOW 1361kg: Cessna 152, 172 & MS.893 Rallye

☐ CS-AUO	Cessna A185F Skywagon	18502324	N53028	0074		1 CO IO-520-D	1520	5 Pax		
☐ CS-AYQ	Partenavia P.68B	204	G-BNXN	0079	0097	2 LY IO-360-A1B6	1960	5 Pax		for sale

ATA-AEROCONDOR – Transportes Aéreos, Lda = 2B / ARD (Subsidiary of Aerocondor, Lda & Escola de Aviacao Aerocondor, Lda) — **Cascais-Tires, Funchal, Lisbon & Seia**

Aerodromo Municipal de Cascais-Tires, P-2775 S. Domingos de Rana, Portugal ☎ (1) 444 26 68 Tx: 15288 eaa p Fax: (1) 444 44 44 SITA: LISOW2B
F: 1984 ⁂ 74 Head: Victor Joao Lopes de Brito IATA: 088 ICAO: AEROCONDOR Net: http://www.aerocondor.com Aircraft below MTOW 1361 kg: Cessna 152, 172, Hughes 269C (300C), Mooney M20J/252SE, Piper PA-18 & PA-25.

☐ CS-AVL	Beech Duchess 76	ME-332	N6718D	0080		2 LY O-360-A1G6D	1769	Y3 / Trainer		
☐ CS-ART	Beech Baron 58	TH-461	D-IFBF	0074		2 CO IO-520-C	2449	Y5 / Photo		dmgd 0098/being repaired Cascais-Tires
☐ CS-AHW	Cessna 414	414-0280	N1565T	0072		2 CO TSIO-520-J	2880	Y5 / Photo		occ lst Imaer Portugal
☐ CS-DCF	Piper PA-31-350 Navajo Chieftain	31-8052174	PH-ECO	0080	0897	2 LY TIO-540-J2BD	3342	Y10 / Freighter		
☐ CS-AYT	Dornier 228-200	8084	VP-FBK	0086	0692	2 GA TPE331-5-252D	5700	Y19 / Freighter		lsf Euroleasing
☐ CS-TGG	Dornier 228-202K	8160	D-CORA*	0088	0095	2 GA TPE331-5-252D	6200	Y19 / Freighter		lsf Erskine Investiments Ltd
☐ CS-TMH	Shorts 360-200 (SD3-60 Variant 100)	SH3694	G-BMNJ	0086	0995	2 PWC PT6A-65AR	11999	Y36		lsf Lynrise Air Lease
☐ CS-TMN	Shorts 360-100 (SD3-60 Variant 100)	SH3638	G-ISLE	0084	1298	2 PWC PT6A-65R	11999	Y36 / Freighter		
☐ CC-CCS	Consolidated PBY-6A Catalina	2043	CC-CNF	0046	0598	2 PW R-1830-92	15000	Tanker		34 / lsf ASPAR / rebuilt 1988
☐ CC-CDT	Consolidated 28-5ACF Catalina	CV-332	F-YCHB	0045	0598	2 PW R-1830-92	15000	Tanker		32 / lsf ASPAR
☐ CC-CNP	Consolidated PBY-6A Catalina	2029	EC-FXN	0046	0598	2 PW R-1830-92	15000	Tanker		35 / lsf ASPAR

EAST ASIA AIRLINES, Ltd (Linhas Aéreas Asia Oriental, Lda dba/Assoc.with STDM,Macau/Chiyoda Trading, Tokyo & Japan Royal Airlines,Tokyo) — **Macau Heliport & Hong Kong Heliport**

Macau Maritime Terminal, Avenida de Amizade, Macau, Macau ☎ 72 59 39 Tx: none Fax: 72 59 42 SITA: n/a
F: 1990 ⁂ 130 Head: Andrew Tse Net: n/a

☐ CS-MHF	Sikorsky S-76C+	760474		0097	1097	2 TU Arriel 2S1	5307	12 Pax		
☐ CS-MHG	Sikorsky S-76C+	760475		0097	1097	2 TU Arriel 2S1	5307	12 Pax		
☐ CS-MHH	Sikorsky S-76C+	760476		0097	1097	2 TU Arriel 2S1	5307	12 Pax		

ERFOTO – Fotografia Aérea, Lda — **Cascais-Tires**

Praceta do Abraao 4B e 5B, P-2745-233 Queluz, Portugal ☎ (1) 430 05 79 Tx: none Fax: (1) 430 05 80 SITA: n/a
F: 1994 ⁂ 5 Head: Dr. Cal Ferreira ICAO: ERFOTO Net: n/a

☐ CS-AUW	Cessna T210L Turbo Centurion II	21060642	N1606X	0075	0094	1 CO TSIO-520-RCH	1723	Photo / Survey		

EUROHELI – Transportes Aéreos, Lda — **Cascais-Tires**

Av. Eng. Duarte Pacheco, Torre 2-17°, Amorelras, P-1070 Lisboa, Portugal ☎ (1) 387 10 10 Tx: none Fax: (1) 387 59 05 SITA: n/a
F: 1995 ⁂ 4 Head: Dr. Joao P. Guimaraes Net: n/a

☐ CS-HDJ	Eurocopter (Aerosp.) AS355F1 Ecureuil 2	5092	I-ELDI	0081	0695	2 AN 250-C20F	2400	6 Pax		for sale
☐ CS-	Agusta A109C					2 AN 250-C20R/1	2720	4 Pax		oo-delivery 0099

FAP – Força Aérea Portuguesa, Transport Fleet = AFP (Portuguese Air Force) — **Lisbon/Lajes-Azores/Montijo/Sintra**

Av. Leite Vasconcelos-Alfragide, P-2720 Amadora, Portugal ☎ (1) 472 35 00 Tx: none Fax: (1) 471 87 83 SITA: n/a
F: 1952 ⁂ n/a Head: n/a ICAO: PORTUGUESE AIR FORCE Net: n/a VIP, SAR, Photo Survey, Liaison & Fisheries Patrol-Transport Fleet branch (Esq.401/502/504/711) of the Air Force,a military organisation which beside military duties also conducting non-commercial VIP, Photo Survey, Liaison & Fisheries Patrol flights for the Government & other agencies. Lockheed Hercules opb TAM-Transp. Aéreos Militares (Esq.501) – see under TAM.

☐ 13701	Reims/Cessna FTB337G Super Skymaster	FTB3370002	CS-AAY	0075	0075	2 CO TSIO-360-D	2100	Liaison		Esquadra 505, Sintra
☐ 13704	Reims/Cessna FTB337G Super Skymaster	FTB3370005	CS-AKQ	0075	0075	2 CO TSIO-360-D	2100	Liaison		Esquadra 505, Sintra
☐ 13705	Reims/Cessna FTB337G Super Skymaster	FTB3370006	CS-ALL	0075	0075	2 CO TSIO-360-D	2100	Liaison		Esquadra 505, Sintra
☐ 13706	Reims/Cessna FTB337G Super Skymaster	FTB3370007	CS-ANX	0075	0075	2 CO TSIO-360-D	2100	Liaison		Esquadra 505, Sintra
☐ 13709	Reims/Cessna FTB337G Super Skymaster	FTB3370010	CS-ANZ	0075	0075	2 CO TSIO-360-D	2100	Liaison		Esquadra 505, Sintra
☐ 13710	Reims/Cessna FTB337G Super Skymaster	FTB3370011	CS-APK	0075	0075	2 CO TSIO-360-D	2100	Liaison		Esquadra 505, Sintra
☐ 13711	Reims/Cessna FTB337G Super Skymaster	FTB3370012	CS-APL	0075	0075	2 CO TSIO-360-D	2100	Liaison		Esquadra 505, Sintra
☐ 13713	Reims/Cessna FTB337G Super Skymaster	FTB3370014	CS-AAC	0075	0075	2 CO TSIO-360-D	2100	Liaison		Esquadra 505, Sintra
☐ 13715	Reims/Cessna FTB337G Super Skymaster	FTB3370016	CS-AAN	0075	0075	2 CO TSIO-360-D	2100	Liaison		Esquadra 505, Sintra
☐ 13729	Reims/Cessna FTB337G Super Skymaster	FTB3370030	CS-ABN	0075	0075	2 CO TSIO-360-D	2100	Liaison		Esquadra 505, Sintra
☐ 13730	Reims/Cessna FTB337G Super Skymaster	FTB3370031	CS-ABP	0075	0075	2 CO TSIO-360-D	2100	Liaison		Esquadra 505, Sintra
☐ 13732	Reims/Cessna FTB337G Super Skymaster	FTB3370033	CS-ABS	0075	0075	2 CO TSIO-360-D	2100	Liaison		Esquadra 505, Sintra
☐ 16501	CASA EC-212-A1 Galaktron Srs 100	13	6501	0074	1074	2 GA TPE331-5-251C	6300	ECM/miltrans/VIP		Esquadra 502,Sintra/cvtd 212-A1 Aviocar
☐ 16502	CASA EC-212-A1 Galaktron Srs 100	14	6502	0074	1074	2 GA TPE331-5-251C	6300	ECM/miltrans/VIP		Esquadra 502,Sintra/cvtd 212-A1 Aviocar
☐ 16503	CASA 212-A1 Aviocar Srs 100	17	6503	0074	1174	2 GA TPE331-5-251C	6300	NavTrainer/miltr		Esquadra 502, Sintra
☐ 16504	CASA 212-A1 Aviocar Srs 100	18	6504	0074	0175	2 GA TPE331-5-251C	6300	miltrans / VIP		Esquadra 502, Sintra
☐ 16505	CASA 212-A2 Aviocar Srs 100	25	6505	0075	0475	2 GA TPE331-5-251C	6300	miltrans / VIP		Esquadra 502, Sintra
☐ 16506	CASA 212-A2 Aviocar Srs 100	26	6506	0075	0575	2 GA TPE331-5-251C	6300	miltrans / VIP		Esquadra 502, Sintra
☐ 16507	CASA 212-A2 Aviocar Srs 100	28	6507	0075	0675	2 GA TPE331-5-251C	6300	miltrans / VIP		Esquadra 502, Sintra
☐ 16508	CASA 212-A2 Aviocar Srs 100	29	6508	0075	0675	2 GA TPE331-5-251C	6300	miltrans / VIP		Esquadra 502, Sintra
☐ 16509	CASA 212-A2 Aviocar Srs 100	32	6509	0075	0775	2 GA TPE331-5-251C	6300	miltrans / VIP		Esquadra 502, Sintra
☐ 16510	CASA 212-A2 Aviocar Srs 100	33	6510	0075	0675	2 GA TPE331-5-251C	6300	Photo Surveyer		Esquadra 401, Sintra
☐ 16511	CASA 212-A2 Aviocar Srs 100	35	6511	0075	1075	2 GA TPE331-5-251C	6300	miltrans / VIP		Esquadra 502, Sintra
☐ 16512	CASA 212-A2 Aviocar Srs 100	36	6512	0075	1075	2 GA TPE331-5-251C	6300	Fisheries Patrol		Esquadra 401, Sintra
☐ 16513	CASA 212-A2 Aviocar Srs 100	37	6513	0075	1175	2 GA TPE331-5-251C	6300	miltrans / VIP		Esquadra 711, Lajes-Azores
☐ 16514	CASA 212-A2 Aviocar Srs 100	38	6514	0075	1175	2 GA TPE331-5-251C	6300	miltrans / VIP		Esquadra 711, Lajes-Azores
☐ 16515	CASA 212-A2 Aviocar Srs 100	41	6515	0075	0176	2 GA TPE331-5-251C	6300	miltrans / VIP		Esquadra 711, Lajes-Azores
☐ 16517	CASA 212-A2 Aviocar Srs 100	49	6517	0076	0376	2 GA TPE331-5-251C	6300	miltrans / VIP		Esquadra 711, Lajes-Azores
☐ 16519	CASA 212-A2 Aviocar Srs 100	53	6519	0076	0276	2 GA TPE331-5-251C	6300	Photo Surveyer		Esquadra 401, Sintra
☐ 16520	CASA 212-A2 Aviocar Srs 100	54	6520	0076	0476	2 GA TPE331-5-251C	6300	miltrans / VIP		Esquadra 711, Lajes-Azores
☐ 16521	CASA 212-B2 Aviocar Srs 100	56	6521	0076	0776	2 GA TPE331-5-251C	6300	miltrans / VIP		Esquadra 502, Sintra
☐ 16522	CASA 212-B2 Aviocar Srs 100	57	6522	0076	0776	2 GA TPE331-5-251C	6300	Photo Surveyer		Esquadra 401, Sintra
☐ 16523	CASA 212-B2 Aviocar Srs 100	61	6523	0076	0776	2 GA TPE331-5-251C	6300	Photo Surveyer		Esquadra 401, Sintra
☐ 16524	CASA 212-B2 Aviocar Srs 100	62	6524	0076	1076	2 GA TPE331-5-251C	6300	Photo Surveyer		Esquadra 401, Sintra / Mad-tail boom
☐ 17201	CASA 212M Aviocar Srs 300 (Patrullero)	459		0095	0095	2 GA TPE331-10R-512/3C	8100	Fisheries Patrol		Esquadra 401, Sintra
☐ 17202	CASA 212M Aviocar Srs 300 (Patrullero)	460		0095	0095	2 GA TPE331-10R-512/3C	8100	Fisheries Patrol		Esquadra 401, Sintra
☐ 19502	Eurocopter (Aerosp.) SA330S-1 Puma	1002	9502	0069	0469	2 TU Makila 101	7400	milt/SAR/EMS/VIP		Esquadra 751, Montijo / cvtd SA330J
☐ 19503	Eurocopter (Aerosp.) SA330S-1 Puma	1009	9503	0069	0869	2 TU Makila 101	7400	milt/SAR/EMS/VIP		Esquadra 751, Montijo / cvtd SA330J
☐ 19504	Eurocopter (Aerosp.) SA330S-1 Puma	1004	9504	0069	1069	2 TU Makila 101	7400	milt/SAR/EMS/VIP		Esquadra 751, Montijo / cvtd SA330J
☐ 19505	Eurocopter (Aerosp.) SA330S-1 Puma	1011	9505	0069	1069	2 TU Makila 101	7400	milt/SAR/EMS/VIP		Esquadra 751, Montijo / cvtd SA330J
☐ 19506	Eurocopter (Aerosp.) SA330S-1 Puma	1019	9506	0069	1169	2 TU Makila 101	7400	milt/SAR/EMS/VIP		Esquadra 711, Lajes-Azores/cvtd SA330J
☐ 19508	Eurocopter (Aerosp.) SA330S-1 Puma	1040	9508	0070	0470	2 TU Makila 101	7400	milt/SAR/EMS/VIP		Esquadra 711, Lajes-Azores/cvtd SA330J
☐ 19509	Eurocopter (Aerosp.) SA330S-1 Puma	1046	9509	0070	0570	2 TU Makila 101	7400	milt/SAR/EMS/VIP		Esquadra 751, Montijo / cvtd SA330J
☐ 19511	Eurocopter (Aerosp.) SA330S-1 Puma	1059	9511	0070	1070	2 TU Makila 101	7400	milt/SAR/EMS/VIP		Esquadra 711, Lajes-Azores/cvtd SA330J
☐ 19512	Eurocopter (Aerosp.) SA330S-1 Puma	1065	9512	0070	1070	2 TU Makila 101	7400	milt/SAR/EMS/VIP		Esquadra 751, Montijo / cvtd SA330J
☐ 19513	Eurocopter (Aerosp.) SA330S-1 Puma	1270	9513	0071	0071	2 TU Makila 101	7400	milt/SAR/EMS/VIP		Esquadra 711, Lajes-Azores/cvtd SA330J
☐ 17103	Dassault Falcon 20D (C)	217	8103	0069	0385	2 GE CF700-2D	13000	VIP/Calibrator		Esquadra 504, Lisbon / cvtd 20D
☐ 17401	Dassault Falcon 50	195	7401	0089	0090	3 GA TFE731-3-1C	18500	VIP		Esquadra 504, Lisbon
☐ 17402	Dassault Falcon 50	198	7402	0089	0090	3 GA TFE731-3-1C	18500	VIP		Esquadra 504, Lisbon
☐ 17403	Dassault Falcon 50	221	7403	0091	0091	3 GA TFE731-3-1C	18500	VIP		Esquadra 504, Lisbon

FERMENA – Importaçoes, Exportaçoes, Representaçoes, Lda — **Cascais-Tires / Porto**

Parque Oceano, Lote 10 R/C, Loja, Santo Amaro de Oeiras, P-2780 Oeiras, Portugal ☎ (1) 441 86 92 Tx: none Fax: (1) 441 86 92 SITA: n/a
F: 1995 ⁂ n/a Head: Cmdte. Fernado Pestana Net: n/a

☐ CS-DCB	Cessna 421B Golden Eagle	421B0548	G-OLDE	0074	1297	2 CO GTSIO-520-H	3379	5 Pax / Frtr		opf pvt

93 registration type of aircraft cn/fn ex/ex* mfd del powered by mtow kg configuration selcal name/fln/specialitites/remarks

HELIATLANTIS – Turismo em Helicopteros, Lda

Funchal

Entrada da Pontinha, Cais de Contentores, P-9000 Funchal, (Madeira), Portugal ☎ (91) 23 28 82 Tx: none Fax: (91) 23 28 04 SITA: n/a
F: 1993 👥 4 Head: Dr. Sergio Marques Net: n/a

☐ CS-HCY	Eurocopter (Aerosp.) AS350B Ecureuil	1730	G-DSAM	0083	0893	1 TU Arriel 1B	1950	5 Pax		lsf Madtrans-Planeamento & Gestao Lda

HELIAVIA – Transporte Aéreo, Lda = HEA

Lisbon

Rua Nova de S. Mamede 28, P-1250 Lisboa, Portugal ☎ (1) 847 47 16 Tx: none Fax: (1) 847 50 42 SITA: LISKOXH
F: 1972 👥 12 Head: Hipolito Pires ICAO: HELIAVIA Net: n/a

☐ CS-HCP	Eurocopter (Aerosp.) AS350BA Ecureuil	2551	F-WYMX*	0091	0693	1 TU Arriel 1B	2100	5 Pax		Marta
☐ CS-ATG	Dassault Falcon 20F	264	F-GJJS	0071	0493	2 GE CF700-2D2	13000	9 Pax		Bezas
☐ CS-TMJ	Dassault Falcon 50	190	I-CAFE	0089	0696	2 GA TFE731-3-1C	18500	10 Pax		

HELIBRAVO Aviaçao, Lda = HIB

Cascais-Tires

Rua de S. Paulo No. 12-2., P-1200 Lisboa, Portugal ☎ (1) 445 11 45 Tx: none Fax: (1) 445 11 45 SITA: n/a
F: 1990 👥 6 Head: Joao Maria Bravo ICAO: HELIBRAVO Net: n/a Aircraft below MTOW 1361kg: Robinson R22 & R44

☐ CS-HED	Eurocopter (Aerosp.) AS350B2 Ecureuil	2669	D-HJOE	0092	0097	1 TU Arriel 1D1	2250	5 Pax		

HELIPORTUGAL – Trabalhos e Transporte Aéreo, Rep., Imp. e Exp., Lda = HPL

Cascais-Tires / Famalicao

Hangar No. 3, Aeródromo Municipal de Cascais-Tires, P-2785-632 S. Domingos de Rana, Portugal ☎ (1) 445 15 75 Tx: none Fax: (1) 444 80 67 SITA: n/a
F: 1982 👥 24 Head: Dr. Pedro Silveira ICAO: HELIPORTUGAL Net: n/a Aircraft below MTOW 1361kg: Robinson R44

☐ CS-HAX	MD Helicopters MD 500D (Hughes 369D)	1129D	D-HJUX	0081	0682	1 AN 250-C20B	1361	4 Pax		
☐ CS-HBL	MD Helicopters MD 500E (Hughes 369E)	0377E		0089	0590	1 AN 250-C20B	1361	4 Pax		
☐ CS-HBN	MD Helicopters MD 500E (Hughes 369E)	0333E	N500AH	0089	0690	1 AN 250-C20B	1361	4 Pax		
☐ CS-HCE	MD Helicopters MD 500D (Hughes 369D)	1200856D	G-JIMI	0080	0392	1 AN 250-C20B	1361	4 Pax		damaged/being repaired at Cascais-Tires
☐ CS-HDK	Eurocopter (Aerosp.) AS350BA Ecureuil	1871	D-HHFZ	0085	1298	1 TU Arriel 1B	2100	6 Pax		cvtd AS350B
☐ CS-HEL	Eurocopter (Aerosp.) AS350B2 Ecureuil	2594	D-HEPB	0091	0798	1 TU Arriel 1D1	2250	6 Pax		
☐ F-GKAS	Eurocopter (Aerosp.) AS350B1 Ecureuil	2224		0089	0596	1 TU Arriel 1D	2200	6 Pax		lsf SHP

HELISUL – Sociedade de meios aéreos, Lda = HSU

Cascais-Tires & Lisbon

Hangar 5, Aerodromo Municipal de Cascais-Tires, P-2785-632 S. Domingos de Rana, Portugal ☎ (1) 445 38 40 Tx: none Fax: (1) 445 38 42 SITA: n/a
F: 1996 👥 12 Head: Luis Tavares ICAO: HELIS Net: n/a

☐ CS-HCL	Bell 206B JetRanger III	2587	N5014L	0079	0095	1 AN 250-C20B	1451	4 Pax		
☐ CS-HDV	Agusta-Bell 206B JetRanger III	8591	G-BWZB	0080	0997	1 AN 250-C20B	1451	4 Pax		
☐ CS-HEC	Eurocopter (Aerosp.) AS350BA Ecureuil	2245	EC-FGD	0089	0198	1 TU Arriel 1B	2100	5 Pax		cvtd AS350B
☐ N67SH	Agusta A109C	7622		0090	1298	2 AN 250-C20R/1	2720	4 Pax		lsf Sloane Helicopters Inc. / opf pvt
☐ CS-HEJ	Bell 212	30684	EC-GHO	0075	0998	2 PWC PT6T-3 TwinPac	5080	14 Pax		lsf HSE / opf Fire Fighting Nat. Corps
☐ CS-AYY	Cessna 501 Citation I/SP	501-0183 / 567	ZS-KPA	0080	0198	2 PWC JT15D-1A	5375	7 Pax / Frtr		
☐ CS-DBM	Cessna 500 Citation	500-0200	N96EA	0074	1298	2 PWC JT15D-1	5216	7 Pax		lsf / opf Tiner-Const. e Obras

HTA Helicopteros – Actividade e Serviço Aéreo, Lda = AHT

Morgado de Apra-Loulé

Casa da Lagoa, Estrada Vale do Lobo 890A, P-8135 Almancil, Portugal ☎ (936) 45 00 32 Tx: none Fax: (89) 39 86 57 SITA: n/a
F: 1996 👥 3 Head: Cmdte. Miguel Barros ICAO: HELIAPRA Net: n/a

☐ CS-HEK	Bell 206B JetRanger III	2914	N628OJ	0080	1298	1 AN 250-C20B	1451	4 Pax		
☐ CS-HEE	Eurocopter (Aerosp.) AS355F1 Ecureuil 2	5006		0081	0098	2 AN 250-C20F	2400	5 Pax		

IMAER PORTUGAL – Técnicas de Fotografia e Detecçao Remota, Lda (Subsidiary of ATA-Aerocondor)

Cascais-Tires

Rua Dr. Carlos Torre d'Assunçao, Lote 3, Lojas B/C, P-2725 Mem Martins, Portugal ☎ (1) 920 71 75 Tx: none Fax: (1) 920 27 85 SITA: n/a
F: 1990 👥 7 Head: Tcor. Silva e Castro Net: n/a

☐ CS-AHW	Cessna 414	414-0280	N1565T	0072	0097	2 CO TSIO-520-J	2880	Photo		occ lsf ARD

INTER CHARTERS, Ltda (Member of Grupo ASAS)

Lisbon

Avenida Fontes Pereira de Melo 35, P-1000 Lisboa, Portugal ☎ (1) 352 66 30 Tx: none Fax: (1) 352 88 76 SITA: n/a
F: 1993 👥 23 Head: José Antonio André Viegas Net: n/a Presently being set-up. Intends to start charter operations in April 2000 with Airbus Industrie A320 or Boeing 737-300 aircraft.

JET ASIA, Ltd

Macau

1st Floor, 747-Hangar, PO Box 28, International Airport, Macau, Macau ☎ 86 11 16 Tx: none Fax: 86 11 21 SITA: n/a
F: 1998 👥 n/a Head: Américo Silva Net: n/a

☐ CS-	Hawker 800XP					2 GA TFE731-5BR-1H	12701	Executive		oo-delivery 0099
☐ CS-MAC	Canadair CL-601-3R (CL-600-2B16) Challen.	5178	C-FWGE*	0095	1098	2 GE CF34-3A1	20457	Executive		lsf STDM-Soc.Turismo/Diversoes de Macau

LEAVIA – Escola de Aviaçao, S.A. (formerly Vega, S.A. / Subsidiary of Grupo Auto-Leauto)

Cascais-Tires

Aérodromo Municipal de Cascais-Tires, P-2775 S. Domingos de Rana, Portugal ☎ (1) 444 37 29 Tx: none Fax: (1) 445 07 35 SITA: n/a
F: 1993 👥 n/a Head: T Cdr. Bernardo Lima de Oliveira Net: n/a Aircraft below MTOW 1361kg: Cessna 150, 152, 172 & Socata TB9 Tampico

☐ CS-AGW	Piper PA-23-250 Aztec E	27-4665	N14054	0071	0098	2 LY TIO-540-C1A	2359	E5 / Trainer		
☐ CS-ARD	Piper PA-31-325 Navajo C/R	31-7912102	N35379	0079	0095	2 LY TIO-540-F2BD	2948	E7 / Trainer		

MARINHA – Portuguese Navy/Helicopter Air Element = PON

Montijo & Frigates

Esquadrilha de Helicopteros da Marinha, Base Aérea No. 6, P-2870 Montijo, Portugal ☎ (1) 231 10 23 Tx: none Fax: (1) 231 10 23 SITA: n/a
F: 1917 👥 n/a Head: Cap. Frag. Montenegro ICAO: PORTUGUESE NAVY Net: n/a Helicopter Air Element of the Marinha/Portuguese Navy which beside military activities also conducting non-commercial EMS & SAR/EMS duties.

☐ 19202	Westland WG.13 Super Lynx Mk. 95	338	ZH581	0091	0893	2 RR Gem 42-1	5126	SAR / ASW		Esquadrilha de Helicopteros da Marinha
☐ 19203	Westland WG.13 Super Lynx Mk. 95	363	ZH582	0093	1193	2 RR Gem 42-1	5126	SAR / ASW		Esquadrilha de Helicopteros da Marinha
☐ 19204	Westland WG.13 Super Lynx Mk. 95	376	ZH583	0093	1193	2 RR Gem 42-1	5126	SAR / ASW		Esquadrilha de Helicopteros da Marinha
☐ 19205	Westland WG.13 Super Lynx Mk. 95	377	ZH584	0093	1193	2 RR Gem 42-1	5126	SAR / ASW		Esquadrilha de Helicopteros da Marinha

NORVOO – Aviaçao e Serviços, Lda

Maia-Vilar de Luz / Braga

Rua Wenceslau de Morais 61, Sra. Hora, P-4460 Senhora da Hora-Matosinhos, Portugal ☎ (2) 951 67 94 Tx: none Fax: (2) 951 67 94 SITA: n/a
F: 1995 👥 1 Head: Cmdte. Antonio Augusto Aguiar Net: n/a

☐ CS-AKJ	Cessna P206 Super Skylane	P206-0183	N2683X	0065	0096	1 CO IO-520-A	1633	5 Pax/Photo/Para		

OMNI – Aviaçao & Tecnologia, Lda = OAV

Cascais-Tires / Espinho / Santa Comba Dao

Hangar 1, Aerodromo Municipal de Cascais-Tires, P-2775 S. Domingos de Rana, Portugal ☎ (1) 445 86 00 Tx: none Fax: (1) 445 86 86 SITA: n/a
F: 1988 👥 45 Head: Cmte. José Miguel Costa ICAO: OMNI Net: n/a Aircraft / Ag-aircraft below MTOW 1361 / 5000kg: Bell 47G, Cessna 152/172 & Piper PA-36

☐ CS-HCA	Bell 206B JetRanger III	2287	ZS-HHD	0077	0691	1 AN 250-C20B	1451	4 Pax		
☐ CS-HCO	Agusta-Bell 206B JetRanger III	8678	I-BDPL	0085	1195	1 AN 250-C20B	1451	4 Pax		
☐ CS-HDS	Bell 222	47028	G-META	0079	1296	2 LY LTS101-650C.3	3561	9 Pax / EMS		
☐ CS-HDT	Bell 222	47050	G-METC	0081	1296	2 LY LTS101-650C.3	3561	9 Pax / EMS		Rescue 1 / opf Fire-Fighting Nat.Corps
☐ CS-HDU	Bell 222	47055	G-METB	0081	1296	2 LY LTS101-650C.3	3561	9 Pax / EMS		
☐ CS-HDX	Bell 222	47071	N307CK	0081	0697	2 LY LTS101-650C.3	3561	9 Pax / EMS		
☐ CS-HCC	Bell 205A-1	30013	F-GINO	0068	0595	1 LY T5313B	4309	14 Pax		
☐ CS-HDH	Bell 205A-1	30121	N25AL	0073	0696	1 LY T5313B	4309	14 Pax		
☐ CS-HDZ	Bell 205A-1	30293	C-FFHX	0079	0198	1 LY T5317A	4309	14 Pax		opf Fire-Fighting National Corps
☐ CS-HEA	Bell 205A-1	30091	C-GFHQ	0070	0198	1 LY T5313B	4309	14 Pax		opf Fire-Fighting National Corps
☐ CS-HEB	Bell 205A-1	30100	C-GFHU	0070	0198	1 LY T5313B	4309	14 Pax		opf Fire-Fighting National Corps
☐ CS-ASG	Twin (Aero) Turbo Commander 690B	11452	N115SB	0077	1195	2 GA TPE331-5-252K	4683	9 Pax / EMS		
☐ CS-HDY	Bell 212	30591	N72383	0073	0797	2 PWC PT6T-3B TwinPac	5080	14 Pax / EMS		Rescue 2 / opf Fire-Fighting Nat.Corps

PGA PORTUGALIA AIRLINES = NI / PGA (Companhia Portuguesa de Transportes Aéreos, S.A. dba)

Lisbon

Aeroporto de Lisboa, Rua C, Edificio 70, P-1700 Lisboa, Portugal ☎ (1) 842 55 00 Tx: 65139 unit p Fax: (1) 842 56 25 SITA: n/a
F: 1989 👥 750 Head: Joao Ribeiro da Fonseca IATA: 685 ICAO: PORTUGALIA Net: http://www.pga.pt

☐ CS-TPG	Embraer RJ145EP (EMB-145EP)	145014	PT-SYK*	0097	0597	2 AN AE3007A	20990	Y50	AC-RS	Melro
☐ CS-TPH	Embraer RJ145EP (EMB-145EP)	145017	PT-SYN*	0097	0697	2 AN AE3007A	20990	Y50	JM-KP	Pardal
☐ CS-TPI	Embraer RJ145EP (EMB-145EP)	145031		0097	1197	2 AN AE3007A	20990	Y50	AL-DP	Cuco
☐ CS-TPJ	Embraer RJ145EP (EMB-145EP)	145036		0097	1297	2 AN AE3007A	20990	Y50	AL-EP	Chapim
☐ CS-TPK	Embraer RJ145EP (EMB-145EP)	145041		0098	0298	2 AN AE3007A	20990	Y50	FK-PS	Gaio
☐ CS-TPL	Embraer RJ145EP (EMB-145EP)	145051	PT-SZQ*	0098	0498	2 AN AE3007A	20990	Y50	FM-PQ	Pisco
☐ CS-TPA	Fokker 100 (F28 Mk0100)	11257	PH-LMF*	0089	0690	2 RR Tay 650-15	44450	CY101	AH-FS	Albatroz / lsf GECA
☐ CS-TPB	Fokker 100 (F28 Mk0100)	11262	PH-EZE*	0090	0690	2 RR Tay 650-15	44450	CY101	AH-GR	Pelicano / lsf GECA
☐ CS-TPC	Fokker 100 (F28 Mk0100)	11287	PH-LML*	0090	0191	2 RR Tay 650-15	44450	CY101	AH-GS	Flamingo / lsf GECA
☐ CS-TPD	Fokker 100 (F28 Mk0100)	11317	PH-LNA*	0091	0592	2 RR Tay 650-15	44450	CY101	CS-FH	Condor / lsf GECA
☐ CS-TPE	Fokker 100 (F28 Mk0100)	11342	PH-LNJ	0092	0593	2 RR Tay 650-15	44450	CY101	EQ-DS	Gaviao / lsf GECA
☐ CS-TPF	Fokker 100 (F28 Mk0100)	11258	PH-FZD*	0089	1294	2 RR Tay 650-15	44450	CY101	HQ-AD	Grifo / lsf GECA

PORTO JATO – Aviaçao Civil, Lda (formerly Air Santos – Transportes Aéreos, Lda)

Porto

Antiga Aerogare, 1. Piso, Salas 46/47, Aeroporto Francisco Sa Carneiro, P-4470 Maia, Portugal ☎ (2) 948 80 91 Tx: none Fax: (2) 948 80 91 SITA: n/a
F: 1990 👥 n/a Head: Ten. Cor. Moreira dos Santos Net: n/a

☐ EC-GMG	Fairchild (Swearingen) SA226TC Metro II	TC-371	OY-BJT	0080	0099	2 GA TPE331-3UW-303G	5670	Y18 / Freighter		occlsf/jtlyopw Intermed.Aérea/tb CS-reg

94 registration type of aircraft cn/fn ex/ex* mfd del powered by mtow kg configuration selcal name/fln/specialitites/remarks

SATA Air Açores - Serviço Açoreano de Transportes Aéreos, E.P. = SP / SAT (Sister co. of SATA International) **Ponta Delgada**

Avenida Infante D. Henrique 55, P-9500 Ponta Delgada, (S. Miguel Azores), Portugal ☎ (96) 20 54 14 Tx: none Fax: (96) 28 23 56 SITA: n/a
F: 1941 n/a Head: Eng. Manuel Cansado IATA: 737 ICAO: SATA Net: http://www.virtualazores.com/sata

☐ CS-TGO	Dornier 228-202	8119	D-CMUC	0087	1293	2 GA TPE331-5-252D	6200	Y17		lsf Dornier Luftfahrt GmbH / cvtd -201
☐ CS-TGL	BAe ATP	2019	G-BRTG*	0089	1289	2 PWC PW126	22930	Y64		Santa Maria
☐ CS-TGM	BAe ATP	2030	G-11-030*	0090	1290	2 PWC PW126	22930	Y64		Graciosa
☐ CS-TGN	BAe ATP	2031	G-11-031*	0090	1290	2 PWC PW126	22930	Y64		Flores

SATA International - Serviço e Transportes Aéreos, S.A. = S4 / RZO (Sister co. of SATA Air Açores) **Ponta Delgada, Lisbon & Funchal**

Avenida Infante D. Henrique 55-4, P-9500 Ponta Delgada, (S. Miguel Azores), Portugal ☎ (96) 20 54 14 Tx: none Fax: (96) 28 23 56 SITA: n/a
F: 1998 n/a Head: Eng. Manuel Cansado IATA: 331 ICAO: AIR AZORES Net: http://www.sata.pt

☐ CS-TGP	Boeing 737-3Q8	24131 / 1541	OO-LTX	0088	0398	2 CFMI CFM56-3B2	62000	C12Y130	KS-GR	Corvo / lsf POLA
☐ CS-TGQ	Boeing 737-36N	28570 / 3010		0098	0398	2 CFMI CFM56-3C1	62822	C12Y130	HS-LQ	Sao Jorge / lsf GECA
☐ CS-TGR	Boeing 737-3Y0	24902 / 1973	9V-TRB	0091	0199	2 CFMI CFM56-3B2	61235	C12Y130	FJ-HQ	Pico / lsf GECA

TAC - Air Centro, SA (formerly TAC – Transportes Aéreos do Centro, Lda) **Cascais-Tires**

Aerodromo Municipal de Cascais-Tires, P-2775 S. Domingos de Rana, Portugal ☎ (1) 445 03 59 Tx: none Fax: (1) 445 63 69 SITA: n/a
F: 1987 3 Head: Georgino Santos Silva Net: n/a Ag-aircraft below MTOW 5000kg: Piper PA-25 & PA-36

☐ CS-AVM	Piper PA-31-350 Navajo Chieftain	31-7752159	N503SC	0077	0391	2 LY TIO-540-J2BD	3175	9 Pax / Frtr		

TAM - Transportes Aéreos Militares = AFP (Esquadra 501 of the Força Aérea Portuguesa / Portuguese Air Force) **Montijo & Lisbon**

Comando Operacional da Força Aérea (COFA), Monsanto, P-1500 Lisboa, Portugal ☎ (1) 778 09 73 Tx: none Fax: (1) 471 32 37 SITA: n/a
F: 1952 n/a Head: n/a ICAO: PORTUGUESE AIR FORCE Net: n/a Branch of the Portuguese Air Force conducting non-commerical relief/aid/humanitarian flights as well as military passenger & cargo flights.

☐ 16801	Lockheed L-382C (C-130H-30) Hercules	73D-4749	6801	0077	0877	4 AN T56-A-15	79380	Frtr/Y88orY112		OGMA cvtd C-130H
☐ 16802	Lockheed L-382C (C-130H-30) Hercules	73D-4753	6802	0078	0478	4 AN T56-A-15	79380	Frtr/Y88orY112		OGMA cvtd C-130H
☐ 16803	Lockheed L-382C (C-130H) Hercules	78D-4772	6803	0078	0478	4 AN T56-A-15	79380	Frtr / Y88		
☐ 16804	Lockheed L-382C (C-130H) Hercules	78D-4777	6804	0078	0678	4 AN T56-A-15	79380	Frtr / Y88		
☐ 16805	Lockheed L-382C (C-130H) Hercules	78D-4778	6805	0078	0678	4 AN T56-A-15	79380	Frtr / Y88		
☐ 16806	Lockheed L-382T (C-130H-30) Hercules	25F-5264	6806	0091	1091	4 AN T56-A-15	79380	Frtr/Y88orY112		

TAP AIR PORTUGAL = TP / TAP (Transportes Aéreos Portugueses, S.A. dba / Member of The Qualiflyer Group) **Lisbon**

Edificio 25, Aeroporto de Lisboa, P-1704 Lisboa Codex, Portugal ☎ (1) 841 50 00 Tx: 12231 taplis p Fax: (1) 841 50 95 SITA: n/a
F: 1945 7450 Head: Eng. Manuel Ferreira Lima IATA: 047 ICAO: AIR PORTUGAL Net: http://www.tap-airportugal.pt
Scheduled inter-island services in Madeira are operated by ATA-AEROCONDOR with Shorts 360 aircraft using TP flight numbers.

☐ CS-TIB	Boeing 737-382	24365 / 1695		0089	0389	2 CFMI CFM56-3B2	62000	CY132	BL-MR	Açores / lsf ILFC
☐ CS-TIC	Boeing 737-382	24366 / 1699		0089	0489	2 CFMI CFM56-3B2	62000	CY132	EH-FM	Algarve / lsf PEGA / Fly Algarve-colors
☐ CS-TIG	Boeing 737-3K9	24213 / 1794		0089	0593	2 CFMI CFM56-3B2	62000	CY132	BL-QS	lsf BAVA
☐ CS-TIH	Boeing 737-3K9	24214 / 1796		0089	0493	2 CFMI CFM56-3B2	62000	CY132	BL-RS	lsf BAVA
☐ CS-TIK	Boeing 737-382	25161 / 2226		0092	0292	2 CFMI CFM56-3B2	62000	CY132	AR-GH	Costa do Estoril / lsf ILFC
☐ CS-TIN	Boeing 737-33A	23827 / 1444	9H-ACS	0087	1195	2 CFMI CFM56-3B2	62000	CY132	KS-GL	lsf NorwayBank consortium
☐ CS-TIO	Boeing 737-33A	23830 / 1462	9H-ACT	0088	1195	2 CFMI CFM56-3B2	62000	CY132	KS-GM	lsf NorwayBank consortium
☐ CS-TTA	Airbus Industrie A319-111	750	D-AVYO*	0097	1297	2 CFMI CFM56-5B5/P	68000	CY132	HR-ES	Vieira da Silva
☐ CS-TTB	Airbus Industrie A319-111	755	D-AVYJ*	0097	1297	2 CFMI CFM56-5B5/P	68000	CY132	HS-GR	Gago Coutinho
☐ CS-TTC	Airbus Industrie A319-111	763	D-AVYS*	0098	0198	2 CFMI CFM56-5B5/P	68000	CY132	LP-AB	Fernando Pessoa / lsf ILFC
☐ CS-TTD	Airbus Industrie A319-111	790	D-AVYC*	0098	0398	2 CFMI CFM56-5B5/P	68000	CY132	FH-PS	Amadeo de Souza-Cardoso / lsf ILFC
☐ CS-TTE	Airbus Industrie A319-111	821	D-AVYN*	0098	0698	2 CFMI CFM56-5B5/P	68000	CY132	EP-KM	Francisco d'Ollanda
☐ CS-TTF	Airbus Industrie A319-111	837	D-AVYL*	0098	0698	2 CFMI CFM56-5B5/P	68000	CY132	QR-EP	Calouste Gulbenkian
☐ CS-TTG	Airbus Industrie A319-111	906	D-AVYN*	0098	1198	2 CFMI CFM56-5B5/P	68000	CY132		Humberto Delgado
☐ CS-TTH	Airbus Industrie A319-111	917	D-AVYJ*	0098	1198	2 CFMI CFM56-5B5/P	68000	CY132		Antonio Sergio
☐ CS-TTI	Airbus Industrie A319-111	933	D-AVYP*	0098	1298	2 CFMI CFM56-5B5/P	68000	CY132		Eca de Queiros
☐ CS-TTJ	Airbus Industrie A319-111	979				2 CFMI CFM56-5B5/P	68000	CY132		oo-delivery 0499
☐ CS-TTK	Airbus Industrie A319-111	1034				2 CFMI CFM56-5B5/P	68000	CY132		oo-delivery 0699
☐ CS-TTL	Airbus Industrie A319-111	1100				2 CFMI CFM56-5B5/P	68000	CY132		oo-delivery 1099
☐ CS-TTM	Airbus Industrie A319-111	1106				2 CFMI CFM56-5B5/P	68000	CY132		oo-delivery 1099
☐ CS-TTN	Airbus Industrie A319-111	1111				2 CFMI CFM56-5B5/P	68000	CY132		oo-delivery 1199
☐ CS-TTO	Airbus Industrie A319-111	1120				2 CFMI CFM56-5B5/P	68000	CY132		oo-delivery 1299
☐ CS-MAH	Airbus Industrie A320-232	805	F-WWID*	0098	0698	2 IAE V2527-A5	73500	CY156	JP-CF	Ilha de Madeira / lsf AMU
☐ CS-TNA	Airbus Industrie A320-211	185	F-WWDB*	0092	0492	2 CFMI CFM56-5A1	73500	CY156	BS-AH	Grao Vasco / lsf BAVA
☐ CS-TNB	Airbus Industrie A320-211	191	F-WWDH*	0091	0492	2 CFMI CFM56-5A1	73500	CY156	BS-AJ	Gil Vicente / lsf BAVA
☐ CS-TNC	Airbus Industrie A320-211	234	F-WWDF*	0091	0392	2 CFMI CFM56-5A1	73500	CY156	BS-AK	Pero da Covilha / lsf GATX
☐ CS-TND	Airbus Industrie A320-211	235	F-WWDM*	0091	0392	2 CFMI CFM56-5A1	73500	CY156	BS-AL	Garcia de Orta / lsf GATX
☐ CS-TNE	Airbus Industrie A320-211	395	F-WWBJ*	0092	0393	2 CFMI CFM56-5A1	73500	CY156	EJ-LR	Sa de Miranda / lsf GATX
☐ CS-TNF	Airbus Industrie A320-211	407	F-WWDH*	0093	0493	2 CFMI CFM56-5A1	73500	CY156	EJ-LS	Fernao Lopes / lsf GATX
☐ CS-TNG	Airbus Industrie A320-214	945	F-WWIX*	0099	0299	2 CFMI CFM56-5B4/P	73500	CY156		Mouzinho da Silveira / lsf ILFC
☐ CS-TNH	Airbus Industrie A320-214	960	F-WWBH*	0099	0399	2 CFMI CFM56-5B4/P	73500	CY156		
☐ CS-TNI	Airbus Industrie A320-214	982				2 CFMI CFM56-5B4/P	73500	CY156		oo-delivery 0599
☐ CS-TNJ	Airbus Industrie A320-214	1001				2 CFMI CFM56-5B4/P	73500	CY156		oo-delivery 0699
☐ CS-TNK	Airbus Industrie A320-214					2 CFMI CFM56-5B4/P	73500	CY156		oo-delivery 0000
☐ CS-TNL	Airbus Industrie A320-214					2 CFMI CFM56-5B4/P	73500	CY156		oo-delivery 0001
☐ CS-TNM	Airbus Industrie A320-214					2 CFMI CFM56-5B4/P	73500	CY156		oo-delivery 0001
☐ CS-	Airbus Industrie A321-211					2 CFMI CFM56-5B3/P	89000	CY190		oo-delivery 0700
☐ CS-	Airbus Industrie A321-211					2 CFMI CFM56-5B3/P	89000	CY190		oo-delivery 1200
☐ CS-TEH	Airbus Industrie A310-304	483	F-WWCS*	0088	1088	2 GE CF6-80C2A2	157000	C37Y178	BM-AR	Bartolomeu Dias / lsf NBB Lisbon Lease
☐ CS-TEI	Airbus Industrie A310-304	495	F-WWCO*	0089	0489	2 GE CF6-80C2A2	157000	C37Y178	BM-AS	Fernao de Magalhaes / lsf Fg Echo Lsg
☐ CS-TEJ	Airbus Industrie A310-304	494	F-WWCM*	0089	0389	2 GE CF6-80C2A2	157000	C37Y178	BM-CR	Pedro Nunes / lsf D.A.P. Lease
☐ CS-TEW	Airbus Industrie A310-304	541	F-WWCR*	0090	0590	2 GE CF6-80C2A2	157000	C37Y178	BM-CS	Vasco da Gama / lsf D.T.P. Lease
☐ CS-TEX	Airbus Industrie A310-304	565	F-WWCC*	0091	0391	2 GE CF6-80C2A2	157000	C37Y178	AF-JS	Joao XXI / lsf ILFC
☐ CS-TOA	Airbus Industrie A340-312	041	F-WWJB*	0094	1294	4 CFMI CFM56-5C3	257000	C42Y238	FS-AK	Fernao Mendes Pinto
☐ CS-TOB	Airbus Industrie A340-312	044	F-WWJN*	0094	1294	4 CFMI CFM56-5C3	257000	C42Y238	GS-AL	D. Joao de Castro
☐ CS-TOC	Airbus Industrie A340-312	079	F-WWJS*	0095	0495	4 CFMI CFM56-5C3	257000	C42Y238	HS-FM	Wenceslau de Moraes
☐ CS-TOD	Airbus Industrie A340-312	091	F-WWJA*	0395	0495	4 CFMI CFM56-5C3	257000	C42Y238	HS-FP	D. Francisco de Almeida

VINAIR - Aeroserviços, S.A. = VIN (formerly Vinair Helicopteros, Lda / Associated with Grupo Siva, S.A.) **Cascais-Tires**

Aerodromo Municipal de Cascais-Tires, P-2775 S. Domingos de Rana, Portugal ☎ (1) 444 32 95 Tx: none Fax: (1) 445 30 38 SITA: n/a
F: 1990 4 Head: Antonio Remédios ICAO: VINAIR Net: http://www.vinair.pt

☐ CS-HDP	Eurocopter (Aerosp.) AS355N Ecureuil 2	5570	N888B	0093	0896	2 TU Arrius 1A	2540	5 Pax		
☐ CS-	Agusta A109E Power	11041				2 PWC PW206C	2850			oo-delivery 0099
☐ CS-TMK	Dassault Falcon 900B	66	F-GJPM	0090	1296	3 GA TFE731-5BR-1C	21099	14 Pax	LQ-JP	lsf BFCE Bail / cvtd 900

CU = CUBA (Republic of Cuba) (Republica de Cuba)

Capital: Havanna Official Language: Spanish Population: 11,5 million Square Km: 110861 Dialling code: +53 Year established: 1902 Acting political head: Dr. Fidel Castro Ruz (President)

AEROCARIBBEAN = CRN (Empresa Aero Caribbean, S.A. dba) **Havana-Jose Marti Int'l**

Calle 23, No. 113, Vedado, La Habana, Cuba ☎ (7) 33 70 96 Tx: 512191 aeroca cu Fax: (7) 33 50 16 SITA: n/a
F: 1982 245 Head: Alberto Sanchez ICAO: AEROCARIBBEAN Net: http://www.cubaweb.cu

☐ CU-T1203	Yakovlev 40	9641450		0076		3 IV AI-25	16000	Y32		lst Oriental as YV-598C
☐ CU-T1211	Yakovlev 40	9731554		0077	0095	3 IV AI-25	16000	Y32		
☐ CU-T1212	Yakovlev 40	9731754		0077	0092	3 IV AI-25	16000	Y32		lst Oriental as YV-599C
☐ CU-T1213	Yakovlev 40	9731954		0077	0095	3 IV AI-25	16000	Y32		
☐ CU-T1220	Yakovlev 40	9841059		0078	0090	3 IV AI-25	16000	Y32		std SCU
☐ CU-T1221	Yakovlev 40	9841159	YV-594C	0078	0090	3 IV AI-25	16000	Y32		lst Oriental de Aviacion as YV-594C
☐ CU-T1296	ATR 42-300	009	F-WQGV	0086	0698	2 PWC PW120	16700	Y46		
☐ CU-T1297	ATR 42-300	014	F-WQIE	0086	0798	2 PWC PW120	16700	Y46		
☐ CU-T925	Ilyushin 14M	7343202	CU-F925	0857		2 SH ASh-82T	17250	Y40		
☐ CU-T882	Antonov 24B	67302602		0066	0094	2 IV AI-24-II	21000	Y50		
☐ CU-T110	Antonov 26	6710	CU-T1228	0078	0084	2 IV AI-24VT	24000	Combi		
☐ CU-T111	Antonov 26	7207	YV-600C	0078	0084	2 IV AI-24VT	24000	Combi		
☐ CU-T112	Antonov 26	7303	CCCP-47334	0079	0084	2 IV AI-24VT	24000	Combi		std HAV
☐ CU-T115	Antonov 26	6803	CU-T1231	0078	0084	2 IV AI-24VT	24000	Combi		std HAV
☐ CU-C132	Ilyushin 18D (F)	188010805	LZ-AZZ	0568	1295	4 IV AI-20M	64000	Freighter		cvtd Ilyushin 18D
☐ CU-C900	Ilyushin 18D	188011104	CU-T900	0068	0091	4 IV AI-20M	64000	Freighter		std HAV
☐ CU-T1268	Ilyushin 18D	188010804	CCCP-74256	0068	0091	4 IV AI-20M	64000	Y100		
☐ CU-T1269	Ilyushin 18V	185007801	CCCP-75562	0065	0090	4 IV AI-20M	64000	Y100		special sea & palms-colors
☐ CU-T131	Ilyushin 18D	188010904	LZ-AZR	0568	1295	4 IV AI-20M	64000	Y100		

AEROGAVIOTA = GTV (Empresa de Aviacion Aerogaviota, SA dba) **Havana-Jose Marti Int'l & -Baracoa & Varadero-Int'l**

Avda 47, No. 2814, Reparto Kolhy, La Habana, Cuba ☎ (7) 81 30 68 Tx: n/a Fax: (7) 33 26 21 SITA: n/a
F: 1994 n/a Head: n/a ICAO: GAVIOTA Net: n/a

☐ CU-T1415	PZL Mielec (Antonov) An-2			0070	0098	1 SH ASh-62IR	5500	Y11		

95 registration type of aircraft cn/fn ex/ex* mfd del powered by mtow kg configuration selcal name/fln/specialitites/remarks

☐ CU-H400	Mil Mi-8P	40736		0088		2 IS TV2-117A	12000	Y24		
☐ CU-H401	Mil Mi-8	40729		0088		2 IS TV2-117A	12000	Y24		
☐ CU-H402	Mil Mi-8	40725		0088		2 IS TV2-117A	12000	Y24		
☐ CU-H403	Mil Mi-8T	40725		0088		2 IS TV2-117A	12000	Y24		
☐ CU-H404	Mil Mi-8	40726		0088		2 IS TV2-117A	12000	Y24		
☐ CU-H405	Mil Mi-8	40738		0088		2 IS TV2-117A	12000	Y24		
☐ CU-H406	Mil Mi-8	41910		0088		2 IS TV2-117A	12000	Y24		
☐ CU-H407	Mil Mi-8T	9733011		0073		2 IS TV2-117A	12000	Y24		
☐ CU-H408	Mil Mi-8					2 IS TV2-117A	12000	Y24		
☐ CU-H409	Mil Mi-8T	9754850		0075		2 IS TV2-117A	12000	Y24		
☐ CU-H410	Mil Mi-8T	40733		0088		2 IS TV2-117A	12000	Y24		
☐ CU-H411	Mil Mi-8	40732		0088		2 IS TV2-117A	12000	Y24		
☐ CU-H412	Mil Mi-8	40739		0088		2 IS TV2-117A	12000	Y24		
☐ CU-H414	Mil Mi-8	40728		0088		2 IS TV2-117A	12000	Y24		
☐ CU-H415	Mil Mi-8	40734		0088		2 IS TV2-117A	12000	Y24		
☐ CU-T1232	Yakovlev 40	9011060		0080		3 IV AI-25	16000	Y32		
☐ CU-T1448	Yakovlev 40	9011160		0080		3 IV AI-25	16000	Y32		
☐ CU-T1449	Yakovlev 40	9021260		0080		3 IV AI-25	16000	Y32		
☐ CU-T1450	Yakovlev 40	9021360		0080		3 IV AI-25	16000	Y32		
☐ CU-T1452	ATR 42-300	015	F-WQIQ	0086	1198	2 PWC PW120	16700	Y46		
☐ CU-F1444	Antonov 30			0078	0098	2 IV AI-24T	23000	Photo/Survey		
☐ CU-T1445	Antonov 30			0078	0097	2 IV AI-24T	23000	Survey / Combi		
☐ CU-T1238	Antonov 26	7803	CCCP-47324	0079		2 IV AI-24VT	24000	Combi		
☐ CU-T1239	Antonov 26	7907	CCCP-47325	0079		2 IV AI-24VT	24000	Combi		
☐ CU-T1240	Antonov 26B	11210		0081		2 IV AI-24VT	24000	Combi		
☐ CU-T1241	Antonov 26B	11301		0081		2 IV AI-24VT	24000	Combi		
☐ CU-T1401	Antonov 26B	12604		0081		2 IV AI-24VT	24000	Combi		
☐ CU-T1402	Antonov 26B	12605		0083		2 IV AI-24VT	24000	Combi		
☐ CU-T1403	Antonov 26B	12905		0083		2 IV AI-24VT	24000	Combi		
☐ CU-T1404	Antonov 26B	12906		0083		2 IV AI-24VT	24000	Combi		
☐ CU-T1405	Antonov 26B	13501		0083	0097	2 IV AI-24VT	24000	Combi		
☐ CU-T1406	Antonov 26B	13502		0083		2 IV AI-24VT	24000	Combi		
☐ CU-T1408	Antonov 26	6903	CCCP-47328	0078		2 IV AI-24VT	24000	Combi		
☐ CU-T1420	Antonov 26	6607	CCCP-47324	0078		2 IV AI-24VT	24000	Combi		
☐ CU-T1421	Antonov 26	6610	CCCP-47325	0078		2 IV AI-24VT	24000	Combi		
☐ CU-T1423	Antonov 26	3806		0076		2 IV AI-24VT	24000	Combi		
☐ CU-T1425	Antonov 26	6904	CCCP-47329	0078		2 IV AI-24VT	24000	Combi		
☐ CU-T1426	Antonov 26	5603	CCCP-47323	0077		2 IV AI-24VT	24000	Combi		
☐ CU-T1428	Antonov 26B	11303		0081		2 IV AI-24VT	24000	Combi		
☐ CU-T1429	Antonov 26	7006	CCCP-47331	0079		2 IV AI-24VT	24000	Combi		
☐ CU-T1432	Antonov 26	7306	CCCP-47335	0079		2 IV AI-24VT	24000	Combi		
☐ CU-T1433	Antonov 26	7309	CCCP-47336	0079		2 IV AI-24VT	24000	Combi		
☐ CU-T1434	Antonov 26	7701	CCCP-47338	0079		2 IV AI-24VT	24000	Combi		
☐ CU-T1435	Antonov 26	7702	CCCP-47339	0079		2 IV AI-24VT	24000	Combi		

AEROTAXI = CNI (Division of ENSA – Empresa Nacional de Servicios Aéreos) **Cayo Largo, Varadero-Int'l & -Downtown**

Calle 27 No 102e/M y N, Vedado, La Habana, Cuba ☎ (7) 32 25 15 Tx: 511196 cu Fax: (7) 33 30 82 SITA: n/a
F: n/a ✈✈✈ n/a Head: Benigno Miranda ICAO: SERAER Net: n/a

☐ CU-T1078	PZL Mielec (Antonov) An-2	1G116-30		0070		1 SH ASh-62IR	5500	11 Pax		
☐ CU-T1081	PZL Mielec (Antonov) An-2	1G116-41		0070		1 SH ASh-62IR	5500	11 Pax		
☐ CU-T1085	PZL Mielec (Antonov) An-2	1G115-54		0070		1 SH ASh-62IR	5500	11 Pax		
☐ CU-T1086	PZL Mielec (Antonov) An-2	1G115-60		0070		1 SH ASh-62IR	5500	11 Pax		
☐ CU-T1089	PZL Mielec (Antonov) An-2	1G116-13		0070		1 SH ASh-62IR	5500	11 Pax		
☐ CU-T1090	PZL Mielec (Antonov) An-2	1G116-08		0070		1 SH ASh-62IR	5500	11 Pax		
☐ CU-T1091	PZL Mielec (Antonov) An-2	1G116-04		0070		1 SH ASh-62IR	5500	11 Pax		Cayo Largo / Panorama windows (modif.)
☐ CU-T1094	PZL Mielec (Antonov) An-2	1G116-16		0070		1 SH ASh-62IR	5500	11 Pax		
☐ CU-T1095	PZL Mielec (Antonov) An-2	1G116-09		0070		1 SH ASh-62IR	5500	11 Pax		
☐ CU-T1097	PZL Mielec (Antonov) An-2	1G116-07		0070		1 SH ASh-62IR	5500	11 Pax		
☐ CU-T1099	PZL Mielec (Antonov) An-2	1G120-33		0071		1 SH ASh-62IR	5500	11 Pax		
☐ CU-T1104	PZL Mielec (Antonov) An-2	1G120-18		0070		1 SH ASh-62IR	5500	11 Pax		
☐ CU-T1105	PZL Mielec (Antonov) An-2	1G120-05		0070		1 SH ASh-62IR	5500	11 Pax		
☐ CU-T1106	PZL Mielec (Antonov) An-2	1G120-08		0070		1 SH ASh-62IR	5500	11 Pax		Panorama windows (modif.)
☐ CU-T1114	PZL Mielec (Antonov) An-2	1G120-09		0070		1 SH ASh-62IR	5500	11 Pax		
☐ CU-T1118	PZL Mielec (Antonov) An-2	1G120-12		0070		1 SH ASh-62IR	5500	11 Pax		
☐ CU-T1119	PZL Mielec (Antonov) An-2	1G120-20		0070		1 SH ASh-62IR	5500	11 Pax		
☐ CU-T1168	PZL Mielec (Antonov) An-2	1G232-08		0088		1 SH ASh-62IR	5500	11 Pax		
☐ CU-T1169	PZL Mielec (Antonov) An-2	1G232-13		0088		1 SH ASh-62IR	5500	11 Pax		
☐ CU-T1174	PZL Mielec (Antonov) An-2	1G232-04		0088		1 SH ASh-62IR	5500	11 Pax		
☐ CU-T1175	PZL Mielec (Antonov) An-2	1G232-01		0088		1 SH ASh-62IR	5500	11 Pax		
☐ CU-T1179	PZL Mielec (Antonov) An-2	1G232-05		0088		1 SH ASh-62IR	5500	11 Pax		
☐ CU-T1181	PZL Mielec (Antonov) An-2	1G232-15		0088		1 SH ASh-62IR	5500	11 Pax		
☐ CU-T1183	PZL Mielec (Antonov) An-2	1G231-31		0088		1 SH ASh-62IR	5500	11 Pax		
☐ CU-T1191	PZL Mielec (Antonov) An-2	1G231-32		0088		1 SH ASh-62IR	5500	11 Pax		Panorama windows (modif.)
☐ CU-T1400	PZL Mielec (Antonov) An-2	1G115-57		0070		1 SH ASh-62IR	5500	11 Pax		
☐ CU-T1410	PZL Mielec (Antonov) An-2	1G120-14		0070		1 SH ASh-62IR	5500	11 Pax		
☐ CU-T1411	PZL Mielec (Antonov) An-2	1G120-25		0070		1 SH ASh-62IR	5500	11 Pax		
☐ CU-T1412	PZL Mielec (Antonov) An-2	1G115-55		0070		1 SH ASh-62IR	5500	11 Pax		Panorama windows (modif.)
☐ CU-T1416	PZL Mielec (Antonov) An-2	1G120-03		0070		1 SH ASh-62IR	5500	11 Pax		
☐ CU-T1418	PZL Mielec (Antonov) An-2	1G120-06		0070		1 SH ASh-62IR	5500	11 Pax		
☐ CU-T1514	PZL Mielec (Antonov) An-2	1G234-13		0089		1 SH ASh-62IR	5500	11 Pax		
☐ CU-T1516	PZL Mielec (Antonov) An-2	1G234-15		0089		1 SH ASh-62IR	5500	11 Pax		
☐ CU-T1518	PZL Mielec (Antonov) An-2	1G234-12		0092		1 SH ASh-62IR	5500	11 Pax		
☐ CU-T1529	PZL Mielec (Antonov) An-2	1G177-36		0077		1 SH ASh-62IR	5500	11 Pax		Panorama windows (modif.)
☐ CU-T1530	PZL Mielec (Antonov) An-2	1G120-10	CU-T1113	0070		1 SH ASh-62IR	5500	11 Pax		
☐ CU-T1531	PZL Mielec (Antonov) An-2	1G116-39		0070		1 SH ASh-62IR	5500	11 Pax		Panorama windows (modif.)
☐ CU-T310	PZL Mielec (Antonov) An-2	1G116-38		0070		1 SH ASh-62IR	5500	11 Pax		
☐ CU-T312	PZL Mielec (Antonov) An-2	1G116-40		0070		1 SH ASh-62IR	5500	11 Pax		Panorama windows (modif.) / std HAV
☐ CU-T695	PZL Mielec (Antonov) An-2	1G116-53		0070		1 SH ASh-62IR	5500	11 Pax		Panorama windows (modif.)
☐ CU-T123	Boeing (Douglas) DC-3C (C-47A-10-DK)	12445	D2-FDK	0044	0097	2 PW R-1830	11884	28 Pax		
☐ CU-T124	Boeing (Douglas) DC-3C (C-47B-25-DK)	32664	D2-EPL	0045	0097	2 PW R-1830	11884	28 Pax		
☐ CU-T127	Boeing (Douglas) DC-3A (C-53D-DO)	11645	N6102	0043	0095	2 PW R-1830	11884	28 Pax		

CUBANA de Aviacion, S.A. = CU / CUB **Havana-Jose Marti Int'l**

Calle 23 No. 64, Vedado, La Habana 10400, Cuba ☎ (7) 33 49 49 Tx: none Fax: (7) 33 33 23 SITA: HAVDDCU
F: 1929 ✈✈✈ 2400 Head: Heriberto Prieto IATA: 136 ICAO: CUBANA Net: http://www.cubana.cu Beside aircraft listed, also leases Boeing 767-300 & DC-10-30 from EUROFLY (I-) & AOM French Airlines (F-) when required.

☐ CU-T1286	Fokker F27 Friendship 600 (F27 Mk600)	10332	EC-BMS	0967	0694	2 RR Dart 532-7	19731	Y44		cvtd 400
☐ CU-T1287	Fokker F27 Friendship 600 (F27 Mk600)	10343	EC-BMT	1167	0894	2 RR Dart 532-7	19731	Y44		cvtd 400
☐ CU-T1288	Fokker F27 Friendship 600 (F27 Mk600)	10347	EC-BMU	0168	0794	2 RR Dart 532-7	19731	Y44		cvtd 400
☐ CU-T1289	Fokker F27 Friendship 600 (F27 Mk600)	10348	EC-BOA	0068	0294	2 RR Dart 532-7	19731	Y44		
☐ CU-T1290	Fokker F27 Friendship 600 (F27 Mk600)	10352	EC-BOB	0068	0394	2 RR Dart 532-7	19731	Y44		
☐ CU-T1260	Antonov 24RV	57310307		0075	0684	2 IV AI-24VT	21800	Y48		La Pinta
☐ CU-T1266	Antonov 24RV	57310107	CCCP-46533	0075	0387	2 IV AI-24VT	21800	Y48		
☐ CU-T1267	Antonov 24RV	47309907	CCCP-46696	0074	0387	2 IV AI-24VT	21800	Y48		
☐ CU-T1294	Antonov 24RV	27308105	YL-LCF	0072	0596	2 IV AI-24VT	21800	Y48		
☐ CU-T1295	Antonov 24RV	27307508	RA-47691	0072	0497	2 IV AI-24VT	21800	Y48		
☐ CU-T1277	Yakovlev 42D	4520423016238		0090	0990	3 LO D-36	56500	Y120		Santiago de Cuba
☐ CU-T1278	Yakovlev 42D	4520423016269		0090	1090	3 LO D-36	56500	Y120		
☐ CU-T1279	Yakovlev 42D	4520424914057		0091	0891	3 LO D-36	56500	Y120		
☐ CU-T1285	Yakovlev 42D	4520424914068		0089	0791	3 LO D-36	56500	Y120		std SCU
☐ EI-TLH	Airbus Industrie A320-231	247	G-OALA	0091	1198	2 IAE V2500-A1	75500	Y180	JR-DQ	lsf / opb TLA
☐ EI-TLJ	Airbus Industrie A320-231	257	N257RX	0091	1198	2 IAE V2500-A1	75500	Y180	GH-LM	lsf / opb TLA
☐ CU-T1222	Tupolev 154B-2	447		0080	1280	3 KU NK-8-2U	98000	Y140		
☐ CU-T1253	Tupolev 154B-2	576		0083	0583	3 KU NK-8-2U	98000	Y140		
☐ CU-T1256	Tupolev 154B-2	599		0083	0684	3 KU NK-8-2U	98000	Y140		Ciudad La Habana
☐ CU-T1265	Tupolev 154M	751		0087	0787	3 SO D-30KU-154-II	100000	Y140		
☐ CU-T1275	Tupolev 154M	777		0088	0788	3 SO D-30KU-154-II	100000	Y140		
☐ CU-T1217	Ilyushin 62M	3933232		0079	0779	4 SO D-30KU	170000	C12Y150		
☐ CU-T1218	Ilyushin 62M	2035657		0080	0580	4 SO D-30KU	170000	C12Y150		
☐ CU-T1225	Ilyushin 62M	3139845		0081	0681	4 SO D-30KU	170000	C12Y150		
☐ CU-T1259	Ilyushin 62M	3445111		0084	0784	4 SO D-30KU	170000	C12Y150		

96 registration type of aircraft cn/fn ex/ex* mfd del powered by mtow kg configuration selcal name/fln/specialitites/remarks

☐ CU-T1280	Ilyushin 62M	3749648		0087	0087	4 SO D-30KU	170000	C12Y150		15 de Febrero
☐ CU-T1282	Ilyushin 62M	2052436		0090	0990	4 SO D-30KU	170000	C12Y150		
☐ CU-T1283	Ilyushin 62M	4053823		0090	0091	4 SO D-30KU	170000	C12Y150		
☐ CU-T1284	Ilyushin 62M	4053732		0090	0091	4 SO D-30KU	170000	C12Y150		
☐ CU-C1258	Ilyushin 76MD	0043454615	CU-T1258	0084	1194	4 SO D-30KP	190000	Freighter		
☐ CU-T1271	Ilyushin 76MD	0053459767	CU-T1271	0485		4 SO D-30KP	190000	Freighter		

CX = URUGUAY (Republic of Uruguay) (Republica de Uruguay)

Capital: Montevideo Official Language: Spanish Population: 3,5 million Square Km: 177414 Dialling code: +598 Year established: 1828 Acting political head: Julio Maria Sanguinetti (President)

AEROMAS — Montevideo-Carrasco

Aeropuerto Internacional de Carrasco, Montevideo-Carrasco, Uruguay ☎ (2) 601 44 59 Tx: none Fax: (2) 601 44 59 SITA: n/a
F: 1988 ⁂ 15 Head: Daniel Dalmas Net: n/a Aircraft below MTOW 1361kg: Cessna 182

☐ CX-BDI	Piper PA-23-250 Aztec B	27-2265		0062		2 LY O-540-A1D5	2177			
☐ CX-BRM	Beech Excalibur Queenaire 8800	LD-200	N326JB	0065		2 LY IO-720-A1B	3992			cvtd Queen Air 65-A80
☐ LV-VHO	Beech King Air B90	LJ-428	N74GR	0068		2 PWC PT6A-20	4377			lsf pvt
☐ CX-MAS	Embraer 110P1 Bandeirante (EMB-110P1)	110393	N91DA	0082	0198	2 PWC PT6A-34	5900	Y15/Frtr/EMS		

CELTA Taxi Aéreo (Compania Eolo, Ltda – Transporte Aereo dba) — Montevideo-Carrasco

Cebollati 1706, Ap. 903, Montevideo, Uruguay ☎ (2) 601 46 97 Tx: none Fax: (2) 601 46 97 SITA: n/a
F: 1984 ⁂ 5 Head: Jorge y Carlos Schneckenburger Net: n/a Aircraft below MTOW 1361 kg: Beech Bonanza H35.

☐ CX-BQS	Cessna 337G Super Skymaster	33701591	N72456	0074	0592	2 CO IO-360-G	2100			
☐ CX-BRB	Cessna 337G Super Skymaster II	33701602	N112GT	0075		2 CO IO-360-G	2100			
☐ CX-BCO	Cessna 310H	310H0114		0063		2 CO IO-470-D	2313			
☐ LV-GNE	Beech Twin Bonanza D50C	DH-294		0061		2 LY GO-480-G2D6	2858			lsf pvt
☐ LV-APU	Beech Queen Air B80 (65-B80)	LD-461		0072		2 LY IGSO-540-A1D	3992			lsf pvt

COTASA Taxi Aéreo, S. en C. (Compania de Transporte Aéreo y Servicios Afines dba) — Montevideo-Carrasco

Rincon 539 P.B., Montevideo, Uruguay ☎ (2) 95 33 02 Tx: 6589 sas uy Fax: (2) 95 60 97 SITA: n/a
F: 1961 ⁂ 2 Head: n/a Net: n/a

☐ CX-BKT	Piper PA-34-200T Seneca II	34-7870466		0078		2 CO TSIO-360-E	2073			COTASA Taxi Aéreo / wfu/retired Melilla
☐ CX-BJZ	Piper PA-23-250 Aztec F	27-7854120		0078		2 LY IO-540-C4B5	2359			

PLUNA – Primeras Lineas Uruguayas de Navegacion Aérea, SA = PU / PUA (Associated with Varig, Brazil) — Montevideo-Carrasco

Colonia 1013-1021, Casilla Correo 1360, Montevideo, Uruguay ☎ (2) 98 06 06 Tx: 23187 pluna uy Fax: (2) 92 14 78 SITA: n/a
F: 1936 ⁂ 850 Head: Juan Piaggio IATA: 286 ICAO: PLUNA Net: n/a

☐ CX-BON	Boeing 737-2A3 (A)	22737 / 830	PH-TSI	0082	0182	2 PW JT8D-9A	53070	Y122	LM-CD	Genera José Artigas
☐ CX-BOO	Boeing 737-2A3 (A)	22738 / 834	PH-TSA	0082	0182	2 PW JT8D-9A	53070	Y122	AC-DG	Brig. Gen. Juan A. Lavallejo
☐ CX-BOP	Boeing 737-2A3 (A)	22739 / 844	PH-TSB	0082	0282	2 PW JT8D-9A	53070	Y122	AC-DH	General Fructuoso Rivera
☐ CX-FAT	Boeing 737-2Q8 (A)	21518 / 522	PP-VPD	0078	0298	2 PW JT8D-17	52390	Y109	ER-DP	lsf VRG/spec.cs by Artist Carlos Vilaro
☐ PP-VMI	Boeing 737-241 (A)	21004 / 390		0074	1198	2 PW JT8D-17A	52390	Y109	HL-DM	lsf VRG

PROGRESO AEROSERVICIOS — Montevideo-Angel S. Adami & Punta del Este-El Jaguel

Avda Brasil sn, C.P. 90300, Progreso, (Dpto Canelones), Uruguay ☎ (32) 88 888 Tx: none Fax: (32) 89 000 SITA: n/a
F: 1984 ⁂ 17 Head: Néstor Hugo Santos Russi Net: n/a Aircraft below MTOW 1361 kg: Cessna 182, Piper PA-25, Robinson R22 & R44

☐ CX-BMS	Piper PA-32-301 Saratoga	32-8006040		0080		1 LY IO-540-K1G5	1633			
☐ CX-BOQ	Cessna U206G Stationair 6 II	U20604476		0078		1 CO IO-520-F	1633			
☐ CX-BJF	Piper PA-23-250 Aztec F	27-7654074		0076		2 LY IO-540-C4B5	2359			

TAMU – Transporte Aéreo Militar Uruguayo (Commercial division of Fuerza Aerea Uruguaya) — Montevideo-Carrasco

Colonia 959, Montevideo, Uruguay ☎ (2) 90 19 38 Tx: 22457 fau uy Fax: (2) 92 09 45 SITA: n/a
F: 1970 ⁂ 35 Head: Tte. Cnel. (Av.) Alvaro Gestido Net: n/a

☐ CX-BJB	Embraer 110C Bandeirante (EMB-110C)	110081	PT-GJK	0075	0975	2 PWC PT6A-27	5600			T-582
☐ CX-BJC	Embraer 110C Bandeirante (EMB-110C)	110082	PT-GJL	0075	1175	2 PWC PT6A-27	5600			T-583
☐ CX-BJJ	Embraer 110C Bandeirante (EMB-110C)	110076	PT-GJI	0075	0975	2 PWC PT6A-27	5600			T-580
☐ CX-BKF	Embraer 110B1 Bandeirante (EMB-110B1)	110187		0078	0878	2 PWC PT6A-27	5600			T-585
☐ CX-BOG	CASA 212 Aviocar Srs 200	187		0081	0781	2 GA TPE331-10-501C	7450			T-531
☐ CX-BPI	CASA 212 Aviocar Srs 200	189		0081	0881	2 GA TPE331-10-501C	7450			T-532
☐ CX-BPJ	CASA 212 Aviocar Srs 200	198		0081	1181	2 GA TPE331-10-501C	7450			T-533
☐ CX-BHW	Fokker F27 Friendship 100 (F27 Mk100)	10202	PH-FDR*	0062	0370	2 RR Dart 514-7	18370			T-561

TRANS AMERICA, S.A. — Montevideo-Carrasco

Florida 1280, Apto 202, Montevideo, Uruguay ☎ (2) 902 02 12 Tx: none Fax: (9) 902 27 50 SITA: n/a
F: n/a ⁂ n/a Head: Attilio Bonelli Net: n/a

☐ CX-TAA	Fairchild (Swearingen) SA227AC Metro III	AC-647	N184SW	0086	0598	2 GA TPE331-11U-611G	6577	Y19		lsf Aero Century IV Inc.

TRANSCONTINENTAL SUR, Srl. = TCT — Montevideo-Carrasco

Aeropuerto Internacional de Carrasco, Hangar 2, Montevideo, Uruguay ☎ (2) 601 48 77 Tx: none Fax: (2) 601 48 95 SITA: n/a
F: 1996 ⁂ 33 Head: Washington Hugo Martinez Villar ICAO: TRANS-CONT Net: n/a

☐ CX-BSB	Boeing 707-321C	18766 / 372	P4-CCG	0064	0697	4 PW JT3D-3B (HK2/COM)	146500	Freighter	CF-EJ	lsf Race Aviation
☐ CX-BSI	Boeing 707-347C	20315 / 824	N108RA	0069	0996	4 PW JT3D-3B	151046	Freighter	FM-HL	lsf Race Aviation

C2 = NAURU (Republic of Nauru)

Capital: Yaren Official Language: English Population: 0,1 million Square Km: 21 Dialling code: +674 Year established: 1968 Acting political head: Kinza Clodumar (President)

AIR NAURU = ON / RON (Nauru Air Corporation dba) — Nauru

International Airport, Nauru, Nauru ☎ 444 31 68 Tx: 33081 govnaru zv Fax: 444 31 73 SITA: INUOCON
F: 1970 ⁂ 258 Head: Michael Aroi IATA: 123 ICAO: AIR NAURU Net: n/a

☐ VH-RON	Boeing 737-4L7	26960 / 2483	C2-RN10	0093	0693	2 CFMI CFM56-3C1	68038	F14C12Y96	CS-FJ	

C3 = ANDORRA Prinicipality of Andorra (Principat d'Andorra / Principauté d'Andorre)

Capital: Andorra la Vella Official Language: Catalan, Spanish, French Population: 0,1 million Square Km: 715 Dialling code: +376 Year established: 1278 Acting political head: Marc Folné Molne (Prime Minister)

HELIAND, SA — La Massana-Heliport

Avda San Antoni s/n, Edifici Comabella, La Massana, Andorra ☎ 83 54 61 Tx: none Fax: 83 64 61 SITA: n/a
F: 1995 ⁂ 6 Head: Jaume Comabella Net: n/a

☐ F-GHCC	Eurocopter (Aerosp.) SA315B Lama	2474	N49504	0077	0895	1 TU Artouste IIIB	1950			lst/opb SAF Helicotères

HELITRANS, SL — La Massana-Heliport

Avda. Carlemany 32, Escaldes, Andorra ☎ 86 65 66 Tx: none Fax: 86 02 64 SITA: n/a
F: 1997 ⁂ n/a Head: Xavier Goya Net: n/a Operates aerial work & charter flights with Bell & Kamov helicopters, leased from other companies when required.

C5 = GAMBIA (Republic of The Gambia)

Capital: Banjul Official Language: English, Mandingo, Wolof Population: 1,2 million Square Km: 11295 Dialling code: +220 Year established: 1965 Acting political head: Lieutenant Yayah Jammeh (President)

MAHFOOZ AVIATION (Gambia), Ltd = M2 / MZS — Jeddah (Saudi Arabia)

PO Box 6664, Jeddah 21452, Saudi Arabia ☎ (2) 651 05 50 Tx: 601585 samic sj Fax: (2) 651 07 96 SITA: n/a
F: 1992 ⁂ 93 Head: Mahfooz Salim Bin Mahfooz ICAO: MAHFOOZ Net: n/a

☐ C5-DMB	Boeing 727-228	20411 / 847	TT-DMB	0070	1293	3 PW JT8D-7B	78018	Y152		
☐ C5-DSZ	Boeing 727-228	20470 / 853	TT-DSZ	0071	1293	3 PW JT8D-7B	78018	F12Y134		
☐ C5-SMM	Boeing 727-251	19973 / 665	HK-3871X	0068	1196	3 PW JT8D-7B / -9A	78245	F16Y138		
☐ C5-AMM	Boeing 707-323B	20176 / 817	N712PC	0069	0895	4 PW JT3D-3B (HK2/COM)	146500	Y185	AG-EL	
☐ C5-BIN	Boeing 707-323B	20172 / 804	N711PC	0069	0895	4 PW JT3D-3B (HK2/COM)	146500	Y185	AG-EK	
☐ C5-MBM	Boeing 707-347C	19966 / 743	OD-AGU	0068	1298	4 PW JT3D-3B (HK2/COM)	146500	Freighter 40t	EG-CH	

C6 = BAHAMAS (Commonwealth of the Bahamas)

Capital: Nassau Official Language: English Population: 0,3 million Square Km: 13878 Dialling code: +1-242 Year established: 1973 Acting political head: Hubert Alexander Ingraham (Prime Minister)

ABACO AIR, Ltd — Marsh Harbour

PO Box AB-492, Marsh Harbour, (Abaco), Bahamas ☎ (242) 367-2266 Tx: none Fax: (242) 367-3256 SITA: n/a
F: 1977 ⁂ 12 Head: Andrew Kelly Net: n/a

☐ C6-BFR	Twin (Aero) Commander 500	500-825	N846VK	0059	0789	2 LY O-540-A2B	2722	6 Pax		
☐ C6-BFS	Twin (Aero) Commander 500	500-685	N6285B	0058	0590	2 LY O-540-A2B	2722	6 Pax		
☐ C6-BFQ	Britten-Norman BN-2A-8 Islander	347	N69HA	0073	1294	2 LY O-540-E4C5	2858	9 Pax		

97 registration type of aircraft cn/fn ex/вх* mfd del powered by mtow kg configuration selcal name/fln/specialitites/remarks

BAHAMASAIR = UP / BHS (Bahamasair Holdings, Ltd dba) — Nassau

PO Box N-4881, Nassau, Bahamas ☎ (242) 377-8451 Tx: 20239 bs Fax: (242) 377-8550 SITA: n/a
F: 1973 ⁂ 650 Head: Lester Turncuet IATA: 111 ICAO: BAHAMAS Net: n/a
Beside aircraft listed, some scheduled flights are operated on behalf of Bahamasair by CONGO AIR (with Metro II) & SKY UNLIMITED (with Beech C99) – for details see under those carriers.

□ C6-BFK	Shorts 360-200 (SD3-60)	SH3693	N695PC	0086	0597	2 PWC PT6A-65AR	11999	Y36		lsf Lynrise Air Lease
□ C6-BFT	Shorts 360-200 (SD3-60)	SH3690	N690PC	0086	0494	2 PWC PT6A-65AR	11999	Y36		
□ C6-BFW	Shorts 360-200 (SD3-60)	SH3691	N360PC	0086	0595	2 PWC PT6A-65AR	11999	Y36		
□ C6-BFG	De Havilland DHC-8-311 Dash 8	288	C-GESR*	0091	0891	2 PWC PW123	18643	Y50		
□ C6-BFH	De Havilland DHC-8-311 Dash 8	291	C-GFOD*	0091	0991	2 PWC PW123	18643	Y50		
□ C6-BFI	De Havilland DHC-8-311 Dash 8	295	C-GFHZ*	0091	1091	2 PWC PW123	18643	Y50		
□ C6-BFN	De Havilland DHC-8-301 Dash 8	159	N801XV	0089	0590	2 PWC PW123	18643	Y50		lsf Aviaco Leasing
□ C6-BFO	De Havilland DHC-8-301 Dash 8	164	N802XV	0089	0590	2 PWC PW123	18643	Y50		lsf Aviaco Leasing
□ C6-BFJ	Boeing 737-201	20211 / 141	N211US	0069	1295	2 PW JT8D-9A	49442	Y120		
□ C6-BGK	Boeing 737-275 (A)	22086 / 667	C-GLPW	0080	1297	2 PW JT8D-9A	53070	Y120		
□ C6-BGL	Boeing 737-275 (A)	22087 / 673	C-GMPW	0080	1297	2 PW JT8D-9A	53070	Y120		

CARIBBEAN AVIATION, Ltd — Nassau

PO Box CB-13949, Nassau, Bahamas ☎ (242) 377-3317 Tx: none Fax: (242) 362-2561 SITA: n/a
F: 1995 ⁂ n/a Head: Randy Butler Net: n/a

□ C6-BFZ	Piper PA-31-350 Navajo Chieftain	31-7852021	N27475	0078		2 LY TIO-540-J2BD	3175			lsf Berries Co. Ltd
□ C6-BGC	Piper PA-31-350 Navajo Chieftain	31-7305071		0073		2 LY TIO-540-J2BD	3175			lsf KMC Ventures
□ C6-BGE	Cessna 404 Titan II	404-0223	N728AC	0078	1298	2 CO GTSIO-520-M	3810			

CAT ISLAND AIR, Ltd — Nassau

PO Box CB-11150, Nassau, Bahamas ☎ (242) 377-3318 Tx: none Fax: (242) 377-3320 SITA: n/a
F: 1997 ⁂ n/a Head: Albert Rolle Net: n/a

□ G-JBAC	Embraer 110P1 Bandeirante (EMB-110P1)	110249	G-BGYV	0080	0098	2 PWC PT6A-34	5670	Y19		lsf BACL
□ N360CL	Embraer 110P1 Bandeirante (EMB-110P1)	110287	N63CZ	0080		2 PWC PT6A-34	5670	Y19		lsf Asahi Enterprises Inc.

CHEROKEE AIR, Ltd – Flight Service — Marsh Harbour

PO Box AB-20485, Marsh Harbour, (Abaco), Bahamas ☎ (242) 367-2089 Tx: none Fax: (242) 367-2530 SITA: n/a
F: 1987 ⁂ n/a Head: Faron S. Sawyer Net: n/a

□ C6-BGQ	Piper PA-23-250 Aztec F	27-7954042	N2337M	0079	0287	2 LY IO-540-C4B5	2359			
□ C6-BGR	Piper PA-23-250 Aztec E	27-7305079	N40266	0073	0988	2 LY IO-540-C4B5	2359			
□ C6-BGS	Piper PA-23-250 Aztec F	27-7854067	N17MR	0078	0696	2 LY IO-540-C4B5	2359			

CLEARE AIR, Ltd — Nassau

PO Box N-9430, Nassau, Bahamas ☎ (242) 377-0341 Tx: none Fax: (242) 377-3296 SITA: n/a
F: n/a ⁂ n/a Head: Durae Cleare Net: n/a

□ N72199	Cessna 337G Super Skymaster	33701540		0073	0497	2 CO IO-360-G	2100			lsf Caribbean Air Inc.
□ N27540	Piper PA-31-350 Navajo Chieftain	31-7852056		0078		2 LY TIO-540-J2BD	3175			lsf Caribbean Air Inc.

ISLAND WINGS — Stella Maris

PO Box LI-30137, Stella Maris, (Long Island), Bahamas ☎ (242) 357-1021 Tx: none Fax: (242) 338-2022 SITA: n/a
F: n/a ⁂ n/a Head: Marty Fox Net: n/a

□ N139BP	Piper PA-23-250 Aztec D	27-4535		0070		2 LY IO-540-C4B5	2359			lsf Charlie Lima Corp.

L.B. Limited = 7Z / LBH (formerly Laker Airways (Bahamas), Ltd) — Freeport & Fort Lauderdale-Hollywood Int'l, FL

1170 Lee Wagener Blvd, Suite 200, Fort Lauderdale, FL 33315, USA ☎ (954) 359-0199 Tx: none Fax: (954) 359-7698 SITA: FLLOO7Z
F: 1992 ⁂ 60 Head: Sir Freddie A. Laker IATA: 569 ICAO: LAKER BAHAMAS Net: n/a

□ N552NA	Boeing 727-2J7 (A)	20706 / 949	OY-SBA	0073	1293	3 PW JT8D-15	86409	Y175		Lucayan Princess-Vacations / lsf CIRR
□ N553NA	Boeing 727-2J7 (A)	20707 / 953	OY-SBB	0073	1293	3 PW JT8D-15 (HK3/FDX)	86409	Y175		Bahamian Princess-Vacations / lsf CIRR

LEAIR CHARTER, Ltd — Nassau

PO Box N-7050, Nassau, Bahamas ☎ (242) 377-2356 Tx: none Fax: (242) 377-2357 SITA: n/a
F: n/a ⁂ n/a Head: Larry Brown Net: n/a

□ N62568	Piper PA-23-250 Aztec F	27-7654049		0076	1292	2 LY IO-540-C4B5	2359			lsf Alaskas Inc.
□ N63717	Piper PA-31-310 Navajo	31-7712037		0077	0990	2 LY TIO-540-A2C	2948			lsf Alaskas Inc.

MAJOR'S AIR SERVICES, Ltd — Freeport

PO Box F-41282, Freeport, (Grand Bahama), Bahamas ☎ (242) 352-5778 Tx: none Fax: (242) 352-5788 SITA: n/a
F: n/a ⁂ n/a Head: Roosevelt Major Net: n/a

□ N141RM	Beech C99 Airliner	U-231	N229BH	0086	0996	2 PWC PT6A-36	5126	Y15		lsf Raytheon Aircraft Receivables Corp.

PARADISE ISLAND HELICOPTERS, Ltd — Nassah-Private Heliport

PO Box N-3725, Nassau, Bahamas ☎ (242) 363-4016 Tx: none Fax: (242) 363-4016 SITA: n/a
F: 1997 ⁂ n/a Head: Mike Rent Net: n/a

□ C6-BGB	Bell 206B JetRanger III	2650	N206HV	0079	0297	1 AN 250-C20B	1451			

SANDPIPER AIR (4 Way Charter, Co. Ltd dba) — Nassau

PO Box CB-13838, Nassau, Bahamas ☎ (242) 377-5751 Tx: none Fax: (242) 377-3143 SITA: n/a
F: 1990 ⁂ 24 Head: Kevin Turnquest Net: http://www.sandpiperair.com

□ N3945C	Cessna 402B	402B0822		0074	0097	2 CO TSIO-520-E	2858			lsf Sandpiper Aviation Inc.
□ N5715C	Cessna 402C II	402C0024		0078	0097	2 CO TSIO-520-VB	3107			lsf Johan Pat Inc.
□ N61PB	Cessna 402C II	402C0298		0080	0097	2 CO TSIO-520-VB	3107			lsf J&H Aviation Enterprises Inc.
□ N7827Q	Cessna 402B II	402B1308		0077	0598	2 CO TSIO-520-E	2858			lsf J&H Aviation Enterprises Inc.
□ N98756	Cessna 402B II	402B1068		0076	0097	2 CO TSIO-520-E	2858			lsf N98756 Inc.

SKY UNLIMITED, Ltd — Nassau

PO Box N-10859, Nassau, Bahamas ☎ (242) 377-8993 Tx: none Fax: (242) 377-3107 SITA: n/a
F: n/a ⁂ n/a Head: Heuter Rolle Net: n/a

□ N42517	Beech C99 Airliner	U-165	PT-LUW	0081	1295	2 PWC PT6A-36	5126	Y15		lsf Sky Unlimited Inc.
□ N38SU	Beech 1900C-1 Airliner	UC-38	N32018	0088	0798	2 PWC PT6A-65B	7530	Y19		lsf Raytheon Aircraft Credit Corp.

STELLA MARIS AVIATION (Division of Stella Maris Inn & Estate) — Stella Maris

PO Box LI-30105, Stella Maris, (Long Island), Bahamas ☎ (242) 338-2051 Tx: none Fax: (242) 338-2052 SITA: n/a
F: 1992 ⁂ n/a Head: Jorge Friese Net: n/a

□ N6292J	Piper PA-34-200T Seneca II	34-7670278		0076	1092	2 CO TSIO-360-E	2073			
□ N50WC	Piper PA-31-310 Navajo	31-309		0068	0293	2 LY TIO-540-A1A	2948			

TAINO AIR SERVICES, Ltd (formerly LucayaAir/Lucaya Enterprises, Inc.) — Freeport

PO Box F-44006, Freeport, (Grand Bahama), Bahamas ☎ (242) 352-8885 Tx: none Fax: (242) 352-5175 SITA: n/a
F: 1959 ⁂ 20 Head: John Martin Net: n/a

□ N282GA	Cessna 402C II	402C0119	N282PB	0079	0095	2 CO TSIO-520-VB	3107			lsf Johan Pat Inc.
□ N402MF	Cessna 402C II	402C0624	N52PB	0081	0095	2 CO TSIO-520-VB	3107			lsf J&H Enterprises Inc.

C9 = MOZAMBIQUE (Republic of Mozambique) (Republica de Moçambique)

Capital: Maputo Official Language: Portuguese Population: 19,0 million Square Km: 801590 Dialling code: +258 Year established: 1975 Acting political head: Major-General Joaquim Alberto Chissano (President)

LAM – Linhas Aéreas de Moçambique = TM / LAM (formerly DETA – Linhas Aéreas de Moçambique) — Maputo

PO Box 2060, Maputo, Mozambique ☎ (1) 46 51 43 Tx: 6386 mpmtm mo Fax: (1) 46 51 34 SITA: n/a
F: 1936 ⁂ 1230 Head: José Ricardo Zuzarte Viegas IATA: 068 ICAO: MOZAMBIQUE Net: n/a Aircraft below MTOW 1361kg: Aerospatiale (Socata) TB10 Tobago.
Beside aircraft listed, also uses a Boeing 747SP-44 lsf/opb SOUTH AFRICAN (ZS-) for a weekly Lisbon service.

□ C9-ATB	Partenavia P.68C-TC	359-40-TC		0086		2 LY TIO-360-C1A6D	1990	Y6		
□ C9-ATK	Partenavia P.68C	223	G-OJCT	0080		2 LY IO-360-A1B6	1990	Y5		
□ C9-ATO	Partenavia P.68C	287	N39274	0083		2 LY IO-360-A1B6	1990	Y6		
□ C9-MEG	Partenavia P.68C	307	I-VIPX	0084		2 LY IO-360-A1B6	1990	Y6		
□ C9-MEA	Cessna 402C II	402C0055	ZS-KET	0079		2 CO TSIO-520-VB	3107	Y9		
□ C9-MEC	Cessna 402C II	402C0636		0082		2 CO TSIO-520-VB	3107	Y9		
□ C9-MEE	Cessna 402C III	402C0802	N1233K	0084		2 CO TSIO-520-VB	3107	Y9		
□ C9-MEF	Cessna 402C II	402C0204	N2713K	0080		2 CO TSIO-520-VB	3107	Y9		
□ C9-ASV	Beech King Air 200C	BL-21	N3831T	0081		2 PWC PT6A-41	5670	Y12 or C8		
□ C9-ASX	Beech King Air 200C	BL-32	N821CA	0081		2 PWC PT6A-41	5670	Y12 or C8		
□ C9-AST	CASA 212-CC22 Aviocar Series 200	167	HB-LMH	0080	0388	2 GA TPE331-10-501C	7450	Freighter		
□ C9-ASU	CASA 212-CC34 Aviocar Series 200	195	HB-LNG	0081	0388	2 GA TPE331-10-501C	7450	Freighter		

98 registration type of aircraft cn/fn ex/ex* mfd del powered by mtow kg configuration selcal name/fln/specialitites/remarks

☐ C9-ATM	CASA 212-CC46 Aviocar Series 200	308	F-GELO	0083	1089	2 GA TPE331-10-511C	7450	Freighter		
☐ C9-ATY	CASA 212-CD63 Aviocar Series 200	291	OO-FKY	0083	0391	2 GA TPE331-10R-512C	7450	Freighter		opf UN
☐ 3D-ALM	Fokker 100 (F28 Mk0100)	11335	PH-EZR*	0091	1096	2 RR Tay 650-15	44452	F12Y85		Lumbeluzi / lsf RSN
☐ C9-BAA	Boeing 737-2B1	20280 / 224		0069	1269	2 PW JT8D-9	46947	Y112		
☐ C9-BAC	Boeing 737-2B1C (A)	20536 / 289		0071	1071	2 PW JT8D-9	49442	Y112 / Frtr		
☐ ZS-SRA	Boeing 767-2B1 (ER)	26471 / 511		0093	0893	2 PW PW4056	175540	F10C28Y154	ES-LQ	lst SAA

NATAIR — Maputo

PO Box 2500, Maputo, Mozambique ☎ (1) 46 54 78 Tx: n/a Fax: (1) 46 54 80 SITA: n/a
F: n/a ⚲⚲⚲ n/a Head: n/a Net: n/a

☐ C9-EDM	Piper PA-34-220T Seneca III	34-8133214	N8429G	0081		2 CO TSIO-360-KB	2155			
☐ C9-ASL	Piper PA-31-350 Navajo Chieftain	31-8052004	N31PA	0080		2 LY TIO-540-J2BD	3175			

SABIN AIR — Maputo & Beira

PO Box 1599, Maputo, Mozambique ☎ (1) 46 51 08 Tx: n/a Fax: (1) 46 50 11 SITA: n/a
F: 1990 ⚲⚲⚲ 33 Head: Carlos Goncalves Net: n/a Aircraft below MTOW 1361kg: AA1 & AA5B (Trainers).

☐ C9-TAB	Twin (Aero) Commander 500B	500B-1463-164	3D-GAT	0064		2 LY IO-540-B1C	3062			
☐ C9-SAB	Piper PA-31-350 Navajo Chieftain	31-7552061	9Q-CSG	0075		2 LY TIO-540-J2BD	3175			
☐ 3D-NVA	Let 410UVP-E3	882035	2035	0088	1097	2 WA M-601E	6400	Y15		
☐ 3D-NVC	Let 410UVP	831033	RA-67405	0083	0096	2 WA M-601D	5800	Y15		Sluffy
☐ N40593	IAI 1121 Jet Commander	1121-41		0066	0394	2 GE CJ610-1	7938			

TTA – Empresa Nacional de Transporte e Trabalho Aéreo, S.A.R.L. = TTA — Maputo

PO Box 2054, Maputo, Mozambique ☎ (1) 49 17 65 Tx: 6539 tta mo Fax: (1) 49 17 63 SITA: n/a
F: 1980 ⚲⚲⚲ 375 Head: Estevao Alberto Jr. ICAO: TRANSAERO Net: n/a

☐ C9-AMH	Piper PA-32-300C Cherokee SIX	32-40682	ZS-IGO	0069		1 LY IO-540-K1A5	1542			
☐ C9-ALS	Britten-Norman BN-2A-6 Islander	174	G-AYDL*	0070		2 LY O-540-E4C5	2858			
☐ C9-AME	Britten-Norman BN-2A-6 Islander	118	G-AYIV*	0069		2 LY O-540-E4C5	2858			
☐ C9-AOV	Britten-Norman BN-2A-3 Islander	624	G-AYJF*	0070		2 LY IO-540-K1B5	2858			
☐ C9-APD	Britten-Norman BN-2A-9 Islander	683	G-AZXO*	0072		2 LY O-540-E4C5	2858			
☐ C9-APO	Britten-Norman BN-2A-2 Islander	687	G-AZXT*	0073		2 LY IO-540-K1B5	2858			
☐ C9-TAH	Britten-Norman BN-2T Turbine Islander	2120	G-BJEE*	0081		2 AN 250-B17C	3175			cvtd BN-2A-26
☐ C9-TAJ	Britten-Norman BN-2T Turbine Islander	2124	G-BJEJ*	0082		2 AN 250-B17C	3175			cvtd BN-2A-26
☐ C9-TAK	Britten-Norman BN-2T Turbine Islander	2121	G-BJEF*	0081		2 AN 250-B17C	3175			cvtd BN-2A-26

UNIQUE AIR CHARTER, S.A. (Subsidiary of Scan Air Charter Ltd, Swaziland/formerly Scan Transportes Aéreos, SA) — Maputo

PO Box 2276, Maputo, Mozambique ☎ (1) 46 55 92 Tx: none Fax: (1) 46 55 25 SITA: n/a
F: 1991 ⚲⚲⚲ 4 Head: Felicity V. Hermansson Net: n/a

☐ C9-STB	Cessna 402B	402B0613	3D-JBM	0074	0091	2 CO TSIO-520-E	2858			

D = GERMANY (Federal Republic of Germany) (Bundesrepublik Deutschland)

Capital: Berlin + Bonn Official Language: German Population: 85,0 million Square Km: 356945 Dialling code: +49 Year established: 1949 Acting political head: Gerhard Schröder (Federal Chancellor)

Government / Corporate / Executive / VIP Aircraft

German Air Force / Luftwaffe uses the ICAO code GAF and ICAO call sign GERMAN AIR FORCE.

☐ D-BEJR	Dornier 328JET (328-300)	3102		0098		2 PWC PW306B	14990	Testbed		Dornier / 2nd Prototype
☐ D-BJET	Dornier 328JET (328-300)	3002	D-CATI	0092		2 PWC PW306B	14990	Testbed		Dornier / Prototype / cvtd 328-110
☐ D-BWAL	Dornier 328JET (328-300)	3099		0098		2 PWC PW306B	14990	Testbed		Dornier / 3rd Prototype
☐ D-CLBA	Beech Beechjet 400A	RK-25	N81918	0092	0494	2 PWC JT15D-5	7303	Liasion / VIP		LBA Luftfahrt-Bundesamt
☐ 10+02	Boeing 707-307C	19998 / 750		0068	1068	4 PW JT3D-3B (HK2/COM)	146500	VIP / mil trans	CK-AE	Hans Grade / Luftwaffe
☐ 10+03	Boeing 707-307C	19999 / 756		0068	1068	4 PW JT3D-3B (HK2/COM)	146500	VIP / mil trans	CK-AF	August Euler / Luftwaffe
☐ 10+21	Airbus Industrie A310-304 (ET)	498	D-AOAA	0089	0891	2 GE CF6-80C2A2	157000	VIP	BM-PS	Luftwaffe
☐ 10+22	Airbus Industrie A310-304 (ET)	499	D-AOAB	0089	0891	2 GE CF6-80C2A2	157000	VIP	BM-QR	Luftwaffe
☐ 10+23	Airbus Industrie A310-304 (ET)	503	D-AOAC	0089	0991	2 GE CF6-80C2A2	157000	mil trans	BM-QS	Kurt Schumacher / Luftwaffe
☐ 10+24	Airbus Industrie A310-304 (F)	434	D-AIDA	0087	1196	2 GE CF6-80C2A2	153000	VIP/Combi/miltr	PS-AH	Luftwaffe / cvtd -304
☐ 10+25	Airbus Industrie A310-304	484	D-AIDB	0088	0896	2 GE CF6-80C2A2	153000	VIP / mil trans	PS-AJ	Luftwaffe
☐ 10+26	Airbus Industrie A310-304	522	D-AIDE	0089	0998	2 GE CF6-80C2A2	153000	VIP / mil trans		Luftwaffe
☐ 10+27	Airbus Industrie A310-304	523	D-AIDI	0090	1198	2 GE CF6-80C2A2	153000	VIP / mil trans		Luftwaffe
☐ 11+01	Tupolev 154M	799	DDR-SFA	0089	1090	3 SO D-30KU-154-II	100000	VIP / mil trans	AC-BG	Luftwaffe
☐ 12+01	Canadair CL-601-1A (CL-600-2A12) Challen.	3031	C-GCTB*	0084		2 GE CF34-1A	19550	VIP / mil trans	CJ-FK	Luftwaffe
☐ 12+02	Canadair CL-601-1A (CL-600-2A12) Challen.	3040	N608CL	0085		2 GE CF34-1A	19550	VIP / mil trans	CJ-FL	Luftwaffe
☐ 12+03	Canadair CL-601-1A (CL-600-2A12) Challen.	3043	N609CL	0085		2 GE CF34-1A	19550	VIP / mil trans	CJ-FM	Luftwaffe
☐ 12+04	Canadair CL-601-1A (CL-600-2A12) Challen.	3049	N610CL	0085		2 GE CF34-1A	19550	VIP / mil trans	CJ-GL	Luftwaffe
☐ 12+05	Canadair CL-601-1A (CL-600-2A12) Challen.	3053	N604CL	0086		2 GE CF34-1A	19550	VIP / mil trans	CJ-GM	Luftwaffe
☐ 12+06	Canadair CL-601-1A (CL-600-2A12) Challen.	3056	N612CL	0086		2 GE CF34-1A	19550	VIP / mil trans	CJ-HL	Luftwaffe
☐ 12+07	Canadair CL-601-1A (CL-600-2A12) Challen.	3059	N614CL	0086		2 GE CF34-1A	19550	VIP / mil trans	CJ-KL	Luftwaffe

ABC NORDFLUG, GmbH & Co. KG — Hamburg

Messberg 4, D-20095 Hamburg, Germany ☎ (40) 30 29 11 00 Tx: none Fax: (40) 30 29 11 01 SITA: n/a
F: 1988 ⚲⚲⚲ 4 Head: Willers Jessen Net: n/a

☐ D-IWHL	Cessna 525 CitationJet	525-0029	N13308	0093	0495	2 WRR FJ44-1A	4717	5 Pax		lsf pvt

ACH HAMBURG Flug, GmbH & Co. (formerly ACH Air Cargo Hamburg, GmbH & Co.) — Hamburg

Flughafen Gebäude 347, D-22335 Hamburg, Germany ☎ (40) 500 42 39 Tx: none Fax: (40) 50 75 10 92 SITA: n/a
F: 1990 ⚲⚲⚲ 9 Head: Hanna & Werner Daniels Net: n/a

☐ D-IBPN	Beech Baron 58P	TJ-424	N6526S	0082	0098	2 CO TSIO-520-WB	2812	4 Pax		lsf Air Charter Bremen
☐ D-IAGB	Beech King Air F90	LA-38	N888EM	0080		2 PWC PT6A-135	4967	6 Pax		lsf pvt
☐ D-IIWB	Beech King Air C90B	LJ-1340	N10799	0093	0098	2 PWC PT6A-21	4581	6 Pax		lsf GML Leasing
☐ D-ISTB	Beech King Air F90-1	LA-227	N330VP	0085	1298	2 PWC PT6A-135A	4967	6 Pax		lsf pvt
☐ D-IDBU	Piper PA-42-720 Cheyenne IIIA	42-5501029	N700CC	0585		2 PWC PT6A-61	5080	8 Pax		lsf Beate Uhse GmbH
☐ D-IBMP	Beech King Air B200	BB-1284	N6321V	0087	0198	2 PWC PT6A-42	5670	9 Pax		lsf B200 Flughcarter Leer GmbH

ACM Air Charter Luftfahrt, GmbH = BVR (formerly ACM Air Charter Minninger, GmbH) — Karlsruhe/Baden-Baden

Hangar D 415, D-77836 Rheinmünster, Germany ☎ (7229) 30 220 Tx: none Fax: (7229) 30 22 11 SITA: FKBACXH
F: 1992 ⚲⚲⚲ 18 Head: Thomas Minninger ICAO: BAVARIAN Net: n/a

☐ D-IPSY	Beech King Air B200	BB-1591		0097	0198	2 PWC PT6A-42	5670			lsf W&K Vermögensverwaltung
☐ D-CACM	Cessna 650 Citation VII	650-7039	N12643	0094	0495	2 GA TFE731-4R-2S	10180			lsf pvt
☐ D-CAYK	Cessna 650 Citation III	650-0187	N78PT	0090	0198	2 GA TFE731-3B-100S	9979			lsf Break Point Aircraft Ltd
☐ D-ASTS	Canadair CL-604 (CL-600-2B16) Challen.	5378	C-GDBZ*	0098	1298	2 GE CF34-3B	21863			lsf BAVA

ADAC Luftrettung, GmbH (Division of ADAC-Allgemeiner Deutscher Automobil-Club) — Munich

Am Westpark 8, D-81373 München, Germany ☎ (89) 76 76 21 24 Tx: 529231 ad Fax: (89) 76 76 28 35 SITA: n/a
F: 1982 ⚲⚲⚲ 65 Head: Gerhard Kugler Net: n/a Non-profit organisation. Additional ambulance aircraft are lsf / opb Aero-Dienst (Learjet 35A, BA 125-1000B & Beech 350) when required – see under that company.

☐ D-HDMA	Eurocopter (MBB) BO105CBS	S-414		0078	1181	2 AN 250-C20B	2400	EMS		
☐ D-HDPS	Eurocopter (MBB) BO105CBS	S-570		0082	0882	2 AN 250-C20B	2400	EMS		
☐ D-HEIM	Eurocopter (MBB) BO105CBS	S-672	N4573T	0084	0887	2 AN 250-C20B	2500	EMS		
☐ D-HELM	Eurocopter (MBB) BO105CBS	S-861		0091	1291	2 AN 250-C20B	2500	EMS		
☐ D-HEMS	Eurocopter (MBB) BO105CBS	S-615		0083	0583	2 AN 250-C20B	2400	EMS		
☐ D-HGAB	Eurocopter (MBB) BO105CBS	S-848	D-HFHF	0091	0591	2 AN 250-C20B	2500	EMS		
☐ D-HGYN	Eurocopter (MBB) BO105CBS	S-661		0083	1183	2 AN 250-C20B	2400	EMS		
☐ D-HHBG	Eurocopter (MBB) BO105CBS	S-625	VH-NSL	0083	1289	2 AN 250-C20B	2500	EMS		lst MAA Medical Air Assistance
☐ D-HHIT	Eurocopter (MBB) BO105CBS	S-872	N5096Y	0092	0195	2 AN 250-C20B	2500	EMS		
☐ D-HLFB	Eurocopter (MBB) BO105CBS	S-868	N3203K	0091	1095	2 AN 250-C20B	2500	EMS		
☐ D-HLRG	Eurocopter (MBB) BO105CBS	S-603	D-HDQZ	0083	0283	2 AN 250-C20B	2400	EMS		
☐ D-HOFF	Eurocopter (MBB) BO105CBS	S-612	D-HDSH	0083	0383	2 AN 250-C20B	2400	EMS		
☐ D-HUHN	Eurocopter (MBB) BO105CBS	S-867	N32022	0091	0496	2 AN 250-C20B	2500	EMS		
☐ D-HUPE	Eurocopter (MBB) BO105CBS	S-871	N4346G	0091	1196	2 AN 250-C20B	2500	EMS		
☐ D-HEUR	Eurocopter EC135T1	0042		0098	0198	2 TU Arrius 2B1	2720	EMS		
☐ D-HJAR	Eurocopter EC135T1	0044		0098	0198	2 TU Arrius 2B1	2720	EMS		
☐ D-HRET	Eurocopter EC135P1	0045		0098	0198	2 PWC PW206B	2720	EMS		
☐ D-HRHM	Eurocopter EC135T1	0027		0097	0897	2 TU Arrius 2B	2720	EMS		
☐ D-HSOS	Eurocopter EC135P1	0071		0098	0998	2 PWC PW206B	2720	EMS		
☐ D-HITH	MD Helicopters MD 900 Explorer	900-00029	N9125N	0095	0398	2 PWC PW206A	2835	EMS		lsf Air Lloyd
☐ D-HMDX	MD Helicopters MD 900 Explorer	900-00036	N9198Y	0096	0497	2 PWC PW206A	2835	EMS		lsf Air Lloyd
☐ D-HBAY	Eurocopter (MBB) BK117B-2	7205	LN-OSY	0090	0197	2 LY LTS101-750B.1	3350	EMS		cvtd B-1
☐ D-HBKK	Eurocopter (MBB) BK117B-2	7009		0083	0487	2 LY LTS101-750B.1	3350	EMS		cvtd BK117A-3

99 registration type of aircraft cn/fn ex/ex* mfd del powered by mtow kg configuration selcal name/fln/specialitites/remarks

☐ D-HBND	Eurocopter (MBB) BK117B-2	7056	OO-XCY	0085	0690	2 LY LTS101-750B.1	3350	EMS		cvtd BK117A-3
☐ D-HBRE	Eurocopter (MBB) BK117B-2	7184	G-HMBB	0088	0697	2 LY LTS101-750B.1	3350	EMS		
☐ D-HDAC	Eurocopter (MBB) BK117B-2	7005	D-HBKG	0082	0284	2 LY LTS101-750B.1	3350	EMS		cvtd BK117A-3
☐ D-HLTB	Eurocopter (MBB) BK117B-2	7224	N8196H	0091	0691	2 LY LTS101-750B.1	3350	EMS		cvtd BK117B-1
☐ D-HMUS	Eurocopter (MBB) BK117A-4	7031		0084	1098	2 LY LTS101-650B.1	3200	EMS		
☐ D-HMUZ	Eurocopter (MBB) BK117A-4	7100	D-HBPU	0087	0697	2 LY LTS101-650B.1	3200	EMS		
☐ D-HSFB	Eurocopter (MBB) BK117B-2	7240	D-HFIE	0094	0594	2 LY LTS101-750B.1	3350	EMS		

ADVANCE AIR Luftfahrt, GmbH & Co. Charter KG — Karlsruhe/Baden-Baden

Bussardweg 8, D-76199 Karlsruhe, Germany ☎ (721) 989 00 99 Tx: none Fax: (721) 88 33 87 SITA: n/a
F: 1997 n/a Head: n/a Net: n/a

☐ D-IFDK	Cessna 421C Golden Eagle III	421C0445	SE-IHO	0078	0498	2 CO GTSIO-520-L	3379			

AERO-DIENST, GmbH Executive Jet Service = ADN (Member of JET Europe) — Nuremberg

Postfach 99 01 31, D-90411 Nürnberg, Germany ☎ (911) 93 560 Tx: 622531z aero d Fax: (911) 935 64 08 SITA: NUEADCR
F: 1958 140 Head: Wolfgang Wenck ICAO: AERODIENST Net: n/a On order (Letter of Intent): 1 Bell 609 (tilt-rotor) for delivery 2001

☐ D-IILG	Beech King Air 300LW	FA-63	D-ILLG	0085		2 PWC PT6A-60A	5670	Executive		lsf Eisenwerk T. Loos GmbH
☐ D-CADN	Beech King Air 350 (B300)	FL-101	N82311	0093	0694	2 PWC PT6A-60A	6800	EMS ADAC		lsf R&R Flugzeugvermiet.GmbH / opf ADAC
☐ D-CCBW	Beech King Air 350 (B300)	FL-46	N81623	0091		2 PWC PT6A-60A	6800	Executive		lsf R&R Flugzeugvermietungs GmbH & Co.
☐ D-CSKY	Beech King Air 350 (B300)	FL-130		0095		2 PWC PT6A-60A	6800	EMS ADAC		lsf Intro Verwaltungs-GmbH / opf ADAC
☐ D-CDWN	Learjet 35A	35A-175		0078		2 GA TFE731-2-2B	8165	Executive / EMS		lsf Eder Maschinenfabrik GmbH
☐ D-CBWW	Hawker 1000B (BAe 125-1000B)	259028	G-5-749*	0092		2 PWC PW305	13999	EMS ADAC		lsf LFL Luftfahrzeug Leasing/opf ADAC

AEROLINE, GmbH — Westerland

Flughafen, D-25980 Westerland, Germany ☎ (4651) 78 77 Tx: none Fax: (4651) 92 97 07 SITA: n/a
F: 1992 5 Head: Daniela Kohnen Net: n/a Aircraft below MTOW 1361kg: Cessna 172 & Piper PA-28.

☐ D-ICWS	Reims/Cessna FT337GP Press. Skymaster	FP3370014		0075		2 CO TSIO-360-C	2130			lsf KT Kraftwerk / lic.blt cn P337-0195
☐ D-GFPG	Partenavia P.68B	170		0079		2 LY IO-360-A1B6	1960			lsf pvt

AERO LLOYD = YP / AEF (Aero Lloyd Flugreisen, GmbH & Co. Luftverkehrs KG dba / Affiliated with Aero Leasing International, GmbH) — Frankfurt

Lessingstr. 7-9, D-61440 Oberursel, Germany ☎ (6171) 62 500 Tx: 410555 d Fax: (6171) 62 51 19 SITA: FRAZZYP
F: 1981 1050 Head: Dipl. Ing. Reinhard B. Kipke IATA: 633 ICAO: AERO LLOYD Net: http://www.aerolloyd.de

☐ D-AGWB	Boeing (Douglas) MD-83 (DC-9-83)	49846 / 1581		0389	1090	2 PW JT8D-219	72575	Y165	DQ-EG	Eltville am Rhein
☐ D-ALLE	Boeing (Douglas) MD-83 (DC-9-83)	49449 / 1354		0387	0387	2 PW JT8D-219	72575	Y167	JL-BH	lsf DAL Operating-Leasing / Trigema-cs
☐ D-ALLF	Boeing (Douglas) MD-83 (DC-9-83)	49602 / 1435		1287	1287	2 PW JT8D-219	72575	Y167	JL-BK	lsf Chricor Equipment Finance Inc.
☐ D-ALLO	Boeing (Douglas) MD-83 (DC-9-83)	53012 / 1736		0690	0790	2 PW JT8D-219	72575	Y167	EH-LQ	
☐ D-ALLQ	Boeing (Douglas) MD-83 (DC-9-83)	53014 / 1740		0890	0890	2 PW JT8D-219	72575	Y167	EH-PQ	Leipzig / lsf DAL Operating-Leasing
☐ D-ALLR	Boeing (Douglas) MD-83 (DC-9-83)	53015 / 1818	N13627*	0191	0691	2 PW JT8D-219	72575	Y167	AF-DR	lsf GATX
☐ D-ALLV	Boeing (Douglas) MD-83 (DC-9-83)	49620 / 1484	EI-BTV	0588	0495	2 PW JT8D-219	72575	Y165	AQ-GH	lsf GECA
☐ D-ALAA	Airbus Industrie A320-232	565	F-WWDR*	0196	0196	2 IAE V2527-A5	75500	Y174	JS-DH	Halle (Saale) / lsf ILFC
☐ D-ALAB	Airbus Industrie A320-232	575	F-WWDU*	0396	0396	2 IAE V2527-A5	75500	Y174	JS-DK	lsf BAVA
☐ D-ALAC	Airbus Industrie A320-232	580	F-WWDV*	0396	0496	2 IAE V2527-A5	75500	Y174	JS-DL	to be lst LTU as D-ALTA 0599
☐ D-ALAD	Airbus Industrie A320-232	661	F-WWDK*	0397	0397	2 IAE V2527-A5	75500	Y174	BE-FJ	lsf ILFC
☐ D-ALAE	Airbus Industrie A320-232	659	F-WWIV*	0397	0397	2 IAE V2527-A5	75500	Y174	BE-GM	lsf Merlan-Mobilien-Verwaltungs GmbH
☐ D-ALAF	Airbus Industrie A320-232	667	F-WWBC*	0497	0497	2 IAE V2527-A5	75500	Y174	JL-BD	lsf ILFC
☐ D-ALAJ	Airbus Industrie A320-232	990				2 IAE V2527-A5	75500	Y174		oo-delivery 0599
☐ D-ALAG	Airbus Industrie A321-231	787	D-AVZL*	0098	0398	2 IAE V2533-A5	89000	Y210	LM-EJ	Stadt Linz / lsf ILFC
☐ D-ALAH	Airbus Industrie A321-231	792	D-AVZM*	0098	0398	2 IAE V2533-A5	89000	Y210	CF-GK	Trigema-colors
☐ D-ALAI	Airbus Industrie A321-231	954		0099	0299	2 IAE V2533-A5	89000	Y210		lsf ILFC / Trigema-colors
☐ D-ALAK	Airbus Industrie A321-231	1004				2 IAE V2533-A5	89000	Y210		to be lsf ILFC 0599
☐ D-	Airbus Industrie A321-231					2 IAE V2533-A5	89000	Y210		oo-delivery 0300
☐ D-	Airbus Industrie A321-231					2 IAE V2533-A5	89000	Y210		to be lsf ILFC 0400
☐ D-	Airbus Industrie A321-231					2 IAE V2533-A5	89000	Y210		to be lsf ILFC 0400
☐ D-	Airbus Industrie A321-231					2 IAE V2533-A5	89000	Y210		to be lsf ILFC 0201
☐ D-	Airbus Industrie A321-231					2 IAE V2533-A5	89000	Y210		oo-delivery 0301
☐ D-	Airbus Industrie A321-231					2 IAE V2533-A5	89000	Y210		to be lsf ILFC 0901

AERORENT, GmbH — Hamburg

c/o Michael Krystek, Buchenkamp 22, D-38126 Braunschweig, Germany ☎ (531) 592 50 16 Tx: none Fax: none SITA: n/a
F: 1994 n/a Head: Michael Krystek Net: n/a

☐ D-IIAS	Cessna 421C Golden Eagle III	421C1055	HB-LQH	0081		2 CO GTSIO-520-N	3379			lsf W.H. Janssen Treuhand GmbH

AEROTEC, GmbH (Aerotec Technische Handels- & Vertriebs GmbH dba) — Rothenburg, Halle-Oppin & Hof

Friedensstrasse 113, D-02929 Rothenburg, Germany ☎ (35891) 46 600 Tx: none Fax: (35891) 46 609 SITA: n/a
F: 1993 n/a Head: Jürgen Nappe Net: n/a

☐ D-HZPF	PZL Swidnik (Mil) Mi-2	563402034	LSK-302	0074		2 IS GTD-350-III	3550	6 Pax or Cargo		
☐ D-HZPO	PZL Swidnik (Mil) Mi-2	543048083	DDR-VGK	0073		2 IS GTD-350-III	3550	6 Pax or Cargo		
☐ S9-TBK	Let 410UVP-E3	871939	1939	0987	0097	2 WA M-601E	6400	Freighter/Para		lsf ATEC
☐ D-HOZI	Mil Mi-8S	0826	DDR-VHI	0068		2 IS TV2-117A (G)	12000	Utility		
☐ D-HOZJ	Mil Mi-8T	10520	DDR-VHJ	0073		2 IS TV2-117A (G)	12000	Utility		std Halle-Oppin
☐ S9-TAH	Mil Mi-8T	10549	93+37	0077		2 IS TV2-117A (G)	12000	Utility		lsf ATEC
☐ S9-TAF	Isolair (Mil Mi-14BT) Terminator II	34011	95+10	0085		2 IS TV3-117MT-3	14000	Water Bomber		Amphibian / lsf ATEC
☐ S9-TAG	Isolair (Mil Mi-14BT) Terminator II	34012	95+11	1085		2 IS TV3-117MT-3	14000	Water Bomber		Amphibian / lsf ATEC
☐ S9-TAI	Isolair (Mil Mi-14BT) Terminator II	34013	95+12	0085		2 IS TV3-117MT-3	14000	Water Bomber		Amphibian / lsf ATEC / std Halle-Oppin
☐ S9-TAJ	Isolair (Mil Mi-14BT) Terminator II	34010	95+09	0085		2 IS TV3-117MT-3	14000	Water Bomber		Amphibian / lsf ATEC

AEROTEC AIRWAYS, GmbH & Co. KG (Sister company of Aerotec GmbH, Rothenburg) — Rothenburg

Friedensstrasse 113, D-02929 Rothenburg, Germany ☎ (35891) 46 600 Tx: none Fax: (35891) 46 609 SITA: n/a
F: 1993 n/a Head: Jürgen Nappe Net: n/a

☐ D-GLAD	Piper PA-34-200T Seneca II	34-7970427	LX-YES	0079	1097	2 CO TSIO-360-EB1	1999			
☐ D-COXC	Let 410UVP	820925	DDR-SXC	0082		2 WA M-601D	6000	Y16 / Frtr		lsf UVW-Leasing GmbH
☐ OY-TCL	Let 410UVP-E20C	912533	OK-WDL	0091	0296	2 WA M-601E	6400	Y19 / Frtr		lsf NAC Holding ApS
☐ OY-TCM	Let 410UVP-E20C	912532	OK-WDJ	0091	0896	2 WA M-601E	6600	Y19 / Frtr		lsf NAC Holding ApS/sub-lst Aero Andes

AEROWEST Braunschweig, GmbH (formerly Aerowest Flugcharter, GmbH) — Hannover

Postfach 420248, D-30662 Hannover-Flughafen, Germany ☎ (511) 973 03 30 Tx: 9230918 awb d Fax: (511) 72 18 06 SITA: n/a
F: 1965 n/a Head: Martin Ewers Net: http://www.aw-aerowest.com Aircraft below MTOW 1361kg: Cessna 172 & 182

☐ D-ICHS	Cessna 425 Conquest I	425-0233	N80938	0085		2 PWC PT6A-112	3900			
☐ D-CDUW	Cessna 560 Citation V	560-0099	OE-GPA	0090	0698	2 PWC JT15D-5A	7212			

AEROWEST Flug Center, GmbH — Braunschweig

Lilienthalplatz 5, D-38108 Braunschweig, Germany ☎ (531) 35 13 30 Tx: none Fax: (531) 35 30 29 SITA: n/a
F: 1980 3 Head: Manfred Müller Net: n/a

☐ D-IAFC	Cessna T303 Crusader	T30300244	N9959C	0083		2 CO TSIO-520-AE	2336			lsf Tipair Reisen GmbH
☐ D-IGCW	Cessna T303 Crusader	T30300177	N9457C	0082		2 CO TSIO-520-AE	2336			lsf HLW Leasing GmbH

AEROWEST PHOTOGRAMMETRIE H. Benfer, GmbH — Dortmund-Wickede

Flugplatz 8, D-44319 Dortmund, Germany ☎ (231) 21 25 93 Tx: none Fax: (231) 21 81 69 SITA: n/a
F: 1970 50 Head: Ralf Benfer Net: n/a

☐ D-IAPD	Cessna 404 Titan II	404-0679	N679R	0080	1192	2 CO GTSIO-520-M	3810	Photo / Survey		

AFC Alster-Flug-Center Lamz, GmbH — Hamburg

Flughafengebäude 347 (GAT), D-22335 Hamburg, Germany ☎ (40) 500 01 47 Tx: none Fax: (40) 500 08 16 SITA: n/a
F: 1984 5 Head: Dieter Lamz Net: n/a Aircraft below MTOW 1361kg: Cessna 172

☐ D-ILMS	Cessna 421C Golden Eagle III	421C0891	N919PW	0080		2 CO GTSIO-520-L	3379			

AFS-Airway Flight Service, GmbH & Co. KG — Bad Nauheim/Reichelsheim

Hessenstr. 23, D-65719 Hofheim-Wollau, Germany ☎ (6122) 91 32 17 Tx: none Fax: (6122) 91 32 38 SITA: n/a
F: 1994 n/a Head: Frank Müller Net: n/a

☐ D-HRMM	Bell 206B JetRanger III	4339		0095		1 AN 250-C20J	1450			lsf Gerd Müller Ingeneirubau GmbH
☐ D-IHMM	Piper PA-31T1 Cheyenne I	31T-8104066	N82LC	0081		2 PWC PT6A-11	3946			

AGRARFLUG HELILIFT, GmbH & Co. KG (formerly Agrarflug Ahlen, GmbH & Co. KG) — Ahlen

Warendorferstrasse 190, D-59227 Ahlen, Germany ☎ (2382) 82 082 Tx: none Fax: (2382) 24 14 SITA: n/a
F: 1975 25 Head: Klaus Beese Net: n/a Aircraft below MTOW 1361 kg: Cessna 172, 182 & Pitts S-2B

☐ D-HAFA	Bell 206B JetRanger	124	G-HELO	0067	0892	1 AN 250-C20	1451			cvtd 206A
☐ D-HAFD	Agusta-Bell 206B JetRanger II	8534	G-BMCH	0077	1292	1 AN 250-C20	1451			
☐ D-HAFI	Agusta-Bell 206B JetRanger III	8492	OE-BXT	0075	0394	1 AN 250-C20B	1451			cvtd JetRanger

100 registration type of aircraft cn/fn ex/ex* mfd del powered by mtow kg configuration selcal name/fln/specialitites/remarks

☐ D-HAFY	Agusta-Bell 206B JetRanger III	8654		0084		1 AN 250-C20B	1451			
☐ D-GAFA	Piper PA-34-200T Seneca II	34-7970218	N2247Z	0079	1192	2 CO TSIO-360-EB1	1999			
☐ D-HAFU	Eurocopter (Aerosp.) AS350B Ecureuil	1788		0084		1 TU Arriel 1B	1950			
☐ D-HAFH	Bell 205A-1	30291	SE-HVT	0079	1293	1 LY T5313B	4309			
☐ D-HAFL	Bell 205A-1	30056	LN-ORY	0069	0695	1 LY T5313B	4309			
☐ D-HAFM	Bell 205A-1	30101	VR-BFW	0071		1 LY T5313B	4309			
☐ D-HAFR	Bell 205A-1	30318	N8227H	0080	0889	1 LY T5313B	4309			
☐ D-HOOK	Bell 205A-1	30206	N205AH	0075		1 LY T5313B	4309			
☐ D-HAFG	Agusta-Bell 212	5629		0076	0199	2 PWC PT6T-3 TwinPac	5080			
☐ D-HAFS	Bell 212	30655	ZK-HNK	0074	0394	2 PWC PT6T-3 TwinPac	5080			lsf VR-Leasing
☐ D-HAFV	Agusta-Bell 212	5504	I-AGUV	0072	0495	2 PWC PT6T-3 TwinPac	5080			lsf VR-Leasing GmbH

AIR ALBATROS, GmbH — Essen-Muelheim

Brunshofstrasse 1, D-45470 Mülheim/Ruhr, Germany ☎ (208) 37 01 91 Tx: none Fax: (208) 75 51 01 SITA: n/a
F: 1995 n/a Head: Lothar Steinbiss Net: n/a Operates sightseeing flights (with Antonov 2) only.

☐ D-FKMC	Antonov An-2	17612	LSK-454	0057	1195	1 SH ASh-62IR	5500	9 Pax		Baronesse
☐ D-FONE	Antonov An-2	18118	DDR-SKE	0057	0495	1 SH ASh-62IR	5500	9 Pax		Roter Baron

AIR-BERLIN, GmbH & Co. Luftverkehrs KG = AB / BER (formerly Air Berlin, Inc.) — Berlin-Tegel

Flughafen-Tegel, D-13405 Berlin, Germany ☎ (30) 41 01 27 81 Tx: 307429 abgl d Fax: (30) 413 20 03 SITA: TXLEXAB
F: 1978 400 Head: Joachim Hunold IATA: 745 ICAO: AIR BERLIN Net: n/a

☐ D-ABAB	Boeing 737-4K5	24769 / 1839	N11AB	0090	0490	2 CFMI CFM56-3C1	68000	Y167	BG-JQ	lsf KG Aircraft Leasing Co. Ltd
☐ D-ABAE	Boeing 737-46J	27171 / 2465		0093	0493	2 CFMI CFM56-3C1	68000	Y167	DR-AG	lsf Euconus Flugzeugleasing GmbH
☐ D-ABAG	Boeing 737-46J	27213 / 2585		0094	0394	2 CFMI CFM56-3C1	68000	Y167	FJ-ER	lsf Euconus Flugzeugleasing GmbH
☐ D-ABAH	Boeing 737-46J	27826 / 2694		0095	0295	2 CFMI CFM56-3C1	68000	Y167	FP-CG	lsf Euconus Flugzeugleasing GmbH
☐ D-ABAI	Boeing 737-46J	28038 / 2794		0096	0596	2 CFMI CFM56-3C1	68000	Y167	KP-MR	
☐ D-ABAK	Boeing 737-46J	28271 / 2801		0096	0696	2 CFMI CFM56-3C1	68000	Y167	KR-GJ	lsf J. Hunold & Co. Flugzeugvermietung
☐ D-ABAL	Boeing 737-46J	28334 / 2802		0096	0696	2 CFMI CFM56-3C1	68000	Y167	LQ-HR	lsf J. Hunold & Co. Flugzeugvermietung
☐ D-ABAM	Boeing 737-46J	28867 / 2879		0097	0497	2 CFMI CFM56-3C1	68000	Y167	KS-PR	lsf AB Dritte Flugzeugvermietung
☐ D-ABAN	Boeing 737-86J	28068 / 36	N35153*	0098	0598	2 CFMI CFM56-7B27	78245	Y184	DH-CS	lsf AB Erste Flugzeugvermietung
☐ D-ABAO	Boeing 737-86J	28069 / 42	N5573B*	0098	0598	2 CFMI CFM56-7B27	78245	Y184	FH-GQ	lsf J. Hunold & Co. Flugzeugvermietung
☐ D-ABAP	Boeing 737-86J	28070 / 106		0098	1098	2 CFMI CFM56-7B27	78245	Y184		lsf J. Hunold & Co. Flugzeugvermietung
☐ D-ABAQ	Boeing 737-86J	28071 / 133		1098	1098	2 CFMI CFM56-7B27	78245	Y184		lsf J. Hunold & Co. Flugzeugvermietung
☐ D-ABAR	Boeing 737-86J	28072 / 147	N1786B*	1198	1198	2 CFMI CFM56-7B27	78245	Y184		lsf J. Hunold & Co. Flugzeugvermietung
☐ D-ABAS	Boeing 737-86J	28073 / 200	N1795B*	0099	0299	2 CFMI CFM56-7B27	78245	Y184		
☐ D-ABAT	Boeing 737-86J	29120 / 202	N1786B*	0099	0299	2 CFMI CFM56-7B27	78245	Y184		
☐ D-ABAU	Boeing 737-86J	29121				2 CFMI CFM56-7B27	78245	Y184		oo-delivery 0799
☐ D-ABAV	Boeing 737-86J					2 CFMI CFM56-7B27	78245	Y184		oo-delivery 0002
☐ D-ABAW	Boeing 737-86J					2 CFMI CFM56-7B27	78245	Y184		oo-delivery 0002

AIRCHARTER Flugservice, GmbH & Co. KG (formerly Aircharter Heinz Conzelmann) — Donaueschingen

Boschstr. 13, D-78655 Dunningen, Germany ☎ (7403) 91 30 16 Tx: none Fax: (7403) 91 30 17 SITA: n/a
F: 1992 2 Head: Detlef Keinath Net: http://www.aircharter.de

☐ D-IEAH	Beech King Air C90A	LJ-1216	N1562Z	0089		2 PWC PT6A-21	4377			lsf Fischerwerke Artur Fischer GmbH

AIR CONNECT Houfek, GmbH — Hamburg

Richthofenstr. 5, D-25436 Uetersen, Germany ☎ (40) 50 75 10 87 Tx: none Fax: (40) 50 75 10 88 SITA: n/a
F: 1986 4 Head: Ralph Houfek Net: n/a

☐ D-IFUN	Beech King Air C90	LJ-874	N44486	0079		2 PWC PT6A-21	4377			

AIR EVEX, GmbH = EVE (formerly EVEX-Fluggesellschaft, mbH & Co. KG) — Duesseldorf

Flughafen, Halle 3, D-40474 Düsseldorf, Germany ☎ (211) 421 66 60 Tx: 8581458 evex d Fax: (211) 454 19 02 SITA: n/a
F: 1975 13 Head: Beethold Kelsch ICAO: SUNBEAM Net: n/a

☐ D-IJYP	Cessna 525 CitationJet	525-0165		0096		2 WRR FJ44-1A	4717			lsf AL Leasing
☐ D-IRKE	Cessna 525 CitationJet	525-0123		0095	0196	2 WRR FJ44-1A	4717			lsf H.D.E. Air
☐ D-CTAN	Cessna 560 Citation V	560-0150		0091	0192	2 PWC JT15D-5A	7212			lsf Barclays Industrie Leasing
☐ D-CDEN	Learjet 31A	31A-049		0091	0292	2 GA TFE731-2-3B	7484			lsf H.D.E. Air

AIR EVEX WESTFALIA, GmbH & Co. KG — Paderborn-Lippstadt

Flughafen Paderborn-Lippstadt, D-33142 Büren-Ahden, Germany ☎ (2955) 77 444 Tx: none Fax: (2955) 69 00 SITA: n/a
F: 1992 5 Head: Dieter Pape Net: n/a

☐ D-FUNY	Pilatus PC-6/B2-H4 Turbo Porter	894		0093		1 PWC PT6A-27	2800			lsf Funy Flugzeug-Vermietung GmbH&Co.KG
☐ D-IERI	Beech King Air B100	BE-29	N7729B	0077		2 GA TPE331-6-252B	5352			lsf Warsteiner Charterflug
☐ D-IKIW	Beech King Air C90	LJ-641	N7128H	0074	0898	2 PWC PT6A-20	4377			
☐ D-IFLY	De Havilland DHC-6 Twin Otter 300	628	LN-BNT	0079		2 PWC PT6A-27	5670			lsf Fly Flugzeug-Vermietung GmbH&Co. KG
☐ D-ISKY	De Havilland DHC-6 Twin Otter 300	462	C-GGVX	0075	0395	2 PWC PT6A-27	5670			lsf Sky Flugzeug-Vermietung GmbH&Co.KG

AIR LLOYD Deutsche Helicopter Flugservice, GmbH — Bonn-Hangelar & Halle-Oppin

Flugplatz Bonn-Hangelar, D-53757 St. Augustin, Germany ☎ (2241) 23 070 Tx: none Fax: (2241) 23 07 30 SITA: n/a
F: 1963 25 Head: Wolfgang Schad Net: n/a Aircraft below MTOW 1361 kg: Bell 47G / T, Robinson R22 & R44.

☐ D-HMOE	MD Helicopters MD 500D (Hughes 369D)	911077D	D-HMAU	0081	0098	1 AN 250-C20B	1361			
☐ D-HAKY	Bell 206B JetRanger III	2687	OE-DXU	0079		1 AN 250-C20B	1451			
☐ D-HIPY	Bell 206B JetRanger III	4186		0091		1 AN 250-C20J	1451			
☐ D-HITH	MD Helicopters MD 900 Explorer	900-00029	N9125N	0095	0398	2 PWC PW206A	2835	EMS		lst ADAC Luftrettung
☐ D-HMDX	MD Helicopters MD 900 Explorer	900-00036	N9198Y	0096	0497	2 PWC PW206A	2835	EMS		lst ADAC Luftrettung

AIR SERVICE WILDGRUBER, GmbH — Friedrichshafen-Löwental

Flugplatz Löwental, D-88046 Friedrichshafen, Germany ☎ (7541) 28 158 Tx: none Fax: (7541) 28 158 SITA: n/a
F: 1991 3 Head: Jan Wildgruber Net: n/a

☐ D-FDFF	Pilatus PC-6/B1-H2 Turbo Porter	629	HB-FDF	0068	0798	1 PWC PT6A-20	2200	Para		lsf pvt
☐ D-IDHC	De Havilland DHC-6 Twin Otter 100	71	C-FCIJ	0067	0691	2 PWC PT6A-20	5260	Pax/Cargo/Para		

AIRSHIP Air Service, GmbH — Berlin-Schoenefeld

Flughafen Schönefeld, D-12527 Berlin, Germany ☎ (30) 60 91 38 00 Tx: none Fax: (30) 60 91 38 02 SITA: n/a
F: 1992 n/a Head: Michael Kozak Net: n/a Aircraft below MTOW 1361kg: Cessna 150/152/172 & HOAC DV20

☐ D-EGUT	Cessna TR182 Turbo Skylane RG II	R18200668	N9204R	0079		1 LY O-540-L3C5D	1406			lsf pvt
☐ D-GAKK	Piper PA-34-200T Seneca II	34-7770097	D-IKKD	0076		2 CO TSIO-360-EB	1999			lsf pvt

AIR TRAFFIC, GmbH - Executive Jet Service = ATJ — Duesseldorf

Flughafen Halle 3, D-40474 Düsseldorf, Germany ☎ (211) 421 66 42 Tx: 8584755 airt d Fax: (211) 436 02 52 SITA: n/a
F: 1969 12 Head: Rüdiger Streffing & Georg Knaak ICAO: SNOOPY Net: n/a

☐ D-INWK	Fairchild (Swearingen) SA226T Merlin IIIA	T-255	N5349M	0075		2 GA TPE331-3U-303G	5670			lsf Rudas Studios KG
☐ D-CGPD	Learjet 35A	35A-202	N499G	0078		2 GA TFE731-2-2B	8300			lsf Knaak/Steffing Gbr
☐ D-CHPD	Learjet 35A	35A-309	N100MN	0080	0790	2 GA TFE731-2-2B	7824			lsf Knaak/Steffing Gbr
☐ D-CLUE	Cessna 650 Citation III	650-0174	N674CC	0089		2 GA TFE731-3B-100S	9980			lsf GEG KG

ALBATROS FLUGDIENST, GmbH & Co. KG — Oldenburg-Hatten

Flugplatz, D-26209 Hatten, Germany ☎ (4481) 92 79 76 Tx: none Fax: (4481) 92 79 77 SITA: n/a
F: n/a n/a Head: Angelika Winters Net: n/a Aircraft below MTOW 1361kg: Piper PA-28

☐ D-EEMJ	Piper PA-32R-300 Lance	32R-7780175	N1682H	0077		1 LY IO-540-K1G5D	1633			lsf pvt
☐ D-GDDC	Piper PA-34-200T Seneca II	34-7770016	D-IMGU	0076		2 CO TSIO-360-EB	1999			lsf pvt

ALPHA AIR Luftfahrt, GmbH — Paderborn

Flugplatzstr. 33, D-33142 Büren-Ahden, Germany ☎ (2955) 77 410 Tx: none Fax: (2955) 77 409 SITA: n/a
F: 1988 n/a Head: Mrs. Adelheid Leber Net: n/a

☐ D-IANA	Beech King Air B200	BB-1517	N3217V	0095	0196	2 PWC PT6A-42	5670			lsf KLW Mietflug

ALPHAFLUG (Alphaflug Pilotenausbildung & Flugbetriebs, GmbH dba) — Stuttgart

Postfach 23 02 43, D-70622 Stuttgart, Germany ☎ (711) 948 49 28 Tx: none Fax: (711) 797 00 57 SITA: n/a
F: 1984 3 Head: Manfred Rappold Net: n/a Aircraft below MTOW 1361kg: Cessna 150/152/172 & 182.

☐ D-IAFM	Cessna 414	414-0354	N1574T	0072		2 CO TSIO-520-J	2880			

AMADEUS FLUGDIENST, GmbH & Co. KG — Hahn

Flughafen Hahn, Geb. 510, D-55483 Lautzenhausen, Germany ☎ (6543) 50 91 19 Tx: none Fax: (6543) 50 91 18 SITA: n/a
F: 1996 n/a Head: Jörg Kunkel Net: n/a Aircraft below MTOW 1361kg: Cessna 172

☐ D-EIFC	Reims/Cessna FR182 Skylane RG II	FR182-0002		0078		1 LY O-540-J3C5D	1406			
☐ D-INPA	Cessna 421B Golden Eagle	421B0647	OE-FVW	0074	0697	2 CO GTSIO-520-H	3379			

101 registration type of aircraft cn/fn ex/ex* mfd del powered by mtow kg configuration selcal name/fln/specialitites/remarks

ARCUS-AIR Logistic, GmbH & Co. KG. — Mannheim

Lütticher Str. 12, D-53842 Troisdorf, Germany ☎ (2241) 95 25 30 Tx: none Fax: (2241) 40 61 28 SITA: n/a
F: 1973 n/a Head: Erhard Ding Net: n/a All flights are operated by COSMOS AIR under ZE flight numbers and are conducted exclusively for Arcus-Air Logistic with ARCUS-AIR titles.

☐ D-IAAD	Reims/Cessna F406 Caravan II	F406-0047	N6589A	0091	0392	2 PWC PT6A-112	4468	Y9 / Freighter		lst / opb Cosmos Air
☐ D-CAAM	Dornier 228-212	8205		0091	1191	2 GA TPE331-5A-252D	6575	Y17 / Freighter		lst / opb Cosmos Air
☐ D-CUTT	Dornier 228-212	8200		0091	1191	2 GA TPE331-5A-252D	6575	Y17 / Freighter		lst / opb Cosmos Air

ATEC Flugcharter, GmbH & Co. KG — Kiel

Eekbrook 15, D-24159 Kiel, Germany ☎ (431) 369 19 40 Tx: none Fax: (431) 369 19 50 SITA: n/a
F: 1978 3 Head: Horst Schoen Net: n/a

☐ D-IDIT	Cessna 414 II	414-0953	N9KJ	0077		2 CO TSIO-520-NB	2880			

ATF Air Transport Flug, GmbH & Co. KG — Bindlach

Flugplatz Strasse 1, D-95463 Bindlach, Germany ☎ (9221) 97 460 Tx: none Fax: (9221) 97 46 99 SITA: n/a
F: 1976 7 Head: Christian Schneider Net: n/a

☐ D-IHDE	Beech King Air C90	LJ-725		0077		2 PWC PT6A-21	4377			

ATLAS AIR SERVICE, GmbH – AAS — Ganderkesee

PO Box 1201, D-27777 Ganderkesee, Germany ☎ (4222) 450 Tx: none Fax: (4222) 45 50 SITA: n/a
F: 1970 50 Head: Michael Laux Net: http://www.atlas-air-service.de Aircraft below MTOW 1361kg: Cessna 182

☐ D-IRGW	Cessna 425 Conquest I	425-0165	N425SP	0082	1197	2 PWC PT6A-112	3901			lsf Weber Vertrieb Int'l B.V.
☐ D-IFAN	Cessna 525 CitationJet	525-0214		0097	0997	2 WRR FJ44-1A	4717			lsf pvt
☐ D-CMIC	Cessna 560XL Citation Excel	560-5021	N5244F*	0098	0599	2 PWC PW545A	8709			lsf pvt

AUGSBURG AIRWAYS, GmbH = IQ / AUB (Team Lufthansa) — Augsburg

(Subsidiary of Interot Spedition, GmbH / formerly Interot Airways, GmbH & Interot Air Service)
Stephingergraben 12, D-86152 Augsburg, Germany ☎ (821) 310 98 79 Tx: 533836 inair d Fax: (821) 310 98 93 SITA: AGBSPIQ
F: 1988 330 Head: Olaf Dlugi IATA: 614 ICAO: AUGSBURG AIR Net: n/a
Scheduled services are operated in conjunction with Lufthansa as a Team franchise partner (in full Team Lufthansa colors & titles) using LH flight numbers.

☐ D-BAGB	De Havilland DHC-8-103 Dash 8	306	C-GFOD*	0091	1191	2 PWC PW121	15650	C37		Philippine Welser / op in Team LH cs
☐ D-BDUS	De Havilland DHC-8-106 Dash 8	253	OE-LLL	0090	1096	2 PWC PW121	16500	C37		lsf TYR/cvtd -103/op in Team LH colors
☐ D-BFRA	De Havilland DHC-8-102 Dash 8	243	OE-LLI	0090	0397	2 PWC PW120A	15650	C37	AM-KP	lsf ELVE / op in Team Lufthansa colors
☐ D-BHAL	De Havilland DHC-8-202 Dash 8Q	463	C-GFOD*	0097	1297	2 PWC PW123D	16500	C37		lsf BAWAG Mobilien Lsg/op in Team LH-cs
☐ D-BIER	De Havilland DHC-8-103 Dash 8	310	OE-LEA	0091	0892	2 PWC PW121	15650	C37		lsf ELVE/cvtd -102/op in Team LH colors
☐ D-BIRT	De Havilland DHC-8-103 Dash 8	260	C-GFOD*	0091	0291	2 PWC PW121	15650	C37		Agnes Bernauer
☐ D-	De Havilland DHC-8-202 Dash 8Q					2 PWC PW123D	16500	C37		oo-delivery 0899/to be op in Team LH-cs
☐ D-BACH	De Havilland DHC-8-314 Dash 8	365		0093	0893	2 PWC PW123B	19500	C50		Kaiser Augustus / op in Team LH colors
☐ D-BHAM	De Havilland DHC-8-311 Dash 8	313	OE-LEC	0092	1097	2 PWC PW123	19500	C50		lsf ELVE / op in Team Lufthansa colors
☐ D-BHAS	De Havilland DHC-8-311 Dash 8Q	503	C-GDLD*	0097	0198	2 PWC PW123	18600	C50		lsf BAWAG Mobilien Lsg/op in Team LH-cs
☐ D-BHAT	De Havilland DHC-8-311 Dash 8Q	505	C-GDFT*	0097	0198	2 PWC PW123	18600	C50		lsf BAWAG Mobilien Lsg/op in Team LH-cs
☐ D-BKIM	De Havilland DHC-8-311 Dash 8	356	C-GFOD*	0393	1096	2 PWC PW123	19500	C50		lsf GECA / op in Team Lufthansa colors
☐ D-BLEJ	De Havilland DHC-8-314 Dash 8Q	521	C-FDHU*	0098	0299	2 PWC PW123B	19500	C50		lsf BAWAG Mob/op in Team LH-cs/cvtd-311
☐ D-BMUC	De Havilland DHC-8-314 Dash 8	350	C-GUAY	0093	0396	2 PWC PW123B	19500	C50		lsf ELVE
☐ D-BPAD	De Havilland DHC-8-314 Dash 8Q	523	C-FDHW*	0099	1098	2 PWC PW123B	18600	C50		lsf BAWAG Mob/op in Team LH-cs/cvtd-311
☐ D-	De Havilland DHC-8-314 Dash 8Q					2 PWC PW123B	19500	C50		oo-delivery 0200/to be op in Team LH-cs
☐ D-	De Havilland DHC-8-314 Dash 8Q					2 PWC PW123B	19500	C50		oo-delivery 0300/to be op in Team LH-cs
☐ D-	De Havilland DHC-8-314 Dash 8Q					2 PWC PW123B	19500	C50		oo-delivery 0300/to be op in Team LH-cs

AUGUSTA AIR Luftfahrtunternehmen Hans Schneider = AUF — Augsburg, Koeln & Braunschweig

(Affiliated with Beechcraft Vertrieb & Service, GmbH)
Flughafenstr. 5, D-86169 Augsburg, Germany ☎ (821) 700 31 47 Tx: none Fax: (821) 700 31 53 SITA: n/a
F: 1985 7 Head: Max Bauer ICAO: AUGUSTA Net: n/a

☐ D-ICBC	Beech King Air 300LW	FA-227	N81418	0093	0195	2 PWC PT6A-60A	5670			lsf Kronospan GmbH
☐ D-CAAA	Beech King Air 350 (B300)	FL-116	N350EA	0094	0498	2 PWC PT6A-60A	6800			
☐ D-CBBB	Beech King Air 350 (B300)	FL-120	N1512H	0094	0195	2 PWC PT6A-60A	6800			
☐ D-CHSW	Beech Beechjet 400A	RK-84	N8138M	0094	0395	2 PWC JT15D-5	7303			

AVANTI AIR, GmbH & Co. KG = EEX — Frankfurt

Am Kraftenborn 10, D-63654 Büdingen, Germany ☎ (6041) 82 730 Tx: none Fax: (6041) 82 73 99 SITA: FRAAACR
F: 1994 10 Head: Markus Baumann ICAO: EUROEXPRESS Net: http://www.avantiair.com

☐ D-IJCL	Piaggio P.180 Avanti	1017	N14P	0092	0897	2 PWC PT6A-66	5238			lsf Diskont & Kredit AG
☐ D-ICHG	Beech King Air B200	BB-1400	N8085D	0091		2 PWC PT6A-42	5670			lsf Diskont & Kredit AG
☐ D-CARA	Beech 1900C Airliner	UB-59	N72391	0086	1296	2 PWC PT6A-65B	7530			lsf Diskont & Kredit AG
☐ D-CBSF	Beech 1900D Airliner	UE-8	N55778	0092	0198	2 PWC PT6A-67D	7690			lsf Diskont & Kredit AG

BADEN AIR, GmbH — Karlsruhe/Baden-Baden

Baden-Baden Airport, Geb. B-410, D-77836 Rheinmünster, Germany ☎ (7229) 66 23 00 Tx: none Fax: (7229) 66 23 09 SITA: n/a
F: 1998 n/a Head: Michael Kürvers Net: n/a

☐ D-BOBO	De Havilland DHC-8-102 Dash 8	153	C-GFOD*	0089	0798	2 PWC PW120A	15650	Y36		lst / opb RUS in Baden Air-colors

BADENIA WINGS — Karlsruhe/Baden-Baden

(Division of Flugservice GmbH/affiliated with Air Charter Badenia Flugzeugvercharterung GmbH)
Flugplatz Karlsruhe, D-76287 Rheinstetten, Germany ☎ (721) 51 70 35 Tx: none Fax: (721) 51 74 23 SITA: n/a
F: 1992 5 Head: Jürgen Gossweiler Net: n/a Aircraft below MTOW 1361kg: Cessna 150, 152, 172, Piper PA-28 & Socata TB9.

☐ D-	Beech King Air 200	BB-				2 PWC PT6A-41	5670			oo-delivery 0099

BAL Bremerhaven Airline, GmbH — Bremerhaven

Flughafen Luneort, D-27572 Bremerhaven, Germany ☎ (471) 971 21 00 Tx: none Fax: (471) 971 21 02 SITA: n/a
F: 1997 3 Head: Bernd Boettcher Net: n/a

☐ D-IAAI	Britten-Norman BN-2B-26 Islander	2167	N405RM	0085	0897	2 LY O-540-E4C5	2814			
☐ D-IABB	Beech King Air C90A	LJ-1235	N1569N	0090		2 PWC PT6A-21	4581			lsf Gardinen & Stoff Boettcher GmbH

BAVARIA International Aircraft Leasing, GmbH & Co. KG = (BAVA) — Munich

(formerly Bavaria Flug, GmbH & Co.)
Denningerstr. 165, D-81925 München, Germany ☎ (89) 923 82 37 Tx: none Fax: (89) 923 83 80 SITA: n/a
F: 1965 7 Head: Robert Salzl & Karsten Sensenh Net: n/a
New aircraft leasing and financing company. Owner/lessor of following (main) aircraft types: Airbus A320, Boeing 717 (on order), 737-200, -300 & -700.
Aircraft leased from BAVA are listed and mentioned as such under the leasing carriers.

BETZLER HELI-LINE — Aschaffenburg-Grossostheim

Flugplatz, D-63762 Grossostheim, Germany ☎ (6026) 99 49 49 Tx: none Fax: (6026) 99 49 50 SITA: n/a
F: 1995 n/a Head: Volker Betzler Net: n/a

☐ D-HHBI	Bell 206BR+ JetRanger III	4210		0092		1 AN 250-C20R/4	1450			occ lst Heli Team, Austria / cvtd 206B

BIN AIR Aero Service, GmbH — Munich

Maria-Probst-Str. 22, D-80939 München, Germany ☎ (89) 318 90 90 Tx: none Fax: (89) 31 89 09 55 SITA: n/a
F: 1995 n/a Head: Eugen Pansow Net: n/a

☐ D-ICRK	Fairchild (Swearingen) SA226TC Metro II	TC-333	4X-CSD	0080	1297	2 GA TPE331-3UW-303G	5670	Y18		lsf LHG Leasing

BIZAIR Flug, GmbH — Berlin-Tempelhof

Darwinstr. 4, D-10589 Berlin, Germany ☎ (30) 344 82 55 Tx: none Fax: (30) 344 60 20 SITA: n/a
F: 1991 7 Head: Andreas Peter Net: n/a

☐ D-ISAZ	Beech King Air B200	BB-983	N983EB	0081		2 PWC PT6A-42	5670			lsf Diskont & Kredit AG

BMW FLUGDIENST = BMW — Munich

(Division of BMW)
General Aviation Terminal, Postfach GAT, D-85356 München, Germany ☎ (89) 97 59 74 00 Tx: none Fax: (89) 97 59 74 06 SITA: n/a
F: 1987 n/a Head: Capt. Gisbert Gaiber ICAO: BMW-FLIGHT Net: n/a Non-commercial flight department conducting corporate flights exclusively for its parent company only.

☐ D-CBMW	Hawker 800XP	258345	D-CBMV	0097	0598	2 GA TFE731-5BR-1H	12701	Executive		
☐ N414BM	GAC G-IV Gulfstream IV (SP)	1214	N405GA	0093	1293	2 RR Tay 611-8	33838	Corporate	FH-QS	lsf BMW Operations Corp.

BRITANNIA AIRWAYS, GmbH = BN / DBY — Berlin-Schoenefeld

(Subsidiary of Britannia Airways Ltd, Great Britain)
Zeppelinstr. 3, D-15732 Waltersdorf, Germany ☎ (33762) 55 900 Tx: none Fax: (33762) 55 90 77 SITA: SXFOOBY
F: 1997 200 Head: Peter Steiner ICAO: WINDSOR Net: n/a

☐ D-AGYC	Boeing 767-304 (ER)	28041 / 614	G-OBYC	0096	0498	2 GE CF6-80C2B7F	186880	Y328	JR-AE	lsf BAL
☐ D-AGYE	Boeing 767-304 (ER)	28979 / 691	G-OBYE	0298	1098	2 GE CF6-80C2B7F	186880	Y328	LM-RS	lsf BAL
☐ D-AGYF	Boeing 767-304 (ER)	28208 / 705	G-OBYF	0098	0698	2 PW PW4060	186880	Y328	BG-KP	lsf BAL
☐ D-AGYH	Boeing 767-304 (ER)	28883 / 737	G-OBYH	0099	0399	2 GE CF6-80C2B7F	186880	Y328		lsf BAL

102 registration type of aircraft cn/fn ex/ex* mfd del powered by mtow kg configuration selcal name/fln/specialitites/remarks

BSF Hubschrauber-Dienste, GmbH (Subsidiary of BSF Berliner Spezialflug, AG) — Berlin-Schoenefeld

Wasmannsdorferstrasse, D-15831 Diepensee, Germany ☎ (30) 633 85 46 Tx: n/a Fax: (30) 633 85 46 SITA: n/a
F: n/a ✈✈✈ n/a Head: n/a Net: n/a Aircraft below MTOW 1361kg: Hughes 269C (300C).

☐ D-HEAS	Bell 206B JetRanger III	4163	LN-OBE	0091		1 AN 250-C20J	1451			lsf Diskont & Kredit AG
☐ D-HBHB	Bell 206L-3 LongRanger III	51545	C-FMEA*	0091		1 AN 250-C30P	1882			lsf Diskont & Kredit AG
☐ D-HOXC	Mil Mi-8T	10583	DDR-SPC	0077		2 IS TV2-117A (G)	12000			
☐ D-HOXP	Mil Mi-8T	105102	DDR-SPP	0084		2 IS TV2-117A (G)	12000			lsf Adler Air Leasing
☐ D-HOXQ	Mil Mi-8T	105103	DDR-SJA	0084		2 IS TV2-117A (G)	12000			lsf Adler Air Leasing

BSF Luftbild & Vermessungen, GmbH (Subsidiary of BSF Berliner Spezialflug, AG) — Berlin-Schoenefeld

Wasmannsdorferstrasse, D-15831 Diepensee, Germany ☎ (30) 633 84 04 Tx: none Fax: (30) 633 84 14 SITA: n/a
F: 1978 ✈✈✈ 20 Head: Dipl. Ing. Horst Huth Net: n/a

☐ D-EIHW	Cessna TU206G Turbo Stationair 6 II	U20606114		0081		1 CO TSIO-520-M	1633	Photo/Survey/Pax		lsf Diskont & Kredit AG
☐ D-EBMW	Cessna 207 Skywagon	20700088	OE-DEV	0069		1 CO IO-520-F	1724	Photo/Survey		lsf Diskont & Kredit AG
☐ D-EBSD	Cessna 207A Stationair 8 II	20700644	N207PP	0080		1 CO IO-520-F	1724	Photo/Survey		lsf Diskont & Kredit AG

BUSINESS AIR CHARTER, GmbH — Gera

Ronneburger Strasse 74, D-07546 Gera, Germany ☎ (365) 43 99 90 Tx: none Fax: (365) 439 99 22 SITA: n/a
F: 1997 ✈✈✈ n/a Head: Gerd Breckle Net: http://www.business-air-charter.de

☐ D-IAMB	Beech King Air 200	BB-790	F-GIAX	0080		2 PWC PT6A-41	5670			lsf Aero-Flugcharter GmbH
☐ D-CAMM	Beech King Air 350 (B300)	FL-64		0091		2 PWC PT6A-60A	6804			lsf Aero-Flugcharter GmbH

BUSINESSWINGS Luftfahrtunternehmen, GmbH (formerly Aerotrans Flugcharter, GmbH & Aero Fallschirm-Sport, GmbH) — Kassel-Calden

Verkehrslandeplatz Kassel-Calden, D-34379 Calden, Germany ☎ (5674) 99 930 Tx: none Fax: (5674) 99 93 33 SITA: n/a
F: 1989 ✈✈✈ 3 Head: Willi Roland Net: n/a

☐ D-FALK	Cessna 208 Caravan I	20800023	N9354F	0085		1 PWC PT6A-114	3311			
☐ D-IVER	De Havilland DHC-6 Twin Otter 300	411	SE-IYP	0074	0593	2 PWC PT6A-27	5675			

CANAIR Luftfahrtunternehmen — Hamburg

Dammtorstr. 20, D-20354 Hamburg, Germany ☎ (40) 34 43 08 Tx: none Fax: (40) 34 07 14 SITA: n/a
F: 1990 ✈✈✈ 4 Head: Stefan Hinners Net: n/a Aircraft below MTOW 1361kg: Cessna 172

☐ D-GIWA	Piper PA-34-200T Seneca II	34-8070145	D-IEWA	0080	0998	2 CO TSIO-360-EB1	1999			
☐ D-IBJH	Cessna T303 Crusader	T30300297	N5433V	0084		2 CO TSIO-520-AE	2336			lsf BSR Naturstein-Aufbereitungs-GmbH

CCF manager airline, GmbH = CCF (formerly Cologne Commercial Flight Reise- und Industrieflug, GmbH) — Cologne

Postfach 98 01 23, D-51129 Köln, Germany ☎ (2203) 952 80 Tx: 884265 ccf d Fax: (2203) 952 86 SITA: n/a
F: 1984 ✈✈✈ 10 Head: Harald Kaempf ICAO: TOMCAT Net: n/a

☐ D-ICVW	Cessna 421C Golden Eagle II	421C0260	N6146G	0077		2 CO GTSIO-520-L	3379	6 Pax		lsf pvt
☐ D-IAAC	Cessna 441 Conquest II (Super 8)	441-0073	N88834	0078		2 GA TPE331-8-511S	4468	9 Pax / EMS		lsf pvt / cvtd Conquest II
☐ D-CCCF	Cessna 550 Citation II	550-0189	HB-VGP	0080	0197	2 PWC JT15D-4	6600	8 Pax		lsf pvt

CENTRAL AIR FLUGCHARTER, GmbH — Kassel-Calden

Ederweg 2, D-34379 Calden, Germany ☎ (5674) 67 32 Tx: none Fax: (5674) 40 52 SITA: n/a
F: 1998 ✈✈✈ n/a Head: Hermann Krug Net: n/a

☐ D-IKOB	Beech King Air B200	BB-921		0081	1298	2 PWC PT6A-42	5670			

CHALLENGE AIR Luftverkehrs, GmbH — Cologne-Bonn

Steinstr. 2-4, D-53844 Troisdorf, Germany ☎ (2241) 98 70 Tx: none Fax: (2241) 98 71 95 SITA: n/a
F: 1996 ✈✈✈ 8 Head: Peter Finkel Net: n/a

☐ D-IRIS	Beech King Air F90-1	LA-229	N7209Z	0084		2 PWC PT6A-135A	4967			lsf pvt
☐ D-BSNA	Canadair CL-600S (CL-600-1A11) Challenger	1066	N51TJ	0082		2 LY ALF502L-2C	18643			lsf pvt

CHARTERFLUG STAHNKE — Altenburg-Nobitz

Mühlweg 4b, D-09385 Erlbach-Kirchberg, Germany ☎ (37295) 40 490 Tx: none Fax: (37295) 40 491 SITA: n/a
F: 1992 ✈✈✈ n/a Head: Gregor Stahnke Net: n/a Aircraft below MTOW 1361kg: Cessna 172

☐ D-IHDS	Cessna T310R II	310R0658	N98242	0077		2 CO TSIO-520-B	2495			

CHARTER SERVICE HETZLER Luftfahrtunternehmen, GmbH — Frankfurt

Flughafen, Gebäude 514, D-60549 Frankfurt/Main, Germany ☎ (69) 95 29 70 70 Tx: 4032099 flug d Fax: (69) 51 80 20 SITA: n/a
F: n/a ✈✈✈ n/a Head: Helmut Hetzler Net: n/a Company is also conducting flights on behalf of CHARTERFLUG ROYAL GmbH (air charter brokerage), Frankfurt.

☐ D-IMME	Cessna 551 Citation II/SP	551-0400	N280JS	0082	0391	2 PWC JT15D-4	5670	9 Pax		lsf AGV Verm. / cvtd Ce 550 cn 550-0359

CIRRUS AIRLINES, Luftfahrt GmbH = C9 / RUS — Saarbrücken-Ensheim

Flughafen, D-66131 Saarbrücken, Germany ☎ (6893) 80 040 Tx: none Fax: (6893) 80 04 20 SITA: SCNOPC9
F: 1991 ✈✈✈ n/a Head: Gerd Brandecker IATA: 251 ICAO: CIRRUS AIR Net: n/a

☐ D-IHRA	Piaggio P.180 Avanti	1019		0092		2 PWC PT6A-66	4944	Y8		lsf HA-RA Umwelt- & Reinigungstechnik
☐ D-ICIR	Beech King Air B200	BB-1051	N6912T	0083		2 PWC PT6A-42	5670	Y10		lsf pvt
☐ D-IAWA	Cessna 551 Citation II/SP	551-0421	N550RD	0082		2 PWC JT15D-4	5670	Y8		lsf pvt / cvtd Ce550 cn550-0422
☐ D-CCON	Learjet 55	55-098	N726L	0084	0098	2 GA TFE731-3AR-2B	9752	Y7		lsf pvt
☐ D-BOBL	De Havilland DHC-8-102 Dash 8	225	C-GFQL*	0090	0498	2 PWC PW120A	15650	Y36		lsf pvt
☐ D-BOBO	De Havilland DHC-8-102 Dash 8	153	C-GFOD*	0089	0998	2 PWC PW120A	15650	Y36		lsf/opf Baden Air in Baden Air-colors
☐ D-BOBY	De Havilland DHC-8-102 Dash 8	177	C-GFQL*	0089	0398	2 PWC PW120A	15650	Y36		lsf pvt

COMAIR REISE & CHARTER, GmbH — Vilshofen

Flugplatz, D-94474 Vilshofen, Germany ☎ (851) 80 61 10 Tx: none Fax: (8541) 87 47 SITA: n/a
F: 1990 ✈✈✈ 4 Head: Rudolf Deglmann Net: n/a

☐ D-IHBP	Beech King Air C90B	LJ-1424	N3252J	0095	1295	2 PWC PT6A-21	4581			

COMFORT-AIR Luftfahrtunternehmen, GmbH & Co. KG (formerly Comfort-Air Flugzeugvermietungs, GmbH & Co. KG) — Munich

Normannenstr. 22, D-81925 München, Germany ☎ (89) 998 39 30 Tx: none Fax: (89) 99 83 93 33 SITA: n/a
F: 1978 ✈✈✈ 3 Head: Rudolf Neumeyr Net: n/a

☐ D-ITSV	Cessna 525 CitationJet	525-0084		0094		2 WRR FJ44-1A	4717			lsf pvt
☐ D-CLEO	Cessna 560 Citation V	560-0159	N68MA	0092	0398	2 PWC JT15D-5A	7212			lsf pvt

CONDOR = DE / CFG (Condor Flugdienst, GmbH dba / Subsidiary of Lufthansa) — Frankfurt

Postfach 1164, D-65440 Kelsterbach, Germany ☎ (6107) 93 90 Tx: n/a Fax: (6107) 93 95 20 SITA: n/a
F: 1961 ✈✈✈ 2250 Head: Dr. D.Kirchner & R.V.Oertzen & F.Schoib IATA: 881 ICAO: CONDOR Net: n/a

☐ D-ABNA	Boeing 757-230	24737 / 267		0090	0390	2 PW PW2040	103900	Y210	FQ-AK	lsf Lufthansa Leasing
☐ D-ABNB	Boeing 757-230	24738 / 274		0090	0490	2 PW PW2040	103900	Y210	FQ-AL	lsf Lufthansa Leasing
☐ D-ABNC	Boeing 757-230	24747 / 275		0090	0490	2 PW PW2040	103900	Y210	FQ-AM	lsf Lufthansa Leasing
☐ D-ABND	Boeing 757-230	24748 / 285		0090	0590	2 PW PW2040	103900	Y210	FQ-AP	lsf Lufthansa Leasing
☐ D-ABNE	Boeing 757-230	24749 / 295	N35153*	0090	0790	2 PW PW2040	103900	Y210	FQ-BC	lsf Lufthansa Leasing
☐ D-ABNF	Boeing 757-230	25140 / 382		0091	0791	2 PW PW2040	103900	Y210	BF-MQ	lsf Havel Aircraft Ltd / Rizzi Bird cs
☐ D-ABNH	Boeing 757-230	25436 / 419		0092	0192	2 PW PW2040	113400	Y207	AJ-BR	
☐ D-ABNI	Boeing 757-230	25437 / 422		0092	0192	2 PW PW2040	103900	Y210	AJ-BS	lsf Spruce Operation Co. Ltd
☐ D-ABNK	Boeing 757-230	25438 / 428		0092	0292	2 PW PW2040	103900	Y210	AJ-CR	lsf Mosel & Lahn Aircraft Ltd
☐ D-ABNL	Boeing 757-230	25439 / 437		0092	0392	2 PW PW2040	103900	Y210	AJ-CS	
☐ D-ABNM	Boeing 757-230	25440 / 443		0092	0492	2 PW PW2040	103900	Y210	AJ-DR	lsf DIA Ltd
☐ D-ABNN	Boeing 757-230	25441 / 446		0092	0492	2 PW PW2040	113400	Y207	AJ-DS	
☐ D-ABNO	Boeing 757-230	25901 / 464		0092	0692	2 PW PW2040	103900	Y210	LM-ES	
☐ D-ABNP	Boeing 757-230	26433 / 521		0093	0293	2 PW PW2040	113400	Y207	CP-AR	
☐ D-ABNR	Boeing 757-230	26434 / 532		0093	0393	2 PW PW2040	113400	Y207	CP-AS	
☐ D-ABNS	Boeing 757-230	26435 / 537		0093	0493	2 PW PW2040	113400	Y207	CP-RS	
☐ D-ABNT	Boeing 757-230	26436 / 587	N1790B*	0094	0394	2 PW PW2040	103900	Y210	EP-LR	lsf Lufthansa Leasing
☐ D-ABNX	Boeing 757-27B	24838 / 302	PH-AHL	0090	1090	2 RR RB211-535E4	103900	Y210	KQ-JM	for sale 1199
☐ D-ABOA	Boeing 757-330	29016 / 804	N757X*	0098	0399	2 RR RB211-535E4-B	122470	Y250		
☐ D-ABOB	Boeing 757-330	29017 / 810	N6067B*	0099	0399	2 RR RB211-535E4-B	122470	Y250		
☐ D-ABOC	Boeing 757-330	29015 / 818	N6069D*	0099	0399	2 RR RB211-535E4-B	122470	Y250		
☐ D-ABOE	Boeing 757-330	29012 / 839	N1012N*	0099	0499	2 RR RB211-535E4-B	122470	Y250		
☐ D-ABOF	Boeing 757-330	29013				2 RR RB211-535E4-B	122470	Y250		oo-delivery 0599
☐ D-ABOG	Boeing 757-330	29014				2 RR RB211-535E4-B	122470	Y250		oo-delivery 0799
☐ D-ABOH	Boeing 757-330	30030				2 RR RB211-535E4-B	122470	Y250		oo-delivery 0799
☐ D-ABOI	Boeing 757-330					2 RR RB211-535E4-B	122470	Y250		oo-delivery 0200
☐ D-ABOJ	Boeing 757-330					2 RR RB211-535E4-B	122470	Y250		oo-delivery 0300

103 registration type of aircraft cn/fn ex/ex* mfd del powered by mtow kg configuration selcal name/fln/specialitites/remarks

☐ D-ABOK	Boeing 757-330					2 RR RB211-535E4-B	122470	Y250		oo-delivery 0400
☐ D-ABOL	Boeing 757-330					2 RR RB211-535E4-B	122470	Y250		oo-delivery 0500
☐ D-ABOM	Boeing 757-330					2 RR RB211-535E4-B	122470	Y250		oo-delivery 0600
☐ D-ABON	Boeing 757-330					2 RR RB211-535E4-B	122470	Y250		oo-delivery 0700
☐ D-ABUA	Boeing 767-330 (ER)	26991 / 455		0092	1092	2 PW PW4060	184600	C24Y245	LM-BR	lsf NBB Frankfurt Lease
☐ D-ABUB	Boeing 767-330 (ER)	26987 / 466		0092	1292	2 PW PW4060	184600	C24Y245	LM-BS	lsf CG-Kumiai
☐ D-ABUC	Boeing 767-330 (ER)	26992 / 470		0092	0193	2 PW PW4060	184600	C24Y245	CM-PR	lsf NBB Bonn Lease
☐ D-ABUD	Boeing 767-330 (ER)	26983 / 471		0092	0193	2 PW PW4060	184600	C24Y245	CM-PS	lsf NBB Bonn Lease
☐ D-ABUE	Boeing 767-330 (ER)	26984 / 518	N1788B*	0093	1093	2 PW PW4060	184600	C24Y245	CM-QR	lsf Lufthansa Leasing
☐ D-ABUF	Boeing 767-330 (ER)	26985 / 537		0094	0494	2 PW PW4060	184600	C24Y245	CM-QS	
☐ D-ABUH	Boeing 767-330 (ER)	26986 / 553	N6046P*	0094	0993	2 PW PW4060	184600	C24Y245	CM-RS	
☐ D-ABUI	Boeing 767-330 (ER)	26988 / 562		0095	0195	2 PW PW4060	184600	C24Y245	DF-LQ	
☐ D-ABUZ	Boeing 767-330 (ER)	25209 / 382		0091	0791	2 PW PW4060	184600	C24Y245	AE-JS	
☐ D-ADQO	Boeing (Douglas) DC-10-30	46596 / 301		0079	1279	3 GE CF6-50C2	263100	Y370	FL-AD	for sale to OAE as N630AX, 0699
☐ D-ADSO	Boeing (Douglas) DC-10-30	48252 / 342		0081	0181	3 GE CF6-50C2	263100	Y370	BL-CD	for sale 1099

CONDOR BERLIN, GmbH = CIB (Subsidiary of Condor Flugdienst, GmbH) — Berlin-Schoenefeld

Flughafen Schönefeld, D-12521 Berlin, Germany ☎ (30) 88 75 52 10 Tx: none Fax: (30) 88 75 52 19 SITA: SXFUODE
F: 1997 ⁂ n/a Head: Peter Lini ICAO: CONDOR BERLIN Net: n/a

☐ D-AICA	Airbus Industrie A320-212	774	F-WWDN*	0098	0298	2 CFMI CFM56-5A3	77000	Y174	JK-DP	
☐ D-AICB	Airbus Industrie A320-212	793	F-WWDU*	0098	0398	2 CFMI CFM56-5A3	77000	Y174	JK-EP	
☐ D-AICC	Airbus Industrie A320-212	809	F-WWIE*	0098	0498	2 CFMI CFM56-5A3	77000	Y174		
☐ D-AICD	Airbus Industrie A320-212	884	F-WWDE*	0098	1098	2 CFMI CFM56-5A3	77000	Y174		
☐ D-AICE	Airbus Industrie A320-212	894	F-WWDI*	0098	1098	2 CFMI CFM56-5A3	77000	Y174		
☐ D-AICF	Airbus Industrie A320-212	905	F-WWDP*	0098	1198	2 CFMI CFM56-5A3	77000	Y174		
☐ D-AICG	Airbus Industrie A320-212	957	F-WWBE*	0099	0399	2 CFMI CFM56-5A3	77000	Y174		
☐ D-AICH	Airbus Industrie A320-212	971		0099	0399	2 CFMI CFM56-5A3	77000	Y174		
☐ D-AICI	Airbus Industrie A320-212					2 CFMI CFM56-5A3	77000	Y174		oo-delivery 1100
☐ D-AICJ	Airbus Industrie A320-212					2 CFMI CFM56-5A3	77000	Y174		oo-delivery 1200
☐ D-AICK	Airbus Industrie A320-212					2 CFMI CFM56-5A3	77000	Y174		oo-delivery 0101
☐ D-AICL	Airbus Industrie A320-212					2 CFMI CFM56-5A3	77000	Y174		oo-delivery 0401

CONSETA Luftfahrt, GmbH = COC (formerly Conseta Luftverkehrs, GmbH) — Saarbruecken-Ensheim

Flughafen Saarbrücken, D-66131 Saarbrücken-Ensheim, Germany ☎ (6893) 83 368 Tx: none Fax: (6893) 80 04 25 SITA: n/a
F: n/a ⁂ 5 Head: Gerd Brandecker ICAO: CONSETA AIR Net: n/a

☐ D-IEKG	Beech King Air C90	LJ-867	HB-GIH	0079		2 PWC PT6A-21	4377			lsf pvt
☐ D-IUDE	Beech King Air C90B	LJ-1323	N90KA	0093	0998	2 PWC PT6A-21	4581			lsf Wolfgang Preinfalk GmbH

CONTACT AIR Interregional = KIS (Team Lufthansa) (ContactAir Flugdienst, GmbH & Co. KG dba) — Stuttgart

Postfach 23 04 42, D-70624 Stuttgart, Germany ☎ (711) 16 76 50 Tx: none Fax: (711) 167 65 65 SITA: n/a
F: 1974 ⁂ 260 Head: Gunther Eheim ICAO: CONTACTAIR Net: n/a
Scheduled services are operated in conjunction with Lufthansa as a Team franchise partner (in full Team Lufthansa colors & titles) using LH flight numbers.

☐ D-AFFI	Fokker 50 (F27 Mk050)	20272	PH-LXL*	0093	0996	2 PWC PW125B	20820	C50	DS-EK	lsf CLH / op in Team Lufthansa colors
☐ D-AFFX	Fokker 50 (F27 Mk050)	20142	EC-GAF	0088	1296	2 PWC PW125B	20820	C50		lsf CLH / op in Team Lufthansa colors
☐ D-AFFY	Fokker 50 (F27 Mk050)	20141	EC-GAE	0088	1196	2 PWC PW125B	20820	C50		lsf CLH / op in Team Lufthansa colors
☐ D-AFFZ	Fokker 50 (F27 Mk050)	20133	EC-GAD	0088	1096	2 PWC PW125B	20820	C50		lsf CLH / op in Team Lufthansa colors
☐ D-AFKK	Fokker 50 (F27 Mk050)	20205	PH-EXN*	0090	1096	2 PWC PW125B	20820	C50	KL-CH	lsf CLH / op in Team Lufthansa colors
☐ D-AFKL	Fokker 50 (F27 Mk050)	20213	PH-EXC*	0091	0596	2 PWC PW125B	20820	C50	KL-CJ	lsf CLH / op in Team Lufthansa colors
☐ D-AFKM	Fokker 50 (F27 Mk050)	20214	PH-EXD*	0091	0696	2 PWC PW125B	20820	C50	KL-CM	lsf CLH / op in Team Lufthansa colors
☐ D-AFKN	Fokker 50 (F27 Mk050)	20223	PH-EXX*	0091	0197	2 PWC PW125B	20820	C50	LM-BD	lsf CLH / op in Team Lufthansa colors
☐ D-AFKO	Fokker 50 (F27 Mk050)	20234	PH-JXO*	0091	0197	2 PWC PW125B	20820	C50	LM-BE	lsf CLH / op in Team Lufthansa colors
☐ D-AFKP	Fokker 50 (F27 Mk050)	20235	PH-EXE*	0091	0297	2 PWC PW125B	20820	C50	LM-BF	lsf CLH / op in Team Lufthansa colors
☐ D-AFKU	Fokker 50 (F27 Mk050)	20236	PH-JXL*	0092	0397	2 PWC PW125B	20820	C50	LM-BG	lsf CLH / op in Team Lufthansa colors

CORNELIUS HUBSCHRAUBER — St. Peter-Ording

Vörreeg 6, D-27804 Berne, Germany ☎ (4406) 93 930 Tx: none Fax: (4406) 93 930 SITA: n/a
F: n/a ⁂ n/a Head: Walter H. Hölter Net: n/a Aircraft below MTOW 1361kg: Enstrom F28A, Hughes 269C (300C) & 369HS (500C)

☐ D-HCHS	MD Helicopters MD 500E (Hughes 369E)	0230E	OE-XXL	0087		1 AN 250-C20B	1400			

COSMOS AIR Luftfahrtunternehmen, GmbH = ZE / AZE (Associated with Arcus-Air Logistics, GmbH & Co. KG) — Mannheim

Flugplatz, D-68163 Mannheim-Neuostheim, Germany ☎ (621) 42 60 40 Tx: none Fax: (621) 426 04 26 SITA: MHGDRZE
F: 1997 ⁂ 70 Head: Gerhard Brandecker & Manfred Dambach IATA: 583 ICAO: COSY Net: http://www.cosmos-air.de

☐ D-IAAD	Reims/Cessna F406 Caravan II	F406-0047	N6589A	0091	0497	2 PWC PT6A-112	4468	Y9 / Freighter		lsf / opf Arcus-Air
☐ D-CAAM	Dornier 228-212	8205		0091	0497	2 GA TPE331-5A-252D	6575	Y17 / Freighter		lsf / opf Arcus-Air
☐ D-CUTT	Dornier 228-212	8200		0091	0497	2 GA TPE331-5A-252D	6575	Y17 / Freighter		lsf / opf Arcus-Air
☐ D-COSA	Dornier 328-110	3085	D-CDXR*	0097	0497	2 PWC PW119B	13990	Y31		Mannheim / lsf Bahag AG
☐ D-	Dornier 328-110					2 PWC PW119B	13990	Y31		oo-delivery 0499

CYCON CITY CONNECTION, GmbH — Moenchengladbach

Flughafen Mönchengladbach, Am Flughafen 34, D-41006 Mönchengladbach, Germany ☎ (2161) 66 64 04 Tx: none Fax: (2161) 66 49 51 SITA: n/a
F: 1996 ⁂ n/a Head: Bernhild Melcher Net: http://www.cycon-flug.de Aircraft below MTOW 1361kg: Cessna 152, 172 & Piper PA-28

☐ D-IPMG	Cessna T303 Crusader	T30300222	N121JH	0083		2 CO TSIO-520-AE	2336			lsf IKB Leasing GmbH
☐ D-IWAL	Beech King Air F90	LA-100	HB-GHP	0080		2 PWC PT6A-135	4967			lsf Willi Waldhausen

DAIMLERCHRYSLER AVIATION (Division of DaimlerChrysler AG) — Stuttgart

c/o DaimlerChrysler AG, D-70546 Stuttgart, Germany ☎ (711) 179 39 70 Tx: none Fax: (711) 179 86 10 SITA: n/a
F: 1999 ⁂ n/a Head: Frank Rösler Net: n/a Operates non-commercial personnel-transfer-flights for the DaimlerChrysler group of companies. Flights are contracted out to TRANSMERIDIAN (N) until delivery of its A319CJ.

☐ D-	Airbus Industrie A319-132 (CJ)					2 IAE V2524-A5	70000	Corporate		oo-delivery 1299
☐ N573DC	Airbus Industrie A320-232	573	CS-MAD	0096	0299	2 IAE V2527-A5	77000	Corporate 50Pax		lsf / opb TRZ

DAS Duscholux Flugbetrieb, GmbH — Mannheim

Flugplatz Neuostheim, D-68163 Mannheim, Germany ☎ (621) 41 34 60 Tx: none Fax: (621) 41 24 86 SITA: n/a
F: n/a ⁂ n/a Head: n/a Net: n/a

☐ D-IDUX	Cessna 340A II	340A0934		0079		2 CO TSIO-520-NB	2717			
☐ D-IDAG	Cessna 525 CitationJet	525-0144		0096	0796	2 WRR FJ44-1A	4717			

DEUTSCHE BA Luftfahrt, GmbH = DI / BAG (Subsidiary of British Airways, Plc) — Munich

Postfach 23 16 24, D-85325 München-Flughafen, Germany ☎ (89) 97 59 15 00 Tx: none Fax: (89) 97 59 15 03 SITA: MUCWWDI
F: 1992 ⁂ 800 Head: Carl H. Michel IATA: 944 ICAO: SPEEDWAY Net: http://www.deutsche-ba.de

☐ D-ADBA	Boeing 737-3L9	26441 / 2250	OY-MAL	0092	0692	2 CFMI CFM56-3B2	58849	Y136	LQ-KM	Metropolis / lsf DAN / Popart-colors
☐ D-ADBC	Boeing 737-3L9	26442 / 2277	OY-MAM	0092	0692	2 CFMI CFM56-3B2	58849	Y136	LQ-KS	Enzian / lsf DAN / Bavaria-colors
☐ D-ADBG	Boeing 737-3L9	25125 / 2059	OY-MMW	0091	1092	2 CFMI CFM56-3B2	58849	Y136	LQ-PR	Edelweiss / lsf DAN / Bavaria-colors
☐ D-ADBH	Boeing 737-3L9	27336 / 2587	OY-MAO	0094	0196	2 CFMI CFM56-3C1	58849	Y136	LQ-PS	Bavaria / lsf Heller Fin. / Bavaria-cs
☐ D-ADBI	Boeing 737-3L9	27337 / 2594	OY-MAP	0094	0496	2 CFMI CFM56-3C1	58849	Y136	LR-AB	Phantasia / lsf Heller Fin. / Popart-cs
☐ D-ADBK	Boeing 737-31S	29055 / 2923		0897	0897	2 CFMI CFM56-3C1	58849	Y136	CH-JR	Aurora / lsf DSF&Leasing/Bauhaus-cs
☐ D-ADBL	Boeing 737-31S	29056 / 2928		0997	0997	2 CFMI CFM56-3C1	58849	Y136	CH-JS	Himmelsstürmer / lsfDSF&Lsg/Bauhaus-cs
☐ D-ADBM	Boeing 737-31S	29057 / 2942		1097	1097	2 CFMI CFM56-3C1	58849	Y136	CH-KP	Schrifttanz / lsfDSF&Lsg/Calligraphy-cs
☐ D-ADBN	Boeing 737-31S	29058 / 2946		1197	1197	2 CFMI CFM56-3C1	58849	Y136	DH-KR	Wolkenschreiber / lsfDSF&Lsg/Callig.-cs
☐ D-ADBO	Boeing 737-31S	29059 / 2967		1297	1297	2 CFMI CFM56-3C1	58849	Y136	CH-KS	Himmelsbrief / lsf DSF&L./Calligraphy-cs
☐ D-ADBP	Boeing 737-31S	29060 / 2979		1297	1297	2 CFMI CFM56-3C1	58849	Y136	CJ-ER	Federtraum / lsf DSF&Lsg/Calligraphy-cs
☐ D-ADBQ	Boeing 737-31S	29099 / 2982		0198	0198	2 CFMI CFM56-3C1	58849	Y136	CJ-FR	Paradiesvogel / lsf DSF&Lsg / Popart-cs
☐ D-ADBR	Boeing 737-31S	29100 / 2984		0198	0198	2 CFMI CFM56-3C1	58849	Y136	CJ-FS	Sternschnuppe / lsf DSF&Lsg/Bauhaus-cs
☐ D-ADBS	Boeing 737-31S	29116 / 3005		0398	0398	2 CFMI CFM56-3C1	58849	Y136	CK-DP	Rheingold / lsf DSF & Lsg / Bauhaus-cs
☐ D-ADBT	Boeing 737-31S	29264 / 3070	N1795B*	0098	0998	2 CFMI CFM56-3C1	58849	Y136	LP-EM	Phantasia / lsf DSF&Lsg/Avignon-colors
☐ D-ADBU	Boeing 737-31S	29265 / 3073	N1787B*	0098	0998	2 CFMI CFM56-3C1	58849	Y136	LP-MR	Kosmopolit / lsf DSF&Lsg/Avignon-colors
☐ D-ADBV	Boeing 737-31S	29266 / 3092	N1786B*	0099	0299	2 CFMI CFM56-3C1	56998	Y136	CG-RS	Sterntaler / lsf GECA/Bauhaus-colors
☐ D-ADBW	Boeing 737-31S	29267 / 3093	N60436*	0099	0299	2 CFMI CFM56-3C1	56998	Y136	LR-AC	Wolkenreiter / lsf GECA/Bauhaus-colors

DEUTSCHE RETTUNGSFLUGWACHT, e.V. – DRF = DV / AMB (German Air-Rescue) (Eine Initiative der Björn Steiger Stiftung, e.V.) — Stuttgart

Postfach 230423, D-70624 Stuttgart, Germany ☎ (711) 70 070 Tx: 7255255 drf d Fax: (711) 700 20 09 SITA: STRAA1I
F: 1972 ⁂ 166 Head: Siegfried Steiger ICAO: CIVIL AIR AMBULANCE Net: n/a

☐ D-HAMB	Eurocopter (MBB) BO105CBS	S-205	HB-XFN	0076		2 AN 250-C20B	2500	EMS		
☐ D-HCCA	Eurocopter (MBB) BO105CBS	S-147	N90740	0074		2 AN 250-C20B	2500	EMS		lst Norsk Luftambulanse
☐ D-HDML	Eurocopter (MBB) BO105CBS	S-438		0080		2 AN 250-C20B	2500	EMS		
☐ D-HEEE	Eurocopter (MBB) BO105CBS	S-713	LX-HAR	0085		2 AN 250-C20B	2500	EMS		
☐ D-HFFF	Eurocopter (MBB) BO105CBS	S-811		0089		2 AN 250-C20B	2500	EMS		

104 registration type of aircraft cn/fn ex/ex* mfd del powered by mtow kg configuration selcal name/fln/specialitites/remarks

☐ D-HFHL	Eurocopter (MBB) BO105CBS	S-854		0091	0591	2 AN 250-C20B	2500	EMS		
☐ D-HIII	Eurocopter (MBB) BO105CBS	S-874	N3203L	0091	0994	2 AN 250-C20B	2500	EMS		
☐ D-HJJJ	Eurocopter (MBB) BO105CBS	S-741		0086		2 AN 250-C20B	2500	EMS		
☐ D-HLLL	Eurocopter (MBB) BO105CBS	S-875	N4345F	0091	1094	2 AN 250-C20B	2500	EMS		
☐ D-HPPP	Eurocopter (MBB) BO105CBS	S-734	C-GJDA	0086	0592	2 AN 250-C20B	2500	EMS		
☐ D-HYYY	Eurocopter EC135P1	0006		0096	0796	2 PWC PW206B	2720	EMS		
☐ D-HAWK	Eurocopter (MBB) BK117B-2	7225		0091		2 LY LTS101-750B.1	3350	EMS		cvtd BK117B-1
☐ D-HBBB	Eurocopter (MBB) BK117B-2	7220	LN-OSV	0091	0299	2 LY LTS101-750B.1	3350	EMS		cvtd BK117B-1
☐ D-HDDD	Eurocopter (MBB) BK117C-1	7507	N6096U	0093	0798	2 TU Arriel 1E2	3350	EMS		
☐ D-HECE	Eurocopter (MBB) BK117B-2	7244	D-HFII	0093	0198	2 LY LTS101-750B.1	3350	EMS		occ lst HTM Helicopter Travel Munich
☐ D-HIMB	Eurocopter (MBB) BK117B-2	7185	JY-ACC	0090		2 LY LTS101-750B.1	3350	EMS		cvtd BK117B-1
☐ D-HIMU	Eurocopter (MBB) BK117B-2	7204		0091	1193	2 LY LTS101-750B.1	3350	EMS		cvtd BK117B-1
☐ D-HMMM	Eurocopter (MBB) BK117B-2	7228	SE-JBC	0085	0299	2 LY LTS101-750B.1	3350	EMS		cvtd BK117B-1
☐ D-HMUF	Eurocopter (MBB) BK117B-2	7105	D-HBPZ	0086	0598	2 LY LTS101-650B.1	3350	EMS		cvtd BK117A-4
☐ D-HQQQ	Eurocopter (MBB) BK117B-2	7071	D-HECC	0086	0299	2 LY LTS101-650B.1	3350	EMS		lsf Eurocopter Deutschl./cvtd BK117A-3
☐ D-HSSS	Eurocopter (MBB) BK117B-2	7245		0093	0293	2 LY LTS101-750B.1	3350	EMS		
☐ D-HTTT	Eurocopter (MBB) BK117B-2	7246		0093	0293	2 LY LTS101-750B.1	3350	EMS		
☐ D-HUUU	Eurocopter (MBB) BK117B-2	7242	N3202U	0091	0694	2 LY LTS101-750B.1	3350	EMS		cvtd BK117B-1
☐ D-HWWW	Eurocopter (MBB) BK117B-2	7248		0093	0193	2 LY LTS101-750B.1	3350	EMS		
☐ D-CAVE	Learjet 35A	35A-423	N200TC	0081		2 GA TFE731-2-2B	8301	EMS	FP-CH	lsf Avia Luftreederei GmbH
☐ D-CCAA	Learjet 35A	35A-315	N662AA	0080		2 GA TFE731-2-2B	8301	EMS	BK-DL	

DFKW-Helicopter Service, GmbH

Rendsburg-Schachtholm

Flugplatz Rendsburg-Schachtholm, D-24797 Hörsten, Germany ☎ (4337) 13 20 Tx: none Fax: (4337) 91 98 30 SITA: n/a
F: 1997 n/a Head: Ludwig Wagatha Net: n/a Aircraft below MTOW 1361kg: Hughes 269C (300C)

☐ D-HMOT	Bell 206B JetRanger III	3947		0086		1 AN 250-C20J	1450			lsf LGS Leasing GmbH
☐ D-HAAN	Euroc.(Helibras/Aerosp.)HB350BA Esquilo	1580 / HB1038	PT-HMB	0090	0098	1 TU Arriel 1B	2100			lsf Meravo

DHD DEUTSCHER HELIKOPTER DIENST, GmbH (formerly Delta Avia Fluggeräte, GmbH & Sales Service)

Ochtendung

Heliport, D-56299 Ochtendung, Germany ☎ (2625) 6005 Tx: 863420 delta d Fax: (2625) 6009 SITA: n/a
F: 1981 37 Head: Kurt Behrens Net: n/a Aircraft below MTOW 1361 kg: Hughes 269C (300C).

☐ D-HERD	MD Helicopters MD 500D (Hughes 369D)	790543D	SE-HNO	0079		1 AN 250-C20B	1361			lsf AL Aviation Leasing GmbH
☐ D-HFLY	MD Helicopters MD 500E (Hughes 369E)	0312E	HA-MSK	0088		1 AN 250-C20B	1361			lsf pvt
☐ D-HFOX	MD Helicopters MD 500D (Hughes 369D)	380289D	ZK-HLP	0078		1 AN 250-C20B	1361			lsf AL Aviation Leasing GmbH
☐ D-HING	MD Helicopters MD 500D (Hughes 369D)	470120D	CS-HCT	0077		1 AN 250-C20B	1361			lsf AL Aviation Leasing GmbH
☐ D-HJUX	MD Helicopters MD 500D (Hughes 369D)	890583D	ZK-HNS	0079	1292	1 AN 250-C20B	1361			lsf LFL Luftfahrzeug Leasing GmbH
☐ D-HMIK	MD Helicopters MD 500D (Hughes 369D)	1270251D	CS-HCX	0078		1 AN 250-C20B	1361			lsf AL Aviation Leasing GmbH
☐ D-HOBY	MD Helicopters MD 500D (Hughes 369D)	1070215D	VH-HRJ	0077		1 AN 250-C20B	1361			
☐ D-HPET	MD Helicopters MD 500D (Hughes 369D)	370095D	OE-KXL	0077		1 AN 250-C20B	1361			lsf Frankfurter Leasing GmbH
☐ D-HSUR	MD Helicopters MD 500D (Hughes 369D)	500702D	CS-HCU	0080		1 AN 250-C20B	1361			
☐ D-HULF	MD Helicopters MD 500E (Hughes 369E)	0150E	G-BMFW	0085		1 AN 250-C20B	1361			lsf AL Aviation Leasing GmbH

DHD HELISERVICE, GmbH (Subsidiary of DHD Deutscher Helikopter Dienst, GmbH)

Gross Kreutz

Am Bahnhof, D-14550 Gross Kreutz, Germany ☎ (3357) 24 57 Tx: n/a Fax: (3357) 24 68 SITA: n/a
F: 1991 n/a Head: Kurt Behrens Net: n/a Aircraft below MTOW 1361kg: Hughes 269C (300C).

☐ D-HEBI	Bell 206B JetRanger III	3662	G-BSBJ	0082	1096	1 AN 250-C20J	1451			lsf pvt

DIAMOND AIR SERVICE, GmbH

Egelsbach

Hessenauer Str. 2, D-65468 Trebur, Germany ☎ (6103) 94 130 Tx: none Fax: (6103) 45 402 SITA: n/a
F: 1990 2 Head: Christian Dries Net: n/a

☐ D-IWSH	Beech King Air B200	BB-1462	N82425	0093		2 PWC PT6A-42	5670			lsf MKG Leasing GmbH

DIRECT AIR, GmbH Luftfahrtunternehmen

Stuttgart

DIRECT AIR

Herdweg 20, D-70174 Stuttgart, Germany ☎ (711) 163 87 40 Tx: none Fax: (711) 29 16 55 SITA: n/a
F: 1992 5 Head: Klaus Vetterle Net: http://www.directair.de

☐ D-ILEH	Cessna 421C Golden Eagle III	421C0459	PH-IPH	0078		2 CO GTSIO-520-L	3379			lsf pvt

DLR Flugbetriebe = GPL (Subsidiary of DLR – Deutsches Zentrum für Luft- und Raumfahrt, e.V.)

Oberpfaffenhofen

DLR

Hauptabteilung Flugbetriebe Oberpfaffenhofen, D-82234 Wessling, Germany ☎ (8153) 28 29 71 Tx: none Fax: (8153) 28 13 46 SITA: n/a
F: 1967 60 Head: Volkert Harbers Net: n/a Aircraft below MTOW 1361 kg: DG-300,LFU-205,Robin DR-400 & S-H Janus. Non-commercial German Aerospace Research Establishment.

☐ D-EEFB	Cessna 207A Stationair 8 II	20700601	N73512	0080		1 CO IO-520-F	1724	Surveyer		Pollution & remote sensing
☐ D-EOUK	Cessna 207 Skywagon	20700008	HB-CUK	0069		1 CO IO-520-F	1724	Astro training		
☐ D-HDDP	Eurocopter (MBB) BO105C	S-123		0074		2 AN 250-C20	2300	Avn research		
☐ D-FDLR	Cessna 208B Grand Caravan	208B0708		0098	1198	1 PWC PT6A-114A	3969	Surveyer		
☐ D-CALM	Dornier 228-101	7051		0085	0885	2 GA TPE331-5-252D	5980	Surveyer		Pollution & remote sensing
☐ D-CAWI	Dornier 228-101	7014	D-IAWI	0083		2 GA TPE331-5-252D	6800	Survey/Polar res		Polar 2 / opf AWI / Wheel-Skis
☐ D-CICE	Dornier 228-101	7073		0085		2 GA TPE331-5-252D	6800	Survey/Polar res		Polar 4 / opf AWI / Wheel-Skis
☐ D-CODE	Dornier 228-101	7083		0086	0886	2 GA TPE331-5-252D	5980	Avn research		
☐ D-CFFU	Dornier 228-212	8180		0091	0991	2 GA TPE331-5A-252D	6400	Surveyer		Pollution & remote sensing
☐ D-CMET	Dassault Falcon 20E-5	329	F-WRQV*	0075		2 GA TFE731-5BR-2C	13200	Surveyer		Pollution & remote sensing / cvtd 20E
☐ D-ADAM	VFW-614	G17	D-BABP	0078	0985	2 RR M45H Mk. 501	19950	Avn research		

DONAU-AIR-SERVICE, GmbH

Mengen

Postfach 6, D-72510 Stetten a.k.M., Germany ☎ (7573) 53 57 Tx: none Fax: (7573) 808 SITA: n/a
F: 1969 3 Head: Gerhard Mogg Net: n/a Aircraft below MTOW 1361 kg: Cessna 150/152/172 & SC01B Gyro Flug

☐ D-GMYU	Beech Duchess 76	ME-330	OE-FEW	0080		2 LY O-360-A1G6D	1769			
☐ D-IDAS	Cessna 421C Golden Eagle III	421C0855	OY-SUI	0080		2 CO GTSIO-520-L	3379			
☐ D-FKME	Antonov An-2T	17805	LSK 457	0057	0292	1 SH ASh-62IR	5500			

DSF FLUGDIENST, AG & Co. KG – DeutschSchweizer Flugdienst

Frankfurt & Reichelsheim

Schwedenpfad 10, D-61348 Bad Homburg, Germany ☎ (6172) 23 549 Tx: n/a Fax: (6172) 22 600 SITA: n/a
F: 1978 11 Head: n/a Net: n/a

☐ D-ILCE	Piper PA-31T1 Cheyenne I	31T-8004053		0080		2 PWC PT6A-11	3946			

EAE European Air Express, GmbH = 3D

Moenchengladbach Dusseldorf Express

Flughafenstr. 79, D-41066 Mönchengladbach, Germany ☎ (2161) 66 990 Tx: none Fax: (2161) 669 91 11 SITA: n/a
F: 1999 n/a Head: Peter Hauptvogel Net: n/a

☐ PH-DMO	Fokker 50 (F27 Mk050)	20103	OY-MBM	0087	0299	2 PWC PW125B	20820	Y50		lsf DNM

EAS Egle Air Service, GmbH & Co. KG

Karlsruhe/Baden-Baden

EAS EGLE AIR SERVICE

Baden Airpark-Sektor C, Summersite Avenue 312, D-77836 Rheinmünster, Germany ☎ (7229) 66 24 40 Tx: none Fax: (7229) 66 24 46 SITA: n/a
F: 1978 8 Head: Bernd H. Egle Net: n/a

☐ D-HIEV	Bell 206B JetRanger III	2967	N2JC	0080	0692	1 AN 250-C20B	1451			
☐ D-HBAP	Bell 407	53208		0097	1297	1 AN 250-C47B	2268			lsf Baden-Airpark AG
☐ D-HEBB	Bell 407	53336		0098	0199	1 AN 250-C47B	2268			

EAS Executive-Air-Service Flug, GmbH & Co KG

Mannheim-Neuostheim

Josef-Braun-Ufer 13, D-68165 Mannheim, Germany ☎ (621) 422 84 40 Tx: none Fax: (621) 422 84 30 SITA: n/a
F: 1985 n/a Head: Horst Kutschbach Net: n/a

☐ D-IDSM	Beech King Air B200	BB-1259	N734P	0086		2 PWC PT6A-42	5670			lsf Diringer & Scheidelbauunternehmung
☐ D-ILIN	Beech King Air 200	BB-545	OY-CBY	0079		2 PWC PT6A-41	5670			

E.C.C.S. AIR & CARGO SERVICE, GmbH (Express Cargo Charter Service dba)

Koblenz

Hauptstr. 26A, D-56593 Niedersteinebach, Germany ☎ (2687) 27 15 Tx: none Fax: (2687) 27 19 SITA: n/a
F: 1997 n/a Head: Manfed Nimführ Net: n/a

☐ D-HASP	MD Helicopters MD 500E (Hughes 369E)	0325E	I-BNAR	0089	0797	1 AN 250-C20R2	1361			

EFS Flug Service, GmbH = FSD

Duesseldorf

Flughafen, Halle 1, D-40474 Düsseldorf, Germany ☎ (211) 45 10 31 Tx: 8586280 efs d Fax: (211) 421 66 01 SITA: n/a
F: 1980 5 Head: Jürgen Böck ICAO: FLUGSERVICE Net: n/a

☐ D-FDHM	Pilatus PC-6/C1-H2 Turbo Porter	688	HB-FEG	0069		1 GA TPE331-1-100	2200			lsf Diskont & Kredit AG
☐ D-IATC	Cessna 500 Citation	500-0116	EC-CJH	0073		2 PWC JT15D-1A	5216			lsf AL Aviation Leasing GmbH

105 registration type of aircraft cn/fn ex/ex* mfd del powered by mtow kg configuration selcal name/fln/specialitites/remarks

EIS Aircraft, GmbH
Dahlem

Flugplatz, D-53949 Dahlem, Germany ☎ (2447) 80 80 Tx: none Fax: (2447) 81 13 SITA: n/a
F: 1998 ⁂ n/a Head: Hansjörg Brandt Net: n/a Private operator conducting target towing flights for the Luftwaffe / German Air Force.

☐ D-FAMT	Pilatus PC-9/B	164	HB-HQK*	0088	0299	1 PWC PT6A-62	2900	target towing		lsf FFL Flugzeug Leasing/opf Luftwaffe
☐ D-FBMT	Pilatus PC-9/B	165	HB-HQL*	0088	0299	1 PWC PT6A-62	2900	target towing		lsf FFL Flugzeug Leasing/opf Luftwaffe
☐ D-FCMT	Pilatus PC-9/B	166		0088	0299	1 PWC PT6A-62	2900	target towing		lsf FFL Flugzeug Leasing/opf Luftwaffe
☐ D-FDMT	Pilatus PC-9/B	167	HB-HPI*	0090	0299	1 PWC PT6A-62	2900	target towing		lsf FFL Flugzeug Leasing/opf Luftwaffe
☐ D-FEMT	Pilatus PC-9/B	168		0090	0299	1 PWC PT6A-62	2900	target towing		lsf FFL Flugzeug Leasing/opf Luftwaffe
☐ D-FFMT	Pilatus PC-9/B	169		0090	0299	1 PWC PT6A-62	2900	target towing		lsf FFL Flugzeug Leasing/opf Luftwaffe
☐ D-FGMT	Pilatus PC-9/B	170		0090	0299	1 PWC PT6A-62	2900	target towing		lsf FFL Flugzeug Leasing/opf Luftwaffe
☐ D-FHMT	Pilatus PC-9/B	171	D-FLFA	0090	0299	1 PWC PT6A-62	2900	target towing		lsf FFL Flugzeug Leasing/opf Luftwaffe
☐ D-FIMT	Pilatus PC-9/B	172		0090	0299	1 PWC PT6A-62	2900	target towing		lsf FFL Flugzeug Leasing/opf Luftwaffe
☐ D-FJMT	Pilatus PC-9/B	173		0090	0299	1 PWC PT6A-62	2900	target towing		lsf FFL Flugzeug Leasing/opf Luftwaffe

ELBE HELICOPTER Rainer Zemke, GmbH & Co. KG (Sister company of Rhein-Ruhr Helicopter Rainer Zemke)
Dresden

Flughafen Dresden, D-01109 Dresden, Germany ☎ (351) 886 43 21 Tx: none Fax: (351) 886 43 22 SITA: n/a
F: 1990 ⁂ n/a Head: Rainer Zemke Net: n/a

☐ D-HMIT	Agusta-Bell 206B JetRanger III	8256	F-GBRE	0070		1 AN 250-C20B	1451			lsf Diskont & Kredit AG / cvtd 206A
☐ D-HELB	Bell 222B	47154	JA9691	0088	0295	2 LY LTS101-750C.1	3742			lsf AL Aviation Leasing GmbH

ERSTER FFC HALLE e.V. (Member of 1. Fallschirmsportclub Halle e.V.)
Halle-Oppin

Flugplatz, D-06188 Oppin, Germany ☎ (345) 804 63 05 Tx: none Fax: none SITA: n/a
F: 1990 ⁂ n/a Head: Klaus Garbe Net: n/a Registered club organisation conducting non-profit para- & sightseeing flights primarily for its members.

☐ D-FWJK	PZL Mielec (Antonov) An-2T	1G142-34	DDR-WJK	0073		1 SH ASh-62IR	5500	Para/sightseeing		

EURO FLUGDIENST Gerhard Spinker
Arnsberg

Stennert 8, D-59439 Holzwickede, Germany ☎ (2377) 72 27 Tx: none Fax: (2377) 73 55 SITA: n/a
F: 1984 ⁂ 3 Head: Gerhard Spinker Net: n/a

☐ D-GGTT	Piper PA-34-220T Seneca III	34-8333115	N43129	0083		2 CO TSIO-360-KB	1999			lsf Werbi-Flugdienst
☐ D-ILUB	Cessna 340	3400076	N4090L	0072		2 CO TSIO-520-K	2710			lsf pvt

EUROFLUG FREIBURG Gerhard Frenzel
Freiburg

Flugplatz, Hangar 1, Hermann-Mitsch-Strasse, D-79108 Freiburg i.Br., Germany ☎ (761) 50 86 86 Tx: none Fax: (761) 50 64 05 SITA: n/a
F: 1989 ⁂ 5 Head: Gerhard Frenzel Net: n/a

☐ D-IBHK	Beech King Air 200	BB-366	N1230	0078		2 PWC PT6A-41	5670			

EUROHELI Helicopterdienste, GmbH
Tippenricht

In der Alting 7, D-90596 Schwanstetten, Germany ☎ (9170) 95 452 Tx: none Fax: (9170) 95 453 SITA: n/a
F: 1996 ⁂ 6 Head: Peter Nowotny Net: http://www.euroheli.de

☐ D-HEEH	Eurocopter (Aerosp.) AS350B2 Ecureuil	1598	N65452	0082		1 TU Arriel 1D1	2250			lsf pvt / cvtd AS350B
☐ D-HEUH	Eurocopter (Aerosp.) AS355F2 Ecureuil 2	5155		0082		2 AN 250-C20F	2500			lsf Schmidt Bank Leasing GmbH/cvtd355F1

EUROSENSE, GmbH
Cologne

Unnauer Weg 17, D-50767 Köln, Germany ☎ (221) 79 80 31 Tx: n/a Fax: (221) 79 66 88 SITA: n/a
F: 1964 ⁂ 7 Head: Dipl.-Geograph Hubert Minten Net: n/a

☐ D-IARC	Cessna 404 Titan II	404-0020	OO-GIS	0076	0893	2 CO GTSIO-520-M	3810	Photo/remote sen		

EUROWINGS = EW / EWG (Eurowings Luftverkehrs AG, Eurowings Flug GmbH & Eurowings Aviation GmbH dba/Subs.of Dr.A.Knauf GmbH & Co.)
Nuremberg

Flughafenstrasse 100, D-90411 Nürnberg, Germany ☎ (911) 36 560 Tx: 622583 nfd d Fax: (911) 365 62 03 SITA: n/a
F: 1993 ⁂ 1600 Head: Reinhard Santner IATA: 104 ICAO: EUROWINGS Net: http://www.eurowings.de
Two aircraft are operated on a code-share agreement with AIR FRANCE (in full such colors & both titles) & using AF flight numbers.

☐ D-BCRO	ATR 42-300 (QC)	122	F-WWES*	0089	0193	2 PWC PW120	16700	Y46 / Frtr		Lippstadt
☐ D-BCRP	ATR 42-300 (QC)	158	F-WWEE*	0089	0193	2 PWC PW120	16700	Y46 / Frtr		
☐ D-BCRQ	ATR 42-300	233	F-WWEO*	0091	0193	2 PWC PW120	16700	Y46		
☐ D-BCRR	ATR 42-300	255	F-WWEC*	0091	0193	2 PWC PW120	16700	Y46		
☐ D-BCRS	ATR 42-300	287	F-WWLL*	0092	0193	2 PWC PW120	16700	Y46		
☐ D-BCRT	ATR 42-300	289	F-WWLN*	0092	0193	2 PWC PW120	16700	Y46		
☐ D-BDDD	ATR 42-300	110	F-WWEG*	0088	0193	2 PWC PW120	16700	Y48		
☐ D-BEEE	ATR 42-300	121	F-WWER*	0088	0193	2 PWC PW120	16700	Y48		lsf Lease Trend GmbH
☐ D-BFFF	ATR 42-300	130	F-WWEC*	0089	0193	2 PWC PW120	16700	Y48		
☐ D-BGGG	ATR 42-300	148	F-WWEU*	0089	0193	2 PWC PW120	16700	Y48		lsf Lease Trend GmbH
☐ D-BHHH	ATR 42-300	173	F-WWED*	0089	0193	2 PWC PW120	16700	Y48		lsf Commerzleasing GmbH & Co.
☐ D-BJJJ	ATR 42-300	278	F-WWEC*	0091	0193	2 PWC PW120	16700	Y48		
☐ D-BKKK	ATR 42-500	532	F-WWLP*	0097	1097	2 PWC PW127E	18600	Y48		
☐ D-BLLL	ATR 42-500	549	F-WWLB*	0097	1097	2 PWC PW127E	18600	Y48		lsf Lombard Leasing GmbH
☐ D-BMMM	ATR 42-500	546	F-WWLE*	0097	1197	2 PWC PW127E	18600	Y48		lsf LFL Luftfahrzeug Leasing GmbH
☐ D-BNNN	ATR 42-500	551	F-WWLL*	0097	1297	2 PWC PW127E	18600	Y48		
☐ D-BOOO	ATR 42-500	559	F-WWLM*	0097	0198	2 PWC PW127E	18600	Y48		
☐ D-AEWG	ATR 72-212	347	F-WWEC*	0093	0293	2 PWC PW127	21500	Y68		
☐ D-AEWH	ATR 72-212	359	F-WWEV*	0093	0493	2 PWC PW127	21500	Y68		
☐ D-AEWI	ATR 72-212	404	F-WWLO*	0094	0394	2 PWC PW127	21500	Y68		
☐ D-AEWK	ATR 72-212	446	F-WWEA*	0095	0495	2 PWC PW127	21500	Y68		lsf BKL Knauf Leasing
☐ D-ANFA	ATR 72-202	224	F-WWEQ*	0091	0193	2 PWC PW124B	21500	Y68		
☐ D-ANFB	ATR 72-202	229	F-WWEX*	0091	0193	2 PWC PW124B	21500	Y68		
☐ D-ANFC	ATR 72-202	237	F-WWEG*	0091	0193	2 PWC PW124B	21500	Y68		lsf Lease Trend GmbH
☐ D-ANFD	ATR 72-202	256	F-WWEE*	0091	0193	2 PWC PW124B	21500	Y68		
☐ D-ANFE	ATR 72-202	294	F-WWLS*	0092	0193	2 PWC PW124B	21500	Y68		
☐ D-ANFF	ATR 72-202	292	F-WWLT*	0092	0193	2 PWC PW124B	21500	Y68		lsf LFL Luftfahrzeug Leasing GmbH
☐ D-ACFA	BAe 146-200	E2200	G-BTVT	0091	1094	4 LY ALF502R-5	42184	Y92		lsf BAMJ
☐ D-AEWD	BAe 146-200	E2069	OO-DJC	0087	0397	4 LY ALF502R-5	40596	Y92		lsf Lombard Leasing GmbH / op in AFR-cs
☐ D-AEWE	BAe 146-200	E2077	OO-DJD	0087	0497	4 LY ALF502R-5	42184	Y92		lsf Lombard Leasing GmbH / op in AFR-cs
☐ D-AJET	BAe 146-200	E2201	G-6-201*	0091	0495	4 LY ALF502R-5	42184	Y98	BS-LR	lsf LeaseTrend Leasing
☐ D-ALOA	BAe 146-200A	E2066	N356BA	0086	1297	4 LY ALF502R-5	42184	Y98		lsf BAMJ
☐ D-AZUR	BAe 146-200A	E2060	N352BA	0086	1197	4 LY ALF502R-5	42184	Y92		lsf BAMJ
☐ D-AEWA	BAe 146-300	E3163	G-BTJG	0090	0396	4 LY ALF502R-5-10	44225	Y98		lsf BAMJ
☐ D-AEWB	BAe 146-300	E3183	G-BUHB	0090	0896	4 LY ALF502R-5	44225	Y98		lsf BAMJ
☐ D-AHOI	BAe 146-300	E3187	G-BSYT	0090	1297	4 LY ALF502R-5	44225	Y98		lsf BAMJ
☐ D-AQUA	BAe 146-300	E3118	G-OAJF	0088	1297	4 LY ALF502R-5	43100	Y98		lsf BAMJ
☐ D-AKNF	Airbus Industrie A319-112	646	F-AVYB*	0097	0197	2 CFMI CFM56-5B6/P	70000	Y142	LQ-BD	Albrecht Dürer / lsf LeaseAir GmbH&Co.
☐ D-AKNG	Airbus Industrie A319-112	654	D-AVYX*	0097	0397	2 CFMI CFM56-5B6/P	70000	Y142	LQ-EH	Johann Wolfgang von Goethe / lsfLse.Air
☐ D-AKNH	Airbus Industrie A319-112	794	D-AVYD*	0098	0398	2 CFMI CFM56-5B6/P	70000	Y142	LQ-AK	Heinrich Heine / lsf Mobilien Leasing
☐ D-AKNI	Airbus Industrie A319-112	1016				2 CFMI CFM56-5B6/P	70000	Y142		oo-delivery 0499
☐ D-AKNK	Airbus Industrie A319-112					2 CFMI CFM56-5B6/P	70000	Y142		oo-delivery 0300

EXPRESS AIRWAYS, GmbH = EPA (Member of Farnair Europe, European Aviation Alliance)
Hahn

Flughafen Hahn, Geb. 417, D-55483 Lautzenhausen, Germany ☎ (6543) 98 73 00 Tx: none Fax: (6543) 987 30 33 SITA: n/a
F: 1998 ⁂ n/a Head: Harald Schwertfeger ICAO: EXPRESS FARNER Net: n/a

☐ D-AAAC	Fokker F27 Friendship 500 (F27 Mk500)	10448	HB-ITY	0071	0299	2 RR Dart 532-7R	20820	Freighter		lsf FAT / op in Farnair Europe-colors

FAI AIRSERVICE, AG = IFA (Assoc. with IFA Int'l Flug Ambulanz e.V./formerly FAI Flight-Ambulance-Service-Int'l)
Nuremberg

Flughafenstr. 100 (GAT), D-90411 Nürnberg, Germany ☎ (911) 36 00 90 Tx: none Fax: (911) 360 09 59 SITA: NUEFAXH
F: 1987 ⁂ 15 Head: Inge Axtmann ICAO: FRANKEN-AIR Net: http://www.fai-airservice.com

☐ D-ISSS	Cessna 500 Citation I	500-0392	I-FLYB	0078	0998	2 PWC JT15D-1A	5375			lsf AL Aviation Leasing GmbH
☐ D-CFAI	Cessna S550 Citation S/II	S550-0134	N134QS	0087	0598	2 PWC JT15D-4B	6900			
☐ D-CIFA	Cessna 550 Citation II	550-0378	OH-CAT	0080	0199	2 PWC JT15D-4	6700			

FDZ Flugdienst Zwickau, GmbH
Zwickau

Marienstr. 32, D-08056 Zwickau, Germany ☎ (375) 28 11 21 Tx: none Fax: (375) 28 11 21 SITA: n/a
F: 1992 ⁂ 5 Head: Dipl. Ing. René Nedoluha Net: n/a

☐ D-HMIC	MD Helicopters MD 500E (Hughes 369E)	0362E	OE-XKK	0089	0797	1 AN 250-C20R2	1361			

FFD Franken Flug Dienst (Luftfahrtunternehmen Manfred Thonius dba)
Nuremberg

Linderweg 8, D-90574 Rosstal, Germany ☎ (9127) 95 12 51 Tx: none Fax: (9127) 95 12 52 SITA: n/a
F: 1996 ⁂ n/a Head: Manfred Thonius Net: n/a

☐ D-IMMB	Beech King Air 300LW	FA-152	N7241V	0088		2 PWC PT6A-60A	5670	8 Pax		lsf pvt

106 registration type of aircraft cn/fn ex/ex* mfd del powered by mtow kg configuration selcal name/fln/specialitites/remarks

FFH Flugdienst Freiburg Harter — Freiburg

Flugplatz, Postfach 702, D-79007 Freiburg i.Br., Germany ☎ (761) 50 05 79 Tx: 772853 maeco d Fax: (761) 50 65 79 SITA: n/a
F: 1962 ⁂ 15 Head: Heinz Harter Net: n/a Aircraft below MTOW 1361 kg: Cessna 150, 172 & Piper PA-28.

☐ D-IDXQ	Piper PA-31-310 Navajo	*31-294*	*N9227Y*	*0068*		*2 LY TIO-540-A1B*	*2948*	*8 Pax*		

FILDER AIR SERVICE, GmbH - FAS = NRX — Nuremberg

Hirschau 3, D-90607 Rückersdorf, Germany ☎ (911) 570 07 71 Tx: none Fax: (911) 570 07 73 SITA: n/a
F: n/a ⁂ n/a Head: Kai Schröder ICAO: NORIS Net: n/a

☐ D-CNRX	BAe 3102 Jetstream 31	*616*	*G-BKUY*	*0083*	*1097*	*2 GA TPE331-10UR-513H*	*7059*	*Y18*		*lsf pvt*
☐ D-	BAe 3103 Jetstream 31	*610*	*SE-KHC*	*0083*	*0499*	*2 GA TPE331-10UR-513H*	*6950*	*Y18*		

FISCHER-FLUG, GmbH — Lahr

Hollerweg 7, D-77654 Offenburg, Germany ☎ (781) 948 35 53 Tx: none Fax: (781) 948 35 51 SITA: n/a
F: 1986 ⁂ 1 Head: Matthias Fischer Net: n/a

☐ D-ILLF	Beech King Air B200	*BB-1568*	*N1067V*	*0097*	*0797*	*2 PWC PT6A-42*	*5670*			

FJS-HELICOPTER LUFTTRANSPORT, GmbH — Damme, Neubrandenburg & Schwerin

Bendiktstr. 17, D-49401 Damme, Germany ☎ (5491) 44 45 Tx: none Fax: (5491) 42 00 SITA: n/a
F: 1993 ⁂ 8 Head: Franz-Josef Strathausen Net: n/a

☐ D-HENA	Eurocopter (Aerosp.) AS350B Ecureuil	*1781*	*OE-KXC*	*0084*	*0798*	*1 TU Arriel 1B*	*1950*			*lsf pvt*
☐ D-HFJS	Eurocopter (Aerosp.) AS350B Ecureuil	*2014*	*CS-HBF*	*0087*		*1 TU Arriel 1B*	*1950*			
☐ D-HJIM	Eurocopter (Aerosp.) AS350BA Ecureuil	*1302*	*F-GCVD*	*0080*	*1296*	*1 TU Arriel 1B*	*2100*			*lsf VR-Leasing GmbH / cvtd AS350B*
☐ D-HLEA	Eurocopter (Aerosp.) AS350BA Ecureuil	*2532*	*VR-HJF*	*0091*		*1 TU Arriel 1B*	*2100*			*lsf VR-Leasing GmbH*

FLM AVIATION (FLM Flugschule Lufttaxi E.O. & St. Mohrdieck, KG dba) — Hartenholm & Kiel

Boelckestr. 100, D-24159 Kiel, Germany ☎ (431) 32 38 28 Tx: none Fax: (431) 32 17 15 SITA: n/a
F: 1973 ⁂ n/a Head: Stefan Mohrdieck Net: http://www.flm-aviation.com Aircraft below MTOW 1361kg: Cessna 150 & Piper PA-28

☐ D-GBRD	Partenavia P.68B	*14*	*OY-DZR*	*0073*	*0697*	*2 LY IO-360-A1B*	*1960*	*Y5*		*lsf pvt*
☐ D-IFFB	Beech King Air 300LW	*FA-224*	*N56449*	*0092*	*0098*	*2 PWC PT6A-60A*	*5670*	*Y10*		*lsf SAG-Strathmann AG & Co.*
☐ D-CSAG	Beech 1900D Airliner	*UE-*		*0093*		*2 PWC PT6A-67D*	*7688*	*Y19*		*oo-delivery 0699*

FLN Frisia-Luftverkehr GmbH Norddeich (Associated with OLT Ostfriesische Lufttransport, GmbH) — Norddeich

Postfach 1160, Flugplatz, D-26501 Norden, Germany ☎ (4931) 93 320 Tx: none Fax: (4931) 93 32 23 SITA: n/a
F: 1969 ⁂ 12 Head: Tjado Ihmels & Hans Lothar Graw Net: http://www.reederei-frisia.de Aircraft below MTOW 1361 kg: Cessna F172.

☐ D-IBNF	Britten-Norman BN-2B-26 Islander	*2205*	*G-BOMG**	*0089*	*0589*	*2 LY O-540-E4C5*	*2994*			Norddeich
☐ D-IFKU	Britten-Norman BN-2B-20 Islander	*2290*	*G-BVXY**	*0096*	*0696*	*2 LY IO-540-K1B5*	*2994*			Norderney
☐ D-IFLN	Britten-Norman BN-2B-20 Islander	*2241*	*G-BSPU**	*0091*	*0691*	*2 LY IO-540-K1B5*	*2994*			Norden

FLUGBEREITSCHAFT, GmbH (Sister company of Flugbereitschaft Baden-Baden, GmbH) — Karlsruhe/Baden-Baden

Flugplatz Baden, D-76287 Rheinstetten, Germany ☎ (721) 95 16 40 Tx: none Fax: (721) 951 64 11 SITA: n/a
F: 1968 ⁂ n/a Head: Heinz Kirchner Net: n/a Aircraft below MTOW 1361 kg: Cessna 150, 172 & 182.

☐ D-IKHO	Cessna 340	*3400250*	*N69428*	*0073*		*2 CO TSIO-520-K*	*2710*			
☐ D-IHEF	Cessna 414	*414-0456*	*N1663T*	*0073*		*2 CO TSIO-520-N*	*2880*			
☐ D-IEFB	Beech King Air B200	*BB-897*	*N200TM*	*0081*		*2 PWC PT6A-42*	*5670*			
☐ D-ICTA	Cessna 551 Citation II/SP	*551-0051*	*N6863C*	*0081*		*2 PWC JT15D-4*	*5670*			

FLUGBEREITSCHAFT BADEN-BADEN, GmbH (Sister company of Flugbereitschaft, GmbH) — Karlsruhe/Baden-Baden

Flugplatz Baden, D-76287 Rheinstetten, Germany ☎ (721) 95 16 40 Tx: none Fax: (721) 951 64 11 SITA: n/a
F: 1997 ⁂ n/a Head: Heinz Kirchner Net: n/a

☐ D-AMIM	Canadair CL-604 (CL-600-2B16) Challen.	*5317*	*C-FYXC**	*0096*	*0297*	*2 GE CF34-3B*	*21863*	*Executive 11Pax*		*lsf FlowTec Technologie Import*

FLUG-CENTER WORMS (Division of Flug- und Trainings-Center Worms Flugschule, GmbH) — Worms

Flugplatz, D-67547 Worms, Germany ☎ (6241) 55 580 Tx: none Fax: (6241) 24 855 SITA: n/a
F: 1984 ⁂ 15 Head: Gisela Martin Net: n/a

☐ D-GEJL	Piper PA-34-200T Seneca II	*34-7870265*	*N31744*	*0077*		*2 CO TSIO-360-EB*	*1999*			*lsf pvt*

FLUGDIENST BAYREUTH, GmbH & Co. KG. — Bayreuth

Bindlacher Str. 4, D-95448 Bayreuth, Germany ☎ (921) 798 22 21 Tx: none Fax: (921) 798 22 20 SITA: n/a
F: n/a ⁂ n/a Head: Roland Weidmann Net: n/a Aircraft below MTOW 1361kg: Bell 47G-3B-1

☐ D-HSBA	Bell 206B JetRanger III	*3640*	*G-IMLH*	*0083*	*0493*	*1 AN 250-C20J*	*1451*			*occ lsf/jtly opw Grasberger GmbH*

FLUGDIENST CARLOS DE PILAR — Munich

Prof.-Kurt-Huberstr. 18, D-82166 Gräfelfing, Germany ☎ (89) 854 23 03 Tx: none Fax: (89) 85 31 76 SITA: n/a
F: 1986 ⁂ 6 Head: Carlos de Pilar Net: n/a Aircraft below MTOW 1361kg: Cessna 177

☐ D-ELAE	Piper PA-32RT-300 Lance II	*32R-7885128*	*N31740*	*0078*		*1 LY IO-540-K1G5D*	*1633*			
☐ D-EBAM	Cessna 210L Centurion II	*21061120*	*N210GV*	*0075*	*1098*	*1 CO IO-520-L*	*1724*			
☐ D-EEXG	Cessna T210L Turbo Centurion II	*21059508*	*N4608Q*	*0072*	*1098*	*1 CO TSIO-520-H*	*1724*			
☐ D-IIRC	Piper PA-31T2 Cheyenne II XL	*31T-1166008*	*N362AB*	*0084*		*2 PWC PT6A-135*	*4297*			*lsf Alpha Aviation Vermietungs GmbH*
☐ N794A	Piper PA-42-720 Cheyenne IIIA	*42-5501015*	*D-ILSW*	*0084*		*2 PWC PT6A-61*	*5080*			*lsf FSBU Trustee*

FLUGDIENST FEHLHABER, GmbH = FFG — Cologne-Bonn

Jägerweg 5, D-53577 Neustadt / Wied, Germany ☎ (2683) 32 070 Tx: none Fax: (2683) 32 499 SITA: n/a
F: 1970 ⁂ 20 Head: Wolfgang Fehlhaber ICAO: WITCHCRAFT Net: n/a

☐ D-INUS	Reims/Cessna F406 Caravan II	*F406-0043*		*0090*	*0890*	*2 PWC PT6A-112*	*4468*	*Y12orFrtr 1,3t*		
☐ D-ISHY	Reims/Cessna F406 Caravan II	*F406-0027*	*PH-FWH*	*0088*	*1295*	*2 PWC PT6A-112*	*4468*	*Y12orFrtr 1,3t*		

FLUGSERVICE SOEMMERDA, GmbH — Soemmerda-Dermsdorf

Am Flugplatz, D-99625 Dermsdorf, Germany ☎ (3635) 48 23 88 Tx: none Fax: (3635) 48 23 84 SITA: n/a
F: 1992 ⁂ n/a Head: Michael Schunke Net: http://www.flugservice-soemmerda.de/ Aircraft below MTOW 1361kg: Cessna 150, 172 & 182

☐ D-IBHE	Cessna 310R II	*310R0066*	*N3370Q*	*0074*		*2 CO IO-520-M*	*2495*			*lsf pvt*
☐ D-IJET	Piper PA-31T1 Cheyenne I	*31T-8104042*		*0081*		*2 PWC PT6A-11*	*3946*			*lsf LGS Leasing*

FLY FTI = FTI (Div. of Frosch Touristik, GmbH / Associated with Airtours International) — Munich

Nymphenburger Str. 1, D-80335 München, Germany ☎ (89) 25 25 51 10 Tx: none Fax: (89) 25 25 52 01 SITA: n/a
F: 1998 ⁂ n/a Head: Dietmar Gunz ICAO: FROG-LINE Net: n/a

☐ D-ACAF	Airbus Industrie A320-231	*444*	*TC-ONF*	*0093*	*0499*	*2 IAE V2500-A1*	*77000*	*Y180*		*lsf ORIX*
☐ D-AFRO	Airbus Industrie A320-231	*230*	*A4O-MA*	*0091*	*0499*	*2 IAE V2500-A1*	*77000*	*Y180*		*lsf ORIX*
☐ D-AFTI	Airbus Industrie A320-231	*338*	*N302ML*	*0092*	*0499*	*2 IAE V2500-A1*	*77000*	*Y180*		*lsf ORIX*

FREUNDE DER ANTONOW, e.V. — Muehldorf

Postfach 11 05, D-85729 Ismaning, Germany ☎ (89) 96 50 96 Tx: n/a Fax: (89) 96 79 49 SITA: n/a
F: 1993 ⁂ n/a Head: Paul Hoffmann & Klaus Gallin Net: n/a

☐ D-FWJM	PZL Mielec (Antonov) An-2T	*1G166-38*	*DDR-WJM*	*0075*		*1 SH ASh-62IR*	*5500*	*sightseeing/Para*		*lsf Fallschirmsportclub Dresden*

FRIESENFLUG, GmbH & Co. KG — Westerland-Sylt

Flughafen Gebäude 101a, D-25980 Westerland (Sylt), Germany ☎ (4651) 12 11 Tx: none Fax: (4651) 24 052 SITA: n/a
F: 1964 ⁂ n/a Head: Peter Siemi Net: n/a Aircraft below MTOW 1361kg: Cessna 172 & 182.

☐ D-ECMB	Cessna 207 Skywagon	*20700195*		*0071*		*1 CO IO-520-F*	*1724*			

GAS Air Service, GmbH & Co. KG — Muenster-Osnabrueck

Postfach 1240, D-49198 Dissen, Germany ☎ (5421) 320 Tx: none Fax: (5421) 32 191 SITA: n/a
F: 1993 ⁂ n/a Head: Franz Gausepohl Net: n/a

☐ D-CGGG	Learjet 31A	*31A-042*		*0091*	*0798*	*2 GA TFE731-2-3B*	*7484*			

GEOCART HERTEN (Geocart Herten Ingenieurgesellschaft für Vermessung, Photogrammetrie & Fernerkundung dba) — Marl-Loemuehle

Nimrodstr. 60, D-45699 Herten, Germany ☎ (2366) 84 281 Tx: none Fax: (2366) 10 95 22 SITA: n/a
F: 1966 ⁂ n/a Head: Heinrich Kiski Net: n/a

☐ D-IBWF	Cessna 402B	*402B0221*		*0072*		*2 CO TSIO-520-E*	*2858*	*Photo*		

GEODATA (Luftbildabteilung der Kreller, KG) — Egelsbach

Flugplatz, D-63329 Egelsbach, Germany ☎ (6103) 49 000 Tx: none Fax: (6103) 44 521 SITA: n/a
F: 1953 ⁂ n/a Head: Sabine Kreller-Fay Net: http://www.kreller.de/

☐ D-ENIF	Cessna P206A Super Skylane	*P206-0252*	*N4652F*	*0066*		*1 CO IO-520-A*	*1633*	*Photo / Survey*		*lsf Roeder Praezision GmbH*
☐ D-IGEO	Cessna 402C II	*402C0409*	*N6785Z*	*0080*	*0292*	*2 CO TSIO-520-VB*	*3107*	*Photo*		

107 registration type of aircraft *cn/fn* *ex/ex** *mfd* *del* *powered by* *mtow kg* *configuration* *selcal* *name/fln/specialitites/remarks*

GEOPLANA (Geoplana Ingenieursges. mbH für Photogrammetrie & Geowissenschaftliche Standort- / Umweltplanung) — Schwaebisch Hall-Hessent

Buechlesweg 17, D-71672 Marbach, Germany ☎ (7144) 83 33 30 Tx: none Fax: (7144) 833 33 99 SITA: n/a
F: 1964 ⁂ 12 Head: Jens-P.Knittel Net: n/a

☐ D-IHBB	Cessna 340A II	340A0217	I-CCTT	0076		2 CO TSIO-520-N	2853	Photo / Survey		lsf Staedte-Verlag

GERMAN FLIGHT INSPECTION = FII (FII Flight Inspection Int'l GmbH dba/Ass. with Avionik Zentrum Braunschwei GmbH/formerly DFMG Deutsche Flugmess GmbH) — Braunschweig

Hermann-Blenk-Strasse 38, D-38108 Braunschweig, Germany ☎ (531) 23 52 70 Tx: none Fax: (531) 235 27 99 SITA: n/a
F: 1994 ⁂ 30 Head: Horst Nickolai ICAO: FLIGHT CHECKER Net: n/a Operates calibration flights for the German Air Navigation Services (DFS), Federal Armed Forces (Bundeswehr) & third parties.

☐ D-CACB	Beech King Air 200T	BT-27	N7244N	0083		2 PWC PT6A-41	6350	Calibrator		cvtd 200 cn BB-1105
☐ D-CFMC	Beech King Air 300	FA-104	N310VE	0086	0698	2 PWC PT6A-60A	6350	Calibrator		
☐ D-CFMA	Beech King Air 350 (B300)	FL-76	N8274U	0092		2 PWC PT6A-60A	6350	Calibrator		
☐ D-CFMB	Beech King Air 350 (B300)	FL-97	N8297L	0093		2 PWC PT6A-60A	6350	Calibrator		

GERMANIA Fluggesellschaft mbH = ST / GMI (Subsidiary of SAT Fluggesellschaft mbH) — Berlin-Tegel & Koeln

Flughafen Tegel, Hangar N1, D-13405 Berlin, Germany ☎ (30) 41 01 35 08 Tx: none Fax: (30) 41 01 35 00 SITA: TXLDDST
F: 1978 ⁂ 335 Head: Dr. Hinrich Bischoff ICAO: GERMANIA Net: n/a 6 Boeing 737-75B are wet-lst/opf LTU (in Germania or TUI-colors).

☐ D-AGEJ	Boeing 737-3L9	24221 / 1604	OY-MMR	0088	0392	2 CFMI CFM56-3B2	62822	Y144	HJ-DM	lsf SAT Flug GmbH
☐ D-AGEK	Boeing 737-3M8	25015 / 1991	N799BB	0091	0996	2 CFMI CFM56-3B2	63276	Y144	AP-FS	
☐ D-AGEL	Boeing 737-75B	28110 / 5	N1791B*	0098	1298	2 CFMI CFM56-7B22	69399	Y144	PR-DF	lsf SAT Flug GmbH
☐ D-AGEM	Boeing 737-75B	28099 / 13	N3502P*	0098	0398	2 CFMI CFM56-7B22	69399	Y144	PR-DG	lsf SAT Flug GmbH / op in TUI-colors
☐ D-AGEN	Boeing 737-75B	28100 / 16	N1789B*	0098	0398	2 CFMI CFM56-7B22	69399	Y144	PR-DH	lsf SAT Flug GmbH / op in TUI-colors
☐ D-AGEO	Boeing 737-75B	28101 / 17	N5573K*	0098	0498	2 CFMI CFM56-7B22	69399	Y144	PR-DJ	
☐ D-AGEP	Boeing 737-75B	28102 / 18	N5573B*	0098	0398	2 CFMI CFM56-7B22	69399	Y144	PR-DK	lsf SAT Flug GmbH / op in TUI-colors
☐ D-AGEQ	Boeing 737-75B	28103 / 23		0098	0798	2 CFMI CFM56-7B22	69399	Y144	PR-DL	lsf SAT Flug GmbH
☐ D-AGER	Boeing 737-75B	28107 / 27	N1002R*	0098	0698	2 CFMI CFM56-7B22	69399	Y144	PR-DM	
☐ D-AGES	Boeing 737-75B	28108 / 28		0098	0698	2 CFMI CFM56-7B22	69399	Y144	PR-DQ	lsf pvt
☐ D-AGET	Boeing 737-75B	28109 / 31		0098	0398	2 CFMI CFM56-7B22	69399	Y144	PR-DS	lsf SAT Flug GmbH
☐ D-AGEU	Boeing 737-75B	28104 / 39		0098	0498	2 CFMI CFM56-7B22	69399	Y144	PR-EF	lsf SAT Flug GmbH
☐ D-AGEV	Boeing 737-75B	28105 / 66		0098	0698	2 CFMI CFM56-7B22	69399	Y144	PR-EG	
☐ D-AGEW	Boeing 737-75B	28106 / 68		0098	0798	2 CFMI CFM56-7B22	69399	Y144	PR-EH	lsf SAT Flug GmbH
☐ D-AGEY	Boeing 737-73S	29076 / 98	N102UN	0098	0399	2 CFMI CFM56-7B24	69400	Y144		lsf PEMB / op in TUI-colors
☐ D-AGEZ	Boeing 737-73S	29077 / 104	N103UN	0098	0399	2 CFMI CFM56-7B24	69400	Y144		lsf PEMB / op in TUI-colors

GERMAN OPERATING AIRCRAFT LEASING GmbH & Co. KG = (GOAL) (Joint venture between Lufthansa & KGAL-KG Allgemeine Leasing) — Gruenwald

Tölzer Strasse 15, D-82031 Grünwald, Germany ☎ (89) 64 14 31 07 Tx: none Fax: (89) 64 14 32 20 SITA: n/a
F: 1998 ⁂ n/a Head: Dirk Gerlach & Ulrich Berger Net: http://www.kgal.de Used aircraft leasing company.
Owner/lessor of following (main) aircraft types: Airbus Industrie A310-300, Boeing 737-300 & other surplus ex Lufthansa-aircraft. Aircraft lsf German Operating Aircraft are listed & mentioned as lsf GOAL under the leasing carriers.

GFD Gesellschaft für Flugzieldarstellung mbH = GFD — Hohn AFB

Flugplatz Hohn, D-24806 Hohn bei Rendsburg, Germany ☎ (4335) 92 020 Tx: 299855 d Fax: (4335) 92 02 15 SITA: n/a
F: 1989 ⁂ 55 Head: Klaus Menzel & Werner Heck ICAO: KITE Net: n/a Private operator conducting target towing & demonstration flights for the Marine/Naval Aviation, the Air Force & the anti-aircraft defense.

☐ D-CARL	Learjet 35A	35A-387		0081	1191	2 GA TFE731-2-2B	8900	target towing		
☐ D-CGFA	Learjet 35A	35A-179	N801PF	0078	0997	2 GA TFE731-2-2B	8890	target towing		
☐ D-CGFB	Learjet 35A	35A-268	N2U	0079	0897	2 GA TFE731-2-2B	8890	target towing		
☐ D-CGFC	Learjet 35A	35A-331	N435JW	0080	0797	2 GA TFE731-2-2B	8890	target towing		
☐ D-CGFD	Learjet 35A	35A-139	N15SC	0077	1191	2 GA TFE731-2-2B	8900	target towing		
☐ D-CGFE	Learjet 36A	36A-062	N4291N*	0089	1289	2 GA TFE731-2-2B	8900	target towing		
☐ D-CGFF	Learjet 36A	36A-063	N1048X*	0089	0290	2 GA TFE731-2-2B	8900	target towing		

GRASBERGER, GmbH - Helikopter Fluggesellschaft — Oedheim

Falkensteiner Str. 37, D-74229 Oedheim, Germany ☎ (7136) 21 424 Tx: none Fax: (7136) 22 783 SITA: n/a
F: 1974 ⁂ 8 Head: Volker Grasberger Net: n/a Aircraft below MTOW 1361kg: Bell 47G, Hiller UH-12E & Robinson R22 & R44

☐ D-HSBA	Bell 206B JetRanger III	3640	G-IMLH	0083	0493	1 AN 250-C20J	1451			occ lst/jtly opw Flugdienst Bayreuth

GRENZLAND AIR SERVICE, GmbH = GZA (formerly Grenzland-Flug Thesing & Co. GmbH) — Stadtlohn & Twente (Netherlands)

Flugplatz Stadtlohn-Wenningfeld, D-48703 Stadtlohn, Germany ☎ (2563) 93 230 Tx: none Fax: (2563) 93 23 20 SITA: n/a
F: 1969 ⁂ 20 Head: Rainald Schulte ICAO: GRENZLAND Net: n/a

☐ D-IGAS	Cessna 525 CitationJet	525-0223		0097	1297	2 WRR FJ44-1A	4717	6 Pax		lsf Roller-Game B.V.
☐ D-IGZA	Cessna 525 CitationJet	525-0260	N5197A*	0098	0698	2 WRR FJ44-1A	4717	6 Pax		lsf Roller-Game B.V.
☐ D-IHOL	Cessna 525 CitationJet	525-0229		0097	0399	2 WRR FJ44-1A	4717	6 Pax		lsf Roller-Game B.V.
☐ D-CGAS	Cessna 550 Citation II	550-0443	OY-CYT	0082	1197	2 PWC JT15D-4	6600	10 Pax		
☐ D-CWOL	Hawker 800B (BAe 125-800B)	258235	OY-RAA	0093	0199	2 GA TFE731-5R-1H	12428	12 Pax		

HAGELABWEHRFLUG, Hagelforschungsverein Rosenheim e.V. — Vogtareuth-Rosenheim

Landkreis Rosenheim, Landratsamt, Wittelsbacherstr. 53, D-83022 Rosenheim, Germany ☎ (8031) 39 23 77 Tx: none Fax: (8031) 12 177 SITA: n/a
F: 1975 ⁂ n/a Head: Georg Vogl Net: n/a Local government institution conducting non-commercial meteorological research flights & flight missions to avert imminent hail-showers.

☐ D-GITY	Partenavia P.68C-TC	360-41-TC	HB-LRK	0086	0596	2 LY TIO-360-C1A6D	1990	Meteo Research		
☐ D-GOGO	Partenavia P.68C-TC	343-31-TC		0085	0988	2 LY TIO-360-C1A6D	1990	Meteo Research		

HAGELABWEHR MUEHLDORF-ALTOETTING, GmbH — Mühldorf

c/o Helmut Huber, Strass Nr. 15, D-84419 Obertaufkirchen, Germany ☎ (8082) 14 50 Tx: none Fax: none SITA: n/a
F: 1980 ⁂ n/a Head: Helmut Huber Net: n/a Operates flight missions under contract to the local government of Landkreis Mühldorf-Altötting, to avert imminent hail-showers.

☐ D-EBDE	Piaggio FWP.149D	131	KB+108	0060	0995	1 LY GO-480-B1A6	1820	Meteo Research		

HAHN AIR BUSINESSLINE, GmbH & Co. KG = HR / HHN (formerly Hahn Air, GmbH & Co. KG) — Hahn

Flughafen Hahn, Halle 814, D-55483 Lautzenhausen, Germany ☎ (6543) 50 92 63 Tx: none Fax: (6543) 98 01 36 SITA: n/a
F: 1994 ⁂ 12 Head: Gerd Schäfer IATA: 169 ICAO: ROOSTER Net: n/a Aircraft below MTOW 1361kg: Cessna 150, 152 & 172

☐ D-ICRF	Cessna 404 Titan II	404-0406	N8776K	0079	0895	2 CO GTSIO-520-M	3810	Y9		
☐ D-IOLB	Cessna 404 Titan II	404-0691	SE-IVG	0080	0696	2 CO GTSIO-520-M	3810	Y9		
☐ D-IESS	Fairchild (Swearingen) SA226TC Metro II	TC-338	N90141	0080	0697	2 GA TPE331-3U-304G	5670	Y14		
☐ D-CABE	Fairchild (Swearingen) SA227AC Metro III	AC-523	N3109C*	0082	1197	2 GA TPE331-11U-611G	6577	Y19		
☐ D-CSAL	Fairchild (Swearingen) SA227AC Metro III	AC-601	I-FSAH	0084	1197	2 GA TPE331-11U-611G	6577	Y19		

HAHN HELICOPTER FLUGDIENSTE, GmbH — Hahn

Flughafen Hahn/Gebäude 669, D-55483 Lautzenhausen, Germany ☎ (6543) 98 90 99 Tx: none Fax: (6543) 50 92 74 SITA: n/a
F: 1995 ⁂ n/a Head: Uwe Weber Net: n/a Aircraft below MTOW 1361kg: Hughes 269C (300C)

☐ D-HAHN	Eurocopter (Aerosp.) AS350B2 Ecureuil	9003		0098	0498	1 TU Arriel 1D1	2250			lsf Schmidt Bank Leasing GmbH
☐ D-HBAS	Eurocopter (Aerosp.) AS350B1 Ecureuil	2204	F-GHFL	0089		1 TU Arriel 1D	2200			lsf pvt
☐ D-HUBW	Eurocopter (Aerosp.) AS350B2 Ecureuil	2105	G-PLME	0088		1 TU Arriel 1D1	2250			

HAL Holstenair Lübeck, Luftverkehrsservice GmbH & Co. Betriebs KG = HTR — Luebeck

Blankenseer Str. 101, D-23562 Lübeck, Germany ☎ (451) 58 90 30 Tx: none Fax: (451) 58 16 19 SITA: n/a
F: 1990 ⁂ 32 Head: Hartmut Euer ICAO: HOLSTEN Net: n/a Private operator conducting target towing flights for the Luftwaffe / German Air Force.

☐ D-CHAL	IAI 1124 Westwind	207	N666K	0077		2 GA TFE731-3-1G	10659	target towing		lsf FFL Flugzeug Leasing/opf Luftwaffe
☐ D-CHBL	IAI 1124 Westwind	226	N120S	0077		2 GA TFE731-3-1G	10659	target towing		lsf FFL Flugzeug Leasing/opf Luftwaffe
☐ D-CHCL	IAI 1124 Westwind I	277	N504JC	0080		2 GA TFE731-3-1G	10700	target towing		lsf FFL Flugzeug Leasing/opf Luftwaffe
☐ D-CHDL	IAI 1124 Westwind	199	N999MS	0076		2 GA TFE731-3-1G	10700	target towing		lsf FFL Flugzeug Leasing/opf Luftwaffe

HAMBURGER AIR CHARTER Erich Wagner, GmbH & Co. KG — Hamburg

Albert-Schweitzer-Ring 1, D-22045 Hamburg, Germany ☎ (40) 50 75 10 87 Tx: none Fax: (40) 50 75 10 88 SITA: n/a
F: 1989 ⁂ 1 Head: Erich Wagner Net: n/a

☐ D-ICPA	Piper PA-31T Cheyenne II	31T-8120025	N290CM	0081		2 PWC PT6A-28	4082			

HAMBURG INTERNATIONAL Luftfahrt, GmbH = HHI (Subsidiary of Ettlinger Schmider Kleiser Holding) — Hamburg

Obere Haupt Str. 3, D-22335 Hamburg, Germany ☎ (40) 50 05 01 20 Tx: none Fax: (40) 50 05 01 11 SITA: n/a
F: 1998 ⁂ n/a Head: Norbert Greller ICAO: LOBSTER Net: n/a

☐ D-ASKH	Boeing 737-73S	29082 / 229				2 CFMI CFM56-7B24	69400	Y148		to be lsf PEMB 0499

HANSA LUFTBILD, GmbH (German Air Surveys) — Muenster-Osnabrueck

Elbestr. 5, D-48145 Münster, Germany ☎ (251) 23 300 Tx: 892645 hlb d Fax: (251) 233 01 12 SITA: n/a
F: 1923 ⁂ 200 Head: Dr. Ralf Schroth Net: http://www.hansaluftbild.de

☐ D-EAOO	Cessna T210N Turbo Centurion II	21063856	N6289C	0080		1 CO TSIO-520-CE	1814	Photo / Survey		
☐ D-IBGF	Cessna 402B	402B0802	C-GGUZ	0075		2 CO TSIO-520-E	2858	Photo / Survey		lsf Photogrammetrie GmbH
☐ D-IHLB	Cessna 402B II	402B1340	N6377X	0078	0193	2 CO TSIO-520-E	2858	Photo / Survey		
☐ D-IDOS	Cessna 404 Titan II	404-0665	N5375C	0080		2 CO GTSIO-520-M	3810	Photo / Survey		

108 registration type of aircraft cn/fn ex/ex* mfd del powered by mtow kg configuration selcal name/fln/specialitites/remarks

HANSEFLUG, GmbH — Lübeck

Resebergweg 30, D-23569 Lübeck, Germany ☎ (451) 30 88 52 Tx: none Fax: (451) 30 68 52 SITA: n/a
F: 1992 ⁂ n/a Head: Ronald Stuht Net: n/a

☐ D-FJKA	Antonov An-2	19318	DDR-WJP	0058		1 SH ASh-62IR	5500			

HAPAG-LLOYD Flug, GmbH = HF / HLF (Subsidiary of Hapag-Lloyd, AG) — Hannover

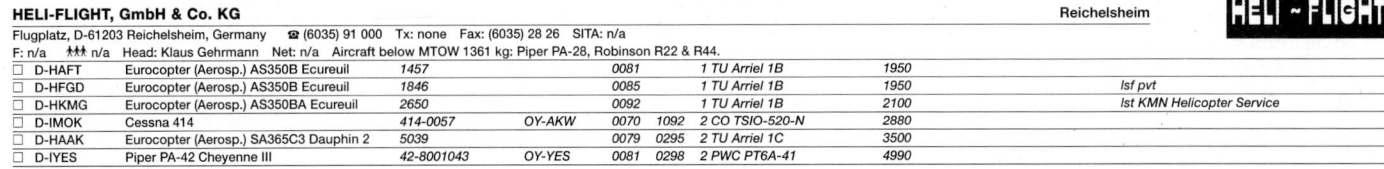

Postfach 42 02 40, D-30662 Hannover, Germany ☎ (511) 97 270 Tx: 924036 hlfl d Fax: (511) 97 27 494 SITA: n/a
F: 1972 ⁂ 1500 Head: Wolfgang Kurth IATA: 617 ICAO: HAPAG LLOYD Net: http://www.hapag-lloyd.com

☐ D-AHLF	Boeing 737-5K5	24927 / 1968		0090	1290	2 CFMI CFM56-3C1	59000	Y128	HL-FQ	lsf Defag
☐ D-AHLI	Boeing 737-5K5	25037 / 2022		0091	0491	2 CFMI CFM56-3C1	59000	Y128	HL-GQ	lsf Defag
☐ D-AHLN	Boeing 737-5K5	25062 / 2044		0091	0591	2 CFMI CFM56-3C1	59000	Y128	HL-JQ	lsf Defag
☐ D-AHLG	Boeing 737-4K5	26316 / 2711		0095	0495	2 CFMI CFM56-3C1	68000	Y167	HQ-CS	lsf ILFC
☐ D-AHLJ	Boeing 737-4K5	24125 / 1687		0089	0389	2 CFMI CFM56-3C1	68000	Y167	HL-DP	lsf Defag
☐ D-AHLK	Boeing 737-4K5	24126 / 1697		0089	0489	2 CFMI CFM56-3C1	68000	Y167	HL-EP	lsf Defag
☐ D-AHLL	Boeing 737-4K5	24127 / 1707		0089	0489	2 CFMI CFM56-3C1	68000	Y167	HL-FP	lsf Defag
☐ D-AHLM	Boeing 737-4K5	27102 / 2394		0092	0393	2 CFMI CFM56-3C1	68000	Y167	HL-AR	lsf Defag
☐ D-AHLO	Boeing 737-4K5	24128 / 1715		0089	0589	2 CFMI CFM56-3C1	68000	Y167	HL-GP	lsf Defag
☐ D-AHLS	Boeing 737-4K5	27074 / 2281		0092	0592	2 CFMI CFM56-3C1	68000	Y167	HL-BR	lsf Defag
☐ D-AHLT	Boeing 737-4K5	27830 / 2670		0094	1194	2 CFMI CFM56-3C1	68000	Y167	BD-CP	lsf Defag
☐ D-AHLU	Boeing 737-4K5	27831 / 2677		0094	1294	2 CFMI CFM56-3C1	68000	Y167	BD-EP	lsf Defag
☐ D-AHFA	Boeing 737-8K5	27981 / 7	N737BX*	0098	1298	2 CFMI CFM56-7B27	78245	Y184	NONE	lsf Defag
☐ D-AHFB	Boeing 737-8K5	27982 / 8	N35030*	0098	1298	2 CFMI CFM56-7B27	78245	Y184	NONE	lsf Defag
☐ D-AHFC	Boeing 737-8K5	27977 / 9	N5573P*	0098	0498	2 CFMI CFM56-7B27	78245	Y184	NONE	lsf Defag
☐ D-AHFD	Boeing 737-8K5	27978 / 40	N35161*	0098	0498	2 CFMI CFM56-7B27	78245	Y184	NONE	lsf Defag
☐ D-AHFE	Boeing 737-8K5	27979 / 44	N3502P*	0098	0598	2 CFMI CFM56-7B27	78245	Y184	NONE	lsf Defag
☐ D-AHFF	Boeing 737-8K5	27980 / 45	N3509J*	0098	0598	2 CFMI CFM56-7B27	78245	Y184	NONE	lsf Defag
☐ D-AHFG	Boeing 737-8K5	27989 / 59		0098	0698	2 CFMI CFM56-7B27	78245	Y184	NONE	lsf Defag
☐ D-AHFH	Boeing 737-8K5	27983				2 CFMI CFM56-7B27	78245	Y184	NONE	oo-delivery 0699
☐ D-AHFI	Boeing 737-8K5	27984				2 CFMI CFM56-7B27	78245	Y184	NONE	oo-delivery 0899
☐ D-AHFJ	Boeing 737-8K5	27990				2 CFMI CFM56-7B27	78245	Y184	NONE	oo-delivery 1099
☐ D-AHFK	Boeing 737-8K5	27991				2 CFMI CFM56-7B27	78245	Y184	NONE	oo-delivery 1299
☐ D-	Boeing 737-8Q8	28228				2 CFMI CFM56-7B27	78245	Y184	NONE	to be lsf ILFC 0200
☐ D-	Boeing 737-8K5					2 CFMI CFM56-7B27	78245	Y184	NONE	oo-delivery 0300
☐ D-	Boeing 737-8K5					2 CFMI CFM56-7B27	78245	Y184	NONE	oo-delivery 0500
☐ D-	Boeing 737-8K5					2 CFMI CFM56-7B27	78245	Y184	NONE	oo-delivery 0700
☐ D-	Boeing 737-8K5					2 CFMI CFM56-7B27	78245	Y184	NONE	oo-delivery 0900
☐ D-	Boeing 737-8K5					2 CFMI CFM56-7B27	78245	Y184	NONE	oo-delivery 1100
☐ D-	Boeing 737-8K5					2 CFMI CFM56-7B27	78245	Y184	NONE	oo-delivery 0101
☐ D-	Boeing 737-8K5					2 CFMI CFM56-7B27	78245	Y184	NONE	oo-delivery 0301
☐ D-	Boeing 737-8K5					2 CFMI CFM56-7B27	78245	Y184	NONE	oo-delivery 0501
☐ D-	Boeing 737-8K5					2 CFMI CFM56-7B27	78245	Y184	NONE	oo-delivery 0701
☐ D-	Boeing 737-8K5					2 CFMI CFM56-7B27	78245	Y184	NONE	oo-delivery 1001
☐ D-AHLV	Airbus Industrie A310-204 (winglets)	430	F-WWBL*	0087	0288	2 GE CF6-80C2A2	134000	Y264	HL-AP	lsf Defag
☐ D-AHLW	Airbus Industrie A310-204 (winglets)	427	F-WWBK*	0087	0188	2 GE CF6-80C2A2	134000	Y264	HL-BP	lsf Defag
☐ D-AHLX	Airbus Industrie A310-204 (winglets)	487	F-WWBO*	0089	1288	2 GE CF6-80C2A2	134000	Y264	HL-BS	lsf Defag
☐ D-AHLZ	Airbus Industrie A310-204 (winglets)	468	F-WWBM*	0088	0388	2 GE CF6-80C2A2	134000	Y264	HL-CP	lsf Defag
☐ D-AHLA	Airbus Industrie A310-304	520	F-WWCI*	0089	1089	2 GE CF6-80C2A2	157000	Y264	HL-AQ	lsf Defag
☐ D-AHLB	Airbus Industrie A310-304	528	F-WWCE*	0090	0190	2 GE CF6-80C2A2	157000	Y264	HL-BQ	lsf Defag
☐ D-AHLC	Airbus Industrie A310-308	620	F-WWCC*	0091	0192	2 GE CF6-80C2A8	161000	Y264	HL-AS	lsf Defag
☐ D-ASRA	Airbus Industrie A310-322	399	HB-IPF	0085		2 PW JT9D-7R4E1	150000	Y264		to be lsf ILFC 0599
☐ D-ASRB	Airbus Industrie A310-322	412	HB-IPK	0086		2 PW JT9D-7R4E1	153000	Y254		to be lsf ILFC 0699

HCG Heli-Charter GmbH & Co. Verwaltungs-KG — Berlin-Tempelhof

Kurfürstendamm 219, D-10719 Berlin, Germany ☎ (30) 69 51 30 40 Tx: none Fax: (30) 69 51 30 41 SITA: n/a
F: 1992 ⁂ n/a Head: Günter Mahler Net: n/a

☐ D-HWLL	Bell 206B JetRanger III	2359	N119AJ	0078		1 AN 250-C20B	1450			
☐ D-HWPP	Bell 206L-3 LongRanger III	51480	C-FKKE	0091		1 AN 250-C30P	1882			

HDM-FLUGSERVICE, GmbH — Nuremberg/Berlin/Bad Berka/Munich & Regensburg

Flughafenstr. 100, D-90411 Nürnberg, Germany ☎ (911) 52 75 70 Tx: none Fax: (911) 527 57 32 SITA: n/a
F: 1972 ⁂ 35 Head: Dieter Dust Net: n/a

☐ D-HHCC	Bell 412HP	36066		0093	0194	2 PWC PT6T-3BE TwinPac	5398	EMS		
☐ D-HHUU	Bell 412HP	36057	N6162A*	0092	0793	2 PWC PT6T-3BE TwinPac	5398	EMS		
☐ D-HHVV	Bell 412HP	36059	N6173A*	0093	0893	2 PWC PT6T-3BE TwinPac	5398	EMS		
☐ D-HHXX	Bell 412HP	36076	OE-XMM	0093	0596	2 PWC PT6T-3BE TwinPac	5398	EMS		
☐ D-HHYY	Bell 412HP	36051	N4382A*	0092	0193	2 PWC PT6T-3BE TwinPac	5398	EMS		
☐ D-HHZZ	Bell 412HP	36065	OE-XNN	0093	0296	2 PWC PT6T-3BE TwinPac	5398	EMS		

HELGOLAND AIRLINES, GmbH & Co. KG = LE (formerly IAAI Air Service, GmbH) — Wilhelmshaven-Mariensiel

Flugplatz Wilhelmshaven-Mariensiel, D-26452 Sande, Germany ☎ (4421) 92 600 Tx: none Fax: (4421) 92 60 10 SITA: n/a
F: 1993 ⁂ 22 Head: Dr. Johannes A. Angerer Net: n/a Aircraft below MTOW 1361kg: Cessna 172 & Piper PA-28

☐ D-IAEB	Britten-Norman BN-2A-8 Islander	218	OH-BNB	0070		2 LY O-540-E4C5	2810			
☐ D-IORF	Britten-Norman BN-2A-26 Islander	2020	N100DA	0079	0794	2 LY O-540-E4C5	2810			
☐ D-IORE	Cessna 404 Titan II	404-0604	I-NARA	0080	0994	2 CO GTSIO-520-M	3810			

HELI AIR Zagel, Lufttransporte AG — Hersbruck-Private Heliport

Friedrichstr. 3, D-91217 Hersbruck, Germany ☎ (9151) 83 540 Tx: none Fax: (9151) 83 54 44 SITA: n/a
F: 1997 ⁂ 12 Head: Wolfgang Zagel Net: n/a

☐ D-HFZA	Kaman K-1200 K-Max	A94-0018		0096	0097	1 LY T5317A-1	2948			

HELI CARGO HELICOPTER SERVICE, GmbH — Hahn

Kirchgasse 20, D-55487 Laufersweiler, Germany ☎ (6543) 25 65 Tx: none Fax: (6543) 25 65 SITA: n/a
F: 1998 ⁂ n/a Head: Freimuth Stephan Net: n/a

☐ D-HFSJ	Eurocopter (Aerosp.) SA316B Alouette III	2244	OE-OXW	0076	1198	1 TU Artouste IIIB	2200	Utility		

HELI-CHARTER Rammelsberg, GmbH & Co. KG — Siegerland

Werftstr. 1, Siegerlandflughafen, D-57299 Burbach, Germany ☎ (2736) 50 601 Tx: none Fax: (2736) 50 602 SITA: n/a
F: 1992 ⁂ 8 Head: Dirk Rammelsberg Net: n/a

☐ D-HEND	Eurocopter (Aerosp.) AS350B1 Ecureuil	1707	F-WQDO	0083	0098	1 TU Arriel 1D	2200			lsf pvt
☐ D-HRAM	Eurocopter (Aerosp.) AS350B Ecureuil	2591		0092	0892	1 TU Arriel 1B	1950			
☐ D-HHRR	Eurocopter (Aerosp.) AS355F1 Ecureuil 2	5086	N5781P	0081	1294	2 AN 250-C20F	2400			

HELICOPTER-SERVICE WASSERTHAL, GmbH – HSW — Hamburg

Kätnerweg 43, D-22393 Hamburg, Germany ☎ (40) 640 10 81 Tx: none Fax: (40) 640 12 32 SITA: n/a
F: 1970 ⁂ 12 Head: Claus Wasserthal Net: n/a

☐ D-HABB	Bell 206L-1 LongRanger II	45783	N102RD	0083	1191	1 AN 250-C28B	1882			
☐ D-HHHS	Bell 206L-3 LongRanger III	51454	SE-HVG	0091	0498	1 AN 250-C30P	1880			
☐ D-HHRW	Bell 206LR+ LongRanger	45082	N16762	0077		1 AN 250-C20R	1814			Pop-out floats/cvtd 206L
☐ D-HHCW	Bell 407	53058		0096	1296	1 AN 250-C47B	2268			
☐ D-HHBW	Eurocopter (MBB) BO105CBS-5	S-346	N6170K	0077	0793	2 AN 250-C20B	2500			Pop-out floats / Cargo sling
☐ D-HIBY	Eurocopter (MBB) BO105D	S-75	HB-XLV	0073		2 AN 250-C20	2500			Pop-out floats / Cargo sling

HELI-FLIGHT, GmbH & Co. KG — Reichelsheim

Flugplatz, D-61203 Reichelsheim, Germany ☎ (6035) 91 000 Tx: none Fax: (6035) 28 26 SITA: n/a
F: n/a ⁂ n/a Head: Klaus Gehrmann Net: n/a Aircraft below MTOW 1361 kg: Piper PA-28, Robinson R22 & R44.

☐ D-HAFT	Eurocopter (Aerosp.) AS350B Ecureuil	1457		0081		1 TU Arriel 1B	1950			
☐ D-HFGD	Eurocopter (Aerosp.) AS350B Ecureuil	1846		0085		1 TU Arriel 1B	1950			lsf pvt
☐ D-HKMG	Eurocopter (Aerosp.) AS350BA Ecureuil	2650		0092		1 TU Arriel 1B	2100			lst KMN Helicopter Service
☐ D-IMOK	Cessna 414	414-0057	OY-AKW	0070	1092	2 CO TSIO-520-N	2880			
☐ D-HAAK	Eurocopter (Aerosp.) SA365C3 Dauphin 2	5039		0079	0295	2 TU Arriel 1C	3500			
☐ D-IYES	Piper PA-42 Cheyenne III	42-8001043	OY-YES	0081	0298	2 PWC PT6A-41	4990			

HELIKOPTER GESCHAEFTSREISEN, GmbH — Lintel-Heliport

Neuenkirchener Landstr. 86, D-33378 Rheda-Wiedenbrück, Germany ☎ (5242) 52 52 Tx: none Fax: (5252) 78 90 SITA: n/a
F: 1984 ⁂ n/a Head: Josef Wiedeler Net: n/a

☐ D-HKLW	Bell 206L-3 LongRanger III	51206	N3205J	0087		1 AN 250-C30P	1882			

109 registration type of aircraft cn/fn ex/ex* mfd del powered by mtow kg configuration selcal name/fln/specialitites/remarks

HELI-RENT Helicopter-Service & Flugschule (Florian Larcherdinger dba) — Ascholding-Heliport

Gartenstr. 1, D-83623 Ascholding, Germany ☎ (8171) 29 400 Tx: n/a Fax: (8171) 29 565 SITA: n/a
F: 1986 ⁂ 6 Head: Peter Thoma Net: n/a

☐ D-HGMS	Bell 206B JetRanger III	4373		0095	1295	1 AN 250-C20B	1450			lsf Pfister GmbH
☐ D-HMCB	Bell 206B JetRanger III	4120		0090		1 AN 250-C20B	1450			lsf MMM Multi Media Marketing GmbH
☐ D-HOMF	Bell 206B JetRanger II	1987	N9932K	0075		1 AN 250-C20	1450			lsf pvt
☐ D-HWFW	Bell 206BR+ JetRanger III	4159	HB-XYF	0091		1 AN 250-C20R/4	1450			lsf pvt / cvtd 206B
☐ D-HALT	Bell 206L-3 LongRanger III	51578	C-FNLC*	0092		1 AN 250-C30P	1882			
☐ D-HPRO	Bell 407	53196		0097	1098	1 AN 250-C47B	2268			lsf pvt

HELISERVICE Helicopter Service Mitte, GmbH = HSM — Egelsbach, Frankfurt, Hassfurt & BG Unfallklinik Murnau

Postfach 1102, D-63323 Egelsbach, Germany ☎ (6103) 94 150 Tx: none Fax: (6103) 45 253 SITA: n/a
F: 1987 ⁂ 30 Head: Eberhard Herr ICAO: LIFESTAR Net: http://www.heliservice.com Aircraft below MTOW 1361kg: Robinson R22 & Schweizer 300CB

☐ D-HDPB	Bell 206B JetRanger III	4151	OH-HTS	0091	0198	1 AN 250-C20J	1450			lsf Columbus Leasing GmbH
☐ D-HHSM	Bell 222B	47139	N91GC	0083	0890	2 LY LTS101-750C.1	3742			lst HSD Hubschrauber
☐ D-HNIC	Bell 222B	47142	N811CE	0084	0492	2 LY LTS101-750C.1	3742			lst HSD Hubschrauber
☐ D-HUKM	Bell 222U	47501	N222AD	0083	1195	2 LY LTS101-750C.1	3742			lsf DVL Deutsche Verkehrs-Leasing GmbH

HELITEAM SUED — Munich

Bürgermeister-Graf-Ring 10, D-82538 Geretsried-Gelting, Germany ☎ (8171) 41 990 Tx: none Fax: (8171) 41 99 20 SITA: n/a
F: 1997 ⁂ n/a Head: Peter Thoma Net: n/a

☐ D-HLKB	Bell 206B JetRanger III	4209		0092		1 AN 250-C20J	1450			
☐ D-HUTA	Bell 407	53158		0097		1 AN 250-C47B	2268			lsf LFL Luftfahrzeug Leasing GmbH

HELI UNIONAIR, Fluggesellschaft mbH (formerly Heli Union (Deutschland), GmbH) — Ottensoos, Berlin-Tempelhof & Leipzig

Bräunleinsberg 25, D-91242 Ottensoos, Germany ☎ (9123) 96 810 Tx: none Fax: (9123) 96 81 10 SITA: n/a
F: 1989 ⁂ 11 Head: Johannes Krüger Net: n/a

☐ D-HESA	Agusta-Bell 206B JetRanger	8373		0074		1 AN 250-C20	1451			lsf AL Aviation Leasing GmbH
☐ D-HHUD	Bell 206B JetRanger III	2327	N700WD	0078		1 AN 250-C20B	1451			lsf AL Aviation Leasing GmbH
☐ D-HGAP	Eurocopter (Aerosp.) SA315B Lama	2625	N27387	0082	0598	1 TU Artouste IIIB1	1950			lsf AL Aviation Leasing GmbH
☐ D-HHUB	Eurocopter (Aerosp.) AS350B2 Ecureuil	2406	HB-XVD	0091	0395	1 TU Arriel 1D1	2250			lsf AL Aviation Leasing GmbH
☐ D-HIFA	Eurocopter (MBB) BO105CBS-4	S-550	LN-OSQ	0082		2 AN 250-C20B	2500	EMS		lst IFA International Flug Ambulanz
☐ D-HFAI	Eurocopter (Aerosp.) AS355F1 Ecureuil 2	5009	N5774M	0081	0697	2 AN 250-C20F	2400	EMS		lsf Deutsche Leasing/sublst IFA Int'l

HELIX Flug, GmbH — Oppin

Flugplatz, D-06188 Oppin, Germany ☎ (7942) 20 66 Tx: none Fax: (7942) 20 69 SITA: n/a
F: n/a ⁂ n/a Head: Ahim Wittmann & Tillmann Frohmeier Net: n/a

☐ D-HIIX	Eurocopter (Aerosp.) AS350B2 Ecureuil	9005		0098	0199	1 TU Arriel 1D1	2250			
☐ D-HLIX	Eurocopter (Aerosp.) AS350BA Ecureuil	1525	F-GBMR	0082	1295	1 TU Arriel 1B	2100			cvtd AS350B

HFS Helicopter Flug-Service, GmbH — Kassel-Calden

Flugplatzstr. 41, D-34379 Calden, Germany ☎ (5674) 824 Tx: none Fax: (5674) 820 SITA: n/a
F: 1983 ⁂ 28 Head: Elke Püschel-Braun Net: n/a Aircraft below MTOW 1361kg: Hughes 269C (300C)

☐ D-HHFS	Bell 206B JetRanger III	2757	G-SHJJ	0079	0489	1 AN 250-C20B	1451			
☐ D-HFSB	Eurocopter (Aerosp.) AS350B2 Ecureuil	2371		0090	0990	1 TU Arriel 1D1	2250			
☐ D-HFSC	Eurocopter (Aerosp.) AS350B Ecureuil	1737	SE-HNF	0083	0893	1 TU Arriel 1B	1950			
☐ D-HFSF	Eurocopter (Aerosp.) AS350B Ecureuil	1690	D-HALL	0083	0295	1 TU Arriel 1B	1950			
☐ D-HHWW	Eurocopter (Aerosp.) AS350B2 Ecureuil	2437		0091	1091	1 TU Arriel 1D1	2250			

HIMMELSSCHREIBER Azur, GmbH — Hamburg-Harbour

Flughafen Fuhlsbüttel, GFZ Geb. 175, D-22335 Hamburg, Germany ☎ (40) 50 75 21 09 Tx: none Fax: (40) 50 75 14 61 SITA: n/a
F: 1993 ⁂ 6 Head: Jörg Steber Net: n/a Aircraft below MTOW 1361kg: Piper PA-12

☐ D-FVIP	De Havilland DHC-2 Beaver I	1512	N6246X	0062	1195	1 PW R-985-AN1	2309	7 Pax		Floats
☐ N423RS	Consolidated PBY-5A Catalina	48423	N4002A	0040	1097	2 PW R-1830-92S	13835	Patrol / 10 Pax		lsf Cat.Angels Ltd/Amph./opf Greenpeace

HSC Helicopter Charter-Service — Saarbruecken

Scheidter Str. 130, D-66123 Saarbrücken, Germany ☎ (681) 36 011 Tx: none Fax: (681) 36 012 SITA: n/a
F: 1994 ⁂ n/a Head: Dr. Rolf Eicholz Net: n/a

☐ D-HBAD	Bell 206B JetRanger III	3819	N3203Z	0084		1 AN 250-C20J	1450			

HSD Hubschrauber-Sonder-Dienst Flugbetriebs-GmbH & Co. — Harste Heliport

An der Burg 4-8, D-37120 Harste, Germany ☎ (5593) 92 920 Tx: none Fax: (5593) 92 92 29 SITA: n/a
F: 1985 ⁂ 28 Head: Kai Scheithauer Net: http://www.hsd-online.de

☐ D-HAFC	Agusta-Bell 206B JetRanger	8323	OE-BXR	0072	1089	1 AN 250-C20	1450			lsf Deutsche Leasing
☐ D-HHSJ	Bell 206L-4 LongRanger IV	52022	N6227Q*	0093	0793	1 AN 250-C30P	2018			lsf OFRA Systembau GmbH & Co.
☐ D-HSDD	MD Helicopters MD 900 Explorer	900-00026	N9094T	0096	0296	2 PWC PW206A	2720			
☐ D-HHSC	Bell 222A	47080	N131GS	0082	0197	2 LY LTS101-650C.3A	3560			lsf Rosental Finanz-Beratung
☐ D-HHSH	Bell 222SP	47063	N82NR	0081	1291	2 AN 250-C30G	3560			lsf LGS Leasing / cvtd 222
☐ D-HHSM	Bell 222B	47139	N91GC	0083		2 LY LTS101-750C.1	3742			lsf Heliservice Heli. Service Mitte
☐ D-HKSL	Bell 222A	47079	N66UT	0082	0688	2 LY LTS101-650C.3A	3560			lsf Deutsche Leasing
☐ D-HNIC	Bell 222B	47142	N811CE	0084		2 LY LTS101-750C.1	3742			lsf Helicopter Heli. Service Mitte
☐ D-HTIM	Bell 222B	47153	JA9668	0087		2 LY LTS101-750C.1	3742			lsf LGS Leasing
☐ D-HVUM	Bell 222SP	47052	N3899G	0080	0593	2 AN 250-C30G	3560			lsf LGS Leasing / cvtd 222

HTM Helicopter Travel Munich, GmbH — Munich

Flughafen München, D-85356 München, Germany ☎ (89) 97 59 75 70 Tx: none Fax: (89) 97 59 75 76 SITA: n/a
F: 1997 ⁂ n/a Head: Hans Ostler Net: http://www.helitravel.de

☐ D-HOTT	Bell 206L-3 LongRanger III	51587	C-FNOQ*	0092		1 AN 250-C30P	1882			lsf pvt
☐ D-HHBP	Eurocopter (Aerosp.) AS350B Ecureuil	1973		0086	0598	1 TU Arriel 1B	1950			
☐ D-HECE	Eurocopter (MBB) BK117B-2	7244	D-HFII	0093	0098	2 LY LTS101-750B.1	3350	EMS		occ lsf AMB

IFAG – Ilyushin 18 Flight Association Germany, e.V. — Berlin-Schönefeld

Flughafen Berlin-Schönefeld, D-12521 Berlin, Germany ☎ (30) 60 91 54 38 Tx: none Fax: (30) 60 91 54 39 SITA: n/a
F: 1998 ⁂ n/a Head: Mario Böhme Net: n/a Non-commercial association. Inteds to acquire an Ilyushin 18 during 1999 & conducting nostalgia sightseeing & demonstation flights.

IFA International Flug Ambulanz e.V. (Associated with FAI Flight-Ambulance-Service International) — Leipzig

Postfach 30, Flughafen, D-04029 Leipzig-Halle, Germany ☎ (341) 424 11 15 Tx: none Fax: (341) 424 11 23 SITA: n/a
F: 1991 ⁂ n/a Head: Jürgen Schlögel Net: n/a

☐ D-HIFA	Eurocopter (MBB) BO105CBS-4	S-550	LN-OSQ	0082	0294	2 AN 250-C20B	2500	EMS		lsf Heli Unionair
☐ D-HFAI	Eurocopter (Aerosp.) AS355F1 Ecureuil 2	5009	N5774M	0081	0697	2 AN 250-C20F	2400	EMS		lsf Heli Unionair

INDUSTRIE-FLUG OTT, GmbH & Co. Flugcharter KG — Stuttgart

Postfach 9, D-74357 Bönnigheim, Germany ☎ (7127) 74 98 Tx: 724911 aman d Fax: (7127) 89 395 SITA: n/a
F: 1978 ⁂ 3 Head: Hanns A. Pielenz Net: n/a

☐ D-IHAN	Beech King Air B200	BB-1478	N8150N	0094	0396	2 PWC PT6A-42	5675			

ISARFLUG, GmbH — Munich

Lohstr. 30b, D-85445 Schweig/Flughafen München, Germany ☎ (8122) 93 481 Tx: none Fax: (8122) 93 482 SITA: n/a
F: 1973 ⁂ 5 Head: Jürgen Ebenhöh Net: n/a

☐ D-IEBE	Beech King Air C90A	LJ-1267	A6-FAE	0090	0196	2 PWC PT6A-21	4581			lsf SüdLeasing GmbH

JET CONNECTION Businessflight, AG — Frankfurt

Abraham Lincoln Strasse 16, D-65189 Wiesbaden, Germany ☎ (611) 976 50 40 Tx: none Fax: (611) 976 50 45 SITA: FRAJTCR
F: 1997 ⁂ 15 Head: Tilman Danker Net: http://www.jetconnection.com

☐ D-CUTE	Learjet 55	55-013	N82679	0081	0097	2 GA TFE731-3AR-2B	9800	8 Pax		lsf Disko Leasing GmbH
☐ D-CLUB	Learjet 45	45-044				2 GA TFE731-20	9163	8 Pax		oo-delivery 0699
☐ D-CSIX	Learjet 60	60-120	N120LJ*	0098	0798	2 PWC PW305A	10319	8 Pax		

JOY-AIR Flugcharter (Division of TEMA-Technologie- & Management-Beratung, GmbH) — Stuttgart

Kirchentellinsfurterstr. 31, D-72127 Kusterdingen, Germany ☎ (7071) 33 527 Tx: none Fax: (7071) 35 347 SITA: n/a
F: 1975 ⁂ n/a Head: Stephan Wawrzinek Net: n/a

☐ D-EXOT	Piper PA-46-310P Malibu	46-8508010	N4378T	0085		1 CO TSIO-520-BE	1860			lsf pvt
☐ D-IWAS	Cessna T303 Crusader	T30300111	N3701C	0082		2 CO TSIO-520-AE	2336			lsf SüdLeasing GmbH

110 registration type of aircraft cn/fn ex/ex* mfd del powered by mtow kg configuration selcal name/fln/specialitites/remarks

JUERG PUENTENER SURVEYS — Egelsbach

Seztgerweg 11, D-55294 Bodenheim, Germany ☎ (6135) 50 85 Tx: none Fax: (6135) 65 32 SITA: n/a
F: 1993 ☗☗☗ n/a Head: Jürg Püntener Net: n/a

☐ D-EAJP	Cessna TU206G Turbo Stationair 6 II	*U20604465*	*N756YK*	*0078*	*0392*	*1 CO TSIO-520-M*	*1633*	*Photo / Survey*		

KAZ BILDMESS, GmbH – Foto & Survey Flug (Subsidiary of Rheinbraun AG) — Leipzig

Karl-Rothe-Str. 10-14, D-04105 Leipzig, Germany ☎ (341) 566 94 57 Tx: none Fax: (341) 566 92 00 SITA: n/a
F: 1991 ☗☗☗ n/a Head: Dr. Herbert Krausz Net: n/a

☐ D-FOTO	Cessna 208 Caravan I	*20800192*	*N9773F*	*0090*	*0492*	*1 PWC PT6A-114*	*3311*	*Photo / Survey*		*lsf Rheinbraun AG*

KBA Kieler Business Air, GmbH & Co. KG = KEL — Kiel

Flughafen, D-24159 Kiel, Germany ☎ (431) 32 96 40 Tx: none Fax: (431) 32 49 12 SITA: n/a
F: 1994 ☗☗☗ n/a Head: Bernd Jürgensen ICAO: KIEL AIR Net: n/a

☐ D-EDOO	Commander (Rockwell) 114	*14273*	*N14GR*	*0077*		*1 LY IO-540-T4A5D*	*1424*			
☐ D-IKBJ	Beech King Air B200	*BB-1209*	*N46GA*	*0085*	*0196*	*2 PWC PT6A-42*	*5670*			*lsf AL Aviation Leasing GmbH*

KIRBERGER AVIATION (Kirberger & Partner Aviation, Service & Consulting, GmbH dba) — Burbach

Flughafenstrasse, D-57299 Burbach, Germany ☎ (2736) 61 98 Tx: none Fax: (2736) 81 89 SITA: n/a
F: 1992 ☗☗☗ 16 Head: Walter Kirberger Net: n/a Aircraft below MTOW 1361kg: Socata TB9

☐ D-ICFG	Cessna 340A II	*340A0537*	*N4345C*	*0078*		*2 CO TSIO-520-NB*	*2717*	*Y6*		*lsf Walter Feickert GmbH*
☐ D-CALY	Dornier 228-212	*8155*	*D-CAOS**	*0089*	*0098*	*2 GA TPE331-5A-252D*	*6400*	*Y18*		*lsf Dornier Luftfahrt GmbH*

KMN-Helicopter Service, GmbH — Sommerland-Heliport

Kamerlandstr. 14, D-25358 Sommerland, Germany ☎ (4126) 38 903 Tx: none Fax: (4126) 38 904 SITA: n/a
F: 1997 ☗☗☗ 4 Head: Walter Koopmann Net: n/a

☐ D-HKMG	Eurocopter (Aerosp.) AS350BA Ecureuil	*2650*		*0092*		*1 TU Arriel 1B*	*2100*			*lsf Heli-Flight*

KURI-FLUGDIENST, GmbH & Co. KG — Friedrichshafen

Ehlersstrasse 11, D-88046 Friedrichshafen, Germany ☎ (7541) 26 464 Tx: 734308 flugfd Fax: (7541) 26 408 SITA: n/a
F: 1976 ☗☗☗ 4 Head: Rechtsanwalt Christian Kubon Net: n/a

☐ D-IFME	Cessna 414A Chancellor II	*414A0120*	*N5645C*	*0078*		*2 CO TSIO-520-N*	*3062*	*5 Pax*		
☐ D-CHZF	Cessna 550 Citation Bravo	*550-0866*		*0099*	*0299*	*2 PWC PW530A*	*6713*	*8 Pax*		
☐ D-ICUR	Cessna 551 Citation II/SP	*551-0029*	*N500ER*	*0080*		*2 PWC JT15D-4*	*5670*	*8 Pax*		

LEIPZIG-DRESDEN FLUG (Flugschule Leipzig-Dresden, GmbH dba) — Gera

Polenzer Strasse, D-04821 Brandis, Germany ☎ (172) 364 45 55 Tx: none Fax: (341) 224 22 73 SITA: n/a
F: n/a ☗☗☗ n/a Head: Günther Storch Net: n/a Aircraft below MTOW 1361kg: Piper PA-28

☐ D-GAAA	Piper PA-44-180 Seminole	*44-7995174*	*N3001H*	*0079*		*2 LY O-360-E1A6D*	*1724*			*lsf ITB Ingenieurgesellschaft*
☐ D-ILEI	Cessna T303 Crusader	*T30300102*	*N3141C*	*0082*		*2 CO TSIO-520-AE*	*2336*			*lsf Commerzleasing GmbH*

LFH Luftverkehr Friesland Harle (Luftverkehr Friesland Brunzema & Partner, KG dba) — Wittmund-Harle

Flugplatz Harle, D-26409 Wittmund, Germany ☎ (4464) 948 10 Tx: none Fax: (4464) 94 81 81 SITA: n/a
F: 1983 ☗☗☗ 14 Head: Jan-Lüppen Brunzema Net: n/a Aircraft below MTOW 1361 kg: Cessna 172.

☐ D-IHER	Britten-Norman BN-2A-8 Islander	*377*	*G-BBUA*	*0073*	*1297*	*2 LY O-540-E4C5*	*2812*			
☐ D-ILFA	Britten-Norman BN-2B-26 Islander	*2243*	*G-BSWO**	*0091*	*0791*	*2 LY O-540-E4C5*	*2994*			
☐ D-ILFB	Britten-Norman BN-2B-26 Islander	*2271*	*G-BUBO**	*0094*	*0296*	*2 LY O-540-E4C5*	*2994*			
☐ D-ILFH	Britten-Norman BN-2B-26 Islander	*2212*	*G-BPXS**	*0089*	*0190*	*2 LY O-540-E4C5*	*2994*			

LGM Luftfahrt GmbH Mannheim — Mannheim

Flughafen Neuostheim, D-68163 Mannheim, Germany ☎ (621) 41 60 34 Tx: none Fax: (621) 41 60 35 SITA: n/a
F: 1980 ☗☗☗ 15 Head: Michael Held Net: n/a Aircraft below MTOW 1361kg: Robinson R22 & R44.

☐ D-HJET	Bell 206B JetRanger III	*3777*	*HB-XSB*	*0083*	*0997*	*1 AN 250-C20J*	*1450*			*lsf SSS Helikopter GmbH*
☐ D-GILD	Piper PA-34-200T Seneca II	*34-7570164*	*N33805*	*0075*		*2 CO TSIO-360-E*	*1999*			*lsf pvt*
☐ D-HBNE	Eurocopter (MBB) BK117A-4	*7057*		*0086*		*2 LY LTS101-650B.1*	*3200*			*lsf pvt*
☐ D-HIMT	Eurocopter (MBB) BK117B-2	*7203*		*0093*		*2 LY LTS101-750B.1*	*3350*			*lsf Eurocopter Deutschland / cvtd B-1*

LGW Luftfahrtgesellschaft Walter, mbH = HE / LGW — Dortmund-Wickede

Flugplatz 11, D-44319 Dortmund, Germany ☎ (231) 21 980 Tx: 822122 lgw d Fax: (231) 21 27 98 SITA: n/a
F: 1980 ☗☗☗ 28 Head: Bernd Walter ICAO: WALTER Net: n/a

☐ D-IKBA	Dornier 228-200	*8066*	*HB-LPC*	*0085*	*0596*	*2 GA TPE331-5-252D*	*5700*	*Y19*		*lsf Dornier / cvtd -201*
☐ D-ILWB	Dornier 228-200	*8035*	*D-CDIZ*	*0084*	*1193*	*2 GA TPE331-5-252D*	*5700*	*Y19*		*cvtd -201*
☐ D-ILWD	Dornier 228-200	*8069*	*D-CHOF*	*0085*	*0592*	*2 GA TPE331-5-252D*	*5700*	*Y19*		*cvtd -202*
☐ D-ILWS	Dornier 228-200	*8002*	*OY-CHJ*	*0082*	*0695*	*2 GA TPE331-5-252D*	*5700*	*Y19*		
☐ D-IMIK	Dornier 228-200	*8058*	*D-CMIC*	*0085*	*1195*	*2 GA TPE331-5-252D*	*5700*	*Y19*		*lsf pvt / cvtd -202*

LIPS FLUGDIENST, GmbH — Leipzig

Gittelstr. 42, D-04347 Leipzig, Germany ☎ (341) 393 91 70 Tx: none Fax: (341) 393 91 72 SITA: n/a
F: 1991 ☗☗☗ n/a Head: Guido Felder Net: n/a Aircraft below MTOW 1361kg: Cessna 150, 172 & MS893E

☐ D-GILA	Partenavia P.68B	*52*		*0076*	*0597*	*2 LY IO-360-A1B6*	*1990*			

LTO Lufttransport Osnabrück-Münster, GmbH (formerly Luft-Taxi Osnabrück) — Muenster-Osnabrueck

Flughafen Münster-Osnabrück, D-48268 Greven, Germany ☎ (2571) 91 166 Tx: none Fax: (2571) 91 164 SITA: n/a
F: 1970 ☗☗☗ 6 Head: Hans-Joachim Peters Net: n/a

☐ D-IMWK	Fairchild (Swearingen) SA227TT Merlin 300	*TT-529A*	*N3109S*	*0085*		*2 GA TPE331-10U-513G*	*5670*	*9 Pax*		*lsf Wilhelm Karmann GmbH*
☐ D-ILTC	Cessna 551 Citation II/SP	*551-0617*	*N617CM*	*0089*	*1091*	*2 PWC JT15D-4*	*5670*	*7 Pax*		

LTU International Airways = LT / LTU (LTU Lufttransport-Unternehmen, GmbH & Co. KG dba / Member of European Leisure Group) — Duesseldorf

Halle 8, Flughafen, D-40474 Düsseldorf, Germany ☎ (211) 941 88 88 Tx: 8584361 ltu d Fax: (211) 941 88 81 SITA: DUSXRLT
F: 1955 ☗☗☗ 2770 Head: Peter Haslebacher IATA: 266 ICAO: LTU Net: http://www.ltu.de
Beside aircraft listed, also uses 6 Boeing 737-75B, lsf/opb GERMANIA (in Germania or TUI-colors). For details – see under that company.

☐ D-ALTA	Airbus Industrie A320-232	*580*	*D-ALAC*	*0396*		*2 IAE V2527-A5*	*75500*	*Y174*		*to be lsf AEF 0599*
☐ D-AMUG	Boeing 757-2G5	*29488 / 830*		*1098*	*1098*	*2 RR RB211-535E4*	*115700*	*Y210*		
☐ D-AMUH	Boeing 757-2G5	*29489 / 834*		*1198*	*1198*	*2 RR RB211-535E4*	*115700*	*Y210*		
☐ D-AMUI	Boeing 757-2G5	*28112 / 708*		*0096*	*0496*	*2 RR RB211-535E4*	*115700*	*Y210*	*JS-FP*	
☐ D-AMUK	Boeing 757-225	*22689 / 117*	*EC-ETZ*	*0086*	*1093*	*2 RR RB211-535E4*	*108860*	*Y210*	*CL-AG*	
☐ D-AMUM	Boeing 757-2G5	*24451 / 227*		*0089*	*0589*	*2 RR RB211-535E4*	*108860*	*Y210*	*BQ-AL*	
☐ D-AMUQ	Boeing 757-2G5	*26278 / 671*		*0095*	*0495*	*2 RR RB211-535E4*	*115700*	*Y210*	*GS-KR*	*lsf ILFC*
☐ D-AMUU	Boeing 757-225	*22688 / 115*	*EC-FIY*	*0086*	*0190*	*2 RR RB211-535E4*	*108860*	*Y210*	*CE-BL*	
☐ D-AMUV	Boeing 757-2G5	*23928 / 146*		*0087*	*1087*	*2 RR RB211-535E4*	*115700*	*Y210*	*EP-AH*	
☐ D-AMUW	Boeing 757-2G5	*23929 / 153*		*0087*	*1187*	*2 RR RB211-535E4*	*108860*	*Y210*	*EP-AJ*	
☐ D-AMUX	Boeing 757-2G5	*23983 / 161*		*0088*	*0388*	*2 RR RB211-535E4*	*115700*	*Y210*	*EP-AK*	
☐ D-AMUY	Boeing 757-2G5	*24176 / 173*		*0088*	*0488*	*2 RR RB211-535E4*	*115700*	*Y210*	*EP-AL*	
☐ D-AMUZ	Boeing 757-2G5	*24497 / 228*		*0089*	*0589*	*2 RR RB211-535E4*	*108860*	*Y210*	*BQ-AM*	
☐ EC-EFX	Boeing 757-2G5	*23118 / 36*	*D-AMUR*	*0084*	*0584*	*2 RR RB211-535C*	*108860*	*Y219*	*CM-EL*	*lst LTE*
☐ EC-EGH	Boeing 757-2G5	*23119 / 51*	*EC-116*	*0085*	*0285*	*2 RR RB211-535C*	*108860*	*Y219*	*CM-FH*	*lst LTE*
☐ EC-ENQ	Boeing 757-2G5	*23651 / 116*	*EC-256*	*0086*	*1286*	*2 RR RB211-535C*	*108860*	*Y219*	*CM-EJ*	*lst LTE*
☐ D-AMUJ	Boeing 767-3G5 (ER)	*28111 / 612*		*0096*	*0496*	*2 PW PW4060*	*186900*	*C18Y244*	*JS-FM*	
☐ D-AMUN	Boeing 767-3G5 (ER)	*24259 / 268*		*0089*	*0689*	*2 PW PW4060*	*184600*	*C18Y244*	*EJ-CP*	
☐ D-AMUO	Boeing 767-3G5 (ER)	*29435 / 720*		*0998*	*0998*	*2 PW PW4060*	*184600*	*C18Y244*		
☐ D-AMUP	Boeing 767-33A (ER)	*25531 / 423*		*0092*	*0392*	*2 PW PW4060*	*184600*	*C18Y244*	*BS-PQ*	
☐ D-AMUR	Boeing 767-3G5 (ER)	*24257 / 251*	*N6046P**	*0089*	*0289*	*2 PW PW4060*	*184600*	*C18Y244*	*EJ-AP*	
☐ D-AMUS	Boeing 767-3G5 (ER)	*24258 / 255*		*0089*	*0289*	*2 PW PW4060*	*184600*	*C18Y244*	*EJ-BP*	
☐ D-AERD	Airbus Industrie A330-322	*143*	*9M-MKY*	*0096*	*1198*	*2 PW PW4168*	*212000*	*F12C30Y256*		*lsf ILFC*
☐ D-AERF	Airbus Industrie A330-322	*082*	*F-WWKD**	*1194*	*1294*	*2 PW PW4168*	*212000*	*Y387*	*GR-LM*	
☐ D-AERG	Airbus Industrie A330-322	*072*	*F-WWKY**	*0195*	*0295*	*2 PW PW4168*	*212000*	*Y387*	*GR-LP*	*lsf ILFC*
☐ D-AERH	Airbus Industrie A330-322	*087*	*F-WWKF**	*0395*	*0395*	*2 PW PW4168*	*212000*	*Y387*	*GR-LQ*	
☐ D-AERK	Airbus Industrie A330-322	*120*	*F-WWKN**	*0296*	*0396*	*2 PW PW4168*	*217000*	*Y387*	*GR-MP*	*lsf JL Emi Lease Co. Ltd*
☐ D-AERQ	Airbus Industrie A330-322	*127*	*F-WWKO**	*0196*	*0296*	*2 PW PW4168*	*217000*	*Y387*	*GR-MQ*	*lsf FI Elm Leasing Ltd*
☐ D-AERS	Airbus Industrie A330-322	*171*	*F-WWKM**	*0497*	*0497*	*2 PW PW4168*	*217000*	*Y387*	*GR-MS*	

LUFT-CHARTER-EMSLAND, GmbH — Nordhorn

Hohenfelstr. 23, D-49809 Lingen, Germany ☎ (591) 59 184 Tx: n/a Fax: (591) 47 271 SITA: n/a
F: 1995 ☗☗☗ 7 Head: Elisabeth Klaus-Lucas Net: n/a

☐ D-IFBU	Piper PA-31-310 Navajo	*31-8012050*	*N3557W*	*0080*		*2 LY TIO-540-A2C*	*2948*			

111 registration type of aircraft cn/fn ex/ex* mfd del powered by mtow kg configuration selcal name/fln/specialitites/remarks

LUFTHANSA = LH / DLH (Deutsche Lufthansa, AG dba / Member of Star Alliance) **Frankfurt/Berlin/Cologne/Hamburg/Munich** **Lufthansa**

Postfach 63 03 00, D-22313 Hamburg, Germany ☎ (40) 50 700 Tx: 212277 d Fax: (40) 50 70 44 01 SITA: FRASELH
F: 1954 ✈✈✈ 25000 Head: Juergen Weber IATA: 220 ICAO: LUFTHANSA Net: http://www.lufthansa.com

Scheduled commuter/feeder services are operated on behalf of Lufthansa (using LH flight numbers) by: LUFTHANSA CITYLINE (Avro RJ85 & Canadair 100), TEAM LUFTHANSA franchise partners:
AIR LITTORAL (CRJ100), AUGSBURG AIRWAYS (DHC-8) & CIMBER AIR (ATR42) & CONTACT AIR (Fokker 50). For details – see under each company.
Scheduled all-cargo services are operated by LUFTHANSA CARGO (using LH-flight numbers) with Boeing 737F/747F & McDonnell Douglas DC-8F - for details see under that company.

☐ D-ABFL	Boeing 737-230 (A)	22120 / 715	VT-MGA	0081	0281	2 PW JT8D-15	50900	F8Y103	AG-CM	std SXF / for sale
☐ D-ABFM	Boeing 737-230 (A)	22121 / 720	VT-MGB	0081	0281	2 PW JT8D-15	50900	F8Y103		std HAM / for sale
☐ D-ABFN	Boeing 737-230 (A)	22122 / 721	VT-MGC	0081	0281	2 PW JT8D-15	50900	F8Y103		std SXF / for sale
☐ D-ABIA	Boeing 737-530	24815 / 1933	N3521N*	0090	1290	2 CFMI CFM56-3B1	54000	CY103	NONE	Greifswald / lsf CIT FSC
☐ D-ABIB	Boeing 737-530	24816 / 1958		0090	1290	2 CFMI CFM56-3B1	54000	CY103	NONE	Esslingen / lsf CIT FSC
☐ D-ABIC	Boeing 737-530	24817 / 1967		0090	1290	2 CFMI CFM56-3B1	54000	CY103	NONE	Krefeld / lsf CIT FSC
☐ D-ABID	Boeing 737-530	24818 / 1974		0091	0191	2 CFMI CFM56-3B1	54000	CY103	NONE	Aachen
☐ D-ABIE	Boeing 737-530	24819 / 1979		0091	0191	2 CFMI CFM56-3B1	54000	CY103	NONE	Hildesheim
☐ D-ABIF	Boeing 737-530	24820 / 1985		0091	0191	2 CFMI CFM56-3B1	54000	CY103	NONE	Landau
☐ D-ABIH	Boeing 737-530	24821 / 1993		0091	0291	2 CFMI CFM56-3B1	54000	CY103	NONE	Bruchsal
☐ D-ABII	Boeing 737-530	24822 / 1997		0090	0291	2 CFMI CFM56-3B1	54000	CY103	NONE	Lörrach
☐ D-ABIK	Boeing 737-530	24823 / 2000		0091	0291	2 CFMI CFM56-3B1	54000	CY103	NONE	Rastatt
☐ D-ABIL	Boeing 737-530	24824 / 2006		0091	0391	2 CFMI CFM56-3B1	54000	CY103	NONE	Memmingen
☐ D-ABIM	Boeing 737-530	24937 / 2011		0091	0391	2 CFMI CFM56-3B1	54000	CY103	NONE	Salzgitter
☐ D-ABIN	Boeing 737-530	24938 / 2023		0091	0491	2 CFMI CFM56-3B1	54000	CY103	NONE	Langenhagen
☐ D-ABIO	Boeing 737-530	24939 / 2031		0091	0491	2 CFMI CFM56-3B1	54000	CY103	NONE	Wesel
☐ D-ABIP	Boeing 737-530	24940 / 2034		0091	0491	2 CFMI CFM56-3B1	54000	CY103	NONE	Oberhausen
☐ D-ABIR	Boeing 737-530	24941 / 2042		0091	0591	2 CFMI CFM56-3B1	54000	CY103	NONE	Anklam
☐ D-ABIS	Boeing 737-530	24942 / 2048		0091	0591	2 CFMI CFM56-3B1	54000	CY103	NONE	Rendsburg
☐ D-ABIT	Boeing 737-530	24943 / 2049		0091	0591	2 CFMI CFM56-3B1	54000	CY103	NONE	Neumünster
☐ D-ABIU	Boeing 737-530	24944 / 2051		0091	0591	2 CFMI CFM56-3B1	54000	CY103	NONE	Limburg
☐ D-ABIW	Boeing 737-530	24945 / 2063		0091	0691	2 CFMI CFM56-3B1	54000	CY103	NONE	Bad Nauheim
☐ D-ABIX	Boeing 737-530	24946 / 2070		0091	0691	2 CFMI CFM56-3B1	54000	CY103	NONE	Iserlohn
☐ D-ABIY	Boeing 737-530	25243 / 2086		0091	0791	2 CFMI CFM56-3B1	54000	CY103	NONE	Lingen
☐ D-ABIZ	Boeing 737-530	25244 / 2098		0091	0891	2 CFMI CFM56-3B1	54000	CY103	NONE	Kirchheim unter Teck
☐ D-ABJA	Boeing 737-530	25270 / 2116		0091	0991	2 CFMI CFM56-3B1	54000	CY103	NONE	Bad Segeberg
☐ D-ABJB	Boeing 737-530	25271 / 2117		0091	0991	2 CFMI CFM56-3B1	54000	CY103	NONE	Rheine
☐ D-ABJC	Boeing 737-530	25272 / 2118		0091	0991	2 CFMI CFM56-3B1	54000	CY103	NONE	Erding
☐ D-ABJD	Boeing 737-530	25309 / 2122		0091	0991	2 CFMI CFM56-3B1	54000	CY103	NONE	Freising
☐ D-ABJE	Boeing 737-530	25310 / 2126		0091	0991	2 CFMI CFM56-3B1	54000	CY103	NONE	Ingelheim am Rhein
☐ D-ABJF	Boeing 737-530	25311 / 2128		0091	1091	2 CFMI CFM56-3B1	54000	CY103	NONE	Aalen
☐ D-ABJH	Boeing 737-530	25357 / 2141		0091	1091	2 CFMI CFM56-3B1	54000	CY103	NONE	Heppenheim/Bergstrasse
☐ D-ABJI	Boeing 737-530	25358 / 2151		0091	1091	2 CFMI CFM56-3B1	54000	CY103	NONE	Siegburg
☐ D-ABEA	Boeing 737-330	24565 / 1818		0090	0290	2 CFMI CFM56-3B1	57600	CY123	NONE	Saarbrücken
☐ D-ABEB	Boeing 737-330	25148 / 2077		0091	0791	2 CFMI CFM56-3B1	57600	CY123	NONE	Xanten
☐ D-ABEC	Boeing 737-330	25149 / 2081		0091	0791	2 CFMI CFM56-3B1	57600	CY123	NONE	Karlsruhe
☐ D-ABED	Boeing 737-330	25215 / 2082		0091	0791	2 CFMI CFM56-3B1	57600	CY123	NONE	Hagen
☐ D-ABEE	Boeing 737-330	25216 / 2084		0091	0791	2 CFMI CFM56-3B1	57600	CY123	NONE	Ulm
☐ D-ABEF	Boeing 737-330	25217 / 2094		0091	0791	2 CFMI CFM56-3B1	57600	CY123	NONE	Weiden i. d. Obf.
☐ D-ABEH	Boeing 737-330	25242 / 2102		0091	0891	2 CFMI CFM56-3B1	57600	CY123	NONE	Bad Kissingen
☐ D-ABEI	Boeing 737-330	25359 / 2158		0091	1191	2 CFMI CFM56-3B1	57600	CY123	NONE	Bamberg
☐ D-ABEK	Boeing 737-330	25414 / 2164		0091	1191	2 CFMI CFM56-3B1	57600	CY123	NONE	Wuppertal
☐ D-ABEL	Boeing 737-330	25415 / 2175		0091	1291	2 CFMI CFM56-3B1	57600	CY123	NONE	Pforzheim
☐ D-ABEM	Boeing 737-330	25416 / 2182		0091	1291	2 CFMI CFM56-3B1	57600	CY123	NONE	Eberswalde-Finow
☐ D-ABEN	Boeing 737-330	26428 / 2196		0092	0192	2 CFMI CFM56-3B1	57600	CY123	NONE	Neubrandenburg
☐ D-ABEO	Boeing 737-330	26429 / 2207		0092	0292	2 CFMI CFM56-3B1	57600	CY123	NONE	Plauen
☐ D-ABEP	Boeing 737-330	26430 / 2216		0092	0392	2 CFMI CFM56-3B1	57600	CY123	NONE	Naumburg (Saale)
☐ D-ABER	Boeing 737-330	26431 / 2242		0092	0392	2 CFMI CFM56-3B1	57600	CY123	NONE	Merseburg
☐ D-ABES	Boeing 737-330	26432 / 2247		0092	0392	2 CFMI CFM56-3B1	57600	CY123	NONE	Köthen/Anhalt
☐ D-ABET	Boeing 737-330	27903 / 2682		0094	0195	2 CFMI CFM56-3B1	57600	CY123	NONE	Gelsenkirchen
☐ D-ABEU	Boeing 737-330	27904 / 2691		0095	0295	2 CFMI CFM56-3B1	57600	CY123	NONE	Goslar
☐ D-ABEW	Boeing 737-330	27905 / 2705		0095	0395	2 CFMI CFM56-3B1	57600	CY128	NONE	Detmold
☐ D-ABWC	Boeing 737-330 (QC)	23835 / 1465		0087	0393	2 CFMI CFM56-3B2	59000	CY121/Freighter	NONE	lsf Condor Leasing / cvtd -330
☐ D-ABWD	Boeing 737-330 (QC)	23836 / 1508		0088	0393	2 CFMI CFM56-3B2	59000	CY121/Freighter	NONE	Westerland/Sylt / lsfCondorLsg/cvtd-330
☐ D-ABWE	Boeing 737-330 (QC)	23837 / 1514		0088	0393	2 CFMI CFM56-3B2	59000	CY121/Freighter	NONE	Görlitz / lsf Condor Leasing/cvtd -330
☐ D-ABWF	Boeing 737-330 (QC)	24283 / 1677		0089	0393	2 CFMI CFM56-3B2	59000	CY121/Freighter	NONE	Rüdesheim a.R. / lsf CondorAc./cvtd-330
☐ D-ABWH	Boeing 737-330	24284 / 1685		0089	1293	2 CFMI CFM56-3B2	57600	CY123	NONE	Rothenburg o.d.Tauber / lsf Crane Ac.
☐ D-ABXA	Boeing 737-330 (QC)	23522 / 1246		0086	0886	2 CFMI CFM56-3B1	59000	CY121/Freighter	NONE	Giessen / cvtd -330
☐ D-ABXB	Boeing 737-330 (QC)	23523 / 1271		0086	0986	2 CFMI CFM56-3B1	59000	CY121/Freighter	NONE	Passau / cvtd -330
☐ D-ABXC	Boeing 737-330 (QC)	23524 / 1272		0086	0986	2 CFMI CFM56-3B1	59000	CY121/Freighter	NONE	Delmenhorst / cvtd -330
☐ D-ABXD	Boeing 737-330	23525 / 1278	TF-ABL	0086	1086	2 CFMI CFM56-3B1	57600	CY123	NONE	Siegen
☐ D-ABXE	Boeing 737-330	23526 / 1282		0086	1086	2 CFMI CFM56-3B1	57600	CY128	NONE	Hamm
☐ D-ABXF	Boeing 737-330	23527 / 1285		0086	1086	2 CFMI CFM56-3B1	57600	CY123	NONE	Minden
☐ D-ABXH	Boeing 737-330	23528 / 1290		0086	1186	2 CFMI CFM56-3B1	57600	CY123	NONE	Cuxhaven
☐ D-ABXI	Boeing 737-330	23529 / 1293		0086	1186	2 CFMI CFM56-3B1	57600	CY123	NONE	Berchtesgaden
☐ D-ABXK	Boeing 737-330	23530 / 1297		0086	1186	2 CFMI CFM56-3B1	57600	CY123	NONE	Ludwigsburg
☐ D-ABXL	Boeing 737-330	23531 / 1307		0086	1286	2 CFMI CFM56-3B1	57600	CY123	NONE	Neuss
☐ D-ABXM	Boeing 737-330	23871 / 1433		0087	0887	2 CFMI CFM56-3B1	57600	CY123	NONE	Herford
☐ D-ABXN	Boeing 737-330	23872 / 1447		0087	1087	2 CFMI CFM56-3B1	57600	CY123	NONE	Böblingen
☐ D-ABXO	Boeing 737-330	23873 / 1489		0088	0188	2 CFMI CFM56-3B1	57600	CY123	NONE	Schwäbisch-Gmünd
☐ D-ABXP	Boeing 737-330	23874 / 1495		0088	0188	2 CFMI CFM56-3B1	57600	CY123	NONE	Fulda
☐ D-ABXR	Boeing 737-330	23875 / 1500		0088	0288	2 CFMI CFM56-3B1	57600	CY123	NONE	Celle / lsf GOAL
☐ D-ABXS	Boeing 737-330	24280 / 1656		0089	0189	2 CFMI CFM56-3B1	57600	CY123	NONE	Sindelfingen
☐ D-ABXT	Boeing 737-330	24281 / 1664		0089	0189	2 CFMI CFM56-3B1	57600	CY123	NONE	Reutlingen
☐ D-ABXU	Boeing 737-330	24282 / 1671		0089	0289	2 CFMI CFM56-3B1	57600	CY123	NONE	Seeheim-Jugenheim
☐ D-ABXW	Boeing 737-330	24561 / 1785		0089	1089	2 CFMI CFM56-3B1	57600	CY123	NONE	Hanau
☐ D-ABXX	Boeing 737-330	24562 / 1787		0089	1089	2 CFMI CFM56-3B1	57600	CY123	NONE	Bad Homburg v.d. Höhe
☐ D-ABXY	Boeing 737-330	24563 / 1801		0090	0190	2 CFMI CFM56-3B1	57600	CY123	NONE	Hof
☐ D-ABXZ	Boeing 737-330	24564 / 1807		0090	0190	2 CFMI CFM56-3B1	57600	CY123	NONE	Bad Mergentheim
☐ D-ABKL	Boeing 737-430	27007 / 2367		0092	1092	2 CFMI CFM56-3C1	65100	Y167		lst SXS as TC-SUS
☐ D-AILA	Airbus Industrie A319-114	609	D-AVYF*	0096	0796	2 CFMI CFM56-5A5	68000	CY126	NONE	Frankfurt (Oder)
☐ D-AILB	Airbus Industrie A319-114	610	D-AVYG*	0096	0896	2 CFMI CFM56-5A5	68000	CY126	NONE	Lutherstadt Wittenberg
☐ D-AILC	Airbus Industrie A319-114	616	D-AVYI*	0096	0996	2 CFMI CFM56-5A5	68000	CY126	NONE	Rüsselsheim
☐ D-AILD	Airbus Industrie A319-114	623	D-AVYL*	0096	1096	2 CFMI CFM56-5A5	68000	CY126	NONE	Dinkelsbühl
☐ D-AILE	Airbus Industrie A319-114	627	D-AVYO*	0096	1196	2 CFMI CFM56-5A5	68000	CY126	NONE	Kelsterbach
☐ D-AILF	Airbus Industrie A319-114	636	D-AVYS*	0096	1296	2 CFMI CFM56-5A5	68000	CY126	NONE	Trier
☐ D-AILH	Airbus Industrie A319-114	641	D-AVYV*	0097	0197	2 CFMI CFM56-5A5	68000	CY126	NONE	Norderstedt
☐ D-AILI	Airbus Industrie A319-114	651	D-AVYY*	0097	0297	2 CFMI CFM56-5A5	68000	CY126	NONE	Ingoldstadt
☐ D-AILK	Airbus Industrie A319-114	679	D-AVYG*	0097	0597	2 CFMI CFM56-5A5	68000	CY126	NONE	Landshut
☐ D-AILL	Airbus Industrie A319-114	689	D-AVYL*	0097	0697	2 CFMI CFM56-5A5	68000	CY126	NONE	Marburg
☐ D-AILM	Airbus Industrie A319-114	694	D-AVYR*	0097	0797	2 CFMI CFM56-5A5	68000	CY126	NONE	Friedrichshafen
☐ D-AILN	Airbus Industrie A319-114	700	D-AVYU*	0097	0997	2 CFMI CFM56-5A5	68000	CY126	NONE	Idar-Oberstein
☐ D-AILP	Airbus Industrie A319-114	717	D-AVYA*	0097	0897	2 CFMI CFM56-5A5	68000	CY126	NONE	Tübingen
☐ D-AILR	Airbus Industrie A319-114	723	D-AVYD*	0097	0997	2 CFMI CFM56-5A5	68000	CY126	NONE	Tegernsee
☐ D-AILS	Airbus Industrie A319-114	729	D-AVYF*	0097	1097	2 CFMI CFM56-5A5	68000	CY126	NONE	Heide
☐ D-AILT	Airbus Industrie A319-114	738	D-AVYN*	0097	1197	2 CFMI CFM56-5A5	68000	CY126	NONE	Straubing
☐ D-AILU	Airbus Industrie A319-114	744	D-AVYI*	0097	1197	2 CFMI CFM56-5A5	68000	CY126	NONE	Verden
☐ D-AILW	Airbus Industrie A319-114	853	D-AVYO*	0098	0798	2 CFMI CFM56-5A5	68000	CY126	NONE	Donaueschingen
☐ D-AILX	Airbus Industrie A319-114	860	D-AVYS*	0098	0798	2 CFMI CFM56-5A5	68000	CY126	NONE	Fellbach
☐ D-AILY	Airbus Industrie A319-114	875	D-AVYC*	0098	0998	2 CFMI CFM56-5A5	68000	CY126	NONE	Schweinfurt
☐ D-AIPA	Airbus Industrie A320-211	069	F-WWII*	0089	1089	2 CFMI CFM56-5A1	73500	CY144	DG-KQ	Buxtehude
☐ D-AIPB	Airbus Industrie A320-211	070	F-WWIJ*	0089	1089	2 CFMI CFM56-5A1	73500	CY144	DG-LQ	Heidelberg
☐ D-AIPC	Airbus Industrie A320-211	071	F-WWIO*	0089	1189	2 CFMI CFM56-5A1	73500	CY144	DG-MQ	Braunschweig
☐ D-AIPD	Airbus Industrie A320-211	072	F-WWIP*	0089	1189	2 CFMI CFM56-5A1	73500	CY144	DG-PQ	Freiburg
☐ D-AIPE	Airbus Industrie A320-211	078	F-WWIU*	0089	1289	2 CFMI CFM56-5A1	73500	CY144	DH-AQ	Kassel
☐ D-AIPF	Airbus Industrie A320-211	083	F-WWDE*	0090	0190	2 CFMI CFM56-5A1	73500	CY144	DH-BQ	Leipzig
☐ D-AIPH	Airbus Industrie A320-211	086	F-WWDJ*	0090	0190	2 CFMI CFM56-5A1	73500	CY144	DH-CQ	Münster
☐ D-AIPK	Airbus Industrie A320-211	093	F-WWDQ*	0090	0290	2 CFMI CFM56-5A1	73500	CY144	DH-EQ	Wiesbaden
☐ D-AIPL	Airbus Industrie A320-211	094	F-WWDR*	0090	0290	2 CFMI CFM56-5A1	73500	CY144	DH-FQ	Ludwigshafen am Rhein
☐ D-AIPM	Airbus Industrie A320-211	104	F-WWIG*	0090	0390	2 CFMI CFM56-5A1	73500	CY144	DH-GQ	Troisdorf
☐ D-AIPP	Airbus Industrie A320-211	110	F-WWID*	0090	0890	2 CFMI CFM56-5A1	73500	CY144	DH-KQ	Starnberg
☐ D-AIPR	Airbus Industrie A320-211	111	F-WWIE*	0090	0890	2 CFMI CFM56-5A1	73500	CY144	DH-LQ	Kaufbeuren
☐ D-AIPS	Airbus Industrie A320-211	116	F-WWIK*	0090	0990	2 CFMI CFM56-5A1	73500	CY144	DH-MQ	Augsburg

112 registration type of aircraft *cn/fn* *ex/ex** *mfd* *del* *powered by* *mtow kg* *configuration* *selcal* name/fln/*specialitites/remarks*

	registration	type of aircraft	cn/fn	ex/ex*	mfd	del	powered by	mtow kg	configuration	selcal	name/fln/specialitites/remarks
☐	D-AIPT	Airbus Industrie A320-211	117	F-WWIL*	0090	0990	2 CFMI CFM56-5A1	73500	CY144	DH-PQ	Cottbus
☐	D-AIPU	Airbus Industrie A320-211	135	F-WWDB*	0090	1290	2 CFMI CFM56-5A1	73500	CY144	HL-GK	Dresden
☐	D-AIPW	Airbus Industrie A320-211	137	F-WWDD*	0090	1290	2 CFMI CFM56-5A1	73500	CY144	HL-GM	Schwerin
☐	D-AIPX	Airbus Industrie A320-211	147	F-WWDN*	0091	0291	2 CFMI CFM56-5A1	73500	CY144	HL-JK	Mannheim
☐	D-AIPY	Airbus Industrie A320-211	161	F-WWIA*	0091	0391	2 CFMI CFM56-5A1	73500	CY144	DE-MQ	Magdeburg
☐	D-AIPZ	Airbus Industrie A320-211	162	F-WWDS*	0091	0391	2 CFMI CFM56-5A1	73500	CY144	DE-PQ	Erfurt
☐	D-AIQA	Airbus Industrie A320-211	172	F-WWIK*	0091	0491	2 CFMI CFM56-5A1	73500	CY144	DF-AQ	Mainz
☐	D-AIQB	Airbus Industrie A320-211	200	F-WWDJ*	0091	0691	2 CFMI CFM56-5A1	73500	CY144	DF-BQ	Bielefeld
☐	D-AIQC	Airbus Industrie A320-211	201	F-WWDL*	0091	0691	2 CFMI CFM56-5A1	73500	CY144	DF-CQ	Zwickau
☐	D-AIQD	Airbus Industrie A320-211	202	F-WWDM*	0091	0691	2 CFMI CFM56-5A1	73500	CY144	DF-EQ	Jena
☐	D-AIQE	Airbus Industrie A320-211	209	F-WWDY*	0091	0791	2 CFMI CFM56-5A1	73500	CY144	DF-GQ	Gera
☐	D-AIQF	Airbus Industrie A320-211	216	F-WWDR*	0091	0791	2 CFMI CFM56-5A1	73500	CY144	DF-HQ	Halle a. d. Saale
☐	D-AIQH	Airbus Industrie A320-211	217	F-WWDS*	0091	0891	2 CFMI CFM56-5A1	73500	CY144	DF-JQ	Dessau
☐	D-AIQK	Airbus Industrie A320-211	218	F-WWDX*	0091	0891	2 CFMI CFM56-5A1	73500	CY144	DF-KQ	Rostock
☐	D-AIQL	Airbus Industrie A320-211	267	F-WWDY*	0092	0192	2 CFMI CFM56-5A1	73500	CY144	BK-EL	Stralsund
☐	D-AIQM	Airbus Industrie A320-211	268	F-WWIB*	0092	0192	2 CFMI CFM56-5A1	73500	CY144	BK-EH	Nordenham
☐	D-AIQN	Airbus Industrie A320-211	269	F-WWIC*	0092	0192	2 CFMI CFM56-5A1	73500	CY144	BK-EJ	Laupheim
☐	D-AIQP	Airbus Industrie A320-211	346	F-WWDX*	0092	0992	2 CFMI CFM56-5A1	73500	CY144	BK-FG	Suhl
☐	D-AIQR	Airbus Industrie A320-211	382	F-WWIZ*	0092	0193	2 CFMI CFM56-5A1	73500	CY144	CP-BS	Lahr/Schwarzwald
☐	D-AIQS	Airbus Industrie A320-211	401	F-WWBD*	0093	0393	2 CFMI CFM56-5A1	73500	CY144	CP-DR	Eisenach
☐	D-AIRA	Airbus Industrie A321-131	458	F-WWIQ*	0094	0194	2 IAE V2530-A5	83000	CY182	DF-LQ	Finkenwerder
☐	D-AIRB	Airbus Industrie A321-131	468	F-WWIS*	0094	0294	2 IAE V2530-A5	83000	CY182	DF-MQ	Baden-Baden
☐	D-AIRC	Airbus Industrie A321-131	473	D-AVZC*	0094	0294	2 IAE V2530-A5	83000	CY182	DF-PQ	Erlangen
☐	D-AIRD	Airbus Industrie A321-131	474	D-AVZD*	0094	0394	2 IAE V2530-A5	83000	CY182	DG-AQ	Coburg
☐	D-AIRE	Airbus Industrie A321-131	484	D-AVZF*	0094	0494	2 IAE V2530-A5	83000	CY182	DG-BQ	Osnabrück
☐	D-AIRF	Airbus Industrie A321-131	493	D-AVZH*	0094	0594	2 IAE V2530-A5	83000	CY182	DG-CQ	Kempten
☐	D-AIRH	Airbus Industrie A321-131	412	F-WWIC*	0093	0794	2 IAE V2530-A5	83000	CY182	DG-EQ	Garmisch-Partenkirchen
☐	D-AIRK	Airbus Industrie A321-131	502	D-AVZL*	0094	0794	2 IAE V2530-A5	83000	CY182	DG-FQ	Freudenstadt/Schwarzwald
☐	D-AIRL	Airbus Industrie A321-131	505	D-AVZM*	0094	0994	2 IAE V2530-A5	83000	CY182	DG-HQ	Kulmbach
☐	D-AIRM	Airbus Industrie A321-131	518	D-AVZT*	0095	0295	2 IAE V2530-A5	83000	CY182	DG-JQ	Darmstadt
☐	D-AIRN	Airbus Industrie A321-131	560	D-AVZK*	0095	1295	2 IAE V2530-A5	83000	CY182	CK-GH	Kaiserslautern
☐	D-AIRO	Airbus Industrie A321-131	563	D-AVZN*	0095	1295	2 IAE V2530-A5	83000	CY182	CK-GJ	Konstanz
☐	D-AIRP	Airbus Industrie A321-131	564	D-AVZL*	0096	0196	2 IAE V2530-A5	83000	CY182	CK-HJ	Lüneburg
☐	D-AIRR	Airbus Industrie A321-131	567	D-AVZM*	0096	0196	2 IAE V2530-A5	83000	CY182	CK-HM	Wismar
☐	D-AIRS	Airbus Industrie A321-131	595	D-AVZX*	0096	0496	2 IAE V2530-A5	83000	CY182	CL-AJ	Husum / *lsf Lufthansa Leasing*
☐	D-AIRT	Airbus Industrie A321-131	652	D-AVZI*	0097	0397	2 IAE V2530-A5	83000	CY182	CL-AK	Regensburg
☐	D-AIRU	Airbus Industrie A321-131	692	D-AVZT*	0097	0797	2 IAE V2530-A5	83000	CY182	CL-BD	Würzburg
☐	D-AIRW	Airbus Industrie A321-131	699	D-AVZY*	0097	0897	2 IAE V2530-A5	83000	CY182	FJ-KM	Heilbronn / *lsf Lufthansa Leasing*
☐	D-AIRX	Airbus Industrie A321-131	887	D-AVZI*	0098	1098	2 IAE V2530-A5	83000	CY182	FK-AB	Weimar
☐	D-AIRY	Airbus Industrie A321-131	901	D-AVZK*	0098	1198	2 IAE V2530-A5	83000	CY182	BK-EM	Flensburg
☐	D-AISB	Airbus Industrie A321-231	1080				2 IAE V2533-A5	89000			*oo-delivery 0999*
☐	D-AISC	Airbus Industrie A321-231	1161				2 IAE V2533-A5	89000			*oo-delivery 0100*
☐	D-AISD	Airbus Industrie A321-231	1190				2 IAE V2533-A5	89000			*oo-delivery 0200*
☐	D-AISE	Airbus Industrie A321-231	1211				2 IAE V2533-A5	89000			*oo-delivery 0400*
☐	D-AISF	Airbus Industrie A321-231	1267				2 IAE V2533-A5	89000			*oo-delivery 0600*
☐	D-AISG	Airbus Industrie A321-231	1309				2 IAE V2533-A5	89000			*oo-delivery 0800*
☐	D-AIDD	Airbus Industrie A310-304	488	F-WWCE*	0089	0389	2 GE CF6-80C2A2	125000	CY222	HM-FL	Emden
☐	D-AIDF	Airbus Industrie A310-304	524	F-WWCA*	0089	1289	2 GE CF6-80C2A2	138600	CY222	BL-AH	Aschaffenburg
☐	D-AIDH	Airbus Industrie A310-304	527	F-WWCD*	0090	0190	2 GE CF6-80C2A2	125000	CY222	FJ-GH	Wetzlar
☐	D-AIDL	Airbus Industrie A310-304	547	F-WWCU*	0090	1190	2 GE CF6-80C2A2	153000	C62Y116	FJ-CD	Oberstdorf
☐	D-AIAH	Airbus Industrie A300-603 (A300B4-603)	380	F-WWAA*	0087	0387	2 GE CF6-80C2A3	165000	C53Y191	HJ-EF	Lindau / Bodensee
☐	D-AIAI	Airbus Industrie A300-603 (A300B4-603)	391	F-WWAL*	0087	0387	2 GE CF6-80C2A3	165000	F10C54Y132	HJ-EG	Erbach / Odenwald
☐	D-AIAK	Airbus Industrie A300-603 (A300B4-603)	401	F-WWAO*	0087	0487	2 GE CF6-80C2A3	165000	F10C54Y132	HJ-EK	Kronberg im Taunus
☐	D-AIAL	Airbus Industrie A300-603 (A300B4-603)	405	F-WWAP*	0087	0487	2 GE CF6-80C2A3	165000	F10C54Y132	HJ-EL	Stade
☐	D-AIAM	Airbus Industrie A300-603 (A300B4-603)	408	F-WWAQ*	0087	0487	2 GE CF6-80C2A3	165000	F10C54Y132	HJ-EM	Rosenheim
☐	D-AIAN	Airbus Industrie A300-603 (A300B4-603)	411	F-WWAR*	0087	0687	2 GE CF6-80C2A3	150000	CY270	HJ-FG	Nördlingen
☐	D-AIAP	Airbus Industrie A300-603 (A300B4-603)	414	F-WWAS*	0087	0687	2 GE CF6-80C2A3	150000	CY270	HJ-FK	Donauwörth
☐	D-AIAR	Airbus Industrie A300-603 (A300B4-603)	546	F-WWAP*	0090	0290	2 GE CF6-80C2A3	150000	CY270	DE-AQ	Bingen am Rhein
☐	D-AIAS	Airbus Industrie A300-603 (A300B4-603)	553	F-WWAX*	0090	0390	2 GE CF6-80C2A3	150000	CY270	DE-BQ	Mönchengladbach
☐	D-AIAT	Airbus Industrie A300-603 (A300B4-603)	618	F-WWAM*	0091	1191	2 GE CF6-80C2A3	150000	CY270	BF-PQ	Bottrop
☐	D-AIAU	Airbus Industrie A300-603 (A300B4-603)	623	F-WWAT*	0092	0192	2 GE CF6-80C2A3	150000	CY270	BG-AQ	Bocholt
☐	D-AIAW	Airbus Industrie A300-605R (A300B4-605R)	764	F-WWAJ*	0096	0796	2 GE CF6-80C2A5	170500	F10C54Y132	LR-KM	Witten / *lsf ILFC*
☐	D-AIAX	Airbus Industrie A300-605R (A300B4-605R)	773	F-WWAO*	0096	1296	2 GE CF6-80C2A5	170500	F10C54Y136	LR-KP	Fürth / *lsf Lufthansa Leasing*
☐	D-AIBA	Airbus Industrie A340-211	008	F-WWJA*	0093	0193	4 CFMI CFM56-5C2	257000	F8C42Y162	LM-AR	Nuernberg / *lsf NBB Lse/StarAlliance-cs*
☐	D-AIBC	Airbus Industrie A340-211	011	F-WWJD*	0093	0493	4 CFMI CFM56-5C2	257000	F8C42Y162	LM-CR	Leverkusen / *lsf NBB Dusseldorf Lease*
☐	D-AIBD	Airbus Industrie A340-211	018	F-WWJI*	0093	0793	4 CFMI CFM56-5C2	257000	F8C42Y162	LM-CS	Essen
☐	D-AIBE	Airbus Industrie A340-211	019	F-WWJJ*	0093	0893	4 CFMI CFM56-5C2	257000	F8C42Y162	LM-DR	Stuttgart
☐	D-AIBF	Airbus Industrie A340-211	006	F-WWBE*	0093	1193	4 CFMI CFM56-5C2	257000	F8C42Y162	LM-DS	Lübeck
☐	D-AIBH	Airbus Industrie A340-211	021	F-WWJL*	0093	1093	4 CFMI CFM56-5C2	257000	F8C42Y162	LM-ER	Bremerhaven
☐	D-AIGA	Airbus Industrie A340-311	020	F-WWJK*	0093	1293	4 CFMI CFM56-5C2	257000	F10C42Y197	LM-FS	Oldenburg / *lsf Lufthansa Leasing*
☐	D-AIGB	Airbus Industrie A340-311	024	F-WWJO*	0093	1193	4 CFMI CFM56-5C2	257000	F8C42Y197	LM-GR	Recklinghausen / *lsf Lufthansa Leasing*
☐	D-AIGC	Airbus Industrie A340-311	027	F-WWJR*	0093	1293	4 CFMI CFM56-5C2	257000	F10C42Y197	LM-GS	Wilhelmshaven / *lsf Lufthansa Leasing*
☐	D-AIGD	Airbus Industrie A340-311	028	F-WWJS*	0094	0194	4 CFMI CFM56-5C2	257000	F8C42Y197	LM-HR	Remscheid
☐	D-AIGE	Airbus Industrie A340-313					4 CFMI CFM56-5C4	271000	F8C42Y197		*oo-delivery 1200*
☐	D-AIGF	Airbus Industrie A340-311	035	F-WWJV*	0094	0594	4 CFMI CFM56-5C2	257000	F8C42Y197	LM-HS	Göttingen
☐	D-AIGG	Airbus Industrie A340-313					4 CFMI CFM56-5C4	271000	F8C42Y197		*oo-delivery 0101*
☐	D-AIGH	Airbus Industrie A340-311	052	F-WWJQ*	0094	0894	4 CFMI CFM56-5C2	257000	F8C42Y197	CM-LS	Koblenz
☐	D-AIGI	Airbus Industrie A340-311	053	F-WWJJ*	0094	1094	4 CFMI CFM56-5C2	257000	F10C42Y197	CP-BR	Worms / *lsf Lufthansa Leasing*
☐	D-AIGK	Airbus Industrie A340-311	056	F-WWJK*	0094	1294	4 CFMI CFM56-5C2	257000	F8C42Y197	LM-AS	Bayreuth / *lsf Airbus Industrie*
☐	D-AIGL	Airbus Industrie A340-313	135	F-WWJS*	0096	0596	4 CFMI CFM56-5C4	257000	F8C42Y197	JR-CK	Herne
☐	D-AIGM	Airbus Industrie A340-313	158	F-WWJN*	0097	0197	4 CFMI CFM56-5C4	257000	F8C42Y197	LS-DQ	Wolfsburg
☐	D-AIGN	Airbus Industrie A340-313	213	F-WWJM*	0098	0398	4 CFMI CFM56-5C4	257000	F8C42Y197	JK-FR	Solingen
☐	D-AIGO	Airbus Industrie A340-313	233	F-WWJJ*	0098	0898	4 CFMI CFM56-5C4	257000	F8C42Y197		Offenbach
☐	D-AIGP	Airbus Industrie A340-313	252	F-WWJM*	0098	1298	4 CFMI CFM56-5C4	257000	F8C42Y197		Paderborn
☐	D-AIGR	Airbus Industrie A340-313	274				4 CFMI CFM56-5C4	257000	F8C42Y197		*oo-delivery 0599*
☐	D-AIGS	Airbus Industrie A340-313	297				4 CFMI CFM56-5C4	271000	F8C42Y197		*oo-delivery 1099*
☐	D-AIGT	Airbus Industrie A340-313	304				4 CFMI CFM56-5C4	271000	F8C42Y197		*oo-delivery 1299*
☐	D-AIGU	Airbus Industrie A340-313					4 CFMI CFM56-5C4	271000	F8C42Y197		*oo-delivery 0200*
☐	D-AIGV	Airbus Industrie A340-313					4 CFMI CFM56-5C4	271000	F8C42Y197		*oo-delivery 0300*
☐	D-AIGW	Airbus Industrie A340-313					4 CFMI CFM56-5C4	271000	F8C42Y197		*oo-delivery 0300*
☐	D-AIGX	Airbus Industrie A340-313					4 CFMI CFM56-5C4	271000	F8C42Y197		*oo-delivery 0900*
☐	D-AIGY	Airbus Industrie A340-313					4 CFMI CFM56-5C4	271000	F8C42Y197		*oo-delivery 1100*
☐	D-AIGZ	Airbus Industrie A340-313					4 CFMI CFM56-5C4	271000	F8C42Y197		*oo-delivery 1200*
☐	D-ABYM	Boeing 747-230B (M)	21588 / 342		0078	1078	4 GE CF6-50E2	362900	F8C50Y326	CG-AD	Schleswig-Holstein
☐	D-ABYP	Boeing 747-230B	21590 / 348	N8291V*	0079	0379	4 GE CF6-50E2	362900	F8C50Y330	FM-EL	Niedersachsen
☐	D-ABYQ	Boeing 747-230B	21591 / 350		0078	1278	4 GE CF6-50E2	362900	F8C50Y326	CG-AE	
☐	D-ABYR	Boeing 747-230B (M)	21643 / 352		0079	0179	4 GE CF6-50E2	362900	F8C50Y326	CG-AF	Nordrhein-Westfalen
☐	D-ABYX	Boeing 747-230B (M)	22670 / 550		0082	0282	4 GE CF6-50E2	377800	F8C50Y326	CG-FL	
☐	D-ABZD	Boeing 747-230B	23407 / 639	N6005C*	0086	0486	4 GE CF6-50E2	377800	F8C50Y326	AF-KM	Kiel
☐	D-ABZE	Boeing 747-230B (M)	23509 / 663	N6038E*	0087	0187	4 GE CF6-50E2	377800	F8C50Y326	CD-HL	
☐	D-ABZH	Boeing 747-230B	23622 / 665	N6046P*	0087	0287	4 GE CF6-50E2	377800	F12C56Y318	FM-DK	
☐	D-AIHA	Airbus Industrie A340-642					4 RR Trent 556	365000			*oo-delivery 0703*
☐	D-AIHB	Airbus Industrie A340-642					4 RR Trent 556	365000			*oo-delivery 0803*
☐	D-AIHC	Airbus Industrie A340-642					4 RR Trent 556	365000			*oo-delivery 0903*
☐	D-AIHD	Airbus Industrie A340-642					4 RR Trent 556	365000			*oo-delivery 1103*
☐	D-AIHE	Airbus Industrie A340-642					4 RR Trent 556	365000			*oo-delivery 1103*
☐	D-AIHF	Airbus Industrie A340-642					4 RR Trent 556	365000			*oo-delivery 1203*
☐	D-AIHH	Airbus Industrie A340-642					4 RR Trent 556	365000			*oo-delivery 0104*
☐	D-AIHI	Airbus Industrie A340-642					4 RR Trent 556	365000			*oo-delivery 0304*
☐	D-AIHK	Airbus Industrie A340-642					4 RR Trent 556	365000			*oo-delivery 0404*
☐	D-AIHL	Airbus Industrie A340-642					4 RR Trent 556	365000			*oo-delivery 0504*
☐	D-ABTA	Boeing 747-430 (M)	24285 / 747		0089	0989	4 GE CF6-80C2B1F	385600	F16C64Y310	BK-GH	Sachsen
☐	D-ABTB	Boeing 747-430 (M)	24286 / 749		0089	1289	4 GE CF6-80C2B1F	385600	F16C64Y310	BK-HL	Brandenburg
☐	D-ABTC	Boeing 747-430 (M)	24287 / 754		0090	0290	4 GE CF6-80C2B1F	385600	F20C75Y165/Plt	BK-JM	Mecklenburg-Vorpommern
☐	D-ABTD	Boeing 747-430 (M)	24715 / 785		0090	0490	4 GE CF6-80C2B1F	385600	F20C75Y165/Plt	BL-AE	Hamburg
☐	D-ABTE	Boeing 747-430 (M)	24966 / 846	N6046P*	0091	0491	4 GE CF6-80C2B1F	394600	F16C64Y310	BF-JQ	Sachsen-Anhalt / *lsf AeroCrane Leasing*
☐	D-ABTF	Boeing 747-430 (M)	24967 / 848		0091	0491	4 GE CF6-80C2B1F	394600	F20C75Y165/Plt	BF-KQ	Thüringen / *lsf Ward FSC Ltd*
☐	D-ABTH	Boeing 747-430 (M)	25047 / 856		0091	0691	4 GE CF6-80C2B1F	394600	F20C75Y165/Plt	BF-LQ	Duisburg / *lsf Overseas Leasing One FSC*
☐	D-ABVA	Boeing 747-430	23816 / 723	N6055X*	0089	0589	4 GE CF6-80C2B1F	385600	F16C64Y292	AL-DH	Berlin

☐ D-ABVB	Boeing 747-430	23817 / 700	N5573S*	0088	0989	4 GE CF6-80C2B1F	385600	F16C64Y292	AL-DJ	Bonn
☐ D-ABVC	Boeing 747-430	24288 / 757		0089	1089	4 GE CF6-80C2B1F	385600	F16C64Y292	AL-DK	Baden-Württemberg
☐ D-ABVD	Boeing 747-430	24740 / 786	N60668*	0090	0590	4 GE CF6-80C2B1F	394600	F16C64Y292	AL-DM	Bochum
☐ D-ABVE	Boeing 747-430	24741 / 787		0090	0590	4 GE CF6-80C2B1F	394600	F16C64Y292	AL-EG	Potsdam
☐ D-ABVF	Boeing 747-430	24761 / 796	N6018N*	0090	0790	4 GE CF6-80C2B1F	394600	F16C64Y292	AL-EH	Frankfurt am Main
☐ D-ABVG	Boeing 747-430					4 GE CF6-80C2B1F	385600	F16C64Y310		oo-delivery 0302
☐ D-ABVH	Boeing 747-430	25045 / 845		0091	0491	4 GE CF6-80C2B1F	394600	F16C64Y292	FL-CD	Düsseldorf / lsf Luke FSC Ltd
☐ D-ABVI	Boeing 747-430	29872				4 GE CF6-80C2B1F	385600	F16C64Y310		oo-delivery 0102
☐ D-ABVK	Boeing 747-430	25046 / 847	N6009F*	0091	0491	4 GE CF6-80C2B1F	394600	F16C64Y292	FH-JM	Hannover / lsf Tower FSC Ltd
☐ D-ABVL	Boeing 747-430	26425 / 898	N60659*	0092	0292	4 GE CF6-80C2B1F	385600	F16C64Y310	EM-AL	München / lsf Overseas Leasing Four FSC
☐ D-ABVM	Boeing 747-430	29101 / 1143		0098	0298	4 GE CF6-80C2B1F	385600	F16C64Y310		Hessen
☐ D-ABVN	Boeing 747-430	26427 / 915		0092	0592	4 GE CF6-80C2B1F	385600	F16C64Y292	CG-AL	Dortmund / lsf DB Export-Leasing GmbH
☐ D-ABVO	Boeing 747-430	28086 / 1080		0096	0596	4 GE CF6-80C2B1F	385600	F16C64Y292	JQ-LR	Mülheim a.d. Ruhr / lsf Lufthansa Lsng
☐ D-ABVP	Boeing 747-430	28284 / 1103		0097	0297	4 GE CF6-80C2B1F	385600	F16C64Y292	MR-DG	Bremen
☐ D-ABVR	Boeing 747-430	28285 / 1106		0097	0397	4 GE CF6-80C2B1F	385600	F16C64Y292	MR-DH	Köln
☐ D-ABVS	Boeing 747-430	28286 / 1109		0097	0497	4 GE CF6-80C2B1F	385600	F16C64Y292	MR-DJ	Saarland
☐ D-ABVT	Boeing 747-430	28287 / 1110		0097	0497	4 GE CF6-80C2B1F	385600	F16C64Y292	MR-DK	Rheinland Pfalz / lsf Lufthansa Leasing
☐ D-ABVU	Boeing 747-430	28492 / 1191		1298	1298	4 GE CF6-80C2B1F	385600	F16C64Y310	CD-AP	
☐ D-ABVW	Boeing 747-430	28493 / 1205		0099	0399	4 GE CF6-80C2B1F	385600	F16C64Y310	BS-PR	
☐ D-ABVX	Boeing 747-430	29868				4 GE CF6-80C2B1F	385600	F16C64Y310		oo-delivery 1299
☐ D-ABVY	Boeing 747-430	29869				4 GE CF6-80C2B1F	385600	F16C64Y310		oo-delivery 0101
☐ D-ABVZ	Boeing 747-430	29870				4 GE CF6-80C2B1F	385600	F16C64Y310		oo-delivery 0201

LUFTHANSA Cargo, AG = LH / GEC (Subsidiary of Lufthansa / formerly Lufthansa Cargo Airlines, GmbH & German Cargo Services, GmbH) — Frankfurt — Lufthansa Cargo

Postfach 1244, D-65441 Kelsterbach, Germany ☎ (69) 696 54 37 Tx: 4189142 gcs d Fax: (69) 696 68 86 SITA: n/a
F: 1977 ⁂ 700 Head: Wilhelm Althen IATA: 020 ICAO: LUFTHANSA CARGO Net: http://www.lhcargo.com
Beside aircraft listed, also uses 1-2 Boeing 737-230F lsf / opb AIR ATLANTA ICELANDIC (TF-) & 1 Airbus Ind. A300B4-203 (F) lsf / opb HEAVYLIFT CARGO (G-) when required.

☐ D-ALCA	Boeing (Douglas) MD-11F	48781 / 625	N9020Q*	0398	0698	3 GE CF6-80C2D1F	285990	Freighter 91,7t	AC-EP	
☐ D-ALCB	Boeing (Douglas) MD-11F	48782 / 626	N9166N*	0098	0698	3 GE CF6-80C2D1F	285990	Freighter 91,7t	AC-HP	
☐ D-ALCC	Boeing (Douglas) MD-11F	48783 / 627		0098	0898	3 GE CF6-80C2D1F	285990	Freighter 91,7t	AD-HQ	Karl-Ulrich Garnadt
☐ D-ALCD	Boeing (Douglas) MD-11F	48784 / 628		0098	0998	3 GE CF6-80C2D1F	285990	Freighter 91,7t		
☐ D-ALCE	Boeing (Douglas) MD-11F	48785 / 629		0098	1098	3 GE CF6-80C2D1F	285990	Freighter 91,7t		
☐ D-ALCF	Boeing (Douglas) MD-11F					3 GE CF6-80C2D1F	285990	Freighter 91,7t		oo-delivery 0899
☐ D-ALCG	Boeing (Douglas) MD-11F					3 GE CF6-80C2D1F	285990	Freighter 91,7t		oo-delivery 1099
☐ D-ALCH	Boeing (Douglas) MD-11F					3 GE CF6-80C2D1F	285990	Freighter 91,7t		oo-delivery 1299
☐ D-ALCI	Boeing (Douglas) MD-11F					3 GE CF6-80C2D1F	285990	Freighter 91,7t		oo-delivery 0100
☐ D-ALCJ	Boeing (Douglas) MD-11F					3 GE CF6-80C2D1F	285990	Freighter 91,7t		oo-delivery 0200
☐ D-ALCK	Boeing (Douglas) MD-11F					3 GE CF6-80C2D1F	285990	Freighter 91,7t		oo-delivery 0300
☐ D-ALCL	Boeing (Douglas) MD-11F					3 GE CF6-80C2D1F	285990	Freighter 91,7t		oo-delivery 0101
☐ D-ALCM	Boeing (Douglas) MD-11F					3 GE CF6-80C2D1F	285990	Freighter 91,7t		oo-delivery 0201
☐ D-ALCN	Boeing (Douglas) MD-11F					3 GE CF6-80C2D1F	285990	Freighter 91,7t		oo-delivery 0301
☐ D-ABYO	Boeing 747-230F (SCD)	21592 / 347		0078	0593	4 GE CF6-50E2	371900	Freighter	CG-AK	America / lsf Lufthansa Leasing
☐ D-ABYT	Boeing 747-230B (SF)	22363 / 490		0080	0890	4 GE CF6-50E2	377800	Freighter	BL-AF	cvtd -230B (M)
☐ D-ABYU	Boeing 747-230F (SCD)	22668 / 538	N1785B*	0081	0593	4 GE CF6-50E2	377800	Freighter	GJ-AL	Asia / lsf Lufthansa Leasing
☐ D-ABYW	Boeing 747-230B (SF)	22669 / 549		0081	0191	4 GE CF6-50E2	377800	Freighter	CH-AB	cvtd -230B (M)
☐ D-ABYY	Boeing 747-230B (SF)	22671 / 574		0082	1191	4 GE CF6-50E2	377800	Freighter	FL-BK	lsf Citibank / cvtd -230B (M)
☐ D-ABYZ	Boeing 747-230B (SF)	23286 / 614	I-DEMX	0085	0394	4 GE CF6-50E2	377800	Freighter	HM-AJ	lsf Lufthansa Leasing/cvtd -230B (M)
☐ D-ABZA	Boeing 747-230B (SF)	23287 / 617	N6038E*	0085	0593	4 GE CF6-50E2	377800	Freighter	HM-CE	lsf Lufthansa Leasing/cvtd -230B (M)
☐ D-ABZB	Boeing 747-230F (SCD)	23348 / 625	N747MC	0085	0593	4 GE CF6-50E2	377800	Freighter	AF-KL	New York
☐ D-ABZC	Boeing 747-230B (SF)	23393 / 633	N6046P*	0086	0593	4 GE CF6-50E2	377800	Freighter	CD-JL	cvtd -230B (M)
☐ D-ABZF	Boeing 747-230F (SCD)	23621 / 660	N6046P*	0086	0593	4 GE CF6-50E2	377800	Freighter	FM-DJ	Africa / special Service Revolution-cs
☐ D-ABZI	Boeing 747-230F (SCD)	24138 / 706	N6005C*	0088	0593	4 GE CF6-50E2	377800	Freighter	FJ-LM	Australia

LUFTHANSA CityLine, GmbH = CL / CLH (Subsidiary of Deutsche Lufthansa AG / formerly DLT Deutsche Luftverkehrs GmbH & OLT) — Cologne & Munich — Lufthansa CityLine

Heinrich Steinmann Strasse, D-51147 Köln, Germany ☎ (2203) 59 60 Tx: none Fax: (2203) 59 68 01 SITA: CGNDDCL
F: 1958 ⁂ 1700 Head: Karl-Heinz Köpfle & Georg Steinbacher IATA: 683 ICAO: HANSALINE Net: http://www.lhcityline.com/
Beside aircraft listed, also uses 5 BAe 146-200 lsf/opb DEBONAIR (G-) in Lufthansa CityLine-colors. For details – see under that company.

☐ D-AFFI	Fokker 50 (F27 Mk050)	20272	PH-LXL*	0093	1093	2 PWC PW125B	20820	C50	DS-EK	lsf Montale Verwaltung / sub-lst KIS
☐ D-AFFX	Fokker 50 (F27 Mk050)	20142	EC-GAF	0088	1288	2 PWC PW125B	20820	C50		lst KIS
☐ D-AFFY	Fokker 50 (F27 Mk050)	20141	EC-GAE	0088	1288	2 PWC PW125B	20820	C50		lst KIS
☐ D-AFFZ	Fokker 50 (F27 Mk050)	20133	EC-GAD	0088	1088	2 PWC PW125B	20820	C50		lst KIS
☐ D-AFKK	Fokker 50 (F27 Mk050)	20205	PH-EXN*	0090	1290	2 PWC PW125B	20820	C50	KL-CH	lst KIS
☐ D-AFKL	Fokker 50 (F27 Mk050)	20213	PH-EXC*	0091	0491	2 PWC PW125B	20820	C50	KL-CJ	lst KIS
☐ D-AFKM	Fokker 50 (F27 Mk050)	20214	PH-EXD*	0091	0491	2 PWC PW125B	20820	C50	KL-CM	lsf Lufthansa Leasing / sub-lst KIS
☐ D-AFKN	Fokker 50 (F27 Mk050)	20223	PH-EXX*	0091	0791	2 PWC PW125B	20820	C50	LM-BD	lsf Lufthansa Leasing / sub-lst KIS
☐ D-AFKO	Fokker 50 (F27 Mk050)	20234	PH-JXO*	0091	1291	2 PWC PW125B	20820	C50	LM-BE	lsf Lufthansa Leasing / sub-lst KIS
☐ D-AFKP	Fokker 50 (F27 Mk050)	20235	PH-EXE*	0091	1291	2 PWC PW125B	20820	C50	LM-BF	lsf Lufthansa Leasing / sub-lst KIS
☐ D-AFKU	Fokker 50 (F27 Mk050)	20236	PH-JXL*	0092	0292	2 PWC PW125B	20820	C50	LM-BG	lsf Miso-Verwaltung / sub-lst KIS
☐ D-ACJA	Canadair Regional Jet 100LR (CL-600-2B19)	7122	C-FMKT*	0096	0696	2 GE CF34-3A1	24000	C50	LM-BG	lsf Lufthansa Leasing
☐ D-ACJB	Canadair Regional Jet 100LR (CL-600-2B19)	7128	C-FMMQ*	0096	0896	2 GE CF34-3A1	24000	C50	LM-BJ	lsf Lufthansa Leasing
☐ D-ACJC	Canadair Regional Jet 100LR (CL-600-2B19)	7130	C-FMMW*	0096	0896	2 GE CF34-3A1	24000	C50	AC-GJ	lsf Lufthansa Leasing
☐ D-ACJD	Canadair Regional Jet 100LR (CL-600-2B19)	7135	C-FMNH*	0096	0996	2 GE CF34-3A1	24000	C50	AC-GK	lsf Lufthansa Leasing
☐ D-ACJE	Canadair Regional Jet 100LR (CL-600-2B19)	7165	C-FMNH*	0097	0397	2 GE CF34-3A1	24000	C50	AC-GL	
☐ D-ACJF	Canadair Regional Jet 100LR (CL-600-2B19)	7200		0097	1097	2 GE CF34-3A1	24000	C50	AC-GM	
☐ D-ACJG	Canadair Regional Jet 100LR (CL-600-2B19)	7220	C-FMMW*	0098	0298	2 GE CF34-3A1	24000	C50	AC-JH	
☐ D-ACJH	Canadair Regional Jet 100LR (CL-600-2B19)	7266		0098	1098	2 GE CF34-3A1	24000	C50		special 40th anniversary-colors
☐ D-ACJI	Canadair Regional Jet 100LR (CL-600-2B19)	7282	C-FNMY*	0098	0199	2 GE CF34-3A1	24000	C50		
☐ D-ACJJ	Canadair Regional Jet 100LR (CL-600-2B19)	7298		0099	0399	2 GE CF34-3A1	24000	C50		
☐ D-ACJK	Canadair Regional Jet 100LR (CL-600-2B19)					2 GE CF34-3A1	24000	C50		oo-delivery 0200
☐ D-ACJL	Canadair Regional Jet 100LR (CL-600-2B19)					2 GE CF34-3A1	24000	C50		oo-delivery 0500
☐ D-ACJM	Canadair Regional Jet 100LR (CL-600-2B19)					2 GE CF34-3A1	24000	C50		oo-delivery 0500
☐ D-ACJN	Canadair Regional Jet 100LR (CL-600-2B19)					2 GE CF34-3A1	24000	C50		oo-delivery 0800
☐ D-ACJO	Canadair Regional Jet 100LR (CL-600-2B19)					2 GE CF34-3A1	24000	C50		oo-delivery 0800
☐ D-ACJP	Canadair Regional Jet 100LR (CL-600-2B19)					2 GE CF34-3A1	24000	C50		oo-delivery 1100
☐ D-ACJQ	Canadair Regional Jet 100LR (CL-600-2B19)					2 GE CF34-3A1	24000	C50		oo-delivery 1100
☐ D-ACJR	Canadair Regional Jet 100LR (CL-600-2B19)					2 GE CF34-3A1	24000	C50		oo-delivery 0101
☐ D-ACJS	Canadair Regional Jet 100LR (CL-600-2B19)					2 GE CF34-3A1	24000	C50		oo-delivery 0301
☐ D-ACJT	Canadair Regional Jet 100LR (CL-600-2B19)					2 GE CF34-3A1	24000	C50		oo-delivery 0401
☐ D-ACLA	Canadair Regional Jet 100LR (CL-600-2B19)	7004	C-GRJJ*	0092	1092	2 GE CF34-3A1	24000	C50	CK-MR	lsf JL Silvia Lease Co. Ltd/cvtd 100ER
☐ D-ACLB	Canadair Regional Jet 100LR (CL-600-2B19)	7005	C-GRJN*	0092	1192	2 GE CF34-3A1	24000	C50	CK-MS	lsf JL Petra Lease Co. Ltd/cvtd 100ER
☐ D-ACLC	Canadair Regional Jet 100LR (CL-600-2B19)	7006	C-GRJO*	0092	1292	2 GE CF34-3A1	24000	C50	CK-PR	lsf JL Rita Lease Co. Ltd/cvtd 100ER
☐ D-ACLD	Canadair Regional Jet 100LR (CL-600-2B19)	7009	C-FMKW*	0092	0193	2 GE CF34-3A1	24000	C50	CK-PS	lsf JL Lisa Lease Co. Ltd / cvtd 100ER
☐ D-ACLE	Canadair Regional Jet 100LR (CL-600-2B19)	7010	C-GRJW*	0092	0293	2 GE CF34-3A1	24000	C50	CK-QR	lsf JL Vera Lease Co. Ltd / cvtd 100ER
☐ D-ACLF	Canadair Regional Jet 100LR (CL-600-2B19)	7015	C-FMLQ*	0093	0493	2 GE CF34-3A1	24000	C50	CK-QS	lsf Lufthansa Leasing / cvtd 100ER
☐ D-ACLG	Canadair Regional Jet 100LR (CL-600-2B19)	7016	C-FMLS*	0093	0593	2 GE CF34-3A1	24000	C50	CK-RS	lsf JL Rosa Lease / cvtd 100ER
☐ D-ACLH	Canadair Regional Jet 100LR (CL-600-2B19)	7007	C-FMKV*	0093	0593	2 GE CF34-3A1	24000	C50	CL-AR	lsf JL Eva Lease Co. Ltd / cvtd 100ER
☐ D-ACLI	Canadair Regional Jet 100LR (CL-600-2B19)	7019	C-FMLV*	0093	0793	2 GE CF34-3A1	24000	C50	CL-AS	lsf Lufthansa Leasing / cvtd 100ER
☐ D-ACLJ	Canadair Regional Jet 100LR (CL-600-2B19)	7021	C-FMML*	0093	0793	2 GE CF34-3A1	24000	C50	CL-BR	lsf Munda Verwaltung / cvtd 100ER
☐ D-ACLK	Canadair Regional Jet 100LR (CL-600-2B19)	7023	C-FMMQ*	0093	0993	2 GE CF34-3A1	24000	C50	CL-BS	lsf Lufthansa Leasing / cvtd 100ER
☐ D-ACLL	Canadair Regional Jet 100LR (CL-600-2B19)	7024	C-FMMT*	0093	1093	2 GE CF34-3A1	24000	C50	CL-DR	lsf JL Sarah Lease Co. Ltd / cvtd 100ER
☐ D-ACLM	Canadair Regional Jet 100LR (CL-600-2B19)	7025		0093	1093	2 GE CF34-3A1	24000	C50	CL-DS	lsf JL Lena Lease Co. Ltd / cvtd 100ER
☐ D-ACLN	Canadair Regional Jet 100LR (CL-600-2B19)	7039	OE-LRQ	0094	0594	2 GE CF34-3A1	24000	C50	CL-ER	lst Bombardier/S.Winds,LV-YLA/cvtd100ER
☐ D-ACLO	Canadair Regional Jet 100LR (CL-600-2B19)	7041	F-GPYZ	0094	0694	2 GE CF34-3A1	24000	C50	CL-ES	lst Bombardier/S.Winds,LV-WXT/cvtd100ER
☐ D-ACLP	Canadair Regional Jet 100LR (CL-600-2B19)	7064	C-FMNX*	0095	0495	2 GE CF34-3A1	24000	C50	CL-FR	lsf JL Anna Lease Co. Ltd / cvtd 100ER
☐ D-ACLQ	Canadair Regional Jet 100LR (CL-600-2B19)	7073	C-FMKF*	0095	0695	2 GE CF34-3A1	24000	C50	CL-FS	lsf JL Carina Lease Co. Ltd/cvtd 100ER
☐ D-ACLR	Canadair Regional Jet 100LR (CL-600-2B19)	7086		0095	1195	2 GE CF34-3A1	24000	C50	CL-GR	lsf JL Laura Lease Co. Ltd
☐ D-ACLS	Canadair Regional Jet 100LR (CL-600-2B19)	7090		0095	1195	2 GE CF34-3A1	24000	C50	CL-GS	lsf JL Tanja Lease Co. Ltd
☐ D-ACLT	Canadair Regional Jet 100LR (CL-600-2B19)	7093		0095	1295	2 GE CF34-3A1	24000	C50	CL-HR	lsf JL Ulla Lease Co. Ltd
☐ D-ACLU	Canadair Regional Jet 100LR (CL-600-2B19)	7104	C-FXPI*	0096	0396	2 GE CF34-3A1	24000	C50	CL-HS	lsf Lufthansa Leasing
☐ D-ACLV	Canadair Regional Jet 100LR (CL-600-2B19)	7113	C-FMMQ*	0096	0596	2 GE CF34-3A1	24000	C50	DS-ER	lsf Lufthansa Leasing
☐ D-ACLW	Canadair Regional Jet 100LR (CL-600-2B19)	7114	C-FMMT*	0096	0596	2 GE CF34-3A1	24000	C50	DS-FG	lsf Lufthansa Leasing
☐ D-ACLX	Canadair Regional Jet 100LR (CL-600-2B19)	7036	OE-LRC	0094	1095	2 GE CF34-3A1	24000	C50	LM-BK	lsf LDA / cvtd 100ER
☐ D-ACLY	Canadair Regional Jet 100LR (CL-600-2B19)	7119	C-FMND*	0096	0596	2 GE CF34-3A1	24000	C50	LM-CE	lsf Lufthansa Leasing
☐ D-ACLZ	Canadair Regional Jet 100LR (CL-600-2B19)	7121	C-FMNQ*	0096	0696	2 GE CF34-3A1	24000	C50	LM-CG	lsf Lufthansa Leasing
☐ D-	Canadair Regional Jet 700					2 GE CF34-8C1	32900	C70		oo-delivery 0201
☐ D-	Canadair Regional Jet 700					2 GE CF34-8C1	32900	C70		oo-delivery 0201
☐ D-	Canadair Regional Jet 700					2 GE CF34-8C1	32900	C70		oo-delivery 0201
☐ D-	Canadair Regional Jet 700					2 GE CF34-8C1	32900	C70		oo-delivery 0501

114 registration type of aircraft cn/fn ex/ex* mfd del powered by mtow kg configuration selcal name/fln/specialitites/remarks

☐ D-	Canadair Regional Jet 700					2 GE CF34-8C1	32900	C70		oo-delivery 1101
☐ D-	Canadair Regional Jet 700					2 GE CF34-8C1	32900	C70		oo-delivery 1101
☐ D-	Canadair Regional Jet 700					2 GE CF34-8C1	32900	C70		oo-delivery 0202
☐ D-	Canadair Regional Jet 700					2 GE CF34-8C1	32900	C70		oo-delivery 0202
☐ D-	Canadair Regional Jet 700					2 GE CF34-8C1	32900	C70		oo-delivery 0502
☐ D-	Canadair Regional Jet 700					2 GE CF34-8C1	32900	C70		oo-delivery 0502
☐ D-AVRA	Avro RJ85 (Cityliner) (Avro 146-RJ85)	E2256	G-6-256*	0094	1194	4 LY LF507-1F	44000	C80		lsf Lufthansa Leasing
☐ D-AVRB	Avro RJ85 (Cityliner) (Avro 146-RJ85)	E2253	G-6-253*	0094	1294	4 LY LF507-1F	44000	C80		lsf Lufthansa Leasing
☐ D-AVRC	Avro RJ85 (Cityliner) (Avro 146-RJ85)	E2251	G-6-251*	0095	0395	4 LY LF507-1F	44000	C80		lsf Lufthansa Leasing
☐ D-AVRD	Avro RJ85 (Cityliner) (Avro 146-RJ85)	E2257	G-6-257*	0095	0395	4 LY LF507-1F	44000	C80		lsf Lufthansa Leasing
☐ D-AVRE	Avro RJ85 (Cityliner) (Avro 146-RJ85)	E2261	G-6-261*	0095	0395	4 LY LF507-1F	44000	C80		lsf Lufthansa Leasing
☐ D-AVRF	Avro RJ85 (Cityliner) (Avro 146-RJ85)	E2269	G-JAYV*	0095	0695	4 LY LF507-1F	44000	C80		lsf Lufthansa Leasing
☐ D-AVRG	Avro RJ85 (Cityliner) (Avro 146-RJ85)	E2266	G-6-266*	0095	0995	4 LY LF507-1F	44000	C80		lsf Lufthansa Leasing
☐ D-AVRH	Avro RJ85 (Cityliner) (Avro 146-RJ85)	E2268	G-OCLH*	0095	1095	4 LY LF507-1F	44000	C80		lsf Lufthansa Leasing
☐ D-AVRI	Avro RJ85 (Cityliner) (Avro 146-RJ85)	E2270	G-CLHX*	0095	1295	4 LY LF507-1F	44000	C80		lsf Lufthansa Leasing
☐ D-AVRJ	Avro RJ85 (Cityliner) (Avro 146-RJ85)	E2277	G-BWKY	0096	0296	4 LY LF507-1F	44000	C80		
☐ D-AVRK	Avro RJ85 (Cityliner) (Avro 146-RJ85)	E2278	G-6-278*	0096	0396	4 LY LF507-1F	44000	C80		
☐ D-AVRL	Avro RJ85 (Cityliner) (Avro 146-RJ85)	E2285	G-6-285*	0096	0396	4 LY LF507-1F	44000	C80		
☐ D-AVRM	Avro RJ85 (Cityliner) (Avro 146-RJ85)	E2288	G-6-288*	0096	0596	4 LY LF507-1F	44000	C80		
☐ D-AVRN	Avro RJ85 (Cityliner) (Avro 146-RJ85)	E2293	G-6-293*	0096	0996	4 LY LF507-1F	44000	C80		
☐ D-AVRO	Avro RJ85 (Cityliner) (Avro 146-RJ85)	E2246	G-6-246*	0094	1094	4 LY LF507-1F	44000	C80		lsf Lufthansa Leasing
☐ D-AVRP	Avro RJ85 (Cityliner) (Avro 146-RJ85)	E2303	G-6-303*	0097	0297	4 LY LF507-1F	44000	C80		
☐ D-AVRQ	Avro RJ85 (Cityliner) (Avro 146-RJ85)	E2304	G-6-304*	0097	0397	4 LY LF507-1F	44000	C80		
☐ D-AVRR	Avro RJ85 (Cityliner) (Avro 146-RJ85)	E2317	G-6-317*	0097	1297	4 LY LF507-1F	44000	C80		

LUFTHANSA Flight Training, GmbH (Subsidirary of Deutsche Lufthansa, AG / formerly Lufthansa Verkehrsfliegerschule) — Bremen

PF 286136, D-28361 Bremen, Germany ☎ (421) 55 920 Tx: none Fax: (421) 559 28 12 SITA: n/a
F: 1956 ♟♟♟ 126 Head: Lothar Martin ICAO: LUFTHANSA Net: n/a Trainer-Aircraft below MTOW 5000kg: Beechcraft Bonanza A36AT & Piper PA-34-220T Seneca V

☐ D-IOSA	Piper PA-42-720 Cheyenne IIIA	42-5501041		0087	0587	2 PWC PT6A-61	5080	Trainer		
☐ D-IOSB	Piper PA-42-720 Cheyenne IIIA	42-5501042		0087	0587	2 PWC PT6A-61	5080	Trainer		
☐ D-IOSC	Piper PA-42-720 Cheyenne IIIA	42-5501043		0087	0987	2 PWC PT6A-61	5080	Trainer		

LUFTHANSA Traditionsflug, GmbH – LTG (Subsidiary of Deutsche Lufthansa, AG) — Frankfurt

Lufthansa Traditionsflug

Lufthansa Basis Abt. FRAZU/T, D-60546 Frankfurt, Germany ☎ (69) 696 41 05 Tx: 411763 (att frazu-t) Fax: (69) 696 52 11 SITA: n/a
F: 1986 ♟♟♟ 3 Head: Capt. Heinz-Dieter Bonsmann Net: n/a Non-profit organisation aircraft occasionally leased from LH Berlin Foundation.

☐ D-CDLH	Junkers Ju52/3m	130714	N52JU	0036	0686	3 PW R-1340-S1H1G	10500	16 Pax		D-AQUI Berlin-Tempelhof

LUFTTAXI FLUG, GmbH = LTF — Dortmund

Flugplatz, D-44319 Dortmund, Germany ☎ (231) 921 33 65 Tx: none Fax: (231) 921 33 66 SITA: n/a
F: 1995 ♟♟♟ 21 Head: Ingo Schnitger ICAO: GARFIELD Net: http://www.lufttaxi.de

☐ D-IGEL	Cessna 340A II	340A1231	OE-FSA	0081		2 CO TSIO-520-NB	2717			lsf RCU GmbH & Co. Leasing KG
☐ D-IAAT	Cessna 421C Golden Eagle III	421C0496	N8482N	0078		2 CO GTSIO-520-L	3379			lsf pvt
☐ D-IKRP	Cessna 421C Golden Eagle II	421C0214	TC-DBH	0077	0898	2 CO GTSIO-520-L	3379			lsf LION Electronics
☐ D-IEGA	Cessna 441 Conquest II	441-0193	OE-FRZ	0080	0598	2 GA TPE331-10N-514S	4468			
☐ D-IDBW	Cessna 525 CitationJet	525-0044	N55DG	0093	0199	2 WRR FJ44-1A	4717			lsf pvt
☐ D-IMON	Beech King Air 200	BB-276		0076	0798	2 PWC PT6A-41	5670			lsf pvt

MAPS Geosystems, GmbH (Affiliated with MAPS (UAE), Sharjah/UAE & MAPS Sàrl, Beirut/Lebanon) — Sharjah (UAE)

MAPS geosystems

Truderinger Str. 13, D-81677 München, Germany ☎ (89) 47 20 83 Tx: none Fax: (89) 47 34 35 SITA: n/a
F: 1974 ♟♟♟ 30 Head: Rolf Becker & Gerhard Thaller Net: http://www.maps-geosystems.com

☐ N756NT	Cessna TU206G Turbo Stationair 6 II	U20604230		0077	1291	1 CO TSIO-520-M	1633	Photo/Survey		lsf MAPS Geosystems Inc.
☐ N900TB	Piper PA-31P Comanchero	31P-7400227		0074	0593	2 PWC PT6A-135	3538	Photo/Survey		lsf MAPS Geosyst.Inc./cvtd Press.Navajo

MEDIAIR, GmbH — Vilshofen

Haidenburger Str. 2, D-94501 Aidenbach, Germany ☎ (8543) 12 88 Tx: none Fax: (8543) 22 26 SITA: n/a
F: 1996 ♟♟♟ n/a Head: Dr. Peter Fricke Net: n/a

☐ D-ETSI	Piper PA-46-310P Malibu	46-8508012	HB-PKY	0085	1196	1 CO TSIO-520-BE	1860			
☐ D-INNN	Piper PA-31T Cheyenne II	31T-8120102	N822SW	0083	0598	2 PWC PT6A-28	4082			lsf Raiffeisenbank Vilshofener Land

MERAVO Luftreederei Fluggesellschaft, mbH (Affiliated with HPS-Helicopter-Leasing, GmbH) — Oedheim

meravo

Flugplatz, D-74229 Oedheim, Germany ☎ (7136) 6051 Tx: none Fax: (7136) 23 315 SITA: n/a
F: 1960 ♟♟♟ 32 Head: Dipl. Ing. (FH) Bernd Hauber Net: n/a Aircraft below MTOW 1361 kg: Bell Agusta-Bell & Bell Soloy 47.

☐ D-HAUE	Bell 206B JetRanger III	4195		0091	0292	1 AN 250-C20B	1451			lsf HPS-Helicopter-Leasing
☐ D-HAUO	Bell 206B JetRanger III	2311	EC-FBX	0077	0992	1 AN 250-C20B	1451			lsf HPS-Heli-Lsng/sublst Ruescher Heli.
☐ D-HEKW	Bell 206B JetRanger II	2101		0076		1 AN 250-C20	1451			lsf HPS-Helicopter-Leasing
☐ D-HMEI	Bell 206B JetRanger III	2550		0078		1 AN 250-C20B	1451			lsf HPS-Helicopter-Leasing
☐ D-HAUV	Eurocopter EC120B Colibri	1010		0098	0998	1 TU Arrius 2F	1680			lsf HPS-Helicopter-Leasing
☐ D-HAUA	Bell 206L-3 LongRanger III	51328	N21AH	0089	0391	1 AN 250-C30P	1882			lsf HPS-Helicopter-Leasing
☐ D-HAAM	Eurocopter (Aerosp.) AS350B Ecureuil	1910		0086		1 TU Arriel 1B	1950			
☐ D-HAAN	Euroc.(Helibras/Aerosp.)HB350BA Esquilo	1580 / HB1038	PT-HMB	0090		1 TU Arriel 1B	2100			lst DFKW-Helicopter Service
☐ D-HAPI	Eurocopter (Aerosp.) AS350B Ecureuil	1184		0079		1 TU Arriel 1B	1950			lsf HPS-Helicopter-Leasing
☐ D-HAUK	Eurocopter (Aerosp.) AS350BA Ecureuil	1750	D-HFFG	0084	0493	1 TU Arriel 1B	2100			cvtd AS350B
☐ D-HAUM	Eurocopter (Aerosp.) AS350B1 Ecureuil	1939	D-HAUX	0086		1 TU Arriel 1D	2200			rebuilt
☐ D-HAUN	Eurocopter (Aerosp.) AS350B Ecureuil	2056		0087		1 TU Arriel 1B	1950			lsf HPS-Helicopter-Leasing
☐ D-HAUR	Eurocopter (Aerosp.) AS350B2 Ecureuil	2394	HB-XUY	0090	0993	1 TU Arriel 1D1	2250			lsf HPS-Helicopter-Leasing
☐ D-HAUU	Eurocopter (Aerosp.) AS350B1 Ecureuil	2072	D-HAUZ	0088	0897	1 TU Arriel 1D	2200			rebuilt
☐ D-HCOR	Eurocopter (Aerosp.) AS350B Ecureuil	1601		0082		1 TU Arriel 1B	1950			lsf pvt
☐ D-HELI	Eurocopter (Aerosp.) AS350BA Ecureuil	1241	F-WZFL*	0080		1 TU Arriel 1B	2100			lsf HPS-Helicopter-Leasing/cvtd AS350B
☐ D-HHDD	Eurocopter (Aerosp.) AS350B Ecureuil	1825		0085		1 TU Arriel 1B	1950			
☐ D-HAUD	Eurocopter (Aerosp.) AS355N Ecureuil 2	5538	F-WYMA*	0092	0393	2 TU Arrius 1A	2540			
☐ D-HAAH	Eurocopter (Aerosp.) SA360C Dauphin	1005	N47287	0076		1 TU Astazou XVIIIA	3000			lsf HPS-Helicopter-Leasing
☐ D-HAAL	Eurocopter (Aerosp.) SA360C Dauphin	1030		0084		1 TU Astazou XVIIIA	3000			lsf HPS-Helicopter-Leasing
☐ D-HAUL	Eurocopter (Aerosp.) SA360C Dauphin	1009	F-GCMG	0076		1 TU Astazou VIIIA	3100			
☐ D-HAUP	Eurocopter (Aerosp.) SA360C Dauphin	1018	JA9244	0079		1 TU Astazou XVIIIA	3000			
☐ D-HAUS	Eurocopter (Aerosp.) SA360C Dauphin	1022	JA9277	0078		1 TU Astazou XVIIIA	3000			
☐ D-HAUG	Sikorsky S-58C	58-836	B-15/OT-ZKP	0056		1 WR R-1820	5897			lsf HPS-Helicopter-Leasing

MFS Manager Flugservice, GmbH (Subsidiary of Unternehmensgruppe Geitlinger, GmbH) — Saarbruecken

Kaiserstr. 74, D-66424 Homburg, Germany ☎ (6841) 50 54 Tx: none Fax: (6841) 50 59 SITA: n/a
F: 1980 ♟♟♟ 4 Head: Manfred Weisbrodt Net: n/a

☐ D-IGOB	Piaggio P.180 Avanti	1016	I-PJAT*	0092	1292	2 PWC PT6A-66	4944			lsf PBG GmbH

MHS HELICOPTER-FLUGSERVICE, GmbH & Co. KG — Munich

Ganghoferstr. 1B, D-82216 Maisach, Germany ☎ (89) 97 33 30 Tx: none Fax: (89) 973 33 33 SITA: n/a
F: 1976 ♟♟♟ 8 Head: Heico Zimmer Net: n/a

☐ D-HISF	Bell 407	53039	N1164Z	0096	1296	1 AN 250-C47B	2268			lsf pvt
☐ D-HBRK	Agusta A109C	7646	N1YE	0091	0992	2 AN 250-C20R/1	2720			
☐ D-HOBM	Agusta A109E Power	11007	HB-XQH	0097	1297	2 PWC PW206C	2850			lsf Metro GmbH & Co. KG

MODERN AIR, GmbH — Zweibruecken

Flughafen, D-66482 Zweibrücken, Germany ☎ (6332) 97 46 40 Tx: none Fax: (6332) 97 46 49 SITA: n/a
F: 1998 ♟♟♟ n/a Head: Walter Meier Net: n/a Presently being set-up. Intends to start operations in autumn 1999.

☐ D-	Dornier 328JET (328-300)					2 PWC PW306B	14990	Y32		oo-delivery 0799
☐ D-	Dornier 328JET (328-300)					2 PWC PW306B	14990	Y32		oo-delivery 0899
☐ D-	Dornier 328JET (328-300)					2 PWC PW306B	14990	Y32		oo-delivery 1099
☐ D-	Dornier 328JET (328-300)					2 PWC PW306B	14990	Y32		oo-delivery 1299
☐ D-	Dornier 328JET (328-300)					2 PWC PW306B	14990	Y32		oo-delivery 0100
☐ D-	Dornier 328JET (328-300)					2 PWC PW306B	14990	Y32		oo-delivery 0200
☐ D-	Dornier 328JET (328-300)					2 PWC PW306B	14990	Y32		oo-delivery 0300
☐ D-	Dornier 328JET (328-300)					2 PWC PW306B	14990	Y32		oo-delivery 0500
☐ D-	Dornier 328JET (328-300)					2 PWC PW306B	14990	Y32		oo-delivery 0600
☐ D-	Dornier 328JET (328-300)					2 PWC PW306B	14990	Y32		oo-delivery 0700

115 registration | type of aircraft | cn/fn | ex/ex* | mfd | del | powered by | mtow kg | configuration | selcal | name/fln/specialitites/remarks

MSR-Flug Charter, GmbH = EBF — Muenster-Osnabrueck

Flughafen Münster-Osnabrück, D-48268 Greven, Germany ☎ (2571) 91 151 Tx: none Fax: (2571) 91 211 SITA: n/a
F: 1978 ☧ n/a Head: Heiner Schulte ICAO: SKYRUNNER Net: n/a

☐ D-INGI	Cessna 340A II	340A0037	N98569	0076		2 CO TSIO-520-N	2853			lsf pvt
☐ D-IOAA	Cessna 421C Golden Eagle III	421C0861	OE-FBL	0080		2 CO GTSIO-520-L	3379			lsf pvt
☐ D-ICMF	Cessna 425 Conquest I	425-0102	N151GA	0081		2 PWC PT6A-112	3900			lsf pvt
☐ D-IPOS	Cessna 425 Conquest I	425-0120	N425R	0082		2 PWC PT6A-112	3900			lsf Dr. Peters GmbH
☐ D-IAMM	Cessna 525 CitationJet	525-0041	HB-VJQ	0093		2 WRR FJ44-1A	4717			lsf MSK-Verpackungs Systeme GmbH
☐ D-ICGT	Cessna 525 CitationJet	525-0164		0096		2 WRR FJ44-1A	4717			lsf AGIB AG

MTM Aviation, GmbH = MTM — Munich

Postfach 231855, D-85327 München, Germany ☎ (89) 97 85 20 Tx: 526705 mtm d Fax: (89) 970 18 81 SITA: MUCASXH
F: 1980 ☧ 50 Head: Werner Bader ICAO: AVITRANS Net: n/a On order (Letter of Intent): 1 Dornier 328JET for delivery 1999

☐ D-IFES	Beech King Air 200	BB-827		0081		2 PWC PT6A-41	5675	Y8 / EMS		
☐ D-CATL	Learjet 55	55-051	N55KD	0082	0195	2 GA TFE731-3AR-2B	9752	Y7 / EMS		
☐ D-CLIP	Learjet 55	55-004	N24CK	0081		2 GA TFE731-3A-2B	9752	Y8 / EMS	FG-BK	
☐ D-COOL	Learjet 55	55-052	N551DB	0082	0992	2 GA TFE731-3AR-2B	9752	Y7 / EMS		
☐ D-CMTM	Dornier 328-110	3094		0098	0398	2 PWC PW119B	13990	Y30		Bavarian Star / lsf Millennium Leasing
☐ D-CMUC	Dornier 328-110	3096		0098	0598	2 PWC PW119B	13990	Y30		lsf Millennium Leasing
☐ D-BUSY	Canadair CL-600S (CL-600-1A11) Challenger	1070	N670CL	0082	0193	2 LY ALF502L-2C	18711	Y10-16 / EMS		

NASKE AIR = HC / HCN (formerly Braunschweig-Flug Ortwin R. Naske) — Hannover

Nachtweide 95, D-39124 Magdeburg, Germany ☎ (391) 259 98 55 Tx: none Fax: (391) 259 98 75 SITA: n/a
F: 1976 ☧ 12 Head: Capt. Ortwin R. Naske ICAO: NASKE AIR Net: n/a

☐ D-CBNA	Dassault Falcon 20C	63	PH-LPS	0066		2 GE CF700-2D2	12100	14 Pax		

NIGHTEXPRESS Luftverkehrs, GmbH = EXT — Frankfurt

Geb. 511, Raum 3056, D-60549 Frankfurt-Flughafen, Germany ☎ (69) 69 04 57 51 Tx: none Fax: (69) 69 02 21 01 SITA: n/a
F: 1984 ☧ 15 Head: Matthias Duckart & Yvonne E. Boag ICAO: EXECUTIVE Net: n/a

☐ D-INAB	Cessna 402B	402B0921	N87116	0075		2 CO TSIO-520-E	2858	Freighter		
☐ D-IBEX	Beech 99 Airliner	U-45	N42948	0068	0894	2 PWC PT6A-20	4722	Freighter		
☐ D-IEXB	Beech 99 Airliner	U-70	G-NUIT	0068	0193	2 PWC PT6A-20	4722	Freighter		
☐ D-CCAS	Shorts 360-300 (SD3-60)	SH3737	G-OLBA	0088	1296	2 PWC PT6A-67R	12300	Y35		lst RAS Flug

NORDAVIA Flug, GmbH = NIA — Hamburg

Innocentiastr. 32, D-20144 Hamburg, Germany ☎ (40) 44 00 40 Tx: none Fax: (40) 45 84 33 SITA: HAMNACR
F: 1976 ☧ 8 Head: Helmut C. Heidemann ICAO: NORDAVIA Net: http://www.nordavia.com

☐ D-IBAR	Beech King Air B200	BB-1280		0087	0297	2 PWC PT6A-42	5675	8-9 Pax		lsf Lindner GmbH / jtly opw Westavia

NORTHERN AIR CHARTER, ApS & Co KG = NAG — Flensburg

Flugplatz Schäferhaus, Lecker Chaussee 127, D-24941 Flensburg, Germany ☎ (461) 91 920 Tx: none Fax: (461) 95 279 SITA: n/a
F: 1991 ☧ 3 Head: Heiko Harms ICAO: STARDUST Net: n/a Aircraft below MTOW 1361kg: Cessna 150/177, DH82 & Piper J3C

☐ D-IHBL	Fairchild (Swearingen) SA227TT Merlin 300	TT-512A	N123GM	0082	1298	2 GA TPE331-10U-513G	5670			lsf Egon Oldendorff Ohg
☐ D-CCCC	Fairchild (Swearingen) SA227AT Merlin IVC	AT-511	N600N	0082	0097	2 GA TPE331-11U-611G	6577			lsf Northern Air Freight Vercharterung
☐ G-BXLM	BAe 3108 Jetstream 31	645	PH-KJA	0084	0997	2 GA TPE331-10UG-513H	6899			lsf Jet Partner Aviation Ltd

OFR Ostseeflug Rügen, GmbH — Guettin

Flugplatz Güttin, D-18573 Güttin-Rügen, Germany ☎ (38306) 20 311 Tx: none Fax: (38306) 12 89 SITA: n/a
F: 1996 ☧ n/a Head: Gerhard Kleinert Net: n/a Aircraft below MTOW 1361kg: Cessna 172

☐ D-EBBG	Cessna 207 Skywagon	20700108		0069	0997	1 CO IO-520-F	1724			

OHLAIR Charterflug, GmbH & Co. KG — Kiel

Boelckestr. 100, D-24159 Kiel-Holtenau, Germany ☎ (431) 32 99 50 Tx: none Fax: (431) 329 95 10 SITA: n/a
F: 1981 ☧ 3 Head: Bernd Radeck Net: n/a Aircraft below MTOW 1361 kg: Cessna 172 & Grob G115.

☐ D-GAFY	Cessna 337A Super Skymaster	337-0389		0066		2 CO IO-360-C	1905			
☐ D-IOHL	Cessna 441 Conquest II	441-0357	PH-BMP	0086	1293	2 GA TPE331-8-403S	4468			

OLT Ostfriesische Lufttransport, GmbH = OL / OLT (Associated with OFD-Ostfriesischer Flug Dienst / Subsidiary of EMS, AG) — Emden & Bremen

Postfach 1154, Flugplatz, D-26691 Emden, Germany ☎ (4921) 89 920 Tx: 27884 olteme d Fax: (4921) 89 92 22 SITA: EMEOLLH
F: 1958 ☧ 80 Head: Dip. Kfm. Bernhard W. Brons IATA: 704 ICAO: OLTRA Net: n/a Aircraft below MTOW 1361kg: Cessna 172.
Flights with Metro II aircraft are operated by OLT but under the colours of ROA Roland Air (subsidiary company). For administration details see under ROA.

☐ D-ECDJ	Cessna 207 Skywagon	20700176	N1576U	0070		1 CO IO-520-F	1724	Y6		
☐ D-IFBN	Britten-Norman BN-2B-26 Islander	2185	G-BLNF*	0087	0896	2 LY O-540-E4C5	2812	Y8		
☐ D-IFOX	Britten-Norman BN-2B-26 Islander	2186	G-BLNG*	0087		2 LY O-540-E4C5	2812	Y8		
☐ D-IOLA	Britten-Norman BN-2B-26 Islander	2187	G-BLNH*	0087		2 LY O-540-E4C5	2812	Y8		
☐ D-IBOS	Cessna 404 Titan II	404-0809	SE-IRB	0081		2 CO GTSIO-520-M	3810	Y9		
☐ D-FOLE	Cessna 208B Grand Caravan	208B0523		0096	0496	1 PWC PT6A-114A	3969	Y10		
☐ D-COLB	Fairchild (Swearingen) SA227AC Metro III	AC-754B	N54NE	0090	1196	2 GA TPE331-11U-612G	7257	Y19		opf ROA in ROA colors
☐ D-COLC	Fairchild (Swearingen) SA227AC Metro III	AC-689	N706C	0087	0795	2 GA TPE331-11U-611G	6577	Y18		opf ROA in ROA colors
☐ D-COLD	Fairchild (Swearingen) SA227AC Metro III	AC-421B	SE-LIM	0081	0498	2 GA TPE331-11U-612G	7260	Y19		opf ROA in ROA cs/cvtd 226AT cn AT-070
☐ D-COLT	Fairchild (Swearingen) SA227AC Metro III	AC-690	N715C	0087	0795	2 GA TPE331-11U-611G	6577	Y18		opf ROA in ROA colors

OSTSEEFLUG, GmbH — Rostock-Laage

Flughafen Rostock-Laage, D-18299 Weitendorf, Germany ☎ (38454) 21 125 Tx: none Fax: (38454) 21 126 SITA: n/a
F: 1992 ☧ n/a Head: Wernfried Remae Net: n/a Aircraft below MTOW 1361kg: Cessna 172/177, HOAC DV20 & Socata TB9

☐ D-GIOR	Piper PA-34-200T Seneca II	34-7570119	D-ICOR	0075		2 CO TSIO-360-EB	1999			lsf pvt
☐ D-GUTE	Piper PA-34-200T Seneca II	34-7770382	N44989	0077		2 CO TSIO-360-E	1999			lsf WVPG Wärmeversorgungsgesellschaft

PHOENIX AIR, GmbH = PAM (formerly PAS Phoenix Air Service, GmbH) — Munich

Erlenweg 6, D-85551 Kirchheim, Germany ☎ (89) 97 59 75 50 Tx: none Fax: (89) 97 59 75 52 SITA: n/a
F: 1979 ☧ 8 Head: Bernd Schaufuss ICAO: PHOENIX Net: http://www.phoenixair.com

☐ D-CAPO	Learjet 35A	35A-159	N93CK	0078		2 GA TFE731-2-2B	8301	Executive	EM-AJ	
☐ D-COSY	Learjet 35A	35A-415	N125AX	0081	0197	2 GA TFE731-2-2B	8301	Executive	EM-AK	

PRIVATE WINGS Flugcharter, GmbH — Berlin-Tempelhof

Tempelhofer Damm 1-7 A1, D-12101 Berlin, Germany ☎ (30) 69 51 25 91 Tx: none Fax: (30) 69 51 22 60 SITA: n/a
F: 1991 ☧ 15 Head: Peter Gatz & Andreas Wagner Net: n/a

☐ D-CINA	Beech King Air 350 (B300)	FL-7	N5668F	0090	0098	2 PWC PT6A-60A	6800			lsf AL Aviation Leasing GmbH / CargoPod
☐ D-COLA	Beech King Air 350 (B300)	FL-75	HB-GJB	0092	1197	2 PWC PT6A-60A	6800			lsf AL Aviation Leasing GmbH / CargoPod
☐ D-COKE	Learjet 35A	35A-447	N300FN	0081	0996	2 GA TFE731-2-2B	8300			lsf AL Aviation Leasing GmbH

QUELLE FLUG, GmbH (Subsidiary of Grossversandhaus Quelle Gustav Schickedanz, KG) — Nuremberg

Nürnberger Str. 91-95, D-90762 Fürth, Germany ☎ (911) 529 80 15 Tx: 626851 qu d Fax: (911) 35 60 55 SITA: n/a
F: n/a ☧ n/a Head: n/a Net: n/a

☐ D-CMAD	Learjet 55C	55-143	N10871	0090		2 GA TFE731-3AR-3B	9750			lsf Degenova Beteiligungs GmbH

QUICK AIR JET CHARTER, GmbH = QAJ (Sister company of Quick Air Service, GmbH & Co. Luftfahrt KG) — Cologne

Flughafen Köln/Bonn, Hangar 3, D-51147 Köln, Germany ☎ (2203) 95 57 00 Tx: 8874606 qas d Fax: (2203) 955 70 20 SITA: n/a
F: 1995 ☧ n/a Head: Jürgen Bauch ICAO: DAGOBERT Net: n/a

☐ D-CFTG	Learjet 35A	35A-204	N277AM	0078		2 GA TFE731-2-2B	8300	8 Pax	EP-BD	lsf pvt
☐ D-CJPG	Learjet 35A	35A-108	N86PC	0077		2 GA TFE731-2-2B	8300	8 Pax	HQ-MP	lsf pvt
☐ D-CCGN	Learjet 55	55-017	N760AQ	0081		2 GA TFE731-3AR-2B	9750	8 Pax	BE-AF	lsf pvt

QUICK AIR SERVICE, GmbH & Co. Luftfahrt KG – QAS (Sister company of Quick Air Jet Charter, GmbH) — Cologne

Flughafen Köln/Bonn, Hangar 3, D-51147 Köln, Germany ☎ (2203) 95 57 00 Tx: 8874606 qas d Fax: (2203) 955 70 20 SITA: n/a
F: 1986 ☧ 11 Head: Jürgen Bauch ICAO: DAGOBERT Net: n/a

☐ D-ICDU	Piper PA-31T2 Cheyenne II XL	31T-1166003	N2604R	0084		2 PWC PT6A-135	4297	6 Pax		lsf pvt
☐ D-IQAS	Piper PA-42-1000 Cheyenne 400LS	42-5527022	N551AC	0085	0497	2 GA TPE331-14A-801Y	5468	7 Pax		

RALL-AIR Luftbild, GmbH — Stuttgart

Flughafen, D-70629 Stuttgart, Germany ☎ (711) 948 48 43 Tx: none Fax: (711) 79 35 62 SITA: n/a
F: 1960 ☧ 4 Head: Walter Rall Net: n/a Aircraft below MTOW 1361 kg: Cessna 172.

☐ D-EAWB	Cessna TP206C Super Skylane	P206-0451	N8651Z	0068		1 CO TSIO-520-C	1633	Surveyer		

116 registration type of aircraft cn/fn ex/ex* mfd del powered by mtow kg configuration selcal name/fln/specialitites/remarks

RAS Flug, GmbH = RW / RLD (Subsidiary of LTU Lufttransport-Unternehmen GmbH & Co. KG / formerly RAS Rheinland Air Service, GmbH) — Duesseldorf & Moenchengladbach

Diessemer Bruch 112, D-47805 Krefeld, Germany ☎ (211) 421 66 21 Tx: none Fax: (211) 43 99 14 SITA: n/a
F: 1973 👥 65 Head: Johannes J.T. Turzer IATA: 586 ICAO: RHEINLAND Net: n/a

☐ D-CCAS	Shorts 360-300 (SD3-60)	SH3737	G-OLBA	0088	0193	2 PWC PT6A-67R	12300	Y35		lsf EXT
☐ D-CRAS	Shorts 360-300 (SD3-60)	SH3744	N825BE	0088	0297	2 PWC PT6A-67R	12300	Y35		lsf Shorts

RAS Ruppiner Air Service, GmbH — Berlin-Schoenefeld & Fehrbellin

Betziner Weg, Flugplatz, D-16833 Fehrbellin, Germany ☎ (33932) 71 865 Tx: none Fax: (3393) 35 97 57 SITA: n/a
F: 1994 👥 n/a Head: Frank Hellberg Net: n/a Aircraft below MTOW 1361kg: Cessna 152, HOAC DV20, MS893, TB10 & Zlin Z37

☐ SE-GUF	Cessna U206G Stationair 6	U20603596	N7272N	0077	1097	1 CO IO-520-F	1633			
☐ D-FOND	Antonov An-2P	19508	DDR-SKD	0058		1 SH ASh-62IR	5500			lsf pvt

REGIO-AIR, GmbH - Mecklenburger Flugdienst = RAG — Trollenhagen

Flughafenstrasse, D-17039 Trollenhagen, Germany ☎ (395) 469 19 90 Tx: none Fax: (395) 422 92 91 SITA: n/a
F: 1993 👥 3 Head: Hubert Goller ICAO: GERMAN LINK Net: n/a

☐ D-IBIJ	Cessna 402B	402B0327	YU-BIJ	0073		2 CO TSIO-520-E	2858			lsf pvt

RHEIN-RUHR HELICOPTER Rainer Zemke (Sister company of Elbe Helicopter Rainer Zemke, GmbH & Co. KG) — Moenchengladbach

Flugplatz-Terminal, D-41066 Mönchengladbach, Germany ☎ (2161) 66 66 36 Tx: n/a Fax: (2161) 66 44 06 SITA: n/a
F: 1977 👥 4 Head: Rainer Zemke Net: n/a

☐ D-HASA	Bell 206L-3 LongRanger III	51278	G-SEAN	0089		1 AN 250-C30P	1882			lsf Werit-Kunststoffwerke W. Schneider
☐ D-HEPY	Bell 206L-3 LongRanger III	51260	C-FDFM*	0088		1 AN 250-C30P	1882			lsf SHS Schloemann-Siemag AG
☐ D-HFKB	Bell 206L-1 LongRanger II	45374		0080		1 AN 250-C28B	1882			lsf AL Aviation Leasing GmbH
☐ D-HBEN	Bell 407	53153		0097		1 AN 250-C47B	2268			
☐ D-HMON	Bell 407	53001	N407BT	0096	0199	1 AN 250-C47B	2268			
☐ D-HARO	Eurocopter (MBB) BO105CBS-4	S-831	OE-XFS	0090		2 AN 250-C20B	2500			lsf AL Aviation Leasing GmbH
☐ D-HTIB	Eurocopter (MBB) BK117A-3	7022	EC-EZT	0083	0998	2 LY LTS101-650B.1	3200			
☐ D-HCAN	Bell 222UT	47548	N222HW	0085	0496	2 LY LTS101-750C.1	3742			lsf AL Aviation Leasing GmbH
☐ D-HTEN	Bell 222U	47549	JA9628	0086	0996	2 LY LTS101-750C.1	3560			lsf Raiffeisen Bank Waidring

RH-FLUGDIENST, GmbH — Aschaffenburg & Michelstadt

Weinberg Str. 28, D-64823 Gross-Umstadt, Germany ☎ (6078) 73 306 Tx: none Fax: (6078) 73 900 SITA: n/a
F: 1997 👥 8 Head: Dr. Gerhard Illing & Veit Illing Net: n/a

☐ D-HILV	MD Helicopters MD 500E (Hughes 369E)	0323E	HB-XVF	0089	1097	1 AN 250-C20R2	1361			
☐ D-HLIA	MD Helicopters MD 500D (Hughes 369D)	500717D	N1099Z	0080	1097	1 AN 250-C20B	1361			lsf LGS Leasing GmbH
☐ D-ILEN	Cessna T303 Crusader	T30300301	N5526V	0084		2 CO TSIO-520-AE	2336			

RIEKER AIR SERVICE, GmbH — Stuttgart

Postfach 23 03 28, D-70623 Stuttgart, Germany ☎ (711) 948 44 04 Tx: none Fax: (711) 948 44 05 SITA: n/a
F: 1976 👥 10 Head: Harald Rieker Net: n/a

☐ D-IEIR	Cessna 501 Citation I/SP	501-0259	N501MS	0083	0591	2 PWC JT15D-1A	5375			
☐ D-IEAR	Cessna 551 Citation II/SP	551-0018	N387MA	0079		2 PWC JT15D-4	5670			

RK-FLUGDIENST (Reservisten-Kameradschaft/Reservistenverband der Bundeswehr dba) — Uetersen

Haderslebenerstr. 19, D-25421 Pinneberg, Germany ☎ (4101) 79 750 Tx: none Fax: (4101) 79 75 29 SITA: n/a
F: 1998 👥 n/a Head: Hagen Hamm Net: n/a Operates historical show- & nostalgia charter-flights with vintage aircraft. Is doing also goodwill-publicity for the German Army and the Flying Service towards the young generation.

☐ D-ICDY	Dornier DO 28D-2 Skyservant	4164	58+89	0073	0698	2 LY IGSO-540-A1E	3862			

ROA Roland Air, Flugverkehrs- & Vertriebs GmbH (Subsidiary of OLT Ostfriesische Lufttransport GmbH) — Bremen

Hermann Köhl Strasse, Flughafendamm, D-28199 Bremen, Germany ☎ (421) 55 55 90 Tx: none Fax: (421) 55 30 92 SITA: BREOLLH
F: 1990 👥 5 Head: Dipl. Kfm. Gerd Weber Net: n/a
Flights (with 3 Metro II aircraft) are operated by OLT under OL flight numbers but under the marketing name & colours of ROA. ROA is acting as handling agent at Bremen.

☐ D-COLB	Fairchild (Swearingen) SA227AC Metro III	AC-754B	N54NE	0090	1196	2 GA TPE331-11U-612G	7257	Y19		opb OLT in ROA colors
☐ D-COLC	Fairchild (Swearingen) SA227AC Metro III	AC-689	N706C	0087	0795	2 GA TPE331-11U-611G	6577	Y18		opb OLT in ROA colors
☐ D-COLD	Fairchild (Swearingen) SA227AC Metro III	AC-421B	SE-LIM	0081	0498	2 GA TPE331-11U-612G	7260	Y19		opb OLT in ROA cs/cvtd 226AT cn AT-070
☐ D-COLT	Fairchild (Swearingen) SA227AC Metro III	AC-690	N715C	0087	0795	2 GA TPE331-11U-611G	6577	Y18		opb OLT in ROA colors

ROTORFLUG, GmbH — Friedrichsdorf-Heliport Burgholzhausen

Postfach 1428, D-61365 Friedrichsdorf, Germany ☎ (6007) 10 32 Tx: none Fax: (6007) 71 61 SITA: n/a
F: 1972 👥 19 Head: Klaus Walther & Karl Mannheim Net: n/a

☐ D-HARD	Bell 206B JetRanger	486	N2288W	0069		1 AN 250-C20	1450	4 Pax		lsf Diskont & Kredit AG / cvtd 206A
☐ D-HOCH	Agusta-Bell 206B JetRanger III	8405	G-BHSM	0074	0097	1 AN 250-C20B	1450	4 Pax		lsf IGW Leasing GmbH / cvtd JetRanger
☐ D-HONY	Bell 206B JetRanger III	2433	N5002U	0078		1 AN 250-C20B	1450	4 Pax		lsf Diskont & Kredit AG
☐ D-HOON	Agusta-Bell 206B JetRanger III	8597		0080		1 AN 250-C20B	1450	4 Pax		lsf Diskont & Kredit AG
☐ D-HORG	Agusta-Bell 206B JetRanger	8375	G-BBXN	0069		1 AN 250-C20	1450	4 Pax		lsf pvt
☐ D-HRFB	Bell 206B JetRanger III	3665	G-OPWL	0082	0492	1 AN 250-C20J	1450	4 Pax		lsf pvt
☐ D-HAAC	Agusta A109C MAX	7642	N1FD	0091	0192	2 AN 250-C20R/1	2720	EMS		lsf pvt
☐ D-HAAP	Agusta A109C	7617	JA9987	0090	1096	2 AN 250-C20R/1	2720	6 Pax		lsf pvt
☐ D-HAMF	Agusta A109A	7217	N77HG	0081	0691	2 AN 250-C20B	2600	6 Pax / EMS		lsf AL Aviation Leasing
☐ D-HAZI	Agusta A109A II	7303	N109MB	0083		2 AN 250-C20B	2600	6 Pax / EMS		
☐ D-HFMW	Agusta A109A II	7307	G-JLCY	0083	0391	2 AN 250-C20B	2600	6 Pax / EMS		lsf pvt
☐ D-HLAT	Agusta A109C	7612	3A-MIS	0089	0097	2 AN 250-C20R/1	2720	6 Pax		lsf LAT Fernmelde-Montagen
☐ D-HMOD	Agusta A109A	7139	SE-HGM	0078	0995	2 AN 250-C20B	2600	6 Pax / EMS		lsf AL Aviation Leasing GmbH

RWL-Luftfahrtgesellschaft, mbH & Co. KG = RWL — Moenchengladbach

Flugplatz, RWL-Center, D-41066 Mönchengladbach, Germany ☎ (2161) 68 900 Tx: 852193 rwl d Fax: (2161) 68 90 90 SITA: n/a
F: 1972 👥 42 Head: Werner Küper ICAO: RHEINTRAINER Net: n/a Aircraft below MTOW 1361 kg: Cessna 150, 152, 172, 182 & Piper PA-28.

☐ D-GACH	Piper PA-44-180 Seminole	44-7995292	OE-FBN	0079	0498	2 LY O-360-E1A6D	1724			
☐ D-GOFW	Piper PA-44-180 Seminole	44-7995123	N3011C	0079		2 LY O-360-E1A6D	1724			
☐ D-GWPL	Piper PA-34-220T Seneca III	34-8433005	N4323Y	0083	0397	2 CO TSIO-360-KB	1999			
☐ D-GEMC	Partenavia P.68B	200		0079		2 LY IO-360-A1B6	1960			lsf pvt
☐ D-IJGW	Cessna 425 Conquest I	425-0193	N1221X	0084		2 PWC PT6A-112	3900			lsf Tobaccoland GmbH

SAFARI AIR (Rolf Schauss Flugdienst, GmbH dba) — Saarlouis-Dueren

Flugplatz Saarlouis-Düren, D-66798 Wallerfangen, Germany ☎ (172) 682 23 34 Tx: none Fax: (6837) 16 00 SITA: n/a
F: 1992 👥 1 Head: Rolf Schauss Net: n/a

☐ D-FAIR	Antonov An-2	17205	LSK 450	0057	0892	1 SH ASh-62IR	5500	9 Pax		lsf Excolo Kunststoffverwertung GmbH

SENATOR AVIATION Charter, GmbH = SNA — Hamburg, Koeln & Berlin-Tempelhof

Geschäftsfliegerzentrum, Hamburg Flughafen, Geb. 347, D-22335 Hamburg, Germany ☎ (40) 50 05 35 70 Tx: none Fax: (40) 50 75 10 89 SITA: CGNSACR
F: 1985 👥 13 Head: Michael Hitgen ICAO: SENATOR Net: http://www.guides.com/acg/senator

☐ D-CFCF	Learjet 35A	35A-413	N27KG	0081		2 GA TFE731-2-2B	8300			lsf Sybera GmbH
☐ D-CITY	Learjet 35A	35A-177	N174CP	0078		2 GA TFE731-2-2B	8300		BM-AH	lsf pvt

SFD Stuttgarter Flugdienst, GmbH (Affiliated with ContactAir) — Stuttgart

Postfach 23 01 06, D-70621 Stuttgart, Germany ☎ (711) 990 50 96 Tx: none Fax: (711) 990 50 98 SITA: n/a
F: 1954 👥 8 Head: Bernd Pleuger Net: http://www.stuttgarterflugdienst.de

☐ D-IBAD	Beech King Air B200	BB-1229		0085		2 PWC PT6A-42	5670	9 Pax		lsf Eheim GmbH & Co. KG
☐ D-CSFD	Cessna S550 Citation S/II	S550-0148	ZS-IDC	0088	1297	2 PWC JT15D-4B	6900	9 Pax		lsf Eheim GmbH & Co. KG
☐ D-ILAN	Cessna 551 Citation II/SP	551-0614		0089	0195	2 PWC JT15D-4	5670	8 Pax		lsf Eheim GmbH & Co. KG
☐ D-CHDE	Cessna 560 Citation V	560-0031	N1229F	0089	0097	2 PWC JT15D-5A	7212	8 Pax		lsf BBP-Kunststoffwerk Marbach Baier

SFS Siebertz Flight Service (formerly Luftfahrerschule Hans Langenbach Luftfahrtunternehmen) — Dinslaken/Schwarze Heide

Flugplatz Dinslaken/Schwarze Heide, D-46569 Hünxe, Germany ☎ (2858) 473 Tx: none Fax: (2858) 82 833 SITA: n/a
F: 1975 👥 8 Head: Peter Siebertz Net: n/a Aircraft below MTOW 1361kg: Cessna 150/172, DA20 Katana, Piper PA-28 & Robin 2160

☐ D-ECKA	Beech Bonanza P35	D-7194		0063	1088	1 CO IO-470-N	1417	3 Pax		
☐ D-GETT	Piper PA-34-200T Seneca II	34-7770376	D-IETT	0077	0598	2 CO TSIO-360-E	1999	4 Pax		lsf pvt
☐ D-FKMB	Antonov An-2	17308	LSK-451	0057	0493	1 SH ASh-62IR	5250	9 Pax		silencer System Gomolzig
☐ D-FKMD	Antonov An-2	17812	LSK-456	0057	0494	1 SH ASh-62IR	5250	9 Pax		silencer system Gomolzig

SGDA-Luftfahrtunternehmen (Division of SGDA-Sanierungsgesellschaft für Deponien & Altlasten mbH) — Zella-Mehlis Heliport

Bahnhofstr. 65, D-98544 Zella-Mehlis, Germany ☎ (3682) 89 04 10 Tx: none Fax: (3682) 89 04 11 SITA: n/a
F: 1996 👥 n/a Head: Wolfgang Marr Net: n/a

☐ D-HSGD	Bell 206B JetRanger III	3119	N5754J	0080		1 AN 250-C20B	1450			

117 registration type of aircraft cn/fn ex/ex* mfd del powered by mtow kg configuration selcal name/fln/specialitites/remarks

SILVER BIRD Charterflug, OHG (Sister company of Flugschule Silver Bird, e.V.)
Flughafen, GAT, D-28199 Bremen, Germany ☎ (421) 55 66 12 Tx: none Fax: (421) 55 67 87 SITA: n/a
Bremen
F: 1995 ♦♦♦ 5 Head: Peter Döllner Net: n/a

registration	type of aircraft	cn/fn	ex/ex*	mfd	del	powered by	mtow kg	configuration	name/fln/specialitites/remarks
☐ D-IFFI	Cessna 421C Golden Eagle II	421C0107	SE-IKU	0076		2 CO GTSIO-520-L	3379		lsf pvt
☐ D-IDIX	Beech King Air C90B	LJ-1495	N919SA	0097	0398	2 PWC PT6A-21	4581		lsf Friedel Dix KG
☐ D-ITLL	Beech King Air F90	LA-192	N17TS	0083	1098	2 PWC PT6A-135	4967		lsf Tamsen Vermögensverwaltung

SILVER CLOUD AIR, GmbH (formerly BFS Business Flugservice, GmbH)
Waldspitzweg 3, D-67105 Schifferstadt, Germany ☎ (6235) 93 03 33 Tx: none Fax: (6235) 93 02 46 SITA: n/a
Speyer
F: 1994 ♦♦♦ 2 Head: Alfred Kirstein Net: http://www.sc-cir.de

☐ D-IHEB	Cessna 525 CitationJet	525-0064		0094		2 WRR FJ44-1A	4717		lsf Fortuna-Werbung GmbH
☐ D-IBFS	Beech King Air B200	BB-1349	N200KG	0090		2 PWC PT6A-42	5675		lsf Heberger-Bau GmbH

SKY JET FLUGSERVICE, GmbH & Co. KG
Augustaplatz 8, D-76530 Baden-Baden, Germany ☎ (7221) 36 601 Tx: none Fax: (7221) 38 822 SITA: n/a
Karlsruhe/Baden-Baden
F: 1976 ♦♦♦ n/a Head: Karlheinz Kögel Net: n/a

☐ VP-CKK	Beech Beechjet 400A	RK-200	N200NA*	0098	1098	2 PWC JT15D-5	7303		

SKYLINE FLIGHTS, GmbH = SLF
Postfach 420265, D-30662 Hannover-Flughafen, Germany ☎ (511) 73 70 00 Tx: 210464 skyl d Fax: (511) 73 85 06 SITA: HAJSKYX
Hannover
F: 1997 ♦♦♦ 10 Head: Wolfgang Schwark ICAO: SKYSHIP Net: http://www.skyline-flights.de

☐ D-ICGA	Piper PA-31T2 Cheyenne II XL	31T-8166056	N550TL	0082	0299	2 PWC PT6A-135	4297		
☐ D-ICGB	Piper PA-42-720 Cheyenne IIIA	42-5501007	N834CM	0084	0299	2 PWC PT6A-61	5080		
☐ D-IHLA	Piper PA-42-720 Cheyenne IIIA	42-5501001	N842PC	0083	0299	2 PWC PT6A-61	5080		
☐ D-CWAY	Learjet 55	55-107	N304AT	0084	0297	2 GA TFE731-3AR-2B	9750		lsf SüdLeasing GmbH

SKYLINE HELICOPTER Flugbetriebs, GmbH
Buchwaldstr. 23, D-63303 Dreieich, Germany ☎ (6103) 94 76 26 Tx: none Fax: (6103) 94 76 25 SITA: n/a
Egelsbach
F: 1996 ♦♦♦ 5 Head: Michael Bitschnau Net: n/a

☐ D-HHMP	Bell 206B JetRanger III	3823		0084		1 AN 250-C20J	1450		lsf pvt

SKYTEAM, GmbH = XST (Subsidiary of E.C.C.S. Air & Cargo Service, GmbH)
Kleiner Kornweg 26-28, D-65451 Kelsterbach, Germany ☎ (6107) 77 000 Tx: none Fax: (6107) 77 00 19 SITA: n/a
Frankfurt
F: 1998 ♦♦♦ n/a Head: Manfed Nimführ ICAO: SKYTEAM Net: n/a

☐ D-ACCS	Fokker F27 Friendship 500 (F27 Mk500)	10434	N981MA	0070	0398	2 RR Dart 532-7R	20820	Freighter	
☐ D-ADUP	Fokker F27 Friendship 500 (F27 Mk500)	10686	OE-IPN	0085	0698	2 RR Dart 552-7R	20820	Y50	lsf A.R.P. Aviation B.V.

SLS Saechsische Luftfahrt-Service, GmbH
Postfach 25, D-01917 Kamenz, Germany ☎ (3578) 31 50 57 Tx: none Fax: (3578) 31 50 94 SITA: n/a
Kamenz SLS SÄCHSISCHE LUFTFAHRT
F: 1991 ♦♦♦ n/a Head: Claus Rippl Net: n/a Aircraft below MTOW 1361kg: Zlin 43

☐ D-ICAL	Cessna T310Q	310Q0250	N7750Q	0071		2 CO TSIO-520-B	2495		lsf Nagel Ingenieur-Bau-GmbH
☐ D-FKMA	Antonov An-2T	117411	LSK 440	0062	0292	1 SH ASh-62IR	5500		

S.P. HELICOPTER SERVICE, GmbH (formerly S.P. Luftbild, GmbH)
Heliport, PO Box 29, D-53541 Linz/Rhein, Germany ☎ (2644) 56 080 Tx: none Fax: (2644) 56 08 40 SITA: n/a
Dattenberg
F: 1975 ♦♦♦ 75 Head: Heinz-Josef Schneider Net: n/a Aircraft below MTOW 1361 kg: Hughes 269B (300B) & Hughes 269C (300C).

☐ D-HSPO	MD Helicopters MD 500E (Hughes 369E)	0207E	HA-MSF	0087	0294	1 AN 250-C20R2	1361		lsf Diskont & Kredit AG
☐ D-HUTE	MD Helicopters MD 500E (Hughes 369E)	0203E	HA-MSB	0087	0294	1 AN 250-C20B	1361		
☐ D-HCOL	Eurocopter (Aerosp.) AS350B2 Ecureuil	2814	F-WYMI*	0094	1094	1 TU Arriel 1D1	2250		lsf Diskont & Kredit AG
☐ D-HERI	Eurocopter (Aerosp.) AS350B2 Ecureuil	2827	N60972	0094	0795	1 TU Arriel 1D1	2250		Erich / lsf Diskont & Kredit AG

S.P. LUFTBILD, GmbH (Subsidiary of S.P. Helicopter Service, GmbH)
Bassenheimerstrasse, D-56648 Saffig, Germany ☎ (33731) 15 325 Tx: none Fax: (33731) 15 217 SITA: n/a
Saffig
F: 1991 ♦♦♦ n/a Head: Andreas Klein Net: n/a Aircraft below MTOW 1361kg: Hughes 269C (300C).

☐ D-HMMW	Eurocopter (Aerosp.) AS350B2 Ecureuil	2727	F-WYMT*	0093	0993	1 TU Arriel 1D1	2250		

SYLT FLUGCHARTER, GmbH
Keitumer Landstrasse 5-7, D-25980 Tinnum (Sylt), Germany ☎ (4651) 25 656 Tx: none Fax: (4651) 29 190 SITA: n/a
Westerland-Sylt
F: 1981 ♦♦♦ n/a Head: Bernd Hake Net: n/a

☐ D-IAHB	Cessna 414	414-0547	N1990G	0074		2 CO TSIO-520-J	2880		lsf pvt
☐ D-IAVB	Cessna 525 CitationJet	525-0172	N172CJ	0097	0797	2 WRR FJ44-1A	4717		lsf AVB Vermietung

TAG Teuto Airways Germany, AG = TEU (Sister company of Teuto Air)
Flughafenstr. 33, D-33142 Büren-Ahden, Germany ☎ (2955) 79 90 01 Tx: none Fax: (2955) 77 47 40 SITA: n/a
Paderborn
F: 1998 ♦♦♦ n/a Head: Klaus Müller ICAO: TEUTO AIR Net: n/a

☐ D-CTAG	Shorts 330-100 (SD3-30 Variant 100)	SH3042	G-BHHU	0080	0895	2 PWC PT6A-45R	10250	Freighter	lsf EBR GmbH

TAL Transair Luftreederei, GmbH (Associated with RAS Flug, GmbH)
Postfach 4063, D-40851 Ratingen, Germany ☎ (2102) 93 25 15 Tx: none Fax: (2102) 93 25 20 SITA: n/a
Duesseldorf
F: 1980 ♦♦♦ 5 Head: Peter Eichhof Net: n/a

☐ D-IKAF	Cessna 421B Golden Eagle	421B0377	OE-FLD	0073		2 CO GTSIO-520-H	3379		lsf pvt

TAUNUS AIR, GmbH & Co KG = TAQ
Fischer Strasse 7, D-65187 Wiesbaden, Germany ☎ (611) 84 00 96 Tx: none Fax: (611) 84 00 66 SITA: n/a
Frankfurt *taunus air*
F: 1990 ♦♦♦ 12 Head: Georg Pätzold & Bernd Jung ICAO: TAUNUSAIR Net: n/a

☐ D-CCAY	Learjet 35A	35A-112	N3810G	0077		2 GA TFE731-2-2B	8300	Executive	lsf G. Pätzold Flugzeugvermietung
☐ D-CCCA	Learjet 35A	35A-160		0078		2 GA TFE731-2-2B	8300	Executive	lsf G. Pätzold Flugzeugvermietung
☐ D-CGRC	Learjet 35A	35A-223	N215JW	0079	0591	2 GA TFE731-2-2B	8300	Photo / Survey	lsf G. Pätzold Flugzeugvermietung

TEMPELHOF EXPRESS, GmbH – TEX = FC / SBY (formerly TAL Thuringia Airlines, GmbH)
Flughafen Berlin-Tempelhof, Gebäudeteil A1, Raum 2651, D-12101 Berlin, Germany ☎ (30) 69 51 30 60 Tx: none Fax: (30) 69 51 30 61 SITA: ERFOWFC
Berlin-Tempelhof
F: 1996 ♦♦♦ 21 Head: Henning Romberg IATA: 859 ICAO: BRANDY Net: n/a

☐ D-CATS	Dornier 328-110	3009		0094	0197	2 PWC PW119B	13990	Y30	lsf pvt / cvtd-100

TERRA-BILDMESSFLUG, GmbH
Schumannstr. 21, D-71672 Marbach, Germany ☎ (7144) 83 12 44 Tx: none Fax: (7144) 83 12 46 SITA: n/a
Aalen
F: 1992 ♦♦♦ n/a Head: Ulrich Sach Net: n/a

☐ D-ELYK	Cessna TU206G Turbo Stationair 6 II	U20606285	N6466Z	0081		1 CO TSIO-520-M	1633	Photo / Survey	lsf VR-Leasing GmbH
☐ D-IGPS	Cessna T303 Crusader	T30300308	N303PK	0084	0195	2 CO TSIO-520-AE	2336	Photo / Survey	

TEUTO AIR Lufttransporte, GmbH (Sister co. of TAG Teuto Airways Germany, AG / formerly Teuto Air Luftaxi, GmbH)
Flughafenstr. 33, D-33142 Büren-Ahden, Germany ☎ (2955) 79 9001 Tx: none Fax: (2955) 77 4740 SITA: n/a
Paderborn
F: 1971 ♦♦♦ 5 Head: Klaus Müller Net: n/a

☐ D-HHSW	Bell 206L-1 LongRanger II	45193	G-DWMI	0078	0098	1 AN 250-C28B	1882		lsf EBR Vertriebs GmbH
☐ D-HASI	Bell 407	53062		0096	1296	1 AN 250-C47B	2268		lsf Diskont & Kredit AG

THENAIR, KG
Obererlachenweg 7, D-96145 Sesslach-Gemünda, Germany ☎ (9567) 226 Tx: none Fax: (9567) 242 SITA: n/a
Coburg & Erfurt THENAIR
F: 1956 ♦♦♦ 5 Head: Heinrich Then Net: n/a

☐ D-IMTM	Cessna 551 Citation II/SP	551-0009	N1959E	0079		2 PWC JT15D-4	5670		dmgd 290896/being repaired/restored

TOPOGRAMM Gesellschaft für Erderkundung & Rauminformation, mbH
Salzgraben 2, D-82362 Weilheim, Germany ☎ (881) 93 100 Tx: n/a Fax: (881) 93 10 27 SITA: n/a
Oberpfaffenhofen
F: 1988 ♦♦♦ 8 Head: Dr. H. Schmidt von Braun Net: n/a

☐ D-	Dornier 228-100					2 GA TPE331-5-252D	5670	Exper./Research	oo-delivery 0099

TRANSAER COLOGNE, GmbH (Subsidiary of Transaer International Airlines Ltd, Ireland)
Postfach 980246, D-51130 Koeln, Germany ☎ (2203) 40 47 40 Tx: none Fax: (2203) 40 47 43 SITA: n/a
Cologne
F: 1998 ♦♦♦ n/a Head: Alexander Schmitz & Mal Corrigan Net: http://www.transaer.de

☐ EI-TLR	Airbus Industrie A320-231	414	B-HYR	0093	0499	2 IAE V2500-A1	75500	Y180	lsf TLA

TRANSAVIA Luftfahrtunternehmen, GmbH — Worms

Flugplatz Worms, D-67346 Speyer, Germany ☎ (6241) 88 775 Tx: 461300 d Fax: (6241) 88 775 SITA: n/a
F: 1986 15 Head: Hans J. Deyerler Net: n/a Aircraft below MTOW 1361kg: Cessna 150/172 & Piper PA-28.

☐ D-GGRO	Piper PA-34-200T Seneca II	34-7570322	N4354X	0075		2 CO TSIO-360-E	1999			
☐ D-IDVL	Beech Queen Air 65	LC-148		0062	0292	2 LY IGSO-480-A1B6	3493			
☐ D-IDEY	Beech Queen Air 65-88	LP-5	N881E	0066		2 LY IGSO-540-A1D	3992			
☐ D-IDAK	Beech King Air C90	LJ-647	LX-DAK	0075		2 PWC PT6A-20A	4377			lsf Air 7 SA

TRAVEL AIR Flug, GmbH & Co. KG = TAX (Subsidiary of EFS Flug Service, GmbH) — Duesseldorf

Flughafen, Halle 1, D-40474 Düsseldorf, Germany ☎ (211) 43 30 40 Tx: 8586280 efs d Fax: (211) 421 66 01 SITA: n/a
F: 1978 2 Head: Jürgen Böck ICAO: TRAVEL AIR Net: n/a Operates airtaxi/charter flights with Cessna 500/551 Citation aircraft leased from EFS Flug Service when required.

TRIPLE ALPHA Avianti Aviation Aachen Luftfahrtges. mbH — Moenchengladbach / Duesseldorf & Cologne-Bonn

Schumanstr. 29, D-52146 Würselen, Germany ☎ (2405) 44 670 Tx: none Fax: (2405) 44 67 20 SITA: n/a
F: 1996 10 Head: Hans Pfeiffer & Erik Scheidt ICAO: CAROLUS Net: n/a

☐ D-GIXB	Piper PA-34-220T Seneca III	34-8233151	SE-IXB	0082		2 CO TSIO-360-KB	1999			lsf pvt
☐ D-GZZZ	Piper PA-34-200T Seneca II	34-7970490		0079		2 CO TSIO-360-EB	1999			lsf pvt
☐ D-IWET	Cessna 421C Golden Eagle III	421C1257	TC-BKT	0082	0298	2 CO GTSIO-520-NB	3379			lsf pvt
☐ D-IKOP	Cessna 525 CitationJet	525-0016	N216CJ	0093		2 WRR FJ44-1A	4717			lsf Bau & Umwelttechnologie Kahlen

VHM Schul- und Charterflug, GmbH (Die Regenbogenflotte) — Essen-Muelheim

Brunshofstrasse 1, D-45470 Mülheim/Ruhr, Germany ☎ (208) 99 23 40 Tx: 856313 vhm d Fax: (208) 992 35 20 SITA: n/a
F: 1976 10 Head: Dipl. Ing. Wolfgang Vautz Net: n/a Aircraft below MTOW 1361 kg: Cessna 152, 172, Enstrom F28F, Socata TB9 / TB200 & Hot air balloons Cameron 4000 & Schroeder 3000

☐ D-EVHM	Socata TB 20 Trinidad	1837		0098	0498	1 LY IO-540-C4D5D	1400			
☐ D-EVTZ	Socata TB 20 Trinidad	1767		0096	0496	1 LY IO-540-C4D5D	1400			
☐ D-EWVZ	Socata TB 20 Trinidad	1711		0095	0795	1 LY IO-540-C4D5D	1400			
☐ D-GIGI	Piper PA-34-220T Seneca III	34-8233117	HB-LNF	0082		2 CO TSIO-360-KB	1999			
☐ D-INAL	Cessna 414A Chancellor III	414A0500		0080		2 CO TSIO-520-NB	3062			
☐ D-INOS	Cessna 421C Golden Eagle III	421C1252	N6787L	0082		2 CO GTSIO-520-N	3379			lsf GFK Mobilien GmbH
☐ D-IVHM	Beech King Air B200	BB-1369	N778HP	0090	0296	2 PWC PT6A-42	5670			
☐ D-IVHN	Beech King Air B200	BB-1124	N678EB	0083	0498	2 PWC PT6A-42	5670			

VIBRO AIR FLUGSERVICE, GmbH (formerly Allkauf Flugservice, GmbH) — Moenchengladbach

Reyerhütte 51, D-41065 Mönchengladbach, Germany ☎ (2161) 66 32 52 Tx: none Fax: (2161) 66 48 01 SITA: n/a
F: 1994 n/a Head: Michael Viehof Net: n/a

☐ D-IALL	Cessna 525 CitationJet	525-0143	D-IOMP	0096	0797	2 WRR FJ44-1A	4717			lsf Vibro Beteiligungs GmbH
☐ D-IAFF	Beech King Air C90A	LJ-1229	N422TW	0090		2 PWC PT6A-21	4581			lsf Vibro Beteiligungs GmbH
☐ D-IAKK	Beech King Air B200	BB-1265	N550TF	0087		2 PWC PT6A-42	5675			lsf Vibro Beteiligungs GmbH
☐ D-ITAB	Beech King Air B200	BB-1166	N717RM	0083		2 PWC PT6A-42	5675			lsf Trajan-Bauregie GmbH

WDL Aviation, GmbH = WDL (Sister company of Westdeutsche Luftwerbung Theodor Wüllenkemper GmbH & Co. KG) — Cologne & Essen-Muelheim & Frankfurt

Postfach 98 02 67, D-51130 Köln, Germany ☎ (2203) 96 70 Tx: 8874690 d Fax: (2203) 96 71 05 SITA: CGNWECR
F: 1991 n/a Head: Walter Böhnke ICAO: WDL Net: n/a

☐ D-CVIP	Learjet 55	55-109	N348HM	0084	0798	2 GA TFE731-3AR-2B	9752	Y7		
☐ D-ADEP	Fokker F27 Friendship 600 (F27 Mk600)	10318	OY-CCK	0067	0998	2 RR Dart 532-7	20412	Freighter		
☐ D-ADOP	Fokker F27 Friendship 600 (F27 Mk600)	10316	OY-BVF	0067	0694	2 RR Dart 532-7	20450	Freighter		Bassan
☐ D-AELC	Fokker F27 Friendship 600 (F27 Mk600)	10438	OY-SLG	0070	0991	2 RR Dart 532-7	20410	Freighter		
☐ D-AELD	Fokker F27 Friendship 600 (F27 Mk600)	10442	OY-SLF	0070	0791	2 RR Dart 532-7	20410	Freighter		Jägermeister
☐ D-AELE	Fokker F27 Friendship 600 (F27 Mk600)	10477	OY-SLE	0072	0491	2 RR Dart 532-7	20410	Freighter		
☐ D-AELF	Fokker F27 Friendship 600 (F27 Mk600)	10323	PH-FKT	0067	1193	2 RR Dart 532-7	20410	Freighter		
☐ D-AELG	Fokker F27 Friendship 400 (F27 Mk400)	10338	VR-BLZ	0067	1193	2 RR Dart 532-7	20410	Freighter		
☐ D-AELH	Fokker F27 Friendship 400 (F27 Mk400)	10340	VR-BLX	0067	0794	2 RR Dart 532-7	20410	Freighter		Jule
☐ D-AELI	Fokker F27 Friendship 600 (F27 Mk600)	10514	N60AN	0075	1194	2 RR Dart 532-7	20410	Freighter		
☐ D-AELJ	Fokker F27 Friendship 600 (F27 Mk600)	10342	F-BYAB	0067	0695	2 RR Dart 532-7	20410	Freighter		
☐ D-AELK	Fokker F27 Friendship 600 (F27 Mk600)	10361	F-GCJV	0068	0795	2 RR Dart 532-7	20410	Freighter		Petra
☐ D-AELM	Fokker F27 Friendship 600 (F27 Mk600)	10450	OY-CCL	0070	1297	2 RR Dart 532-7	20410	Freighter		
☐ D-AISY	Fokker F27 Friendship 600 (F27 Mk600)	10391	OY-CCR	0069	0598	2 RR Dart 532-7	20410	Freighter		
☐ D-BAKB	Fokker F27 Friendship 600 (F27 Mk600)	10261	F-GHRC	0064	0595	2 RR Dart 532-7	19730	Freighter		cvtd -200
☐ D-BAKC	Fokker F27 Friendship 600 (F27 Mk600)	10195	F-GFJS	0062	1095	2 RR Dart 532-7	19730	Freighter		
☐ D-BAKD	Fokker F27 Friendship 600 (F27 Mk600)	10179	F-GKJC	0061	0196	2 RR Dart 532-7	19370	Freighter		lst White Eagle as SP-FNF / cvtd -200
☐ D-AWDL	BAe 146-100	E1011	G-UKJF	0083	0798	4 LY ALF502R-5	37308	Y73		
☐ D-AWUE	BAe 146-200	E2050	PK-PJP	0086	0199	4 LY ALF502R-5	42184	Y98		

WDL Luftschiff, GmbH (Sister company of Westdeutsche Luftwerbung Theodor Wüllenkemper GmbH & Co. KG/formerly WDL Flugdienst GmbH) — Essen-Muelheim

Flughafen Essen-Mülheim, D-45470 Mülheim-Ruhr, Germany ☎ (208) 37 80 80 Tx: 856810 wdl d Fax: (208) 378 08 33 SITA: n/a
F: 1955 n/a Head: Theodor Wüllenkemper Net: n/a Aircraft below MTOW 1361kg: Cessna 172 & Piper PA-18

☐ D-LDFO	Luftschiff WDL 1	101A	JA1002*	0081		2 CO IO-360-C	5443	Advertising		Fuji titles
☐ D-LDFQ	Luftschiff WDL 1B	106	JA1007	0089	0895	2 CO IO-360-CB	6212	Advertising		
☐ D-LDFR	Luftschiff WDL 1B	107	JA1008	0090	0893	2 CO IO-360-CB	6212	Advertising		

WESTAVIA, GmbH (Subsidiary of Nordavia Flug, GmbH / formerly Borussia Flug, GmbH) — Moenchengladbach

Flughafen Terminal, D-41066 Mönchengladbach, Germany ☎ (2161) 66 56 23 Tx: 852222 fmgh d Fax: (2161) 66 59 54 SITA: n/a
F: 1982 3 Head: Rolf Schumann Net: n/a

☐ D-IHAK	Cessna 421C Golden Eagle II	421C0128	N3876C	0076		2 CO GTSIO-520-L	3379			lsf pvt
☐ D-IBAR	Beech King Air B200	BB-1280		0087		2 PWC PT6A-42	5675			jtly opw Nordavia Flug

WESTFLUG AACHEN Luftfahrt, GmbH = WFA — Aachen-Merzbrueck

Flugplatz Merzbrück, D-52146 Würselen, Germany ☎ (2405) 48 510 Tx: n/a Fax: (2405) 48 51 87 SITA: n/a
F: 1963 28 Head: Walter Kampsmann ICAO: WESTFLUG Net: http://www.westflug.ac/net.de Aircraft below MTOW 1361 kg: Cessna 150, 152, 172, HOAC DU20 & Piper PA-28

☐ D-GCCF	Piper PA-34-200T Seneca II	34-8070001	N45123	0080		2 CO TSIO-360-EB	1999			lsf pvt
☐ D-ICLY	Cessna T303 Crusader	T30300159	N6588C	0082		2 CO TSIO-520-AE	2336			lsf pvt
☐ D-IVIN	Cessna 525 CitationJet	525-0188		0097		2 WRR FJ44-1A	4717			lsf FL-Air Luftfahrt GmbH & Co.

WESTKUESTENFLUG Lange, GmbH — Wyk auf Foehr

Flugplatz, D-25938 Wyk auf Föhr, Germany ☎ (4681) 81 39 Tx: none Fax: (4681) 26 70 SITA: n/a
F: 1985 2 Head: Oluf Lange Net: n/a Aircraft below MTOW 1361 kg: Cessna 172 & Maule MX7-180.

☐ D-ECMX	Cessna 207 Skywagon	20700194		0071		1 CO IO-520-F	1724			

WIKING FLIGHT SERVICE, GmbH — Hannover

Karl-Wiechert-Allee 4, D-30625 Hannover, Germany ☎ (511) 72 80 70 Tx: none Fax: (511) 73 66 36 SITA: n/a
F: 1989 6 Head: Heinrich Sikora & Joachim Kopatzki Net: http://www.wikingflight.com

☐ D-CCAT	IAI 1125 Astra SP	059	N4341S	0092		2 GA TFE731-3A-200G	11190			lsf Preussag AG

WIKING HELIKOPTER Service, GmbH = WHS (Subsidiary of Helikopter Service, A.S. Norway & VTG, GmbH / Member of Preussag Group) — Wilhelmshaven-Mariensiel

Nagelsweg 34, D-20097 Hamburg, Germany ☎ (40) 23 54 43 00 Tx: none Fax: (40) 23 54 43 10 SITA: n/a
F: 1975 60 Head: Rolf Schneider ICAO: WEEKING Net: n/a

☐ D-HOSA	Sikorsky S-76A+	760093	G-BVCW	0080		2 TU Arriel 1S	4899	EMS		cvtd S-76A
☐ D-HOSB	Sikorsky S-76A+	760191		0081		2 TU Arriel 1S	4899			cvtd S-76A
☐ D-HOSC	Sikorsky S-76A+	760032	N4937M	0079		2 TU Arriel 1S	4899			cvtd S-76A
☐ D-HOSD	Sikorsky S-76A+	760150	N75GY	0080		2 TU Arriel 1S	4899			cvtd S-76A
☐ D-HOSF	Sikorsky S-76B	760413	N5006B*	0093	0693	2 PWC PT6B-36A	5307			lsf SILEX Mobilien-Verwaltungs GmbH
☐ D-HOBB	Bell 212	30612	LN-OSM	0074		2 PWC PT6T-3 TwinPac	5080			lst Helicsa as EC-EEQ

WINDROSE AIR Flugcharter, GmbH (Sister company of Windrose Air Jetcharter, GmbH) — Berlin-Tempelhof

Tempelhofer Damm 1-7, D-12101 Berlin, Germany ☎ (30) 69 51 24 00 Tx: none Fax: (30) 69 51 24 04 SITA: n/a
F: 1991 5 Head: Thomas Stillmann Net: n/a

☐ D-ICCC	Cessna 500 Citation	500-0269	N5269J	0075		2 PWC JT15D-1A	5216			lsf AL Aviation Leasing GmbH

WINDROSE AIR Jetcharter, GmbH (Sister company of Windrose Air Flugcharter, GmbH) — Berlin-Tempelhof

Tempelhofer Damm 1-7, D-12101 Berlin, Germany ☎ (30) 69 51 24 00 Tx: none Fax: (30) 69 51 24 04 SITA: n/a
F: 1991 n/a Head: Thomas Stillmann Net: n/a

☐ D-CAWA	Cessna 550 Citation II	550-0596	N96TD	0088	1297	2 PWC JT15D-4	6033			lsf AL Aviation Leasing GmbH
☐ D-CKKK	Learjet 60	60-144	N60144	0099	0399	2 PWC PW305A	10659			

119 registration type of aircraft cn/fn ex/ex* mfd del powered by mtow kg configuration selcal name/fln/specialitites/remarks

WM AERO CHARTER, GmbH (jointly operated with PACT-Proair Charter Transport, Filderstadt)

Karlsruhe/Baden-Baden

In der Au 12, D-76307 Karlsbad, Germany ☎ (1805) 95 99 59 Tx: none Fax: (711) 708 39 11 SITA: STRPACR
F: 1998 ⁂ n/a Head: Dr. Bernd Wildenmann Net: http://www.wm-aero.de

☐ D-ICLE	Beech King Air C90	LJ-1002	N643PU	0082	0198	2 PWC PT6A-21	4581			
☐ D-ICKM	Beech King Air B200	BB-1005	OE-FKW	0082	1198	2 PWC PT6A-42	5670			
☐ D-ICWM	Beech King Air B200C	BL-49	N51CV	0082	0199	2 PWC PT6A-42	5670			

ZOLLERN FLUGDIENSTE, GmbH – ZFD

Mengen

ZOLLERN

Postfach 220, D-72481 Sigmaringen, Germany ☎ (7571) 70 203 Tx: none Fax: (7571) 70 330 SITA: n/a
F: 1978 ⁂ 2 Head: Friedr. Wilhelm Fürst von Hohenzollern Net: n/a Aircraft below MTOW 1361kg: Piper PA-28.

☐ D-IPRC	Cessna 340A II	340A1248	N87453	0081	1298	2 CO TSIO-520-NB	2717	6 Pax		
☐ D-IFHZ	Piper PA-31T1A Cheyenne IA	31T-1104016	N91201	0084		2 PWC PT6A-11	3946	5 Pax / Frtr		

DQ = FIJI (Republic of Fiji) (Na Matanitu ko Viti)

Capital: Suva Official Language: English, Fijian, Hindi Population: 0,8 million Square Km: 18274 Dialling code: +679 Year established: 1970 Acting political head: General-Brigadier Sitivena Rabuka (Prime Minister)

AIR FIJI, Ltd = PC / FAJ (formerly Fiji Air, Ltd & Air Pacific, Ltd)

Suva-Nausori

PO Box 1259, Suva, Fiji ☎ 47 87 99 Tx: 2258 fj Fax: 40 04 37 SITA: n/a
F: 1967 ⁂ 55 Head: Manasa Baravilala IATA: 677 ICAO: FIJIAIR Net: n/a

☐ DQ-FBS	Beech Baron C55 (95-C55)	TE-446	VH-DEZ	0067	0372	2 CO IO-520-C	2404	Y5		
☐ DQ-FET	Britten-Norman BN-2A-21 Islander	661	ZK-NNE	0071	0297	2 LY IO-540-K1B5	2994	Y9		
☐ DQ-FIC	Britten-Norman BN-2A-20 Islander	511	ZK-KHB	0076	0297	2 LY IO-540-K1B5	2994	Y9		
☐ DQ-FHC	Harbin Yunshuji Y12 II	0056		0091	0192	2 PWC PT6A-27	5300	Y17		Danny Jorgensen
☐ DQ-FHF	Harbin Yunshuji Y12 II	0047	B-531L	0091	0297	2 PWC PT6A-27	5300	Y17		Waisale Serevi
☐ DQ-FSC	Harbin Yunshuji Y12 II	0048		0093	1097	2 PWC PT6A-27	5300	Y17		
☐ DQ-	Harbin Yunshuji Y12 II	0057	9M-TAB	0091	0499	2 PWC PT6A-27	5300	Y17		
☐ DQ-	Harbin Yunshuji Y12 II	0058	9M-TAE	0293	0499	2 PWC PT6A-27	5300	Y17		
☐ DQ-AFN	Embraer 110P1 Bandeirante (EMB-110P1)	110416	N130EM	0083	0994	2 PWC PT6A-34	5670	Y15		Ratu ni Ceva
☐ DQ-AFO	Embraer 110P1 Bandeirante (EMB-110P1)	110419	EI-BVX	0083	0795	2 PWC PT6A-34	5670	Y15		
☐ DQ-LCM	Embraer 110P1 Bandeirante (EMB-110P1)	110410	VH-XFN	0082	0198	2 PWC PT6A-34	5670	Y15		
☐ DQ-YES	Embraer 110P2 Bandeirante (EMB-110P2)	110307	VH-FNR	0080	1198	2 PWC PT6A-34	5670	Y15		
☐ DQ-AFM	De Havilland DHC-6 Vista Liner 310	448	N234SA	0075	1293	2 PWC PT6A-27	5670	Y19		cvtd Twin Otter
☐ DQ-FIL	De Havilland DHC-6 Twin Otter 200	221	C-FQIM	0069	0297	2 PWC PT6A-20	5252	Y19		

AIR KATAFANGA, Ltd (Affiliated with Katafanga Resort/Subsidiary of J&S Miller, Ltd)

Suva

PO Box 14993, Suva, Fiji ☎ 30 73 33 Tx: none Fax: 30 73 34 SITA: n/a
F: 1995 ⁂ n/a Head: John Miller Net: n/a

☐ DQ-FIK	Piper PA-31-350 Navajo Chieftain	31-7752090	N7088C	0077	0695	2 LY TIO-540-J2BD	3175			

AIR PACIFIC, Ltd = FJ / FJI (formerly Fiji Airways, Ltd / Associated with Qantas Airways, Ltd)

Nadi-Int'l

AIR PACIFIC

PO Box 9266, Nadi Airport, Fiji ☎ 72 07 77 Tx: none Fax: 72 06 86 SITA: NANPDFJ
F: 1951 ⁂ 700 Head: Gerald Barrack IATA: 260 ICAO: PACIFIC Net: http://supersite.net/airpn2/docs/home.htm

☐ DQ-FJB	Boeing 737-5Y0	26067 / 2304		0092	0692	2 CFMI CFM56-3C1	60555	C8Y100	CR-DP	Island of Taveuni / lsf GECA
☐ DQ-FJD	Boeing 737-33A	27285 / 2608	N102AN	0094	0195	2 CFMI CFM56-3C1	61235	C8Y118	CQ-DR	lsf AWAS/sub-lst/jtly opw Royal Tongan
☐ DQ-FJF	Boeing 737-7X2	28878 / 96	N1786B*	0098	0998	2 CFMI CFM56-7B24	70080			Island of Koro / lsf APL Finance Ltd
☐ DQ-FJG	Boeing 737-8X2	29968				2 CFMI CFM56-7B26	79015			oo-delivery 0599
☐ DQ-FJH	Boeing 737-8X2	29969				2 CFMI CFM56-7B26	79015			oo-delivery 0899
☐ DQ-FJC	Boeing 767-3X2 (ER)	26260 / 552		0094	0994	2 GE CF6-80C2B6	172365	C18Y245	FS-DG	Island of Vanua Levu / lsf ILFC
☐ DQ-FJE	Boeing 747-238B	22614 / 464	VH-EBR	0080	0896	4 RR RB211-524D4	377842	C23Y421	DK-EM	Island of Viti Levu / lsf QFA
☐ DQ-FJI	Boeing 747-238B	22145 / 410	VH-EBQ	0079	1298	4 RR RB211-524D4	377842	C23Y421	DK-FM	lsf QFA

AIR WAKAYA (Wakaya Club, Ltd dba)

Suva-Nausori

PO Box 15424, Suva, Fiji ☎ 44 03 54 Tx: none Fax: 44 04 06 SITA: n/a
F: 1989 ⁂ 5 Head: Ken Christoffersen Net: n/a

☐ DQ-FHG	Britten-Norman BN-2B-26 Islander	2230	G-BSAC*	0090	0392	2 LY O-540-E4C5	2994			lsf Wakaya Club Ltd

AVIATION SERVICES FIJI, Ltd

Suva

PO Box 11808, Suva, Fiji ☎ 34 05 75 Tx: none Fax: 40 04 54 SITA: n/a
F: 1997 ⁂ n/a Head: Maurita Sigli Net: n/a

☐ DQ-FID	Piper PA-23-250 Aztec D	27-3941	VH-MGJ	0068	0798	2 LY IO-540-C4B5	2359			

ISLAND HOPPER (Pacific Crown Aviation (Fiji), Ltd dba)

Nadi-Int'l

PO Box 9622, Nadi Airport, Fiji ☎ 72 04 10 Tx: none Fax: 72 01 72 SITA: n/a
F: 1976 ⁂ 14 Head: Ian Simpson Net: n/a

☐ DQ-FDH	Eurocopter (Aerosp.) AS350D Squirrel	1182	N3599T	0079	0580	1 LY LTS101-600A.2	1950			
☐ DQ-FIH	Eurocopter (Aerosp.) AS350BA Squirrel	2164	JA9789	0088	0194	1 TU Arriel 1B	2100			cvtd AS350B
☐ DQ-FKH	Eurocopter (Aerosp.) AS350B1 Squirrel	1992	F-GEOC	0087	0697	1 TU Arriel 1D	2200			

SUNFLOWER AIRLINES, Limited = PI / SUF (Subsidiary of Colombine Holdings (Fiji), Ltd)

Nadi-Int'l

PO Box 9452, Nadi Airport, Fiji ☎ 72 35 55 Tx: 5183 sunair fj Fax: 72 00 85 SITA: NANRMPI
F: 1980 ⁂ 80 Head: Donald Ian Collingwood IATA: 252 ICAO: SUNFLOWER Net: http://www.fiji.to

☐ DQ-FCX	Britten-Norman BN-2A-27 Islander	833	G-BEMJ	0077	0685	2 LY O-540-E4C5	2994	Y9		Adi Yasawa / lsf Colombine Holdings
☐ DQ-FDV	Britten-Norman BN-2A-26 Islander	41	9M-MDA	0068	0184	2 LY O-540-E4C5	2994	Y9		Bui Nigone / lsf Colombine Holdings
☐ DQ-FDW	Britten-Norman BN-2A-26 Islander	602	9M-MDC	0069	0183	2 LY O-540-E4C5	2994	Y9		Adi Makutu / lsf Colombine Holdings
☐ DQ-FIN	Britten-Norman BN-2A-26 Islander	159	VH-ISA	0070	0397	2 LY O-540-E4C5	2994	Y9		lsf Island Supplies (Fiji) Ltd
☐ DQ-FEW	Beech Excalibur Queenaire 8800	LD-168	YJ-RV17	0065	0290	2 LY IO-720-A1B	3992	Y9		cvtd Queen Air 65-A80
☐ DQ-FEY	De Havilland DHC-6 Twin Otter 210	87	N64NB	0067	0690	2 PWC PT6A-20	5252	Y18		Spirit of the North / lsfColom./cvtd-100
☐ DQ-FEZ	De Havilland DHC-6 Twin Otter 210	9	F-OCFJ	0066	1090	2 PWC PT6A-20	5252	Y18		Spirit of the West / lsfCol.Hd/cvtd-100
☐ DQ-FIE	De Havilland DHC-6 Twin Otter 310	660	N933LC	0079	0194	2 PWC PT6A-27	5670	Y18		Spirit of Nadi / lsf Colombine Holdings
☐ DQ-FIJ	Shorts 330-100 (SD3-30)	SH3060	G-BIFK	0080	0895	2 PWC PT6A-45R	10250	Y30		Spirit of Rotuma
☐ DQ-SUN	Shorts 330-100 (SD3-30)	SH3056	VH-HUS	0080	1298	2 PWC PT6A-45R	10250	Y30		

TURTLE AIRWAYS, Ltd = TLT

Nadi-Int'l

Turtle Airways

Private Mail Bag 0355, Nadi Airport, Fiji ☎ 72 29 88 Tx: 5180 tia fj Fax: 72 03 46 SITA: n/a
F: 1978 ⁂ 30 Head: John G. Pettitt ICAO: TURTLE Net: n/a

☐ DQ-FDB	Cessna U206G Stationair 6 II	U20604151	ZK-EKI	0077	0979	1 CO IO-520-F	1633			Floats
☐ DQ-FDU	Cessna U206G Stationair 6 II	U20604381	N756VB	0078	0883	1 CO IO-520-F	1633			Floats
☐ DQ-FEM	Cessna U206G Stationair 6 II	U20606650	N9771Z	0082	0387	1 CO IO-520-F	1633			Floats
☐ DQ-FEX	Cessna U206G Stationair 6 II	U20605706	ZK-FHE	0480	1290	1 CO IO-520-F	1633			Floats
☐ DQ-TAL	De Havilland DHC-2 Beaver I	1255	C-GLED	0057	0998	1 PW R-985	2313			Floats

D2 = ANGOLA (Republic of Angola) (Republica de Angola)

Capital: Luanda Official Language: Portuguese Population: 11,5 million Square Km: 1246700 Dialling code: +244 Year established: 1975 Acting political head: José Eduardo dos Santos (President)

Government / Corporate / Executive / VIP Aircraft

☐ D2-EAG	Yakovlev 40	9230122		0072		3 IV AI-25	16000	VIP		Gvmt
☐ D2-ECB	GAC G-1159A Gulfstream III	474	N311GA*	0086		2 RR Spey 511-8	31615	VIP	AM-BP	Cunene / Gvmt
☐ D2-ECC	Tupolev 134A	49830		0077		2 SO D-30-II	49000	VIP		Gvmt
☐ D2-TPR	Boeing 707-3J6B	20715 / 870	B-2404	0973	0295	4 PW JT3D-7 (HK2/COM)	151046	VIP	HK-BJ	Gvmt

AIR NACOIA Exploraçao de Aeronaves, Lda = ANL (Subsidiary of Nacoia, Lda)

Luanda

Rua Comandante Che Guevara 61-1e Andar, Apart. 1, Luanda, Angola ☎ (2) 33 17 11 Tx: none Fax: (2) 39 54 77 SITA: n/a
F: 1993 ⁂ 40 Head: Salvador Silva ICAO: AIR NACOIA Net: n/a

☐ D2-FAS	Boeing 727-227 (A)	20773 / 983	N552PE	0073	0994	3 PW JT8D-9A	79651	Freighter		
☐ D2-FAV	Boeing 707-321C	18717 / 366	HK-3232X	0464	1096	4 PW JT3D-3B (HK2/COM)	145331	Freighter	JK-CL	lst AGO

ALADA – Empresa de Transportes Aéreos, Lda = RAD

Luanda

CP 12261, Luanda, Angola ☎ (2) 32 45 05 Tx: none Fax: (2) 32 45 05 SITA: n/a
F: 1995 ⁂ 70 Head: Adelino Gomez Riberio, Jr. ICAO: AIR ALADA Net: n/a

☐ D2-FAP	Antonov 32B	2903		0091		2 IV AI-20D	27000	Combi		
☐ D2-FAX	Antonov 32B			0091	0098	2 IV AI-20D	27000	Combi		
☐ D2-FAJ	Antonov 12B				0098	4 IV AI-20M	61000	Freighter		
☐ D2-FAO	Antonov 12BP	402812	7T-WAG/591	0064	0096	4 IV AI-20M	61000	Freighter		
☐ D2-FAR	Antonov 12BP	402810	7T-WAE/550	0064	0096	4 IV AI-20K	61000	Freighter		
☐ D2-FAW	Antonov 12BP	402605	7T-WAC/514	0064		4 IV AI-20M	61000	Freighter		

120 registration type of aircraft cn/fn ex/ex* mfd del powered by mtow kg configuration selcal name/fln/specialitites/remarks

ANGOLA AIR CHARTER, Ltd – AAC = AGO (Subsidiary of TAAG Angola Airlines)   Luanda

CP 3010, Luanda, Angola ☎ (2) 32 53 77 Tx: none Fax: (2) 35 05 59 SITA: n/a
F: n/a ♦♦♦ 300 Head: n/a ICAO: ANGOLA CHARTER Net: n/a

registration	type of aircraft	cn/fn	ex/ex*	mfd	del	powered by	mtow kg	configuration	selcal	name/fln/specialitites/remarks
☐ D2-TBI	Boeing 737-214	19681 / 68	N7380F	0068	0594	2 PW JT8D-9A	49442	Y130		lsf Aviation Consultants
☐ PJ-TAC	Lockheed L-382G (L-100-30) Hercules	70C-5225	N4161T	0091	0196	4 AN 501-D22A	70307	Freighter		lsf Frameair
☐ D2-TJC	Boeing 727-23 (F)	19180 / 251	9Q-CSY	0066	0595	3 PW JT8D-7B	76884	Freighter		cvtd -23
☐ D2-FAV	Boeing 707-321C	18717 / 366	HK-3232X	0464	0498	4 PW JT3D-3B (HK2/COM)	145331	Freighter	JK-CL	lsf ANL
☐ D2-TOK	Boeing 707-324C	19869 / 700	S7-2HM	0068	0791	4 PW JT3D-3B (HK2/COM)	151046	Freighter	HM-AC	lsf EQUA
☐ D2-TOL	Boeing 707-347C	19963 / 723	N1501W	0068	0092	4 PW JT3D-3B	151046	Freighter	BH-DF	Cidade de Luanda/City of Luanda
☐ D2-TON	Boeing 707-324C	19871 / 711	S7-4HM	0068	0691	4 PW JT3D-3B (HK2/COM)	151046	Freighter	BM-DL	lsf EQUA

ECOMEX AIR CARGO, Lda = ECX   Luanda

Rua Comandante Valodia 179, Luanda, Angola ☎ (2) 34 06 92 Tx: none Fax: (2) 34 06 92 SITA: n/a
F: 1993 ♦♦♦ 13 Head: Mateus J.M. da Graça ICAO: AIR ECOMEX Net: n/a   Suspended own cargo flights (with Antonov 12 aircraft) in 1998. Intends to restart with leased freighter-aircraft.

INTERTRANSIT   Luanda

Aeroporto 4 de Fevereiro, Luanda, Angola ☎ (2) 32 38 95 Tx: none Fax: (2) 32 38 95 SITA: n/a
F: n/a ♦♦♦ n/a Head: n/a Net: n/a

registration	type of aircraft	cn/fn	ex/ex*	mfd	del	powered by	mtow kg	configuration	selcal	name/fln/specialitites/remarks
☐ D2-ERG	Bell 206B JetRanger III	4215		0592		1 AN 250-C20J	1451			
☐ ZS-MEU	Beech Baron 58	TH-1051		0079		2 CO IO-520-CB	2449			lsf Beechcraft
☐ D2-EMX	Beech King Air 200	BB-480	ZS-MJH	0079		2 PWC PT6A-41	5670			Rita Yara
☐ D2-EXR	Hawker 403B (HS 125-403B)	25215	ZS-NPV	0069	0197	2 RR Viper 522	10705			

SAL – Sociedade de Aviaçao Ligeira, SA   Luanda

CP 2560, Luanda, Angola ☎ (2) 39 46 40 Tx: n/a Fax: (2) 33 52 25 SITA: n/a
F: 1992 ♦♦♦ 182 Head: Pimentel Araujo Net: n/a Aircraft / Ag-aircraft below MTOW 1361/5000kg: Ayres Turbo Trush SR34, Cessna 172 & 188.

registration	type of aircraft	cn/fn	ex/ex*	mfd	del	powered by	mtow kg	configuration	selcal	name/fln/specialitites/remarks
☐ D2-ECN	Reims/Cessna F406 Caravan II	F406-0002	PH-MNS	0086		2 PWC PT6A-112	4468	Y10 / Freighter		lsf Iber Aviation Ltd
☐ D2-ECO	Reims/Cessna F406 Caravan II	F406-0011	D-IDAA	0087		2 PWC PT6A-112	4468	C8		lsf Iber Aviation Ltd
☐ D2-ECP	Reims/Cessna F406 Caravan II	F406-0016	PH-LAS	0087		2 PWC PT6A-112	4468	Y10 / Freighter		lsf Iber Aviation Ltd
☐ D2-ECQ	Reims/Cessna F406 Caravan II	F406-0019	G-CVAN	0087		2 PWC PT6A-112	4468	Y10 / Freighter		lsf Iber Aviation Ltd
☐ D2-ECX	Beech King Air B200	BB-1362	N1565F	0090		2 PWC PT6A-42	5670	C7		lsf B.N.A.
☐ D2-ECY	Beech King Air B200C	BL-135	S9-NAP	0090		2 PWC PT6A-42	5670	Y7 / Freighter		lsf G.I.A.S.
☐ D2-EOD	Shorts Skyvan 3 Variant 200 (SC-7)	SH1938	CR-LOD	0074		2 GA TPE331-2-201A	6123	Y15 / Freighter		
☐ D2-ECW	Beech King Air 350 (B300)	FL-102	S9-TAP	0093		2 PWC PT6A-60A	6804	C8		lsf G.I.A.S.
☐ D2-ECZ	Beech King Air 350 (B300)	FL-59	S9-NAY	0091	0593	2 PWC PT6A-60A	6804	C8		lsf Ministerio Territ.

SAVANAIR, Lda = SVN   Luanda

Largo Amilcar Cabral 14-2° Andar, Luanda, Angola ☎ (2) 39 67 56 Tx: none Fax: (2) 39 36 63 SITA: n/a
F: 1994 ♦♦♦ 50 Head: Luis R.C. Paiva ICAO: SAVANAIR Net: n/a Operates cargo flights with Antonov 12 aircraft, leased from SANTA CRUZ IMPERIAL (EL-), when required.

SONAIR – Helipetrol (Sonangol Aeronautica dba / division of Sonangol State Corporaçion)   Luanda

CP 1316, Luanda, Angola ☎ (2) 32 16 32 Tx: 3148 sonang Fax: (2) 32 15 21 SITA: n/a
F: 1979 ♦♦♦ 250 Head: Salgado Costa Net: n/a

registration	type of aircraft	cn/fn	ex/ex*	mfd	del	powered by	mtow kg	configuration	selcal	name/fln/specialitites/remarks
☐ D2-ESX	Socata TB 21 Trinidad TC	1568		0093	0097	1 LY TIO-540-AB1AD	1400	Y4		
☐ D2-EQD	Eurocopter (Aerosp.) AS365N2 Dauphin 2	6521		0097	0097	2 TU Arriel 1C2	4250	Y12		
☐ D2-EQE	Eurocopter (Aerosp.) AS365N2 Dauphin 2	6531	F-GJIK	0097	0398	2 TU Arriel 1C2	4250	Y12		
☐ D2-EVE	Eurocopter (Aerosp.) AS365N2 Dauphin 2	6418	F-GHRZ	0091		2 TU Arriel 1C2	4250	Y12		
☐ D2-EVF	Eurocopter (Aerosp.) AS365N2 Dauphin 2	6410	F-GHRX	0091		2 TU Arriel 1C2	4250	Y12		
☐ ZS-RHB	Sikorsky S-76A++	760109	VH-EMX	0080	0097	2 TU Arriel 1S1	4899	Y12		lsf Court Helicopters / cvtd S-76A
☐ D2-ESO	Beech King Air B200C	BL-127		0086		2 PWC PT6A-42	5670	Y8		Luanda
☐ D2-ESQ	Beech King Air B200	BB-1407		0091		2 PWC PT6A-42	5670	Y7		Luanda
☐ D2-EST	Beech King Air B200	BB-1348	S9-NAO	0089		2 PWC PT6A-42	5670	Y9		Cobo
☐ D2-EVA	De Havilland DHC-6 Twin Otter 310	728	V2-LDD	0081	0498	2 PWC PT6A-27	5670	Y19		
☐ D2-EVB	De Havilland DHC-6 Twin Otter 310	810	V2-LDH	0084	0498	2 PWC PT6A-27	5670	Y19		
☐ D2-EVC	De Havilland DHC-6 Twin Otter 310	809	V2-LDG	0084	0498	2 PWC PT6A-27	5670	Y19		
☐ D2-EVH	De Havilland DHC-6 Twin Otter 310	511	HB-LOM	0076	1198	2 PWC PT6A-27	5670	Y19		
☐ S9-CAM	Beech King Air 350 (B300)	FL-163	N1057Q	0097	0597	2 PWC PT6A-60A	6804	Y8		lsf Golfo Int'l Air Services
☐ D2-ESV	Dassault Falcon 20F-5	262	F-GHVR	0071	0295	2 GA TFE731-5BR-2C	13200	Y10		cvtd 20F
☐ D2-ESN	Fokker F27 Friendship 500 (F27 Mk500)	10610	PH-FTY*	0081	0481	2 RR Dart 536-7R	20412	Y42		Kwanda
☐ D2-ESR	Fokker 50 (F27 Mk050)	20240	PH-RRK*	0092	0992	2 PWC PW125B	20820	Y45		Lombo Este
☐ D2-ESW	Fokker 50 (F27 Mk050)	20241	PH-RRM*	0092	0596	2 PWC PW125B	20820	Y45		lsf Golfo Int'l Air Services
☐ D2-ESU	Boeing 727-23 (F)	19431 / 372	N516FE	0067	0295	3 PW JT8D-7A	76657	Freighter		cvtd -23
☐ D2-EVD	Boeing 727-29C	19403 / 435	CB-02	0067	0299	3 PW JT8D-7A	76657	Y128		
☐ D2-EVG	Boeing 727-29C	19402 / 415	N70PA	0067	0299	3 PW JT8D-7A	76657	Y128		

TAAG Angola Airlines / Linhas Aéreas de Angola = DT / DTA (formerly DTA – Linhas Aéreas de Angola)   Luanda

CP 3010, Luanda, Angola ☎ (2) 33 23 87 Tx: 3442 an Fax: (2) 39 22 29 SITA: n/a
F: 1938 ♦♦♦ 4530 Head: Julio Sampaio Almeida IATA: 118 ICAO: DTA Net: n/a

registration	type of aircraft	cn/fn	ex/ex*	mfd	del	powered by	mtow kg	configuration	selcal	name/fln/specialitites/remarks
☐ D2-TFM	Fokker F27 Maritime 200MAR (F27 Mk200MAR)	10595	D2-MEF	0080	0388	2 RR Dart 536-7R	19051	Y44		
☐ D2-TFQ	Fokker F27 Friendship 600 (F27 Mk600)	10423	D2-TAE	0069	0278	2 RR Dart 532-7	19731	Y44		
☐ D2-TFR	Fokker F27 Friendship 600 (F27 Mk600)	10457	D2-TMB	0071	0571	2 RR Dart 532-7	19731	Y44		
☐ D2-TFS	Fokker F27 Troopship 400M (F27 Mk400M)	10561	FAPA T-101	0077	0783	2 RR Dart 536-7R	19731	Freighter		
☐ D2-TFW	Fokker F27 Friendship 500 (F27 Mk500)	10608	PH-FSK*	0081	0483	2 RR Dart 536-7R	20412	Y48		
☐ D2-TBC	Boeing 737-2M2C (A)	21173 / 447	D2-TAB	0076	0576	2 PW JT8D-17	53070	Y78 / Plt	BF-HM	
☐ D2-TBD	Boeing 737-2M2 (A)	21723 / 567	D2-TAH	0079	0479	2 PW JT8D-17	53070	Y128	BE-HL	Joao Paulo II
☐ D2-TBO	Boeing 737-2M2 (A)	22776 / 891	N1782B*	0082	1182	2 PW JT8D-17	53070	Y128	BH-EJ	
☐ D2-TBP	Boeing 737-2M2 (A)	23220 / 1084		0185	0285	2 PW JT8D-17A	53070	Y128	FH-LM	Nelson Mandela
☐ D2-TBX	Boeing 737-2M2 (A)	23351 / 1117		0085	0685	2 PW JT8D-17A	53070	Y128	EG-AJ	
☐ D2-TOP	Boeing 707-382B	20136 / 803	CS-TBE	0069	0683	4 PW JT3D-3B	151046	F10Y138	EG-AL	
☐ D2-TIF	Ilyushin 62M	4648525		0086	0086	4 SO D-30KU	167000	Y168		
☐ D2-TIG	Ilyushin 62M	4750919		0087	0587	4 SO D-30KU	167000	Y168		
☐ D2-TEA	Boeing 747-312 (M)	23410 / 653	9V-SKN	0886	0797	4 PW JT9D-7R4G2	377842	Combi	KL-DG	Cidade de Kuito / lst Sonangol State Co

TRANS AIR WELWITCHIA, Lda = TWW (Sister company of A. Welwitchia-Sociedade de Comercio Geral, Lda)   Luanda

Aeroporto 4 de Fevereiro, Luanda, Angola ☎ (2) 39 63 32 Tx: n/a Fax: (2) 39 32 87 SITA: n/a
F: n/a ♦♦♦ n/a Head: n/a ICAO: WELWITCHIA Net: n/a Operates charter flights with Antonov 32 aircraft, leased from Ukraine Air Alliance (UR-) when required.

D4 = CAPE VERDE ISLANDS (Republic of Cape Verde) (Republica de Cabo Verde)

Capital: Praia Official Language: Portuguese Population: 0,4 million Square Km: 4033 Dialling code: +238 Year established: 1975 Acting political head: Antonio Mascarenhas Monteiro (President)

CABO VERDE EXPRESS   Sal

CP 50, Sal, Ilha do Sal, Cape Verde Islands ☎ 41 26 00 Tx: none Fax: 41 26 00 SITA: n/a
F: 1998 ♦♦♦ n/a Head: Jean-Christophe Bartz Net: n/a

registration	type of aircraft	cn/fn	ex/ex*	mfd	del	powered by	mtow kg	configuration	selcal	name/fln/specialitites/remarks
☐ D4-CBJ	Cessna 208B Grand Caravan	208B0336	N1040W	0093	0698	1 PWC PT6A-114A	3969			

GUARDA COSTEIRA DE CABO VERDE – Airwing   Praia

c/o Ministry of Transport & Infrastructure, Boeira, Ilha do Santiago, Cape Verde Islands ☎ 61 34 22 Tx: none Fax: 61 53 58 SITA: n/a
F: n/a ♦♦♦ n/a Head: Cmdt Major Elseu Sousa Lopes Net: n/a Non-commercial government organisation conducting SAR/Patrol, cargo & passenger flights.

registration	type of aircraft	cn/fn	ex/ex*	mfd	del	powered by	mtow kg	configuration	selcal	name/fln/specialitites/remarks
☐ FAC-03	Embraer 110P1 Bandeirante (EMB-110P1)	110479	2337	0088	0095	2 PWC PT6A-34	6000	SAR/Frtr/19Pax		
☐ D4-CBC	Dornier 228-201	8091	D-CEDS*	0086	1192	2 GA TPE331-5-252D	5980	SAR/Frtr/19Pax		Garca Boeira

TACV – CABO VERDE AIRLINES = VR / TCV (Transportes Aéreos de Cabo Verde dba)   Praia

Caixa Postal 1, Praia, Ilha do Santiago, Cape Verde Islands ☎ 61 58 13 Tx: 6065 tacv cv Fax: 61 35 85 SITA: RAICAVR
F: 1955 ♦♦♦ 600 Head: Alfredo M. Carvalho IATA: 696 ICAO: TRANSVERDE Net: n/a

registration	type of aircraft	cn/fn	ex/ex*	mfd	del	powered by	mtow kg	configuration	selcal	name/fln/specialitites/remarks
☐ D4-CAY	De Havilland DHC-6 Twin Otter 300	663	CR-CAY	0080	0280	2 PWC PT6A-27	5670	Y20		
☐ D4-CBE	ATR 42-320	382	F-WWEA*	0094	1194	2 PWC PW121	16700	Y46		Joaquim Ribeiro
☐ D4-CBF	ATR 42-320	386	F-WWEK*	0094	1294	2 PWC PW121	16700	Y46		Rebil
☐ D4-CBH	ATR 42-320	415	F-WWLA*	0097	0797	2 PWC PW121	16700	Y46		Alex
☐ D4-CBG	Boeing 757-2Q8	27599 / 696		0096	0396	2 PW PW2037	115666	F20Y165	MQ-ER	lsf ILFC

D6 = COMOROS (Federal Islamic Republic of the Comoros) (Jumhuriya al-Qumur al-Itthadiya al-Islamiya)

This country uses a country prefix (nationality mark) not notified to the ICAO
Capital: Moroni Official Language: Comor, Arabic, French Population: 0,8 million Square Km: 1862 Dialling code: +269 Year established: 1975 Acting political head: Mohamed Taki Abdoulkarim (President)

COMORES AIR SERVICE (formerly Aero Comores)   Moroni-Int'l Prince Said

BP 277, Moroni, Comores ☎ 73 33 66 Tx: none Fax: 73 32 38 SITA: n/a
F: 1996 ♦♦♦ n/a Head: John Cleave Net: n/a

registration	type of aircraft	cn/fn	ex/ex*	mfd	del	powered by	mtow kg	configuration	selcal	name/fln/specialitites/remarks
☐ 5Y-NIK	Let 410UVP-E9	912619	OK-WDW	0091	0097	2 WA M-601E	6400	Y17		lsf Mombasa Air Service

121 registration type of aircraft cn/fn ex/ex* mfd del powered by mtow kg configuration selcal name/fln/specialitites/remarks

EC = SPAIN (Kingdom of Spain) (Reino de Espana)

Capital: Madrid Official Language: Spanish Population: 39,7 million Square Km: 504750 Dialling code: +34 Year established: 1479 Acting political head: José Maria Aznar (Prime Minister)

Government / Corporate / Executive / VIP Aircraft

AME-Aeronave Militar Espanola, Ministerio de Defensa = ICAO 3 letter-code AME & call sing AIRMIL

registration	type of aircraft	cn/fn	ex/ex*	mfd	del	powered by	mtow kg	configuration	name/fln/specialitites/remarks
EC-DNB	CASA 212 Aviocar Srs 200	178		0081	0096	2 GA TPE331-10-501C	7450	Surveyer	SVA-Servicio de Vigilancia Aduanero
EC-DRO	CASA 212 Aviocar Srs 200	247		0082	0782	2 GA TPE331-10-501C	7450	Surveyer	SVA-Servicio de Vigilancia Aduanero
EC-DTL	CASA 212 Aviocar Srs 200	311		0083	0783	2 GA TPE331-10R-501C	7450	Surveyer	SVA-Servicio de Vigilancia Aduanero
EC-ECD	CASA 212 Aviocar Srs 200	359		0087	0387	2 GA TPE331-10R-512C	7450	Surveyer	SVA-Servicio de Vigilancia Aduanero
EC-FAP	CASA 212 Aviocar Srs 200	323		0084	1290	2 GA TPE331-10R-512C	7450	Surveyer	SVA-Servicio de Vigilancia Aduanero
EC-FAQ	CASA 212 Aviocar Srs 200	261	LV-AYL	0084	1290	2 GA TPE331-10R-512C	7450	Surveyer	SVA-Servicio de Vigilancia Aduanero
T11-1	Dassault Falcon 20E	253	EC-BZV	0071	0678	2 GE CF700-2D2	13000	Calibrator	408-10/csEC-ZCJ / AME/Ejercito del Aire
T11-5	Dassault Falcon 20F	475	F-WJML*	0085	0988	2 GE CF700-2D2	13000	VIP	45-05/cs EC-ZCN / AME/Ejercito del Aire
T16-1	Dassault Falcon 50	84	F-WZHK*	0081	0283	3 GA TFE731-3-1C	17600	VIP	45-20/cs EC-ZCP / AME/Ejercito del Aire
T17-2	Boeing 707-331C (KC-137E)	18757 / 387	N792TW	0064	0789	4 PW JT3D-3B	151046	Tanker	45-11 / AME/Ejercito del Aire/cvtd-331C
T17-3	Boeing 707-368C (KC-137E)	21367 / 922	N7667B	0077	0290	4 PW JT3D-3B	151046	VIP	45-12 / AME/Ejercito del Aire/cvtd-368C
T18-1	Dassault Falcon 900	38		0088	0488	2 GA TFE731-5AR-1C2	20638	VIP / miltrans	45-40 / AME/Ejercito del Aire
T18-2	Dassault Falcon 900	90	F-WWFG*	0091	0291	2 GA TFE731-5AR-1C2	20638	VIP / miltrans	45-41 / AME/Ejercito del Aire
T19C-01	CASA (IPTN) CN235-10	C013		0088	1288	2 GE CT7-7A	15100	VIP / miltrans	35-60 / AME/Ejercito del Aire
T19C-02	CASA (IPTN) CN235-10	C014		0088	1288	2 GE CT7-7A	15100	VIP / miltrans	35-61 / AME/Ejercito del Aire
TM11-2	Dassault Falcon 20D	222	EC-BXV	0071	0678	2 GE CF700-2D2	13000	Calibrator	45-03/cs EC-ZCK / AME/Ejercito del Aire
TM11-3	Dassault Falcon 20D	219	EC-BVV	0070	0678	2 GE CF700-2D2	13000	Calibrator	45-04/cs EC-ZCL / AME/Ejercito del Aire
TM11-4	Dassault Falcon 20E	332	EC-CTV	0075	0678	2 GE CF700-2D2	13000	Calibrator	408-11/csEC-ZCI / AME/Ejercito del Aire
TM17-4	Boeing 707-351C (KC-137E)	19164 / 508	SX-DBO	0066	0496	4 PW JT3D-3B	151091	Tanker/miltrans	408-21 / AME/Ejerc. del Aire/cvtd-351C

AERODROMO DE LA MANCHA, S.L. = MAM

La Mancha

Orense 10, E-28020 Madrid, Spain ☎ (91) 677 05 58 Tx: none Fax: (91) 677 05 58 SITA: n/a
F: 1993 5 Head: Francisco Torres Arias ICAO: AEROMAN Net: n/a

registration	type of aircraft	cn/fn	ex/ex*	mfd	del	powered by	mtow kg
EC-EFH	Twin (Aero) Turbo Commander 690A	11130	N111VS	0073	0887	2 GA TPE331-5-251K	4683

AERONOVA, S.L. = OVA

Valencia-Manises

Avda del Cid 144, E-46014 Valencia, Spain ☎ (96) 154 45 49 Tx: none Fax: (96) 370 60 05 SITA: n/a
F: 1996 n/a Head: Alejandro J. Lopez ICAO: AERONOVA Net: n/a

registration	type of aircraft	cn/fn	ex/ex*	mfd	del	powered by	mtow kg	configuration
EC-CTG	Piper PA-31P Pressurized Navajo	31P-7530017	N54946	0075	0096	2 LY TIGO-541-E1A	3538	5 Pax/Freighter
EC-GVE	Fairchild (Swearingen) SA227AC Metro III	AC-669	N2702Z	0087	0698	2 GA TPE331-11U-611G	6577	19 Pax/Freighter

AEROVENTO, S.A. = VET

Pamplona-Noain

Iturrama 13, E-31007 Pamplona, Spain ☎ (948) 16 87 94 Tx: none Fax: (948) 16 87 95 SITA: n/a
F: 1997 6 Head: Enrique Urdanoz ICAO: AEROVENTO Net: http://www.cin.es/aerovento

registration	type of aircraft	cn/fn	ex/ex*	mfd	del	powered by	mtow kg	configuration	name/fln/specialitites/remarks
EC-GOY	Beech King Air C90	LJ-527	N55SG	0071	0997	2 PWC PT6A-20	4377	Executive	
N19WP	Fairchild (Swearingen) SA226TC Metro II	TC-390	C-FBWY	0081	0399	2 GA TPE331-10UA-511G	5670	Freighter	lsf GAS Wilson Inc. / to be EC re-reg.

AIR ATLANTIC, S.L. = QD / RCU (Member of Grupo Boluda)

Gran Canaria-Gando

San Diego No. 13, Portal 1-2A, E-35200 Telde (Gran Canaria), Spain ☎ (928) 68 01 90 Tx: none Fax: (928) 68 33 65 SITA: n/a
F: 1992 70 Head: Eduardo Gomez Martinez IATA: 850 ICAO: AIR COURIER Net: http://www.airatlantic.com

registration	type of aircraft	cn/fn	ex/ex*	mfd	del	powered by	mtow kg	configuration	name/fln/specialitites/remarks
EC-GDV	Fairchild (Swearingen) SA226AT Merlin IV	AT-043	EC-975	0076	0495	2 GA TPE331-10UA-511G	5670	EMS	opf SUC-Servicio de Urgencias Canario
EC-GJX	Fairchild (Swearingen) SA227DC Metro 23	DC-855B	EC-395	0094	0796	2 GA TPE331-12U-701G	7484	Y19 / Combi	
F-GTRB	Fairchild (Swearingen) SA227AC Metro III	AC-519	EC-GJV	0082	0698	2 GA TPE331-11U-611G	6577	Y19 / Combi	lsf FEU
EC-GZL	Beech 1900D Airliner	UE-335	N23269	0098	1298	2 PWC PT6A-67D	7688	Y19 / Combi	lsf Raytheon Aircraft Receivables Corp.

AIR EUROPA = UX / AEA (Div.of Globalia Corporacion Empresarial SA/Sister co. of Air Europa Express)

Palma-Son Sant Joan & Gran Canaria-Gando

air europa

Gran Via Asima 23, Poligono Son Castello, E-07009 Palma de Mallorca, Spain ☎ (971) 17 81 00 Tx: 69158 e Fax: (971) 43 15 00 SITA: PMIMMUX
F: 1986 3480 Head: Juan José Hidalgo Acera IATA: 996 ICAO: EUROPA Net: http://www.aireuropa.es
Turboprop commuter flights are operated under a franchise agreement with AIR EUROPA EXPRESS (with BAe ATP) using UX flight numbers – for details see under that company.

registration	type of aircraft	cn/fn	ex/ex*	mfd	del	powered by	mtow kg	configuration	selcal	name/fln/specialitites/remarks
EC-FJZ	Boeing 737-3Y0	23923 / 1540	EC-898	0488	1191	2 CFMI CFM56-3B2	62822	Y148	LS-CR	lsf GECA
EC-FKI	Boeing 737-375	23707 / 1388	EC-782	0587	0587	2 CFMI CFM56-3B2	62822	Y148	LS-CK	Virgen de la Vega / lsf GECA
EC-FKJ	Boeing 737-3Y0	23749 / 1389	EC-781	0587	0587	2 CFMI CFM56-3B2	62822	Y148	LS-CM	Virgen de la Pena de Francia / lsf GECA
EC-FUT	Boeing 737-3Q8	26293 / 2541	EC-520	1093	1193	2 CFMI CFM56-3C1	63276	Y148	DS-CP	lsf ILFC / Andalucia-stickers
EC-FYF	Boeing 737-3Q8	26301 / 2623	EC-547	0694	0694	2 CFMI CFM56-3C1	63276	Y148	FS-BP	Canarias / lsf ILFC / Andalucia-stickers
EC-GEQ	Boeing 737-3Y0	23750 / 1431	EC-135	0887	1095	2 CFMI CFM56-3B1	61235	Y148	LS-CP	Salamanca / lsf CITG / Marini-stickers
EC-GEU	Boeing 737-375	23808 / 1434	EC-136	0987	1095	2 CFMI CFM56-3B1	61235	Y148	LS-CQ	Lugo / lsf Intec
EC-GFU	Boeing 737-3Y0	24256 / 1629	EC-204	1188	0194	2 CFMI CFM56-3B1	61235	Y148	LS-DR	lsf BBAM / Andalucia-stickers
EC-GGO	Boeing 737-3M8	24376 / 1717	EC-238	0589	0496	2 CFMI CFM56-3B2	62142	Y148	EG-BD	lsf Avn Investing Co.B.V./Andalucia-st.
EC-GHD	Boeing 737-3M8	25071 / 2039	EC-262	0591	0596	2 CFMI CFM56-3B2	62142	Y148	EF-GK	lsf Marubeni Plc / Andalucia-stickers
EC-GMY	Boeing 737-36Q	28658 / 2865		0397	0497	2 CFMI CFM56-3C1	63276	Y148	BR-AS	lsf BOUL
EC-GNU	Boeing 737-36Q	28660 / 2883		0597	0597	2 CFMI CFM56-3C1	63276	Y148	BQ-LR	lsf BOUL
EC-FXP	Boeing 737-4Q8	24706 / 1996	EC-644	0291	0594	2 CFMI CFM56-3C1	62822	Y162	BG-FP	Villanueva del Conde / lsf TRIT
EC-FXQ	Boeing 737-4Q8	24707 / 2057	EC-645	0691	0594	2 CFMI CFM56-3C1	62822	Y162	BF-PS	lsf ILFC
EC-FZZ	Boeing 737-4Y0	24686 / 1861	EC-772	0590	1294	2 CFMI CFM56-3C1	64636	Y162	LS-DE	Baleares / lsf Al-Rahji
EC-GAZ	Boeing 737-4Y0	24906 / 2009	EC-850	0291	0595	2 CFMI CFM56-3C1	64636	CY150	LS-DF	lsf GECA/sub-lst/opf IBE in Iberia-cs
EC-GBN	Boeing 737-4Y0	24912 / 2064	EC-851	0591	0495	2 CFMI CFM56-3C1	64636	CY150	LS-DG	lsf GECA/sub-lst/opf IBE in Iberia-cs
EC-GPI	Boeing 737-46Q	28661 / 2910		0797	0797	2 CFMI CFM56-3C1	65091	CY150	BR-CD	lsf BOUL/sub-lst/opf IBE in Iberia-cs
EC-GUO	Boeing 737-4Q8	26285 / 2416	N402KW	0193	0598	2 CFMI CFM56-3C1	68038	Y162	LS-DH	lsf ILFC
EC-	Boeing 737-85P	28381				2 CFMI CFM56-7B26	78245	Y184		to be lsf ITOH 0499
EC-	Boeing 737-85P	28382				2 CFMI CFM56-7B26	78245	Y184		to be lsf ITOH 0499
EC-	Boeing 737-85P	28383				2 CFMI CFM56-7B26	78245	Y184		to be lsf ITOH 0499
EC-	Boeing 737-85P	28384				2 CFMI CFM56-7B26	78245	Y184		to be lsf ITOH 1199
EC-	Boeing 737-85P	28385				2 CFMI CFM56-7B26	78245	Y184		to be lsf ITOH 1199
EC-	Boeing 737-85P	28386				2 CFMI CFM56-7B26	78245	Y184		to be lsf ITOH 1199
EC-	Boeing 737-85P	28387				2 CFMI CFM56-7B26	78245	Y184		to be lsf ITOH 0200
EC-	Boeing 737-85P	28388				2 CFMI CFM56-7B26	78245	Y184		to be lsf ITOH 0400
EC-	Boeing 737-85P	28535				2 CFMI CFM56-7B26	78245	Y184		to be lsf ITOH 0400
EC-	Boeing 737-85P	28536				2 CFMI CFM56-7B26	78245	Y184		to be lsf ITOH 0400
EC-FEE	Boeing 757-236	25053 / 358	EC-667	0491	0491	2 RR RB211-535E4	113398	CY200	FM-LQ	lsf CITG/sub-lst/opf IBE in Iberia-cs
EC-FEF	Boeing 757-236	24794 / 278	EC-669	0490	0491	2 RR RB211-535E4	113398	CY200	LQ-EK	lsf TOMB/sub-lst/opf IBE in Iberia-cs
EC-FFK	Boeing 757-236	24122 / 187	EC-744	0788	0691	2 RR RB211-535E4	113398	CY200	BP-HM	lsf INGL/sub-lst/opf IBE in Iberia-cs
EC-GBX	Boeing 757-236	25597 / 441	EC-897	0492	0595	2 RR RB211-535E4	113398	CY200	HS-GK	lsf Geonet/sub-lst/opf IBE in Iberia-cs
EC-GCA	Boeing 757-236	22185 / 34	EC-845	0384	0695	2 RR RB211-535C	108862	CY200	HS-FR	lsf Finova/sub-lst/opf IBE in Iberia-cs
EC-GCB	Boeing 757-236	23227 / 57	EC-847	0385	0495	2 RR RB211-535C	104550	CY200	HS-GJ	lsf PEGA/sub-lst/opf IBE in Iberia-cs
EC-GHM	Boeing 767-204 (ER)	24457 / 256	EC-276	0389	0496	2 GE CF6-80A2	163294	Y254	JR-AG	Palma de Mallorca / lsf GECA
EC-GOJ	Boeing 767-204 (ER)	23072 / 107	ZK-NBI	0285	0797	2 GE CF6-80A2	163294	Y253	JP-FR	lsf Heller Finance / cvtd -204
EC-GSU	Boeing 767-3Y0 (ER)	26206 / 487	HL7269	0593	0398	2 GE CF6-80C2B4F	185065	CY211	AK-BS	lsf GECA/sub-lst/opf IBE in Iberia-cs
EC-GTI	Boeing 767-3Y0 (ER)	26207 / 503	HL7286	0793	0398	2 GE CF6-80C2B4F	185065	CY211	BS-HJ	lsf GECA/sub-lst/opf IBE in Iberia-cs

AIR EUROPA EXPRESS = PMI (Div.of Globalia Corporacion Empresarial SA/Sister co.of Air Europa)

Palma-Son Sant Joan & Barcelona-El Prat

Calle Ereos 39, 3rd Floor, E-07009 Palma de Mallorca, Spain ☎ (971) 43 13 46 Tx: none Fax: (971) 43 40 18 SITA: n/a
F: 1996 125 Head: Juan Socastro ICAO: AIR REGIONAL Net: http://www.aireuropa.es Flights are operated under a franchise agreement with AIR EUROPA using their IATA Code UX.

registration	type of aircraft	cn/fn	ex/ex*	mfd	del	powered by	mtow kg	configuration	name/fln/specialitites/remarks
EC-GSE	BAe ATP	2038	EC-GKJ	0091	1196	2 PWC PW126	22930	Y64	lsf BAMT
EC-GSF	BAe ATP	2039	EC-GKI	0091	1196	2 PWC PW126	22930	Y64	lsf BAMT
EC-GSG	BAe ATP	2041	EC-GLC	0091	0197	2 PWC PW126	22930	Y64	lsf BAMT
EC-GSH	BAe ATP	2043	EC-GNI	0091	0497	2 PWC PW126	22930	Y64	lsf BAMT
EC-GSI	BAe ATP	2044	EC-GNJ	0091	0497	2 PWC PW126	22930	Y64	lsf BAMT
EC-GUX	BAe ATP	2024	G-OEDJ	0090	0698	2 PWC PW126	22930	Y64	lsf BAMT
EC-GYE	BAe ATP	2007	G-BTPA	0088	1098	2 PWC PW126	22930	Y64	lsf BAMT
EC-GYF	BAe ATP	2010	G-BTPC	0088	1098	2 PWC PW126	22930	Y64	lsf BAMT
EC-GYR	BAe ATP	2011	G-BTPD	0089	1298	2 PWC PW126	22930	Y64	lsf BAMT
EC-GZH	BAe ATP	2012	G-BTPE	0089	1298	2 PWC PW126	22930	Y64	lsf BAMT

AIR MALLORCA, S.L.

Palma-Son Sant Joan

Juan Alcover 32, E-07006 Palma de Mallorca, Spain ☎ (971) 46 71 62 Tx: none Fax: (971) 46 73 92 SITA: n/a
F: 1986 3 Head: Honorino Nunez Net: n/a

registration	type of aircraft	cn/fn	ex/ex*	mfd	del	powered by	mtow kg	configuration
EC-DYT	Cessna 340A II	340A0687	G-VELT	0079	0486	2 CO TSIO-520-NB	2717	5 Pax/Freighter

AIRNOR – Aeronaves del Noroeste, S.L. = ENW (formerly Aeronor)

Ponteareas Heliport-Pontevedra

Helipuerto de Guillade, E-36860 Ponteareas (Pontevedra), Spain ☎ (986) 65 36 36 Tx: none Fax: (986) 65 38 35 SITA: n/a
F: 1988 7 Head: Julio Dorado ICAO: AIRNOR Net: http://www.cibermedia.com/airnor Aircraft below MTOW 1361kg: Cessna 172 & Robinson R22.

registration	type of aircraft	cn/fn	ex/ex*	mfd	del	powered by	mtow kg	configuration
EC-ERE	Eurocopter (Aerosp.) AS350B Ecureuil	1865	D-HGBA	0087	0393	1 TU Arriel 1B	1950	5 Pax
EC-EGZ	Eurocopter (Aerosp.) SA316B Alouette III	2319	HB-XRY	0076	0392	1 TU Artouste IIIB	2200	5 Pax

AIR NOSTRUM, Lineas Aéreas del Mediterraneo S.A. = YW / ANS (Iberia Regional) — Valencia-Manises

Calle Francisco Valldecabres 31, E-46940 Manises (Valencia), Spain ☎ (96) 196 02 00 Tx: none Fax: (96) 196 09 87 SITA: n/a
F: 1994 ✈✈✈ 725 Head: Carlos Bertomeu IATA: 694 ICAO: NOSTRUM AIR Net: http://www.airnostrum.com
All scheduled services are operated under a franchise agreement with IBERIA as IBERIA REGIONAL (most in such colors & both titles) and using IB flight numbers.

□ EC-GBG	Fokker 50 (F27 Mk050)	20109	EC-868	0089	0395	2 PWC PW125B	20820	Y50		Roble / lsf Frevag Group
□ EC-GBH	Fokker 50 (F27 Mk050)	20159	EC-869	0089	0595	2 PWC PW125B	20820	Y50		Encina / lsf Frevag/opin IB Regional-cs
□ EC-GDD	Fokker 50 (F27 Mk050)	20160	EC-871	0089	0795	2 PWC PW125B	20820	Y50		Olmo / lsf Frevag Group
□ EC-GFP	Fokker 50 (F27 Mk050)	20239	EC-152	0092	0795	2 PWC PW125B	20820	Y50		Nogal / lsf PLMI/op in IB Regional-cs
□ EC-GHB	Fokker 50 (F27 Mk050)	20257	EC-282	0092	0596	2 PWC PW125B	20820	Y50		Aladierno / lsf PLMI/op in IB Regio.-cs
□ EC-GHC	Fokker 50 (F27 Mk050)	20262	EC-287	0092	0596	2 PWC PW125B	20820	Y50		Sabina / lsf PLMI/op in IB Regional-cs
□ EC-GJI	Fokker 50 (F27 Mk050)	20258	EC-284	0092	0896	2 PWC PW125B	20820	Y50		Enebro / lsf PLMI/op in IB Regional-cs
□ EC-GJY	Fokker 50 (F27 Mk050)	20265	D-AFFH	0093	1096	2 PWC PW125B	20820	Y50		Naranjo / lsf PLMI/op in IB Regional-cs
□ EC-GKE	Fokker 50 (F27 Mk050)	20263	D-AFFG	0093	1296	2 PWC PW125B	20820	Y50		Limonero / lsf PLMI/opin IB Regional-cs
□ EC-GKU	Fokker 50 (F27 Mk050)	20273	D-AFFJ	0093	1296	2 PWC PW125B	20820	Y50		Alamo / lsf PLMI / op in IB Regional-cs
□ EC-GKV	Fokker 50 (F27 Mk050)	20274	D-AFFK	0093	1296	2 PWC PW125B	20820	Y50		Arce / lsf PLMI / op in IB Regional-cs
□ EC-GKX	Fokker 50 (F27 Mk050)	20275	D-AFFL	0093	1296	2 PWC PW125B	20820	Y50		Cedro / lsf PLMI / op in IB Regional-cs
□ EC-GQI	Fokker 50 (F27 Mk050)	20251	PH-WXH	0092	1097	2 PWC PW125B	20820	Y50		Palmera / lsf AFTR/op in IB Regional-cs
□ EC-GQT	Fokker 50 (F27 Mk050)	20136	5Y-BFM	0088	1197	2 PWC PW125B	20820	Y50		Fresno / lsf AFTR/op in IB Regional-cs
□ EC-GRY	Fokker 50 (F27 Mk050)	20280	PH-LXU	0093	0198	2 PWC PW127B	20820	Y50		Morera / lsf AFTR/op in IB Regional-cs
□ EC-GRZ	Fokker 50 (F27 Mk050)	20282	PH-MXE	0093	0198	2 PWC PW127B	20820	Y50		Abedul / lsf AFTR/op in IB Regional-cs
□ EC-GTE	Fokker 50 (F27 Mk050)	20203	PH-DMG	0090	0798	2 PWC PW125B	20820	Y50		Acacia / lsf DNM / op in IB Regional-cs
□ EC-	Fokker 50 (F27 Mk050)					2 PWC PW125B	20820	Y50		to be lsd 0599/tb op in IB Regional-cs
□ EC-	Fokker 50 (F27 Mk050)					2 PWC PW125B	20820	Y50		to be lsd 0699/tb op in IB Regional-cs
□ EC-GQS	ATR 72-211	147	EI-CBC	0089	0398	2 PWC PW127	21500	Y70		lsf GECA/cvtd -201/op in IB Regional-cs
□ EC-GQU	ATR 72-201	198	F-WQGC	0090	1297	2 PWC PW124B	21500	Y70		lsf A.T.R. / op in IB Regional-cs
□ EC-GQV	ATR 72-201	210	F-WQGE	0091	1297	2 PWC PW124B	21500	Y70		lsf A.T.R. / op in IB Regional-cs
□ EC-GUL	ATR 72-211	150	EI-CBD	0090	0598	2 PWC PW127	21500	Y70		lsf GECA/cvtd -201/op in IB Regional-cs
□ EC-	ATR 72-500 (72-212A)	578				2 PWC PW127F	22500	Y70		oo-delivery 0499/tbop in IB Regional-cs
□ EC-	ATR 72-500 (72-212A)	580				2 PWC PW127F	22500	Y70		oo-delivery 0499/tbop in IB Regional-cs
□ EC-	ATR 72-500 (72-212A)					2 PWC PW127F	22500	Y70		oo-delivery 0899/tbop in IB Regional-cs
□ EC-	ATR 72-500 (72-212A)					2 PWC PW127F	22500	Y70		oo-delivery 0999/tbop in IB Regional-cs
□ EC-	ATR 72-500 (72-212A)					2 PWC PW127F	22500	Y70		oo-delivery 0200/tbop in IB Regional-cs
□ EC-GTG	Canadair Regional Jet 100ER (CL-600-2B19)	7020	F-GNME	0093	0398	2 GE CF34-3A1	23133	Y50		Sorolla / lsf LIT/op in IB Regional-cs
□ EC-GYI	Canadair Regional Jet 200ER (CL-600-2B19)	7249	C-GDDM*	0098	1098	2 GE CF34-3B1	23133	Y50		op in IB Regional-colors
□ EC-GZA	Canadair Regional Jet 200ER (CL-600-2B19)	7252	C-GDDO*	0098	1298	2 GE CF34-3B1	23133	Y50		op in IB Regional-colors
□ EC-	Canadair Regional Jet 200ER (CL-600-2B19)					2 GE CF34-3B1	23133	Y50		oo-delivery 0699/tbop in IB Regional-cs
□ EC-	Canadair Regional Jet 200ER (CL-600-2B19)					2 GE CF34-3B1	23133	Y50		oo-delivery 1099/tbop in IB Regional-cs
□ EC-	Canadair Regional Jet 200ER (CL-600-2B19)					2 GE CF34-3B1	23133	Y50		oo-delivery 1199/tbop in IB Regional-cs

AIR PLUS COMET = 2Z / MPD (Air Comet, S.A. dba/Member of Grupo Marsans/formerly Magic Airlines, S.A.) — Madrid-Barajas

Edificio Barajas I, Calle Trespaderne 29, E-28042 Madrid, Spain ☎ (91) 329 49 29 Tx: none Fax: (91) 329 35 11 SITA: n/a
F: 1996 ✈✈✈ 150 Head: José Maria Llodra ICAO: RED COMET Net: n/a

□ EC-GMU	Airbus Industrie A310-324 (ET)	451	N571SW	0088	0397	2 PW PW4152	153000	F12Y241	MR-FS	
□ EC-GOT	Airbus Industrie A310-324 (ET)	455	N572SW	0088	0697	2 PW PW4152	153000	F12Y241	MR-GH	Andalucia sob hay una
□ EC-	Airbus Industrie A310-324 (ET)	542	N824PA	0090		2 PW PW4152	153000	F12Y241		to be lsf PART 0599

AMBULANCIAS INSULARES, S.A. = AIM (Affiliated with Centro Servicios Medicos, S.A.) — Palma-Son Sant Joan

Ca'n Valero 36, Poligono Ca'n Valero, E-07011 Palma de Mallorca, Spain ☎ (971) 26 37 59 Tx: n/a Fax: (971) 49 00 08 SITA: n/a
F: 1978 ✈✈✈ n/a Head: Dr. José Maria Garcia Ruiz ICAO: AMBUL-INSU Net: n/a

□ EC-FFZ	Britten-Norman BN-2B-26 Islander	2224	EC-750	0089	0691	2 LY O-540-E4C5	2994	EMS		
□ EC-EFS	Twin (Aero) Turbo Commander 690	11034	N400JJ	0072	1087	2 GA TPE331-5-251K	4649	EMS		

ARTAC AVIACION, S.L. = AVS — Madrid-Barajas

Terminal de Aviacion General, Aeropuerto de Barajas, E-28042 Madrid, Spain ☎ (91) 393 69 24 Tx: none Fax: (91) 393 64 47 SITA: n/a
F: 1994 ✈✈✈ 33 Head: Rosa Maria Bejarano ICAO: ARTAC Net: n/a

□ EC-GEN	Fairchild (Swearingen) SA227AC Metro III	AC-688	EC-126	0087	1095	2 GA TPE331-11U-612G	6577	Combi		
□ EC-GJM	Fairchild (Swearingen) SA227BC Metro III	BC-772B	EC-307	0091	0796	2 GA TPE331-11U-611G	7257	Combi		

AUDELI, S.A. = ADI (Audeli Air Express / Audeli Executive Jet) — Madrid-Barajas

Castrobarto 10, Piso 1°, Of. 5, E-28042 Madrid, Spain ☎ (91) 329 30 70 Tx: none Fax: (91) 329 46 30 SITA: n/a
F: 1987 ✈✈✈ 25 Head: Juan Pericas Vila ICAO: AUDELI Net: n/a Freighter services are operated under the marketing name AUDELI AIR EXPRESS and executive services under the marketing name AUDELI EXECUTIVE JET.

□ EC-EDC	Dassault Falcon 20C	6	N750SS	0065	0787	2 GE CF700-2D2	13000	Executive		
□ EC-EHC	Dassault Falcon 20D (C)	46	N46VG	0066	0288	2 GE CF700-2D2	13000	Freighter		cvtd Falcon 20C

AVIACO – Aviacion y Comercio, S.A. = AO / AYC (Subsidiary of Iberia) — Madrid-Barajas

AVIACO

Maudes 51, Edificio Minister, E-28003 Madrid, Spain ☎ (91) 453 10 00 Tx: 27641 aomad e Fax: (91) 533 46 13 SITA: MADDDAO
F: 1948 ✈✈✈ 1700 Head: Juan Losa IATA: 110 ICAO: AVIACO Net: http://www.aviaco.com
All scheduled flights are operated in conjunction with IBERIA using IB-flight numbers. Expected to be fully integrated into IBERIA & all aircraft repainted into Iberia-cs during 1999.

□ EC-BIH	Boeing (Douglas) DC-9-32	47076 / 134		0067	0784	2 PW JT8D-9A (HK3/ABS)	49895	CY110	FG-CE	Roncesvalles
□ EC-BIK	Boeing (Douglas) DC-9-32	47080 / 164		0067	0582	2 PW JT8D-9A (HK3/ABS)	49895	CY110	FG-CK	Castillo de Guanapay
□ EC-BIP	Boeing (Douglas) DC-9-32	47091 / 206		0067	0580	2 PW JT8D-9A (HK3/ABS)	49895	CY110	DM-EG	Castillo de Monteagudo
□ EC-BQY	Boeing (Douglas) DC-9-32	47455 / 579		0070	0484	2 PW JT8D-9A	49895	CY110	HL-AJ	Mar Menor
□ EC-BYE	Boeing (Douglas) DC-9-32	47504 / 651		0071	0690	2 PW JT8D-9A (HK3/ABS)	48988	CY110	AF-DJ	Cala Galdana
□ EC-BYF	Boeing (Douglas) DC-9-32	47542 / 652		0172	0891	2 PW JT8D-9A (HK3/ABS)	48988	CY110	AF-DK	Hernan Cortes
□ EC-BYI	Boeing (Douglas) DC-9-32	47452 / 660		0472	0791	2 PW JT8D-9A (HK3/ABS)	48988	CY110	AF-EG	Pedro de Valdivia
□ EC-BYJ	Boeing (Douglas) DC-9-32	47461 / 663		0572	0791	2 PW JT8D-9A (HK3/ABS)	48988	CY110	AF-EH	Ciudad de Salamanca
□ EC-CGN	Boeing (Douglas) DC-9-32	47637 / 731		0074	0674	2 PW JT8D-9A (HK3/ABS)	49895	CY110	DE-GJ	Martin Alonso Pinzon
□ EC-CGO	Boeing (Douglas) DC-9-32	47640 / 734		0074	0674	2 PW JT8D-9A (HK3/ABS)	49895	CY110	DE-GK	Pedro Alonso Nino
□ EC-CGP	Boeing (Douglas) DC-9-32	47642 / 749		0074	1074	2 PW JT8D-9A (HK3/ABS)	49895	CY110	DE-GL	Juan Sebastian Elcano
□ EC-CGQ	Boeing (Douglas) DC-9-32	47643 / 750		0074	1074	2 PW JT8D-9A (HK3/ABS)	49895	CY110	DE-GM	Alonso de Ojeda
□ EC-CGR	Boeing (Douglas) DC-9-32	47644 / 767		0075	0275	2 PW JT8D-9A	49895	CY110	DE-HJ	Francisco de Orellana
□ EC-CLD	Boeing (Douglas) DC-9-32	47675 / 782		0775	0775	2 PW JT8D-9A	49895	CY110	DE-HL	Hernando de Soto
□ EC-CTR	Boeing (Douglas) DC-9-34F (CF)	47702 / 817	N19B*	0076	0576	2 PW JT8D-17	54885	CY110	DE-JL	lst IBE
□ EC-CTS	Boeing (Douglas) DC-9-34F (CF)	47704 / 819		0476	0576	2 PW JT8D-17	54885	CY110	DE-JM	Francisco de Pizarro
□ EC-CTU	Boeing (Douglas) DC-9-34F (CF)	47707 / 823		0076	0776	2 PW JT8D-17	54885	CY110	DF-AC	Pedro de Alvarado
□ EC-DGC	Boeing (Douglas) DC-9-34	48104 / 928		1079	1179	2 PW JT8D-17	54885	CY110	DL-EM	Castillo de Sotomayor
□ EC-DGD	Boeing (Douglas) DC-9-34	48105 / 929		0079	1279	2 PW JT8D-17	54885	CY110	DM-EH	Castillo de Arcos
□ EC-DGE	Boeing (Douglas) DC-9-34	48106 / 933		0079	0180	2 PW JT8D-17	54885	CY110	DM-FK	Castillo de Bellver
□ EC-FGM	Boeing (Douglas) MD-88 (DC-9-88)	53193 / 1890	EC-751	0091	0891	2 PW JT8D-217C	64410	CY155	JP-GQ	Torre de Hércules
□ EC-FHG	Boeing (Douglas) MD-88 (DC-9-88)	53194 / 1911	EC-752	0891	0991	2 PW JT8D-217C	64410	CY155	JP-HQ	La Almudaina / special Canarias-cs
□ EC-FIG	Boeing (Douglas) MD-88 (DC-9-88)	53195 / 1929	EC-753	0091	1191	2 PW JT8D-217C	64410	CY155	JP-KQ	Penon de Ifach
□ EC-FIH	Boeing (Douglas) MD-88 (DC-9-88)	53196 / 1930	EC-754	1091	1191	2 PW JT8D-217C	64410	CY155	JP-LQ	Albaicin
□ EC-FJE	Boeing (Douglas) MD-88 (DC-9-88)	53197 / 1940	EC-755	0091	1291	2 PW JT8D-217C	64410	CY155	JP-MQ	Gibralfaro
□ EC-FLK	Boeing (Douglas) MD-88 (DC-9-88)	53304 / 1975	EC-946	0092	0392	2 PW JT8D-217C	64410	CY155	KL-BQ	Palacio de la Magdalena
□ EC-FLN	Boeing (Douglas) MD-88 (DC-9-88)	53303 / 1974	EC-945	0092	0392	2 PW JT8D-217C	64410	CY155	KL-AQ	Puerta de Tierra
□ EC-FND	Boeing (Douglas) MD-88 (DC-9-88)	53305 / 2001	EC-964	0092	0692	2 PW JT8D-217C	64410	CY155	KL-CQ	Playa de la Concha
□ EC-FOF	Boeing (Douglas) MD-88 (DC-9-88)	53307 / 2015	EC-966	0092	0892	2 PW JT8D-217C	64410	CY155	KL-EQ	Cesar Manrique Lanzarote
□ EC-FOG	Boeing (Douglas) MD-88 (DC-9-88)	53306 / 2014	EC-965	0092	0792	2 PW JT8D-217C	64410	CY155	KL-DQ	La Giralda
□ EC-FOZ	Boeing (Douglas) MD-88 (DC-9-88)	53308 / 2022	EC-987	0092	0992	2 PW JT8D-217C	64410	CY155	KL-FQ	Montjuic
□ EC-FPD	Boeing (Douglas) MD-88 (DC-9-88)	53309 / 2023	EC-988	0092	0992	2 PW JT8D-217C	64410	CY155	KL-GQ	Lago de Coradonga
□ EC-FPJ	Boeing (Douglas) MD-88 (DC-9-88)	53310 / 2024	EC-989	0092	1092	2 PW JT8D-217C	64410	CY155	KL-HQ	Ria de Vigo

AVIALSA T-35 — Valencia-Manises

Bloque técnico, Aeropuerto de Valencia, E-46940 Manises, Spain ☎ (96) 370 95 00 Tx: none Fax: (96) 152 36 76 SITA: n/a
F: 1988 ✈✈✈ 25 Head: Vicente Huerta Dominguez Net: n/a Ag-aircraft below MTOW 5000kg: PZL M-18A

□ EC-ETU	Cessna 337G Super Skymaster	33701573	N6AX	0074	0590	2 CO IO-360-G	2100	Surveyer/Tanker		
□ EC-GDS	Air Tractor AT-802	802-0018	EC-881	0095	1195	1 PWC PT6A-67AG	7257	Tanker		
□ EC-GFX	Air Tractor AT-802	802-0027	N6065G*	0096	0496	1 PWC PT6A-67AG	7257	Tanker		
□ EC-GGY	Air Tractor AT-802	802-0031	N6097U*	0096	0696	1 PWC PT6A-67AG	7257	Tanker		
□ EC-GHL	Air Tractor AT-802	802-0032	N61289*	0096	0996	1 PWC PT6A-67AG	7257	Tanker		

AVISER, S.A. - Aviacion Sanitaria = AVH — Sant Cugat H.G.C.-Heliport & Circuit de Catalunya-Heliport

AVISER

Hospital General de Catalunya, C/Gomera sn, E-08190 Sant Cugat del Valles (Barcelona), Spain ☎ (93) 675 45 11 Tx: none Fax: (93) 675 20 06 SITA: n/a
F: 1988 ✈✈✈ 15 Head: Luis Freixa Figuerola ICAO: AVISER Net: n/a

□ EC-ERD	Eurocopter (Aerosp.) AS350B Ecureuil	1530	G-JORR	0081	1189	1 TU Arriel 1B	1950	EMS		opf Reial Automobil Club de Catalunya
□ EC-EVM	Eurocopter (Aerosp.) AS350B2 Ecureuil	2312		0090	0490	1 TU Arriel 1D1	2250	EMS		opf Reial Automobil Club de Catalunya
□ EC-FAL	Eurocopter (Aerosp.) SA316C Alouette III	2146	EC-555	0074	1290	1 TU Artouste IIID	2250	EMS		std Circuit de Catalunya / for sale
□ EC-GUH	Eurocopter (Aerosp.) AS355F2 Ecureuil 2	5474	N6040U	0491	0498	2 AN 250-C20F	2540	EMS		opf Reial Automobil Club de Catalunya

123 registration | type of aircraft | cn/fn | ex/ex* | mfd | del | powered by | mtow kg | configuration | selcal | name/fln/specialitites/remarks

AZIMUT, S.A. = AZT — Madrid-Cuatro Vientos

Marques de Urquijo 11, E-28008 Madrid, Spain ☎ (91) 541 05 00 Tx: none Fax: (91) 542 51 12 SITA: n/a
F: 1969 20 Head: Antonio Madrid Ortega ICAO: AZIMUT Net: n/a

registration	type of aircraft	cn/fn	ex/ex*	mfd	del	powered by	mtow kg	configuration	selcal	name/fln/specialitites/remarks
☐ EC-CNC	Cessna 310Q II	310Q1123	N1272G	0074	0375	2 CO IO-470-VO	2404	Photo		
☐ EC-DET	Cessna T310R II	310R0644	N98907	0077	0179	2 CO TSIO-520-B	2495	Photo		
☐ EC-EAH	Cessna T310R II	310R1271	N6104C	0078	0986	2 CO TSIO-520-B	2495	Photo		

BASAER - Baquero Servicios Aéreos, S.L. — Cordoba

Avda de Libia sn, E-14014 Cordoba, Spain ☎ (957) 25 31 72 Tx: none Fax: (957) 43 23 01 SITA: n/a
F: 1982 4 Head: Javier Baquero Bejarzno Net: n/a Ag-aircraft below MTOW 5000kg: Cessna A188 & Piper PA-25

registration	type of aircraft	cn/fn	ex/ex*	mfd	del	powered by	mtow kg	configuration	selcal	name/fln/specialitites/remarks
☐ EC-GGB	Boeing (Douglas) DC-7C	45112 / 736	EC-888	0056	0795	4 WR R-3350	64864	Tanker		opf DGCN-DirGen.Conservacion Naturalez
☐ EC-GGC	Boeing (Douglas) DC-7C	45215 / 913	EC-889	0057	0695	4 WR R-3350	64864	Tanker		opf DGCN-DirGen.Conservacion Naturaleza

BINTER CANARIAS, S.A. = NT / IBB (Compania de Aviacion Regional para Canarias dba/Subs.of Iberia) — Gran Canaria-Gando & Tenerife-Los Rodeos

Aeropuerto de Gando, Parcela 9 del Zima, E-35230 Gran Canaria, Spain ☎ (928) 57 96 01 Tx: none Fax: (928) 57 96 03 SITA: n/a
F: 1988 300 Head: Gregorio Garcia Ruiz IATA: 474 Net: n/a All scheduled flights are operated in conjunction with IBERIA using IB-flight numbers.

registration	type of aircraft	cn/fn	ex/ex*	mfd	del	powered by	mtow kg	configuration	selcal	name/fln/specialitites/remarks
☐ EC-ESS	ATR 72-202	154	EC-383	0089	1289	2 PWC PW124B	21500	Y68		
☐ EC-EUJ	ATR 72-202	157	EC-384	0089	0290	2 PWC PW124B	21500	Y68		
☐ EC-EYK	ATR 72-202	183	EC-515	0090	0890	2 PWC PW124B	21500	Y68		
☐ EC-FIV	ATR 72-201	260	EC-873	0091	1291	2 PWC PW124B	21500	Y68		
☐ EC-FJX	ATR 72-201	267	EC-874	0091	1291	2 PWC PW124B	21500	Y68		
☐ EC-FKQ	ATR 72-201	276	EC-935	0091	0192	2 PWC PW124B	21500	Y68		
☐ EC-GQF	ATR 72-202	489	F-WWLJ*	0096	1097	2 PWC PW124B	21500	Y68		
☐ EC-GRP	ATR 72-202	488	F-WWLI*	0096	1297	2 PWC PW124B	21500	Y68		
☐ EC-GRU	ATR 72-202	493	F-WWLN*	0097	1297	2 PWC PW124B	21500	Y68		

BINTER MEDITERRANEO, S.A. = AX / BIM (Compania de Aviacion Regional del Mediterraneo dba / Subsidiary of Iberia) — Malaga-Picasso

Binter Mediterráneo

Aeropuerto de Malaga, Antiquo Edificio Salidas Nacionales, Muelle B, E-29004 Malaga, Spain ☎ (95) 204 83 90 Tx: none Fax: (95) 204 83 92 SITA: n/a
F: 1989 75 Head: Gregorio Garcia Ruiz ICAO: BINTER Net: n/a All scheduled flights are operated in conjunction with IBERIA using IB-flight numbers.

registration	type of aircraft	cn/fn	ex/ex*	mfd	del	powered by	mtow kg	configuration	selcal	name/fln/specialitites/remarks
☐ EC-FAC	CASA (IPTN) CN-235-100	C029	EC-009	0090	1090	2 GE CT7-9C	15100	Y40		
☐ EC-FAD	CASA (IPTN) CN-235-100	C018		0090	0990	2 GE CT7-9C	15100	Y40		
☐ EC-FBC	CASA (IPTN) CN-235-100	C033	EC-013	0090	1290	2 GE CT7-9C	15100	Y40		Ciudad Autonoma de Melilla
☐ EC-HAU	CASA (IPTN) CN-235-200	C030	LV-VHM	0090	0990	2 GE CT7-9C	15800	Y44		cvtd -100
☐ EC-HAV	CASA (IPTN) CN-235-200	C032	LV-VGV	0090	1290	2 GE CT7-9C	15800	Y40		cvtd -100

BOREAL AVIACION, S.L. — Madrid-Barajas

Av. de Valdelaparra 27, Neisa Norte, Ed. 2, Loc. 8, E-28100 Alcobendas (Madrid), Spain ☎ (91) 661 06 95 Tx: none Fax: (91) 661 92 48 SITA: n/a
F: 1995 4 Head: Raul Delgado Net: n/a

registration	type of aircraft	cn/fn	ex/ex*	mfd	del	powered by	mtow kg	configuration	selcal	name/fln/specialitites/remarks
☐ EC-EMH	Cessna 402B	402B0534	N101GP	0073	0095	2 CO TSIO-520-E	2858	8 Pax		

CANARIAS REGIONAL AIR, S.A. = FW / CNM — Tenerife-Los Rodeos

Avda. Generalisimo 8, E-38400 Puerto de la Cruz, (Tenerife), Spain ☎ (922) 37 26 56 Tx: none Fax: (922) 38 84 82 SITA: n/a
F: 1997 50 Head: D. Juan Manuel Socastro Gonzalez IATA: 233 ICAO: CANARIAS AIR Net: n/a Suspended operations 310199 (with BAe ATP aircraft). Intends to restart with Boeing 737-300.

CATAIR Lineas Aéreas — Gerona-Costa Brava

Calle Pelayo No.40, atico 2, E-08001 Barcelona, Spain ☎ (93) 889 36 36 Tx: none Fax: (93) 889 36 36 SITA: n/a
F: 1997 5 Head: J.M. Pare Subiranas Net: n/a Presently being set-up. Intends to start operations during 1999 with 1 Embraer 120 Brasilia aircraft.

CEGISA (Subs. of Comair, Emaer & Gestair / Member of Gestair Interholding) — Salamanca-Matacan

Carretera de Madrid Km 14, Matacan, E-37001 Salamanca, Spain ☎ (923) 30 62 52 Tx: none Fax: (923) 30 62 84 SITA: n/a
F: 1995 30 Head: Francisco Martinez Bernalte Net: http://www.gestair.es/cegisa

registration	type of aircraft	cn/fn	ex/ex*	mfd	del	powered by	mtow kg	configuration	selcal	name/fln/specialitites/remarks
☐ EC-GBP	Canadair CL-215 (CL-215-1A10)	1031	UD.13-3	0073	0096	2 PW R-2800-CA3	17100	Tanker		Amphibian
☐ EC-GBQ	Canadair CL-215 (CL-215-1A10)	1033	UD.13-5	0073	0096	2 PW R-2800-CA3	17100	Tanker		Amphibian
☐ EC-GBR	Canadair CL-215 (CL-215-1A10)	1051	UD.13-11	0076	0096	2 PW R-2800-CA3	17100	Tanker		Amphibian
☐ EC-GBS	Canadair CL-215 (CL-215-1A10)	1052	UD.13-12	0076	0096	2 PW R-2800-CA3	17100	Tanker		Amphibian
☐ EC-GBT	Canadair CL-215 (CL-215-1A10)	1054	UD.13-14	0077	0096	2 PW R-2800-CA3	17100	Tanker		Amphibian

CENTER VOL, S.A. Helicopters (Viatges Center Vol, S.A. dba) — Gerona-Costa Brava

Aeropuerto de Girona, E-17185 Girona, Spain ☎ (972) 47 42 04 Tx: none Fax: (972) 47 42 59 SITA: n/a
F: 1991 7 Head: Pedro Macia Net: n/a Aircraft below MTOW 1361kg: Robinson R22.

registration	type of aircraft	cn/fn	ex/ex*	mfd	del	powered by	mtow kg	configuration	selcal	name/fln/specialitites/remarks
☐ EC-FEV	Bell 206B JetRanger	1162	C-GZPX	0073	0591	1 AN 250-C20	1451	4 Pax		

CLIPPER NATIONAL AIR, S.A. = ORO (formerly C.N. Air, S.A.) — Barcelona-El Prat

Tuset 30, 3.P, E-08006 Barcelona, Spain ☎ (93) 218 23 21 Tx: none Fax: (93) 218 22 23 SITA: n/a
F: 1992 10 Head: Antonio Martinez Garcia ICAO: CAPRI Net: n/a

registration	type of aircraft	cn/fn	ex/ex*	mfd	del	powered by	mtow kg	configuration	selcal	name/fln/specialitites/remarks
☐ EC-GOK	Mitsubishi MU-2J (MU-2B-35)	635	OY-ARV	0074	0497	2 GA TPE331-6-251M	4899	EMS / Executive		
☐ EC-GTS	Cessna 500 Citation	500-0038	N407SC	0072	0498	2 PWC JT15D-1	5216	Executive		
☐ EC-	Cessna 500 Citation	500-0209	N800AV	0074	0499	2 PWC JT15D-1	5216	Executive		

CYGNUS AIR, S.A. = RGN (Subs.of Gestair Interholding/formerly Regional Lineas Aéreas, S.A.) — Madrid-Barajas

Calle Aguetol 7, 1.Planta, E-28042 Madrid, Spain ☎ (91) 746 15 33 Tx: none Fax: (91) 746 15 32 SITA: MADHDGP
F: 1994 50 Head: Jesus M. Macarron ICAO: REGIONAL LINEAS Net: n/a

registration	type of aircraft	cn/fn	ex/ex*	mfd	del	powered by	mtow kg	configuration	selcal	name/fln/specialitites/remarks
☐ EC-EMD	Boeing (Douglas) DC-8-62F	46023 / 407	EC-217	0068	1198	4 PW JT3D-7 (HK3/BAC)	151953	Freighter	GL-CE	lst / opf IBE in Iberia-cs / cvtd -62
☐ EC-EMX	Boeing (Douglas) DC-8-62F	45921 / 322	EC-230	0067	1198	4 PW JT3D-7 (HK3/BAC)	151953	Freighter	GL-CD	lst / opf IBE in Iberia-cs / cvtd -62

D.G.T. - Servicio de Helicopteros (Helicopter division of the Direccion General de Trafico, part of the Ministerio del Interior) — Marid-Cuatro Vientos

Aeropuerto de Cuatro Vientos, Apartado 27022, E-28080 Madrid, Spain ☎ (91) 508 27 10 Tx: none Fax: (91) 508 96 17 SITA: n/a
F: 1978 60 Head: Manuel Guillen Garcia Net: n/a
State organisation conducting non-commerical road patrol & other mission flights from central base Madrid-Cuatro Vientos & sub-bases at Barcelona, Valencia, Malaga & Sevilla.

registration	type of aircraft	cn/fn	ex/ex*	mfd	del	powered by	mtow kg	configuration	selcal	name/fln/specialitites/remarks
☐ EC-ELN	Eurocopter (Aerosp.) AS350B1 Ecureuil	2128	F-WYMJ*	0088	1288	1 TU Arriel 1D	2200	Patrol		
☐ EC-ELO	Eurocopter (Aerosp.) AS350B2 Ecureuil	2129		0088	1288	1 TU Arriel 1D1	2250	Patrol		
☐ EC-ERR	Eurocopter (Aerosp.) AS350B2 Ecureuil	2271		0088	0190	1 TU Arriel 1D1	2250	Patrol		cvtd AS350B
☐ EC-FGS	Eurocopter (Aerosp.) AS350B2 Ecureuil	2537		0091	1091	1 TU Arriel 1D1	2250	Patrol		
☐ EC-FIB	Eurocopter (Aerosp.) AS350B2 Ecureuil	2558	EC-853	0091	1291	1 TU Arriel 1D1	2250	Patrol		
☐ EC-FJV	Eurocopter (Aerosp.) AS350B2 Ecureuil	2580		1291	0192	1 TU Arriel 1D1	2250	Patrol		
☐ EC-FOQ	Eurocopter (Aerosp.) AS350B2 Ecureuil	2639		0092	0992	1 TU Arriel 1D1	2250	Patrol		
☐ EC-FQH	Eurocopter (Aerosp.) AS350B2 Ecureuil	2674		0092	1092	1 TU Arriel 1D1	2250	Patrol		
☐ EC-CBY	Eurocopter (Aerosp.) SA319B Alouette III	2021		0073	0078	1 TU Astazou XIVB	2250	Patrol		
☐ EC-EBH	Eurocopter (Aerosp.) SA316B Alouette III	1783	ZIMB AF	0070	0687	1 TU Artouste IIIB	2200	Patrol		
☐ EC-EBI	Eurocopter (Aerosp.) SA316B Alouette III	1783	314	0068	0687	1 TU Artouste IIIB	2200	Patrol		
☐ EC-FXO	Eurocopter (Aerosp.) SA319B Alouette III	2227	HD.16-5	0075	0794	1 TU Astazou XIVB	2250	Patrol		
☐ EC-FYI	Eurocopter (Aerosp.) SA319B Alouette III	2256	HD.16-7	0075	0994	1 TU Astazou XIVB	2250	Patrol		
☐ EC-GAJ	Eurocopter (Aerosp.) SA319B Alouette III	2212	HD.16-4	0075	0495	1 TU Astazou XIVB	2250	Patrol		
☐ EC-FTX	Eurocopter (Aerosp.) AS355N Ecureuil 2	5550	F-WYMU*	0093	1193	2 TU Arrius 1A	2540	Patrol		
☐ EC-FUH	Eurocopter (Aerosp.) AS355N Ecureuil 2	5554	F-WYMB*	0093	1293	2 TU Arrius 1A	2540	Patrol		
☐ EC-GVH	Eurocopter (Aerosp.) AS355N Ecureuil 2	5656		0098	0998	2 TU Arrius 1A	2540	Patrol		

EAC - European Air Cargo, Sl. — Palma de Mallorca

Aptdo. 197, C/Pintor Jorge Juan 17-7-4, E-07015 Palma de Mallorca, Spain ☎ (971) 70 71 48 Tx: none Fax: (971) 70 71 49 SITA: n/a
F: 1992 23 Head: Capt. B.G. Lwowski Hofmann Net: n/a Beside Aircraft sourcing & leasing, Government & Aviation consulting, Airport planning & consulting, also operates cargo-charter flights with Antonov 12/22/124 & Ilyushin 76-aircraft, leased from other companies when required.

ERA - European Regions Airlines, S.A. = EA / EUA — Palma-Son Sant Joan & Victoria-Foronda

Son Garcias del Pinar s/n, E-07007 Coll d'En Rabassa, Spain ☎ (971) 42 86 68 Tx: none Fax: (971) 42 98 77 SITA: n/a
F: 1998 35 Head: Joaquin Torrebella IATA: 382 ICAO: GOLDEN ANGEL Net: n/a

registration	type of aircraft	cn/fn	ex/ex*	mfd	del	powered by	mtow kg	configuration	selcal	name/fln/specialitites/remarks
☐ EC-GZI	Embraer RJ145EU (EMB-145EU)	145098	PT-SBU*	0098	1298	2 AN AE3007A	19990	Y50		
☐ EC-GZU	Embraer RJ145EU (EMB-145EU)	145106		0099	0199	2 AN AE3007A	19990	Y50		

EURO CONTINENTAL AIR, S.L. = ECN — Barcelona-El Prat

Plaza Brasilia 2, E-08860 Castelldefels (Barcelona), Spain ☎ (93) 635 02 25 Tx: none Fax: (93) 635 02 26 SITA: n/a
F: 1997 n/a Head: n/a ICAO: EURO CONTINENTAL Net: http://www.eurocontinental.com

registration	type of aircraft	cn/fn	ex/ex*	mfd	del	powered by	mtow kg	configuration	selcal	name/fln/specialitites/remarks
☐ EC-GPS	Fairchild (Swearingen) SA227AC Metro III	AC-722	N439MA	0088	0897	2 GA TPE331-11U-612G	6577	Y19 / Freighter		

FAASA AVIACION - Fumigacion Aérea Andaluza, S.A. = FAM

Palma del Rio-Cordoba, Salamanca & Badajoz

Alamillos 18, E-14700 Palma de Rio (Cordoba), Spain ☎ (957) 71 04 60 Tx: none Fax: (957) 71 06 87 SITA: n/a
F: 1967 ♟♟♟ 70 Head: Sebastian Almagro ICAO: FAASA Net: n/a Aircraft/Ag-aircraft below MTOW 1361/5000kg: Cessna 152, Grumman G-164A/B/C & Piper PA-25

☐ EC-FGL	Bell 206L-3 LongRanger III	51379	N65108	0090	0991	1 AN 250-C30P	1882	6 Pax / EMS		
☐ EC-DVR	Agusta A109A	7231		0085	0093	2 AN 250-C20B	2600	EMS		opf OGI Andalucia
☐ EC-EOI	Bell UH-1B (204)	408	N5023U	0062	0589	1 LY T5311D	3856			
☐ EC-EOX	Bell UH-1B (204)	1214	N90632	0065	0989	1 LY T5311D	3856			
☐ EC-GAS	Bell 205A-1	30081	EC-844	0070	0495	1 LY T5313B	4309			
☐ EC-GDM	Bell UH-1H (205)	5398	N205UD	0067	0695	1 LY T53-L-13	4309			
☐ EC-GDN	Bell UH-1H (205)	5721	N6190P	0067	0695	1 LY T53-L-13	4309			
☐ EC-GDO	Bell UH-1H (205)	8800	N205UE	0067	0695	1 LY T53-L-13	4309			
☐ EC-GKY	Bell UH-1H (205)	13274	HE.10B-37	0073	0096	1 LY T53-L-13	4309			
☐ EC-GKZ	Bell UH-1H (205)	13275	HE.10B-38	0073	0096	1 LY T53-L-13	4309			
☐ EC-GOE	Bell UH-1H (205)	5272	N19UH	0067	0097	1 LY T53-L-13	4309			
☐ EC-GOF	Bell UH-1H (205)	5580	N15UH	0067	0097	1 LY T53-L-13	4309			
☐ EC-GOG	Bell UH-1H (205)	9960	N17UH	0068	0097	1 LY T53-L-13	4309			
☐ EC-GOH	Bell UH-1H (205)	10484	N16UH	0069	0097	1 LY T53-L-13	4309			
☐ EC-CHE	Beech King Air A100	B-195	E23-2	0074		2 PWC PT6A-28	5216	8 Pax / EMS		opf Junta de Andalucia

FLIGHTLINE, S.L. = FTL

Barcelona-El Prat

Calle Industria 131, Entresuelo 3A, E-08025 Barcelona, Spain ☎ (93) 435 99 40 Tx: none Fax: (93) 347 36 34 SITA: n/a
F: 1994 ♟♟♟ 5 Head: Jorge Casas Pérez ICAO: FLIGHT-AVIA Net: n/a

☐ EC-GDR	Fairchild (Swearingen) SA226AT Merlin IVA	AT-074	EC-702	0080	0199	2 GA TPE331-3U-303G	5670	Freighter		
☐ EC-GFK	Fairchild (Swearingen) SA226AT Merlin IVA	AT-062	EC-125	0077	1195	2 GA TPE331-3UW-304G	5670	Y19/Frtr 1,3t		
☐ EC-GBB	Beech King Air 200	BB-182	EC-727	0076	0096	2 PWC PT6A-41	5670	C8		lsf P.M.S. S.A.

FUTURA International Airways = FH / FUA (Compania Hispano Irlandesa de Aviacion SA dba/Subs.of Aer Lingus & Belton Air SA)

Palma-Son Sant Joan & Tenerife-Reina Sofia

Gran Via Asima 17, E-07009 Palma de Mallorca, Spain ☎ (971) 43 20 53 Tx: 68 597 fua e Fax: (971) 43 44 01 SITA: n/a
F: 1989 ♟♟♟ 350 Head: William Walsh ICAO: FUTURA Net: n/a

☐ EC-GNZ	Boeing 737-4Y0	25178 / 2199	D-ABAD	0091	0497	2 CFMI CFM56-3C1	68038	Y170	JQ-HM	lsf GECA
☐ EC-GRX	Boeing 737-46B	24123 / 1663	G-OBMN	0089	1297	2 CFMI CFM56-3C1	65770	Y170	LR-EF	lsf BBAM
☐ EC-GUG	Boeing 737-4S3	25116 / 2061	EI-CNE	0591	0195	2 CFMI CFM56-3C1	64636	Y170	FP-MR	lsf KM Association
☐ EC-GUI	Boeing 737-4Y0	24690 / 1885	EI-COU	0090	1290	2 CFMI CFM56-3C1	68038	Y170	EG-BF	lsf GECA
☐ EC-GVB	Boeing 737-4Y0	24689 / 1883	PT-TDD	0090	0790	2 CFMI CFM56-3C1	68038	Y170	AQ-GM	lsf GECA
☐ EC-GXR	Boeing 737-4Y0	24685 / 1859	PT-TDB	0090	0590	2 CFMI CFM56-3C1	68038	Y170	HR-KP	lsf GECA
☐ EC-GYK	Boeing 737-4Y0	24688 / 1876	G-OABF	0090	1094	2 CFMI CFM56-3C1	65770	Y170	LP-AJ	lsf GECA
☐ EC-HAN	Boeing 737-4Q8	25740 / 2461	TC-JED	0093	0299	2 CFMI CFM56-3C1	68038	Y170		lsf ILFC
☐ EC-	Boeing 737-4Y0	25180 / 2201	EI-CNF	0092	0192	2 CFMI CFM56-3C1	65770	Y170	JR-BE	lsf GECA/sublst TBA as PT-TDG in winter
☐ EC-	Boeing 737-46B	24124 / 1679	SU-SAB	0089	0694	2 CFMI CFM56-3C1	65770	Y170	JM-KR	lsf ANAU/sublst EIN as EI-CRC in winter
☐ EC-	Boeing 737-4Y0	24545 / 1805	G-OABE	0090	0290	2 CFMI CFM56-3C1	65770	Y170	HR-KM	lsf GECA/sublst TBA as PT-TDE in winter
☐ EC-	Boeing 737-86N					2 CFMI CFM56-7B26	78245	Y184		to be lsf GECA 1199
☐ EC-	Boeing 737-86N					2 CFMI CFM56-7B26	78245	Y184		to be lsf GECA 1299
☐ EC-	Boeing 737-86N					2 CFMI CFM56-7B26	78245	Y184		to be lsf GECA 0300
☐ EC-	Boeing 737-86N					2 CFMI CFM56-7B26	78245	Y184		to be lsf GECA 0400

GESTAIR Executive Jet, S.A. = GP / GES (Member of JET Europe/Sub.of Gestair Interholding)

Barcelona/Burgos/La Coruna/Madrid/Palma/Sevilla

Calle Aguetol 7, 1.Planta, E-28042 Madrid, Spain ☎ (91) 329 30 31 Tx: 44558 gstr e Fax: (91) 329 33 23 SITA: MADHDGP
F: 1977 ♟♟♟ 180 Head: Jesus M. Macarron ICAO: GESTAIR Net: http://www.gestair.es

☐ EC-FZP	Cessna 525 CitationJet	5250065	EC-704	0094	0994	2 WRR FJ44-1A	4717	Executive		
☐ EC-GIE	Cessna 525 CitationJet	525-0133	EC-261	0096	0896	2 WRR FJ44-1A	4717	Executive		
☐ EC-GOV	Cessna 560 Citation V Ultra	560-0419		0597	0697	2 PWC JT15D-5D	7394	Executive		
☐ EC-GIB	IAI 1124A Westwind I	335	EC-254	0081	0996	2 GA TFE731-3-1G	10659	Executive / EMS	MR-GS	
☐ EC-GSL	IAI 1124A Westwind II	353	C-GRGE	0081	0298	2 GA TFE731-3-1G	10659	Executive		
☐ EC-ELK	Hawker 800B (BAe 125-800B)	258022	EC-193	0084	0296	2 GA TFE731-5R-1H	12428	Executive	BF-GH	
☐ EC-GNK	Dassault Falcon 2000	37	F-WWMH*	0097	0597	2 CFE CFE738-1-1B	16238	Executive		
☐ EC-GPN	Dassault Falcon 50	204	VP-CGP	0090	0897	3 GA TFE731-3-1C	18500	Executive		
☐ EC-GTR	Dassault Falcon 50EX	268	F-WWHS*	0498	0498	3 GA TFE731-40	18500	Executive		
☐ EC-	Canadair CL-604 (CL-600-2B16) Challen.					2 GE CF34-3B	21909	Executive		oo-delivery 1199
☐ EC-FPI	Dassault Falcon 900	115	EC-235	0092	0992	3 GA TFE731-5AR-1C	20639	Executive	BD-LP	
☐ EC-GMO	Dassault Falcon 900EX	6	F-OIBL	0197	0297	3 GA TFE731-60-1C	22226	Executive	HR-FG	
☐ EC-FRV	GAC (Grumman) G-1159B Gulfstream IIB	237	EC-363	0079	0393	2 RR Spey 511-8	31615	Executive	GJ-BC	cvtd G-1159
☐ N101GA	GAC G-IV Gulfstream IV	1109	V8-007	0889	1098	2 RR Tay 611-8	33203	Executive		lsf Telefonica Internacional SA

HELI CANARIAS, S.A. (Subsidiary of Z1 Alerta y Control, S.A.)

Las Palmas de Gran Canaria-Heliport

Avda. Presidente Alvear 56, 6th Floor, E-35007 Las Palmas de Gran Canaria, Spain ☎ (928) 27 69 73 Tx: none Fax: (928) 22 48 45 SITA: n/a
F: 1997 ♟♟♟ 3 Head: José Juan Ramirez Net: n/a Presently being set-up. Intends to start operations in 1999 with Agusta A109 or Eurocopter SA365 helicopters.

HELICASA - Helicopteros de Cataluna, S.A.

Barcelona-Parets Heliport

Callse Tuset 23, At., E-08006 Barcelona, Spain ☎ (93) 414 19 70 Tx: none Fax: (93) 414 75 83 SITA: n/a
F: 1998 ♟♟♟ 6 Head: N. Tosca Net: n/a

☐ EC-FYA	Agusta-Bell 206B JetRanger III	8647	I-DACF	0084	0698	1 AN 250-C20B	1451	4 Pax		
☐ EC-FHI	Eurocopter (Aerosp.) SA319B Alouette III	2369	H-66	0079	0698	1 TU Astazou XIVB	2250	5 Pax		
☐ EC-FHJ	Eurocopter (Aerosp.) SA319B Alouette III	2322	H-60	0079	0698	1 TU Astazou XIVB	2250	5 Pax		
☐ EC-FJA	Eurocopter (Aerosp.) SA319B Alouette III	2297	EC-746	0076	0698	1 TU Astazou XIVB	2250	5 Pax		

HELICSA - Helicopteros, S.A. = HHH (Associated with Helikopter Service A/S, Norway & Schreiner B.V., Netherlands)

Albacete-Helicsa Heliport

Calle Musgo 3, Urbanizacion La Florida, E-28023 Aravaca (Madrid), Spain ☎ (91) 307 67 68 Tx: none Fax: (91) 307 60 49 SITA: n/a
F: 1965 ♟♟♟ 182 Head: Antonio Dominguez Arqués ICAO: HELICSA Net: n/a Aircraft below MTOW 1361kg: Bell 47G-4.

☐ EC-DUA	Agusta-Bell 206B JetRanger III	8665		0083	0097	1 AN 250-C20B	1450	4 Pax		lsf Senasa / opf Escuela Helicsa
☐ EC-EEC	Eurocopter (Aerosp.) SA316B Alouette III	1912		0071	0489	1 TU Artouste IIIB	2200	6 Pax		lst Z1 Alerta y Control
☐ EC-DVK	Eurocopter (MBB) BO105CB	S-630	D-HDSZ*	0085	0785	2 AN 250-C20B	2500	Survey/Patrol		Argos I / opf Vigilancia Aduanera
☐ EC-DVL	Eurocopter (MBB) BO105CB	S-631	D-HDTA*	0085	0785	2 AN 250-C20B	2500	Survey/Patrol		Argos II / opf Vigilancia Aduanera
☐ EC-ECH	Eurocopter (MBB) BO105CB	S-667	D-HDUI*	0085	0487	2 AN 250-C20B	2500	Survey/Patrol		Argos IV / opf Vigilancia Aduanera
☐ EC-FFV	Eurocopter (MBB) BO105CBS	S-852	D-HFHJ*	0091	0791	2 AN 250-C20B	2500	Survey/Patrol		opf Vigilancia Aduanera
☐ EC-DZX	Eurocopter (Aerosp.) AS355F1 Ecureuil 2	5243		0082	0097	2 AN 250-C20F	2400			lst Heli Europa
☐ EC-GHY	Eurocopter (Aerosp.) AS355F1 Ecureuil 2	5089	EC-391	1081	0197	2 AN 250-C20F	2400	EMS / Patrol		opf Bomberos Comunidad Auton. de Madrid
☐ EC-ESX	Eurocopter (MBB) BK117B-1	7176		0089	0090	2 LY LTS101-750B.1	3200	Survey/Patrol		opf Vigilancia Aduanera
☐ EC-DXM	Eurocopter (Aerosp.) SA365C2 Dauphin 2	5007	PH-SSL	0078	0785	2 TU Arriel 1A2	3500	9 Pax		opf Repsol/Off shore-ops
☐ EC-DYU	Eurocopter (Aerosp.) SA365C1 Dauphin 2	5053	PH-SSC	0079	0386	2 TU Arriel 1A1	3400	9 Pax		opf Repsol/Off shore-ops
☐ EC-FOX	Eurocopter (Aerosp.) SA365C2 Dauphin 2	5024	EC-136	0079	0692	2 TU Arriel 1A2	3500	EMS		opf Sanitaria
☐ EC-GCZ	Eurocopter (Aerosp.) SA365C2 Dauphin 2	5037	EC-887	0079	0795	2 TU Arriel 1A2	3500	EMS		opf C.A. de Canarias/Urgencias 061
☐ EC-GJE	Eurocopter (Aerosp.) SA365N1 Dauphin 2	6308	LX-HUM	0088	0796	2 TU Arriel 1C1	4100	EMS		opf C.A. de Canarias/Urgencias 061
☐ EC-GXY	Eurocopter (Aerosp.) SA365N1 Dauphin 2	6242	N12AE	0088	0098	2 TU Arriel 1C1	4100	EMS		opf Sanitaria
☐ SE-JAE	Eurocopter (Aerosp.) AS365N2 Dauphin 2	6416		0091	0998	2 TU Arriel 1C2	4250	SAR		lsf Helic.Rental Group/opf XuntaGalicia
☐ EC-EEQ	Bell 212	30612	D-HOBB	0074	0787	2 PWC PT6T-3 TwinPac	5080	EMS		lsf Wik.H./opf CA de Canarias/Prot.Civ.
☐ EC-FBL	Bell 212	30558	EC-553	0072	1190	2 PWC PT6T-3 TwinPac	5080	SAR		opf Xunta, Galicia/Conselleria de Pesca
☐ EC-FBM	Bell 212	30574	EC-552	0073	1190	2 PWC PT6T-3 TwinPac	5080	SAR		opf Xunta de Galicia/Conselleria Pesca
☐ EC-GIC	Bell 212	30775	LN-OQD	0076	0796	2 PWC PT6T-3 TwinPac	5080			
☐ EC-GLS	Bell 212	31155	OY-HCU	0081	0397	2 PWC PT6T-3B TwinPac	5080	SAR		lsf GRL
☐ EC-GVP	Bell 212	30572	LN-OQG	0073	0398	2 PWC PT6T-3 TwinPac	5080	SAR / Utility		opf Bomberos CAM
☐ EC-GXA	Bell 212	30812	LN-OQJ	0076	0798	2 PWC PT6T-3 TwinPac	5080	SAR / Utility		
☐ EC-GSK	Bell 412	33092	SE-HVL	0082	0698	2 PWC PT6T-3B TwinPac	5262	SAR		lsf Osterm./opf Xunta,Galicia/Con.Pesca
☐ EC-FJJ	Sikorsky S-61N	61299	EC-862	0066	1091	2 GE CT58-140-2	9299	SAR		opf SASEMAR-Co.de Salvamentos Maritimos
☐ EC-FMZ	Sikorsky S-61N	61361	LN-ORH	0066	0492	2 GE CT58-140-2	9299	SAR		opf SASEMAR-Co.de Salvamentos Maritimos
☐ EC-FTB	Sikorsky S-61N	61741	LN-OSY	0076	0593	2 GE CT58-140-2	9299	SAR		opf SASEMAR-Co.de Salvamentos Maritimos
☐ EC-FVO	Sikorsky S-61N	61756	EC-575	0075	0294	2 GE CT58-140-2	9299	SAR		opf SASEMAR-Co.de Salvamentos Maritimos
☐ EC-FZJ	Sikorsky S-61N	61758	EC-717	0076	1094	2 GE CT58-140-2	9299	SAR		opf SASEMAR-Co.de Salvamentos Maritimos

HELI EUROPA, S.A.

Santiago-Lavacolla

Edificio de Campo, E-15820 Aeropuerto de Lavacolla, Spain ☎ (981) 54 77 45 Tx: none Fax: (981) 54 77 45 SITA: n/a
F: 1989 ♟♟♟ 3 Head: José Lopez Candal Net: n/a Aircraft below MTOW 1361kg: Bell 47G-4

☐ EC-FHX	Bell 206B JetRanger III	3786	G-OCAP	0084	1191	1 AN 250-C20J	1451	4 Pax		
☐ EC-DZX	Eurocopter (Aerosp.) AS355F1 Ecureuil 2	5243		0082	0298	2 AN 250-C20F	2400	5 Pax		lsf Helicsa

HELI-IBERICA, S.A. = HRA

Madrid-Barajas & Cuatro Vientos

Apartado Correos 116019, E-28080 Madrid, Spain ☎ (91) 307 67 20 Tx: n/a Fax: (91) 307 60 49 SITA: n/a
F: 1986 ♟♟♟ 7 Head: J.M. Garcia-Sahagun ICAO: ERICA Net: n/a

☐ EC-FFX	Cessna 411	411-0085	N7385U	0065	0291	2 CO GTSIO-520-C	2948	Executive		

125 registration type of aircraft cn/fn ex/ex* mfd del powered by mtow kg configuration selcal name/fln/specialitites/remarks

HELIMAR – Helicopteros del Mare Nostrum, S.A.

Valledolid/Pamplona-Noain/Madrid-Cuatro Vientos

Dr. Gil y Morte 4, E-46007 Valencia, Spain ☎ (96) 341 35 50 Tx: 61470 hemar e Fax: (96) 341 26 53 SITA: n/a
F: 1981 22 Head: José Maria Montalt Sauri Net: n/a Aircraft below MTOW 1361kg: Agusta & Bell 47G-3B.

□ EC-DNU	Eurocopter (Aerosp.) AS350B Ecureuil	1475	F-WZFH*	0081	0781	1 TU Arriel 1B	1950		
□ EC-DYK	Eurocopter (Aerosp.) AS350B Ecureuil	1863		0085	0286	1 TU Arriel 1B	1950		
□ EC-FME	Eurocopter (Aerosp.) AS350B2 Ecureuil	2448	F-GKLR	0091	0492	1 TU Arriel 1D1	2250		
□ EC-FUF	Eurocopter (Aerosp.) AS350B Ecureuil	2596	EC-427	0092	0094	1 TU Arriel 1B	1950		
□ EC-FXH	Eurocopter (Aerosp.) AS350B2 Ecureuil	2638	EC-545	0092	1194	1 TU Arriel 1D1	2250		
□ EC-GDL	Eurocopter (Aerosp.) AS350B2 Ecureuil	2879		0095	0895	1 TU Arriel 1D1	2250	Patrol / Survey	opf Policia Foral de Navarra
□ EC-GDP	Eurocopter (Aerosp.) AS350B2 Ecureuil	2886		0095	0095	1 TU Arriel 1D1	2250	Patrol / Survey	opf Policia Foral de Navarra
□ EC-GIY	Eurocopter (Aerosp.) AS350B2 Ecureuil	2175	OY-HEP	0089	0896	1 TU Arriel 1D1	2250		cvtd AS350B
□ EC-EVS	Bell UH-1B (204)	893	EC-463	0062	0790	1 LY T53-L-11D	3856		
□ EC-EXO	Bell UH-1B (204)	202	EC-436	0060	0890	1 LY T53-L-11D	3856		
□ EC-GIZ	Bell UH-1H (205)	5631	N6738B	0067	0896	1 LY T53-L-13	4309		
□ EC-GJA	Bell UH-1H (205)	5387	N205UD	0067	0096	1 LY T53-L-13	4309		
□ EC-GJB	Bell UH-1H (205)	9262	N8154S	0067	0096	1 LY T53-L-13	4309		

HELISERVICES – Helieuropa Services, S.A. (Associated with Bristow Group)

BCN-Sabadell/Marbella Heliport & MAD-Cuatro Vientos

Plaza Doctor Ignacio Barraquer 6, Ent. 3, E-08029 Barcelona, Spain ☎ (93) 419 20 34 Tx: none Fax: (93) 419 18 36 SITA: n/a
F: 1987 25 Head: Pedro Saenz Maturana Net: n/a Aircraft below MTOW 1361kg: Agusta-Bell & Bell 47G-3

□ EC-FCP	Agusta-Bell 206B JetRanger	8006	G-BPIB	0067	0695	1 AN 250-C20	1451	4 Pax / Survey	cvtd 206A
□ EC-FRS	Bell 206L-1 LongRanger II	45412	HK-3166X	0080	0098	1 AN 250-C28B	1882	6 Pax	
□ EC-GDJ	Bell UH-1H (205)	5320	66-837	0066	0098	1 LY T53-L-13B	4309	Utility	lsf Tragsa
□ EC-GJL	Agusta-Bell 205A-1	4010	Z.10-5	0066	0096	1 LY T5313B	4310	Utility	

HELISUR – Helicopteros del Sur, S.L.

Cordoba

Urbanizacion Los Angeles, Camelia 14, E-41907 Valencina de la Concepcion (Sevilla), Spain ☎ (95) 471 53 31 Tx: none Fax: (95) 471 34 86 SITA: n/a
F: 1989 5 Head: Antonio Luis Ortiz Diaz Net: n/a Aircraft below MTOW 1361kg: Tomcat 6B

□ EC-EEN	Agusta-Bell 204B	3002	HB-XCG	0062		1 RR Gnome H.1200-610	3856		
□ EC-EKA	Bell UH-1B (204)	313	N9050Q	0061	0088	1 LY T5311D	3856		
□ EC-EKC	Bell UH-1B (204)	684	N394HP	0062	0588	1 LY T5311D	3856		
□ EC-GOD	Bell UH-1H (205)	4787	N92820	0065	0497	1 LY T53-L-13A	4309		

HELISURESTE – Helicopteros del Sureste, S.A. = UV / HSE

Alicante-San Vicente Heliport/Malaga/Sevilla/Valencia

Camino del Reloj sn, E-03690 San Vicente, (Alicante), Spain ☎ (96) 566 38 35 Tx: 66012 bnysa e Fax: (96) 566 59 24 SITA: n/a
F: 1983 67 Head: D. Luis Minano Sanvalero IATA: 662 ICAO: HELISURESTE Net: http://www.helisureste.com

□ EC-DEK	Agusta-Bell 206B JetRanger III	8568		0079		1 AN 250-C20B	1451	4 Pax	
□ EC-EBF	Agusta-Bell 206B JetRanger III	8704		0085	0287	1 AN 250-C20J	1451	4 Pax	
□ EC-FCO	Bell 206L-3 LongRanger III	51179	N52CH	0086	0491	1 AN 250-C30P	1882	EMS	opf Junta de Extremadura
□ EC-FFQ	Bell 206L-3 LongRanger III	51463	N6635Y	0091	0596	1 AN 250-C30P	1882	6 Pax	opf Junta de Extremadura in summer
□ EC-FOL	Bell 206L-3 LongRanger III	51417	N6605R	0090	0792	1 AN 250-C30P	1882	6 Pax	opf Junta de Extremadura in summer
□ EC-FRY	Bell 206L-3 LongRanger III	51330	N43904	0090	0293	1 AN 250-C30P	1882	6 Pax	opf Generalitat Valenziana
□ EC-FTM	Bell 206L-4 LongRanger IV	52024		0093	0993	1 AN 250-C30P	2018	6 Pax	opf Junta de Extremadura in summer
□ EC-GCU	Bell 206LT TwinRanger	52105	EC-843	0094	0295	2 AN 250-C20R	2018	EMS	opf 061 Andalucia
□ EC-GEA	Bell 206L-3 LongRanger III	51196	N54CH	0091	0995	1 AN 250-C30P	1882	EMS	opf Govern Balear
□ EC-GNR	Bell 206LT TwinRanger	52051	N41060	0093	0597	2 AN 250-C20R	2018	EMS	opf 061 Andalucia
□ EC-DNM	Agusta A109A	7222	N4210X	0081		2 AN 250-C20B	2600	EMS	opf 061 Andalucia
□ EC-DZT	Agusta A109A	7159	HB-XIU	0078	0786	2 AN 250-C20B	2600	EMS	opf Generalitat Valenciana
□ EC-ETF	Agusta A109C	7605	3A-MOR	0089	0390	2 AN 250-C20R/1	2720	EMS	opf Diputacion de Alicante
□ EC-FQJ	Agusta A109C	7664	N1YU	0092	0992	2 AN 250-C20R/1	2720	Fishery Patrol	Alcotan I / opf Sec.Gen.Pesca Maritima
□ EC-FUY	Agusta A109C	7670	EC-453	0093	1093	2 AN 250-C20R/1	2720	Fisher Patrol	Alcotan II / opf Sec.Gen.Pesca Maritima
□ EC-GCQ	Agusta A109C	7665	EC-895	0092	0595	2 AN 250-C20R/1	2720	Fishery Patrol	AlcotanIII / opf Sec.Gen.Pesca Maritima
□ EC-GQX	Agusta A109E Power	11013		1097	0198	2 PWC PW206C	2850	EMS	lsf Metro GmbH & Co. KG / opf SERCAM
□ EC-GRA	Agusta A109C	7676	EC-GJD	0093	0898	2 AN 250-C20R/1	2720	Executive	opf pvt
□ I-SOCC	Agusta A109A II MAX	7399	N1VG	0087	0097	2 AN 250-C20R/1	2720	EMS	lsf Agusta SpA / opf 061 Andalucia
□ EC-GAA	Bell 205A-1	30134	EC-756	0073	1094	1 LY T5313B	4309	Utility	opf Junta de Andalucia
□ EC-GHO	Bell 212	30684	EC-FYC	0075	0097	2 PWC PT6T-3 TwinPac	5080	Rescue	lst HSU as CS-HEJ
□ EC-GHP	Bell 212	30557	EC-FYB	0073	0097	2 PWC PT6T-3 TwinPac	5080	Utility	opf Generalitat Valenciana
□ EC-GVV	Bell 212	30584	N58121	0073	0698	2 PWC PT6T-3 TwinPac	5080	Utility	opf Generalitat Valenciana
□ EC-GXG	Bell 212	30759	N21601	0076	0598	2 PWC PT6T-3 TwinPac	5080	Utility	
□ EC-FEL	Agusta-Bell 412SP	25576	EC-607	0089	0491	2 PWC PT6T-3B TwinPac	5398	EMS/Rescue	opf C.A. de Madrid
□ EC-FTN	Bell 412SP	36006	C-GOPP	0090	0693	2 PWC PT6T-3B TwinPac	5398	Rescue	opf Proteccion Civil Tenerife
□ EC-GBE	Agusta-Bell 412	25503	EC-757	0083	0595	2 PWC PT6T-3B TwinPac	5262	Utility	
□ EC-GOP	Bell 412HP	36031	N4603T	0091	0597	2 PWC PT6T-3BE TwinPac	5398	EMS	opf 061 Andalucia
□ EC-GPA	Bell 412HP	36071	N7238Y	0093	0997	2 PWC PT6T-3BE TwinPac	5398	12 Pax	

HELISWISS IBERICA, S.A. = HSW (Subsidiary of Heliswiss-Schweiz. Helikopter, AG / formerly Aercombi, S.A.)

Barcelona-Parets Heliport & Baqueira-Beret

Poligono Industrial Can Volart, E-08150 Parets del Valles (Barcelona), Spain ☎ (93) 573 00 63 Tx: none Fax: (93) 562 47 08 SITA: n/a
F: 1981 31 Head: Narciso Tosca Rovira ICAO: IBERSWISS Net: http://www.heliswiss.es Aircraft below MTOW 1361kg: Robinson R22

□ EC-GQH	Bell 206B JetRanger	578	HB-XDH	0070	0997	1 AN 250-C20	1450	4 Pax	cvtd 206A
□ EC-FPS	Eurocopter (Aerosp.) SA315B Lama	2402	HB-XVN	0074	0692	1 TU Artouste IIIB1	1950	5 Pax	
□ EC-EVA	Eurocopter (Aerosp.) AS350B Ecureuil	1345	HB-XMA	0080	0590	1 TU Arriel 1B	1950	5 Pax	
□ EC-FMA	Eurocopter (Aerosp.) SA316B Alouette III	2341	HB-XVQ	0078	0091	1 TU Artouste IIIB	2200	5 Pax	

HISPANICA DE AVIACION, S.A.

Madrid-Cuatro Vientas

Avenida del Valle 13, Oficina 204, E-28003 Madrid, Spain ☎ (91) 553 85 01 Tx: none Fax: (91) 554 18 19 SITA: n/a
F: 1986 10 Head: J. Ignacio del Corral Net: n/a Aircraft below MTOW 1361 kg: Bell 47G-2.

□ EC-EKO	Bell 206B JetRanger III	2406	N50006	0078	0988	1 AN 250-C20J	1451	4 Pax	
□ EC-FVS	Bell 206B JetRanger III	4012	N323BH	0088	0494	1 AN 250-C20J	1451	4 Pax	
□ EC-EES	Bell 206L LongRanger	45153	N16942	0078	0787	1 AN 250-C20B	1814	6 Pax	

IBERIA Lineas Aéreas de Espana, S.A. = IB / IBE

Madrid-Barajas

130 Calle Velazquez, E-28006 Madrid, Spain ☎ (91) 587 87 87 Tx: 27775 ibmad e Fax: (91) 587 58 84 SITA: n/a
F: 1927 22450 Head: Xabier de Irala Estevez IATA: 075 ICAO: IBERIA Net: http://www.iberia.com/

Some domestic/regional flights are operated on behalf of Iberia/in conjunction with (using IB-flight numbers): AIR NOSTRUM, AVIACO, BINTER CANARIAS & BINTER MEDITERRANEO – for details, see under each company. Beside aircraft listed, also uses 1-2 Boeing 747-200F lsf/opb ATLAS AIR (N, in partial Iberia-colors) for all-cargo services, when required. For details – see under Atlas Air.

□ EC-BIM	Boeing (Douglas) DC-9-32	47088 / 180		1067	1067	2 PW JT8D-7B	48988	CY105	FG-CM	Ciudad de Santander
□ EC-BIR	Boeing (Douglas) DC-9-32	47093 / 237		0168	0168	2 PW JT8D-7B	48988	CY105	FG-DK	Ciudad de Valencia
□ EC-BQV	Boeing (Douglas) DC-9-32	47453 / 565		1269	0170	2 PW JT8D-7B	48988	CY105	HL-AF	Ciudad de Ibiza / based MIA
□ EC-BQZ	Boeing (Douglas) DC-9-32	47456 / 580		0370	0370	2 PW JT8D-7B	48988	CY105	HL-AK	Ciud. de Sta Cruz de La Palma
□ EC-CTR	Boeing (Douglas) DC-9-34F (CF)	47702 / 817	N19B*	0076	0891	2 PW JT8D-17	54885	CY105	DE-JL	Hernan Cortes / lsf AYC/based MIA
□ EC-CTT	Boeing (Douglas) DC-9-34F (CF)	47706 / 821		0076	0891	2 PW JT8D-17	54885	CY105	DF-AB	Pedro de Valdivia / based MIA
□ EC-DGB	Boeing (Douglas) DC-9-34	48103 / 925		0079	0891	2 PW JT8D-17	54885	CY105	DL-EK	Castillo de Javier / based MIA
□ EC-EXF	Boeing (Douglas) MD-87 (DC-9-87)	49832 / 1703	EC-295	0490	0590	2 PW JT8D-217C	61689	CY109	BQ-HM	Ciudad de Pamplona
□ EC-EXG	Boeing (Douglas) MD-87 (DC-9-87)	49833 / 1706	EC-296	0490	0590	2 PW JT8D-217C	61689	CY109	BQ-HP	Ciudad de Almeria
□ EC-EXM	Boeing (Douglas) MD-87 (DC-9-87)	49835 / 1717	EC-298	0090	0690	2 PW JT8D-217C	61689	CY109	BQ-JL	Ciudad de Zaragoza
□ EC-EXN	Boeing (Douglas) MD-87 (DC-9-87)	49836 / 1721	EC-299	0590	0790	2 PW JT8D-217C	61689	CY109	BQ-JM	Ciudad de Badajoz
□ EC-EXR	Boeing (Douglas) MD-87 (DC-9-87)	49834 / 1714	EC-297	0590	0690	2 PW JT8D-217C	61689	CY109	BQ-JK	Ciudad de Oviedo
□ EC-EXT	Boeing (Douglas) MD-87 (DC-9-87)	49837 / 1730	EC-300	0690	0790	2 PW JT8D-217C	61689	CY109	BQ-JP	Ciudad de Albacete
□ EC-EYB	Boeing (Douglas) MD-87 (DC-9-87)	49838 / 1733	EC-301	0690	0890	2 PW JT8D-217C	61689	CY109	BQ-KL	Cangas de Onis
□ EC-EYX	Boeing (Douglas) MD-87 (DC-9-87)	49839 / 1739	EC-302	0790	0890	2 PW JT8D-217C	61689	CY109	BQ-KM	Ciudad de Caceres
□ EC-EYY	Boeing (Douglas) MD-87 (DC-9-87)	49840 / 1745	EC-303	0790	0890	2 PW JT8D-217C	61689	CY109	BQ-KP	Ciudad de Barcelona
□ EC-EYZ	Boeing (Douglas) MD-87 (DC-9-87)	49841 / 1751	EC-304	0890	0990	2 PW JT8D-217C	61689	CY109	BQ-LM	Ciudad de Las Palmas
□ EC-EZA	Boeing (Douglas) MD-87 (DC-9-87)	49842 / 1763	EC-305	0990	0990	2 PW JT8D-217C	61689	CY109	BQ-LP	Ciudad de Segovia
□ EC-EZS	Boeing (Douglas) MD-87 (DC-9-87)	49843 / 1771	EC-306	0990	1090	2 PW JT8D-217C	61689	CY109	BQ-MP	Ciudad de Mahon
□ EC-FEY	Boeing (Douglas) MD-87 (DC-9-87)	53208 / 1865	EC-634	0091	0691	2 PW JT8D-217C	61689	CY109	AP-LR	Ciudad de Jaen
□ EC-FEZ	Boeing (Douglas) MD-87 (DC-9-87)	53207 / 1862	EC-633	0491	0691	2 PW JT8D-217C	61689	CY109	AP-KS	Ciudad de Malaga
□ EC-FFA	Boeing (Douglas) MD-87 (DC-9-87)	53209 / 1867	EC-635	0591	0791	2 PW JT8D-217C	61689	CY109	AP-LS	Ciudad de Avila
□ EC-FFH	Boeing (Douglas) MD-87 (DC-9-87)	53211 / 1874	EC-637	0591	0691	2 PW JT8D-217C	61689	CY109	AP-MS	Ciudad de Logrono
□ EC-FFI	Boeing (Douglas) MD-87 (DC-9-87)	53210 / 1871	EC-636	0591	0691	2 PW JT8D-217C	61689	CY109	AP-MR	Ciudad de Cuenca
□ EC-FHD	Boeing (Douglas) MD-87 (DC-9-87)	53212 / 1877	EC-638	0691	0791	2 PW JT8D-217C	61689	CY109	AP-QR	Ciudad de Leon
□ EC-FHK	Boeing (Douglas) MD-87 (DC-9-87)	53213 / 1879	EC-639	0091	0791	2 PW JT8D-217C	61689	CY109	AP-QS	Ciudad de Tarragona
□ EC-GRK	Boeing (Douglas) MD-87 (DC-9-87)	49827 / 1654	EC-EUE	1289	0490	2 PW JT8D-217C	61689	CY109	BQ-GM	Ciudad de Sevilla / lsf Julyco
□ EC-GRL	Boeing (Douglas) MD-87 (DC-9-87)	49828 / 1667	EC-EUD	0190	0490	2 PW JT8D-217C	61689	CY109	BQ-GP	Ciudad de Toledo / lsf Julyco
□ EC-GRM	Boeing (Douglas) MD-87 (DC-9-87)	49829 / 1678	EC-EUC	0290	0390	2 PW JT8D-217C	61689	CY109	BQ-HJ	Ciudad de Burgos / lsf Julyco
□ EC-GRN	Boeing (Douglas) MD-87 (DC-9-87)	49830 / 1684	EC-EUL	0090	0490	2 PW JT8D-217C	61689	CY109	BQ-HK	Ciudad de Cadiz / lsf Julyco
□ EC-GRO	Boeing (Douglas) MD-87 (DC-9-87)	49831 / 1688	EC-EVB	0090	0490	2 PW JT8D-217C	61689	CY109	BQ-HL	Arrecife de Lanzarote / lsf Julyco

126 registration type of aircraft cn/fn ex/ex* mfd del powered by mtow kg configuration selcal name/fln/specialitites/remarks

registration	type of aircraft	cn/fn	ex/ex*	mfd	del	powered by	mtow kg	configuration	selcal	name/fln/specialitites/remarks
☐ EC-GAZ	Boeing 737-4Y0	24906 / 2009	EC-850	0291	0398	2 CFMI CFM56-3C1	64636	CY150	LS-DF	lsf / opb AEA in Iberia-colors
☐ EC-GBN	Boeing 737-4Y0	24912 / 2064	EC-851	0591	0398	2 CFMI CFM56-3C1	64636	CY150	LS-DG	lsf / opb AEA in Iberia-colors
☐ EC-GPI	Boeing 737-46Q	28661 / 2910		0797	0498	2 CFMI CFM56-3C1	65091	CY150	BR-CD	lsf / opb AEA in Iberia-colors
☐ EC-	Airbus Industrie A319-111					2 CFMI CFM56-5B5/P	64000			to be lsf ILFC 0100
☐ EC-	Airbus Industrie A319-111					2 CFMI CFM56-5B5/P	64000			to be lsf ILFC 0200
☐ EC-	Airbus Industrie A319-111					2 CFMI CFM56-5B5/P	64000			to be lsf ILFC 0400
☐ EC-	Airbus Industrie A319-111					2 CFMI CFM56-5B5/P	64000			to be lsf ILFC 1100
☐ EC-	Airbus Industrie A319-111					2 CFMI CFM56-5B5/P	64000			to be lsf ILFC 0101
☐ EC-	Airbus Industrie A319-111					2 CFMI CFM56-5B5/P	64000			to be lsf ILFC 0301
☐ EC-	Airbus Industrie A319-111					2 CFMI CFM56-5B5/P	64000			to be lsf ILFC 0301
☐ EC-	Airbus Industrie A319-111					2 CFMI CFM56-5B5/P	64000			to be lsf ILFC 0501
☐ EC-	Airbus Industrie A319-111					2 CFMI CFM56-5B5/P	64000			to be lsf ILFC 0901
☐ EC-FCB	Airbus Industrie A320-211	158	EC-579	0090	0391	2 CFMI CFM56-5A1	73500	CY147	GP-FQ	Montana de Covadonga
☐ EC-FDA	Airbus Industrie A320-211	176	EC-581	0090	0491	2 CFMI CFM56-5A1	73500	CY147	AH-JS	Lagunas de Ruidera
☐ EC-FDB	Airbus Industrie A320-211	173	EC-580	0090	0491	2 CFMI CFM56-5A1	73500	CY147	AH-JR	Lago de Sanabria
☐ EC-FGH	Airbus Industrie A320-211	223	EC-585	0091	0891	2 CFMI CFM56-5A1	73500	CY147	AH-LP	Caldera de Taburiente
☐ EC-FGR	Airbus Industrie A320-211	224	EC-586	0091	0991	2 CFMI CFM56-5A1	73500	CY147	AH-LR	Dehesa de Moncayo
☐ EC-FGU	Airbus Industrie A320-211	199	EC-583	0091	0791	2 CFMI CFM56-5A1	73500	CY147	AH-KR	Sierra Espuna
☐ EC-FGV	Airbus Industrie A320-211	207	EC-584	0091	0791	2 CFMI CFM56-5A1	73500	CY147	AH-KS	Monfrague
☐ EC-FIA	Airbus Industrie A320-211	240	EC-587	0091	1091	2 CFMI CFM56-5A1	73500	CY147	AH-LS	Isla de la Cartuja
☐ EC-FIC	Airbus Industrie A320-211	241	EC-588	0091	1091	2 CFMI CFM56-5A1	73500	CY147	AH-MP	Sierra de Grazalema
☐ EC-FKD	Airbus Industrie A320-211	264	EC-880	0091	0192	2 CFMI CFM56-5A1	73500	CY147	CD-HR	Monte Alhoya
☐ EC-FLP	Airbus Industrie A320-211	266	EC-881	0091	0292	2 CFMI CFM56-5A1	73500	CY147	CD-HS	Torcal de Antequera
☐ EC-FLQ	Airbus Industrie A320-211	274	EC-882	0091	0292	2 CFMI CFM56-5A1	73500	CY147	CD-JR	Dunas de Liencres
☐ EC-FML	Airbus Industrie A320-211	303	EC-883	0092	0592	2 CFMI CFM56-5A1	73500	CY147	CD-LR	Hayedo de Tejera Negra
☐ EC-FMN	Airbus Industrie A320-211	312	EC-884	0092	0592	2 CFMI CFM56-5A1	73500	CY147		Cadi Moixero
☐ EC-FNR	Airbus Industrie A320-211	323	EC-885	0092	0792	2 CFMI CFM56-5A1	73500	CY147		Monte de Valle
☐ EC-FQY	Airbus Industrie A320-211	356	EC-886	0092	0193	2 CFMI CFM56-5A1	73500	CY147	CD-KS	Joan Miro
☐ EC-GRE	Airbus Industrie A320-211	134	EC-FAS	0090	1290	2 CFMI CFM56-5A1	73500	CY147	GP-BQ	Sierra de Cazorla / lsf Julyco
☐ EC-GRF	Airbus Industrie A320-211	136	EC-FBQ	0090	0191	2 CFMI CFM56-5A1	73500	CY147	GP-CQ	Montseny / lsf Julyco
☐ EC-GRG	Airbus Industrie A320-211	143	EC-FBS	0090	0191	2 CFMI CFM56-5A1	73500	CY147	GP-DQ	Timanfaya / lsf Julyco
☐ EC-GRH	Airbus Industrie A320-211	146	EC-FBR	0090	0291	2 CFMI CFM56-5A1	73500	CY147	GP-EQ	Sierra de Segura / lsf Julyco
☐ EC-GRI	Airbus Industrie A320-211	177	EC-FEO	0091	0691	2 CFMI CFM56-5A1	73500	CY147	AH-KP	Delta del Ebro / lsf Julyco
☐ EC-GRJ	Airbus Industrie A320-211	246	EC-FKH	0091	0192	2 CFMI CFM56-5A1	73500	CY147	AH-MR	Canon de Rio Lobos / lsf Julyco
☐ EC-	Airbus Industrie A320-214					2 CFMI CFM56-5B4/P	73500	CY150		to be lsf ILFC 0599
☐ EC-	Airbus Industrie A320-214					2 CFMI CFM56-5B4/P	73500	CY150		to be lsf SALE 0599
☐ EC-	Airbus Industrie A320-214					2 CFMI CFM56-5B4/P	73500	CY150		oo-delivery 0899
☐ EC-	Airbus Industrie A320-214					2 CFMI CFM56-5B4/P	73500	CY150		oo-delivery 0899
☐ EC-	Airbus Industrie A320-214					2 CFMI CFM56-5B4/P	73500	CY150		oo-delivery 0999
☐ EC-	Airbus Industrie A320-214					2 CFMI CFM56-5B4/P	73500	CY150		to be lsf SALE 0999
☐ EC-	Airbus Industrie A320-214					2 CFMI CFM56-5B4/P	73500	CY150		oo-delivery 1099
☐ EC-	Airbus Industrie A320-214					2 CFMI CFM56-5B4/P	73500	CY150		to be lsf ILFC 1099
☐ EC-	Airbus Industrie A320-214					2 CFMI CFM56-5B4/P	73500	CY150		oo-delivery 1199
☐ EC-	Airbus Industrie A320-214					2 CFMI CFM56-5B4/P	73500	CY150		oo-delivery 1299
☐ EC-	Airbus Industrie A320-214					2 CFMI CFM56-5B4/P	73500	CY150		to be lsf ILFC 0400
☐ EC-	Airbus Industrie A320-214					2 CFMI CFM56-5B4/P	73500	CY150		oo-delivery 0500
☐ EC-	Airbus Industrie A320-214					2 CFMI CFM56-5B4/P	73500	CY150		to be lsf ILFC 0500
☐ EC-	Airbus Industrie A320-214					2 CFMI CFM56-5B4/P	73500	CY150		to be lsf ILFC 0500
☐ EC-	Airbus Industrie A320-214					2 CFMI CFM56-5B4/P	73500	CY150		oo-delivery 0600
☐ EC-	Airbus Industrie A320-214					2 CFMI CFM56-5B4/P	73500	CY150		oo-delivery 0700
☐ EC-	Airbus Industrie A320-214					2 CFMI CFM56-5B4/P	73500	CY150		oo-delivery 0800
☐ EC-	Airbus Industrie A320-214					2 CFMI CFM56-5B4/P	73500	CY150		oo-delivery 0900
☐ EC-	Airbus Industrie A320-214					2 CFMI CFM56-5B4/P	73500	CY150		oo-delivery 0201
☐ EC-	Airbus Industrie A320-214					2 CFMI CFM56-5B4/P	73500	CY150		to be lsf ILFC 0201
☐ EC-	Airbus Industrie A320-214					2 CFMI CFM56-5B4/P	73500	CY150		oo-delivery 0501
☐ EC-	Airbus Industrie A320-214					2 CFMI CFM56-5B4/P	73500	CY150		to be lsf ILFC 0501
☐ EC-	Airbus Industrie A320-214					2 CFMI CFM56-5B4/P	73500	CY150		oo-delivery 0801
☐ EC-	Airbus Industrie A320-214					2 CFMI CFM56-5B4/P	73500	CY150		oo-delivery 1001
☐ EC-	Airbus Industrie A320-214					2 CFMI CFM56-5B4/P	73500	CY150		oo-delivery 1101
☐ EC-	Airbus Industrie A320-214					2 CFMI CFM56-5B4/P	73500	CY150		oo-delivery 1201
☐ EC-	Airbus Industrie A320-214					2 CFMI CFM56-5B4/P	73500	CY150		oo-delivery 0502
☐ EC-	Airbus Industrie A320-214					2 CFMI CFM56-5B4/P	73500	CY150		oo-delivery 0602
☐ EC-	Airbus Industrie A320-214					2 CFMI CFM56-5B4/P	73500	CY150		oo-delivery 0702
☐ EC-	Airbus Industrie A320-214					2 CFMI CFM56-5B4/P	73500	CY150		oo-delivery 0702
☐ EC-	Airbus Industrie A320-214					2 CFMI CFM56-5B4/P	73500	CY150		oo-delivery 0802
☐ EC-	Airbus Industrie A320-214					2 CFMI CFM56-5B4/P	73500	CY150		oo-delivery 0902
☐ EC-	Airbus Industrie A320-214					2 CFMI CFM56-5B4/P	73500	CY150		oo-delivery 1002
☐ EC-	Airbus Industrie A320-214					2 CFMI CFM56-5B4/P	73500	CY150		oo-delivery 1102
☐ EC-	Airbus Industrie A320-214					2 CFMI CFM56-5B4/P	73500	CY150		oo-delivery 1202
☐ EC-	Airbus Industrie A320-214					2 CFMI CFM56-5B4/P	73500	CY150		oo-delivery 1202
☐ EC-	Airbus Industrie A320-214					2 CFMI CFM56-5B4/P	73500	CY150		oo-delivery 0503
☐ EC-	Airbus Industrie A320-214					2 CFMI CFM56-5B4/P	73500	CY150		oo-delivery 0803
☐ EC-	Airbus Industrie A320-214					2 CFMI CFM56-5B4/P	73500	CY150		oo-delivery 0104
☐ EC-	Airbus Industrie A320-214					2 CFMI CFM56-5B4/P	73500	CY150		oo-delivery 0304
☐ EC-	Airbus Industrie A321-211					2 CFMI CFM56-5B3/P	89000	CY186		oo-delivery 0599
☐ EC-	Airbus Industrie A321-211					2 CFMI CFM56-5B3/P	89000	CY186		oo-delivery 0699
☐ EC-	Airbus Industrie A321-211					2 CFMI CFM56-5B3/P	89000	CY186		oo-delivery 0700
☐ EC-	Airbus Industrie A321-211					2 CFMI CFM56-5B3/P	89000	CY186		oo-delivery 1100
☐ EC-	Airbus Industrie A321-211					2 CFMI CFM56-5B3/P	89000	CY186		oo-delivery 1200
☐ EC-	Airbus Industrie A321-211					2 CFMI CFM56-5B3/P	89000	CY186		oo-delivery 0701
☐ EC-	Airbus Industrie A321-211					2 CFMI CFM56-5B3/P	89000	CY186		oo-delivery 0801
☐ EC-	Airbus Industrie A321-211					2 CFMI CFM56-5B3/P	89000	CY186		oo-delivery 0202
☐ EC-	Airbus Industrie A321-211					2 CFMI CFM56-5B3/P	89000	CY186		oo-delivery 0402
☐ EC-	Airbus Industrie A321-211					2 CFMI CFM56-5B3/P	89000	CY186		oo-delivery 0702
☐ EC-	Airbus Industrie A321-211					2 CFMI CFM56-5B3/P	89000	CY186		oo-delivery 1002
☐ EC-	Airbus Industrie A321-211					2 CFMI CFM56-5B3/P	89000	CY186		oo-delivery 1102
☐ EC-	Airbus Industrie A321-211					2 CFMI CFM56-5B3/P	89000	CY186		oo-delivery 0103
☐ EC-	Airbus Industrie A321-211					2 CFMI CFM56-5B3/P	89000	CY186		oo-delivery 0503
☐ EC-	Airbus Industrie A321-211					2 CFMI CFM56-5B3/P	89000	CY186		oo-delivery 0803
☐ EC-	Airbus Industrie A321-211					2 CFMI CFM56-5B3/P	89000	CY186		oo-delivery 1103
☐ EC-	Airbus Industrie A321-211					2 CFMI CFM56-5B3/P	89000	CY186		oo-delivery 1203
☐ EC-	Airbus Industrie A321-211					2 CFMI CFM56-5B3/P	89000	CY186		oo-delivery 0504
☐ EC-	Airbus Industrie A321-211					2 CFMI CFM56-5B3/P	89000	CY186		oo-delivery 0604
☐ EC-CBA	Boeing 727-256 (A)	20595 / 905	N1787B*	0072	0573	3 PW JT8D-9	83552	CY153	AD-GL	Vascongadas
☐ EC-CBF	Boeing 727-256 (A)	20600 / 912	N1789B*	0072	0373	3 PW JT8D-9	83552	CY153	AD-CK	Gran Canaria
☐ EC-CBG	Boeing 727-256 (A)	20601 / 913	N1790B*	0072	0373	3 PW JT8D-9	83552	CY153	AD-CJ	Extremadura
☐ EC-CFA	Boeing 727-256 (A)	20811 / 1003		0073	0174	3 PW JT8D-9	83552	CY153	AD-BF	Jerez Xeres Sherry
☐ EC-CFB	Boeing 727-256 (A)	20812 / 1004		0074	0174	3 PW JT8D-9	83552	CY164	AD-CG	Rioja
☐ EC-CFC	Boeing 727-256 (A)	20813 / 1005		0074	0174	3 PW JT8D-9	83552	CY164	AD-EF	Tarragona
☐ EC-CFD	Boeing 727-256 (A)	20814 / 1006		0074	0274	3 PW JT8D-9	83552	CY164	AD-FG	Montilla-Moriles
☐ EC-CFE	Boeing 727-256 (A)	20815 / 1007		0074	0274	3 PW JT8D-9	83552	CY164	AD-FJ	Penedes
☐ EC-CFF	Boeing 727-256 (A)	20816 / 1008		0074	0274	3 PW JT8D-9	83552	CY164	AD-GH	Valdepenas
☐ EC-CFG	Boeing 727-256 (A)	20817 / 1009		0074	0374	3 PW JT8D-9	83552	CY164	AD-GJ	La Mancha
☐ EC-CFH	Boeing 727-256 (A)	20818 / 1010		0074	0374	3 PW JT8D-9	83552	CY164	AD-LM	Priorato
☐ EC-CFI	Boeing 727-256 (A)	20819 / 1018		0074	0474	3 PW JT8D-9	83552	CY164	AE-BD	Carinena
☐ EC-CFK	Boeing 727-256 (A)	20821 / 1035		0074	0574	3 PW JT8D-9	83552	CY164	AE-CD	Ribeiro
☐ EC-CID	Boeing 727-256 (A)	20974 / 1077		0074	1074	3 PW JT8D-9	83552	CY164	JK-BD	Malaga
☐ EC-CIE	Boeing 727-256 (A)	20975 / 1080		0074	1074	3 PW JT8D-9	83552	CY164	EG-HL	Esparragosa
☐ EC-DCC	Boeing 727-256 (A)	21609 / 1369		0078	0778	3 PW JT8D-9	83552	CY153	BH-EK	Albarino
☐ EC-DCD	Boeing 727-256 (A)	21610 / 1380		0078	0878	3 PW JT8D-9	83552	CY153	BH-EL	Chacoli-Txakoli
☐ EC-DCE	Boeing 727-256 (A)	21611 / 1382		0078	0978	3 PW JT8D-9	83552	CY153	BH-EM	Mentrida
☐ EC-DDX	Boeing 727-256 (A)	21779 / 1498		0079	0679	3 PW JT8D-9	83552	CY153	DJ-FK	Monasterio de Poblet
☐ EC-DDZ	Boeing 727-256 (A)	21781 / 1501		0079	0779	3 PW JT8D-9	83552	CY153	DJ-FM	Murallas de Avila
☐ EC-GCI	Boeing 727-256 (A)	20598 / 910	EC-CBD	0072	0473	3 PW JT8D-9	83552	CY153	AD-CH	Murcia / lsf Boeing
☐ EC-GCJ	Boeing 727-256 (A)	20602 / 914	N8281B	0072	0173	3 PW JT8D-9	83552	CY153	AD-BE	Galicia / lsf Boeing
☐ EC-GCK	Boeing 727-256 (A)	20603 / 915	EC-CBI	0072	0273	3 PW JT8D-9	83552	CY153	AD-CF	Asturias / lsf Boeing
☐ EC-GCL	Boeing 727-256 (A)	20604 / 916	EC-CBJ	0073	0173	3 PW JT8D-9	83552	CY153	AD-CG	Andalucia / lsf Boeing
☐ EC-GCM	Boeing 727-256 (A)	20606 / 937	EC-CBL	0073	0473	3 PW JT8D-9	83552	CY153	AD-GL	Tenerife / lsf Boeing
☐ EC-GSX	Boeing 727-256 (A)	20594 / 885	YV-126C	0072	0572	3 PW JT8D-9	83442	CY153	AF-GM	std OPF / for sale

☐ EC-GSY	Boeing 727-256 (A)	20597 / 909	YV-127C	0072	0473	3 PW JT8D-9	83552	CY153	AD-FH	std OPF / for sale
☐ EC-GSZ	Boeing 727-256 (A)	20599 / 911	YV-129C	0072	0373	3 PW JT8D-9	83552	CY153	AD-CL	std OPF / for sale
☐ EC-GTA	Boeing 727-256 (A)	20605 / 921	YV-128C	0073	0273	3 PW JT8D-9	83552	CY153	AD-CH	std OPF / for sale
☐ EC-FEE	Boeing 757-236	25053 / 358	EC-667	0491	1098	2 RR RB211-535E4	113398	CY200	FM-LQ	lsf / opb AEA in Iberia-colors
☐ EC-FEF	Boeing 757-236	24794 / 278	EC-669	0490	1098	2 RR RB211-535E4	113398	CY200	LQ-EK	lsf / opb AEA in Iberia-cs
☐ EC-FFK	Boeing 757-236	24122 / 187	EC-744	0788	0398	2 RR RB211-535E4	113398	CY200	BP-HM	lsf / opb AEA in Iberia-colors
☐ EC-FTR	Boeing 757-256	26239 / 553	EC-420	0093	0693	2 RR RB211-535E4	99790	CY200		Sierra de Guadarrama
☐ EC-FXU	Boeing 757-256	26240 / 561	EC-616	0093	0893	2 RR RB211-535E4	99790	CY200		Xacobeo 93
☐ EC-FXV	Boeing 757-256	26241 / 572	EC-618	0093	0893	2 RR RB211-535E4	99790	CY200	DJ-MR	Argentina
☐ EC-FYJ	Boeing 757-256	26242 / 593	EC-608	0094	0794	2 RR RB211-535E4	99790	CY200	DJ-MS	Venezuela
☐ EC-FYK	Boeing 757-256	26243 / 603	EC-609	0094	0794	2 RR RB211-535E4	99790	CY200	DJ-PR	Chile / lsf ITOH
☐ EC-FYM	Boeing 757-256	26245 / 617	EC-611	0094	0894	2 RR RB211-535E4	99790	CY200		México / lsf SUNR
☐ EC-FYN	Boeing 757-256	26246 / 620	EC-612	0094	0894	2 RR RB211-535E4	99790	CY200		Costa Rica / lsf Mitsubishi Corp.
☐ EC-GBX	Boeing 757-236	25597 / 441	EC-897	0492	0298	2 RR RB211-535E4	113398	CY200	HS-GK	lsf / opb AEA in Iberia-colors
☐ EC-GCA	Boeing 757-236	22185 / 34	EC-845	0384	1097	2 RR RB211-535C	108862	CY200	HS-FR	lsf / opb AEA in Iberia-colors
☐ EC-GCB	Boeing 757-236	23227 / 57	EC-847	0385	1097	2 RR RB211-535C	104550	CY200	HS-GJ	lsf / opb AEA in Iberia-colors
☐ EC-GZY	Boeing 757-256	26247				2 RR RB211-535E4	99790	CY200		oo-delivery 0499
☐ EC-GZZ	Boeing 757-256	26248				2 RR RB211-535E4	99790	CY200		oo-delivery 0499
☐ EC-HAA	Boeing 757-256	26249				2 RR RB211-535E4	99790	CY200		oo-delivery 0899
☐ EC-	Boeing 757-256					2 RR RB211-535E4	99790	CY200		oo-delivery 0999
☐ EC-	Boeing 757-256					2 RR RB211-535E4	99790	CY200		oo-delivery 1199
☐ EC-	Boeing 757-256					2 RR RB211-535E4	99790	CY200		oo-delivery 1199
☐ EC-	Boeing 757-256					2 RR RB211-535E4	99790	CY200		oo-delivery 1299
☐ EC-	Boeing 757-256					2 RR RB211-535E4	99790	CY200		oo-delivery 1299
☐ EC-	Boeing 757-256					2 RR RB211-535E4	99790	CY200		oo-delivery 0300
☐ EC-	Boeing 757-256					2 RR RB211-535E4	99790	CY200		oo-delivery 0400
☐ EC-	Boeing 757-256					2 RR RB211-535E4	99790	CY200		oo-delivery 0700
☐ EC-	Boeing 757-256					2 RR RB211-535E4	99790	CY200		oo-delivery 0800
☐ EC-	Boeing 757-256					2 RR RB211-535E4	99790	CY200		oo-delivery 0800
☐ EC-	Boeing 757-256					2 RR RB211-535E4	99790	CY200		oo-delivery 0900
☐ EC-	Boeing 757-256					2 RR RB211-535E4	99790	CY200		oo-delivery 1100
☐ EC-	Boeing 757-256					2 RR RB211-535E4	99790	CY200		oo-delivery 1200
☐ EC-EMD	Boeing (Douglas) DC-8-62F	46023 / 407	EC-217	0068	1188	4 PW JT3D-7 (HK3/BAC)	151953	Freighter	GL-CE	lsf / opb RGN in Iberia-cs / cvtd -62
☐ EC-EMX	Boeing (Douglas) DC-8-62F	45921 / 322	EC-230	0067	1188	4 PW JT3D-7 (HK3/BAC)	151953	Freighter	GL-CD	lsf / opb RGN in Iberia-cs / cvtd -62
☐ EC-DLF	Airbus Industrie A300B4-120	133	F-WZEB*	0081	0381	2 PW JT9D-59A	157500	C35Y221	DL-CH	Canadas del Teide
☐ EC-DLG	Airbus Industrie A300B4-120	135	F-WZEA*	0081	0481	2 PW JT9D-59A	157500	C35Y221	EJ-CM	Tablas de Daimiel
☐ EC-DLH	Airbus Industrie A300B4-120	136	F-WZEN*	0081	0481	2 PW JT9D-59A	157500	C35Y221	FG-AE	Aigues Tortes
☐ EC-DNQ	Airbus Industrie A300B4-120	156	F-WZMF*	0081	0282	2 PW JT9D-59A	157500	C35Y221	AL-BE	Islas Cies
☐ EC-DNR	Airbus Industrie A300B4-120	170	F-WZMQ*	0082	0282	2 PW JT9D-59A	157500	C35Y221	AL-BF	Ordesa
☐ EC-EON	Airbus Industrie A300B4-203	076	EC-273	0079	0489	2 GE CF6-50C	157500	C35Y221	EG-HJ	Penalara / cvtd -2C
☐ EC-GSU	Boeing 767-3Y0 (ER)	26206 / 487	HL7269	0593	0398	2 GE CF6-80C2B4F	185065	CY211	AK-BS	lsf / opb AEA in Iberia-colors
☐ EC-GTI	Boeing 767-3Y0 (ER)	26207 / 503	HL7286	0793	0398	2 GE CF6-80C2B4F	185065	CY211	BS-HJ	lsf / opb AEA in Iberia-colors
☐ EC-CEZ	Boeing (Douglas) DC-10-30	47980 / 150		0074	0574	3 GE CF6-50C	251701	F10C23Y235	KM-AJ	Costa del Azahar
☐ EC-DEA	Boeing (Douglas) DC-10-30	47982 / 279		0079	0579	3 GE CF6-50C	251744	F10C23Y235	DH-GM	Rias Gallegas
☐ EC-DHZ	Boeing (Douglas) DC-10-30	47834 / 324		0080	0680	3 GE CF6-50C	251744	F10C23Y235	EL-BM	Costas Canarias
☐ EC-GNG	Boeing (Douglas) DC-10-30	46953 / 225	YV-139C	0076	0576	3 GE CF6-50C	251744	F10C23Y235	DG-AK	Cornisa Cantabrica
☐ EC-GTB	Boeing (Douglas) DC-10-30	46556 / 146	YV-134C	0074	0898	3 GE CF6-50C	251744	F10C23Y235		
☐ EC-GTD	Boeing (Douglas) DC-10-30	46982 / 290	YV-137C	0079	0898	3 GE CF6-50C	251744	F10C23Y235		
☐ EC-GGS	Airbus Industrie A340-313	125	EC-154	0096	0296	4 CFMI CFM56-5C4	260000	F5C42Y202	DJ-RS	Concha Espina
☐ EC-GHX	Airbus Industrie A340-313	134	EC-155	0096	0596	4 CFMI CFM56-5C4	260000	F5C42Y202	DK-AR	Rosalia de Castro
☐ EC-GJT	Airbus Industrie A340-313	145	EC-156	0096	0996	4 CFMI CFM56-5C4	260000	F5C42Y202	DK-AS	Rosa Chacel
☐ EC-GLE	Airbus Industrie A340-313	146	EC-157	0096	1096	4 CFMI CFM56-5C4	260000	F5C42Y202	DK-BR	Concepcion Arenal
☐ EC-GPB	Airbus Industrie A340-313	193	F-WWJR*	0097	1097	4 CFMI CFM56-5C4	275000	F5C42Y202	HS-MR	Teresa de Avila
☐ EC-GQK	Airbus Industrie A340-313	197	F-WWJL*	0097	1197	4 CFMI CFM56-5C4	275000	F5C24Y202	HS-PR	Emilia Pardo Bazan
☐ EC-GUP	Airbus Industrie A340-313	217	F-WWJG*	0098	0598	4 CFMI CFM56-5C4	275000	F5C42Y202		Agustina de Aragon
☐ EC-GUQ	Airbus Industrie A340-313	221	F-WWJA*	0098	0698	4 CFMI CFM56-5C4	275000	F5C42Y202		Beatriz Galindo
☐ EC-	Airbus Industrie A340-313					4 CFMI CFM56-5C4	275000	F5C42Y202		oo-delivery 1199
☐ EC-	Airbus Industrie A340-313					4 CFMI CFM56-5C4	275000	F5C42Y202		oo-delivery 0200
☐ EC-	Airbus Industrie A340-313					4 CFMI CFM56-5C4	275000	F5C42Y202		oo-delivery 0300
☐ EC-	Airbus Industrie A340-313					4 CFMI CFM56-5C4	275000	F5C42Y202		oo-delivery 0400
☐ EC-	Airbus Industrie A340-313					4 CFMI CFM56-5C4	275000	F5C42Y202		oo-delivery 0201
☐ EC-	Airbus Industrie A340-313					4 CFMI CFM56-5C4	275000	F5C42Y202		oo-delivery 0301
☐ EC-DIA	Boeing 747-256B	22238 / 450		0080	0580	4 PW JT9D-7Q	371946	F12C30Y374	EJ-GL	Tirso de Molina
☐ EC-DIB	Boeing 747-256B	22239 / 451		0080	0580	4 PW JT9D-7Q	371946	F12C30Y374	EK-CJ	Cervantes
☐ EC-DLC	Boeing 747-256B (M)	22454 / 509		0081	0281	4 PW JT9D-7Q3	371946	F12C30Y374	AE-BJ	Francisco de Quevedo / cvtd -256B
☐ EC-DLD	Boeing 747-256B (M)	22455 / 515		0081	0381	4 PW JT9D-7Q3	371946	F12C30Y374	AG-BC	Lope de Vega / cvtd -256B
☐ EC-DNP	Boeing 747-256B	22764 / 554	N8296V*	0082	0282	4 PW JT9D-7Q3	371946	F12C30Y374	AH-LM	Juan Ramon Jimenez
☐ EC-EEK	Boeing 747-256B (M)	24071 / 699	EC-136	0088	0488	4 PW JT9D-7Q3	371946	F12C30Y238/Plts	AG-DL	Garcia Lorca
☐ EC-GAG	Boeing 747-256B	20137 / 173	EC-765	0071	0172	4 PW JT9D-7A	351534	F8C30Y374	HL-BD	Calderon de la Barca / lsf Boeing
☐ TF-ABA	Boeing 747-267B	22530 / 531	B-HID	0681	1198	4 RR RB211-524C2	377842	F12C32Y336		lsf / opb ABD in Iberia-colors
☐ TF-ABP	Boeing 747-267B	22429 / 493	B-HIC	1280	0199	4 RR RB211-524C4	377842	F12C32Y336		lsf / opb ABD in Iberia-colors

IBERTRANS AEREA, S.L. = IBT — Madrid-Barajas

Calle Gonzalo de Cespedes 7, 1C, E-28042 Madrid, Spain ☎ (91) 329 55 34 Tx: none Fax: (91) 329 47 03 SITA: n/a
F: 1991 ♟♟♟ 60 Head: Miguel Alemany ICAO: IBERTRANS Net: n/a Beside aircraft listed, also uses leased aircraft from other Spanish & French companies when required.

☐ EC-GQA	Embraer 120ER Brasilia (EMB-120ER)	120027	EC-GMT	0086	0397	2 PWC PW118	11990	Freighter		Margarita Tur / cvtd 120RT
☐ EC-GTJ	Embraer 120RT Brasilia (EMB-120RT)	120024	N72157	0086	0198	2 PWC PW118	11500	Freighter		Silvia Torras
☐ LX-LGK	Embraer 120ER Brasilia (EMB-120ER)	120261	PT-SUH*	0091	0399	2 PWC PW118	11990	Freighter/Y29		lsf Flamingo Air Leasing / cvtd 120RT

IBERWORLD, S.A. = TY / IWD (Subsidiary of Grupo Viajes Iberia) — Palma-Son Sant Joan

Avenida Portugal 5-4P, E-07012 Palma de Mallorca, Spain ☎ (971) 72 20 63 Tx: none Fax: (971) 71 31 84 SITA: n/a
F: 1998 ♟♟♟ n/a Head: Cassimiro Bermudez Net: n/a

☐ EC-GLT	Airbus Industrie A320-231	314	N314RX	0092	0498	2 IAE V2500-A1	75500	Y180	KS-CL	lsf FCL
☐ EC-GUR	Airbus Industrie A320-231	308	G-BXRW	0092	0598	2 IAE V2500-A1	75500	Y180		lsf FCL
☐ EC-GZD	Airbus Industrie A320-214	879	F-WWDD*	0098	1298	2 CFMI CFM56-5B4/P	77000	Y180	BQ-AP	lsf GECA
☐ EC-GZE	Airbus Industrie A320-214	888	F-WWDG*	0098	1298	2 CFMI CFM56-5B4/P	77000	Y180		lsf GECA
☐ EC-	Airbus Industrie A320-200					2	77000	Y180		oo-delivery 1001
☐ EC-	Airbus Industrie A320-200					2	77000	Y180		oo-delivery 1101
☐ EC-HAL	Airbus Industrie A310-324	594	LX-TXA	0091	0298	2 PW PW4152	160000	Y254		lsf Kerino Investments

INSTITUT CARTOGRAFICO DE CATALUNIA – Negociat de Vols = ICC — Barcelona-El Prat

Parc de Montjuic, E-08038 Barcelona, Spain ☎ (93) 370 37 06 Tx: none Fax: (93) 370 37 06 SITA: n/a
F: 1982 ♟♟♟ 250 Head: Josef Ventura ICAO: CARTO Net: n/a Non-commercial regional organisation conducting cartography & photo flights for the Autonomous Comunity of Catalonia and other customers on request.

☐ EC-DTS	Partenavia P.68 Observer	324-17-OB		0084	0284	2 LY IO-360-A1B6	1960	Photo / Carto		01
☐ EC-EDN	Cessna 501 Citation I/SP	501-0010	VH-POZ	0077	0787	2 PWC JT15D-1A	5375	Photo / Carto		02

INTERMEDIACION AEREA, S.L. — Barcelona-El Prat

Tillers 45, E-08960 Sant Just Desvern (Barcelona), Spain ☎ (93) 372 55 10 Tx: none Fax: (93) 372 55 10 SITA: n/a
F: 1997 ♟♟♟ n/a Head: Juan Comabella Net: n/a

☐ EC-GMG	Fairchild (Swearingen) SA226TC Metro II	TC-371	OY-BJT	0080	0297	2 GA TPE331-3UW-303G	5670	Y18 / Freighter		occ lst/jtly opw Porto Jato

LTE International Airways, S.A. = XO / LTE (Subsidiary of LTU, Germany) — Palma de Mallorca, Gran Canaria & Tenerife

Calle del Ter 27, Poligono de Son Fuster, E-07009 Palma de Mallorca, Spain ☎ (971) 47 57 00 Tx: 68660 lteop e Fax: (971) 47 88 74 SITA: PMIDZXO
F: 1987 ♟♟♟ 170 Head: Lazaro Ros ICAO: FUN JET Net: n/a

☐ EC-EFX	Boeing 757-2G5	23118 / 36	D-AMUR	0084	1087	2 RR RB211-535C	108860	Y219	CM-EL	lsf LTU
☐ EC-EGH	Boeing 757-2G5	23119 / 51	EC-116	0085	1287	2 RR RB211-535C	108860	Y219	CM-FH	lsf LTU
☐ EC-ENQ	Boeing 757-2G5	23651 / 116	EC-256	0086	0489	2 RR RB211-535C	108860	Y219	CM-EJ	lsf LTU

MAC AVIATION, S.L. = MAQ — Zaragoza

Zurita 14, Bajos, E-50001 Zaragoza, Spain ☎ (976) 32 65 29 Tx: none Fax: (976) 31 77 20 SITA: n/a
F: 1986 ♟♟♟ 8 Head: Isabel Mangas ICAO: MAQ Net: n/a

☐ EC-EGY	Learjet 25D	25D-373	N29EW	0085	0288	2 GE CJ610-8A	6804	Executive / EMS		

MARINA AEROSERVICE, S.A. — Malaga-Picasso

Edificio Marina Marbella, Puerto Pesquero s/n, E-29600 Marbella, Spain ☎ (95) 282 53 46 Tx: none Fax: (95) 282 27 37 SITA: n/a
F: 1990 ♟♟♟ 2 Head: Lars Sundberg Net: n/a

☐ EC-DGG	Piper PA-34-200T Seneca II	34-7670161	HB-LHU	0076	1293	2 CO TSIO-360-EB	2073	5 Pax		

128 registration type of aircraft cn/fn ex/ex* mfd del powered by mtow kg configuration selcal name/fln/specialitites/remarks

MAYORAL = MYO (Dominguez Toledo, S.A. dba / Member of Grupo Mayoral / formerly Como Aerotaxi) **Malaga-Picasso**

Camino de los Prados 1, E-29006 Malaga, Spain ☎ (95) 204 86 09 Tx: none Fax: (95) 204 86 12 SITA: n/a
F: 1995 ☻ 9 Head: Brian Davies ICAO: MAYORAL Net: n/a

	registration	type of aircraft	cn/fn	ex/ex*	mfd	del	powered by	mtow kg	configuration	selcal	remarks
☐	EC-DHF	Piper PA-31T Cheyenne II	31T-7920073	N23699	0079		2 PWC PT6A-28	4082	6 Pax		
☐	EC-DQG	Aerospatiale SN601 Corvette	27	F-BVPH	0076		2 PWC JT15D-4	7000	8 Pax		

NAYSA Aerotaxis - Navegacion y Servicios Aéreos Canarios, S.A. = NAY **Gran Canaria-Gando**

Aeropuerto de Gran Canaria, Apartado de Correos 39, E-35230 Gando (Gran Canaria), Spain ☎ (928) 57 91 94 Tx: none Fax: (928) 57 91 96 SITA: n/a
F: 1969 ☻ 50 Head: Miguel Luis Ramon ICAO: NAYSA Net: n/a

	registration	type of aircraft	cn/fn	ex/ex*	mfd	del	powered by	mtow kg	configuration	selcal	remarks
☐	EC-GTM	Beech 1900C Airliner	UB-30	N7210R	0084	0997	2 PWC PT6A-65B	7530	Freighter		lsf Raytheon Aircraft Credit Corp.
☐	EC-GUD	Beech 1900C-1 Airliner	UC-156	N156YV	0591	1197	2 PWC PT6A-65B	7530	Y19 / Freighter		lsf Raytheon Aircraft Credit Corp.
☐	EC-GZG	Beech 1900C-1 Airliner	UC-161	N55635	0091	0898	2 PWC PT6A-65B	7530	Y19 / Freighter		lsf Raytheon Aircraft Credit Corp.
☐	N122GP	Beech 1900C-1 Airliner	UC-124		0090	1198	2 PWC PT6A-65B	7530	Y19 / Freighter		lsf Raytheon Aircraft Credit Corp.

NOREST AIR, S.L. = NRT **BCN-El Prat/Palma-Son Sant Joan/Menorca-Sant Lluis**

Casa Llobet, E-25657 Biscarri (Lerida), Spain ☎ (973) 25 20 65 Tx: none Fax: (973) 25 23 91 SITA: n/a
F: 1996 ☻ 5 Head: Fco Aubets Puig ICAO: NORESTAIR Net: n/a

	registration	type of aircraft	cn/fn	ex/ex*	mfd	del	powered by	mtow kg	configuration	selcal	remarks
☐	EC-CEY	Piper PA-34-200 Seneca	34-7350311	N56279	0073	0096	2 LY IO-360-C1E6	1905	5 Pax/Freighter		
☐	EC-CUT	Cessna 340 II	340-0303	ECT-538	0073	0096	2 CO TSIO-520-K	2710	5 Pax		
☐	EC-EYR	Cessna 340A II	340A0608	N8668R	0079	0096	2 CO TSIO-520-NB	2717	5 Pax/Freighter		

PAN AIR Lineas Aéreas, S.A. = PV / PNR **Madrid-Barajas**

Edif.de Servicios Generales, 6.Pl, Of.609, Aeropuerto de Barajas, E-28042 Madrid, Spain ☎ (91) 393 82 00 Tx: none Fax: (91) 393 82 08 SITA: n/a
F: 1988 ☻ 150 Head: Nicolas Valero IATA: 562 ICAO: SKYJET Net: n/a

	registration	type of aircraft	cn/fn	ex/ex*	mfd	del	powered by	mtow kg	configuration	selcal	remarks
☐	EC-ELT	BAe 146-200 (QT)	E2102	EC-198	0088	1088	4 LY ALF502R-5	42184	Freighter	AQ-HL	lsf/opf TNT Int'l in TNT-cs/cvtd -200
☐	EC-EPA	BAe 146-200 (QT)	E2089	EC-281	0087	0689	4 LY ALF502R-5	42184	Freighter	AQ-MP	lsf/opf TNT Int'l in TNT-cs/cvtd -200
☐	EC-FVY	BAe 146-200 (QT)	E2117	EC-615	0088	0494	4 LY ALF502R-5	42184	Freighter	FQ-LM	lsf/opf TNT Int'l in TNT-cs/cvtd -200
☐	EC-FZE	BAe 146-200 (QT)	E2105	EC-719	0088	1094	4 LY ALF502R-5	42184	Freighter	AQ-HM	lsf/opf TNT Int'l in TNT-cs/cvtd -200
☐	EC-GQO	BAe 146-200 (QT)	E2086	D-ADEI	0088	1197	4 LY ALF502R-5	42184	Freighter	CF-AP	lsf/opf TNT Int'l in TNT-cs/cvtd -200
☐	EC-GQP	BAe 146-200 (QT)	E2100	D-ANTJ	0088	1097	4 LY ALF502R-5	42184	Freighter	AQ-HK	lsf/opf TNT Int'l in TNT-cs/cvtd -200
☐	EC-FFY	BAe 146-300 (QT)	E3154	EC-712	0089	0990	4 LY ALF502R-5	44225	Freighter	CM-PQ	lsf/opf TNT Int'l in TNT-cs/cvtd -300

PANORAMA = PNM (Pablo E. Devoto Bevacqua dba) **Malaga-Picasso**

Aeropuerto de Malaga, Terminal de Aviacion General, E-29004 Malaga, Spain ☎ (95) 204 82 82 Tx: none Fax: (95) 204 82 83 SITA: n/a
F: 1995 ☻ n/a Head: Pablo E. Devoto Bevacqua ICAO: PANORAMA Net: n/a Aircraft below MTOW 1361kg: Cessna 150 & Rockwell Commander 112

	registration	type of aircraft	cn/fn	ex/ex*	mfd	del	powered by	mtow kg	configuration	selcal	remarks
☐	EC-DDL	Piper PA-32R-300 Lance	32R-7780238	N2267Q	0077	0095	1 LY IO-540-K1G5D	1633	5 Pax		

SAESA - Servicios Aéreos Espanoles, S.A. = SSS **Madrid-Cuatro Vientos & Tenerife-Los Rodeos**

Aeropuerto Cuatro Vientos, Hangar 8, E-28044 Madrid, Spain ☎ (91) 508 91 70 Tx: none Fax: (91) 508 70 55 SITA: n/a
F: 1989 ☻ 19 Head: Jacinto Moras Olmedo ICAO: SAESA Net: n/a Aircraft below MTOW 1361kg: MS894E & Rallye 180T

	registration	type of aircraft	cn/fn	ex/ex*	mfd	del	powered by	mtow kg	configuration	selcal	remarks
☐	EC-ERK	Bell 204 (UH-1E)	6069	N151LC	0070		1 LY T53-L-13	3856			
☐	EC-370	Bell UH-1H (205)	5057	N2218N	0065	0196	1 LY T53-L-13A	4309			
☐	EC-GOC	Bell UH-1H (205)		EC-360	0073	0096	1 LY T53-L-13A	4309			
☐	EC-EVK	Consolidated PBY-5A Catalina	2008	EC-359	0043	0790	2 PW R-1830-92S	13835	Tanker		Amphibian / opf ICONA-Inst.Cons.Natur.
☐	EC-FMC	Consolidated PBY-5A Catalina	2134	EC-940	0043	0791	2 PW R-1830-92S	13835	Tanker		Amphibian / opf ICONA-Inst.Cons.Natur.

SEVEN AIR, Compania Canaria de Transporte Aéreo, S.A. **Gran Canaria-Gando & Tenerife-Los Rodeos**

Villalba Hervas 5-2, E-38002 Santa Cruz, (Tenerife), Spain ☎ (922) 53 41 50 Tx: none Fax: (922) 29 68 90 SITA: n/a
F: 1998 ☻ 20 Head: Gabriel Garcia-Casado Net: n/a

	registration	type of aircraft	cn/fn	ex/ex*	mfd	del	powered by	mtow kg	configuration	selcal	remarks
☐	EC-FIO	GAC (Grumman) G-159 (F/SCD) Gulfstream I	040	EC-493	0060	0399	2 RR Dart 529-8X	16329	Freighter		cvtd G-159
☐	EC-GYL	Fokker F27 Friendship 500 (F27 Mk500)	10381	G-BVOM	0069	1298	2 RR Dart 536-7	19731	Y52		
☐	EC-	Fokker F27 Friendship 500 (F27 Mk500)	10427	G-BVRN	0070	0499	2 RR Dart 532-7	19731	Y52		

SKY HELICOPTEROS, S.A. **Palma-Son Bonet**

Aerodromo de Son Bonet, E-07009 Pont d'Inca, Palma de Mallorca, Spain ☎ (971) 79 40 40 Tx: none Fax: (971) 79 53 18 SITA: n/a
F: 1992 ☻ 7 Head: Christine Martine Net: n/a Aircraft below MTOW 1361kg: Robinson R22.

	registration	type of aircraft	cn/fn	ex/ex*	mfd	del	powered by	mtow kg	configuration	selcal	remarks
☐	EC-GEH	Bell 206B JetRanger II	2201	EC-972	0077	1095	1 AN 250-C20	1451	4 Pax		

SKY SERVICES AVIATION, S.L. = SKT (formerly Multiavionica, S.L.) **Madrid-Barajas**

Calle Santander 3, Planta 14, E-28003 Madrid, Spain ☎ (91) 535 06 22 Tx: none Fax: (91) 535 07 25 SITA: n/a
F: 1992 ☻ 15 Head: Jacinto Arguello ICAO: STAR-JET Net: n/a

	registration	type of aircraft	cn/fn	ex/ex*	mfd	del	powered by	mtow kg	configuration	selcal	remarks
☐	EC-GXX	Learjet 35A	35A-263	N37FN	0079	0898	2 GA TFE731-2-2B	8301	Executive		
☐	EC-HAI	Learjet 55	55-112	N7AU	0085	0199	2 GA TFE731-3AR-2B	9752	Executive		

SPANAIR, S.A. = JK / JKK (Associated with Scandinavian SAS & Viajes Marsans, S.A.) **Palma-Son Sant Joan**

Aeropuerto de Palma de Mallorca, Apartado de Correos 50086, E-07000 Palma de Mallorca, Spain ☎ (971) 74 50 20 Tx: 69994 spair e Fax: (971) 49 25 53 SITA: PMIMMJK
F: 1987 ☻ 1700 Head: Gonzalo Pascual Arias IATA: 680 ICAO: SPANAIR Net: http://www.spanair.com
Intends to lease additional 6 MD-82/83 from Alaska Airlines & China Eastern in second half of 1999. LoI for up to 45 Airbus 319/320/321 for delivery starting September 2000

	registration	type of aircraft	cn/fn	ex/ex*	mfd	del	powered by	mtow kg	configuration	selcal	remarks
☐	EC-GKF	Boeing (Douglas) MD-87 (DC-9-87)	49389 / 1333	SE-DHG	0087	0397	2 PW JT8D-219	67875	Y137	CF-BP	Sundream / lsf Air Trade Capital
☐	EC-GKG	Boeing (Douglas) MD-87 (DC-9-87)	49706 / 1614	SE-DHI	0989	1196	2 PW JT8D-219	67875	Y137	DE-HM	Sunshine / lsf Air Trade Capital
☐	EC-FTS	Boeing (Douglas) MD-83 (DC-9-83)	49621 / 1495	EC-479	0088	0788	2 PW JT8D-219	72575	Y170	EH-MP	Sunbird / lsf Uninter Leasing
☐	EC-FXA	Boeing (Douglas) MD-83 (DC-9-83)	49938 / 1785	EC-592	1090	0394	2 PW JT8D-219	72575	Y170	AC-QS	Sunstar / lsf GECA
☐	EC-FXI	Boeing (Douglas) MD-83 (DC-9-83)	49630 / 1591	EC-638	0489	0589	2 PW JT8D-219	72575	Y170	EG-AS	Sunseeker / lsf Finova Capital Ltd
☐	EC-FXY	Boeing (Douglas) MD-83 (DC-9-83)	49627 / 1580	EC-646	0389	0489	2 PW JT8D-219	72575	Y170	EG-AR	Sunbeam / lsf GECA
☐	EC-FZC	Boeing (Douglas) MD-83 (DC-9-83)	49790 / 1643	EC-742	0989	1089	2 PW JT8D-219	72575	Y170	JQ-AP	Sunflower / lsf GECA
☐	EC-GAT	Boeing (Douglas) MD-83 (DC-9-83)	49709 / 1542	EC-835	1188	0395	2 PW JT8D-219	72575	Y170	HS-DL	Sunmyth / lsf GECA
☐	EC-GBA	Boeing (Douglas) MD-83 (DC-9-83)	49626 / 1538	EC-805	1088	0495	2 PW JT8D-219	72575	Y170	HS-DM	Sungod / lsf GECA
☐	EC-GCV	Boeing (Douglas) MD-82 (DC-9-82)	53165 / 2042	EC-894	0092	0695	2 PW JT8D-217C	67812	Y170	HS-GL	Sunburst / lsf GECA
☐	EC-GGV	Boeing (Douglas) MD-83 (DC-9-83)	49791 / 1644	EC-166	0989	0496	2 PW JT8D-219	72575	Y170	KS-BJ	Sunbow / lsf GECA
☐	EC-GHE	Boeing (Douglas) MD-83 (DC-9-83)	49398 / 1332	EC-245	1186	0496	2 PW JT8D-219	72575	Y170	MQ-LR	Sunset / lsf GECA
☐	EC-GHH	Boeing (Douglas) MD-83 (DC-9-83)	49578 / 1455	EC-291	0388	0696	2 PW JT8D-219	72575	Y170	MS-EL	Sundance / lsf GECA
☐	EC-GNY	Boeing (Douglas) MD-83 (DC-9-83)	49396 / 1305	N396GE	0886	0497	2 PW JT8D-219	72575	Y170	BG-AE	Sunflash / lsf GECA
☐	EC-GOM	Boeing (Douglas) MD-83 (DC-9-83)	49579 / 1465	EC-EIG	0388	0488	2 PW JT8D-219	72575	Y170	EH-KP	Sunlight / lsf Finans Skandic
☐	EC-GOU	Boeing (Douglas) MD-83 (DC-9-83)	53198 / 1847	SE-DLS	0391	0697	2 PW JT8D-219	72575	Y170	QR-JP	Sunlover / lsf GECA
☐	EC-GQG	Boeing (Douglas) MD-83 (DC-9-83)	49577 / 1454	EC-FSY	0288	0388	2 PW JT8D-219	72575	Y170	EH-JP	Sunrise / lsf Finans Skandic
☐	EC-GQZ	Boeing (Douglas) MD-82 (DC-9-82)	49571 / 1458	HB-INY	0088	1197	2 PW JT8D-217C	67812	Y151	QR-JM	Sunbear / lsf Flightlease / cvtd-81
☐	EC-GTO	Boeing (Douglas) MD-82 (DC-9-82)	49570 / 1440	HB-INX	0088	0398	2 PW JT8D-217C	67812	Y151	BG-JR	Sunjet / lsf Air Fleet Credit Corp.
☐	EC-GVI	Boeing (Douglas) MD-83 (DC-9-83)	49936 / 1778	EI-CPA	1090	0698	2 PW JT8D-219	72575	Y170	EH-LP	Sunup / lsf GECA
☐	EC-GVO	Boeing (Douglas) MD-83 (DC-9-83)	49642 / 1421	N462GE	1187	0698	2 PW JT8D-219	72575	Y170		Sunspot / lsf GECA
☐	EC-GXU	Boeing (Douglas) MD-83 (DC-9-83)	49622 / 1498	EC-FTT	0688	0892	2 PW JT8D-219	72575	Y170	AF-DS	Sunray / lsf Finans Skandic
☐	EC-HBP	Boeing (Douglas) MD-83 (DC-9-83)	49629 / 1583	HB-IKP	0389	0499	2 PW JT8D-219	72575	Y170		lsf Credit Agricole
☐	EC-	Boeing (Douglas) MD-82 (DC-9-82)	53148 / 2072	HL7548	0093		2 PW JT8D-217C	67812	Y170		to be lsf GECA 0599 / ex KAL
☐	EC-FCU	Boeing 767-3Y0 (ER)	24999 / 354	EC-547	0091	0291	2 PW PW4060	184612	C18Y248	MQ-AF	Baleares / lsf GECA
☐	EC-FHA	Boeing 767-3Y0 (ER)	25000 / 386	EC-548	0091	0891	2 PW PW4060	184612	C18Y248	EG-BR	Canarias / lsf BBAM

SPASA - Servicios Politecnicos Aéreos, S.A. = SPS **Madrid-Cuatro Vientos**

Calle Esteban Arteaga 3, Entreplanta derechz, E-28019 Madrid, Spain ☎ (91) 560 57 17 Tx: n/a Fax: (91) 469 49 06 SITA: n/a
F: 1985 ☻ n/a Head: Pepe Lopez Brotons ICAO: SALDUERO Net: n/a

	registration	type of aircraft	cn/fn	ex/ex*	mfd	del	powered by	mtow kg	configuration	selcal	remarks
☐	EC-BSZ	Piper PA-23-250 Aztec D	27-4364	N6993Y	0069		2 LY IO-540-C4B5	2359	Photo / Survey		
☐	EC-CAC	Piper PA-23-250 Aztec E	27-4770	N14212	0072	0585	2 LY IO-540-C4B5	2359	Photo / Survey		
☐	EC-CDZ	Piper PA-23-250 Turbo Aztec E	27-7305111	N40296	0073		2 LY TIO-540-C1A	2359	Photo / Survey		
☐	EC-ESZ	Piper PA-23-250 Turbo Aztec E	27-7305201	D-IGAU	0073	0290	2 LY TIO-540-C1A	2359	Photo / Survey		

SWIFT AIR, S.A. = SWT **Madrid-Barajas & Vitoria-Foranda**

Ing. Torres Quevedo 14, Poligono Fin de Semana, Ctra. Madrid-Barcelona Km 13.400, E-28022 Madrid, Spain ☎ (91) 329 46 93 Tx: none Fax: (91) 329 57 20 SITA: n/a
F: 1986 ☻ 125 Head: Salvador Moreno Gonzalez-Aller ICAO: SWIFT Net: http://www.swiftair.com

	registration	type of aircraft	cn/fn	ex/ex*	mfd	del	powered by	mtow kg	configuration	selcal	remarks
☐	EC-EZD	Fairchild (Swearingen) SA226TC Metro II	TC-314	EC-487	0079	0790	2 GA TPE331-10UA-511G	5670	Freighter		op in DHL-colors
☐	EC-FPC	Fairchild (Swearingen) SA226TC Metro IIA	TC-408	EC-243	0081	0892	2 GA TPE331-10UA-511G	6001	Freighter		
☐	EC-FUX	Fairchild (Swearingen) SA226AT Merlin IVA	AT-038	EC-509	0075	1093	2 GA TPE331-3UW-303G	5670	Freighter		lsf BCS
☐	EC-FZB	Fairchild (Swearingen) SA226TC Metro II	TC-221	EC-666	0075	0794	2 GA TPE331-3UW-303G	5670	Freighter		lsf BCS
☐	EC-GBI	Fairchild (Swearingen) SA226AT Merlin IVA	AT-041	EC-867	0075	0495	2 GA TPE331-3UW-303G	5670	Freighter		lsf BCS / op in DHL-colors
☐	EC-FSV	Fairchild (Swearingen) SA227AC Metro III	AC-461B	EC-437	0081	0793	2 GA TPE331-11U-611G	7257	Freighter/Y19		
☐	EC-GUS	Fairchild (Swearingen) SA227AC Metro III	AC-648	N2685L	0086	0598	2 GA TPE331-11U-611G	6577	Freighter		lsf Finova Capital Corp.
☐	EC-GXE	Fairchild (Swearingen) SA227AC Metro III	AC-694	N457AM	0088	0798	2 GA TPE331-11U-612G	6577	Freighter		lsf Finova Capital Corp.
☐	EC-GYB	Fairchild (Swearingen) SA227AC Metro III	AC-699	N458AM	0088	0998	2 GA TPE331-11U-612G	6577	Freighter		lsf Finova Capital Corp.
☐	EC-GBF	Convair 580 (F) (SCD)	458	EC-830	0057	0395	2 AN 501-D13	24766	Freighter		lsf BCS/cvtd 440-97/op in DHL-colors
☐	EC-GDY	Convair 580 (F) (SCD)	25	EC-943	0052	0795	2 AN 501-D13	26379	Freighter		lsf BCS/cvtd 340-31/op in DHL-colors
☐	EC-GHN	Convair 580 (F) (SCD)	186	EC-255	0053	0396	2 AN 501-D13	26379	Freighter		lsf BCS/cvtd 440-31/op in DHL-colors
☐	EC-GKH	Convair 580 (F) (SCD)	135	OO-DHD	0053	1196	2 AN 501-D13	24766	Freighter		lsf BCS/cvtd 340-48/op in DHL-colors

☐ EC-GSJ	Convair 580 (F) (SCD)	130	OO-HUB	0053	0298	2 AN 501-D13	24766	Freighter		lsf BCS/cvtd 340-47/op in DHL-colors
☐ EC-HAH	Boeing 727-223 (F) (A)	21084 / 1199	OO-DHV	0476	0299	3 PW JT8D-9A (HK3/FDX)	78457	Freighter		lsf BCS / cvtd -223 / op in DHL-colors

SYMBOL, S.A. - Compania de Aviacion = SYB (Division of Symbol Publicidad, S.A.)

Valencia-Manises

Aeropuerto de Valencia, Bloco Tecnico, E-46940 Manises (Valencia), Spain ☎ (96) 152 11 85 Tx: none Fax: (96) 274 14 16 SITA: n/a

F: 1981 ⁂ 15 Head: Carlos Escobar ICAO: SYMBOLAIR Net: n/a Aircraft below MTOW 1361kg: Piper PA-18

☐ EC-BRA	Piper PA-23-250 Aztec D	27-4127	N6849Y	0069		2 LY IO-540-C4B5	2359	5 Pax		
☐ EC-EQK	Cessna 310R II	310R1610	N36873	0079		2 CO IO-520-MB	2495			

TADAIR, S.A. = TDC

Barcelona-Sabadell & -El Prat

Mallorca 319, E-08037 Barcelona, Spain ☎ (93) 712 36 08 Tx: none Fax: (93) 712 29 49 SITA: n/a

F: 1990 ⁂ 60 Head: Paco Irigoyen ICAO: TADAIR Net: http://www.tadair.es Aircraft below MTOW 1361kg: Mooney M20, Piper PA-18 & PA-25

☐ EC-BCB	Beech Travel Air D95A	TD-635	D-GARE	0065		2 LY IO-360-B1B	1905	5 Pax		
☐ EC-CGE	Piper PA-34-200 Seneca	34-7350324	N56378	0073	0095	2 LY IO-360-C1E6	1905	Freighter		
☐ EC-CKI	Piper PA-34-200 Seneca	34-7450122	N41469	0074		2 LY IO-360-C1E6	1905	Freighter		
☐ EC-CDS	Piper PA-31-310 Navajo B	31-7300951	N7561L	0073		2 LY TIO-540-A2C	2948	Freighter		opf Nacex Servicio Express
☐ EC-EZE	Fairchild (Swearingen) SA226TC Metro II	TC-319	EC-488	0079	1298	2 GA TPE331-10UA-511G	5670	Freighter		
☐ EC-GKR	Fairchild (Swearingen) SA227AC Metro III	AC-620	N174SW	0085	1196	2 GA TPE331-11U-611G	6577	Freighter/19Pax		

TAF HELICOPTERS, S.A. = HET

Barcelona-Sabadell

Apartad de correus 1063, E-08204 Sabadell (Barcelona), Spain ☎ (93) 712 00 12 Tx: none Fax: (93) 712 37 22 SITA: n/a

F: 1954 ⁂ 30 Head: Eduardo Miralta ICAO: HELITAF Net: n/a Aircraft below MTOW 1361 kg: Hughes 269B (300) Helicopters which operates on behalf of Generalitat de Catalunya are using the call sign BOMBEROS.

☐ EC-DRG	Eurocopter (Aerosp.) AS350B Ecureuil	1597		0082	0782	1 TU Arriel 1B	1950	5 Pax		
☐ EC-EZP	Eurocopter (Aerosp.) AS350B Ecureuil	2413	EC-562	0090	0091	1 TU Arriel 1B	1950	5 Pax		
☐ EC-FOA	Eurocopter (Aerosp.) AS350BA Ecureuil	2626	EC-990	0092	0692	1 TU Arriel 1B	2100	5 Pax		
☐ EC-DSU	Eurocopter (MBB) BO105CBS-5	S-623	D-HDSS*	0083	0983	2 AN 250-C20B	2500	EMS/Rescue		02 / opf Generalitat de Catalunya
☐ EC-FYV	Eurocopter (MBB) BO105CBS-5	S-896	EC-705	0094	1294	2 AN 250-C20B	2500	EMS/Rescue		01 / opf Generalitat de Catalunya
☐ EC-GUZ	Eurocopter (Aerosp.) AS355F2 Ecureuil 2	5454	N26ET	0090	0598	2 AN 250-C20F	2540	5 Pax		
☐ EC-EVT	Eurocopter (MBB) BK117A-4	7074	D-HBNV*	0086	0790	2 LY LTS101-650B.1	3200	EMS/Rescue		03 / opf Generalitat de Catalunya
☐ EC-FQO	Bell 205A-1	30011	N43162	0062	0293	1 LY T5313B	4309	Utility		
☐ EC-GPP	Bell 205A-1	30290	EC-GCG	0079	0495	1 LY T5313B	4309	Utility		
☐ SE-HMS	Bell 205A-1	30256	N16750	0077	0697	1 LY T5313B	4309	Utility		lsf Sterner Aero AB
☐ SE-HMT	Bell 205A-1	30180	N68HJ	0075	0396	1 LY T5313B	4309	Utility		lsf Sterner Aero AB

TASA - Trabajos Aéreos, S.A. = TGE

Madrid-Cuatro Vientos

Avda de America 47, E-28002 Madrid, Spain ☎ (91) 413 57 41 Tx: none Fax: (91) 519 25 40 SITA: n/a

F: 1973 ⁂ 5 Head: D. Antonio Flores Alvarez ICAO: TASA Net: n/a Aircraft below MTOW 1361kg: Piper PA-18 & PA-28

☐ EC-CJE	Cessna 402B	402B0531	N69396	0073	0574	2 CO TSIO-520-E	2858	Photo/Survey		
☐ EC-DKP	Cessna 402C II	402C0275	N2757A	0080	0880	2 CO TSIO-520-VB	3107	Photo/Survey		

TAS - Transportes Aéreos del Sur, S.A. = HSS (Associated with HELISURESTE – Helicopteros del Sureste, SA)

Sevilla-San Pablo & -Heliport Cartuja

Helipuerto Isla de la Cartuja, Ronda de la Esposicion s/n, E-41092 Sevilla, Spain ☎ (95) 446 26 16 Tx: none Fax: (95) 446 00 38 SITA: n/a

F: 1989 ⁂ 25 Head: Manuel Cano ICAO: TAS Net: n/a Aircraft below MTOW 1361kg: Bell 47G, Enstrom F28A, Optica OA7 & PZL-104 Wilga 80

☐ EC-DOL	Agusta-Bell 206B JetRanger III	8615		0081		1 AN 250-C20B	1451	4 Pax		
☐ EC-EUT	Bell 206L-3 LongRanger III	51337	N8212U	0090	0590	1 AN 250-C30P	1882	6 Pax		
☐ EC-GHS	Partenavia P.68 Observer	329-20-OB	G-OBSV	0085	0896	2 LY IO-360-A1B6	1960	Photo / Survey		opf Baleares Gvmt / based Ibiza
☐ EC-GPK	Bell 412	33048	N16HW	0081	0098	2 PWC PT6T-3B TwinPac	5262	Utility		
☐ EC-GHZ	Beech King Air 200	BB-555	D-IFOR	0079	0796	2 PWC PT6A-41	5670	10 Pax / EMS		
☐ EC-GSQ	Beech King Air 350 (B300)	FL-128	N128FL	0094	0298	2 PWC PT6A-60A	6804	Executive / EMS		

TAVASA - Trabajos Aéreos Vascongados, S.A.

Bilbao-Sondika

Apartado de Correos 206, E-48080 Bilbao (Vizcaya), Spain ☎ (94) 453 05 08 Tx: 32525 amaz e Fax: (94) 471 00 11 SITA: n/a

F: 1981 ⁂ 22 Head: José Manuel Alegria Artiach Net: n/a Aircraft below MTOW 1361kg: Socata MS893E

☐ EC-EOF	Eurocopter (Aerosp.) SA315B Lama	2261	F-GEJS	0072	0589	1 TU Artouste IIIB	1950	4 Pax		
☐ EC-ERZ	Eurocopter (Aerosp.) AS350B2 Ecureuil	2261		0089	0290	1 TU Arriel 1D1	2250	Police Patrol		opf Gobierno Vasco-Ertzaintza/cvtd350B1
☐ EC-ESA	Eurocopter (Aerosp.) AS350B2 Ecureuil	2260	F-WYMF*	0089	0190	1 TU Arriel 1D1	2250	5 Pax		cvtd AS350B1
☐ EC-EHO	Eurocopter (Aerosp.) SA316B Alouette III	1585	F-GEPJ	0069	0488	1 TU Artouste IIIB1	2200	5 Pax		
☐ EC-GMZ	Eurocopter EC135T1	0016		0097	0397	2 TU Arrius 2B1	2720	Police Patrol		opf Gobierno Vasco-Ertzaintza
☐ EC-GNA	Eurocopter EC135T1	0017		0097	0397	2 TU Arrius 2B1	2720	Police Patrol		opf Gobierno Vasco-Ertzaintza
☐ EC-EBB	Eurocopter (Aerosp.) SA365C3 Dauphin 2	5013	F-GBOU	0079	1286	2 TU Arriel 1C	3500	Police Patrol		opf Gobierno Vasco-Ertzaintza
☐ EC-EGV	Eurocopter (Aerosp.) SA365C3 Dauphin 2	5032	F-GBTB	0079	0288	2 TU Arriel 1C	3500	Police Patrol		opf Gobierno Vasco-Ertzaintza
☐ EC-ERY	Sikorsky S-76A+	760037	EC-364	0079	0890	2 TU Arriel 1S	4864	EMS/Rescue/VIP		cvtd 76A/opf C.A.de Cantabria/based SDR

TOP FLY, S.L. = TLY

Barcelona-Sabadell

Aeropuerto de Sabadell, Apartado 1037, E-08204 Sabadell (Barcelona), Spain ☎ (93) 712 23 60 Tx: none Fax: (93) 712 04 98 SITA: n/a

F: 1993 ⁂ 11 Head: Jorge Garcia Veguin ICAO: TOPFLY Net: http://www.topfly.com. Aircraft below MTOW 1361kg: Cessna 172, Piper PA-18 & Robinson R22

☐ EC-DND	Reims/Cessna FR182 Skylane RG II	FR182-0021	N9012F	0079	1197	1 LY O-540-J3C5D	1406	3 Pax		
☐ EC-GDB	Agusta-Bell 206B JetRanger	8095	EC-913	0068	1097	1 AN 250-C20	1451	4 Pax		cvtd 206A
☐ EC-EYV	Piper PA-34-220T Seneca III	34-8233109		0082	0094	2 CO TSIO-360-KB	2031	4 Pax/Freighter		

TRABAJOS AEREOS ESPEJO, S.L.

Cordoba

José Maria Valdenebro 27, E-14004 Cordoba, Spain ☎ (957) 23 71 42 Tx: n/a Fax: (957) 41 14 61 SITA: n/a

F: 1992 ⁂ n/a Head: Fernando Espejo Net: n/a

☐ EC-EJH	Cessna TU206G Turbo Stationair 6 II	U20604172	N756LH	0077	0692	1 CO TSIO-520-M	1633			
☐ EC-FMX	Piper PA-34-200T Seneca II	34-7970396	N606RH	0079	0592	2 CO TSIO-360-EB1	2073			

TRAGSA - Empresa de transformacion agraria, S.A.

Madrid-Cuatro Vientos

Hangar 3, Aeropuerto Cuatro Vientos, E-28044 Madrid, Spain ☎ (91) 508 80 46 Tx: none Fax: (91) 508 72 91 SITA: n/a

F: 1994 ⁂ 11 Head: Luis Molano Bernardino Net: n/a

☐ EC-GAO	Eurocopter (Aerosp.) SA316B Alouette III	2324	EC-801	0077	0295	1 TU Artouste IIIB	2200	5 Pax		
☐ EC-GDJ	Bell UH-1H (205)	5320	66-837	0066	0795	1 LY T53-L-13B	4309	Utility		lst Heliservices
☐ EC-GDK	Bell UH-1H (205)	5639	N82814	0066	0795	1 LY T53-L-13B	4309	Utility		
☐ EC-GIU	Bell UH-1H (205)	5265	N12UH	0066	0696	1 LY T53-L-13B	4309	Utility		
☐ EC-GIV	Bell UH-1H (205)	12481	N11UH	0070	0696	1 LY T53-L-13B	4309	Utility		
☐ EC-GUT	Bell UH-1H (205)	13367	N21UH	0073	0098	1 LY T53-L-13	4309	Utility		
☐ EC-GXF	Bell UH-1H (205)	12604	N22UH	0070	0798	1 LY T53-L-13	4309	Utility		

TRANSAVIATION, S.A. = TVT

Madrid-Barajas

Calle Geminis 33, bajo, E-28042 Barajas (Madrid), Spain ☎ (91) 305 61 57 Tx: none Fax: (91) 305 80 63 SITA: n/a

F: 1994 ⁂ 14 Head: Julian Bravo ICAO: TRANSAVIATION Net: n/a

☐ EC-FQX	Lockheed L-1329 JetStar II	5202 / 25	EC-232	0076	0094	4 GA TFE731-3-1K	20185	Executive 10Pax		

TURISVOL HELICOPTERS

Costa Brava-Centre Heliport

Apartado de Correos 181, E-17250 Platja d'Aro, Girona, Spain ☎ (972) 81 71 23 Tx: none Fax: (972) 85 22 10 SITA: n/a

F: 1997 ⁂ 3 Head: Josep Gelabert Net: n/a

☐ EC-GCN	Bell 206B JetRanger III	2545	G-WOSP	0078	0097	1 AN 250-C20B	1451	4 Pax		

VICTOR ECHO, S.A. = VEE

Barcelona-El Prat

Avda de la Riera 21, E-08961 Sant Just Desvern (Barcelona), Spain ☎ (93) 298 43 36 Tx: none Fax: (93) 298 43 37 SITA: n/a

F: 1997 ⁂ 5 Head: Josep Ventura Sala ICAO: VICTOR ECHO Net: n/a

☐ EC-BBZ	Piper PA-23-250 Aztec C	27-2938	N5805Y	0065	0097	2 LY IO-540-C4B5	2359	5 Pax/Freighter		
☐ EC-FCC	Cessna 402B II	402B1013	N113JG	0074	0898	2 CO TSIO-520-E	2858	7 Pax/Freighter		

ZONA BLAVA, S.L. = OZB

Barcelona-Sabadell

Calle Servia 6, Baixos, E-08041 Barcelona, Spain ☎ (93) 436 44 12 Tx: $one Fax: (93) 435 80 75 SITA: n/a

F: 1996 ⁂ n/a Head: Mr. Mauri ICAO: ZONA BLAVA Net: n/a

☐ EC-FKK	Cessna 401	401-0279	EC-EXH	0068		2 CO TSIO-520-E	2858	6 Pax		TV Aerial Support

Z1 Alerta y Control, S.A.

Gran Canaria-El Berriel

Calle Presidente Alvear 52, 6a Planta, E-35007 Las Palmas de Gran Canaria, Spain ☎ (928) 27 69 73 Tx: none Fax: (928) 22 48 45 SITA: n/a

F: 1994 ⁂ 3 Head: José Juan Ramizez Net: n/a Aircraft below MTOW 1361kg: Westland-Bell 47G-4A

☐ EC-EEC	Eurocopter (Aerosp.) SA316B Alouette III	1912		0071	0798	1 TU Artouste IIIB	2200	6 Pax / Patrol		lsf Helicsa

ZOREX AIR TRANSPORT = ORZ (Zorex, S.A. dba)

Madrid-Barajas

Carrera de San Jeronimo 17, 2B, E-28014 Madrid, Spain ☎ (91) 369 02 72 Tx: none Fax: (91) 369 02 54 SITA: n/a

F: 1997 ⁂ 12 Head: Santiago Zorrilla ICAO: ZOREX Net: n/a

☐ EC-GPE	Fairchild (Swearingen) SA226TC Metro II	TC-273	OY-JER	0078	0997	2 GA TPE331-10UA-511G	5670	Airtaxi/Frtr		lsf Bent Dall ApS

130 registration type of aircraft cn/fn ex/ex* mfd del powered by mtow kg configuration selcal name/fln/specialitites/remarks

EI = EIRE (Eire / Ireland))

The semi-official names 'Poblacht na h'Eireann', 'Republic of Eire' and 'Republic of Ireland' are often used both to emphasize the independence of the country and to distinguish Ireland from Northern Ireland which stayed with the United Kingdom when Ireland became independent)
Capital: Dublin Official Language: English, Gaelic Population: 3,6 million Square Km: 70284 Dialling code: +353 Year established: 1919 Acting political head: Berti Ahern (Prime Minister)

Government / Corporate / Executive / VIP Aircraft

☐ 240	Beech King Air 200	BB-672		0080		2 PWC PT6A-41	5670	VIP		Irish Air Corps/Aer-chor na h-Eireann
☐ 251	GAC G-IV Gulfstream IV	1160	N17584*	0091	1291	2 RR Tay 611-8	33203	VIP		Irish Air Corps/Aer-chor na h-Eireann

AER ARANN = RE / REA (Galway Aviation Services, Ltd / Comharbairt Gaillimh Teo dba) — Dublin & Galway

International House, Corballis Park, Dublin Airport, (Co. Dublin), Ireland ☎ (1) 814 52 41 Tx: none Fax: (1) 814 52 50 SITA: n/a
F: 1969 ⁂ 20 Head: Eugene O'Kelly & Padraig O'Ceidigh IATA: 809 ICAO: AER ARANN Net: n/a

☐ EI-AYN	Britten-Norman BN-2A-8 Islander	704	G-BBFJ	0074		2 LY O-540-E4C5	2858	Y9		
☐ EI-BCE	Britten-Norman BN-2A-26 Islander	519	G-BDUV	0076		2 LY O-540-E4C5	2994	Y9		
☐ EI-CPR	Shorts 360-200 (SD3-60 Variant 100)	SH3713	G-OBOH	0087	0299	2 PWC PT6A-65AR	11999	Y36		lsf RPX

AER ATLANTIC = RDK (Irish Air Transport, Ltd dba / Member of Atlantic Group / formerly Irish Air Tours) — Dublin

Park House, Corballis Park, Dublin Airport, (Co. Dublin), Ireland ☎ (1) 844 41 59 Tx: none Fax: (1) 844 40 81 SITA: n/a
F: 1991 ⁂ n/a Head: Marian Knopek ICAO: IRISH TOURS Net: n/a

☐ EI-CNM	Piper PA-31-350 Navajo Chieftain	31-7305107	N12014	0073	1296	2 LY TIO-540-J2BD	3175			

AER LINGUS, Plc = EI / EIN (Aer Lingus Commuter) — Dublin

PO Box 180, Dublin Airport, (Co. Dublin), Ireland ☎ (1) 705 22 22 Tx: 25101 alt ei Fax: (1) 705 38 32 SITA: n/a
F: 1936 ⁂ 6200 Head: Bernie Cahill IATA: 053 ICAO: SHAMROCK Net: http://www.aerlingus.ie
Domestic & & flights to United Kingdom (other than London) with Fokker 50 & BAe 146 aircraft are operated under the marketing name AER LINGUS COMMUTER (carrying such titles).

☐ EI-FKA	Fokker 50 (F27 Mk050)	20118	PH-LMA*	0087	0189	2 PWC PW125B	20820	Y50		St. Fintan / Fionntain
☐ EI-FKB	Fokker 50 (F27 Mk050)	20119	PH-LMB*	0088	0289	2 PWC PW125B	20820	Y50		St. Fergal / Fearghal
☐ EI-FKC	Fokker 50 (F27 Mk050)	20177	PH-EXC*	0090	0290	2 PWC PW125B	20820	Y50		St. Fidelma / Fiedeilme
☐ EI-FKD	Fokker 50 (F27 Mk050)	20181	PH-EXG*	0090	0490	2 PWC PW125B	20820	Y50		St. Mel
☐ EI-FKE	Fokker 50 (F27 Mk050)	20208	PH-EXA*	0091	0191	2 PWC PW125B	20820	Y50		St. Pappin / Paipan
☐ EI-FKF	Fokker 50 (F27 Mk050)	20209	PH-EXE*	0091	0291	2 PWC PW125B	20820	Y50		St. Ultan
☐ EI-CSK	BAe 146-200	E2062	N810AS	0086	0498	4 LY ALF502R-5	40750	Y93		St. Ciara / lsf BAMJ
☐ EI-CSL	BAe 146-200	E2074	N812AS	0087	0598	4 LY ALF502R-5	40750	Y93		St. Cormac / lsf BAMJ
☐ EI-CLG	BAe 146-300	E3131	G-BRAB	0089	0695	4 LY ALF502R-5	41750	Y110		St. Finbarr / Fionnbar / lsf BAMJ
☐ EI-CLH	BAe 146-300	E3146	G-BOJJ	0090	0695	4 LY ALF502R-5	41750	Y110		St. Aoife / lsf BAMJ
☐ EI-CLI	BAe 146-300	E3159	G-BVSA	0090	0495	4 LY ALF502R-5	41750	Y110		St. Eithne / lsf BAMJ
☐ EI-CLJ	BAe 146-300	E3155	G-BTNU	0090	0396	4 LY ALF502R-5	41750	Y110		St. Senan / Seanan / lsf BAMJ
☐ EI-CLY	BAe 146-300	E3149	G-BTZN	0089	0497	4 LY ALF502R-5	41750	Y110		St. Eugene / Eoghan / lsf BAMJ
☐ EI-CTM	BAe 146-300	E3129	G-JEAL	0089	0399	4 LY ALF502R-5	41750	Y110		St. Fiacre / Fiachra / lsf BAMJ
☐ EI-CDA	Boeing 737-548	24878 / 1939	EI-BXE	0090	1090	2 CFMI CFM56-3B1	55000	CY117	AC-FQ	St. Columba / Colum / tblst RSL 0699
☐ EI-CDB	Boeing 737-548	24919 / 1970	EI-BXF	0090	1290	2 CFMI CFM56-3B1	55000	CY117	AC-GQ	St. Albert / Ailbhe
☐ EI-CDC	Boeing 737-548	24968 / 1975	EI-BXG	0091	0191	2 CFMI CFM56-3B1	55000	CY117	AC-HQ	St. Munchin / Maincin
☐ EI-CDD	Boeing 737-548	24989 / 1989	EI-BXH	0091	0291	2 CFMI CFM56-3B1	55000	CY117	AC-JQ	St. Macartan / Macarthaln
☐ EI-CDE	Boeing 737-548	25115 / 2050	PT-SLM	0091	0591	2 CFMI CFM56-3B1	55000	CY117	JM-EQ	St. Jarlath / Iarflaith
☐ EI-CDF	Boeing 737-548	25737 / 2232		0092	0392	2 CFMI CFM56-3B1	55000	CY117	BD-GR	St. Cronan
☐ EI-CDG	Boeing 737-548	25738 / 2261		0092	0492	2 CFMI CFM56-3B1	55000	CY117	BD-FS	St. Moling
☐ EI-CDH	Boeing 737-548	25739 / 2271		0092	0492	2 CFMI CFM56-3B1	55000	CY117	BD-GS	St. Ronan
☐ EI-BXA	Boeing 737-448	24474 / 1742		0089	0789	2 CFMI CFM56-3B2	65000	CY156	JM-GP	St. Conleth / Connlaodh
☐ EI-BXB	Boeing 737-448	24521 / 1788		0089	1089	2 CFMI CFM56-3B2	65000	CY156	JM-HP	St. Gall
☐ EI-BXC	Boeing 737-448	24773 / 1850		0090	0490	2 CFMI CFM56-3B2	65000	CY156	GQ-HP	St. Brendan / Breandan
☐ EI-BXD	Boeing 737-448	24866 / 1867		0090	0690	2 CFMI CFM56-3B2	65000	CY156	GQ-JK	St. Colman
☐ EI-BXI	Boeing 737-448	25052 / 2036		0091	0491	2 CFMI CFM56-3B2	65000	CY156	GQ-JL	St. Finnian
☐ EI-BXK	Boeing 737-448	25736 / 2269		0092	0492	2 CFMI CFM56-3B2	65000	CY156	BD-HR	St. Caimin / lst RYN in winter
☐ EI-CRC	Boeing 737-46B	24124 / 1679	EC-GNC	0089	1098	2 CFMI CFM56-3C1	65770	Y170	JM-KR	lsf FUA / sub-lst RYN in winter
☐ EI-	Airbus Industrie A320-214					2 CFMI CFM56-5B4/P	73500	CY150		oo-delivery 0400
☐ EI-	Airbus Industrie A320-214					2 CFMI CFM56-5B4/P	73500	CY150		oo-delivery 1000
☐ EI-	Airbus Industrie A320-214					2 CFMI CFM56-5B4/P	73500	CY150		oo-delivery 0001
☐ EI-	Airbus Industrie A320-214					2 CFMI CFM56-5B4/P	73500	CY150		oo-delivery 0001
☐ EI-	Airbus Industrie A320-214					2 CFMI CFM56-5B4/P	73500	CY150		oo-delivery 0002
☐ EI-	Airbus Industrie A320-214					2 CFMI CFM56-5B4/P	73500	CY150		oo-delivery 0002
☐ EI-CPC	Airbus Industrie A321-211	815	D-AVZT*	0098	0598	2 CFMI CFM56-5B3/P	89000	CY193	AQ-GH	St. Fergus / Feargus / lsf ILFC
☐ EI-CPD	Airbus Industrie A321-211	841	D-AVZA*	0098	0698	2 CFMI CFM56-5B3/P	89000	CY193		St. Davnet / Damhnat / lsf ILFC
☐ EI-CPE	Airbus Industrie A321-211	926	D-AVZQ*	0098	1298	2 CFMI CFM56-5B3/P	89000	CY193		St. Enda / Eanna
☐ EI-CPF	Airbus Industrie A321-211	991		0099	0399	2 CFMI CFM56-5B3/P	89000	CY193		St. Ita / lsf ILFC
☐ EI-CPG	Airbus Industrie A321-211	1023				2 CFMI CFM56-5B3/P	89000	CY193		oo-delivery 0599
☐ EI-CPH	Airbus Industrie A321-211	1094				2 CFMI CFM56-5B3/P	89000	CY193		oo-delivery 1099
☐ EI-CRK	Airbus Industrie A330-301	070	F-WWKV*	0094	1194	2 GE CF6-80E1A2	215000	C24Y303	DP-CR	St. Brigid / Brighid / lsf ILFC
☐ EI-DUB	Airbus Industrie A330-301	055	F-WWKP*	0094	0594	2 GE CF6-80E1A2	215000	C24Y303	DJ-GR	St. Patrick / Padraig / lsf ILFC
☐ EI-JFK	Airbus Industrie A330-301	086	F-GMDE	0095	0795	2 GE CF6-80E1A2	215000	C36Y279	JS-AP	St. Colmcille
☐ EI-ORD	Airbus Industrie A330-301	059	F-GMDD	0694	0697	2 GE CF6-80E1A2	215000	C24Y303	QR-KP	St. Maeve / Maedbh
☐ EI-SHN	Airbus Industrie A330-301	054	F-WWKJ*	0294	0594	2 GE CF6-80E1A2	215000	C36Y279	DG-JQ	St. Flannan / lsf ILFC
☐ EI-LAX	Airbus Industrie A330-202	269		0099	0499	2 GE CF6-80E1A4	232000	C24Y251		St. Mella
☐ EI-	Airbus Industrie A330-202					2 GE CF6-80E1A4	230000	C24Y255		to be lsf ILFC 0500
☐ N272WA	Boeing (Douglas) MD-11	48437 / 506		0093		3 PW PW4460	280320	C24Y296	GH-AS	St.Kilian/Cilian / tblsf/opb WOA05-1099

AER TURAS Teoranta = ATT — Dublin

Corballis Park, Dublin Airport, (Co. Dublin), Ireland ☎ (1) 844 41 31 Tx: 33393 att ei Fax: (1) 844 60 49 SITA: DUBYQEI
F: 1962 ⁂ 60 Head: John J. Harnett ICAO: AERTURAS Net: n/a

☐ EI-BNA	Boeing (Douglas) DC-8-63F (CF)	45989 / 371	LX-ACV	0068	1082	4 PW JT3D-7 (HK3/BAC)	161025	Freighter	EF-JL	City of Dublin
☐ EI-CGO	Boeing (Douglas) DC-8-63F	45924 / 392	N353AS	0868	0489	4 PW JT3D-7 (HK3/BAC)	161025	Freighter	EG-AF	cvtd -63
☐ EI-CNN	Lockheed L-1011-385-1 TriStar 1	193K-1024	VR-HHV	0273	0497	3 RR RB211-22B	195045	Y342	BH-DL	lsf Equis Finance Group/opf TBG Airways

AIR CONTRACTORS (Ireland), Ltd = AG / ABR (Subsidiary of CMB, Belgium & Safair, South Africa / formerly Hunting Cargo Airlines (Ireland) Ltd) — Dublin

The Plaza, New Street, Swords, (Co. Dublin), Ireland ☎ (1) 812 19 51 Tx: none Fax: (1) 812 19 69 SITA: n/a
F: 1993 ⁂ n/a Head: Hugh Flynn IATA: 914 ICAO: CONTRACT Net: n/a

☐ ZS-RSI	Lockheed L-382G (L-100-30) Hercules	31C-4600	F-GIMV	0075	0396	4 AN 501-D22A	70307	Freighter		lsf SFR
☐ EI-HCA	Boeing 727-225 (F)	20382 / 825	N8839E	0070	0494	3 PW JT8D-7B (HK3/FDX)	80559	Freighter		Eagle / lsf TTC Hunt II Lsng/cvtd -225
☐ EI-HCB	Boeing 727-223 (F)	19492 / 652	N6817	1168	0895	3 PW JT8D-7B (HK3/FDX)	80559	Freighter		lsf TTC Hunt II Leasing Corp./cvtd -223
☐ EI-HCC	Boeing 727-223 (F)	19480 / 545	N6805	0368	0995	3 PW JT8D-7B (HK3/FDX)	80559	Freighter		lsf TT Hunt II Leasing Corp./cvtd -223
☐ EI-HCD	Boeing 727-223 (F)	20185 / 710	N6832	0469	1195	3 PW JT8D-7B (HK3/FDX)	80559	Freighter		lsf TTC Hunt II Leasing Corp./cvtd -223
☐ EI-HCI	Boeing 727-223 (F)	20183 / 705	N6830	0469	0595	3 PW JT8D-7B (HK3/FDX)	80559	Freighter		lsf TTC Hunt II Leasing Corp./cvtd -223
☐ EI-LCH	Boeing 727-281 (F)	20466 / 865	N903PG	0071	0295	3 PW JT8D-7B (HK3/FDX)	80559	Freighter		Sylvia / lsf TTC Hunt II Lsng/cvtd -281
☐ EI-EAA	Airbus Industrie A300B4-203 (F)	150	SU-BCC	0081	0498	2 GE CF6-50C2	165000	Freighter		lsf Pyramid Lsng/cvtd -203/op in DHL-cs
☐ EI-EAB	Airbus Industrie A300B4-203 (F)	199	F-WQFO	0082	0598	2 GE CF6-50C2	165000	Freighter		lsf Pyramid Lsng/cvtd -203/op in DHL-cs
☐ EI-EAC	Airbus Industrie A300B4-203 (F)	250	N10970	0083	1198	2 GE CF6-50C2	165000	Freighter		lsf Household Comm/cvtd-203/opin DHL-cs
☐ EI-EAD	Airbus Industrie A300B4-203 (F)	289	N13972	0083	1198	2 GE CF6-50C2	165000	Freighter		lsf Pyramid Lsng/cvtd -203/op in DHL-cs
☐ EI-EAT	Airbus Industrie A300B4-203 (F)	116	D-ASAY	0080	1297	2 GE CF6-50C2	165000	Freighter		lsf Pyramid Lsng/cvtd -203/op in DHL-cs

AIRLINK AIRWAYS, Ltd = HYR — Dublin

256 Charlemont, Griffith Avenue, Dublin 9, (Co. Dublin), Ireland ☎ (1) 836 86 93 Tx: none Fax: (1) 836 86 93 SITA: n/a
F: 1993 ⁂ 5 Head: Capt. L. Mulligan ICAO: HIGHFLYER Net: n/a

☐ EI-CIJ	Cessna 340 II	340-0304	G-BBVE	0073	0793	2 CO TSIO-520-K	2710			

BOND HELICOPTERS (Ireland), Ltd (Subsidiary of Bond Helicopters, Ltd) — Shannon, Dublin & Cork

Shannon Airport, (Co. Clare), Ireland ☎ (61) 47 46 90 Tx: none Fax: (61) 47 45 66 SITA: n/a
F: 1996 ⁂ n/a Head: Capt. Mike Shaw Net: n/a

☐ EI-MIP	Eurocopter (Aerosp.) SA365N Dauphin 2	6119	G-BLEY	0084	0496	2 TU Arriel 1C	4000	12 Pax		opf Marathon Oil & adhoc-charters
☐ EI-CNL	Sikorsky S-61N	61746	G-BDDA	0075	1296	2 GE CT58-140-1	9299	SAR / Utility		Oil&Gas Support/Standby for Marine-IMES
☐ EI-MES	Sikorsky S-61N	61776	G-BXAE	0077	0197	2 GE CT58-140-2	9299	SAR		opf Marine-IMES Rescue
☐ EI-SAR	Sikorsky S-61N	61143	G-AYOM	0062	0598	2 GE CT58-140-1	9299	SAR		opf Marine-IMES Rescue

CELTIC HELICOPTERS, Ltd — Knocksedan Heliport

Celtic Heliport, Knocksedan, Dublin Airport, Swords, (Co. Dublin), Ireland ☎ (1) 890 13 49 Tx: none Fax: (1) 890 13 65 SITA: n/a
F: 1985 ⁂ 8 Head: Ciaran Haughey Net: n/a

☐ EI-BYJ	Bell 206B JetRanger II	1897	N49725	0076	0689	1 AN 250-C20	1451			
☐ EI-CAW	Bell 206B JetRanger	780	N2947W	0072		1 AN 250-C20	1451			
☐ EI-CHV	Agusta A109A	7149	VR-BMM	0078	0693	2 AN 250-C20B	2600			

131 registration type of aircraft cn/fn ex/ex* mfd del powered by mtow kg configuration selcal name/fln/specialitites/remarks

CITYJET = WX / BCY (Business City Direct, Plc dba) — Dublin

The Atirum, Level 5, Terminal Building, Dublin Airport, (Co. Dublin), Ireland ☎ (1) 844 55 88 Tx: none Fax: (1) 844 45 88 SITA: n/a
F: 1993 👥 320 Head: Patrick Byrne IATA: 689 ICAO: CITY-IRELAND Net: n/a
One aircraft is operated on a code-share agreement with AIR FRANCE (in full such colors & both titles) & using AF flight numbers.

registration	type of aircraft	cn/fn	ex/ex*	mfd	del	powered by	mtow kg	configuration	selcal	name/fln/specialitites/remarks
☐ EI-CPM	Saab 2000	*2000-028*	*SE-KCF*	*0095*	*0398*	*2 AN AE2100A*	*22800*	*Y50*		*lsf Saab Aircraft Credit AB*
☐ EI-CPQ	Saab 2000	*2000-013*	*F-GTSA*	*0095*	*0498*	*2 AN AE2100A*	*22800*	*Y50*		*lsf Saab/sub-lst/opf RGI in Regional-cs*
☐ EI-CPW	Saab 2000	*2000-016*	*F-GTSC*	*0095*	*0698*	*2 AN AE2100A*	*22800*	*Y50*		*lsf Saab Aircraft Credit AB*
☐ EI-CPY	BAe 146-100	*E1003*	*N246SS*	*0082*	*0798*	*4 LY ALF502R-5*	*38101*	*Y77*		*lsf BAMJ*
☐ EI-CMS	BAe 146-200	*E2044*	*N184US*	*0085*	*0496*	*4 LY ALF502R-5*	*40597*	*Y81*		*lsf USAL*
☐ EI-CMY	BAe 146-200	*E2039*	*N177US*	*0085*	*0696*	*4 LY ALF502R-5*	*40597*	*Y81*		*lsf USAL*
☐ EI-CNB	BAe 146-200	*E2046*	*N187US*	*0085*	*0896*	*4 LY ALF502R-5*	*40597*	*Y81*		*lsf USAL*
☐ EI-CNQ	BAe 146-200	*E2031*	*G-OWLD*	*0085*	*1196*	*4 LY ALF502R-5*	*40597*	*Y81*		*op in Air France Express-colors*

ELVEDEN INVESTMENT, Ltd = (ELVE) (Sister company of Tyrolean Airways, Austria) — Dublin

PO Box 2751, Dublin 1, (Co. Dublin), Ireland ☎ (1) 74 07 77 Tx: n/a Fax: (1) 74 30 50 SITA: n/a
F: n/a 👥 n/a Head: n/a Net: n/a New and used aircraft leasing, sales and financing company.
Owner / lessor of following (main) aircraft types: De Havilland DHC-8-100/300. Aircraft leased from ELVE are listed and mentioned as such under the leasing carriers.

E.U. AIR (European United Air, Ltd dba) — Dublin

9-11 Village Centre, Lucan, (Co. Dublin), Ireland ☎ (1) 621 96 95 Tx: none Fax: (1) 621 97 05 SITA: n/a
F: 1998 👥 n/a Head: Capt. Roger James Net: n/a

registration	type of aircraft	cn/fn	ex/ex*	mfd	del	powered by	mtow kg	configuration	selcal	name/fln/specialitites/remarks
☐ EI-COV	Hawker 700B (HS 125-700B)	*257178*	*N621S*	*0082*	*0598*	*2 GA TFE731-3R-1H*	*11567*			*lsf Wilton Bridge Ltd*

GE CAPITAL AVIATION SERVICES, Ltd = GCC = (GECA) (Subsidiary of General Electric Credit Corporation – GECC) — Shannon

GPA House, Shannon, (Co. Clare), Ireland ☎ (61) 36 00 00 Tx: none Fax: (61) 36 08 88 SITA: n/a
F: n/a 👥 n/a Head: Neill Green ICAO: GECAS Net: n/a New and used aircraft leasing, sales and financing company. Delivery flights are made under the name AIR TARA (an internal division) using the ICAO Code AGP.
Owner / Lessor of following (main) aircraft types A300-200, A320-200, A321-200, ATR42/72, BAe 111-200/400, Boeing 737-200/300/400/500/600/ 700/800, 747-200, 767-200/300, 777-200,
De Havilland DHC-8, McDonnell Douglas DC-8-71/73, DC-9-10/30, MD-80, MD-11 & Lockheed L-1011. Aircraft leased from GECA are listed and mentioned as such under the leasing carriers.

HELICOPTER SERVICES IRELAND — Dublin

32B Ashbrook, Grovenor Road, Rathgar, Dublin 6, (Co. Dublin), Ireland ☎ (1) 496 60 88 Tx: none Fax: (1) 496 27 30 SITA: n/a
F: 1997 👥 n/a Head: Capt. Paul Wynne Net: n/a

registration	type of aircraft	cn/fn	ex/ex*	mfd	del	powered by	mtow kg	configuration	selcal	name/fln/specialitites/remarks
☐ EI-ONE	Bell 206B JetRanger	*1761*	*EI-CJM*	*0075*	*0097*	*1 AN 250-C20*	*1451*			*lsf pvt*
☐ EI-PMI	Agusta-Bell 206B JetRanger III	*8614*	*EI-BLG*	*0081*	*0097*	*1 AN 250-C20B*	*1451*			*lsf Ping Golf Equipment Ltd*

IRISH HELICOPTERS, Ltd (Subsidiary of Bristow Helicopters, Ltd) — Dublin

Westpoint Hangar, Coultry, Swords, (Co. Dublin), Ireland ☎ (1) 844 45 00 Tx: none Fax: (1) 844 45 05 SITA: n/a
F: 1968 👥 7 Head: Ian Dunn Net: http://www.iol.ie/irishhelicopter

registration	type of aircraft	cn/fn	ex/ex*	mfd	del	powered by	mtow kg	configuration	selcal	name/fln/specialitites/remarks
☐ EI-BKT	Agusta-Bell 206B JetRanger III	*8562*	*D-HAFD*	*0078*	*0481*	*1 AN 250-C20B*	*1451*	*4 Pax*		
☐ EI-BLD	Eurocopter (MBB) BO 105DB	*S-381*	*D-HDLQ*	*0079*	*0781*	*2 AN 250-C20B*	*2300*	*4 Pax*		
☐ EI-LIT	Eurocopter (MBB) BO105CBS	*S-434*	*A6-DBH*	*0080*	*0296*	*2 AN 250-C20B*	*2500*	*4 Pax*		

OMEGA AIR, Ltd = (OMEG) — Dublin

Collinstown Cross, Dublin Airport, (Co. Dublin), Ireland ☎ (1) 837 66 22 Tx: 91636 omeg ei Fax: (1) 837 44 70 SITA: n/a
F: 1980 👥 n/a Head: n/a Net: n/a Used aircraft leasing, sales and financing company.
Owner / Lessor of following (main) aircraft types: Boeing 707 & McDonnell Douglas DC-10-40F. Aircraft leased from OMEG are listed and mentioned as such under the leasing carriers.

ORIX Aviation Systems, Ltd = (ORIX) (Subsidiary of Orix Corp., Tokyo/Japan) — Dublin

2nd Floor, IFSC House, Custom House Docks, Dublin 1, (Co. Dublin), Ireland ☎ (1) 670 06 33 Tx: 91807 orix ei Fax: (1) 670 03 44 SITA: n/a
F: 1991 👥 20 Head: Yoshio Ono Net: n/a New & used aircraft leasing and financing company.
Owner / lessor of following (main) aircraft types: Airbus Industrie A320-231. Aircraft leased from ORIX are listed and mentioned as such under the leasing carriers.

PEMBROKE CAPITAL, Ltd = (PEMB) (Subsidiary of Pembroke Group) — Dublin

Pembroke House, 33-41 Lower Mount Street, Dublin, Ireland ☎ (1) 661 09 00 Tx: none Fax: (1) 661 28 48 SITA: n/a
F: 1993 👥 25 Head: Shane Cooke Net: n/a New and used aircraft leasing, sales and financing company.
Owner / lessor of following (main) aircraft types: Boeing 737-300/500/700 & 717-200 (on order). Aircraft leased from Pembroke Capital are listed and mentioned as lsf PEMB under the leasing carriers.

PREMIER HELICOPTERS, Ltd (formerley ACE Helicopters, Ltd) — Dublin

Bond Road, East Wall, Dublin 3, (Co. Dublin), Ireland ☎ (41) 22 845 Tx: none Fax: (41) 82 256 SITA: n/a
F: 1997 👥 n/a Head: John O'Sullivan Net: n/a

registration	type of aircraft	cn/fn	ex/ex*	mfd	del	powered by	mtow kg	configuration	selcal	name/fln/specialitites/remarks
☐ EI-ECA	Agusta A109A II	*7387*	*N109RP*	*0087*	*0297*	*2 AN 250-C20B*	*2600*			*lsf Blackdrive Ltd*

RYANAIR, Ltd = FR / RYR — Dublin

Dublin Airport, (Co. Dublin), Ireland ☎ (1) 844 44 00 Tx: 33588 frop ei Fax: (1) 844 44 01 SITA: DUBHQFR
F: 1985 👥 950 Head: David Bondermann IATA: 224 ICAO: RYANAIR Net: http://www.iminet.com/SMS/Ryan/index.html

registration	type of aircraft	cn/fn	ex/ex*	mfd	del	powered by	mtow kg	configuration	selcal	name/fln/specialitites/remarks
☐ EI-CJC	Boeing 737-204 (A)	*22640 / 867*	*G-BJCV*	*0582*	*0194*	*2 PW JT8D-15*	*55110*	*Y130*		
☐ EI-CJD	Boeing 737-204 (A)	*22966 / 946*	*G-BKHE*	*0283*	*0294*	*2 PW JT8D-15A*	*55110*	*Y130*		*Eircell-colors*
☐ EI-CJE	Boeing 737-204 (A)	*22639 / 863*	*G-BJCU*	*0482*	*0394*	*2 PW JT8D-15*	*55110*	*Y130*		*Jaguar-colors*
☐ EI-CJF	Boeing 737-204 (A)	*22967 / 953*	*G-BTZF*	*0383*	*0394*	*2 PW JT8D-15*	*55110*	*Y130*		
☐ EI-CJG	Boeing 737-204 (A)	*22058 / 629*	*G-BGYK*	*0180*	*0394*	*2 PW JT8D-15*	*55110*	*Y130*		
☐ EI-CJH	Boeing 737-204 (A)	*22057 / 621*	*G-BGYJ*	*0180*	*0394*	*2 PW JT8D-15A*	*55110*	*Y130*		
☐ EI-CJI	Boeing 737-2E7 (A)	*22875 / 917*	*G-BMDF*	*1082*	*0794*	*2 PW JT8D-15*	*58105*	*Y130*	*JL-BF*	
☐ EI-CKP	Boeing 737-2K2 (A)	*22296 / 668*	*PH-TVS*	*0680*	*1094*	*2 PW JT8D-15*	*56472*	*Y130*	*HM-BE*	
☐ EI-CKQ	Boeing 737-2K2 (A)	*22906 / 888*	*PH-TVU*	*0682*	*0395*	*2 PW JT8D-15*	*56472*	*Y130*	*LM-CD*	
☐ EI-CKR	Boeing 737-2K2 (A)	*22025 / 647*	*PH-TVR*	*0380*	*0595*	*2 PW JT8D-15A*	*56472*	*Y130*	*HM-BD*	
☐ EI-CKS	Boeing 737-2T5 (A)	*22023 / 636*	*PH-TVX*	*0280*	*0695*	*2 PW JT8D-15*	*56472*	*Y130*		
☐ EI-CNT	Boeing 737-230 (A)	*22115 / 694*	*D-ABFC*	*0080*	*1296*	*2 PW JT8D-15 (HK3/NOR)*	*54204*	*Y130*		*Sun/New of the World-colors*
☐ EI-CNV	Boeing 737-230 (A)	*22128 / 752*	*D-ABFX*	*0481*	*0397*	*2 PW JT8D-15*	*54204*	*Y130*		
☐ EI-CNW	Boeing 737-230 (A)	*22133 / 772*	*D-ABHC*	*0781*	*0597*	*2 PW JT8D-15*	*54204*	*Y130*		
☐ EI-CNX	Boeing 737-230 (A)	*22127 / 745*	*D-ABFW*	*0481*	*0797*	*2 PW JT8D-15*	*54204*	*Y130*		*Tipperary Crystal-colors*
☐ EI-CNY	Boeing 737-230 (A)	*22113 / 649*	*D-ABFB*	*0480*	*1097*	*2 PW JT8D-15 (HK3/NOR)*	*54204*	*Y130*		*Kilkenny-The Cream of Irish Beer-colors*
☐ EI-CNZ	Boeing 737-230 (A)	*22126 / 735*	*D-ABFU*	*0481*	*1197*	*2 PW JT8D-15 (HK3/NOR)*	*54204*	*Y130*		
☐ EI-COA	Boeing 737-230 (A)	*22637 / 848*	*CS-TES*	*0082*	*1297*	*2 PW JT8D-17A*	*54204*	*Y130*		*lsf ICCO*
☐ EI-COB	Boeing 737-230 (A)	*22124 / 727*	*D-ABFR*	*0381*	*0198*	*2 PW JT8D-15 (HK3/NOR)*	*51990*	*Y130*		
☐ EI-CON	Boeing 737-2T5 (A)	*22396 / 730*	*PK-RIW*	*0081*	*0698*	*2 PW JT8D-15 (HK3/NOR)*	*54204*	*Y130*		
☐ EI-COX	Boeing 737-230 (A)	*22123 / 726*	*D-ABFP*	*0381*	*0198*	*2 PW JT8D-15 (HK3/NOR)*	*51990*	*Y130*		
☐ EI-CSA	Boeing 737-8AS	*29916 / 210*		*0099*	*0399*	*2 CFMI CFM56-7B24*	*70522*	*Y189*		
☐ EI-CSB	Boeing 737-8AS	*29917*				*2 CFMI CFM56-7B24*	*70522*	*Y189*		*oo-delivery 0699*
☐ EI-CSC	Boeing 737-8AS	*29918*				*2 CFMI CFM56-7B24*	*70522*	*Y189*		*oo-delivery 0699*
☐ EI-CSD	Boeing 737-8AS	*29919*				*2 CFMI CFM56-7B24*	*70522*	*Y189*		*oo-delivery 0899*
☐ EI-CSE	Boeing 737-8AS	*29920*				*2 CFMI CFM56-7B24*	*70522*	*Y189*		*oo-delivery 0999*
☐ EI-CSF	Boeing 737-8AS	*29921*				*2 CFMI CFM56-7B24*	*70522*	*Y189*		*oo-delivery 0500*
☐ EI-CSG	Boeing 737-8AS	*29922*				*2 CFMI CFM56-7B24*	*70522*	*Y189*		*oo-delivery 0500*
☐ EI-CSH	Boeing 737-8AS	*29923*				*2 CFMI CFM56-7B24*	*70522*	*Y189*		*oo-delivery 0600*
☐ EI-CSI	Boeing 737-8AS	*29924*				*2 CFMI CFM56-7B24*	*70522*	*Y189*		*oo-delivery 0600*
☐ EI-CSJ	Boeing 737-8AS	*29925*				*2 CFMI CFM56-7B24*	*70522*	*Y189*		*oo-delivery 0600*
☐ EI-CSM	Boeing 737-8AS					*2 CFMI CFM56-7B24*	*70522*	*Y189*		*oo-delivery 1200*
☐ EI-CSN	Boeing 737-8AS					*2 CFMI CFM56-7B24*	*70522*	*Y189*		*oo-delivery 1200*
☐ EI-CSO	Boeing 737-8AS					*2 CFMI CFM56-7B24*	*70522*	*Y189*		*oo-delivery 1200*
☐ EI-CSP	Boeing 737-8AS					*2 CFMI CFM56-7B24*	*70522*	*Y189*		*oo-delivery 0101*
☐ EI-CSQ	Boeing 737-8AS					*2 CFMI CFM56-7B24*	*70522*	*Y189*		*oo-delivery 0101*
☐ EI-CSR	Boeing 737-8AS					*2 CFMI CFM56-7B24*	*70522*	*Y189*		*oo-delivery 1201*
☐ EI-CSS	Boeing 737-8AS					*2 CFMI CFM56-7B24*	*70522*	*Y189*		*oo-delivery 1201*
☐ EI-CST	Boeing 737-8AS					*2 CFMI CFM56-7B24*	*70522*	*Y189*		*oo-delivery 1201*
☐ EI-CSV	Boeing 737-8AS					*2 CFMI CFM56-7B24*	*70522*	*Y189*		*oo-delivery 0002*
☐ EI-CSW	Boeing 737-8AS					*2 CFMI CFM56-7B24*	*70522*	*Y189*		*oo-delivery 0002*
☐ EI-CSX	Boeing 737-8AS					*2 CFMI CFM56-7B24*	*70522*	*Y189*		*oo-delivery 0002*
☐ EI-CSY	Boeing 737-8AS					*2 CFMI CFM56-7B24*	*70522*	*Y189*		*oo-delivery 0002*
☐ EI-CSZ	Boeing 737-8AS					*2 CFMI CFM56-7B24*	*70522*	*Y189*		*oo-delivery 0002*
☐ EI-CTA	Boeing 737-8AS					*2 CFMI CFM56-7B24*	*70522*	*Y189*		*oo-delivery 0003*
☐ EI-CTB	Boeing 737-8AS					*2 CFMI CFM56-7B24*	*70522*	*Y189*		*oo-delivery 0003*

SHANNONAIR LEASING, Ltd = (SNNL) (Member of IAS Group) — Shannon

IAS House, Shannon Business Park, Shannon, (Co. Clare), Ireland ☎ (61) 676 79 65 Tx: 72066 ias ei Fax: (61) 676 76 23 SITA: n/a
F: 1988 👥 35 Head: Eoin Colley Net: n/a Used aircraft leasing, sales and financing company.
Owner / Lessor of following (main) aircraft types: Airbus A300B4-100, Boeing 727-200, 737-200, 747-200 & McDonnell Douglas DC-10-30. Aircraft leased from SNNL are listed and mentioned as such under the leasing carriers.

SUNROCK AIRCRAFT, Corp. Ltd = (SUNR) (Member of Nissho Iwai Group) — Dublin

Russell House, Russell Court, Harcourt Street, Dublin 2, (Co. Dublin), Ireland ☎ (1) 478 54 10 Tx: 32316 sacl ei Fax: (1) 478 54 15 SITA: n/a
F: 1990 👥 n/a Head: Nobutoshi Gonda Net: n/a New and used aircraft leasing, sales and financing company.
Owner / lessor of following (main) aircraft types: Boeing 737-300/400/500, Boeing 757-200 & Boeing 767-300. Aircraft leased from SUNR are listed and mentioned as such under the leasing carriers.

TRANSAER International Airlines, Ltd = TLA (Member of the Translift Group / formerly Translift Airways, Ltd) **Dublin**

TransAer

Transaer House, Dublin Airport, (Co. Dublin), Ireland ☎ (1) 808 08 00 Tx: none Fax: (1) 808 08 01 SITA: DUBSST7
F: 1991 ⁂ 200 Head: Patrick J. McGoldrick IATA: 839 ICAO: TRANSLIFT Net: n/a

registration	type of aircraft	cn/fn	ex/ex*	mfd	del	powered by	mtow kg	configuration	selcal	name/fln/specialitites/remarks
☐ EI-TLE	Airbus Industrie A320-231	429	D-AORX	0093	1093	2 IAE V2500-A1	77000	Y180	GJ-AC	lsf ORIX / sub-lst / opf BAL -1099
☐ EI-TLF	Airbus Industrie A320-231	476	F-WWBR*	0094	0694	2 IAE V2500-A1	75500	Y180	CR-DK	lsf ORIX / sub-lst / opf BAL -1099
☐ EI-TLG	Airbus Industrie A320-231	428	C-GMPG	0094	0594	2 IAE V2500-A1	77000	Y180	CR-EH	lsf ILFC / sub-lst / opf TRZ in winter
☐ EI-TLH	Airbus Industrie A320-231	247	G-OALA	0091	1294	2 IAE V2500-A1	75500	Y180	JR-DQ	lsf ORIX / sub-lst / opf CUB
☐ EI-TLI	Airbus Industrie A320-231	405	N141LF	0093	0595	2 IAE V2500-A1	75500	Y180	JQ-CR	lsf ILFC / sub-lst / opf TRZ in winter
☐ EI-TLJ	Airbus Industrie A320-231	257	N257RX	0091	1295	2 IAE V2500-A1	75500	Y180	GH-LM	lsf ORIX / sub-lst / opf CUB
☐ EI-TLO	Airbus Industrie A320-232	758	F-WWDC*	0097	0198	2 IAE V2527-A5	77000	Y180	CR-EH	lsf SALE / sub-lst / opf BAL -1099
☐ EI-TLP	Airbus Industrie A320-232	760	F-WWDD*	0097	0198	2 IAE V2527-A5	75500	Y180	BJ-DE	lsf ILFC / sub-lst / opf LAV
☐ EI-TLR	Airbus Industrie A320-231	414	B-HYR	0093	0698	2 IAE V2500-A1	75500	Y180		lsf ILFC / sub-lst Transaer Cologne
☐ EI-TLS	Airbus Industrie A320-231	430	B-HYS	0093	0898	2 IAE V2500-A1	75500	Y180		lsf ILFC / sub-lst / opf VEX
☐ EI-	Airbus Industrie A320-232					2 IAE V2527-A5	77000	Y180		to be lsf SALE 0499
☐ EI-CJK	Airbus Industrie A300B4-103	020	F-BUAR	0075	0895	2 GE CF6-50C2	157500	Y314	AC-LM	lsf GECA / cvtd -2C
☐ EI-TLB	Airbus Industrie A300B4-103	012	F-GIJU	0075	0496	2 GE CF6-50C2	157500	Y314	JK-AM	lsf GECA / cvtd -2C
☐ EI-TLK	Airbus Industrie A300B4-203	161	N226GE	0081	0397	2 GE CF6-50C2	165000	Y314	BJ-AN	lsf POLA
☐ EI-TLL	Airbus Industrie A300B4-203	158	N225GE	0081	0697	2 GE CF6-50C2	165000	Y314	KL-EF	lsf POLA/to be sub-lst/opf VEX 06-1099
☐ EI-TLM	Airbus Industrie A300B4-203	046	RP-C8882	0377	0997	2 GE CF6-50C2	165000	Y314	DH-AK	lsf GECA / cvtd -103
☐ EI-TLQ	Airbus Industrie A300B4-203	131	6Y-JMK	0080	0498	2 GE CF6-50C2	165000	Y314	AD-FL	lsf GECA

VIRGIN EXPRESS (Ireland), Ltd = VK / VEI (Sister company of Virgin Express, Belgium / Member of Virgin Group) **Shannon**

Virgin House, Shannon Airport, (Co. Clare), Ireland ☎ (61) 70 44 90 Tx: none Fax: (61) 70 44 50 SITA: SNNOOTV
F: 1998 ⁂ n/a Head: Richard M. Branson ICAO: GREEN ISLE Net: n/a

registration	type of aircraft	cn/fn	ex/ex*	mfd	del	powered by	mtow kg	configuration	selcal	name/fln/specialitites/remarks
☐ EI-TVN	Boeing 737-36N	28586 / 3090	N1786B*	0199	0199	2 CFMI CFM56-3C1	61235	Y144		lsf GECA
☐ EI-TVA	Boeing 737-43Q	28489 / 2827	B-18671	0096	1198	2 CFMI CFM56-3C1	62822	Y170		lsf GECA
☐ EI-TVB	Boeing 737-43Q	28493 / 2838	B-18676	0096	1298	2 CFMI CFM56-3C1	62822	Y170		lsf BOUL

WESTAIR AVIATION, Ltd = EFF (Leoni Aviation, Ltd dba) **Shannon**

South East Ramp, Shannon Airport, (Co. Clare), Ireland ☎ (61) 47 51 66 Tx: none Fax: (61) 47 45 44 SITA: n/a
F: 1976 ⁂ 30 Head: Capt. Bryan A. Carpenter ICAO: EMERALD Net: n/a Aircraft below MTOW 1361 kg: Piper PA-38 & Robinson R22.

registration	type of aircraft	cn/fn	ex/ex*	mfd	del	powered by	mtow kg	configuration	selcal	name/fln/specialitites/remarks
☐ EI-BXX	Agusta-Bell 206B JetRanger III	8560	G-JMVB	0078	1188	1 AN 250-C20B	1451			
☐ EI-EEC	Piper PA-23-250 Aztec E	27-7554045	G-SATO	0075	0292	2 LY IO-540-C4B5	2359			
☐ EI-WAC	Piper PA-23-250 Aztec E	27-4683	G-AZBK	0071	0595	2 LY IO-540-C4B5	2359			
☐ EI-BOR	Bell 222A	47021	LN-OSB	0080		2 LY LTS101-650C.3	3561			
☐ EI-TAR	Bell 222A	47029	N121NN	0080	0998	2 LY LTS101-650C.3	3561			
☐ EI-WAV	Bell 430	49028	N4213V*	0097	1197	2 AN 250-C40	4082			
☐ N80JN	Mitsubishi MU-2J (MU-2B-35)	626	EC-GLU	0073	1298	2 GA TPE331-6-251M	4899			
☐ EI-WHE	Beech King Air B200	BB-1569	VP-CHE	0097	0598	2 PWC PT6A-42	5670			
☐ EI-WDC	Hawker 3B (HS 125-3B)	25132	G-OCBA	0067	1094	2 RR Viper 522	9843			
☐ EI-WGV	GAC G-V Gulfstream V	505	N505GV*	0097	1097	2 BR BR710A1-10	41232			

EK = ARMENIA (Republic of Armenia) (Hayastani Hanrapetutyun)

Capital: Yerevan Official Language: Armenian Population: 3,8 million Square Km: 29800 Dialling code: +374 Year established: 1990 Acting political head: Robert Kocharyan (President)

ARARAT AVIA, State Joint-Stock Company = 4A / ARK (Ararat Airlines) (Sister company of Armenian Airlines) **Yerevan-Erebuni**

Prospekt Arshakunyats 135, 375004 Yerevan, Armenia ☎ (2) 56 71 08 Tx: none Fax: (2) 50 52 19 SITA: n/a
F: 1998 ⁂ n/a Head: Sergei L. Vantsyan IATA: 444 ICAO: ARARAT AVIA Net: n/a Most aircraft are still in ex Armenian Airlines colors but will be repainted in due course.

registration	type of aircraft	cn/fn	ex/ex*	mfd	del	powered by	mtow kg	configuration	selcal	name/fln/specialitites/remarks
☐ EK-87316	Yakovlev 40	9331529	CCCP-87316	0773	0198	3 IV AI-25	17200	Y36		
☐ EK-87536	Yakovlev 40	9520142	CCCP-87536	0775	0198	3 IV AI-25	17200	Y34		lsf IRE as EP-DMS
☐ EK-87937	Yakovlev 40	9740856	CCCP-87937	0178	0198	3 IV AI-25	17200	Y34		lst IRE as EP-DAZ
☐ EK-88157	Yakovlev 40	9611146	CCCP-88157	0376	0198	3 IV AI-25	17200	Y36		
☐ EK-88167	Yakovlev 40	9610147	CCCP-88167	0476	0198	3 IV AI-25	17200	Y36		
☐ EK-88199	Yakovlev 40	9630149	CCCP-88199	0876	0198	3 IV AI-25	17200	Y34		
☐ EK-88250	Yakovlev 40	9710452	CCCP-88250	0177	0198	3 IV AI-25	17200	Y36		
☐ EK-88262	Yakovlev 40K	9711752	CCCP-88262	0477	0198	3 IV AI-25	17200	Y36		
☐ EK-46711	Antonov 24B		RA-46711	1169	0198	2 IV AI-24	21800	Y48		
☐ EK-49275	Antonov 24T		RA-49275	0669	0198	2 IV AI-24VT	22500	Y44		
☐ EK-11351	Antonov 12BP	4341910		0064	0098	4 IV AI-20M	64000	Freighter		

ARAX AIRWAYS = RXR **Yerevan-Zvartnots**

Zvartnots Airport, 375042 Yerevan, Armenia ☎ (2) 28 26 41 Tx: none Fax: (2) 28 26 41 SITA: n/a
F: 1995 ⁂ n/a Head: David Tovmasyan ICAO: ARAX AIR Net: n/a

registration	type of aircraft	cn/fn	ex/ex*	mfd	del	powered by	mtow kg	configuration	selcal	name/fln/specialitites/remarks
☐ EK-85607	Tupolev 154M	702	RA-85607	1184	0695	3 SO D-30KU-154-II	100000	Y160		
☐ EK-85803	Tupolev 154M	822	RA-85803	1189	0796	3 SO D-30KU-154-II	100000	Y164		

ARMENIAN AIRLINES = R3 / RME (formerly Aeroflot Armenian directorate) **Yerevan-Zvartnots**

Zvartnots Airport, 375042 Yerevan, Armenia ☎ (2) 22 54 44 Tx: 243152 port Fax: (2) 15 13 93 SITA: n/a
F: 1993 ⁂ n/a Head: Tigran M. Achoyan IATA: 956 ICAO: ARMENIAN Net: n/a

registration	type of aircraft	cn/fn	ex/ex*	mfd	del	powered by	mtow kg	configuration	selcal	name/fln/specialitites/remarks
☐ EK-65044	Tupolev 134A-3	49450	CCCP-65044	1276	0393	2 SO D-30-III	49000	Y72		
☐ EK-65072	Tupolev 134A-3	49972	CCCP-65072	0777	0393	2 SO D-30-III	49000	VIP		
☐ EK-65822	Tupolev 134A-3	09071	CCCP-65822	0574	0393	2 SO D-30-III	49000	Y72		
☐ EK-65831	Tupolev 134A-3	17102	CCCP-65831	0774	0393	2 SO D-30-III	49000	Y72		
☐ EK-65848	Tupolev 134A-3	23136	CCCP-65848	1274	0393	2 SO D-30-III	49000	Y72		
☐ EK-65975	Tupolev 134A-3	3352006	CCCP-65975	0973	0393	2 SO D-30-III	49000	Y72		
☐ EK-85166	Tupolev 154B-1	166	CCCP-85166	0876	0393	3 KU NK-8-2U	98000	F12Y126		
☐ EK-85200	Tupolev 154B-1	200	CCCP-85200	0377	0393	3 KU NK-8-2U	98000	Combi Y62&Cargo		
☐ EK-85279	Tupolev 154B-2	279	CCCP-85279	0578	0393	3 KU NK-8-2U	98000	Y155		
☐ EK-85403	Tupolev 154B-2	403	CCCP-85403	0380	0393	3 KU NK-8-2U	98000	Y155		
☐ EK-85442	Tupolev 154B-2	442	CCCP-85442	0980	0393	3 KU NK-8-2U	98000	Y145		
☐ EK-85536	Tupolev 154B-2	536	CCCP-85536	0482	0393	3 KU NK-8-2U	100000	F12Y126		
☐ EK-85566	Tupolev 154B-2	566	CCCP-85566	1282	0393	3 KU NK-8-2U	100000	F12Y126		
☐ F-OGYW	Airbus Industrie A310-222	276	F-WGYN	0083	0798	2 PW JT9D-7R4E1	142000	F30Y159		lsf Airbus Industrie Financial Services
☐ EK-86117	Ilyushin 86	51483209085	CCCP-86117	0691	0393	4 KU NK-86	215000	Y306		
☐ EK-86118	Ilyushin 86	51483209086	CCCP-86118	0891	0393	4 KU NK-86	215000	Y306		

AVIA-URARTU = URT **Yerevan-Erebuni**

Prospekt Arshakunyats 135, 375004 Erevan, Armenia ☎ (2) 23 40 02 Tx: none Fax: n/a SITA: n/a
F: 1996 ⁂ n/a Head: n/a ICAO: URARTU AIR Net: n/a

registration	type of aircraft	cn/fn	ex/ex*	mfd	del	powered by	mtow kg	configuration	selcal	name/fln/specialitites/remarks
☐ EK-98116	Antonov 24T					2 IV AI-24VT	22500	Combi		

DVIN-AVIA, Joint-Stock Company = DVN (Dvin-Air) **Yerevan-Erebuni**

Ul. Tznabyab 32, Apt. 17, 375010 Yerevan, Armenia ☎ (2) 52 63 81 Tx: none Fax: (2) 52 18 12 SITA: n/a
F: 1996 ⁂ n/a Head: Artashes Gevorgyan ICAO: DVIN-AVIA Net: n/a

registration	type of aircraft	cn/fn	ex/ex*	mfd	del	powered by	mtow kg	configuration	selcal	name/fln/specialitites/remarks
☐ EK-87359	Yakovlev 40	9340831	ER-87359	1073	0097	3 IV AI-25	17200	Y36		lst IRQ as EP-TQA
☐ EK-87662	Yakovlev 40	9240625	RA-87662	0072	0096	3 IV AI-25	17200	VIP 15 Pax		
☐ EK-11029	Antonov 12B	7344908	RA-11029	0067	0098	4 IV AI-20M	61000	Freighter		
☐ EK-11030	Antonov 12B	9346208		0069	0099	4 IV AI-20M	61000	Freighter		

YER-AVIA = ERV (Yerevan-Avia / Yerevan Aviation) **Yerevan-Zvartnots**

Busand Street 1/3, 375010 Yerevan, Armenia ☎ (2) 58 01 21 Tx: none Fax: (2) 56 75 11 SITA: n/a
F: 1992 ⁂ n/a Head: Arsen Aslanian IATA: 998 ICAO: YEREVAN-AVIA Net: n/a

registration	type of aircraft	cn/fn	ex/ex*	mfd	del	powered by	mtow kg	configuration	selcal	name/fln/specialitites/remarks
☐ EK-86724	Ilyushin 76M	073410284	CCCP-86724	0277		4 SO D-30KP	170000	Freighter		lst IRP as EP-TPZ
☐ EK-86817	Ilyushin 76M	063407191	CCCP-86817	0376		4 SO D-30KP	170000	Freighter		lst IRP as EP-TPO

EL = LIBERIA (Republic of Liberia)

Capital: Monrovia Official Language: English Population: 3,0 million Square Km: 111369 Dialling code: +231 Year established: 1847 Acting political head: Charles Gankay Taylor (President)

ALES AIRLINES **Turin & Milan-Linate**

Operations office: c/o Mr. A. Cardoni, Casale Molino 1, I-13060 Graglia, Italy ☎ (336) 46 17 76 Tx: none Fax: (336) 56 31 50 SITA: n/a
F: 1997 ⁂ n/a Head: Alessandro Cardoni Net: n/a

registration	type of aircraft	cn/fn	ex/ex*	mfd	del	powered by	mtow kg	configuration	selcal	name/fln/specialitites/remarks
☐ EL-CAR	Yakovlev 40	9412030	RA-87351	0074	0097	3 IV AI-25	16800	Executive		

EAGLE AVIATION, Inc. **Jeddah (Saudi Arabia)**

Saudi Arabian Operations Office:, PO Box 15664, Jeddah 21454, Saudi Arabia ☎ (2) 685 04 81 Tx: none Fax: (2) 622 18 82 SITA: n/a
F: 1996 ⁂ 65 Head: Manuel Garbaccio Net: n/a Operates non-commercial corporate flights exclusively for member companies of the Al Amrani Group of Companies.

registration	type of aircraft	cn/fn	ex/ex*	mfd	del	powered by	mtow kg	configuration	selcal	name/fln/specialitites/remarks
☐ PK-PJA	GAC G-1159A Gulfstream III	395	N1761Q	0083	0098	2 RR Spey 511-8	31615	Corporate 14 Pax		lsf PAS / opf Mouawad Co.

registration	type of aircraft	cn/fn	ex/ex*	mfd	del	powered by	mtow kg	configuration	selcal	name/fln/specialitites/remarks
☐ EL-LIB	BAe (BAC) One-Eleven 412EB	111	F-WQFM	0067	0296	2 RR Spey 511-14	40597	Corporate 15Pax		opf Al-Hamrani Group of Companies
☐ F-OHLE	Airbus Industrie A300B4-103	031	EL-LIC	0076	0398	2 GE CF6-50C2	157500	Y290		Sultana / lsf Ham Loc / cvtd -2C

LIBERIA WORLD AIRLINES, Inc. = LWA

Ostend (Belgium)

European Headquarters:, PO Box 24, Hangar 5, B-8400 Ostend Airport, Belgium   ☎ (59) 80 26 23   Tx: 82341 libwa b   Fax: (59) 80 78 42   SITA: n/a
F: 1974   ♦♦♦ 65   Head: Duane Egli   Net: n/a

☐ EL-AJO	Boeing (Douglas) DC-8-55F (JT)	45683 / 208	9Q-CKI	0064	0687	4 PW JT3D-3B (HK2/QNC)	147418	Freighter		DH-BE
☐ EL-AJQ	Boeing (Douglas) DC-8-55F (JT)	45858 / 274	5N-ATY	0066	0993	4 PW JT3D-3B (HK2)	147418	Freighter		BL-FK

LOTUS AIRWAYS

Dubai (UAE)

U.A.E. Operations office:, PO Box 32670, Dubai, United Arab Emirates   ☎ (4) 27 49 58   Tx: none   Fax: (4) 22 41 97   SITA: n/a
F: 1998   ♦♦♦ n/a   Head: Gopal Revankar   Net: n/a

☐ EL-ALA	Antonov 12B	00347305	RA-12991	0070	0598	4 IV AI-20M	64000	Freighter		

OCCIDENTAL AIRLINES, Ltd = OCT

Ostend

European Headquarters:, Box 32, Ostend Int'l Airport, B-8400 Ostend Airport, Belgium   ☎ (59) 51 42 40   Tx: none   Fax: (59) 51 01 03   SITA: OSTOAXH
F: 1995   ♦♦♦ 35   Head: n/a   ICAO: OCCIDENTAL   Net: n/a   Suspended operations 0199 (with Boeing 707C aircraft). Intents to re-start.

SANTA CRUZ IMPERIAL AIRLINES – SCI = SNZ (Division of Flying Dolphin)

Sharjah (UAE)

U.A.E. Operations Office:, PO Box 60315, Dubai, United Arab Emirates   ☎ (4) 82 19 67   Tx: none   Fax: (4) 82 18 06   SITA: DXBTOC7
F: 1996   ♦♦♦ n/a   Head: Abdulla bin Zayed   ICAO: SANTA CRUZ   Net: n/a

☐ EL-ALF	Antonov 24RV			0097		2 IV AI-24T	21800	Y48 / Freighter		
☐ EL-ASA	Antonov 24B	87304504	UR-49258	0068	0398	2 IV AI-24	21000	Y48 / Freighter		lsf UDD
☐ EL-ALT	Antonov 26	9807	UR-26004	0080	0598	2 IV AI-24VT	24000	Combi		lsf UFA
☐ EL-ANZ	Antonov 26B	13906	RA-26172	0083	0097	2 IV AI-24VT	24000	Combi		lsf SCI
☐ EL-AKY	Antonov 8	0G3410	4R-EXA	0059	0096	2 IV AI-20D	38000	Freighter		
☐ EL-AKZ	Antonov 8	OD3450	RA-69353	0059	0096	2 IV AI-20D	38000	Freighter		
☐ EL-ALC	Antonov 8	OI3410		0059	0097	2 IV AI-20D	38000	Freighter		
☐ EY-ALE	Antonov 8	1U3460	EL-ALE	0059	0096	2 IV AI-20D	38000	Freighter		
☐ EL-ALB	Antonov 12BP	402108	RA-12116	0062	0096	4 IV AI-20M	64000	Freighter		
☐ EL-ALJ	Antonov 12BP	8346202	RA-12191	0068	0097	4 IV AI-20M	61000	Freighter		lsf SCI
☐ EL-ASC	Antonov 12B			0097		4 IV AI-20M	64000	Freighter		
☐ EL-ASJ	Antonov 12B			0098		4 IV AI-20M	64000	Freighter		
☐ EY-ASS	Antonov 12BP	3340909	EL-ASS	0063	0097	4 IV AI-20M	64000	Freighter		
☐ EL-ADY	Ilyushin 18V	182004804	3D-ALQ	0562	0098	4 IV AI-20M	64000	Combi		
☐ EL-AHO	Ilyushin 18V	183006205	YR-IME	0563	0098	4 IV AI-20M	64000	Combi		
☐ EL-ALD	Ilyushin 18E	185008601	LZ-BEW	0065	0098	4 IV AI-20K	64000	Combi		
☐ EL-ALW	Ilyushin 18V	182004904	RA-75825	0062	0097	4 IV AI-20M	64000	Combi		
☐ EL-ARK	Ilyushin 18E	185008603	LZ-BEZ	0065	0098	4 IV AI-20K	64000	Combi		
☐ A6-ZYD	Boeing 707-3J6C	20718 / 872	B-513L	0073	0398	4 PW JT3D-7	152000	Freighter		

SKYAIR CARGO = TAW (Transway Air Services, Inc. dba/Managed by Skyair Cargo Services (UK), Ltd)

Sharjah (UAE)

European Headquarters:, Maples King House, 55-57 Park Royal Road, London NW10 7JH, Great Britain   ☎ (181) 961 09 32   Tx: 916843 skyair g   Fax: (181) 961 09 56   SITA: LONSACR
F: 1988   ♦♦♦ 17   Head: Roger Sherman   Net: n/a

☐ EL-JNS	Boeing 707-323C	18689 / 354	N902RQ	0063	1188	4 PW JT3D-3B (HK2/COM)	151953	Freighter		BJ-GM

WEASUA AIRTRANSPORT, Co. – WAT = WTC

Freetown & Monrovia-Sprigg Payne

Lungi-Int'l Airport, Freetown, Sierra Leone   ☎ (25) 421   Tx: none   Fax: (25) 421   SITA: n/a
F: n/a   ♦♦♦ n/a   Head: n/a   ICAO: WATCO   Net: n/a

☐ EL-MCA	Cessna 402B	402B0600		0074		2 CO TSIO-520-E	2858			
☐ UN-46699	Antonov 24RV	47309910	CCCP-46699	0074	0597	2 IV AI-24VT	21800	Y48		lsf KZK

EP = IRAN (Islamic Republic of Iran) (Joumhouri-e-Islami-e-Iran)

Capital: Tehran   Official Language: Farsi   Population: 73,0 million   Square Km: 1648000   Dialling code: +98   Year established: 1502   Acting political head: Zayed Mohammed Khatami (President)

Government / Corporate / Executive / VIP Aircraft

☐ EP-AGA	Boeing 737-286 (A)	21317 / 483		0077	0377	2 PW JT8D-15	49442	VIP		Gvmt
☐ EP-FIC	Dassault Falcon 20E	334	F-WRQU*	0075	1075	2 GE CF700-2D2	13000	Calibrator		CAO Civil Aviation Organization
☐ EP-FID	Dassault Falcon 20E	338	F-WMKG*	0075	0176	2 GE CF700-2D2	13000	Calibrator		CAO Civil Aviation Organization
☐ EP-GDS	Boeing 727-81	19557 / 405	1002	0067	0674	3 PW JT8D-7	72802	VIP	DE-GJ	Gvmt / std THR
☐ EP-PLN	Boeing 727-30	18363 / 35	EP-SHP	0064	0374	3 PW JT8D-7	72802	VIP	DK-AB	Palestine / std THR
☐ 1001	Boeing 707-386C	21396 / 928	EP-NHY	0078	0778	4 PW JT3D-3B	151477	VIP		Islamic Republic of Iran Air Force
☐ 1002	Boeing 707-370C	20890 / 891	YI-AGF	0074	0091	4 PW JT3D-7	151091	VIP	AL-DJ	Islamic Republic of Iran Air Force

ATLAS AIR = IRH (Atlas Aviation Group dba)

Tehran

PO Box 19395-6768, Tehran, Iran   ☎ (21) 877 11 36   Tx: 217151 i   Fax: (21) 877 47 99   SITA: n/a
F: 1995   ♦♦♦ 73   Head: Al-Akbar Golrounia   Net: n/a

☐ EP-ALE	Ilyushin 76TD	0043453575	RA-76477	0784	0998	4 SO D-30KP	190000	Freighter		lsf ILV
☐ EP-ALF	Ilyushin 76TD	0033448407	RA-76474	0983	0998	4 SO D-30KP	190000	Freighter		lsf ILV
☐ EP-ALG	Ilyushin 76TD	0033448404	RA-76473	1083	1098	4 SO D-30KP	190000	Freighter		lsf ILV
☐ EP-ALI	Ilyushin 76TD	1003499994	RA-76796	0390	0199	4 SO D-30KP	190000	Freighter		
☐ EP-ALJ	Ilyushin 76TD	0013434018	RA-86896	1181	1298	4 SO D-30KP	190000	Freighter		lsf / cvtd MD

BON AIR – Bonyad Airlines = IRJ (Subsidiary of B & J Foundation)

Tehran

PO Box 14155-6355, Tehran, Iran   ☎ (21) 890 05 90   Tx: 216982 bona ir   Fax: (21) 890 49 93   SITA: n/a
F: 1994   ♦♦♦ 250   Head: J. Mossadeghi   ICAO: BON AIR   Net: n/a

☐ EP-BOA	Yunshuji Y8F-100			0098	0098	4 WJ 6A	61000	Freighter 16t		
☐ EP-BOJ	Tupolev 154M	904	RA-85722	0092	0096	3 SO D-30KU-154-II	100000	Y164		lsf MVD
☐ EP-BOM	Tupolev 154M	891	RA-85715	0091	0096	3 SO D-30KU-154-II	100000	Y164		lsf MVD
☐ EP-BON	Tupolev 154M	929	RA-85746	0092	0096	3 SO D-30KU-154-II	100000	Y164		lsf MVD

CASPIAN AIRLINES = CPN

Tehran

Enghlab Avenue, Kalege Cross, Apt No. 1020, Tehran 11339, Iran   ☎ (21) 645 69 52   Tx: none   Fax: (21) 67 85 47   SITA: n/a
F: 1993   ♦♦♦ n/a   Head: Mahmud Rajabian   ICAO: CASPIAN   Net: n/a

☐ EP-CPB	Yakovlev 42D	4520421219029	UR-42410	0092		3 LO D-36	56500	Y120		lsf UDN
☐ EP-CPC	Yakovlev 42D	4520421401018	UR-42449	0094		3 LO D-36	56500	Y120		lsf UDN
☐ EP-CPE	Yakovlev 42D	4520423219102	UR-42416	0092		3 LO D-36	56500	Y120		lsf UDN
☐ YA-TAR	Tupolev 154M	748		0087	0098	3 SO D-30KU-154-II	100000	Y164		lsf AFG

HELICOPTER SERVICES ORGANIZATION – H.S.O. (formerly Helicopter Aviation Service, SA)

Tehran

No. 37, 7th Street, Sarafraz Street, Motahari Avenue, Tehran 15876, Iran   ☎ (21) 873 74 44   Tx: 224470 ir   Fax: (21) 873 96 71   SITA: n/a
F: 1965   ♦♦♦ 350   Head: Mahmood Hajighasemali   Net: n/a

☐ EP-HCG	Eurocopter (Aerosp.) SA315B Lama	2440		0076		1 TU Artouste IIIB	1950			
☐ EP-HTW	Eurocopter (Aerosp.) SA315B Lama	2384		0075		1 TU Artouste IIIB	1950			
☐ EP-HBH	Eurocopter (Aerosp.) SA316B Alouette III	1061		0062		1 TU Artouste IIIB	2200			cvtd SE3160
☐ EP-HBN	Eurocopter (Aerosp.) SA316B Alouette III	2236		0075		1 TU Artouste IIIB	2200			
☐ EP-HBO	Eurocopter (Aerosp.) SA316B Alouette III	2198		0074		1 TU Artouste IIIB	2200			
☐ EP-HGA	Eurocopter (Aerosp.) SA316B Alouette III	1777		0071		1 TU Artouste IIIB	2200			
☐ EP-HGB	Eurocopter (Aerosp.) SA316B Alouette III	1932	PH-SCG	0071		1 TU Artouste IIIB	2200			
☐ EP-HGE	Eurocopter (Aerosp.) SA316B Alouette III	2339		0078		1 TU Artouste IIIB	2200			
☐ EP-HSF	Eurocopter (Aerosp.) SA316B Alouette III	1487		0068		1 TU Artouste IIIB	2200			cvtd SE3160
☐ EP-HSG	Eurocopter (Aerosp.) SA316B Alouette III	1496		0068		1 TU Artouste IIIB	2200			cvtd SE3160
☐ EP-HSH	Eurocopter (Aerosp.) SA316B Alouette III	1519		0069		1 TU Artouste IIIB	2200			cvtd SE3160
☐ EP-HSJ	Eurocopter (Aerosp.) SA316B Alouette III	1633		0069		1 TU Artouste IIIB	2200			cvtd SE3160
☐ EP-HSO	Eurocopter (Aerosp.) SA316B Alouette III	1951	F-WIEK*	0072		1 TU Artouste IIIB	2200			
☐ EP-HSS	Eurocopter (Aerosp.) SA316B Alouette III	2136	PH-SCN	0074		1 TU Artouste IIIB	2200			
☐ EP-HST	Eurocopter (Aerosp.) SA316B Alouette III	2153	PH-SCO	0074		1 TU Artouste IIIB	2200			
☐ EP-HSU	Eurocopter (Aerosp.) SA316B Alouette III	2154	PH-SAU	0074		1 TU Artouste IIIB	2200			
☐ EP-HSY	Eurocopter (Aerosp.) SA316B Alouette III	5199	F-WTNP*	0075		1 TU Artouste IIIB	2200			
☐ EP-HTB	Eurocopter (Aerosp.) SA316B Alouette III	1942		0071		1 TU Artouste IIIB	2200			
☐ EP-HTC	Eurocopter (Aerosp.) SA316B Alouette III	2246	F-WTNS*	0075		1 TU Artouste IIIB	2200			
☐ EP-HTE	Eurocopter (Aerosp.) SA316B Alouette III	2258	F-WXFP*	0075		1 TU Artouste IIIB	2200			
☐ EP-HTR	Eurocopter (Aerosp.) SA316B Alouette III	5260	F-WTNZ*	0075		1 TU Artouste IIIB	2200			
☐ EP-HTT	Eurocopter (Aerosp.) SA316B Alouette III	5253	F-WTNZ*	0075		1 TU Artouste IIIB	2200			
☐ EP-HTX	Eurocopter (Aerosp.) SA316B Alouette III	2231	F-WXFU*	0075		1 TU Artouste IIIB	2200			
☐ EP-HTO	Bell 205A-1	30163	N64743	0074		1 LY T5313B	4309			

☐ EP-HTQ	Bell 205A-1	30189	N90039	0075		1 LY T5313B	4309			
☐ EP-HBJ	Bell 212	30504		0071		2 PWC PT6T-3 TwinPac	5080			
☐ EP-HTN	Bell 212	30885	N5009K	0078		2 PWC PT6T-3 TwinPac	5080			
☐ EP-HUA	Bell 212	31176	HB-XPO	0081		2 PWC PT6T-3B TwinPac	5080			
☐ EP-HUB	Bell 412	33016	HB-XNB	0081		2 PWC PT6T-3B TwinPac	5398			
☐ EP-HGC	Eurocopter (Aerosp.) SA330G Puma	1287		0075		2 TU Turmo IVA	7400			

IRAN AIR – The Airline of The Islamic Republic of Iran = IR / IRA

Tehran

PO Box 13185-775, Tehran, Iran ☎ (21) 91 11 Tx: 212795 iran i Fax: (21) 600 32 48 SITA: n/a

F: 1962 ⁂ 11460 Head: S.H. Shafti IATA: 096 ICAO: IRANAIR Net: n/a

☐ EP-IDA	Fokker 100 (F28 Mk0100)	11292	PH-LMG*	0090	0990	2 RR Tay 650-15	44452	Y104		
☐ EP-IDB	Fokker 100 (F28 Mk0100)	11299	PH-LMO*	0090	1290	2 RR Tay 650-15	44452	Y104	EH-AM	
☐ EP-IDC	Fokker 100 (F28 Mk0100)	11267	PH-LMH*	0090	1190	2 RR Tay 650-15	44452	Y104	EH-AL	
☐ EP-IDD	Fokker 100 (F28 Mk0100)	11294	PH-LMM*	0090	0191	2 RR Tay 650-15	44452	Y104	EH-BC	
☐ EP-IDF	Fokker 100 (F28 Mk0100)	11298	PH-LMN*	0090	0291	2 RR Tay 650-15	44452	Y104	EH-BD	
☐ EP-IDG	Fokker 100 (F28 Mk0100)	11302	PH-LMW*	0091	0491	2 RR Tay 650-15	44452	Y104	EH-BG	
☐ EP-IRF	Boeing 737-286 (A)	20498 / 283		0071	0771	2 PW JT8D-15	49442	Y115	GK-AJ	Bisotun
☐ EP-IRH	Boeing 737-286C (A)	20500 / 286		0071	0971	2 PW JT8D-15	51936	Y115	GK-AM	Ray
☐ EP-IRI	Boeing 737-286C (A)	20740 / 321		0073	0573	2 PW JT8D-15	52390	Y115	GK-LM	Chel-Stotun
☐ EP-IRB	Boeing 727-86	19172 / 323		0066	1066	3 PW JT8D-7B	72575	Y116	GK-AC	Abadan
☐ EP-IRC	Boeing 727-86	19816 / 505		0067	1267	3 PW JT8D-7B	72575	Y116	GK-AD	Ramsar
☐ EP-IRP	Boeing 727-286 (A)	20945 / 1048		0074	0674	3 PW JT8D-15	86406	Y157	GJ-FH	
☐ EP-IRR	Boeing 727-286 (A)	20946 / 1052		0074	0774	3 PW JT8D-15	86406	Y157	GJ-FK	
☐ EP-IRS	Boeing 727-286 (A)	20947 / 1070		0074	0974	3 PW JT8D-15	86406	Y157	GJ-FL	
☐ EP-IRT	Boeing 727-286 (A)	21078 / 1114		0075	0375	3 PW JT8D-15	86406	Y157	GJ-AH	
☐ EP-IRK	Boeing 707-321C	19267 / 541	N445PA	0066	0375	4 PW JT3D-3B	151477	Freighter	GK-AE	
☐ EP-IRL	Boeing 707-386C	20287 / 832		0069	1269	4 PW JT3D-3B	151477	Y180	GK-AF	Apadana
☐ EP-IRM	Boeing 707-386C	20288 / 839		0070	0370	4 PW JT3D-3B	151477	Y180	GK-AH	Ekbatana
☐ EP-IRN	Boeing 707-386C	20741 / 866	N1785B*	0073	0573	4 PW JT3D-3B	151477	Y180	GK-DF	Pasargad
☐ EP-IBR	Airbus Industrie A300B2-203	061	F-WZEK*	0079	0380	2 GE CF6-50C2	142000	Y280	FK-JL	
☐ EP-IBS	Airbus Industrie A300B2-203	080	F-WZEO*	0080	0480	2 GE CF6-50C2	142000	Y280	FK-JM	
☐ EP-IBT	Airbus Industrie A300B2-203	185	F-WZMB*	0082	0482	2 GE CF6-50C2	142000	Y280		
☐ EP-IBV	Airbus Industrie A300B2-203	187	F-WZMD*	0082	0582	2 GE CF6-50C2	142000	Y280		
☐ EP-IBZ	Airbus Industrie A300B2-203	226	F-WZME*	0082	0183	2 GE CF6-50C2	142000	Y280		
☐ EP-IBA	Airbus Industrie A300-605R (A300B4-605R)	723	F-WWAL*	0094	1294	2 GE CF6-80C2A5	170500	C22Y239	AQ-FJ	
☐ EP-IBB	Airbus Industrie A300-605R (A300B4-605R)	727	F-WWAZ*	0094	1294	2 GE CF6-80C2A5	170500	C22Y239	AQ-FK	
☐ EP-IAA	Boeing 747SP-86	20998 / 275		0075	0376	4 PW JT9D-7F	303907	C22Y283	GJ-AD	Kurdistan
☐ EP-IAB	Boeing 747SP-86	20999 / 278		0076	0576	4 PW JT9D-7F	303907	C22Y283	GJ-AE	Khorasan
☐ EP-IAC	Boeing 747SP-86	21093 / 307		0077	0577	4 PW JT9D-7F	303907	C22Y283	GJ-AF	Fars
☐ EP-IAD	Boeing 747SP-86	21758 / 371	N1800B*	0079	0779	4 PW JT9D-7F	303907	C22Y283	BH-AM	
☐ EP-IAG	Boeing 747-286B (M)	21217 / 291		0076	1076	4 PW JT9D-7F	351534	C22Y419	AL-EK	Azarabadegan
☐ EP-IAH	Boeing 747-286B (M)	21218 / 300		0077	0377	4 PW JT9D-7F	351534	C22Y419	AL-EM	
☐ EP-IAM	Boeing 747-186B	21759 / 381	N5573P*	0079	0879	4 PW JT9D-7F	333390	C22Y419	BH-CF	
☐ EP-ICC	Boeing 747-2J9F	21514 / 343	5-8116	0078	1180	4 PW JT9D-7F	364240	Freighter	AG-CD	

IRAN AIR TOURS, Co. = IRB (Joint venture of Iran Air & Tajikistan Airlines)

Tehran & Mashad

191 Motahari Avenue, Dr. Moffateh Road, Tehran 15879, Iran ☎ (21) 875 83 91 Tx: 213956 irat ir Fax: (21) 875 58 84 SITA: n/a

F: 1992 ⁂ 600 Head: S.K. Ghaffar Net: n/a

☐ EP-YAA	Yakovlev 42D	4520422219055	RA-42412	0592	0097	3 LO D-36	57500	Y120		lsf CHB
☐ EP-YAB	Yakovlev 42D	4520422219066	RA-42413	0792	0097	3 LO D-36	57500	Y120		lsf CHB
☐ EP-YAC	Yakovlev 42D	4520424116698	RA-42408	0192	0097	3 LO D-36	56500	Y120		lsf CHB
☐ EP-ITV	Tupolev 154M	810	RA-85660	0089	0095	3 SO D-30KU-154-II	100000	Y164		lsf BTK
☐ EP-MAJ	Tupolev 154M	719	RA-85818	1285	0096	3 SO D-30KU-154-II	100000	Y164		lsf OMS
☐ EP-MAK	Tupolev 154M	884	RA-85709	0991	0097	3 SO D-30KU-154-II	100000	Y164		lsf SBI
☐ EP-MAN	Tupolev 154M	961	RA-85802	1293	0097	3 SO D-30KU-154-II	100000	Y164		lsf CHF
☐ EP-MAP	Tupolev 154M	923	RA-85766	1092	0097	3 SO D-30KU-154-II	100000	Y164		lsf CHF
☐ EP-MAR	Tupolev 154M	932	RA-85750	1092	0096	3 SO D-30KU-154-II	100000	Y164		lsf OMS
☐ EP-MAS	Tupolev 154M	866	RA-85693	0391	0098	3 SO D-30KU-154-II	100000	Y164		lsf SBI
☐ EP-MAT	Tupolev 154M	928	RA-85745	0992	0098	3 SO D-30KU-154-II	100000	Y166		lsf OMS
☐ EP-MAZ	Tupolev 154M	857	RA-85687	1190	1098	3 SO D-30KU-154-II	100000	Y164		lsf SBI
☐ EP-MBA	Tupolev 154M	860	RA-85689	1290	0098	3 SO D-30KU-154-II	100000	Y164		lsf BTK
☐ EP-MBB	Tupolev 154M	821	RA-85830	1189	1198	3 SO D-30KU-154-II	100000	Y164		lsf OMS

IRAN ASSEMAN AIRLINES – IAA = IRC

Tehran

PO Box 13145-1476, Tehran, Iran ☎ (21) 640 02 57 Tx: 212575 atxi ir Fax: (21) 640 43 18 SITA: THRIAY7

F: 1980 ⁂ 900 Head: Ali Abedzadeh Net: n/a

☐ EP-DED	Piper PA-31-350 Navajo Chieftain	31-7652137	N59880	0076		2 LY TIO-540-J2BD	3175	Y9		
☐ EP-PAK	Piper PA-31-350 Navajo Chieftain	31-7552103	N61386	0075		2 LY TIO-540-J2BD	3175	Y9		
☐ EP-PAM	Piper PA-31-350 Navajo Chieftain	31-7552109	N61397	0075		2 LY TIO-540-J2BD	3175	Y9		
☐ EP-PAF	Britten-Norman BN-2A-3 Islander	655	G-AYXG	0071		2 LY IO-540-K1B5	2858	Y9		
☐ EP-PAG	Britten-Norman BN-2A-3 Islander	665	G-AZDP	0071		2 LY IO-540-K1B5	2858	Y9		
☐ EP-AGY	Dassault Falcon 20E	286	F-WRQU*	0073		2 GE CF700-2D2	13000	Executive		
☐ EP-FIE	Dassault Falcon 20E	251	EP-VAP	0071		2 GE CF700-2D2	13000	Executive		
☐ EP-FIF	Dassault Falcon 20E	320	EP-AHV	0075		2 GE CF700-2D2	13000	EMS		
☐ EP-SEA	Dassault Falcon 20F	367	F-WRQR*	0077		2 GE CF700-2D2	13000	Executive		
☐ EP-ATR	ATR 42-320	291	F-WWLZ*	0092	0493	2 PWC PW121	16700	Y48		
☐ EP-ATA	ATR 72-212	334	F-WWLQ*	0093	1093	2 PWC PW127	21500	Y70		
☐ EP-ATH	ATR 72-212	339	F-WWLU*	0093	1093	2 PWC PW127	21500	Y70		
☐ EP-ATS	ATR 72-212	391	F-WWED*	0093	1293	2 PWC PW127	21500	Y70		
☐ EP-ATZ	ATR 72-212	398	F-WWEK*	0093	0194	2 PWC PW127	21500	Y70		
☐ F-OIRA	ATR 72-500 (72-212A)	562	F-WWLZ*			2 PWC PW127F	22500	Y70		oo-delivery 0499
☐ F-OIRB	ATR 72-500 (72-212A)	573	F-WWEK*			2 PWC PW127F	22500	Y70		oo-delivery 0499
☐ EP-PAT	Fokker F28 Fellowship 4000 (F28 Mk4000)	11164	PH-ZCA*	0081	0581	2 RR Spey 555-15H	33110	Y85		
☐ EP-PAU	Fokker F28 Fellowship 4000 (F28 Mk4000)	11166	PH-ZCB*	0081	0681	2 RR Spey 555-15H	33110	Y85		
☐ EP-PAX	Fokker F28 Fellowship 1000C (F28 Mk1000C)	11102	F-GEXX	0076	0492	2 RR Spey 555-15	29480	Y65		
☐ EP-PAZ	Fokker F28 Fellowship 1000 (F28 Mk1000)	11104	F-GIAK	0076	0593	2 RR Spey 555-15	29480	Y65		
☐ EP-PBJ	Fokker F28 Fellowship 4000 (F28 Mk4000)	11135	F-GDFD	0079	0394	2 RR Spey 555-15H	33110	Y85		
☐ F-GDUZ	Fokker F28 Fellowship 4000 (F28 Mk4000)	11144	5N-ANV	0079	0394	2 RR Spey 555-15H	33110	Y85		lsf Locaterme
☐ EP-ASA	Boeing 727-228 (A)	22081 / 1594	LX-IRA	0080	1094	3 PW JT8D-15A	86409	Y184	EK-BL	
☐ EP-ASB	Boeing 727-228 (A)	22082 / 1603	LX-IRB	0080	1094	3 PW JT8D-15A	86409	Y184	EK-BG	
☐ EP-ASC	Boeing 727-228 (A)	22084 / 1638	LX-IRC	0080	1094	3 PW JT8D-15A	86409	Y184	EK-AJ	
☐ EP-ASD	Boeing 727-228 (A)	22085 / 1665	LX-IRD	0080	1094	3 PW JT8D-15A	86409	Y184	EK-GH	

IRANIAN AIR TRANSPORT, Co. – IATC = IRG

Ahwaz

125 V.Dastgerd (ex Zafar) Street, D.R.Shariati Ave, PO Box 1863, Tehran, Iran ☎ (21) 222 80 44 Tx: none Fax: (21) 227 15 54 SITA: n/a

F: 1992 ⁂ 200 Head: A.M. Alikhani ICAO: NAFT Net: n/a

☐ EP-IOP	De Havilland DHC-6 Twin Otter 300	577		0078	0392	2 PWC PT6A-27	5670	Y19		
☐ EP-IOS	Fokker F27 Friendship 300 (F27 Mk300)	10151	PH-IOS	0060	0392	2 RR Dart 514-7	18370	Y44		
☐ EP-GAS	Fokker 50 (F27 Mk050)	20224	PH-JXA*	0091	0392	2 PWC PW125B	20820	Y50		
☐ EP-OIL	Fokker 50 (F27 Mk050)	20222	PH-LNZ*	0091	0392	2 PWC PW125B	20820	Y50		

KISH AIR = IRK (Subsidiary of Kish Development Organisation)

Tehran

PO Box 19697-4639, Tehran, Iran ☎ (21) 877 61 84 Tx: 226124 kc ir Fax: (21) 877 66 30 SITA: n/a

F: n/a ⁂ 220 Head: Capt. Yadulla Khalili ICAO: KISHAIR Net: n/a

☐ EP-LBJ	Yakovlev 40	9642051	RA-88247	1276	0098	3 IV AI-25	16800	Y36		lsf VGV
☐ EP-LBK	Yakovlev 40	9620947	RA-88171	0376	0098	3 IV AI-25	17200	Y36		lsf VGV
☐ EP-LAZ	Tupolev 154M	976	RA-85792	1293	0397	3 SO D-30KU-154-II	100000	Y166		lsf BRZ
☐ EP-LBG	Tupolev 154M	706	LZ-BTI	1284	0098	3 SO D-30KU-154-II	100000	Y166		lsf LAZ
☐ EP-LBH	Tupolev 154M	913	RA-85731	0592	0098	3 SO D-30KU-154-II	100000	Y166		lsf BRZ
☐ EP-LBL	Tupolev 154M	754	LZ-BTH	0388	0098	3 SO D-30KU-154-II	100000	Y166		lsf LAZ

MAHAN AIR = IRM

Kerman

PO Box 76135-1663, Kerman, Iran ☎ (341) 26 43 12 Tx: 342863 mal ir Fax: (341) 26 30 50 SITA: n/a

F: 1993 ⁂ 300 Head: Asghar Bank ICAO: MAHAN AIR Net: n/a

☐ EP-ARG	Tupolev 154M	899	SU-OAD	0392	0393	3 SO D-30KU-154-II	100000	Y160		
☐ EP-JAZ	Tupolev 154M	898	SU-OAC	0392	0393	3 SO D-30KU-154-II	100000	Y160		
☐ EP-JAY	Ilyushin 76TD	1013409297	SU-OAA	1291	0393	4 SO D-30KP	190000	Freighter		
☐ EP-MAH	Ilyushin 76TD	1013409321	SU-OAB	0091	0393	4 SO D-30KP	190000	Freighter		

135 registration type of aircraft cn/fn ex/ex* mfd del powered by mtow kg configuration selcal name/fln/specialitites/remarks

NAVID AIR = IRI (Navidtec Air Services Company dba)
Karaj-Payam Int'l

95 Golab Street, Mohammed Ali Jinnah Blvd., Tehran 14515-711, Iran ☎ (1) 822 66 77 Tx: 216586 nvtg ir Fax: (1) 820 67 62 SITA: n/a
F: 1992 ♦♦♦ 75 Head: Eng. Reza Nayeri ICAO: NAVID Net: n/a

registration	type of aircraft	cn/fn	ex/ex*	mfd	del	powered by	mtow kg	configuration	selcal	name/fln/specialitites/remarks
☐ EP-NAB	Mil Mi-8MTV-1	95932	RA-27108	0092		2 IS TV3-117VM	13000	Freighter		
☐ EP-NAC	Mil Mi-8T	99254442	RA-27024	0092		2 IS TV2-117A	12000	VIP		
☐ EP-NAD	Mil Mi-8T	99254471	RA-27025	0092		2 IS TV2-117A	12000	VIP		
☐ EP-NAA	Mil Mi-8AMT (Mi-171)	59489602238	RA-25520	0092		2 IS TV3-117VM	13000	Freighter		

NCC – National Cartographic Center/Flight Dept.
Tehran

PO Box 13185-1684, Tehran, Iran ☎ (21) 600 00 31 Tx: none Fax: (21) 600 19 71 SITA: n/a
F: n/a ♦♦♦ n/a Head: n/a Net: n/a Non-commercial state organisation conducting photo & survey flights.

registration	type of aircraft	cn/fn	ex/ex*	mfd	del	powered by	mtow kg	configuration	selcal	name/fln/specialitites/remarks
☐ EP-TCC	Dornier 228-212	8195	D-CNCC*	0092	1092	2 GA TPE331-5A-252D	6400	Photo/Survey		
☐ EP-THA	Dornier 228-212	8207	D-CIME*	0092	1192	2 GA TPE331-5A-252D	6400	Photo/Survey		
☐ EP-TKH	Dornier 228-212	8204	D-CIMO*	0092	1192	2 GA TPE331-5A-252D	6400	Photo/Survey		
☐ EP-TZA	Dornier 228-212	8208	D-CIMU*	0092	1192	2 GA TPE331-5A-252D	6400	Photo/Survey		

PARIZ AIR = IRE
Tehran

435 Satarkhan Ave., Tehran 14547, Iran ☎ (21) 822 17 71 Tx: none Fax: (21) 821 19 69 SITA: n/a
F: 1997 ♦♦♦ n/a Head: Mohammad Ali Azidhak ICAO: PARIZAIR Net: n/a

registration	type of aircraft	cn/fn	ex/ex*	mfd	del	powered by	mtow kg	configuration	selcal	name/fln/specialitites/remarks
☐ EP-DAZ	Yakovlev 40	9740856	EK-87937	0178	0098	3 IV AI-25	17200	Y34		Isf ARK
☐ EP-DMS	Yakovlev 40	9520142	EK-87536	0775	0098	3 IV AI-25	17200	Y34		Isf ARK

PAYAM AVIATION SERVICES, Co. = IRP (formerly IPTAS-Iranian Post & Telecom Aviation Services)
Karaj-Payam Int'l

No. 3 Topchhi Street, Dr. Shariati Avenue, Tehran 16765-3166, Iran ☎ (21) 876 30 45 Tx: 223486 tci air Fax: (21) 811 36 50 SITA: n/a
F: 1990 ♦♦♦ 240 Head: Capt. Hossein Arzegar IATA: 158 ICAO: PAYAMAIR Net: n/a Beside aircraft listed, also leases Ilyushin 76MD from ATI AIRCOMPANY (UR-) when required.

registration	type of aircraft	cn/fn	ex/ex*	mfd	del	powered by	mtow kg	configuration	selcal	name/fln/specialitites/remarks
☐ EP-TPC	Bell 212	30516	6-9202	0271	0098	2 PWC PT6T-3 TwinPac	5080	Utility		
☐ EP-TPD	Bell 412SP	33117	A7-HBA	0085	0098	2 PWC PT6T-3B TwinPac	5398	Utility		
☐ EP-TPA	Embraer 110P1 Bandeirante (EMB-110P1)	110438	VH-LVJ	0084	0492	2 PWC PT6A-34	5670	Freighter		Kerman
☐ EP-TPG	Embraer 110P1 Bandeirante (EMB-110P1)	110386	VH-LVH	0084	0392	2 PWC PT6A-34	5670	Freighter		Esfahan
☐ EP-TPM	Embraer 110P1 Bandeirante (EMB-110P1)	110453	VH-ABD	0084	0393	2 PWC PT6A-34	5670	Freighter		Tehran
☐ EP-TPS	Embraer 110P1 Bandeirante (EMB-110P1)	110423	VH-LVI	0083	0392	2 PWC PT6A-34	5670	Freighter		Semnan
☐ EP-TPT	Embraer 110P1 Bandeirante (EMB-110P1)	110442	VH-LVK	0084	0492	2 PWC PT6A-34	5670	Freighter		Kashan
☐ 6-9101	Bell 214B BigLifter	28002		0175	0098	1 LY T5508D	6123	VIP		Isf Army
☐ EP-TPO	Ilyushin 76M	063407191	EK-86817	0376	0097	4 SO D-30KP	170000	Freighter		Isf ERV
☐ EP-TPZ	Ilyushin 76M	073410284	EK-86724	0277	0197	4 SO D-30KP	170000	Freighter		Isf ERV

QESHM AIRLINES = IRQ (Faraz Qeshm Airlines dba)
Tehran

PO Box 15875-1548, Tehran, Iran ☎ (21) 872 48 71 Tx: none Fax: (21) 872 48 74 SITA: n/a
F: 1993 ♦♦♦ n/a Head: n/a ICAO: FARAZ AIR Net: n/a

registration	type of aircraft	cn/fn	ex/ex*	mfd	del	powered by	mtow kg	configuration	selcal	name/fln/specialitites/remarks
☐ EP-TQA	Yakovlev 40	9340831	EK-87359	1073	0098	3 IV AI-25	17200	Y36		Isf DVN
☐ EP-TQD	Tupolev 154M	940	RA-	0092	0098	3 SO D-30KU-154-II	102000	Y166		
☐ EP-TQE	Tupolev 154M	940	RA-85758	0092	0098	3 SO D-30KU-154-II	102000	Y166		Isf AKZ

SAFIRAN AIRLINES = SFN
Tehran

PO Box 15855-389, Tehran, Iran ☎ (21) 883 96 68 Tx: 226243 airs ir Fax: (21) 883 95 50 SITA: n/a
F: 1988 ♦♦♦ 35 Head: Mohammad Bagher Nahvi ICAO: SAFIRAN Net: n/a Operates charter flights with Antonov 124, Boeing 707C & Ilyushin 76 freighter aircraft, leased from other companies when required.

SAFIRAN AIR LINES

SAHA AIR = IRZ
Tehran

PO Box 13865-164, Tehran, Iran ☎ (21) 669 62 00 Tx: 226342 saha ir Fax: (21) 669 80 16 SITA: n/a
F: 1990 ♦♦♦ n/a Head: Capt. A. Saedi ICAO: SAHA Net: n/a

registration	type of aircraft	cn/fn	ex/ex*	mfd	del	powered by	mtow kg	configuration	selcal	name/fln/specialitites/remarks
☐ EP-SHL	Fokker F27 Friendship 600 (F27 Mk600)	10474	5-8801	0072	0092	2 RR Dart 532-7R	19731	Y44		
☐ EP-SHM	Fokker F27 Friendship 600 (F27 Mk600)	10475	5-8802	0072	0092	2 RR Dart 532-7R	19731	Y44.		
☐ EP-SHN	Fokker F27 Troopship 400M (F27 Mk400M)	10491	5-8811	0072	0092	2 RR Dart 532-7R	19731	Y44		
☐ EP-SHO	Fokker F27 Troopship 400M (F27 Mk400M)	10480	5-8814	0072	0092	2 RR Dart 532-7R	19731	Y44		
☐ EP-SHE	Boeing 707-3J9C	21127 / 915	5-8311	0076	0091	4 PW JT3D-3B	151477	Y160		
☐ EP-SHG	Boeing 707-3J9C	20830 / 876	5-8301	0074	0091	4 PW JT3D-3B	151477	Y160		
☐ EP-SHJ	Boeing 707-3J9C	20833 / 890	5-8304	0074	0091	4 PW JT3D-3B	151477	Y160		
☐ EP-SHK	Boeing 707-3J9C	21128 / 917	5-8312	0076	0091	4 PW JT3D-3B	151477	Y160		
☐ EP-SHP	Boeing 707-3J9C	21123 / 908	5-8307	0076	0092	4 PW JT3D-7	151477	Y160		
☐ EP-SHA	Boeing 747-2J9F	21507 / 340	5-8115	0078	0091	4 PW JT9D-7F	364240	Freighter	AG-BM	
☐ EP-SHB	Boeing 747-2J9F	21486 / 315	5-8113	0077	0091	4 PW JT9D-7F	364240	Freighter	AK-JL	
☐ EP-SHD	Boeing 747-131 (SF)	20081 / 85	5-8105	0070	0091	4 PW JT9D-7A	332937	Freighter		cvtd -131
☐ EP-SHH	Boeing 747-2J9F	21487 / 319	5-8114	0278	0095	4 PW JT9D-7F	364240	Freighter		

TA-AIR AIRLINE = IRF
Tehran

No. 3 Kooh-e-Noor Street, Motahari Street, Tehran, Iran ☎ (21) 873 14 95 Tx: none Fax: (21) 875 35 06 SITA: n/a
F: 1998 ♦♦♦ n/a Head: n/a ICAO: TA-AIR Net: n/agg2Presently being set-up. Intends to start domestic & international passenger flights during 1999.

TARA AIRLINES, Ltd = IRR
Bandar Abbas

296 Taleghani Ave., Tehran 15717, Iran ☎ (21) 884 48 02 Tx: 214393 mrx ir Fax: (21) 882 29 96 SITA: n/a
F: 1993 ♦♦♦ 30 Head: Payam Mohebi ICAO: TARAIR Net: n/a

registration	type of aircraft	cn/fn	ex/ex*	mfd	del	powered by	mtow kg	configuration	selcal	name/fln/specialitites/remarks
☐ EP-TRA	Kamov Ka-32	8902	RA-31071	0992	0097	2 IS TV3-117V	12600	Utility / 15 Pax		Isf SOC
☐ EP-TRM	Kamov Ka-32	8604	RA-31582	0691	0097	2 IS TV3-117V	12600	Utility / 15 Pax		Isf SOC
☐ EP-TRZ	Kamov Ka-32	8901	RA-31070	0992	0097	2 IS TV3-117V	12600	Utility / 15 Pax		Isf SOC

ER = MOLDOVA (Republic of Moldova) (Republica Moldova)

Capital: Kishinev/Chisinau Official Language: Romanian Population: 4,5 million Square Km: 33700 Dialling code: +373 Year established: 1991 Acting political head: Petru Lucinschi (President)

Government / Corporate / Executive / VIP Aircraft

registration	type of aircraft	cn/fn	ex/ex*	mfd	del	powered by	mtow kg	configuration	selcal	name/fln/specialitites/remarks
☐ ER-72932	Antonov 72	39572070696	CCCP-72932	0087		2 LO D-36	34500	Freighter		Ministry of Defence
☐ ER-72933	Antonov 72		CCCP-72933	0090		2 LO D-36	34500	Freighter		Ministry of Defence
☐ ER-72935	Antonov 72		CCCP-72935	0090		2 LO D-36	34500	Freighter		Ministry of Defence

AERIANTUR-M AIRLINES = TUM
Chisinau

Airport, MD-2026 Chisinau, Moldova ☎ (2) 52 60 64 Tx: none Fax: (2) 52 60 64 SITA: n/a
F: 1994 ♦♦♦ n/a Head: n/a ICAO: AIR-EM Net: n/a Operates charter flights with Antonov 72/74 & Tupolev 134/154 aircraft leased from other companies when required.

AEROCOM = MCC
Chisinau

Chisinau Airport, MD-2026 Chisinau, Moldova ☎ (2) 21 93 98 Tx: none Fax: (2) 52 95 60 SITA: n/a
F: 1998 ♦♦♦ n/a Head: V.V. Podarilov Net: n/a

registration	type of aircraft	cn/fn	ex/ex*	mfd	del	powered by	mtow kg	configuration	selcal	name/fln/specialitites/remarks
☐ ER-AFU	Antonov 24RV	27308010	RA-46482	0972	0098	2 IV AI-24VT	21800	Y48		
☐ ER-ADT	Antonov 12BP	2340605	CCCP-11382	0862	0098	4 IV AI-20M	61000	Freighter		

AERODACIA = DCA
Balti

Str. Stefan cel Marc 6/2, MD-3100 Balti, Moldova ☎ (31) 22 380 Tx: none Fax: (32) 23 219 SITA: n/a
F: 1998 ♦♦♦ n/a Head: n/a ICAO: AERODACIA Net: n/a Operates charter flights with aircraft leased from other companies when required.

AGROAVIA (formerly AEN)
Chisinau

Chisinau Airport, MD-2026 Chisinau, Moldova ☎ (2) 52 59 11 Tx: none Fax: (2) 52 40 40 SITA: n/a
F: n/a ♦♦♦ n/a Head: Oleg Shpacovich Net: n/a

registration	type of aircraft	cn/fn	ex/ex*	mfd	del	powered by	mtow kg	configuration	selcal	name/fln/specialitites/remarks
☐ ER-19106	Kamov Ka-26	7102208	CCCP-19106	1271		2 VE M-14V-26	3250	Utility		
☐ ER-19262	Kamov Ka-26	7102004	CCCP-19262	0871		2 VE M-14V-26	3250	Utility		
☐ ER-19274	Kamov Ka-26	7001204	CCCP-19274	0870		2 VE M-14V-26	3250	Utility		
☐ ER-19282	Kamov Ka-26	7001606	CCCP-19282	1270		2 VE M-14V-26	3250	Utility		
☐ ER-19292	Kamov Ka-26	7101805	CCCP-19292	0371		2 VE M-14V-26	3250	Utility		
☐ ER-19294	Kamov Ka-26	7101807	CCCP-19294	0471		2 VE M-14V-26	3250	Utility		
☐ ER-19296	Kamov Ka-26	7101809	CCCP-19296	0571		2 VE M-14V-26	3250	Utility		
☐ ER-19298	Kamov Ka-26	7101903	CCCP-19298	0571		2 VE M-14V-26	3250	Utility		
☐ ER-19316	Kamov Ka-26	7203105	CCCP-19316	1272		2 VE M-14V-26	3250	Utility		
☐ ER-19323	Kamov Ka-26	7303206	CCCP-19323	0373		2 VE M-14V-26	3250	Utility		
☐ ER-19327	Kamov Ka-26	7303309	CCCP-19327	0473		2 VE M-14V-26	3250	Utility		
☐ ER-19328	Kamov Ka-26	7303310	CCCP-19328	0473		2 VE M-14V-26	3250	Utility		
☐ ER-19329	Kamov Ka-26	7303401	CCCP-19329	0473		2 VE M-14V-26	3250	Utility		
☐ ER-19330	Kamov Ka-26	7303402	CCCP-19330	0473		2 VE M-14V-26	3250	Utility		
☐ ER-19343	Kamov Ka-26	7303509	CCCP-19343	0673		2 VE M-14V-26	3250	Utility		
☐ ER-19344	Kamov Ka-26	7303510	CCCP-19344	0673		2 VE M-14V-26	3250	Utility		
☐ ER-19345	Kamov Ka-26	7303601	CCCP-19345	0773		2 VE M-14V-26	3250	Utility		

☐ ER-19346	Kamov Ka-26	7303602	CCCP-19346	0773		2 VE M-14V-26	3250	Utility		
☐ ER-19347	Kamov Ka-26	7303603	CCCP-19347	0773		2 VE M-14V-26	3250	Utility		
☐ ER-19356	Kamov Ka-26	7202307	CCCP-19356	0272		2 VE M-14V-26	3250	Utility		
☐ ER-19358	Kamov Ka-26	7202309	CCCP-19358	0272		2 VE M-14V-26	3250	Utility		
☐ ER-19360	Kamov Ka-26	7202401	CCCP-19360	0372		2 VE M-14V-26	3250	Utility		
☐ ER-19369	Kamov Ka-26	7202508	CCCP-19369	0572		2 VE M-14V-26	3250	Utility		
☐ ER-19370	Kamov Ka-26	7202509	CCCP-19370	0672		2 VE M-14V-26	3250	Utility		
☐ ER-19377	Kamov Ka-26	7202701	CCCP-19377	0872		2 VE M-14V-26	3250	Utility		
☐ ER-19378	Kamov Ka-26	7202702	CCCP-19378	0972		2 VE M-14V-26	3250	Utility		
☐ ER-19381	Kamov Ka-26	7202705	CCCP-19381	0972		2 VE M-14V-26	3250	Utility		
☐ ER-19385	Kamov Ka-26	7202709	CCCP-19385	0972		2 VE M-14V-26	3250	Utility		
☐ ER-19387	Kamov Ka-26	7202801	CCCP-19387	0972		2 VE M-14V-26	3250	Utility		
☐ ER-19406	Kamov Ka-26	7404320	CCCP-19406	0574		2 VE M-14V-26	3250	Utility		
☐ ER-19416	Kamov Ka-26	7404410	CCCP-19416	0674		2 VE M-14V-26	3250	Utility		
☐ ER-19466	Kamov Ka-26	7303802	CCCP-19466	0973		2 VE M-14V-26	3250	Utility		
☐ ER-19467	Kamov Ka-26	7303803	CCCP-19467	0973		2 VE M-14V-26	3250	Utility		
☐ ER-19475	Kamov Ka-26	7303904	CCCP-19475	1273		2 VE M-14V-26	3250	Utility		
☐ ER-19476	Kamov Ka-26	7303905	CCCP-19476	1273		2 VE M-14V-26	3250	Utility		
☐ ER-19486	Kamov Ka-26	7404101	CCCP-19486	0274		2 VE M-14V-26	3250	Utility		
☐ ER-19494	Kamov Ka-26	7404110	CCCP-19494	0374		2 VE M-14V-26	3250	Utility		
☐ ER-19496	Kamov Ka-26	7404202	CCCP-19496	0374		2 VE M-14V-26	3250	Utility		
☐ ER-19500	Kamov Ka-26	7404206	CCCP-19500	0374		2 VE M-14V-26	3250	Utility		
☐ ER-19502	Kamov Ka-26	7404208	CCCP-19502	0374		2 VE M-14V-26	3250	Utility		
☐ ER-19503	Kamov Ka-26	7404301	CCCP-19503	0374		2 VE M-14V-26	3250	Utility		
☐ ER-19505	Kamov Ka-26	7404315	CCCP-19505	0574		2 VE M-14V-26	3250	Utility		
☐ ER-19506	Kamov Ka-26	7404316	CCCP-19506	0574		2 VE M-14V-26	3250	Utility		
☐ ER-19507	Kamov Ka-26	7404317	CCCP-19507	0574		2 VE M-14V-26	3250	Utility		
☐ ER-19518	Kamov Ka-26	7404509	CCCP-19518	0874		2 VE M-14V-26	3250	Utility		
☐ ER-19521	Kamov Ka-26	7404513	CCCP-19521	0974		2 VE M-14V-26	3250	Utility		
☐ ER-19534	Kamov Ka-26	7404607	CCCP-19534	0974		2 VE M-14V-26	3250	Utility		
☐ ER-19547	Kamov Ka-26	7404706	CCCP-19547	1174		2 VE M-14V-26	3250	Utility		
☐ ER-19611	Kamov Ka-26	7505014	CCCP-19611	0675		2 VE M-14V-26	3250	Utility		
☐ ER-19622	Kamov Ka-26	7505110	CCCP-19622	0875		2 VE M-14V-26	3250	Utility		
☐ ER-24073	Kamov Ka-26	6900602	CCCP-24073	0870		2 VE M-14V-26	3250	Utility		
☐ ER-24092	Kamov Ka-26	7001107	CCCP-24092	0770		2 VE M-14V-26	3250	Utility		

AIR MOLDOVA = 9U / MLD (Sister company of Air Moldova International) — Chisinau

Chisinau Airport, MD-2026 Chisinau, Moldova ☎ (2) 52 55 02 Tx: 163169 ptb Fax: (2) 52 60 51 SITA: KIVCS9U
F: 1992 n/a Head: Peter A. Ceban IATA: 572 ICAO: AIR MOLDOVA Net: n/a

☐ ER-46376	Antonov 24B	07306009	CCCP-46376	0470	0092	2 IV AI-24	21000	Y48		
☐ ER-46414	Antonov 24B	87304009	CCCP-46414	0268	0092	2 IV AI-24	21000	Y48		
☐ ER-46417	Antonov 24B	87304102	CCCP-46417	0268	0092	2 IV AI-24	21000	Y44		
☐ ER-46508	Antonov 24RV	37308404	CCCP-46508	0273	0092	2 IV AI-24VT	21800	Y44		
☐ ER-46685	Antonov 24RV	47309710	CCCP-46685	0874	0092	2 IV AI-24VT	21800	Y40		
☐ ER-47698	Antonov 24RV	27307605	CCCP-47698	0272	0092	2 IV AI-24VT	21800	Y44		
☐ ER-26046	Antonov 26B	10807	CCCP-26046	0281	0092	2 IV AI-24VT	24000	Freighter		
☐ ER-26059	Antonov 26B	11104	CCCP-26059	0581	0092	2 IV AI-24VT	24000	Freighter		
☐ ER-26204	Antonov 26B	14103	CCCP-26204	0585	0092	2 IV AI-24VT	24000	Freighter		
☐ ER-65036	Tupolev 134A-3	48700	CCCP-65036	0876	0092	2 SO D-30-III	47800	Y76		
☐ ER-65050	Tupolev 134A-3	49756	CCCP-65050	0377	0092	2 SO D-30-III	47000	Y76		
☐ ER-65051	Tupolev 134A-3	49758	CCCP-65051	0377	0092	2 SO D-30-III	47000	Y76		
☐ ER-65071	Tupolev 134A-3	49915	CCCP-65071	0777	0092	2 SO D-30-III	47600	Y76		lst GAK
☐ ER-65094	Tupolev 134A-3	60255	CCCP-65094	0378	0092	2 SO D-30-III	47600	VIP C36		opf Gvmt
☐ ER-65140	Tupolev 134A-3	60932	CCCP-65140	1278	0092	2 SO D-30-III	47600	Y76		
☐ ER-65707	Tupolev 134A-3	63435	CCCP-65707	1080	0092	2 SO D-30-III	47600	Y76		
☐ ER-65791	Tupolev 134A-3	63110	CCCP-65791	0280	0092	2 SO D-30-III	49000	Y76		
☐ ER-65897	Tupolev 134A-3	42210	CCCP-65897	1175	0092	2 SO D-30-III	47000	Y76		

AIR MOLDOVA INTERNATIONAL, SA = 3R / MLV (Sister company of Air Moldova) — Chisinau

Chisinau Airport, Hotel 4th Floor, MD-2026 Chisinau, Moldova ☎ (2) 52 99 60 Tx: none Fax: (2) 52 64 11 SITA: KIVDG3R
F: 1995 120 Head: Viorel Ous IATA: 283 ICAO: MOLDOVAINTERNATIONAL Net: http://www.ami.md

☐ ER-87230	Yakovlev 40	9541542	UR-87230	0075	0096	3 IV AI-25	16800	Y32		lsf UKR-Kirovograd Aviation Enterprise
☐ ER-46464	Antonov 24RV	27307810	UR-46464	0572	0098	2 IV AI-24VT	21800	Y48		
☐ ER-42409	Yakovlev 42D	4520421216709	UR-42409	0392	0096	3 LO D-36	56500	C12Y84		lsf UDN

CRI-COSTA = FCC — Chisinau

77 Stefan cel Marc bul, MD-2012 Chisinau, Moldova ☎ (2) 24 72 54 Tx: none Fax: none SITA: n/a
F: 1998 n/a Head: n/a ICAO: CRI-COSTA Net: n/a Operates charter flights with aircraft leased from other companies when required.

MOLDAEROSERVICE = MLE — Balti

Airport, MD-3100 Balti, Moldova ☎ (31) 23 310 Tx: none Fax: (31) 23 319 SITA: n/a
F: n/a n/a Head: Vitalie Povonschi ICAO: MOLDAERO Net: n/a

☐ ER-15796	PZL Swidnik (Mil) Mi-2	522850033	CCCP-15796	0473		2 IS GTD-350-4	3550	Utility		
☐ ER-20121	PZL Swidnik (Mil) Mi-2	543022073	CCCP-20121	0773		2 IS GTD-350-4	3550	Utility		
☐ ER-20164	PZL Swidnik (Mil) Mi-2	523430034	CCCP-20164	0374		2 IS GTD-350-4	3550	Utility		
☐ ER-20170	PZL Swidnik (Mil) Mi-2	523437034	CCCP-20170	0374		2 IS GTD-350-4	3550	Utility		
☐ ER-20204	PZL Swidnik (Mil) Mi-2	526843100	CCCP-20204	1180		2 IS GTD-350-4	3550	Utility		
☐ ER-20223	PZL Swidnik (Mil) Mi-2	527012011	CCCP-20223	0781		2 IS GTD-350-4	3550	Utility		
☐ ER-20257	PZL Swidnik (Mil) Mi-2	547215071	CCCP-20257	0781		2 IS GTD-350-4	3550	Utility		
☐ ER-20289	PZL Swidnik (Mil) Mi-2	547408111	CCCP-20289	1281		2 IS GTD-350-4	3550	Utility		
☐ ER-20293	PZL Swidnik (Mil) Mi-2	527428121	CCCP-20293	0182		2 IS GTD-350-4	3550	Utility		
☐ ER-20680	PZL Swidnik (Mil) Mi-2	526645050	CCCP-20680	0680		2 IS GTD-350-4	3550	Utility		
☐ ER-20726	PZL Swidnik (Mil) Mi-2	527543032	CCCP-20726	0382		2 IS GTD-350-4	3550	Utility		
☐ ER-20727	PZL Swidnik (Mil) Mi-2	527544032	CCCP-20727	0382		2 IS GTD-350-4	3550	Utility		
☐ ER-20728	PZL Swidnik (Mil) Mi-2	527545032	CCCP-20728	0382		2 IS GTD-350-4	3550	Utility		
☐ ER-20739	PZL Swidnik (Mil) Mi-2	547636052	CCCP-20739	0582		2 IS GTD-350-4	3550	Utility		
☐ ER-20740	PZL Swidnik (Mil) Mi-2	547637052	CCCP-20740	0582		2 IS GTD-350-4	3550	Utility		
☐ ER-20819	PZL Swidnik (Mil) Mi-2	528023013	CCCP-20819	0283		2 IS GTD-350-4	3550	Utility		
☐ ER-20820	PZL Swidnik (Mil) Mi-2	528024013	CCCP-20820	0283		2 IS GTD-350-4	3550	Utility		
☐ ER-20821	PZL Swidnik (Mil) Mi-2	528025013	CCCP-20821	0283		2 IS GTD-350-4	3550	Utility		
☐ ER-20830	PZL Swidnik (Mil) Mi-2	548103033	CCCP-20830	0383		2 IS GTD-350-4	3550	Utility		
☐ ER-23211	PZL Swidnik (Mil) Mi-2	5210132037	CCCP-23211	0387		2 IS GTD-350-4	3550	Utility		
☐ ER-23237	PZL Swidnik (Mil) Mi-2	5210238057	CCCP-23237	0687		2 IS GTD-350-4	3550	Utility		
☐ ER-23238	PZL Swidnik (Mil) Mi-2	5210239057	CCCP-23238	0687		2 IS GTD-350-4	3550	Utility		
☐ ER-23264	PZL Swidnik (Mil) Mi-2	5210338087	CCCP-23264	0987		2 IS GTD-350-4	3550	Utility		
☐ ER-23265	PZL Swidnik (Mil) Mi-2	5210339087	CCCP-23265	0987		2 IS GTD-350-4	3550	Utility		
☐ ER-23313	PZL Swidnik (Mil) Mi-2	529144045	CCCP-23313	0485		2 IS GTD-350-4	3550	Utility		
☐ ER-23334	PZL Swidnik (Mil) Mi-2	529223055	CCCP-23334	0585		2 IS GTD-350-4	3550	Utility		
☐ ER-23429	PZL Swidnik (Mil) Mi-2	529344085	CCCP-23429	0885		2 IS GTD-350-4	3550	Utility		
☐ ER-23469	PZL Swidnik (Mil) Mi-2	526208069	CCCP-23469	0679		2 IS GTD-350-4	3550	Utility		
☐ ER-23470	PZL Swidnik (Mil) Mi-2	526209069	CCCP-23470	0779		2 IS GTD-350-4	3550	Utility		
☐ ER-23471	PZL Swidnik (Mil) Mi-2	526210069	CCCP-23471	0679		2 IS GTD-350-4	3550	Utility		
☐ ER-01762	PZL Mielec (Antonov) An-2	1G107-09	CCCP-01762	0669		1 SH ASh-62IR	5500	Utility		
☐ ER-02499	PZL Mielec (Antonov) An-2	1G119-42	CCCP-02499	1070		1 SH ASh-62IR	5500	Utility		
☐ ER-07206	PZL Mielec (Antonov) An-2	1G146-35	CCCP-07206	0473		1 SH ASh-62IR	5500	Utility		
☐ ER-07351	PZL Mielec (Antonov) An-2	1G149-55	CCCP-07351	0873		1 SH ASh-62IR	5500	Utility		
☐ ER-32274	PZL Mielec (Antonov) An-2	1G96-36	CCCP-32274	0768		1 SH ASh-62IR	5500	Utility		
☐ ER-32424	PZL Mielec (Antonov) An-2	1G105-05	CCCP-32424	1268		1 SH ASh-62IR	5500	Utility		
☐ ER-33643	PZL Mielec (Antonov) An-2	1G233-33	CCCP-33643	0189		1 SH ASh-62IR	5500	Utility		
☐ ER-33645	PZL Mielec (Antonov) An-2	1G233-35	CCCP-33645	0189		1 SH ASh-62IR	5500	Utility		
☐ ER-33646	PZL Mielec (Antonov) An-2	1G233-36	CCCP-33646	0189		1 SH ASh-62IR	5500	Utility		
☐ ER-33648	PZL Mielec (Antonov) An-2	1G233-38	CCCP-33648	0189		1 SH ASh-62IR	5500	Utility		
☐ ER-35531	PZL Mielec (Antonov) An-2	1G114-43	CCCP-35531	0370		1 SH ASh-62IR	5500	Utility		
☐ ER-35538	PZL Mielec (Antonov) An-2	1G114-50	CCCP-35538	0370		1 SH ASh-62IR	5500	Utility		
☐ ER-26068	Antonov 26B	11308	CCCP-26068	0781		2 IV AI-24VT	24000	Freighter		

MOLDAVIAN AIRLINES = 2M / MDV — Chisinau

Chisinau Airport, MD-2026 Chisinau, Moldova ☎ (2) 52 93 56 Tx: none Fax: (2) 52 50 64 SITA: KIVDC2M
F: 1994 120 Head: Nicolae Petrov IATA: 860 ICAO: MOLDAVIAN Net: n/a

☐ ER-SGA	Saab 340B	340B-168	ER-ASA	1089	0397	2 GE CT7-9B	13155	Y33		

137 registration type of aircraft cn/fn ex/ex* mfd del powered by mtow kg configuration selcal name/fln/specialitites/remarks

registration	type of aircraft	cn/fn	ex/ex*	mfd	del	powered by	mtow kg	configuration	selcal	name/fln/specialitites/remarks
☐ ER-JGD	Yakovlev 40	9421334	RA-88307	0674	0098	3 IV AI-25	17200	Y30		
☐ ER-JGE	Yakovlev 40	9810757	RA-87210	0478	0098	3 IV AI-25	17200	Y32		
☐ ER-TCF	Tupolev 134A-3	62390	ER-AAZ	0779	0097	2 SO D-30-III	49000	C12Y56		

RENAN = RAN

Chisinau

Belinskogo 59/55, MD-2008 Chisinau, Moldova ☎ (2) 52 61 24 Tx: none Fax: (2) 52 61 28 SITA: n/a
F: 1994 ⁂ 79 Head: Andrei G. Grosul ICAO: RENAN Net: n/a

☐ ER-LIA	Let 410UVP	810623	UR-67022	0481	0097	2 WA M-601D	5800	Y15		
☐ ER-JGA	Yakovlev 40	9521640	RA-87514	0575	0097	3 IV AI-25	16800	Y32		
☐ ER-AFY	Antonov 24RV	47309809	YR-AMY	1074	0398	2 IV AI-24VT	21800	Y48		
☐ ER-ADI	Antonov 32B	3205	RA-48140	0193	0096	2 IV AI-20D	27000	Y40 / Freighter		
☐ ER-AFA	Antonov 32B	3406	ER-ADA	0693	0096	2 IV AI-20D	27000	Y40 / Freighter		
☐ ER-AFM	Antonov 32B	3305	ER-ACM	0493	0095	2 IV AI-20D	27000	Y40 / Freighter		
☐ ER-AEJ	Antonov 72	36572094889	ER-ACA	0192	0595	2 LO D-36	31200	Y30 / Freighter		fn 13-08
☐ ER-AER	Antonov 72	36572094888	ER-ACF	1291	1294	2 LO D-36	31200	Y30 / Freighter		
☐ ER-AEN	Antonov 74	36547095898	ER-ACN	0392	0195	2 LO D-36	34800	Y10 / Freighter		
☐ ER-ICG	Ilyushin 18V	184007301	YR-IMG	0464	0398	4 IV AI-20M	64000	Y109 / Freighter		
☐ ER-ICJ	Ilyushin 18D	186009102	YR-IMJ	0566	0097	4 IV AI-20M	64000	Y109 / Freighter		
☐ ER-ICL	Ilyushin 18D	187009903	YR-IML	0467	0398	4 IV AI-20M	64000	Y109 / Freighter		

SALVIRAJ = VRA (formerly Viraj-Avia, S.A.)

Bendery

24/47 Lenin Street, MD-3200 Bendery, Moldova ☎ (32) 23 468 Tx: none Fax: (32) 43 154 SITA: n/a
F: 1997 ⁂ n/a Head: n/a ICAO: VIRAJ Net: n/a Operates charter flights with aircraft leased from other companies when required.

SUD AEROCARGO = KSA

Cahul

Airport, MD-3900 Cahul, Moldavia ☎ (39) 26 744 Tx: none Fax: (39) 20 844 SITA: n/a
F: 1997 ⁂ n/a Head: n/a ICAO: SUDCARGO Net: n/a Operates charter flights with aircraft leased from other companies when required.

TANDEM-AERO, Srl. = TDM

Chisinau

Bd. Negruzzi 10, MD-2026 Chisinau, Moldova ☎ (2) 26 41 39 Tx: none Fax: (2) 26 43 29 SITA: n/a
F: 1998 ⁂ n/a Head: n/a ICAO: TANDEM Net: n/a Operates charter flights with aircraft leased from other companies when required.

TIRAMAVIA, Ltd = TVI (formerly Mikma, Ltd)

Chisinau

Airport, Dachia 60/5, Of. 115, MD-2026 Chisinau, Moldova ☎ (2) 52 68 13 Tx: none Fax: (2) 52 68 13 SITA: n/a
F: 1998 ⁂ 40 Head: Mikhail Kopichinskhi ICAO: TIRAMAVIA Net: n/a

☐ ER-AFS	Antonov 24B	87304507	RA-46553	0768	0098	2 IV AI-24	21000	Y48		
☐ ER-AFP	Antonov 26B	11902	UR-26097	0182	0098	2 IV AI-24VT	24000	Freighter		
☐ ER-AFT	Antonov 26B	13403	UR-26578	0184	0098	2 IV AI-24VT	24000	Freighter		
☐ ER-ACB	Antonov 12BP	2340608		0862	0098	4 IV AI-20M	61000	Freighter		
☐ ER-ACH	Antonov 12BP	4342209	2209	0764	0098	4 IV AI-20M	61000	Freighter		
☐ ER-ACL	Antonov 12BP	0901306		1260	0098	4 IV AI-20M	61000	Freighter		

VALAN International Cargo Charter = VLN

Chisinau

Zelinsky Str. 36/3-29, MD-2038 Chisinau, Moldova ☎ (2) 52 50 48 Tx: none Fax: (2) 52 49 19 SITA: KIVVN9U
F: 1993 ⁂ n/a Head: Alexander V. Zagrebelny ICAO: VALAN Net: n/a

☐ ER-07863	PZL Mielec (Antonov) An-2TP	1G170-22		0776	0093	1 SH ASh-62IR	5500	Combi		
☐ ER-AKA	PZL Mielec (Antonov) An-28	1AJ010-02	UR-28956	0991	0098	2 GS TVD-10B	6500	Y17		
☐ ER-ADB	Antonov 32B	3009	UR-48073	0492	0096	2 IV AI-20D	27000	Freighter		
☐ ER-AEC	Antonov 32B	3003	ER-ADC	0392	0095	2 IV AI-20D	27000	Combi		lst Africa Cargo Air
☐ ER-AET	Antonov 32	2105	RA-69310	0889	0098	2 IV AI-20D	27000	Freighter		

VICHI = VIH

Chisinau

Strada Hinçesti 84, MD-2021 Chisinau, Moldova ☎ (2) 78 12 49 Tx: none Fax: (2) 23 35 33 SITA: n/a
F: 1993 ⁂ n/a Head: Petr G. Yerkhan ICAO: VICHI Net: n/a

☐ ER-75929	Ilyushin 18D	187010505		1267	0093	4 IV AI-20M	64000	Freighter/Y105		

ES = ESTONIA (Republic of Estonia) (Eesti Vabariik)

Capital: Tallinn Official Language: Estonian Population: 1,7 million Square Km: 45215 Dialling code: +372 Year established: 1990 Acting political head: Lennart Meri (President)

AIR LIVONIA, Ltd = LIV (formerly Baltic Aeroservice)

Pärnu

Eametsa k., EE-80044 Pärnu, Estonia ☎ (44) 75 000 Tx: none Fax: (44) 75 002 SITA: n/a
F: 1997 ⁂ n/a Head: Ants Aringo ICAO: LIVONIA Net: n/a

☐ YL-KAB	PZL Mielec (Antonov) An-28	1AJ009-15	CCCP-28949	0090	0098	2 GS TVD-10B	6500	Y17		lsf RAK

AVIES Air Company = AIA (AVIES Lennukompanii)

Tallinn-Ylemiste

AvieS

Lennujaama 2, EE-11101 Tallinn, Estonia ☎ 638 80 22 Tx: none Fax: (2) 21 29 51 SITA: n/a
F: 1991 ⁂ 23 Head: Valentin Manusha ICAO: AVIES Net: n/a

☐ ES-PAH	Piper PA-31-350 Navajo Chieftain	31-7405156	SE-GDI	0073	0492	2 LY TIO-540-J2BD	3175	8 Pax		
☐ ES-PLB	Let 410UVP	851413	LY-AVY	0085	0299	2 WA M-601D	5800	15 Pax		
☐ ES-PLI	Let 410UVP	851438	LY-AIL	0085	0797	2 WA M-601D	5800	15 Pax		lsf Forex Lissingu AS
☐ ES-PVV	Learjet 55	55-011	N200BA	0081	0498	2 GA TFE731-3AR-2B	9752	8 Pax		lsf Hoiuliisingu AS

EE AERONAUTIKA-KLUBI

Tallinn

Lennujaama 2, EE-11101 Tallinn, Estonia ☎ 638 83 91 Tx: none Fax: 625 82 03 SITA: n/a
F: n/a ⁂ n/a Head: Tonis Lepp Net: n/a Aircraft below MTOW 1361kg: Piper PA-28 & Robinson R22

☐ ES-FPM	Piper PA-34-200T Seneca II	34-8070191	D-GLHW	0080	0797	2 CO L/TSIO-360-EB	1999			

ELK AIRWAYS – Estonian Aviation Company = S8 / ELK (ELK-Eesti Lennukompanii)

Tallinn-Ylemiste

ELK AIRWAYS

26 Majaka Street, EE-11412 Tallinn, Estonia ☎ 638 09 72 Tx: 173051 tllak ee Fax: 638 09 75 SITA: n/a
F: 1991 ⁂ 96 Head: Priit Louk IATA: 520 ICAO: ELKA Net: n/a

☐ ES-LLB	Let 410UVP-E20C	912608	OK-WDG*	0091	0893	2 WA M-601E	6400	Y19		
☐ ES-LLC	Let 410UVP-E20C	912609	OK-WDH*	0091	1093	2 WA M-601E	6400	Y19		
☐ ES-LLD	Let 410UVP	841317	UR-67492	0084	1298	2 WA M-601D	5800	Y17		lsf Universal Leasing
☐ YL-LDC	Antonov 26B	12010	CCCP-26109	0082	0098	2 IV AI-24VT	24000	Freighter		
☐ ES-LTA	Tupolev 134A-3	60195	LY-ABG	0078	0897	2 SO D-30-III	49000	Y76		
☐ ES-LTP	Tupolev 154M	909	CCCP-85727	0092	0092	3 SO D-30KU-154-II	100000	Y164		

ENIMEX, Ltd = ENI

Tallinn-Ylemiste

Pae str. 12, EE-11414 Tallinn, Estonia ☎ 638 04 39 Tx: none Fax: 638 00 28 SITA: n/a
F: 1994 ⁂ 62 Head: Andrei Kislyi ICAO: ENIMEX Net: http://www.enimex.ee

☐ ES-NOA	PZL Mielec (Antonov) An-28	1AJ004-08	UR-28759	0087	1298	2 GS TVD-10B	6500	Combi		
☐ YL-KAD	PZL Mielec (Antonov) An-28	1AJ004-02	RA-28753	0087	1098	2 GS TVD-10B	6500	Combi		lsf RAK
☐ YL-KAF	PZL Mielec (Antonov) An-28	1AJ009-09	RA-28943	0090	1098	2 GS TVD-10B	6500	Combi		lsf RAK
☐ ES-NOB	Antonov 72	36572070695	CCCP-72931	0089	0495	2 LO D-36	34800	Combi		
☐ ES-NOC	Antonov 72	36572010952		0086	1098	2 LO D-36	34800	Freighter		fn 02-04 / lsf ANTK Antonov
☐ ES-NOG	Antonov 72	36572080786	RA-72942	0089	0997	2 LO D-36	34800	Combi		lsf Uhisliisingu AS
☐ ES-NOK	Antonov 72	36572080780	RA-72039	0089	0297	2 LO D-36	34800	Combi		
☐ ES-NOL	Antonov 72	36572080789	UR-72004	0087	0796	2 LO D-36	34800	Combi		

ESTONIAN AIR = OV / ELL (Eesti Lennuliinide AS Estonian Air dba)

Tallinn-Ylemiste

Lennujaama 2, EE-11101 Tallinn, Estonia ☎ 640 11 00 Tx: none Fax: 631 27 40 SITA: TLLAPOV
F: 1991 ⁂ 350 Head: Borge Thornbech IATA: 960 ICAO: ESTONIAN Net: n/a

☐ ES-AFK	Fokker 50 (F27 Mk050)	20126	OY-MMI	0088	1096	2 PWC PW125B	20820	CY56		lsf DAN
☐ ES-AFL	Fokker 50 (F27 Mk050)	20127	OY-MMJ	0088	1096	2 PWC PW125B	20820	CY56		lsf DAN
☐ ES-ABC	Boeing 737-5Q8	26324 / 2735		0095	0695	2 CFMI CFM56-3C1	52389	CY108	HS-KL	Koit / lsf ILFC
☐ ES-ABD	Boeing 737-5Q8	26323 / 2770		0196	0296	2 CFMI CFM56-3C1	52389	CY108	HS-KM	Hämarik / lsf ILFC
☐ ES-ABE	Boeing 737-5L9	28083 / 2784	OY-APA	0096	1098	2 CFMI CFM56-3C1	52389	CY107		lsf DAN

PAKKER AVIO, Ltd = PKR

Tartu

Tartu Airport, Torvandi, EE-61701 Tartu, Estonia ☎ (7) 35 12 29 Tx: none Fax: (7) 35 12 29 SITA: n/a
F: n/a ⁂ n/a Head: Endel Käärt ICAO: PAKKER AVIO Net: n/a Aircraft below MTOW 1361kg: Cessna 152 & 172

☐ ES-ECA	Cessna 310K	310K0161	SE-GTY	0066	0897	2 CO IO-470-V	2359			lsf HP Liising AS

STATE AVIATION GROUP

Tallin-Ylemiste

Süsta 15, EE-11712 Tallinn, Estonia ☎ 639 95 10 Tx: none Fax: 639 95 09 SITA: n/a
F: 1994 ⁂ 35 Head: Arvo Palumäe Net: n/a Non-commercial government organisation conducting border guard/patrol, rescue & transport flights.

☐ ES-PLW	Let 410UVP	810726	ES-EPA	0081	0993	2 WA M-601D	6000	SAR/Patrol/EMS		
☐ ES-PLY	Let 410UVP	810727	ES-EPI	0081	0994	2 WA M-601D	6000	SAR/Patrol/EMS		
☐ ES-PMC	Mil Mi-8T	10579	93+71	0077	1195	2 IS TV2-117A	12000	SAR		
☐ ES-PMD	Mil Mi-8T	10595	D-HOXE	0079	1195	2 IS TV2-117A	12000	SAR		

ET = ETHIOPIA (Federal Democratic Republic of Ethiopia)

Capital: Addis Ababa Official Language: Amharic Population: 62,0 million Square Km: 1104300 Dialling code: +251 Year established: 1855 Acting political head: Meles Zenawi (President)

ETHIOPIAN AIRLINES Enterprise = ET / ETH (formerly Ethiopian Airlines Corporation) — Addis Ababa

PO Box 1755, Addis Ababa, Ethiopia ☎ (1) 61 22 22 Tx: 21012 ethair Fax: (1) 61 14 74 SITA: ADDDZET
F: 1945 ⁂ 3300 Head: HE Ato. S. Abraha IATA: 071 ICAO: ETHIOPIAN Net: n/a Ag-Aircraft/Trainer-aircraft below MTOW 1361/5000kg: Ayres S2R-T34, Cessna 172/185/A188B, Piper PA-23/PA-34 & Schweizer G-164BT Eshet

☐	ET-AIM	De Havilland DHC-6 Twin Otter 300	815	C-GDCZ*	0085	0385	2 PWC PT6A-27	5670	Y18		
☐	ET-AIN	De Havilland DHC-6 Twin Otter 300	816	C-GDFT*	0085	0385	2 PWC PT6A-27	5670	Y18		
☐	ET-AIT	De Havilland DHC-6 Twin Otter 300	820	C-GDNG*	0085	0585	2 PWC PT6A-27	5670	Y18		
☐	ET-AIU	De Havilland DHC-6 Twin Otter 300	822	C-GFJQ	0085	0785	2 PWC PT6A-27	5670	Y18		lst Ethiopian Air Force
☐	ET-AIX	De Havilland DHC-6 Twin Otter 300	835	C-GDFT*	0087	0187	2 PWC PT6A-27	5670	Y18		
☐	ET-AJC	ATR 42-320	071	F-WWEZ*	0088	0388	2 PWC PW121	16150	Y46		std / for sale
☐	ET-AJD	ATR 42-320	076	F-WWEB*	0088	0388	2 PWC PW121	16150	Y46		
☐	ET-AHJ	De Havilland DHC-5A Buffalo	102A	C-GBXL*	0081	0681	2 GE CT64-820-4	18597	Y38 / Frtr		
☐	ET-AKR	Fokker 50 (F27 Mk050)	20313	PH-LOP*	0096	0996	2 PWC PW127B	20820	Y50		
☐	ET-AKS	Fokker 50 (F27 Mk050)	20328	PH-EXB*	0097	0597	2 PWC PW127B	20820	Y50		
☐	ET-AKT	Fokker 50 (F27 Mk050)	20331	PH-EXC*	0096	1296	2 PWC PW127B	20820	Y50		
☐	ET-AKU	Fokker 50 (F27 Mk050)	20333	PH-EXD*	0097	0297	2 PWC PW127B	20820	Y50		
☐	ET-AKV	Fokker 50 (F27 Mk050)	20335	PH-EXE*	0097	0497	2 PWC PW127B	20820	Y50		
☐	ET-AJB	Boeing 737-260 (A)	23915 / 1583		0088	0788	2 PW JT8D-17A	53070	F8Y107	DK-EL	
☐	ET-AJK	Lockheed L-382G (L-100-30) Hercules	67C-5022	N4272M*	0085	0788	4 AN 501-D22A	70307	Freighter		lsf Ministry of Transport
☐	ET-AKG	Lockheed L-382G (L-100-30) Hercules	72C-5306		0092	1292	4 AN 501-D22A	70307	Freighter		lsf Ministry of Transport
☐	ET-AJS	Boeing 757-260PF	24845 / 300	N3519L*	0090	0890	2 PW PW2040	115666	Freighter	KQ-HJ	
☐	ET-AJX	Boeing 757-260	25014 / 348		0091	0291	2 PW PW2040	115666	F16C39Y96	DJ-KQ	
☐	ET-AKC	Boeing 757-260	25353 / 408		0091	1191	2 PW PW2040	115666	F16C39Y96	DJ-LQ	
☐	ET-AKE	Boeing 757-260	26057 / 444		0092	0492	2 PW PW2040	115666	F16C39Y96	DJ-MQ	
☐	ET-AKF	Boeing 757-260	26058 / 496		0092	1092	2 PW PW2040	115666	F16C39Y96	DJ-CP	
☐	ET-AIV	Boeing 707-327C	19531 / 646	OD-AGZ	0067	0585	4 PW JT3D-3B	151046	Freighter	AH-CJ	
☐	ET-AIE	Boeing 767-260 (ER)	23106 / 90	N1792B*	0084	0584	2 PW JT9D-7R4E	156489	F12C48Y126	CM-AJ	
☐	ET-AIF	Boeing 767-260 (ER)	23107 / 93	N6065Y*	0084	0684	2 PW JT9D-7R4E	156489	F12C48Y126	CM-AK	
☐	ET-AKW	Boeing 767-33A (ER)	25346 / 403	V8-RBE	0091	0497	2 PW PW4056	172365	F12C48Y126	AH-DG	lsf BBAM
☐	ET-ALC	Boeing 767-33A (ER)	28043 / 734		0199	0199	2 PW PW4060	172365	F12C48Y126		lsf AWAS

MAF Ethiopia – Mission Aviation Fellowship (Branch of MAF Europe) — Addis Ababa

PO Box 7716, Addis Ababa, Ethiopia ☎ (1) 51 84 82 Tx: none Fax: (1) 51 40 47 SITA: n/a
F: n/a ⁂ n/a Head: n/a Net: n/a Non-commercial mulitnational ecclesiastical consortium conducting flights for relief & development agencies & missions in remote areas of third world countries.

☐	N9750F	Cessna 208 Caravan I	20800172		0089	0098	1 PWC PT6A-114	3629			lsf Project Air Inc. / to be ET re-reg.

MIDROC AVIATION (Subsidiary of Midroc Construction) — Addis Ababa & Jeddah (Saudi Arabia)

PO Box 8677, Addis Ababa, Ethiopia ☎ (1) 61 22 22 Tx: none Fax: (1) 51 35 93 SITA: n/a
F: 1997 ⁂ n/a Head: n/a Net: n/a Operates non-commercial passenger / EMS & cargo flights for its parent company only.

☐	ET-AKY	De Havilland DHC-8-202 Dash 8Q	475	C-GDKL*	0098	0498	2 PWC PW123D	16465	Y29/Combi/Frtr		lsf Midroc Leasing Inc., Bahamas
☐	ET-AKZ	De Havilland DHC-8-202 Dash 8Q	469	C-GLOT*	0098	0498	2 PWC PW123D	16465	Y29/Combi/Frtr		lsf Midroc Leasing Inc., Bahamas

EW = BELARUS (Republic of Belarus) (Respublika Belarus)

Capital: Minsk Official Language: Russian Population: 10,4 million Square Km: 207600 Dialling code: +375 Year established: 1991 Acting political head: Alexander Lukashenko (President)

Government / Corporate / Executive / VIP Aircraft

☐	EW-63955	Tupolev 134A	63955	CCCP-63955	0082		2 SO D-30-II	49000	VIP		Ministry of Defence

BAS – Belarussky aviatsionny servis (Subsidiary of Overhaul plant no. 407) — Minsk 1

Ul. Aerodromnaya 10, 220600 Minsk, Belarus ☎ (17) 225 05 56 Tx: none Fax: (17) 224 05 51 SITA: n/a
F: 1995 ⁂ n/a Head: Arkady G. Yamov Net: n/a

☐	EW-87657	Yakovlev 40	9020409	I-JAKA	0570		3 IV AI-25	16100	Y30		

BELAIR Belarussian Airlines = BLI — Minsk 2

Ul. Korotkevicha 5, 220039 Minsk, Belarus ☎ (17) 222 57 02 Tx: none Fax: (17) 222 75 09 SITA: n/a
F: 1991 ⁂ n/a Head: Yevgeni A. Kuzmin ICAO: AIR BELARUS Net: n/a

☐	EW-65565	Tupolev 134A	63998	CCCP-65565	0283	0092	2 SO D-30-II	49000	Y64		lst CHZ as RA-65565
☐	EW-76837	Ilyushin 76TD	1023409316	CCCP-76837	0092	0092	4 SO D-30KP	190000	Freighter		lst AZZ as ST-APS

BELAVIA Belarusian Airlines = B2 / BRU (NAK Belavia) — Minsk 1 & -2

Ul. Nemiga 14, 220004 Minsk, Belarus ☎ (17) 279 17 92 Tx: none Fax: (17) 279 17 42 SITA: MSQCDB2
F: 1993 ⁂ n/a Head: Anatoly N. Gusarov IATA: 628 ICAO: BELARUS AVIA Net: n/a

☐	EW-88187	Yakovlev 40	9620748	CCCP-88187	0876		3 IV AI-25	16800	Y30		
☐	EW-88202	Yakovlev 40	9630449	ER-88202	0876		3 IV AI-25	17200	Y30		
☐	EW-46359	Antonov 24B	07305809	UR-46359	0270		2 IV AI-24-II	21000	Y48		
☐	EW-46375	Antonov 24B	07306008	CCCP-46375	0470		2 IV AI-24-II	21000	Y48		
☐	EW-46498	Antonov 24RV	27308301	CCCP-46498	1272		2 IV AI-24VT	21800	Y48		
☐	EW-46615	Antonov 24RV	37308702	CCCP-46615	0573		2 IV AI-24VT	21800	Y48		
☐	EW-47291	Antonov 24RV	07306601	CCCP-47291	1170		2 IV AI-24VT	21800	Y48		
☐	EW-47825	Antonov 24B	17307206	TC-ANK	0971		2 IV AI-24-II	21800	Y48		
☐	EW-26112	Antonov 26B	12109	CCCP-26112	0582		2 IV AI-24VT	24000	Freighter		
☐	EW-26127	Antonov 26B	12701	CCCP-26127	1282		2 IV AI-24VT	24000	Freighter		
☐	EW-65082	Tupolev 134A	60081	CCCP-65082	0077		2 SO D-30-II	49000	Y76		
☐	EW-65085	Tupolev 134A	60123	CCCP-65085	0077		2 SO D-30-II	49000	CY68		
☐	EW-65106	Tupolev 134A	60315	CCCP-65106	0078		2 SO D-30-II	49000	CY68		
☐	EW-65108	Tupolev 134A	60332	CCCP-65108	0078		2 SO D-30-II	49000	CY68		
☐	EW-65133	Tupolev 134A-3	60645	CCCP-65133	0078		2 SO D-30-III	49000	CY68		
☐	EW-65145	Tupolev 134A	60985	CCCP-65145	0079		2 SO D-30-II	49000	CY68		
☐	EW-65149	Tupolev 134A	61033	CCCP-65149	0079		2 SO D-30-II	49000	CY68		
☐	EW-65754	Tupolev 134A	62154	CCCP-65754	0079		2 SO D-30-II	49000	CY68		
☐	EW-65772	Tupolev 134A-3	62472	CCCP-65772	0079		2 SO D-30-III	49000	CY68		
☐	EW-65821	Tupolev 134A	08060	CCCP-65821	0074		2 SO D-30-II	47000	Y76		
☐	EW-85411	Tupolev 154B-2	411	CCCP-85411	0080		3 KU NK-8-2U	98000	Y164		
☐	EW-85419	Tupolev 154B-2	419	CCCP-85419	0080		3 KU NK-8-2U	98000	Y164		
☐	EW-85465	Tupolev 154B-2	465	CCCP-85465	0080		3 KU NK-8-2U	100000	Y164		
☐	EW-85509	Tupolev 154B-2	509	CCCP-85509	0081		3 KU NK-8-2U	100000	Y164		
☐	EW-85538	Tupolev 154B-2	538	4W-85538	0082		3 KU NK-8-2U	100000	Y164		
☐	EW-85545	Tupolev 154B-2	545	CCCP-85545	0082		3 KU NK-8-2U	100000	Y164		
☐	EW-85580	Tupolev 154B-2	580	CCCP-85580	0083		3 KU NK-8-2U	100000	Y164		
☐	EW-85581	Tupolev 154B-2	581	CCCP-85581	0083		3 KU NK-8-2U	100000	Y164		
☐	EW-85582	Tupolev 154B-2	582	CCCP-85582	0083		3 KU NK-8-2U	100000	Y164		std MSQ
☐	EW-85591	Tupolev 154B-2	591	CCCP-85591	0083		3 KU NK-8-2U	100000	Y164		
☐	EW-85593	Tupolev 154B-2	593	CCCP-85593	0083		3 KU NK-8-2U	100000	Y164		std MSQ
☐	EW-85703	Tupolev 154M	878	CCCP-85703	0091		3 SO D-30KU-154-II	100000	Y164 or F12Y120		
☐	EW-85706	Tupolev 154M	881	CCCP-85706	0091		3 SO D-30KU-154-II	100000	Y164 or F12Y120		
☐	EW-85741	Tupolev 154M	896	ES-LTR	0091	0498	3 SO D-30KU-154-II	100000	Y164 or F12Y120		
☐	EW-85748	Tupolev 154M	924	CCCP-85748	1092		3 SO D-30KU-154-II	100000	Y164 or F12Y120		
☐	EW-85815	Tupolev 154M	1010		0095	0895	3 SO D-30KU-154-II	100000	VIP 49 Pax		opf Gvmt / Belarus-titles

GOMELAVIA = YD / GOM (Gomel Airlines) (formerly part of Belavia) — Gomel

Gomel Airport, 246011 Gomel, Belarus ☎ (232) 53 14 15 Tx: none Fax: (232) 53 64 14 SITA: n/a
F: 1996 ⁂ n/a Head: Valery N. Kulakovsky ICAO: GOMEL Net: n/a

☐	EW-14126	PZL Swidnik (Mil) Mi-2	5210838029	CCCP-14126	0289	0096	2 IS GTD-350-4	3550	Utility		
☐	EW-14158	PZL Swidnik (Mil) Mi-2	5210443117	CCCP-14158	1287	0096	2 IS GTD-350-4	3550	Utility		
☐	EW-14159	PZL Swidnik (Mil) Mi-2	5210444117	CCCP-14159	1287	0096	2 IS GTD-350-4	3550	Utility		
☐	EW-14199	PZL Swidnik (Mil) Mi-2	5410940069	CCCP-14199	0689	0096	2 IS GTD-350-4	3550	Utility		
☐	EW-14200	PZL Swidnik (Mil) Mi-2	5410941069	CCCP-14200	0689	0096	2 IS GTD-350-4	3550	Utility		
☐	EW-14213	PZL Swidnik (Mil) Mi-2	5211048129	CCCP-14213	1289	0096	2 IS GTD-350-4	3550	Utility		
☐	EW-14216	PZL Swidnik (Mil) Mi-2	5211101119	CCCP-14216	1289	0096	2 IS GTD-350-4	3550	Utility		
☐	EW-14251	PZL Swidnik (Mil) Mi-2	5211138050	CCCP-14251	0590	0096	2 IS GTD-350-4	3550	Utility		
☐	EW-15624	PZL Swidnik (Mil) Mi-2	5210039126	CCCP-15624	1286	0096	2 IS GTD-350-4	3550	Utility		
☐	EW-15633	PZL Swidnik (Mil) Mi-2	5210104017	CCCP-15633	0187	0096	2 IS GTD-350-4	3550	Utility		
☐	EW-20371	PZL Swidnik (Mil) Mi-2	529818066	CCCP-20371	0686	0096	2 IS GTD-350-4	3550	Utility		
☐	EW-20737	PZL Swidnik (Mil) Mi-2	527634052	CCCP-20737	0582	0096	2 IS GTD-350-4	3550	Utility		

139 registration type of aircraft cn/fn ex/ex* mfd del powered by mtow kg configuration selcal name/fln/specialitites/remarks

☐ EW-20913	PZL Swidnik (Mil) Mi-2	528545024	CCCP-20913	0484	0096	2 IS GTD-350-4	3550	Utility		
☐ EW-20961	PZL Swidnik (Mil) Mi-2	549517115	CCCP-20961	1185	0096	2 IS GTD-350-4	3550	Utility		
☐ EW-23232	PZL Swidnik (Mil) Mi-2	5210233057	CCCP-23232	0587	0096	2 IS GTD-350-4	3550	Utility		
☐ EW-23291	PZL Swidnik (Mil) Mi-2	529112025	CCCP-23291	0285	0096	2 IS GTD-350-4	3550	Utility		
☐ EW-17869	PZL Mielec (Antonov) An-2	1G205-10	CCCP-17869	1083	0096	1 SH ASh-62IR	5500	Utility		
☐ EW-17983	PZL Mielec (Antonov) An-2	1G210-07	CCCP-17983	0984	0096	1 SH ASh-62IR	5500	Utility		
☐ EW-40622	PZL Mielec (Antonov) An-2	1G213-29	CCCP-40622	0585	0096	1 SH ASh-62IR	5500	Utility		
☐ EW-43951	PZL Mielec (Antonov) An-2	1G210-28	CCCP-43951	0984	0096	1 SH ASh-62IR	5500	Utility		
☐ EW-54901	PZL Mielec (Antonov) An-2	1G186-49	CCCP-54901	0380	0096	1 SH ASh-62IR	5500	Utility		
☐ EW-62660	PZL Mielec (Antonov) An-2	1G178-52	CCCP-62660	0278	0096	1 SH ASh-62IR	5500	Utility		
☐ EW-71168	PZL Mielec (Antonov) An-2	1G200-11	CCCP-71168	1182	0096	1 SH ASh-62IR	5500	Utility		
☐ EW-81539	PZL Mielec (Antonov) An-2	1G208-43	CCCP-81539	0684	0096	1 SH ASh-62IR	5500	Utility		
☐ EW-84730	PZL Mielec (Antonov) An-2	1G201-48	CCCP-84730	0283	0096	1 SH ASh-62IR	5500	Utility		
☐ EW-46304	Antonov 24B	97305204	CCCP-46304	0469	0096	2 IV AI-24-II	21800	Y48		
☐ EW-46483	Antonov 24RV	27308101	CCCP-46483	0972	0096	2 IV AI-24VT	21800	Y48		lst LNS
☐ EW-46631	Antonov 24RV	37308810	CCCP-46631	0873	0096	2 IV AI-24VT	21800	Y48		
☐ EW-46829	Antonov 24RV	17306706	CCCP-46829	0371	0096	2 IV AI-24VT	21800	Y48		
☐ EW-46835	Antonov 24RV	17306802	CCCP-46835	0371	0096	2 IV AI-24VT	21800	Y48		
☐ EW-47697	Antonov 24RV	27307604	CCCP-47697	0272	0096	2 IV AI-24VT	21800	Y48		
☐ EW-47808	Antonov 24RV	17306910	CCCP-47808	0571	0096	2 IV AI-24VT	21800	Y48		
☐ EW-65049	Tupolev 134A	49755	CCCP-65049	0076	0096	2 SO D-30-II	49000	Y76		
☐ EW-65676	Tupolev 134A	1351502	CCCP-65676	0071	0096	2 SO D-30-II	47000	Y76		
☐ EW-85757	Tupolev 154M	939	RA-85757	0092	1296	3 SO D-30KU-154-II	100000	Y164		lst ITX

MOGILEVAVIA = MOG (formerly part of Belavia) — **Mogilev**

Mogilev Airport, 212031 Mogilev, Belarus ☎ (222) 26 12 69 Tx: none Fax: (222) 26 62 70 SITA: n/a
F: n/a ⁂ n/a Head: Vladimir V. Nekhaev ICAO: MOGILEV Net: n/a Some aircraft are still in former Belavia or Aeroflot colors but will be repainted in due course.

☐ EW-87320	Yakovlev 40	9331929	CCCP-87320	0873		3 IV AI-25	16800	Y36		
☐ EW-87330	Yakovlev 40	9510139	CCCP-87330	0275		3 IV AI-25	16800	Y36		
☐ EW-87419	Yakovlev 40	9421134	CCCP-87419	0574		3 IV AI-25	16800	Y36		lst GIE
☐ EW-87577	Yakovlev 40	9220922	CCCP-87577	0572		3 IV AI-25	16800	Y27		
☐ EW-87658	Yakovlev 40	9240225	CCCP-87658	1072		3 IV AI-25	16800	Y27		
☐ EW-88161	Yakovlev 40	9611546	CCCP-88161	0876		3 IV AI-25	16800	Y32		

TECHAVIASERVICE, Joint-Stock Company = BTS (Associated with Lukoil Co., Russia) — **Minsk 2**

Ul. Avakyana 30a, 220065 Minsk, Belarus ☎ (17) 213 11 25 Tx: none Fax: (17) 217 43 00 SITA: n/a
F: 1994 ⁂ n/a Head: Vladimir Ya. Zhigachev ICAO: TECHSERVICE Net: n/a

☐ EW-11365	Antonov 12BP	5343109	09 YELLOW	0665	0096	4 IV AI-20M	61000	Freighter		
☐ EW-11371	Antonov 12BP	4342108	08 YELLOW	0664	0096	4 IV AI-20K	61000	Freighter		

TRANS AVIA EXPORT Cargo Airlines = AL / TXC — **Minsk-Machulishchy**

Ul. Zakharova 44, 220034 Minsk, Belarus ☎ (17) 227 51 01 Tx: n/a Fax: (17) 236 36 41 SITA: n/a
F: 1992 ⁂ 560 Head: Viktor S. Bulankin ICAO: TRANSEXPORT Net: n/a

☐ EW-78765	Ilyushin 76MD	0083486590	CCCP-78765	0088	0093	4 SO D-30KP	190000	Freighter		
☐ EW-78769	Ilyushin 76MD	0083487607	CCCP-78769	0088	0095	4 SO D-30KP	190000	Freighter		
☐ EW-78779	Ilyushin 76MD	0083489662	CCCP-78779	0088	0095	4 SO D-30KP	190000	Freighter		
☐ EW-78787	Ilyushin 76MD	0083490698	CCCP-78787	0088	0095	4 SO D-30KP	190000	Freighter		
☐ EW-78793	Ilyushin 76MD	0093490721	CCCP-78793	0088	0096	4 SO D-30KP	190000	Freighter		
☐ EW-78799	Ilyushin 76MD	0093491754	CCCP-78799	1188	0095	4 SO D-30KP	190000	Freighter		lst ESL
☐ EW-78801	Ilyushin 76MD	0093492763	CCCP-78801	0089	0095	4 SO D-30KP	190000	Freighter		lst AYZ / fn 7001
☐ EW-78802	Ilyushin 76MD	0093492771	CCCP-78802	0089	0096	4 SO D-30KP	190000	Freighter		
☐ EW-78808	Ilyushin 76MD	0093493794	CCCP-78808	0089	0093	4 SO D-30KP	190000	Freighter		lst ESL
☐ EW-78819	Ilyushin 76MD	0093495883	CCCP-78819	0089	0093	4 SO D-30KP	190000	Freighter		lst ESL
☐ EW-78826	Ilyushin 76MD	1003499991	CCCP-78826	0090	0093	4 SO D-30KP	190000	Freighter		lst ESL
☐ EW-78827	Ilyushin 76MD	1003499997	CCCP-78827	0090	0093	4 SO D-30KP	190000	Freighter		lst AYZ / fn 7510
☐ EW-78828	Ilyushin 76MD	1003401004	CCCP-78828	0090	0093	4 SO D-30KP	190000	Freighter		lst SEV
☐ EW-78836	Ilyushin 76MD	0093499986	CCCP-78836	0090	0093	4 SO D-30KP	190000	Freighter		
☐ EW-78839	Ilyushin 76MD	1003402047	CCCP-78839	0090	0093	4 SO D-30KP	190000	Freighter		lst ESL
☐ EW-78843	Ilyushin 76MD	1003403082	CCCP-78843	0090	0093	4 SO D-30KP	190000	Freighter		lst ESL
☐ EW-78848	Ilyushin 76MD	1003405159	CCCP-78848	0090	0093	4 SO D-30KP	190000	Freighter		
☐ EW-78849	Ilyushin 76MD	1013405192	CCCP-78849	0091	0093	4 SO D-30KP	190000	Freighter		fn 8008

WINGS = VGS — **Minsk**

Ul. Aerodromnaya 4, 220065 Minsk, Belarus ☎ (17) 222 57 33 Tx: none Fax: (17) 269 20 64 SITA: n/a
F: 1993 ⁂ n/a Head: Viktor Yasinsky ICAO: AERO WINGS Net: n/a

☐ EW-11322	Antonov 12BP	0901409	CCCP-11322	0060		4 IV AI-20M	61000	Freighter		lst ADB as UR-11322

EX = KYRGYZSTAN (Republic of Kyrgyzstan) (Kyrgyz Respublikasy)

Capital: Bishkek Official Language: Kyrghiz Population: 5,0 million Square Km: 198500 Dialling code: +996 Year established: 1991 Acting political head: Askar Akayev (President)

KYRGHYZSTAN AIRLINES = K2 / KGA (Kyrgyzstan Aba Zholdoru) — **Bishkek-Manas, Karakol & Osh**

Manas Airport, 720062 Bishkek, Kyrgyzstan ☎ (3312) 25 77 55 Tx: 245166 port kh Fax: (3312) 25 71 62 SITA: n/a
F: 1992 ⁂ n/a Head: Timur Muratov IATA: 758 ICAO: KYRGYZ Net: n/a Beside aircraft listed, also owns 55 Antonov 2 aircraft, most of them are stored.

☐ EX-23305	PZL Swidnik (Mil) Mi-2	529126035	CCCP-23305	0385	0092	2 IS GTD-350-4	3550	Utility		
☐ EX-23316	PZL Swidnik (Mil) Mi-2	529147045	CCCP-23316	0485	0092	2 IS GTD-350-4	3550	Utility		
☐ EX-23415	PZL Swidnik (Mil) Mi-2	538937114	CCCP-23415	1184	0092	2 IS GTD-350-4	3550	Utility		
☐ EX-23477	PZL Swidnik (Mil) Mi-2	526236079	CCCP-23477	0879	0092	2 IS GTD-350-4	3550	Utility		
☐ EX-23497	PZL Swidnik (Mil) Mi-2	526314099	CCCP-23497	0979	0092	2 IS GTD-350-4	3550	Utility		
☐ EX-23520	PZL Swidnik (Mil) Mi-2	525923128	CCCP-23520	1278	0092	2 IS GTD-350-4	3550	Utility		
☐ EX-28728	PZL Mielec (Antonov) An-28	1AJ007-13	CCCP-28728	0090	0092	2 GS TVD-10B	6500	Y17		
☐ EX-28729	PZL Mielec (Antonov) An-28	1AJ007-14	CCCP-28729	0090	0092	2 GS TVD-10B	6500	Y17		
☐ EX-28738	PZL Mielec (Antonov) An-28	1AJ008-01	CCCP-28738	0090	0092	2 GS TVD-10B	6500	Y17		
☐ EX-28917	PZL Mielec (Antonov) An-28	1AJ008-03	CCCP-28917	0090	0092	2 GS TVD-10B	6500	Y17		
☐ EX-28934	PZL Mielec (Antonov) An-28	1AJ008-21	CCCP-28934	0090	0092	2 GS TVD-10B	6500	Y17		
☐ EX-28946	PZL Mielec (Antonov) An-28	1AJ009-12	CCCP-28946	0090	0092	2 GS TVD-10B	6500	Y17		
☐ EX-22329	Mil Mi-8T	7154	CCCP-22329	0077	0092	2 IS TV2-117A	12000	Utility		
☐ EX-22398	Mil Mi-8T	7407	CCCP-22398	0077	0092	2 IS TV2-117A	12000	Utility		
☐ EX-22621	Mil Mi-8T	7968	CCCP-22621	0080	0092	2 IS TV2-117A	12000	Utility		
☐ EX-22835	Mil Mi-8T	7635	CCCP-22835	0078	0092	2 IS TV2-117A	12000	Utility		
☐ EX-24690	Mil Mi-8T	9815750	CCCP-24690	0081	0092	2 IS TV2-117A	12000	Utility		
☐ EX-25148	Mil Mi-8MTV-1	96155		1293	1293	2 IS TV3-117MT	13000	VIP		
☐ EX-25178	Mil Mi-8MTV-1	95488	CCCP-25178	0990	0092	2 IS TV3-117MT	13000	Utility		
☐ EX-25180	Mil Mi-8MTV-1	95490	CCCP-25180	0990	0092	2 IS TV3-117MT	13000	Utility		
☐ EX-25182	Mil Mi-8MTV-1	95521	CCCP-25182	0990	0092	2 IS TV3-117MT	13000	Utility		
☐ EX-25428	Mil Mi-8MTV-1	95460	CCCP-25428	0990	0092	2 IS TV3-117MT	13000	Utility		
☐ EX-25791	Mil Mi-8T	4524	CCCP-25791	0074	0092	2 IS TV2-117A	12000	Utility		
☐ EX-25920	Mil Mi-8T	5555	CCCP-25920	0075	0092	2 IS TV2-117A	12000	Utility		
☐ EX-87250	Yakovlev 40	9310726	CCCP-87250	0073	0092	3 IV AI-25	16800	Y32		
☐ EX-87259	Yakovlev 40	9311626	CCCP-87259	0073	0092	3 IV AI-25	16800	Y32		
☐ EX-87275	Yakovlev 40	9311127	CCCP-87275	0073	0092	3 IV AI-25	16800	Y32		
☐ EX-87293	Yakovlev 40	9320828	CCCP-87293	0073	0092	3 IV AI-25	16800	Y32		
☐ EX-87331	Yakovlev 40	9510239	CCCP-87331	0075	0092	3 IV AI-25	16800	Y32		
☐ EX-87354	Yakovlev 40	9330331	CCCP-87354	0073	0092	3 IV AI-25	16800	Y32		std Bishkek
☐ EX-87366	Yakovlev 40	9341631	CCCP-87366	0073	0092	3 IV AI-25	16800	Y32		
☐ EX-87379	Yakovlev 40	9411030	CCCP-87379	0074	0092	3 IV AI-25	16800	VIP		
☐ EX-87412	Yakovlev 40	9420434	CCCP-87412	0074	0092	3 IV AI-25	16800	Y32		
☐ EX-87426	Yakovlev 40	9420235	CCCP-87426	0074	0092	3 IV AI-25	16800	Y32		
☐ EX-87442	Yakovlev 40	9431935	CCCP-87442	0074	0092	3 IV AI-25	16800	Y32		
☐ EX-87445	Yakovlev 40	9430236	CCCP-87445	0074	0092	3 IV AI-25	16800	Y32		
☐ EX-87470	Yakovlev 40	9441537	CCCP-87470	0074	0092	3 IV AI-25	16800	Y32		
☐ EX-87529	Yakovlev 40	9521141	CCCP-87529	0075	0092	3 IV AI-25	16800	Y32		
☐ EX-87538	Yakovlev 40	9530342	CCCP-87538	0075	0092	3 IV AI-25	16800	Y32		
☐ EX-87555	Yakovlev 40	9210621	CCCP-87555	0072	0092	3 IV AI-25	16800	Y32		
☐ EX-87561	Yakovlev 40	9211221	CCCP-87561	0072	0092	3 IV AI-25	16800	Y32		
☐ EX-87571	Yakovlev 40	9221521	CCCP-87571	0072	0092	3 IV AI-25	16800	Y32		
☐ EX-87589	Yakovlev 40	9220123	CCCP-87589	0072	0072	3 IV AI-25	16800	Y32		
☐ EX-87631	Yakovlev 40	9131219	CCCP-87631	0071	0092	3 IV AI-25	16800	Y32		
☐ EX-87632	Yakovlev 40	9131319	CCCP-87632	0071	0092	3 IV AI-25	16800	Y32		

140 registration type of aircraft cn/fn ex/ex* mfd del powered by mtow kg configuration selcal name/fln/specialitites/remarks

	registration	type of aircraft	cn/fn	ex/ex*	mfd	del	powered by	mtow kg	configuration	selcal	name/fln/specialitites/remarks
☐	EX-87664	Yakovlev 40	9240825	CCCP-87664	0072	0092	3 IV AI-25	16800	Y32		
☐	EX-87820	Yakovlev 40	9231224	CCCP-87820	0072	0092	3 IV AI-25	16800	Y32		
☐	EX-87836	Yakovlev 40	9240226	CCCP-87836	0072	0092	3 IV AI-25	16800	Y32		
☐	EX-26036	Antonov 26B	10606	CCCP-26036	0080	0092	2 IV AI-24VT	24000	Freighter		
☐	EX-65111	Tupolev 134A-3	60346	CCCP-65111	0078	0092	2 SO D-30-III	49000	Y76		
☐	EX-65119	Tupolev 134A-3	60475	CCCP-65119	0078	0092	2 SO D-30-III	49000	VIP		
☐	EX-65125	Tupolev 134A-3	60575	CCCP-65125	0078	0092	2 SO D-30-III	49000	Y76		
☐	EX-65778	Tupolev 134A-3	62590	CCCP-65778	0079	0092	2 SO D-30-III	49000	Y76		
☐	EX-65779	Tupolev 134A-3	62602	CCCP-65779	0079	0092	2 SO D-30-III	49000	Y76		
☐	EX-65789	Tupolev 134A-3	62850	CCCP-65789	0080	0092	2 SO D-30-III	49000	Y76		
☐		Airbus Industrie A319-132					2 IAE V2524-A5	64000			to be lsf Debis AirFinance 0601
☐		Airbus Industrie A319-132					2 IAE V2524-A5	64000			to be lsf Debis AirFinance 1001
☐	F-OHGA	Airbus Industrie A320-231	478	D-AWWW	0094	0698	2 IAE V2500-A1	77000	C20Y126		lsf Debis Aircraft Leasing XIX B.V.
☐	EX-85252	Tupolev 154B-1	252	CCCP-85252	0077	0092	3 KU NK-8-2U	98000	Y164		
☐	EX-85259	Tupolev 154B-1	259	CCCP-85259	0077	0092	3 KU NK-8-2U	98000	Y164		
☐	EX-85294	Tupolev 154B-1	294	CCCP-85294	0078	0092	3 KU NK-8-2U	98000	Y164		
☐	EX-85313	Tupolev 154B-2	313	CCCP-85313	0078	0092	3 KU NK-8-2U	98000	Y164		
☐	EX-85369	Tupolev 154B-2	369	CCCP-85369	0079	0092	3 KU NK-8-2U	98000	Y164		
☐	EX-85444	Tupolev 154B-2	444	CCCP-85444	0080	0092	3 KU NK-8-2U	98000	Y164		
☐	EX-85491	Tupolev 154B-2	491	CCCP-85491	0081	0092	3 KU NK-8-2U	100000	Y164		
☐	EX-85497	Tupolev 154B-2	497	CCCP-85497	0081	0092	3 KU NK-8-2U	100000	Y164		
☐	EX-85519	Tupolev 154B-2	519	CCCP-85519	0081	0092	3 KU NK-8-2U	100000	Y164		
☐	EX-85590	Tupolev 154B-2	590	CCCP-85590	0083	0092	3 KU NK-8-2U	100000	Y164		
☐	EX-85718	Tupolev 154M	900	CCCP-85718	0091	0092	3 SO D-30KU-154-II	100000	Y164		
☐	EX-85762	Tupolev 154M	945	RA-85762	0092	0092	3 SO D-30KU-154-II	100000	Y164		
☐	EX-76815	Ilyushin 76TD	1013409310	CCCP-76815	0091	0092	4 SO D-30KP	198000	Freighter		

EY = TAJIKISTAN (Republic of Tajikistan) (Cumhurii Toçikiston)

Capital: Dushanbe Official Language: Tadzhik Population: 7,0 million Square Km: 143100 Dialling code: +7 Year established: 1991 Acting political head: Imam Ali S. Rahmanov (President)

TAJIKISTAN AIRLINES = 7J / TZK (formerly Tajik Air / part of Aeroflot Tajikistan Directorate) Dushanbe & Khudzhand

Ul. Titova 32/1, 734006 Dushanbe, Tajikistan ☎ (3772) 51 00 41 Tx: none Fax: (3772) 51 00 41 SITA: n/a

F: n/a 👪 n/a Head: Mirzo A. Mastangulov IATA: 502 ICAO: TAJIKISTAN Net: n/a Some aircraft are still in Aeroflot colours but will be repainted in due course.

	registration	type of aircraft	cn/fn	ex/ex*	mfd	del	powered by	mtow kg	configuration	selcal	name/fln/specialitites/remarks
☐	EY-28704	PZL Mielec (Antonov) An-28	1AJ006-14	CCCP-28704	0789		2 GS TVD-10B	6500	Y17		
☐	EY-28705	PZL Mielec (Antonov) An-28	1AJ006-15	CCCP-28705	0789		2 GS TVD-10B	6500	Y17		
☐	EY-28724	PZL Mielec (Antonov) An-28	1AJ007-09	CCCP-28724	0190		2 GS TVD-10B	6500	Y17		
☐	EY-28734	PZL Mielec (Antonov) An-28	1AJ007-19	CCCP-28734	0490		2 GS TVD-10B	6500	Y17		
☐	EY-28735	PZL Mielec (Antonov) An-28	1AJ007-22	CCCP-28735	0490		2 GS TVD-10B	6500	Y17		
☐	EY-28736	PZL Mielec (Antonov) An-28	1AJ007-24	CCCP-28736	0490		2 GS TVD-10B	6500	Y17		
☐	EY-28750	PZL Mielec (Antonov) An-28	1AJ003-14	CCCP-28750	0587		2 GS TVD-10B	6500	Y17		
☐	EY-28751	PZL Mielec (Antonov) An-28	1AJ003-15	CCCP-28751	0687		2 GS TVD-10B	6500	Y17		
☐	EY-28757	PZL Mielec (Antonov) An-28	1AJ005-03	CCCP-28757	0488		2 GS TVD-10B	6500	Y17		
☐	EY-28762	PZL Mielec (Antonov) An-28	1AJ004-11	CCCP-28762	1187		2 GS TVD-10B	6500	Y17		
☐	EY-28791	PZL Mielec (Antonov) An-28	1AJ005-24	CCCP-28791	0189		2 GS TVD-10B	6500	Y17		
☐	EY-28921	PZL Mielec (Antonov) An-28	1AJ008-07	CCCP-28921	0790		2 GS TVD-10B	6500	Y17		
☐	EY-22691	Mil Mi-8T	8150	CCCP-22691	1280		2 IS TV2-117A	12000	Y28		
☐	EY-22826	Mil Mi-8T	7626	CCCP-22826	0978		2 IS TV2-117A	12000	Y28		
☐	EY-22838	Mil Mi-8T	7638	CCCP-22838	1078		2 IS TV2-117A	12000	Y28		
☐	EY-24404	Mil Mi-8T	98625146	CCCP-24404	0386		2 IS TV2-117A	12000	Y28		
☐	EY-24495	Mil Mi-8T	98628987	CCCP-24495	0187		2 IS TV2-117A	12000	Y28		
☐	EY-25149	Mil Mi-8MTV-1	95190	CCCP-25149	0190		2 IS TV3-117MT	13000	Y28		
☐	EY-25167	Mil Mi-8MTV-1	95378	CCCP-25167	0690		2 IS TV3-117MT	13000	Y28		
☐	EY-25169	Mil Mi-8MTV-1	95380	CCCP-25169	0690		2 IS TV3-117MT	13000	Y28		
☐	EY-25438	Mil Mi-8MTV-1	95549	CCCP-25438	1290		2 IS TV3-117MT	13000	Y28		
☐	EY-25549	Mil Mi-8T	2885	CCCP-25549	0372		2 IS TV2-117A	12000	Y28		
☐	EY-25635	Mil Mi-8T	3048	CCCP-25635	0672		2 IS TV2-117A	12000	Y28		
☐	EY-25713	Mil Mi-8T	4192	CCCP-25713	1173		2 IS TV2-117A	12000	Y28		
☐	EY-87214	Yakovlev 40K	9640851	HA-LJB	1276		3 IV AI-25	16800	Y21		
☐	EY-87217	Yakovlev 40	9510340	CCCP-87217	0375		3 IV AI-25	16800	Y21		
☐	EY-87269	Yakovlev 40	9310527	CCCP-87269	0273		3 IV AI-25	16800	Y32		
☐	EY-87310	Yakovlev 40	9321327A	CCCP-87310	0673		3 IV AI-25	16800	Y32		
☐	EY-87313	Yakovlev 40	9330829	CCCP-87313	0773		3 IV AI-25	16800	Y36		
☐	EY-87356	Yakovlev 40	9340531	CCCP-87356	1073		3 IV AI-25	16800	Y36		
☐	EY-87434	Yakovlev 40	9431035	CCCP-87434	0774		3 IV AI-25	16800	Y36		
☐	EY-87446	Yakovlev 40	9430336	CCCP-87446	0874		3 IV AI-25	16800	Y36		
☐	EY-87461	Yakovlev 40	9432036	CCCP-87461	1074		3 IV AI-25	16800	Y36		
☐	EY-87522	Yakovlev 40	9520441	CCCP-87522	0675		3 IV AI-25	16800	Y36		
☐	EY-87554	Yakovlev 40	9210521	CCCP-87554	0272		3 IV AI-25	16800	Y32		
☐	EY-87666	Yakovlev 40	9241025	CCCP-87666	1172		3 IV AI-25	16800	Y32		
☐	EY-87697	Yakovlev 40	9910205	CCCP-87697	0369		3 IV AI-25	16800	Y32		
☐	EY-87827	Yakovlev 40	9241924	CCCP-87827	1072		3 IV AI-25	16800	Y32		
☐	EY-87835	Yakovlev 40	9240126	CCCP-87835	1272		3 IV AI-25	16800	Y32		
☐	EY-87922	Yakovlev 40K	9731355	CCCP-87922	1077		3 IV AI-25	16800	Y36		
☐	EY-87963	Yakovlev 40K	9831058	CCCP-87963	0878		3 IV AI-25	16800	Y36		
☐	EY-87967	Yakovlev 40K	9831158	CCCP-87967	0878		3 IV AI-25	16800	Y36		
☐	EY-88196	Yakovlev 40	9631648	CCCP-88196	0776		3 IV AI-25	16800	Y36		
☐	EY-88267	Yakovlev 40K	9720553	CCCP-88267	0477		3 IV AI-25	16800	Y36		
☐	EY-46365	Antonov 24B	07305906	CCCP-46365	0370		2 IV AI-24	21000	Y52		
☐	EY-46399	Antonov 24B	07306303	CCCP-46399	0770		2 IV AI-24	21000	Y52		
☐	EY-46595	Antonov 24B	97305105	CCCP-46595	0369		2 IV AI-24	21000	Y52		
☐	EY-46602	Antonov 24RV	37308509	CCCP-46602	0473		2 IV AI-24VT	21000	Y52		lst DAO
☐	EY-47693	Antonov 24RV	27307510	CCCP-47693	0172		2 IV AI-24VT	21800	Y52		lst DAO
☐	EY-26205	Antonov 26B	14107	CCCP-26205	0685		2 IV AI-24VT	24000	Cargo&Y19 Combi		
☐	EY-26658	Antonov 26	7904	CCCP-26658	0379		2 IV AI-24VT	24000	Cargo&Y19 Combi		
☐	EY-65003	Tupolev 134A-3	44040	CCCP-65003	1275		2 SO D-30-III	49000	Y80		
☐	EY-65022	Tupolev 134A	48395	ES-AAE	0576	0197	2 SO D-30-II	47000	Y80		
☐	EY-65763	Tupolev 134A-3	62299	CCCP-65763	0579		2 SO D-30-III	49000	Y80		lst SND
☐	EY-65788	Tupolev 134A-3	62835	CCCP-65788	0280		2 SO D-30-III	49000	Y80		lst SND
☐	EY-65814	Tupolev 134A-3	4352208	CCCP-65814	0374		2 SO D-30-III	49000	Y80		
☐	EY-65820	Tupolev 134A-3	08056	CCCP-65820	0474		2 SO D-30-III	49000	Y80		std MSQ
☐	EY-65835	Tupolev 134A-3	17112	CCCP-65835	0874		2 SO D-30-III	49000	Y8		
☐	EY-65876	Tupolev 134A-3	31220	CCCP-65876	0575		2 SO D-30-III	49000	Y80		
☐	EY-85247	Tupolev 154B-1	247	CCCP-85247	1277		3 KU NK-8-2U	98000	Y167		
☐	EY-85251	Tupolev 154B-1	251	CCCP-85251	1277		3 KU NK-8-2U	100000	Y167		
☐	EY-85385	Tupolev 154B-2	385	CCCP-85385	1279		3 KU NK-8-2U	100000	Y167		lst JAK as UN-85385
☐	EY-85406	Tupolev 154B-2	406	CCCP-85406	0480		3 KU NK-8-2U	98000	Y167		
☐	EY-85440	Tupolev 154B-2	440	CCCP-85440	0880		3 KU NK-8-2U	100000	Y167		
☐	EY-85466	Tupolev 154B-2	466	CCCP-85466	1281		3 KU NK-8-2U	100000	Y167		
☐	EY-85469	Tupolev 154B-2	469	CCCP-85469	0181		3 KU NK-8-2U	100000	Y167		
☐	EY-85475	Tupolev 154B-2	475	CCCP-85475	0281		3 KU NK-8-2U	102000	Y167		
☐	EY-85487	Tupolev 154B-2	487	CCCP-85487	0881		3 KU NK-8-2U	100000	Y167		
☐	EY-85511	Tupolev 154B-2	511	CCCP-85511	1081		3 KU NK-8-2U	100000	Y152		
☐	EY-85691	Tupolev 154M	864	CCCP-85691	0291		3 SO D-30KU-154-II	100000	Y167		lst DAO
☐	EY-85692	Tupolev 154M	865	CCCP-85692	0291		3 SO D-30KU-154-II	100000	Y167		
☐	EY-85717	Tupolev 154M	897	CCCP-85717	1291		3 SO D-30KU-154-II	100000	Y167		

EZ = TURKMENISTAN (Türkmenistan) (Cumhurii Türkmenistan)

(Republic of Turkmenistan)
Capital: Ashkhabad Official Language: Turkmen Population: 4,3 million Square Km: 488100 Dialling code: +993 Year established: 1991 Acting political head: General Saparmurad A. Niyazov (President)

TURKMENISTAN/AKHAL Aircompany = T5 / AKH (Member of Turkmenistan Airlines Concern) Ashkhabad

Airport, 744008 Ashkhabad, Turkmenistan ☎ (1) 35 60 84 Tx: 228112 akhal su Fax: (1) 39 07 84 SITA: n/a

F: 1992 👪 n/a Head: B.N. Nepesov IATA: 542 ICAO: AKHAL Net: n/a

	registration	type of aircraft	cn/fn	ex/ex*	mfd	del	powered by	mtow kg	configuration	selcal	name/fln/specialitites/remarks
☐	EZ-S701	Sikorsky S-76C+	760463		1096	1096	2 TU Arriel 2S1	5307	VIP 5 Pax		
☐	EZ-S702	Sikorsky S-76C+	760461		1096	1096	2 TU Arriel 2S1	5307	Y8		
☐	EZ-22291	Mil Mi-8T	6979	CCCP-22291	0377	0092	2 IS TV2-117A	12000	Freighter		
☐	EZ-22292	Mil Mi-8T	6889	CCCP-22292	0377	0092	2 IS TV2-117A	12000	Freighter		
☐	EZ-22597	Mil Mi-8T	7892	CCCP-22597	1279	0092	2 IS TV2-117A	12000	Freighter		
☐	EZ-22645	Mil Mi-8T	8030	CCCP-22645	0780	0092	2 IS TV2-117A	12000	Freighter		

☐ EZ-22698	Mil Mi-8T	8157	CCCP-22698	0181	0092	2 IS TV2-117A	12000	Freighter		
☐ EZ-24624	Mil Mi-8T	8253	CCCP-24624	0681	0092	2 IS TV2-117A	10800	Freighter		
☐ EZ-24625	Mil Mi-8T	8254	CCCP-24625	0681	0092	2 IS TV2-117A	12000	Freighter		
☐ EZ-25829	Mil Mi-8T	4566	CCCP-25829	0874	0092	2 IS TV2-117A	12000	Freighter		
☐ EZ-25830	Mil Mi-8T	4567	CCCP-25830	0874	0092	2 IS TV2-117A	12000	Freighter		
☐ EZ-25911	Mil Mi-8PS	5195	CCCP-25911	0576	0092	2 IS TV2-117A	12000	VIP 8 Pax		
☐ EZ-25956	Mil Mi-8T	5595	CCCP-25956	0675	0092	2 IS TV2-117A	12000	Freighter		
☐ EZ-25960	Mil Mi-8T	5806	TC-HUS	0775	0092	2 IS TV2-117A	12000	Freighter		
☐ EZ-25979	Mil Mi-8T	7509	CCCP-25979	0378	0092	2 IS TV2-117A	12000	Freighter		
☐ EZ-25980	Mil Mi-8T	7510	CCCP-25980	0378	0092	2 IS TV2-117A	12000	Freighter		
☐ EZ-25981	Mil Mi-8T	7511	CCCP-25981	0378	0092	2 IS TV2-117A	12000	Freighter		
☐ EZ-B021	Hawker 1000B (BAe 125-1000B)	259029	G-5-751*	1292	1292	2 PWC PW305	14062	VIP 7 Pax	DR-CF	
☐ EZ-46206	Antonov 24B	67302804	CCCP-46206	0966	0092	2 IV AI-24T	21000	Y52		
☐ EZ-46228	Antonov 24B	77303108	CCCP-46228	0267	0092	2 IV AI-24T	21000	Y52		
☐ EZ-46274	Antonov 24B	77303607	CCCP-46274	0867	0092	2 IV AI-24-II	21000	Y48		
☐ EZ-46348	Antonov 24B	97305707	CCCP-46348	1269	0092	2 IV AI-24T	21000	Y48		
☐ EZ-46398	Antonov 24B	07306302	CCCP-46398	0770	0092	2 IV AI-24T	21000	Y52		
☐ EZ-46490	Antonov 24RV	27308108	CCCP-46490	1072	0092	2 IV AI-24T	21800	Y44		
☐ EZ-46512	Antonov 24RV	37308408	CCCP-46512	0778	0092	2 IV AI-24T	21800	Y48		
☐ EZ-46592	Antonov 24B	97305102	CCCP-46592	0269	0092	2 IV AI-24T	21000	Y48		
☐ EZ-46680	Antonov 24RV	47309702	CCCP-46680	0774	0092	2 IV AI-24T	21800	Y48		
☐ EZ-47301	Antonov 24RV	57310205	CCCP-47301	0475	0092	2 IV AI-24T	21800	Y48		
☐ EZ-47314	Antonov 24RV	57310501	CCCP-47314	1275	0092	2 IV AI-24T	21800	Y48		
☐ EZ-47322	Antonov 24RV	67310508	CCCP-47322	0576	0092	2 IV AI-24T	21800	Y48		
☐ EZ-47784	Antonov 24B	89901509	CCCP-47784	0368	0092	2 IV AI-24T	21000	Y48		
☐ EZ-21194	Mil Mi-6	2680909V	CCCP-21194	0062	0092	2 SO D-25V	42500	Freighter		
☐ EZ-42404	Yakovlev 42D	4520422116617	CCCP-42404	0691	0092	3 LO D-36	56500	Y120		
☐ EZ-J672	Yakovlev 42D	4520421316562		0493	0593	3 LO D-36	56500	Y120		
☐ EZ-J673	Yakovlev 42D	4520421316574		0393	0393	3 LO D-36	56500	Y120		
☐ EZ-J674	Yakovlev 42D	4520421319020		0093	0393	3 LO D-36	56500	Y120		
☐ EZ-A001	Boeing 737-341	26855 / 2305	EK-A001	0692	1192	2 CFMI CFM56-3B2	62822	C16Y102	FP-BS	
☐ EZ-A002	Boeing 737-332	25994 / 2439	N301DE	0393	0894	2 CFMI CFM56-3C1	60750	C12Y106	EP-FJ	
☐ EZ-A003	Boeing 737-332	25995 / 2455	N302DE	0493	0894	2 CFMI CFM56-3C1	60750	C12Y106	EP-FK	
☐ EZ-85241	Tupolev 154B-1	241	CCCP-85241	1077	0092	3 KU NK-8-2U	98000	Y152		
☐ EZ-85246	Tupolev 154B-1	246	CCCP-85246	1177	0092	3 KU NK-8-2U	98000	Y152		
☐ EZ-85250	Tupolev 154B-1	250	4K-85250	1277	0092	3 KU NK-8-2U	98000	Y152		
☐ EZ-85345	Tupolev 154B-2	345	CCCP-85345	0579	0092	3 KU NK-8-2U	98000	Y152		
☐ EZ-85383	Tupolev 154B-2	383	CCCP-85383	1279	0092	3 KU NK-8-2U	98000	Y164		
☐ EZ-85394	Tupolev 154B-2	394	CCCP-85394	0180	0092	3 KU NK-8-2U	98000	Y152		
☐ EZ-85410	Tupolev 154B-2	410	CCCP-85410	0480	0092	3 KU NK-8-2U	98000	Y164		
☐ EZ-85492	Tupolev 154B-2	492	CCCP-85492	0581	0092	3 KU NK-8-2U	98000	Y152		
☐ EZ-85507	Tupolev 154B-2	507	CCCP-85507	0981	0092	3 KU NK-8-2U	100000	Y164		
☐ EZ-85532	Tupolev 154B-2	532	CCCP-85532	0382	0092	3 KU NK-8-2U	100000	Y152		
☐ EZ-85549	Tupolev 154B-2	549	CCCP-85549	0882	0092	3 KU NK-8-2U	98000	Y152		
☐ EZ-85560	Tupolev 154B-2	560	CCCP-85560	1182	0092	3 KU NK-8-2U	98000	Y152		
☐ EZ-A010	Boeing 757-23A	25345 / 412	N58AW	1191	1293	2 RR RB211-535E4	100244	VIP 36 Pax	FP-CR	
☐ EZ-A011	Boeing 757-22K	28336 / 725		0096	0996	2 RR RB211-535E4	110223	C16Y173	LR-DJ	
☐ EZ-A012	Boeing 757-22K	28337 / 726		0096	0996	2 RR RB211-535E4	110223	C16Y173	LR-DK	
☐ EZ-F421	Ilyushin 76TD	10234498978	CCCP-76421	1292	0293	4 SO D-30KP	190000	Freighter		
☐ EZ-F422	Ilyushin 76TD	1023410348	CCCP-76830	0592	0693	4 SO D-30KP	190000	Freighter		
☐ EZ-F423	Ilyushin 76TD	1033418608		0093	0695	4 SO D-30KP	190000	Freighter		
☐ EZ-F424	Ilyushin 76TD	1033418592		1293	0394	4 SO D-30KP	190000	Freighter		
☐ EZ-F425	Ilyushin 76TD	1023410336	CCCP-76816	0392	0394	4 SO D-30KP	190000	Freighter		
☐ EZ-F426	Ilyushin 76TD	1033418609		0093	0695	4 SO D-30KP	190000	Freighter		
☐ EZ-F427	Ilyushin 76TD	1033418620		1193	0597	4 SO D-30KP	190000	Freighter		
☐ EZ-F428	Ilyushin 76TD	1043418624		0094	0695	4 SO D-30KP	190000	Freighter		

TURKMENISTAN/KHAZAR Aircompany = KHR (Member of Turkmenistan Airlines Concern) Turkmenbashi

Airport, 745007 Turkmenbashi, Turkmenistan ☎ (43222) 74 087 Tx: n/a Fax: n/a SITA: n/a
F: n/a ✈✈✈ n/a Head: Alexander Zakharenko ICAO: KHAZAR Net: n/a

☐ EZ-02547	PZL Mielec (Antonov) An-2	1G121-31	CCCP-02547	0071		1 SH ASh-62IR	5250	Freighter		
☐ EZ-02716	PZL Mielec (Antonov) An-2	1G124-22	CCCP-02716	0071		1 SH ASh-62IR	5250	Freighter		
☐ EZ-07390	PZL Mielec (Antonov) An-2	1G150-25	CCCP-07390	0073		1 SH ASh-62IR	5250	Freighter		
☐ EZ-07464	PZL Mielec (Antonov) An-2	1G151-39	CCCP-07464	0073		1 SH ASh-62IR	5250	Y12		
☐ EZ-07469	PZL Mielec (Antonov) An-2	1G151-44	CCCP-07469	0073		1 SH ASh-62IR	5250	Y12		
☐ EZ-07562	PZL Mielec (Antonov) An-2	1G156-02	CCCP-07562	0074		1 SH ASh-62IR	5250	Freighter		
☐ EZ-07771	PZL Mielec (Antonov) An-2	1G161-46	CCCP-07771	0075		1 SH ASh-62IR	5250	Freighter		
☐ EZ-07779	PZL Mielec (Antonov) An-2	1G161-54	CCCP-07779	0075		1 SH ASh-62IR	5250	Freighter		
☐ EZ-09684	PZL Mielec (Antonov) An-2	1G76-18	CCCP-09684	0066		1 SH ASh-62IR	5250	Y12		
☐ EZ-33368	PZL Mielec (Antonov) An-2	1G226-27	CCCP-33368	0086		1 SH ASh-62IR	5250	Freighter		
☐ EZ-35054	PZL Mielec (Antonov) An-2	1G110-20	CCCP-35054	0069		1 SH ASh-62IR	5250	Freighter		
☐ EZ-35404	Antonov An-2	113247318	CCCP-35404	0060		1 SH ASh-62IR	5250	Freighter		
☐ EZ-35448	Antonov An-2	113547320	CCCP-35448	0060		1 SH ASh-62IR	5250	Freighter		
☐ EZ-41254	PZL Mielec (Antonov) An-2	1G185-03	CCCP-41254	0079		1 SH ASh-62IR	5250	Freighter		
☐ EZ-62564	PZL Mielec (Antonov) An-2	1G176-33	CCCP-62564	0077		1 SH ASh-62IR	5250	Y12		
☐ EZ-62565	PZL Mielec (Antonov) An-2	1G176-34	CCCP-62565	0077		1 SH ASh-62IR	5250	Freighter		
☐ EZ-62608	PZL Mielec (Antonov) An-2	1G177-49	CCCP-62608	0077		1 SH ASh-62IR	5250	Y12		
☐ EZ-70200	PZL Mielec (Antonov) An-2	1G138-18	CCCP-70200	0072		1 SH ASh-62IR	5250	Freighter		
☐ EZ-84684	PZL Mielec (Antonov) An-2	1G192-02	CCCP-84684	0080		1 SH ASh-62IR	5250	Freighter		
☐ EZ-46284	Antonov 24B	77303706	CCCP-46284	1067		2 IV AI-24-II	21000	Y48		
☐ EZ-46314	Antonov 24B	97305310	CCCP-46314	0669		2 IV AI-24T	21000	Y48		
☐ EZ-46433	Antonov 24B	87304303	CCCP-46433	0468		2 IV AI-24-II	21000	Y48		
☐ EZ-46598	Antonov 24B	97305108	CCCP-46598	0369		2 IV AI-24T	21000	Y48		
☐ EZ-47806	Antonov 24RV	17306908	CCCP-47806	0471		2 IV AI-24T	21800	Y52		
☐ EZ-26055	Antonov 26	11001	CCCP-26055	0381		2 IV AI-24VT	24000	Freighter		
☐ EZ-26512	Antonov 26	6809	CCCP-26512	0778		2 IV AI-24VT	24000	Freighter		
☐ EZ-26524	Antonov 26	7105	CCCP-26524	0978		2 IV AI-24VT	24000	Freighter		
☐ EZ-26527	Antonov 26	7209	CCCP-26527	1078		2 IV AI-24VT	24000	Freighter		
☐ EZ-26633	Antonov 26	5910	CCCP-26633	1277		2 IV AI-24VT	24000	Freighter		

TURKMENISTAN/LEBAP Aircompany = LEB (Member of Turkmenistan Airlines Concern) Chardzhou

Airport, 746106 Chardzhou, Turkmenistan ☎ (422) 21 032 Tx: n/a Fax: (422) 21 636 SITA: n/a
F: n/a ✈✈✈ n/a Head: Beymurad Saparov ICAO: LEBAP Net: n/a

☐ EZ-20299	PZL Swidnik (Mil) Mi-2	537434121	CCCP-20299	0081		2 IS GTD-350-4	3550	Y6		
☐ EZ-20300	PZL Swidnik (Mil) Mi-2	537435121	CCCP-20300	0081		2 IS GTD-350-4	3550	Y6		
☐ EZ-20303	PZL Swidnik (Mil) Mi-2	547438121	CCCP-20303	0081		2 IS GTD-350-4	3550	Y6		
☐ EZ-20790	PZL Swidnik (Mil) Mi-2	537902102	CCCP-20790	0082		2 IS GTD-350-4	3550	Y6		
☐ EZ-20791	PZL Swidnik (Mil) Mi-2	537903102	CCCP-20791	0082		2 IS GTD-350-4	3550	Y6		
☐ EZ-20793	PZL Swidnik (Mil) Mi-2	537905102	CCCP-20793	0082		2 IS GTD-350-4	3550	Y6		
☐ EZ-20853	PZL Swidnik (Mil) Mi-2	548134043	CCCP-20853	0083		2 IS GTD-350-4	3550	Y6		
☐ EZ-20854	PZL Swidnik (Mil) Mi-2	548135043	CCCP-20854	0083		2 IS GTD-350-4	3550	Y6		
☐ EZ-20855	PZL Swidnik (Mil) Mi-2	548136043	CCCP-20855	0083		2 IS GTD-350-4	3550	Y6		
☐ EZ-20890	PZL Swidnik (Mil) Mi-2	538329093	CCCP-20890	0083		2 IS GTD-350-4	3550	Y6		
☐ EZ-20891	PZL Swidnik (Mil) Mi-2	538330093	CCCP-20891	0083		2 IS GTD-350-4	3550	Y6		
☐ EZ-02576	PZL Mielec (Antonov) An-2	1G120-36	CCCP-02576	0071		1 SH ASh-62IR	5250	Y12		
☐ EZ-07437	PZL Mielec (Antonov) An-2	1G151-12	CCCP-07437	0073		1 SH ASh-62IR	5250	Y12		
☐ EZ-07477	PZL Mielec (Antonov) An-2	1G151-52	CCCP-07477	0073		1 SH ASh-62IR	5250	Y12		
☐ EZ-07607	PZL Mielec (Antonov) An-2	1G156-47	CCCP-07607	0074		1 SH ASh-62IR	5250	Frtr / Sprayer		
☐ EZ-07630	PZL Mielec (Antonov) An-2	1G156-70	CCCP-07630	0074		1 SH ASh-62IR	5250	Frtr / Sprayer		
☐ EZ-16088	PZL Mielec (Antonov) An-2	1G164-42	CCCP-16088	0075		1 SH ASh-62IR	5250	Frtr / Sprayer		
☐ EZ-17784	PZL Mielec (Antonov) An-2	1G203-45	CCCP-17784	0083		1 SH ASh-62IR	5250	Frtr / Sprayer		
☐ EZ-17785	PZL Mielec (Antonov) An-2	1G203-46	CCCP-17785	0083		1 SH ASh-62IR	5250	Frtr / Sprayer		
☐ EZ-17804	PZL Mielec (Antonov) An-2	1G204-05	CCCP-17804	0083		1 SH ASh-62IR	5250	Frtr / Sprayer		
☐ EZ-31464	PZL Mielec (Antonov) An-2	1G198-29	CCCP-31464	0082		1 SH ASh-62IR	5250	Frtr / Sprayer		
☐ EZ-35115	PZL Mielec (Antonov) An-2	1G111-41	CCCP-35115	0069		1 SH ASh-62IR	5250	Frtr / Sprayer		
☐ EZ-40301	PZL Mielec (Antonov) An-2	1G221-31	CCCP-40301	0086		1 SH ASh-62IR	5250	Frtr / Sprayer		
☐ EZ-40372	PZL Mielec (Antonov) An-2	1G222-51	CCCP-40372	0086		1 SH ASh-62IR	5250	Frtr / Sprayer		
☐ EZ-40899	PZL Mielec (Antonov) An-2	1G215-36	CCCP-40899	0085		1 SH ASh-62IR	5250	Frtr / Sprayer		
☐ EZ-40961	PZL Mielec (Antonov) An-2	1G217-01	CCCP-40961	0085		1 SH ASh-62IR	5250	Frtr / Sprayer		
☐ EZ-44606	PZL Mielec (Antonov) An-2	1G86-23	CCCP-44606	0065		1 SH ASh-62IR	5250	Frtr / Sprayer		

142 registration type of aircraft cn/fn ex/ex* mfd del powered by mtow kg configuration selcal name/fln/specialitites/remarks

☐ EZ-54793	PZL Mielec (Antonov) An-2	*1G183-57*	*CCCP-54793*	*0079*		*1 SH ASh-62IR*	*5250*	*Frtr / Sprayer*		
☐ EZ-54794	PZL Mielec (Antonov) An-2	*1G183-58*	*CCCP-54794*	*0079*		*1 SH ASh-62IR*	*5250*	*Frtr / Sprayer*		
☐ EZ-54795	PZL Mielec (Antonov) An-2	*1G183-59*	*CCCP-54795*	*0079*		*1 SH ASh-62IR*	*5250*	*Frtr / Sprayer*		
☐ EZ-54801	PZL Mielec (Antonov) An-2	*1G184-08*	*CCCP-54801*	*0079*		*1 SH ASh-62IR*	*5250*	*Frtr / Sprayer*		
☐ EZ-54802	PZL Mielec (Antonov) An-2	*1G184-09*	*CCCP-54802*	*0079*		*1 SH ASh-62IR*	*5250*	*Frtr / Sprayer*		
☐ EZ-56406	PZL Mielec (Antonov) An-2	*1G180-36*	*CCCP-56406*	*0078*		*1 SH ASh-62IR*	*5250*	*Frtr / Sprayer*		
☐ EZ-56418	PZL Mielec (Antonov) An-2	*1G181-02*	*CCCP-56418*	*0078*		*1 SH ASh-62IR*	*5250*	*Frtr / Sprayer*		
☐ EZ-62513	PZL Mielec (Antonov) An-2	*1G175-36*	*CCCP-62513*	*0077*		*1 SH ASh-62IR*	*5250*	*Frtr / Sprayer*		
☐ EZ-62543	PZL Mielec (Antonov) An-2	*1G176-06*	*CCCP-62543*	*0077*		*1 SH ASh-62IR*	*5250*	*Frtr / Sprayer*		
☐ EZ-68144	PZL Mielec (Antonov) An-2	*1G196-37*	*CCCP-68144*	*0081*		*1 SH ASh-62IR*	*5250*	*Frtr / Sprayer*		
☐ EZ-70608	PZL Mielec (Antonov) An-2	*1G128-17*	*CCCP-70608*	*0071*		*1 SH ASh-62IR*	*5250*	*Frtr / Sprayer*		
☐ EZ-84528	PZL Mielec (Antonov) An-2	*1G188-53*	*CCCP-84528*	*0080*		*1 SH ASh-62IR*	*5250*	*Frtr / Sprayer*		
☐ EZ-84686	PZL Mielec (Antonov) An-2	*1G192-04*	*CCCP-84686*	*0080*		*1 SH ASh-62IR*	*5250*	*Frtr / Sprayer*		
☐ EZ-84687	PZL Mielec (Antonov) An-2	*1G192-05*	*CCCP-84687*	*0080*		*1 SH ASh-62IR*	*5250*	*Frtr / Sprayer*		
☐ EZ-22699	Mil Mi-8	*8158*	*CCCP-22699*	*0080*		*2 IS TV2-117A*	*12000*	*Freighter*		
☐ EZ-22763	Mil Mi-8	*9831150*	*CCCP-22763*	*0083*		*2 IS TV2-117A*	*12000*	*Freighter*		
☐ EZ-24615	Mil Mi-8	*8243*	*CCCP-24615*	*0081*		*2 IS TV2-117A*	*12000*	*Freighter*		
☐ EZ-24619	Mil Mi-8	*8247*	*CCCP-24619*	*0081*		*2 IS TV2-117A*	*12000*	*Freighter*		
☐ EZ-24688	Mil Mi-8	*9815748*	*CCCP-24688*	*0081*		*2 IS TV2-117A*	*12000*	*Freighter*		
☐ EZ-24697	Mil Mi-8	*98103221*	*CCCP-24697*	*0081*		*2 IS TV2-117A*	*12000*	*Freighter*		
☐ EZ-24701	Mil Mi-8	*98103235*	*CCCP-24701*	*0081*		*2 IS TV2-117A*	*12000*	*Freighter*		
☐ EZ-25347	Mil Mi-8	*98206680*	*CCCP-25347*	*0082*		*2 IS TV2-117A*	*12000*	*Freighter*		
☐ EZ-25348	Mil Mi-8	*98206685*	*CCCP-25348*	*0082*		*2 IS TV2-117A*	*12000*	*Freighter*		
☐ EZ-25368	Mil Mi-8	*98206881*	*CCCP-25368*	*0082*		*2 IS TV2-117A*	*12000*	*Freighter*		
☐ EZ-25395	Mil Mi-8	*98208235*	*CCCP-25395*	*0082*		*2 IS TV2-117A*	*12000*	*Freighter*		
☐ EZ-L481	Mil Mi-8MTV-1	*96143*		*0093*		*2 IS TV3-117VM*	*13000*	*Freighter*		
☐ EZ-L482	Mil Mi-8MTV-1	*96144*		*0093*		*2 IS TV3-117VM*	*13000*	*Freighter*		
☐ EZ-L483	Mil Mi-8MTV-1	*96145*		*0093*		*2 IS TV3-117VM*	*13000*	*Freighter*		
☐ EZ-87338	Yakovlev 40	*9510739*	*CCCP-87338*	*0175*		*3 IV AI-25*	*16100*	*Y36*		
☐ EZ-87387	Yakovlev 40	*9411832*	*CCCP-87387*	*0274*		*3 IV AI-25*	*16100*	*Y36*		
☐ EZ-87409	Yakovlev 40	*9420134*	*CCCP-87409*	*0574*		*3 IV AI-25*	*16100*	*Y36*		
☐ EZ-87427	Yakovlev 40	*9420335*	*CCCP-87427*	*0674*		*3 IV AI-25*	*16100*	*Y36*		
☐ EZ-87531	Yakovlev 40	*9521341*	*CCCP-87531*	*0775*		*3 IV AI-25*	*16100*	*Y36*		
☐ EZ-87548	Yakovlev 40	*9531342*	*CCCP-87548*	*0875*		*3 IV AI-25*	*16100*	*Y36*		
☐ EZ-87668	Yakovlev 40	*9021460*	*CCCP-87668*	*0680*		*3 IV AI-25*	*16100*	*VIP 16 Pax*		
☐ EZ-88169	Yakovlev 40	*9610747*	*CCCP-88169*	*0476*		*3 IV AI-25*	*16100*	*Y36*		
☐ EZ-88178	Yakovlev 40	*9631847*	*CCCP-88178*	*0676*		*3 IV AI-25*	*16100*	*Y36*		
☐ EZ-88230	Yakovlev 40	*9641950*	*CCCP-88230*	*1276*		*3 IV AI-25*	*16100*	*Y36*		

E3 = ERITREA (State of Eritrea) (Dawlat al Eritrea)

Capital: Asmara Official Language: Arabic, Tigrinya, Gurage Population: 4,0 million Square Km: 117600 Dialling code: +291 Year established: 1993 Acting political head: Issaias Afwerki (President)

ASMARA AIR SERVICE (Air Service of The Municipality of Asmara) — Asmara

PO Box 1590, Asmara, Eritrea ☎ (1) 12 10 37 Tx: none Fax: (1) 12 10 37 SITA: n/a
F: 1994 ⁂ n/a Head: n/a Net: n/a

☐ E3-AAA	Dornier DO 28D-2 Skyservant	*4175*	*E3-IAAS*	*0073*	*0494*	*2 LY IGSO-540-A1E*	*3842*	*10 Pax*		Asmara
☐ E3-AAB	Dornier DO 28D-2 Skyservant	*4192*	*E3-IADE*	*0073*	*0594*	*2 LY IGSO-540-A1E*	*3842*	*10 Pax*		Dekemhare / *longrange-tanks*
☐ E3-AAD	Dornier DO 28D-2 Skyservant	*4191*	*E3-IAME*	*0073*	*0594*	*2 LY IGSO-540-A1E*	*3842*	*10 Pax*		Mendefera / *longrange-tanks*
☐ E3-AAF	Dornier DO 28D-2 Skyservant	*4083*	*E3-IAAB*	*0071*	*0494*	*2 LY IGSO-540-A1E*	*3842*	*10 Pax*		Asab
☐ E3-AAG	Dornier DO 28D-2 Skyservant	*4163*	*58+88*	*0073*		*2 LY IGSO-540-A1E*	*3842*	*10 Pax*		*std Germany*

BIK SURVEYS (Braeumer Ingenier Korporation dba / Sister company of BIK, Germany) — Asmara

PO Box 1590, Asmara, Eritrea ☎ (1) 12 10 37 Tx: none Fax: (1) 12 10 37 SITA: n/a
F: 1994 ⁂ 15 Head: Burkhard Braeumer Net: n/a

☐ E3-AAC	Dornier DO 28D-2 Skyservant	*4179*	*E3-IAMA*	*0073*	*0394*	*2 LY IGSO-540-A1E*	*3842*	*Photo/Survey*		Massawa
☐ E3-AAE	Dornier DO 28D-2 Skyservant	*4180*	*E3-IANA*	*0073*	*0394*	*2 LY IGSO-540-A1E*	*3842*	*Photo/Survey*		Nacfa

RED SEA AIR = 7R / ERT (Eritrean Airlines dba) — Asmara

PO Box 222, Asmara, Eritrea ☎ (1) 12 55 00 Tx: none Fax: (1) 12 54 65 SITA: n/a
F: 1992 ⁂ n/a Head: Abraha Ghirmazion ICAO: ERITREAN Net: n/a

☐ YR-JBA	BAe (BAC) One-Eleven 528FL	*234*	*G-BJRT*	*0071*	*1298*	*2 RR Spey 514-14DW*	*44000*	*C20Y55*		*lsf MDJ*

F = FRANCE (French Republic) (République Française)

(incl. "Overseas Departments" Departements d'Outre Mer: Guadeloupe + Saint Barthelemy, Guyane, Martinique, Réunion & French "Territorial Units" Collectivités territoriales: Mayotte, Saint-Pierre + Miquelon; & Overseas Territories (Territoires d Outre-Mer): New Caledonia (Nouvelle Calédonie), Polynesia (Polynésie)
Capital: Paris Official Language: French Population: 58,0 million Square Km: 551700 Dialling code: +33 Year established: 843 Acting political head: Jacques Chirac (President)

Polynesia (Polynésie)
Capital: Papeete Official Language: French Population: 0,3 million Square Km: 3521 Dialling code: +689 Acting political head: Gaston Flosse (Prime Minister)
Caledonia (Nouvelle Calédonie)
Capital: Nouméa Official Language: French Population: 0,2 million Square Km: 19058 Dialling code: +687 Acting political head: Didier Cultiaux (High Commissioner)
Guadeloupe & Saint-Barthelemy
Capital: Basse Terre Official Language: French Population: 0,5 million Square Km: 1780 Dialling code: +590 Acting political head: Jacques Chirac (President)
Guyane
Capital: Cayenne Official Language: French Population: 0,2 million Square Km: 91000 Dialling code: +594 Acting political head: Jacques Chirac (President)
Martinique
Capital: Fort-de-France Official Language: French Population: 0,4 million Square Km: 1102 Dialling code: +596 Acting political head: Jacques Chirac (President)
Mayotte
Capital: Dzaoudzi Official Language: French Population: 0,2 million Square Km: 374 Dialling code: +262 Acting political head: Jacques Chirac (President)
Réunion
Capital: Saint-Denis Official Language: French Population: 0,7 million Square Km: 2512 Dialling code: +262 Acting political head: Jacques Chirac (President)
Saint-Pierre & Miquelon
Capital: Saint-Pierre Official Language: French Population: 0,2 million Square Km: 242 Dialling code: +508 Acting political head: Jacques Chirac (President)
Wallis + Futuna
Capital: Matâ-Utu Official Language: French Population: 0,1 million Square Km: 274 Dialling code: +681 Acting political head: Claude Pierret (Supreme Administrator)

Government / Corporate / Executive / VIP Aircraft

ETOM = Escadron de Transport d'Outre-mer (Provided by COTAM - Commandement du Transport Aérien Militaire).

☐ F-RADA	Airbus Industrie A310-304	*421*	*F-ODVD*	*0387*	*1193*	*2 GE CF6-80C2A2*	*157000*	*VIP / miltrans*	*FK-MR*	*Armée de l'Air / CoTAM ET3/60 CDG*
☐ F-RADB	Airbus Industrie A310-304	*422*	*F-ODVE*	*0387*	*1193*	*2 GE CF6-80C2A2*	*157000*	*VIP / miltrans*	*FK-MS*	*Armée de l'Air / CoTAM ET3/60 CDG*
☐ F-RAFF	Boeing (Douglas) DC-8-72F (CF)	*46130 / 542*	*OH-LFY*	*0069*	*0181*	*4 CFMI CFM56-2C*	*152000*	*F8Y154 / Frtr*	*BG-AK*	*A.de l'Air/CoTAM ET3/60CDG/cvtd-62F(CF)*
☐ F-RAFG	Boeing (Douglas) DC-8-72F (CF)	*46013 / 427*	*OH-LFT*	*0069*	*1181*	*4 CFMI CFM56-2C*	*152000*	*F8Y154 / Frtr*	*BG-AL*	*A.de l'Air/CoTAM ET3/60CDG/cvtd-62F(CF)*
☐ F-RAFI	Dassault Falcon 50	*5*	*F-WZHB**	*0080*		*3 GA TFE731-3-1C*	*17600*	*VIP*	*DJ-GL*	Rambouillet / *A.del'Air / GLAM Villa.*
☐ F-RAFJ	Dassault Falcon 50	*78*	*F-GEOY*	*0081*		*3 GA TFE731-3-1C*	*17600*	*VIP*	*DJ-GM*	*Armée de l'Air / GLAM Villacoublay*
☐ F-RAFK	Dassault Falcon 50	*27*	*F-WGTG**	*0080*	*0090*	*3 GA TFE731-3-1C*	*18500*	*VIP*	*JL-DE*	*Armée de l'Air / GLAM Villacoublay*
☐ F-RAFL	Dassault Falcon 50	*34*	*F-WEFS**	*0081*	*0090*	*3 GA TFE731-3-1C*	*18500*	*VIP*	*JL-CQ*	*Armée de l'Air / GLAM Villacoublay*
☐ F-RAFM	Dassault Falcon 20C	*238*	*F-WRQP**	*0071*		*2 GE CF700-2C*	*12400*	*VIP*		*Armée de l'Air / GLAM Villacoublay*
☐ F-RAFN	Dassault Falcon 20C	*93*	*F-RBQA*	*0067*		*2 GE CF700-2C*	*12400*	*VIP*		*Armée de l'Air / GLAM Villacoublay*
☐ F-RAFP	Dassault Falcon 900	*2*	*F-GFJC*	*0086*		*3 GA TFE731-5A-1C2*	*20638*	*VIP*		*Armée de l'Air / GLAM Villacoublay*
☐ F-RAFQ	Dassault Falcon 900	*4*	*F-WWFA**	*0086*		*3 GA TFE731-5A-1C2*	*20638*	*VIP*	*JK-FL*	*Armée de l'Air / GLAM Villacoublay*
☐ F-RAFR	Eurocopter (Aerosp.) SA330BA Puma	*1257*	*F-ZKBA*	*0074*		*2 TU Turmo IIIC4*	*6400*	*VIP*		Carrousel / *Armée de l'Air/GLAM 1/60*
☐ F-RAFY	Eurocopter (Aerosp.) AS332L Super Puma	*2233*		*0087*		*2 TU Makila 1A*	*8600*	*VIP*		*Armée de l'Air / GLAM 1/60 Villa.*
☐ F-WWAI	Airbus Industrie A340-311	*001*		*0091*		*4 CFMI CFM56-5C2*	*257000*	*Testbed*	*AJ-DM*	*Airbus Industrie/1st prototype*
☐ F-WWEY	ATR 72-201	*098*		*0088*	*1088*	*2 PWC PW124B*	*21500*	*Testbed*		*ATR 1st prototype*
☐ F-WWFT	Airbus Industrie A320-131	*001*	*F-WWAI**	*0087*		*2 IAE V2500-A1*	*68000*	*Testbed / Demo*		*cvtd -111/Airbus Ind./1st prototype*
☐ F-WWKA	Airbus Industrie A330-202	*181*		*0897*		*2 GE CF6-80E1A2*	*230000*	*Testbed*		*Airbus Industrie / Prototype*
☐ 167	Dassault Falcon 20C	*167*	*F-RAFL*	*0068*		*2 GE CF700-2C*	*12400*	*VIP*		*Armée de l'Air / GLAM Villacoublay*
☐ 268	Dassault Falcon 20C	*268*	*F-RAFK*	*0072*		*2 GE CF700-2C*	*12400*	*VIP*		*Armée de l'Air / GLAM Villacoublay*

AEROLYON = 4Q / AEY — Lyon-Satolas

BP 138, F-69125 Lyon-Satolas, France ☎ 472 22 73 00 Tx: none Fax: 472 22 73 10 SITA: LYSOO4Q
F: 1996 ⁂ 100 Head: Jean-Louis Chicon ICAO: AEROLYON Net: n/a

☐ F-BTDD	Boeing (Douglas) DC-10-30	*46963 / 244*		*0077*	*0197*	*3 GE CF6-50C2*	*263084*	*Y356*		

AERO NORD 186532 — Caen-Carpiquet

Aéroport de Caen-Carpiquet, F-14650 Carpiquet, France ☎ 231 26 62 06 Tx: none Fax: 231 26 62 06 SITA: n/a
F: 1995 ⁂ n/a Head: Bernard Tampon Net: n/a

☐ F-GFVT	Dornier DO 27Q-5	*2062*	*F-BKVT*	*0060*		*2 LY GO-480-B1A6*	*1850*	*5 Pax*		Sentimental Journey

143 registration type of aircraft *cn/fn* *ex/ex** *mfd* *del* *powered by* *mtow kg* *configuration* *selcal* *name/fln/specialitites/remarks*

AEROPE 3S AVIATION = OPE (formerly 3S Aviation) **Pontoise-Cormeilles**

Aérodrome de Pontoise-Cormeilles, F-95650 Boissy l'Aillerie, France ☎ (1) 30 32 60 75 Tx: none Fax: (1) 30 32 18 60 SITA: n/a
F: 1988 ⁂ 17 Head: Mme. Sedillot ICAO: PONTOISAIR Net: n/a

☐ F-GCFZ	Agusta-Bell 206B JetRanger III	8578		0079	0097	1 AN 250-C20B	1451	4 Pax		lsf Finloc
☐ F-GFHQ	Beech King Air B90	LJ-347	N777SB	0068		2 PWC PT6A-20	4377	9 Pax		lsf Soder Bail

AERO SERVICES EXECUTIVE, Sarl = W4 / BES (formerly Wallisair) **Paris-Le Bourget**

Hangar H5, Zone Aviation d'Affaires, F-93350 Le Bourget Aéroport, France ☎ (1) 48 35 87 77 Tx: 234710 f Fax: (1) 48 35 87 76 SITA: n/a
F: 1985 ⁂ 30 Head: Philippe d'Aprile ICAO: BIRD EXPRESS Net: n/a

☐ F-GGPR	Beech King Air 200	BB-681	LN-AXA	0080		2 PWC PT6A-41	5670	7 or 10 Pax		lsf BNP Bail
☐ F-GFMD	Dassault Falcon 10	136	F-WZGS*	0081		2 GA TFE731-2-1C	8500	7 Pax		lsf CIP Transports
☐ F-GFPF	Dassault Falcon 10	68	N80MP	0075		2 GA TFE731-2-1C	8500	8 Pax		lsf BNP Bail
☐ F-GYSL	Dassault Falcon 20F-5	341	F-OHCJ*	0076		2 GA TFE731-5BR-2C	13200	9 Pax		lsf Berlys Aero / cvtd 20F
☐ F-GGCP	Dassault Falcon 50	9		0080		3 GA TFE731-3-1C	17600	9 Pax	EF-LM	lsf Loxxia

AERO SOTRAVIA (Subsidiary of Sotravia, SA – Société de Travail Aérien de l'Ile de France) **Nangis les Loges**

Aérodrome de Nangis les Loges, CD 56, F-77370 Clos-Fontaine, France ☎ (1) 64 60 92 85 Tx: 690981 f aerodsa Fax: (1) 64 60 92 87 SITA: n/a
F: 1961 ⁂ 7 Head: Jean Pelletier Net: n/a Aircraft below MTOW 1361 kg: Cessna 172 & Socata Rallyes.

☐ F-GCPO	Piper PA-34-200T Seneca II	34-8070358	N8266V	0080		2 CO TSIO-360-EB1	2073			
☐ F-GDQF	Piper PA-34-200T Seneca II	34-7770337	HB-LIY	0077		2 CO TSIO-360-EB1	2073			
☐ F-GDHD	Britten-Norman BN-2A-9 Islander	591	9Q-CMJ	0077		2 LY O-540-E4C5	2858			
☐ F-BMSK	Dornier DO 28A-1	3055	D-IBOR	0065		2 LY O-540-A1D	2450			
☐ F-GMLJ	Cessna 414	414-0635	I-CCEE	0075		2 CO TSIO-520-J	2880			

AERO 34 (Compagnie d'Hélicoptères Aero 34 dba) **Montpellier**

Aéroport de Montpellier-Méditerranée, F-34134 Mauguio Cédex, France ☎ 467 65 18 55 Tx: none Fax: 467 65 84 02 SITA: n/a
F: 1981 ⁂ n/a Head: Arnold Félix Net: n/a

☐ F-GHTU	Eurocopter (Aerosp.) SE3130 Alouette II	1429	ALAT	0060		1 TU Artouste IIC6	1500			

AERO VISION = AOV **Toulouse-Blagnac**

31 Allée des Vignes, F-31770 Colomiers, France ☎ 561 30 40 58 Tx: n/a Fax: 561 30 41 77 SITA: n/a
F: 1994 ⁂ 6 Head: Patrick Piallat ICAO: AEROVISION Net: n/a

☐ F-BUQP	Aerospatiale SN601 Corvette	4	F-WUQP*	0074		2 PWC JT15D-4	7000	12 Pax		lsf pvt
☐ F-GPLA	Aerospatiale SN601 Corvette	28	F-BTTL	0076		2 PWC JT15D-4	7000	12 Pax		

AIGLE AZUR = AAF (formerly Lucas Aigle Azur) **Pontoise-Cormeilles-en-Vexin**

Aéroport de Paris-Pontoise, BP 24, F-95301 Cergy Pontoise Cédex, France ☎ (1) 34 41 70 50 Tx: 605322 f aiglazu Fax: (1) 30 32 28 28 SITA: n/a
F: 1970 ⁂ 40 Head: Pierre Guichet ICAO: AIGLE AZUR Net: n/a

☐ F-GMJD	Boeing 737-2K5 (A)	22599 / 814	D-AHLG	0081	0393	2 PW JT8D-17	58105	Y129	EM-AD	lsf BNP Bail SA / sub-lsf/opf CRL

AIRAILES = LSF (formerly Stylair) **Colmar-Houssen**

Aéroport Colmar-Houssen, 41 Rte de Strasbourg, F-68000 Colmar, France ☎ 389 47 94 44 Tx: none Fax: 389 47 99 14 SITA: n/a
F: 1991 ⁂ 6 Head: Brigitte Stoffel ICAO: EOLE Net: n/a

☐ F-GCGA	Beech King Air C90	LJ-894		0080		2 PWC PT6A-21	4377			lsf Fédébail
☐ F-GNEG	Beech King Air B200	BB-1377	HB-GIR	0090		2 PWC PT6A-42	5670			lsf ING Lease France SA

AIR ANGOULEME = AGL **Angoulème-Brie-Champniers**

Aéroport d'Angouleme, F-16430 Champniers, France ☎ 545 69 81 92 Tx: none Fax: 545 69 92 27 SITA: n/a
F: 1976 ⁂ 3 Head: Jean Prayssinhes ICAO: AIR ANGOULEME Net: n/a Aircraft below MTOW 1361kg: Agusta-Bell 47G-2 & Schweizer 269C (300C)

☐ F-GCMP	Agusta-Bell 206B JetRanger III	8592		0080		1 AN 250-C20B	1450	4 Pax		lsf pvt
☐ F-GIJQ	Eurocopter (Aerosp.) AS350B Ecureuil	1647	EI-BYT	0079		1 TU Arriel 1B	1950	5 Pax		
☐ F-GJAB	Eurocopter (Aerosp.) AS350B Ecureuil	1174	N3599U	0079		1 TU Arriel 1B	1950	5 Pax		

AIR ARCHIPELS = RHL (Sister company of Air Tahiti) **Papeete-Faaa**

BP 6019, F-98702 Faaa Aéroport, (Tahiti), Polynésie Française ☎ 86 42 62 Tx: none Fax: 86 42 69 SITA: n/a
F: 1996 ⁂ 8 Head: Marel Galenon ICAO: ARCHIPELS Net: n/a

☐ F-ODUJ	Cessna 441 Conquest II	441-0264	G-EVNS	0082		2 GA TPE331-10-403S	4468			lsf pvt
☐ F-OHJK	Beech King Air B200	BB-1544	N1094S	0096	0497	2 PWC PT6A-42	5670			lsf Airinvest

AIR ATLANTIQUE = KI / APB **La Rochelle-Laleu & Cherbourg-Maupertus**

Aéroport de La Rochelle-Laleu, F-17043 La Rochelle, France ☎ 546 00 37 70 Tx: none Fax: 546 67 23 29 SITA: n/a
F: 1963 ⁂ n/a Head: Jacques Mosse ICAO: CHARENTE Net: n/a

☐ F-GGLK	ATR 42-300	022	OH-LTB	0086	0398	2 PWC PW120	16900	Y46		lsf / opf LIB
☐ F-GIIA	ATR 42-300	018	TR-LEW	0086	0493	2 PWC PW120	16700	Y50		lsf ATR
☐ F-GIRC	ATR 42-300	033	F-WIAF	0086	0897	2 PWC PW120	16900	Y46		lsf / opf LIB
☐ F-GKND	ATR 42-300	231		0091	0998	2 PWC PW120	16900	Y46		lsf / opf LIB

AIR AUSTRAL = UU / REU (Associated with Air France / formerly Air Réunion) **St. Denis-Gillot**

BP 611, F-97473 St. Denis Cédex, Réunion ☎ 93 10 10 Tx: 916236 re Fax: 29 28 95 SITA: RUNGVUU
F: 1975 ⁂ 140 Head: Gérard Etheve IATA: 760 ICAO: REUNION Net: n/a

☐ F-ODZJ	Boeing 737-53A	24877 / 1943	F-GHXN	0090	1290	2 CFMI CFM56-3C1	60554	Y120		lsf R. Garros Bail
☐ F-ODZY	Boeing 737-33A	27452 / 2679		0094	1294	2 CFMI CFM56-3C1	61235	Y133		lsf Mascareignes Aviation
☐ F-ODZZ	Boeing 737-39M	28898 / 2906	N1786B*	0797	0797	2 CFMI CFM56-3C1	61235	Y133		lsf Snc Austral Investissements

AIR BOR = BRI (Commercial divison of Air Bor Flying School) **Dijon-Longvic**

Aéroport de Dijon-Longvic, F-21600 Dijon, France ☎ 380 65 25 55 Tx: none Fax: 380 66 67 66 SITA: n/a
F: 1989 ⁂ 17 Head: Bernard Borella & Julie Perrod ICAO: AIR BOR Net: n/a

☐ F-GINJ	Beech Baron 58	TH-539	F-OANJ	0074		2 CO IO-520-C	2450	4 Pax		
☐ F-BXSK	Piper PA-31T Cheyenne II	31T-7620020		0076		2 PWC PT6A-28	4082	6 Pax		
☐ F-BTQP	Beech King Air 90 (65-90)	LJ-40	I-GNIS	0065		2 PWC PT6A-6	4218	8 Pax		lsf Air Bourgogne Service

AIR BOURGOGNE EUROPE = ABY **Chalon**

BP 376, F-71109 Chalon sur Saone, France ☎ 611 37 88 28 Tx: none Fax: 385 41 68 14 SITA: n/a
F: 1997 ⁂ n/a Head: Edmond Dombek ICAO: BOURGOGNE Net: n/a

☐ F-GIFC	Beech King Air B90	LJ-456	D-ILTY	0069	0097	2 PWC PT6A-20	4381			lsf Bail Equipement

AIR BRETAGNE **Noyal-Pontivy**

Parc Pompidou, F-56036 Vannes Cédex, France ☎ 297 47 20 47 Tx: none Fax: 297 47 03 82 SITA: n/a
F: 1996 ⁂ 11 Head: Jean-Marc Le Rouzic Net: n/a

☐ F-GHHV	Beech King Air A100	B-91	N9050V	0071	0098	2 PWC PT6A-28	5216			lsf Snc GIN Finances
☐ F-GXAB	Beech King Air A100	B-193	EC-CHD	0074	0098	2 PWC PT6A-28	5216			lsf Union Finloc

AIRBUS TRANSPORT INTERNATIONAL, Snc. = BGA (Subsidiary of G.I.E. Airbus Industrie) **Toulouse-Blagnac**

5 Av. Gabriel Clerc, F-31707 Blagnac Cédex, France ☎ 561 93 43 62 Tx: n/a Fax: 561 93 46 11 SITA: n/a
F: 1996 ⁂ 85 Head: Louis Germain ICAO: SUPER TRANSPORT Net: n/a
Subsidiary of Aribus Industrie conducting non-commercial cargo flights for the group, transporting aircraft parts to the final assembly sites. Beside this aircraft are also available/used for commercial cargo charter flights.

☐ F-GSTA	Airbus Ind.A300-608ST Beluga (A300-600ST)	655 / 1	F-WAST*	0095	1196	2 GE CF6-80C2A8	153000	Freighter	KR-JL	Super Transporter 1
☐ F-GSTB	Airbus Ind.A300-608ST Beluga (A300-600ST)	751 / 2	F-WSTB*	0096	1196	2 GE CF6-80C2A8	155000	Freighter	BJ-AR	Super Transporter 2
☐ F-GSTC	Airbus Ind.A300-608ST Beluga (A300-600ST)	765 / 3	F-WSTC*	0097	0597	2 GE CF6-80C2A8	155000	Freighter	LP-AE	Super Transporter 3 / lsf BBV Leasing
☐ F-GSTD	Airbus Ind.A300-608ST Beluga (A300-600ST)	776 / 4	F-WSTD*	0098	0698	2 GE CF6-80C2A8	155000	Freighter	AE-CQ	Super Transporter 4 / lsf BBV Leasing
☐ F-GSTF	Airbus Ind.A300-608ST Beluga (A300-600ST)	796 / 4				2 GE CF6-80C2A8	155000	Freighter		Super Transporter 5 / oo-delivery 0001

AIR CALEDONIE = TY / TPC (Société Calédonienne de Transports Aériens dba) **Noumea-Magenta**

BP 212, Aérodrome de Magenta, F-98800 Nouméa, Nouvelle Calédonie ☎ 25 03 00 Tx: none Fax: 25 48 69 SITA: NOUTYSB
F: 1955 ⁂ 210 Head: Olivier Razavet IATA: 190 ICAO: AIRCAL Net: http://www.air-caledonie.nc

☐ F-ODYB	Dornier 228-212	8191	D-CORK*	0090	0790	2 GA TPE331-5A-252D	6400	Y19		
☐ F-ODGN	ATR 42-320	097		0088	0688	2 PWC PW121	16700	Y46		lsf Caledonie Bail / cvtd -300
☐ F-ODYD	ATR 42-320	221		0090	1290	2 PWC PW121	16700	Y48		lsf Caledonie 2005 / cvtd -300
☐ F-ODYE	ATR 42-300	335	F-WWLW*	0092	0293	2 PWC PW120	16700	Y48		lsf Caledonie Investissements II
☐ F-OIAM	ATR 42-320	403	F-WWLD*	0094	1297	2 GE PW121	16700	Y48		lsf Sna Calaero

AIRCALIN – Air Calédonie International = SB / ACI **Noumea-La Tontouta**

8 Rue Fréderic-Surleau, BP 3736, F-98800 Nouméa, Nouvelle Calédonie ☎ 26 55 46 Tx: none Fax: 27 27 72 SITA: NOUDGSB
F: 1983 ⁂ 175 Head: Charles Lavoix IATA: 063 ICAO: AIRCALIN Net: n/a

☐ F-OCQZ	De Havilland DHC-6 Twin Otter 300	412		0074		2 PWC PT6A-27	5670	Y19		
☐ F-ODGX	Boeing 737-33A	24094 / 1729		0089	0689	2 CFMI CFM56-3B2	62822	CY127	FQ-BD	lsf Caledonie Investissement

144 registration type of aircraft cn/fn ex/ex* mfd del powered by mtow kg configuration selcal name/fln/specialitites/remarks

AIR CALYPSO = KLY

Pointe à Pitre-Raizet

Aéroport du Raizet, Zone Sud, F-97139 Abymes, Guadeloupe ☎ 89 27 69 Tx: none Fax: 93 73 14 SITA: n/a
F: 1997 ✈✈✈ n/a Head: Simon Hayot ICAO: LYPSO Net: n/a

registration	type of aircraft	cn/fn	ex/ex*	mfd	del	powered by	mtow kg	configuration	selcal	name/fln/specialitites/remarks
☐ F-OHQF	Shorts 360-300 (SD3-60)	SH3743	N824BE	0088	1097	2 PWC PT6A-67R	12292	Y36		lsf Lynrise Air Lease
☐ F-OHQG	Shorts 360-300 (SD3-60)	SH3721	N121PC	0087	1297	2 PWC PT6A-67R	12292	Y36		lsf Lynrise Air Lease
☐ F-OHQH	Shorts 360-300 (SD3-60)	SH3722	N722PC	0087	0198	2 PWC PT6A-67R	12292	Y36		lsf Lynrise Air Lease

AIR ENTREPRISE = AEN

Paris-Le Bourget

Bâtiment, Zone d'Aviation d'Affaires, F-93350 Le Bourget, France ☎ (1) 48 35 98 99 Tx: 236482 f Fax: (1) 48 35 93 18 SITA: LBGOOKD
F: 1969 ✈✈✈ 52 Head: Rene Micaud ICAO: ENTREPRISE Net: http://www.air-entreprise.com

registration	type of aircraft	cn/fn	ex/ex*	mfd	del	powered by	mtow kg	configuration	selcal	name/fln/specialitites/remarks
☐ F-GMCP	Piaggio P.180 Avanti	1022		0093	0893	2 PWC PT6A-66	5239	9 Pax		
☐ F-GNAE	Piaggio P.180 Avanti	1020		0093	0193	2 PWC PT6A-66	5239	9 Pax		
☐ F-GFDH	Aerospatiale SN601 Corvette	13	N601AN	0075	0098	2 PWC JT15D-4	7000	10 Pax		lsf Eurocopter France
☐ F-GILM	Aerospatiale SN601 Corvette	32	EC-DUF	0076		2 PWC JT15D-4	7000	9 Pax		lsf West Indies Finance Ltd
☐ F-GJAS	Aerospatiale SN601 Corvette	8	6V-AEA	0074	0098	2 PWC JT15D-4	7000	11 Pax		lsf Europeenne de Credit
☐ F-GKGA	Aerospatiale SN601 Corvette	11	F-WFPD	0075	0098	2 PWC JT15D-4	7000	10 Pax		
☐ F-GMCK	Dassault Falcon 2000	46	F-WWMN	0097	1297	2 CFE CFE738-1-1B	16238	9 Pax		lsf Ridgedale Ltd
☐ F-GMGA	Dassault Falcon 50	51	N52DQ	0081	0493	3 GA TFE731-3-1C	18500	10 Pax	AE-JK	

AIR FRANCE = AF / AFR (Member of Groupe Air France)

Paris-Orly & -Charles de Gaulle

45 rue de Paris, F-95747 Roissy-CDG, France ☎ (1) 41 56 78 00 Tx: 200666 f afpar Fax: (1) 41 56 70 29 SITA: n/a
F: 1933 ✈✈✈ 46400 Head: Jean-Cyril Spinetta IATA: 057 ICAO: AIRFRANS Net: http://www.airfrance.fr
Beside aircraft listed, additional are operated on a franchise or code-share agreement on behalf of AIR FRANCE (in full such colors & both titles) using AF flight numbers by:
AIR LITTORAL (Fokker 70/100), BRIT AIR (ATR42&72/CRJ100), CITYJET (BAe 146), GILL AIRWAYS (ATR42/Fokker 100), JERSEY EUROPEAN (BAe 146), L'AEROPOSTALE (B737-300), PROTEUS (DO328) & REGIONAL AIRLINES (EMB145 & Saab 2000). For details – see under each company.

registration	type of aircraft	cn/fn	ex/ex*	mfd	del	powered by	mtow kg	configuration	selcal	name/fln/specialitites/remarks
☐ F-BPUA	Fokker F27 Friendship 500 (F27 Mk500)	10369	PH-FMR*	0068	0968	2 RR Dart 532-7	19990	Mail		opf Admin. Postale / Poste cs
☐ F-BPUC	Fokker F27 Friendship 500 (F27 Mk500)	10373	PH-FMV*	0068	1068	2 RR Dart 532-7	19990	Mail		opf Admin. Postale / Poste cs
☐ F-BPUD	Fokker F27 Friendship 500 (F27 Mk500)	10374	PH-FMW*	0068	1068	2 RR Dart 532-7	19990	Mail		opf Admin. Postale / Poste cs
☐ F-BPUE	Fokker F27 Friendship 500 (F27 Mk500)	10377	PH-FMZ*	0068	1168	2 RR Dart 532-7	19990	Mail		opf Admin. Postale / Poste cs
☐ F-BPUF	Fokker F27 Friendship 500 (F27 Mk500)	10378	PH-FNA*	0068	1168	2 RR Dart 532-7	19990	Mail		opf Admin. Postale / Poste cs
☐ F-BPUG	Fokker F27 Friendship 500 (F27 Mk500)	10379	PH-FNB*	0068	1268	2 RR Dart 532-7	19990	Mail		opf Admin. Postale / Poste cs
☐ F-BPUH	Fokker F27 Friendship 500 (F27 Mk500)	10382	PH-FNE*	0069	0169	2 RR Dart 532-7	19990	Mail		opf Admin. Postale / Poste cs
☐ F-BPUJ	Fokker F27 Friendship 500 (F27 Mk500)	10390	PH-FNN*	0069	0369	2 RR Dart 532-7	19990	Mail		opf Admin. Postale / Poste cs
☐ F-GPXA	Fokker 100 (F28 Mk0100)	11487	PH-EZW*	0095	0997	2 RR Tay 650-15	44450	Y109		lsf Lufthansa Leasing
☐ F-GPXB	Fokker 100 (F28 Mk0100)	11492	PH-EZK*	0095	0997	2 RR Tay 650-15	44450	Y109		lsf Lufthansa Leasing
☐ F-GPXC	Fokker 100 (F28 Mk0100)	11493	PH-EZY*	0095	0997	2 RR Tay 650-15	44450	Y109		lsf Lufthansa Leasing
☐ F-GPXD	Fokker 100 (F28 Mk0100)	11494	PH-EZO*	0095	0997	2 RR Tay 650-15	44450	Y109		lsf Lufthansa Leasing
☐ F-GPXE	Fokker 100 (F28 Mk0100)	11495	PH-EZP*	0095	0997	2 RR Tay 650-15	44450	Y109		lsf Lufthansa Leasing
☐ F-GBYA	Boeing 737-228 (A)	23000 / 930	N1787B*	0082	1282	2 PW JT8D-15A	52000	CY114	EK-AH	
☐ F-GBYB	Boeing 737-228 (A)	23001 / 936		0083	0183	2 PW JT8D-15A	52000	CY114	EK-AL	
☐ F-GBYC	Boeing 737-228 (A)	23002 / 937		0083	0183	2 PW JT8D-15A	52000	CY114	EK-AM	
☐ F-GBYD	Boeing 737-228 (A)	23003 / 939		0083	0283	2 PW JT8D-15A	52000	CY114	EK-DF	
☐ F-GBYF	Boeing 737-228 (A)	23005 / 943		0083	0283	2 PW JT8D-15A	52000	CY114	EK-FM	
☐ F-GBYG	Boeing 737-228 (A)	23006 / 944		0083	0283	2 PW JT8D-15A	52000	CY114	EK-HL	lsf Fleet National Bank Assocation
☐ F-GBYJ	Boeing 737-228 (A)	23009 / 958		0083	0483	2 PW JT8D-15A	52000	CY114	HK-AL	
☐ F-GBYK	Boeing 737-228 (A)	23010 / 959		0083	0583	2 PW JT8D-15A	52000	CY114	HK-AM	
☐ F-GBYL	Boeing 737-228 (A)	23011 / 971		0083	0683	2 PW JT8D-15A	52000	CY114	EK-GL	
☐ F-GBYM	Boeing 737-228 (A)	23349 / 1135		0085	0785	2 PW JT8D-15A	52000	CY114	EJ-AC	
☐ F-GBYN	Boeing 737-228 (A)	23503 / 1256		0086	0886	2 PW JT8D-15A	52000	CY114	HM-AG	
☐ F-GBYO	Boeing 737-228 (A)	23504 / 1267		0086	0886	2 PW JT8D-15A	52000	CY114	EK-DM	
☐ F-GBYP	Boeing 737-228 (A)	23792 / 1397		0087	0687	2 PW JT8D-15A	52000	CY114	EK-BJ	
☐ F-GBYQ	Boeing 737-228 (A)	23793 / 1426		0087	0887	2 PW JT8D-15A	52000	CY114	EK-AD	
☐ F-GFLV	Boeing 737-2K5 (A)	22597 / 773	EC-DTR	0081	0388	2 PW JT8D-15A	57000	CY114	AG-DM	
☐ F-GFLX	Boeing 737-2K5 (A)	22598 / 792	EC-DUB	0081	0288	2 PW JT8D-15A	57000	CY114	AJ-EF	
☐ F-GHXM	Boeing 737-53A	24788 / 1921		0090	0395	2 CFMI CFM56-3C1	52000	CY112		lsf Laure Bail
☐ F-GJNA	Boeing 737-528	25206 / 2099		0091	0891	2 CFMI CFM56-3C1	52000	CY112	EH-JK	
☐ F-GJNB	Boeing 737-528	25227 / 2108		0091	0891	2 CFMI CFM56-3C1	52000	CY112	EH-GK	
☐ F-GJNC	Boeing 737-528	25228 / 2170		0091	1191	2 CFMI CFM56-3C1	52000	CY112	BH-AE	lsf Sandhill Finance Ltd
☐ F-GJND	Boeing 737-528	25229 / 2180		0091	1291	2 CFMI CFM56-3C1	52000	CY112	JM-AH	lsf Piedmont Finance Ltd
☐ F-GJNE	Boeing 737-528	25230 / 2191		0092	0192	2 CFMI CFM56-3C1	52000	CY112		
☐ F-GJNF	Boeing 737-528	25231 / 2208		0092	0192	2 CFMI CFM56-3C1	52000	CY112	JL-FG	
☐ F-GJNG	Boeing 737-528	25232 / 2231		0092	0392	2 CFMI CFM56-3C1	52000	CY112	JM-AG	lsf Golf 737 Bail I
☐ F-GJNH	Boeing 737-528	25233 / 2251		0092	0392	2 CFMI CFM56-3C1	52000	CY112	DJ-HQ	lsf Golf 737 Bail 1
☐ F-GJNI	Boeing 737-528	25234 / 2411		0092	0193	2 CFMI CFM56-3C1	52000	CY112		
☐ F-GJNJ	Boeing 737-528	25235 / 2428		0093	0293	2 CFMI CFM56-3C1	52000	CY112	CR-JK	
☐ F-GJNK	Boeing 737-528	25236 / 2443		0093	0393	2 CFMI CFM56-3C1	52000	CY112	CR-JL	lsf ST Orchid Co. Ltd
☐ F-GJNM	Boeing 737-528	25237 / 2464		0093	0493	2 CFMI CFM56-3C1	52000	CY112	CR-JM	lsf SCL Bronze Co. Ltd
☐ F-GJNN	Boeing 737-528	27304 / 2572		0094	0294	2 CFMI CFM56-3C1	52000	CY112	EH-GS	lsf FC Uncle Leasing Ltd
☐ F-GJNO	Boeing 737-528	27305 / 2574		0094	0294	2 CFMI CFM56-3C1	52000	CY112	EH-JP	lsf FC Voice Leasing Ltd
☐ F-GJNS	Boeing 737-53S	29073 / 3083	N1786B*	1198	1198	2 CFMI CFM56-3C1	52000	CY112		lsf PEMB
☐ F-GJNT	Boeing 737-53S	29074 / 3086	N1786B*	0098	1298	2 CFMI CFM56-3C1	52000	CY112		lsf PEMB
☐ F-GJNU	Boeing 737-53S	29075		0099	0399	2 CFMI CFM56-3C1	52000	CY112		lsf PEMB
☐ F-	Boeing 737-548	26287 / 2427	EI-CDS	0093		2 CFMI CFM56-3B1	52000	CY112		to be lsf ILFC 0499
☐ F-GFUA	Boeing 737-33A	23635 / 1436	G-OUTA	0088	0791	2 CFMI CFM56-3B1	58970	CY130	EL-AD	lsf AWAS
☐ F-GFUD	Boeing 737-33A	24027 / 1597		0088	0391	2 CFMI CFM56-3B1	58970	CY130	HJ-AE	lsf AWAS
☐ F-GFUJ	Boeing 737-33A	25118 / 2065		0091	0691	2 CFMI CFM56-3B1	58970	Y141		lsf AWAS / based FDF/PTP
☐ F-GHVM	Boeing 737-33A	24026 / 1595	G-MONT	0088	1191	2 CFMI CFM56-3B1	58970	CY130	FL-DG	lsf AWAS
☐ F-GHVN	Boeing 737-33A	25138 / 2153	F-OGRT	0091	1091	2 CFMI CFM56-3B1	58970	CY130		
☐ F-GHVO	Boeing 737-33A	24025 / 1556	G-MONU	0088	1191	2 CFMI CFM56-3B1	58970	CY130	FL-CH	lsf NORD
☐ F-GRFA	Boeing 737-36N	28672 / 2976	N1786B*	1297	0198	2 CFMI CFM56-3C1	58970	CY130	EK-AF	lsf GECA
☐ F-GRFB	Boeing 737-36N	28673 / 2995		0098	0298	2 CFMI CFM56-3C1	58970	CY130		lsf GECA
☐ F-GRFC	Boeing 737-36N	28569 / 2996		0098	0298	2 CFMI CFM56-3C1	58970	CY130	EK-BD	lsf GECA
☐ F-GPMA	Airbus Industrie A319-113	598	D-AVYD*	0096	0997	2 CFMI CFM56-5A4	64000	CY135		
☐ F-GPMB	Airbus Industrie A319-113	600	D-AVYC*	0096	0997	2 CFMI CFM56-5A4	64000	CY135		
☐ F-GPMC	Airbus Industrie A319-113	608	D-AVYE*	0096	0997	2 CFMI CFM56-5A4	64000	CY135		
☐ F-GPMD	Airbus Industrie A319-113	618	D-AVYJ*	0096	0997	2 CFMI CFM56-5A4	64000	CY135		
☐ F-GPME	Airbus Industrie A319-113	625	D-AVYQ*	0096	0997	2 CFMI CFM56-5A4	64000	CY135	AD-HK	
☐ F-GPMF	Airbus Industrie A319-113	637	D-AVYT*	0096	0997	2 CFMI CFM56-5A4	64000	CY135		
☐ F-GPMG	Airbus Industrie A319-113	644	D-AVYA*	0097	0997	2 CFMI CFM56-5A4	64000	CY135		lsf ILFC
☐ F-GPMH	Airbus Industrie A319-113	647	D-AVYD*	0097	0997	2 CFMI CFM56-5A4	64000	CY135		lsf ILFC
☐ F-GPMI	Airbus Industrie A319-113	660	D-AVYC*	0097	0997	2 CFMI CFM56-5A4	64000	CY135		lsf ILFC
☐ F-GRHA	Airbus Industrie A319-111	938	D-AVYS*	0099	0199	2 CFMI CFM56-5B5/P	64000	CY135		lsf ILFC
☐ F-	Airbus Industrie A319-111	985				2 CFMI CFM56-5B5/P	64000	CY135		oo-delivery 0399
☐ F-	Airbus Industrie A319-111	998				2 CFMI CFM56-5B5/P	64000	CY135		to be lsf ILFC 0499
☐ F-	Airbus Industrie A319-111	1000				2 CFMI CFM56-5B5/P	64000	CY135		to be lsf ILFC 0499
☐ F-	Airbus Industrie A319-111	1020				2 CFMI CFM56-5B5/P	64000	CY135		oo-delivery 0599
☐ F-	Airbus Industrie A319-111	1025				2 CFMI CFM56-5B5/P	64000	CY135		oo-delivery 0599
☐ F-	Airbus Industrie A319-111					2 CFMI CFM56-5B5/P	64000	CY135		to be lsf ILFC 0699
☐ F-	Airbus Industrie A319-111					2 CFMI CFM56-5B5/P	64000	CY135		to be lsf ILFC 0799
☐ F-	Airbus Industrie A319-111					2 CFMI CFM56-5B5/P	64000	CY135		to be lsf ILFC 1099
☐ F-	Airbus Industrie A319-111					2 CFMI CFM56-5B5/P	64000	CY135		oo-delivery 0000
☐ F-	Airbus Industrie A319-111					2 CFMI CFM56-5B5/P	64000	CY135		oo-delivery 0000
☐ F-	Airbus Industrie A319-111					2 CFMI CFM56-5B5/P	64000	CY135		oo-delivery 0000
☐ F-	Airbus Industrie A319-111					2 CFMI CFM56-5B5/P	64000	CY135		oo-delivery 0000
☐ F-	Airbus Industrie A319-111					2 CFMI CFM56-5B5/P	64000	CY135		oo-delivery 0000
☐ F-	Airbus Industrie A319-111					2 CFMI CFM56-5B5/P	64000	CY135		to be lsf ILFC 0200
☐ F-	Airbus Industrie A319-111					2 CFMI CFM56-5B5/P	64000	CY135		oo-delivery 0001
☐ F-	Airbus Industrie A319-111					2 CFMI CFM56-5B5/P	64000	CY135		oo-delivery 0001
☐ F-	Airbus Industrie A319-111					2 CFMI CFM56-5B5/P	64000	CY135		oo-delivery 0001
☐ F-	Airbus Industrie A319-111					2 CFMI CFM56-5B5/P	64000	CY135		oo-delivery 0001
☐ F-	Airbus Industrie A319-111					2 CFMI CFM56-5B5/P	64000	CY135		oo-delivery 0001
☐ F-	Airbus Industrie A319-111					2 CFMI CFM56-5B5/P	64000	CY135		oo-delivery 0002
☐ F-	Airbus Industrie A319-111					2 CFMI CFM56-5B5/P	64000	CY135		oo-delivery 0002
☐ F-GFKA	Airbus Industrie A320-111	005	F-WWDI*	0088	0388	2 CFMI CFM56-5A1	66000	CY159	CD-FP	Ville de Paris / lsf Durus Verwaltung
☐ F-GFKB	Airbus Industrie A320-111	007	F-WWDJ*	0088	0588	2 CFMI CFM56-5A1	66000	CY159	CD-GP	Ville de Rome / lsf Orado Verwaltung
☐ F-GFKD	Airbus Industrie A320-111	014	F-WWDO*	0088	1088	2 CFMI CFM56-5A1	66000	CY159	CD-JP	Ville de Londres
☐ F-GFKE	Airbus Industrie A320-111	019		0088	1088	2 CFMI CFM56-5A1	66000	CY159	CD-HP	Ville de Bonn
☐ F-GFKF	Airbus Industrie A320-111	020		0089	0289	2 CFMI CFM56-5A1	66000	CY159	CD-KP	Ville de Madrid
☐ F-GFKG	Airbus Industrie A320-111	021		0089	0289	2 CFMI CFM56-5A1	66000	CY159	CD-LP	Ville de Amsterdam
☐ F-GFKH	Airbus Industrie A320-211	061		0089	0889	2 CFMI CFM56-5A1	73000	CY159	GQ-AB	Ville de Bruxelles / lsf OBNV Finance

registration	type of aircraft	cn/fn	ex/ex*	mfd	del	powered by	mtow kg	configuration	selcal	name/fln/specialitites/remarks
☐ F-GFKI	Airbus Industrie A320-211	062		0089	0889	2 CFMI CFM56-5A1	73000	CY159	GQ-AC	Ville de Lisbonne
☐ F-GFKJ	Airbus Industrie A320-211	063		0089	0989	2 CFMI CFM56-5A1	73000	CY159	GQ-AD	Ville de Copenhague / lsf OBNV Finance
☐ F-GFKK	Airbus Industrie A320-211	100		0090	0390	2 CFMI CFM56-5A1	65000	CY159	GQ-AE	Ville d'Athenes / lsf STL Partenairs
☐ F-GFKL	Airbus Industrie A320-211	101		0090	0390	2 CFMI CFM56-5A1	73000	CY159	JL-FH	Ville de Dublin / lsf Clemence Bail
☐ F-GFKM	Airbus Industrie A320-211	102		0090	0390	2 CFMI CFM56-5A1	73000	CY159	DK-FJ	Ville de Luxembourg / lsf Marie Bail
☐ F-GFKN	Airbus Industrie A320-211	128		0090	0191	2 CFMI CFM56-5A1	73000	CY159	GQ-CD	
☐ F-GFKO	Airbus Industrie A320-211	129		0090	1190	2 CFMI CFM56-5A1	73000	CY159	GQ-CE	lsf Eiffel Aircraft Ltd
☐ F-GFKP	Airbus Industrie A320-211	133		0090	1290	2 CFMI CFM56-5A1	73000	CY159	EK-HL	Ville de Nice / lsf Versailles Aircraft
☐ F-GFKQ	Airbus Industrie A320-111	002	F-WWDA*	0087	0291	2 CFMI CFM56-5A1	66000	CY159	EH-GM	Ville de Berlin
☐ F-GFKR	Airbus Industrie A320-211	186		0091	0591	2 CFMI CFM56-5A1	65000	CY159	DJ-AQ	Ville de Barceloune
☐ F-GFKS	Airbus Industrie A320-211	187		0091	0591	2 CFMI CFM56-5A1	65000	CY159	DJ-BQ	
☐ F-GFKT	Airbus Industrie A320-211	188		0091	0591	2 CFMI CFM56-5A1	65000	CY159	DJ-CQ	Ville de Lyon / lsf DB Export Leasing
☐ F-GFKU	Airbus Industrie A320-211	226		0091	0991	2 CFMI CFM56-5A1	65000	CY159	DJ-EQ	Ville de Manchester / lsf DB Export Lsg
☐ F-GFKV	Airbus Industrie A320-211	227		0091	0991	2 CFMI CFM56-5A1	65000	CY159	DJ-FQ	Ville de Bordeaux / lsf DB Exp.Lsg
☐ F-GFKX	Airbus Industrie A320-211	228		0091	0991	2 CFMI CFM56-5A1	73000	CY159	JM-AF	Ville de Francfort
☐ F-GFKY	Airbus Industrie A320-211	285		0092	0292	2 CFMI CFM56-5A1	73000	CY159	BM-KR	Ville de Toulouse
☐ F-GFKZ	Airbus Industrie A320-211	286		0092	0392	2 CFMI CFM56-5A1	73000	CY159	GM-HL	Ville de Turin
☐ F-GGEA	Airbus Industrie A320-111	010	F-WWDL*	0088	0997	2 CFMI CFM56-5A1	68000	CY159		
☐ F-GGEB	Airbus Industrie A320-111	012	F-WWDM*	0088	0997	2 CFMI CFM56-5A1	68000	CY159		
☐ F-GGEC	Airbus Industrie A320-111	013	F-WWDN*	0088	0997	2 CFMI CFM56-5A1	68000	CY159		
☐ F-GGEE	Airbus Industrie A320-111	016	F-WWDQ*	0089	0997	2 CFMI CFM56-5A1	68000	CY159		lsf Dia ITF Ltd
☐ F-GGEF	Airbus Industrie A320-111	004	F-WWDC*	0087	0997	2 CFMI CFM56-5A1	68000	CY159		lsf Dia LAI Ltd
☐ F-GGEG	Airbus Industrie A320-111	003	F-WWDB*	0087	0997	2 CFMI CFM56-5A1	68000	CY159		lsf STL Inter I Co Ltd
☐ F-GHQA	Airbus Industrie A320-211	033	F-GGEF	0089	0997	2 CFMI CFM56-5A1	68000	CY159		lsf Gie ITAB 320
☐ F-GHQB	Airbus Industrie A320-211	036	F-GGEG	0089	0997	2 CFMI CFM56-5A1	68000	CY159		lsf Gie ITAB 320
☐ F-GHQC	Airbus Industrie A320-211	044	F-GGEH	0089	0997	2 CFMI CFM56-5A1	68000	CY159		lsf Gie ITAB 320
☐ F-GHQD	Airbus Industrie A320-211	108		0090	0997	2 CFMI CFM56-5A1	68000	CY159		lsf STL Aircraft Co Ltd
☐ F-GHQE	Airbus Industrie A320-211	115		0090	0997	2 CFMI CFM56-5A1	68000	CY159		lsf AI Leasing Co Ltd
☐ F-GHQF	Airbus Industrie A320-211	130		0090	0997	2 CFMI CFM56-5A1	68000	CY159		lsf Gie ITAB 320
☐ F-GHQG	Airbus Industrie A320-211	155		0091	0997	2 CFMI CFM56-5A1	68000	CY159		
☐ F-GHQH	Airbus Industrie A320-211	156		0091	0997	2 CFMI CFM56-5A1	68000	CY159		
☐ F-GHQI	Airbus Industrie A320-211	184		0091	0997	2 CFMI CFM56-5A1	68000	CY159		lsf Gie ITAB 320
☐ F-GHQJ	Airbus Industrie A320-211	214		0091	0997	2 CFMI CFM56-5A1	68000	CY159		
☐ F-GHQK	Airbus Industrie A320-211	236		0091	0997	2 CFMI CFM56-5A1	73500	CY159		
☐ F-GHQL	Airbus Industrie A320-211	239		0091	0997	2 CFMI CFM56-5A1	68000	CY159		lsf AI Lease Co Ltd
☐ F-GHQM	Airbus Industrie A320-211	237		0091	0997	2 CFMI CFM56-5A1	68000	CY159		
☐ F-GHQO	Airbus Industrie A320-211	278		0092	0997	2 CFMI CFM56-5A1	68000	CY159		lsf Lucky Leasing Co Ltd
☐ F-GHQP	Airbus Industrie A320-211	337		0092	0997	2 CFMI CFM56-5A1	68000	CY159		lsf ORIX
☐ F-GHQQ	Airbus Industrie A320-211	352		0092	0997	2 CFMI CFM56-5A1	68000	CY159		
☐ F-GHQR	Airbus Industrie A320-211	377		0092	0997	2 CFMI CFM56-5A1	68000	CY159		
☐ F-GJVA	Airbus Industrie A320-211	144	F-WWDK*	0091	0997	2 CFMI CFM56-5A1	68000	CY159		lsf GATX
☐ F-GJVB	Airbus Industrie A320-211	145	F-WWDL*	0091	0997	2 CFMI CFM56-5A1	68000	CY159		lsf GATX
☐ F-GJVC	Airbus Industrie A320-211	204		0091	0997	2 CFMI CFM56-5A1	68000	CY159		
☐ F-GJVD	Airbus Industrie A320-211	211		0091	0997	2 CFMI CFM56-5A1	73500	CY159		
☐ F-GJVE	Airbus Industrie A320-211	215		0091	0997	2 CFMI CFM56-5A1	73500	CY159		lsf ILFC
☐ F-GJVF	Airbus Industrie A320-211	244		0091	0997	2 CFMI CFM56-5A1	73500	CY159		lsf ILFC
☐ F-GJVG	Airbus Industrie A320-211	270		0091	0997	2 CFMI CFM56-5A1	68000	CY159		lsf ILFC
☐ F-GJVW	Airbus Industrie A320-211	491	F-WWBS*	0094	0997	2 CFMI CFM56-5A1	73500	CY159		lsf ILFC
☐ F-GJVZ	Airbus Industrie A320-211	085	F-WWDF*	0089	0997	2 CFMI CFM56-5A1	73500	CY159		lsf GECA
☐ F-GKXA	Airbus Industrie A320-211	287		0092	0392	2 CFMI CFM56-5A1	65000	CY159	DM-LR	Ville de Nantes
☐ F-GLGG	Airbus Industrie A320-212	203	ZS-NZP	0091	0594	2 CFMI CFM56-5A3	77000	CY159	EK-CD	lsf GECA
☐ F-GLGH	Airbus Industrie A320-212	220	ZS-NZR	0091	0694	2 CFMI CFM56-5A3	77000	CY159	FL-KM	lsf GECA
☐ F-GMZA	Airbus Industrie A321-111	498	D-AVZK*	0094	0997	2 CFMI CFM56-5B1	78000	CY189		lsf FT Global Leasing Ltd
☐ F-GMZB	Airbus Industrie A321-111	509	D-AVZN*	0094	0997	2 CFMI CFM56-5B1	78000	CY189		
☐ F-GMZC	Airbus Industrie A321-111	521	D-AVZW*	0095	0997	2 CFMI CFM56-5B1	78000	CY189		
☐ F-GMZD	Airbus Industrie A321-111	529	D-AVZA*	0095	0997	2 CFMI CFM56-5B1	78000	CY189		
☐ F-GMZE	Airbus Industrie A321-111	544	D-AVZF*	0095	0997	2 CFMI CFM56-5B1	78000	CY189		
☐ F-GTAA	Airbus Industrie A321-211	674	D-AVZP*	0097	0597	2 CFMI CFM56-5B3/P	89000	CY189		lsf GATX
☐ F-GTAB	Airbus Industrie A321-211	675	D-AVZS*	0097	0597	2 CFMI CFM56-5B3/P	89000	CY189		lsf GATX
☐ F-GTAC	Airbus Industrie A321-211	684	D-AVZQ*	0097	0697	2 CFMI CFM56-5B3/P	89000	CY189		lsf GATX
☐ F-GTAD	Airbus Industrie A321-211	777	D-AVZI*	0098	0298	2 CFMI CFM56-5B3/P	89000	CY189	EK-BF	
☐ F-GTAE	Airbus Industrie A321-211	796	D-AVZN*	0097	0398	2 CFMI CFM56-5B3/P	89000	CY189	EK-BM	
☐ F-GTAF	Airbus Industrie A321-211	761	D-AVZJ*	0098	0298	2 CFMI CFM56-5B3/P	89000	CY189	EK-DG	lsf GATX
☐ F-GTAG	Airbus Industrie A321-211	956		0099	0399	2 CFMI CFM56-5B3/P	89000	CY189		
☐ F-GTAH	Airbus Industrie A321-211					2 CFMI CFM56-5B3/P	89000	CY189		oo-delivery 0000
☐ F-GTAI	Airbus Industrie A321-211					2 CFMI CFM56-5B3/P	89000	CY189		oo-delivery 0000
☐ F-GTAJ	Airbus Industrie A321-211					2 CFMI CFM56-5B3/P	89000	CY189		oo-delivery 0000
☐ F-GTAK	Airbus Industrie A321-211					2 CFMI CFM56-5B3/P	89000	CY189		oo-delivery 0000
☐ F-GEMA	Airbus Industrie A310-203	316		0084	0484	2 GE CF6-80A3	142000	C40Y124	EH-LM	
☐ F-GEMB	Airbus Industrie A310-203	326		0084	0684	2 GE CF6-80A3	142000	C40Y124	JM-BC	
☐ F-GEMC	Airbus Industrie A310-203	335		0084	0684	2 GE CF6-80A3	142000	C40Y124	AK-FJ	
☐ F-GEMD	Airbus Industrie A310-203	355		0084	0185	2 GE CF6-80A3	142000	C40Y124	EJ-AG	
☐ F-GEME	Airbus Industrie A310-203	369		0085	0485	2 GE CF6-80A3	142000	C40Y124	EK-BC	
☐ F-GEMF	Airbus Industrie A310-203	172	F-WZLI	0082	0386	2 GE CF6-80A3	142000	Y225	EH-GJ	lst KYV as TC-JYK / cvtd A310-221
☐ F-GEMG	Airbus Industrie A310-203	454		0088	0388	2 GE CF6-80A3	142000	C40Y124	CD-EP	
☐ F-GEMN	Airbus Industrie A310-304	502	F-WWCD*	0089	0889	2 GE CF6-80C2A2	152000	C40Y127	GQ-BM	
☐ F-GEMO	Airbus Industrie A310-304	504	F-WWCF*	0089	0889	2 GE CF6-80C2A2	152000	C40Y127	GQ-BP	
☐ F-GEMP	Airbus Industrie A310-304	550		0090	1290	2 GE CF6-80C2A2	152000	C40Y127	JL-GK	
☐ F-GEMQ	Airbus Industrie A310-304	551		0091	0291	2 GE CF6-80C2A2	152000	C40Y127	CP-HQ	
☐ F-GHGF	Boeing 767-3Q8 (ER)	24745 / 355		0091	1091	2 PW PW4060	184600	C25Y185	HP-LM	lsf ILFC
☐ F-GHGG	Boeing 767-3Q8 (ER)	24746 / 378		0091	1191	2 PW PW4060	184600	C25Y185	JK-AP	lsf BBAM
☐ F-GHGH	Boeing 767-37E (ER)	25077 / 385		0091	0891	2 PW PW4060	184600	C25Y185	JK-BP	
☐ F-GHGI	Boeing 767-328 (ER)	27135 / 493		0093	0593	2 GE CF6-80C2B6F	184600	C25Y185	BM-HR	lsf Florita Finance Ltd
☐ F-GHGJ	Boeing 767-328 (ER)	27136 / 497		0093	0593	2 GE CF6-80C2B6F	184600	C25Y185	BM-HS	lsf NBB Paris Lease Co Ltd
☐ F-BTSC	Aerospatiale / BAe Concorde 101	203	F-WTSC*	0075	1080	4 RR Olympus 593-610	185070	R100	EJ-AD	
☐ F-BTSD	Aerospatiale / BAe Concorde 101	213	N94SD	0078	0580	4 RR Olympus 593-610	185070	R100	HL-FG	
☐ F-BVFA	Aerospatiale / BAe Concorde 101	205	N94FA	0075	1275	4 RR Olympus 593-610	185070	R100	DH-AB	
☐ F-BVFB	Aerospatiale / BAe Concorde 101	207	N94FB	0076	0476	4 RR Olympus 593-610	185070	R100	DG-KL	
☐ F-BVFC	Aerospatiale / BAe Concorde 101	209	N94FC	0076	0876	4 RR Olympus 593-610	185070	R100	DG-KM	
☐ F-BVFF	Aerospatiale / BAe Concorde 101	215		0078	1080	4 RR Olympus 593-610	185070	R100	AK-HJ	
☐ F-GSPA	Boeing 777-228 (ER)	29002 / 129		0098	0398	2 GE GE90-92B	294200	F12C56Y202	EK-CM	
☐ F-GSPB	Boeing 777-228 (ER)	29003 / 133		0098	0498	2 GE GE90-92B	294200	F12C56Y202	FL-CM	
☐ F-GSPC	Boeing 777-228 (ER)	29004 / 138		0098	0598	2 GE GE90-92B	294200	F12C56Y202		
☐ F-GSPD	Boeing 777-228 (ER)	29005 / 187		1298	0199	2 GE GE90-92B	294200	F12C56Y202		
☐ F-GSPE	Boeing 777-228 (ER)	29006 / 189		0199	0199	2 GE GE90-92B	294200	F12C56Y202		
☐ F-GSPF	Boeing 777-228 (ER)	29007				2 GE GE90-92B	294200	F12C56Y202		oo-delivery 0499
☐ F-GSPG	Boeing 777-228 (ER)	27609 / 195		0299	0299	2 GE GE90-92B	294200	F12C56Y202		lsf ILFC
☐ F-GSPH	Boeing 777-228 (ER)	28675				2 GE GE90-92B	294200	F12C56Y202		to be lsf ILFC 0599
☐ F-GSPI	Boeing 777-228 (ER)					2 GE GE90-92B	294200	F12C56Y202		oo-delivery 0100
☐ F-GSPJ	Boeing 777-228 (ER)					2 GE GE90-92B	294200	F12C56Y202		oo-delivery 0300
☐ F-GSPK	Boeing 777-228 (ER)					2 GE GE90-92B	294200	F12C56Y202		oo-delivery 0600
☐ F-GLZA	Airbus Industrie A340-311	005	F-WWCA*	0092	0893	4 CFMI CFM56-5C2	257000	F6C42Y204	AK-GJ	lsf Marseilles Ac./tb cvtd to-312, 260t
☐ F-GLZB	Airbus Industrie A340-311	007		0093	0293	4 CFMI CFM56-5C2	257000	F6C42Y204	BM-GS	lsf Farukon Leasing/tb cvtd to-312,260t
☐ F-GLZC	Airbus Industrie A340-311	029		0093	0993	4 CFMI CFM56-5C2	257000	F6C42Y204	BM-JR	lsf NBB Cannes Lse/tb cvtd to -312,260t
☐ F-GLZG	Airbus Industrie A340-311	049		0094	0494	4 CFMI CFM56-5C2	257000	F6C42Y204	GM-DF	lsf Oryx Lynx/to be cvtd to -312, 260t
☐ F-GLZH	Airbus Industrie A340-311	078		0095	0795	4 CFMI CFM56-5C2	257000	F6Y42Y204	HL-FJ	lsf BBV Leasing/to be cvtd to -312,260t
☐ F-GLZI	Airbus Industrie A340-311	084		0095	0895	4 CFMI CFM56-5C2	257000	F6C42Y204	AK-GH	lsf BBV Leasing/to be cvtd to -312,260t
☐ F-GLZJ	Airbus Industrie A340-313	186		0097	0997	4 CFMI CFM56-5C4	271000	F6C42Y204	EH-GJ	lsf DB Export Leasing GmbH
☐ F-GLZK	Airbus Industrie A340-313	207		0097	0198	4 CFMI CFM56-5C4	271000	F6C42Y204	AQ-PS	
☐ F-GLZL	Airbus Industrie A340-313	210		0098	0298	4 CFMI CFM56-5C4	271000	F6C42Y204	JK-CP	
☐ F-GLZM	Airbus Industrie A340-313	237		0098	1098	4 CFMI CFM56-5C4	271000	F6C42Y204		lsf Sylvie Bail
☐ F-GLZN	Airbus Industrie A340-313	245		0098	1198	4 CFMI CFM56-5C4	271000	F6C42Y204		
☐ F-GLZO	Airbus Industrie A340-313	246		0098	1298	4 CFMI CFM56-5C4	271000	F6C42Y204		
☐ F-GLZP	Airbus Industrie A340-313	260		0099	0299	4 CFMI CFM56-5C4	271000	F6C42Y204		
☐ F-GLZQ	Airbus Industrie A340-313	289				4 CFMI CFM56-5C4	271000	F6C42Y204		oo-delivery 0899
☐ F-GLZR	Airbus Industrie A340-313	310				4 CFMI CFM56-5C4	271000	F6C42Y204		oo-delivery 1299
☐ F-GLZS	Airbus Industrie A340-313					4 CFMI CFM56-5C4	271000	F6C42Y204		oo-delivery 0600
☐ F-GLZT	Airbus Industrie A340-313					4 CFMI CFM56-5C4	271000	F6C42Y204		oo-delivery 0600
☐ F-GNIF	Airbus Industrie A340-313	168		0097	0497	4 CFMI CFM56-5C4	271000	F6C42Y204	EH-KS	lsf ILFC
☐ F-GNIG	Airbus Industrie A340-313	174		0097	0597	4 CFMI CFM56-5C4	271000	F6C42Y204	EH-LP	lsf ILFC

☐ F-BPVJ	Boeing 747-128	20541 / 200	N28903	0072	0273	4 PW JT9D-7	332900	F6C62Y274	DG-BM	
☐ F-BPVL	Boeing 747-128	20798 / 224	N88931*	0074	0374	4 PW JT9D-7	332900	F6C62Y274	EK-DJ	Jumbo
☐ F-BPVM	Boeing 747-128	20799 / 227	N63305	0073	1273	4 PW JT9D-7	332900	F6C62Y274	EK-FH	
☐ F-BPVP	Boeing 747-128	20954 / 252		0074	0375	4 PW JT9D-7	332900	F6C62Y274	EK-CG	
☐ F-BPVR	Boeing 747-228F (SCD)	21255 / 295	N1783B*	0076	1076	4 GE CF6-50E2	371900	Freighter	EK-GH	lsf AFPL
☐ F-BPVS	Boeing 747-228B (M)	21326 / 303		0077	0477	4 GE CF6-50E2	362900	F8C41Y182/Plts	EJ-AL	lsf AFPL
☐ F-BPVT	Boeing 747-228B (M)	21429 / 313		0077	0977	4 GE CF6-50E2	362900	F8C41Y182/Plts	EJ-AM	lsf AFPL
☐ F-BPVU	Boeing 747-228B (M)	21537 / 333	N1252E	0078	0878	4 GE CF6-50E2	362900	F8C41Y182/Plts	EJ-BD	
☐ F-BPVX	Boeing 747-228B (M)	21731 / 364		0079	0379	4 GE CF6-50E2	362900	F8C41Y182/Plts	EJ-BC	lsf BBAM
☐ F-BPVY	Boeing 747-228B	21745 / 370		0079	0479	4 GE CF6-50E2	371900	F8C41Y324	EJ-BM	
☐ F-BPVZ	Boeing 747-228F (SCD)	21787 / 398		0079	0979	4 GE CF6-50E2	371900	Freighter	EJ-AK	lsf AFPL
☐ F-GBOX	Boeing 747-2B3F (SCD)	21835 / 388		0079	0192	4 GE CF6-50E2	371900	Freighter	EJ-GK	lsf Arkia Leasing
☐ F-GCBA	Boeing 747-228B	21982 / 428		0080	0280	4 GE CF6-50E2	371900	F8C41Y324	EJ-BL	lsf AFPL
☐ F-GCBB	Boeing 747-228B (M)	22272 / 463	N1289E	0080	0780	4 GE CF6-50E2	362900	F8C41Y182/Plts	EK-GJ	lsf WTC Trustee
☐ F-GCBD	Boeing 747-228B (SF)	22428 / 503	N1305E	0080	0381	4 GE CF6-50E2	377800	Freighter	EJ-AH	cvtd -228B (M)
☐ F-GCBE	Boeing 747-228F (SCD)	22678 / 535	N4508E	0081	0981	4 GE CF6-50E2	371900	Freighter	JL-FK	lsf Bank of New York Trustee
☐ F-GCBF	Boeing 747-228B (M)	22794 / 558	N4506H	0082	0382	4 GE CF6-50E2	377800	F16C44Y192/Plts	JL-EM	lsf The Bank of New York
☐ F-GCBG	Boeing 747-228F (SCD)	22939 / 569	N4544F	0082	1082	4 GE CF6-50E2	371900	Freighter	EH-KL	lsf First Trust of CA
☐ F-GCBH	Boeing 747-228B (SF)	23611 / 656	N6046P*	0086	0986	4 GE CF6-50E2	377800	Freighter	FM-BK	cvtd -228B (M)
☐ F-GCBI	Boeing 747-228B (M)	23676 / 661	N6009F*	0086	1086	4 GE CF6-50E2	377800	F16C44Y192/Plts	BF-GK	
☐ F-GCBJ	Boeing 747-228B (M)	24067 / 698	N6018N*	0088	0388	4 GE CF6-50E2	377800	F16C44Y192/Plts	EK-GM	
☐ F-GCBK	Boeing 747-228F (SCD)	24158 / 714	N6055X*	0088	0988	4 GE CF6-50E2	377800	Freighter	JL-EK	lsf AFPL
☐ F-GCBL	Boeing 747-228F (SCD)	24735 / 772		0090	0290	4 GE CF6-50E2	377800	Freighter	EF-DK	lsf PBA Foreign Sales Corp.
☐ F-GCBM	Boeing 747-228F (SCD)	24879 / 822		0090	0192	4 GE CF6-50E2	377800	Freighter	EJ-FM	lsf USW FCS One
☐ F-GPAN	Boeing 747-2B3F (SCD)	21515 / 337	N1780B*	0078	0386	4 GE CF6-50E2	371900	Freighter	FM-BL	
☐ F-BTDG	Boeing 747-2B3B (M) (SUD)	22514 / 518		0081	0192	4 GE CF6-50E2	362900	F8C41Y324	KM-BD	cvtd -2B3B (M)
☐ F-BTDH	Boeing 747-2B3B (M) (SUD)	22515 / 521		0081	0192	4 GE CF6-50E2	362900	F8C41Y182/Plt	KM-BF	cvtd -2B3B (M)
☐ F-GETA	Boeing 747-3B3 (M)	23413 / 632	N6009F*	0086	0192	4 GE CF6-50E2	362900	C22Y486	FL-DJ	Big Boss
☐ F-GETB	Boeing 747-3B3 (M)	23480 / 641	N6018N*	0086	1191	4 GE CF6-50E2	362900	C22Y486	FL-DK	
☐ F-GEXA	Boeing 747-4B3	24154 / 741		0089	0192	4 GE CF6-80C2B1F	394600	F13C56Y322	HP-JL	lsf TLC Asset Co Ltd
☐ F-GEXB	Boeing 747-4B3 (M)	24155 / 864		0091	0192	4 GE CF6-80C2B1F	394600	F13C56Y322	HP-JM	
☐ F-GISA	Boeing 747-428 (M)	25238 / 872		0091	0991	4 GE CF6-80C2B1F	394600	F13C56Y182/Plts	CP-FQ	
☐ F-GISB	Boeing 747-428 (M)	25302 / 884		0091	1191	4 GE CF6-80C2B1F	394600	F13C56Y182/Plts	CP-GQ	
☐ F-GISC	Boeing 747-428 (M)	25599 / 899		0092	0292	4 GE CF6-80C2B1F	394600	F13C56Y182/Plts	AF-BR	
☐ F-GISD	Boeing 747-428 (M)	25628 / 934		0092	0992	4 GE CF6-80C2B1F	385600	F13C56Y182/Plts	AQ-RS	
☐ F-GISE	Boeing 747-428 (M)	25630 / 960		0093	0293	4 GE CF6-80C2B1F	385600	F13C56Y182/Plts	DG-CM	lsf Wrightbrothers Ltd
☐ F-GITA	Boeing 747-428	24969 / 836		0091	0291	4 GE CF6-80C2B1F	371900	F13C56Y322	CP-DQ	lsf Wingtip Finance Ltd
☐ F-GITB	Boeing 747-428	24990 / 843	N6009F*	0091	0491	4 GE CF6-80C2B1F	371900	F13C56Y322	CP-EQ	lsf USW FSC Three Ltd
☐ F-GITC	Boeing 747-428	25344 / 889		0091	1291	4 GE CF6-80C2B1F	385600	F13C56Y322	CP-JQ	
☐ F-GITD	Boeing 747-428	25600 / 901		0092	0292	4 GE CF6-80C2B1F	371900	F13C56Y322	AF-BS	
☐ F-GITE	Boeing 747-428	25601 / 906		0092	0392	4 GE CF6-80C2B1F	371900	F13C56Y322	AF-CR	
☐ F-GITF	Boeing 747-428	25602 / 909		0092	0492	4 GE CF6-80C2B1F	371900	F13C56Y322	AF-CS	lsf CIT FSC Twelve Ltd

AIR GAMA

Niort-Souche

Aéroport de Souche, F-79000 Niort, France ☎ 549 28 12 28 Tx: none Fax: 549 28 14 46 SITA: n/a
F: 1989 ✱✱✱ 5 Head: Christian Ribbe Net: n/a

☐ F-BTEL	Cessna F550 Citation II	550-0190	N98715	0080		2 PWC JT15D-4	5700	8 Pax		lsf Air Delta 79
☐ F-GGGA	Cessna F550 Citation II	550-0586	N1301N	0088		2 PWC JT15D-4	5700	8 Pax		lsf Locanorm

AIR GEFCO = GEF (Affiliated with Sté Gefco)

Paris-Le Bourget

75 Avenue de la Grande-Armée, F-75116 Paris, France ☎ (1) 40 67 27 27 Tx: 290436 f gef Fax: (1) 45 00 13 75 SITA: n/a
F: 1977 ✱✱✱ 4 Head: François Valentin ICAO: AIR GEFCO Net: n/a

☐ F-GPSA	Dassault Falcon 50	123	N211EF	0082		3 GA TFE731-3-1C	17600	10 Pax		

AIR GUADELOUPE = TX / FWI (Caribienne de Transport Aérien dba)

Pointe à Pitre-Le Raizet

Aéroport du Raizet, F-97139 Abymes, Guadeloupe ☎ 82 47 22 Tx: 919008 gl ptpdog Fax: 83 70 03 SITA: n/a
F: 1970 ✱✱✱ 170 Head: François Paneole IATA: 427 ICAO: FRENCH WEST Net: n/a

☐ F-OGES	De Havilland DHC-6 Twin Otter 300	254	N302MA	0069	0370	2 PWC PT6A-27	5670	Y19		lst BTH
☐ F-OGIZ	De Havilland DHC-6 Twin Otter 300	675		0080	0380	2 PWC PT6A-27	5670	Y19		lst BTH
☐ F-ODUN	Dornier 228-212	8197	D-CATS*	0090	0498	2 GA TPE331-5A-252D	6400	Y19		lsf Sodap
☐ F-OGOF	Dornier 228-202K	8143	D-CBCB*	0088	0988	2 GA TPE331-5-252D	6200	Y19		
☐ F-OGOH	Dornier 228-202K	8173	D-CBDS*	0089	0689	2 GA TPE331-5-252D	6200	Y19		
☐ F-OGOZ	Dornier 228-202K	8161	D-CBDR*	0089	0097	2 GA TPE331-5-252D	6200	Y19		lsf Sodeta
☐ F-OGPI	Dornier 228-202K	8169	D-COCA*	0089	0890	2 GA TPE331-5-252D	6200	Y19		
☐ F-OGVA	Dornier 228-212	8236	D-CBDB*	0096	1296	2 GA TPE331-5AB-252D	6400	Y19		lsf Caribaero 1
☐ F-OGVE	Dornier 228-212	8237	D-CBDD*	0096	1296	2 GA TPE331-5AB-252D	6400	Y19		lsf Unimat
☐ F-OGXG	Dornier 228-212	8176	D-CBDG*	0095	1295	2 GA TPE331-5A-252D	6400	Y19		lsf Caribaero 1
☐ F-OHQJ	Dornier 228-212	8239		0097	1297	2 GA TPE331-5AB-252D	6400	Y19		lsf Caribaero 5
☐ F-OHQK	Dornier 228-212	8238		0097	1297	2 GA TPE331-5AB-252D	6400	Y19		lsf Caribaero 8
☐ F-OGNE	ATR 42-300	026		0086	1086	2 PWC PW120	16700	Y50 / Combi		lsf A.I.R.
☐ F-OHQL	ATR 42-500	524	F-WWEF*	0097	1297	2 PWC PW127E	18600	Y46		lsf Caribaero 6/sub-lst Air Martinique
☐ F-OHQV	ATR 42-500	571	F-WWEM*	0098	1298	2 PWC PW127E	18600	Y46		lsf Caribaero / sub-lst Air Martinique
☐ F-OGUO	ATR 72-212	475	F-WWEH*	0096	1296	2 PWC PW127	21500	Y70		lsf Caribaero 3
☐ F-OGXF	ATR 72-212	461	F-WWLP*	0095	0296	2 PWC PW127	21500	Y70		lsf Caribaero 1
☐ TF-ELM	Boeing 737-2M8 (A)	21736 / 557	F-GLXG	0079	1298	2 PW JT8D-15	54204	Y131		lsf ICB

AIR GUYANE = GUY

Cayenne-Rochambeau

Aéroport de Cayenne Rochambeau, F-97351 Matoury, Guyane ☎ 35 65 55 Tx: 910619 fg Fax: 35 65 06 SITA: n/a
F: 1980 ✱✱✱ 60 Head: Jean Pierre Prevot ICAO: AIR GUYANE Net: n/a Ag-Aircraft below MTOW 5000 kg: Ayres Trush S2R/Turbo Trush A34AG & Cessna T188C AgHusky.

☐ F-OGOD	Cessna 208 Caravan I	20800166		0089		1 PWC PT6A-114	3629	Y9 / Freighter		lsf Natiolocation
☐ F-OGOG	Reims/Cessna F406 Caravan II	F406-0026		0088		2 PWC PT6A-112	4465	Y12		lsf BNP Bail
☐ F-OGVS	Reims/Cessna F406 Caravan II	F406-0061	N3121X	0091		2 PWC PT6A-112	4468	Y12		ING Lease France SA
☐ F-OGJV	De Havilland DHC-6 Twin Otter 300	422	EC-CJI	0074		2 PWC PT6A-27	5670	Y19		

AIR JET = AIJ (Subsidiary of TNT Express Worldwide)

Paris-CDG

BP 10297, F-95700 Roissy CDG, France ☎ (1) 49 19 73 00 Tx: none Fax: (1) 48 62 50 80 SITA: CDGBCCR
F: 1979 ✱✱✱ 97 Head: Roger Caille ICAO: AIR JET Net: http://www.airjet.fr/

☐ F-GLNI	BAe 146-200 (QC)	E2188	G-BTDO*	0091	1091	4 LY ALF502R-5	42184	Y94 / Frtr 10t	BQ-KS	lsf BAMJ / cvtd -200
☐ F-GMMP	BAe 146-200 (QC)	E2176	G-BWLG	0090	0496	4 LY ALF502R-5	42184	Y94 / Frtr 10t		lsf BAMJ / cvtd -200
☐ F-GOMA	BAe 146-200 (QC)	E2211	G-6-211*	0093	0694	4 LY ALF502R-5	42184	Y94 / Frtr 10t		lsf BAMJ / cvtd -200

AIRLEC AIR ESPACE, S.A. = ARL

Bordeaux

Zone d'Aviation Générale, F-33700 Merignac-Cédex 05, France ☎ 556 34 02 14 Tx: none Fax: 556 55 98 18 SITA: n/a
F: 1997 ✱✱✱ 6 Head: Patric Tiba ICAO: AIRLEC Net: n/a

☐ F-GEPE	Piper PA-31T Cheyenne II	31T-7720031	HB-LIW	0077		2 PWC PT6A-28	4082	6 Pax		lsf Natiolocation
☐ F-GGRV	Piper PA-31T Cheyenne II	31T-7720036	N41RC	0077	0098	2 PWC PT6A-28	4082	6 Pax		lsf Natiolocation
☐ F-GGVG	Fairchild (Swearingen) SA226T Merlin IIIB	T-293	D-IBBB	0078	0098	2 GA TPE331-10U-512G	5670	8 Pax		lsf PEA

AIR LIBERTE = IJ / LIB (Subsidiary of British Airways, Plc)

Paris-Orly

Immeuble Le Delta, 3 Rue du Pont des Halles, F-94656 Rungis Cédex, France ☎ (1) 49 79 23 00 Tx: 263795 f Fax: (1) 46 87 28 83 SITA: n/a
F: 1987 ✱✱✱ 2600 Head: Lofti Belhassine IATA: 718 ICAO: AIR LIBERTE Net: http://www.w3i.com/eng/transp/airlib.htm Some scheduled services are operated on a franchise agreement with BRITISH AIRWAYS (in full such colors & both titles) & using BA flight numbers. Beside aircraft listed, additional are operated on a franchise code-share agreement (in AIR LIBERTE colors & flight numbers) by: FLANDRE AIR (with Beech 1900C-1/1900D & Embraer 120ER). for details – see under that company.

☐ F-GGLK	ATR 42-300	022	OH-LTB	0086	1097	2 PWC PW120	16900	Y50		lsf Aircr.Int'l Renting/sub-lst/opb APB
☐ F-GIRC	ATR 42-300	033	F-WIAF	0086	1097	2 PWC PW120	16900	Y46		lsf Aircr.Int'l Renting/sub-lst/opb APB
☐ F-GKNB	ATR 42-300	226		0091	1097	2 PWC PW120	16900	Y46		lsf Prop Bail / sub-lst / opb OPN
☐ F-GKNC	ATR 42-300	230		0091	1097	2 PWC PW120	16900	Y46		lsf Prop Bail / sub-lst / opb OPN
☐ F-GKND	ATR 42-300	231		0091	1097	2 PWC PW120	16900	Y46		lsf Prop Bail / sub-lst/opb APB
☐ F-GPZB	ATR 42-300	027	F-OGOE	0086	1097	2 PWC PW120	16700	Y50		lsf Aircraft Int'l Renting Ltd
☐ F-GKOA	ATR 72-202	201		0091	1097	2 PWC PW124B	21500	Y70		lsf South East Leasing Ltd
☐ F-GKOB	ATR 72-202	232		0091	1097	2 PWC PW124B	21500	Y70		lsf Worldwide Leasing Ltd
☐ F-GDUS	Fokker F28 Fellowship 2000 (F28 Mk2000)	11053	5N-ANB	0072	1097	2 RR Spey 555-15	29480	Y79		
☐ F-GDUT	Fokker F28 Fellowship 2000 (F28 Mk2000)	11091	5N-ANH	0075	1097	2 RR Spey 555-15	29480	Y79		
☐ F-GDUU	Fokker F28 Fellowship 2000 (F28 Mk2000)	11108	5N-ANI	0076	1097	2 RR Spey 555-15	29480	CY74		
☐ F-GDUV	Fokker F28 Fellowship 2000 (F28 Mk2000)	11109	5N-ANJ	0076	1097	2 RR Spey 555-15	29480	CY79		
☐ F-GIOA	Fokker 100 (F28 Mk0100)	11261	PH-EZK*	0089	1097	2 RR Tay 620-15	44455	CY105		lsf CLS Amethyst Leasing
☐ F-GIOG	Fokker 100 (F28 Mk0100)	11364	PH-EZA*	0091	1097	2 RR Tay 620-15	44455	Y105		lsf Jet Trading & Leasing Co. Ltd
☐ F-GIOH	Fokker 100 (F28 Mk0100)	11424	PH-LXV*	0092	1097	2 RR Tay 650-15	44455	CY105		lsf Transregiolise

147 registration type of aircraft cn/fn ex/ex* mfd del powered by mtow kg configuration selcal name/fln/specialitites/remarks

registration	type of aircraft	cn/fn	ex/ex*	mfd	del	powered by	mtow kg	configuration	selcal	name/fln/specialitites/remarks
☐ F-GIOI	Fokker 100 (F28 Mk0100)	11433	PH-MXA*	0093	1097	2 RR Tay 650-15	44455	CY105		lsf Barclays Bail/1789 Rights of Man-cs
☐ F-GIOJ	Fokker 100 (F28 Mk0100)	11454	PH-EZF*	0093	1097	2 RR Tay 650-15	44455	CY105		lsf Jet 11-12
☐ F-GIOK	Fokker 100 (F28 Mk0100)	11455	PH-EZG*	0093	1097	2 RR Tay 650-15	44455	CY105		lsf Jet 11-12
☐ F-GNLG	Fokker 100 (F28 Mk0100)	11363	D-ADFE	0091	1097	2 RR Tay 620-15	44455	CY105		lsf Jet Trading & Leasing Co. Ltd
☐ F-GNLH	Fokker 100 (F28 Mk0100)	11311	D-ADFB	0091	1097	2 RR Tay 620-15	43995	CY105		lsf Jet Trading & Leasing Co. Ltd
☐ F-GNLI	Fokker 100 (F28 Mk0100)	11315	D-ADFC	0091	1097	2 RR Tay 620-15	44225	CY105		lsf Jet Trading & Leasing Co. Ltd
☐ F-GNLJ	Fokker 100 (F28 Mk0100)	11344	D-ADFD	0091	1097	2 RR Tay 620-15	43995	CY105		lsf Jet Fonce Bail
☐ F-GNLK	Fokker 100 (F28 Mk0100)	11307	D-ADFA	0090	1097	2 RR Tay 620-15	44455	CY105		lsf Jet Trading & Leasing Co. Ltd
☐ F-GFZB	Boeing (Douglas) MD-83 (DC-9-83)	49707 / 1487		0588	0788	2 PW JT8D-219	72575	CY159		lsf ILFC
☐ F-GHEB	Boeing (Douglas) MD-83 (DC-9-83)	49822 / 1539		1088	1288	2 PW JT8D-219	72575	CY159	HM-GP	lsf ILFC
☐ F-GHED	Boeing (Douglas) MD-83 (DC-9-83)	49576 / 1422	EI-BWE	0087	0189	2 PW JT8D-219	72575	CY159	CP-BQ	lsf GIE Libellule 1
☐ F-GHEI	Boeing (Douglas) MD-83 (DC-9-83)	49968 / 1668		1289	0290	2 PW JT8D-219	72575	CY159	DQ-GL	lsf ILFC
☐ F-GHEK	Boeing (Douglas) MD-83 (DC-9-83)	49823 / 1540	N83MV	1088	0390	2 PW JT8D-219	72575	CY159	DM-AG	lsf ILFC
☐ F-GHHO	Boeing (Douglas) MD-83 (DC-9-83)	49985 / 1838		0291	0391	2 PW JT8D-219	72575	CY159	AE-CR	lsf GIE Alizé
☐ F-GHHP	Boeing (Douglas) MD-83 (DC-9-83)	49986 / 1842		0391	0491	2 PW JT8D-219	72575	CY159	AE-CS	lsf GIE Alizé
☐ F-GJHQ	Boeing (Douglas) MD-83 (DC-9-83)	49668 / 1467	N63050	0088	0397	2 PW JT8D-219	72575	CY159	AC-BE	lsf GECA / cvtd MD-82
☐ F-GPZA	Boeing (Douglas) MD-83 (DC-9-83)	49943 / 1887	EI-CBX	0091	0498	2 PW JT8D-219	72575	CY159		lsf GECA / La Pyramide du Louvre-cs
☐ F-GRML	Boeing (Douglas) MD-83 (DC-9-83)	49628 / 1582	F-WQFN	0389	1298	2 PW JT8D-219	72575	CY159		lsf Greencow Ltd / L'esprit Liberté-cs
☐ F-GPVA	Boeing (Douglas) DC-10-30	47956 / 181	OH-LHA	1174	0696	3 GE CF6-50C2	259500	C19Y310	BH-CG	lsf CLPK Ac.Funding/L'esprit Liberté-cs
☐ F-GPVC	Boeing (Douglas) DC-10-30 (ER)	48265 / 345	N345HC	1080	0196	3 GE CF6-50C2B	267600	C19Y310	CH-LM	lsf FSBU Trustee / cvtd DC-10-30
☐ F-GPVD	Boeing (Douglas) DC-10-30	47865 / 135	OH-LHD	1173	0794	3 GE CF6-50C2	256300	C19Y310	BE-AK	lsf CLPK Aircraft Funding

AIR LITTORAL = FU / LIT (Air Littoral Express) (Member of SAir Group & The Qualiflyer Group) — **Montpellier-Méditerranée & Nice-Cote d'Azur**

417 rue Samuel Morse Le Millenaire II, F-34961 Montpellier Cedex 2, France ☎ 467 20 67 20 Tx: 490601 f air lit Fax: 467 64 10 61 SITA: n/a

F: 1972 ⁂ 1300 Head: Marc Dufour IATA: 659 ICAO: AIR LITTORAL Net: n/a Regional cargo flights (with Beech 1900) are operated under the name AIR LITTORAL EXPRESS (an internal division, same headquarters). Some aircraft are operated on a franchise agreement with AIR FRANCE LUFTHANSA (as TEAM LUFTHANSA), in full such colors & both titles & using AF or LH flight numbers.

registration	type of aircraft	cn/fn	ex/ex*	mfd	del	powered by	mtow kg	configuration	selcal	name/fln/specialitites/remarks
☐ F-GPYS	Beech 1900C-1 Airliner	UC-69	N69ZR	0689	0996	2 PWC PT6A-65B	7529	Freighter		lsf Raytheon Aircraft Credit Corp.
☐ F-GPYT	Beech 1900C-1 Airliner	UC-80	N80ZR	0989	0996	2 PWC PT6A-65B	7529	Freighter		lsf Raytheon Aircraft Credit Corp.
☐ F-GPYU	Beech 1900C-1 Airliner	UC-109	N109YV	0490	0896	2 PWC PT6A-65B	7529	Freighter		lsf Raytheon Aircraft Credit Corp.
☐ F-GPYV	Beech 1900C-1 Airliner	UC-121	N121ZR	0890	0896	2 PWC PT6A-65B	7529	Freighter		lsf Raytheon Aircraft Credit Corp.
☐ F-GPYX	Beech 1900C-1 Airliner	UC-111	N111YV	0590	0896	2 PWC PT6A-65B	7529	Freighter		lsf Raytheon Aircraft Credit Corp.
☐ F-GPYY	Beech 1900C-1 Airliner	UC-115	N115YV	0790	0896	2 PWC PT6A-65B	7529	Freighter		lsf Raytheon Aircraft Credit Corp.
☐ F-GPYA	ATR 42-500	457	F-WWET*	0095	0396	2 PWC PW127E	18600	Y46		lsf Brice Bail
☐ F-GPYB	ATR 42-500	480	F-WWLZ*	0096	0396	2 PWC PW127E	18600	Y46		lsf Brice Bail
☐ F-GPYC	ATR 42-500	484	F-WWEB*	0096	0396	2 PWC PW127E	18600	Y46		lsf Brice Bail
☐ F-GPYD	ATR 42-500	490	F-WWLJ*	0096	0396	2 PWC PW127E	18600	Y46		lsf Brice Bail
☐ F-GPYF	ATR 42-500	495	F-WWLM*	0096	0496	2 PWC PW127E	18600	Y46		Marie Sara / lsf Brice Bail
☐ F-GPYG	ATR 42-500	516	F-WWLU*	0096	1096	2 PWC PW127E	18600	Y46		lsf Bruce Bail
☐ F-GPYH	ATR 42-500	522	F-WWLC*	0096	1196	2 PWC PW127E	18600	Y46		lsf Bruce Bail
☐ F-GPYI	ATR 42-500	526	F-WWLM*	0096	1296	2 PWC PW127E	18600	Y46		lsf Bruce Bail
☐ F-GPYJ	ATR 42-500	530	F-WWLH*	0096	0197	2 PWC PW127E	18600	Y46		lsf Bruce Bail
☐ F-GPYK	ATR 42-500	537	F-WWLC*	0097	0297	2 PWC PW127E	18600	Y46		lsf Brice Bail
☐ F-GPYL	ATR 42-500	542	F-WWLB*	0097	0397	2 PWC PW127E	18600	Y46		lsf GIE Callen
☐ F-GPYM	ATR 42-500	520	F-WWLR*	0097	0397	2 PWC PW127E	18600	Y46		lsf GIE Callen
☐ F-GPYN	ATR 42-500	539	F-WWLO*	0097	0397	2 PWC PW127E	18600	Y46		lsf GIE Callen
☐ F-GPYO	ATR 42-500	544	F-WWLH*	0097	0397	2 PWC PW127E	18600	Y46		lsf GIE Callen
☐ F-GLIJ	Canadair Regional Jet 100ER (CL-600-2B19)	7081		0095	1095	2 GE CF34-3A1	23133	Y50		lsf Bombardier Capital
☐ F-GLIK	Canadair Regional Jet 100ER (CL-600-2B19)	7084	C-FMMT*	0095	1095	2 GE CF34-3A1	23133	Y50		lsf Bombardier Capital
☐ F-GLIY	Canadair Regional Jet 100ER (CL-600-2B19)	7053	C-FMMQ*	0094	1294	2 GE CF34-3A1	23133	Y50		lsf Nocean Corp. / op in Team LH-cs
☐ F-GLIZ	Canadair Regional Jet 100ER (CL-600-2B19)	7057	C-FMMY*	0095	0195	2 GE CF34-3A1	23133	Y50		lsf Genese Corp.
☐ F-GNME	Canadair Regional Jet 100ER (CL-600-2B19)	7020		0093	1093	2 GE CF34-3A1	23133	Y50		lsf Gie RJ Fin / sub-lst ANS as EC-GTG
☐ F-GNMN	Canadair Regional Jet 100ER (CL-600-2B19)	7003	C-GVRJ*	0090	1093	2 GE CF34-3A1	23133	Y50		lsf RJ Fin / sub-lst Southern Winds
☐ F-GPTB	Canadair Regional Jet 100ER (CL-600-2B19)	7177		0097	0797	2 GE CF34-3A1	23133	Y50		lsf Gie Lerins
☐ F-GPTC	Canadair Regional Jet 100ER (CL-600-2B19)	7182		0097	0797	2 GE CF34-3A1	23133	Y50		lsf Gie Lerins
☐ F-GPTD	Canadair Regional Jet 100ER (CL-600-2B19)	7184		0097	0797	2 GE CF34-3A1	23133	Y50		lsf Gie Lerins
☐ F-GPTE	Canadair Regional Jet 100ER (CL-600-2B19)	7183		0097	0797	2 GE CF34-3A1	23133	Y50		lsf Gie Lerins
☐ F-GPTF	Canadair Regional Jet 100ER (CL-600-2B19)	7197		0097	1097	2 GE CF34-3A1	23133	Y50		lsf Gie Lerins / op in Team LH-cs
☐ F-GPTG	Canadair Regional Jet 100ER (CL-600-2B19)	7223		0098	0298	2 GE CF34-3A1	23133	Y50		lsf Bombardier Capital Inc.
☐ F-GPTH	Canadair Regional Jet 100ER (CL-600-2B19)					2 GE CF34-3A1	23133	Y50		oo-delivery 0599
☐ F-GPTI	Canadair Regional Jet 100ER (CL-600-2B19)					2 GE CF34-3A1	23133	Y50		oo-delivery 0599
☐ F-GPTJ	Canadair Regional Jet 100ER (CL-600-2B19)					2 GE CF34-3A1	23133	Y50		oo-delivery 0699
☐ F-GPTK	Canadair Regional Jet 100ER (CL-600-2B19)					2 GE CF34-3A1	23133	Y50		oo-delivery 0799
☐ F-GPYP	Canadair Regional Jet 100ER (CL-600-2B19)	7126	C-FMML*	0096	0796	2 GE CF34-3A1	23133	Y50		lsf Gie RJ Fin / op in Team LH-colors
☐ F-GPYQ	Canadair Regional Jet 100ER (CL-600-2B19)	7144	C-FMMT*	0096	0197	2 GE CF34-3A1	23133	Y50		lsf Regional Aircraft Finance B.V.
☐ F-GPYR	Canadair Regional Jet 100ER (CL-600-2B19)	7164	C-FMND*	0097	0397	2 GE CF34-3A1	23133	Y50		lsf Regional Aircraft Finance B.V.
☐ F-GLIS	Fokker 70 (F28 Mk0070)	11540	PH-RRS	0095	0595	2 RR Tay 620-15	36740	Y79		lsf AFTR / op in AF Express-colors
☐ F-GLIT	Fokker 70 (F28 Mk0070)	11541	PH-RRT	0095	0595	2 RR Tay 620-15	36740	Y79		lsf AFTR / op in AF Express-colors
☐ F-GLIU	Fokker 70 (F28 Mk0070)	11543	PH-RRU	0095	0695	2 RR Tay 620-15	36740	Y79		lsf AFTR / op in AF Express-colors
☐ F-GLIV	Fokker 70 (F28 Mk0070)	11556	PH-RRV	0095	1095	2 RR Tay 620-15	36740	Y79		lsf AFTR / op in AF Express-colors
☐ F-GLIX	Fokker 70 (F28 Mk0070)	11558	PH-RRW	0095	1195	2 RR Tay 620-15	36740	Y79		lsf AFTR / op in AF Express-colors
☐ F-GLIR	Fokker 100 (F28 Mk0100)	11509	PH-EZF*	0095	0395	2 RR Tay 650-15	44450	Y109		lsf AFTR

AIR MARTINIQUE (Subsidiary of Air Guadeloupe) — **Fort de France-Le Lamentin**

Aéroport de Lamentin, F-97232 Le Lamentin, Martinique ☎ 51 08 09 Tx: 912048 mr airmar Fax: 51 59 27 SITA: n/a

F: 1981 ⁂ 100 Head: Guy Aurore Net: n/a

registration	type of aircraft	cn/fn	ex/ex*	mfd	del	powered by	mtow kg	configuration	selcal	name/fln/specialitites/remarks
☐ F-OHQL	ATR 42-500	524	F-WWEF*	0097	1297	2 PWC PW127E	18600	Y46		lsf FWI
☐ F-OHQV	ATR 42-500	571	F-WWEM*	0098	1298	2 PWC PW127E	18600	Y46		lsf FWI

AIR MEDITERRANEE = BIE — **Tarbes**

Aéroport Tarbes-Ossun-Lourdes, F-65290 Juillan, France ☎ 562 32 92 00 Tx: none Fax: 562 32 08 24 SITA: LDEAMCR

F: 1997 ⁂ 46 Head: Antoine Ferretti ICAO: MEDITERRANEE Net: n/a

registration	type of aircraft	cn/fn	ex/ex*	mfd	del	powered by	mtow kg	configuration	selcal	name/fln/specialitites/remarks
☐ F-GCJL	Boeing 737-222	19067 / 71	N9029U	0068	0498	2 PW JT8D-9A (HK3/NOR)	49442	Y130		
☐ F-GCSL	Boeing 737-222	19066 / 69	N9028U	0068	0299	2 PW JT8D-7B	49442	Y130		lsf EUL
☐ F-GOAF	Boeing 737-242C	19847 / 84	N847TA	0068	0897	2 PW JT8D-9A (HK3/NOR)	53070	Y130 / Frtr		lsf TAT SA

AIR MEDITERRANEE CORSE — **Propriano**

Lieudit Tavaria, F-20100 Propriano, France ☎ 495 76 00 57 Tx: none Fax: 495 73 45 02 SITA: n/a

F: 1996 ⁂ n/a Head: n/a Net: n/a

registration	type of aircraft	cn/fn	ex/ex*	mfd	del	powered by	mtow kg	configuration	selcal	name/fln/specialitites/remarks
☐ F-BSTD	Cessna 421B Golden Eagle	421B0106	N8076Q	0071		2 CO GTSIO-520-H	3289	7 Pax		lsf Aeronautique Financement

AIR MOOREA = TAH (Subsidiary of Air Tahiti) — **Papeete-Faaa**

BP 6019, F-98702 Faaa Aéroport, (Tahiti), Polynésie Française ☎ 86 41 00 Tx: none Fax: 86 42 69 SITA: n/a

F: 1968 ⁂ 80 Head: Marcel Galenon ICAO: AIR MOOREA Net: n/a

registration	type of aircraft	cn/fn	ex/ex*	mfd	del	powered by	mtow kg	configuration	selcal	name/fln/specialitites/remarks
☐ F-ODUP	Britten-Norman BN-2B-26 Islander	2219	G-BRGB*	0090	0490	2 LY O-540-E4C5	2812	Y9		lsf Moorea Bail
☐ F-ODUQ	Britten-Norman BN-2B-26 Islander	2220	G-BRGC*	0090	0590	2 LY O-540-E4C5	2812	Y9		lsf Moorea Bail
☐ F-ODUR	Britten-Norman BN-2B-26 Islander	2217	G-BRFZ*	0090	0590	2 LY O-540-E4C5	2812	Y9		lsf Moorea Bail
☐ F-ODBN	De Havilland DHC-6 Twin Otter 300	470		0075	0791	2 PWC PT6A-27	5670	Y19		
☐ F-OHJF	De Havilland DHC-6 Twin Otter 300	500	N929MA	0076	1195	2 PWC PT6A-27	5670	Y19		

AIR NORMANDIE = ID / RNO (Normandie Aviation, SA dba) — **Le Havre-Octeville**

Aéroport du Havre, F-76620 Le Havre, France ☎ 232 85 38 53 Tx: none Fax: 232 85 38 51 SITA: LEHIDIJ

F: 1991 ⁂ 70 Head: Jean Borie ICAO: NORMANDIE Net: http://www.ibsfr.com/airno/

registration	type of aircraft	cn/fn	ex/ex*	mfd	del	powered by	mtow kg	configuration	selcal	name/fln/specialitites/remarks
☐ F-BXAP	Beech King Air C90	LJ-522	D-IHVB	0071		2 PWC PT6A-20	4377	Y7		lsf Bail Ouest
☐ F-BXSL	Beech King Air C90	LJ-648		0074		2 PWC PT6A-20A	4377	Y7		lst RNO
☐ F-GEJV	Beech King Air A100	B-129	N235B	0072		2 PWC PT6A-28	5216	Y12		lsf BNP Bail
☐ F-GELL	Beech King Air E90	LW-88	9Q-CTQ	0073		2 PWC PT6A-28	4581	Y7		
☐ F-GJAD	Beech King Air E90	LW-3	N888BH	0072		2 PWC PT6A-28	4581	Y7		lsf Credit de l'Est
☐ F-GJDG	Cessna 500 Citation I	500-0312	N82AT	0076		2 PWC JT15D-1A	5375	Y6		lsf Gin Finances
☐ F-BVET	Beech King Air 200	BB-21		0074	0098	2 PWC PT6A-41	5670			lsf Commerciale de Metaux & Minerais
☐ F-GHSV	Beech King Air 200	BB-622	N212BF	0080		2 PWC PT6A-41	5670	Y9		lsf Sodelem
☐ F-GMCR	Beech King Air 200	BB-424	D-IGRO	0078		2 PWC PT6A-41	5670	Y9		lsf Ligier Jet Air
☐ F-GMCS	Beech Catpass 250	BB-688	N250TR	0080		2 PWC PT6A-41	5670	Y12		lsf Bail Equipement/cvtd King Air 200
☐ F-GMVH	BAe 3206 Jetstream 32	974	G-BURU	0092	1098	2 GA TPE331-12UAR-701H	7350	Y19		lsf RGI
☐ F-GMVJ	BAe 3206 Jetstream 32	976	G-BUUZ	0092	0097	2 GA TPE331-12UAR-701H	7350	Y19		lsf RGI
☐ F-GMVL	BAe 3206 Jetstream 32	978	G-31-978*	0092	0098	2 GA TPE331-12UAR-701H	7350	Y19		lsf RGI
☐ F-GMVM	BAe 3206 Jetstream 32	979	G-31-979*	0093	0398	2 GA TPE331-12UAR-701H	7350	Y19		lsf RGI
☐ F-GMVN	BAe 3206 Jetstream 32	980	G-31-980*	0093	0399	2 GA TPE331-12UAR-701H	7350	Y19		lsf RGI
☐ F-GMVO	BAe 3206 Jetstream 32	982	G-31-982*	0093	1096	2 GA TPE331-12UAR-701H	7350	Y19		Charente / lsf RGI

AIR OPEN SKY, S.A. = OPN
Paris-CDG & Metz

BP 10256, F-95704 Roissy-CDG Cédex, France ☎ (1) 48 16 11 11 Tx: none Fax: (1) 48 16 11 92 SITA: n/a
F: 1998 ⁂ 80 Head: Stéphane Brun ICAO: AIR SKY Net: n/a

☐ F-GEQJ	ATR 42-300	*008*	*PH-ATR*	*0086*	*1198*	*2 PWC PW120*	*16700*	*Y46 / Freighter*		*lsf ATR*
☐ F-GKNB	ATR 42-300	*226*		*0091*	*1098*	*2 PWC PW120*	*16900*	*Y46*		*lsf / opf LIB*
☐ F-GKNC	ATR 42-300	*230*		*0091*	*1098*	*2 PWC PW120*	*16900*	*Y46*		*lsf / opf LIB*

AIR POITIERS = FUR
Poitiers-Biard

Aéroport de Poitiers-Biard, BP1067, F-86061 Poitiers Cédex 09, France ☎ 549 37 93 65 Tx: n/a Fax: 549 37 93 63 SITA: n/a
F: 1993 ⁂ 2 Head: n/a ICAO: FUTUROSCOPE Net: http://www.airpoitiers.fr

☐ F-GETI	Beech King Air F90	*LA-19*	*N90NS*	*0079*		*2 PWC PT6A-135*	*4967*	*9 Pax*		*lsf Locavi*
☐ F-GHUV	Beech King Air E90	*LW-278*	*N700MA*	*0078*		*2 PWC PT6A-28*	*4581*	*9 Pax*		*lsf Slibail*
☐ F-GSMC	Cessna F500 Citation	*500-0308*	*F-GMLH*	*0076*		*2 PWC JT15D-1A*	*5375*	*6 Pax*		*lsf Air Stream*

AIR PROVENCE INTERNATIONAL = APR (formerly Compagnie Air Provence Int'l / Société Nouvelle d'Exploitation Air Provence Int'l dba)
Marseille-Marignane & Paris-LBG

BP 33, Aéroport, Centre Aviation Générale, F-13728 Marignane Cédex, France ☎ 442 14 30 83 Tx: none Fax: 442 89 65 40 SITA: MRSMDCR
F: 1978 ⁂ 110 Head: Jean P. Rozan ICAO: AIR PROVENCE Net: n/a

☐ F-GFEF	GAC (Grumman) G-159 Gulfstream I	*122*	*N707MP*	*0063*	*1287*	*2 RR Dart 529-8H*	*15240*	*Y19*		*lsf Minière de Trebas*
☐ F-GFGT	GAC (Grumman) G-159 Gulfstream I	*005*	*N159AJ*	*0059*	*0987*	*2 RR Dart 529-8E/X*	*15240*	*Y24 / Freighter*		*lsf Minière de Trebas*
☐ F-GFGV	GAC (Grumman) G-159 Gulfstream I	*044*	*N717RD*	*0060*	*0887*	*2 RR Dart 529-8H*	*15240*	*Y24 / Freighter*		Le Provençal Club / *lsf Min.de Trebas*
☐ F-GFIB	GAC (Grumman) G-159 Gulfstream I	*071*	*N222EF*	*0061*		*2 RR Dart 529-8X*	*15240*	*Y24 / Freighter*		
☐ F-GFMH	GAC (Grumman) G-159 Gulfstream I	*020*	*N732US*	*0059*	*1189*	*2 RR Dart 529-8E/H*	*16330*	*Y24*		*lsf Minière de Trebas*
☐ F-GGGY	GAC (Grumman) G-159 Gulfstream I	*080*	*N200GJ*	*0061*	*0390*	*2 RR Dart 529-8X*	*15240*	*Y19*		Le Francilien / *lsf Min.de Trebas*
☐ F-GODD	BAe (HS) 748-245 Srs 2A	*1658 / 134*	*G-BFLL*	*0068*	*0695*	*2 RR Dart 534-2*	*20183*	*Freighter*		*lsf Wisdom Investments Ltd*
☐ F-GPDC	BAe (HS) 748-232 Srs 2A	*1612 / 83*	*G-AZSU*	*0067*	*0495*	*2 RR Dart 534-2*	*20183*	*Freighter*		*lsf Wisdom Investments Ltd*
☐ F-GBRQ	Fairchild Ind. FH-227B	*562*	*PT-LCU*	*0067*	*0296*	*2 RR Dart 532-7*	*19990*	*Y48*		*lsf Wisdom Investments Ltd*
☐ F-GCLM	Fairchild Ind. FH-227B	*544*	*N4225*	*0067*	*0296*	*2 RR Dart 532-7*	*19990*	*Y48*		*lsf Wisdom Investments Ltd*

AIR SAINT BARTHELEMY = OJ / BTH (Sté Commerciale Aeronautique dba / Member of Groupe Air Guadeloupe)
Saint Barthelemy

St. Jean, F-97133 Saint Barthelemy, Guadeloupe ☎ 27 71 90 Tx: none Fax: 27 67 03 SITA: n/a
F: 1995 ⁂ n/a Head: Eric Koury IATA: 981 ICAO: BARTHS Net: n/a Beside aircraft listed, additional (Cessna 208B Grand Caravan I) are lsf AIR SAINT MARTIN when required.

☐ F-OGES	De Havilland DHC-6 Twin Otter 300	*254*	*N302MA*	*0069*	*0097*	*2 PWC PT6A-27*	*5670*	*Y19*		*lsf FWI*
☐ F-OGIZ	De Havilland DHC-6 Twin Otter 300	*675*		*0080*	*0095*	*2 PWC PT6A-27*	*5670*	*Y19*		*lsf AGU*

AIR SAINT MARTIN = S6 / ASM (SCTA-Sté Caribéenne de Transport Aérien dba/Member of Groupe Air Guadeloupe)
Pointe à Pitre/Fort de France/St.Martin/St.Barthelemy

Immeuble Le Lieu No. 1 & 11, F-97139 Les Abymes, Guadeloupe ☎ 82 96 63 Tx: none Fax: 91 49 69 SITA: n/a
F: 1991 ⁂ 45 Head: Raphael Koury IATA: 707 ICAO: AIR SAINT MARTIN Net: n/a

☐ F-OGXI	Cessna 208B Grand Caravan	*208B0485*	*N2647Y*	*0095*	*0196*	*1 PWC PT6A-114A*	*3969*	*Y9*		*lsf ING Lease*
☐ F-OGXJ	Cessna 208B Grand Caravan	*208B0497*	*N12289*	*0095*	*0296*	*1 PWC PT6A-114A*	*3969*	*Y9*		*lsf ING Lease*
☐ F-OGXK	Cessna 208B Grand Caravan	*208B0459*	*N2646X*	*0095*	*0296*	*1 PWC PT6A-114A*	*3969*	*Y9*		*lsf ING Lease*
☐ F-OGXX	Cessna 208B Grand Caravan	*208B0557*	*N1268N*	*0096*	*1296*	*1 PWC PT6A-114A*	*3969*	*Y9*		*lsf ING Lease*
☐ F-OGXY	Cessna 208B Grand Caravan	*208B0574*	*N1207A*	*0096*	*1296*	*1 PWC PT6A-114A*	*3969*	*Y9*		*lsf ING Lease*
☐ F-OGXZ	Cessna 208B Grand Caravan	*208B0586*	*N12160*	*0096*	*1296*	*1 PWC PT6A-114A*	*3969*	*Y9*		*lsf ING Lease*
☐ F-OHQM	Cessna 208B Grand Caravan	*208B0726*		*0098*	*1298*	*1 PWC PT6A-114A*	*3969*	*Y9*		*lsf Snc Antillaero*
☐ F-OHQN	Cessna 208B Grand Caravan	*208B0715*	*N1258H**	*0098*	*1298*	*1 PWC PT6A-114A*	*3969*	*Y9*		*lsf Snc Antillaero*

AIR SAINT-PIERRE, SA = PJ / SPM (Partenaire CANADIEN / CANADIAN Partner)
St. Pierre

BP 4225, F-97500 St. Pierre, St. Pierre and Miquelon Isles ☎ 41 27 20 Tx: 914422 qn briand Fax: 41 23 36 SITA: n/a
F: 1964 ⁂ 38 Head: Remy L. Briand IATA: 638 ICAO: SAINT-PIERRE Net: http://205.250.151.22/aspweb
Scheduled services with ATR 42 aircraft are operated in conjunction with Canadian / Canadian as a Partenaire CANADIEN / CANADIAN Partner (in own cs) using CP flt no's.

☐ F-OBYN	Piper PA-31-350 Navajo Chieftain	*31-8152005*	*N4046M*	*0080*		*2 LY TIO-540-J2BD*	*3175*	*Y7*		
☐ F-OHGL	ATR 42-320	*323*	*F-WWET**	*0093*	*1293*	*2 PWC PW121*	*16700*	*Y48*		*lsf St. Pierre Investissements*

AIR SERVICE 51 (Affiliated with Ets Collard SàRL)
Bouzy

BP 1 Bouzy, F-51150 Tours-sur-Marne, France ☎ 326 57 01 12 Tx: none Fax: 326 57 09 87 SITA: n/a
F: 1983 ⁂ 3 Head: A. Collard Net: n/a

☐ F-GFFU	Eurocopter (Aerosp.) AS350B Ecureuil	*2083*		*0088*		*1 TU Arriel 1B*	*1950*	*5 Pax*		
☐ F-GSMU	Eurocopter EC135T1	*0043*		*0098*	*0398*	*2 TU Arrius 2B1*	*2720*			*lsf Eurocopter Deutschland*

AIR SERVICES
Noumea-Magenta

BP 14383, F-98803 Nouméa, Nouvelle Calédonie ☎ 27 51 06 Tx: none Fax: n/a SITA: n/a
F: 1997 ⁂ n/a Head: n/a Net: n/a

☐ F-ODYQ	Socata TB 20 Trinidad	*1118*	*VH-LQJ*	*0090*	*0097*	*1 LY IO-540-C4D5D*	*1400*			*lsf SàRL TAT*
☐ F-OIAC	Piper PA-34-200 Seneca	*34-7350277*	*VH-RRS*	*0073*	*0097*	*2 LY IO-360-C1E6*	*1905*			

AIR SERVICE VOSGES = VGE (Associated with CCI Chambre de Commerce et d'Industrie, Epinal)
Epinal-Mirecourt

BP 96, F-88003 Epinal Cédex, France ☎ 329 35 18 14 Tx: 960536 f chamco Fax: 329 64 01 88 SITA: n/a
F: 1976 ⁂ n/a Head: François Renolleau ICAO: AIR SERVICE VOSGES Net: n/a

☐ F-GFVO	Piper PA-31T Cheyenne II	*31T-7920049*	*N500FC*	*0079*		*2 PWC PT6A-28*	*4082*	*6 Pax*		
☐ F-GDAK	Beech King Air F90	*LA-141*		*0081*		*2 PWC PT6A-135*	*4967*	*9 Pax*		

AIRSTAR (Subsidiary of Savoie Hélicoptères)
Chambéry

BP 64, F-73212 Aime Cédex, France ☎ 479 55 69 73 Tx: 980469 f Fax: 479 09 77 50 SITA: n/a
F: 1981 ⁂ n/a Head: Raymond Prevot Net: n/a Aircraft below MTOW 1361kg: Bellanca 7GCBC

☐ F-GFEM	Piper PA-34-200T Seneca II	*34-8170017*	*N82772*	*0081*		*2 CO TSIO-360-EB1*	*2073*	*5 Pax*		

AIR TAHITI = VT / VTA (formerly Air Polynésie)
Papeete-Faaa

BP 6722, F-98702 Faaa Aéroport, (Tahiti), Polynésie Française ☎ 86 40 00 Tx: none Fax: 86 40 69 SITA: PPTDAVT
F: 1958 ⁂ 770 Head: Christian Vernaudon IATA: 135 ICAO: AIR TAHITI Net: http://www.aboveall.com/tt/TTPG02A.html

☐ F-OHAA	Dornier 228-212	*8198*	*D-CDWK**	*0090*	*1190*	*2 GA TPE331-5A-252D*	*6400*	*Y19*		*lsf Moorea Bail*
☐ F-OHAF	Dornier 228-212	*8199*	*D-CBDZ**	*0091*	*0392*	*2 GA TPE331-5A-252D*	*6400*	*Y19*		*lsf Tahiti Investissements I*
☐ F-GNPL	ATR 42-300	*063*	*F-ODUC*	*0087*	*1187*	*2 PWC PW120*	*16700*	*Y46*		*lst CLG -0699*
☐ F-OHJB	ATR 42-500	*513*	*F-WWLL**	*0096*	*1196*	*2 PWC PW127E*	*18600*	*Y48*		*lsf Airinvest 42-96-1*
☐ F-OHJC	ATR 42-500	*528*	*F-WWLF**	*0096*	*1296*	*2 PWC PW127E*	*18600*	*Y48*		*lsf Airinvest 42-96-2*
☐ F-OHJD	ATR 42-500	*556*	*F-WWLM**	*0097*	*0697*	*2 PWC PW127E*	*18600*	*Y48*		*lsf GIE Tahiti 2009*
☐ F-OHAT	ATR 72-202	*365*	*F-WWEM**	*0093*	*0693*	*2 PWC PW124B*	*21500*	*Y66*		Moeata
☐ F-OHJA	ATR 72-202	*456*	*F-WWLN**	*0095*	*0595*	*2 PWC PW124B*	*21500*	*Y66*		*lsf ATR 72-95*
☐ F-OHJN	ATR 72-500 (72-212A)	*535*	*F-WWEC**	*0097*	*1197*	*2 PWC PW127F*	*22500*	*Y66*		*lsf Vavin Tahiti Bail*
☐ F-OHJO	ATR 72-500 (72-212A)	*553*	*F-WWLC**	*0098*	*0698*	*2 PWC PW127F*	*22500*	*Y66*		*lsf SA-Air Bail*
☐ F-OHJT	ATR 72-500 (72-212A)			*0099*		*2 PWC PW127F*	*22500*	*Y66*		*oo-delivery 0000*
☐ F-OHJU	ATR 72-500 (72-212A)	*563*	*F-WWEA**	*0098*	*1298*	*2 PWC PW127F*	*22500*	*Y66*		*lsf Doumer Tahiti Bail*

AIR TAHITI NUI = TN / THT
Papeete-Faaa

BP 1673, F-98713 Papéeté, (Tahiti), Polynésie Française ☎ 46 02 02 Tx: none Fax: 460 29 02 SITA: n/a
F: 1998 ⁂ n/a Head: Jacques Bankir IATA: 244 ICAO: TAHITI AIRLINES Net: n/a

☐ F-OITN	Airbus Industrie A340-211	*031*	*F-GLZD*	*0093*	*1198*	*4 CFMI CFM56-5C2*	*257000*	*Y286*		*lsf Airbus Industrie Financial Services*

AIR TOULOUSE INTERNATIONAL = SH / TLE (Societe Nouvelle Air Toulouse International dba)
Toulouse-Blagnac

BP 44, F-31702 Blagnac Cédex, France ☎ 561 16 76 00 Tx: none Fax: 561 16 76 99 SITA: TLSDESH
F: 1969 ⁂ 147 Head: François Hersen IATA: 887 ICAO: AIR TOULOUSE Net: n/a

☐ F-GPPF	Dassault Falcon 50	*65*	*N1EV*	*0082*	*0996*	*3 GA TFE731-3-1C*	*17600*	*Executive*		*lsf Slibail Location*
☐ F-GEXI	Boeing 737-2L9 (A)	*22406 / 690*	*G-BNGK*	*0080*	*0996*	*2 PW JT8D-17*	*58105*	*Y131*		*lsf Alter Bail Aviation*
☐ F-GHXK	Boeing 737-2A1 (A)	*21599 / 514*	*N171AW*	*0078*	*0595*	*2 PW JT8D-17*	*54204*	*Y131*		*lsf Alter Bail Aviation*
☐ F-GHXL	Boeing 737-2S3 (A)	*21775 / 570*	*G-BMOR*	*0079*	*0395*	*2 PW JT8D-17*	*54204*	*Y131*		*lsf Alter Bail Aviation*
☐ F-GLXF	Boeing 737-219 (A)	*22657 / 846*	*G-BJXJ*	*0082*	*0395*	*2 PW JT8D-15*	*54204*	*Y131*		*lsf Alter Bail Aviation*
☐ F-GLXH	Boeing 737-2D6 (A)	*20544 / 290*	*G-BMMZ*	*0071*	*0493*	*2 PW JT8D-9A*	*54253*	*Y131*		*lsf Localease Aviation B.V.*

AIR TURQUOISE = TUQ
Noumea-Magenta

7 Rue du Pasteur Maurice Leenhardt, F-98800 Nouméa, Nouvelle Calédonie ☎ 25 91 01 Tx: n/a Fax: 25 91 01 SITA: n/a
F: 1995 ⁂ n/a Head: François Gastine ICAO: AIR TURQUOISE Net: n/a

☐ F-OHYA	Cessna U206F Stationair II	*U20603130*	*N52EC*	*0076*	*0795*	*1 CO IO-520-F*	*1656*			*Amphibian*

AIRWAYS, SA = WAY
Agen-La Garenne

Château Lalande, F-82340 Donzac, France ☎ 553 68 18 18 Tx: n/a Fax: 553 96 95 48 SITA: n/a
F: 1987 ⁂ 8 Head: Michel Malecot ICAO: GARONNE Net: n/a

☐ F-GIII	Piper PA-31T Cheyenne II	*31T-8020037*	*N805SW*	*0080*		*2 PWC PT6A-28*	*4082*			*lsf Locabail*
☐ F-GKRR	Piper PA-31T Cheyenne II	*31T-8120015*	*N107TT*	*0081*		*2 PWC PT6A-28*	*4082*			

149 registration type of aircraft *cn/fn* *ex/ex** *mfd* *del* *powered by* *mtow kg* *configuration* *selcal* *name/fln/specialitites/remarks*

ALSAIR, SA = LSR (Member of Industriegruppe Knauf) — Colmar-Houssen

Aéroport de Colmar-Houssen, F-68000 Colmar, France ☎ 389 41 41 95 Tx: 871294 f Fax: 389 24 09 08 SITA: n/a
F: 1982 ⁂ 13 Head: Jean Marie Joubert ICAO: ALSAIR Net: n/a

☐ F-GEOU	Beech King Air C90	LJ-941	N3804C	0080		2 PWC PT6A-21	4377	9 Pax		
☐ F-GIAL	Beech King Air 200	BB-844	SE-IGV	0081		2 PWC PT6A-41	5670	12 Pax		
☐ F-GJMJ	Beech King Air 200	BB-1032	I-CUVI	0082	0989	2 PWC PT6A-42	5670	11 Pax		
☐ F-GLTK	Cessna F550 Citation II	550-0609	D-CHOP	0089	0098	2 PWC JT15D-4	5700	9 Pax		lsf Snc Knauf Trade

ALTAGNA (Sister company of Air Provence International) — Bastia-Poretta

Aéroport de Bastia-Poretta, F-20290 Borgo, France ☎ 495 38 36 33 Tx: n/a Fax: 495 38 33 15 SITA: n/a
F: 1987 ⁂ 3 Head: Jean Pierre Rozan Net: n/a

☐ F-BOSY	Beech King Air A90 (65-A90)	LJ-128	D-IMTW	0066		2 PWC PT6A-20	4213	7 Pax		lsf Bail Equipement

AOM French Airlines = IW / AOM (AOM-Minerve, SA dba/Member of The Qualiflyer Group/Subs. of SAirGroup & Marine-Wendel Group) — Paris-Orly

BP 854, F-94551 Orly Aérogare Cédex, France ☎ (1) 49 79 10 00 Tx: 263050 f airom Fax: (1) 49 79 10 12 SITA: ORSKIW
F: 1992 ⁂ 1450 Head: Alexandre Couvelaire IATA: 646 ICAO: FRENCH LINES Net: http://www.aom.com

☐ F-GHOL	Boeing 737-53C	24825 / 1894		0090	0498	2 CFMI CFM56-3C1	52000	CY112	GP-HJ	lsf EUL
☐ F-GHUL	Boeing 737-53C	24826 / 2041		0091	0498	2 CFMI CFM56-3C1	52000	CY112		lsf EUL
☐ F-GINL	Boeing 737-53C	24827 / 2243		0092	0498	2 CFMI CFM56-3C1	52000	CY112		lsf EUL
☐ F-GGMA	Boeing (Douglas) MD-83 (DC-9-83)	49399 / 1343	EI-BTL	0187	0192	2 PW JT8D-219	72480	C16Y139	BG-AJ	lsf Athena Lise
☐ F-GGMB	Boeing (Douglas) MD-83 (DC-9-83)	49617 / 1464		0088	0192	2 PW JT8D-219	72480	C16Y139	EP-AC	lsf Athena Fl
☐ F-GGMD	Boeing (Douglas) MD-83 (DC-9-83)	49618 / 1611		0689	0192	2 PW JT8D-219	72480	Y169	AB-FQ	lsf T.L.C. Property Co. Ltd
☐ F-GGME	Boeing (Douglas) MD-83 (DC-9-83)	49855 / 1728		0090	0192	2 PW JT8D-219	72480	Y169	AC-KQ	lsf Athena Aviation Ltd
☐ F-GGMF	Boeing (Douglas) MD-83 (DC-9-83)	53463 / 2089		0094	1094	2 PW JT8D-219	72480	C16Y139	HK-CR	lsf TLC Crocus Ltd
☐ F-GRMC	Boeing (Douglas) MD-83 (DC-9-83)	53466 / 2101		0094	1294	2 PW JT8D-219	72480	C16Y139	HK-DS	lsf ORIX Altair Corp.
☐ F-GRMG	Boeing (Douglas) MD-83 (DC-9-83)	53464 / 2091		0094	1094	2 PW JT8D-219	72480	C16Y139	HK-CS	lsf TLC Daffodil Ltd
☐ F-GRMH	Boeing (Douglas) MD-83 (DC-9-83)	53465 / 2093		1094	1294	2 PW JT8D-219	72480	C16Y139	HK-DR	lsf Virgo Ltd
☐ F-GRMI	Boeing (Douglas) MD-83 (DC-9-83)	53488 / 2134		0096	0396	2 PW JT8D-219	72575	C16Y139	LR-HK	lsf SL Condor Ltd
☐ F-GRMJ	Boeing (Douglas) MD-83 (DC-9-83)	53520 / 2137		0096	0496	2 PW JT8D-219	72575	C16Y139	LR-HQ	lsf ORIX Carina Corp.
☐ F-BTDE	Boeing (Douglas) DC-10-30	46853 / 134	N54639	0073	0393	3 GE CF6-50C2	263084	C42Y275	HJ-AF	lsf Batide Bail
☐ F-GHOI	Boeing (Douglas) DC-10-30	46870 / 217	OY-KDA	0075	0594	3 GE CF6-50C2	263084	C42Y275	GM-HL	lsf Daiichi Research Institute Co. Ltd
☐ F-GKMY	Boeing (Douglas) DC-10-30	47815 / 325	SE-DFF	1279	0192	3 GE CF6-50C2B	267620	C42Y275	CG-DM	lsf Gekamy
☐ F-GLMX	Boeing (Douglas) DC-10-30	47814 / 315	LN-RKC	0080	0192	3 GE CF6-50C2B	267620	C42Y275	CH-BL	lsf Transinvest I
☐ F-GNDC	Boeing (Douglas) DC-10-30	47849 / 213	F-GDJK	0075	1293	3 GE CF6-50C2	263084	C42Y275	EL-GH	lsf AOM Finance SA/special bird-colors
☐ F-GNEM	Boeing (Douglas) DC-10-30	46892 / 204	TU-TAM	0075	0792	3 GE CF6-50C2	263084	C42Y275	BE-DK	lsf RKA
☐ F-GTDF	Boeing (Douglas) DC-10-30	46854 / 193	N54649	0075	1194	3 GE CF6-50C2	263084	C42Y275	FL-CM	lsf GATX
☐ F-GTDG	Boeing (Douglas) DC-10-30	46997 / 288	TU-TAN	0079	0295	3 GE CF6-50C2	263084	C42Y275	BL-EG	lsf Tutane Leasing
☐ F-GTDH	Boeing (Douglas) DC-10-30	46851 / 85	F-BTDC	0073	0395	3 GE CF6-50C2R	263084	C42Y275	BJ-HL	lsf AFR
☐ F-GTDI	Boeing (Douglas) DC-10-30	46890 / 77	TU-TAL	0073	0696	3 GE CF6-50C	256280	C42Y252	BK-DJ	lsf AOM Finance SA
☐ F-ODLX	Boeing (Douglas) DC-10-30	46872 / 233	SE-DFE	0076	0192	3 GE CF6-50C	256280	C42Y275	AG-FH	Diamant / lsf AOM Finance SA
☐ F-ODLY	Boeing (Douglas) DC-10-30	46954 / 227	SE-DFH	0076	0192	3 GE CF6-50C	256280	Y344	AC-FL	Turquoise / lsf AOM Finance SA
☐ F-ODLZ	Boeing (Douglas) DC-10-30	46869 / 174	SE-DFD	0074	0192	3 GE CF6-50C2	263084	C42Y275	AC-HK	Saphir / lsf KS DC-10-30 I
☐ F-GLZE	Airbus Industrie A340-211	038		0094	0399	4 CFMI CFM56-5C2	257000	C36Y242		lsf Airbus Industrie Financial Services
☐ F-GLZF	Airbus Industrie A340-211	043		0094	0299	4 CFMI CFM56-5C2	257000	C36Y242		lsf Airbus Industrie Financial Services

ARCHIPEL — Paris-Le Bourget

6 rue Jean Gougon, F-75008 Paris, France ☎ (1) 45 61 03 03 Tx: none Fax: (1) 45 62 97 44 SITA: n/a
F: 1998 ⁂ n/a Head: Xavier Leny Net: n/a

☐ F-BUIB	Cessna 207 Skywagon	20700217	N1617U	0072	0098	1 CO IO-520-F	1724			lsf T.F.C. Textron

ATLANTIQUE AIR ASSISTANCE – AAA = TLB — Nantes-Atlantique

BP 4, F-49600 Beaupréau, France ☎ 241 63 05 50 Tx: none Fax: 241 63 53 77 SITA: n/a
F: 1989 ⁂ 6 Head: A. Besseau ICAO: TRIPLE-A Net: n/a

☐ F-GIZB	Beech King Air C90	LJ-955	N768SB	0081	0293	2 PWC PT6A-21	4377	Y8		
☐ F-GNBR	Beech 1900D Airliner	UE-327	N23154*	0098	0998	2 PWC PT6A-67D	7688	Y19		lsf Raytheon Airliner Lease Corp.

ATLANTIQUE HELICOPTERE — Nantes-Atlantique

32 rue de la Bouqinière, F-44200 Nantes, France ☎ 240 84 80 80 Tx: none Fax: 240 84 80 80 SITA: n/a
F: 1998 ⁂ n/a Head: Eric Oger Net: n/a Aircraft below MTOW 1361kg: Robinson R22

☐ F-GHDR	Agusta-Bell 206B JetRanger III	8693		0086	0098	1 AN 250-C20J	1451			lsf Eurl Aerozais

AVDEF – Aviation Défense Service (formerly Precision Air Services) — Nimes-Garons

Zone Aeroportuaire, Nimes Arles Camargue, F-30800 St. Gilles, France ☎ 466 70 74 10 Tx: 490573 f Fax: 466 70 12 22 SITA: n/a
F: 1989 ⁂ 42 Head: Henri Bret Net: n/a

☐ F-GBPZ	Beech King Air C90	LJ-860		0079		2 PWC PT6A-21	4377	8 Pax		
☐ F-GIDV	Beech King Air 200	BB-590	I-ALGH	0080		2 PWC PT6A-41	5670	9 Pax		lsf Bail Ecureuil
☐ F-BVPR	Dassault Falcon 10	5	F-WVPR	0075	0399	2 GA TFE731-2-1C	8500	7 Pax		lsf Unimat
☐ F-GPAA	Dassault Falcon 20C	103	G-FRAV	0067	0493	2 GE CF700-2D2	13000	Target towing		lsf BNP Bail
☐ F-GPAB	Dassault Falcon 20F	254	G-FRAC	0071	0195	2 GE CF700-2D2	13000	9 Pax		lsf Unionfin

AVIALIM — Limoges-Bellegarde

Aéroport de Limoges Bellegarde, F-87100 Limoges, France ☎ 555 48 05 61 Tx: n/a Fax: 555 48 05 51 SITA: n/a
F: n/a ⁂ n/a Head: n/a Net: n/a

☐ F-GPJD	Beech King Air E90	LW-328	N551M	0079	0797	2 PWC PT6A-28	4581	9 Pax		
☐ F-GQJD	Beech King Air C90	LJ-667	G-BMZD	0075	0298	2 PWC PT6A-21	4377	6 Pax		

AVIASUD Aérotaxi = AVU (Member of Air Provence International Group) — Nice-Cote d'Azur

Aéroport Nice-Cote d'Azur, F-06056 Nice Cédex, France ☎ 493 21 34 50 Tx: 461090 f aviasud Fax: 493 21 34 47 SITA: n/a
F: 1973 ⁂ 8 Head: Mme Denise Arnaud ICAO: AVIASUD Net: n/a

☐ F-GEXL	Beech King Air 200	BB-202	N2425X	0076	0595	2 PWC PT6A-41	5670	Y10		lsf Minière de Trebas

AVIATION SANS FRONTIERES France – A.S.F. (Affiliated with Aviation sans Frontières, Belgium) — Paris-Orly & Overseas

Orly Fret 768, Batiment 351, F-94398 Orly Aérogare Cédex, France ☎ (1) 49 75 74 37 Tx: n/a Fax: (1) 49 75 74 33 SITA: n/a
F: 1980 ⁂ 3 Head: Marcel Poulet Net: n/a Non-commercial organisation conducting flights for relief & development agencies & missions in remote areas of third world countries.

☐ F-OHLG	Cessna 208 Caravan I	20800061	N9463F	0085	1192	1 PWC PT6A-114	3629			
☐ F-OHKF	De Havilland DHC-6 Twin Otter 200	149	F-GELV	0068	0694	2 PWC PT6A-20	5252			

AVIAZUR = VZR (formerly Air Avia) — Noumea-Magenta

BP 1116, F-98845 Nouméa Cédex, Nouvelle Calédonie ☎ 25 37 09 Tx: none Fax: 25 46 62 SITA: n/a
F: 1983 ⁂ 10 Head: Christophe Panchou ICAO: IAZUR Net: n/a

☐ F-ODYV	Beech Duchess 76	ME-171	VH-JKE	0079	0193	2 LY O-360-A1G6D	1769	3 Pax		
☐ F-ODYF	Britten-Norman BN-2A-26 Islander	309	G-BADK	0072	0891	2 LY O-540-E4C5	2812	8 Pax		lsf Air Pacifique Aviation
☐ F-OIAR	Britten-Norman BN-2T Turbine Islander	2287	G-BVSK	0095	1296	2 AN 250-B17C	3175	9 Pax		
☐ F-ODYZ	Reims/Cessna F406 Caravan II	F406-0057	N31226	0090	1293	2 PWC PT6A-112	4468	12 Pax		lsf Locazur

BEL AIR – Ile de France = FBR — Paris-Orly

95-97 Ave de la Victoire, F-94310 Orly, France ☎ (1) 48 53 76 00 Tx: none Fax: (1) 48 53 76 39 SITA: PARBLCR
F: 1994 ⁂ 170 Head: Bruno Carrier ICAO: EUROBELAIR Net: n/a

☐ F-GKZL	Boeing (Douglas) MD-83 (DC-9-83)	49402 / 1261	D-ALLD	0386	0398	2 PW JT8D-219	72575	Y169		lsf Aircraft 49402 Inc.
☐ F-GCGQ	Boeing 727-227 (A)	20609 / 892	N411BN	0072	0397	3 PW JT8D-9A	83000	Y182	LQ-BE	La Nef
☐ F-GGGR	Boeing 727-2H3 (A)	20822 / 996	PH-AHD	0073	0895	3 PW JT8D-9A	86296	Y182		Villa Squeville

BOOGIE PERFORMANCE, E.U.R.L. — Cap

31 Cote des Lauriers Tins, F-34980 Montferrier-Lez, France ☎ 467 59 87 82 Tx: none Fax: 467 59 96 14 SITA: n/a
F: 1997 ⁂ n/a Head: n/a Net: n/a Operates para-flights (FF Parachutisme) for club-members only.

☐ F-GOGN	CASA 212-CB Aviocar Srs 100	92	TC-AOC	0077	0597	2 GA TPE331-5-251C	6500	Para		

BRIT AIR = DB / BZH — Morlaix-Ploujean

Aéroport, BP 156, F-29204 Morlaix Cédex, France ☎ 298 62 10 22 Tx: 941688 f britair Fax: 298 62 77 97 SITA: MXNEDDB
F: 1973 ⁂ 700 Head: Xavier Leclerq IATA: 750 ICAO: BRIT AIR Net: n/a
Some aircraft are operated on a franchise agreement with AIR FRANCE as AIR FRANCE by Brit Air (in full such colors & both titles) & using AF flight numbers.

☐ F-GGLR	ATR 42-300	043		0087	0387	2 PWC PW120	16700	Y46		op in Air France-colors
☐ F-GHJE	ATR 42-300	070	F-WWEW*	0088	0396	2 PWC PW120	16700	Y50		lsf Unimat
☐ F-GHPI	ATR 42-300	214	F-WWEB*	0090	1190	2 PWC PW120	16700	Y48		lsf BNP Lease / op in Air France-colors
☐ F-GHPK	ATR 42-300	218	F-WWEC*	0090	1190	2 PWC PW120	16700	Y48		lsf Dolmen Bail / op in Air France-cs
☐ F-GHPS	ATR 42-300	006	B-2206	0086	0391	2 PWC PW120	16700	Y48		lsf BNP Bail / op in Air France-colors

150 registration type of aircraft cn/fn ex/ex* mfd del powered by mtow kg configuration selcal name/fln/specialitites/remarks

☐ F-GHPY	ATR 42-300	321	F-WWES*	0093	0393	2 PWC PW120	16700	Y46		lsf GIE 42 / op in Air France-colors
☐ F-GHPZ	ATR 42-300	005	F-WGZH*	0085	0990	2 PWC PW120	16700	Y46		lsf BNP Lease / op in Air France-colors
☐ F-GLIA	ATR 42-300	010	F-GDXL*	0086	0386	2 PWC PW120	16700	Y50		lsf Aviation Ent. / op in Air France-cs
☐ F-GLIB	ATR 42-300	025	F-GHME	0086	0189	2 PWC PW120	16700	Y50		lsf Aviation Ent. / op in Air France-cs
☐ F-GHPU	ATR 72-201	227		0091	0391	2 PWC PW124B	21500	Y68		lsf Bail Equipement/op in Air France-cs
☐ F-GHPV	ATR 72-201	234		0091	0591	2 PWC PW124B	21500	Y68		lsf Bail Ouest / op in Air France-cs
☐ F-GRJA	Canadair Regional Jet 100ER (CL-600-2B19)	7070	C-FMKW*	0095	0695	2 GE CF34-3A1	23133	Y50		op in Air France-colors
☐ F-GRJB	Canadair Regional Jet 100ER (CL-600-2B19)	7076	C-FMLS*	0095	0895	2 GE CF34-3A1	23133	Y50		lsf Ergie Lise / op in Air France-cs
☐ F-GRJC	Canadair Regional Jet 100ER (CL-600-2B19)	7085		0095	1095	2 GE CF34-3A1	23133	Y50		lsf St. Laurent / op in Air France-cs
☐ F-GRJD	Canadair Regional Jet 100ER (CL-600-2B19)	7088	C-FMLU*	0095	1195	2 GE CF34-3A1	23133	Y50		lsf St. Laurent / op in Air France-cs
☐ F-GRJE	Canadair Regional Jet 100ER (CL-600-2B19)	7106		0096	0496	2 GE CF34-3A1	23133	Y50		lsf St. Laurent / op in Air France-cs
☐ F-GRJF	Canadair Regional Jet 100ER (CL-600-2B19)	7108	C-FMLU*	0096	0396	2 GE CF34-3A1	23133	Y50		lsf St. Laurent / op in Air France-cs
☐ F-GRJG	Canadair Regional Jet 100ER (CL-600-2B19)	7143	C-FMMQ*	0796	1096	2 GE CF34-3A1	23133	Y50		lsf Saint Gonven / op in Air France-cs
☐ F-GRJH	Canadair Regional Jet 100ER (CL-600-2B19)	7162		0097	0397	2 GE CF34-3A1	23133	Y50		lsf Saint Gonven / op in Air France-cs
☐ F-GRJI	Canadair Regional Jet 100ER (CL-600-2B19)	7147	C-FZAL*	0096	1296	2 GE CF34-3A1	23133	Y50		lsf Saint Gonven
☐ F-GRJJ	Canadair Regional Jet 100ER (CL-600-2B19)	7190	C-GBFF*	0097	1097	2 GE CF34-3A1	23133	Y50		lsf Guengat / op in Air France-colors
☐ F-GRJK	Canadair Regional Jet 100ER (CL-600-2B19)	7219	C-FMMQ	0098	0298	2 GE CF34-3A1	23133	Y50		lsf Guengat / op in Air France-colors
☐ F-GRJL	Canadair Regional Jet 100ER (CL-600-2B19)	7221		0098	0298	2 GE CF34-3A1	23133	Y50		lsf Guengat / op in Air France-colors
☐ F-GRJM	Canadair Regional Jet 100ER (CL-600-2B19)	7222		0098	0398	2 GE CF34-3A1	23133	Y50		lsf Guengat / op in Air France-colors
☐ F-GRJN	Canadair Regional Jet 100ER (CL-600-2B19)	7262	C-FMLT*	0098	1098	2 GE CF34-3A1	23133	Y50		op in Air France-colors
☐ F-GRJO	Canadair Regional Jet 100ER (CL-600-2B19)	7296		0099	0199	2 GE CF34-3A1	23133	Y50		
☐ F-GRJP	Canadair Regional Jet 100ER (CL-600-2B19)					2 GE CF34-3A1	23133	Y50		oo-delivery 0499
☐ F-GRJQ	Canadair Regional Jet 100ER (CL-600-2B19)					2 GE CF34-3A1	23133	Y50		oo-delivery 0499
☐ F-GRJR	Canadair Regional Jet 100ER (CL-600-2B19)					2 GE CF34-3A1	23133	Y50		oo-delivery 0599
☐ F-GRJS	Canadair Regional Jet 100ER (CL-600-2B19)					2 GE CF34-3A1	23133	Y50		oo-delivery 0999
☐ F-GRJT	Canadair Regional Jet 100ER (CL-600-2B19)					2 GE CF34-3A1	23133	Y50		oo-delivery 0200
☐ F-	Canadair Regional Jet 700					2 GE CF34-8C1	32885	Y70		oo-delivery 0001
☐ F-	Canadair Regional Jet 700					2 GE CF34-8C1	32885	Y70		oo-delivery 0001
☐ F-	Canadair Regional Jet 700					2 GE CF34-8C1	32885	Y70		oo-delivery 0001
☐ F-	Canadair Regional Jet 700					2 GE CF34-8C1	32885	Y70		oo-delivery 0001

CARAIBES AIR TRANSPORT — Fort de France-Le Lamentin

Aéroport de Fort-de-France, F-97232 Le Lamentin, Martinique ☎ 51 17 27 Tx: none Fax: 51 39 04 SITA: n/a

F: 1998 👥 n/a Head: Jean-Paul Dubeuil Net: n/a

☐ F-OGOV	Britten-Norman BN-2A-26 Islander	399	G-BJWP	0074	0098	2 LY O-540-E4C5	2812	Y9		
☐ F-OGUD	Cessna 208 Caravan I	20800210	N9794F	0091	0098	1 PWC PT6A-114	3629	Y9		lsf Union Stars Aviation SA
☐ F-OGVJ	Cessna 208B Grand Caravan	208B0363	N1116H	0093	0098	1 PWC PT6A-114A	3969	Y9		lsf Airema SàRL
☐ F-OGOX	Beech King Air C90	LJ-668	F-GGMO	0075	0098	2 PWC PT6A-21	4377	Y6		lsf Union Stars Aviation SA
☐ F-OGPQ	Beech King Air 200	BB-192	F-GLIF	0076	0098	2 PWC PT6A-21	5670	Y8		lsf Union Stars Aviation SA
☐ F-GGKA	De Havilland DHC-6 Twin Otter 300	381	TZ-ACD	0073	0098	2 PWC PT6A-27	5670	Y18		lsf Caraibes Air Services
☐ F-ODZF	Dornier 228-201	8107	LN-NVH	0087	0098	2 GA TPE331-5-252D	5980	Y19		lsf Union Stars Aviation SA
☐ F-ODZG	Dornier 228-202K	8123	N2255E	0087	0098	2 GA TPE331-5-252D	6200	Y19		lsf Union Stars Aviation SA
☐ F-ODZH	Dornier 228-202K	8077	N2255Y	0085	0098	2 GA TPE331-5-252D	6200	Y19		lsf Union Stars Aviation SA / cvtd -201
☐ F-OGOL	Dornier 228-202K	8139	D-CACC*	0087	1098	2 GA TPE331-5-252D	6200	Y19		lsf Air Vendée Investissements SA

CARIBBEAN HELICOPTERS — Saint Barthelemy

Saint-Jean-Espace Neptune, F-97098 Saint Barthelemy Cédex, Guadeloupe ☎ 25 66 57 Tx: none Fax: 29 66 58 SITA: n/a

F: 1994 👥 n/a Head: François Cahen Net: n/a Aircraft below MTOW 1361kg: Bell 47G-2

☐ F-GNFP	Bell 206B JetRanger	1148	G-HUMT	0073		1 AN 250-C20	1451			lsf KN Helicopter

CARRY AIR = EEC — Lyon-Bron

Aeroport de Bron, F-69500 Bron, France ☎ 472 14 16 50 Tx: none Fax: 472 14 16 59 SITA: n/a

F: 1997 👥 3 Head: Olivier Biseau ICAO: QUICK SPEED Net: http://www.net-on-line.net/carry_air/

☐ F-GHDQ	Cessna TR182 Skylane RG II	R18201331	N2330S	0079		1 LY O-540-L3C5D	1406	3 Pax		lsf Serdag
☐ F-GBVS	Piper PA-30-160 Twin Comanche B	30-1293	I-KLKL	0066		2 LY IO-320-C1A	1688	3 Pax		
☐ F-GNBA	Beech King Air A90 (65-A90)	LJ-311	HB-GIN	0067	0097	2 PWC PT6A-20	4377	8 Pax		lsf Serdag

C.A.T.E.X., S.A. - Compagnie Aérien de Transport Executif = TEX — Saint-Etienne

Aéroport de Saint-Etienne, F-42160 Andrezieux-Boutheon, France ☎ 477 36 54 11 Tx: none Fax: 477 36 62 07 SITA: EBUTXCR

F: 1989 👥 10 Head: Jean N. Herbaud ICAO: CATEX Net: n/a

☐ F-GELT	Dassault Falcon 100	211	F-WZGT*	0086		2 GA TFE731-2-1C	8755	8 Pax		lsf Barclays Bail

CHALAIR = M6 / CLG — Caen-Carpiquet

Aéroport de Caen-Carpiquet, F-14650 Carpiquet, France ☎ 231 71 26 26 Tx: none Fax: 231 71 26 27 SITA: n/a

F: 1986 👥 25 Head: n/a ICAO: CHALLAIR Net: n/a

☐ F-GCCB	Cessna 310Q II	310Q0925	PH-PLE	0074		2 CO IO-470-VO	2404	Y5		
☐ F-GETJ	Beech King Air E90	LW-296	N207CP	0078		2 PWC PT6A-28	4581	Y8		
☐ F-GGLV	Beech King Air A100	B-150	N51BL	0073		2 PWC PT6A-28	5216	Y10		
☐ F-GJJJ	Beech King Air A100	B-196	N773SK	0074		2 PWC PT6A-28	5216	Y12		
☐ F-GKSP	Beech King Air C90A	LJ-1409		0095		2 PWC PT6A-21	4581	Y6		lsf SàRL Afl
☐ F-GHVV	Beech King Air 200	BB-676	N1362B	0080		2 PWC PT6A-41	5670	Y10		
☐ F-GIJB	Beech King Air 200	BB-13	N83MA	0074	1091	2 PWC PT6A-41	5670	Y10		
☐ F-GKCV	Beech King Air 200	BB-251	I-BMPE	0077		2 PWC PT6A-41	5670	Y11		
☐ F-GHVG	Fairchild (Swearingen) SA227AC Metro III	AC-499	SE-KHH	0082	0993	2 GA TPE331-11U-611G	6577	Y18		lsf Unimat
☐ F-GNPL	ATR 42-300	063	F-ODUC	0087	0697	2 PWC PW120	16700	Y46		lsf VTA -0699

CHALLENG'AIR = (CHAL) — Toussus-le-Noble

Aérodrome de Toussus-le-Noble, Zone Ouest-Parcelle 309, F-78117 Chateaufort, France ☎ (1) 39 56 85 25 Tx: none Fax: (1) 39 56 44 02 SITA: PARCHCR

F: 1989 👥 n/a Head: Daniel Schutz Net: n/a New & used aircraft leasing & sales company.

Owner/lessor of following (main) aircraft types: Airbus A300B4, Boeing 727-200 & 737-200/300. Aircraft leased from Challeng'Air are listed & mentioned as lsf CHAL under the leasing carriers.

CHAMPAGNE AIRLINES = CPH (Sister company of Heli Champagne Arden) — Reims-Champagne

Aéroport de Reims-Champagne, F-51450 Betheny, France ☎ 326 50 78 78 Tx: none Fax: 326 50 18 28 SITA: n/a

F: 1998 👥 n/a Head: Gilles Poncin ICAO: CHAMPAGNE Net: n/a

☐ F-GFIR	Beech King Air B90	LJ-434		0069		2 PWC PT6A-20	4377	8 Pax		
☐ F-GIML	Beech King Air E90	LW-180	N2180L	0076		2 PWC PT6A-28	4581	8 Pax		

CNET Opérations Aériennes = CNT (Centre National d'Etudes des Télécommunications dba) — Lannion-Servel

2 Av. P. Marzin, F-22307 Lannion, France ☎ 296 05 11 11 Tx: 740675 Fax: 296 05 27 35 SITA: LAIFTCR

F: n/a 👥 n/a Head: Jean Guiomar ICAO: KNET Net: n/a Non-commercial state organisation conducting transport flights for telecommunication support purposes.

☐ F-SEBP	Eurocopter (Aerosp.) AS350B Ecureuil	1115	N8TV	0079	0090	1 TU Arriel 1B	1950	Utility		
☐ F-SEBK	ATR 42-320	264	F-WQCH	0092	1195	2 PWC PW121	16700	Y46		

COMPAGNIE AERONAUTIQUE EUROPEENNE - CAE = FEU — Marseille-Marignane

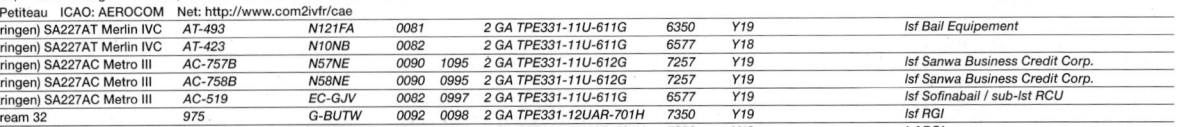

BP 127, Aéroport Marseille Provence, F-13729 Marignane Cédex, France ☎ 442 77 47 77 Tx: 402024 f Fax: 442 77 47 70 SITA: n/a

F: 1991 👥 20 Head: Charles Petiteau ICAO: AEROCOM Net: http://www.com2ivfr/cae

☐ F-GGLG	Fairchild (Swearingen) SA227AT Merlin IVC	AT-493	N121FA	0081		2 GA TPE331-11U-611G	6350	Y19		lsf Bail Equipement
☐ F-GHVF	Fairchild (Swearingen) SA227AT Merlin IVC	AT-423	N10NB	0082		2 GA TPE331-11U-611G	6577	Y18		
☐ F-GJPN	Fairchild (Swearingen) SA227AC Metro III	AC-757B	N57NE	0090	1095	2 GA TPE331-11U-612G	7257	Y19		lsf Sanwa Business Credit Corp.
☐ F-GPSN	Fairchild (Swearingen) SA227AC Metro III	AC-758B	N58NE	0090	0995	2 GA TPE331-11U-612G	7257	Y19		lsf Sanwa Business Credit Corp.
☐ F-GTRB	Fairchild (Swearingen) SA227AC Metro III	AC-519	EC-GJV	0082	0997	2 GA TPE331-11U-611G	6577	Y19		lsf Sofinabail / sub-lst RCU
☐ F-GMVI	BAe 3206 Jetstream 32	975	G-BUTW	0092	0098	2 GA TPE331-12UAR-701H	7350	Y19		lsf RGI
☐ F-GMVK	BAe 3206 Jetstream 32	977	G-BUVD	0093	0398	2 GA TPE331-12UAR-701H	7350	Y19		lsf RGI
☐ F-GMVP	BAe 3206 Jetstream 32	970	G-BUVC	0092	0098	2 GA TPE331-12UAR-701H	7350	Y19		lsf RGI

COMPAGNIE CORSE MEDITERRANEE = XK / CCM — Ajaccio

BP 505, F-20186 Ajaccio Cédex, France ☎ 495 29 05 00 Tx: 460166 f Fax: 495 29 05 05 SITA: AJADGXK

F: 1989 👥 420 Head: François Mosconi IATA: 146 ICAO: CORSICA Net: n/a

☐ F-GKPC	ATR 72-102	171	F-WWEA*	0090	0690	2 PWC PW124B	21500	Y68		
☐ F-GKPD	ATR 72-102	177	F-WWEH*	0090	0590	2 PWC PW124B	21500	Y68		lsf Corse Bail
☐ F-GKPE	ATR 72-102	192	F-WWEE*	0091	0391	2 PWC PW124B	21500	Y68		lsf Piana Bail
☐ F-GKPF	ATR 72-102	222		0091	0491	2 PWC PW124B	21500	Y68		
☐ F-GKPH	ATR 72-202	352	F-WWEJ*	0093	0393	2 PWC PW124B	21500	Y68		lsf Corsica Bail
☐ F-GKHD	Fokker 100 (F28 Mk0100)	11381	HB-IVI	0092	0696	2 RR Tay 620-15	44455	Y109		lsf TAT SA
☐ F-GKHE	Fokker 100 (F28 Mk0100)	11386	HB-IVK	0092	0696	2 RR Tay 620-15	44455	Y109		lsf TAT SA
☐ F-GMPG	Fokker 100 (F28 Mk0100)	11362	PH-EZT*	0091	0492	2 RR Tay 620-15	43090	Y109		lsf Campo dell'Oro Bail

151 registration type of aircraft cn/fn ex/ex* mfd del powered by mtow kg configuration selcal name/fln/specialitites/remarks

CORSAIR = SS / CRL (formerly Corse-Air International) — Paris-Orly

24 Rue Saarinen, Silic 221, F-94528 Rungis Silic Cédex, France ☎ (1) 49 79 49 89 Tx: 263459 f Fax: (1) 49 79 49 98 SITA: ORYOOSS
F: 1981 ♦♦♦ 1130 Head: Jacques Maillot ICAO: CORSAIR Net: http://www.corsair-info.com

registration	type of aircraft	cn/fn	ex/ex*	mfd	del	powered by	mtow kg	configuration	selcal	name/fln/specialitites/remarks
☐ F-GMJD	Boeing 737-2K5 (A)	22599 / 814	D-AHLG	0081	0497	2 PW JT8D-17	58105	Y129	EM-AD	lsf/opb AAF
☐ F-GFUG	Boeing 737-4B3	24750 / 1916		0090	0292	2 CFMI CFM56-3C1	68038	Y173	GM-DF	lsf Nouvelles Frontières Aviation
☐ F-GFUH	Boeing 737-4B3	24751 / 2107		0091	1092	2 CFMI CFM56-3C1	68038	Y173	CD-MP	lsf Nouvelles Frontières Aviation
☐ F-	Airbus Industrie A330-243	285				2 RR Trent 772B-60	230000	Y356		oo-delivery 0699
☐ F-	Airbus Industrie A330-243					2 RR Trent 772B-60	230000	Y356		oo-delivery 0200
☐ F-GTOM	Boeing 747SP-44	21253 / 293	LX-ACO	0076	1094	4 PW JT9D-7J	315700	C20Y323	GM-DJ	
☐ F-GKLJ	Boeing 747-121	19660 / 50	LX-GCV	0070	0691	4 PW JT9D-7A	332936	C16Y508	CL-DG	
☐ F-GLNA	Boeing 747-206B	20399 / 156	PH-BUE	0071	1292	4 PW JT9D-7J	362873	C27Y512	CK-EJ	
☐ F-GPJM	Boeing 747-206B	20427 / 170	PH-BUG	0071	0295	4 PW JT9D-7J	351533	C27Y512	CJ-GK	
☐ F-GSEA	Boeing 747-312	23032 / 603	N121KG	0084	0897	4 PW JT9D-7R4G2	377842	C25Y555	GK-AJ	
☐ F-GSUN	Boeing 747-312	23030 / 593	N119KE	0084	1095	4 PW JT9D-7R4G2	377842	C25Y555	CE-FL	

CORSE HELICOPTERES — Ajaccio-Campo dell'Oro   corse hélicoptères

Aéroport Campo dell'Oro, Aviation Géneralé, F-20090 Ajaccio, France ☎ 495 23 56 46 Tx: none Fax: 495 23 57 47 SITA: n/a
F: 1985 ♦♦♦ 8 Head: Pierre Massimi Net: n/a

registration	type of aircraft	cn/fn	ex/ex*	mfd	del	powered by	mtow kg	configuration	selcal	name/fln/specialitites/remarks
☐ F-GFCV	Eurocopter (Aerosp.) SA315B Lama	2497	N49531	0077		1 TU Artouste IIIB1	1950	4 Pax		
☐ F-GMJT	Eurocopter (Aerosp.) SE313B Alouette II	1115	F-SEBN	0057		1 TU Artouste IIC6	1600	4 Pax		
☐ F-GMCZ	Eurocopter (Aerosp.) AS350B2 Ecureuil	2641	D-HWPW	0092	0194	1 TU Arriel 1D1	2250	5 Pax		

CROSSAIR EUROPE = QE / ECC (ECA-European Continental Airways dba / Associated with Crossair, Switzerland) — Basel/Mulhouse-EuroAirport

Aéroport de Bale-Mulhouse, Bat.du Catering, F-68300 St. Louis, France ☎ 389 90 40 87 Tx: none Fax: 389 90 40 89 SITA: MLHDGQE
F: 1998 ♦♦♦ 38 Head: Philip Perrin de Nelle IATA: 894 ICAO: CIGOGNE Net: n/a

registration	type of aircraft	cn/fn	ex/ex*	mfd	del	powered by	mtow kg	configuration	selcal	name/fln/specialitites/remarks
☐ F-GPKD	Saab 340B (Cityliner)	340B-173	HB-AKD	0089	0398	2 GE CT7-9B	13155	Y33		lsf CRX
☐ F-GPKG	Saab 340B (Cityliner)	340B-185	HB-AKG	0090	0398	2 GE CT7-9B	13155	Y33		lsf CRX

DARTA Aero Charter = DRT — Paris-Le Bourget

Aéroport du Bourget, Zone Aviation d'Affaires, F-93350 Le Bourget, France ☎ (1) 48 62 54 54 Tx: 235664 f Fax: (1) 48 62 41 43 SITA: n/a
F: 1972 ♦♦♦ 25 Head: Yves Darnaudet ICAO: DARTA Net: http://www.aero-charter-darta.com

registration	type of aircraft	cn/fn	ex/ex*	mfd	del	powered by	mtow kg	configuration	selcal	name/fln/specialitites/remarks
☐ F-GKIR	Cessna F500 Citation I	500-0361	N90EB	0077		2 PWC JT15D-1A	5375	7 Pax		lsf Location L'Industrie Aerienne
☐ F-GEPY	Beech King Air 200	BB-779	N811CB	0080		2 PWC PT6A-41	5670	8 Pax		lsf Nyco SA
☐ F-GHOC	Beech King Air 200	BB-406	G-OEMS	0078		2 PWC PT6A-41	5670	9 Pax		lsf Locavia
☐ F-GJYD	Cessna F550 Citation II	T550-0415	N1949M	0082	0391	2 PWC JT15D-4	6033	8 Pax		lsf Soderlocation
☐ F-GKBC	Dassault Falcon 10	99	N67JW	0077		2 GA TFE731-2-1C	8500	7 Pax		lsf Sofinabail

DASSAULT FALCON SERVICE = EFS (formerly Europe Falcon Service) — Paris-Le Bourget

BP 10, F-93352 Le Bourget Cédex, France ☎ (1) 49 34 20 20 Tx: 235671 f efs ops Fax: (1) 49 34 20 90 SITA: n/a
F: 1967 ♦♦♦ 450 Head: Jean-François Georges ICAO: AIR FALCON Net: n/a

registration	type of aircraft	cn/fn	ex/ex*	mfd	del	powered by	mtow kg	configuration	selcal	name/fln/specialitites/remarks
☐ F-GHSK	Dassault Falcon 100	218	F-WZGB*	0089		2 GA TFE731-2-1C	8755	7 Pax		lsf Sofinabail
☐ F-GBTM	Dassault Falcon 20GF	397	F-WBTM*	0080		2 GA ATF3-6A-4C	14515	8 Pax		cvtd 20F
☐ F-GEFS	Dassault Falcon 20F	486	F-WLCV*	0083		2 GE CF700-2D2	13000	10 Pax		
☐ F-GHDT	Dassault Falcon 20C-5	176	F-WGTM*	0069	0191	2 GA TFE731-5AR-2C	13200	10 Pax	AR-DP	cvtd Falcon 20C
☐ F-GHPA	Dassault Falcon 20C	170	I-EKET	0069		2 GE CF700-2C	12000	9 Pax		
☐ F-GOBZ	Dassault Falcon 20E-5	293	F-WQBN	0073	1297	2 GA TFE731-5AR-2C	13200	10 Pax		lsf Bizjet SA / cvtd 20E
☐ F-GSXF	Dassault Falcon 20E-5	315	F-SEBI	0074	0798	2 GA TFE731-5AR-2C	13200	10 Pax		cvtd 20E
☐ F-GOJT	Dassault Falcon 200	501	F-WWGP*	0085		2 GA ATF3-6A-4C	14515	10 Pax		
☐ F-GSAA	Dassault Falcon 2000	36	F-WWMA*	0097	0697	2 CFE CFE738-1-1B	16238	8 Pax		lsf Snc Air Co.
☐ F-GOAL	Dassault Falcon 50	131	F-WGTF*	0083		3 GA TFE731-3-1C	18500	9 Pax		lsf Continent Hypermarches
☐ F-GIDE	Dassault Falcon 900	1	F-WIDE*	0084		3 GA TFE731-5A-1C2	20638	14 Pax	AJ-CH	
☐ F-GLGY	Dassault Falcon 900	11	UN-89002	0087	1096	3 GA TFE731-5AR-1C	21092	14 Pax		
☐ F-GUEQ	Dassault Falcon 900B	167	F-WWFO*	0098	0398	3 GA TFE731-5BR-1C	21099	VIP		lsf GE167/opf Gvmt of Equatorial Guinea

DK FLIGHT — Nancy

10 Rue Poirel, F-54000 Nancy, France ☎ 383 35 70 35 Tx: none Fax: 383 35 70 35 SITA: n/a
F: 1996 ♦♦♦ n/a Head: n/a Net: n/a

registration	type of aircraft	cn/fn	ex/ex*	mfd	del	powered by	mtow kg	configuration	selcal	name/fln/specialitites/remarks
☐ F-BRNO	Beech King Air B90	LJ-482	HB-GEE	0069		2 PWC PT6A-20	4377			

DOUANES FRANCAISES – Brigade de Surveillance Aérienne = FDO — Paris-Dugny/Le Bourget

Base Aeronavale, BP 24, F-93440 Dugny, France ☎ (1) 49 92 93 50 Tx: none Fax: (1) 49 92 93 66 SITA: n/a
F: 1960 ♦♦♦ n/a Head: Gérard Plez ICAO: FRENCH CUSTOM Net: n/a Aircraft below MTOW 1361kg: Socata MS893E Rallye 180 & 235
Non commercial government-organisation conducting survey/patrol & passenger flights (from 10 main bases) for customs purposes.

registration	type of aircraft	cn/fn	ex/ex*	mfd	del	powered by	mtow kg	configuration	selcal	name/fln/specialitites/remarks
☐ F-ZBEM	Socata TB 20 Trinidad	384		0083	0184	1 LY IO-540-C4D5D	1400			
☐ F-ZBDV	Eurocopter (Aerosp.) AS350BA Ecureuil	1157	F-GCFR	0079	0480	1 TU Arriel 1B	2100			cvtd AS350B
☐ F-ZBFH	Eurocopter (Aerosp.) AS350BA Ecureuil	2110	JA8771	0088	0995	1 TU Arriel 1B	2100			cvtd AS350B
☐ F-ZBDZ	Cessna 310R II	310R0569	F-GAJI	0076	1081	2 CO IO-520-M	2495			
☐ F-ZBAC	Eurocopter (Aerosp.) AS355F2 Ecureuil 2	5026	C-GFSI	0081	0792	2 AN 250-C20F	2540			cvtd AS355F1
☐ F-ZBAD	Eurocopter (Aerosp.) AS355F2 Ecureuil 2	5156	N5796A	0082	0792	2 AN 250-C20F	2540			cvtd AS355F1
☐ F-ZBEF	Eurocopter (Aerosp.) AS355F2 Ecureuil 2	5236		0082	1282	2 AN 250-C20F	2540			cvtd AS355F1
☐ F-ZBEJ	Eurocopter (Aerosp.) AS355F1 Ecureuil 2	5003	F-WZKI	0081	0583	2 AN 250-C20F	2400			
☐ F-ZBEK	Eurocopter (Aerosp.) AS355F2 Ecureuil 2	5298		0083	0184	2 AN 250-C20F	2540			cvtd AS355F1
☐ F-ZBEL	Eurocopter (Aerosp.) AS355F2 Ecureuil 2	5299		0083	0184	2 AN 250-C20F	2540			cvtd AS355F1
☐ F-ZBDW	Cessna 404 Titan II	404-0640	F-BIPJ	0080	1080	2 CO GTSIO-520-M	3810			
☐ F-ZBDY	Cessna 404 Titan II	404-0815	F-GCVR	0081	0781	2 CO GTSIO-520-M	3810			
☐ F-ZBER	Cessna 404 Titan II	404-0608	F-GAMZ	0080	0487	2 CO GTSIO-520-M	3810			
☐ F-ZBFZ	Piper PA-31T Cheyenne II	31T-8120064	F-WFLQ	0081	0490	2 PWC PT6A-28	4082			
☐ F-ZBAB	Reims/Cessna F406 Vigilant PolMar II	F406-0025	F-GEUL	0088	1088	2 PWC PT6A-112	4468	Survey/Patrol		
☐ F-ZBBB	Reims/Cessna F406 Vigilant PolMar II	F406-0039	F-WZDS	0089	0489	2 PWC PT6A-112	4468	Survey/Patrol		
☐ F-ZBCE	Reims/Cessna F406 Vigilant PolMar II	F406-0042	F-GKRA	0089	1193	2 PWC PT6A-112	4468	Survey/Patrol		
☐ F-ZBCF	Reims/Cessna F406 Vigilant SurMar	F406-0077	F-WZDZ	0095	0995	2 PWC PT6A-112	4468	Survey/Patrol		
☐ F-ZBCG	Reims/Cessna F406 Vigilant PolMar II	F406-0066	F-WZDT	0093	1193	2 PWC PT6A-112	4468	Survey/Patrol		
☐ F-ZBCH	Reims/Cessna F406 Vigilant SurMar	F406-0075		0094	0195	2 PWC PT6A-112	4468	Survey/Patrol		
☐ F-ZBCI	Reims/Cessna F406 Vigilant PolMar II	F406-0070		0093	1193	2 PWC PT6A-112	4468	Survey/Patrol		
☐ F-ZBCJ	Reims/Cessna F406 Vigilant SurMar	F406-0074		0094	1294	2 PWC PT6A-112	4468	Survey/Patrol		
☐ F-ZBEP	Reims/Cessna F406 Vigilant PolMar II	F406-0006		0085	1285	2 PWC PT6A-112	4468	Survey/Patrol		
☐ F-ZBES	Reims/Cessna F406 Vigilant PolMar II	F406-0017		0085	1087	2 PWC PT6A-112	4468	Survey/Patrol		
☐ F-ZBFA	Reims/Cessna F406 Vigilant PolMar I	F406-001	F-GGRA	0085	0388	2 PWC PT6A-112	4468	Survey/Patrol		
☐ F-ZBGA	Reims/Cessna F406 Vigilant SurMar	F406-0086		0098	1298	2 PWC PT6A-112	4468	Survey/Patrol		

EJA FRANCE = AEJ (Air Affaires EJA International dba / Member of Groupe Transair) — Paris-Le Bourget   EJA FRANCE

BP 174, F-93352 Le Bourget Aéroport, France ☎ (1) 48 35 99 45 Tx: 233746 f Fax: (1) 48 35 91 25 SITA: n/a
F: 1962 ♦♦♦ 10 Head: Jean Michel Delval Net: n/a

registration	type of aircraft	cn/fn	ex/ex*	mfd	del	powered by	mtow kg	configuration	selcal	name/fln/specialitites/remarks
☐ F-GKJL	Cessna 560 Citation V	560-0093		0091		2 PWC JT15D-5A	7212	7 Pax		lsf BNP Bail

ESMA Compagnie Aérienne de Transport Public-Vols d'Affaires (Div.of Ecole Superieure des Métiers de l'Aeron./Subs.of Air Littoral) — Montpellier, Lyon, Paris & Nice   ESMA

Aéroport de Montpellier-Méditerranée, F-34130 Mauguio, France ☎ 467 20 67 00 Tx: none Fax: 467 22 29 26 SITA: n/a
F: 1994 ♦♦♦ 50 Head: Marc Dufour Net: n/a

registration	type of aircraft	cn/fn	ex/ex*	mfd	del	powered by	mtow kg	configuration	selcal	name/fln/specialitites/remarks
☐ F-BUOS	Beech Baron 58	TH-401		0073		2 CO IO-520-C	2450			

EURALAIR International = RN / EUL (Member of JET Europe) — Paris-Le Bourget   euralair

Aéroport du Bourget, Zone Nord, F-93350 Le Bourget, France ☎ (1) 49 34 62 00 Tx: 230662 f eurlrdg Fax: (1) 49 34 63 00 SITA: n/a
F: 1963 ♦♦♦ 250 Head: Antoine de Bizemont ICAO: EURALAIR Net: n/a

registration	type of aircraft	cn/fn	ex/ex*	mfd	del	powered by	mtow kg	configuration	selcal	name/fln/specialitites/remarks
☐ F-GKGL	Cessna 560 Citation V	560-0058	N2686Y*	0090	0690	2 PWC JT15D-5A	7212	8 Pax		
☐ F-GKHL	Cessna 560 Citation V	560-0059	N2687L*	0090	0690	2 PWC JT15D-5A	7212	8 Pax		lsf SA Tournées Charles Baret
☐ F-GCSL	Boeing 737-222	19066 / 69	N9028U	0068	0480	2 PW JT8D-7B	49442	Y130		lsf BIE
☐ F-GFYL	Boeing 737-2A9C	20205 / 242	N383PA	0070	0488	2 PW JT8D-9A (HK3/NOR)	54432	Y130	KR-AH	lsf Hallett Investments B.V.
☐ F-GJDL	Boeing 737-210C	20440 / 256	N200NE	0070	1288	2 PW JT8D-9A (HK3/NOR)	52390	Y130	KR-AJ	
☐ F-GHOL	Boeing 737-53C	24825 / 1894		0090	0790	2 CFMI CFM56-3C1	52000	CY112	GP-HJ	lsf Floreal Bail / sub-lst AOM
☐ F-GHUL	Boeing 737-53C	24826 / 2041		0091	0591	2 CFMI CFM56-3C1	52000	CY112	GP-HK	lsf Germinal Bail / sub-lst AOM
☐ F-GINL	Boeing 737-53C	24827 / 2243		0092	0392	2 CFMI CFM56-3C1	52000	CY112		lsf Prairial Bail / sub-lst AOM
☐ F-GRNA	Boeing 737-85F	28823 / 174	N1784B*	0099	0199	2 CFMI CFM56-7B26	78245	Y184		lsf GATX
☐ F-GRNC	Boeing 737-85F	28821 / 151	N1786B*	0098	1298	2 CFMI CFM56-7B26	78245	Y184		lsf GATX / op in Voyages FRAM-colors

FINIST' AIR = FTR — Brest-Guipavas & Belle-Ile   finist'Air

Aéroport de Brest-Guipavas, F-29490 Guipavas, France ☎ 298 84 64 87 Tx: 940500 f ccibapt Fax: 298 84 64 60 SITA: n/a
F: 1982 ♦♦♦ 12 Head: Robert Le Thous Net: n/a

registration	type of aircraft	cn/fn	ex/ex*	mfd	del	powered by	mtow kg	configuration	selcal	name/fln/specialitites/remarks
☐ F-GHGZ	Cessna 208 Caravan I	20800188		0090	0790	1 PWC PT6A-114	3629	9 Pax		
☐ F-GJFI	Cessna 208B Grand Caravan	208B0230	N208GC	0090	0691	1 PWC PT6A-114A	3969	9 Pax		

registration   type of aircraft   cn/fn   ex/ex*   mfd   del   powered by   mtow kg   configuration   selcal   name/fln/specialitites/remarks

FLANDRE AIR = IX / FRS
Lille-Lesquin

Flandre AIR

BP 202, F-59812 Lesquin Cédex, France ☎ 320 90 78 90 Tx: 810921 fast f Fax: 320 90 78 82 SITA: LILFAIX
F: 1976 ⭑⭑⭑ 220 Head: Luc Delesalle IATA: 972 ICAO: FLANDRAIR Net: n/a All scheduled flights are operated in conjunction with AIR LIBERTE (in full such colors & both titles), using IJ flight numbers.

	registration	type of aircraft	cn/fn	ex/ex*	mfd	del	powered by	mtow kg	configuration	selcal	name/fin/specialtites/remarks
☐	F-GHSE	Beech 1900C-1 Airliner	UC-172		0091	1091	2 PWC PT6A-65B	7530	Y19		lsf Raytheon Airc./op in Air Liberté-cs
☐	F-GHSI	Beech 1900C-1 Airliner	UC-173		0091	1091	2 PWC PT6A-65B	7530	Y19		lsf Raytheon Airc./op in Air Liberté-cs
☐	F-GLPL	Beech 1900C-1 Airliner	UC-92	N15382	0089	0993	2 PWC PT6A-65B	7530	Y19		lsf Raytheon Airc./op in Air Liberté-cs
☐	F-GLND	Beech 1900D Airliner	UE-196	N3234G*	0096	0296	2 PWC PT6A-67D	7688	Y19		lsf BNP Lease / op in Air Liberté-cs
☐	F-GLNE	Beech 1900D Airliner	UE-197	N3234U*	0096	0296	2 PWC PT6A-67D	7688	Y19		lsf Unimat / op in Air Liberté-cs
☐	F-GLNF	Beech 1900D Airliner	UE-69	YR-RLA	0093	0596	2 PWC PT6A-67D	7688	Y19		lsf Raytheon Airc./op in Air Liberté-cs
☐	F-GLNH	Beech 1900D Airliner	UE-73	YR-RLB	0093	0596	2 PWC PT6A-67D	7688	Y19		lsf Raytheon Airc./op in Air Liberté-cs
☐	F-GLNJ	Beech 1900D Airliner	UE-258	N10936*	0096	0997	2 PWC PT6A-67D	7688	Y19		lsf Raytheon Airc./op in Air Liberté-cs
☐	F-GLNK	Beech 1900D Airliner	UE-269	N11017*	0097	0497	2 PWC PT6A-67D	7688	Y19		lsf Raytheon Airc./op in Air Liberté-cs
☐	F-GGTD	Embraer 120ER Brasilia (EMB-120ER)	120129	PT-SNV*	0089	0594	2 PWC PW118	11990	Y30		lsf Locmat/cvtd RT/op in Air Liberté-cs
☐	F-GHEX	Embraer 120ER Brasilia (EMB-120ER)	120209	PT-SSD*	0090	0893	2 PWC PW118	11990	Y30		lsf BFCEBail/cvtdRT/opin Air Liberté-cs
☐	F-GHEY	Embraer 120ER Brasilia (EMB-120ER)	120214	PT-SSI*	0090	0893	2 PWC PW118	11990	Y30		lsf BFCEBail/cvtdRT/opin Air Liberté-cs
☐	F-GHIA	Embraer 120ER Brasilia (EMB-120ER)	120154	PT-SPT*	0089	0197	2 PWC PW118	11990	Y30		lsf A.T.R./cvtd RT/op in Air Liberté-cs
☐	F-GHIB	Embraer 120ER Brasilia (EMB-120ER)	120162	PT-SQA*	0089	0197	2 PWC PW118	11990	Y30		lsf A.T.R./cvtd RT/op in Air Liberté-cs
☐	F-GIVK	Embraer 120ER Brasilia (EMB-120ER)	120112	C-FKOE	0088	0594	2 PWC PW118	11990	Y30		lsf ActiLoc./cvtdRT/opin Air Liberté-cs
☐	F-GIYH	Embraer 120ER Brasilia (EMB-120ER)	120239	LX-LGL	0091	0998	2 PWC PW118	11990	Y30	AQ-ER	lsf Flamingo Air Lsng/cvtd RT/white-cs
☐	F-GJAK	Embraer 120ER Brasilia (EMB-120ER)	120215	PT-SSJ*	0090	0197	2 PWC PW118	11990	Y30		lsf A.T.R./cvtd RT/op in Air Liberté-cs
☐	F-	Embraer RJ135 (EMB-135)					2 AN AE3007A3	19000	Y37		oo-delivery 0999/tbop in Air Liberté-cs
☐	F-	Embraer RJ135 (EMB-135)					2 AN AE3007A3	19000	Y37		oo-delivery 1199/tbop in Air Liberté-cs
☐	F-	Embraer RJ135 (EMB-135)					2 AN AE3007A3	19000	Y37		oo-delivery 0100/tbop in Air Liberté-cs
☐	F-	Embraer RJ135 (EMB-135)					2 AN AE3007A3	19000	Y37		oo-delivery 0300/tbop in Air Liberté-cs
☐	F-	Embraer RJ135 (EMB-135)					2 AN AE3007A3	19000	Y37		oo-delivery 0500/tbop in Air Liberté-cs
☐	F-	Embraer RJ135 (EMB-135)					2 AN AE3007A3	19000	Y37		oo-delivery 0700/tbop in Air Liberté-cs
☐	F-	Embraer RJ135 (EMB-135)					2 AN AE3007A3	19000	Y37		oo-delivery 0900/tbop in Air Liberté-cs
☐	F-	Embraer RJ135 (EMB-135)					2 AN AE3007A3	19000	Y37		oo-delivery 1100/tbop in Air Liberté-cs
☐	F-	Embraer RJ135 (EMB-135)					2 AN AE3007A3	19000	Y37		oo-delivery 0401/tbop in Air Liberté-cs
☐	F-	Embraer RJ135 (EMB-135)					2 AN AE3007A3	19000	Y37		oo-delivery 0801/tbop in Air Liberté-cs

FRANCE DAKOTA (DC3 SA Publi-Air dba / formerly France DC-3)
Paris-Orly

c/o DC3 SA Publi-Air, Rue Victor Masse 25, F-75009 Paris, France ☎ (1) 45 26 18 62 Tx: none Fax: (1) 53 20 08 13 SITA: n/a
F: 1991 ⭑⭑⭑ n/a Head: Sabine Fourquez Net: n/a

	registration	type of aircraft	cn/fn	ex/ex*	mfd	del	powered by	mtow kg	configuration	selcal	name/fin/specialtites/remarks
☐	F-GDPP	Boeing (Douglas) DC-3C (C-47A-1-DL)	9172	TL-AAX	0043	0591	2 PW R-1830-90D	11880	26 Pax		

FRANCE EUROPE AVIAJET = FEJ
Angers & Paris-Le Bourget

FRANCE EUROPE AVIAJET

B.P. 7, Soucelles, F-49140 Seiches-sur-Loir, France ☎ 241 21 05 05 Tx: none Fax: 241 32 29 89 SITA: n/a
F: 1981 ⭑⭑⭑ 3 Head: Claude Bremond ICAO: AVIAJET Net: n/a

	registration	type of aircraft	cn/fn	ex/ex*	mfd	del	powered by	mtow kg	configuration	selcal	name/fin/specialtites/remarks
☐	F-GFEA	Piper PA-31T Cheyenne II	31T-7620011	N76PT	0076	0085	2 PWC PT6A-28	4082	6 Pax		

GALLIC AVIATION = GLI
Paris-Le Bourget

158 Rue de la Pompe, F-75116 Paris, France ☎ (1) 45 53 27 50 Tx: 642100 f Fax: (1) 45 53 22 20 SITA: PARGACR
F: 1974 ⭑⭑⭑ 18 Head: Daniel Weiss ICAO: GALLIC Net: n/a Operates airtaxi/charter flights, current with aircraft leased from other companies when required. On option: 2 Dornier 328JET.

GUYANE AERO SERVICES
Cayenne-Rochambeau

Aéroport de Rochambeau, F-97351 Matoury, Guyane ☎ 35 61 62 Tx: none Fax: 35 84 50 SITA: n/a
F: 1983 ⭑⭑⭑ 8 Head: Guy Buirette Net: n/a

	registration	type of aircraft	cn/fn	ex/ex*	mfd	del	powered by	mtow kg	configuration	selcal	name/fin/specialtites/remarks
☐	F-OGKY	Cessna 182R Skylane B	18268540	N9498X	0085		1 CO O-470-U	1406	3 Pax		
☐	F-OGNQ	Cessna U206G Stationair 6 II	U20607015	N9302W	0086		1 CO IO-520-F	1633	5 Pax		lsf Travaux Publics & de Mines
☐	F-OGVI	Cessna U206G Stationair 6 II	U20604849	N734LN	0079	1093	1 CO IO-520-F	1633	5 Pax		
☐	F-OGXD	Cessna U206G Stationair 6 II	U20605007	N4622U	0079	0596	1 CO IO-520-F	1633	5 Pax		lsf Air Fregate
☐	F-OGXM	Pilatus PC-6/B2-H4 Turbo Porter	915		0096	0696	1 PWC PT6A-27	2800	9 Pax		lsf SCBP Banque Populaire
☐	F-OHQO	Pilatus PC-6/B2-H4 Turbo Porter	924		0098	0798	1 PWC PT6A-27	2800	9 Pax		lsf Sodelem SA

HELI AIR MEDITERRANEE
Cannes

144 Rue Buffon, F-06110 Le Cannet, France ☎ 493 60 10 20 Tx: none Fax: 493 60 19 90 SITA: n/a
F: 1996 ⭑⭑⭑ n/a Head: Claude Leguezec Net: n/a

	registration	type of aircraft	cn/fn	ex/ex*	mfd	del	powered by	mtow kg	configuration	selcal	name/fin/specialtites/remarks
☐	F-GQFH	Bell 206B JetRanger III	2270	F-WQFH	0077	0996	1 AN 250-C20B	1451			

HELI ALPES (Member of Groupe SAF)
Annecy-Meythet

BP 1016, Aérodrome d'Annecy-Meythet, F-74966 Meythet Cédex, France ☎ 450 27 35 45 Tx: none Fax: 450 27 31 24 SITA: n/a
F: 1972 ⭑⭑⭑ 6 Head: Eric Fraissinet Net: n/a Aircraft below MTOW 1361 kg: Jodel D140 & Robinson R22 Beta.

	registration	type of aircraft	cn/fn	ex/ex*	mfd	del	powered by	mtow kg	configuration	selcal	name/fin/specialtites/remarks
☐	F-GHCO	Eurocopter (Aerosp.) AS350B Ecureuil	1467	LN-OTC	0081		1 TU Arriel 1B	1950	5 Pax		lsf SAF

HELI BOURGOGNE
St. Florentin

Aerodrome de St. Florentin Cheu, F-89600 St. Florentin, France ☎ 386 35 06 16 Tx: none Fax: 386 43 73 19 SITA: n/a
F: 1989 ⭑⭑⭑ 3 Head: n/a Net: n/a Aircraft below MTOW 1361kg: Hughes 269C (300C)

	registration	type of aircraft	cn/fn	ex/ex*	mfd	del	powered by	mtow kg	configuration	selcal	name/fin/specialtites/remarks
☐	F-BVUN	Bell 206B JetRanger	247	D-HAMO	0068		1 AN 250-C20	1451			lsf Euromaintenance Helic. / cvtd 206A

HELICAP = HLC
Paris-Issy les Moulineaux / Toulouse-Blagnac

Héliport de Paris, 4 Avenue de la Porte de Sèvres, F-75015 Paris, France ☎ (1) 45 57 75 51 Tx: none Fax: 45 54 12 55 SITA: n/a
F: 1977 ⭑⭑⭑ 38 Head: Jean Capoulade ICAO: HELICAP Net: n/a

	registration	type of aircraft	cn/fn	ex/ex*	mfd	del	powered by	mtow kg	configuration	selcal	name/fin/specialtites/remarks
☐	F-GHRH	Eurocopter (Aerosp.) AS350B Ecureuil	2504		0091		1 TU Arriel 1B	1950	5 Pax		lsf FinPayelle
☐	F-GHYL	Eurocopter (Aerosp.) AS350BA Ecureuil	2632		0092	0592	1 TU Arriel 1B	2100	5 Pax		
☐	F-GMCJ	Eurocopter EC135T1	0020		0097	0797	2 TU Arrius 2B	2720	6 Pax		lsf SNVB Financements
☐	F-GMHC	Eurocopter EC135T1	0036		0097	1297	2 TU Arrius 2B	2720	6 Pax		
☐	F-GMHD	Eurocopter EC135T1	0037		0097	1297	2 TU Arrius 2B	2720	6 Pax		lsf FinPayelle
☐	F-GMHE	Eurocopter EC135T1	0048		0098	0398	2 TU Arrius 2B	2720	6 Pax		lsf SNVB Financements
☐	F-GMHF	Eurocopter EC135T1	0056		0098	0098	2 TU Arrius 2B	2720	6 Pax		lsf Bail Expansion
☐	F-GMHG	Eurocopter EC135T1	0066		0098	0798	2 TU Arrius 2B	2720	6 Pax		lsf Cofranteg
☐	F-GMHJ	Eurocopter EC135T1	0032		0097	1197	2 TU Arrius 2B	2720	6 Pax		lsf Bail Expansion
☐	F-GMHK	Eurocopter EC135T1	0081		0099	0299	2 TU Arrius 2B	2720	6 Pax		
☐	F-GMJC	Eurocopter EC135T1	0026		0097	0997	2 TU Arrius 2B	2720	6 Pax		lsf Confranteg
☐	F-GMOM	Eurocopter EC135T1	0023		0097	0597	2 TU Arrius 2B	2720	6 Pax		lsf FinPayelle
☐	F-GMON	Eurocopter EC135T1	0024		0097	0697	2 TU Arrius 2B	2720	6 Pax		lsf FinPayelle

HELI CHAMPAGNE ARDEN – HCA (Sister company of Champagne Airlines / formerly Heli Arden)
Reims-Prunay & Charleville

Aérodrome de Reims-Prunay, F-51360 Prunay, France ☎ 326 61 70 47 Tx: none Fax: 326 61 70 98 SITA: n/a
F: 1993 ⭑⭑⭑ 14 Head: Gilles Poncin Net: n/a

	registration	type of aircraft	cn/fn	ex/ex*	mfd	del	powered by	mtow kg	configuration	selcal	name/fin/specialtites/remarks
☐	F-GHLR	Bell 206B JetRanger III	2718	N2761B	0079		1 AN 250-C20B	1451	4 Pax		
☐	F-GDRQ	Eurocopter (Aerosp.) AS350B Ecureuil	1832		0085		1 TU Arriel 1B	1950	5 Pax		
☐	F-GIAD	Eurocopter (Aerosp.) AS350B Ecureuil	2112		0088	0098	1 TU Arriel 1B	1950	5 Pax		lsf pvt
☐	F-GIYG	Eurocopter (Aerosp.) AS350B Ecureuil	1410	HB-XLZ	0081		1 TU Arriel 1B	1950	5 Pax		lsf BNP Lease
☐	F-GKCN	Eurocopter (Aerosp.) AS350B Ecureuil	1098	N3596D	0079		1 TU Arriel 1B	1950	5 Pax		lsf T.F.C. Textron / cvtd AS350D
☐	F-GIBI	Eurocopter (Aerosp.) AS355F1 Ecureuil 2	5027	D-HAST	0081	0098	2 AN 250-C20F	2400	5 Pax		lsf Lombard Financement

HELICOCEAN = OCE (Soc. Michel Pentecost Mines dba)
Nouméa-Magenta

BP C2, F-98800 Nouméa Cédex, Nouvelle Calédonie ☎ 25 72 00 Tx: 3051 nm penocea Fax: 25 72 72 SITA: n/a
F: 1970 ⭑⭑⭑ 8 Head: Michel Pentecost ICAO: HELIOCEAN Net: n/a

	registration	type of aircraft	cn/fn	ex/ex*	mfd	del	powered by	mtow kg	configuration	selcal	name/fin/specialtites/remarks
☐	F-ODGQ	Eurocopter (Aerosp.) AS350B Ecureuil	2263		0089		1 TU Arriel 1B	1950	5 Pax		lsf Minière du Sud Pacifique
☐	F-ODYP	Eurocopter (Aerosp.) AS350B1 Ecureuil	2303		0089	0190	1 TU Arriel 1D	2200	5 Pax		
☐	F-OIAG	Eurocopter (Aerosp.) AS350B2 Ecureuil	2170		0089	1096	1 TU Arriel 1D1	2250	5 Pax		
☐	F-OIAJ	Eurocopter (Aerosp.) AS350BA Ecureuil	1296	F-OIAE	0079	0580	1 TU Arriel 1B	2100	5 Pax		lsf pvt / cvtd AS350A
☐	F-OIAU	Eurocopter (Aerosp.) AS350B2 Ecureuil	2978		0097	0497	1 TU Arriel 1D1	2250	6 Pax		lsf pvt

HELICOPTERE SERVICE
Montpellier-l'Or

HÉLICOPTÈRE SERVICE

Aérodrome de Montpellier l'Or, F-34130 Candillargues, France ☎ 467 29 21 70 Tx: none Fax: 467 29 21 80 SITA: n/a
F: 1984 ⭑⭑⭑ 5 Head: Pierre Galipon Net: n/a

	registration	type of aircraft	cn/fn	ex/ex*	mfd	del	powered by	mtow kg	configuration	selcal	name/fin/specialtites/remarks
☐	F-GILX	Eurocopter (Aerosp.) SA315B Lama	2366	N62190	0074		1 TU Artouste IIIB1	1950	4 Pax		lsf Locavia
☐	F-GIMY	Eurocopter (Aerosp.) AS350B2 Ecureuil	1799	F-WYMP*	0086		1 TU Arriel 1D1	2250	5 Pax		lsf Bail Ouest / cvtd AS350B
☐	F-GIPY	Eurocopter (Aerosp.) AS350B2 Ecureuil	2033	LN-OCA	0087	0591	1 TU Arriel 1D1	2250	5 Pax		lsf Geopatagonia, Argentina

HELI-COURLIS (formerly Heli-Courly)
Lyon-Bron

Héli-Courlis

Aéroport de Lyon-Bron, F-69500 Bron, France ☎ 466 23 91 23 Tx: none Fax: 466 64 95 78 SITA: n/a
F: 1981 ⭑⭑⭑ 2 Head: Michel Dreyfus Net: n/a

	registration	type of aircraft	cn/fn	ex/ex*	mfd	del	powered by	mtow kg	configuration	selcal	name/fin/specialtites/remarks
☐	F-GJYG	Eurocopter (Aerosp.) AS350B Ecureuil	1244	N3607C	0080	0590	1 TU Arriel 1B	1950	5 Pax		

HELIDAN, SàRL
Toussus-le-Noble

Hangar 110, Aérodrome Toussus-le-Noble, F-78117 Chateaufort, France ☎ (1) 39 56 16 92 Tx: none Fax: (1) 39 56 29 36 SITA: n/a
F: 1986 �△☆ 5 Head: Eric Parthuisot Net: n/a Aircraft below MTOW 1361kg: Bell 47G-2

registration	type of aircraft	cn/fn	ex/ex*	mfd	del	powered by	mtow kg	configuration	selcal	name/fln/specialitites/remarks
☐ F-GHVQ	Eurocopter (Aerosp.) SE313B Alouette II	1398		0060		1 TU Artouste IIC6	1600	4 Pax		lsf pvt
☐ F-GIJL	Eurocopter (Aerosp.) SE313B Alouette II	1556		0061		1 TU Artouste IIC6	1600	4 Pax		
☐ F-GPEP	Eurocopter (Aerosp.) SE313B Alouette II	1666		0062	0097	1 TU Artouste IIC6	1600	4 Pax		lsf pvt

HELI EUROPE
Lognes

42 rue du Bac, F-75007 Paris, France ☎ (1) 60 17 40 40 Tx: none Fax: (1) 60 17 41 41 SITA: n/a
F: 1998 ☆☆☆ n/a Head: François Maeght Net: n/a Aircraft below MTOW 1361kg: Robinson R22 & R44

registration	type of aircraft	cn/fn	ex/ex*	mfd	del	powered by	mtow kg	configuration	selcal	name/fln/specialitites/remarks
☐ F-GPPE	Agusta A109A	7173	F-WQBP	0080		2 AN 250-C20B	2600			lsf T.F.C. Textron

HELIFRANCE = HFR
Paris-Issy les Moulineaux & Toussus-Le-Noble

4 Ave. de la Porte de Sèvres, F-75015 Paris, France ☎ (1) 45 57 53 67 Tx: 201774 f helifra Fax: (1) 45 54 18 81 SITA: n/a
F: 1980 ☆☆☆ 23 Head: Joel Bastien ICAO: HELIFRANCE Net: n/a

registration	type of aircraft	cn/fn	ex/ex*	mfd	del	powered by	mtow kg	configuration	selcal	name/fln/specialitites/remarks
☐ F-GCJC	Eurocopter (Aerosp.) AS350B Ecureuil	1257		0080		1 TU Arriel 1B	1950	5 Pax		
☐ F-GECM	Eurocopter (Aerosp.) AS350B Ecureuil	1792		0084		1 TU Arriel 1B	1950	5 Pax		lsf BNP Bail
☐ F-GEJB	Eurocopter (Aerosp.) AS350B Ecureuil	1669		0082		1 TU Arriel 1B	1950	5 Pax		lsf BNP Bail
☐ F-GFED	Eurocopter (Aerosp.) AS350B Ecureuil	1473	D-HHPS	0081		1 TU Arriel 1B	1950	5 Pax		lsf BNP Bail
☐ F-GHMQ	Eurocopter (Aerosp.) AS350B2 Ecureuil	2525		0091		1 TU Arriel 1D1	2250	5 Pax		lsf SC Cavok
☐ F-GIHI	Eurocopter (Aerosp.) AS350B1 Ecureuil	2086		0088		1 TU Arriel 1D	2200	5 Pax		
☐ F-GHMC	Eurocopter (Aerosp.) AS355F2 Ecureuil 2	5108	N57902	0081		2 AN 250-C20F	2540	5 Pax		lsf BNP Bail

HELI-INTER, SA = HIN (Affiliated with Business Express)
Cergy-Pontoise

BP 55, F-95312 Cergy-Pontoise Cédex, France ☎ (1) 30 37 30 00 Tx: 697482 f heli int Fax: (1) 34 64 55 27 SITA: n/a
F: 1976 ☆☆☆ 40 Head: Claude A. d'Albronn ICAO: HELI INTER Net: n/a
Helicopters are operated from several bases. Each base operate under a tradename: HELI-INTER AQUITAINE (Biarritz & Bordeaux), HELI-INTER ASSISTANCE (Narbonne), HELI-INTER BRETAGNE (Dinard),
HELI-INTER LORRAINE (Metz), HELI-INTER MIDI PYRENEES (Toulouse/Labège) HELI-INTER NORMANDIE (Deauville), HELI-INTER PARIS (Cergy), HELI-INTER PROVENCE ALPES (Aix-en-Provence) & HELI-INTER RIVIERA (Cannes).

registration	type of aircraft	cn/fn	ex/ex*	mfd	del	powered by	mtow kg	configuration	selcal	name/fln/specialitites/remarks
☐ F-GGTJ	Eurocopter (Aerosp.) SA342J Gazelle	1473	C-GVWC	0078		1 TU Astazou XIVH	1900	4 Pax		lsf Credit de l'Est
☐ F-GCGZ	Eurocopter (Aerosp.) AS350B Ecureuil	1068	TJ-AFU	0079		1 TU Arriel 1B1	1950	5 Pax		lsf Location Moderne
☐ F-GEHN	Eurocopter (Aerosp.) AS350B Ecureuil	1027	F-ODIO	0078		1 TU Arriel 1B	1950	5 Pax		lsf BNP Bail
☐ F-GEHV	Eurocopter (Aerosp.) AS350B Ecureuil	1454	N5786B	0081		1 TU Arriel 1B1	1950	5 Pax		lsf Concorde Equipement
☐ F-GEHZ	Eurocopter (Aerosp.) AS350B Ecureuil	1291	N803DB	0080		1 TU Arriel 1B	1950	5 Pax		lsf Natiolocation
☐ F-GFZC	Eurocopter (Aerosp.) AS350B Ecureuil	2163		0089	0098	1 TU Arriel 1B	1950	5 Pax		lsf Midor SA
☐ F-GGTQ	Eurocopter (Aerosp.) AS350B Ecureuil	1147	N35978	0079		1 TU Arriel 1B	1950	5 Pax		lsf BNP Bail
☐ F-GHAK	Eurocopter (Aerosp.) AS350B Ecureuil	1631	LN-OPQ	0082		1 TU Arriel 1B	1950	5 Pax		lsf Procredit-Probail
☐ F-GKLL	Eurocopter (Aerosp.) AS350B Ecureuil	1202	SE-HKH	0079		1 TU Arriel 1B	1950	5 Pax		lsf BNP Bail
☐ F-GOUT	Eurocopter (Aerosp.) AS355F1 Ecureuil 2	5141	N5793Y	0082	0896	2 AN 250-C20F	2400	5 Pax		lsf BNP Bail

HELI-INTER GUYANE = HIG (Subsidiary of Héli-Inter, SA)
Cayenne-Rochambeau & Saint-Martin/Guadeloupe

Aéroport de Rochambeau, F-97300 Cayenne, Guyane ☎ 35 62 31 Tx: none Fax: 35 82 56 SITA: n/a
F: 1977 ☆☆☆ 10 Head: C.A. D'Albronn ICAO: INTER GUYANE Net: n/a

registration	type of aircraft	cn/fn	ex/ex*	mfd	del	powered by	mtow kg	configuration	selcal	name/fln/specialitites/remarks
☐ F-GHFJ	Eurocopter (Aerosp.) AS350B1 Ecureuil	2127	LN-OTP	0089		1 TU Arriel 1D	2200	5 Pax		
☐ F-GHUM	Eurocopter (Aerosp.) AS350BA Ecureuil	1448		0080		1 TU Arriel 1B	2100	5 Pax		lsf SCBP Banque Populaire / cvtd AS350B
☐ F-OGRY	Eurocopter (Aerosp.) AS350B2 Ecureuil	2577		0091		1 TU Arriel 1D1	2250	5 Pax		lsf pvt
☐ F-OGUZ	Eurocopter (Aerosp.) AS350B2 Ecureuil	2684		0092		1 TU Arriel 1D1	2250	5 Pax		lsf Slibail
☐ F-OGVR	Eurocopter (Aerosp.) AS350B2 Ecureuil	2773		0093		1 TU Arriel 1D1	2250	5 Pax		lsf BNP Bail
☐ F-OGXC	Eurocopter (Aerosp.) AS350BA Ecureuil	1300	F-GJHI	0080		1 TU Arriel 1B	2100	5 Pax		lsf Slibail / cvtd AS350B
☐ F-GDLV	Eurocopter (Aerosp.) AS355F1 Ecureuil 2	5265	F-WZKM	0083		2 AN 250-C20F	2500	5 Pax		lsf Concorde Equipement
☐ F-GFEY	Eurocopter (Aerosp.) AS355F Ecureuil 2	5046	N57826	0081		2 AN 250-C20F	2300	5 Pax		lsf Slibail
☐ F-OGOU	Eurocopter (Aerosp.) AS355F1 Ecureuil 2	5051	C-GLCA	0081		2 AN 250-C20F	2400	5 Pax		lsf Natio Equipement
☐ F-GIIP	Eurocopter (Aerosp.) SA365C3 Dauphin 2	5022	G-BJKA	0079	0991	2 TU Arriel 1C	3500	8 Pax		lsf Slibail
☐ F-GIPI	Eurocopter (Aerosp.) SA365C3 Dauphin 2	5020	G-BGKM	0079		2 TU Arriel 1C	3500	8 Pax		lsf Slibail
☐ F-GPUM	Eurocopter (Aerosp.) SA330J Puma	1652	HB-XUV	0081	0996	2 TU Turmo IVC	7400	Utility		lsf Snc Rorota

HELI-INTER POLYNESIE (Subsidiary of Héli-Inter, SA)
Papeete-Faaa

BP 424, F-98713 Papéeté, (Tahiti), Polynésie Française ☎ 81 99 00 Tx: none Fax: 81 99 99 SITA: n/a
F: 1994 ☆☆☆ 15 Head: Hugues Rauly Net: n/a

registration	type of aircraft	cn/fn	ex/ex*	mfd	del	powered by	mtow kg	configuration	selcal	name/fln/specialitites/remarks
☐ F-GIHD	Eurocopter (Aerosp.) AS350B Ecureuil	1100	N3598X	0079		1 TU Arriel 1B1	1950	5 Pax		lsf Soder Bail
☐ F-ODUS	Eurocopter (Aerosp.) AS350B Ecureuil	2098		0088		1 TU Arriel 1B	1950	5 Pax		lsf Fodus
☐ F-OHAM	Eurocopter (Aerosp.) AS350BA Ecureuil	2633	F-WYMP*	0092		1 TU Arriel 1B	2100	5 Pax		lsf BNP Bail
☐ F-GDFA	Eurocopter (Aerosp.) AS355F1 Ecureuil 2	5018		0081		2 AN 250-C20F	2400	5 Pax		lsf Snc St. Elie
☐ F-GFEX	Eurocopter (Aerosp.) AS355F1 Ecureuil 2	5217	ZS-HKZ	0082		2 AN 250-C20F	2400	6 Pax		lsf Slibail
☐ F-GSAS	Eurocopter (Aerosp.) AS355F1 Ecureuil 2	5159	N5796B	0082		2 AN 250-C20F	2400	5 Pax		lsf Banque Populaire

HELILAGON
Altiport Eperon

Altiport de l'Eperon, F-97460 Saint Paul, Réunion ☎ 55 55 55 Tx: none Fax: 22 86 78 SITA: n/a
F: 1985 ☆☆☆ 23 Head: Jean Marie Lavaivre Net: n/a

registration	type of aircraft	cn/fn	ex/ex*	mfd	del	powered by	mtow kg	configuration	selcal	name/fln/specialitites/remarks
☐ F-ODLI	Eurocopter (Aerosp.) AS350B1 Ecureuil	2063	F-WYMC	0087		1 TU Arriel 1D	2200	6 Pax		lsf Reunion Location Conseil
☐ F-ODLL	Eurocopter (Aerosp.) AS350BA Ecureuil	1192	N215EH	0079		1 TU Arriel 1B	2100	6 Pax		cvtd AS350B
☐ F-OHSC	Eurocopter (Aerosp.) AS350B2 Ecureuil	2333	HB-XVV	0590	1097	1 TU Arriel 1D1	2250	6 Pax		lsf Snc Choucas
☐ F-GJKL	Eurocopter (Aerosp.) SA316B Alouette III	5277	F-ODLH	0076		1 TU Artouste IIIB1	2200	6 Pax		
☐ F-GKTS	Eurocopter (Aerosp.) AS355F2 Ecureuil 2	5081	HB-XPF	0081		2 AN 250-C20F	2540	6 Pax		lsf Anthurium Loc. / cvtd AS355F1
☐ F-ODZV	Eurocopter (Aerosp.) AS355F2 Ecureuil 2	5310	JA9611	0084	1095	2 AN 250-C20F	2540	6 Pax		lsf Combavas Location / cvtd AS355F1

HELI-LOC
Renneville

Hélistation de Renneville, F-31290 Renneville, France ☎ 561 27 79 83 Tx: none Fax: 562 71 02 93 SITA: n/a
F: 1993 ☆☆☆ 11 Head: Bernhard Spors Net: n/a

registration	type of aircraft	cn/fn	ex/ex*	mfd	del	powered by	mtow kg	configuration	selcal	name/fln/specialitites/remarks
☐ F-GGCI	Eurocopter (Aerosp.) SE313B Alouette II	1050		0057		1 TU Artouste IIC5	1600			lsf Lardy Helico Service
☐ F-GLXL	Eurocopter (Aerosp.) SE3130 Alouette II	1612	76+25	0062		1 TU Artouste IIC6	1500			lst Heli Pyrenees
☐ F-GNEA	Eurocopter (Aerosp.) SE313B Alouette II	1841	FAP9208	0063		1 TU Artouste IIC6	1600			

HELI MONTAGNE (Flying division of Commerc'Air, S.A.)
Albertville-Tournon / Gap / Grimaud-Heliport

Aérodrome d'Albertville-Tournon, F-73460 Frontenex, France ☎ 479 38 44 07 Tx: n/a Fax: 479 38 61 17 SITA: n/a
F: 1990 ☆☆☆ 11 Head: Claude Evangelisti Net: n/a

registration	type of aircraft	cn/fn	ex/ex*	mfd	del	powered by	mtow kg	configuration	selcal	name/fln/specialitites/remarks
☐ F-GDUE	Eurocopter (Aerosp.) SE313B Alouette II	1457 / 243		0060	0193	1 TU Artouste IIC6	1600			
☐ F-GIXV	Eurocopter (Aerosp.) SA315B Lama	2029A	F-OGVY	0073	0895	1 TU Artouste IIIB1	1950			lsf Fin Air Trade
☐ F-GDXR	Eurocopter (Aerosp.) AS350B Ecureuil	1912	F-OGNB	0086		1 TU Arriel 1B	1950			
☐ F-GLNG	Eurocopter (Aerosp.) AS350B Ecureuil	1415	F-OGNY	0081	1097	1 TU Arriel 1B	1950			
☐ F-GNBT	Eurocopter (Aerosp.) AS350B3 Ecureuil	3095		0098	0598	1 TU Arriel 2B	2250			lst Textron Finance
☐ F-GPFE	Eurocopter (Aerosp.) AS350B2 Ecureuil	2621	G-BWAZ	0092	0697	1 TU Arriel 1D1	2250			lsf Locavia
☐ F-GOLE	Eurocopter (Aerosp.) SA316B Alouette III	1353	ALAT	0066	0596	1 TU Artouste IIIB1	2200			
☐ F-GTCE	Eurocopter (Aerosp.) SA316B Alouette III	1271	F-GJCX	0065	0495	1 TU Artouste IIIB1	2200			
☐ F-GTJE	Eurocopter (Aerosp.) AS355N Ecureuil 2	5646		0098	0698	2 TU Arrius 1A	2540			
☐ F-GTVE	Eurocopter (Aerosp.) AS355F2 Ecureuil 2	5378	DQ-FGH	0088	1297	2 AN 250-C20F	2540			

HELI OCEAN (Aero Systems Heli Ocean Helicoptères dba)
Nantes-Atlantique

CP 52, F-44340 Bouguenais, France ☎ 240 05 22 11 Tx: none Fax: 240 05 22 02 SITA: n/a
F: 1987 ☆☆☆ 4 Head: Patrick Durieux Net: http://www.aerosystemes.com

registration	type of aircraft	cn/fn	ex/ex*	mfd	del	powered by	mtow kg	configuration	selcal	name/fln/specialitites/remarks
☐ F-GJIM	Eurocopter (Aerosp.) AS350B Ecureuil	1489	N5434T	0081		1 TU Arriel 1B	1950	5 Pax		lsf Jet Systems
☐ F-OIAH	Eurocopter (Aerosp.) AS350B2 Ecureuil	9004		0098	0898	1 TU Arriel 1D1	2250	5 Pax		

HELIPACA (formerly Helivar)
Fréjus

Rue Jean Carra 1, F-83600 Fréjus, France ☎ 494 17 18 19 Tx: none Fax: 494 17 30 11 SITA: n/a
F: 1990 ☆☆☆ 8 Head: Lionel Dominique Net: n/a

registration	type of aircraft	cn/fn	ex/ex*	mfd	del	powered by	mtow kg	configuration	selcal	name/fln/specialitites/remarks
☐ F-BIPH	Eurocopter (Aerosp.) SA318C Alouette II	1773	F-ZBBA	0062		1 TU Astazou IIA2	1650			
☐ F-GFPQ	Eurocopter (Aerosp.) SA318C Alouette II	2247	C-FQMQ	0071		1 TU Astazou IIA2	1650			
☐ F-GKOT	Eurocopter (Aerosp.) SE313B Alouette II	1243	ALAT	0059		1 TU Artouste IIC6	1600			
☐ F-GHFR	Eurocopter (Aerosp.) AS350BA Ecureuil	1374	N5779W	0080		1 TU Arriel 1B	2100			cvtd AS350B
☐ F-GHIR	Eurocopter (Aerosp.) AS350B1 Ecureuil	1980	N160BC	0087		1 TU Arriel 1D	2200			lsf BNP Bail
☐ LX-HAH	Bell 205A-1	30096	C-GEAH	0071	0696	1 LY T5313B	4309			lsf Eagle Copters Ltd
☐ LX-HFZ	Bell 205A-1	30168	HB-XFZ	0374	0091	1 LY T5313B	4309			lsf Heli Europe SA / rebuilt
☐ LX-HOR	Bell 205A-1	30159	C-GMOR	0074	0696	1 LY T5313B	4309			lsf Eagle Copters Ltd
☐ LX-HRI	Bell 205A-1	30019	HB-XRI	0268	0091	1 LY T5313B	4309			lsf Heli Europe SA
☐ LX-HXU	Bell 205A-1	30288	HB-XXU	0079	0091	1 LY T5313B	4309			lsf Heli Europe SA
☐ LX-HEP	Bell 212	30972	N606LH	0079	1097	2 PWC PT6T-3 TwinPac	5080			lsf Heli Europe SA

HELI PACIFIC – Tahiti Hélicoptères
Papeete-Faaa

BP 6109, F-98702 Faaa Aéroport, (Tahiti), Polynésie Française ☎ 85 68 00 Tx: n/a Fax: 85 68 08 SITA: n/a
F: 1983 ♦♦♦ 4 Head: P. Galipon Net: n/a

registration	type of aircraft	cn/fn	ex/ex*	mfd	del	powered by	mtow kg	configuration	selcal	name/fln/specialitites/remarks
☐ F-ODUM	Eurocopter (Aerosp.) AS350B Ecureuil	1834	VH-LEW	0085		1 TU Arriel 1B	1950	6 Pax		

HELI-PARTENAIRES, S.A. (formerly Heli Rhone Alpes)
St. Chamond-l'Horme

BP 214, F-42408 Saint Chamond, France ☎ 477 31 55 80 Tx: 900752 f Fax: 477 31 27 51 SITA: n/a
F: n/a ♦♦♦ 2 Head: Robert Guerra Net: n/a

registration	type of aircraft	cn/fn	ex/ex*	mfd	del	powered by	mtow kg	configuration	selcal	name/fln/specialitites/remarks
☐ F-GKMB	Eurocopter (Aerosp.) AS350B Ecureuil	2304	F-WYMD	0089		1 TU Arriel 1B	1950	5 Pax		lsf Loc Heli

HELI PERIGORD
Bergerac-Roumanire

Route d'Agen, F-24100 Bergerac, France ☎ 553 63 19 96 Tx: 570556 f Fax: 553 27 15 74 SITA: n/a
F: 1982 ♦♦♦ 4 Head: Gérard Crouzet Net: n/a

registration	type of aircraft	cn/fn	ex/ex*	mfd	del	powered by	mtow kg	configuration	selcal	name/fln/specialitites/remarks
☐ F-GCVF	Agusta-Bell 206B JetRanger III	8607		0080		1 AN 250-C20B	1451	4 Pax		
☐ F-GPGC	Bell 206LT TwinRanger	52069	N41061	0094	0097	2 AN 250-C20R	2018	6 Pax		
☐ F-GKHP	Eurocopter (Aerosp.) AS350B Ecureuil	2357		0090	0590	1 TU Arriel 1B	1950	6 Pax		lsf Camebail
☐ F-GLHP	Eurocopter (Aerosp.) AS350B2 Ecureuil	2609		0092	0292	1 TU Arriel 1D1	2250	6 Pax		
☐ F-GFCP	Eurocopter (Aerosp.) AS355F2 Ecureuil 2	5292	F-WYMI	0083		2 AN 250-C20F	2540	5 Pax		cvtd AS355F1
☐ F-GIHU	Eurocopter (Aerosp.) AS355F2 Ecureuil 2	5513	XC-EDM	0091	1296	2 AN 250-C20F	2540	5 Pax		

HELI PLAISANCE – HEP
Lognes-Emerainville

Aérodrome de Lognes-Emerainville, F-77322 Marne La Vallée Cédex, France ☎ (1) 60 06 35 37 Tx: none Fax: (1) 64 80 78 77 SITA: n/a
F: 1975 ♦♦♦ 4 Head: Roland Patriarca Net: n/a

registration	type of aircraft	cn/fn	ex/ex*	mfd	del	powered by	mtow kg	configuration	selcal	name/fln/specialitites/remarks
☐ F-GDQR	Eurocopter (Aerosp.) SA318C Alouette II	2262	C-FMQP	0072		1 TU Astazou IIA2	1650	4 Pax		
☐ F-GRUE	Eurocopter (Aerosp.) AS350B2 Ecureuil	2462	F-GHUP	0391	0198	1 TU Arriel 1D1	2250	5 Pax		lsf Bail Materiel SA

HELI-PROTECTION, SA (Subsidiary of Heli-Union & Conair Aviation, Ltd)
Grenoble-Le Versoud

4 Avenue de la Porte-de-Sèvres, F-75015 Paris, France ☎ (1) 53 78 08 18 Tx: 205897 f heli a Fax: (1) 53 78 08 16 SITA: n/a
F: 1990 ♦♦♦ 5 Head: Jean-Pierre Duchanoy Net: n/a

registration	type of aircraft	cn/fn	ex/ex*	mfd	del	powered by	mtow kg	configuration	selcal	name/fln/specialitites/remarks
☐ F-GHHQ	Bell 205A-1	30092	C-GVHX	0070	0091	1 LY T5317A	4309	Tanker		lsf BNP Bail
☐ F-GHHR	Bell 205A-1	30223	C-GFHN	0076	0091	1 LY T5317A	4309	Tanker		lsf BNP Bail

HELI PYRENEES
Perpignan

Aéroport de Perpignan Rivesaltes, F-66000 Perpignan, France ☎ 468 52 26 60 Tx: none Fax: 468 52 58 18 SITA: n/a
F: 1993 ♦♦♦ 19 Head: n/a Net: n/a Aircraft below MTOW 1361kg: Agusta-Bell 47G

registration	type of aircraft	cn/fn	ex/ex*	mfd	del	powered by	mtow kg	configuration	selcal	name/fln/specialitites/remarks
☐ F-GDQL	Eurocopter (Aerosp.) SE313B Alouette II	1250		0059		1 TU Artouste IIC6	1600			
☐ F-GLXL	Eurocopter (Aerosp.) SE3130 Alouette II	1612	76+25	0062		1 TU Artouste IIC6	1500			lsf Heli-Loc
☐ F-ODZP	Eurocopter (Aerosp.) SE3130 Alouette II	1573		0061		1 TU Artouste IIC6	1500			lsf Heli Blue
☐ F-ODZR	Eurocopter (Aerosp.) SE3130 Alouette II	1359		0060		1 TU Artouste IIC6	1500			lsf Heli Blue
☐ F-GMHP	Eurocopter (Aerosp.) SA316B Alouette III	1780	EC-FST	0071	0796	1 TU Artouste IIIB	2200			
☐ F-GMTA	Eurocopter (Aerosp.) SE3160 Alouette III	1535	F-WQFJ	0069	1096	1 TU Artouste IIIB1	2100			

HELI REUNION
St. Denis-Gillot

BP 332, F-97468 St. Denis, Réunion ☎ 93 11 11 Tx: 916322 f Fax: 29 51 70 SITA: n/a
F: 1993 ♦♦♦ 15 Head: Laurent Popineau Net: n/a

registration	type of aircraft	cn/fn	ex/ex*	mfd	del	powered by	mtow kg	configuration	selcal	name/fln/specialitites/remarks
☐ F-GDQN	Eurocopter (Aerosp.) SA318C Alouette II	2059	C-FZHM	0069		1 TU Astazou IIA2	1650			lsf Aero Finances
☐ F-ODLC	Eurocopter (Aerosp.) SA315B Lama	2635		0082	1097	1 TU Artouste IIIB	1950			lsf BNP Bail
☐ F-ODLE	Eurocopter (Aerosp.) SA315B Lama	2250 / 25	5V-MAJ	0072		1 TU Artouste IIIB1	1950			lsf Aero Finances / cvtd Alouette II
☐ F-ODLU	Eurocopter (Aerosp.) AS350B1 Ecureuil	2242		0089		1 TU Arriel 1D	2200			lsf BNP Bail
☐ F-ODLJ	Eurocopter (Aerosp.) SA365C3 Dauphin 2	5079	D-HMKB	0085		2 TU Arriel 1C	3500			lsf BNP Bail
☐ F-OHSB	Eurocopter (Aerosp.) SA365C3 Dauphin 2	5014	G-BFVW	0079	0797	2 TU Arriel 1C	3500			lsf Dauphin des Mascareignes

HELI SECURITE
Helistation de Grimaud

BP 39, F-83316 Grimaud Cédex, France ☎ 494 43 39 30 Tx: none Fax: 494 43 39 60 SITA: n/a
F: 1998 ♦♦♦ n/a Head: René Romet Net: n/a

registration	type of aircraft	cn/fn	ex/ex*	mfd	del	powered by	mtow kg	configuration	selcal	name/fln/specialitites/remarks
☐ F-GFAQ	Eurocopter (Aerosp.) AS350B1 Ecureuil	2048		0087	0098	1 TU Arriel 1D	2200			lsf BNP Bail
☐ F-GNLP	Eurocopter (Aerosp.) AS350B Ecureuil	1848	HB-XRO	0085	0098	1 TU Arriel 1B	1950			lsf Slibail

HELITIME
Deauville-Hotel l'Amirauté & Corneville-Risle

BP 2, F-27500 Corneville s/Risle, France ☎ 232 57 00 38 Tx: 180635 f Fax: 232 57 02 01 SITA: n/a
F: 1983 ♦♦♦ 3 Head: Pierre Le Foll Net: n/a

registration	type of aircraft	cn/fn	ex/ex*	mfd	del	powered by	mtow kg	configuration	selcal	name/fln/specialitites/remarks
☐ F-BKMR	Agusta-Bell 206B JetRanger	8313		0072		1 AN 250-C20	1450	4 Pax		
☐ F-GDQX	Agusta-Bell 206B JetRanger II	8517	3A-MFC	0076		1 AN 250-C20	1450	4 Pax		lsf Technimat

HELI-UNION = HLU (Affil.with Corse Helicoptères, Heli-Protection, Heli-Union France & Int'l, Oya Helicoptères)
Paris-Heliport

4, Avenue de la Porte-de-Sèvres, F-75015 Paris, France ☎ (1) 53 78 08 18 Tx: 270168 f helidg Fax: (1) 53 78 08 19 SITA: n/a
F: 1961 ♦♦♦ 350 Head: Christophe de Courlon ICAO: HELI UNION Net: n/a
Associated or subs. companies in: Angola, Argentina, Bolivia, Brazil Cameroon, Congo, Ecuador, Gabon, Guyane, Ivory Coast, Luxembourg, Myanmar, Peru, Spain, Tunisia, Venezuela & Vietnam.
Additional main sub-bases are at Grenoble, Tarbes, Ile d'Yeu & Cayenne (Guyane).

registration	type of aircraft	cn/fn	ex/ex*	mfd	del	powered by	mtow kg	configuration	selcal	name/fln/specialitites/remarks
☐ F-BIFT	Eurocopter (Aerosp.) SA315B Lama	05		0060		1 TU Artouste IIIB1	1950	4 Pax		
☐ F-BVEU	Eurocopter (Aerosp.) SA315B Lama	2379		0074		1 TU Artouste IIIB	1950	4 Pax		
☐ F-GAMB	Eurocopter (Aerosp.) SA315B Lama	2457		0076		1 TU Artouste IIIB	1950	4 Pax		
☐ F-GDFX	Eurocopter (Aerosp.) SA315B Lama	2629	LX-HUC	0082		1 TU Artouste IIIB	1950	4 Pax		lst Helicopteros Marinos
☐ F-GEJU	Eurocopter (Aerosp.) SA315B Lama	2295	N62886	0072		1 TU Artouste IIIB	1950	4 Pax		
☐ F-GHUF	Eurocopter (Aerosp.) SA315B Lama	2540	N9006S	0078		1 TU Artouste IIIB1	1950	4 Pax		
☐ F-GIIB	Eurocopter (Aerosp.) SA315B Lama	2461	CS-HBR	0076		1 TU Artouste IIIB	1950	4 Pax		
☐ F-GJGF	Eurocopter (Aerosp.) SA315B Lama	2617	VT-BKM	0081		1 TU Artouste IIIB1	1950	4 Pax		lst Helicopteros Marinos
☐ F-GKSF	Eurocopter (Aerosp.) SA315B Lama	2471	N471E	0077		1 TU Artouste IIIB	1950	4 Pax		lst Helicopteros Marinos
☐ F-GLHD	Eurocopter (Aerosp.) SA315B Lama	2647	VT-VKT	0082		1 TU Artouste IIIB1	1950	4 Pax		
☐ F-GDAM	Eurocopter (Aerosp.) AS350BA Ecureuil	1449		0081		1 TU Arriel 1B	2100	5 Pax		cvtd AS350B
☐ F-GIAN	Eurocopter (Aerosp.) AS350BA Ecureuil	1911	3A-MMD	0086		1 TU Arriel 1B	2100	5 Pax		cvtd AS350B
☐ F-GIZF	Eurocopter (Aerosp.) AS350B3 Ecureuil	3083		0098	0098	1 TU Arriel 2B	2250	5 Pax		
☐ F-GIZG	Eurocopter (Aerosp.) AS350B3 Ecureuil	3084		0098	0098	1 TU Arriel 2B	2250	5 Pax		
☐ F-BSUQ	Eurocopter (Aerosp.) SA316B Alouette III	1779	HC-BOX	0071		1 TU Artouste IIIB	2200	6 Pax		
☐ F-BUAV	Eurocopter (Aerosp.) SE3160 Alouette III	1683	HC-BMP	0070		1 TU Artouste IIIB	2200	6 Pax		
☐ F-GEOY	Eurocopter (Aerosp.) SA316B Alouette III	5397	HC-BPZ	0078		1 TU Artouste IIIB1	2200	6 Pax		
☐ F-GIQL	Eurocopter (Aerosp.) SA316B Alouette III	1836	EC-FEM	0071	1097	1 TU Artouste IIIB1	2200	6 Pax		
☐ F-GCQR	Eurocopter (Aerosp.) SA365C2 Dauphin 2	5054		0080		2 TU Arriel 1A2	3500	9 Pax		lst Oya Helicopteres
☐ F-GEDE	Eurocopter (Aerosp.) SA365C2 Dauphin 2	5078		0083		2 TU Arriel 1A2	3500	9 Pax		
☐ F-GEPN	Eurocopter (Aerosp.) SA365C2 Dauphin 2	5073	D-HELY	0082		2 TU Arriel 1A2	3500	9 Pax		
☐ F-GERJ	Eurocopter (Aerosp.) SA365N Dauphin 2	6066	F-ODRA	0083		2 TU Arriel 1C	4000	9 Pax		
☐ F-GFBM	Eurocopter (Aerosp.) SA365C2 Dauphin 2	5070	F-OAYC	0081		2 TU Arriel 1A2	3500	9 Pax		lst Helicopteros Marinos
☐ F-GFCH	Eurocopter (Aerosp.) SA365C2 Dauphin 2	5072	F-OCCD	0081		2 TU Arriel 1A2	3500	9 Pax		
☐ F-GFEC	Eurocopter (Aerosp.) SA365C2 Dauphin 2	5071	F-ODBV	0081		2 TU Arriel 1A2	3500	9 Pax		
☐ F-GFPA	Eurocopter (Aerosp.) SA365C2 Dauphin 2	5063	LV-AIE	0080		2 TU Arriel 1A2	3500	9 Pax		lst Helicopteros Marinos
☐ F-GFPB	Eurocopter (Aerosp.) SA365C2 Dauphin 2	5064	F-ODNJ	0080		2 TU Arriel 1A2	3500	9 Pax		
☐ F-GFYU	Eurocopter (Aerosp.) SA365N Dauphin 2	6082	F-ODTC	0084		2 TU Arriel 1C	4000	9 Pax		
☐ F-GHXF	Eurocopter (Aerosp.) SA365C2 Dauphin 2	5017	LV-AID	0079		2 TU Arriel 1A2	3500	9 Pax		
☐ F-GIVE	Eurocopter (Aerosp.) SA365C2 Dauphin 2	5052	D-HLTD	0081		2 TU Arriel 1A2	3500	9 Pax		
☐ F-GIZU	Eurocopter (Aerosp.) AS365N2 Dauphin 2	6540		0098	0798	2 TU Arriel 1C	4250	11 Pax		
☐ F-GJDV	Eurocopter (Aerosp.) SA365N Dauphin 2	6065	I-SINV	0083	0895	2 TU Arriel 1C	4000	9 Pax		
☐ F-GKCU	Eurocopter (Aerosp.) SA365N Dauphin 2	6011	PH-SEC	0082		2 TU Arriel 1C	4000	9 Pax		
☐ F-GMAY	Eurocopter (Aerosp.) SA365N Dauphin 2	6137		0085	0396	2 TU Arriel 1C	4000	9 Pax		
☐ F-GMHI	Eurocopter (Aerosp.) SA365N Dauphin 2	6037	PH-SED	0083		2 TU Arriel 1C	4000	9 Pax		
☐ LX-HUN	Eurocopter (Aerosp.) AS365N2 Dauphin 2	6468	F-GJBU	0094		2 TU Arriel 1C2	4250	11 Pax		lst Heli Union Int'l
☐ LX-HUA	Sikorsky S-76A+	760170	F-GKSI	0081	0097	2 TU Arriel 1S	4763	12 Pax		lst Heli Union Int'l / cvtd S-76A
☐ LX-HUD	Sikorsky S-76A++	760042	F-GILD	0079	0792	2 TU Arriel 1S1	4763	12 Pax		lst Heli Union Int'l / cvtd S-76A
☐ LX-HUE	Sikorsky S-76A+	760186	F-GDHU	0082	0792	2 TU Arriel 1S	4763	12 Pax		lst Heli Union Int'l
☐ F-BXOY	Eurocopter (Aerosp.) SA330J Puma	1358	PT-HTY	0075		2 TU Turmo IVC	7400	17 Pax		lst ICARO, Ecuador
☐ F-GBGU	Eurocopter (Aerosp.) SA330J Puma	1571	PT-HUL	0078		2 TU Turmo IVC	7400	17 Pax		lst Helivia as PT-HAO
☐ F-GBTF	Eurocopter (Aerosp.) SA330J Puma	1307	HC-BPJ	0075		2 TU Turmo IVC	7400	17 Pax		
☐ F-GEHU	Eurocopter (Aerosp.) SA330J Puma	1309	I-EHPG	0076		2 TU Turmo IVC	7400	17 Pax		
☐ F-GEQI	Eurocopter (Aerosp.) SA330J Puma	1590	PT-HTJ	0078		2 TU Turmo IVC	7400	17 Pax		lst Helivia as PT-YAW
☐ F-GIMI	Eurocopter (Aerosp.) SA330J Puma	1099	PH-SAZ	0074		2 TU Turmo IVC	7400	17 Pax		
☐ LX-HUL	Eurocopter (Aerosp.) SA330J Puma	1583	F-GHYR	0078		2 TU Turmo IVC	7400	17 Pax		lst Heli Union Int'l

HEX'AIR = UD / HER
Le Puy-Loudes

Aéroport Le Puy-Loudes, F-43320 Loudes, France ☎ 471 08 62 28 Tx: 990534 f Fax: 471 08 04 10 SITA: n/a
F: 1991 ♦♦♦ 5 Head: Pierre Bernard IATA: 848 ICAO: HEX AIRLINE Net: n/a

registration	type of aircraft	cn/fn	ex/ex*	mfd	del	powered by	mtow kg	configuration	selcal	name/fln/specialitites/remarks
☐ F-GOPE	Beech 1900D Airliner	UE-103	N82930	0094	1194	2 PWC PT6A-67D	7688	Y19		La Fayette

ICARE FRANCHE COMTE = FRC

Montbeliard

Aerodrome de Montbéliard, F-25420 Courcelles-lès-Montbéliard, France ☎ 381 90 41 89 Tx: none Fax: 384 23 96 70 SITA: n/a
F: 1993 ⁂ 2 Head: Fréderic Petit ICAO: FRANCHE COMTE Net: http://www.pro.wanadoo.fr/icare.fc

☐ F-BTMH	Piper PA-34-200 Seneca	*34-7250135*		*0072*		*2 LY IO-360-C1E6*	*1905*			
☐ F-GIFB	Beech King Air B90	*LJ-453*	*D-ILTO*	*0069*		*2 PWC PT6A-20*	*4377*			

IGN FRANCE – Institut Géographique National

Creil

Service des Activités Aériennes, Aérodrome de Creil, F-60107 Creil, France ☎ 344 25 41 09 Tx: 150158 f ign saa Fax: 344 25 78 90 SITA: n/a
F: 1945 ⁂ 90 Head: Mr. Jacqmin Net: n/a Non-commercial state organisation, conducting surveying and photo flights. F27 is operated for ARAT-Aviation de Recherche Atmospherique et de Teledetection.

☐ F-GALN	Beech King Air 200T	*BT-1*		*0076*		*2 PWC PT6A-41*	*6350*	*Surveyer*		*cvtd 200 cn BB-186*
☐ F-GALP	Beech King Air 200T	*BT-2*		*0076*		*2 PWC PT6A-41*	*6350*	*Surveyer*		*cvtd 200 cn BB-203*
☐ F-GMLT	Beech King Air 200T	*BT-34*	*N56361**	*0092*	*0793*	*2 PWC PT6A-41*	*6350*	*Surveyer*		*cvtd 200 cn BB-1426*
☐ F-BMSS	Dassault Falcon 20F	*2 / 402*	*F-WMSS**	*0065*		*2 GE CF700-2D2*	*13000*	*Surveyer*		
☐ F-BYAO	Fokker F27 Friendship 700 (F27 Mk700)	*10127*	*F-WYAO*	*0059*	*0486*	*2 RR Dart 514-7*	*18370*	*Surveyer*		*opf ARAT / cvtd 100 / long nose probe*

JEAN BORIES, Transports Public-Travaux Aériens

Pont-sur-Yonne

Aérodrome de Pont-sur-Yvonne, F-89140 Gisy les Nobles, France ☎ 386 67 21 40 Tx: none Fax: 386 65 75 98 SITA: n/a
F: 1982 ⁂ 9 Head: Jean Bories Net: n/a Aircraft / Ag-aircraft below MTOW 1361 / 5000kg: Agusta-Bell 47G, Bell 47G & Cessna A188B

☐ F-GHSF	Eurocopter (Aerosp.) SE313B Alouette II	*1297*	*ALAT*	*0059*		*1 TU Artouste IIC6*	*1600*			
☐ F-GJBN	Eurocopter (Aerosp.) SE313B Alouette II	*1619*	*ALAT*	*0061*		*1 TU Artouste IIC6*	*1600*			
☐ F-GIYB	Eurocopter (Aerosp.) AS355F1 Ecureuil 2	*5142*	*N5793Z*	*0282*	*0098*	*2 AN 250-C20F*	*2400*			
☐ F-GPNA	Eurocopter (Aerosp.) AS355F1 Ecureuil 2	*5207*	*N5802B*	*0082*	*0796*	*2 AN 250-C20F*	*2400*			*lsf Locmat*

JET SYSTEMS

Le Mans-Arnage

Aérodrome Le Mans-Arnage, F-72100 Le Mans, France ☎ 243 72 07 70 Tx: 720015 f Fax: 243 72 25 14 SITA: n/a
F: 1986 ⁂ 17 Head: Patrick Durieux Net: n/a Aircraft below MTOW 1361kg: Agusta-Bell 47G-2.

☐ F-GKLS	Agusta-Bell 206B JetRanger	*8441*	*G-JERY*	*0075*		*1 AN 250-C20*	*1450*	*4 Pax*		*lsf Aero Services*
☐ F-GKML	Eurocopter (Aerosp.) SE313B Alouette II	*1430*	*ALAT*	*0060*		*1 TU Artouste IIC6*	*1600*	*4 Pax*		*lsf SàRL Over Ground Effect*
☐ F-GCVU	Bell 206L-1 LongRanger II	*45456*	*HB-XLO*	*0080*		*1 AN 250-C28B*	*1882*	*6 Pax*		
☐ F-GIGA	Eurocopter (Aerosp.) AS350B Ecureuil	*1804*	*D-HOUA*	*0084*		*1 TU Arriel 1B*	*1950*	*5 Pax*		*lsf Procredit*
☐ F-GJIM	Eurocopter (Aerosp.) AS350B Ecureuil	*1489*	*N5434T*	*0081*		*1 TU Arriel 1B*	*1950*	*5 Pax*		*lsf Procredit / sub-lst Heli Ocean*
☐ I-AGKB	Agusta A109K2	*10028*		*0096*	*0097*	*2 TU Arriel 1K1*	*2850*	*EMS*		*lsf Agusta SpA*

JET SYSTEMS HELICOPTERES SERVICE

Valence-Chabeuil

Les Gonnards, F-26120 Chabeuil, France ☎ 475 85 43 20 Tx: none Fax: 475 85 43 55 SITA: n/a
F: 1987 ⁂ 6 Head: Jose-Anne Moulin Net: n/a

☐ F-GHST	Bell 206B JetRanger	*1104*	*D-HOCH*	*0073*		*1 AN 250-C20*	*1451*	*4 Pax*		*lsf Assoc. les Montgolfières du Nord*
☐ F-GGDH	Eurocopter (Aerosp.) SE313B Alouette II	*1103*	*ALAT*	*0057*		*1 TU Artouste IIC6*	*1600*	*4 Pax*		
☐ F-GJBR	Eurocopter (Aerosp.) SE313B Alouette II	*1357*	*ALAT*	*0060*		*1 TU Artouste IIC5*	*1600*	*4 Pax*		
☐ F-GKRF	Eurocopter (Aerosp.) SA342J Gazelle	*1058*	*C-FEMF*	*0073*		*1 TU Astazou XIVH*	*1900*	*4 Pax*		*lsf SàRL BTAS*
☐ F-GINV	Eurocopter (Aerosp.) AS350B Ecureuil	*1153*		*0079*		*1 TU Arriel 1B*	*1950*	*EMS*		
☐ F-GKJE	Eurocopter (Aerosp.) AS350BA Ecureuil	*1144*	*N350AJ*	*0079*		*1 TU Arriel 1B*	*2100*	*5 Pax*		*lsf Slibail / cvtd AS350B*

KYRNAIR = KYN

Ajaccio-Campo dell'Oro

Aéroport Campo dell'Oro, F-20090 Ajaccio, France ☎ 495 10 60 80 Tx: none Fax: 495 10 60 98 SITA: AJAOPKH
F: 1986 ⁂ 50 Head: Jean-Pierre & Raymond Thouement ICAO: GOLDBIRD Net: n/a Aircraft below MTOW 1361kg: Cessna 172 & 182.

☐ F-GKII	Beech King Air 200	*BB-515*	*N200HC*	*0079*		*2 PWC PT6A-41*	*5670*	*Y11*		*lsf Novabail*
☐ F-GKYN	ATR 42-300	*095*	*F-ODUL*	*0088*	*0397*	*2 PWC PW120*	*16700*	*Y46*		*lsf Pacifique Lise*

L'AEROPOSTALE = ARP (Société d'Exploitation Aeropostale dba / formerly ICS Inter Ciel Service / Associated with La Poste & Air France Group)

Paris-CDG

BP 10454, F-95708 Roissy-CDG, France ☎ (1) 48 62 80 05 Tx: 263414 f Fax: (1) 48 62 80 24 SITA: n/a
F: 1986 ⁂ 390 Head: Martin Vial ICAO: AEROPOSTE Net: n/a
Some passenger flights with Boeing 737-300 aircraft are operated on behalf of AIR FRANCE (some in full such colors & both titles) & using AF-flight numbers.

☐ F-GFVI	Boeing 737-230C	*20256 / 238*	*N304XV*	*0070*	*0988*	*2 PW JT8D-9A (HK3/AVA)*	*53750*	*Freighter*	*NONE*	
☐ F-GGVP	Boeing 737-2K2C (A)	*20943 / 405*	*VT-EKC*	*0075*	*0990*	*2 PW JT8D-15 (HK3/AVA)*	*53750*	*Freighter*	*NONE*	
☐ F-GGVQ	Boeing 737-2K2C (A)	*20944 / 408*	*VT-EKD*	*0075*	*1190*	*2 PW JT8D-15 (HK3/AVA)*	*53750*	*Y130/Freighter*	*NONE*	
☐ F-GIXA	Boeing 737-2K2C (A)	*20836 / 354*	*PH-TVC*	*0074*	*1289*	*2 PW JT8D-15A (HK3/AVA)*	*53750*	*Y130/Freighter*	*NONE*	
☐ F-GFUE	Boeing 737-3B3 (QC)	*24387 / 1693*		*0089*	*0292*	*2 CFMI CFM56-3B1*	*61235*	*Y147/Freighter*	*NONE*	*cvtd -3B3*
☐ F-GFUF	Boeing 737-3B3 (QC)	*24388 / 1725*		*0089*	*0392*	*2 CFMI CFM56-3B1*	*61235*	*Y147/Freighter*	*NONE*	*cvtd -3B3 / op in Air France-colors*
☐ F-GIXB	Boeing 737-33A (QC)	*24789 / 1953*	*F-OGSD*	*0090*	*0191*	*2 CFMI CFM56-3C1*	*58967*	*Y147/Freighter*	*NONE*	*lsf CL Jet Ltd / cvtd -33A*
☐ F-GIXC	Boeing 737-38B (QC)	*25124 / 2047*	*F-OGSS*	*0091*	*1291*	*2 CFMI CFM56-3C1*	*58967*	*Y147/Freighter*	*NONE*	*lsf Champs Elysees Lsng Co./cvtd -38B*
☐ F-GIXD	Boeing 737-33A (QC)	*25744 / 2198*	*N3213T*	*0091*	*0092*	*2 CFMI CFM56-3C1*	*58967*	*Y147/Freighter*	*NONE*	*lsf CIT FSC Eleven Ltd/cvtd -33A*
☐ F-GIXE	Boeing 737-3B3 (QC)	*26850 / 2235*	*N854WT*	*0092*	*0392*	*2 CFMI CFM56-3C1*	*58967*	*Y147/Freighter*	*NONE*	*lsf CIT FSC Fourteen Ltd/cvtd -3B3*
☐ F-GIXF	Boeing 737-3B3 (QC)	*26851 / 2267*	*N4361V*	*0092*	*0492*	*2 CFMI CFM56-3C1*	*58967*	*Y147/Freighter*	*NONE*	*lsf CIT FSC Fifteen Ltd/cvtd -3B3*
☐ F-GIXG	Boeing 737-382 (QC)	*24364 / 1657*	*F-OGSX*	*0089*	*0694*	*2 CFMI CFM56-3B1*	*61235*	*Y147/Freighter*	*NONE*	*lsf SPC Aircraft Holding / cvtd -382*
☐ F-GIXH	Boeing 737-3S3 (QC)	*23788 / 1393*	*N271LF*	*0087*	*1194*	*2 CFMI CFM56-3B2*	*63276*	*Y147/Freighter*	*NONE*	*lsf ILFC / cvtd -3S3*
☐ F-GIXI	Boeing 737-348 (QC)	*23809 / 1458*	*F-OGSY*	*0087*	*0195*	*2 CFMI CFM56-3B1*	*61235*	*Y147/Freighter*	*NONE*	*lsf NBB Buckingham Lease / cvtd -348*
☐ F-GIXJ	Boeing 737-3Y0 (QC)	*23685 / 1357*	*G-MONH*	*0087*	*0495*	*2 CFMI CFM56-3B1*	*61235*	*Freighter*	*NONE*	*cvtd -3Y0*
☐ F-GIXK	Boeing 737-33A (QC)	*24028 / 1599*	*G-MONP*	*0088*	*0495*	*2 CFMI CFM56-3B1*	*61235*	*Freighter*	*NONE*	*lsf Transcontinental Avn / cvtd -33A*
☐ F-GIXL	Boeing 737-348 (QC)	*23810 / 1474*	*F-OHCS*	*0087*	*0195*	*2 CFMI CFM56-3B1*	*61235*	*Y147/Freighter*	*NONE*	*lsf NBB Kensington Lease / cvtd -348*
☐ F-GIXO	Boeing 737-3Q8 (QC)	*24132 / 1555*	*N241LF*	*0088*	*0196*	*2 CFMI CFM56-3B2*	*63276*	*Y147/Freighter*	*NONE*	*lsf ILFC / cvtd -3Q8*
☐ F-GIXP	Boeing 737-3M8 (QC)	*24021 / 1630*	*9V-SQZ*	*0088*	*0896*	*2 CFMI CFM56-3B2*	*63276*	*Y147/Freighter*	*NONE*	*lsf INGO / cvtd -3M8*
☐ F-GKDY	Boeing 727-225 (F) (A)	*22438 / 1685*	*N807EA*	*0080*	*0695*	*3 PW JT8D-15A (HK3/FDX)*	*88400*	*Freighter*		*lsf PEGA / cvtd -225*
☐ F-GKDZ	Boeing 727-225 (F) (A)	*22441 / 1695*	*N810EA*	*0080*	*0595*	*3 PW JT8D-15A (HK3/FDX)*	*88400*	*Freighter*		*lsf PEGA / cvtd -225*
☐ F-GOZA	Airbus Industrie A300B4-103 (F)	*148*	*SX-BEG*	*0581*	*0399*	*2 GE CF6-50C2*	*157500*	*Freighter*		*lsf Aircargo Capital / cvtd -102/3*
☐ F-GOZB	Airbus Industrie A300B4-103 (F)	*184*	*SX-BEH*	*0382*		*2 GE CF6-50C2*	*157500*	*Freighter*		*tblsf Aircargo Capital 0099/cvtd -102/3*
☐ F-GOZC	Airbus Industrie A300B4-103 (F)	*189*	*SX-BEI*	*0482*		*2 GE CF6-50C2*	*157500*	*Freighter*		*tblsf Aircargo Capital 0099/cvtd -102/3*

LEADAIR-UNIJET, SA = LEA

Paris-Le Bourget

BP 184, Aéroport du Bourget, F-93352 Le Bourget Cédex, France ☎ (1) 48 35 90 90 Tx: 234176 f Fax: (1) 48 35 90 65 SITA: n/a
F: 1968 ⁂ 33 Head: Dannys Famin ICAO: LEADAIR Net: n/a

☐ F-GGMV	Beech King Air 200	*BB-616*	*SE-IUN*	*0080*		*2 PWC PT6A-41*	*5670*	*9 Pax*		*lsf Sofinabail*
☐ F-BJLH	Dassault Falcon 10	*1*	*F-BSQU*	*0073*		*2 GA TFE731-2-1C*	*8500*	*7 Pax*		*lsf Slibail*
☐ F-GDLR	Dassault Falcon 10	*121*	*HB-VFT*	*0078*		*2 GA TFE731-2-1C*	*8500*	*7 Pax*		*lsf Slibail*
☐ F-GJLL	Dassault Falcon 10	*22*	*N48JC*	*0074*		*2 GA TFE731-2-1C*	*8755*	*7 Pax*		*lsf Slibail*
☐ F-GNDZ	Dassault Falcon 10	*17*	*EC-949*	*0074*	*0792*	*2 GA TFE731-2-1C*	*8500*	*7 Pax*		*lsf Groupe André*
☐ F-GGVB	Dassault Falcon 50	*11*	*N5739*	*0081*		*3 GA TFE731-3-1C*	*17600*	*9 Pax*		*lsf Bollore Technologies*
☐ F-HAXA	Dassault Falcon 900EX	*12*	*F-WQBL*	*0097*	*1298*	*3 GA TFE731-60-1C*	*22226*	*14 Pax*		*lsf Axa Réassurance*

LOCAVIA FRANCE

Nantes-Atlantique

Aérodrome de Cholet, F-49300 Cholet, France ☎ 240 05 13 47 Tx: none Fax: 241 71 14 05 SITA: n/a
F: 1982 ⁂ 9 Head: Muriel Verrier Net: n/a

☐ F-GBLU	Beech King Air C90	*LJ-822*		*0079*		*2 PWC PT6A-21*	*4377*	*9 Pax*		*lsf Prestations Location*
☐ F-GFHC	Beech King Air C90	*LJ-717*	*N200BX*	*0077*		*2 PWC PT6A-21*	*4377*	*9 Pax*		*lsf Locavia*
☐ F-GKEL	Beech King Air A100	*B-228*	*N23868*	*0076*		*2 PWC PT6A-28*	*5216*	*12 Pax*		*lsf Locavia*

LOCAVIONS AERO SERVICES = PAU

Pau

Aéroport d'Uzein, F-64230 Sauvagnon, France ☎ 559 33 18 74 Tx: none Fax: 559 33 79 12 SITA: n/a
F: 1996 ⁂ n/a Head: n/a ICAO: ADOUR Net: n/a

☐ F-GCLH	Piper PA-31T Cheyenne II	*31T-8020044*	*N2330V*	*0080*		*2 PWC PT6A-28*	*4082*	*7 Pax*		*lsf SA Alarme Service France*

MANAG'AIR = MRG

Amiens-Glisy

Aéroport d'Amiens Glisy, RN29, F-80440 Glisy, France ☎ 322 38 12 34 Tx: n/a Fax: 322 38 16 76 SITA: n/a
F: 1995 ⁂ n/a Head: Albert Ruoso ICAO: MANAG'AIR Net: n/a

☐ F-BXSN	Beech King Air E90	*LW-175*		*0076*		*2 PWC PT6A-28*	*4581*	*8 Pax*		*lsf Air Picardie Investissement*

MG-AVIATION = MGM (formerly Marie Galante Aviation)

Marie Galante

Immeuble Ferdinand Le Maistre, Rue Jeanne d'Arc, F-97112 Grand Bourg de Marie Galante, Guadeloupe ☎ 97 77 02 Tx: none Fax: 97 76 89 SITA: n/a
F: 1995 ⁂ n/a Head: n/a ICAO: MARIE GALANTE Net: n/a

☐ F-OGVX	Partenavia P.68B	*39*	*G-BFVO*	*0075*	*0395*	*2 LY IO-360-A1B6*	*1990*			

MICHELIN AIR SERVICES

Clermont-Ferrand

23 Place des Carmes Déchaux, F-63000 Clermont-Ferrand, France ☎ 473 60 44 61 Tx: none Fax: 473 60 44 69 SITA: n/a
F: 1998 ⁂ n/a Head: Henri Perrier Net: n/a

☐ F-GOPM	Dassault Falcon 20E	*302*	*F-WQBM*	*0074*	*0098*	*2 GE CF700-2D2*	*13000*			*lsf BNP Lease*

156 registration type of aircraft *cn/fn* *ex/ex** *mfd* *del* *powered by* *mtow kg* *configuration* *selcal* *name/fln/specialitites/remarks*

MONT-BLANC HELICOPTERES — Annemasse

Rue Germain Sommeiller, Aérodrome d'Annemasse, F-74100 Annemasse, France ☎ 450 92 78 21 Tx: none Fax: 450 38 01 01 SITA: n/a
F: 1980 ☤☤☤ 15 Head: Marc Blanc Net: http://www.montblanc-helicopteres.fr Aircraft below MTOW 1361kg: Robinson R22

☐ F-GHFI	Eurocopter (Aerosp.) SA315B Lama	2476	D-HLEO	0076		1 TU Artouste IIIB1	1950	4 Pax		lsf Bail Materiel
☐ F-GIBK	Eurocopter (Aerosp.) SA315B Lama	2287 / 41	F-GEHY	0072		1 TU Artouste IIIB1	1950	4 Pax		lsf Helicom / cvtd Alouette II
☐ F-GRRB	Eurocopter (Aerosp.) SA315B Lama	2475	F-SEBO	0077	0497	1 TU Artouste IIIB1	1950	4 Pax		lsf Helicom
☐ F-GFPM	Eurocopter (Aerosp.) AS350BA Ecureuil	1833		0086		1 TU Arriel 1B	2100	5 Pax		lsf Helicom / cvtd AS350B
☐ F-GHUT	Eurocopter (Aerosp.) AS350B2 Ecureuil	2545		0091	0991	1 TU Arriel 1D1	2250	5 Pax		lsf Pozzi Rent Snc
☐ F-GIDR	Eurocopter (Aerosp.) AS350BA Ecureuil	1993	N350TC	0087	0097	1 TU Arriel 1B	2100	5 Pax		lsf Victoria Heli.Services / cvtd 350B
☐ F-GJAM	Eurocopter (Aerosp.) AS350BA Ecureuil	1866	D-HILF	0085		1 TU Arriel 1B	2100	5 Pax		lsf Alfox
☐ F-GJJH	Eurocopter (Aerosp.) AS350B2 Ecureuil	2584		0092	0292	1 TU Arriel 1D1	2250	5 Pax		lsf Bail Equipement
☐ F-GKBE	Eurocopter (Aerosp.) AS350B2 Ecureuil	2503		0091	0791	1 TU Arriel 1D1	2250	5 Pax		lsf Helicom
☐ F-GMHR	Eurocopter (Aerosp.) AS350B2 Ecureuil	1921	OY-HEJ	0086	0794	1 TU Arriel 1D1	2250	5 Pax		lsf Heligral
☐ F-GTOY	Eurocopter (Aerosp.) AS350B Ecureuil	1030	C-FBKW	0078		1 TU Arriel 1B	1950	5 Pax		lsf Helidream
☐ F-GIVL	Eurocopter (Aerosp.) AS355N Ecureuil 2	5603		0096	0696	2 TU Arrius 1A	2540	5 Pax		lsf Solair

NICE HELICOPTERES = JX — Nice-Cote d'Azur

Aéroport Nice-Cote d'Azur, F-06281 Nice Cédex 3, France ☎ 493 21 34 32 Tx: none Fax: 493 21 35 64 SITA: n/a
F: 1985 ☤☤☤ 4 Head: Annie-Claire Benchimol IATA: 179 Net: n/a

☐ F-GEPU	Eurocopter (Aerosp.) SA315B Lama	2641	G-BNHZ	0082		1 TU Artouste IIIB	1950	4 Pax		
☐ F-GMBN	Eurocopter (Aerosp.) AS350B Ecureuil	1794	3A-MFC	0084	0695	1 TU Arriel 1B	1950	5 Pax		
☐ F-GMBO	Eurocopter (Aerosp.) AS350B2 Ecureuil	2253	SE-HUS	0089	0596	1 TU Arriel 1D1	2250	5 Pax		cvtd AS350B

OCCITANIA JET FLEET = OJF — Paris-Le Bourget

21 Avenue Georges V, F-75008 Paris, France ☎ (1) 48 64 29 99 Tx: none Fax: (1) 48 64 36 80 SITA: n/a
F: 1997 ☤☤☤ n/a Head: Alain Regourd ICAO: OCCITANIA Net: n/a

☐ F-GLPJ	Beech 1900C-1 Airliner	UC-40	OY-BVG	0088	1198	2 PWC PT6A-65B	7530	19 Pax		lsf Regourd Aviation
☐ F-GNPM	Beech 1900C-1 Airliner	UC-153	N153YV	0491	0798	2 PWC PT6A-65B	7530	19 Pax		lsf Raytheon Aircraft Credit Corp.
☐ F-GMOT	Dassault Falcon 50	111	N50AH	0082	1098	3 GA TFE731-3-1C	17600	10 Pax		lsf Gridley Finance Ltd
☐ F-GSER	Dassault Falcon 50	2	F-BINR	0078	0497	3 GA TFE731-3-1C	17600	10 Pax		lsf Regourd Aviation

OYA HELICOPTERES (Subsidiary of Héli-Union) — L'Ile d'Yeu-Le Grand Phare

BP 100, F-85350 L'Ile d'Yeu, France ☎ 251 59 22 22 Tx: none Fax: 251 59 20 77 SITA: n/a
F: 1989 ☤☤☤ 10 Head: Jean-Pierre Duchanoy Net: n/a

☐ F-GCQR	Eurocopter (Aerosp.) SA365C2 Dauphin 2	5054		0080		2 TU Arriel 1A2	3500	9 Pax		lsf Heli-Union

OYONNAIR, SàRL — Oyonnax-Arbent

6 rue du Moulin, F-01115 Bellignat-Oyonnax Cédex, France ☎ 474 73 59 43 Tx: none Fax: 474 77 80 66 SITA: n/a
F: 1989 ☤☤☤ n/a Head: Michel Maradan Net: n/a

☐ F-GNMA	Beech King Air C90A	LJ-1299	N8253D	0092		2 PWC PT6A-21	4581	8 Pax		lsf Bail Equipement

PAN EUROPEENNE AIR SERVICE = PEA — Chambéry-Aix les Bains

Aéroport Chambéry Aix les Bains, F-73420 Le Viviers-du-Lac, France ☎ 479 54 42 68 Tx: 309636 f paneuro Fax: 479 54 46 45 SITA: n/a
F: 1977 ☤☤☤ n/a Head: Bernard Guichon Net: n/a

☐ F-GGVG	Fairchild (Swearingen) SA226T Merlin IIIB	T-293	D-IBBB	0078		2 GA TPE331-10U-512G	5670	8 Pax		lst ARL
☐ F-BTME	Beech 99 Airliner	U-79	N100GP	0069	0084	2 PWC PT6A-20	4717	15 Pax		lst Taxi Air Fret
☐ F-GFPE	Beech 99 Airliner	U-21	OO-WAY	0068	1186	2 PWC PT6A-20	4717	15 Pax		lst Taxi Air Fret
☐ F-BXSL	Beech King Air C90	LJ-648		0074		2 PWC PT6A-20A	4377	9 Pax		lst RNO
☐ F-GGLA	Beech King Air 200	BB-744	F-GGPJ	0080	0098	2 PWC PT6A-41	5670	8 Pax		
☐ F-GUPE	Beech 1900D Airliner	UE-248	N10882*	0096	0197	2 PWC PT6A-67D	7688	19 Pax		

PARIS HELICOPTERE SYSTEM - P.H.S. — Paris-Le Bourget & Beauvais-Tillé

Zone d'Aviation d'Affaires, F-93350 Aéroport du Bourget, France ☎ (1) 48 35 90 44 Tx: none Fax: (1) 48 35 90 61 SITA: n/a
F: 1990 ☤☤☤ n/a Head: Eric & Charles Aguettant Net: http://www.paris-helicopteres.com

☐ F-GFHM	Eurocopter (Aerosp.) AS350B Ecureuil	1560	F-WYMB	0082		1 TU Arriel 1B	1950	5 Pax		
☐ F-GHPH	Eurocopter (Aerosp.) AS350B2 Ecureuil	2365		0090		1 TU Arriel 1D1	2250	5 Pax		lsf Locabail
☐ F-GETR	Eurocopter (Aerosp.) AS355F2 Ecureuil 2	5060	F-OBUU	0081	0097	2 AN 250-C20F	2540	5 Pax		lsf BNP Lease

PONAIR — Vannes-Meucon

Aérodrome de Vannes-Meucon, F-56250 Monterblanc, France ☎ 297 60 62 60 Tx: none Fax: 297 60 69 91 SITA: n/a
F: 1994 ☤☤☤ n/a Head: Daniel Manoury Net: n/a

☐ F-GCTM	Eurocopter (Aerosp.) AS350B Ecureuil	1453		0081		1 TU Arriel 1B	1950			lsf Novaleasing

PREST'AFFAIR — Lille-Lesquin

Aeroport de Lille, F-59810 Lesquin, France ☎ 320 49 67 90 Tx: none Fax: 320 96 61 43 SITA: n/a
F: 1996 ☤☤☤ n/a Head: Nicolas Collignon Net: n/a

☐ F-GCVY	Agusta-Bell 206B JetRanger III	8623		0081		1 AN 250-C20B	1450			
☐ F-GHCS	Beech King Air 200	BB-303	N18345	0078		2 PWC PT6A-41	5670			

PROCOPTERE — Beaune-Challenges

Aerodrome de Beaune-Challenges, F-21200 Beaune, France ☎ 380 24 62 26 Tx: n/a Fax: 380 24 95 23 SITA: n/a
F: 1992 ☤☤☤ 7 Head: J.M. Redon Net: n/a Aircraft below MTOW 1361kg: Bell 47G

☐ F-GHUQ	Eurocopter (Aerosp.) SE313B Alouette II	1242	ALAT	0059		1 TU Artouste IIC6	1600			

PROTEUS AIRLINES = YS / PRB (Associated with Delta Air Lines, Inc. / formerly Proteus Air System) — Dijon-Longvic & Lyon-Satolas

24 rue de la redoute, BP 76, F-21850 Saint Apollinaire, France ☎ 380 60 93 60 Tx: none Fax: 380 60 93 70 SITA: n/a
F: 1986 ☤☤☤ 300 Head: Franklin Devaux IATA: 977 ICAO: PROTEUS Net: n/a Some aircraft are operated on a franchise agreement with AIR FRANCE in full such colors & both titles & using AF flight numbers.

☐ F-GNAD	Beech 1900C-1 Airliner	UC-58	N1568G	0389	0597	2 PWC PT6A-65B	7530	Y19		lsf Raytheon Aircraft Credit Corp.
☐ F-GNAH	Beech 1900C-1 Airliner	UC-131	N15486	0090	0897	2 PWC PT6A-65B	7530	Y19		lsf Raytheon Aircraft Credit Corp.
☐ F-GNAJ	Beech 1900C-1 Airliner	UC-163	N163AM	0691	0897	2 PWC PT6A-65B	7530	Y19		lsf Raytheon Aircraft Credit Corp.
☐ F-GNYL	Beech 1900C-1 Airliner	UC-134	N134YV	1290	0597	2 PWC PT6A-65B	7530	Y19		Ville d'Annecy / lsf Raytheon Aircraft
☐ F-GMAD	Beech 1900D Airliner	UE-290	N18153*	0097	1297	2 PWC PT6A-67D	7688	Y19		Ville de Rodez / lsf Franco-American Ls
☐ F-GPBM	Beech 1900D Airliner	UE-305	N22546*	0098	0498	2 PWC PT6A-67D	7688	Y19		lsf Beechcraft UE-305 Leasing Inc.
☐ F-GPSD	Beech 1900D Airliner	UE-303	N11249*	0098	0498	2 PWC PT6A-67D	7688	Y19		Ville de Dijon / lsf Franco-Kansas Lse
☐ F-GREA	Beech 1900D Airliner	UE-307	N22761*	0098	0598	2 PWC PT6A-67D	7688	Y19		Ville de Chambery / lsf BeechUE-307Lsng
☐ F-GRMD	Beech 1900D Airliner	UE-296	N21572*	0097	0198	2 PWC PT6A-67D	7688	Y19		Ville de St.Etienne / lsf Intl LseCorp.
☐ F-GRPM	Beech 1900D Airliner	UE-300	N22120*	0098	0198	2 PWC PT6A-67D	7688	Y19		Ville de Reims / lsf Kansas Beech Lsng
☐ F-GRYL	Beech 1900D Airliner	UE-301	N22161*	0098	0198	2 PWC PT6A-67D	7688	Y19		Ville d'Avignon / lsf Rayth.-Kansas Lse
☐ F-GSFD	Beech 1900D Airliner	UE-252	N10907*	0096	0397	2 PWC PT6A-67D	7688	Y18		lsf Raytheon Aircr.Credit/op in AFR-cs
☐ F-GUCB	Beech 1900D Airliner	UE-308	N22841*	0098	0498	2 PWC PT6A-67D	7688	Y19		lsf Beechcraft U-308 Lsng/op in AFR-cs
☐ F-GNBS	Dornier 328-110	3053	D-CDXU*	0096	0396	2 PWC PW119B	13990	Y31		lsf Deut.Structured Fin. / op in AFR-cs
☐ F-GNPA	Dornier 328-110	3063	D-CDXK*	0096	0396	2 PWC PW119B	13990	Y31		lsf Deut.Structured Fin. / op in AFR-cs
☐ F-GNPR	Dornier 328-110	3088	D-CDXU*	0098	0398	2 PWC PW119B	13990	Y31		lsf Dornier Luftfahrt GmbH/op in AFR-cs
☐ F-GOAC	Dornier 328-110	3084	D-CDXI*	0097	0997	2 PWC PW119B	13990	Y31		lsf Dornier Luftfahrt GmbH/op in AFR-cs
☐ F-GOFB	Dornier 328-110	3087	D-CDXK*	0098	0398	2 PWC PW119B	13990	Y31		lsf Dornier Luftfahrt GmbH/op in AFR-cs
☐ F-GTJL	Dornier 328-110	3089		0098	0998	2 PWC PW119B	13990	Y31		lsf Dornier Luftfahrt GmbH/op white-cs
☐ F-	Dornier 328JET (328-300)					2 PWC PW306B	14990	Y32		oo-delivery 0499
☐ F-	Dornier 328JET (328-300)					2 PWC PW306B	14990	Y32		oo-delivery 0999
☐ F-	Dornier 328JET (328-300)					2 PWC PW306B	14990	Y32		oo-delivery 0300
☐ F-	Dornier 328JET (328-300)					2 PWC PW306B	14990	Y32		oo-delivery 0400
☐ F-	Dornier 328JET (328-300)					2 PWC PW306B	14990	Y32		oo-delivery 0500
☐ F-	Dornier 328JET (328-300)					2 PWC PW306B	14990	Y32		oo-delivery 0600

PROTEUS HELICOPTERES (Sister company of Proteus Airlines / formerly Tecnavia Aeronautique) — Lyon-Satolas

Aéroport Dijon-Bourgogne, BP 25, F-21601 Longvic Cédex, France ☎ 380 63 13 58 Tx: none Fax: 380 63 13 60 SITA: n/a
F: 1985 ☤☤☤ 21 Head: Bernard Stouff Net: n/a

☐ F-GEQE	Bell 206B JetRanger III	3163	N555BA	0080		1 AN 250-C20B	1450	4 Pax		lsf pvt
☐ F-GJLJ	Bell 206B JetRanger III	2748	YU-HCI	0079	0098	1 AN 250-C20B	1451	4 Pax		lsf pvt
☐ F-GLEF	Agusta A109E Power	11027		0098	0199	2 PWC PW206C	2850	EMS SAMU 61		lsf Longvic Heli
☐ F-GLEG	Agusta A109E Power	11030		0098	0199	2 PWC PW206C	2850	EMS SAMU 26		
☐ F-GLEH	Agusta A109E Power	11037		0098	0299	2 PWC PW206C	2850	EMS SAMU 28		
☐ F-GNGR	Agusta A109K2	10017	OO-AAU	0093	0498	2 TU Arriel 1K1	2850	EMS SAMU		opf SAMU/Conseil General de l'Orne
☐ F-GLOR	Eurocopter EC135T1	0041		0098	0498	2 TU Arrius 2B	2720	EMS SAMULorraine		lsf Eurocopter Deutschland

PROVENCE AERO SERVICE - PAS = RPA (Member of Groupe SAF) — Castellet

Aerodrome de Castellet, 3250 Route des Hauts de Camd, F-83330 Castellet, France ☎ 479 38 48 29 Tx: none Fax: 479 08 33 57 SITA: n/a
F: 1986 ☤☤☤ 20 Head: Eric Fraissinet ICAO: AIRPASS Net: n/a Uses helicopters from the SAF fleet when required.

157 registration type of aircraft cn/fn ex/ex* mfd del powered by mtow kg configuration selcal name/fln/specialitites/remarks

PYRENEES HELICO SERVICES

Pau-Pyrenees & Agen-La Garenne

6 rue Clabe, F-64450 Theze, France ☎ 559 33 97 50 Tx: none Fax: 559 33 72 14 SITA: n/a
F: 1990 ⁂ 6 Head: Maurice Crouail Net: n/a Aircraft below MTOW 1361kg: Agusta-Bell 47G-2

registration	type of aircraft	cn/fn	ex/ex*	mfd	del	powered by	mtow kg	configuration	selcal	name/fln/specialitites/remarks
☐ F-GHTO	Eurocopter (Aerosp.) SE313B Alouette II	1021		0056		1 TU Artouste IIC5	1600			
☐ F-GDFM	Eurocopter (Aerosp.) AS350B Ecureuil	1007	G-BGHG	0078	0098	1 TU Arriel 1B	1950			lsf BNP Bail

REGIONAL AIRLINES, S.A. = VM / RGI

Nantes-Atlantique

Aéroport Nantes Atlantique, F-44340 Bouguenais, France ☎ 240 13 53 00 Tx: none Fax: 240 13 53 08 SITA: NTEPFVM
F: 1992 ⁂ 650 Head: Jean-Paul Dubreuil IATA: 982 ICAO: REGIONAL Net: http://www.regionalairlines.com
Some aircraft are operated on code-sharing agreement with AIR FRANCE (in full such colors & both titles) & using AF flight numbers.

registration	type of aircraft	cn/fn	ex/ex*	mfd	del	powered by	mtow kg	configuration	selcal	name/fln/specialitites/remarks
☐ F-GMVH	BAe 3206 Jetstream 32	974	G-BURU	0092	0293	2 GA TPE331-12UAR-701H	7350	Y19		lsf BAMT / sub-lst RNO
☐ F-GMVI	BAe 3206 Jetstream 32	975	G-BUTW	0092	0193	2 GA TPE331-12UAR-701H	7350	Y19		lsf BAMT / sub-lst FEU
☐ F-GMVJ	BAe 3206 Jetstream 32	976	G-BUUZ	0092	0393	2 GA TPE331-12UAR-701H	7350	Y19		lsf BAMT / sub-lst RNO
☐ F-GMVK	BAe 3206 Jetstream 32	977	G-BUVD	0093	0493	2 GA TPE331-12UAR-701H	7350	Y19		lsf BAMT / sub-lst FEU
☐ F-GMVL	BAe 3206 Jetstream 32	978	G-31-978*	0092	0493	2 GA TPE331-12UAR-701H	7350	Y19		lsf BAMT / sub-lst RNO
☐ F-GMVM	BAe 3206 Jetstream 32	979	G-31-979*	0093	0593	2 GA TPE331-12UAR-701H	7350	Y19		lsf BAMT / sub-lst RNO
☐ F-GMVN	BAe 3206 Jetstream 32	980	G-31-980*	0093	0993	2 GA TPE331-12UAR-701H	7350	Y19		lsf BAMT / sub-lst RNO
☐ F-GMVO	BAe 3206 Jetstream 32	982	G-31-982*	0093	0194	2 GA TPE331-12UAR-701H	7350	Y19		Charente / lsf BAMT / sub-lst RNO
☐ F-GMVP	BAe 3206 Jetstream 32	970	G-BUVC	0092	0994	2 GA TPE331-12UAR-701H	7350	Y19		lsf BAMT / sub-lst FEU
☐ F-GFEO	Embraer 120ER Brasilia (EMB-120ER)	120062	PT-SKF*	0087	1097	2 PWC PW118	11990	Y30		lsf A.I.R. / cvtd 120RT
☐ F-GFEQ	Embraer 120ER Brasilia (EMB-120ER)	120097	PT-SMP*	0088	1097	2 PWC PW118	11990	Y30		lsf A.I.R. / cvtd 120RT
☐ F-GFER	Embraer 120ER Brasilia (EMB-120ER)	120099	PT-SMR*	0088	1097	2 PWC PW118	11990	Y30		lsf A.I.R. / cvtd 120RT
☐ F-GTSG	Embraer 120ER Brasilia (EMB-120ER)	120087	PH-BRS	0088	0398	2 PWC PW118	11990	Y30		lsf Gie Regiair / cvtd 120RT
☐ F-GTSH	Embraer 120ER Brasilia (EMB-120ER)	120104	OO-DTH	0088	0398	2 PWC PW118	11990	Y30		lsf Gie Regiair / cvtd 120RT
☐ F-GTSI	Embraer 120ER Brasilia (EMB-120ER)	120123	OO-DTJ	0089	0498	2 PWC PW118	11990	Y30		lsf Gie Regiair / cvtd 120RT
☐ F-GTSJ	Embraer 120ER Brasilia (EMB-120ER)	120176	OO-DTL	0090	0398	2 PWC PW118	11990	Y30		lsf Gie Regiair / cvtd 120RT
☐ F-GTSK	Embraer 120ER Brasilia (EMB-120ER)	120213	OO-MTD	0090	0298	2 PWC PW118	11990	Y30		lsf Gie Regiair / cvtd 120RT
☐ F-GHVS	Saab 340B	340B-230	SE-G30*	0191	0192	2 GE CT7-9B	13155	Y35		lsf VAG Sverige AB -0699
☐ F-GMVY	Saab 340B	340B-363	SE-C63*	0094	0994	2 GE CT7-9B	13155	Y35		lsf Nordbanken Finans AB -0399
☐ F-GTSF	Saab 340B	340B-318	EC-GMI	0092	0194	2 GE CT7-9B	13155	Y35		lsf Finans Skandic AB -1099
☐ F-GRGP	Embraer RJ135 (EMB-135)					2 AN AE3007A3	19000	Y37		oo-delivery 1099
☐ F-GRGQ	Embraer RJ135 (EMB-135)					2 AN AE3007A3	19000	Y37		oo-delivery 1299
☐ F-GRGR	Embraer RJ135 (EMB-135)					2 AN AE3007A3	19000	Y37		oo-delivery 0300
☐ F-GRGS	Embraer RJ135 (EMB-135)					2 AN AE3007A3	19000	Y37		oo-delivery 0600
☐ F-GRGT	Embraer RJ135 (EMB-135)					2 AN AE3007A3	19000	Y37		oo-delivery 0900
☐ F-GRGA	Embraer RJ145EU (EMB-145EU)	145008	PT-SYE*	0097	0597	2 AN AE3007A	19990	Y50		lsf Samba Aviation B.V.
☐ F-GRGB	Embraer RJ145EU (EMB-145EU)	145010	PT-SYG*	0097	0697	2 AN AE3007A	19990	Y50		lsf Samba Aviation B.V.
☐ F-GRGC	Embraer RJ145EU (EMB-145EU)	145012	PT-SYI*	0097	0697	2 AN AE3007A	19990	Y50		lsf Samba Aviation/op in Air France-cs
☐ F-GRGD	Embraer RJ145EU (EMB-145EU)	145043	PT-SZI*	0098	0298	2 AN AE3007A	19990	Y50		lsf Samba Aviation B.V.
☐ F-GRGE	Embraer RJ145EU (EMB-145EU)	145047	PT SZM*	0098	0398	2 AN AE3007A	19990	Y50		lsf Samba Aviation B.V.
☐ F-GRGF	Embraer RJ145EU (EMB-145EU)	145050	PT-SZP*	0098	0498	2 AN AE3007A	19990	Y50		lsf Samba Aviation B.V.
☐ F-GRGG	Embraer RJ145EU (EMB-145EU)	145118		0099	0399	2 AN AE3007A	19990	Y50		lsf Samba Aviation B.V.
☐ F-GRGH	Embraer RJ145EU (EMB-145EU)	145120		0099	0399	2 AN AE3007A	19990	Y50		lsf Samba Aviation B.V.
☐ F-GRGI	Embraer RJ145EU (EMB-145EU)					2 AN AE3007A	19990	Y50		oo-delivery 0699
☐ F-GRGJ	Embraer RJ145EU (EMB-145EU)					2 AN AE3007A	19990	Y50		oo-delivery 0300
☐ F-GRGK	Embraer RJ145EU (EMB-145EU)					2 AN AE3007A	19990	Y50		oo-delivery 0300
☐ F-GRGL	Embraer RJ145EU (EMB-145EU)					2 AN AE3007A	19990	Y50		oo-delivery 0500
☐ F-GRGM	Embraer RJ145EU (EMB-145EU)					2 AN AE3007A	19990	Y50		oo-delivery 0600
☐ F-GRGN	Embraer RJ145EU (EMB-145EU)					2 AN AE3007A	19990	Y50		oo-delivery 0700
☐ F-GRGO	Embraer RJ145EU (EMB-145EU)					2 AN AE3007A	19990	Y50		oo-delivery 0800
☐ F-GMVB	Saab 2000	2000-019	SE-019*	0095	0695	2 AN AE2100A	22800	Y53		lsf Nordbanken Finans AB
☐ F-GMVC	Saab 2000	2000-021	SE-021*	0095	0895	2 AN AE2100A	22800	Y53		lsf Nordbanken Finans AB
☐ F-GMVD	Saab 2000	2000-034	SE-034*	0096	0396	2 AN AE2100A	22800	Y53		lsf Nordbanken Fin./op in Air France-cs
☐ F-GMVE	Saab 2000	2000-040	SE-040*	0096	1096	2 AN AE2100A	22800	Y53		lsf Nordbanken Finans AB
☐ F-GMVF	Saab 2000	2000-045	SE-045*	0097	0397	2 AN AE2100A	22800	Y53		lsf Saab Aircraft Credit AB
☐ F-GMVG	Saab 2000	2000-049	SE-049*	0097	0897	2 AN AE2100A	22800	Y53		lsf Saab Aircraft Credit AB
☐ F-GTSB	Saab 2000	2000-014	D-ADSB	0095	0597	2 AN AE2100A	22800	Y50		lsf DB Export-Leasing GmbH
☐ EI-CPQ	Saab 2000	2000-013	F-GTSA	0095	0597	2 AN AE2100A	22800	Y50		lsf / opb BCY in Regional-colors

RHONAIR EXECUTIVE = RHO

Valence-Chabeuil

Aéroport de Valence-Chabeuil, F-26120 Chabeuil, France ☎ 475 85 42 14 Tx: none Fax: 475 85 44 56 SITA: n/a
F: 1995 ⁂ 3 Head: Roland Orfila Net: n/a

registration	type of aircraft	cn/fn	ex/ex*	mfd	del	powered by	mtow kg	configuration	selcal	name/fln/specialitites/remarks
☐ F-GGRD	Cessna 340A II	340A0944	N2744Z	0080	0995	2 CO TSIO-520-NB	2717	5 Pax		

SAF HELICOPTERES, S.A. = SHP (formerly SAF-Service Aérien Français, SA & Société Aérienne Française d'Exploitation)

Albertville-Tournon & Courchevel

BP 39, Aérodrome Albertville-Tournon, F-73460 Frontenex, France ☎ 479 38 48 29 Tx: 309960 f saf Fax: 479 38 48 42 SITA: n/a
F: 1983 ⁂ 45 Head: Eric Fraissinet ICAO: SAF Net: n/a Aircraft below MTOW 1361 kg: Robinson R22.
The name "Air Courchevel" is used for some marketing purposes. Rescue / EMS services are operated on behalf of SECOURS AERIEN FRANCAIS (an Air Rescue association).

registration	type of aircraft	cn/fn	ex/ex*	mfd	del	powered by	mtow kg	configuration	selcal	name/fln/specialitites/remarks
☐ F-GFMK	Bell 206B JetRanger III	2386	N777TE	0078		1 AN 250-C20B	1451	3 Pax		lsf Artemis Aviation & Finance
☐ F-GECT	Eurocopter (Aerosp.) SA315B Lama	2666		0085		1 TU Artouste IIIB1	1950	4 Pax		lsf Sliba
☐ F-GFCM	Eurocopter (Aerosp.) SA315B Lama	2226	G-BLLX	0071		1 TU Artouste IIIB	1950	4 Pax		lsf Sliba
☐ F-GHCC	Eurocopter (Aerosp.) SA315B Lama	2474	N49504	0077		1 TU Artouste IIIB	1950	4 Pax		lsf/opf Heliand
☐ F-GHCI	Eurocopter (Aerosp.) SA315B Lama	1819 / 11	TR-LXB	0076		1 TU Artouste IIIB1	1950	4 Pax		lsf BNP Bail/cvtd Alouette II
☐ F-GHCO	Eurocopter (Aerosp.) AS350B Ecureuil	1467	LN-OTC	0081		1 TU Arriel 1B	1950	5 Pax		lsf Artemis Afin / sub-lst Heli Alpes
☐ F-GIRF	Eurocopter (Aerosp.) AS350B2 Ecureuil	2411		0090	1190	1 TU Arriel 1D1	2250	5 Pax		lsf Sliba
☐ F-GJCP	Eurocopter (Aerosp.) AS350B1 Ecureuil	2172		0089		1 TU Arriel 1D	2200	5 Pax		lsf BNP Bail
☐ F-GKAS	Eurocopter (Aerosp.) AS350B1 Ecureuil	2224		0089		1 TU Arriel 1D	2200	5 Pax		lst HPL
☐ F-GKHA	Eurocopter (Aerosp.) AS350B2 Ecureuil	2359		0090		1 TU Arriel 1D1	2250	5 Pax		lsf Locafrance Equipement
☐ F-BPPH	Eurocopter (Aerosp.) SA316B Alouette III	2245		0076		1 TU Artouste IIIB	2200	6 Pax		
☐ F-GIIE	Eurocopter (Aerosp.) SA316B Alouette III	1885		0071		1 TU Artouste IIIB	2200	6 Pax		lsf Sliba
☐ N4442F	Bell 407	53294		0098	1198	1 AN 250-C47B	2268	6 Pax		lsf TFC Rotor Inc.
☐ F-GJAX	Eurocopter (Aerosp.) AS355N Ecureuil 2	5543	I-IIII*	0093	0097	2 TU Arrius 1A	2540	5 Pax		lsf Artemis Aviation & Finance
☐ F-GJFU	Eurocopter (Aerosp.) AS355F1 Ecureuil 2	5079	G-BUZI	0081	0797	2 AN 250-C20F	2400	5 Pax		lsf Artemis Aviation & Finance
☐ F-GJGU	Eurocopter (Aerosp.) AS355F1 Ecureuil 2	5095	N7090T	0081	0797	2 AN 250-C20F	2400	5 Pax		lsf Artemis Aviation & Finance
☐ F-GKLP	Eurocopter (Aerosp.) AS355F1 Ecureuil 2	5014	F-OGPY	0081	0098	2 AN 250-C20F	2400	5 Pax		

SAINT BARTH COMMUTER = PV

Saint Barthelemy

Aéroport Gustave III, F-97133 St. Barthelemy, Guadeloupe ☎ 27 54 54 Tx: none Fax: 27 54 58 SITA: n/a
F: 1995 ⁂ 6 Head: Bruno Masens Net: n/a

registration	type of aircraft	cn/fn	ex/ex*	mfd	del	powered by	mtow kg	configuration	selcal	name/fln/specialitites/remarks
☐ F-OGXA	Britten-Norman BN-2A-26 Islander	788	D-IHUG	0076	1095	2 LY O-540-E4C5	2858	Y9		
☐ F-OGXB	Britten-Norman BN-2A-2 Islander	303	D-IHVH	0072	0695	2 LY IO-540-K1B5	2858	Y9		
☐ F-OHQW	Britten-Norman BN-2A-26 Islander	3009	D-IORC	0084	1198	2 LY O-540-E4C5	2812	Y9		

SAVOIE AIRLINES, S.A.

Courchevel

c/o Solair Plus, Batiment Hera, F-74166 Archamps, France ☎ 450 31 52 10 Tx: none Fax: 450 95 28 45 SITA: n/a
F: 1998 ⁂ n/a Head: Jean Schianchi Net: n/a

registration	type of aircraft	cn/fn	ex/ex*	mfd	del	powered by	mtow kg	configuration	selcal	name/fln/specialitites/remarks
☐ F-GJDS	De Havilland DHC-6 Twin Otter 300	375	TR-LDH	0073	0299	2 PWC PT6A-27	5670	Y19		lsf Satair Craft

SAVOIE HELICOPTERES (Compagnie Savoie Helicoptère dba)

Chambéry

BP 64, F-73212 Aime Cédex, France ☎ 479 55 69 73 Tx: 980469 f Fax: 479 09 77 50 SITA: n/a
F: 1990 ⁂ 3 Head: Raymond Prevot Net: n/a

registration	type of aircraft	cn/fn	ex/ex*	mfd	del	powered by	mtow kg	configuration	selcal	name/fln/specialitites/remarks
☐ F-GEST	Eurocopter (Aerosp.) SA341G Gazelle	1113	EC-CUA	0074		1 TU Astazou IIIA	1800	4 Pax		lsf Snc Parcim
☐ F-GHSN	Eurocopter (Aerosp.) AS350B Ecureuil	1905	N37AW	0086		1 TU Arriel 1B	1950	5 Pax		lsf BNP Bail

SECURITE CIVILE – Groupement Moyens Aériens (Fire Service) (Division of Ministère de l'Intérieur)

Marseille-Marignane & Nimes

1 Place Beauvau, F-75800 Paris, France ☎ (1) 56 04 75 06 Tx: 611390 f cosec a Fax: (1) 56 04 74 63 SITA: n/a
F: 1957 ⁂ 350 Head: Frédéric Dohet Net: n/a Non-commercial state organisation conducting sea & mountain rescue flights, ambulance missions and forest fire fighting.

registration	type of aircraft	cn/fn	ex/ex*	mfd	del	powered by	mtow kg	configuration	selcal	name/fln/specialitites/remarks
☐ F-ZBBN	Eurocopter (Aerosp.) AS350B1 Ecureuil	1951	F-ZKBT	0087	0687	1 TU Arriel 1D	2200	Rescue		
☐ F-ZBEA	Eurocopter (Aerosp.) AS350B Ecureuil	1003	F-GBBQ	0078	0782	1 TU Arriel 1B	1950	Logistic		
☐ F-ZBFC	Eurocopter (Aerosp.) AS350B1 Ecureuil	2109		0088	0789	1 TU Arriel 1D	2200	Rescue		
☐ F-ZBFD	Eurocopter (Aerosp.) AS350B1 Ecureuil	2114	F-GIRO	0088	0689	1 TU Arriel 1D	2200	Rescue		
☐ F-ZBFT	Eurocopter (Aerosp.) AS350B2 Ecureuil	2380		0090	0790	1 TU Arriel 1D1	2250	Rescue		
☐ F-ZBAF	Eurocopter (Aerosp.) SA316B Alouette III	1075	F-RAFO	0063	0781	1 TU Artouste IIIB	2200	Rescue		cvtd SE3160
☐ F-ZBAH	Eurocopter (Aerosp.) SA316B Alouette III	1790	EI-AVI	0071	0973	1 TU Artouste IIIB	2200	Rescue		
☐ F-ZBAJ	Eurocopter (Aerosp.) SA316B Alouette III	2224		0075	0275	1 TU Artouste IIIB	2200	Rescue		
☐ F-ZBAK	Eurocopter (Aerosp.) SA316B Alouette III	1076	F-RAFP	0063	0781	1 TU Artouste IIIB	2200	Rescue		cvtd SE3160
☐ F-ZBAN	Eurocopter (Aerosp.) SE316B Alouette III	1115	F-RAFQ	0063	0981	1 TU Artouste IIIB	2200	Rescue		cvtd SE3160
☐ F-ZBAV	Eurocopter (Aerosp.) SA316B Alouette III	2252		0076	0276	1 TU Artouste IIIB	2200	Rescue		

☐ F-ZBAW	Eurocopter (Aerosp.) SA316B Alouette III	2306		0076	0576	1 TU Artouste IIIB	2200	Rescue		
☐ F-ZBBC	Eurocopter (Aerosp.) SA316B Alouette III	1791		0071	0671	1 TU Artouste IIIB	2200	Rescue		
☐ F-ZBBP	Eurocopter (Aerosp.) SA316B Alouette III	1795		0071	0571	1 TU Artouste IIIB	2200	Rescue		
☐ F-ZBBQ	Eurocopter (Aerosp.) SA316B Alouette III	1798		0071	0771	1 TU Artouste IIIB	2200	Rescue		
☐ F-ZBBS	Eurocopter (Aerosp.) SA316B Alouette III	1978		0072	0672	1 TU Artouste IIIB	2200	Rescue		
☐ F-ZBDC	Eurocopter (Aerosp.) SA316B Alouette III	1435		0067	1167	1 TU Artouste IIIB	2200	Rescue		
☐ F-ZBDE	Eurocopter (Aerosp.) SA316B Alouette III	1630	FAP 9331	0070	1077	1 TU Artouste IIIB	2200	Rescue		cvtd SE3160
☐ F-ZBDF	Eurocopter (Aerosp.) SA316B Alouette III	1646	FAP 9346	0070	1077	1 TU Artouste IIIB	2200	Rescue		cvtd SE3160
☐ F-ZBDG	Eurocopter (Aerosp.) SA316B Alouette III	1749	FAP 9357	0070	1077	1 TU Artouste IIIB	2200	Rescue		cvtd SE3160
☐ F-ZBDH	Eurocopter (Aerosp.) SA316B Alouette III	1784	FAP 9366	0070	1077	1 TU Artouste IIIB	2200	Rescue		cvtd SE3160
☐ F-ZBDI	Eurocopter (Aerosp.) SA316B Alouette III	1878	FAP 9388	0071	1077	1 TU Artouste IIIB	2200	Rescue		cvtd SE3160
☐ F-ZBDJ	Eurocopter (Aerosp.) SA316B Alouette III	1879	FAP 9389	0071	1077	1 TU Artouste IIIB	2200	Rescue		cvtd SE3160
☐ F-ZBDL	Eurocopter (Aerosp.) SA316B Alouette III	1611	XC-FAR	0069	0690	1 TU Artouste IIIB	2200	Rescue		rebuilt
☐ F-ZBDM	Eurocopter (Aerosp.) SA316B Alouette III	1610	XC-FAS	0069	0978	1 TU Artouste IIIB	2200	Rescue		
☐ F-ZBDN	Eurocopter (Aerosp.) SA316B Alouette III	1854	XC-FIB	0071	0578	1 TU Artouste IIIB	2200	Rescue		
☐ F-ZBDQ	Eurocopter (Aerosp.) SA316B Alouette III	2357		0078	0578	1 TU Artouste IIIB	2200	Rescue		
☐ F-ZBFL	Eurocopter (Aerosp.) SE316B Alouette III	1121	ALAT	0063	0393	1 TU Artouste IIIB	2200	Rescue		cvtd SE3160
☐ F-ZBFM	Eurocopter (Aerosp.) SE316B Alouette III	1280	ALAT	0065	0393	1 TU Artouste IIIB	2200	Rescue		cvtd SE3160
☐ F-ZBFU	Eurocopter (Aerosp.) SA316B Alouette III	5386	F-GBLC	0078	0992	1 TU Artouste IIIB	2200	Rescue		
☐ F-	Eurocopter (MBB) BK117C-2					2 TU Arriel 1E2	3500	Rescue		oo-delivery 0099
☐ F-	Eurocopter (MBB) BK117C-2					2 TU Arriel 1E2	3500	Rescue		oo-delivery 0099
☐ F-	Eurocopter (MBB) BK117C-2					2 TU Arriel 1E2	3500	Rescue		oo-delivery 0000
☐ F-	Eurocopter (MBB) BK117C-2					2 TU Arriel 1E2	3500	Rescue		oo-delivery 0000
☐ F-	Eurocopter (MBB) BK117C-2					2 TU Arriel 1E2	3500	Rescue		oo-delivery 0000
☐ F-	Eurocopter (MBB) BK117C-2					2 TU Arriel 1E2	3500	Rescue		oo-delivery 0000
☐ F-	Eurocopter (MBB) BK117C-2					2 TU Arriel 1E2	3500	Rescue		oo-delivery 0000
☐ F-	Eurocopter (MBB) BK117C-2					2 TU Arriel 1E2	3500	Rescue		oo-delivery 0001
☐ F-	Eurocopter (MBB) BK117C-2					2 TU Arriel 1E2	3500	Rescue		oo-delivery 0001
☐ F-	Eurocopter (MBB) BK117C-2					2 TU Arriel 1E2	3500	Rescue		oo-delivery 0001
☐ F-	Eurocopter (MBB) BK117C-2					2 TU Arriel 1E2	3500	Rescue		oo-delivery 0001
☐ F-	Eurocopter (MBB) BK117C-2					2 TU Arriel 1E2	3500	Rescue		oo-delivery 0001
☐ F-	Eurocopter (MBB) BK117C-2					2 TU Arriel 1E2	3500	Rescue		oo-delivery 0002
☐ F-	Eurocopter (MBB) BK117C-2					2 TU Arriel 1E2	3500	Rescue		oo-delivery 0002
☐ F-	Eurocopter (MBB) BK117C-2					2 TU Arriel 1E2	3500	Rescue		oo-delivery 0002
☐ F-	Eurocopter (MBB) BK117C-2					2 TU Arriel 1E2	3500	Rescue		oo-delivery 0002
☐ F-	Eurocopter (MBB) BK117C-2					2 TU Arriel 1E2	3500	Rescue		oo-delivery 0002
☐ F-	Eurocopter (MBB) BK117C-2					2 TU Arriel 1E2	3500	Rescue		oo-delivery 0003
☐ F-	Eurocopter (MBB) BK117C-2					2 TU Arriel 1E2	3500	Rescue		oo-delivery 0003
☐ F-	Eurocopter (MBB) BK117C-2					2 TU Arriel 1E2	3500	Rescue		oo-delivery 0003
☐ F-	Eurocopter (MBB) BK117C-2					2 TU Arriel 1E2	3500	Rescue		oo-delivery 0003
☐ F-	Eurocopter (MBB) BK117C-2					2 TU Arriel 1E2	3500	Rescue		oo-delivery 0003
☐ F-	Eurocopter (MBB) BK117C-2					2 TU Arriel 1E2	3500	Rescue		oo-delivery 0004
☐ F-	Eurocopter (MBB) BK117C-2					2 TU Arriel 1E2	3500	Rescue		oo-delivery 0004
☐ F-	Eurocopter (MBB) BK117C-2					2 TU Arriel 1E2	3500	Rescue		oo-delivery 0004
☐ F-	Eurocopter (MBB) BK117C-2					2 TU Arriel 1E2	3500	Rescue		oo-delivery 0004
☐ F-	Eurocopter (MBB) BK117C-2					2 TU Arriel 1E2	3500	Rescue		oo-delivery 0004
☐ F-	Eurocopter (MBB) BK117C-2					2 TU Arriel 1E2	3500	Rescue		oo-delivery 0005
☐ F-	Eurocopter (MBB) BK117C-2					2 TU Arriel 1E2	3500	Rescue		oo-delivery 0005
☐ F-	Eurocopter (MBB) BK117C-2					2 TU Arriel 1E2	3500	Rescue		oo-delivery 0005
☐ F-	Eurocopter (MBB) BK117C-2					2 TU Arriel 1E2	3500	Rescue		oo-delivery 0005
☐ F-	Eurocopter (MBB) BK117C-2					2 TU Arriel 1E2	3500	Rescue		oo-delivery 0005
☐ F-ZBEC	Eurocopter (Aerosp.) SA365C1 Dauphin 2	5027	N122ME	0079	0483	2 TU Arriel 1A1	3400	Rescue		
☐ F-ZBED	Eurocopter (Aerosp.) SA365C1 Dauphin 2	5040		0079	0782	2 TU Arriel 1A1	3400	Rescue		
☐ F-ZBEV	Eurocopter (Aerosp.) SA365C1 Dauphin 2	5043	F-GBEP	0079	0787	2 TU Arriel 1A1	3400	Rescue		
☐ F-ZBFJ	Beech King Air B200	BB-1102	D-IWAN	0083	0294	2 PWC PT6A-42	5670	Logistic		98
☐ F-ZBFK	Beech King Air B200	BB-876	F-GHSC	0081	0490	2 PWC PT6A-42	5670	Logistic		97
☐ F-ZBAU	Conair Firecat	009	F-WZLQ	0058	0582	2 WR R-1820-82	11793	Tanker		02 / cvtd DHC CS2F-1 Tracker DHC-32
☐ F-ZBAA	Conair Turbo Firecat	027	F-WEOL	0057	0693	2 PWC PT6A-67AF	11793	Tanker		22 / cvtd Grumman US-2B Tracker cn 456
☐ F-ZBAP	Conair Turbo Firecat	026	F-ZBDA	0057	0992	2 PWC PT6A-67AF	11793	Tanker		12 / cvtd Grumman US-2B Tracker cn 567
☐ F-ZBBL	Conair Turbo Firecat	024	F-WEOK	0058	0791	2 PWC PT6A-67AF	11793	Tanker		19 / cvtd Grumman US-2B Tracker cn 626
☐ F-ZBCZ	Conair Turbo Firecat	036	F-ZBCA	0060	0896	2 PW R-982-C9HE2	11793	Tanker		77 / cvtd DHC CS2F-2 Tracker cn DHC-94
☐ F-ZBEH	Conair Turbo Firecat	035	F-WEOJ	0057	0791	2 PWC PT6A-67AF	11793	Tanker		20 / cvtd Grumman S2F-1 Tracker cn 410
☐ F-ZBET	Conair Turbo Firecat	028	F-WEOJ	0057	0789	2 PWC PT6A-67AF	11793	Tanker		15 / cvtd Grumman S2F-1 Tracker cn 710
☐ F-ZBEW	Conair Turbo Firecat	025	F-WEOL	0058	0694	2 PWC PT6A-67AF	11793	Tanker		11 / cvtd Grumman S2F-1 Tracker cn 621
☐ F-ZBEY	Conair Turbo Firecat	017	C-WEOK	0057	0784	2 PWC PT6A-67AF	11793	Tanker		07 / cvtd Grumman S2 Tracker cn 400
☐ F-ZBFE	Conair Turbo Firecat	032	F-WEOK	0057	0789	2 PWC PT6A-67AF	11793	Tanker		17 / cvtd Grumman S2F-1 Tracker cn 656
☐ F-ZBEG	Canadair CL-415 (CL-215-6B11)	2015	C-FXBH*	1295	0396	2 PWC PW123AF	19890	Tanker		39 / Amphibian
☐ F-ZBEO	Canadair CL-415 (CL-215-6B11)	2011	C-FWPD*	0995	1195	2 PWC PW123AF	19890	Tanker		36 / Amphibian
☐ F-ZBEU	Canadair CL-415 (CL-215-6B11)	2024	C-FZDE*	0996	0697	2 PWC PW123AF	19890	Tanker		42 / Amphibian
☐ F-ZBEZ	Canadair CL-415 (CL-215-6B11)	2018	C-FXBX*	0196	0696	2 PWC PW123AF	19890	Tanker		41 / Amphibian
☐ F-ZBFN	Canadair CL-415 (CL-215-6B11)	2006	C-FVUK*	0695	0795	2 PWC PW123AF	19890	Tanker		33 / Amphibian
☐ F-ZBFP	Canadair CL-415 (CL-215-6B11)	2002	C-FBET*	0394	0696	2 PWC PW123AF	19890	Tanker		31 / Amphibian
☐ F-ZBFS	Canadair CL-415 (CL-215-6B11)	2001	C-GSCT*	1193	0795	2 PWC PW123AF	19890	Tanker		32 / Amphibian
☐ F-ZBFV	Canadair CL-415 (CL-215-6B11)	2013	C-FWPE*	0595	1295	2 PWC PW123AF	19890	Tanker		37 / Amphibian
☐ F-ZBFW	Canadair CL-415 (CL-215-6B11)	2014	C-FWZH*	1195	0396	2 PWC PW123AF	19890	Tanker		38 / Amphibian
☐ F-ZBFX	Canadair CL-415 (CL-215-6B11)	2007	C-FVUJ*	0695	0795	2 PWC PW123AF	19890	Tanker		34 / Amphibian
☐ F-ZBFY	Canadair CL-415 (CL-215-6B11)	2010	C-FVDY*	0395	0696	2 PWC PW123AF	19890	Tanker		35 / Amphibian
☐ F-ZBFF	Conair Firebomber (Fokker F27 Mk600)	10432 / 3	C-FGDS	0070	0790	2 RR Dart 532-7R	20412	Tanker		71 / cvtd F27 Friendship
☐ F-ZBFG	Conair Firebomber (Fokker F27 Mk600)	10440 / 2	C-FBDY	0070	0790	2 RR Dart 532-7R	20412	Tanker		72 / cvtd F27 Friendship

SEFA – Service d'Exploitation de la Formation Aéronautique (Division of DGAC-Dirèction Générale de l'Aviation Civile/formerly SFACT) **Muret, Toulouse & St. Yan**

BP 80, Aérodrome, F-31607 Muret Cedex, France ☎ 562 14 78 78 Tx: none Fax: 562 16 79 79 SITA: n/a
F: n/a 👥 n/a Head: Gerard Lefevre ICAO: SEFA Net: http://www.ourworld.compuserve.com/sefa
Trainer-aircraft below MTOW 5000kg: Beechcraft Baron 58, Cessna 310R, MS893 Rallye, Robin R2160 & Socata TB-10/20. Non-commercial state organisation conducting training, calibrating and VIP missions.

☐ F-ASFA	Beech King Air E90	LW-47		0073	0673	2 PWC PT6A-28	4585	Calibrator/VIP		
☐ F-GJFA	Beech King Air B200	BB-1270	N30391	0087	0589	2 PWC PT6A-42	5670	Calibrator/VIP		
☐ F-GJFC	Beech King Air B200	BB-1347		0089	0190	2 PWC PT6A-42	5670	Calibrator/VIP		
☐ F-GJFD	Beech King Air B200	BB-1379		0090	0990	2 PWC PT6A-42	5670	Calibrator/VIP		
☐ F-GJFE	Beech King Air B200	BB-1399		0091	0491	2 PWC PT6A-42	5670	Calibrator/VIP		
☐ F-GSFA	Beech King Air B200	BB-1244	G-RIOO	0086	0192	2 PWC PT6A-42	5670	Calibrator/VIP		
☐ F-GFJH	ATR 42-300	049		0087	0991	2 PWC PW120	16150	Calibrator		Aviation Civile-titles

SINAIR = SIN **Grenoble-St. Geoirs**

Aéroport de Grenoble, F-38590 St. Etienne de St. Geoirs, France ☎ 476 65 42 99 Tx: 320193 f sinair Fax: 476 65 59 71 SITA: n/a
F: 1981 👥 9 Head: Jean Claude Sinour ICAO: SINAIRLINE Net: n/a

☐ F-GKID	Cessna F500 Citation I	500-0319	N9MA	0076	0590	2 PWC JT15D-1A	5216	7 Pax		
☐ F-GSIN	Beech King Air 200	BB-239	G-WWHL	0077		2 PWC PT6A-41	5670	11 Pax		

SPHAIR Société Française de Photographies Aériennes **Toulouse-Blagnac**

SPHAIR

4 Av. Didier Daurat Prolongée, Z.I. de Montaudran, F-31400 Toulouse Cédex, France ☎ 561 20 44 49 Tx: none Fax: 561 80 23 73 SITA: n/a
F: 1975 👥 5 Head: Christian Gout Net: n/a

☐ F-GBLZ	Cessna TU206G Turbo Stationair 6 II	U20605151		0079		1 CO TSIO-520-M	1633	Photo		
☐ F-GLGC	Piper PA-31-350 Navajo Chieftain	31-8052149	N3279H	0080	1292	2 LY TIO-540-J2BD	3175	Photo		

STAR AIRLINES = 2R / SEU (Société de Transport Aérien Regional dba/Subsidiary of Look Voyages & Transat/formerly STAR Europe) **Paris-CDG**

Immeuble Horizon, 10 Allée Bienvenue, F-93885 Noisy-le-Grand, France ☎ (1) 48 15 90 00 Tx: none Fax: (1) 48 15 90 10 SITA: n/a
F: 1995 👥 180 Head: Cédric Pastour IATA: 473 ICAO: STARWAY Net: n/a

☐ F-GRSD	Airbus Industrie A320-214	653	F-WWIF*	0096	0297	2 CFMI CFM56-5B4-2	77000	Y180	EQ-CS	lsf GATX
☐ F-GRSE	Airbus Industrie A320-214	657	F-WWIR*	0097	0297	2 CFMI CFM56-5B4-2	77000	Y180	EQ-DF	lsf GATX
☐ F-GRSG	Airbus Industrie A320-214	737	F-WWBS*	0097	1197	2 CFMI CFM56-5B4/P	77000	Y180	JP-EH	lsf GECA
☐ F-GRSH	Airbus Industrie A320-214	749	F-WWIK*	0097	1297	2 CFMI CFM56-5B4/P	77000	Y180		lsf GECA
☐ F-GRSI	Airbus Industrie A320-214	973				2 CFMI CFM56-5B4/P	77000	Y180		to be lsf ILFC 0499
☐ C-GTSR	Lockheed L-1011-385-3 TriStar 500	293B-1239	CS-TEA	0082	1298	3 RR RB211-524B4-02	231332	C19Y290	HJ-CM	lsf TSC

STAR SERVICE INTERNATIONAL = SSD **Orleans**

Les 4 Vents Airport, F-45550 St. Denis de l'Hotel, France ☎ 238 59 09 69 Tx: none Fax: 238 59 09 75 SITA: n/a
F: 1987 👥 2 Head: José Delot ICAO: STAR SERVICE Net: n/a

☐ F-GEQM	Mitsubishi MU-2B-60 Marquise	790SA	N279MA	0080		2 GA TPE331-10-511M	5250	8 Pax		

159 registration type of aircraft cn/fn ex/ex* mfd del powered by mtow kg configuration selcal name/fln/specialitites/remarks

TAB HELICOPTERES (SàRL Travaux Aériens Bouquemont dba) — Coligny

12 Av. de la Gare Coligny, Val des Marais, F-51130 Vertus, France ☎ 326 52 18 49 Tx: n/a Fax: 326 52 24 99 SITA: n/a
F: 1975 ⁂ 2 Head: n/a Net: n/a

☐ F-GFII	MD Helicopters MD 500D (Hughes 369D)	1290628D	N58357	0079		1 AN 250-C20B	1361			

TAXI AIR FRET, S.A. — Paris-Le Bourget & Toussus-le-Noble

Aéroport de Toussus-le-Noble, Hangar 230, F-78117 Chateaufort, France ☎ (1) 39 56 87 55 Tx: none Fax: (1) 39 56 88 28 SITA: n/a
F: 1992 ⁂ n/a Head: Christian Rosa Net: n/a

☐ F-GGAT	Piper PA-31T Cheyenne II	31T-7820010	D-IFPD	0078	0098	2 PWC PT6A-28	4082	6 Pax/Freighter		lsf Bail Materiel
☐ F-BTME	Beech 99 Airliner	U-79	N100GP	0069	0098	2 PWC PT6A-20	4717	15 Pax/Freighter		lsf PEA
☐ F-GFPE	Beech 99 Airliner	U-21	OO-WAY	0068	0097	2 PWC PT6A-20	4717	9 Pax/Freighter		lsf PEA

THS HELICOPTERES - Trans Hélicoptère Service = THZ — Lyon

Terminal SAR, Aéroport de Lyon-Bron, F-69500 Bron, France ☎ 478 26 63 33 Tx: none Fax: 478 26 32 43 SITA: n/a
F: 1985 ⁂ 15 Head: Michel Dreyfus ICAO: LYON HELIJET Net: http://www.mediartis.fr/ths

☐ F-GDHX	Eurocopter (Aerosp.) AS350B Ecureuil	1662		0082		1 TU Arriel 1B	1950	5 Pax		lsf SC MSI
☐ F-GEFI	Eurocopter (Aerosp.) AS350B Ecureuil	1787	D-HHCC	0084	0797	1 TU Arriel 1B	1950	5 Pax		
☐ F-GKYG	Eurocopter (Aerosp.) AS350B Ecureuil	1536	JA9315	0082		1 TU Arriel 1B	1950	5 Pax		lsf Bail Equipement
☐ F-GFAB	Eurocopter (Aerosp.) AS355F1 Ecureuil 2	5165	F-ODOM	0082		2 AN 250-C20F	2400	5 Pax		lsf Locavia
☐ F-GERS	Beech King Air 200	BB-753	N3705B	0080		2 PWC PT6A-41	5670	11 Pax		lsf Localease
☐ LX-THS	Cessna F550 Citation II	550-0074	D-CIFA	0079	0198	2 PWC JT15D-4	5670	8 Pax		lsf LXA
☐ F-GPFD	Dassault Falcon 100	221	OE-GHA	0090	0596	2 GA TFE731-2-1C	8300	8 Pax		lsf Avion Ecco
☐ F-GHPB	Dassault Falcon 100	215		0089		2 GA TFE731-2-1C	8755	8 Pax		lsf Starngate Ltd
☐ F-GLMD	Dassault Falcon 20C-5	117	EC-FJP	0067	0894	2 GA TFE731-5AR-2C	13200	9 Pax		lsf Dobson Mnmg/sub-lst THS / cvtd 20C

TRANSCARAIBES AIR INTERNATIONAL = DZ / NOE — Saint Barthelemy

Les Terrasses de St. Jean, F-97133 St. Barthelemy, Guadeloupe ☎ 27 93 36 Tx: none Fax: 27 93 38 SITA: n/a
F: 1995 ⁂ n/a Head: n/a ICAO: FRENCH HOPPER Net: http://www.stbarths.transcaraibes.html

☐ F-GHJM	Cessna 207A Stationair 8 II	20700635	F-OGJM	0080		1 CO IO-520-F	1724			lsf pvt
☐ F-OGVN	Partenavia P.68B	155	F-GBLY	0078		2 LY IO-360-A1B6	1960			lsf pvt

TRANSPORT AIR = TSI — Roanne-Renaison

2 rue du Coulaire, F-84370 Bedarrides, France ☎ 490 84 06 40 Tx: none Fax: 490 33 16 72 SITA: n/a
F: 1997 ⁂ 5 Head: Louis J. Tartevet Net: n/a

☐ F-BSRE	Cessna 414	414-0156	N8226Q	0071	0098	2 CO TSIO-520-J	2880	5 Pax		

VIKING HELICOPTERS — Fecamp

Z.I. Babeuf St. Leonard, F-74600 Fécamp, France ☎ 235 10 23 57 Tx: none Fax: 235 29 34 78 SITA: n/a
F: 1991 ⁂ n/a Head: Dominique Acheray Net: n/a Aircraft below MTOW 1361kg: Robinson R22

☐ F-BSGB	Agusta-Bell 206B JetRanger	8325		0072		1 AN 250-C20	1450	4 Pax		lsf pvt
☐ F-GIVH	Bell 206B JetRanger III	4176		0091		1 AN 250-C20J	1451	4 Pax		
☐ F-GOPY	Bell 206B JetRanger III	2584	G-RSMA	0079	0498	1 AN 250-C20B	1451	4 Pax		
☐ F-GIGT	Eurocopter (Aerosp.) AS355F1 Ecureuil 2	5023	N355F	0081	0096	2 AN 250-C20F	2400	5 Pax		

WANAIR, SàRL — Papeete-Faaa

BP 6806, F-98702 Faaa, (Tahiti), Polynésie Française ☎ 85 55 54 Tx: none Fax: 85 55 56 SITA: n/a
F: 1987 ⁂ 6 Head: Robert Wan Net: n/a

☐ F-OHRT	Beech King Air 300LW	FA-226	N80907	0093	0296	2 PWC PT6A-60A	5670	Y10		lsf Snc Erlair
☐ F-OHRU	Cessna 560 Citation V Ultra	560-0407	N1218Y*	0097	0597	2 PWC JT15D-5D	7394	Y9		lsf Jetperle Snc
☐ F-OHRX	Beech 1900D Airliner	UE-282	N11296*	0097	1198	2 PWC PT6A-67D	7688	Y19		lsf Perline Snc

WESTAIR — Brest

Aéroport International Brest, F-29490 Guipavas, France ☎ 298 84 89 66 Tx: none Fax: 298 84 89 60 SITA: n/a
F: 1995 ⁂ 8 Head: Patric Wormser Net: n/a Operates charter flights with Boeing 737-200 aircraft, leased from AIR MEDITERRANEE when required.

YANKEE DELTA = DYT — Rennes

1 Place des Lanvadières, F-91450 Soisy-sur-Seine, France ☎ 299 30 34 79 Tx: none Fax: 299 35 38 49 SITA: n/a
F: 1997 ⁂ n/a Head: Mme Anne Duval ICAO: DUVALAIR Net: n/a

☐ F-GHTA	Piper PA-31T Cheyenne II	31T-7820015	N107BK	0078	0097	2 PWC PT6A-28	4082	Y6		

G = GREAT BRITAIN (United Kingdom of GreatBritain & NorthernIreland)

(including Bailiwicks of Guernsey and Jersey & the Isle of Man)
Capital: London Official Language: English Population: 59,0 million Square Km: 242432 Dialling code: +44 Year established: 1066 Acting political head: Tony Blair (Prime Minister)

Guernsey
Capital: St. Peter Port Official Language: English, French Population: 0,1 million Square Km: 87 Dialling code: +44-1481 Acting political head: Sir Peter Crill (Bailiff)
Isle of Man
Capital: Douglas Official Language: English, Manx Population: 0,1 million Square Km: 572 Dialling code: +44 Acting political head: Air Marshal Sir Laurence Jones (Governor)
Jersey
Capital: St. Helier Official Language: English, French Population: 0,1 million Square Km: 108 Dialling code: +44-1534 Acting political head: Graham Dorey (Bailiff)

Government / Corporate / Executive / VIP Aircraft

☐ G-XXEA	Sikorsky S-76C+	760492		0098	1298	2 TU Arriel 2S1	5307	VIP		Queen's Flight
☐ XX105	BAe (BAC) One-Eleven 201AC	008	G-ASJD	0064	0497	2 RR Spey 511-14	35833	Calib./Research	FH-AG	DERA Aircraft & Eng.Dept, Boscombe Down
☐ XX507	Hawker CC2A (HS 125-F600B)	256006		0073	0473	2 GA TFE731-3R-1H	11567	VIP / Liaison	AH-CK	RAF, 32 (The Royal) Sqn. / cvtd -CC2
☐ XX508	Hawker CC2A (HS 125-F600B)	256008		0073	0473	2 GA TFE731-3R-1H	11567	VIP / Liaison	AH-CL	RAF, 32 (The Royal) Sqn. / cvtd -CC2
☐ XX919	BAe (BAC) One-Eleven 402AP	091	PI-C1121	0066	0497	2 RR Spey 511-14	40143	Calib./Research	FH-AG	DERA Aircraft & Eng.Dept, Boscombe Down
☐ ZD620	Hawker CC3 (HS 125-700B)	257181	G-5-16*	0082	0283	2 GA TFE731-3R-1H	11567	VIP / Liaison	DJ-FH	RAF, 32 (The Royal) Sqn.
☐ ZD621	Hawker CC3 (HS 125-700B)	257190		0082	0383	2 GA TFE731-3R-1H	11567	VIP / Liaison	DJ-FK	RAF, 32 (The Royal) Sqn.
☐ ZD703	Hawker CC3 (HS 125-700B)	257183	G-5-20*	0082	0283	2 GA TFE731-3R-1H	11567	VIP / Liaison	DJ-FM	RAF, 32 (The Royal) Sqn.
☐ ZD704	Hawker CC3 (HS 125-700B)	257194		0082	0383	2 GA TFE731-3R-1H	11567	VIP / Liaison	DJ-FL	RAF, 32 (The Royal) Sqn.
☐ ZE395	Hawker CC3 (HS 125-700B)	257205	G-5-19*	0083	0083	2 GA TFE731-3R-1H	11567	VIP / Liaison	AH-DF	RAF, 32 (The Royal) Sqn.
☐ ZE396	Hawker CC3 (HS 125-700B)	257211	G-5-11*	0084	0085	2 GA TFE731-3R-1H	11567	VIP / Liaison	AH-DJ	RAF, 32 (The Royal) Sqn.
☐ ZE432	BAe (BAC) One-Eleven 479FU	250	DQ-FBV	0073	0384	2 RR Spey 511-14DW	44679	Research/Tanker		A & AEE / ETPS Boscombe Down
☐ ZE433	BAe (BAC) One-Eleven 479FU	245	DQ-FBQ	0072	0497	2 RR Spey 511-14DW	44679	Radar trials		Air Fleet Department / opf Ferranti,EDI
☐ ZE700	BAe 146-C1 (Srs. 100)	E1021	G-6-021*	0084	0486	4 LY ALF502R-5	38102	VIP	LM-BD	RAF Queen's Flight
☐ ZE701	BAe 146-C1 (Srs. 100)	E1029	G-6-029*	0085	0786	4 LY ALF502R-5	38102	VIP	LM-BE	RAF Queen's Flight
☐ ZE702	BAe 146-C1 (Srs. 100)	E1124	G-6-124*	0090	0191	4 LY ALF502R-5	38102	VIP	EM-BQ	RAF Queen's Flight
☐ ZH763	BAe (BAC) One-Eleven 539GL	263	G-BGKE	0080	0497	2 RR Spey 512-14DW	44000	Research		DERA Aircraft & Eng.Dept, Boscombe Down

AB AIRLINES, Plc = 7L / AZX (formerly Air Bristol, Ltd) — Bristol-Filton & London-Stansted

Enterprise House, London Stansted Airport, Stansted, Essex CM24 1QW, Great Britain ☎ (1279) 66 34 79 Tx: none Fax: (1279) 68 04 43 SITA: n/a
F: 1993 ⁂ 90 Head: Brian G. Beal IATA: 698 ICAO: AZTEC AIR Net: http://www.abairlines.com

☐ G-AVMN	BAe (BAC) One-Eleven 510ED	142		0068	0597	2 RR Spey 512-14DW(HK2)	41950	Y104		lsf EAF
☐ G-AVMW	BAe (BAC) One-Eleven 510ED	150		0069	0597	2 RR Spey 512-14DW(HK2)	43550	Y104		lsf EAF
☐ G-OABA	Boeing 737-33A	24097 / 1741	VT-JAD	0089	0598	2 CFMI CFM56-3B2	61235	Y145		lsf AWAS
☐ G-OABL	Boeing 737-33A	24096 / 1739	VT-JAC	0089	0598	2 CFMI CFM56-3B2	61235	Y145		lsf AWAS / sub-lst DEB
☐ G-	Boeing 737-7AB					2 CFMI CFM56-7B24	69400			oo-delivery 0101
☐ G-	Boeing 737-7AB					2 CFMI CFM56-7B24	69400			oo-delivery 0601
☐ G-	Boeing 737-7AB					2 CFMI CFM56-7B24	69400			oo-delivery 0002
☐ G-	Boeing 737-7AB					2 CFMI CFM56-7B24	69400			oo-delivery 0002
☐ G-	Boeing 737-7AB					2 CFMI CFM56-7B24	69400			oo-delivery 0003
☐ G-	Boeing 737-7AB					2 CFMI CFM56-7B24	69400			oo-delivery 0003

AEROFILMS, Ltd (Subsidiary of Hunting Plc) — Cranfield

Cranfield Airfield, Cranfield, Bedfordshire MK43 0JR, Great Britain ☎ (1234) 75 26 20 Tx: none Fax: (1234) 75 26 21 SITA: n/a
F: 1919 ⁂ n/a Head: Larry Whitmore Net: n/a

☐ G-FOTO	Piper PA-E23-250 Aztec F	27-7654089	G-BJDH	0076		2 LY IO-540-C4B5	2266	Aerial Photo		
☐ G-AWNT	Britten-Norman BN-2A Islander	32		0068		2 LY O-540-E4C5	2722	Aerial Photo		

AEROFLOAT, Ltd — Glasgow

General Aviation Terminal, Glasgow Airport, Paisley, Strathclyde PA3 2TF, Scotland, Great Britain ☎ (141) 887 05 06 Tx: n/a Fax: (141) 887 05 06 SITA: n/a
F: 1991 ⁂ 3 Head: Capt. Robert Swainston Net: n/a

☐ G-SEAI	Cessna U206G Stationair	U20604059	N756FQ	0077		1 CO IO-550-C	1724			Amphibian

160 registration type of aircraft cn/fn ex/ex* mfd del powered by mtow kg configuration selcal name/fln/specialitites/remarks

AEROMEGA HELICOPTERS = OMG (Aeromega, Ltd dba) Stapleford

Stapleford Aerodrome, Stapleford Tawney, Essex RM4 1RL, Great Britain ☎ (1708) 68 83 61 Tx: none Fax: (1708) 68 85 66 SITA: n/a
F: 1979 ⁂ 19 Head: Kit Pemberton ICAO: OMEGA Net: http://www.aeromega.co.uk Beside helicopters listed, additional (AS350B2) are leased from GROENLANDSFLY (OY-) when required.

☐ G-LGRM	Bell 206B JetRanger	1376	G-OBRU	0074	0098	1 AN 250-C20	1451			
☐ G-OMDR	Agusta-Bell 206B JetRanger III	8610	G-HRAY	0081	1297	1 AN 250-C20B	1451			
☐ G-OVBJ	Bell 206B JetRanger III	2734	G-BXDS	0079	0497	1 AN 250-C20B	1451			
☐ G-BXIB	Bell 206L-3 LongRanger III	51300	EC-EQQ	0089		1 AN 250-C30P	1882			
☐ G-EYRE	Bell 206L-1 LongRanger II	45229	G-STVI	0081		1 AN 250-C28B	1882			lsf Hideroute Ltd
☐ G-OCRP	Bell 206L-1 LongRanger II	45232	G-BWCU	0079	0595	1 AN 250-C28B	1882			lst Island Aviation as V4-AAB
☐ G-BWZC	Eurocopter (Aerosp.) AS355F1 Tw.Squirrel	5185	G-MOBZ	0082	1195	2 AN 250-C20F	2400			lsf Castle Aviation
☐ G-EPOL	Eurocopter (Aerosp.) AS355F1 Tw.Squirrel	5302	G-SASU	0083		2 AN 250-C20F	2400			opf Essex Police Air Support Unit
☐ G-OTSP	Eurocopter (Aerosp.) AS355F1 Tw.Squirrel	5177	G-XPOL	0082	0491	2 AN 250-C20F	2400			

AIR CAERNARFON, Ltd (Subsidiary of Atlantic Holdings) Caernarfon

Caernarfon Airport, Dinas Dinlle, Caernarfon, Gwynedd LL54 5TP, Wales, Great Britain ☎ (1286) 83 08 00 Tx: none Fax: (1286) 83 02 80 SITA: n/a
F: 1986 ⁂ 6 Head: E.V. Aggett Net: n/a Aircraft below MTOW 1361kg: Cessna 172, Piper PA-28 & Robin HR200

☐ G-AIDL	BAe (DH) DH.89A Dragon Rapide	6968	TX310	0046		2 Gipsy Queen 3	2722			occ lst Atlantic Air Transport Ltd

AIR CARE (South West), Ltd = WCI Plymouth

Unit 10, Plymouth City Airport, Crownhill, Plymouth, Devon PL6 8BW, Great Britain ☎ (1752) 77 71 77 Tx: none Fax: (1752) 77 72 77 SITA: n/a
F: 1990 ⁂ 3 Head: Michael J. Raymont ICAO: DRAKE Net: n/a

☐ G-BBZI	Piper PA-31-310 Navajo B	31-7401211	N7590L	0073		2 LY TIO-540-A2C	2948			
☐ G-NAVO	Piper PA-31-310 Navajo	31-8212031	G-BMPV	0082	0296	2 LY TIO-540-A2C	2948			

AIR CAVREL, Ltd = ACL (Subsidiary of ACS-Air Charter Service) Manston-Kent Int'l

Riverview House, 20 Old Bridge Street, Hampton Wick, Kingston-upon-Thames, Surrey KT1 4BU, Great Britain ☎ (181) 943 99 66 Tx: 921096 acs g Fax: (181) 943 97 97 SITA: STNFFCR
F: 1996 ⁂ 15 Head: Chris Leach ICAO: CAVREL Net: http://www.aircharter.co.uk

☐ G-BITW	Shorts 330-200 (SD3-30 Variant 100)	SH3070	G-EASI	0081	1297	2 PWC PT6A-45R	10387	Freighter		
☐ G-DACS	Shorts 330-200 (SD3-30 Variant 100)	SH3089	C-GLAL	0082	0698	2 PWC PT6A-45R	10387	Freighter		

AIR COMMUTER = RGM (Rangemile, Ltd dba) Coventry

Coventry Airport, Coventry, Warwickshire CV8 3AZ, Great Britain ☎ (1203) 30 44 52 Tx: none Fax: (1203) 63 90 31 SITA: n/a
F: 1959 ⁂ n/a Head: Capt. Peter A. Jones ICAO: RANGEMILE Net: n/a

☐ G-IMGL	Beech King Air B200	BB-1564	VP-CMA	0097	0897	2 PWC PT6A-42	5670			

AIRFOYLE, Ltd = GS / UPA (Affiliated with AirFoyle Executive, Ltd) London-Luton & Leeds-Bradford

Halcyon House, Luton Airport, Luton, Bedfordshire LU2 9LU, Great Britain ☎ (1582) 41 97 92 Tx: 825538 afoyle g Fax: (1582) 40 09 58 SITA: LTNHOGS
F: 1978 ⁂ 135 Head: William R.C. (Christopher) Foyle ICAO: FOYLE Net: http://www.airfoyle.co.uk
Additional freighter aircraft (Antonov 12/22/124/225) are marketed and (as required) operated in conjunction with ANTONOV DESIGN BUREAU (UR-) For aircraft details – see under that co.

☐ G-TNTA	BAe 146-200 (QT)	E2056	N146QT*	0085	0487	4 LY ALF502R-5	42184	Freighter	BH-CP	lsf/opf TNT Int'l in TNT-cs/cvtd -200
☐ G-TNTB	BAe 146-200 (QT)	E2067	G-5-067*	0087	0987	4 LY ALF502R-5	42184	Freighter	BH-DP	lsf/opf TNT Int'l in TNT-cs/cvtd -200
☐ G-TJPM	BAe 146-300 (QT)	E3150	SE-DIM	0089	0794	4 LY ALF502R-5	44225	Freighter	MQ-DG	lsf/opf TNT Int'l in TNT-cs/cvtd-300
☐ G-TNTE	BAe 146-300 (QT)	E3153	G-BRPW*	0089	0690	4 LY ALF502R-5	44225	Freighter	CM-LQ	lsf/opf TNT Int'l in TNT-cs/cvtd -300
☐ G-TNTG	BAe 146-300 (QT)	E3182	G-BSUY*	0091	1091	4 LY ALF502R-5	44225	Freighter	AR-DJ	lsf/opf TNT Int'l in TNT-cs/cvtd -300
☐ G-TNTK	BAe 146-300 (QT)	E3186	G-BSXL*	0091	1091	4 LY ALF502R-5	44225	Freighter	AR-DK	lsf/opf TNT Int'l in TNT-cs/cvtd -300
☐ G-TNTL	BAe 146-300 (QT)	E3168	RP-C479	0090	0394	4 LY ALF502R-5	44225	Freighter	AE-QS	lsf/opf TNT Int'l in TNT-cs/cvtd -300
☐ G-TNTR	BAe 146-300 (QT)	E3151	SE-DIT	0090	0794	4 LY ALF502R-5	44225	Freighter	MQ-DH	lsf/opf TNT Int'l in TNT-cs/cvtd -300

AIRFOYLE CHARTER AIRLINES, Ltd = UPD (Sister company of Airfoyle, Ltd) London-Luton

Halcyon House, Luton Airport, Luton, Bedfordshire LU2 9LU, Great Britain ☎ (1582) 41 97 92 Tx: 825538 afoyle g Fax: (1582) 40 09 58 SITA: LTNHOGS
F: 1994 ⁂ 118 Head: William R.C. (Christopher) Foyle ICAO: BROADSWORD Net: http://www.airfoyle.co.uk

☐ G-COLB	Boeing 737-3Q8	26283 / 2383	N373TA	1092	0898	2 CFMI CFM56-3C1	62142	Y136		lsf / opf CLA in Color Air-colors
☐ G-COLC	Boeing 737-3Q8	26286 / 2424	N374TA	0293	0898	2 CFMI CFM56-3C1	62142	Y136		lsf / opf CLA in Color Air-colors
☐ G-COLE	Boeing 737-3Q8	24962 / 2139	PP-VOX	0091	1198	2 CFMI CFM56-3C1	61235	Y136		lsf / opf CLA in Color Air-colors
☐ G-SWJW	Airbus Industrie A300B4-203FF	302	OH-LAB	0084	0598	2 GE CF6-50C2	165000	Y317	ER-LQ	lsf / opf SCY in Air Scandic-colors
☐ G-TTMC	Airbus Industrie A300B4-203FF	299	OH-LAA	0084	0498	2 GE CF6-50C2	165000	Y317	ER-DS	lsf / opf SCY in Air Scandic-colors

AIR HANSON, Ltd = AHL (Subsidiary of The Lynton Group, Inc.) Blackbushe

Business Aviation Centre, Blackbushe Airport, Camberley, Surrey GU17 9LG, Great Britain ☎ (1252) 89 00 89 Tx: 858329 hanson g Fax: (1252) 86 42 96 SITA: n/a
F: 1971 ⁂ 70 Head: Chris Tennant ICAO: AIR HANSON Net: n/a

☐ G-BWVE	Bell 206B JetRanger III	3394	G-BOSX	0081		1 AN 250-C20J	1451			lsf Bartlett Industrial Holdings Ltd
☐ G-BOYF	Sikorsky S-76B	760343		0088		2 PWC PT6B-36A	5307			lsf Darley Stud Management Co. Ltd
☐ G-BUXB	Sikorsky S-76A	760086	VR-CCZ	0080		2 AN 250-C30S	4763			
☐ G-OAUS	Sikorsky S-76A	760219	N3122M	0082		2 AN 250-C30S	4763			lsf Darley Stud Management Co. Ltd

AIR HARRODS, Ltd London-Stansted

First Avenue, London Stansted Airport, Stansted, Essex CM24 1QQ, Great Britain ☎ (1279) 66 08 00 Tx: none Fax: (1279) 66 08 80 SITA: n/a
F: 1996 ⁂ n/a Head: Steve Grimes Net: http://www.metrofbo.com

☐ G-HARO	Eurocopter (Aerosp.) AS355F2 Tw.Squirrel	5364	G-DAFT	0087	0896	2 AN 250-C20F	2540			
☐ G-SMAF	Sikorsky S-76A++	760149	N130TL	0081	0398	2 TU Arriel 1S1	4899			cvtd S-76A

AIR KILROE, Ltd = AKL Manchester

Manchester Airport, Hangar 4, Western Maintenance Area, Manchester M90 5PF, Great Britain ☎ (161) 436 20 55 Tx: 665525 airtax g Fax: (161) 499 18 90 SITA: n/a
F: 1976 ⁂ 40 Head: Brian Hetherington ICAO: KILRO Net: http://www.airkilroe.co.uk

☐ G-IJYS	BAe 3102 Jetstream 31 (Formula I)	715	G-BTZT*	0086	1192	2 GA TPE331-10UR-513H	6950	VIP 9 Pax		Flying Scotsman
☐ G-OAKI	BAe 3102 Jetstream 31	718	N417MX	0086	0692	2 GA TPE331-10UF-513H	6950	18 Pax		
☐ G-OAKJ	BAe 3202 Jetstream 32	795	G-BOTJ*	0088	0989	2 GA TPE331-12UAR-701H	7350	18 Pax		

AIRLONG CHARTER, Ltd Norwich

Riverview, Woods End, Bramerton, Norwich NR14 7ED, Great Britain ☎ (1508) 53 83 46 Tx: n/a Fax: (1508) 53 83 46 SITA: n/a
F: 1994 ⁂ n/a Head: Capt. G. Long Net: n/a

☐ G-BCRP	Piper PA-E23-250 Aztec E	27-7305082	N40269	0073	0797	2 LY IO-540-C4B5	2359			

AIR MED = MCD (Air Medical, Ltd dba) Oxford & London-Stansted

The Old Farmhouse, Oxford Airport, Oxfordshire OX5 1RA, Great Britain ☎ (1865) 84 28 87 Tx: none Fax: (1865) 37 06 42 SITA: n/a
F: 1986 ⁂ 13 Head: Rod Paris ICAO: AIR MED Net: http://www.airmed.co.uk

☐ G-BDUN	Piper PA-34-200T Seneca II	34-7570163	SE-GIA	0075		2 CO TSIO-360-E	1999	EMS		
☐ G-BFLH	Piper PA-34-200T Seneca II	34-7870065	N2126M	0077		2 CO TSIO-360-E	1999	EMS		
☐ G-BMDK	Piper PA-34-220T Seneca III	34-8133155	ZS-LOS	0082		2 CO TSIO-360-KB	2155	EMS		
☐ G-BXXY	Piper PA-34-220T Seneca III	34-8333061	PH-TLN	0083	0798	2 CO TSIO-360-KB	2155	EMS		
☐ G-PZAZ	Piper PA-31-350 Navajo Chieftain	31-7405214	G-VTAX	0074	0397	2 LY TIO-540-J2BD	3175	EMS		
☐ G-PZIZ	Piper PA-31-350 Navajo Chieftain	31-7405429	G-CAFZ	0074	1098	2 LY TIO-540-J2BD	3175	EMS		

AIR NOVA, Plc Liverpool

Bldg 9, Liverpool Speke Airport, Liverpool L24 1YD, Great Britain ☎ (151) 427 79 07 Tx: none Fax: (151) 427 79 08 SITA: n/a
F: 1986 ⁂ n/a Head: Rod Mackay Net: n/a

☐ G-GILT	Cessna 421C Golden Eagle III	421C0515	G-BMZC	0078	1096	2 CO GTSIO-520-L	3379			

AIR SCANDIC International Aviation, Oy = SCY (Air Scandic, AB dba) Manchester & Newcastle

4A Britannia Place, Bath Street, St. Helier JE2 4SU, Jersey, Channel Islands ☎ (1534) 87 08 87 Tx: none Fax: (1534) 51 90 44 SITA: n/a
F: 1997 ⁂ n/a Head: Gunnar Ohlsson ICAO: AIRSCAN Net: n/a

☐ G-SWJW	Airbus Industrie A300B4-203FF	302	OH-LAB	0084	0598	2 GE CF6-50C2	165000	Y317	ER-LQ	lst / opb UPD in Air Scandic-colors
☐ G-TTMC	Airbus Industrie A300B4-203FF	299	OH-LAA	0084	0498	2 GE CF6-50C2	165000	Y317	ER-DS	lst / opb UPD in Air Scandic-colors

AIR TAXIS = ATX (Warwickshire Aerocentre, Ltd dba) Birmingham

Old Firewatch, Hangar Road, Birmingham Airport, Birmingham B26 3QN, Great Britain ☎ (121) 782 10 11 Tx: none Fax: (121) 782 42 56 SITA: n/a
F: 1991 ⁂ 3 Head: Jon D. Poole ICAO: AIRTAX Net: http://www.airtaxco.uk Aircraft below MTOW 1361kg: AA5B, Cessna 152/172 & Piper PA-38.

☐ G-BNEN	Piper PA-34-200T Seneca II	34-8070262	N8232V	0080		2 CO TSIO-360-EB1	1999			
☐ G-BVYF	Piper PA-31-350 Navajo Chieftain	31-7952102	G-SAVE	0079		2 LY TIO-540-J2BD	3175			

AIRTOURS INTERNATIONAL = VZ / AIH (Airtours International Airways, Ltd dba / Subsidiary of Airtours, Plc) Manchester

Parkway 3, Parkway Business Centre, 300 Princess Road, Manchester M14 7QU, Great Britain ☎ (161) 232 66 00 Tx: none Fax: (161) 232 66 10 SITA: MANDDVZ
F: 1986 ⁂ 1940 Head: David Crossland IATA: 727 ICAO: KESTREL Net: n/a

☐ G-COEZ	Airbus Industrie A320-231	179	OY-CNH	0091	0297	2 IAE V2500-A1	75500	Y180	KS-BP	lsf Sigmund Leasing Ltd
☐ G-CRPH	Airbus Industrie A320-231	424	F-WQBB	0093	0495	2 IAE V2500-A1	75500	Y180	JM-AS	lsf Hare Ltd / sub-lst Skyservice USA

161 registration type of aircraft cn/fn ex/ex* mfd del powered by mtow kg configuration selcal name/fln/specialitites/remarks

☐ G-DACR	Airbus Industrie A320-212	349	G-OEXC	0092	0296	2 CFMI CFM56-5A3	77000	Y177	KS-BQ	lsf GPAA Funding / sub-lst VKG, OY-CNR
☐ G-DJAR	Airbus Industrie A320-231	164	OY-CNE	0091	0397	2 IAE V2500-A1	75500	Y180	KS-CE	lsf Frid Leasing Ltd
☐ G-DRVE	Airbus Industrie A320-212	221	F-GLGI	0091	0596	2 CFMI CFM56-5A3	77000	Y177		lsf GECC / sub-lst VKG as OY-CNB
☐ G-EPFR	Airbus Industrie A320-231	437	C-FTDF	0093	1197	2 IAE V2500-A1	75500	Y180	AQ-GH	lsf ORIX
☐ G-HBAP	Airbus Industrie A320-212	294	G-HAGT	0092	0296	2 CFMI CFM56-5A3	77000	Y177		lsf GPAA Funding / sub-lst VKG, OY-CNP
☐ G-JANM	Airbus Industrie A320-212	301	G-KMAM	0092	1195	2 CFMI CFM56-5A3	77000	Y177	KS-BM	lsf Airplanes A320Ltd/sublst VKG,OY-CNM
☐ G-JDFW	Airbus Industrie A320-212	299	G-SCSR	0092	1195	2 CFMI CFM56-5A3	77000	Y177	KS-BL	lsf ALPS 94/1 / sub-lst VKG as OY-CNW
☐ G-RDVE	Airbus Industrie A320-231	163	OY-CND	0091	0297	2 IAE V2500-A1	75500	Y180	KS-CD	lsf Beowolf Leasing Ltd
☐ G-RRJE	Airbus Industrie A320-212	222	F-GLGJ	0091	0596	2 CFMI CFM56-5A3	77000	Y177		lsf GECC / sub-lst VKG as OY-CNC
☐ G-SUEE	Airbus Industrie A320-231	363	G-IEAG	0092	0993	2 IAE V2500-A1	75500	Y180	DS-AL	lsf Wing Aerospace
☐ G-TICL	Airbus Industrie A320-231	169	OY-CNG	0091	1296	2 IAE V2500-A1	75500	Y180	KS-BM	lsf Odin Leasing Ltd
☐ G-TMDP	Airbus Industrie A320-231	168	OY-CNF	0091	1196	2 IAE V2500-A1	75500	Y180	KS-BL	lsf LOKI Leasing Ltd
☐ G-TPTT	Airbus Industrie A320-212	348	F-GLGE	0092	0296	2 CFMI CFM56-5A3	75500	Y180		lsf GPAA Funding / cvtd -211
☐ G-VCED	Airbus Industrie A320-231	193	OY-CNI	0091	0197	2 IAE V2500-A1	75500	Y180	KS-BQ	lsf Thor Leasing Ltd
☐ G-YJBM	Airbus Industrie A320-231	362	G-IEAF	0093	0993	2 IAE V2500-A1	75500	Y180	DS-AK	lsf ALPS 94/1
☐ G-JSJX	Airbus Industrie A321-211	808	D-AVZP*	0098	0498	2 CFMI CFM56-5B3/P	89000	Y220	LR-MP	lsf GATX
☐ G-VOLH	Airbus Industrie A321-211	823	D-AVZX*	0098	0598	2 CFMI CFM56-5B3/P	89000	Y220	LR-MQ	lsf GATX
☐ G-JALC	Boeing 757-225	22194 / 5	N504EA	0082	0295	2 RR RB211-535E4	104326	Y233	HS-AL	lsf Anfield Ltd
☐ G-LCRC	Boeing 757-23A (ET)	24636 / 259	G-IEAB	0090	1093	2 RR RB211-535E4	108860	Y233	LQ-GM	lsf AWAS
☐ G-MCEA	Boeing 757-225	22200 / 20	N510EA	0083	0295	2 RR RB211-535E4	104326	Y233	HS-AM	lsf Goodison Ltd
☐ G-PIDS	Boeing 757-225	22195 / 6	N505EA	0082	0195	2 RR RB211-535E4	104326	Y233	HS-AK	lsf Elland Ltd
☐ G-RJGR	Boeing 757-225	22197 / 8	N701MG	0082	1094	2 RR RB211-535E4	104326	Y233	HS-AJ	lsf Ewood Ltd
☐ G-WJAN	Boeing 757-21K	28674 / 746		0097	0397	2 RR RB211-535E4	108860	Y233	AP-BE	
☐ G-DAJC	Boeing 767-31K (ER)	27206 / 533		0094	0494	2 GE CF6-80C2B7F	184612	Y326	FP-ES	lsf Bluebird Leasing
☐ G-DIMB	Boeing 767-31K (ER)	28865 / 657		0097	0497	2 GE CF6-80C2B7F	184612	Y326	DG-EF	
☐ G-SJMC	Boeing 767-31K (ER)	27205 / 528	N6038E*	0094	0394	2 GE CF6-80C2B7F	184612	Y326	FP-ER	lsf Crown Green Ltd
☐ G-MDBD	Airbus Industrie A330-243	266				2 RR Trent 772B-60	230000	C49Y311		oo-delivery 0699
☐ G-MLJL	Airbus Industrie A330-243	254				2 RR Trent 772B-60	230000	C49Y311		oo-delivery 0699
☐ G-	Airbus Industrie A330-243	301				2 RR Trent 772B-60	230000	C49Y311		oo-delivery 1099
☐ G-	Airbus Industrie A330-243	309				2 RR Trent 772B-60	230000	C49Y311		oo-delivery 1199
☐ OY-CNO	Boeing (Douglas) DC-10-30	46990 / 260	XA-SYE	0078	0498	3 GE CF6-50C2	259455	Y359	DM-EF	lsf VKG / to be re-reg. G-BYDA

AIR 2000, Ltd = DP / AMM (Subsidiary of First Choice Holidays, Plc.) — Manchester & Gatwick

First Choice House, London Road, Crawley, West Sussex RH10 2GX, Great Britain ☎ (1293) 51 89 66 Tx: 878434 ammhdq g Fax: (1293) 58 87 57 SITA: MANOODP
F: 1986 ⁂ 1500 Head: Kenneth Smith IATA: 091 ICAO: JET SET Net: http://www.air2000.ltd.uk

☐ G-OOAA	Airbus Industrie A320-231	291	F-WWBZ*	0092	0492	2 IAE V2500-A1	75500	Y180	CQ-PR	lsf ORIX
☐ G-OOAB	Airbus Industrie A320-231	292	F-WWDN*	0092	0492	2 IAE V2500-A1	75500	Y180	CQ-PS	lsf ORIX
☐ G-OOAC	Airbus Industrie A320-231	327	F-WWDQ*	0092	0892	2 IAE V2500-A1	75500	Y180	CR-DQ	lsf ORIX
☐ G-OOAD	Airbus Industrie A320-231	336	F-WWIG*	0092	0892	2 IAE V2500-A1	75500	Y180	CR-DS	lsf ORIX
☐ G-OOAE	Airbus Industrie A321-211	852	D-AVZG*	0098	0798	2 CFMI CFM56-5B3/P	89000	Y220	HQ-JL	lsf Abbotsbury Ltd
☐ G-OOAF	Airbus Industrie A321-211	677	G-UNID	0097	1098	2 CFMI CFM56-5B3/P	89000	Y220		lsf Eagardon Ltd
☐ G-OOAH	Airbus Industrie A321-211	781	G-UNIE	0098	1098	2 CFMI CFM56-5B3/P	89000	Y220	EP-GK	lsf GECA
☐ G-OOAJ	Airbus Industrie A321-211	1017		0099	0499	2 CFMI CFM56-5B3/P	89000	Y220		lsf GECA
☐ G-OOOA	Boeing 757-28A	23767 / 127	C-FOOA	0387	0487	2 RR RB211-535E4	108862	Y233	AP-DK	lsf ILFC
☐ G-OOOB	Boeing 757-28A	23822 / 130	C-FOOB	0487	0487	2 RR RB211-535E4	108862	Y233	AP-DL	lsf CE Fin.Lsg/lst ROY,C-FRYH in winter
☐ G-OOOC	Boeing 757-28A (ER)	24017 / 162	C-FXOC	0388	0388	2 RR RB211-535E4	113398	Y233	AM-DP	lsf BBAM/sublst ROY as C-FRYL in winter
☐ G-OOOD	Boeing 757-28A	24235 / 180	C-FXOD	0588	0588	2 RR RB211-535E4	108862	Y233	BC-JP	lsf BBAM/sublst ROY as C-GRYU in winter
☐ G-OOOG	Boeing 757-23A (ER)	24292 / 219	C-FOOG	0389	0389	2 RR RB211-535E4	113398	Y233	BQ-FK	lsf AWAS/sublst ROY as C-GRYY in winter
☐ G-OOOI	Boeing 757-23A (ER)	24289 / 209	N510SK	0389	1089	2 RR RB211-535E4	108862	Y233	MQ-EP	lsf AWAS
☐ G-OOOJ	Boeing 757-23A (ER)	24290 / 212	N510FP	0389	1089	2 RR RB211-535E4	108862	Y233	MQ-LP	lsf AWAS
☐ G-OOOS	Boeing 757-236 (ER)	24397 / 221	G-BRJD	0089	0591	2 RR RB211-535E4	113398	Y233	BQ-AC	lsf Phoenix III Investment
☐ G-OOOU	Boeing 757-2Y0 (ER)	25240 / 388		0091	1091	2 RR RB211-535E4	113398	Y233	BL-DS	lsf Buckingham Partners
☐ G-OOOV	Boeing 757-225	22211 / 74	N521EA	0085	1291	2 RR RB211-535E4	104326	Y233	CE-BG	lsf GATX
☐ G-OOOW	Boeing 757-225	22611 / 75	N522EA	0085	0192	2 RR RB211-535E4	104326	Y233	CE-BH	lsf GATX
☐ G-OOOX	Boeing 757-2Y0 (ER)	26158 / 526		0093	0293	2 RR RB211-535E4	113398	Y233	DH-FS	lsf ALPS-94-1
☐ G-OOOY	Boeing 757-28A (ER)	28203 / 802		0098	0598	2 RR RB211-535E4	104326	Y233	PQ-CD	lsf ILFC
☐ G-OOAL	Boeing 767-38A (ER)	29617		0099	0399	2 GE CF6-80C2B7F	186880	C38Y274		lsf GECA
☐ G-OOAN	Boeing 767-39H (ER)	26256 / 484	G-UKLH	0093	1298	2 GE CF6-80C2B6F	184612	Y327	CR-EQ	Caribbean Star / lsf ILFC
☐ G-OOAO	Boeing 767-39H (ER)	26257 / 488	G-UKLI	0093	1298	2 GE CF6-80C2B6F	184612	Y327	CR-ES	Atlantic Star / lsf ILFC
☐ G-	Boeing 767-38A (ER)					2 GE CF6-80C2B7F	186880	Y327		to be lsf GECA 0400
☐ G-	Airbus Industrie A330-223	320				2 PW PW4168A	230000	Y380		oo-delivery 0200
☐ G-	Airbus Industrie A330-223	330				2 PW PW4168A	230000	Y380		oo-delivery 0300

ALAN MANN HELICOPTERS, Ltd = AMH (Member of Alan Mann Group) — Fairoaks

Fairoaks Airport, Chobham, Woking, Surrey GU24 8HU, Great Britain ☎ (1276) 85 77 77 Tx: 858492 amsale g Fax: (1276) 85 62 41 SITA: n/a
F: 1968 ⁂ 40 Head: Alan Mann ICAO: MANN Net: http://www.alanmann.co.uk Aircraft below MTOW 1361 kg: Bell 47G-5A.

☐ G-BXLI	Bell 206B JetRanger III	4041	N206JR	0089		1 AN 250-C20J	1451			opf Williams Grand Prix Engineering Ltd
☐ G-OAMG	Bell 206B JetRanger III	2901	G-COAL	0080		1 AN 250-C20B	1451			
☐ G-TREE	Bell 206B JetRanger III	2826	N2779U	0079		1 AN 250-C20B	1451			lsf LGH Aviation Ltd
☐ G-COPT	Eurocopter (Aerosp.) AS350B Squirrel	2168	9M-FSA	0088	0298	1 TU Arriel 1B	1950			lsf Owenlars Ltd
☐ G-FFRI	Eurocopter (Aerosp.) AS355F1 Tw.Squirrel	5120	G-GLOW	0182		2 AN 250-C20F	2400			lsf Ford Farm Racing

AL-KHARAFI AVIATION 2000, Ltd (Subsidiary of Mohamed Abdul Mohsin Al-Kharafi & Son) — Kuwait & London

Operations Office:, PO Box 886, Safat, 13009 Kuwait, Kuwait ☎ 481 36 22 Tx: none Fax: 482 01 70 SITA: n/a
F: 1998 ⁂ n/a Head: Kamal Darwish Net: n/a Operates non-commerical corporate flights for its owners only.

☐ G-OMAK	Airbus Industrie A319-132 (CJ)	913	F-WWIF*	0098	1298	2 IAE V2524-A5	70000	VIP 30 Pax		

ALL CHARTER, Ltd = BLA — Bournemouth

Hangar 600, Bournemouth Int'l Airport, Christchurch, Dorset BH23 6DF, Great Britain ☎ (1202) 58 02 04 Tx: 41552 lahurn g Fax: (1202) 57 00 69 SITA: n/a
F: 1982 ⁂ 6 Head: W.G. Booth ICAO: ALL CHARTER Net: n/a

☐ G-BEVG	Piper PA-34-200T Seneca II	34-7570060	VQ-SAM	0075		2 CO TSIO-360-E	2073			lsf Aranair Ltd

ALM Aircraft Leasing & Management = (ALMA) — London-Gatwick

First Point, Buckingham Gate, South Terminal, London-Gatwick Airport, West Sussex RH6 0NT, Great Britain ☎ (1293) 56 76 56 Tx: 878896 airlsg g Fax: (1293) 56 78 21 SITA: n/a
F: 1987 ⁂ 8 Head: Stephen L. Vella Net: http://www.alm-lease.co.uk New & used aircraft leasing, sales and financing company.
Manages (principally on behalf of banks) following main aircraft types: Airbus Industrie A320, Boeing 737 & Fokker 50. Aircraft leased through ALM are listed and mentioned as lsf ALMA under the leasing carriers.

ANGLO AMERICAN AIRMOTIVE, Ltd = MOU — Bournemouth

Bournemouth Int'l Airport, Bldg. 602, Christchurch, Dorset BH23 6NE, Great Britain ☎ (1202) 57 00 23 Tx: none Fax: (1202) 57 02 03 SITA: n/a
F: n/a ⁂ 35 Head: Kenneth W. Norms ICAO: BLACKADDER Net: n/a Aircraft below MTOW 1361kg: Cessna 152 / 172 & Piper PA-28

☐ G-ONPA	Piper PA-31-350 Navajo Chieftain	31-7952110	N89PA	0079	0598	2 LY TIO-540-J2BD	3175			

ANT AVIATION, Ltd (formerly Ashley Norman Thorpe Aviation, Ltd) — Cambridge

Manor Farm Stud, High Street, Chippenham, Ely, Cambs CB7 5PR, Great Britain ☎ (1638) 72 08 88 Tx: n/a Fax: (1638) 72 13 10 SITA: n/a
F: n/a ⁂ n/a Head: Capt. Karl Ratcliffe Net: n/a

☐ G-BEHU	Piper PA-34-200T Seneca II	34-7670265	N6175J	0076		2 CO TSIO-360-E	1999			dmgd 0198 / wfu

ARAVCO, Ltd = ARV — Farnborough

Farnborough Airport, Farnborough, Hampshire GU14 6XA, Great Britain ☎ (1252) 55 40 00 Tx: 859200 aravco g Fax: (1252) 37 77 10 SITA: n/a
F: 1976 ⁂ 20 Head: Capt. John Brodhurst ICAO: ARAVCO Net: n/a

☐ G-BTAB	Hawker 800B (BAe 125-800B)	258088	G-BOOA	0087		2 GA TFE731-5R-1H	12428	Executive		opf Dean Finance Ltd
☐ G-RCEJ	Hawker 800B (BAe 125-800B)	258021		0085	0695	2 GA TFE731-5R-1H	12428	Executive		
☐ G-TCDI	Hawker F403B (HS 125-F403B)	25248	N792A	0071	1096	2 GA TFE731-3R-1H	10569	Executive		cvtd 125-403B
☐ G-MAAH	BAe (BAC) One-Eleven 488GH	259	PK-TAL	0078	1098	2 RR Spey 511-14DW	44679	Executive		

ATLANTIC AIRLINES = AAG (Atlantic Air Transport Ltd dba/Subs.of Atlantic Holdings/formerly dba Air Corbière, Air Atlantique, Atlantic Airways & Cargo) — Coventry

Coventry Airport, Baginton, Coventry CV8 3AZ, Great Britain ☎ (1203) 30 75 66 Tx: 311260 aat cvt g Fax: (1203) 63 90 37 SITA: CVTFSBD
F: 1974 ⁂ 235 Head: Michael Collett ICAO: ATLANTIC Net: n/a

☐ G-BODY	Cessna 310R II	310R1503	N4897A	0079		2 CO IO-520-M	2495	Y5 / Trainer		
☐ G-SOUL	Cessna 310R II	310R0140	N5020J	0075		2 CO IO-520-M	2495	Y5 / AerialPhoto		
☐ G-EYES	Cessna 402C II	402C0008	SE-IRU	0078		2 CO TSIO-520-VB	3107	Y9 / Patrol		
☐ G-NOSE	Cessna 402B	402B0823	N98AR	0075		2 CO TSIO-520-E	2858	Y9 / Surveyer		
☐ G-BCEN	Britten-Norman BN-2A-26 Islander	403	4X-AYG	0074		2 LY O-540-E4C5	2994	Patrol / SAR		opf HM Coastguard
☐ G-NERC	Piper PA-31-350 Navajo Chieftain	31-7405402	G-BBXX	0074		2 LY TIO-540-J2BD	3175	Surveyer		opf Natural Environment ResearchCouncil
☐ G-EXEX	Cessna 404 Titan II	404-0037	SE-GZF	0077		2 CO GTSIO-520-M	3810	Surveyer	EG-AM	Pollution&RadarControl/opf Dept of Trsp
☐ G-MIND	Cessna 404 Titan II	404-0004	G-SKKC	0076	0493	2 CO GTSIO-520-M	3810	Y9		
☐ G-TASK	Cessna 404 Titan II	404-0829	PH-MPC	0082	0293	2 CO GTSIO-520-M	3810	Surveyer		Pollution&RadarControl/opf Dept of Trsp

162 registration type of aircraft cn/fn ex/ex* mfd del powered by mtow kg configuration selcal name/fln/specialitites/remarks

☐ G-LEAF	Reims/Cessna F406 Caravan II	*F406-0018*	*EI-CKY*	*0087*	*0396*	*2 PWC PT6A-112*	*4468*	*Y9 / Frtr 1,5t*		
☐ G-LOFT	Cessna 500 Citation I	*500-0331*	*LN-NAT*	*0076*		*2 PWC JT15D-1A*	*5375*	*C5*		
☐ N22GA	Cessna 550 Citation II	*550-0031*	*RP-C296*	*0078*	*0098*	*2 PWC JT15D-4*	*6032*	*C6*		*lsf Ilmor Engineering Inc.*
☐ G-BUKA	Fairchild (Swearingen) SA227AC Metro III	*AC-706B*	*ZK-NSQ*	*0088*	*0592*	*2 GA TPE331-11U-612G*	*7257*	*Y19 / Frtr 2,1t*		
☐ G-APRS	Scottish Aviation Twin Pioneer 3	*561*	*G-BCWF*	*0059*	*1293*	*2 ALV Leonides 531-8B*	*6622*	*Y16*		*RAF-Empire Test Pilots School-colors*
☐ G-AMCA	Boeing (Douglas) DC-3C (C-47B-30-DK)	*32966*	*KN487*	*0045*		*2 PW R-1830*	*12700*	*Sprayer*		*Pollution Control/opf Dept of Transport*
☐ G-AMHJ	Boeing (Douglas) DC-3C (C-47A-25-DK)	*13468*	*SU-AZI*	*0042*		*2 PW R-1830*	*12700*	*Sprayer*		*Pollution Control/opf Dept of Transport*
☐ G-AMPO	Boeing (Douglas) DC-3C (C-47B-30-DK)	*33185*	*LN-RTO*	*0045*		*2 PW R-1830*	*12700*	*Sprayer*		*std Coventry*
☐ G-AMPY	Boeing (Douglas) DC-3C (C-47B-15-DK)	*26569*	*N15751*	*0042*		*2 PW R-1830*	*12700*	*Sprayer*		*Pollution Control/opf Dept of Transport*
☐ G-AMPZ	Boeing (Douglas) DC-3C (C-47B-30-DK)	*32872*	*EI-BDT*	*0045*	*0990*	*2 PW R-1830*	*12700*	*Y30 / Frtr 3,6t*		*RAF Transport Command KN442-colors*
☐ G-AMRA	Boeing (Douglas) DC-3C (C-47B-15-DK)	*26735*	*XE280*	*0044*	*1081*	*2 PW R-1830*	*12700*	*Freighter 3,6t*		
☐ G-AMSV	Boeing (Douglas) DC-3C (C-47B-25-DK)	*32820*	*KN397*	*0044*		*2 PW R-1830*	*12700*	*Sprayer*		*Pollution Control/opf Dept of Transport*
☐ G-AMYJ	Boeing (Douglas) DC-3C (C-47B-25-DK)	*32716*	*SU-AZF*	*0044*	*0290*	*2 PW R-1830*	*12700*	*Sprayer*		*std Coventry*
☐ G-ANAF	Boeing (Douglas) DC-3C (C-47B-35-DK)	*33436*	*N170GP*	*0045*		*2 PW R-1830*	*12700*	*Freighter*		*opf Racal Avionics*
☐ G-APSA	Boeing (Douglas) DC-6A	*45497 / 995*	*4W-ABQ*	*0658*	*0287*	*4 PW R-2800-CB3*	*47083*	*Freighter 13t*	*EG-AH*	
☐ G-SIXC	Boeing (Douglas) DC-6A/B	*45550 / 1032*	*N93459*	*0058*	*0387*	*4 PW R-2800-CB3*	*47083*	*Freighter 13t*		*cvtd DC-6B*
☐ G-FIJR	Lockheed L-188PF Electra	*1138*	*EI-HCF*	*0061*	*1097*	*4 AN 501-D13A*	*52617*	*Freighter 14,5t*		*cvtd L-188C*
☐ G-FIJV	Lockheed L-188C (F) Electra	*1129*	*EI-HCE*	*0060*	*0998*	*4 AN 501-D13A*	*52617*	*Freighter 14,5t*		*cvtd L-188A*
☐ G-FIZU	Lockheed L-188C (F) Electra	*2014*	*EI-CHY*	*0060*	*0998*	*4 AN 501-D13A*	*52617*	*Freighter 14,5t*		*cvtd L-188C*
☐ G-LOFB	Lockheed L-188C (F) Electra	*1131*	*N667F*	*0060*	*0694*	*4 AN 501-D13A*	*52617*	*Freighter 14,5t*		*cvtd -188C*
☐ G-LOFC	Lockheed L-188C (F) Electra	*1100*	*N665F*	*0059*	*0695*	*4 AN 501-D13A*	*52617*	*Freighter 14,5t*		*cvtd -188A*
☐ G-LOFD	Lockheed L-188A (F) Electra	*1143*	*LN-FOG*	*0061*	*0597*	*4 AN 501-D13A*	*52617*	*Freighter 14,5t*		*cvtd L-188A*
☐ G-LOFE	Lockheed L-188C (F) Electra	*1144*	*EI-CET*	*0061*	*0998*	*4 AN 501-D13A*	*52617*	*Freighter 14,5t*		*cvtd L-188C*

ATLANTA HELICOPTERS (Global), Ltd — Bristol

The Hangars, Bristol Airport, Bristol BS48 3EP, Great Britain ☎ (1275) 47 44 56 Tx: none Fax: (1275) 47 44 53 SITA: n/a
F: 1996 n/a Head: Mrs. Tracy Batten Net: n/a Aircraft below MTOW 1361kg: Robinson R22

☐ G-BARP	Bell 206B JetRanger	*967*	*N18092*	*0073*		*1 AN 250-C20*	*1451*			*occ lsf SWEB Helicopter*
☐ G-MFMF	Bell 206B JetRanger III	*3569*	*G-BJNJ*	*0081*		*1 AN 250-C20J*	*1451*			*occ lsf SWEB Helicopter*
☐ G-XXIV	Agusta-Bell 206B JetRanger III	*8717*		*0089*		*1 AN 250-C20J*	*1451*			*lsf Hampton Printing (Bristol) Ltd*

AURIGNY AIR SERVICES, Ltd = GR / AUR (Subsidiary of Aurigny Aviation Holdings, Ltd / Member of the Exxtor Group of Companies) — Guernsey & Alderney

Grande Rue, St. Martin, Guernsey, Channel Islands ☎ (1481) 66 444 Tx: none Fax: (1481) 66 446 SITA: n/a
F: 1968 150 Head: Andrew R. Round IATA: 924 ICAO: AYLINE Net: n/a

☐ G-BDTN	Britten-Norman BN-2A Mk.III-2 Trislander	*1026*	*S7-AAN*	*0076*	*0387*	*3 LY O-540-E4C5*	*4536*	*Y16*		
☐ G-BDTO	Britten-Norman BN-2A Mk.III-2 Trislander	*1027*	*G-RBSI*	*0076*	*1184*	*3 LY O-540-E4C5*	*4536*	*Y16*		*Mercury Asset Management-colors*
☐ G-BDWV	Britten-Norman BN-2A Mk.III-2 Trislander	*1035*	*8P-ASF*	*0076*	*1284*	*3 LY O-540-E4C5*	*4536*	*Y16*		
☐ G-BEPH	Britten-Norman BN-2A Mk.III-2 Trislander	*1052*	*S7-AAG*	*0076*	*0587*	*3 LY O-540-E4C5*	*4536*	*Y16*		*Steeple Finance-colors*
☐ G-BEPI	Britten-Norman BN-2A Mk.III-2 Trislander	*1053*		*0077*	*1083*	*3 LY O-540-E4C5*	*4536*	*Y16*		*SG Hambros Private Banking in the CI-cs*
☐ G-BEVT	Britten-Norman BN-2A Mk.III-2 Trislander	*1057*		*0077*	*0783*	*3 LY O-540-E4C5*	*4536*	*Y16*		*Islands'Insurance-colors*
☐ G-JOEY	Britten-Norman BN-2A Mk.III-2 Trislander	*1016*	*G-BDGG*	*0075*	*0679*	*3 LY O-540-E4C5*	*4536*	*Y16*		
☐ G-OCTA	Britten-Norman BN-2A Mk.III-2 Trislander	*1008*	*VR-CAA*	*0075*	*0691*	*3 LY O-540-E4C5*	*4536*	*Y16*		*ITEX Technology with Confidence-colors*
☐ G-XTOR	Britten-Norman BN-2A Mk.III-2 Trislander	*1065*		*0096*	*0496*	*3 LY O-540-E4C5*	*4536*	*Y16*		
☐ G-BVMX	Shorts 360-300 (SD3-60 Variant 100)	*SH3751*	*G-BPFS*	*0088*	*0598*	*2 PWC PT6A-67R*	*12292*	*Y36*		*lsf Lynrise Air Lease*

AVIA SPECIAL (Avia Special, Ltd dba) — White Waltham

2 Brookside, Hatfield, Hertfordshire AL10 9RR, Great Britain ☎ (1707) 26 27 74 Tx: none Fax: (1707) 25 14 05 SITA: n/a
F: 1975 6 Head: James M.K. Black Net: n/a Aircraft below MTOW 1361kg: DH-82A Tiger Moth, Mudry CP.10B & Zlin Z526. Operates para & vintage pleasure flights.

☐ HA-MKE	PZL Mielec (Antonov) An-2	*1G158-34*	*UR-07714*	*0074*		*1 SH ASh-62IR*	*5500*	*12 Pax / Para*		*lsf pvt*
☐ HA-MKF	PZL Mielec (Antonov) An-2	*1G233-43*	*OM-248*	*0088*		*1 SH ASh-62IR*	*5500*	*12 Pax / Para*		*lsf pvt*

AVIATION BEAUPORT, Ltd - A.B. AIR TAXI = AVB — Jersey

States of Jersey Airport, St. Peter, Jersey, Channel Islands ☎ (1534) 42 128 Tx: 4192255 belair g Fax: (1534) 44 272 SITA: n/a
F: 1969 20 Head: G.A. Graham ICAO: BEAUPAIR Net: n/a

☐ G-BGTT	Cessna 310R II	*310R1641*	*N1AN*	*0079*		*2 CO IO-520-MB*	*2495*	*5 Pax*		
☐ G-KIWI	Cessna 404 Titan II	*404-0644*	*G-BHNI*	*0080*		*2 CO GTSIO-520-M*	*3810*	*11 Pax*		
☐ G-BJIR	Cessna 550 Citation II	*550-0296*	*N6888C*	*0081*		*2 PWC JT15D-4*	*6033*	*8 Pax*		*lsf Gator Aviation Ltd*

AVIATION INVESTOR SERVICES, Ltd = (AVIS) (Associated with Aviation Investors International Inc., USA) — Cayman Islands

European Office:, 59 Hyde Park Gate, Suite 18, London SW7 5ED, Great Britain ☎ (171) 584 72 36 Tx: none Fax: (171) 589 34 52 SITA: n/a
F: 1993 n/a Head: Maxime Sadowsky Net: n/a New and used aircraft leasing, sales and financing company. Owner / lessor of the following (main) aircraft types:
Boeing 737-300/400, 757-200, 767-300ER, DHC-7/DHC-8, Fokker 50, McDonnell Douglas DC-10-30 & MD-83. Aircraft leased from AVIS are listed and mentioned as such under the leasing carriers.

AVON AVIATION, Ltd (Subsidiary of TBI, Ltd) — Cardiff & Bristol

The Court House, 110 High Street, Nailsea, Bristol, Avon BS48 1AH, Great Britain ☎ (1275) 81 07 67 Tx: none Fax: (1275) 85 83 68 SITA: n/a
F: 1999 n/a Head: n/a Net: n/a Presently being set-up. Intends to start operations during 1999 with a BAe (BAC) One-Eleven 500 aircraft.

AWYR CYMRU CYF — Mid Wales-Welshpool

Westham, Arbory Road, Castletown IM9 1ND, Isle of Man ☎ (1624) 82 25 14 Tx: none Fax: (1624) 82 29 81 SITA: n/a
F: 1998 n/a Head: Kevin M. Curran Net: n/a

☐ G-BWHF	Piper PA-31-325 Navajo C/R	*31-7612076*	*F-GECA*	*0076*	*0098*	*2 LY TIO-540-F2BD*	*2948*			

BAC EXPRESS AIRLINES, Ltd = RPX (Subsidiary of BAC Group Limited / formerly BAC Aircraft, Ltd) — London-Gatwick

BAC House, Bonehurst Road, Horley, Surrey RH6 8QG, Great Britain ☎ (1293) 82 16 21 Tx: 877087 flybac g Fax: (1293) 82 12 04 SITA: LGWRPXH
F: 1992 80 Head: Neil Dickson ICAO: RAPEX Net: http://www.bacexpress.com

☐ G-BMAR	Shorts 360-100 (SD3-60 Variant 100)	*SH3633*	*G-14-3633**	*0084*	*1298*	*2 PWC PT6A-65R*	*11999*	*Y36 / Freighter*		
☐ G-CEAL	Shorts 360-300 (SD3-60 Variant 100)	*SH3761*	*N161CN*	*1189*	*0197*	*2 PWC PT6A-67R*	*12292*	*Y39 / Freighter*		*lsf BACL*
☐ G-CLAS	Shorts 360-200 (SD3-60 Variant 100)	*SH3635*	*EI-BEK*	*0084*	*1195*	*2 PWC PT6A-65AR*	*11999*	*Y36 / Freighter*		City of Cardiff / *lsf BACL*
☐ G-OBOH	Shorts 360-200 (SD3-60 Variant 100)	*SH3713*	*G-BNDJ**	*0087*	*1096*	*2 PWC PT6A-65AR*	*11999*	*Y36 / Freighter*		*lsf BACL / sub-lst REA as EI-CPR*
☐ G-OCEA	Shorts 360-300 (SD3-60 Variant 100)	*SH3762*	*N162CN*	*1289*	*0497*	*2 PWC PT6A-67R*	*12292*	*Y39 / Freighter*		*lsf BACL*
☐ G-OJSY	Shorts 360-100 (SD3-60 Variant 100)	*SH3603*	*N368MQ*	*0082*	*1195*	*2 PWC PT6A-65R*	*11999*	*Y36 / Freighter*		*lsf BACL*
☐ G-VBAC	Shorts 360-300 (SD3-60 Variant 100)	*SH3736*	*VH-MJU*	*0088*	*0997*	*2 PWC PT6A-67R*	*12292*	*Y39 / Freighter*		*lsf BACL*
☐ G-BMXD	Fokker F27 Friendship 500 (F27 Mk500)	*10417*	*TF-FLR*	*0069*	*1298*	*2 RR Dart 532-7*	*19731*	*Freighter*		Scottish Trader
☐ G-BVOB	Fokker F27 Friendship 500 (F27 Mk500)	*10366*	*PH-FMN*	*0068*	*1297*	*2 RR Dart 536-7*	*19731*	*Freighter*		
☐ G-JEAD	Fokker F27 Friendship 500RF (F27 Mk500RF)	*10627*	*VH-EWU*	*0083*	*0897*	*2 RR Dart 532-7*	*19731*	*Freighter*		Midland Trader / *lsf JEA*

BAC LEASING, Ltd = (BACL) (Subsidiary of BAC Group Limited) — London-Gatwick

BAC House, Bonehurst Road, Horley, Surrey RH6 8QG, Great Britain ☎ (1293) 82 08 18 Tx: none Fax: (1293) 82 07 20 SITA: n/a
F: 1985 10 Head: David Robinson Net: n/a Used aircraft leasing, sales, financing, remarketing & startup airline consultory company.
Owner / lessor of following (main) aircraft types: DHC-6 Twin Otter, Embraer 110 Bandeirante, Fokker F27-500/-600 & Shorts 330/360. Aircraft leased from BACL are listed and mentioned as such under the leasing carriers.

BBC AIR, Ltd — Compton Abbas

PO Box 1840, Wells, Somerset, Great Britain ☎ (1258) 83 05 15 Tx: none Fax: (1749) 67 77 87 SITA: n/a
F: 1997 n/a Head: Roger Collins Net: n/a

☐ G-HBBC	BAe (DH) 104 Dove 8	*04211*	*VP961*	*0048*		*2 Gipsy Queen 70 Mk.3*	*4150*	*10 Pax*		

BENAIR, Ltd = INI (Member of Martini Group of Companies / formerly Martini Airfreight Services, Ltd) — Manchester & Edinburgh

Unit 13, Peerglow Ind. Estate, Park Road, West Timperley, Altrinchaw, Cheshire WA14 5QH, Great Britain ☎ (161) 962 22 27 Tx: none Fax: (161) 962 22 28 SITA: n/a
F: 1996 30 Head: Shane A. Martin ICAO: MARTINI Net: n/a Operates small-package cargo-flights for the Martini Group of Companies & Newspaper, Royal Mail & contract cargo & passenger flights with
Cessna 208B & Reims/Cessna F406 aircraft, leased from AVIATION CENTER WEST (OY-) & HANGAR 5 AIRSERVICES NORWAY (LN-) when required.

BIGGIN HILL HELICOPTERS (The Hughes Helicopter Company Ltd dba) — Biggin Hill

Building 158A, Biggin Hill Airport, Westerham, Kent TN16 3BN, Great Britain ☎ (1959) 54 08 03 Tx: none Fax: (1959) 57 11 76 SITA: n/a
F: 1994 n/a Head: Chris Stepto ICAO: HELISPEED Net: http://www.bhh.co.uk Aircraft below MTOW 1361kg: Hughes 269C (300C) & 369HS (500C)

☐ G-OTDB	MD Helicopters MD 500E (Hughes 369E)	*0204E*	*G-BXUR*	*0087*	*0498*	*1 AN 250-C20B*	*1361*			*lsf Helisport Ltd*
☐ G-CHGL	Bell 206B JetRanger	*1669*	*G-BPNG*	*0075*	*1097*	*1 AN 250-C20*	*1451*			*lsf Helisport Ltd*
☐ G-CRPS	Bell 206B JetRanger II	*1967*	*A6-BCC*	*0076*	*0997*	*1 AN 250-C20*	*1451*			*lsf Helisport Ltd*
☐ G-DBHH	Agusta-Bell 206B JetRanger	*8111*	*G-AWVO*	*0069*	*0596*	*1 AN 250-C20*	*1451*			*lsf UK Helicopter Charter / cvtd 206A*
☐ G-JWLS	Bell 206B JetRanger	*1114*	*G-BSXE*	*0073*		*1 AN 250-C20*	*1451*			*lsf JWL Services*
☐ G-WLLY	Bell 206B JetRanger	*405*	*G-OBHH*	*0069*	*0396*	*1 AN 250-C20*	*1361*			*lsf Blue Five Aviation Ltd / cvtd 206A*

BKS SURVEYS, Ltd — Belfast-Int'l

47 Ballycairn Road, Coleraine, Londonderry BT51 3HZ, Northern Ireland, Great Britain ☎ (1265) 52 311 Tx: none Fax: (1265) 57 637 SITA: n/a
F: n/a n/a Head: Lynn E. Neill Net: n/a

☐ G-BKVT	Piper PA-23-250 Aztec F	*27-7754002*	*G-HARV*	*0076*	*0698*	*2 LY IO-540-C4B5*	*2359*	*Photo / Survey*		

163 registration type of aircraft cn/fn ex/ex* mfd del powered by mtow kg configuration selcal name/fln/specialitites/remarks

BLACKPOOL AIR CHARTER, Ltd (Subsidiary of Justgold, Ltd) — Blackpool

Blackpool Airport, Blackpool, Lancashire FY4 2QS, Great Britain ☎ (1253) 34 18 71 Tx: 677289 batair g Fax: (1253) 34 15 67 SITA: n/a
F: 1986 ⁂ 10 Head: Capt. William Brian Bateson Net: n/a

registration	type of aircraft	cn/fn	ex/ex*	mfd	del	powered by	mtow kg	configuration	selcal	name/fln/specialities/remarks
☐ G-ARJS	Piper PA-23-160 Apache G	23-1977		0061		2 LY O-320-B3B	1724			

BOND HELICOPTERS, Ltd = BND (Member of Helicopter Services Group, Norway / formerly Management Aviation, Ltd & North Scottish Helicopters, Ltd) — Aberdeen

Bond

Aberdeen Airport East, Dyce, Aberdeen AB2 0DU, Scotland, Great Britain ☎ (1224) 72 55 05 Tx: 739794 bondab g Fax: (1224) 72 24 25 SITA: n/a
F: 1961 ⁂ 710 Head: Stephen W. Bond ICAO: BOND Net: n/a

registration	type of aircraft	cn/fn	ex/ex*	mfd	del	powered by	mtow kg	configuration	selcal	name/fln/specialities/remarks
☐ G-AZOR	Eurocopter (MBB) BO105DB	S-20	EC-DOE	0071	1086	2 AN 250-C20B	2400	4 Pax / EMS		
☐ G-BAFD	Eurocopter (MBB) BO105DB	S-35	D-HDAO*	0072	0489	2 AN 250-C20B	2400	4 Pax / EMS		
☐ G-BAMF	Eurocopter (MBB) BO105DB	S-36	D-HDAM*	0072	1184	2 AN 250-C20B	2400	4 Pax		
☐ G-BATC	Eurocopter (MBB) BO105DB	S-45	D-HDAW*	0074	1184	2 AN 250-C20B	2400	4 Pax / EMS		
☐ G-BTHV	Eurocopter (MBB) BO105DBS-4	S-855	D-HMBV	0091	0497	2 AN 250-C20B	2500	EMS		opf West Midlands Air Ambulance
☐ G-BUIB	Eurocopter (MBB) BO105DBS-4	S-138/911	G-BDYZ	0092	0592	2 AN 250-C20B	2400	4 Pax / EMS		remanufactured BO105D cn S-138
☐ G-BUTN	Eurocopter (MBB) BO105DBS-4	S-34/912	G-AZTI	0092	0193	2 AN 250-C20B	2400	4 Pax / EMS		remanufactured BO105D cn S-34
☐ G-BUXS	Eurocopter (MBB) BO105DBS-4	S-41/913	G-PASA	0093	0593	2 AN 250-C20B	2400	4 Pax / EMS		remanufactured BO105D cn S-41
☐ G-CDBS	Eurocopter (MBB) BO105DBS-4	S-738	D-HDRZ*	0085	0989	2 AN 250-C20B	2400	EMS		opf Cornwall Air Ambulance
☐ G-DCCH	Eurocopter (MBB) BO105DBS-4	S-770	D-HDYF*	0086	0098	2 AN 250-C20B	2500	EMS		opf Devon Air Ambulance
☐ G-DNLB	Eurocopter (MBB) BO105DBS-4	S-60/850	G-BUDP	0092	0492	2 AN 250-C20B	2400	4 Pax		remanufactured BO105D cn S-60
☐ G-SPOL	Eurocopter (MBB) BO105DBS-4	S-392	VR-BGV	0079	0196	2 AN 250-C20B	2300	Patrol/Survey		opf Strathclyde Police ASU
☐ G-THLS	Eurocopter (MBB) BO105DBS-4	S-80/859	G-BCXO	0092	0292	2 AN 250-C20B	2400	4 Pax		reman.BO105D cn S-80/opf Trinity House
☐ G-WMAA	Eurocopter (MBB) BO105DBS-4	S-135/914	G-PASB	0093	0994	2 AN 250-C20B	2400	EMS		reman.105D cnS-135/opf West Midl.AirAmb
☐ G-BKXD	Eurocopter (Aerosp.) SA365N Dauphin 2	6088	F-WMHD*	0083	1184	2 TU Arriel 1C	4000	12 Pax		
☐ G-BLEZ	Eurocopter (Aerosp.) SA365N Dauphin 2	6131		0084	1184	2 TU Arriel 1C	4000	12 Pax		
☐ G-BLUM	Eurocopter (Aerosp.) SA365N Dauphin 2	6101		0085	0185	2 TU Arriel 1C	4000	12 Pax		
☐ G-BLUN	Eurocopter (Aerosp.) SA365N Dauphin 2	6114	PH-SSS	0085	1294	2 TU Arriel 1C	4000	12 Pax		
☐ G-BTEU	Eurocopter (Aerosp.) AS365N2 Dauphin 2	6392		0090	0291	2 TU Arriel 1C2	4250	12 Pax		
☐ G-BTNC	Eurocopter (Aerosp.) AS365N2 Dauphin 2	6409		0091	0691	2 TU Arriel 1C2	4250	12 Pax		
☐ G-BTUX	Eurocopter (Aerosp.) AS365N2 Dauphin 2	6424		0091	0991	2 TU Arriel 1C2	4250	12 Pax		
☐ G-NTWO	Eurocopter (Aerosp.) AS365N2 Dauphin 2	6358		0090	0990	2 TU Arriel 1C2	4250	12 Pax		
☐ ZJ164	Eurocopter (Aerosp.) AS365N2 Dauphin 2	6406	G-BTLC	0091	0491	2 TU Arriel 1C2	4250	12 Pax		opf Royal Navy-Flag Officer Sea Trng
☐ ZJ165	Eurocopter (Aerosp.) AS365N2 Dauphin 2	6372	G-NTOO	0090	1090	2 TU Arriel 1C2	4250	12 Pax		opf Royal Navy-Flag Officer Sea Trng
☐ G-BHGK	Sikorsky S-76A+	760049		0080	1186	2 TU Arriel 1S	4899	12 Pax		cvtd S-76A
☐ G-BMAL	Sikorsky S-76A+	760120		0080	1184	2 TU Arriel 1S	4899	12 Pax		cvtd S-76A
☐ G-BOND	Sikorsky S-76A+	760036	N4931Y	0080	1185	2 TU Arriel 1S	4899	12 Pax		cvtd S-76A
☐ G-SSSC	Sikorsky S-76C	760408		0093	1093	2 TU Arriel 1S1	5307	12 Pax		
☐ G-SSSD	Sikorsky S-76C	760415		0093	1093	2 TU Arriel 1S1	5307	12 Pax		
☐ G-SSSE	Sikorsky S-76C	760416		0093	1193	2 TU Arriel 1S1	5307	12 Pax		
☐ G-PUMA	Eurocopter (Aerosp.) AS332L Super Puma	2038	F-WMHB*	0083	0185	2 TU Makila 1A	8600	18 Pax		
☐ G-PUMB	Eurocopter (Aerosp.) AS332L Super Puma	2075		0083	0185	2 TU Makila 1A	8600	18 Pax		
☐ G-PUMD	Eurocopter (Aerosp.) AS332L Super Puma	2077	F-WXFD*	0083	0485	2 TU Makila 1A	8600	18 Pax		
☐ G-PUME	Eurocopter (Aerosp.) AS332L Super Puma	2091		0083	1184	2 TU Makila 1A	8600	18 Pax		
☐ G-PUMG	Eurocopter (Aerosp.) AS332L Super Puma	2018	F-ODOS	0082	0485	2 TU Makila 1A	8600	18 Pax		
☐ G-PUMH	Eurocopter (Aerosp.) AS332L Super Puma	2101		0083	0485	2 TU Makila 1A	8600	18 Pax		
☐ G-PUMI	Eurocopter (Aerosp.) AS332L Super Puma	2170		0085	0186	2 TU Makila 1A	8600	18 Pax		
☐ G-PUMM	Eurocopter (Aerosp.) AS332L2 S.Puma II	2477		0098	0798	2 TU Makila 1A2	9150	18 Pax		
☐ G-PUMO	Eurocopter (Aerosp.) AS332L2 S.Puma II	2467		0098	0998	2 TU Makila 1A2	9150	18 Pax		

BOURNEMOUTH HELICOPTERS, Ltd — Bournemouth

Hangar 600, Bournemouth Int'l Airport, Christchurch, Dorset BH23 6SE, Great Britain ☎ (1202) 59 08 00 Tx: none Fax: (1202) 59 08 00 SITA: n/a
F: 1994 ⁂ n/a Head: Gary Ellson Net: n/a Aircraft below MTOW 1361kg: Robinson R22

registration	type of aircraft	cn/fn	ex/ex*	mfd	del	powered by	mtow kg	configuration	selcal	name/fln/specialities/remarks
☐ G-SPYI	Bell 206B JetRanger III	3689	G-BVRC	0082		1 AN 250-C20J	1451			lsf pvt
☐ G-BAGL	Eurocopter (Aerosp.) SA341G Gazelle	1067		0073		1 TU Astazou IIIA	1800			lsf Triangle Computer Services Ltd

BRISTOW HELICOPTERS, Ltd = BHL (British Executive Air Services) (Associated with Air Logistics/Offshore Logistics Inc., USA) — Redhill & Aberdeen

BRISTOW HELICOPTERS LIMITED

Redhill Aerodrome, Redhill, Surrey RH1 5JZ, Great Britain ☎ (1737) 82 23 53 Tx: 21913 brstow g Fax: (1737) 82 26 94 SITA: n/a
F: 1953 ⁂ 2000 Head: Peter Buckley ICAO: BRISTOW Net: n/a Aircraft below MTOW 1361 kg: Robinson R22 & Slingsby T67C. Associated and subsidiary companies in Australia, Bermuda, Malaysia, Nigeria, Singapore, Trinidad & USA. Some business is done under the name BEAS-BRITISH EXECUTIVE AIR SERVICES, Ltd (affiliated company, same headquarters & fleet).

registration	type of aircraft	cn/fn	ex/ex*	mfd	del	powered by	mtow kg	configuration	selcal	name/fln/specialities/remarks
☐ G-AVII	Agusta-Bell 206B JetRanger	8011		0067	0367	1 AN 250-C20	1451			cvtd 206A
☐ G-BAUN	Bell 206B JetRanger	464	5N-BAY	0068	1292	1 AN 250-C20	1451			cvtd 206A
☐ G-REEM	Eurocopter (Aerosp.) AS355F1 Tw.Squirrel	5175	G-EMAN	0082		2 AN 250-C20F	2400			opf pvt
☐ G-BHBF	Sikorsky S-76A+	760022	N4247S	0079	1179	2 TU Arriel 1S	4899			Spirit of Paris / cvtd S-76A
☐ G-BIBG	Sikorsky S-76A+	760083		0080	1091	2 TU Arriel 1S	4899			Loch Seaforth / cvtd S-76A
☐ G-BIEJ	Sikorsky S-76A+	760097		0080	1080	2 TU Arriel 1S	4899			Glenlossie / cvtd S-76A
☐ G-BISZ	Sikorsky S-76A+	760156		0081	0381	2 TU Arriel 1S	4899			cvtd S-76A
☐ G-BITR	Sikorsky S-76A+	760157	PT-HRW	0081	1085	2 TU Arriel 1S	4899			Glenlassaugh / cvtd S-76A
☐ G-BJFL	Sikorsky S-76A+	760056	N106BH	0080	0981	2 TU Arriel 1S	4899			Glen Moray / cvtd S-76A
☐ G-BJGX	Sikorsky S-76A+	760026	N103BH	0079	0981	2 TU Arriel 1S	4899			Glen Elgin / cvtd S-76A
☐ G-BJVX	Sikorsky S-76A+	760100	N108BH	0080	0182	2 TU Arriel 1S	4899			cvtd S-76A
☐ G-BVKR	Sikorsky S-76A+	760115	734	0080	0394	2 TU Arriel 1S	4899			cvtd S-76A
☐ G-BXZS	Sikorsky S-76A+	760287	N190AL	0086	0998	2 TU Arriel 1S	4899			cvtd S-76A
☐ G-DRNT	Sikorsky S-76A+	760201	N93WW	0081	0598	2 TU Arriel 1S	4899			cvtd S-76A
☐ G-BALZ	Bell 212	30542	EC-GCR	0072	1095	2 PWC PT6T-3 TwinPac	5080			based Bangladesh
☐ G-BCMC	Bell 212	30639	EC-GCS	0074	1095	2 PWC PT6T-3 TwinPac	5080			lst APSA as HK-4103X
☐ G-BFER	Bell 212	30835	N18099	0077	1177	2 PWC PT6T-3 TwinPac	5080			
☐ G-BGLJ	Bell 212	30548	EC-295	0072	0396	2 PWC PT6T-3 TwinPac	5080			
☐ G-BIXV	Bell 212	30870	N16931	0078	0581	2 PWC PT6T-3 TwinPac	5080			
☐ G-BWLE	Bell 212	31225	N4247M	0082	0196	2 PWC PT6T-3B TwinPac	5080			
☐ G-BXIK	Bell 212	31191	SE-HVB	0081	0697	2 PWC PT6T-3B TwinPac	5080			lst Deccan Aviation as VT-DAM
☐ ZH814	Bell 212	30512	G-BGMH	0071		2 PWC PT6T-3 TwinPac	5080			opf Army Air Corps, No 7 Flt,bsd Brunei
☐ ZH815	Bell 212	30668	G-BGCZ	0074		2 PWC PT6T-3 TwinPac	5080			opf Army Air Corps, No 7 Flt,bsd Brunei
☐ ZH816	Bell 212	30549	G-BGMC	0072		2 PWC PT6T-3 TwinPac	5080			opf Army Air Corps, No 7 Flt,bsd Brunei
☐ G-BKFN	Bell 214ST	28109	LZ-CAW	0082	1195	2 GE CT7-2A	7938			
☐ G-BKFP	Bell 214ST	28110		0082	0882	2 GE CT7-2A	7938			
☐ G-BLPM	Eurocopter (Aerosp.) AS332L Tiger	2122	LN-ONB	0084		2 TU Makila 1A	8600			
☐ G-BLRY	Eurocopter (Aerosp.) AS332L Tiger	2111	LN-ONA	0084		2 TU Makila 1A	8600			lst Norsk Helikopter as LN-ONA
☐ G-BLXR	Eurocopter (Aerosp.) AS332L Tiger	2154		0085	0585	2 TU Makila 1A	8600			Cromarty
☐ G-BLXS	Eurocopter (Aerosp.) AS332L Tiger	2157		0085	0585	2 TU Makila 1A	8600			lst Norsk Helikopter as LN-OND
☐ G-BMCW	Eurocopter (Aerosp.) AS332L Tiger	2161	F-WYMG*	0085	1085	2 TU Makila 1A	8600			based China
☐ G-BMCX	Eurocopter (Aerosp.) AS332L Tiger	2164		0085	1085	2 TU Makila 1A	8600			Lossiemouth
☐ G-BRXU	Eurocopter (Aerosp.) AS332L Tiger	2092	VH-BHV	0084	0390	2 TU Makila 1A	8600			
☐ G-BTCT	Eurocopter (Aerosp.) AS332L Tiger	2129	HP-1012	0084	0191	2 TU Makila 1A	8600			
☐ G-BWMG	Eurocopter (Aerosp.) AS332L Tiger	2046	OY-HMG	0083	0296	2 TU Makila 1A	8600			Catterline
☐ G-BWWI	Eurocopter (Aerosp.) AS332L Tiger	2040	OY-HMF	0083	0996	2 TU Makila 1A	8600			Johnshaven
☐ G-BWZX	Eurocopter (Aerosp.) AS332L Tiger	2120	F-WQDX	0084	1296	2 TU Makila 1A	8600			
☐ G-TIGB	Eurocopter (Aerosp.) AS332L Tiger	2023	G-BJXC	0082	0382	2 TU Makila 1A	8600			City of Aberdeen
☐ G-TIGC	Eurocopter (Aerosp.) AS332L Tiger	2024	G-BJYH	0082	0482	2 TU Makila 1A	8600			Royal Burgh of Montrose / based Vietnam
☐ G-TIGE	Eurocopter (Aerosp.) AS332L Tiger	2028	G-BJYT	0082	0482	2 TU Makila 1A	8600			City of Dundee
☐ G-TIGF	Eurocopter (Aerosp.) AS332L Tiger	2030	F-WKQJ*	0082	0482	2 TU Makila 1A	8600			Peterhead
☐ G-TIGG	Eurocopter (Aerosp.) AS332L Tiger	2032	F-WXFT*	0082	0482	2 TU Makila 1A	8600			Mac Duff
☐ G-TIGI	Eurocopter (Aerosp.) AS332L Tiger	2036	F-WTNP*	0082	0482	2 TU Makila 1A	8600			Fraserburgh / based China
☐ G-TIGJ	Eurocopter (Aerosp.) AS332L Tiger	2042	VH-BHT	0082	0698	2 TU Makila 1A	8600			
☐ G-TIGL	Eurocopter (Aerosp.) AS332L Tiger	2050		0082	0482	2 TU Makila 1A	8600			Portsoy
☐ G-TIGM	Eurocopter (Aerosp.) AS332L Tiger	2045		0082	0482	2 TU Makila 1A	8600			Banff
☐ G-TIGO	Eurocopter (Aerosp.) AS332L Tiger	2061	F-WMHH*	0083	0283	2 TU Makila 1A	8600			Royal Burgh of Arbroath
☐ G-TIGP	Eurocopter (Aerosp.) AS332L Tiger	2064		0083	0283	2 TU Makila 1A	8600			Carnoustie / based China
☐ G-TIGR	Eurocopter (Aerosp.) AS332L Tiger	2071	F-WTNW*	0083	0383	2 TU Makila 1A	8600			Stoneheaven / based China
☐ G-TIGS	Eurocopter (Aerosp.) AS332L Tiger	2086		0083	0583	2 TU Makila 1A	8600			Findochty
☐ G-TIGT	Eurocopter (Aerosp.) AS332L Tiger	2078		0083	0583	2 TU Makila 1A	8600			Portknockie
☐ G-TIGU	Eurocopter (Aerosp.) AS332L Tiger	2096		0083	0184	2 TU Makila 1A	8600			Branderburgh
☐ G-TIGV	Eurocopter (Aerosp.) AS332L Tiger	2099	LN-ONC	0083	0191	2 TU Makila 1A	8600			Burghead
☐ G-TIGW	Eurocopter (Aerosp.) AS332L Tiger	2059		0083	0284	2 TU Makila 1A	8600			Nairn
☐ G-BBHL	Sikorsky S-61N	61712	N4032S	0073	1173	2 GE CT58-140-1	9299			Glamis / opf HM Coastguard
☐ G-BBHM	Sikorsky S-61N	61713	8Q-HUM	0073	0593	2 GE CT58-140-2	9299			Braemer
☐ G-BBVA	Sikorsky S-61N	61718		0074	0274	2 GE CT58-140-2	9299			Vega
☐ G-BCLC	Sikorsky S-61N	61737		0074	0175	2 GE CT58-140-2	9299			Craigievar / HM Coastguard cs
☐ G-BCLD	Sikorsky S-61N	61739		0074	0275	2 GE CT58-140-2	9299			Slains / based Falkland Islands
☐ G-BDIJ	Sikorsky S-61N	61751	9M-AYF	0075	0684	2 GE CT58-140-2	9299			Crathes / HM Coastguard cs
☐ G-BDOC	Sikorsky S-61N	61765		0076	0376	2 GE CT58-140-2	9299			Tolquhoun / HM Coastguard cs

☐ G-BFMY	Sikorsky S-61N	61745	N4040S	0075	0378	2 GE CT58-140-2	9299			Diamond / based Falkland Islands
☐ G-BFRI	Sikorsky S-61N	61809		0078	0378	2 GE CT58-140-2	9299			Braerich / based Falkland Islands
☐ G-BGWJ	Sikorsky S-61N	61819		0079		2 GE CT58-140-2	9299			Monadh Mor
☐ G-BGWK	Sikorsky S-61N	61820	N1346C	0079		2 GE CT58-140-2	9299			
☐ G-BHOF	Sikorsky S-61N	61824	LN-ONK	0080	0695	2 GE CT58-140-2	9299			
☐ G-BHOG	Sikorsky S-61N	61825		0080	0380	2 GE CT58-140-2	9299			lst Aeroleo as PT-YEK
☐ G-BHOH	Sikorsky S-61N	61827		0080	0480	2 GE CT58-140-2	9299			Ben Avon
☐ G-BIMU	Sikorsky S-61N	61752	N8511Z	0075	0590	2 GE CT58-140-2	9299			HM Coastguard cs
☐ G-BPWB	Sikorsky S-61N	61822	EI-BHO	0079	0597	2 GE CT58-140-2	9299			Druminnor / HM Coastguard cs
☐ G-BXSN	Sikorsky S-61N	61761	EI-BLY	0077	0298	2 GE CT58-140-1	9299			

BRITANNIA AIRWAYS, Ltd = BY / BAL (Member of Thomson Travel Group / formerly Euravia (London), Ltd) **London-Luton**

Luton Airport, Luton, Bedfordshire LU2 9ND, Great Britain ☎ (1582) 42 41 55 Tx: 82239 ltnby g Fax: (1582) 45 85 94 SITA: n/a
F: 1961 ⁂ 3200 Head: Roger Burnell IATA: 754 ICAO: BRITANNIA Net: n/a

☐ EI-TLE	Airbus Industrie A320-231	429	D-AORX	0093	0599	2 IAE V2500-A1	77000	Y180	GJ-AC	lsf / opb TLA -1099
☐ EI-TLF	Airbus Industrie A320-231	476	F-WWBR*	0094	0599	2 IAE V2500-A1	75500	Y180	CR-DK	lsf / opb TLA -1099
☐ EI-TLO	Airbus Industrie A320-232	758	F-WWDC*	0097	0599	2 IAE V2527-A5	77000	Y180	CR-EH	lsf / opb TLA -1099
☐ G-	Boeing 737-804					2 CFMI CFM56-7B26	78245	Y189		oo-delivery 0300
☐ G-	Boeing 737-804					2 CFMI CFM56-7B26	78245	Y189		to be lsf ILFC 0300
☐ G-	Boeing 737-804					2 CFMI CFM56-7B26	78245	Y189		to be lsf ILFC 0400
☐ G-	Boeing 737-804					2 CFMI CFM56-7B26	78245	Y189		to be lsf ILFC 0400
☐ G-	Boeing 737-804					2 CFMI CFM56-7B26	78245	Y189		oo-delivery 0500
☐ OY-SEA	Boeing 737-8Q8	28213 / 50	N3521N*	0098	0698	2 CFMI CFM56-7B26	78245	Y189	HK-BL	lsf / opb SEA in Britannia-colors
☐ G-BXOL	Boeing 757-23A (ET)	24528 / 250	SE-DSM	0089	1197	2 RR RB211-535E4	112699	Y235	MS-GP	lsf TOMB
☐ G-BYAD	Boeing 757-204 (ET)	26963 / 450		0092	0592	2 RR RB211-535E4	112699	Y235	BQ-RS	
☐ G-BYAE	Boeing 757-204 (ET)	26964 / 452		0092	0592	2 RR RB211-535E4	112699	Y235	BR-AJ	
☐ G-BYAF	Boeing 757-204 (ET)	26266 / 514		0092	0193	2 RR RB211-535E4	112699	Y235	AC-BF	lsf ILFC
☐ G-BYAG	Boeing 757-204	26965 / 517		0093	0193	2 RR RB211-535E4	103699	Y235	AD-EH	
☐ G-BYAH	Boeing 757-204	26966 / 520		0093	0293	2 RR RB211-535E4	103699	Y235	AE-GH	lsf Thomson Int'l Finance AG
☐ G-BYAI	Boeing 757-204	26967 / 522		0093	0393	2 RR RB211-535E4	103699	Y235	HL-BM	
☐ G-BYAJ	Boeing 757-204 (ET)	25623 / 528		0093	0393	2 RR RB211-535E4	112699	Y235	DF-AB	lsf ILFC
☐ G-BYAK	Boeing 757-204	26267 / 538		0093	0493	2 RR RB211-535E4	103699	Y235	DF-KM	lsf ILFC
☐ G-BYAL	Boeing 757-204	25626 / 549		0093	0593	2 RR RB211-535E4	103699	Y235	DG-BC	lsf ILFC
☐ G-BYAM	Boeing 757-2T7	23895 / 132	G-DRJC	0087	0393	2 RR RB211-535E4	103699	Y235	FH-CK	lsf Nimbus Aviation Ltd
☐ G-BYAN	Boeing 757-204	27219 / 596		0094	0194	2 RR RB211-535E4	103699	Y235	EH-FG	lsf ILFC
☐ G-BYAO	Boeing 757-204	27235 / 598		0094	0294	2 RR RB211-535E4	103699	Y235	EL-GJ	lsf ITID Leasing AG
☐ G-BYAP	Boeing 757-204	27236 / 600		0094	0294	2 RR RB211-535E4	103699	Y235	EM-AD	
☐ G-BYAR	Boeing 757-204	27237 / 602		0094	0394	2 RR RB211-535E4	103699	Y235	EM-AG	
☐ G-BYAS	Boeing 757-204	27238 / 604		0094	0394	2 RR RB211-535E4	103699	Y235	EM-DH	
☐ G-BYAT	Boeing 757-204	27208 / 606		0094	0394	2 RR RB211-535E4	103699	Y235	EM-DL	lsf ILFC
☐ G-BYAU	Boeing 757-204	27220 / 618		0094	0594	2 RR RB211-535E4	103699	Y235	FG-BE	lsf ILFC
☐ G-BYAW	Boeing 757-204	27234 / 663		0095	0495	2 RR RB211-535E4	103699	Y235	CL-GJ	Eric Morecambe, O.B.E.
☐ G-BYAX	Boeing 757-204	28834 / 850		0299	0299	2 RR RB211-535E4	103699	Y235		lsf ILFC
☐ G-BYAY	Boeing 757-204	28836				2 RR RB211-535E4	103699	Y235		to be lsf ILFC 0499
☐ SE-DUN	Boeing 757-225	22612 / 114	G-OOOM	0086	0798	2 RR RB211-535E4	109317	Y223	FH-MQ	lsf BLX
☐ G-BNYS	Boeing 767-204 (ER)	24013 / 210	N6009F*	0088	0388	2 GE CF6-80A2	158699	Y274	CH-EM	
☐ G-BOPB	Boeing 767-204 (ER)	24239 / 243	N6009F*	0088	1188	2 GE CF6-80A2	158699	Y274	CJ-BF	Capitan Sir Ross Smith
☐ G-BRIF	Boeing 767-204 (ER)	24736 / 296		0090	0390	2 GE CF6-80A2	158699	Y274	EG-KL	Lord Horatio Nelson
☐ G-BRIG	Boeing 767-204 (ER)	24757 / 299		0090	0490	2 GE CF6-80A2	158699	Y274	EG-KM	Eglantyne Jebb
☐ G-BYAA	Boeing 767-204 (ER)	25058 / 362	PH-AHM	0091	0491	2 GE CF6-80C2	158699	Y274	CD-JM	Sir Matt Busby, C.B.E.
☐ G-BYAB	Boeing 767-204 (ER)	25139 / 373		0091	0691	2 GE CF6-80C2	158699	Y274	CD-KM	Brian Johnston, C.B.E. MC
☐ G-BXOP	Boeing 767-3S1 (ER)	25221 / 384	N770TA	0891	0298	2 GE CF6-80C2B6F	172365	Y328	AQ-KR	lsf TAI / sub-lst BLX
☐ G-OBYA	Boeing 767-304 (ER)	28039 / 610	D-AGYA	0096	0596	2 GE CF6-80C2B7F	186880	Y328	JR-AC	lsf MCC Leasing (No. 18) Ltd
☐ G-OBYB	Boeing 767-304 (ER)	28040 / 613		0096	0596	2 GE CF6-80C2B7F	186880	Y328	JR-AD	Bobby Moore, O.B.E.
☐ G-OBYC	Boeing 767-304 (ER)	28041 / 614		0096	0596	2 GE CF6-80C2B7F	186880	Y328	JR-AE	lst DBY as D-AGYC
☐ G-OBYD	Boeing 767-304 (ER)	28042 / 649		0097	0397	2 GE CF6-80C2B7F	186880	Y328	JR-AF	lsf ALE-Four Ltd
☐ G-OBYE	Boeing 767-304 (ER)	28979 / 691		0298	0298	2 GE CF6-80C2B7F	186880	Y328	LM-RS	lst DBY as D-AGYE
☐ G-OBYF	Boeing 767-304 (ER)	28208 / 705		0098	0698	2 PW PW4060	186880	Y328	BG-KP	lsf ILFC / sub-lst DBY as D-AGYF
☐ G-OBYG	Boeing 767-304 (ER)	29137 / 733		1298	0199	2 GE CF6-80C2B7F	186880	Y328	JR-EF	lsf ILFC
☐ G-OBYH	Boeing 767-304 (ER)	28883 / 737		0099	0299	2 GE CF6-80C2B7F	186880	Y328		lsf ILFC / sub-lst DBY as D-AGYH

BRITISH AEROSPACE ASSET MANAGEMENT – Jets = (BAMJ) (Division of British Aerospace / formerly Asset Management Organisation) **Hatfield**

1 Bishop Square, St. Albans Road West, Hatfield, Hertfordshire AL10 9NE, Great Britain ☎ (1707) 27 17 77 Tx: none Fax: (1707) 25 55 55 SITA: n/a
F: 1993 ⁂ 60 Head: David Singleton Net: http://www.bae.co.uk New & used aircraft management, leasing, sales, financing & remarketing company.
Owner / lessor of following (main) aircraft types: BAe 146. Aircraft leased from BAe Asset Management–Jets are listed and mentioned as lsf BAMJ under the leasing carriers.

BRITISH AEROSPACE Corporate Flight Operations = BAE (Division of British Aerospace, Plc) **Warton**

BAe Military Aircraft, Warton Aerodrome, Preston, Lancashire PR4 1AX, Great Britain ☎ (1772) 85 37 99 Tx: n/a Fax: (1772) 85 52 40 SITA: n/a
F: n/a ⁂ n/a Head: C.J. Yeo Net: n/a Non-commercial flight operations department within BAe conducting corporate flights exclusively for BAe requirements.

☐ G-CORP	BAe ATP	2037	G-BTNK	0091	0398	2 PWC PW126A	22930	Y64		
☐ G-BLRA	BAe 146-100	E1017	N117TR	0084	1097	4 LY ALF502R-5	38101	Y76		

BRITISH AIRWAYS, Plc = BA / BAW (Member of Oneworld Alliance) **London-Heathrow / -Gatwick & Manchester**

Waterside PO Box 365, Harmondsworth UB7 0GB, Great Britain ☎ (181) 759 55 11 Tx: 8813983 bawysc g Fax: (181) 562 99 30 SITA: LHRPRBA
F: 1974 ⁂ 53000 Head: Robert Ayling IATA: 125 ICAO: SPEEDBIRD & SHUTTLE Net: http://www.britishairways.com
Beside aircraft listed, additional aircraft are operated on a franchise agreement with BRITISH AIRWAYS (in full such colors & both titles & using BA-flight numbers by: BRITISH REGIONAL AIRLINES (G-, with BAe J41/ATP & Embraer RJ145), BRITISH MEDITERRANEAN (G-, with A320), BRYMON AIRWAYS (G-, with DHC-8-300), CITYFLYER EXPRESS (G-, with ATR42-300, ATR72-200 & Avro RJ100), COMAIR (ZS-, with Boeing 737-200 & Boeing 727-200), GBAIRWAYS (G-, with Boeing 737-300/-400), LOGANAIR (G-, with BN-2B, DHC-6-300 & Shorts 360), MAERSK AIR (G- with BAe J41, Boeing 737-500 & Canadair RJ200), SUN-AIR (OY-, with BAe J31/J41 & ATP). For details – see under each company. For all-cargo services Airbus A300B4, Boeing 747-400F & McDonnell Douglas DC-8F-54 are lsf/opb CHANNEL EXPRESS (G-), ATLAS AIR (N) & AFRICAN INT'L (3D-), when required.
Regional hubs from Gatwick & Manchester are operated by internal subsidiaries BRITISH AIRWAYS (European Operations at Gatwick) Ltd & BRITISH AIRWAYS REGIONAL, Ltd. Flights to Taiwan are operated under the name BRITISH ASIA AIRWAYS (with such titles & logo). All same headquarters. Aircraft used by them are marked as such.

☐ G-BGDA	Boeing 737-236 (A)	21790 / 599	N1285E*	0079	1281	2 PW JT8D-15A	52750	CY112		lsf BOUL/opb Euro LGW/Ndebele Martha-cs
☐ G-BGDE	Boeing 737-236 (A)	21794 / 643		0080	0380	2 PW JT8D-15A	52750	CY112		lsf BOUL/opb Euro LGW/Sterntaler-cs
☐ G-BGDF	Boeing 737-236 (A)	21795 / 645		0080	0380	2 PW JT8D-15A	52750	CY112		lsfBOUL/opbEuroLGW/DelftblueDaybreak-cs
☐ G-BGDJ	Boeing 737-236 (A)	21799 / 660		0080	0580	2 PW JT8D-15A	50000	CY108		lsf BOUL / opb Regional / Nami Tsuru-cs
☐ G-BGDL	Boeing 737-236 (A)	21801 / 669		0080	0680	2 PW JT8D-15A	52750	CY112		lsf BOUL/opb Euro LGW/BenyhoneTartan-cs
☐ G-BGDO	Boeing 737-236 (A)	21803 / 677		0080	0780	2 PW JT8D-15A	50000	CY108		lsf POLA/opb Regional/Whale Rider-cs
☐ G-BGDR	Boeing 737-236 (A)	21805 / 697		0080	0980	2 PW JT8D-15A	52750	CY114		lsf BOUL / opb Euro LGW / Colum-cs
☐ G-BGDS	Boeing 737-236 (A)	21806 / 699		0080	0980	2 PW JT8D-15A	54204	CY112		lsf BOUL
☐ G-BGDT	Boeing 737-236 (A)	21807 / 710		0080	1180	2 PW JT8D-15A	48000	CY108		lsf PEGA/opb Regional/Animals&Trees-cs
☐ G-BGJE	Boeing 737-236 (A)	22026 / 644		0080	0380	2 PW JT8D-15A	52750	CY114		lsf TRIT / opb Euro LGW / Rendezvous-cs
☐ G-BKYA	Boeing 737-236 (A)	23159 / 1047		0084	0984	2 PW JT8D-15A	48000	CY108		Ariel / opb Regional
☐ G-BKYB	Boeing 737-236 (A)	23160 / 1053		0084	0984	2 PW JT8D-15A	50000	CY108		opb Regional / Blue Poole-colors
☐ G-BKYE	Boeing 737-236 (A)	23163 / 1058		0084	1184	2 PW JT8D-15A	48000	CY108		opb Regional / Water Dreaming-colors
☐ G-BKYH	Boeing 737-236 (A)	23166 / 1067		0084	1284	2 PW JT8D-15A	48000	CY108		Hotspur / opb Regional
☐ G-BKYI	Boeing 737-236 (A)	23167 / 1074		0084	0185	2 PW JT8D-15A	50000	CY108		River Waveney / opb Regional
☐ G-BKYK	Boeing 737-236 (A)	23169 / 1081		0085	0285	2 PW JT8D-15A	50000	CY108		River Foyle / opb Reg. / for PEGA 0898
☐ G-BKYL	Boeing 737-236 (A)	23170 / 1086		0085	0285	2 PW JT8D-15A	52750	CY108		Titania / opb Regional / for PEGA 0998
☐ G-BKYM	Boeing 737-236 (A)	23171 / 1088		0085	0385	2 PW JT8D-15A	48000	CY108		Moonshine / opb Regional/for PEGA 0798
☐ G-BKYN	Boeing 737-236 (A)	23172 / 1091		0085	0385	2 PW JT8D-15A	50000	CY108		Prince Hal / opb Regional
☐ G-BKYO	Boeing 737-236 (A)	23225 / 1102		0085	0485	2 PW JT8D-15A	50000	CY108		Oberon / opb Regional / for PEGA 1098
☐ G-BKYP	Boeing 737-236 (A)	23226 / 1105		0085	0485	2 PW JT8D-15A	50000	CY108		opb Regional / Nami Tsuru-colors
☐ G-OAMS	Boeing 737-37Q	28548 / 2961		0097	1297	2 CFMI CFM56-3B2	54672	CY126	CJ-GS	lsf Novel/opb Regional/Rendezvous-cs
☐ G-ODUS	Boeing 737-36Q	28659 / 2880	D-ADBX	0097	0398	2 CFMI CFM56-3B2	54672	CY126	CS-BR	lsf BOUL / opb Regional / Nami Tsuru-cs
☐ G-OFRA	Boeing 737-36Q	29327 / 3023		0098	0598	2 CFMI CFM56-3B2	54672	CY126	DE-AP	lsf BOUL / opb Regional / Bauhaus-cs
☐ G-OHAJ	Boeing 737-36Q	29141 / 3035		0098	0698	2 CFMI CFM56-3B2	54672	CY126		lsfBOUL/opbRegional/DelftblueDaybreak-cs
☐ G-OMUC	Boeing 737-36Q	29405 / 3047		0698	0698	2 CFMI CFM56-3B2	54672	CY126		lsf BOUL / opb Regional / Colum-cs
☐ G-XBHX	Boeing 737-36N	28572 / 3031		0098	0598	2 CFMI CFM56-3B2	54672	CY126	FR-BM	lsf GECA/opb Regional / Grand Union-cs
☐ G-XMAN	Boeing 737-36N	28573 / 3041		0098	0698	2 CFMI CFM56-3B2	54672	CY126	MR-CP	lsfGECA/opbRegional/Golden Khokhloma-cs
☐ G-BSNV	Boeing 737-4Q8	25168 / 2210		0092	1192	2 CFMI CFM56-3C1	62800	CY147	AS-HJ	lsf ILFC / opb Euro LGW
☐ G-BSNW	Boeing 737-4Q8	25169 / 2237		0092	1192	2 CFMI CFM56-3C1	62800	CY147	AS-HK	lsf ILFC / opb Euro LGW
☐ G-BUHJ	Boeing 737-4Q8	25164 / 2447		0093	0393	2 CFMI CFM56-3C1	62800	CY147	FH-AE	lsf ILFC / opb Euro LGW
☐ G-BUHK	Boeing 737-4Q8	26289 / 2486		0093	0693	2 CFMI CFM56-3C1	62800	CY147	FH-AJ	lsf ILFC / opb Euro LGW
☐ G-BVNM	Boeing 737-4S3	24163 / 1700	G-BPKA	0089	0292	2 CFMI CFM56-3C1	62800	CY147	CJ-GQ	lsfLanieAc/EuroLGW/Pause to Remember-cs
☐ G-BVNN	Boeing 737-4S3	24164 / 1702	G-BPKB	0089	1192	2 CFMI CFM56-3C1	62800	CY147	CJ-GR	lsf Lanie Aircraft / opb Euro LGW
☐ G-BVNO	Boeing 737-4S3	24167 / 1736	G-BPKE	0089	1192	2 CFMI CFM56-3C1	62800	CY150	CJ-GS	lsfLanieAc./opbEu.LGW/BenyhoneTartan-cs
☐ G-DOCA	Boeing 737-436	25267 / 2131		0091	1091	2 CFMI CFM56-3C1	62820	CY141		River Ballinderry / opb Regional MAN
☐ G-DOCB	Boeing 737-436	25304 / 2144		0091	1091	2 CFMI CFM56-3C1	62820	CY141		Wings-colors

165 registration type of aircraft cn/fn ex/ex* mfd del powered by mtow kg configuration selcal name/fln/specialitites/remarks

registration	type of aircraft	cn/fn	ex/ex*	mfd	del	powered by	mtow kg	configuration	selcal	name/fln/specialitites/remarks
☐ G-DOCC	Boeing 737-436	25305 / 2147		0091	1091	2 CFMI CFM56-3C1	62820	CY141		Blue Poole-colors
☐ G-DOCD	Boeing 737-436	25349 / 2156		0091	1191	2 CFMI CFM56-3C1	62820	CY141		Animals & Trees-colors
☐ G-DOCE	Boeing 737-436	25350 / 2167		0091	1191	2 CFMI CFM56-3C1	62820	CY141		Blomsterang-colors
☐ G-DOCF	Boeing 737-436	25407 / 2178		0091	1291	2 CFMI CFM56-3C1	62820	CY141		opb Euro LGW / Koguty Lowickie-colors
☐ G-DOCG	Boeing 737-436	25408 / 2183		0091	1291	2 CFMI CFM56-3C1	62820	CY141		Chelsea Rose-colors
☐ G-DOCH	Boeing 737-436	25428 / 2185		0091	1291	2 CFMI CFM56-3C1	62820	CY141		opb Euro LGW / Grand Union-colors
☐ G-DOCI	Boeing 737-436	25839 / 2188		0092	0192	2 CFMI CFM56-3C1	62820	CY141		River Carron
☐ G-DOCJ	Boeing 737-436	25840 / 2197		0092	0192	2 CFMI CFM56-3C1	62820	CY141		BenyhoneTartan/Mountain of the Birds-cs
☐ G-DOCK	Boeing 737-436	25841 / 2222		0092	0292	2 CFMI CFM56-3C1	62820	CY141		River Lochay
☐ G-DOCL	Boeing 737-436	25842 / 2228		0092	0392	2 CFMI CFM56-3C1	62820	CY147		opb Euro LGW / Ndebele Martha-colors
☐ G-DOCM	Boeing 737-436	25843 / 2244		0092	0392	2 CFMI CFM56-3C1	62820	CY147		opb Euro LGW / Rendezvous-colors
☐ G-DOCN	Boeing 737-436	25848 / 2379		0092	1092	2 CFMI CFM56-3C1	62820	CY147		River Ottery / opb Euro LGW
☐ G-DOCO	Boeing 737-436	25849 / 2381		0092	1092	2 CFMI CFM56-3C1	62820	CY147		River Parrett / opb Euro LGW
☐ G-DOCP	Boeing 737-436	25850 / 2386		0092	1192	2 CFMI CFM56-3C1	62820	CY147		River Swift / opb Euro LGW
☐ G-DOCR	Boeing 737-436	25851 / 2387		0092	1192	2 CFMI CFM56-3C1	62820	CY147		River Tavy / opb Euro LGW
☐ G-DOCS	Boeing 737-436	25852 / 2390		0092	1292	2 CFMI CFM56-3C1	62820	CY147		River Teifi / opb Euro LGW
☐ G-DOCT	Boeing 737-436	25853 / 2409		0092	1292	2 CFMI CFM56-3C1	62820	CY141		Crossing Borders-colors
☐ G-DOCU	Boeing 737-436	25854 / 2417		0092	0193	2 CFMI CFM56-3C1	62820	CY141		Ndebele Martha-colors
☐ G-DOCV	Boeing 737-436	25855 / 2420		0193	0193	2 CFMI CFM56-3C1	62820	CY141		BenyhoneTartan/Mountain of the Birds-cs
☐ G-DOCW	Boeing 737-436	25856 / 2422		0093	0293	2 CFMI CFM56-3C1	62820	CY141		Rendezvous-colors
☐ G-DOCX	Boeing 737-436	25857 / 2451		0093	0393	2 CFMI CFM56-3C1	62820	CY141		Colum-colors
☐ G-DOCY	Boeing 737-436	25844 / 2514	OO-LTQ	0093	0993	2 CFMI CFM56-3C1	62820	CY147		River Weaver
☐ G-DOCZ	Boeing 737-436	25858 / 2522	EC-FXJ	0093	1093	2 CFMI CFM56-3C1	62820	CY147		opb Euro LGW
☐ G-GBTA	Boeing 737-436	25859 / 2532	G-BVHA	0093	1193	2 CFMI CFM56-3C1	62820	CY141		opb Euro LGW / Youm-al-Suq-colors
☐ G-GBTB	Boeing 737-436	25860 / 2545	OO-LTS	0093	1293	2 CFMI CFM56-3C1	62820	CY147		opb Euro LGW
☐ G-EUPA	Airbus Industrie A319-131	1082				2 IAE V2522-A5	64000	CY126		oo-delivery 0999
☐ G-EUPB	Airbus Industrie A319-131	1115				2 IAE V2522-A5	64000	CY126		oo-delivery 1199
☐ G-EUPC	Airbus Industrie A319-131	1116				2 IAE V2522-A5	64000	CY126		oo-delivery 0100
☐ G-EUPD	Airbus Industrie A319-131					2 IAE V2522-A5	64000	CY126		oo-delivery 0200
☐ G-EUPE	Airbus Industrie A319-131					2 IAE V2522-A5	64000	CY126		oo-delivery 0300
☐ G-EUPF	Airbus Industrie A319-131					2 IAE V2522-A5	64000	CY126		oo-delivery 0400
☐ G-EUPG	Airbus Industrie A319-131					2 IAE V2522-A5	64000	CY126		oo-delivery 0500
☐ G-EUPH	Airbus Industrie A319-131					2 IAE V2522-A5	64000	CY126		oo-delivery 0600
☐ G-EUPI	Airbus Industrie A319-131					2 IAE V2522-A5	64000	CY126		oo-delivery 0700
☐ G-EUPJ	Airbus Industrie A319-131					2 IAE V2522-A5	64000	CY126		oo-delivery 0800
☐ G-EUPK	Airbus Industrie A319-131					2 IAE V2522-A5	64000	CY126		oo-delivery 0900
☐ G-EUPL	Airbus Industrie A319-131					2 IAE V2522-A5	64000	CY126		oo-delivery 1000
☐ G-EUPM	Airbus Industrie A319-131					2 IAE V2522-A5	64000	CY126		oo-delivery 1100
☐ G-EUPN	Airbus Industrie A319-131					2 IAE V2522-A5	64000	CY126		oo-delivery 1200
☐ G-EUPO	Airbus Industrie A319-131					2 IAE V2522-A5	64000	CY126		oo-delivery 0101
☐ G-EUPP	Airbus Industrie A319-131					2 IAE V2522-A5	64000	CY126		oo-delivery 0201
☐ G-EUPR	Airbus Industrie A319-131					2 IAE V2522-A5	64000	CY126		oo-delivery 0301
☐ G-EUPS	Airbus Industrie A319-131					2 IAE V2522-A5	64000	CY126		oo-delivery 0401
☐ G-EUPT	Airbus Industrie A319-131					2 IAE V2522-A5	64000	CY126		oo-delivery 0501
☐ G-EUPU	Airbus Industrie A319-131					2 IAE V2522-A5	64000	CY126		oo-delivery 0601
☐ G-EUPV	Airbus Industrie A319-131					2 IAE V2522-A5	64000	CY126		oo-delivery 0701
☐ G-EUPW	Airbus Industrie A319-131					2 IAE V2522-A5	64000	CY126		oo-delivery 0801
☐ G-EUPX	Airbus Industrie A319-131					2 IAE V2522-A5	64000	CY126		oo-delivery 0901
☐ G-EUPY	Airbus Industrie A319-131					2 IAE V2522-A5	64000	CY126		oo-delivery 1001
☐ G-EUPZ	Airbus Industrie A319-131					2 IAE V2522-A5	64000	CY126		oo-delivery 1101
☐ G-	Airbus Industrie A319-131					2 IAE V2522-A5	64000	CY126		oo-delivery 1201
☐ G-	Airbus Industrie A319-131					2 IAE V2522-A5	64000	CY126		oo-delivery 0002
☐ G-	Airbus Industrie A319-131					2 IAE V2522-A5	64000	CY126		oo-delivery 0002
☐ G-	Airbus Industrie A319-131					2 IAE V2522-A5	64000	CY126		oo-delivery 0002
☐ G-	Airbus Industrie A319-131					2 IAE V2522-A5	64000	CY126		oo-delivery 0002
☐ G-	Airbus Industrie A319-131					2 IAE V2522-A5	64000	CY126		oo-delivery 0002
☐ G-	Airbus Industrie A319-131					2 IAE V2522-A5	64000	CY126		oo-delivery 0002
☐ G-	Airbus Industrie A319-131					2 IAE V2522-A5	64000	CY126		oo-delivery 0002
☐ G-	Airbus Industrie A319-131					2 IAE V2522-A5	64000	CY126		oo-delivery 0002
☐ G-	Airbus Industrie A319-131					2 IAE V2522-A5	64000	CY126		oo-delivery 0003
☐ G-	Airbus Industrie A319-131					2 IAE V2522-A5	64000	CY126		oo-delivery 0003
☐ G-	Airbus Industrie A319-131					2 IAE V2522-A5	64000	CY126		oo-delivery 0003
☐ G-	Airbus Industrie A319-131					2 IAE V2522-A5	64000	CY126		oo-delivery 0003
☐ G-	Airbus Industrie A319-131					2 IAE V2522-A5	64000	CY126		oo-delivery 0003
☐ G-BUSB	Airbus Industrie A320-111	006	F-WWDD*	0087	0388	2 CFMI CFM56-5A1	68000	CY149	CH-BP	Koguty Lowickie-colors
☐ G-BUSC	Airbus Industrie A320-111	008	F-WWDE*	0088	0688	2 CFMI CFM56-5A1	68000	CY149	CH-DP	British Olympic-colors
☐ G-BUSD	Airbus Industrie A320-111	011	F-WWDF*	0088	0788	2 CFMI CFM56-5A1	68000	CY149	CH-EP	Isle of Mull
☐ G-BUSE	Airbus Industrie A320-111	017	F-WWDG*	0088	1288	2 CFMI CFM56-5A1	68000	CY149	CH-FP	BenyhoneTartan/Mountain of the Birds-cs
☐ G-BUSF	Airbus Industrie A320-111	018	F-WWDH*	0089	0589	2 CFMI CFM56-5A1	68000	CY149	EQ-DL	Isle of Man
☐ G-BUSG	Airbus Industrie A320-211	039	F-WWDM*	0089	0589	2 CFMI CFM56-5A1	73500	CY149	EQ-DM	Sterntaler-colors
☐ G-BUSH	Airbus Industrie A320-211	042	F-WWDT*	0089	0689	2 CFMI CFM56-5A1	73500	CY149	EQ-DP	Isle of Jura
☐ G-BUSI	Airbus Industrie A320-211	103	F-WWDB*	0090	0390	2 CFMI CFM56-5A1	73500	CY149	EQ-FG	Wings-colors
☐ G-BUSJ	Airbus Industrie A320-211	109	F-WWIC*	0090	0890	2 CFMI CFM56-5A1	73500	CY149	EQ-FH	Water Dreaming-colors
☐ G-BUSK	Airbus Industrie A320-211	120	F-WWIN*	0090	1090	2 CFMI CFM56-5A1	73500	CY149	EQ-FJ	Nami Tsuru-colors
☐ G-EUOA	Airbus Industrie A320-232					2 IAE V2527-A5	73500	CY156		oo-delivery 0002
☐ G-EUOB	Airbus Industrie A320-232					2 IAE V2527-A5	73500	CY156		oo-delivery 0002
☐ G-EUOC	Airbus Industrie A320-232					2 IAE V2527-A5	73500	CY156		oo-delivery 0002
☐ G-EUOD	Airbus Industrie A320-232					2 IAE V2527-A5	73500	CY156		oo-delivery 0002
☐ G-EUOE	Airbus Industrie A320-232					2 IAE V2527-A5	73500	CY156		oo-delivery 0002
☐ G-EUOF	Airbus Industrie A320-232					2 IAE V2527-A5	73500	CY156		oo-delivery 0002
☐ G-EUOG	Airbus Industrie A320-232					2 IAE V2527-A5	73500	CY156		oo-delivery 0002
☐ G-EUOH	Airbus Industrie A320-232					2 IAE V2527-A5	73500	CY156		oo-delivery 0002
☐ G-EUOI	Airbus Industrie A320-232					2 IAE V2527-A5	73500	CY156		oo-delivery 0002
☐ G-EUOJ	Airbus Industrie A320-232					2 IAE V2527-A5	73500	CY156		oo-delivery 0002
☐ G-EUOK	Airbus Industrie A320-232					2 IAE V2527-A5	73500	CY156		oo-delivery 0003
☐ G-EUOL	Airbus Industrie A320-232					2 IAE V2527-A5	73500	CY156		oo-delivery 0003
☐ G-EUOM	Airbus Industrie A320-232					2 IAE V2527-A5	73500	CY156		oo-delivery 0003
☐ G-EUON	Airbus Industrie A320-232					2 IAE V2527-A5	73500	CY156		oo-delivery 0003
☐ G-EUOO	Airbus Industrie A320-232					2 IAE V2527-A5	73500	CY156		oo-delivery 0003
☐ G-EUOP	Airbus Industrie A320-232					2 IAE V2527-A5	73500	CY156		oo-delivery 0003
☐ G-EUOR	Airbus Industrie A320-232					2 IAE V2527-A5	73500	CY156		oo-delivery 0003
☐ G-EUOS	Airbus Industrie A320-232					2 IAE V2527-A5	73500	CY156		oo-delivery 0003
☐ G-EUOT	Airbus Industrie A320-232					2 IAE V2527-A5	73500	CY156		oo-delivery 0003
☐ G-EUOU	Airbus Industrie A320-232					2 IAE V2527-A5	73500	CY156		oo-delivery 0003
☐ G-BIKA	Boeing 757-236	22172 / 9		0082	0383	2 RR RB211-535C	99700	CY180	KL-AF	Blue Poole-colors
☐ G-BIKB	Boeing 757-236	22173 / 10		0082	0183	2 RR RB211-535C	99700	CY180	KL-AG	Chelsea Rose-colors
☐ G-BIKC	Boeing 757-236	22174 / 11		0082	0183	2 RR RB211-535C	99700	Y195	KL-AH	Ndebele Emmly-colors
☐ G-BIKD	Boeing 757-236	22175 / 13		0083	0383	2 RR RB211-535C	99700	Y195	KL-AJ	Caernafon Castle
☐ G-BIKF	Boeing 757-236	22177 / 16		0083	0483	2 RR RB211-535C	99700	CY180	KL-AM	Wanula Dreaming-colors
☐ G-BIKG	Boeing 757-236	22178 / 23		0083	0883	2 RR RB211-535C	99700	Y195	KL-BC	Stirling Castle
☐ G-BIKH	Boeing 757-236	22179 / 24		0083	1083	2 RR RB211-535C	99700	CY180	KL-BD	Golden Khokhloma-colors
☐ G-BIKI	Boeing 757-236	22180 / 25		0083	1183	2 RR RB211-535C	99700	CY180	KL-BE	Tintagel Castle
☐ G-BIKJ	Boeing 757-236	22181 / 29		0083	0184	2 RR RB211-535C	99700	Y195	KL-BF	Waves of the City-colors
☐ G-BIKK	Boeing 757-236	22182 / 30		0084	0284	2 RR RB211-535C	99700	CY180	KL-BG	Eilean Donan Castle
☐ G-BIKL	Boeing 757-236	22183 / 32		0084	0284	2 RR RB211-535C	99700	CY180	KL-BH	BenyhoneTartan/Mountain of the Birds-cs
☐ G-BIKM	Boeing 757-236	22184 / 33	N8293V*	0084	0384	2 RR RB211-535C	99700	CY180	FM-HL	Glamis Castle
☐ G-BIKN	Boeing 757-236	22186 / 50		0085	0186	2 RR RB211-535C	99700	CY180	FM-JK	Bodiam Castle
☐ G-BIKO	Boeing 757-236	22187 / 52		0085	0285	2 RR RB211-535C	99700	CY180	FM-JL	Harlech Castle
☐ G-BIKP	Boeing 757-236	22188 / 54		0085	0385	2 RR RB211-535C	99700	CY180	GH-AB	Enniskillen Castle
☐ G-BIKR	Boeing 757-236	22189 / 58		0085	0385	2 RR RB211-535C	99700	CY180	GH-AC	Bamburgh Castle
☐ G-BIKS	Boeing 757-236	22190 / 63		0085	0585	2 RR RB211-535C	99700	CY180	GH-AD	Corfe Castle
☐ G-BIKT	Boeing 757-236	23398 / 77		0085	1185	2 RR RB211-535C	99700	CY180	GH-AE	Crossing Borders-colors
☐ G-BIKU	Boeing 757-236	23399 / 78		0085	1185	2 RR RB211-535C	99700	CY180	FM-KL	Inveraray Castle
☐ G-BIKV	Boeing 757-236	23400 / 81		0085	1285	2 RR RB211-535C	99700	CY180	EF-GL	Raglan Castle
☐ G-BIKW	Boeing 757-236	23492 / 89		0086	0386	2 RR RB211-535C	99700	Y195	BD-EJ	Ndebele Martha-colors
☐ G-BIKX	Boeing 757-236	23493 / 90		0086	0386	2 RR RB211-535C	99700	Y195	BD-EK	Delftblue Daybreak-colors
☐ G-BIKY	Boeing 757-236	23533 / 93		0086	0386	2 RR RB211-535C	99700	CY180	BD-EL	Primavera-colors
☐ G-BIKZ	Boeing 757-236	23532 / 98		0086	0586	2 RR RB211-535C	99700	CY180	BD-AL	Kenilworth Castle
☐ G-BMRA	Boeing 757-236	23710 / 123		0087	0387	2 RR RB211-535C	99700	CY180	BD-CE	Paithani-colors
☐ G-BMRB	Boeing 757-236	23975 / 145		0087	0987	2 RR RB211-535C	99700	CY180	CD-FG	Colchester Castle

registration	type of aircraft	cn/fn	ex/ex*	mfd	del	powered by	mtow kg	configuration	selcal	name/fln/specialitites/remarks
☐ G-BMRC	Boeing 757-236	24072 / 160		0088	0188	2 RR RB211-535C	99700	CY180	CD-EH	British Olympic-colors
☐ G-BMRD	Boeing 757-236	24073 / 166		0088	0288	2 RR RB211-535C	99700	CY180	KM-DG	Chelsea Rose-colors
☐ G-BMRE	Boeing 757-236	24074 / 168		0088	0388	2 RR RB211-535C	99700	CY180	KM-DL	Rendezvous-colors
☐ G-BMRF	Boeing 757-236	24101 / 175		0088	0588	2 RR RB211-535C	99700	CY180	AM-JK	Water Dreaming-colors
☐ G-BMRG	Boeing 757-236	24102 / 179		0088	0588	2 RR RB211-535C	99700	CY180	BD-AM	Rendezvous-colors
☐ G-BMRH	Boeing 757-236	24266 / 210		0089	0289	2 RR RB211-535C	99700	CY180	AC-JL	Nalanji Dreaming-colors
☐ G-BMRI	Boeing 757-236	24267 / 211		0089	0289	2 RR RB211-535C	99700	CY180	AM-GH	Blomsterang-colors
☐ G-BMRJ	Boeing 757-236	24268 / 214		0089	0289	2 RR RB211-535C	99700	CY180	AD-BK	Grand Union-colors
☐ G-BPEA	Boeing 757-236 (ET)	24370 / 218		0089	0289	2 RR RB211-535E4	108800	CY180	AK-HL	Kidwelly Castle / lsf BBAM/opb Euro LGW
☐ G-BPEB	Boeing 757-236 (ET)	24371 / 225		0089	0489	2 RR RB211-535E4	108800	CY180	BF-GK	lsf BBAM / opb Euro LGW
☐ G-BPEC	Boeing 757-236 (ET)	24882 / 323		0090	1190	2 RR RB211-535E4	99700	CY180	AC-JM	Sir Simon Rattle
☐ G-BPED	Boeing 757-236 (ET)	25059 / 363		0091	0591	2 RR RB211-535E4	99700	Y201	BD-FJ	Koguty Lowickie-colors
☐ G-BPEE	Boeing 757-236 (ET)	25060 / 364		0091	0591	2 RR RB211-535E4	99700	CY180	AM-DH	Robert Louis Stevenson
☐ G-BPEF	Boeing 757-236 (ET)	24120 / 174	G-BOHC	0088	0592	2 RR RB211-535E4	108800	CY180	BP-HK	lsf BBAM / opb Euro LGW
☐ G-BPEI	Boeing 757-236	25806 / 601		0094	0394	2 RR RB211-535E4	99700	CY180	AL-BG	Winchester Castle
☐ G-BPEJ	Boeing 757-236	25807 / 610		0094	0494	2 RR RB211-535E4	99700	CY180	DH-EF	Castell Dinas Bran / Llangollen Castle
☐ G-BPEK	Boeing 757-236	25808 / 665		0095	0395	2 RR RB211-535E4	99700	CY180	EF-HM	Cardew Castle
☐ G-CPEL	Boeing 757-236	24398 / 224	N602DF	0089	0892	2 RR RB211-535E4	99700	CY180	BQ-AD	Animals & Trees-colors
☐ G-CPEM	Boeing 757-236	28665 / 747		0097	0397	2 RR RB211-535E4	99700	CY180		Blue Poole-colors
☐ G-CPEN	Boeing 757-236	28666 / 751		0097	0497	2 RR RB211-535E4	99700	CY180		
☐ G-CPEO	Boeing 757-236	28667 / 762		0097	0797	2 RR RB211-535E4	99700	CY180	BF-DS	Whale Rider-colors
☐ G-CPEP	Boeing 757-2Y0	25268 / 400	C-GTSU	0091	0497	2 RR RB211-535E4	99700	Y201	AL-CR	Colum-colors
☐ G-CPER	Boeing 757-236	29113 / 784		1297	1297	2 RR RB211-535E4	99700	Y201	AM-DF	Wings-colors
☐ G-CPES	Boeing 757-236	29114 / 793		0098	0398	2 RR RB211-535E4	99700	Y201	BM-DP	Wings-colors
☐ G-CPET	Boeing 757-236	29115 / 798		0098	0598	2 RR RB211-535E4	99700	Y201	BM-EP	Sterntaler-colors
☐ G-CPEU	Boeing 757-236					2 RR RB211-535E4	99700	CY180		oo-delivery 0499
☐ G-CPEV	Boeing 757-236					2 RR RB211-535E4	99700	CY180		oo-delivery 0499
☐ G-CPEW	Boeing 757-236					2 RR RB211-535E4	99700	CY180		oo-delivery 0599
☐ G-CPEX	Boeing 757-236					2 RR RB211-535E4	99700	CY180		oo-delivery 0699
☐ G-CPEY	Boeing 757-236					2 RR RB211-535E4	99700	CY180		oo-delivery 0699
☐ G-CPEZ	Boeing 757-236					2 RR RB211-535E4	99700	CY180		oo-delivery 0699
☐ G-BNWA	Boeing 767-336 (ER)	24333 / 265	N6009F*	0089	0490	2 RR RB211-524H	158000	CY256	HP-BC	City of Brussels
☐ G-BNWB	Boeing 767-336 (ER)	24334 / 281	N6046P*	0090	0290	2 RR RB211-524H	158000	CY256	HP-BD	Chelsea Rose-colors
☐ G-BNWC	Boeing 767-336 (ER)	24335 / 284		0090	0290	2 RR RB211-524H	158000	CY256	HP-BE	Rendezvous-colors
☐ G-BNWD	Boeing 767-336 (ER)	24336 / 286	N6018N*	0090	0290	2 RR RB211-524H	158000	CY252	HP-BF	Martha Masanabo-colors
☐ G-BNWE	Boeing 767-336 (ER)	24337 / 288		0090	0390	2 RR RB211-524H	158000	CY252	HP-BG	Chelsea Rose-colors
☐ G-BNWF	Boeing 767-336 (ER)	24338 / 293	N1788B*	0090	0690	2 RR RB211-524H	158000	CY252	HP-BJ	Benyhone Tartan-colors
☐ G-BNWG	Boeing 767-336 (ER)	24339 / 298		0090	0790	2 RR RB211-524H	158000	CY252	HP-BK	Waves of the City-colors
☐ G-BNWH	Boeing 767-336 (ER)	24340 / 335	N6005C*	0090	1090	2 RR RB211-524H	172300	F10C42Y141	HP-BL	Waves of the City-colors
☐ G-BNWI	Boeing 767-336 (ER)	24341 / 342		0090	1290	2 RR RB211-524H	181400	CY213	HP-BM	City of Madrid
☐ G-BNWJ	Boeing 767-336 (ER)	24342 / 363		0091	0491	2 RR RB211-524H	158000	CY252	HP-CD	Golden Khokhloma-colors
☐ G-BNWK	Boeing 767-336 (ER)	24343 / 364		0091	0491	2 RR RB211-524H	158000	CY247	HP-CE	Column-colors
☐ G-BNWL	Boeing 767-336 (ER)	25203 / 365		0091	0491	2 RR RB211-524H	158000	CY256	EK-FQ	City of Luxembourg
☐ G-BNWM	Boeing 767-336 (ER)	25204 / 376		0091	0691	2 RR RB211-524H	181400	CY213	EK-GQ	City of Toulouse
☐ G-BNWN	Boeing 767-336 (ER)	25444 / 398		0091	1091	2 RR RB211-524H	158000	CY252	EK-HQ	City of Berlin
☐ G-BNWO	Boeing 767-336 (ER)	25442 / 418		0092	0392	2 RR RB211-524H	181400	CY213	EK-JQ	City of Barcelona
☐ G-BNWP	Boeing 767-336 (ER)	25443 / 419		0092	0392	2 RR RB211-524H	158000	CY252	EK-LQ	Rendezvous-colors
☐ G-BNWR	Boeing 767-336 (ER)	25732 / 421		0092	0392	2 RR RB211-524H	181400	CY213	EK-MQ	Chelsea Rose-colors
☐ G-BNWS	Boeing 767-336 (ER)	25826 / 473	N6018N*	0093	0293	2 RR RB211-524H	158000	CY252	EK-PQ	City of Oporto
☐ G-BNWT	Boeing 767-336 (ER)	25828 / 476		0093	0293	2 RR RB211-524H	158000	CY252	EL-AQ	City of Cork
☐ G-BNWU	Boeing 767-336 (ER)	25829 / 483		0093	0393	2 RR RB211-524H	181400	CY213	EL-BQ	Blomsterang-colors
☐ G-BNWV	Boeing 767-336 (ER)	27140 / 490		0093	0493	2 RR RB211-524H	158000	CY247	EL-CQ	City of Bonn
☐ G-BNWW	Boeing 767-336 (ER)	25831 / 526		0094	0294	2 RR RB211-524H	158000	CY252	AC-LM	City of Marseille
☐ G-BNWX	Boeing 767-336 (ER)	25832 / 529		0094	0394	2 RR RB211-524H	158000	CY252	AG-HL	City of Bilbao
☐ G-BNWY	Boeing 767-336 (ER)	25834 / 608	N5005C*	0096	0496	2 RR RB211-524H	158000	CY252	AG-JK	City of Helsinki
☐ G-BNWZ	Boeing 767-336 (ER)	25733 / 648		0097	0297	2 RR RB211-524H	158000	CY252	AL-BS	
☐ G-BZHA	Boeing 767-336 (ER)	29230 / 702	N60668*	0098	0598	2 RR RB211-524H3	158000	CY252	CH-GP	Wings-colors
☐ G-BZHB	Boeing 767-336 (ER)	29231 / 704		0098	0598	2 RR RB211-524H3	158000	CY252		Delftblue Daybreak-colors
☐ G-BZHC	Boeing 767-336 (ER)	29232 / 708		0698	0698	2 RR RB211-524H3	158000	CY252		Nami Tsuru-colors
☐ G-BOAA	BAe / Aerospatiale Concorde 102	206	G-N94AA	0075	0176	4 RR Olympus 593-610	185070	R100	BD-CM	Union Flag-colors
☐ G-BOAB	BAe / Aerospatiale Concorde 102	208	G-N94AB	0076	0976	4 RR Olympus 593-610	185070	R100	BD-EG	
☐ G-BOAC	BAe / Aerospatiale Concorde 102	204	G-N81AC	0075	0276	4 RR Olympus 593-610	185070	R100	BD-FH	Union Flag-colors
☐ G-BOAD	BAe / Aerospatiale Concorde 102	210	G-N94AD	0076	1276	4 RR Olympus 593-610	185070	R100	BD-AK	Union Flag-colors
☐ G-BOAE	BAe / Aerospatiale Concorde 102	212	G-N94AE	0077	0777	4 RR Olympus 593-610	185070	R100	BD-CF	Union Flag-colors
☐ G-BOAF	BAe / Aerospatiale Concorde 102	216	G-BFKX	0079	0680	4 RR Olympus 593-610	185070	R100	AG-EJ	Union Flag-colors
☐ G-BOAG	BAe / Aerospatiale Concorde 102	214	G-BFKW	0078	0280	4 RR Olympus 593-610	185070	R100	BH-FJ	
☐ G-RAES	Boeing 777-236 (ER)	27491 / 76		0097	0697	2 GE GE90-85B	267619	F14C56Y197	GK-ES	Delftblue Daybreak-colors
☐ G-VIIA	Boeing 777-236 (ER)	27483 / 41	N5022E*	1096	0797	2 GE GE90-85B	267619	F14C56Y197	GK-AS	Waves of the City-colors
☐ G-VIIB	Boeing 777-236 (ER)	27484 / 49	N5023Q*	0096	0597	2 GE GE90-85B	267619	F14C56Y197	GK-BR	
☐ G-VIIC	Boeing 777-236 (ER)	27485 / 53	N5016R*	0096	0297	2 GE GE90-85B	267619	F14C56Y197	GK-BS	
☐ G-VIID	Boeing 777-236 (ER)	27486 / 56		0097	0297	2 GE GE90-85B	267619	F14C56Y197	GK-CR	
☐ G-VIIE	Boeing 777-236 (ER)	27487 / 58		0097	0297	2 GE GE90-85B	267619	F14C56Y197	GK-CS	
☐ G-VIIF	Boeing 777-236 (ER)	27488 / 61		0097	0397	2 GE GE90-85B	267619	F14C56Y197	GK-DR	
☐ G-VIIG	Boeing 777-236 (ER)	27489 / 65		0097	0497	2 GE GE90-85B	267619	F14C56Y197	GK-DS	
☐ G-VIIH	Boeing 777-236 (ER)	27490 / 70		0097	0597	2 GE GE90-85B	267619	F14C56Y197	GK-ER	
☐ G-VIIJ	Boeing 777-236 (ER)	27492 / 111		0097	1297	2 GE GE90-85B	267619	F14C56Y197	GK-FR	BenyhoneTartan/Mountain of the Birds-cs
☐ G-VIIK	Boeing 777-236 (ER)	28840 / 117		0098	0298	2 GE GE90-85B	267619	F14C56Y197	GK-FS	Animals & Trees-colors
☐ G-VIIL	Boeing 777-236 (ER)	27493 / 127		0098	0398	2 GE GE90-85B	267619	F14C56Y197	GK-HR	Wings-colors
☐ G-VIIM	Boeing 777-236 (ER)	28841 / 130		0098	0398	2 GE GE90-85B	267619	F14C56Y197	GK-AR	Nami Tsuru-colors
☐ G-VIIN	Boeing 777-236 (ER)	29319 / 157		0898	0898	2 GE GE90-85B	267619	F14C56Y197		Whale Rider-colors
☐ G-VIIO	Boeing 777-236 (ER)	29320 / 182		0199	0199	2 GE GE90-85B	267619	F14C56Y197		Chelsea Rose-colors
☐ G-VIIP	Boeing 777-236 (ER)	29321 / 193		0099	0299	2 GE GE90-85B	267619	F14C56Y197		
☐ G-VIIR	Boeing 777-236 (ER)	29322		0099	0399	2 GE GE90-85B	267619	F14C56Y197		
☐ G-VIIS	Boeing 777-236 (ER)	29323		0099	0499	2 GE GE90-85B	267619	F14C56Y197		
☐ G-VIIT	Boeing 777-236 (ER)					2 GE GE90-85B	267619	F14C56Y197		oo-delivery 0599
☐ G-VIIU	Boeing 777-236 (ER)					2 GE GE90-85B	267619	F14C56Y197		oo-delivery 0599
☐ G-VIIV	Boeing 777-236 (ER)					2 GE GE90-85B	267619	F14C56Y197		oo-delivery 1099
☐ G-VIIW	Boeing 777-236 (ER)					2 GE GE90-85B	267619	F14C56Y197		oo-delivery 1299
☐ G-VIIX	Boeing 777-236 (ER)					2 GE GE90-85B	267619	F14C56Y197		oo-delivery 0100
☐ G-VIIY	Boeing 777-236 (ER)					2 GE GE90-85B	267619	F14C56Y197		oo-delivery 0200
☐ G-YMMA	Boeing 777-236 (ER)					2 RR Trent 895	294200			oo-delivery 0300
☐ G-YMMB	Boeing 777-236 (ER)					2 RR Trent 895	294200			oo-delivery 0400
☐ G-YMMC	Boeing 777-236 (ER)					2 RR Trent 895	294200			oo-delivery 0600
☐ G-YMMD	Boeing 777-236 (ER)					2 RR Trent 895	294200			oo-delivery 0700
☐ G-YMME	Boeing 777-236 (ER)					2 RR Trent 895	294200			oo-delivery 0800
☐ G-YMMF	Boeing 777-236 (ER)					2 RR Trent 895	294200			oo-delivery 1000
☐ G-YMMG	Boeing 777-236 (ER)					2 RR Trent 895	294200			oo-delivery 1200
☐ G-YMMH	Boeing 777-236 (ER)					2 RR Trent 895	294200			oo-delivery 0201
☐ G-YMMI	Boeing 777-236 (ER)					2 RR Trent 895	294200			oo-delivery 0301
☐ G-YMMJ	Boeing 777-236 (ER)					2 RR Trent 895	294200			oo-delivery 0401
☐ G-YMMK	Boeing 777-236 (ER)					2 RR Trent 895	294200			oo-delivery 0601
☐ G-YMML	Boeing 777-236 (ER)					2 RR Trent 895	294200			oo-delivery 0801
☐ G-YMMM	Boeing 777-236 (ER)					2 RR Trent 895	294200			oo-delivery 1001
☐ G-YMMN	Boeing 777-236 (ER)					2 RR Trent 895	294200			oo-delivery 1201
☐ G-YMMO	Boeing 777-236 (ER)					2 RR Trent 895	294200			oo-delivery 0002
☐ G-YMMP	Boeing 777-236 (ER)					2 RR Trent 895	294200			oo-delivery 0002
☐ G-ZZZA	Boeing 777-236	27105 / 6	N77779*	0095	0596	2 GE GE90-76B	242670	F14C56Y197	GJ-BS	Sir Frank Whittle
☐ G-ZZZB	Boeing 777-236	27106 / 10	N77771*	0095	0397	2 GE GE90-76B	242670	F14C56Y197	GJ-CR	Sir William Sefton Brancker
☐ G-ZZZC	Boeing 777-236	27107 / 15	N5014K*	0095	1195	2 GE GE90-76B	242670	F14C56Y197	GJ-CS	Rendezvous-colors
☐ G-ZZZD	Boeing 777-236	27108 / 17		0095	1295	2 GE GE90-76B	242670	F14C56Y197	GJ-DR	Orville Wright / Wilbur Wright
☐ G-ZZZE	Boeing 777-236	27109 / 19		0095	0196	2 GE GE90-76B	242670	F14C56Y197	GJ-DS	Sir John Alock/Sir Arthur Whitten-Brown
☐ G-BEBL	Boeing (Douglas) DC-10-30	46949 / 179	N54643*	0076	0488	3 GE CF6-50C2	259455	F12C35Y162	AM-CL	Forest of Dean / std LGW / for sale
☐ G-BHDH	Boeing (Douglas) DC-10-30	47816 / 316		0080	0488	3 GE CF6-50C2	259455	F12C35Y162	BE-CK	Benmore Forest / for sale
☐ G-BHDI	Boeing (Douglas) DC-10-30	47831 / 327		0080	0488	3 GE CF6-50C2	259455	F12C35Y162	DG-FJ	Forest of Ae / for sale
☐ G-BHDJ	Boeing (Douglas) DC-10-30	47840 / 337	N19B*	0080	0488	3 GE CF6-50C2	259455	F12C35Y162	DH-CL	Glen Cap Forest / for sale
☐ G-DCIO	Boeing (Douglas) DC-10-30	48277 / 354		0081	0488	3 GE CF6-50C2	259455	F12C35Y162	DH-FJ	Epping Forest / for sale
☐ G-MULL	Boeing (Douglas) DC-10-30	47888 / 291	YA-LAS	0079	0488	3 GE CF6-50C2	259455	F12C35Y162	AM-DF	New Forest / for sale
☐ G-NIUK	Boeing (Douglas) DC-10-30	46932 / 158	9Q-CLT	0074	0488	3 GE CF6-50C2	259455	C32Y279	DH-CJ	Loch Loyal / for sale
☐ G-AWNE	Boeing 747-136	19765 / 109		0071	0474	4 PW JT9D-7A	332937	F14C76Y266	BD-EF	Derwent Water
☐ G-AWNF	Boeing 747-136	19766 / 111		0071	0474	4 PW JT9D-7A	332937	F14C76Y266	BE-GH	Blagdon Lake / lsf AARL

☐ G-AWNH	Boeing 747-136	20270 / 169		0071	0474	4 PW JT9D-7A	332937	F14C76Y266	BE-KM	Devoke Water / lsf AARL
☐ G-AWNM	Boeing 747-136	20708 / 210		0073	0474	4 PW JT9D-7A	332937	F14C76Y266	EF-HL	Ullswater / lsf AARL
☐ G-AWNN	Boeing 747-136	20809 / 220		0073	0474	4 PW JT9D-7A	332937	F14C76Y266	KM-CG	Loweswater / lsf AARL
☐ G-AWNO	Boeing 747-136	20810 / 222		0073	0474	4 PW JT9D-7A	332937	F14C76Y266	KM-CH	Grafham Water / lsf AARL
☐ G-AWNP	Boeing 747-136	20952 / 246		0074	1174	4 PW JT9D-7A	332937	F14C76Y266	KM-CJ	Hanningfield Water / lsf AARL
☐ G-BBPU	Boeing 747-136	20953 / 248		0074	0375	4 PW JT9D-7A	332937	F14C76Y266	BD-CH	Virginia Water / lsf AARL
☐ G-BDPV	Boeing 747-136	21213 / 281		0076	0476	4 PW JT9D-7A	332937	F14C76Y266	BD-CL	Blea Water / lsf AARL
☐ G-BDXA	Boeing 747-236B	21238 / 292	N1790B*	0076	0777	4 RR RB211-524D4	371945	F14C64Y298	BD-CJ	City of Peterborough / lsf ICCO
☐ G-BDXB	Boeing 747-236B	21239 / 302	N8280V*	0077	0677	4 RR RB211-524D4	371945	F14C64Y298	BD-AJ	City of Liverpool
☐ G-BDXC	Boeing 747-236B	21240 / 305		0077	0677	4 RR RB211-524D4	371945	F14C64Y298	AM-HK	City of Manchester
☐ G-BDXD	Boeing 747-236B	21241 / 317	N8285V*	0077	0478	4 RR RB211-524D4	371945	C47Y378	AM-GJ	Blue Poole-colors
☐ G-BDXE	Boeing 747-236B	21350 / 321		0078	0378	4 RR RB211-524D4	371945	C47Y378	BD-AG	City of Glasgow
☐ G-BDXF	Boeing 747-236B	21351 / 323		0078	0478	4 RR RB211-524D4	371945	C47Y378	BD-FL	City of York
☐ G-BDXG	Boeing 747-236B	21536 / 328		0078	0678	4 RR RB211-524D4	371945	C47Y378	BD-CK	Blomsterang-colors
☐ G-BDXH	Boeing 747-236B	21635 / 365		0079	0379	4 RR RB211-524D4	371945	F14C76Y266	BD-EH	City of Elgin
☐ G-BDXI	Boeing 747-236B	21830 / 430		0080	0380	4 RR RB211-524D4	371945	F14C64Y298	EF-DL	City of Cambridge
☐ G-BDXJ	Boeing 747-236B	21831 / 440	N1792B*	0080	0580	4 RR RB211-524D4	371945	F14C64Y298	AG-FL	City of Birmingham
☐ G-BDXK	Boeing 747-236B	22303 / 495		0081	0383	4 RR RB211-524D4	371945	F14C64Y298	BD-GL	Chelsea Rose-colors
☐ G-BDXL	Boeing 747-236B	22305 / 506	N8280V*	0081	0384	4 RR RB211-524D4	371945	F14C64Y298	CJ-DL	City of Winchester
☐ G-BDXM	Boeing 747-236B (M)	23711 / 672	N6055X*	0087	0287	4 RR RB211-524D4	377842	F14C64Y298	CD-FH	City of Derby
☐ G-BDXN	Boeing 747-236B (M)	23735 / 674	N6046P*	0087	0387	4 RR RB211-524D4	377842	F14C64Y298	CJ-DM	City of Stoke on Trent
☐ G-BDXO	Boeing 747-236B	23799 / 677	N6055X*	0087	0487	4 RR RB211-524D4	371945	F14C64Y298	KM-DJ	Paithani-colors
☐ G-BDXP	Boeing 747-236B (M)	24088 / 697	N6009F*	0088	0288	4 RR RB211-524D4	377842	F14C64Y298	AM-GK	City of Salisbury
☐ G-BNLA	Boeing 747-436	23908 / 727	N60665*	0089	0689	4 RR RB211-524H2	396893	F14C55Y332	BP-AF	Chelsea Rose-colors
☐ G-BNLB	Boeing 747-436	23909 / 730		0089	0789	4 RR RB211-524H2	396893	F18C55Y332	BP-AG	City of Edinburgh
☐ G-BNLC	Boeing 747-436	23910 / 734		0089	0789	4 RR RB211-524H2	396893	F14C55Y332	BP-AH	City of Cardiff / Dinas Caerdydd
☐ G-BNLD	Boeing 747-436	23911 / 744	N6018N*	0089	0989	4 RR RB211-524H2	396893	F14C55Y332	BP-AJ	Delftblue Daybreak-colors
☐ G-BNLE	Boeing 747-436	24047 / 753		0089	1189	4 RR RB211-524H2	396893	F18C55Y332	BP-AK	City of Newcastle
☐ G-BNLF	Boeing 747-436	24048 / 773		0090	0290	4 RR RB211-524H2	396893	F18C55Y332	BP-AL	City of Leeds
☐ G-BNLG	Boeing 747-436	24049 / 774		0090	0290	4 RR RB211-524H2	396893	F14C55Y332	BP-AM	Whale Rider-colors
☐ G-BNLH	Boeing 747-436	24050 / 779		0090	0390	4 RR RB211-524H2	396893	F14C55Y332	BP-CD	Wings-colors
☐ G-BNLI	Boeing 747-436	24051 / 784		0090	0490	4 RR RB211-524H2	396893	F14C55Y332	BP-CE	Benyhone Tartan-colors
☐ G-BNLJ	Boeing 747-436	24052 / 789	N60668*	0090	0590	4 RR RB211-524H2	396893	F14C55Y332	BP-CF	Ndebele Martha-colors
☐ G-BNLK	Boeing 747-436	24053 / 790	N6009F*	0090	0590	4 RR RB211-524H2	396893	F18C55Y332	BP-CG	Water Dreaming-colors
☐ G-BNLL	Boeing 747-436	24054 / 794		0090	0690	4 RR RB211-524H2	396893	F18C55Y332	BP-CH	Chelsea Rose-colors
☐ G-BNLM	Boeing 747-436	24055 / 795	N6009F*	0090	0690	4 RR RB211-524H2	396893	F18C55Y332	BP-CJ	Ndebele Martha-colors
☐ G-BNLN	Boeing 747-436	24056 / 802		0090	0790	4 RR RB211-524H2	396893	F14C55Y332	BP-CK	Nalanji Dreaming-colors
☐ G-BNLO	Boeing 747-436	24057 / 817		0090	1090	4 RR RB211-524H2	396893	F14C55Y332	BP-CL	Ndebele Emmly-colors
☐ G-BNLP	Boeing 747-436	24058 / 828		0090	1290	4 RR RB211-524H2	396893	F18C55Y332	BP-CM	City of Aberdeen
☐ G-BNLR	Boeing 747-436	24447 / 829	N6005C*	0091	0191	4 RR RB211-524H2	396893	F18C55Y332	BD-FM	Rendezvous-colors
☐ G-BNLS	Boeing 747-436	24629 / 841		0091	0391	4 RR RB211-524H2	396893	F14C55Y332	EQ-BP	Wanula Dreaming-colors
☐ G-BNLT	Boeing 747-436	24630 / 842		0091	0391	4 RR RB211-524H2	396893	F14C55Y332	EQ-CD	Koguty Lowickle-colors
☐ G-BNLU	Boeing 747-436	25406 / 895		0092	0192	4 RR RB211-524H2	396893	F14C55Y332	BR-AC	City of Bangor
☐ G-BNLV	Boeing 747-436	25427 / 900		0092	0292	4 RR RB211-524H2	396893	F18C55Y332	BR-AD	City of Exeter
☐ G-BNLW	Boeing 747-436	25432 / 903		0092	0392	4 RR RB211-524H2	396893	F18C55Y332	BR-AE	City of Norwich
☐ G-BNLX	Boeing 747-436	25435 / 908		0092	0492	4 RR RB211-524H2	396893	F18C55Y332	BR-AF	Waves of the City-colors
☐ G-BNLY	Boeing 747-436	27090 / 959	N60659*	0093	0293	4 RR RB211-524H2	396893	F18C55Y332	BR-AG	City of Swansea
☐ G-BNLZ	Boeing 747-436	27091 / 964		0093	0393	4 RR RB211-524H2	396893	F18C64Y318	BR-AH	Animals & Trees-colors
☐ G-BYGA	Boeing 747-436	28855 / 1190		1298	1298	4 RR RB211-524H2	396893	F14C55Y340		Chelsea Rose-colors
☐ G-BYGB	Boeing 747-436	28856 / 1194		0199	0199	4 RR RB211-524H2	396893	F14C55Y340		Column-colors
☐ G-BYGC	Boeing 747-436	25823 / 1195		0199	0199	4 RR RB211-524H2	396893	F14C55Y340		Chelsea Rose-colors
☐ G-BYGD	Boeing 747-436	28857 / 1196		0199	0199	4 RR RB211-524H2	396893	F14C55Y340		Rendezvous-colors
☐ G-BYGE	Boeing 747-436	28858 / 1198		0099	0299	4 RR RB211-524H2	396893	F14C55Y340		
☐ G-BYGF	Boeing 747-436	25824 / 1200		0299	0299	4 RR RB211-524H2	396893	F14C55Y340		
☐ G-BYGG	Boeing 747-436					4 RR RB211-524H2	396893	F14C55Y340		oo-delivery 0599
☐ G-CIVA	Boeing 747-436	27092 / 967		0093	0393	4 RR RB211-524H2	396893	F18C55Y332	AK-QR	C'of St.Davids/DinasTyddesi / BrAsia-cs
☐ G-CIVB	Boeing 747-436	25811 / 1018		0094	0294	4 RR RB211-524H2	396893	F18C55Y332	AK-QS	City of Lichfield
☐ G-CIVC	Boeing 747-436	25812 / 1022		0094	0294	4 RR RB211-524H2	396893	F14C55Y332	AK-RS	City of St. Andrews
☐ G-CIVD	Boeing 747-436	27349 / 1048		0094	1294	4 RR RB211-524H2	396893	F14C55Y332	FP-HR	City of Coventry
☐ G-CIVE	Boeing 747-436	27350 / 1050		0094	1294	4 RR RB211-524H2	396893	F14C55Y332	FP-GR	City of Sunderland / British Asia-colors
☐ G-CIVF	Boeing 747-436	25434 / 1058		0095	0395	4 RR RB211-524H2	381017	F14C55Y340	BG-KQ	City of St. Albans
☐ G-CIVG	Boeing 747-436	25813 / 1059	N6009F*	0095	0495	4 RR RB211-524H2	381017	F14C55Y340	BG-LS	City of Wells
☐ G-CIVH	Boeing 747-436	25809 / 1078		0096	0496	4 RR RB211-524H2	381017	F14C55Y340	BG-MR	City of Hereford
☐ G-CIVI	Boeing 747-436	25814 / 1079		0096	0596	4 RR RB211-524H2	381017	F14C55Y340	BG-MS	City of Gloucester
☐ G-CIVJ	Boeing 747-436	25817 / 1102		0097	0297	4 RR RB211-524H2	396893	F14C55Y332	BG-PQ	
☐ G-CIVK	Boeing 747-436	25818 / 1104		0097	0297	4 RR RB211-524H2	396893	F14C55Y332	BG-PR	
☐ G-CIVL	Boeing 747-436	27478 / 1108		0097	0397	4 RR RB211-524H2	396893	F14C55Y332	BH-MP	
☐ G-CIVM	Boeing 747-436	28700 / 1116		0097	0697	4 RR RB211-524H2	396893	F14C55Y332	CJ-GQ	Nami Tsuru-colors
☐ G-CIVN	Boeing 747-436	28848 / 1129		0997	0997	4 RR RB211-524H2	396893	F14C55Y332	BF-KS	Delftblue Daybreak-colors
☐ G-CIVO	Boeing 747-436	28849 / 1135	N6046P*	0097	1297	4 RR RB211-524H2	396893	F14C55Y332	BF-PR	BenyhoneTartan/Mountain of the Birds-cs
☐ G-CIVP	Boeing 747-436	28850 / 1144		0098	0298	4 RR RB211-524H2	396893	F14C55Y332	CL-HJ	Column-colors
☐ G-CIVR	Boeing 747-436	25820 / 1146		0098	0398	4 RR RB211-524H2	396893	F14C55Y332	CL-AP	Nami Tsuru-colors
☐ G-CIVS	Boeing 747-436	28851 / 1148		0098	0398	4 RR RB211-524H2	396893	F14C55Y332	CL-BP	Whale Rider-colors
☐ G-CIVT	Boeing 747-436	25821 / 1149		0098	0398	4 RR RB211-524H2	396893	F14C55Y332	CL-DP	Delftblue Daybreak-colors
☐ G-CIVU	Boeing 747-436	25810 / 1154		0098	0498	4 RR RB211-524H2	396893	F14C55Y332	CL-EP	Wings-colors
☐ G-CIVV	Boeing 747-436	25819 / 1156	N6009F*	0098	0598	4 RR RB211-524H2	396893	F14C55Y340	CL-FP	Rendezvous-colors
☐ G-CIVW	Boeing 747-436	25822 / 1157		0098	0598	4 RR RB211-524H2	396893	F14C55Y340	CP-HM	BenyhoneTartan/Mountain of the Birds-cs
☐ G-CIVX	Boeing 747-436	28852 / 1172		0098	0998	4 RR RB211-524H2	396893	F14C55Y340		Nami Tsuru-colors
☐ G-CIVY	Boeing 747-436	28853 / 1178		0998	0998	4 RR RB211-524H2	396893	F14C55Y340		Whale Rider-colors
☐ G-CIVZ	Boeing 747-436	28854 / 1183		1098	1098	4 RR RB211-524H2	396893	F14C55Y340		Benyhone Tartan-colors

BRITISH INTERNATIONAL = BS / BIH (Brintel Helicopters Ltd dba/Subs.of CHC Helicopter Corp./formerly British Airways Helicopters) **Aberdeen / Sumburgh / Beccles & Penzance**

Buchan Road, Aberdeen Airport, Dyce, Aberdeen AB2 0BZ, Scotland, Great Britain ☎ (1224) 77 13 53 Tx: none Fax: (1224) 77 16 32 SITA: n/a
F: 1947 ✈✈✈ 320 Head: Neil Calvert ICAO: BRINTEL Net: n/a

☐ G-BVCX	Sikorsky S-76A+	760183	N951L	0081	0993	2 TU Arriel 1S	4899	12 Pax	cvtd S-76A
☐ G-CHCD	Sikorsky S-76A+	760101	G-CBJB	0080	0198	2 TU Arriel 1S	4899	12 Pax	cvtd S-76A
☐ G-ATBJ	Sikorsky S-61N	61269		0065		2 GE CT58-140-2	9299	23 Pax	
☐ G-ATFM	Sikorsky S-61N	61270	CF-OKY	0065		2 GE CT58-140-2	9299	23 Pax	
☐ G-AYOY	Sikorsky S-61N	61476		0070		2 GE CT58-140-1	9299	23 Pax	
☐ G-BCEA	Sikorsky S-61N	61721		0074		2 GE CT58-140-1	9299	23 Pax	
☐ G-BCEB	Sikorsky S-61NM	61454	N4023S	0072		2 GE CT58-140-2	9299	23 Pax	
☐ G-BEIC	Sikorsky S-61N	61222	N307Y	0064		2 GE CT58-140-1	9299	23 Pax	
☐ G-BEWM	Sikorsky S-61N	61772		0077		2 GE CT58-140-1	9299	23 Pax	
☐ G-BFFJ	Sikorsky S-61N	61777	N6231	0078		2 GE CT58-140-2	9299	23 Pax	
☐ G-BFFK	Sikorsky S-61N	61778		0078		2 GE CT58-140-1	9299	23 Pax	
☐ G-BKZE	Eurocopter (Aerosp.) AS332L Super Puma	2102	F-WKQE*	0083		2 TU Makila 1A	8600	19 Pax	
☐ G-BKZG	Eurocopter (Aerosp.) AS332L Super Puma	2106		0083		2 TU Makila 1A	8600	19 Pax	
☐ G-BKZH	Eurocopter (Aerosp.) AS332L Super Puma	2107		0083		2 TU Makila 1A	8600	19 Pax	
☐ G-BOZK	Eurocopter (Aerosp.) AS332L Super Puma	2179	LN-OMQ	0088		2 TU Makila 1A	8600	19 Pax	
☐ G-BSOI	Eurocopter (Aerosp.) AS332L Super Puma	2063	C-GSLE	0083		2 TU Makila 1A	8600	19 Pax	
☐ G-BUZD	Eurocopter (Aerosp.) AS332L Super Puma	2069	C-GSLJ	0083	0293	2 TU Makila 1A	8600	19 Pax	
☐ G-BWHN	Eurocopter (Aerosp.) AS332L Super Puma	2017	C-GSLC	0082	1095	2 TU Makila 1A	8600	19 Pax	
☐ G-CHCA	Eurocopter (Aerosp.) AS332L Super Puma	2007	F-WQDZ	0081	0398	2 TU Makila 1A	8600	19 Pax	cvtd AS332C
☐ G-CHCB	Eurocopter (Aerosp.) AS332L Super Puma	2015	C-GQYX	0082	0398	2 TU Makila 1A	8600	19 Pax	cvtd AS332C
☐ G-CHCC	Eurocopter (Aerosp.) AS332L Super Puma	2087	N25AN	0083	0398	2 TU Makila 1A	8600	19 Pax	
☐ G-TIGZ	Eurocopter (Aerosp.) AS332L Super Puma	2115	C-GQKK	0084		2 TU Makila 1A	8600	19 Pax	

BRITISH MEDITERRANEAN AIRWAYS, Ltd = KJ / LAJ **London-Heathrow**

Cirrus House, Bedfont Road, London Heathrow Airport, Staines, Middlesex TW19 7NL, Great Britain ☎ (1784) 26 63 01 Tx: none Fax: (1784) 26 63 57 SITA: LHRKZKJ
F: 1994 ✈✈✈ 200 Head: Lord Alexander Hesketh IATA: 436 ICAO: BEE MED Net: n/a Scheduled svcs are operated on a franchise agreement with BRITISH AIRWAYS in full such colors (& both titles) & using BA-flight numbers.

☐ G-MEDA	Airbus Industrie A320-231	480	N480RX	0094	1094	2 IAE V2500-A1	75500	C22Y102		lsf ORIX / BA Whale Rider-colors
☐ G-MEDB	Airbus Industrie A320-231	376	3B-RGY	0092	0497	2 IAE V2500-A1	75500	C22Y102		lsf Debis AirFinance / BA Rendezvous-cs
☐ G-MEDD	Airbus Industrie A320-231	386	3B-RGZ	0092	0497	2 IAE V2500-A1	75500	F8C16Y102	FR-AE	lsf DebisAirFin./BA Crossing Borders-cs

BRITISH MIDLAND = BD / BMA (British Midland Airways Ltd dba/Member of British Midland Group/Assoc. with Scandinavian – SAS/formerly Derby Airways) **East Midlands**

Donington Hall, Castle Donington, Derbyshire DE74 2SB, Great Britain ☎ (1332) 85 40 00 Tx: 37172 bmaobd g Fax: (1332) 85 46 62 SITA: EMACOBD
F: 1938 ✈✈✈ 5000 Head: Sir Michael Bishop, CBE IATA: 236 ICAO: MIDLAND Net: http://www.iflybritishmidland.com
Commuter flights are operated on behalf of British Midland by BRITISH MIDLAND COMMUTER (with Saab 340 & Embraer 145), using BD-flight numbers. For details – see under that company.

☐ G-BVTE	Fokker 70 (F28 Mk0070)	11538	PH-EZX*	0095	0495	2 RR Tay 620-15	36899	CY74	lsf East Midlands Aircraft Finance

168 registration type of aircraft cn/fn ex/ex* mfd del powered by mtow kg configuration selcal name/fln/specialitites/remarks

EDINBURGH AIR CHARTER, Ltd = EDC — Edinburgh

Eastfield Avenue, Edinburgh Airport, Edinburgh EH12 9DN, Scotland, Great Britain ☎ (131) 339 80 08 Tx: none Fax: (131) 339 40 59 SITA: n/a
F: 1990 ☗☗☗ 14 Head: John Easson ICAO: SALTIRE Net: n/a

☐ G-BWYE	Cessna 310R II	310R1654	F-GBPE	0079	0996	2 CO IO-520-M	2495			
☐ G-BWYH	Cessna 310R II	310R1640	F-GBPC	0079	1096	2 CO IO-520-M	2495			
☐ G-FISH	Cessna 310R II	310R1845	N2740Y	0079		2 CO IO-520-M	2495			lsf pvt
☐ G-TKPZ	Cessna 310R II	310R1225	G-BRAH	0077	0894	2 CO IO-520-M	2495			
☐ G-BXJA	Cessna 402B	402B0356	N5753M	0073	0797	2 CO TSIO-520-E	2858			lsf Air Ward Ltd
☐ G-DOBN	Cessna 402B II	402B1243	N24PL	0077	0496	2 CO TSIO-520-E	2858			
☐ G-ILGW	Cessna 404 Titan II	404-0690	D-ILGW	0080	0198	2 CO GTSIO-520-M	3810			

ELECTRA AVIATION, Ltd - EAL = (ELEC) (Subsidiary of Aviation Holdings, PLC) — London & Wilmington, DE (USA)

65 Kingsway, London WC2B 6QT, Great Britain ☎ (171) 831 17 71 Tx: none Fax: (171) 831 61 45 SITA: n/a
F: 1987 ☗☗☗ 2 Head: Simon H. Frost Net: n/a Used aircraft leasing, sales and financing company.
Owner / lessor of following (main) aircraft types: Airbus A300B4, McDonnell Douglas DC-9-30, MD-82 & DC-10-30. Aircraft leased from ELEC are listed and mentioned as such under the leasing carriers.

ELITE HELICOPTERS (Solent Helicopters, Ltd dba) — White Waltham & Nottingham

White Waltham Airfield, Maidenhead, Berks SL6 3NJ, Great Britain ☎ (1628) 82 81 88 Tx: none Fax: (1628) 82 81 22 SITA: n/a
F: 1994 ☗☗☗ 18 Head: Glenn Curtis Net: http://ourworld.compuserve.com/homepage/helifl

☐ G-BLCA	Bell 206B JetRanger III	3443	N20982	0081		1 AN 250-C20B	1451			lsf RMH Stainless Ltd
☐ G-BYBA	Agusta-Bell 206B JetRanger III	8596	G-BHXV	0080	0098	1 AN 250-C20B	1451			lsf R. Forests Ltd
☐ G-HMPH	Bell 206B JetRanger	1232	G-BBUY	0073		1 AN 250-C20	1451			lsf Mightycraft Ltd
☐ G-JBDB	Agusta-Bell 206B JetRanger	8238	G-OOPS	0070		1 AN 250-C20	1451			lsf Brad Helicopters Ltd
☐ G-LTEK	Bell 206B JetRanger II	2034	G-BMIB	0076		1 AN 250-C20	1451			lsf Stuart Aviation Ltd
☐ G-OCBB	Bell 206B JetRanger	969	G-BASE	0073		1 AN 250-C20	1451			lsf Helispeed Ltd
☐ G-WIZZ	Agusta-Bell 206B JetRanger II	8540		0077		1 AN 250-C20	1451			lsf Cavenhurst Ltd

EMERALD AIRWAYS, Ltd = G3 / JEM (formerly Janes Aviation 748, Ltd) — Liverpool

48 High Road, Benfleet, Essex SS7 5LH, Great Britain ☎ (151) 448 08 44 Tx: 627774 emrld g Fax: (151) 448 05 49 SITA: n/a
F: 1987 ☗☗☗ 115 Head: Andrew Janes IATA: 938 ICAO: GEMSTONE Net: n/a

☐ G-ATMI	BAe (HS) 748-225 Srs 2A	1592 / 62	VP-LIU	0066	0792	2 RR Dart 534-2	19995	Freighter		Old Ben / Reed Aviation-Freight co.-cs
☐ G-ATMJ	BAe (HS) 748-225 Srs 2A	1593 / 63	VP-LAJ	0066	0792	2 RR Dart 534-2	19995	Freighter		
☐ G-AVXI	BAe (HS) 748-238 Srs 2A	1623 / 122		0068	1098	2 RR Dart 534-2	20183	Freighter		
☐ G-AVXJ	BAe (HS) 748-238 Srs 2A	1624 / 137		0069	1098	2 RR Dart 534-2	20183	Freighter		
☐ G-AYIM	BAe (HS) 748-270 Srs 2A	1687 / 167	CS-TAG	0070	0694	2 RR Dart 534-2	19995	Freighter		
☐ G-BEJD	BAe (HS) 748-105 Srs 1	1543 / 10	LV-HHE	0062	0792	2 RR Dart 514	17916	Freighter		Sisyphus / Reed Aviation-Freight co.-cs
☐ G-BGMN	BAe (HS) 748-347 Srs 2A	1766 / 250	PK-OCH	0079	1098	2 RR Dart 534-2	21092	Y48		
☐ G-BGMO	BAe (HS) 748-347 Srs 2A	1767 / 256	ZK-MCB	0079	0296	2 RR Dart 534-2	20183	Y48		
☐ G-BIUV	BAe (HS) 748-275 Srs 2A (SCD)	1701 / 178	5W-FAN	0071	0792	2 RR Dart 534-2	19995	Freighter		cvtd Srs 2A
☐ G-BPDA	BAe (HS) 748-334 Srs 2A	1756 / 227	G-GLAS	0077	0192	2 RR Dart 535-2	19995	Freighter		John J.Goodall / Reed Avn-Freight co.cs
☐ G-BVOU	BAe (HS) 748-270 Srs 2A	1721 / 197	CS-TAH	0073	0694	2 RR Dart 534-2	19995	Freighter		
☐ G-BVOV	BAe (HS) 748-372 Srs 2A	1777 / 258	CS-TAO	0080	0694	2 RR Dart 535-2	19995	Freighter		
☐ G-EMRD	BAe (HS) 748-378 Srs 2B	1797 / 278	G-HDBD	0084	0796	2 RR Dart 536-2	20000	Y48		
☐ G-OPFW	BAe (HS) 748-266 Srs 2A	1714 / 193	G-BMFT	0072	0398	2 RR Dart 534-2	19995	Freighter		Parcelforce-colors
☐ G-OSOE	BAe (HS) 748-242 Srs 2A	1697 / 170	G-AYYG	0071	1096	2 RR Dart 534-2	20183	Freighter		Securicor Omega Express-colors
☐ G-SOEI	BAe (HS) 748-242 Srs 2A	1689 / 186	ZK-DES	0071	0298	2 RR Dart 534-2	20183	Y48		

EURO EXECUTIVE JET, Ltd — Oxford

The Farm House, Oxford Airport, Kidlington, Oxfordshire OX5 1RA, Great Britain ☎ (1865) 84 75 01 Tx: none Fax: (1865) 84 75 02 SITA: n/a
F: 1998 ☗☗☗ n/a Head: Stephen Loveridge Net: n/a Operates charter flights with the AOC currently using from OXAERO.

☐ C-CITZ	Bell 206B JetRanger II	1997	G-BRTB	0076	0998	1 AN 250-C20	1451			
☐ G-CITI	Cessna 501 Citation I/SP	501-0084	VP-CDM	0079	0798	2 PWC JT15D-1	5375			lst Oxaero

EUROJET AVIATION, Ltd = GOJ — Birmingham, Belfast, Gloucester & Dublin

NCP Building, Old Terminal, Birmingham International Airport, Birmingham B26 3QJ, Great Britain ☎ (121) 782 17 00 Tx: 747747 gojops g Fax: (121) 782 17 11 SITA: n/a
F: 1991 ☗☗☗ 35 Head: Graeme Campbell ICAO: GOJET Net: n/a

☐ G-DCDB	Bell 407	53137	N7238A	0097	0097	1 AN 250-C47B	2268			
☐ G-OEJA	Cessna 500 Citation	500-0264	F-GLJA	0075	0896	2 PWC JT15D-1A	5375			
☐ G-ESTA	Cessna 550 Citation II	550-0127	G-GAUL	0080	0098	2 PWC JT15D-4	6033			lsf Executive Aviation Services Ltd
☐ G-OCDB	Cessna 550 Citation II	550-0601	G-ELOT	0089		2 PWC JT15D-4	6033			lsf Paycourt Ltd

EUROPEAN AIRCHARTER - EAC = EAF (European Aviation Air Charter, Ltd dba / Subsidiary of European Aviation, Ltd) — Bournemouth

European House, Bournemouth Int'l Airport, Christchurch, Dorset BH23 6EA, Great Britain ☎ (1202) 58 11 11 Tx: none Fax: (1202) 57 83 33 SITA: BOHEACR
F: 1993 ☗☗☗ 350 Head: Paul G. Stoddart ICAO: EUROCHARTER Net: n/a

☐ G-AVMH	BAe (BAC) One-Eleven 510ED	136		0068	0893	2 RR Spey 512-14DW(HK2)	41950	Y104		lsf European Aviation Ltd
☐ G-AVMI	BAe (BAC) One-Eleven 510ED	137		0068	0893	2 RR Spey 512-14DW(HK2)	43550	C70		The Rome Express / lsf European Avn
☐ G-AVMK	BAe (BAC) One-Eleven 510ED	139		0068	0693	2 RR Spey 512-14DW(HK2)	41950	Y104		lsf European Aviation Ltd
☐ G-AVML	BAe (BAC) One-Eleven 510ED	140		0068	0693	2 RR Spey 512-14DW(HK2)	43550	Y104		lsf European Aviation Ltd
☐ G-AVMM	BAe (BAC) One-Eleven 510ED	141		0068	0693	2 RR Spey 512-14DW(HK2)	41950	Y104		lsf European Aviation Ltd
☐ G-AVMN	BAe (BAC) One-Eleven 510ED	142		0068	0893	2 RR Spey 512-14DW(HK2)	41950	Y104		lsf European Aviation Ltd / sub-lst AZX
☐ G-AVMP	BAe (BAC) One-Eleven 510ED	144		0068	0893	2 RR Spey 512-14DW(HK2)	41950	Y104		The Madrid Express / lsf Euro.Avn Ltd
☐ G-AVMS	BAe (BAC) One-Eleven 510ED	146		0069	0893	2 RR Spey 512-14DW(HK2)	43550	Y104		lsf European Aviation Ltd
☐ G-AVMT	BAe (BAC) One-Eleven 510ED	147		0069	0893	2 RR Spey 512-14DW(HK2)	43550	Y104		lsf European Aviation Ltd
☐ G-AVMW	BAe (BAC) One-Eleven 510ED	150		0069	0693	2 RR Spey 512-14DW(HK2)	41950	Y104		lsf European Aviation Ltd / sub-lst AZX
☐ G-AVMY	BAe (BAC) One-Eleven 510ED	152		0069	0693	2 RR Spey 512-14DW(HK2)	43550	Y104		lsf European Aviation Ltd
☐ G-AVMZ	BAe (BAC) One-Eleven 510ED	153		0069	0693	2 RR Spey 512-14DW	43550	Y104		lsf European Aviation Ltd
☐ G-AWYV	BAe (BAC) One-Eleven 501EX	178		0069	0894	2 RR Spey 512-14DW(HK2)	41950	Y104		lsf European Aviation Ltd
☐ G-AXLL	BAe (BAC) One-Eleven 523FJ	193	OB-R-1173	0069	1294	2 RR Spey 512-14DW(HK2)	45200	Y104		lsf European Aviation Ltd
☐ G-AYOP	BAe (BAC) One-Eleven 530FX	233		0071	0894	2 RR Spey 512-14DW(HK2)	45200	Y104		lsf European Aviation Ltd / cvtd -518FG
☐ G-AZMF	BAe (BAC) One-Eleven 530FX	240	7Q-YKJ	0072	1094	2 RR Spey 512-14DW(HK2)	41950	VIP E50		lsf European Aviation Ltd
☐ G-CEAC	Boeing 737-229C (A)	21738 / 576	OO-SDR	0079		2 PW JT8D-15/15A	52750	Y130		tblsf European Aviation Ltd 0099/ex SAB
☐ G-CEAD	Boeing 737-229 (A)	21137 / 421	OO-SDM	0075		2 PW JT8D-15/15A	54200	Y130		tblsf European Aviation Ltd 0099/ex SAB
☐ G-	Boeing 737-229 (A)	20911 / 360	OO-SDE	0074		2 PW JT8D-15/15A	54200	Y130		tblsf European Aviation Ltd 0099
☐ G-	Boeing 737-229 (A)	20907 / 351	OO-SDA	0074		2 PW JT8D-15 (HK3/NOR)	52750	Y130		tblsf European Aviation Ltd 0000/ex SAB
☐ G-	Boeing 737-229 (A)	20910 / 358	OO-SDD	0074		2 PW JT8D-15 (HK3/NOR)	52750	Y130		tblsf European Aviation Ltd 0000/ex SAB
☐ G-	Boeing 737-229 (A)	20912 / 365	OO-SDF	0074		2 PW JT8D-15/15A	52750	Y130		tblsf European Aviation Ltd 0000/ex SAB
☐ G-	Boeing 737-229 (A)	21135 / 418	OO-SDG	0075		2 PW JT8D-15/15A	52750	Y130		tblsf European Aviation Ltd 0000/ex SAB
☐ G-	Boeing 737-229 (A)	21136 / 420	OO-SDL	0075		2 PW JT8D-15/15A	52750	Y130		tblsf European Aviation Ltd 0000/ex SAB
☐ G-	Boeing 737-229 (A)	21176 / 431	OO-SDN	0075		2 PW JT8D-15/15A	54200	Y130		tblsf European Aviation Ltd 0000/ex SAB
☐ G-	Boeing 737-229 (A)	21177 / 433	OO-SDO	0075		2 PW JT8D-15/15A	54200	Y130		tblsf European Aviation Ltd 0000/ex SAB
☐ G-	Boeing 737-229C (A)	20915 / 401	OO-SDJ	0075		2 PW JT8D-15/15A	52750	Y130		tblsf European Aviation Ltd 0000/ex SAB
☐ G-	Boeing 737-229C (A)	20916 / 403	OO-SDK	0075		2 PW JT8D-15/15A	52750	Y130		tblsf European Aviation Ltd 0000/ex SAB
☐ G-	Boeing 737-229C (A)	21139 / 437	OO-SDP	0075		2 PW JT8D-15/15A	52750	Y130		tblsf European Aviation Ltd 0000/ex SAB

EUROPE ELITE = Y6 / VIP — London-Heathrow

25 Thurloe Street, South Kensington, London SW7 2LH, Great Britain ☎ (171) 225 13 45 Tx: none Fax: (171) 225 14 50 SITA: n/a
F: 1996 ☗☗☗ n/a Head: John Beveridge ICAO: VESTAL Net: n/a Presently being set-up. Intends to start operations during 1999 with Boeing 757 aircraft.

EUROSCOT AIRWAYS, Ltd = MY / EUJ — Bournemouth

Bournemouth International Airport, Christchurch, Dorset BH23 6SE, Great Britain ☎ (1202) 36 42 65 Tx: none Fax: (1202) 36 42 72 SITA: BOHRRMY
F: 1997 ☗☗☗ 14 Head: Jack Romero IATA: 866 ICAO: SCOTAIR Net: http://www.euroscot.com

☐ G-BXXA	ATR 72-202	301	F-WQGJ	0092	0898	2 PWC PW124B	21500	Y66		lsf/opb GIL in EUJ-colors
☐ G-	Fokker 100 (F28 Mk0100)					2 RR Tay 650-15	44452	Y100		to be leased 0599

FALCON JET CENTRE, Ltd = FJC (Division AM Group of Companies) — London-Heathrow

No. 2 Maintenance Area, London Heathrow Airport, Hounslow, Middlesex TW6 3AE, Great Britain ☎ (181) 897 60 21 Tx: 932879 falcon g Fax: (181) 897 76 38 SITA: n/a
F: 1975 ☗☗☗ 22 Head: Simon Ford ICAO: FALCONJET Net: n/a

☐ G-BJDJ	Hawker 700B (HS 125-700B)	257142	G-RCDI	0081	1296	2 GA TFE731-3R-1H	11567	Executive		
☐ G-BGOP	Dassault Falcon 20F	406	F-WMKF*	0079		2 GE CF700-2D2	13000	Executive		opf Nissan (UK) Ltd

FAST HELICOPTERS, Ltd = FHL — Thruxton

Thruxton Aerodrome, Thruxton, nr. Andover, Hampshire SP11 8PW, Great Britain ☎ (1264) 77 25 08 Tx: none Fax: (1264) 77 38 24 SITA: n/a
F: 1986 ☗☗☗ n/a Head: Capt. Michael Green ICAO: FINDON Net: http://www.fast-helicopters.co.uk/ Aircraft below MTOW 1361 kg: Robinson R22

☐ G-BVGA	Bell 206B JetRanger III	2922	N54AJ	0080		1 AN 250-C20B	1451			
☐ G-BXKL	Bell 206B JetRanger III	3006	N5735Y	0080	1297	1 AN 250-C20B	1451			lsf Swattons Aviation Ltd
☐ G-DNCN	Agusta-Bell 206A JetRanger	8185	9H-AAJ	0070	1297	1 AN 250-C18B	1361			
☐ G-PORT	Bell 206B JetRanger III	2784	N37AH	0079		1 AN 250-C20B	1451			lsf Image Computer Systems Ltd
☐ G-OLDN	Bell 206L LongRanger	45077	G-TBCA	0077		1 AN 250-C20B	1814			lsf Gulfstream Air Services (UK) Ltd

173 registration type of aircraft cn/fn ex/ex* mfd del powered by mtow kg configuration selcal name/fln/specialitites/remarks

FIRFAX AIR CHARTER (Firfax Aviation, Ltd dba) — Staverton

High Street, Avening, Tetbury, Gloucestershire GL8 8LU, Great Britain ☎ (1452) 71 78 00 Tx: none Fax: (1452) 71 78 20 SITA: n/a
F: 1997 n/a Head: Richard Smith Net: n/a

☐ G-BVES	Cessna 340A II	*340A0077*	*N1378G*	*0076*		*2 CO TSIO-520-N*	*2717*			

FIRST CITY AIR, Plc = MBL — Westland Heliport

Westland Heliport, Lombard Road, London SW11 3RE, Great Britain ☎ (171) 223 80 00 Tx: none Fax: (171) 223 81 11 SITA: n/a
F: 1993 5 Head: Malcolm Thwaites ICAO: FIRST CITY Net: n/a

☐ G-MANN	Eurocopter (Aerosp.) SA341G Gazelle	*1295*	*G-BKLW*	*0075*		*1 TU Astazou IIIA*	*1800*			

FLIGHTLINE, Ltd = FLT (Palmair Flightline) — Southend & London-Stansted

Viscount House, Southend Airport, Southend-on-Sea, Essex SS2 6YF, Great Britain ☎ (1702) 54 30 00 Tx: none Fax: (1702) 54 77 78 SITA: SENFLCR
F: 1989 120 Head: Ian Stewart ICAO: FLIGHTLINE Net: n/a PALMAIR FLIGHTLINE is the marketing name (painted on 1 BAe 146) used for flights in conjunction with associate company BATH TRAVEL.
2 aircraft are op. on a wet-lease agreement on behalf of AZZURRAIR (in Alitalia-colors) & SWISSAIR (in Swissair Express-colors) using AZ & SR flight numbers.

☐ G-OFLT	Embraer 110P1 Bandeirante (EMB-110P1)	*110211*	*G-MOBL*	*0079*	*1290*	*2 PWC PT6A-34*	*5670*	*Y19 / Freighter*		
☐ G-FLTA	BAe 146-200	*E2048*	*N189US*	*0085*	*0298*	*4 LY ALF502R-5*	*40597*	*CY82*		*lsf Alpine Aviation/op in SR Express-cs*
☐ G-OZRH	BAe 146-200	*E2047*	*N188US*	*0085*	*0196*	*4 LY ALF502R-5*	*40597*	*Y98*		
☐ G-TBIC	BAe 146-200	*E2025*	*N167US*	*0084*	*1296*	*4 LY ALF502R-5*	*40597*	*CY94*		*lsf TBI Plc / op in AZI/Alitalia-colors*
☐ G-BPNT	BAe 146-300	*E3126*		*0089*	*0493*	*4 LY ALF502R-5*	*43091*	*Y110*		*lsf BAMJ/opf Bath Travel/Palmair-titles*

FLIGHT PRECISION, Ltd = CLB — Teesside

Hangar 360, Teesside Airport, Darlington DL2 1NJ, Great Britain ☎ (1325) 33 29 33 Tx: none Fax: (1325) 33 35 91 SITA: n/a
F: 1996 n/a Head: Colin Chitty ICAO: CALIBRATOR Net: n/a Private company, conducting calibration-, navigation- and flight-inspection-flights for the Civil Aviation Authority, Royal Air Force & independent airfields.

☐ G-FCAL	Cessna 441 Conquest II	*441-0293*	*C-FMHD*	*0083*	*1096*	*2 GA TPE331-8-403S*	*4468*	*Calibrator*		*lsf Cobham Leasing Ltd*
☐ G-FPLC	Cessna 441 Conquest II	*441-0207*	*G-FRAX*	*0081*	*1096*	*2 GA TPE331-8-403S*	*4468*	*Calibrator*		
☐ G-FPLA	Beech King Air B200	*BB-944*	*N31WL*	*0082*	*1297*	*2 PWC PT6A-42*	*5670*	*Calibrator*		*lsf Cobham Leasing Ltd*
☐ G-FPLB	Beech King Air B200	*BB-1048*	*N739WG*	*0082*	*1297*	*2 PWC PT6A-42*	*5670*	*Calibrator*		*lsf Cobham Leasing Ltd*

FLYING COLOURS Airlines, Ltd = MT / FCL (Subsidiary of Thomas Cook Group, Ltd) — Manchester & London-Gatwick

Building 79, Terminal 2, Manchester Airport, M90 4FX, Great Britain ☎ (161) 489 57 57 Tx: none Fax: (161) 489 57 58 SITA: n/a
F: 1996 700 Head: Errol Cossey ICAO: COLOURS Net: n/a

☐ G-BXKC	Airbus Industrie A320-214	*730*	*F-WWBQ**	*0097*	*1198*	*2 CFMI CFM56-5B4*	*77000*	*Y180*	*RS-EH*	*lsf GECA / sub-lst RYN in winter*
☐ G-BXKD	Airbus Industrie A320-214	*735*	*F-WWBV**	*0097*	*1198*	*2 CFMI CFM56-5B4*	*77000*	*Y180*	*RS-EJ*	*lsf GECA / sub-lst RYN in winter*
☐ G-BXRW	Airbus Industrie A320-231	*308*	*EC-GNB*	*0092*	*1198*	*2 IAE V2500-A1*	*75500*	*Y180*	*FG-AR*	*lsf ORIX / sub-lst IWD as EC-GUR*
☐ G-BXRX	Airbus Industrie A320-231	*314*	*N314RX*	*0092*	*1198*	*2 IAE V2500-A1*	*75500*	*Y180*	*FG-AS*	*lsf ORIX / sub-lst IWD as EC-GLT*
☐ N714AW	Airbus Industrie A320-214	*714*	*G-BXKA**	*0097*	*1198*	*2 CFMI CFM56-5B4*	*77000*	*Y180*	*RS-EF*	*lsf GECA / sub-lst RYN in winter*
☐ N716AW	Airbus Industrie A320-214	*716*	*G-BXKB**	*0097*	*1198*	*2 CFMI CFM56-5B4*	*77000*	*Y180*	*RS-EG*	*lsf GECA / sub-lst RYN in winter*
☐ G-FCLA	Boeing 757-28A	*27621 / 738*	*N1789B**	*0097*	*0297*	*2 RR RB211-535E4*	*102060*	*Y235*	*QS-DE*	*lsf ILFC*
☐ G-FCLB	Boeing 757-28A	*28164 / 749*	*N751NA*	*0097*	*0397*	*2 RR RB211-535E4*	*102060*	*Y235*	*QS-DF*	*lsf ILFC*
☐ G-FCLC	Boeing 757-28A	*28166 / 756*		*0597*	*0597*	*2 RR RB211-535E4*	*105688*	*Y235*	*QS-DG*	*lsf ILFC*
☐ G-FCLD	Boeing 757-25F (ET)	*28718 / 752*		*0097*	*0497*	*2 RR RB211-535E4*	*111580*	*Y235*	*QS-DH*	*lsf GATX*
☐ G-FCLE	Boeing 757-28A	*28171 / 805*		*0598*	*0598*	*2 RR RB211-535E4*	*99338*	*Y235*	*CH-JQ*	*lsf ILFC*
☐ G-FCLF	Boeing 757-28A	*28835*				*2 RR RB211-535E4*	*113398*	*Y235*		*to be lsf ILFC 0699*
☐ G-FCLG	Boeing 757-28A	*24367 / 208*	*N701LF*	*0089*	*1298*	*2 RR RB211-535E4*	*113398*	*Y235*		*lsf ILFC*
☐ G-FCLH	Boeing 757-28A	*26274 / 676*	*N751LF*	*0095*		*2 RR RB211-535E4*	*113398*	*Y235*		*to be lsf ILFC 0599 / ex TSO*
☐ G-FCLI	Boeing 757-28A	*26275 / 672*	*N651LF*	*0095*		*2 RR RB211-535E4*	*113398*	*Y235*		*to be lsf ILFC 0599 / ex TSO*
☐ G-FCLJ	Boeing 757-2Y0	*26160 / 555*	*N160GE*	*0094*		*2 RR RB211-535E4*	*113398*	*Y235*		*to be lsf GECA 0499*
☐ G-FCLK	Boeing 757-2Y0	*26161 / 557*	*N161GE*	*0094*		*2 RR RB211-535E4*	*113398*	*Y235*		*to be lsf GECA 0499*
☐ C-FOOE	Boeing 757-28A	*24369 / 226*		*0089*		*2 RR RB211-535E4*	*113398*	*Y226*	*JL-MP*	*to be lsf CMM in summer, 05-1099*

FORDAIR = FOB (Division of Ford Motor, Co. Ltd) — London-Stansted

Hangar 2, Stocking Wood, Stansted Airport, Essex CM24 1QU, Great Britain ☎ (1279) 66 56 00 Tx: 81449 g Fax: (1279) 66 56 54 SITA: n/a
F: 1967 n/a Head: Capt. Robert Gardner ICAO: FORDAIR Net: n/a Private, non-commercial company conducting corporate flights for itself only.

☐ G-JETI	Hawker 800B (BAe 125-800B)	*258056*		*0086*	*1097*	*2 GA TFE731-5R-1H*	*12483*	*Corporate*		
☐ VP-BOO	Boeing (Douglas) MD-87 (DC-9-87)	*49778 / 1646*	*VR-BOO*	*1089*	*1292*	*2 PW JT8D-219*	*63503*	*Corporate 115Pax*	*AH-JK*	*lsf Interlocutory Ltd*
☐ VP-BOP	Boeing (Douglas) MD-87 (DC-9-87)	*49725 / 1552*	*VR-BOP*	*1288*	*0293*	*2 PW JT8D-219*	*63503*	*Corporate 115Pax*		*lsf Interlocutory Ltd*

FORD HELICOPTERS, Ltd (Affiliated with maintenance company March Helicopters, Ltd) — Northampton-Sywell

Northampton-Sywell Aerodrome, Northampton, Northamptonshire NN6 0BN, Great Britain ☎ (1604) 49 31 37 Tx: none Fax: (1604) 79 00 51 SITA: n/a
F: 1980 7 Head: Alan Ford Net: http://www.helicopter-sales.co.uk/charter.htm

☐ G-OFHL	Eurocopter (Aerosp.) AS350B Squirrel	*1805*	*EI-BPM*	*0084*	*0693*	*1 TU Arriel 1B*	*1950*			

FORMULA 1 – Flight Operations (Flight Operations-division of Formula 1 Administration, Ltd) — Biggin Hill

c/o Formula 1 Administration Ltd, 6 Princes Gate, London SW7 1, Great Britain ☎ (1959) 54 06 79 Tx: none Fax: (1959) 54 06 82 SITA: n/a
F: 1992 2 Head: Ross Mercer Net: n/a Operates non-commercial corporate flights to transport Formula 1 personnel between the European Grand Prix-circuits.

☐ N2FU	Learjet 31	*31-027*	*N30LJ*	*0090*	*0792*	*2 GA TFE731-2-3B*	*7484*	*Corporate 5 Pax*		*lsf Wilmington Trust Co.*
☐ N12FU	Learjet 60	*60-027*	*N4230S*	*0094*	*1296*	*2 PWC PW305A*	*10659*	*Corporate 8 Pax*		*lsf Wilmington Trust Co.*
☐ G-OFOA	BAe 146-100	*E1006*	*G-BKMN*	*0083*	*0298*	*4 LY ALF502R-3A*	*37310*	*Corporate F7Y60*		

F R AVIATION, Ltd – FRA = FRA (Flight Refuelling, Ltd dba / Member of the Cobham Group) — Bournemouth

Bournemouth-Hurn Airport, Christchurch, Dorset BH23 6NE, Great Britain ☎ (1202) 40 90 00 Tx: 41147 frhurn g Fax: (1202) 58 09 36 SITA: n/a
F: 1965 200 Head: Michael Knight ICAO: RUSHTON Net: n/a Operates aircraft on contract basis for the MoD, NATO and specialist contractors. Also maintains and operates military aircraft for MoD.

☐ G-AZXA	Beech Baron C55 (95-C55)	*TE-72*	*SE-EXZ*	*0066*		*2 CO IO-520-C*	*2404*	*Target towing*		*lsf Cobham Leasing Ltd*
☐ G-FRBY	Beech Baron E55	*TE-868*	*N78PS*	*0072*		*2 CO IO-520-C*	*2404*	*Target towing*		*lsf Cobham Leasing Ltd*
☐ G-MAFF	Britten-Norman BN-2T Turbine Islander	*2119*	*G-BJED*	*0081*		*2 AN 250-B17C*	*3175*	*Surveyer*		*lsf Cobham Lsng/cvtd BN-2B-26/Fish.Pat.*
☐ G-FRAZ	Cessna 441 Conquest II	*441-0035*	*SE-GYC*	*0078*		*2 GA TPE331-8-403S*	*4468*	*Target towing*		*lsf Cobham Leasing Ltd*
☐ G-MAFE	Dornier 228-202K	*8009*	*G-OALF*	*0083*	*1292*	*2 GA TPE331-5-252D*	*6200*	*Surveyer*		*lsf Cobham Leasing Ltd/Fisheries Patrol*
☐ G-MAFI	Dornier 228-200	*8115*	*D-CAAE**	*0087*	*0387*	*2 GA TPE331-5-252D*	*5700*	*Surveyer*		*lsf Cobham Leasing Ltd/Fisheries Patrol*
☐ G-OMAF	Dornier 228-200	*8112*	*D-CAAD**	*0087*	*0287*	*2 GA TPE331-5-252D*	*5700*	*Surveyer*		*lsf Cobham Leasing Ltd/Fisheries Patrol*
☐ G-FFRA	Dassault Falcon 20D (C)	*132*	*N902FR*	*0068*		*2 GE CF700-2D2*	*13000*	*TS Trainer*		*lsf Cobham Leasing Ltd*
☐ G-FRAD	Dassault Falcon 20E	*304*	*G-BCYF*	*0075*		*2 GE CF700-2D2*	*13000*	*Target towing*		*lsf Cobham Leasing Ltd*
☐ G-FRAE	Dassault Falcon 20E	*280*	*N910FR*	*0073*		*2 GE CF700-2D2*	*13000*	*Target towing*		*lsf Cobham Leasing Ltd*
☐ G-FRAF	Dassault Falcon 20E	*295*	*N911FR*	*0074*		*2 GE CF700-2D2*	*13000*	*Target towing*		*lsf Cobham Leasing Ltd*
☐ G-FRAH	Dassault Falcon 20D (C)	*223*	*N900FR*	*0070*		*2 GE CF700-2D2*	*13000*	*TS Trainer*		*lsf Cobham Leasing Ltd*
☐ G-FRAI	Dassault Falcon 20E (C)	*270*	*N901FR*	*0070*		*2 GE CF700-2D2*	*13000*	*TS Trainer*		*lsf Cobham Leasing Ltd*
☐ G-FRAJ	Dassault Falcon 20E (C)	*20*	*N903FR*	*0066*		*2 GE CF700-2D2*	*13000*	*TS Trainer*		*lsf Cobham Leasing Ltd*
☐ G-FRAK	Dassault Falcon 20D (C)	*213*	*N905FR*	*0070*		*2 GE CF700-2D2*	*13000*	*TS Trainer*		*lsf Cobham Leasing Ltd / opf AVDEF*
☐ G-FRAL	Dassault Falcon 20D (C)	*151*	*N904FR*	*0068*		*2 GE CF700-2D2*	*13000*	*TS Trainer*		*lsf Cobham Leasing Ltd*
☐ G-FRAM	Dassault Falcon 20D (C)	*224*	*N907FR*	*0070*		*2 GE CF700-2D2*	*13000*	*EW Trainer*		*lsf Cobham Leasing Ltd*
☐ G-FRAO	Dassault Falcon 20D (C)	*214*	*N906FR*	*0070*		*2 GE CF700-2D2*	*13000*	*TS Trainer*		*lsf Cobham Leasing Ltd*
☐ G-FRAP	Dassault Falcon 20D (C)	*207*	*N908FR*	*0070*		*2 GE CF700-2D2*	*13000*	*EW Trainer*		*lsf Cobham Leasing Ltd*
☐ G-FRAR	Dassault Falcon 20D (C)	*209*	*N909FR*	*0070*		*2 GE CF700-2D2*	*13000*	*EW Trainer*		*lsf Cobham Leasing Ltd*
☐ G-FRAS	Dassault Falcon 20C	*82*	*CAF 117501*	*0067*	*1090*	*2 GE CF700-2D2*	*13000*	*Trainer*		*lsf Cobham Leasing Ltd*
☐ G-FRAT	Dassault Falcon 20C	*87*	*CAF 117502*	*0067*	*1190*	*2 GE CF700-2D2*	*13000*	*Trainer*		*lsf Cobham Leasing Ltd*
☐ G-FRAU	Dassault Falcon 20C	*97*	*CAF 117504*	*0067*	*1190*	*2 GE CF700-2D2*	*13000*	*Trainer*		*lsf Cobham Leasing Ltd*
☐ G-FRAW	Dassault Falcon 20C	*114*	*CAF 117507*	*0067*	*0990*	*2 GE CF700-2D2*	*13000*	*Trainer*		*lsf Cobham Leasing Ltd*
☐ G-FRBA	Dassault Falcon 20D	*178*	*OH-FFA*	*0070*	*0796*	*2 GE CF700-2D2*	*13000*	*Target towing*		*lsf Cobham Leasing Ltd*

GAMA AVIATION, Ltd = GMA — Fairoaks

Fairoaks Airport, Chobham, Woking, Surrey GU24 8HX, Great Britain ☎ (1276) 85 69 61 Tx: 859482 gama g Fax: (1276) 85 84 85 SITA: n/a
F: 1983 12 Head: Marwan A. Khalek ICAO: GAMA Net: n/a

☐ G-OSCA	Cessna 500 Citation	*500-0270*	*G-SWET*	*0075*		*2 PWC JT15D-1*	*5216*	*7 Pax*		*lsf Oscar Aviation Ltd*
☐ G-BPPM	Beech King Air B200	*BB-1044*	*N7061T*	*0082*		*2 PWC PT6A-42*	*5670*	*10 Pax*		
☐ G-HAMA	Beech King Air 200	*BB-30*	*N244JB*	*0075*		*2 PWC PT6A-41*	*5670*	*10 Pax*		
☐ G-SBAS	Beech King Air B200	*BB-1007*	*SE-IVZ*	*0082*		*2 PWC PT6A-42*	*5670*	*11 Pax*		
☐ G-JETG	Learjet 35A	*35A-324*	*G-JETN*	*0080*	*1097*	*2 GA TFE731-2-2B*	*8165*	*8 Pax*		
☐ G-LJET	Learjet 35A	*35A-643*	*N39418*	*0088*	*1097*	*2 GA TFE731-2-2B*	*8301*	*8 Pax*		

GB AIRWAYS, Ltd = GT / GBL (Member of Bland Group Companies / Associated with British Airways, Plc) — London-Gatwick

Iain Stewart Centre, Beehive Ring Road South, Gatwick Airport, West Sussex RH6 0PB, Great Britain ☎ (1293) 66 42 39 Tx: none Fax: (1293) 66 42 18 SITA: LGWDQGT
F: 1931 510 Head: Joseph J. Gaggero, CBE IATA: 171 ICAO: GEEBEE AIRWAYS Net: n/a
Scheduled services are operated on a franchise agreement with BRITISH AIRWAYS (in full such colors & both titles) & using BA-flight numbers.

☐ G-OGBB	Boeing 737-34S	*29108 / 2983*		*0198*	*0198*	*2 CFMI CFM56-3C3*	*59647*	*CY130*		*op in BA Dove-colors*
☐ G-OGBC	Boeing 737-34S	*29109 / 3001*	*N1787B**	*0298*	*0298*	*2 CFMI CFM56-3C3*	*59647*	*CY130*		*op in BA Flowers of Mazowsze-colors*
☐ G-OGBD	Boeing 737-3L9	*27833 / 2688*	*OY-MAR*	*0195*	*0398*	*2 CFMI CFM56-3C1*	*59647*	*CY130*		*lsf ORIX / op in BA Martha Masanabo-cs*
☐ G-OGBE	Boeing 737-3L9	*27834 / 2692*	*OY-MAS*	*0095*	*1198*	*2 CFMI CFM56-3C1*	*59647*	*CY130*		*lsf Sanwa/op in BA Crossing Borders-cs*

174 registration type of aircraft *cn/fn* *ex/ex** *mfd* *del* *powered by* *mtow kg* *configuration* *selcal* *name/fln/specialitites/remarks*

registration	type of aircraft	cn/fn	ex/ex*	mfd	del	powered by	mtow kg	configuration	selcal	name/fln/specialitites/remarks
☐ G-BNNK	Boeing 737-4Q8	24069 / 1635		1288	0495	2 CFMI CFM56-3C1	62800	CY150	JP-CH	lsf ILFC/op in BA Waves of the City-cs
☐ G-BNNL	Boeing 737-4Q8	24070 / 1665		0189	0395	2 CFMI CFM56-3C1	62800	CY150	JP-CK	lsf ILFC / op in BA Chelsea Rose-cs
☐ G-BUHL	Boeing 737-4S3	25134 / 2083	9M-MLH	0691	0396	2 CFMI CFM56-3C1	62800	CY146	AK-HM	lsf ILFC / op in BA Wings-colors
☐ G-OGBA	Boeing 737-4S3	25596 / 2255	G-OBMK	0392	0497	2 CFMI CFM56-3C1	62800	CY150	AK-HM	lsf ILFC / op in BA Waves & Cranes-cs
☐ G-TREN	Boeing 737-4S3	24796 / 1887	G-BRKG	0690	0497	2 CFMI CFM56-3C1	62800	CY150	AR-KQ	lsf ILFC / op in BA Blue Poole-colors
☐ G-	Airbus Industrie A320-232					2 IAE V2527-A5	73500	CY159		oo-delivery 0001/to be op in BA-colors
☐ G-	Airbus Industrie A320-232					2 IAE V2527-A5	73500	CY159		oo-delivery 0001/to be op in BA-colors
☐ G-	Airbus Industrie A320-232					2 IAE V2527-A5	73500	CY159		oo-delivery 0001/to be op in BA-colors
☐ G-	Airbus Industrie A320-232					2 IAE V2527-A5	73500	CY159		oo-delivery 0002/to be op in BA-colors
☐ G-	Airbus Industrie A320-232					2 IAE V2527-A5	73500	CY159		oo-delivery 0002/to be op in BA-colors
☐ G-	Airbus Industrie A320-232					2 IAE V2527-A5	73500	CY159		oo-delivery 0002/to be op in BA-colors
☐ G-	Airbus Industrie A320-232					2 IAE V2527-A5	73500	CY159		oo-delivery 0002/to be op in BA-colors
☐ G-	Airbus Industrie A320-232					2 IAE V2527-A5	73500	CY159		oo-delivery 0003/to be op in BA-colors
☐ G-	Airbus Industrie A320-232					2 IAE V2527-A5	73500	CY159		oo-delivery 0003/to be op in BA-colors

GILL AIRWAYS = 9C / GIL (Gill Aviation Ltd dba / Subsidiary of New Aviation Holdings Ltd / formerly GillAir) — Newcastle

Newcastle International Airport, Newcastle, Tyne & Wear NE13 8BT, Great Britain ☎ (191) 214 66 00 Tx: 537313 gilair g Fax: (191) 214 66 99 SITA: NCLRR9C
F: 1969 ⁂ 300 Head: William Price IATA: 786 ICAO: GILLAIR Net: n/a
Some aircraft are operated on a franchise agreement with AIR FRANCE & KLM uk in full such colors & both titles), using AF & UK flight-numbers.

registration	type of aircraft	cn/fn	ex/ex*	mfd	del	powered by	mtow kg	configuration	selcal	name/fln/specialitites/remarks
☐ G-BLZT	Shorts 360-100 (SD3-60 Variant 100)	SH3676		0085	1294	2 PWC PT6A-65R	11999	Y35		
☐ G-BNYI	Shorts 360-300 (SD3-60 Variant 100)	SH3731	N360CC	0087	0598	2 PWC PT6A-67R	12292	Y35		lsf Lynrise Air Lease
☐ G-DASI	Shorts 360-100 (SD3-60 Variant 100)	SH3606	G-14-3606*	0083	0495	2 PWC PT6A-65R	11999	Y35		
☐ G-OLAH	Shorts 360-100 (SD3-60 Variant 100)	SH3604	G-BPCO	0082	0491	2 PWC PT6A-65R	11999	Y35		
☐ G-RMCT	Shorts 360-100 (SD3-60 Variant 100)	SH3656	EI-BPD	0084	0294	2 PWC PT6A-65AR	11999	Y35		
☐ G-BVJP	ATR 42-300	371	F-WWLN*	0094	0494	2 PWC PW120	16700	Y48		
☐ G-BXBV	ATR 42-300	245	TS-LBA	0092	0597	2 PWC PW120	16700	Y48		lsf TUI
☐ G-ORFH	ATR 42-300	346	F-WWEI*	0093	1293	2 PWC PW120	16700	Y48		lsf Malfed Lsng / op in Air France-cs
☐ G-WFEP	ATR 42-300	149	N4210G	0089	0298	2 PWC PW120	16700	Y48		lsf Renaiss.Lsng / op in KLM uk-colors
☐ G-BWDA	ATR 72-202	444	F-WWEQ*	0095	0695	2 PWC PW124B	21500	Y66		
☐ G-BWDB	ATR 72-202	449	F-WWEE*	0095	0695	2 PWC PW124B	21500	Y66		Spirit of Newcastle
☐ G-BXXA	ATR 72-202	301	F-WQGJ	0092	0698	2 PWC PW124B	21500	Y66		lst/opf EUJ in EUJ-colors
☐ G-BXYV	ATR 72-202	322	B-22708	0092	0998	2 PWC PW124B	21500	Y66		
☐ G-BYDN	Fokker 100 (F28 Mk0100)	11329	N130ML	0091	0599	2 RR Tay 650-15	44452	Y100		lsf Debis AirFinance/opin Air France-cs
☐ G-BYDO	Fokker 100 (F28 Mk0100)	11323	N131ML	0090	0499	2 RR Tay 650-15	44452	Y100		lsf Debis AirFinance/opin Air France-cs
☐ G-BYDP	Fokker 100 (F28 Mk0100)	11321	F-WQJA	0090	0399	2 RR Tay 650-15	44452	Y100		lsf Debis AirFinance/opin Air France-cs

GM AIRLINES, Ltd (Subsidiary of GMH – General Mediterranean Holding) — Ostend & Accra

European HQ:, 364-366 Kensington High Street, London W14 8NS, Great Britain ☎ (171) 602 70 55 Tx: none Fax: (171) 603 55 33 SITA: n/a
F: n/a ⁂ 4 Head: Dr. Charles L. Panayides Net: n/a

registration	type of aircraft	cn/fn	ex/ex*	mfd	del	powered by	mtow kg	configuration	selcal	name/fln/specialitites/remarks
☐ N359PA	Boeing 727-230 (A)	20789 / 1015	D-ABSI	0074	0690	3 PW JT8D-15	82781	Corporate	BK-EL	Naghan/opf GMH-GenMed.Holding/opb CCL
☐ 9G-ADM	Boeing 707-321C	19369 / 648	9G-ADL	1167	0690	4 PW JT3D-3B (HK2/COM)	151092	Freighter	KM-CF	Garissa / opb CCL

GO Fly, Ltd = OG / GOE (Subsidiary of British Airways, Plc) — London-Stansted

Enterprise House, London Stansted Airport, Stansted, Essex CM24 1SB, Great Britain ☎ (1279) 66 63 33 Tx: none Fax: (1279) 68 17 62 SITA: n/a
F: 1998 ⁂ 150 Head: Barbara Cassini ICAO: GO-FLIGHT Net: http://www.go-fly.com

registration	type of aircraft	cn/fn	ex/ex*	mfd	del	powered by	mtow kg	configuration	selcal	name/fln/specialitites/remarks
☐ G-IGOA	Boeing 737-3Y0	24678 / 1853	EI-BZK	0090	0798	2 CFMI CFM56-3B1	56472	Y148		lsf GECA / sky blue underside-colors
☐ G-IGOC	Boeing 737-3Y0	24546 / 1811	EI-BZH	0089	0598	2 CFMI CFM56-3B1	56472	Y148	LP-KS	lsf GECA / purple underside-colors
☐ G-IGOE	Boeing 737-3Y0	24547 / 1813	EI-BZI	0089	0598	2 CFMI CFM56-3B1	56472	Y148	LQ-AH	lsf GECA / magenta underside-colors
☐ G-IGOF	Boeing 737-3Q8	24698 / 1846	PK-GWF	0090	0598	2 CFMI CFM56-3B1	58000	Y148	FL-GQ	lsf INGO / green underside-colors
☐ G-IGOG	Boeing 737-3Y0	23927 / 1580	F-GLLE	0788	0998	2 CFMI CFM56-3B1	56472	Y148		lsf BBAM / red underside-colors
☐ G-IGOH	Boeing 737-3Y0	23926 / 1562	F-GLLD	0588	1198	2 CFMI CFM56-3B1	56472	Y148		lsf GECA / olive green underside-colors
☐ G-IGOI	Boeing 737-33A	24092 / 1669	G-OBMD	0089	1198	2 CFMI CFM56-3B1	56472	Y148		yellow underside-colors
☐ G-IGOJ	Boeing 737-36N	28872 / 3082	N1795B*	0098	1198	2 CFMI CFM56-3C1	56472	Y148		lsf GECA
☐ G-IGOK	Boeing 737-36N	28594				2 CFMI CFM56-3C1	56472	Y148		to be lsf GECA 0099
☐ G-IGOL	Boeing 737-36N	28596				2 CFMI CFM56-3C1	56472	Y148		to be lsf GECA 0099
☐ G-IGOM	Boeing 737-36N	28599				2 CFMI CFM56-3C1	56472	Y148		to be lsf GECA 0099
☐ G-IGOP	Boeing 737-36N	28602				2 CFMI CFM56-3C1	56472	Y148		to be lsf GECA 0099
☐ G-IGOR	Boeing 737-36N	28606				2 CFMI CFM56-3C1	56472	Y148		to be lsf GECA 0099

GOLD AIR INTERNATIONAL, Ltd = GDA — Cambridge & Biggin Hill

Cambridge Airport, Newmarket Road, Cambridge CB5 8RX, Great Britain ☎ (1223) 29 47 77 Tx: none Fax: (1223) 29 35 73 SITA: n/a
F: 1996 ⁂ n/a Head: John Mason ICAO: GOLDAIR Net: n/a

registration	type of aircraft	cn/fn	ex/ex*	mfd	del	powered by	mtow kg	configuration	selcal	name/fln/specialitites/remarks
☐ G-HFTG	Piper PA-23-250 Aztec E	27-7405378	G-BSOB	0074	0199	2 LY IO-540-C4B5	2359			
☐ G-OLDA	Piper PA-31-350 Navajo Chieftain	31-8052038	G-BNDS	0080		2 LY TIO-540-J2BD	3175			lsf Owen Air Ltd
☐ G-OLDB	Piper PA-31-350 Navajo Chieftain	31-8152014	OY-SKY	0080	0597	2 LY TIO-540-J2BD	3175			lsf Shed Three Ltd
☐ G-OSGB	Piper PA-31-350 Navajo Chieftain	31-7952155	G-YSKY	0079		2 LY TIO-540-J2BD	3175			
☐ G-BDYF	Cessna 421C Golden Eagle II	421C0055	N98468	0076	0199	2 CO GTSIO-520-L	3379			
☐ G-FTAX	Cessna 421C Golden Eagle II	421C0308	N8363G	0077	0199	2 CO GTSIO-520-L	3379			lsf CRV Leasing
☐ G-JDTI	Cessna 421C Golden Eagle III	421C1226	N42E	0082	0199	2 CO GTSIO-520-L	3379			lsf MCP Aviation (Charter) Ltd
☐ G-BVRS	Beech King Air B90	LJ-481	G-KJET	0069		2 PWC PT6A-20	4377			lsf The Eight Blew Ltd
☐ G-OLDZ	Beech King Air 200	BB-828	G-MCEO	0081	0696	2 PWC PT6A-41	5670			lst Shed One Ltd
☐ G-REBK	Beech King Air B200	BB-1202	D-IHAP	0084	0597	2 PWC PT6A-42	5670			lsf Planstable Enterprises Ltd
☐ G-BFRM	Cessna 550 Citation II	550-0027	N527CC	0079	0199	2 PWC JT15D-4	6033			lsf Marshall of Cambridge Aerospace Ltd
☐ G-JETJ	Cessna 550 Citation II	550-0154	G-EJET	0080	0199	2 PWC JT15D-4	6033			
☐ G-OJPB	Hawker F600B (HS 125-F600B)	25258	VP-CJP	0071	0199	2 GA TFE731-3R-1H	11567			cvtd -600B

GOLDEN AIRWAYS, Ltd — Peterborough-Conington

1-3 Sterling Court, Loddington, Kettering, Northamptonshire NN14 1RZ, Great Britain ☎ (1536) 71 35 55 Tx: none Fax: (1536) 71 33 99 SITA: n/a
F: 1997 ⁂ n/a Head: Peter Wardle Net: n/a

registration	type of aircraft	cn/fn	ex/ex*	mfd	del	powered by	mtow kg	configuration	selcal	name/fln/specialitites/remarks
☐ G-BCPO	Partenavia P.68B	27		0075		2 LY IO-360-A1B6	1990			
☐ G-PEAT	Cessna 421B Golden Eagle	421B0432	G-BBIJ	0073		2 CO GTSIO-520-H	3379			

GO ONE AIR = GK (Go One Airways, Ltd dba) — London-Gatwick

318 Earlsfield Road, London SW18 3EJ, Great Britain ☎ (181) 874 83 29 Tx: none Fax: (181) 877 07 94 SITA: n/a
F: 1994 ⁂ n/a Head: n/a IATA: 274 Net: n/a Presently being set-up. Intends to start scheduled services to the Middle East with aircraft type not yet finalized.

GRAFF AVIATION, Ltd — Coventry

6/7 New Bond Street, London W1Y 9PE, Great Britain ☎ (171) 584 85 71 Tx: none Fax: (171) 581 34 15 SITA: n/a
F: 1984 ⁂ n/a Head: Laurence Graff Net: http://www.graff-uk.com

registration	type of aircraft	cn/fn	ex/ex*	mfd	del	powered by	mtow kg	configuration	selcal	name/fln/specialitites/remarks
☐ G-RAFF	Learjet 35A	35A-504	N8568B	0084		2 GA TFE731-2-2B	8165			

GRAMPIAN HELICOPTERS = GMR (Grampian Helicopter Charter, Ltd dba) — Inverurie

PO Box 11, Inverurie, Grampian AB51 9ZL, Scotland, Great Britain ☎ (1467) 63 30 40 Tx: none Fax: (1467) 63 30 30 SITA: n/a
F: 1991 ⁂ n/a Head: Robert Constable ICAO: GRAMAIR Net: n/a Aircraft below MTOW 1361kg: Robinson R22

registration	type of aircraft	cn/fn	ex/ex*	mfd	del	powered by	mtow kg	configuration	selcal	name/fln/specialitites/remarks
☐ G-GHCL	Bell 206B JetRanger	925	G-SHVV	0073	0792	1 AN 250-C20	1451			lst Scotia Helicopters
☐ G-OGHL	Eurocopter (Aerosp.) AS355F1 Tw.Squirrel	5164	N5796S	0382	0497	2 AN 250-C20F	2400			

HEAVYLIFT CARGO AIRLINES = NP / HLA (a Trafalgar House Company / formerly TAC HeavyLift) — London-Stansted & Southend

Stansted Airport, Stansted, Essex CM24 1QW, Great Britain ☎ (1279) 68 06 11 Tx: 817618 hlaops g Fax: (1279) 68 06 15 SITA: STNHONP
F: 1978 ⁂ 150 Head: Michael Hayles ICAO: HEAVYLIFT Net: n/a Beside aircraft listed: 6 Antonov 124 are managed/jointly operated by subsidiary HEAVYLIFT-VOLGA DNPER Ltd (same headquarters) together with VOLGA DNEPR, Russia. For fleet details – Volga Dnepr (RA-). Additional aircraft (Antonov 124, Ilyushin 76, Lockheed Hercules) are leased from ROSSIYA (RA), AIRSTAN (RA-) & PELITA AIR (PK-) when required.

registration	type of aircraft	cn/fn	ex/ex*	mfd	del	powered by	mtow kg	configuration	selcal	name/fln/specialitites/remarks
☐ RA-12995	Antonov 12B	00347402	CCCP-12995	0070	1296	4 IV AI-20M	61000	Freighter		lsf PLK
☐ G-BEPS	Shorts SC.5 Belfast	SH.1822	G-52-13*	0066		4 RR Tyne 515-101W	104780	Freighter	EF-CG	
☐ G-HLFT	Shorts SC.5 Belfast	SH.1819	XR365	0064		4 RR Tyne 515-101W	104780	Freighter	EF-CD	St. George
☐ G-HLAA	Airbus Industrie A300B4-203 (F)	047	EI-TLN	0077	1097	2 GE CF6-50C2	165000	Freighter	EF-CL	lsf CSAV / cvtd -203
☐ G-HLAB	Airbus Industrie A300B4-203 (F)	045	N743SC	0077	0298	2 GE CF6-50C2	165000	Freighter	DJ-EF	lsf CSAV / cvtd -203
☐ G-HLAC	Airbus Industrie A300B4-203 (F)	074	N829SC	0079	1298	2 GE CF6-50C2	165000	Freighter		lsf CSAV / cvtd -203
☐ G-HLAD	Airbus Industrie A300B4-203 (F)	154	N820SC	0781		2 GE CF6-50C2	165000	Freighter		to be lsf CSAV 0499 / cvtd -203
☐ RA-76401	Ilyushin 76TD	1023412399	CCCP-76401	0792	0795	4 SO D-30KP	190000	Freighter		lsf VDA

HELICENTRE, Ltd — Blackpool

Blackpool Airport, Blackpool, Lancashire FY4 2QY, Great Britain ☎ (1253) 34 30 82 Tx: n/a Fax: (1253) 40 73 51 SITA: n/a
F: 1991 ⁂ n/a Head: Geoff Hopkins Net: n/a Aircraft below MTOW 1361kg: Robinson R22.

registration	type of aircraft	cn/fn	ex/ex*	mfd	del	powered by	mtow kg	configuration	selcal	name/fln/specialitites/remarks
☐ G-BBCA	Bell 206B JetRanger	1101	N18091	0073		1 AN 250-C20	1451			lsf Kelly Trucks Ltd
☐ G-BPWI	Bell 206B JetRanger III	3087	9M-BSR	0080		1 AN 250-C20B	1451			lsf pvt
☐ G-TOYZ	Bell 206B JetRanger III	3949	G-RGER	0086		1 AN 250-C20J	1451			lsf pvt

HELICOPTER TRAINING & HIRE, Ltd = MVK
Belfast-Int'l

Helicopter Centre, General Aviation Building, Belfast International Airport, Belfast BT29 4JT, Northern Ireland, Great Britain ☎ (1849) 45 36 63 Tx: none Fax: (1849) 42 32 33 SITA: n/a
F: 1992 ⁂ 10 Head: Stewart Smiley ICAO: MAVRIK Net: n/a Aircraft below MTOW 1361kg: Robinson R22 & R44

☐ G-CORT	Agusta-Bell 206B JetRanger III	8739		0092	0696	1 AN 250-C20R/4	1451			

HELIJET AVIATION (Yorkshire Helicopters (Leeds), Ltd dba)
Leeds/Bradford

Leeds Heliport, Harrogate Road, Leeds LS19 7XS, Great Britain ☎ (113) 250 05 88 Tx: none Fax: (113) 250 81 61 SITA: n/a
F: 1996 ⁂ n/a Head: Mike D. Thorpe Net: n/a

☐ G-BTFY	Bell 206B JetRanger	1714	N49590	0074	1096	1 AN 250-C20	1451			
☐ G-RAMI	Bell 206B JetRanger III	2955	N1080N	0079	1096	1 AN 250-C20B	1451			
☐ G-OSAL	Cessna 421C Golden Eagle II	421C0218	OY-BEC	0077	1096	2 CO GTSIO-520-L	3379			

HELISCOTT, Ltd (Associated with Peter Scott Agric, Ltd)
Walton Wood

Walton Wood Airfield, Thorpe Audlin, Pontefract, West Yorkshire WF8 3HQ, Great Britain ☎ (1977) 62 13 78 Tx: none Fax: (1977) 62 08 68 SITA: n/a
F: 1980 ⁂ 7 Head: Capt. Peter E. Scott Net: http://www.heliscott.co.uk Aircraft below MTOW 1361kg: Robinson R22.

☐ G-BAML	Bell 206B JetRanger	36	N7844S	0067		1 AN 250-C20	1451			cvtd 206A

HIGHLAND AIRWAYS, Ltd = RLB (Subsidiary of Atlantic Holdings / formerly Air Alba, Ltd)
Inverness

HIGHLAND AIRWAYS

Inverness Airport, Dalcross, Inverness IV1 2JB, Scotland, Great Britain ☎ (1667) 46 26 64 Tx: none Fax: (1667) 46 26 96 SITA: n/a
F: 1991 ⁂ 8 Head: Alan Mossman ICAO: HIWAY Net: n/a

☐ G-RICK	Beech Baron B55 (95-B55)	TC-1472	G-BAAG	0072		2 CO IO-470-L	2313	Y5		lsf James Jack (Invergordon) Ltd
☐ G-TWIG	Reims/Cessna F406 Caravan II	F406-0014	PH-FWD	0087	1098	2 PWC PT6A-112	4468	Y12		

HUNTING AVIATION, Ltd = NVL (formerly Field Aircraft Services / Member of Hunting Group)
Kidlington

HUNTING AVIATION

Bldg 29, East Midlands Airport, Derby DE74 2SL, Great Britain ☎ (1332)810910ext3729 Tx: none Fax: (1753) 85 00 06 SITA: n/a
F: n/a ⁂ n/a Head: Tim Anderson ICAO: NAVCAL Net: n/a

☐ G-BVXW	Shorts Skyvan 3 Variant 100 (SC-7)	SH1889	LX-DEF	0071	1195	2 GA TPE331-2-201A	6215	Para		
☐ G-PIGY	Shorts Skyvan 3 Variant 100 (SC-7)	SH1943	LX-JUL	1175	0495	2 GA TPE331-2-201A	5670	Para		

I.D.S. Aircraft, Ltd = IDS
Bournemouth

Citation Centre, Hangar 266, Bournemouth Int'l Airport, Christchurch, Dorset BH23 6NW, Great Britain ☎ (1202) 59 01 00 Tx: none Fax: (1202) 58 15 79 SITA: n/a
F: 1968 ⁂ 18 Head: Arthur I. Sutherland ICAO: FANJET Net: n/a

☐ G-JETA	Cessna 550 Citation II	550-0094	N26630	0079		2 PWC JT15D-4	6033	Executive		

INTERFLIGHT = IFT (Interflight (Air Charter), Ltd dba)
London-Gatwick

Room 76A, The Beehive, Gatwick Airport, West Sussex RH6 0LA, Great Britain ☎ (1293) 54 04 09 Tx: 87407 infly g Fax: (1293) 56 73 58 SITA: n/a
F: 1980 ⁂ 22 Head: Simon P. Masey ICAO: INTERFLIGHT Net: n/a

☐ G-IFTC	Hawker F3B/RA (HS 125-F3B/RA	25171	G-OPOL	0069	0794	2 GA TFE731-3R-1H	10706			lsf Albion Aviation Management/cvtd -3B
☐ G-IFTE	Hawker 700B (HS 125-700B)	257037	G-BFVI	0078		2 GA TFE731-3R-1H	11567			lsf Albion Aviation Management Ltd
☐ G-PLGI	Hawker 700B (HS 125-700B)	257034	N510HS	0078	0795	2 GA TFE731-3R-1H	11567			lsf Polygram Record Operations Ltd

ISLAND AVIATION AND TRAVEL, Ltd = IOM
Isle of Man

Isle of Man (Ronaldsway) Airport, Ballasalla IM9 2JE, Isle of Man ☎ (1624) 82 39 80 Tx: 629439 g Fax: (1624) 82 49 46 SITA: n/a
F: 1984 ⁂ 9 Head: John Critchley ICAO: ISLE AVIA Net: n/a

☐ G-ASRH	Piper PA-30-160 Twin Comanche	30-368		0064		2 LY IO-320-B1A	1633			
☐ G-BIYO	Piper PA-31-310 Navajo C	31-7912022	PH-ECG	0079	0393	2 LY TIO-540-A2C	2950			lsf Executive Jet Leasing Ltd

ISLES OF SCILLY SKY BUS, Ltd = 5Y / IOS (Subsidiary of Isles of Scilly Steamship Company)
St. Just

Landsend Aerodrome, St. Just, Penzance, Cornwall TR19 7RL, Great Britain ☎ (1736) 78 70 17 Tx: none Fax: (1736) 78 83 66 SITA: n/a
F: 1984 ⁂ 50 Head: Michael Hicks ICAO: SCILLONIA Net: n/a

☐ G-BUBN	Britten-Norman BN-2B-26 Islander	2270		0093	0395	2 LY O-540-E4C5	2994			
☐ G-SBUS	Britten-Norman BN-2A-26 Islander	3013	G-BMMH	0086		2 LY O-540-E4C5	2994			
☐ G-SSKY	Britten-Norman BN-2A-26 Islander	2247		0091	0592	2 LY O-540-E4C5	2994			
☐ G-BIHO	De Havilland DHC-6 Twin Otter 310	738	A6-ADB	0081	0494	2 PWC PT6A-27	5670			

JERSEY EUROPEAN AIRWAYS, Ltd – JEA = JY / JEA (Member of the Walker Aviation Group of Companies)
Exeter

JERSEY EUROPEAN

Hangar 3, Exeter Airport, Exeter, Devon EX5 2BD, Great Britain ☎ (1392) 36 66 69 Tx: 42763 jeaops g Fax: (1392) 36 61 51 SITA: EXTOOJY
F: 1979 ⁂ 600 Head: Jack Walker IATA: 267 ICAO: JERSEY Net: http://www.jersey-european.co.uk
Some aircraft are operated on a franchise agreement with AIR FRANCE (in full such colors & both titles) & using AF-flight numbers.

☐ G-BKMX	Shorts 360-100 (SD3-60 Variant 100)	SH3608	G-14-3608*	0083	1098	2 PWC PT6A-65R	11999	Y36		
☐ G-OBHD	Shorts 360-200 (SD3-60 Variant 100)	SH3714	G-BNDK	0087	0387	2 PWC PT6A-65AR	11999	Y36		
☐ G-OBLK	Shorts 360-200 (SD3-60 Variant 100)	SH3712	G-BNDI	0087	0287	2 PWC PT6A-65AR	11999	Y36		
☐ G-JEAD	Fokker F27 Friendship 500RF (F27 Mk500RF)	10627	VH-EWU	0083	1190	2 RR Dart 532-7	19731	Freighter		lst RPX
☐ G-JEAE	Fokker F27 Friendship 500RF (F27 Mk500RF)	10633	VH-EWV	0083	1290	2 RR Dart 532-7	19731	Y48		
☐ G-JEAF	Fokker F27 Friendship 500RF (F27 Mk500RF)	10637	OY-SRD	0083	1290	2 RR Dart 532-7	20412	Y48		
☐ G-JEAG	Fokker F27 Friendship 500 (F27 Mk500)	10639	D-ADAP	0082	1190	2 RR Dart 532-7	19731	Y48		
☐ G-JEAH	Fokker F27 Friendship 500RF (F27 Mk500RF)	10669	VH-EWY	0084	0890	2 RR Dart 532-7	19999	Y48		
☐ G-JEAI	Fokker F27 Friendship 500RF (F27 Mk500RF)	10672	VH-EWZ	0084	0890	2 RR Dart 532-7	19731	Y48		
☐ G-JEAP	Fokker F27 Friendship 500 (F27 Mk500)	10459	9Q-CBI	0071	0495	2 RR Dart 532-7	19999	Freighter		lst EXS
☐ G-JEAO	BAe 146-100	E1010	G-UKPC	0083	0994	4 LY ALF502R-5	37308	Y74		lsf BAMJ / op in Air France-colors
☐ G-JEAT	BAe 146-100	E1071	N171TR	0087	1096	4 LY ALF502R-5	37308	Y74		
☐ G-JEAU	BAe 146-100	E1035	N135TR	0086	0197	4 LY ALF502R-5	37308	Y74		
☐ G-JEAJ	BAe 146-200	E2099	G-OLCA	0088	0393	4 LY ALF502R-5	42184	Y100		Pride of Guernsey / lsf BAMJ
☐ G-JEAK	BAe 146-200	E2103	G-OLCB	0088	0393	4 LY ALF502R-5	42184	Y100		Pride of Birmingham / lsf BAMJ
☐ G-JEAR	BAe 146-200	E2018	G-HWPB	0083	1195	4 LY ALF502R-5	40595	Y99		lsf BAMJ / op in Air France-colors
☐ G-JEAS	BAe 146-200	E2020	G-OLHB	0084	0296	4 LY ALF502R-5	42184	Y99		op in Air France-colors
☐ G-JEAV	BAe 146-200	E2064	N764BA	0086	0697	4 LY ALF502R-5	42184	Y99		lsf BAMJ
☐ G-JEAW	BAe 146-200	E2059	N759BA	0086	0897	4 LY ALF502R-5	42184	Y99		lsf BAMJ
☐ G-JEAX	BAe 146-200	E2136	N136JV	0089	0298	4 LY ALF502R-5	40595	Y99		lsf BAMJ
☐ G-JEAM	BAe 146-300	E3128	G-BTJT	0089	0593	4 LY ALF502R-5	43091	Y112		Pride of Jersey / lst BRT
☐ G-JEBA	BAe 146-300	E3181	HS-TBL	0091	0698	4 LY ALF502R-5	43091	Y112		lsf Walker Avn Fin./op in Air France-cs
☐ G-JEBB	BAe 146-300	E3185	HS-TBK	0091	0698	4 LY ALF502R-5	43091	Y112		lsf Walker Avn Fin./op in Air France-cs
☐ G-JEBC	BAe 146-300	E3189	HS-TBO	0091	0698	4 LY ALF502R-5	43091	Y112		lsf Walker Aviation Finance Ltd
☐ G-JEBD	BAe 146-300	E3191	HS-TBJ	0091	0798	4 LY ALF502R-5	43091	Y112		lsf Walker Aviation Finance Ltd
☐ G-JEBE	BAe 146-300	E3206	HS-TBM	0092	0698	4 LY ALF502R-5	43091	Y112		lsf Walker Aviation Finance Ltd

KEENAIR CHARTER, Ltd = JFK
Liverpool

Bldg 39, Liverpool Airport South Terminal, Speke, Liverpool L24 1YD, Great Britain ☎ (151) 448 03 03 Tx: none Fax: (151) 448 09 09 SITA: n/a
F: 1994 ⁂ 8 Head: Martin R. Keen ICAO: KEENAIR Net: n/a

☐ G-AZLJ	Britten-Norman BN-2A Mk.III-1 Trislander	319	G-OREG	0072	1096	3 LY O-540-E4C5	4536	Freighter		lsf Hebridean Air Services Ltd
☐ G-BGYT	Embraer 110P1 Bandeirante (EMB-110P1)	110234	N104VA	0079	1197	2 PWC PT6A-34	5670	Freighter		lsf Thonhill Aviation Ltd
☐ G-FLTY	Embraer 110P1 Bandeirante (EMB-110P1)	110215	G-ZUSS	0079	0098	2 PWC PT6A-34	5670	Y19 / Freighter		lsf Thornhill Aviation Ltd

KLM uk = UK / UKA (Air UK, Ltd dba / Subsidiary of KLM-Royal Dutch Airlines)
Norwich & London-Stansted

KLM uk

Stansted House, Stansted Airport, Stansted, Essex CM24 1AE, Great Britain ☎ (1279) 66 04 00 Tx: 817052 stnops g Fax: (1279) 66 03 30 SITA: n/a
F: 1980 ⁂ 2000 Head: Floris J. van Pallandt IATA: 130 ICAO: UKAY Net: http://www.klmuk.com
Beside aircraft listed, also uses an ATR42-300 wet-leased/opb GILL AIRWAYS (in KLM uk) colors on week-days. For details – see under that company.

☐ G-UKTA	Fokker 50 (F27 Mk050)	20246	PH-KXF	0092	0394	2 PWC PW125B	20820	CY50		City of Norwich / lsf Abbey Nat'l Lsng
☐ G-UKTB	Fokker 50 (F27 Mk050)	20247	PH-KXG	0092	0494	2 PWC PW125B	20820	CY50		City of Aberdeen / lsf Abbey Nat'l Lsng
☐ G-UKTC	Fokker 50 (F27 Mk050)	20249	PH-KXH	0092	0694	2 PWC PW125B	20820	CY50		City of Bradford / lsf Abbey Nat'l Leasing
☐ G-UKTD	Fokker 50 (F27 Mk050)	20256	PH-KXT	0092	0594	2 PWC PW125B	20820	CY50		City of Leeds / lsf Abbey National Lsng
☐ G-UKTE	Fokker 50 (F27 Mk050)	20270	PH-LXJ	0092	1094	2 PWC PW125B	20820	CY50		City of Hull / lsf Abbey National Lsng
☐ G-UKTF	Fokker 50 (F27 Mk050)	20271	PH-LXK	0093	1094	2 PWC PW125B	20820	CY50		City of York / lsf Abbey National Lsng
☐ G-UKTG	Fokker 50 (F27 Mk050)	20276	PH-LXP	0093	1194	2 PWC PW125B	20820	CY50		City of Durham / lsf Abbey National Lsng
☐ G-UKTH	Fokker 50 (F27 Mk050)	20277	PH-LXR	0093	1294	2 PWC PW125B	20820	CY50		City of Amsterdam / lsf Abbey Nat'l Lsng
☐ G-UKTI	Fokker 50 (F27 Mk050)	20279	PH-LXT*	0093	0395	2 PWC PW125B	20820	CY50		City of Stavanger / lsf Abbey Nat'l Lsg
☐ G-UKTJ	ATR 72-202	509		0097	1297	2 PWC PW124B	21500	CY66		
☐ G-UKTK	ATR 72-202	519	F-WWLQ*	0098	0198	2 PWC PW124B	21500	CY66		
☐ G-UKTL	ATR 72-202	523	F-WWLD	0098	0398	2 PWC PW124B	21500	CY66		
☐ G-UKTM	ATR 72-202	508	F-WWLU*	0096	0498	2 PWC PW124B	21500	CY66		
☐ G-UKTN	ATR 72-202	496	F-WWLT*	0096	0698	2 PWC PW124B	21500	CY66		
☐ G-BSNR	BAe 146-300	E3165	EC-FGT	0090	1194	4 LY ALF502R-5	41750	CY108	BJ-AR	lsf BAMJ
☐ G-BSNS	BAe 146-300	E3169	EC-FHU	0090	1094	4 LY ALF502R-5	41750	CY108	BJ-AS	lsf BAMJ
☐ G-BTTP	BAe 146-300	E3203	G-6-203*	0091	1093	4 LY ALF502R-5	41750	CY108		lsf BAMJ
☐ G-BUHC	BAe 146-300	E3193	G-BTMI	0092	0395	4 LY ALF502R-5	41750	CY108		lsf BAMJ
☐ G-UKAC	BAe 146-300	E3142	G-5-142*	0089	1189	4 LY ALF502R-5	41750	CY108		lsf Wilmington Trust Co.

176 registration type of aircraft cn/fn ex/ex* mfd del powered by mtow kg configuration selcal name/fln/specialitites/remarks

	registration	type of aircraft	cn/fn	ex/ex*	mfd	del	powered by	mtow kg	configuration	selcal	name/fln/specialitites/remarks
☐	G-UKAG	BAe 146-300	E3162	G-6-162*	0090	0191	4 LY ALF502R-5	41750	CY108		lsf BAMJ
☐	G-UKHP	BAe 146-300	E3123	G-5-123*	0089	0289	4 LY ALF502R-5	41750	CY108		lsf BAMJ
☐	G-UKID	BAe 146-300	E3157	G-6-157*	0090	0390	4 LY ALF502R-5	41750	CY108		lsf Wilmington Trust Co.
☐	G-UKRC	BAe 146-300	E3158	G-BSMR*	0091	0291	4 LY ALF502R-5	41750	CY108		lsf BAMJ
☐	G-UKSC	BAe 146-300	E3125	G-5-125*	0089	0389	4 LY ALF502R-5	41750	CY108		The City of Innsbruck / lsf BAMJ
☐	G-UKFA	Fokker 100 (F28 Mk0100)	11246	N602RP	0089	0792	2 RR Tay 620-15	41995	CY99		lsf ILFC
☐	G-UKFB	Fokker 100 (F28 Mk0100)	11247	N602TR	0089	0792	2 RR Tay 620-15	41995	CY99		lsf ILFC
☐	G-UKFC	Fokker 100 (F28 Mk0100)	11263	N602DG	0089	0792	2 RR Tay 620-15	41995	CY99		lsf ILFC
☐	G-UKFD	Fokker 100 (F28 Mk0100)	11259	C-FICP	0089	0792	2 RR Tay 620-15	41995	CY99		lsf ILFC
☐	G-UKFE	Fokker 100 (F28 Mk0100)	11260	C-FICQ	0089	0792	2 RR Tay 620-15	41995	CY99		lsf ILFC
☐	G-UKFF	Fokker 100 (F28 Mk0100)	11274	PH-ZCK	0089	0194	2 RR Tay 620-15	44450	CY99		lsf AFTR
☐	G-UKFG	Fokker 100 (F28 Mk0100)	11275	PH-ZCL	0089	1193	2 RR Tay 620-15	41995	CY99		lsf AFTR
☐	G-UKFH	Fokker 100 (F28 Mk0100)	11277	PH-ZCM	0089	0993	2 RR Tay 620-15	41995	CY99		lsf AFTR
☐	G-UKFI	Fokker 100 (F28 Mk0100)	11279	PH-ZCN	0089	1093	2 RR Tay 620-15	41995	CY99		lsf AFTR
☐	G-UKFJ	Fokker 100 (F28 Mk0100)	11248	F-GIOV	0088	0196	2 RR Tay 620-15	44450	CY99		lsf ILFC
☐	G-UKFK	Fokker 100 (F28 Mk0100)	11249	F-GIOX	0088	0196	2 RR Tay 620-15	44450	CY99		
☐	G-UKFL	Fokker 100 (F28 Mk0100)	11268	PH-KLC	0088	0897	2 RR Tay 620-15	44450	CY99		
☐	G-UKFM	Fokker 100 (F28 Mk0100)	11269	PH-KLD	0088	1098	2 RR Tay 620-15	44450	CY99		
☐	G-UKFN	Fokker 100 (F28 Mk0100)	11270	PH-KLE	0088	0697	2 RR Tay 620-15	44450	CY99		
☐	G-UKFO	Fokker 100 (F28 Mk0100)	11271	PH-KLG	0089	1097	2 RR Tay 620-15	44450	CY99		
☐	G-UKFP	Fokker 100 (F28 Mk0100)	11272	PH-KLH	0089	1098	2 RR Tay 620-15	44450	CY99		
☐	G-UKFR	Fokker 100 (F28 Mk0100)	11273	PH-KLI	0089	0397	2 RR Tay 620-15	44450	CY99		

LOGANAIR, Ltd = LOG — Glasgow

St. Andrews Drive, Glasgow Abbotsinch Airport, Paisley, Renfrewshire PA3 2TG, Great Britain ☎ (141) 848 75 94 Tx: 778246 loggla g Fax: (141) 887 60 20 SITA: n/a
F: 1962 ⁂ 200 Head: Scott Brier ICAO: LOGAN Net: n/a
All scheduled services are operated on a franchise agreement with BRITISH AIRWAYS (in full such colors & both titles) & using BA-flight numbers.

☐	G-BJOP	Britten-Norman BN-2B-26 Islander	2132		0082	0984	2 LY O-540-E4C5	2994	Y9		Capt.E.E.Fresson, OBE / BA-cs
☐	G-BLDV	Britten-Norman BN-2B-26 Islander	2179	D-INEY	0085	0796	2 LY O-540-E4C5	2994	Y9		BA BenyhoneTartan/Mtn of Many Birds-cs
☐	G-BLNJ	Britten-Norman BN-2B-26 Islander	2189		0086	1287	2 LY O-540-E4C5	2994	Y9		E.L.Gander Dower,Esq. / BA-cs
☐	G-BLNW	Britten-Norman BN-2B-26 Islander	2197		0087	1288	2 LY O-540-E4C5	2994	EMS		Sister Jean Kennedy / Scottish Amb.-cs
☐	G-BPCA	Britten-Norman BN-2B-26 Islander	2198	G-BLNX	0087	0288	2 LY O-540-E4C5	2994	EMS		Capt.David Barclay,MBE / Scott.Amb.-cs
☐	G-BVVK	De Havilland DHC-6 Twin Otter 310	666	LN-BEZ	0079	1294	2 PWC PT6A-27	5670	Y19		British Airways-colors
☐	G-BNMT	Shorts 360-300 (SD3-60 Variant 100)	SH3723	N160DD	0087	1098	2 PWC PT6A-67R	12292	Y34		lsf Lynrise / BA Koguty Lowickie-cs
☐	G-BNMU	Shorts 360-300 (SD3-60 Variant 100)	SH3724	N161DD	0087	1198	2 PWC PT6A-67R	12292	Y34		lsf Lynrise Air Lease / BA Column-cs
☐	G-BPFN	Shorts 360-300 (SD3-60 Variant 100)	SH3747	N747HH	0088	0898	2 PWC PT6A-67R	12292	Y34		BA Benyhone Tartan/Mtn of the Birds-cs

LOMAS HELICOPTERS = LMS (Lomas Brothers, Ltd dba) — Exeter

Lake Abbotsham, Bideford, North Devon EX39 5BQ, Great Britain ☎ (1237) 42 10 54 Tx: none Fax: (1237) 42 40 60 SITA: n/a
F: 1989 ⁂ 3 Head: David Lomas ICAO: LOMAS Net: http://www.gratton.co.uk/lomas Aircraft below MTOW 1361 kg: Robinson R22

☐	G-OGOA	Eurocopter (Aerosp.) AS350B Squirrel	1745	G-PLMD	0084		1 TU Arriel 1B	1950			

LONDON EXECUTIVE AVIATION, Ltd – LEA = LNX — London-City, London-Stansted & Stapleford

London-City Airport, Royal Docks, London E16 2PX, Great Britain ☎ (171) 474 33 44 Tx: none Fax: (171) 474 55 66 SITA: n/a
F: 1990 ⁂ 30 Head: George Galanopoulos ICAO: LONEX Net: http://www.flylea.com

☐	G-BASX	Piper PA-34-200 Seneca	34-7350123	N15781	0073		2 LY IO-360-C1E6	1905	5 Pax		
☐	G-BGLW	Piper PA-34-200 Seneca	34-7250132	OY-BDZ	0072	0596	2 LY IO-360-C1E6	1905	5 Pax		
☐	G-CHEM	Piper PA-34-200T Seneca II	34-8170032	N8292Y	0081	0398	2 CO TSIO-360-EB	2073	5 Pax		
☐	G-ELBC	Piper PA-34-200 Seneca	34-7350021	G-BANS	0073	0496	2 LY IO-360-C1E6	1905	5 Pax		opf LBC Radio London Lookout
☐	G-EXEC	Piper PA-34-200 Seneca	34-7450072	OY-BGU	0074		2 LY IO-360-C1E6	1905	5 Pax		lsf Sky Air Travel Ltd
☐	G-SSFC	Piper PA-34-200 Seneca	34-7450016	G-BBXG	0074	0496	2 LY IO-360-C1E6	1905	5 Pax		
☐	G-TEST	Piper PA-34-200 Seneca	34-7450116	OO-RPW	0074	0496	2 LY IO-360-C1E6	1905	5 Pax		
☐	G-BLFZ	Piper PA-31-310 Navajo C	31-7912106	PH-RWS	0079		2 LY TIO-540-A2C	2948	7 Pax		
☐	G-ISFC	Piper PA-31-310 Navajo B	31-7300970	G-BNEF	0073	0496	2 LY TIO-540-A2C	2948	7 Pax		
☐	G-MOHS	Piper PA-31-350 Navajo Chieftain	31-8152115	G-BWOC	0081	0496	2 LY TIO-540-J2BD	3175	9 Pax		lsf Sky Air Travel Ltd
☐	G-MRMR	Piper PA-31-350 Navajo Chieftain	31-7952092	OH-PRE	0079	0897	2 LY TIO-540-J2BD	3175	9 Pax		lsf MRMR Flight Services
☐	G-FRYI	Beech King Air 200	BB-210	G-OAVX	0076		2 PWC PT6A-41	5670	8 Pax		
☐	G-FJET	Cessna 550 Citation II	550-0419	G-DCFR	0082		2 PWC JT15D-4	6033	7 Pax		lsf Worldstage Ltd
☐	G-SPUR	Cessna 550 Citation II	550-0714	N593EM	0092	1098	2 PWC JT15D-4	6033	7 Pax		lsf Amsail Ltd

LOTHIAN HELICOPTERS, Ltd (formerly dba Helicopter Tours UK) — Edinburgh

2 Roseneath Place, Edinburgh, Scotland EH9 1JB, Great Britain ☎ (131) 228 99 99 Tx: none Fax: (131) 228 99 88 SITA: n/a
F: n/a ⁂ n/a Head: Ian Grindlay Net: n/a

☐	G-IANG	Bell 206L LongRanger	45132	SE-HSV	0077	1297	1 AN 250-C20B	1815			

LOVE AIR = 4J / LOV (Scheduled services & Charter-division of London Flight Centre (Stansted), Ltd) — London-Stansted & Biggin Hill

Bldg 44, London-Stansted-Airport, Stansted, Essex CM24 1QE, Great Britain ☎ (1279) 68 01 44 Tx: none Fax: (1279) 68 03 56 SITA: n/a
F: 1982 ⁂ 60 Head: Capt. Nigel J. Harris ICAO: LOVEAIR Net: n/a

☐	G-BEZL	Piper PA-31-310 Navajo C	31-7712054	SE-GPA	0077	1092	2 LY TIO-540-A2C	2948			
☐	G-EEAC	Piper PA-31-310 Navajo	31-761	G-SKKA	0071	0597	2 LY TIO-540-A2C	2948			
☐	G-HVRD	Piper PA-31-350 Navajo Chieftain	31-7305052	SE-GDP	0073		2 LY TIO-540-J2BD	3175			
☐	G-LOVA	BAe 3102 Jetstream 31	640	G-OAKA	0084	0598	2 GA TPE331-10UR-513H	6950			

LYNTON AVIATION, Ltd = LYN (Subsidiary of The Lynton Group, Inc.) — Denham & Oxford

Denham Airfield, Uxbridge, Middlesex UB9 5DF, Great Britain ☎ (1895) 83 50 00 Tx: none Fax: (1895) 83 25 64 SITA: n/a
F: 1982 ⁂ 59 Head: Chris Tennant ICAO: LYNTON Net: n/a

☐	G-BSYI	Eurocopter (Aerosp.) AS355F1 Tw.Squirrel	5197	M-MJI	0082		2 AN 250-C20F	2400			opf pvt
☐	G-DOOZ	Eurocopter (Aerosp.) AS355F2 Tw.Squirrel	5367	G-BNSX	0087		2 AN 250-C20F	2540			opf pvt
☐	G-JETU	Eurocopter (Aerosp.) AS355F2 Tw.Squirrel	5450	VR-CET	0090	0596	2 AN 250-C20F	2540			lsf Debis Financial Services Ltd
☐	G-OITN	Eurocopter (Aerosp.) AS355F1 Tw.Squirrel	5088	N400HH	0081		2 AN 250-C20F	2400			opf Independent Television News Ltd
☐	G-XCEL	Eurocopter (Aerosp.) AS355F1 Tw.Squirrel	5324	G-HBAC	0085		2 AN 250-C20F	2400			lsf Tri-Ventures Group Ltd
☐	G-BURS	Sikorsky S-76A+	760040	G-OHTL	0080		2 TU Arriel 1S	4763			opf pvt / cvtd S-76A
☐	G-OPWH	Dassault Falcon 900B	151	F-WWFK*	0095	1195	3 GA TFE731-5BR-1C	21099		AK-PS	lsf Aviation Partnership

MAERSK AIR, Ltd = VB / MSK (Member of Maersk Air Group) — Birmingham

Maersk Air House, 2245-49 Coventry Road, Sheldon, Birmingham B26 3NG, Great Britain ☎ (121) 743 90 90 Tx: 337215 beafwd g Fax: (121) 604 90 20 SITA: n/a
F: 1993 ⁂ 380 Head: Gert Kristensen IATA: 702 ICAO: BLUESTAR Net: http://www.maersk-air.ltd.uk
Scheduled services are operated on a franchise agreement with BRITISH AIRWAYS (in full such colors & both titles) & using BA-flight numbers.

☐	G-MSKJ	BAe 4100 Jetstream 41	41034	N434JX	0094	0996	2 GA TPE331-14HR-805H	10886	Y29		lsf BAMT / op in BA Ndebele-colors
☐	G-MSKK	Canadair Regional Jet 200LR (CL-600-2B19)	7226	C-GCBS*	0098	0598	2 GE CF34-3B1	23995	CY50		op in BA Wings-colors
☐	G-MSKL	Canadair Regional Jet 200LR (CL-600-2B19)	7247	C-FMML*	0098	0798	2 GE CF34-3B1	23995	CY50		op in BA Ndebele Emmly-colors
☐	G-MSKM	Canadair Regional Jet 200LR (CL-600-2B19)	7248	C-FMMN*	0098	0798	2 GE CF34-3B1	23995	CY50		op in BA Sterntaler-colors
☐	G-MSKN	Canadair Regional Jet 200LR (CL-600-2B19)	7283		0099	0199	2 GE CF34-3B1	23995	CY50		op in BA Chelsea Rose-colors
☐	G-MSKO	Canadair Regional Jet 200LR (CL-600-2B19)	7299		0099	0299	2 GE CF34-3B1	23995	CY50		op in BA Crossing Borders-colors
☐	G-MSKP	Canadair Regional Jet 200LR (CL-600-2B19)					2 GE CF34-3B1	23995	CY50		oo-delivery 0899/to be op in BA-colors
☐	G-MSKR	Canadair Regional Jet 200LR (CL-600-2B19)					2 GE CF34-3B1	23995	CY50		oo-delivery 0300/to be op in BA-colors
☐	G-MSKS	Canadair Regional Jet 200LR (CL-600-2B19)					2 GE CF34-3B1	23995	CY50		oo-delivery 0400/to be op in BA-colors
☐	G-MSKA	Boeing 737-5L9	24859 / 1919	OY-MAC	0090	1096	2 CFMI CFM56-3B1	60555	CY114	MQ-HP	op in BA Blue Poole-colors
☐	G-MSKB	Boeing 737-5L9	24928 / 1961	OY-MAD	0090	1196	2 CFMI CFM56-3B1	60555	CY114	MQ-JK	op in BA Column-colors
☐	G-MSKC	Boeing 737-5L9	25066 / 2038	OY-MAE	0091	1296	2 CFMI CFM56-3B1	55566	CY114	CR-GP	lsf DAN / op in BA Waves of the City-cs
☐	G-MSKD	Boeing 737-5L9	24778 / 1816	HL7230	0090	0198	2 CFMI CFM56-3B1	55566	CY114	MS-BQ	lsf DAN / op in BA Whale Rider-colors
☐	G-MSKE	Boeing 737-5L9	28084 / 2788	OY-APB	0096	0199	2 CFMI CFM56-3C1	54884	CY114		lsf DAN/op in BA Delftblue Daybreak-cs

MAGEC AVIATION, Ltd = MGC (Subsidiary of The Lynton Group, Inc.) — London-Luton

London-Luton-Airport, Luton, Bedfordshire LU2 9NT, Great Britain ☎ (1582) 24 182 Tx: 82185 magec g Fax: (1582) 45 54 53 SITA: n/a
F: 1989 ⁂ 126 Head: Capt. D.E. White ICAO: MAGEC Net: http://www.magec.co.uk

☐	G-OCAA	Hawker 700B (HS 125-700B)	257091	G-BHLF	0080		2 GA TFE731-3R-1H	11567			
☐	G-OMGD	Hawker 700B (HS 125-700B)	257184	9K-AGA	0082	1294	2 GA TFE731-3R-1H	11567		EL-BC	
☐	G-OMGE	Hawker 800B (BAe 125-800B)	258197	G-BTMG*	0091	0791	2 GA TFE731-5R-1H	12428			lsf Marconda Services Ltd
☐	G-OMGG	Hawker 800B (BAe 125-800B)	258058	N125JW	0086	1194	2 GA TFE731-5R-1H	12428		AP-HL	
☐	HZ-OFC3	Dassault Falcon 900B	133	F-GODE	0093	0294	3 GA TFE731-5BR-1C	21099		CJ-ES	lsf Olayan Finance Co.

MANHATTAN AIR, Ltd = MHN — Blackbushe

PO Box 138, Camberley, Surrey GU17 9YY, Great Britain ☎ (1252) 89 05 00 Tx: 858144 manhat g Fax: (1252) 87 59 00 SITA: n/a
F: 1993 ⁂ 12 Head: Trevor Jones ICAO: MANHATTAN Net: n/a

☐	G-BVMA	Beech King Air 200	BB-797	G-VPLC	0081	0993	2 PWC PT6A-41	5670			
☐	G-BXMA	Beech King Air 200	BB-726	N622JA	0080	0797	2 PWC PT6A-41	5670			

MANX AIRLINES, Ltd = JE / MNX (Skianyn Vannin – Wings of Man) (Member of British Regional Airlines (Holdings) Ltd)

Isle of Man

Isle of Man (Ronaldsway) Airport, Ballasalla IM9 2JE, Isle of Man ☎ (1624) 82 60 00 Tx: 629683 manx g Fax: (1624) 82 60 01 SITA: IOMOWJE
F: 1982 ♦♦♦ 570 Head: Sir Michael Bishop IATA: 916 ICAO: MANX Net: http://www.manx-airlines.com

registration	type of aircraft	cn/fn	ex/ex*	mfd	del	powered by	mtow kg	configuration	selcal	name/fln/specialitites/remarks
☐ G-MAJA	BAe 4100 Jetstream 41	41032	G-4-032*	0093	0594	2 GA TPE331-14G/HR-802H	10433	Y29		
☐ G-MANA	BAe ATP	2056	G-LOGH	0094	0394	2 PWC PW126	22930	Y68		
☐ G-MANB	BAe ATP	2055	G-LOGG	0093	0294	2 PWC PW126	22930	Y68		
☐ G-MANC	BAe ATP	2054	G-LOGF	0093	0394	2 PWC PW126	22930	Y68		
☐ G-MANU	BAe ATP	2008	G-BUUP	0088	0494	2 PWC PW126	22930	Y68		white colors
☐ G-MIMA	BAe 146-200	E2079	G-CNMF	0087	0393	4 LY ALF502R-5	40750	Y95		Caaig Vanninagh / Chough of Mann

MAYFAIR Dove Aviation (W.G.T. Pritchard dba)

Biggin Hill

6 Victoria Road, Horley, Surrey RH6 9BN, Great Britain ☎ (1293) 82 23 19 Tx: n/a Fax: (1293) 82 23 19 SITA: n/a
F: 1993 ♦♦♦ 6 Head: Chris Wadlow Net: n/a

registration	type of aircraft	cn/fn	ex/ex*	mfd	del	powered by	mtow kg	configuration	selcal	name/fln/specialitites/remarks
☐ G-OPLC	BAe (DH) 104 Dove 8	04212	G-BLRB	0048		2 Gipsy Queen 70 Mk.3	4150			

MEDICAL AVIATION SERVICES, Ltd – MAS = MCL (Affiliated with Police Aviation Services, Ltd/Subsidiary of Bombardier Services Group)

Gloucester-Staverton

Gloucester Airport, Staverton, Cheltenham, Gloucestershire GL6 6SS, Great Britain ☎ (1452) 85 79 99 Tx: none Fax: (1452) 85 78 88 SITA: n/a
F: 1986 ♦♦♦ n/a Head: Capt. Mark Trumble ICAO: MEDIC Net: n/a
Operates medical/EMS flights with Eurocopter AS355F1 / BO105DBS & Pilatus Britten-Norman Islander aircraft in conjunction with POLICE AVIATION SERVICES, Ltd – for fleet details – see under that company.

MILLENNIUM EXECUTIVE AIR CHARTER, Ltd (Subsidiary of Osprey Aviation, Ltd)

Southampton

Southampton Airport, Southampton, Hampshire S018 2HG, Great Britain ☎ (1703) 48 37 00 Tx: 477237 g Fax: (1703) 61 78 39 SITA: SOUGFCR
F: 1996 ♦♦♦ n/a Head: Paul Emms Net: n/a

registration	type of aircraft	cn/fn	ex/ex*	mfd	del	powered by	mtow kg	configuration	selcal	name/fln/specialitites/remarks
☐ G-DJLW	Hawker 3B/RA (HS 125-3B/RA)	25140	G-AVVB	0068		2 RR Viper 522	10342			

MONARCH AIRLINES, Ltd = ZB / MON (Member of Globus Gateway Group)

London-Luton

Luton Airport, Luton, Bedfordshire LU2 9NU, Great Britain ☎ (1582) 40 00 00 Tx: 825624 ltnmon g Fax: (1582) 40 13 06 SITA: LTNAPZB
F: 1967 ♦♦♦ 2100 Head: Daniel L. Bernstein IATA: 974 ICAO: MONARCH Net: http://www.Monarch-Airlines.com

registration	type of aircraft	cn/fn	ex/ex*	mfd	del	powered by	mtow kg	configuration	selcal	name/fln/specialitites/remarks
☐ G-MONW	Airbus Industrie A320-212	391	F-WWDQ*	0093	0293	2 CFMI CFM56-5A3	77000	Y180	DQ-RS	lsf GECA / cvtd -211
☐ G-MONX	Airbus Industrie A320-212	392	F-WWDR*	0092	0393	2 CFMI CFM56-5A3	77000	Y180	DR-AB	lsf GECA / cvtd -211
☐ G-MONZ	Airbus Industrie A320-212	446	F-WWDJ*	0093	1093	2 CFMI CFM56-5A3	77000	Y180	FH-LR	lsf ILFC/sublst SSV as C-FTDI in winter
☐ G-MPCD	Airbus Industrie A320-212	379	C-FTDU	0092	0394	2 CFMI CFM56-5A3	77000	Y180	AE-FQ	
☐ G-OZBB	Airbus Industrie A320-212	389	C-FTDW	0094	0394	2 CFMI CFM56-5A3	77000	Y180	AE-GQ	lst SSV as C-FTDW in winter
☐ G-MARA	Airbus Industrie A321-231	983		0099	0399	2 IAE V2533-A5	89000	Y220	CM-HR	
☐ G-OJEG	Airbus Industrie A321-231	1015		0099	0499	2 IAE V2533-A5	89000	Y220	GS-DE	
☐ G-OZBC	Airbus Industrie A321-231	633	D-ASSE*	0096	0497	2 IAE V2533-A5	89000	Y220	PR-DE	lsf ILFC
☐ G-DAJB	Boeing 757-2T7	23770 / 125		0087	0387	2 RR RB211-535E4	113400	Y235	GK-FL	
☐ G-MONB	Boeing 757-2T7	22780 / 15		0083	0383	2 RR RB211-535E4	108860	Y235	GK-BL	
☐ G-MONC	Boeing 757-2T7	22781 / 18	PH-AHO	0083	0483	2 RR RB211-535E4	108860	Y235	GK-CJ	
☐ G-MOND	Boeing 757-2T7	22960 / 19	D-ABNZ	0083	0583	2 RR RB211-535E4	108860	Y235	CE-AP	
☐ G-MONE	Boeing 757-2T7	23293 / 56		0085	0385	2 RR RB211-535E4	108860	Y235	CE-BP	
☐ G-MONJ	Boeing 757-2T7	24104 / 170		0088	0488	2 RR RB211-535E4	113400	Y235	GK-DE	
☐ G-MONK	Boeing 757-2T7	24105 / 172		0088	0488	2 RR RB211-535E4	113400	Y235	GK-CF	
☐ G-MAJS	Airbus Industrie A300-605R (A300B4-605R)	604	F-WWAX*	0091	0491	2 GE CF6-80C2A5	171700	Y361	AG-PR	
☐ G-MONR	Airbus Industrie A300-605R (A300B4-605R)	540	VH-YMJ	0989	0390	2 GE CF6-80C2A5	171700	Y361	JQ-EH	
☐ G-MONS	Airbus Industrie A300-605R (A300B4-605R)	556	VH-YMK	0290	0490	2 GE CF6-80C2A5	171700	Y361	JQ-EK	
☐ G-OJMR	Airbus Industrie A300-605R (A300B4-605R)	605	F-WWAY*	0091	0591	2 GE CF6-80C2A5	171700	Y361	AG-PS	
☐ G-EOMA	Airbus Industrie A330-243	265				2 RR Trent 772B-60	230000	C51Y323	CM-HQ	oo-delivery 0699
☐ G-SMAN	Airbus Industrie A330-243	261				2 RR Trent 772B-60	230000	C51Y323	CM-GQ	oo-delivery 0699
☐ G-DMCA	Boeing (Douglas) DC-10-30	48266 / 348	N3016Z	1180	0396	3 GE CF6-50C2	259455	Y361	CL-DF	lsf Sky Leasing Inc.

MULTIFLIGHT, Ltd

Leeds/Bradford

Leeds/Bradford Airport, Yeadon, Leeds LS19 7YG, Great Britain ☎ (113) 238 71 00 Tx: none Fax: (113) 239 13 26 SITA: n/a
F: 1997 ♦♦♦ n/a Head: Catherine Wickett Net: n/a

registration	type of aircraft	cn/fn	ex/ex*	mfd	del	powered by	mtow kg	configuration	selcal	name/fln/specialitites/remarks
☐ G-ECOS	Eurocopter (Aerosp.) AS355F1 Tw.Squirrel	5300	G-DOLR	0083	0797	2 AN 250-C20F	2400			
☐ G-BXXV	Eurocopter EC135T1	0049		0098	0998	2 TU Arrius 2B	2720			
☐ N365EL	Eurocopter (Aerosp.) AS365N2 Dauphin 2	6431	JA6673	0091	0798	2 TU Arriel 1C2	4250			lsf Multiflight Aviation Inc.
☐ G-MLTI	Dassault Falcon 900B	164	F-WWFC*	0097	0697	3 GA TFE731-5BR-1C	21099			

NATIONAL GRID HELICOPTERS = GRD (Division of National Grid Company, Plc)

Oxford & Woodford

National Stores, Old Milton Road, Didcot, Oxfordshire OX11 7HH, Great Britain ☎ (118) 928 59 02 Tx: none Fax: (118) 928 59 05 SITA: n/a
F: 1967 ♦♦♦ n/a Head: Dave Bedford ICAO: GRID Net: n/a

registration	type of aircraft	cn/fn	ex/ex*	mfd	del	powered by	mtow kg	configuration	selcal	name/fln/specialitites/remarks
☐ G-GRID	Eurocopter (Aerosp.) AS355F1 Tw.Squirrel	5012	TG-BOS	0081		2 AN 250-C20F	2400			
☐ G-LINE	Eurocopter (Aerosp.) AS355N Tw.Squirrel	5566		0094	0794	2 TU Arrius 1A	2540			
☐ G-WIRE	Eurocopter (Aerosp.) AS355F1 Tw.Squirrel	5312	G-CEGB	0084		2 AN 250-C20F	2400			

NORTHERN EXECUTIVE AVIATION, Ltd = NV / NEX

Manchester & London-Luton

Business Aviation Centre, Hangar 7, Fairey's Way, Manchester Airport West M90 5NE, Great Britain ☎ (161) 436 66 66 Tx: 668777 neamcr g Fax: (161) 436 34 50 SITA: n/a
F: 1962 ♦♦♦ 30 Head: David L. Antrobus ICAO: NEATAX Net: n/a

registration	type of aircraft	cn/fn	ex/ex*	mfd	del	powered by	mtow kg	configuration	selcal	name/fln/specialitites/remarks
☐ G-HUGG	Learjet 35A	35A-432	VR-CAD	0081	0496	2 GA TFE731-2-2B	8165			lsf 1427 Ltd
☐ G-LEAR	Learjet 35A	35A-265	N1462B	0079		2 GA TFE731-2-2B	8165			
☐ G-MURI	Learjet 35A	35A-646	N712JB	0088	0198	2 GA TFE731-2-2B	8301			lsf G-MURI Ltd
☐ G-ZENO	Learjet 35A	35A-429	G-GAYL	0081		2 GA TFE731-2-2B	8165			
☐ G-EVES	Dassault Falcon 900B	165	F-WWFD*	0097	1197	3 GA TFE731-5BR-1C	21099			

OPERATIONAL SUPPORT SERVICES, Ltd – OSS (Member of the McAlpine Group of Companies)

Hayes

Swallowfield Way, Hayes, Middlesex UB3 1SP, Great Britain ☎ (181) 848 96 47 Tx: none Fax: (181) 569 32 30 SITA: n/a
F: 1990 ♦♦♦ 28 Head: Christopher Forrest ICAO: MACLINE Net: n/a

registration	type of aircraft	cn/fn	ex/ex*	mfd	del	powered by	mtow kg	configuration	selcal	name/fln/specialitites/remarks
☐ G-BOOV	Eurocopter (Aerosp.) AS355F2 Tw.Squirrel	5374		0088		2 AN 250-C20F	2540			opf Merseyside Police ASU
☐ G-BXBT	Eurocopter (Aerosp.) AS355F1 Tw.Squirrel	5262	G-TMMC	0083	0296	2 AN 250-C20F	2400			
☐ G-CCAO	Eurocopter (Aerosp.) AS355F1 Tw.Squirrel	5077	G-SETA	0081		2 AN 250-C20F	2400			
☐ G-DANS	Eurocopter (Aerosp.) AS355F2 Tw.Squirrel	5480	G-BTNM	0091		2 AN 250-C20F	2540			opf Frewton Ltd
☐ G-DANZ	Eurocopter (Aerosp.) AS355N Tw.Squirrel	5658		0098	0998	2 TU Arrius 1A	2540			
☐ G-FTWO	Eurocopter (Aerosp.) AS355F2 Tw.Squirrel	5347	G-OJOR	0086		2 AN 250-C20F	2540			
☐ G-GMPA	Eurocopter (Aerosp.) AS355F2 Tw.Squirrel	5409	G-BPOI	0089		2 AN 250-C20F	2540			opf Greater Manchester Police ASU
☐ G-LOUN	Eurocopter (Aerosp.) AS355N Tw.Squirrel	5627		0097	0197	2 TU Arrius 1A	2540			opf Loune Ltd
☐ G-OILX	Eurocopter (Aerosp.) AS355F1 Tw.Squirrel	5327	G-RMGN	0085		2 AN 250-C20F	2400			
☐ ZJ139	Eurocopter (Aerosp.) AS355F1 Tw.Squirrel	5325	G-NUTZ	0085	0296	2 AN 250-C20F	2400			opf RAF 32 (The Royal) Squadron
☐ ZJ140	Eurocopter (Aerosp.) AS355F1 Tw.Squirrel	5303	G-FFHI	0083	0296	2 AN 250-C20F	2400			opf RAF 32 (The Royal) Squadron
☐ G-CCAU	Eurocopter EC135T1	0040		0098	0698	2 TU Arrius 2B	2720			opf Central Counties Police

OXAERO = OXE (Oxford Aero Charter, Ltd dba)

Oxford

The Farmhouse, Oxford Airport, Kidlington, Oxfordshire OX5 1RA, Great Britain ☎ (1865) 37 42 62 Tx: none Fax: (1865) 37 42 63 SITA: n/a
F: 1979 ♦♦♦ 8 Head: Alex Durand ICAO: OXOE Net: n/a

registration	type of aircraft	cn/fn	ex/ex*	mfd	del	powered by	mtow kg	configuration	selcal	name/fln/specialitites/remarks
☐ G-CITI	Cessna 501 Citation I/SP	501-0084	VP-CDM	0079	0798	2 PWC JT15D-1	5375			lsf London Executive Jet
☐ G-ORJB	Cessna 500 Citation I	500-0364	G-OKSP	0077		2 PWC JT15D-1A	5375			lsf L'Equipe Air Ltd

OXFORD HELICOPTERS = WDK (Oxford Air Services, Ltd dba)

Oxford

The Business Aviation Centre, Oxford Airport, Kidlington, Oxford OX5 1RA, Great Britain ☎ (1865) 37 07 39 Tx: none Fax: (1865) 37 04 78 SITA: n/a
F: 1994 ♦♦♦ 9 Head: Michael Hampton ICAO: WOODSTOCK Net: n/a

registration	type of aircraft	cn/fn	ex/ex*	mfd	del	powered by	mtow kg	configuration	selcal	name/fln/specialitites/remarks
☐ G-UEST	Bell 206B JetRanger	1484	G-RYOB	0074		1 AN 250-C20	1451			lsf pvt
☐ G-BRVO	Eurocopter (Aerosp.) AS350B Squirrel	2315		0090		1 TU Arriel 1B	1950			lsf Malcolm Wilson (Motorsport) Ltd
☐ G-EJOC	Eurocopter (Aerosp.) AS350B Squirrel	1465	G-GEDS	0081		1 TU Arriel 1B	1950			lsf Elmsdale (UK) Ltd
☐ G-NEXT	Eurocopter (Aerosp.) AS355F1 Tw.Squirrel	5115	G-WDKR	0081		2 AN 250-C20F	2400			lsf RCR Aviation Ltd
☐ N766AM	Eurocopter (Aerosp.) AS355N Tw.Squirrel	5601	F-WQDA	0094		2 TU Arrius 1A	2540			lsf Beacon Energy Aviation

PDG HELICOPTERS = PDG (PLM/Dollar Group, Ltd dba)

Inverness & Glasgow

The Heliport, Dalcross (Airport) Industrial Estate, Inverness, Highland IV1 2JB, Scotland, Great Britain ☎ (1667) 46 27 40 Tx: none Fax: (1667) 46 23 76 SITA: n/a
F: 1995 ♦♦♦ 53 Head: Jerry Francis ICAO: OSPREY Net: http://www.weblink.co.uk/leisure/tgal/pdgheli.

registration	type of aircraft	cn/fn	ex/ex*	mfd	del	powered by	mtow kg	configuration	selcal	name/fln/specialitites/remarks
☐ G-AYMW	Bell 206B JetRanger	587		0070	0995	1 AN 250-C20	1451			cvtd 206A
☐ G-BEWY	Bell 206B JetRanger	348	G-CULL	0069	0995	1 AN 250-C20	1451			cvtd 206A
☐ G-LAMA	Eurocopter (Aerosp.) SA315B Lama	2348	SE-HET	0073	0097	1 TU Artouste IIIB	1950			
☐ G-BMAV	Eurocopter (Aerosp.) AS350B Squirrel	1089		0079	1298	1 TU Arriel 1B	1950			
☐ G-BVJE	Eurocopter (Aerosp.) AS350B1 Squirrel	1991	SE-HRS	0087	0995	1 TU Arriel 1B	2200			lsf I.S. & G. Steel Stockholders Ltd
☐ G-BXGA	Eurocopter (Aerosp.) AS350B2 Squirrel	2493	OO-RCH	0091	0498	1 TU Arriel 1D1	2250			
☐ G-PLMB	Eurocopter (Aerosp.) AS350B Squirrel	1207	G-BMMB	0079	0995	1 TU Arriel 1B	1950			

registration	type of aircraft	cn/fn	ex/ex*	mfd	del	powered by	mtow kg	configuration	selcal	name/fln/specialitites/remarks
☐ G-PLMC	Eurocopter (Aerosp.) AS350B Squirrel	1731	G-BKUM	0083	0995	1 TU Arriel 1B	1950			
☐ G-PLMH	Eurocopter (Aerosp.) AS350B2 Squirrel	2156	F-WQDJ*	0089	0995	1 TU Arriel 1D1	2250			cvtd AS350B
☐ G-BPRJ	Eurocopter (Aerosp.) AS355F1 Tw.Squirrel	5201	N368E	0082	0995	2 AN 250-C20F	2400			
☐ G-BVLG	Eurocopter (Aerosp.) AS355F1 Tw.Squirrel	5011	N57745	0080		2 AN 250-C20F	2400			
☐ G-PLMI	Eurocopter (Aerosp.) SA365C1 Dauphin 2	5001	F-GFYH	0077	0995	2 TU Arriel 1A1	3400			

PENNINE HELICOPTERS, Ltd

Saddleworth

Oakdene Farm, Stanedge, Saddleworth, Lancashire OL3 5LU, Great Britain ☎ (1457) 82 01 52 Tx: n/a Fax: (1457) 82 01 53 SITA: n/a

F: 1991 ⁂ n/a Head: Capt. Chris J. Ruddy Net: n/a Aircraft below MTOW 1361kg: Hughes 269C (300C).

registration	type of aircraft	cn/fn	ex/ex*	mfd	del	powered by	mtow kg	configuration	selcal	name/fln/specialitites/remarks
☐ G-LEEZ	Bell 206L-1 LongRanger II	45761	G-BPCT	0083		1 AN 250-C28B	1882			

POLICE AVIATION SERVICES = PLC (Bombardier Services UK Ltd dba/Affiliated with Medical Aviation Services Ltd)

Gloucester-Staverton

Gloucester Airport, Staverton, Cheltenham, Gloucestershire GL51 6SS, Great Britain ☎ (1452) 85 79 99 Tx: none Fax: (1452) 85 78 88 SITA: n/a

F: 1984 ⁂ 120 Head: Capt. Mark Trumble ICAO: SPECIAL Net: n/a Fleet is operated in conjunction with MEDICAL AVIATION SERVICES, Ltd (EMS flights).

registration	type of aircraft	cn/fn	ex/ex*	mfd	del	powered by	mtow kg	configuration	selcal	name/fln/specialitites/remarks
☐ G-PASC	Eurocopter (MBB) BO105DBS-4	S-421	G-BNPS	0080		2 AN 250-C20B	2500	EMS		opf Lincolnshire Air Ambulance
☐ G-PASD	Eurocopter (MBB) BO105DBS-4	S-656	G-BNRS	0084		2 AN 250-C20B	2500	EMS		
☐ G-PASG	Eurocopter (MBB) BO105DBS-4	S-819	G-MHSL	0090	0395	2 AN 250-C20B	2500	Patrol / EMS		
☐ G-PASX	Eurocopter (MBB) BO105DBS-4	S-814		0089	1289	2 AN 250-C20B	2500	Patrol / EMS		opf Sussex Police H/C Unit
☐ G-WYPA	Eurocopter (MBB) BO105DBS-4	S-815		0089		2 AN 250-C20B	2500	Patrol / EMS		opf West Yorkshire Police ASU
☐ G-CAMB	Eurocopter (Aerosp.) AS355F2 Tw.Squirrel	5416	N813LP	0089	1296	2 AN 250-C20F	2540	Patrol / EMS		opf Cambridge Police ASU
☐ G-CPOL	Eurocopter (Aerosp.) AS355F1 Tw.Squirrel	5007	N5775T	0081	1195	2 AN 250-C20F	2400	Patrol / EMS		opf Chiltern Police ASU / cvtd AS355E
☐ G-KGMT	Eurocopter (Aerosp.) AS355F1 Tw.Squirrel	5042	G-PASE	0081	0790	2 AN 250-C20F	2400	EMS		opf Kent Air Ambulance
☐ G-NAAS	Eurocopter (Aerosp.) AS355F1 Tw.Squirrel	5203	G-BPRG	0082	0794	2 AN 250-C20F	2400	EMS		opf Northumbria Air Ambulance
☐ G-OASP	Eurocopter (Aerosp.) AS355F2 Tw.Squirrel	5479	F-GJAJ	0091	0895	2 AN 250-C20F	2540	Patrol / EMS		opf Western Counties Police ASU
☐ G-PASF	Eurocopter (Aerosp.) AS355F1 Tw.Squirrel	5033	G-SCHU	0081		2 AN 250-C20F	2400	Patrol / EMS		opf Northumbria Police ASU
☐ G-PASH	Eurocopter (Aerosp.) AS355F1 Tw.Squirrel	5040	F-GHLI	0081	0596	2 AN 250-C20F	2400	Patrol / EMS		
☐ G-SYPA	Eurocopter (Aerosp.) AS355F2 Tw.Squirrel	5193	LV-WHC	0083	0996	2 AN 250-C20F	2540	Patrol / EMS		opf South Yorks. Police ASU/cvtd 355F1
☐ G-TVPA	Eurocopter (Aerosp.) AS355F1 Tw.Squirrel	5181	G-BPRI	0082		2 AN 250-C20F	2400	Patrol / EMS		opf Chiltern Police ASU
☐ G-WMPA	Eurocopter (Aerosp.) AS355F2 Tw.Squirrel	5401		0089		2 AN 250-C20F	2540	Patrol / EMS		opf West Midlands Police ASU
☐ G-BXZK	MD Helicopters MD 902 Explorer (900 Adv.)	900-00057	N9238T*	0098	0898	2 PWC PW206E	2840	Patrol / EMS		opf Dorset Police ASU
☐ G-PASS	MD Helicopters MD 902 Explorer (900 Adv.)	900-00056	N9234P*	0098	1098	2 PWC PW206E	2840	Patrol / EMS		opf Sussex Police
☐ G-WPAS	MD Helicopters MD 902 Explorer (900 Adv.)	900-00053		0098	0798	2 PWC PW206E	2840	Patrol / EMS		opf Wiltshire Police ASU
☐ G-BJSA	Britten-Norman BN-2A-26 Islander	46	HB-LIC	0069	0395	2 LY O-540-E4C5	2994	EMS		
☐ G-CHES	Britten-Norman BN-2A-26 Islander	2011	G-PASY	0077		2 LY O-540-E4C5	2994	Patrol / EMS		opf The Cheshire Constabulary
☐ G-NESU	Britten-Norman BN-2B-20 Islander	2260	G-BTVN	0092	0296	2 LY IO-540-K1B5	2994	Patrol / EMS		opf North East Police ASU
☐ G-PASV	Britten-Norman BN-2B-21 Islander	2157	G-BKJH	0091	0395	2 LY IO-540-K1B5	2994	EMS		
☐ G-DCPA	Eurocopter (MBB) BK117C-1	7511	D-HECU	0095		2 TU Arriel 1E2	3350	Patrol / EMS		opf Devon & Cornwall Police
☐ G-PASU	Britten-Norman BN-2T Turbine Islander	2144	5T-BSA	0084	0395	2 AN 250-B17C	3175	EMS		cvtd 2B-26

POLO AVIATION, Ltd = CUK

Bristol

Plot 4, Cargo Village, Bristol Airport, Avon BS19 3DY, Great Britain ☎ (1275) 47 41 00 Tx: none Fax: (1275) 47 25 26 SITA: n/a

F: 1994 ⁂ 7 Head: P.J. Hall ICAO: CHUKKA Net: http://www.bengrove.u-net.com/polo.htm Beside helicopters listed, leases additional (Eurocopter AS355F Twin Squirrel) from SWEB Helicopter Unit when required.

registration	type of aircraft	cn/fn	ex/ex*	mfd	del	powered by	mtow kg	configuration	selcal	name/fln/specialitites/remarks
☐ G-OCST	Agusta-Bell 206B JetRanger III	8694	VR-CDG	0086		1 AN 250-C20J	1451			lsf Fieldgrove Trading

POPLAR AVIATION, Ltd

Elmsett

Poplar Hall, Elmsett, Ipswich, Suffolk IP7 6LN, Great Britain ☎ (1473) 82 41 16 Tx: none Fax: (1473) 82 28 96 SITA: n/a

F: 1980 ⁂ 12 Head: Tony D. Gray Net: n/a Aircraft below MTOW 1361 kg: Cessna 172.

registration	type of aircraft	cn/fn	ex/ex*	mfd	del	powered by	mtow kg	configuration	selcal	name/fln/specialitites/remarks
☐ G-BASM	Piper PA-34-200 Seneca	34-7350120	N16272	0073		2 LY IO-360-C1E6	1905			

PREMIAIR CHARTER, Ltd = SUZ

Southampton

c/o Osprey Aviation, Ltd, Executive Jet Centre, Southampton Airport, Hampshire S018 2HG, Great Britain ☎ (1703) 48 37 00 Tx: 477237 g Fax: (1703) 62 96 84 SITA: n/a

F: 1996 ⁂ n/a Head: Mrs. Susan Barralet ICAO: SUZY Net: n/a

registration	type of aircraft	cn/fn	ex/ex*	mfd	del	powered by	mtow kg	configuration	selcal	name/fln/specialitites/remarks
☐ G-BFBU	Partenavia P.68B	24	SE-FTM	0074		2 LY IO-360-A1B6	1960			

RAVENAIR = RVR (formerly Executive Air Tours / Cheshire Flying Services, Ltd dba)

Manchester

Hangar 522, Southside, Manchester Int'l Airport, Wilmslow, Cheshire SK9 4LL, Great Britain ☎ (161) 436 88 48 Tx: none Fax: (161) 499 16 32 SITA: n/a

F: 1982 ⁂ 25 Head: Jeffrey T. Nuttall ICAO: RAVEN Net: http://www.ravenair.co.uk Aircraft below MTOW 1361 kg: Piper PA-28 & PA-38.

registration	type of aircraft	cn/fn	ex/ex*	mfd	del	powered by	mtow kg	configuration	selcal	name/fln/specialitites/remarks
☐ G-RVRB	Piper PA-34-200T Seneca II	34-7970440	G-BTAJ	0079		2 CO TSIO-360-EB	2073			
☐ G-ORVR	Partenavia P.68B	115	G-BFBD	0077	1095	2 LY IO-360-A1B6	1990			
☐ G-BAVZ	Piper PA-23-250 Aztec E	27-7305045	N40241	0073		2 LY IO-540-C4B5	2359			
☐ G-BBGB	Piper PA-23-250 Aztec E	27-7305004	N40206	0073		2 LY IO-540-C4B5	2359			
☐ G-RVRC	Piper PA-23-250 Aztec E	27-7405336	G-BNPD	0074	1097	2 LY IO-540-C4B5	2359			
☐ G-RVRD	Piper PA-23-250 Aztec E	27-4634	G-BRAV	0071	0298	2 LY IO-540-C4B5	2359			

REDHILL CHARTERS = RHC (Redhill Aviation, Ltd dba / Affiliated with Redhill School of Flying, Ltd & Redhill Flying Club)

Redhill

Redhill Aerodrome, Redhill, Surrey RH1 5JY, Great Britain ☎ (1737) 82 29 59 Tx: none Fax: (1737) 82 21 63 SITA: n/a

F: 1984 ⁂ 6 Head: Capt. Zahurul Islam ICAO: REDAIR Net: n/a

registration	type of aircraft	cn/fn	ex/ex*	mfd	del	powered by	mtow kg	configuration	selcal	name/fln/specialitites/remarks
☐ G-BOJK	Piper PA-34-220T Seneca III	3433020	G-BRUF	0086		2 CO TSIO-360-KB	1999			
☐ G-OMAR	Piper PA-34-220T Seneca III	34-8233142	N82033	0082		2 CO TSIO-360-KB	1999			
☐ G-OJIL	Piper PA-31-350 Navajo Chieftain	31-7652175	OY-BTP	0076	0597	2 LY TIO-540-J2BD	3175			

REDHILL HELICOPTER CENTRE

Redhill

Hangar 1, Aerodrome, King's Mill Lane, Redhill, Surrey RH1 5JY, Great Britain ☎ (1737) 82 32 82 Tx: none Fax: (1737) 82 31 18 SITA: n/a

F: 1972 ⁂ n/a Head: Martin Leworthy Net: n/a

registration	type of aircraft	cn/fn	ex/ex*	mfd	del	powered by	mtow kg	configuration	selcal	name/fln/specialitites/remarks
☐ G-STER	Bell 206B JetRanger III	4116	OO-EGA	0090		1 AN 250-C20J	1451			lsf pvt

RELIEF TRANSPORT SERVICES, Ltd = RTS

Manston-Kent Int'l

Vallance Byways, Lowfield Heath Road, Charlwood, Horley, Surrey RH6 0BT, Great Britain ☎ (1293) 86 22 55 Tx: 877372 g Fax: (1293) 86 25 33 SITA: LGWRLXH

F: 1981 ⁂ 10 Head: Barry Keating ICAO: RELIEF Net: n/a Operates relief cargo flights with temporarily leased aircraft as required.

RM AVIATION, Ltd = RMN (formerly RAM Aviation, Ltd)

London-Luton

RM House, Letchmore Heath, Hertfordshire WD2 8ES, Great Britain ☎ (1923) 85 24 24 Tx: none Fax: (1923) 85 79 33 SITA: n/a

F: 1974 ⁂ 6 Head: Peter Roberts ICAO: ROMAN Net: n/a Currently operates under the AOC-Air Operators Certificate of Westair Aviation Ltd, Ireland.

registration	type of aircraft	cn/fn	ex/ex*	mfd	del	powered by	mtow kg	configuration	selcal	name/fln/specialitites/remarks
☐ G-RIBV	Cessna 560 Citation V	560-				2 PWC JT15D-5A	7212			oo-delivery 0099

ROYAL AIR FORCE – Air Transport/Air-to-Air Refuelling Fleet = RR / RRR

Brize Norton

Movements Resources, HQ38GP, RAF High Wycombe, Buckinghamshire HP14 4UE, Great Britain ☎ (1494) 46 14 61 Tx: none Fax: (1494) 49 60 77 SITA: n/a

F: 1918 ⁂ n/a Head: RAF officer (changes in intervals) ICAO: ASCOT Net: n/a RAF division conducting semi-civilian scheduled passenger/cargo flights to selected destinations & VIP missions for the government.

Civilians to fly on RAF scheduled flts to the Falklands have to contact: Falkland Islands Government Office, Westminster, London. Phone: (171) 222 25 42, Fax: (171) 222 23 75.

registration	type of aircraft	cn/fn	ex/ex*	mfd	del	powered by	mtow kg	configuration	selcal	name/fln/specialitites/remarks
☐ XR807	BAe (Vickers) VC10 C1K Srs. 1180	827		0066	1166	4 RR Conway Mk.301	145000	Pax/Frtr/Tanker	AJ-KM	Thomas Gray VC / cvtd C1/1106
☐ XR808	BAe (Vickers) VC10 C1K Srs. 1180	828		0066	0766	4 RR Conway Mk.301	145000	Pax/Frtr/Tanker	BK-CL	Kenneth Campbell VC / cvtd C1/1106
☐ XR810	BAe (Vickers) VC10 C1K Srs. 1180	830		0066	1266	4 RR Conway Mk.301	145000	Pax/Frtr/Tanker	BL-GK	David Lord VC / cvtd C1/1106
☐ XV101	BAe (Vickers) VC10 C1K Srs. 1180	831		0067	0167	4 RR Conway Mk.301	145000	Pax/Frtr/Tanker	BL-HJ	Lance Hawker VC / cvtd C1/1106
☐ XV102	BAe (Vickers) VC10 C1K Srs. 1180	832		0067	0567	4 RR Conway Mk.301	145000	Pax/Frtr/Tanker	BL-HK	Guy Gibson VC / cvtd C1/1106
☐ XV103	BAe (Vickers) VC10 C1K Srs. 1180	833		0067	0767	4 RR Conway Mk.301	145000	Pax/Frtr/Tanker	CF-AB	Edward Mannock VC / cvtd C1/1106
☐ XV104	BAe (Vickers) VC10 C1K Srs. 1180	834		0067	0867	4 RR Conway Mk.301	145000	Pax/Frtr/Tanker	CF-AE	James McCudden VC / cvtd C1/1106
☐ XV105	BAe (Vickers) VC10 C1K Srs. 1180	835		0067	1067	4 RR Conway Mk.301	145000	Pax/Frtr/Tanker	CF-AH	Albert Ball VC / cvtd C1/1106
☐ XV106	BAe (Vickers) VC10 C1K Srs. 1180	836		0067	1267	4 RR Conway Mk.301	145000	Pax/Frtr/Tanker	CF-DE	Thomas Mottershead VC / cvtd C1/1106
☐ XV107	BAe (Vickers) VC10 C1K Srs. 1180	837		0068	0468	4 RR Conway Mk.301	145000	Pax/Frtr/Tanker	CF-DM	James Nicolson VC / cvtd C1/1106
☐ XV108	BAe (Vickers) VC10 C1K Srs. 1180	838		0068	0668	4 RR Conway Mk.301	145000	Pax/Frtr/Tanker	EG-AK	William Rh. Moorhouse VC / cvtd C1/1106
☐ XV109	BAe (Vickers) VC10 C1K Srs. 1180	839		0068	0868	4 RR Conway Mk.301	145000	Pax/Frtr/Tanker	EG-AL	Arthur Scarf VC / cvtd C1/1106
☐ ZD948	Lockheed L-1011-385-3 TriStar KC Mk 1	193V-1157	G-BFCA	0078	0383	3 RR RB211-524B4	245000	Pax/Tanker/Frtr	DH-KL	cvtd TriStar 500
☐ ZD949	Lockheed L-1011-385-3 TriStar K Mk 1	193V-1159	G-BFCB	0079	0383	3 RR RB211-524B4	245000	Pax / Tanker	DH-KM	cvtd TriStar 500
☐ ZD950	Lockheed L-1011-385-3 TriStar KC Mk 1	193V-1164	G-BFCC	0079	0283	3 RR RB211-524B4	245000	Pax/Tanker/Frtr	DJ-AB	cvtd TriStar 500
☐ ZD951	Lockheed L-1011-385-3 TriStar K Mk 1	193V-1165	G-BFCD	0079	0383	3 RR RB211-524B4	245000	Pax / Tanker	DJ-AH	cvtd TriStar 500
☐ ZD952	Lockheed L-1011-385-3 TriStar KC Mk 1	193V-1168	G-BFCE	0079	0383	3 RR RB211-524B4	245000	Pax/Tanker/Frtr	DJ-BC	cvtd TriStar 500
☐ ZD953	Lockheed L-1011-385-3 TriStar KC Mk 1	193V-1174	G-BFCF	0080	0283	3 RR RB211-524B4	245000	Pax/Tanker/Frtr	DJ-AE	cvtd TriStar 500
☐ ZE704	Lockheed L-1011-385-3 TriStar C Mk 2	193Y-1186	N508PA	0080	1184	3 RR RB211-524B4	228600	Pax	LM-BJ	cvtd TriStar 500
☐ ZE705	Lockheed L-1011-385-3 TriStar C Mk 2	193Y-1188	N509PA	0080	1284	3 RR RB211-524B4	228600	Pax	LM-BK	cvtd TriStar 500
☐ ZE706	Lockheed L-1011-385-3 TriStar C Mk 2A	193Y-1177	N503PA	0079	0385	3 RR RB211-524B4	245000	Pax	LM-DG	cvtd TriStar 500

SABRE AIRWAYS, Ltd = SBE

London-Gatwick

Mitre Court, Fleming Way, Crawley, West Sussex RH10 2NJ, Great Britain ☎ (1293) 41 07 27 Tx: 877147 sabre g Fax: (1293) 41 07 37 SITA: LGWOOTJ

F: 1994 ⁂ 200 Head: Keith Newnham ICAO: SABRE Net: n/a

registration	type of aircraft	cn/fn	ex/ex*	mfd	del	powered by	mtow kg	configuration	selcal	name/fln/specialitites/remarks
☐ G-OJSW	Boeing 737-8Q8	28218 / 160		0098	1298	2 CFMI CFM56-7B26	78245	Y189		lsf ILFC
☐ G-OKDN	Boeing 737-8Q8	28226 / 77		0098	0798	2 CFMI CFM56-7B26	78245	Y189		lsf ILFC

☐ G-	Boeing 737-81Q	29049				2 CFMI CFM56-7B26	78245	Y189		to be lsf TOMB 1199
☐ G-	Boeing 737-81Q	29051				2 CFMI CFM56-7B26	78245	Y189		to be lsf TOMB 0200
☐ G-BNNI	Boeing 727-276 (A)	20950 / 1081	VH-TBK	0074	0395	3 PW JT8D-15 (HK3/FDX)	86409	Y187		Lady Patricia / lsf Arkia Leasing
☐ G-BPND	Boeing 727-2D3 (A)	21021 / 1082	OK-EGK	0074	0495	3 PW JT8D-17A	86409	Y187		Katie / lsf PLMI

SCOTIA HELICOPTERS, Ltd (Associated with Grampian Helicopters) — **Cumbernauld**

Cumbernauld Airport, Ward Park North, Cumbernauld, Strathclyde, Scotland G68 0HH, Great Britain ☎ (1236) 78 01 40 Tx: none Fax: (1236) 78 16 46 SITA: n/a
F: 1996 n/a Head: Ian McNab Net: n/a Aircraft below MTOW 1361kg: Robinson R22

☐ G-GHCL	Bell 206B JetRanger	925	G-SHVV	0073		1 AN 250-C20	1451			lsf Grampian Helicopters

SEAFLITE, Ltd — **Loch Earn-SPB**

Loch Earn SPB, Edwample Mill House, Loch Earn Head, Scotland FK19 8QE, Great Britain ☎ (1567) 83 03 84 Tx: none Fax: (1567) 83 04 44 SITA: n/a
F: 1991 n/a Head: Capt. Anthony F. Allen Net: n/a Aircraft below MTOW 1361kg: Cessna FR172F & Piper PA-18 (on Floats).

☐ G-BVER	De Havilland DHC-2 Beaver I	1648	G-BTDM	0066		1 PW R-985-AN14B	2308			painted in AAC cs as XV268
☐ G-DHCB	De Havilland DHC-2 Beaver I	1450	G-BTDL	0060		1 PW R-985-AN14B	2308			Floats

SENAIR CHARTER, Ltd = SEN — **Coventry**

Coventry Airport, Baginton, Coventry CV8 3AZ, Great Britain ☎ (1203) 30 25 53 Tx: n/a Fax: (1203) 63 93 48 SITA: n/a
F: n/a n/a Head: M.L. Ballinger ICAO: SENEX Net: n/a Aircraft below MTOW 1361kg: Piper PA-28 & PA-38.

☐ G-SENX	Piper PA-34-200T Seneca II	34-7870356	G-DARE	0078	0595	2 CO TSIO-360-EB1A	1999			

SHELL AIRCRAFT, Ltd = SHE — **London-Heathrow & Africa**

Cardinal Point, Newall Road, London Heathrow Airport, Hounslow, Middlesex TW6 2HF, Great Britain ☎ (181) 759 05 22 Tx: none Fax: (181) 730 52 34 SITA: n/a
F: 1927 n/a Head: Brian Humphries ICAO: SHELL Net: n/a Operates non-commercial corporate flights exclusively for its owners.

☐ VP-BSA	Dassault Falcon 50	196	D-BNTH	0089	0198	3 GA TFE731-3-1D	18500	Corporate		
☐ VP-BSL	Dassault Falcon 50	209	N96DS	0090	0798	3 GA TFE731-3-1D	18500	Corporate		
☐ G-DNVT	GAC G-IV Gulfstream IV	1078	N17589*	0088	0889	2 RR Tay 611-8	33204	Corporate		

SIROCCO AEROSPACE INTERNATIONAL (U.K.), Ltd = (SIRO) (Subsidiary of Kato Aromatic & Cairo Bank) — **London**

46 Grosvenor Street, London W1, Great Britain ☎ (171) 204 01 20 Tx: none Fax: (171) 204 01 21 SITA: n/a
F: 1996 n/a Head: Ibrahim Kamel Net: n/a New and used aircraft leasing, sales and financing company.
Owner / lessor of following (main) aircraft types: Tupolev 204 / 204C. Aircraft leased from Sirocco Aerospace are listed and mentioned as lsf SIRO under the leasing carriers.

SKYDRIFT AIRCHARTER, Ltd = DFT — **Norwich**

Terminal Building, Airport, Norwich, Norfolk NR6 6EP, Great Britain ☎ (1603) 40 74 24 Tx: none Fax: (1603) 41 86 87 SITA: n/a
F: 1988 15 Head: Travis A. Taberham ICAO: SKYDRIFT Net: n/a

☐ G-TABS	Embraer 110P1 Bandeirante (EMB-110P1)	110212	G-PBAC	0079	0098	2 PWC PT6A-34	5670			lsf Thornhill Aviation Ltd

SKYHOPPER, Ltd (formerly Virgin Helicopters, Ltd & McCarthy Helicopter Services) — **Wycombe Air Park**

Wycombe-Airport nr. Marlow, Buckinghamshire S07 5D0, Great Britain ☎ (1494) 45 11 11 Tx: none Fax: (1494) 45 06 27 SITA: n/a
F: 1979 n/a Head: Mark Bunce Net: http://www.skyhopper.co.uk Aircraft below MTOW 1361kg: Robinson R22 & R44

☐ G-BUZZ	Agusta-Bell 206B JetRanger	8178	F-GAMS	0069		1 AN 250-C20	1451			cvtd 206A
☐ G-HEBE	Bell 206B JetRanger III	3745	CS-HDN	0083	0098	1 AN 250-C20J	1451			lsf MGGR (UK) Ltd
☐ G-NEUF	Bell 206L-1 LongRanger II	45548	G-BVVV	0080	1198	1 AN 250-C28B	1882			lsf Vendle Roberts Ltd
☐ G-BPRL	Eurocopter (Aerosp.) AS355F1 Tw.Squirrel	5154	N362E	0083		2 AN 250-C20F	2400			
☐ G-TOPC	Eurocopter (Aerosp.) AS355F1 Tw.Squirrel	5313	I-LGOG	0082	0797	2 AN 250-C20F	2400			

SKY-TREK AIRLINES = UKT (Atlantic Bridge Aviation, Ltd dba) — **Lydd**

Lydd-Airport, Lydd, Kent TN29 9QL, Great Britain ☎ (1797) 32 00 00 Tx: none Fax: (1797) 32 10 55 SITA: n/a
F: 1996 n/a Head: Jonathan Gordon ICAO: CLOUD Net: http://www.lydd-airport.co.uk

☐ G-BDOT	Britten-Norman BN-2A Mk.III-2 Trislander	1025	ZK-SFF	0076	0397	3 LY O-540-E4C5	4536	Y16		
☐ G-BEDP	Britten-Norman BN-2A Mk.III-2 Trislander	1039	ZK-SFG	0076	1296	3 LY O-540-E4C5	4536	Y16		
☐ G-OJAV	Britten-Norman BN-2A Mk.III-2 Trislander	1024	G-BDOS	0076	1196	3 LY O-540-E4C5	4536	Y16		

SLOANE HELICOPTERS, Ltd = SLN (Sloane Aviation, Ltd dba) — **Sywell**

Sywell Aerodrome, Sywell, Northamptonshire NN6 0BN, Great Britain ☎ (1604) 79 05 95 Tx: none Fax: (1604) 79 09 88 SITA: n/a
F: 1969 n/a Head: David George ICAO: SLOANE Net: http://www.sloanehelicopters.com Aircraft below MTOW 1361kg: Robinson R22

☐ G-FOXM	Bell 206B JetRanger	1514	G-STAK	0074		1 AN 250-C20	1451			
☐ G-OBYT	Agusta-Bell 206B JetRanger	8237	G-BNRC	0070	0698	1 AN 250-C20	1451			
☐ G-BXCB	Agusta A109A II	7347	F-GJSH	0085		2 AN 250-C20B	2600			
☐ G-GVIP	Agusta A109E Power	11024		0098	0798	2 PWC PW206C	2850			
☐ G-JRSL	Agusta A109E Power	11036		0098	1198	2 PWC PW206C	2850			
☐ G-SLNE	Agusta A109A II	7393	G-EEVS	0087	0796	2 AN 250-C20B	2600			

SOUTH COAST AIRWAYS, Ltd = GAD (Seasonal April-November ops only) — **Bournemouth**

73 Gladstone Road, Boscombe, Bournemouth, Dorset BH7 6HD, Great Britain ☎ (1202) 30 48 55 Tx: none Fax: (1202) 30 48 55 SITA: n/a
F: 1995 6 Head: Andrew Dixon ICAO: SOUTHCOAST Net: n/a Seasonal (April-November) operations only.

☐ G-DAKK	Boeing (Douglas) DC-3C (C-47A-35-DL)	9798	F-GEOM	0042	0496	2 PW R-1830	12700	Y32		lsf Meridian Aircraft Ltd

SOUTH EAST REGIONAL POLICE - Air Support Unit (Joint operation of Metropolitan Police & Surrey Police) — **Loughton-Lippitts Hill & Fairoaks**

Lippitts Hill Camp, High Beech, Loughton, Essex IG10 4AL, Great Britain ☎ (181) 508 84 17 Tx: none Fax: (181) 502 33 91 SITA: n/a
F: 1973 n/a Head: Insp. Phil Whitelaw Net: n/a Police unit, conducting non-commercial patrol & survey flights exclusively for police purposes.

☐ G-SEPA	Eurocopter (Aerosp.) AS355N Tw.Squirrel	5525	G-METD	0092	0893	2 TU Arrius 1A	2540	Patrol/Survey		
☐ G-SEPB	Eurocopter (Aerosp.) AS355N Tw.Squirrel	5574	G-BVSE	0094	0395	2 TU Arrius 1A	2540	Patrol/Survey		
☐ G-SEPC	Eurocopter (Aerosp.) AS355N Tw.Squirrel	5596	G-BWGV	0095	0296	2 TU Arrius 1A	2540	Patrol/Survey		

SOUTHERN AIR, Ltd = HSN — **Shoreham & Goodwood**

The Flight Centre, Shoreham Airport, Shoreham-by-Sea, West Sussex BN4 5FF, Great Britain ☎ (1273) 46 16 61 Tx: 877246 southn g Fax: (1273) 46 44 74 SITA: n/a
F: 1974 50 Head: Wayne Chandler ICAO: HELI SOUTHERN Net: n/a Aircraft below MTOW 1361kg: Enstrom F28/280/480 & Hughes 369HS (500C).
Uses additional helicopters for short periods as company is also aircraft sales-agent & dealer.

☐ G-JEKP	Agusta-Bell 206B JetRanger III	8598	D-HMSF	0080	0297	1 AN 250-C20B	1451			lsf pvt

STARSPEED, Ltd = SSP — **Blackbushe**

11 Little Bookham Street, Bookham, Surrey KT23 3AA, Great Britain ☎ (700) 77 82 77 Tx: none Fax: (1372) 45 90 68 SITA: n/a
F: 1978 4 Head: David Voy ICAO: STARSPEED Net: n/a

☐ G-ROIN	Eurocopter (Aerosp.) AS350BA Squirrel	2344	F-GMAR	0090	0098	1 TU Arriel 1B	2100			lsf CCB Aviation / cvtd AS350B
☐ G-LENI	Eurocopter (Aerosp.) AS355F1 Tw.Squirrel	5311	G-ZFDB	0084		2 AN 250-C20F	2400			lsf Grid Aviation Ltd
☐ G-NOIR	Bell 222A	47031	G-OJLC	0080		2 LY LTS101-650C.3	3561			lsf Arlington Securities Plc

STEPHENSON AVIATION, Ltd (A Luke Holdings Group Company) — **Chichester-Goodwood**

Hangar 3, Goodwood Airfield, Chichester, West Sussex PO18 0PH, Great Britain ☎ (1243) 53 01 65 Tx: none Fax: (1243) 53 99 21 SITA: n/a
F: 1993 11 Head: Martin Luke Net: n/a Aircraft below MTOW 1361kg: Enstrom F-28A/F

☐ G-BOLO	Bell 206B JetRanger	1522	N59409	0074		1 AN 250-C20	1451			lsf Hargreaves Construction Co. Ltd
☐ G-LILY	Bell 206B JetRanger III	4107	G-NTBI	0090		1 AN 250-C20J	1451			lsf pvt

STERLING HELICOPTERS, Ltd = GPH — **Norwich**

Hangar E, Gambling Close, Norwich Airport, Norwich, Norfolk NR6 6EG, Great Britain ☎ (1603) 41 71 56 Tx: none Fax: (1603) 41 07 91 SITA: n/a
F: 1989 20 Head: Gerry Hermer ICAO: SILVERLINE Net: http://www.flysterling.com Aircraft below MTOW 1361kg: Hughes 269C (300C).

☐ G-BNYD	Bell 206B JetRanger II	1911	N3254P	0076		1 AN 250-C20	1451			
☐ G-BTHY	Bell 206B JetRanger III	2290	N6606M	0077		1 AN 250-C20B	1451			lsf pvt
☐ G-BXNS	Bell 206B JetRanger III	2385	N16822	0078	1197	1 AN 250-C20B	1451			
☐ G-BXNT	Bell 206B JetRanger III	2398	N94CA	0078	1197	1 AN 250-C20B	1451			
☐ G-BFYA	Eurocopter (MBB) BO105DB	S-321	D-HJET	0077	0395	2 AN 250-C20B	2400			
☐ G-TOPS	Eurocopter (Aerosp.) AS355F1 Tw.Squirrel	5151	G-BPRH	0082	0494	2 AN 250-C20F	2400			
☐ G-OMNH	Beech King Air 200	BB-108	N108BM	0076	0898	2 PWC PT6A-41	5670			lsf Maynard & Harris Holdings Ltd

STREAMLINE AVIATION = SSW (Streamline Aviation (SW), Ltd dba) — **Exeter**

12 Kingfisher Court, Venny Bridge, Pinhoe, Exeter, Devon EX4 8JN, Great Britain ☎ (1392) 46 60 33 Tx: none Fax: (1392) 46 60 55 SITA: n/a
F: 1990 50 Head: Bernard Haddican ICAO: STREAMLINE Net: n/a

☐ G-LEDN	Shorts 330-200 (SD3-30 Variant 100)	SH3064	5N-AOX	0081	0393	2 PWC PT6A-45R	10387	Freighter		
☐ G-SSWT	Shorts 330-200 (SD3-30 Variant 100)	SH3095	4X-CSQ	0083	0698	2 PWC PT6A-45R	10387	Freighter		
☐ G-SSWU	Shorts 330-200 (SD3-30 Variant 100)	SH3076	C-FYXF	0081	0199	2 PWC PT6A-45R	10387	Freighter		

SUCKLING AIRWAYS = CB / SAY (Suckling Aviation Int'l, Ltd dba) — **Cambridge**

Cambridge Airport, Cambridge CB5 8RT, Great Britain ☎ (1223) 29 25 25 Tx: none Fax: (1223) 29 21 60 SITA: n/a
F: 1984 65 Head: Capt. Roy G. Suckling IATA: 969 ICAO: SUCKLING Net: n/a

☐ G-BMMR	Dornier 228-200	8063	D-IAOT*	0086	0486	2 GA TPE331-5-252D	5700	Y19		
☐ G-BUXT	Dornier 228-202K	8065	D-CBOL	0086	0593	2 GA TPE331-5-252D	6200	Y19		
☐ G-BWIR	Dornier 328-110	3023	D-CDXF*	0095	1095	2 PWC PW119B	13990	Y31		cvtd -100

180 registration type of aircraft cn/fn ex/ex* mfd del powered by mtow kg configuration selcal name/fln/specialitites/remarks

☐ G-BWWT	Dornier 328-110	3022	D-CDXO*	0095	1196	2 PWC PW119B	13990	Y31		cvtd -100
☐ G-BYHF	Dornier 328-110	3050	N350AD	0095	0399	2 PWC PW119B	13990	Y31		

SWEB HELICOPTER UNIT = ELE (South Western Helicopters, Ltd dba / Subsidiary of South West Electricity, Plc) Bristol

Bristol Airport, Lulsgate, Bristol, Avon BS19 3DP, Great Britain ☎ (1275) 47 27 13 Tx: 44298 swebhq g Fax: (1275) 47 48 16 SITA: n/a
F: 1963 ⁂ 11 Head: Capt. R. Malone ICAO: ELECTRICITY Net: n/a

☐ G-BARP	Bell 206B JetRanger	967	N18092	0073		1 AN 250-C20	1451			occ lst Atlanta Helicopters
☐ G-MFMF	Bell 206B JetRanger III	3569	G-BJNJ	0081		1 AN 250-C20J	1451			occ lst Atlanta Helicopters
☐ G-LECA	Eurocopter (Aerosp.) AS355F1 Tw.Squirrel	5043	G-BNBK	0081		2 AN 250-C20F	2400			
☐ G-OHMS	Eurocopter (Aerosp.) AS355F1 Tw.Squirrel	5194	N367E	0082	0690	2 AN 250-C20F	2400			

TG AVIATION, Ltd = TGC Manston-Kent Int'l

Kent Int'l Airport, Manston, Kent CT12 5BP, Great Britain ☎ (1843) 82 36 56 Tx: 965446 kiaops g Fax: (1843) 82 20 24 SITA: n/a
F: 1982 ⁂ 18 Head: Capt. Edward Girdler ICAO: THANET Net: http://www.tgaviation.demon.co.uk

☐ G-BSUW	Piper PA-34-200T Seneca II	34-7870081	N2360M	0077		2 CO TSIO-360-EB1	1999	5 Pax		
☐ G-BFTT	Cessna 421C Golden Eagle III	421C0462	N6789C	0077		2 CO GTSIO-520-L	3379	6 Pax		lsf P&B Metal Components Ltd

TIGER HELICOPTERS, Ltd Shobdon

Shobdon Aerodrome, Shobdon, Hertfordshire HR6 9NR, Great Britain ☎ (1568) 70 80 28 Tx: none Fax: (1568) 70 80 05 SITA: n/a
F: 1992 ⁂ n/a Head: Capt. Alan L. Ramsden Net: http://www.yell.co.uk/sites/tiger-helicopters/

☐ G-BLGV	Bell 206B JetRanger	982	5B-JSB	0073		1 AN 250-C20	1451			lsf Part Reward Ltd
☐ G-BORV	Bell 206B JetRanger II	2202	C-GVTY	0077		1 AN 250-C20	1451			lsf Rosenberg Helicopters
☐ G-JAHL	Bell 206B JetRanger III	3565	N666ST	0081	0198	1 AN 250-C20B	1451			lsf Jet Air Helicopters

TITAN AIRWAYS, Ltd = AWC (Member of 3i Group) London-Stansted

Enterprise House, London-Stansted Airport, Stansted, Essex CM24 1QW, Great Britain ☎ (1279) 68 06 16 Tx: none Fax: (1279) 68 01 10 SITA: STNTACR
F: 1988 ⁂ 85 Head: Gene H. Willson ICAO: ZAP Net: http://www.titan-airways.co.uk

☐ G-ZAPI	Cessna 500 Citation I	500-0404	G-BHTT	0080	0994	2 PWC JT15D-1A	5375	Y5		
☐ G-ZAPD	Shorts 360-300 (SD3-60)	SH3741	G-OLGW	0088	0892	2 PWC PT6A-67R	12292	Y39		
☐ G-BUPS	ATR 42-300	109	DQ-FEP	0088	0694	2 PWC PW120	16700	Y46		lsf GECA
☐ G-ZAPJ	ATR 42-300	113	EI-CIQ	0088	0595	2 PWC PW120	16700	Y46		lsf GECA
☐ G-ZAPK	BAe 146-200 (QC)	E2148	G-BTIA	0088	0496	4 LY ALF502R-5	42184	Y80 / Frtr		cvtd -200
☐ G-ZAPL	BAe 146-200	E2030	G-WLCY	0085	0597	4 LY ALF502R-5	40597	Y80		special surrealistic-colors

TNT International Aviation Services – Global Express Logistics & Mail = NTR (Division of TNT Express Worldwide) Liege (Belgium)

Stead House, 2-6 Frances Road, Windsor, Berkshire SL4 3AA, Great Britain ☎ (1753) 84 21 68 Tx: 846980 tntias g Fax: (1753) 85 81 58 SITA: LONTN7X
F: 1987 ⁂ 100 Head: Bob O'Donnell ICAO: NITRO Net: http://www.tntew.com All aircraft are operated by the following associated companies:
AIRFOYLE Luton (G-), CHANNEL EXPRESS Bournemouth (G-), MISTRAL AIR Rome (I-), PACIFIC EAST ASIA Manila (RP-), PAN AIR Madrid (EC-) & STERLING EUROPEAN (OY-). For additional details – see under each carrier.

☐ G-TNTA	BAe 146-200 (QT)	E2056	N146QT*	0085	0487	4 LY ALF502R-5	42184	Freighter	BH-CP	lst/opb UPA / cvtd -200
☐ G-TNTB	BAe 146-200 (QT)	E2067	G-5-067*	0087	0987	4 LY ALF502R-5	42184	Freighter	BH-DP	lst/opb UPA / cvtd -200
☐ EC-ELT	BAe 146-200 (QT)	E2102	EC-198	0088	1088	4 LY ALF502R-5	42184	Freighter	AQ-HL	lst/opb PNR / cvtd -200
☐ EC-EPA	BAe 146-200 (QT)	E2089	EC-281	0087	0388	4 LY ALF502R-5	42184	Freighter	AQ-MP	lst/opb PNR / cvtd -200
☐ EC-FVY	BAe 146-200 (QT)	E2117	EC-615*	0088	0589	4 LY ALF502R-5	42184	Freighter	FQ-LM	lst/opb PNR/cvtd-200
☐ EC-FZE	BAe 146-200 (QT)	E2105	EC-719	0088	1188	4 LY ALF502R-5	42184	Freighter	AQ-HM	lst/opb PNR / cvtd -200
☐ EC-GQO	BAe 146-200 (QT)	E2086	D-ADEI	0088	0288	4 LY ALF502R-5	42184	Freighter	CF-AP	lsf Nordbanken Fin/lst/opb PNR/cvtd-200
☐ EC-GQP	BAe 146-200 (QT)	E2100	D-ANTJ	0088	0988	4 LY ALF502R-5	42184	Freighter	AQ-HK	lst/opb PNR/cvtd-200
☐ I-TNTC	BAe 146-200 (QT)	E2078	G-5-078*	0087	1287	4 LY ALF502R-5	42184	Freighter	BH-EP	lst/opb MSA / cvtd -200
☐ RP-C481	BAe 146-200 (QT)	E2109	G-TNTD	0088	1288	4 LY ALF502R-5	42184	Freighter	AQ-HP	lst/opb PEC / cvtd -200
☐ RP-C482	BAe 146-200 (QT)	E2112	F-GTNU	0088	0189	4 LY ALF502R-5	42184	Freighter	AQ-JK	lst/opb PEC/cvtd-200
☐ G-TJPM	BAe 146-300 (QT)	E3150	SE-DIM	0089	1289	4 LY ALF502R-5	44225	Freighter	MQ-DG	lst/opb UPA / cvtd -300
☐ G-TNTE	BAe 146-300 (QT)	E3153	G-BRPW*	0089	0690	4 LY ALF502R-5	44225	Freighter	CM-LQ	lst/opb UPA / cvtd -300
☐ G-TNTG	BAe 146-300 (QT)	E3182	G-BSUY*	0091	1091	4 LY ALF502R-5	44225	Freighter	AR-DJ	lst/opb UPA / cvtd -300
☐ G-TNTK	BAe 146-300 (QT)	E3186	G-BSXL*	0091	1091	4 LY ALF502R-5	44225	Freighter	AR-DK	lst/opb UPA / cvtd -300
☐ G-TNTL	BAe 146-300 (QT)	E3168	RP-C479	0090	1290	4 LY ALF502R-5	44225	Freighter	AE-QS	lst/opb UPA / cvtd -300
☐ G-TNTM	BAe 146-300 (QT)	E3166	RP-C480	0090	1290	4 LY ALF502R-5	44225	Freighter	AE-RS	lst/opb MSA / cvtd -300
☐ G-TNTR	BAe 146-300 (QT)	E3151	SE-DIT	0090	0290	4 LY ALF502R-5	44225	Freighter	MQ-DH	lst/opb UPA / cvtd -300
☐ EC-FFY	BAe 146-300 (QT)	E3154	EC-712	0089	0990	4 LY ALF502R-5	44225	Freighter	CM-PQ	lst/opb PNR / cvtd -200
☐ N6809	Boeing 727-223 (F)	19484 / 560		0468	0596	3 PW JT8D-9 (HK3/FDX)	80966	Freighter	BK-EL	lsf KHA/sub-lst/opb PEC / cvtd -223
☐ OY-SER	Boeing 727-232 (F) (A)	20639 / 927	N16784	0073	0698	3 PW JT8D-15 (HK3/FDX)	86409	Freighter		lsf PACA / sub-lst/opb SNB / cvtd -232
☐ OY-SES	Boeing 727-251 (F)	19977 / 690	N258US	0269	0398	3 PW JT8D-7B (HK3/FDX)	78245	Freighter		lsf PEGA / sub-lst/opf SNB / cvtd -251
☐ OY-SET	Boeing 727-227 (F) (A)	21245 / 1202	EI-PAK	0076	0396	3 PW JT8D-7B (HK3/FDX)	80558	Freighter		lsf Wren Eq./sub-lst/opb SNB / cvtd-227
☐ OY-SEU	Boeing 727-243 (F) (A)	21269 / 1230	EI-EWW	0076	1197	3 PW JT8D-7B (HK3/FDX)	80558	Freighter		lsf WrenEquip./sub-lst/opb SNB/cvtd-243
☐ OY-SEV	Boeing 727-281 (F)	20571 / 884	EI-SKY	0072	0595	3 PW JT8D-7B (HK3/FDX)	80558	Freighter		lsfPACA/lst/opbSNB inSkyPak cs/cvtd-281
☐ OY-SEW	Boeing 727-287 (F) (A)	21688 / 1415	N920PG	0078	0997	3 PW JT8D-7B (HK3/FDX)	80558	Freighter		lsf PACA/sub-lst/opb SNB/cvtd -287
☐ OY-SEY	Boeing 727-224 (F) (A)	20659 / 979	N29730	1073	0297	3 PW JT8D-7B (HK3/FDX)	78245	Freighter	FG-HM	lsf Naabi Ltd/sub-lst/opb SNB/cvtd -224
☐ OY-TNT	Boeing 727-281 (F)	20725 / 958	EI-TNT	0073	0295	3 PW JT8D-7B (HK3/FDX)	80558	Freighter		lsf PACA / sub-lst/opb SNB / cvtd -281
☐ G-BYDH	Airbus Industrie A300B4-203 (F)	210	F-WHPK	0082	0199	2 GE CF6-50C2	165000	Freighter		lst / opb EXS / cvtd -203
☐ G-CEXI	Airbus Ind.A300B4-203 (F) (Eurofreighter)	121	D-ASAA	0080	0998	2 GE CF6-50C2	165000	Freighter		lsf / opb EXS / cvtd -203
☐	Airbus Industrie A300B4-203 (F)	227	N223KW	0083		2 GE CF6-50C2	165000	Freighter		oo-delivery 0899 / cvtd -203
☐	Airbus Industrie A300B4-203 (F)	247	N247TN	0083		2 GE CF6-50C2	165000	Freighter		oo-delivery 1099 / cvtd -203

TRACE WORLDWIDE, Ltd Biggin Hill

Flight Inspection Division, Bldg. 526, Biggin Hill Airport, Westerham, Kent TN16 3BN, Great Britain ☎ (1959) 57 07 00 Tx: none Fax: (1959) 54 06 68 SITA: n/a
F: n/a ⁂ n/a Head: John Gurney Net: n/a

☐ G-HCTL	Piper PA-31-350 Navajo Chieftain	31-7952097	G-BGOY	0079	0797	2 LY TIO-540-J2BD	3175	Calibrator		

TRANSCITY AIRLINES, Ltd London-Stansted

26 Christchurch Road, Sidcup, Kent DA15 7HQ, Great Britain ☎ (181) 300 35 94 Tx: none Fax: (181) 300 88 11 SITA: n/a
F: 1996 ⁂ n/a Head: Geoff Simmonds Net: n/a Presently being set-up. Intends to start operations during 1999 with 1 BAe Jetstream 31 aircraft.

VERITAIR, Ltd (Subsidiary of CHC Helicopter Corp., Canada) Cardiff Heliport

Cardiff Heliport, Foreshore Road, East Moors, Cardiff, South Glamorgan CF1 5LZ, Wales, Great Britain ☎ (1222) 46 58 80 Tx: none Fax: (1222) 48 75 06 SITA: n/a
F: 1982 ⁂ 7 Head: Capt. Julian Verity ICAO: VERITAIR Net: n/a

☐ G-BTKL	Eurocopter (MBB) BO105DBS-4	S-422	D-HDMU	0080		2 AN 250-C20B	2500			
☐ G-SAEW	Eurocopter (Aerosp.) AS355F2 Tw.Squirrel	5435	N244BB	0089	1296	2 AN 250-C20F	2540			opf South & East Wales Police

VIRGIN ATLANTIC = VS / VIR (Virgin Atlantic Airways, Ltd dba / Member of Virgin Group) London-Gatwick & -Heathrow

The Office, Crawley Business Quarter, Manor Royal, Crawley, West Sussex RH10 2NU, Great Britain ☎ (1293) 56 23 45 Tx: 877077 virair g Fax: (1293) 56 17 21 SITA: n/a
F: 1984 ⁂ 4800 Head: Richard M. Branson IATA: 932 ICAO: VIRGIN Net: http://www.fly.virgin.com

☐ G-OUZO	Airbus Industrie A320-231	449	EI-VIR	0093	0495	2 IAE V2500-A1	75500	F14Y138	JP-MR	Spirit of Melina / lsf ORIX
☐ G-VAEL	Airbus Industrie A340-311	015	F-WWJG*	0093	1293	4 CFMI CFM56-5C2	257000	C40W28Y187	EJ-MS	Maiden Toulouse
☐ G-VAIR	Airbus Industrie A340-313	164	F-WWJA*	0097	0497	4 CFMI CFM56-5C4	262000	C40W28Y187	MR-KP	Maiden Tokyo / lsf ILFC
☐ G-VBUS	Airbus Industrie A340-311	013	F-WWJE*	0093	1193	4 CFMI CFM56-5C2	257000	C40W28Y187	EJ-MR	Lady in Red
☐ G-VELD	Airbus Industrie A340-313	214	F-WWJY*	0098	0398	4 CFMI CFM56-5C4	262000	C40W28Y187	PS-LM	African Queen / lsf ILFC
☐ G-VFAR	Airbus Industrie A340-313	225	F-WWJZ*	0098	0698	4 CFMI CFM56-5C4	262000	C40W28Y187	PS-LQ	Diana
☐ G-VFLY	Airbus Industrie A340-311	058	F-WWJE*	0094	1094	4 CFMI CFM56-5C2	257000	C40W28Y187	EJ-PS	Dragon Lady
☐ G-VHOL	Airbus Industrie A340-311	002	F-WWAS*	0092	0597	4 CFMI CFM56-5C2	257000	C40W28Y187	AR-KM	Jetstreamer
☐ G-VSEA	Airbus Industrie A340-311	003	F-WWDA*	0092	0797	4 CFMI CFM56-5C2	257000	C40W28Y187	MR-KQ	Plane Sailing
☐ G-VSKY	Airbus Industrie A340-311	016	F-WWJH*	0093	0294	4 CFMI CFM56-5C2	257000	C40W28Y187	EJ-PR	China Girl
☐ G-VSUN	Airbus Industrie A340-313	114	F-WWJI*	0196	0496	4 CFMI CFM56-5C4	257000	C40W28Y187	HR-PS	First Lady / lsf ILFC
☐ G-VBEE	Boeing 747-219B	22723 / 527	ZK-NZW	0081	0399	4 RR RB211-524D4	377842	C28W36Y358		
☐ G-VCAT	Boeing 747-267B	22872 / 566	B-HIE	0782	1098	4 RR RB211-524D4	377842			Wild Thing
☐ G-VGIN	Boeing 747-243B	19732 / 134	N747BL	0071	0186	4 PW JT9D-7J	362873	C52W30Y281	BH-JM	Scarlet Lady
☐ G-VIBE	Boeing 747-219B	22791 / 568	ZK-NZZ	0082		4 RR RB211-524D4	377842			oo-delivery 0999 / ex ANZ
☐ G-VIRG	Boeing 747-287B	21189 / 274	N354AS	0075	0684	4 PW JT9D-7J	362873	C52W30Y281	BH-JL	Maiden Voyager
☐ G-VJFK	Boeing 747-238B	20842 / 238	VH-EBH	0074	0291	4 PW JT9D-7J	362873	C50W30Y294	BK-FL	Boston Belle
☐ G-VLAX	Boeing 747-238B	20921 / 241	VH-EBI	0074	0591	4 PW JT9D-7J	362873	C50W30Y294	BK-FM	California Girl
☐ G-VPUF	Boeing 747-219B	22725 / 563	ZK-NZY	0082		4 RR RB211-524D4	377842			oo-delivery 0200 / ex ANZ
☐ G-VRUM	Boeing 747-267B	23048 / 582	B-HIF	0583	1098	4 RR RB211-524D4	377842			Calypso Queen
☐ G-VSSS	Boeing 747-219B	22724 / 528	ZK-NZX	0081		4 RR RB211-524D4	377842			oo-delivery 0500 / ex ANZ
☐ G-VZZZ	Boeing 747-219B	22722 / 523	ZK-NZV	0081	0799	4 RR RB211-524D4	377842	C28W36Y358		
☐ G-	Airbus Industrie A340-642					4 RR Trent 556	365000			oo-delivery 0002
☐ G-	Airbus Industrie A340-642					4 RR Trent 556	365000			oo-delivery 0002
☐ G-	Airbus Industrie A340-642	383				4 RR Trent 556	365000			oo-delivery 0302
☐ G-	Airbus Industrie A340-642					4 RR Trent 556	365000			oo-delivery 0003
☐ G-	Airbus Industrie A340-642					4 RR Trent 556	365000			oo-delivery 0003

181 registration type of aircraft cn/fn ex/ex* mfd del powered by mtow kg configuration selcal name/fln/specialitites/remarks

registration	type of aircraft	cn/fn	ex/ex*	mfd	del	powered by	mtow kg	configuration	selcal	name/fln/specialitites/remarks
☐ G-	Airbus Industrie A340-642					4 RR Trent 556	365000			oo-delivery 0003
☐ G-	Airbus Industrie A340-642					4 RR Trent 556	365000			oo-delivery 0003
☐ G-	Airbus Industrie A340-642					4 RR Trent 556	365000			oo-delivery 0004
☐ G-	Airbus Industrie A340-642					4 RR Trent 556	365000			oo-delivery 0004
☐ G-	Airbus Industrie A340-642					4 RR Trent 556	365000			oo-delivery 0004
☐ G-VAST	Boeing 747-41R	28757 / 1117		0697	0697	4 GE CF6-80C2B1F	377842	C48W22Y340	MR-KL	Ladybird
☐ G-VBIG	Boeing 747-4Q8	26255 / 1081		0596	0696	4 GE CF6-80C2B1F	377842	C12W20Y461	HR-PQ	Tinker Belle / lsf ILFC
☐ G-VFAB	Boeing 747-4Q8	24958 / 1028		0094	0494	4 GE CF6-80C2B1F	377842	C48W22Y340	EJ-QR	Lady Penelope / lsf ILFC
☐ G-VHOT	Boeing 747-4Q8	26326 / 1043		0094	1094	4 GE CF6-80C2B1F	377842	C48W22Y340	EJ-QS	Tubular Belle / lsf ILFC
☐ G-VTOP	Boeing 747-4Q8	28194 / 1100		0097	0197	4 GE CF6-80C2B1F	377842	C48W22Y340	MR-JS	Virginia Plain / lsf ILFC
☐ G-VXLG	Boeing 747-41R	29406 / 1177		0998	0998	4 GE CF6-80C2B1F	377842	C48W22Y340	PS-LR	Ruby Tuesday

VIRGIN HEMS (London), Ltd – Helicopter Emergency Medical Service — London-The Royal London Hospital Helipad

The Helipad, The Royal London Hospital, Whitechapel, London E1 1BB, Great Britain ☎ (171) 247-67224 Tx: none Fax: (171) 247 67 64 SITA: n/a
F: 1988 ⁂ 7 Head: Capt. Geoff Newman ICAO: MEDIVAC Net: http://www.hems-london.virgin.net

registration	type of aircraft	cn/fn	ex/ex*	mfd	del	powered by	mtow kg	configuration	selcal	name/fln/specialitites/remarks
☐ G-HEMS	Eurocopter (Aerosp.) SA365N Dauphin 2	6009	N365AN	0082		2 TU Arriel 1C	4000	Ambulance		lsf Virgin Executive Aviation Ltd

VIRGIN SUN, Ltd = V2 (Subsidiary of Virgin Holidays / Member of Virgin Group) — London-Gatwick

Virgin Holidays, The Galleria, Station Road, Crawley, West Sussex RH10 1WW, Great Britain ☎ (1293) 61 62 61 Tx: none Fax: (1293) 53 69 57 SITA: n/a
F: 1998 ⁂ n/a Head: Richard M. Branson Net: n/a

registration	type of aircraft	cn/fn	ex/ex*	mfd	del	powered by	mtow kg	configuration	selcal	name/fln/specialitites/remarks
☐ G-VMED	Airbus Industrie A320-214	978		0499	0499	2 CFMI CFM56-5B4	77000	Y180		Mediterreanen Maiden / lsf GECA
☐ G-VTAN	Airbus Industrie A320-214	764	G-BXTA	0498	0499	2 CFMI CFM56-5B4	77000	Y180	CG-MR	Sunshine Girl / lsf GECA

WESTAIR FLYING SERVICES, Ltd (Air Charter and Travel, Ltd dba) — Blackpool

Blackpool Airport, Blackpool, Lancashire FY4 2QX, Great Britain ☎ (1253) 42 660 Tx: none Fax: (1253) 40 11 21 SITA: n/a
F: 1938 ⁂ 25 Head: John Westoby Net: n/a

registration	type of aircraft	cn/fn	ex/ex*	mfd	del	powered by	mtow kg	configuration	selcal	name/fln/specialitites/remarks
☐ G-AZFR	Cessna 401B	401B0121	N9781Q	0071		2 CO TSIO-520-E	2858			

WEST MIDLANDS POLICE – Air Operations Unit — Birmingham

Hangar Road, Birmingham International Airport, Birmingham B26 3QB, Great Britain ☎ (121) 712 60 12 Tx: none Fax: (121) 712 60 11 SITA: n/a
F: 1989 ⁂ n/a Head: Sgt Scott McKenna Net: n/a Police unit, conducting non-commercial patrol/survey/EMS flights exclusively for police purposes.

registration	type of aircraft	cn/fn	ex/ex*	mfd	del	powered by	mtow kg	configuration	selcal	name/fln/specialitites/remarks
☐ G-WMPA	Eurocopter (Aerosp.) AS355F2 Tw.Squirrel	5401		0089		2 AN 250-C20F	2540	Survey / EMS		opb Police Aviation Services

WOODGATE AVIATION (IOM), Ltd = WOD — Isle of Man

Isle of Man (Ronaldsway) Airport, Ballasalla IM9 2AS, Isle of Man ☎ (1624) 82 37 07 Tx: none Fax: (1624) 82 23 46 SITA: n/a
F: 1969 ⁂ 4 Head: Capt. John Moon ICAO: WOODAIR Net: n/a

registration	type of aircraft	cn/fn	ex/ex*	mfd	del	powered by	mtow kg	configuration	selcal	name/fln/specialitites/remarks
☐ G-CALL	Piper PA-23-250 Aztec F	27-7754061	N62826	0077		2 LY IO-540-C4B5	2359	Pax/Frtr/Survey		
☐ G-CITY	Piper PA-31-350 Navajo Chieftain	31-7852136	N27741	0078		2 LY TIO-540-J2BD	3175	Pax/Frtr/EMS		

WOODGATE EXECUTIVE AIR CHARTER (UK), Ltd = WOD (Sister company of Woodgate Aviation (IOM), Ltd / formerly Woodgate Executive Air Charter (UK), Ltd) — Belfast-Int'l

Belfast International Airport, Belfast BT29 4AA, Northern Ireland, Great Britain ☎ (1849) 42 24 78 Tx: none Fax: (1849) 45 26 49 SITA: n/a
F: 1969 ⁂ 5 Head: Capt. Allan John Keen ICAO: WOODAIR Net: n/a

registration	type of aircraft	cn/fn	ex/ex*	mfd	del	powered by	mtow kg	configuration	selcal	name/fln/specialitites/remarks
☐ G-LIDE	Piper PA-31-350 Navajo Chieftain	31-7852156	N27800	0078		2 LY TIO-540-J2BD	3175	Pax/Frtr/EMS		lsf Keen Leasing Ltd
☐ G-BEFO	Britten-Norman BN-2A Mk.III-2 Trislander	1041	5H-AZP	0079	0695	3 LY O-540-E4C5	4536	Pax/Frtr		lsf Keen Leasing Ltd
☐ G-WEAC	Britten-Norman BN-2A Mk.III-2 Trislander	1042	5H-AZD	0079	1294	3 LY O-540-E4C5	4536	Pax/Frtr		lsf Keen Leasing Ltd

YORKSHIRE HELICOPTER Centre, Ltd — Swinton-Heliport

6 Swinton Meadows, Swinton, Mexborough, South Yorkshire S64 8AB, Great Britain ☎ (1709) 57 17 20 Tx: none Fax: (1709) 57 17 21 SITA: n/a
F: 1989 ⁂ 6 Head: David Ness Net: n/a

registration	type of aircraft	cn/fn	ex/ex*	mfd	del	powered by	mtow kg	configuration	selcal	name/fln/specialitites/remarks
☐ G-BWZW	Bell 206B JetRanger	12	G-CTEK	0067	1196	1 AN 250-C20	1451			cvtd 206A
☐ G-OJCB	Agusta-Bell 206B JetRanger II	8554		0078		1 AN 250-C20	1451			
☐ G-SHCC	Bell 206B JetRanger III	1172	N280C	0073	1292	1 AN 250-C20B	1451			cvtd JetRanger

HA = HUNGARY (Hungarian Republic) (Magyar Köztarsasag)

Capital: Budapest Official Language: Hungarian Population: 10,6 million Square Km: 93033 Dialling code: +36 Year established: 1001 Acting political head: Viktor Orban (Prime Minister)

AERO ESZTERGOM = EGM (Commercial division of Aeroclub Esztergom) — Esztergom

PO Box 66, H-2501 Esztergom, Hungary ☎ (33) 31 44 79 Tx: none Fax: (33) 31 14 43 SITA: n/a
F: n/a ⁂ n/a Head: Gabor Kraszlan ICAO: AERO ESTERGOM Net: n/a

registration	type of aircraft	cn/fn	ex/ex*	mfd	del	powered by	mtow kg	configuration	selcal	name/fln/specialitites/remarks
☐ HA-LDF	Let 200D Morava	171408		0062		2 WA M-337	1950			
☐ HA-LDG	Let 200D Morava	171411	S5-CAH	0062		2 WA M-337	1950			
☐ HA-YCD	Piper PA-23-250 Aztec E	27-4700	OH-PKS	0071		2 LY IO-540-C4B5	2359			
☐ HA-ABA	PZL Mielec (Antonov) An-2	1G234-23		0089		1 SH ASh-62IR	5500			
☐ HA-ABJ	PZL Mielec (Antonov) An-2	1G201-40	RA-84722	0083		1 SH ASh-62IR	5500			
☐ HA-ABP	PZL Mielec (Antonov) An-2	1G185-52	RA-54885	0080		1 SH ASh-62IR	5500			
☐ HA-ANI	PZL Mielec (Antonov) An-2	1G132-55		0071		1 SH ASh-62IR	5500			

AEROTRADERS, Ltd — Budapest-Ferihegy & Esztergom

c/o TPG Airways Hungary, Ltd, Kossuth Lajos utca 97, H-1181 Budapest, Hungary ☎ (1) 295 35 35 Tx: none Fax: (1) 295 35 35 SITA: BUDAP8X
F: 1992 ⁂ n/a Head: Thomas Pakuts, Jr. Net: n/a Beside airtaxi flights with PA-32, also operates cargo flights with Antonov 12/22/26/32/72/74/124 & Ilyushin 18/76 freighters leased from other companies when required.

registration	type of aircraft	cn/fn	ex/ex*	mfd	del	powered by	mtow kg	configuration	selcal	name/fln/specialitites/remarks
☐ HA-API	Piper PA-32-300 Cherokee SIX	32-40220	N4149W	0067		1 LY IO-540-K1A5	1542			lst/jtly opw TPG Airways

AIR HUNGARIA Air Transport, Co. Ltd = AHN — Budapest-Ferihegy

Csiky Ut. 18, H-1194 Budapest, Hungary ☎ (1) 280 00 32 Tx: none Fax: (1) 280 88 66 SITA: QIFALMA
F: 1993 ⁂ 50 Head: Tatjana Mazalin ICAO: AIR HUNGARIA Net: n/a Operates cargo & passenger flights with Antonov 124, Ilyushin 76 & Tupolev 154M aircraft, leased from other companies when required.

AIR SERVICE HUNGARY – Repülőgépes Szolgalat Allami Vallat = RSZ (formerly MEM Repülőgépes Szolgalat) — Budapest-Budaörs

Kőérberki Ut. 36, H-1112 Budapest XI, Hungary ☎ (1) 185 13 44 Tx: 226031 rszdp h Fax: (1) 68 81 17 SITA: n/a
F: 1959 ⁂ 90 Head: Zoltan Jancsi ICAO: HUNSER Net: n/a

registration	type of aircraft	cn/fn	ex/ex*	mfd	del	powered by	mtow kg	configuration	selcal	name/fln/specialitites/remarks
☐ HA-MSH	MD Helicopters MD 500E (Hughes 369E)	0309E		0088		1 AN 250-C20B	1361			
☐ HA-MBN	PZL Mielec (Antonov) An-2R	1G166-32		0076		1 SH ASh-62IR	5500			
☐ HA-MBR	PZL Mielec (Antonov) An-2R	1G168-14		0076		1 SH ASh-62IR	5500			
☐ HA-MDG	PZL Mielec (Antonov) An-2R	1G181-38		0078		1 SH ASh-62IR	5500			
☐ HA-MDK	PZL Mielec (Antonov) An-2R	1G181-42		0078		1 SH ASh-62IR	5500			
☐ HA-MDM	PZL Mielec (Antonov) An-2R	1G183-20		0079		1 SH ASh-62IR	5500			
☐ HA-MDN	PZL Mielec (Antonov) An-2R	1G183-21		0079		1 SH ASh-62IR	5500			
☐ HA-MDP	PZL Mielec (Antonov) An-2R	1G185-44		0079		1 SH ASh-62IR	5500			
☐ HA-MDQ	PZL Mielec (Antonov) An-2R	1G185-45		0079		1 SH ASh-62IR	5500			
☐ HA-MEO	PZL Mielec (Antonov) An-2R	1G190-24		0081		1 SH ASh-62IR	5500			
☐ HA-MHT	PZL Mielec (Antonov) An-2R	1G155-11		0074		1 SH ASh-62IR	5500			
☐ HA-MHU	PZL Mielec (Antonov) An-2R	1G155-12		0074		1 SH ASh-62IR	5500			
☐ HA-MHV	PZL Mielec (Antonov) An-2R	1G154-05		0074		1 SH ASh-62IR	5500			
☐ HA-MHW	PZL Mielec (Antonov) An-2R	1G158-60		0074		1 SH ASh-62IR	5500			
☐ HA-YHB	PZL Mielec (Antonov) An-2PF	1G181-44		0078		1 SH ASh-62IR	5500			
☐ HA-YHD	PZL Mielec (Antonov) An-2PF	1G187-36		0080		1 SH ASh-62IR	5500			
☐ HA-YHE	PZL Mielec (Antonov) An-2PF	1G187-37		0080		1 SH ASh-62IR	5500			
☐ HA-YFC	Let 410FG	851528		0085		2 WA M-601D	5800	Aerial mapping		Glazed nose

BUDAPEST AIRCRAFT SERVICES, Ltd = BPS — Budapest-Ferihegy

PO Box 175, H-1675 Budapest, Hungary ☎ (1) 296 80 62 Tx: none Fax: (1) 296 76 10 SITA: n/a
F: 1991 ⁂ 28 Head: Capt. Zoltan Armai ICAO: BASE Net: n/a

registration	type of aircraft	cn/fn	ex/ex*	mfd	del	powered by	mtow kg	configuration	selcal	name/fln/specialitites/remarks
☐ HA-BDA	Eurocopter (Aerosp.) AS350B Ecureuil	2472		0591	0791	1 TU Arriel 1B	1950	EMS		opf OMSz-Hungarian Air Ambulance
☐ HA-BDB	Eurocopter (Aerosp.) AS350B Ecureuil	2607		0392	0392	1 TU Arriel 1B	1950	EMS		opf OMSz-Hungarian Air Ambulance
☐ HA-BDC	Eurocopter (Aerosp.) AS350B Ecureuil	1715	D-HLOS	0083	0894	1 TU Arriel 1B	1950	EMS		opf OMSz-Hungarian Air Ambulance
☐ HA-BCA	PZL Swidnik Mi-2	516301099		0979	0180	2 IS GTD-350P	3550	EMS		opf OMSz-Hungarian Air Ambulance
☐ HA-BCD	PZL Swidnik Mi-2	517537032		0382	0582	2 IS GTD-350P	3550	EMS		opf OMSz-Hungarian Air Ambulance
☐ HA-YHG	PZL Mielec (Antonov) An-2PF	1G234-08		1289	1289	1 SH ASh-62IR	5500	Pax / EMS		opf OMSz-Hungarian Air Ambulance
☐ HA-LAF	Let 410UVP-E8A	902518		0090	0191	2 WA M-601E	6400	Y15/Calibrator		opf LRI Air Traffic & Airport Admin.
☐ HA-LAV	Let 410UVP-E	892215	RA-67604	0089	0097	2 WA M-601E	6400	Y19		lst TDR
☐ HA-YFD	Let 410UVP-E17	892324		1189	0590	2 WA M-601E	6400	Y19 / EMS		lst TDR

BUSINESS AIR, Kft. = BHU — Budapest-Budaörs

PO Box 32, H-2043 Budaörs 3, Hungary ☎ (76) 49 70 53 Tx: none Fax: (76) 49 70 54 SITA: n/a
F: 1993 ⁂ 8 Head: Lafos Vlaszak ICAO: BUSINESS HUNGARY Net: n/a

registration	type of aircraft	cn/fn	ex/ex*	mfd	del	powered by	mtow kg	configuration	selcal	name/fln/specialitites/remarks
☐ HA-ACT	Beech Duke B60	P-434	N9046Z	0077	0395	2 LY TIO-541-E1C4	3073	6 Pax		
☐ HA-LAN	Let 410UVP	851408	UR-67504	0085	0095	2 WA M-601D	6000	17 Pax		
☐ HA-LAP	Let 410UVP				0096	2 WA M-601D	6000	17 Pax		

FARNER AIR TRANSPORT Hungary, Kft. = FAH (Member of Farnair Europe, European Aviation Alliance / formerly Nawa Air) — **Budapest-Ferihegy**

PO Box 173, H-1701 Budapest, Hungary ☎ (1) 282 92 86 Tx: 202596 h Fax: (1) 177 21 83 SITA: n/a
F: 1990 👥 19 Head: Mihaly Fabian ICAO: BLUE STRIP Net: n/a

☐ HA-ACN	Cessna 402B II	*402B1037*	*OO-SVD*	*0076*		*2 CO TSIO-520-E*	*2858*	*Photo / Survey*		*opf Eurosense Hungary*
☐ HA-LAD	Let 410UVP-E8	*902516*		*0090*	*0093*	*2 WA M-601E*	*6400*	*Y19 / Freighter*		*op in Farnair Europe-colors*
☐ HA-LAE	Let 410UVP-E8	*902517*		*0090*	*0093*	*2 WA M-601E*	*6400*	*Y19 / Freighter*		*op in Farnair Europe-colors*
☐ HA-LAQ	Let 410UVP	*841332*	*332*	*0084*	*0096*	*2 WA M-601D*	*6000*	*Y19 / Freighter*		*lst LSU*
☐ HA-LAR	Let 410UVP-E	*871923*	*923*	*0087*	*0096*	*2 WA M-601E*	*6400*	*Y19 / Freighter*		*lst LSU*
☐ HA-LAS	Let 410UVP-E	*871924*	*924*	*0087*	*0096*	*2 WA M-601E*	*6400*	*Y19 / Freighter*		*op in Farnair Europe-colors*
☐ HA-FAB	Fokker F27 Friendship 500 (F27 Mk500)	*10370*	*HB-ISY*	*0068*	*0998*	*2 RR Dart 532-7R*	*20820*	*Freighter*		*lsf FAT / op in Farnair Europe-colors*

G1 Kereskedelmi és Szolgaltato, Rt. = GCV — **Budapest-Ferihegy**

Törökvész u 30/a, H-1022 Budapest, Hungary ☎ (1) 212 40 22 Tx: none Fax: (1) 212 40 23 SITA: n/a
F: 1995 👥 5 Head: Attila Molnar ICAO: GEE-BIRD Net: n/a

☐ HA-ACV	GAC (Grumman) G-159 Gulfstream I	*102*	*N48CQ*	*0063*	*1195*	*2 RR Dart 529-8X*	*16329*	*F16*		

HELI HUNGARY, Kft. (Subsidiary of Heli Holland Holding, B.V.) — **Budapest-Budaörs**

Pf. 13, H-8617 Köröshegy, Hungary ☎ (84) 34 11 58 Tx: none Fax: (84) 34 11 58 SITA: n/a
F: 1998 👥 3 Head: Matyiko Ferenc Net: n/a

☐ HA-LFS	Agusta-Bell 206A JetRanger	*8108*	*PH-HHG*	*0068*	*1298*	*1 AN 250-C18*	*1361*			

HUK Hungarian-Ukrainian Airlines, Co. Ltd = HUK (formerly Hungarian-Ukrainian Heavy Lift, Co. Ltd) — **Budapest-Ferihegy**

Ferihegy-Airport 1, H-1185 Budapest, Hungary ☎ (1) 296 78 60 Tx: none Fax: (1) 296 78 60 SITA: n/a
F: 1991 👥 n/a Head: Istvan Virag ICAO: BIG BIRD Net: n/a

☐ HA-TCB	Ilyushin 76TD	*1013408257*	*UR-78736*	*0091*		*4 SO D-30KP*	*190000*	*Freighter*		

INDICATOR AVIATION, Inc. = IDR — **Budapest-Budaörs**

Varosmajor u. 30, H-1122 Budapest, Hungary ☎ (1) 202 62 84 Tx: none Fax: (1) 202 62 84 SITA: n/a
F: 1990 👥 32 Head: Kalman Horti ICAO: INDICATOR Net: n/a Aircraft / Trainer-aircraft below MTOW 1361/5000kg: Cessna 150/172/182, Maule M7-235 & Zlin Z37A

☐ HA-YDE	Pilatus PC-6/B2-H2 Turbo Porter	*814*		*0081*		*1 PWC PT6A-27*	*2200*	*Photo/Survey*		*lsf ABKS/Central Org.for Flood Prot.*
☐ HA-LAG	Let 410UVP	*800425*	*CCCP-67159*	*0080*		*2 WA M-601D*	*5800*	*Y15*		

JETSTREAM AIR, Ltd = JSH (formerly Jetstream, Ltd) — **Budapest-Farkashegy**

Dohany u. 29, H-1075 Budapest, Hungary ☎ (1) 342 87 85 Tx: n/a Fax: (1) 122 55 47 SITA: n/a
F: 1992 👥 5 Head: Tibor Herkely ICAO: STREAM-AIR Net: n/a Aircraft below MTOW 1361kg: Cessna 172, Maule M5-235 & Piper PA-28

☐ HA-LFP	Soko (Eurocopter/Aerosp.) SA341G Gazelle	*008*		*0073*	*0097*	*1 TU Astazou IIIA*	*1800*			
☐ HA-ACG	Cessna 402B II	*402B1222*	*N4421Z*	*0077*	*1292*	*2 CO TSIO-520-E*	*2858*			
☐ HA-ACF	Cessna 421	*421-0048*	*N4048L*	*0067*	*1292*	*2 CO GTSIO-520-D*	*3084*			

LINAIR-HUNGARIAN REGIONAL AIRLINES, Ltd = LIN (Magyar Regionalis Légitarsasag, Kft dba) — **Budapest-Ferihegy**

Ecsedhaca Street 23, H-1171 Budapest, Hungary ☎ (1) 296 77 91 Tx: n/a Fax: (1) 296 78 91 SITA: n/a
F: 1994 👥 20 Head: Tamas Kovacs ICAO: LINAIR Net: n/a

☐ HA-LRA	Yakovlev 40	*9440837*	*OK-EED*	*0074*	*0097*	*3 IV AI-25*	*16000*	*VIP C21*		*opf LRI Air Traffic & Airport Admin.*
☐ HA-YLR	Yakovlev 40	*9541044*		*0075*	*0097*	*3 IV AI-25*	*15890*	*Calibrator*		*opf LRI Flight Inspection Service*

MALEV Hungarian Airlines, Plc = MA / MAH (Magyar Légiközlekedési Vallalat dba / formerly Maszovlet) — **Budapest-Ferihegy**

Roosevelt tér 2, H-1051 Budapest V, Hungary ☎ (1) 295 35 35 Tx: 224954 malev h Fax: (1) 266 77 75 SITA: n/a
F: 1946 👥 3300 Head: Csaba Siklos IATA: 182 ICAO: MALEV Net: http://osgweb.com/airlines/malev/index.html

☐ HA-LMA	Fokker 70 (F28 Mk0070)	*11564*	*PH-EZR**	*0095*	*1295*	*2 RR Tay 620-15*	*36740*	*CY75*		*lsf ILFC*
☐ HA-LMB	Fokker 70 (F28 Mk0070)	*11565*	*PH-EZX**	*0096*	*0296*	*2 RR Tay 620-15*	*36740*	*CY75*		*lsf ILFC*
☐ HA-LMC	Fokker 70 (F28 Mk0070)	*11569*	*PH-EZA**	*0096*	*0396*	*2 RR Tay 620-15*	*36740*	*CY75*	*CS-KQ*	*lsf ILFC*
☐ HA-LMD	Fokker 70 (F28 Mk0070)	*11563*	*PH-WXD*	*0095*	*1097*	*2 RR Tay 620-15*	*38100*	*CY67*		*lsf AFTR*
☐ HA-LME	Fokker 70 (F28 Mk0070)	*11575*	*PH-WXB*	*0096*	*1097*	*2 RR Tay 620-15*	*38100*	*CY67*		*lsf AFTR*
☐ HA-LMF	Fokker 70 (F28 Mk0070)	*11571*	*PH-RVE*	*0096*	*0498*	*2 RR Tay 620-15*	*38100*	*CY67*		*lsf AFTR*
☐ HA-LEI	Boeing 737-2T4 (A)	*22803 / 906*	*B-614L*	*0083*	*0295*	*2 PW JT8D-17A*	*56472*	*CY110*	*AC-FG*	*lsf GECA*
☐ HA-LEK	Boeing 737-2K9 (A)	*23404 / 1176*	*VR-BMX*	*0085*	*0694*	*2 PW JT8D-15A*	*53070*	*CY110*	*BK-JM*	*lsf BAVA*
☐ HA-LEM	Boeing 737-2T4 (A)	*22804 / 908*	*B-615L*	*0083*	*0395*	*2 PW JT8D-17A*	*56472*	*CY110*	*AE-BH*	*lsf GECA*
☐ HA-LEP	Boeing 737-5K5	*24776 / 1848*	*D-AHLE*	*0090*	*1298*	*2 CFMI CFM56-3C1*	*59000*	*CY110*		*lsf Defag Leasing Co.*
☐ HA-LER	Boeing 737-5K5	*24926 / 1966*	*D-AHLD*	*0090*	*1298*	*2 CFMI CFM56-3C1*	*59000*	*CY110*		*lsf Defag Leasing Co.*
☐ HA-LED	Boeing 737-3Y0	*24909 / 2021*		*0091*	*0491*	*2 CFMI CFM56-3C1*	*61235*	*CY128*	*GK-EQ*	*lsf GECA*
☐ HA-LEF	Boeing 737-3Y0	*24914 / 2054*		*0091*	*0591*	*2 CFMI CFM56-3C1*	*61235*	*CY128*	*GK-FQ*	*lsf BBAM*
☐ HA-LEG	Boeing 737-3Y0	*24916 / 2066*		*0091*	*0691*	*2 CFMI CFM56-3C1*	*61235*	*CY128*	*GK-HQ*	Szent Istvan-SanctusStephanus / *lsfGECA*
☐ HA-LEJ	Boeing 737-3Q8	*26303 / 2635*		*0094*	*0794*	*2 CFMI CFM56-3C1*	*56472*	*CY128*	*CS-KQ*	*lsf ILFC*
☐ HA-LEN	Boeing 737-4Y0	*26069 / 2352*	*UR-GAA*	*0092*	*0195*	*2 CFMI CFM56-3C1*	*68038*	*CY150*	*DE-BS*	*lsf GECA*
☐ HA-LEO	Boeing 737-4Y0	*26071 / 2361*	*UR-GAB*	*0092*	*1294*	*2 CFMI CFM56-3C1*	*68038*	*CY150*	*CS-MP*	*lsf GECA*
☐ HA-LCO	Tupolev 154B-2	*473*		*0080*	*0281*	*3 KU NK-8-2U*	*100000*	*CY143 or 155*	*CS-PR*	
☐ HA-LCR	Tupolev 154B-2	*543*		*0082*	*0582*	*3 KU NK-8-2U*	*100000*	*CY143 or 155*	*DE-AR*	
☐ HA-LCU	Tupolev 154B-2	*531*	*CCCP-85531*	*0081*	*0788*	*3 KU NK-8-2U*	*100000*	*CY143 or 155*	*DE-AS*	
☐ HA-LCV	Tupolev 154B-2	*544*	*CCCP-85544*	*0082*	*0888*	*3 KU NK-8-2U*	*100000*	*CY143 or 155*	*DE-BR*	
☐ HA-LHA	Boeing 767-27G (ER)	*27048 / 475*	*N6009F**	*0093*	*0493*	*2 GE CF6-80C2B4F*	*175500*	*CY197*	*CP-DS*	
☐ HA-LHB	Boeing 767-27G (ER)	*27049 / 482*	*N60668**	*0093*	*0493*	*2 GE CF6-80C2B4F*	*175500*	*CY197*	*CP-ER*	

SZER-BON, Rt. = HSB — **Debrecen**

Hargita u. Hrsz. 2816, H-2011 Budkalasz, Hungary ☎ (26) 34 15 97 Tx: none Fax: (26) 34 15 97 SITA: n/a
F: n/a 👥 n/a Head: n/a ICAO: SARBON Net: n/a

☐ HA-BFR	PZL Swidnik (Mil) Mi-2	*528021013*	*EW-20817*	*0083*		*2 IS GTD-350-4*	*3550*	*Utility*		

TPG AIRWAYS Hungary, Ltd — **Budapest-Ferihegy & Esztergom**

Kossuth Lajos utca 97, H-1181 Budapest, Hungary ☎ (1) 295 35 35 Tx: none Fax: (1) 295 35 35 SITA: BUDTO8X
F: 1990 👥 n/a Head: Gabor Halmagyi Net: n/a
Beside airtaxi flights with PA-32, also operates charter flights with Tupolev 134A in conjuction with ATYRAN & KAZAIR WEST (UN-) but intends to start own charter flights during 1999 with 1 Boeing 737-400 & 2 Fokker 70 aircraft.

☐ HA-API	Piper PA-32-300 Cherokee SIX	*32-40220*	*N4149W*	*0067*		*1 LY IO-540-K1A5*	*1542*			*lsf/jtly opw Aerotraders*

HB = SWITZERLAND (Swiss Confederation) (Schweiz. Eidgenossenschaft)

(official name of country is in German, French + Italian: Schweiz. Eidgenossenschaft / Confédération Suisse / Confederazione Svizzera) (including: Principality of Liechtenstein)
Capital: Berne Official Language: German, French, Italian Population: 7,5 million Square Km: 41293 Dialling code: +41 Year established: 1291 Acting political head: Mrs Ruth Dreifuss (Federal President)

Liechtenstein
Capital: Vaduz Official Language: German Population: 0,1 million Square Km: 161 Dialling code: +41 Acting political head: Mario Frick (Prime Minister)

AERO LOCARNO, SA — **Locarno**

Aeroporto Cantonale, CH-6596 Gordola, Switzerland ☎ (91) 745 20 27 Tx: 846093 adlo ch Fax: (91) 745 47 47 SITA: n/a
F: 1984 👥 8 Head: Urs Frischknecht Net: n/a Aircraft below MTOW 1361kg: CAP10B, Cessna 152/172 & Piper PA-28

☐ HB-LQQ	Piper PA-34-200T Seneca II	*34-7570281*	*N1544X*	*0075*		*2 CO L/TSIO-360-EB*	*1999*			
☐ HB-FKH	Pilatus PC-6/B2-H4 Turbo Porter	*865*		*0689*		*1 PWC PT6A-27*	*2800*			*lsf Para-Centro SA Locarno*
☐ HB-FKM	Pilatus PC-6/B2-H4 Turbo Porter	*873*		*0990*		*1 PWC PT6A-27*	*2800*			*lsf Para-Centro SA Locarno*

AFLAG Air Finanz & Leasing, AG — **Zurich**

c/o Dr. Walter H. Meier, Bienenstr. 1, CH-8004 Zürich, Switzerland ☎ (1) 493 56 94 Tx: n/a Fax: (1) 492 66 56 SITA: n/a
F: 1983 👥 3 Head: Hans-Rudolf Walti Net: n/a

☐ HB-VJB	Cessna 501 Citation I/SP	*501-0067*	*VR-BLW*	*0078*		*2 PWC JT15D-1*	*5670*			*lsf Sius AG*

AIR ENGIADINA – The Swiss Regional Airline = RQ / RQX (AE Air Engiadina, AG Regionalfluggesellschaft dba) — **Berne & Geneva**

Flugplatzstr. 11, CH-3123 Belp, Switzerland ☎ (31) 960 12 11 Tx: none Fax: (31) 960 12 17 SITA: BRNTSRQ
F: 1987 👥 120 Head: Dietmar Leitgeb IATA: 834 ICAO: ENGIADINA Net: http://www.airengiadina.ch

☐ HB-AEE	Dornier 328-110	*3005*	*D-CITA**	*0093*	*1093*	*2 PWC PW119B*	*13990*	*Y31*		City of Berne / *lsfDo-Lease AG/cvtd-100*
☐ HB-AEF	Dornier 328-110	*3017*	*D-CDHB**	*0094*	*0894*	*2 PWC PW119B*	*13990*	*Y31*		City of Thun / *lsf BBV Lsng / cvtd -100*
☐ HB-AEG	Dornier 328-110	*3011*	*D-CDOG**	*0094*	*0395*	*2 PWC PW119B*	*13990*	*Y31*		Ville de Fribourg / *lsfDo-Lse/cvtd-100*
☐ HB-AEH	Dornier 328-110	*3036*	*D-CDXB**	*0095*	*1095*	*2 PWC PW119B*	*13990*	*Y31*		Ville de Neuchatel

AIR FRIBOURG SERVICES, SA — **Ecuvillens**

Aérodrome, CH-1730 Ecuvillens, Switzerland ☎ (26) 411 12 14 Tx: none Fax: (26) 411 35 35 SITA: n/a
F: 1987 👥 1 Head: Denis Rossier Net: n/a Aircraft below MTOW 1361kg: Cessna 172.

☐ HB-CQC	Cessna R182 Skylane RG II	*R18202034*	*N6474T*	*0086*		*1 LY O-540-J3C5D*	*1406*			
☐ HB-LSC	Piper PA-34-220T Seneca III	*34-8333004*	*N8240G*	*0082*	*0298*	*2 CO L/TSIO-360-KB*	*2155*			

183 registration type of aircraft *cn/fn* *ex/ex** *mfd* *del* *powered by* *mtow kg* *configuration* *selcal* *name/fln/specialitites/remarks*

AIR-GLACIERS, SA = GB / AGV — Sion, Lauterbrunnen & Saanen

Case postale 34, CH-1951 Sion, Switzerland ☎ (27) 329 14 15 Tx: none Fax: (27) 329 14 29 SITA: SIRAGBH
F: 1965 ⁂ 100 Head: Bruno Bagnoud ICAO: AIR GLACIERS Net: n/a Aircraft below MTOW 1361 kg: Piper PA-18 Super Cub 150.

☐ HB-XNU	Agusta-Bell 206B JetRanger III	*8289*	*D-HASA*	*0071*		*1 AN 250-C20B*	*1451*	*4 Pax*		*cvtd 206A*
☐ HB-XYX	Bell 206B JetRanger	*831*	*C-FFGN*	*0072*		*1 AN 250-C20*	*1451*	*4 Pax*		
☐ HB-XEO	Eurocopter (Aerosp.) SA315B Lama	*2321*	*F-BUYA*	*0073*		*1 TU Artouste IIIB*	*1950*	*4 Pax*		
☐ HB-XIB	Eurocopter (Aerosp.) SA315B Lama	*2531*		*0079*		*1 TU Artouste IIIB*	*1950*	*4 Pax*		
☐ HB-XJN	Eurocopter (Aerosp.) SA315B Lama	*2609*	*I-BREY*	*0081*	*0796*	*1 TU Artouste IIIB*	*1950*	*4 Pax*		
☐ HB-XOY	Eurocopter (Aerosp.) SA315B Lama	*2508*	*ZK-HNV*	*0078*		*1 TU Artouste IIIB*	*1950*	*4 Pax*		
☐ HB-XRE	Eurocopter (Aerosp.) SA315B Lama	*2462*	*N47319*	*0076*		*1 TU Artouste IIIB*	*1950*	*4 Pax*		
☐ HB-XRL	Eurocopter (Aerosp.) SA315B Lama	*2291*	*C-GDWD*	*0072*		*1 TU Artouste IIIB*	*1950*	*4 Pax*		
☐ HB-XRN	Eurocopter (Aerosp.) SA315B Lama	*2309*	*N6390*	*0073*		*1 TU Artouste IIIB*	*1950*	*4 Pax*		
☐ HB-XTO	Eurocopter (Aerosp.) SA315B Lama	*2633*	*LN-OTE*	*0082*	*0389*	*1 TU Artouste IIIB*	*1950*	*4 Pax*		
☐ HB-XTU	Eurocopter (Aerosp.) SA315B Lama	*2614*	*F-GEHJ*	*0081*	*0589*	*1 TU Artouste IIIB*	*1950*	*4 Pax*		
☐ HB-XTW	Eurocopter (Aerosp.) SA315B Lama	*2537*	*F-GCLB*	*0078*	*0889*	*1 TU Artouste IIIB1*	*1950*	*4 Pax*		
☐ HB-XVL	Eurocopter (Aerosp.) SA315B Lama	*2334*	*N62250*	*0073*	*0490*	*1 TU Artouste IIIB*	*1950*	*4 Pax*		
☐ HB-XXJ	Eurocopter (Aerosp.) SA315B Lama	*1155 / 16*	*F-GFFG*	*0081*	*0291*	*1 TU Artouste IIIB*	*1950*	*4 Pax*		*cvtd Alouette II*
☐ HB-CGW	Cessna U206G Stationair 6 II	*U20604822*	*D-ELML*	*0079*		*1 CO IO-520-F*	*1633*	*5 Pax*		
☐ HB-XCB	Eurocopter (Aerosp.) SE3160 Alouette III	*1259*		*0065*		*1 TU Artouste IIIB*	*2200*	*6 Pax*		
☐ HB-XJR	Eurocopter (Aerosp.) SA316B Alouette III	*1781*	*I-LESY*	*0071*	*0197*	*1 TU Artouste IIIB*	*2200*	*6 Pax*		
☐ HB-XNZ	Eurocopter (Aerosp.) SA316B Alouette III	*1071*	*LX-EEE*	*0062*		*1 TU Artouste IIIB*	*2200*	*6 Pax*		*cvtd SE3160*
☐ HB-XOE	Eurocopter (Aerosp.) SE3160 Alouette III	*1019*	*LX-AAA*	*0062*		*1 TU Artouste IIIB*	*2100*	*6 Pax*		
☐ HB-XOF	Eurocopter (Aerosp.) SE3160 Alouette III	*1439*	*LX-OOO*	*0067*		*1 TU Artouste IIIB*	*2100*	*6 Pax*		
☐ HB-XXC	Eurocopter (Aerosp.) SA316B Alouette III	*1592*	*OE-EXT*	*0069*	*0891*	*1 TU Artouste IIIB*	*2200*	*6 Pax*		
☐ HB-FCT	Pilatus PC-6/B2-H2 Turbo Porter	*637*		*0067*		*1 PWC PT6A-27*	*2200*	*7 Pax*		
☐ HB-FDU	Pilatus PC-6/B1-H2 Turbo Porter	*663*		*0068*		*1 PWC PT6A-20*	*2200*	*7 Pax*		
☐ HB-FFW	Pilatus PC-6/B2-H2 Turbo Porter	*735*		*0070*		*1 PWC PT6A-27*	*2200*	*7 Pax*		
☐ HB-XQZ	MD Helicopters MD 900 Explorer	*900-00037*	*N9199X*	*0096*	*0199*	*2 PWC PW206A*	*2835*			*lsf HL Le Mirador International SA*
☐ HB-GHT	Beech King Air C90	*LJ-944*	*G-PTER*	*0081*		*2 PWC PT6A-21*	*4377*	*7 Pax*		
☐ HB-GHW	Beech King Air C90A	*LJ-1089*	*N46KA*	*0085*	*0589*	*2 PWC PT6A-21*	*4377*	*7 Pax*		
☐ HB-GIL	Beech King Air 200	*BB-194*	*N502EB*	*0077*		*2 PWC PT6A-21*	*5670*	*9 Pax*		
☐ HB-GJI	Beech King Air 200	*BB-451*	*D-IBOW*	*0079*	*0396*	*2 PWC PT6A-41*	*5670*	*9 Pax*		
☐ HB-VIF	Learjet 36A	*36A-057*		*0086*	*0496*	*2 GA TFE731-2-2B*	*8301*	*6 Pax / EMS*	*GH-CM*	

AIR GRISCHA Helikopter, AG — Untervaz-Heliport & San Vittore

Postfach, CH-7204 Untervaz, Switzerland ☎ (81) 322 57 57 Tx: 74574 airgr ch Fax: (81) 322 50 00 SITA: n/a
F: 1976 ⁂ 30 Head: Hans Kueng Net: n/a

☐ HB-XZB	Agusta-Bell 206B JetRanger III	*8735*		*0092*		*1 AN 250-C20R*	*1451*			
☐ HB-XFE	Eurocopter (Aerosp.) SA315B Lama	*2436*		*0075*		*1 TU Artouste IIIB*	*1950*			
☐ HB-XMC	Eurocopter (Aerosp.) SA315B Lama	*2527*	*ZK-HNW*	*0078*		*1 TU Artouste IIIB*	*1950*			
☐ HB-XND	Eurocopter (Aerosp.) SA315B Lama	*2624*		*0082*		*1 TU Artouste IIIB*	*1950*			
☐ HB-XRF	Eurocopter (Aerosp.) SA315B Lama	*2490*	*OE-KXD*	*0076*	*0489*	*1 TU Artouste IIIB*	*1950*			
☐ HB-XTN	Eurocopter (Aerosp.) SA315B Lama	*2407*	*N62345*	*0074*	*0989*	*1 TU Artouste IIIB*	*1950*			
☐ HB-XYR	Eurocopter (Aerosp.) AS350B2 Ecureuil	*2420*	*N6037N*	*0091*	*0891*	*1 TU Arriel 1D1*	*2250*			

AIRLINA, SA — Zurich

Morgentalstr. 2, CH-8108 Dällikon, Switzerland ☎ (81) 844 04 45 Tx: n/a Fax: (81) 844 51 00 SITA: n/a
F: 1988 ⁂ 4 Head: Markus Hummel Net: n/a

☐ HB-LPK	Cessna 340A II	*340A0235*	*D-IEVO*	*0677*		*2 CO TSIO-520-N*	*2717*			

AIRPORT HELICOPTER BASEL, Müller & Co. = AHE (formerly Airport Helicopter Basel Schaub & Müller) — Basel/Mulhouse-EuroAirport

Postfach 219, CH-4030 Basel-Flughafen, Switzerland ☎ (61) 325 48 88 Tx: n/a Fax: (61) 325 48 90 SITA: n/a
F: 1993 ⁂ n/a Head: Hans-Rudolf Müller ICAO: AIRPORT HELICOPTER Net: n/a Aircraft below MTOW 1361kg: Bell 47G & Robinson R22

☐ HB-XMT	Bell 206B JetRanger III	*866*	*D-HKLI*	*0073*		*1 AN 250-C20B*	*1451*			*cvtd JetRanger*
☐ HB-XXO	Bell 206B JetRanger III	*3595*	*N101DG*	*0082*	*1097*	*1 AN 250-C20B*	*1451*			

AIRPORT HELICOPTER ZUERICH, AG — Zurich

Postfach 9, CH-8058 Zürich-Flughafen, Switzerland ☎ (1) 905 33 33 Tx: none Fax: (1) 905 30 30 SITA: n/a
F: 1995 ⁂ 4 Head: Marlies Vollenweider Net: http://members.zol.com/airpheli

☐ HB-XJX	Bell 407	*53169*		*0097*	*0797*	*1 AN 250-C47B*	*2268*			*lsf Deep Blue Technology AG*
☐ HB-XQY	Bell 407	*53299*	*N8226X**	*0098*	*1198*	*1 AN 250-C47B*	*2268*			*lsf Deep Blue Technology AG*
☐ HB-ZBA	Bell 407	*53324*	*C-GEGC**	*0098*	*1298*	*1 AN 250-C47B*	*2268*			*lsf Deep Blue Technology AG*

AIR ZERMATT, AG – Oberwalliser Lufttransportunternehmen = AZF — Zermatt-Heliport, Raron & Sion

Heliport, CH-3920 Zermatt, Switzerland ☎ (027) 967 34 87 Tx: none Fax: (027) 967 40 04 SITA: n/a
F: 1968 ⁂ 50 Head: Reinhard Meichtry ICAO: AIR ZERMATT Net: http://www.rhone.ch/airzermatt

☐ HB-XFX	Eurocopter (Aerosp.) SA315B Lama	*2445*		*0076*		*1 TU Artouste IIIB1*	*1950*			
☐ HB-XII	Eurocopter (Aerosp.) SA315B Lama	*2551*		*0079*		*1 TU Artouste IIIB1*	*1950*			
☐ HB-XSW	Eurocopter (Aerosp.) SA315B Lama	*2563*		*0079*		*1 TU Artouste IIIB1*	*1950*			
☐ HB-XTY	Eurocopter (Aerosp.) SA315B Lama	*2645*	*LN-OMO*	*0083*		*1 TU Artouste IIIB1*	*1950*			
☐ HB-XXE	Eurocopter (Aerosp.) SA315B Lama	*2331 / 35*		*0072*	*0790*	*1 TU Artouste IIIB1*	*1950*			*cvtd Alouette II*
☐ HB-XSU	Eurocopter (Aerosp.) AS350B2 Ecureuil	*2115*		*0088*		*1 TU Arriel 1D1*	*2250*			*cvtd AS350B1*
☐ HB-XDA	Eurocopter (Aerosp.) SA316B Alouette III	*1609*		*0069*		*1 TU Artouste IIIB1*	*2200*			
☐ HB-XQD	Eurocopter (Aerosp.) SA316B Alouette III	*1324*		*0065*	*1097*	*1 TU Artouste IIIB1*	*2200*			

ALBEN WATCH, Co. Sarl. – Taxi Aérien — La Chaux-de-Fonds/Les Eplatures

Rue Numa-Droz 12, CH-2300 La Chaux-de-Fonds, Switzerland ☎ (32) 926 82 55 Tx: 952120 lsgc ch Fax: (32) 926 79 00 SITA: n/a
F: 1982 ⁂ n/a Head: René Ferner Net: n/a

☐ HB-LMS	Piper PA-34-220T Seneca III	*34-8133105*		*0081*		*2 CO L/TSIO-360-KB*	*1999*	*5 Pax*		

ALPAR, Flug- & Flugplatzgesellschaft AG = LAX — Berne

CH-3123 Belp, (BE), Switzerland ☎ (31) 960 22 22 Tx: none Fax: (31) 960 22 25 SITA: n/a
F: 1929 ⁂ 33 Head: Eva Staehelin ICAO: ALPAR Net: n/a Aircraft below MTOW 1361 kg: Cessna 172, FFA AS202/15 & Piper PA-28

☐ HB-CHB	Cessna FR182 Skylane RG II	*FR18200043*	*G-ILLI*	*0078*		*1 LY O-540-J3C5D*	*1405*			
☐ HB-CLU	Cessna R182 Skylane RG II	*R18201776*	*N4848T*	*0081*	*0790*	*1 LY O-540-J3C5D*	*1406*			
☐ HB-PGY	Piper PA-28-236 Dakota	*28-8311009*		*0082*		*1 LY O-540-J3A5D*	*1361*			

ALPINE Fluggesellschaft (Associated with Motorfluggruppe Obersimmental & Montorfluggruppe Saanen) — Zweisimmen & Saanen

Postfach 419, CH-3770 Zweisimmen, Switzerland ☎ (33) 722 18 38 Tx: none Fax: (33) 722 18 38 SITA: n/a
F: 1997 ⁂ n/a Head: Herbert Messerli Net: n/a Aircraft below MTOW 1361kg: Piper PA-28

☐ HB-PKJ	Piper PA-32-301T Turbo Saratoga	*32-8224007*	*N824MC*	*0082*	*0097*	*1 LY TIO-540-S1AD*	*1633*			*lsf Motorfluggruppe Obersimmental*

ALPLINER, AG Rundflüge & Airtaxi = ALP — Zurich

Zelglistr. 13, CH-5615 Fahrwangen, Switzerland ☎ (56) 667 23 30 Tx: none Fax: (56) 667 21 65 SITA: n/a
F: 1989 ⁂ 3 Head: Motty Bar-On ICAO: ALPLINER Net: http://www.alpliner.ch

☐ HB-PES	Piper PA-32R-301 Saratoga SP	*32R-8013042*	*N81437*	*0080*		*1 LY IO-540-K1G5D*	*1633*			

ASCOAVIA, SA — Ascona

Via Aerodromo, CH-6612 Ascona, Switzerland ☎ (91) 791 84 34 Tx: 846123 lszd ch Fax: (91) 791 84 34 SITA: n/a
F: 1980 ⁂ 3 Head: Mario Totaro Net: n/a Aircraft below MTOW 1361kg: Piper PA-18

☐ HB-LLM	Piper PA-34-200T Seneca II	*34-7970108*	*N2077N*	*0079*		*2 CO L/TSIO-360-EB*	*2073*			
☐ HB-LRU	Piper PA-34-220T Seneca III	*3433171*	*I-CGAQ*	*0089*	*0193*	*2 CO L/TSIO-360-KB*	*2155*			

AVCON, AG = VCN (Avcon, Ltd Aviation Consulting dba) — Zurich

Postfach 1, CH-8058 Zürich-Flughafen, Switzerland ☎ (1) 804 16 16 Tx: 829196 avc ch Fax: (1) 804 16 17 SITA: ZRH25SR
F: 1988 ⁂ 16 Head: Fred Muggli ICAO: AVCON Net: http://www.avcon.ch Aviation Consulting & Aircraft Management company. Air Taxi services are managed for & operated in conjunction with other carriers. In addition to the listed commercially operated aircraft also offers management support to over 40 executive aircraft on behalf of private companies.

☐ HB-LNX	Piper PA-31T2 Cheyenne II XL	*31T-8166050*	*N700XL*	*0082*		*2 PWC PT6A-135*	*4297*	*7 Pax*		*jtly opw Transwing*
☐ HB-FOE	Pilatus PC-12	*102*		*0094*	*0898*	*1 PWC PT6A-67B*	*4100*	*9 Pax*		*jtly opw Belnet Air Services*
☐ HB-IMJ	GAC G-V Gulfstream V	*517*	*N517GA**	*0098*	*0598*	*2 BR BR710A1-10*	*41050*	*16 Pax*		*jtly opw G5 Executive*

AVILU, SA — Lugano-Agno

Aerodromo Comunale Lugano, CH-6982 Agno, Switzerland ☎ (91) 59 39 34 Tx: n/a Fax: (91) 50 68 60 SITA: n/a
F: 1963 ⁂ 6 Head: D. Rusca Net: n/a Aircraft below MTOW 1361 kg: Cessna 150/152, FFA AS202-180 Bravo, Piper PA-28 & Socata TB10.

☐ HB-LOG	Piper PA-34-200T Seneca II	*34-7870415*	*OE-FSS*	*0078*		*2 CO L/TSIO-360-EB*	*1999*			*lsf Akzenta Holding AG*

184 registration type of aircraft cn/fn ex/ex* mfd del powered by mtow kg configuration selcal name/fln/specialitites/remarks

AVISTO, Ltd (Aviation Support & Trading Organisation dba) — Africa

Postfach 61, CH-8154 Oberglatt, Switzerland ☎ (1) 850 57 57 Tx: 826982 avi ch Fax: (1) 850 57 58 SITA: n/a
F: 1990 ⁂ 40 Head: Franz Fassbind Net: n/a Commercial contract-operator with ad-hoc bases in Africa.

☐ HB-AAM	Shorts 360-300 (SD3-60)	SH3763	G-BRMY	0089	0990	2 PWC PT6A-67R	12292	Y39		opf Sirte Oil Co.
☐ HB-AAS	Fokker F28 Fellowship 2000 (F28 Mk2000)	11110	F-GDUX	0076	0091	2 RR Spey 555-15	29480	Y65		opf Sirte Oil Co.

BALAIR/CTA Leisure, AG = BB / BBB (Subsidiary of SAir Lines / Member of European Leisure Group) — Zurich

Postfach, CH-8058 Zürich-Flughafen, Switzerland ☎ (1) 812 30 70 Tx: none Fax: (1) 812 92 12 SITA: ZRHBOSR
F: 1997 ⁂ 200 Head: Stefan Helsing IATA: 290 ICAO: BALAIR Net: http://www.balair-cta.ch

☐ HB-IPL	Airbus Industrie A310-325 (ET)	640	F-WWCL*	0092	1197	2 PW PW4156A	164000	C34Y187	BJ-CQ	lsf GATX till 1199
☐ HB-IPM	Airbus Industrie A310-325 (ET)	642	F-WWCX*	0092	1197	2 PW PW4156A	164000	C34Y187	BJ-DQ	lsf GATX till 0999
☐ EI-CJA	Boeing 767-35H (ER)	26387 / 445	S7-AAQ	0092		2 GE CF6-80C2B6	185065	C24Y245		to be lsf AEL 0999
☐ EI-CJB	Boeing 767-35H (ER)	26388 / 456	S7-AAV	0092		2 GE CF6-80C2B6	185065	C24Y245		to be lsf AEL 0999

BB HELI, AG — Zurich

Gotthelfstr. 41, CH-8172 Niederglatt, Switzerland ☎ (1) 850 45 50 Tx: none Fax: (1) 850 45 55 SITA: n/a
F: 1991 ⁂ 8 Head: Markus Baumann Net: http://www.bbheli.ch

☐ HB-XUW	Agusta-Bell 206B JetRanger III	8722		0090	0298	1 AN 250-C20J	1451			
☐ HB-XXN	Bell 206B JetRanger III	4123		0090		1 AN 250-C20R	1451			
☐ HB-ZBB	Eurocopter EC120B Colibri	067				1 TU Arrius 2F	1680			oo-delivery 1099

BELNET AIR SERVICES (Division of Belnet, SA) — Lausanne

Rte Monts-de-Lavaux 36, CH-1092 Belmont-sur-Lausanne, Switzerland ☎ (21) 728 47 43 Tx: none Fax: (21) 728 27 07 SITA: n/a
F: 1994 ⁂ 1 Head: Andreas Eggenberger Net: n/a

☐ HB-FOE	Pilatus PC-12	102		0094	0898	1 PWC PT6A-67B	4100	9 Pax		jtly opw Avcon

BENAVIA, S.A. = BEA — Geneva & Africa

Avenue Louis-Casai 79, CH-1216 Cointrin, Switzerland ☎ (22) 799 05 00 Tx: none Fax: (22) 799 05 01 SITA: n/a
F: 1997 ⁂ n/a Head: Kjetil Korneliussen ICAO: BENAVIA Net: n/a

☐ HB-FKO	Pilatus PC-6/B2-H4 Turbo Porter	874	V5-ODH	0090	0299	1 PWC PT6A-27	2800			lsf Imaginair SA
☐ HB-FKZ	Pilatus PC-6/B2-H4 Turbo Porter	892		0093	0299	1 PWC PT6A-27	2800			lsf Imaginair SA
☐ HB-LSP	De Havilland DHC-6 Twin Otter 300	288	VH-TGC	0070	0898	2 PWC PT6A-27	5670			lsf Topscore Management S.A.
☐ HB-LSU	De Havilland DHC-6 Twin Otter 300	277	N615BA	0070	1298	2 PWC PT6A-27	5670			lsf Topscore Mngmt/sublst Tassili Airl.
☐ HB-LSV	De Havilland DHC-6 Twin Otter 300	281	VH-TGH	0070	1298	2 PWC PT6A-27	5670			lsf Topscore Management S.A.
☐ HB-LSY	De Havilland DHC-6 Twin Otter 300	283	N616BA	0070	1298	2 PWC PT6A-27	5670			lsf Topscore Management S.A.
☐ N612BA	De Havilland DHC-6 Twin Otter 300	600	HI-685CA	0078	0598	2 PWC PT6A-27	5670			lsf Topscore Aviation Inc.
☐ HB-IVX	De Havilland DHC-7-102 Dash 7	091	SU-MAC	0082	0399	4 PWC PT6A-50	19958			lsf DK Aviation

BMG Burgener Helikopter-Transporte (Division of BMG Burgener Metall- und Glasbau, AG) — Zurich

Riederweg 1, CH-8302 Kloten, Switzerland ☎ (1) 814 33 35 Tx: none Fax: (1) 814 33 24 SITA: n/a
F: 1995 ⁂ 3 Head: Felix Burgener Net: n/a

☐ HB-XLJ	Eurocopter (Aerosp.) AS350B2 Ecureuil	2811		0094	0095	1 TU Arriel 1D1	2250			

BOHAG Berner Oberländer Helikopter, AG — Gsteigwiler- & Zweisimmen-Heliport

Postfach 1, CH-3814 Gsteigwiler, Switzerland ☎ (33) 828 90 00 Tx: none Fax: (33) 828 90 10 SITA: n/a
F: 1972 ⁂ 20 Head: Daniel Hofer Net: http://www.interlakentourism.ch/bohag

☐ HB-XIA	Eurocopter (Aerosp.) SA315B Lama	2552		0079		1 TU Artouste IIIB	1950			
☐ HB-XTM	Eurocopter (Aerosp.) SA315B Lama	2654	LN-OMW	0084	0189	1 TU Artouste IIIB	1950			
☐ HB-XNS	Eurocopter (Aerosp.) SA319B Alouette III	2389		0082	1097	1 TU Astazou XIVB	2250			
☐ HB-XQC	Bell 407	53132		0097	0597	1 AN 250-C47B	2268			

BONSAI HELIKOPTER, AG — St. Gallen-Altenrhein

Postfach 5126, CH-6000 Luzern 5, Switzerland ☎ (79) 432 81 81 Tx: none Fax: (41) 410 26 07 SITA: n/a
F: 1993 ⁂ 3 Head: Rudolf Schmid Net: http://www.bonsaiheli.ch Aircraft below MTOW 1361kg: Robinson R22

☐ HB-ZBD	Eurocopter EC120B Colibri	1009		0098	1098	1 TU Arrius 2F	1680			opf Colibri Helikopter AG

CAT AVIATION, AG = CAZ — Zurich

Postfach 1411, CH-8058 Zürich-Flughafen, Switzerland ☎ (1) 814 00 66 Tx: 829462 cat ch Fax: (1) 813 77 41 SITA: ZRHOOXH
F: 1987 ⁂ 10 Head: Helene Niedhart ICAO: EUROCAT Net: n/a

☐ HB-VIS	Cessna 550 Citation II	550-0447	N12482	0082		2 PWC JT15D-4	6033	8 Pax		
☐ HB-VHV	Hawker 800A (BAe 125-800A)	258153	G-5-627*	0089	0197	2 GA TFE731-5R-1H	12428	8 Pax		

CLASSIC AIR, AG = CLC — Zurich

Ackerstr. 2, CH-8180 Bülach, Switzerland ☎ (1) 860 44 24 Tx: 829396 clc ch Fax: (1) 860 47 07 SITA: n/a
F: 1985 ⁂ 25 Head: Bruno Dobler ICAO: CLASSIC AIR Net: http://www.classic-air.ch

☐ HB-ISB	Boeing (Douglas) DC-3C (C-47-DL)	4666	C-FTAS	0042	0186	2 PW R-1830-92	11884	28 Pax		
☐ HB-ISC	Boeing (Douglas) DC-3C (C-47A-45-DL)	9995	N88YA	0043	0986	2 PW R-1830-92	11884	28 Pax		

CORPAVIA JETS, SA (Associated with Corpavia Club) — Geneva & Vienna-Schwechat

Rue des Bains 35, CH-1205 Genève, Switzerland ☎ (22) 809 07 70 Tx: none Fax: (22) 809 07 67 SITA: n/a
F: 1995 ⁂ n/a Head: n/a Net: n/a Operates executive charters exclusively for Members of the Corpavia Club.

☐ HB-VLM	Beech Beechjet 400A	RK-66	N400Y	0093	1295	2 PWC JT15D-5	7303	Executive		lst/opb MGR for Corpavia Jets
☐ HB-VLN	Beech Beechjet 400A	RK-94	N3051S	0094	1295	2 PWC JT15D-5	7303	Executive		lst/opb MGR for Corpavia Jets

CROSSAIR = LX / CRX (Crossair,Limited Company for Regional European Air Transport dba/Subs.of SAirLines/Member of SAirGroup) — Basel/Mulhouse-EuroAirport

Postfach, CH-4002 Basel, Switzerland ☎ (61) 325 25 25 Tx: none Fax: (61) 325 32 68 SITA: BSLDDLX
F: 1975 ⁂ 2800 Head: Moritz Suter IATA: 724 ICAO: CROSSAIR Net: http://www.crossair.ch

☐ HB-AKA	Saab 340B (Cityliner)	340B-160	SE-F60*	0089	0989	2 GE CT7-9B	13155	Y33		
☐ HB-AKB	Saab 340B (Cityliner)	340B-161	SE-F61*	0089	0989	2 GE CT7-9B	13155	Y33		
☐ HB-AKC	Saab 340B (Cityliner)	340B-164	SE-F64*	0089	1089	2 GE CT7-9B	13155	Y33		
☐ HB-AKD	Saab 340B (Cityliner)	340B-173	SE-F73*	0089	1289	2 GE CT7-9B	13155	Y33		lst Crossair Europe as F-GPKD
☐ HB-AKE	Saab 340B (Cityliner)	340B-176	SE-F76*	0089	0290	2 GE CT7-9B	13155	Y33		
☐ HB-AKF	Saab 340B (Cityliner)	340B-182	SE-F82*	0090	0590	2 GE CT7-9B	13155	Y33		lsf Cinderella Aviation Llc
☐ HB-AKG	Saab 340B (Cityliner)	340B-185	SE-F85*	0090	0490	2 GE CT7-9B	13155	Y33		lst Crossair Europe as F-GPKG
☐ HB-AKH	Saab 340B (Cityliner)	340B-200	SE-E02*	0090	0890	2 GE CT7-9B	13155	Y33		lsf Cinderella Aviation Llc
☐ HB-AKI	Saab 340B (Cityliner)	340B-208	SE-G08*	0090	1090	2 GE CT7-9B	13155	Y33		lsf Cinderella Aviation Llc
☐ HB-AKK	Saab 340B (Cityliner)	340B-213	SE-G13*	0090	1190	2 GE CT7-9B	13155	Y33		lsf Cinderella Aviation Llc
☐ HB-AKL	Saab 340B (Cityliner)	340B-215	SE-G15*	0090	1290	2 GE CT7-9B	13155	Y33		
☐ HB-AKM	Saab 340B (Cityliner)	340B-221	SE-G21*	0090	0191	2 GE CT7-9B	13155	Y33		
☐ HB-AKN	Saab 340B (Cityliner)	340B-225	SE-G25*	0091	0291	2 GE CT7-9B	13155	Y33		
☐ HB-AKO	Saab 340B (Cityliner)	340B-228	SE-G28*	0091	0391	2 GE CT7-9B	13155	Y33		
☐ HB-IYA	Saab 2000 (Concordino)	2000-056	SE-056*	0098	0498	2 AN AE2100A	22800	Y50		EuroCross-colors on port-side
☐ HB-IYB	Saab 2000 (Concordino)	2000-057	SE-057*	0098	0698	2 AN AE2100A	22800	Y50		
☐ HB-IYC	Saab 2000 (Concordino)	2000-058	SE-058*	0098	0998	2 AN AE2100A	22999	Y50		
☐ HB-IYD	Saab 2000 (Concordino)	2000-059	SE-059*	0099	1198	2 AN AE2100A	22999	Y50		special Sion 2000-colors
☐ HB-IYE	Saab 2000 (Concordino)	2000-060	SE-060*	0099	0299	2 AN AE2100A	22999	Y50		
☐ HB-IYF	Saab 2000 (Concordino)	2000-061	SE-061*	0099	0399	2 AN AE2100A	22999	Y50		
☐ HB-IYG	Saab 2000 (Concordino)	2000-062				2 AN AE2100A	22999	Y50		oo-delivery 0699
☐ HB-IYH	Saab 2000 (Concordino)	2000-063				2 AN AE2100A	22999	Y50		oo-delivery 0799
☐ HB-IZA	Saab 2000 (Concordino)	2000-004	SE-004*	0094	0995	2 AN AE2100A	22800	Y50		
☐ HB-IZB	Saab 2000 (Concordino)	2000-005	SE-005*	0094	1094	2 AN AE2100A	22800	Y50		lsf Huskvarna Aircraft Ltd
☐ HB-IZC	Saab 2000 (Concordino)	2000-006	SE-006*	0094	0894	2 AN AE2100A	22800	Y50		lsf Stockholm Aircraft Ltd
☐ HB-IZD	Saab 2000 (Concordino)	2000-007	SE-007*	0094	0994	2 AN AE2100A	22800	Y50		lsf Goteborg Aircraft Ltd
☐ HB-IZE	Saab 2000 (Concordino)	2000-008	SE-008*	0094	0994	2 AN AE2100A	22800	Y50		lsf Uppsala Aircraft Ltd
☐ HB-IZF	Saab 2000 (Concordino)	2000-009	SE-009*	0094	1094	2 AN AE2100A	22800	Y50		lsf Arboga Aircraft Ltd
☐ HB-IZG	Saab 2000 (Concordino)	2000-010	SE-010*	0095	0195	2 AN AE2100A	22800	Y50		lsf SL Scorpio Ltd
☐ HB-IZH	Saab 2000 (Concordino)	2000-011	SE-011*	0095	0295	2 AN AE2100A	22800	Y50		lsf SL Capricorn Aircraft Ltd
☐ HB-IZI	Saab 2000 (Concordino)	2000-012	SE-012*	0095	0395	2 AN AE2100A	22800	Y50		lsf SL Aquarius Aircraft Ltd
☐ HB-IZJ	Saab 2000 (Concordino)	2000-015	SE-015*	0095	0495	2 AN AE2100A	22800	Y50		lsf SL Pisces Aircraft Ltd
☐ HB-IZK	Saab 2000 (Concordino)	2000-018	SE-018*	0095	0695	2 AN AE2100A	22800	Y50		lsf SL Garnet Ltd
☐ HB-IZL	Saab 2000 (Concordino)	2000-022	SE-022*	0095	0995	2 AN AE2100A	22800	Y50		
☐ HB-IZM	Saab 2000 (Concordino)	2000-024	SE-024*	0095	1095	2 AN AE2100A	22800	Y50		
☐ HB-IZN	Saab 2000 (Concordino)	2000-026	SE-026*	0095	1295	2 AN AE2100A	22800	Y50		
☐ HB-IZO	Saab 2000 (Concordino)	2000-029	SE-029*	0095	1295	2 AN AE2100A	22800	Y50		
☐ HB-IZP	Saab 2000 (Concordino)	2000-031	SE-031*	0096	0296	2 AN AE2100A	22800	Y50		

185 registration type of aircraft cn/fn ex/ex* mfd del powered by mtow kg configuration selcal name/fln/specialitites/remarks

☐	HB-IZQ	Saab 2000 (Concordino)	2000-032	SE-032*	0096	0296	2 AN AE2100A	22800	Y50		
☐	HB-IZR	Saab 2000 (Concordino)	2000-033	SE-033*	0096	0396	2 AN AE2100A	22800	Y50		
☐	HB-IZS	Saab 2000 (Concordino)	2000-035	SE-035*	0096	0496	2 AN AE2100A	22800	Y50		
☐	HB-IZT	Saab 2000 (Concordino)	2000-036	SE-036*	0096	0496	2 AN AE2100A	22800	Y50		
☐	HB-IZU	Saab 2000 (Concordino)	2000-037	SE-037*	0096	0596	2 AN AE2100A	22800	Y50		
☐	HB-IZV	Saab 2000 (Concordino)	2000-038	SE-038*	0096	0896	2 AN AE2100A	22800	Y50		
☐	HB-IZW	Saab 2000 (Concordino)	2000-039	SE-039*	0096	1096	2 AN AE2100A	22800	Y50		
☐	HB-IZX	Saab 2000 (Concordino)	2000-041	SE-041*	0096	1196	2 AN AE2100A	22800	Y50		
☐	HB-IZY	Saab 2000 (Concordino)	2000-047	SE-047*	0097	0597	2 AN AE2100A	22800	Y50		
☐	HB-IZZ	Saab 2000 (Concordino)	2000-048	SE-048*	0097	0697	2 AN AE2100A	22800	Y50		25th Concordino-sticker
☐	HB-IXF	Avro RJ85 (Jumbolino) (Avro 146-RJ85)	E2226	G-CROS*	0093	0493	4 LY LF507-1F	43998	CY82		
☐	HB-IXG	Avro RJ85 (Jumbolino) (Avro 146-RJ85)	E2231	G-6-231*	0093	0593	4 LY LF507-1F	43998	CY82		
☐	HB-IXH	Avro RJ85 (Jumbolino) (Avro 146-RJ85)	E2233	G-6-233*	0093	0693	4 LY LF507-1F	43998	CY82		
☐	HB-IXK	Avro RJ85 (Jumbolino) (Avro 146-RJ85)	E2235	G-6-235*	0093	0793	4 LY LF507-1F	43998	CY82		
☐	HB-IXM	Avro RJ100 (Jumbolino) (Avro 146-RJ100)	E3291	G-6-291*	0096	0896	4 LY LF507-1F	46039	CY97		
☐	HB-IXN	Avro RJ100 (Jumbolino) (Avro 146-RJ100)	E3286	G-6-286*	0096	0796	4 LY LF507-1F	46039	CY97		
☐	HB-IXO	Avro RJ100 (Jumbolino) (Avro 146-RJ100)	E3284	G-6-284*	0096	0596	4 LY LF507-1F	46039	CY97		lsf Kulan Mobilien
☐	HB-IXP	Avro RJ100 (Jumbolino) (Avro 146-RJ100)	E3283	G-6-283*	0096	0496	4 LY LF507-1F	46039	CY97		lsf Kulan Mobilien Verwaltungs GmbH
☐	HB-IXQ	Avro RJ100 (Jumbolino) (Avro 146-RJ100)	E3282	G-6-282*	0096	0396	4 LY LF507-1F	46039	CY97		lsf Kulan Mobilien Verwaltungs GmbH
☐	HB-IXR	Avro RJ100 (Jumbolino) (Avro 146-RJ100)	E3281	G-6-281*	0096	0296	4 LY LF507-1F	46039	CY97		lsf Kulan Mobilien Verwaltung
☐	HB-IXS	Avro RJ100 (Jumbolino) (Avro 146-RJ100)	E3280	G-6-280*	0096	0296	4 LY LF507-1F	46039	CY97		lsf Euler Verwaltungs GmbH
☐	HB-IXT	Avro RJ100 (Jumbolino) (Avro 146-RJ100)	E3259	G-BVYS*	0095	1295	4 LY LF507-1F	46039	CY97		lsf Harpalus/Möwe Air Lsng GmbH & Co.KG
☐	HB-IXU	Avro RJ100 (Jumbolino) (Avro 146-RJ100)	E3276	G-6-276*	0095	1295	4 LY LF507-1F	46039	CY97		lsf Melik Mobilien- Verwaltungs GmbH
☐	HB-IXV	Avro RJ100 (Jumbolino) (Avro 146-RJ100)	E3274	G-6-274*	0095	1295	4 LY LF507-1F	46039	CY97		lsf Laurus Mobilien- Verwaltungs GmbH
☐	HB-IXW	Avro RJ100 (Jumbolino) (Avro 146-RJ100)	E3272	G-6-272*	0095	1095	4 LY LF507-1F	46039	CY97		lsf Lakuna Mobilien-Verwaltungs GmbH
☐	HB-IXX	Avro RJ100 (Jumbolino) (Avro 146-RJ100)	E3262	G-6-262*	0095	1095	4 LY LF507-1F	46039	CY97		lsf Metra Mobilien-Verwaltungs GmbH
☐	HB-IYW	Avro RJ100 (Jumbolino) (Avro 146-RJ100)	E3359	G-6-359*	0099	0399	4 LY LF507-1F	46039	CY97		
☐	HB-IYX	Avro RJ100 (Jumbolino) (Avro 146-RJ100)	E3357	G-6-357*	0099	0399	4 LY LF507-1F	46039	CY97		
☐	HB-IYY	Avro RJ100 (Jumbolino) (Avro 146-RJ100)	E3339	G-6-339*	0098	1298	4 LY LF507-1F	46039	CY97		EuroCross-colors on port-side
☐	HB-IYZ	Avro RJ100 (Jumbolino) (Avro 146-RJ100)	E3338	G-6-338*	0098	1198	4 LY LF507-1F	46039	CY97		
☐	HB-INR	Boeing (Douglas) MD-82 (DC-9-82)	49277 / 1181		0085	1295	2 PW JT8D-219	67812	CY156	FM-AK	lsf SAT Flug GmbH / cvtd MD-81
☐	HB-INV	Boeing (Douglas) MD-83 (DC-9-83)	49359 / 1349		0287	1095	2 PW JT8D-219	72575	CY156	DF-HL	lsf SAT Flug GmbH / cvtd MD-81/82
☐	HB-INW	Boeing (Douglas) MD-83 (DC-9-83)	49569 / 1405		0087	1195	2 PW JT8D-219	72575	CY156	FM-AC	lsf SAT Flug GmbH / cvtd MD-82
☐	HB-INZ	Boeing (Douglas) MD-83 (DC-9-83)	49572 / 1468		0088	1095	2 PW JT8D-219	72575	CY156	CL-JM	lsf SAT Flug GmbH / cvtd MD-81/82
☐	HB-ISX	Boeing (Douglas) MD-83 (DC-9-83)	49844 / 1579		0389	0496	2 PW JT8D-219	72575	CY156	DH-BJ	lsf SAT Flug GmbH / cvtd MD-81/82
☐	HB-ISZ	Boeing (Douglas) MD-83 (DC-9-83)	49930 / 1720		0590	1195	2 PW JT8D-219	72575	CY156	FM-CK	lsf SAT Flug GmbH
☐	HB-IUG	Boeing (Douglas) MD-83 (DC-9-83)	53149 / 1817		0191	0396	2 PW JT8D-219	72575	Y161	DF-BL	lsf SAT Flug GmbH / cvtd MD-81/82
☐	HB-IUH	Boeing (Douglas) MD-83 (DC-9-83)	53150 / 1831		0091	0396	2 PW JT8D-219	72575	Y161	DF-BM	lsfSAT Flug GmbH/cvtd81/82/McDonalds-cs
☐	HB-IUM	Boeing (Douglas) MD-83 (DC-9-83)	49847 / 1585	D-AGWC	0389	1197	2 PW JT8D-219	72575	CY156		lsf Mycal Finance Co. Ltd
☐	HB-IUN	Boeing (Douglas) MD-83 (DC-9-83)	49769 / 1559	D-ALLK	1288	0298	2 PW JT8D-219	72575	Y161		lsf GECA
☐	HB-IUO	Boeing (Douglas) MD-83 (DC-9-83)	49857 / 1687	D-ALLN	0290	0498	2 PW JT8D-219	72575	CY156		lsf GECA
☐	HB-IUP	Boeing (Douglas) MD-83 (DC-9-83)	49856 / 1675	D-ALLM	1289	0199	2 PW JT8D-219	72575	CY156		lsf GECA

EAGLE AIR SERVICE, AG = EAB
Berne

Flughafen Bern-Belpmoos, CH-3123 Belp, Switzerland ☎ (31) 961 72 62 Tx: none Fax: (31) 961 72 63 SITA: n/a
F: 1980 ⁂ 5 Head: Walter Gosteli ICAO: SWISS EAGLE Net: n/a

☐	HB-VKP	Cessna 550 Citation II	550-0622	N826EW	0089	0298	2 PWC JT15D-4	6577			
☐	HB-VMJ	Cessna S550 Citation S/II	S550-0029	N608LB	0085	0399	2 PWC JT15D-4B	6668			
☐	HB-VLV	Cessna 560 Citation V	560-0077	N42NA	0090	0497	2 PWC JT15D-5A	7394			

EASYJET SWITZERLAND = BH / EZS (Associated with EasyJet Airline, GB / formerly TEA Switzerland)
Geneva & Zurich

CP 831, CH-1215 Genève-Aéroport, Switzerland ☎ (22) 717 80 05 Tx: none Fax: (22) 717 80 54 SITA: GVATOBH
F: 1988 ⁂ 105 Head: Jean-Marc Thevenaz ICAO: TOPSWISS Net: n/a

☐	HB-IIB	Boeing 737-3M8	24024 / 1689		0289	0389	2 CFMI CFM56-3B2	63276	Y149	EP-GH	Isle of Avalon / lsf GECA
☐	HB-IIE	Boeing 737-3Q8	26307 / 2664	N721LF	1194	1194	2 CFMI CFM56-3C1	63276	Y148	GR-KL	lsf ILFC
☐	HB-III	Boeing 737-33V					2 CFMI CFM56-3C1	56999	Y149		to be lsf EZY 0699
☐	HB-IIJ	Boeing 737-33V					2 CFMI CFM56-3C1	56999	Y149		to be lsf EZY 1099

EAT Executive Air Transport, AG = EXZ
Zurich & Riyadh

Postfach, CH-8058 Zürich-Flughafen, Switzerland ☎ (1) 803 07 77 Tx: 828630 fiba ch Fax: (1) 803 04 44 SITA: n/a
F: 1988 ⁂ 15 Head: John Rageth ICAO: EXECUTIVE ZURICH Net: http://www.guides.com/acg/eat/
In addition to the listed commercially operated aircraft also operates a number of Boeing 727-100/737-200, Canadair 601 Challenger,Cessna 550 & 560 aircraft on behalf of private companies.

☐	HB-VKB	Cessna 525 CitationJet	525-0037		0093	1293	2 WRR FJ44-1A	4717	Executive		

EDELWEISS AIR, AG = EDW (Subsidiary of Kuoni Reisen Holding, AG)
Zurich

Postfach, CH-8058 Zürich-Flughafen, Switzerland ☎ (1) 816 50 60 Tx: none Fax: (1) 816 50 61 SITA: n/a
F: 1995 ⁂ 100 Head: Capt. Niklaus Grob ICAO: EDELWEISS Net: http://www.edelweissair.ch

☐	HB-IHX	Airbus Industrie A320-214	942	F-WWIU*	0099	0199	2 CFMI CFM56-5B4/2P	77000	CY164	AF-DQ	Calvaro / lsf Alp Air Holdings Ltd
☐	HB-IHY	Airbus Industrie A320-214	947	F-WWIY*	0099	0299	2 CFMI CFM56-5B4/2P	77000	CY164	AF-GQ	Upali / lsf Alp Air Holdings Ltd
☐	HB-IHZ	Airbus Industrie A320-214	1026				2 CFMI CFM56-5B4/2P	77000	CY164	AF-HQ	Victoria / oo-delivery 0699

EFOS FLIGHT-CHARTER, AG
Zurich

Flughafenstr. 14, CH-8302 Kloten, Switzerland ☎ (1) 813 52 92 Tx: 825567 efos ch Fax: (1) 813 55 35 SITA: n/a
F: 1976 ⁂ 3 Head: Konrad F. Schutzbach Net: n/a Aircraft below MTOW 1361 kg: Piper PA-28.

☐	HB-GOD	Beech Travel Air 95	TD-247		0059		2 LY O-360-A1A	1814			lsf Hevent-Air GmbH/for lease/IFR-trng
☐	HB-LEL	Piper PA-34-200 Seneca	34-7350313	N56296	0073		2 LY IO-360-C1E6	1905			for lease / IFR-training
☐	HB-LOR	Piper PA-23-250 Turbo Aztec E	27-7305192	D-IFGE	0073		2 LY TIO-540-C1A	2359			for lease / IFR-training
☐	HB-LKU	Cessna 340A III Rob. STOL/RAM	340A0493	N6322X	0078		2 CO TSIO-520-NBR	2853			for lease / Airtaxi
☐	HB-LHW	Cessna 402B	402B0926	N87130	0075		2 CO TSIO-520-E	2858			for lease / Airtaxi
☐	HB-GJG	Beech E18S	BA-328	N328N	0058	0198	2 PW R-985-AN14B	4581			lsf/opf Adventure Flight AG

ELITICINO, SA
Locarno

Casella postale, CH-6596 Gordola, Switzerland ☎ (91) 745 22 22 Tx: none Fax: (91) 745 10 25 SITA: n/a
F: 1966 ⁂ 16 Head: Martino Albertalli Net: n/a Additional helicopters lsf Heliswiss and Air Grischa when required.

☐	HB-XDN	Eurocopter (Aerosp.) SA315B Lama	2232		0071		1 TU Artouste IIIB	1950			
☐	HB-XPK	Eurocopter (Aerosp.) AS350B1 Ecureuil	1903		0086		1 TU Arriel 1D	2200			
☐	HB-XIQ	Eurocopter (Aerosp.) AS355N Ecureuil 2	5557	VR-BQM	0094	1194	2 TU Arrius 1A	2540			lsf pvt

FARNER AIR TRANSPORT, AG = FAT (Member of Farnair Europe, European Aviation Alliance)
Basel/Mulhouse-EuroAirport

Postfach, CH-4030 Basel-Flughafen, Switzerland ☎ (61) 325 30 67 Tx: 965643 fatb ch Fax: (61) 325 48 24 SITA: HDQ20SR
F: 1984 ⁂ 66 Head: Guy Girard ICAO: FARNER Net: n/a

☐	HB-AAZ	Fokker F27 Friendship 400 (F27 Mk400)	10268	F-BRQL	0065	0396	2 RR Dart 532-7	19731	Y34		lsf/opf Swiss Government in UN-colors
☐	HB-ILJ	Fokker F27 Friendship 500 (F27 Mk500)	10596	F-SEBJ	0080	0396	2 RR Dart 532-7R	20412	Y50		op in Farnair Europe-colors
☐	HB-ILQ	Fokker F27 Friendship 500 (F27 Mk500)	10389 / 528	F-BPUI	0069	0295	2 RR Dart 532-7R	20820	Freighter		op in Farnair Europe-colors
☐	HB-ISQ	Fokker F27 Friendship 500 (F27 Mk500)	10447 / 506	F-BSUM	0070	0294	2 RR Dart 532-7R	20820	Freighter		op in Farnair Europe-colors
☐	HB-ISY	Fokker F27 Friendship 500 (F27 Mk500)	10370	F-BPUB	0068	0594	2 RR Dart 532-7R	20820	Freighter		lst FAH as HA-FAB
☐	HB-ITY	Fokker F27 Friendship 500 (F27 Mk500)	10448	F-BSUN	0071	0797	2 RR Dart 532-7R	20820	Freighter		lst EPA as D-AAAC
☐	PH-JLN	Fokker F27 Friendship 500 (F27 Mk500)	10449	F-BSUO	0071	0298	2 RR Dart 532-7R	20820	Freighter		lst FRN

FFA Air-Travel = FFA (Division of Flugplatz St.Gallen-Altenrhein AG)
St. Gallen-Altenrhein

Flugplatz St. Gallen-Altenrhein, CH-9423 Altenrhein, Switzerland ☎ (71) 858 53 63 Tx: 881557 ch Fax: (71) 858 53 35 SITA: n/a
F: 1971 ⁂ 6 Head: Thomas Hiestand ICAO: FAIRTRAVEL Net: n/a

☐	HB-LRY	Piper PA-34-220T Seneca III	3433132	N9191P	0088	0992	2 CO TSIO-360-KB	2155			
☐	HB-GEV	Beech King Air A90 (65-A90)	LJ-215	D-IEVW	0067		2 PWC PT6A-20	4218			

FLITE vols touristiques (Ecole d'Aviation Générale Flite, SA dba)
Sion

Aéroport Civil, CH-1950 Sion, Switzerland ☎ (27) 322 55 85 Tx: none Fax: (27) 322 04 72 SITA: n/a
F: 1982 ⁂ 7 Head: Henri Chollet Net: n/a

☐	HB-LMV	Piper PA-34-220T Seneca III	34-8133177		0081		2 CO L/TSIO-360-KB	1999			

FLUGSCHULE EICHENBERGER, AG – Airtaxi (Affiliated with Eichenberger Aviation, AG)
Buttwil & Zurich

Flugplatz, CH-5632 Buttwil, Switzerland ☎ (56) 675 50 50 Tx: 827964 lszu ch Fax: (56) 675 50 55 SITA: n/a
F: 1969 ⁂ 25 Head: Werner Eichenberger Net: n/a Aircraft below MTOW 1361 kg: Cessna 150/152/172/172RG, Enstrom F28C/280C, Grob 115, Piper J3C, PZL-104, S205-18/R, Varga 2150 & 2180.

☐	HB-XXY	Bell 206B JetRanger III	4131	D-HHBI	0090		1 AN 250-C20R	1451			lsf pvt
☐	HB-CJI	Cessna U206G Turbine Stationair 6 II	U20605938	N6527X	0081	0391	1 AN 250-C20S	1633			Soloy cvtd

186 registration type of aircraft cn/fn ex/ex* mfd del powered by mtow kg configuration selcal name/fln/specialitites/remarks

FLYING DEVIL, SA — Lausanne

Av. Tissot 2, CH-1001 Lausanne, Switzerland ☎ (21) 340 03 04 Tx: n/a Fax: (21) 323 99 20 SITA: n/a
F: 1995 n/a Head: Daniel Vidoudez Net: n/a

registration	type of aircraft	cn/fn	ex/ex*	mfd	del	powered by	mtow kg	configuration	selcal	name/fln/specialitites/remarks
☐ HB-FLI	Pilatus PC-6/B2-H4 Turbo Porter	893	F-GONE	0093	1294	1 PWC PT6A-27	2800			
☐ HB-GJH	Beech King Air C90	LJ-972	N18080	0081	1098	2 PWC PT6A-21	4581			lsf Happy Lines SA

FLYING RANCH, AG — Triengen

Postfach 234, CH-6234 Triengen, Switzerland ☎ (41) 933 38 80 Tx: none Fax: (41) 933 27 43 SITA: n/a
F: 1989 n/a Head: Bruno Müller Net: n/a Aircraft below MTOW 1361kg: Cessna 172.

registration	type of aircraft	cn/fn	ex/ex*	mfd	del	powered by	mtow kg	configuration	selcal	name/fln/specialitites/remarks
☐ HB-NCH	Commander (Rockwell) 114	14050		0076		1 LY IO-540-T4A5D	1424			

FUCHS HELIKOPTER — Schindellegi-Heliport

Friesischwand 1, CH-8834 Schindellegi, Switzerland ☎ (1) 787 05 05 Tx: none Fax: (1) 787 05 19 SITA: n/a
F: 1974 6 Head: Lisa Stokmaier-Fuchs Net: n/a Aircraft below MTOW 1361 kg: Hughes 269C (300C) & 269D (330)

registration	type of aircraft	cn/fn	ex/ex*	mfd	del	powered by	mtow kg	configuration	selcal	name/fln/specialitites/remarks
☐ HB-XYP	MD Helicopters MD 520N (Hughes 500N)	LN052	N5204P	0093	0294	1 AN 250-C20R2	1520			
☐ HB-XQB	MD Helicopters MD 600N (Hughes 600N)	RN007	N92007	0097	0298	1 AN 250-C47M	1860			
☐ HB-XJF	MD Helicopters MD 900 Explorer	900-00017	N9213Z	0095	0895	2 PWC PW206A	2722			

GATX Flightlease Management, GmbH = (GATX) (Joint venture between GATX Capital (a GATX Corp. Company) & Flighlease AG (a SAirGroup Company)) — Zurich

Postfach, CH-8058 Zürich-Flughafen, Switzerland ☎ (1) 812 40 20 Tx: none Fax: (1) 812 93 33 SITA: n/a
F: 1998 n/a Head: Alan C. Coe & Hans-Jörg Hunziker Net: n/a New and used aircraft leasing, sales and financing company.
Owner / lessor of following (main) aircraft types: Airbus Industrie A300/310/319/320/321/330/340-600 (o.o.), Boeing 727/737/747/757/767, DC-9/DC-10/MD-11/MD-82 & MD-83.
Aircraft leased from GATX Flightlease are listed and mentioned as lsf GATX under the leasing carriers.

G5 EXECUTIVE, AG = EXH — Zurich

Postfach 1, CH-8058 Zürich-Flughafen, Switzerland ☎ (1) 804 20 90 Tx: none Fax: (1) 804 20 99 SITA: n/a
F: 1998 n/a Head: Peter Fried ICAO: ALIEN Net: n/a

registration	type of aircraft	cn/fn	ex/ex*	mfd	del	powered by	mtow kg	configuration	selcal	name/fln/specialitites/remarks
☐ HB-IMJ	GAC G-V Gulfstream V	517	N517GA*	0098	0598	2 BR BR710A1-10	41050	16 Pax		lsf Sky Unlimited AG/jtly opw G5 Avcon

GOFIR, SA – Aerotaxi = GOI — Lugano-Agno

Aeroporto, CH-6982 Agno, Switzerland ☎ (91) 605 45 42 Tx: none Fax: (91) 604 68 52 SITA: n/a
F: 1983 4 Head: Daniel Rusca ICAO: SWISS HAWK Net: n/a

registration	type of aircraft	cn/fn	ex/ex*	mfd	del	powered by	mtow kg	configuration	selcal	name/fln/specialitites/remarks
☐ HB-GHK	Twin (Aero) Jetprop Commander 1000 (695A)	96023	ZS-KZV	0082		2 GA TPE331-10-511K	5080			

GRIBAIR, AG — Berne

Flughafen Bern-Belpmoos, CH-3123 Belp, Switzerland ☎ (31) 961 04 91 Tx: n/a Fax: (32) 652 63 67 SITA: n/a
F: 1962 3 Head: Hugo Dobler Net: http://www.swissonline.ch/gribair Aircraft below MTOW 1361 kg: Piper PA-28.

registration	type of aircraft	cn/fn	ex/ex*	mfd	del	powered by	mtow kg	configuration	selcal	name/fln/specialitites/remarks
☐ HB-LEU	Piper PA-34-200 Seneca	34-7450076	N40751	0073		2 LY L/IO-360-C1E6	1905			
☐ HB-LMC	Piper PA-34-200 Seneca	34-7450008	OO-GPA	0074		2 LY L/IO-360-C1E6	1905			lsf pvt
☐ HB-LQJ	Piper PA-34-200 Seneca	34-7350164	D-GNUT	0073	0198	2 LY L/IO-360-C1E6	1905			lsf Meliga Habillement Horloger SA

HELI BERNINA, AG = HEB (Associated with HELOG, AG and HELI-LINTH, AG) — Samedan

Postfach, CH-7503 Samedan, Switzerland ☎ (81) 852 46 77 Tx: none Fax: (81) 852 39 04 SITA: n/a
F: 1985 8 Head: Hansueli Bärfuss ICAO: HELIBERNINA Net: n/a

registration	type of aircraft	cn/fn	ex/ex*	mfd	del	powered by	mtow kg	configuration	selcal	name/fln/specialitites/remarks
☐ HB-XPD	Eurocopter (Aerosp.) SA315B Lama	2167 / 22	F-WIPE*	0083	0585	1 TU Artouste IIIB	1950			cvtd Alouette II
☐ HB-XUA	Eurocopter (Aerosp.) SA315B Lama	2595	F-GHCP	0080	0589	1 TU Artouste IIIB	1950			
☐ HB-XXL	Eurocopter (Aerosp.) AS350B2 Ecureuil	2432		0090	1190	1 TU Arriel 1D1	2250			
☐ HB-XZJ	Eurocopter (Aerosp.) AS350B2 Ecureuil	2585	F-WYMG*	0091	0697	1 TU Arriel 1D1	2250			

HELICOPTERE SERVICE, S.A. — Sion

Aéroport Civil, CH-1951 Sion, Switzerland ☎ (27) 323 66 66 Tx: none Fax: (27) 323 66 73 SITA: n/a
F: 1998 n/a Head: Richard Christian Net: n/a

registration	type of aircraft	cn/fn	ex/ex*	mfd	del	powered by	mtow kg	configuration	selcal	name/fln/specialitites/remarks
☐ HB-XPJ	Eurocopter (Aerosp.) SA315B Lama	2368	9M-SAB	0073	0498	1 TU Artouste IIIB	1950			
☐ HB-XQV	Bell 407	53259		0098	0698	1 AN 250-C47B	2268			

HELI GOTTHARD, AG — Erstfeld-Heliport

Pfaffenmatt, CH-6472 Erstfeld, Switzerland ☎ (41) 880 21 22 Tx: none Fax: (41) 880 21 66 SITA: n/a
F: 1984 10 Head: Franz Steinegger Net: n/a Aircraft below MTOW 1361kg: Hughes 269C (300C)

registration	type of aircraft	cn/fn	ex/ex*	mfd	del	powered by	mtow kg	configuration	selcal	name/fln/specialitites/remarks
☐ HB-XXP	Eurocopter (Aerosp.) AS350B2 Ecureuil	2461		0091	0391	1 TU Arriel 1D1	2250			occ lst Lions Air
☐ HB-ZBH	Eurocopter (Aerosp.) AS350B3 Ecureuil	3190		0099	0499	1 TU Arriel 2B	2250			

HELIKOPTER SERVICE TRIET, AG — St. Gallen-Altenrhein

Flughafen St. Gallen-Altenrhein, CH-9423 Altenrhein, Switzerland ☎ (71) 855 70 10 Tx: none Fax: (71) 855 70 11 SITA: n/a
F: 1985 10 Head: Roland Triet Net: n/a Aircraft below MTOW 1361kg: Hughes 269C (300C).

registration	type of aircraft	cn/fn	ex/ex*	mfd	del	powered by	mtow kg	configuration	selcal	name/fln/specialitites/remarks
☐ HB-XPL	Eurocopter (Aerosp.) SA315B Lama	2560	OE-EXD	0079		1 TU Artouste IIIB	1950			
☐ HB-XYT	Eurocopter (Aerosp.) SA315B Lama	2439	D-HBRA	0075	0492	1 TU Artouste IIIB	1950			

HELI-LINK HELIKOPTER, AG = HLK — St. Gallen-Altenrhein & Zurich

Postfach, CH-8058 Zürich-Airport, Switzerland ☎ (1) 810 83 83 Tx: none Fax: (1) 920 37 36 SITA: n/a
F: 1990 n/a Head: Hanspeter Candrian ICAO: HELILINK Net: http://www.heli-link.ch

registration	type of aircraft	cn/fn	ex/ex*	mfd	del	powered by	mtow kg	configuration	selcal	name/fln/specialitites/remarks
☐ HB-XMJ	Bell 206B JetRanger III	4302	N112AJ	0094	0594	1 AN 250-C20R	1451			
☐ HB-XVS	Bell 206L-3 LongRanger III	51358	N7133D	0090	0790	1 AN 250-C30P	1882			
☐ HB-XDJ	Eurocopter (Aerosp.) SA365N Dauphin 2	6151	F-OHCF	0085	0297	2 TU Arriel 1C	4000			
☐ HB-XQS	Eurocopter (Aerosp.) AS365N3 Dauphin 2	6539		0098	0698	2 TU Arriel 2C	4250			lsf Sun Heli Est.

HELI-LINTH, AG — Mollis

Flugplatz, CH-8753 Mollis, Switzerland ☎ (55) 612 33 33 Tx: none Fax: (55) 612 26 82 SITA: n/a
F: 1972 12 Head: Peter Kolesnik Net: n/a Aircraft below MTOW 1361kg: Piper PA-18

registration	type of aircraft	cn/fn	ex/ex*	mfd	del	powered by	mtow kg	configuration	selcal	name/fln/specialitites/remarks
☐ HB-XQJ	Eurocopter (Aerosp.) AS350B3 Ecureuil	3093		0098	0698	1 TU Arriel 2B	2250			
☐ HB-XUK	Eurocopter (Aerosp.) AS350B2 Ecureuil	2330		0090	0390	1 TU Arriel 1D1	2250			
☐ HB-XUU	Eurocopter (Aerosp.) AS350B2 Ecureuil	2598	F-WYME*	0092		1 TU Arriel 1D1	2250			

HELIMISSION (Stiftung Helimission Ernst Tanner) — Africa & Asia

Bleiche 336, CH-9043 Trogen, Switzerland ☎ (71) 343 71 71 Tx: 883933 heta ch Fax: (71) 343 71 70 SITA: n/a
F: 1971 17 Head: Ernst Tanner Net: n/a Aircraft below MTOW 1361kg: Bell 47G-4A (Trainer, based USA) Non-commercial organisation conducting flights for missionaries & relief work.

registration	type of aircraft	cn/fn	ex/ex*	mfd	del	powered by	mtow kg	configuration	selcal	name/fln/specialitites/remarks
☐ HB-XDY	Agusta-Bell 206B JetRanger III	8335		0072		1 AN 250-C20B	1451	5 Pax		based Kenya / cvtd JetRanger
☐ HB-XLL	Agusta-Bell 206B JetRanger III	8609	P2-XLL	0080		1 AN 250-C20B	1451	5 Pax		
☐ HB-XSH	Bell 206B JetRanger III	2337	N215GP	0078		1 AN 250-C20B	1451	5 Pax		based Kenya
☐ HB-XQP	Bell 206L-4 LongRanger IV	52016	D-HOBC	0093	0198	1 AN 250-C30P	2018	7 Pax		based Irian Jaya/Indonesia
☐ HB-XQQ	Bell 206L-4 LongRanger IV	52167	N72167	0096	0698	1 AN 250-C30P	2018	7 Pax		based Cameroon
☐ HB-XSP	Bell 206L-3 LongRanger III	51158	N3199J	0085		1 AN 250-C30P	1882	7 Pax		
☐ HB-XON	Eurocopter (Aerosp.) AS350B Ecureuil	1104	I-LILL	0079		1 TU Arriel 1B	1950	6 Pax		based Madagascar
☐ HB-XPN	Eurocopter (Aerosp.) AS350B Ecureuil	1328	F-GCQU	0080		1 TU Arriel 1B	1950	6 Pax		

HELI PARTNER, GmbH — Sitterdorf

Frauenfelderstr. 49, CH-8370 Sirnach, Switzerland Tx: n/a Fax: n/a SITA: n/a
F: 1997 n/a Head: Willi Hefel Net: n/a

registration	type of aircraft	cn/fn	ex/ex*	mfd	del	powered by	mtow kg	configuration	selcal	name/fln/specialitites/remarks
☐ HB-XQO	Bell 206B JetRanger III	3934	OE-XRH	0087	0598	1 AN 250-C20J	1451			

HELI REZIA, AG/SA — Ambri

C.P. 10, CH-6775 Ambri, Switzerland ☎ (91) 873 66 66 Tx: none Fax: (91) 873 66 69 SITA: n/a
F: 1989 15 Head: Renato Belloli & David Bernasocchi Net: n/a

registration	type of aircraft	cn/fn	ex/ex*	mfd	del	powered by	mtow kg	configuration	selcal	name/fln/specialitites/remarks
☐ HB-XQI	Agusta-Bell 206B JetRanger	8326	I-MIPE	0072	0298	1 AN 250-C20	1450			lsf South Alps Maintenance
☐ HB-XQU	Eurocopter (Aerosp.) AS350B2 Ecureuil	2629	OE-XHK	0092	0698	1 TU Arriel 1D1	2250			
☐ HB-XVM	Eurocopter (Aerosp.) AS350B2 Ecureuil	2399		0090	0797	1 TU Arriel 1D1	2250			lsf Griti SA
☐ HB-XYS	Eurocopter (Aerosp.) AS350B2 Ecureuil	2637		0092	0797	1 TU Arriel 1D1	2250			lsf Griti SA

HELISWISS-Schweiz. Helikopter, AG = HSI — Berne

Flugplatz Bern, CH-3123 Belp, Switzerland ☎ (31) 818 88 88 Tx: 911655 helis ch Fax: (31) 818 88 89 SITA: n/a
F: 1953 62 Head: Dr. Jürg Riedi ICAO: HELISWISS Net: n/a Aircraft below MTOW 1361kg: Hughes 269C (300C)

registration	type of aircraft	cn/fn	ex/ex*	mfd	del	powered by	mtow kg	configuration	selcal	name/fln/specialitites/remarks
☐ HB-XLA	Agusta-Bell 206B JetRanger III	8616		0981	0981	1 AN 250-C20B	1451			
☐ HB-XPQ	Agusta-Bell 206B JetRanger III	8606	OE-DXV	1080	0386	1 AN 250-C20B	1451			
☐ HB-XSI	Bell 206B JetRanger III	3091	EC-GNO	0080	0887	1 AN 250-C20B	1451			

registration	type of aircraft	cn/fn	ex/ex*	mfd	del	powered by	mtow kg	configuration	selcal	name/fln/specialitites/remarks
☐ HB-XUE	Bell 206B JetRanger III	3080	OE-KXR	0780	0589	1 AN 250-C20B	1451			
☐ HB-XHD	Eurocopter (Aerosp.) SA315B Lama	2460	OE-EXL	1276	0378	1 TU Artouste IIIB	1950			
☐ HB-XHN	Eurocopter (Aerosp.) SA315B Lama	1083	F-BIEC	0074	0092	1 TU Artouste IIIB	1950			
☐ HB-XPP	Eurocopter (Aerosp.) SA315B Lama	2679	OE-XPP	0085	0092	1 TU Artouste IIIB	1950			
☐ HB-XTC	Eurocopter (Aerosp.) SA315B Lama	2521	N90016	0378	0888	1 TU Artouste IIIB	1950			
☐ HB-XTD	Eurocopter (Aerosp.) SA315B Lama	2596	N70283	0181	0988	1 TU Artouste IIIB	1950			
☐ HB-XVV	Eurocopter (Aerosp.) SA315B Lama	2382	OE-OXB	0074	0297	1 TU Artouste IIIB	1950			
☐ HB-XXS	Eurocopter (Aerosp.) SA315B Lama	2470	OE-OXI	0077	0497	1 TU Artouste IIIB	1950			lsf Helitrade AG
☐ HB-XJW	Eurocopter (Aerosp.) AS350B Ecureuil	1802	OE-KXB	0084	0597	1 TU Arriel 1B	1950			
☐ HB-XUZ	Eurocopter (Aerosp.) AS350B2 Ecureuil	2381		0990	0990	1 TU Arriel 1D1	2250			
☐ HB-XVZ	Bell 214B-1 BigLifter	28048	LN-OPV	0080	0499	1 LY T5508D	5670			
☐ HB-XKE	Kamov Ka-32A	8709	RA-31587	0092	0696	2 IS TV3-117VMA	11000			

HELIT HELICOPTERES, SA — La Chaux-de-Fonds

Ave LéopoldRobert 161, CH-2300 La Chaux-de-Fonds, Switzerland ☎ (32) 926 60 60 Tx: none Fax: (32) 926 56 32 SITA: n/a
F: 1997 ♟♟♟ n/a Head: Daniel Terraz Net: n/a

☐ HB-XQG	MD Helicopters MD 500E (Hughes 369E)	0419E	D-HJAA	0090	0797	1 AN 250-C20B	1361			lsf Breitling SA
☐ HB-ZBI	MD Helicopters MD 520N (Hughes 500N)	LN037	N520N	0092	0199	1 AN 250-C20R	1520			lsf Swissrotor SàRL

HELITRANS, AG — Basel/Mulhouse-EuroAirport

EuroAirport Basel-Mulhouse-Freiburg, CH-4030 Basel, Switzerland ☎ (61) 325 39 33 Tx: none Fax: (61) 325 39 33 SITA: n/a
F: 1990 ♟♟♟ 3 Head: Rudolf Waldmeier Net: n/a

☐ HB-XSL	Bell 206B JetRanger	1516	D-HCBB	0074		1 AN 250-C20	1451			lst Lions Air

HELI-TV, SA — Lugano-Agno

Aeroporto, CH-6527 Londrino, Switzerland ☎ (91) 873 40 40 Tx: none Fax: (91) 873 40 44 SITA: n/a
F: 1981 ♟♟♟ 35 Head: Ing. Giovanni Frapolli Net: http://www.heli.tv.ch/com Aircraft below MTOW 1361 kg: Hughes 269C (300C).

☐ HB-XJJ	Eurocopter (Aerosp.) SE3130 Alouette II	1903	V-57	0064	0697	1 TU Artouste IIC5	1500	4 Pax		lsf pvt
☐ HB-XPY	Eurocopter (Aerosp.) SA315B Lama	2542	N9007N	0078		1 TU Artouste IIIB	1950	4 Pax/cargosling		
☐ HB-XRA	Eurocopter (Aerosp.) SA315B Lama	1542 / 17	F-GHCG	0081	0789	1 TU Artouste IIIB	1950	4 Pax/Cargosling		
☐ HB-XSV	Eurocopter (Aerosp.) SA315B Lama	2421	LN-ORU	0075		1 TU Artouste IIIB	1950	4 Pax/Cargosling		
☐ HB-XSO	Eurocopter (Aerosp.) AS350B2 Ecureuil	1950	D-HACC	0086		1 TU Arriel 1D1	2250	5 Pax/Cargosling		cvtd AS350B1
☐ HB-XJK	Eurocopter (Aerosp.) SA319B Alouette III	2273	I-OYEN	0075	0596	1 TU Astazou XIVB	2250			
☐ HB-XNE	Eurocopter (Aerosp.) AS332C1 Super Puma	2002	F-WZJM*	0080	0199	2 TU Makila 1A1	8600			lsf Helog

HELOG, AG – Helikopter-Transporte = HLG — Küssnacht a.R.-Heliport Haltikon

Heliport Haltikon, CH-6403 Küssnacht a.R., Switzerland ☎ (41) 854 08 54 Tx: none Fax: (41) 854 08 55 SITA: n/a
F: 1981 ♟♟♟ 30 Head: Beat Ruckli ICAO: HELOG Net: http://www.helog.ch Additional helicopters lsf Heli Bernina (AS350B1 & SA315B) when required.

☐ HB-XZU	Eurocopter (Aerosp.) SA315B Lama	2522	JA9190	0078	0993	1 TU Artouste IIIB	1950			
☐ HB-XNE	Eurocopter (Aerosp.) AS332C1 Super Puma	2002	F-WZJM*	0080	0782	2 TU Makila 1A1	8600			lst Heli-TV
☐ HB-XVY	Eurocopter (Aerosp.) AS332C Super Puma	2033	N5795P	0082	0590	2 TU Makila 1A	8600			occ lst Helog SA, France

IBM EUROFLIGHT = BBL (Member of IBM International Business Machines Corporation) — Paris-Le Bourget (F)

Z.I. Nord, Aeroport du Bourget, F-93350 Le Bourget, France ☎ (1) 49 34 68 99 Tx: none Fax: (1) 48 35 96 46 SITA: n/a
F: 1965 ♟♟♟ n/a Head: Bernard Picard ICAO: BLUE Net: n/a Operates non-commercial corporate flights exclusively fot the IBM Group of Companies only.

☐ N161EU	Dassault Falcon 20F-5	485	F-WLCT	0084	1289	2 GA TFE731-5AR-2C	13200	Corporate		lsf IBM Credit Corp. / cvtd 20F
☐ HB-IVM	Dassault Falcon 2000	55	F-WWMM*	0097	0698	2 CFE CFE738-1-1B	16556	Corporate		lsf Covalind SA
☐ HB-IVN	Dassault Falcon 2000	61	F-WWME*	0098	0898	2 CFE CFE738-1-1B	16556	Corporate		lsf Covalind SA

JET AVIATION BUSINESS JETS, AG = PP / PJS (Associated with Jet Aviation Int'l Inc., USA / formerly Private Jet Services, AG) — Zurich

Postfach 1347, CH-8058 Zürich-Flughafen, Switzerland ☎ (1) 816 48 48 Tx: 825655 jbj ch Fax: (1) 816 48 88 SITA: ZRHPJPP
F: 1973 ♟♟♟ 180 Head: Theo Staub ICAO: JET AVIATION Net: http://www.jetaviation.com In addition to the listed commercially operated aircraft also offers management, operational, technical or administrative support to over 120 F-, HB-, HZ-, N, OE-, VH-, VP-B & VP-C registered executive aircraft on behalf of private companies or carriers.

☐ HB-VGS	Cessna 550 Citation II	550-0183	N98630	0080		2 PWC JT15D-4	6577	Executive		
☐ HB-VLP	Cessna 650 Citation VII	650-7064	N52626*	0096	0696	2 GA TFE731-4R-2S	10183	Executive		
☐ HB-ILK	Canadair CL-601-1A (CL-600-2A12) Challen.	3033		0084		2 GE CF34-1A	19550	Executive	DH-AE	lsf Credit Suisse Leasing
☐ HB-IVP	Canadair CL-604 (CL-600-2B16) Challen.	5369	C-GCQB*	0098	0998	2 GE CF34-3B	21909	Executive		lsf Credit Suisse Leasing

JET BUSINESS, S.A. = JBS — Sion

Rte de l'Aéroport, CH-1950 Sion, Switzerland ☎ (27) 322 85 80 Tx: none Fax: (27) 322 88 81 SITA: n/a
F: 1994 ♟♟♟ n/a Head: Philippe Horowicz ICAO: JET SKY Net: n/a

☐ HB-LRL	Cessna 421B Golden Eagle	421B0398	N205PV	0073	0598	2 CO GTSIO-520-H	3379			

JETCLUB, AG – Executive Aircraft Charter & Management = JCS — Zurich

Postfach 99, CH-8058 Zürich-Flughafen, Switzerland ☎ (1) 816 90 10 Tx: 825126 ch Fax: (1) 816 90 19 SITA: ZRHJCXH
F: 1994 ♟♟♟ 35 Head: Greg Sutton ICAO: JETCLUB Net: http://www.jetclub.com Also conducting fleet management for a number of executive jets (Falcon 900B & Gulfstream IVSP) for non-commercial private owners.

☐ HB-IVS	Canadair CL-601-3R (CL-600-2B16) Challen.	5166	9M-NSK	0094	1098	2 GE CF34-3A1	20457	Executive		lsf MWM AG
☐ HB-IBX	GAC G-IV Gulfstream IV	1183	VR-BDC	0092	0397	2 RR Tay 611-8	33204	Executive	GR-FK	lsf Jet Leasing Establishment

JETCOM, SA = JCA — Geneva

Case postale 570, CH-1215 Genève-Aéroport 15, Switzerland ☎ (22) 798 64 21 Tx: none Fax: (22) 798 00 78 SITA: n/a
F: 1983 ♟♟♟ 9 Head: Jean-Claude Kaufmann ICAO: JETCOM Net: n/a

☐ F-GLMD	Dassault Falcon 20C-5	117	EC-FJP	0067	0098	2 GA TFE731-5AR-2C	13200	9 Pax		lsf THZ / cvtd 20C

JU-AIR (Verein der Freunde der Schweizerischen Fliegertruppe – VFL dba) — Duebendorf-AFB

Postfach, CH-8600 Dübendorf 1, Switzerland ☎ (1) 823 20 83 Tx: none Fax: (1) 823 26 53 SITA: n/a
F: 1982 ♟♟♟ 5 Head: Kurt Waldmeier Net: http://www.ju-air.com

☐ HB-HOP	Junkers Ju 52/3m G4E	6610	A-703	0039		3 BMW 132A3	10500	17 Pax		lsf Bundesamt für Militärfl./IWC-colors
☐ HB-HOS	Junkers Ju 52/3m G4E	6580	A-701	0039		3 BMW 132A3	10500	17 Pax		Purple Milka-colors
☐ HB-HOT	Junkers Ju 52/3m G4E	6595	A-702	0039		3 BMW 132A3	10500	17 Pax		lsf Bundesamt für Militärflugzeuge
☐ HB-HOY	CASA 352-L (Junkers Ju 52/3m G4E)	96	D-CIAK	0049	1291	3 BMW 132A3	10500	17 Pax		

KRUMMEN AIR TAXI, AG — Neuchatel

Postfach, CH-3210 Kerzers, Switzerland ☎ (31) 750 22 00 Tx: none Fax: (31) 755 69 00 SITA: n/a
F: 1993 ♟♟♟ 1 Head: Peter Krummen Net: n/a

☐ HB-LLW	Piper PA-34-200T Seneca II	34-8070170	N8176T	0080		2 CO L/TSIO-360-EB	2073			

LEMANAIR, S.A. = LMR (Sister company of Lemanair Executive, S.A.) — Geneva

Case postale 483, CH-1215 Genève-Aéroport 15, Switzerland ☎ (22) 717 84 00 Tx: none Fax: (22) 717 84 02 SITA: n/a
F: 1994 ♟♟♟ 85 Head: Christian S. Valentiny ICAO: LEMANAIR Net: http://www.lemanair.com

☐ HB-JFA	Embraer RJ145EU (EMB-145EU)	145159				2 AN AE3007A1	19990	C50		oo-delivery 0899
☐ HB-JFB	Embraer RJ145EU (EMB-145EU)	145175				2 AN AE3007A1	19990	C50		oo-delivery 1099
☐ HB-JFC	Embraer RJ145EP (EMB-145EP)	145191				2 AN AE3007A1	20990	C50		oo-delivery 1299
☐ HB-JFD	Embraer RJ145EP (EMB-145EP)					2 AN AE3007A1	20990	C50		oo-delivery 0000
☐ HB-JFE	Embraer RJ145EP (EMB-145EP)					2 AN AE3007A1	20990	C50		oo-delivery 0000

LEMANAIR EXECUTIVE, S.A. = LMX (Sister company of Lemanair, S.A.) — Geneva

Case postale 483, CH-1215 Genève-Aéroport 15, Switzerland ☎ (22) 717 84 00 Tx: none Fax: (22) 717 84 02 SITA: n/a
F: 1997 ♟♟♟ 6 Head: Christian S. Valentiny ICAO: LEMANAIR Net: n/a

☐ HB-LIP	Piper PA-34-200T Seneca II	34-7770198	N2798Q	0077	1298	2 CO L/TSIO-360-EB	1999	Executive		lsf Lemanair Trading S.A.
☐ HB-VKQ	Cessna 550 Citation II	550-0211	N77PR	0081	0399	2 PWC JT15D-4	6033	Executive		

LEOPAIR, SA = LEO — Geneva

Case postale 1081, CH-1211 Genève 5, Switzerland ☎ (22) 798 21 10 Tx: none Fax: (22) 791 02 14 SITA: n/a
F: 1984 ♟♟♟ 6 Head: André Cougn ICAO: LEOPAIR Net: n/a

☐ HB-VKK	Cessna 500 Citation	500-0178	I-FBCK	0074	0392	2 PWC JT15D-1	5216	Y6		

LIONS AIR, AG = LEU — Zurich

Postfach 233, CH-8058 Zürich-Flughafen, Switzerland ☎ (1) 818 88 88 Tx: 822457 leu ch Fax: (1) 818 88 99 SITA: n/a
F: 1987 ♟♟♟ 20 Head: Jürg Fleischmann ICAO: LIONSAIR Net: n/a

☐ HB-XSL	Bell 206B JetRanger	1516	D-HCBB	0074		1 AN 250-C20	1451			lsf Helitrans
☐ HB-XJC	Eurocopter (Aerosp.) AS350B2 Ecureuil	2382	G-BWLI	0090	0396	1 TU Arriel 1D1	2250			
☐ HB-XXP	Eurocopter (Aerosp.) AS350B2 Ecureuil	2461		0091	0099	1 TU Arriel 1D1	2250			occ lsf Heli Gotthard
☐ HB-VIC	Cessna 501 Citation I/SP	501-0098	N144AR	0079		2 PWC JT15D-1	5375			lsf TASair Aviation SA

registration	type of aircraft	cn/fn	ex/ex*	mfd	del	powered by	mtow kg	configuration	selcal	name/fln/specialitites/remarks
☐ HB-VMG	IAI 1125A Astra SPX	105	N217PT	0098	0199	2 GA TFE731-40R-200G	11700			lsf TASair Aviation SA
☐ N65TD	IAI 1125A Astra SPX	093		0097	0098	2 GA TFE731-40R-200G	11700			lsf LDG Investment
☐ HB-	IAI 1126 Galaxy	024				2 PWC PW406A	15173			oo-delivery 0400
☐ N505GA	IAI 1126 Galaxy	005	4X-IGB*	0098	0199	2 PWC PW406A	15173			lsf Fytosan .

MOTORFLUGGRUPPE OBERENGADIN
Samedan

Flugplatz, CH-7503 Samedan, Switzerland ☎ (82) 65 433 Tx: 852436 ch Fax: (82) 64 314 SITA: n/a
F: 1979 ᚙᚙᚙ n/a Head: Alfred Riederer Net: n/a Aircraft below MTOW 1361 kg: Cessna 172.

registration	type of aircraft	cn/fn	ex/ex*	mfd	del	powered by	mtow kg	configuration	selcal	name/fln/specialitites/remarks
☐ HB-PHW	Piper PA-28-236 Dakota	27-7911212			0079	1 LY O-540-J3A5D	1361			
☐ HB-LOA	Partenavia P.68B	35			0075	2 LY IO-360-A1B6	1960			

MOUNTAIN FLYERS 80, Ltd
Berne

Postfach 69, CH-3123 Belp, Switzerland ☎ (31) 819 60 30 Tx: none Fax: (31) 819 60 58 SITA: n/a
F: 1980 ᚙᚙᚙ 3 Head: Ueli Soltermann Net: n/a Aircraft below MTOW 1361kg: Robinson R22.

registration	type of aircraft	cn/fn	ex/ex*	mfd	del	powered by	mtow kg	configuration	selcal	name/fln/specialitites/remarks
☐ HB-XSM	Agusta-Bell 206B JetRanger III	8550	OE-BXW	0078		1 AN 250-C20B	1451			
☐ HB-XYW	Bell 206B JetRanger III	4180		0091	0298	1 AN 250-C20R	1451			lsf pvt
☐ HB-XOO	Eurocopter (Aerosp.) SA319B Alouette III	1959	D-HAAK	0072	0298	1 TU Astazou XIVB	2250			

POCAIR S.A.
La Chaux-de-Fonds/Les Eplatures

Bd des Eplatures 42, CH 2304 La Chaux-de-Fonds, Switzerland ☎ (32) 924 02 94 Tx: none Fax: (32) 926 20 28 SITA: n/a
F: 1989 ᚙᚙᚙ n/a Head: Pierre-Olivier Chave Net: n/a

registration	type of aircraft	cn/fn	ex/ex*	mfd	del	powered by	mtow kg	configuration	selcal	name/fln/specialitites/remarks
☐ HB-GGP	Beech Baron 58P	TJ-157			0078	2 CO TSIO-520-L	2767			

PRIVATAIR, SA = PTI (formerly Petrolair, SA & Petrolair System, SA)
Geneva & Athens

Case postale 53, CH-1216 Cointrin, Switzerland ☎ (22) 929 27 39 Tx: none Fax: (22) 929 27 57 SITA: n/a
F: 1977 ᚙᚙᚙ 40 Head: Ian McGrath ICAO: PRIVATAIR Net: http://www.privatair.com Company conducting non-commercial corporate flights for itself & commercial luxury charter flights.

registration	type of aircraft	cn/fn	ex/ex*	mfd	del	powered by	mtow kg	configuration	selcal	name/fln/specialitites/remarks
☐ HB-ITX	GAC G-IV Gulfstream IV	1093	VR-BLC	0089	0290	2 RR Tay 611-8	32590	F10	GJ-CQ	
☐ HB-IIN	Boeing 737-3L9	27924 / 2760	OY-MAT	0095	0198	2 CFMI CFM56-3C1	63276	F44		lsf Interaviation Holdings Ltd
☐ HB-	Boeing 737-700 (BBJ)					2 CFMI CFM56-7B26	77564	VIP		oo-delivery 1099
☐ HB-	Boeing 737-700 (BBJ)					2 CFMI CFM56-7B26	77564	VIP		oo-delivery 1199
☐ HB-IEE	Boeing 757-23A	24527 / 249	HB-IHU	0089	1089	2 RR RB211-535E4	99790	F60	LQ-KP	

RABBIT-AIR, AG = RBB (Associated with ABB)
Zurich

Postfach 295, CH-8058 Zürich-Flughafen, Switzerland ☎ (1) 816 44 77 Tx: n/a Fax: (1) 816 45 38 SITA: n/a
F: 1989 ᚙᚙᚙ 10 Head: C. Ronchetti ICAO: RABBIT Net: n/a Company holds an airtaxi/charter licence however currently conducting non-commercial corporate flights for its owner company only.

registration	type of aircraft	cn/fn	ex/ex*	mfd	del	powered by	mtow kg	configuration	selcal	name/fln/specialitites/remarks
☐ HB-IAX	Dassault Falcon 2000	33	F-WWME*	0096	1296	2 CFE CFE738-1-1B	16556	Corporate		
☐ HB-IAY	Dassault Falcon 2000	34	F-WWMF*	0096	1296	2 CFE CFE738-1-1B	16556	Corporate		
☐ HB-IAQ	Dassault Falcon 900EX	35	N2BD	0098	1098	3 GA TFE731-60-1C	22226	Corporate		lsf B.G. Investments Ltd, Bermuda

RHEIN-HELIKOPTER, AG
Balzers-Heliport

Schifflände 2, FL-9496 Balzers, Liechtenstein ☎ (75) 384 22 77 Tx: none Fax: (75) 384 28 79 SITA: n/a
F: 1983 ᚙᚙᚙ 12 Head: David Vogt Net: n/a

registration	type of aircraft	cn/fn	ex/ex*	mfd	del	powered by	mtow kg	configuration	selcal	name/fln/specialitites/remarks
☐ HB-XRD	Eurocopter (Aerosp.) SA315B Lama	2400	OE-EXV	0074		1 TU Artouste IIIB	1950	4 Pax		
☐ HB-XQR	Eurocopter (Aerosp.) AS350B2 Ecureuil	9000		0098	0698	1 TU Arriel 1D1	2250	5 Pax		

ROTEX Helicopter, AG
Balzers-Heliport

Schifflände 2, FL-9496 Balzers, Liechtenstein ☎ (75) 384 35 35 Tx: none Fax: (75) 384 35 61 SITA: n/a
F: 1997 ᚙᚙᚙ 11 Head: Heinz Leibundgut Net: http://www.rotex-helicopter.ch

registration	type of aircraft	cn/fn	ex/ex*	mfd	del	powered by	mtow kg	configuration	selcal	name/fln/specialitites/remarks
☐ HB-XQA	Kaman K-1200 K-Max	A94-0008	N136KA	0094	0497	1 LY T5317A-1	2722			

RUNDFLUG MFGZ (Division of Motorfluggruppe Zürich)
Zurich

Postfach 1456, CH-8058 Zürich-Flughafen, Switzerland ☎ (1) 814 26 20 Tx: none Fax: (1) 814 16 29 SITA: n/a
F: 1978 ᚙᚙᚙ 18 Head: Richard Frank Net: n/a

registration	type of aircraft	cn/fn	ex/ex*	mfd	del	powered by	mtow kg	configuration	selcal	name/fln/specialitites/remarks
☐ HB-PCU	Piper PA-32-300 Cherokee SIX	32-7840097	N9382C	0078		1 LY IO-540-K1G5	1542	6 Pax		

SECURITE CIVILE Genève – Service Hélicoptère (formerly Protection Civile)
Geneva

Route H.C. Forestier 32, CH-1217 Meyrin, Switzerland ☎ (22) 798 61 31 Tx: none Fax: (22) 782 40 20 SITA: n/a
F: 1971 ᚙᚙᚙ 6 Head: François Gindre Net: n/a

registration	type of aircraft	cn/fn	ex/ex*	mfd	del	powered by	mtow kg	configuration	selcal	name/fln/specialitites/remarks
☐ HB-XVB	Eurocopter (Aerosp.) AS350B2 Ecureuil	2340		0090	0590	1 TU Arriel 1D1	2250	EMS		

SEEHOLZER-AIR
Triengen

Rebmattweg 10, CH-6402 Merlischachen, Switzerland ☎ (41) 850 02 92 Tx: none Fax: none SITA: n/a
F: 1989 ᚙᚙᚙ n/a Head: Jakob Seeholzer Net: n/a

registration	type of aircraft	cn/fn	ex/ex*	mfd	del	powered by	mtow kg	configuration	selcal	name/fln/specialitites/remarks
☐ HB-CQB	Cessna A185F Skywagon II	18504093	N60998	0080		1 CO IO-520-D	1520	Wheel-Skis		
☐ HB-CWZ	Cessna A185F Skywagon	18502641	N4879C	0075		1 CO IO-520-D	1520	Wheel-Skis		

SERVAIR, AG = SWZ (formerly Servair Private Charter, AG)
Zurich

CH-5467 Fisibach, (AG), Switzerland ☎ (1) 858 30 70 Tx: none Fax: (1) 858 30 71 SITA: n/a
F: 1980 ᚙᚙᚙ 8 Head: M. Helbling ICAO: SWISSBIRD Net: n/a

registration	type of aircraft	cn/fn	ex/ex*	mfd	del	powered by	mtow kg	configuration	selcal	name/fln/specialitites/remarks
☐ HB-VLY	Cessna 550 Citation II	550-0430	N1278	0082	1097	2 PWC JT15D-4	6033			
☐ HB-VMH	Cessna 550 Citation II	550-0649	N44LQ	0090	0299	2 PWC JT15D-4	6577			

SIRIUS, AG
Zurich

Bleicherweg 58, CH-8057 Zürich, Switzerland ☎ (1) 814 05 43 Tx: n/a Fax: (1) 813 13 44 SITA: n/a
F: 1967 ᚙᚙᚙ 4 Head: Quirino Riva Net: n/a

registration	type of aircraft	cn/fn	ex/ex*	mfd	del	powered by	mtow kg	configuration	selcal	name/fln/specialitites/remarks
☐ HB-VLW	Beech Beechjet 400A	RK-103	D-CIGM	0095	0797	2 PWC JT15D-5	7303			

SKY JET, AG
Zurich

Postfach 305, CH-8008 Zürich, Switzerland ☎ (1) 252 22 26 Tx: 817427 crhg ch Fax: (1) 252 25 63 SITA: n/a
F: 1974 ᚙᚙᚙ 2 Head: R. Iten Net: n/a

registration	type of aircraft	cn/fn	ex/ex*	mfd	del	powered by	mtow kg	configuration	selcal	name/fln/specialitites/remarks
☐ HB-VKW	Hawker 800A (BAe 125-800A)	258246	N387H	0093	0194	2 GA TFE731-5R-1H	12428			

SKY WORK, AG = SRK
Berne

Flughafen Bern-Belp, CH-3123 Belp, Switzerland ☎ (31) 961 00 00 Tx: 911944 ch Fax: (31) 961 64 44 SITA: n/a
F: 1983 ᚙᚙᚙ 6 Head: Alex Gribi ICAO: SKYFOX Net: n/a

registration	type of aircraft	cn/fn	ex/ex*	mfd	del	powered by	mtow kg	configuration	selcal	name/fln/specialitites/remarks
☐ HB-VLE	Cessna 500 Citation Eagle	500-0313	N313BA	0076	0395	2 PWC JT15D-1A	5670			lsf Spring Air AG / cvtd Citation I
☐ HB-VIO	Cessna 551 Citation II/SP	551-0205	N342DA	0080		2 PWC JT15D-4	5670			
☐ HB-VLS	Cessna 550 Citation II	550-0196	N400DK	0080	0297	2 PWC JT15D-4	6033			
☐ HB-VLZ	Cessna 560 Citation V Ultra	560-0446		0097	1297	2 PWC JT15D-5D	7394			lsf Sarena Jet AG

SPEEDWINGS, SA = SPW
Geneva

Case postale 785, CH-1215 Genève 15, Switzerland ☎ (22) 717 84 80 Tx: none Fax: (22) 717 84 81 SITA: GVAWOSR
F: 1989 ᚙᚙᚙ 15 Head: François Allaz ICAO: SPEEDWING Net: http://www.speedwings.ch

registration	type of aircraft	cn/fn	ex/ex*	mfd	del	powered by	mtow kg	configuration	selcal	name/fln/specialitites/remarks
☐ HB-VDO	Cessna 551 Citation II/SP	551-0133	I-JESA	0079	0298	2 PWC JT15D-4	5670			
☐ HB-VLQ	Cessna 550 Citation II	550-0324	I-JESJ	0081	0897	2 PWC JT15D-4	6033			
☐ HB-VCN	Sabreliner 65 (Rockwell NA265-65)	465-32	N303A	0080	0298	2 GA TFE731-3R-1D	10886			

STAC Service des transports aériens de la confédération = FOC (Lufttransportdienst des Bundes / Federal Air Transport Service)
Berne-Belp

c/o BAZL Bundesamt für Zivilluftfahrt, Bundesbasis Belp, CH-3123 Belp, Switzerland ☎ (31) 818 50 00 Tx: none Fax: (31) 818 50 01 SITA: n/a
F: 1970 ᚙᚙᚙ 4 Head: Stefan Wenger ICAO: STAC Net: n/a Non-commercial Federal organisation conducting VIP and transport flights for the Swiss Government.

registration	type of aircraft	cn/fn	ex/ex*	mfd	del	powered by	mtow kg	configuration	selcal	name/fln/specialitites/remarks
☐ HB-XVA	Eurocopter (Aerosp.) AS350B2 Ecureuil	2387	F-WYME*	0090	1090	1 TU Arriel 1D1	2250	VIP		
☐ HB-XQE	Agusta A109E Power	11016		0098	0598	2 PWC PW206C	2850	VIP		
☐ HB-XPE	Eurocopter (Aerosp.) SA365N Dauphin 2	6146		0085		2 TU Arriel 1C	4000	VIP		
☐ HB-GDL	Beech King Air B200	BB-1079	HB-GDI	0082		2 PWC PT6A-42	5670	VIP		

SWIFT COPTERS, S.A.
Geneva

Case Postale 168, CH-1215 Genève-Aéroport 15, Switzerland ☎ (22) 717 83 83 Tx: none Fax: (22) 717 83 80 SITA: n/a
F: 1996 ᚙᚙᚙ 8 Head: Jean-Marc Régis Net: http://www.swiftcopters.ch Aircraft below MTOW 1361kg: Hughes 296C (300C)

registration	type of aircraft	cn/fn	ex/ex*	mfd	del	powered by	mtow kg	configuration	selcal	name/fln/specialitites/remarks
☐ HB-XCJ	Eurocopter (Aerosp.) AS350B2 Ecureuil	2557	F-GJOK	0091	0796	1 TU Arriel 1D1	2250			lsf Immo-Copters SA
☐ HB-XRK	Agusta A109A II	7352	I-AGSC	0086	0796	2 AN 250-C20B	2600			
☐ HB-XQW	Eurocopter (Aerosp.) SA365N1 Dauphin 2	6350	JA6609	0090	0598	2 TU Arriel 1C1	4100			lsf Immo-Copters SA
☐ HB-ZBG	Eurocopter (Aerosp.) SA365N1 Dauphin 2	6251	N600GN	0087	0299	2 TU Arriel 1C1	4100			lsf Algum Ltd

registration   type of aircraft   cn/fn   ex/ex*   mfd   del   powered by   mtow kg   configuration   selcal   name/fln/specialitites/remarks

SWISSAIR = SR / SWR (Swissair Asia & Express) (Schweiz.Luftverkehr AG dba/Member of The Qualiflyer Group & SAirGroup/Subs. of SAirLines) Zurich

Postfach, CH-8058 Zürich-Flughafen, Switzerland ☎ (1) 812 12 12 Tx: 52407 srf ch Fax: (1) 810 80 46 SITA: ZRHDPSR

F: 1931 ✝✝✝ 19100 Head: Philippe Bruggisser IATA: 085 ICAO: SWISSAIR Net: http://www.swissair.com Some passenger flights are operated on behalf of Swissair by CROSSAIR (with Avro RJ85/100, McDonnell Douglas MD-82/83 & Saab 340B/2000); all-cargo flights by GEMINI AIR CARGO (DC-10-30F) using SR-flight numbers. For fleet details – see under each company.

SWISSAIR ASIA is the name used for flights to Taiwan (same headquarters). 2 MD-11 are painted with Swissair Asia titles & colors.

SWISSAIR EXPRESS is the marketing name for flights operated on behalf of Swissair in Swissair Express colors & both titles by DEBONAIR (G) & FLIGHTLINE (G) - see under both companies.

☐	HB-IPR	Airbus Industrie A319-112	1018				2 CFMI CFM56-5B6/2P	64000	CY126		to be lsf GATX 0599
☐	HB-IPS	Airbus Industrie A319-112	734	D-AVYZ*	0097	1097	2 CFMI CFM56-5B6/2P	64000	CY126	QS-KP	Weiach / lsf GATX
☐	HB-IPT	Airbus Industrie A319-112	727	D-AVYC*	0097	0997	2 CFMI CFM56-5B6/2P	64000	CY126	QS-KL	Stadel / lsf GATX
☐	HB-IPU	Airbus Industrie A319-112	713	D-AVYB*	0097	0897	2 CFMI CFM56-5B6/2P	64000	CY126	QS-KM	Hochfelden / lsf GATX
☐	HB-IPV	Airbus Industrie A319-112	578	F-WWTA*	0096	0496	2 CFMI CFM56-5B6/2P	64000	CY126	DP-FQ	Rümlang / lsf GATX
☐	HB-IPW	Airbus Industrie A319-112	588	D-AVYB*	0096	0596	2 CFMI CFM56-5B6/2P	64000	CY126	DP-FS	Bachenbülach / lsf GATX
☐	HB-IPX	Airbus Industrie A319-112	612	D-AVYH*	0096	0896	2 CFMI CFM56-5B6/2P	64000	CY126	DP-GQ	Steinmaur / lsf GATX
☐	HB-IPY	Airbus Industrie A319-112	621	D-AVYK*	0096	1096	2 CFMI CFM56-5B6/2P	64000	CY126	DP-HQ	Höri / lsf GATX
☐	HB-IPZ	Airbus Industrie A319-112	629	D-AVYR*	0096	1196	2 CFMI CFM56-5B6/2P	64000	CY126	DP-LS	Oberglatt / lsf GATX
☐	HB-IJA	Airbus Industrie A320-214	533	F-WWIF*	0095	0595	2 CFMI CFM56-5B4/2	73500	CY150	FR-HP	Opfikon / lsf GATX
☐	HB-IJB	Airbus Industrie A320-214	545	F-WWII*	0095	0895	2 CFMI CFM56-5B4/2	73500	CY150	FR-HQ	Embrach / lsf GATX
☐	HB-IJC	Airbus Industrie A320-214	548	F-WWIJ*	0095	0995	2 CFMI CFM56-5B4/2	73500	CY150	FR-HS	Winkel / lsf GATX
☐	HB-IJD	Airbus Industrie A320-214	553	F-WWIE*	0095	1095	2 CFMI CFM56-5B4/2	73500	CY150	FR-JK	Regensdorf / lsf GATX
☐	HB-IJE	Airbus Industrie A320-214	559	F-WWIP*	0095	1195	2 CFMI CFM56-5B4/2	73500	CY150	FR-JL	Dübendorf / lsf GATX
☐	HB-IJF	Airbus Industrie A320-214	562	F-WWDQ*	0095	1295	2 CFMI CFM56-5B4/2	73500	CY150	FR-JM	Bellevue / lsf GATX
☐	HB-IJG	Airbus Industrie A320-214	566	F-WWIN*	0096	0196	2 CFMI CFM56-5B4/2	73500	CY150	FR-JP	Illnau-Effretikon / lsf GATX
☐	HB-IJH	Airbus Industrie A320-214	574	F-WWDN*	0096	0296	2 CFMI CFM56-5B4/2	73500	CY150	FR-JO	Wangen-Brüttisellen / lsf GATX
☐	HB-IJI	Airbus Industrie A320-214	577	F-WWDT*	0096	0396	2 CFMI CFM56-5B4/2	73500	CY150	FR-JS	Binningen / lsf GATX
☐	HB-IJJ	Airbus Industrie A320-214	585	F-WWIV*	0096	0596	2 CFMI CFM56-5B4/2	73500	CY150	FR-KL	Dietlikon / lsf GATX
☐	HB-IJK	Airbus Industrie A320-214	596	F-WWBH*	0096	0696	2 CFMI CFM56-5B4/2	73500	CY150	DM-PQ	Genthod / lsf GATX
☐	HB-IJL	Airbus Industrie A320-214	603	F-WWBK*	0096	0796	2 CFMI CFM56-5B4/2	73500	CY150	DM-PS	Bassersdorf / lsf GATX
☐	HB-IJM	Airbus Industrie A320-214	635	F-WWDD*	0096	1196	2 CFMI CFM56-5B4/2	73500	CY150	DM-QR	Wallisellen / lsf GATX
☐	HB-IJN	Airbus Industrie A320-214	643	F-WWDI*	0096	1296	2 CFMI CFM56-5B4/2	73500	CY150	DP-AS	Meyrin / lsf GATX
☐	HB-IJO	Airbus Industrie A320-214	673	F-WWBF*	0097	0497	2 CFMI CFM56-5B4/2P	73500	CY150	DP-CQ	Grand-Saconnex / lsf GATX
☐	HB-IJP	Airbus Industrie A320-214	681	F-WWBH*	0097	0597	2 CFMI CFM56-5B4/2P	73500	CY150	DP-EQ	Vernier / lsf GATX
☐	HB-IJQ	Airbus Industrie A320-214	701	F-WWDL*	0097	0697	2 CFMI CFM56-5B4/2P	73500	CY150	QS-JP	Niederhasli / lsf GATX
☐	HB-IJR	Airbus Industrie A320-214	703	F-WWDS*	0097	0797	2 CFMI CFM56-5B4/2P	73500	CY150	QS-JR	Aire-La-Ville / lsf GATX
☐	HB-IJS	Airbus Industrie A320-214	782	F-WWDS*	0098	0398	2 CFMI CFM56-5B4/2P	73500	CY150		Neerach / lsf GATX
☐	HB-IJT	Airbus Industrie A320-214	870	F-WWBX*	0098	0499	2 CFMI CFM56-5B4/2P	73500	CY150		Champagne / lsf GATX
☐	HB-IOA	Airbus Industrie A321-111	517	D-AVZS*	0094	0195	2 CFMI CFM56-5B1/2	83000	CY186	FR-KM	Neuchatel / lsf GATX
☐	HB-IOB	Airbus Industrie A321-111	519	D-AVZU*	0094	0295	2 CFMI CFM56-5B1/2	83000	CY186	FR-KP	Aargau / lsf GATX
☐	HB-IOC	Airbus Industrie A321-111	520	D-AVZV*	0095	0395	2 CFMI CFM56-5B1/2	83000	CY186	FR-KQ	Lausanne / lsf GATX
☐	HB-IOD	Airbus Industrie A321-111	522	D-AVZX*	0095	0495	2 CFMI CFM56-5B1/2	83000	CY186	FR-KS	Kloten / lsf GATX
☐	HB-IOE	Airbus Industrie A321-111	535	D-AVZC*	0095	0695	2 CFMI CFM56-5B1/2	83000	CY186	FR-LM	Solothurn / lsf GATX
☐	HB-IOF	Airbus Industrie A321-111	541	D-AVZE*	0095	0795	2 CFMI CFM56-5B1/2	83000	CY186	FR-LP	Winterthur / lsf GATX
☐	HB-IOG	Airbus Industrie A321-111	642	D-AVZH*	0097	0197	2 CFMI CFM56-5B1/2	83000	CY186	FR-LQ	Bülach / lsf GATX
☐	HB-IOH	Airbus Industrie A321-111	664	D-AVZL*	0097	0397	2 CFMI CFM56-5B1/P	83000	CY186	FR-LS	Würenlos / lsf GATX
☐	HB-IOI	Airbus Industrie A321-111	827	D-AVZY*	0098	0598	2 CFMI CFM56-5B1/2P	83000	CY186	HS-PR	lsf GATX
☐	HB-IOJ	Airbus Industrie A321-111	891	D-AVZJ*	0098	1198	2 CFMI CFM56-5B1/2P	83000	CY186		lsf GATX
☐	HB-IOK	Airbus Industrie A321-111	987		0099	0399	2 CFMI CFM56-5B1/2P	83000	CY186		lsf GATX
☐	HB-IOL	Airbus Industrie A321-111					2 CFMI CFM56-5B1/2P	83000	CY186		to be lsf GATX 1299
☐	HB-IPG	Airbus Industrie A310-322	404	F-WWCD*	0085	1285	2 PW JT9D-7R4E1	150000	F16C54Y105	DG-BK	Zug / lsf GATX -0699/for ILFC
☐	HB-IPN	Airbus Industrie A310-325 (ET)	672	F-WWCD*	0093	1195	2 PW PW4156A	164000	C42Y151	BJ-EQ	lsf GATX -0999 / for Airbus Ind.
☐	HB-IQA	Airbus Industrie A330-223	229	F-WWKS*	0098	0998	2 PW PW4168A	230000	F10C48Y166		Sion 2006 / lsf GATX
☐	HB-IQB	Airbus Industrie A330-223	240	F-WWKZ*	0098	1198	2 PW PW4168A	230000	F10C48Y166		Glarus / lsf GATX
☐	HB-IQC	Airbus Industrie A330-223	249	F-WWKI*	0098	1298	2 PW PW4168A	230000	F10C48Y166		Zug / lsf GATX
☐	HB-IQD	Airbus Industrie A330-223	253	F-WWKM*	0099	0299	2 PW PW4168A	230000	F10C48Y166		Liechtenstein / lsf GATX
☐	HB-IQE	Airbus Industrie A330-223	255	F-WWKB*	0099	0399	2 PW PW4168A	230000	F10C48Y166		Appenzell i.Rh. / lsf GATX
☐	HB-IQF	Airbus Industrie A330-223	262	F-WWKS*	0099	099	2 PW PW4168A	230000	F10C48Y166		lsf GATX
☐	HB-IQG	Airbus Industrie A330-223	275				2 PW PW4168A	230000	F10C48Y166		to be lsf GATX 0599
☐	HB-IQH	Airbus Industrie A330-223	288				2 PW PW4168A	230000	F10C48Y166		to be lsf GATX 0799
☐	HB-IQI	Airbus Industrie A330-223	291				2 PW PW4168A	230000	F10C48Y166		to be lsf GATX 0899
☐	HB-IQJ	Airbus Industrie A330-223	294				2 PW PW4168A	230000	F10C48Y166		to be lsf GATX 0899
☐	HB-IQK	Airbus Industrie A330-223	303				2 PW PW4168A	230000	F10C48Y166		to be lsf GATX 1099
☐	HB-IQL	Airbus Industrie A330-223	308				2 PW PW4168A	230000	F10C48Y166		to be lsf GATX 1199
☐	HB-IQM	Airbus Industrie A330-223	311				2 PW PW4168A	230000	F10C48Y166		to be lsf GATX 1299
☐	HB-IQN	Airbus Industrie A330-223	342				2 PW PW4168A	230000	F10C48Y166		to be lsf GATX 0500
☐	HB-IQO	Airbus Industrie A330-223	349				2 PW PW4168A	230000	F10C48Y166		to be lsf GATX 0700
☐	HB-IWA	Boeing (Douglas) MD-11	48443 / 458	N517MD*	0291	0391	3 PW PW4462	285990	F12C49Y180	AF-HQ	Obwalden / lsf GATX -0002-4/for FDX
☐	HB-IWB	Boeing (Douglas) MD-11	48444 / 459		0391	0391	3 PW PW4462	285990	F12C49Y180	AF-JQ	Graubünden / lsf GATX -0002-4/for FDX
☐	HB-IWC	Boeing (Douglas) MD-11	48445 / 460		0491	0491	3 PW PW4462	285990	F12C49Y180	AF-KQ	Schaffhausen / lsf GATX -0002-4/for FDX
☐	HB-IWD	Boeing (Douglas) MD-11	48446 / 463		0591	0591	3 PW PW4462	285990	F12C49Y180	AF-LQ	Thurgau / lsf GATX -0002-4/for FDX
☐	HB-IWE	Boeing (Douglas) MD-11	48447 / 464		0691	0691	3 PW PW4462	285990	F12C49Y180	AF-MQ	Nidwalden / lsf GATX -0002-4/for FDX
☐	HB-IWG	Boeing (Douglas) MD-11	48452 / 472		0991	0991	3 PW PW4462	285990	F12C49Y180	AG-BQ	lsf GATX -0002-4/for FDX/SR Asia-colors
☐	HB-IWH	Boeing (Douglas) MD-11	48453 / 473		0991	1091	3 PW PW4462	285990	F12C49Y180	AG-CQ	St. Gallen / lsf GATX -0002-4/for FDX
☐	HB-IWI	Boeing (Douglas) MD-11	48454 / 477		1091	1191	3 PW PW4462	285990	F12C49Y180	AG-DQ	Uri / lsf GATX -0002-4/for FDX
☐	HB-IWK	Boeing (Douglas) MD-11	48455 / 487		0192	0292	3 PW PW4462	283722	F12C49Y180	AG-EQ	Fribourg / lsf GATX -0002-4/for FDX
☐	HB-IWL	Boeing (Douglas) MD-11	48456 / 494		0392	0492	3 PW PW4462	285990	F12C49Y180	AG-FQ	Appenzell a.Rh. / lsfGATX-0002-4/forFDX
☐	HB-IWM	Boeing (Douglas) MD-11	48457 / 498		0492	0692	3 PW PW4462	283722	F12C49Y180	AG-HQ	Jura / lsf GATX -0002-4/for FDX
☐	HB-IWN	Boeing (Douglas) MD-11	48539 / 571		0694	0794	3 PW PW4462	285990	F12C49Y180	AG-JQ	lsf GATX -0002-4/for FDX/SR Asia-colors
☐	HB-IWO	Boeing (Douglas) MD-11	48540 / 611		0097	0397	3 PW PW4462	285990	F12C49Y180	MS-DE	Schwyz / lsf GATX -0002-4/for FDX
☐	HB-IWP	Boeing (Douglas) MD-11	48634 / 614		0097	0797	3 PW PW4462	285990	F12C49Y180	MS-DF	Basel-Land / lsf GATX -0002-4/for FDX
☐	HB-IWQ	Boeing (Douglas) MD-11	48541 / 621		1197	1297	3 PW PW4462	285990	F12C49Y180	MS-DG	Valais / lsf GATX -0002-4/for FDX
☐	HB-IWR	Boeing (Douglas) MD-11	48484 / 484	D-AERB	1291	1098	3 PW PW4462	283722	F12C49Y180		Bern / lsf GATX -0002-4/for FDX
☐	HB-IWS	Boeing (Douglas) MD-11	48485 / 502	D-AERW	0592	1198	3 PW PW4462	283722	F12C49Y180		Ticino / lsf GATX -0002-4/for FDX
☐	HB-IWT	Boeing (Douglas) MD-11	48486 / 509	D-AERX	0092	1198	3 PW PW4462	283722	F12C49Y180		Basel / lsf GATX -0002-4/for FDX
☐	HB-IWU	Boeing (Douglas) MD-11	48538 / 533	D-AERZ	0193	1098	3 PW PW4462	283722	F12C49Y180		Luzern / lsf GATX -0002-4/for FDX
☐	HB-	Airbus Industrie A340-642					4 RR Trent 556	365000			to be lsf GATX 0402
☐	HB-	Airbus Industrie A340-642					4 RR Trent 556	365000			to be lsf GATX 0502
☐	HB-	Airbus Industrie A340-642					4 RR Trent 556	365000			to be lsf GATX 0602
☐	HB-	Airbus Industrie A340-642					4 RR Trent 556	365000			to be lsf GATX 0702
☐	HB-	Airbus Industrie A340-642					4 RR Trent 556	365000			to be lsf GATX 0802
☐	HB-	Airbus Industrie A340-642					4 RR Trent 556	365000			to be lsf GATX 0003
☐	HB-	Airbus Industrie A340-642					4 RR Trent 556	365000			to be lsf GATX 0003
☐	HB-	Airbus Industrie A340-642					4 RR Trent 556	365000			to be lsf GATX 0003
☐	HB-	Airbus Industrie A340-642					4 RR Trent 556	365000			to be lsf GATX 0003
☐	HB-IGD	Boeing 747-357 (M)	22705 / 576	N1784B*	0083	0383	4 PW JT9D-7R4G2	371945	F18C66Y181/Plts	DE-GK	Basel / lsf GATX till 0799
☐	HB-IGE	Boeing 747-357	22995 / 585	N221GE	0083	1283	4 PW JT9D-7R4G2	371945	F18C66Y312	DE-GL	Genève / lsf GATX till 0100
☐	HB-IGF	Boeing 747-357	22996 / 586	N221GF	0083	1183	4 PW JT9D-7R4G2	371945	F18C66Y312	CM-DE	Zürich / lsf GATX till 1299

SWISS AIR-AMBULANCE, Ltd = SAZ (Schweiz. Luft-Ambulanz, AG) (Subsidiary of Swiss Air-Rescue – Schweiz. Rettungsflugwacht / REGA) Zurich

Postfach, CH-8058 Zürich-Flughafen, Switzerland ☎ (1) 654 33 11 Tx: 815815 reg ch Fax: (1) 654 33 22 SITA: n/a

F: 1952 ✝✝✝ 250 Head: Kurt Bolliger ICAO: SWISS AMBULANCE Net: http://www.swiss-air-ambulance.com REGA means: Schweiz. Rettungsflugwacht / Garde Aérienne Suisse de Sauvetage / Guardia Aerea Svizzera di soccorso / Swiss Air-Rescue. Helicopters are operates from bases at: Basel, Berne, Erstfeld, Gsteigwiler, Lausanne, Locarno, Samedan, St. Gallen, Untervaz & Zurich.

☐	HB-XWA	Agusta A109K2	10001		0091	1291	2 TU Arriel 1K1	2850	Ambulance		
☐	HB-XWB	Agusta A109K2	10002		0092	0492	2 TU Arriel 1K1	2850	Ambulance		
☐	HB-XWC	Agusta A109K2	10003		0092	0093	2 TU Arriel 1K1	2850	Ambulance		
☐	HB-XWD	Agusta A109K2	10004		0092	0792	2 TU Arriel 1K1	2850	Ambulance		
☐	HB-XWG	Agusta A109K2	10007		0093	0693	2 TU Arriel 1K1	2850	Ambulance		
☐	HB-XWH	Agusta A109K2	10008		0093	1193	2 TU Arriel 1K1	2850	Ambulance		
☐	HB-XWI	Agusta A109K2	10009		0093	1193	2 TU Arriel 1K1	2850	Ambulance		
☐	HB-XWJ	Agusta A109K2	10010		0094	0794	2 TU Arriel 1K1	2850	Ambulance		
☐	HB-XWK	Agusta A109K2	10011		0094	1294	2 TU Arriel 1K1	2850	Ambulance		
☐	HB-XWL	Agusta A109K2	10012		0094	0994	2 TU Arriel 1K1	2850	Ambulance		
☐	HB-XWM	Agusta A109K2	10013		0094	1294	2 TU Arriel 1K1	2850	Ambulance		
☐	HB-XWN	Agusta A109K2	10014		0095	1295	2 TU Arriel 1K1	2850	Ambulance		
☐	HB-XWO	Agusta A109K2	10015		0095	0595	2 TU Arriel 1K1	2850	Ambulance		
☐	HB-XWP	Agusta A109K2	10027		0095	0795	2 TU Arriel 1K1	2850	Ambulance		
☐	HB-VIK	Hawker 800B (BAe 125-800B)	258091	G-5-560*	0087		2 GA TFE731-5R-1H	12428	Ambulance	CK-FP	
☐	HB-VIL	Hawker 800B (BAe 125-800B)	258097		0087		2 GA TFE731-5R-1H	12428	Ambulance	CK-GP	
☐	HB-IKT	Canadair CL-601-3A (CL-600-2B16) Challen.	5003	N778XX	0087	0091	2 GE CF34-3A	19550	Ambulance	CH-LR	

190 registration type of aircraft cn/fn ex/ex* mfd del powered by mtow kg configuration selcal name/fln/specialitites/remarks

SWISS AIR FORCE = SUI (Einsatzstelle Lufttransport, Alpnach) — Berne

Einsatzstelle Lufttransport, CH-6055 Alpnach, Switzerland ☎ (41) 672 56 20 Tx: none Fax: (41) 670 19 63 SITA: n/a
F: n/a ✈✈✈ n/a Head: n/a ICAO: AIRFORCE SWITZERLAND Net: n/a Non-commercial military organisation conducting photo/calibration, survey VIP-transport flights for the Swiss Government and its agencies.

☐ HB-LID	De Havilland DHC-6 Twin Otter 300	466	C-GPXO-X*	0076	0576	2 PWC PT6A-27	5670	Calibrator		opf Schweiz. Grundbuch-Vermessung
☐ HB-GII	Beech Super King Air 350C (B300C)	FN-1		0093	1193	2 PWC PT6A-60A	6804	Photo/Survey		opf Bundesamt für Landestopographie
☐ T-781	Learjet 35A	35A-068	HB-VEM	0076		2 GA TFE731-2-2B	8301	VIP		
☐ T-783	Dassault Falcon 50	67	HB-IEP	0081	0196	3 GA TFE731-3-1C	17600	VIP		

SWISS WORLD AIRWAYS, S.A. - SWA = SO / SWO — Geneva

Case Postale 792, CH-1215 Genève-Aéroport, Switzerland ☎ (22) 717 84 90 Tx: none Fax: (22) 717 84 94 SITA: n/a
F: 1997 ✈✈✈ n/a Head: Pierre A Porta IATA: 681 ICAO: SWISSWORLD Net: n/a Suspended operations (with Boeing 767-200 aircraft) 021298. Intends to restart.

TAG AVIATION, S.A. = FP / FPG (Member of TAG Group / formerly Aeroleasing, SA & ALG Aeroleasing, AG) — Geneva

Case postale 36, CH-1215 Genève-Aéroport, Switzerland ☎ (22) 717 00 00 Tx: 415731 plane ch Fax: (22) 717 00 07 SITA: GVAOPFP
F: 1966 ✈✈✈ 190 Head: Ernst Saxer ICAO: TAG AVIATION Net: http://www.tagaviation.com Also operates a number of non-commercial executive aircraft on behalf of private private companies.

☐ HB-VIP	Cessna 550 Citation II	550-0469	VR-BIZ	0083	0296	2 PWC JT15D-4	6033	Exec 7-8 Pax		
☐ HB-VIT	Cessna 550 Citation II	550-0197	N44FC	0080	0591	2 PWC JT15D-4	6033	Exec 7-8 Pax		
☐ HB-VJI	Learjet 31	31-011		0089	0889	2 GA TFE731-2-3B	7711	Exec 7-8 Pax		lsf TAG Leasing S.A.
☐ HB-VLR	Learjet 31A	31A-127	N80727	0096	0197	2 GA TFE731-2-3B	7711	Exec 7-8 Pax	GH-DK	
☐ HB-VJJ	Learjet 35A	35A-649		0089		2 GA TFE731-2-2B	8301	Exec 7-8 Pax	AC-BQ	lsf TAG Leasing S.A.
☐ HB-VJK	Learjet 35A	35A-651		0089	0989	2 GA TFE731-2-2B	8301	Exec 7-8 Pax	AC-EQ	
☐ HB-VJL	Learjet 35A	35A-653		0089	1189	2 GA TFE731-2-2B	8301	Exec 7-8 Pax	AC-DQ	
☐ HB-VKE	Dassault Falcon 10	7	D-CASH	0074	0691	2 GA TFE731-2-1C	8500	Exec 7-8 Pax		lsf Ilta Trade Finance SA
☐ HB-VJV	Dassault Falcon 20E-5	237	VR-BKH	0071	0290	2 GA TFE731-5AR-2C	13200	Exec 9 Pax	DM-GL	cvtd 20E
☐ HB-VKO	Dassault Falcon 20F-5	257	F-GKDD	0071	0392	2 GA TFE731-5AR-2C	13200	Exec 9 Pax	DM-GH	lsf TAG Leasing S.A. / cvtd 20F
☐ HB-IAZ	Dassault Falcon 2000	30	F-WWMB*	0096	1296	2 CFE CFE738-1-1B	16238	Exec 10-13 Pax	FJ-HS	lsf Alag AG
☐ HB-IBH	Dassault Falcon 2000	42	F-WWMG*	0096	0897	2 CFE CFE738-1-1B	16556	Exec 10-13 Pax	BM-PR	lsf UBS Leasing S.A.
☐ HB-IVR	Canadair CL-604 (CL-600-2B16) Challen.	5318	HB-IKQ	0096	0198	2 GE CF34-3B	21863	Exec 11 Pax	FS-CR	lsf Sintez SA
☐ HB-IAH	Dassault Falcon 900EX	28	F-WWFZ*	0098	1198	3 GA TFE731-60-1C	22226	Exec 12 Pax	FS-DH	lsf Credit Suisse Leasing
☐ HB-IDJ	Canadair Regional Jet 100SE (CL-600-2B19)	7136	VP-CRJ	0096	0198	2 GE CF34-3B1	24041	Exec 16 Pax	AB-DH	lsf TAG Aviation Services Ltd
☐ HB-IVU	Canadair Regional Jet 100SE (CL-600-2B19)	7176	N176SE	0097	0299	2 GE CF34-3B1	24041	Exec 16 Pax		lsf Credit Suisse Leasing

TARMAC AVIATION, SA — Lugano

Via Aeroporto, CH-6982 Agno, Switzerland ☎ (91) 605 30 77 Tx: none Fax: (91) 605 31 52 SITA: n/a
F: 1984 ✈✈✈ 5 Head: Rolf Marending Net: n/a

☐ HB-XXW	Eurocopter (Aerosp.) AS350B2 Ecureuil	2405	N450HH	0090	0391	1 TU Arriel 1D1	2250			
☐ HB-LGR	Cessna 340	3400068	N5916M	0072		2 CO TSIO-520-K	2710			lsf pvt

TRANS-HELI AIR-GLACIERS, SA (Subsidiary of Air-Glaciers, SA / formerly Trans-Heli, SA) — Collombey-Heliport & Lausanne-Blécherette

Rue Pré-du-Pont, CH-1868 Collombey, Switzerland ☎ (24) 473 70 70 Tx: none Fax: (24) 473 70 71 SITA: n/a
F: 1972 ✈✈✈ 11 Head: Pierre Belaieff Net: n/a Beside helicopters listed, uses additional (SA315B Lama) from AIR-GLACIERS when required.

☐ HB-XGP	Eurocopter (Aerosp.) SA315B Lama	2349	F-BVUG*	0073		1 TU Artouste IIIB	1950			

TRANSWING, AG — Basel/Mulhouse-EuroAirport & Berne

Sonnmattstr. 2, CH-3415 Hasle-Rüegsau, Switzerland ☎ (34) 461 52 25 Tx: none Fax: (34) 461 52 25 SITA: n/a
F: 1992 ✈✈✈ n/a Head: Andreas Ramseier Net: n/a

☐ HB-LNX	Piper PA-31T2 Cheyenne II XL	31T-8166050	N700XL	0082		2 PWC PT6A-135	4297	7 Pax		jtly opw Avcon

ZIMEX AVIATION, Ltd = C4 / IMX (Subsidiary of Zimex Aviation Holding, AG) — Zurich & Overseas

Postfach, CH-8058 Zürich-Flughafen, Switzerland ☎ (1) 815 53 20 Tx: 816091 air ch Fax: (1) 815 53 21 SITA: n/a
F: 1969 ✈✈✈ 180 Head: Hannes Ziegler ICAO: ZIMEX Net: n/a

☐ HB-LQW	Partenavia AP68TP-300 Spartacus	8001		0084	0789	2 AN 250-B17C	2600	Surveyer		
☐ HB-FEZ	Pilatus PC-6/B2-H4 Turbo Porter	699		1069		1 PWC PT6A-27	2800			cvtd B2-H2
☐ HB-FFA	Pilatus PC-6/B2-H4 Turbo Porter	700		0069		1 PWC PT6A-27	2800			cvtd B2-H2
☐ HB-FFI	Pilatus PC-6/B2-H4 Turbo Porter	671		0068	1172	1 PWC PT6A-27	2800			cvtd B2-H2
☐ HB-FFV	Pilatus PC-6/B2-H4 Turbo Porter	817	9Q-CTH	1282	0488	1 PWC PT6A-27	2800			cvtd B2-H2
☐ HB-FGA	Pilatus PC-6/B2-H4 Turbo Porter	726	F-GAMV	0071	1080	1 PWC PT6A-27	2800			cvtd B2-H2
☐ HB-FGI	Pilatus PC-6/B2-H4 Turbo Porter	810		0081	0881	1 PWC PT6A-27	2800			cvtd B2-H2
☐ HB-FHZ	Pilatus PC-6/B2-H4 Turbo Porter	840	ZS-MTP	0084	1292	1 PWC PT6A-27	2800			cvtd B2-H2
☐ HB-FIE	Pilatus PC-6/B2-H4 Turbo Porter	748	A4O-AL	0075	0384	1 PWC PT6A-27	2800			cvtd B2-H2
☐ HB-FKF	Pilatus PC-6/B2-H4 Turbo Porter	815	G-OAPA	0082	0188	1 PWC PT6A-27	2800			cvtd B2-H2
☐ HB-FKR	Pilatus PC-6/B2-H4 Turbo Porter	872		0090	0196	1 PWC PT6A-27	2800			
☐ HB-FLA	Pilatus PC-6/B2-H4 Turbo Porter	905		1293	0294	1 PWC PT6A-27	2800			
☐ HB-FLB	Pilatus PC-6/B2-H4 Turbo Porter	906		0194	0394	1 PWC PT6A-27	2800			
☐ HB-FLE	Pilatus PC-6/B2-H4 Turbo Porter	912		1294	0196	1 PWC PT6A-27	2800			
☐ HB-FLG	Pilatus PC-6/B2-H4 Turbo Porter	910		0596	0297	1 PWC PT6A-27	2800			
☐ HB-FLH	Pilatus PC-6/B2-H4 Turbo Porter	918		0097	0497	1 PWC PT6A-27	2800			lsf Pilatus Flugzeugwerke AG
☐ HB-GJD	Beech King Air 200C	BL-7	F-GJBJ	0080	0093	2 PWC PT6A-41	5670			
☐ HB-LOK	De Havilland DHC-6 Twin Otter 300	658	D-IASL	0080	0984	2 PWC PT6A-27	5670			
☐ HB-LPA	De Havilland DHC-6 Twin Otter 300	657	SE-GXN	1179	0286	2 PWC PT6A-27	5670			
☐ HB-LQV	De Havilland DHC-6 Twin Otter 300	643	5Y-LQV	0079	0489	2 PWC PT6A-27	5670			lsf Debis Leasing AG
☐ HB-LRF	De Havilland DHC-6 Twin Otter 300	794	N794CC	0082	0290	2 PWC PT6A-27	5670			
☐ HB-LRN	De Havilland DHC-6 Twin Otter 300	636	PK-YPE	0079	0191	2 PWC PT6A-27	5670			lsf Credit Suisse Leasing
☐ HB-LRO	De Havilland DHC-6 Twin Otter 300	523	F-GKTO	0077	0591	2 PWC PT6A-27	5670			lsf Credit Suisse Leasing / rebuit 1991
☐ HB-LRR	De Havilland DHC-6 Twin Otter 300	505	5Y-KZT	0076	0791	2 PWC PT6A-27	5670			lsf Credit Suisse Leasing
☐ HB-LRS	De Havilland DHC-6 Twin Otter 300	502	5Y-UAU	0976	0791	2 PWC PT6A-27	5670			
☐ HB-LSN	De Havilland DHC-6 Twin Otter 300	695	C-FZSP	0080	0497	2 PWC PT6A-27	5670			lsf Beau Del Leasing Inc.

HC = ECUADOR (Republic of Ecuador) (Republica de Ecuador)

Capital: Quito Official Language: Spanish Population: 12,0 million Square Km: 283561 Dialling code: +593 Year established: 1809 Acting political head: Jamil Mahuad (President)

Government / Corporate / Executive / VIP Aircraft

☐ FAE001	BAe (HS) 748-267 Srs 2A	1684 / 155	HC-AUK	0070	1170	2 RR Dart 534-2	20183	VIP / 20 Pax		FAE684 / Fuerza Aérea Ecuatoriana

AECA - Aeroservicios Ecuatorianos, CA = EAE — Guayaquil

Apartado 4113, Guayaquil, Ecuador ☎ (4) 28 81 10 Tx: n/a Fax: (4) 28 16 38 SITA: n/a
F: n/a ✈✈✈ n/a Head: Capt. Alfredo F. del Monaco ICAO: AECA Net: n/a Aircraft below MTOW 1361 kg: Cessna 182.

☐ HC-AKG	Piper PA-23-250 Aztec C	27-2926		0065		2 LY IO-540-C4B5	2359			
☐ HC-BEJ	Cessna 310R II	310R0971		0077		2 CO IO-520-M	2495			
☐ HC-BJN	Cessna 402B	402B0241		0072		2 CO TSIO-520-E	2858			
☐ HC-BGP	Boeing 707-321C	19273 / 580	N451RN	0567	0394	4 PW JT3D-3B (HK2/COM)	146149	Freighter	GL-HM	
☐ HC-BTB	Boeing 707-330C	18937 / 451	LZ-PVA	0065	1196	4 PW JT3D-3B (HK2/COM)	146500	Freighter		lsf Air Taxi International

AEROGAL - Aerolineas Galapagos, SA — Shell-Mera & Quito

PO Box 17-01-2444, Quito, Ecuador ☎ (2) 44 19 50 Tx: 22205 aerogal ed Fax: (2) 43 04 87 SITA: n/a
F: 1986 ✈✈✈ 20 Head: Carlos Serrano Ordonez Net: n/a

☐ HC-BNV	Dornier DO 28D-2 Skyservant	4343	D-IAYB	0079		2 LY IGSO-540-A1E	4142			
☐ HC-BOK	Dornier DO 28D-2 Skyservant	4305	D-IDLH	0075		2 LY IGSO-540-A1E	4142			
☐ HC-BQS	Dornier DO 28D-2 Skyservant	4306	D-IAEG	0075		2 LY IGSO-540-A1E	4142			
☐ HC-BSL	Fairchild Ind. F-27F	56	N28FA	0059	0393	2 RR Dart 529-7E	19051			cvtd F-27A
☐ HC-BSV	Fairchild Ind. F-27F	71	N870H	0059	1093	2 RR Dart 529-7E	19051			cvtd F-27A

ALAS DE SOCORRO (Wings of Help) — Shell Mera (Pastaza)

Casilla 6228, Quito, Ecuador ☎ (2) 79 51 83 Tx: n/a Fax: n/a SITA: n/a
F: n/a ✈✈✈ n/a Head: n/a Net: n/a Non-commercial development company conducting relief missions in remote aereas.

☐ HC-BAB	Cessna A185F Skywagon	18502669		0075		1 CO IO-520-D	1520			
☐ HC-BND	Cessna A185F Skywagon II	18503929		0079		1 CO IO-520-D	1520			
☐ HC-BLP	Cessna TU206G Turbo Stationair 6 II	U20606449		0082		1 CO TSIO-520-M	1633			
☐ HC-BMO	Cessna TU206G Turbo Stationair 6 II	U20605349	N6150U	0080		1 CO TSIO-520-M	1633			
☐ HC-BQV	Cessna TU206G Turbo Stationair 6 II	U20606662	N9791Z	0082	0691	1 CO TSIO-520-M	1633			
☐ HC-BXB	Cessna TU206G Turbo Stationair 6 II	U20604322	N756SP	0078	0097	1 CO TSIO-520-M	1633			
☐ HC-BXK	Cessna TU206G Turbo Stationair 6 II	U20604404	N756SP	0078	0097	1 CO TSIO-520-M	1633			

AUSTRO AEREO, S.A. — Cuenca

Hermano Miguel 542, Cuenca, (Guayas), Ecuador ☎ (7) 86 87 48 Tx: none Fax: (7) 84 86 59 SITA: n/a
F: 1996 ✈✈✈ 47 Head: John Mora IATA: 312 Net: n/a

☐ HC-BXC	Fairchild Ind. FH-227B	533	F-WQFK	0067	0597	2 RR Dart 532-7	19888	Y44		Ciudad de Cuenca

191 registration type of aircraft cn/fn ex/ex* mfd del powered by mtow kg configuration selcal name/fln/specialitites/remarks

CEDTA – Compania Ecuatoriana de Transportes Aéreos, CA — Guayaquil

Casilla Correo 4400, Guayaquil, Ecuador ☎ (4) 30 19 54 Tx: n/a Fax: (4) 32 73 36 SITA: n/a
F: 1950 👥 15 Head: Arturo Serrano ICAO: CEDTA Net: n/a

☐ HC-BDX	Britten-Norman BN-2A Islander	51	F-OGEB	0069		2 LY O-540-E4C5	2722	9 Pax		Senor de la Buena Esperanza

ECUATORIANA de Aviacion, S.A. = EU / EEA (Subsidiary of VASP, Brazil / formerly Empresa Ecuatoriana de Aviacion, SA) — Quito

Colon y Reina Victoria, Condominio Almagro, CP505, Quito, Ecuador ☎ (2) 56 30 03 Tx: 21143 eea ed Fax: (2) 56 39 20 SITA: UICDDEU
F: 1957 👥 n/a Head: Davidson Botelho IATA: 341 ICAO: ECUATORIANA Net: n/a

☐ HC-BVM	Boeing 727-2M7 (A)	21502 / 1339	N725RW	0578	1096	3 PW JT8D-17R	88360			lsf PACA
☐ HC-BVT	Boeing 727-287 (A)	22603 / 1732	N914PG	0081	0197	3 PW JT8D-17	86411			lsf PACA
☐ HC-BXU	Boeing 727-287 (A)	21689 / 1427	N915PG	0078	1097	3 PW JT8D-17	86411			lsf PACA
☐ PP-SFH	Airbus Industrie A310-304	552	F-GKTD	0090	1097	2 GE CF6-80C2A2	157000		LQ-CJ	lsf VSP
☐ PP-SFB	Boeing (Douglas) DC-10-30	46575 / 57	HC-BKO	0072	0083	3 GE CF6-50C	256284	C18Y251	AE-CG	lsf VSP

ECUAVIA, Ltda — Guayaquil

PO Box 3364, Aeropuerto Simon Bolivar, Guayaquil, Ecuador ☎ (4) 28 96 28 Tx: 043464 ecuvia ed Fax: (4) 28 22 52 SITA: n/a
F: 1949 👥 25 Head: Ing. Carlos L. Estrada ICAO: ECUAVIA Net: n/a Aircraft/Ag-aircraft below MTOW 1361/5000 kg: Bell 47J, Piper PA-14, PA-18 & PA-28

☐ HC-BJC	Bell 206B JetRanger III	3375	N2067V	0080		1 AN 250-C20B	1451			
☐ HC-BJP	Piper PA-44-180 Seminole	44-8195023		0081		2 LY O-360-E1A6D	1724			
☐ HC-BDY	Piper PA-34-200T Seneca II	34-7770328		0077		2 CO TSIO-360-E	2073			
☐ HC-BTJ	Cessna 550 Citation II	550-0016	N276AL	0078	0794	2 PWC JT15D-4	6033			

HELIPET – Helicopteros Petroleros, SA (formerly Ecuavia Oriente, SA – EOSA) — Quito

PO Box 17-01-3418, Quito, Ecuador ☎ (2) 24 74 15 Tx: none Fax: (2) 43 07 13 SITA: n/a
F: 1988 👥 69 Head: Capt. Gerardo Arias Net: n/a

☐ HC-BIK	Bell 206B JetRanger III	856	N14818	0072		1 AN 250-C20B	1451	4 Pax		cvtd JetRanger
☐ HC-BUY	Eurocopter (Aerosp.) SA315B Lama	2014 / 6	N2128Z	0068	1095	1 TU Artouste IIIB1	1950	4 Pax		cvtd SA318C Alouette II
☐ HC-BNJ	Bell 206L-1 LongRanger II	45191	N5007X	0078		1 AN 250-C28B	1882	6 Pax		
☐ HC-BQP	Bell 206L-1 LongRanger II	45588	N55EA	0081		1 AN 250-C28B	1882	6 Pax		

ICARO – Instituto Civil Aeronautico, SA (Associated with Héli-Union, France) — Quito & Coca

Casilla 4996 C.C.I., Quito, Ecuador ☎ (2) 43 98 68 Tx: n/a Fax: (2) 43 98 67 SITA: n/a
F: 1971 👥 60 Head: Capt. Guido Saltos M. Net: n/a Aircraft below MTOW 1361 kg: Cessna 172.

☐ HC-BXA	Bell 206L-3 LongRanger III	51606	C-FLYO	0092	0397	1 AN 250-C30P	1882			
☐ HC-BPF	Twin (Aero) Turbo Commander 690A	11235	N57235	0075		2 GA TPE331-5-251K	4649			
☐ HC-BPX	Twin (Aero) Turbo Commander 690A	11187	N440CA	0074		2 GA TPE331-5-251K	4649			
☐ HC-BVP	Cessna 500 Citation I	500-0389	ANE-201	0078	0097	2 PWC JT15D-1A	5375			
☐ HC-BSR	Beech Catpass 200	BB-483	N27BG	0079	0893	2 PWC PT6A-41	5675			cvtd King Air 200
☐ F-BXOY	Eurocopter (Aerosp.) SA330J Puma	1358	PT-HTY	0075	0398	2 TU Turmo IVC	7400			lsf HLU
☐ HC-	Beech 1900D Airliner	UE-317	N22908*	0098	0798	2 PWC PT6A-67D	7688			

LAN ECUADOR – Lineas Aéreas Nacionales Ecuador, SA — Guayaquil

Avenida de Las Americas sn, Casilla 10908, Guayaquil, Ecuador ☎ (4) 28 08 98 Tx: 42705 lanelu ed Fax: (4) 28 39 54 SITA: n/a
F: 1966 👥 27 Head: Mario Roche León Net: n/a Aircraft / Ag-Aircraft below MTOW 1361 / 5000 kg: Air Tractor AT-402B/AT-502B & Grumman G-164A/B

☐ HC-BQA	Cessna T337H Super Skymaster II	33701947		0080		2 CO TSIO-360-HB	2100			
☐ HC-BUS	Piper PA-31T2 Cheyenne II XL	31T-8166064	N7194Y	0081	0695	2 PWC PT6A-135	4297			

LANSA – Lineas Aéreas Nacionales, SA — Guayaquil

Casilla Correo 4400, Guayaquil, Ecuador ☎ (4) 30 12 61 Tx: n/a Fax: (4) 32 73 36 SITA: n/a
F: 1966 👥 10 Head: Arturo Serrano ICAO: LANSA Net: n/a

☐ HC-BHC	Britten-Norman BN-2A Islander	59	N863JA	0069		2 LY O-540-E4C5	2722	9 Pax		

NICA Taxi Aéreo (Nacional Importadora Compañia Anonima dba) — Bahia de Caraquez

Casilla 17-01-222, Quito, Ecuador ☎ (2) 23 75 47 Tx: 22745 olaray ed Fax: (2) 50 23 99 SITA: n/a
F: 1983 👥 12 Head: Dr. Jorge W. Lara Net: n/a Aircraft below MTOW 1361 kg: Cessna 172 & Mooney M20.

☐ HC-BOD	Piper PA-32-300 Cherokee SIX	32-40531	N4193R	0068		1 LY IO-540-K1A5	1542	5 Pax		

PETROPRODUCCION – Unidad de Aviacion (Division of Petroecuador / formerly Petroecuador-TEXACO, Petroamazonas & CEPE-TEXACO) — Quito & Lago Agrio

Pasaje Amazonas sn y Rio Arajuno, Quito, Ecuador ☎ (2) 43 99 85 Tx: n/a Fax: (2) 44 91 69 SITA: n/a
F: 1970 👥 34 Head: Capt. Victor Ayala C. Net: n/a Private, non-commercial company conducting corporate flights for itself only.

☐ HC-BJS	Pilatus PC-6/B2-H2 Turbo Porter	724	N2386	0071	0081	1 PWC PT6A-27	2770	Corporate 9 Pax		
☐ HC-BHD	Fairchild Ind. F-27J	122	N994	0066	0081	2 RR Dart 532-7	19091	Corporate 31 Pax		
☐ HC-AYM	Fairchild Ind. FH-227E	511	N7805M	0066	1072	2 RR Dart 532-7L	19773	Corporate 38 Pax		cvtd FH227C / std OPF

SAETA Air Ecuador = EH / SET (Sociedad Anonima Ecuatoriana de Transportes Aéreos, S.A. dba) — Quito

Avenida C.J. Arosemena KM 2.5, Guayaquil, Ecuador ☎ (4) 20 02 77 Tx: 22570 dunn ed Fax: (4) 20 51 15 SITA: n/a
F: 1967 👥 600 Head: Roberto D. Barreiro IATA: 156 ICAO: SAETA Net: http://www.saeta.com.ec

☐ HC-BUJ	Airbus Industrie A320-232	527	F-WWDI*	0095	0395	2 IAE V2527-A5	77000	Y150		lsf ILFC
☐ HC-BUM	Airbus Industrie A320-232	530	F-WWDP*	0095	0595	2 IAE V2527-A5	77000	Y150		Pichinca / lsf ILFC
☐ HC-BJL	Boeing 727-95	19596 / 479	PP-VLR	0067	1081	3 PW JT8D-9A	76657	Y108		partly lst/jointly opw SAN
☐ HC-BPL	Boeing 727-31	18753 / 83	N846TW	0064	1288	3 PW JT8D-7	72802	Y108		std GYE
☐ HC-BRG	Boeing 727-282 (A)	20973 / 1099	CS-TBS	0075	1191	3 PW JT8D-17	86409	Y162	DM-GK	
☐ HC-BVY	Boeing 727-251 (A)	21505 / 1391	N294US	0978	0497	3 PW JT8D-15/-15A	80059	Y162		lsf Airlease Finance

SAN – Servicios Aéreos Nacionales, S.A. = WB / SAN — Guayaquil

Avenida C.J. Arosemena KM 2.5, Guayaquil, Ecuador ☎ (4) 20 02 77 Tx: 043275 sangye ed Fax: (4) 20 11 53 SITA: n/a
F: 1964 👥 140 Head: Patricio Suarez IATA: 739 ICAO: AEREOS Net: n/a

☐ HC-BJL	Boeing 727-95	19596 / 479	PP-VLR	0067	1095	3 PW JT8D-9A	76657	Y108		partly lsf/jtly opw SAETA

SERVICIO AEREO MISIONAL – S.A.M. (Div.of Mision Salesiana de Oriente/Assoc.with Min.Educacion/Min.Salud/Fed. Centros Shuar) — Macas (Morona-Santiago)

Casilla 692, Quito, Ecuador ☎ (2) 55 10 12 Tx: none Fax: (7) 70 02 59 SITA: n/a
F: 1975 👥 10 Head: P. Barale Adriano Net: n/a

☐ HC-BTC	Helio HT-295 Trigear Courier	1717	N7711Y	0074	0194	1 LY GO-480-G1D6	1633	5 Pax		
☐ HC-BUG	Helio HT-295 Trigear Courier	1703	N68870	0074	1294	1 LY GO-480-G1D6	1633	5 Pax		
☐ HC-BNT	Dornier DO 28D-2 Skyservant	4342	D-IAYA	0078		2 LY IGSO-540-A1E	4015	12 Pax		

TAME – Transportes Aéreos Mercantiles Ecuatorianos, CA = EQ / TAE (Commercial div.of Fuerza Aérea Ecuatoriana/formerly TAME-Transp. Aéreos Militares Ecuatorianos, CA) — Quito

Avenida Amazonas 1354, PO Box 17-07-8736, Quito, Ecuador ☎ (2) 50 93 75 Tx: 22567 tame ed Fax: (2) 56 10 52 SITA: n/a
F: 1962 👥 730 Head: Gen. Julio Espinosa IATA: 269 ICAO: TAME Net: n/a

☐ FAE447	De Havilland DHC-6 Twin Otter 300	832		0086	0187	2 PWC PT6A-27	5670	Y19		occ lsf Fuerza Aérea Ecuatoriana
☐ FAE448	De Havilland DHC-6 Twin Otter 300	833		0086	0187	2 PWC PT6A-27	5670	Y19		occ lsf Fuerza Aérea Ecuatoriana
☐ FAE449	De Havilland DHC-6 Twin Otter 300	834		0086	0187	2 PWC PT6A-27	5670	Y19		occ lsf Fuerza Aérea Ecuatoriana
☐ HC-AUD	BAe (HS) 748-246 Srs 2A	1682 / 168		0070	1070	2 RR Dart 534-2	20183	Y38		FAE682
☐ HC-BEY	BAe (HS) 748-285 Srs 2A (SCD)	1739 / 220		0076	0476	2 RR Dart 534-2	20183	Y38		FAE739
☐ HC-BMD	Fokker F28 Fellowship 4000 (F28 Mk4000)	11220	PH-ZCH*	0084	1285	2 RR Spey 555-15P	33112	Y85		FAE220 / Ciudad de Loja
☐ HC-	Fokker F28 Fellowship 4000 (F28 Mk4000)	11112	SE-DGE	0076	0299	2 RR Spey 555-15P	33112	Y85		
☐ HC-BLE	Boeing 727-134	19691 / 487	RP-C1240	0067	0684	3 PW JT8D-7A	76657	Y123		FAE691
☐ HC-BLF	Boeing 727-134	19692 / 498	RP-C1241	0067	0784	3 PW JT8D-9A	76657	Y123		FAE692
☐ HC-BLV	Boeing 727-17	20328 / 806	G-BKCG	0070	0485	3 PW JT8D-9A	76657	Y126		FAE328
☐ HC-BHM	Boeing 727-2T3 (A)	22078 / 1644	N1293E*	0080	0980	3 PW JT8D-17	88452	Y173		FAE078 / Cotopaxi
☐ HC-BRI	Boeing 727-230 (A)	20560 / 887	D-ABHI	0072	1291	3 PW JT8D-15	82350	F8Y128	HM-BK	FAE560
☐ HC-BSC	Boeing 727-230 (A)	20788 / 1011	D-ABRI	0074	0193	3 PW JT8D-15	82782	F8Y128		FAE788
☐ HC-	Boeing 727-230 (A)	21618 / 1404	TC-AFT	0078	0299	3 PW JT8D-15	82782	Y170		
☐ HC-	Boeing 727-230 (A)	21620 / 1419	TC-AFO	0078	0299	3 PW JT8D-15 (HK3/FDX)	82782	Y170		

TAO – Transportes Aéreos Orientales, Cia Ltda — Quito & Rio Amazonas

PO Box 2568, Quito, Ecuador ☎ (2) 44 67 80 Tx: none Fax: (2) 44 67 79 SITA: n/a
F: 1949 👥 10 Head: Cap. Gonzalo Ruales Net: n/a Suspended operations in 1998 (with Cessna 206 aircraft). Intends to restart during 1999.

TRANS AM Cia Aero Express DHL = RTM — Guayaquil

Aeropuerto Simon Bolivar, Guayaquil, Ecuador ☎ (4) 28 25 10 Tx: 43879 ed Fax: (4) 28 24 77 SITA: n/a
F: 1991 👥 n/a Head: Luis Grudena ICAO: AERO TRANSAM Net: n/a

☐ HC-BSS	Dassault Falcon 20C	150	TG-RBW	0068	0893	2 GE CF700-2D2	13000	Freighter		opf DHL
☐ HC-BUP	Dassault Falcon 20D	200	YV-200C	0069	0095	2 GE CF700-2D2	12400	Freighter		opf DHL

VIP – Vuelos Internos Privados (Subsidiary of Prodepro, S.A.) — Guayaquil

Galleria Colon, Local 17, Hotel Hilton, Guayaquil, Ecuador ☎ (4) 28 99 20 Tx: none Fax: (4) 68 90 17 SITA: n/a
F: 1997 👥 40 Head: Mauricio Pinto Net: http://www.vipec.com

☐ HC-BXO	Dornier 328-120	3076	D-CDXE*	0096	0797	2 PWC PW119C	13990	Y32		

192 registration type of aircraft cn/fn ex/ex* mfd del powered by mtow kg configuration selcal name/fln/specialitites/remarks

HH = HAITI (Republic of Haiti) (République d'Haïti)
Capital: Port-au-Prince) Official Language: French Population: 7,5 million Square Km: 27750 Dialling code: +509 Year established: 1804 Acting political head: René Préval (President)

AIR D'AYITI (Haiti Aviation, S.A. dba)   Port-au-Prince & Miami-Int'l (FL/USA)
219 NE 422nd Terrace, Miami, FL 33138, USA ☎ (305) 751-3434 Tx: none Fax: (305) 751-2424 SITA: n/a
F: 1998 ✦✦✦ n/a Head: Charles Boyd Net: n/a

☐ N369FA	Boeing 727-2K5 (A)	21851 / 1551	ZS-OAZ	0079	1298	3 PW JT8D-17 (HK3/FDX)	86409	Y170	occ lsf / opb FAO

AIR HAITI = HJA   Port-au-Prince & Miami-Int'l (FL/USA)
PO Box 520612, Miami, FL 33152-0612, USA ☎ (305) 871-1249 Tx: none Fax: (305) 871-8245 SITA: n/a
F: n/a ✦✦✦ n/a Head: Lionel Augustin ICAO: AIR HAITI Net: n/a Operates cargo flights with McDonnell Douglas DC-8F, leased from FINE AIR (N), when required.

HAITI AIR FREIGHT International, SA = HLS   Port-au-Prince & Miami-Int'l, FL   ≡≡≡ HAITI AIR FREIGHT
PO Box 590626, Miami, FL 33159, USA ☎ (305) 871-5814 Tx: none Fax: (305) 871-1879 SITA: n/a
F: 1977 ✦✦✦ 50 Head: Smith Augustin Net: n/a Operates cargo flights with aircraft leased from U.S. companies when required.

HI = DOMINICAN REPUBLIC (Republica Dominicana)
Capital: Santo Domingo) Official Language: Spanish Population: 8,0 million Square Km: 48734 Dialling code: +1-809 Year established: 1844 Acting political head: Leonel Fernandez (President)

AEROCHAGO Airlines, SA = AHG   Santo Domingo-Las Americas
Aeropuerto Int'l Las Americas, Zona de Carga, Santo Domingo, Dominican Republic ☎ (809) 549-0709 Tx: none Fax: (809) 549-0708 SITA: n/a
F: n/a ✦✦✦ n/a Head: Pedro Rodriguez IATA: 198 ICAO: AEROCHAGO Net: n/a Beside aircraft listed, leases McDonnell Douglas DC-8F from Miami-based US-companies when required.

☐ HI-583CT	Lockheed L-1049B (C-121J) Super Const.	4137	N2114Z	0054	0190	4 WR R-3350	58967	Freighter	std SDQ

AERODOMCA – Aeronaves Dominicanas, C. por A.   Santo Domingo-Herrera
Aeropuerto de Herrera, Avenida Luperon, Santo Domingo, Dominican Republic ☎ (809) 567-1984 Tx: none Fax: (809) 566-6558 SITA: n/a
F: 1980 ✦✦✦ n/a Head: n/a Net: n/a Aircraft below MTOW 1361kg: Cessna 172

☐ HI-482CT	Piper PA-32-300 Cherokee SIX	32-40011		0066		1 LY IO-540-K1A5	1542		
☐ HI-528CT	Cessna 207 Skywagon	20700112	N1502U	0069		1 CO IO-520-F	1724		
☐ HI-562CT	Cessna 207A Stationair 7 II	20700487		0078		1 CO IO-520-F	1724		
☐ HI-634CT	Twin (Aero) Shrike Commander 500S	3121	N803AC	0072		2 LY IO-540-E1B5	3062		
☐ HI-582CA	BAe (DH) 114 Riley Heron	14060	HI-582CT	0057		4 LY IO-540-K1C5	6124		cvtd Srs 2B

AERO INTER, SA   Santiago
Cibao Int'l Airport, Ave Bartolome Colon, Santiago, Dominican Republic ☎ (809) 581-8272 Tx: n/a Fax: (809) 241-0075 SITA: n/a
F: 1982 ✦✦✦ n/a Head: Alejandro Brown Net: n/a Aircraft below MTOW 1361kg: Cessna 172

☐ HI-506CT	Piper PA-34-200T Seneca II	34-7970075	N2134G	0079		2 CO TSIO-360-EB	2073		

AEROMAR AIRLINES = BQ / ROM (Aeromar, C por A dba)   Santo Domingo-Las Americas
PO Box 11, Aeropuerto Las Americas, Santo Domingo, Dominican Republic ☎ (809) 549-0281 Tx: none Fax: (809) 542-0152 SITA: n/a
F: n/a ✦✦✦ n/a Head: n/a IATA: 926 ICAO: BRAVO QUEBEC Net: n/a Beside aircraft listed, also leases Boeing (Douglas) DC-8F for US-cargo services from other companies when required.

☐ HI-592CT	Boeing (Douglas) DC-6A	45110 / 768	HI-596CA	0257	1288	4 PW R-2800	47083	Freighter	std SDQ
☐ N203AV	Boeing 727-259 (A)	22474 / 1688		0080	0199	3 PW JT8D-17R (HK3/FDX)	86637	Y163	lsf / opb FAO
☐ N266US	Boeing 727-251	19985 / 745		0869	1198	3 PW JT8D-9A	82780	Y166	Lillian / lsf / opb FAO

AIR ATLANTIC DOMINICANA = LU   Santo Domingo
Av. 27 de Febrero esq. Tiradentes, Apto 105, Plaza Merengue, Santo Domingo, Dominican Republic ☎ (809) 472-1441 Tx: none Fax: (809) 472-1622 SITA: n/a
F: 1996 ✦✦✦ n/a Head: Carlos Cevalier IATA: 849 Net: n/a

☐ XA-SYI	Boeing 727-247	20264 / 756	N324AS	0069	0898	3 PW JT8D-15	78245	Y167	EK-BG	Carlos 1 / lsf GRO

AIR CENTURY, S.A.   Santo Domingo-Herrera
Aeropuerto de Herrera, Avenida Luperon, Santo Domingo, Dominican Republic ☎ (809) 567-6778 Tx: none Fax: (809) 567-2705 SITA: n/a
F: 1992 ✦✦✦ 28 Head: n/a Net: n/a Aircraft below MTOW 1361kg: Cessna 150 & Piper PA-28

☐ HI-490TX	Piper PA-34-200 Seneca	34-7250052		0072		2 LY IO-360-C1E6	1814		
☐ HI-491CA	Piper PA-34-200 Seneca	34-7350056		0073		2 LY IO-360-C1E6	1905		
☐ HI-607CT	Piper PA-34-200 Seneca	34-7250355		0072		2 LY IO-360-C1E6	1905		
☐ HI-671CA	Let 410UVP	800413	N41431	0080	1096	2 WA M-601D	5800		

AIR SANTO DOMINGO = EX / SDO (Aerolineas Santo Domingo, S.A. dba / Subsidiary of Air Europa)   Santo Domingo-Herrera
Edificio JP, Ave. 27 de Febrero 272, esq. Calle Seminario, Santo Domingo, Dominican Republic ☎ (809) 683-8428 Tx: none Fax: (809) 683-8436 SITA: SDQSDUX
F: 1996 ✦✦✦ n/a Head: n/a IATA: 309 ICAO: AERO DOMINGO Net: n/a

☐ HI-676CA	Let 410UVP	851340	HI-676SP	0085	0497	2 WA M-601D	5800		Puerto Plata
☐ HI-679CA	Let 410UVP-E3	882023	HI-679SP	0088	0497	2 WA M-601E	6400		
☐ HI-680CA	Let 410UVP-E3	882024	HI-680SP	0088	0497	2 WA M-601E	6400		
☐ HI-681CA	Let 410UVP-E3	882025	HI-681SP	0088	0497	2 WA M-601E	6400		Puerto Cana

AIR TAXI, C por A   Santo Domingo-Herrera
Ave. Nunez de Caceres 2, Los Prados, Apartado Postal 229-9, Santo Domingo, Dominican Republic ☎ (809) 227-8333 Tx: n/a Fax: (809) 227-8038 SITA: n/a
F: 1979 ✦✦✦ n/a Head: Jimmy Butler Net: n/a

☐ HI-314CA	Piper PA-32-300 Cherokee SIX	32-7840048		0078		1 LY IO-540-K1G5	1542		
☐ HI-555CA	Piper PA-34-200 Seneca	34-7250118		0072		2 LY IO-360-C1E6	1814		
☐ HI-551CA	Britten-Norman BN-2A-21 Islander	410	HH-CNA	0077		2 LY IO-540-K1B5	2994		
☐ HI-593CA	Britten-Norman BN-2A-26 Islander	2005	N7134A	0077	0291	2 LY O-540-E4C5	2858		
☐ HI-640CA	Britten-Norman BN-2A-21 Islander	849	A2-AEA	0077	0093	2 LY IO-540-K1B5	2994		

APA International Air, SA = 7P / APY   Santo Domingo-Las Americas   ЯРЯ INTERNATIONAL AIR
PO Box 524039, Miami, FL 33152, USA ☎ (305) 805-0425 Tx: none Fax: (305) 805-0427 SITA: n/a
F: 1980 ✦✦✦ n/a Head: Rafael Trujillo IATA: 917 ICAO: APA INTERNACIONAL Net: n/a
Scheduled flights are operated with Boeing 727-200 aircraft, lsf/opb SKY TREK INTERNTIONAL AIRLINES (N) when required.

CARIBAIR, SA   Santo Domingo-Herrera
Aeropuerto de Herrera, Avenida Luperon, Santo Domingo, Dominican Republic ☎ (809) 567-2394 Tx: none Fax: (809) 567-7033 SITA: n/a
F: 1983 ✦✦✦ 60 Head: Rafael Rosado Fermin Net: n/a

☐ HI-520CA	Piper PA-32R-300 Lance	32R-7780240		0077		1 LY IO-540-K1G5D	1633		
☐ HI-326CA	Piper PA-34-200T Seneca II	34-7970276		0079		2 CO TSIO-360-E	2073		
☐ HI-569CT	Piper PA-31-310 Navajo	31-700	HI-569CA	0070		2 LY TIO-540-A2C	2948		
☐ HI-585CA	Piper PA-31-310 Navajo B	31-850	N333GT	0072		2 LY TIO-540-A2C	2948		
☐ HI-653CA	Britten-Norman BN-2A-26 Islander	8	N28BN	0067	0792	2 LY O-540-E4C5	2994		
☐ HI-666CT	Let 410UVP	851517	RA-67550	0085	0096	2 WA M-601D	5800		
☐ S9-TAU	Let 410UVP-E9A	882039	OK-TDB	0088		2 WA M-601E	6400		lsf ATEC
☐ S9-TAV	Let 410UVP-E9A	882040	OK-TDG	0088		2 WA M-601E	6400		lsf ATEC

COTURISCA   Santo Domingo-Herrera
Edo.Centro Coordinador Empresarial,, Av.Nunez de Caceres, Fso.Guarocuya,Fl.Millon, Santo Domingo, Dominican Republic ☎ (809) 683-3660 Tx: none Fax: (809) 683-3651 SITA: n/a
F: n/a ✦✦✦ 17 Head: Huascar M. Rodriguez Net: http://www.coturisca.com/ Aircraft below MTOW 1361kg: Cessna 172

☐ HI-419CT	Bell 206B JetRanger III	3757	HI-437	0083		1 AN 250-C20J	1451	4 Pax	
☐ HI-686SP	Bell 206B JetRanger III	4015	N5371M	0088	0797	1 AN 250-C20J	1451	4 Pax	
☐ HI-505TX	Eurocopter (MBB) BO105CBS	S-343	N6BX	0077		2 AN 250-C20B	2500	4 Pax	
☐ HI-687SP	Eurocopter (MBB) BO105LS-A3	2035	N105LH	0091	0097	2 AN 250-C28C	2600	4 Pax	
☐ HI-396CT	Piper PA-31-350 Navajo Chieftain	31-8252047		0082	0097	2 LY TIO-540-J2BD	3175	7 Pax	

DOMINAIR = YU / ADM (Aerolineas Dominicanas, SA – ADSA dba)   Santiago   DOMINAIR AEROLINEAS DOMINICANAS
Aeropuerto Int'l Cibao, Apartado 202, Santiago, Dominican Republic ☎ (809) 583-3410 Tx: none Fax: (809) 582-1674 SITA: n/a
F: 1974 ✦✦✦ 28 Head: José A. Bermudez IATA: 725 ICAO: DOMINAIR Net: n/a Operates scheduled services with DHC-8 aircraft leased from and operated by LIAT (V2-) as required.

DOMINICANA DE AVIACION = DOA (Compania Dominicana de Aviacion, C por A dba)   Santo Domingo-Las Americas
Apartado Postal 1415, Santo Domingo, Dominican Republic ☎ (809) 533-4281 Tx: none Fax: (809) 535-1656 SITA: n/a
F: 1944 ✦✦✦ 580 Head: Dr. Rodolfo Rincon ICAO: DOMINICANA Net: n/a Operates passenger flights with Boeing 727/737/767 aircraft leased from TAESA (XA-), Avatlantic (N) & Air Europe (I) when required.

HISPANIOLA AIRWAYS, C. por A. = HIS   Puerto Plata & Miami-Int'l, FL
PO Box 524211, Miami, Florida 33152, USA ☎ (305) 591-1704 Tx: none Fax: (305) 591-1706 SITA: n/a
F: n/a ✦✦✦ 25 Head: Jacques Bernateau ICAO: HISPANIOLA Net: n/a Operates cargo & passenger flights, currently with aircraft leased from other companies when required.

JET EXPRESO, S.A. — Santo Domingo-Herrera

Aeropuerto de Herrera, Avenida Luperon, Hangar 1, Parte Oeste, Santo Domingo, Dominican Republic ☎ (809) 563-4360 Tx: none Fax: none SITA: n/a
F: 1984 n/a Head: Narcisco Sajour Net: n/a Aircraft below MTOW 1361kg: Beechcraft A24R & Piper PA-28

☐ HI-570CA	Cessna 205 (210-5)	205-0336		0063		1 CO IO-470-S	1497			

QUEEN AIR, Aeronaves Queen, S.A. = 5G / QNA — Santo Domingo-Las Americas

Av. 27 de Febrero Esq., Local 202, 2P., Tiradentes Plaza Merengue, Santo Domingo, Dominican Republic ☎ (809) 685-2168 Tx: none Fax: (809) 686-1091 SITA: n/a
F: 1998 n/a Head: Julio Rosario IATA: 396 ICAO: QUEEN AIR Net: n/a Operates passenger flights with Airbus Industrie A320 aircraft, lsf/opb TRANSMERIDIAN AIRLINES (N), when required.

SAP – Servicios Aéreos Profesionales, SA — Santo Domingo-Herrera

Aeropuerto de Herrera, Avenida Luperon, Santo Domingo, Dominican Republic ☎ (809) 565-2448 Tx: none Fax: (809) 540-4667 SITA: n/a
F: 1983 n/a Head: José Miguel Patin Hernandez Net: n/a Aircraft below MTOW 1361kg: Cessna 172

☐ HI-331CT	Cessna U206G Stationair 6 II	U20604778		0078		1 CO IO-520-D	1633	Y5		
☐ HI-510CA	Cessna U206F Stationair	U20601796		0072		1 CO IO-520-F	1633	Y5		lsf Rutas Turisticas
☐ HI-650CT	Cessna 210K Centurion	21059349		0070		1 CO IO-520-L	1724	Y5		
☐ HI-636CT	Britten-Norman BN-2A-21 Islander	625	CS-AQP	0072	0393	2 LY IO-540-K1B5	2994	Y9		
☐ HI-624CT	De Havilland DHC-6 Twin Otter 100	72	C-GZFP	0067	1091	2 PWC PT6A-20	5252	Y20		
☐ HI-644CT	De Havilland DHC-6 Twin Otter 200	46	CS-TFG	0067	0095	2 PWC PT6A-20	5252	Y20		lsf World Jet Inc. / cvtd -100
☐ HI-665CT	Let 410UVP-E	902433	RA-67640	0090	0096	2 WA M-601E	6400	Y19		
☐ HI-670CT	Let 410UVP	831105	S9-TAZ	0083	0496	2 WA M-601D	6000	Y19		
☐ S9-TAR	Let 410UVP	831106	D-COXE	0083	0095	2 WA M-601D	6000	Y19		lsf ATEC
☐ S9-TAW	Let 410UVP	831107	D-COXF	0083	0096	2 WA M-601D	6000	Y17		lsf ATEC
☐ S9-TBC	Let 410UVP	851439	CCCP-67532	0085	0096	2 WA M-601D	6000	Y19		City of Frankfurt / lsf ATEC
☐ TG-TJI	Let 410UVP-E	902502	RA-67649	0090	0096	2 WA M-601E	6400	Y19		lsf Tikal Agency
☐ N10759	Beech 1900D Airliner	UE-264		0097	0797	2 PWC PT6A-67D	7688	Y19		El Sereno IV / lsf Corp. 385 Inc.
☐ N10876	Beech 1900D Airliner	UE-241		0096	0697	2 PWC PT6A-67D	7688	Y19		lsf Raytheon Aircraft Credit Corp.
☐ HI-657CT	Shorts 360-200 (SD3-60)	SH3672	B-3605	0085	1195	2 PWC PT6A-65AR	11999	Y38		
☐ HI-658CT	Shorts 360-200 (SD3-60)	SH3674	B-3607	0085	1195	2 PWC PT6A-65AR	11999	Y38		
☐ N980TT	GAC (Grumman) G-159 Gulfstream I	323	N22320	0065	0096	2 RR Dart 529-8X	15921	Y14		lsf Bradley Flying Service Inc.

TAINO AIRLINES, SA = TIN — Santo Domingo-Las Americas

Calle Gustavo Meijia Ricart 93, Plaza Piantini, 2do piso, Santo Domingo, Dominican Republic ☎ (809) 549-0324 Tx: none Fax: (809) 549-0325 SITA: n/a
F: 1974 n/a Head: Juan Carlos Hernandez ICAO: TAINO Net: n/a Operates charter flights, currently with Convair 240 aircraft leased from Trans Florida Airlines (N) when required.

HK = COLOMBIA (Republic of Colombia) (Republica de Colombia)

Capital: Bogota Official Language: Spanish Population: 41,0 million Square Km: 1138914 Dialling code: +57 Year established: 1810 Acting political head: Andres Pastrana (President)

Government / Corporate / Executive / VIP Aircraft

☐ FAC0001	Fokker F28 Fellowship 1000 (F28 Mk1000)	11992	PH-EXA*	0070	0271	2 RR Spey 555-15	30164	Frtr / VIP		Fuerza Aérea Colombiana
☐ FAC002	Bell 212	30511	N7070J	0071		2 PWC PT6T-3 TwinPac	5080	VIP		Fuerza Aérea Colombiana
☐ FAC004	Bell 412					2 PWC PT6T-3B TwinPac	5398	VIP		Fuerza Aérea Colombiana
☐ FAC1201	Boeing 707-373C	19716 / 644	HL7425	0067	1283	4 PW JT3D-3B	152409	VIP / Combi	BC-EG	Fuerza Aérea Colombiana
☐ FAC1211	Cessna 550 Citation II	550-0582		0088		2 PWC JT15D-4	6033	VIP		Fuerza Aérea Colombiana
☐ HK-2777G	De Havilland DHC-6 Twin Otter 300	727	N214FC	0080	0782	2 PWC PT6A-27	5670	Liasion		Policia Nacional Fondo Rotatorio
☐ HK-3000G	Piper PA-42 Cheyenne III	42-8001062		0082		2 PWC PT6A-41	5080	Executive		DAAC / Aerocivil
☐ HK-3381G	Piper PA-42-720 Cheyenne IIIA	42-5501039	N9126B	0087	1187	2 PWC PT6A-61	5080	Executive/VIP		Idema

ACES Colombia – Aerolineas Centrales de Colombia, SA = VX / AES — Medellin

Calle 49 No. 50-21, Edif. del Café, Piso 34, Apartado Aéreo 6503, Medellin (Antioquia), Colombia ☎ (4) 511 41 11 Tx: 65224 aces co Fax: (4) 251 16 77 SITA: n/a
F: 1971 1850 Head: Mario Gomez IATA: 137 ICAO: ACES Net: n/a

☐ HK-1980	De Havilland DHC-6 Twin Otter 300	510		0076	1176	2 PWC PT6A-27	5670	Y20		
☐ HK-2381	De Havilland DHC-6 Twin Otter 300	644		0079	1079	2 PWC PT6A-27	5670	Y20		
☐ HK-2445	De Havilland DHC-6 Twin Otter 300	684	C-GCGP*	0080	0680	2 PWC PT6A-27	5670	Y20		
☐ HK-2547	De Havilland DHC-6 Twin Otter 300	717		0080	1180	2 PWC PT6A-27	5670	Y20		
☐ HK-2548	De Havilland DHC-6 Twin Otter 300	718	C-GDIW*	0080	1180	2 PWC PT6A-27	5670	Y20		
☐ HK-2603	De Havilland DHC-6 Twin Otter 300	749		0081	0581	2 PWC PT6A-27	5670	Y20		
☐ HK-2669	De Havilland DHC-6 Twin Otter 300	760		0081	0581	2 PWC PT6A-27	5670	Y20		
☐ HK-2670	De Havilland DHC-6 Twin Otter 300	767		0081	0981	2 PWC PT6A-27	5670	Y20		
☐ HK-3777X	De Havilland DHC-6 Twin Otter 300	477	N7138K	0076	1092	2 PWC PT6A-27	5670	Y20		
☐ HK-3678X	ATR 42-320	261	F-WWEI*	0091	1291	2 PWC PW121	16700	Y48		lsf GECA
☐ HK-3684X	ATR 42-320	284	F-WWLJ*	0092	0292	2 PWC PW121	16700	Y48		lsf GECA
☐ HK-3943X	ATR 42-320	142	EI-BXS	0089	0894	2 PWC PW121	16700	Y46		lsf GECA / cvtd -300
☐ HK-4035X	ATR 42-320	259	N99838	0092	0895	2 PWC PW121	16700	Y46		lsf BTA
☐ VP-BNH	ATR 42-320	296	VR-BNH*	0092	1192	2 PWC PW121	16700	Y48		lsf GECA
☐ VP-BOG	ATR 42-320	333	VR-BOG*	0093	0793	2 PWC PW121	16700	Y48		lsf GECA
☐	Airbus Industrie A320-233					2 IAE V2527E-A5	77000	Y150		oo-delivery 0004
☐	Airbus Industrie A320-233					2 IAE V2527E-A5	77000	Y150		oo-delivery 0004
☐	Airbus Industrie A320-233					2 IAE V2527E-A5	77000	Y150		oo-delivery 0004
☐	Airbus Industrie A320-233					2 IAE V2527E-A5	77000	Y150		oo-delivery 0004
☐ VP-BVA	Airbus Industrie A320-233	739	F-WWBX*	0097	1197	2 IAE V2527E-A5	77000	Y150		Manizales del Alma / lsf SPC Abuela Ltd
☐ VP-BVB	Airbus Industrie A320-233	743	F-WWIF*	0097	1197	2 IAE V2527E-A5	77000	Y150		lsf SPC Abuela Ltd
☐ VP-BVC	Airbus Industrie A320-233	839	F-WWBE*	0098	0798	2 IAE V2527E-A5	77000	Y150	QR-LP	lsf SPC Abuela Ltd
☐ VP-BVD	Airbus Industrie A320-233	892	F-WWDF*	0098	1098	2 IAE V2527E-A5	77000	Y150		lsf Debis AirFinance
☐ VP-BVF	Airbus Industrie A320-233	1085				2 IAE V2527E-A5	77000	Y150		oo-delivery 1099
☐ VP-BVG	Airbus Industrie A320-233	1110				2 IAE V2527E-A5	77000	Y150		oo-delivery 1199
☐ VP-BVH	Airbus Industrie A320-233	1125				2 IAE V2527E-A5	77000	Y150		oo-delivery 1299
☐ HK-3738X	Boeing 727-227 (A)	21997 / 1573	N306AS	0080	0692	3 PW JT8D-17R	86409	C98		lsf Bankers Trust Co.
☐ HK-3977X	Boeing 727-277 (A)	20548 / 907	N274WC	0072	1294	3 PW JT8D-17	86863	C98		lsf ARON
☐ HK-3998X	Boeing 727-225 (A)	20620 / 903	N8858E	0072	0295	3 PW JT8D-15	86409	Y155	GH-AM	lsf Aerocar Aviation Corp.
☐ HK-4010X	Boeing 727-243 (A)	21267 / 1228	N574PE	0076	0595	3 PW JT8D-9A	79605	Y155	BF-CJ	lsf Aerocar Aviation Corp.

ADES Colombia – Aerolineas del Este, Ltda — Villavicencio

Apartado Aéreo 2851, Villavicencio, (Meta), Colombia ☎ (86) 64 80 26 Tx: 2851 Fax: (86) 64 80 51 SITA: n/a
F: 1975 25 Head: Ricardo Bernal Blanco Net: n/a

☐ HK-1721	Cessna A185F Skywagon	18502636	N4868C	0075		1 CO IO-520-D	1520			
☐ HK-2279	Cessna U206G Stationair 6 II	CU20604885		0079		1 CO IO-520-F	1633			
☐ HK-2430	Cessna TU206G Turbo Stationair 6 II	CU20605166		0079		1 CO TSIO-520-M	1633			
☐ HK-1149	Boeing (Douglas) DC-3C (C-47B-15-DK)	26593	N69	0044	0096	2 PW R-1830-94	11431	Freighter		

AEROATLANTICO Colombia – Aerovias del Atlantico, Ltda = AOK — Barranquilla

Aeropuerto Ernesto Cortissoz, Hangar 1, Apartado Aéreo 118, Barranquilla (Atlantico), Colombia ☎ (5) 42 19 62 Tx: none Fax: (5) 42 05 18 SITA: n/a
F: 1980 24 Head: Luis Alfredo Gallego Ramos Net: n/a Aircraft below MTOW 1361 kg: Piper PA-28.

☐ HK-2447	AAC (Piper) Aerostar 601P	61P-0777-8063388	N3635D	0080		2 LY IO-540-S1A5	2722			
☐ HK-2963	Piper PA-31T2 Cheyenne II XL	31T-8166053	N174CC	0081		2 PWC PT6A-135	4297			lsf Supertiendas y Droguerias Olimpicas

AEROCOL Colombia – Aerotaxi del Oriente Colombiano, Ltda — El Yopal

Aeropuerto El Yopal, Yopal, (Casanare), Colombia ☎ (87) 55 86 95 Tx: none Fax: (87) 55 86 95 SITA: n/a
F: 1989 n/a Head: Dario Perez Rivera Net: n/a Aircraft below MTOW 1361kg: Cessna 172

☐ HK-2097	Cessna U206G Stationair 6 II	CU20604135		0077		1 CO IO-520-F	1633			
☐ HK-2827	Cessna U206G Stationair 6 II	CU20606551		0082		1 CO IO-520-F	1633			

AEROCORALES Colombia — Cartagena

Aeropuerto Rafael Nunez, A.A. 40049, Cartagena, Colombia ☎ (53) 662 22 00 Tx: n/a Fax: (53) 66 56 65 SITA: n/a
F: n/a n/a Head: Jaime Cuellar Alvarez Net: n/a

☐ HK-2222	Piper PA-31-350 Navajo Chieftain	31-7852169		0078		2 LY TIO-540-J2BD	3175			
☐ HK-3309	Cessna 208 Caravan I	C20800098		0086		1 PWC PT6A-114	3629			

AEROLLANO Colombia – Aerovias del Llano, Ltda — Villavicencio (Meta) & Trinidad (Casanare)

Aeropuerto Vanguardia, Villavicencio, (Meta), Colombia ☎ (86) 64 82 15 Tx: n/a Fax: (86) 64 82 15 SITA: n/a
F: n/a n/a Head: Pedro Villalba Herrera Net: n/a Aircraft below MTOW 1361 kg: Cessna 182.

☐ HK-1604	Piper PA-32-300C Cherokee SIX	32-40970		0070		1 LY IO-540-K1A5	1542			
☐ HK-2852	Cessna TU206G Turbo Stationair 6 II	CU20606641		0082		1 CO TSIO-520-M	1633			
☐ HK-2990	Cessna TU206G Turbo Stationair 6 II	CU20606471		0083		1 CO TSIO-520-M	1633			
☐ HK-3512	Cessna 441 Conquest II	441-0261	N261DW	0082		2 GA TPE331-8-403S	4468			

194 registration type of aircraft cn/fn ex/ex* mfd del powered by mtow kg configuration selcal name/fln/specialitites/remarks

AEROMEL Colombia - Aeromel Aerotaxi, Ltda — Bogota-Eldorado

Aeropuerto Eldorado, Entrada 1, Interior 25, Santafé de Bogota, (D.E.), Colombia ☎ (1) 413 95 80 Tx: none Fax: (1) 413 91 84 SITA: n/a
F: 1992 n/a Head: Jeiner de Jesus Jaramillo Toro Net: n/a

registration	type of aircraft	cn/fn	ex/ex*	mfd	del	powered by	mtow kg	configuration	selcal	name/fln/specialitites/remarks
☐ HK-3058	Piper PA-34-220T Seneca III	34-8333083		0083		2 CO TSIO-360-KB	2155			

AEROREPUBLICA, S.A. = P5 / RPB — Bogota-Eldorado

Carrera 10a, No 27-51, Oficina 303, Santafé de Bogota, (D.E.), Colombia ☎ (1) 281 51 99 Tx: none Fax: (1) 283 16 80 SITA: n/a
F: 1992 630 Head: Alfonso Avila Velandia IATA: 845 ICAO: AEROREPUBLICA Net: n/a

registration	type of aircraft	cn/fn	ex/ex*	mfd	del	powered by	mtow kg	configuration	selcal	name/fln/specialitites/remarks
☐ HK-3905X	Boeing (Douglas) DC-9-31	47399 / 430	YV-818C	0069	0394	2 PW JT8D-17	47627	Y105	CJ-AK	Suzette
☐ HK-3906X	Boeing (Douglas) DC-9-31	47401 / 444	YV-819C	0369	0494	2 PW JT8D-17	47627	Y105	CJ-AM	
☐ HK-3926X	Boeing (Douglas) DC-9-32	47231 / 396	N285AW	1068	0594	2 PW JT8D-9A	48989	Y107		
☐ HK-3927X	Boeing (Douglas) DC-9-32	47519 / 615	N29LR	1270	0794	2 PW JT8D-15	48989	Y107		
☐ HK-3928X	Boeing (Douglas) DC-9-32	47311 / 398	N286AW	1068	0994	2 PW JT8D-17 / -17A	48989	Y107		Miguel Angel
☐ HK-3963X	Boeing (Douglas) DC-9-32	47437 / 544	I-RIZL	1069	1194	2 PW JT8D-15	48989	Y107		
☐ HK-3964X	Boeing (Douglas) DC-9-32	47434 / 537	I-RIZJ	0969	1294	2 PW JT8D-15	48989	Y107		
☐ HK-4084X	Boeing (Douglas) DC-9-31	47330 / 407	YV-770C	1068	0796	2 PW JT8D-9A	47627	Y105		
☐ HK-4155X	Boeing (Douglas) DC-9-32	47524 / 632	N27522	0071	0598	2 PW JT8D-9A	49895	Y107		lsf TRIT
☐ HK-3840X	Boeing 727-46	18879 / 254	HR-ALZ	0466	0593	3 PW JT8D-7B / -9A	76884	Y119		Ines

AEROSOL Colombia - Aerovias Sol de Colombia, Ltda — Bogota-Eldorado & Villavicencio

Aeropuerto Eldorado, Entrada 1, Interior 4, Apartado Aéreo 151110, Santafé de Bogota (D.E.), Colombia ☎ (1) 413 85 90 Tx: n/a Fax: none SITA: n/a
F: n/a n/a Head: Hernan Suarez Loaiza Net: n/a

registration	type of aircraft	cn/fn	ex/ex*	mfd	del	powered by	mtow kg	configuration	selcal	name/fln/specialitites/remarks
☐ HK-3969X	Convair 580 (F) (SCD)	466	HP-1222CTH	0057	1194	2 AN 501-D13	24766	Freighter		cvtd CV440-59
☐ HK-1700	Boeing (Douglas) DC-6BF	44419 / 491	N4419R	0054	0097	4 PW R-2800	45360	Freighter		cvtd DC-6B

AEROSUCRE, S.A. = 6N / KRE — Barranquilla & Bogota-Eldorado

Avenida Eldorado No. 97-36, Santafé de Bogota, (D.E.), Colombia ☎ (1) 413 97 08 Tx: n/a Fax: (1) 413 94 42 SITA: n/a
F: 1969 239 Head: Capt. Jorge Solano Recio ICAO: AEROSUCRE Net: n/a

registration	type of aircraft	cn/fn	ex/ex*	mfd	del	powered by	mtow kg	configuration	selcal	name/fln/specialitites/remarks
☐ HK-3805X	Aerosp. (Sud) SE210 Caravelle 10B3 (F)	257	OY-STF	0069	1292	2 PW JT8D-7	55000	Freighter	BG-KM	cvtd 10B3
☐ HK-3806X	Aerosp. (Sud) SE210 Caravelle 10B3 (F)	262	F-GHKM	0069	1292	2 PW JT8D-7	55000	Freighter		cvtd 10B3
☐ HK-1717	Boeing 727-21 (F)	18993 / 215	N315PA	0065	0492	3 PW JT8D-7A	73028	Freighter	EK-CF	cvtd -21
☐ HK-3667X	Boeing 727-23 (F)	19430 / 366	N934FT	0066	1091	3 PW JT8D-7B	76884	Freighter	BH-GM	cvtd -23
☐ HK-727	Boeing 727-59 (F)	19127 / 243		0066	0592	3 PW JT8D-7	73028	Freighter	FK-AM	cvtd -59
☐ HK-3985X	Boeing 727-224	20465 / 814	N32723	0072	0395	3 PW JT8D-9A	78245	Freighter	DM-EK	cvtd -2F2

AEROTACA Colombia - Aerotranportes Casanare, S.A. = ATK (formerly Aerotaxi Casanare, S.A.) — Bogota-Eldorado & El Yopal (Casanare)

Aeropuerto El Dorado, Entrada 1, Interior 20, Santafé de Bogota, (D.E.), Colombia ☎ (1) 413 90 40 Tx: none Fax: (1) 413 52 56 SITA: n/a
F: 1965 128 Head: Antonio Urdaneta ICAO: AEROTACA Net: n/a

registration	type of aircraft	cn/fn	ex/ex*	mfd	del	powered by	mtow kg	configuration	selcal	name/fln/specialitites/remarks
☐ HK-2760	De Havilland DHC-6 Twin Otter 300	777		0081		2 PWC PT6A-27	5670	Y20		
☐ HK-3523	De Havilland DHC-6 Twin Otter 300	608	N784DL	0079	0989	2 PWC PT6A-27	5670	Y20		
☐ HK-1411	Fairchild Ind. FH-227D	575	N2743R	0068	0093	2 RR Dart 532-7L	20638	Y38		

AEROTAXI DEL QUINDIO, Ltda — Armenia

Escera 15, 10-23, Local 106, Armenia, Colombia ☎ (67) 46 34 56 Tx: none Fax: (67) 45 04 48 SITA: n/a
F: n/a n/a Head: Jorgé Alonso Andrade Net: n/a

registration	type of aircraft	cn/fn	ex/ex*	mfd	del	powered by	mtow kg	configuration	selcal	name/fln/specialitites/remarks
☐ HK-3705	Beech King Air 200	BB-63	N10DM	0075		2 PWC PT6A-41	5670			
☐ HK-3654	Beech King Air 300	FA-101	HK-3509	0086		2 PWC PT6A-60A	6350			
☐ HK-3828	Beech King Air 300	FA-10	N13PD	0084		2 PWC PT6A-60A	6350			

AEROVANGUARDIA Colombia - Aerovias Vanguardia, Ltda — Villavicencio

Aeropuerto Vanguardia, Hangar 1, Villavicencio, (Meta), Colombia ☎ (86) 64 81 22 Tx: n/a Fax: none SITA: n/a
F: 1993 n/a Head: Francisco Simon Garcia Net: n/a Aircraft below MTOW 1361kg: Cessna 172.

registration	type of aircraft	cn/fn	ex/ex*	mfd	del	powered by	mtow kg	configuration	selcal	name/fln/specialitites/remarks
☐ HK-3894	Beech King Air B200	BB-1049	F-GMLP	0082		2 PWC PT6A-42	5670			
☐ HK-1503	Boeing (Douglas) DC-3C (C-47B-50-DK)	34331	N54336	0043	0093	2 PW R-1830	12202	Freighter		El Viejto

AEROVILLA Colombia - Aerovilla Ltda — Villavicencio

Aeropuerto Vanguardia, Entrada principal, Villavicencio, (Meta), Colombia ☎ (86) 64 81 10 Tx: n/a Fax: none SITA: n/a
F: n/a n/a Head: Victor Villalobos Net: n/a Aircraft below MTOW 1361kg: Cessna 172 & 182

registration	type of aircraft	cn/fn	ex/ex*	mfd	del	powered by	mtow kg	configuration	selcal	name/fln/specialitites/remarks
☐ HK-3292	Boeing (Douglas) DC-3C (C-47A-80-DL)	19661	C-GABG	0044		2 PW R-1830-92	12202	Freighter		

AEROVUELOS Colombia - Aerovuelos y Servicios, Ltda — Bogota-Eldorado

Aeropuerto Eldorado, Entrada 2 Int. 2, Of. 220, Santafé de Bogota, (D.E.), Colombia ☎ (1) 413 94 25 Tx: none Fax: (1) 413 87 28 SITA: n/a
F: 1987 12 Head: Leonor Martinez Sepulveda Net: n/a

registration	type of aircraft	cn/fn	ex/ex*	mfd	del	powered by	mtow kg	configuration	selcal	name/fln/specialitites/remarks
☐ HK-2307	Piper PA-32RT-300T Turbo Lance II	32R-7987122		0079		1 LY TIO-540-S1AD	1633			
☐ HK-2713	Piper PA-34-220T Seneca III	34-8133241		0081		2 CO TSIO-360-KB	2155			lsf Aeroamazonas Ltda
☐ HK-1094	Beech Queen Air B80 (65-B80)	LD-312		0066		2 LY IGSO-540-A1D	3992			
☐ HK-3025	Piper PA-31T Cheyenne II	31T-8120062		0081		2 PWC PT6A-28	4082			
☐ HK-2050	De Havilland DHC-6 Twin Otter 300	562		0078	0093	2 PWC PT6A-27	5670			lsf pvt
☐ HK-4002	Let 410UVP-E	861810	CCCP-67597	0086	0395	2 WA M-601E	6400			
☐ HK-4013	Let 410UVP-E	861601	CCCP-67561	0086	0795	2 WA M-601E	6400			

AIR COLOMBIA, Ltda — Bogota-Eldorado & Villavicencio

Apto Eldorado, Entrada 1, Interior 21, A.A. 151702, Santafé de Bogota, (D.E.), Colombia ☎ (1) 413 98 03 Tx: n/a Fax: (1) 413 97 74 SITA: n/a
F: 1980 17 Head: Mayor Luis Hernan Wilson Net: n/a

registration	type of aircraft	cn/fn	ex/ex*	mfd	del	powered by	mtow kg	configuration	selcal	name/fln/specialitites/remarks
☐ HK-3293	Boeing (Douglas) DC-3C (C-47A-1-DL)	9186	N46877	0043		2 PW R-1830-92	12202	Freighter		
☐ HK-4046X	Boeing (Douglas) DC-6A (C-118B)	43708 / 347	HK-3531X	0053	0095	4 PW R-2800	47083	Freighter		
☐ HK-3973X	Boeing 727-123	19838 / 551	N1964	0368	1196	3 PW JT8D-7B	72847	Freighter		

AIRES Colombia - Aerovias de Integracion Regional, SA = 4C / ARE — Bogota-Eldorado

Avenida Eldorado, Entrada 1, Hangar Aires, Apartado Aéreo 44120, Santafé de Bogota, (D.E.), Colombia ☎ (1) 413 90 24 Tx: 44406 asex co Fax: (1) 413 88 51 SITA: n/a
F: 1981 400 Head: Mrs. Guiomar P. Echeverri ICAO: AIRES Net: n/a

registration	type of aircraft	cn/fn	ex/ex*	mfd	del	powered by	mtow kg	configuration	selcal	name/fln/specialitites/remarks
☐ HK-2741	Embraer 110P1 Bandeirante (EMB-110P1)	110380	PT-SEX*	0081	1281	2 PWC PT6A-34	5900	Y19		Rodrigo Lara Bonilla
☐ HK-2856	Embraer 110P1 Bandeirante (EMB-110P1)	110406	PT-SFW*	0082	0782	2 PWC PT6A-34	5900	Y19		
☐ HK-3942X	De Havilland DHC-8-103 Dash 8	136	N4101T	0089	0694	2 PWC PW121	15649	Y37		Rodrigo Lara Bonilla / lsf AGES
☐ HK-3946X	De Havilland DHC-8-103 Dash 8	076	N4101Z	0087	0694	2 PWC PW121	15649	Y37		lsf AGES
☐ HK-3951X	De Havilland DHC-8-301 Dash 8	184	N184CL	0089	0994	2 PWC PW123	18643	Y50		lsf AGES
☐ HK-3952X	De Havilland DHC-8-301 Dash 8	169	N169CL	0089	0994	2 PWC PW123	18643	Y50		Gustavo Arcunduaga / lsf AGES
☐ HK-4030X	De Havilland DHC-8-301 Dash 8	100	N100CQ	0088	0895	2 PWC PW123	18643	Y50		lsf AGES
☐ HK-3637X	Fairchild Ind. F-27J	64	N270VR	0059	0691	2 RR Dart 532-7	19051	Y43		lsf Northern Aviation Inc./cvtd F-27A

AIR PEREIRA Colombia - Transportes Aéreos Air Pereira, Ltda — Pereira

Aeropuerto Matecana Bodega 3, Local 4, Pereira, Colombia ☎ (63) 26 10 66 Tx: n/a Fax: none SITA: n/a
F: n/a n/a Head: Juan Carlos Kafruny Net: n/a

registration	type of aircraft	cn/fn	ex/ex*	mfd	del	powered by	mtow kg	configuration	selcal	name/fln/specialitites/remarks
☐ HK-2645	Piper PA-34-220T Seneca III	34-8133125		0081		2 CO TSIO-360-KB	2155			

ALCOM Colombia - Aerolineas Comerciales del Meta, Ltda — Villavicencio

300mts antes del Aeropuerto Vanguardia, Entrada Principal, Villavicencio (Meta), Colombia ☎ (86) 64 82 00 Tx: none Fax: (86) 64 82 00 SITA: n/a
F: 1990 6 Head: Carlos Alberto Rivera Bueno Net: n/a

registration	type of aircraft	cn/fn	ex/ex*	mfd	del	powered by	mtow kg	configuration	selcal	name/fln/specialitites/remarks
☐ HK-3349	Boeing (Douglas) DC-3C (C-47A-DK)	11825	FAE 92066	0043	0097	2 PW R-1830-92	12202			
☐ HK-4045	Boeing (Douglas) DC-3C (C-47B-1-DK)	25808	N10004	0044		2 PW R-1830	12202			

ALIANSA Colombia - Aerolineas Andinas, SA — Villavicencio

Cra. 19, No. 34-09, Aeropuerto Vanguardia, Villavicencio, (Meta), Colombia ☎ (86) 64 80 24 Tx: none Fax: (86) 64 81 17 SITA: n/a
F: 1991 16 Head: Capt. Jorge Luis Alvarez Rodriguez Net: n/a

registration	type of aircraft	cn/fn	ex/ex*	mfd	del	powered by	mtow kg	configuration	selcal	name/fln/specialitites/remarks
☐ HK-2581	Boeing (Douglas) DC-3C (C-47B-23-DK)	27006	N94470	0043	1295	2 PW R-1830	12202	Freighter		rebuilt 1992
☐ HK-2820	Boeing (Douglas) DC-3C (C-47A-90-DL)	20171	N151D	0043	0091	2 PW R-1830	12202	Freighter		
☐ HK-3037	Boeing (Douglas) DC-3C (C-47A-90-DL)	20548	N17779	0043	0097	2 PW R-1830-92	11884	Freighter		
☐ HK-337	Boeing (Douglas) DC-3C (C-47A-DK)	11831	PJ-ALP	0043	0493	2 PW R-1830	12202	Freighter		rebuilt 1992

ALICOL Colombia - Aerolineas Intercolombianas, Ltda — Villavicencio

Calle 38, No. 30A-64, Oficina 801, Villavicencio, (Meta), Colombia ☎ (86) 62 41 67 Tx: n/a Fax: (86) 62 41 67 SITA: n/a
F: n/a n/a Head: Orlando Blanco Lopez Net: n/a Aircraft below MTOW 1361kg: Cessna 172 & 180.

registration	type of aircraft	cn/fn	ex/ex*	mfd	del	powered by	mtow kg	configuration	selcal	name/fln/specialitites/remarks
☐ HK-1152	Cessna 185A Skywagon	185-0492		0062		1 CO IO-470-F	1451			std VVC
☐ HK-2159	Cessna TU206G Turbo Stationair 6 II	CU20604327		0078		1 CO TSIO-520-M	1633			
☐ HK-3461	Twin (Aero) Jetprop Commander 980 (695)	95043	N74CD	0080		2 GA TPE331-10-511K	4683			
☐ HK-140	Boeing (Douglas) DC-3A-447	6354	C-140	0043	0095	2 PW R-1830	12202			lsf pvt
☐ HK-3176	Boeing (Douglas) DC-3C (C-47A-80-DL)	19606	FAC1122	0043	0092	2 PW R-1830	11431			

APSA Colombia – Aeroexpreso Bogota, S.A. = ABO (Associated with Aero Mercantil, S.A.) — **Bogota-Guayamaral & Bogota-Heliport**

Carrera 3A No. 56-19, Apartado Aéreo 6781, Santafé de Bogota, (D.E.), Colombia ☎ (1) 211 81 00 Tx: 44581 lave co Fax: (1) 212 89 52 SITA: n/a
F: 1978 ☗☗☗ 160 Head: Capt. Jaime Roberto Nino ICAO: AEROEXPRESO Net: n/a

☐ HK-4050X	Eurocopter (MBB) BO105C	*S-110*	*N3532T*	*0274*	*1195*	*2 AN 250-C20B*	*2400*			
☐ HK-4051X	Eurocopter (MBB) BO105C	*S-113*	*N3535T*	*0573*	*1195*	*2 AN 250-C20B*	*2400*			
☐ HK-3811	Britten-Norman BN-2A-26 Islander	*2040*	*TF-ARA*	*0088*		*2 LY O-540-E4C5*	*2994*			
☐ HK-3736X	Bell 212	*31144*	*N3895P*	*0080*		*2 PWC PT6T-3 TwinPac*	*5080*			
☐ HK-3737X	Bell 212	*31153*	*N3895U*	*0080*		*2 PWC PT6T-3 TwinPac*	*5080*			
☐ HK-3802X	Bell 212	*30817*	*N16785*	*0077*		*2 PWC PT6T-3 TwinPac*	*5080*			
☐ HK-3937X	Bell 212	*30932*	*N4425S*	*0079*	*0794*	*2 PWC PT6T-3 TwinPac*	*5080*			
☐ HK-3989X	Bell 212	*30869*	*N25FJ*	*0078*	*0195*	*2 PWC PT6T-3 TwinPac*	*5080*			
☐ HK-4076X	Bell 212	*30826*	*N62AL*	*0077*	*0596*	*2 PWC PT6T-3 TwinPac*	*5080*			
☐ HK-4087X	Bell 212	*30934*	*N68AL*	*0079*	*0996*	*2 PWC PT6T-3 TwinPac*	*5080*			
☐ HK-4103X	Bell 212	*30639*	*G-BCMC*	*0074*	*0397*	*2 PWC PT6T-3 TwinPac*	*5080*			*lsf BHL*
☐ HK-3796	Beech Catpass 200	*BB-264*	*C-FCGV*	*0077*	*1192*	*2 PWC PT6A-41*	*5670*			*cvtd King Air 200*
☐ HK-3990X	Beech Catpass 200	*BB-1376*	*N914YW*	*0090*	*0195*	*2 PWC PT6A-42*	*5670*			*cvtd King Air B200*
☐ N147BJ	Beech Beechjet 400A	*RK-147*		*0097*	*0897*	*2 PWC JT15D-5*	*7303*			*lsf Raytheon Aircraft Credit Corp.*
☐ HK-3983	Learjet 35A	*35A-259*	*N259HA*	*0079*	*1194*	*2 GA TFE731-2-2B*	*8301*			

ARALL Colombia – Aerolineas Llaneras, Ltda — **Villavicencio**

Carrera 39 No. 33B-51, Apartado Aéreo 2387, Villavicencio (Meta), Colombia ☎ (86) 64 80 44 Tx: n/a Fax: none SITA: n/a
F: 1980 ☗☗☗ 8 Head: Sergio Cruz Zapata Net: n/a Aircraft below MTOW 1361 kg: Cessna R172.

☐ HK-1231	Cessna TU206D Turbo Skywagon	*U206-1391*		*0069*		*1 CO TSIO-520-C*	*1633*			
☐ HK-2257	Cessna U206G Stationair 6 II	*CU20604600*		*0078*		*1 CO IO-520-F*	*1633*			
☐ HK-2708	Cessna U206G Stationair 6 II	*CU20606167*		*0081*		*1 CO IO-520-F*	*1633*			
☐ HK-2735	Cessna TU206G Turbo Stationair 6 II	*CU20606320*		*0081*		*1 CO TSIO-520-M*	*1633*			
☐ HK-2868	Cessna TU206G Turbo Stationair 6 II	*CU20606626*		*0082*		*1 CO TSIO-520-M*	*1633*			
☐ HK-1018	De Havilland DHC-2 Beaver I	*93*	*HK-240*	*0051*		*1 PW R-985*	*2313*			
☐ HK-2373	De Havilland DHC-2 Beaver I	*61*	*HK-84*	*0051*		*1 PW R-985*	*2313*			
☐ HK-2890	Britten-Norman BN-2B-27 Islander	*2111*	*N3235G*	*0081*		*1 LY O-540-E4C5*	*2885*			*dmgd 230594 / std VVC*

ARCA Colombia – Aerovias Colombianas, Ltda = AKC — **Bogota-Eldorado**

Calle 19 No 8-81, Oficina 303, Santafé de Bogota, (D.E.), Colombia ☎ (1) 334 76 51 Tx: 45319 arca co Fax: (1) 284 34 76 SITA: n/a
F: 1954 ☗☗☗ n/a Head: Capt. Hernando Gutierrez S. ICAO: ARCA Net: n/a Suspended operations (with DC-8F) 0197. Intends to restart in 1999 with Freighter-aircraft.

ASUR Colombia – Aerovias del Sur, Ltda — **Cali**

Aeropuerto Alfonso Bonilla Aragon, Cali, Colombia ☎ none Tx: none Fax: none SITA: n/a
F: n/a ☗☗☗ n/a Head: Ivan Rodriguez Rodriguez Net: n/a

☐ HK-1703	Boeing (Douglas) DC-6A (C-118B)	*43716 / 369*	*N96258*	*0053*		*4 PW R-2800*	*47083*	*Freighter*		
☐ HK-3301	Boeing (Douglas) DC-6A (C-118A-DO)	*44637 / 576*	*N4241C*	*0053*		*4 PW R-2800*	*47083*	*Freighter*		

ATC Colombia – Aero Transcolombiana de Carga, S.A. = TCO — **Bogota-Eldorado**

Bodega 5, Aeropuerto Eldorado, Santafé de Bogota (D.E.), Colombia ☎ (571) 414 80 70 Tx: n/a Fax: (571) 413 54 31 SITA: n/a
F: 1992 ☗☗☗ 120 Head: Carlos F. Child IATA: 826 ICAO: TRANSCOLOMBIA Net: n/a

☐ HK-3816X	Boeing (Douglas) DC-8-51F	*45685 / 204*	*HI-588CA*	*0064*	*0293*	*4 PW JT3D-3B (HK2/BAC)*	*125191*	*Freighter*		*lsf Agro Air Associates / cvtd DC-8-51*
☐ N507DC	Boeing (Douglas) DC-8-51F	*45855 / 281*	*C-FFQI*	*0066*	*0296*	*4 PW JT3D-3B (HK2/BAC)*	*125191*	*Freighter*	*JK-DE*	*lsf FBF / cvtd -51*
☐ N508DC	Boeing (Douglas) DC-8-51F	*45935 / 330*	*C-FFSB*	*0066*	*0197*	*4 PW JT3D-3B (HK2/BAC)*	*125191*	*Freighter*	*JK-DF*	*lsf FBF / cvtd -51*

AVIANCA Colombia – Aerovias Nacionales de Colombia, S.A. = AV / AVA — **Bogota-Eldorado & Barranquilla**

Avenida Eldorado No. 93-30, Piso 4, Bloque 1, Santafé de Bogota, (D.E.), Colombia ☎ (1) 413 95 11 Tx: 41453 edav co Fax: (1) 269 91 31 SITA: n/a
F: 1919 ☗☗☗ 3400 Head: Augusto Lopez IATA: 134 ICAO: AVIANCA Net: http://www.vip-ve.com/avianca/aviindex.htm

☐ PH-AVG	Fokker 50 (F27 Mk050)	*20278*	*PH-LXS**	*0093*	*0593*	*2 PWC PW127B*	*20820*	*Y50*		*lsf AFTR*
☐ PH-AVH	Fokker 50 (F27 Mk050)	*20281*		*0093*	*0593*	*2 PWC PW127B*	*20820*	*Y50*		*lsf AFTR*
☐ PH-AVJ	Fokker 50 (F27 Mk050)	*20285*		*0093*	*1193*	*2 PWC PW127B*	*20820*	*Y50*		*lsf AFTR*
☐ PH-AVN	Fokker 50 (F27 Mk050)	*20296*		*0093*	*1193*	*2 PWC PW127B*	*20820*	*Y50*		*lsf AFTR*
☐ PH-AVO	Fokker 50 (F27 Mk050)	*20297*		*0093*	*1193*	*2 PWC PW127B*	*20820*	*Y50*		*lsf AFTR*
☐ PH-LXW	Fokker 50 (F27 Mk050)	*20266*		*0093*	*0593*	*2 PWC PW127B*	*20820*	*Y50*		*lsf AFTR*
☐ PH-MXJ	Fokker 50 (F27 Mk050)	*20288*		*0094*	*1294*	*2 PWC PW127B*	*20820*	*Y50*		*lsf AFTR*
☐ PH-MXS	Fokker 50 (F27 Mk050)	*20299*		*0094*	*0594*	*2 PWC PW127B*	*20820*	*Y50*		*lsf AFTR*
☐ PH-MXT	Fokker 50 (F27 Mk050)	*20300*		*0094*	*0894*	*2 PWC PW127B*	*20820*	*Y50*		*lsf AFTR*
☐ PH-MXZ	Fokker 50 (F27 Mk050)	*20301*		*0094*	*0794*	*2 PWC PW127B*	*20820*	*Y50*		*lsf AFTR*
☐ HK-4137X	Boeing (Douglas) MD-83 (DC-9-83)	*53190 / 2148*	*N190AN*	*0096*	*0298*	*2 PW JT8D-219*	*72575*	*C12Y140*		*lsf AWAS*
☐ HK-4165X	Boeing (Douglas) MD-83 (DC-9-83)	*53093 / 2066*	*N873RA*	*0093*	*1098*	*2 PW JT8D-219*	*72575*	*C12Y140*		*lsf AWAS*
☐ EI-CBR	Boeing (Douglas) MD-83 (DC-9-83)	*49939 / 1787*		*1090*	*0392*	*2 PW JT8D-219*	*72575*	*C12Y140*	*AC-DE*	Ciudad de Bucaramanga / *lsf GECA*
☐ EI-CBS	Boeing (Douglas) MD-83 (DC-9-83)	*49942 / 1799*		*0090*	*0392*	*2 PW JT8D-219*	*72575*	*C12Y140*		Ciudad de Cucuta / *lsf GECA*
☐ EI-CBY	Boeing (Douglas) MD-83 (DC-9-83)	*49944 / 1888*		*0091*	*0292*	*2 PW JT8D-219*	*72575*	*C12Y140*		Ciudad de Barranquilla / *lsf GECA*
☐ EI-CBZ	Boeing (Douglas) MD-83 (DC-9-83)	*49945 / 1889*		*0091*	*0292*	*2 PW JT8D-219*	*72575*	*C12Y140*		Ciudad Santiago de Cali / *lsf GECA*
☐ EI-CCC	Boeing (Douglas) MD-83 (DC-9-83)	*49946 / 1898*		*0091*	*0392*	*2 PW JT8D-219*	*72575*	*C12Y140*		Ciudad de Pereira / *lsf GECA*
☐ EI-CCE	Boeing (Douglas) MD-83 (DC-9-83)	*49947 / 1900*		*0091*	*0392*	*2 PW JT8D-219*	*72575*	*C12Y140*		Ciudad de Medellin / *lsf GECA*
☐ EI-CDY	Boeing (Douglas) MD-83 (DC-9-83)	*49948 / 1905*		*0091*	*0492*	*2 PW JT8D-219*	*72575*	*C12Y140*		Ciudad de Santa Marta / *lsf GECA*
☐ EI-CEP	Boeing (Douglas) MD-83 (DC-9-83)	*53122 / 1984*		*0092*	*0492*	*2 PW JT8D-219*	*72575*	*C12Y140*		San Andres Isla / *lsf GECA*
☐ EI-CEQ	Boeing (Douglas) MD-83 (DC-9-83)	*53123 / 1987*		*0092*	*0592*	*2 PW JT8D-219*	*72575*	*C12Y140*		Ciudad de Leticia / *lsf GECA*
☐ EI-CER	Boeing (Douglas) MD-83 (DC-9-83)	*53125 / 1993*		*0092*	*0692*	*2 PW JT8D-219*	*72575*	*C12Y140*		Ciudad de Monteria / *lsf GECA*
☐ EI-CFZ	Boeing (Douglas) MD-83 (DC-9-83)	*53120 / 1964*	*N6206F**	*0092*	*0792*	*2 PW JT8D-219*	*72575*	*C12Y140*		Ciudad San Juan de Pasto / *lsf GECA*
☐ HK-2151X	Boeing 727-2A1 (A)	*21343 / 1320*		*0078*	*1078*	*3 PW JT8D-17R*	*86637*	*Y170*		*lsf Aviation Equipment Services Inc.*
☐ HK-2152X	Boeing 727-2A1 (A)	*21344 / 1322*		*0078*	*1178*	*3 PW JT8D-17R*	*86637*	*Y170*		*lsf Aviation Equipment Services Inc.*
☐ HK-3480X	Boeing 727-2H3 (A)	*20739 / 952*	*N726VA*	*0073*	*0489*	*3 PW JT8D-9A*	*86637*	*Y165*		*lsf North American Air Svc/Bancoquia-cs*
☐ EI-CEY	Boeing 757-2Y0	*26152 / 478*		*0092*	*0892*	*2 RR RB211-535E4*	*113398*	*C12Y164*	*CR-HP*	*lsf GECA*
☐ EI-CEZ	Boeing 757-2Y0	*26154 / 486*		*0092*	*0992*	*2 RR RB211-535E4*	*113398*	*C12Y164*	*CR-HQ*	*lsf GECA*
☐ N321LF	Boeing 757-2Q8	*26269 / 612*		*0094*	*0896*	*2 RR RB211-535E4*	*115666*	*C12Y164*		*lsf ILFC*
☐ N987AN	Boeing 757-2Y0 (ET)	*25494 / 611*		*0094*	*0494*	*2 RR RB211-535E4*	*113398*	*C12Y164*		*lsf AWAS*
☐ N985AN	Boeing 767-259 (ER)	*24618 / 292*		*0090*	*0290*	*2 PW PW4056*	*159211*	*C23Y156*	*GL-EJ*	Cristobal Colon / *lsf WTC Trustee*
☐ N986AN	Boeing 767-259 (ER)	*24835 / 321*		*0090*	*0890*	*2 PW PW4056*	*159211*	*C23Y156*	*GK-DF*	Amerigo Vespucio / *lst WTC Trustee*
☐ N988AN	Boeing 767-284 (ER)	*24742 / 303*	*VH-RMA*	*0090*	*0297*	*2 PW PW4056*	*175540*	*C23Y156*	*GS-PR*	*lsf Bay 2 Bay Leasing Llc*
☐ N984AN	Boeing 767-383 (ER)	*24357 / 262*	*LN-RCB*	*0089*	*0894*	*2 PW PW4060*	*184612*	*C24Y187*	*BQ-GK*	*lsf PEGA*

AVIAPA Colombia – Aerovias del Pacifico, Ltda — **Pereira**

Aeropuerto Matecana, Hangar 7, Pereira, Colombia ☎ (63) 26 66 66 Tx: none Fax: (63) 26 66 66 SITA: n/a
F: n/a ☗☗☗ n/a Head: Capt. Carlos A. Acelas F. Net: n/a

☐ HK-4004X	Dornier DO 28D-2 Skyservant	*4182*	*D-IEDH*	*0073*		*2 LY IGSO-540-A1E*	*3842*			
☐ HK-4005X	Dornier DO 28D-2 Skyservant	*4136*		*0071*		*2 LY IGSO-540-A1E*	*3842*			

AVIEL Colombia – Aviones Ejecutivos, Ltda — **Bogota-Eldorado**

Aeropuerto Eldorado, Entrada 2, Int. 1, Of. 227, Santafé de Bogota, (D.E.), Colombia ☎ (1) 413 85 82 Tx: n/a Fax: none SITA: n/a
F: n/a ☗☗☗ n/a Head: Jairo Forero Pulido Net: n/a

☐ HK-3403	MD Helicopters MD 530F (Hughes 369FF)	*0056FF*		*0088*		*1 AN 250-C30*	*1406*			
☐ HK-3311	Bell 206L-3 LongRanger III	*51195*	*N32041*	*0087*		*1 AN 250-C30P*	*1882*			
☐ HK-3312	Bell 206L-3 LongRanger III	*51211*		*0087*		*1 AN 250-C30P*	*1882*			
☐ HK-574	Piper PA-23-250 Aztec C	*27-3752*	*HC-ANG*	*0067*		*2 LY IO-540-J4A5*	*2359*			*std BOG*
☐ HK-2281	Twin (Aero) Turbo Commander 690	*11033*	*N100DG*	*0072*		*2 GA TPE331-5-251K*	*4649*			
☐ HK-3218	Twin (Aero) Jetprop Commander 1000 (695A)	*96061*	*N184BB*	*0083*		*2 GA TPE331-10-501K*	*5080*			

BPX Colombia – BP Exploration Company Colombia, Ltda = BPX — **Bogota-Eldorado**

Officio Seguro de Commercio/Dept. Vuelos, Carrera Novena 9902, 4P, Santafé de Bogota, Colombia ☎ (1) 618 27 77 Tx: none Fax: (1) 413 51 87 SITA: n/a
F: n/a ☗☗☗ 31 Head: Enrique Pinto Net: n/a Operates non-commercial corporate flights for itself only.

☐ HK-3704X	Beech Catpass 250	*BB-1392*	*N8026J*	*0090*	*0292*	*2 PWC PT6A-41*	*5670*	*Corporate 13Pax*		*cvtd King Air B200*
☐ HK-3997W	De Havilland DHC-8-202 Dash 8	*391*	*C-GFBW**	*0095*	*0495*	*2 PWC PW123D*	*16465*	*Corporate 39Pax*		

CARICARGA COLOMBIA – Cali Cargo, Ltda — **Bogota-Eldorado & Cali**

Aeropuerto Alfonso B. Aragon, Cali, Colombia ☎ (2) 441 70 41 Tx: n/a Fax: (2) 441 70 41 SITA: n/a
F: n/a ☗☗☗ n/a Head: Armando Gutierrez Fernandez Net: n/a

☐ HK-4007X	Antonov 32B	*3303*	*UR-48019*	*0094*	*0095*	*2 IV AI-20D*	*27000*	*Freighter 6,7t*		
☐ HK-4009X	Antonov 32B	*3410*	*UR-48022*	*0094*	*0095*	*2 IV AI-20D*	*27000*	*Freighter 6,7t*		
☐ HK-4052X	Antonov 32	*1805*	*YN-CBU*	*0088*	*0096*	*2 IV AI-20D*	*27000*	*Freighter 6,7t*		

196 registration | type of aircraft | cn/fn | ex/ex* | mfd | del | powered by | mtow kg | configuration | selcal | name/fln/specialitites/remarks

CENTRAL CHARTER de Colombia, S.A. = AJS (formerly Aeroejecutivos Colombia – Aeroservicios Ejecutivos, SA) — Bogota-Eldorado

Aeropuerto Eldorado Entrada 2, Int. 1, Apartado Aéreo 15115, Santafé de Bogota (D.E.), Colombia ☎ (1) 413 95 30 Tx: 45404 aeroe co Fax: (1) 413 95 50 SITA: n/a
F: 1979 ⁂ 50 Head: Fernando Munoz Merizalde ICAO: AEROEJECUTIVOS Net: n/a

☐ HK-3504	Beech King Air B200	BB-1063	N256L	0082	0789	2 PWC PT6A-42	5670			
☐ HK-4016X	Learjet 55	55-041	N550RH	0082	0595	2 GA TFE731-3A-2B	8845			
☐ HK-3971X	IAI 1124A Westwind II	306		0081		2 GA TFE731-3-1G	10659			

CORAL Colombia – Coronado Aerolineas, Ltda = CRA — Villavicencio

Hangar 1, Aeropuerto Vanguardia, Villavicencio, (Meta), Colombia ☎ (86) 63 56 43 Tx: n/a Fax: (86) 63 54 22 SITA: n/a
F: 1986 ⁂ n/a Head: Raul Antonio Coronado Cubillos ICAO: CORAL Net: n/a

☐ HK-851	Curtiss C-46A-60-CS Commando	383	HP-217	0045		2 PW R-2800-51	21772	Freighter		

EL DORADO Colombia – Lineas Aereas El Dorado, Ltda = EDR — Villavicencio

Aeropuerto Vanguardia, Villavicencio, (Meta), Colombia ☎ (86) 64 80 79 Tx: none Fax: none SITA: n/a
F: n/a ⁂ n/a Head: Chela Maria Vengoechea de Galvez ICAO: ELDORADO Net: n/a

☐ HK-122	Boeing (Douglas) DC-3C (C-47-DL)	4414	C-122	0042		2 PW R-1830-92	12202	Freighter		
☐ HK-2666	Boeing (Douglas) DC-3C (C-47A-60-DL)	10201	C-GSTA	0042		2 PW R-1830	12202	Freighter		

FRONTERA Colombia – Aeroexpreso de la Frontera, Ltda — Villavicencio & Rondon

Aeropuerto Vanguardia, Villavicencio, (Meta), Colombia ☎ (86) 64 80 57 Tx: none Fax: n/a SITA: n/a
F: n/a ⁂ n/a Head: Luis Hernando Marroquin Net: n/a Aircraft below MTOW 1361kg: Cessna 172, 180, 182 & Piper PA-28.

☐ HK-2835	Piper PA-34-220T Seneca III	34-8233129		0082		2 CO TSIO-360-KB	2155			
☐ HK-3539	Cessna 208 Caravan I	C20800165		0089		1 PWC PT6A-114	3629			
☐ HK-1344	Twin (Aero) Super Commander 680	680-498-168	FAC 554	0056		2 LY GSO-480-B1A6	3175			

HELICOL Colombia – Helicopteros Nacionales de Colombia, SA = HEL (Subsidiary of Avianca Colombia) — Barranquilla / Bogota-Eldorado & Medellin-Olaya Herrera

Helicol

Cra. 13 No. 28-17, Piso 6, Santafé de Bogota, (D.E.), Colombia ☎ (1) 287 60 30 Tx: 41225 hl co Fax: (1) 287 49 18 SITA: n/a
F: 1955 ⁂ 600 Head: Nicanor Isaza Restrepo ICAO: HELICOL Net: n/a

☐ HK-2374E	Bell 206B JetRanger III	2774		0079	1079	1 AN 250-C20B	1451			
☐ HK-3357G	Bell 206L-3 LongRanger III	51231		1287	0294	1 AN 250-C30P	1882	VIP		opf Svcs Seccional de Salud Antioquia
☐ HK-3619X	Bell 206L-1 LongRanger II	45632	N206TT	0080	0291	1 AN 250-C28B	1882			lsf Latin American Air Service
☐ HK-3633X	Bell 206L-1 LongRanger II	45510	N57497	0079	0591	1 AN 250-C28B	1882			lsf Latin American Air Service
☐ HK-3725X	Bell 206L-3 LongRanger III	51201	N63WM	0187	0592	1 AN 250-C30P	1882			lsf Latin American Air Service
☐ HK-3754X	Bell 206L-3 LongRanger III	51591		0792	0892	1 AN 250-C30P	1882			lsf Latin American Air Service
☐ HK-3792X	Bell 206L-3 LongRanger III	51592		0792	0193	1 AN 250-C30P	1882			lsf Latin American Air Service
☐ HK-3823X	Bell 206L-1 LongRanger II	45507	HK-3156E	0080	1284	1 AN 250-C28B	1882			lsf Bell Helicopter Textron
☐ HK-3825X	Bell 206L-3 LongRanger III	51234	N75AJ	0088	0293	1 AN 250-C30P	1882			lsf Cadena Radical Colombiana
☐ HK-2610	Eurocopter (Aerosp.) AS350B Ecureuil	1339		0179	1180	1 TU Arriel 1B	1950			
☐ HK-4024X	Eurocopter (Aerosp.) AS355F1 Ecureuil 2	5126	HK-3589X	0379	0890	2 AN 250-C20F	2400			lsf North American Air Service
☐ HK-1346E	Bell 205A-1	30062	N2253W	0070	1073	1 LY T5313B	4309			
☐ HK-3183X	Bell 212	32137	N21505	0081	0985	2 PWC PT6T-3 TwinPac	5080			lsf Latin American Air Service
☐ HK-3303X	Bell 212	30654	N59608	1074	0487	2 PWC PT6T-3 TwinPac	5080			lsf Latin American Air Service
☐ HK-3336X	Bell 212	31207	N2180J	0081	1187	2 PWC PT6T-3 TwinPac	5080			lsf Latin American Air Service
☐ HK-3899X	Bell 212	30915	N5009N	0179	0194	2 PWC PT6T-3 TwinPac	5080			lsf Petroleum Helicopters, USA
☐ HK-3900X	Bell 212	30989	N1074C	0280	0194	2 PWC PT6T-3 TwinPac	5080			lsf Petroleum Helicopters, USA
☐ HK-4031X	Bell 212	31203	HK-3184X	0081	0795	2 PWC PT6T-3 TwinPac	5080			lsf Latin American Air Service
☐ HK-3578G	Bell 412	33203		0190	1290	2 PWC PT6T-3B TwinPac	5398	VIP		opf Gobernacion de Antioquia
☐ HK-3749X	Beech King Air 200	BB-363	N1014K	0478	0893	2 PWC PT6A-41	5670			lsf Latin American Air Service
☐ HK-2439	De Havilland DHC-6 Twin Otter 300	668	9H-AAS	0480	0580	2 PWC PT6A-27	5670			
☐ HK-2553	De Havilland DHC-6 Twin Otter 300	719		1080	1180	2 PWC PT6A-27	5670			lsf Petroleum Helicopters de Colombia
☐ HK-4018X	De Havilland DHC-6 Twin Otter 300	754	HK-3021X	0381	0483	2 PWC PT6A-27	5670			lsf Latin American Air Service
☐ HK-4019X	De Havilland DHC-6 Twin Otter 300	781	HK-2970X	0282	0483	2 PWC PT6A-27	5670			lsf Latin American Air Service
☐ 8P-KAM	Cessna 650 Citation III	650-0119		0986	0893	2 GA TFE731-3C-100S	9979			lsf Petroleum Helicopters de Colombia
☐ HK-3879X	Mil Mi-8MTV-1	96006		0992	1193	2 IS TV3-117VM	13000			lsf Latin American Air Service
☐ HK-3880X	Mil Mi-8MTV-1	96016		1092	1193	2 IS TV3-117VM	13000			lsf Latin American Air Service
☐ HK-3882X	Mil Mi-8MTV-1	96018		1092	1193	2 IS TV3-117VM	13000			lsf Latin American Air Service
☐ HK-3889X	Mil Mi-8MTV-1	95839		0292	1293	2 IS TV3-117VM	13000			lsf Latin American Air Service
☐ HK-3890X	Mil Mi-8MTV-1	95973		0792	1293	2 IS TV3-117VM	13000			lsf Latin American Air Service
☐ HK-3897X	Mil Mi-8MTV-1	96154		0793	1293	2 IS TV3-117VM	13000			lsf Latin American Air Service
☐ HK-3898X	Mil Mi-8MTV-1	96156		0793	1293	2 IS TV3-117VM	13000			lsf Latin American Air Service
☐ HK-4022X	GAC (Grumman) G-159 Gulfstream I	190	HK-3579X	0468	0790	2 RR Dart 529-8X	15422			lsf Latin American Air Service
☐ HK-3111G	De Havilland DHC-7-102 Dash 7	087	C-GFBW*	0682	0284	4 PWC PT6A-50	19958	Corporate		opf Intercor/Carbocol Colombia
☐ HK-3340W	De Havilland DHC-7-102 Dash 7	108	C-GFBW*	1085	0587	4 PWC PT6A-50	19958	Corporate		opf Intercor/Carbocol Colombia
☐ 8P-MAK	GAC G-IV Gulfstream IV	1186	N479GA*	0193	0193	2 RR Tay 611-8	33203			lsf A.L.N. Ltd

HELITAXI Colombia – Helitaxi, Ltda — Bogota-Guaymaral & -Eldorado

HELITAXI LTDA.

Aeropuerto Eldorado, Nueva Zona de Aviacion General, Hangar 19, Santafé de Bogota (D.E.), Colombia ☎ (571) 547 24 14 Tx: none Fax: (571) 414 86 50 SITA: n/a
F: 1982 ⁂ 240 Head: German Ricardo Rodgriguez Melo Net: n/a

☐ HK-2175	MD Helicopters MD 500D (Hughes 369D)	1080360D		0078		1 AN 250-C20B	1361	5 Pax		
☐ HK-2529	Bell 206B JetRanger III	3057		0080		1 AN 250-C20B	1451	5 Pax		
☐ HK-3353	Bell 206L-3 LongRanger III	51177		0086		1 AN 250-C30P	1882	6 Pax		
☐ HK-3727	Bell 206L-3 LongRanger III	51525	N3215K*	0091	0096	1 AN 250-C30P	1882	6 Pax		
☐ HK-3262	Bell 222UT	47556		0086		2 LY LTS101-750C.1	3742	7 Pax		
☐ HK-3416	Bell 222UT	47534	N227DC	0085	0096	2 LY LTS101-750C.1	3742	7 Pax		
☐ HK-2455	Piper PA-31T Cheyenne II XL	31T-8020047		0080		2 PWC PT6A-135	4082	6 Pax		cvtd Cheyenne II
☐ HK-3466	Twin (Aero) Turbo Commander 690A	11165	N690LP	0074	0989	2 GA TPE331-5-251K	4649	6 Pax		
☐ HK-3250	Bell 212	31219	HC-BSI	0082		2 PWC PT6T-3 TwinPac	5080	13 Pax		
☐ HK-3709	Bell 212	30586	HK-3185X	0073		2 PWC PT6T-3 TwinPac	5080	13 Pax		
☐ HK-3723	Bell 212	32122	N1080V	0079		2 PWC PT6T-3 TwinPac	5080	13 Pax		
☐ HK-3742	Bell 212	30847		0077		2 PWC PT6T-3 TwinPac	5080	13 Pax		
☐ HK-4025	Bell 212	31143	HC-BSQ	0080	0093	2 PWC PT6T-3B TwinPac	5080	13 Pax		
☐ HK-3854	Beech King Air 200	BB-135	N535E	0076	0097	2 PWC PT6A-41	5670			
☐ HK-3400	Cessna 550 Citation II	550-0363	N444CC	0082		2 PWC JT15D-4	6033	10 Pax		
☐ HK-3988	Beech King Air 350 (B300)	FL-18	N80CK	0090	0097	2 PWC PT6A-60A	6804			
☐ HK-3888	Mil Mi-8MTV-1	95838		0292	0096	2 IS TV3-117MT-3	13000	28 Pax		
☐ HK-3908	Mil Mi-8MTV-1	95823		1291	0096	2 IS TV3-117MT-3	13000	28 Pax		
☐ HK-3910	Mil Mi-8MTV-1	96008		0992	0096	2 IS TV3-117MT-3	13000	28 Pax		
☐ HK-3911	Mil Mi-8MTV-1	96124		0493	0096	2 IS TV3-117MT-3	13000	28 Pax		
☐ HK-3730	Mil Mi-17	95728		0092	0092	2 IS TV3-117MT-3	13000	28 Pax		
☐ HK-3731X	Mil Mi-17	95586		0092	0092	2 IS TV3-117MT-3	13000	28 Pax		
☐ HK-3732X	Mil Mi-17	95729		0092	0092	2 IS TV3-117MT-3	13000	28 Pax		
☐ HK-3758X	Mil Mi-17	95908	HC-BSG	0092	0092	2 IS TV3-117MT-3	13000	28 Pax		
☐ HK-3779X	Mil Mi-17	95645		0092	0092	2 IS TV3-117MT-3	13000	28 Pax		
☐ HK-3780X	Mil Mi-17	95909		0092	0092	2 IS TV3-117MT-3	13000	28 Pax		
☐ HK-3782X	Mil Mi-17	95910	HC-BSH	0092	0092	2 IS TV3-117MT-3	13000	28 Pax		
☐ HK-3862	Mil Mi-17	95923		0092	0093	2 IS TV3-117MT-3	13000	28 Pax		
☐ HK-3863	Mil Mi-17	95894		0092	0093	2 IS TV3-117MT-3	13000	28 Pax		
☐ HK-3864	Mil Mi-17	95893		0092	0093	2 IS TV3-117MT-3	13000	28 Pax		
☐ HK-3865	Mil Mi-17	95892		0092	0093	2 IS TV3-117MT-3	13000	28 Pax		

HELIVALLE Colombia – Helicopteros del Valle, Ltda — Palmira (Valle)

HELIVALLE

Carrera 11 No. 86-60, Oficina 202, Apartado Aéreo 91747, Santafé de Bogota (D.E.), Colombia ☎ (1) 257 06 35 Tx: 45167 helva co Fax: (1) 218 86 89 SITA: n/a
F: 1965 ⁂ 65 Head: Miguel Roberto Espitita E. Net: n/a Aircraft below MTOW 1361 kg: Bell 47 Soloy

☐ HK-2383E	Bell 206B JetRanger III	2841		0079		1 AN 250-C20B	1451			
☐ HK-3838X	Bell 206L-4 LongRanger IV	52008		0092	0093	1 AN 250-C30P	2018			
☐ HK-3978X	Bell 206L-3 LongRanger III	51446		0091		1 AN 250-C30P	1882			
☐ HK-4015X	Bell 206L-4 LongRanger IV	52092	N2468G	0094	0595	1 AN 250-C30P	2018			
☐ HK-3603	Piper PA-31T2 Cheyenne II XL	31T-8166034	N730PC	0081		2 PWC PT6A-135	4297			
☐ HK-3693X	Piper PA-42 Cheyenne III	42-8001075	N4998M	0082	0093	2 PWC PT6A-41	5080			
☐ HK-3849X	Bell 212	30926	PT-HPZ	0079		2 PWC PT6T-3 TwinPac	5080			
☐ HK-4026X	Bell 212	35055	N4354J	0092		2 PWC PT6T-3B TwinPac	5080			

INTERAMERICANA Colombia – Interamericana de Aviacion, SA = IIA — Bogota-Eldorado

INTERAMERICANA

Avenida Eldorado, Entrada 1, Interior 12, Apartado Aéreo 90277, Santafé de Bogota (D.E.), Colombia ☎ (1) 413 94 00 Tx: 45606 ideav co Fax: (1) 413 80 36 SITA: n/a
F: n/a ⁂ n/a Head: Gabriel Nunez ICAO: INTERAMERICANA Net: n/a

☐ HK-1848	Piper PA-23-250 Turbo Aztec E	27-7554122	N54825	0075		2 LY TIO-540-C1A	2359			
☐ HK-2491	Beech King Air E90	LW-183	YV-940P	0076		2 PWC PT6A-28	4581			
☐ HK-2489	Beech King Air 200	BB-393	N2014K	0078		2 PWC PT6A-41	5670			

197 registration type of aircraft cn/fn ex/ex* mfd del powered by mtow kg configuration selcal name/fln/specialitites/remarks

INTERANDES Colombia – Compañia Interandina de Aviacion, SA = IAN

Bogota-Eldorado & Guaymaral

Aeropuerto Eldorado, Entrada 2, Apartado Aéreo 040350, Santafé de Bogota (D.E.), Colombia ☎ (1) 413 88 35 Tx: 45220 auhg co Fax: (1) 413 87 95 SITA: n/a
F: 1979 👥 20 Head: Alvaro & Duenas Acero ICAO: INTERANDES Net: n/a

registration	type of aircraft	cn/fn	ex/ex*	mfd	del	powered by	mtow kg	configuration	selcal	name/fln/specialitites/remarks
☐ HK-3457	Cessna 441 Conquest II	441-0359	N4CS	0086	0189	2 GA TPE331-8-403S	4468			
☐ HK-3607X	Cessna 550 Citation II	550-0040	N900LC	0079	1290	2 PWC JT15D-4	6033			lsf Cessna Fin./cvtd Ce 551 cn 551-0085

INTERCONTINENTAL Colombia – Intercontinental de Aviacion, SA = RS / ICT (formerly Aeropesca Colombia)

Bogota-Eldorado

Avenida Eldorado, Entrada No. 2, Interior 6, Apartado Aéreo 151005, Santafé de Bogota (D.E.), Colombia ☎ (1) 413 88 88 Tx: 42241 inavi co Fax: (1) 413 84 58 SITA: n/a
F: 1965 👥 650 Head: Capt. Luis H. Zia IATA: 608 ICAO: CONTAVIA Net: http://www.insite-network.com/Inter/

registration	type of aircraft	cn/fn	ex/ex*	mfd	del	powered by	mtow kg	configuration	selcal	name/fln/specialitites/remarks
☐ HK-4061X	De Havilland DHC-8-301 Dash 8	192	C6-BFL	0090	0396	2 PWC PW123	18643	Y50		lsf Aviaco Traders Int'l
☐ HK-4062X	De Havilland DHC-8-301 Dash 8	196	C6-BFM	0090	0496	2 PWC PW123	18643	Y50		lsf Aviaco Traders Int'l
☐ HK-2865X	Boeing (Douglas) DC-9-15	45722 / 55	FAC1142	1066	1282	2 PW JT8D-7B	41141	Y83		lsf Largo Leasing
☐ HK-3752X	Boeing (Douglas) DC-9-15	45781 / 101	N1067T	0467	0892	2 PW JT8D-7B	41141	Y83		lsf Largo Leasing
☐ HK-3827X	Boeing (Douglas) DC-9-15	47048 / 35	G-BMAA	0766	0393	2 PW JT8D-7B	41141	Y83		lsf Largo Leasing
☐ HK-3859X	Boeing (Douglas) DC-9-14	45843 / 28	N8962	0466	1093	2 PW JT8D-7B	41141	Y83		lsf Transpacific Leasing
☐ HK-3891X	Boeing (Douglas) DC-9-15	45776 / 72	YV-857C	1266	0193	2 PW JT8D-7B	41141	Y83		lsf Largo Leasing
☐ HK-3958X	Boeing (Douglas) DC-9-15	45738 / 54	G-BMAB	1066	0894	2 PW JT8D-7A	41141	Y83		lsf Transpacific Leasing
☐ HK-4056X	Boeing (Douglas) DC-9-14	45712 / 6	G-BMAH	0865	1195	2 PW JT8D-7B	41141	Y83		lsf Transpacific Leasing / std BOG
☐ XA-SSW	Boeing (Douglas) DC-9-14	45735 / 25	HK-3867X	0466	0393	2 PW JT8D-7B	41141	Y83		lsf Largo Leasing / sub-lst CBE
☐ XA-SVZ	Boeing (Douglas) DC-9-15	47125 / 388	HK-3486X	0968	1289	2 PW JT8D-7B	41141	Y83		lsf Largo Leasing / sub-lst CBE
☐ XA-SXS	Boeing (Douglas) DC-9-14	45713 / 9	G-BMAI	0166	0495	2 PW JT8D-7A	41141	Y83		lsf Transpacific Leasing / sub-lst TEJ
☐ XA-SXT	Boeing (Douglas) DC-9-15	45719 / 18	G-BMAG	0166	0395	2 PW JT8D-7A	41141	Y83		lsf Transpacific Leasing / sub-lst TEJ
☐ XA-SXV	Boeing (Douglas) DC-9-14	45715 / 10	HK-3830X	0166	0793	2 PW JT8D-7B	41141	Y83		lsf Largo Leasing / sub-lst TEJ
☐ XA-SYF	Boeing (Douglas) DC-9-15	45780 / 93	HK-3710X	0367	0492	2 PW JT8D-7B	41141	Y83		lsf Largo Leasing / sub-lst TEJ
☐ XA-SZC	Boeing (Douglas) DC-9-15	45739 / 56	G-BMAC	1066	0895	2 PW JT8D-7A	41141	Y83		lsf Transpacific Leasing / sub-lst TEJ
☐ XA-TBX	Boeing (Douglas) DC-9-14	45716 / 13	HK-3833X	0166	0393	2 PW JT8D-7B	41141	Y83		lsf Largo Leasing / sub-lst CBE
☐ XA-TGJ	Boeing (Douglas) DC-9-15	45783 / 128	HK-3720X	0667	0592	2 PW JT8D-7B	41141	Y83		lst CBE as XA-TGJ

LACOL Colombia – Lineas Aéreas Colombianas, Ltda = LAE

Villavicencio

Calle 38 No. 31-41, Oficina 305, Edificio Parque Santander, Villavicencio (Meta), Colombia ☎ (86) 64 81 97 Tx: none Fax: (86) 64 81 97 SITA: n/a
F: 1982 👥 15 Head: Jorge Antonio Ronado Amaris ICAO: LACOL Net: n/a

registration	type of aircraft	cn/fn	ex/ex*	mfd	del	powered by	mtow kg	configuration	selcal	name/fln/specialitites/remarks
☐ HK-124	Boeing (Douglas) DC-3C (C-47-DL)	4349	C-124	0042		2 PW R-1830-92	12202	Freighter		std BOG / being restored
☐ HK-3215	Boeing (Douglas) DC-3C (C-47B-5-DK)	26111	N124SF	0044		2 PW R-1830-92	12202	Freighter		Capt. Miguel Angel Rodado A. / std VVC

LANC Colombia – Lineas Aéreas Norte de Colombia, Ltda

Cartagena

La Matuna Cra. 10A, No. 32C-24, Local 26, Cartagena, (Bolivar), Colombia ☎ (5) 664 08 83 Tx: n/a Fax: n/a SITA: n/a
F: n/a 👥 n/a Head: Carlos Alberto Gaviria Olano Net: n/a

registration	type of aircraft	cn/fn	ex/ex*	mfd	del	powered by	mtow kg	configuration	selcal	name/fln/specialitites/remarks
☐ HK-2497	Boeing (Douglas) DC-3C (C-47B-20-DK)	27079	N423MB	0044	0094	2 PW R-1830-94	11431	Freighter		Capt.Pin / lsfpvt/stdVVC/being restored
☐ HK-3948X	Aerosp. (Sud) SE210 Caravelle 10B1R	255	HK-3939X	0069	0894	2 PW JT8D-7B	53000	Freighter		

LANS Colombia – Lineas Aéreas Norte de Santander, Ltda

Cucuta

Calle 9, No. 11E-52, Cucuta, Colombia ☎ (75) 27 56 96 Tx: n/a Fax: (75) 87 56 97 SITA: n/a
F: n/a 👥 n/a Head: Capt. José Rafael Ramirez Yanez Net: n/a

registration	type of aircraft	cn/fn	ex/ex*	mfd	del	powered by	mtow kg	configuration	selcal	name/fln/specialitites/remarks
☐ HK-2876	Piper PA-32-301T Turbo Saratoga	32-8224013		0082		1 LY TIO-540-S1AD	1633			
☐ HK-4040X	Piper PA-34-200T Seneca II	34-7670333		0076	0995	2 CO TSIO-360-E	2073			
☐ HK-1021	Piper PA-23-250 Aztec B	27-2465		0063		2 LY O-540-A1D5	2177			
☐ HK-4039X	Piper PA-23-250 Aztec F	27-7654195		0076	0995	2 LY IO-540-C4B5	2359			

LAP Colombia – Lineas Aéreas Petroleras, SA = APT

Bogota-Eldorado

Avenida Eldorado, Entrada 1, Int. 7, Apartado Aéreo 151227, Santafé de Bogota (D.E.), Colombia ☎ (1) 413 52 58 Tx: 43434 pspcl co Fax: (1) 413 86 35 SITA: n/a
F: 1976 👥 56 Head: Samuel Arturo Diaz ICAO: LAP Net: n/a Aircraft below MTOW 1361 kg: Bell 47G.

registration	type of aircraft	cn/fn	ex/ex*	mfd	del	powered by	mtow kg	configuration	selcal	name/fln/specialitites/remarks
☐ HK-2757	Eurocopter (Aerosp.) SA315B Lama	2613		0081		1 TU Artouste IIIB	1950			
☐ HK-2349	Piper PA-34-200T Seneca II	34-7970376		0079		2 CO TSIO-360-EB1	2073			
☐ HK-1379	Piper PA-31-310 Navajo	31-131		0068		2 LY TIO-540-A1A	2948			
☐ HK-2503	Piper PA-31-310 Navajo	31-8012056		0080		2 LY TIO-540-A2C	2948			
☐ HK-2504	Piper PA-31-310 Navajo	31-8012083		0080		2 LY TIO-540-A2C	2948			
☐ HK-1514	Boeing (Douglas) DC-3A (C-53D-DO)	11741	N100RW	0042		2 PW R-1830-94	11431			

LATINA Colombia – Latina de Aviacion, Ltda

Villavicencio & Bogota-Eldorado

Aeropuerto Eldorado, Nt.1, Int. 25, Santafé de Bogota, (D.E.), Colombia ☎ (1) 413 95 80 Tx: none Fax: (1) 413 95 80 SITA: n/a
F: 1994 👥 n/a Head: Esper Arbey Andrade Polania Net: n/a

registration	type of aircraft	cn/fn	ex/ex*	mfd	del	powered by	mtow kg	configuration	selcal	name/fln/specialitites/remarks
☐ HK-4066X	PZL Mielec M-28 Skytruck	EJE001-02		0096	0096	2 PWC PT6A-65B	7000			
☐ HK-4143X	Beech 1900C-1 Airliner	UC-39	N39019	0088	0198	2 PWC PT6A-65B	7530			lsf Raytheon Aircraft Receivables Corp.
☐ HK-4173X	Beech 1900C-1 Airliner	UC-14	N38015	0087	1298	2 PWC PT6A-65B	7530			lsf Raytheon Aircraft Receivables Corp.
☐ HK-1212	Boeing (Douglas) DC-3-455	4987	N76B	0042	0094	2 PW R-1830-90D	12202			La Viga / lsf pvt

LINEAS AEREAS SURAMERICANAS, S.A. = LAU

Bogota-Eldorado

Aeropuerto Eldorado, Entrada 2, Interior 7, Apartado Aéreo 98971, Santafé de Bogota (D.E.), Colombia ☎ (1) 413 95 15 Tx: 43320 lasur co Fax: (1) 413 96 08 SITA: n/a
F: 1986 👥 67 Head: Luis E. Prieto ICAO: SURAMERICANO Net: n/a Beside aircraft listed, also uses 2-3 Boeing 747-200F, lsf/opb ATLAS AIR (N), when required.

registration	type of aircraft	cn/fn	ex/ex*	mfd	del	powered by	mtow kg	configuration	selcal	name/fln/specialitites/remarks
☐ HK-3756X	Aerospatiale (Sud) SE210 Caravelle 10B3	259	TC-JUN	0069	0992	2 PW JT8D-7B	56000	Freighter		El Sultan
☐ HK-3837X	Aerospatiale (Sud) SE210 Caravelle 10B1R	250	TC-ALA	0070	0393	2 PW JT8D-7B	53000	Freighter		Atatürk
☐ HK-3932X	Aerospatiale (Sud) SE210 Caravelle 10B1R	201	F-RAFH	0066	0794	2 PW JT8D-7B	53000	Freighter		Napoleon B.
☐ HK-1271	Boeing 727-24C	19524 / 428	N5475	0067	0194	3 PW JT8D-7B	77111	Freighter		Pegassus
☐ HK-1273	Boeing 727-24C	19526 / 442	N8320	0076	0294	3 PW JT8D-7B	77111	Freighter		Voyager
☐ HK-3814X	Boeing 727-25 (F)	18270 / 79	N5111Y	0064	1292	3 PW JT8D-7B	76657	Freighter		Skipper / cvtd -25
☐ HK-4154X	Boeing 727-51 (F)	18804 / 162	N5607	0065	0698	3 PW JT8D-7B (HK3/RAI)	76657	Freighter		lsf Flying Cargo / cvtd -51

SADELCA Colombia – Sociedad Aérea del Caqueta, Ltda = SDK

Villavicencio & Neiva

Aeropuerto Vanguardia, Apartado Aéreo 3151, Villavicencio, (Meta), Colombia ☎ (86) 64 80 25 Tx: n/a Fax: (86) 64 82 75 SITA: n/a
F: 1974 👥 22 Head: Miguel Parra ICAO: SADELCA Net: n/a

registration	type of aircraft	cn/fn	ex/ex*	mfd	del	powered by	mtow kg	configuration	selcal	name/fln/specialitites/remarks
☐ HK-2664	Boeing (Douglas) DC-3C (C-47A-75-DL)	19433	C-FXPK	0043	0093	2 PW R-1830-92	12202			Angela Sofia
☐ HK-3286	Boeing (Douglas) DC-3C (C-47-DL)	6144	HP-86	0042		2 PW R-1830-90	12202	Freighter		Liliana
☐ HK-3994	Boeing (Douglas) DC-3C (C-47-DL)	4319	N2111M	0042		2 PW R-1830-92	11431	Freighter 3t		Miguel Angel
☐ HK-4006X	Antonov 32B	3409	UR-48023	0094	0096	2 IV AI-20D	27000	Freighter 6,7t		
☐ HK-4117X	Antonov 32B	2909	RA-48071	0092	0097	2 IV AI-20D	27000	Freighter 6,7t		
☐ HK-4136X	Antonov 32B	2509	ER-AES	0090	0097	2 IV AI-20D	27000	Freighter 6,7t		

SAEP – SERVICIOS AEREOS PETROLEROS Colombia = KSP (Servicios Aéreos Especializados en Transportes Petroleros, SA dba)

Bogota-Eldorado

Av. Eldorado, Entrada No. 1, Int. 13, Apartado Aéreo 55534, Santafé de Bogota (D.F.), Colombia ☎ (1) 413 90 28 Tx: none Fax: (1) 413 54 34 SITA: n/a
F: 1980 👥 24 Head: Dra. Liliana Ortega Salcedo ICAO: SAEP Net: n/a

registration	type of aircraft	cn/fn	ex/ex*	mfd	del	powered by	mtow kg	configuration	selcal	name/fln/specialitites/remarks
☐ HK-2006	Boeing (Douglas) DC-3C	43086	N43A	0046	0080	2 PW R-1830-92	11431	Freighter 3t		std BOG
☐ HK-2494	Boeing (Douglas) DC-3C (TC-47B-30-DK)	33105	N87611	0044	0080	2 PW R-1830-92	11431	Freighter 3t		std BOG
☐ HK-2663	Boeing (Douglas) DC-3C (C-47A-10-DK)	12352	C-FXUS	0042	0092	2 PW R-1830-92	12202	Freighter 3t		std BOG
☐ HK-3348	Boeing (Douglas) DC-3A (C-53D-DO)	11775	FAE 11775	0043	0091	2 PW R-1830-92	11431	Freighter 3t		std BOG
☐ HK-3350	Boeing (Douglas) DC-3-454	4993	FAE 1969	0037	0091	2 PW R-1830-92	11431	Freighter 3t		std BOG
☐ HK-4011X	Antonov 32B	3208	UR-48007	0094	0495	2 IV AI-20D	27000	Freighter 6,7t		
☐ HK-4012X	Antonov 32B	3504	UR-48025	0095	0495	2 IV AI-20D	27000	Freighter 6,7t		

SALLA Colombia – Servicios Aéreos del Lllano, Ltda

Villavicencio

Aeropuerto Vanguardia, Villavicencio, (Meta), Colombia ☎ (86) 64 82 15 Tx: n/a Fax: (86) 64 82 15 SITA: n/a
F: n/a 👥 n/a Head: Edgar Diario Zambrano Delgado Net: n/a Aircraft below MTOW 1361kg: Cessna 172.

registration	type of aircraft	cn/fn	ex/ex*	mfd	del	powered by	mtow kg	configuration	selcal	name/fln/specialitites/remarks
☐ HK-3140	Cessna 210N Centurion II	C21064822		0083		1 CO IO-520-L	1724			
☐ HK-2937	Cessna T303 Crusader	CT30300152		0082		2 CO TSIO-520-AE	2336			
☐ HK-2275	Cessna 402C II	C402C0022		0079		2 CO TSIO-520-VB	3107			

SAM Colombia = MM / SAM (Sociedad Aeronautica de Medellin Consolidada, SA dba/Subsidiary of Avianca Colombia)

Medellin

Apartado Aéreo 1085, Medellin, (Antioquia), Colombia ☎ (4) 251 55 44 Tx: none Fax: (4) 251 07 11 SITA: n/a
F: 1946 👥 430 Head: Dr. Gustavo A. Lenis IATA: 334 ICAO: SAM Net: n/a

registration	type of aircraft	cn/fn	ex/ex*	mfd	del	powered by	mtow kg	configuration	selcal	name/fln/specialitites/remarks
☐ HK-	Cessna 208B Grand Caravan					1 PWC PT6A-114A	3969	Y9		oo-delivery 0099
☐ HK-	Cessna 208B Grand Caravan					1 PWC PT6A-114A	3969	Y9		oo-delivery 0099
☐ N504MM	Avro RJ100 (Avro 146-RJ100)	E3221	G-OIII	0093	1294	4 LY LF507-1F	46040	Y100		lsf FSBU Trustee
☐ N505MM	Avro RJ100 (Avro 146-RJ100)	E3242	G-6-242*	0094	0894	4 LY LF507-1F	46040	Y100		lsf FSBU Trustee
☐ N506MM	Avro RJ100 (Avro 146-RJ100)	E3244	G-6-244*	0094	0994	4 LY LF507-1F	46040	Y100		lsf FSBU Trustee
☐ N507MM	Avro RJ100 (Avro 146-RJ100)	E3245	G-6-245*	0094	0994	4 LY LF507-1F	46040	Y100		lsf FSBU Trustee
☐ N508MM	Avro RJ100 (Avro 146-RJ100)	E3247	G-6-247*	0094	0994	4 LY LF507-1F	46040	Y100		lsf FSBU Trustee

N509MM	Avro RJ100 (Avro 146-RJ100)	E3248	G-6-248*	0094	1094	4 LY LF507-1F	46040	Y100		lsf FSBU Trustee
N510MM	Avro RJ100 (Avro 146-RJ100)	E3250	G-6-250*	0094	1094	4 LY LF507-1F	46040	Y100		lsf FSBU Trustee
N511MM	Avro RJ100 (Avro 146-RJ100)	E3255	G-6-255*	0094	1294	4 LY LF507-1F	46040	Y100		lsf FSBU Trustee
N512MM	Avro RJ100 (Avro 146-RJ100)	E3263	G-6-263*	0095	0995	4 LY LF507-1F	46040	Y100		lsf FSBU Trustee

SAS Colombia – Servicio Aéreo de Santander, Ltda — Bogota-Eldorado

Calle 72, No 10-03, Of. 102, Santafe de Bogota, (D.E.), Colombia ☎ (1) 210 41 47 Tx: n/a Fax: (1) 210 41 45 SITA: n/a
F: 1986 👥 n/a Head: Alfonso Fonseca Sanchez Net: n/a Aircraft below MTOW 1361kg: Cessna 172 & Piper PA-28.

HK-3364	Twin (Aero) Jetprop Commander 1000 (695A)	96001	N333UP	0082	0988	2 GA TPE331-10-501K	5080			
HK-3463	Beech King Air 300	FA-39	G-SRES	0085		2 PWC PT6A-60A	6350			

SATENA – Servicio de Aeronavegacion a Territorios Nacionales = NSE — Bogota-Eldorado

Avenida Eldorado, Entrada 1, Interior 11, Apartado Aéreo 11163, Santafé de Bogota (D.E.), Colombia ☎ (1) 413 84 38 Tx: 42332 sat co Fax: (1) 413 81 78 SITA: n/a
F: 1962 👥 350 Head: Maj. Gen. German Castro ICAO: SATENA Net: http://www.satena.com
Commercial wing of FAC-Fuerza Aérea Colombiana which operates scheduled flights to remote parts of Colombia.

FAC-1156	CASA 212 Aviocar Srs 300	370		0087	1287	2 GA TPE331-10R-512/3C	7700			Vaupes
FAC-1157	CASA 212 Aviocar Srs 300	372		0087	1287	2 GA TPE331-10R-512/3C	7700			Amazonas
FAC-1160	Dornier 328-120	3079	D-CDXB*	0096	1196	2 PWC PW119C	13990	Y31		Maipures
FAC-1161	Dornier 328-120	3080	D-CDXH*	0096	1196	2 PWC PW119C	13990	Y31		La Macarena
FAC-1162	Dornier 328-120	3082	D-CDXP*	0096	1296	2 PWC PW119C	13990	Y31		Bahia Solano
FAC-1163	Dornier 328-120	3081	D-CDXM*	0096	0398	2 PWC PW119C	13990	Y31		
FAC-1164	Dornier 328-120	3092	D-CDXO*	0097	0398	2 PWC PW119C	13990	Y31		
FAC-1165	Dornier 328-120	3103	D-CDXR*	0098	0698	2 PWC PW119C	13990	Y31		
FAC-1141	Fokker F28 Fellowship 3000C (F28 MK3000C)	11162	PH-EZL*	0080	0285	2 RR Spey 555-15H	33112			El Llanero
FAC-1146	Boeing 727-95 (F)	19595 / 467	HK-3771X	0067	0996	3 PW JT8D-7B	76884	Freighter		cvtd -95

SEARCA, Ltda – Servicio Aéreo de Capurgana, Ltda = SRC — Medellin-Enrique Olaya Herrera

Aeropuerto Olaya Herrera, Cra.67, 4-21, Hangar 40, Apartado Aéreo 75754, Medellin, Colombia ☎ (4) 285 89 79 Tx: none Fax: (4) 285 89 79 SITA: n/a
F: 1992 👥 30 Head: Jorge Alberto Campillo-Velez ICAO: SEARCA Net: n/a

HK-3953	Dornier DO 28D-2 Skyservant	4196		0073	0994	2 LY IGSO-540-A1E	3842			
HK-3967	Dornier DO 28D-2 Skyservant	4188	YS-401P	0073	1194	2 LY IGSO-540-A1E	3842			
HK-4108	Beech King Air 200	BB-60	N530JA	0075	0497	2 PWC PT6A-41	5670			
HK-4038	Let 410UVP	851323	OK-022	0085	0095	2 WA M-601D	5800			
HK-4048	Let 410UVP-E	912626	TG-TJT	0091	1095	2 WA M-601E	6400			
HK-4094	Let 410UVP-E	861707	N5857T	0086	1196	2 WA M-601E	6400			
HK-4105	Let 410UVP-E	861613	CCCP-67573	0086	0197	2 WA M-601E	6400			

SEC Colombia – Servicio Espelializado de Carga Aérea, Ltda = SEZ — Bogota-Eldorado

Avenida Eldorado, Entrada 1, Interior 12, Terminal Aéreo Simon Bolivar, Santafé de Bogota (D.E.), Colombia ☎ n/a Tx: none Fax: none SITA: n/a
F: 1991 👥 20 Head: Lidia Leon Pachon ICAO: SEC-CARGO Net: n/a

HK-3686	Cessna 208 Caravan I	20800044	CP-2149	0075		1 PWC PT6A-114	3629	Freighter		
HK-3666	Convair 580	18	N580SC	0054	0491	2 AN 501-D13	24766	Executive		cvtd CV340-31
HK-3674	Convair 580 (F) (SCD)	496	YV-83C	0053	1092	2 AN 501-D13	24766	Freighter		cvtd CV440-62

SELVA Colombia – Servicios Aéreos del Vaupes, Ltda = SDV — Villavicencio

Calle 40 No. 32-50, Oficina 805, Apartado Aéreo 2214, Villavicencio (Meta), Colombia ☎ (86) 62 66 24 Tx: none Fax: (86) 64 80 47 SITA: n/a
F: 1978 👥 42 Head: José Joaquin Carvajal Amariles ICAO: SELVA Net: n/a

HK-4008X	Antonov 32B	3402	UR-48020	0094	0097	2 IV AI-20D	27000	Freighter 6,7t		lsf Aviant-Kiev Aviation Plant

TAERCO, Ltda – Taxi Aéreo Colombiano, Ltda — Villavicencio (Meta) & Yopal (Casanare)

Cra. 42B, No. 33B-11, (602), Edif. Rice B. Barzal, Villavicencio, (Meta), Colombia ☎ (86) 64 80 22 Tx: none Fax: (86) 64 81 15 SITA: n/a
F: 1974 👥 18 Head: German Medina Medina Net: n/a Aircraft below MTOW 1361 kg: Piper PA-28.

HK-1506	Cessna U206F Stationair	CU20602554		0074		1 CO IO-520-F	1633			
HK-1664	Cessna U206F Stationair	U20602257	N1555U	0074		1 CO IO-520-F	1633			
HK-1924	Cessna TU206F Turbo Stationair II	CU20603272		0076		1 CO TSIO-520-F	1633			
HK-2182	Cessna U206G Stationair 6 II	CU20604400		0078		1 CO IO-520-F	1633			std VVC
HK-2310	Cessna U206G Stationair 6 II	CU20604882	N734VS	0079		1 CO IO-520-F	1633			
HK-2915	Cessna U206G Stationair 6 II	CU20606675		0082		1 CO IO-520-F	1633			lsf pvt
HK-3066	Cessna U206G Stationair 6 II	CU20606720		0083		1 CO IO-520-F	1633			
HK-1315	Boeing (Douglas) DC-3C (C-47-DL)	4307	PP-ANG	0042		2 PW R-1830-92	12202	Freighter		

TAGUA Colombia – Taxi Aéreo del Guaviare, Ltda — Villavicencio

Calle 40 No. 31-14, Villavicencio, (Meta), Colombia ☎ (86) 64 41 06 Tx: n/a Fax: (86) 62 34 75 SITA: n/a
F: n/a 👥 n/a Head: Hernando Gonzalez Villamizar Net: n/a Aircraft below MTOW 1361 kg: Cessna 170 & 172.

HK-1832	Cessna U206F Stationair II	CU20603179		0076		1 CO IO-520-F	1633			

TAMPA Colombia = QT / TPA (Transportes Aéreos Mercantiles Panamericanos, SA dba / Associated with Martinair, Netherlands) — Medellin

Carrera 76 No. 34A-61, Apartado Aéreo 494, Medellin, (Antioquia), Colombia ☎ (4) 250 29 39 Tx: 66601 tampa co Fax: (4) 250 56 39 SITA: n/a
F: 1973 👥 750 Head: Fabio Echeverry IATA: 729 ICAO: TAMPA Net: n/a

HK-3333X	Boeing 707-321C	18714 / 362	N228VV	0264	0487	4 PW JT3D-3B (HK2/COM)	145331	Freighter	CE-GH	lsf Comtran
HK-3604X	Boeing 707-324C	19352 / 576	N707PM	0467	1190	4 PW JT3D-3B (HK2/COM)	145331	Freighter	EK-BD	lsf Comtran
HK-3785X	Boeing (Douglas) DC-8-71F	46066 / 462	N8099U	0769	1092	4 CFMI CFM56-2C	147418	Freighter	AD-BE	lsf GECA / cvtd DC-8-61/-71
HK-3786X	Boeing (Douglas) DC-8-71F	45849 / 289	N8074U	0467	1192	4 CFMI CFM56-2C	147418	Freighter	AC-GK	lsf GECA / cvtd DC-8-61/-71
HK-4176X	Boeing (Douglas) DC-8-71F	45945 / 337	N945GE	0068	1198	4 CFMI CFM56-2C	147418	Freighter		lsf GECA / cvtd -61/-71

TCA Colombia – Transporte Aéreo del Casanare, Ltda — Villavicencio

Calle 49, No. 33-18, Villavicencio, (Meta), Colombia ☎ n/a Tx: none Fax: none SITA: n/a
F: n/a 👥 n/a Head: Ana Maria Medina Tobar Net: n/a

HK-3199	Boeing (Douglas) DC-3C (C-47B-5-DK)	26044	FAC1123	0044	0097	2 PW R-1830	12202			
HK-3462	Boeing (Douglas) DC-3A (C-53D-DO)	11759	N130W	0043	0094	2 PW R-1830	12202			

TRANSAMAZONICA Colombia – Transporte Aéreo de la Amazonia, Ltda = TAZ — Villavicencio

Aeropuerto Vanguardia, Apartado Aéreo 2344, Villavicencio, (Meta), Colombia ☎ (86) 64 80 76 Tx: n/a Fax: (86) 64 87 76 SITA: n/a
F: n/a 👥 n/a Head: Uber Enrique Velez Rojas ICAO: AMAZON Net: n/a

HK-1175	Boeing (Douglas) DC-3C (C-47A-90-DL)	20432	N5592A	0043		2 PW R-1830	12202			std VVC / being restored
HK-3359	Boeing (Douglas) DC-3C (C-47B-45-DK)	34295	C-FTFV	0045		2 PW R-1830	12202			
HK-3360	Boeing (Douglas) DC-3C (C-47B-30-DK)	33052	N893	0044		2 PW R-1830	12202			

TRANSOCEANICA Colombia – Transoceanica de Aviacion, Ltda — Barranquilla

Aeropuerto Ernesto Cortizos, Oficina Terminal de Carga, Barranquilla, Colombia ☎ (5) 54 05 51 Tx: none Fax: (1) 248 85 57 SITA: n/a
F: 1993 👥 n/a Head: Rosalba Almeida Narvaez Net: n/a

HK-3530X	Boeing (Douglas) DC-6A (C-118B)	43672 / 268	N2097G	0052	0195	4 PW R-2800	47083	Freighter		lsf Universal, Panama
HK-3892X	Boeing (Douglas) DC-6B	45514 / 1014	N843TA	0758	0294	4 PW R-2800	45359	Freighter		lsf Alpes Aviation, Miami / std BOG

TRANS ORIENTE Colombia – T.A. Regular Secundario Oriental, SA — Villavicencio

Apartado Aéreo 2851, Villavicencio, (Meta), Colombia ☎ (86) 64 80 26 Tx: n/a Fax: (86) 64 80 51 SITA: n/a
F: 1990 👥 15 Head: Teresa Uribe de Bernal Net: n/a

HK-3981	Dornier DO 28D-2 Skyservant	4162	D-IDND	0072	0094	2 LY IGSO-540-A1E	3842			
HK-3982	Dornier DO 28D-2 Skyservant	4169	D-IDNC	0073	0094	2 LY IGSO-540-A1E	3842			
HK-3991	Dornier DO 28D-2 Skyservant	4148	D-IDNF	0071	0094	2 LY IGSO-540-A1E	3842			
HK-3992	Dornier DO 28D-2 Skyservant	4161	D-IDNE	0072	0094	2 LY IGSO-540-A1E	3842			

HL = KOREA (Republic of Korea) (Taehan Min-guk)

Capital: Seoul Official Language: Korean Population: 46,0 million Square Km: 99016 Dialling code: +82 Year established: 1948 Acting political head: Kim Dae Jung (President)

Government / Corporate / Executive / VIP Aircraft

HL5214	BAe 3202 Jetstream 32	945	G-BTYU*	0091	0192	2 GA TPE331-12UAR-701H	7350	Corporate 12 Pax		Dong-Ah Group
85101	Boeing 737-3Z8	23152 / 1073		0085	0185	2 CFMI CFM56-3B1	61235	VIP		Gvmt / opb Korea Air Force

AIR KOREA, Co. Ltd. = AKA (Member of Han Gin Group) — Seoul & Pusan

281 Konghang-Dong, Gangseo-Ku, Seoul, Republic of Korea ☎ (2) 660 63 50 Tx: n/a Fax: (2) 660 66 67 SITA: n/a
F: n/a 👥 40 Head: Ha Ryong Jung Net: n/a

HL9115	MD Helicopters MD 500D (Hughes 369D)	1100840D	81-0159	0080	0881	1 AN 250-C20B	1361			
HL9207	Eurocopter (MBB) BO105C	S-390	N2304H	0078	1078	2 AN 250-C20B	2400			
HL9227	Kawasaki (Eurocopter/MBB) BK117B-1	1004	JA9613	0084	0285	2 LY LTS101-750B.1	3200			cvtd BK117

199 registration type of aircraft cn/fn ex/ex* mfd del powered by mtow kg configuration selcal name/fln/specialitites/remarks

☐ HL5107	Cessna 208 Caravan I	20800238	N9842F*	0094	0894	1 PWC PT6A-114	3629			
☐ HL9229	Eurocopter (Aerosp.) SA365N Dauphin 2	6113	F-WYMW*	0085	1285	2 TU Arriel 1C	4000			
☐ HL9230	Eurocopter (Aerosp.) SA365N Dauphin 2	6128	F-WYMP*	0086	0486	2 TU Arriel 1C	4000			
☐ HL9234	Eurocopter (Aerosp.) SA365N Dauphin 2	6219		0085	0387	2 TU Arriel 1C	4000			
☐ HL9201	Eurocopter (Aerosp.) AS332L1 Super Puma	2355	F-WYME*	0092	0492	2 TU Makila 1A1	8600			

ASIANA AIRLINES, Inc. = OZ / AAR (Member of Kumho Group)

Seoul

Asiana

47 Ose-Dong, Kangseo-ku, Seoul 135270, Republic of Korea ☎ (2) 669 50 99 Tx: k29883 asiana Fax: (2) 669 51 30 SITA: n/a
F: 1988 ✱✱✱ 5000 Head: Dr. Seong Yawing & Jung Koo Park IATA: 988 ICAO: ASIANA Net: http://www.asiana.co.kr/english/

☐ HL7232	Boeing 737-58E	25767 / 2614		0094	0594	2 CFMI CFM56-3C1	60554	Y130	DR-KP	
☐ HL7233	Boeing 737-58E	25768 / 2724		0095	0595	2 CFMI CFM56-3C1	60554	Y130	GR-FQ	lsf INGO
☐ HL7250	Boeing 737-58E	25769 / 2737		0095	0795	2 CFMI CFM56-3C1	60554	Y130	HQ-MS	
☐ HL7227	Boeing 737-48E	25764 / 2314		0092	0792	2 CFMI CFM56-3C1	64637	Y168	CH-DS	
☐ HL7228	Boeing 737-48E	25765 / 2335		0092	0792	2 CFMI CFM56-3C1	64637	Y168	CH-ER	
☐ HL7235	Boeing 737-4Q8	26308 / 2665		0094	1094	2 CFMI CFM56-3C1	64637	Y168	GS-AB	lsf ILFC
☐ HL7251	Boeing 737-4Y0	23869 / 1639		0088	1288	2 CFMI CFM56-3C1	64637	Y168	AQ-EF	lsf BBAM
☐ HL7253	Boeing 737-4Y0	23977 / 1655		0089	0189	2 CFMI CFM56-3C1	64637	Y168	AQ-EH	lsf GECA
☐ HL7254	Boeing 737-4Y0	23978 / 1659		0089	0189	2 CFMI CFM56-3C1	64637	Y168	AQ-EJ	lsf GECA
☐ HL7257	Boeing 737-4Y0	24469 / 1749		0089	0789	2 CFMI CFM56-3C1	64637	Y168	GQ-KP	lsf GECA
☐ HL7258	Boeing 737-4Y0	24493 / 1751		0089	0789	2 CFMI CFM56-3C1	64637	Y168	GQ-LM	lsf GECA
☐ HL7259	Boeing 737-4Y0	24494 / 1757		0089	0889	2 CFMI CFM56-3C1	64637	Y168	GQ-LP	lsf GECA
☐ HL7260	Boeing 737-4Y0	24520 / 1803		0090	0190	2 CFMI CFM56-3C1	64637	Y168	GQ-MP	lsf GECA
☐ HL7508	Boeing 737-48E	25772 / 2791		0096	0596	2 CFMI CFM56-3C1	64637	Y168		lsf OZ Alpha Leasing Ltd
☐ HL7509	Boeing 737-48E	28198 / 2806		0096	0796	2 CFMI CFM56-3C1	64637	Y168		lsf ILFC
☐ HL7510	Boeing 737-48E	25771 / 2816		0096	0996	2 CFMI CFM56-3C1	64637	Y168		
☐ HL7511	Boeing 737-48E	27630 / 2848		0097	0197	2 CFMI CFM56-3C1	64637	Y168		lsf ILFC
☐ HL7512	Boeing 737-48E	27632 / 2857		0097	0297	2 CFMI CFM56-3C1	64637	Y168		lsf ILFC
☐ HL7513	Boeing 737-48E	25776 / 2860		0097	0397	2 CFMI CFM56-3C1	64637	Y168		lsf OZ Gamma Leasing Ltd
☐ HL7517	Boeing 737-48E	25774 / 2909		0797	0797	2 CFMI CFM56-3C1	64637	Y168		
☐ HL7518	Boeing 737-48E	28053 / 2954		0097	1197	2 CFMI CFM56-3C1	64637	Y168		lsf ILFC
☐ HL7588	Airbus Industrie A321-131	771	D-AVZE*	0098	0398	2 IAE V2530-A5	83000	C12Y183		
☐ HL	Airbus Industrie A321-131					2 IAE V2530-A5	83000	C12Y183		oo-delivery 00XX
☐ HL	Airbus Industrie A321-131					2 IAE V2530-A5	83000	C12Y183		oo-delivery 00XX
☐ HL	Airbus Industrie A321-131					2 IAE V2530-A5	83000	C12Y183		oo-delivery 00XX
☐ HL	Airbus Industrie A321-131					2 IAE V2530-A5	83000	C12Y183		oo-delivery 00XX
☐ HL	Airbus Industrie A321-131					2 IAE V2530-A5	83000	C12Y183		oo-delivery 00XX
☐ HL	Airbus Industrie A321-131					2 IAE V2530-A5	83000	C12Y183		oo-delivery 00XX
☐ HL	Airbus Industrie A321-131					2 IAE V2530-A5	83000	C12Y183		oo-delivery 00XX
☐ HL	Airbus Industrie A321-131					2 IAE V2530-A5	83000	C12Y183		oo-delivery 00XX
☐ HL	Airbus Industrie A321-131					2 IAE V2530-A5	83000	C12Y183		oo-delivery 00XX
☐ HL	Airbus Industrie A321-131					2 IAE V2530-A5	83000	C12Y183		oo-delivery 00XX
☐ F-OHRC	Airbus Industrie A321-131	855	F-WWDS*	0098	1298	2 IAE V2530-A5	83000	C12Y183		lsf Airbus Industrie Financial Services
☐ HL7247	Boeing 767-38E	25757 / 523		0094	0194	2 GE CF6-80C2B2F	159211	C18Y242	EQ-FR	
☐ HL7248	Boeing 767-38E	25758 / 582		0095	0795	2 GE CF6-80C2B2F	159211	C18Y242	GS-AD	
☐ HL7249	Boeing 767-3Q8 (ER)	26265 / 570		0095	0395	2 GE CF6-80C2B4F	184612	C18Y229		lsf ILFC
☐ HL7263	Boeing 767-38E	24797 / 328		0090	0990	2 GE CF6-80C2B2F	159211	C18Y242	FK-MQ	
☐ HL7264	Boeing 767-38E	24798 / 331		0090	1090	2 GE CF6-80C2B2F	159211	C18Y242	FK-PQ	
☐ HL7506	Boeing 767-38EF (ER)	25760 / 639		0096	1296	2 GE CF6-80C2B7F	185066	Freighter		lsf OZ Gamma Leasing Ltd
☐ HL7507	Boeing 767-38EF (ER)	25761 / 616	N6005C*	0096	0896	2 GE CF6-80C2B7F	185066	Freighter		lsf OZ Alpha Leasing Ltd
☐ HL7514	Boeing 767-38E	25763 / 656		0097	0497	2 GE CF6-80C2B2F	159211	C18Y232		lsf OZ Everest Leasing Ltd
☐ HL7515	Boeing 767-38E	25762 / 658	N6055X*	0097	0597	2 GE CF6-80C2B2F	159211	C18Y242		lsf OZ Delta Leasing Ltd
☐ HL7516	Boeing 767-38E	25759 / 668		0797	0797	2 GE CF6-80C2B2F	159211	C18Y242		lsf OZ Everest Leasing Ltd
☐ HL7528	Boeing 767-38E	29129 / 693	N6005C*			2 GE CF6-80C2B2F	159211	C18Y242		oo-delivery 0099
☐ HL	Boeing 767-38EF (ER)					2 GE CF6-80C2B7F	185066	Freighter		oo-delivery 00XX
☐ HL	Boeing 767-38E					2 GE CF6-80C2B2F	159211	C18Y242		oo-delivery 00XX
☐ HL	Boeing 767-38E					2 GE CF6-80C2B2F	159211	C18Y242		oo-delivery 00XX
☐ HL	Boeing 767-38E					2 GE CF6-80C2B2F	159211	C18Y242		oo-delivery 00XX
☐ HL	Airbus Industrie A330-321					2 PW PW4164	212000			oo-delivery 00XX
☐ HL	Airbus Industrie A330-321					2 PW PW4164	212000			oo-delivery 00XX
☐ HL	Airbus Industrie A330-321					2 PW PW4164	212000			oo-delivery 00XX
☐ HL	Airbus Industrie A330-223					2 PW PW4168A	230000			oo-delivery 00XX
☐ HL	Airbus Industrie A330-223					2 PW PW4168A	230000			oo-delivery 00XX
☐ HL	Airbus Industrie A330-223					2 PW PW4168A	230000			oo-delivery 00XX
☐ HL	Boeing 777-28E (ER)					2 PW PW4090	286897			to be lsf ILFC 1099
☐ HL	Boeing 777-28E (ER)					2 PW PW4090	286897			oo-delivery 00XX
☐ HL	Boeing 777-28E (ER)					2 PW PW4090	286897			oo-delivery 00XX
☐ HL	Boeing 777-28E (ER)					2 PW PW4090	286897			oo-delivery 00XX
☐ HL	Boeing 777-28E (ER)					2 PW PW4090	286897			oo-delivery 00XX
☐ HL	Boeing 777-28E (ER)					2 PW PW4090	286897			oo-delivery 00XX
☐ HL	Boeing 777-28E (ER)					2 PW PW4090	286897			oo-delivery 00XX
☐ HL	Boeing 777-38E					2 PW PW4098	299371			oo-delivery 00XX
☐ HL	Boeing 777-38E					2 PW PW4098	299371			oo-delivery 00XX
☐ HL	Boeing 777-38E					2 PW PW4098	299371			oo-delivery 00XX
☐ HL	Boeing 777-38E					2 PW PW4098	299371			oo-delivery 00XX
☐ HL	Boeing 777-38E					2 PW PW4098	299371			oo-delivery 00XX
☐ HL	Boeing 777-38E					2 PW PW4098	299371			oo-delivery 00XX
☐ HL	Boeing 777-38E					2 PW PW4098	299371			oo-delivery 00XX
☐ HL	Boeing 777-38E					2 PW PW4098	299371			oo-delivery 06XX
☐ HL7413	Boeing 747-48E (M)	25405 / 880		0091	1191	4 GE CF6-80C2B1F	394625	F16C46Y236 / Plt	BH-FS	
☐ HL7414	Boeing 747-48E (M)	25452 / 892		0091	0192	4 GE CF6-80C2B1F	394625	F16C46Y236 / Plt	BR-CS	
☐ HL7415	Boeing 747-48E (M)	25777 / 946		0092	1292	4 GE CF6-80C2B1F	394625	F16C46Y236 / Plt	CS-FQ	
☐ HL7417	Boeing 747-48E	25779 / 1006		0093	1293	4 GE CF6-80C2B1F	394625		DS-CR	
☐ HL7418	Boeing 747-48E	25780 / 1035	N6018N*	0094	0994	4 GE CF6-80C2B1F	394625		GR-KQ	
☐ HL7419	Boeing 747-48EF (SCD)	25781 / 1044		0094	1194	4 GE CF6-80C2B1F	394625	Freighter	AF-KR	lsf Seagalt Aircraft Ltd
☐ HL7420	Boeing 747-48EF (SCD)	25783 / 1064		0095	0695	4 GE CF6-80C2B1F	394625	Freighter	GS-AC	lsf Eagle Aircraft Ltd
☐ HL7421	Boeing 747-48E (M)	25784 / 1086		0096	0896	4 GE CF6-80C2B1F	394625	F16C46Y236 / Plt		
☐ HL7422	Boeing 747-48EF (SCD)	28367 / 1096		0096	1296	4 GE CF6-80C2B1F	394625	Freighter		lsf SALE
☐ HL7423	Boeing 747-48E (M)	25782 / 1115		0597	0597	4 GE CF6-80C2B1F	394625	F16C46Y236 / Plt		lsf OZ Delta Leasing Ltd
☐ HL7426	Boeing 747-48EF (SCD)	27603				4 GE CF6-80C2B1F	394625	Freighter		to be lsf ILFC 0499
☐ HL	Boeing 747-48E (M)	28551 / 1131	N6055X*	0097		4 GE CF6-80C2B1F	394625			oo-delivery 0099
☐ HL	Boeing 747-48E	28552 / 1160	N6018N*	0098		4 GE CF6-80C2B1F	394625			oo-delivery 0099
☐ HL	Boeing 747-48E					4 GE CF6-80C2B1F	394625			oo-delivery 00XX
☐ HL	Boeing 747-48E					4 GE CF6-80C2B1F	394625			oo-delivery 00XX
☐ HL	Boeing 747-48E					4 GE CF6-80C2B1F	394625			oo-delivery 00XX
☐ HL	Boeing 747-48E (M)					4 GE CF6-80C2B1F	394625			oo-delivery 00XX
☐ HL	Boeing 747-48E					4 GE CF6-80C2B1F	394625			oo-delivery 00XX

CITI AIR

Seoul

Suat 1821, Changkang, Bldg 22, Dong-Woa-Dong, Mapo-ku, Seoul, Republic of Korea ☎ (2) 32 72 81 20 Tx: n/a Fax: (2) 32 72 81 25 SITA: n/a
F: n/a ✱✱✱ n/a Head: n/a Net: n/a

☐ HL9221	PZL Swidnik W-3AM Sokol	370703	SP-SYH (1)*	0096	0296	2 PZL-10W	6400			
☐ HL9222	PZL Swidnik W-3AM Sokol	370704	SP-SYH (2)*	0096	0596	2 PZL-10W	6400			
☐ HL9259	PZL Swidnik W-3AM Sokol	370803	SP-SYN (1)*	0097	0797	2 PZL-10W	6400			
☐ HL9262	PZL Swidnik W-3AM Sokol	370805	SP-SYN (3)*	0098	0398	2 PZL-10W	6400			

HELI KOREA, Co. Ltd (Associated with Samju Co.)

Seoul

282-16 Dae Hwadong, Daeduck Gu, Daejgon, Republic of Korea ☎ (42) 633 89 00 Tx: none Fax: (42) 624 84 00 SITA: n/a
F: 1996 ✱✱✱ 30 Head: Kyong-Jo Min Net: n/a

☐ HL9103	MD Helicopters MD 500D (Hughes 369D)	1260043D		0076	0096	1 AN 250-C20B	1361			
☐ HL9121	MD Helicopters MD 500D (Hughes 369D)	1054D		0082	0096	1 AN 250-C20B	1361			
☐ HL9129	MD Helicopters MD 500D (Hughes 369D)	1226D	90-0170	0084	0096	1 AN 250-C20B	1361			
☐ HL9138	MD Helicopters MD 500E (Hughes 369E)	0199E	N298E	0086	0497	1 AN 250-C20R	1361			
☐ HL9132	Bell 214B-1 BigLifter	28044	HB-XYG	0079	0896	1 LY T5508D	5670			
☐ HL9136	Bell 214B-1 BigLifter	28051	N103RA	0080	0197	1 LY T5508D	5670			

KCAB FLIGHT INSPECTION (Division of Ministry of Transport/Korea Civil Aviation Bureau)

Seoul

Flight Inspection Div., Seoul Regional Aviation Adm., Kimpo Int'l Airport, 274 Gwahae-dong Gangseo-gu, Seoul 157711, Republic of Korea ☎ (2) 660 21 62 Tx: none Fax: (2) 662 08 81 SITA: n/a
F: n/a ✱✱✱ n/a Head: Kim Seung Hwan Net: n/a Non-commercial national organisation conducting flight inspection missions.

☐ HL7577	Canadair CL-601-3R (CL-600-2B16) Challen.	5182	C-FVZC*	0095	0596	2 GE CF34-3A1	20457	Calibrator		

200 registration type of aircraft cn/fn ex/ex* mfd del powered by mtow kg configuration selcal name/fln/specialitites/remarks

KOREAN AIR = KE / KAL (Member of the Han Jin Group / formerly Korean Air Lines – KAL)

CPO Box 864, 41-3, Seosomun-dong, Chung-gu, Seoul, Republic of Korea ☎ (2) 656 78 05 Tx: k27526 kalho Fax: (2) 656 78 70 SITA: n/a

F: 1962 👥 16000 Head: Yang Ho Cho IATA: 180 ICAO: KOREANAIR Net: http://www.koreanair.com Trainer-aircraft below MTOW 5000kg: Piper PA-34

	registration	type of aircraft	cn/fn	ex/ex*	mfd	del	powered by	mtow kg	configuration	selcal	name/fln/specialitites/remarks
☐	HL9225	MD Helicopters MD 900 Explorer	900-00032	N9132N*	0096	0696	2 PWC PW206A	2722	Y7		
☐	HL5253	CASA 212-CB16 Aviocar Srs 100	125		0079	0580	2 GA TPE331-5-251C	6500	Y17 / Freighter		
☐	HL7501	Cessna 560 Citation V Ultra	560-0292	N1295N*	0095	0695	2 PWC JT15D-5D	7394	Trainer / Exec		
☐	HL7502	Cessna 560 Citation V Ultra	560-0294	N1295Y*	0095	0695	2 PWC JT15D-5D	7394	Trainer / Exec		
☐	HL7503	Cessna 560 Citation V Ultra	560-0297	N1296N*	0095	0795	2 PWC JT15D-5D	7394	Trainer / Exec		
☐	HL7504	Cessna 560 Citation V Ultra	560-0300	N1297V*	0095	0795	2 PWC JT15D-5D	7394	Trainer / Exec		
☐	HL7222	GAC G-IV Gulfstream IV	1188	N482GA*	0093	1194	2 RR Tay 611-8	33203	Executive		
☐	HL7206	Fokker 100 (F28 Mk0100)	11378	PH-KXA*	0092	0492	2 RR Tay 650-15	44452	Y109		
☐	HL7207	Fokker 100 (F28 Mk0100)	11387	PH-KXB*	0092	0692	2 RR Tay 650-15	44452	Y109		
☐	HL7208	Fokker 100 (F28 Mk0100)	11388	PH-KXC*	0092	0692	2 RR Tay 650-15	44452	Y109		
☐	HL7209	Fokker 100 (F28 Mk0100)	11432	PH-EZJ*	0092	0193	2 RR Tay 650-15	44452	Y109		
☐	HL7210	Fokker 100 (F28 Mk0100)	11438	PH-EZL*	0093	0293	2 RR Tay 650-15	44452	Y109		
☐	HL7211	Fokker 100 (F28 Mk0100)	11439	PH-EZM*	0093	0393	2 RR Tay 650-15	44452	Y109		
☐	HL7212	Fokker 100 (F28 Mk0100)	11476	PH-EZY*	0093	1093	2 RR Tay 650-15	44452	Y109		
☐	HL7213	Fokker 100 (F28 Mk0100)	11504	PH-EZP*	0094	0494	2 RR Tay 650-15	44452	Y109		
☐	HL7214	Fokker 100 (F28 Mk0100)	11513	PH-EZI*	0094	0494	2 RR Tay 650-15	44452	Y109		
☐	HL7215	Fokker 100 (F28 Mk0100)	11519	PH-EZK*	0094	0994	2 RR Tay 650-15	44452	Y109		
☐	HL7216	Fokker 100 (F28 Mk0100)	11522	PH-EZG*	0094	1294	2 RR Tay 650-15	44452	Y109		lsf ORIX
☐	HL7217	Fokker 100 (F28 Mk0100)	11523	PH-EZM*	0095	0195	2 RR Tay 650-15	44452	Y109		lsf ORIX
☐	HL	Boeing 737-76N					2 CFMI CFM56-7B24	69400			to be lsf GECA 0400
☐	HL	Boeing 737-76N					2 CFMI CFM56-7B24	69400			to be lsf GECA 0600
☐	HL	Boeing 737-76N					2 CFMI CFM56-7B24	69400			to be lsf GECA 0800
☐	HL	Boeing 737-76N					2 CFMI CFM56-7B24	69400			to be lsf GECA 1000
☐	HL	Boeing 737-76N					2 CFMI CFM56-7B24	69400			to be lsf GECA 0301
☐	HL	Boeing 737-76N					2 CFMI CFM56-7B24	69400			to be lsf GECA 0901
☐	HL	Boeing 737-76N					2 CFMI CFM56-7B24	69400			to be lsf GECA 1001
☐	HL	Boeing 737-76N					2 CFMI CFM56-7B24	69400			to be lsf GECA 1201
☐	HL7225	Boeing (Douglas) MD-82 (DC-9-82)	53467 / 2102		0094	1294	2 PW JT8D-217C	67812	Y164		
☐	HL7236	Boeing (Douglas) MD-82 (DC-9-82)	53468 / 2114		0095	0795	2 PW JT8D-217C	67812	Y164		
☐	HL7237	Boeing (Douglas) MD-82 (DC-9-82)	53469 / 2116		0095	0795	2 PW JT8D-217C	67812	Y164		
☐	HL7541	Boeing (Douglas) MD-82 (DC-9-82)	49373 / 1201	HL7272	0085	0885	2 PW JT8D-217A	67812	Y164		lsf GECA
☐	HL7542	Boeing (Douglas) MD-82 (DC-9-82)	49374 / 1208	HL7273	0085	0885	2 PW JT8D-217A	67812	Y164		lsf GECA
☐	HL7543	Boeing (Douglas) MD-82 (DC-9-82)	49416 / 1271	HL7275	0086	0586	2 PW JT8D-217A	67812	Y164		lsf GECA
☐	HL7544	Boeing (Douglas) MD-82 (DC-9-82)	49417 / 1278	HL7276	0086	0686	2 PW JT8D-217A	67812	Y164		lsf GECA
☐	HL7545	Boeing (Douglas) MD-82 (DC-9-82)	49418 / 1394	HL7282	0087	0887	2 PW JT8D-217A	67812	Y164		lsf GECA
☐	HL7546	Boeing (Douglas) MD-82 (DC-9-82)	49419 / 1403	HL7283	0087	0987	2 PW JT8D-217A	67812	Y164		lsf GECA
☐	HL7547	Boeing (Douglas) MD-82 (DC-9-82)	53147 / 2069	HL7203	0093	0993	2 PW JT8D-217C	67812	Y164		lsf GECA
☐	HL7548	Boeing (Douglas) MD-82 (DC-9-82)	53148 / 2072	HL7204	0093	1193	2 PW JT8D-217C	67812	Y164	HM-CL	lsf GECA - 0599 / for JKK
☐	HL7570	Boeing (Douglas) MD-83 (DC-9-83)	53485 / 2128		0096	0196	2 PW JT8D-219	72575	Y160		
☐	HL7571	Boeing (Douglas) MD-83 (DC-9-83)	53486 / 2130		0096	0296	2 PW JT8D-219	72575	Y160		
☐	HL7572	Boeing (Douglas) MD-83 (DC-9-83)	53487 / 2132		0096	0396	2 PW JT8D-219	72575	Y160		
☐	HL	Boeing 737-8B5					2 CFMI CFM56-7B26	78245			oo-delivery 0800
☐	HL	Boeing 737-8B5					2 CFMI CFM56-7B26	78245			oo-delivery 1200
☐	HL	Boeing 737-8B5					2 CFMI CFM56-7B26	78245			oo-delivery 0001
☐	HL	Boeing 737-8B5					2 CFMI CFM56-7B26	78245			oo-delivery 0001
☐	HL	Boeing 737-8B5					2 CFMI CFM56-7B26	78245			oo-delivery 0002
☐	HL	Boeing 737-8B5					2 CFMI CFM56-7B26	78245			oo-delivery 0002
☐	HL	Boeing 737-9B5					2 CFMI CFM56-7B26	79016			oo-delivery 0002
☐	HL	Boeing 737-9B5					2 CFMI CFM56-7B26	79016			oo-delivery 0002
☐	HL	Boeing 737-9B5					2 CFMI CFM56-7B26	79016			oo-delivery 0002
☐	HL	Boeing 737-9B5					2 CFMI CFM56-7B26	79016			oo-delivery 0002
☐	HL	Boeing 737-9B5					2 CFMI CFM56-7B26	79016			oo-delivery 0003
☐	HL	Boeing 737-9B5					2 CFMI CFM56-7B26	79016			oo-delivery 0003
☐	HL	Boeing 737-9B5					2 CFMI CFM56-7B26	79016			oo-delivery 0003
☐	HL	Boeing 737-9B5					2 CFMI CFM56-7B26	79016			oo-delivery 0003
☐	HL	Boeing 737-9B5					2 CFMI CFM56-7B26	79016			oo-delivery 0003
☐	HL	Boeing 737-9B5					2 CFMI CFM56-7B26	79016			oo-delivery 0004
☐	HL	Boeing 737-9B5					2 CFMI CFM56-7B26	79016			oo-delivery 0004
☐	HL	Boeing 737-9B5					2 CFMI CFM56-7B26	79016			oo-delivery 0004
☐	HL	Boeing 737-9B5					2 CFMI CFM56-7B26	79016			oo-delivery 0004
☐	HL	Boeing 737-9B5					2 CFMI CFM56-7B26	79016			oo-delivery 0004
☐	HL	Boeing 737-9B5					2 CFMI CFM56-7B26	79016			oo-delivery 0005
☐	HL	Boeing 737-9B5					2 CFMI CFM56-7B26	79016			oo-delivery 0005
☐	HL7278	Airbus Industrie A300F4-203	277	F-WZME*	0083	0886	2 GE CF6-50C2	165000	Freighter	BC-AP	cvtd A300C4-203
☐	HL7279	Airbus Industrie A300F4-203	292	F-WZMS*	0084	0886	2 GE CF6-50C2	165000	Freighter	BC-DP	cvtd A300C4-203
☐	HL7239	Airbus Industrie A300-622R (A300B4-622R)	627	F-WWAD*	0092	0392	2 PW PW4158	170500	F24Y232		
☐	HL7240	Airbus Industrie A300-622R (A300B4-622R)	631	F-WWAB*	0092	0592	2 PW PW4158	170500	F24Y232		
☐	HL7241	Airbus Industrie A300-622R (A300B4-622R)	662	F-WWAT*	0092	0193	2 PW PW4158	170500	F18Y234	BH-AR	
☐	HL7242	Airbus Industrie A300-622R (A300B4-622R)	685	F-WWAG*	0093	0493	2 PW PW4158	170500	Y292	FH-AM	
☐	HL7243	Airbus Industrie A300-622R (A300B4-622R)	692	F-WWAR*	0093	0693	2 PW PW4158	170500	Y292	KL-HJ	
☐	HL7244	Airbus Industrie A300-622R (A300B4-622R)	722	F-WWAH*	0094	0394	2 PW PW4158	170500	F18Y234		
☐	HL7245	Airbus Industrie A300-622R (A300B4-622R)	731	F-WWAK*	0094	0594	2 PW PW4158	170500	F18Y234		
☐	HL7280	Airbus Industrie A300-622 (A300B4-622)	361	F-WWAE*	0085	0887	2 PW PW4158	165000	F24Y232	FH-BG	cvtd A300-620
☐	HL7281	Airbus Industrie A300-622 (A300B4-622)	365	F-WWAF*	0085	0887	2 PW PW4158	165000	F24Y232	FH-CD	cvtd A300-620
☐	HL7287	Airbus Industrie A300-622 (A300B4-622)	358	F-WZYC*	0085	0388	2 PW PW4158	165000	F24Y232	KL-AP	cvtd A300-620
☐	HL7290	Airbus Industrie A300-622 (A300B4-622)	388	F-WWAB*	0086	0389	2 PW PW4158	165000	F24Y232		cvtd A300-620
☐	HL7291	Airbus Industrie A300-622 (A300B4-622)	417	F-WWAT*	0087	0489	2 PW PW4158	165000	F24Y232	DQ-MP	
☐	HL7294	Airbus Industrie A300-622R (A300B4-622R)	560	F-WWAZ*	0090	0690	2 PW PW4158	170500	F24Y232		
☐	HL7295	Airbus Industrie A300-622R (A300B4-622R)	582	F-WWAM*	0091	0291	2 PW PW4158	170500	F24Y232		
☐	HL7297	Airbus Industrie A300-622R (A300B4-622R)	609	F-WWAE*	0091	0791	2 PW PW4158	170500	F24Y232	KM-CF	
☐	HL7298	Airbus Industrie A300-622R (A300B4-622R)	614	F-WWAZ*	0091	0991	2 PW PW4158	170500	F24Y232	AS-BE	
☐	HL7299	Airbus Industrie A300-622R (A300B4-622R)	717	F-WWAY*	0093	0194	2 PW PW4158	170500	F18Y234		
☐	HL7519	Airbus Industrie A300-622R (A300B4-622R)	611	VH-IWD	0091	0797	2 PW PW4158	171700	F24Y234		lsf AWAS
☐	HL7520	Airbus Industrie A300-622R (A300B4-622R)	613	VH-IGF	0091	0797	2 PW PW4158	171700	F24Y234		lsf AWAS
☐	HL7521	Airbus Industrie A300-622R (A300B4-622R)	657	PK-GAP	0092	0897	2 PW PW4158	171700	F24Y234		lsf JFSS
☐	HL7523	Airbus Industrie A300-622R (A300B4-622R)	659	PK-GAQ	0092	0997	2 PW PW4158	171700	F24Y234		lsf JFSS
☐	HL7529	Airbus Industrie A300-622R (A300B4-622R)	477	HL7288	0088	1188	2 PW PW4158	170500	F24Y234	AQ-CK	
☐	HL7535	Airbus Industrie A300-622R (A300B4-622R)	543	HL7292	0090	0190	2 PW PW4158	170500	F24Y234	LQ-HJ	
☐	HL7536	Airbus Industrie A300-622R (A300B4-622R)	554	HL7293	0090	0390	2 PW PW4158	170500	F24Y234	LQ-HK	
☐	HL7537	Airbus Industrie A300-622R (A300B4-622R)	479	HL7289	0088	1288	2 PW PW4158	170500	F24Y234		
☐	HL7580	Airbus Industrie A300-622R (A300B4-622R)	756	F-WWAB*	0095	1195	2 PW PW4158	171700	F24Y234		lsf CBF
☐	HL7581	Airbus Industrie A300-622R (A300B4-622R)	762	F-WWAZ*	0095	0196	2 PW PW4158	171700	F24Y234		lsf CBF
☐	HL7524	Airbus Industrie A330-322	206	HL7552	0098	0698	2 PW PW4168	217000	FCY296		
☐	HL7525	Airbus Industrie A330-322	219	F-WWKO*	0098	0698	2 PW PW4168	217000	FCY296		
☐	HL7540	Airbus Industrie A330-322	241	F-WWKF*	0098	1198	2 PW PW4168	217000	FCY296		
☐	HL7550	Airbus Industrie A330-322	162	F-WWKK*	0097	0397	2 PW PW4168	217000	FCY296		
☐	HL7551	Airbus Industrie A330-322	172	F-WWKI*	0097	0597	2 PW PW4168	217000	FCY296		
☐	HL	Airbus Industrie A330-323	267				2 PW PW4168A	230000	FCY296		oo-delivery 0499
☐	HL	Airbus Industrie A330-323	256	F-WWKN*			2 PW PW4168A	230000	FCY296		oo-delivery 0899
☐	HL	Airbus Industrie A330-323					2 PW PW4168A	230000	FCY296		oo-delivery 00XX
☐	HL	Airbus Industrie A330-323					2 PW PW4168A	230000	FCY296		oo-delivery 00XX
☐	HL	Airbus Industrie A330-323					2 PW PW4168A	230000	FCY296		oo-delivery 00XX
☐	HL7526	Boeing 777-2B5 (ER)	27947 / 148	N50217*	0098	1298	2 PW PW4090	267619	F12C28Y261		
☐	HL7530	Boeing 777-2B5 (ER)	27945 / 59		0097	0397	2 PW PW4090	267619	F12C28Y261	PR-BE	lsf KE Appollo Leasing Ltd
☐	HL7531	Boeing 777-2B5 (ER)	27946 / 62		0097	0397	2 PW PW4090	267619	F12C28Y261	PR-BF	lsf KE Appollo Leasing Ltd
☐	HL	Boeing 777-2B5 (ER)					2 PW PW4090	267619	F12C28Y261		oo-delivery 0699
☐	HL7538	Airbus Industrie A330-223	222	F-WWKP*	0098	0898	2 PW PW4168A	230000	FCY245		lsf Debis AirFinance
☐	HL7539	Airbus Industrie A330-223	226	F-WWKR*	0098	0998	2 PW PW4168A	230000	FCY245		lsf Debis AirFinance
☐	HL	Airbus Industrie A330-223	258	F-WWKQ*			2 PW PW4168A	230000	FCY245		oo-delivery 0499
☐	HL7532	Boeing 777-3B5	28371 / 162				2 PW PW4098	299371			oo-delivery 0499
☐	HL7533	Boeing 777-3B5	27948 / 178				2 PW PW4098	299371			oo-delivery 0499
☐	HL7534	Boeing 777-3B5	27950 / 120	N5020K*			2 PW PW4098	299371			oo-delivery 0699
☐	HL	Boeing 777-3B5					2 PW PW4098	299371			oo-delivery 0300
☐	HL	Boeing 777-3B5					2 PW PW4098	299371			oo-delivery 0500
☐	HL	Boeing 777-3B5					2 PW PW4098	299371			oo-delivery 0600
☐	HL	Boeing 777-3B5					2 PW PW4098	299371			oo-delivery 1000

☐ HL	Boeing 777-3B5					2 PW PW4098	299371			oo-delivery 1100
☐ HL7371	Boeing (Douglas) MD-11	48407 / 456		0090	0291	3 PW PW4460	280320	F20C30Y223	MQ-FK	
☐ HL7372	Boeing (Douglas) MD-11 (F)	48408 / 457		0091	0191	3 PW PW4460	280320	Freighter	MQ-FL	cvtd MD-11
☐ HL7373	Boeing (Douglas) MD-11 (F)	48409 / 490		0092	0392	3 PW PW4460	280320	Freighter	AS-BC	cvtd MD-11
☐ HL7374	Boeing (Douglas) MD-11 (F)	48410 / 495		0092	0592	3 PW PW4460	280320	Freighter	AS-BD	cvtd MD-11
☐ HL7375	Boeing (Douglas) MD-11	48523 / 516		0092	1092	3 PW PW4460	280320	F20C30Y223	BH-AS	
☐ HL7405	Boeing 747-2B5F (SCD)	24195 / 718	HL7475	0088	1088	4 PW JT9D-7R4G2	377842	Freighter	KL-CP	lsf K.I. Freight Ltd
☐ HL7408	Boeing 747-2B5F (SCD)	24196 / 720	HL7476	0088	1289	4 PW JT9D-7R4G2	377842	Freighter	KL-DP	
☐ HL7424	Boeing 747-2S4F (SCD)	22169 / 472	HL7474	0080	0985	4 PW JT9D-7Q	371946	Freighter	BC-FK	lsf SCT Air Co.
☐ HL7441	Boeing 747-230F	20373 / 168	D-ABYE	0071	1278	4 PW JT9D-7A	351534	Freighter	FH-BL	
☐ HL7443	Boeing 747-2B5B	21772 / 363		0079	0379	4 PW JT9D-7A	351534	F12C24Y342	GK-FJ	
☐ HL7451	Boeing 747-2B5F (SCD)	22480 / 448		0080	0680	4 PW JT9D-7Q	371946	Freighter	JM-HK	
☐ HL7452	Boeing 747-2B5F (SCD)	22481 / 454	N5573F*	0080	0680	4 PW JT9D-7Q	371946	Freighter	JM-HL	
☐ HL7454	Boeing 747-2B5B (SF)	22482 / 484		0080	1180	4 PW JT9D-7Q	371946	Freighter	KL-AC	cvtd -2B5B
☐ HL7458	Boeing 747-2B5B (SF)	22485 / 513		0081	0481	4 PW JT9D-7Q	371946	Freighter	AC-GH	cvtd -2B5B
☐ HL7459	Boeing 747-2B5F (SCD)	22486 / 520		0081	0581	4 PW JT9D-7Q	371946	Freighter	AC-KL	
☐ HL7471	Boeing 747-273C	20652 / 211	N748WA	0073	0485	4 PW JT9D-7A	351534	Freighter	HM-JL	
☐ HL7469	Boeing 747-3B5	22489 / 611	N6009F*	0085	0485	4 PW JT9D-7R4G2	377842	F16C37Y369	GK-BF	
☐ HL7470	Boeing 747-3B5 (M)	24194 / 713	N6038E*	0088	0888	4 PW JT9D-7R4G2	377842	F16C38Y238/Plts	KL-BP	
☐ HL7402	Boeing 747-4B5	26407 / 1155	N6038E*	0098	1298	4 PW PW4056	385554			
☐ HL7403	Boeing 747-4B5F (SCD)	26408 / 1163	N60659*	0098	1298	4 PW PW4056	385554	Freighter		
☐ HL7404	Boeing 747-4B5	26409 / 1170	N6009F*	0098	1298	4 PW PW4056	385554			
☐ HL7407	Boeing 747-4B5	24198 / 729	HL7477	0089	0689	4 PW PW4056	385554	F16C65Y310	KL-EP	lsf K.I. Freight Ltd
☐ HL7409	Boeing 747-4B5	24199 / 739	HL7478	0089	0789	4 PW PW4056	385554	F16C65Y310	KL-FP	
☐ HL7412	Boeing 747-4B5	24200 / 748	HL7479	0089	0989	4 PW PW4056	385554	F16C65Y310	KL-GP	
☐ HL7460	Boeing 747-4B5	26404 / 1107		0097	0397	4 PW PW4056	385554		BH-FR	lsf KE Appollo Leasing Ltd
☐ HL7461	Boeing 747-4B5	26405 / 1118		0697	0697	4 PW PW4056	385554		BH-JQ	
☐ HL7462	Boeing 747-4B5F (SCD)	26406 / 1123		0797	0797	4 PW PW4056	385554	Freighter		
☐ HL7472	Boeing 747-4B5	26403 / 1095		0096	1196	4 PW PW4056	385554		PR-BC	
☐ HL7473	Boeing 747-4B5	28335 / 1098		0096	1296	4 PW PW4056	385554		PR-BD	
☐ HL7480	Boeing 747-4B5 (M)	24619 / 793	N6009F*	0090	0690	4 PW PW4056	385554	F16C65Y310	MQ-FG	
☐ HL7481	Boeing 747-4B5	24621 / 830		0091	0191	4 PW PW4056	385554	F16C65Y310	MQ-FJ	
☐ HL7482	Boeing 747-4B5	25205 / 853		0091	0591	4 PW PW4056	385554	F16C65Y310	CJ-FG	
☐ HL7483	Boeing 747-4B5	25275 / 874		0091	0991	4 PW PW4056	385554	F16C65Y310	AR-QS	
☐ HL7484	Boeing 747-4B5	26392 / 893		0092	0192	4 PW PW4056	385554	F16C66Y310	BG-QS	lsf OLC Air Leasing
☐ HL7485	Boeing 747-4B5	26395 / 922		0092	0692	4 PW PW4056	385554	F16C66Y310	BG-RS	
☐ HL7486	Boeing 747-4B5	26396 / 951		0092	0193	4 PW PW4056	385554	F16C66Y310	CM-KS	
☐ HL7487	Boeing 747-4B5	26393 / 958		0093	0293	4 PW PW4056	385554	F16C65Y310	CM-LR	
☐ HL7488	Boeing 747-4B5	26394 / 986		0093	0793	4 PW PW4056	385554	F16C66Y310	BP-LR	
☐ HL7489	Boeing 747-4B5	27072 / 1013		0094	0194	4 PW PW4056	385554		ES-CJ	
☐ HL7490	Boeing 747-4B5	27177 / 1019		0094	0294	4 PW PW4056	385554		ES-CK	
☐ HL7491	Boeing 747-4B5	27341 / 1037		0094	0794	4 PW PW4056	385554		EG-DR	
☐ HL7492	Boeing 747-4B5	26397 / 1055		0095	0295	4 PW PW4056	385554		EK-CR	
☐ HL7493	Boeing 747-4B5	26398 / 1057		0095	0395	4 PW PW4056	385554		AH-PS	
☐ HL7494	Boeing 747-4B5	27662 / 1067		0095	0895	4 PW PW4056	385554		JQ-ER	
☐ HL7495	Boeing 747-4B5	28096 / 1073		0095	1295	4 PW PW4056	385554		JQ-ES	
☐ HL7496	Boeing 747-4B5	26400 / 1083		0096	0696	4 PW PW4056	385554		KS-MP	
☐ HL7497	Boeing 747-4B5F (SCD)	26401 / 1087		0096	0996	4 PW PW4056	385554	Freighter		
☐ HL7498	Boeing 747-4B5	26402 / 1092		0096	1096	4 PW PW4056	385554		BP-LR	
☐ HL	Boeing 747-4B5					4 PW PW4056	385554			oo-delivery 0699
☐ HL	Boeing 747-4B5F (SCD)					4 PW PW4056	385554	Freighter		oo-delivery 0799
☐ HL	Boeing 747-4B5					4 PW PW4056	385554			oo-delivery 00XX

SAMSUNG AEROSPACE – Transportation division (Division of Samsung Aerospace Industries, Ltd

Seoul

Samsung Life Bldg, 150-2ka, Taepyung-ro, Chung-ku, Seoul 100716, Republic of Korea ☎ (2) 36 62 15 62 Tx: none Fax: (2) 36 62 89 16 SITA: n/a
F: n/a 👪 n/a Head: Kim Lee-Hong Net: n/a Operates non-commercial corporate for itself & commercial charter flights.

☐ HL9203	Eurocopter (Aerosp.) AS365N2 Dauphin 2	6469	F-WYMT*	0094	0894	2 TU Arriel 1C2	4250			
☐ HL9204	Eurocopter (Aerosp.) AS365N2 Dauphin 2	6470		0094	0894	2 TU Arriel 1C2	4250			
☐ HL9205	Eurocopter (Aerosp.) AS365N2 Dauphin 2	6471	F-WYMA*	0094	1094	2 TU Arriel 1C2	4250			
☐ HL9206	Eurocopter (Aerosp.) AS365N2 Dauphin 2	6472		0094	1094	2 TU Arriel 1C2	4250			
☐ HL9208	Eurocopter (Aerosp.) AS365N2 Dauphin 2	6473		0094	1094	2 TU Arriel 1C2	4250			
☐ HL9253	Bell 412EP	36128	N62739	0096	1196	2 PWC PT6T-3D TwinPac	5398	EMS		
☐ HL7301	Dassault Falcon 900B	156	N202FJ	0096	0896	3 GA TFE731-5BR-1C	21099			
☐ HL9261	Mil Mi-26TC	071217		0097	1097	2 LO D-136	49750			

SEOUL AIR INTERNATIONAL, Ltd – SAI = SHI

Seoul

C.P.O. Box 10352, Seoul 100699, Republic of Korea ☎ (2) 699 09 91 Tx: k28226 Fax: (2) 699 09 54 SITA: n/a
F: 1972 👪 60 Head: S.Y. Roh ICAO: SEOUL AIR Net: n/a

☐ HL9135	MD Helicopters MD 520N (Hughes 500N)	LN044	TG-DIS	0093	1196	1 AN 250-C20R	1520			
☐ HL9243	Kawasaki (Eurocopter/MBB) BK117B-1	1025	JA9904	0089	0590	2 LY LTS101-750B.1	3200			
☐ HL9215	Bell 222	47056		0081	0481	2 LY LTS101-650C.3	3561			
☐ HL9116	Bell 214B-1 BigLifter	28058	N514RM	0080	0394	1 LY T5508D	5670			
☐ HL9133	Bell 214B-1 BigLifter	28021	N114RM	0077	1096	1 LY T5508D	5670			
☐ HL5224	BAe 3112 Jetstream 31	783	C-FCOE	1087	0295	2 GA TPE331-10UGR-514H	6950			
☐ HL5225	BAe 3112 Jetstream 31	786	C-FIOE	1187	0195	2 GA TPE331-10UGR-514H	6950			

HP = PANAMA (Republic of Panama) (Republica de Panama)

Capital: Panama City Official Language: Spanish Population: 2,6 million Square Km: 77082 Dialling code: +507 Year established: 1903 Acting political head: Ernesto Perez Balladares (President)

Government / Corporate / Executive / VIP Aircraft

☐ HP-1A	GAC (Grumman) G-1159 Gulfstream II	078	N90HH	0068		2 RR Spey 511-8	29393	VIP		Direccion de Aeronautica Civil
☐ HP-AIA	Sikorsky S-76C	760386	N5007R	0091		2 TU Arriel 1S1	5307	VIP		Direccion de Aeronautica Civil

AEREO TAXI INTERNACIONAL, SA

Panama-Marco A. Gelabert

Apartado 55-0960, Paitilla, Panama (Panama), Republic of Panama ☎ 264 27 76 Tx: n/a Fax: 226 34 22 SITA: n/a
F: 1988 👪 35 Head: José Ivanhoe de Roux Net: n/a Aircraft below MTOW 1361kg: Cessna 182

☐ HP-1323XI	Bell 206B JetRanger II	2089	N16674	0076	1096	1 AN 250-C20	1451			
☐ HP-1153XI	Britten-Norman BN-2A-26 Islander	672	HP-1153PS	0072		2 LY O-540-E4C5	2994			
☐ HP-1209XI	Britten-Norman BN-2A-8 Islander	296	HR-ALP	0071	0092	2 LY O-540-E4C5	2858			
☐ HP-1232XI	Britten-Norman BN-2A Islander	612	HP-1232TN	0070		2 LY O-540-E4C5	2858			lsf PARSA
☐ HP-987XI	Britten-Norman BN-2A Islander	61	HP-987TN	0069		2 LY O-540-E4C5	2858			lsf PARSA

AEROPERLAS, S.A. = WL / APP

Panama-Marcos A. Gelabert

Apartado 6-3596, El Dorado, (Panama), Republic of Panama ☎ 263 53 63 Tx: 2870 conta pg Fax: 223 06 06 SITA: n/a
F: 1969 👪 240 Head: George F. Novey ICAO: AEROPERLAS Net: http://www.pananet.com/aeroperlas Some services are operated under the name AEROLINEAS PACIFICO ATLANTICO S.A. (same headquarters & fleet).

☐ HP-1336APP	Beech King Air A100	B-173	C-FJFH	0073	0897	2 PWC PT6A-28	5216			
☐ HP-1267APP	De Havilland DHC-6 Twin Otter 300	624	C-FTOT	0078	1294	2 PWC PT6A-27	5670			
☐ HP-1276APP	De Havilland DHC-6 Twin Otter 300	445	C-FVBH	0075	0495	2 PWC PT6A-27	5670			
☐ HP-1281APP	De Havilland DHC-6 Twin Otter 300	407	C-FVFK	0074	0595	2 PWC PT6A-27	5670			
☐ HP-1283APP	De Havilland DHC-6 Twin Otter 300	269	C-GKBO	0069	0595	2 PWC PT6A-27	5670			
☐ HP-1308APP	De Havilland DHC-6 Twin Otter 300	402	N546N	0074	0396	2 PWC PT6A-27	5670			
☐ HP-747APP	De Havilland DHC-6 Twin Otter 300	403		0074	0274	2 PWC PT6A-27	5670			Isla del Rey
☐ HP-1251APP	Shorts 360-200 (SD3-60)	SH3610	N715NC	0083	0394	2 PWC PT6A-65AR	11999			
☐ HP-1280APP	Shorts 360-200 (SD3-60)	SH3665	N190SB	0085	0495	2 PWC PT6A-65AR	11999			
☐ HP-1315APP	Shorts 360-200 (SD3-60)	SH3614	N363MQ	0083	0396	2 PWC PT6A-65AR	11999			
☐ HP-1317APP	Shorts 360-200 (SD3-60)	SH3602	N360MQ	0082	0596	2 PWC PT6A-65AR	11999			lst La Costena, Nicaragua
☐ HP-1318APP	Shorts 360-200 (SD3-60)	SH3612	N362MQ	0083	0596	2 PWC PT6A-65AR	11999			lst La Costena, Nicaragua
☐ HP-1319APP	Shorts 360-200 (SD3-60)	SH3607	N361MQ	0083	0696	2 PWC PT6A-65AR	11999			

ANSA – Aerolineas Nacionales, S.A.

Panama-Marcos A. Gelabert

Apartado 6-8463, El Dorado, (Panama), Republic of Panama ☎ 226 68 81 Tx: none Fax: 226 40 70 SITA: n/a
F: 1983 👪 n/a Head: José Ivanhoe De Roux Net: n/a

☐ HP-1220KN	Britten-Norman BN-2A-7 Islander	242	N4278B	0070	1192	2 LY O-540-E4C5	2858			lsf Admin. de Aeronaves

AVIATUR – Aviacion de Turismo, S.A.

Panama-Marcos A. Gelabert

Apartado 0832-1658 WTC, Panama City, (Panama), Republic of Panama ☎ 270 17 48 Tx: none Fax: 315 03 16 SITA: n/a
F: 1994 👪 n/a Head: Zosimo Guardia V. Net: n/a

☐ HP-1332AR	Cessna U206G Stationair 6 II	U20604857	C-GNTB	0079	0697	1 CO IO-520-F	1633			lsf Aircraft Leasing Int'l Inc.

202 registration type of aircraft cn/fn ex/ex* mfd del powered by mtow kg configuration selcal name/fln/specialitites/remarks

registration	type of aircraft	cn/fn	ex/ex*	mfd	del	powered by	mtow kg	configuration	selcal	name/fln/specialitites/remarks
☐ HP-668AR	Twin (Aero) Shrike Commander 500S	500S-1862-41	HP-668	0069		2 LY IO-540-E1B5	3062			
☐ HP-1284AR	Britten-Norman BN-2A-26 Islander	170	N140FS	0070	0695	2 LY O-540-E4C5	2994			lsf Aircraft Leasing Int'l Inc.
☐ HP-1312AR	Britten-Norman BN-2A-6 Islander	641	D-IORS	0071	0496	2 LY O-540-E4C5	2812			lsf Aircraft Leasing Int'l Inc.
☐ HP-1345AR	Cessna 208B Grand Caravan	208B0380	YN-CEJ	0093	0498	1 PWC PT6A-114A	3969			lsf Aircraft Leasing Int'l Inc.
☐ HP-1360AR	Cessna 208B Grand Caravan	208B0719		0098	1298	1 PWC PT6A-114A	3969			lsf Caravan Investment Inc.

CARGO THREE, Inc. = CTW — Panama-Tocumen Int'l

Apartado Postal 2472, Panama 9A, (Panama), Republic of Panama ☎ 238 40 91 Tx: none Fax: 238 44 17 SITA: n/a
F: 1990 ⁂ 25 Head: Francisco Giraldo IATA: 413 ICAO: THIRD CARGO Net: n/a

☐ HP-1221CTW	Convair 580 (F) (SCD)	169	HP-1221CTH	0054	0592	2 AN 501-D13	24766	Freighter		Peter / lsf Tobalcri SA / cvtd CV340-31

COCLESANA DE AVIACION, S.A. — Penonome

Aeropuerto, Penonomé, (Coclé), Republic of Panama ☎ 213 05 42 Tx: none Fax: 213 05 42 SITA: n/a
F: n/a ⁂ n/a Head: n/a Net: n/a

☐ HP-1223CC	MD Helicopters MD 500D (Hughes 369D)	1100842D	C-GPDH	0080		1 AN 250-C20B	1361			lsf Northern Mountain Helicopters
☐ HP-1240CC	MD Helicopters MD 500D (Hughes 369D)	1270249D	C-GSZT	0078		1 AN 250-C20B	1361			lsf Northern Mountain Helicopters
☐ HP-1253CC	MD Helicopters MD 500D (Hughes 369D)	711031D	C-GESC	0081		1 AN 250-C20B	1361			lsf Northern Mountain Helicopters
☐ HP-1278CC	MD Helicopters MD 500D (Hughes 369D)	280260D	C-GRLC	0078		1 AN 250-C20B	1361			lsf Northern Mountain Helicopters
☐ HP-1306CC	MD Helicopters MD 500D (Hughes 369D)	1193D	N32CL	0082		1 AN 250-C20B	1361			
☐ HP-1268CC	Bell 206B JetRanger III	2387	C-GNME	0078		1 AN 250-C20B	1451			lsf Northern Mountain Helicopters
☐ HP-1351CC	Bell 206B JetRanger	291	C-GTQD	0068	0598	1 AN 250-C20	1451			lsf Northern Montain Heli. / cvtd 206A
☐ HP-763CC	Piper PA-34-200T Seneca II	34-8070268		0080		2 CO TSIO-360-EB	2073			lsf Geo Air SA
☐ HP-1349CC	Eurocopter (Aerosp.) AS350B Ecureuil	1317	C-FPTR	0080	0598	1 TU Arriel 1B	1950			lsf Northern Mountain Helicopters

COPA Panama - Compania Panamena de Aviacion, SA = CM / CMP (Associated with Continental Airlines Inc., USA) — Panama-Tocumen Int'l

Apartado Postal 1572, Panama 1, (Panama), Republic of Panama ☎ 227 25 22 Tx: 2893 copapty pg Fax: 227 19 52 SITA: PMDHCM
F: 1947 ⁂ 1600 Head: Alberto Motta IATA: 230 ICAO: COPA Net: http://www.copaair.com

☐ HP-1134CMP	Boeing 737-230C	20253 / 223	N301XV	1269	0288	2 PW JT8D-9	54204	Freighter		lsf FSBU Trustee
☐ HP-1163CMP	Boeing 737-204 (A)	21693 / 541	G-BFVA	1178	0890	2 PW JT8D-15	55111	C8Y106		lsf FSBU Trustee
☐ HP-1195CMP	Boeing 737-204 (A)	20806 / 338	G-BAZG	0174	0991	2 PW JT8D-15	55111	C8Y106		lsf FSBU Trustee
☐ HP-1234CMP	Boeing 737-2S3 (A)	22660 / 849	VR-HYK	0382	0593	2 PW JT8D-15	55111	C8Y106	BK-CJ	lsf Interlease Management
☐ HP-1245CMP	Boeing 737-2H6 (A)	22620 / 822	9M-MBK	1281	1093	2 PW JT8D-15	54204	C8Y106	CG-DE	lsf Interlease Management
☐ HP-1255CMP	Boeing 737-2P6 (A)	21359 / 500	HR-SHQ	0977	0494	2 PW JT8D-15	53070	C8Y106	CH-JK	lsf POLA
☐ HP-1288CMP	Boeing 737-219 (A)	22088 / 676	N318CM	0680	0695	2 PW JT8D-15	53297	C8Y106		lsf IAI Pacific Leasing
☐ HP-1297CMP	Boeing 737-219 (A)	21645 / 535	N237TA	1078	0195	2 PW JT8D-15	53070	C8Y106		lsf Int'l Aircraft Investors
☐ HP-1311CMP	Boeing 737-2H6C (A)	21109 / 436	N124GU	1075	0693	2 PW JT8D-15	54204	C8Y106		lsf CITG
☐ HP-1322CMP	Boeing 737-2P5 (A)	22667 / 794	AP-BEV	0981	1196	2 PW JT8D-15	52616	C8Y106		lsf FSBU Trustee
☐ HP-1324CMP	Boeing 737-2P5 (A)	23113 / 1010	AP-BEW	0084	1296	2 PW JT8D-15	51563	C8Y106		lsf FSBU Trustee
☐ HP-1339CMP	Boeing 737-2P6 (A)	21677 / 538	EI-CKW	1178	0198	2 PW JT8D-15	53070	C8Y106		lsf GECA
☐ HP-1340CMP	Boeing 737-2P6 (A)	21612 / 528	EI-CKK	0878	0198	2 PW JT8D-15	53070	C8Y106		lsf GECA
☐ HP-	Boeing 737-71Q					2 CFMI CFM56-7B24	69400	C8Y106		to be lsf TOMB 0499
☐ HP-	Boeing 737-71Q					2 CFMI CFM56-7B24	69400	C8Y106		to be lsf TOMB 0799
☐ HP-	Boeing 737-76N					2 CFMI CFM56-7B24	69400	C8Y106		to be lsf GECA 1099
☐ HP-	Boeing 737-700					2 CFMI CFM56-7B24	69400	C8Y106		oo-delivery 1099
☐ HP-	Boeing 737-76N					2 CFMI CFM56-7B24	69400	C8Y106		to be lsf GECA 1199
☐ HP-	Boeing 737-700					2 CFMI CFM56-7B24	69400	C8Y106		oo-delivery 0200
☐ HP-	Boeing 737-700					2 CFMI CFM56-7B24	69400	C8Y106		oo-delivery 0400
☐ HP-	Boeing 737-700					2 CFMI CFM56-7B24	69400	C8Y106		oo-delivery 0500
☐ HP-	Boeing 737-700					2 CFMI CFM56-7B24	69400	C8Y106		oo-delivery 0900
☐ HP-	Boeing 737-700					2 CFMI CFM56-7B24	69400	C8Y106		oo-delivery 0101
☐ HP-	Boeing 737-700					2 CFMI CFM56-7B24	69400	C8Y106		oo-delivery 0501
☐ HP-	Boeing 737-700					2 CFMI CFM56-7B24	69400	C8Y106		oo-delivery 0801

DHL Aero Expreso, S.A. = DS / DAE (Subsidiary of DHL WorldWide, Netherlands) — Panama-Tocumen Int'l

Apartado Aéreo 11491, Panama City 6, (Panama), Republic of Panama ☎ 238 42 06 Tx: none Fax: 238 41 49 SITA: PTYSNER
F: 1996 ⁂ 68 Head: Steve Getzler IATA: 992 Net: n/a

☐ HP-1310DAE	Boeing 727-264 (F) (A)	20894 / 1047	N9184X	0074	0496	3 PW JT8D-17R (HK3/FDX)	83552	Freighter		El Gato / cvtd -264

HELICOPTEROS EJECUTIVOS, S.A. — Panama-Marcos A. Gelabert

193 Balboa Ancon, Panama City, (Panama), Republic of Panama ☎ 261 59 16 Tx: none Fax: 261 58 21 SITA: n/a
F: n/a ⁂ n/a Head: n/a Net: n/a

☐ HP-3077DD	Bell 407	53308		0098	1298	1 AN 250-C47B	2268			

HELIPAN, Corp. — Panama-Marcos A. Gelabert

U.S. office: 1917 NW 82nd Ave., Miami, FL 33126, USA ☎ Panama 226 12 63 Tx: none Fax: Panama 226 10 39 SITA: n/a
F: n/a ⁂ n/a Head: n/a Net: n/a Aircraft below MTOW 1361kg: Robinson R22 & R44

☐ HP-1321HC	Bell 206B JetRanger	303	C-GPYT	0068		1 AN 250-C20	1451			cvtd 206A

MK AVIATION, S.A. = (MKAV) (formerly Aeronautics & Astronautics Services, Inc.) — Panama

PO Box 6-308, El Dorado, (Panama), Republic of Panama ☎ 269 52 11 Tx: 2808 emkay pg Fax: 269 14 73 SITA: n/a
F: 1978 ⁂ 11 Head: Mordechai Kraselnick Net: n/a Used aircraft leasing, sales and financing company.
Owner /Lessor of the following (main) aircraft types: Boeing 707-320C, 727-100, DC-9-15 & DC-10-10 / 30. Aircraft leased from MK Aviation are listed and mentioned as lsf MKAV under the leasing carriers.

PACIFIC INTERNATIONAL AIRLINES = PFC — Panama-Tocumen Int'l

Apartado Postal 1592, Panama 9A, (Panama), Republic of Panama ☎ 226 32 11 Tx: none Fax: 226 40 12 SITA: n/a
F: 1993 ⁂ 22 Head: Capt. Guillermo Rodriguez IATA: 993 ICAO: PACIFIC INT'L Net: n/a

☐ HP-1229PFC	Boeing 727-23 (F)	18429 / 26	N517FE	0063	0793	3 PW JT8D-7B	76884	Freighter		cvtd -23
☐ HP-1299PFC	Boeing 727-23 (F)	18435 / 51	N518PM	0064	0995	3 PW JT8D-7B	76884	Freighter		cvtd -23

PANAVIA PANAMA, SA — Panama-Tocumen Int'l

Apartado 8140030, Zona 14/1, Panama City, (Panama), Republic of Panama ☎ 238 45 03 Tx: none Fax: 238 45 09 SITA: n/a
F: 1994 ⁂ n/a Head: n/a Net: n/a

☐ HP-1261PVI	Boeing 727-25 (F)	18965 / 205	N8141N	0065	1294	3 PW JT8D-7B	72756	Freighter		lsf Aero Inversiones SA / cvtd -25

PARSA, SA — Panama-Marcos A. Gelabert

Apartado 9-001, Zona 9, Panama, (Panama), Republic of Panama ☎ 226 38 03 Tx: n/a Fax: 226 34 22 SITA: n/a
F: 1980 ⁂ 26 Head: José Ivanhoe De Roux Net: n/a

☐ HP-775PS	Piper PA-34-200T Seneca II	34-7670306		0076		2 CO TSIO-360-E	2073			
☐ HP-1016PS	Britten-Norman BN-2A-27 Islander	628	N268BN	0071		2 LY O-540-E4C5	2994			
☐ HP-1232XI	Britten-Norman BN-2A Islander	612	HP-1232TN	0070		2 LY O-540-E4C5	2858			lst Aereo Taxi Internacional
☐ HP-987XI	Britten-Norman BN-2A Islander	61	HP-987TN	0069		2 LY O-540-E4C5	2858			lst Aereo Taxi Internacional
☐ HP-899PS	Britten-Norman BN-2A Mk.III-1 Trislander	1007	HP-899CH	0075		3 LY O-540-E4C5	4536			

HR = HONDURAS (Republic of Honduras) (Republica de Honduras)

Capital: Tegucigalpa Official Language: Spanish Population: 6,0 million Square Km: 112088 Dialling code: +504 Year established: 1821 Acting political head: Carlos Roberto Flores Facussé (President)

Government / Corporate / Executive / VIP Aircraft

☐ HR-001	IAI 1123 Jet Commander	183	FAH318	0075		2 GE CJ610-9	9389	VIP		Fuerza Aérea Hondurena
☐ HR-002	IAI 1124A Westwind II	333	4X-CTA*	0081		2 GA TFE731-3-1G	10659	VIP		Fuerza Aérea Hondurena
☐ HR-EMA	Lockheed L-188A Electra	1028	555	0059	0492	4 AN 501-D13	51256	VIP		Gvmt / opb Fuerza Aérea Hondurena

AEROLINEAS SOSA, Sarl = P4 — La Ceiba

Avenida San Isidro, Frente al Parque Central, La Ceiba, Honduras ☎ 43 18 94 Tx: none Fax: 43 18 94 SITA: n/a
F: 1984 ⁂ n/a Head: Juan Antonio Sosa B. ICAO: SOSA Net: n/a

☐ HR-AJM	Cessna U206G Stationair	U20603524	N8771Q	0077		1 CO IO-520F	1633			
☐ HR-AQR	Let 410UVP	851516	CCCP-67549	0085	0096	2 WA M-601D	5800			

ISLENA AIRLINES = ISV (Islena de Inversiones, SA de CV dba / Member of Groupo TACA) — La Ceiba

PO Box 402, Frente Parque Central, Avda San Isidro, La Ceiba, Honduras ☎ 440 08 26 Tx: none Fax: 441 25 27 SITA: n/a
F: 1982 ⁂ 250 Head: Arturo A. Wood Net: n/a Aircraft below MTOW 1361 kg: Cessna 182.

☐ HR-IAA	Embraer 110P2 Bandeirante (EMB-110P2)	110153	N2932C	0078	0690	2 PWC PT6A-34	5670	Y20		
☐ HR-IAV	Embraer 110P2 Bandeirante (EMB-110P2)	110146	N717GA	0077	1194	2 PWC PT6A-34	5670	Y20		
☐ HR-IAR	Let 410UVP	800506	RA-67035	0080	0094	2 WA M-601D	5800	Y18		
☐ HR-IAZ	Let 410UVP	831137	TG-TJB	0083	0097	2 WA M-601D	5800	Y18		
☐ HR-IBB	Let 410UVP	831136	HI-674CT	0083	0997	2 WA M-601D	5800	Y18		
☐ HR-IBC	Let 410UVP	851404	HI-677CA	0085	0097	2 WA M-601D	5800	Y18		
☐ HR-IAP	Shorts 360-100 (SD3-60)	SH3616	N345MV	0083	0493	2 PWC PT6A-65R	11999	Y39		
☐ HR-IAW	Shorts 360-100 (SD3-60)	SH3669	N361PA	0085	0195	2 PWC PT6A-65R	11999	Y39		
☐ HR-ALM	ATR 42-320	392	F-WQIF	0095	1298	2 PWC PW121	16700	Y50		lsf ATR

☐ HR-IAX	ATR 42-300	004	F-WEGD*	0085	0496	2 PWC PW120	16700	Y50		
☐ HR-IAY	ATR 42-300	120	F-WQHM	0089	0497	2 PWC PW120	16700	Y50		
☐ HR-	ATR 42-320	093	TG-AGA	0088		2 PWC PW121	16700	Y50		to be lsf ATR 0099
☐ HR-	ATR 42-320	066	TG-AFA	0087		2 PWC PW121	16700	Y50		to be lsf ATR 0099 / cvtd -300

SETCO – Servicios Ejecutivos Turisticos Commander — Tegucigalpa

Aeropuerto Toncontin, Tegucigalpa, Honduras ☎ 33 17 12 Tx: none Fax: 33 20 41 SITA: n/a
F: 1981 ⁂ n/a Head: Capt. Ricardo Ynestrosa Net: n/a

☐ HR-AFB	Twin (Aero) Shrike Commander 500S	3268	HR-315	0076		2 LY IO-540-E1B5	3062			
☐ HR-AFC	Twin (Aero) Shrike Commander 500S	3271	HR-317	0076		2 LY IO-540-E1B5	3062			
☐ HR-AKF	Twin (Aero) Commander 560E	560E-592	N6215B	0058		2 LY GO-480-G1B6	2948			
☐ HR-AKM	Twin (Aero) Shrike Commander 500S	3098	TG-CNA	0071		2 LY IO-540-E1B5	3062			
☐ HR-AAJ	Twin (Aero) Turbo Commander 690A	11233	N9192N	0075		2 GA TPE331-5-251K	4649			
☐ HR-AJY	Boeing (Douglas) DC-3C (C-47-DL)	6068	HP-665	0042		2 PW R-1830	12202			std TGU
☐ HR-ALU	Boeing (Douglas) DC-3C (C-47)					2 PW R-1830	12202			std TGU

HS = THAILAND (Kingdom of Thailand) (Prathet T'hai)

Capital: Bangkok Official Language: Thai Population: 59,0 million Square Km: 513115 Dialling code: +66 Year established: 1782 Acting political head: Chuan Leekpai (Prime Minister)

Government / Corporate / Executive / VIP Aircraft

☐ HS-DCA	BAe 3200 Jetstream 32	960	G-BUDJ*	0092	0792	2 GA TPE331-12UAR-701H	7350	Liaison/19 Pax		Department of Aviation
☐ HS-DCB	Beech King Air 200	BB-132	HS-FFI	0076	0779	2 PWC PT6A-41	5670	Liaison/8 Pax		Department of Aviation
☐ HS-DCF	Beech King Air B200	BB-1315	HS-AFI	0089	0590	2 PWC PT6A-42	6350	Liaison/9 Pax		Department of Aviation
☐ HS-DCG	Cessna 650 Citation VII	650-7071		0096	0896	2 GA TFE731-4R-2S	10180	Calibrator		Department of Aviation
☐ 1060	BAe 4100 Jetstream 41	41060	G-BWGW*	0095	1295	2 GA TPE331-14GR-805H	10886	VIP / mil trans		Royal Thai Army
☐ 1094	BAe 4100 Jetstream 41	41094	G-BWTZ*	0096	1196	2 GA TPE331-14GR-805H	10886	VIP / mil trans		Royal Thai Army
☐ 11-111	BAe (HS) 748-208 Srs 2A	1570 / 48	HS-TAF	0064	0165	2 RR Dart 533-2	20183	VIP		Royal Thai Air Force/Royal Flight
☐ 22-222	Boeing 737-2Z6 (A)	23059 / 980	N45733*	0083	1283	2 PW JT8D-15	52390	VIP		Royal Thai Air Force/Royal Flight
☐ 29-999	Fairchild (Swearingen) SA226AT Merlin IVA	AT-065		0078		2 GA TPE331-3U-303G	5670	VIP		Royal Thai Air Force/Royal Flight
☐ 44-444	Airbus Industrie A310-324	591	F-WWCH*	0091	1191	2 PW PW4152	157000	VIP	EJ-FL	HS-TYQ / Royal Thai Air Force/Royal Flt
☐ 55-555	Boeing 737-4Z6	27906 / 2698		0095	0295	2 CFMI CFM56-3C1	64637	VIP	EK-AL	HS-RTA / Gvmt
☐ 99-999	BAe (HS) 748-208 Srs 2A	1715 / 198	HS-TAF	0072	0173	2 RR Dart 533-2	20183	VIP		Royal Thai Air Force/Royal Flight

ANGEL AIRLINES, Co. Ltd = 8G / NGE (Subsidiary of JVK Holdings) — Bangkok-Int'l

222 Krungtherp Kreetha Road, Huamark Sub-Distr., Bangkapi District, Bangkok 10000, Thailand ☎ (2) 535 62 87 Tx: none Fax: (2) 535 62 89 SITA: n/a
F: 1998 ⁂ n/a Head: n/a IATA: 958 ICAO: ANGEL AIR Net: n/a

☐ 9M-MFE	Boeing 737-5H6	26454 / 2511		0093	0998	2 CFMI CFM56-3C1	52389	F16Y88		lsf MAS

BANGKOK AIR = PG / BKP (Bangkok Airways, Co. Ltd dba / Subsidiary of Bangkok United Mechanical Co. Ltd) — Bangkok-Int'l

60 Queen Sirikit National, Convention Center, New Rajadapisek Road, Klongioey, Bangkok 10110, Thailand ☎ (2) 229 34 56 Tx: n/a Fax: (2) 229 34 54 SITA: BKKRRPG
F: 1968 ⁂ 657 Head: Dr. Prasert Prasarttong-Osoth IATA: 829 ICAO: BANGKOK AIR Net: n/a

☐ HS-PGG	ATR 42-320	078	F-WQBQ	0088	0497	2 PWC PW121	16700	Y46		lsf GIE Dorabella / cvtd -300
☐ HS-PGA	ATR 72-202	373	F-WWEU*	0093	1094	2 PWC PW124B	21500	Y70		lsf Grampas Ltd
☐ HS-PGB	ATR 72-202	367	F-WWEX*	0093	1194	2 PWC PW124B	21500	Y70		lsf Grampas Ltd
☐ HS-PGC	ATR 72-202	452	F-WWEW*	0095	0695	2 PWC PW124B	21500	Y70		lsf GIE Dorabella
☐ HS-PGD	ATR 72-202	455	F-WWLM*	0095	0795	2 PWC PW124B	21500	Y70		lsf GIE Dorabella
☐ HS-PGE	ATR 72-202	450	F-WWEH*	0095	1195	2 PWC PW124B	21500	Y70		lsf GIE Dorabella
☐ HS-PGF	ATR 72-202	477	F-WWEI*	0096	1196	2 PWC PW124B	21500	Y70		lsf GIE Dorabella
☐ HS-PGH	ATR 72-212	469	F-OHLC	0095	1298	2 PWC PW127	21500	Y70		lsf ATR

ORIENT THAI AIRLINES, Co. Ltd = OX / OEA (formerly Orient Express Air, Co. Ltd & Cambodia Int'l Airlines, Co. Ltd) — Bangkok

138/70 17th Floor, Jewellery Center, Siphaya, Bangkok 10500, Thailand ☎ (2) 267 32 10 Tx: none Fax: (2) 267 32 16 SITA: n/a
F: 1992 ⁂ n/a Head: Udom Tantiprasongchai ICAO: ORIENT EXPRESS Net: n/a

☐ HS-LTA	Lockheed L-1011-385-1 TriStar 1	193A-1043	N143MC	0773	0896	3 RR RB211-22B	195045	C49Y250		lst / opf MNA
☐ HS-LTB	Lockheed L-1011-385-1 TriStar 1	193A-1055	N155MC	1273	1096	3 RR RB211-22B	195045	C49Y250		occ lst/jtly opw KMP

PB AIR, Ltd = PBA — Bangkok

1001 Samsen Road, Bangkok 10300, Thailand ☎ (2) 669 20 66 Tx: none Fax: (2) 669 20 92 SITA: n/a
F: 1991 ⁂ 30 Head: Dr. Piya Bhirombhakdi ICAO: PEEBEE AIR Net: n/a

☐ HS-PBB	Dornier 328-110	3072	D-CDXY*	0096	1096	2 PWC PW119B	13990	Y30 or VIP C20		

SIAM LAND FLYING, Co. Ltd — Bangkok-Int'l

171 Domestic Terminal, Room 3602, Vibhavadi Ransit Road, Bangkok 10210, Thailand ☎ (2) 535 47 34 Tx: none Fax: (2) 535 43 55 SITA: n/a
F: 1991 ⁂ 16 Head: n/a Net: n/a

☐ HS-SLB	Beech King Air C90A	LJ-1243	HS-TFH	0090	1095	2 PWC PT6A-21	4377			
☐ HS-SLA	Beech King Air 350 (B300)	FL-53	HS-TFI	0091	0795	2 PWC PT6A-60A	6350			

SI-CHANG FLYING SERVICE, Co Ltd = SCR — Bangkok-Int'l

12th Floor, 26/40 Orakarn Bldg, Chidlom Road, Pathumwan, Bangkok 10330, Thailand ☎ (2) 655 01 86 Tx: none Fax: (2) 251 32 23 SITA: n/a
F: 1990 ⁂ 21 Head: Chira Ratanarat ICAO: SICHART Net: http://www.sino.net/sichang/

☐ HS-SFA	Kawasaki (Eurocopter/MBB) BK117B-1	1067		0090	0191	2 LY LTS101-750B.1	3200			
☐ HS-SFB	Kawasaki (Eurocopter/MBB) BK117B-1	1078	JQ1078*	0091	0591	2 LY LTS101-750B.1	3200			

THAI AIRWAYS INTERNATIONAL, Public Co. Ltd. = TG / THA (Member of Star Alliance / formerly Thai Airways International, Ltd) — Bangkok-Int'l

89 Vibhavadi Rangsit Super Highway, PO Box 1075 G.P.O., Bangkok 10900, Thailand ☎ (2) 513 01 21 Tx: 82359 thanter th Fax: (2) 513 01 83 SITA: n/a
F: 1959 ⁂ 11300 Head: Mahidol Chantrangkurn IATA: 217 ICAO: THAI Net: http://www.thaiair.com Also uses a Boeing 747-200F lsf/opb ATLAS AIR (N) in Thai-colors for cargo flights. For details – see under that company.

☐ HS-TRA	ATR 72-201	164	F-WWEO*	0090	0290	2 PWC PW124B	21500	Y64		Lampang
☐ HS-TRB	ATR 72-201	167	F-WWEU*	0090	0490	2 PWC PW124B	21500	Y64		Chai Nat
☐ HS-TDA	Boeing 737-4D7	24830 / 1899		0090	0890	2 CFMI CFM56-3C1	64637	C12Y138	EH-JL	Songkhla
☐ HS-TDB	Boeing 737-4D7	24831 / 1922		0090	0990	2 CFMI CFM56-3C1	64637	C12Y138	EH-JM	Phuket
☐ HS-TDC	Boeing 737-4D7	25321 / 2113		0091	0991	2 CFMI CFM56-3C1	64637	C12Y138	EH-KL	Narathiwat
☐ HS-TDD	Boeing 737-4D7	26611 / 2318		0092	0792	2 CFMI CFM56-3C1	64637	C12Y138	EH-KM	Chumphon
☐ HS-TDE	Boeing 737-4D7	26612 / 2330		0092	0792	2 CFMI CFM56-3C1	64637	C12Y138	EH-LM	Surin
☐ HS-TDF	Boeing 737-4D7	26613 / 2338		0092	0892	2 CFMI CFM56-3C1	64637	C12Y138	EJ-AD	Si Sa Ket
☐ HS-TDG	Boeing 737-4D7	26614 / 2481		0093	0593	2 CFMI CFM56-3C1	64637	C12Y138	EJ-AF	Kalasin
☐ HS-TDH	Boeing 737-4D7	28703 / 2962		0097	1297	2 CFMI CFM56-3C1	64637	C12Y138	EJ-FM	Lop Buri
☐ HS-TDJ	Boeing 737-4D7	28704 / 2968		0097	1297	2 CFMI CFM56-3C1	64637	C12Y138	EJ-GH	Nakhon Chaisi
☐ HS-TDK	Boeing 737-4D7	28701 / 2977		0097	0198	2 CFMI CFM56-3C1	64637	C12Y138	EJ-GM	Sri Surat
☐ HS-TDL	Boeing 737-4D7	28702 / 2978		0097	0198	2 CFMI CFM56-3C1	64637	C12Y138	EJ-KM	Srikarn
☐ HS-TIC	Airbus Industrie A310-204 (winglets)	424	F-WWCM*	0086	0488	2 GE CF6-80C2A2	142000	Y265	EL-CH	Ratchaburi
☐ HS-THP	Airbus Industrie A300B4-103	084	HS-TGP	0079	0879	2 GE CF6-50C2	157500	C43Y180	EJ-FL	Srisubhan / cvtd A300B4-2C/for Airbus99
☐ HS-THR	Airbus Industrie A300B4-103	085	HS-TGR	0079	0979	2 GE CF6-50C2	157500	C43Y180	EJ-FG	Thepamart / cvtdA300B4-2C/for Airbus99
☐ HS-THT	Airbus Industrie A300B4-203	141	HS-TGT	0081	0581	2 GE CF6-50C2	165000	C43Y180	EJ-DM	Jiraprabha / for Airbus 0099
☐ HS-THW	Airbus Industrie A300B4-203	149	HS-TGW	0081	0981	2 GE CF6-50C2	165000	C43Y180	EK-AB	Srisachanalai / for Airbus/DHL 0099
☐ HS-TAA	Airbus Industrie A300-601 (A300B4-601)	368	F-WWAG*	0085	0985	2 GE CF6-80C2A1	165000	C46Y201	CJ-FL	Suwannaphum
☐ HS-TAB	Airbus Industrie A300-601 (A300B4-601)	371	F-WWAH*	0085	0985	2 GE CF6-80C2A1	165000	C46Y201	CJ-FM	Sri Anocha
☐ HS-TAC	Airbus Industrie A300-601 (A300B4-601)	377	F-WWAI*	0085	1285	2 GE CF6-80C2A1	165000	C46Y201	CJ-GL	Sri Ayutthaya
☐ HS-TAD	Airbus Industrie A300-601 (A300B4-601)	384	F-WWAK*	0085	0286	2 GE CF6-80C2A1	165000	C46Y201	CJ-GM	U Thong
☐ HS-TAE	Airbus Industrie A300-601 (A300B4-601)	395	F-WWAM*	0086	1086	2 GE CF6-80C2A1	165000	C46Y201	CJ-HK	Sukhothai
☐ HS-TAF	Airbus Industrie A300-601 (A300B4-601)	398	F-WWAN*	0086	1286	2 GE CF6-80C2A1	165000	C46Y201	CJ-HL	Ratchasima
☐ HS-TAG	Airbus Industrie A300-605R (A300B4-605R)	464	F-WWAL*	0088	0888	2 GE CF6-80C2A5	170500	C46Y201	CJ-HM	Srinapha
☐ HS-TAH	Airbus Industrie A300-605R (A300B4-605R)	518	F-WWAE*	0089	0689	2 GE CF6-80C2A5	170500	C46Y201	CJ-KL	Napachinda
☐ HS-TAK	Airbus Industrie A300-622R (A300B4-622R)	566	F-WWAB*	0090	1090	2 PW PW4158	170500	C46Y201	CJ-KM	Phaya Thai
☐ HS-TAL	Airbus Industrie A300-622R (A300B4-622R)	569	F-WWAD*	0090	1190	2 PW PW4158	170500	C46Y201	CK-AH	Sri Trang
☐ HS-TAM	Airbus Industrie A300-622R (A300B4-622R)	577	F-WWAG*	0090	1290	2 PW PW4158	170500	C46Y201	CK-AJ	Chiang Mai
☐ HS-TAN	Airbus Industrie A300-622R (A300B4-622R)	628	F-WWAE*	0092	0492	2 PW PW4158	170500	C46Y201	CK-AL	Chiang Rai
☐ HS-TAO	Airbus Industrie A300-622R (A300B4-622R)	629	F-WWAF*	0092	0492	2 PW PW4158	170500	C46Y201	CJ-FK	Chanthaburi / Star Alliance-colors
☐ HS-TAP	Airbus Industrie A300-622R (A300B4-622R)	635	F-WWAP*	0092	0692	2 PW PW4158	170500	C46Y201	EK-AJ	Pathum Thani
☐ HS-TAR	Airbus Industrie A300-622R (A300B4-622R)	681	F-WWAB*	0093	0393	2 PW PW4158	170500	C46Y201	CJ-GP	Yasothon
☐ HS-TAS	Airbus Industrie A300-622R (A300B4-622R)	705	F-WWAT*	0093	1093	2 PW PW4158	170500	C46Y201	CJ-HP	Yala
☐ HS-TAT	Airbus Industrie A300-622R (A300B4-622R)	782	F-WWAY*	0098	1298	2 PW PW4158	170500	C46Y201	LS-AP	Srimuang
☐ HS-TAW	Airbus Industrie A300-622R (A300B4-622R)	784	F-WWAL*	0098	1298	2 PW PW4158	170500	C46Y201	LS-AQ	Suranarre
☐ HS-TAX	Airbus Industrie A300-622R (A300B4-622R)	785	F-WWAO*	0098	1298	2 PW PW4158	170500	C46Y201	LS-AR	
☐ HS-TAY	Airbus Industrie A300-622R (A300B4-622R)	786	F-WWAQ*	0098	1298	2 PW PW4158	170500	C46Y201	LS-BC	Srisoonthorn
☐ HS-TAZ	Airbus Industrie A300-622R (A300B4-622R)	787	F-WWAB*	0098	1298	2 PW PW4158	170500	C46Y201	LS-BD	

204 registration type of aircraft cn/fn ex/ex* mfd del powered by mtow kg configuration selcal name/fln/specialitites/remarks

□ HS-TEA	Airbus Industrie A330-321	050	F-WWKI*	0094	0195	2 PW PW4164	212000	C50Y265	EL-DH	Manorom
□ HS-TEB	Airbus Industrie A330-321	060	F-WWKQ*	0094	1294	2 PW PW4164	212000	C50Y265	EL-DJ	Ski Sakhon
□ HS-TEC	Airbus Industrie A330-321	062	F-WWKR*	0095	1294	2 PW PW4164	212000	C50Y265	EL-DK	Bang Rachan
□ HS-TED	Airbus Industrie A330-321	064	F-WWKS*	0095	0295	2 PW PW4164	212000	C50Y265	EL-DM	Don Chedi
□ HS-TEE	Airbus Industrie A330-321	065	F-WWKT*	0095	0195	2 PW PW4164	212000	C50Y265	EL-GH	Kusuman
□ HS-TEF	Airbus Industrie A330-321	066	F-WWKJ*	0095	0395	2 PW PW4164	212000	C50Y265	EF-KP	Song Dao
□ HS-TEG	Airbus Industrie A330-321	112	F-WWKM*	0095	1095	2 PW PW4164	212000	C50Y265	EF-KR	Lam Plai Mat
□ HS-TEH	Airbus Industrie A330-321	122	F-WWKG*	0095	1295	2 PW PW4164	212000	C50Y265	EF-KS	Sai Puri
□ HS-TEJ	Airbus Industrie A330-322	209	F-WWKN*	0098	0898	2 PW PW4168	212000	C50Y265	LP-DG	Sudawadi / lsf Debis AirFinance
□ HS-TEK	Airbus Industrie A330-322	224	F-WWKD*	0098	1298	2 PW PW4168	212000	C50Y265	LP-DH	Srichulalak
□ HS-TEL	Airbus Industrie A330-322	231	F-WWKU*	0098	0998	2 PW PW4168	212000	C50Y265	LP-EH	Thepamart
□ HS-TEM	Airbus Industrie A330-323	279				2 PW PW4168A	230000	C50Y265		oo-delivery 0899
□ HS-TJA	Boeing 777-2D7	27726 / 25		0096	0396	2 RR Trent 875	242671	C55Y303	DP-GR	Lamphun
□ HS-TJB	Boeing 777-2D7	27727 / 32		0096	0696	2 RR Trent 875	242671	C55Y303	DP-GS	Uthai Thani
□ HS-TJC	Boeing 777-2D7	27728 / 44		0096	1096	2 RR Trent 875	242671	C55Y303	DP-HR	Nakhon Nayok
□ HS-TJD	Boeing 777-2D7	27729 / 51		0096	1296	2 RR Trent 875	242671	C55Y303	DP-HS	Mukdahan
□ HS-TJE	Boeing 777-2D7	27730 / 89		0897	0897	2 RR Trent 875	242671	C55Y303	EF-LR	Chaiyaphum / lsf Palomino Leasing Ltd
□ HS-TJF	Boeing 777-2D7	27731 / 95		0997	0997	2 RR Trent 875	242671	C55Y303	EF-LS	Pahnom Sarakham / lsf Mustang Lsng Ltd
□ HS-TJG	Boeing 777-2D7	27732 / 100		1097	1097	2 RR Trent 875	247208	C55Y303	EG-AP	Pattani
□ HS-TJH	Boeing 777-2D7	27733 / 113		0097	0198	2 RR Trent 875	247208	C55Y303	EG-DP	Suphan Buri
□ HS-TKA	Boeing 777-3D7	29150 / 156	N5028Y*	0098	1298	2 RR Trent 892	299371	C51Y289	GK-CL	Sriwanna
□ HS-TKB	Boeing 777-3D7	29151 / 170		0098	1298	2 RR Trent 892	299371	C51Y289	GK-CM	Chainarai
□ HS-TKC	Boeing 777-3D7					2 RR Trent 892	299371	C51Y289	GK-DH	oo-delivery 1099
□ HS-TKD	Boeing 777-3D7					2 RR Trent 892	299371	C51Y289	GK-EF	oo-delivery 1199
□ HS-TKE	Boeing 777-3D7					2 RR Trent 892	299371	C51Y289	GK-EH	oo-delivery 1000
□ HS-TKF	Boeing 777-3D7					2 RR Trent 892	299371	C51Y289	GK-EJ	oo-delivery 1100
□ HS-TMD	Boeing (Douglas) MD-11	48416 / 466		0091	0691	3 GE CF6-80C2D1F	277273	F10C42Y233	EL-CD	Phra Nakhon
□ HS-TME	Boeing (Douglas) MD-11	48417 / 467		0091	0791	3 GE CF6-80C2D1F	277273	F10C42Y233	EL-CH	Pathumwan
□ HS-TMF	Boeing (Douglas) MD-11	48418 / 501		0092	0792	3 GE CF6-80C2D1F	277273	F10C42Y233	EL-CK	Phichit
□ HS-TMG	Boeing (Douglas) MD-11	48451 / 505		0092	0792	3 GE CF6-80C2D1F	277273	F10C42Y233	EL-CM	Nakhon Sawan
□ HS-TGD	Boeing 747-3D7	23721 / 681	N6046P*	0087	1287	4 GE CF6-80C2B1	377842	F18C62Y325	GK-DL	Suchada
□ HS-TGE	Boeing 747-3D7	23722 / 688	N60668*	0087	1287	4 GE CF6-80C2B1	377842	F18C62Y325	GK-DM	Chutamat
□ HS-TGH	Boeing 747-4D7	24458 / 769		0090	0290	4 GE CF6-80C2B1F	385553	F18C62Y325	FJ-AM	Chaiprakarn
□ HS-TGJ	Boeing 747-4D7	24459 / 777		0090	0390	4 GE CF6-80C2B1F	385553	F18C62Y325	FJ-BC	Hariphunchai
□ HS-TGK	Boeing 747-4D7	24993 / 833		0091	0191	4 GE CF6-80C2B1F	385553	F18C62Y325	FJ-AL	Alongkorn
□ HS-TGL	Boeing 747-4D7	25366 / 890		0091	1291	4 GE CF6-80C2B1F	385553	F18C62Y325	FJ-AC	Theparat
□ HS-TGM	Boeing 747-4D7	27093 / 945		0092	1192	4 GE CF6-80C2B1F	385553	F18C62Y325	DP-JR	Chao Phraya
□ HS-TGN	Boeing 747-4D7	26615 / 950		0092	1292	4 GE CF6-80C2B1F	385553	F18C62Y325	DP-JS	Simongkhon
□ HS-TGO	Boeing 747-4D7	26609 / 1001		0093	1093	4 GE CF6-80C2B1F	385553	F18C62Y325	DP-KR	Bowonrangsi
□ HS-TGP	Boeing 747-4D7	26610 / 1047		0094	1194	4 GE CF6-80C2B1F	385553	F18C62Y325	DP-KS	Thepprasit
□ HS-TGR	Boeing 747-4D7	27723 / 1071		0095	1195	4 GE CF6-80C2B1F	385553	F18C62Y325	DS-BM	Siriwatthana
□ HS-TGT	Boeing 747-4D7	26616 / 1097		0096	1296	4 GE CF6-80C2B1F	385553	F18C62Y325	FJ-AB	Watthanothai
□ HS-TGW	Boeing 747-4D7	27724 / 1111		0097	0497	4 GE CF6-80C2B1F	385553	F18C62Y325	EK-DQ	Visuthakasatriya
□ HS-TGX	Boeing 747-4D7	27725 / 1134		0097	1197	4 GE CF6-80C2B1F	385553	F18C62Y325	EK-DS	Sirisobhakya
□ HS-TGY	Boeing 747-4D7	28705 / 1164	N60697*	0098	1298	4 GE CF6-80C2B1F	385553	F18C62Y325	AK-DP	Dararasmi
□ HS-TGZ	Boeing 747-4D7	28706				4 GE CF6-80C2B1F	385553	F18C62Y325	AK-LP	oo-delivery 0599

THAI AVIATION SERVICES, Co. Ltd (Associated with Canadian Helicopters, Ltd) — Songkhla

Box 22, Songkhla 90000, Thailand ☎ (74) 32 48 45 Tx: none Fax: (74) 32 48 47 SITA: n/a
F: n/a ✈ n/a Head: Jim Whitley Net: n/a

□ HS-HTG	Sikorsky S-76A++	760187	C-FCHG	0081	0597	2 TU Arriel 1S1	4763			lsf Canadian Helicopters / cvtd S-76A
□ HS-HTM	Sikorsky S-76A	760044	C-GIMM	0080	0693	2 AN 250-C30	4763			lsf Canadian Helicopters
□ HS-HTX	Sikorsky S-76A+	760213	C-GIMX	0081	1196	2 TU Arriel 1S	4763			lsf Canadian Helicopters / cvtd S-76A
□ HS-HTC	Sikorsky S-61N	61722	C-GARC	0074	0693	2 GE CT58-140-1	9318			lsf Canadian Helicopters
□ HS-HTH	Sikorsky S-61N	61815	C-GOLH	0078	0197	2 GE CT58-140-1	9318			lsf Canadian Helicopters

THAI FLYING HELICOPTER SERVICE, Co Ltd = TFH (Affiliated with Thai Flying Service, Co Ltd) — Bangkok-Int'l

171 Domestic Terminal, Room 208, Vibhavadi Ransit Road, Bangkok 10210, Thailand ☎ (2) 535 49 36 Tx: 20542 thaifly th Fax: (2) 535 49 45 SITA: n/a
F: 1989 ✈ 26 Head: Thidej Maithai ICAO: THAI HELICOPTER Net: n/a

□ HS-NMB	Eurocopter (Aerosp.) AS355N Ecureuil 2	5582	F-OHNC	1194	0195	2 TU Arrius 1A	2540			

THAI FLYING SERVICE, Co. Ltd (Affiliated with Thai Flying Helicopter Service, Co Ltd) — Bangkok-Int'l

171 Domestic Terminal, Room 208, Vibhavadi Ransit Road, Bangkok 10210, Thailand ☎ (2) 535 49 36 Tx: 20542 thaifly th Fax: (2) 996 85 22 SITA: n/a
F: 1981 ✈ 59 Head: Thidej Maithai Net: n/a

□ HS-TFA	Piper PA-34-200T Seneca II	34-7670361	HS-CHK	0076	0281	2 CO TSIO-360-E	2073			
□ HS-TFK	Piper PA-34-200T Seneca II	34-7870416		0078	0397	2 CO TSIO-360-E	2073			
□ HS-TFE	Piper PA-23-250 Aztec F	27-7954045		0079	0392	2 LY TIO-540-C1A	2359			
□ HS-TFG	Twin (Aero) Turbo Commander 690B	11482	N745T	0078	0491	2 GA TPE331-5-251K	4683			
□ HS-ITD	Beech King Air 350 (B300)	FL-151	N10817	0097	0497	2 PWC PT6A-60A	6804			lsf Italian/Thai Development Co.
□ 9G-AYO	Boeing 707-323C	19519 / 619	EL-RDS	0067	0199	4 PW JT3D-7 (HK2/COM)	146500	Freighter		lsf/jtly opw GHN for Jea-Sin Group

HV = VATICAN (State of the Vatican City) (Status Civitatis Vaticanae)

The country's name in Italian is: Stato dellaCitta del Vaticano
Capital: Vaticano Official Language: Italian, Latin Population: 0.1 million Square Km: 1 Dialling code: +39 Acting political head: John Paul II (Pope)

At present there is no licenced commercial air operator in this country

HZ = SAUDI ARABIA (Kingdom of Saudi Arabia) (al Mamlaka al Arabiya as-Sa'udiya)

Capital: Riyadh Official Language: Arabic Population: 20,0 million Square Km: 2149690 Dialling code: +966 Year established: 1932 Acting political head: Fahd bin Abdul-Aziz as-Sa'ud (King)

Government / Corporate / Executive / VIP Aircraft

□ HZ-103	GAC G-1159A Gulfstream III	453	N332GA*	0085		2 RR Spey 511-8	31615	VIP		Royal Embassy of Saudi Arabia
□ HZ-104	Hawker 800A (BAe 125-800A)	258115	G-BPGR*	0089		2 GA TFE731-5R-1H	12428	VIP		Royal Saudi Air Force
□ HZ-105	Hawker 800A (BAe 125-800A)	258118	G-BPGT*	0089		2 GA TFE731-5R-1H	12428	VIP		Royal Saudi Air Force
□ HZ-106	Learjet 35A	35A-374		0081		2 GA TFE731-2-2B	8301	VIP		Royal Saudi Air Force
□ HZ-107	Learjet 35A	35A-375		0081		2 GA TFE731-2-2B	8301	VIP		Royal Saudi Air Force
□ HZ-108	GAC G-1159A Gulfstream III	353	HZ-BSA	0083		2 RR Spey 511-8	30935	VIP	AG-CF	Royal Embassy of Saudi Arabia
□ HZ-109	Hawker 800A (BAe 125-800A)	258146	G-5-703*	0089		2 GA TFE731-5R-1H	12428	VIP		Royal Saudi Air Force
□ HZ-110	Hawker 800A (BAe 125-800A)	258148	G-BPYE*	0089	0889	2 GA TFE731-5R-1H	12428	VIP		Royal Saudi Air Force
□ HZ-123	Boeing 707-138B	17696 / 29	N138MJ	0059	0987	4 PW JT3D-1 (Q)	116574	VIP	AC-GJ	Royal Embassy of Saudi Arabia
□ HZ-124	Airbus Industrie A340-213	004	F-WWBA*	0092	0297	4 CFMI CFM56-5C4	257000	VIP	PR-FG	Royal Embassy of Saudi Arabia/cvtd -211
□ HZ-AB3	Boeing 727-2U5 (A/RE) (Super 27/winglets)	22362 / 1657		0080	0794	3 PW JT8D-217C/17 (BFG)	89448	Executive		Al-Anwa Establishment / cvtd -2U5
□ HZ-ABM2	BAe (BAC) One-Eleven 401AK	060	HZ-MAA	0066	0693	2 RR Spey 511-14	40597	Executive		private
□ HZ-ADC	GAC G-IV Gulfstream IV	1037	N17588*	0088		2 RR Tay 610-8	33203	VIP	AM-BL	Air Defence Command
□ HZ-DG1	Boeing 727-51	19124 / 347	N604NA	0066	0187	3 PW JT8D-7B (HK3/FDX)	72802	Executive	AE-DP	Dallah Albaraka
□ HZ-HE4	Boeing 727-29C	19987 / 634	N444SA	0068	0782	3 PW JT8D-7	76884	Executive	EM-BK	private
□ HZ-HR1	Boeing 727-2K5 (A)	21853 / 1640	LX-MMM	0080	0292	3 PW JT8D-17	89000	Executive	AE-FM	Jet Financing Inc. / opb Matrix Group
□ HZ-HR3	Boeing 727-2Y4 (A)	22968 / 1815	HZ-RH3	0082	0183	3 PW JT8D-15	89358	Executive	AD-BC	private
□ HZ-KA4	Boeing 720-047B	18453 / 314	N93147	0062	0678	4 PW JT3D-3B (Q)	106142	Executive	CK-AB	private
□ HZ-KA8	Fokker F27 Friendship 600 (F27 Mk600)	10304	VH-FNO	0066	0194	2 RR Dart 532-7	20412	Executive		private
□ HZ-KB1	BAe (BAC) One-Eleven 414EG	158	HZ-AB1	0070	0794	2 RR Spey 511-14	40143	Executive	DL-AH	Al Tameer Company
□ HZ-MAJ	BAe (BAC) One-Eleven 401AK	088	HZ-NIR	0066	0882	2 RR Spey 511-14	40597	Executive	AJ-FL	Jarallah Corp. / std GVA
□ HZ-MIS	Boeing 737-2K5 (A)	22600 / 816	D-AHLH	0081	0293	2 PW JT8D-17 (HK3/NOR)	58105	Executive	BG-EF	private
□ HZ-PC2	Beech 1900C-1 Airliner	UC-4	N3078C*	0087	0190	2 PWC PT6A-65B	7530	Executive		CAA
□ HZ-PCA	GAC (Grumman) G-1159 Gulfstream II	179	HZ-CAD	0076		2 RR Spey 511-8	29393	Executive		DCA
□ HZ-RC3	GAC G-1159A Gulfstream III	331	N17LB	0081		2 RR Spey 511-8	30935	VIP	AJ-EL	Royal Commission
□ HZ-SG1	Dornier 228-201	8044	D-COKI*	0084	0285	2 GA TPE331-5-252D	5980	VIP		Ministry of Information
□ HZ-SG2	Dornier 228-201	8045	D-COKO*	0085	0485	2 GA TPE331-5-252D	5980	VIP		Ministry of Information
□ HZ-TAM	Antonov 32	2708		0091		2 IV AI-20D	27000	Corporate Frtr		private
□ HZ-TBA	Boeing 737-205 (A)	23468 / 1262	N891FS	0086	1293	2 PW JT8D-17A	56472	Executive	AD-BM	Al Maha / private
□ 101	Lockheed L-1329 JetStar 8	5129	N7974S	0068		4 PW JT12A-8	19005	VIP		Royal Saudi Air Force
□ 102	Lockheed L-1329 JetStar 8	5130	103	0068		4 PW JT12A-8	19005	VIP		Royal Saudi Air Force

ARABIAN HELICOPTERS, Ltd — Dhahran

Box 619, Dhahran, Saudi Arabia ☎ (3) 857 17 79 Tx: n/a Fax: (3) 857 13 47 SITA: n/a
F: n/a ✈ n/a Head: Larry Edeal Net: n/a

□ N62200	Bell 212	35065		0093	0993	2 PWC PT6T-3B TwinPac	5080			lsf ARAC Services Inc.

205 registration type of aircraft cn/fn ex/ex* mfd del powered by mtow kg configuration selcal name/fln/specialitites/remarks

KINGDOM HOLDING – Flight Dept. (Flight Dept. of Kingdom Holding Company) Riyadh

PO Box 8653, Riyadh 11492, Saudi Arabia ☎ (1) 488 11 11 Tx: none Fax: (1) 481 13 62 SITA: n/a
F: n/a 👥 16 Head: Capt. Bill Moersis Net: n/a Operates non-commercial VIP flights for its parent company & member companies of the group, including Kingdom Entertainment.

☐ HZ-WBT2	Boeing 727-95	19252 / 327	HZ-WBT	0066	0698	3 PW JT8D-7A (HK3/FDX)	72802	VIP	DH-FL	
☐ N255KD	Boeing 767-3P6 (ER)	27255 / 525	A4O-GX	0093	1196	2 GE CF6-80C2B4	175540	VIP		lsf Kingdom XI (USA) Ltd

MID EAST JET, Inc. (formerly Skyways International, Inc.) Jeddah

PO Box 9935, Jeddah 21423, Saudi Arabia ☎ (2) 682 42 03 Tx: none Fax: (2) 682 48 27 SITA: n/a
F: 1990 👥 n/a Head: Khurshid Mahmood Kahn Net: n/a Operates non-commercial VIP flights under contract to private clients only.

☐ VP-BNA	Boeing 727-21	19262 / 426	VR-BNA	0067	0692	3 PW JT8D-7B (HK3/FDX)	72802	VIP	DF-AH	lsf Skyjet Ltd
☐ N757MA	Boeing 757-24Q	28463 / 739		0097	0197	2 PW PW2040	113398	VIP 45 Pax		lsf FSBU Trustee
☐ N767KS	Boeing 767-29N (ER)	28270 / 629		0096	1096	2 GE CF6-80C2B4	175540	VIP 45 Pax		lsf FSBU Trustee
☐ N777AS	Boeing 777-24Q (ER)	29271 / 174		1198	1198	2 GE GE90-92B	294200	VIP		

SAUDI ARABIAN Airlines = SV / SVA (formerly SAUDIA Saudi Arabian Airlines) Jeddah

SAUDI ARABIAN AIRLINES
الخطوط الجوية العربية السعودية

PO Box 620, Jeddah 21231, Saudi Arabia ☎ (2) 686 00 00 Tx: 601007 comm sj Fax: (2) 686 45 52 SITA: n/a
F: 1945 👥 24000 Head: HRH Prince Sultan Bin Abdul Aziz IATA: 065 ICAO: SAUDIA Net: http://www.saudiarabian-airlines.com
Executive services are operated by Special Flight Services (an internal division of Saudi Arabian Airlines). Additional (Boeing 747) are seasonally (hadj) lsf/opb AIR ATLANTA ICELANDIC (TF-) & TOWER AIR (N), when required.

☐ HZ-ATO	De Havilland DHC-6 Twin Otter 300	836	C-GDCZ*	0088	0688	2 PWC PT6A-27	5670	Executive		
☐ HZ-AFP	Cessna 550 Citation II	550-0472	N12511*	0084		2 PWC JT15D-4	6033	Executive	JM-GK	
☐ HZ-AFQ	Cessna 550 Citation II	550-0473	N12513*	0084		2 PWC JT15D-4	6033	Executive	JM-GL	
☐ HZ-AFA2	Canadair CL-604 (CL-600-2B16) Challen.	5320	N605CC	0096	0397	2 GE CF34-3B	21863	Executive		
☐ HZ-AFT	Dassault Falcon 900	21	F-WWFJ*	0087		3 GA TFE731-5AR-1C2	20638	Executive	CE-KP	
☐ HZ-AFZ	Dassault Falcon 900	61	HZ-AB2	0089		3 GA TFE731-5AR-1C2	20638	Executive	BH-EQ	
☐ HZ-AFH	GAC (Grumman) G-1159 Gulfstream II	171	N17585*	0075		2 RR Spey 511-8	29393	Executive	CM-EF	
☐ HZ-AFI	GAC (Grumman) G-1159 Gulfstream II (TT)	201	N17585*	0077		2 RR Spey 511-8	29710	Executive	DE-CJ	
☐ HZ-AFJ	GAC (Grumman) G-1159 Gulfstream II (TT)	203	N17587*	0077		2 RR Spey 511-8	29710	Executive	DE-CM	
☐ HZ-AFK	GAC (Grumman) G-1159 Gulfstream II (TT)	239	N17582*	0079		2 RR Spey 511-8	29710	Executive	DE-AL	
☐ HZ-AFN	GAC G-1159A Gulfstream III	364	N1761D*	0083		2 RR Spey 511-8	30935	Executive	EM-HJ	
☐ HZ-AFR	GAC G-1159A Gulfstream III	410	N350GA*	0084		2 RR Spey 511-8	30935	Executive	AJ-EM	
☐ HZ-AFU	GAC G-IV Gulfstream IV	1031	N434GA*	0087	0790	2 RR Tay 610-8	33203	Executive	JQ-FL	
☐ HZ-AFV	GAC G-IV Gulfstream IV	1035	N435GA*	0088		2 RR Tay 610-8	33203	Executive	JQ-FK	
☐ HZ-AFW	GAC G-IV Gulfstream IV	1038	N438GA*	0088		2 RR Tay 611-8	33203	Executive	JQ-FM	
☐ HZ-AFX	GAC G-IV Gulfstream IV	1143	N410GA*	0090	0391	2 RR Tay 611-8	33203	Executive	EM-HK	
☐ HZ-AFY	GAC G-IV Gulfstream IV	1166	HZ-SAR	0091		2 RR Tay 611-8	33203	Executive	CJ-MR	
☐ HZ-MFL	GAC G-IV Gulfstream IV	1128	N429GA*	0090	0291	2 RR Tay 611-8	33203	Executive	EF-CK	
☐ HZ-AGA	Boeing 737-268C (A)	20574 / 294		0072	0372	2 PW JT8D-15	53070	F14Y88	CG-BH	
☐ HZ-AGB	Boeing 737-268C (A)	20575 / 295		0072	0472	2 PW JT8D-15	53070	F14Y88	CG-BJ	
☐ HZ-AGC	Boeing 737-268 (A)	20576 / 297		0072	0572	2 PW JT8D-15	53070	F14Y88	CG-BK	
☐ HZ-AGD	Boeing 737-268 (A)	20577 / 298		0072	0572	2 PW JT8D-15	53070	F14Y88	CG-BL	
☐ HZ-AGE	Boeing 737-268 (A)	20578 / 299		0072	0572	2 PW JT8D-15	53070	F14Y88	CG-BM	
☐ HZ-AGF	Boeing 737-268 (A)	20882 / 356		0074	0574	2 PW JT8D-15	53070	F14Y88	CG-KM	
☐ HZ-AGG	Boeing 737-268 (A)	20883 / 366		0074	0774	2 PW JT8D-15	53070	F14Y88	CG-LM	
☐ HZ-AGH	Boeing 737-268 (A)	21275 / 467		0076	0776	2 PW JT8D-15	53070	F14Y88	CM-GH	
☐ HZ-AGI	Boeing 737-268 (A)	21276 / 468		0076	0876	2 PW JT8D-15	53070	F14Y88	CM-GJ	
☐ HZ-AGJ	Boeing 737-268 (A)	21277 / 469		0076	0876	2 PW JT8D-15	53070	F14Y88	CM-GK	
☐ HZ-AGK	Boeing 737-268 (A)	21280 / 471		0076	1176	2 PW JT8D-15	53070	F14Y88	CM-HK	
☐ HZ-AGL	Boeing 737-268 (A)	21281 / 472		0076	1076	2 PW JT8D-15	53070	F14Y88	CM-JK	
☐ HZ-AGN	Boeing 737-268 (A)	21283 / 477	N1243E*	0076	1276	2 PW JT8D-15	53070	F14Y88	CG-EF	
☐ HZ-AGO	Boeing 737-268 (A)	21360 / 485		0077	0377	2 PW JT8D-15	53070	F14Y88	DF-AK	
☐ HZ-AGP	Boeing 737-268 (A)	21361 / 488		0077	0477	2 PW JT8D-15	53070	F14Y88	DF-AL	
☐ HZ-AGQ	Boeing 737-268 (A)	21362 / 511		0078	0378	2 PW JT8D-15	53070	F14Y88	DF-AM	
☐ HZ-AGR	Boeing 737-268 (A)	21653 / 531		0078	0978	2 PW JT8D-15	53070	F14Y88	CM-AH	
☐ HZ-AGS	Boeing 737-268 (A)	21654 / 532		0078	0978	2 PW JT8D-15	53070	F14Y88	DF-AJ	
☐ HZ-AP2	Boeing (Douglas) MD-90-30					2 IAE V2525-D5	70760	F18Y103	PS-GR	oo-delivery 0100
☐ HZ-AP3	Boeing (Douglas) MD-90-30					2 IAE V2525-D5	70760	F18Y103	PS-HJ	oo-delivery 0100
☐ HZ-AP4	Boeing (Douglas) MD-90-30					2 IAE V2525-D5	70760	F18Y103	PS-HK	oo-delivery 0200
☐ HZ-APA	Boeing (Douglas) MD-90-30	53491 / 2191		0097	1298	2 IAE V2525-D5	70760	F18Y103	PS-DM	
☐ HZ-APB	Boeing (Douglas) MD-90-30	53492 / 2205		0097	0498	2 IAE V2525-D5	70760	F18Y103	PS-DQ	
☐ HZ-APC	Boeing (Douglas) MD-90-30	53493 / 2209		0097	0498	2 IAE V2525-D5	70760	F18Y103	PS-DR	
☐ HZ-APD	Boeing (Douglas) MD-90-30	53494 / 2213		0098	0598	2 IAE V2525-D5	70760	F18Y103	PS-EF	
☐ HZ-APE	Boeing (Douglas) MD-90-30	53495 / 2215		0098	0598	2 IAE V2525-D5	70760	F18Y103	PS-EG	
☐ HZ-APF	Boeing (Douglas) MD-90-30	53496 / 2216		0098	0698	2 IAE V2525-D5	70760	F18Y103	PS-EH	
☐ HZ-APG	Boeing (Douglas) MD-90-30	53497 / 2219		0098	0698	2 IAE V2525-D5	70760	F18Y103	PS-EJ	
☐ HZ-APH	Boeing (Douglas) MD-90-30	53498 / 2221				2 IAE V2525-D5	70760	F18Y103	PS-EK	oo-delivery 0499
☐ HZ-API	Boeing (Douglas) MD-90-30	53499 / 2223		0098	0698	2 IAE V2525-D5	70760	F18Y103	PS-EL	
☐ HZ-APJ	Boeing (Douglas) MD-90-30	53500 / 2225		0098	0698	2 IAE V2525-D5	70760	F18Y103	PS-EM	
☐ HZ-APK	Boeing (Douglas) MD-90-30	53501 / 2226		0098	0998	2 IAE V2525-D5	70760	F18Y103	PS-EQ	
☐ HZ-APL	Boeing (Douglas) MD-90-30	53502 / 2227		0098	0998	2 IAE V2525-D5	70760	F18Y103	PS-ER	
☐ HZ-APM	Boeing (Douglas) MD-90-30	53503 / 2229		0098	1098	2 IAE V2525-D5	70760	F18Y103	PS-FG	
☐ HZ-APN	Boeing (Douglas) MD-90-30	53504 / 2230		0098	1198	2 IAE V2525-D5	70760	F18Y103	PS-FH	
☐ HZ-APO	Boeing (Douglas) MD-90-30	53505 / 2231	N9012S*	0098	1198	2 IAE V2525-D5	70760	F18Y103	PS-FJ	
☐ HZ-APP	Boeing (Douglas) MD-90-30	53506 / 2232		0098	1198	2 IAE V2525-D5	70760	F18Y103	PS-FK	
☐ HZ-APQ	Boeing (Douglas) MD-90-30	53507 / 2235		0098	1198	2 IAE V2525-D5	70760	F18Y103	PS-FL	
☐ HZ-APR	Boeing (Douglas) MD-90-30	53508 / 2237		0098	1198	2 IAE V2525-D5	70760	F18Y103	PS-FM	
☐ HZ-APS	Boeing (Douglas) MD-90-30	53509				2 IAE V2525-D5	70760	F18Y103	PS-FQ	oo-delivery 0599
☐ HZ-APT	Boeing (Douglas) MD-90-30	53510				2 IAE V2525-D5	70760	F18Y103	PS-FR	oo-delivery 0699
☐ HZ-APU	Boeing (Douglas) MD-90-30	53511				2 IAE V2525-D5	70760	F18Y103	PS-GH	oo-delivery 0799
☐ HZ-APV	Boeing (Douglas) MD-90-30	53512				2 IAE V2525-D5	70760	F18Y103	PS-GJ	oo-delivery 0899
☐ HZ-APW	Boeing (Douglas) MD-90-30	53513				2 IAE V2525-D5	70760	F18Y103	PS-GK	oo-delivery 0999
☐ HZ-APX	Boeing (Douglas) MD-90-30	53514				2 IAE V2525-D5	70760	F18Y103	PS-GL	oo-delivery 1099
☐ HZ-APY	Boeing (Douglas) MD-90-30	53515				2 IAE V2525-D5	70760	F18Y103	PS-GM	oo-delivery 1199
☐ HZ-APZ	Boeing (Douglas) MD-90-30	53516				2 IAE V2525-D5	70760	F18Y103	PS-GQ	oo-delivery 1299
☐ HZ-AJA	Airbus Industrie A300-620 (A300B4-620)	284	F-WZLS*	0083	0684	2 PW JT9D-7R4H1	165000	F26Y232	BM-DE	
☐ HZ-AJB	Airbus Industrie A300-620 (A300B4-620)	294	F-WZYA*	0083	0484	2 PW JT9D-7R4H1	165000	F26Y232	CJ-BE	
☐ HZ-AJC	Airbus Industrie A300-620 (A300B4-620)	301	F-WZYB*	0084	0384	2 PW JT9D-7R4H1	165000	F26Y232	CJ-BG	
☐ HZ-AJD	Airbus Industrie A300-620 (A300B4-620)	307	F-WZYC*	0084	0484	2 PW JT9D-7R4H1	165000	F26Y232	CJ-BH	
☐ HZ-AJE	Airbus Industrie A300-620 (A300B4-620)	312	F-WZYD*	0084	0484	2 PW JT9D-7R4H1	165000	F26Y232	CJ-BK	
☐ HZ-AJF	Airbus Industrie A300-620 (A300B4-620)	317	F-WZYE*	0084	0484	2 PW JT9D-7R4H1	165000	F26Y232	CL-HK	
☐ HZ-AJG	Airbus Industrie A300-620 (A300B4-620)	321	F-WZYF*	0084	0584	2 PW JT9D-7R4H1	165000	F26Y232	DE-BG	
☐ HZ-AJH	Airbus Industrie A300-620 (A300B4-620)	336	F-WZYI*	0084	0784	2 PW JT9D-7R4H1	165000	F26Y232	DE-BL	
☐ HZ-AJI	Airbus Industrie A300-620 (A300B4-620)	341	F-WZYJ*	0084	0884	2 PW JT9D-7R4H1	165000	F26Y232	DE-BM	
☐ HZ-AJJ	Airbus Industrie A300-620 (A300B4-620)	348	F-WZYL*	0084	0884	2 PW JT9D-7R4H1	165000	F26Y232	DE-CF	
☐ HZ-AJK	Airbus Industrie A300-620 (A300B4-620)	351	F-WZYB*	0084	1084	2 PW JT9D-7R4H1	165000	F26Y232	JM-FL	
☐ HZ-AHA	Lockheed L-1011-385-1-15 TriStar 200	193S-1110	N64854*	0075	0675	3 RR RB211-524B-02	211374	F30C43Y141	BM-GH	cvtd 100 / std/for sale
☐ HZ-AHB	Lockheed L-1011-385-1-15 TriStar 200	193S-1116		0075	0775	3 RR RB211-524B-02	211374	F30C43Y141	BM-GJ	cvtd 100 / std/for sale
☐ HZ-AHC	Lockheed L-1011-385-1-15 TriStar 200	193S-1137		0076	0576	3 RR RB211-524B-02	211374	F30C43Y141	CL-HM	cvtd 100 / std/for sale
☐ HZ-AHD	Lockheed L-1011-385-1-15 TriStar 200	193S-1144	N48354*	0076	0577	3 RR RB211-524B-02	211374	F30C43Y141	CL-KM	std/for sale
☐ HZ-AHE	Lockheed L-1011-385-1-15 TriStar 200	193B-1124	N31032	0076	0276	3 RR RB211-524B-02	211374	F30C43Y141	CM-FG	cvtd 1/100 / std/for sale
☐ HZ-AHF	Lockheed L-1011-385-1-15 TriStar 200	193B-1130	N31033	0076	0276	3 RR RB211-524B-02	211374	F30C43Y141	CM-FJ	cvtd 1/100 / std/for sale
☐ HZ-AHG	Lockheed L-1011-385-1-15 TriStar 200	193S-1148		0077	1077	3 RR RB211-524B-02	211374	F30C43Y141	CG-EH	std/for sale
☐ HZ-AHH	Lockheed L-1011-385-1-15 TriStar 200	193S-1149		0077	1277	3 RR RB211-524B-02	211374	F30C43Y141	CG-FH	std/for sale
☐ HZ-AHI	Lockheed L-1011-385-1-15 TriStar 200	193S-1160		0078	1278	3 RR RB211-524B-02	211374	F30C43Y141	DF-BC	std/for sale
☐ HZ-AHJ	Lockheed L-1011-385-1-15 TriStar 200	193S-1161		0078	0379	3 RR RB211-524B-02	211374	F30C43Y141	DF-BE	std/for sale
☐ HZ-AHL	Lockheed L-1011-385-1-15 TriStar 200	193S-1170		0079	0979	3 RR RB211-524B-02	211374	F30C43Y141	DE-BH	std/for sale
☐ HZ-AHM	Lockheed L-1011-385-1-15 TriStar 200	193S-1171		0079	1079	3 RR RB211-524B-02	211374	F30C43Y141	DE-BJ	std/for sale
☐ HZ-AHN	Lockheed L-1011-385-1-15 TriStar 200	193S-1175		0080	1080	3 RR RB211-524B-02	211374	F30C43Y141	DJ-EG	std/for sale
☐ HZ-AHO	Lockheed L-1011-385-1-15 TriStar 200	193S-1187		0080	0980	3 RR RB211-524B-02	211374	F30C43Y141	DJ-EH	std/for sale
☐ HZ-AHP	Lockheed L-1011-385-1-15 TriStar 200	193S-1190		0080	0980	3 RR RB211-524B-02	211374	F30C43Y141	DJ-EK	std/for sale
☐ HZ-AHQ	Lockheed L-1011-385-1-15 TriStar 200	193S-1192		0080	0281	3 RR RB211-524B-02	211374	F30C43Y141	DJ-EL	std/for sale
☐ HZ-AHR	Lockheed L-1011-385-1-15 TriStar 200	193S-1214		0081	0881	3 RR RB211-524B-02	211374	F30C43Y141	BM-DF	std/for sale
☐ HZ-AKA	Boeing 777-268 (ER)	28344 / 98	N50217*	0097	1297	2 GE GE90-92B	286897	F30C31Y183	PS-BF	
☐ HZ-AKB	Boeing 777-268 (ER)	28345 / 99	N5023Q*	0097	1297	2 GE GE90-92B	286897	F30C31Y183	PS-BG	
☐ HZ-AKC	Boeing 777-268 (ER)	28346 / 101		0097	1297	2 GE GE90-92B	286897	F30C31Y183	PS-BH	
☐ HZ-AKD	Boeing 777-268 (ER)	28347 / 103		0097	1297	2 GE GE90-92B	286897	F30C31Y183	PS-BJ	
☐ HZ-AKE	Boeing 777-268 (ER)	28348 / 109		0098	0198	2 GE GE90-92B	286897	F30C31Y183	PS-BK	
☐ HZ-AKF	Boeing 777-268 (ER)	28349 / 114		0098	0298	2 GE GE90-92B	286897	F30C31Y183	PS-BL	
☐ HZ-AKG	Boeing 777-268 (ER)	28350 / 119		0098	0398	2 GE GE90-92B	286897	F30C31Y183	PS-BM	
☐ HZ-AKH	Boeing 777-268 (ER)	28351 / 124		0098	0498	2 GE GE90-92B	286897	F30C31Y183	PS-BQ	
☐ HZ-AKI	Boeing 777-268 (ER)	28352 / 143		0098	0698	2 GE GE90-92B	286897	F30C31Y183	PS-BR	

206 registration type of aircraft cn/fn ex/ex* mfd del powered by mtow kg configuration selcal name/fln/specialitites/remarks

☐ HZ-AKJ	Boeing 777-268 (ER)	28353 / 147		0098	0798	2 GE GE90-92B	286897	F30C31Y183	PS-CD	
☐ HZ-AKK	Boeing 777-268 (ER)	28354 / 154		0098	0998	2 GE GE90-92B	286897	F30C31Y183	PS-CE	
☐ HZ-AKL	Boeing 777-268 (ER)	28355 / 166		0098	1198	2 GE GE90-92B	286897	F30C31Y183	PS-CF	
☐ HZ-AKM	Boeing 777-268 (ER)	28356 / 175		0098	1298	2 GE GE90-92B	286897	F30C31Y183	PS-CG	
☐ HZ-AKN	Boeing 777-268 (ER)	28357 / 181		1298	1298	2 GE GE90-92B	286897	F30C31Y183	PS-CH	
☐ HZ-AKO	Boeing 777-268 (ER)	28358 / 186		0199	0199	2 GE GE90-92B	286897	F30C31Y183	PS-CJ	
☐ HZ-AKP	Boeing 777-268 (ER)	28359				2 GE GE90-92B	286897	F30C31Y183	PS-CK	oo-delivery 0499
☐ HZ-AKQ	Boeing 777-268 (ER)	28360				2 GE GE90-92B	286897	F30C31Y183	PS-CL	oo-delivery 0799
☐ HZ-AKR	Boeing 777-268 (ER)	28361				2 GE GE90-92B	286897	F30C31Y183	PS-CM	oo-delivery 0999
☐ HZ-AKS	Boeing 777-268 (ER)	28362				2 GE GE90-92B	286897	F30C31Y183	PS-CQ	oo-delivery 1199
☐ HZ-AKT	Boeing 777-268 (ER)	28363				2 GE GE90-92B	286897	F30C31Y183	PS-CR	oo-delivery 0300
☐ HZ-AKU	Boeing 777-268 (ER)	28364				2 GE GE90-92B	286897	F30C31Y183	PS-DE	oo-delivery 0800
☐ HZ-AKV	Boeing 777-268 (ER)	28365				2 GE GE90-92B	286897	F30C31Y183	PS-DF	oo-delivery 0701
☐ HZ-AKW	Boeing 777-268 (ER)	28366				2 GE GE90-92B	286897	F30C31Y183	PS-DG	oo-delivery 0901
☐ HZ-ANA	Boeing (Douglas) MD-11F	48773 / 609	N90187*	0097	1297	3 GE CF6-80C2D1F	285990	Freighter	PS-DH	
☐ HZ-ANB	Boeing (Douglas) MD-11F	48775 / 616		0797	1297	3 GE CF6-80C2D1F	285990	Freighter	PS-DJ	
☐ HZ-ANC	Boeing (Douglas) MD-11F	48776 / 617	N91078*	0897	1297	3 GE CF6-80C2D1F	285990	Freighter	PS-DK	
☐ HZ-AND	Boeing (Douglas) MD-11F	48777 / 618	N9166N*	0097	0198	3 GE CF6-80C2D1F	285990	Freighter	PS-DL	
☐ HZ-AIF	Boeing 747SP-68	22503 / 529		0081	0681	4 RR RB211-524C2	317515	F18C28Y222	EF-CJ	
☐ HZ-AIA	Boeing 747-168B	22498 / 512	N8281V*	0081	0481	4 RR RB211-524C2	340194	F18C24Y327	EF-AB	
☐ HZ-AIB	Boeing 747-168B	22499 / 517		0081	0481	4 RR RB211-524C2	340194	F18C24Y327	EF-AC	
☐ HZ-AIC	Boeing 747-168B	22500 / 522		0081	0581	4 RR RB211-524C2	340194	F18C24Y327	EF-BD	
☐ HZ-AID	Boeing 747-168B	22501 / 525		0081	0581	4 RR RB211-524C2	340194	F18C24Y327	EF-BC	
☐ HZ-AIE	Boeing 747-168B	22502 / 530	N8284V*	0081	0781	4 RR RB211-524C2	340194	F18C24Y327	EF-CH	
☐ HZ-AIG	Boeing 747-168B	22747 / 551		0081	0182	4 RR RB211-524C2	340194	F18C24Y327	EM-HL	
☐ HZ-AII	Boeing 747-168B	22749 / 557		0082	0482	4 RR RB211-524C2	340194	F18C24Y327	EM-JL	
☐ HZ-AIU	Boeing 747-268F (SCD)	24359 / 724	N6018N*	0089	0189	4 RR RB211-524D4	377842	Freighter	CM-HJ	
☐ HZ-AIK	Boeing 747-368	23262 / 616	N6005C*	0085	0785	4 RR RB211-524D4	377842	F36C38Y319	AF-GH	
☐ HZ-AIL	Boeing 747-368	23263 / 619	N6009F*	0085	0885	4 RR RB211-524D4	377842	F36C38Y319	AF-GJ	
☐ HZ-AIM	Boeing 747-368	23264 / 620	N6046P*	0085	0885	4 RR RB211-524D4	377842	F36C38Y319	AF-GK	
☐ HZ-AIN	Boeing 747-368	23265 / 622	N6046P*	0085	1285	4 RR RB211-524D4	377842	F36C38Y319	AF-JL	
☐ HZ-AIO	Boeing 747-368	23266 / 624	N6005C*	0085	1085	4 RR RB211-524D4	377842	F36C38Y319	AF-JM	
☐ HZ-AIP	Boeing 747-368	23267 / 630	N6055X*	0086	0186	4 RR RB211-524D4	377842	F36C38Y319	CF-DH	
☐ HZ-AIQ	Boeing 747-368	23268 / 631	N6005C*	0086	0386	4 RR RB211-524D4	377842	F36C38Y319	CF-DL	
☐ HZ-AIR	Boeing 747-368	23269 / 643	N6038E*	0086	0786	4 RR RB211-524D4	377842	F36C38Y319	CF-EG	
☐ HZ-AIS	Boeing 747-368	23270 / 645	N6046P*	0086	0886	4 RR RB211-524D4	377842	F36C38Y319	CF-EH	
☐ HZ-AIT	Boeing 747-368	23271 / 652	N6038N*	0086	1186	4 RR RB211-524D4	377842	F36C38Y319	CF-GM	
☐ HZ-AIV	Boeing 747-468	28339 / 1122	N6005C*	0097	1297	4 GE CF6-80C2B1F	396893	F36C32Y290	PS-AQ	
☐ HZ-AIW	Boeing 747-468	28340 / 1138		0098	0298	4 GE CF6-80C2B1F	396893	F36C32Y290	PS-AR	
☐ HZ-AIX	Boeing 747-468	28341 / 1182		0098	1198	4 GE CF6-80C2B1F	396893	F36C32Y290	PS-BC	
☐ HZ-AIY	Boeing 747-468	28342				4 GE CF6-80C2B1F	396893	F36C32Y290	PS-BD	oo-delivery 0699
☐ HZ-AIZ	Boeing 747-468					4 GE CF6-80C2B1F	396893	F36C32Y290	PS-BE	oo-delivery 0601

SAUDI ARABIAN VIP Aircraft (VIP-division of Saudi Arabian Airlines) **Riyadh**

PO Box 620, Jeddah 21231, Saudi Arabia ☎ (2) 686 00 00 Tx: 601007 comm sj Fax: (2) 686 45 52 SITA: n/a

F: n/a ✈✈✈ n/a Head: HRH Prince Sultan Bin Abdul Aziz ICAO: SAUDI GREEN FLIGHT Net: n/a Operates non-commercial VIP and EMS-Aeromedical Evacuation flights on behalf of the Royal Family.

☐ HZ-MS1	Learjet 35A	35A-467	N3796Q*	0082	0482	2 GA TFE731-2-2B	8301	EMS		
☐ HZ-MS4	GAC (Grumman) G-1159 Gulfstream II	103	N833GA	0071	0185	2 RR Spey 511-8	29393	EMS	AF-BH	
☐ HZ-MSD	GAC (Grumman) G-1159 Gulfstream II	256	N17581*	0080	0980	2 RR Spey 511-8	29393	EMS	BF-AL	
☐ HZ-MS3	GAC G-1159A Gulfstream III	385	N1761K*	0083	0784	2 RR Spey 511-8	30935	EMS	CD-AG	
☐ HZ-HM4	Boeing 737-268 (A)	22050 / 622	HZ-AGT	0079	0180	2 PW JT8D-15 (HK3/NOR)	53070	VIP	DE-BK	
☐ HZ-117	Lockheed L-382G (L-100-30) Hercules	63C-4954		0083	0883	4 AN 501-D22A	70307	VIP		
☐ HZ-128	Lockheed L-382G (L-100-30) Hercules	60C-4950	MS 5	0084	0984	4 AN 501-D22A	70307	Mobile Hospital	CF-AL	
☐ HZ-129	Lockheed L-382G (L-100-30) Hercules	61C-4957	MS 10	0085	1285	4 AN 501-D22A	70307	Mobile Hospital	AC-EF	
☐ MS 14	Lockheed L-382G (L-100-30) Hercules	61C-4960	HZ-MS14	0086	0386	4 AN 501-D22A	70307	Mobile Hospital		
☐ MS 6	Lockheed L-382G (L-100-30) Hercules	60C-4952	HZ-MS6	0084	1084	4 AN 501-D22A	70307	Mobile Hospital		
☐ MS 8	Lockheed L-382T (C-130H-30) Hercules	55E-4986	HZ-MS8	0084	1284	4 AN T56-A-15	70307	Mobile Hospital		
☐ MS 9	Lockheed L-382G (L-100-30) Hercules	61C-4956	HZ-MS9	0085	1285	4 AN 501-D22A	70307	Mobile Hospital		
☐ HZ-114	Lockheed L-382C (VC-130H) Hercules	4E-4843	HZ-HM5	0080	0780	4 AN 501-D22A	70307	VIP	FL-BG	
☐ HZ-115	Lockheed L-382C (VC-130H) Hercules	4E-4845	HZ-HM6	0080	0780	4 AN 501-D22A	70307	VIP	JL-KM	
☐ HZ-116	Lockheed L-382C (VC-130H) Hercules	26D-4915	N4185M*	0082	0982	4 AN 501-D22A	70307	VIP	DE-GH	
☐ MS 19	Lockheed L-382C (VC-130H) Hercules	93D-4837	HZ-MS19	0081	0981	4 AN 501-D22A	70307	Mobile Hospital		
☐ MS 21	Lockheed L-382C (VC-130H) Hercules	32E-4918	HZ-MS21	0083	0783	4 AN 501-D22A	70307	Mobile Hospital		
☐ MS 7	Lockheed L-382C (VC-130H) Hercules	26E-4922	HZ-MS7	0084	1284	4 AN 501-D22A	70307	Mobile Hospital		
☐ HZ-OCV	Boeing 727-21	19006 / 262	HZ-TFA	0066	0296	3 PW JT8D-7B (HK3/FDX)	72802	VIP		
☐ HZ-HMED	Boeing 757-23A	25495 / 599	N275AW	0094	0395	2 RR RB211-535E4	108862	Mobile Hospital		
☐ HZ-HM2	Boeing 707-368C	21081 / 903	HZ-HM1	0075	0975	4 PW JT3D-3B (HK2/COM)	151046	VIP	BM-FJ	
☐ HZ-HM3	Boeing 707-368C	21368 / 925	HZ-ACK	0077	0779	4 PW JT3D-3B (HK2/COM)	151046	VIP	CG-FK	
☐ HZ-HM5	Lockheed L-1011-385-3 TriStar 500	193G-1250	N5129K	0083	1189	3 RR RB211-524B4	231332	VIP	BM-EJ	
☐ HZ-HM6	Lockheed L-1011-385-3 TriStar 500	293A-1249	VR-CZZ	0583	0294	3 RR RB211-524B4	231332	VIP	BM-EL	
☐ HZ-HM8	Boeing (Douglas) MD-11	48532 / 532	N9093P	0093	1093	3 PW PW4460	283722	VIP		
☐ HZ-HM9	Boeing (Douglas) MD-11	48533 / 544	N9020Z	0093	1293	3 PW PW4460	283722	VIP		
☐ HZ-AIJ	Boeing 747SP-68	22750 / 560	N6046P*	0082	0582	4 RR RB211-524C2	317515	VIP	EM-KL	
☐ HZ-HM1B	Boeing 747SP-68	21652 / 329	HZ-HM1	0078	0779	4 RR RB211-524C2	317515	VIP	DE-BF	
☐ HZ-HM1A	Boeing 747-3G1	23070 / 592	N1784B*	0083	1283	4 PW JT9D-7R4G2	377842	VIP	DE-BC	

SAUDI ARAMCO AVIATION (Aviation Department of Saudi ARAMCO – Saudi Arabian Oil Company) **Dhahran**

PO Box 80, Dhahran 31311, Saudi Arabia ☎ (3) 877 40 61 Tx: none Fax: (3) 877 47 53 SITA: n/a

F: 1944 ✈✈✈ 525 Head: M.I. Snobar Net: n/a Saudi company conducting passenger, cargo & medevac flights in support of coporate oil production activities.

☐ N719H	Bell 206L-3 LongRanger III	51451		0091	0791	1 AN 250-C20P	1882	Corporate		lsf ARAMCO Associated Company, USA
☐ N722H	Bell 206L-3 LongRanger III	51452		0091	0791	1 AN 250-C20P	1882	Corporate		lsf ARAMCO Associated Company, USA
☐ N726H	Bell 206L-3 LongRanger III	51548		0092	0492	1 AN 250-C20P	1882	Corporate		lsf ARAMCO Associated Company, USA
☐ N727H	Bell 206L-3 LongRanger III	51550		0092	0492	1 AN 250-C20P	1882	Corporate		lsf ARAMCO Associated Company, USA
☐ N728H	Bell 206L-3 LongRanger III	51553		0092	0492	1 AN 250-C20P	1882	Corporate		lsf ARAMCO Associated Company, USA
☐ N731H	Bell 206L-3 LongRanger III	51562	N4338X	0092	0793	1 AN 250-C20P	1882	Corporate		lsf ARAMCO Associated Company, USA
☐ N732H	Bell 206L-3 LongRanger III	51607	N6180Q	0092	0593	1 AN 250-C20P	1882	Corporate		lsf ARAMCO Associated Company, USA
☐ N701H	Bell 212	35096	N6276N	0096	0696	2 PWC PT6T-3B TwinPac	5080	Corporate		lsf ARAMCO Associated Company, USA
☐ N705H	Bell 212	35088		0095	0795	2 PWC PT6T-3B TwinPac	5080	Corporate		lsf ARAMCO Associated Company, USA
☐ N735H	Bell 212	35046		0091	1291	2 PWC PT6T-3B TwinPac	5080	Corporate		lsf ARAMCO Associated Company, USA
☐ N736H	Bell 212	35048		0091	1291	2 PWC PT6T-3B TwinPac	5080	Corporate		lsf ARAMCO Associated Company, USA
☐ N748H	Bell 212	35060		0093	0693	2 PWC PT6T-3B TwinPac	5080	Corporate		lsf ARAMCO Associated Company, USA
☐ N749H	Bell 212	35061		0093	0693	2 PWC PT6T-3B TwinPac	5080	Corporate		lsf ARAMCO Associated Company, USA
☐ N754H	Bell 212	35034		0091	0791	2 PWC PT6T-3B TwinPac	5080	Corporate		lsf ARAMCO Associated Company, USA
☐ N708H	Bell 412EP	36198		0398	0698	2 PWC PT6T-3DF TwinPac	5398	Corporate		lsf ARAMCO Associated Company, USA
☐ N709H	Bell 412EP	36199		0398	0698	2 PWC PT6T-3DF TwinPac	5398	Corporate		lsf ARAMCO Associated Company, USA
☐ N660MA	De Havilland DHC-6 Twin Otter 300	231		0069	0769	2 PWC PT6A-27	5670	Corporate		lsf ARAMCO Associated Company, USA
☐ N663MA	De Havilland DHC-6 Twin Otter 300	593		0078	0778	2 PWC PT6A-27	5670	Corporate		lsf ARAMCO Associated Company, USA
☐ N704H	Bell 214ST	28108		0082	0983	2 GE CT7-2A	7938	Corporate		lsf ARAMCO Associated Company, USA
☐ N745H	Bell 214ST	28197	N6667Y	0091	1093	2 GE CT7-2A	7938	Corporate		lsf ARAMCO Associated Company, USA
☐ N746H	Bell 214ST	28200	N66675	0091	1093	2 GE CT7-2A	7938	Corporate		lsf ARAMCO Associated Company, USA
☐ N824H	Bell 214ST	28119	A4O-CK	0683	0498	2 GE CT7-2A	7938	Corporate		lsf ARAMCO Associated Company, USA
☐ N825H	Bell 214ST	28137	A4O-CN	0694	0498	2 GE CT7-2A	7938	Corporate		lsf ARAMCO Associated Company, USA
☐ N308A	Cessna 550 Citation II	550-0703		0092	1292	2 PWC JT15D-4	6033	Corporate		lsf ARAMCO Associated Company, USA
☐ N661MA	Air Tractor AT-802A	802A-0057		0097	0198	1 PWC PT6A-67AG	7257	Corp. Sprayer		lsf ARAMCO Associated Company, USA
☐ N662MA	Air Tractor AT-802	802-0037		0096	0896	1 PWC PT6A-67AG	7257	Corp. Sprayer		lsf ARAMCO Associated Company, USA
☐ N710A	Hawker 800B (BAe 125-800B)	258110	D-CMIR	0089	0395	2 GA TFE731-5R-1H	12428	Corporate		lsf ARAMCO Associated Company, USA
☐ N724A	De Havilland DHC-8-202 Dash 8Q	440	C-GFBW*	0096	0996	2 PWC PW123D	16465	Corporate Combi		lsf ARAMCO Associated Company, USA
☐ N725A	De Havilland DHC-8-202 Dash 8Q	441	C-GFCF*	0096	0996	2 PWC PW123D	16465	Corporate Combi		lsf ARAMCO Associated Company, USA
☐ N759A	De Havilland DHC-8-202 Dash 8Q	435		0096	0596	2 PWC PW123D	16465	Corporate Combi		lsf ARAMCO Associated Company, USA
☐ N107A	GAC G-IV Gulfstream IV	1070	N407GA*	0088	0988	2 RR Tay 611-8	31615	Corporate	CF-BH	lsf ARAMCO Associated Company, USA
☐ N765A	GAC G-IV Gulfstream IV	1069	N459GA*	0088	0988	2 RR Tay 611-8	31615	Corporate	CF-AK	lsf ARAMCO Associated Company, USA
☐ N713A	Boeing 737-205 (A)	23467 / 1245	JA8577	0086	1297	2 PW JT8D-17	56472	Corporate Y110		lsf ARAMCO Associated Company, USA
☐ N714A	Boeing 737-2T4 (A)	23405 / 1178	N701ML	0085	1291	2 PW JT8D-15A	56472	Corporate Y110		lsf ARAMCO Associated Company, USA
☐ N715A	Boeing 737-2S2C (A)	21928 / 603	N204FE	0079	1280	2 PW JT8D-17	56472	Corp.Y119orFrtr	BK-DM	lsf ARAMCO Associated Company, USA
☐ N716A	Boeing 737-2S2C (A)	21929 / 608	N205FE	0079	0181	2 PW JT8D-17	56472	Corp.Y119orFrtr	CH-DF	lsf ARAMCO Associated Company, USA
☐ N719A	Boeing 737-2X2 (A)	22679 / 807	DQ-FDM	0081	0790	2 PW JT8D-17	56472	Corporate Y110		lsf ARAMCO Associated Company, USA
☐ N720A	Boeing 737-2S2C (A)	21926 / 597	N201FE	0079	1081	2 PW JT8D-17	56472	Corp.Y119orFrtr		lsf ARAMCO Associated Company, USA
☐ N	Boeing 737-700					2 CFMI CFM56-7B26	69400	Corporate		tblsf ARAMCO Associated Co., USA 0900
☐ N	Boeing 737-700					2 CFMI CFM56-7B26	69400	Corporate		tblsf ARAMCO Associated Co., USA 1000
☐ N	Boeing 737-700					2 CFMI CFM56-7B26	69400	Corporate		tblsf ARAMCO Associated Co., USA 0001

207 registration type of aircraft cn/fn ex/ex* mfd del powered by mtow kg configuration selcal name/fln/specialitites/remarks

☐ N	Boeing 737-700C					2 CFMI CFM56-7B26	69400	Corporate / Frtr		tblsf ARAMCO Associated Co., USA 0001
☐ N	Boeing 737-700C					2 CFMI CFM56-7B26	69400	Corporate / Frtr		tblsf ARAMCO Associated Co., USA 0001
☐ N728A	Boeing (Douglas) DC-8-72	46081 / 471	N8971U	0069	0182	4 CFMI CFM56-2C	158757	Corporate F31	CF-BJ	lsf ARAMCO Ass. Co., USA / cvtd DC-8-62

SNAS AVIATION, Ltd = RSE — Riyadh & Bahrain

PO Box 22199, Riyadh 11495, Saudi Arabia ☎ (1) 462 19 19 Tx: n/a Fax: (1) 462 03 71 SITA: n/a
F: n/a 👥 n/a Head: n/a IATA: 952 ICAO: RED SEA Net: n/a

☐ HZ-SN8	Fairchild (Swearingen) SA227AT Merlin IVC	AT-434B	N3110F	0082	0488	2 GA TPE331-11U-611G	7257	Freighter		lst / joint opw DHL Aviation
☐ HZ-SN10	Fairchild (Swearingen) SA227AC Metro III	AC-769B	HZ-SN1	0091	0391	2 GA TPE331-11U-612G	7257	Freighter		lst / joint opw DHL Aviation
☐ HZ-SN7	Fairchild (Swearingen) SA227AC Metro III	AC-565	N3113G*	0083	0284	2 GA TPE331-11U-612G	7257	Freighter		lst / joint opw DHL Aviation
☐ HZ-SN11	Convair 580 (F) (SCD)	385	C-FKFA	0056	0791	2 AN 501-D13	26379	Freighter		lst/joint opw DHL Aviation/cvtd 440-32
☐ HZ-SN14	Convair 580 (F) (SCD)	361	OO-DHJ	0056	1095	2 AN 501-D13H	26379	Freighter		lst/joint opw DHL Aviation/cvtd 440-12

H4 = SOLOMON ISLANDS

Capital: Honiara Official Language: English Population: 0,4 million Square Km: 28896 Dialling code: +677 Year established: 1978 Acting political head: Solomon Mamoloni (Prime Minister)

AIR TRANSPORT, Ltd (formerly Heli Solomons) — Honiara-Henderson Int'l

PO Box 766, Honiara, Solomon Islands ☎ 36 033 Tx: n/a Fax: 36 713 SITA: n/a
F: n/a 👥 n/a Head: Dick Grouse Net: n/a

☐ H4-HSB	Bell 206B JetRanger	485	VH-JWF	0069	0090	1 AN 250-C20	1451			cvtd 206A

PACIFIC AIR EXPRESS (Solomon Islands), Ltd = PAQ — Honiara

PO Box 103, Airport, Honiara, Solomon Islands ☎ 39 248 Tx: none Fax: 39 343 SITA: n/a
F: 1993 👥 28 Head: Gary J. Clifford ICAO: SOLPAC Net: n/a

☐ H4-PAE	Boeing 727-281 (F) (A)	21455 / 1316	N528JS	0078	1096	3 PW JT8D-17	78472	Freighter		Spirit of Laulasi / lsf T.P.A./cvtd-281

SOLOMONS - Solomon Airlines, Ltd = IE / SOL (formerly Solair) — Honiara-Henderson Int'l

PO Box 23, Honiara, Solomon Islands ☎ 36 704 Tx: none Fax: 36 572 SITA: HIRDZIE
F: 1968 👥 150 Head: Gideon Zoloveke, Jr. IATA: 193 ICAO: SOLOMON Net: n/a Aircraft below MTOW 1361kg: Aerospatiale TB9 Tampico

☐ H4-AAH	Britten-Norman BN-2A-8 Islander	75	VH-TZH	0069		2 LY O-540-E4C5	2858	Y9		
☐ H4-AAI	Britten-Norman BN-2A-9 Islander	355	N355BN	0073		2 LY O-540-E4C5	2858	Y9		
☐ H4-FNT	De Havilland DHC-6 Twin Otter 310	280	VH-FNT	0070	1297	2 PWC PT6A-34	5670	Y19		
☐ H4-SIB	De Havilland DHC-6 Twin Otter 310	256	N661MA	0070	0987	2 PWC PT6A-27	5670	Y19		
☐ H4-SID	De Havilland DHC-6 Twin Otter 310	442	VH-XFE	0075	1194	2 PWC PT6A-27	5670	Y19		
☐ VH-TJB	Boeing 737-376	24296 / 1653		0088	0694	2 CFMI CFM56-3C1	61235	F8CY108	EG-DM	Guadalcanal / lsf/jtly opw QFA

I = ITALY (Italian Republic) (Repubblica Italiana)

Capital: Rome Official Language: Italian Population: 58,0 million Square Km: 301268 Dialling code: +39 Year established: 1861 Acting political head: Massimo D'Alema (Prime Minister)

Government / Corporate / Executive / VIP Aircraft

☐ MM	Airbus Industrie A319-100 (CJ)					2	70000	VIP 50 Pax		oo-del.1199/Aeronautica Militare Ital.
☐ MM	Dassault Falcon 900EX					3 GA TFE731-60-1C	22226	VIP / mil trans		oo-del.0999/Aeronautica Militare Ital.
☐ MM	Airbus Industrie A319-100 (CJ)					2	70000	VIP 50 Pax		oo-del.0800/Aeronautica Militare Ital.
☐ MM	Dassault Falcon 900EX					3 GA TFE731-60-1C	22226	VIP / mil trans		oo-del.1199/Aeronautica Militare Ital.
☐ MM	ATR 42-400 (MP)	466	F-WQJC*			2 PWC PW121A	17900	MaritPatrol/VIP		Ital.A.F./Guardia di Finanza/oo-del. 99
☐ MM61948	Piaggio PD-808	506		0069	0069	2 RR Viper 526	8165	VIP / mil trans		Aeronautica Militare Italiana
☐ MM61949	Piaggio PD-808	507		0069	0069	2 RR Viper 526	8165	VIP / mil trans		Aeronautica Militare Italiana
☐ MM61950	Piaggio PD-808	508		0069	0069	2 RR Viper 526	8165	VIP / mil trans		Aeronautica Militare Italiana
☐ MM61951	Piaggio PD-808	509		0069	0069	2 RR Viper 526	8165	VIP / mil trans		Aeronautica Militare Italiana
☐ MM62012	Boeing (Douglas) DC-9-32	47595 / 709		0074	0174	2 PW JT8D-9	48988	EMS/VIP/miltrans	BD-GJ	Aeronautica Militare Italiana
☐ MM62013	Boeing (Douglas) DC-9-32	47600 / 710	N54635*	0074	0374	2 PW JT8D-9	48988	EMS/VIP/miltrans	AB-CE	Aeronautica Militare Italiana
☐ MM62020	Dassault Falcon 50	151	F-WPXD*	0085	1185	3 GA TFE731-3-1C	17600	VIP / mil trans	AB-CH	Aeronautica Militare Italiana
☐ MM62021	Dassault Falcon 50	155	F-WPXH*	0085	1285	3 GA TFE731-3-1C	17600	VIP / mil trans		Aeronautica Militare Italiana
☐ MM62022	GAC G-1159A Gulfstream III	451	N330GA*	0085	0985	2 RR Spey 511-8	31615	VIP / mil trans	AB-CD	Aeronautica Militare Italiana
☐ MM62025	GAC G-1159A Gulfstream III	479	N317GA*	0086	1286	2 RR Spey 511-8	31615	VIP / mil trans	AB-CG	Aeronautica Militare Italiana
☐ MM62026	Dassault Falcon 50	193	F-WWHH*	0089	1289	3 GA TFE731-3-1C	17600	VIP / mil trans	AB-CH	Aeronautica Militare Italiana
☐ MM62029	Dassault Falcon 50	211	F-WWHR*	0091	0091	3 GA TFE731-3-1C	17600	VIP / mil trans		Aeronautica Militare Italiana
☐ MM62165	ATR 42-400 (MP)	500	F-WWEW*	0096	1296	2 PWC PW121A	17900	MaritPatrol/VIP		GF-13 / Italian A.F./Guardia di Finanza
☐ MM62166	ATR 42-400 (MP)	502	F-WWEM*	0097	0497	2 PWC PW121A	17900	MaritPatrol/VIP		GF-14 / Italian A.F./Guardia di Finanza

AAAV Flight Inspection Branch (Division of Azienda Autonoma Assistenza al Volo) — Rome-Ciampino

Via Salaria 716, I-00138 Roma, Italy ☎ (06) 79 34 07 03 Tx: none Fax: (06) 79 34 06 91 SITA: n/a
F: 1981 👥 52 Head: Cpt. S. Giuliano Net: n/a Non-commercial government organisation conducting aeronautical flight inspection missions.

☐ I-AVGM	Cessna 550 Citation II	550-0492		0084	0584	2 PWC JT15D-4	6033	Calibrator		
☐ I-AVRM	Cessna 550 Citation II	550-0491		0084	0584	2 PWC JT15D-4	6033	Calibrator		
☐ I-AVVM	Cessna S550 Citation S/II	S550-0062	N12715*	0085	0186	2 PWC JT15D-4B	6668	Calibrator		

ACTION AIR, Srl. = ORS — Milan-Linate

Piazza E. Duse 4, I-20122 Milano, Italy ☎ (02) 70 10 06 08 Tx: none Fax: (02) 76 01 42 49 SITA: n/a
F: 1989 👥 2 Head: n/a ICAO: AVIATION SERVICE Net: n/a

☐ I-ALPG	Cessna 551 Citation II/SP	551-0355	N551AS	0081		2 PWC JT15D-4	5670	9 Pax		lsf Desio & Brianza Leasing

AERMARCHE, SpA. = MMC — Ancona-Falconara

Viale Aristide Meloni 47, I-60044 Fabriano, (AN), Italy ☎ (071) 918 87 91 Tx: n/a Fax: (071) 918 84 13 SITA: n/a
F: n/a 👥 7 Head: n/a ICAO: AERMARCHE Net: n/a

☐ I-ECUR	Eurocopter (Aerosp.) AS355F1 Ecureuil 2	5285	I-BSBS	0083		2 AN 250-C20F	2300			
☐ I-AGFA	Eurocopter (Aerosp.) SA365N1 Dauphin 2	6229		0089		2 TU Arriel 1C1	4100			
☐ I-CMUT	Dassault Falcon 20F	389	F-WRQV*	0079		2 GE CF700-2D2	13000			lsf Centro Leasing

AERNORD, SpA = AED (Associated with Elilombardia, SpA) — Clusone

Eliporto, I-24023 Clusone, (BG), Italy ☎ (0346) 23 737 Tx: 211584 i Fax: (0346) 22 003 SITA: n/a
F: 1981 👥 14 Head: Ing. Stefano Bongiovanni ICAO: AERNSPA Net: n/a

☐ I-ETIB	Eurocopter (Aerosp.) SA315B Lama	2090 / 14		0080		1 TU Artouste IIIB	1950			
☐ I-ETID	Eurocopter (Aerosp.) SA315B Lama	2615	F-GDFB	0081		1 TU Artouste IIIB	1950			
☐ I-FVBD	Eurocopter (Aerosp.) SA315B Lama	2620		0082		1 TU Artouste IIIB1	1950			
☐ I-IBLE	Eurocopter (Aerosp.) SA315B Lama	2483		0077		1 TU Artouste IIIB	1950			
☐ I-LAZZ	Eurocopter (Aerosp.) SA315B Lama	2653		0084		1 TU Artouste IIIB1	1950			
☐ I-SADG	Eurocopter (Aerosp.) AS350B3 Ecureuil					1 TU Arriel 2B	2250			oo-delivery 0099

AEROCENTRO VARESINO, Srl. (formerly Pubbli Aer Foto di Mario Mazzucchelli E.C.S.N.C.) — Venegono (VA)

Via Silvio Pellico 24, I-21040 Venegono Inferiore, (MI), Italy ☎ (0368) 342 39 08 Tx: none Fax: (02) 469 01 30 SITA: n/a
F: 1965 👥 5 Head: Giancarla Besozzi ICAO: PUBLAERO Net: n/a Aircraft below MTOW 1361 kg: Cessna F172H (Photo).

☐ I-ALJK	Cessna 337A Super Skymaster	337-0471	N5371S	0066		2 CO IO-360-C/D	1905	Photo		

AERONIKE FLIGHT SERVICES — Cagliari-Elmas

Casella Postale 22, Aeroporto Civile di Elmas, I-09134 Cagliari, (CA), Italy ☎ (070) 24 00 39 Tx: n/a Fax: (070) 24 00 39 SITA: n/a
F: n/a 👥 n/a Head: n/a Net: n/a Aircraft below MTOW 1361kg: Maule MX7-180, Piper PA-18 & SIAI 205-20R

☐ I-RTAA	Partenavia P.68B Victor	181		0079		2 LY IO-360-A1B6	1990			

AEROVENETA, Srl. = EVT — Verona-Villafranca

Aeroporto V. Catullo di Verona Villafranca, I-37060 Caselle di Sommacampagna, (VR), Italy ☎ (045) 861 90 65 Tx: none Fax: (045) 861 90 63 SITA: n/a
F: 1988 👥 28 Head: Dott. Alessandro Aichner ICAO: AEROVENETA Net: n/a

☐ I-ELEM	Eurocopter (Aerosp.) AS350B1 Ecureuil	2095		0087		1 TU Arriel 1D	2200			
☐ I-ELTE	Eurocopter (Aerosp.) AS350B Ecureuil	1477	HB-XMI	0081		1 TU Arriel 1B	1950			lsf Sef Leasing
☐ I-GICO	Eurocopter (Aerosp.) AS350B1 Ecureuil	2229		0089		1 TU Arriel 1D	2200			lsf Heliport Srl.
☐ I-MAIC	Eurocopter (Aerosp.) AS350B2 Ecureuil	1942	LV-AZX	0087		1 TU Arriel 1D1	2250			lsf Palladio Leasing
☐ I-VREM	Eurocopter (Aerosp.) AS355F1 Ecureuil 2	5297	F-GEHL	0083		2 AN 250-C20F	2400	EMS		lsf San Paolo Lsnt/opf Verona Emergenza
☐ I-VRVR	Eurocopter (Aerosp.) AS355F1 Ecureuil 2	5180		0082		2 AN 250-C20F	2400			
☐ I-LEOG	Agusta A109C	7602		0088	0098	2 AN 250-C20R/1	2720			lsf San Paolo Leasint
☐ I-BKBS	Eurocopter (MBB) BK117C-1	7504	D-HOTZ	0096	1297	2 TU Arriel 1E2	3350	EMS		lsf SanPaolo Lsnt/opf Brescia Emergenza
☐ D-HECD	Eurocopter (MBB) BK117C-1	7500		0092		2 TU Arriel 1E2	3350	EMS		lsf Eurocopter Deut./opf Croce Bianca
☐ D-HSML	Eurocopter (MBB) BK117C-1	7514	N40027	0095	1296	2 TU Arriel 1E2	3350	EMS		lsf Eurocopter Deut./opf Croce Bianca

AIR ABRUZZO, Srl — L'Aquila-Preturo

Aeroporto l'Aquila-Preturo, I-67010 L'Aquila, (PE), Italy ☎ (0862) 46 14 74 Tx: none Fax: (0862) 31 16 47 SITA: n/a
F: 1980 👥 7 Head: Giorgio Zecca Net: n/a Aircraft below MTOW 1361kg: Aviamilano P.19, Piper PA-18 & Robinson R22.

☐ I-PRSC	Piper PA-34-200 Seneca	34-7450154	N41853	0074		2 LY IO-360-C1E6	1905			

208 registration type of aircraft cn/fn ex/ex* mfd del powered by mtow kg configuration selcal name/fln/specialitites/remarks

AIR COLUMBIA, Srl. = ACO — Perugia & Pescara

Aeroporto Civile, Via Tiburtina 384, I-65129 Pescara, (PE), Italy ☎ (085) 54 241 Tx: n/a Fax: (085) 431 03 36 SITA: n/a
F: 1984 ⁂ n/a Head: Ing. Giuseppe Spadaccini ICAO: SPADA Net: n/a Aircraft below MTOW 1361kg: Cessna 172, Piper PA-28 & SIAI F260.

☐ I-SEPA	Partenavia P.68	08		1272		2 LY IO-360-A1B	1960			
☐ I-AEAL	Cessna 500 Citation	500-0053	HB-VGO	0072		2 PWC JT15D-1A	5216			lsf Leasing Roma SpA

AIR DOLOMITI, SpA – Linee Aeree Regionali Europee = EN / DLA (Member of EBM Group) — Trieste

Via Aquileia 46, I-34077 Ronchi dei Legionari, (GO), Italy ☎ (0481) 47 77 11 Tx: 460493 i Fax: (0481) 47 45 40 SITA: TRSMTEN
F: 1989 ⁂ 320 Head: Dr. Alcide Leali IATA: 101 ICAO: DOLOMITI Net: n/a

☐ I-ADLF	ATR 42-500	462	F-OHFF	0095	1095	2 PWC PW127E	18600	Y46		
☐ I-ADLG	ATR 42-500	476	F-OHFG	0095	1195	2 PWC PW127E	18600	Y46		
☐ I-ADLH	ATR 42-500	445	F-OHFM	0095	0497	2 PWC PW127E	18600	Y46		lsf Locafit
☐ I-ADLI	ATR 42-500	515	F-OHFN	0097	0497	2 PWC PW127E	18600	Y46		lsf Locafit
☐ I-ADLL	ATR 42-500	518	F-OHFP	0097	0498	2 PWC PW127E	18600	Y46		
☐ F-OHFA	ATR 42-320	363	F-WWLC*	0093	1293	2 PWC PW121	16900	Y46		lsf Ludovica Leasing Ltd
☐ F-OHFB	ATR 42-320	366	F-WWLE*	0093	1293	2 PWC PW121	16900	Y46		lsf Ludovica Leasing Ltd
☐ F-OHFC	ATR 42-320	351	F-WWER*	0094	0394	2 PWC PW121	16900	Y46		lsf Ludovica Leasing Ltd
☐ F-OHFD	ATR 42-320	374	F-WWLQ*	0094	0494	2 PWC PW121	16900	Y46		lsf Ludovica Leasing Ltd
☐ F-OHFE	ATR 42-320	378	F-WWLA*	0094	0694	2 PWC PW121	16900	Y46		lsf Ludovica Leasing Ltd
☐ I-ADLM	ATR 72-500 (72-212A)	543	F-WWLB*	0098	0398	2 PWC PW127F	22500	Y64		lsf Locafit
☐ I-ADLN	ATR 72-500 (72-212A)	557	F-WWLV*	0098	0698	2 PWC PW127F	22500	Y64		lsf Locafit
☐ I-ADLO	ATR 72-500 (72-212A)	585	F-WWEQ*	0099	0399	2 PWC PW127F	22500	Y64		

AIR EUROPE, SpA = PE / AEL (Member of European Leisure Group / formerly Flying Services, Srl.) — Milan-Malpensa

Via Carlo Noe' 3, I-21013 Gallarate, (VA), Italy ☎ (0331) 77 21 11 Tx: 315050 i Fax: (0331) 77 63 30 SITA: n/a
F: 1989 ⁂ 450 Head: Lupo Rattazzi IATA: 667 ICAO: AIR EUROPE Net: n/a

☐ I-MAWW	Beech Baron 58P	TJ-55		0076		2 CO TSIO-520-L	2767	Freighter / Y4		
☐	Airbus Industrie A320-212	131	F-GLGM	0090		2 CFMI CFM56-5A3	77000			to be lsf GATX 0599
☐	Airbus Industrie A320-212	132	F-GLGN	0090		2 CFMI CFM56-5A3	77000			to be lsf GATX 0599
☐	Airbus Industrie A320-212					2 CFMI CFM56-5A3	77000			to be lsf GATX 0599
☐	Airbus Industrie A320-212					2 CFMI CFM56-5A3	77000			to be lsf GATX 0599
☐	Airbus Industrie A320-212					2 CFMI CFM56-5A3	77000			to be lsf GATX 0599
☐ EI-CIY	Boeing 767-330 (ER)	25208 / 381	D-ABUY	0091	1293	2 PW PW4060	184612	C24Y245	AE-JR	lsf KB Flygplanet III
☐ EI-CJA	Boeing 767-35H (ER)	26387 / 445	S7-AAQ	0092	0892	2 GE CF6-80C2B6	185065	C24Y245	CS-HP	lsf ITOH / to be sub-lst BBB 0999
☐ EI-CJB	Boeing 767-35H (ER)	26388 / 456	S7-AAV	0092	1092	2 GE CF6-80C2B6	185065	C24Y245	CS-HQ	lsf ITOH / to be sub-lst BBB 0999
☐ EI-CLS	Boeing 767-352 (ER)	26262 / 583	N171LF	0095	0695	2 PW PW4062	184612	C24Y245	HS-JP	lsf ILFC
☐ EI-CMQ	Boeing 767-352 (ER)	27993 / 619		0096	0696	2 PW PW4062	184612	C24Y245	KR-JM	lsf ILFC
☐ EI-CNS	Boeing 767-3Q8 (ER)	27600 / 655	N6005C*	0097	0497	2 GE CF6-80C2B6	185065	C24Y245	QS-EL	lsf ILFC
☐ EI-CPV	Boeing 767-38E (ER)	25132 / 417	N132KR	0092	0698	2 GE CF6-80C2B4F	184612	C24Y245	AQ-FG	lsf ILFC
☐ I-	Boeing 777-2Q8 (ER)					2 PW PW4090	294200			to be lsf ILFC 0799
☐ I-	Boeing 777-2Q8 (ER)					2 PW PW4090	294200			to be lsf ILFC 1099

AIR GREEN, Srl. — Robassomero (TO)

Via Fiano 63 / 1, I-10070 Robassomero, (TO), Italy ☎ (011) 923 63 70 Tx: 225295 airg i Fax: (011) 923 58 85 SITA: n/a
F: 1985 ⁂ 15 Head: Airaudi Mauro Net: n/a Aircraft below MTOW 1361kg: Robinson R22.

☐ I-ETIA	Eurocopter (Aerosp.) SA315B Lama	2548		0079	0097	1 TU Artouste IIIB	1950			
☐ I-GREN	Eurocopter (Aerosp.) SA315B Lama	2482	N223RM	0077		1 TU Artouste IIIB1	1950			
☐ I-MURE	Eurocopter (Aerosp.) SA315B Lama	2509	N72590	0078		1 TU Artouste IIIB1	1950			
☐ I-OLEY	Eurocopter (Aerosp.) SA315B Lama	2369		0074		1 TU Artouste IIIB1	1950			
☐ I-ORLY	Eurocopter (Aerosp.) SA315B Lama	2627		0082		1 TU Artouste IIIB1	1950			
☐ I-PATI	Eurocopter (Aerosp.) SA315B Lama	2651		0084		1 TU Artouste IIIB1	1950			
☐ I-AFCN	Eurocopter (Aerosp.) AS350B1 Ecureuil	1997	JA9461	0087		1 TU Arriel 1D	2200			
☐ I-VIOU	Eurocopter (Aerosp.) SA316B Alouette III	2179		0074		1 TU Artouste IIIB1	2200			
☐ I-AIRR	Agusta-Bell 412	25577	HB-XVU	0089	0797	2 PWC PT6T-3B TwinPac	5398			lsf Findata Finanziamenti SpA
☐ I-AIVO	Bell 412	33014	HB-XRP	0081	0597	2 PWC PT6T-3B TwinPac	5400			lsf Locat
☐ I-GONI	Agusta-Bell 412	25506		0084		2 PWC PT6T-3B TwinPac	5400			

AIR MACH, Srl (formerly Air Mac, Srl / Affiliated with AFE, SpA & Associated with Genavia) — Novi Ligure-E. Mossi

Aeroporto E.Mossi, Via Mazzini, I-15067 Novi Ligure, (AL), Italy ☎ (0143) 74 45 55 Tx: none Fax: (0143) 74 52 15 SITA: n/a
F: 1981 ⁂ 9 Head: Paolo Mossi Net: n/a Aircraft below MTOW 1361kg: DH82A, Piper PA-18 / PA-22 & Stampe SV4C.

☐ I-OBSR	Partenavia P.68 Observer	236-01-OB		0080		2 LY IO-360-A1B6	1960	Photo / Survey		

AIR ONE, SpA = AP / ADH (Subsidiary of Toto, SpA / formerly Aliadriatica, SpA) — Rome-Fiumicino & Pescara

Via Sardegna 14, I-00187 Roma, Italy ☎ (06) 488 36 42 Tx: none Fax: (06) 488 36 45 SITA: ROMKKAP
F: 1983 ⁂ 400 Head: Giovanni Sebastiani IATA: 867 ICAO: HERON Net: http://www.air-one.com

☐ I-ELBA	Beech Baron B55 (95-B55)	TC-1291	HB-GEF	0069		2 CO IO-470-L	2313	Y6		
☐ I-ALKA	Cessna 550 Citation II	550-0351	N99KW	0082	0189	2 PWC JT15D-4	6033	Y9		lsf Leasing Roma SpA
☐ I-TIAR	Boeing (Douglas) DC-9-15F (RC)	47015 / 156	N72AF	0067	0297	2 PW JT8D-7B	41141	Y85		lsf Centro Investimenti Srl.
☐ I-JETA	Boeing 737-229 (A)	21839 / 593	OO-SBS	0079	0794	2 PW JT8D-15	52753	Y120		
☐ I-JETC	Boeing 737-230 (A)	23153 / 1075	D-ABMA	0085	0497	2 PW JT8D-15 (HK3/NOR)	54204	Y120		
☐ I-JETD	Boeing 737-230 (A)	23158 / 1089	D-ABMF	0085	0897	2 PW JT8D-15 (HK3/NOR)	54204	Y120		lsf San Paolo Leasint SpA
☐ EI-CLW	Boeing 737-3Y0	25187 / 2248	XA-SAB	0092	1195	2 CFMI CFM56-3C1	62822	Y148		lsf GECA
☐ EI-CLZ	Boeing 737-3Y0	25179 / 2205	XA-RJR	0092	0895	2 CFMI CFM56-3C1	62822	Y148		lsf GECA
☐ F-GKTA	Boeing 737-3M8	24413 / 1884		0090	0596	2 CFMI CFM56-3B2	61235	Y149	CE-DG	lsf Alter Bail Aviation
☐ F-GKTB	Boeing 737-3M8	24414 / 1895		0090	0596	2 CFMI CFM56-3B2	61235	Y149	CE-GH	lsf Alter Bail Aviation
☐ EI-COH	Boeing 737-430	27001 / 2316	D-ABKB	0092	0797	2 CFMI CFM56-3C1	65090	Y153		lsf GATX
☐ EI-COI	Boeing 737-430	27002 / 2323	D-ABKC	0092	0797	2 CFMI CFM56-3C1	65090	Y153		lsf Adrienne Enterprises
☐ EI-COJ	Boeing 737-430	27005 / 2359	D-ABKK	0092	0797	2 CFMI CFM56-3C1	65090	Y153		lsf Adrienne Enterprises
☐ EI-COK	Boeing 737-430	27003 / 2328	D-ABKD	0092	0298	2 CFMI CFM56-3C1	65090	Y153		lsf GATX
☐ EI-CPU	Boeing 737-430	27004 / 2344	D-ABKF	0092	0598	2 CFMI CFM56-3C1	65090	Y153		lsf GATX

AIR SERVICE CENTER, Srl. – A.S.C. = RCX — Arena Po (PV)

Via Begoglio 19, I-27047 Santa Maria della Versa, (PV), Italy ☎ (0385) 27 21 17 Tx: none Fax: (0385) 27 23 57 SITA: n/a
F: 1987 ⁂ 15 Head: //www.airservicecenter.com ICAO: SERVICE CENTER Net: n/a Aircraft below MTOW 1361 kg: Hughes 269C (300C).

☐ I-GRAE	Eurocopter (Aerosp.) SA315B Lama	1807 / 37	HB-XYQ	0076	0097	1 TU Artouste IIIB1	1950			lsf Helinord / cvtd Alouette II
☐ I-AMVE	Eurocopter (Aerosp.) AS350B2 Ecureuil	2640	F-WYMQ	0092		1 TU Arriel 1D1	2250			
☐ I-AMVG	Eurocopter (Aerosp.) AS350B3 Ecureuil	3071		0098	0398	1 TU Arriel 2B	2250			lsf Sanpaolo Leasint SpA
☐ I-REIL	Eurocopter (Aerosp.) AS350B2 Ecureuil	2379		0090	0198	1 TU Arriel 1D1	2250			

AIR SICILIA, SpA = BM / SIC — Catania & Palermo

Via G. La Rosa N. 23, I-91014 Caltagirrone (Catania), Italy ☎ (0933) 26 714 Tx: none Fax: (0933) 23 737 SITA: n/a
F: 1994 ⁂ n/a Head: Giacomo Babbucci IATA: 243 ICAO: AIR SICILIA Net: n/a

☐ I-ATRM	ATR 42-300	114	F-WWEK*	0088	0495	2 PWC PW120	16700	Y46		
☐ F-OHFH	ATR 42-300	067	I-ATRK	0088	0396	2 PWC PW120	16150	Y46		Peter Pan / lsf ATR Lease
☐ EI-CRN	Boeing 737-228 (A)	23008 / 952	F-GBYI	0083	0299	2 PW JT8D-15A	52000	CY114		lsf Rancemont Lease

AIRUMBRIA, Srl. = UMB — Perugia

Aeroporto S. Egidio, I-06080 Perugia-S. Egidio, (PG), Italy ☎ (075) 592 80 84 Tx: none Fax: (075) 592 80 87 SITA: n/a
F: 1992 ⁂ n/a Head: Fortunato Ragusa ICAO: AIR UMBRIA Net: n/a

☐ I-VVEE	Beech Baron 58P	TJ-320	N3707N	0081		2 CO TSIO-520-WB	2812	5 Pax		
☐ I-RAGC	Piper PA-31-350 Navajo Chieftain	31-7552024	9Q-CSI	0075		2 LY TIO-540-J2BD	3175	6 Pax		
☐ CS-AZL	Boeing (Douglas) DC-3C (C-47B-10-DK)	26244	9Q-CGW	0044		2 PW R-1830	12202	24 Pax		

AIR VALLEE, SpA – Services Aériens du Val d'Aoste = DO / RVL — Aosta

Localita Aeroporto, I-11020 Saint-Christophe, (AO), Italy ☎ (0165) 23 69 66 Tx: none Fax: (0165) 32 529 SITA: n/a
F: 1987 ⁂ 5 Head: Ing. Gianfranco Marten Perolino ICAO: AIR VALLEE Net: n/a

☐ I-ASIO	Eurocopter (Aerosp.) SA315B Lama	1923 / 21	D-HODU	0083	0097	1 TU Artouste IIIB1	1950			cvtd Alouette II
☐ I-LURY	Eurocopter (Aerosp.) SA316B Alouette III	1365	HB-XPB	0066	0097	1 TU Artouste IIIB1	2200			
☐ I-PIAH	Beech King Air 200	BB-777		0080		2 PWC PT6A-41	5670			
☐ I-AIRW	Learjet 31	31-025	N39399	0090	0691	2 GA TFE731-2-3B	7484			

AIR WALSER, Srl. — Crodo-Private Heliport

Frazione Monte Piano, I-28862 Crodo, (VB), Italy ☎ (0324) 61 88 89 Tx: none Fax: (0324) 61 88 89 SITA: n/a
F: 1997 ⁂ n/a Head: Luigi Castellano Net: n/a

☐ I-BXXB	Eurocopter (Aerosp.) SA315B Lama	2453	HB-XGG	0076	0898	1 TU Artouste IIIB1	1950			
☐ I-BXWA	Eurocopter (Aerosp.) SA316B Alouette III	1307	F-GIBY	0065	0897	1 TU Artouste IIIB1	2200			

209 registration type of aircraft cn/fn ex/ex* mfd del powered by mtow kg configuration selcal name/fln/specialitites/remarks

AIRWAY, Srl. — Lasa-Private Heliport

Zona Industriale 35, I-39023 Lasa, (BZ), Italy ☎ (0473) 62 66 67 Tx: none Fax: (0473) 62 66 91 SITA: n/a
F: 1997 ✈ n/a Head: Helmut Zingerle Net: n/a

registration	type of aircraft	cn/fn	ex/ex*	mfd	del	powered by	mtow kg	configuration	selcal	name/fln/specialitites/remarks
☐ I-APUS	Eurocopter (Aerosp.) SA315B Lama	*2539*	*VR-HIL*	*0078*	*0097*	*1 TU Artouste IIIB1*	*1950*			
☐ I-	Eurocopter (Aerosp.) AS350B2 Ecureuil		*HB-*	*0089*		*1 TU Arriel 1D1*	*2250*			*oo-delivery 0099*

ALBA SERVIZI TRASPORTI, SpA (Associated with Fininvest Group) — Milan-Linate

Via Paleocapa 3, I-20121 Milano, (MI), Italy ☎ (02) 21 021 Tx: n/a Fax: (02) 76 11 11 10 SITA: n/a
F: n/a ✈ n/a Head: n/a Net: n/a

registration	type of aircraft	cn/fn	ex/ex*	mfd	del	powered by	mtow kg	configuration	selcal	name/fln/specialitites/remarks
☐ I-SPOT	Agusta-Bell 412SP	*25601*		*0089*		*2 PWC PT6T-3B TwinPac*	*5400*			*lsf Fininvest*
☐ I-BAEL	Dassault Falcon 20F	*426*	*N416RM*	*0080*		*2 GE CF700-2D2*	*13000*			
☐ I-MADU	GAC G-1159A Gulfstream III	*448*	*N225SB*	*0085*		*2 RR Spey 511-8*	*31615*			
☐ I-LUBI	GAC G-IV Gulfstream IV	*1123*	*N457GA**	*0090*		*2 RR Tay 611-8*	*33203*			

ALI CAPITOL, SpA = ALJ (Affiliated with Air Capitol, Srl-Flying school / formerly ALI Aero Leasing Italiana, SpA) — Rome-Ciampino

Aeroporto Ciampino-Ovest, I-00040 Roma, Italy ☎ (06) 79 49 43 69 Tx: none Fax: (06) 79 49 43 69 SITA: n/a
F: 1977 ✈ 80 Head: Giuseppe Ciarrapico Net: n/a

registration	type of aircraft	cn/fn	ex/ex*	mfd	del	powered by	mtow kg	configuration	selcal	name/fln/specialitites/remarks
☐ I-LIAD	Learjet 35A	*35A-111*	*OE-GMA*	*0077*		*2 GA TFE731-2-2B*	*8301*			
☐ I-LIAB	Dassault Falcon 20C	*172*	*F-BRHB*	*0068*		*2 GE CF700-2D2*	*13000*			
☐ I-LIAC	Dassault Falcon 20D	*234*	*D-COLL*	*0070*		*2 GE CF700-2D2*	*13000*			

ALIDAUNIA, Srl. = D4 / LID — Foggia-Gino Lisa

Via degli Aviatori, Aeroporto Civile Gino Lisa, I-71100 Foggia, (FG), Italy ☎ (0881) 61 79 61 Tx: 810341 alida i Fax: (0881) 61 96 60 SITA: n/a
F: 1976 ✈ 18 Head: Roberto Pucillo ICAO: LID Net: http://www.alidaunia.com Aircraft below MTOW 1361 kg: Partenavia P.66B

registration	type of aircraft	cn/fn	ex/ex*	mfd	del	powered by	mtow kg	configuration	selcal	name/fln/specialitites/remarks
☐ I-AGSE	Agusta A109A II	*7354*		*0086*		*2 AN 250-C20B*	*2600*			
☐ I-AGSH	Agusta A109A II	*7384*		*0087*		*2 AN 250-C20B*	*2600*			
☐ I-MSTR	Agusta A109A	*7227*	*N4256P*	*0083*		*2 AN 250-C20B*	*2600*			
☐ I-RMDV	Sikorsky S-76A	*760235*	*N760P*	*0084*		*2 AN 250-C30S*	*4763*			

ALIEUROPE, Srl. = TOO — Uggiate Trevano-Heliport

Via Albertolli 5, I-21000 Como, (CO), Italy ☎ (031) 24 33 72 Tx: none Fax: (031) 24 33 79 SITA: n/a
F: 1992 ✈ 5 Head: Franco Noe ICAO: ALIEUROPE Net: n/a

registration	type of aircraft	cn/fn	ex/ex*	mfd	del	powered by	mtow kg	configuration	selcal	name/fln/specialitites/remarks
☐ I-ALWE	Eurocopter (Aerosp.) AS350BA AStar	*2468*	*C-FJXY*	*0091*	*1197*	*1 TU Arriel 1B*	*2100*			*cvtd AS350B*
☐ I-LAMO	Eurocopter (Aerosp.) AS350B1 Ecureuil	*2171*		*0089*	*0097*	*1 TU Arriel 1D*	*2200*			
☐ I-RECL	Eurocopter (Aerosp.) AS350B2 Ecureuil	*2107*	*OE-OXC*	*0088*	*0798*	*1 TU Arriel 1D1*	*2250*			*cvtd AS350B1*
☐ I-AXLE	Agusta A109A II Plus	*7436*		*0089*	*0098*	*2 AN 250-C20R/1*	*2600*			
☐ I-	Agusta A109E Power					*2 PWC PW206C*	*2850*			*oo-delivery 0099*

ALIFOTO — Torino

Corso Tassoni Alessandro 4, I-10143 Torino, (TO), Italy ☎ (011) 749-5362 Tx: n/a Fax: n/a SITA: n/a
F: n/a ✈ n/a Head: n/a Net: n/a

registration	type of aircraft	cn/fn	ex/ex*	mfd	del	powered by	mtow kg	configuration	selcal	name/fln/specialitites/remarks
☐ I-GRAD	Partenavia P.68C-TC	*222*		*0080*		*2 LY TIO-360-C1A6D*	*1990*	*Photo*		

ALIPARMA, Srl. = PAJ — Parma

Via A.M. Adorni 1, I-43100 Parma, Italy ☎ (0521) 98 27 11 Tx: 530336 i Fax: (0521) 98 26 94 SITA: n/a
F: 1986 ✈ 6 Head: Luciano Caldarini ICAO: ALIPARMA Net: n/a

registration	type of aircraft	cn/fn	ex/ex*	mfd	del	powered by	mtow kg	configuration	selcal	name/fln/specialitites/remarks
☐ I-IPIZ	Beech Beechjet 400A	*RK-29*	*N15693*	*0092*		*2 PWC JT15D-5*	*7303*	*9 Pax*		
☐ I-OTTY	Beech Beechjet 400	*RJ-25*	*N125RJ*	*0087*	*0198*	*2 PWC JT15D-5*	*7158*	*9 Pax*		*lsf Italease*

ALISERIO, SpA = ALL — Milan-Linate

Viale Aviazione 65, I-20138 Milano, (MI), Italy ☎ (02) 70 10 01 90 Tx: 331875 aliser i Fax: (02) 76 11 11 17 SITA: n/a
F: 1967 ✈ 10 Head: Dott. Ettore Rossi ICAO: ALISERIO Net: n/a

registration	type of aircraft	cn/fn	ex/ex*	mfd	del	powered by	mtow kg	configuration	selcal	name/fln/specialitites/remarks
☐ I-ALSI	Beech Beechjet 400	*RJ-31*	*N5450M*	*0087*	*1089*	*2 PWC JT15D-5*	*7158*	*9 Pax*		

ALITALIA – Linee Aeree Italiane, SpA = AZ / AZA (Alitalia Team) (Subsidiary of IRI – Istituto per la Ricostruzione Industriale, SpA) — Rome-Fiumicino

Centro Direzionale, Viale Alessandro Marchetti 111, I-00148 Roma, Italy ☎ (06) 65 621 Tx: 656211 romaz i Fax: (06) 65 62 47 33 SITA: n/a
F: 1957 ✈ 19000 Head: Fausto Cereti IATA: 055 ICAO: ALITALIA Net: http://www.alitalia.it A number of MCDonnell Douglas MD-82 & all Airbus Ind. A321 & Boeing 767-300 (ER) are operated by ALITALIA TEAM SpA, an internal operating subsidiary. Aircraft marked as such. Some regional flights are operated on behalf of ALITALIA under the marketing name ALITALIA EXPRESS (and in such colors) by: AZZURRAIR (Avro RJ70/RJ85), MINERVA (Dornier 328) & subsidiary ALITALIA EXPRESS (ATR42/72) using AZ-flight numbers. Some intercontinental & all cargo flights are operated on behalf of Alitalia by: EUROFLY (Boeing 767-300) & ATLAS AIR (N, Boeing 747-200F). For details – see under each company.

registration	type of aircraft	cn/fn	ex/ex*	mfd	del	powered by	mtow kg	configuration	selcal	name/fln/specialitites/remarks
☐ I-TREQ	Piper PA-42-720 Cheyenne IIIA	*42-5501046*		*0087*	*0687*	*2 PWC PT6A-61*	*5080*	*Trainer*		
☐ I-TRER	Piper PA-42-720 Cheyenne IIIA	*42-5501047*		*0087*	*0787*	*2 PWC PT6A-61*	*5080*	*Trainer*		
☐ I-DACM	Boeing (Douglas) MD-82 (DC-9-82)	*49971 / 1755*		*0890*	*0990*	*2 PW JT8D-217C*	*66678*	*Y163*		La Spezia / *lsf Cofiri Leasing*
☐ I-DACN	Boeing (Douglas) MD-82 (DC-9-82)	*49972 / 1757*		*0090*	*0990*	*2 PW JT8D-217C*	*66678*	*Y163*		Rieti / *lsf Cofiri Leasing*
☐ I-DACP	Boeing (Douglas) MD-82 (DC-9-82)	*49973 / 1762*		*0090*	*0990*	*2 PW JT8D-217C*	*66678*	*Y163*		Padova
☐ I-DACQ	Boeing (Douglas) MD-82 (DC-9-82)	*49974 / 1774*		*1090*	*1090*	*2 PW JT8D-217C*	*66678*	*CY133*		Taranto
☐ I-DACR	Boeing (Douglas) MD-82 (DC-9-82)	*49975 / 1775*		*0090*	*1090*	*2 PW JT8D-217C*	*66678*	*CY133*		Carrara
☐ I-DACS	Boeing (Douglas) MD-82 (DC-9-82)	*53053 / 1806*		*0090*	*1290*	*2 PW JT8D-217C*	*66678*	*CY133*		Maratea
☐ I-DACT	Boeing (Douglas) MD-82 (DC-9-82)	*53054 / 1856*		*0091*	*0591*	*2 PW JT8D-217C*	*66678*	*CY133*		Valtellina
☐ I-DACU	Boeing (Douglas) MD-82 (DC-9-82)	*53055 / 1857*		*0091*	*0591*	*2 PW JT8D-217C*	*66678*	*Y163*		Brindisi
☐ I-DACV	Boeing (Douglas) MD-82 (DC-9-82)	*53056 / 1880*		*0091*	*0691*	*2 PW JT8D-217C*	*66678*	*Y163*		Riccione
☐ I-DACW	Boeing (Douglas) MD-82 (DC-9-82)	*53057 / 1894*		*0091*	*0891*	*2 PW JT8D-217C*	*66678*	*CY133*		Vieste
☐ I-DACX	Boeing (Douglas) MD-82 (DC-9-82)	*53060 / 1944*		*0091*	*1291*	*2 PW JT8D-217C*	*66678*	*CY133*		Piacenza / *opb Team*
☐ I-DACY	Boeing (Douglas) MD-82 (DC-9-82)	*53059 / 1942*		*0091*	*1291*	*2 PW JT8D-217C*	*66678*	*CY133*		Novara / *opb Team*
☐ I-DACZ	Boeing (Douglas) MD-82 (DC-9-82)	*53058 / 1927*		*0091*	*1091*	*2 PW JT8D-217C*	*66678*	*CY133*		Castelfidardo
☐ I-DAND	Boeing (Douglas) MD-82 (DC-9-82)	*53061 / 1957*		*0092*	*0192*	*2 PW JT8D-217C*	*66678*	*Y163*		Bolzano
☐ I-DANF	Boeing (Douglas) MD-82 (DC-9-82)	*53062 / 1960*		*0092*	*0192*	*2 PW JT8D-217C*	*66678*	*Y163*		Sassari
☐ I-DANG	Boeing (Douglas) MD-82 (DC-9-82)	*53176 / 1972*		*0192*	*0292*	*2 PW JT8D-217C*	*66678*	*Y163*		Benevento
☐ I-DANH	Boeing (Douglas) MD-82 (DC-9-82)	*53177 / 1973*		*0092*	*0392*	*2 PW JT8D-217C*	*66678*	*Y163*		Massina
☐ I-DANL	Boeing (Douglas) MD-82 (DC-9-82)	*53178 / 1994*		*0092*	*0492*	*2 PW JT8D-217C*	*66678*	*Y163*		Cosenza
☐ I-DANM	Boeing (Douglas) MD-82 (DC-9-82)	*53179 / 1997*		*0492*	*0592*	*2 PW JT8D-217C*	*66678*	*CY133*		Vicenza
☐ I-DANP	Boeing (Douglas) MD-82 (DC-9-82)	*53180 / 2002*		*0592*	*0692*	*2 PW JT8D-217C*	*66678*	*CY133*		Fabriano
☐ I-DANQ	Boeing (Douglas) MD-82 (DC-9-82)	*53181 / 2005*		*0692*	*0692*	*2 PW JT8D-217C*	*66678*	*Y163*		Lecce
☐ I-DANR	Boeing (Douglas) MD-82 (DC-9-82)	*53203 / 2007*		*0092*	*0792*	*2 PW JT8D-217C*	*66678*	*Y163*		Matera / *opb Team*
☐ I-DANU	Boeing (Douglas) MD-82 (DC-9-82)	*53204 / 2009*		*0092*	*0792*	*2 PW JT8D-217C*	*66678*	*Y163*		Trapani
☐ I-DANV	Boeing (Douglas) MD-82 (DC-9-82)	*53205 / 2028*		*0092*	*0992*	*2 PW JT8D-217C*	*66678*	*CY133*		Forte dei Marmi / *lsf Cofiri Leasing*
☐ I-DANW	Boeing (Douglas) MD-82 (DC-9-82)	*53206 / 2034*		*0092*	*1192*	*2 PW JT8D-217C*	*66678*	*CY133*		Siena
☐ I-DATA	Boeing (Douglas) MD-82 (DC-9-82)	*53216 / 2048*		*0093*	*0393*	*2 PW JT8D-217C*	*66678*	*CY133*		Gubbio
☐ I-DATB	Boeing (Douglas) MD-82 (DC-9-82)	*53221 / 2079*		*0094*	*0494*	*2 PW JT8D-217C*	*66678*	*CY133*		Bergamo
☐ I-DATC	Boeing (Douglas) MD-82 (DC-9-82)	*53222 / 2080*		*0094*	*0594*	*2 PW JT8D-217C*	*66678*	*Y163*		Foggia / *opb Team*
☐ I-DATD	Boeing (Douglas) MD-82 (DC-9-82)	*53223 / 2081*		*0094*	*0594*	*2 PW JT8D-217C*	*66678*	*CY133*		Savona
☐ I-DATE	Boeing (Douglas) MD-82 (DC-9-82)	*53217 / 2053*		*0093*	*0493*	*2 PW JT8D-217C*	*66678*	*Y163*		Grosseto
☐ I-DATF	Boeing (Douglas) MD-82 (DC-9-82)	*53224 / 2084*		*0094*	*0694*	*2 PW JT8D-217C*	*66678*	*CY133*		Vittorio Veneto / *opb Team*
☐ I-DATG	Boeing (Douglas) MD-82 (DC-9-82)	*53225 / 2086*		*0094*	*0794*	*2 PW JT8D-217C*	*66678*	*CY133*		Arezzo
☐ I-DATH	Boeing (Douglas) MD-82 (DC-9-82)	*53226 / 2087*		*0094*	*0794*	*2 PW JT8D-217C*	*66678*	*CY133*		Pescara / *opb Team*
☐ I-DATI	Boeing (Douglas) MD-82 (DC-9-82)	*53218 / 2060*		*0093*	*0593*	*2 PW JT8D-217C*	*66678*	*Y163*		Siracusa
☐ I-DATJ	Boeing (Douglas) MD-82 (DC-9-82)	*53227 / 2103*		*0095*	*0195*	*2 PW JT8D-217C*	*66678*	*CY133*		Lunigiana / *opb Team*
☐ I-DATK	Boeing (Douglas) MD-82 (DC-9-82)	*53228 / 2104*		*0095*	*0195*	*2 PW JT8D-217C*	*66678*	*CY133*		Ravenna / *opb Team*
☐ I-DATL	Boeing (Douglas) MD-82 (DC-9-82)	*53229 / 2105*		*0095*	*0295*	*2 PW JT8D-217C*	*66678*	*CY133*		Alghero / *opb Team*
☐ I-DATM	Boeing (Douglas) MD-82 (DC-9-82)	*53230 / 2106*		*0095*	*0295*	*2 PW JT8D-217C*	*66678*	*CY133*		Cividale del Friuli / *opb Team*
☐ I-DATN	Boeing (Douglas) MD-82 (DC-9-82)	*53231 / 2107*		*0095*	*0395*	*2 PW JT8D-217C*	*66678*	*CY133*		Sondrio / *opb Team*
☐ I-DATO	Boeing (Douglas) MD-82 (DC-9-82)	*53219 / 2062*		*0093*	*0693*	*2 PW JT8D-217C*	*66678*	*CY133*		Reggio Emilia / *opb Team*
☐ I-DATP	Boeing (Douglas) MD-82 (DC-9-82)	*53232 / 2108*		*0095*	*0495*	*2 PW JT8D-217C*	*66678*	*CY133*		Latina / *opb Team*
☐ I-DATQ	Boeing (Douglas) MD-82 (DC-9-82)	*53233 / 2110*		*0095*	*0495*	*2 PW JT8D-217C*	*66678*	*CY133*		Modena / *opb Team*
☐ I-DATR	Boeing (Douglas) MD-82 (DC-9-82)	*53234 / 2111*		*0095*	*0595*	*2 PW JT8D-217C*	*66678*	*CY133*		Livorno / *opb Team*
☐ I-DATS	Boeing (Douglas) MD-82 (DC-9-82)	*53235 / 2113*		*0095*	*0695*	*2 PW JT8D-217C*	*66678*	*CY133*		Foligno / *opb Team*
☐ I-DATU	Boeing (Douglas) MD-82 (DC-9-82)	*53220 / 2073*		*1193*	*0494*	*2 PW JT8D-217C*	*66678*	*CY133*		Verona
☐ I-DAVA	Boeing (Douglas) MD-82 (DC-9-82)	*49215 / 1253*		*0186*	*0286*	*2 PW JT8D-217A*	*66678*	*Y163*		Cuneo
☐ I-DAVB	Boeing (Douglas) MD-82 (DC-9-82)	*49216 / 1262*		*0286*	*0386*	*2 PW JT8D-217A*	*66678*	*CY133*		Ferrara
☐ I-DAVC	Boeing (Douglas) MD-82 (DC-9-82)	*49217 / 1268*		*0086*	*0486*	*2 PW JT8D-217A*	*66678*	*Y163*		Lucca
☐ I-DAVD	Boeing (Douglas) MD-82 (DC-9-82)	*49218 / 1274*		*0086*	*0586*	*2 PW JT8D-217A*	*66678*	*Y163*		Mantova
☐ I-DAVF	Boeing (Douglas) MD-82 (DC-9-82)	*49219 / 1310*		*0086*	*1086*	*2 PW JT8D-217A*	*66678*	*Y163*		Oristano
☐ I-DAVG	Boeing (Douglas) MD-82 (DC-9-82)	*49220 / 1319*		*1086*	*1186*	*2 PW JT8D-217A*	*66678*	*CY133*		Pesaro
☐ I-DAVH	Boeing (Douglas) MD-82 (DC-9-82)	*49221 / 1330*		*1186*	*0187*	*2 PW JT8D-217A*	*66678*	*CY133*		Salerno / *lsf San Paolo Leasint*
☐ I-DAVI	Boeing (Douglas) MD-82 (DC-9-82)	*49430 / 1334*		*0086*	*0187*	*2 PW JT8D-217A*	*66678*	*CY133*		Assisi
☐ I-DAVJ	Boeing (Douglas) MD-82 (DC-9-82)	*49431 / 1377*		*0087*	*0687*	*2 PW JT8D-217A*	*66678*	*CY133*		Parma
☐ I-DAVK	Boeing (Douglas) MD-82 (DC-9-82)	*49432 / 1378*		*0087*	*0687*	*2 PW JT8D-217A*	*66678*	*CY133*		Pompei
☐ I-DAVL	Boeing (Douglas) MD-82 (DC-9-82)	*49433 / 1428*		*0088*	*0188*	*2 PW JT8D-217A*	*66678*	*Y163*		Reggio Calabria

☐	I-DAVM	Boeing (Douglas) MD-82 (DC-9-82)	49434 / 1446		0088	0388	2 PW JT8D-217A	66678	CY133		Caserta
☐	I-DAVN	Boeing (Douglas) MD-82 (DC-9-82)	49435 / 1504		0088	1088	2 PW JT8D-217C	66678	Y163		Volterra / lsf SIPA S.A.
☐	I-DAVP	Boeing (Douglas) MD-82 (DC-9-82)	49549 / 1544		0088	1288	2 PW JT8D-217C	66678	Y163		Gorizia
☐	I-DAVR	Boeing (Douglas) MD-82 (DC-9-82)	49550 / 1584		0089	0489	2 PW JT8D-217C	66678	Y163		Pisa
☐	I-DAVS	Boeing (Douglas) MD-82 (DC-9-82)	49551 / 1586		0089	0589	2 PW JT8D-217C	66678	Y163		Catania
☐	I-DAVT	Boeing (Douglas) MD-82 (DC-9-82)	49552 / 1597		0589	0689	2 PW JT8D-217C	66678	Y163		Como
☐	I-DAVU	Boeing (Douglas) MD-82 (DC-9-82)	49794 / 1600		0089	0689	2 PW JT8D-217C	66678	Y163		Udine
☐	I-DAVV	Boeing (Douglas) MD-82 (DC-9-82)	49795 / 1639		0089	1089	2 PW JT8D-217C	66678	Y163		Pavia
☐	I-DAVW	Boeing (Douglas) MD-82 (DC-9-82)	49796 / 1713		0090	0590	2 PW JT8D-217C	66678	Y163		Camerino / lsf Cofiri Leasing
☐	I-DAVX	Boeing (Douglas) MD-82 (DC-9-82)	49969 / 1719		0090	0690	2 PW JT8D-217C	66678	Y163		Asti / lsf Cofiri Leasing
☐	I-DAVZ	Boeing (Douglas) MD-82 (DC-9-82)	49970 / 1737		0090	0790	2 PW JT8D-217C	66678	Y163		Brescia / lsf Cofiri Leasing
☐	I-DAWA	Boeing (Douglas) MD-82 (DC-9-82)	49192 / 1126	N19B*	0083	1283	2 PW JT8D-217A	66678	CY133		Roma
☐	I-DAWB	Boeing (Douglas) MD-82 (DC-9-82)	49197 / 1138		0084	0584	2 PW JT8D-217A	66678	CY133		Cagliari
☐	I-DAWC	Boeing (Douglas) MD-82 (DC-9-82)	49198 / 1142		0584	0684	2 PW JT8D-217A	66678	CY133		Campobasso
☐	I-DAWD	Boeing (Douglas) MD-82 (DC-9-82)	49199 / 1143		0584	0684	2 PW JT8D-217A	66678	CY133		Catanzaro
☐	I-DAWE	Boeing (Douglas) MD-82 (DC-9-82)	49193 / 1127	N13627*	0083	1283	2 PW JT8D-217A	66678	CY133		Milano
☐	I-DAWF	Boeing (Douglas) MD-82 (DC-9-82)	49200 / 1147		0084	0784	2 PW JT8D-217A	66678	CY133		Firenze
☐	I-DAWG	Boeing (Douglas) MD-82 (DC-9-82)	49201 / 1148		0084	0784	2 PW JT8D-217A	66678	CY133		L'Aquila
☐	I-DAWH	Boeing (Douglas) MD-82 (DC-9-82)	49202 / 1170		0084	1184	2 PW JT8D-217A	66678	CY133		Palermo
☐	I-DAWI	Boeing (Douglas) MD-82 (DC-9-82)	49194 / 1130		0184	0284	2 PW JT8D-217A	66678	CY133		Ancona
☐	I-DAWJ	Boeing (Douglas) MD-82 (DC-9-82)	49203 / 1174		0084	1284	2 PW JT8D-217A	66678	CY133		Genova
☐	I-DAWL	Boeing (Douglas) MD-82 (DC-9-82)	49204 / 1179		0085	0285	2 PW JT8D-217A	66678	CY133		Perugia
☐	I-DAWM	Boeing (Douglas) MD-82 (DC-9-82)	49205 / 1184		0085	0285	2 PW JT8D-217A	66678	CY133		Potenza
☐	I-DAWO	Boeing (Douglas) MD-82 (DC-9-82)	49195 / 1136		0084	0584	2 PW JT8D-217A	66678	CY133		Bari
☐	I-DAWP	Boeing (Douglas) MD-82 (DC-9-82)	49206 / 1188		0085	0385	2 PW JT8D-217A	66678	CY133		Torino
☐	I-DAWQ	Boeing (Douglas) MD-82 (DC-9-82)	49207 / 1189		0085	0385	2 PW JT8D-217A	66678	CY133		Trieste
☐	I-DAWR	Boeing (Douglas) MD-82 (DC-9-82)	49208 / 1190		0285	0385	2 PW JT8D-217A	66678	CY133		Venezia
☐	I-DAWS	Boeing (Douglas) MD-82 (DC-9-82)	49209 / 1191		0085	0485	2 PW JT8D-217A	66678	CY133		Aosta
☐	I-DAWT	Boeing (Douglas) MD-82 (DC-9-82)	49210 / 1192		0085	0485	2 PW JT8D-217A	66678	Y163		Napoli
☐	I-DAWU	Boeing (Douglas) MD-82 (DC-9-82)	49196 / 1137		0084	0584	2 PW JT8D-217A	66678	CY133		Bologna
☐	I-DAWV	Boeing (Douglas) MD-82 (DC-9-82)	49211 / 1202		0085	0585	2 PW JT8D-217A	66678	Y163		Trento
☐	I-DAWW	Boeing (Douglas) MD-82 (DC-9-82)	49212 / 1233		0085	1185	2 PW JT8D-217A	66678	Y163		Riace
☐	I-DAWY	Boeing (Douglas) MD-82 (DC-9-82)	49213 / 1243		1185	1285	2 PW JT8D-217A	66678	Y163		Agrigento
☐	I-DAWZ	Boeing (Douglas) MD-82 (DC-9-82)	49214 / 1245		0085	1285	2 PW JT8D-217A	66678	Y163		Avellino
☐	I-BIKA	Airbus Industrie A320-214	951	F-WWBT*	0099	0399	2 CFMI CFM56-5B4/P	73500	CY147		
☐	I-BIKB	Airbus Industrie A320-214					2 CFMI CFM56-5B4/P	73500	CY147		oo-delivery 0500
☐	I-BIKC	Airbus Industrie A320-214					2 CFMI CFM56-5B4/P	73500	CY147		oo-delivery 0400
☐	I-BIKD	Airbus Industrie A320-214					2 CFMI CFM56-5B4/P	73500	CY147		oo-delivery 0400
☐	I-BIKE	Airbus Industrie A320-214	999				2 CFMI CFM56-5B4/P	73500	CY147		oo-delivery 0599
☐	I-BIKF	Airbus Industrie A320-214					2 CFMI CFM56-5B4/P	73500	CY147		oo-delivery 0500
☐	I-BIKG	Airbus Industrie A320-214					2 CFMI CFM56-5B4/P	73500	CY147		oo-delivery 0500
☐	I-BIKI	Airbus Industrie A320-214					2 CFMI CFM56-5B4/P	73500	CY147		oo-delivery 0100
☐	I-BIKL	Airbus Industrie A320-214					2 CFMI CFM56-5B4/P	73500	CY147		oo-delivery 0601
☐	I-BIKM	Airbus Industrie A320-214					2 CFMI CFM56-5B4/P	73500	CY147		oo-delivery 0002
☐	I-BIKN	Airbus Industrie A320-214					2 CFMI CFM56-5B4/P	73500	CY147		oo-delivery 0002
☐	I-BIKO	Airbus Industrie A320-214					2 CFMI CFM56-5B4/P	73500	CY147		oo-delivery 0200
☐	I-BIKP	Airbus Industrie A320-214					2 CFMI CFM56-5B4/P	73500	CY147		oo-delivery 0002
☐	I-BIKQ	Airbus Industrie A320-214					2 CFMI CFM56-5B4/P	73500	CY147		oo-delivery 0002
☐	I-BIKR	Airbus Industrie A320-214					2 CFMI CFM56-5B4/P	73500	CY147		oo-delivery 0003
☐	I-BIKS	Airbus Industrie A320-214					2 CFMI CFM56-5B4/P	73500	CY147		oo-delivery 0003
☐	I-BIKT	Airbus Industrie A320-214					2 CFMI CFM56-5B4/P	73500	CY147		oo-delivery 0003
☐	I-BIKU	Airbus Industrie A320-214					2 CFMI CFM56-5B4/P	73500	CY147		oo-delivery 0500
☐	I-BIKV	Airbus Industrie A320-214					2 CFMI CFM56-5B4/P	73500	CY147		oo-delivery 0003
☐	I-BIXA	Airbus Industrie A321-112	477	D-AVZE*	0094	0394	2 CFMI CFM56-5B2	83000	CY187		Piazza del Duomo-Milano / opb Team
☐	I-BIXB	Airbus Industrie A321-112	524	D-AVZY*	0095	0595	2 CFMI CFM56-5B2	83000	CY187		Piazza Castello-Torino / opb Team
☐	I-BIXC	Airbus Industrie A321-112	526	D-AVZZ*	0095	0595	2 CFMI CFM56-5B2	83000	CY187	CH-FL	Piazza del Campo-Siena / opb Team
☐	I-BIXD	Airbus Industrie A321-112	532	D-AVZB*	0095	0695	2 CFMI CFM56-5B2	83000	CY187		Piazza Pretorio-Palermo / opb Team
☐	I-BIXE	Airbus Industrie A321-112	488	D-AVZG*	0094	0594	2 CFMI CFM56-5B2	83000	CY187		Piazza di Spagna-Roma / opb Team
☐	I-BIXF	Airbus Industrie A321-112	515	D-AVZQ*	0095	0995	2 CFMI CFM56-5B2	83000	CY187		Pz.Maggiore-Bologna / opb Team/cvtd-111
☐	I-BIXG	Airbus Industrie A321-112	516	D-AVZR*	0095	0995	2 CFMI CFM56-5B2	83000	CY187		Pz.dei Miracoli-Pisa / opbTeam/cvtd-111
☐	I-BIXH	Airbus Industrie A321-112	940	D-AVZS*	0099	0199	2 CFMI CFM56-5B2	83000	CY187		opb Team
☐	I-BIXI	Airbus Industrie A321-112	494	D-AVZI*	0094	0694	2 CFMI CFM56-5B2	83000	CY187		Piazza San Marco-Venezia / opb Team
☐	I-BIXJ	Airbus Industrie A321-112	959		0099	0399	2 CFMI CFM56-5B2	83000	CY187		opb Team
☐	I-BIXK	Airbus Industrie A321-112					2 CFMI CFM56-5B2	83000	CY187		oo-delivery 0400 / to be opb Team
☐	I-BIXL	Airbus Industrie A321-112	513	D-AVZO*	0095	0196	2 CFMI CFM56-5B2	83000	CY187		Pz.Duomo-Lecce / lsfNBB/opbTeam/cvtd111
☐	I-BIXM	Airbus Industrie A321-112	514	D-AVZP*	0095	0296	2 CFMI CFM56-5B2	83000	CY187		S.Francesco-Assisi / lsfNBB/opbTeam/cv111
☐	I-BIXN	Airbus Industrie A321-112	576	D-AVZR*	0096	0396	2 CFMI CFM56-5B2	83000	CY187		Pz.del Duomo-Catania / lsf NBB/opb Team
☐	I-BIXO	Airbus Industrie A321-112	495	D-AVZJ*	0094	0794	2 CFMI CFM56-5B2	83000	CY187		Piazza Plebiscito-Napoli / opb Team
☐	I-BIXP	Airbus Industrie A321-112	583	D-AVZT*	0096	0496	2 CFMI CFM56-5B2	83000	CY187		Carlo Morelli / lsf NBB Lease/opb Team
☐	I-BIXQ	Airbus Industrie A321-112	586	D-AVZU*	0096	0297	2 CFMI CFM56-5B2	83000	CY187		Domenico Colapietro / lsf NBB/opb Team
☐	I-BIXR	Airbus Industrie A321-112	593	D-AVZW*	0096	0297	2 CFMI CFM56-5B2	83000	CY187		Piazza del Campidoglio-Roma / opb Team
☐	I-BIXS	Airbus Industrie A321-112	599	D-AVZZ*	0096	0497	2 CFMI CFM56-5B2	83000	CY187	CF-JM	Piazza S.Martino-Lucca / opb Team
☐	I-BIXT	Airbus Industrie A321-112	765	D-AVZW*	0098	0198	2 CFMI CFM56-5B2	83000	CY187		Piazza della Signoria-Vizenza / opbTeam
☐	I-BIXU	Airbus Industrie A321-112	434	D-AVZB*	0093	1194	2 CFMI CFM56-5B2	83000	CY187		Pz del.Signoria-Firenze / cvtd 111/Team
☐	I-BIXV	Airbus Industrie A321-112	819	D-AVZU*	0098	0598	2 CFMI CFM56-5B2	83000	CY187		Pzz.del Rinaccimento-Urbino / opb Team
☐	I-BIXZ	Airbus Industrie A321-112	848	D-AVZC*	0098	0798	2 CFMI CFM56-5B2	83000	CY187		Piazza del Duomo-Orvieto / opb Team
☐	I-	Airbus Industrie A321-112					2 CFMI CFM56-5B2	83000	CY187		oo-delivery 0002 / to be opb Team
☐	I-	Airbus Industrie A321-112					2 CFMI CFM56-5B2	83000	CY187		oo-delivery 0003 / to be opb Team
☐	I-BUSM	Airbus Industrie A300B2-203	049	N291EA	0077	0988	2 GE CF6-50C2	142000	Y296	JM-BE	Raffaello / std FCO/for sale
☐	I-BUSN	Airbus Industrie A300B2-203	051	N292EA	0078	1288	2 GE CF6-50C2	142000	Y296	JM-BF	Giotto / std FCO/for sale
☐	I-BUSP	Airbus Industrie A300B4-103	067	N207EA	0078	1188	2 GE CF6-50C2	157500	Y296	CH-EK	Masaccio / std FCO/for sale
☐	I-BUSQ	Airbus Industrie A300B4-103	118	N401UA	0080	0489	2 GE CF6-50C2	157500	Y296	CH-FJ	Michelangelo / std FCO/for sale
☐	I-BUSR	Airbus Industrie A300B4-103	120	N402UA	0080	0489	2 GE CF6-50C2	157500	Y296	CH-FK	Cimabue / std FCO/for sale
☐	I-BUST	Airbus Industrie A300B4-203	068	N403UA	0079	0789	2 GE CF6-50C2	165000	C70Y169	HL-AB	Piero Francesca / cvtd-103/std FCO/FS
☐	I-DEIB	Boeing 767-33A (ER)	27376 / 560	G-OITA	0094	0195	2 GE CF6-80C2B6F	184612	C25Y198	JK-HL	Pier Paolo Racchetti / lsf AWAS/opbTeam
☐	I-DEIC	Boeing 767-33A (ER)	27377 / 561	G-OITB	0094	0195	2 GE CF6-80C2B6F	184612	C25Y202	JM-BH	Alberto Nassetti / lsf AWAS/opb Team
☐	I-DEID	Boeing 767-33A (ER)	27468 / 584	G-OITC	0095	0695	2 GE CF6-80C2B6F	184612	C25Y202	JM-BK	Marco Polo / lsf AWAS / opb Team
☐	I-DEIF	Boeing 767-33A (ER)	27908 / 578	G-OITF	0095	0895	2 GE CF6-80C2B6F	184612	C25Y202	JM-BL	Cristoforo Colombo / lsf SALE/opb Team
☐	I-DEIG	Boeing 767-33A (ER)	27918 / 603	G-OITG	0096	0296	2 GE CF6-80C2B6F	184612	C25Y202	JM-DE	Francesco Agello / lsf SALE / opb Team
☐	I-DEIL	Boeing 767-33A (ER)	28147 / 611	G-OITL	0096	0496	2 GE CF6-80C2B6F	184612	C25Y202	JM-DK	Arturo Ferrarin / lsf SALE / opb Team
☐	EI-CRL	Boeing 767-36M (ER)	30008 /				2 GE CF6-80C2B6F	184612	C25Y202		to be lsf GECA 0599 / opb Team
☐	EI-CRM	Boeing 767-36M (ER)	30009 /				2 GE CF6-80C2B6F	184612	C25Y202		to be lsf GECO 0599 / opb Team
☐	I-DUPA	Boeing (Douglas) MD-11F (C)	48426 / 468	N9020Z*	0092	0392	3 GE CF6-80C2D1F	280320	F12C24Y174/Plts	FK-DJ	Gioacchino Rossini / opb Team
☐	I-DUPB	Boeing (Douglas) MD-11	48431 / 534		0093	0493	3 GE CF6-80C2D1F	280320	F12C24Y215	FK-EJ	Pietro Mascagni / opb Team
☐	I-DUPC	Boeing (Douglas) MD-11	48581 / 565		0094	0594	3 GE CF6-80C2D1F	283722	F12C24Y215	FK-EM	V. Bellini / opb Team
☐	I-DUPD	Boeing (Douglas) MD-11	48630 / 567		0094	0694	3 GE CF6-80C2D1F	283722	F12C24Y215	FK-DE	G. Donizetti / opb Team
☐	I-DUPE	Boeing (Douglas) MD-11F (C)	48427 / 471	N9020Z*	0091	1191	3 GE CF6-80C2D1F	280320	F12C24Y174/Plts	FK-DL	Giuseppe Verdi / opb Team
☐	I-DUPI	Boeing (Douglas) MD-11F (C)	48428 / 474		0091	1291	3 GE CF6-80C2D1F	280320	F12C24Y174/Plts	FK-DM	Giacomo Puccini / opb Team
☐	I-DUPO	Boeing (Douglas) MD-11F (C)	48429 / 500		0092	0792	3 GE CF6-80C2D1F	280320	F12C24Y174/Plts	FK-EG	Nicolo Paganini / lsf Cofiri / opb Team
☐	I-DUPU	Boeing (Douglas) MD-11F (C)	48430 / 508		0092	0892	3 GE CF6-80C2D1F	280320	F12C24Y174/Plts	FK-EH	Antonio Vivaldi / lsf Spei Lsg/opb Team
☐	I-DEMC	Boeing 747-243B (SF)	22506 / 492		0080	1180	4 GE CF6-50E2	362874	Freighter	EJ-HM	Atlante / lsf Cofiri Lsg/cvtd -243B (M)
☐	I-DEMF	Boeing 747-243B (M)	22508 / 499		0080	1280	4 GE CF6-50E2	362874	C36Y368	EK-HM	Portofino / lsf Leasing Roma
☐	I-DEMG	Boeing 747-243B	22510 / 533		0081	0881	4 GE CF6-50E2	362874	C36Y368	EK-LM	Cervinia / lsf IN Leasing
☐	I-DEML	Boeing 747-243B	22511 / 536		0081	0981	4 GE CF6-50E2	362874	C36Y368	FK-DG	Sorrento
☐	I-DEMN	Boeing 747-243B	22512 / 542		0081	1181	4 GE CF6-50E2	362874	C36Y368	JK-GH	Porto Cervo
☐	I-DEMP	Boeing 747-243B	22513 / 546		0081	1281	4 GE CF6-50E2	362874	C36Y368	JK-GL	Capri
☐	I-DEMR	Boeing 747-243F (SCD)	22545 / 545		0081	1281	4 GE CF6-50E2	377842	Freighter	EJ-KL	Titano
☐	I-DEMS	Boeing 747-243B	22969 / 575	N8289V*	0083	0283	4 GE CF6-50E2	362874	C36Y368	FK-GJ	Argentario / Bulgari Watch-colors
☐	I-DEMV	Boeing 747-243B	23301 / 618	N6018N*	0085	0785	4 GE CF6-50E2	371946	C36Y368	EK-JM	Sestriere
☐	I-DEMY	Boeing 747-230B	21589 / 345	D-ABYN	1178	0790	4 GE CF6-50E2	362874	C36Y368	EK-JL	Asolo

ALITALIA EXPRESS, SpA = XM / SMX (Subsidiary of Alitalia-Linee Aeree Italiane, SpA) **Rome-Fiumicino**

Centro Direzionale, Viale Alessandro Marchetti 111, I-00148 Roma, Italy ☎ (06) 65 591 Tx: none Fax: (06) 655 15 02 SITA: QLTXMAZ

F: 1997 ⁂ 290 Head: Massimo Chieli ICAO: CEE-CEE EXPRESS Net: n/a Flights are operated on behalf/in conjunction with ALITALIA using AZ-flight numbers.

☐	I-ATRD	ATR 42-300	032	F-WWEN*	0086	1097	2 PWC PW120	16700	Y46		Lago Trasimeno
☐	I-ATRF	ATR 42-300	034	F-WWEP*	0086	1097	2 PWC PW120	16700	Y46		Flumendosa
☐	I-ATRG	ATR 42-300	042	F-WWEW*	0087	1097	2 PWC PW120	16700	Y46		Lago Maggiore
☐	I-ATRJ	ATR 42-300	057	F-WWEL*	0087	1097	2 PWC PW120	16700	Y46		Lago di Bolsena
☐	I-ATRL	ATR 42-300	068	F-WWES*	0088	1097	2 PWC PW120	16700	Y46		Fiume Adige
☐	I-ATRN	ATR 42-300	020	SX-BIX	0086	1097	2 PWC PW120	16700	Y46		Fiume Arno
☐	I-ATRP	ATR 42-300	021	SX-BIY	0086	1097	2 PWC PW120	16700	Y46		Lago di Garda

211 registration type of aircraft cn/fn ex/ex* mfd del powered by mtow kg configuration selcal name/fln/specialitites/remarks

registration	type of aircraft	cn/fn	ex/ex*	mfd	del	powered by	mtow kg	configuration	selcal	name/fln/specialitites/remarks
☐ I-NOWA	ATR 42-300	051	F-WWEF*	0087	1097	2 PWC PW120	16700	Y46		Fiume Po
☐ I-NOWT	ATR 42-300	054	F-WWEI*	0087	1097	2 PWC PW120	16700	Y46		Fiume Tevere
☐ EI-CLB	ATR 72-212	423	F-WWEB*	0094	1097	2 PWC PW127	21500	Y66		Lago di Bracciano / Isf Tarquin Ltd
☐ EI-CLC	ATR 72-212	428	F-WWEF*	0095	1097	2 PWC PW127	21500	Y66		Fiume Simeto / Isf Tarquin Ltd
☐ EI-CLD	ATR 72-212	432	F-WWEL*	0095	1097	2 PWC PW127	21500	Y66		Fiume Piave / Isf Tarquin Ltd
☐ EI-CMJ	ATR 72-212	467	F-WHLU*	0095	1097	2 PWC PW127	21500	Y66		Fiume Volturno / Isf Tarquin Ltd
☐ I-	ATR 72-500 (72-212)					2 PWC PW127F	22500	Y66		oo-delivery 0799
☐ I-	ATR 72-500 (72-212)					2 PWC PW127F	22500	Y66		oo-delivery 0999
☐ I-	ATR 72-500 (72-212)					2 PWC PW127F	22500	Y66		oo-delivery 1299

ALIVEN, Srl. = LVN — Verona

Via P. Bembo 70, I-37062 Dossobuono, (VR), Italy ☎ (045) 861 92 15 Tx: n/a Fax: (045) 861 92 14 SITA: n/a
F: 1984 ⁂ 4 Head: Capt. Mauro Cittadini ICAO: ALIVEN Net: http://www.easynet.it/aliven

☐ I-FARN	Cessna 500 Citation I	500-0401	N2651	0080	0198	2 PWC JT15D-1A	5375	Executive		Isf Locafit
☐ I-ZOOM	Learjet 35A	35A-135	N11AK	0077	1295	2 GA TFE731-2-2B	8302	Exec / EMS		Isf Locat

ALPI EAGLES, SpA = E8 / ELG — Venice-Marco Polo & Verona-Villafranca

Via Mattei 1, I-30020 Marcon, (VE), Italy ☎ (041) 599 77 77 Tx: 483025 eagles i Fax: (041) 599 77 08 SITA: n/a
F: 1979 ⁂ 16 Head: Avv. Ennio Arengi IATA: 789 ICAO: ALPI EAGLES Net: n/a Aircraft below MTOW 1361kg: Siai F260C

☐ I-MALL	Agusta A109E Power	11023		0098	0098	2 PWC PW206C	2850	Executive		Isf Alicante Srl.
☐ I-ALPN	Piaggio P.180 Avanti	1015		0092	0593	2 PWC PT6A-66	5239	Executive		Isf ABF Leasing SpA
☐ I-ALPR	Learjet 55	55-078	N56TG	0083	0790	2 GA TFE731-3AR-2B	9752	Executive		Isf Locat
☐ I-ALPK	Fokker 100 (F28 Mk0100)	11244	HB-IVA	0088	0696	2 RR Tay 620-15	44450	C28Y57		Sant Antonio / Isf San Paolo Leasint
☐ I-ALPL	Fokker 100 (F28 Mk0100)	11250	F-WQHG	0088	0696	2 RR Tay 620-15	44450	C28Y57		San Marco / Isf San Paolo Leasint
☐ I-ALPQ	Fokker 100 (F28 Mk0100)	11256	F-WQFP	0088	0597	2 RR Tay 620-15	44450	C28Y57		San Pietro / Isf San Paolo Leasint SpA
☐ I-ALPS	Fokker 100 (F28 Mk0100)	11254	HB-IVF	0088	0896	2 RR Tay 620-15	44450	C28Y57		Isf San Paolo Leasint SpA
☐ I-ALPX	Fokker 100 (F28 Mk0100)	11251	F-WQFL	0088	0297	2 RR Tay 620-15	44450	C28Y57		San Vincenzo / Isf Ithifly SpA
☐ I-ALPZ	Fokker 100 (F28 Mk0100)	11252	HB-IVD	0088	0996	2 RR Tay 620-15	44450	C28Y57		Isf Ithifly SpA

ATAL Milano, Srl. = IOI — Milan-Bresso

Via Locatelli 6, I-20124 Milano, (MI), Italy ☎ (02) 66 50 16 42 Tx: none Fax: (02) 66 50 16 42 SITA: n/a
F: 1954 ⁂ 4 Head: Enrico Davide Genovesi ICAO: ATALMILANO Net: n/a Aircraft below MTOW 1361kg: Agusta-Bell 47J, Breda Nardi NH-300C & Schweizer 269C (300C)

☐ I-SOUL	Bell 206B JetRanger	1599	I-MIBE	0075		1 AN 250-C20	1450			
☐ I-FAIV	Agusta-Bell 204B	3048	OE-EXO	0063	0098	1 RR Gnome H.1200-610	3856			

AVIO NORD, Srl. = FNM — Milan-Linate

Piazzale Cadorna 14, I-20123 Milano, Italy ☎ (02) 86 27 24 Tx: n/a Fax: (02) 869 37 10 SITA: n/a
F: 1989 ⁂ n/a Head: Daniele Paggiaro Net: http://www.ferrovienord.it

☐ I-CRMD	Agusta A109A II	7301		0085		2 AN 250-C20B	2600			

AVIORIPRESE JET EXECUTIVE, SpA = VJG (formerly Aviopriprese, Srl.) — Naples-Capodichino

Aeroporto di Capodichino, I-80144 Napoli, (NA), Italy ☎ (081) 584 43 19 Tx: n/a Fax: (081) 584 14 81 SITA: n/a
F: n/a ⁂ n/a Head: n/a ICAO: AVIORIPRESE Net: n/a

☐ I-AVJC	Bell 206B JetRanger III	1491	N777FL	0074		1 AN 250-C20B	1450			cvtd JetRanger
☐ I-GJUL	Partenavia P.68B	206		0079		2 LY IO-360-A1B6	1990			
☐ I-OBPC	Partenavia P.68 Observer	261-08-OB		0083		2 LY IO-360-A1B6	1960			
☐ I-AVJJ	Agusta A109A	7154	I-CELB	0078	0798	2 AN 250-C20B	2600			
☐ I-CBLT	Agusta A109A	7175		0080		2 AN 250-C20B	2600			
☐ I-DCVM	Agusta A109A	7109		0075		2 AN 250-C20B	2600			Isf Compagnia Regionale Leasing
☐ I-AVJE	Learjet 25D	25D-254	N973	0078		2 GE CJ610-8A	6804			
☐ I-AVJG	Learjet 35A	35A-189	N727JP	0078	1196	2 GA TFE731-2-2B	7711			Isf Locat

AVIOSARDA AIRLINES = DF / ADZ (Aviosarda, Srl. dba) — Olbia

Aeroporto Olbia-Costa Smeralda, I-07026 Olbia, (SS), Italy ☎ (0789) 64 50 17 Tx: none Fax: (0789) 68 035 SITA: n/a
F: n/a ⁂ n/a Head: Antonio Depau ICAO: AVIOSARDA Net: n/a Suspended operations (with ATR42 aircraft) 1098. Intends to re-start.

AZZURRAAIR, SpA = ZS / AZI (Alitalia Express) (Associated with Air Malta, Co. Ltd) — Bergamo-Orio Al Serio

Viale Papa Giovanni 48, I-24100 Bergamo, Italy ☎ (035) 416 03 11 Tx: none Fax: (035) 416 03 00 SITA: n/a
F: 1995 ⁂ 70 Head: Dominic R. Attard IATA: 864 ICAO: AZZURRA AIR Net: n/a All aircraft are in ALITALIA EXPRESS-colors with both titles and are partly operated in conjunction with/on behalf of ALITALIA as ALITALIA EXPRESS, using AZ-flight numbers. Beside aircraft listed, a BAe 146-200 is lsf/opb FLIGHTLINE (G-) under a wet-lease agreement. For details – see under that company.

☐ EI-COQ	Avro RJ70 (Avro 146-RJ70)	E1254	9H-ACM	0094	1097	4 LY LF507-1F	43091	CY82		Isf Peregrine Aviation / AZ Express-cs
☐ EI-CPJ	Avro RJ70 (Avro 146-RJ70)	E1258	9H-ACN	0094	0398	4 LY LF507-1F	43091	CY82		Puglia / Isf Peregrine / AZ Express-cs
☐ EI-CPK	Avro RJ70 (Avro 146-RJ70)	E1260	9H-ACO	0094	0398	4 LY LF507-1F	43091	CY82		Calabria / Isf Peregrine/AZ Express-cs
☐ EI-CPL	Avro RJ70 (Avro 146-RJ70)	E1267	9H-ACP	0095	0398	4 LY LF507-1F	43091	CY82		Isf Peregrine Aviation / AZ Express-cs
☐ EI-CNI	Avro RJ85 (Avro 146-RJ85)	E2299	G-6-299*	0096	1196	4 LY LF507-1F	43998	CY92		Lombardia / Isf Peregrine/AZ Express-cs
☐ EI-CNJ	Avro RJ85 (Avro 146-RJ85)	E2300	G-6-300*	0096	1296	4 LY LF507-1F	43998	CY92		Piemonte / Isf Peregrine/AZ Express-cs
☐ EI-CNK	Avro RJ85 (Avro 146-RJ85)	E2306	G-6-306*	0097	0597	4 LY LF507-1F	43998	CY92		Lazio / Isf Peregrine / AZ Express-cs

BENAIR, SpA = BEI (Member of Benetton Group) — Treviso

Via Villa Minelli 1, I-31050 Ponzano Veneto, (TV), Italy ☎ (0422) 26 36 36 Tx: none Fax: (0422) 43 09 85 SITA: n/a
F: 1990 ⁂ 16 Head: Sergio Valori ICAO: BENAIR Net: http://www.benairmall.it

☐ I-ASAZ	Cessna 550 Citation II	550-0432	N432CC	0082		2 PWC JT15D-4	6033			
☐ I-BETV	Cessna 650 Citation III	650-0104	N13195	0086		2 GA TFE731-3B-100S	9979		AD-BK	
☐ I-BEWW	Canadair CL-601-3A (CL-600-2B16) Chal.	5020	C-FBKR	0088		2 GE CF34-3A	20457		AH-CF	

BESIT, Srl. - Servizi Aerei = BST — Olbia

Aeroporto Costa Smeralda, I-07026 Olbia, (SS), Sardinia, Italy ☎ (0789) 67 042 Tx: n/a Fax: (0789) 69 149 SITA: n/a
F: n/a ⁂ 8 Head: n/a ICAO: BESIT Net: n/a

☐ I-NARB	Fairchild (Swearingen) SA226AT Merlin IV	AT-020	N747BD	0074		2 GA TPE331-3U-303G	5670	Freighter		Cises
☐ I-NARC	Fairchild (Swearingen) SA226AT Merlin IV	AT-035	N90090	0075		2 GA TPE331-3U-303G	5670	Freighter		Isf Desio & Brianza Leasing
☐ I-NARW	Fairchild (Swearingen) SA226AT Merlin IV	AT-058	D-ICFB	0077		2 GA TPE331-3U-303G	5670	Freighter		
☐ I-BSTS	Fairchild (Swearingen) SA227AC Metro III	AC-603	N3117S	0084	0298	2 GA TPE331-11U-611G	6577	Y19		Ist Locafit

BLUE PANORAMA AIRLINES, SpA = 9S / BPA (Subsidiary of Astra Travel) — Rome-Fiumicino

Via L. Bissolati 76, I-00187 Roma, Italy ☎ (06) 42 01 29 53 Tx: none Fax: (06) 42 00 31 16 SITA: n/a
F: 1998 ⁂ n/a Head: Franco Pecci ICAO: BLUE JET Net: n/a

☐ XA-SWO	Boeing 737-33A	27284 / 2606	CS-TKF	0094	0499	2 CFMI CFM56-3B2	62822	Y148		Isf BPA
☐ D-AHLR	Boeing 737-4K5	24901 / 1854		0090	1298	2 CFMI CFM56-3C1	68000	Y167		Isf Defag Leasing Co.

CAF, Srl. - Consorzio Aeromobili Fiat = AFF (Member of Gruppo Fiat) — Turin-Caselle

Aeroporto "Città di Torino", I-10072 Caselle Torinese, (TO), Italy ☎ (011) 996 18 27 Tx: n/a Fax: (011) 996 24 84 SITA: n/a
F: n/a ⁂ n/a Head: n/a ICAO: AEROCAF Net: n/a

☐ I-FLYK	Dassault Falcon 20E	241	HZ-PL7	0071	0096	2 GE CF700-2D2	13000			Isf Eurofly Service
☐ I-CAFD	Dassault Falcon 50	183	F-WWHF*	0088		2 GA TFE731-3-1C	18500			Isf Italease

C.A.I. - Compagnia Aeronautica Italiana, SpA = KVY — Rome-Ciampino

Aeroporto Ciampino Ovest, I-00040 Roma, Italy ☎ (06) 79 34 03 41 Tx: 613298 cai i Fax: (06) 79 49 26 95 SITA: n/a
F: 1979 ⁂ 25 Head: n/a ICAO: KILO VICTOR Net: n/a

☐ I-DPCA	Agusta A109A II	7322	MM81223	0086		2 AN 250-C20B	2600	EMS		opf Protezione Civile
☐ I-DPCB	Agusta A109A II	7323	MM81224	0086		2 AN 250-C20B	2600	EMS		opf Protezione Civile
☐ I-DPCC	Agusta A109A	7226	MM80752	0081		2 AN 250-C20B	2600	EMS		opf Protezione Civile
☐ I-DPCJ	Agusta A109K2	10034		0097	1097	2 TU Arriel 1K1	2850	EMS		opf Protezione Civile
☐ I-SAME	Dassault Falcon 50	37	F-WZMH*	0081		3 GA TFE731-3-1C	17600	Executive		
☐ I-DIES	Dassault Falcon 900	30	F-WGTH*	0088	0595	3 GA TFE731-5AR-1C	21092	Executive		
☐ I-FICV	Dassault Falcon 900	54	F-WWFC*	0089	0189	3 GA TFE731-5AR-1C	20638	Executive	AK-HM	
☐ I-NUMI	Dassault Falcon 900	89	F-WWFB*	0091	0291	3 GA TFE731-5AR-1C	20638	Executive	AK-HM	

CIOCCO TRAVEL (Il Ciocco International Travel Service, Srl. dba) — Lucca

Castelvecchio Pascoli, I-55020 Barga, (LU), Italy ☎ (0583) 71 91 Tx: 500447 ciocco i Fax: (0583) 72 31 97 SITA: n/a
F: n/a ⁂ n/a Head: n/a Net: n/a Aircraft below MTOW 1361kg: Robinson R22.

☐ I-CIOH	Eurocopter (Aerosp.) SA365N Dauphin 2	6004	F-WZJS*	0080		2 TU Arriel 1C	4000			

COMPAGNIA GENERALE RIPRESEAEREE, SpA = CGR

Parma

Via Cremonese 35A, I-43010 Fontana, (PR), Italy ☎ (0521) 99 49 48 Tx: 530464 cgr pr i Fax: (0521) 99 28 03 SITA: n/a
F: 1969 ♦♦♦ n/a Head: Licinio Ferretti ICAO: COMPRIP Net: n/a

	registration	type of aircraft	cn/fn	ex/ex*	mfd	del	powered by	mtow kg	configuration	selcal	name/fln/specialtites/remarks
☐	I-LJFE	Aeronautica Macchi AL.60-B2	89 / 269		0069		1 CO TSIO-470-B	1746			
☐	I-ANCP	Partenavia P.68B	17		0074		2 LY IO-360-A1B6	1960			
☐	I-ATAT	Partenavia P.68C-TC	254-14-TC		0081		2 LY TIO-360-C1A6D	1990			
☐	I-GIFE	Partenavia P.68C	335		0085		2 LY IO-360-A1B6	1990			
☐	I-LYFE	Partenavia P.68	12		0073		2 LY IO-360-A1B	1960			
☐	I-BGFE	Piper PA-31-350 Navajo Chieftain	31-7652043	N59772	0075		2 LY TIO-540-J2BD	3175			
☐	I-MAFE	CASA 212-CC Aviocar Srs 200	273	EC-DVD	0084	0393	2 GA TPE331-10-501C	7700			
☐	I-BMFE	Learjet 25C	25C-146	N6KJ	0073		2 GE CJ610-6	6804			
☐	I-BLUB	Cessna 650 Citation VI	650-0216	N68269	0092		2 GA TFE731-3B-100S	9979			lsf Barilla Servizi Finanziari

CONDOMETT, Srl. = OND

Fidenza Heliport

Via Coduro 3A, I-43036 Fidenza, (PR), Italy ☎ (0524) 81 048 Tx: none Fax: (0524) 52 54 29 SITA: n/a
F: 1969 ♦♦♦ 4 Head: Antonino Besagni ICAO: CONDOMETT Net: n/a

☐	I-OMET	Eurocopter (Aerosp.) AS350B Ecureuil	2490	F-WYMQ*	0091		1 TU Arriel 1B	1950			
☐	I-VBIT	Eurocopter (Aerosp.) AS350B Ecureuil	1553		0082		1 TU Arriel 1B	1950			

CORPO FORESTALE DELLO STATO – CFS (Division of Ministerio dell'Agricoltura e delle Foreste)

Rome-Urbe & -Ciampino

Centro Operativo Aeromobili, Via Salaria 825, I-00138 Roma, Italy ☎ (06) 812 02 44 Tx: n/a Fax: (06) 886 04 01 SITA: n/a
F: n/a ♦♦♦ n/a Head: n/a Net: n/a Aircraft below MTOW 1361kg: Hughes 369HS (500C). Non-commercial state organisation conducting surveillance flights for the protection of Italian forests.

☐	I-CFSD	Breda Nardi (Hughes) NH-500D	BH-01		0080	0780	1 AN 250-C20B	1360			CFS-04
☐	I-CFSE	Breda Nardi (Hughes) NH-500D	BH-02		0080	0780	1 AN 250-C20B	1360			CFS-05
☐	I-CFSF	Breda Nardi (Hughes) NH-500D	BH-03		0080	0780	1 AN 250-C20B	1360			CFS-06
☐	I-CFSG	Breda Nardi (Hughes) NH-500D	BH-04		0081	1181	1 AN 250-C20B	1360			CFS-07
☐	I-CFSH	Breda Nardi (Hughes) NH-500D	BH-05		0081	1181	1 AN 250-C20B	1360			CFS-08
☐	I-CFSI	Breda Nardi (Hughes) NH-500D	BH-06		0081	1181	1 AN 250-C20B	1360			CFS-09
☐	I-CFSK	Breda Nardi (Hughes) NH-500D	BH-07		0083	1083	1 AN 250-C20B	1360			CFS-10
☐	I-CFSL	Breda Nardi (Hughes) NH-500D	BH-15		0085	0186	1 AN 250-C20B	1360			CFS-11
☐	I-CFSM	Breda Nardi (Hughes) NH-500D	BH-16		0086	0486	1 AN 250-C20B	1360			CFS-12
☐	I-CFSN	Breda Nardi (Hughes) NH-500D	BH-17		0086	0786	1 AN 250-C20B	1360			CFS-13
☐	I-CFAA	Agusta-Bell 412SP	25610		0091	0991	2 PWC PT6T-3B TwinPac	5400			CFS-20 / lsf Banca Nazionale dell'Agri.
☐	I-CFAB	Agusta-Bell 412SP	25614		0091	0991	2 PWC PT6T-3B TwinPac	5400			CFS-21 / lsf Banca Nazionale dell'Agri.
☐	I-CFAC	Agusta-Bell 412SP	25615		0091	1191	2 PWC PT6T-3B TwinPac	5400			CFS-22 / lsf Banca Nazionale dell'Agri.
☐	I-CFAD	Agusta-Bell 412SP	25618		0091	1191	2 PWC PT6T-3B TwinPac	5400			CFS-23 / lsf Banca Nazionale dell'Agri.
☐	I-CFSJ	Agusta-Bell 412	25561		0088	1288	2 PWC PT6T-3B TwinPac	5260			CFS-14
☐	I-CFSO	Agusta-Bell 412	25562		0088	1288	2 PWC PT6T-3B TwinPac	5260			CFS-15
☐	I-CFSP	Agusta-Bell 412	25563		0088	0189	2 PWC PT6T-3B TwinPac	5260			CFS-16
☐	I-CFSW	Agusta-Bell 412	25564		0089	0789	2 PWC PT6T-3B TwinPac	5260			CFS-18
☐	I-CFSX	Agusta-Bell 412	25572		0088	0189	2 PWC PT6T-3B TwinPac	5260			CFS-19
☐	I-CFST	Canadair CL-215 (CL-215-1A10)	1072	MM62019	0082	0787	2 PW R-2800-CA3	19731	Tanker		2 / opb SISAM
☐	I-CFSZ	Canadair CL-215 (CL-215-1A10)	1108	C-FFYO*	0088	1288	2 PW R-2800-CA3	19731	Tanker		4 / opb SISAM

E.A.S. Aeroservizi – Executive Aviation Services = GDM (E.A.S. di Peruffo Giorgio e C., Sas dba)

Vicenza

Via S. Antonino 59, I-36100 Vicenza, (VI), Italy ☎ (0444) 92 36 36 Tx: 482104 i Fax: (0444) 92 39 98 SITA: n/a
F: 1993 ♦♦♦ 10 Head: Capt. Giorgio Peruffo ICAO: AEROSERVIZI Net: n/a

☐	I-OTEL	Cessna 501 Citation I/SP	501-0048	N414CC	0078	0098	2 PWC JT15D-1A	5375			lsf Italfly Srl.4
☐	I-MOCO	Learjet 35A	35A-445	HB-VHG	0081		2 GA TFE731-2-2B	8301			lsf Locat

ELIABRUZZO, Srl.

San Martino sulla Marrucina

Zona Industriale Loc. Campotrino, I-66010 San Martino sulla Marrucina, (CH), Italy ☎ (0871) 85 351 Tx: n/a Fax: (0871) 80 03 70 SITA: n/a
F: n/a ♦♦♦ n/a Head: n/a Net: n/a

☐	I-ELBR	Eurocopter (Aerosp.) AS350B2 Ecureuil	2502		0091		1 TU Arriel 1D1	2250			

ELICAMPIGLIO, Srl.

Madonna di Campiglio

Via Monte Spinale 1/B, I-38084 Madonna di Campiglio, (TN), Italy ☎ (0465) 44 33 22 Tx: none Fax: (0465) 44 32 66 SITA: n/a
F: 1993 ♦♦♦ 3 Head: Gino Bresadold Net: n/a

☐	I-ISAF	Eurocopter (Aerosp.) SA315B Lama	2148 / 23		0086		1 TU Artouste IIIB1	1950			cvtd SA318C

ELIDOLOMITI, Srl = EDO

Belluno Heliport

Via Caduti XIV Settembre 1944, I-32100 Belluno, (BL), Italy ☎ (0437) 31 620 Tx: 440201 elidol i Fax: (0437) 34 924 SITA: n/a
F: 1983 ♦♦♦ 26 Head: Dr. Natale Menegus ICAO: ELIDOLOMITI Net: n/a

☐	I-FLAR	Eurocopter (Aerosp.) SA315B Lama	2662		0085		1 TU Artouste IIIB1	1950			
☐	I-EFCN	Eurocopter (Aerosp.) AS350B Ecureuil	1445		0081		1 TU Arriel 1B	1950			lsf Elicortina Srl.
☐	I-FLAO	Eurocopter (Aerosp.) AS350B2 Ecureuil	2097		0088		1 TU Arriel 1D1	2250			cvtd AS350B1
☐	I-FLAP	Eurocopter (Aerosp.) AS350B2 Ecureuil	2487	G-BTLS	0091		1 TU Arriel 1D1	2250			lsf Bipiemme Leasing
☐	I-AGKK	Agusta A109K2	10021		0094	0994	2 TU Arriel 1K1	2720	EMS		Falco

ELI FLY, SpA = EBS

Esine Heliport

Via Casa Bianca 2, I-25040 Esine, (BS), Italy ☎ (0364) 46 387 Tx: 305068 elifly i Fax: (0364) 46 64 96 SITA: n/a
F: 1983 ♦♦♦ 10 Head: Com.te Francesco Comensoli ICAO: ELIFLY Net: n/a Aircraft below MTOW 1361 kg: Breda Nardi NH-300C & Hughes 269C (300C)

☐	I-SOCO	Eurocopter (Aerosp.) SA315B Lama	2183 / 39	F-GMET	0070	0697	1 TU Artouste IIIB1	1950			cvtd Alouette II
☐	I-VIOL	Eurocopter (Aerosp.) SA315B Lama	2501		0077		1 TU Artouste IIIB1	1950			
☐	F-OIOM	Eurocopter (Aerosp.) SA315B Lama	2423	EC-DNZ	0075	0098	1 TU Artouste IIIB	1950			lsf Textron Finance
☐	I-DASO	Eurocopter (Aerosp.) SA316B Alouette III	1318	F-GJCY	0065	1195	1 TU Artouste IIIB1	2200			
☐	I-DJNO	Eurocopter (Aerosp.) SA316B Alouette III	5411	F-WTNB*	0082		1 TU Artouste IIIB	2200			
☐	F-OIOL	Bell 412SP	33160	N4380K	0087	0898	2 PWC PT6T-3B TwinPac	5262			lsf Textron Finance / sub-lst Freeair

ELIFRIULIA, Srl. = EFG

Trieste

Aeroporto, I-34077 Ronchi dei Legionari, (GO), Italy ☎ (0481) 77 89 01 Tx: 460680 elifri i Fax: (0481) 77 89 03 SITA: n/a
F: 1971 ♦♦♦ 18 Head: Marco Coloatto ICAO: ELIFRIULIA Net: n/a Aircraft below MTOW 1361 kg: Robinson R22 & R44.

☐	I-KGKM	Eurocopter (Aerosp.) SA315B Lama	1241 / 48		0065	0796	1 TU Artouste IIIB1	1950	4 Pax		cvtd Alouette II
☐	I-EQUR	Eurocopter (Aerosp.) AS350B2 Ecureuil	2579		0091	1291	1 TU Arriel 1D1	2250	5 Pax		
☐	I-HOOK	Eurocopter (Aerosp.) AS350B3 Ecureuil	3090		0098	0698	1 TU Arriel 2B	2250	5 Pax		
☐	I-ORAO	Eurocopter (Aerosp.) AS355N Ecureuil 2	5583		0095	0695	2 TU Arrius 1A	2540	5 Pax		
☐	I-HEMS	Eurocopter EC135T1	0035		0097	1297	2 TU Arrius 2B	2720	6 Pax / EMS		
☐	I-HIFI	Eurocopter EC135T1	0085		0098	1298	2 TU Arrius 2B	2720	6 Pax / EMS		

ELILARIO, SpA = ELC

Colico (LC) & Caiolo (SO)

Zona Industriale, I-23823 Colico, (LC), Italy ☎ (0341) 94 01 26 Tx: 380242 helser i Fax: (0341) 93 05 36 SITA: n/a
F: 1978 ♦♦♦ 35 Head: n/a ICAO: ELILARIO Net: n/a Aircraft below MTOW 1361 kg: Agusta-Bell 47J.

☐	I-AVIF	Eurocopter (Aerosp.) SA315B Lama	2566		0080		1 TU Artouste IIIB1	1950			
☐	I-ELPA	Eurocopter (Aerosp.) SA315B Lama	2568	F-GCFO	0079		1 TU Artouste IIIB1	1950			
☐	I-EPEP	Eurocopter (Aerosp.) SA315B Lama	2661		0083		1 TU Artouste IIIB1	1950			
☐	I-ICGR	Eurocopter (Aerosp.) SA315B Lama	2671		0086		1 TU Artouste IIIB1	1950			
☐	I-LOGI	Eurocopter (Aerosp.) SA315B Lama	2489	N49521	0077		1 TU Artouste IIIB1	1950			
☐	I-AIOI	Eurocopter (Aerosp.) AS350B2 Ecureuil	2535		0091		1 TU Arriel 1D1	2250			lsf Locfin
☐	I-HEDD	Eurocopter (Aerosp.) AS350B2 Ecureuil	2479	F-WYMU*	0091		1 TU Arriel 1D1	2250			lsf Desio & Brianza Leasing
☐	I-CRSR	Eurocopter (Aerosp.) SA316B Alouette III	1949	F-OCUR	0073		1 TU Artouste IIIB1	2200			
☐	I-ELTO	Eurocopter (Aerosp.) SA316B Alouette III	2310	N9002G	0074		1 TU Artouste IIIB1	2200			
☐	I-AGKL	Agusta A109K2	10020		0095		2 TU Arriel 1K1	2720			
☐	I-CRBM	Agusta A109C	7623	I-CRBN	0090		2 AN 250-C20R/1	2720			
☐	I-DVCM	Agusta A109A	7156		0080		2 AN 250-C20B	2600			
☐	I-PCLE	Agusta A109A	7164		0080		2 AN 250-C20B	2600			
☐	I-AGSF	Agusta-Bell 412	25542		0087		2 PWC PT6T-3B TwinPac	5260			
☐	I-AGUI	Agusta-Bell 412	25507	11337	0082	0097	2 PWC PT6T-3B TwinPac	5260			
☐	I-CGCL	Agusta-Bell 412SP	25600		0089		2 PWC PT6T-3B TwinPac	5400			
☐	I-MAGM	Agusta-Bell 412SP	25602		0089		2 PWC PT6T-3B TwinPac	5260			
☐	I-SEIQ	Agusta-Bell 412SP	25603		0090		2 PWC PT6T-3B TwinPac	5400			lsf Siam Leasing SpA
☐	I-	Agusta-Bell 412EP					2 PWC PT6T-3D TwinPac	5400			oo-delivery 0099

ELILIGURIA INTERNATIONAL, Srl. = HLL (Associated with Heli Air Monaco / formerly Eliliguria, Srl.)

Albenga

Aeroporto, I-17038 Villanova-Albenga, Italy ☎ (0182) 58 29 06 Tx: none Fax: (0182) 58 20 17 SITA: n/a
F: 1985 ♦♦♦ 10 Head: Ing. Davide Viziano ICAO: ELILIGURIA Net: n/a Aircraft below MTOW 1361kg: Robinson R22

☐	I-ELIL	Eurocopter (Aerosp.) AS350BA Ecureuil	1091	3A-MMB	0079	0496	1 TU Arriel 1B	2100			cvtd AS350B

ELILOMBARDA, Srl. Calcinate del Pesce

Via Lungolago Duca degli Abruzzi 45, I-21100 Calcinate del Pesce, (VA), Italy ☎ (0332) 31 05 68 Tx: 312543 elilom i Fax: (0332) 31 33 70 SITA: n/a
F: 1978 ⁂ 21 Head: Alessandro Papis Net: n/a

☐ I-DACD	Agusta A109A II	7258		0082		2 AN 250-C20B	2600	Executive		
☐ I-MABR	Eurocopter (MBB) BK117A-4	7047	D-HBMV	0086		2 LY LTS101-650B.1	3200	EMS		cvtd A-3
☐ I-BRMA	Agusta-Bell 412	25626		0092		2 PWC PT6T-3B TwinPac	5400	Offshore		lsf San Paolo Leasint
☐ I-POPA	Bell 412SP	33199	N14UV	0089	0098	2 PWC PT6T-3B TwinPac	5400	EMS / Offshore		lsf Locafit
☐ I-RECE	Agusta-Bell 412	25571		0088		2 PWC PT6T-3B TwinPac	5260	EMS / Offshore		

ELILOMBARDIA, SpA = ELB Clusone Heliport

Via Lama 1, I-24023 Clusone (BG), (BG), Italy ☎ (0346) 22 449 Tx: 211584 i Fax: (0346) 22 003 SITA: n/a
F: 1978 ⁂ 12 Head: Ing. Stefano Bongiovanni ICAO: ELILOMBARDIA Net: n/a

☐ I-FVDB	Eurocopter (Aerosp.) SA315B Lama	2636		0082		1 TU Artouste IIIB1	1950			
☐ I-GELP	Eurocopter (Aerosp.) SA315B Lama	2237	TG-H-FEM-CP	0072		1 TU Artouste IIIB1	1950			

ELIMEDITERRANEA, Srl. = MEE San Benedetto del Tronto

Viale de Gasperi 27, I-63039 San Benedetto del Tronto, (AP), Italy ☎ (0735) 78 00 85 Tx: n/a Fax: (0735) 78 04 21 SITA: n/a
F: n/a ⁂ n/a Head: n/a ICAO: ELIMEDITERRANEA Net: n/a

☐ I-GLTS	Eurocopter (Aerosp.) AS350B2 Ecureuil	2627		0092	0693	1 TU Arriel 1D1	2250			
☐ I-MEDT	Eurocopter (Aerosp.) AS350B2 Ecureuil	2766	F-WYMI*	0093	0794	1 TU Arriel 1D1	2250			

ELINORD - Servizi Aerotrasporti Milano, Srl. (Associated with Elilario) Milan-Bresso

Viale Don Minzoni 61, I-20091 Bresso, (MI), Italy ☎ (02) 610 23 16 Tx: none Fax: none SITA: n/a
F: 1972 ⁂ 3 Head: Com.te Enrico Pozzi Net: n/a Aircraft below MTOW 1361kg: Bell 47G-2.

☐ I-PRVV	Eurocopter (Aerosp.) SA315B Lama	2418		0075		1 TU Artouste IIIB	1950			

ELIOS, Srl = VUL S. Agata li Battiati

Via G. d'Annunzio 6/8, I-95131 San Agata di Battiati, (CT), Italy ☎ (095) 21 30 96 Tx: none Fax: (095) 725 25 41 SITA: n/a
F: 1986 ⁂ 10 Head: Michele Pennisi ICAO: ELIOS Net: n/a Aircraft below MTOW 1361kg: Bredanardi-Hughes 300C & Hughes 269C (300C)

☐ I-TOMA	Agusta-Bell 206B JetRanger III	8736		0092	0392	1 AN 250-C20R/4	1450			
☐ I-TOLU	Agusta A109A II Plus	7424		0090		2 AN 250-C20R/1	2600			

ELIOSSOLA, Srl. = EOS Crevoladossola

S.S. Sempione 208, I-28035 Crevoladossola, (VB), Italy ☎ (0324) 33 134 Tx: none Fax: (0324) 33 82 02 SITA: n/a
F: 1993 ⁂ 3 Head: Ing. Ugo Brusa ICAO: ELIOSSOLA Net: n/a

☐ I-AMAY	Eurocopter (Aerosp.) SA315B Lama	2607		0081		1 TU Artouste IIIB1	1950			
☐ I-FLAI	Eurocopter (Aerosp.) SA315B Lama	2605	F-GDCX	0081		1 TU Artouste IIIB1	1950			

ELIPIU', Srl. = IEP Lorla (TV)

Via Zaccaria Bricito 31A, I-36061 Bassano del Grappa, (VI), Italy ☎ (0423) 45 63 94 Tx: none Fax: (0423) 45 63 89 SITA: n/a
F: n/a ⁂ n/a Head: n/a ICAO: ELIPIU Net: n/a Aircraft below MTOW 1361kg: Robinson R22 & R44

☐ I-EPIA	Agusta-Bell 206B JetRanger III	8701	F-GEJM	0086	0997	1 AN 250-C20J	1451			
☐ I-EPIB	Bell 407	53260	C-GDSZ*	0098	0998	1 AN 250-C47B	2268			lsf Italease

ELISERVIZI ITALIANI, Srl. = ESI (Associated with H.T. Heli Transport / formerly ESI & Aerossola) Masera-Heliport, Biella & Champoluc

Via Paolo Ferraris 15, Localita SNAM, I-28855 Ossola, (VB), Italy ☎ (0324) 35 395 Tx: none Fax: (0324) 35 283 SITA: n/a
F: 1975 ⁂ 23 Head: Pierleoni Pietro ICAO: ELISERVIZI Net: n/a Aircraft below MTOW 1361kg: Robinson R22.

☐ I-MROS	Eurocopter (Aerosp.) SA315B Lama	2498	G-BMUC	0077		1 TU Artouste IIIB1	1950			
☐ I-SESI	Eurocopter (Aerosp.) SA315B Lama	2053 / 20	N29907	0069		1 TU Artouste IIIB1	1950			cvtd SA318C
☐ I-TALE	Eurocopter (Aerosp.) SA315B Lama	2025 / 26		0068		1 TU Artouste IIIB1	1950			cvtd SA318C Alouette II
☐ I-HEVL	Eurocopter (Aerosp.) SA316B Alouette III	1081	F-GSOS	0063		1 TU Artouste IIIB1	2200			cvtd SE3160
☐ I-VALL	Eurocopter (Aerosp.) SA316B Alouette III	1374		0072	0097	1 TU Artouste IIIB1	2200			cvtd SE3160
☐ I-VLLE	Eurocopter (Aerosp.) SA319B Alouette III	1999	HB-XUM	0075	0497	1 TU Astazou XIVB	2250			lsf HT-Heli Training Srl.

ELISONDRIO, Srl Sondrio-Caiolo

Via Pedemontana, I-23010 Caiolo, (SO), Italy ☎ (0342) 35 52 68 Tx: none Fax: (0342) 35 52 68 SITA: n/a
F: 1988 ⁂ 5 Head: Nera Massimo Net: n/a Aircraft below MTOW 1361kg: Robinson R22.

☐ I-SOND	Eurocopter (Aerosp.) SA315B Lama	2481	N221RM	0077		1 TU Artouste IIIB1	1950			

ELISUSA, Srl. = LDO Gravere Heliport

Via Nazionale 12, I-10050 Gravere, (TO), Italy ☎ (0122) 31 920 Tx: none Fax: (0122) 31 920 SITA: n/a
F: n/a ⁂ n/a Head: n/a ICAO: ELISUSA Net: n/a

☐ I-BRAL	Eurocopter (Aerosp.) AS350B Ecureuil	1904		0086	0097	1 TU Arriel 1B	1950			lsf Locat

ELISYSTEM, SpA = EEI (Affiliated with Elisystem Eliagricola, SpA) Rivanazzano

Via F. Baracca 11, I-27055 Rivanazzano, (PV), Italy ☎ (0383) 84 44 40 Tx: none Fax: (0383) 91 591 SITA: n/a
F: 1973 ⁂ 15 Head: Rossi Piero ICAO: ELISYSTEM Net: n/a Aircraft below MTOW 1361kg: Hughes 269C & Bredanardi-Hughes 300C.

☐ I-ANBE	MD Helicopters MD 500D (Hughes 369D)	1127D	N5183Y	0082		1 AN 250-C20B	1361			
☐ I-CRMC	Eurocopter (Aerosp.) AS350B Ecureuil	1272	F-GCJZ	0080	0097	1 TU Arriel 1B	1950			
☐ I-GLGM	Eurocopter (Aerosp.) AS350B2 Ecureuil	2332		0090	0097	1 TU Arriel 1D1	2250			
☐ I-MIAE	Eurocopter (Aerosp.) AS350BA Ecureuil	1774	N8837K	0084		1 TU Arriel 1B	2100			lsf Fiscambi Leasing SpA / cvtd AS350B
☐ I-SILL	Eurocopter (Aerosp.) AS350B2 Ecureuil	2456	F-WYMT*	0091	0097	1 TU Arriel 1D1	2250			lsf San Paolo Leasint SpA
☐ I-	Eurocopter (Aerosp.) AS350B3 Ecureuil					1 TU Arriel 2B	2250			oo-delivery 0099

ELITALIANA, SpA = ETI (Associated with Freeair, SpA) Tarquinia

c/o Freeair, SpA, Strada Litoranea, Local San Girogio, I-01016 Tarquinia, (VT), Italy ☎ (0766) 84 32 18 Tx: 843217 i Fax: (0766) 84 32 17 SITA: n/a
F: 1964 ⁂ 26 Head: n/a ICAO: ELITALIANA Net: n/a

☐ I-DESO	Agusta A109A II Plus	7401		0088		2 AN 250-C20R/1	2600			lsf Romaleasing
☐ I-FREF	Bell 430	49023	N7204R*	0098	0898	2 AN 250-C40	4082	EMS Piemonte Reg		lsf Freeair
☐ I-AGSO	Agusta-Bell 412SP	25560		0088		2 PWC PT6T-3B TwinPac	5260	EMS Piemonte Reg		

ELITELLINA, Srl. = FGS Sondrio & Gordona

Via delle Orobie, I-23100 Sondrio, (SO), Italy ☎ (0342) 21 33 36 Tx: n/a Fax: (0342) 21 97 99 SITA: n/a
F: 1977 ⁂ 11 Head: Guido Fratta ICAO: ELITELLINA Net: n/a

☐ I-AFET	Eurocopter (Aerosp.) SA315B Lama	2663		0085		1 TU Artouste IIIB1	1950			
☐ I-BLIP	Eurocopter (Aerosp.) SA315B Lama	2495		0077		1 TU Artouste IIIB	1950			
☐ I-IRPI	Eurocopter (Aerosp.) SA315B Lama	2672		0086		1 TU Artouste IIIB1	1950			

ELITORINO, Srl = ELW Torino-Caselle

Aeroprto Citta di Torino, I-10072 Caselle, (TO), Italy ☎ (011) 470 37 97 Tx: none Fax: (011) 470 39 38 SITA: n/a
F: 1988 ⁂ 4 Head: Geom. Giampiero Brach Prever ICAO: ELITORINO Net: n/a Aircraft below MTOW 1361kg: Bredanardi NH300C.

☐ I-GPBP	Eurocopter (Aerosp.) AS350B2 Ecureuil	2345	I-BPGP	0090	0790	1 TU Arriel 1D1	2250	5 Pax		lsf Locat

ELIVIT, Srl. Naples-Capodichino

Via Caracciolo 10, I-80122 Napoli, Italy ☎ (081) 738 72 57 Tx: none Fax: (081) 738 72 57 SITA: n/a
F: 1988 ⁂ 6 Head: n/a Net: n/a

☐ I-CELF	Bell 206B JetRanger	1605	N77884	0074		1 AN 250-C20	1450			

ETI 2000, Srl. = MJM Quart Heliport

Localita Lillaz, I-11020 Quart, (AO), Italy ☎ (0165) 76 54 17 Tx: none Fax: (0165) 76 54 18 SITA: n/a
F: 1993 ⁂ 8 Head: Marco Jans ICAO: ELCO Net: n/a

☐ I-APEX	Eurocopter (Aerosp.) SA315B Lama	2491	F-GFCA	0076		1 TU Artouste IIIB1	1950			
☐ I-DENY	Eurocopter (Aerosp.) SA315B Lama	2525	G-BMKT	0078	0098	1 TU Artouste IIIB1	1950			

EURAVIATION, Srl = EVN Milan-Linate

Via Conservatorio 11, I-20122 Milano, (MI), Italy ☎ (02) 70 20 99 87 Tx: none Fax: (02) 70 20 99 87 SITA: n/a
F: 1987 ⁂ 11 Head: Ing. Enzo Nardi ICAO: EURAVIATION Net: http://space.tin.it/viaggi/enardi

☐ I-ABCA	Beech Bonanza F33A	CE-235	HB-EHH	0068		1 CO IO-520-B	1496			
☐ I-AMAG	Beech Bonanza F33A	CE-650	D-ELKA	0076		1 CO IO-520-BA	1542			
☐ I-GIPA	Beech Baron 58P	TJ-148	N48TX	0078		2 CO TSIO-520-WB	2812			
☐ I-NIAR	Cessna 551 Citation II/SP	551-0056	N214AM	0081	0597	2 PWC JT15D-4	5670			lsf Arni Srl.

EURECA, Srl. - European Regional Carrier = F4 / URE (formerly International Flying Services, Srl.) Bergamo-Orio al Serio

Hangar 39, Aeroporto, I-24050 Orio al Serio, (BG), Italy ☎ (035) 420 39 11 Tx: 305184 flyser i Fax: (035) 31 46 15 SITA: BGYFJF4
F: 1989 ⁂ 41 Head: Cesare Musumeci IATA: 514 ICAO: EURECA Net: n/a

☐ I-TASE	Twin (Aero) Turbo Commander 690A	11260	N324BT	0075		2 GA TPE331-5-251K	4649	Freighter / Y7		
☐ I-FSAD	Fairchild (Swear.) SA227AT Expediter IVC	AT-440B	N36JP	0081		2 GA TPE331-11U-611G	7257	Freighter		lsf Desio & Brianza Leasing

214 registration type of aircraft cn/fn ex/ex* mfd del powered by mtow kg configuration selcal name/fln/specialitites/remarks

☐ I-FSTK	Fokker F27 Friendship 600 (F27 Mk600)	10409	OY-FCM	0069	0397	2 RR Dart 532-7R	20412	Freighter		
☐ SE-KZE	Fokker F27 Friendship 100 (F27 Mk100)	10248	LN-SUL	0064	0797	2 RR Dart 514-7	18370	Y44		lsf SAE Swe Aviation Europe AB
☐ SE-KZG	Fokker F27 Friendship 100 (F27 Mk100)	10287	LN-NPM	0065	1197	2 RR Dart 514-7	18370	Y44		lsf SAE Swe Aviation Europe AB

EUROFLY, SpA = GJ / EEZ (Member of Gruppo Alitalia / Associated with Olivetti & Crediop) — Bergamo-Orio al Serio

Via 24 Maggio 6, I-20099 Sesto San Giovanni, (MI), Italy ☎ (02) 24 445 Tx: none Fax: (02) 24 44 55 53 SITA: TRNEAAZ
F: 1989 ⁂ 70 Head: Angelo Fornasari ICAO: SIRIOFLY Net: n/a Beside aircraft listed, leases additional McDonnell Douglas MD-82 from Alitalia when required.

☐ I-FLYY	Boeing (Douglas) DC-9-51	47754 / 856	N56UA	0477	1189	2 PW JT8D-17	54885	Y139		lsf Isefi Internazionale
☐ I-FLYZ	Boeing (Douglas) DC-9-51	47697 / 816	N54UA	0376	1189	2 PW JT8D-17	54885	Y139	AB-CD	lsf Isefi Internazionale
☐ EI-CEK	Boeing (Douglas) MD-83 (DC-9-83)	49631 / 1596	EC-FMY	0589	0394	2 PW JT8D-219	72575	Y164	CF-RS	lsf GECA
☐ EI-CMM	Boeing (Douglas) MD-83 (DC-9-83)	49937 / 1784	G-COES	1090	0296	2 PW JT8D-219	72575	Y164	AK-LS	lsf GECA
☐ EI-CMZ	Boeing (Douglas) MD-83 (DC-9-83)	49390 / 1269	9Y-THN	0086	0796	2 PW JT8D-219	72575	Y164	BJ-AE	lsf GECA
☐ EI-CNR	Boeing (Douglas) MD-83 (DC-9-83)	53199 / 1968	SE-DLU	0092	0497	2 PW JT8D-219	72575	Y164		lsf GECA
☐ EI-CPB	Boeing (Douglas) MD-83 (DC-9-83)	49940 / 1788	TC-IND	0090	0498	2 PW JT8D-219	72575	Y164		lsf GECA
☐ EI-CRD	Boeing 767-31B (ER)	26259 / 534	B-2565	0094	1198	2 GE CF6-80C2B6F	184612	C24Y230		lsf ILFC
☐ EI-CRF	Boeing 767-31B (ER)	25170 / 542	B-2566	0094	1298	2 GE CF6-80C2B6F	184612	C24Y230		lsf ILFC
☐ EI-CRO	Boeing 767-3Q8 (ER)	29383		0099		2 GE CF6-80C2B6F	184612	C24Y230		to be lsf ILFC 1199

EUROFLY SERVICE, SpA = EEU (Subsidiary of Pirelli) — Torino-Caselle

Aeroporto "Città di Torino", I-10072 Caselle Torinese, (TO), Italy ☎ (011) 567 80 55 Tx: 214375 eurfly i Fax: (011) 567 83 37 SITA: n/a
F: 1978 ⁂ 49 Head: Domenico Osella ICAO: EUROFLY Net: n/a

☐ I-IDAG	Cessna 525 CitationJet	525-0093	N5151S	0095		2 WRR FJ44-1A	4717			
☐ I-TYKE	Learjet 31A	31A-120	N5020Y	0096	0996	2 GA TFE731-2-3B	7711			lsf Fincaer Servizi SpA
☐ I-FLYH	Learjet 35A	35A-498	N8564P	0083		2 GA TFE731-2-2B	8301			
☐ I-FLYJ	Learjet 55	55-084	N740AC	0083	0495	2 GA TFE731-3AR-2B	9752			
☐ I-LOOK	Learjet 55	55-021	EI-BSA	0082		2 GA TFE731-3AR-2B	9752			
☐ I-GASD	Cessna 650 Citation III	650-0037	N37VP	0084	1296	2 GA TFE731-3B-100S	9752			lsf Gretair Srl.
☐ I-FLYK	Dassault Falcon 20E	241	HZ-PL7	0071	0889	2 GE CF700-2D2	13000			
☐ I-REAL	Dassault Falcon 20E	267	F-WRQZ*	0072	0096	2 GE CF700-2D2	13000			lsf Rusconi Editore SpA
☐ I-EDIK	Dassault Falcon 50	132	F-WPXF*	0084		3 GA TFE731-3-1C	17600			
☐ I-LXGR	GAC G-IV Gulfstream IV (SP)	1234	N924ML	0093	0396	2 RR Tay 611-8	33838		GR-EK	lsf Luxottica Leasing

EUROJET ITALIA, Srl = ERJ — Milan-Linate & Genova

Viale dell'Aviazione 65, I-20138 Milano, (MI), Italy ☎ (02) 76 11 00 50 Tx: 360385 eurojt i Fax: (02) 76 11 04 78 SITA: n/a
F: 1987 ⁂ 21 Head: Dott. Edoardo Rubino ICAO: JET ITALIA Net: n/a

☐ I-EDEM	Cessna 525 CitationJet	525-0155	N155CJ	0096	0197	2 WRR FJ44-1A	4717			lsf Ritmo Srl.
☐ I-GCFA	Beech Beechjet 400	RJ-44	N3144A	0088	0097	2 PWC JT15D-5	7158			
☐ I-AGEN	Learjet 35A	35A-491	N485	0083	0189	2 GA TFE731-2-2B	8301			
☐ PH-OMC	Dassault Falcon 20F	239	I-AGEC	0070	0294	2 GE CF700-2D2	13000			

EVIN AIR = EVI (Evin Evoluzioni Industriali, Srl. dba) — Florence

Via Camalfi 2, I-52020 Castelfranco di Sopra, Italy ☎ (055) 914 99 05 Tx: none Fax: (055) 914 90 80 SITA: n/a
F: n/a ⁂ n/a Head: n/a ICAO: EVIN AIR Net: n/a

☐ I-LLEO	Bell 206B JetRanger III	4077	N63AJ	0089		1 AN 250-C20J	1450			lsf Adriatica Finanziaria SpA

FEDERICO II AIRWAYS, SpA = 2D / FDE — Foggia

c/o Palazzo Amgas, Via Manfredi 58, I-71100 Foggia, (FG), Italy ☎ (0881) 76 00 43 Tx: none Fax: (0881) 76 00 50 SITA: n/a
F: 1998 ⁂ n/a Head: Ronzo Orlando IATA: 822 ICAO: FEDEREAGLE Net: n/a

☐ D-CHIC	Dornier 328-110	3021	D-CDXQ	0095	0998	2 PWC PW119B	13990	Y31		San Giovanni Rotondo / lsfMilleniumLsg

FLY JET, Srl. = FJT — Turin-Caselle

Aeroporto "Città di Torino", I-10072 Caselle Torinese, (TO), Italy ☎ (011) 470 45 59 Tx: n/a Fax: (011) 470 45 59 SITA: n/a
F: n/a ⁂ n/a Head: n/a ICAO: FLY JET Net: n/a

☐ I-FJTO	Cessna 550 Citation II	550-0679		0091		2 PWC JT15D-4	6395			

FREEAIR, SpA — Tarquinia

Strada Litoranea, Local San Giorgio, I-01016 Tarquinia, (VT), Italy ☎ (0766) 84 32 18 Tx: 843217 i Fax: (0766) 84 32 17 SITA: n/a
F: 1995 ⁂ n/a Head: Carmelo Stanziola Net: n/a Aircraft below MTOW 1361kg: Hughes 269C (300C) & Robinson R22

☐ I-FREB	Bell 206B JetRanger III	3105	I-MIAB	0080	0895	1 AN 250-C20B	1451			
☐ I-HPWG	Bell 206B JetRanger III	3297	I-MIGE	0081		1 AN 250-C20B	1451			lsf Locat
☐ I-COOP	Eurocopter (Aerosp.) SA315B Lama	2668		0085		1 TU Artouste IIIB1	1950			lsf Cooperleasing
☐ I-FREC	Bell 407	53241	C-GBLC*	0098	0998	1 AN 250-C47B	2268			lsf Green Fly
☐ I-CMDV	Agusta A109A	7128		0078	0097	2 AN 250-C20B	2600			
☐ I-SEIA	Agusta A109A II	7388		0087	0097	2 AN 250-C20B	2600	EMS		lsf S.E.I. SpA
☐ I-SEID	Agusta A109A II MAX	7429	N1VQ	0088	0097	2 AN 250-C20R/1	2600	EMS		lsf C.S.A. Srl.
☐ I-FREF	Bell 430	49023	N7204R*	0098	0898	2 AN 250-C40	4082	EMS Piemonte Reg		118 / lst Elitaliana
☐ I-FREG	Bell 430	49025	N7244N*	0098	0898	2 AN 250-C40	4082	EMS Piemonte Reg		
☐ I-FREM	Bell 212	30685	C-GCVF	0075	0898	2 PWC PT6T-3 TwinPac	5080			lsf Eagle Copters Ltd
☐ F-OIOL	Bell 412SP	33160	N4380K	0087	0098	2 PWC PT6T-3B TwinPac	5262			lsf Eli-Fly

GANDALF AIRLINES = G7 — Bergamo-Orio al Serio

Via Aeroporto, I-24050 Orio al Serio, (BG), Italy ☎ (035) 459 50 11 Tx: none Fax: (035) 424 33 07 SITA: n/a
F: 1998 ⁂ n/a Head: Luciano di Fazio Net: n/a

☐ D-CGAN	Dornier 328-110	3112		0098	0399	2 PWC PW119B	13990	Y32		lsf Dornier
☐ D-CGAO	Dornier 328-110	3113		0098	0499	2 PWC PW119B	13990	Y32		lsf Dornier
☐	Dornier 328JET (328-300)					2 PWC PW306B	14990	Y32		oo-delivery 0999
☐	Dornier 328JET (328-300)					2 PWC PW306B	14990	Y32		oo-delivery 0999
☐	Dornier 328JET (328-300)					2 PWC PW306B	14990	Y32		oo-delivery 1199
☐	Dornier 328JET (328-300)					2 PWC PW306B	14990	Y32		oo-delivery 1199

HELITALIA, SpA = HIT (Associated with Bristow Helicopters Ltd, Great Britain) — Florence

Via del Termine 11, I-50127 Florence, Italy ☎ (055) 30 83 23 Tx: none Fax: (055) 30 83 21 SITA: n/a
F: 1994 ⁂ 54 Head: Ing. Giulio C. Valdonio ICAO: HELITALIA Net: n/a

☐ I-CARR	Agusta A109A II	7319		0085		2 AN 250-C20B	2600	EMS		
☐ I-HBHA	Agusta A109K2	10023		0095	0895	2 TU Arriel 1K1	2850	EMS		
☐ I-HBHB	Agusta A109K2	10025		0095	0097	2 TU Arriel 1K1	2850	EMS		
☐ I-BKBO	Eurocopter (MBB) BK117B-1	7199	N54114	0089	0096	2 LY LTS101-750B.1	3200	Offshore		
☐ I-HBHC	Eurocopter (MBB) BK117B-2	7251	D-HITZ	0095	0096	2 LY LTS101-750B.1	3350	EMS		lsf Eligestione
☐ I-HBAS	Sikorsky S-76A++	760298	VR-HZC	0085	0896	2 TU Arriel 1S1	4899	Offshore		cvtd S-76A
☐ I-HBBS	Sikorsky S-76A+	760114	G-BVKP	0080	1297	2 TU Arriel 1S	4899	Offshore		cvtd S-76A

HELIWEST, Srl. — Isola d'Asti

Via Fiera 1, I-14057 Isola d'Asti, (AT), Italy ☎ (0141) 59 59 85 Tx: none Fax: (0141) 59 59 95 SITA: n/a
F: n/a ⁂ 14 Head: Luciano Villani Net: n/a Aircraft below MTOW 1361kg: Hughes 269C (300C) & Piper PA-28

☐ I-MAEL	Eurocopter (Aerosp.) SA315B Lama	2510	F-GEEZ	0077	0097	1 TU Artouste IIIB1	1950			lsf CTE-Cost.Tecno Elettriche SpA
☐ I-OLLY	Eurocopter (Westland) SA341G Gazelle	WA.1065	F-GBMC	0073		1 TU Astazou IIIA	1800			
☐ I-LASD	Eurocopter (Aerosp.) AS350B2 Ecureuil	2410	F-GHHL	0090	1296	1 TU Arriel 1D1	2250			
☐ I-LASP	Eurocopter (Aerosp.) AS350B1 Ecureuil	1822	JA9779	0086	0194	1 TU Arriel 1D	2200			
☐ I-LTOP	Eurocopter (Aerosp.) AS355F1 Ecureuil 2	5106	N5792X	0081	0097	2 AN 250-C20F	2400			lsf Desio & Brianza Leasing SpA

ICARO, Srl – Impresa Commerciale Aeronautica Romagnola = ICA — Forli

Aeroporto L. Ridolfi, I-47100 Forli, (FO), Italy ☎ (0543) 78 05 04 Tx: none Fax: (0543) 78 05 04 SITA: n/a
F: 1982 ⁂ 8 Head: Capt. Egisto Bernucci ICAO: ICARFLY Net: n/a Aircraft below MTOW 1361kg: GA F20/F22, Piper PA-28 & SIAI F.260

☐ I-PEGA	Cessna 500 Citation	500-0081	HB-VDA	0073		2 PWC JT15D-1A	5216	7 Pax		
☐ N70WA	Cessna 500 Citation I	500-0320	I-NORT	0076	1297	2 PWC JT15D-1A	5375	7 Pax		lsf Wrangler Aviation Corp.
☐ I-VICY	Fairchild (Swearingen) SA227DC Metro 23	DC-849B	N451LA	0094	0797	2 GA TPE331-12UHR-701G	7485	Y19		lsf Leasing Roma SpA

ICARUS Elicotteri = IUS (Icarus Societa Cooperativa, A.R.L. dba) — Lametia Terme (CZ)

Via Siena 16, I-89018 Villa San Giovanni, (RC), Italy ☎ (0965) 79 51 10 Tx: n/a Fax: (0968) 53 963 SITA: n/a
F: 1986 ⁂ 10 Head: Luciano Ottana ICAO: ICARUS Net: http://www.calnet.it./aziende/icarus Aircraft below MTOW 1361kg: Breda Nardi NH300C

☐ I-BLUX	Eurocopter (Aerosp.) AS350B2 Ecureuil	2506	SE-JAF	0091	0893	1 TU Arriel 1D1	2250			
☐ I-NDIO	Eurocopter (Aerosp.) AS350B1 Ecureuil	2308		0089		1 TU Arriel 1D	2200			

INTERJET, Srl. = MTF (Associated with Meccanica Aeronautica, Srl.) — Bologna

Via Belvedere 23, I-41014 Castelvetro di Modena, (MO), Italy ☎ (059) 75 46 11 Tx: 510345 i Fax: (059) 75 46 99 SITA: n/a
F: 1984 ⁂ 3 Head: Aldo Balugani ICAO: INTERJET Net: n/a

☐ I-CREM	Dassault Falcon 10	161	N50SL	0380		2 GA TFE731-2-1C	8500	8 Pax		

215 registration type of aircraft cn/fn ex/ex* mfd del powered by mtow kg configuration selcal name/fln/specialitites/remarks

ITALAIR, SpA = B8 / DRG Rome-Fiumicino

Via G.F. Ingrassia 15, I-00152 Roma, Italy ☎ (06) 58 20 53 41 Tx: none Fax: (06) 58 20 95 90 SITA: n/a
F: 1996 n/a Head: Dario Brugnoli IATA: 823 ICAO: ITALAIR Net: n/a

☐ EI-CBK	ATR 42-300	199	F-WWEM*	0090	0998	2 PWC PW120	16700	Y48		lsf GECA
☐ EI-COD	ATR 42-300	052	N4203G	0087	0797	2 PWC PW120	16700	Y48		lsf A.T.R.
☐ EI-CPT	ATR 42-300	191	C-GIQS	0090	0898	2 PWC PW120	16700	Y48		lsf GECA

ITALY FIRST, SpA Rimini

Corso d'Augusto 115, I-47037 Rimini, Italy ☎ (0541) 27 756 Tx: none Fax: (0541) 53 955 SITA: n/a
F: 1998 n/a Head: Stefano Patacconi Net: n/a Presently being set-up. Intends to start operations in November 1999 with Boeing 737-300/400 aircraft.

JET A-1, Srl Reggio Emilia

Via del Buracchione 10, I-42020 Reggio Emilia, (RE), Italy ☎ (0522) 56 91 45 Tx: n/a Fax: (0522) 56 98 08 SITA: n/a
F: 1987 n/a Head: C. Battisti Net: n/a Aircraft below MTOW 1361 kg: Enstrom 280FX / F28F & Hughes 269C (300C).

☐ I-BNAP	Breda Nardi (Hughes) NH-500D	BH-12		0085		1 AN 250-C20B	1360			lsf Italease

LAUDA AIR, SpA = L4 / LDI (Associated with Lauda Air, Austria & ITC&P) Milan-Malpensa

Aeroporto Milano-Malpensa, Strada Provinciale 52, I-21010 Vizzola-Ticino, (VA), Italy ☎ (0331) 23 04 44 Tx: none Fax: (0331) 23 04 67 SITA: n/a
F: 1992 90 Head: Niki Lauda IATA: 372 ICAO: LAUDA ITALY Net: n/a Beside aircraft listed, additional aircraft (Boeing 737/767) are leased from sister company LAUDA AIR, Austria (OE-), when required.

☐ OE-LAS	Boeing 767-33A (ER)	27909 / 591		0095	0199	2 PW PW4056	186880	C24Y220	JS-MQ	Ayrton Senna / lsf LDA
☐ OE-LAT	Boeing 767-31A (ER)	25273 / 393	PH-MCK	1291	0393	2 PW PW4060	184612	C24Y234	DH-BC	Enzo Ferrari / lsf LDA

MED AIRLINES, SpA = M8 / MDS Palermo

Via Foro 5, I-90146 Palermo, (PA), Italy ☎ (091) 54 59 99 Tx: none Fax: (091) 54 59 51 SITA: n/a
F: 1997 n/a Head: Franco Castiglione ICAO: MIZAIR Net: n/a

☐ F-OHLA	ATR 42-320	031	F-WQHR	0086	0498	2 PWC PW121	16700	Y50		lsf A.T.R. / cvtd -300
☐ SE-LSH	Saab 2000	2000-052	SE-052	0097	0198	2 AN AE2100A	22800	Y53		lsf Saab Aircraft Credit AB/tbr I-MEDD
☐ SE-LSI	Saab 2000	2000-050	SE-050	0097	0498	2 AN AE2100A	22800	Y53		lsf Saab Aircraft Credit AB

MERIDIANA, SpA = IG / ISS (Subsidiary of Fimpar / formerly Alisarda, SpA) Olbia & Florence

Zona Industriale A, I-07026 Olbia, (SS), Sardinia, Italy ☎ (0789) 52 600 Tx: none Fax: (0789) 52 802 SITA: n/a
F: 1963 1200 Head: Franco Trivi IATA: 191 ICAO: MERAIR Net: n/a

☐ I-SARB	Bell 412	33078		0082	0682	2 PWC PT6T-3B TwinPac	5260	Y13		
☐ I-FLRE	BAe 146-200	E2210	G-BVMP	0092	0594	4 LY ALF502R-5	38986	CY84		
☐ I-FLRI	BAe 146-200	E2220	G-BVMT	0093	0794	4 LY ALF502R-5	38986	CY84		
☐ I-FLRO	BAe 146-200	E2227	G-BVMS	0094	0694	4 LY ALF502R-5	38986	CY84		
☐ I-FLRU	BAe 146-200	E2204	I-FLRA	0092	0494	4 LY ALF502R-5	38986	CY84		
☐ I-SMEE	Boeing (Douglas) DC-9-51	47656 / 783	EC-ENZ	0075	1089	2 PW JT8D-17	52163	Y125	DH-BJ	
☐ I-SMEJ	Boeing (Douglas) DC-9-51	47657 / 787	OY-CTB	0075	0689	2 PW JT8D-17	52163	Y125	BC-FG	
☐ I-SMEO	Boeing (Douglas) DC-9-51	47655 / 763	OY-CTA	0075	0689	2 PW JT8D-17	52163	Y125	JM-CG	
☐ I-SMEB	Boeing (Douglas) MD-82 (DC-9-82)	53064 / 1908	B-28001	0091	0598	2 PW JT8D-217C	67812	Y165		
☐ I-SMEC	Boeing (Douglas) MD-83 (DC-9-83)	49808 / 1836	N183NA	0091	0998	2 PW JT8D-219	72575	Y165		lsf ILFC
☐ I-SMED	Boeing (Douglas) MD-83 (DC-9-83)	53182 / 2069	N875RA	0093	0499	2 PW JT8D-219	72575	Y165		lsf AWAS
☐ I-SMEL	Boeing (Douglas) MD-82 (DC-9-82)	49247 / 1151	HB-IKK	0084	0984	2 PW JT8D-217A	67812	Y165		
☐ I-SMEM	Boeing (Douglas) MD-82 (DC-9-82)	49248 / 1152	HB-IKL	0084	0984	2 PW JT8D-217A	67812	Y165		
☐ I-SMEP	Boeing (Douglas) MD-82 (DC-9-82)	49740 / 1618		0089	0889	2 PW JT8D-217C	62959	Y165		
☐ I-SMER	Boeing (Douglas) MD-82 (DC-9-82)	49901 / 1766	N6202S*	0990	0391	2 PW JT8D-217C	62959	Y165		
☐ I-SMES	Boeing (Douglas) MD-82 (DC-9-82)	49902 / 1948		0091	0492	2 PW JT8D-217C	62959	Y165		
☐ I-SMET	Boeing (Douglas) MD-82 (DC-9-82)	49531 / 1362		0087	0587	2 PW JT8D-217A	67812	Y165		
☐ I-SMEV	Boeing (Douglas) MD-82 (DC-9-82)	49669 / 1493		0088	0788	2 PW JT8D-217A	67812	Y165		
☐ EI-	Boeing (Douglas) MD-83 (DC-9-83)	49951 / 1915	HB-IKN	0091		2 PW JT8D-219	72575	Y165		to be lsf GECA 0499
☐ EI-CIW	Boeing (Douglas) MD-83 (DC-9-83)	49785 / 1628	HL7271	0089	0697	2 PW JT8D-217C	72575	Y165		lsf GECA
☐ EI-CKM	Boeing (Douglas) MD-83 (DC-9-83)	49792 / 1655	TC-INC	1089	0398	2 PW JT8D-219	72575	Y165	AK-LR	lsf GECA
☐ EI-CRE	Boeing (Douglas) MD-83 (DC-9-83)	49854 / 1601	D-ALLL	0589	1298	2 PW JT8D-219	72575	Y165		lsf Crane Aircraft 49854 Llc
☐ EI-CRH	Boeing (Douglas) MD-83 (DC-9-83)	49935 / 1773	HB-IKM	0990	0299	2 PW JT8D-219	72575	Y165		lsf GECA
☐ EI-CRJ	Boeing (Douglas) MD-83 (DC-9-83)	53013 / 1738	D-ALLP	0790	0399	2 PW JT8D-219	72575	Y165		lsf Valcara Intl Ltd
☐ PH-SEZ	Boeing (Douglas) MD-82 (DC-9-82)	49903 / 1949	N3010C	0091	0493	2 PW JT8D-217C	62959	Y165		lsf Air Finance Holland

MINERVA AIRLINES, SpA = Q2 / MTC Trieste

Via Tambarin 38, I-34077 Ronchi dei Legionari, (GO), Italy ☎ (0481) 77 27 11 Tx: none Fax: (0481) 47 49 99 SITA: TRSWWQ2
F: 1996 120 Head: Dr. Mario Rosconi ICAO: AIR MINERVA Net: n/a Some aircraft are operated in conjunction with/on behalf of Alitalia as ALITALIA EXPRESS (in full such colors & both titles) & using AZ-flight numbers.

☐ D-CPRP	Dornier 328-110	3066	D-CDXL*	0096	0596	2 PWC PW119B	13990	Y32		lsf D.S.F. & Leasing GmbH & Co.
☐ D-CPRS	Dornier 328-110	3046	D-CDXM*	0096	1096	2 PWC PW119B	13990	Y32		lsf Millennium Lsng/op in AZ Express-cs
☐ D-CPRT	Dornier 328-110	3042	D-CDXI*	0097	0397	2 PWC PW119B	13990	Y32		lsf Millennium Leasing
☐ D-CPRU	Dornier 328-110	3091		0097	0997	2 PWC PW119B	13990	Y32		lsf Millennium Leasing
☐ D-CPRV	Dornier 328-110	3093	D-CDXD*	0097	1297	2 PWC PW119B	13990	Y32		lsf Millennium Lsng/op in AZ Express-cs
☐ D-CPRX	Dornier 328-110	3101		0098	1098	2 PWC PW119B	13990	Y32		lsf Millennium Lsng/op in AZ Express-cs

MINILINER, Srl. = MNL (Farnair Europe) (Member of Farnair Europe, European Aviation Alliance) Bergamo-Orio al Serio

Via Aeroporto 13, Casella Postale 21, I-24050 Orio al Serio, (BG), Italy ☎ (035) 31 68 65 Tx: none Fax: (035) 31 82 24 SITA: n/a
F: 1981 25 Head: Giuseppe Berlusconi ICAO: MINILINER Net: http://www.farnair.com

☐ I-MLQT	Fokker F27 Friendship 400 (F27 Mk400)	10295	HB-ITQ	0066	0096	2 RR Dart 532-7R	20412	Freighter		op in Farnair Europe-colors
☐ PH-FNV	Fokker F27 Friendship 500 (F27 Mk500)	10397	F-BPUK	0069	0098	2 RR Dart 532-7R	20820	Freighter		lsf FRN in Farnair Europe-colors

MISTRAL AIR, Srl. = MSA Rome-Ciampino

Aeroporto Ciampino Ovest, Palazzina N.131, I-00040 Roma, Italy ☎ (06) 79 34 06 14 Tx: 616123 mistr i Fax: (06) 79 34 09 01 SITA: n/a
F: 1980 55 Head: Werner Romanello ICAO: AIRMERCI Net: n/a

☐ I-ATPI	Beech Bonanza F33A	CE-464		0073		1 CO IO-520-BA	1542	Trainer		
☐ I-TNTC	BAe 146-200 (QT)	E2078	G-5-078*	0087	1287	4 LY ALF502R-5	42184	Freighter	BH-EP	lsf/opf TNT Traco in TNT-cs/cvtd -200
☐ G-TNTM	BAe 146-300 (QT)	E3166	RP-C480	0090	0397	4 LY ALF502R-5	44225	Freighter	AE-RS	lsf/opf TNT in TNT-cs/cvtd -300

NAUTA, Srl. = DLO Treviso

Via P.M. Pennacchi 1, I-31100 Treviso, Italy ☎ (0422) 30 40 64 Tx: none Fax: (0422) 42 16 10 SITA: n/a
F: n/a n/a Head: n/a ICAO: NAUTA Net: n/a

☐ I-DLON	Learjet 35A	35A-346	N35AJ	0080		2 GA TFE731-2-2B	8301			

PALIO AIR SERVICE, SpA = PLS Prato (PO)

Via de Fossi 14, I-50100 Prato Firenze, (PO), Italy ☎ (0574) 62 30 64 Tx: 575420 palair i Fax: (0574) 62 40 72 SITA: n/a
F: 1985 n/a Head: Nicola Rossi ICAO: PALIO Net: n/a Aircraft below MTOW 1361kg: Robinson R22

☐ I-ATOM	Eurocopter (Aerosp.) SA341G Gazelle	1073	F-BXPG	0073		1 TU Astazou IIIA	1800			lsf Locat
☐ I-TEST	Eurocopter (Aerosp.) AS355F1 Ecureuil 2	5119	N5791Z	0082		2 AN 250-C20F	2400			lsf Locat

PANAIR Compagnia Aerea Mediterranea, Srl. = PIT (formerly Panair Int'l, Srl.) Rome-Ciampino & Palermo

Aeroporto Ciampino Ovest, I-00040 Roma, Italy ☎ (06) 79 34 05 33 Tx: 616109 panain i Fax: (06) 79 34 03 82 SITA: n/a
F: 1979 25 Head: S.re Travagliante ICAO: PANAIRCAM Net: n/a

☐ I-AMCU	Cessna 500 Citation	500-0109	G-RAVY	0073		2 PWC JT15D-1	5216			lsf In Leasing
☐ I-AUNY	Cessna 501 Citation I/SP	501-0213	N6785D	0081		2 PWC JT15D-1A	5375			
☐ I-UUNY	Cessna 500 Citation I	500-0358	SE-DEP	0077		2 PWC JT15D-1A	5375			lsf Sicil Fly
☐ I-FLYD	Cessna 550 Citation II	550-0393	N12GK	0081		2 PWC JT15D-4	6033			
☐ I-PNCA	Cessna 550 Citation II	550-0235	N67SG	0081		2 PWC JT15D-4	6033			lsf Romaleasing

ROSSI, Srl. Brescia-Montichiari

Via S. Zeno 40, I-25125 Brescia, (BS), Italy ☎ (030) 22 00 68 Tx: 301322 rossi i Fax: (030) 242 12 01 SITA: n/a
F: n/a n/a Head: Luigi Rossi Net: n/a

☐ I-EJRA	Cessna 402B	402B0918	N82931	0075		2 CO TSIO-520-E	2858	Photo		
☐ I-ISOR	Cessna 402B	402B0438		0073		2 CO TSIO-520-E	2858	Photo / Survey		

S.A.M., Srl. - Società Aerea Meridionale Bellizzi (SA)

Via Olmo 24, I-84092 Bellizzi, (SA), Italy ☎ (0828) 35 41 55 Tx: 770143 i Fax: (0828) 35 42 11 SITA: n/a
F: 1989 8 Head: Guido Rainone ICAO: UNIRAI Net: n/a Aircraft below MTOW 1361kg: Robinson R22.

☐ I-CSAM	Eurocopter (Aerosp.) AS350B1 Ecureuil	2233		0089		1 TU Arriel 1D	2200	VIP / Utility		
☐ I-DSAM	Eurocopter (Aerosp.) AS350B1 Ecureuil	2296	F-WYMA*	0089		1 TU Arriel 1D	2200	EMS		
☐ I-VIMU	Eurocopter (Aerosp.) AS355F2 Ecureuil 2	5443		0090	0098	2 AN 250-C20F	2540	EMS		

SARDAIRLINE, So. Coop. Arl. = SAP Cagliari

Viale Ciusa 16, I-09131 Cagliari, Italy ☎ (070) 24 11 73 Tx: none Fax: (070) 24 04 92 SITA: n/a
F: 1995 n/a Head: n/a ICAO: SARDAIR Net: n/a

☐ I-DEPE	Britten-Norman BN-2B-26 Islander	2253	G-BTLY*	0091	0595	2 LY O-540-E4C5	2810	Y9		lsf Codit

216 registration type of aircraft cn/fn ex/ex* mfd del powered by mtow kg configuration selcal name/fln/specialitites/remarks

SERIB WINGS, Srl. = ISW

Turin-Caselle

Via Rocca Vecchia 2, I-27029 Vigevano, (PV), Italy ☎ (0381) 77 441 Tx: none Fax: (0381) 77 443 SITA: n/a

F: 1988 ⚹⚹⚹ 12 Head: n/a ICAO: SERIB Net: n/a

☐ I-SWAB	Fairchild (Swearingen) SA226TC Metro II	*TC-402*	*OO-JJJ*	*0081*	*0591*	*2 GA TPE331-3UW-304G*	*5670*	*Y19*		

SIRIO, SpA = SIO

Milan-Linate

Viale dell'Aviazone 65, I-20138 Milano, Italy ☎ (02) 70 20 99 66 Tx: none Fax: (02) 70 20 99 60 SITA: n/a

F: n/a ⚹⚹⚹ n/a Head: n/a ICAO: SIRIO Net: n/a

☐ I-DDVE	Eurocopter (Aerosp.) AS365N2 Dauphin 2	*6414*	*G-CBRA*	*0092*	*0098*	*2 TU Arriel 1C2*	*4250*			*lsf Del.Air Srl.*
☐ I-SDFG	Hawker 800A (BAe 125-800A)	*258136*	*N452SM*	*0088*	*0796*	*2 GA TFE731-5R-1H*	*12249*			*lsf Trevi SpA*

SOREM – Società Richerche Esperienze Meteorologiche, Srl.

Rome-Ciampino

Aeroporto Ciampino, Bldg. 131, I-00040 Ciampino, Italy ☎ (06) 79 34 82 26 Tx: none Fax: (06) 79 34 06 87 SITA: n/a

F: n/a ⚹⚹⚹ n/a Head: Sebastiano Nervo Net: n/a

☐ I-CFST	Canadair CL-215 (CL-215-1A10)	*1072*	*MM62019*	*0082*	*0098*	*2 PW R-2800-CA3*	*19731*	*Tanker*		*2 / opf Corpo Forestale Statale*
☐ I-CFSZ	Canadair CL-215 (CL-215-1A10)	*1108*	*C-FFYO**	*0088*	*0098*	*2 PW R-2800-CA3*	*19731*	*Tanker*		*4 / opf Corpo Forestale Statale*
☐ I-SISB	Canadair CL-215 (CL-215-1A10)	*1034*	*UD.13-6*	*0074*	*0199*	*2 PW R-2800-CA3*	*19731*	*Tanker*		*6 / Amphibian*
☐ I-SISC	Canadair CL-215 (CL-215-1A10)	*1038*	*UD.13-10*	*0074*	*0199*	*2 PW R-2800-CA3*	*19731*	*Tanker*		*7 / Amphibian*
☐ I-DPCD	Canadair CL-415 (CL-215-6B11)	*2003*	*C-FTUA**	*0094*	*0098*	*2 PWC PW123AF*	*19890*	*Tanker*		*Amphibian / opf Protezione Civile*
☐ I-DPCE	Canadair CL-415 (CL-215-6B11)	*2004*	*C-FTUS**	*0094*	*0098*	*2 PWC PW123AF*	*19890*	*Tanker*		*Amphibian / opf Protezione Civile*
☐ I-DPCN	Canadair CL-415 (CL-215-6B11)	*2008*	*C-FUAK**	*0095*	*0098*	*2 PWC PW123AF*	*19890*	*Tanker*		*Amphibian / opf Protezione Civile*
☐ I-DPCO	Canadair CL-415 (CL-215-6B11)	*2009*	*C-FVRA**	*0095*	*0098*	*2 PWC PW123AF*	*19890*	*Tanker*		*Amphibian / opf Protezione Civile*
☐ I-DPCP	Canadair CL-415 (CL-215-6B11)	*2020*	*C-FYCY**	*0096*	*0098*	*2 PWC PW123AF*	*19890*	*Tanker*		*Amphibian / opf Protezione Civile*
☐ I-DPCQ	Canadair CL-415 (CL-215-6B11)	*2021*	*C-FYDA**	*0096*	*0098*	*2 PWC PW123AF*	*19890*	*Tanker*		*Amphibian / opf Protezione Civile*
☐ I-DPCR	Canadair CL-415 (CL-215-6B11)	*2035*	*C-GCXG**	*0098*	*0798*	*2 PWC PW123AF*	*19890*	*Tanker*		*Amphibian / opf Protezione Civile*
☐ I-DPCS	Canadair CL-415 (CL-215-6B11)	*2036*	*C-GDHW**	*0098*	*0798*	*2 PWC PW123AF*	*19890*	*Tanker*		*Amphibian / opf Protezione Civile*
☐ I-DPCT	Canadair CL-415 (CL-215-6B11)			*0098*	*1098*	*2 PWC PW123AF*	*19890*	*Tanker*		*Amphibian / opf Protezione Civile*
☐ I-DPCU	Canadair CL-415 (CL-215-6B11)			*0098*	*1098*	*2 PWC PW123AF*	*19890*	*Tanker*		*Amphibian / opf Protezione Civile*

STAR WORK SKY, Sas – S.W.S. = SWP

Predosa Heliport

Via Case Sparse 69, I-15077 Predosa, (AL), Italy ☎ (0131) 71 513 Tx: none Fax: (0131) 71 513 SITA: n/a

F: 1981 ⚹⚹⚹ 3 Head: Giorgio Subrero ICAO: STAR WORK Net: n/a

☐ I-NJNO	Eurocopter (Aerosp.) SA318C Alouette II	*1804*	*F-BMRG*	*0062*		*1 TU Astazou IIA*	*1650*			
☐ I-SERY	Eurocopter (Aerosp.) SA315B Lama	*2603*	*F-GDCY*	*0081*		*1 TU Artouste IIIB1*	*1950*			
☐ I-NARE	Eurocopter (Aerosp.) AS350B Ecureuil	*1266*		*0080*		*1 TU Arriel 1B*	*1950*			

TELLAIR, S.A.

Bergamo-Orio al Serio

Via Girella 2, CH-6814 Lugano-Lamone, Switzerland ☎ (91) 960 21 70 Tx: none Fax: (91) 960 21 79 SITA: n/a

F: 1997 ⚹⚹⚹ n/a Head: Renzo Bianchini Net: http://www.tellair.com Presently being set-up. Intends to start operations (under the flight code & in conjunction with EURECA) during 99 with Jetstream 31 (to be lsf Filder Air Service, D).

UMBRIA FLY, Srl. = UFI

Rome-Urbe

Via Salaria 825, I-00138 Roma, Italy ☎ (06) 88 64 14 41 Tx: n/a Fax: (06) 812 31 37 SITA: n/a

F: 1992 ⚹⚹⚹ 3 Head: C.te Giampaolo Serantoni ICAO: UMBRIA FLY Net: n/a Aircraft below MTOW 1361kg: Partenavia P.57 & Piper PA-18

☐ I-RICI	Cessna 182R Skylane II	*18268105*	*N9909H*	*0081*		*1 CO O-470-U*	*1406*	*3 Pax*		*lsf C.G.A.*
☐ I-NEGL	Cessna 421A	*421A0138*	*OO-EDB*	*0069*		*2 CO GTSIO-520-D*	*3105*	*7 Pax*		*lsf Lirfly Trade Express*

VIGILI DEL FUOCO – Sez. Elicotteri (Helicopter Fire Service) (Div.of Dir.Generale Dip'mento Protezione Civile&Servizio Antincendio & Ministero dell'Interno)

Rome-Ciampino

DGPCSA, Palazzo Viminale, I-00184 Roma, Italy ☎ (06) 46 52 93 11 Tx: none Fax: (06) 46 52 94 04 SITA: n/a

F: n/a ⚹⚹⚹ n/a Head: D.I. Demetrio Teodoracopulos Net: n/a Non-commercial national organisation conducting fire-fighting missions.

The helicopters are allocated to 12 units/Nuclei Elicotteri based at Arezzo, Bari, Bologna, Catania, Genoa, Pescara, Rome-Ciampino, Sassari, Salerno, Torino, Varese & Venice. Former I-VF registrations are still used as callsign.

☐ VF-10	Agusta-Bell 206B JetRanger II	*8514*	*I-VFEA*	*0075*	*0276*	*1 AN 250-C20*	*1450*			
☐ VF-12	Agusta-Bell 206B JetRanger	*8058*	*I-VFER*	*0068*	*1068*	*1 AN 250-C20*	*1450*			
☐ VF-14	Agusta-Bell 206B JetRanger III	*8650*	*I-VFAA*	*0082*	*0782*	*1 AN 250-C20B*	*1450*			
☐ VF-15	Agusta-Bell 206B JetRanger III	*8651*	*I-VFAB*	*0082*	*0782*	*1 AN 250-C20B*	*1450*			
☐ VF-16	Agusta-Bell 206B JetRanger III	*8653*	*I-VFAC*	*0082*	*0782*	*1 AN 250-C20B*	*1450*			
☐ VF-18	Agusta-Bell 206B JetRanger III	*8655*	*I-VFAD*	*0082*	*0782*	*1 AN 250-C20B*	*1450*			
☐ VF-19	Agusta-Bell 206B JetRanger III	*8656*	*I-VFAE*	*0082*	*0782*	*1 AN 250-C20B*	*1450*			
☐ VF-20	Agusta-Bell 206B JetRanger III	*8659*	*I-VFAF*	*0082*	*0882*	*1 AN 250-C20B*	*1450*			
☐ VF-21	Agusta-Bell 206B JetRanger III	*8660*	*I-VFAG*	*0082*	*1182*	*1 AN 250-C20B*	*1450*			
☐ VF-22	Agusta-Bell 206B JetRanger III	*8662*	*I-VFAH*	*0082*	*1182*	*1 AN 250-C20B*	*1450*			
☐ VF-23	Agusta-Bell 206B JetRanger III	*8663*	*I-VFAI*	*0082*	*1182*	*1 AN 250-C20B*	*1450*			
☐ VF-24	Agusta-Bell 206B JetRanger III	*8664*	*I-VFAL*	*0082*	*1182*	*1 AN 250-C20B*	*1450*			
☐ VF-25	Agusta-Bell 206B JetRanger III	*8667*	*I-VFAM*	*0082*	*1282*	*1 AN 250-C20B*	*1450*			
☐ VF-26	Agusta-Bell 206B JetRanger III	*8670*	*I-VFAN*	*0082*	*1282*	*1 AN 250-C20B*	*1450*			
☐ VF-27	Agusta-Bell 206B JetRanger III	*8671*	*I-VFAO*	*0082*	*1282*	*1 AN 250-C20B*	*1450*			
☐ VF-28	Agusta-Bell 206B JetRanger III	*8673*	*I-VFAP*	*0082*	*0183*	*1 AN 250-C20B*	*1450*			
☐ VF-30	Agusta-Bell 204VF	*3093*	*I-VFMB*	*0063*		*1 GE T58-GE-3*	*3856*			
☐ VF-31	Agusta-Bell 204VF	*3135*	*I-VFMC*	*0064*		*1 GE T58-GE-3*	*3856*			
☐ VF-32	Agusta-Bell 204VF	*3143*	*I-VFMD*	*0064*		*1 GE T58-GE-3*	*3856*			
☐ VF-33	Agusta-Bell 204VF	*3149*	*I-VFME*	*0064*		*1 GE T58-GE-3*	*3856*			
☐ VF-34	Agusta-Bell 204VF	*3148*	*I-VFMF*	*0064*		*1 GE T58-GE-3*	*3856*			
☐ VF-35	Agusta-Bell 204VF	*3214*	*I-VFMG*	*0065*		*1 GE T58-GE-3*	*3856*			
☐ VF-36	Agusta-Bell 204VF	*3215*	*I-VFMH*	*0065*		*1 GE T58-GE-3*	*3856*			
☐ VF-37	Agusta-Bell 204VF	*3219*	*I-VFML*	*0065*		*1 GE T58-GE-3*	*3856*			
☐ VF-39	Agusta-Bell 204VF	*3223*	*I-VFMP*	*0065*		*1 GE T58-GE-3*	*3856*			
☐ VF-40	Agusta-Bell 204VF	*3225*	*I-VFMR*	*0065*		*1 GE T58-GE-3*	*3856*			
☐ VF-42	Agusta-Bell 204VF	*3227*	*I-VFMT*	*0065*		*1 GE T58-GE-3*	*3856*			
☐ VF-04	Agusta-Bell 205A-1	*4502*	*I-VFES*	*0071*	*0471*	*1 LY T5313B*	*4310*			
☐ VF-50	Agusta-Bell 412	*25501*	*I-VFOB*	*0084*	*1184*	*2 PWC PT6T-3B TwinPac*	*5400*			
☐ VF-51	Agusta-Bell 412	*25559*	*I-VFOC*	*0088*		*2 PWC PT6T-3B TwinPac*	*5400*			
☐ VF-52	Agusta-Bell 412	*25543*	*I-VFOD*	*0086*		*2 PWC PT6T-3B TwinPac*	*5400*			
☐ VF-53	Agusta-Bell 412	*25544*	*I-VFOE*	*0086*		*2 PWC PT6T-3B TwinPac*	*5400*			
☐ VF-54	Agusta-Bell 412	*25545*	*I-VFOF*	*0086*		*2 PWC PT6T-3B TwinPac*	*5400*			
☐ VF-55	Agusta-Bell 412	*25558*	*I-VFOG*	*0088*		*2 PWC PT6T-3B TwinPac*	*5400*			
☐ VF-56	Agusta-Bell 412	*25620*	*I-VFOH*	*0092*	*0392*	*2 PWC PT6T-3B TwinPac*	*5400*			
☐ VF-57	Agusta-Bell 412	*25622*	*I-VFOI*	*0092*	*0392*	*2 PWC PT6T-3B TwinPac*	*5400*			
☐ VF-58	Agusta-Bell 412EP	*25904*	*I-VFOL*	*0096*	*0097*	*2 PWC PT6T-3D TwinPac*	*5400*			
☐ VF-59	Agusta-Bell 412EP	*25905*	*I-VFOM*	*0096*	*0097*	*2 PWC PT6T-3D TwinPac*	*5400*			
☐ VF-60	Agusta-Bell 412EP	*25906*	*I-VFON*	*0097*	*0097*	*2 PWC PT6T-3D TwinPac*	*5400*			
☐ VF-61	Agusta-Bell 412EP	*25907*	*I-VFOP*	*0097*	*0097*	*2 PWC PT6T-3D TwinPac*	*5400*			

VIGILI DEL FUOCO TRENTO – Nucleo Elicotteri (Division of the Provincia Autonoma di Trento, Serv. Antincendi)

Trento

Aeroporto G. Caproni, I-38100 Trento (TN), Italy ☎ (0461) 49 23 60 Tx: none Fax: (0461) 94 45 88 SITA: n/a

F: 1958 ⚹⚹⚹ 16 Head: Sandro Rossato (Director Operativo) Net: n/a Non-commercial organisation of the Province of Trento conducting fire-fighting, search & rescue, EMS & civil protection flight missions.

☐ I-PELL	Eurocopter (Aerosp.) SA315B Lama	*2621*		*0082*	*0095*	*1 TU Artouste IIIB*	*1950*			
☐ I-SINE	Eurocopter (Aerosp.) SA316B Alouette III	*1203*	*I-SIBE*	*0064*	*0080*	*1 TU Artouste IIIB1*	*2200*	*SAR / EMS*		
☐ I-PATE	Eurocopter (Aerosp.) AS365N2 Dauphin 2	*6356*		*0090*	*1290*	*2 TU Arriel 1C2*	*4250*	*SAR / EMS*		

VOLARE AIRLINES, SpA = 8D / VLE (Member of SAirGroup)

Verona

Corso Garibaldi 186, I-36016 Tiene (VI), Italy ☎ (0445) 80 01 00 Tx: none Fax: (0445) 80 01 01 SITA: n/a

F: 1997 ⚹⚹⚹ n/a Head: Vincenzo Soddu ICAO: REVOLA Net: n/a

☐ F-GJVU	Airbus Industrie A320-211	*436*	*G-BXAT*	*0093*	*0298*	*2 CFMI CFM56-5A1*	*77000*	*Y180*	*PR-CE*	*lsf GATX*
☐ F-GJVX	Airbus Industrie A320-211	*420*	*PH-GCX*	*0093*	*0398*	*2 CFMI CFM56-5A1*	*77000*	*Y180*		*lsf GATX*
☐ F-OHFT	Airbus Industrie A320-212	*343*	*G-UKLK*	*0092*	*1198*	*2 CFMI CFM56-5A3*	*75500*	*Y180*		*lsf GATX*

VULCAN AIR, SpA = CDF (formerly Samanta, SpA)

Naples-Capodichino

Via G. Pascoli 7, I-80026 Casoria, (NA), Italy ☎ (081) 591 82 37 Tx: none Fax: (081) 591 81 72 SITA: n/a

F: 1989 ⚹⚹⚹ 85 Head: Carlo de Feo Net: http://www.vulancair.com

☐ I-AITE	Partenavia AP68TP-600 Viator	*9006*		*0088*		*2 AN 250-B17C*	*3000*	*Surveyer/Trainer*		*lsf Alenia SpA*
☐ I-AITT	Partenavia AP68TP-300 Spartacus	*8011*		*0087*		*2 AN 250-B17C*	*2600*	*TPF Trainer*		
☐ I-ODUE	Partenavia P.68 Observer 2	*384-01-OB2*		*0088*		*2 LY IO-360-A1B6*	*2084*	*Surveyer/Trainer*		
☐ I-SMTA	Partenavia P.68 Observer 2	*393-04-OB2*		*0091*		*2 LY IO-360-A1B6*	*2084*	*Surveyer/Trainer*		
☐ I-TLRN	Partenavia AP68TP-600 Viator	*9005*	*I-RAIL*	*0092*	*0597*	*2 AN 250-B17C*	*3000*	*Surveyer/Trainer*		*lsf Finmeccanica SpA*
☐ I-VULA	SIAI-Marchetti SF.600A Canguro	*010*		*0090*	*0097*	*2 AN 250-B17F*	*2800*	*TPF Trainer*		
☐ I-VULB	SIAI-Marchetti SF.600 Canguro	*006*	*I-CNGT*	*0086*	*0097*	*2 AN 250-B17C*	*2800*	*TPF Trainer*		
☐ I-VULC	Learjet 35A	*35A-421*	*N413JP*	*0081*	*0397*	*2 GA TFE731-2-2B*	*8165*	*TPF Trainer*		*lsf Locat*

217 registration type of aircraft *cn/fn* *ex/ex** *mfd* *del* *powered by* *mtow kg* *configuration* *selcal* *name/fln/specialitites/remarks*

JA = JAPAN (Nihon Koku)

Capital: Tokyo Official Language: Japanese Population: 125,0 million Square Km: 377815 Dialling code: +81 Year established: 660 Acting political head: Keizo Obuchi (Prime Minister)

Government / Corporate / Executive / VIP Aircraft

registration	type of aircraft	cn/fn	ex/ex*	mfd	del	powered by	mtow kg	configuration	selcal	name/fln/specialitites/remarks
00001	Eurocopter (Aerosp.) AS332L Super Puma	2162	JA9629	0085	0186	2 TU Makila 1A	8600	VIP		Hato / Japan Ground Self-Defence Force
00002	Eurocopter (Aerosp.) AS332L Super Puma	2168	JA9630	0085	0286	2 TU Makila 1A	8600	VIP		Hibari / Japan Ground Self-Defence Force
00003	Eurocopter (Aerosp.) AS332L Super Puma	2125	JA9631	0085	0386	2 TU Makila 1A	8600	VIP		Kamome / Japan Ground Self-Defence Force
20-1101	Boeing 747-47C	24730 / 816	JA8091	0091	0492	4 GE CF6-80C2B1F	363000	VIP	AB-CQ	Japan Air Self-Defence Force
20-1102	Boeing 747-47C	24731 / 839	JA8092	0091	0492	4 GE CF6-80C2B1F	363000	VIP	AB-DQ	Japan Air Self-Defence Force

ACE HELICOPTER, Co. Ltd (formerly Nihon Norin Helicopter, Co. Ltd)

Kawagoe

1610 Yanagihara Furuyahongo, Kawagoe-shi, Saitama-ken 350-0002, Japan ☎ (3) 35 03 55 51 Tx: none Fax: (3) 32 22 41 50 SITA: n/a

F: n/a 🚶 400 Head: Tsutou Ono Net: n/a Aircraft below MTOW 1361 kg: Bell & Kawasaki-Bell & Soloy-Bell 47G, Hiller UH-12E & Hughes 269C (300C).

registration	type of aircraft	cn/fn	ex/ex*	mfd	del	powered by	mtow kg	configuration	selcal	name/fln/specialitites/remarks
JA6042	MD Helicopters MD 500E (Hughes 369E)	0421E		0090	1190	1 AN 250-C20B	1361			
JA6069	MD Helicopters MD 500E (Hughes 369E)	0409E		0090	0291	1 AN 250-C20B	1361			
JA6105	MD Helicopters MD 500E (Hughes 369E)	0492E		0091		1 AN 250-C20B	1361			
JA6106	MD Helicopters MD 500E (Hughes 369E)	0496E		0091		1 AN 250-C20B	1361			
JA6107	MD Helicopters MD 500E (Hughes 369E)	0497E		0091		1 AN 250-C20B	1361			
JA9385	MD Helicopters MD 500D (Hughes 369D)	1080378D	N58230	0078		1 AN 250-C20B	1361			
JA9386	MD Helicopters MD 500D (Hughes 369D)	490490D	N58287	0079		1 AN 250-C20B	1361			
JA9387	MD Helicopters MD 500D (Hughes 369D)	1280433D	N58283	0078		1 AN 250-C20B	1361			
JA9415	MD Helicopters MD 500D (Hughes 369D)	800778D	N1102A	0080		1 AN 250-C20B	1361			
JA9417	MD Helicopters MD 500D (Hughes 369D)	1087D	N5114Y	0081		1 AN 250-C20B	1361			
JA9418	MD Helicopters MD 500E (Hughes 369E)	0152E		0086		1 AN 250-C20B	1361			
JA9419	MD Helicopters MD 500D (Hughes 369D)	1098D	N51338	0081		1 AN 250-C20B	1361			
JA9420	MD Helicopters MD 500D (Hughes 369D)	1099D	N5124X	0081		1 AN 250-C20B	1361			lsf Mitsui Lease Jigyo
JA9436	MD Helicopters MD 500D (Hughes 369D)	1190627D	N58355	0080		1 AN 250-C20B	1361			
JA9482	MD Helicopters MD 500E (Hughes 369E)	0219E	N1601U	0087		1 AN 250-C20B	1361			lsf Katsuhiko Nonome
JA9483	MD Helicopters MD 500E (Hughes 369E)	0222E	N1602B	0087		1 AN 250-C20B	1361			
JA9723	MD Helicopters MD 500E (Hughes 369E)	0022E		0084	0292	1 AN 250-C20B	1361			
JA9804	MD Helicopters MD 500E (Hughes 369E)	0326E		0089		1 AN 250-C20B	1361			lsf Mitsui Lease Jigyo
JA9805	MD Helicopters MD 500E (Hughes 369E)	0327E		0089	0489	1 AN 250-C20B	1361			lsf Mitsui Lease Jigyo
JA9806	MD Helicopters MD 500E (Hughes 369E)	0328E		0089	0489	1 AN 250-C20B	1361			lsf Mitsui Lease Jigyo
JA9899	MD Helicopters MD 500E (Hughes 369E)	0394E		0090	0790	1 AN 250-C20B	1361			
JA6022	Bell 206B JetRanger III	4129	N6504J	0091		1 AN 250-C20J	1451			lsf ITC Leasing
JA6061	Bell 206B JetRanger III	4145		0091	0491	1 AN 250-C20J	1451			
JA6063	Bell 206B JetRanger III	4147		0091	0491	1 AN 250-C20J	1451			
JA6064	Bell 206B JetRanger III	4150		0091	0491	1 AN 250-C20J	1451			
JA6109	Bell 206B JetRanger III	4165	N4304F*	0091		1 AN 250-C20J	1451			lsf Kogin Lease
JA6113	Bell 206B JetRanger III	4192		0091		1 AN 250-C20J	1451			
JA9475	Bell 206B JetRanger III	3396	N2140X	0081		1 AN 250-C20B	1451			lsf Higashi Nihon Jyutaku
JA9480	Bell 206B JetRanger III	3944	N3203L	0087		1 AN 250-C20J	1451			
JA9490	Bell 206B JetRanger III	3052	N1031R	0080	0792	1 AN 250-C20B	1451			lsf Mitsui Lease Jigyo
JA9751	Bell 206B JetRanger III	2654	N2747W	0079	0493	1 AN 250-C20B	1451			lsf Mitsui Lease Jigyo
JA9817	Bell 206B JetRanger III	4054		0089		1 AN 250-C20J	1451			
JA9864	Bell 206B JetRanger III	4081		0090		1 AN 250-C20J	1451			lsf ITC Leasing
JA9865	Bell 206B JetRanger III	4082		0090		1 AN 250-C20J	1451			lsf Crown Leasing
JA9866	Bell 206B JetRanger III	4083		0090		1 AN 250-C20J	1451			lsf Kogin Lease
JA9867	Bell 206B JetRanger III	4084		0090		1 AN 250-C20J	1451			lsf Kogin Lease
JA9868	Bell 206B JetRanger III	4085		0090		1 AN 250-C20J	1451			lsf Kogin Lease
JA9869	Bell 206B JetRanger III	4086		0090		1 AN 250-C20J	1451			lsf Kogin Lease
JA6121	MD Helicopters MD 520N (Hughes 500N)	LN034		0092		1 AN 250-C20R	1520			lsf Takeda
JA6050	Eurocopter (Aerosp.) AS350B Ecureuil	2425		0090	1290	1 TU Arriel 1B	1950			
JA9235	Eurocopter (Aerosp.) AS350B Ecureuil	1130		0079		1 TU Arriel 1B	1950			
JA9309	Eurocopter (Aerosp.) AS350B Ecureuil	1527		0081		1 TU Arriel 1B	1950			
JA9357	Eurocopter (Aerosp.) AS350B Ecureuil	1725		0083		1 TU Arriel 1B	1950			
JA9803	Eurocopter (Aerosp.) AS350B Ecureuil	2181		0089	0490	1 TU Arriel 1B	1950			
JA6629	Eurocopter (Aerosp.) AS355F2 Ecureuil 2	5446		0090		2 AN 250-C20F	2540			
JA6630	Eurocopter (Aerosp.) AS355F2 Ecureuil 2	5447		0090		2 AN 250-C20F	2540			
JA9592	Eurocopter (Aerosp.) AS355F1 Ecureuil 2	5295		0083		2 AN 250-C20F	2400			cvtd AS355F
JA9653	Eurocopter (Aerosp.) AS355F1 Ecureuil 2	5055	N5795T	0081		2 AN 250-C20F	2400			lsf ITC Leasing
JA9670	Eurocopter (Aerosp.) AS355F2 Ecureuil 2	5365		0087	0691	2 AN 250-C20F	2540			
JA9910	Eurocopter (Aerosp.) AS355F1 Ecureuil 2	5005	9V-BNA	0081	0991	2 AN 250-C20F	2400			
JA9696	Kawasaki (Eurocopter/MBB) BK117A-4	1017		0088		2 LY LTS101-650B.1	3200			lsf Subaru Kosan
JA9125	Fuji-Bell 204B	CH-33		0074		1 KA KT5311A	3856			
JA9203	Fuji-Bell 204B-2	CH-46		0078		1 KA KT5313B	3856			
JA9257	Fuji-Bell 204B-2	CH-51		0080		1 KA KT5313B	3856			
JA6175	Fuji-Bell 205B	01		0095		1 LY T5317B	4763			lsf ITC Leasing
JA9854	Bell 205B	30188	N394EH	0075	0891	1 LY T5513B	4763			lsf Mitsui Lease Jigyo / cvtd 205A-1
JA9446	Bell 214B BigLifter	28032	N4434D	0078		1 LY T5508D	7257			

AERO ASAHI, Corp. – Asahi Koyo

Tokyo-Heliport & Osaka-Yao

Sunshine 60, 43rd Floor, 1-1-3 Higashi-Ikebukuro, Toshima-ku, Tokyo 170-6070, Japan ☎ (3) 39 88 95 72 Tx: none Fax: (3) 39 88 28 48 SITA: n/a

F: 1955 🚶 n/a Head: Toru Nakahura Net: http://www.owl.or.jp/aeroasahi/ Aircraft below MTOW 1361 kg: Cessna 150 & 172.

registration	type of aircraft	cn/fn	ex/ex*	mfd	del	powered by	mtow kg	configuration	selcal	name/fln/specialitites/remarks
JA6136	Bell 206B JetRanger III	4294		0094	0494	1 AN 250-C20J	1451			
JA6137	Bell 206B JetRanger III	4295		0094	0494	1 AN 250-C20J	1451			
JA6138	Bell 206B JetRanger III	4296		0094	0494	1 AN 250-C20J	1451			
JA6150	Bell 206B JetRanger III	4326	N20334	0094	0395	1 AN 250-C20J	1451			
JA6164	Bell 206B JetRanger III	4327	N20887	0094	0395	1 AN 250-C20J	1451			
JA6165	Bell 206B JetRanger III	4328	N20956	0094	0395	1 AN 250-C20J	1451			
JA6179	Bell 206B JetRanger III	4387	N9210T	0096	0496	1 AN 250-C20J	1451			
JA6180	Bell 206B JetRanger III	4388	N92110	0096	0496	1 AN 250-C20J	1451			
JA6192	Bell 206B JetRanger III	4437		0097	0097	1 AN 250-C20J	1450			lsf Yamamizu Kaiun
JA6193	Bell 206B JetRanger III	4438		0097	0097	1 AN 250-C20J	1450			lsf Yamamizu Kaiun
JA6500	Bell 206B JetRanger III	4456		0097	0198	1 AN 250-C20J	1451			
JA9169	Bell 206B JetRanger II	2112		0076		1 AN 250-C20	1451			
JA9186	Bell 206B JetRanger III	2263		0077		1 AN 250-C20B	1451			
JA9194	Bell 206B JetRanger III	2318		0078		1 AN 250-C20B	1451			
JA9199	Bell 206B JetRanger III	2366		0078		1 AN 250-C20B	1451			
JA9200	Bell 206B JetRanger III	2369		0078		1 AN 250-C20B	1451			
JA9210	Bell 206B JetRanger III	2477		0078		1 AN 250-C20B	1451			
JA9232	Bell 206B JetRanger III	2685		0079		1 AN 250-C20B	1451			lsf Asahi Helicopter
JA9256	Bell 206B JetRanger III	3007		0080		1 AN 250-C20B	1451			
JA9266	Bell 206B JetRanger III	3135		0080		1 AN 250-C20B	1451			
JA9270	Bell 206B JetRanger III	3192		0080		1 AN 250-C20B	1451			
JA9283	Bell 206B JetRanger III	3251		0081		1 AN 250-C20B	1451			
JA9285	Bell 206B JetRanger III	3257		0081		1 AN 250-C20B	1451			
JA9287	Bell 206B JetRanger III	3263		0081		1 AN 250-C20B	1451			
JA9300	Bell 206B JetRanger III	3383		0081		1 AN 250-C20B	1451			
JA9310	Bell 206G JetRanger III	3555		0081		1 AN 250-C20B	1451			
JA9335	Bell 206B JetRanger III	3638		0082		1 AN 250-C20B	1451			
JA9384	Bell 206B JetRanger III	3300	N2039S	0081		1 AN 250-C20B	1451			
JA9405	Bell 206B JetRanger III	2280	N44SM	0077		1 AN 250-C20B	1451			
JA9406	Bell 206B JetRanger III	3008	N206E	0080		1 AN 250-C20B	1451			
JA9456	Bell 206B JetRanger III	3355	N811PC	0081		1 AN 250-C20B	1451			
JA9469	Bell 206B JetRanger III	3561	N831DP	0081		1 AN 250-C20B	1451			
JA9223	Eurocopter (Aerosp.) AS350B Ecureuil	1077		0079		1 TU Arriel 1B	1950			
JA9224	Eurocopter (Aerosp.) AS350B Ecureuil	1088		0079		1 TU Arriel 1B	1950			
JA9252	Eurocopter (Aerosp.) AS350B Ecureuil	1238		0080		1 TU Arriel 1B	1950			
JA9303	Eurocopter (Aerosp.) AS350B Ecureuil	1505		0081		1 TU Arriel 1B	1950			
JA9313	Eurocopter (Aerosp.) AS350B Ecureuil	1535		0082		1 TU Arriel 1B	1950			
JA9316	Eurocopter (Aerosp.) AS350B Ecureuil	1541		0082		1 TU Arriel 1B	1950			
JA9326	Eurocopter (Aerosp.) AS350B Ecureuil	1557		0082		1 TU Arriel 1B	1950			
JA9343	Eurocopter (Aerosp.) AS350B Ecureuil	1671		0083		1 TU Arriel 1B	1950			
JA9352	Eurocopter (Aerosp.) AS350B Ecureuil	1684		0083		1 TU Arriel 1B	1950			
JA9467	Eurocopter (Aerosp.) AS350B Ecureuil	1995		0087		1 TU Arriel 1B	1950			lsf Koseido Kaihatsu
JA9468	Eurocopter (Aerosp.) AS350B Ecureuil	1994		0087	0889	1 TU Arriel 1B	1950			
JA9807	Eurocopter (Aerosp.) AS350B Ecureuil	2190		0089		1 TU Arriel 1B	1950			lsf Tokyo Soko Unyu
JA6725	Eurocopter (Aerosp.) AS355F2 Ecureuil 2	5555		0093	1293	2 AN 250-C20F	2540			

☐ JA9573	Eurocopter (Aerosp.) AS355F1 Ecureuil 2	5125		0082		2 AN 250-C20F	2400			cvtd AS355F
☐ JA9580	Eurocopter (Aerosp.) AS355F2 Ecureuil 2	5218		0082		2 AN 250-C20F	2540			cvtd AS355F1
☐ JA9587	Eurocopter (Aerosp.) AS355F1 Ecureuil 2	5275		0082		2 AN 250-C20F	2400			cvtd AS355F
☐ JA9590	Eurocopter (Aerosp.) AS355F1 Ecureuil 2	5279		0083		2 AN 250-C20F	2400			cvtd AS355F
☐ JA9601	Eurocopter (Aerosp.) AS355F2 Ecureuil 2	5304		0083		2 AN 250-C20F	2540			cvtd AS355F1
☐ JA9639	Eurocopter (Aerosp.) AS355F2 Ecureuil 2	5323		0086		2 AN 250-C20F	2540			cvtd AS355F1
☐ JA9952	Eurocopter (Aerosp.) AS355F2 Ecureuil 2	5294		0083	0489	2 AN 250-C20F	2540			cvtd AS355F1
☐ JA6757	MD Helicopters MD 900 Explorer	900-00018		0095	0895	2 PWC PW206A	2722			
☐ JA6789	MD Helicopters MD 900 Explorer	900-00028		0096	0596	2 PWC PW206A	2722			
☐ JA6790	MD Helicopters MD 900 Explorer	900-00024	N90375	0096	0796	2 PWC PW206A	2722			
☐ JA6906	MD Helicopters MD 900 Explorer	900-00055		0098	0698	2 PWC PW206A	2722			
☐ JA9586	Kawasaki (Eurocopter/MBB) BK117A-3	1001	JQ1001*	0082		2 LY LTS101-650B.1	3200			cvtd BK117
☐ JA9615	Kawasaki (Eurocopter/MBB) BK117A-3	1008		0082		2 LY LTS101-650B.1	3200			cvtd BK117
☐ JA5200	Twin (Aero) Shrike Commander 500S	3149	N9180N	0073		2 LY IO-540-E1B5	3062			
☐ JA5313	Twin (Aero) Shrike Commander 500S	3296	N12LD	0077	0893	2 LY IO-540-E1B5	3062			
☐ JA6734	Bell 230	23020	N5292B	0094	0794	2 AN 250C-30G2	3810			lsf Mitsui Bussan Aerospace
☐ JA6026	Fuji-Bell 204B-2	CH-58		0091	0491	1 KA KT5313B	3856			
☐ JA9148	Fuji-Bell 204B-2	CH-37		0074		1 KA KT5313B	3856			
☐ JA9155	Fuji-Bell 204B-2	CH-38		0076	0994	1 KA KT5313B	3856			
☐ JA9163	Fuji-Bell 204B-2	CH-39		0076		1 KA KT5313B	3856			
☐ JA6900	Bell 430	49030	N72073*	0097	1197	2 AN 250-C40	4082			
☐ JA6181	Fuji-Bell 205B	02		0095		1 LY T5317B	4763			
☐ JA6612	Sikorsky S-76A	760064	N1546Z	0080	0690	2 AN 250-C30S	4672			
☐ JA6693	Sikorsky S-76C	760388		0091	1091	2 TU Arriel 1S1	5307			
☐ JA6788	Sikorsky S-76C+	760459		0096	1097	2 TU Arriel 2S1	5307			
☐ JA6901	Sikorsky S-76C+	760482		0098	0398	2 TU Arriel 2S1	5307			
☐ JA9603	Sikorsky S-76A	760234		0083	1089	2 AN 250-C30S	4672			lsf Mitsui Lease Jigyo
☐ JA8870	Piper PA-42-1000 Cheyenne 400LS	42-5527040	N9219G	0088	1097	2 GA TPE331-114	5466			
☐ JA9572	Bell 412	33051	B-12127	0081		2 PWC PT6T-3B TwinPac	5398			
☐ JA9584	Bell 412	33030	N2196K	0081		2 PWC PT6T-3B TwinPac	5398			
☐ JA9599	Bell 412	33066	N3886W	0082		2 PWC PT6T-3B TwinPac	5398			lsf Asahi Helicopter
☐ JA9616	Bell 412SP	33109	9M-SSQ	0084	0993	2 PWC PT6T-3B TwinPac	5398			
☐ JA01TM	Cessna 560 Citation V Ultra	560-0403		0097	1197	2 PWC JT15D-5D	7394			
☐ JA6658	Eurocopter (Aerosp.) SA330J Puma	1627	N627E	0080	0990	2 TU Turmo IVC	7400			
☐ JA6732	Eurocopter (Aerosp.) SA330J Puma	1227	I-EHPE	0073	0394	2 TU Turmo IVC	7400			
☐ JA9541	Eurocopter (Aerosp.) SA330J Puma	1589		0079		2 TU Turmo IVC	7400			lsf Mitsui Shintaku Ginko
☐ JA9542	Eurocopter (Aerosp.) SA330J Puma	1604		0079		2 TU Turmo IVC	7400			lsf Asahi Helicopter
☐ JA9612	Eurocopter (Aerosp.) AS332L Super Puma	2131		0084		2 TU Makila 1A	8600			
☐ JA9635	Eurocopter (Aerosp.) AS332L Super Puma	2097	C-GSNA	0083		2 TU Makila 1A	8600			lsf Mitsui Lease Jigyo
☐ JA9690	Eurocopter (Aerosp.) AS332L Super Puma	2089	C-GQCO	0083		2 TU Makila 1A	8600			lsf Mitsui Lease Jigyo

AIR DOLPHIN, Co. Ltd

Okinawa-Naha

306-1 Kagamizu, Naha, Okinawa 901-0142, Japan ☎ (98) 858 73 51 Tx: none Fax: (98) 858 73 52 SITA: n/a

F: 1994 👥 n/a Head: n/a Net: n/a Aircraft below MTOW 1361 kg: Cessna 172.

☐ JA3428	Cessna P206C Super Skylane	P206-0517	N1610C	0068	0294	1 CO IO-520-A	1633			
☐ JA5306	Britten-Norman BN-2B-26 Islander	2236	G-BSPO*	0091	0098	2 LY O-540-E4C5	2812			
☐ JA5232	Cessna 402B	402B0555	N2965Q	0074	0294	2 CO TSIO-520-E	2858			

AIR NIPPON, Co. Ltd – ANK Air Nippon, K.K. = EL / ANK (Associated with All Nippon Airways – ANA/formerly Nihon Kinkyori Airways, Co. Ltd)

Tokyo-Haneda

2-5 Kasumigaseki, 3-chome, Chiyoda-ku, Tokyo 100-0013, Japan ☎ (3) 54 62 19 11 Tx: 2422124 anktyo j Fax: (3) 54 62 19 50 SITA: n/a

F: 1974 👥 1200 Head: Akio Kondo IATA: 768 ICAO: ANK AIR Net: n/a Beside aircraft listed, additional aircraft (Boeing 767-381) are lsf All Nippon Airways (with additional ANK-titles) when required.

☐ JA8797	De Havilland DHC-6 Twin Otter 300	285	9V-BCL	0070	0374	2 PWC PT6A-27	5670	Y19		
☐ JA8799	De Havilland DHC-6 Twin Otter 300	420	C-GOWO*	0074	0874	2 PWC PT6A-27	5670	Y19		
☐ JA8722	NAMC YS-11A-213	2078		0068	0991	2 RR Dart 543-10J/K	24500	Y64		lsf ANA
☐ JA8727	NAMC YS-11A-213	2095		0069		2 RR Dart 543-10J/K	24500	Y64		
☐ JA8729	NAMC YS-11A-213	2097		0069		2 RR Dart 543-10J/K	24500	Y64		
☐ JA8734	NAMC YS-11A-213	2103		0069	0489	2 RR Dart 543-10J/K	24500	Y64		
☐ JA8735	NAMC YS-11A-213	2108		0069	0488	2 RR Dart 543-10J/K	24500	Y64		
☐ JA8744	NAMC YS-11A-513	2116		0069	0991	2 RR Dart 543-10J/K	24500	Y64		
☐ JA8761	NAMC YS-11A-513	2133		0070	1091	2 RR Dart 543-10J/K	24500	Y64		lsf ANA
☐ JA8772	NAMC YS-11A-523	2146	JQ2146*	0070	0188	2 RR Dart 543-10J/K	24500	Y64		
☐ JA8453	Boeing 737-281 (A)	21767 / 585		0079	0992	2 PW JT8D-17	49987	Y126		lsf ANA
☐ JA8454	Boeing 737-281 (A)	21768 / 586		0079	0992	2 PW JT8D-17	49987	Y126		lsf ANA
☐ JA8456	Boeing 737-281 (A)	21770 / 588		0079	0391	2 PW JT8D-17	49987	Y126		lsf ANA
☐ JA300K	Boeing 737-54K	27434 / 2872		0097	0597	2 CFMI CFM56-3C1	48988	Y126		
☐ JA301K	Boeing 737-54K	27435 / 2875		0597	0597	2 CFMI CFM56-3C1	48988	Y126		
☐ JA302K	Boeing 737-54K	28990 / 3002		0098	0398	2 CFMI CFM56-3C1	48988	Y126		
☐ JA303K	Boeing 737-54K	28991 / 3017		0098	0498	2 CFMI CFM56-3C1	48988	Y126		lsf Sky Dolphin & others
☐ JA304K	Boeing 737-54K	28992 / 3030		0098	0598	2 CFMI CFM56-3C1	48988	Y126		lsf MNE Lease
☐ JA305K	Boeing 737-54K	28993 / 3075	N1781B*	0098	1098	2 CFMI CFM56-3C1	48988	Y126		lsf Star Dolphin & others
☐ JA8195	Boeing 737-54K	27433 / 2815		0096	0996	2 CFMI CFM56-3C1	52390	Y126		lsf Air Dolphin Leasing
☐ JA8196	Boeing 737-54K	27966 / 2824		0096	1096	2 CFMI CFM56-3C1	52390	Y126		
☐ JA8404	Boeing 737-54K	27381 / 2708	N35108*	0095	0495	2 CFMI CFM56-3C1	48988	Y126		
☐ JA8419	Boeing 737-54K	27430 / 2723		0095	0795	2 CFMI CFM56-3C1	48988	Y126		lsf Mitsui Lease Jigyo
☐ JA8500	Boeing 737-54K	27431 / 2751		0095	0995	2 CFMI CFM56-3C1	48988	Y126		lsf Sumigin Lease
☐ JA8504	Boeing 737-54K	27432 / 2783		0096	0596	2 CFMI CFM56-3C1	48988	Y126		
☐ JA8595	Boeing 737-54K	28461 / 2850		0097	0297	2 CFMI CFM56-3C1	48988	Y126		
☐ JA8596	Boeing 737-54K	28462 / 2853		0097	0297	2 CFMI CFM56-3C1	48988	Y126		lsf J.L. Hawk Lease
☐ JA8387	Airbus Industrie A320-211	196	F-WWDE*	0091	0792	2 CFMI CFM56-5A1	67000	Y166		lsf ANA
☐ JA8389	Airbus Industrie A320-211	219	F-WWDZ*	0091	1193	2 CFMI CFM56-5A1	67000	Y166		lsf ANA
☐ JA8390	Airbus Industrie A320-211	245	F-WWDE*	0091	0693	2 CFMI CFM56-5A1	67000	Y166		lsf ANA
☐ JA8391	Airbus Industrie A320-211	300	F-WWDD*	0092	0693	2 CFMI CFM56-5A1	67000	Y166		lsf ANA

AIR OKHOTSK, Co. Ltd – AOH

Hokkaido-Memanbetsu

Chuo 258-1, Memanbetsu Aiport, Abashiri-Gun, Hokkaido 099-2371, Japan ☎ (1527) 43 705 Tx: n/a Fax: (1527) 43 987 SITA: n/a

F: 1978 👥 n/a Head: Noriyuki Fuchu Net: n/a Aircraft below MTOW 1361kg: Cessna 172

☐ JA5236	Cessna 402B	402B0597	N3739C	0074		2 CO TSIO-520-EB	2858			

ALL NIPPON AIRWAYS – ANA = NH / ANA (Zen Nippon Kuyu, K.K.)

Tokyo-Haneda

2-5 Kasumigaseki, 3-chome, Chiyoda-ku, Tokyo 100-6090, Japan ☎ (3) 35 80 47 11 Tx: 2223064 anahon j Fax: (3) 35 92 30 39 SITA: n/a

F: 1952 👥 13800 Head: Takaya Sugiura IATA: 205 ICAO: ALL NIPPON Net: http://www.ana.co.jp

☐ JA8871	Piper PA-42-720 Cheyenne IIIA	42-5501048	N92264*	0090	0390	2 PWC PT6A-61	5080	Trainer		
☐ JA8872	Piper PA-42-720 Cheyenne IIIA	42-5501049	N92266*	0090	0490	2 PWC PT6A-61	5080	Trainer		
☐ JA8873	Piper PA-42-720 Cheyenne IIIA	42-5501050	N92275*	0090	0590	2 PWC PT6A-61	5080	Trainer		
☐ JA8874	Piper PA-42-720 Cheyenne IIIA	42-5501058	N9194X*	0091	0491	2 PWC PT6A-61	5080	Trainer		
☐ JA8722	NAMC YS-11A-213	2078		0068	0968	2 RR Dart 543-10J/K	24500	Y64		lst ANK
☐ JA8761	NAMC YS-11A-513	2133		0070	0270	2 RR Dart 543-10J/K	24500	Y64		lst ANK
☐ JA8453	Boeing 737-281 (A)	21767 / 585		0079	0779	2 PW JT8D-17	49987	Y126		lst ANK
☐ JA8454	Boeing 737-281 (A)	21768 / 586		0079	0779	2 PW JT8D-17	49987	Y126		lst ANK
☐ JA8456	Boeing 737-281 (A)	21770 / 588		0079	0779	2 PW JT8D-17	49987	Y126		lst ANK
☐ JA8300	Airbus Industrie A320-211	549	F-WWIU*	0095	0995	2 CFMI CFM56-5A1	67000	Y166		lsf Kogin Lease
☐ JA8304	Airbus Industrie A320-211	531	F-WWDY*	0095	0595	2 CFMI CFM56-5A1	67000	Y166		lsf Fuyo Sogo Lease
☐ JA8313	Airbus Industrie A320-211	534	F-WWBC*	0095	0595	2 CFMI CFM56-5A1	67000	Y166		lsf Global & Sumishin Lease
☐ JA8381	Airbus Industrie A320-211	138	F-WWDE*	0090	0191	2 CFMI CFM56-5A1	67000	Y166		
☐ JA8382	Airbus Industrie A320-211	139	F-WWDF*	0090	0191	2 CFMI CFM56-5A1	67000	Y166		
☐ JA8383	Airbus Industrie A320-211	148	F-WWDO*	0090	0291	2 CFMI CFM56-5A1	67000	Y166		lsf Sumishin Lease
☐ JA8384	Airbus Industrie A320-211	151	F-WWDR*	0091	0391	2 CFMI CFM56-5A1	67000	Y166		lsf Sumishin Lease
☐ JA8385	Airbus Industrie A320-211	167	F-WWIE*	0091	0491	2 CFMI CFM56-5A1	67000	Y166		lsf Sumishin Lease
☐ JA8386	Airbus Industrie A320-211	170	F-WWII*	0091	0491	2 CFMI CFM56-5A1	67000	Y166		lsf Sumishin Lease
☐ JA8387	Airbus Industrie A320-211	196	F-WWDE*	0091	0691	2 CFMI CFM56-5A1	67000	Y166		lst ANK
☐ JA8388	Airbus Industrie A320-211	212	F-WWIG*	0091	0791	2 CFMI CFM56-5A1	67000	Y166		
☐ JA8389	Airbus Industrie A320-211	219	F-WWDZ*	0091	0891	2 CFMI CFM56-5A1	67000	Y166		lst ANK
☐ JA8390	Airbus Industrie A320-211	245	F-WWDE*	0091	1191	2 CFMI CFM56-5A1	67000	Y166		lst ANK
☐ JA8391	Airbus Industrie A320-211	300	F-WWDD*	0092	0492	2 CFMI CFM56-5A1	67000	Y166		lst ANK
☐ JA8392	Airbus Industrie A320-211	328	F-WWDR*	0092	0692	2 CFMI CFM56-5A1	67000	Y166		
☐ JA8393	Airbus Industrie A320-211	365	F-WWBZ*	0092	1192	2 CFMI CFM56-5A1	67000	Y166		lsf Kogin Lease
☐ JA8394	Airbus Industrie A320-211	383	F-WWBF*	0093	0193	2 CFMI CFM56-5A1	67000	Y166		lsf ORIX
☐ JA8395	Airbus Industrie A320-211	413	F-WWIM*	0093	0493	2 CFMI CFM56-5A1	67000	Y166		lsf ORIX

219 registration type of aircraft cn/fn ex/ex* mfd del powered by mtow kg configuration selcal name/fln/specialitites/remarks

registration	type of aircraft	cn/fn	ex/ex*	mfd	del	powered by	mtow kg	configuration	selcal	name/fln/specialitites/remarks
☐ JA8396	Airbus Industrie A320-211	482	F-WWIO*	0094	0894	2 CFMI CFM56-5A1	67000	Y166		
☐ JA8400	Airbus Industrie A320-211	554	F-WWIG*	0095	1195	2 CFMI CFM56-5A1	67000	Y166		lsf Nihon Lease
☐ JA8609	Airbus Industrie A320-211	501	F-WWIN*	0094	1294	2 CFMI CFM56-5A1	67000	Y166		lsf Sumisho Lease
☐ JA8654	Airbus Industrie A320-211	507	F-WWBT*	0094	0295	2 CFMI CFM56-5A1	67000	Y166		lsf Sumigin Lease
☐ JA8946	Airbus Industrie A320-211	669	F-WWBD*	0097	0497	2 CFMI CFM56-5A1	67000	Y166		lsf FI Honey Leasing
☐ JA8947	Airbus Industrie A320-211	685	F-WWDR*	0097	0697	2 CFMI CFM56-5A1	67000	Y166		lsf Marmaid Leasing
☐ JA8997	Airbus Industrie A320-211	658	F-WWIU*	0097	0297	2 CFMI CFM56-5A1	67000	Y166		lsf FI Lemon Leasing
☐ JA101A	Airbus Industrie A321-131	802	D-AVZO*	0098	0398	2 IAE V2530-A5	83000	Y191	LR-GK	special filmroll-colors
☐ JA102A	Airbus Industrie A321-131	811	D-AVZR*	0098	0498	2 IAE V2530-A5	83000	Y191	LR-GK	lsf Spider Leasing/special filmroll-cs
☐ JA104A	Airbus Industrie A321-131	963				2 IAE V2530-A5	83000	Y191		oo-delivery 0499
☐ JA105A	Airbus Industrie A321-131	1008				2 IAE V2530-A5	83000	Y191		oo-delivery 0999
☐ JA	Airbus Industrie A321-131					2 IAE V2530-A5	83000	Y191		oo-delivery 0300
☐ JA	Airbus Industrie A321-131					2 IAE V2530-A5	83000	Y191		oo-delivery 0900
☐ JA	Airbus Industrie A321-131					2 IAE V2530-A5	83000	Y191		oo-delivery 0001
☐ JA8238	Boeing 767-281	23140 / 106	N6067B*	0084	0285	2 GE CF6-80A	126960	Y234		lsf Marubeni Aerospace
☐ JA8239	Boeing 767-281	23141 / 108	N5573K*	0085	0385	2 GE CF6-80A	126960	Y234		lsf KC Five
☐ JA8240	Boeing 767-281	23142 / 110	N6038E*	0085	0485	2 GE CF6-80A	126960	Y234		lsf Marubeni Aerospace
☐ JA8241	Boeing 767-281	23143 / 114	N6018N*	0085	0585	2 GE CF6-80A	126960	Y234		lsf KC Five
☐ JA8242	Boeing 767-281	23144 / 115	N6038E*	0085	0685	2 GE CF6-80A	126960	Y234		lsf KC Five
☐ JA8243	Boeing 767-281	23145 / 116	N6005C*	0085	0985	2 GE CF6-80A	126960	Y234		lsf Marubeni Aerospace
☐ JA8244	Boeing 767-281	23146 / 121	N6055X*	0085	1085	2 GE CF6-80A	126960	Y234		lsf KC Six
☐ JA8245	Boeing 767-281	23147 / 123	N6005C*	0085	1185	2 GE CF6-80A	126960	Y234		lsf Marubeni Aerospace
☐ JA8251	Boeing 767-281	23431 / 143	N6009F*	0086	0686	2 GE CF6-80A	126960	Y234		lsf KC Six
☐ JA8252	Boeing 767-281	23432 / 145	N6005C*	0086	0786	2 GE CF6-80A	126960	Y234		lsf Marubeni Aerospace
☐ JA8254	Boeing 767-281	23433 / 167	N6038E*	0087	0487	2 GE CF6-80A	126960	Y234		
☐ JA8255	Boeing 767-281	23434 / 171	N6046P*	0087	0487	2 GE CF6-80A	126960	Y234		
☐ JA8485	Boeing 767-281	23016 / 80	N1788B*	0084	0284	2 GE CF6-80A	126960	Y234		lsf KC Three / for ABX as N783AX, 0099
☐ JA8486	Boeing 767-281	23017 / 82	N56807*	0084	0384	2 GE CF6-80A	126960	Y234		lsf KC Three / for ABX as N784AX, 0099
☐ JA8487	Boeing 767-281	23018 / 84	N1781B*	0084	0484	2 GE CF6-80A	126960	Y234		lsf KC Three / for ABX as N785AX, 0099
☐ JA8488	Boeing 767-281	23019 / 85	N1791B*	0084	0584	2 GE CF6-80A	126960	Y234		lsf Marubeni Aero.for ABX,N786AX,0099
☐ JA8489	Boeing 767-281	23020 / 96	N1784B*	0084	0784	2 GE CF6-80A	126960	Y234		lsf KC Three / for ABX as N787AX, 0000
☐ JA8490	Boeing 767-281	23021 / 103	N1785B*	0084	1084	2 GE CF6-80A	126960	Y234		lsf KC Three / for ABX as N788AX, 0000
☐ JA8491	Boeing 767-281	23022 / 104	N1792B*	0084	1184	2 GE CF6-80A	126960	Y234		lsf K.C. Four
☐ JA601A	Boeing 767-381	27943 / 669		0097	0897	2 GE CF6-80C2B6	130952	Y288		lsf F.I. Strawberry Leasing & others
☐ JA602A	Boeing 767-381	27944 / 684		0198	0198	2 GE CF6-80C2B6	130952	Y288		
☐ JA8256	Boeing 767-381	23756 / 176	N6005C*	0087	0787	2 GE CF6-80C2B2	130952	Y288		
☐ JA8257	Boeing 767-381	23757 / 177	N6038E*	0087	0787	2 GE CF6-80C2B2	130952	Y288		
☐ JA8258	Boeing 767-381	23758 / 179	N6055X*	0087	0787	2 GE CF6-80C2B2	130952	Y288		
☐ JA8259	Boeing 767-381	23759 / 185	N6038E*	0087	0987	2 GE CF6-80C2B2	130952	Y288		
☐ JA8271	Boeing 767-381	24002 / 199	N60668*	0088	0288	2 GE CF6-80C2B2	130952	Y288		
☐ JA8272	Boeing 767-381	24003 / 212	N6038E*	0088	0488	2 GE CF6-80C2B2	130952	Y288		
☐ JA8273	Boeing 767-381	24004 / 218	N6055X*	0088	0588	2 GE CF6-80C2B2	130952	Y288		
☐ JA8274	Boeing 767-381	24005 / 222	N6046P*	0088	0688	2 GE CF6-80C2B2	130952	Y288	AS-QR	
☐ JA8275	Boeing 767-381	24006 / 223	N6018N*	0088	0688	2 GE CF6-80C2B2	130952	Y288	DF-KP	
☐ JA8285	Boeing 767-381	24350 / 245	N1789B*	0089	0489	2 GE CF6-80C2B2	130952	Y288		
☐ JA8286	Boeing 767-381 (ER)	24400 / 269		0089	0689	2 GE CF6-80C2B6	156489	C22Y209	AE-FM	
☐ JA8287	Boeing 767-381	24351 / 271		0089	0789	2 GE CF6-80C2B2	130952	Y288		
☐ JA8288	Boeing 767-381	24415 / 276		0089	0889	2 GE CF6-80C2B2	130952	Y288		
☐ JA8289	Boeing 767-381	24416 / 280		0089	0989	2 GE CF6-80C2B2	130952	Y288		
☐ JA8290	Boeing 767-381	24417 / 290		0090	0190	2 GE CF6-80C2B2	130952	Y288		
☐ JA8291	Boeing 767-381	24755 / 295		0090	0390	2 GE CF6-80C2B2	130952	Y288		
☐ JA8322	Boeing 767-381	25618 / 458		0092	1092	2 GE CF6-80C2B2	130952	Y288		lsf Global Lease & others
☐ JA8323	Boeing 767-381 (ER)	25654 / 463		0092	1192	2 GE CF6-80C2B6	156489	C18Y227	AS-PQ	lsf Fuyo Sogo Lease
☐ JA8324	Boeing 767-381	25655 / 465		0092	1192	2 GE CF6-80C2B2	130952	Y288		lsf Mitsui Lease Jigyo
☐ JA8342	Boeing 767-381	27445 / 573		0095	0495	2 GE CF6-80C2B2	130952	Y288		lsf Kogin Lease
☐ JA8356	Boeing 767-381	25136 / 379		0091	0791	2 GE CF6-80C2B2	130952	Y288	DF-JP	
☐ JA8357	Boeing 767-381	25293 / 401		0091	1191	2 GE CF6-80C2B2	130952	Y288		
☐ JA8358	Boeing 767-381	25616 / 432		0092	0592	2 GE CF6-80C2B2	130952	Y288	AS-MR	
☐ JA8359	Boeing 767-381	25617 / 439		0092	0692	2 GE CF6-80C2B2	130952	Y288		
☐ JA8360	Boeing 767-381	25055 / 352		0091	0291	2 GE CF6-80C2B2	130952	Y288		
☐ JA8362	Boeing 767-381 (ER)	24632 / 285		0089	1089	2 GE CF6-80C2B6	156489	C22Y209	AE-FK	
☐ JA8363	Boeing 767-381	24756 / 300		0090	0490	2 GE CF6-80C2B2	130952	Y288		
☐ JA8368	Boeing 767-381	24880 / 336		0090	1190	2 GE CF6-80C2B2	130952	Y288		
☐ JA8567	Boeing 767-381	25656 / 510		0093	0893	2 GE CF6-80C2B2	130952	Y288		lsf Nihon Lease
☐ JA8568	Boeing 767-381	25657 / 515		0093	0993	2 GE CF6-80C2B2	130952	Y288		lsf Diamond Lease
☐ JA8569	Boeing 767-381	27050 / 516		0093	1293	2 GE CF6-80C2B2	130952	Y288		lsf Fuyo Sogo Lease/Pocket Monsters-cs
☐ JA8578	Boeing 767-381	25658 / 519		0093	1193	2 GE CF6-80C2B2	130952	Y288		lsf Sumisho Lease / Pocket Monsters-cs
☐ JA8579	Boeing 767-381	25659 / 520		0093	1293	2 GE CF6-80C2B2	130952	Y288		lsf Kogin Lease
☐ JA8664	Boeing 767-381 (ER)	27339 / 556		0094	1094	2 GE CF6-80C2B6	181436	C22Y209		lsf ORIX
☐ JA8669	Boeing 767-381	27444 / 567		0095	0395	2 GE CF6-80C2B2	130952	Y288		lsf K.C. Air Lease
☐ JA8670	Boeing 767-381	25660 / 539		0094	0594	2 GE CF6-80C2B2	130952	Y288		
☐ JA8674	Boeing 767-381	25661 / 543		0094	0694	2 GE CF6-80C2B2	130952	Y288		lsf Fuyo Sogo Lease
☐ JA8677	Boeing 767-381	25662 / 551		0094	0894	2 GE CF6-80C2B2	130952	Y288		lsf Kogin Lease
☐ JA8970	Boeing 767-381	25619 / 645		0097	0297	2 GE CF6-80C2B6	130952	Y288		lsf FI Orchad Leasing & others
☐ JA8971	Boeing 767-381	27942 / 651		0097	0397	2 GE CF6-80C2B6	133809	Y288		
☐ JA701A	Boeing 777-281	27938 / 77		0697	0697	2 PW PW4074	229518	C18Y361		lsf Alpine Rose & others
☐ JA702A	Boeing 777-281	27033 / 75		0697	0697	2 PW PW4074	229518	C18Y361		
☐ JA703A	Boeing 777-281	27034 / 81	N50217*	0097	0897	2 PW PW4074	229518	C18Y361		lsf SBL Aqua Marine & others
☐ JA704A	Boeing 777-281	27035 / 131		0098	0398	2 PW PW4074	229518	C18Y361		lsf Phoenix Leasing & others
☐ JA705A	Boeing 777-281	29029 / 137		0098	0498	2 PW PW4074	229518	C18Y361		lsf JL Seagull Lease & others
☐ JA706A	Boeing 777-281	27036 / 141		0098	0598	2 PW PW4074	229518	C18Y361		
☐ JA8197	Boeing 777-281	27027 / 16	N5016R*	0095	1095	2 PW PW4074	202937	C18Y361		lsf Sumishin Lease & others
☐ JA8198	Boeing 777-281	27028 / 21		0095	1295	2 PW PW4074	202937	C18Y361		lsf Sumigin Lease
☐ JA8199	Boeing 777-281	27029 / 29		0096	0596	2 PW PW4074	202937	C18Y361		lsf Sumishin Lease & others
☐ JA8967	Boeing 777-281	27030 / 37		0096	0896	2 PW PW4074	229518	C18Y361		
☐ JA8968	Boeing 777-281	27031 / 38		0096	0896	2 PW PW4074	229518	C18Y361		lsf Diamond Lease
☐ JA8969	Boeing 777-281	27032 / 50		0096	1296	2 PW PW4074	229518	C18Y361		lsf F.I. Kiwi Leasing & others
☐ JA	Boeing 777-281 (ER)					2 PW PW4090	294200			oo-delivery 0799
☐ JA	Boeing 777-281 (ER)					2 PW PW4090	294200			oo-delivery 0999
☐ JA	Boeing 777-281					2 PW PW4074	229518	C18Y361		oo-delivery 0000
☐ JA	Boeing 777-281					2 PW PW4074	202937	C18Y361		oo-delivery 0000
☐ JA	Boeing 777-281					2 PW PW4074	229518	C18Y361		oo-delivery 0000
☐ JA	Boeing 777-281					2 PW PW4074	202937	C18Y361		oo-delivery 0000
☐ JA	Boeing 777-281					2 PW PW4074	229518	C18Y361		oo-delivery 0000
☐ JA751A	Boeing 777-381	28272 / 142		0098	0698	2 PW PW4090	263084			lsf Anacreon Leasing & others / spec.cs
☐ JA752A	Boeing 777-381	28274 / 160		0898	0898	2 PW PW4090	263084			lsf FO Serenade Leasing & others
☐ JA753A	Boeing 777-381	28273 / 132		0098	0798	2 PW PW4090	263084			lsf Orix Skyblue
☐ JA754A	Boeing 777-381	27939 / 172		1098	1098	2 PW PW4090	263084			lsf Orix Skylark
☐ JA	Boeing 777-381	28275	N5017Q*	1197		2 PW PW4090	263084			oo-delivery 0599
☐ JA	Boeing 777-381					2 PW PW4090	263084			oo-delivery 1199
☐ JA	Boeing 777-381					2 PW PW4090	263084			oo-delivery 0400
☐ JA	Boeing 777-381					2 PW PW4090	263084			oo-delivery 0700
☐ JA	Airbus Industrie A340-313					4 CFMI CFM56-5C4	275000			oo-delivery 0200
☐ JA	Airbus Industrie A340-313					4 CFMI CFM56-5C4	275000			oo-delivery 0300
☐ JA	Airbus Industrie A340-313					4 CFMI CFM56-5C4	275000			oo-delivery 1100
☐ JA	Airbus Industrie A340-313					4 CFMI CFM56-5C4	275000			oo-delivery 0301
☐ JA	Airbus Industrie A340-313					4 CFMI CFM56-5C4	275000			oo-delivery 1001
☐ JA8135	Boeing 747SR-81	21606 / 360		0079	0379	4 GE CF6-45A2	258911	C20Y508		lsf NI Aircraft Leasing
☐ JA8138	Boeing 747SR-81	21924 / 420		0079	0180	4 GE CF6-45A2	258911	C20Y508		lsf Showa Lease
☐ JA8139	Boeing 747SR-81	21925 / 422		0080	0280	4 GE CF6-45A2	258911	C20Y508	AE-BL	lsf Showa Lease
☐ JA8145	Boeing 747SR-81	22291 / 453		0080	0580	4 GE CF6-45A2	258911	C20Y508		lsf Showa Lease
☐ JA8146	Boeing 747SR-81	22292 / 456		0080	0680	4 GE CF6-45A2	258911	C20Y508		
☐ JA8147	Boeing 747SR-81	22293 / 477	N5973L*	0080	1180	4 GE CF6-45A2	258911	C20Y508		
☐ JA8148	Boeing 747SR-81	22294 / 481		0080	1180	4 GE CF6-45A2	258911	C20Y508		
☐ JA8152	Boeing 747SR-81	22594 / 511		0081	0681	4 GE CF6-45A2	258911	C20Y508		
☐ JA8153	Boeing 747SR-81	22595 / 516		0081	0581	4 GE CF6-45A2	258911	C20Y508		
☐ JA8156	Boeing 747SR-81	22709 / 541	N5573B*	0081	0782	4 GE CF6-45A2	258911	C20Y508	AC-PR	
☐ JA8157	Boeing 747SR-81	22710 / 544		0081	0682	4 GE CF6-45A2	340194	F16C32Y326	AE-BD	
☐ JA8159	Boeing 747SR-81	22712 / 572		0082	0783	4 GE CF6-45A2	258911	C20Y508		

☐ JA8174	Boeing 747-281B	23501 / 648	N6055X*	0086	0686	4 GE CF6-50E2	377842	F24C88Y214	AE-FH	lsf Orix Aircraft
☐ JA8175	Boeing 747-281B	23502 / 649	N60659*	0086	0786	4 GE CF6-50E2	377842	F24C88Y214	AE-FJ	lsf Orix Aircraft
☐ JA8181	Boeing 747-281B	23698 / 667	N6055C*	0086	1286	4 GE CF6-50E2	377842	F24C88Y214	AE-BF	being cvtd to (SF)
☐ JA8182	Boeing 747-281B	23813 / 683	N60659*	0087	0787	4 GE CF6-50E2	377842	F24C88Y214	AE-BG	
☐ JA8190	Boeing 747-281B	24399 / 750		0089	0889	4 GE CF6-50E2	377842	F24C88Y214	GK-BC	
☐ JA401A	Boeing 747-481	28282 / 1133		0097	1197	4 GE CF6-80C2B1F	394625		MQ-FR	
☐ JA402A	Boeing 747-481	28283 / 1142		0198	0198	4 GE CF6-80C2B1F	394625		MQ-FS	
☐ JA403A	Boeing 747-481	29262 / 1199		0299	0299	4 GE CF6-80C2B1F	394625	F19C86Y260		
☐ JA404A	Boeing 747-481	29263				4 GE CF6-80C2B1F	394625	F19C86Y260		oo-delivery 0300
☐ JA8094	Boeing 747-481	24801 / 805		0090	0890	4 GE CF6-80C2B1F	394625	C27Y443	GK-BD	
☐ JA8095	Boeing 747-481	24833 / 812		0090	1090	4 GE CF6-80C2B1F	394625	F19C86Y260	AS-MP	
☐ JA8096	Boeing 747-481	24920 / 832		0091	0291	4 GE CF6-80C2B1F	394625	C27Y523	AC-LR	
☐ JA8097	Boeing 747-481	25135 / 863		0091	0791	4 GE CF6-80C2B1F	394625	F19C86Y260	AC-LS	
☐ JA8098	Boeing 747-481	25207 / 870		0091	0891	4 GE CF6-80C2B1F	394625	F19C86Y260	AC-MR	
☐ JA8099	Boeing 747-481 (D)	25292 / 891		0092	0192	4 GE CF6-80C2B1F	276555	C27Y542	AE-BK	
☐ JA8955	Boeing 747-481	25639 / 914		0092	0592	4 GE CF6-80C2B1F	394625	F19C86Y260	FR-BH	cvtd -481 (D)
☐ JA8956	Boeing 747-481 (D)	25640 / 920		0092	0692	4 GE CF6-80C2B1F	276555	C27Y542	AC-LR	
☐ JA8957	Boeing 747-481	25642 / 927		0092	0792	4 GE CF6-80C2B1F	394625	F19C86Y260	MQ-ES	cvtd -481 (D)
☐ JA8958	Boeing 747-481	25641 / 928	N6009F*	0092	0892	4 GE CF6-80C2B1F	394625	F19C86Y260	AS-MQ	lsf Afuko
☐ JA8959	Boeing 747-481 (D)	25646 / 952		0093	0193	4 GE CF6-80C2B1F	276555	C27Y542	AB-CM	
☐ JA8960	Boeing 747-481	25643 / 972		0093	0593	4 GE CF6-80C2B1F	394625	F19C86Y260		lsf Sumisho Lease & others
☐ JA8961	Boeing 747-481 (D)	25644 / 975		0093	0593	4 GE CF6-80C2B1F	276555	C27Y542		lsf Mitsui Lease Jigyo
☐ JA8962	Boeing 747-481	25645 / 979		0093	0693	4 GE CF6-80C2B1F	394625	F19C86Y260	AS-PR	lsf Beta Aircraft
☐ JA8963	Boeing 747-481 (D)	25647 / 991	N6055X*	0093	0893	4 GE CF6-80C2B1F	276555	C27Y542		lsf Fuyo Sogo Lease
☐ JA8964	Boeing 747-481 (D)	27163 / 996	N5573S*	0094	0394	4 GE CF6-80C2B1F	276918	C27Y542		lsf Diamond Lease
☐ JA8965	Boeing 747-481 (D)	27436 / 1060		0095	0495	4 GE CF6-80C2B1F	276918	C27Y542		lsf Sumigin Lease / Pocket Monsters-cs
☐ JA8966	Boeing 747-481 (D)	27442 / 1066	N6018N*	0095	1295	4 GE CF6-80C2B1F	276555	C27Y542		lsf Fuyo Sogo Lease

ALL NIPPON HELICOPTER, Co. Ltd – ANH (Subsidiary of All Nippon Airways – ANA) — Tokyo-Heliport

Tokyo Heliport, 4-chome, Shin-kiba, Kotoku, Tokyo 136-0082, Japan ☎ (3) 35 21 11 37 Tx: n/a Fax: (3) 35 21 11 65 SITA: n/a
F: 1986 ⁂ 50 Head: Katuaki Kumagae Net: n/a Beside main base at Tokyo-Heliport, helicopters are based at Fukuoka, Hiroshima, Nagoya, Okinawa, Osaka, Sapporo, Sendai & Shizuoka.

☐ JA6638	Eurocopter (Aerosp.) AS355F2 Ecureuil 2	5449		0090		2 AN 250-C20F	2540			lsf Naka Nihon Air Service
☐ JA6645	Eurocopter (Aerosp.) AS355F2 Ecureuil 2	5461		0091		2 AN 250-C20F	2540			lsf Zen Nikku Shoji
☐ JA6670	Eurocopter (Aerosp.) AS355F2 Ecureuil 2	5488		0091		2 AN 250-C20F	2540			lsf Zen Nikku Shoji Aircraft
☐ JA6697	Eurocopter (Aerosp.) AS355F2 Ecureuil 2	5524		0092	1092	2 AN 250-C20F	2540			lsf Toho Koku
☐ JA9905	Eurocopter (Aerosp.) AS355F2 Ecureuil 2	5384		0088		2 AN 250-C20F	2540			lsf Naka Nihon Air Service
☐ JA9967	Eurocopter (Aerosp.) AS355F2 Ecureuil 2	5422		0089		2 AN 250-C20F	2540			
☐ JA9977	Eurocopter (Aerosp.) AS355F2 Ecureuil 2	5426		0090		2 AN 250-C20F	2540			lsf Naka Nihon Air Service
☐ JA6675	Eurocopter (Aerosp.) AS365N2 Dauphin 2	6419		0091		2 TU Arriel 1C2	4250			lsf Zen Nikku Shoji Aircraft
☐ JA6677	Eurocopter (Aerosp.) AS365N2 Dauphin 2	6420		0091	0891	2 TU Arriel 1C2	4250			lsf Naka Nihon Air Service
☐ JA6753	Eurocopter (Aerosp.) AS365N2 Dauphin 2	6484		0095	0695	2 TU Arriel 1C2	4250			
☐ JA6770	Eurocopter (Aerosp.) AS365N2 Dauphin 2	6501		0096	0396	2 TU Arriel 1C2	4250			

AMAKUSA AIRLINES, Co. Ltd — Kumamoto

901-23 Sugidou, Mashiki-machi Kamimashihki-gun, Kumamoto 861-2205, Japan ☎ (96) 286 08 80 Tx: none Fax: (96) 286 88 66 SITA: n/a
F: 1998 ⁂ 12 Head: Hiroki Uozumi Net: n/a Presently being set-up. Intends to start operations in spring 2000.

☐ JA	De Havilland DHC-8-103 Dash 8Q					2 PWC PW121	15649	Y39		oo-delivery 0300

ASIA AIR SURVEY, Co. Ltd – Asia Kosoku, K.K. — Tokyo-Chofu

ASIA AIR SURVEY

Shinjuku-Kofu Bldg, 8F, 2-18, Shinjuku-4, Shinjuku-ku, Tokyo 160, Japan ☎ (3) 53 79 21 55 Tx: 2423201 asiako j Fax: (3) 53 79 21 56 SITA: n/a
F: 1949 ⁂ 1301 Head: Hiroshi Tsuda Net: n/a

☐ JA3856	Cessna TU206G Turbo Stationair 6 II	U20605374		0080		1 CO TSIO-520-M	1633	Surveyer		
☐ JA8600	Twin (Aero) Jetprop Commander 980 (695)	95070	N35SA	0081	0795	2 GA TPE331-10-511K	4683	Surveyer		
☐ JA8604	Twin (Aero) Jetprop Commander 980 (695)	95044	N65664	0080	0194	2 GA TPE331-10-511K	4683	Surveyer		

DAI-ICHI KOKU – First Flying, Co. Ltd — Osaka-Yao

Kuko 2-12, Yao-shi, Osaka 581-0043, Japan ☎ (729) 91 29 61 Tx: none Fax: (729) 91 05 75 SITA: n/a
F: n/a ⁂ n/a Head: Toshio Yoshida Net: n/a Aircraft below MTOW 1361 kg: Cessna 172

☐ JA3746	Cessna TU206F Turbo Stationair II	U20602818	N35944	0075		1 CO TSIO-520-C	1633			
☐ JA3804	Cessna TU206G Turbo Stationair 6 II	U20604244	N756PH	0078		1 CO TSIO-520-M	1633			

DIAMOND AIR SERVICE, Co. Ltd – DAS (Division of Mitsubishi Heavy Industries Ltd) — Nagoya

1 Toyaba, Toyoyama-cho, Nishikasuga-gun, Aichi Pref. 480-0293, Japan ☎ (568) 29 00 20 Tx: none Fax: (568) 29 00 21 SITA: n/a
F: 1989 ⁂ 142 Head: Hiroshi Hayafuji Net: n/a

☐ JA8431	GAC (Grumman) G-1159 Gulfstream II	141	N17584*	0074	1295	2 RR Spey 511-8	28123	Testbed / Exec		lsf MHI Finance

EXCEL AIR SERVICE, Inc. – EXAS (Excel Koku) (Subsidiary of Hirose & Co. Ltd) — Urayasu Heliport

14 Chidori, Urayasu-shi, Chiba Pref. 279-0032, Japan ☎ (47) 380 11 11 Tx: none Fax: (47) 380 11 12 SITA: n/a
F: 1991 ⁂ 32 Head: Yasuhito Nakachi Net: n/a

☐ JA6764	Eurocopter (Aerosp.) AS355F2 Ecureuil 2	5518	F-OHNK	0092		2 AN 250-C20F	2540			lsf Sumigin Lease
☐ JA9957	Eurocopter (Aerosp.) AS355F2 Ecureuil 2	5415		0089		2 AN 250-C20F	2540			lsf Yukio Sato
☐ JA6647	Eurocopter (Aerosp.) AS365N2 Dauphin 2	6387		0090		2 TU Arriel 1C2	4250			lsf Sumisho Lease
☐ JA9953	Sikorsky S-76A	760192	N400MB	0081		2 AN 250-C30S	4536			

HANKYU KOKU – Hankyu Airlines, Co. Ltd (Associated with Hankyu Railways Group) — Osaka-Yao

6F Hankyu Corp. Building, 1-16-1 Shibata, Kita-ku, Osaka 530-0012, Japan ☎ (6) 63 73 16 61 Tx: 5234026 j Fax: (6) 63 73 16 60 SITA: n/a
F: 1960 ⁂ 93 Head: Shintara Nanba Net: n/a Aircraft below MTOW 1361 kg: Cessna 172 & Kawasaki-Hughes 369HS (500C)

☐ JA9279	Kawasaki-Hughes 369D	6708		0081		1 AN 250-C20B	1361			lsf Asahi Lease
☐ JA9485	MD Helicopters MD 500D (Hughes 369D)	510978	N3999T	0081		1 AN 250-C20B	1361			
☐ JA3719	Cessna T207 Turbo Skywagon	20700262	N1662U	0074		1 CO TSIO-520-G	1724			
☐ JA9241	Eurocopter (Aerosp.) AS350B Ecureuil	1119		0079		1 TU Arriel 1B	1950			
☐ JA9347	Eurocopter (Aerosp.) AS350B Ecureuil	1694		0083		1 TU Arriel 1B	1950			
☐ JA9393	Eurocopter (Aerosp.) AS350B Ecureuil	1800		0085	0791	1 TU Arriel 1B	1950			
☐ JA9395	Eurocopter (Aerosp.) AS350B Ecureuil	1808		0085		1 TU Arriel 1B	1950			
☐ JA9407	Eurocopter (Aerosp.) AS350B Ecureuil	1829		0085		1 TU Arriel 1B	1950			
☐ JA9491	Eurocopter (Aerosp.) AS350B Ecureuil	2039		0087		1 TU Arriel 1B	1950			lsf Noritsu Koki & Shima Seiki
☐ JA9733	Eurocopter (Aerosp.) AS350B Ecureuil	2078		0088		1 TU Arriel 1B	1950			
☐ JA9831	Eurocopter (Aerosp.) AS350B Ecureuil	2237		0089		1 TU Arriel 1B	1950			
☐ JA9878	Eurocopter (Aerosp.) AS350B Ecureuil	2313		0090		1 TU Arriel 1B	1950			
☐ JA6718	Eurocopter (Aerosp.) AS355F2 Ecureuil 2	5519		0092	0993	2 AN 250-C20F	2540			
☐ JA6738	Eurocopter (Aerosp.) AS355N Ecureuil 2	5578		0094	0595	2 TU Arrius 1A	2540			
☐ JA9588	Eurocopter (Aerosp.) AS355F1 Ecureuil 2	5286		0083	0389	2 AN 250-C20F	2400			cvtd AS355F
☐ JA9591	Eurocopter (Aerosp.) AS355F1 Ecureuil 2	5284		0083		2 AN 250-C20F	2400			cvtd AS355F
☐ JA9636	Eurocopter (Aerosp.) AS355F1 Ecureuil 2	5319		0086		2 AN 250-C20F	2400			
☐ JA9903	Eurocopter (Aerosp.) SA365N Dauphin 2	6079		0083		2 TU Arriel 1C	3850			
☐ JA9920	Eurocopter (Aerosp.) SA365N1 Dauphin 2	6312		0088	0392	2 TU Arriel 1C1	4100			

HARLEQUIN AIR, Corp. = JH / HLQ (Subsidiary of Japan Air System) — Fukuoka

Fukuoka Int'l Airport, 767-1 Shimousui, Hakata-ku, Fukuoka 812, Japan ☎ (92) 623 80 91 Tx: none Fax: (92) 623 12 30 SITA: n/a
F: 1997 ⁂ n/a Head: n/a ICAO: HARLEQUIN Net: n/a

☐ JA8552	Boeing (Douglas) MD-81 (DC-9-81)	53297 / 2040		0093	0198	2 PW JT8D-217A/C	63503			lsf JAS
☐ JA8550	Boeing (Douglas) DC-10-30	48315 / 436		0088	1297	3 GE CF6-50C2	267619		JP-CQ	lsf JAS

HOKKAIDO AIR SYSTEM – HAS (Joint venture between Japan Air System & Hokkaido Prefectual Government) — Sapporo

Sapporo-shi, Shigashi-ku, Hokkadama-cho, Airport, Sapporo 063, Japan ☎ (11) 781 12 47 Tx: none Fax: (11) 784 17 16 SITA: n/a
F: 1997 ⁂ n/a Head: n/a Net: n/a

☐ JA01HC	Saab 340B (Plus)	340B-432	SE-B32*	0098	0298	2 GE CT7-9B	12927	Y36		
☐ JA02HC	Saab 340B (Plus)	340B-440	SE-B40*	0098	0698	2 GE CT7-9B	12927	Y36		

HOKKAIDO INTERNATIONAL AIRLINES, Co. Ltd – AIR DO = HD / ADO — Sapporo

1-23 Nishi 6, Cho-me, Chou-Ku, Sapporo, Hokkaido 060, Japan ☎ (3) 57 08 70 70 Tx: none Fax: (3) 57 08 70 72 SITA: n/a
F: 1997 ⁂ n/a Head: Maski Nakatani ICAO: AIR DO Net: n/a

☐ JA98AD	Boeing 767-33A (ER)	27476 / 687	N767AN	0098	1298	2 GE CF6-80C2B7F	130952	Y286		lsf AWAS

HOKKAIDO KOKU – Hokkaido Aviation, Co. Ltd — Sapporo

63 Okada-cho, Higashi-ku, Sapporo-shi, Hokkaido 062-0938, Japan ☎ (11) 781 12 47 Tx: none Fax: (11) 784 17 16 SITA: n/a
F: n/a ⁂ n/a Head: Seiichro Yamamoto Net: n/a Aircraft below MTOW 1361 kg: Cessna 172.

☐ JA3872	Cessna TU206G Turbo Stationair 6 II	U20605605	N5262X	0080		1 CO TSIO-520-M	1633			

221 registration type of aircraft cn/fn ex/ex* mfd del powered by mtow kg configuration selcal name/fln/specialitites/remarks

☐ JA3884	Cessna TU206G Turbo Stationair 6 II	U20606143	N1589C	0081		1 CO TSIO-520-M	1633			
☐ JA3899	Cessna TU206G Turbo Stationair 6 II	U20606481	N1687C	0082		1 CO TSIO-520-M	1633			
☐ JA3950	Cessna TU206G Turbo Stationair 6 II	U20606843	N1583C	0084		1 CO TSIO-520-M	1633			
☐ JA6098	Eurocopter (Aerosp.) AS350B2 Ecureuil	2541		0091	1091	1 TU Arriel 1D1	2250			
☐ JA6182	Eurocopter (Aerosp.) AS350B2 Ecureuil	2929		0096	0596	1 TU Arriel 1D1	2250			
☐ JA9327	Eurocopter (Aerosp.) AS350B Ecureuil	1603		0082		1 TU Arriel 1B	1950			Birugo
☐ JA9423	Eurocopter (Aerosp.) AS350B Ecureuil	1880		0086		1 TU Arriel 1B	1950			Besta
☐ JA6731	Eurocopter (Aerosp.) AS355N Ecureuil 2	5562		0093	0394	2 TU Arrius 1A	2540			
☐ JA001H	Eurocopter (Aerosp.) AS365N2 Dauphin 2	6498		0096	0197	2 TU Arriel 1C2	4250			

HONDA KOKU – Honda Airways, Co. Ltd

Saitama-Honda Airport

53-1 Demaru-shimogo, Kawashima-cho, Hikigun, Saitama-ken 350-0141, Japan ☎ (492) 99 11 11 Tx: none Fax: (492) 97 81 20 SITA: n/a

F: 1964 ⁂ 250 Head: Takeshi Minowa Net: n/a Aircraft below MTOW 1361 kg: Cessna 172 & Slingsby T67M.

☐ JA3729	Cessna TU206F Turbo Stationair II	U20602719	N33298	0075		1 CO TSIO-520-C	1633			
☐ JA4000	Cessna TU206G Turbo Stationair 6 II	U20604629	N9980M	0078		1 CO TSIO-520-M	1633			
☐ JA9367	Eurocopter (Aerosp.) AS350B Ecureuil	1746		0084		1 TU Arriel 1B	1950			
☐ JA9438	Eurocopter (Aerosp.) AS350B Ecureuil	1946		0086		1 TU Arriel 1B	1950			lsf Kanematsu Sogo Finance
☐ JA9773	Eurocopter (Aerosp.) AS350B Ecureuil	2141		0088		1 TU Arriel 1B	1950			lsf Eiko Seminar
☐ JA9823	Eurocopter (Aerosp.) AS350B Ecureuil	2223		0089		1 TU Arriel 1B	1950			lsf Honda Finance
☐ JA9577	Eurocopter (Aerosp.) SA365N Dauphin 2	6051		0082	0590	2 TU Arriel 1C	3850			

IMPERIAL KOKU – Imperial Air Line, Co. Ltd

Tokyo-Heliport

Tokyo Heliport, 14 Shin-kubo, 4-chome, Kotoku, Tokyo 136-0082, Japan ☎ (3) 35 22 17 01 Tx: n/a Fax: (3) 35 22 17 05 SITA: n/a

F: 1960 ⁂ 65 Head: Kazuo Fuji Net: n/a Aircraft below 1361 kg: Bell & Kawasaki-Bell 47G & Hiller UH-12E.

☐ JA9448	Bell 206B JetRanger III	3806	N206JG	0084		1 AN 250-C20J	1451			lsf Helicopter Leasing Int'l
☐ JA9702	Bell 206B JetRanger III	3967		0087		1 AN 250-C20J	1451			lsf Tonichi Finance
☐ JA9497	Eurocopter (Aerosp.) AS350B1 Ecureuil	2043		0087		1 TU Arriel 1D	2200			lsf Higashi Nihon Jyutaku

J-AIR (JAL Flight Academy dba / Subsidiary of Japan Airlines – JAL)

Nagasaki

c/o JAL, Tokyo Bldg, 7-3 Marunouchi, 2-chome, Chiyoda-ku, Tokyo 100-0002, Japan ☎ (3) 32 84 26 10 Tx: 2466361 jaltyo j Fax: (3) 32 84 26 59 SITA: n/a

F: 1991 ⁂ 112 Head: Masashi Obuse Net: n/a Operates commuter flights on behalf of Japan Airlines – JAL using JL flight numbers.

☐ JA8590	BAe 3217 Jetstream 32	986	G-31-986*	0096	0596	2 GA TPE331-12UAR-701H	7350	Y19		lsf Kanematsu Sogo Finance
☐ JA8591	BAe 3217 Jetstream 32	985	G-31-985*	0096	0997	2 GA TPE331-12UAR-701H	7350	Y19		lsf Kanematsu Sogo Finance
☐ JA8865	BAe 3217 Jetstream 32	981	G-31-981*	0093	0893	2 GA TPE331-12UAR-701H	7350	Y19		lsf Nikko Lease
☐ JA8876	BAe 3217 Jetstream 32	923	G-31-923*	0091	0491	2 GA TPE331-12UAR-701H	7350	Y19		lsf Nikko Lease
☐ JA8877	BAe 3217 Jetstream 32	925	G-31-925*	0091	0491	2 GA TPE331-12UAR-701H	7350	Y19		lsf Nikko Lease

JAL Express, Co. Ltd = JC / JEX (Subsidiary of Japan Airlines, Co. Ltd)

Tokyo-Haneda

2-4-11, Higashi-Shinagawa, Shinagawa-ku, Tokyo 140-0002, Japan ☎ (3) 54 60 31 91 Tx: 2466361 jaltyo j Fax: (3) 45 60 59 29 SITA: n/a

F: 1997 ⁂ n/a Head: Susumu Yamaji ICAO: JANEX Net: n/a

☐ JA8991	Boeing 737-446	27916 / 2718		0095	0597	2 CFMI CFM56-3C1	62822	Y150	GR-JL	
☐ JA8992	Boeing 737-446	27917 / 2729	N1792B*	0095	0597	2 CFMI CFM56-3C1	62822	Y150		

JANET HELICOPTER

Futuba Heliport

Futuba-cho, Kitakomagun Yamanashi 445-Yuan, Utsunomiya 407-0100, Japan ☎ (296) 44 71 51 Tx: none Fax: (551) 28 72 79 SITA: n/a

F: n/a ⁂ n/a Head: n/a Net: n/a Aircraft below MTOW 1361kg: Enstrom 480 & Robinson R22

☐ JA6058	Eurocopter (Aerosp.) AS350B Ecureuil	2453		0091	0496	1 TU Arriel 1B	1950			

JAPAN AIR CHARTER, Co. Ltd – JAZ = JZ / JAZ (Subsidiary of Japan Airlines – JAL)

Tokyo-Haneda / Narita & Fukuoka

2-4-11, Higashi-Shinagawa, Shinagawa-ku, Tokyo 140-0002, Japan ☎ (3) 54 60 31 91 Tx: none Fax: (3) 54 60 59 29 SITA: n/a

F: 1990 ⁂ 360 Head: Shinzo Sudo ICAO: JAPAN CHARTER Net: n/a

☐ JA8539	Boeing (Douglas) DC-10-40 (I)	47822 / 304		0080	1090	3 PW JT9D-59A	251744	Y300	CD-GL	Super Resort Express colors
☐ JA8541	Boeing (Douglas) DC-10-40 (I)	47824 / 308	N10020*	0080	0495	3 PW JT9D-59A	251744	C41Y227	CD-GH	lst JAL
☐ JA8544	Boeing (Douglas) DC-10-40 (I)	47852 / 340		0080	1193	3 PW JT9D-59A	251744	Y300	EJ-AM	Super Resort Express colors
☐ JA8547	Boeing (Douglas) DC-10-40 (I)	47856 / 366		0081	0495	3 PW JT9D-59A	251744	Y300	EG-KM	Super Resort Express colors
☐ JA8110	Boeing 747-246B	20504 / 181		0072	1195	4 PW JT9D-7AW	351534	C34Y393	GM-BK	lst JAL
☐ JA8111	Boeing 747-246B	20505 / 182		0072	0497	4 PW JT9D-7AW	351534	C16Y444	GM-BL	lst JAL
☐ JA8114	Boeing 747-246B	20530 / 196	N1800B*	0072	0497	4 PW JT9D-7AW	351534	C16Y444	DM-HL	lst JAL
☐ JA8116	Boeing 747-146	20532 / 199		0072	1196	4 PW JT9D-7A	332937	F22C74Y256	GM-AL	lst JAL
☐ JA8127	Boeing 747-246B	21031 / 255		0075	1090	4 PW JT9D-7A	351534	F22C92Y232	JL-BF	lst JAL

JAPAN AIR COMMUTER, Co. Ltd – JAC = 3X / JAC (Nihon Air Commuter) (Subsidiary of Japan Air System – JAS)

Kagoshima

Kagoshima Airport Bldg., 822 Fumoto Mizobe-cho, Aira-gun, Kagoshima-ken 899-6495, Japan ☎ (995) 58 21 51 Tx: 2225182 gzjd j Fax: (995) 58 39 04 SITA: n/a

F: 1983 ⁂ 210 Head: Yoshitomi Ono ICAO: COMMUTER Net: n/a

☐ JA001C	Saab 340B	340B-419	SE-B19*	0097	0697	2 GE CT7-9B	12927	Y36		
☐ JA8594	Saab 340B	340B-399	SE-C99*	0096	0696	2 GE CT7-9B	12927	Y36		
☐ JA8642	Saab 340B	340B-365	SE-C65*	0094	1294	2 GE CT7-9B	12927	Y36		lsf Tajima Kuko Terminal
☐ JA8649	Saab 340B	340B-368	SE-C68*	0095	0695	2 GE CT7-9B	12927	Y36		lsf Central Lease
☐ JA8703	Saab 340B	340B-355	SE-C55*	0093	0194	2 GE CT7-9B	12927	Y36		lsf Nihon Lease
☐ JA8704	Saab 340B	340B-361	SE-C61*	0094	0195	2 GE CT7-9B	12927	Y36		lsf Mitsui Lease Jigyo
☐ JA8886	Saab 340B	340B-281	SE-G81*	0092	0292	2 GE CT7-9B	12927	Y36		lsf Mitsui Lease Jigyo
☐ JA8887	Saab 340B	340B-308	SE-C08*	0092	0892	2 GE CT7-9B	12927	Y36		lsf Diamond Lease
☐ JA8888	Saab 340B	340B-331	SE-C31*	0093	0293	2 GE CT7-9B	12927	Y36		lsf Kogin Lease
☐ JA8900	Saab 340B	340B-378	SE-C78*	0095	1295	2 GE CT7-9B	12927	Y36		lsf Kogin Lease
☐ JA8717	NAMC YS-11A-500	2092		0069	0292	2 RR Dart 542-10J/K	24500	Y64		lsf JAS / cvtd -217
☐ JA8759	NAMC YS-11A-500	2152	JQ2152*	0070	0793	2 RR Dart 542-10J/K	24500	Y64		lsf JAS / cvtd -227
☐ JA8763	NAMC YS-11A-500	2135	JQ2135*	0070		2 RR Dart 542-10J/K	24500	Y64		lsf JAS / cvtd -227
☐ JA8766	NAMC YS-11A-500	2142	JQ2142*	0070		2 RR Dart 542-10J/K	24500	Y64		lsf JAS / cvtd -227
☐ JA8771	NAMC YS-11A-500	2149		0070		2 RR Dart 542-10J/K	24500	Y64		lsf JAS / cvtd -227
☐ JA8776	NAMC YS-11A-500	2157		0071	0593	2 RR Dart 542-10J/K	24500	Y64		lsf JAS / cvtd -227
☐ JA8777	NAMC YS-11A-500	2163		0071		2 RR Dart 542-10J/K	24500	Y64		lsf JAS / cvtd -227
☐ JA8781	NAMC YS-11A-500	2166		0071		2 RR Dart 542-10J/K	24500	Y64		lsf JAS / cvtd -217
☐ JA8788	NAMC YS-11A-500	2176		0073		2 RR Dart 542-10J/K	24500	Y64		lsf JAS / cvtd -217
☐ JA8805	NAMC YS-11A-500	2055	PP-CTF	0067	0095	2 RR Dart 542-10J/K	24500	Y64		lsf JAS / cvtd -202
☐ JA8809	NAMC YS-11A-500	2054	PP-CTE	0067	0095	2 RR Dart 542-10J/K	24500	Y64		lsf JAS / cvtd -202

JAPAN AIRLINES, Co. Ltd – JAL = JL / JAL (Nihon Koku, K.K.)

Tokyo-Haneda / Narita

2-4-11, Higashi-Shinagawa, Shinagawa-ku, Tokyo 140-0002, Japan ☎ (3) 54 60 31 91 Tx: 2466361 jaltyo j Fax: (3) 45 60 59 29 SITA: n/a

F: 1951 ⁂ 21000 Head: Susumu Yamaji IATA: 131 ICAO: JAPANAIR Net: http://www.jal.co.jp/ Commuter flights are operated on behalf of Japan Airlines by J-AIR (subsidiary, with Jetstream 31) – see under that carrier.

Additional aircraft (Boeing 747 & McDonnell Douglas DC-10) are lsf Japan Air Charter & Japan Asia Airways when required – see under both carriers.

☐ JA8993	Boeing 737-446	28087 / 2812		0096	0896	2 CFMI CFM56-3C1	62822	Y150		lsf Marubeni Aerospace
☐ JA8994	Boeing 737-446	28097 / 2907	N1786B*	0797	0797	2 CFMI CFM56-3C1	62822	Y150		lsf Zonet Aviation Financial Service
☐ JA8995	Boeing 737-446	28831 / 2911		0797	0797	2 CFMI CFM56-3C1	62822	Y150		lsf Zonet Aviation Financial Service
☐ JA8996	Boeing 737-446	28832 / 2953	N1786B*	0097	1197	2 CFMI CFM56-3C1	62822	Y150		lsf Zonet Aviation Financial Service
☐ JA8998	Boeing 737-446	28994 / 3044		0098	0698	2 CFMI CFM56-3C1	62822	Y150		
☐ JA8999	Boeing 737-446	29864				2 CFMI CFM56-3C1	62822	Y150		oo-delivery 0699
☐ JA8231	Boeing 767-246	23212 / 117	N6046P*	0085	0785	2 PW JT9D-7R4D	136077	Y219	EH-BJ	lsf Nikko Lease
☐ JA8232	Boeing 767-246	23213 / 118	N6038E*	0085	0885	2 PW JT9D-7R4D	136077	Y219	EH-BK	
☐ JA8233	Boeing 767-246	23214 / 122	N6038E*	0085	1185	2 PW JT9D-7R4D	136077	Y219	EH-BL	
☐ JA8234	Boeing 767-346	23216 / 148	N6005C*	0086	0986	2 PW JT9D-7R4D	142972	C16Y254	EH-CD	
☐ JA8235	Boeing 767-346	23217 / 150	N60659*	0086	1086	2 PW JT9D-7R4D	142972	C16Y254	EH-CF	lsf Kowa Fudosan
☐ JA8236	Boeing 767-346	23215 / 132	N767S*	0086	1286	2 PW JT9D-7R4D	142972	C16Y254	EH-BM	lsf World Corp.
☐ JA8253	Boeing 767-346	23645 / 174	N6038E*	0087	0687	2 PW JT9D-7R4D	142972	C16Y254	GJ-FH	
☐ JA8264	Boeing 767-346	23965 / 186	N6018N*	0087	0987	2 PW JT9D-7R4D	142972	C24Y209	DF-KL	
☐ JA8265	Boeing 767-346	23961 / 192	N6005C*	0087	1187	2 PW JT9D-7R4D	142972	C16Y254	GK-AB	
☐ JA8267	Boeing 767-346	23962 / 193	N6038E*	0087	1287	2 PW JT9D-7R4D	142972	C16Y254	JL-BM	
☐ JA8268	Boeing 767-346	23963 / 224	N6055X*	0088	0688	2 PW JT9D-7R4D	142972	C16Y254	GM-CE	
☐ JA8269	Boeing 767-346	23964 / 225	N6046P*	0088	0688	2 PW JT9D-7R4D	142972	C16Y254	GM-CF	
☐ JA8299	Boeing 767-346	24498 / 277	N6055X*	0089	0889	2 PW JT9D-7R4D	142972	C16Y254	GM-BD	lsf Kogin Lease
☐ JA8364	Boeing 767-346	24782 / 327		0090	0990	2 PW JT9D-7R4D	142972	C16Y254	KQ-JL	lsf Nikko Lease
☐ JA8365	Boeing 767-346	24783 / 329		0090	0990	2 PW JT9D-7R4D	142972	C16Y254	MQ-JL	lsf Nikko Lease
☐ JA8397	Boeing 767-346	27311 / 547		0094	0894	2 GE CF6-80C2B2	133809	C16Y254	ES-FQ	
☐ JA8398	Boeing 767-346	27312 / 548		0094	0894	2 GE CF6-80C2B2	133809	C16Y254	ES-FR	lsf Fuyo Sogo Lease
☐ JA8399	Boeing 767-346	27313 / 554		0094	1094	2 GE CF6-80C2B2	133809	C16Y254	ES-GH	lsf Diamond Lease
☐ JA8975	Boeing 767-346	27658 / 581		0095	0695	2 GE CF6-80C2B2	133809	C16Y254	HJ-CS	
☐ JA8980	Boeing 767-346	28837 / 673		0997	0997	2 GE CF6-80C2B2	142972	C16Y254		

222 registration type of aircraft cn/fn ex/ex* mfd del powered by mtow kg configuration selcal name/fln/specialitites/remarks

	registration	type of aircraft	cn/fn	ex/ex*	mfd	del	powered by	mtow kg	configuration	selcal	name/fln/specialitites/remarks
☐	JA8986	Boeing 767-346	28838 / 680		0097	1297	2 GE CF6-80C2B2	130952	C16Y254		
☐	JA8987	Boeing 767-346	28553 / 688		0098	0298	2 GE CF6-80C2B2	130952	C16Y254		lsf JAA
☐	JA8981	Boeing 777-246	27364 / 23		0096	0296	2 PW PW4084	229518	C12Y375		Sirius
☐	JA8982	Boeing 777-246	27365 / 26		0096	0396	2 PW PW4084	229518	C12Y375		Vega
☐	JA8983	Boeing 777-246	27366 / 39		0096	0996	2 PW PW4084	229518	C12Y375		Altair
☐	JA8984	Boeing 777-246	27651 / 68		0097	0497	2 PW PW4084	229518	C12Y375		Betelgeuse / lsf Skywalk Lsng & others
☐	JA8985	Boeing 777-246	27652 / 72		0597	0597	2 PW PW4084	229518	C12Y375		Procyon
☐	JA8989	Boeing 777-246					2 PW PW4084	229518	C12Y375		oo-delivery 0401
☐	JA8990	Boeing 777-246					2 PW PW4084	229518	C12Y375		oo-delivery 0401
☐	JA	Boeing 777-246					2 PW PW4084	229518	C12Y375		oo-delivery 0699
☐	JA	Boeing 777-246					2 PW PW4084	229518	C12Y375		oo-delivery 0001
☐	JA	Boeing 777-246					2 PW PW4084	229518	C12Y375		oo-delivery 0001
☐	JA8531	Boeing (Douglas) DC-10-40 (I)	46923 / 216	N8703Q*	0076	0497	3 PW JT9D-59A	251744	C48Y225	JL-BK	lsf JAA
☐	JA8532	Boeing (Douglas) DC-10-40 (I)	46660 / 220	N8705Q*	0076	0497	3 PW JT9D-59A	251744	C48Y225	FJ-KL	lsf JAA / cvtd DC-10-40 (D)
☐	JA8534	Boeing (Douglas) DC-10-40 (I)	46913 / 206	N54652*	0075	0797	3 PW JT9D-59A	251744	C48Y225	FJ-KM	lsf JAA
☐	JA8535	Boeing (Douglas) DC-10-40 (I)	46662 / 230	N19B*	0076	0876	3 PW JT9D-59A	251744	F14C88Y137	DH-GK	
☐	JA8536	Boeing (Douglas) DC-10-40 (D)	46966 / 262		0078	1178	3 PW JT9D-59A	201849	C18Y300	FH-AC	
☐	JA8537	Boeing (Douglas) DC-10-40 (I)	46967 / 265		0077	0497	3 PW JT9D-59A	251744	C48Y225	FH-AD	lsf JAA / cvtd DC-10-40 (D)
☐	JA8538	Boeing (Douglas) DC-10-40 (I)	46974 / 274		0079	0479	3 PW JT9D-59A	251744	F14C88Y137	FH-AG	
☐	JA8540	Boeing (Douglas) DC-10-40 (D)	47823 / 306		0079	0180	3 PW JT9D-59A	201849	C18Y300	CD-GM	
☐	JA8541	Boeing (Douglas) DC-10-40 (I)	47824 / 308	N10020*	0080	0380	3 PW JT9D-59A	251744	C41Y227	CD-GH	lsf JAZ
☐	JA8542	Boeing (Douglas) DC-10-40 (I)	47825 / 310		0080	0480	3 PW JT9D-59A	251744	C48Y227	CD-GJ	
☐	JA8543	Boeing (Douglas) DC-10-40 (I)	47826 / 313		0080	0580	3 PW JT9D-59A	251744	F14C88Y137	CD-GK	cvtd DC-10-40 (D)
☐	JA8545	Boeing (Douglas) DC-10-40 (I)	47853 / 343		0080	1280	3 PW JT9D-59A	251744	C48Y227	JK-CG	
☐	JA8546	Boeing (Douglas) DC-10-40 (D)	47855 / 349	N13627*	0081	0381	3 PW JT9D-59A	201849	C18Y300	EJ-BD	
☐	JA8548	Boeing (Douglas) DC-10-40 (D)	47857 / 367		0082	0182	3 PW JT9D-59A	201849	C18Y300	DJ-FG	
☐	JA8549	Boeing (Douglas) DC-10-40 (D)	48301 / 381		0083	0383	3 PW JT9D-59A	201849	C18Y300	DF-JK	
☐	JA8941	Boeing 777-346	28393 / 152		0098	0798	2 PW PW4090	263084			lsf Camper Leasing & others
☐	JA8942	Boeing 777-346	28394 / 158	N5028Y*	0898	0898	2 PW PW4090	263084			Spica / lsf FO Harvest Leasing & Others
☐	JA8943	Boeing 777-346	28395 / 196		0299	0299	2 PW PW4090	263084			Arcturus
☐	JA8944	Boeing 777-346	28396				2 PW PW4090	263084			oo-delivery 0499
☐	JA8945	Boeing 777-346	28397				2 PW PW4090	263084			oo-delivery 0899
☐	JA8580	Boeing (Douglas) MD-11	48571 / 552		0093	1193	3 PW PW4460	273289	F12C47Y180	DR-EF	Tufted Puffin / lsf Diamond Lease
☐	JA8581	Boeing (Douglas) MD-11	48572 / 556	N90187*	0093	1293	3 PW PW4460	273289	F12C47Y180	DR-EG	Fairy Pitia / lsf Fuyo Sogo Lease
☐	JA8582	Boeing (Douglas) MD-11	48573 / 559	N90187*	0093	0394	3 PW PW4460	280320	F12C47Y180	DR-EH	Red Crowned Crane
☐	JA8583	Boeing (Douglas) MD-11	48574 / 566		0094	0894	3 PW PW4460	280320	F12C47Y180	FQ-LS	Golden Eagle / lsf Diamond Lease
☐	JA8584	Boeing (Douglas) MD-11	48575 / 568		0094	0994	3 PW PW4460	280320	F12C47Y180	FQ-MR	Okinawa Rail / lsf Kogin Lease & others
☐	JA8585	Boeing (Douglas) MD-11	48576 / 574		0095	0495	3 PW PW4460	273289	F12C47Y180	FQ-MS	lsf Diamond Lease
☐	JA8586	Boeing (Douglas) MD-11	48577 / 583		0095	0495	3 PW PW4460	280320	F12C47Y180	FQ-PR	
☐	JA8587	Boeing (Douglas) MD-11	48578 / 588		0095	0695	3 PW PW4460	280320	F12C47Y180	FQ-PS	Pryer's Woodpecker / lsf Diamond Lease
☐	JA8588	Boeing (Douglas) MD-11	48579 / 599		0096	0496	3 PW PW4460	280320	F12C47Y180	FR-AB	lsf Diamond Lease & others
☐	JA8589	Boeing (Douglas) MD-11	48774 / 610		0097	0597	3 PW PW4460	280320	F12C47Y180	FR-AC	Rock Ptarmigan / lsf Dia Leasing & others
☐	JA8104	Boeing 747-246B	19823 / 116		0071	0271	4 PW JT9D-7AW	351534	F22Y74C256	FK-GM	lsf Ryoshin Lease
☐	JA8105	Boeing 747-246B	19824 / 122		0071	0371	4 PW JT9D-7AW	351534	F22C106Y216	GK-AD	lsf Ryoshin Lease / Super Resort Exp.cs
☐	JA8106	Boeing 747-246B	19825 / 137		0071	0571	4 PW JT9D-7AW	351534	F22C34Y320	GK-AE	lsf Ryoshin Lease / Super Resort Exp.cs
☐	JA8108	Boeing 747-246B	20333 / 166		0071	1171	4 PW JT9D-7AW	351534	F22C59Y256	GK-AH	lsf Ryoshin Lease
☐	JA8110	Boeing 747-246B	20504 / 181		0072	0372	4 PW JT9D-7AW	351534	C34Y393	GM-BK	lsf JAZ
☐	JA8111	Boeing 747-246B	20505 / 182		0072	0372	4 PW JT9D-7AW	351534	C16Y444	GM-BL	lsf JAZ / Super Resort Express-colors
☐	JA8114	Boeing 747-246B	20530 / 196	N1800B*	0072	1172	4 PW JT9D-7AW	351534	C16Y444	DM-HL	lsf JAZ / Super Resort Express-colors
☐	JA8115	Boeing 747-146	20531 / 197		0072	1072	4 PW JT9D-7A	332937	F8Y454	GM-AK	lsf Ryoshin Lease / Super Resort Exp.cs
☐	JA8116	Boeing 747-146	20532 / 199		0072	1272	4 PW JT9D-7A	332937	F22C74Y256	GM-AL	lsf JAZ / Super Resort Expr. cs
☐	JA811J	Boeing 747-246F (SCD)	22989 / 571	N211JL	0082	1282	4 PW JT9D-7Q	377842	Freighter	EG-JL	lsf Nikko Lease / Super Logistics color
☐	JA8123	Boeing 747-246F (SCD)	21034 / 243		0074	0974	4 PW JT9D-7AW	351534	Freighter	JL-AK	lsf Sumisho Lease
☐	JA8127	Boeing 747-246B	21031 / 255		0075	0575	4 PW JT9D-7A	351534	F22C92Y232	JL-BF	lsf JAZ
☐	JA8128	Boeing 747-146	21029 / 259		0075	1198	4 PW JT9D-7A	332937	F12C42Y353	JL-BG	lsf JAA
☐	JA8130	Boeing 747-246B	21679 / 376		0079	0679	4 PW JT9D-7Q	362874	F22C90Y216	GH-BF	
☐	JA8131	Boeing 747-246B	21680 / 380		0079	0679	4 PW JT9D-7Q	362874	F22C90Y216	GH-BJ	Super Resort Express colors
☐	JA8132	Boeing 747-246F	21681 / 382	N1782B*	0079	0779	4 PW JT9D-7Q	371946	Freighter	GH-BK	lsf Showa Lease
☐	JA8140	Boeing 747-246B	22064 / 407		0079	1179	4 PW JT9D-7Q	362874	F22C90Y216	GH-BL	
☐	JA8141	Boeing 747-246B	22065 / 411		0079	1279	4 PW JT9D-7Q	362874	F22C90Y216	GH-BM	Super Resort Express colors
☐	JA8149	Boeing 747-246B	22478 / 489		0081	0381	4 PW JT9D-7Q	351534	C30Y397	EJ-AH	lsf Ryoshin Lease / Super Resort Exp.cs
☐	JA8150	Boeing 747-246B	22479 / 496	N1783B*	0081	0381	4 PW JT9D-7Q	351534	C30Y397	EJ-AK	lsf Ryoshin Lease / Super Resort Exp.cs
☐	JA8154	Boeing 747-246B	22745 / 547		0081	1181	4 PW JT9D-7Q	362874	F22C90Y216	EG-JK	lsf Niaruko Aviation / sub-lst JAA
☐	JA8160	Boeing 747-221F (SCD)	21744 / 392	N905PA	0079	1092	4 PW JT9D-7Q	362874	Freighter	DG-BC	lsf Nikko Lease / Super Logistics cs
☐	JA8161	Boeing 747-246B	22990 / 579	N6046B*	0083	0683	4 PW JT9D-7R4G2	377842	F32C124Y110	GK-KL	
☐	JA8162	Boeing 747-246B	22991 / 581	N5573K*	0083	0683	4 PW JT9D-7R4G2	377842	F32C124Y110	GK-AC	
☐	JA8164	Boeing 747-146B (SR)	23150 / 601	N1781B*	0084	1284	4 PW JT9D-7A	272155	C22Y511	DJ-BC	
☐	JA8165	Boeing 747-221F (SCD)	21743 / 384	N904PA	0079	1283	4 PW JT9D-7Q	362874	Freighter	FK-DH	lsf Sumisho Lease
☐	JA8169	Boeing 747-246B	23389 / 635	N6018N*	0086	0386	4 PW JT9D-7R4G2	377842	F32C124Y110	DJ-BF	
☐	JA8170	Boeing 747-146B (SR / SUD)	23390 / 636	N6009F*	0086	0386	4 PW JT9D-7A	272155	C25Y538	GJ-HK	
☐	JA8171	Boeing 747-246F (SCD)	23391 / 654	N6038E*	0086	0886	4 PW JT9D-7R4G2	377842	Freighter	GM-BH	lsf Showa Lease / Super Logistics cs
☐	JA8176	Boeing 747-146B (SR / SUD)	23637 / 655	N60668*	0086	0986	4 PW JT9D-7A	272155	C25Y538	GJ-HL	
☐	JA8180	Boeing 747-246F (SCD)	23641 / 684		0087	0887	4 PW JT9D-7R4G2	377842	Freighter	CJ-DE	lsf Sumigin Lease / Super Logistics cs
☐	JA8193	Boeing 747-212B (SF)	21940 / 457	9V-SQO	0080	0691	4 PW JT9D-7Q	294835	Freighter	BE-DG	lsf Nikko Lease / cvtd -212B
☐	JA8937	Boeing 747-246F (SCD)	22477 / 494	N740SJ	0081	0199	4 PW JT9D-7Q	371946	Freighter		
☐	JA812J	Boeing 747-346	23067 / 588	N212JL	0083	1183	4 PW JT9D-7R4G2	371946	F33C102Y184	DJ-GH	
☐	JA813J	Boeing 747-346	23068 / 589	N213JL	0083	1283	4 PW JT9D-7R4G2	371946	F33C102Y184	GJ-HM	
☐	JA8163	Boeing 747-346	23149 / 599	N5573B*	0084	1284	4 PW JT9D-7R4G2	371946	F33C102Y184	CJ-BL	
☐	JA8166	Boeing 747-346	23151 / 607	N1786B*	0085	0285	4 PW JT9D-7R4G2	371946	F33C102Y184	CJ-BM	Super Resort Express-colors
☐	JA8173	Boeing 747-346	23482 / 640	N6009F*	0086	0486	4 PW JT9D-7R4G2	371946	F33C102Y184	BK-CD	
☐	JA8177	Boeing 747-346	23638 / 658	N6009F*	0086	1086	4 PW JT9D-7R4G2	371946	F33C102Y184	FK-HJ	
☐	JA8178	Boeing 747-346	23639 / 664	N6009F*	0086	1286	4 PW JT9D-7R4G2	371946	F33C102Y184	EG-HM	
☐	JA8179	Boeing 747-346	23640 / 668	N6009F*	0087	0287	4 PW JT9D-7R4G2	371946	F33C102Y184	JK-CL	
☐	JA8183	Boeing 747-346	23967 / 692	N6005C*	0087	1287	4 PW JT9D-7R4G2	371946	F33C102Y184	GJ-FM	cvtd -346 (SR)
☐	JA8184	Boeing 747-346 (SR)	23968 / 693	N6055X*	0088	0188	4 PW JT9D-7R4G2	272155	C18Y538	GM-DE	
☐	JA8185	Boeing 747-346	23969 / 691	N6005C*	0088	0388	4 PW JT9D-7R4G2	371946	F33C102Y184	DJ-GK	
☐	JA8186	Boeing 747-346 (SR)	24018 / 694	N6018N*	0088	0288	4 PW JT9D-7R4G2	272155	C25Y538	DJ-AE	Super Resort Express-colors
☐	JA8187	Boeing 747-346 (SR)	24019 / 695	N6038E*	0088	0288	4 PW JT9D-7R4G2	272155	C25Y538	BK-CG	Super Resort Express-colors
☐	JA8071	Boeing 747-446	24423 / 758		0090	0190	4 GE CF6-80C2B1F	394625	FC60Y324	DG-AE	
☐	JA8072	Boeing 747-446	24424 / 760		0090	0190	4 GE CF6-80C2B1F	394625	FC60Y324	DG-AH	
☐	JA8073	Boeing 747-446	24425 / 767		0090	0290	4 GE CF6-80C2B1F	394625	FC60Y324	DJ-HK	lsf Nikko Lease
☐	JA8074	Boeing 747-446	24426 / 768		0090	0290	4 GE CF6-80C2B1F	394625	FC60Y324	FK-BL	
☐	JA8075	Boeing 747-446	24427 / 780		0090	0390	4 GE CF6-80C2B1F	394625	FC60Y324	CH-DJ	
☐	JA8076	Boeing 747-446	24777 / 797	N6046P*	0090	0790	4 GE CF6-80C2B1F	394625	FC60Y324	FQ-DK	lsf Nikko Lease
☐	JA8077	Boeing 747-446	24784 / 798		0090	0790	4 GE CF6-80C2B1F	394625	FC60Y324	FQ-DJ	lsf Nikko Lease
☐	JA8078	Boeing 747-446	24870 / 821	N60697*	0090	1190	4 GE CF6-80C2B1F	394625	FC60Y324	MQ-JP	lsf Nikko Lease
☐	JA8079	Boeing 747-446	24885 / 824	N6005C*	0090	1290	4 GE CF6-80C2B1F	394625	FC60Y324	MQ-KL	lsf Nikko Lease
☐	JA8080	Boeing 747-446	24886 / 825		0090	1290	4 GE CF6-80C2B1F	394625	FC60Y324	MQ-KP	lsf Nikko Lease
☐	JA8081	Boeing 747-446	25064 / 851		0091	0591	4 GE CF6-80C2B1F	385560	FC60Y324	CJ-PQ	
☐	JA8082	Boeing 747-446	25212 / 871		0091	0891	4 GE CF6-80C2B1F	394625	FC60Y324	FG-AQ	
☐	JA8083	Boeing 747-446 (D)	25213 / 844	N60668*	0091	1091	4 GE CF6-80C2B1F	272155	C24Y544	CH-LP	
☐	JA8084	Boeing 747-446 (D)	25214 / 879		0091	1091	4 GE CF6-80C2B1F	272155	C24Y544	CP-KM	
☐	JA8085	Boeing 747-446	25260 / 876		0091	0991	4 GE CF6-80C2B1F	394625	FC60Y324	EP-HQ	lsf Sumigin Lease
☐	JA8086	Boeing 747-446	25308 / 885		0091	1191	4 GE CF6-80C2B1F	394625	FC60Y324	EP-JQ	
☐	JA8087	Boeing 747-446	26346 / 897		0092	0292	4 GE CF6-80C2B1F	394625	FC60Y324	EP-KQ	lsf N.I. Aircraft Leasing
☐	JA8088	Boeing 747-446	26341 / 902		0092	0292	4 GE CF6-80C2B1F	394625	FC60Y324	EP-LQ	lsf Kogin Lease
☐	JA8089	Boeing 747-446	26342 / 905		0092	0392	4 GE CF6-80C2B1F	394625	FC60Y324	EP-MQ	lsf N.I. Aircraft Leasing
☐	JA8090	Boeing 747-446 (D)	26347 / 907		0092	0392	4 GE CF6-80C2B1F	272155	C24Y544	FG-BQ	lsf N.I. Aircraft Leasing
☐	JA8901	Boeing 747-446	26343 / 918		0092	0692	4 GE CF6-80C2B1F	394625	FC60Y324	BR-CK	
☐	JA8902	Boeing 747-446	26344 / 929	N6018N*	0092	0892	4 GE CF6-80C2B1F	394625	FC60Y324	BR-CL	
☐	JA8903	Boeing 747-446 (D)	26345 / 935		0092	0992	4 GE CF6-80C2B1F	272155	C24Y544	BR-CM	lsf Kogin Lease
☐	JA8904	Boeing 747-446 (D)	26348 / 941		0092	1192	4 GE CF6-80C2B1F	272155	C24Y544	BR-CP	
☐	JA8905	Boeing 747-446 (D)	26349 / 948		0092	1292	4 GE CF6-80C2B1F	272155	C24Y544	BR-CQ	
☐	JA8906	Boeing 747-446	26350 / 961		0093	0393	4 GE CF6-80C2B1F	394625	FC60Y324	CR-MQ	lsf Charlotte Aircraft
☐	JA8907	Boeing 747-446 (D)	26351 / 963		0093	0393	4 GE CF6-80C2B1F	272155	C24Y544	CR-MS	lsf Sumigin Lease
☐	JA8908	Boeing 747-446 (D)	26352 / 978		0093	0693	4 GE CF6-80C2B1F	272155	C24Y544	CR-PQ	lsf Kogin Lease
☐	JA8909	Boeing 747-446	26353 / 980		0093	0693	4 GE CF6-80C2B1F	394625	FC60Y324	CR-PS	
☐	JA8910	Boeing 747-446	26355 / 1024		0094	0394	4 GE CF6-80C2B1F	394625	FC60Y324	DS-BR	
☐	JA8911	Boeing 747-446	26356 / 1026		0094	0394	4 GE CF6-80C2B1F	394625	FC60Y324	EL-QS	

☐	JA8912	Boeing 747-446	27099 / 1031		0094	0594	4 GE CF6-80C2B1F	376482	FC60Y324	ES-CP	lsf Illinois Aircraft Leasing
☐	JA8913	Boeing 747-446	26359 / 1153		0098	0498	4 GE CF6-80C2B1F	376482	FC60Y324	ES-CQ	
☐	JA8914	Boeing 747-446	26360 / 1166		0098	0798	4 GE CF6-80C2B1F	376482	FC60Y324		
☐	JA8915	Boeing 747-446	26361 / 1188		1198	1198	4 GE CF6-80C2B1F	394625	FC60Y324		
☐	JA8916	Boeing 747-446	26362				4 GE CF6-80C2B1F	394625	FC60Y324		oo-delivery 0499
☐	JA8917	Boeing 747-446	29899				4 GE CF6-80C2B1F	394625	FC60Y324		oo-delivery 0499
☐	JA8918	Boeing 747-446					4 GE CF6-80C2B1F	394625	FC60Y324		oo-delivery 1099
☐	JA8919	Boeing 747-446					4 GE CF6-80C2B1F	394625	FC60Y324		oo-delivery 1099
☐	JA8920	Boeing 747-446					4 GE CF6-80C2B1F	394625	FC60Y324		oo-delivery 0000
☐	JA8921	Boeing 747-446					4 GE CF6-80C2B1F	394625	FC60Y324		oo-delivery 0000
☐	JA8922	Boeing 747-446					4 GE CF6-80C2B1F	394625	FC60Y324		oo-delivery 0000
☐	JA8923	Boeing 747-446					4 GE CF6-80C2B1F	394625	FC60Y324		oo-delivery 0000
☐	JA8924	Boeing 747-446					4 GE CF6-80C2B1F	394625	FC60Y324		oo-delivery 0000
☐	JA8925	Boeing 747-446					4 GE CF6-80C2B1F	394625	FC60Y324		oo-delivery 0001
☐	JA8926	Boeing 747-446					4 GE CF6-80C2B1F	394625	FC60Y324		oo-delivery 0001
☐	JA8927	Boeing 747-446					4 GE CF6-80C2B1F	394625	FC60Y324		oo-delivery 0001
☐	JA8928	Boeing 747-446					4 GE CF6-80C2B1F	394625	FC60Y324		oo-delivery 0001
☐	JA8929	Boeing 747-446					4 GE CF6-80C2B1F	394625	FC60Y324		oo-delivery 0001
☐	JA8930	Boeing 747-446					4 GE CF6-80C2B1F	394625	FC60Y324		oo-delivery 1000

JAPAN AIR SYSTEM, Co. Ltd – JAS = JD / JAS (Nihon Air System) (formerly TOA Domestic Airlines – TDA) **Tokyo-Haneda**

JAS M1 Building, 5-1 Hanedakuko, 3-chome, Ota-ku, Tokyo 144-0041, Japan ☎ (3) 54 73 40 00 Tx: 2225182 tdatyo j Fax: (3) 54 73 40 09 SITA: n/a
F: 1964 ⁂ 5600 Head: Hiromi Funabiki IATA: 234 ICAO: AIR SYSTEM Net: http://www.jas.co.jp

☐	JA5311	Beech Baron 58	TH-1656	N55602*	0092	0692	2 CO IO-520-CB	2495	Trainer/5 Pax		
☐	JA8717	NAMC YS-11A-500	2092		0069	0269	2 RR Dart 542-10J/K	24500	Y64		Aso / lst JAC / cvtd -217
☐	JA8759	NAMC YS-11A-500	2152	JQ2152*	0070	1270	2 RR Dart 542-10J/K	24500	Y64		Daisetsu / lst JAC / cvtd -227
☐	JA8763	NAMC YS-11A-500	2135	JQ2135*	0070	0470	2 RR Dart 542-10J/K	24500	Y64		Erabu / lst JAC / cvtd -227
☐	JA8766	NAMC YS-11A-500	2142	JQ2142*	0070	0770	2 RR Dart 542-10J/K	24500	Y64		Tokunoshima / lst JAC / cvtd -227
☐	JA8768	NAMC YS-11A-500	2147	PK-IYS	0070	0178	2 RR Dart 542-10J/K	24500	Y64		Rikuchuu / lst JAC / cvtd -227
☐	JA8771	NAMC YS-11A-500	2149		0070	0970	2 RR Dart 542-10J/K	24500	Y64		Akiyoshi / lst JAC / cvtd -227
☐	JA8776	NAMC YS-11A-500	2157		0071	0571	2 RR Dart 542-10J/K	24500	Y64		Shiretoko / lst JAC / cvtd -227
☐	JA8777	NAMC YS-11A-500	2163		0071	0371	2 RR Dart 542-10J/K	24500	Y64		Setouchi / lst JAC / cvtd -227
☐	JA8781	NAMC YS-11A-500	2166		0071	1071	2 RR Dart 542-10J/K	24500	Y64		Kunisaki / lst JAC / cvtd -217
☐	JA8788	NAMC YS-11A-500	2176		0073	0373	2 RR Dart 542-10J/K	24500	Y64		Oga / lst JAC / cvtd -217
☐	JA8805	NAMC YS-11A-500	2055	PP-CTF	0067	1177	2 RR Dart 542-10J/K	24500	Y64		Ibusuki / lst JAC / cvtd -202
☐	JA8809	NAMC YS-11A-500	2054	PP-CTE	0067	0179	2 RR Dart 542-10J/K	24500	Y64		Ikoma / lst JAC / cvtd -202
☐	JA8278	Boeing (Douglas) MD-87 (DC-9-87)	49464 / 1476		0088	0688	2 PW JT8D-217A/C	56699	Y134		
☐	JA8279	Boeing (Douglas) MD-87 (DC-9-87)	49465 / 1604		0089	0989	2 PW JT8D-217A/C	56699	Y134		
☐	JA8280	Boeing (Douglas) MD-87 (DC-9-87)	49466 / 1727		0090	0790	2 PW JT8D-217A/C	56699	Y134		
☐	JA8281	Boeing (Douglas) MD-87 (DC-9-87)	49467 / 1742		0090	0890	2 PW JT8D-217A/C	56699	Y134		
☐	JA8370	Boeing (Douglas) MD-87 (DC-9-87)	53039 / 1881		0091	0691	2 PW JT8D-217A/C	56699	Y134		lsf Mitsui Lease Jigyo
☐	JA8371	Boeing (Douglas) MD-87 (DC-9-87)	53040 / 1897		0091	0891	2 PW JT8D-217A/C	56699	Y134		lsf Mitsui Lease Jigyo
☐	JA8372	Boeing (Douglas) MD-87 (DC-9-87)	53041 / 1945		0091	1291	2 PW JT8D-217A/C	56699	Y134		
☐	JA8373	Boeing (Douglas) MD-87 (DC-9-87)	53042 / 1969	N90126*	0092	0392	2 PW JT8D-217A/C	56699	Y134		
☐	JA8260	Boeing (Douglas) MD-81 (DC-9-81)	49461 / 1359		0087	0587	2 PW JT8D-217A/C	63503	Y163	JP-BQ	lsf ORIX
☐	JA8261	Boeing (Douglas) MD-81 (DC-9-81)	49462 / 1477		0088	0688	2 PW JT8D-217A/C	63503	Y163		lsf Air Star
☐	JA8262	Boeing (Douglas) MD-81 (DC-9-81)	49463 / 1488		0088	0788	2 PW JT8D-217A/C	63503	Y163		lsf Intec Lease
☐	JA8294	Boeing (Douglas) MD-81 (DC-9-81)	49820 / 1598		0089	0689	2 PW JT8D-217A/C	63503	Y163		
☐	JA8295	Boeing (Douglas) MD-81 (DC-9-81)	49821 / 1615		0089	0889	2 PW JT8D-217A/C	63503	Y163		lsf Air Eagle
☐	JA8296	Boeing (Douglas) MD-81 (DC-9-81)	49907 / 1734		0090	0790	2 PW JT8D-217A/C	63503	Y163		
☐	JA8297	Boeing (Douglas) MD-81 (DC-9-81)	49908 / 1749		0090	0890	2 PW JT8D-217A/C	63503	Y163		
☐	JA8374	Boeing (Douglas) MD-81 (DC-9-81)	53043 / 1982		0092	0392	2 PW JT8D-217A/C	63503	Y163		
☐	JA8460	Boeing (Douglas) MD-81 (DC-9-81)	48031 / 969		0081	0481	2 PW JT8D-217A/C	63503	Y163		lsf JFS Holding Co.
☐	JA8461	Boeing (Douglas) MD-81 (DC-9-81)	48032 / 978		0081	0681	2 PW JT8D-217A/C	63503	Y163		lsf JFS Holding Co.
☐	JA8462	Boeing (Douglas) MD-81 (DC-9-81)	48033 / 988		0081	0781	2 PW JT8D-217A/C	63503	Y163		lsf JFS Holding Co.
☐	JA8496	Boeing (Douglas) MD-81 (DC-9-81)	49280 / 1194		0085	0485	2 PW JT8D-217A/C	63503	Y163		lsf Air Star
☐	JA8497	Boeing (Douglas) MD-81 (DC-9-81)	49281 / 1200		0085	0585	2 PW JT8D-217A/C	63503	Y163		
☐	JA8498	Boeing (Douglas) MD-81 (DC-9-81)	49282 / 1282	N6202S*	0086	0686	2 PW JT8D-217A/C	63503	Y163		lsf IBJ & Diamond & Japan Leasing
☐	JA8499	Boeing (Douglas) MD-81 (DC-9-81)	49283 / 1299		0086	0986	2 PW JT8D-217A/C	63503	Y163		lsf Mitsui & Sumisho & SB Leasing
☐	JA8552	Boeing (Douglas) MD-81 (DC-9-81)	53297 / 2040		0093	0193	2 PW JT8D-217A/C	63503	Y163		lst HLQ
☐	JA8553	Boeing (Douglas) MD-81 (DC-9-81)	53298 / 2045		0093	0193	2 PW JT8D-217A/C	63503	Y163		
☐	JA8554	Boeing (Douglas) MD-81 (DC-9-81)	53299 / 2075		0093	1293	2 PW JT8D-217A/C	63503	Y163		lsf Nihon Lease
☐	JA8555	Boeing (Douglas) MD-81 (DC-9-81)	53300 / 2076		0094	0594	2 PW JT8D-217A/C	63503	Y163		lsf Nihon Lease
☐	JA8556	Boeing (Douglas) MD-81 (DC-9-81)	53301 / 2082		0094	0694	2 PW JT8D-217A/C	63503	Y163		lsf Mitsui Lease Jigyo
☐	JA8557	Boeing (Douglas) MD-81 (DC-9-81)	53302 / 2085		0094	0694	2 PW JT8D-217A/C	63503	Y163		lsf Sumigin Lease
☐	JA001D	Boeing (Douglas) MD-90-30	53555 / 2210		0097	1197	2 IAE V2525-D5	70760	Y166		
☐	JA002D	Boeing (Douglas) MD-90-30	53556 / 2207		0097	1297	2 IAE V2525-D5	70760	Y166		
☐	JA003D	Boeing (Douglas) MD-90-30	53557 / 2211		0097	1297	2 IAE V2525-D5	70760	Y166		lsf Sony Finance Int'l
☐	JA004D	Boeing (Douglas) MD-90-30	53558 / 2212		0097	1297	2 IAE V2525-D5	70760	Y166		lsf Kogin Lease
☐	JA005D	Boeing (Douglas) MD-90-30	53559 / 2236		0098	0798	2 IAE V2525-D5	70760	Y166		
☐	JA006D	Boeing (Douglas) MD-90-30	53560 / 2245		0098	1098	2 IAE V2525-D5	70760	Y166		
☐	JA8004	Boeing (Douglas) MD-90-30	53359 / 2184		0097	0697	2 IAE V2525-D5	70760	Y166		
☐	JA8020	Boeing (Douglas) MD-90-30	53360 / 2190		0097	0797	2 IAE V2525-D5	70760	Y166		
☐	JA8029	Boeing (Douglas) MD-90-30	53361 / 2202		0097	1097	2 IAE V2525-D5	70760	Y166		lsf Central Lease & others
☐	JA8062	Boeing (Douglas) MD-90-30	53352 / 2098		0695	0695	2 IAE V2525-D5	70760	Y166		
☐	JA8063	Boeing (Douglas) MD-90-30	53353 / 2120		0995	0995	2 IAE V2525-D5	70760	Y166		
☐	JA8064	Boeing (Douglas) MD-90-30	53354 / 2125		1295	1295	2 IAE V2525-D5	70760	Y166		
☐	JA8065	Boeing (Douglas) MD-90-30	53355 / 2131		0096	0396	2 IAE V2525-D5	70760	Y166		
☐	JA8066	Boeing (Douglas) MD-90-30	53356 / 2157		0096	1096	2 IAE V2525-D5	70760	Y166		
☐	JA8069	Boeing (Douglas) MD-90-30	53357 / 2164		0096	1296	2 IAE V2525-D5	70760	Y166		
☐	JA8070	Boeing (Douglas) MD-90-30	53358 / 2179		0097	0597	2 IAE V2525-D5	70760	Y166		
☐	JA8237	Airbus Industrie A300B4-2C (SCD)	256	F-WZMA*	0083	0386	2 GE CF6-50C2R	150000	Y298		lsf SB Gen.&Sumisho Leasing/cvtd C4-203
☐	JA8263	Airbus Industrie A300B4-2C	151	VH-TAB	0081	0387	2 GE CF6-50C2R	150000	C32Y223 or Y283	JP-EQ	lsf Sumigin Lease / cvtd B4-203
☐	JA8276	Airbus Industrie A300B4-2C	169	D-AHLJ	0081	0488	2 GE CF6-50C2R	150000	Y298		lsf Sumigin Lease / cvtd B4-203
☐	JA8277	Airbus Industrie A300B4-2C	174	D-AHLK	0081	0388	2 GE CF6-50C2R	150000	C32Y223 or Y283	JP-FQ	lsf Diamond Lease / cvtd B4-203
☐	JA8292	Airbus Industrie A300B4-2C	110	PP-CLB	0080	0489	2 GE CF6-50C2R	150000	Y298		lsf Sumigin Lease / cvtd B4-203
☐	JA8293	Airbus Industrie A300B4-2C	194	PP-VNE	0082	1289	2 GE CF6-50C2R	165000	Y298		lsf Kogin Lease / cvtd B4-203
☐	JA8369	Airbus Industrie A300B4-2C	239	SU-GAA	0083	0990	2 GE CF6-50C2R	165000	Y298	AC-FK	cvtd B4-203
☐	JA8464	Airbus Industrie A300B2K-3C	082	F-WZEQ*	0080	1080	2 GE CF6-50C2R	137000	Y298		lsf Mitsui Lease Jigyo
☐	JA8465	Airbus Industrie A300B2K-3C	089	F-WZEF*	0080	1280	2 GE CF6-50C2R	137000	Y298		
☐	JA8466	Airbus Industrie A300B2K-3C	090	F-WZEG*	0080	1280	2 GE CF6-50C2R	137000	Y298		lsf Mitsui Lease Jigyo
☐	JA8471	Airbus Industrie A300B2K-3C	160	F-WZMI*	0081	1181	2 GE CF6-50C2R	137000	Y298		
☐	JA8472	Airbus Industrie A300B2K-3C	163	F-WZMJ*	0081	1281	2 GE CF6-50C2R	137000	Y298		
☐	JA8473	Airbus Industrie A300B2K-3C	176	F-WZMU*	0082	0282	2 GE CF6-50C2R	137000	Y298		
☐	JA8476	Airbus Industrie A300B2K-3C	209	F-WZMH*	0083	0383	2 GE CF6-50C2R	137000	Y298		
☐	JA8477	Airbus Industrie A300B2K-3C	244	F-WZMS*	0083	0583	2 GE CF6-50C2R	137000	Y298		
☐	JA8478	Airbus Industrie A300B2K-3C	253	F-WZMX*	0083	0683	2 GE CF6-50C2R	137000	Y298		
☐	JA8560	Airbus Industrie A300B4-2C	178	F-BVGS	0082	1291	2 GE CF6-50C2R	165000	Y298		lsf Diamond Lease / cvtd B4-203
☐	JA011D	Airbus Industrie A300-622R (A300B4-622R)	783	F-WWAA*	0098	0598	2 PW PW4158	171700	Y308		lsf Nichimen Corp. / std XLW
☐	JA8375	Airbus Industrie A300-622R (A300B4-622R)	602	F-WWAT*	0091	0491	2 PW PW4158	144000	Y308	AB-QR	lsf Mitsui Lease Jigyo
☐	JA8376	Airbus Industrie A300-622R (A300B4-622R)	617	F-WWAK*	0091	1191	2 PW PW4158	144000	Y308	AB-QS	
☐	JA8377	Airbus Industrie A300-622R (A300B4-622R)	621	F-WWAA*	0091	0192	2 PW PW4158	144000	Y308	AB-RS	
☐	JA8527	Airbus Industrie A300-622R (A300B4-622R)	724	F-WWAQ*	0095	0495	2 PW PW4158	171700	Y308		
☐	JA8529	Airbus Industrie A300-622R (A300B4-622R)	729	F-WWAM*	0094	0594	2 PW PW4158	171700	Y308		lsf Nihon Lease
☐	JA8558	Airbus Industrie A300-622R (A300B4-622R)	637	F-WWAX*	0092	0792	2 PW PW4158	144000	Y308	AC-DR	
☐	JA8559	Airbus Industrie A300-622R (A300B4-622R)	641	F-WWAM*	0092	0992	2 PW PW4158	144000	Y308	AB-QS	
☐	JA8561	Airbus Industrie A300-622R (A300B4-622R)	670	F-WWAD*	0092	0193	2 PW PW4158	144000	C52Y193	AC-DR	
☐	JA8562	Airbus Industrie A300-622R (A300B4-622R)	679	F-WWAL*	0092	0393	2 PW PW4158	144000	Y308	AC-DR	special Pocari Sweat-colors
☐	JA8563	Airbus Industrie A300-622R (A300B4-622R)	683	F-WWAJ*	0093	0693	2 PW PW4158	144000	Y308		
☐	JA8564	Airbus Industrie A300-622R (A300B4-622R)	703	F-WWAO*	0094	1294	2 PW PW4158	171700	Y308		lsf Mitsui Lease Jigyo
☐	JA8565	Airbus Industrie A300-622R (A300B4-622R)	711	F-WWAE*	0093	1293	2 PW PW4158	171700	Y308	AC-DR	lsf Sumigin Lease
☐	JA8566	Airbus Industrie A300-622R (A300B4-622R)	730	F-WWAV*	0094	0995	2 PW PW4158	171700	Y308		
☐	JA8573	Airbus Industrie A300-622R (A300B4-622R)	737	F-WWAF*	0094	0994	2 PW PW4158	171700	Y308	AC-DR	
☐	JA8574	Airbus Industrie A300-622R (A300B4-622R)	740	F-WWAG*	0094	1194	2 PW PW4158	171700	Y308		
☐	JA8657	Airbus Industrie A300-622R (A300B4-622R)	753	F-WWAD*	0096	0596	2 PW PW4158	171700	Y308		lsf Kogin Lease
☐	JA8659	Airbus Industrie A300-622R (A300B4-622R)	770	F-WWAQ*	0096	0696	2 PW PW4158	171700	Y308		lsf Kogin Lease
☐	JA	Airbus Industrie A300-622R (A300B4-622R)					2 PW PW4158	171700	Y308		oo-delivery 0100
☐	JA007D	Boeing 777-289	27639 / 134		0098	0498	2 PW PW4074	229518	F12C38Y330		
☐	JA008D	Boeing 777-289	27640 / 146		0098	0698	2 PW PW4074	229518	F12C38Y330		
☐	JA009D	Boeing 777-289	27641 / 159	N5017V*	0098	0998	2 PW PW4074	229518	F12C38Y330		lsf Sony Finance & others

224 registration type of aircraft cn/fn ex/ex* mfd del powered by mtow kg configuration selcal name/fln/specialitites/remarks

registration	type of aircraft	cn/fn	ex/ex*	mfd	del	powered by	mtow kg	configuration	selcal	name/fln/specialitites/remarks
☐ JA010D	Boeing 777-289	27642				2 PW PW4074	229518	F12C38Y330		oo-delivery 0599
☐ JA8977	Boeing 777-289	27636 / 45		0096	1296	2 PW PW4074	229518	F12C38Y330		lsf Sumigin Lease
☐ JA8978	Boeing 777-289	27637 / 79		0697	0697	2 PW PW4074	229518	F12C38Y330		
☐ JA8979	Boeing 777-289	27638 / 107		1197	1197	2 PW PW4074	229518	F12C38Y330		
☐ JA8550	Boeing (Douglas) DC-10-30	48315 / 436		0088	0488	3 GE CF6-50C2	267619	C41Y235	JP-CQ	lsf Rainbow Leasing / sub-lst HLQ
☐ JA8551	Boeing (Douglas) DC-10-30	48316 / 437	HL7329	0088	0788	3 GE CF6-50C2	267619	C41Y235	JP-DQ	lsf Mitsui Lease Jigyo

JAPAN ASIA AIRWAYS, Co. Ltd – JAA = EG / JAA (Nihon Asia Koku)

Tokyo-Narita

Yurakucho Denki Bldg, Minami-kan 7-1, Yurakucho, 1-chome, Tokyo 100-0006, Japan ☎ (3) 32 84 29 74 Tx: none Fax: (3) 32 84 29 80 SITA: n/a

F: 1975 ✝✝✝ 900 Head: Noboru Okamura IATA: 688 ICAO: ASIA Net: http://www.asiannet.com/taiwan/jaa Additional aircraft (Boeing 747 & DC-10) are lsf Japan Airlines when required.

registration	type of aircraft	cn/fn	ex/ex*	mfd	del	powered by	mtow kg	configuration	selcal	name/fln/specialitites/remarks
☐ JA8266	Boeing 767-346	23966 / 191	N6018N*	0087	0497	2 PW JT9D-7R4D	151953	C24Y209	DH-KM	
☐ JA8976	Boeing 767-346	27659 / 667		0797	0797	2 GE CF6-80C2B2	130952	C16Y254		
☐ JA8987	Boeing 767-346	28553 / 688		0098	0298	2 GE CF6-80C2B2	130952	C16Y254		lsf JAL
☐ JA8531	Boeing (Douglas) DC-10-40 (I)	46923 / 216	N8703Q*	0076	1287	3 PW JT9D-59A	251744	C48Y225	JL-BK	lst JAL
☐ JA8532	Boeing (Douglas) DC-10-40 (I)	46660 / 220	N8705Q*	0076	1086	3 PW JT9D-59A	251744	C48Y225	FJ-KL	lst JAL / cvtd DC-10-40 (D)
☐ JA8534	Boeing (Douglas) DC-10-40 (I)	46913 / 206	N54652*	0075	1186	3 PW JT9D-59A	251744	C48Y225	FJ-KM	lst JAL
☐ JA8537	Boeing (Douglas) DC-10-40 (I)	46967 / 265		0077	1188	3 PW JT9D-59A	251744	C48Y225	FH-AD	lst JAL / cvtd DC-10-40 (D)
☐ JA8128	Boeing 747-146	21029 / 259		0075	1186	4 PW JT9D-7A	332937	F12C42Y353	JL-BG	lst JAL
☐ JA8129	Boeing 747-246B	21678 / 361		0079	1188	4 PW JT9D-7AW	351534	F12C42Y353	GM-BC	
☐ JA8154	Boeing 747-246B	22745 / 547		0081	1298	4 PW JT9D-7Q	362874	F22C90Y216	EG-JK	lsf JAL
☐ JA8155	Boeing 747-246B	22746 / 548		0081	0292	4 PW JT9D-7Q	362874	F22C90Y216	EG-KL	
☐ JA8189	Boeing 747-346	24156 / 716	N6046P*	0088	1088	4 PW JT9D-7R4G2	310710	F12C48Y384	GJ-FK	

JAPAN REGIONAL AIRLINES, Co. Ltd – JRA (Subs.of Nishi-Nihon Medical Services, Co.Ltd/Member of Yosinaga Enterprises Group/formerly Hirokoo Airlines)

Yamaguchi-Ube

625-17, Oki-Ube, Ube City 755-0007, Yamaguchi Pref., Japan ☎ (836) 35 36 01 Tx: none Fax: (836) 35 36 02 SITA: n/a

F: 1985 ✝✝✝ 26 Head: Kozou Yoshinaga Net: n/a Aircraft below MTOW 1361kg: Cessna 172

registration	type of aircraft	cn/fn	ex/ex*	mfd	del	powered by	mtow kg	configuration	selcal	name/fln/specialitites/remarks
☐ JA8229	Cessna 208 Caravan I	20800137	N1570C	0088		1 PWC PT6A-114	3629	Y9		lsf Nishin Nihon Iryo Service
☐ JA8890	Cessna 208 Caravan I	20800195	N9776F*	0090		1 PWC PT6A-114	3629	Y9		lsf Shikoku Iryo Service
☐ JA8835	Dornier 228-200	8007	D-IDID*	0083	0095	2 GA TPE331-5-252D	5700	Y19		lsf Nishi Nihon Medical Service
☐ JA8836	Dornier 228-200	8019	D-IBLJ*	0083	0095	2 GA TPE331-5-252D	5700	Y19		lsf Nishi Nihon Medical Service
☐ JA8866	Dornier 228-200	8124	D-IAHD*	0087	0095	2 GA TPE331-5-252D	5700	Y19		lsf Shikoku Iryo Service

JAPAN ROYAL HELICOPTER, Co. Ltd – JRH (formerly Light Air Network, Co. Ltd & Royal Airline, Co. Ltd)

Tokyo-Heliport

4-19 Shinkiba Koto-ku, Tokyo 136-0082, Japan ☎ (3) 35 21 73 31 Tx: n/a Fax: (3) 35 21 73 30 SITA: n/a

F: 1968 ✝✝✝ 66 Head: n/a Net: n/a

registration	type of aircraft	cn/fn	ex/ex*	mfd	del	powered by	mtow kg	configuration	selcal	name/fln/specialitites/remarks
☐ JA6101	Bell 206B JetRanger III	4164	N4303V	0491		1 AN 250-C20J	1451			lsf Tuzome Shida
☐ JA6129	Eurocopter (Aerosp.) SA315B Lama	1318 / 43		1159		1 TU Artouste IIIB1	1950			lsf Nozaki Sangyo / cvtd Alouette II
☐ JA6135	Eurocopter (Aerosp.) SA315B Lama	2252 / 45		0071	1293	1 TU Artouste IIIB1	1950			lsf Mitsui Lease Jigyo/cvtd Alouette II
☐ JA6143	Eurocopter (Aerosp.) SA315B Lama	2155 / 46	F-GJLD	0372		1 TU Artouste IIIB1	1950			cvtd Alouette II
☐ JA9397	Eurocopter (Aerosp.) SA315B Lama	2656		0085		1 TU Artouste IIIB1	1950			
☐ JA9399	Eurocopter (Aerosp.) SA315B Lama	2657		0085		1 TU Artouste IIIB1	1950			
☐ JA9798	Eurocopter (Aerosp.) SA315B Lama	2272 / 29	C-FEZO	0072		1 TU Artouste IIIB1	1950			cvtd Alouette II
☐ JA6049	Eurocopter (Aerosp.) AS350B Ecureuil	2435		0090		1 TU Arriel 1B	1950			
☐ JA9353	Eurocopter (Aerosp.) AS350B Ecureuil	1686	F-WZFL*	0083		1 TU Arriel 1B	1950			
☐ JA9366	Eurocopter (Aerosp.) AS350B Ecureuil	1736		0083		1 TU Arriel 1B	1950			
☐ JA6798	Bell 230	23026	N7904F	0994		2 AN 250C-30G2	3810			lsf Mitsui Bussan
☐ JA9314	Fuji-Bell 204B-2	CH-53		0084		1 KA KT5313B	3856			
☐ JA6184	Kaman K-1200 K-Max	A94-0012		0095	0496	1 LY T5317A-1	2722			lsf Kyokuto Boeki
☐ JA6200	Kaman K-1200 K-Max	A94-0020		1296		1 LY T5317A-1	2722			lsf Kyokuto Boeki
☐ JA6189	Bell 214B BigLifter	28039		0878		1 LY T5508D	7257			

JAPAN TRANSOCEAN AIR, Co. Ltd – JTA = NU / JTA (Associated with Japan Airlines / formerly Southwest Air Lines, Co. Ltd)

Okinawa-Naha

306-1 Kagamizu, Naha, Okinawa 901-0142, Japan ☎ (98) 857 21 14 Tx: 795477 swal aaj Fax: (98) 857 02 93 SITA: n/a

F: 1967 ✝✝✝ 760 Head: Keiivhi Inamine IATA: 353 ICAO: JAI OCEAN Net: n/a

registration	type of aircraft	cn/fn	ex/ex*	mfd	del	powered by	mtow kg	configuration	selcal	name/fln/specialitites/remarks
☐ JA8802	De Havilland DHC-6 Twin Otter 300	492	C-GPBR	0076	0776	2 PWC PT6A-27	5670	Y19		lst Ryukyu Air Commuter
☐ JA8808	De Havilland DHC-6 Twin Otter 300	604	C-GQWL	0078	1078	2 PWC PT6A-27	5670	Y19		lst Ryukyu Air Commuter
☐ JA8710	NAMC YS-11A-500	2090		0068	1268	2 RR Dart 542-10J/K	24500	Y64		cvtd -214
☐ JA8794	NAMC YS-11A-500	2083	PP-CTL	0068	1073	2 RR Dart 542-10J/K	24500	Y64		cvtd -202
☐ JA8250	Boeing 737-2Q3 (A)	23481 / 1241		0086	0686	2 PW JT8D-17	52390	Y130		
☐ JA8282	Boeing 737-2Q3 (A)	24103 / 1565		0088	0688	2 PW JT8D-17	52390	Y130		lsf N.I. Aircraft Leasing
☐ JA8366	Boeing 737-205 (A)	23469 / 1266	LN-SUV	0086	0590	2 PW JT8D-17	49442	Y130	AL-CG	lsf Ryuichi Matsuda Leasing
☐ JA8467	Boeing 737-2Q3 (A)	22367 / 706		0080	1180	2 PW JT8D-17	52390	Y130		
☐ JA8475	Boeing 737-2Q3 (A)	22736 / 896		0082	1082	2 PW JT8D-17	52390	Y130		
☐ JA8492	Boeing 737-2Q3 (A)	23117 / 1033		0084	0684	2 PW JT8D-17	52390	Y130		
☐ JA8528	Boeing 737-205 (A)	23464 / 1223	LN-SUA	0086	0693	2 PW JT8D-17	49442	Y124	AL-CD	lsf Tomen Corp.
☐ JA8523	Boeing 737-4Q3	26603 / 2618		0094	0694	2 CFMI CFM56-3C1	62822	Y150		lsf N.I. Aircraft Leasing
☐ JA8524	Boeing 737-4Q3	26604 / 2684		0095	0295	2 CFMI CFM56-3C1	62822	Y150		lsf Nikko Lease
☐ JA8525	Boeing 737-4Q3	26605 / 2752		0095	0995	2 CFMI CFM56-3C1	62822	Y150		lsf Marubeni Aerospace
☐ JA8526	Boeing 737-4Q3	26606 / 2898		0697	0697	2 CFMI CFM56-3C1	62822	Y150		lsf Nikko Lease
☐ JA8597	Boeing 737-4Q3	27660 / 3043		0098	0698	2 CFMI CFM56-3C1	62822	Y150		
☐ JA8938	Boeing 737-4Q3	29485 / 3085		1198	1198	2 CFMI CFM56-3C1	62822	Y150		lsf Nikko Lease
☐ JA8939	Boeing 737-4Q3	29486 / 3088	N1800B*	0199	0199	2 CFMI CFM56-3C1	62822	Y150		
☐ JA8940	Boeing 737-4Q3	29487				2 CFMI CFM56-3C1	62822	Y150		oo-delivery 0099
☐ JA8953	Boeing 737-4K5	24129 / 1783	D-AHLP	0089	0198	2 CFMI CFM56-3C1	62822	Y150		Papas Island / lsf Nikko Lease
☐ JA8954	Boeing 737-4K5	24130 / 1827	D-AHLQ	0090	1298	2 CFMI CFM56-3C1	62822	Y150		lsf Central Lease

JCAB FLIGHT INSPECTION (Division of Ministry of Transport/Japan Civil Aviation Bureau)

Tokyo-Haneda

Operations & Flight Inspection Division, 1-3 Kasumigaseki, 2-chome, Chiyoda-ku, Tokyo 100-8989, Japan ☎ (3) 35 80 31 11 Tx: none Fax: (3) 35 81 58 49 SITA: n/a

F: 1961 ✝✝✝ 67 Head: Nobuo Ochi Net: n/a Non-commercial national organisation conducting flight inspection missions.

registration	type of aircraft	cn/fn	ex/ex*	mfd	del	powered by	mtow kg	configuration	selcal	name/fln/specialitites/remarks
☐ JA003G	Saab 2000	2000-051	SE-051*	0098	0598	2 AN AE2100A	22800	Calibrator		
☐ JA004G	Saab 2000	2000-054	SE-054*	0098	0698	2 AN AE2100A	22800	Calibrator		
☐ JA8709	NAMC YS-11A-212	2084	PP-SMN	0068	1085	2 RR Dart 542-10J/K	24500	Calibrator		
☐ JA8711	NAMC YS-11-115	2048		0067	0472	2 RR Dart 542-10J/K	23500	Calibrator		
☐ JA8712	NAMC YS-11-115	2049		0067	0472	2 RR Dart 542-10J/K	23500	Calibrator		
☐ JA8720	NAMC YS-11-118	2047		0067	0868	2 RR Dart 542-10J/K	23500	Calibrator		
☐ JA001G	GAC G-IV Gulfstream IV	1190	N403GA*	0093	0993	2 RR Tay 611-8	33203	Calibrator		
☐ JA002G	GAC G-IV Gulfstream IV	1244	N404GA*	0095	1195	2 RR Tay 611-8	33203	Calibrator		

KAGOSHIMA KOKUSAI KOKU – Kagoshima Kokusai Air, Co. Ltd

Kagoshima

Iwasaki Bldg 5, Yamashita-cho, 9-chome, Kagoshima-shi, Kagoshima 892-0816, Japan ☎ (992) 22 88 28 Tx: n/a Fax: (992) 23 10 55 SITA: n/a

F: 1966 ✝✝✝ 20 Head: Tadakazu Okayama Net: n/a Aircraft below MTOW 1361 kg: Cessna 172.

registration	type of aircraft	cn/fn	ex/ex*	mfd	del	powered by	mtow kg	configuration	selcal	name/fln/specialitites/remarks
☐ JA9195	Bell 206B JetRanger III	2321		0078		1 AN 250-C20B	1451			
☐ JA9288	Bell 206B JetRanger III	3260		0081		1 AN 250-C20B	1451			lsf Crown Leasing
☐ JA9815	Bell 206B JetRanger III	4047	C-FEUD*	0089		1 AN 250-C20J	1451			lsf Mitsui Lease Jigyo
☐ JA6096	Eurocopter (Aerosp.) AS350B Ecureuil	2529		0091		1 TU Arriel 1B	1950			lsf Kogin Lease

KANKO, K.K. – KSK (Subsidiary of Keihan Electric Railway, K.K / formerly Kansai Kosoku, K.K.)

Osaka-Yao

2-2-48 Katamachi, Miyakojima-ku, Sumitomo Seimei Kyobashi Building, Osaka 534-0025, Japan ☎ (6) 351 11 31 Tx: none Fax: (6) 351 11 91 SITA: n/a

F: 1928 ✝✝✝ 252 Head: Akihiko Iwauchi Net: n/a Aircraft below MTOW 1361 kg: Cessna 172.

registration	type of aircraft	cn/fn	ex/ex*	mfd	del	powered by	mtow kg	configuration	selcal	name/fln/specialitites/remarks
☐ JA3720	Cessna T207 Turbo Skywagon	20700264	N1664U	0074		1 CO TSIO-520-G	1724	Photo / Survey		

KAWASAKI HELICOPTER SYSTEM, Ltd – KHS (Subsidiary of Kawasaki Heavy Industries, Ltd/formerly Airlift, Co. Ltd)

Gifu

1-Kawasaki-cho, Kakamigahara-shi, Gifu 504-0971, Japan ☎ (583) 82 56 51 Tx: none Fax: (583) 82 29 72 SITA: n/a

F: 1967 ✝✝✝ 150 Head: Hideto Kaneko Net: n/a

registration	type of aircraft	cn/fn	ex/ex*	mfd	del	powered by	mtow kg	configuration	selcal	name/fln/specialitites/remarks
☐ JA9189	Kawasaki-Hughes 369D (500D)	6701		0079		1 AN 250-C20B	1361	5 Pax		
☐ JA9226	Kawasaki-Hughes 369D (500D)	6702		0079	0895	1 AN 250-C20B	1361	5 Pax		
☐ JA6628	Kawasaki (Eurocopter/MBB) BK117B-1	1064		0090	0392	2 LY LTS101-750B.1	3200	7 Pax		
☐ JA9614	Kawasaki (Eurocopter/MBB) BK117B-2	1009		0085		2 LY LTS101-750B.1	3350	7 Pax		cvtd BK117B-1
☐ JA9699	Kawasaki (Eurocopter/MBB) BK117A-4	1016		0088	0393	2 LY LTS101-650B.1	3200	7 Pax		lsf Kunihiro Ando
☐ JA9508	Kawasaki-Vertol 107-IIA	4014		0068		2 GE CT58-IHI-140-1	8618	25 Pax		Kiso
☐ JA9509	Kawasaki-Vertol 107-IIA	4013		0068		2 GE CT58-140-1	8618	25 Pax		Nagara
☐ JA9555	Kawasaki-Vertol 107-IIA	4130		0080		2 GE CT58-IHI-140-1	8618	25 Pax		Mino

KAWASAKI KOKU

Tokyo-Chofu

Chofu Airport, 1060 Nishi-machi, Chofu-shi, Tokyo 182-0032, Japan ☎ (422) 31 96 33 Tx: n/a Fax: n/a SITA: n/a

F: n/a ✝✝✝ n/a Head: n/a Net: n/a Aircraft below MTOW 1361 kg: Cessna 172.

registration	type of aircraft	cn/fn	ex/ex*	mfd	del	powered by	mtow kg	configuration	selcal	name/fln/specialitites/remarks
☐ JA3513	Cessna TP206D Turbo Skylane	P206-0585	N1753C	0069		1 CO TSIO-520-C	1633			
☐ JA3818	Cessna TU206G Turbo Stationair 6 II	U20604670	N1671C	0079		1 CO TSIO-520-M	1633			
☐ JA3917	Cessna TU206G Turbo Stationair 6 II	U20606536	N1701C	0082		1 CO TSIO-520-M	1633			

KAWASAKI LEASING International = (KAWA)

Tokyo

Shuwa Shiba Park Bldg, 2-4-1 Shibakoen, Minato-ku, Tokyo 105, Japan ☎ (3) 35 78 60 15 Tx: n/a Fax: (3) 35 78 60 89 SITA: n/a
F: n/a ⁂ n/a Head: n/a Net: n/a New and used aircraft leasing, sales and financing company.
Owner / lessor of following (main) aircraft types: Airbus Industrie A320 & Boeing 757. Aircraft leased from KAWA are listed and mentioned as such under the leasing carriers.

KITA NIHON KOKU – Kita Japan Aviation

Sendai

4 Kitanaganuma, Aza Gou Shimono, Iwanuma City, Miyagi 989-2421, Japan ☎ (223) 24 22 22 Tx: n/a Fax: (223) 22 36 85 SITA: n/a
F: n/a ⁂ n/a Head: n/a Net: n/a Aircraft below MTOW 1361kg: Cessna 172

☐ JA5234	Piper PA-34-200 Seneca	*34-7450011*	*N56640*	*0073*	*0396*	*2 LY IO-360-C1E6*	*1905*			

KOKUSAI KOKU YUSO, K.K. – ATK Air Transport Kokusai, Co. Ltd

Tokyo-Chofu

Chofu Airport, 1060 Nishi-machi, Chofu-shi, Tokyo 182-0032, Japan ☎ (422) 32 22 11 Tx: n/a Fax: (422) 32 71 29 SITA: n/a
F: 1961 ⁂ 42 Head: Jiro Minami Net: n/a Aircraft below MTOW 1361 kg: Cessna 172

☐ JA3688	Cessna TU206F Turbo Stationair	*U20602155*	*N1719C*	*0073*		*1 CO TSIO-520-C*	*1633*			
☐ JA3717	Cessna TU206F Turbo Stationair	*U20602480*	*N1137V*	*0074*		*1 CO TSIO-520-C*	*1633*			
☐ JA3979	Cessna TU206G Turbo Stationair 6 II	*U20605640*	*N5321X*	*0080*	*1095*	*1 CO TSIO-520-M*	*1633*			
☐ JA3700	Cessna T207 Turbo Skywagon	*20700238*	*N1571C*	*0074*		*1 CO TSIO-520-G*	*1724*			

KYOKUSHIN AIR – KOK

Niigata

Niigata Airport, Matsuhama-chou, Niigata City 950-0001, Japan ☎ (25) 273 03 12 Tx: n/a Fax: (25) 273 03 04 SITA: n/a
F: 1996 ⁂ 17 Head: Koichiro Takano Net: n/a

☐ JA5321	Britten-Norman BN-2B-20 Islander	*2272*	*G-BUBP**	*0095*	*0895*	*2 LY IO-540-K1B5*	*2976*			*lsf Tokyo Lease*

KYORITSU KOKU SATSUEI – JAP Joint Air Photo, Co. Ltd

Tokyo-Chofu

1-43-3 Fuda, Chofu-shi, Tokyo 182-0024, Japan ☎ (424) 81 13 01 Tx: none Fax: (424) 81 13 03 SITA: n/a
F: 1972 ⁂ 40 Head: Tadashi Hanei Net: n/a

☐ JA3847	Cessna TU206G Turbo Stationair 6 II	*U20604780*	*N1872C*	*0079*		*1 CO TSIO-520-M*	*1633*	*Photo / Survey*		*lsf Koku Kaihatsu*
☐ JA4028	Cessna TU206G Turbo Stationair 6 II	*U20605416*	*N6312U*	*0080*		*1 CO TSIO-520-M*	*1633*	*Photo / Survey*		
☐ JA3710	Cessna T207 Turbo Skywagon	*20700242*	*N1583C*	*0074*		*1 CO TSIO-520-G*	*1724*	*Photo / Survey*		*lsf Koku Kaihatsu*
☐ JA8891	Cessna 208 Caravan I	*20800199*	*N9782F**	*0090*		*1 PWC PT6A-114*	*3629*	*Photo / Survey*		*lsf Nozaki Sangyo*
☐ JA8895	Cessna 208 Caravan I	*20800208*	*N9792F**	*0092*		*1 PWC PT6A-114*	*3629*	*Photo / Survey*		*lsf Nihon Cable*
☐ JA8897	Cessna 208 Caravan I	*20800220*	*N9816F**	*0093*		*1 PWC PT6A-114*	*3629*	*Photo / Survey*		
☐ JA5082	Twin (Aero) Commander 680E	*1005-43*	*N6186X*	*0061*		*2 LY GSO-480-B1A6*	*3629*	*Photo / Survey*		

MARITIME SAFETY AGENCY – MSA (Kaijo Hoan Cho)

Tokyo-Haneda 海 上 保 安 庁

Aviation Division, 1-3 Kasumigaseki, 2-chome, Chiyoda-ku, Tokyo 100, Japan ☎ (3) 35 91 63 61 Tx: n/a Fax: (3) 35 91 63 61 SITA: n/a
F: n/a ⁂ 12000 Head: Eturo Honda Net: n/a Aircraft below MTOW 1361kg: Hughes 369HS (500C). Non-commercial national organisation conducting non-military surveillance & SAR missions from 14 airbases.

☐ JA6082	Bell 206B JetRanger III	*4149*		*0091*	*0691*	*1 AN 250-C20J*	*1451*	*Survey/Patrol*		
☐ JA6176	Bell 206B JetRanger III	*4380*	*N91940*	*0096*	*0296*	*1 AN 250-C20J*	*1451*	*Survey/Patrol*		
☐ JA6177	Bell 206B JetRanger III	*4381*	*N9195B*	*0096*	*0296*	*1 AN 250-C20J*	*1451*	*Survey/Patrol*		
☐ JA6178	Bell 206B JetRanger III	*4383*	*N9202H*	*0096*	*0296*	*1 AN 250-C20J*	*1451*	*Survey/Patrol*		
☐ JA9119	Bell 206B JetRanger	*947*	*N58064*	*0073*		*1 AN 250-C20*	*1451*	*Survey/Patrol*		Abi
☐ JA3790	Cessna U206G Stationair	*U20603958*	*N756BK*	*0077*		*1 CO IO-520-F*	*1633*	*Survey/Patrol*		Setotsubame
☐ JA6755	Sikorsky S-76C	*760431*		*0095*	*1195*	*2 TU Arriel 1S1*	*5307*	*Survey/Patrol*		
☐ JA6903	Sikorsky S-76C+	*760483*		*0098*	*1098*	*2 TU Arriel 2S1*	*5307*	*Survey/Patrol*		
☐ JA6904	Sikorsky S-76C+	*760484*		*0098*	*1098*	*2 TU Arriel 2S1*	*5307*	*Survey/Patrol*		
☐ JA9532	Bell 212	*30889*		*0078*		*2 PWC PT6T-3 TwinPac*	*5080*	*Survey/Patrol*		
☐ JA9533	Bell 212	*30892*		*0078*		*2 PWC PT6T-3 TwinPac*	*5080*	*Survey/Patrol*		
☐ JA9534	Bell 212	*30894*		*0078*		*2 PWC PT6T-3 TwinPac*	*5080*	*Survey/Patrol*		
☐ JA9536	Bell 212	*30900*		*0078*		*2 PWC PT6T-3 TwinPac*	*5080*	*Survey/Patrol*		
☐ JA9538	Bell 212	*30904*		*0078*		*2 PWC PT6T-3 TwinPac*	*5080*	*Survey/Patrol*		Setozuru
☐ JA9540	Bell 212	*30922*		*0079*		*2 PWC PT6T-3 TwinPac*	*5080*	*Survey/Patrol*		
☐ JA9550	Bell 212	*31105*		*0080*		*2 PWC PT6T-3 TwinPac*	*5080*	*Survey/Patrol*		
☐ JA9559	Bell 212	*31178*		*0081*		*2 PWC PT6T-3 TwinPac*	*5080*	*Survey/Patrol*		
☐ JA9560	Bell 212	*31179*		*0081*		*2 PWC PT6T-3 TwinPac*	*5080*	*Survey/Patrol*		
☐ JA9561	Bell 212	*31181*		*0081*		*2 PWC PT6T-3 TwinPac*	*5080*	*Survey/Patrol*		
☐ JA9562	Bell 212	*31182*		*0081*		*2 PWC PT6T-3 TwinPac*	*5080*	*Survey/Patrol*		Kamitaka 1
☐ JA9563	Bell 212	*31184*	*N18095*	*0081*		*2 PWC PT6T-3 TwinPac*	*5080*	*Survey/Patrol*		
☐ JA9564	Bell 212	*31185*	*N18090*	*0081*		*2 PWC PT6T-3 TwinPac*	*5080*	*Survey/Patrol*		
☐ JA9565	Bell 212	*31186*	*N18092*	*0081*		*2 PWC PT6T-3 TwinPac*	*5080*	*Survey/Patrol*		
☐ JA9566	Bell 212	*31187*	*N18091*	*0081*		*2 PWC PT6T-3 TwinPac*	*5080*	*Survey/Patrol*		
☐ JA9574	Bell 212	*31216*		*0082*		*2 PWC PT6T-3B TwinPac*	*5080*	*Survey/Patrol*		
☐ JA9575	Bell 212	*31218*		*0082*		*2 PWC PT6T-3B TwinPac*	*5080*	*Survey/Patrol*		
☐ JA9594	Bell 212	*31222*		*0082*		*2 PWC PT6T-3B TwinPac*	*5080*	*Survey/Patrol*		
☐ JA9595	Bell 212	*31226*		*0082*		*2 PWC PT6T-3B TwinPac*	*5080*	*Survey/Patrol*		
☐ JA9607	Bell 212	*31268*		*0084*		*2 PWC PT6T-3B TwinPac*	*5080*	*Survey/Patrol*		
☐ JA9617	Bell 212	*31265*		*0084*		*2 PWC PT6T-3B TwinPac*	*5080*	*Survey/Patrol*		
☐ JA9618	Bell 212	*31266*		*0084*		*2 PWC PT6T-3B TwinPac*	*5080*	*Survey/Patrol*		
☐ JA9619	Bell 212	*31267*		*0084*		*2 PWC PT6T-3B TwinPac*	*5080*	*Survey/Patrol*		
☐ JA9684	Bell 212	*31294*		*0088*		*2 PWC PT6T-3B TwinPac*	*5080*	*Survey/Patrol*		
☐ JA9929	Bell 212	*31301*		*0088*	*0389*	*2 PWC PT6T-3B TwinPac*	*5080*	*Survey/Patrol*		Setotsuru
☐ JA9930	Bell 212	*31302*		*0088*	*0389*	*2 PWC PT6T-3B TwinPac*	*5080*	*Survey/Patrol*		
☐ JA9931	Bell 212	*31303*		*0088*	*0389*	*2 PWC PT6T-3B TwinPac*	*5080*	*Survey/Patrol*		
☐ JA6713	Bell 412	*36052*	*N5092J**	*0093*	*1093*	*2 PWC PT6T-3BE TwinPac*	*5398*	*Survey/Patrol*		Hoshizuna
☐ JA6714	Bell 412	*36053*	*N5091H**	*0093*	*1093*	*2 PWC PT6T-3BE TwinPac*	*5398*	*Survey/Patrol*		
☐ JA6756	Bell 412EP	*36096*	*N2291W**	*0095*	*1095*	*2 PWC PT6T-3D TwinPac*	*5398*	*Survey/Patrol*		
☐ JA6795	Bell 412EP	*36120*	*N9215T**	*0096*	*0297*	*2 PWC PT6T-3D TwinPac*	*5398*	*Survey/Patrol*		
☐ JA6796	Bell 412EP	*36121*	*N92155**	*0096*	*0297*	*2 PWC PT6T-3D TwinPac*	*5398*	*Survey/Patrol*		
☐ JA8810	Beech King Air 200T	*BT-5*	*N2071C*	*0079*		*2 PWC PT6A-41*	*6350*	*Survey/Patrol*		*cvtd 200 cn BB-469*
☐ JA8811	Beech King Air 200T	*BT-6*	*N2071D*	*0079*		*2 PWC PT6A-41*	*6350*	*Survey/Patrol*		*cvtd 200 cn BB-489*
☐ JA8812	Beech King Air 200T	*BT-7*	*N2071X*	*0079*		*2 PWC PT6A-41*	*6350*	*Survey/Patrol*		*cvtd 200 cn BB-510*
☐ JA8813	Beech King Air 200T	*BT-8*	*N2071Y*	*0079*		*2 PWC PT6A-41*	*6350*	*Survey/Patrol*		*cvtd 200 cn BB-530*
☐ JA8814	Beech King Air 200T	*BT-9*	*N2071Z*	*0079*		*2 PWC PT6A-41*	*6350*	*Survey/Patrol*		Sakura-jima / *cvtd 200 cn BB-551*
☐ JA8815	Beech King Air 200T	*BT-11*	*N60576*	*0080*		*2 PWC PT6A-41*	*6350*	*Survey/Patrol*		*cvtd 200 cn BB-573*
☐ JA8816	Beech King Air 200T	*BT-12*	*N60581*	*0080*		*2 PWC PT6A-41*	*6350*	*Survey/Patrol*		*cvtd 200 cn BB-591*
☐ JA8817	Beech King Air 200T	*BT-13*	*N60587*	*0080*		*2 PWC PT6A-41*	*6350*	*Survey/Patrol*		*cvtd 200 cn BB-609*
☐ JA8818	Beech King Air 200T	*BT-14*	*N6059C*	*0080*		*2 PWC PT6A-41*	*6350*	*Survey/Patrol*		*cvtd 200 cn BB-627*
☐ JA8819	Beech King Air 200T	*BT-15*	*N6059D*	*0080*		*2 PWC PT6A-41*	*6350*	*Survey/Patrol*		Pikari / *cvtd 200 cn BB-647*
☐ JA8820	Beech King Air 200T	*BT-16*	*N60603*	*0080*		*2 PWC PT6A-41*	*6350*	*Survey/Patrol*		*cvtd 200 cn BB-665*
☐ JA8824	Beech King Air 200T	*BT-17*	*N3718Q*	*0081*		*2 PWC PT6A-41*	*6350*	*Survey/Patrol*		*cvtd 200 cn BB-798*
☐ JA8829	Beech King Air 200T	*BT-22*	*N1841K*	*0082*		*2 PWC PT6A-41*	*6350*	*Survey/Patrol*		*cvtd 200 cn BB-991*
☐ JA8833	Beech King Air 200T	*BT-28*	*N1846M*	*0083*		*2 PWC PT6A-41*	*6350*	*Survey/Patrol*		*cvtd 200 cn BB-1117*
☐ JA8854	Beech King Air B200T	*BT-31*	*N72392*	*0087*		*2 PWC PT6A-42*	*6350*	*Survey/Patrol*		*cvtd B200 cn BB-1264*
☐ JA8860	Beech King Air B200T	*BT-32*	*N3184A*	*0088*		*2 PWC PT6A-42*	*6350*	*Survey/Patrol*		*cvtd B200 cn BB-1289*
☐ JA6685	Eurocopter (Aerosp.) AS332L1 Super Puma	*2332*		*0091*	*0492*	*2 TU Makila 1A1*	*8600*	*Survey/Patrol*		Wakataka
☐ JA6686	Eurocopter (Aerosp.) AS332L1 Super Puma	*2350*		*0091*	*0492*	*2 TU Makila 1A1*	*8600*	*Survey/Patrol*		Umitaka
☐ JA6805	Eurocopter (Aerosp.) AS332L1 Super Puma	*2448*	*F-WQDA**	*0096*	*0597*	*2 TU Makila 1A1*	*8600*	*Survey/Patrol*		Wakawashi
☐ JA6806	Eurocopter (Aerosp.) AS332L1 Super Puma	*2451*	*F-WQDB**	*0097*	*0597*	*2 TU Makila 1A1*	*8600*	*Survey/Patrol*		
☐ JA8951	Saab 340B (Plus SAR-200)	*340B-385*	*SE-C85**	*0096*	*0397*	*2 GE CT7-9B*	*12927*	*Survey/Patrol*		MA951
☐ JA8952	Saab 340B (Plus SAR-200)	*340B-405*	*SE-B05**	*0097*	*0397*	*2 GE CT7-9B*	*12927*	*Survey/Patrol*		
☐ JA8570	Dassault Falcon 900	*53*	*N438FJ**	*0089*	*0989*	*3 GA TFE731-5AR-1C2*	*20638*	*Survey/Patrol*		
☐ JA8571	Dassault Falcon 900	*56*	*N440FJ**	*0089*	*0989*	*3 GA TFE731-5AR-1C2*	*20638*	*Survey/Patrol*		
☐ JA8701	NAMC YS-11A-207	*2093*		*0069*	*0369*	*2 RR Dart 542-10J/K*	*24500*	*Survey/Patrol*		
☐ JA8702	NAMC YS-11A-207	*2175*		*0071*	*1171*	*2 RR Dart 542-10J/K*	*24500*	*Survey/Patrol*		
☐ JA8780	NAMC YS-11A-213	*2164*		*0071*	*0379*	*2 RR Dart 542-10J/K*	*24500*	*Survey/Patrol*		LA780
☐ JA8782	NAMC YS-11A-213	*2167*		*0072*	*0279*	*2 RR Dart 542-10J/K*	*24500*	*Survey/Patrol*		
☐ JA8791	NAMC YS-11A-213	*2177*		*0073*	*1278*	*2 RR Dart 542-10J/K*	*24500*	*Survey/Patrol*		

NAGASAKI AIRWAYS, Co. Ltd – NAW (Nagasaki Koku)

Nagasaki

593-2 Mishima-cho, Omura-shi, Nagasaki 856-0816, Japan ☎ (957) 53 66 92 Tx: none Fax: (957) 53 65 92 SITA: n/a
F: 1961 ⁂ 62 Head: Hideaki Matsushima Net: n/a Aircraft below MTOW 1361 kg: Cessna 172.

☐ JA3792	Cessna TU206G Turbo Stationair	*U20603553*	*N8829Q*	*0076*	*0280*	*1 CO TSIO-520-M*	*1633*			
☐ JA5284	Britten-Norman BN-2A-26 Islander	*2037*	*G-BNEB**	*0087*	*0487*	*2 LY O-540-E4C5*	*2812*			
☐ JA5298	Britten-Norman BN-2B-26 Islander	*2209*	*G-BPLR**	*0089*	*1089*	*2 LY O-540-E4C5*	*2812*			
☐ JA5316	Britten-Norman BN-2B-20 Islander	*2240*	*G-BSPT**	*0093*	*0693*	*2 LY IO-540-K1B5*	*2976*			
☐ JA5318	Britten-Norman BN-2B-20 Islander	*2267*	*G-BUBJ**	*0094*	*0794*	*2 LY IO-540-K1B5*	*2976*			
☐ JA5323	Britten-Norman BN-2B-20 Islander	*2291*	*G-BVYD**	*0096*	*0796*	*2 LY IO-540-K1B5*	*2976*			

226 registration type of aircraft *cn/fn* *ex/ex** *mfd* *del* *powered by* *mtow kg* *configuration* *selcal* name/fln/*specialitites/remarks*

NAKA NIHON AIR SERVICE, Co. Ltd – Naka Nihon Koku (Member of Meitetsu Group / Subsidiary of Nagoya Railway, Co. Ltd) Nagoya

NAKANIHON AIR SERVICE

Nagoya Int'l Airport, Toyoyama-cho, Nishi Kasugai-gun, Aichi-Pref. 480-0202, Japan ☎ (568) 28 21 51 Tx: 4485832 nnk j Fax: (568) 28 56 77 SITA: n/a
F: 1953 ⁂ 490 Head: Satoshi Hasegawa Net: n/a Aircraft below MTOW 1361 kg: Kawasaki-Bell 47G & Cessna 172/177/182.

☐ JA6167	Bell 206B JetRanger III	4345		0095	0695	1 AN 250-C20J	1451			
☐ JA9102	Bell 206B JetRanger	989		0073		1 AN 250-C20	1451			
☐ JA9144	Bell 206B JetRanger III	1876		0075		1 AN 250-C20B	1451			cvtd JetRanger
☐ JA9168	Bell 206B JetRanger III	2108		0077		1 AN 250-C20B	1451			cvtd JetRanger II
☐ JA9181	Bell 206B JetRanger III	2236		0077		1 AN 250-C20B	1451			
☐ JA9182	Bell 206B JetRanger III	2242		0077		1 AN 250-C20B	1451			
☐ JA9196	Bell 206B JetRanger III	2333		0078		1 AN 250-C20B	1451			
☐ JA9249	Bell 206B JetRanger III	2894		0080		1 AN 250-C20B	1451			
☐ JA9291	Bell 206B JetRanger III	3323	N2009H	0081		1 AN 250-C20B	1451			
☐ JA9292	Bell 206B JetRanger III	3326		0081		1 AN 250-C20B	1451			
☐ JA9305	Bell 206B JetRanger III	3495	N21793	0081		1 AN 250-C20B	1451			
☐ JA9396	Bell 206B JetRanger III	3423	N2072D	0081		1 AN 250-C20B	1451			
☐ JA9449	Bell 206B JetRanger III	2837	N1067V	0079		1 AN 250-C20B	1451			
☐ JA9453	Bell 206B JetRanger III	3564	HK-2855X	0081		1 AN 250-C20B	1451			
☐ JA9486	Bell 206B JetRanger III	3206	N84BL	0080		1 AN 250-C20B	1451			
☐ JA9725	Bell 206B JetRanger III	3488	N37BL	0081		1 AN 250-C20B	1451			
☐ JA9739	Bell 206B JetRanger III	3493	N2198B	0081		1 AN 250-C20B	1451			
☐ JA9745	Bell 206B JetRanger III	3987		0087		1 AN 250-C20J	1451			
☐ JA9746	Bell 206B JetRanger III	3667	N3172R	0082		1 AN 250-C20J	1451			
☐ JA9802	Bell 206B JetRanger III	4037		0088		1 AN 250-C20J	1451			
☐ JA9704	Eurocopter (Aerosp.) SA315B Lama	2652	N5804X	0083		1 TU Artouste IIIB1	1950			
☐ JA9754	Eurocopter (Aerosp.) SA315B Lama	2655	N58041	0083		1 TU Artouste IIIB1	1950			
☐ JA3619	Cessna TU206F Turbo Stationair	U20601746	N1588C	0072		1 CO TSIO-520-C	1633			
☐ JA3699	Cessna TU206F Turbo Stationair	U20602295	N1576C	0074		1 CO TSIO-520-C	1633			
☐ JA3959	Cessna TU206G Turbo Stationair 6 II	U20605024	N4645U	0079	0398	1 CO TSIO-520-M	1633			
☐ JA9289	Bell 206L-1 LongRanger II	45566	N5760Y*	0081		1 AN 250-C28B	1882			
☐ JA9360	Bell 206L-1 LongRanger II	45762	N31774	0083		1 AN 250-C28B	1882			
☐ JA9308	Eurocopter (Aerosp.) AS350B Ecureuil	1529		0081		1 TU Arriel 1B	1950			
☐ JA9318	Eurocopter (Aerosp.) AS350B Ecureuil	1570		0082		1 TU Arriel 1B	1950			
☐ JA9332	Eurocopter (Aerosp.) AS350B Ecureuil	1627		0082		1 TU Arriel 1B	1950			
☐ JA9338	Eurocopter (Aerosp.) AS350B Ecureuil	1632		0082		1 TU Arriel 1B	1950			
☐ JA9350	Eurocopter (Aerosp.) AS350B Ecureuil	1676		0083		1 TU Arriel 1B	1950			
☐ JA9351	Eurocopter (Aerosp.) AS350B Ecureuil	1685		0083		1 TU Arriel 1B	1950			
☐ JA9398	Eurocopter (Aerosp.) AS350B Ecureuil	1806		0085		1 TU Arriel 1B	1950			
☐ JA9403	Eurocopter (Aerosp.) AS350B Ecureuil	1819		0085		1 TU Arriel 1B	1950			
☐ JA9411	Eurocopter (Aerosp.) AS350B Ecureuil	1844		0085		1 TU Arriel 1B	1950			
☐ JA9427	Eurocopter (Aerosp.) AS350B Ecureuil	1885		0086		1 TU Arriel 1B	1950			
☐ JA9428	Eurocopter (Aerosp.) AS350B Ecureuil	1886		0086		1 TU Arriel 1B	1950			
☐ JA9429	Eurocopter (Aerosp.) AS350B Ecureuil	1914		0086		1 TU Arriel 1B	1950			
☐ JA9451	Eurocopter (Aerosp.) AS350B Ecureuil	1971		0086		1 TU Arriel 1B	1950			
☐ JA9712	Eurocopter (Aerosp.) AS350B Ecureuil	2059		0087		1 TU Arriel 1B	1950			
☐ JA9743	Eurocopter (Aerosp.) AS350B1 Ecureuil	2077		0088	0896	1 TU Arriel 1D	2200			
☐ JA9793	Eurocopter (Aerosp.) AS350B1 Ecureuil	2155		0088		1 TU Arriel 1D	2200			lsf H.M.C.
☐ JA5287	Cessna T303 Crusader	T30300188	N9571C	0083	0997	2 CO TSIO-520-AE	2336			
☐ JA6602	Eurocopter (Aerosp.) AS355F2 Ecureuil 2	5433		0089	0995	2 AN 250-C20F	2540			
☐ JA6603	Eurocopter (Aerosp.) AS355F2 Ecureuil 2	5437		0090		2 AN 250-C20F	2540			
☐ JA6638	Eurocopter (Aerosp.) AS355F2 Ecureuil 2	5449		0090	1090	2 AN 250-C20F	2540			lst All Nippon Helicopter
☐ JA6689	Eurocopter (Aerosp.) AS355F2 Ecureuil 2	5507		0091	1191	2 AN 250-C20F	2540			
☐ JA6778	Eurocopter (Aerosp.) AS355N Ecureuil 2	5605		0095	1295	2 TU Arrius 1A	2540			
☐ JA9905	Eurocopter (Aerosp.) AS355F2 Ecureuil 2	5384		0088	0892	2 AN 250-C20F	2540			lst All Nippon Helicopter
☐ JA9963	Eurocopter (Aerosp.) AS355F2 Ecureuil 2	5414		0089		2 AN 250-C20F	2540			
☐ JA9977	Eurocopter (Aerosp.) AS355F2 Ecureuil 2	5426		0090		2 AN 250-C20F	2540			lst All Nippon Helicopter
☐ JA6677	Eurocopter (Aerosp.) AS365N2 Dauphin 2	6420		0091	0891	2 TU Arriel 1C2	4250			lst All Nippon Helicopter
☐ JA9913	Eurocopter (Aerosp.) SA365N Dauphin 2	6220		0088		2 TU Arriel 1C	4000			
☐ JA5264	Cessna 404 Titan II	404-0065	N5448G	0077		2 CO GTSIO-520-M	3810			
☐ JA5267	Cessna 404 Titan II	404-0627	N5046B	0080		2 CO GTSIO-520-M	3810			
☐ JA9165	Fuji-Bell 204B-2	CH-40		0077		1 KA KT5313B	3856			
☐ JA9221	Fuji-Bell 204B-2	CH-48		0079		1 KA KT5313B	3856			
☐ JA9264	Fuji-Bell 204B-2	CH-52		0080	0791	1 KA KT5313B	3856			
☐ JA9383	Fuji-Bell 204B-2	CH-54		0084		1 KA KT5313B	3856			
☐ JA9478	Fuji-Bell 204B-2	CH-57		0087		1 KA KT5313B	3856			
☐ JA8899	Cessna 208B Grand Caravan	208B0246	N5127B	0090	0397	1 PWC PT6A-114A	3969			
☐ JA05TV	Bell 430	49031	N7208H*	0097	1197	2 AN 250-C40	4082			
☐ JA121T	Bell 430	49009	N62837*	0096	0397	2 AN 250-C40	4082			
☐ JA9546	Bell 212	30975		0079		2 PWC PT6T-3 TwinPac	5080			
☐ JA6767	Bell 412EP	36108		0095	1195	2 PWC PT6T-3D TwinPac	5400			
☐ JA9268	Bell 214B BigLifter	28053	N18091	0080		1 LY T5508D	7257			
☐ JA9324	Bell 214B BigLifter	28070		0082		1 LY T5508D	7257			
☐ JA8705	Beech King Air B200	BB-1431	N82696	0092	0594	2 PWC PT6A-42	5670			
☐ JA119N	Cessna 560 Citation V	560-0067	N45BA	0090	0697	2 PWC JT15D-5A	7212			
☐ JA6717	Eurocopter (Aerosp.) AS332L1 Super Puma	2394		0193	0393	2 TU Makila 1A1	8600			
☐ JA6787	Eurocopter (Aerosp.) AS332L1 Super Puma	2439		0096	0396	2 TU Makila 1A1	8600			
☐ JA9660	Eurocopter (Aerosp.) AS332L Super Puma	2095	N5803C	0084		2 TU Makila 1A	8600			
☐ JA9965	Eurocopter (Aerosp.) AS332L1 Super Puma	2174		0089	0889	2 TU Makila 1A1	8600			

NAL – Naka Nihon Air Line Service, Co. Ltd (Associated with Naka Nihon Air Service & All Nippon Airways/Member of Meitetsu Group) Nagoya

NAL

Nagoya Airport, Toyoyama-cho, Nishikasugai-Gun 480-0202, (Aichi-Pref.), Japan ☎ (568) 28 54 05 Tx: none Fax: (568) 28 54 15 SITA: n/a
F: 1988 ⁂ 106 Head: Takehiko Kaito Net: n/a

☐ JA8200	Fokker 50 (F27 Mk050)	20307	PH-JCN*	0095	1295	2 PWC PW125B	19950	Y56		lsf Meitetsu Sogo Kigyo
☐ JA8875	Fokker 50 (F27 Mk050)	20196	PH-LMS*	0090	1190	2 PWC PW125B	19950	Y56		lsf Meitetsu Sogo Kigyo
☐ JA8889	Fokker 50 (F27 Mk050)	20259	PH-EXX	0092	0892	2 PWC PW125B	19950	Y56		lsf Meitetsu Sogo Kigyo

NANKI KOKU, K.K. – Nanki Airways Nanki Shirahama

5-10-3, Misono-cho, Wakayama 640-8331, Japan ☎ (734) 32 43 11 Tx: n/a Fax: n/a SITA: n/a
F: n/a ⁂ n/a Head: Yoshio Ogawa Net: n/a Aircraft below MTOW 1361 kg: Cessna 172 & 177.

☐ JA3429	Cessna TU206C Super Skywagon	U206-1198	N29262	0068		1 CO TSIO-520-C	1633			

NATIONAL AEROSPACE LABORATORY Flight Research – NAL Sendai

7-chome, 44-1 Jindaiji-higashi-machi, Chofu-shi, Tokyo 182, Japan ☎ (422) 47 59 11 Tx: none Fax: (422) 49 88 13 SITA: n/a
F: n/a ⁂ n/a Head: Toshio Bando Net: n/a Non-commercial national organisation conducting aerial flight research & survey missions.

☐ JA8858	Dornier 228-200	8128	N111AL	0087	0388	2 GA TPE331-5-252D	5700	Surveyer		

NIHON HELICOPTER – Japan Helicopter, K.K. Ryugasaki

Tokyo Heliport, Shin-Kiba, 4-chome, Koto-ku, Tokyo 136-0082, Japan ☎ (3) 35 21 82 10 Tx: n/a Fax: (3) 35 21 82 61 SITA: n/a
F: n/a ⁂ 36 Head: Seiki Watanabe Net: n/a Aircraft below MTOW 1361 kg: Hughes & Kawasaki-Hughes 369HS (500C).

☐ JA9445	Eurocopter (Aerosp.) AS350B Ecureuil	1964		0086		1 TU Arriel 1B	1950			lsf Nozaki Sangyo
☐ JA9843	Eurocopter (Aerosp.) AS350B Ecureuil	2259		0089		1 TU Arriel 1B	1950			lsf Orix Alpha

NIPPON CARGO AIRLINES, Co. Ltd – NCA = KZ / NCA (Associated with All Nippon Airways – ANA) Tokyo-Narita

NCA Nippon Cargo Airlines

Shin-Kasumigaseki Building 10F, 3-2, Kasumigaseki 3-chome, Chiyoda-ku, Tokyo 100-0013, Japan ☎ (3) 35 07 41 00 Tx: none Fax: (3) 35 07 41 69 SITA: TYOBAKZ
F: 1978 ⁂ 670 Head: Jiro Nemoto IATA: 933 Net: http://www.aranet.or.jp/nca/

☐ JA8158	Boeing 747SR-81 (SF)	22711 / 559		0082	1293	4 GE CF6-45A2	268011	Freighter	HJ-CF	cvtd -81
☐ JA8167	Boeing 747-281F (SCD)	23138 / 604	N6066Z*	0084	1284	4 GE CF6-50E2	377842	Freighter	JK-BL	
☐ JA8168	Boeing 747-281F (SCD)	23139 / 608	N6046P*	0085	0385	4 GE CF6-50E2	377842	Freighter	JK-BM	
☐ JA8172	Boeing 747-281F (SCD)	23350 / 623	N6018N*	0085	1085	4 GE CF6-50E2	377842	Freighter	JK-BC	lsf Zen Nikku Shoji
☐ JA8188	Boeing 747-281F (SCD)	23919 / 689	N6009F*	0088	0188	4 GE CF6-50E2	377842	Freighter	AE-CJ	
☐ JA8191	Boeing 747-281F (SCD)	24576 / 818		0090	1190	4 GE CF6-50E2	377842	Freighter	JK-CD	
☐ JA8192	Boeing 747-2D3B (SF)	22579 / 514	G-CITB	0081	0897	4 GE CF6-50E2	377842	Freighter	AC-MS	cvtd -2D3B
☐ JA8194	Boeing 747-281F (SCD)	25171 / 886		0091	1191	4 GE CF6-50E2	377842	Freighter	AF-JK	

NISHI NIHON KUYU – Nishi Nihon Air Lines, Co. Ltd Fukuoka

7-11 Tenjin, 4-chome, Chuo-ku, Fukuoka 810-0001, Japan ☎ (92) 761 62 57 Tx: n/a Fax: (92) 711 76 28 SITA: n/a
F: 1953 ⁂ 110 Head: Kiyoharu Ueda Net: n/a Aircraft below MTOW 1361 kg: Cessna 172P, Kawasaki-Bell 47G & Kawasaki-Hughes 369HS (500C).

☐ JA001W	MD Helicopters MD 500E (Hughes 369E)	0533E	N92053	0096	0297	1 AN 250-C20B	1361			
☐ JA6117	Eurocopter (Aerosp.) SA315B Lama	2020 / 13		0077	0292	1 TU Artouste IIIB	1950			cvtd Alouette II

227 registration type of aircraft cn/fn ex/ex* mfd del powered by mtow kg configuration selcal name/fln/specialitites/remarks

registration	type of aircraft	cn/fn	ex/ex*	mfd	del	powered by	mtow kg	configuration	selcal	name/fln/remarks
☐ JA9080	Eurocopter (Aerosp.) SA315B Lama	2268		0072		1 TU Artouste IIIB	1950			
☐ JA9106	Eurocopter (Aerosp.) SA315B Lama	2361		0073		1 TU Artouste IIIB	1950			
☐ JA9135	Eurocopter (Aerosp.) SA315B Lama	2386		0074		1 TU Artouste IIIB	1950			
☐ JA3730	Cessna TU206F Turbo Stationair II	U20602786	N35894	0075		1 CO TSIO-520-C	1633			
☐ JA3868	Cessna TU206G Turbo Stationair 6 II	U20605868	N1851C	0080		1 CO TSIO-520-M	1633			
☐ JA6047	Eurocopter (Aerosp.) AS350B Ecureuil	2428		0090	1290	1 TU Arriel 1B	1950			
☐ JA6132	Eurocopter (Aerosp.) AS350BA Ecureuil	2764		0094	1094	1 TU Arriel 1B	2100			
☐ JA6146	Eurocopter (Aerosp.) AS350BA Ecureuil	2842		0094	0496	1 TU Arriel 1B	2100			
☐ JA9307	Eurocopter (Aerosp.) AS350B Ecureuil	1524		0081		1 TU Arriel 1B	1950			
☐ JA9312	Eurocopter (Aerosp.) AS350B Ecureuil	1534		0082		1 TU Arriel 1B	1950			
☐ JA9402	Eurocopter (Aerosp.) AS350B Ecureuil	1821		0085		1 TU Arriel 1B	1950			
☐ JA9495	Eurocopter (Aerosp.) AS350B Ecureuil	2028		0087		1 TU Arriel 1B	1950			
☐ JA9761	Eurocopter (Aerosp.) AS350B Ecureuil	2116		0088		1 TU Arriel 1B	1950			
☐ JA6745	Eurocopter (Aerosp.) AS355N Ecureuil 2	5575		0094	1095	2 TU Arrius 1A	2540			
☐ JA6027	Fuji-Bell 204B-2	CH-59		0091	0391	1 KA KT5313B	3856			
☐ JA9439	Fuji-Bell 204B-2	CH-56		0086		1 KA KT5313B	3856			

OSAKA KOKU, K.K. - Osaka Aviation, Co. Ltd — Osaka-Yao

Yao Airport, Kuko 2-12, Yao-shi, Osaka 581-0043, Japan ☎ (729) 91 29 00 Tx: 5353833 oskav j Fax: (729) 91 27 14 SITA: n/a
F: 1968 staff 21 Head: Toshiyuki Itoi Net: n/a Aircraft below MTOW 1361 kg: Cessna 172, Robinson R22B & R44.

registration	type of aircraft	cn/fn	ex/ex*	mfd	del	powered by	mtow kg	configuration	selcal	name/fln/remarks
☐ JA3672	Cessna TU206F Turbo Stationair	U20602038	N1659C	0073		1 CO TSIO-520-C	1633			
☐ JA3779	Cessna TU206F Turbo Stationair II	U20603437	N1941C	0076		1 CO TSIO-520-C	1633			
☐ JA6660	Kawasaki (Eurocopter/MBB) BK117B-1	1073		0091		2 LY LTS101-750B.1	3200			lsf Himeji Central Park

RAC - Ryukyu Air Commuter, Co. Ltd (Subsidiary of Japan Transocean Air, Co. Ltd) — Okinawa-Naha

306-1 Kagamizu, Naha, Okinawa, Okinawa 901-0142, Japan ☎ (98) 858 96 64 Tx: none Fax: (98) 858 65 60 SITA: n/a
F: 1985 staff 82 Head: Masayoshi Asato Net: n/a

registration	type of aircraft	cn/fn	ex/ex*	mfd	del	powered by	mtow kg	configuration	selcal	name/fln/remarks
☐ JA5281	Britten-Norman BN-2B-26 Islander	2154	N667J	0082		2 LY O-540-E4C5	2812	Y9		
☐ JA5282	Britten-Norman BN-2B-26 Islander	2129	N665J	0082		2 LY O-540-E4C5	2812	Y9		
☐ JA8802	De Havilland DHC-6 Twin Otter 300	492	C-GPBR	0076	1192	2 PWC PT6A-27	5670	Y19		lsf Japan Transocean
☐ JA8808	De Havilland DHC-6 Twin Otter 300	604	C-GQWL	0078	1192	2 PWC PT6A-27	5670	Y19		lsf Japan Transocean
☐ JA8972	De Havilland DHC-8-103 Dash 8Q	472	C-GDKL*	0097	0397	2 PWC PW121	14969	Y39		
☐ JA8973	De Havilland DHC-8-103 Dash 8Q	501	C-GDLD*	0097	1097	2 PWC PW121	14969	Y39		
☐ JA8974	De Havilland DHC-8-103 Dash 8Q					2 PWC PW121	15649	Y39		oo-delivery 1299
☐ JA	De Havilland DHC-8-103 Dash 8Q					2 PWC PW121	15649	Y39		oo-delivery 0302

SAGAWA HELICOPTER EXPRESS = SHX (Sagawa Koku, K.K. / Sagawa Air Services, Co. Ltd dba / Member of Sagawa Express Group) — Tokyo-Heliport

Shinkiba 4-chome, Koto-ku, Tokyo 136-0082, Japan ☎ (3) 55 69 20 23 Tx: none Fax: (3) 55 69 20 25 SITA: n/a
F: 1989 staff 110 Head: Hirofumi Maeda Net: n/a

registration	type of aircraft	cn/fn	ex/ex*	mfd	del	powered by	mtow kg	configuration	selcal	name/fln/remarks
☐ JA9375	Bell 206B JetRanger III	3790		0384	1289	1 AN 250-C20J	1451			
☐ JA9376	Bell 206B JetRanger III	3791		0384	1289	1 AN 250-C20J	1451			
☐ JA9378	Bell 206B JetRanger III	3793		0384	1289	1 AN 250-C20J	1451			
☐ JA9379	Bell 206B JetRanger III	3794		0384	1289	1 AN 250-C20J	1451			
☐ JA6128	Eurocopter (Aerosp.) SA315B Lama	1854 / 44		0563	0993	1 TU Artouste IIIB1	1950			lsf Zen Nikku Shoji / cvtd Alouette II
☐ JA6141	Eurocopter (Aerosp.) SA315B Lama	2456	XC-BOH	0176	0394	1 TU Artouste IIIB1	1950			lsf Nozaki Sangyo
☐ JA6044	Eurocopter (Aerosp.) AS350B Ecureuil	2427		1190	0191	1 TU Arriel 1B	1950			lsf Nozaki Sangyo
☐ JA6068	Eurocopter (Aerosp.) AS350B Ecureuil	2457		0291	0591	1 TU Arriel 1B	1950			lsf Marunaka
☐ JA6090	Eurocopter (Aerosp.) AS350B Ecureuil	2485		0891	0493	1 TU Arriel 1B	1950			lsf Nozaki Sangyo
☐ JA9273	Eurocopter (Aerosp.) AS350B Ecureuil	1407		0181	1289	1 TU Arriel 1B	1950			
☐ JA9281	Eurocopter (Aerosp.) AS350B Ecureuil	1429		0281	1289	1 TU Arriel 1B	1950			
☐ JA9337	Eurocopter (Aerosp.) AS350B Ecureuil	1637		1082	1289	1 TU Arriel 1B	1950			
☐ JA9348	Eurocopter (Aerosp.) AS350B Ecureuil	1712		0583	1289	1 TU Arriel 1B	1950			
☐ JA9368	Eurocopter (Aerosp.) AS350B Ecureuil	1776		0484	1289	1 TU Arriel 1B	1950			
☐ JA9370	Eurocopter (Aerosp.) AS350B Ecureuil	1777		0484	1289	1 TU Arriel 1B	1950			
☐ JA9862	Eurocopter (Aerosp.) AS350B Ecureuil	2274		1189	0690	1 TU Arriel 1B	1950			
☐ JA9871	Eurocopter (Aerosp.) AS350B Ecureuil	2299		1289	0690	1 TU Arriel 1B	1950			
☐ JA6616	Sikorsky S-76A+	760366		1090	1190	2 TU Arriel 1S	4536			
☐ JA6640	Sikorsky S-76A+	760369		1090	1190	2 TU Arriel 1S	4536			

SHIKOKU KOKU - SKK Shikoku Air Service, Co. Ltd — Takamatsu

1-5 Bancho, 1-chome, Takamatsu-shi, Kagawa 760-0017, Japan ☎ (878) 51 75 00 Tx: none Fax: (878) 51 75 47 SITA: n/a
F: 1956 staff 100 Head: Syohei Kato Net: n/a Aircraft below MTOW 1361 kg: Cessna 172

registration	type of aircraft	cn/fn	ex/ex*	mfd	del	powered by	mtow kg	configuration	selcal	name/fln/remarks
☐ JA6119	Eurocopter (Aerosp.) SA315B Lama	1234 / 38	F-GKGC	0065		1 TU Artouste IIIB	1950			cvtd Alouette II
☐ JA9191	Eurocopter (Aerosp.) SA315B Lama	2524		0078		1 TU Artouste IIIB	1950			
☐ JA6108	Eurocopter (Aerosp.) AS350B Ecureuil	2528		0091	1091	1 TU Arriel 1B	1950			
☐ JA9267	Eurocopter (Aerosp.) AS350B Ecureuil	1383		0080		1 TU Arriel 1B	1950			
☐ JA9336	Eurocopter (Aerosp.) AS350B Ecureuil	1628		0082		1 TU Arriel 1B	1950			
☐ JA9401	Eurocopter (Aerosp.) AS350B Ecureuil	1807		0085		1 TU Arriel 1B	1950			
☐ JA9421	Eurocopter (Aerosp.) AS350B Ecureuil	1862		0085		1 TU Arriel 1B	1950			
☐ JA9984	Kawasaki (Eurocopter/MBB) BK117B-1	1039		0090		2 LY LTS101-750B.1	3200			lsf Hyaku Jyu Yon Lease
☐ JA6722	Eurocopter (Aerosp.) SA330J Puma	1585	F-WYMC	0078		2 TU Turmo IVC	7400			lsf Sumigin Lease
☐ JA6777	Eurocopter (Aerosp.) AS332L1 Super Puma	2005	F-WZLB	0082		2 TU Makila 1A1	8600			lsf Sumigin Lease / cvtd AS332L

SHINCHUO KOKU, K.K. - NCA New Central Aviation, Co. Ltd — Niijima

3177 Honda-cho, Ryugasaki-shi, Ibaraki 301-0806, Japan ☎ (297) 62 12 71 Tx: n/a Fax: (297) 62 12 75 SITA: n/a
F: 1979 staff 37 Head: Haruo Wakabayashi Net: n/a Aircraft below MTOW 1361 kg: Cessna 152 & 172.

registration	type of aircraft	cn/fn	ex/ex*	mfd	del	powered by	mtow kg	configuration	selcal	name/fln/remarks
☐ JA3453	Cessna TU206C Super Skywagon	U206-1218	N1775C	0068	0994	1 CO TSIO-520-C	1633			
☐ JA3669	Cessna TU206F Turbo Stationair	U20601964	N1704C	0073	0994	1 CO TSIO-520-C	1633			
☐ JA4002	Cessna TU206G Turbo Stationair 6 II	U20606975	N1643C	0086	0994	1 CO TSIO-520-M	1633			
☐ JA5195	Britten-Norman BN-2A-20 Islander	302	G-AZUR*	0072		2 LY IO-540-K1B5	2976			
☐ JA5290	Britten-Norman BN-2B-20 Islander	2172	G-BKOI*	0083		2 LY IO-540-K1B5	2994			
☐ JA5305	Britten-Norman BN-2B-20 Islander	2239	G-BSPS*	0091	0591	2 LY IO-540-K1B5	2976			lsf Mitsui Lease Jigyo
☐ JA5319	Britten-Norman BN-2B-20 Islander	2268	G-BUBK*	0095	0496	2 LY IO-540-K1B5	2976			lsf Crown Leasing
☐ JA5320	Britten-Norman BN-2B-20 Islander	2269	G-BUBM*	0093	1294	2 LY IO-540-K1B5	2976			lsf ITC Leasing

SHIN-NIHON HELICOPTER, Co. Ltd (Subsidiary of Chubu & Tokyo Electric Power, Co. Ltd) — Tokyo-Heliport

3-6 Ginza, 4-chome, Chuo-ku, Tokyo 104-0061, Japan ☎ (3) 35 67 32 06 Tx: 2524796 snk j Fax: (3) 35 67 37 45 SITA: n/a
F: 1960 staff 123 Head: Masaji Hori Net: n/a Aircraft below MTOW 1361 kg: Hughes & Kawasaki-Hughes 369HS (500C).

registration	type of aircraft	cn/fn	ex/ex*	mfd	del	powered by	mtow kg	configuration	selcal	name/fln/remarks
☐ JA6055	Bell 206L-3 LongRanger III	51393		0091	0291	1 AN 250-C30P	1882			
☐ JA9472	Bell 206L-3 LongRanger III	51204		0087		1 AN 250-C30P	1882			
☐ JA9473	Bell 206L-3 LongRanger III	51205		0087		1 AN 250-C30P	1882			
☐ JA9710	Bell 206L-3 LongRanger III	51220		0087		1 AN 250-C30P	1882			
☐ JA9711	Bell 206L-3 LongRanger III	51221		0087		1 AN 250-C30P	1882			
☐ JA9796	Bell 206L-3 LongRanger III	51265		0088	0189	1 AN 250-C30P	1882			
☐ JA9845	Bell 206L-3 LongRanger III	51306		0089	1189	1 AN 250-C30P	1882			
☐ JA9846	Bell 206L-3 LongRanger III	51309		0089	1189	1 AN 250-C30P	1882			
☐ JA9847	Bell 206L-3 LongRanger III	51319		0089	1290	1 AN 250-C30P	1882			
☐ JA6728	Eurocopter (MBB) BO105LS-A3	2042	C-GFUI	0093		2 AN 250-C28C	2600			lsf Tokyo Denryokoku
☐ JA6746	Eurocopter (MBB) BO105LS-A3	2050	C-GGKQ	0093		2 AN 250-C28C	2600			lsf Chubu Denryoku
☐ JA6715	Kawasaki (Eurocopter/MBB) BK117B-1	1088		0093	0993	2 LY LTS101-750B.1	3200			
☐ JA9145	Fuji-Bell 204B-2	CH-36		0076		1 KA KT5313B	3856			cargo hook
☐ JA9177	Fuji-Bell 204B-2	CH-45		0077		1 KA KT5313B	3856			cargo hook
☐ JA9188	Bell 214B BigLifter	28023		0078	1092	1 LY T5508D	7257			
☐ JA9228	Bell 214B BigLifter	28046	N5019F	0079		1 LY T5508D	7257			cargo hook
☐ JA6721	Eurocopter (Aerosp.) AS332L1 Super Puma	2406		0094	0194	2 TU Makila 1A1	8600			
☐ JA6741	Eurocopter (Aerosp.) AS332L1 Super Puma	2413		0095	0395	2 TU Makila 1A1	8600			

SHOWA AVIATION, Co. Ltd - Showa Koku, K.K. — Osaka-Yao

Shimanouchi 1-19-21, Chuo-ku, Osaka 542-0082, Japan ☎ (6) 271 06 00 Tx: 5222444 tski j Fax: (6) 251 64 78 SITA: n/a
F: 1968 staff 31 Head: Hiroo Sasaki Net: n/a Aircraft below MTOW 1361 kg: Cessna 172.

registration	type of aircraft	cn/fn	ex/ex*	mfd	del	powered by	mtow kg	configuration	selcal	name/fln/remarks
☐ JA5257	Cessna 404 Titan II	404-0041	N5423G	0077		2 CO GTSIO-520-M	3810	Surveyer		1 camera hole
☐ JA8828	Fairchild (Swearingen) SA226AT Merlin IV	AT-016	N76MX	0074		2 GA TPE331-3U-303G	5670	9 Pax / Surveye		3 large camera holes

SKYMARK AIRLINES, Co. Ltd = BC / SKY (Subsidiary of HIS Travel Group) — Osaka-Itami

Sumitomoseimei Humamatsucho, Bldg. 1F, 1-22-5 Hamamatsucho, Minato-ku, Tokyo 105-0013, Japan ☎ (3) 54 02 67 67 Tx: none Fax: (3) 54 02 67 74 SITA: n/a
F: 1997 staff n/a Head: Hideo Sawada ICAO: SKYMARK Net: n/a

registration	type of aircraft	cn/fn	ex/ex*	mfd	del	powered by	mtow kg	configuration	selcal	name/fln/remarks
☐ JA767A	Boeing 767-3Q8 (ER)	27616 / 714		0898	0898	2 GE CF6-80C2B6F	130952	C12Y297	HR-MP	lsf ILFC / DirecTV-colors
☐ JA767B	Boeing 767-3Q8 (ER)	27617 / 722		1098	1098	2 GE CF6-80C2B6F	130952	C12Y297	FJ-PS	lsf ILFC / Microsoft-colors

TOHO KOKU, K.K. – Toho Air Service, Co. Ltd Tokyo-Chofu

11-25 Osawa, 6-chome, Mitaki-shi, Tokyo 181-0015, Japan ☎ (422) 31 55 05 Tx: n/a Fax: (422) 33 05 05 SITA: n/a
F: 1959 ⁂ 128 Head: Kei Fujiwara Net: n/a Aircraft below MTOW 1361 kg: Cessna 172, 175, Hiller UH-12E, Hughes 269C (300C) & Kawasaki-Bell 47G.

registration	type of aircraft	cn/fn	ex/ex*	mfd	del	powered by	mtow kg	configuration	selcal	name/fln/specialitites/remarks
☐ JA9192	Eurocopter (Aerosp.) SA315B Lama	2479		0078		1 TU Artouste IIIB	1950			
☐ JA9193	Eurocopter (Aerosp.) SA315B Lama	2506		0078		1 TU Artouste IIIB	1950			lsf Nozaki Sangyo
☐ JA9826	Eurocopter (Aerosp.) SA315B Lama	1421 / 31	FAP60-601	0071	0496	1 TU Artouste IIIB	1950			cvtd Alouette II
☐ JA9263	Eurocopter (Aerosp.) AS350B Ecureuil	1311		0080		1 TU Arriel 1B	1950			
☐ JA9333	Eurocopter (Aerosp.) AS350B Ecureuil	1616		0082		1 TU Arriel 1B	1950			lsf Crown Leasing
☐ JA9340	Eurocopter (Aerosp.) AS350B Ecureuil	1645		0082		1 TU Arriel 1B	1950			
☐ JA9341	Eurocopter (Aerosp.) AS350B Ecureuil	1655		0082		1 TU Arriel 1B	1950			lsf ITC Leasing
☐ JA9345	Eurocopter (Aerosp.) AS350B Ecureuil	1660		0082		1 TU Arriel 1B	1950			lsf ITC Leasing
☐ JA9371	Eurocopter (Aerosp.) AS350B Ecureuil	1783		0084		1 TU Arriel 1B	1950			lsf Crown Leasing
☐ JA9389	Eurocopter (Aerosp.) AS350B Ecureuil	1785		0084	0492	1 TU Arriel 1B	1950			
☐ JA9784	Eurocopter (Aerosp.) AS350B Ecureuil	2173		0089	0396	1 TU Arriel 1B	1950			
☐ JA9820	Eurocopter (Aerosp.) AS350B Ecureuil	2197		0089	0995	1 TU Arriel 1B	1950			
☐ JA9839	Eurocopter (Aerosp.) AS350B Ecureuil	2284		0089		1 TU Arriel 1B	1950			lsf Dai Nippon Consultant
☐ JA6697	Eurocopter (Aerosp.) AS355F2 Ecureuil 2	5524		0092	1092	2 AN 250-C20F	2540			lst All Nippon Helicopter
☐ JA9570	Eurocopter (Aerosp.) AS355F1 Ecureuil 2	5140		0082		2 AN 250-C20F	2400			lsf Nozaki Sangyo / cvtd AS355F
☐ JA6656	Eurocopter (Aerosp.) AS365N2 Dauphin 2	6370		0090	0897	2 TU Arriel 1C2	4250			
☐ JA9968	Eurocopter (Aerosp.) AS365N1 Dauphin 2	6333		0089	0997	2 TU Arriel 1C1	4100			
☐ JA9558	Eurocopter (Aerosp.) SA330J Puma	1637		0081	1193	2 TU Turmo IVC	7400			
☐ JA9672	Eurocopter (Aerosp.) AS332L Super Puma	2173		0087		2 TU Makila 1A	8600			lsf Crown Leasing

TOHOKU AIR SERVICE (Subsidiary of Tohoku Electric) Sendai-Heliport

7-1, Ichibancho 3-chome, Aopbaku, Sendai-shi, Miyagi-ken 980-0811, Japan ☎ (22) 247 54 42 Tx: none Fax: (22) 304 10 92 SITA: n/a
F: n/a ⁂ n/a Head: n/a Net: n/a Aircraft below MTOW 1361kg: Hughes 369HS (500C)

registration	type of aircraft	cn/fn	ex/ex*	mfd	del	powered by	mtow kg	configuration	selcal	name/fln/specialitites/remarks
☐ JA6702	Eurocopter (MBB) BO105CBS-4	S-882	D-HFNN*	0093		2 AN 250-C20B	2500			lsf Higashi Nihon Kogyo
☐ JA6735	Eurocopter (MBB) BO105CBS-4	S-890	*	0094		2 AN 250-C20B	2500			Oshidori-3 / lsf Higashi Nihon Kogyo
☐ JA6752	Eurocopter (MBB) BO105CBS-4	S-901	*	0095		2 AN 250-C20B	2500			Oshidori-4 / lsf Higashi Nihon Kogyo
☐ JA9997	Eurocopter (MBB) BO105CBS-4	S-824	D-HFCH*	0090	0392	2 AN 250-C20B	2500			Oshidori-1
☐ JA6620	Kawasaki (Eurocopter/MBB) BK117B-2	1062		0090		2 LY LTS101-750B.1	3350			Bandai / cvtd BK117B-1
☐ JA6654	Kawasaki (Eurocopter/MBB) BK117B-2	1102		0091		2 LY LTS101-750B.1	3350			lsf Miyagi Authorities / cvtd BK117B-1
☐ JA9926	Kawasaki (Eurocopter/MBB) BK117B-2	1028		0089		2 LY LTS101-750B.1	3350			Towada / cvtd BK117B-1
☐ JA6680	Eurocopter (Aerosp.) AS365N2 Dauphin 2	6411		0091		2 TU Arriel 1C2	4250			lsf Tohoku Denryoku
☐ JA330T	Eurocopter (Aerosp.) SA330J Puma	1324	F-GIFV	0075	1096	2 TU Turmo IVC	7400			

TOHOKU SOKURYO, K.K. – Tohoku Survey, Co. Ltd Aomori

2-16 Gappo, 1-chome, Aomori-shi, Aomori 030-0902, Japan ☎ (177) 41 83 31 Tx: n/a Fax: n/a SITA: n/a
F: n/a ⁂ n/a Head: Masatsugo Arima Net: n/a

registration	type of aircraft	cn/fn	ex/ex*	mfd	del	powered by	mtow kg	configuration	selcal	name/fln/specialitites/remarks
☐ JA3773	Cessna TU206F Turbo Stationair II	U20603496	N8743Q	0076		1 CO TSIO-520-C	1633	Photo/Survey		
☐ JA5230	Twin (Aero) Commander 685	685-12055	N57066	0074	0893	2 CO GTSIO-520-K	4082	Photo/survey		1 camera hole

JU = MONGOLIA (State of Mongolia)

This country uses country prefixes (nationality marks) not notified to the ICAO
Capital: Ulaanbaatar Official Language: Mongolian Population: 2,4 million Square Km: 1566500 Dialling code: +976 Year established: 1921 Acting political head: Tsakhiagiin Elbegdorj (Prime Minister)

EASTERN AIRLINES = ERN Ulaanbaatar

PO Box 112, Ulaanbaatar, Mongolia ☎ (1) 32 40 31 Tx: none Fax: (1) 31 37 85 SITA: n/a
F: 1997 ⁂ n/a Head: n/a ICAO: EASTERN AIRCO Net: n/a

registration	type of aircraft	cn/fn	ex/ex*	mfd	del	powered by	mtow kg	configuration	selcal	name/fln/specialitites/remarks
☐ JU-9050	NAMC YS-11A-500	2158	N107SD	0071	0698	2 RR Dart 542-10J/K	24500	Y64		cvtd -213

HANGARD AVIATION, Ltd = HGD Ulaanbaatar

Buyant-Ukhaa-34, Ulaanbaatar 210734, Mongolia ☎ (1) 31 13 33 Tx: none Fax: (1) 32 01 38 SITA: n/a
F: 1983 ⁂ n/a Head: n/a ICAO: HANGARD Net: n/a

registration	type of aircraft	cn/fn	ex/ex*	mfd	del	powered by	mtow kg	configuration	selcal	name/fln/specialitites/remarks
☐ MT-7048	Antonov 24B	07306307	RA-47269	0070		2 IV AI-24	21000	Y48		to be re-reg. JU-7048

MIAT – Mongolian Airlines = OM / MGL (Mongolyn Irgeniy Agaaryn Teever dba) Ulaanbaatar

Buyant-Ukhaa-34, Ulaanbaatar 210734, Mongolia ☎ (1) 37 97 01 Tx: 79226 miat mh Fax: none SITA: n/a
F: 1956 ⁂ n/a Head: Darjagiin Surenkhorloo IATA: 289 ICAO: MONGOL AIR Net: n/a

registration	type of aircraft	cn/fn	ex/ex*	mfd	del	powered by	mtow kg	configuration	selcal	name/fln/specialitites/remarks
☐ JU-5070	PZL Mielec (Antonov) An-2					1 SH ASh-62IR	5500	Y12 / Frtr		
☐ JU-5071	PZL Mielec (Antonov) An-2					1 SH ASh-62IR	5500	Y12 / Frtr		
☐ JU-1024	Mil Mi-8T	20409	MONG-20409	0085		2 IS TV2-117A	12000	Y20		
☐ 20411	Mil Mi-8T	20411	MONG-20411	0085		2 IS TV2-117A	12000	Y20		
☐ MONG-20410	Mil Mi-8T	20410	BNMAU410	0085		2 IS TV2-117A	12000	Y20		
☐ JU-1001	Antonov 24B	47301204	MT-1001	0064		2 IV AI-24-II	21000	Y50		
☐ JU-1002	Antonov 24B	77303302	MT-1002	0067		2 IV AI-24-II	21000	Y50		
☐ JU-1003	Antonov 24RV	07306207	MT-1003	0070		2 IV AI-24VT	21800	Y50		
☐ JU-1004	Antonov 24RV	17306807	MT-1004	0071		2 IV AI-24VT	21800	Y50		
☐ JU-1005	Antonov 24RV	47309310	MT-1005	0073		2 IV AI-24VT	21800	Y50		
☐ JU-1006	Antonov 24RV	47309807	MT-1006	0074		2 IV AI-24VT	21800	Y50		
☐ JU-1007	Antonov 24RV	57310102	MT-1007	0075		2 IV AI-24VT	21800	Y50		
☐ JU-1009	Antonov 24RV	57310104	MT-1009	0075		2 IV AI-24VT	21800	Y50		
☐ JU-1010	Antonov 24RV	57310209	MT-1010	0075		2 IV AI-24VT	21800	Y50		
☐ JU-1011	Antonov 24RV	57310301	MT-1011	0075		2 IV AI-24VT	21800	Y50		
☐ JU-1027	Antonov 24B	67302510	MT-1027	0066		2 IV AI-24-II	21000	Y50		
☐ BNMAU-1506	Antonov 30	1506	MT-1016	0078		2 IV AI-24VT	23000	Surveyer		to be re-reg. JU-1016
☐ JU-1012	Antonov 26	3009	MT-1012	0075		2 IV AI-24VT	24000	Combi		
☐ JU-1013	Antonov 26	3010	MT-1013	0075		2 IV AI-24VT	24000	Combi		
☐ JU-1014	Antonov 26B	14101	MT-1014	0084		2 IV AI-24VT	24000	Combi		
☐ JU-1036	Boeing 727-281 (A)	20572 / 881	MT-1036	0072	0594	3 PW JT8D-9A	86410	Y166	AE-FK	
☐ JU-1037	Boeing 727-281 (A)	20573 / 888	MT-1037	0072	0594	3 PW JT8D-9A	86410	Y166	AE-FL	
☐ JU-1054	Boeing 727-281	20435 / 787	MT-1054	0071	0792	3 PW JT8D-9A	78019	Y166		
☐ F-OHPT	Airbus Industrie A310-304	526	F-WHPT	0090	0598	2 GE CF6-80C2A2	153000	F10C40Y120		lsf Airbus Ind.Finan.Svcs / tbr JU-1069

JY = JORDAN (Hashemite Kingdom of Jordan) (al-Mamlaka al-Urdunniyah al-Hashemiyah)

Capital: Amman Official Language: Arabic Population: 5,5 million Square Km: 97740 Dialling code: +962 Year established: 1918 Acting political head: Abdullah II (Abdullah bin Hussein bin Talal bin Abdullah) (King)

Government / Corporate / Executive / VIP Aircraft

registration	type of aircraft	cn/fn	ex/ex*	mfd	del	powered by	mtow kg	configuration	selcal	name/fln/specialitites/remarks
☐ JY-HKJ	Lockheed L-1011-385-3 TriStar 500	293A-1247	N64854*	0083	0684	3 RR RB211-524B4	224982	VIP	DK-HJ	Gvmt / for sale
☐ JY-RAY	GAC G-IV Gulfstream IV	1202	V8-009	0093	0198	2 RR Tay 611-8	33203	VIP		Gvmt

ARAB WINGS, Ltd = AWS (Sister company of Royal Wings / Subsidiary of Royal Jordanian) Amman

PO Box 341018, Amman 11134, Jordan ☎ (6) 489 19 94 Tx: 21608 wings jo Fax: (6) 489 31 58 SITA: AMMCDRJ
F: 1975 ⁂ 35 Head: Ahed Quntar ICAO: ARAB WINGS Net: http://arabwings.com.jo

registration	type of aircraft	cn/fn	ex/ex*	mfd	del	powered by	mtow kg	configuration	selcal	name/fln/specialitites/remarks
☐ JY-AFG	Cessna 340A III	340A1806	N1230V	0084		2 CO TSIO-520-NB	2717	4 Pax		
☐ JY-AFH	Sabreliner 75A (Rockwell NA265-80)	380-57	HZ-RBH	0077		2 GE CF700-2D2	10433	8 Pax		
☐ JY-AFP	Sabreliner 75A (Rockwell NA265-80)	380-62		0078		2 GE CF700-2D2	10433	7 Pax	BC-GK	

HMS AIRWAYS Amman, London-Stansted & Paris-Le Bourget

Operational HQ: c/o Int'l Jet Services, 8th Floor, Regal House, 70 London Road, Twickenham, Middx. TW1 4QZ, Great Britain ☎ (181) 892 38 72 Tx: none Fax: (181) 255 36 00 SITA: n/a
F: 1996 ⁂ n/a Head: Hany Salam Net: n/a Operates non-commercial executive flights for a private customer only.

registration	type of aircraft	cn/fn	ex/ex*	mfd	del	powered by	mtow kg	configuration	selcal	name/fln/specialitites/remarks
☐ JY-HS1	Boeing 727-76 (winglets)	20228 / 766	VR-CHS	0069	0296	3 PW JT8D-7B	79379	Executive	EL-BK	opf pvt
☐ JY-HS2	Boeing 727-2L4 (A) (winglets)	21010 / 1100	VR-CCA	0075	0496	3 PW JT8D-17	90628	Executive	FG-BJ	opf pvt

ROYAL JORDANIAN = RJ / RJA (formerly ALIA – The Royal Jordanian Airline) Amman

PO Box 302, Amman, Jordan ☎ (6) 445 12 61 Tx: 21932 rjmat jo Fax: (6) 445 33 44 SITA: AMMDDRJ
F: 1963 ⁂ 5000 Head: Nader Aldahabi IATA: 512 ICAO: JORDANIAN Net: http://www.rja.com.jo/info/rj.html On order (Letter of Intent): 5 Airbus Industrie A340 for delivery 1999-2000.

registration	type of aircraft	cn/fn	ex/ex*	mfd	del	powered by	mtow kg	configuration	selcal	name/fln/specialitites/remarks
☐ F-OGYA	Airbus Industrie A320-212	087	F-WWDM*	0090	0390	2 CFMI CFM56-5A3	73500	F12Y132	CK-GH	Cairo / lsf Jordair Bail / cvtd -211
☐ F-OGYB	Airbus Industrie A320-212	088	F-WWDN*	0090	0490	2 CFMI CFM56-5A3	73500	F12Y132	CK-JL	Baghdad / lsf Jordair Bail / cvtd -211
☐ F-OGYC	Airbus Industrie A320-212	569	F-WWDG*	0096	0396	2 CFMI CFM56-5A3	73500	F12Y132	AE-BS	lsf Jordair Bail
☐ 7T-VJE	Airbus Industrie A310-203	295	5A-DLA	0083	0895	2 GE CF6-80A3	142000	F12Y195	DK-GH	lsf DAH
☐ 7T-VJF	Airbus Industrie A310-203	306	5A-DLB	0084	0894	2 GE CF6-80A3	142000	F12Y195	DK-GJ	lsf DAH
☐ JY-AJN	Boeing 707-3J6C	20720 / 874	B-2414	0073	0995	4 PW JT3D-7 (HK2/COM)	151046	Freighter	EL-AB	
☐ JY-AJO	Boeing 707-3J6C	20723 / 879	B-2420	0074	0995	4 PW JT3D-7 (HK2/COM)	151046	Freighter	EJ-DG	
☐ JY-AGS	Airbus Industrie A310-304	598	HC-BRP	0091	1098	2 GE CF6-80C2A2	157000	F16Y188		lsf ILFC
☐ JY-AGT	Airbus Industrie A310-308	663	9K-ALC	0093	1198	2 GE CF6-80C2A8	157000	F16Y188		lsf KAC
☐ F-ODVF	Airbus Industrie A310-304	445		0288	0288	2 GE CF6-80C2A2	153000	F16Y188	FH-CM	Princess Raiyah / lsf Royal Jord. Bail
☐ F-ODVG	Airbus Industrie A310-304	490		0189	0289	2 GE CF6-80C2A2	153000	F16Y188	HJ-AC	Prince Faisal / lsf Royal Jord. Bail
☐ F-ODVH	Airbus Industrie A310-304	491		0189	0389	2 GE CF6-80C2A2	153000	F16Y188	DF-JM	Prince Hamzeh / lsf Royal Jord. Bail
☐ F-ODVI	Airbus Industrie A310-304	531		0090	0390	2 GE CF6-80C2A2	153000	F16Y188	AE-GH	Princess Haya / lsf Royal Jord. Bail

registration	type of aircraft	cn/fn	ex/ex*	mfd	del	powered by	mtow kg	configuration	selcal	name/fln/specialitites/remarks
☐ JY-AGA	Lockheed L-1011-385-3 TriStar 500	293A-1217		0981	0981	3 RR RB211-524B4	231332	F12Y225	DG-AL	Amman
☐ JY-AGB	Lockheed L-1011-385-3 TriStar 500	293A-1219		1081	1081	3 RR RB211-524B4	231332	F12Y225	DG-AM	Princess Alia

ROYAL WINGS = AWS (Sister company of Arab Wings / Subsidiary of Royal Jordanian)
Amman

PO Box 341018, Amman, Jordan ☎ (6) 489 19 94 Tx: none Fax: (6) 489 31 58 SITA: n/a
F: 1995 ♦♦♦ 115 Head: Ahed Quntar ICAO: ROYAL WINGS Net: http://www.royalwings.com.jo

registration	type of aircraft	cn/fn	ex/ex*	mfd	del	powered by	mtow kg	configuration	selcal	name/fln/specialitites/remarks
☐ JY-RWA	De Havilland DHC-8-311 Dash 8	286	C-FXGF	0091	0196	2 PWC PW123	18643	Y50		lsf Bombardier
☐ JY-RWB	De Havilland DHC-8-315 Dash 8	401	N7985B	0095	0198	2 PWC PW123B	19500	Y50		lsf Bombardier / cvtd -311

J2 = DJIBOUTI (Republic of Djibouti) (al-Jumhouriya al-Djibouti)
Capital: Djibouti Official Language: Arabic, French Population: 0,6 million Square Km: 23200 Dialling code: +253 Year established: 1977 Acting political head: Hassan Gouled Aptidon (President)

Government / Corporate / Executive / VIP Aircraft

registration	type of aircraft	cn/fn	ex/ex*	mfd	del	powered by	mtow kg	configuration	selcal	name/fln/specialitites/remarks
☐ J2-KBA	Dassault Falcon 50	71	YI-ALB	0082	1287	2 GA TFE731-3-1C	17600	VIP		Gvmt

AIR DJIBOUTI – Red Sea Airlines = DY / DJU
Djibouti

BP 499, Djibouti, Djibouti ☎ 35 67 23 Tx: none Fax: 35 67 34 SITA: n/a
F: n/a ♦♦♦ n/a Head: n/a IATA: 213 ICAO: AIR DJIB Net: n/a

registration	type of aircraft	cn/fn	ex/ex*	mfd	del	powered by	mtow kg	configuration	selcal	name/fln/specialitites/remarks
☐ F-OHPQ	Airbus Industrie A310-222	318	F-WGYQ	0084	0798	2 PW JT9D-7R4E1	142000	C30Y159		lsf Airbus Industrie Financial Services

DAALLO AIRLINES = D3 / DAO
Djibouti & Dubai (UAE)

BP 2565, Djibouti, Djibouti ☎ 35 34 01 Tx: none Fax: 35 17 65 SITA: n/a
F: 1992 ♦♦♦ n/a Head: Mohamed I. Yassin IATA: 991 ICAO: DALO AIRLINES Net: n/a

registration	type of aircraft	cn/fn	ex/ex*	mfd	del	powered by	mtow kg	configuration	selcal	name/fln/specialitites/remarks
☐ RA-67565	Let 410UVP-E	861605	CCCP-67565	0086	0097	2 WA M-601E	6400	Y19		lsf OAO
☐ EY-46602	Antonov 24RV	37308509	CCCP-46602	0473	0097	2 IV AI-24VT	21000	Y52		lsf TZK
☐ EY-47693	Antonov 24RV	27307510	CCCP-47693	0172	0095	2 IV AI-24VT	21800	Y52		lsf TZK
☐ EY-85691	Tupolev 154M	864	CCCP-85691	0291		3 SO D-30KU-154-II	100000	Y170		lsf TZK

DJIBOUTI AIRLINES = DJB
Djibouti

BP 2240, Djibouti, Djibouti ☎ 35 10 06 Tx: n/a Fax: 35 24 29 SITA: n/a
F: 1996 ♦♦♦ n/a Head: n/a ICAO: DJIBOUTI AIR Net: n/a Operates passenger flights with Antonov 24 & Ilyushin 18 aircraft, leased from other companies when required.

J3 = GRENADA (State of Grenada)
Capital: St. George's Official Language: English Population: 0,2 million Square Km: 344 Dialling code: +1-473 Year established: 1974 Acting political head: Keith Mitchell (Prime Minister)

AIRLINES OF CARRIACOU, Ltd = C4 / COU
Grenada-Point Salines Int'l

PO Box 805, St. George's, Grenada ☎ (473) 444-1475 Tx: none Fax: (473) 444-2898 SITA: n/a
F: 1992 ♦♦♦ 18 Head: Capt. Arthur W. Bain IATA: 484 ICAO: AIR CARRIACOU Net: n/a

registration	type of aircraft	cn/fn	ex/ex*	mfd	del	powered by	mtow kg	configuration	selcal	name/fln/specialitites/remarks
☐ J3-GAF	Britten-Norman BN-2B-26 Islander	2025	G-UERN	0080	0693	2 LY O-540-E4C5	2994	Y9		lsf Wetlease Ltd of Antilles Management
☐ J3-GAG	Britten-Norman BN-2A Islander	163	V2-LAG	0070	0093	2 LY O-540-E4C5	2858	Y9		lsf LIA
☐ J3-GAH	Britten-Norman BN-2A-26 Islander	570	C-GGVJ	0077	0195	2 LY O-540-E4C5	2994	Y9		lsf Wetlease Ltd of Antilles Management

J5 = GUINEA BISSAU (Republic of Guinea Bissau) (Republica da Guiné Bissau)
Capital: Bissau Official Language: Portuguese Population: 1,1 million Square Km: 36125 Dialling code: +245 Year established: 1973 Acting political head: Brig.-Gen. Joao Bernardo Vieira (President)

AIR BISSAU = GBU (formerly TAGB – Transportes Aéreos da Guine-Bissau)
Bissau

Caixa Postal 3, Bissau, Guinea Bissau ☎ 20 12 77 Tx: none Fax: 25 10 08 SITA: n/a
F: 1975 ♦♦♦ n/a Head: Baba Jahate ICAO: TRANSBISSAU Net: n/a
Suspended own operations. All operations were transferred under a co-operation-contract to TACV Cabo Verde Airlines. Intends to restart its own operations during 1999.

J6 = ST. LUCIA (State of St. Lucia)
Capital: Castries Official Language: English Population: 0,2 million Square Km: 622 Dialling code: +1-758 Year established: 1979 Acting political head: Kenny Anthony (Prime Minister)

EAGLE AIR SERVICES (St. Lucia), Ltd.
Castries-Vigie

Box 838, Castries, St. Lucia ☎ (758) 452-1900 Tx: none Fax: (758) 452-9683 SITA: n/a
F: 1988 ♦♦♦ 7 Head: Capt. Ewart F. Hinkson Net: n/a

registration	type of aircraft	cn/fn	ex/ex*	mfd	del	powered by	mtow kg	configuration	selcal	name/fln/specialitites/remarks
☐ J6-SLT	Britten-Norman BN-2A-26 Islander	741	V2-LDV	0075	0593	2 LY O-540-E4C5	2994	Y9		
☐ J6-SLY	Britten-Norman BN-2A-26 Islander	384	8R-GFL	0074	0090	2 LY O-540-E4C5	2994	Y9		

HELENAIR, Corp. Ltd = 2Y / HCL
Castries-Vigie

Box 253, Castries, St. Lucia ☎ (758) 452-1958 Tx: none Fax: (758) 452-1958 SITA: n/a
F: 1987 ♦♦♦ 30 Head: Capt. Joaquin A. Willie IATA: 687 ICAO: HELENCORP Net: n/a

registration	type of aircraft	cn/fn	ex/ex*	mfd	del	powered by	mtow kg	configuration	selcal	name/fln/specialitites/remarks
☐ J6-AAL	De Havilland DHC-6 Twin Otter 300	532	C-GQKZ	0077	1297	2 PWC PT6A-27	5670	Y19		lsf KBA
☐ J6-AAH	Beech 1900C-1 Airliner	UC-146	N146YV	0291	0697	2 PWC PT6A-65B	7530	Y19		lsf Raytheon Aircraft Credit Corp.
☐ J6-AAI	Beech 1900C-1 Airliner	UC-143	N143AM	0191	0797	2 PWC PT6A-65B	7530	Y19		lsf Raytheon Aircraft Credit Corp.
☐ J6-AAJ	Beech 1900C-1 Airliner	UC-164	N164YV	0791	1197	2 PWC PT6A-65B	7530	Y19		lsf Raytheon Aircraft Credit Corp.

SAINT LUCIA HELICOPTERS, Inc.
Castries-Vigie

PO Box 2047, Castries, St. Lucia ☎ (758) 453-6950 Tx: none Fax: (758) 453-6590 SITA: n/a
F: 1990 ♦♦♦ n/a Head: n/a Net: n/a

registration	type of aircraft	cn/fn	ex/ex*	mfd	del	powered by	mtow kg	configuration	selcal	name/fln/specialitites/remarks
☐ N2635Z	Bell 206B JetRanger	852			0072	1 AN 250-C20	1451			lsf Rotorcraft Partnerships
☐ N42AH	Bell 206B JetRanger III	2935			0080	1 AN 250-C20B	1451			lsf Rotorcraft Partnerships

J7 = DOMINICA (Commonwealth of Dominica)
Capital: Roseau Official Language: English Population: 0,1 million Square Km: 751 Dialling code: +1-767 Year established: 1978 Acting political head: Edison James (Prime Minister)

DJIBOUTI AIRLINES = DJB
Djibouti

BP 2240, Djibouti, Djibouti ☎ 35 10 06 Tx: n/a Fax: 35 24 29 SITA: n/a
F: 1996 ♦♦♦ n/a Head: n/a ICAO: DJIBOUTI AIR Net: n/a

registration	type of aircraft	cn/fn	ex/ex*	mfd	del	powered by	mtow kg	configuration	selcal	name/fln/specialitites/remarks
☐ J2-KBC	Let 410UVP-E	912537	CCCP-67669	0091	0096	2 WA M-601E	6400	Y19		
☐ ST-APZ	Ilyushin 18D	187010004	RA-75449	0067	0098	4 IV AI-20M	64000	Y100		lsf RMY

J8 = ST. VINCENT & GRENADINES (State of St. Vincent & Grenadines)
Capital: Kingstown Official Language: English Population: 0,2 million Square Km: 388 Dialling code: +1-809 Year established: 1979 Acting political head: Sir James F. Mitchell (Prime Minister)

MUSTIQUE AIRWAYS, Ltd = Q4 / MAW
St. Vincent

PO Box 1232, Kingstown, St. Vincent & Grenadines ☎ (784) 458-4380 Tx: 7542 charter vq Fax: (784) 456-4586 SITA: n/a
F: 1979 ♦♦♦ 55 Head: Jonathan Palmer ICAO: MUSTIQUE Net: http://www.mustique.com

registration	type of aircraft	cn/fn	ex/ex*	mfd	del	powered by	mtow kg	configuration	selcal	name/fln/specialitites/remarks
☐ J8-VBD	Twin (Aero) Commander 500U	500U-1670-18	N75CG	0066	1296	2 LY IO-540-E1A5	3062	Y5		
☐ J8-VAH	Britten-Norman BN-2B-26 Islander	2018	VP-VAH	0079	0582	2 LY O-540-E4C5	2994	Y9		
☐ J8-VAM	Britten-Norman BN-2B-26 Islander	2165	N670J	0083	0886	2 LY O-540-E4C5	2994	Y9		lsf Locaiman Ltd
☐ J8-VAZ	Embraer 110P1 Bandeirante (EMB-110P1)	110304	G-BVRT	0080	0496	2 PWC PT6A-34	5670	Y19		lsf Jonathan B. Palmer Esq.

SVG AIR = SVD (St. Vincent Grenadines Air (1990), Ltd dba)
St. Vincent

PO Box 39, Kingstown, St. Vincent & Grenadines ☎ (784) 456-5610 Tx: none Fax: (784) 458-4697 SITA: n/a
F: n/a ♦♦♦ n/a Head: Paul Gravel ICAO: GRENADINES Net: http://www.duhe.com/svgair

registration	type of aircraft	cn/fn	ex/ex*	mfd	del	powered by	mtow kg	configuration	selcal	name/fln/specialitites/remarks
☐ J8-VAQ	Cessna 402B II STOL	402B1038	N400XY	0076	0890	2 CO TSIO-520-E	2858			
☐ J8-VAX	Twin (Aero) Shrike Commander 500S	500S-1869-45	N9033N	0069	1294	2 LY IO-540-E1B5	3062			
☐ J8-VAY	Twin (Aero) Commander 500U	500U-1637-2	N6531V	0066	0296	2 LY IO-540-E1A5	3062			
☐ J8-VAW	Britten-Norman BN-2A-27 Islander	868	C-FSTJ	0080	0694	2 LY O-540-E4C5	2885			

LN = NORWAY (Kingdom of Norway) (Kongeriket Norge)
Capital: Oslo Official Language: Norwegian Population: 4,5 million Square Km: 323878 Dialling code: +47 Year established: 1814 Acting political head: Kjell Magne Bondevik (Prime Minister)

Government / Corporate / Executive / VIP Aircraft
ROYAL NORWEGIAN AIR FORCE uses the ICAO three-letter-code: NOW and call sign: NORWEGIAN.

registration	type of aircraft	cn/fn	ex/ex*	mfd	del	powered by	mtow kg	configuration	selcal	name/fln/specialitites/remarks
☐ 0125	Dassault Falcon 20C-5	125	LN-FOE	0067		2 GE TFE731-5BR-2C	13200	VIP / mil trans		Royal Norwegian Air Force / cvtd 20C

AGDERFLY, A/S = AGD
Kristiansand-Kjevik

Kristiansand Lufthavn, N-4750 Kjevik, Norway ☎ 38 06 31 11 Tx: none Fax: 38 06 31 60 SITA: n/a
F: 1976 ♦♦♦ n/a Head: Ola Rustenberg ICAO: AGDERFLY Net: n/a Aircraft below MTOW 1361kg: Fuji FA-200 & Piper PA-28

registration	type of aircraft	cn/fn	ex/ex*	mfd	del	powered by	mtow kg	configuration	selcal	name/fln/specialitites/remarks
☐ LN-VYM	Gulfstream American GA-7 Cougar	GA7-0047	N760GA	0078		2 LY O-320-D1D	1725			

AIRCONTACTGRUPPEN, A/S = (AIRG) (Affiliated with Aircontact, A/S / Aircontact Aviation Management, A/S) — Oslo

PO Box 1447 Vika, N-0115 Oslo, Norway ☎ 22 55 40 50 Tx: 19918 airgt n Fax: 22 55 05 92 SITA: n/a
F: 1962 ♟♟♟ n/a Head: Dag Tveteras Net: n/a New and used aircraft leasing, sales and financing company. Owner / lessor of following (main) aircraft types: Boeing 737-300, Boeing 767-200 & Lockheed Hercules.
Business is handled by affiliated companies: Boeing by AIRCONTACT AVIATION MANAGEMENT, A/S and Lockheed by AIRCONTACT, A/S (all same headquarters).
Aircraft leased from AIRG are listed an mentioned as such under the leasing carriers.

AIRLIFT, A/S — Foerde

Foerde Lufthavn, N-6815 Bygstad, Norway ☎ 57 71 81 00 Tx: none Fax: 57 71 81 01 SITA: n/a
F: 1986 ♟♟♟ 75 Head: Lars Kleivan Net: n/a

registration	type of aircraft	cn/fn	ex/ex*	mfd	del	powered by	mtow kg	remarks
☐ LN-OMS	MD Helicopters MD 500D (Hughes 369D)	*911067D*	*SE-HMB*	*0081*	*0496*	*1 AN 250-C20B*	*1361*	*lst Helikopterteneste*
☐ LN-OCE	Eurocopter (Aerosp.) SA315B Lama	*2179*	*5V-MAF*	*0071*	*0496*	*1 TU Artouste IIIB1*	*1950*	*lst Helikopterteneste*
☐ LN-OMU	Eurocopter (Aerosp.) SA315B Lama	*2643*	*F-WXFC**	*0083*	*0496*	*1 TU Artouste IIIB1*	*1950*	*lst Helikopterteneste*
☐ LN-OPU	Eurocopter (Aerosp.) SA315B Lama	*2316 / 33*	*HB-XVW*	*0073*	*0395*	*1 TU Artouste IIIB*	*1950*	*cvtd Alouette II*
☐ LN-OCD	Eurocopter (Aerosp.) AS350B1 Ecureuil	*2207*		*0089*	*0496*	*1 TU Arriel 1D*	*2200*	*lst Helikopterteneste*
☐ LN-OCF	Eurocopter (Aerosp.) AS350B2 Ecureuil	*2478*		*0091*	*0496*	*1 TU Arriel 1D1*	*2250*	*lst Helikopterteneste*
☐ LN-OMB	Eurocopter (Aerosp.) AS350B2 Ecureuil	*2514*	*F-WYMO**	*0091*	*0791*	*1 TU Arriel 1D1*	*2250*	
☐ LN-OPK	Eurocopter (Aerosp.) AS350B3 Ecureuil	*3091*		*0098*	*0798*	*1 TU Arriel 2B*	*2250*	*lsf ABN Amro Bank AB*
☐ LN-OPP	Eurocopter (Aerosp.) AS350B1 Ecureuil	*2080*		*0088*		*1 TU Arriel 1D*	*2200*	
☐ LN-OPS	Eurocopter (Aerosp.) AS350B Ecureuil	*1849*	*SE-HTS*	*0085*	*0196*	*1 TU Arriel 1B*	*1950*	
☐ LN-OPT	Eurocopter (Aerosp.) AS350B1 Ecureuil	*1881*	*D-HHPS*	*0086*		*1 TU Arriel 1D*	*2200*	
☐ LN-OPV	Eurocopter (Aerosp.) AS350B2 Ecureuil	*2378*	*HB-XUS*	*0090*		*1 TU Arriel 1D1*	*2250*	*lsf Heliflight, A/S*
☐ LN-OSM	Eurocopter (Aerosp.) AS350B1 Ecureuil	*1966*	*SE-HUT*	*0086*	*0199*	*1 TU Arriel 1D*	*2200*	
☐ LN-OPL	Eurocopter (Aerosp.) SA365N1 Dauphin 2	*6346*	*F-WQDP*	*0088*	*1196*	*2 TU Arriel 1C1*	*4100*	
☐ LN-OPM	Eurocopter (Aerosp.) SA365N1 Dauphin 2	*6264*	*CS-HCG*	*0088*	*1196*	*2 TU Arriel 1C1*	*4100*	
☐ LN-OPQ	Eurocopter (Aerosp.) SA365N1 Dauphin 2	*6319*	*G-THGS*	*0089*	*0993*	*2 TU Arriel 1C1*	*4100*	
☐ LN-OLK	Bell 212	*30722*	*C-GOKT*	*0075*	*1295*	*2 PWC PT6T-3 TwinPac*	*5080*	
☐ LN-OMX	Eurocopter (Aerosp.) AS332L1 Super Puma	*2351*	*G-BTNZ*	*0091*	*0497*	*2 TU Makila 1A1*	*8600*	

AIR TEAM, A/S = 8W / TTX — Notodden

Merdeveien 18B, N-3670 Notodden, Norway ☎ 35 02 50 00 Tx: none Fax: 35 02 50 06 SITA: n/a
F: 1978 ♟♟♟ 5 Head: Ivar A. Joergensen ICAO: AIR TEAM Net: n/a Aircraft below MTOW 1361kg: Socata TB-9.

registration	type of aircraft	cn/fn	ex/ex*	mfd	del	powered by	mtow kg	remarks
☐ LN-KLK	Piper PA-34-200T Seneca II	*34-7570028*	*SE-GIC*	*0075*		*2 CO TSIO-360-E*	*1999*	*lsf First Estate A/S*
☐ SE-ILY	Piper PA-31-350 Navajo Chieftain	*31-7852051*	*G-FTTA*	*0078*		*2 LY TIO-540-J2BD*	*3175*	*lsf Arne Otto Myklebust A/S*
☐ LN-KCG	Beech King Air C90	*LJ-768*	*OY-SBU*	*0078*		*2 PWC PT6A-21*	*4377*	*lsf J-Invest A/S*

ARCTIC AIR, A/S — Alta & Kautokeino

Postboks 2037, N-9501 Alta, Norway ☎ 78 48 78 00 Tx: none Fax: 78 48 78 00 SITA: n/a
F: 1995 ♟♟♟ 3 Head: Marit Karlsen Net: http://www.arcticnet.no/arctic.air

registration	type of aircraft	cn/fn	ex/ex*	mfd	del	powered by	mtow kg	remarks
☐ LN-OTL	Bell 206B JetRanger	*234*	*OH-HHW*	*0068*	*0798*	*1 AN 250-C20*	*1451*	*lsf ABN Amro Bank AB / cvtd 206A*
☐ LN-FAY	Cessna U206G Stationair 6 II	*U20604326*		*0078*	*0596*	*1 CO IO-520-F*	*1633*	

BRAATHEN LEASING, A/S = (BRAL) (Sister company of Braathens, ASA) — Oslo

PO Box 55, N-1330 Fornebu, Norway ☎ 67 59 71 30 Tx: 71595 buosl n Fax: 67 59 73 87 SITA: n/a
F: 1986 ♟♟♟ n/a Head: Hans A. Groetterud Net: n/a Boeing 767 leasing is done jointly with Int'l Lease Finance Corp. by associate company PACIFIC OCEAN LEASING Ltd = (PACO) (same headquarters).
New and used aircraft leasing, sales and financing company. Owner/Lessor of following (main) aircraft types: Boeing 737-200, -400, -500 & 767-200. Aircraft leased from BRAL are listed and mentioned as such under leasing carriers.

BRAATHENS, ASA = BU / BRA (Assoc. with KLM / formerly Braathens S.A.F.E.-South-American & Far East Airtransport, A/S) — Oslo-Fornebu & Stavanger-Sola

Postboks 55, N-1330 Fornebu, Norway ☎ 67 59 70 00 Tx: 71595 buosl n Fax: 67 59 13 09 SITA: OSLDPBU
F: 1946 ♟♟♟ 5800 Head: Erik G. Braathen IATA: 154 ICAO: BRAATHENS Net: http://www.braathens.no/

registration	type of aircraft	cn/fn	ex/ex*	mfd	del	powered by	mtow kg	configuration	selcal	name/fln/specialitites/remarks
☐ LN-BRC	Boeing 737-505	*24650 / 1792*	*N5573K**	*0090*	*0390*	*2 CFMI CFM56-3C1*	*60554*	*Y125*	*GQ-EF*	Hakon IV Hakonsson
☐ LN-BRD	Boeing 737-505	*24651 / 1842*		*0090*	*0490*	*2 CFMI CFM56-3C1*	*60554*	*Y125*	*GQ-EH*	Harald Gille / *lsf INGO*
☐ LN-BRF	Boeing 737-505	*24652 / 1917*	*D-ACBA*	*0090*	*0990*	*2 CFMI CFM56-3C1*	*57833*	*Y125*	*BJ-LQ*	Magnus Lagaboter / *lsf CITG*
☐ LN-BRG	Boeing 737-505	*24272 / 1923*		*0090*	*0990*	*2 CFMI CFM56-3C1*	*52843*	*Y125*	*BJ-MQ*	Oystein Magnusson
☐ LN-BRH	Boeing 737-505	*24828 / 1925*	*D-ACBB*	*0090*	*1090*	*2 CFMI CFM56-3C1*	*57833*	*Y125*	*BJ-PQ*	Haakon den gode / *lsf CITG*
☐ LN-BRJ	Boeing 737-505	*24273 / 2018*	*D-ACBC*	*0091*	*0391*	*2 CFMI CFM56-3C1*	*52843*	*Y119*	*CQ-RS*	Magnus Barfot
☐ LN-BRK	Boeing 737-505	*24274 / 2035*		*0091*	*0491*	*2 CFMI CFM56-3C1*	*52843*	*Y119*	*AR-LP*	Olav Tryggvason / *lsf ORIX*
☐ LN-BRM	Boeing 737-505	*24645 / 2072*		*0091*	*0691*	*2 CFMI CFM56-3C1*	*52843*	*Y119*	*AR-LQ*	Olav den Hellige
☐ LN-BRN	Boeing 737-505	*24646 / 2138*		*0091*	*1091*	*2 CFMI CFM56-3C1*	*52843*	*Y119*	*AR-LS*	Hakon Herdebrei
☐ LN-BRO	Boeing 737-505	*24647 / 2143*		*0091*	*1091*	*2 CFMI CFM56-3C1*	*52843*	*Y119*	*AR-MP*	Magnus Haraldsson
☐ LN-BRR	Boeing 737-505	*24648 / 2213*		*0092*	*0292*	*2 CFMI CFM56-3C1*	*52843*	*Y119*	*AR-MQ*	Halvdan Svarte
☐ LN-BRS	Boeing 737-505	*24649 / 2225*		*0092*	*0292*	*2 CFMI CFM56-3C1*	*52843*	*Y119*	*AR-MS*	Olav Kyrre
☐ LN-BRT	Boeing 737-505	*25789 / 2229*		*0092*	*0292*	*2 CFMI CFM56-3C1*	*57833*	*Y125*	*AR-PQ*	Sigurd Jorsalfar / *lsf INGO*
☐ LN-BRU	Boeing 737-505	*25790 / 2245*		*0092*	*0392*	*2 CFMI CFM56-3C1*	*57833*	*Y125*	*AR-PS*	Eirik Magnusson
☐ LN-BRV	Boeing 737-505	*25791 / 2351*		*0092*	*0892*	*2 CFMI CFM56-3C1*	*57833*	*Y125*	*BG-KS*	Hakon Sverresson / *lsf Sanwa*
☐ LN-BRW	Boeing 737-505	*25792 / 2353*		*0092*	*0992*	*2 CFMI CFM56-3C1*	*60554*	*Y131*		*lsf BRA Cayman 1 / sub-lst CXA B-2591*
☐ LN-BRX	Boeing 737-505	*25797 / 2434*		*0093*	*0293*	*2 CFMI CFM56-3C1*	*52843*	*Y125*	*DE-JR*	Sigurd Munn
☐ LN-BRY	Boeing 737-505	*27155 / 2449*		*0093*	*0493*	*2 CFMI CFM56-3C1*	*60554*	*Y131*		*lst CXA as B-2593*
☐ LN-BRZ	Boeing 737-505	*27153 / 2516*		*0093*	*0993*	*2 CFMI CFM56-3C1*	*60554*	*Y131*		*lsf BRA Cayman 3/sub-lst CXA as B-2592*
☐ LN-BUA	Boeing 737-505	*26297 / 2578*		*0094*	*0294*	*2 CFMI CFM56-3C1*	*60554*	*Y125*		*lsf ILFC / sub-lst CXA B-2529*
☐ LN-BUC	Boeing 737-505	*26304 / 2649*		*0094*	*0994*	*2 CFMI CFM56-3C1*	*52843*	*Y125*	*ER-DQ*	Magnus Erlingsson / *lsf ILFC*
☐ LN-BUD	Boeing 737-505	*25794 / 2803*		*0096*	*0796*	*2 CFMI CFM56-3C1*	*52843*	*Y125*	*LR-AK*	Inge Krokrygg
☐ LN-BUE	Boeing 737-505	*27627 / 2800*		*0096*	*0696*	*2 CFMI CFM56-3C1*	*52843*	*Y125*	*LR-AM*	Erling Skjalgsson / *lsf ILFC*
☐ LN-BUG	Boeing 737-505	*27631 / 2866*		*0097*	*0297*	*2 CFMI CFM56-3C1*	*52843*	*Y125*	*AM-BR*	Oystein Haraldsson / *lsf ILFC*
☐ LN-TUA	Boeing 737-705	*28211 / 33*		*0098*	*0498*	*2 CFMI CFM56-7B24*	*64864*	*Y134*	*BH-LP*	Ingeborg Eriksdatter / *lsf ILFC*
☐ LN-TUB	Boeing 737-705	*29089 / 83*		*0098*	*0898*	*2 CFMI CFM56-7B24*	*60328*	*Y134*	*GH-LQ*	
☐ LN-TUC	Boeing 737-705	*29090 / 109*	*N1786B**	*0998*	*0998*	*2 CFMI CFM56-7B24*	*60328*	*Y134*	*GH-MQ*	
☐ LN-TUD	Boeing 737-705	*28217 / 142*	*N1786B**	*0098*	*1198*	*2 CFMI CFM56-7B24*	*64864*	*Y134*	*GH-PQ*	*lsf ILFC*
☐ LN-TUE	Boeing 737-705	*29091 / 230*		*0099*	*0399*	*2 CFMI CFM56-7B24*	*60328*	*Y134*	*HM-JP*	
☐ LN-TUF	Boeing 737-705	*28222 / 245*		*0099*	*0499*	*2 CFMI CFM56-7B24*	*60328*	*Y134*	*HQ-CR*	*lsf ILFC*
☐ LN-TUG	Boeing 737-705	*29092 / 260*		*0099*	*0499*	*2 CFMI CFM56-7B24*	*60328*	*Y134*	*HQ-BS*	
☐ LN-TUI	Boeing 737-705					*2 CFMI CFM56-7B24*	*60328*	*Y134*		*oo-delivery 0200*
☐ LN-TUK	Boeing 737-705					*2 CFMI CFM56-7B24*	*60328*	*Y134*		*oo-delivery 0300*
☐ LN-	Boeing 737-705					*2 CFMI CFM56-7B24*	*60282*	*Y134*		*to be lsf ILFC 0400*
☐ LN-	Boeing 737-705					*2 CFMI CFM56-7B24*	*60282*	*Y134*		*to be lsf ILFC 1000*
☐ LN-BRA	Boeing 737-405	*24270 / 1726*		*0089*	*0689*	*2 CFMI CFM56-3C1*	*67998*	*Y156*	*JM-DP*	Eirik Blodoks
☐ LN-BRB	Boeing 737-405	*24271 / 1738*		*0089*	*0689*	*2 CFMI CFM56-3C1*	*67998*	*Y156*	*JM-DQ*	Inge Bardsson
☐ LN-BRE	Boeing 737-405	*24643 / 1860*		*0090*	*0590*	*2 CFMI CFM56-3C1*	*67998*	*Y156*	*GQ-EJ*	Hakon V Magnusson / *lsf BBAM*
☐ LN-BRI	Boeing 737-405	*24644 / 1938*	*9M-MLL*	*0090*	*1090*	*2 CFMI CFM56-3C1*	*65317*	*Y156*	*BP-KQ*	Harald Harfagre / *lsf K.R. Partners*
☐ LN-BRP	Boeing 737-405	*25303 / 2137*	*9M-MLK*	*0091*	*1091*	*2 CFMI CFM56-3C1*	*67998*	*Y156*	*AR-DS*	Harald Hardrade / *lsf Lillehammer Co.*
☐ LN-BRQ	Boeing 737-405	*25348 / 2148*		*0091*	*1091*	*2 CFMI CFM56-3C1*	*65317*	*Y156*	*AR-EF*	Harald Grafell
☐ LN-BUF	Boeing 737-405	*25795 / 2867*		*0097*	*0497*	*2 CFMI CFM56-3C1*	*64863*	*Y156*	*AM-EP*	Magnus den gode / *lsf CITG*

COAST AIR, K/S = BX / CST — Haugesund-Karmoey

Postboks 126, N-4262 Avaldsnes, Norway ☎ 52 83 41 10 Tx: none Fax: 52 84 03 74 SITA: n/a
F: 1988 ♟♟♟ 30 Head: Harry Aase IATA: 970 ICAO: COAST CENTER Net: http://www.coastair.no

registration	type of aircraft	cn/fn	ex/ex*	mfd	del	powered by	mtow kg	configuration	name/fln/specialitites/remarks
☐ LN-FAJ	BAe 3100 Jetstream 31	*621*	*G-BTXL*	*0083*	*1093*	*2 GA TPE331-10UF-513H*	*6999*	*Y19*	Bokn / *lsf Vestfly K/S*
☐ LN-FAL	BAe 3100 Jetstream 31	*604*	*OY-CLC*	*0082*	*1297*	*2 GA TPE331-10UF-512H*	*6900*	*Y19*	Utsira / *lsf Vestfly K/S*
☐ LN-FAM	BAe 3100 Jetstream 31	*740*	*C-GJPO*	*0087*	*1194*	*2 GA TPE331-10UGR-516H*	*6999*	*Y19*	Feoy
☐ LN-FAV	BAe 3100 Jetstream 31	*606*	*OY-CLB*	*0082*	*1297*	*2 GA TPE331-10UR-516H*	*6900*	*Y19*	Bomlo / *lsf Vestfly K/S*
☐ LN-FAZ	BAe 3100 Jetstream 31	*749*	*C-GJPU*	*0087*	*1194*	*2 GA TPE331-10UGR-516H*	*6999*	*Y19*	Rovcer

COLOR AIR, A/S = CLA (Subsidiary of Color Line / formerly Scan Express Airlines, A/S) — Oslo-Gardermoen

PO Box A, N-2061 Gardermoen, Norway ☎ 63 94 71 00 Tx: none Fax: 63 94 71 10 SITA: n/a
F: 1993 ♟♟♟ 170 Head: Morten Andersen ICAO: PENNANT Net: http://www.colorair.no

registration	type of aircraft	cn/fn	ex/ex*	mfd	del	powered by	mtow kg	configuration	remarks
☐ G-COLB	Boeing 737-3Q8	*26283 / 2383*	*N373TA*	*1092*	*0898*	*2 CFMI CFM56-3C1*	*62142*	*Y136*	*lsf ILFC/sublst/opb UPD in Color Air-cs*
☐ G-COLC	Boeing 737-3Q8	*26286 / 2424*	*N374TA*	*0293*	*0898*	*2 CFMI CFM56-3C1*	*62142*	*Y136*	*lsf ILFC/sublst/opb UPD in Color Air-cs*
☐ G-COLE	Boeing 737-3Q8	*24962 / 2139*	*PP-VOX*	*0091*	*1198*	*2 CFMI CFM56-3C1*	*61235*	*Y136*	*lsf GECA/sublst/opb UPD in Color Air-cs*

CORONET NORGE, A/S — Oslo-Fornebu SPB & Notodden

Postboks 2486 Solli, N-0202 Oslo, Norway ☎ 67 80 50 33 Tx: none Fax: 67 80 50 39 SITA: n/a
F: 1969 ♟♟♟ n/a Head: Christian Hagemann Net: http://www.coronet.no

registration	type of aircraft	cn/fn	ex/ex*	mfd	del	powered by	mtow kg	remarks
☐ LN-NAA	Cessna U206F Stationair II	*U20603199*	*N11KB*	*0076*	*0498*	*1 CO IO-520-F*	*1633*	*lsf pvt / Floats*
☐ LN-SEA	Cessna 208 Caravan I	*20800173*	*OY-IRP*	*0089*	*0498*	*1 PWC PT6A-114*	*3630*	Cindy / *lsf AS Br.Michaelsen/Amphibian*

DAKOTA NORWAY (Stiftelsen Dakota Norway) — Sandefjord-Torp

Sandefjord Lufthavn, N-3233 Sandefjord, Norway ☎ 33 47 03 00 Tx: none Fax: 33 46 26 06 SITA: n/a
F: n/a ♟♟♟ n/a Head: n/a Net: n/a Non-profit organisation conducting historical DC-3 flights.

registration	type of aircraft	cn/fn	ex/ex*	mfd	del	powered by	mtow kg
☐ LN-WND	Boeing (Douglas) DC-3A (C-53D-DO)	*11750*	*DO-9*	*0043*		*2 PW R-1830*	*11431*

EUROPEAN FLIGHT CENTER, A/S (formerly European Helicopter Center, A/S) **Sandefjord-Torp**

Sandefjord lufthavn, N-3233 Sandefjord, Norway ☎ 33 47 00 50 Tx: none Fax: 33 47 02 12 SITA: n/a
F: 1996 ⁂ 20 Head: Ole Aronsen Net: n/a Aircraft below MTOW 1361kg: Robinson R22 & R44

☐ LN-OAC	Eurocopter (Aerosp.) AS350B2 Ecureuil	*2511*	*D-HMIR*	*0091*	*0897*	*1 TU Arriel 1D1*	*2250*			*lsf ABN Amro Bank AB*

FIRDAFLY, A/S (Seasonal April-October ops only) **Sandane-Sjoflyplass**

Postboks 183, N-6860 Sandane, Norway ☎ 57 86 53 88 Tx: none Fax: 57 86 53 20 SITA: n/a
F: 1976 ⁂ 6 Head: Hakon Lundestad Net: n/a

☐ LN-ALX	Cessna U206G Stationair 6 II	*U20605407*	*N6300U*	*0080*		*1 CO IO-520-F*	*1633*			*Floats*
☐ LN-BFQ	Cessna U206D Super Skywagon	*U206-1352*	*N72286*	*0069*		*1 CO IO-520-F*	*1633*			*Floats*

FJELLANGER-WIDEROE, A/S **Oslo-Fornebu**

Postboks 190, N-1330 Fornebu, Norway ☎ 67 58 70 00 Tx: none Fax: 67 58 70 01 SITA: n/a
F: 1935 ⁂ 220 Head: Reidar W. Bye Net: n/a

☐ LN-MTA	Cessna U206G Stationair 6 II	*U20605641*	*N5322X*	*0080*	*0095*	*1 CO IO-520-F*	*1633*	*Photo*		
☐ LN-SFT	Fairchild (Swearingen) SA226T Merlin IIIB	*T-342*	*N342NX*	*0080*	*1288*	*2 GA TPE331-10U-512G*	*6350*	*Photo / Survey*		*Pollution Control*
☐ LN-FAH	Twin (Aero) Turbo Commander 690B	*11367*	*OY-BEJ*	*0077*		*2 GA TPE331-5-251K*	*4649*	*Photo*		
☐ LN-FWA	Twin (Aero) Jetprop Commander 840 (690C)	*11681*	*SE-IUV*	*0081*	*0692*	*2 GA TPE331-5-254K*	*4683*	*Photo*		

FJELLFLY **Hovden**

Postboks 45, N-4695 Hovden i Setesdal, Norway ☎ 37 93 96 07 Tx: none Fax: 37 93 98 44 SITA: n/a
F: 1977 ⁂ 6 Head: Einar A. Andersen Net: n/a Aircraft below MTOW 1361 kg: Hughes 269C (300C).

☐ LN-OHR	Bell 206B JetRanger III	*2491*	*OY-HDJ*	*0078*	*0797*	*1 AN 250-C20B*	*1451*			*lsf Hovden Helicopter & Rotor A/S*
☐ LN-ALC	Cessna U206G Stationair	*U20603657*	*N7426N*	*0082*		*1 CO IO-520-F*	*1633*			*lsf Hiltec Marine A/S/Floats/Wheel-Skis*
☐ LN-ALD	Cessna U206G Stationair	*U20603628*	*N7355N*	*0082*		*1 CO IO-520-F*	*1633*			*lsf Fjellfly Invest / Floats/Wheel-Skis*
☐ LN-HAM	Cessna U206F Stationair II	*U20602689*	*N33244*	*0075*		*1 CO IO-520-F*	*1633*			*lsf pvt / Floats/Wheel-Skis*

FONNAFLY Sjö, A/S = NOF **Rosendal / Bergen / Voss**

n/n, N-5470 Rosendal, Norway ☎ 53 48 02 22 Tx: 42872 harbo n Fax: 53 48 19 86 SITA: n/a
F: 1971 ⁂ 7 Head: Jostein Nerhus ICAO: FONNA Net: n/a

☐ LN-BFP	Cessna U206F Stationair	*U20601928*		*0073*		*1 CO IO-520-F*	*1633*			Fonna 13 / *lsf pvt / Floats*
☐ LN-HAI	Cessna U206F Stationair II	*U20603058*	*N4696Q*	*0076*		*1 CO IO-520-F*	*1633*			Fonna 15 / *lsf pvt / Floats*
☐ LN-HON	Cessna U206G Stationair 6 II	*U20605475*		*0080*		*1 CO IO-520-F*	*1633*			Fonna 17 / *lsf pvt / Floats*
☐ LN-HOZ	Cessna U206G Stationair 6 II	*U20604279*	*SE-GYK*	*0078*		*1 CO IO-520-F*	*1633*			Fonna 14 / *lsf pvt / Floats*
☐ LN-IKA	Cessna TU206G Turbo Stationair 6 II	*U20606251*	*N6356Z*	*0081*		*1 CO TSIO-520-M*	*1633*			Fonna 11 / *Floats*
☐ LN-MAQ	Cessna U206G Stationair 6	*U20603733*	*SE-GZY*	*0077*		*1 CO IO-520-F*	*1633*			Fonna 12 / *lsf pvt / Floats*
☐ LN-TEP	Cessna U206G Stationair 6 II	*U20605186*	*N5305U*	*0079*		*1 CO IO-520-F*	*1633*			Fonna 10 / *lsf Voss Fly A/S / Floats*

FOTONOR, A/S **Sandefjord-Torp**

Postboks 1310, N-3205 Sandefjord, Norway ☎ 33 42 08 00 Tx: none Fax: 33 42 08 01 SITA: n/a
F: 1985 ⁂ 15 Head: Oivind Aase Net: n/a Aircraft below MTOW 1361kg: Cessna 177RG.

☐ LN-NAB	Piper PA-31-310 Navajo	*31-8012029*	*OY-BYJ*	*0080*	*0294*	*2 LY TIO-540-A2C*	*3103*			
☐ LN-NPZ	Piper PA-31-310 Navajo C	*31-7512051*		*0075*	*0195*	*2 LY TIO-540-A2C*	*3103*			

GOFJELD-FLY, A/S **Oslo-Fornebu**

Postboks 132, N-1330 Fornebu, Norway ☎ 67 53 02 31 Tx: none Fax: none SITA: n/a
F: n/a ⁂ n/a Head: n/a Net: n/a

☐ LN-LMJ	Cessna U206C Super Skywagon	*U206-1163*	*N29205*	*0068*		*1 CO IO-520-F*	*1633*			*Floats*

GUARD AIR, A/S = FB / JAP **Oslo-Gardermoen & Skien**

Peder Bogensvei 4B, N-3215 Sandefjord, Norway ☎ 33 42 78 80 Tx: none Fax: 33 48 28 01 SITA: n/a
F: 1993 ⁂ 23 Head: Tor Espen Braten ICAO: GUARD AIR Net: n/a

☐ LN-BEN	Cessna T210M Turbo Centurion II	*21061584*	*OH-CHP*	*0076*	*0096*	*1 CO TSIO-520-R*	*1724*	*Photo / Survey*		
☐ LN-BEP	Piper PA-31-310 Navajo B	*31-7300915*		*0073*	*0096*	*2 LY TIO-540-A2C*	*2948*	*Photo / Survey*		
☐ LN-FKE	Piper PA-31-310 Navajo	*31-293*	*SE-FFE*	*0068*	*0097*	*2 LY TIO-540-A1B*	*2948*	*Photo / Survey*		*lsf pvt*
☐ LN-BER	Dornier 228-212	*8192*	*F-ODYC*	*0090*	*0997*	*2 GA TPE331-5A-252D*	*6400*	*Y19/Frtr/Photo*		
☐ TF-ELH	Dornier 228-201	*8070*	*SE-KVV*	*0085*	*0298*	*2 GA TPE331-5-252D*	*6200*	*Y19/Frtr/Photo*		*lsf ICB*

HANGAR 5 AIRSERVICES NORWAY, A/S = HAX (Subsidiary of Hangar 5 Airservice, ApS, Denmark) **Oslo-Gardermoen**

Postboks 28, N-2060 Gardermoen-Lufthavn, Norway ☎ 63 97 85 55 Tx: none Fax: 63 97 80 86 SITA: n/a
F: 1995 ⁂ 15 Head: Trond E. Torgersen ICAO: SCOOP Net: n/a Aircraft below MTOW 1361kg: Cessna 172

☐ LN-PBD	Cessna 208 Caravan I	*20800105*	*OY-TCA*	*0086*		*1 PWC PT6A-114*	*3630*	*Freighter*		*lsf Alebco Corp. ApS*
☐ LN-PBB	Cessna 208B Grand Caravan	*208B0302*	*OY-TCB*	*0092*		*1 PWC PT6A-114A*	*3969*	*Freighter*		*lsf Alebco Corp. ApS*
☐ LN-PBE	Cessna 208B Grand Caravan	*208B0587*		*0092*	*0197*	*1 PWC PT6A-114A*	*3969*	*Freighter*		*lsf Alebco Corp. ApS*
☐ SE-DRT	Cessna 500 Citation Eagle	*500-0311*	*N39RE*	*0076*	*0097*	*2 PWC JT15D-1A*	*5670*			*lsf Alebco Corp. ApS / cvtd Citation*

HELIFLY, A/S **Jarlsberg & Sandefjord-Torp**

Postboks 31, N-3170 Sem, Norway ☎ 33 38 04 00 Tx: none Fax: 33 38 09 50 SITA: n/a
F: 1989 ⁂ 16 Head: Torgeir Jacobsen Net: http://www.helifly.no

☐ LN-OME	MD Helicopters MD 500E (Hughes 369E)	*0335E*	*N10NT*	*0089*	*1295*	*1 AN 250-C20R2*	*1361*			
☐ LN-OMP	MD Helicopters MD 500E (Hughes 369E)	*0177E*	*SE-HRB*	*0086*		*1 AN 250-C20B*	*1361*			*lsf Air Prospekt A/S*
☐ LN-OMG	Eurocopter (Aerosp.) SA315B Lama	*2443*	*SE-HGY*	*0076*	*0395*	*1 TU Artouste IIIB*	*1950*			
☐ LN-OTE	Eurocopter (Aerosp.) SA315B Lama	*2338 / 36*	*SE-JDN*	*0073*	*0698*	*1 TU Artouste IIIB1*	*1950*			*cvtd Alouette II*
☐ LN-OML	MD Helicopters MD 520N (Hughes 500N)	*LN054*	*SE-JBF*	*0093*		*1 AN 250-C20R2*	*1520*			*lsf Stang Eiendom A/S*

HELIKOPTER SERVICE, AS = L5 / HKS (Subsidiary of Helikopter Services Group, ASA) **Stavanger-Sola / Bergen-Flesland & BNN/BOO/FRO/KSU**

Postboks 522, N-4055 Stavanger Lufthavn, Norway ☎ 51 94 10 00 Tx: 76431 norep n Fax: 51 94 13 20 SITA: n/a
F: 1956 ⁂ 900 Head: Jakob Bae ICAO: HELIBUS Net: http://www.hesgrp.com

☐ LN-OMJ	Eurocopter (Aerosp.) AS365N2 Dauphin 2	*6301*	*F-WQEZ*	*0087*	*1196*	*2 TU Arriel 1C2*	*4250*	*SAR*		*lsf Eurocopter France*
☐ LN-OMN	Eurocopter (Aerosp.) AS365N2 Dauphin 2	*6423*	*F-GHXG*	*0091*	*0493*	*2 TU Arriel 1C2*	*4250*	*SAR*		*lsf Heliwest A/S*
☐ LN-	Eurocopter (Aerosp.) AS365N4 Dauphin 2					*2 TU Arriel 2C*	*4800*			*oo-delivery 0099*
☐ LN-	Eurocopter (Aerosp.) AS365N4 Dauphin 2					*2 TU Arriel 2C*	*4800*			*oo-delivery 0099*
☐ LN-	Eurocopter (Aerosp.) AS365N4 Dauphin 2					*2 TU Arriel 2C*	*4800*			*oo-delivery 0099*
☐ LN-	Eurocopter (Aerosp.) AS365N4 Dauphin 2					*2 TU Arriel 2C*	*4800*			*oo-delivery 0099*
☐ LN-	Eurocopter (Aerosp.) AS365N4 Dauphin 2					*2 TU Arriel 2C*	*4800*			*oo-delivery 0099*
☐ LN-	Eurocopter (Aerosp.) AS365N4 Dauphin 2					*2 TU Arriel 2C*	*4800*			*oo-delivery 0099*
☐ LN-OMM	Bell 214ST	*28199*		*0089*	*0590*	*2 GE CT7-2A*	*7938*	*SAR*		
☐ LN-OBF	Eurocopter (Aerosp.) AS332L1 Super Puma	*2381*	*F-WTNH**	*0092*	*1293*	*2 TU Makila 1A1*	*8600*			*lsf Helicopter Lease Int'l (Three) Ltd*
☐ LN-OBQ	Eurocopter (Aerosp.) AS332L1 Super Puma	*2312*		*0690*	*1293*	*2 TU Makila 1A1*	*8600*			*lsf Helicopter Lease Int'l (One) Ltd*
☐ LN-ODA	Eurocopter (Aerosp.) AS332L Super Puma	*2073*	*G-PUML*	*0083*		*2 TU Makila 1A*	*8600*			
☐ LN-OHA	Eurocopter (Aerosp.) AS332L2 S.Puma II	*2396*		*0093*	*0893*	*2 TU Makila 1A2*	*9150*			*lsf Heliwest A/S*
☐ LN-OHB	Eurocopter (Aerosp.) AS332L2 S.Puma II	*2398*	*F-WYMD**	*0093*	*1293*	*2 TU Makila 1A2*	*9150*			*lsf Heliwest A/S*
☐ LN-OHC	Eurocopter (Aerosp.) AS332L2 S.Puma II	*2393*		*0095*	*0795*	*2 TU Makila 1A2*	*9150*			*lsf Helicopter Leasing (Jersey) Ltd*
☐ LN-OHD	Eurocopter (Aerosp.) AS332L2 S.Puma II	*2395*		*0097*	*0397*	*2 TU Makila 1A2*	*9150*			*lsf FinansSkandic AB*
☐ LN-OHE	Eurocopter (Aerosp.) AS332L2 S.Puma II	*2474*		*0098*	*0598*	*2 TU Makila 1A2*	*9300*			*lsf Helicopter Lease Int'l (Four) Ltd*
☐ LN-OHF	Eurocopter (Aerosp.) AS332L2 S.Puma II	*2484*		*0098*	*1198*	*2 TU Makila 1A2*	*9150*			*lsf Helicopter Lease Int'l (Three) Ltd*
☐ LN-OHG	Eurocopter (Aerosp.) AS332L2 S.Puma II	*2493*		*0099*	*0199*	*2 TU Makila 1A2*	*9150*			*lsf Helicopter Lease Int'l (Five) Ltd*
☐ LN-OMF	Eurocopter (Aerosp.) AS332L Super Puma	*2067*	*G-PUMK*	*0083*		*2 TU Makila 1A*	*8600*			
☐ LN-OMH	Eurocopter (Aerosp.) AS332L Super Puma	*2113*	*HZ-RH4*	*0084*		*2 TU Makila 1A*	*8600*			
☐ LN-OMI	Eurocopter (Aerosp.) AS332L Super Puma	*2123*	*G-PUMJ*	*0084*	*0084*	*2 TU Makila 1A*	*8600*			
☐ LN-OMT	Eurocopter (Aerosp.) AS332L1 Super Puma	*2468*		*0097*	*1297*	*2 TU Makila 1A1*	*8600*			*lsf FinansSkandic AB*
☐ LN-OPH	Eurocopter (Aerosp.) AS332L1 Super Puma	*2347*		*0091*		*2 TU Makila 1A1*	*8600*			*lsf GE Capital Services (EEF) Ltd*
☐ C-GQCH	Eurocopter (Aerosp.) AS332L Super Puma	*2139*	*LN-OLF*	*0085*		*2 TU Makila 1A*	*8600*			*lst CHI*
☐ C-GTCH	Eurocopter (Aerosp.) AS332L Super Puma	*2048*	*LN-OMD*	*0082*		*2 TU Makila 1A*	*8600*			*lst CHI*
☐ C-GVCH	Eurocopter (Aerosp.) AS332L Super Puma	*2074*	*LN-OLA*	*0083*		*2 TU Makila 1A*	*8600*			*lst CHI*
☐ OY-HMH	Eurocopter (Aerosp.) AS332L Super Puma	*2053*	*LN-OME*	*0083*		*2 TU Makila 1A*	*8600*			*lst Maersk Helicopters*
☐ OY-HMI	Eurocopter (Aerosp.) AS332L Super Puma	*2103*	*LN-OLD*	*0084*		*2 TU Makila 1A*	*8600*			*lst Maersk Helicopters*
☐ OY-HMJ	Eurocopter (Aerosp.) AS332L Super Puma	*2082*	*LN-OLB*	*0083*		*2 TU Makila 1A*	*8600*			*lst Maersk Helicopters*
☐ VH-LAF	Eurocopter (Aerosp.) AS332L1 Super Puma	*2319*	*LN-OBT*	*0890*	*1293*	*2 TU Makila 1A1*	*8600*			*lst Lloyd Helicopters*
☐ VH-LAG	Eurocopter (Aerosp.) AS332L1 Super Puma	*2352*	*LN-OBU*	*0091*	*1293*	*2 TU Makila 1A1*	*8600*			*lst Lloyd Helicopters*
☐ VH-LHG	Eurocopter (Aerosp.) AS332L1 Super Puma	*2317*	*LN-OBR*	*0790*	*1293*	*2 TU Makila 1A1*	*8600*			*lst Lloyd Helicopters*
☐ LN-OQB	Sikorsky S-61N	*61807*		*0078*		*2 GE CT58-140-2*	*9299*			
☐ LN-OQM	Sikorsky S-61N	*61764*		*0077*		*2 GE CT58-140-2*	*9299*			
☐ LN-OQQ	Sikorsky S-61N	*61814*	*OY-HGG*	*0078*		*2 GE CT58-140-2*	*9299*			
☐ LN-OQU	Sikorsky S-61N	*61816*		*0078*		*2 GE CT58-140-2*	*9299*			
☐ LN-ORC	Sikorsky S-61N	*61817*		*0078*		*2 GE CT58-140-2*	*9299*			
☐ LN-OSJ	Sikorsky S-61N	*61715*	*N53094*	*0074*		*2 GE CT58-140-2*	*9299*			
☐ LN-OST	Sikorsky S-61N	*61738*		*0074*		*2 GE CT58-140-2*	*9299*			
☐ OY-HDO	Sikorsky S-61N	*61740*	*LN-OSU*	*0075*		*2 GE CT58-140-2*	*9299*			*lst GRL*
☐ PT-YCF	Sikorsky S-61N	*61757*	*LN-OQH*	*0076*		*2 GE CT58-140-2*	*9299*			*lst Aeroleo Taxi Aéreo*

232 registration type of aircraft *cn/fn* *ex/ex** *mfd* *del* *powered by* *mtow kg* *configuration* *selcal* *name/fln/specialitites/remarks*

HELIKOPTERTENESTE, A/S (Subsidiary of Airlift, A/S)

Kinsarvik

Head office, N-5780 Kinsarvik, Norway ☎ 53 66 33 00 Tx: none Fax: 53 66 34 50 SITA: n/a
F: 1982 ⁂ 16 Head: Arne Mehl Net: n/a

☐ LN-OMS	MD Helicopters MD 500D (Hughes 369D)	911067D	SE-HMB	0081		1 AN 250-C20B	1361			lsf Airlift
☐ LN-OCE	Eurocopter (Aerosp.) SA315B Lama	2179	5V-MAF	0071	0390	1 TU Artouste IIIB1	1950			lsf Airlift
☐ LN-OMU	Eurocopter (Aerosp.) SA315B Lama	2643	F-WXFC*	0083		1 TU Artouste IIIB1	1950			lsf Airlift
☐ LN-OCD	Eurocopter (Aerosp.) AS350B1 Ecureuil	2207		0089	0589	1 TU Arriel 1D	2200			lsf Airlift
☐ LN-OCF	Eurocopter (Aerosp.) AS350B2 Ecureuil	2478		0091	0591	1 TU Arriel 1D1	2250			lsf Airlift

HELI-TEAM, A/S

Stangnes Syd-Harstad

Postboks 2019, N-9401 Harstad, Norway ☎ 77 07 15 77 Tx: none Fax: 77 07 12 88 SITA: n/a
F: 1988 ⁂ 6 Head: Mrs Bente Slatto Steien Net: n/a

☐ LN-ORH	Eurocopter (Aerosp.) AS350B2 Ecureuil	2843	OY-HJC	0095	0797	1 TU Arriel 1D1	2250			
☐ LN-ORJ	Eurocopter (Aerosp.) AS350B1 Ecureuil	2212	N501RP	0089	1093	1 TU Arriel 1D	2200			
☐ LN-ORT	Eurocopter (Aerosp.) AS350B2 Ecureuil	1883	N48CD	0086	0596	1 TU Arriel 1D1	2250			ex Heli-Team / cvtd AS350B

HELITOURIST, A/S

Aurland

Postboks 98, N-5745 Aurland, Norway ☎ 57 63 13 00 Tx: none Fax: 57 63 13 01 SITA: n/a
F: n/a ⁂ 8 Head: Leif Turlid Net: n/a

☐ LN-ORA	Eurocopter (Aerosp.) SA315B Lama	2665	F-GECS	0085	0895	1 TU Artouste IIIB1	1950			
☐ LN-ORD	Eurocopter (Aerosp.) SA315B Lama	2172 / 18	F-GHCJ	0081	0596	1 TU Artouste IIIB1	1950			cvtd Alouette II

HELI-TRANS, A/S = 5H / HTA

Trondheim-Vaernes

Trondheim Lufthavn-Vaernes, N-7500 Stjoerdal, Norway ☎ 74 82 28 25 Tx: none Fax: 74 82 76 25 SITA: n/a
F: n/a ⁂ 15 Head: Ivar Hustad ICAO: SCANBIRD Net: n/a Aircraft below MTOW 1361kg: Hughes 369HS (500C).

☐ LN-OMY	Eurocopter (Aerosp.) AS350BA Ecureuil	1017	SE-HIA	0078	1093	1 TU Arriel 1B	2100			cvtd AS350B
☐ LN-OPC	Eurocopter (Aerosp.) AS350BA Ecureuil	1845	OE-KXF	0085	0597	1 TU Arriel 1B	2100			cvtd AS350B
☐ LN-AZN	Piper PA-31-310 Navajo	31-475	OY-AZN	0069		2 LY TIO-540-A1A	2948			lsf Air Pegaus A/S
☐ LN-HTA	Dornier 228-202	8127	D-CBDE	0087	0597	2 GA TPE331-5-252D	6200			lsf Deutsche Financial Services Corp.

HESNES AIR, A/S

Sandefjord-Torp

Postboks 40 Teie, N-3106 Tonsberg, Norway ☎ 33 30 44 73 Tx: none Fax: 33 32 30 30 SITA: n/a
F: 1996 ⁂ 2 Head: Trond Brygard Net: n/a

☐ LN-OMW	MD Helicopters MD 500E (Hughes 369E)	0498E	SE-JBA	0092		1 AN 250-C20R	1361			
☐ LN-ORK	Eurocopter (Aerosp.) AS350BA Ecureuil	1056	SE-JDE	0079	0398	1 TU Arriel 1B	2100			cvtd AS350B

KATO AIR, A/S = KAT

Harstad-Evenes

Harstad/Narvik lufthavn, Evenes, N-8534 Liland, Norway ☎ 77 08 13 80 Tx: none Fax: 77 08 13 85 SITA: n/a
F: 1995 ⁂ 8 Head: Torlaug Karlsen ICAO: KATO-AIR Net: n/a Aircraft below MTOW 1361kg: Cessna 172

☐ LN-KKK	Piper PA-34-220T Seneca III	3449010	SE-KEP	0097	0798	2 CO TSIO-360-KB	2155			lsf ABN Amro Bank AB
☐ LN-TSC	Piper PA-31-350 Navajo Chieftain	31-7852119	N27720	0078		2 LY TIO-540-J2BD	3175			
☐ LN-KJK	Cessna 208B Grand Caravan	208B0554	N1267A	0096	0297	1 PWC PT6A-114A	3969			
☐ LN-HTB	Dornier 228-100	7005	D-IDOM	0082	0098	2 GA TPE331-5-252D	5670			lsf Bedriftsfinans A/S

LOFOTFLY, A/S (Seasonal summer ops only)

Svolvaer

Postboks 45, N-8301 Svolvaer, Norway ☎ 76 07 27 11 Tx: none Fax: 76 07 27 11 SITA: n/a
F: 1991 ⁂ 2 Head: Robert Johansen Net: n/a

☐ LN-DBF	Cessna U206B Super Skywagon	U206-0779	N3479L	0067	0794	1 CO IO-550-F	1633			Floats

LOKENFLY

Oslo-Gardermoen & Kjeller

Gamle Trondheimsvei 66, N-2020 Skedsmokorset, Norway ☎ 63 87 61 57 Tx: none Fax: 63 87 88 43 SITA: n/a
F: 1992 ⁂ 1 Head: Ole E. Loken Net: n/a

☐ LN-ALI	Piper PA-34-200T Seneca II	34-7970259	N2822A	0079		2 CO TSIO-360-E	1999			

LUFTTRANSPORT, A/S = LTR (Subsidiary of Helikopter Service, A/S)

Tromso & AES/BNN/FBU/KKN/LYR

Postboks 2500, N-9005 Tromso, Norway ☎ 77 60 83 00 Tx: 65885 lufta n Fax: 77 60 83 83 SITA: n/a
F: 1955 ⁂ 123 Head: Bjorn Moe ICAO: LUFTTRANSPORT Net: http://www.lufttransport.no

☐ LN-OSF	Eurocopter (Aerosp.) SA315B Lama	2580		0079		1 TU Artouste IIIB	1950			
☐ LN-OTB	Eurocopter (Aerosp.) SA315B Lama	2604		0081	0491	1 TU Artouste IIIB1	1950			
☐ LN-OLG	Eurocopter (Aerosp.) AS350B2 Ecureuil	2198		0089		1 TU Arriel 1D1	2250			cvtd AS350B1 / opf Police
☐ LN-OPB	Eurocopter (Aerosp.) AS350B1 Ecureuil	1940		0086	0995	1 TU Arriel 1D	2200			lsf Caseb Invest A/S / sub-lst HFL
☐ LN-OPE	Eurocopter (Aerosp.) AS350B1 Ecureuil	2183		0089	0995	1 TU Arriel 1D	2200			lsf KS Ecureuil / sub-lst HFL
☐ LN-OTA	Eurocopter (Aerosp.) AS350B1 Ecureuil	1902	SE-JAC	0086	0197	1 TU Arriel 1D	2200			lsf Troms Heli A/S / sub-lst HFL
☐ LN-OLN	Eurocopter (Aerosp.) SA365N Dauphin 2	6115	G-BLUO	0085		2 TU Arriel 1C	4000	EMS		
☐ LN-OLT	Eurocopter (Aerosp.) SA365N Dauphin 2	6140	G-BLUP	0085		2 TU Arriel 1C	4000	EMS		
☐ LN-OPD	Eurocopter (Aerosp.) SA365N Dauphin 2	6067		0083	0995	2 TU Arriel 1D	4000	EMS		
☐ LN-MOA	Beech King Air 200	BB-582	N78LB	0080	0995	2 PWC PT6A-41	5670			
☐ LN-MOB	Beech King Air 200	BB-584	N400WP	0080	0995	2 PWC PT6A-41	5670	EMS		
☐ LN-MOC	Beech King Air B200	BB-1449	N200KA	0093	0995	2 PWC PT6A-42	5670	EMS		lsf Finova Capital Corp.
☐ LN-MOD	Beech King Air B200	BB-1459	N8163R	0093	0995	2 PWC PT6A-42	5670	EMS		
☐ LN-MOE	Beech King Air B200	BB-1460	N8164G	0093	0995	2 PWC PT6A-42	5670	EMS		lsf Finova Capital Corp.
☐ LN-MOF	Beech King Air B200	BB-1461	N8261E	0093	0995	2 PWC PT6A-42	5670	EMS		lsf Finova Capital Corp.
☐ LN-MOG	Beech King Air B200	BB-1465	N8214T	0093	0995	2 PWC PT6A-42	5670	EMS		lsf Finova Capital Corp.
☐ LN-MOH	Beech King Air B200	BB-1466	N8216Z	0093	0995	2 PWC PT6A-42	5670	EMS		lsf Finova Capital Corp.
☐ LN-MOI	Beech King Air B200	BB-1470	N8225Z	0093	0995	2 PWC PT6A-42	5670	EMS		lsf Finova Capital Corp.
☐ LN-LYR	Dornier 228-202K	8166	D-CICA	0088	0594	2 GA TPE331-5-252D	6200			lsf Dornier Luftfahrt GmbH

MASTER AVIATION, A/S = MSD

Sandefjord-Torp

Postboks 123, N-1330 Fornebu, Norway ☎ 33 48 60 30 Tx: none Fax: 33 48 60 31 SITA: n/a
F: 1994 ⁂ 21 Head: Alf Remseth ICAO: MASTER AIR Net: n/a Aircraft below MTOW 1361kg: Cessna 172

☐ LN-TWC	Piper PA-44-180 Seminole	44-7995289	N7174Q	0079		2 LY O-360-E1A6D	1724			lsf Stenhjem Invest A/S
☐ LN-VIU	Beech King Air 200	BB-216	OY-AUZ	0077	0898	2 PWC PT6A-41	5670			lsf Scan Equipment Norway-Remseth

MIDT-FLY, A/S

Steinkjer

Bolas, N-7700 Steinkjer, Norway ☎ 74 14 33 44 Tx: none Fax: 74 16 77 66 SITA: n/a
F: 1996 ⁂ 2 Head: Ernst Bolas Net: n/a

☐ LN-BOL	Cessna U206G Stationair 6 II	U20605504	SE-INO	0080	0498	1 CO IO-520-F	1633			
☐ LN-HPO	Cessna U206G Stationair	U20603816	TF-HRO	0077	0997	1 CO IO-520-F	1633			

NOR AVIATION, A/S = NOO

Oslo-Fornebu

Postboks 50, N-1330 Fornebu, Norway ☎ 67 53 40 60 Tx: none Fax: 67 53 04 50 SITA: n/a
F: 1996 ⁂ 40 Head: Tor Bratli ICAO: MIDNIGHT Net: http://www.noravition.no

☐ LN-NOA	Beech King Air B200	BB-829	N829AJ	0080	0297	2 PWC PT6A-42	5670	EMS		lsf Sundt A/S
☐ LN-NLC	Cessna 650 Citation III	650-0028	N328QS	0084	0297	2 GA TFE731-3B-100S	9752	EMS	GS-MP	lsf Petter C.G. Sundt A/S
☐ LN-NLD	Cessna 650 Citation III	650-0070	N370TG	0085	0297	2 GA TFE731-3B-100S	9752	EMS		lsf Petter C.G. Sundt A/S

NORDIC AVIATION RESOURCES, Ltd (Subsidiary of Luftfartverket)

Oslo-Fornebu

PO Box 8124 DEP, N-0032 Oslo, Norway ☎ 22 94 23 71 Tx: none Fax: 22 94 23 53 SITA: n/a
F: 1997 ⁂ n/a Head: Trond Nordeng Net: n/a Aircraft below MTOW 1361kg: Hughes 269C (300C)

☐ LN-ILS	De Havilland DHC-8-103 Dash 8	396		0095	0498	2 PWC PW121	15650	Calibrator		opf Luftfartverket

NORDLANDSFLY, A/S

Mosjoen

Postboks 171, N-8651 Mosjoen, Norway ☎ 75 18 95 00 Tx: none Fax: 75 18 95 01 SITA: n/a
F: 1985 ⁂ 2 Head: Anne Sevenusen Net: n/a

☐ LN-OCC	MD Helicopters MD 500E (Hughes 369E)	0252E		0087		1 AN 250-C20B	1361			lsf KS Nesseby Invest A/S
☐ LN-OSK	MD Helicopters MD 500E (Hughes 369E)	0261E	SE-HSR	0088	0392	1 AN 250-C20B	1361			
☐ LN-ODD	Eurocopter (Aerosp.) SA315B Lama	2578	SE-HRX	0079	0698	1 TU Artouste IIIB	1950			lsf Lama Invest A/S

NORSK FLYTJENESTE, A/S = NIR (Subsidiary of Nyge Aero, AB)

Sandefjord-Torp

Sandefjord Lufthavn, N-3233 Sandefjord, Norway ☎ 33 47 02 30 Tx: none Fax: 33 47 02 20 SITA: n/a
F: 1961 ⁂ 12 Head: Tor Lundstrom ICAO: NORSEMAN Net: n/a Aircraft below MTOW 1361kg: Slingsby T67M200 Company operates Air Target Support flights for the Royal Norwegian Armed Forces.

☐ LN-HAE	Cessna 310R II	310R0525	TF-EUT	0076		2 CO IO-520-M	2495			
☐ LN-HPT	Cessna 310R II	310R0083	OY-BIW	0075	1289	2 CO IO-520-M	2495			
☐ LN-MAJ	Cessna 310R II	310R0627	N98871	0076		2 CO IO-520-M	2495			
☐ LN-NPX	Cessna 310P	310P0229	N5729M	0069		2 CO IO-470-VO	2359			

233 registration type of aircraft cn/fn ex/ex* mfd del powered by mtow kg configuration selcal name/fln/specialitites/remarks

NORSK HELIKOPTER, A/S = NOR (Associated with Bristow Helicopters)

Stavanger-Sola

Postboks 171, N-4050 Sola, Norway ☎ 51 64 66 00 Tx: none Fax: 51 64 66 99 SITA: n/a
F: 1993 ✝✝✝ 93 Head: Graham Vavangas ICAO: NORSK Net: n/a

registration	type of aircraft	cn/fn	ex/ex*	mfd	del	powered by	mtow kg	configuration	selcal	name/fin/specialitites/remarks
LN-ONZ	Sikorsky S-76C+	760456		0096	0796	2 TU Arriel 2S1	5307			lsf Sikorsky Export Corp.
LN-OBA	Eurocopter (Aerosp.) AS332L1 Super Puma	2384		0092	0096	2 TU Makila 1A1	8600			lsf Brilog Leasing Ltd
LN-OLC	Eurocopter (Aerosp.) AS332L Super Puma	2083	JA6782	0083	0798	2 TU Makila 1A	8600			lsf Brig-Log Leasing Ltd
LN-ONA	Eurocopter (Aerosp.) AS332L Tiger	2111	G-BLRY	0084	0497	2 TU Makila 1A	8600			lsf Bristow Helicopters
LN-OND	Eurocopter (Aerosp.) AS332L Tiger	2157	G-BLXS	0085	0897	2 TU Makila 1A	8600			lsf Bristow Helicopters
LN-ONH	Eurocopter (Aerosp.) AS332L2 S.Puma II	2488		0099	0299	2 TU Makila 1A2	9150			lsf Brig-Log Leasing Ltd

NORSK LUFTAMBULANSE, A/S = DOC (Norwegian Air Ambulance)

Oslo-Fornebu   Norsk Luftambulanse

Postboks 27, N-1330 Fornebu, Norway ☎ 67 59 27 59 Tx: none Fax: 67 59 27 58 SITA: n/a
F: 1978 ✝✝✝ 110 Head: Per Arne Gulvik ICAO: HELIDOC Net: http://www.sol.no/nla

registration	type of aircraft	cn/fn	ex/ex*	mfd	del	powered by	mtow kg	configuration	selcal	name/fin/specialitites/remarks
LN-OSB	Eurocopter (MBB) BO105CBS-4	S-606	N2913Z	0082		2 AN 250-C20B	2500	EMS		lsf GE Capital Equipment Finance AB
LN-OSE	Eurocopter (MBB) BO105CBS-4	S-634	N2784V	0083		2 AN 250-C20B	2500	EMS		lsf GE Capital Equipment Finance AB
LN-OSI	Eurocopter (MBB) BO105CBS-4	S-609	N29144	0083		2 AN 250-C20B	2500	EMS		lsf GE Capital Equipment Finance AB
LN-OSZ	Eurocopter (MBB) BO105CBS-4	S-666	N4573A	0084	0691	2 AN 250-C20B	2500	EMS		lsf GE Capital Equipment Finance AB
LN-OTD	Eurocopter (MBB) BO105CBS-4	S-433	D-HDMG	0081		2 AN 250-C20B	2500	EMS		lsf GE Capital Equipment Finance AB
D-HCCA	Eurocopter (MBB) BO105CBS	S-147	N90740	0074	0098	2 AN 250-C20B	2500	EMS		lsf AMB
LN-OOA	Eurocopter EC135P1					2 PWC PW206B	2720	EMS		oo-delivery 1099

NORWEGIAN AIR SHUTTLE, A/S = NAX

Oslo-Fornebu, Bergen, Stavanger & Trondheim

Postboks 115, N-1331 Fornebu, Norway ☎ 67 58 37 77 Tx: none Fax: 67 58 32 77 SITA: n/a
F: 1993 ✝✝✝ 90 Head: Stig Willassen ICAO: NOR SHUTTLE Net: n/a

registration	type of aircraft	cn/fn	ex/ex*	mfd	del	powered by	mtow kg	configuration	selcal	name/fin/specialitites/remarks
LN-BBA	Fokker 50 (F27 Mk050)	20130	PH-EXC*	0088	0193	2 PWC PW125B	20820	Y50		lsf Elcon Finans A/S
LN-BBB	Fokker 50 (F27 Mk050)	20131	PH-EXE*	0088	0193	2 PWC PW125B	20820	Y50		lsf Elcon Finans A/S
LN-BBC	Fokker 50 (F27 Mk050)	20134	PH-EXH*	0088	0193	2 PWC PW125B	20820	Y50		lsf Elcon Finans A/S
LN-KKA	Fokker 50 (F27 Mk050)	20117	PH-DLT	0088	0295	2 PWC PW125B	20820	Y50		lsf Heller Financial Inc.
LN-KKD	Fokker 50 (F27 Mk050)	20230	PT-SLR	0091	0898	2 PWC PW125B	20820	Y50		lsf Brazilian Aircraft Fin. VII B.V.
LN-KKE	Fokker 50 (F27 Mk050)	20226	PT-SLQ	0091	1098	2 PWC PW125B	20820	Y50		lsf Brazilian Aircraft Fin. VIII B.V.

SCANDINAVIAN AIRLINES SAS & SCANDINAVIAN COMMUTER – see under SE-markings

TEDDY AIR, A/S = ZJ / TED

Skien   TEDDY AIR

Voldsveien 200, N-3729 Skien, Norway ☎ 35 54 66 00 Tx: none Fax: 35 54 67 40 SITA: n/a
F: 1990 ✝✝✝ 32 Head: Tollef Dale ICAO: TEDDYS Net: http://www.teddyair.com

registration	type of aircraft	cn/fn	ex/ex*	mfd	del	powered by	mtow kg	configuration	selcal	name/fin/specialitites/remarks
LN-TDY	Embraer 110P1 Bandeirante (EMB-110P1)	110456	N220EB	0084	0595	2 PWC PT6A-34	5670	Y15		
SE-LEP	Saab SF340A	340A-127	B-12200	0088	0298	2 GE CT7-5A2	12700	Y36		lsf / opb GAO
SE-LES	Saab SF340A	340A-129	B-12299	0088	0398	2 GE CT7-5A2	12700	Y37		lsf / opb GAO

TRANS WING, A/S = TWG

Oslo-Gardermoen

Postboks 41, N-2060 Gardermoen-Lufthavn, Norway ☎ 63 97 88 40 Tx: none Fax: 63 97 88 65 SITA: n/a
F: 1986 ✝✝✝ 15 Head: Per Marius Nilsen ICAO: TRANSWING CARGO Net: n/a

registration	type of aircraft	cn/fn	ex/ex*	mfd	del	powered by	mtow kg	configuration	selcal	name/fin/specialitites/remarks
LN-TWD	Cessna 208B Grand Caravan	208B0266		0091	0791	1 PWC PT6A-114A	3969	Freighter		

VALDRESFLY, A/S = VLF

Oslo-Fornebu & Stenhuset-SPB   Valdresfly

Oksenoeyveien 10, N-1330 Fornebu, Norway ☎ 67 58 35 88 Tx: none Fax: 67 58 36 44 SITA: n/a
F: 1983 ✝✝✝ 4 Head: Tund Hagsveen ICAO: VALFLY Net: n/a

registration	type of aircraft	cn/fn	ex/ex*	mfd	del	powered by	mtow kg	configuration	selcal	name/fin/specialitites/remarks
TF-ELF	Dornier 228-201	8046	LN-NVC	0084		2 GA TPE331-5-252D	5980	Y19		lsf ICB

WIDEROE Flyveselskap, ASA = WF / WIF (Associated with Scandinavian SAS)

Bodö, Florö, Hammerfest & Sandefjord   Wideroe

Postboks 247, N-8001 Bodo, Norway ☎ 75 51 35 00 Tx: 78509 wifly n Fax: 75 51 35 81 SITA: n/a
F: 1934 ✝✝✝ 865 Head: Per Arne Watle IATA: 701 ICAO: WIDEROE Net: http://www.wideroe.no

registration	type of aircraft	cn/fn	ex/ex*	mfd	del	powered by	mtow kg	configuration	selcal	name/fin/specialitites/remarks
LN-WFD	De Havilland DHC-6 Twin Otter 300	700		0080	0780	2 PWC PT6A-27	5670	Y19		
LN-WIA	De Havilland DHC-8-103 Dash 8	359	C-GHRI*	0093	0593	2 PWC PW121	15650	Y37		Nordland
LN-WIB	De Havilland DHC-8-103 Dash 8	360	C-GFBW*	0093	0593	2 PWC PW121	15650	Y37		Finnmark
LN-WIC	De Havilland DHC-8-103 Dash 8	367	C-GDNG*	0093	1093	2 PWC PW121	15650	Y37		Sogn og Fjordane
LN-WID	De Havilland DHC-8-103 Dash 8	369	C-FDHD*	0093	1193	2 PWC PW121	15650	Y37		More og Romsdal
LN-WIE	De Havilland DHC-8-103 Dash 8	371	C-GFYI*	0093	0194	2 PWC PW121	15650	Y37		Hordaland
LN-WIF	De Havilland DHC-8-103 Dash 8	372	C-GFOD*	0093	0194	2 PWC PW121	15650	Y37		Nord-Trondelag
LN-WIG	De Havilland DHC-8-103 Dash 8	382	C-GLOT*	0094	0694	2 PWC PW121	15650	Y37		Troms
LN-WIH	De Havilland DHC-8-103 Dash 8	383	C-GFYI*	0094	0794	2 PWC PW121	15650	Y37		Oslo
LN-WII	De Havilland DHC-8-103 Dash 8	384	C-GFOD*	0094	0894	2 PWC PW121	15650	Y37		Nordkapp
LN-WIJ	De Havilland DHC-8-103 Dash 8	386		0094	0994	2 PWC PW121	15650	Y37		Hammerfest
LN-WIK	De Havilland DHC-8-103 Dash 8	394	C-GDNG*	0095	0195	2 PWC PW121	15650	Y37		Bodo
LN-WIL	De Havilland DHC-8-103 Dash 8	398	C-GFCF*	0095	0395	2 PWC PW121	15650	Y37		Floro
LN-WIM	De Havilland DHC-8-103 Dash 8	403	C-GDIU*	0095	0695	2 PWC PW121	15650	Y37		Vesterälen
LN-WIN	De Havilland DHC-8-103 Dash 8	409		0095	0895	2 PWC PW121	15650	Y37		Lofoten
LN-WIO	De Havilland DHC-8-103 Dash 8	417		0095	1295	2 PWC PW121	15650	Y37		Akershus
LN-WIP	De Havilland DHC-8-103 Dash 8	239	C-FXNE	0090	0396	2 PWC PW121	15650	Y37		Alstahaug / cvtd -106
LN-WIR	De Havilland DHC-8-103 Dash 8	273	C-FZNU	0091	1296	2 PWC PW121	15650	Y37		
LN-WFA	De Havilland DHC-8-311 Dash 8	342	C-FTUY	0092	0395	2 PWC PW123	19500	Y50		lsf GECA
LN-WFB	De Havilland DHC-8-311 Dash 8	293	PH-SDS	0092	0396	2 PWC PW123	19500	Y50		lsf GECA
LN-WFC	De Havilland DHC-8-311 Dash 8	236	D-BEYT	0090	0796	2 PWC PW123	19500	Y50		
LN-WFE	De Havilland DHC-8-311 Dash 8Q	491	C-GFCA*	0097	0598	2 PWC PW123	19500	Y50		
LN-WFH	De Havilland DHC-8-311 Dash 8Q	238	C-FZOH	0090	1296	2 PWC PW123	19500	Y50		
LN-WFO	De Havilland DHC-8-311 Dash 8Q	493	C-GERC*	0097	0598	2 PWC PW123	19500	Y50		
LN-WFP	De Havilland DHC-8-311 Dash 8Q	495	C-GFUM*	0097	0598	2 PWC PW123	19500	Y50		
LN-WFR	De Havilland DHC-8-315 Dash 8	385	N383DC	0094	1098	2 PWC PW123B	19500	Y50		lsf Bombardier Inc. / cvtd -314
LN-	De Havilland DHC-8-401 Dash 8Q					2 PWC PW150A	26989	Y70		oo-delivery 0999

LV = ARGENTINA (Republic of Argentina) (Republica de Argentina)

Capital: Buenos Aires   Official Language: Spanish   Population: 35,0 million   Square Km: 2766889   Dialling code: +54   Year established: 1816   Acting political head: Carlos Menem (President)

Government / Corporate / Executive / VIP Aircraft

ICAO code is used: FAG for Fuerza Aerea Argentina, ICAO call sign: FUAE.

registration	type of aircraft	cn/fn	ex/ex*	mfd	del	powered by	mtow kg	configuration	selcal	name/fin/specialitites/remarks
AE-175	Sabreliner 75A (Rockwell NA265-80)	380-13	N65761	0074		2 GE CF700-2D2	10433	VIP		Ejército Argentino
GN708	Sabreliner 75A (Rockwell NA265-80)	380-4	N11887	0074	0098	2 GE CF700-2D2	10433	VIP		Gendarmeria Nacional
H-01	Sikorsky S-70A	707023			0094	2 GE T700-GE-701A	9979	VIP		Malvinas Argentinas / Fuerza Aérea Arg.
H-02	Sikorsky S-76B	760337	N984	0086	0096	2 PWC PT6B-36A	5307	VIP		Presidencia de la Nacion
H-03	Sikorsky S-61R	61378	H-02	0068		2 GE T58-GE-5	10002	VIP		Fuerza Aérea Argentina
LQ-MBS	FMA IA.50 Guarani II	024		0070		2 TU Bastan VIA	7750	MEDEVAC		Ministerio de Accion Social
LQ-MLV	Fairchild (Swearingen) SA226TC Metro II	TC-257	LV-PAO	0078	1278	2 GA TPE331-3UW-303G	5670	MEDEVAC		Ministerio de Accion Social
LQ-MRM	Cessna 500 Citation I	500-0386	LV-PAX	0078		2 PWC JT15D-1A	5375	VIP		Policia Federal
LV-AIT	Learjet 35A	35A-408	LV-POG	0081		2 GA TFE731-2-2B	8165	VIP		Provincia de Tierra del Fuego
LV-ASZ	IAI 102 Arava	067	LV-POA	0080	0783	2 PWC PT6A-34	6804	VIP		Provincia de Formosa
LV-LRC	Learjet 24D	24D-316	T-03	0075		2 GE CJ610-6	6123	VIP		Provincia de La Rioja
LV-MHP	IAI 102 Arava	041	LV-PZU	0078	0478	2 PWC PT6A-34	6804	VIP		Provincia de Salta
LV-MRR	IAI 102 Arava	052	LV-PAP	0078	1278	2 PWC PT6A-34	6804	VIP / Tanker		Provincia de Misiones
LV-MRS	IAI 102 Arava	053	LV-PAR	0078	1278	2 PWC PT6A-34	6804	VIP		Provincia de Misiones
LV-WEJ	Cessna 550 Citation II	550-0724	LV-PGU	0093		2 PWC JT15D-4	6033	VIP		Provincia de Buenos Aires
LV-WJO	Cessna 550 Citation II	550-0728	N728CC*	0094		2 PWC JT15D-4	6033	VIP		Provincia de Corrientes
LV-WLS	Cessna 560 Citation V Ultra	560-0289		0095	0495	2 PWC JT15D-5D	7394	VIP		Provincia de Santa Cruz
LV-WPE	Beech Beechjet 400A	RK-104	LV-PLT	0095	0596	2 PWC JT15D-5	7303	VIP		Provincia de Chubut
LV-WPM	Beech Catpass 250	BB-729	N743R	0080	0995	2 PWC PT6A-41	5670	VIP		Provincia de La Pampa/cvtd King Air 200
LV-YHC	Cessna 550 Citation II	550-0715	LV-PNL	0093	0098	2 PWC JT15D-4	6033	VIP		Gobernacion de San Juan
T-01	Boeing 757-23A	25487 / 470		0092	0792	2 RR RB211-535E4	113398	VIP	DH-ES	Virgen de Lujan / Fuerza Aérea Argent.
T-02	Fokker F28 Fellowship 1000 (F28 Mk1000)	11048	LV-LZN	0072	1277	2 RR Spey 555-15	28576	VIP		Patagonia / Fuerza Aérea Argentina
T-03	Fokker F28 Fellowship 1000 (F28 Mk1000)	11028	T-04	0070	1270	2 RR Spey 555-15	28576	VIP		Presidente Tte.Gral.Juan D. Peron / FAA
T-10	Learjet 60	60-140	N140LJ*	0098	1298	2 PWC PW305A	10659	VIP		Fuerza Aérea Argentina
T-11	Sabreliner 75A (Rockwell NA265-80)	380-3	T-10	0074		2 GE CF700-2D2	10433	VIP		Fuerza Aérea Argentina

AERO ANDES, S.A.

Buenos Aires-Aeroparque J. Newbery

Lavalle 548, 5F, B, 1047 Buenos Aires, Argentina ☎ (1) 478 19 55 Tx: none Fax: (1) 372 80 97 SITA: n/a
F: 1992 ✝✝✝ n/a Head: Cesar Fabre Net: n/a

registration	type of aircraft	cn/fn	ex/ex*	mfd	del	powered by	mtow kg	configuration	selcal	name/fin/specialitites/remarks
OY-TCM	Let 410UVP-E20C	912532	OK-WDJ	0091	0097	2 WA M-601E	6600	Y19 / Frtr		lsf Aerotec Airways
RA-67599	Let 410UVP-E	871812	CCCP-67599	0087	0099	2 WA M-601E	6400	Y19		lsf Let

registration   type of aircraft   cn/fn   ex/ex*   mfd   del   powered by   mtow kg   configuration   selcal   name/fin/specialitites/remarks

AEROLINEAS ARGENTINAS, SA = AR / ARG (Subsidiary of Interinvest)

Buenos Aires-Ministro Pistarini & Aeroparque J. Newbery

Bouchard 547, 1043 Buenos Aires, Argentina ☎ (1) 317 30 00 Tx: 181812 baar ar Fax: (1) 320 21 35 SITA: n/a
F: 1949 ✦✦✦ 5180 Head: Diego Cousino IATA: 044 ICAO: ARGENTINA Net: http://www.aerolineas.com.ar
Some domestic feeder flights are operated by SOUTHERN WINDS as a AEROLINEAS ARGENTINAS CONNECTION-carrier. For details – see under that carrier.
On order (MoU/Letter of Intent): 6 Airbus Industrie A340-600 for delivery starting 2004.

registration	type of aircraft	cn/fn	ex/ex*	mfd	del	powered by	mtow kg	configuration	selcal	name/fln/specialitites/remarks
☐ LV-JMW	Boeing 737-287	20403 / 236		0070	0270	2 PW JT8D-9A	49442	C8Y103	CJ-GK	Ciudad de Mar del Plata
☐ LV-JMX	Boeing 737-287	20404 / 243		0070	0370	2 PW JT8D-9A	49442	C8Y103	CJ-HK	Ciudad de Bariloche
☐ LV-JMY	Boeing 737-287	20405 / 248		0070	0470	2 PW JT8D-9A	49442	C8Y103	CJ-HM	Ciudad de Posadas
☐ LV-JMZ	Boeing 737-287	20406 / 261		0070	0770	2 PW JT8D-9A	49442	C8Y103	CJ-KL	Ciudad de Buenos Aires
☐ LV-JND	Boeing 737-287C	20407 / 263		0070	0970	2 PW JT8D-9A	51710	C8Y103	CJ-KM	Ciudad de Comodoro Rivadavia
☐ LV-JTD	Boeing 737-287 (A)	20523 / 285	LV-PRQ	0071	1071	2 PW JT8D-9A	49442	C8Y103	KM-BC	Ciudad de Tucuman
☐ LV-JTO	Boeing 737-287 (A)	20537 / 291		0071	1271	2 PW JT8D-9A	49442	C8Y103	KM-BF	Ciudad de Jujuy
☐ LV-LEB	Boeing 737-287 (A)	20768 / 331		0073	1173	2 PW JT8D-9A	49442	C8Y103	BM-FL	Ciudad de Esquel
☐ LV-LIV	Boeing 737-287 (A)	20965 / 381		0074	1274	2 PW JT8D-9A	52163	C8Y103	EJ-CD	
☐ LV-LIW	Boeing 737-287 (A)	20966 / 387		0074	1274	2 PW JT8D-9A	52163	C8Y103	BM-JL	0800-Volar special colors
☐ LV-WGX	Boeing 737-2P6 (A)	21358 / 498	A4O-BF	0077	0494	2 PW JT8D-15	53070	C8Y103	AG-CE	lsf POLA
☐ LV-WRO	Boeing 737-212	20521 / 288	N161FN	1171	1296	2 PW JT8D-9A	53070	C8Y103	KM-DH	lsf PACA
☐ LV-WSU	Boeing 737-2A8 (A)	21496 / 503	N912PG	0077	0197	2 PW JT8D-17A	52390	C8Y103	DK-CH	lsf PACA
☐ LV-WSY	Boeing 737-281 (A)	20562 / 293	JA8416	0072	0297	2 PW JT8D-17	49377	C8Y103	NONE	
☐ LV-WTG	Boeing 737-2A8 (A)	21498 / 505	N913PG	0077	0297	2 PW JT8D-9A	52390	C8Y103		lsf PACA
☐ LV-WTX	Boeing 737-281 (A)	20561 / 292	LV-PMI	0072	0497	2 PW JT8D-17	49377	C8Y103		
☐ LV-YEB	Boeing 737-2P6 (A)	21733 / 564	EI-CLK	0079	0198	2 PW JT8D-15 (HK3/NOR)	53070	C8Y103		lsf GECA
☐ LV-YIB	Boeing 737-2P6 (A)	21356 / 496	EI-CKL	0077	0398	2 PW JT8D-15 (HK3/NOR)	53070	C8Y103		lsf GECA
☐ LV-ZEC	Boeing 737-236 (A)	21796 / 648	N921PG	0080	0698	2 PW JT8D-15A	52752	C8Y103		lsf PACA
☐ LV-ZIE	Boeing 737-236 (A)	21798 / 658	N922PG	0080	1298	2 PW JT8D-15A	52752	C8Y103		lsf PACA
☐ EI-CNP	Boeing 737-266 (A)	21192 / 451	TF-ABG	0076	0397	2 PW JT8D-17	54204	C8Y103	GM-FJ	lsf GECA
☐ LV-VAG	Boeing (Douglas) MD-83 (DC-9-83)	53117 / 1951	N6202D*	0092	0492	2 PW JT8D-219	72574	C12Y135	PS-JR	cvtd MD-82
☐ LV-VBX	Boeing (Douglas) MD-88 (DC-9-88)	53047 / 2016		0092	0892	2 PW JT8D-219	72574	C12Y131	CP-FS	Parque Nacional Lanin
☐ LV-VBY	Boeing (Douglas) MD-88 (DC-9-88)	53048 / 2030		0092	1292	2 PW JT8D-219	72574	C12Y131	CP-GR	Parque Tierra del Fuego
☐ LV-VBZ	Boeing (Douglas) MD-88 (DC-9-88)	53049 / 2031		0092	1292	2 PW JT8D-219	72574	C12Y131	CP-GS	Parque Baritu
☐ LV-VCB	Boeing (Douglas) MD-88 (DC-9-88)	53351 / 2043		0092	0793	2 PW JT8D-219	72574	C12Y131	CP-HR	Parque Iguazu
☐ LV-VGB	Boeing (Douglas) MD-88 (DC-9-88)	53446 / 2046		0093	0793	2 PW JT8D-219	72574	C12Y131	DS-CL	Parque Nahuel Huapi
☐ LV-VGC	Boeing (Douglas) MD-88 (DC-9-88)	53447 / 2064		0093	0793	2 PW JT8D-219	72574	C12Y131	DS-CM	Parque Calilegua
☐ F-OGYR	Airbus Industrie A310-324 (ET)	456	N819PA	0088	0794	2 PW PW4152	160000	C24Y170	AD-FP	lsf WTC Trustee
☐ F-OGYS	Airbus Industrie A310-324 (ET)	467	N822PA	0088	0794	2 PW PW4152	160000	C24Y170	AD-GP	lsf WTC Trustee
☐ F-OHPF	Airbus Industrie A340-211	063	VR-HMR	0094		4 CFMI CFM56-5C2	257000	CY225		tobe lsf Airbus Ind.Financial Svcs 0099
☐ F-OHPG	Airbus Industrie A340-211	074	F-WHPG	0094		4 CFMI CFM56-5C2	257000	CY225		tobe lsf Airbus Ind.Financial Svcs 0099
☐ F-OHPH	Airbus Industrie A340-211	080	VR-HMT	0095		4 CFMI CFM56-5C2	257000	CY225		tobe lsf Airbus Ind.Financial Svcs 0099
☐ F-OHPI	Airbus Industrie A340-211	085	VR-HMU	0095		4 CFMI CFM56-5C2	257000	CY225		tobe lsf Airbus Ind.Financial Svcs 0099
☐ F-OHPL	Airbus Industrie A340-313	187	F-WWJO*	0097		4 CFMI CFM56-5C4	271000	CY264		tobe lsf Airbus Ind.Financial Svcs 0099
☐ F-OHPM	Airbus Industrie A340-313	196	F-WWJI*	0097		4 CFMI CFM56-5C4	271000	CY264		tobe lsf Airbus Ind.Financial Svcs 0099
☐ F-OHPZ	Airbus Industrie A340-312	036	F-WHPZ*	0097		4 CFMI CFM56-5C3	260000	CY264		tobe lsf Airbus Ind.Financial Svcs 0099
☐ LV-MLO	Boeing 747-287B	21725 / 349		0079	0179	4 PW JT9D-7Q	371952	C46Y346	BM-HL	
☐ LV-MLP	Boeing 747-287B	21726 / 403		0079	1079	4 PW JT9D-7Q	371952	C46Y346	JL-FG	lsf GECA
☐ LV-MLR	Boeing 747-287B	21727 / 404		0079	1079	4 PW JT9D-7Q	371952	C46Y346	JL-FH	
☐ LV-OEP	Boeing 747-287B	22297 / 487		0080	1180	4 PW JT9D-7Q	371952	C46Y346	JM-AC	lsf GECA
☐ LV-OOZ	Boeing 747-287B	22592 / 532		0081	0881	4 PW JT9D-7Q	371952	C46Y346	JM-DH	lsf GECA
☐ LV-OPA	Boeing 747-287B	22593 / 552		0082	0182	4 PW JT9D-7Q	371952	C46Y346	AM-BC	
☐ LV-WYT	Boeing 747-238B	20009 / 147	N307TW	0071	0997	4 PW JT9D-7F	356070	C46Y354	BH-DE	lsf PACA
☐ LV-YPC	Boeing 747-212B	21938 / 436	HL7453	0080	0598	4 PW JT9D-7Q	371946	C46Y354		lsf ILFC
☐ LV-YSB	Boeing 747-257B	20116 / 112	N303TW	0171	0598	4 PW JT9D-7A	351534	C46Y354		lsf PEGA

AEROMIL, SA (Member of Amil Group)

Buenos Aires-Moreno

Maipu 53, Piso P, 1084 Buenos Aires, Argentina ☎ (1) 345 10 00 Tx: n/a Fax: (1) 342 45 23 SITA: n/a
F: 1995 ✦✦✦ 17 Head: Guillermo Anaya Net: n/a

☐ LV-WJX	Eurocopter (MBB) BO105CBS-4	S-86	N73PL	0073	0195	2 AN 250-C20B	2400	EMS		

AEROTRANSPORTES WOLLKOPF, Srl.

Buenos Aires-Aeroparque J. Newbery

Aeroparque Jorge Newbery, 1425 Buenos Aires, Argentina ☎ (1) 47 78 18 84 Tx: none Fax: (1) 47 78 16 90 SITA: n/a
F: 1956 ✦✦✦ n/a Head: n/a

☐ LV-OHD	Beech Baron B55 (95-B55)	TC-2272	LV-PDM	0078		2 CO IO-470-L	2313	5 Pax		
☐ LV-LMV	Beech Baron 58	TH-504		0074		2 CO IO-520-C	2449	5 Pax		
☐ LV-WOZ	Cessna 550 Citation II	550-0626	LV-PLR	0089		2 PWC JT15D-4	6033	8 Pax		
☐ LV-WGO	Cessna 560 Citation V	560-0251	LV-PGZ	0093		2 PWC JT15D-5A	7212	8 Pax		

AEROVIDA, SA

Buenos Aires-Don Torcuato

Aeropuerto Don Torcuato, Sector F, 1611 Don Torcuato, (Buenos Aires), Argentina ☎ (1) 47 41 25 67 Tx: none Fax: (1) 47 48 43 98 SITA: n/a
F: 1986 ✦✦✦ 7 Head: Dr. Guillermo Della Rodolfa Net: n/a

☐ N629SC	Beech King Air A100	B-137	PT-OVQ	0072		2 PWC PT6A-28	5216	EMS		lsf Aero Supreme Inc.
☐ N550CG	Cessna 550 Citation II	550-0095	N100UF	0079		2 PWC JT15D-4	6033	EMS		lsf Aero Supreme Inc.

AEROVIP

Cordoba

Belgrano 875, 1092 Buenos Aires, Argentina ☎ (1) 343 15 40 Tx: none Fax: (1) 343 15 40 SITA: n/a
F: 1996 ✦✦✦ n/a Head: Hernan M. Agote Net: n/a

☐ LV-	BAe 3201 Jetstream 32EP	869	N869AE	0089		2 GA TPE331-12UAR-704H	7350	Y19		to be lsf BAMT 0499 / cvtd 32
☐ LV-	BAe 3201 Jetstream 32EP	931	N931AE	0091		2 GA TPE331-12UAR-704H	7350	Y19		to be lsf BAMT 0499 / cvtd 32

AIRMAN, S.A. = AYM

Buenos Aires-San Fernando

Rafaela 4957, 9C, 1407 Buenos Aires, Argentina ☎ (1) 335 74 48 Tx: none Fax: (1) 335 52 10 SITA: n/a
F: n/a ✦✦✦ n/a Head: Angelo Torriani ICAO: AIRMAN Net: n/a

☐ LV-WSD	Fairchild (Swearingen) SA226TC Metro II	TC-237E	N766AS	0077	1296	2 GA TPE331-3UW-303G	5670*	Y19 / Freighter		
☐ LV-ZEB	Fairchild (Swearingen) SA226TC Metro II	TC-393	N867MA	0080	0698	2 GA TPE331-3UW-304G	5670	Y19 / Freighter		
☐ LV-YIC	Fairchild (Swearingen) SA227AC Metro III	AC-448	LV-PNF	0081	1297	2 GA TPE331-11U-611G	6577	Y19 / Freighter		

AIR SERVICE, S.A.

Buenos Aires-Aeroparque J. Newbery

Cerrito 774, Piso 5, 1425 Buenos Aires, Argentina ☎ (1) 371 13 24 Tx: none Fax: (1) 371 13 24 SITA: n/a
F: 1994 ✦✦✦ 20 Head: Carlos Jimenc Net: n/a

☐ LV-WJP	Beech King Air C90	LJ-529	N78SE	0071	0495	2 PWC PT6A-20	4377	Freighter/Exec		
☐ LV-WMF	Dassault Falcon 20C	9	C-GSKA	0065	0495	2 GE CF700-2D2	12000	Freighter		
☐ LV-WMM	Dassault Falcon 20C	29	C-GSKC	0066	0495	2 GE CF700-2D2	12000	Freighter		

AIR TANGO, S.A.

Buenos Aires-Aeroparque J. Newbery

PO Box 66, Correo de San Isidro, 1642 San Isidro, (Buenos Aires), Argentina ☎ (5411) 47 65 70 30 Tx: none Fax: (5411) 47 65 63 65 SITA: n/a
F: 1993 ✦✦✦ n/a Head: Ramon Chain Net: n/a

☐ LV-WEO	Fairchild (Swearingen) SA226TC Metro II	TC-346	N52EA	0080	1293	2 GA TPE331-10UA-511G	5670	Y19 / Freighter		

ALAS DEL SUR

Buenos Aires-San Fernando

Acceso Norte (Ramal Tigre), Ruta 202, 1646 San Fernando, (Buenos Aires), Argentina ☎ (1) 714 64 24 Tx: none Fax: (1) 714 70 10 SITA: n/a
F: 1995 ✦✦✦ n/a Head: n/a

☐ LV-WRM	Beech King Air B90	LJ-333	OB-1495	0068	1096	2 PWC PT6A-20	4377	Freighter		
☐ LV-WLX	Sabreliner 60 (Rockwell NA265-60)	306-41	N614MM	0069	0495	2 PW JT12A-8	9150	Freighter		
☐ LV-WOF	Sabreliner 60 (Rockwell NA265-60)	306-25	OB-1550	0068	0096	2 PW JT12A-8	9150	Freighter		

AMERICAN FALCON, S.A.

Buenos Aires-Aeroparque J. Newbery & -Ministro Pistarini

Avenida Santa Fe 1713, 4.Piso, 1060 Buenos Aires, Argentina ☎ (1) 811 05 76 Tx: none Fax: (1) 815 66 57 SITA: n/a
F: 1998 ✦✦✦ n/a Head: Emilio J. Dirube Net: n/a

☐ LV-WZC	Fokker F28 Fellowship 1000 (F28 Mk1000)	11017	N802PH	0070	1298	2 RR Spey 555-15	29484	Y62		lsf Capital Airlines Leasing

AMERICAN JET, SA

Buenos Aires-Aeroparque J. Newbery & Neuquen

American Jet

Aeroparque J. Newbery, 1425 Buenos Aires, Argentina ☎ (1) 775 54 87 Tx: n/a Fax: (1) 775 54 36 SITA: n/a
F: 1982 ✦✦✦ n/a Head: Jorge Rodriguez Net: n/a

☐ LV-VDV	Bell 206B JetRanger III	3161	N5758W	0080	1192	1 AN 250-C20B	1451			
☐ LV-VFG	AAC (Ted Smith) Aerostar 601P	61P-0242-039	N601WP	0075	1192	2 LY IO-540-S1A5	2722			
☐ LV-LZR	Cessna 500 Citation I	500-0332	LV-PUY	0076		2 PWC JT15D-1A	5375			
☐ LV-JTZ	Learjet 24D	24D-234	LV-PRA	0071		2 GE CJ610-6	6124			
☐ LV-JXA	Learjet 24D	24D-240	LV-PRB	0071		2 GE CJ610-6	6124			
☐ LV-WTD	Dornier 228-202	8094	D-CDAL	0086	0497	2 GA TPE331-5-252D	6200			lsf Dornier Aviation / cvtd -201

235 registration   type of aircraft   cn/fn   ex/ex*   mfd   del   powered by   mtow kg   configuration   selcal   name/fln/specialitites/remarks

☐ LV-WTV	Dornier 228-202	8093	N228BM	0086	0497	2 GA TPE331-5-252D	6200			lsf Dornier Aviation / cvtd -201
☐ N3027B	Fairchild (Swearingen) SA227DC Metro 23	DC-856B		0094	1196	2 GA TPE331-12U-701G	7484			lsf PC Air Charter Inc.
☐ LV-WBP	Learjet 25G	25G-337	N337GL	0083	0793	2 GE CJ610-8A	7394			
☐ N97AM	Learjet 25C	25C-071	YV-132CP	0071	0096	2 GE CJ610-6	6804			lsf Fairway Aircraft Inc.
☐ N428W	IAI 1124A Westwind II	428	4X-CUO*	0085		2 GA TFE731-3-1G	10659			lsf Fair Sky Corp.
☐ N1125L	IAI 1125 Astra SP	072		0094	0697	2 GA TFE731-3A-200G	10659			lsf Terraire S.A.
☐ N96PC	IAI 1125 Astra	004	4X-CUA*	0086	0096	2 GA TFE731-3A-200G	10659			lsf PC Air Charter Inc.
☐ N908CL	Canadair CL-601-3A (CL-600-2B16) Challen.	5031	N900CL	0089	0198	2 GE CF34-3A	20500			lsf Bombardier Aerospace

ARIES DEL SUR, SA (Subsidiary of IEGSA-International Enterprise Group, SA) — **Buenos Aires-Ministro Pistarini**

Chacabuco 90, Piso 7, 1069 Buenos Aires, Argentina ☎ (1) 345 24 79 Tx: none Fax: (1) 245 24 78 SITA: n/a
F: n/a ⁂ n/a Head: Pedro Rossini Net: n/a Beside aircraft listed, international cargo flights are operated with Boeing 707C, leased from AECA (HC-) when required.

☐ LV-WME	Mitsubishi MU-2F (MU-2B-20)	139	N90SA	0068		2 GA TPE331-1-151A	4500	Freighter/Exec		

ARMADA ARGENTINA – Transportes Aeronavales (Operated by the Comando de Aviacion Naval Argentina) — **Bahia Blanca**

Casilla Postal s/n, 8111 Puerto Belgrano, (Buenos Aires), Argentina ☎ (1) 317 20 00 Tx: none Fax: (1) 328 76 52 SITA: n/a
F: 1963 ⁂ n/a Head: Capt. Hector Dabini Net: n/a As a branch of the Argentine Navy – Transportes Aeronavales provides scheduled flights for cargo, naval personnel and other special passengers.

☐ 0740	Fokker F28 Fellowship 3000M (F28 Mk3000M)	11147	PH-EXW*	0079	0679	2 RR Spey 555-15H	33112	VIP		5-T-10 / Stella Maris
☐ 0741	Fokker F28 Fellowship 3000C (F28 Mk3000C)	11145	LV-RRA	0079	0479	2 RR Spey 555-15H	33112	Y65 / Combi		5-T-20
☐ 0742	Fokker F28 Fellowship 3000MC(F28Mk3000MC)	11150	PH-EXX*	0079	0879	2 RR Spey 555-15H	33112	Y65 / Combi		5-T-21 / Islas Malvinas / cvtd 3000M

AUSTRAL Lineas Aéreas = AU / AUT (Cielos del Sur, S.A. dba / Subsidiary of Andes Holding) — **Buenos Aires-Aeroparque J. Newbery**

Av. Leandre N. Alem 1134, 4.Piso, 1001 Buenos Aires, Argentina ☎ (1) 317 36 00 Tx: n/a Fax: (1) 778 43 08 SITA: n/a
F: 1971 ⁂ 1900 Head: Manuel A. M. Casero IATA: 143 ICAO: AUSTRAL Net: http://www.austral.com.ar

☐ LV-WEH	Boeing (Douglas) DC-9-32	47447 / 563	EC-BQU	0070	1093	2 PW JT8D-7B	48988	Y105	JK-CH	
☐ LV-WFT	Boeing (Douglas) DC-9-32	47365 / 504	EC-BPG	0069	0294	2 PW JT8D-7B	48988	Y105	JK-BG	
☐ LV-WGU	Boeing (Douglas) DC-9-32	47454 / 567	EC-BQX	0170	0494	2 PW JT8D-7B	48988	Y105	HL-AG	
☐ LV-WHL	Boeing (Douglas) DC-9-32	47368 / 505	EC-BPH	0569	0794	2 PW JT8D-7B	48988	Y105	JK-BL	
☐ LV-WIS	Boeing (Douglas) DC-9-32	47312 / 262	EC-BIS	0268	1194	2 PW JT8D-7B	48988	Y105	FG-DL	
☐ LV-WJH	Boeing (Douglas) DC-9-32	47079 / 163	EC-BIJ	0067	1294	2 PW JT8D-7B	48988	Y105	FG-CJ	
☐ LV-WSZ	Boeing (Douglas) DC-9-31	47140 / 212	N8931E	0067	0397	2 PW JT8D-7B	48988	Y105	AL-DM	lsf Boeing Capital Corp.
☐ LV-WTH	Boeing (Douglas) DC-9-31	45839 / 116	N8924E	0067	0497	2 PW JT8D-7B	47627	Y105		lsf Boeing Capital Corp.
☐ LV-YAB	Boeing (Douglas) DC-9-32	47313 / 268	LV-PNG	0268	1197	2 PW JT8D-7B	48988	Y105	FG-DM	
☐ LV-WFN	Boeing (Douglas) MD-81 (DC-9-81)	48025 / 952	N10027	0080	0181	2 PW JT8D-217A	63503	C8Y145		lsf Boeing Capital Corp.
☐ LV-WGM	Boeing (Douglas) MD-83 (DC-9-83)	49784 / 1627	N509MD	0089	0989	2 PW JT8D-219	72574	C8Y145		lsf Boeing Capital Corp.
☐ LV-WGN	Boeing (Douglas) MD-83 (DC-9-83)	49934 / 1764	N907MD	0090	0990	2 PW JT8D-219	72574	C8Y145		lsf Boeing Capital Corp.
☐ LV-WPY	Boeing (Douglas) MD-81 (DC-9-81)	48024 / 948	N10022	0080	0181	2 PW JT8D-217A	63503	C8Y145		lsf Boeing Capital Corp.

BAIRES FLY, S.A. — **Buenos Aires-Aeroparque J. Newbery**

Av. Rafael Obligado sn, Hall Taxis Aéreos, Aerparque Jorge Newbery, 1425 Buenos Aires, Argentina ☎ (1) 47 76 28 00 Tx: none Fax: (1) 47 76 28 00 SITA: n/a
F: 1996 ⁂ n/a Head: n/a Net: n/a

☐ LV-WHG	Fairchild (Swearingen) SA226TC Metro II	TC-344	N44CS	0080	0096	2 GA TPE331-3UW-304G	5670	Y19 / Freighter		
☐ LV-WRA	Fairchild (Swearingen) SA227AC Metro III	AC-429	C-FJLF	0081	0496	2 GA TPE331-11U-611G	6577	Y19 / Freighter		
☐ LV-WTE	Fairchild (Swearingen) SA227AC Metro III	AC-584	LV-PMF	0084	0098	2 GA TPE331-11U-611G	6577	Y19 / Freighter		
☐ LV-ZMG	Fairchild (Swearingen) SA227AC Metro III	AC-425	N721MA	0081	0098	2 GA TPE331-11U-611G	6577	Y19 / Freighter		

BEST FLY, S.A. — **Neuquen**

Aeropuerto Internacional de Neuquen, 8300 Neuquen, Argentina ☎ (99) 632 39 08 Tx: none Fax: (99) 449 01 00 SITA: n/a
F: 1996 ⁂ n/a Head: n/a Net: n/a Aircraft below MTOW 1361kg: Piper PA-28

☐ LV-VFC	Beech King Air E90	LW-339	N290TC	0079		2 PWC PT6A-28	4581			

BLASER AVIACION — **Rio Gallegos**

Perito Moreno 471, 9400 Rio Gallegos, Argentina ☎ (966) 22 672 Tx: n/a Fax: (966) 20 797 SITA: n/a
F: 1993 ⁂ n/a Head: Mario Blaser Net: n/a Aircraft below MTOW 1361kg: Piper PA-28

☐ LV-WIG	Piper PA-31-325 Navajo C/R	31-7512009	N857MC	0075	0994	2 LY TIO-540-F2BD	2948			

CATA Linea Aérea S.A.C.I.F.I. = CTZ (formerly CATA S.A.C.I.F.I. Servicios Aeronauticos) — **Buenos Aires-Aeroparque J. Newbery**

Cerrito 1320, 3° Piso, 1010 Buenos Aires, Argentina ☎ (1) 48 13 14 15 Tx: none Fax: (1) 48 11 29 66 SITA: n/a
F: 1980 ⁂ 200 Head: Roque Pugliese ICAO: CATA Net: http://www.satlink.com/usuarios/c/cataaer

☐ LV-JOJ	Twin (Aero) Hawk Commander 681	681-6007	N9057N	0069	0094	2 GA TPE331-1-151K	4264	Y6		
☐ LV-LRF	Twin (Aero) Turbo Commander 690A	11228	LV-PTJ	0075	0681	2 GA TPE331-5-251K	4683	Y8		
☐ LV-OLS	IAI 102 Arava	046	LV-PIJ	0080	0980	2 PWC PT6A-34	6804	Y19		Jorge Newbery
☐ LV-AZV	Fairchild Ind. F-27J	65	LV-PAD	0059	0787	2 RR Dart 532-7	19051	Y44		cvtd F-27A
☐ LV-AZW	Fairchild Ind. F-27J	70	N279PH	0059	1187	2 RR Dart 532-7	19051	Y44		cvtd F-27A / std Moron
☐ LV-RBO	Fairchild Ind. F-27J	78	LV-PAG	0060	0688	2 RR Dart 532-7	19051	Y44		cvtd F-27A
☐ LV-RLB	Fairchild Ind. F-27J	42	N102FJ	0059	1091	2 RR Dart 532-7	19051	Y44		cvtd F-27
☐ LV-MGV	Fairchild Ind. FH-227B	567	PP-BUH	0067	0297	2 RR Dart 532-7	20412	Y44		
☐ LV-MGW	Fairchild Ind. FH-227B	568	PP-BUI	0067	0297	2 RR Dart 532-7	20412	Y44		

CORONAIRE — **Buenos Aires-Don Torcuato**

Donboco 88, 1876 Bernal, (Buenos Aires), Argentina ☎ (1) 254 63 11 Tx: none Fax: (1) 251 56 67 SITA: n/a
F: 1991 ⁂ 30 Head: Dr. Paul A. Gargano Net: n/a

☐ LV-RZA	Piper PA-31-350 Navajo Chieftain	31-7552091	C-GJGA	0075	1291	2 LY TIO-540-J2BD	3175			
☐ LV-RZB	Fairchild (Swearingen) SA26AT Merlin IIB	T26-143	LV-PFR	0069	1291	2 GA TPE331-1-151G	4536			

CUADRADO Servicios Aéreos — **Buenos Aires-Aeroparque J. Newbery**

Aeroparque Jorge Newbery, 1425 Buenos Aires, Argentina ☎ (1) 773 22 07 Tx: n/a Fax: (1) 771 30 51 SITA: n/a
F: 1961 ⁂ n/a Head: José Cuadrado Net: n/a

☐ LV-LDD	Piper PA-34-200 Seneca	34-7250020	N2689T	0071		2 LY IO-360-C1E6	1905			

DINAR Lineas Aéreas, S.A. = D7 / RDN (Associated with TAC Bus Company) — **Buenos Aires-Aeroparque J. Newbery & Salta**

Carlos Pellegrini 675, 10.Piso, 1009 Buenos Aires, Argentina ☎ (1) 327 11 11 Tx: none Fax: (1) 326 01 34 SITA: n/a
F: 1991 ⁂ 150 Head: Alberto Desimone IATA: 429 ICAO: AERO DINAR Net: n/a

☐ LV-YNA	Boeing (Douglas) DC-9-41	47614 / 747	OH-LNF	0974	0598	2 PW JT8D-17A	51710	Y123		
☐ LV-YOA	Boeing (Douglas) DC-9-41	47606 / 727	OH-LND	0474	0499	2 PW JT8D-17A	51710	Y123		
☐ LV-YPA	Boeing (Douglas) DC-9-41	47613 / 742	OH-LNC	0774	1298	2 PW JT8D-17A	51710	Y123		
☐ LV-WTY	Boeing (Douglas) MD-81 (DC-9-81)	48011 / 994	LV-PMJ	0081	0597	2 PW JT8D-217C	64410	Y147		lsf Boeing Capital Corp.

EMPRESA AEREA HALCON, Srl. — **Buenos Aires-Aeroparque J. Newbery**

Avda. Rafael Obligado sn, Aeroparque J. Newbery, 1425 Buenos Aires, Argentina ☎ (1) 771 84 95 Tx: none Fax: (1) 777 45 74 SITA: n/a
F: 1961 ⁂ 28 Head: Mario Augusto Petit de Meurville Net: http://www.eaereahalcon.com.ar

☐ LV-JHP	Cessna 402	402-0251		0068	0686	2 CO TSIO-520-E	2858			
☐ LV-VHP	Twin (Aero) Hawk Commander 681	681-6014	N88RK	0070	0493	2 GA TPE331-43BL	4264			
☐ LV-WHZ	IAI 1121B Jet Commander	1121-108	N77ST	0067	0794	2 GE CJ610-5	8391			

EXECUTIVE JET, S.A. — **Buenos Aires-Aeroparque J. Newbery**

Coronel Diaz 2581, 4.Piso, 1425 Buenos Aires, Argentina ☎ (1) 777 40 43 Tx: none Fax: (1) 777 40 43 SITA: n/a
F: 1993 ⁂ n/a Head: n/a Net: n/a

☐ LV-WND	Sabreliner 40A (Rockwell NA265-40A)	282-131	N82R	0073	0795	2 PW JT12A-8	8896			
☐ N747E	Sabreliner 40 (Rockwell NA265-40)	282-22	N747	0064	0094	2 PW JT12A-8A	8459			lsf Corporate Flight Inc.

EXPRESS POST, S.A. — **Buenos Aires-Aeroparque J. Newbery**

Juramento 2796, 3.Piso, Depto. D, 1425 Buenos Aires, Argentina ☎ (1) 383 82 77 Tx: none Fax: (1) 383 38 54 SITA: n/a
F: 1995 ⁂ 7 Head: n/a Net: n/a

☐ LV-WFB	Beech King Air C90B	LJ-1414	N3234X	0095	1195	2 PWC PT6A-21	4581			

FEDERAL AVIATION, S.A. — **Buenos Aires-Aeroparque J. Newbery**

Hipolito Yrigoyen 785, 2F, Apdo F, 1086 Buenos Aires, Argentina ☎ (1) 345 55 55 Tx: none Fax: (1) 342 07 47 SITA: n/a
F: 1997 ⁂ n/a Head: Gustavo Adolfo Julia Net: n/a

☐ LV-MML	Piper PA-31-350 Navajo Chieftain	31-7852133		0078	0097	2 LY TIO-540-J2BD	3175			
☐ LV-WLG	Learjet 25D	25D-345	LV-PHU	0081	0097	2 GE CJ610-8A	6804			

FLYMELL, S.A. — **Buenos Aires-Aeroparque J. Newbery**

Gurruchaga 830, 1425 Buenos Aires, Argentina ☎ (1) 777 97 28 Tx: none Fax: (1) 777 45 74 SITA: n/a
F: 1995 ⁂ n/a Head: Mario Petit Net: n/a

☐ LV-WJU	IAI 1123 Jet Commander	1123-179	N1123Y	0075		2 GE CJ610-9	9389			

236 registration type of aircraft cn/fn ex/ex* mfd del powered by mtow kg configuration selcal name/fln/specialitites/remarks

GEOPATAGONIA, Srl. — Comodoro Rivadavia

P. Colello 324, Barrio Industrial, 9000 Comodoro Rivadavia, Argentina ☎ (97) 48 32 68 Tx: none Fax: (97) 47 83 09 SITA: n/a
F: 1994 ⁂ 12 Head: Mario Aragone Net: n/a

☐ LV-WIM	Bell 206B JetRanger III	*2933*	*N1080J*	*0080*	*0094*	*1 AN 250-C20B*	*1451*			
☐ F-GIPY	Eurocopter (Aerosp.) AS350B2 Ecureuil	*2033*	*LN-OCA*	*0087*	*0098*	*1 TU Arriel 1D1*	*2250*			*lsf Helicoptère Service*

HAWK AIR, S.A. — Buenos Aires-Aeroparque J. Newbery

Jean Jaures 834, 1.Piso, 1215 Buenos Aires, Argentina ☎ (1) 962 71 30 Tx: none Fax: (1) 962 68 14 SITA: n/a
F: 1991 ⁂ n/a Head: Libertario Cukierkopf Net: n/a

☐ LV-WHX	Piper PA-31-310 Navajo	*31-353*	*N716DR*	*0069*	*0394*	*2 LY TIO-540-A1A*	*2948*			
☐ LV-WIR	Fairchild (Swearingen) SA226T Merlin III	*T-232*	*N56TA*	*0073*	*1094*	*2 GA TPE331-3U-303G*	*5670*	*Freighter*		
☐ LV-WNC	Fairchild (Swearingen) SA226AT Merlin IVA	*AT-036*	*N642TS*	*0075*	*0795*	*2 GA TPE331-3U-303G*	*5670*	*Freighter*		
☐ LV-WXW	Fairchild (Swearingen) SA226TC Metro II	*TC-419*	*N7205L*	*0081*	*0797*	*2 GA TPE331-3UW-303G*	*5670*	*Freighter*		

HELICOPTEROS MARINOS, SA (Subsidiary of Heli-Union, France) — Buenos Aires-Don Torcuato & Rio Grande

Aeropuerto Don Torcuato, CP 46, 1611 Don Torcuato, (Buenos Aires), Argentina ☎ (1) 741 47 18 Tx: none Fax: (1) 748 68 86 SITA: n/a
F: 1978 ⁂ n/a Head: Ch. de Courlon Net: n/a Aircraft below MTOW 1361kg: Hughes 269C (300C)

☐ LV-WHJ	Eurocopter (Aerosp.) SA315B Lama	*2322*	*F-GIDU*	*0073*	*0594*	*1 TU Artouste IIIB1*	*1950*	*4 Pax*		
☐ F-GDFX	Eurocopter (Aerosp.) SA315B Lama	*2629*	*LX-HUC*	*0082*	*0098*	*1 TU Artouste IIIB*	*1950*	*4 Pax*		*lsf Heli-Union*
☐ F-GJGF	Eurocopter (Aerosp.) SA315B Lama	*2617*	*VT-BKM*	*0081*	*0097*	*1 TU Artouste IIIB1*	*1950*	*4 Pax*		*lsf Heli-Union*
☐ F-GKSF	Eurocopter (Aerosp.) SA315B Lama	*2471*	*N471E*	*0077*		*1 TU Artouste IIIB*	*1950*	*4 Pax*		*lsf Heli-Union*
☐ F-GFBM	Eurocopter (Aerosp.) SA365C2 Dauphin 2	*5070*	*F-OAYC*	*0081*	*0096*	*2 TU Arriel 1A2*	*3500*	*9 Pax*		*lsf Heli-Union*
☐ F-GFPA	Eurocopter (Aerosp.) SA365C2 Dauphin 2	*5063*	*LV-AIE*	*0080*		*2 TU Arriel 1A2*	*3500*	*9 Pax*		*lsf Heli-Union*

HELICORP - Helicopter Corporation, SA — Buenos Aires-Torcuato

Avenida Leandro N. Alem 592, Piso 13, 1001 Buenos Aires, Argentina ☎ (1) 432 00 42 Tx: none Fax: (1) 432 64 30 SITA: n/a
F: 1993 ⁂ n/a Head: Alberto Shebar Net: n/a

☐ LV-WFY	Bell 206B JetRanger III	*3071*	*C-FKCH*	*0080*	*1193*	*1 AN 250-C20B*	*1451*			
☐ LV-WHR	Bell 206L-3 LongRanger III	*51210*	*N3205W*	*0087*	*0694*	*1 AN 250-C30P*	*1882*			

HELYJET, S.A. — Buenos Aires-San Fernando

Esmeralda 1320, 5P, Apartado A, 1007 Buenos Aires, Argentina ☎ (1) 43 22 91 00 Tx: none Fax: (1) 43 27 04 04 SITA: n/a
F: 1996 ⁂ n/a Head: n/a Net: http://www.helyjet.com

☐ LV-YBL	Fairchild (Swearingen) SA227AC Metro III	*AC-746B*	*N46NE*	*0089*	*0997*	*2 GA TPE331-11U-612G*	*7257*			*lsf Joda Partnership*
☐ LV-WRE	Learjet 25D	*25G-355*	*N355AM*	*0082*	*1096*	*2 GE CJ610-8A*	*6804*			*lsf Joda Partnership*
☐ LV-WXY	Learjet 25D	*25G-357*	*N27KG*	*0083*	*1096*	*2 GE CJ610-8A*	*6804*			*lsf Joda Partnership*

HIGH LEVEL, S.A. — Buenos Aires-San Fernando

Aeropuerto, Acceso Norte (Ramaltiore), Ruta 202, 1646 San Fernando (Buenos Aires), Argentina ☎ (1) 714 61 65 Tx: none Fax: (1) 714 66 85 SITA: n/a
F: 1996 ⁂ n/a Head: Barry Melborne Hussey Net: n/a

☐ LV-WWX	GAC (Grumman) G-159 Gulfstream I		*N*		*0097*	*2 RR Dart 529-8X*	*16329*			

KAIKEN Lineas Aéreas = KJI (Valls Lineas Aéreas y Servicios, Srl. dba) — Rio Grande

Perito Moreno 937, 9420 Rio Grande, (Tierra del Fuego), Argentina ☎ (964) 22 710 Tx: none Fax: (964) 30 665 SITA: n/a
F: 1990 ⁂ 80 Head: Oscar N. Valls IATA: 088 Net: n/a

☐ LV-LAO	Cessna 310Q	*310Q0477*	*LV-PSC*	*0072*		*2 CO IO-470-VO*	*2404*	*Y5*		
☐ LV-WDU	Fairchild (Swearingen) SA226TC Metro II	*TC-310*	*N242AM*	*0079*	*1193*	*2 GA TPE331-10UA-511G*	*5670*	*Y19*		Ciudad de Ushuaia / *std/for sale*
☐ LV-WDV	Fairchild (Swearingen) SA226TC Metro II	*TC-271*	*N102GS*	*0079*	*1193*	*2 GA TPE331-10UA-511G*	*5670*	*Y19*		Ciudad de Rio Grande
☐ LV-WIY	Fairchild (Swearingen) SA226TC Metro II	*TC-307*	*N334BA*	*0079*	*1194*	*2 GA TPE331-10UA-511G*	*5670*	*Y19*		Ciudad de Tolhuin / *std/for sale*
☐ LV-WON	Saab SF340A	*340A-075*	*LV-PLP*	*0086*	*0598*	*2 GE CT7-5A2*	*12700*	*Y34*		*lsf Saab Aircraft Credit AB*
☐ LV-WXE	Saab SF340A	*340A-072*	*LV-PMO*	*0086*	*0697*	*2 GE CT7-5A2*	*12700*	*Y34*		El Mapuche / *lsf Lambert Leasing Inc.*
☐ LV-WYS	Saab SF340A	*340A-069*	*LV-PMZ*	*0086*	*0997*	*2 GE CT7-5A2*	*12700*	*Y34*		El Yagan / *lsf Lambert Leasing Inc.*
☐ LV-WIN	De Havilland DHC-7-102 Dash 7	*041*	*C-FTAW*	*0081*	*0994*	*4 PWC PT6A-50*	*19958*	*Y50*		El Patagonico / *std/for sale*
☐ LV-WJF	De Havilland DHC-7-102 Dash 7	*029*	*LV-PHS*	*0080*	*0195*	*4 PWC PT6A-50*	*19958*	*Y50*		El Antartico / *std/for sale*

LADE - Lineas Aéreas del Estado = LDE (Operated by the Fuerza Aérea Argentina/I Brigada Aérea/II Escuadron de Transporte) — Buenos Aires-Aeroparque J. Newbery & Comodoro Rivadavia

Peru 714, 1068 Buenos Aires, Argentina ☎ (1) 361 70 71 Tx: 122040 ar Fax: (1) 362 48 99 SITA: n/a
F: 1940 ⁂ 450 Head: Comodoro Guillermo José Testoni ICAO: LADE Net: n/a Operates scheduled flights to commercially unprofitable destinations. Aircraft are owned by & operated in full Fuerza Aérea Argentina/I Brigada Aérea colors & titles. Additional aircraft (FMA IA-50 & Lockheed C-130H Hercules) are occasionally used from Fuerza Aérea Argentina transport units.

☐ T-82	De Havilland DHC-6 Twin Otter 200	*167*		*0068*	*1168*	*2 PWC PT6A-20*	*5252*	*Y19*		
☐ T-84	De Havilland DHC-6 Twin Otter 200	*172*		*0068*	*1268*	*2 PWC PT6A-20*	*5252*	*Y19*		
☐ T-85	De Havilland DHC-6 Twin Otter 200	*173*		*0068*	*1268*	*2 PWC PT6A-20*	*5252*	*Y19*		
☐ T-86	De Havilland DHC-6 Twin Otter 200	*225*		*0069*	*1069*	*2 PWC PT6A-20*	*5252*	*Y19*		
☐ T-90	De Havilland DHC-6 Twin Otter 200	*178*	*LV-JMR*	*0068*	*1082*	*2 PWC PT6A-20*	*5252*	*Y19*		
☐ T-41	Fokker F27 Friendship 600 (F27 Mk600)	*10345*	*T-80*	*0067*	*0868*	*2 RR Dart 532-7*	*20412*	*Y44/Frtr/Combi*		*cvtd 400*
☐ T-42	Fokker F27 Friendship 600 (F27 Mk600)	*10346*	*T-79*	*0067*	*0868*	*2 RR Dart 532-7*	*20412*	*Y44/Frtr/Combi*		*cvtd 400*
☐ T-43	Fokker F27 Friendship 600 (F27 Mk600)	*10451*	*PH-EXA**	*0071*	*1271*	*2 RR Dart 532-7*	*20412*	*Y44/Frtr/Combi*		
☐ T-44	Fokker F27 Friendship 600 (F27 Mk600)	*10454*	*PH-EXB**	*0071*	*1271*	*2 RR Dart 532-7*	*20412*	*Y44/Frtr/Combi*		
☐ T-45	Fokker F27 Friendship 600 (F27 Mk600)	*10368*	*TC-79*	*0068*	*0876*	*2 RR Dart 532-7*	*20412*	*Y44/Frtr/Combi*		*cvtd 400*
☐ TC-52	Fokker F28 Fellowship 1000C (F28 Mk1000C)	*11074*	*LV-RCS*	*0073*	*0175*	*2 RR Spey 555-15*	*29484*	*Y65/Frtr/Combi*		*cvtd -1000*
☐ TC-53	Fokker F28 Fellowship 1000C (F28 Mk1000C)	*11020*	*PH-EXX**	*0070*	*0575*	*2 RR Spey 555-15*	*29484*	*Y65/Frtr/Combi*		*cvtd -1000*
☐ TC-54	Fokker F28 Fellowship 1000C (F28 Mk1000C)	*11018*	*LV-VCS*	*0069*	*0775*	*2 RR Spey 555-15*	*29484*	*Y65/Frtr/Combi*		*cvtd -1000*
☐ TC-55	Fokker F28 Fellowship 1000C (F28 Mk1000C)	*11024*	*PH-EXZ**	*0070*	*1075*	*2 RR Spey 555-15*	*29484*	*Y65/Frtr/Combi*		*cvtd -1000*
☐ LV-ISD	Boeing 707-387B	*19241 / 555*	*TC-95*	*0067*	*0183*	*4 PW JT3D-3B*	*150547*	*Y174/Frtr/Combi*		
☐ LV-LGO	Boeing 707-372C	*20076 / 721*	*TC-93*	*0068*	*1282*	*4 PW JT3D-3B*	*150547*	*Y174/Frtr/Combi*		
☐ LV-WXL	Boeing 707-365C	*19590 / 654*	*JY-AJM*	*0067*	*0997*	*4 PW JT3D-3B (HK2/COM)*	*148642*	*Y174/Frtr/Combi*		
☐ TC-91	Boeing 707-387B (SCD)	*21070 / 897*	*T-91*	*0075*	*0675*	*4 PW JT3D-3B*	*150547*	*Y174/Frtr/Combi*		

LAER - Lineas Aéreas Entre Rios, S.A. (formerly SAPER – Servicio Aéreo de la Provincia de Entre Rios / Subsidiary of Salero II, S.A.) — Parana

Aeropuerto Gral. Urquiza, 3100 Parana, (Entre Rios), Argentina ☎ (43) 24 38 50 Tx: n/a Fax: (43) 24 33 20 SITA: n/a
F: 1967 ⁂ 74 Head: Roberto Neira Net: n/a

☐ LV-VEI	BAe 3212 Jetstream 32	*830*	*C-GBDR*	*0088*	*1092*	*2 GA TPE331-12UAR-705H*	*7350*	*Y19*		Rio Parana / *lsf BAMT*
☐ LV-VEJ	BAe 3212 Jetstream 32	*831*	*C-GDBR*	*0088*	*1092*	*2 GA TPE331-12UAR-705H*	*7350*	*Y19*		Rio Uruguay / *lsf BAMT*
☐ LV-WCZ	BAe 3212 Jetstream 32	*832*	*LV-PGO*	*0089*	*0993*	*2 GA TPE331-12UAR-705H*	*7350*	*Y19*		Rio Gualeguay / *lsf BAMT*
☐ LV-	BAe 3201 Jetstream 32	*824*	*N3108*	*0088*		*2 GA TPE331-12UAR-705H*	*7350*	*Y19*		*to be lsf BAMT 0499*
☐ LV-YJA	ATR 42-300	*038*	*F-WQGK*	*0087*	*0498*	*2 PWC PW120*	*16700*	*Y46*		Rio Guayquiraro / *lsf ATR*
☐ LV-ZNV	ATR 42-320	*072*	*XA-TGR*	*0088*	*1298*	*2 PWC PW121*	*16700*	*Y46*		Rio de la Plata / *lsf ATR / cvtd -300*

LAPA - Lineas Aéreas Privadas Argentinas, SA = MJ / LPR — Buenos Aires-Aeroparque J. Newbery

Av. Santa Fe 1970, 2 Piso, 1123 Buenos Aires, Argentina ☎ (1) 819 52 72 Tx: none Fax: (1) 814 21 00 SITA: n/a
F: 1977 ⁂ 460 Head: Capt. Gustavo A. Deutsch IATA: 069 ICAO: LAPA Net: n/a

☐ LV-WIJ	Cessna 560 Citation V	*560-0265*		*0093*	*0994*	*2 PWC JT15D-5A*	*7212*	*Executive*		
☐ LV-VGF	Boeing 737-2M6 (A)	*21138 / 422*	*ZK-NAL*	*0075*	*0293*	*2 PW JT8D-15*	*53070*	*Y120*	*GH-KM*	Altair / *lsf AFIN*
☐ LV-WBO	Boeing 737-244	*20330 / 257*	*ZS-SBP*	*0070*	*0793*	*2 PW JT8D-9*	*47174*	*Y120*	*BM-JK*	
☐ LV-WFX	Boeing 737-2P6 (A)	*21357 / 497*	*A4O-BE*	*0077*	*0294*	*2 PW JT8D-15*	*53070*	*Y120*	*GH-FL*	Adhara / *lsf POLA*
☐ LV-WJS	Boeing 737-2S3 (A)	*22278 / 646*	*LV-PHT*	*0080*	*0195*	*2 PW JT8D-15*	*53070*	*Y120*		Antares / *lsf GECA*
☐ LV-WNA	Boeing 737-2T4 (A)	*22368 / 707*	*EI-BOM*	*0080*	*0895*	*2 PW JT8D-15 (HK3/NOR)*	*54431*	*Y120*		*lsf GECA*
☐ LV-WNB	Boeing 737-2T4 (A)	*22369 / 708*	*EI-BON*	*0080*	*0895*	*2 PW JT8D-15*	*54431*	*Y120*		*lsf GECA*
☐ LV-WPA	Boeing 737-2T4C (A)	*23065 / 989*	*N675MA*	*0083*	*0496*	*2 PW JT8D-17A*	*56472*	*Y120*	*EK-CG*	Canopus / *lsf GECA*
☐ LV-WRZ	Boeing 737-204C	*20389 / 251*	*F-GGPB*	*0070*	*1296*	*2 PW JT8D-9A*	*53070*	*Y120*		Vega
☐ LV-WSH	Boeing 737-204C	*20282 / 245*	*F-GGPC*	*0070*	*1296*	*2 PW JT8D-9A*	*53070*	*Y120*		*lsf Ardennes Ltd*
☐ LV-WYI	Boeing 737-266 (A)	*21196 / 465*	*LV-PMW*	*0076*	*0897*	*2 PW JT8D-17A*	*54204*	*Y120*		*lsf GECA*
☐ LV-YBS	Boeing 737-266 (A)	*21193 / 453*	*LV-PNI*	*0076*	*0198*	*2 PW JT8D-17A*	*54204*	*Y120*		*lsf GECA*
☐ LV-YGB	Boeing 737-2S3 (A)	*22633 / 746*	*N633GP*	*0081*	*0298*	*2 PW JT8D-15*	*55772*	*Y120*		*lsf GECA*
☐ LV-YXB	Boeing 737-204 (A)	*21335 / 487*	*LV-PNO*	*0077*	*0298*	*2 PW JT8D-15*	*53750*	*Y120*		*lsf TRIT*
☐ LV-YZA	Boeing 737-204 (A)	*21336 / 489*	*LV-PNS*	*0077*	*0398*	*2 PW JT8D-15*	*53750*	*Y120*		*lsf TRIT*
☐ LV-YYC	Boeing 737-7Q8	*28210 / 22*	*N801LF*	*0498*	*0798*	*2 CFMI CFM56-7B24*	*69400*	*Y148*		Polaris / *lsf ILFC*
☐ LV-ZHX	Boeing 737-76N	*28577 / 124*	*LV-PNZ*	*0098*	*1198*	*2 CFMI CFM56-7B24*	*69400*	*Y148*		Borealis / *lsf GECA*
☐ LV-	Boeing 737-7Q8					*2 CFMI CFM56-7B24*	*69400*			*to be lsf ILFC 0999*
☐ N331LF	Boeing 737-7Q8	*28219 / 183*	*N1782B*	*0199*	*0199*	*2 CFMI CFM56-7B24*	*69400*			*lsf ILFC*
☐ LV-WMH	Boeing 757-2Q8	*26332 / 688*		*0095*	*0995*	*2 PW PW2040*	*113398*	*Y227*		Sirius / *lsf ILFC*
☐ LV-WTS	Boeing 757-2Q8	*25131 / 458*	*CC-CYH*	*0092*	*0597*	*2 PW PW2040*	*113398*	*Y218*		Anillaco / *lsf ILFC*

LAWSA - Lineas Aéreas Williams, S.A. — Buenos Aires-Aeroparque J. Newbery

Aeroparque Jorge Newbery, 1425 Buenos Aires, Argentina ☎ (1) 777 35 00 Tx: none Fax: (1) 777 35 00 SITA: n/a
F: n/a ⁂ n/a Head: n/a Net: n/a

☐ LV-WGF	Bell 206L-1 LongRanger II	*45635*	*N75AJ*	*0080*	*1197*	*1 AN 250-C28B*	*1882*			
☐ N385PH	Fairchild (Swearingen) SA227AC Metro III	*AC-595*	*N3116L*	*0084*	*0797*	*2 GA TPE331-11U-611G*	*6577*			*lsf Joda Partnership*

237 registration type of aircraft *cn/fn* *ex/ex** *mfd* *del* *powered by* *mtow kg* *configuration* *selcal* *name/fln/specialitites/remarks*

MACAIR JET, S.A.

Buenos Aires-Aeroparque J. Newbery

Av. Rafael Obligado sn, Hall Taxi Aéreos, 1425 Buenos Aires, Argentina ☎ (1) 777 75 14 Tx: none Fax: (1) 777 74 52 SITA: n/a
F: 1996 ⁂ n/a Head: Franco Macri Net: n/a

☐ LV-WFM	Learjet 60	60-024	LV-PGX	0094		2 PWC PW305A	10478			
☐ LV-WOM	GAC G-IV Gulfstream IV (SP)	1274	N458GA	0095	0196	2 RR Tay 611-8	33838			

MALDONADO AIR

Buenos Aires-Don Torcuato

Avda Cabral s/n, 6500 Nueve Vejulio, Argentina ☎ (317) 22 730 Tx: none Fax: (317) 22 730 SITA: n/a
F: 1993 ⁂ n/a Head: Guillermo F. Maldonado Net: n/a

☐ LV-WFU	MD Helicopters MD 500D (Hughes 369D)	290463D	N58277	0079	0094	1 AN 250-C20B	1361			
☐ LV-LSF	Beech Bonanza V35B	D-9749	LV-PTQ	0075	0396	1 CO IO-520-BA	1542			

MEDICORP ARGENTINA

Buenos Aires-San Fernando

Cerrito 836, 7y8 Piso, 1010 Buenos Aires, Argentina ☎ (1) 815 12 77 Tx: n/a Fax: (1) 816 06 70 SITA: n/a
F: 1993 ⁂ n/a Head: n/a Net: n/a

☐ N60BT	Mitsubishi MU-2P (MU-2B-26A)	358SA	C-GIRO	0077	0093	2 GA TPE331-5-252M	4749	EMS		lsf TAM Srl.
☐ LV-WMR	Learjet 24	24-135	N77LB	0066	0094	2 GE CJ610-4	5897	EMS		lsf TAM Srl.

ORION Servicios Aéreos, S.A.

Buenos Aires-Aeroparque J. Newbery

Amemabar 1342, 1426 Buenos Aires, Argentina ☎ (1) 784 39 49 Tx: none Fax: (1) 783 24 57 SITA: n/a
F: n/a ⁂ n/a Head: Alfredo Martinez Net: n/a

☐ LV-WYV	Let 410UVP-E	912603	OK-WDP	0091	0097	2 WA M-601E	6400	Y19		

RACA, SA

Buenos Aires-San Fernando

Ruta 202 y Panamericana, Aeropuerto San Fernando, 1646 San Fernando (Buenos Aires), Argentina ☎ (1) 746 44 77 Tx: n/a Fax: (1) 746 67 84 SITA: n/a
F: 1969 ⁂ 35 Head: Mrs. Isabel Fernandez-Racca Net: n/a Aircraft below MTOW 1361kg: Hughes 369HS (500C).

☐ LV-WEP	MD Helicopters MD 520N (Hughes 500N)	LN039	LV-DMF	0092		1 AN 250-C20R	1520			

RADEAIR, S.A.

Buenos Aires-Aeroparque J. Newbery

Aeroparque Jorge Newbery, Rafael Obligado sn, Hangar 1, 1425 Buenos Aires, Argentina ☎ (1) 777 03 00 Tx: none Fax: (1) 778 05 50 SITA: n/a
F: 1986 ⁂ 15 Head: Miguel Denegri Net: n/a

☐ LV-WIB	Bell 206L-1 LongRanger II	45591	N505BB	0081	0794	1 AN 250-C28B	1882			
☐ LV-WOV	IAI 1124 Westwind I	331	N811VC	0081	0098	2 GA TFE731-3-1G	10659			
☐ N911SP	IAI 1124 Westwind	244	N124PA	0079	0492	2 GA TFE731-3-1G	10365			lsf Free Wind Corp.

RENT-A-PLANE, SA

Buenos Aires-Aeroparque J. Newbery

Aeroparque Jorge Newbery, 1425 Buenos Aires, Argentina ☎ (1) 772 65 73 Tx: none Fax: (1) 778 13 48 SITA: n/a
F: 1976 ⁂ 8 Head: Edgardo Ferreyra Net: n/a

☐ LV-IYO	Twin (Aero) Commander 500U	500U-1673-19	N6529V	0066		2 LY IO-540-E1A5	3062	5 Pax		
☐ LV-MNP	Piper PA-31-310 Navajo C	31-7812122		0078		2 LY TIO-540-A2C	2948	6 Pax		
☐ LV-JLW	Beech Excalibur Queenaire 8200	LC-282		0068		2 LY IO-720-A1B	3719	8 Pax		cvtd Queen Air A65 / std Don Torcuato
☐ LV-ONN	Learjet 35A	35A-355	LV-PJZ	0080		2 GA TFE731-2-2B	8165	8 Pax		lsf Dahm Automotores

ROYAL CLASS, S.A. (Subsidiary of Lanolec, S.A.)

Buenos Aires-Aeroparque J. Newbery

Viamonte 352, Piso 5, Oficina I, 1053 Buenos Aires, Argentina ☎ (11) 47 76 08 88 Tx: none Fax: (11) 47 76 08 88 SITA: n/a
F: 1993 ⁂ 12 Head: n/a Net: n/a

☐ LV-WDR	Cessna 560 Citation V	560-0227	LV-PGR	0093	0095	2 PWC JT15D-5A	7212	VIP / EMS		lsf Landelec S.A.
☐ LV-WMT	Cessna 560 Citation V Ultra	560-0305	LV-PLE	0095	0795	2 PWC JT15D-5D	7394	VIP / EMS		

SAB – Servicio Aéreo Bahiense

Bahia Blanca

Calle Madrid 42, 8000 Bahia Blanca, (Buenos Aires), Argentina ☎ (66) 70 50 73 Tx: none Fax: (91) 54 50 10 SITA: n/a
F: 1990 ⁂ n/a Head: Pablo Fuentes Net: n/a Aircraft below MTOW 1361kg: Cessna 152 & 182.

☐ LV-VFB	Piper PA-34-200T Seneca II	34-8070058	N37TT	0080	0692	2 CO TSIO-360-EB	2073			
☐ LV-JZP	Piper PA-31-310 Navajo	31-429		0069		2 LY TIO-540-A1A	2948			

SAPSA – Servicios Aéreos Patagonicas, S.A. (Alas Rionegrinas) (formerly SAP-Servicios Aéreos Patagonicas, S.E.)

Viedma

Av. San Martin 57, 8500 Viedma, (Rio Negro), Argentina ☎ (920) 21 405 Tx: none Fax: (920) 23 990 SITA: n/a
F: 1990 ⁂ 50 Head: Robert Trappa Net: n/a

☐ LV-JOR	Cessna 402A	402A0129		0069		2 CO TSIO-520-E	2858	Y9		
☐ LV-LTC	Twin (Aero) Turbo Commander 690A	11241	LV-PUB	0075		2 GA TPE331-5-251K	4649	Y8		
☐ LV-RBP	Fairchild (Swearingen) SA227AC Metro III	AC-415	N173MA	0081	0891	2 GA TPE331-11U-611G	6577	Y19		cvtd IIA/cn TC-415
☐ LV-RBR	Fairchild (Swearingen) SA227AC Metro III	AC-416	N177MA	0081	0891	2 GA TPE331-11U-611G	6577	Y19		cvtd IIA/cn TC-416
☐ LV-WAG	Fairchild (Swearingen) SA227AC Metro III	AC-543B	D-CKVW	0083	0593	2 GA TPE331-11U-611G	7257	Y19		cvtd SA227AT

SENMA, S.A.

Buenos Aires-San Fernando & -Aeroparque J. Newbery

Aeropuerto Internacional San Fernando, Acceso norte (ramal Tigre), Ruta 202, 1646 San Fernando (Buenos Aires), Argentina ☎ (1) 714 84 98 Tx: none Fax: (1) 714 23 98 SITA: n/a
F: n/a ⁂ n/a Head: Rodolfo Jose Pereyro Net: n/a

☐ N26974	Fairchild (Swearingen) SA227AC Metro III	AC-664		0086	1198	2 GA TPE331-11U-611G	6577	Freighter / Y19		lsf Joda Partnership
☐ N2698C	Fairchild (Swearingen) SA227AC Metro III	AC-665		0086	0398	2 GA TPE331-11U-611G	6577	Freighter / Y19		lsf Joda Partnership
☐ N31168	Fairchild (Swearingen) SA227AC Metro III	AC-599		0084	0898	2 GA TPE331-11U-611G	6577	Freighter / Y19		lsf Joda Partnership
☐ N3116F	Fairchild (Swearingen) SA227AC Metro III	AC-594		0084	0098	2 GA TPE331-11U-611G	6577	Freighter / Y19		lsf Joda Partnership
☐ N3116Z	Fairchild (Swearingen) SA227AC Metro III	AC-598		0084	0498	2 GA TPE331-11U-611G	6577	Freighter / Y19		lsf Joda Partnership

SERVICIOS ESPECIALES, SA

Mendoza

Miguens 3519, 1644 Victoria, (Buenos Aires), Argentina ☎ (1) 746 36 57 Tx: n/a Fax: (1) 746 36 57 SITA: n/a
F: n/a ⁂ n/a Head: Manuel Prieto Net: n/a Aircraft below MTOW 1361kg: Bell 47G, Hughes 369C (500C) & Piper PA-25

☐ N77HA	AAC (Ted Smith) Aerostar 601	61-0137-075		0073	0095	2 LY IO-540-S1A5	2585			lsf BGM Airborne Surveys Inc.
☐ N9464F	Cessna 208 Caravan I	20800062		0085	0096	1 PWC PT6A-114	3629			lsf BGM Airborne Surveys Inc.
☐ LV-INC	Twin (Aero) Grand Commander 680FL	680FL-1467-90		0064	0096	2 LY IGSO-540-B1A	3856			
☐ N4489L	Cessna 404 Titan II	404-0029		0077	1296	2 CO GTSIO-520-M	3810	Photo/Survey		lsf BGM Airborne Surveys Inc.
☐ LV-WED	Bell 204 (UH-1B)	426	N4242T	0062	1193	1 LY T53-L-11	3856			
☐ LV-WIX	Bell 204 (UH-1B)	1157	N479SA	0064	0994	1 LY T53-L-11	3856	64-14033		
☐ LV-WMS	Bell 204 (UH-1B)	833	63-8611	0063	0095	1 LY T53-L-11	3856			
☐ LV-WPJ	Bell 204 (UH-1B)	505	N489SA	0062	0896	1 LY T53-L-11	3856			

SOUTHERN WINDS, S.A. = A4 / SWD (Aerolineas Argentinas Connection) (formerly Pampas Air)

Cordoba

Avda Colon 540, 5000 Cordoba, Argentina ☎ (51) 24 76 72 Tx: none Fax: (51) 24 72 51 SITA: n/a
F: 1996 ⁂ n/a Head: Juan Maggio IATA: 242 ICAO: SOUTHERN WINDS Net: n/a Flights are operated in conjunction with Aerolineas Argentinas as a AEROLINEAS ARGENTINAS CONNECTION-carrier (both titles on aircraft).

☐ LV-POD	De Havilland DHC-8-102 Dash 8	330	N826MA	0092	0199	2 PWC PW120A	15649	Y37		lsf Bombardier Capital Inc.
☐ LV-YTA	De Havilland DHC-8-102 Dash 8	363	N864MA	0093	0698	2 PWC PW120A	15649	Y37		lsf Bombardier Capital Inc.
☐ LV-YTC	De Havilland DHC-8-102 Dash 8	366	N866MA	0093	0698	2 PWC PW120A	15649	Y37		lsf Bombardier Capital Inc.
☐ LV-ZGB	De Havilland DHC-8-102 Dash 8	364	N865MA	0093	0898	2 PWC PW120A	15649	Y37		lsf Bombardier Capital Inc.
☐ LV-ZLZ	De Havilland DHC-8-102 Dash 8	361	N859MA	0093	1198	2 PWC PW120A	15649	Y37		lsf Bombardier Capital Inc.
☐ LV-WPF	Canadair Regional Jet 100LR (CL-600-2B19)	7115	C-FXPQ*	0096	0796	2 GE CF34-3A1	23995	Y50		Cordoba / lsf Bombardier / cvtd 100ER
☐ LV-WSB	Canadair Regional Jet 100ER (CL-600-2B19)	7154	C-FMOI*	0096	0197	2 GE CF34-3A1	23133	Y50		lsf Bombardier
☐ LV-WXT	Canadair Regional Jet 100LR (CL-600-2B19)	7041	F-GPYZ	0094	0897	2 GE CF34-3A1	23995	Y50		lsf Bombardier Inc./CLH / cvtd 100ER
☐ LV-YLA	Canadair Regional Jet 100LR (CL-600-2B19)	7039	LV-PNT	0094	0498	2 GE CF34-3A1	24000	Y50		lsf Bombardier/CLH / cvtd -100ER
☐ F-GNMN	Canadair Regional Jet 100ER (CL-600-2B19)	7003	C-GVRJ*	0090	0698	2 GE CF34-3A1	23133	Y50		lsf LIT

STAF – Servicios de Transportes Aéreos Fueguinos, SA = FS / STU

Buenos Aires-Ministro Pistarini

Carlos Pelegrini 1063-1B, 1009 Buenos Aires, Argentina ☎ (1) 394 78 23 Tx: n/a Fax: (1) 394 90 67 SITA: n/a
F: 1985 ⁂ n/a Head: Dr. Elbio A.S. Ferrario IATA: 278 ICAO: FUEGUINO Net: n/a Beside aircraft listed, also leases Airbus Industrie A300 & Boeing 757/767 from other companies when required.

☐ N276WA	Boeing (Douglas) MD-11F (CF)	48632 / 582		0095	0898	3 PW PW4462	280320	Freighter		lsf / opb WOA in STAF-colors

TACA – Transporte Aéreo Costa Atlantica, S.A.

Buenos Aires-San Fernando

Casilla Correo 40, 1401 Buenos Aires, Argentina ☎ (1) 307 19 56 Tx: 23891 opr ar Fax: (1) 307 19 56 SITA: n/a
F: 1957 ⁂ 29 Head: Dr. Armando Schlecker Hirsch Net: n/a Beside aircraft listed, also leases Fairchild Metro II from Air Tango & TACA when required.

☐ LV-IXR	Piper PA-32-300 Cherokee SIX	32-753		0066		1 LY IO-540-K1A5	1542			
☐ LV-GXO	Piper PA-23-250 Aztec A	27-249		0060	0490	2 LY O-540-A1B5	2177			
☐ LV-IIL	Cessna 310I	310I0149		0064	0291	2 CO IO-470-U	2313			
☐ LV-CRB	Fairchild C-82A-FA Jet Packet	10071	N8009E	0045		2 PW R-2800-85+J1000jet	24494	Freighter		
☐ LV-PNY	Fairchild C-82A-FA Jet Packet	10045	44-23001	0045		2 PW R-2800-85+J1000jet	24494	Freighter		

TAC – Transportes Aéreos de Catamarca (Division of the Directorate of Aeronautics of the Province of Catamarca)

Catamarca

Dir. Aeronautica, Gen. Navaro y Congresso Central, Villas Cubas, San Fernando del Valle, 4700 Catamarca (Catamarca), Argentina ☎ (833) 37 575 Tx: none Fax: (833) 37 576 SITA: n/a
F: 1993 ⁂ 25 Head: Alvarez Carlos Net: n/a

☐ LV-APF	Piper PA-42 Cheyenne III	42-8001026	LV-DMP	0081		2 PWC PT6A-41	5080	Y9		
☐ LV-WEE	Fairchild (Swearingen) SA227AC Metro III	AC-516	N45ML	0082	1193	2 GA TPE331-11U-611G	6577	Y19		

TAL – Trade Airlines, S.A. — Buenos Aires-Aeroparque J. Newbery

Bartolome Mitre 811, 3P, 1036 Buenos Aires, Argentina ☎ (1) 328 80 78 Tx: none Fax: (1) 328 69 25 SITA: n/a
F: n/a ⁂ n/a Head: Vicente Angelucci Net: n/a

☐ LV-WNY	Fairchild (Swearingen) SA226TC Metro II	TC-313	N230AM	0079	0097	2 GA TPE331-10UA-511G	5670	Y19		Ciudad de Rio Cuarto

TAN – Transportes Aéreos Neuquen, S.A. = T8 / NQN (Subsidiary of VASP, Brazil / formerly TAN-Transportes Aéreos Neuquen, S.E.) — Neuquen

Diagonal 25 de Mayo 180, 8300 Neuquen, (Neuquen), Argentina ☎ (99) 44 06 07 Tx: none Fax: (99) 44 06 07 SITA: n/a
F: 1972 ⁂ 110 Head: Jose Chalen IATA: 249 ICAO: TANEU Net: n/a

☐ LV-MAU	Twin (Aero) Turbo Commander 690B	11394	LV-PVL	0077	0777	2 GA TPE331-5-251K	4683	Y8		Alumine
☐ LV-MAW	Twin (Aero) Turbo Commander 690B	11398	LV-PVN	0077	0777	2 GA TPE331-5-251K	4683	Y8		Collon Cora
☐ LV-AOP	Fairchild (Swearingen) SA227AC Metro III	AC-460	N3029F	0081	1281	2 GA TPE331-11U-601G	6577	Y19		
☐ LV-VDJ	Fairchild (Swearingen) SA227AC Metro III	AC-729	N27283	0089	0992	2 GA TPE331-11U-612G	6577	Y19		
☐ LV-AXV	Saab SF340A	340A-094	SE-E94*	0087	0987	2 GE CT7-5A2	12372	Y34		
☐ LV-YOB	Saab SF340A	340A-033	SE-ISS	0085	1194	2 GE CT7-5A2	12700	Y34		

TAPSA Aviacion – Transportes Aéreos Petroleros, S.A. = TPS — Buenos Aires-Min.Pistarini, Comodoro Rivadavia & Salta

Sarmiento 539, 7 Piso, 1041 Buenos Aires, Argentina ☎ (1) 480 05 72 Tx: n/a Fax: (1) 480 05 52 SITA: n/a
F: 1991 ⁂ n/a Head: Mr. Abrita ICAO: TAPSA Net: n/a

☐ LV-JTA	Cessna 402B	402B0038		0070	1291	2 CO TSIO-520-E	2858			
☐ LV-JYP	Cessna 402B	402B0122		0071	1291	2 CO TSIO-520-E	2858			
☐ LV-MAG	Twin (Aero) Turbo Commander 690B	11392	LV-PVH	0077	0694	2 GA TPE331-5-251K	4683			
☐ LV-MOO	Twin (Aero) Turbo Commander 690B II	11543	LV-PBS	0079	0095	2 GA TPE331-5-251K	4649			
☐ LV-APT	De Havilland DHC-6 Twin Otter 200	138	AE-258	0068	1291	2 PWC PT6A-20	5252			
☐ LV-JMM	De Havilland DHC-6 Twin Otter 200	205	LQ-JMM	0069	1291	2 PWC PT6A-20	5252			
☐ LV-JMN	De Havilland DHC-6 Twin Otter 200	214	LQ-JMN	0069	1291	2 PWC PT6A-20	5252			
☐ LV-JPX	De Havilland DHC-6 Twin Otter 200	185	LQ-JPX	0070	1291	2 PWC PT6A-20	5252			
☐ LV-LNY	De Havilland DHC-6 Twin Otter 200	171	1-G-101	0069	1291	2 PWC PT6A-20	5252			
☐ LV-LSI	De Havilland DHC-6 Twin Otter 300	456	LV-PTW	0075	1291	2 PWC PT6A-27	5670			
☐ LV-LSJ	De Havilland DHC-6 Twin Otter 300	458	LV-PTX	0075	1291	2 PWC PT6A-27	5670			
☐ LV-MAH	De Havilland DHC-6 Twin Otter 300	535	LV-PVF	0077	1291	2 PWC PT6A-27	5670			
☐ LV-WJT	Fairchild (Swearingen) SA227AC Metro III	AC-776B	N776NE	0091	0198	2 GA TPE331-11U-612G	7257	Y19		
☐ LV-MRY	IAI 102 Arava	055	LV-PBO	0078	1291	2 PWC PT6A-34	6804			
☐ LV-WLD	Saab SF340A	340A-013	LV-PHW	0084	0295	2 GE CT7-5A2	12700	Y34		

TARSA – Transportes Angela Rosa, SA — Buenos Aires-Aeroparque J. Newbery

Aeropuerto Jorge Newbery, 1425 Buenos Aires, Argentina ☎ (1) 772 30 22 Tx: n/a Fax: (1) 772 30 22 SITA: n/a
F: 1978 ⁂ 14 Head: Ernesto Gaboto Net: n/a

☐ LV-JJB	Cessna 310N	310N0198		0068		2 CO IO-470-V	2359			
☐ LV-MBZ	AAC (Ted Smith) Aerostar 600A	60-0423-144	N9773Q	0077		2 LY IO-540-K1F5	2495			
☐ LV-MDH	AAC (Ted Smith) Aerostar 601P	61P-0428-158	N9793Q	0077		2 LY IO-540-S1A5	2722			
☐ LV-JTH	Cessna 414	414-0055		0070		2 CO TSIO-520-J	2880			

TIME SAVE AIR — Buenos Aires-San Fernando

Sarmiento 1206, Piso 3, Of. 8, 1058 Buenos Aires, Argentina ☎ (1) 382 42 10 Tx: n/a Fax: (1) 382 42 10 SITA: n/a
F: n/a ⁂ n/a Head: n/a Net: n/a

☐ LV-RAC	Mitsubishi MU-2P (MU-2B-26A)	386SA	N999BE	0078		2 GA TPE331-5-252M	4749			

TRANSPORTES BRAGADO, SA — Buenos Aires-Aeroparque J. Newbery

Bernardo de Irigoyen 190, Piso 8, 1138 Buenos Aires, Argentina ☎ (1) 394 46 73 Tx: n/a Fax: (1) 394 46 36 SITA: n/a
F: 1987 ⁂ n/a Head: n/a Net: n/a

☐ LV-MIF	Piper PA-34-200T Seneca II	34-7870212		0078	0587	2 CO TSIO-360-E	2073			
☐ LV-MGD	Piper PA-31T Cheyenne II	31T-7720059	LV-PXD	0077	1086	2 PWC PT6A-28	4082			

LX = LUXEMBOURG (Grand Duchy of Luxembourg) (Grousherzogdem Letzebuerg / GD du Luxembourg)

Capital: Luxembourg Official Language: Letzeburgish, French Population: 0,4 million Square Km: 2586 Dialling code: +352 Year established: 1815 Acting political head: Jean-Claude Juncker (Prime Minister)

CAE AVIATION, SàRL — Luxembourg

Aéroport, L-1110 Luxembourg, GD Luxembourg ☎ 43 68 11 Tx: 1444 cae lu Fax: 43 68 89 SITA: n/a
F: 1971 ⁂ 20 Head: Bernard J.C. Zeler Net: n/a Ag-Aircraft below MTOW 5000 kg: Cessna A188B AgTruck (Sprayer).

☐ LX-KEV	Britten-Norman BN-2T Turbine Islander	2102	LX-III	1281	0192	2 AN 250-B17C	3175			cvtd BN-2B-26
☐ LX-ABC	Shorts Skyvan 3 Variant 100 (SC-7)	SH1888	PA-51	0071	0695	2 GA TPE331-2-201A	6215			
☐ LX-GHI	Shorts Skyvan 3 Variant 100 (SC-7)	SH1890	PA-53	0071	0795	2 GA TPE331-2-201A	6215			

CARGO LION = TLX (Translux International Airlines, SA dba / Member of the Cargo Lion Group) — Luxembourg

Lion Aviation Bldg., Aéroport, L-1110 Luxembourg, GD Luxembourg ☎ 422 58 51 Tx: none Fax: 422 58 52 22 SITA: LUXCLCR
F: 1992 ⁂ 75 Head: Capt. Bertram G. Pohl ICAO: TRANSLUX Net: http://www.cargolion.com

☐ LX-TLA	Boeing (Douglas) DC-8-62F (CF)	45960 / 347	F-GDJM	0468	0792	4 PW JT3D-7 (HK3/BAC)	158759	Freighter	BG-AM	lsf Guernsey Air Leasing
☐ LX-TLB	Boeing (Douglas) DC-8-62F	45925 / 333	N922BV	0268	0495	4 PW JT3D-7 (HK3/BAC)	151955	Freighter		lsf Guernsey Air Leasing / cvtd -62
☐ LX-TLC	Boeing (Douglas) DC-8-62F	45920 / 319	N924BV	0068	0198	4 PW JT3D-7 (HK3/BAC)	151955	Freighter		lsf ALGI / cvtd -62

CARGOLUX Airlines International, SA = CV / CLX (Associated with Luxair & Swissair) — Luxembourg

Aéroport, L-2990 Luxembourg, GD Luxembourg ☎ 42 111 Tx: 2272 cvlux lu Fax: 43 54 46 SITA: n/a
F: 1970 ⁂ 1000 Head: Heiner Wilkens IATA: 172 ICAO: CARGOLUX Net: http://www.cargolux.com Beside aircraft listed, also uses 2 Boeing 747-400F, lsf/opb ATLAS AIR (N) when required.

☐ LX-FCV	Boeing 747-4R7F (SCD)	25866 / 1002	N1785B*	0093	1193	4 GE CF6-80C2B1F	396893	Freighter	CS-KL	City of Luxembourg / lsf Elena Leasing
☐ LX-GCV	Boeing 747-4R7F (SCD)	25867 / 1008		0093	1293	4 GE CF6-80C2B1F	396893	Freighter	CS-KM	City of Esch/Alzette / lsf GeraldineLsg
☐ LX-ICV	Boeing 747-428F (SCD)	25632 / 968	N6005C*	0093	0995	4 GE CF6-80C2B1F	396893	Freighter	JS-EP	City of Ettelbrück
☐ LX-KCV	Boeing 747-4R7F (SCD)	25868 / 1125		0897	0897	4 GE CF6-80C2B1F	396893	Freighter	CG-KR	
☐ LX-LCV	Boeing 747-4R7F (SCD)	29053 / 1139		1297	1297	4 GE CF6-80C2B1F	396893	Freighter	PS-JL	City of Grevenmacher
☐ LX-MCV	Boeing 747-4R7F (SCD)	29729 / 1189		0098	1298	4 RR RB211-524G/H-T	396893	Freighter		City of Echternach
☐ LX-NCV	Boeing 747-4R7F (SCD)	29730		0099	0399	4 RR RB211-524G/H-T	396893	Freighter		
☐ LX-OCV	Boeing 747-4R7F (SCD)	29731				4 RR RB211-524G/H-T	396893	Freighter		oo-delivery 0899
☐ LX-	Boeing 747-4R7F (SCD)					4 RR RB211-524G/H-T	396893	Freighter		oo-delivery 1099
☐ LX-	Boeing 747-4R7F (SCD)					4 RR RB211-524G/H-T	396893	Freighter		oo-delivery 1099
☐ LX-	Boeing 747-4R7F (SCD)					4 RR RB211-524G/H-T	396893	Freighter		oo-delivery 1199
☐ LX-	Boeing 747-4R7F (SCD)					4 RR RB211-524G/H-T	396893	Freighter		oo-delivery 0602

HELI UNION INTERNATIONAL, SA (Subsidiary of Heli-Union, France) — Luxembourg, Africa & South America

56 bd Napoleon, 1er, L-2210 Luxembourg, GD Luxembourg ☎ 440 95 12 00 Tx: none Fax: 45 75 54 SITA: n/a
F: 1992 ⁂ 2 Head: Christophe de Courlon Net: n/a

☐ LX-HUN	Eurocopter (Aerosp.) AS365N2 Dauphin 2	6468	F-GJBU	0094		2 TU Arriel 1C2	4250	11 Pax		lsf Heli-Union, France
☐ LX-HUA	Sikorsky S-76A+	760170	F-GKSI	0081	1297	2 TU Arriel 1S	4763	12 Pax		lsf Heli-Union, France / cvtd S-76A
☐ LX-HUD	Sikorsky S-76A++	760042	F-GILD	0079	0792	2 TU Arriel 1S1	4763	12 Pax		lsf HLU/sub-lst Court,ZS-RKE/cvtd S-76A
☐ LX-HUE	Sikorsky S-76A+	760186	F-GDHU	0082	0792	2 TU Arriel 1S	4763	12 Pax		lsf Heli-Union, France / cvtd S-76A
☐ LX-HUL	Eurocopter (Aerosp.) SA330J Puma	1583	F-GHYR	0078		2 TU Turmo IVC	7400	17 Pax		lsf Heli-Union, France

LUXAIR Société de Luxembourgeoise Navigation Aérienne, SA = LG / LGL — Luxembourg

BP 2203, L-2987 Luxembourg, GD Luxembourg ☎ 47 981 Tx: 2372 lgddap lu Fax: 47 98 42 89 SITA: LUXSMLG
F: 1962 ⁂ 1660 Head: Jean-Donat Calmes IATA: 149 ICAO: LUXAIR Net: http://www.luxair.lu Beside aircraft listed, also uses a Boeing 767-300 (ER) lsf/opb CITY BIRD (OO-) for scheduled flights to USA when required.

☐ LX-LGT	Embraer RJ145LR (EMB-145LR) (Eurojet)	145076	PT-SAU*	0098	0898	2 AN AE3007A1/2	22000	Y50		Princess Alexandra
☐ LX-LGU	Embraer RJ145LR (EMB-145LR) (Eurojet)	145084		0098	1098	2 AN AE3007A1/2	22000	Y50	KR-DH	Prince Sebastien
☐ LX-LGV	Embraer RJ145LR (EMB-145LR) (Eurojet)					2 AN AE3007A1/2	22000	Y50		oo-delivery 0100
☐ LX-LGW	Embraer RJ145LR (EMB-145LR) (Eurojet)					2 AN AE3007A1/2	22000	Y50		oo-delivery 0200
☐ LX-LGX	Embraer RJ145LR (EMB-145LR) (Eurojet)					2 AN AE3007A1/2	22000	Y50		oo-delivery 0600
☐ LX-LGY	Embraer RJ145LR (EMB-145LR) (Eurojet)					2 AN AE3007A1/2	22000	Y50		oo-delivery 1000
☐ LX-LGZ	Embraer RJ145LR (EMB-145LR) (Eurojet)					2 AN AE3007A1/2	22000	Y50		oo-delivery 0001
☐ LX-LGB	Fokker 50 (F27 Mk050)	20221	PH-EXU*	0091	0691	2 PWC PW125B	20820	Y50	AQ-ES	lsf SL-Done Co Ltd
☐ LX-LGC	Fokker 50 (F27 Mk050)	20168	PH-EXH*	0089	1189	2 PWC PW125B	20820	Y50	JQ-CK	Prince Guillaume / lsf Slux (One)CoLtd
☐ LX-LGD	Fokker 50 (F27 Mk050)	20171	PH-EXJ*	0089	1289	2 PWC PW125B	20820	Y50	JQ-CL	Prince Félix / lsf Slux (One) Co Ltd
☐ LX-LGE	Fokker 50 (F27 Mk050)	20180	PH-EXF*	0090	0390	2 PWC PW125B	20820	Y50	JQ-CM	Prince Louis / lsf Slux (Two) Co Ltd
☐ LX-LGO	Boeing 737-5C9	26438 / 2413		0092	0193	2 CFMI CFM56-3C1	57833	Y121	BQ-ER	Chateau de Clervaux
☐ LX-LGP	Boeing 737-5C9	26439 / 2444		0093	0393	2 CFMI CFM56-3C1	57833	Y121	BQ-ES	Chateau de Bourglinster
☐ LX-LGR	Boeing 737-528	27424 / 2720		0095	0895	2 CFMI CFM56-3C1	54657	Y121	BQ-FS	Chateau de Beaufort / lsf Itochu Lease
☐ LX-LGS	Boeing 737-528	27425 / 2730		0095	0995	2 CFMI CFM56-3C1	53977	Y121	BQ-GR	Chateau de Schengen / lsf ITOH
☐ LX-LGF	Boeing 737-4C9	25429 / 2215		0092	0292	2 CFMI CFM56-3C1	65997	Y165	AQ-FR	Chateau de Vianden / lsf Lux Spring Ltd
☐ LX-LGG	Boeing 737-4C9	26437 / 2249		0092	0392	2 CFMI CFM56-3C1	65997	Y165	AQ-FS	Ch.de Bourscheid / lsf Lux East Ltd

239 registration | type of aircraft | cn/fn | ex/ex* | mfd | del | powered by | mtow kg | configuration | selcal | name/fln/specialitites/remarks

LUXAVIATION, S.A. = LXA   Luxembourg

Aviation Générale, Aéroport, L-1110 Luxembourg, GD Luxembourg   ☎ 425 25 21 Tx: none Fax: 42 71 40 SITA: n/a
F: 1992   ♦♦♦ 10 Head: Nico F. Franck ICAO: RED LION Net: http://www.luxaviation.lu

	registration	type of aircraft	cn/fn	ex/ex*	mfd	del	powered by	mtow kg	configuration	selcal	name/fln/remarks
☐	LX-GDB	Beech King Air 200	BB-397	D-IAMW	0078	0297	2 PWC PT6A-41	5670	10 Pax		
☐	LX-GDL	Cessna F550 Citation II	550-0033	F-WPLT	0078	0296	2 PWC JT15D-4	5670	8 Pax		
☐	LX-THS	Cessna F550 Citation II	550-0074	D-CIFA	0079	0198	2 PWC JT15D-4	5670	8 Pax		lst THZ

LUXEMBOURG AIR RESCUE, a.s. = LUV   Luxembourg

175A rue de Cessange, L-1321 Luxembourg, GD Luxembourg   ☎ 48 90 06 Tx: none Fax: 40 25 63 SITA: n/a
F: 1988   ♦♦♦ 27 Head: René Closter ICAO: LUX RESCUE Net: n/a

☐	OO-EMS	MD Helicopters MD 900 Explorer	900-00020	SE-JCG	0095	0596	2 PWC PW206A	2722	EMS		Christoph Lux 2 / lsf Helifly
☐	LX-RST	Piper PA-31T Cheyenne II	31T-7820027	F-GGPJ	0078		2 PWC PT6A-28	4082	EMS		lsf Creditlease S.A.
☐	LX-TWO	Mitsubishi MU-2B-60 Marquise	1515SA	N802SM	0081	1098	2 GA TPE331-10-511M	5250	EMS		

SOLID'AIR, S.A.   Luxembourg

Rue de Luxembourg, L-5230 Sandweiler, Luxembourg   ☎ 355 22 01 Tx: none Fax: 352 02 10 SITA: n/a
F: 1998   ♦♦♦ n/a Head: Ludovic Sauwen Net: n/a

☐	LX-	Airbus Industrie A310-304 (ET)	595	D-AIDM	0091		2 GE CF6-80C2A2	153000	C22Y195		to be lsf GOAL 0499
☐	LX-	Airbus Industrie A310-304 (ET)	599	D-AIDN	0092		2 GE CF6-80C2A2	153000	C22Y195		to be lsf GOAL 0499

LY = LITHUANIA (Republic of Lithuania) (Lietuvos Respublika)
Capital: Vilnius Official Language: Lithuanian Population: 3,8 million Square Km: 65200 Dialling code: +370 Year established: 1990 Acting political head: Valdas Adamkus (President)

AIR KLAIPEDA = KLD (Klaipedos Avialinijos)   Klaipeda

Jaku pastas, LI-5843 Klaipeda, Lithuania   ☎ (6) 25 44 14 Tx: n/a Fax: (6) 25 52 85 SITA: n/a
F: 1976   ♦♦♦ n/a Head: n/a ICAO: AIR KLAIPEDA Net: n/a

☐	LY-HAI	Kamov Ka-26	7706010	CCCP-24308	0077	0096	2 VE M-14V-26	3250	Y7		
☐	LY-HAK	Kamov Ka-26	7605813	CCCP-24381	0076	0097	2 VE M-14V-26	3250	Y7		
☐	LY-HAN	Kamov Ka-26	7505211	CCCP-19631	0075		2 VE M-14V-26	3250	Y7		
☐	LY-AEK	PZL Mielec (Antonov) An-2	1G168-45	CCCP-82869	0076		1 SH ASh-62IR	5500	Sprayer		
☐	LY-AEL	PZL Mielec (Antonov) An-2	1G171-35	CCCP-92978	0076		1 SH ASh-62IR	5500	Sprayer		
☐	LY-AEN	PZL Mielec (Antonov) An-2	1G182-31	CCCP-56474	0079		1 SH ASh-62IR	5500	Sprayer		
☐	LY-AEO	PZL Mielec (Antonov) An-2	1G185-14	CCCP-54854	0079		1 SH ASh-62IR	5500	Y12		
☐	LY-AES	PZL Mielec (Antonov) An-2	1G191-16	CCCP-84638	0080		1 SH ASh-62IR	5500	Y12		
☐	LY-AEW	PZL Mielec (Antonov) An-2	1G206-60	CCCP-17955	0084		1 SH ASh-62IR	5500	Sprayer		
☐	LY-AFT	PZL Mielec (Antonov) An-2	1G178-16	LY-ACT	0077	0096	1 SH ASh-62IR	5500	Sprayer / Frtr		
☐	LY-AFU	PZL Mielec (Antonov) An-2	1G178-15	LY-ACU	0077	0096	1 SH ASh-62IR	5500	Sprayer / Frtr		
☐	LY-AHH	PZL Mielec (Antonov) An-2	1G212-34	RA-32729	0085	0098	1 SH ASh-62IR	5500	Sprayer / Frtr		
☐	LY-AKA	PZL Mielec (Antonov) An-2	1G197-47	RA-31424	0082	0098	1 SH ASh-62IR	5500	Sprayer / Frtr		
☐	LY-AKB	PZL Mielec (Antonov) An-2	1G230-28	RA-33586	0088	0098	1 SH ASh-62IR	5500	Sprayer / Frtr		

AIR LITHUANIA = TT / KLA (Aviakompanija Lietuva)   Kaunas

Veiveriu 132, LI-3018 Kaunas, Lithuania   ☎ (7) 29 52 03 Tx: none Fax: (7) 22 60 30 SITA: n/a
F: 1991   ♦♦♦ 200 Head: Kestutis Auryla IATA: 843 ICAO: KLA Net: http://www.airlithuania.lt

☐	LY-AAA	Yakovlev 40	9720154	CCCP-88279	0077		3 IV AI-25	16800	Y18		
☐	LY-AAB	Yakovlev 40	9520940	CCCP-87507	0075		3 IV AI-25	16800	Y28		
☐	LY-AAY	Yakovlev 40	9720753	CCCP-88269	0077		3 IV AI-25	16800	Y30		
☐	LY-ARI	ATR 42-300	012A	F-WQBT	0086	0397	2 PWC PW120	16700	Y46		lsf A.I.R.
☐	LY-ABA	Tupolev 134A	3352003	CCCP-65973	0073		2 SO D-30-II	49000	Y68		

AP AIRLINES = AVX (Aviapaslauga)   Kaunas

Veiveriu 132, LI-3018 Kaunas, Lithuania   ☎ (7) 29 54 57 Tx: n/a Fax: (7) 79 98 67 SITA: n/a
F: 1994   ♦♦♦ 10 Head: V. Tamosilinas ICAO: PASLAUGA Net: n/a

☐	LY-AFI	Let 410UVP-E3	872021	2021	0087	0497	2 WA M-601E	6400	Y17		
☐	LY-ASB	Let 410UVP	851426	CCCP-67522	0085		2 WA M-601D	5800	Y15		
☐	LY-AVA	Let 410UVP-E3	882036	2036	0088	0698	2 WA M-601E	6400	Y17		
☐	LY-AVT	Let 410UVP-E3	882033	2033	0088	0298	2 WA M-601E	6400	Y17		
☐	LY-AVX	Let 410UVP-E3	872015	2015	0087	0497	2 WA M-601E	6400	Y17		

AURELA, Co. Ltd = LSK   Vilnius

Rodunes Keles 2-10, LI-2038 Vilnius, Lithuania   ☎ (2) 26 44 30 Tx: none Fax: (2) 26 41 45 SITA: n/a
F: 1996   ♦♦♦ 12 Head: Kazimeras Gudonis ICAO: AURELA Net: n/a

☐	LY-ASK	Tupolev 134A	60054	LY-ABD	0077	0096	2 SO D-30-III	47600	F11C32		

AVIA BALTIKA Aviation Company, Ltd = KAB   Kaunas

Vilniaus str. 86a, LI-4301 Karmelava-Kaunas, Lithuania   ☎ (7) 54 12 30 Tx: none Fax: (7) 39 93 05 SITA: n/a
F: 1991   ♦♦♦ 74 Head: Jurii Borisov ICAO: AVIABALTIKA Net: n/a

☐	LY-HAO	Mil Mi-8T	3029		0072		2 IS TV2-117A	12000	28 Pax		
☐	LY-HAP	Mil Mi-8S	22613		0071		2 IS TV2-117A	12000	VIP 10 Pax		

HELISOTA (formerly Avia Baltika-Servisas)   Kaunas

Bakanausko 29, LI-3018 Kaunas, Lithuania   ☎ (7) 29 17 37 Tx: none Fax: (7) 29 54 20 SITA: n/a
F: 1997   ♦♦♦ n/a Head: n/a Net: n/a

☐	LY-HAQ	Mil Mi-8T	5876		0075	0097	2 IS TV2-117A	12000	24 Pax		

LITHUANIAN AIRLINES – LAL = TE / LIL (Lietuvos Avialinijos)   Vilnius

A. Gustaicio 4, LI-2038 Vilnius Airport, Lithuania   ☎ (2) 30 66 66 Tx: 261135 Fax: (2) 30 61 40 SITA: n/a
F: 1991   ♦♦♦ n/a Head: Stasys Dailydka IATA: 874 ICAO: LITHUANIAN AIR Net: n/a

☐	LY-SBA	Saab 340B	340B-248	EC-349	0091	1296	2 GE CT7-9B	13155	Y33		lsf Nordbanken Finans AB
☐	LY-SBB	Saab 340B	340B-255	OH-FAH	0091	0597	2 GE CT7-9B	13155	Y33		lsf Nordbanken Finans AB
☐	LY-AMB	Lockheed L-1329 JetStar 731	5161 / 15	N99VR	0067		4 GA TFE731-3-1E	20071	EMS / Executive		cvtd JetStar 8
☐	LY-SBC	Saab 2000	2000-025	F-GTSE	0095	1098	2 AN AE2100A	22800	Y50		lsf DB Export-Leasing GmbH
☐	LY-SBD	Saab 2000	2000-023	F-GTSD	0095	1298	2 AN AE2100A	22800	Y50		lsf DB Export-Leasing GmbH
☐	LY-BSD	Boeing 737-2T4 (A)	22701 / 886	N4569N	0082	0695	2 PW JT8D-17	56472	CY110		Steponas Darius
☐	LY-BSG	Boeing 737-2T2 (A)	22793 / 892	N4571M	0082	0995	2 PW JT8D-17	56472	CY110		Stasys Girénas
☐	LY-AAO	Yakovlev 42	4520424606267	CCCP-42339	0086	1091	3 LO D-36	54000	Y120		std Vilnius in ex Aeroflot-colors
☐	LY-AAQ	Yakovlev 42	4520422708295	CCCP-42344	0787	1091	3 LO D-36	54000	Y120		std Vilnius in ex Aeroflot-colors
☐	LY-AAR	Yakovlev 42	4520422708304	CCCP-42345	0087	1091	3 LO D-36	54000	Y120		
☐	LY-AAT	Yakovlev 42	4520424711396	CCCP-42353	1087	1091	3 LO D-36	54000	Y120		std Vilnius in ex Aeroflot-colors
☐	LY-AAU	Yakovlev 42D	4520424711397	CCCP-42354	0087	1091	3 LO D-36	56500	Y108		lst BHO
☐	LY-AAV	Yakovlev 42D	4520424711399	CCCP-42355	0087	1091	3 LO D-36	56500	Y108		lst BHO
☐	LY-AAW	Yakovlev 42D	4520423811417	CCCP-42359	0788	1091	3 LO D-36	56500	Y108		
☐	LY-AAX	Yakovlev 42D	4520424811431	CCCP-42362	1088	1091	3 LO D-36	56500	Y108		std Vilnius

SVEDIJOS PREKES (Lietuvos ir Svedijos SVEDIJOS PREKES dba)   Klaipeda & Vallentuna (Sweden)

Jurininku 12-7, LI-5800 Klaipeda, Lithuania   ☎ (6) 32 06 91 Tx: none Fax: 86) 32 06 91 SITA: n/a
F: n/a   ♦♦♦ n/a Head: n/a Net: n/a

☐	LY-ABJ	PZL Mielec (Antonov) An-2	1G233-23	RA-40402	0088	0496	1 SH ASh-62IR	5500	Freighter/Para		
☐	LY-ABK	PZL Mielec (Antonov) An-2	1G238-11	SE-LCG	0090	0596	1 SH ASh-62IR	5500	Freighter/Para		
☐	LY-ABS	PZL Mielec (Antonov) An-2	1G234-01	SP-FAN	0089	0796	1 SH ASh-62IR	5500	Freighter/Para		
☐	LY-ABT	PZL Mielec (Antonov) An-2	1G233-20	SE-KZV	0088	0796	1 SH ASh-62IR	5500	Freighter/Para		
☐	LY-ABU	PZL Mielec (Antonov) An-2	1G233-24	SE-KZX	0088	0796	1 SH ASh-62IR	5500	Freighter/Para		
☐	LY-ABY	PZL Mielec (Antonov) An-2	1G238-13	SE-LCI	0090	0497	1 SH ASh-62IR	5500	Freighter/Para		
☐	LY-AER	PZL Mielec (Antonov) An-2	1G191-15	CCCP-84637	0080		1 SH ASh-62IR	5500	Freighter/Para		
☐	LY-AET	PZL Mielec (Antonov) An-2	1G192-07	CCCP-84689	0080		1 SH ASh-62IR	5500	Freighter/Para		

LZ = BULGARIA (Republic of Bulgaria) (Republika Balgaria)
Capital: Sofia Official Language: Bulgarian Population: 9,2 million Square Km: 110994 Dialling code: +359 Year established: 1878 Acting political head: Petar Stoyanov (President)

AIR MAX, Ltd = RMX   Plovdiv

73 Persenk Street, BG-1164 Sofia, Bulgaria   ☎ (2) 962 58 08 Tx: none Fax: (9) 963 30 52 SITA: n/a
F: 1996   ♦♦♦ n/a Head: Mrs. Julia Zaprianova ICAO: AEROMAX Net: n/a

☐	LZ-RMB	PZL Swidnik Mi-2	5411114010		0090	0096	2 IS GTD-350P	3550	Y6		
☐	LZ-RMA	Let 410UVP-E3	902523	069	0090	0096	2 WA M-601E	6400	Y19		
☐	LZ-RMC	Let 410UVP-E12	882207	LZ-LSC	0088	0797	2 WA M-601E	6400	Y19		
☐	LZ-RME	Let 410UVP-E3	902524	064	0090	0097	2 WA M-601E	6400	Y19		

AIR SOFIA = CT / SFB

Sofia

64 Patriarch Evtimi Blvd., BG-1000 Sofia, Bulgaria ☎ (2) 981 08 80 Tx: 24332 airsof bg Fax: (2) 980 29 07 SITA: SOFCDCT
F: 1992 ✈✈✈ 350 Head: Georgi Ivanov IATA: 551 ICAO: AIR SOFIA Net: n/a

registration	type of aircraft	cn/fn	ex/BX*	mfd	del	powered by	mtow kg	configuration	selcal	name/fln/specialitites/remarks
☐ LZ-SFH	Antonov 26	*3904*	*RA-26570*	*0076*	*0297*	*2 IV AI-24VT*	*24000*	*Frtr/16 Pax*		*lst Air Mark Aviation, Singapore*
☐ LZ-SFA	Antonov 12BP	*02348007*	*LZ-SGA*	*0072*	*0091*	*4 IV AI-20M*	*61000*	*Freighter*		
☐ LZ-SFJ	Antonov 12BP	*4342105*	*2105*	*0064*	*1097*	*4 IV AI-20M*	*61000*	*Freighter*		
☐ LZ-SFK	Antonov 12BP	*2341901*	*CCCP-11511*	*0062*	*0092*	*4 IV AI-20M*	*61000*	*Freighter*		
☐ LZ-SFL	Antonov 12BP	*4342101*	*Z3-AFA*	*0064*	*0092*	*4 IV AI-20M*	*61000*	*Freighter*		
☐ LZ-SFN	Antonov 12BP	*2340806*	*LZ-FEA*	*0062*	*1094*	*4 IV AI-20M*	*61000*	*Freighter*		*lst / opf RKA*
☐ LZ-SFS	Antonov 12BP	*5344308*	*SP-LZB*	*0065*	*0395*	*4 IV AI-20M*	*61000*	*Freighter*		

BALKAN Bulgarian Airlines = LZ / LAZ (formerly TABSO)

Sofia

Sofia Airport, BG-1540 Sofia, Bulgaria ☎ (2) 66 16 90 Tx: 22342 balkan bg Fax: (2) 72 34 96 SITA: n/a
F: 1947 ✈✈✈ 3890 Head: Valeri Doganov IATA: 196 ICAO: BALKAN Net: n/a

registration	type of aircraft	cn/fn	ex/BX*	mfd	del	powered by	mtow kg	configuration	selcal	name/fln/specialitites/remarks
☐ LZ-ANC	Antonov 24B	*67302808*		*1066*	*0066*	*2 IV AI-24*	*21000*	*Y42*		
☐ LZ-AND	Antonov 24B	*77303301*		*0367*	*0067*	*2 IV AI-24*	*21000*	*Y42*		
☐ LZ-ANL	Antonov 24B	*67302206*	*DM-SBA*	*1265*	*0076*	*2 IV AI-24*	*21000*	*Y42*		
☐ LZ-ANM	Antonov 24B	*77302905*	*SP-LTL*	*1067*	*0087*	*2 IV AI-24*	*21000*	*Y42*		
☐ LZ-ANO	Antonov 24B	*87304406*	*SP-LTM*	*0668*	*0087*	*2 IV AI-24*	*21000*	*Y42*		
☐ LZ-ANS	Antonov 24B	*07306006*	*SP-LTR*	*0470*	*1287*	*2 IV AI-24*	*21000*	*Y42*		
☐ LZ-TUG	Tupolev 134A-3	*49858*	*OK-BYT*	*0077*	*0983*	*2 SO D-30-III*	*49000*	*CY64*		*occ lsf/opb Govmt Flight Wing/cvtd -134*
☐ LZ-BOA	Boeing 737-53A	*24881 / 1945*		*1190*	*1190*	*2 CFMI CFM56-3C1*	*58967*	*CY116*		City of Sofia / *lsf AWAS*
☐ LZ-BOB	Boeing 737-53A	*24921 / 1962*		*1290*	*1290*	*2 CFMI CFM56-3C1*	*58967*	*CY116*		City of Plovdiv / *lsf AWAS*
☐ LZ-BOC	Boeing 737-53A	*25425 / 2177*		*1291*	*1291*	*2 CFMI CFM56-3C1*	*58967*	*CY116*	*BQ-HR*	City of Varna / *lsf AWAS*
☐ LZ-BAC	Antonov 12B	*6343708*		*1265*	*0080*	*4 IV AI-20M*	*64000*	*Freighter*		
☐ LZ-BAE	Antonov 12BP	*402001*		*1063*	*0087*	*4 IV AI-20M*	*64000*	*Freighter*		
☐ LZ-BAF	Antonov 12B	*402408*		*0664*	*0087*	*4 IV AI-20M*	*64000*	*Freighter*		
☐ LZ-BEH	Ilyushin 18D	*186008905*	*SP-LSI*	*0366*	*0091*	*4 IV AI-20M*	*64000*	*Y105/Freighter*		*ex LOT colours*
☐ LZ-BEU	Ilyushin 18V	*183005905*	*4W-ABO*	*0263*	*0984*	*4 IV AI-20M*	*64000*	*Y105/Freighter*		
☐ LZ-BTG	Tupolev 154B	*095*		*0275*	*0075*	*3 KU NK-8-2U*	*98000*	*CY157*		*cvtd 154A*
☐ LZ-BTH	Tupolev 154M	*754*		*0388*	*0088*	*3 SO D-30KU-154-II*	*100000*	*CY157*		*lst IRK as EP-LBL*
☐ LZ-BTI	Tupolev 154M	*706*	*EP-LBC*	*1284*	*0585*	*3 SO D-30KU-154-II*	*100000*	*CY157*		*lst IRK as EP-LBG*
☐ LZ-BTJ	Tupolev 154B-1	*270*		*0878*	*0589*	*3 KU NK-8-2U*	*98000*	*CY157*		
☐ LZ-BTK	Tupolev 154B	*144*		*0376*	*0376*	*3 KU NK-8-2U*	*98000*	*CY157*		
☐ LZ-BTL	Tupolev 154B	*208*		*0477*	*0677*	*3 KU NK-8-2U*	*98000*	*CY157*		
☐ LZ-BTN	Tupolev 154M	*832*		*0390*	*0390*	*3 SO D-30KU-154-II*	*100000*	*CY157*		
☐ LZ-BTO	Tupolev 154B-1	*258*		*0178*	*0278*	*3 KU NK-8-2U*	*98000*	*CY157*		
☐ LZ-BTP	Tupolev 154B-1	*278*		*0578*	*0578*	*3 KU NK-8-2U*	*98000*	*CY157*		
☐ LZ-BTQ	Tupolev 154M	*743*	*EP-LBD*	*1286*	*0087*	*3 SO D-30KU-154-II*	*100000*	*CY157*		
☐ LZ-BTS	Tupolev 154B-2	*422*		*0680*	*0680*	*3 KU NK-8-2U*	*98000*	*CY157*		
☐ LZ-BTT	Tupolev 154B-2	*483*		*0381*	*0481*	*3 KU NK-8-2U*	*98000*	*CY157*		
☐ LZ-BTU	Tupolev 154B-2	*484*		*0481*	*0481*	*3 KU NK-8-2U*	*98000*	*CY157*		
☐ LZ-BTV	Tupolev 154B-2	*569*		*0183*	*0083*	*3 KU NK-8-2U*	*98000*	*CY157*		
☐ LZ-BTW	Tupolev 154M	*707*		*0185*	*0585*	*3 SO D-30KU-154-II*	*100000*	*CY157*		
☐ LZ-BTX	Tupolev 154M	*744*	*EP-LBE*	*0187*	*0087*	*3 SO D-30KU-154-II*	*100000*	*CY157*		
☐ LZ-BTY	Tupolev 154M	*800*		*0389*	*0089*	*3 SO D-30KU-154-II*	*100000*	*CY157*		
☐ LZ-BTZ	Tupolev 154M	*781*		*0088*	*0088*	*3 SO D-30KU-154-II*	*100000*	*C90*		*occ lsf/opb Government Flight Wing*
☐ LZ-LTA	Tupolev 154M	*927*	*UN-85744*	*0092*	*0698*	*3 SO D-30KU-154-II*	*100000*	*Y164*		
☐ LZ-LTB	Tupolev 154B-2	*365*	*RA-85365*	*0079*	*0698*	*3 KU NK-8-2U*	*98000*	*Y164*		*lsf AVL-Arkhangelskie vozdushnye*
☐ LZ-LTC	Tupolev 154M	*974*	*RA-85790*	*0093*	*0299*	*3 SO D-30KU-154-II*	*102000*	*Y164*		*lsf Sakhaavia/Yakutsk Air Enterprise*

BF CARGO = BFB (Bulgarian Flying Cargo dba)

Sofia

1 Kalina Malina Street, 5th Floor, 16ap., BG-1000 Sofia, Bulgaria ☎ (2) 73 12 34 Tx: 24899 bfc bg Fax: (2) 73 11 84 SITA: SOFTOFN
F: 1993 ✈✈✈ n/a Head: Chavdar Kantchev Net: n/a

registration	type of aircraft	cn/fn	ex/BX*	mfd	del	powered by	mtow kg	configuration	selcal	name/fln/specialitites/remarks
☐ LZ-BFD	Antonov 12BP	*5343005*	*RA-98102*	*0065*	*0095*	*4 IV AI-20M*	*61000*	*Freighter*		*lsf Progress*
☐ LZ-BFG	Antonov 12BP	*6344305*	*RA-11650*	*0066*	*0097*	*4 IV AI-20M*	*61000*	*Freighter*		*lsf Progress*

GOVERNMENT FLIGHT WING – Detachment 28

Sofia

Sofia Airport, BG-1540 Sofia, Bulgaria ☎ (2) 71 80 29 Tx: none Fax: (2) 71 70 83 SITA: n/a
F: n/a ✈✈✈ n/a Head: n/a ICAO: BULGARIA Net: n/a Operates non-commercial VIP flights for the government & occasionally sub-charter flights for BALKAN Bulgarian Airlines.

registration	type of aircraft	cn/fn	ex/BX*	mfd	del	powered by	mtow kg	configuration	selcal	name/fln/specialitites/remarks
☐ LZ-BTZ	Tupolev 154M	*781*		*0088*	*0088*	*3 SO D-30KU-154-II*	*100000*	*VIP / C90*		*opf Gvmt/occlst/opf LAZ in LAZ cs*
☐ LZ-TUG	Tupolev 134A-3	*49858*	*OK-BYT*	*0077*	*0983*	*2 SO D-30-III*	*49000*	*VIP / CY64*		*opf Gvmt/occlst/opf LAZ/LAZ cs/cvtd-134*

HELI AIR Services = HLR

Sofia

Sofia Airport-North, BG-1540 Sofia, Bulgaria ☎ (2) 79 50 36 Tx: 24308 helair bg Fax: (2) 79 50 36 SITA: n/a
F: 1990 ✈✈✈ 80 Head: Georgi Spassov ICAO: HELI BULGARIA Net: n/a

registration	type of aircraft	cn/fn	ex/BX*	mfd	del	powered by	mtow kg	configuration	selcal	name/fln/specialitites/remarks
☐ LZ-CCA	Cessna 421C Golden Eagle II	*421C0272*		*0077*	*0098*	*2 CO GTSIO-520-L*	*3379*	*Y6*		
☐ LZ-CAB	Mil Mi-8	*10309*		*0074*		*2 IS TV2-117A*	*12000*	*Y24*		
☐ LZ-CAE	Mil Mi-8P	*10312*		*0075*		*2 IS TV2-117A*	*12000*	*Y26*		*lst Malta Air Charter*
☐ LZ-CAH	Mil Mi-8P	*24024*		*0091*		*2 IS TV2-117A*	*12000*	*Y26*		*lst Malta Air Charter*
☐ LZ-CAL	Mil Mi-8	*10317*		*0081*		*2 IS TV2-117A*	*12000*	*Utility*		
☐ LZ-CAM	Mil Mi-8	*10318*		*0682*		*2 IS TV2-117A*	*12000*	*Y24*		
☐ LZ-CAZ	Mil Mi-8P	*24023*		*0091*		*2 IS TV2-117A*	*12000*	*Y26*		*lst Malta Air Charter*
☐ LZ-CBA	Antonov 26	*8007*	*UR-26659*	*0079*	*0097*	*2 IV AI-24VT*	*24000*	*Freighter*		

HEMUS AIR – Bulgarian Aviation Company = DU / HMS

Sofia

Sofia Airport, BG-1540 Sofia, Bulgaria ☎ (2) 70 20 76 Tx: 22342 hms bg Fax: (2) 79 63 80 SITA: n/a
F: 1986 ✈✈✈ 150 Head: Dimitar Pavlov IATA: 748 ICAO: HEMUS AIR Net: n/a

registration	type of aircraft	cn/fn	ex/BX*	mfd	del	powered by	mtow kg	configuration	selcal	name/fln/specialitites/remarks
☐ LZ-LSB	Let 410UVP-E1	*861802*		*0086*		*2 WA M-601E*	*6400*	*Photo / Y16*		
☐ LZ-DOB	Yakovlev 40	*9340432*		*0073*		*3 IV AI-25*	*16000*	*C18*		
☐ LZ-DOC	Yakovlev 40	*9340532*		*0073*		*3 IV AI-25*	*16000*	*C18*		
☐ LZ-DOE	Yakovlev 40	*9521441*		*0075*		*3 IV AI-25*	*16000*	*Calibrator*		
☐ LZ-DOF	Yakovlev 40	*9521541*		*0075*		*3 IV AI-25*	*16000*	*Y27*		
☐ LZ-DOM	Yakovlev 40	*9620447*		*0076*	*0093*	*3 IV AI-25*	*16000*	*Y32*		*lst ADE*
☐ LZ-DOR	Yakovlev 40	*9231623*		*0072*		*3 IV AI-25*	*16000*	*Y32*		
☐ LZ-DOS	Yakovlev 40	*9231423*		*0072*		*3 IV AI-25*	*16000*	*C16*		
☐ LZ-TUH	Tupolev 134A	*60142*	*OK-HFM*	*0077*	*1197*	*2 SO D-30-II*	*49000*	*Y72*		*lst LBC*
☐ LZ-TUJ	Tupolev 134A	*49913*	*OK-HFL*	*0077*	*1297*	*2 SO D-30-II*	*49000*	*Y72*		*lst LBC*
☐ LZ-TUL	Tupolev 134A-3	*3352303*		*0073*		*2 SO D-30-III*	*49000*	*Y76*		*cvtd Tu-134A*
☐ LZ-TUN	Tupolev 134A-3	*4352307*		*0074*		*2 SO D-30-III*	*49000*	*Y76*		*cvtd Tu-134A*
☐ LZ-TUP	Tupolev 134A	*1351303*	*LZ-D-050*	*0071*	*0097*	*2 SO D-30-II*	*49000*	*Y76*		
☐ LZ-TUT	Tupolev 134B-3	*63987*		*0082*	*0096*	*2 SO D-30-III*	*49000*	*Y76*		*lst LBC*

INTER TRANS AIR = ITT

Sofia

2 Levski Street, BG-1000 Sofia, Bulgaria ☎ (2) 988 24 21 Tx: 25060 bg Fax: (2) 988 44 70 SITA: SOFARXH
F: 1996 ✈✈✈ 30 Head: Vassil Nickolov ICAO: INTER TRANSAIR Net: n/a

registration	type of aircraft	cn/fn	ex/BX*	mfd	del	powered by	mtow kg	configuration	selcal	name/fln/specialitites/remarks
☐ LZ-ITA	Antonov 12BP	*3341004*		*0063*	*0097*	*4 IV AI-20M*	*61000*	*Freighter*		

LADA AIR, Ltd = LDB (Subsidiary of Lada Bulgaria, Ltd)

Sofia

7 Akad. Nikola Obrechkov Street, BG-1113 Sofia, Bulgaria ☎ (2) 973 38 76 Tx: 24364 lada bg Fax: (2) 973 36 69 SITA: n/a
F: 1996 ✈✈✈ 12 Head: Valko Mihaylov ICAO: LADA Net: n/a

registration	type of aircraft	cn/fn	ex/BX*	mfd	del	powered by	mtow kg	configuration	selcal	name/fln/specialitites/remarks
☐ LZ-PIA	Piaggio P.180 Avanti	*1008*	*LZ-VPC*	*0091*	*0096*	*2 PWC PT6A-66*	*5239*	*F7*		

LUCKY AIR = BLF (Bulgarian Lucky Flight dba)

Sofia

19 Ekzarh Joseph Street, BG-1000 Sofia, Bulgaria ☎ (2) 83 34 22 Tx: none Fax: (2) 83 31 67 SITA: n/a
F: 1990 ✈✈✈ n/a Head: Valery Grigorov ICAO: LUCKY AIR Net: n/a

registration	type of aircraft	cn/fn	ex/BX*	mfd	del	powered by	mtow kg	configuration	selcal	name/fln/specialitites/remarks
☐ LZ-VPD	Antonov 24RV	*47309703*	*RA-46681*	*0074*	*0097*	*2 IV AI-24VT*	*21800*	*Y48*		

SCORPION AIR = SPN (Division of Scorpions Company)

Sofia

73 Persenk Street, BG-1164 Sofia, Bulgaria ☎ (2) 962 58 08 Tx: none Fax: (2) 963 30 52 SITA: n/a
F: 1990 ✈✈✈ n/a Head: Milko Sopryanov ICAO: AIR SCORPIC Net: n/a

registration	type of aircraft	cn/fn	ex/BX*	mfd	del	powered by	mtow kg	configuration	selcal	name/fln/specialitites/remarks
☐ LZ-MNG	Let 410UVP	*841326*	*UR-67100*	*0084*	*0096*	*2 WA M-601D*	*5800*	*Y17 / Freighter*		
☐ LZ-MSL	Kamov Ka-32T	*22905*		*0091*		*2 IS TV3-117V*	*11600*	*Utility*		
☐ LZ-MSM	Kamov Ka-32T	*8702*		*0091*		*2 IS TV3-117V*	*11600*	*Utility*		
☐ LZ-MSW	Kamov Ka-32T	*8610*		*0091*		*2 IS TV3-117V*	*11600*	*Utility*		
☐ LZ-MOE	Mil Mi-8MTV-1	*415M01*		*0093*		*2 IS TV3-117MT*	*13000*	*Utility*		
☐ LZ-MOF	Mil Mi-8MTV-1	*103M15*		*0091*		*2 IS TV3-117MT*	*13000*	*Utility*		

registration	type of aircraft	cn/fn	ex	mfd	del	powered by	mtow kg	configuration	selcal	remarks
☐ LZ-MOG	Mil Mi-8MTV-1	415M02		0093		2 IS TV3-117MT	13000	Utility		
☐ LZ-MOH	Mil Mi-8MTV-1	103M14		0091		2 IS TV3-117MT	13000	Utility		
☐ LZ-MSN	Mil Mi-8MTV-1	95919		0092		2 IS TV3-117MT	13000	Utility		
☐ LZ-MNI	Antonov 24B	07305810	040	0070	0097	2 IV AI-24-II	21800	Y48		
☐ LZ-MNH	Antonov 26	6407	UR-26504	0078	0096	2 IV AI-24VT	24000	Freighter		op in DHL-colors
☐ LZ-MNL	Antonov 26	1309	1309	0072	0097	2 IV AI-24VT	24000	Freighter		
☐ LZ-PVM	Antonov 32B	3005	RA-48068	0092	0098	2 IV AI-20D	27000	Freighter		
☐ LZ-PVN	Antonov 32B	3006	RA-48069	0092	0098	2 IV AI-20D	27000	Freighter		
☐ LZ-MNM	Antonov 74	36547098946	UR-74053	0093	0898	2 LO D-36	34800	Combi		lsf UKL
☐ LZ-MOA	Mil Mi-26	226206		0090		2 LO D-136	56000	Utility		
☐ LZ-MOB	Mil Mi-26	226207		0090		2 LO D-136	56000	Utility		

VIA - Air VIA Bulgarian Airways = VL / VIM

Sofia

54 G.M. Dimitrov Blvd, BG-1125 Sofia, Bulgaria ☎ (2) 971 36 25 Tx: 24535 bg Fax: (2) 973 34 54 SITA: SOFTOVL
F: 1990 ⁂ 60 Head: Michael Donsky IATA: 699 Net: n/a

registration	type of aircraft	cn/fn	ex	mfd	del	powered by	mtow kg	configuration	selcal	remarks
☐ LZ-MIG	Tupolev 154M	840		0090	0090	3 SO D-30KU-154-II	100000	Y157		
☐ LZ-MIK	Tupolev 154M	844		0090	0790	3 SO D-30KU-154-II	100000	Y157		
☐ LZ-MIL	Tupolev 154M	845		0090	0090	3 SO D-30KU-154-II	100000	Y157	AE-MS	
☐ LZ-MIR	Tupolev 154M	852		0090	0090	3 SO D-30KU-154-II	100000	Y157		
☐ LZ-MIS	Tupolev 154M	863		0090	0090	3 SO D-30KU-154-II	100000	Y157		
☐ LZ-MIV	Tupolev 154M	920	CCCP-85737	0092	0093	3 SO D-30KU-154-II	100000	Y157		

N = USA (United States of America)

(including Northern Mariana Islands [Commonwealth of the Northern Mariana Islands / Islas Marianas], Guam, Puerto Rico [Commonwealth of Puerto Rico] & US Virgin Islands)
Capital: Washington/DC Official Language: English Population: 264,0 million Square Km: 9363123 Dialling code: +1 Year established: 1776 Acting political head: Bill Clinton (President)

Virgin Islands
Capital: St. John Official Language: English Population: 0,2 million Square Km: 344 Dialling code: +1-340 Acting political head: Roy L. Schneider (Governor)
Guam
Capital: Agana Official Language: English + Chamorro Population: 0,2 million Square Km: 549 Dialling code: +671 Acting political head: Carl T.C. Gutierrez (Governor)
Northern Mariana Islands (Commonwealth of the Northern Mariana Islands) (Islas Marianas)
Capital: Susupe/Saipan Official Language: English Population: 0,1 million Square Km: 475 Dialling code: +670 Acting political head: Pedro Pangelinan Tenorio (Governor)
Puerto Rico (Commonwealth of Puerto Rico) (Estado Libre Asociado de P.R.)
Capital: San Juan Official Language: Spanish + English Population: 4,0 million Square Km: 8897 Dialling code: +1-787 Acting political head: Pedro Rossello (Governor)

Government / Corporate / Executive / VIP Aircraft

ERDA = US Energy Research & Development Administration, MILITARY AIRLIFT COMMAND (MAC – USAF) uses IATA two letter code: MC and ICAO call sign: MAC, USAF Special Air Mission uses ICAO call sign: US. SAM.

registration	type of aircraft	cn/fn	ex	mfd	del	powered by	mtow kg	configuration	selcal	remarks
☐ N10UP	BAe 3101 Jetstream 31	635	N635JX	0084	0697	2 GA TPE331-10UR-513H	6900	Corporate		Union Pacific Resources Company
☐ N1568D	Beech 1900C-1 Airliner	UC-78		0089	0989	2 PWC PT6A-65B	7530	Corporate		Dow Chemical Corp.
☐ N20W	Fairchild Ind. F-27F	97	N2724R	0063	1098	2 RR Dart 529-7E	19051	Executive		Beartooth Communication Company
☐ N2TS	Beech 1900C Airliner	UB-39	N484SS	0085	1097	2 PWC PT6A-65B	7530	Corporate		Sabco Racing Inc.
☐ N305CC	Canadair Regional Jet 100SE (CL-600-2B19)	7099	N253SE	0095	0397	2 GE CF34-3B1	24154	Corporate		Carnival Corp. / lsf FSBU Trustee
☐ N305PA	Boeing (Douglas) DC-9-15	45740 / 62	N911KM	1166	0394	2 PW JT8D-7	41141	Corporate		Pharmair Corp.
☐ N305PC	Beech 1900D Airliner	UE-299		0097	1297	2 PWC PT6A-67D	7688	Corporate		Peabody Western Coal Co/lsf MDFC Equip.
☐ N311AG	Boeing 727-17 (RE) (Super 27)	20512 / 858	N767RV	0071	0586	3 PW JT8D-217C/7B (BFG)	76884	Corporate	FK-EM	Baker Corp. / cvtd -17
☐ N328CP	Dornier 328-120	3077	D-CHIC	0096	0998	2 PWC PW119C	13990	Corporate		BLC Corp.
☐ N368CE	Boeing 737-33A	27456 / 2749	9M-CHG	0095	1298	2 CFMI CFM56-3C1	61235	VIP		Club Excellence Inc./lsf Finova Capital
☐ N37NY	Boeing 737-4Y0	23976 / 1651	N773RA	0088	0596	2 CFMI CFM56-3C1	64637	VIP		MSG Aircraft Leasing Llc/opf NY Knicks
☐ N39MB	Saab SF340A	340A-022	N53LB	0085	0993	2 GE CT7-5A2	12372	Corporate		Mellon Bank N.A.
☐ N40SH	Boeing (Douglas) DC-9-15	45775 / 71	N89SM	0066	1297	2 PW JT8D-7	41141	Executive		JRW Aviation Inc.
☐ N44KS	Saab SF340A	340A-050	N340SA	0086	1096	2 GE CT7-5A2	12372	Corporate		Goodyear Tire & Rubber Company
☐ N4AS	Boeing 737-74U (BBJ)	29233 / 197	N1786B*	0099	0299	2 CFMI CFM56-7B26	69400	Executive		Air Shamrock Inc.
☐ N60FM	Boeing 727-27	19535 / 456	N7294	0067	0196	3 PW JT8D-7B (HK3/FDX)	72802	Corporate	CE-BM	Airfreight Services / lst AIMES Cyprus
☐ N62WH	BAe (BAC) One-Eleven 401AK	078	HZ-TA1	0066	0597	2 RR Spey 511-14	40597	Executive		Air Finance Corp.
☐ N653PC	Dornier 328-110	3027	D-CDHM*	0094	1294	2 PWC PW119B	13990	Corporate 31Pax		Prince Transportation Inc.
☐ N655CC	Canadair Regional Jet 100SE (CL-600-2B19)	7152	N150SE	0096	0298	2 GE CF34-3B1	24154	Corporate		Compaq Computer Corporation
☐ N669JX	BAe 3101 Jetstream 31	669	N409AE	0085	0198	2 GA TPE331-10UF-513H	6950	Corporate		Northwest International Industries Inc.
☐ N698SN	Boeing (Douglas) DC-8-54F (JT)	45886 / 283	N698QS	0066	0498	4 PW JT3D-3B (HK2/QNC)	149685	Testbed		Stage 3 Nacelle Inc.
☐ N707GE	Boeing 707-321 (F)	17608 / 122	N37681	0060	0183	3/1 PW JT4A / CFM56-5B	141521	Engine Testbed	GL-CK	General Electric Co.
☐ N707JT	Boeing 707-138B	18740 / 388	N707XX	0064	0598	4 PW JT3D-1 (Q)	116574	Executive		Jet Clipper Johnny Llc
☐ N707SK	Boeing 707-138B	17702 / 64	N707KS	0059	0687	4 PW JT3D-3B (Q)	116574	VIP	KM-BD	private / cvtd 707-138
☐ N717QS	Boeing 707-3J6B	20717 / 882	B-2408	0074	0795	4 PW JT3D-7 (HK3/BAC)	151046	Testbed		Quiet Skies Inc. / used for HK3-tests
☐ N717XA	Boeing 717-200	55000 / 5001		0998		2 BR BR715	51710	Testbed		Boeing Company / 1st Prototype
☐ N717XB	Boeing 717-200	55001 / 5002		1098		2 BR BR715	51710	Testbed		Boeing Company / 2nd Prototype
☐ N720DC	Boeing 727-77	19253 / 296	N448DR	0066	0695	3 PW JT8D-7	72802	Corporate	CD-BK	Santa Barbara Aerospace
☐ N720JR	Boeing 720-047B	18451 / 307	N2143J	0062	1191	4 PW JT3D-3B (Q)	106141	Executive	CF-KL	JAR Aircraft Services Inc.
☐ N727AK	Boeing 727-51	19123 / 334	XC-UJA	0066	1197	3 PW JT8D-7B (HK3/RAI)	73028	Executive		Marbyia Investments Ltd
☐ N737BG	Boeing 737-247	19612 / 93	N903LC	1168	0898	2 PW JT8D-9A (HK3/AVA)	49442	AvionicsFly.Lab.		Boeing Company / Boeing military-colors
☐ N737BZ	Boeing 737-73Q (BBJ)	29102 / 101		0098	1298	2 CFMI CFM56-7B26	69400	Corporate		Boeing Company
☐ N737CC	Boeing 737-74Q (BBJ)	29135 / 206		0299	0299	2 CFMI CFM56-7B26	69400	Executive		private
☐ N737DX	Boeing 737-408	24804 / 1851	TF-FIC	0090	1298	2 CFMI CFM56-3C1	65990	VIP		Sports Jet Llc
☐ N7470	Boeing 747-121	20235 / 1	N1352B*	0069	0091	4 PW JT9D-7A	332937	Testbed engines		Boeing Co./lsf Museum of Flight Found.
☐ N747GE	Boeing 747-121	19651 / 25	N744PA	0070	0392	4 PW JT9D-7A	332937	Engine Testbed		General Electric Co. / lsf WTC Trustee
☐ N757A	Boeing 757-200 Catfish	22212 / 1		0082	0282	2 PW PW2037	99790	F22Testbed/Proto		Boeing Defense&Space Group/mil.house cs
☐ N767BA	Boeing 767-200	22233 / 1		0081	0981	2 PW JT9D-7R4D	136078	Prototp/Testbed		Boeing Co/Airborne Surveillance Testbed
☐ N770BB	Boeing 757-2J4	25220 / 387	VP-CAU	0091	0498	2 RR RB211-535E4	113398	Executive		Yucaipa Companies Llc
☐ N7771	Boeing 777-200	27116 / 1		0694		2 PW PW4084	233600	Testbed	GR-AB	Boeing Co. / Prototype
☐ N7806M	Fairchild Ind. FH-227D (SCD)	515		0066	0894	2 RR Dart 532-7	20638	Corporate		Lansing Community College/cvtd FH-227B
☐ N896FM	Beech 1900C Airliner	UB-48	N810BE	0085	0596	2 PWC PT6A-65B	7530	Corporate		Intel Corp. / lsf Fleet Capital Corp.
☐ N896SC	Beech 1900C Airliner	UB-40	N809BE	0085	0596	2 PWC PT6A-65B	7530	Corporate		Intel Corp. / lsf Fleet Capital Corp.
☐ N904FH	BAe 3101 Jetstream 31	613	N331BA	0083	0592	2 GA TPE331-10UR-513H	6900	Corporate		Coca-Cola Bottling Co.
☐ N910SF	Boeing (Douglas) DC-10-10	46524 / 65	N124AA	1172	0498	3 GE CF6-6K	195045	Testbed		Sweet Judy / Raytheon Company
☐ 01	GAC VC-20B (G-1159A Gulfstream III)	477	86-0205	0087	0794	2 RR Spey 511-8	31615	VIP	AF-LP	US Coast Guard, Washington
☐ 58-6971	Boeing VC-137B (707-153B)	17926 / 40		0059	0559	4 PW JT3D-3B	117027	VIP / mil trans		USAF/89th Airlift Wing/AMC, cvtd -153
☐ 62-4125	Boeing VC-135B	18465		0062		4 PW JT3D-3B	134717	VIP / mil trans		USAF, 58th MAS, Ramstein AFB
☐ 62-4126	Boeing VC-135B	18466		0062		4 PW JT3D-3B	134717	VIP / mil trans		USAF, 89th Airlift Wing/AMC,Andrews AFB
☐ 62-4127	Boeing VC-135B	18467		0062		4 PW JT3D-3B	134717	VIP / mil trans		USAF, 89th Airlift Wing/AMC,Andrews AFB
☐ 62-4129	Boeing VC-135B	18469		0062		4 PW JT3D-3B	134717	VIP / mil trans		USAF, 89th Airlift Wing/AMC,Andrews AFB
☐ 62-4130	Boeing VC-135B	18470		0062		4 PW JT3D-3B	134717	VIP / mil trans		USAF, 89th Airlift Wing/AMC,Andrews AFB
☐ 71-0874	Boeing (Douglas) C-9A (DC-9-32F)	47467 / 647		0071	1271	2 PW JT8D-9	48988	Ambulance		USAF, 374 TAW, Clark AFB
☐ 71-0876	Boeing (Douglas) C-9A (DC-9-32F)	47475 / 653		0072	0372	2 PW JT8D-9	48988	Ambulance		USAF, 435 TAW, Chievres
☐ 71-0878	Boeing (Douglas) C-9A (DC-9-32F)	47536 / 659		0472	0572	2 PW JT8D-9	48988	Ambulance		USAF, 435 TAW, Rhein-Main AFB
☐ 71-0882	Boeing (Douglas) C-9A (DC-9-32F)	47541 / 670		0072	0872	2 PW JT8D-9	48988	Ambulance		USAF, 435 TAW, Rhein-Main AFB
☐ 72-7000	Boeing VC-137C (707-353B)	20630 / 862	N8459	0072	0872	4 PW JT3D-3B	148778	VIP	AE-HP	USAF, 89th Airlift Wing/AMC,Andrews AFB
☐ 73-1676	Boeing E-4B (747-200B)	20682 / 202		0073	0773	4 GE CF6-50E2	362874	Command Post/VIP		USAF / cvtd E-4A
☐ 73-1677	Boeing E-4B (747-200B)	20683 / 204		0073	1073	4 GE CF6-50E2	362874	Command Post/VIP		USAF / cvtd E-4A
☐ 73-1681	Boeing (Douglas) VC-9C (DC-9-32)	47668 / 765		0075	0275	2 PW JT8D-9 (HK3/ABS)	49895	VIP		USAF, 89th Airlift Wing/AMC,Andrews AFB
☐ 73-1682	Boeing (Douglas) VC-9C (DC-9-32)	47670 / 769		0075	0375	2 PW JT8D-9 (HK3/ABS)	49895	VIP		USAF, 89th Airlift Wing/AMC,Andrews AFB
☐ 73-1683	Boeing (Douglas) VC-9C (DC-9-32)	47671 / 774		0075	0575	2 PW JT8D-9 (HK3/ABS)	49895	VIP		USAF, 89th Airlift Wing/AMC,Andrews AFB
☐ 74-0787	Boeing E-4B (747-200B)	20684 / 232		0074	1074	4 GE CF6-50E2	362874	Command Post/VIP		USAF / cvtd E-4A
☐ 75-0125	Boeing E-4B (747-200B)	20949 / 257		0075	0875	4 GE CF6-50E2	362874	Command Post/VIP		USAF
☐ 82-8000	Boeing VC-25A (747-2G4B)	23824 / 679	N6005C*	0587	0890	4 GE CF6-80C2B1	362874	VIP	AE-FP	USAF Pres Ac / Air Force One
☐ 83-0500	GAC C-20A (G-1159A Gulfstream III)	382	N305GA*	0083	0983	2 RR Spey 511-8	30935	VIP	DM-FL	USAF, 58th MAS, Ramstein AFB
☐ 83-0501	GAC C-20A (G-1159A Gulfstream III)	383	N308GA*	0083	0983	2 RR Spey 511-8	30935	VIP	FH-GK	USAF, 58th MAS, Ramstein AFB
☐ 83-0502	GAC C-20A (G-1159A Gulfstream III)	389	N310GA*	0083	0983	2 RR Spey 511-8	30935	VIP	FL-AC	USAF, 58th MAS, Ramstein AFB
☐ 85-6973	Boeing VC-137C (707-396C)	20043 / 786	OE-IDA	0069	0785	4 PW JT3D-3B	148778	VIP		USAF, 89th Airlift Wing/AMC,Andrews AFB
☐ 86-0201	GAC C-20B (G-1159A Gulfstream III)	470	N344GA*	0087	0587	2 RR Spey 511-8	31615	VIP	AF-GP	USAF, 89th Airlift Wing/AMC,Andrews AFB
☐ 86-0202	GAC C-20B (G-1159A Gulfstream III)	468	N342GA*	0087	0087	2 RR Spey 511-8	31615	VIP	AF-HP	USAF, 89th Airlift Wing/AMC,Andrews AFB
☐ 86-0203	GAC C-20B (G-1159A Gulfstream III)	475	N312GA*	0087	0087	2 RR Spey 511-8	31615	VIP	AF-JP	USAF, 89th Airlift Wing/AMC,Andrews AFB
☐ 86-0204	GAC C-20B (G-1159A Gulfstream III)	476	N314GA*	0087	0087	2 RR Spey 511-8	31615	VIP	AF-KP	USAF, 89th Airlift Wing/AMC,Andrews AFB
☐ 86-0206	GAC C-20B (G-1159A Gulfstream III)	478	N318GA*	0087	0087	2 RR Spey 511-8	31615	VIP	AF-MP	USAF, 89th Airlift Wing/AMC,Andrews AFB
☐ 86-0403	GAC C-20D (G-1159A Gulfstream III)	473	N326GA*	0087	0087	2 RR Spey 511-8	31615	VIP	AF-DP	USAF, 89th Airlift Wing/AMC,Andrews AFB
☐ 89-0266	GAC (Grumman) VC-11A (G-1159 Gulf.II (SP)	045	N51741	0069	1189	2 RR Spey 511-8	29710	VIP		US Army, OSAC PAT, Andrews AFB
☐ 90-0300	GAC C-20G (G-IV Gulfstream IV)	1181	N473GA*	0094	0694	2 RR Tay 611-8	33203	VIP		USAF, 89th Airlift Wing/AMC,Andrews AFB
☐ 92-0375	GAC C-20H (G-IV Gulfstream IV (SP)	1256	N438GA*	0095	1095	2 RR Tay 611-8	33838	VIP		USAF, 89th Airlift Wing/AMC,Andrews AFB
☐ 92-9000	Boeing VC-25A (747-2G4B)	23825 / 685	N60659*	0087	1290	4 GE CF6-80C2B1	362874	VIP	AE-MP	USAF Presidential Aircraft
☐ 96-0112	Beech 1900D Airliner	UE-256	N10931	0096	0397	2 PWC PT6A-67D	7688	VIP / mil trans		US Army / United States of America-TL
☐ 97-0400	GAC C-37A (G-V Gulfstream V)	521	N521GA*	0098	0798	2 BR BR710A1-10	41232	VIP 12 Pax		USAF, 89th Airlift Wing/AMC,Andrews AFB
☐ 97-0401	GAC C-37A (G-V Gulfstream V)	542	N642GA*	0098	0998	2 BR BR710A1-10	41232	VIP 12 Pax		USAF, 89th Airlift Wing/AMC,Andrews AFB
☐ 98-0001	Boeing VC-32A (757-2G4)	29025 / 783	N3519L*	0098	0698	2 PW PW2040	115666	VIP 45 Pax		USAF, 89th Airlift Wing/AMC,Andrews AFB
☐ 98-0002	Boeing VC-32A (757-2G4)	29026 / 787	N3519M*	0098	0598	2 PW PW2040	115666	VIP 45 Pax		USAF, 89th Airlift Wing/AMC,Andrews AFB
☐ 99-0003	Boeing VC-32A (757-2G4)	29027 / 824		0098	1198	2 PW PW2040	115666	VIP 45 Pax		USAF, 89th Airlift Wing/AMC,Andrews AFB
☐ 99-0004	Boeing VC-32A (757-2G4)	29028 / 829		1198	1198	2 PW PW2040	115666	VIP 45 Pax		USAF, 89th Airlift Wing/AMC,Andrews AFB

AAC AIR CHARTER (Anoka Air Charter, Inc. dba) — Minneapolis-Anoka County/Blaine, MN

PO Box 49541, Minneapolis, MN 55449-0541, USA ☎ (612) 783-1866 Tx: none Fax: (612) 783-1633 SITA: n/a
F: 1992 ⁂ 9 Head: Michael Hayes Net: n/a

☐ N830Q	Beech Baron 58	TH-368		0073	0395	2 CO IO-520-CB7	2449	Freighter		lsf Pellco Inc.
☐ N200VW	Piper PA-31-350 Navajo Chieftain	31-8052011		0080	0497	2 LY TIO-540-J2BD	3349	9 Pax		lsf Pellco Inc.
☐ N55CT	Piper PA-31-310 Navajo	31-172		0068	0497	2 LY TIO-540-A2BD	2948	6 Pax		lsf Simcox Aviation Inc.
☐ N633D	Piper PA-31-350 Navajo Chieftain	31-7852098	N63ND	0078	0997	2 LY TIO-540-J2BD	3349	7 Pax		lsf Pellco Inc.

A & P HELICOPTERS, Inc. — Yuba City-Sutter County, CA

728 Aster Court, Yuba City, CA 95991, USA ☎ (530) 673-1966 Tx: none Fax: (530) 671-2049 SITA: n/a
F: 1988 ⁂ 2 Head: Audrey W. Young Net: n/a

☐ N8351F	MD Helicopters MD 500D (Hughes 369D)	170008D		0077	0888	1 AN 250-C20B	1361			

AAR FINANCIAL SERVICES, Corp. – Leasing Operations = (AARL) (Subsidiary of AAR, Corp.) — Wood Dale, IL

One AAR Way, 1100 North Wood Dale Road, Wood Dale, IL 60191, USA ☎ (630) 227-2000 Tx: 190062 aar ut Fax: (630) 227-2089 SITA: n/a
F: n/a ⁂ n/a Head: David Storch Net: n/a Used aircraft leasing, sales and financing company.
Owner / Lessor of the following (main) aircraft types: Airbus Industrie A300B4, Boeing 727-200 & 747-100. Aircraft leased from AARL are listed and mentioned as such under the leasing carriers.

ABC HELITOURS, Inc. — Guam-Tumon Bay Helipad, GU

997 South Marine Drive, Tamuning, GU 96911, USA ☎ 646-6827 Tx: none Fax: 649-9445 SITA: n/a
F: 1990 ⁂ n/a Head: Henry M. Simpson, Jr. Net: n/a

☐ N249HS	Eurocopter (Aerosp.) AS350B AStar	2249		0089	0190	1 TU Arriel 1B	1950			
☐ N31131	Eurocopter (Aerosp.) AS350B AStar	2402	N521AJ	0090	0596	1 TU Arriel 1B	1950			

ABERDEEN FLYING SERVICE, Inc. — Aberdeen-Regional, SD

4430 East Highway 12, Aberdeen, SD 57401, USA ☎ (605) 225-1384 Tx: none Fax: (605) 226-3141 SITA: n/a
F: 1946 ⁂ n/a Head: Mark A. Caven Net: n/a Aircraft below MTOW 1361kg: Cessna 172

☐ N2290H	Cessna 207 Skywagon	20700356		0076	1187	1 CO IO-520-F	1724			
☐ N73266	Cessna 207A Stationair 8 II	20700574		0080	0888	1 CO IO-520-F	1724			
☐ N91060	Cessna T207 Turbo Skywagon	20700047		0069	0491	1 CO TSIO-520-M	1724			
☐ N5179A	Cessna T210N Turbo Centurion II	21063297		0079	0696	2 CO TSIO-520-R	1814			
☐ N732PY	Cessna 210M Centurion II	21061677		0076	0191	1 CO IO-520-L	1724			
☐ N9746C	Cessna T303 Crusader	T30300210		0083	0490	2 CO TSIO-520-AE	2336			
☐ N1306G	Cessna 310Q II	310Q1148		0074	0293	2 CO IO-470-VO	2404			
☐ N6832Y	Cessna 310R II	310R2121		0080	0784	2 CO IO-520-MB	2495			
☐ N5373J	Cessna 402B	402B0367		0073	0691	2 CO TSIO-520-E	2858			
☐ N4057C	Cessna 414A Chancellor III	414A0848		0082	1090	2 CO TSIO-520-NB	3062			

ABILENE AERO, Inc. (Lubbock Aero) — Abilene-Regional & Lubbock-Int'l, TX

2850 Airport Blvd, Abilene, TX 79602, USA ☎ (915) 677-2601 Tx: none Fax: (915) 675-5432 SITA: n/a
F: 1968 ⁂ n/a Head: Ron O. Clark Net: n/a LUBBOCK AERO is the marketing name used for operations from the Lubbock-base (same headquarters & fleet).

☐ N1143T	Beech Bonanza A36	E-1139		0077	0894	1 CO IO-520-BA	1633			
☐ N20530	Beech Bonanza A36	E-1413		0079	0796	1 CO IO-520-BB	1633			
☐ N37AK	Beech Baron 58	TH-517		0074	0396	2 CO IO-520-C	2449			
☐ N66795	Beech Baron 58	TH-1082		0080	0190	2 CO IO-520-CB	2449			
☐ N811PB	Beech Baron 58	TH-194		0072	0297	2 CO IO-520-C	2449			
☐ N79FW	Cessna 414A Chancellor III	414A0278		0079	0994	2 CO TSIO-520-NB	3062			

ABST AVIATION (Terrill L. Abst dba) — Modesto-County/Hrry Sham Field, CA

PO Box 1902, Modesto, CA 95353, USA ☎ (209) 848-3321 Tx: none Fax: none SITA: n/a
F: 1989 ⁂ n/a Head: Terrill L. Abst Net: n/a

☐ N8700Y	Piper PA-30-160 Twin Comanche C	30-1847		0069	1096	2 LY IO-320-B1A	1633			

ACADEMY Airlines = ACD (Airline Aviation Academy, Inc. dba) — Thomaston-Upson County, GA

Box 693, Griffin, GA 30224, USA ☎ (770) 227-2000 Tx: none Fax: (770) 227-8779 SITA: n/a
F: 1967 ⁂ 30 Head: Robert D. McSwiggan ICAO: ACADEMY Net: n/a

☐ N160RL	Beech Baron 58	TH-60	N160YC	0070	0887	2 CO IO-520-C	2449	Freighter		lsf pvt
☐ N41EC	Beech Baron 58	TH-471	N41FC	0074	0484	2 CO IO-520-C	2449	Freighter		lsf pvt
☐ N30TD	Beech E18S	BA-415	N1707H	0059	0786	2 PW R-985	4218	Freighter		lsf pvt
☐ N130D	Boeing (Douglas) DC-3C (C-47A-80-DL)	19800	N55115	0041	0274	2 PW R-1830	12202	Freighter		Animal Crackers / lsf pvt/Animal-colors
☐ N143D	Boeing (Douglas) DC-3A	2054	N2817D	0038	0174	2 PW R-1830	12202	Freighter		Miss Ali-Gator
☐ N232GB	Boeing (Douglas) DC-3C (C-47B-10-DK)	26268	N2005J	0044	0696	2 PW R-1830	12202	Freighter		lsf pvt

ACCESS AIR (Jeflyn Aviation, Inc. dba) — Boise-Air Terminal/Gowen Field, ID

4546 Aeronca Street, Boise, ID 83705, USA ☎ (208) 389-9906 Tx: none Fax: (208) 331-4533 SITA: n/a
F: 1995 ⁂ n/a Head: James N. Hutchens Net: n/a

☐ N717CM	Cessna TU206G Turbo Stationair 6 II	U20605155	N4898U	0079	0497	1 CO TSIO-520-M	1633			
☐ N35CH	Bell 206L-3 LongRanger III	51335		0090	0397	1 AN 250-C30P	1882			lsf Jasco Inc.
☐ N36990	Cessna 414A Chancellor III	414A0504		0080	0098	2 CO TSIO-520-NB	3062			lsf Fisher Sand & Gravel Co.

ACCESSAIR, Inc. = ZA / CYD (Subsidiary of AccessAir Holdings, Inc.) — Des Moines-Int'l, IA

The Ruan Center II, 601 Locust Street, Suite 330, Des Moines, IA 50309, USA ☎ (515) 288-7144 Tx: none Fax: (515) 247-2216 SITA: n/a
F: 1997 ⁂ n/a Head: Roger Pearson IATA: 144 ICAO: CYCLONE Net: n/a

☐ N621AC	Boeing 737-230 (A)	23156 / 1082	D-ABMD	0085	0398	2 PW JT8D-15 (HK3/NOR)	50900			lsf AccessAir Property II Llc
☐ N623AC	Boeing 737-230 (A)	23157 / 1085	D-ABME	0085	0598	2 PW JT8D-15 (HK3/NOR)	50900			lsf AccessAir Property I Llc

ACE AERIAL SERVICE, Inc. — Ukiah-Municipal, CA

1571 South State Street, Ukiah, CA 95482, USA ☎ (707) 462-4527 Tx: none Fax: (707) 462-3155 SITA: n/a
F: 1967 ⁂ n/a Head: Max E. Hartly Net: n/a Aircraft below MTOW 1361kg: Piper PA-28 & Monney M20C

☐ N32523	Piper PA-32-300 Cherokee SIX	32-7540046		0074	0775	1 LY IO-540-K1A5	1542			

ACE AIRCRAFT SERVICES (HAT Aviation, Inc. dba) — Pontiac-Oakland, MI

77 North Johnson Street, Pontiac, MI 48341, USA ☎ (248) 669-3275 Tx: none Fax: (248) 485-3142 SITA: n/a
F: 1991 ⁂ n/a Head: Harley D. Plante, Jr. Net: n/a

☐ N355C	Hamilton Westwind I Tri-gear	BA-700	N995RF	0064	0295	2 PWC PT6A-28	5216	Freighter		lsf Roush Air Inc. / cvtd Beech H18

ACE AVIATION, Corp. (Associated with Parsons Aviation, Inc.) — Parsons-Tri City, KS

Box 833, Parsons, KS 67357, USA ☎ (316) 336-3440 Tx: none Fax: none SITA: n/a
F: 1981 ⁂ n/a Head: Paul Laforge Net: n/a

☐ N26603	Cessna 421C Golden Eagle III	421C0862		0080	0681	2 CO GTSIO-520-L	3379			

ACE AVIATION, Inc. — Belfast-Municipal, ME

PO Box 457, Belfast, ME 04915, USA ☎ (207) 338-2970 Tx: none Fax: (207) 338-3602 SITA: n/a
F: 1979 ⁂ n/a Head: Douglas W. Low Net: http://www.aceaviation.com Aircraft below MTOW 1361kg: Cessna 172

☐ N6918	Piper PA-23-160 Apache	23-2038		0062	0691	2 LY O-320-B	1724			
☐ N4095F	Piper PA-31-310 Navajo	31-8112076		0081	0886	2 LY TIO-540-A2C	2948			

ACE AVIATION, Inc. — Moncks Corner-Berkeley County, SC

PO Box 937, Moncks Corner, SC 29461, USA ☎ (843) 899-7711 Tx: none Fax: none SITA: n/a
F: 1993 ⁂ n/a Head: James C. Davis Net: n/a

☐ N999DS	Cessna 401	401-0074		0067	0597	2 CO TSIO-520-E	2858			

ACE FLIGHT CENTER — St. Thomas-Cyril E. King, VI

PO Box 306962, St. Thomas, VI 00803, USA ☎ (340) 776-4141 Tx: none Fax: (340) 776-4141 SITA: n/a
F: 1990 ⁂ n/a Head: Cleophas U. Hodge Net: n/a

☐ N1119P	Piper PA-23-150 Apache	23-129		0055	0896	2 LY O-320-A1A	1588			
☐ N1202P	Piper PA-23-150 Apache	23-218		0055	0390	2 LY O-320-A1A	1588			
☐ N527PR	Piper PA-23-150 Apache	23-1028		0057	0291	2 LY O-320-A1A	1588			
☐ N91MS	Beech Travel Air 95	TD-82		0058	0396	2 LY O-360-A1A	1814			
☐ N9165Q	Beech Baron 58	TH-131		0071	0496	2 CO IO-520-C	2449			

ACM AVIATION, Inc. — San Jose-Int'l, CA

1475 Airport Boulevard, San Jose, CA 95110, USA ☎ (408) 286-3832 Tx: none Fax: (408) 286-1629 SITA: n/a
F: 1981 ⁂ n/a Head: Standley A. Bac Net: n/a

☐ N2617U	Cessna 501 Citation I/SP	501-0235		0082	1190	2 PWC JT15D-1A	5375			lsf Cavu Inc.

243 registration type of aircraft cn/fn ex/ex* mfd del powered by mtow kg configuration selcal name/fln/specialitites/remarks

☐ N4YS	Beech King Air 350 (B300)	FL-82	N8182C	0092	1294	2 PWC PT6A-60A	6350			lsf WR Fry Trustee
☐ N36MJ	Learjet 36A	36A-036	N610GE	0078	1280	2 GA TFE731-2-2B	8301			
☐ N65KB	Cessna 650 Citation III	650-0199		0091	0296	2 GA TFE731-3B-100S	9979			lsf B & D Aviation Inc.
☐ N620JF	Learjet 60	60-074	N8074W	0096	0696	2 PWC PW305A	10478			lsf Shearwater Air Inc.
☐ N601KJ	Canadair CL-601-3R (CL-600-2B16) Challen.	5187	C-GLXK*	0095	1095	2 GE CF34-3A1	20457			lsf Miranda Int'l Aviation
☐ N900MJ	Dassault Falcon 900	48	N435FJ	0088	0988	3 GA TFE731-5A-1C	20639			

ACTION AIRLINES = AXQ (JIB, Inc. dba) — Groton/New London, CT

Box 117, East Haddam, CT 06423-0117, USA ☎ (860) 448-1646 Tx: none Fax: (860) 446-0130 SITA: n/a
F: 1973 👥 15 Head: John A. Rutledge ICAO: ACTION AIR Net: n/a Aircraft below MTOW 1361 kg: Cessna 172

☐ N660RA	Piper PA-34-200T Seneca II	34-7870354	N36708	0078	0683	2 CO TSIO-360-E	2073			
☐ N797MT	Piper PA-34-200T Seneca II	34-7870433		0078	0597	2 CO TSIO-360-E	2073			
☐ N13878	Piper PA-23-250 Aztec D	27-4513		0071	0195	2 LY IO-540-C4B5	2359			lsf River Valley Aircraft Leasing
☐ N54857	Piper PA-23-250 Aztec E	27-7554157		0075	0195	2 LY IO-540-C4B5	2359			lsf River Valley Aircraft Leasing
☐ N935CA	Piper PA-31T1 Cheyenne I	31T-8004033	XB-FDE	0080	0897	2 PWC PT6A-11	3946			

ACTION AVIATION, Inc. — Renton-Municipal, WA

840 West Perimeter Road, Renton, WA 98055, USA ☎ (206) 255-8800 Tx: none Fax: (206) 255-7997 SITA: n/a
F: 1989 👥 n/a Head: William O. Wiles Net: n/a

☐ N5233Z	Cessna U206G Stationair 6 II	U20606083		0081	0792	1 CO IO-520-F	1633			

ACTION HELICOPTER SERVICE (TSP-Tulsa Security Patrol, Inc. dba) — Tulsa-Security Heliport, OK

PO Box 4158, Tulsa, OK 74159, USA ☎ (918) 584-2431 Tx: none Fax: (918) 583-2726 SITA: n/a
F: 1985 👥 n/a Head: Larry Gass Net: n/a Aircraft below MTOW 1361kg: Bell 47G-3B2 & Hughes 269C (300C)

☐ N2047C	Bell 206B JetRanger III	3319		0081	0390	1 AN 250-C20B	1451			
☐ N206LG	Bell 206B JetRanger III	3577	N206AJ	0082	0286	1 AN 250-C20J	1451			
☐ N206TS	Bell 206B JetRanger III	2381	N76KN	0078	1185	1 AN 250-C20B	1451			
☐ N27629	Bell 206B JetRanger III	2741		0079	0192	1 AN 250-C20B	1451			
☐ N6880J	Piper PA-32R-300 Lance	32R-7680377		0076	0491	1 LY IO-540-K1G5D	1633			
☐ N227H	Bell 206L-3 LongRanger III	51317	C-GHHF	0089	0895	1 AN 250-C30P	1882			
☐ N48EA	Bell 206L-3 LongRanger III	51438	D-HGRO	0091	0897	1 AN 250-C30P	1882			

ADIRONDACK AIR, Inc. — Long Lake-Helms SPB, NY

PO Box 368, Long Lake, NY 12847, USA ☎ (518) 624-5544 Tx: none Fax: (518) 624-2112 SITA: n/a
F: 1997 👥 n/a Head: Gregg R. Spengler Net: n/a

☐ N90YC	De Havilland DHC-2 Beaver I	1338	N67675	0059	0497	1 PW R-985	2309			lsf Northwest Seaplanes / Floats

ADIRONDACK FLYING SERVICE (Lake Placid Airways, Inc. dba) — Lake Placid, NY

PO Box 630, Lake Placid, NY 12946, USA ☎ (518) 523-2473 Tx: none Fax: (518) 523-1905 SITA: n/a
F: 1968 👥 n/a Head: Stephen A. Short Net: n/a Aircraft below MTOW 1361kg: Cessna 177

☐ N33247	Cessna U206F Stationair II	U20602692		0075	0480	1 CO IO-520-F	1633			
☐ N372WP	Cessna 310R II	310R0904		0077	1090	2 CO IO-520-M	2495			
☐ N402AF	Cessna 402B II	402B1337		0078	0198	2 CO TSIO-520-E	2858			
☐ N8091Q	Cessna 402B	402B0369		0073	0592	2 CO TSIO-520-E	2858			

ADIRONDACK HELICOPTERS, Inc. — Remsen-Private Heliport, NY

10482 Bardwells Mill Road, Remsen, NY 13438, USA ☎ (315) 831-5838 Tx: none Fax: none SITA: n/a
F: 1996 👥 n/a Head: Stephen C. Burton Net: n/a

☐ N28373	Bell 206B JetRanger	1496	ZK-HYA	0074	0098	1 AN 250-C20	1451			lsf pvt

ADVANCE LEASING COMPANY = 4G — Nashville-Int'l, TN

PO Box 140865, Nashville, TN 37214-0865, USA ☎ (706) 354-1135 Tx: none Fax: (706) 354-1135 SITA: n/a
F: 1990 👥 n/a Head: Lawrence W. Able Net: n/a

☐ N82178	Lockheed L-382G (L-100-30) Hercules	5048		0085	0090	4 AN 501-D22A	70307	Freighter		lsf Transadvaree Company

ADVENTURE CLUB, Inc. — Morristown-Municipal, NJ

32 Devonshire Drive, Morganville, NJ 07751, USA ☎ (732) 591-8409 Tx: none Fax: none SITA: n/a
F: 1988 👥 n/a Head: John W. Beck Net: http://www.usac.com/charter.html

☐ N1921G	Cessna 310R II	310R0062		0074	0488	2 CO IO-520-M	2495			

ADVENTURE FLOATPLANES, Inc. — West Palm Beach-Spencer Marina, FL

PO Box 20382, West Palm Beach, FL 33416, USA ☎ (561) 842-0034 Tx: none Fax: none SITA: n/a
F: 1994 👥 n/a Head: Richard H. Young, Jr. Net: n/a Aircraft below MTOW 1361kg: Cessna 172 (on Floats)

☐ N5347X	Cessna U206G Stationair 6 II	U20605663		0080	0694	1 CO IO-520-F	1633			Floats

AERIAL SOLUTIONS, Inc. — Tabor City-Private Airstrip, NC

7074 Ramsey Ford Road, Tabor City, NC 28463, USA ☎ (910) 653-2471 Tx: none Fax: (910) 653-9000 SITA: n/a
F: 1985 👥 n/a Head: William C. Cox, III Net: n/a

☐ N112AS	MD Helicopters MD 500D (Hughes 369D)	900808D	N1102N	0080	0587	1 AN 250-C20B	1361			
☐ N11AS	MD Helicopters MD 500D (Hughes 369D)	790541D	N58422	0079	0288	1 AN 250-C20B	1361			
☐ N7148Z	MD Helicopters MD 500D (Hughes 369D)	570136D		0077	0291	1 AN 250-C20B	1361			

AERO AIR, Llc — Portland-Hillsboro, OR

2050 NE 25th Avenue, Hillsboro, OR 97124, USA ☎ (503) 640-3711 Tx: none Fax: (503) 640-0322 SITA: n/a
F: 1935 👥 n/a Head: Norman W. Ralston, Sr. Net: http://www.aeroair.com

☐ N45AE	Learjet 35A	35A-422	N86BL	0081	0698	2 GA TFE731-2-2B	8301			lsf Erickson AA Llc
☐ N163AV	Dassault Falcon 10	163	N163CH	0080	0494	2 GA TFE731-2-1C	8500			lsf Aerovertigo Inc. Trustee
☐ N6458	GAC G-1159A Gulfstream III	349	N6453	0082	1090	2 RR Spey 511-8	30935			lsf Nike Inc.

AEROCENTER, Inc. — Zehphyrhills-Municipal, FL

39317 Air Park Road, Zephyrhills, FL 33540, USA ☎ (941) 782-7789 Tx: none Fax: (941) 783-2043 SITA: n/a
F: 1985 👥 n/a Head: David A. Sullivan Net: n/a

☐ N3019W	Beech King Air C90	LJ-639		0074	1097	2 PWC PT6A-20	4377			

AERO CHARTER, Inc. — Chesterfield-Spirit of St. Louis, MO

501 Turbine Avenue, Chesterfield, MO 63005-3630, USA ☎ (314) 537-0005 Tx: none Fax: (314) 537-9291 SITA: n/a
F: 1978 👥 n/a Head: Robert A. Thomas Net: http://www.aerocharter.com

☐ N328WT	Beech Baron 58	TH-458		0074	1287	2 CO IO-520-C	2449			
☐ N6651X	Beech Baron 58	TH-1043		0079	1090	2 CO IO-520-CB	2449			lsf Aero Sales Inc.
☐ N27316	Piper PA-31-350 Navajo Chieftain	31-7752142		0077	1289	2 LY TIO-540-J2BD	3175			
☐ N350AC	Beech King Air 200	BB-405	N83GB	0078	0895	2 PWC PT6A-41	5670			lsf Aero Sales Inc.
☐ N265M	Sabreliner 65 (Rockwell NA265-65)	465-31	N65FC	0080	0796	2 GA TFE731-3R-1D	10886			lsf Aero Sales Inc.
☐ N570R	Sabreliner 65 (Rockwell NA265-65)	465-75	N2581E	0081	0195	2 GA TFE731-3R-1D	10886			lsf Frontenac Properties Inc.

AEROCOPTERS, Inc. — Seattle-Boeing Field, WA

8013 Perimeter Road South, Boeing Field, Seattle, WA 98108, USA ☎ (206) 763-2177 Tx: none Fax: (206) 763-2281 SITA: n/a
F: 1954 👥 5 Head: Gerald C. Garbell Net: n/a

☐ N1087L	Bell 206B JetRanger III	3004		0080	0680	1 AN 250-C20B	1451			
☐ N2062D	Bell 206B JetRanger III	3334		0081	0881	1 AN 250-C20B	1451			
☐ N58004	Bell 206B JetRanger III	999		0073	0575	1 AN 250-C20B	1451			cvtd JetRanger

AERO DYNAMICS = DYN (Dynamic Ventures, Inc. dba) — Dallas-Love Field, TX

8001 Lemmon Avenue, Suite 276, Dallas, TX 75209, USA ☎ (972) 352-2376 Tx: none Fax: (972) 358-4818 SITA: n/a
F: 1978 👥 n/a Head: Andrew P. Tomiak ICAO: AERO DYNAMIC Net: n/a

☐ N15MD	Beech Baron 58	TH-441		0074	0696	2 CO IO-520-C	2449			lsf CBJJ Enterprises Lc
☐ N48J	Beech Baron 58	TH-409		0074	0497	2 CO IO-520-C	2449			lsf LBL Investments
☐ N35890	Piper PA-31-350 Navajo Chieftain	31-8052139		0080	0091	2 LY TIO-540-J2BD	3175			lsf EZ Co.
☐ N457TC	Piper PA-31T Cheyenne II	31T-8020059	SE-IDM	0080	1296	2 PWC PT6A-28	4082			lsf Brittany Aviation Services Inc.
☐ N300BS	Hawker 700A (HS 125-700A)	257056 / NA0241	N25MK	0079	0890	2 GA TFE731-3R-1H	11249			lsf Tanara Inc.

AERO FLIGHT SERVICE, Inc. = AGY (Subsidiary of Aero Group, Inc.) — Fort Lauderdale-Executive, FL

1995 West Commercial Blvd, Suite I, Fort Lauderdale, FL 33309, USA ☎ (954) 776-1886 Tx: none Fax: (954) 776-3990 SITA: n/a
F: 1976 👥 n/a Head: Gregory D. Smith ICAO: FLIGHT GROUP Net: n/a

☐ N122M	Learjet 23	23-065A	N1GZ	0065	0790	2 GE CJ610-4	5670			lsf Aero Smith Leasing Inc./tbr N156AG
☐ N154AG	Learjet 23	23-034	N24FF	0065	0685	2 GE CJ610-4	5670			lsf Aero Smith Leasing Inc.

244 registration type of aircraft cn/fn ex/ex* mfd del powered by mtow kg configuration selcal name/fln/specialitites/remarks

☐ N155AG	Learjet 25	25-037	N28AA	0069	1186	2 GE CJ610-6	6804			lsf Aero Smith Leasing Inc.
☐ N160AG	Hawker 3A/RA (HS 125-3A/RA)	25160 / NA707	SE-DHH	0068	0194	2 RR Viper 522	10342			
☐ N163AG	Hawker 3A/RA (HS 125-3A/RA)	25169	N122AW	0068	0795	2 RR Viper 522	10342			lsf Nevada Desert Holdings Inc.
☐ N165AG	Hawker 400A (HS 125-400A)	25206 / NA735	XA-ROJ	0069	0496	2 RR Viper 522	10569			

AEROFLITE, Inc. — Marion-Williamson County Regional, IL

300 Aviation Drive, Marion, IL 62959-9540, USA ☎ (618) 993-2764 Tx: none Fax: (618) 997-6925 SITA: n/a
F: 1957 n/a Head: Charles C. Stoker Net: n/a Aircraft below MTOW 1361kg: Piper PA-28-181 & PA-28R-201T

☐ N3014G	Piper PA-28-236 Dakota	28-7911072		0079	0386	1 LY O-540-J3A5D	1361			
☐ N81291	Piper PA-34-200T Seneca II	34-8070037		0079	1279	2 CO TSIO-360-EB	2073			
☐ N14268	Piper PA-23-250 Aztec E	27-4828		0072	0777	2 LY IO-540-C4B5	2359			

AERO FLITE, Inc. — Kingman, AZ

4700 Flightline Drive, Kingman, AZ 86401, USA ☎ (520) 757-1002 Tx: none Fax: (520) 757-2951 SITA: n/a
F: 1966 n/a Head: Matthew J. Ziomek Net: n/a

☐ N82FA	Boeing (Douglas) DC-4 (C-54G-1-DO)	35960 / DO 354	N14BA	0045	0894	4 PW R-2000	32205	Tanker		161
☐ N96358	Boeing (Douglas) DC-4 (C-54E-5-DO)	27284 / DO 230	90398	0045	1077	4 PW R-2000	32205	Tanker		160

AEROFLITE, Inc. — Poplar Bluff-Municipal, MO

PO Box 477, Poplar Bluff, MO 63902, USA ☎ (573) 686-4892 Tx: none Fax: (573) 686-7764 SITA: n/a
F: 1997 n/a Head: J. Scott Saunders Net: n/a

☐ N8387Z	Piper PA-34-220T Seneca III	34-8133093		0081	0697	2 CO TSIO-360-KB	2155			lsf Executive Air Inc.

AERO FREIGHT, Inc. (Aero Executives) — El Paso-Int'l, TX

6775 Convair Road, El Paso, TX 79925, USA ☎ (915) 772-3273 Tx: none Fax: (915) 772-9243 SITA: n/a
F: 1979 16 Head: Gail E. Beach Net: n/a Passenger flights are operated under the marketing name AERO EXECUTIVES (same headquarters & fleet).

☐ XA-SBM	Piper PA-31-350 Navajo Chieftain	31-7852138	N27749	0078		2 LY TIO-540-J2BD	3175			occ lsf/jtly opw Aero Juarez
☐ N251AF	Learjet 25	25-004	N47MJ	0068	0790	2 GE CJ610-6	6804			
☐ N472AF	Boeing (Douglas) DC-3C (C-47A-25-DK)	13485	C-GRSA	0044	1194	2 PW R-1830	12202	Freighter		

AEROGENESIS AVIATION, Inc. — Mason-Jewett Field, MI

659 Eden Road, Mason, MI 48854-9239, USA ☎ (517) 676-4860 Tx: none Fax: (517) 676-4863 SITA: n/a
F: 1994 n/a Head: Eric A. Swanson Net: n/a

☐ N45017	Piper PA-31-350 Navajo Chieftain	31-8052173		0080	0397	2 LY TIO-540-J2BD	3175			
☐ N923CR	Beech King Air C90A	LJ-1074	N6583K	0084	0997	2 PWC PT6A-21	4377			lsf JMS Partners Llc
☐ N200FV	Beech King Air 200	BB-299	N6111	0077	0997	2 PWC PT6A-41	5670			
☐ N211CP	Beech King Air 200	BB-843	N3850K	0081	1196	2 PWC PT6A-41	5670			
☐ N884PG	Beech King Air 200	BB-91	N9CJ	0076	0595	2 PWC PT6A-41	5670			lsf Midway Air Group Inc.

AERO HAVEN, Inc. — Big Bear City, CA

PO Box 2799, Big Bear City, CA 92314-0597, USA ☎ (909) 585-9663 Tx: none Fax: (909) 585-7156 SITA: n/a
F: 1980 7 Head: Michael L. Smith Net: n/a Aircraft below MTOW 1361kg: Cessna 177 & Piper PA-28

☐ N2671S	Cessna 337C Super Skymaster	337-0971		0068	1095	2 CO IO-360-C/D	1996			

AERO INDUSTRIES, Inc. = WAB — Richmond-Int'l, VA

Executive Terminal, 5690 Clarkson Road, Richmond Int'l Arpt., VA 23250-2411, USA ☎ (804) 222-7211 Tx: none Fax: (804) 236-1670 SITA: n/a
F: 1946 n/a Head: John H. Clarke ICAO: WABASH Net: n/a Aircraft below MTOW 1361kg: Piper PA-28.

☐ N1439T	Piper PA-32-260E Cherokee SIX	32-7200039		0072	1072	1 LY O-540-E4B5	1542			
☐ N3073W	Piper PA-32-300 Cherokee SIX	32-7940081		0079	0683	1 LY IO-540-K1G5D	1542			lsf L&J Aviation Llc
☐ N9211K	Piper PA-34-200T Seneca II	34-7670191		0076	1185	2 CO TSIO-360-E	2073			
☐ N27508	Piper PA-31-350 Navajo Chieftain	31-7852031		0078	0884	2 LY TIO-540-J2BD	3175			
☐ N3521S	Piper PA-31-350 Navajo Chieftain	31-7952107		0079	0383	2 LY TIO-540-J2BD	3175			

AEROJET, Inc. (Sapphire Aviation) — West Palm Beach-Int'l, FL

Southern Boulevard 3867, West Palm Beach, FL 33406, USA ☎ (954) 772-5070 Tx: none Fax: (954) 772-2742 SITA: n/a
F: 1991 n/a Head: David O'Donnell Net: n/a Aircraft below MTOW 1361kg: Cessna 172. Some services are marketed under the name SAPPHIRE AVIATION (same headquarters & fleet).

☐ N6866T	Cessna 310D	39166		0060	0996	2 CO IO-470-D	2191			
☐ N57EB	Twin (Aero) Commander 500A	500A-1245-71		0063	0396	2 CO IO-470-M	2835			lsf Consolidated Transport Inc.
☐ N78343	Twin (Aero) Commander 500A	500A-1264-87		0063	1297	2 CO IO-470-M	2835			lsf Consolidated Transport Inc.

AEROLEASE International, Inc. = (AERO) — Miami, FL

6303 Blue Lagoon Drive, Suite 380, Miami, FL 33126, USA ☎ (305) 261-8900 Tx: none Fax: (305) 261-3583 SITA: n/a
F: 1986 9 Head: Michael A. Goldberg Net: n/a Used commercial aircraft leasing, sales and financing company.
Owner / Lessor of the following (main) aircraft types: DC-8-62 & DC-8-63. Aircraft leased from AERO are listed and mentioned as such under the leasing carriers.

AEROMANAGEMENT FLIGHT SERVICES, Inc. — Leesburg-Municipal/Godfrey Field, VA

560 Herndon Parkway, Suite 330, Herndon, VA 20170, USA ☎ (703) 742-0903 Tx: none Fax: (703) 742-0907 SITA: n/a
F: 1992 n/a Head: Bolling Desouza Net: http://www.aeromanagement.com

☐ N901TP	Partenavia AP68TP-600 Viator	9001	I-BAML	0085	0492	2 AN 250-B17C	2850			
☐ N116AM	Learjet 35A	35A-116	I-MMAE	0077	0195	2 GA TFE731-2-2B	8301			
☐ N43TR	Learjet 35A	35A-645		0088	0592	2 GA TFE731-2-2B	8301			

AEROMAP US, Inc. — Anchorage-Merrill Field, AK

2014 Merrill Field Drive, Anchorage, AK 99501, USA ☎ (907) 272-4495 Tx: none Fax: (907) 274-3265 SITA: n/a
F: 1990 n/a Head: Ward Penney Net: n/a

☐ N5750K	Beech Bonanza S35	D-7538		0064	0691	1 CO IO-520-B	1497	Photo / Survey		
☐ N3443Q	Cessna 320E SkyKnight	320E0043		0067	0690	2 CO TSIO-520-B	2404	Photo / Survey		
☐ N4198T	Cessna 320D SkyKnight	320D0098		0066	0690	2 CO TSIO-520-B	2359	Photo / Survey		
☐ N7516Q	Cessna T310Q	310Q0530		0072	0490	2 CO TSIO-520-B	2495	Photo / Survey		

AERO MED (Butterworth Aero Med, Inc. dba / Division of Spectrum Health) — Grand Rapids-Kent County Int'l, MI

100 Michigan N.E., Grand Rapids, MI 49503, USA ☎ (616) 391-5330 Tx: none Fax: (616) 391-5343 SITA: n/a
F: 1987 n/a Head: Ralph N. Rogers Net: n/a

☐ N176AM	Sikorsky S-76A	760260	N902H	0084	0397	2 AN 250-C30	4672	EMS		
☐ N176BA	Sikorsky S-76B	760317	N546D	0085	0494	2 PWC PT6B-36A	5307	EMS		

AERO NATIONAL, Inc. (AAA Air Ambulance) — Washington-County, PA

PO Box 538, Washington, PA 15301, USA ☎ (724) 228-8000 Tx: none Fax: (724) 228-8059 SITA: n/a
F: 1968 n/a Head: L. Michael Sollon Net: http://www.gatewayads.com/32896/aaa.html Uses the service-name AAA AIR AMBULANCE for its EMS-flights.

☐ N2669Z	Cessna 340A II	340A0736		0079	0187	2 CO TSIO-520-NB	2717			lsf pvt
☐ N344HB	Cessna 340A II	340A0539		0078	1290	2 CO TSIO-520-NB	2717			
☐ N4326C	Cessna 340A II	340A0075		0076	1089	2 CO TSIO-520-N	2717			
☐ N69457	Cessna 340 II	340-0309		0073	1287	2 CO TSIO-520-K	2710			lsf pvt
☐ N7632Q	Cessna 340	340-0236		0073	1184	2 CO TSIO-520-K	2710			
☐ N3591P	Piper PA-31-325 Navajo C/R	31-8012081		0080	1091	2 LY TIO-540-F2BD	2948			

AERONAUTICAL CHARTER, Inc. — Punta Gorda-Charlotte County, FL

7355 Utilities Road, Unit C, Punta Gorda, FL 33982, USA ☎ (941) 639-2647 Tx: none Fax: (941) 575-6980 SITA: n/a
F: 1995 n/a Head: Sandra K. Hamouda Net: n/a Aircraft below MTOW 1361kg: Piper PA-28

☐ N444SA	Piper PA-34-200 Seneca	34-7250183		0072	1195	2 LY IO-360-C1E6	1905			lsf Aeronautical Services Inc.

AERONAUTICAL SERVICES, Inc. — Friday Harbour, WA

PO Box 1490, Friday Harbour, WA 98250, USA ☎ (360) 378-3110 Tx: none Fax: (360) 378-3613 SITA: n/a
F: 1973 71 Head: Steve D. Franklin Net: n/a

☐ N1584U	Cessna 207 Skywagon	20700184		0070	0884	1 CO IO-520-F	1724	Freighter/Pax		lst West Isle Air
☐ N2634Y	De Havilland DHC-3 Otter	59	CAF 3692	0054	0488	1 PW R-1340	3629	Freighter		
☐ N357AS	De Havilland DHC-3 Otter	357	CAF 9402	0060	0785	1 PW R-1340	3629	Freighter		
☐ N18R	Beech E18S	BA-312		0057	0589	2 PW R-985-AN14B	4218	Freighter		lst Catalina Flying Boats Inc.
☐ N9375Y	Beech G18S	BA-564		0060	0489	2 PW R-985	4400	Freighter		lst Catalina Flying Boats Inc.
☐ N403JB	Boeing (Douglas) DC-3C (C-47B-45-DK)	34202	N17778	0045	0593	2 PW R-1830-90D	12202	Freighter		lst Catalina Flying Boats Inc.

AERONAUTICS LEASING, Inc. = (ANAU) — Golden, CO

528 Commons Drive, Golden, CO 80401-5746, USA ☎ (970) 526-9534 Tx: 452087 aeron gldn ud Fax: (970) 526-9612 SITA: n/a
F: 1985 n/a Head: Michael A. Chowdry Net: n/a New and used aircraft leasing, sales and financing company.
Owner / lessor of the following (main) aircraft types: Boeing 737-300 / 400 , 747-200, DC-9-30 & DC 10-30. Aircraft leased from ANAU are listed and mentioned as such under the leasing carriers.

245 registration type of aircraft cn/fn ex/ex* mfd del powered by mtow kg configuration selcal name/fln/specialitites/remarks

AERON AVIATION, Corp. = (ARON) Great Neck, NY

420 Great Neck Road, Great Neck, NY 11021, USA ☎ (516) 466-1148 Tx: 645110 grnk Fax: (516) 773-4936 SITA: n/a
F: n/a ☃ n/a Head: Amos Ginor Net: n/a Used aircraft leasing, sales and financing company.
Owner / lessor of following (main) aircraft types: Boeing 727-200 & McDonnell Douglas DC-9-30. Aircraft leased from ARON are listed and mentioned as such under the leasing carriers.

AEROPAC CHARTERS (PC Design, Inc. dba) Manchester, NH

252 Willow Street, Manchester, NH 03103-3316, USA ☎ (603) 647-0544 Tx: none Fax: (603) 647-0360 SITA: n/a
F: 1992 ☃ n/a Head: Raymond R. Boissoneau Net: n/a

N87X	Beech Duke B60	P-470		0077	0889	2 LY TIO-541-E1C4	3073			
N87XX	Beech King Air B100	BE-105	N28PH	0081	1192	2 GA TPE331-6-252B	5352			

AEROPAK, Inc. = STK San Antonio-Int'l, TX

18207 Apache Springs Drive, San Antonio, TX 78259-3606, USA ☎ (210) 494-5233 Tx: none Fax: (210) 494-5233 SITA: n/a
F: 1983 ☃ n/a Head: Jerry W. Oyler ICAO: SAT PAK Net: n/a

N47961	Piper PA-32R-300 Lance	32R-7880029		0078	0890	1 LY IO-540-K1G5D	1633	Freighter		lsf pvt
N6119J	Piper PA-32R-300 Lance	32R-7680306		0076	1286	1 LY IO-540-K1G5D	1633	Freighter		lsf pvt
N67DJ	Piper PA-32-300 Cherokee SIX	32-7840063		0077	0388	1 LY IO-540-K1G5	1542	Freighter		lsf pvt
N69LH	Piper PA-32R-300 Lance	32R-7780323		0077	0489	1 LY IO-540-K1G5D	1633	Freighter		lsf pvt
N9349M	Cessna 207A Stationair 8 II	20700682		0081	0985	1 CO IO-520-F	1724	Freighter		lsf pvt
N103BU	Piper PA-31-350 Navajo Chieftain	31-7405202		0077	0991	2 LY TIO-540-J2BD	3175	Freighter		lsf pvt
N130BV	Piper PA-31-350 Navajo Chieftain	31-7952216		0079	0890	2 LY TIO-540-J2BD	3175	Freighter		lsf pvt
N13AL	Piper PA-31-350 Navajo Chieftain	31-7752009		0077	0889	2 LY TIO-540-J2BD	3175	Freighter		lsf pvt
N203SB	Piper PA-31-350 Navajo Chieftain	31-7852095		0078	0496	2 LY TIO-540-J2BD	3175	Freighter		lsf pvt
N3535S	Piper PA-31-350 Navajo Chieftain	31-7952203		0079	0496	2 LY TIO-540-J2BD	3175	Freighter		lsf pvt
N803CM	Piper PA-31-350 Navajo Chieftain	31-7952030		0079	0592	2 LY TIO-540-J2BD	3175	Freighter		lsf pvt
N1122Y	Cessna 208B Grand Caravan	208B0392		0094	0594	1 PWC PT6A-114A	3969	Freighter		lsf pvt

AERO RESOURCES, Inc. Hazard-Wendell H. Ford, KY

PO Box 2346, Hazard, KY 41701, USA ☎ (606) 439-5140 Tx: none Fax: (606) 436-6671 SITA: n/a
F: 1987 ☃ n/a Head: Jeffery W. Hylton Net: n/a

N77AR	Beech Baron 58	TH-757	N77JC	0076	0987	2 CO IO-520-C	2449			

AERO SPECIALISTS, Inc. Coolidge-Municipal, AZ

5100 North Tumbleweed Road, Eloy, AZ 85231, USA ☎ (520) 466-4711 Tx: none Fax: (520) 466-4720 SITA: n/a
F: 1986 ☃ n/a Head: Lawrence E. Hill Net: n/a

N2625	Beech C-45H (18)	AF-601	52-10671	0052	0187	2 PW R-985	3969	Para		
N86584	Boeing (Douglas) DC-3C (C-53-DO)	4935	42-6483	0042	0987	2 PW R-1830	12202	Para		

AERO SYSTEMS, Inc. Erie-Tri County, CO

2580 South Main Street, Erie, CO 80516, USA ☎ (970) 665-9321 Tx: 9109400990 aero sys Fax: (970) 665-6367 SITA: n/a
F: 1983 ☃ n/a Head: Walter Clement Net: n/a

N2LA	Eurocopter (MBB) BO105CS	S-120	N17242	0074	0188	2 AN 250-C20B	2400			
N15VZ	Twin (Aero) Turbo Commander 690	11035	N882GS	0072	0686	2 GA TPE331-5-251K	4649			

AERO TAXI, Inc. = QKC Wilmington-New Castle County, DE

110 Old Churmans Road, New Castle, DE 19720, USA ☎ (302) 328-3430 Tx: none Fax: (302) 328-5615 SITA: n/a
F: 1953 ☃ n/a Head: Dirk Dinkeloo ICAO: QUAKER CITY Net: n/a

N572T	Beech Bonanza S35	D-7400		0064	0285	1 CO IO-520-B	1497			
N1732E	Cessna 310R II	310R1553		0078	0189	2 CO IO-520-M	2495			
N4939J	Cessna 310R II	310R0120		0074	0483	2 CO IO-520-M	2495			
N5092P	Cessna 310P	310P0057	C-FKBC	0069	0188	2 CO IO-470-VO	2359			
N9621R	Beech G18S	BA-471		0059	0484	2 PW R-985-AN14B	4400	Freighter		
N416W	IAI 1124 Westwind I	416	4X-CUD*	0085	1294	2 GA TFE731-3-1G	10659			lsf AFT Corp.

AERO TAXI ROCKFORD, Inc. Rockford-Greater Rockford, IL

6028 Cessna Drive, Rockford, IL 61109, USA ☎ (815) 963-4444 Tx: none Fax: (815) 963-8885 SITA: n/a
F: 1969 ☃ 20 Head: Richard E. Gibson Net: n/a

N198MA	Mitsubishi MU-2J (MU-2B-35) Cargoliner	563		0072	0487	2 GA TPE331-6-252M	4899	Frtr/Pax		Cavenaugh SCD conversion
N5AP	Mitsubishi MU-2J (MU-2B-35) Cargoliner	604	N300WT	0073	0987	2 GA TPE331-6-252M	4899	Frtr/Pax		Cavenaugh SCD conversion
N1481G	Beech H18	BA-628		0062	0484	2 PW R-985	4491	Freighter		
N279SC	Beech E18S	BA-74		0055	1173	2 PW R-985	4581	Freighter		
N911DG	Dassault Falcon 20C (C)	162	N162CT	0069	0997	2 GE CF700-2D2	13000	Freighter		cvtd Falcon 20
N911RG	Dassault Falcon 20C (C)	144	N800KR	0068	0495	2 GE CF700-2D2	13000	Freighter		cvtd Falcon 20

AERO TECH Flight Service, Inc. Anchorage-Merrill Field, AK

1100 Merrill Field Drive, Anchorage, AK 99501, USA ☎ (907) 279-6558 Tx: none Fax: (907) 279-2818 SITA: n/a
F: 1956 ☃ 22 Head: Richard Ardaiz Net: n/a Aircraft below MTOW 1361 kg: Cessna 172

N153LM	Piper PA-23-250 Aztec F	27-7754019		0077	0682	2 LY IO-540-C4B5	2359	5 Pax		

AERO-TECH SERVICES (Michael Kuhn dba) Smoketown, PA

311 Airport Drive, Airport Complex, Smoketown, PA 17576, USA ☎ (717) 394-2675 Tx: none Fax: (717) 394-5737 SITA: n/a
F: 1982 ☃ n/a Head: Michael L. Kuhn Net: n/a

N40504	Piper PA-23-250 Aztec E	27-7405235		0074	0185	2 LY IO-540-C4B5	2359			
N5FA	AAC (Ted Smith) Aerostar 600A	60-0310-115	N90519	0076	0797	2 LY IO-540-K1F5	2495			lsf pvt
N600VF	AAC (Piper) Aerostar 600A	60-0757-8061229	N6081Z	0080	1291	2 LY IO-540-K1J5	2495			

AERO UNION, Corp. Chico-Municipal, CA

100 Lockheed Avenue, Chico, CA 95926-9098, USA ☎ (530) 896-3000 Tx: 171359 aerounion cic Fax: (530) 893-8585 SITA: n/a
F: 1959 ☃ 160 Head: Victor E. Alvistur Net: http://www.aerounion.com

N4096W	Piper PA-32-300 Cherokee SIX	32-40159		0067	0387	1 LY IO-540-K1A5	1542			
N4112W	Piper PA-32-300 Cherokee SIX	32-40175		0067	0776	1 LY IO-540-K1A5	1542			
N8234Y	Piper PA-30-160 Twin Comanche B	30-1360		0066	0591	2 LY IO-320-B1A	1633			
N5938Y	Piper PA-23-250 Aztec C	27-3103		0065	0978	2 LY IO-540-C4B5	2359			
N701AU	Lockheed P2V-7S (SP-2H) Neptune	726-7190	N920AU	0058	0686	2 WR R-3350	30617	Tanker		01
N702AU	Lockheed P2V-7S (SP-2H) Neptune	726-7218	N716AU	0058	1186	2 WR R-3350	30617	Tanker		
N703AU	Lockheed P2V-7S (SP-2H) Neptune	726-7217	N967LH	0058	1186	2 WR R-3350	30617	Tanker		03
N712AU	Lockheed P2V-7 (P-2H) Neptune	726-7286	N283RR	0058	0588	2 WR R-3350	36287	Tanker		
N713AU	Lockheed P2V-7 (P-2H) Neptune	726-7165	N903LH	0058	1186	2 WR R-3350	36287	Tanker		
N714AU	Lockheed P2V-7 (P-2H) Neptune	726-7224	N339L	0058	1186	2 WR R-3350	36287	Tanker		
N715AU	Lockheed P2V-7 (P-2H) Neptune	726-7228	N343RR	0058	0588	2 WR R-3350	36287	Tanker		
N716AU	Lockheed P2V-7S (SP-2H) Neptune	726-7065	N90YY	0056	0486	2 WR R-3350	30617	Tanker		16
N717AU	Lockheed P2V-7 (P-2H) Neptune	726-7209	N959LH	0058	1186	2 WR R-3350	36287	Tanker		
N718AU	Lockheed P2V-7S (SP-2H) Neptune	726-7214	N964L	0058	1186	2 WR R-3350	30617	Tanker		18
N719AU	Lockheed P2V-7 (P-2H) Neptune	726-7284	N281RR	0058	0788	2 WR R-3350	36287	Tanker		
N720AU	Lockheed P2V-7 (P-2H) Neptune	726-7184	145917	0058	1087	2 WR R-3350	36287	Tanker		
N980AP	Lockheed P2V-7 (P-2H) Neptune	726-7082	140980	0056	0994	2 WR R-3350	36287	Tanker		
N9AU	Lockheed P2V-7 (P-2H) Neptune	726-7039	135596	0056	0786	2 WR R-3350	36287	Tanker		
N11712	Boeing (Douglas) DC-4 (C-54-DO)	3088 / DO 30	HP-434	0043	0277	4 PW R-2000	30241	Tanker		02
N2742G	Boeing (Douglas) DC-4 (C-54G-15-DO)	36089 / DO 483	N54577	0045	0682	4 PW R-2000	30241	Tanker		15
N4958M	Boeing (Douglas) DC-4 (C-54G-5-DO)	36009 / DO 403	N427NA	0045	1279	4 PW R-2000	30241	FTV		
N4994H	Boeing (Douglas) DC-4 (C-54D-5-DC)	10653 / DC 384	42-72548	0045	1078	4 PW R-2000	30241	Freighter		
N62297	Boeing (Douglas) DC-4 (C-54E-15-DO)	27328 / DO 274	90402	0045	1274	4 PW R-2000	30241	Tanker		14
N62342	Boeing (Douglas) DC-4 (C-54D-1-DC)	10613 / DC 344	56497	0045	1275	4 PW R-2000	30241	Tanker		13
N76AU	Boeing (Douglas) DC-4 (C-54D-1-DC)	10547 / DC 278	N62296	0045	1274	4 PW R-2000	30241	Tanker		26
N900AU	Lockheed P-3A (P3V-1) Orion	185-5104	N406TP	0063	1089	4 AN T56-A	47627	Tanker		00
N921AU	Lockheed P-3A (P3V-1) Orion	185-5098	151385	0063	0397	4 AN T56-A	47627	Tanker		21
N922AU	Lockheed P-3A (P3V-1) Orion	185-5100	N181AU	0063	1089	4 AN T56-A	47627	Tanker		22
N923AU	Lockheed P-3A (P3V-1) Orion	185-5085	N185AU	0063	1289	4 AN T56-A	47627	Tanker		23
N925AU	Lockheed P-3A (P3V-1) Orion	185-5074	N183AU	0063	1089	4 AN T56-A	47627	Tanker		25
N926AU	Lockheed P-3B (P3V-1) Orion	185-5171	152731	0063	0297	4 AN T56-A	47627	Tanker		26
N927AU	Lockheed P-3A (P3V-1) Orion	185-5082	N182AU	0063	1089	4 AN T56-A	47627	Tanker		27

AERO WEST (Troutdale Aviation, Inc. dba) Portland-Troutdale, OR

920 NW Perimeter Road, Troutdale, OR 97060, USA ☎ (541) 661-4940 Tx: none Fax: (541) 666-0507 SITA: n/a
F: 1993 ☃ n/a Head: Michael P. Edger Net: n/a Aircraft below MTOW 1361kg: Cessna 172

N357DA	Piper PA-44-180 Seminole	44-7995271		0079	1094	2 LY O-360-E1A6D	1724			lsf pvt

246 registration type of aircraft cn/fn ex/ex* mfd del powered by mtow kg configuration selcal name/fln/specialitites/remarks

☐ N39608	Piper PA-44-180 Seminole	44-7995015		0079	0895	2 LY O-360-E1A6D	1724			lsf Troutdale Aircraft Leasing Co.
☐ N20BC	Piper PA-34-200T Seneca II	34-7570233		0075	0296	2 CO TSIO-360-E	2073			lsf Troutdale Aircraft Leasing Co.
☐ N9451C	Piper PA-34-200T Seneca II	34-7870189		0078	1196	2 CO TSIO-360-E	2073			lsf Troutdale Aircraft Leasing Co.

AEROWEST HELICOPTERS (Aerowest Management Services, Inc. dba / Sister company of Si Nombre Inc.) **Albuquerque-Double Eagle II, NM**

PO Box 508, Corrales, NM 87048-0508, USA ☎ (505) 352-0950 Tx: none Fax: (505) 352-0954 SITA: n/a
F: 1984 ⁂ n/a Head: Donald C. Ambabo Net: n/a

☐ N124DA	Bell 206B JetRanger III	2052		0076	1095	1 AN 250-C20B	1451			cvtd JetRanger II
☐ N2779B	Bell 206B JetRanger III	2819		0079	0593	1 AN 250-C20B	1451			
☐ N913TV	Bell 206B JetRanger III	2392	N5FG	0078	0897	1 AN 250-C20B	1451			lsf MSI Helicopters Inc.

AFG AIR FINANCE, Inc. = (AFGR) (Subsidiary of American Finance Group, Inc. / Affiliated with Investors Asset Holding, Corp.) **Boston, MA**

24 School Street, 7th Floor, Boston, MA 02108, USA ☎ (781) 557-9300 Tx: none Fax: (781) 557-9348 SITA: n/a
F: 1984 ⁂ 92 Head: Jeffrey Zerrer Net: n/a New and used aircraft leasing, sales and financing company.
Owner / lessor of following (main) aircraft types: Boeing 727-200/ 747SP, De Havilland DHC-6, Lockheed L-1011 TriStar, McDonnell Douglas DC-9-30/DC-10-40, Saab SF340 & Shorts 330.
Aircraft leased from AFGR are listed and mentioned as such under the leasing carriers.

AGES AIRCRAFT SALES & LEASING, A Limited Partnership = (AGES) (An affiliate of The AGES Group, A Limited Partnership) **Boca Raton, FL**

645 Park of Commerce Way, Boca Raton, FL 33487, USA ☎ (561) 998-9330 Tx: 314821 Fax: (561) 994-2040 SITA: FLLGDXD
F: 1980 ⁂ 200 Head: David Dornyak Net: n/a New & used aircraft leasing, sales and financing company.
Owner / lessor of following (main) aircraft types: BAe Jetstream 31, Boeing 727-200/737-200/747-100, De Havilland DHC-5, DHC-7 & DHC-8. Aircraft leased from AGES are listed and mentioned as such under the leasing carriers.

AGILE AIR SERVICE, Inc. **Chester-Landing Strip & Manchester, NH**

660 Fremont Road, Chester, NH 03036-4177, USA ☎ (603) 887-3272 Tx: none Fax: (603) 887-3046 SITA: n/a
F: 1987 ⁂ n/a Head: Michael H. Heaton Net: http://www.agileair.com/

☐ N5813T	Cessna 185C Skywagon	185-0713		0064	1087	1 CO IO-470-F	1451			

AGROTORS, Inc. **Gettysburg-Battlefield Heliport, PA**

PO Box 4537, Gettysburg, PA 17325, USA ☎ (717) 334-6777 Tx: none Fax: (717) 334-0854 SITA: n/a
F: 1958 ⁂ 45 Head: Timothy H. Voss Net: n/a

☐ N1097J	MD Helicopters MD 500D (Hughes 369D)	900801D		0080	0288	1 AN 250-C20B	1361			
☐ N369AW	MD Helicopters MD 500D (Hughes 369D)	470117D		0077	1188	1 AN 250-C20B	1361			
☐ N500DC	MD Helicopters MD 500D (Hughes 369D)	290456D		0078	1293	1 AN 250-C20B	1361			
☐ N5027P	MD Helicopters MD 500D (Hughes 369D)	611002D		0081	0387	1 AN 250-C20B	1361			
☐ N5070J	MD Helicopters MD 500D (Hughes 369D)	121096D		0081	0098	1 AN 250-C20B	1361			
☐ N8330P	MD Helicopters MD 500E (Hughes 369E)	0330E	N1606L	0089	0098	1 AN 250-C20B	1361			
☐ N206BX	Bell 206B JetRanger III	2872	C-GAVS	0079	0385	1 AN 250-C20B	1451			
☐ N206BY	Bell 206B JetRanger III	2871	C-GAVQ	0079	0385	1 AN 250-C20B	1451			
☐ N49718	Bell 206B JetRanger II	1917		0076	0786	1 AN 250-C20	1451			
☐ N54AG	Bell OH-58A (206 JetRanger)	41582	N843PD	0072	1097	1 AN 250-C20B	1361			
☐ N58AG	Bell OH-58A (206 JetRanger)	41797	N844PD	0072	1097	1 AN 250-C20B	1361			
☐ N90322	Bell 206B JetRanger	1736		0075	0392	1 AN 250-C20	1451			
☐ N9907K	Bell 206B JetRanger III	2040		0076	1084	1 AN 250-C20B	1451			cvtd JetRanger II
☐ N51AG	Bell UH-1H (205)	13002	70-20178	0070	0895	1 LY T53-L-13	4309			
☐ N52AG	Bell UH-1H (205)	12356	70-15746	0070	0895	1 LY T53-L-13	4309			
☐ N53AG	Bell UH-1H (205)	13287	72-21588	0071	1097	1 LY T53-L-13	4309			
☐ N8530B	Bell 212	30702		0075	1285	2 PWC PT6T-3 TwinPac	5080			
☐ N8530F	Bell 212	30920	N600EA	0079	0293	2 PWC PT6T-3 TwinPac	5080			

AIG AVIATION, Inc. (American International Aviation Corporation dba) **Atlanta-DeKalb Peachtree, GA & Teterboro, NJ**

1175 Peach Street NE, Suite 1000, Atlanta, GA 30361, USA ☎ (770) 458-4915 Tx: none Fax: (770) 458-4915 SITA: n/a
F: 1991 ⁂ n/a Head: J. Douglas Azar Net: n/a

☐ N54HG	Eurocopter (Aerosp.) AS355N TwinStar	5567	N6097U	0094	1194	2 TU Arrius 1A	2540			
☐ N47SE	Sabreliner 65 (Rockwell NA265-65)	465-34	N65TS	0080	1191	2 GA TFE731-3R-1D	10886			

A.I.R., Inc. (Aviation International Rotors, Inc. dba / Sister company of Heavy Lift Helicopters, Inc.) **Apple Valley, CA & Ketchikan, AK**

19378 Central Road, Apple Valley, CA 92307, USA ☎ (760) 240-4247 Tx: none Fax: (760) 240-1202 SITA: n/a
F: 1992 ⁂ n/a Head: Chester C. Rasberry Net: n/a

☐ N104CR	Bell 204B Super	2006	C-GKQH	0063	0794	1 LY T5313B	3856			cvtd 204B
☐ N1177U	Bell 204B Super	2023		0064	0196	1 LY T5313B	3856			cvtd 204B
☐ N415B	Bell 212	30613	N212HV	0074	0895	2 PWC PT6T-3 TwinPac	5080			lsf pvt

AIR ALASKA CARGO, Inc. = SIR (formerly Salair, Inc.) **Seattle-Tacoma Int'l, WA**

6105 East Rutter Ave., Suite 201, Spokane, WA 99212, USA ☎ (509) 532-1000 Tx: none Fax: (509) 532-8000 SITA: n/a
F: 1980 ⁂ n/a Head: Bruce C. Salerno ICAO: SALAIR Net: n/a

☐ N94CF	Convair 440-75 (F) (SCD) Metropolitan	394	SE-FUG	0057	0898	2 PW R-2800	21772	Freighter		lsf Sion Air Express

AIR ALPHA, Inc. **Cincinnati-Municipal/Lunken Field, OH**

PO Box 26130, Cincinnati, OH 45226, USA ☎ (513) 871-1051 Tx: none Fax: (513) 871-3471 SITA: n/a
F: 1977 ⁂ n/a Head: Dwayne D. Alvarez Net: n/a

☐ N333PR	Piper PA-31-350 Navajo Chieftain	31-7305112		0073	0690	2 LY TIO-540-J2BD	3175			

AIR AMBULANCE, Inc. (Affiliated with Hawaii Air Ambulance, Inc.) **Hayward-Air Termianl & Burbank-Glendale Pasadena, CA**

21927 Skywest Drive, Hayward, CA 94541, USA ☎ (925) 786-1592 Tx: none Fax: (925) 782-9337 SITA: n/a
F: 1970 ⁂ 100 Head: Michael N. Cowan Net: n/a

☐ N4686N	Cessna 414A Chancellor III	414A0075		0078	0381	2 CO TSIO-520-N	3062	EMS		lst Hawaii Air Ambulance
☐ N5614C	Cessna 414A Chancellor III	414A0203		0078	0779	2 CO TSIO-520-NB	3062	EMS		lst Hawaii Air Ambulance
☐ N5637C	Cessna 414A Chancellor III	414A0118		0078	0481	2 CO TSIO-520-N	3062	EMS		lst Hawaii Air Ambulance
☐ N5449J	Cessna 421B Golden Eagle	421B0907		0075	0297	2 CO GTSIO-520-H	3379	EMS		lsf pvt
☐ N375CA	Mitsubishi MU-2J (MU-2B-35)	643	N881DT	0074	0192	2 GA TPE331-6-251M	4899	EMS		lsf pvt

AIR AMERICA JET CHARTER, Inc. (Sister company of North American Jet, Inc.) **Houston-William P. Hobby, TX**

9000 Randolph Road, Houston, TX 77061, USA ☎ (713) 640-2900 Tx: none Fax: (713) 640-2193 SITA: n/a
F: 1981 ⁂ n/a Head: William B. McCarter, Jr. Net: n/a

☐ N555MC	Piper PA-31-350 Navajo Chieftain	31-7752154		0077	0594	2 LY TIO-540-J2BD	3175			lsf Mcoco Inc.
☐ N345MC	Learjet 25	25-046	N33PT	0069	0881	2 GE CJ610-6	6804			lsf Mcoco Inc.

AIRATLANTIC AIRLINES, Inc. **Centre Hall-Penns Cave, PA & Newburgh-Stewart Int'l, NY**

Box 165, Centre Hall, PA 16828, USA ☎ (814) 364-1477 Tx: none Fax: (814) 364-1479 SITA: n/a
F: 1979 ⁂ n/a Head: Russell E. Schleiden Net: n/a

☐ N771PC	Piper PA-32-260 Cherokee SIX	32-381		0066	0294	1 LY O-540-E4B5	1542			
☐ N10TG	Twin (Aero) Turbo Commander 680V II	680T-1684-65	N1UT	0067	0896	2 GA TPE331-43BL	4264			
☐ N87WS	Cessna 441 Conquest II	441-0009	N777ED	0078	0490	2 GA TPE331-8-401S	4468			lsf TMG Corp.

AIR AURORA, Inc. = AX / AAI **Chicago-Aurora Municipal, IL**

11407W Irving Park Road, Franklin Park, IL 60131, USA ☎ (847) 957-0900 Tx: none Fax: (847) 957-0902 SITA: n/a
F: 1977 ⁂ n/a Head: Warren Rogers IATA: 386 ICAO: BOREALIS Net: n/a

☐ N8373W	Piper PA-28-181 Cherokee Archer II	28-8190214		0081	0496	1 LY O-360-A4M	1157	Freighter		

AIRBORNE, Inc. **Elmira-Corning Regional, NY**

236 Sing Sing Road, Horseheads, NY 14845, USA ☎ (607) 739-7148 Tx: none Fax: (607) 796-2869 SITA: n/a
F: 1994 ⁂ n/a Head: John H. Dow Net: n/a

☐ N181RB	Dassault Falcon 20C	66	N109RK	0066	0895	2 GE CF700-2D2	12400			lsf International Group Inc.
☐ N281RB	GAC (Grumman) G-1159 Gulfstream II	200	N17GG	0077	0897	2 RR Spey 511-8	29393			lsf International Group Inc.
☐ N776MA	GAC (Grumman) G-1159B Gulfstream IIB	166	XA-SWP	0075	0795	2 RR Spey 511-8	31615			lsf Denison Enterpr. Inc. / cvtd G-1159

AIRBORNE EXPRESS = GB / ABX (ABX Air, Inc. dba / formerly Airborne Express, Inc. / Subsidiary of Airborne Freight, Corp.) **Wilmington-Airborne Airpark, OH**

Air Operations, 145 Hunter Drive, Wilmington, OH 45177, USA ☎ (513) 382-5591 Tx: 214317 airbn exp wim Fax: (513) 382-2452 SITA: n/a
F: 1979 ⁂ 6900 Head: Carl Donaway IATA: 832 ICAO: ABEX Net: http://www.airborne-express.com

☐ N925AX	Boeing (Douglas) DC-9-15	45728 / 14	I-TIGA	0865	0883	2 PW JT8D-7B (HK3/ABS)	41141	Freighter		cvtd -11
☐ N927AX	Boeing (Douglas) DC-9-15	45717 / 20	I-TIGE	0266	0883	2 PW JT8D-7B (HK3/ABS)	41141	Freighter		
☐ N900AX	Boeing (Douglas) DC-9-32	47380 / 514	N1284L	0669	0381	2 PW JT8D-7B (HK3/ABS)	49895	Freighter		
☐ N901AX	Boeing (Douglas) DC-9-32	47381 / 519	N1285L	0769	0381	2 PW JT8D-7B (HK3/ABS)	49895	Freighter		
☐ N902AX	Boeing (Douglas) DC-9-32	47426 / 572	N1286L	0170	1280	2 PW JT8D-7B (HK3/ABS)	49895	Freighter		
☐ N903AX	Boeing (Douglas) DC-9-32	47427 / 573	N1287L	0270	0381	2 PW JT8D-7B (HK3/ABS)	49895	Freighter		

247 registration type of aircraft cn/fn ex/ex* mfd del powered by mtow kg configuration selcal name/fln/specialitites/remarks

☐ N904AX	Boeing (Douglas) DC-9-32F	47040 / 172	N931F	1067	0881	2 PW JT8D-7B (HK3/ABS)	49895	Freighter		cvtd DC-9-32F (CF)
☐ N905AX	Boeing (Douglas) DC-9-32F	47147 / 208	N933F	1067	0781	2 PW JT8D-7B (HK3/ABS)	49895	Freighter		cvtd DC-9-32F (CF)
☐ N906AX	Boeing (Douglas) DC-9-31	47072 / 270	VH-TJM	0268	0382	2 PW JT8D-7B (HK3/ABS)	48988	Freighter		
☐ N907AX	Boeing (Douglas) DC-9-31	47203 / 401	VH-TJN	1068	0682	2 PW JT8D-7B (HK3/ABS)	48988	Freighter		
☐ N908AX	Boeing (Douglas) DC-9-31	47008 / 98	VH-TJK	0467	0183	2 PW JT8D-7B (HK3/ABS)	48988	Freighter		
☐ N909AX	Boeing (Douglas) DC-9-32F	47148 / 246	N934F	0168	0185	2 PW JT8D-7B (HK3/ABS)	48988	Freighter	AE-CF	cvtd DC-9-32F (CF)
☐ N923AX	Boeing (Douglas) DC-9-31	47165 / 260	N8942E	0168	0991	2 PW JT8D-7B (HK3/ABS)	47627	Freighter	AM-BD	
☐ N924AX	Boeing (Douglas) DC-9-31	47403 / 507	N8987E	0569	0991	2 PW JT8D-7B (HK3/ABS)	47627	Freighter	CM-AF	
☐ N928AX	Boeing (Douglas) DC-9-32	47392 / 447	YU-AJB	0169	0685	2 PW JT8D-7B (HK3/ABS)	48988	Freighter		
☐ N929AX	Boeing (Douglas) DC-9-31	45874 / 351	N965ML	0768	1291	2 PW JT8D-7B (HK3/ABS)	47627	Freighter	CH-BE	
☐ N930AX	Boeing (Douglas) DC-9-33F	47363 / 445	N502MD	0169	0384	2 PW JT8D-7B (HK3/ABS)	51710	Freighter		cvtd DC-9-33F (RC)
☐ N931AX	Boeing (Douglas) DC-9-33F	47384 / 543	HB-IFW	0969	0584	2 PW JT8D-7B (HK3/ABS)	51710	Freighter		
☐ N932AX	Boeing (Douglas) DC-9-33F	47465 / 584	N7465B	0370	0185	2 PW JT8D-7B (HK3/ABS)	51710	Freighter		cvtd DC-9-33F (CF)
☐ N933AX	Boeing (Douglas) DC-9-33F	47291 / 343	N94454	0768	0185	2 PW JT8D-7B (HK3/ABS)	51710	Freighter		cvtd DC-9-33F (CF)
☐ N934AX	Boeing (Douglas) DC-9-33F	47462 / 564	N32UA	0269	0387	2 PW JT8D-9 (HK3/ABS)	51710	Freighter		cvtd DC-9-33F (RC)
☐ N935AX	Boeing (Douglas) DC-9-33F	47413 / 521	N939F	0769	0690	2 PW JT8D-11 (HK3/ABS)	51710	Freighter	BC-DL	
☐ N936AX	Boeing (Douglas) DC-9-31	47269 / 371	N970ML	0868	1291	2 PW JT8D-7B (HK3/ABS)	47627	Freighter		
☐ N937AX	Boeing (Douglas) DC-9-31	47074 / 376	N973ML	0068	0192	2 PW JT8D-7B (HK3/ABS)	47627	Freighter		
☐ N938AX	Boeing (Douglas) DC-9-31	47009 / 152	VH-TJL	0867	1086	2 PW JT8D-7B (HK3/ABS)	46720	Freighter		
☐ N939AX	Boeing (Douglas) DC-9-32	47201 / 459	EC-ECU	0269	0389	2 PW JT8D-9 (HK3/ABS)	49895	Freighter		
☐ N941AX	Boeing (Douglas) DC-9-31	47419 / 602	VH-TJQ	0870	0789	2 PW JT8D-7B (HK3/ABS)	46720	Freighter		
☐ N942AX	Boeing (Douglas) DC-9-31	47552 / 640	VH-TJU	1071	1189	2 PW JT8D-7B (HK3/ABS)	46720	Freighter		
☐ N943AX	Boeing (Douglas) DC-9-31	47528 / 617	VH-TJR	0271	0989	2 PW JT8D-7B (HK3/ABS)	46720	Freighter		
☐ N944AX	Boeing (Douglas) DC-9-31	47550 / 623	VH-TJS	0471	0989	2 PW JT8D-7B (HK3/ABS)	46720	Freighter		
☐ N945AX	Boeing (Douglas) DC-9-31	47551 / 634	VH-TJT	0771	1089	2 PW JT8D-7B (HK3/ABS)	46720	Freighter		
☐ N946AX	Boeing (Douglas) DC-9-31	47003 / 86	N535MD	0367	0790	2 PW JT8D-7B (HK3/ABS)	46720	Freighter		
☐ N947AX	Boeing (Douglas) DC-9-31	47004 / 81	N537MD	0467	1290	2 PW JT8D-9 (HK3/ABS)	46720	Freighter		
☐ N948AX	Boeing (Douglas) DC-9-31	47065 / 269	N534MD	0368	1190	2 PW JT8D-7B (HK3/ABS)	46720	Freighter		
☐ N949AX	Boeing (Douglas) DC-9-31	47325 / 515	N540MD	0769	0890	2 PW JT8D-9 (HK3/ABS)	46720	Freighter		
☐ N980AX	Boeing (Douglas) DC-9-32	47176 / 314	N3335L	0468	0491	2 PW JT8D-7A (HK3/ABS)	48988	Freighter		
☐ N981AX	Boeing (Douglas) DC-9-32	47273 / 347	N3337L	0668	0791	2 PW JT8D-7A (HK3/ABS)	48988	Freighter		
☐ N982AX	Boeing (Douglas) DC-9-32	47317 / 385	N1261L	0868	0191	2 PW JT8D-7A (HK3/ABS)	48988	Freighter		
☐ N983AX	Boeing (Douglas) DC-9-32	47257 / 386	N1262L	0968	0291	2 PW JT8D-7A (HK3/ABS)	48988	Freighter		
☐ N984AX	Boeing (Douglas) DC-9-32	47258 / 387	N1263L	0968	0391	2 PW JT8D-7A (HK3/ABS)	48988	Freighter		
☐ N985AX	Boeing (Douglas) DC-9-32	47522 / 606	EC-BYD	0071	0492	2 PW JT8D-7B (HK3/ABS)	48988	Freighter	JK-BH	
☐ N986AX	Boeing (Douglas) DC-9-32	47543 / 654	EC-BYG	0072	0492	2 PW JT8D-9A (HK3/ABS)	48988	Freighter	AF-DL	
☐ N987AX	Boeing (Douglas) DC-9-32	47364 / 484	EC-BPF	0069	0392	2 PW JT8D-7A (HK3/ABS)	48988	Freighter	JK-BE	
☐ N988AX	Boeing (Douglas) DC-9-32	47084 / 179	EC-BIL	0067	0492	2 PW JT8D-7A (HK3/ABS)	48988	Freighter	FG-CL	
☐ N989AX	Boeing (Douglas) DC-9-32	47314 / 279	EC-BIU	0068	0392	2 PW JT8D-7A (HK3/ABS)	48988	Freighter	FG-EH	
☐ N951AX	Boeing (Douglas) DC-9-41	47616 / 759	JA8433	1274	1089	2 PW JT8D-15 (HK3/ABS)	51710	Freighter		
☐ N952AX	Boeing (Douglas) DC-9-41	47615 / 751	JA8432	1074	0191	2 PW JT8D-15 (HK3/ABS)	51710	Freighter		
☐ N953AX	Boeing (Douglas) DC-9-41	47608 / 732	JA8427	0074	0293	2 PW JT8D-15 (HK3/ABS)	51710	Freighter		
☐ N954AX	Boeing (Douglas) DC-9-41	47612 / 736	JA8428	0074	0393	2 PW JT8D-15 (HK3/ABS)	51710	Freighter		
☐ N955AX	Boeing (Douglas) DC-9-41	47619 / 768	JA8436	0275	1291	2 PW JT8D-15 (HK3/ABS)	51710	Freighter		
☐ N956AX	Boeing (Douglas) DC-9-41	47620 / 777	JA8437	0075	0592	2 PW JT8D-15 (HK3/ABS)	51710	Freighter		
☐ N957AX	Boeing (Douglas) DC-9-41	47759 / 871	JA8439	0077	0393	2 PW JT8D-15 (HK3/ABS)	51710	Freighter		
☐ N958AX	Boeing (Douglas) DC-9-41	47760 / 874	JA8440	0078	0596	2 PW JT8D-15 (HK3/ABS)	51710	Freighter		
☐ N959AX	Boeing (Douglas) DC-9-41	47761 / 875	JA8441	0078	1296	2 PW JT8D-15 (HK3/ABS)	51710	Freighter		
☐ N960AX	Boeing (Douglas) DC-9-41	47762 / 876	JA8442	0078	1096	2 PW JT8D-15 (HK3/ABS)	51710	Freighter		
☐ N962AX	Boeing (Douglas) DC-9-41	47768 / 887	JA8449	0078	1096	2 PW JT8D-15 (HK3/ABS)	51710	Freighter		
☐ N963AX	Boeing (Douglas) DC-9-41	47780 / 894	JA8450	0078	0197	2 PW JT8D-15 (HK3/ABS)	51710	Freighter		
☐ N964AX	Boeing (Douglas) DC-9-41	47781 / 895	JA8451	0079	0896	2 PW JT8D-15 (HK3/ABS)	51710	Freighter		
☐ N965AX	Boeing (Douglas) DC-9-41	47498 / 566	SE-DAL	1269	0691	2 PW JT8D-11 (HK3/ABS)	51710	Freighter	AM-CG	
☐ N966AX	Boeing (Douglas) DC-9-41	47510 / 645	OY-KGK	0971	1091	2 PW JT8D-11 (HK3/ABS)	51710	Freighter	BF-AM	
☐ N967AX	Boeing (Douglas) DC-9-41	47509 / 643	SE-DAO	1071	0292	2 PW JT8D-11 (HK3/ABS)	51710	Freighter	BC-GM	
☐ N968AX	Boeing (Douglas) DC-9-41	47499 / 568	SE-DAM	0270	0692	2 PW JT8D-11 (HK3/ABS)	51710	Freighter	AM-CH	
☐ N969AX	Boeing (Douglas) DC-9-41	47464 / 575	SE-DAN	0770	0792	2 PW JT8D-11 (HK3/ABS)	51710	Freighter	AM-CJ	
☐ N970AX	Boeing (Douglas) DC-9-41	47494 / 601	OY-KGI	0770	1092	2 PW JT8D-11 (HK3/ABS)	51710	Freighter	BC-GH	
☐ N971AX	Boeing (Douglas) DC-9-41	47497 / 604	LN-RLB	0870	0193	2 PW JT8D-11 (HK3/ABS)	51710	Freighter	BC-JM	
☐ N973AX	Boeing (Douglas) DC-9-41	47511 / 677	LN-RLU	0072	0193	2 PW JT8D-11 (HK3/ABS)	51710	Freighter	FL-EH	
☐ N974AX	Boeing (Douglas) DC-9-41	47623 / 728	LN-RLS	0474	1197	2 PW JT8D-11 (HK3/ABS)	51710	Freighter		
☐ N975AX	Boeing (Douglas) DC-9-41	47512 / 678	SE-DAP	0072	0493	2 PW JT8D-11 (HK3/ABS)	51710	Freighter	BC-KL	
☐ N976AX	Boeing (Douglas) DC-9-41	47596 / 714	SE-DAR	1273	0399	2 PW JT8D-11 (HK3/ABS)	51710	Freighter		
☐ N977AX	Boeing (Douglas) DC-9-41	47513 / 679	LN-RLX	1172	0296	2 PW JT8D-11 (HK3/ABS)	51710	Freighter		
☐ N978AX	Boeing (Douglas) DC-9-41	47628 / 740	OY-KGN	0774	0398	2 PW JT8D-11 (HK3/ABS)	51710	Freighter		
☐ N979AX	Boeing (Douglas) DC-9-41	47492 / 559	SE-DAK	0070	0195	2 PW JT8D-11 (HK3/ABS)	51710	Freighter		
☐ N990AX	Boeing (Douglas) DC-9-41	47493 / 562	SE-DLC	1269	0195	2 PW JT8D-11 (HK3/ABS)	51710	Freighter		
☐ N841AX	Boeing (Douglas) DC-8-61	45908 / 296	EC-EAM	0867	1287	4 PW JT3D-3B (HK2/BAC)	147418	Freighter		
☐ N842AX	Boeing (Douglas) DC-8-61	46015 / 405	N766RD	1168	1287	4 PW JT3D-3B (HK2/BAC)	147418	Freighter		
☐ N843AX	Boeing (Douglas) DC-8-61	46017 / 418	N64RD	1268	1287	4 PW JT3D-3B (HK2/BAC)	147418	Freighter		
☐ N844AX	Boeing (Douglas) DC-8-61	45848 / 285	JA8050	0267	0288	4 PW JT3D-3B (HK2/BAC)	147418	Freighter		
☐ N845AX	Boeing (Douglas) DC-8-61	46157 / 541	JA8045	1270	0188	4 PW JT3D-3B (HK2/BAC)	147418	Freighter		
☐ N846AX	Boeing (Douglas) DC-8-61	46158 / 543	JA8046	0171	0188	4 PW JT3D-3B (HK2/BAC)	147418	Freighter		
☐ N847AX	Boeing (Douglas) DC-8-61	46031 / 435	N28UA	0169	1287	4 PW JT3D-3B (HK2/BAC)	147418	Freighter		
☐ N848AX	Boeing (Douglas) DC-8-61	46032 / 436	N51UA	0169	1091	4 PW JT3D-3B (HK2/QNC)	147418	Freighter		
☐ N849AX	Boeing (Douglas) DC-8-61F	45891 / 305	N21UA	1067	0495	4 PW JT3D-3B (HK2/QNC)	145286	Freighter		cvtd DC-8-61
☐ N850AX	Boeing (Douglas) DC-8-61	45894 / 297	N915CL	0867	0289	4 PW JT3D-3B (HK2/BAC)	147418	Freighter		
☐ N851AX	Boeing (Douglas) DC-8-61	45940 / 314	N8075U	1267	0689	4 PW JT3D-3B (HK2)	147418	Freighter		
☐ N852AX	Boeing (Douglas) DC-8-61	46016 / 409	TC-MAB	0068	1294	4 PW JT3D-3B (HK2/BAC)	147418	Freighter		
☐ N853AX	Boeing (Douglas) DC-8-61F	46037 / 419	ZP-CCR	0068	0295	4 PW JT3D-3B (HK2/QNC)	147418	Freigher		cvtd DC-8-61
☐ N801AX	Boeing (Douglas) DC-8-62	46077 / 470	N923R	0769	0885	4 PW JT3D-3B (HK3/BAC)	151953	Freighter		
☐ N802AX	Boeing (Douglas) DC-8-62	46134 / 513	N924CL	0470	0186	4 PW JT3D-3B (HK3/BAC)	151953	Freighter		
☐ N803AX	Boeing (Douglas) DC-8-62	45917 / 332	N4761G	0268	0186	4 PW JT3D-3B (HK3/BAC)	151953	Freighter		
☐ N804AX	Boeing (Douglas) DC-8-62	45987 / 366	OH-LFZ	0668	0287	4 PW JT3D-3B (HK3/BAC)	151953	Freighter		
☐ N805AX	Boeing (Douglas) DC-8-62	45906 / 300	N762UA	0867	0287	4 PW JT3D-3B (HK3/BAC)	151953	Freighter		
☐ N808AX	Boeing (Douglas) DC-8-62	45954 / 362	5N-AON	0568	0487	4 PW JT3D-3B (HK3/BAC)	151953	Freighter		
☐ N767AX	Boeing 767-281 (PC)	22785 / 51	JA8479	0083	0897	2 GE CF6-80A	140614	Freighter		cvtd -281
☐ N768AX	Boeing 767-281 (PC)	22786 / 54	JA8480	0083	1197	2 GE CF6-80A	140614	Freighter		cvtd -281
☐ N769AX	Boeing 767-281 (PC)	22787 / 58	JA8481	0083	0398	2 GE CF6-80A	140614	Freighter		cvtd -281
☐ N773AX	Boeing 767-281 (PC)	22788 / 61	JA8482	0083	0598	2 GE CF6-80A	140614	Freighter		cvtd -281
☐ N774AX	Boeing 767-281 (PC)	22789 / 67	JA8483	0083	0898	2 GE CF6-80A	140614	Freighter		cvtd -281
☐ N775AX	Boeing 767-281 (PC)	22790 / 69	JA8484	0083	1198	2 GE CF6-80A	140614	Freighter		cvtd -281
☐ N783AX	Boeing 767-281 (PC)	23016 / 80	JA8485	0084		2 GE CF6-80A	140614	Freighter		oo-delivery 0099 / ex ANA / cvtd -281
☐ N784AX	Boeing 767-281 (PC)	23017 / 82	JA8486	0084		2 GE CF6-80A	140614	Freighter		oo-delivery 0099 / ex ANA / cvtd -281
☐ N785AX	Boeing 767-281 (PC)	23018 / 84	JA8487	0084		2 GE CF6-80A	140614	Freighter		oo-delivery 0099 / ex ANA / cvtd -281
☐ N786AX	Boeing 767-281 (PC)	23019 / 85	JA8488	0084		2 GE CF6-80A	140614	Freighter		oo-delivery 0099 / ex ANA / cvtd -281
☐ N787AX	Boeing 767-281 (PC)	23020 / 96	JA8489	0084		2 GE CF6-80A	140614	Freighter		oo-delivery 0000 / ex ANA / cvtd -281
☐ N788AX	Boeing 767-281 (PC)	23021 / 103	JA8490	0084		2 GE CF6-80A	140614	Freighter		oo-delivery 0000 / ex ANA / cvtd -281
☐ N811AX	Boeing (Douglas) DC-8-63F	46113 / 521	N818EV	0370	0390	4 PW JT3D-7 (HK3/BAC)	161025	Freighter	AJ-GL	cvtd DC-8-63
☐ N812AX	Boeing (Douglas) DC-8-63F	46126 / 524	N819EV	0470	0390	4 PW JT3D-7 (HK3/BAC)	161025	Freighter	AJ-GM	cvtd DC-8-63
☐ N813AX	Boeing (Douglas) DC-8-63	46136 / 509	N795AL	0170	0492	4 PW JT3D-7 (HK3/BAC)	161025	Freighter	AD-GM	
☐ N814AX	Boeing (Douglas) DC-8-63F	46041 / 439	N792AL	1269	1290	4 PW JT3D-7 (HK3/BAC)	161025	Freighter	BC-AF	cvtd DC-8-63
☐ N815AX	Boeing (Douglas) DC-8-63F	46097 / 503	N793AL	0069	0393	4 PW JT3D-7 (HK3/BAC)	161025	Freighter	CL-HM	cvtd DC-8-63 (PF)
☐ N816AX	Boeing (Douglas) DC-8-63F	46093 / 496	N790AL	1169	1090	4 PW JT3D-7 (HK3/BAC)	161025	Freighter	CL-HK	cvtd DC-8-63 (PF)
☐ N817AX	Boeing (Douglas) DC-8-63	45928 / 334	N780AL	1267	0691	4 PW JT3D-7 (HK3/BAC)	161025	Freighter	DL-EF	
☐ N818AX	Boeing (Douglas) DC-8-63	46075 / 484	N512FP	0069	1093	4 PW JT3D-7 (HK3/BAC)	161025	Freighter	BH-CD	
☐ N819AX	Boeing (Douglas) DC-8-63F	45927 / 327	N783AL	0068	0395	4 PW JT3D-7 (HK3/BAC)	161025	Freighter	DL-CM	cvtd DC-8-63
☐ N820AX	Boeing (Douglas) DC-8-63	46155 / 529	C-GQBA	0470	1291	4 PW JT3D-7 (HK3/BAC)	161025	Freighter	BC-GL	
☐ N821AX	Boeing (Douglas) DC-8-63	46116 / 518	C-GQBF	0170	1291	4 PW JT3D-7 (HK3/BAC)	161025	Freighter	BC-KL	
☐ N822AX	Boeing (Douglas) DC-8-63	46079 / 476	N4934Z	0069	1094	4 PW JT3D-7 (HK3/BAC)	161025	Freighter	BC-FG	
☐ N823AX	Boeing (Douglas) DC-8-63	46122 / 506	5Y-ZEB	0069	0194	4 PW JT3D-7 (HK3/BAC)	161025	Freighter	GL-CM	
☐ N824AX	Boeing (Douglas) DC-8-63	46141 / 533	HB-IBF	0070	0194	4 PW JT3D-7 (HK3/BAC)	161025	Freighter	AB-JM	
☐ N825AX	Boeing (Douglas) DC-8-63	46115 / 530	ZP-CCH	0070	0295	4 PW JT3D-7 (HK3/BAC)	158757	Freighter	HM-EG	
☐ N826AX	Boeing (Douglas) DC-8-63F	46061 / 480	N952R	0069	0795	4 PW JT3D-7 (HK3/BAC)	158757	Freighter	FG-AM	cvtd DC-8-63F (CF)
☐ N828AX	Boeing (Douglas) DC-8-63F	45999 / 377	N788AL	0068	0297	4 PW JT3D-7 (HK3/BAC)	161025	Freighter		cvtd DC-8-63

AIRBORNE FIRE ATTACK

Santa Ana-John Wayne/Orange County, CA

43 Fulmer Lane, Eliso Viejo, CA 92656, USA ☎ (949) 588-1130 Tx: none Fax: (949) 588-0011 SITA: n/a
F: 1996 n/a Head: John M. Wells Net: n/a

☐ N324FA	Consolidated 28-5ACF Catalina	2163	C-FPIU	0045	1197	2 PW R-1830	13835	Tanker		115 / lsf Wells Aviation Inc.

248 registration type of aircraft cn/fn ex/ex* mfd del powered by mtow kg configuration selcal name/fln/specialitites/remarks

AIRBORNE FLYING SERVICES, Inc.
Hot Springs-Memorial Field, AR

525 Airport Road, Hot Springs, AR 71913, USA ☎ (870) 624-4545 Tx: none Fax: (870) 624-5550 SITA: n/a
F: 1970 ♦♦♦ n/a Head: Jolly R. Higdon Net: n/a Aircraft below MTOW 1361kg: Cessna 182

☐ N7958D	Beech Baron 58	TH-1019		0079	0596	2 CO IO-520-CB	2449		lsf Tiffany Air Inc.
☐ N9021V	Beech Baron 58	TH-233		0072	1291	2 CO IO-520-C	2404		

AIRBORNE SUPPORT, Inc. (formerly Ag Air, Inc. / Affiliated with EASI-Environmental Aviation Services, Inc.)
Houma-Terrebonne, LA

PO Box 487, Bourg, LA 70343-0487, USA ☎ (504) 851-6391 Tx: none Fax: (504) 851-6393 SITA: n/a
F: 1975 ♦♦♦ n/a Head: Howard Barker

☐ N4994N	Boeing (Douglas) DC-3C (C-47B-1-DK)	25771	N840M	0043	0379	2 PW R-1830	12202	Sprayer	lsf Environmental Aviation Services
☐ N64766	Boeing (Douglas) DC-3C (C-47B-20-DK)	27218	CAF12910	0043	1279	2 PW R-1830	12202	Sprayer	lsf Environmental Aviation Services
☐ N64767	Boeing (Douglas) DC-3C (C-47A-55-DL)	10199	CAF12941	0043	1279	2 PW R-1830	12202	Sprayer	lsf Environmental Aviation Services
☐ N67024	Boeing (Douglas) DC-4 (C-54D-1-DC)	10550 / DC 281	BU50871	0045	1185	4 PW R-2000	30241	Sprayer	lsf Environmental Aviation Services

AIR CAL, Inc.
Burbank-Glendale/Pasadena, CA

615 East Olive F, Burbank, CA 91501, USA ☎ (818) 955-5857 Tx: none Fax: (818) 955-8806 SITA: n/a
F: 1993 ♦♦♦ n/a Head: Conrad C. Lohner Net: n/a

☐ N4510Q	Cessna 402A	402A0010		0069	0993	2 CO TSIO-520-E	2858		lsf pvt

AIRCAM NATIONAL HELICOPTERS (Aircam National Helicopter Services, Inc. dba)
Denver-Centennial, CO

7505 South Peoria Circle, Box D-3, Englewood, CO 80112, USA ☎ (303) 799-0079 Tx: none Fax: (303) 799-0081 SITA: n/a
F: 1987 ♦♦♦ n/a Head: James B. Dirker Net: n/a

☐ N206BD	Bell 206B JetRanger III	4203		0092	1195	1 AN 250-C20J	1451		lsf JBD Enterprises Inc.
☐ N2064S	Bell 206L-4 LongRanger IV	52002		0092	0396	1 AN 250-C30P	2018		lsf JBD Enterprises Inc.
☐ N57905	Eurocopter (Aerosp.) AS355F1 TwinStar	5114		0082	0994	2 AN 250-C20F	2400		lsf JBD Enterprises Inc.
☐ N5802W	Eurocopter (Aerosp.) AS355F1 TwinStar	5221		0082	0895	2 AN 250-C20F	2400		lsf JBD Enterprises Inc.

AIR CARE, Inc.
Rocky Mount-Wilson, NC

PO Box 7668, Rocky Mount, NC 27804, USA ☎ (919) 977-1717 Tx: none Fax: (919) 442-5578 SITA: n/a
F: 1961 ♦♦♦ n/a Head: John B. Williams, Jr. Net: n/a

☐ N123MG	Beech Baron 58P	TJ-115		0078	1196	2 CO TSIO-520-WB	2812		

AIR CARGO CARRIERS, Inc. = SNC
Milwaukee-General Mitchell Int'l, WI

4984 South Howell Avenue, Milwaukee, WI 53207, USA ☎ (920) 482-1711 Tx: none Fax: (920) 482-2038 SITA: n/a
F: 1986 ♦♦♦ 22 Head: James M. Germek ICAO: NIGHT CARGO Net: n/a

☐ N20EF	Fairchild (Swearingen) SA26AT Merlin IIB	T26-157	N20ER	0069	0497	2 GA TPE331-1-151G	4536	Freighter	
☐ N410AC	Shorts Skyvan 3 Variant 100 (SC-7)	SH1883	C-FQSL	0070	0790	2 GA TPE331-2-201A	5670	Freighter	
☐ N731E	Shorts Skyvan 3 Variant 200 (SC-7)	SH1853	N80JJ	0068	0187	2 GA TPE331-2-201A	5670	Freighter	opf Airborne Express
☐ N167RC	Shorts 330-200 (SD3-30)	SH3038	N690RA	0079	0492	2 PWC PT6A-45R	10251	Freighter	
☐ N2629P	Shorts 330-200 (SD3-30)	SH3079	N339MV	0081	0496	2 PWC PT6A-45R	10251	Freighter	
☐ N330AC	Shorts 330-200 (SD3-30)	SH3007	C-GSKW	0076	0594	2 PWC PT6A-45B	10160	Freighter	
☐ N335MV	Shorts 330-200 (SD3-30)	SH3017	PJ-DDA	0078	0196	2 PWC PT6A-45R	10251	Freighter	
☐ N336MV	Shorts 330-200 (SD3-30)	SH3018	PJ-DDB	0078	1292	2 PWC PT6A-45R	10251	Freighter	
☐ N390GA	Shorts 330-200 (SD3-30)	SH3077	4X-CSP	0081	0598	2 PWC PT6A-45R	10387	Freighter	
☐ N55AN	Shorts 330-200 (SD3-30)	SH3025	N373HA	0079	0895	2 PWC PT6A-45R	10387	Freighter	
☐ N936MA	Shorts 330-200 (SD3-30)	SH3036	G-BGNI*	0079	0192	2 PWC PT6A-45R	10251	Freighter	
☐ N937MA	Shorts 330-200 (SD3-30)	SH3040	G-BGZT*	0080	0192	2 PWC PT6A-45R	10251	Freighter	
☐ N938MA	Shorts 330-200 (SD3-30)	SH3046	G-BHJJ*	0080	0192	2 PWC PT6A-45R	10251	Freighter	
☐ N939MA	Shorts 330-200 (SD3-30)	SH3047	G-BHSH*	0080	0192	2 PWC PT6A-45R	10251	Freighter	
☐ N124CA	Shorts 360-100 (SD3-60)	SH3652	G-14-3652*	0084	0895	2 PWC PT6A-65R	11999	Freighter	
☐ N151CA	Shorts 360-100 (SD3-60)	SH3653	G-14-3653*	0084	0695	2 PWC PT6A-65R	11999	Freighter	
☐ N360RW	Shorts 360-100 (SD3-60)	SH3613	C-FCRB	0083	0598	2 PWC PT6A-65R	11999	Freighter	
☐ N4498Y	Shorts 360-100 (SD3-60)	SH3625	G-14-3625*	0083	1195	2 PWC PT6A-65R	11999	Freighter	
☐ N601CA	Shorts 360-100 (SD3-60)	SH3623	G-BKWM	0083	0496	2 PWC PT6A-65R	11999	Freighter	
☐ N691A	Shorts 360-100 (SD3-60)	SH3618	G-BKUG*	0083	0798	2 PWC PT6A-65AR	11999	Freighter	

AIR CARGO EXPRESS = 3K / FXG (Division of Tatonduk Outfitters, Ltd)
Fairbanks-Int'l, AK

PO Box 61680, Fairbanks, AK 99706, USA ☎ (907) 474-3488 Tx: none Fax: (907) 474-4602 SITA: n/a
F: 1994 ♦♦♦ n/a Head: Robert W. Everts ICAO: CARGO EXPRESS Net: n/a

☐ N54514	Curtiss C-46D-10-CU Commando	33285	44-77889	0045	1296	2 PW R-2800	21772	Freighter	
☐ N151	Boeing (Douglas) DC-6BF	45496 / 992	C-GICD	0058	0997	4 PW R-2800-CB16	47083	Freighter	cvtd DC-6B
☐ N251CE	Boeing (Douglas) DC-6A (C-118A-DO)	44613 / 533	USN 153693	0054	1296	4 PW R-2800-CB16	47083	Freighter	
☐ N351CE	Boeing (Douglas) DC-6A (C-118A-DO)	44599 / 505	53-3228	0054	0694	4 PW R-2800-CB16	47083	Freighter	
☐ N555SQ	Boeing (Douglas) DC-6BF	45137 / 830	N37585	0057	0496	4 PW R-2800-CB16	47083	Freighter	cvtd DC-6B
☐ N6586C	Boeing (Douglas) DC-6BF	45222 / 849		0057	0498	4 PW R-2800-CB16	47083	Freighter	cvtd DC-6B
☐ N888DG	Boeing (Douglas) DC-6A (C-118A-DO)	44675 / 642	53-3304	0056	0696	4 PW R-2800-CB16	47083	Freighter	

AIR CARGO EXPRESS, Inc.
Fort Wayne-Int'l, IN

4021 Air Street, Fort Wayne, IN 46809, USA ☎ (219) 747-1963 Tx: none Fax: (219) 747-1967 SITA: n/a
F: 1995 ♦♦♦ n/a Head: Mark C. Spatz Net: n/a

☐ N999TA	Mitsubishi MU-2G (MU-2B-30)	514	N514WG	0070	1095	2 GA TPE331-1-151A	4899	Freighter	
☐ N992TD	Learjet 23	23-035	N100X	0065	0197	2 GE CJ610-4	5670	Freighter	
☐ N993TD	Learjet 24	24-166	N124HF	0068	0997	2 GE CJ610-4	5897	Freighter	
☐ N994TD	Learjet 24	24-179	XA-RQP	0068	0698	2 GE CJ610-4	5897	Freighter	

AIR CARGO MASTERS, Inc.
Sioux Falls-Regional/Joe Foss Field, SD

701 West National Guard Drive, Sioux Falls, SD 57104, USA ☎ (605) 373-0303 Tx: none Fax: (605) 373-9595 SITA: n/a
F: 1993 ♦♦♦ n/a Head: Dennis L. Sherrill Net: http://www.aircargomasters.com

☐ N212BA	Mitsubishi MU-2J (MU-2B-35) Cargoliner	587	N102BH	0073	0295	2 GA TPE331-6-251M	4899	Freighter	Cavenaugh SCD conversion
☐ N300GL	Fairchild (Swearingen) SA226TC Metro II	TC-308	5Y-CNT	0078	0896	2 GA TPE331-10UA-511G	5670	Freighter	lsf Interair Lease Llc
☐ N434MA	Fairchild (Swearingen) SA227AC Metro III	AC-717	N27213	0088	0297	2 GA TPE331-11U-612G	6577	Freighter	lsf Interair Lease Llc
☐ N442MA	Fairchild (Swearingen) SA227AC Metro III	AC-725		0088	0597	2 GA TPE331-11U-612G	6577	Freighter	lsf Dude Inc.
☐ N122GL	Beech 1900C-1 Airliner	UC-122	N195GL	0090	0997	2 PWC PT6A-65B	7530	Freighter	lsf GLA
☐ N162RB	Beech 1900C-1 Airliner	UC-101	N101UE	0090	1297	2 PWC PT6A-65B	7530	Freighter	lsf M&G Air Travel Inc.
☐ N316BH	Beech 1900C Airliner	UB-26	N16RA	0084	0697	2 PWC PT6A-65B	7530	Freighter	lsf Raytheon Aircraft Credit Corp.

AIR CAROLINA, Inc.
Spartanburg-Downtown Municipal, SC

500 Ammons Road, Spartanburg, SC 29306, USA ☎ (864) 574-4857 Tx: none Fax: (864) 574-1886 SITA: n/a
F: 1994 ♦♦♦ n/a Head: David E. Treinis Net: n/a

☐ N7210C	Beech Baron 58	TH-1431		0084	0296	2 CO IO-520-C	2449		

AIR CARRIERS, Inc. = FCI
Bessemer & Birmingham, AL

PO Box 400, Bessemer, AL 35021, USA ☎ (205) 425-9500 Tx: none Fax: (205) 424-7400 SITA: n/a
F: 1989 ♦♦♦ n/a Head: Tommy Morrow ICAO: FAST CHECK Net: http://www.bessemeraviation.com

☐ N101DW	Piper PA-32R-300 Lance	32R-7680399		0076	0695	1 LY IO-540-K1G5D	1633	Freighter	
☐ N38709	Piper PA-32R-300 Lance	32R-7780463		0076	0695	1 LY IO-540-K1G5D	1633	Freighter	
☐ N6190J	Piper PA-32R-300 Lance	32R-7680329		0076	0695	1 LY IO-540-K1G5D	1633	Freighter	
☐ N8337C	Piper PA-32R-300 Lance	32R-7680101		0076	0695	1 LY IO-540-K1G5D	1633	Freighter	
☐ N8554C	Piper PA-32R-300 Lance	32R-7680122		0076	0695	1 LY IO-540-K1G5D	1633	Freighter	
☐ N27JR	Cessna 210L Centurion II	21059706		0072	0795	1 CO IO-520-L	1724	Freighter	
☐ N33JN	Cessna 210L Centurion II	21060993		0075	0795	1 CO IO-520-L	1724	Freighter	
☐ N6554B	Cessna 210M Centurion II	21062785		0078	0795	1 CO IO-520-L	1724	Freighter	
☐ N6585A	Cessna 210N Centurion II	21063554		0079	0795	1 CO IO-520-L	1724	Freighter	
☐ N732QA	Cessna 210M Centurion II	21061679		0076	0795	1 CO IO-520-L	1724	Freighter	
☐ N761PS	Cessna 210M Centurion II	21062415		0077	0795	1 CO IO-520-L	1724	Freighter	
☐ N7761VX	Cessna 210M Centurion II	21062563		0078	0795	1 CO IO-520-L	1724	Freighter	
☐ N9823AR	Cessna 210M Centurion II	21062661		0078	0795	1 CO IO-520-L	1724	Freighter	
☐ N9163M	Cessna 210M Centurion II	21062067		0077	0795	1 CO IO-520-L	1724	Freighter	
☐ N93885	Cessna 210L Centurion II	21060444		0074	0795	1 CO IO-520-L	1724	Freighter	
☐ N2201F	Cessna 310L	310L0001		0067	0795	2 CO IO-470-V	2359	Freighter	
☐ N4140Q	Cessna 310N	310N0040		0068	0490	2 CO IO-470-V	2359	Freighter	
☐ N7742Q	Cessna 310Q	310Q0242		0071	0294	2 CO IO-470-VO	2404	Freighter	
☐ N64754Q	Cessna 310Q	310Q0254		0071	1295	2 CO IO-470-VO	2404	Freighter	
☐ N7940Q	Cessna 310Q	310Q0623		0073	0389	2 CO IO-470-VO	2404	Freighter	
☐ N699RF	AAC (Ted Smith) Aerostar 600A	60-0169-074	N74GD	0074	0496	2 LY IO-540-K1F5	2495	Freighter	
☐ N90404	AAC (Ted Smith) Aerostar 600A	60-0249-102		0075	0696	2 LY IO-540-K1F5	2495	Freighter	
☐ N90676	AAC (Ted Smith) Aerostar 600A	60-0331-122	N906SB	0076	0795	2 LY IO-540-K1F5	2495	Freighter	

registration type of aircraft   cn/fn   ex/ex*   mfd   del   powered by   mtow kg   configuration   selcal   name/fln/specialitites/remarks

☐ N91WW	AAC (Ted Smith) Aerostar 600A	60-0262-105	N90466	0075	0795	2 LY IO-540-K1F5	2495	Freighter		
☐ N8536	Twin (Aero) Shrike Commander 500S	3267		0076	1093	2 LY IO-540-E1B5	3062	Freighter		
☐ N900DT	Twin (Aero) Shrike Commander 500S	3056		0070	0793	2 LY IO-540-E1B5	3062	Freighter		
☐ N9096N	Twin (Aero) Shrike Commander 500S	3076		0070	0793	2 LY IO-540-E1B5	3062	Freighter		
☐ N13RR	Mitsubishi MU-2L (MU-2B-36) Cargoliner	682	N13PR	0075	1094	2 GA TPE331-6-251M	5250	Freighter		Cavenaugh SCD conversion
☐ N503AA	Mitsubishi MU-2J (MU-2B-35) Cargoliner	633	N483MA	0074	0496	2 GA TPE331-6-251M	4899	Freighter		Cavenaugh SCD conversion
☐ N92ST	Mitsubishi MU-2J (MU-2B-35) Cargoliner	610	N342MA	0074	0595	2 GA TPE331-6-251M	4899	Freighter		Cavenaugh SCD conversion

AIR CASTLE, Corp. (Associated with Global Aviation (Singapore) & Hop-A-Jet (Florida) / Member of The Winfair Aviation Alliance) **Teterboro, NJ**

501 Santa Monica Blvd., Suite 703, Santa Monica, CA 90401, USA ☎ (310) 899-5250 Tx: none Fax: (310) 899-5259 SITA: n/a
F: 1990 ⁂ n/a Head: Clifford Russell Net: n/a

☐ N161CC	Cessna 500 Citation	500-0161	C-GHEC	0074	0596	2 PWC JT15D-1	5216	Executive		lsf Interplanetary Aviation Inc.
☐ N358AC	Learjet 35A	35A-427	N42LL	0081	0997	2 GA TFE731-2-2B	7711	Executive		lsf Hop-a-Jet
☐ N710AT	Learjet 35A	35A-337	N337WC	0080	0197	2 GA TFE731-2-2B	7711	Executive		lsf CIT Leasing Corp. / sub-lst GAZ
☐ N950G	Learjet 36A	36A-032	HB-VLK	0077	0197	2 GA TFE731-2-2B	7711	Executive		lsf Global Aviation US Ltd/sub-lst GAZ
☐ N556GA	Learjet 55	55-028	N7244W	0082	0897	2 GA TFE731-3AR-2B	9752	Executive		lsf Hop-A-Jet
☐ N558AC	Learjet 55	55-048	PT-OBS	0082	1197	2 GA TFE731-3A-2B	9752	Executive		
☐ N39CD	Canadair CL-601-1A (CL-600-2A12) Challen.	3030	N34CD	0084	0197	2 GE CF34-1A	19550	Executive		lsf CIT Leasing Corp. / sub-lst GAZ
☐ N651AC	Canadair CL-601-1A (CL-600-2A12) Challen.	3009	N873G	0083	0098	2 GE CF34-1A	19550	Executive		lsf Hop-a-Jet
☐ N875G	Canadair CL-601-1A (CL-600-2A12) Challen.	3019	N375G	0084	0098	2 GE CF34-1A	19550	Executive		lsf General Electric Co.

AIR CENTER HELICOPTERS, Inc. **Fort Worth-Meacham Int'l, TX & St.Thomas-Cyril E. King, VI**

4359 North Main Street, Hangar 19N-A, Fort Worth, TX 76106, USA ☎ (817) 624-6300 Tx: none Fax: (817) 624-6311 SITA: n/a
F: 1986 ⁂ n/a Head: Rodney M. Tinney Net: n/a

☐ N2070U	Bell 206L-1 LongRanger II	45706		0081	1097	1 AN 250-C28B	1882			
☐ N59CH	Bell 206L-1 LongRanger II	45284	N77AH	0079	0497	1 AN 250-C28B	1882			
☐ N4083S	Bell 412	33028	JA9916	0081	0997	2 PWC PT6T-3B TwinPac	5398			

AIR CHARTER (Dejarnette's Enterprises, Inc. dba) **Kansas City-Richards Gebaur, MO**

PO Box 858, Lee's Summit, MO 64063, USA ☎ (816) 525-3330 Tx: none Fax: (816) 525-0454 SITA: n/a
F: 1991 ⁂ n/a Head: Ronald W. DeJarnette, Sr. Net: n/a

☐ N421KC	Cessna 421C Golden Eagle II	421C0028		0075	0895	2 CO GTSIO-520-L	3379			
☐ N580S	Beech King Air B100	BE-77	N55US	0079	0395	2 GA TPE331-6-252B	5352			
☐ N458N	Cessna 550 Citation II	550-0061	N456N	0079	0696	2 PWC JT15D-4	6033			

AIR CHARTER, Ltd **Mosinee-Central Wisconsin, WI**

2318 Mount View Boulevard, Wausau, WI 54403, USA ☎ (715) 842-4507 Tx: none Fax: (715) 848-9146 SITA: n/a
F: 1993 ⁂ n/a Head: Michael E. Turner Net: n/a

☐ N266M	Fairchild (Swear.) SA227TT Merlin IIIC	TT-424	N900AK	0082	0696	2 GA TPE331-10U-513G	5670			

AIR CHARTER EXPRESS (Craig S. Carter dba) **Fort Wayne-Int'l, IN**

11001 West Perimeter Road, Fort Wayne, IN 46809, USA ☎ (219) 747-5600 Tx: none Fax: (219) 747-9356 SITA: n/a
F: 1993 ⁂ 3 Head: Craig S. Carter Net: n/a

☐ N81009	Piper PA-34-200T Seneca II	34-8070004		0080	0693	2 CO TSIO-360-EB	2073			
☐ N27902	Piper PA-31-350 Navajo Chieftain	31-7952037		0078	0894	2 LY TIO-540-J2BD	3175			

AIR CHARTER EXPRESS = FRG (Freight Runners Express, Inc. dba) **Milwaukee-General Mitchell Int'l, WI**

1901 East Layton Avenue, Hangar 4, Milwaukee, WI 53207, USA ☎ (920) 744-5525 Tx: none Fax: (920) 744-4850 SITA: n/a
F: 1983 ⁂ 12 Head: Charles F. Zens, Jr. ICAO: FREIGHT RUNNERS Net: n/a

☐ N1517U	Cessna 207 Skywagon	20700117		0069	1286	1 CO IO-520-F	1724	Freighter		
☐ N1518U	Cessna 207 Skywagon	20700118		0069	0390	1 CO IO-520-F	1724	Freighter		
☐ N337PL	Cessna 402A	402A0039		0069	0390	2 CO TSIO-520-E	2858			
☐ N4504B	Cessna 402B II	402B1370		0078	0892	2 CO TSIO-520-E	2858			
☐ N4532Q	Cessna 402A	402A0032		0069	0789	2 CO TSIO-520-E	2858			
☐ N727CA	Cessna 402A	402A0102	N7802Q	0069	0890	2 CO TSIO-520-E	2858			
☐ N75GB	Cessna 402B	402B0912		0075	0493	2 CO TSIO-520-E	2858			
☐ N199CZ	Beech 99 Airliner	U-30	N3RP	0068	0894	2 PWC PT6A-20	4717	Freighter		
☐ N299CZ	Beech 99 Airliner	U-74	C-FCVJ	0069	0696	2 PWC PT6A-20	4717	Freighter		
☐ N399CZ	Beech B99 Airliner	U-52	ZK-LLA	0068	0296	2 PWC PT6A-28	4944	Freighter		cvtd -99
☐ N499CZ	Beech 99A Airliner	U-81	N36AK	0069	0297	2 PWC PT6A-27	4717	Freighter		
☐ N599CZ	Beech B99 Airliner	U-89	5Y-BJW	0069	0698	2 PWC PT6A-27	4944	Freighter		cvtd 99A

AIR CHARTER EXPRESS, Inc. **San Diego-Montgomery Field, CA**

5133 A. Renaissance Avenue, San Diego, CA 92122, USA ☎ (760) 457-4152 Tx: none Fax: (760) 457-2321 SITA: n/a
F: 1992 ⁂ n/a Head: Robert J. Golo Net: n/a

☐ N101G	Cessna 310R II	310R0017	N1333G	0075	0192	2 CO IO-520-M	2495			
☐ N28RG	Cessna 340A II	340A0347	N555TZ	0077	0396	2 CO TSIO-520-N	2717			
☐ N321DM	Beech King Air E90	LW-250	N600EF	0078	0296	2 PWC PT6A-28	4581			lsf INR Avn/sublst American Jet S. Ant.

AIR CHARTER SERVICE, Inc. **Washington-County, PA**

600 Airport Road, Washington, PA 15301, USA ☎ (724) 222-1025 Tx: none Fax: (724) 228-6275 SITA: n/a
F: 1977 ⁂ n/a Head: Frank Fazzolare, Jr. Net: http://www.webcreations.com/ACS/

☐ N33SB	Beech King Air A90 (65-A90)	LJ-252	N728K	0067	0290	2 PWC PT6A-20	4218			lsf pvt
☐ N77PF	Beech King Air 100	B-70	N25JL	0071	0489	2 PWC PT6A-28	4808			

AIR CHARTERS, Inc. **Griffin-Spalding County, GA**

155 Ward Road, Williamson, GA 30292, USA ☎ (770) 227-8046 Tx: none Fax: (770) 227-8079 SITA: n/a
F: 1996 ⁂ n/a Head: Richard L. Ward Net: http://www.freescape.com/aci

☐ N402B	Cessna 402B II	402B1305		0077	0396	2 CO TSIO-520-E	2858			
☐ N402WR	Cessna 402C II	402C0519		0081	0796	2 CO TSIO-520-VB	3107			

AIRCOASTAL HELICOPTERS, Inc. **West Palm Beach-County Park/Lantana, FL**

2615 Lantana Road, Suite J, Lantana, FL 33462, USA ☎ (561) 642-6840 Tx: none Fax: (561) 642-5393 SITA: n/a
F: 1981 ⁂ n/a Head: Boyce D. Crowe, Jr. Net: http://www.aircoastal.com Aircraft below MTOW 1361kg: Robinson R22

☐ N281CB	Bell 206B JetRanger III	3303		0081	0688	1 AN 250-C20B	1451			
☐ N5005N	Bell 206B JetRanger II	1931		0076	1195	1 AN 250-C20	1451			

AIRCRAFT CHARTER SERVICES (Integrated Airways, Inc. dba) **South Bend-Michiana Regional TC, IN**

4302 Lathrop Street, South Bend, IN 46628, USA ☎ (219) 233-1040 Tx: none Fax: (219) 233-1176 SITA: n/a
F: 1988 ⁂ n/a Head: Michael S. Krueger Net: n/a

☐ N677WC	Cessna 310R II	310R0100		0074	1095	2 CO IO-520-M	2495			
☐ N520AB	Cessna 421C Golden Eagle III	421C0690		0079	0597	2 CO GTSIO-520-L	3379			lsf MTS Leasing

AIRCRAFT SERVICES (Aircraft Services Group, Inc. dba) **Teterboro, NJ**

1032 First Street, Bldg 112, New Windsor, NY 12553, USA ☎ (973) 393-0500 Tx: none Fax: (973) 393-9232 SITA: n/a
F: 1990 ⁂ 10 Head: George A. Reenstra Net: n/a

☐ N206MD	GAC (Grumman) G-1159 Gulfstream II	022	N683FM	0068	0892	2 RR Spey 511-8	28123			lsf GBH Aviation

AIRCRAFT SERVICES OF OHIO COUNTY (Fortener Aviation, Inc. dba) **Hartford-Ohio County, KY**

2260 Country Club Lane, Hartford, KY 42347, USA ☎ (502) 298-3500 Tx: none Fax: (502) 298-9969 SITA: n/a
F: 1988 ⁂ n/a Head: Ronald K. Fortener Net: n/a

☐ N4643Q	Cessna 210L Centurion II	21059543		0072	0593	1 CO IO-520-L	1724			lsf pvt
☐ N5680C	Cessna 414A Chancellor III	414A0218		0079	0988	2 CO TSIO-520-NB	3062			lsf Air Relief Inc.

AIR CRANE, Inc. **Winder-Barrow County, GA**

3250 Claude Brewer Road, Loganville, GA 30249, USA ☎ (770) 466-2129 Tx: none Fax: (770) 466-7257 SITA: n/a
F: 1983 ⁂ n/a Head: John M. Haertsch Net: n/a

☐ N85HJ	Sikorsky S-58D	58-1716	N58WH	0064	1297	1 WR R-1820	5897			
☐ N97AA	Sikorsky S-58E	58-1575	N90807	0062	0996	1 WR R-1820	5897			

AIR DECK, Inc. **Lebanon-Keller Brothers, PA**

351 South Ramona Road, Lebanon, PA 17042, USA ☎ (717) 866-4388 Tx: none Fax: none SITA: n/a
F: 1974 ⁂ n/a Head: Clyde E. Deck Net: n/a

☐ N42866	Piper PA-34-200 Seneca	34-7450173		0074	0674	2 LY IO-360-C1E6	1905			
☐ N414NP	Cessna 414A Chancellor III	414A0313		0079	0690	2 CO TSIO-520-NB	3062			lsf New Penn Motor Express Inc.

250 registration type of aircraft cn/fn ex/ex* mfd del powered by mtow kg configuration selcal name/fln/specialitites/remarks

AIR DESERT PACIFIC, Corp. — La Verne-Brackett Field, CA

1889 McKinley Way, La Verne, CA 91750, USA ☎ (909) 596-6059 Tx: none Fax: (909) 593-2596 SITA: n/a
F: 1990 ⅏ n/a Head: Ari D. Lapin Net: n/a

☐ N626JD	Piper PA-32R-300 Lance	32R-7680084		0076	0191	1 LY IO-540-K1A5D	1633			lsf pvt
☐ N1080U	Piper PA-34-200 Seneca	34-7250083		0072	0493	2 LY IO-360-C1E6	1905			
☐ N410DS	Piper PA-34-200 Seneca	34-7250240		0072	0491	2 LY IO-360-C1E6	1905			lsf pvt
☐ N41298	Piper PA-34-200 Seneca	34-7450106		0074	0495	2 LY IO-360-C1E6	1905			
☐ N41RN	Piper PA-34-200 Seneca	34-7350326		0073	0394	2 LY IO-360-C1E6	1905			
☐ N4551T	Piper PA-34-200 Seneca	34-7250131		0072	0894	2 LY IO-360-C1E6	1905			
☐ N49SA	Piper PA-34-200 Seneca	34-7350057		0073	0594	2 LY IO-360-C1E6	1905			
☐ N5388T	Piper PA-34-200 Seneca	34-7250256		0072	1092	2 LY IO-360-C1E6	1905			lsf pvt
☐ N56974	Piper PA-34-200 Seneca	34-7450044		0074	0793	2 LY IO-360-C1E6	1905			
☐ N57368	Piper PA-34-200 Seneca	34-7450054		0074	0495	2 LY IO-360-C1E6	1905			
☐ N8000N	Piper PA-34-200 Seneca	34-7250167		0072	0192	2 LY IO-360-C1E6	1905			
☐ N6933Y	Piper PA-23-250 Aztec D	27-4290		0069	0395	2 LY IO-540-C4B5	2359			
☐ N57AS	Piper PA-31-310 Navajo	31-113		0068	1094	2 LY TIO-540-A1A	2948			

AIR DIRECT (Rhinelander Flying Service, Inc. dba) — Rhinelander-Oneida County & Wausau-Downtown, WI

PO Box 501, Rhinelander, WI 54501, USA ☎ (715) 369-3131 Tx: none Fax: (715) 365-3461 SITA: n/a
F: 1985 ⅏ n/a Head: Charles P. Turner Net: n/a Aircraft below MTOW 1361kg: Cessna 172

☐ N102CT	Cessna 310R II	310R0136	C-GNKT	0074	1296	2 CO IO-520-M	2495			
☐ N87395	Cessna 310R II	310R0543		0076	0591	2 CO IO-520-M	2495			
☐ N66AT	Piper PA-31-350 Navajo Chieftain	31-7552042	N59928	0075	0490	2 LY TIO-540-J2BD	3175			
☐ N100YR	Cessna 421B Golden Eagle	421B0437		0073	0793	2 CO GTSIO-520-H	3379			

AIR EAST, Inc. — Johnstown-Cambria County, PA

Cambria County Airport, Johnstown, PA 15904, USA ☎ (814) 536-5103 Tx: none Fax: (814) 536-3011 SITA: n/a
F: 1967 ⅏ n/a Head: Benjamin F. McKinney Net: n/a

☐ N264PA	Beech King Air B100	BE-86	N85KA	0080	0496	2 GA TPE331-6-252B	5352			
☐ N922RR	Hawker 400A/731 (HS 125-400A/731)	25195 / NA726	YV-141CP	0069	1295	2 GA TFE731-3R-1H	10568			lsf Reschini Agency Inc./cvtd 125-400A

AIREVAC (A Service of Hillcrest HealthCare) — Tulsa-Int'l, OK

3014 North 74th East Avenue, Tulsa, OK 74115-2317, USA ☎ (918) 836-0576 Tx: none Fax: (918) 836-0579 SITA: n/a
F: 1987 ⅏ 33 Head: Tammy L. Brown Net: http://www.hillcrest.com/services/airevac.html

☐ N176AE	Sikorsky S-76C+	760477		0097	1297	2 TU Arriel 2S1	5307	EMS		lsf Tulsa Industrial Authority

AIR EVAC LIFETEAM & AVIATION (Air Evac EMS, Inc. dba) — West Plains-Municipal &-Ozarks Medical Heliport, MO

1488 West 8th Street, West Plains, MD 65775, USA ☎ (417) 256-0010 Tx: none Fax: (417) 256-0846 SITA: n/a
F: 1985 ⅏ n/a Head: James A. Lentz Net: n/a

☐ N119SD	Bell 206L-1 LongRanger II	45165	N5000J	0078	0591	1 AN 250-C28B	1882			lsf Air Evac Leasing Corp.
☐ N119TA	Bell 206L-1 LongRanger II	45263		0079	0286	1 AN 250-C28B	1882			lsf Air Evac Leasing Corp.
☐ N400EA	Bell 206L-1 LongRanger II	45544	N60DG	0080	1092	1 AN 250-C28B	1882			lsf Air Evac Leasing Corp.
☐ N5753T	Bell 206L-1 LongRanger II	45547		0080	0888	1 AN 250-C28B	1882			lsf Air Evac Leasing Corp.
☐ N911QC	Bell 206L-1 LongRanger II	45224	C-FVEP	0079	0897	1 AN 250-C28B	1882			lsf Air Evac Leasing Corp.
☐ N9900M	Bell 206L-1 LongRanger II	45470	N5747W	0080	1097	1 AN 250-C28B	1882			lsf Air Evac Leasing Corp.
☐ N2889M	Piper PA-34-200T Seneca II	34-7870099		0078	0085	2 CO TSIO-360-E	2073			lsf J.W. Phillips Ltd
☐ N1952S	Beech Baron 58	TH-420		0074	0195	2 CO IO-520-C	2449			lsf Air Evac Leasing Corp.
☐ N915DW	Cessna 421B Golden Eagle	421B0914		0075	0693	2 CO GTSIO-520-H	3379			lsf Air Evac Leasing Corp.

AIREVAC SERVICES, Inc. (Subsidiary of Petroleum Helicopters, Inc. / formerly Samaritan AirEvac) — Phoenix-Sky Harbor Int'l, AZ

2630 Sky Harbor Blvd, Phoenix, AZ 85034-4424, USA ☎ (602) 244-9327 Tx: none Fax: (602) 275-1745 SITA: n/a
F: 1969 ⅏ 200 Head: Pete Sorenson Net: n/a

☐ N131AE	Eurocopter (MBB) BO105CBS-4	S-787	N4391S	0488	0093	2 AN 250-C20B	2500	EMS		lsf/opb Petroleum Helicopters
☐ N133AE	Eurocopter (MBB) BO105CBS-4	S-800	N5418A	0988	0093	2 AN 250-C20B	2500	EMS		lsf/opb Petroleum Helicopters
☐ N135AE	Eurocopter (MBB) BO105CBS-4	S-838	N7171A	0790	0093	2 AN 250-C20B	2500	EMS		lsf/opb Petroleum Helicopters
☐ N137AE	Eurocopter (MBB) BO105CBS-4	S-851	N4193R	0191	0093	2 AN 250-C20B	2500	EMS		lsf/opb Petroleum Helicopters
☐ N132AE	Eurocopter (MBB) BK117B-2	7238	N31502	1091	0093	2 LY LTS101-750B.1	3350	EMS		lsf/opb Petroleum Helicopters/cvtd B-1
☐ N134AE	Eurocopter (MBB) BK117B-2	7237	N3152E	0991	0093	2 LY LTS101-750B.1	3350	EMS		lsf/opb Petroleum Helicopters/cvtd B-1
☐ N136AE	Eurocopter (MBB) BK117B-2	7234	N4280V	0991	0093	2 LY LTS101-750B.1	3350	EMS		lsf/opb Petroleum Helicopters/cvtd B-1
☐ N401PH	Eurocopter (MBB) BK117A-4	7050	N507AL	0485	0093	2 LY LTS101-650B.1	3200	EMS		lsf/opb Petroleum Helicopters
☐ N434AE	Cessna 441 Conquest II	441-0097	N30RP	0079	0194	2 GA TPE331-8-401S	4468	EMS		
☐ N445AE	Cessna 441 Conquest II	441-0043	N445WS	0078	0194	2 GA TPE331-8-401S	4468	EMS		
☐ N687AE	Cessna 441 Conquest II	441-0087	N441DW	0079	0987	2 GA TPE331-8-401S	4468	EMS		
☐ N689AE	Cessna 441 Conquest II	441-0281	N6832C	0082	0490	2 GA TPE331-8-403S	4468	EMS		
☐ N988AE	Cessna 441 Conquest II	441-0175	N2723A	0080	0589	2 GA TPE331-8-401S	4468	EMS		
☐ N110AE	Learjet 35A	35A-155	N110KG	0078	0191	2 GA TFE731-2-2B	8165	EMS		

AIR EVERETT, Inc. — Tampa-Int'l, FL

9210 Adamo Drive, Tampa, FL 33619, USA ☎ (813) 621-7747 Tx: none Fax: (813) 261-4188 SITA: n/a
F: 1995 ⅏ n/a Head: Everett P. Swiger Net: n/a

☐ N177JW	Beech King Air 300	FA-77	N678SB	0085	0195	2 PWC PT6A-60A	6350			

AIR EXCURSIONS (Steve R. Wilson dba) — Gustavus, AK

PO Box 16, Gustavus, AK 99826, USA ☎ (907) 697-2375 Tx: none Fax: (907) 697-2376 SITA: n/a
F: 1990 ⅏ n/a Head: Steve R. Wilson Net: n/a Aircraft below MTOW 1361kg: Cessna 172 & Lake LA4-200

☐ N15950	Piper PA-32-300 Cherokee SIX	32-7340075		0073	1290	1 LY IO-540-K1A5	1542			
☐ N8200M	Piper PA-32-301 Saratoga	32-8006048		0080	0492	1 LY IO-540-K1G5	1633			
☐ N8908N	Piper PA-32-300C Cherokee SIX	32-40695		0069	0596	1 LY IO-540-K1A5	1542			

AIR EXEC, Inc. — Fort Madison-Municipal, IA

50 Airport Road, Fort Madison, IA 52627, USA ☎ (319) 372-1138 Tx: none Fax: (319) 372-3051 SITA: n/a
F: 1983 ⅏ n/a Head: Stephen M. Hohl Net: n/a

☐ N7872Q	Cessna 310Q	310Q0653		0073	0387	2 CO IO-470-VO	2404			
☐ N4735A	Cessna 414A Chancellor III	414A0090		0078	1196	2 CO TSIO-520-N	3062			

AIR FLITE, Inc. — Shawnee-Municipal, OK

2320 Airport Drive, Shawnee, OK 74801, USA ☎ (405) 275-4388 Tx: none Fax: (405) 275-4389 SITA: n/a
F: 1983 ⅏ n/a Head: Mark White Net: n/a Aircraft below MTOW 1361kg: Hughes 269C (300C)

☐ N21MW	Bell 206B JetRanger III	3585	N22591	0082	1187	1 AN 250-C20B	1451			
☐ N255AL	Bell 206L-1 LongRanger II	45602	N39084	0081	1283	1 AN 250-C28B	1882			

AIR FLORIDA Express, Inc. = FD — Miami-Int'l, FL

PO Box 660194, Miami, FL 33266, USA ☎ (305) 888-1979 Tx: none Fax: (305) 888-1952 SITA: n/a
F: 1988 ⅏ n/a Head: Pervez A. Khan Net: n/a

☐ N371R	Cessna 402C II	402C0028		0079	0691	2 CO TSIO-520-VB	3107			
☐ N404PJ	Cessna 402C II	402C0513	TR-LAA	0081	0497	2 CO TSIO-520-VB	3107			
☐ N2099S	Piper PA-31-310 Navajo	31-658		0070	0196	2 LY TIO-540-A1A	2948			lsf Air Florida Airlines Inc.

AIR GERONIMO CHARTER, Inc. — Richmond-Int'l, VA

5745 Huntsman Road, Richmond, VA 23250, USA ☎ (804) 288-1489 Tx: none Fax: (804) 285-3151 SITA: n/a
F: 1994 ⅏ n/a Head: Stanley Navas Net: n/a

☐ N45CP	Learjet 25C (XR)	25C-073	N888DB	0072	0697	2 GE CJ610-6	6804			

AIR GO PACK (Pamela J. Rappa dba) — Port Huron-St. Clair County Int'l, MI

150 North Airport Drive, Port Huron, MI 48074, USA ☎ (810) 364-4282 Tx: none Fax: none SITA: n/a
F: 1997 ⅏ n/a Head: Pamela J. Rappa Net: n/a

☐ N2248R	Cessna T210J Turbo Centurion	T2100398		0069	1097	1 CO TSIO-520-H	1542			

AIR GRAND CANYON, Inc. — Grand Canyon-National Park, AZ

6000 Janine Drive, Prescott, AZ 86301, USA ☎ (520) 776-6000 Tx: none Fax: (520) 776-8099 SITA: n/a
F: 1972 ⅏ 12 Head: Dan C. Lawler Net: http://www.airgrandcanyon.com Aircraft below MTOW 1361 kg: Cessna 182

☐ N1558D	Cessna 195A	7780		0052	0390	1 JA R-755-9	1633			
☐ N3000B	Cessna TU206C Super Skywagon	U206-1077		0068	0788	1 CO TSIO-520-C	1633			
☐ N6308H	Cessna T207A Turbo Stationair 7 II	20700476		0078	1088	1 CO TSIO-520-M	1724			
☐ N6491H	Cessna T207A Turbo Stationair 7 II	20700543		0079	0488	1 CO TSIO-520-M	1724			
☐ N7311U	Cessna T207A Turbo Skywagon	20700395		0077	1083	1 CO TSIO-520-M	1724			
☐ N91085	Cessna T207 Turbo Skywagon	20700066		0069	0691	1 CO TSIO-520-M	1724			
☐ N9527M	Cessna T207A Turbo Stationair 8 II	20700701		0081	1294	1 CO TSIO-520-M	1724			lsf Dalessio Enterprises Inc.

251 registration type of aircraft cn/fn ex/ex* mfd del powered by mtow kg configuration selcal name/fln/specialitites/remarks

AIR JET, Inc.
Raleigh/Durham-Int'l, NC

PO Box 80333, RDU Airport, NC 27623-0333, USA ☎ (919) 831-5679 Tx: none Fax: (919) 833-8432 SITA: n/a
F: 1997 ♦♦♦ n/a Head: Terry B. Lewis Net: n/a

registration	type of aircraft	cn/fn	ex/ex*	mfd	del	powered by	mtow kg	configuration	name/fln/specialitites/remarks
☐ N94AJ	Cessna 500 Citation	500-0024	VH-ICN	0072	0197	2 PWC JT15D-1	5216		

AIR KETCHUM, Inc.
Hailey-Friedman Memorial, ID

PO Box 3300, Ketchum, ID 83340, USA ☎ (208) 788-2494 Tx: none Fax: (208) 788-9713 SITA: n/a
F: 1997 ♦♦♦ n/a Head: Lenard MacIntosh Net: n/a

registration	type of aircraft	cn/fn	ex/ex*	mfd	del	powered by	mtow kg	configuration	name/fln/specialitites/remarks
☐ N3820L	Beech Baron 58P	TJ-341		0081	0297	2 CO TSIO-520-WB	2812		lsf pvt

AIRLINERS OF AMERICA, Inc.
Camarillo, CA

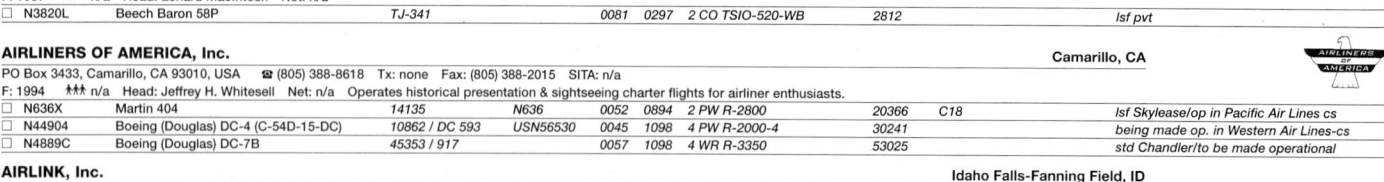

PO Box 3433, Camarillo, CA 93010, USA ☎ (805) 388-8618 Tx: none Fax: (805) 388-2015 SITA: n/a
F: 1994 ♦♦♦ n/a Head: Jeffrey H. Whitesell Net: n/a Operates historical presentation & sightseeing charter flights for airliner enthusiasts.

registration	type of aircraft	cn/fn	ex/ex*	mfd	del	powered by	mtow kg	configuration	name/fln/specialitites/remarks
☐ N636X	Martin 404	14135	N636	0052	0894	2 PW R-2800	20366	C18	lsf Skylease/op in Pacific Air Lines cs
☐ N44904	Boeing (Douglas) DC-4 (C-54D-15-DC)	10862 / DC 593	USN56530	0045	1098	4 PW R-2000-4	30241		being made op. in Western Air Lines-cs
☐ N4889C	Boeing (Douglas) DC-7B	45353 / 917		0057	1098	4 WR R-3350	53025		std Chandler/to be made operational

AIRLINK, Inc.
Idaho Falls-Fanning Field, ID

4030 East Iona Road, Idaho Falls, ID 83401, USA ☎ (208) 523-1597 Tx: none Fax: (208) 523-0361 SITA: n/a
F: 1993 ♦♦♦ n/a Head: Erik C. Gullikson Net: n/a

registration	type of aircraft	cn/fn	ex/ex*	mfd	del	powered by	mtow kg	configuration	name/fln/specialitites/remarks
☐ N129AL	Agusta A109K2	10029	N1YU	0096	0298	2 TU Arriel 1K1	2850	EMS	lsf Agusta Aerosp./opf Air Idaho Rescue

AIR LOGISTICS, Llc = ALG
New Iberia-Air Logistics 2 Heliport, LA

Box 5C, Lafayette, LA 70505, USA ☎ (318) 365-6771 Tx: 586689 Fax: (318) 364-8222 SITA: n/a
F: 1972 ♦♦♦ 415 Head: George M. Small ICAO: AIRLOG Net: n/a

registration	type of aircraft	cn/fn	ex/ex*	mfd	del	powered by	mtow kg	configuration	name/fln/specialitites/remarks
☐ N1078Y	Bell 206B JetRanger III	2924		0080	0989	1 AN 250-C20B	1451		
☐ N113AL	Bell 206B JetRanger III	2380		0078	0478	1 AN 250-C20B	1451		lsf Joseph Murray Trustee
☐ N116AL	Bell 206B JetRanger III	2389		0078	0578	1 AN 250-C20B	1451		
☐ N117AL	Bell 206B JetRanger III	2391		0078	0578	1 AN 250-C20B	1451		
☐ N120AL	Bell 206B JetRanger III	2395	PT-HUF	0078	0578	1 AN 250-C20B	1451		
☐ N20335	Bell 206B JetRanger III	3343		0081	0989	1 AN 250-C20B	1451		
☐ N209AL	Bell 206B JetRanger	1044	N3WP	0073	1277	1 AN 250-C20	1451		
☐ N213AL	Bell 206B JetRanger	1066	N58110	0073	0378	1 AN 250-C20	1451		
☐ N2155Z	Bell 206B JetRanger III	3476		0081	0492	1 AN 250-C20B	1451		
☐ N2295F	Bell 206B JetRanger III	3579		0082	0492	1 AN 250-C20J	1451		
☐ N2299U	Bell 206B JetRanger III	3415		0081	0989	1 AN 250-C20B	1451		
☐ N30AL	Bell 206B JetRanger	1054		0073	0673	1 AN 250-C20	1451		
☐ N360S	Bell 206B JetRanger III	2217	N666TV	0077	0492	1 AN 250-C20B	1451		
☐ N3896W	Bell 206B JetRanger III	3197		0080	0989	1 AN 250-C20B	1451		
☐ N3912Q	Bell 206B JetRanger III	3271		0081	0492	1 AN 250-C20B	1451		
☐ N42AL	Bell 206B JetRanger	918		0072	0173	1 AN 250-C20	1451		
☐ N5008K	Bell 206B JetRanger III	2524		0078	0492	1 AN 250-C20B	1451		
☐ N5011F	Bell 206B JetRanger III	2564		0078	0492	1 AN 250-C20B	1451		
☐ N53AL	Bell 206B JetRanger	1092		0073	0873	1 AN 250-C20	1451		
☐ N56AL	Bell 206B JetRanger	1402		0074	0674	1 AN 250-C20	1451		
☐ N57536	Bell 206B JetRanger III	3124		0080	0989	1 AN 250-C20B	1451		
☐ N57AL	Bell 206B JetRanger	1404		0074	1184	1 AN 250-C20	1451		
☐ N58111	Bell 206B JetRanger	1082		0073	0378	1 AN 250-C20	1451		
☐ N59485	Bell 206B JetRanger	1266		0074	0484	1 AN 250-C20	1451		
☐ N59541	Bell 206B JetRanger	1412		0074	0478	1 AN 250-C20	1451		
☐ N59AL	Bell 206B JetRanger	1422		0074	0674	1 AN 250-C20	1451		
☐ N65AL	Bell 206B JetRanger	1443		0074	1184	1 AN 250-C20	1451		
☐ N90228	Bell 206B JetRanger	1720		0075	0184	1 AN 250-C20	1451		
☐ N1067D	Bell 206L-1 LongRanger II	45435		0080	0880	1 AN 250-C28B	1882		
☐ N1068S	Bell 206L-1 LongRanger II	45436		0080	0880	1 AN 250-C28B	1882		
☐ N1075W	Bell 206L-1 LongRanger II	45377		0080	0993	1 AN 250-C28B	1882		
☐ N1075Y	Bell 206L-1 LongRanger II	45378		0080	0480	1 AN 250-C28B	1882		
☐ N1078N	Bell 206L-1 LongRanger II	45389		0080	0480	1 AN 250-C28B	1882		
☐ N1081G	Bell 206L-1 LongRanger II	45405		0080	0680	1 AN 250-C28B	1882		
☐ N1081K	Bell 206L-1 LongRanger II	45407	PT-HVR	0080	0993	1 AN 250-C28B	1882		
☐ N1084Y	Bell 206L-1 LongRanger II	45433		0080	0880	1 AN 250-C28B	1882		
☐ N170AL	Bell 206L-4 LongRanger IV	52063		0093	0194	1 AN 250-C30P	2018		
☐ N171AL	Bell 206L-4 LongRanger IV	52064		0093	1293	1 AN 250-C30P	2018		
☐ N173AL	Bell 206L-4 LongRanger IV	52066		0093	0194	1 AN 250-C30P	2018		
☐ N174AL	Bell 206L-4 LongRanger IV	52067		0093	0294	1 AN 250-C30P	2018		
☐ N175AL	Bell 206L-4 LongRanger IV	52117		0095	0195	1 AN 250-C30P	2018		
☐ N176AL	Bell 206L-4 LongRanger IV	52146	C-FOFE*	0095	0995	1 AN 250-C30P	2018		
☐ N177AL	Bell 206L-4 LongRanger IV	52157	C-GLZU*	0095	1195	1 AN 250-C30P	2018		
☐ N187AL	Bell 206L-3 LongRanger III	51135	XA-RNM	0085	0895	1 AN 250-C30P	1882		
☐ N2018R	Bell 206L-1 LongRanger II	45681		0081	0187	1 AN 250-C28B	1882		
☐ N206SL	Bell 206L-1 LongRanger II	45245		0079	0989	1 AN 250-C28B	1882		
☐ N2092U	Bell 206L-1 LongRanger II	45697		0081	0492	1 AN 250-C28B	1882		
☐ N27483	Bell 206L-1 LongRanger II	45230		0079	0890	1 AN 250-C28B	1882		
☐ N27545	Bell 206L-1 LongRanger II	45234		0079	0579	1 AN 250-C28B	1882		
☐ N27554	Bell 206L-1 LongRanger II	45246		0079	0890	1 AN 250-C28B	1882		
☐ N2755F	Bell 206L-1 LongRanger II	45237		0079	0579	1 AN 250-C28B	1882		
☐ N2755N	Bell 206L-1 LongRanger II	45243		0079	0579	1 AN 250-C28B	1882		
☐ N2756A	Bell 206L-1 LongRanger II	45256		0079	0779	1 AN 250-C28B	1882		
☐ N2758L	Bell 206L-1 LongRanger II	45266		0079	0779	1 AN 250-C28B	1882		
☐ N2759N	Bell 206L-1 LongRanger II	45271		0079	0879	1 AN 250-C28B	1882		
☐ N2762D	Bell 206L-1 LongRanger II	45280		0079	0492	1 AN 250-C28B	1882		
☐ N3179S	Bell 206L-1 LongRanger II	45781		0083	0989	1 AN 250-C28B	1882		opf Dept. of Interior
☐ N3179V	Bell 206L-1 LongRanger II	45782		0083	0989	1 AN 250-C28B	1882		opf Dept. of Interior
☐ N3184P	Bell 206L-1 LongRanger II	45774		0083	0989	1 AN 250-C28B	1882		
☐ N3185P	Bell 206L-1 LongRanger II	45775		0083	0989	1 AN 250-C28B	1882		
☐ N3186P	Bell 206L-1 LongRanger II	45776		0083	0989	1 AN 250-C28B	1882		
☐ N3188P	Bell 206L-1 LongRanger II	45778		0083	0989	1 AN 250-C28B	1882		
☐ N3190P	Bell 206L-1 LongRanger II	45779		0083	0989	1 AN 250-C28B	1882		
☐ N3192P	Bell 206L-1 LongRanger II	45780	XA-SIP	0083	0989	1 AN 250-C28B	1882		
☐ N3195P	Bell 206L-1 LongRanger II	45789		0083	0989	1 AN 250-C28B	1882		
☐ N3199P	Bell 206L-1 LongRanger II	45790		0083	0989	1 AN 250-C28B	1882		
☐ N343AL	Bell 206L-3 LongRanger III	51372		0090	0790	1 AN 250-C30P	1882		
☐ N344AL	Bell 206L-3 LongRanger III	51374		0090	0790	1 AN 250-C30P	1882		
☐ N348AL	Bell 206L-3 LongRanger III	51386		0090	0890	1 AN 250-C30P	1882		
☐ N349AL	Bell 206L-3 LongRanger III	51388		0090	0990	1 AN 250-C30P	1882		
☐ N350AL	Bell 206L-3 LongRanger III	51429		0090	0191	1 AN 250-C30P	1882		
☐ N351AL	Bell 206L-3 LongRanger III	51431		0090	0191	1 AN 250-C30P	1882		
☐ N355AL	Bell 206L-3 LongRanger III	51444		0091	0391	1 AN 250-C30P	1882		
☐ N359AL	Bell 206L-3 LongRanger III	51461		0091	0491	1 AN 250-C30P	1882		
☐ N362AL	Bell 206L-3 LongRanger III	51471		0091	0591	1 AN 250-C30P	1882		
☐ N364AL	Bell 206L-3 LongRanger III	51434	XA-RVD	0091	1292	1 AN 250-C30P	1882		
☐ N365AL	Bell 206L-3 LongRanger III	51376		0090	0193	1 AN 250-C30P	1882		
☐ N366AL	Bell 206L-3 LongRanger III	51470	XA-RXX	0091	0193	1 AN 250-C30P	1882		
☐ N367AL	Bell 206L-3 LongRanger III	51443	XA-RVX	0091	0193	1 AN 250-C30P	1882		
☐ N41GH	Bell 206L-1 LongRanger II	45502	N5748N	0080	0187	1 AN 250-C28B	1882		
☐ N516EH	Bell 206L-1 LongRanger II	45416		0080	0989	1 AN 250-C28B	1882		
☐ N5734M	Bell 206L-1 LongRanger II	45449		0080	0880	1 AN 250-C28B	1882		
☐ N5734S	Bell 206L-1 LongRanger II	45455		0080	0880	1 AN 250-C28B	1882		
☐ N5740L	Bell 206L-1 LongRanger II	45459		0080	0187	1 AN 250-C28B	1882		
☐ N5749J	Bell 206L-1 LongRanger II	45551		0080	0989	1 AN 250-C28B	1882		
☐ N5750Y	Bell 206L-1 LongRanger II	45517		0080	0394	1 AN 250-C28B	1882		
☐ N57510	Bell 206L-1 LongRanger II	45530		0080	1280	1 AN 250-C28B	1882		
☐ N5751Q	Bell 206L-1 LongRanger II	45524		0080	1280	1 AN 250-C28B	1882		
☐ N5756N	Bell 206L-1 LongRanger II	45546		0080	1280	1 AN 250-C28B	1882		
☐ N5760A	Bell 206L-1 LongRanger II	45538		0080	1280	1 AN 250-C28B	1882		
☐ N407AL	Bell 407	53044		0096	0896	1 AN 250-C47B	2268		
☐ N417AL	Bell 407	53054		0096	0996	1 AN 250-C47B	2268		
☐ N427AL	Bell 407	53107		0097	0297	1 AN 250-C47B	2268		
☐ N437AL	Bell 407	53141		0097	0497	1 AN 250-C47B	2268		
☐ N457AL	Bell 407	53151		0097	0597	1 AN 250-C47B	2268		
☐ N107AL	Eurocopter (MBB) BO105CBS	S-772		0087	0493	2 AN 250-C20B	2400		

N2785R	Eurocopter (MBB) BO105CBS	S-642		0083	0395	2 AN 250-C20B	2400			
N352TT	Eurocopter (MBB) BO105C	S-59	N3527T	1272	0296	2 AN 250-C20B	2400			
N41N	Eurocopter (MBB) BO105CBS	S-344	N777VE	0077	0197	2 AN 250-C20B	2400			
N4572V	Eurocopter (MBB) BO105CBS	S-665		0084	0185	2 AN 250-C20B	2400			
N491HL	Eurocopter (MBB) BO105CBS-2	S-664	N233BK	0084	0091	2 AN 250-C20B	2500			
N493HL	Eurocopter (MBB) BO105CBS-4	S-809	N423HL	0090	0890	2 AN 250-C20B	2500			
N494HL	Eurocopter (MBB) BO105CBS-4	S-813	N234JL	0089	1191	2 AN 250-C20B	2500			
N495HL	Eurocopter (MBB) BO105CBS-4	S-817	N126TP	0090	0790	2 AN 250-C20B	2500			
N496HL	Eurocopter (MBB) BO105CBS-4	S-822	N246HA	0090	0890	2 AN 250-C20B	2500			
N501AL	Eurocopter (MBB) BO105C	S-58	N205BB	1172	0296	2 AN 250-C20B	2400			
N502AL	Eurocopter (MBB) BO105C	S-103	N1818X	1173	0296	2 AN 250-C20B	2400			
N503AL	Eurocopter (MBB) BO105CBS	S-712	HK-3224X	0085	0197	2 AN 250-C20B	2400			
N51948	Eurocopter (MBB) BO105CBS-4	S-774		0088	0292	2 AN 250-C20B	2400			
N5412J	Eurocopter (MBB) BO105CBS-4	S-784		0088	0392	2 AN 250-C20B	2400			
N5416F	Eurocopter (MBB) BO105CBS-4	S-794		0088	0392	2 AN 250-C20B	2400			
N90761	Eurocopter (MBB) BO105CS	S-160	D-HDEA	0074	0296	2 AN 250-C20B	2400			
N372E	Eurocopter (Aerosp.) AS355E TwinStar	5208		0084	0189	2 AN 250-C20F	2300			
N375E	Eurocopter (Aerosp.) AS355F1 TwinStar	5209		0084	0189	2 AN 250-C20F	2300			
N376E	Eurocopter (Aerosp.) AS355F1 TwinStar	5213		0084	0189	2 AN 250-C20F	2300			
N5773X	Eurocopter (Aerosp.) AS355F TwinStar	5004		0081	0881	2 AN 250-C20F	2300			
N5775H	Eurocopter (Aerosp.) AS355F TwinStar	5025		0081	0182	2 AN 250-C20F	2300			
N5787E	Eurocopter (Aerosp.) AS355F TwinStar	5058		0081	0282	2 AN 250-C20F	2300			
N5787T	Eurocopter (Aerosp.) AS355F TwinStar	5080		0081	0282	2 AN 250-C20F	2300			
N5789Y	Eurocopter (Aerosp.) AS355F TwinStar	5094		0081	0282	2 AN 250-C20F	2300			
N1547K	Sikorsky S-76A	760085		0080	1080	2 AN 250-C30S	4672			cvtd S-76/lsf FSBU NA Trustee
N1547N	Sikorsky S-76A	760088		0080	1280	2 AN 250-C30S	4672			cvtd S-76
N164AG	Sikorsky S-76A	760290	N154AE	0084	0597	2 AN 250-C30S	4672			
N376AL	Sikorsky S-76A	760002		0079	0379	2 AN 250-C30S	4672			cvtd S-76
N518AL	Sikorsky S-76A+	760134	G-BVGM	0080	0897	2 TU Arriel 1S	4672			cvtd S-76A
N701AL	Sikorsky S-76A	760238		0084	0684	2 AN 250-C30S	4672			
N702AL	Sikorsky S-76A	760243		0084	0684	2 AN 250-C30S	4672			
N703AL	Sikorsky S-76A	760266		0084	0684	2 AN 250-C30S	4672			
N705AL	Sikorsky S-76A	760267		0084	0684	2 AN 250-C30S	4672			
N707AL	Sikorsky S-76A	760189	N989QS	0082	0294	2 AN 250-C30S	4672			
N709AL	Sikorsky S-76A	760278		0084	1084	2 AN 250-C30S	4672			
N710AL	Sikorsky S-76A	760279		0084	1084	2 AN 250-C30S	4672			
N712AL	Sikorsky S-76A	760280		0084	1084	2 AN 250-C30S	4672			
N717AL	Sikorsky S-76A	760221	G-BWIM	0082	0597	2 AN 250-C30S	4672			
N741SW	Sikorsky S-76A	760070		0080	0989	2 AN 250-C30S	4672			cvtd S-76
N7612L	Sikorsky S-76A	760054		0080	0880	2 AN 250-C30S	4672			cvtd S-76
N768AL	Sikorsky S-76A	760031	VH-EMM	0079	0180	2 AN 250-C30S	4672			cvtd S-76
N769AL	Sikorsky S-76A	760048		0080	0580	2 AN 250-C30S	4672			cvtd S-76
N690L	Piper PA-42-720 Cheyenne IIIA	42-5501020	N623KW	0084	1193	2 PWC PT6A-61	5080			
N24HL	Bell 212	30815	XA-IAY	0077	0493	2 PWC PT6T-3 TwinPac	5080			
N24HS	Bell 212	31147	XA-KUM	0080	0493	2 PWC PT6T-3 TwinPac	5080			
N29AL	Bell 212	30569		0073	0873	2 PWC PT6T-3 TwinPac	5080			
N2071S	Bell 412	33046		0081	0182	2 PWC PT6T-3B TwinPac	5262			
N397AL	Bell 412	36012		0090	0194	2 PWC PT6T-3B TwinPac	5398			
N214EV	Bell 214ST	28117	VH-LHT	0083	1297	2 GE CT7-2A	7938			
N390AL	Bell 214ST	28198	N3217H	0090	0292	2 GE CT7-2A	7938			
N391AL	Bell 214ST	28103	N2091E	0082	0194	2 GE CT7-2A	7938			
N392AL	Bell 214ST	28114	G-BKJD	0082	0897	2 GE CT7-2A	7938			

AIR LOGISTICS OF ALASKA, Inc. (Sister company of Air Logistics, Llc / formerly Heli-Lift, Inc.)

Fairbanks-Metro Field, AK

1915 Donald Ave, Fairbanks, AK 99701, USA ☎ (907) 452-1197 Tx: none Fax: (907) 452-4539 SITA: n/a

F: 1977 46 Head: Lyle M. Rizk Net: n/a

N27574	Bell 206B JetRanger III	2562		0079	0097	1 AN 250-C20B	1451			lsf Offshore Logistics Inc.
N5008G	Bell 206B JetRanger III	2506		0078	0097	1 AN 250-C20B	1451			lsf Offshore Logistics Inc.
N9AT	Bell 206B JetRanger III	3854		0085	0685	1 AN 250-C20J	1451			
N130AL	Bell 206L-3 LongRanger III	51132		0085	0685	1 AN 250-C30P	1882			
N133AL	Bell 206L-3 LongRanger III	51133		0085	0685	1 AN 250-C30P	1882			
N3194P	Bell 206L-1 LongRanger II	45788		0083	0097	1 AN 250-C28B	1882			lsf Offshore Logistics Inc.
N346AL	Bell 206L-3 LongRanger III	51378		0090	0097	1 AN 250-C30P	1882			lsf Offshore Logistics Inc.
N358AL	Bell 206L-3 LongRanger III	51460		0091	0097	1 AN 250-C30P	1882			lsf Offshore Logistics Inc.
N360AL	Bell 206L-3 LongRanger III	51462		0091	0097	1 AN 250-C30P	1882			lsf Offshore Logistics Inc.
N363AL	Bell 206L-3 LongRanger III	51472		0091	0591	1 AN 250-C30P	1882			lsf Offshore Logistics Inc.
N492HL	Eurocopter (MBB) BO105CBS-4	S-803	N124PW	0090	0790	2 AN 250-C20B	2500			

AIR MADURA (Mark Madura, Inc. dba / Seasonal May-October ops only)

Anchorage-Lake Hood SPB, AK

3705 Arctic Blvd, Suite 400, Anchorage, AK 99503, USA ☎ (907) 243-7133 Tx: none Fax: (907) 243-1773 SITA: n/a

F: 1993 n/a Head: Mark R. Madura Net: n/a

N150PL	De Havilland DHC-2 Beaver I	1540	C-FBJZ	0064	0298	1 PW R-985	2309			Floats

AIR MANGO, Ltd

St. Maarten (Netherlands Antilles)

PO Box 37217, Airport Station, San Juan, PR 00973-0217, USA ☎ (787) 752-7621 Tx: none Fax: (787) 752-7621 SITA: n/a

F: 1994 n/a Head: Gordon L. Gray Net: n/a

N63942	Piper PA-23-250 Aztec F	27-7854075		0078	0394	2 LY IO-540-C4B5	2359			

AIR MAUI Helicopter Tours (Aris, Inc. dba / formerly Air Kauai, Inc.)

Kahului-Heliport, HI

Kahului Heliport, Hangar 110, Kahului, HI 96732, USA ☎ (808) 877-7005 Tx: none Fax: (808) 871-7031 SITA: n/a

F: 1994 n/a Head: Steven R. Egger Net: n/a

N4AK	Eurocopter (Aerosp.) AS350BA AStar	2544	N6052B	0091	0194	1 TU Arriel 1B	2100			
N6101Y	Eurocopter (Aerosp.) AS350BA AStar	2833		0094	0196	1 TU Arriel 1B	2100			lsf Geneva Transport Equipment Co.

AIR MED SERVICES, Inc. (Associated with Acadian Ambulance)

Lafayette-Regional, LA

PO Box 98000, Lafayette, LA 70509-8000, USA ☎ (318) 267-3333 Tx: none Fax: (318) 267-1594 SITA: n/a

F: 1989 n/a Head: Roland F. Dugas, Jr. Net: http://www.acadian.com

N84BP	Cessna T210N Turbo Centurion II	21064896		0084	0495	1 CO TSIO-520-R	1814	EMS		lsf Acadian Ambulance Service Inc.
N911LD	Cessna 414A Chancellor III	414A0461	N3928A	0080	0589	2 CO TSIO-520-NB	3062	EMS		lsf Acadian Ambulance Service Inc.
N911ER	Cessna 441 Conquest II	441-0249	N800BN	0082	0193	2 GA TPE331-8-403S	4468	EMS		lsf Acadian Ambulance Service Inc.

AIR METHODS Corporation

Denver-Centennial, CO

7301 South Peoria Street, Englewood, CO 80112, USA ☎ (303) 792-7400 Tx: none Fax: (303) 790-0499 SITA: n/a

F: 1980 n/a Head: George W. Belsey Net: http://www.airmethods.com

N170AM	Bell 206L-3 LongRanger III	51213	N206UM	0087	0188	1 AN 250-C30P	1882			lsf New Air
N206UH	Bell 206L-3 LongRanger III	51167		0086	1291	1 AN 250-C30P	1882			
N3174S	Bell 206L-3 LongRanger III	51036		0082	0283	1 AN 250-C30P	1882			
N3175R	Bell 206L-3 LongRanger III	51039		0082	0683	1 AN 250-C30P	1882			
N5735M	Bell 206L-1 LongRanger II	45446	N781SA	0080	0980	1 AN 250-C28B	1882			
N771AM	Bell 206L-3 LongRanger III	51065		0084	0684	1 AN 250-C30P	1882	EMS AirLife		
N407GA	Bell 407	53104	C-FSPD	0097	0198	1 AN 250-C47B	2268	EMS		lsf Flagstaff Medical Center
N407LN	Bell 407	53181	N5984L	0097	0897	1 AN 250-C47B	2268	EMS LifeNet		lsf / opf Lifenet Inc.
N407LR	Bell 407	53279		0098	0898	1 AN 250-C47B	2268			
N772AL	Bell 407	53040		0096	0896	1 AN 250-C47B	2268	EMS		
N773AL	Bell 407	53160	N176PA	0097	0498	1 AN 250-C47B	2268	EMS		
N911AL	Bell 407	53144	N70829	0097	0597	1 AN 250-C47B	2268	EMS MedCenterAir		lsf Finova Capital/opf NC MedCenter Air
N911WB	Bell 407	53176	N72402	0097	0897	1 AN 250-C47B	2268			lsf FSBU Trustee
N852AL	Cessna 421B Golden Eagle	421B0904	N5446J	0075	0691	2 CO GTSIO-520-H	3379	EMS Air Life OR		opf Air Life of Oregon
N206CM	Bell 222U	47558	N7643S	0086	0294	2 LY LTS101-750C.1	3742			
N208CM	Bell 222U	47518	N773AM	0084	1189	2 LY LTS101-750C.1	3742	EMS		lsf Charlotte Memorial Hospital
N222AM	Bell 222U	47547	N221HX	0086	1298	2 LY LTS101-750C.1	3742			lsf General Electric Capital Corp.
N222LL	Bell 222	47060	N222LG	0081	0690	2 LY LTS101-650C.3	3561	EMS LifeLink III		opf Minneapolis Hospital-consortium
N224LL	Bell 222U	47552	N776AM	0086	1186	2 LY LTS101-750C.1	3742	EMS LifeLink III		opf Minneapolis Hospital-consortium
N225LL	Bell 222U	47539	N101NM	0085	0296	2 LY LTS101-750C.1	3742			
N611SJ	Bell 222U	47564	N222MT	0087	0793	2 LY LTS101-750C.1	3742			
N781SA	Bell 222UT	47537	N274SM	0085	0593	2 LY LTS101-750C.1	3742			
N885AL	Bell 222U	47542	N772AM	0085	0392	2 LY LTS101-750C.1	3742	EMS Air Life OR		opf Air Life of Oregon
N911ED	Bell 222U	47551	N3204L	0086	0886	2 LY LTS101-750C.1	3742			

253 registration type of aircraft cn/fn ex/ex* mfd del powered by mtow kg configuration selcal name/fln/specialitites/remarks

registration	type of aircraft	cn/fn	ex	mfd	del	powered by	mtow kg	configuration	selcal	remarks
☐ N911NM	Bell 222U	47569	N4181X	0088	0992	2 LY LTS101-750C.1	3742			lsf Ventana Leasing Inc.
☐ N299AM	Pilatus PC-12/45	236	HB-FRG*	0098	0299	1 PWC PT6A-67B	4500	EMS		lsf FSBU Trustee
☐ N853AL	Pilatus PC-12/45	168	N168WA	0097	0798	1 PWC PT6A-67B	4500	EMS Air Life OR		lsf St.Charles Med.Ctr/opf Air Life, OR
☐ N376LL	Sikorsky S-76A	760055	C-GRJC	0080	0788	2 AN 250-C30S	4763	EMS		lsf MDFC Equipment Leasing Corp.
☐ N20703	Bell 412	33017		0081	0788	2 PWC PT6T-3B TwinPac	5398	EMS AirLife		opf St. Mary's Hospital
☐ N412FH	Bell 412HP	36027		0091	0991	2 PWC PT6T-3B TwinPac	5398	EMS		lsf Fairfax Hospital System Inc.
☐ N412LG	Bell 412SP	33209		0090	1090	2 PWC PT6T-3B TwinPac	5398	EMS LifeGuard10		lsf Mitsui Capital/opf Carilion Health
☐ N555BA	Bell 412HP	36015		0091	0595	2 PWC PT6T-3B TwinPac	5398			lsf Bexar County Hospital District
☐ N556UH	Bell 412SP	33178	N2024Z	0088	0294	2 PWC PT6T-3B TwinPac	5398	EMS		lsf Bexar County Hospital District
☐ N586AC	Bell 412SP	36009	N402MA	0090	0995	2 PWC PT6T-3B TwinPac	5398	EMS AirCare		lsf Mercy Air / opf NC Baptist Hospital
☐ N778AM	Bell 412	33033	N586AC	0082	0993	2 PWC PT6T-3B TwinPac	5398			
☐ N793DC	Beech King Air B200	BB-1404	N93CD	0091	1091	2 PWC PT6A-42	5670	EMS		lsf Deaconess Medical Center
☐ N91CD	Beech King Air B200	BB-1402	N5516Q	0091	0991	2 PWC PT6A-42	5670	EMS		lsf Deaconess Medical Center

AIRMETRO Helicopters, Inc. — **Haverstraw-Heliport, NY**

23 Thornwood Drive, New City, NY 10956, USA ☎ (212) 883-0999 Tx: none Fax: (212) 288-7503 SITA: n/a
F: 1964 ⁂ 6 Head: Charles J. Zanlunghi Net: n/a

registration	type of aircraft	cn/fn	ex	mfd	del	powered by	mtow kg	configuration	selcal	remarks
☐ N33QP	Bell 206B JetRanger III	2753		0079	0882	1 AN 250-C20B	1451			

AIR MIDWEST, Inc. = ZV / AMW (US Airways Express) (Subsidiary of Mesa Air Group, Inc.) — **Wichita-Mid Continent, KS**

PO Box 7724, Wichita, KS 67277, USA ☎ (316) 942-8137 Tx: none Fax: (316) 945-0947 SITA: n/a
F: 1965 ⁂ 300 Head: Archille R. Paquette IATA: 471 ICAO: AIR MIDWEST Net: http://www.mesa-air.com/amw.htm
All aircraft are operated as US AIRWAYS EXPRESS (in full such colours & both titles), a commuter system to provide feeder connection at US Airways major hubs, using US flight numbers.

registration	type of aircraft	cn/fn	ex	mfd	del	powered by	mtow kg	configuration	selcal	remarks
☐ N139ZV	Beech 1900D Airliner	UE-139		0395	0498	2 PWC PT6A-67D	7688	Y19		lsf ASH/op in US Airways Express-colors
☐ N163YV	Beech 1900D Airliner	UE-163		0895	0895	2 PWC PT6A-67D	7688	Y19		lsf ASH/op in US Airways Express-colors
☐ N166YV	Beech 1900D Airliner	UE-166		0895	0895	2 PWC PT6A-67D	7688	Y19		lsf ASH/op in US Airways Express-colors
☐ N171ZV	Beech 1900D Airliner	UE-171		1095	1095	2 PWC PT6A-67D	7688	Y19		lsf ASH/op in US Airways Express-colors
☐ N174YV	Beech 1900D Airliner	UE-174		1095	1095	2 PWC PT6A-67D	7688	Y19		lsf ASH/op in US Airways Express-colors
☐ N176YV	Beech 1900D Airliner	UE-176		1095	1095	2 PWC PT6A-67D	7688	Y19		lsf ASH/op in US Airways Express-colors
☐ N178YV	Beech 1900D Airliner	UE-178		1195	1195	2 PWC PT6A-67D	7688	Y19		lsf ASH/op in US Airways Express-colors
☐ N182YV	Beech 1900D Airliner	UE-182		1195	1195	2 PWC PT6A-67D	7688	Y19		lsf ASH/op in US Airways Express-colors
☐ N18YV	Beech 1900D Airliner	UE-18		0892	0498	2 PWC PT6A-67D	7688	Y19		lsf ASH/op in US Airways Express-colors
☐ N231YV	Beech 1900D Airliner	UE-231		0896	0896	2 PWC PT6A-67D	7688	Y19		lsf ASH/op in US Airways Express-colors
☐ N233YV	Beech 1900D Airliner	UE-233		0896	0896	2 PWC PT6A-67D	7688	Y19		lsf ASH/op in US Airways Express-colors
☐ N237YV	Beech 1900D Airliner	UE-237		0996	0996	2 PWC PT6A-67D	7688	Y19		lsf ASH/op in US Airways Express-colors
☐ N242YV	Beech 1900D Airliner	UE-242		0996	0996	2 PWC PT6A-67D	7688	Y19		lsf ASH/op in US Airways Express-colors
☐ N244YV	Beech 1900D Airliner	UE-244		1096	1096	2 PWC PT6A-67D	7688	Y19		lsf ASH/op in US Airways Express-colors

AIRNET SYSTEMS, Inc. = USC (formerly U.S. Check Airl., PDQ Air Service,Inc., Wright Int'l Express & Air Continental,Inc.) — **Columbus-Int'l, OH & Dallas-Love Field, TX**

3939 Int'l Gateway, Columbus, OH 43219, USA ☎ (614) 237-2057 Tx: none Fax: (614) 237-1915 SITA: n/a
F: 1978 ⁂ n/a Head: Gerald G. Mercer ICAO: STAR CHECK Net: http://www.airnet.com

registration	type of aircraft	cn/fn	ex	mfd	del	powered by	mtow kg	configuration	selcal	remarks
☐ N3420G	Cessna 310R II	310R1229		0078	0585	2 CO IO-520-M	2495	Freighter		lsf Partnership Foxtrott
☐ N3597G	Cessna 310R II	310R0875		0077	1081	2 CO IO-520-M	2495	Freighter		
☐ N35H	Cessna 310R II	310R0953		0077	0582	2 CO IO-520-M	2495	Freighter		lsf F&V Aircraft Leasing Co.
☐ N3700G	Cessna 310R II	310R0899		0077	0984	2 CO IO-520-M	2495	Freighter		
☐ N37223	Cessna 310R II	310R0963		0077	0283	2 CO IO-520-M	2495	Freighter		
☐ N37575	Cessna 310R II	310R1207		0077	0282	2 CO IO-520-M	2495	Freighter		
☐ N3845G	Cessna 310R II	310R0929		0077	1285	2 CO IO-520-M	2495	Freighter		lsf LOG Aviation Inc.
☐ N5119C	Cessna 310R II	310R1420		0078	0584	2 CO IO-520-M	2495	Freighter		lsf Partnership Echo
☐ N5215C	Cessna 310R II	310R1515		0079	0785	2 CO IO-520-M	2495	Freighter		
☐ N5338C	Cessna 310R II	310R1544		0078	0481	2 CO IO-520-M	2495	Freighter		
☐ N5494J	Cessna 310R II	310R0292		0075	0987	2 CO IO-520-M	2495	Freighter		lsf Partnership Golf
☐ N6121C	Cessna 310R II	310R1288		0078	1084	2 CO IO-520-M	2495	Freighter		
☐ N6122C	Cessna 310R II	310R1290		0078	0283	2 CO IO-520-M	2495	Freighter		
☐ N6160X	Cessna 310R II	310R1305		0078	0184	2 CO IO-520-M	2495	Freighter		
☐ N8521G	Cessna 310R II	310R0931		0077	0583	2 CO IO-520-M	2495	Freighter		
☐ N5740V	Beech Baron C55 (95-C55)	TE-103		0066	0988	2 CO IO-520-C	2404	Freighter		
☐ N158MT	Beech Baron 58	TH-1186		0080	0298	2 CO IO-520-C	2449	Freighter		
☐ N1653W	Beech Baron 58	TH-252		0072	0988	2 CO IO-520-C	2449	Freighter		
☐ N17708	Beech Baron 58	TH-813		0077	0493	2 CO IO-520-C	2449	Freighter		
☐ N1814W	Beech Baron 58	TH-287		0072	0988	2 CO IO-520-C	2449	Freighter		
☐ N1847F	Beech Baron 58	TH-1291		0081	0197	2 CO IO-520-CB	2449	Freighter		lsf Midway Aviation Inc.
☐ N1859K	Beech Baron 58	TH-1299		0081	0197	2 CO IO-520-C	2449	Freighter		lsf Midway Aviation Inc.
☐ N2027V	Beech Baron 58	TH-965		0078	0197	2 CO IO-520-C	2449	Freighter		lsf Midway Aviation Inc.
☐ N2064V	Beech Baron 58	TH-1004		0080	0197	2 CO IO-520-C	2449	Freighter		lsf Midway Aviation Inc.
☐ N26CC	Beech Baron 58	TH-136		0071	0988	2 CO IO-520-C	2449	Freighter		
☐ N2892W	Beech Baron 58	TH-389		0073	0393	2 CO IO-520-C	2449	Freighter		
☐ N33DK	Beech Baron 58	TH-372		0073	0895	2 CO IO-520-C	2449	Freighter		
☐ N33WC	Beech Baron 58	TH-170		0071	0694	2 CO IO-520-C	2449	Freighter		
☐ N36673	Beech Baron 58	TH-1143		0080	0296	2 CO IO-520-CB	2449	Freighter		
☐ N3695V	Beech Baron 58	TH-1183		0080	0197	2 CO IO-520-C	2449	Freighter		lsf Midway Aviation Inc.
☐ N36FS	Beech Baron 58	TH-1084		0080	0996	2 CO IO-520-CB	2449	Freighter		
☐ N3703Q	Beech Baron 58	TH-1189		0080	0197	2 CO IO-520-C	2449	Freighter		lsf Midway Aviation Inc.
☐ N400RP	Beech Baron 58	TH-319		0073	0394	2 CO IO-520-C	2449	Freighter		
☐ N4098S	Beech Baron 58	TH-600		0075	1092	2 CO IO-520-C	2449	Freighter		
☐ N456WW	Beech Baron 58	TH-444		0074	0197	2 CO IO-520-C	2449	Freighter		lsf Midway Aviation Inc.
☐ N4575S	Beech Baron 58	TH-695		0075	0395	2 CO IO-520-C	2449	Freighter		
☐ N4AW	Beech Baron 58	TH-450		0074	0894	2 CO IO-520-C	2449	Freighter		
☐ N525GW	Beech Baron 58	TH-557		0074	0394	2 CO IO-520-C	2449	Freighter		
☐ N58TA	Beech Baron 58	TH-596		0075	0994	2 CO IO-520-C	2449	Freighter		
☐ N58WA	Beech Baron 58	TH-201		0072	0988	2 CO IO-520-C	2449	Freighter		
☐ N6650D	Beech Baron 58	TH-1375		0082	0197	2 CO IO-520-C	2449	Freighter		lsf Midway Aviation Inc.
☐ N6758C	Beech Baron 58	TH-1080		0080	0197	2 CO IO-520-C	2449	Freighter		lsf Midway Aviation Inc.
☐ N696BD	Beech Baron 58	TH-352		0073	0493	2 CO IO-520-C	2449	Freighter		
☐ N7383R	Beech Baron 58	TH-502		0074	0988	2 CO IO-520-C	2449	Freighter		
☐ N78DM	Beech Baron 58	TH-281		0072	0693	2 CO IO-520-C	2449	Freighter		
☐ N78RE	Beech Baron 58	TH-371		0073	0792	2 CO IO-520-C	2449	Freighter		
☐ N858LG	Beech Baron 58	TH-518		0074	1092	2 CO IO-520-C	2449	Freighter		
☐ N9044V	Beech Baron 58	TH-216		0072	0993	2 CO IO-520-C	2404	Freighter		
☐ N9189Q	Beech Baron 58	TH-148		0071	0192	2 CO IO-520-C	2449	Freighter		
☐ N9367Q	Beech Baron 58	TH-192		0072	0192	2 CO IO-520-C	2449	Freighter		
☐ N95BB	Beech Baron 58	TH-333		0073	0595	2 CO IO-520-C	2449	Freighter		
☐ N222KD	AAC (Ted Smith) Aerostar 600A	60-0557-181	N8074J	0078	0495	2 LY IO-540-K1F5	2495	Freighter		
☐ N3643D	AAC (Piper) Aerostar 600A	60-0835-8161238		0081	0289	2 LY IO-540-K1J5	2495	Freighter		
☐ N3645M	AAC (Piper) Aerostar 600A	60-0847-8161243		0081	0895	2 LY IO-540-K1J5	2495	Freighter		
☐ N3645T	AAC (Piper) Aerostar 600A	60-0852-8161244		0081	0988	2 LY IO-540-K1J5	2495	Freighter		
☐ N6069T	AAC (Piper) Aerostar 600A	60-0674-7961212		0079	0289	2 LY IO-540-K1J5	2495	Freighter		
☐ N6076L	AAC (Piper) Aerostar 600A	60-0713-7961221		0079	0988	2 LY IO-540-K1J5	2495	Freighter		
☐ N6078E	AAC (Piper) Aerostar 600A	60-0729-8061226		0080	0988	2 LY IO-540-K1J5	2495	Freighter		
☐ N6892R	AAC (Piper) Aerostar 600A	60-0887-8161251		0081	1290	2 LY IO-540-K1J5	2495	Freighter		
☐ N6896B	AAC (Piper) Aerostar 600A	60-0919-8161260		0081	0289	2 LY IO-540-K1J5	2495	Freighter		
☐ N7512S	AAC (Ted Smith) Aerostar 600A	60-0144-064		0073	0987	2 LY IO-540-K1F5	2495	Freighter		
☐ N8073J	AAC (Ted Smith) Aerostar 600A	60-0556-180		0078	0988	2 LY IO-540-K1F5	2495	Freighter		
☐ N8090J	AAC (Piper) Aerostar 600A	60-0576-7961187		0079	1087	2 LY IO-540-K1J5	2495	Freighter		
☐ N8229J	AAC (Piper) Aerostar 600A	60-0631-7961200	C-GFEI	0079	0187	2 LY IO-540-K1J5	2495	Freighter		
☐ N8248J	AAC (Piper) Aerostar 601B	61-0652-7962140		0079	0289	2 LY IO-540-S1A5	2722	Freighter		
☐ N90349	AAC (Ted Smith) Aerostar 600A	60-0202-090		0075	1287	2 LY IO-540-K1F5	2495	Freighter		
☐ N90437	AAC (Ted Smith) Aerostar 600A	60-0243-100		0075	0988	2 LY IO-540-K1F5	2495	Freighter		
☐ N90609	AAC (Ted Smith) Aerostar 600A	60-0320-118	C-GVLZ	0076	0188	2 LY IO-540-K1F5	2495	Freighter		
☐ N9825Q	AAC (Ted Smith) Aerostar 601B	61-0513-130		0078	0988	2 LY IO-540-S1A5	2722	Freighter		
☐ N22427	Piper PA-31-350 Navajo Chieftain	31-8152065		0081	0595	2 LY TIO-540-J2BD	3175	Freighter		
☐ N225TM	Piper PA-31-350 Navajo Chieftain	31-8152133	XA-MAU	0081	0397	2 LY TIO-540-J2BD	3175	Freighter		
☐ N2KC	Piper PA-31-350 Navajo Chieftain	31-7952217		0079	0594	2 LY TIO-540-J2BD	3175	Freighter		
☐ N3547C	Piper PA-31-350 Navajo Chieftain	31-8052018		0080	0794	2 LY TIO-540-J2BD	3175	Freighter		
☐ N35551	Piper PA-31-350 Navajo Chieftain	31-8052063		0080	0496	2 LY TIO-540-J2BD	3175	Freighter		
☐ N35871	Piper PA-31-350 Navajo Chieftain	31-8052123		0080	1194	2 LY TIO-540-J2BD	3175	Freighter		
☐ N3590D	Piper PA-31-350 Navajo Chieftain	31-8052144		0080	1096	2 LY TIO-540-J2BD	3175	Freighter		
☐ N40919	Piper PA-31-350 Navajo Chieftain	31-8152162		0081	0397	2 LY TIO-540-J2BD	3175	Freighter		
☐ N40978	Piper PA-31-350 Navajo Chieftain	31-8152199		0081	0395	2 LY TIO-540-J2BD	3175	Freighter		
☐ N42HD	Piper PA-31-350 Navajo Chieftain	31-8152031		0081	0796	2 LY TIO-540-J2BD	3175	Freighter		
☐ N4UE	Piper PA-31-350 Navajo Chieftain	31-8152061		0081	0795	2 LY TIO-540-J2BD	3175	Freighter		

☐ N525AA	Piper PA-31-350 Navajo Chieftain	31-8052111		0080	0297	2 LY TIO-540-J2BD	3175	Freighter		
☐ N711LH	Piper PA-31-350 Navajo Chieftain	31-8152174		0081	1194	2 LY TIO-540-J2BD	3175	Freighter		
☐ N100WN	Learjet 25D	25D-288	N40BC	0079	0990	2 GE CJ610-6	6804	Freighter		
☐ N121EL	Learjet 25	25-010	N102PS	0068	1088	2 GE CJ610-6	6804	Freighter		
☐ N228SW	Learjet 25D	25D-228		0077	0389	2 GE CJ610-6	6804	Freighter		
☐ N8MQ	Learjet 25B	25B-085	N8MA	0072	0988	2 GE CJ610-6	6804	Freighter		
☐ N924BW	Learjet 25B	25B-158	N71RB	0074	0890	2 GE CJ610-6	6804	Freighter		
☐ N1140A	Learjet 35	35-045	N304AT	0075	0796	2 GA TFE731-2-2B	8301	Freighter		lsf pvt
☐ N118DA	Learjet 35A	35A-081	JY-AFF	0076	0587	2 GA TFE731-2-2B	8301	Freighter		
☐ N122JW	Learjet 35A	35A-217	N111RF	0078	0795	2 GA TFE731-2-2B	8301	Freighter		
☐ N130F	Learjet 35	35-044		0076	0895	2 GA TFE731-2-2B	8301	Freighter		
☐ N15WH	Learjet 35A	35A-085		0076	0194	2 GA TFE731-2-2B	8301	Freighter		
☐ N279DM	Learjet 35A	35A-214		0078	1096	2 GA TFE731-2-2B	8301	Freighter		
☐ N27BL	Learjet 35A	35A-163	YV-173CP	0078	0589	2 GA TFE731-2-2B	8301	Freighter		
☐ N27TT	Learjet 35A	35A-122	OE-GMP	0077	0395	2 GA TFE731-2-2B	8301	Freighter		
☐ N31WR	Learjet 35A	35A-313	TR-LZI	0080	1194	2 GA TFE731-2-2B	8301	Freighter		
☐ N39DK	Learjet 35A	35A-480	N35CK	0082	1096	2 GA TFE731-2-2B	8301	Freighter		
☐ N400JE	Learjet 35A	35A-120		0077	0194	2 GA TFE731-2-2B	8301	Freighter		
☐ N40AN	Learjet 35A	35A-271	LV-OAS	0079	0597	2 GA TFE731-2-2B	8301	Freighter		
☐ N4358N	Learjet 35	35-065	N425DN	0076	0187	2 GA TFE731-2-2B	8301	Freighter		
☐ N55F	Learjet 35A	35A-147	N717W	0077	0689	2 GA TFE731-2-2B	8301	Freighter		
☐ N64CP	Learjet 35A	35A-264	VR-CDI	0079	1292	2 GA TFE731-2-2B	8301	Freighter		
☐ N700SJ	Learjet 35A	35A-082	N700GB	0076	0194	2 GA TFE731-2-2B	8301	Freighter		
☐ N701AS	Learjet 35	35-047	N13MJ	0076	1086	2 GA TFE731-2-2B	8301	Freighter		
☐ N72JF	Learjet 35A	35A-088	OE-GBR	0076	0194	2 GA TFE731-2-2B	8301	Freighter		
☐ N800AW	Learjet 35A	35A-149	N600AW	0077	0297	2 GA TFE731-2-2B	8301	Freighter		
☐ N8040A	Learjet 35	35-048	F-GHMP	0076	1095	2 GA TFE731-2-2B	8301	Freighter		
☐ N813AS	Learjet 35A	35A-167	N725P	0078	1192	2 GA TFE731-2-2B	8301	Freighter		
☐ N88BG	Learjet 35A	35A-090	I-FIMI	0076	0793	2 GA TFE731-2-2B	8301	Freighter		
☐ N959SA	Learjet 35A	35A-076		0076	1096	2 GA TFE731-2-2B	8301	Freighter		

AIR NEW ENGLAND, Inc.
Vineyard Haven-Marthas Vineyard, MA

PO Box 4656, Vineyard Haven, MA 02568, USA ☎ (508) 693-8899 Tx: none Fax: (508) 693-5557 SITA: n/a
F: 1992 👥 8 Head: Edward B. Stott Net: n/a

☐ N9F	Cessna A185F Skywagon	18502855	N1479F	0075	0094	1 CO IO-520-D2H	1520			lsf Tellairco Inc.
☐ N92P	Piper PA-23-250 Turbo Aztec E	27-4824	N142MC	0072	0094	2 LY TIO-540-C1A	2359			lsf Tellairco Inc.
☐ N88604	Cessna 421C Golden Eagle III	421C0604		0078	0892	2 CO GTSIO-520-L	3379			lsf pvt

AIR ONE HELICOPTERS, Inc.
San Jose-Int'l, CA

1144 Coleman Ave., San Jose, CA 95110, USA ☎ (408) 292-5043 Tx: none Fax: (408) 292-5622 SITA: n/a
F: 1976 👥 n/a Head: George Bumb Net: http://www.airone.com/

☐ N3596B	Eurocopter (Aerosp.) AS350B AStar	1099		0079	0180	1 TU Arriel 1B	1950			cvtd AS350D
☐ N291B	Bell 212	30842	C-GXHS	0077	1296	2 PWC PT6T-3 TwinPac	5080			
☐ N9121Z	Bell 212	30580	C-GJDC	0073	0296	2 PWC PT6T-3 TwinPac	5080			
☐ N47B	Sikorsky S-58BT	58-530	EC-CYJ	0057	0291	1 PWC PT6T TwinPac	5897			cvtd S-58B
☐ N72B	Sikorsky S-58ET	58-1626	EC-DJN	0063	0291	1 PWC PT6T TwinPac	5897			cvtd S-58E

AIR ORLANDO CHARTER, Inc. (Affiliated with Air Orlando, Inc., Air Orlando Sales, Inc. & Ambrose Investments, Inc.)
Orlando-Executive, FL

400 Herndon Avenue, Suite 109, Orlando, FL 32803, USA ☎ (561) 896-0721 Tx: none Fax: (561) 894-6180 SITA: n/a
F: 1987 👥 n/a Head: Raymond Ambrose Net: http://www.airorlando.com

☐ N7244R	Beech Baron 58	TH-558		0074	1095	2 CO IO-520-C	2449			lsf Exec U Flites Inc.

AIR OZARK, Inc.
Springfield-Branson Regional, MO

PO Box 118, Willard, MO 65781, USA ☎ (417) 848-5999 Tx: none Fax: none SITA: n/a
F: 1994 👥 n/a Head: Jack S. Reynolds Net: n/a

☐ N110JR	Piper PA-30-160 Twin Comanche B	30-1029	N7938Y	0066	0694	2 LY IO-320-B1A	1633			lsf pvt

AIRPAC AIRLINES, Inc. = LQ / APC
Seattle-Boeing Field/King County Int'l, WA

7277 Perimeter Road South, Seattle, WA 98108, USA ☎ (206) 762-8006 Tx: none Fax: (206) 762-6357 SITA: n/a
F: 1975 👥 28 Head: Gregory S. Thompson IATA: 856 ICAO: AIRPAC Net: n/a

☐ N36319	Piper PA-34-200T Seneca II	34-7870318		0078	0084	2 CO TSIO-360-E	2073	Freighter		
☐ N4377X	Piper PA-34-200T Seneca II	34-7670035		0076	0578	2 CO TSIO-360-E	2073	Freighter		
☐ N4490F	Piper PA-34-200T Seneca II	34-7670339		0076	0893	2 CO TSIO-360-E	2073	Freighter		
☐ N8107D	Piper PA-34-200T Seneca II	34-8070010		0080	0993	2 CO TSIO-360-EB	2073	Freighter		
☐ N8407C	Piper PA-34-200T Seneca II	34-7670137		0076	1080	2 CO TSIO-360-E	2073	Freighter		
☐ N27594	Piper PA-31-350 Navajo Chieftain	31-7852070		0078	0384	2 LY TIO-540-J2BD	3175	Freighter		
☐ N3582X	Piper PA-31-350 Navajo Chieftain	31-8052105		0080	0990	2 LY TIO-540-J2BD	3175	Freighter		
☐ N36PB	Piper PA-31-350 Navajo Chieftain	31-7405128		0073	0084	2 LY TIO-540-J2BD	3175	Freighter		
☐ N40ST	Piper PA-31-350 Navajo Chieftain	31-7405183		0074	0091	2 LY TIO-540-J2BD	3175	Freighter		lsf Pioneer Leasing
☐ N627HA	Piper PA-31-350 Navajo Chieftain	31-7952241		0079	0990	2 LY TIO-540-J2BD	3175	Freighter		
☐ N777KT	Piper PA-31-350 Navajo Chieftain	31-7552053	N1TW	0075	0681	2 LY TIO-540-J2BD	3175	Freighter		
☐ N41SA	Cessna 404 Titan II	404-0023	N5271J	0077	0485	2 CO GTSIO-520-M	3810	Freighter		
☐ N48SA	Cessna 404 Titan II	404-0417	C-GSPG	0079	0385	2 CO GTSIO-520-M	3810	Freighter		
☐ N5278J	Cessna 404 Titan II	404-0635		0080	0084	2 CO GTSIO-520-M	3810	Freighter		
☐ N2880A	Beech 99 Airliner	U-109		0069	0089	2 PWC PT6A-20	4717	Freighter		

AIRPLANE SERVICES (Carl Spray dba)
Winchester-Municipal, TN

2756 Lockmiller Road, Estill Springs, TN 37330, USA ☎ (931) 967-3130 Tx: none Fax: (931) 967-3130 SITA: n/a
F: 1979 👥 n/a Head: Carl Spray Net: n/a

☐ N8341Y	Piper PA-30-160 Twin Comanche B	30-1487		0067	0185	2 LY IO-320-B1A	1633			

AIRPRO FLIGHT SERVICES (Aircraft Investments, Inc. dba)
Batesville-Regional, AR

1126 Batesville Blvd., Batesville, AR 72501, USA ☎ (870) 251-3900 Tx: none Fax: (870) 251-3896 SITA: n/a
F: 1992 👥 n/a Head: Doyle W. Rogers, Jr. Net: n/a

☐ N618JX	BAe 3101 Jetstream 31	618	N820JS	0083	1096	2 GA TPE331-10UR-513H	6900	C15		
☐ N849JS	BAe 3101 Jetstream 31	812	G-31-812*	0088	0797	2 GA TPE331-10UG-513H	6900	C15		

AIR RACINE (Sylvania Air Travel, Inc. dba)
Racine-John H. Batten, WI

2409 Spring Street, Racine, WI 53405, USA ☎ (920) 637-5354 Tx: none Fax: none SITA: n/a
F: 1968 👥 n/a Head: Theodore B. Harmon Net: n/a

☐ N81TH	Piper PA-34-200T Seneca II	34-7870178		0078	0885	2 CO TSIO-360-E	2073			

AIR RELDAN, Inc.
New Orleans-Lakefront, LA

8227 Lloyd Stearman Drive, New Orleans, LA 70126, USA ☎ (504) 241-9400 Tx: none Fax: (504) 241-9449 SITA: n/a
F: 1982 👥 n/a Head: Neil Nadler Net: n/a Aircraft below MTOW 1361kg: Cessna 177 & Piper PA-28

☐ N304CW	Piper PA-34-200T Seneca II	34-7870153		0078	1187	2 CO TSIO-360-E	2073			
☐ N7090B	Piper PA-31-350 Navajo Chieftain	31-7752075		0077	0892	2 LY TIO-540-J2BD	3175			

AIR RESOURCES HELICOPTERS, Inc.
Santa Ana-John Wayne/Orange County, CA

PO Box 10305, Newport Beach, CA 92658-0305, USA ☎ (949) 442-0480 Tx: none Fax: (949) 442-4483 SITA: n/a
F: 1994 👥 n/a Head: Charles R. MacFarland, Jr. Net: n/a

☐ N3310	Bell 206L-4 LongRanger IV	52094	XA-SWN	0094	0796	1 AN 250-C30P	2018			
☐ N98D	Bell 206L-3 LongRanger III	51350	D-HILF	0090	0897	1 AN 250-C30P	1882			
☐ N351WM	Eurocopter (Aerosp.) AS350B1 AStar	2167		0089	0193	1 TU Arriel 1D	2200			

AIR RESPONSE, Inc.
Mesa-Falcon Field, AZ

4949 East Falcon Drive, Mesa, AZ 85205, USA ☎ (520) 844-0800 Tx: none Fax: (520) 396-8616 SITA: n/a
F: 1986 👥 4 Head: Richard E. Packard Net: n/a

☐ N438NA	Boeing (Douglas) DC-4 (C-54G-10-DO)	36031 / DO 425	USN 45578	0045	0386	4 PW R-2000	30241	Sprayer		
☐ N67017	Boeing (Douglas) DC-4 (C-54B-1-DC)	10438 / DC 169	USN 39122	0042	0586	4 PW R-2000	30241	Sprayer		
☐ N67019	Boeing (Douglas) DC-4 (C-54B-1-DC)	10520 / DC 251	USN 50865	0043	0586	4 PW R-2000	30241	Sprayer		
☐ N99AS	Boeing (Douglas) DC-4 (C-54D-15-DC)	22203 / DC 655	USN 56549	0044	0586	4 PW R-2000	30241	Sprayer		

AIR RESPONSE, Inc.
Denver-Centennial, CO & Albany-County, NY

7211 South Peoria Street, Suite 200, Englewood, CO 80112, USA ☎ (303) 799-0670 Tx: none Fax: (888) 631-6565 SITA: n/a
F: 1986 👥 n/a Head: Louis R. Capece, Jr. Net: n/a

☐ N98600	Cessna 340A II	340A0054		0076	1192	2 CO TSIO-520-N	2717			
☐ N621PG	Piper PA-31-350 Navajo Chieftain	31-7652049		0076	0893	2 LY TIO-540-J2BD	3175			

255 registration type of aircraft cn/fn ex/ex* mfd del powered by mtow kg configuration selcal name/fln/specialitites/remarks

☐ N918WK	Cessna 421B Golden Eagle	421B0956		0075	0295	2 CO GTSIO-520-H	3379			
☐ N3330K	Mitsubishi MU-2J (MU-2B-35)	551	N111WN	0072	0691	2 GA TPE331-6-251M	4899			
☐ N777MR	Learjet 24	24-142	N200NR	0067	1190	2 GE CJ610-6	5897			
☐ N102AR	Learjet 25	25-012	N846YC	0068	0694	2 GE CJ610-6	6804			

AIR ST. THOMAS = ZP / STT (formerly Virgin Air, Inc.) — **St. Thomas-Cyril E. King, VI**

PO Box 302788, St. Thomas, VI 00803, USA ☎ (340) 776-2722 Tx: none Fax: (340) 714-2727 SITA: n/a
F: 1970 👥 20 Head: Paul H. Wikander IATA: 315 ICAO: PARADISE Net: http://www.airstthomas.com

☐ N329SD	Piper PA-23-250 Aztec C	27-3512		0066	0386	2 LY IO-540-C4B5	2359	Y5		
☐ N5623Y	Piper PA-23-250 Aztec C	27-2733		0064	0185	2 LY IO-540-C4B5	2359	Y5		
☐ N6389Y	Piper PA-23-250 Aztec C	27-3675		0067	1296	2 LY IO-540-C4B5	2359	Y5		
☐ N8125F	Cessna 402	402-0231		0068	1191	2 CO TSIO-520-E	2858	Y7		

AIR SAL, Inc. — **Miami-Kendall Tamiami Executive, FL**

14359 SW 127 Street, Miami, FL 33186, USA ☎ (305) 251-1982 Tx: none Fax: (305) 251-1966 SITA: n/a
F: 1984 👥 n/a Head: Bud W. Skinner Net: n/a Aircraft below MTOW 1361kg: Cessna 172

☐ N1869	Beech King Air C90	LJ-520	N880M	0071	0393	2 PWC PT6A-20	4377			lsf Air Sal Leasing Inc.
☐ N4392W	Beech King Air A100	B-192		0074	0992	2 PWC PT6A-28	5216			lsf Air Sal Leasing Inc.
☐ N45RL	Beech King Air C90	LJ-565	N711MP	0072	0393	2 PWC PT6A-20	4377			lsf Air Sal Leasing Inc.
☐ N515AS	Beech King Air A100	B-90	F-GFDV	0071	0992	2 PWC PT6A-28	5216			lsf Air Sal Leasing Inc.
☐ N66KA	Beech King Air C90	LJ-582		0073	0892	2 PWC PT6A-20	4377			lsf Air Sal Leasing Inc.

AIR SAN FRANCISCO (AAA Air Charter, Inc. dba) — **San Francisco-Int'l, CA**

AMR Executive Terminal, Int'l Airport, San Francisco, CA 94128, USA ☎ (650) 877-0300 Tx: none Fax: (650) 877-0307 SITA: n/a
F: 1971 👥 n/a Head: Richard E. Weston Net: n/a

☐ N987S	Cessna 414 II	414-0828		0076	0887	2 CO TSIO-520-N	2880			

AIR SAVANNAH (Aero Medical Transport, Inc. dba) — **Savannah-Int'l, GA**

PO Box 7736, Garden City, GA 31418, USA ☎ (912) 964-5655 Tx: none Fax: (803) 785-5619 SITA: n/a
F: 1987 👥 n/a Head: Robert L. Lacombe Net: n/a

☐ N200WS	Piper PA-34-200 Seneca	34-7450117		0074	0196	2 LY IO-360-C1E6	1905			
☐ N27626	Piper PA-31-325 Navajo C/R	31-7812068		0078	0796	2 LY TIO-540-F2BD	2948			

AIRSCAN, Inc. — **Titusville-Arthur Dunn Air Park, FL**

7017 Challenger Avenue, Titusville, FL 32780, USA ☎ (561) 264-2911 Tx: none Fax: (561) 264-2917 SITA: n/a
F: 1989 👥 n/a Head: John W. Mansur Net: n/a

☐ N5113S	Cessna R182 Skylane RG II	R18201507		0080	1196	1 LY O-540-J3C5D	1406	Survey/Patrol		
☐ N52515	Cessna O-2A (337B) Super Skymaster	M3370048	67-21342	0067	0893	2 CO IO-360-C/D	1950	Survey/Patrol		
☐ N5257G	Cessna O-2A (337B) Super Skymaster	M3370113	67-21407	0067	0893	2 CO IO-360-C/D	1950	Survey/Patrol		
☐ N722AS	Cessna 337G Super Skymaster II	33701823	N1331L	0078	0689	2 CO IO-360-G	2100	Survey/Patrol		
☐ N723AS	Cessna 337G Super Skymaster II	33701648	N44HK8	0075	0689	2 CO IO-360-G	2100	Survey/Patrol		
☐ N724AS	Cessna 337G Super Skymaster II	33701792	N53698	0077	0689	2 CO IO-360-G	2100	Survey/Patrol		
☐ N725AS	Cessna 337G Super Skymaster II	33701671	N53511	0076	0789	2 CO IO-360-G	2100	Survey/Patrol		
☐ N726AS	Cessna 337G Super Skymaster II	33701661	N4AE	0075	0191	2 CO IO-360-G	2100	Survey/Patrol		
☐ N8070L	Cessna 337G Super Skymaster II	33701674		0076	1196	2 CO IO-360-G	2100	Survey/Patrol		
☐ N303ET	Cessna T303 Crusader	T30300036		0082	1196	2 CO TSIO-520-AE	2336	Survey/Patrol		

AIR SERVICES, Inc. — **Traverse City-Cherry Capital, MI**

1026 Hannah Street, Traverse City, MI 49686, USA ☎ (616) 922-0406 Tx: none Fax: (616) 941-8612 SITA: n/a
F: 1994 👥 12 Head: Roy C. Nichols Net: n/a

☐ N7222K	Beech Bonanza A36	E-2164		0084	0991	1 CO IO-550-BB	1633			lsf Nichols Optical Inc.
☐ N5591A	Beech Baron 58	TH-1566		0089	0196	2 CO IO-550-C	2495			
☐ N682DR	Beech King Air 200	BB-130	N323MB	0076	0395	2 PWC PT6A-41	5670			lsf Air Services Brokerage Llc

AIRSERV INTERNATIONAL (Air Serv International, Inc. dba) — **Africa**

PO Box 3041, Redlands, CA 92373, USA ☎ (909) 793-2627 Tx: none Fax: (909) 793-0226 SITA: n/a
F: 1985 👥 n/a Head: Ken Frizzel Net: n/a Non-profit international organisation conducting relief missions in remote aereas.

☐ N756GQ	Cessna TU206G Turbo Stationair 6 II	U20604083		0077	0194	1 CO TSIO-520-M	1633			
☐ N6210Y	Cessna T210N Turbo Centurion II	21064297		0081	0194	1 CO TSIO-520-R	1814			
☐ N9324F	Cessna 208 Caravan I	20800013		0085	1190	1 PWC PT6A-114	3629			
☐ N9732F	Cessna 208 Caravan I	20800156		0089	1289	1 PWC PT6A-114	3629			
☐ N17SE	Beech King Air E90	LW-169	N600KC	0075	0194	2 PWC PT6A-28	4581			
☐ N899AS	De Havilland DHC-6 Twin Otter 300	347	LN-FKB	0072	0288	2 PWC PT6A-27	5670			opf UN
☐ N740GL	Beech King Air 200	BB-650	N33TJ	0080	1195	2 PWC PT6A-41	5670			

AIRSPECT, Inc. (Affiliated with PWM, Inc.) — **Akron-Fulton Int'l, OH**

1600 Triplett Blvd, Akron, OH 44306-3311, USA ☎ (330) 794-8383 Tx: none Fax: (330) 794-8042 SITA: n/a
F: 1976 👥 18 Head: Spasoje Miskovic Net: n/a

☐ N8160R	Beech Baron 58	TH-516		0074	0386	2 CO IO-520-C	2449	5 Pax		
☐ N30TF	Fairchild (Swearingen) SA26AT Merlin IIB	T26-162	C-FTEL	0069	0984	2 GA TPE331-1-151G	4808	6 Pax		lsf PWM Inc.

AIR STAR AIRLINES (Air Star Helicopters, Inc. dba) — **Grand Canyon-National Park, AZ**

PO Box 3379, Grand Canyon, AZ 86023, USA ☎ (520) 638-2622 Tx: none Fax: (520) 638-2607 SITA: n/a
F: 1989 👥 n/a Head: Brad M. Martin Net: http://www.airstar.com

☐ N9962M	Cessna T207A Turbo Stationair 8 II	20700765		0083	0892	1 CO TSIO-520-M	1724			
☐ N31AS	Eurocopter (Aerosp.) AS350B2 AStar	2689	LV-WFD	0092	0697	1 TU Arriel 1D1	2250			
☐ N333AS	Eurocopter (Aerosp.) AS350B2 AStar	2893	N4006G	0095	0296	1 TU Arriel 1D1	2250			
☐ N544AS	Eurocopter (Aerosp.) AS350B2 AStar	2890	N4014J	0095	0496	1 TU Arriel 1D1	2250			

AIRSTAR AVIATION, Inc. — **Van Nuys, CA**

23 Chickasaw Court, Corte Madera, CA 94925, USA ☎ (818) 909-7733 Tx: none Fax: (818) 927-7201 SITA: n/a
F: 1988 👥 n/a Head: Bruce Shinneman Net: n/a

☐ N315AJ	Learjet 24	24-108	N900JA	0066	1097	2 GE CJ610-4	5897			lsf Millenium Jets Inc.

AIR SUNSHINE, Inc. = YI / RSI (Sister company of Tropical Aviation Services, Inc. & Tropical Transport Services, Ltd) — **Fort Lauderdale-Hollywood Int'l, FL**

PO Box 22237, Fort Lauderdale, FL 33335-2237, USA ☎ (954) 434-8900 Tx: none Fax: (954) 359-8229 SITA: n/a
F: 1982 👥 22 Head: Allen Adili IATA: 806 ICAO: AIR SUNSHINE Net: n/a

☐ N122TA	Cessna 402C II	402C0122	N2712P	0079	0597	2 CO TSIO-520-VB	3107	Y9		lsf Tropical Transport Services Ltd
☐ N251RS	Cessna 402C II	402C0251	N166PB	0079	1193	2 CO TSIO-520-VB	3107	Y9		lsf Tropical Aviation Services Inc.
☐ N26548	Cessna 402C II	402C0347		0080	0397	2 CO TSIO-520-VB	3107	Y9		lsf Tropical Transport Services Ltd
☐ N2716L	Cessna 402C II	402C0220		0079	0397	2 CO TSIO-520-VB	3107	Y9		lsf Tropical Transport Services Ltd
☐ N351AB	Cessna 402C II	402C0351	N26629	0080	0392	2 CO TSIO-520-VB	3107	Y9		lsf Tropical Transport Services Ltd
☐ N402RS	Cessna 402C II	402C0402	N2663N	0081	1188	2 CO TSIO-520-VB	3107	Y9		lsf Tropical Transport Services Ltd
☐ N603AB	Cessna 402C II	402C0603	N84PB	0081	0197	2 CO TSIO-520-VB	3107	Y9		lsf Tropical Transport Services Ltd
☐ N123HY	Embraer 110P1 Bandeirante (EMB-110P1)	110321	N619KC	0081	1193	2 PWC PT6A-34	5670	Y15		lsf Tropical Transport Services Ltd

AIR TAHOMA, Inc. = HMA — **San Diego-Int'l/Lindbergh Field, CA**

5469 Kearny Villa Road, Suite 201, San Diego, CA 92123, USA ☎ (760) 560-4544 Tx: none Fax: (760) 560-0664 SITA: n/a
F: 1995 👥 n/a Head: Noel Rude ICAO: TAHOMA Net: n/a

☐ N581P	Convair 580 (F) (SCD)	29	C-FBHW	0052	0295	2 AN 501-D13	26379	Freighter		lsf R&R Holdings Inc. / cvtd CV340-31
☐ N582P	Convair 580	475	N969N	0057	0896	2 AN 501-D13	26379	Freighter		lsf N582P Inc. / cvtd CV 540/CL-66C
☐ N583P	Convair 580 (F) (SCD)	454	C-GKFR	0057	1297	2 AN 501-D13	26379	Freighter		lsf Kasi Leasing Inc. / cvtd 440-0

AIR TEJAS, Inc. (Sister company of Tejas Avionics, Inc.) — **Georgetown-Municipal, TX**

205 Corsair Drive, Georgetown, TX 78628-2308, USA ☎ (512) 863-9567 Tx: none Fax: (512) 863-6986 SITA: n/a
F: 1995 👥 12 Head: John Gruell Net: n/a

☐ N962AT	Beech King Air A90 (65-A90)	LJ-207		0067	1296	2 PWC PT6A-20	4218	Corporate		lsf pvt
☐ N941AT	Boeing (Douglas) DC-3C (C-47A-20-DK)	12907	N6666A	0044	0295	2 PW R-1830	12202	Freighter		Vera Lynn II / lsf pvt

AIRTEX (Division of Spartan Mills) — **Greer-Greenville Spartanburg, SC**

PO Box 12096, Greenville, SC 29612, USA ☎ (864) 879-6000 Tx: none Fax: (864) 879-6215 SITA: n/a
F: 1987 👥 n/a Head: Reginald Gerwig Net: n/a

☐ N48N	Beech King Air B200	BB-969	N188W	0082	0187	2 PWC PT6A-42	5670			

AIR TRAILS, Llc (Million Air Monterey) — **Salinas-Municipal & Monterey-Peninsula, CA**

280 Mortensen Avenue, Salinas, CA 93905, USA ☎ (408) 757-5144 Tx: none Fax: (408) 757-9483 SITA: n/a
F: 1960 👥 n/a Head: Bob Buck Net: n/a Aircraft below MTOW 1361kg: Piper PA-28 FBO services at Monterey, CA are done under the marketing name MILLION AIR MONTEREY (same headquarters & fleet).

☐ N15AT	Cessna 310R II	310R0103	N69611	0074	0196	2 CO IO-520-M	2495			
☐ N63AT	Cessna 340A II	340A0925	N2742B	0080	0596	2 CO TSIO-520-N	2717			
☐ N4AT	Beech King Air 200	BB-281	N315JW	0077	0696	2 PWC PT6A-41	5670			
☐ N561AS	Cessna 550 Citation II	550-0383	N551AB	0080	0198	2 PWC JT15D-4	6033			

256 registration type of aircraft cn/fn ex/ex* mfd del powered by mtow kg configuration selcal name/fln/specialitites/remarks

AIRTRAN AIRWAYS, Inc. = FL / TRS (Subsidiary of AirTran Holdings, Inc./formerly Airtran Airlines, Inc. & Valujet Airlines, Inc.)

Orlando-Int'l, FL & Atlanta-Int'l, GA

AirTran

9955 Airtran Blvd, Orlando, FL 32827, USA ☎ (407) 251-5600 Tx: none Fax: (407) 251-5571 SITA: n/a
F: 1992 ⁂ 3400 Head: Joseph Leonard IATA: 332 ICAO: CITRUS Net: http://www.airtran.com

☐ N132NK	Boeing (Douglas) DC-9-31	47202 / 400	N965VV	0068	1195	2 PW JT8D-7B	46720	C12Y94		lst NKS / to be re-reg.N865AT
☐ N801AT	Boeing (Douglas) DC-9-32	47275 / 363	N901VJ	0868	1093	2 PW JT8D-7B (HK3/ABS)	48988	C12Y94		
☐ N802AT	Boeing (Douglas) DC-9-32	47177 / 330	N902VJ	0668	1093	2 PW JT8D-7B	48988	C12Y94		
☐ N803AT	Boeing (Douglas) DC-9-32	47261 / 411	N903VJ	0168	1193	2 PW JT8D-7B	48988	C12Y94		
☐ N805AT	Boeing (Douglas) DC-9-32	47378 / 508	N905VJ	0769	1293	2 PW JT8D-7B	48988	C12Y94		
☐ N806AT	Boeing (Douglas) DC-9-32	47379 / 509	N906VJ	0769	1293	2 PW JT8D-7B (HK3/ABS)	48988	C12Y94		
☐ N807AT	Boeing (Douglas) DC-9-32	47444 / 578	N907VJ	0470	0194	2 PW JT8D-7B (HK3/ABS)	48988	C12Y94		
☐ N809AT	Boeing (Douglas) DC-9-32	47322 / 456	N909VJ	0269	0294	2 PW JT8D-7B (HK3/ABS)	48988	C12Y94		
☐ N810AT	Boeing (Douglas) DC-9-32	47277 / 379	N910VJ	0168	0394	2 PW JT8D-7B (HK3/ABS)	48988	C12Y94		
☐ N811AT	Boeing (Douglas) DC-9-32	47285 / 414	N911VV	0068	0494	2 PW JT8D-7B (HK3/ABS)	48988	C12Y94		
☐ N813AT	Boeing (Douglas) DC-9-32	47318 / 426	N913VV	1168	0594	2 PW JT8D-7B	48988	C12Y94		
☐ N815AT	Boeing (Douglas) DC-9-32	47443 / 577	N915VV	0070	0794	2 PW JT8D-7B (HK3/ABS)	48988	C12Y94		
☐ N816AT	Boeing (Douglas) DC-9-32	47445 / 585	N916VV	0070	0794	2 PW JT8D-7B (HK3/ABS)	48988	C12Y94		
☐ N817AT	Boeing (Douglas) DC-9-32	47323 / 468	N917VV	0069	1294	2 PW JT8D-7B	48988	C12Y94		
☐ N818AT	Boeing (Douglas) DC-9-32	47320 / 454	N918VV	0069	0195	2 PW JT8D-7B	48988	C12Y94		
☐ N819AT	Boeing (Douglas) DC-9-32	47260 / 410	N919VV	0068	0395	2 PW JT8D-7B	48988	C12Y94		
☐ N821AT	Boeing (Douglas) DC-9-32	47284 / 413	N921VV	0068	1095	2 PW JT8D-7B (HK3/ABS)	48988	C12Y94		
☐ N823AT	Boeing (Douglas) DC-9-32	47529 / 625	N923VV	0271	0995	2 PW JT8D-7B (HK3/ABS)	48988	C12Y94		
☐ N824AT	Boeing (Douglas) DC-9-32	47278 / 380	N924VV	0068	0496	2 PW JT8D-7B (HK3/ABS)	48988	C12Y94		
☐ N825AT	Boeing (Douglas) DC-9-32	47319 / 434	N925VV	0069	0496	2 PW JT8D-7B	48988	C12Y94		
☐ N826AT	Boeing (Douglas) DC-9-32	47359 / 495	N912VV	0069	0594	2 PW JT8D-7B	48988	C12Y94		
☐ N827AT	Boeing (Douglas) DC-9-32	47486 / 628	N914VV	0571	0494	2 PW JT8D-7B (HK3/ABS)	48988	C12Y94		
☐ N828AT	Boeing (Douglas) DC-9-32	47274 / 348	N922VV	0068	0895	2 PW JT8D-7B	48988	C12Y94		
☐ N830AT	Boeing (Douglas) DC-9-32	47723 / 838	N930VV	0076	1294	2 PW JT8D-9A (HK3/ABS)	48988	C12Y94		
☐ N831AT	Boeing (Douglas) DC-9-32	47674 / 793	N931VV	0075	1294	2 PW JT8D-9A (HK3/ABS)	48988	C12Y94		
☐ N832AT	Boeing (Douglas) DC-9-32	47451 / 547	N932VV	0070	1294	2 PW JT8D-9A (HK3/ABS)	48988	C12Y94		
☐ N833AT	Boeing (Douglas) DC-9-32	47489 / 528	N933VV	0869	1294	2 PW JT8D-9A (HK3/ABS)	48988	C12Y94		
☐ N834AT	Boeing (Douglas) DC-9-32	47488 / 527	N934VV	0069	0195	2 PW JT8D-9A (HK3/ABS)	48988	C12Y94		
☐ N835AT	Boeing (Douglas) DC-9-32	47534 / 644	N935VV	0071	0295	2 PW JT8D-9A (HK3/ABS)	48988	C12Y94		
☐ N836AT	Boeing (Douglas) DC-9-32	47397 / 636	N936VV	0071	0395	2 PW JT8D-9A (HK3/ABS)	48988	C12Y94		
☐ N837AT	Boeing (Douglas) DC-9-32	45774 / 336	N937VV	0068	0295	2 PW JT8D-9A (HK3/ABS)	48988	C12Y94		
☐ N838AT	Boeing (Douglas) DC-9-32	47442 / 524	N938VV	0070	1094	2 PW JT8D-9A (HK3/ABS)	48988	C12Y94		
☐ N839AT	Boeing (Douglas) DC-9-32	47089 / 189	N939VV	0067	0296	2 PW JT8D-7B (HK3/ABS)	49898	C12Y94		
☐ N840AT	Boeing (Douglas) DC-9-32	47523 / 593	N940VV	0070	0595	2 PW JT8D-9A (HK3/ABS)	48988	C12Y94		
☐ N845AT	Boeing (Douglas) DC-9-32	47238 / 465	N945VV	0069	0795	2 PW JT8D-9A (HK3/ABS)	48988	C12Y94		
☐ N846AT	Boeing (Douglas) DC-9-32	47226 / 333	N946VV	0068	0296	2 PW JT8D-9A (HK3/ABS)	48988	C12Y94		
☐ N847AT	Boeing (Douglas) DC-9-32	47555 / 667	N947VV	0072	0496	2 PW JT8D-9A (HK3/ABS)	48988	C12Y94		
☐ N848AT	Boeing (Douglas) DC-9-32	47559 / 672	N948VV	0072	1196	2 PW JT8D-9A (HK3/ABS)	48988	C12Y94		
☐ N849AT	Boeing (Douglas) DC-9-32	47484 / 648	N949VV	0071	1096	2 PW JT8D-9A (HK3/ABS)	48988	C12Y94		
☐ N866AT	Boeing (Douglas) DC-9-32	47168 / 423	N966VV	0068	1295	2 PW JT8D-9 (HK3/ABS)	49895	C12Y94		
☐ N867AT	Boeing (Douglas) DC-9-32	47170 / 425	N967VV	0068	1195	2 PW JT8D-9A (HK3/ABS)	49895	C12Y94		
☐ N940AT	Boeing 717-200	55004				2 BR BR715	51710	C12Y105		oo-delivery 0699
☐ N942AT	Boeing 717-200	55005				2 BR BR715	51710	C12Y105		oo-delivery 0799
☐ N943AT	Boeing 717-200	55006				2 BR BR715	51710	C12Y105		oo-delivery 0899
☐ N945AT	Boeing 717-200	55008				2 BR BR715	51710	C12Y105		oo-delivery 0999
☐ N946AT	Boeing 717-200	55009				2 BR BR715	51710	C12Y105		oo-delivery 0999
☐ N947AT	Boeing 717-200	55010				2 BR BR715	51710	C12Y105		oo-delivery 1099
☐ N948AT	Boeing 717-200	55011				2 BR BR715	51710	C12Y105		oo-delivery 1099
☐ N949AT	Boeing 717-200	55003				2 BR BR715	51710	C12Y105		oo-delivery 1199
☐ N950AT	Boeing 717-200	55012				2 BR BR715	51710	C12Y105		oo-delivery 1199
☐ N951AT	Boeing 717-200					2 BR BR715	51710	C12Y105		oo-delivery 1299
☐ N952AT	Boeing 717-200					2 BR BR715	51710	C12Y105		oo-delivery 1299
☐ N953AT	Boeing 717-200					2 BR BR715	51710	C12Y105		oo-delivery 0100
☐ N954AT	Boeing 717-200					2 BR BR715	51710	C12Y105		oo-delivery 0100
☐ N955AT	Boeing 717-200					2 BR BR715	51710	C12Y105		oo-delivery 0200
☐ N956AT	Boeing 717-200					2 BR BR715	51710	C12Y105		oo-delivery 0300
☐ N957AT	Boeing 717-200					2 BR BR715	51710	C12Y105		oo-delivery 0300
☐ N958AT	Boeing 717-200					2 BR BR715	51710	C12Y105		oo-delivery 0400
☐ N959AT	Boeing 717-200					2 BR BR715	51710	C12Y105		oo-delivery 0500
☐ N960AT	Boeing 717-200					2 BR BR715	51710	C12Y105		oo-delivery 0500
☐ N961AT	Boeing 717-200					2 BR BR715	51710	C12Y105		oo-delivery 0600
☐ N963AT	Boeing 717-200					2 BR BR715	51710	C12Y105		oo-delivery 0700
☐ N964AT	Boeing 717-200					2 BR BR715	51710	C12Y105		oo-delivery 0700
☐ N965AT	Boeing 717-200					2 BR BR715	51710	C12Y105		oo-delivery 0800
☐ N966AT	Boeing 717-200					2 BR BR715	51710	C12Y105		oo-delivery 0900
☐ N967AT	Boeing 717-200					2 BR BR715	51710	C12Y105		oo-delivery 0900
☐ N968AT	Boeing 717-200					2 BR BR715	51710	C12Y105		oo-delivery 1000
☐ N969AT	Boeing 717-200					2 BR BR715	51710	C12Y105		oo-delivery 1100
☐ N970AT	Boeing 717-200					2 BR BR715	51710	C12Y105		oo-delivery 1100
☐ N971AT	Boeing 717-200					2 BR BR715	51710	C12Y105		oo-delivery 1200
☐ N972AT	Boeing 717-200					2 BR BR715	51710	C12Y105		oo-delivery 0101
☐ N975AT	Boeing 717-200					2 BR BR715	51710	C12Y105		oo-delivery 0201
☐ N977AT	Boeing 717-200					2 BR BR715	51710	C12Y105		oo-delivery 0301
☐ N978AT	Boeing 717-200					2 BR BR715	51710	C12Y105		oo-delivery 0401
☐ N979AT	Boeing 717-200					2 BR BR715	51710	C12Y105		oo-delivery 0401
☐ N980AT	Boeing 717-200					2 BR BR715	51710	C12Y105		oo-delivery 0501
☐ N981AT	Boeing 717-200					2 BR BR715	51710	C12Y105		oo-delivery 0601
☐ N982AT	Boeing 717-200					2 BR BR715	51710	C12Y105		oo-delivery 0601
☐ N983AT	Boeing 717-200					2 BR BR715	51710	C12Y105		oo-delivery 0701
☐ N984AT	Boeing 717-200					2 BR BR715	51710	C12Y105		oo-delivery 0801
☐ N985AT	Boeing 717-200					2 BR BR715	51710	C12Y105		oo-delivery 0801
☐ N986AT	Boeing 717-200					2 BR BR715	51710	C12Y105		oo-delivery 0901
☐ N987AT	Boeing 717-200					2 BR BR715	51710	C12Y105		oo-delivery 1001
☐ N988AT	Boeing 717-200					2 BR BR715	51710	C12Y105		oo-delivery 1001
☐ N989AT	Boeing 717-200					2 BR BR715	51710	C12Y105		oo-delivery 1101
☐ N990AT	Boeing 717-200					2 BR BR715	51710	C12Y105		oo-delivery 1201
☐ N991AT	Boeing 717-200					2 BR BR715	51710	C12Y105		oo-delivery 1201
☐ N992AT	Boeing 717-200					2 BR BR715	51710	C12Y105		oo-delivery 0002
☐ N993AT	Boeing 717-200					2 BR BR715	51710	C12Y105		oo-delivery 0002
☐ N460AT	Boeing 737-214	20158 / 192	N460AC	0069	1293	2 PW JT8D-9A	49442	C6Y110		lsf AARL
☐ N461AT	Boeing 737-2E1 (A)	20976 / 388	N461AC	0074	0794	2 PW JT8D-9A (HK3/AVA)	52390	C6Y110		lsf POLA
☐ N462AT	Boeing 737-297 (A)	22631 / 894	N730AL	0082	0195	2 PW JT8D-9A (HK3/NOR)	53070	C6Y110	CF-JL	lsf CITG
☐ N464AT	Boeing 737-2L9 (A)	21278 / 479	N358AS	1176	0695	2 PW JT8D-17 (HK3/AVA)	54204	C6Y110		
☐ N465AT	Boeing 737-2L9 (A)	21528 / 517	N359AS	0478	0695	2 PW JT8D-17 (HK3/AVA)	54204	C6Y110		
☐ N466AT	Boeing 737-2L9 (A)	21279 / 480	N737Q	1276	0895	2 PW JT8D-17 (HK3/AVA)	54204	C6Y110	EF-CG	
☐ N467AT	Boeing 737-2T4 (A)	22055 / 633	XA-SLC	0180	1295	2 PW JT8D-15 (HK3/AVA)	54204	C6Y110		lsf CITG
☐ N468AT	Boeing 737-222	19074 / 95	N144AW	0068	0196	2 PW JT8D-9A	49442	C6Y110		
☐ N470AT	Boeing 737-284 (A)	21501 / 492	N310VA	0077	0897	2 PW JT8D-9A (HK3/NOR)	53070	C6Y110		lsf POLA

AIR TRANSPORT, Inc.

Nashua-Boire Field, NH

RFD 3, Box 183, Plymouth, NH 03264, USA ☎ (603) 536-7244 Tx: none Fax: (603) 536-2691 SITA: n/a
F: 1988 ⁂ n/a Head: Lewis E. Marden Net: http://www.flyati.com

☐ N3LH	Piper PA-31-310 Navajo	31-581		0070	0294	2 LY TIO-540-A1A	2948			
☐ N9287Y	Piper PA-31-310 Navajo	31-380		0069	0490	2 LY TIO-540-A1A	2948			

AIR TRANSPORT, Inc. = CYO (Air Med El Paso)

El Paso-Int'l, TX

7007 Boeing Drive, El Paso, TX 79925-1109, USA ☎ (915) 772-1448 Tx: none Fax: (915) 772-1467 SITA: n/a
F: 1979 ⁂ n/a Head: Victoria K. Wingett ICAO: COYOTE Net: n/a
Uses the service-name AIR MED EL PASO for its EMS-operations.

☐ N9683G	Cessna TU206F Turbo Stationair	U20601883		0073	0494	1 CO TSIO-520-F	1633			lsf pvt
☐ N761JP	Cessna T210M Turbo Centurion II	21062296		0077	0889	1 CO TSIO-520-R	1724			lsf pvt
☐ N22WE	Cessna 402B	402B0004	C-GULD	0070	0790	2 CO TSIO-520-E	2858			lsf pvt
☐ N3855C	Cessna 421C Golden Eagle II	421C0121		0076	0190	2 CO GTSIO-520-L	3379			lsf pvt
☐ N77404	Cessna 404 Titan II	404-0005	N3933C	0076	0284	2 CO GTSIO-520-M	3810			lsf pvt
☐ N26AT	Learjet 25B	25B-130	N25PL	0073	0785	2 GE CJ610-6	6804	EMS		lsf NKL Inc.
☐ N273LR	Learjet 25	25-058	N273LP	0070	1192	2 GE CJ610-6	6804	EMS		lsf NKL Corp.
☐ N976BS	Learjet 25	25-016	N8FF	0068	0895	2 GE CJ610-6	6804			lsf pvt

257 registration type of aircraft cn/fn ex/ex* mfd del powered by mtow kg configuration selcal name/fln/specialitites/remarks

AIR TRANSPORT INTERNATIONAL, Llc – ATI = 8C / ATN (Air Traffic Service, Co. dba / Subs.of BAX Global / formerly Interstate Airlines, Inc.) — Little Rock-Adams Field, AR

2800 Cantrell Road, Little Rock, AR 72202, USA ☎ (501) 615-3500 Tx: none Fax: (501) 603-2093 SITA: LITDD8C
F: 1979 ☨☨☨ 450 Head: James J. Bonsall ICAO: AIR TRANSPORT Net: n/a

☐ N861PL	Boeing (Douglas) DC-8-61F	45964 / 364	N47UA	0568	0989	4 PW JT3D-3B (HK2/QNC)	145286	Freighter	EM-AH	cvtd DC-8-61
☐ N820BX	Boeing (Douglas) DC-8-71F	46065 / 460	N8098U	0069	0293	4 CFMI CFM56-2C	147418	Freighter		lsf / opf BAX Global / cvtd -61/-71
☐ N821BX	Boeing (Douglas) DC-8-71F	45811 / 262	N8071U	0067	0293	4 CFMI CFM56-2C	147418	Freighter		lsf / opf BAX Global / cvtd -61/-71
☐ N822BX	Boeing (Douglas) DC-8-71F	45813 / 284	N8073U	0067	0293	4 CFMI CFM56-2C	147418	Freighter	EF-DM	lsf / opf BAX Global / cvtd -61/-71
☐ N823BX	Boeing (Douglas) DC-8-71F	46064 / 459	N8097U	0069	0293	4 CFMI CFM56-2C	147418	Freighter		lsf / opf BAX Global / cvtd -61/-71
☐ N824BX	Boeing (Douglas) DC-8-71F	45946 / 339	N8078U	0068	0293	4 CFMI CFM56-2C	147418	Freighter		lsf / opf BAX Global / cvtd -61/-71
☐ N825BX	Boeing (Douglas) DC-8-71F	45978 / 381	N8088U	0068	0693	4 CFMI CFM56-2C	147418	Freighter		lsf / opf BAX Global / cvtd -61/-71
☐ N826BX	Boeing (Douglas) DC-8-71F	45998 / 399	N8094U	0068	0793	4 CFMI CFM56-2C	147418	Freighter		lsf / opf BAX Global / cvtd -61/-71
☐ N827BX	Boeing (Douglas) DC-8-71F	45971 / 356	SE-DLM	0068	1193	4 CFMI CFM56-2C	148900	Freighter		lsf / opf BAX Global / cvtd -61/-71
☐ N828BX	Boeing (Douglas) DC-8-71F	45993 / 382	N8089U	0068	1193	4 CFMI CFM56-2C	147418	Freighter		lsf / opf BAX Global / cvtd -61/-71
☐ N829BX	Boeing (Douglas) DC-8-71F	45994 / 387	N501SR	0068	1194	4 CFMI CFM56-2C	147418	Freighter		lsf / opf BAX Global / cvtd -61/-71
☐ N830BX	Boeing (Douglas) DC-8-71F	45973 / 358	N783UP	0068	0796	4 CFMI CFM56-2C	147418	Freighter		lsf / opf BAX Global / cvtd -61/-71
☐ N21CX	Boeing (Douglas) DC-8-62F (CF)	45955 / 365	N163CA	0068	1094	4 PW JT3D-7 (HK3/BAC)	151953	Combi C27&10Plt	FJ-BM	cvtd -62
☐ N31CX	Boeing (Douglas) DC-8-62F (CF)	45911 / 318	N1806	0067	1094	4 PW JT3D-7 (HK3/BAC)	151953	Combi C27&10Plt	GK-FH	cvtd -62
☐ N41CX	Boeing (Douglas) DC-8-62F (CF)	46129 / 523	N798AL	0070	1094	4 PW JT3D-7 (HK3/BAC)	151953	Combi C33&10Plt	GK-LM	lsf AERO
☐ N61CX	Boeing (Douglas) DC-8-62F	46142 / 546	OB-1210	0371	1194	4 PW JT3D-3B (HK3/BAC)	151953	Freighter	EM-AB	lsf GMD Inc. / cvtd -62
☐ N728PL	Boeing (Douglas) DC-8-62F	45918 / 353	F-BOLF	0068	0586	4 PW JT3D-3B (HK3/BAC)	151953	Freighter	GK-FL	cvtd -62
☐ N799AL	Boeing (Douglas) DC-8-62F	45922 / 335	RTAF 60-112	0068	0798	4 PW JT3D-7 (HK3/BAC)	151953	Freighter		lsf IALI/sub-lst/opf BAX Gl./cvtd (CF)
☐ N8974U	Boeing (Douglas) DC-8-62F	46110 / 487	HI-576CT	0069	0297	4 PW JT3D-7 (HK3/BAC)	158757	Freighter		lsf IALI / cvtd -62
☐ N786AL	Boeing (Douglas) DC-8-63F	46121 / 500	EI-CAK	0069	0994	4 PW JT3D-7 (HK3/BAC)	161025	Freighter	AD-BH	lsf AERO / cvtd -63
☐ N867BX	Boeing (Douglas) DC-8-63F	46049 / 479	TF-FLC	0069	0197	4 PW JT3D-7 (HK3/BAC)	161025	Freighter		lsf / opf BAX Global / cvtd (CF)
☐ N868BX	Boeing (Douglas) DC-8-63F	46034 / 434	C-FTIL	0069	0197	4 PW JT3D-7 (HK3/BAC)	161025	Freighter		lsf / opf BAX Global / cvtd -63
☐ N869BX	Boeing (Douglas) DC-8-63F	46035 / 438	C-FTIM	0069	0197	4 PW JT3D-7 (HK3/BAC)	161025	Freighter		lsf / opf BAX Global / cvtd -63
☐ N870BX	Boeing (Douglas) DC-8-63F	46036 / 445	C-FTIN	0069	0197	4 PW JT3D-7 (HK3/BAC)	161025	Freighter		lsf / opf BAX Global / cvtd -63
☐ N906R	Boeing (Douglas) DC-8-63F	46087 / 454	N774FT	0069	0795	4 PW JT3D-7 (HK3/BAC)	161025	Freighter	DL-JK	lsf AERO / cvtd (CF)

AIR TRANSPORT SERVICE, Inc. — Postville-Dale Delight, IA

724 Jackson Hollow Drive, Postville, IA 52162, USA ☎ (319) 864-7782 Tx: none Fax: none SITA: n/a
F: 1988 ☨☨☨ n/a Head: Marlin D. Swenson Net: n/a

☐ N8247Q	Cessna 414	414-0252		0072	0792	2 CO TSIO-520-J	2880			

AIR USA, Inc. (Sister company of Argosy Airways) — Burbank-Glendale/Pasadena, CA

4409 Empire Avenue, Burbank, CA 91505, USA ☎ (626) 559-5500 Tx: none Fax: (626) 559-5523 SITA: n/a
F: 1991 ☨☨☨ n/a Head: J. Elliott Black Net: n/a

☐ N7146T	Piper PA-31-350 Navajo Chieftain	31-7305015		0073	0793	2 LY TIO-540-J2BD	3175			

AIR VEGAS, Inc. = 6V / VGA (AVI, Inc. dba) — Las Vegas-Henderson Executive, NV

PO Box 11008, Las Vegas, NV 89111, USA ☎ (702) 736-3599 Tx: none Fax: (702) 361-8967 SITA: n/a
F: 1971 ☨☨☨ 100 Head: James W. Petty ICAO: AIR VEGAS Net: n/a

☐ N272S	Beech Bonanza V35	D-8002		0065	0382	1 CO IO-520-B	1542	Y4		lsf C & M Enterprises
☐ N174AV	Beech C99 Airliner	U-174	N99CJ	0081	0496	2 PWC PT6A-36	5126	Y15		
☐ N189AV	Beech C99 Airliner	U-189	N516DM	0082	0293	2 PWC PT6A-36	5126	Y15		
☐ N191AV	Beech C99 Airliner	U-191	VR-CIB	0082	0195	2 PWC PT6A-36	5126	Y15		
☐ N206AV	Beech C99 Airliner	U-206	N216EE	0083	0397	2 PWC PT6A-36	5126	Y15		
☐ N227AV	Beech C99 Airliner	U-227	N2225H	0084	0297	2 PWC PT6A-36	5126	Y15		
☐ N234AV	Beech C99 Airliner	U-234	N234BH	0086	1192	2 PWC PT6A-36	5126	Y15		
☐ N235AV	Beech C99 Airliner	U-235	N235BH	0086	0194	2 PWC PT6A-36	5126	Y15		
☐ N330AV	Beech C99 Airliner	U-230	N3063W	0086	0195	2 PWC PT6A-36	5126	Y15		
☐ N388AV	Beech C99 Airliner	U-188	N799GL	0082	0393	2 PWC PT6A-36	5126	Y15		

AIRWAY AIR CHARTER, Inc. — Hamilton-Fairfield, OH

2318 Hamilton-Eaton Road, Hamilton, OH 45013, USA ☎ (513) 863-3933 Tx: none Fax: (513) 726-6389 SITA: n/a
F: 1992 ☨☨☨ n/a Head: Virgil L. Wardlow Net: n/a

☐ N3590N	Piper PA-31-350 Navajo Chieftain	31-8052148		0080	0394	2 LY TIO-540-J2BD	3175			

AIRWAYS, Inc. — Lancaster, PA

PO Box 5403, Lancaster, PA 17606, USA ☎ (717) 569-4996 Tx: none Fax: (717) 569-4596 SITA: n/a
F: 1988 ☨☨☨ n/a Head: Ralph E. Herr Net: http://www.flyairways.com Aircraft below MTOW 1361kg: Cessna 172

☐ N21438	Piper PA-44-180 Seminole	44-7995051		0079	0994	2 LY O-360-E1A6D	1724			
☐ N6274X	Cessna 340A II	340A0458		0078	1195	2 CO TSIO-520-NB	2717			

AIRWAY TRANSPORT, Inc. — California City-Municipal, CA

22636 Airport Way 3, California City, CA 93505, USA ☎ (760) 373-4287 Tx: none Fax: (760) 373-1054 SITA: n/a
F: 1984 ☨☨☨ n/a Head: Jan E. Aarvik, Sr. Net: n/a

☐ N7500A	Boeing (Douglas) DC-3A (C-53D-DO)	11693	N777K	0043	0584	2 WR R-1820-202A	12202	Y28		Norge / occ opf Air Cruise America

AIR WEST, Inc. — Mesa-Falcon Field, AZ

4610 Fighter Aces Drive, Mesa, AZ 85215, USA ☎ (602) 396-0688 Tx: none Fax: (602) 985-3691 SITA: n/a
F: 1995 ☨☨☨ n/a Head: Mark T. Wilkinson Net: n/a

☐ N7584Q	Cessna T310Q	310Q0084		0070	0395	2 CO TSIO-520-B	2495			

AIRWST HELICOPTERS, Llc — Phoenix-Deer Valley Municipal, AZ

19208 North 32nd Ave, Phoenix, AZ 85027-8416, USA ☎ (520) 581-8592 Tx: none Fax: (520) 581-5592 SITA: n/a
F: 1994 ☨☨☨ n/a Head: Jeffrey A. Boatman Net: n/a

☐ N59383	Bell 206B JetRanger	1150		0073	1294	1 AN 250-C20	1451			lsf 3M Investments

AIR WISCONSIN AIRLINES, Corp. = ZW / AWI (United Express) — Appleton, WI / Chicago-ORD, IL & Denver, CO

W6390 Challenger Drive, Suite 203, Appleton, WI 54915-9120, USA ☎ (920) 739-5123 Tx: none Fax: (920) 749-4158 SITA: n/a
F: 1965 ☨☨☨ 1700 Head: Geoffrey T. Crowley IATA: 303 ICAO: AIR WISCONSIN Net: http://www.airwis.com
All aircraft are operated as UNITED EXPRESS (in full such colours & titles), a commuter system to provide feeder connection at United Airlines major hubs, using UA flight numbers.

☐ N328MX	Dornier 328-120	3071	D-CDXX*	0096	0498	2 PWC PW119C	13990	Y31		301 / lsf Dornier / op in UA Express-cs
☐ N328PH	Dornier 328-110	3006	D-CDIY*	0093	0498	2 PWC PW119B	13990	Y32		305 / lsf Dornier/cvtd -100/UA Exp.-cs
☐ N329MX	Dornier 328-120	3049	D-CAOS*	0096	0498	2 PWC PW119C	13990	Y31		302 / lsf Dornier / op in UA-Express-cs
☐ N329PH	Dornier 328-110	3007	D-COCI*	0093	0598	2 PWC PW119B	13990	Y32		306 / lsf Dornier/cvtd -100/UA-Exp.-cs
☐ N330MX	Dornier 328-120	3067	D-CDXN*	0096	0498	2 PWC PW119C	13990	Y31		303 / lsf Dornier / op in UA Express-cs
☐ N330PH	Dornier 328-110	3008	D-CDAN*	0093	0598	2 PWC PW119B	13990	Y32		307 / lsf Dornier/cvtd -100/UA Exp.-cs
☐ N331MX	Dornier 328-120	3074	D-CDXA*	0096	0498	2 PWC PW119C	13990	Y31		304 / lsf Dornier / op in UA Express-cs
☐ N332PH	Dornier 328-110	3010	D-CFFA*	0094	0598	2 PWC PW119B	13990	Y32		308 / lsf Dornier/cvtd -100/UA Exp.-cs
☐ N334PH	Dornier 328-110	3012	D-CASI*	0094	0598	2 PWC PW119B	13990	Y32		309 / lsf Dornier/cvtd -100/UA Exp.-cs
☐ N336PH	Dornier 328-110	3014	D-CDHO*	0094	0598	2 PWC PW119B	13990	Y32		310 / lsf Dornier/cvtd -100/UA Exp.-cs
☐ N339PH	Dornier 328-110	3015	D-CARR*	0094	0598	2 PWC PW119B	13990	Y32		311 / lsf Dornier/cvtd -100/UA Exp.-cs
☐ N401AW	Canadair Regional Jet 200LR (CL-600-2B19)	7280	C-FMMW*	0098	1298	2 GE CF34-3B1	23995	Y50		op in United Express-colors
☐ N402AW	Canadair Regional Jet 200LR (CL-600-2B19)	7281	C-FMMX*	0099	1298	2 GE CF34-3B1	23995	Y50		op in United Express-colors
☐ N403AW	Canadair Regional Jet 200LR (CL-600-2B19)	7287		0099	0199	2 GE CF34-3B1	23995	Y50		op in United Express-colors
☐ N404AW	Canadair Regional Jet 200LR (CL-600-2B19)	7288		0099	0499	2 GE CF34-3B1	23995	Y50		op in United Express-colors
☐ N405AW	Canadair Regional Jet 200LR (CL-600-2B19)					2 GE CF34-3B1	23995	Y50		oo-delivery 0100/tbop in United Exp.-cs
☐ N406AW	Canadair Regional Jet 200LR (CL-600-2B19)					2 GE CF34-3B1	23995	Y50		oo-delivery 0300/tbop in United Exp.-cs
☐ N407AW	Canadair Regional Jet 200LR (CL-600-2B19)					2 GE CF34-3B1	23995	Y50		oo-delivery 1000/tbop in United Exp.-cs
☐ N409AW	Canadair Regional Jet 200LR (CL-600-2B19)					2 GE CF34-3B1	23995	Y50		oo-delivery 0301/tbop in United Exp.-cs
☐ N410AW	Canadair Regional Jet 200LR (CL-600-2B19)					2 GE CF34-3B1	23995	Y50		oo-delivery 1001/tbop in United Exp.-cs
☐ N463AP	BAe 146-100A	E1063	N70NA	0086	0491	4 LY ALF502R-5	38102	Y86		op in United Express-colors
☐ N156TR	BAe 146-200A	E2156	N884DV	0089	1196	4 LY ALF502R-5	40597	Y88		lsf BAMJ / op in United Express-colors
☐ N179US	BAe 146-200A	E2041	N358PS	0085	0996	4 LY ALF502R-5	40597	Y88		lsf USAL / op in United Express-colors
☐ N181US	BAe 146-200A	E2042	N359PS	0085	0996	4 LY ALF502R-5	40597	Y88		lsf USAL / op in United Express-colors
☐ N183US	BAe 146-200A	E2043	N360PS	0085	0996	4 LY ALF502R-5	40597	Y88		lsf USAL / op in United Express-colors
☐ N291UE	BAe 146-200A	E2084	N815AS	0087	0498	4 LY ALF502R-5	42184	Y88		lsf BAMJ / op in United Express-colors
☐ N292UE	BAe 146-200A	E2087	N816AS	0087	0498	4 LY ALF502R-5	42184	Y88		lsf BAMJ / op in United Express-colors
☐ N606AW	BAe 146-200A	E2033		0085	0285	4 LY ALF502R-5	40597	Y88	FK-CG	op in United Express-colors
☐ N607AW	BAe 146-200A	E2052	G-5-001*	0085	0186	4 LY ALF502R-5	40597	Y88	FK-DJ	op in United Express-colors
☐ N608AW	BAe 146-200A	E2049	G-5-002*	0086	0486	4 LY ALF502R-5	40597	Y88	GL-BK	op in United Express-colors
☐ N609AW	BAe 146-200A	E2070	G-BNKK*	0087	0687	4 LY ALF502R-5	40597	Y88	GL-AM	op in United Express-colors
☐ N610AW	BAe 146-200A	E2082	G-5-082*	0087	0987	4 LY ALF502R-5	40597	Y88	GL-BC	op in United Express-colors
☐ N814AS	BAe 146-200A	E2080	N290UE	0087	1297	4 LY ALF502R-5	42184	Y88		lsf BAMJ / op in United Express-colors
☐ N611AW	BAe 146-300A	E3120	N146UK*	0088	1288	4 LY ALF502R-5	43084	Y100		Kitty / op in United Express-colors
☐ N612AW	BAe 146-300A	E3122	G-5-122*	0088	1288	4 LY ALF502R-5	43084	Y100	GL-BH	op in United Express-colors
☐ N614AW	BAe 146-300A	E3132	G-5-132*	0089	0589	4 LY ALF502R-5	43084	Y100		op in United Express-colors
☐ N615AW	BAe 146-300A	E3141	G-5-141*	0089	0989	4 LY ALF502R-5	43084	Y100		op in United Express-colors
☐ N616AW	BAe 146-300A	E3145	G-5-145*	0089	1189	4 LY ALF502R-5	43084	Y100		op in United Express-colors

258 registration type of aircraft cn/fn ex/ex* mfd del powered by mtow kg configuration selcal name/fln/specialitites/remarks

AKERS AVIATION (Merle W. Akers dba) — Anchorage-Lake Hood SPB, AK

3031 Bennett Avenue, Anchorage, AK 99517, USA ☎ (907) 243-4802 Tx: none Fax: none SITA: n/a
F: 1994 ♦♦♦ n/a Head: Merle W. Akers Net: n/a

registration	type of aircraft	cn/fn	ex/ex*	mfd	del	powered by	mtow kg	configuration	selcal	name/fln/specialities/remarks
☐ N5077R	Cessna A185F Skywagon	18503000		0076	0294	1 CO IO-520-D	1520			Floats / Wheel-Skis

ALABAMA AIR CHARTER, Inc. (Associated with Aerostar World, Inc. & Flightline of Dothan, Inc.) — Dothan, AL

PO Box 9044, Dothan, AL 36304-1044, USA ☎ (334) 983-5600 Tx: none Fax: (334) 983-4314 SITA: n/a
F: 1995 ♦♦♦ n/a Head: Donald S. Smith Net: n/a

| ☐ N20LR | AAC (Ted Smith) Aerostar 601P | 61P-0192-013 | N20WL | 0075 | 0496 | 2 LY IO-540-S1A5 | 2722 | | | |

ALADDIN AIR SERVICES, Inc. — Bryce Canyon, UT

PO Box 2, Panguitch, UT 84759, USA ☎ (435) 834-5555 Tx: none Fax: (435) 834-5556 SITA: n/a
F: 1995 ♦♦♦ n/a Head: Terry L. Andrews Net: n/a Aircraft below MTOW 1361kg: Cessna 172

| ☐ N5195U | Cessna 206 Super Skywagon | 206-0195 | | 0064 | 0596 | 1 CO IO-520-A | 1588 | | | lsf pvt |

ALAMO JET, Inc. — Fort Lauderdale-Executive, FL

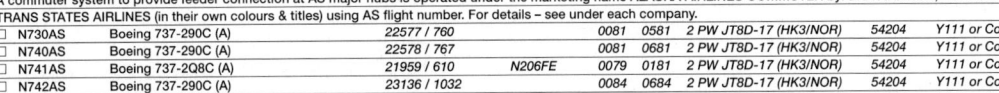

4631 NW 31 Ave, Ste 118, Fort Lauderdale, FL 33309, USA ☎ (954) 771-9511 Tx: none Fax: (954) 771-7159 SITA: n/a
F: 1985 ♦♦♦ 10 Head: David C. Brown Net: http://www.alamojet.com

☐ N355DB	Learjet 55	55-006	N126EL	0081	0689	2 GA TFE731-3AR-2B	9752			
☐ N855DB	Learjet 55	55-062	N292RC	0082	0295	2 GA TFE731-3AR-2B	9752			lsf General Electric Capital Corp.
☐ N955DB	Canadair CL-601-1A (CL-600-2A12) Challen.	3044	N125N	0085	0998	2 GE CF34-1A	19550			lsf NationsBanc Leasing Corp.

ALASKA AIR ADVENTURES (C. Vernon Humble dba) — Anchorage-Lake Hood SPB, AK

200 West 34th Ave., Suite 382, Anchorage, AK 99503, USA ☎ (907) 349-4976 Tx: none Fax: (907) 344-0941 SITA: n/a
F: 1990 ♦♦♦ n/a Head: C. Vernon Humble Net: n/a

| ☐ N47059 | De Havilland DHC-2 Beaver I | 184 | 9J-RGA | 0052 | 0190 | 1 PW R-985 | 2313 | | | Floats / Wheel-Skis |

ALASKA AIRLINES, Inc. = AS / ASA (Subsidiary of Alaska Air Group, Inc.) — Seattle-Tacoma Int'l, WA

PO Box 68900, Seattle, WA 98168, USA ☎ (206) 433-3200 Tx: 32303 Fax: (206) 433-3366 SITA: n/a
F: 1932 ♦♦♦ 6470 Head: John F. Kelly IATA: 027 ICAO: ALASKA Net: http://www.alaskaair.com
A commuter system to provide feeder connection at AS major hubs is operated under the marketing name ALASKA AIRLINES COMMUTER by: ERA AVIATION, HARBOR AIR, HORIZON AIR, PENAIR & TRANS STATES AIRLINES (in their own colours & titles) using AS flight number. For details – see under each company.

registration	type of aircraft	cn/fn	ex/ex*	mfd	del	powered by	mtow kg	configuration	selcal	name/fln/specialities/remarks
☐ N730AS	Boeing 737-290C (A)	22577 / 760		0081	0581	2 PW JT8D-17 (HK3/NOR)	54204	Y111 or Combi		
☐ N740AS	Boeing 737-290C (A)	22578 / 767		0081	0681	2 PW JT8D-17 (HK3/NOR)	54204	Y111 or Combi		
☐ N741AS	Boeing 737-2Q8C (A)	21959 / 610	N206FE	0079	0181	2 PW JT8D-17 (HK3/NOR)	54204	Y111 or Combi		
☐ N742AS	Boeing 737-290C (A)	23136 / 1032		0084	0684	2 PW JT8D-17 (HK3/NOR)	54204	Y111 or Combi		
☐ N743AS	Boeing 737-210C (A)	21821 / 590	N492WC	0079	1084	2 PW JT8D-17 (HK3/NOR)	54204	Y111 or Combi		
☐ N744AS	Boeing 737-210C (A)	21822 / 605	N493WC	0079	1084	2 PW JT8D-17 (HK3/NOR)	54204	Y111 or Combi		
☐ N745AS	Boeing 737-298C (A)	20794 / 346	N87WA	0074	1088	2 PW JT8D-17 (HK3/NOR)	54204	Y111 or Combi		
☐ N746AS	Boeing 737-2X6C (A)	23123 / 1042	N672MA	0084	0494	2 PW JT8D-17A (HK3/NOR)	58060	Y111 or Combi	DG-BH	
☐ N607AS	Boeing 737-790	29751				2 CFMI CFM56-7B24	69400			oo-delivery 0599
☐ N609AS	Boeing 737-790	29752				2 CFMI CFM56-7B24	69400			oo-delivery 0699
☐ N611AS	Boeing 737-790	29753				2 CFMI CFM56-7B24	69400			oo-delivery 0799
☐ N612AS	Boeing 737-790	30162				2 CFMI CFM56-7B24	69400			oo-delivery 0999
☐ N613AS	Boeing 737-790	30163				2 CFMI CFM56-7B24	69400			oo-delivery 1199
☐ N614AS	Boeing 737-790	30343				2 CFMI CFM56-7B24	69400			oo-delivery 0000
☐ N615AS	Boeing 737-790	30344				2 CFMI CFM56-7B24	69400			oo-delivery 0000
☐ N617AS	Boeing 737-790	30164				2 CFMI CFM56-7B24	69400			oo-delivery 0000
☐ N618AS	Boeing 737-790	30165				2 CFMI CFM56-7B24	69400			oo-delivery 0000
☐ N619AS	Boeing 737-790	30166				2 CFMI CFM56-7B24	69400			oo-delivery 0000
☐ N703AS	Boeing 737-490	28893 / 3039		0098	0698	2 CFMI CFM56-3C1	65091	F10Y126		
☐ N705AS	Boeing 737-490	29318 / 3042		0098	0698	2 CFMI CFM56-3C1	65091	F10Y126		
☐ N706AS	Boeing 737-490	28894 / 3050		0098	0798	2 CFMI CFM56-3C1	65091	F10Y126		
☐ N708AS	Boeing 737-490	28895 / 3098		0299	0299	2 CFMI CFM56-3C1	65091	F10Y126		
☐ N709AS	Boeing 737-490	28896		0099	0399	2 CFMI CFM56-3C1	65091	F10Y126		
☐ N713AS	Boeing 737-490	30161				2 CFMI CFM56-3C1	65091	F10Y126		oo-delivery 0899
☐ N754AS	Boeing 737-4Q8	25095 / 2266		0092	0492	2 CFMI CFM56-3C1	65091	F10Y126		Spirit of Alaska
☐ N755AS	Boeing 737-4Q8	25096 / 2278		0092	0592	2 CFMI CFM56-3C1	65091	F10Y126		lsf ILFC
☐ N756AS	Boeing 737-4Q8	25097 / 2299		0092	0692	2 CFMI CFM56-3C1	65091	F10Y126		
☐ N760AS	Boeing 737-4Q8	25098 / 2320		0092	0792	2 CFMI CFM56-3C1	65091	F10Y126		
☐ N762AS	Boeing 737-4Q8	25099 / 2334		0092	0792	2 CFMI CFM56-3C1	65091	F10Y126		
☐ N763AS	Boeing 737-4Q8	25100 / 2346		0092	0892	2 CFMI CFM56-3C1	65091	F10Y126		
☐ N764AS	Boeing 737-4Q8	25101 / 2348		0092	0992	2 CFMI CFM56-3C1	65091	F10Y126		lsf ILFC
☐ N765AS	Boeing 737-4Q8	25102 / 2350		0092	1092	2 CFMI CFM56-3C1	65091	F10Y126		lsf ILFC
☐ N767AS	Boeing 737-490	27081 / 2354		0092	0992	2 CFMI CFM56-3C1	65091	F10Y126		
☐ N768AS	Boeing 737-490	27082 / 2356		0092	0992	2 CFMI CFM56-3C1	65091	F10Y126		
☐ N769AS	Boeing 737-4Q8	25103 / 2552		0093	0393	2 CFMI CFM56-3C1	65091	F10Y126		
☐ N771AS	Boeing 737-4Q8	25104 / 2476		0093	0593	2 CFMI CFM56-3C1	65091	F10Y126		lsf ILFC
☐ N772AS	Boeing 737-4Q8	25105 / 2505		0093	0793	2 CFMI CFM56-3C1	65091	F10Y126		lsf ILFC
☐ N773AS	Boeing 737-4Q8	25106 / 2518		0093	0993	2 CFMI CFM56-3C1	65091	F10Y126		lsf ILFC
☐ N774AS	Boeing 737-4Q8	25107 / 2526		0093	1093	2 CFMI CFM56-3C1	65091	F10Y126		lsf ILFC
☐ N775AS	Boeing 737-4Q8	25108 / 2551		0093	1293	2 CFMI CFM56-3C1	65091	F10Y126		lsf ILFC
☐ N776AS	Boeing 737-4Q8	25109 / 2561		0093	0194	2 CFMI CFM56-3C1	65091	F10Y126		lsf ILFC
☐ N778AS	Boeing 737-4Q8	25110 / 2586		0094	0394	2 CFMI CFM56-3C1	65091	F10Y126		lsf ILFC
☐ N779AS	Boeing 737-4Q8	25111 / 2605		0094	0494	2 CFMI CFM56-3C1	65091	F10Y126		lsf ILFC
☐ N780AS	Boeing 737-4Q8	25112 / 2638		0094	0894	2 CFMI CFM56-3C1	65091	F10Y126		lsf ILFC
☐ N782AS	Boeing 737-4Q8	25113 / 2656		0094	1094	2 CFMI CFM56-3C1	65091	F10Y126		lsf ILFC
☐ N783AS	Boeing 737-4Q8	25114 / 2666		0094	1294	2 CFMI CFM56-3C1	65091	F10Y126		
☐ N784AS	Boeing 737-4Q8	28199 / 2826		0096	1196	2 CFMI CFM56-3C1	65091	F10Y126		lsf ILFC
☐ N785AS	Boeing 737-4Q8	27628 / 2858		0097	0297	2 CFMI CFM56-3C1	65091	F10Y126		lsf ILFC
☐ N786AS	Boeing 737-4S3	24795 / 1870	TF-FIE	0090	0496	2 CFMI CFM56-3C1	65091	F10Y126		
☐ N788AS	Boeing 737-490	28885 / 2891		0097	0697	2 CFMI CFM56-3C1	65091	F10Y126		
☐ N791AS	Boeing 737-490	28886 / 2902		0097	0797	2 CFMI CFM56-3C1	65091	F10Y126		
☐ N792AS	Boeing 737-490	28887 / 2903		0097	0797	2 CFMI CFM56-3C1	65091	F10Y126		
☐ N793AS	Boeing 737-490	28888 / 2990		0098	0298	2 CFMI CFM56-3C1	65091	F10Y126		
☐ N794AS	Boeing 737-490	28889 / 3000		0098	0298	2 CFMI CFM56-3C1	65091	F10Y126		
☐ N795AS	Boeing 737-490	28890 / 3006		0098	0398	2 CFMI CFM56-3C1	65091	F10Y126		
☐ N796AS	Boeing 737-490	28891 / 3027		0098	0598	2 CFMI CFM56-3C1	65091	F10Y126		
☐ N797AS	Boeing 737-490	28892 / 3036		0098	0698	2 CFMI CFM56-3C1	65091	F10Y126		
☐ N799AS	Boeing 737-490	29270 / 3038		0098	0698	2 CFMI CFM56-3C1	65091	F10Y126		
☐ N931AS	Boeing (Douglas) MD-83 (DC-9-83)	49232 / 1178		0085	0285	2 PW JT8D-219	67812	F10Y125		cvtd MD-82
☐ N932AS	Boeing (Douglas) MD-83 (DC-9-83)	49233 / 1203		0085	0685	2 PW JT8D-219	72575	F10Y125		cvtd MD-82
☐ N933AS	Boeing (Douglas) MD-83 (DC-9-83)	49234 / 1204		0085	0685	2 PW JT8D-219	72575	F10Y125		cvtd MD-82
☐ N934AS	Boeing (Douglas) MD-83 (DC-9-83)	49235 / 1234		0085	1185	2 PW JT8D-219	72575	F10Y125		Goodwill Games I
☐ N935AS	Boeing (Douglas) MD-83 (DC-9-83)	49236 / 1235		0085	1285	2 PW JT8D-219	72575	F10Y125		
☐ N937AS	Boeing (Douglas) MD-83 (DC-9-83)	49364 / 1276		0086	0586	2 PW JT8D-219	72575	F10Y125		
☐ N939AS	Boeing (Douglas) MD-83 (DC-9-83)	49657 / 1459		0288	0488	2 PW JT8D-219	72575	F10Y125		lsf ILFC -0099 / for TWA
☐ N942AS	Boeing (Douglas) MD-83 (DC-9-83)	53052 / 1731		0090	0790	2 PW JT8D-219	72575	F10Y125		lsf ILFC
☐ N943AS	Boeing (Douglas) MD-83 (DC-9-83)	53018 / 1779		0090	1190	2 PW JT8D-219	72575	F10Y125		
☐ N944AS	Boeing (Douglas) MD-83 (DC-9-83)	53019 / 1783		0090	1190	2 PW JT8D-219	72575	F10Y125		
☐ N947AS	Boeing (Douglas) MD-83 (DC-9-83)	53020 / 1789		0090	1290	2 PW JT8D-219	72575	F10Y125		
☐ N948AS	Boeing (Douglas) MD-83 (DC-9-83)	53021 / 1801		0090	1290	2 PW JT8D-219	72575	F10Y125		
☐ N949AS	Boeing (Douglas) MD-83 (DC-9-83)	53022 / 1809		0090	1290	2 PW JT8D-219	72575	F10Y125		
☐ N950AS	Boeing (Douglas) MD-83 (DC-9-83)	53023 / 1821		0091	0291	2 PW JT8D-219	72575	F10Y125		
☐ N951AS	Boeing (Douglas) MD-82 (DC-9-82)	49111 / 1064	N781JA	0082	1087	2 PW JT8D-217	66678	F10Y125		
☐ N953AS	Boeing (Douglas) MD-82 (DC-9-82)	49386 / 1287	N784JA	0086	1087	2 PW JT8D-217A	67812	F10Y125		
☐ N954AS	Boeing (Douglas) MD-82 (DC-9-82)	49387 / 1283	N785JA	0086	1087	2 PW JT8D-217A	67812	F10Y125		
☐ N955AS	Boeing (Douglas) MD-82 (DC-9-82)	48080 / 1022	N778JA	0081	1087	2 PW JT8D-217	66678	F10Y125		
☐ N956AS	Boeing (Douglas) MD-82 (DC-9-82)	48079 / 1016	N779JA	0081	1087	2 PW JT8D-217	66678	F10Y125		lsf Aviation Assets 956 Inc.
☐ N957AS	Boeing (Douglas) MD-82 (DC-9-82)	49126 / 1080	N780JA	0082	1087	2 PW JT8D-217	66678	F10Y125		lsf CITG
☐ N958AS	Boeing (Douglas) MD-83 (DC-9-83)	53024 / 1825		0091	0391	2 PW JT8D-219	72575	F10Y125		
☐ N960AS	Boeing (Douglas) MD-83 (DC-9-83)	53074 / 1976		0092	0392	2 PW JT8D-219	72575	F10Y125		
☐ N961AS	Boeing (Douglas) MD-83 (DC-9-83)	53075 / 1977		0092	0392	2 PW JT8D-219	72575	F10Y125		
☐ N962AS	Boeing (Douglas) MD-83 (DC-9-83)	53076 / 1988		0092	0492	2 PW JT8D-219	72575	F10Y125		
☐ N963AS	Boeing (Douglas) MD-83 (DC-9-83)	53077 / 1995		0492	0592	2 PW JT8D-219	72575	F10Y125		
☐ N964AS	Boeing (Douglas) MD-83 (DC-9-83)	53078 / 1996		0092	0692	2 PW JT8D-219	72575	F10Y125		
☐ N965AS	Boeing (Douglas) MD-83 (DC-9-83)	53079 / 2004		0092	0692	2 PW JT8D-219	72575	F10Y125		
☐ N967AS	Boeing (Douglas) MD-82 (DC-9-82)	49103 / 1083	N782JA	0082	1087	2 PW JT8D-217A	67812	F10Y125		lsf INGL
☐ N968AS	Boeing (Douglas) MD-83 (DC-9-83)	53016 / 1850		0091	0991	2 PW JT8D-219	72575	F10Y125		

registration	type of aircraft	cn/fn	ex/ex*	mfd	del	powered by	mtow kg	configuration	selcal	name/fln/specialitites/remarks
☐ N969AS	Boeing (Douglas) MD-83 (DC-9-83)	53063 / 1851		0091	0991	2 PW JT8D-219	72575	F10Y125		
☐ N972AS	Boeing (Douglas) MD-83 (DC-9-83)	53448 / 2074		0094	0394	2 PW JT8D-219	72575	F10Y125		
☐ N973AS	Boeing (Douglas) MD-83 (DC-9-83)	53449 / 2077		0094	0394	2 PW JT8D-219	72575	F10Y125		
☐ N974AS	Boeing (Douglas) MD-83 (DC-9-83)	53450 / 2078		0094	0394	2 PW JT8D-219	72575	F10Y125		
☐ N975AS	Boeing (Douglas) MD-83 (DC-9-83)	53451 / 2083		0094	0594	2 PW JT8D-219	72575	F10Y125		
☐ N976AS	Boeing (Douglas) MD-83 (DC-9-83)	53452 / 2109		0095	0495	2 PW JT8D-219	72575	F10Y125		
☐ N977AS	Boeing (Douglas) MD-83 (DC-9-83)	53453 / 2112		0095	0595	2 PW JT8D-219	72575	F10Y125		
☐ N979AS	Boeing (Douglas) MD-83 (DC-9-83)	53471 / 2139		0096	0596	2 PW JT8D-219	72575	F10Y125		
☐ N981AS	Boeing (Douglas) MD-83 (DC-9-83)	53472 / 2178		0097	0497	2 PW JT8D-219	72575	F10Y125		
☐ N982AS	Boeing (Douglas) MD-83 (DC-9-83)	53473 / 2183		0097	0597	2 PW JT8D-219	72575	F10Y125		
☐ N671AS	Boeing 737-990	30017				2 CFMI CFM56-7B26	79016	FY174		oo-delivery 0001
☐ N672AS	Boeing 737-990	30016				2 CFMI CFM56-7B26	79016	FY174		oo-delivery 0001
☐ N673AS	Boeing 737-990					2 CFMI CFM56-7B26	79016	FY174		oo-delivery 0001
☐ N674AS	Boeing 737-990					2 CFMI CFM56-7B26	79016	FY174		oo-delivery 0002
☐ N675AS	Boeing 737-990					2 CFMI CFM56-7B26	79016	FY174		oo-delivery 0002
☐ N676AS	Boeing 737-990					2 CFMI CFM56-7B26	79016	FY174		oo-delivery 0002
☐ N677AS	Boeing 737-990					2 CFMI CFM56-7B26	79016	FY174		oo-delivery 0002
☐ N678AS	Boeing 737-990					2 CFMI CFM56-7B26	79016	FY174		oo-delivery 0003
☐ N679AS	Boeing 737-990					2 CFMI CFM56-7B26	79016	FY174		oo-delivery 0003
☐ N681AS	Boeing 737-990					2 CFMI CFM56-7B26	79016	FY174		oo-delivery 0003

ALASKA AIR TAXI (Jack B. Barber dba)

Anchorage-Lake Hood SPB, AK

5045 Aircraft Drive, Anchorage, AK 99502, USA ☎ (907) 243-3944 Tx: none Fax: (907) 248-2993 SITA: n/a
F: 1990 ⋀⋀⋀ n/a Head: Jack B. Barber Net: n/a

☐ N732XR	Cessna U206G Stationair 6 II	U20604735		0079	0993	1 CO IO-520-F	1633			Floats / Wheels
☐ N9129M	Cessna U206E Super Skywagon	U20601529		0070	0293	1 CO IO-520-F	1633			Floats / Wheels
☐ N10395	De Havilland DHC-2 Beaver I	1354	CF-MAY	0060	0794	1 PW R-985	2313			lsf B&B Recr. Prop. / Floats/Wheel-Skis
☐ N62197	De Havilland DHC-2 Beaver I	1177	56-419	0057	1293	1 PW R-985	2313			lsf pvt / Floats/Wheel-Skis

ALASKA AIR TRANSIT – AAT (J & M Alaska Air Tours, Inc. dba)

Anchorage-Merrill Field, AK

1000 Merrill Field Drive, Anchorage, AK 99501, USA ☎ (907) 276-5422 Tx: none Fax: (907) 276-5400 SITA: n/a
F: 1992 ⋀⋀⋀ n/a Head: Doug Ferguson Net: n/a

☐ N3974X	Piper PA-34-200T Seneca II	34-7670011		0076	0696	2 CO TSIO-360-E	2073			
☐ N34WM	Piper PA-31-350 Navajo Chieftain	31-7305125		0073	1192	2 LY TIO-540-J2BD	3175			

ALASKA BUSH CARRIER, Inc.

Anchorage-Lake Hood SPB, AK   *Alaska Bush Carrier*

4801 Aircraft Drive, Anchorage, AK 99502, USA ☎ (907) 243-3127 Tx: none Fax: (907) 243-6670 SITA: n/a
F: 1962 ⋀⋀⋀ 5 Head: Patricia D'Aoust Net: n/a

☐ N756HL	Cessna U206G Stationair	U20604103		0077	0694	1 CO IO-520-F	1633			Floats / Wheel-Skis

ALASKA BUSH FLOATPLANE SERVICE, Co. (Seasonal April-September ops only)

Talkeetna, AK

PO Box 264, Talkeetna, AK 99676, USA ☎ (907) 733-1693 Tx: none Fax: none SITA: n/a
F: 1996 ⋀⋀⋀ n/a Head: Elbert G. Sturgis Net: n/a

☐ N1046V	Cessna TU206F Turbo Stationair	U20602418		0074	0396	1 CO TSIO-520-C	1633			Floats

ALASKA CARGO SERVICE – A.C.S. (Donald E. Darden dba)

Dillingham, AK

PO Box 251, Dillingham, AK 99576, USA ☎ (907) 842-5491 Tx: none Fax: (907) 842-2432 SITA: n/a
F: 1982 ⋀⋀⋀ n/a Head: Donald E. Darden Net: n/a

☐ N5322G	De Havilland DHC-3 Otter	128	55-3280	0056	0782	1 PW R-1340	3629	Freighter		

ALASKA CENTRAL EXPRESS, Inc. = KO / AER (Subsidiary of Western States Investment / formerly Yutana Airlines)

Anchorage-Int'l, AK

PO Box 190248, Anchorage, AK 99519, USA ☎ (907) 245-0231 Tx: none Fax: (907) 245-0246 SITA: n/a
F: 1987 ⋀⋀⋀ n/a Head: Donald Swortwood ICAO: ACE AIR Net: n/a

☐ N75941	Cessna 207A Stationair 8 II	20700656		0080	0896	1 CO IO-520-F	1724	Freighter		
☐ N9874M	Cessna 207A Stationair 8 II	20700745		0081	0498	1 CO IO-520-F	1724	Freighter		
☐ N9957M	Cessna 207A Stationair 8 II	20700764		0083	0497	1 CO IO-520-F	1724	Freighter		
☐ N1563C	Beech 1900C-1 Airliner	UC-20	N31187*	0088	0596	2 PWC PT6A-65B	7530	Freighter		
☐ N41UE	Beech 1900C-1 Airliner	UC-41	N219GL	0088	0597	2 PWC PT6A-65B	7530	Freighter		
☐ N45GL	Beech 1900C-1 Airliner	UC-45	OY-CCH	0088	0597	2 PWC PT6A-65B	7530	Freighter		
☐ N5632C	Beech 1900C-1 Airliner	UC-81	N15189*	0089	0596	2 PWC PT6A-65B	7530	Freighter		

ALASKA FLYERS (MAA, Inc. dba / Seasonal April-October ops only)

Kaktovik, AK

PO Box 67, Kaktovik, AK 99747, USA ☎ (907) 640-6324 Tx: none Fax: (907) 640-6218 SITA: n/a
F: 1988 ⋀⋀⋀ 3 Head: Walt Audi Net: n/a Aircraft below MTOW 1361kg: Piper PA-18

☐ N1658U	Cessna 207 Skywagon	20700258		0074	0489	1 CO IO-520-F	1724			

ALASKA FLY'N FISH CHARTERS (Harold J. Laughlin dba / Seasonal May-October ops only)

Juneau-SPB, AK

9604 Kelly Court, Juneau, AK 99801, USA ☎ (907) 780-6409 Tx: none Fax: (907) 780-6411 SITA: n/a
F: 1991 ⋀⋀⋀ n/a Head: Harold J. Laughlin Net: n/a

☐ N8419Q	Cessna U206F Stationair II	U20603279		0076	0593	1 CO IO-550-F	1633			Floats

ALASKA ISLAND AIR, Inc. = AAK (formerly RAM Aviation)

Kotzebue-Ralph Wien Memorial, AK

PO Box 1167, Kotzebue, AK 99752, USA ☎ (907) 442-2468 Tx: none Fax: (907) 442-2205 SITA: n/a
F: 1986 ⋀⋀⋀ n/a Head: Michael A. Spisak ICAO: ALASKA ISLAND Net: n/a

☐ N1047F	Cessna A185F Skywagon	18502704		0075	0896	1 CO IO-520-D	1520			lsf pvt
☐ N185QB	Cessna 185 Skywagon	185-0131		0061	0994	1 CO IO-470-F	1451			lsf pvt
☐ N8013Z	Cessna U206 Super Skywagon	U206-0413		0065	0192	1 CO IO-520-A	1497			lsf pvt
☐ N9647F	Cessna 208 Caravan I	20800111	ZS-LXK	0087	0798	1 PWC PT6A-114	3629			lsf pvt
☐ N32AL	Boeing (Douglas) DC-3C (C-47B-35-DK)	33368	N132AL	0044	0693	2 PW R-1830	12202	Freighter		lsf pvt

ALASKA MOUNTAIN AIR, Inc. (Seasonal May-October ops only)

Palmer, AK

PO Box 1, Palmer, AK 99645, USA ☎ (907) 745-3477 Tx: none Fax: (907) 745-3477 SITA: n/a
F: 1987 ⋀⋀⋀ n/a Head: Charles A. Akers Net: n/a

☐ N5227R	Cessna A185F Skywagon	18503023		0076	0387	1 CO IO-520-D	1520			Floats

ALASKAN AIRVENTURES (Airventures Associates, Inc. dba)

Snowshoe Lake, AK

HC-1, Box 2510, Glennallen, AK 99588-9504, USA ☎ (907) 822-3905 Tx: none Fax: (907) 822-5362 SITA: n/a
F: 1987 ⋀⋀⋀ n/a Head: Clarence P. Bartley, Jr. Net: n/a

☐ N73DA	Cessna 185 Skywagon	185-0119		0061	1088	1 CO IO-470-F	1451			lsf Hennesy Leasing

ALASKA SEAPLANE SERVICE, Llc = UI (formerly Loken Aviation, Inc.)

Juneau-Int'l, AK

8995 Yandukin Drive, Juneau, AK 99801, USA ☎ (907) 789-7880 Tx: none Fax: (907) 789-7076 SITA: n/a
F: 1954 ⋀⋀⋀ n/a Head: Craig Loken Net: n/a Aircraft below MTOW 1361kg: Cessna 180 (on Floats)

☐ N1779U	Cessna 207A Skywagon	20700379		0077	0097	1 CO IO-520-F	1724			lsf pvt
☐ N4794C	De Havilland DHC-2 Beaver I	342	51-16545	0051	0895	1 PW R-985	2313			lsf Inian Inc. / Floats
☐ N60077	De Havilland DHC-2 Beaver I	1419	LV-GLJ	0060	1297	1 PW R-985	2313			lsf Inian Inc. / Floats

ALASKA SKYTREKKING (Customized Alaskan Adventures dba / Seasonal April-September ops only)

Anchorage-Lake Hood SPB, AK

6608 Blackberry, Anchorage, AK 99502, USA ☎ (907) 243-1649 Tx: none Fax: (907) 248-6351 SITA: n/a
F: 1987 ⋀⋀⋀ n/a Head: Charles J. Wirschem Net: n/a Aircraft below MTOW 1361kg: Piper PA-18 (Floats / Wheel-Skis)

☐ N4786Q	Cessna A185F Skywagon II	18503556		0078	0787	1 CO IO-520-D	1520			Floats / Wheel-Skis

ALASKA'S LAKE CLARK INN & AIR (Mark E. Lang dba)

Port Alsworth, AK

1 Lang Lane, Port Alsworth, AK 99653-9999, USA ☎ (907) 781-2224 Tx: none Fax: (907) 781-2252 SITA: n/a
F: 1996 ⋀⋀⋀ n/a Head: Mark E. Lang Net: n/a

☐ N9939Z	Cessna U206G Stationair 6 II	U20606758		0083	1296	1 CO IO-520-F	1633			Floats / Wheel-Skis

ALASKA WEST AIR, Inc. (Affiliated with Alaska West Guides & Outfitters, Inc. & Wolverine Leasing/ Seasonal May-October ops only)

Kenai-Island Lake SPB, AK   ALASKA WEST AIR

PO Box 8553, Nikiski, AK 99635, USA ☎ (907) 776-5147 Tx: n/a Fax: (907) 776-5623 SITA: n/a
F: 1983 ⋀⋀⋀ n/a Head: Danny E. Brewer, Jr. Net: n/a Aircraft below MTOW 1361kg: Piper PA-18 (on Floats)

☐ N115AW	Cessna A185F Skywagon	18502941	N4364R	0076	0687	1 CO IO-520-D	1520			Floats
☐ N1432Z	De Havilland DHC-2 Beaver I	797	54-1668	0054	0787	1 PW R-985	2309			Floats
☐ N211AW	De Havilland DHC-2 Beaver I	1360	CF-XGG	0057	0690	1 PW R-985	2309			Floats
☐ N8134G	De Havilland DHC-2 Beaver I	1410	N90508	0058	1195	1 PW R-985	2309			lsf pvt / Floats
☐ N87AW	De Havilland DHC-3 Turbo Otter	52	C-FMPO	0054	0696	1 PWC PT6A-135A	3629			cvtd Otter

ALERT KRH (Kalispell Regional Hospital dba)

Kalispell-Hospital Helipad, MT

310 Sunnyview Lane, Kalispell, MT 59901, USA ☎ (406) 752-1763 Tx: none Fax: (406) 756-4748 SITA: n/a
F: 1975 ✈ 5 Head: William Diers Net: n/a

☐ N215KH	Bell 206L-3 LongRanger III	51215		0087	0787	1 AN 250-C30P	1882	EMS		

ALEUTIAN AIR, Ltd

Unalaska, AK

PO Box 330, Dutch Harbor, AK 99692, USA ☎ (907) 581-1686 Tx: none Fax: (907) 581-1306 SITA: n/a
F: 1983 ✈ 2 Head: Charles T. Madsen Net: n/a

☐ N686Q	Beech E18S	BA-400		0059	0683	2 PW R-985	4581	7 Pax / Frtr		

ALEXAIR (Alika Aviation, Inc. dba)

Kahului-Heliport, HI & Torrance-Municipal, CA

Hangar 108, Kahului Heliport, Kahului, HI 96732, USA ☎ (808) 871-0792 Tx: none Fax: (808) 871-8193 SITA: n/a
F: 1971 ✈ n/a Head: Shelly A. Alexander Net: n/a Aircraft below MTOW 1361kg: Hughes 369HS (500C)

☐ N58252	MD Helicopters MD 500D (Hughes 369D)	1080364D		0078	1292	1 AN 250-C20B	1361			lsf pvt
☐ N58267	MD Helicopters MD 500D (Hughes 369D)	390473D		0079	1292	1 AN 250-C20B	1361			lsf pvt
☐ N8625F	MD Helicopters MD 500D (Hughes 369D)	470111D		0077	1085	1 AN 250-C20B	1361			lsf pvt
☐ N1404W	Bell 206B JetRanger	298		0068	0987	1 AN 250-C20	1451			lsf pvt / cvtd 206A

ALII AVIATION, Inc.

Hilo-Int'l, HI

PO Box 4248, Hilo, HI 96720, USA ☎ (808) 969-9319 Tx: none Fax: (808) 969-3997 SITA: n/a
F: 1992 ✈ n/a Head: Ray Hodge Net: n/a

☐ N3978Y	Eurocopter (Aerosp.) SA315B Lama	2520		0078		1 TU Artouste IIIB	1950			lsf Roberts Aircraft Co.
☐ N48HJ	Eurocopter (Aerosp.) SA315B Lama	2341		0078		1 TU Artouste IIIB	1950			lsf Roberts Aircraft Co.

ALLEGHENY AIRLINES, Inc. = US / ALO (US Airways Express) (Subsidiary of US Airways Group, Inc.)

Middletown-Harrisburg-Int'l, PA

PO Box 432, Middletown, PA 17057-0432, USA ☎ (717) 944-2781 Tx: 842533 Fax: (717) 944-9183 SITA: n/a
F: 1941 ✈ 1350 Head: Keith D. Houk IATA: 395 ICAO: ALLEGHENY Net: http://www.usairways.com
All aircraft are operated as US AIRWAYS EXPRESS (in full such colours & titles), a commuter system to provide feeder connection at USAir major hubs, using US flight numbers.

☐ N804EX	De Havilland DHC-8-102 Dash 8	227	C-GFYI*	0090	0890	2 PWC PW120A	15649	Y37		op in US Airways Express-colors
☐ N805EX	De Havilland DHC-8-102 Dash 8	228	C-GLOT*	0090	0990	2 PWC PW120A	15649	Y37		op in US Airways Express-colors
☐ N806EX	De Havilland DHC-8-102 Dash 8	263	C-GEVP*	0091	0591	2 PWC PW120A	15649	Y37		op in US Airways Express-colors
☐ N807EX	De Havilland DHC-8-102 Dash 8	292	C-GFQL*	0091	0891	2 PWC PW120A	15649	Y37		op in US Airways Express-colors
☐ N808EX	De Havilland DHC-8-102 Dash 8	299	C-GDKL*	0091	1091	2 PWC PW120A	15649	Y37		op in US Airways Express-colors
☐ N809EX	De Havilland DHC-8-102 Dash 8	302	C-GFYI*	0091	1191	2 PWC PW120A	15649	Y37		op in US Airways Express-colors
☐ N810EX	De Havilland DHC-8-102 Dash 8	308	C-GDKL*	0091	0592	2 PWC PW120A	15649	Y37		op in US Airways Express-colors
☐ N812EX	De Havilland DHC-8-102 Dash 8	312	C-GDNG*	0091	0592	2 PWC PW120A	15649	Y37		op in US Airways Express-colors
☐ N814EX	De Havilland DHC-8-102 Dash 8	318	C-GDNG*	0092	0592	2 PWC PW120A	15649	Y37		op in US Airways Express-colors
☐ N815EX	De Havilland DHC-8-102 Dash 8	321	C-GDFT*	0092	0592	2 PWC PW120A	15649	Y37		op in US Airways Express-colors
☐ N816EX	De Havilland DHC-8-102 Dash 8	329	C-GEVP*	0092	0592	2 PWC PW120A	15649	Y37		op in US Airways Express-colors
☐ N817EX	De Havilland DHC-8-102 Dash 8	191	N810AW	0090	0592	2 PWC PW120A	15649	Y37		op in US Airways Express-colors
☐ N818EX	De Havilland DHC-8-102 Dash 8	235	N812AW	0090	0592	2 PWC PW120A	15649	Y37		op in US Airways Express-colors
☐ N819EX	De Havilland DHC-8-102 Dash 8	016	N803MX	0085	0193	2 PWC PW120A	15649	Y37		cvtd -101 / op in US Airways Express-cs
☐ N820EX	De Havilland DHC-8-102 Dash 8	019	N804MX	0085	0593	2 PWC PW120A	15649	Y37		cvtd -101 / op in US Airways Express-cs
☐ N821EX	De Havilland DHC-8-102 Dash 8	173	N808AW	0089	0393	2 PWC PW120A	15649	Y37		op in US Airways Express-colors
☐ N822EX	De Havilland DHC-8-102 Dash 8	187	N809AW	0089	0693	2 PWC PW120A	15649	Y37		op in US Airways Express-colors
☐ N824EX	De Havilland DHC-8-102 Dash 8	387		0094	0994	2 PWC PW120A	15649	Y37		op in US Airways Express-colors
☐ N824MA	De Havilland DHC-8-102 Dash 8	327	C-GFQL*	0092	0798	2 PWC PW120A	15649	Y37		lsf DHC / op in US Airways Express-cs
☐ N825EX	De Havilland DHC-8-102 Dash 8	388		0094	1094	2 PWC PW120A	15649	Y37		op in US Airways Express-colors
☐ N826EX	De Havilland DHC-8-102 Dash 8	389		0094	1094	2 PWC PW120A	15649	Y37		op in US Airways Express-colors
☐ N827EX	De Havilland DHC-8-102 Dash 8	390		0094	1194	2 PWC PW120A	15649	Y37		op in US Airways Express-colors
☐ N828EX	De Havilland DHC-8-102 Dash 8	392		0094	1294	2 PWC PW120A	15649	Y37		op in US Airways Express-colors
☐ N828MA	De Havilland DHC-8-102 Dash 8	333	C-GEOA*	0092	1298	2 PWC PW120A	15649	Y37		lsf DHC / op in US Airways Express-cs
☐ N829EX	De Havilland DHC-8-102 Dash 8	146	N805AW	0089	0795	2 PWC PW120A	15649	Y37		op in US Airways Express-colors
☐ N829MA	De Havilland DHC-8-102 Dash 8	335	C-GFCF*	0092	1298	2 PWC PW120A	15649	Y37		lsf DHC / op in US Airways Express-cs
☐ N830EX	De Havilland DHC-8-102 Dash 8	155	N806AW	0089	0795	2 PWC PW120A	15649	Y37		op in US Airways Express-colors
☐ N831EX	De Havilland DHC-8-102 Dash 8	160	N807AW	0089	0595	2 PWC PW120A	15649	Y37		op in US Airways Express-colors
☐ N831MA	De Havilland DHC-8-102 Dash 8	339	C-GDFT*	0092	1298	2 PWC PW120A	15649	Y37		lsf DHC / op in US Airways Express-cs
☐ N832EX	De Havilland DHC-8-102 Dash 8	280	N415AW	0091	0495	2 PWC PW120A	15649	Y37		op in US Airways Express-colors
☐ N833EX	De Havilland DHC-8-102 Dash 8	282	N416AW	0091	0495	2 PWC PW120A	15649	Y37		op in US Airways Express-colors
☐ N834EX	De Havilland DHC-8-102 Dash 8	285	N417AW	0091	0495	2 PWC PW120A	15649	Y37		op in US Airways Express-colors
☐ N835EX	De Havilland DHC-8-102 Dash 8	289	N418AW	0091	0495	2 PWC PW120A	15649	Y37		op in US Airways Express-colors
☐ N836EX	De Havilland DHC-8-102 Dash 8	297	N419AW	0091	0495	2 PWC PW120A	15649	Y37		op in US Airways Express-colors
☐ N837EX	De Havilland DHC-8-102 Dash 8	217	N976HA	0090	0197	2 PWC PW120A	15649	Y37		op in US Airways Express-colors
☐ N838EX	De Havilland DHC-8-102 Dash 8	220	N977HA	0090	0197	2 PWC PW120A	15649	Y37		op in US Airways Express-colors
☐ N839EX	De Havilland DHC-8-102 Dash 8	226	N978HA	0090	0497	2 PWC PW120A	15649	Y37		op in US Airways Express-colors
☐ EI-CBJ	De Havilland DHC-8-102 Dash 8	215	C-GFCF*	0090	0393	2 PWC PW120A	15649	Y37		lsf GECA / op in US Airways Express-cs
☐ EI-CHP	De Havilland DHC-8-102 Dash 8	258	VH-FNQ	0091	0693	2 PWC PW120A	15649	Y37		lsf GECA / op in US Airways Express-cs

ALLEGIANT AIR, Inc. (formerly Westjet Express Airlines)

Fesno-Yosemite Int'l, GA

4955 East Anderson, Suite 120, Fresno, CA 93727, USA ☎ (209) 251-2200 Tx: none Fax: (209) 454-7795 SITA: n/a
F: 1998 ✈ n/a Head: Mitchell Allee Net: n/a

☐ N127NK	Boeing (Douglas) DC-9-21	47361 / 488	SE-DBO	0069	0698	2 PW JT8D-11 (HK3/ABS)	44452	Y89		lsf MJG Jet Leasing

ALLEN COUNTY AVIATION, Corp.

Lima-Allen County, OH

700 Airport Drive, Lima, OH 45804, USA ☎ (419) 227-3225 Tx: none Fax: (419) 224-9773 SITA: n/a
F: 1986 ✈ n/a Head: John L. Galvin Net: n/a

☐ N82JG	Beech Baron B55 (95-B55)	TC-2435	N62069	0082	0485	2 CO IO-470-L	2313			
☐ N86JG	Beech King Air C90A	LJ-1076	N69275	0084	0287	2 PWC PT6A-21	4377			

ALLIANCE AIR (G and G Flight, Inc. dba)

Denver-Front Range, CO

10421 East 107th Place, Brighton, CO 80601, USA ☎ (970) 287-5175 Tx: none Fax: (970) 287-5130 SITA: n/a
F: 1993 ✈ n/a Head: Edouard A. Garneau Net: n/a

☐ N670CC	Cessna 401	401-0287		0068	0893	2 CO TSIO-520-E	2858			lsf Alliance Aviation Inc.
☐ N66906	Piper PA-31-350 Navajo Chieftain	31-7405197		0074	0695	2 LY TIO-540-J2BD	3175			lsf Alliance Aviation Inc.

ALLIANT HEALTH SYSTEM, Inc. (Sister company of Central American Airways, Inc.)

Louisville-Bowman Field, KY

Bowman Field, Louisville, KY 40205, USA ☎ (502) 458-3211 Tx: none Fax: (502) 458-1109 SITA: n/a
F: 1985 ✈ n/a Head: Stephen A. Williams Net: n/a

☐ N94KC	Beech King Air 200	BB-172	N68RR	0076	0994	2 PWC PT6A-41	5670	EMS		lsf Alliant Hospitals Inc.

ALLIED AIR FREIGHT, Inc.

Nashua-Boire Field, NH

99 Pine Hill Road, Nashua, NH 03063, USA ☎ (603) 594-8655 Tx: none Fax: (603) 594-0176 SITA: n/a
F: 1996 ✈ 10 Head: Dan Walus Net: n/a

☐ N54AA	Boeing (Douglas) DC-3C (C-47A-10-DK)	12475	C-FGHL	0042	0598	2 PW R-1830	12202	Freighter		
☐ N57NA	Boeing (Douglas) DC-3C (C-47A-80-DL)	19560	FinAF DO-6	0044	0496	2 PW R-1830	12202	Freighter		

ALLIED HELICOPTERS (Allied Helicopter Service, Inc. dba)

Tulsa-Downtown Airpark, OK

PO Box 6216, Tulsa, OK 74148, USA ☎ (918) 425-7558 Tx: none Fax: none SITA: n/a
F: 1949 ✈ n/a Head: Roy B. David Net: n/a Aircraft below MTOW 1361kg: Bell 47G-3B & 47G-4

☐ N59617	Bell 206B JetRanger	1517		0074	0485	1 AN 250-C20	1451			lsf Allied Helicopter Int'l Inc

ALLIED SIGNAL AVIATION SERVICES (Aviation division of Allied Signal, Inc.)

Morristown,NJ / Olathe,KS / Phoenix-Sky Harbor Int'l,AZ

12 Airport Road, Morristown, NJ 07960, USA ☎ (973) 455-4274 Tx: none Fax: (973) 455-5886 SITA: n/a
F: n/a ✈ n/a Head: Skip Penizotto ICAO: BLUE LINE Net: http://www.alliedsignal.com Aircraft below MTOW 5000kg (for Testing & Marketing): Beech 55/90, Cessna 205, MD900, Mooney M20, Piper PA-28 & PA-46
Non-commercial aviation department conducting non-commercial corporate transport, marketing & testing flights for its parent only.

☐ N176AS	Sikorsky S-76B	760465		0097	0897	2 PWC PT6B-36A	5307	Corporate 6Pax		based Morristown
☐ N200ZC	Beech King Air 200	BB-41		0075	1194	2 PWC PT6A-41	5670	Testbed / 10Pax		based Olathe
☐ N670AS	Sabreliner 65 (Rockwell NA265-65)	465-58	N65AM	0081	1094	2 GA TFE731-3R-1D	10886	Demo / 8Pax		based Olathe
☐ N650AS	Cessna 650 Citation VII	650-7053	N344AS	0095	0895	2 GA TFE731-4R-2S	10183	Corporate 8Pax		std Morristown / for sale
☐ N680AS	BAe 4101 Jetstream 41	41030	N410JA	0094	1095	2 GA TPE331-14HR-805H	10886	Corporate 14Pax		lsf MDFC Equipment Leasing / based MMU
☐ N200GT	Dassault Falcon 20C	137	N777PV	0068	1288	2 GE CF700-2D2	12400	Testbed		based Phoenix
☐ N610AS	Dassault Falcon 2000	8	F-WWMF*	0095	1095	2 CFE CFE738-1-1B	16556	Corporate 9Pax	HJ-BE	lsf Bendix Leasing Co. / based MMU
☐ N40AS	Dassault Falcon 50	171	N171FJ	0087	0587	2 GA TFE731-3-1D	17600	Corporate 9Pax		based PHX / to be re-reg. N620AS
☐ N600AS	Dassault Falcon 900EX	17	F-WWFB*	0097	1097	3 GA TFE731-60-1C	22226	Corporate		based Morristown
☐ N580AS	Convair 580	2	N113AP	0152	0192	2 AN 501-D13	24766	Testbed / 16Pax		cvtdCV340-31/based Fort Lauderdale-Exec
☐ N720GT	Boeing 720-051B	18384 / 237	OY-APZ	0061	1187	4 PW JT3D-3B	106594	Engine Testbed		based Phoenix

261 registration type of aircraft cn/fn ex/ex* mfd del powered by mtow kg configuration selcal name/fln/specialitites/remarks

ALL STAR HELICOPTERS, Inc.

Dayton-James M. Cox Int'l, OH

433 North Dixie Drive, Vandalia, OH 45377, USA ☎ (937) 898-8200 Tx: none Fax: (937) 898-8288 SITA: n/a
F: 1994 ⁂ n/a Head: Michael Huffman Net: n/a

☐ N2068W	Bell 206B JetRanger III	3389		0081	0496	1 AN 250-C20B	1451			

ALL-STAR HELICOPTERS, Inc. (Sister company of All-Star Video Productions, Inc.)

Dallas-Love Field, TX

PO Box 1251, Harrison, TX 75001, USA ☎ (214) 956-1810 Tx: none Fax: (214) 956-1813 SITA: n/a
F: 1986 ⁂ n/a Head: Clarence J. Lott Net: n/a

☐ N444MA	Bell 222	47078	XA-SII	0082	0897	2 LY LTS101-650C.3	3561			lsf Mullen Air Inc.

ALLWEST FREIGHT, Inc.

Sterling-South Gasline, AK

PO Box 131, Sterling, AK 99672, USA ☎ (907) 262-5676 Tx: none Fax: (907) 260-5327 SITA: n/a
F: 1997 ⁂ n/a Head: William H. Michel Net: n/a

☐ N73123	Cessna 207A Stationair 7 II	20700561		0079	0897	1 CO IO-550-F	1724			
☐ N549WB	Shorts Skyvan 3 Variant 100 (SC-7)	SH1911	XA-SRD	0073	0497	2 GA TPE331-2-201A	5670	Freighter		

ALOHA AIRLINES, Inc. = AQ / AAH (Subsidiary of Aloha Air Group, Inc. / formerly Trans-Pacific Airlines Ltd)

Honolulu-Int'l, HI

PO Box 30028, Honolulu, HI 96820-0028, USA ☎ (808) 836-4210 Tx: none Fax: (808) 833-3671 SITA: HNLEXAQ
F: 1946 ⁂ 2270 Head: Han H. Ching IATA: 327 ICAO: ALOHA Net: http://www.alohaair.com Aloha commuter services are operated on behalf of Aloha by ISLAND AIR, for details – see under that carrier.

☐ N726AL	Boeing 737-297 (A)	22426 / 738		0081	0688	2 PW JT8D-9A	53070	F10Y111	BL-CH	Lunalilo / lsf POLA
☐ N802AL	Boeing 737-2S5C (A)	22148 / 663	C-GENL	0080	1286	2 PW JT8D-9A	53070	Freighter		Kamehameha Pai'ea / lsf ACG Acquisition
☐ N804AL	Boeing 737-2Q9 (A)	21719 / 551	OO-TEK	0079	0289	2 PW JT8D-9A	54204	F10Y111		Kauikeaouli / lsf ACG Acquisition
☐ N805AL	Boeing 737-2M6C (A)	21809 / 637	V8-UED	0080	0790	2 PW JT8D-15	53070	F10Y103 / Frtr		Hoapili / lsf POLA
☐ N806AL	Boeing 737-2S2C (A)	21927 / 600	CC-CHU	0079	0590	2 PW JT8D-9A	56472	F10Y103 / Frtr	BC-AG	Lot Kapua'iwa
☐ N807AL	Boeing 737-2T4 (A)	23443 / 1151	B-2511	0085	0594	2 PW JT8D-9A	56472	F10Y111		Ke'opuolani / lsf GECA
☐ N808AL	Boeing 737-2T4 (A)	23445 / 1155	B-2514	0085	0694	2 PW JT8D-9A	56472	F10Y111		Kaleleonalani / lsf GECA
☐ N810AL	Boeing 737-2Y5 (A)	24031 / 1523	9H-ABG	0088	0495	2 PW JT8D-9A	56472	F10Y111	CG-JK	Lu'ukia / lsf FSBU Trustee
☐ N816AL	Boeing 737-2X6C (A)	23122 / 1036	TF-ABE	0084	0695	2 PW JT8D-9A	58105	F10Y103 / Frtr	DG-BF	lsf Ajet Inc.
☐ N817AL	Boeing 737-2X6C (A)	23292 / 1113	N674MA	0785	1295	2 PW JT8D-9A	58105	F6Y107 / Frtr	DG-CE	lsf BJet Inc.
☐ N818AL	Boeing 737-230 (A)	22117 / 703	D-ABFF	0081	1096	2 PW JT8D-9A	50900	F10Y111		lsf JETZ
☐ N819AL	Boeing 737-25A (A)	23791 / 1486	N685MA	1287	1295	2 PW JT8D-9A	56472	F6Y110		lsf Boeing Capital Corp.
☐ N820AL	Boeing 737-230 (A)	22138 / 790	D-ABHM	0081	0896	2 PW JT8D-9A	50900	F10Y111		lsf JETZ
☐ N821AL	Boeing 737-230 (A)	23155 / 1079	D-ABMC	0085	0996	2 PW JT8D-9A (HK3/NOR)	50900	F10Y111		lsf Bancorp Leasing Hawaii
☐ N823AL	Boeing 737-230 (A)	23154 / 1078	D-ABMB	0085	0497	2 PW JT8D-9A (HK3/NOR)	50900	F10Y111		lsf JETZ
☐ N824AL	Boeing 737-282 (A)	23045 / 978	CS-TEO	0083	0398	2 PW JT8D-9A	56472	F10Y111		lsf Aircraft No. 2 Llc
☐ N826AL	Boeing 737-282C (A)	23051 / 1002	CS-TEQ	0083	1198	2 PW JT8D-9A	56472	F10Y103 / Frtr		lsf AARL
☐ N827AL	Boeing 737-209 (A)	23913 / 1579	PK-RIO	0688	0698	2 PW JT8D-9A	52390	F10Y111		lsf Airlease Industries Ltd

ALPHA AVIATION, Inc.

Morristown-Moore Murrell, TN

312 Piper Street, Morristown, TN 37814-1020, USA ☎ (423) 581-6583 Tx: none Fax: (423) 581-8029 SITA: n/a
F: 1992 ⁂ 1 Head: Jerry E. Reece Net: n/a

☐ N310KC	Cessna 310R II	310R0697		0076	0193	2 CO IO-520-M	2495			

ALPHA CENTURY AVIATION (Century Aviation, Inc. dba / Sister company of Jet East, Inc.)

Dallas-Love Field, TX

7515 Lemmon Avenue, Hangar P, Dallas, TX 75209, USA ☎ (972) 351-6571 Tx: none Fax: (972) 350-4287 SITA: n/a
F: 1990 ⁂ n/a Head: Aubry Von Rodman Net: n/a In addition to the listed commercially operated aircraft also operates a number of non-commercial executive jets on behalf of private companies.

☐ N195MA	Beech King Air 100	B-20	N49GW	0069	0592	2 PWC PT6A-28	4808			
☐ N444WW	Learjet 25D	25D-283	N312GK	0079	1092	2 GE CJ610-6	6804			

ALPHA JET INTERNATIONAL, Inc. = EHD (Darby Aviation dba)

Muscle Shoals, AL

PO Box 471, Sheffield, AL 35660, USA ☎ (205) 389-3241 Tx: none Fax: (205) 389-3249 SITA: n/a
F: 1947 ⁂ n/a Head: Elton H. Darby ICAO: PLATINUM AIR Net: http://www.alphajet.com

☐ N28ED	Bell 206B JetRanger III	2498		0078	0379	1 AN 250-C20B	1451			lsf pvt
☐ N112ED	Piper PA-31T Cheyenne II	31T-8020060	N703CJ	0080	0181	2 PWC PT6A-28	4082			
☐ N45ED	Learjet 24	24-104	N924ED	0066	0368	2 GE CJ610-4	5897			
☐ N35ED	Learjet 35A	35A-215	N80GD	0079	0287	2 GA TFE731-2-2B	8301			

ALPINE AIR = 5A / AIP (Alpine Aviation, Inc. dba)

Provo-Municipal, UT

3450 West Mike Jense Parkway, Provo, UT 84601, USA ☎ (801) 373-1508 Tx: none Fax: (801) 373-6728 SITA: n/a
F: 1977 ⁂ 32 Head: Eugene R. Mallette IATA: 511 ICAO: ALPINE AIR Net: n/a Aircraft below MTOW 1361kg: Piper PA-28

☐ N31998	Piper PA-32RT-300T Turbo Lance II	32R-7887019		0078	0490	1 LY TIO-540-S1AD	1633	Y6/Freighter		lsf CLB Corp.
☐ N114SA	Piper PA-31-350 Navajo Chieftain	31-8052053		0080	0391	2 LY TIO-540-J2BD	3175	Y8		lsf CLB Corp.
☐ N27367	Piper PA-31-350 Navajo Chieftain	31-7852007		0077	0891	2 LY TIO-540-J2BD	3175	Y8		lsf CLB Corp.
☐ N700TS	Piper PA-31-350 Navajo Chieftain	31-8152157		0081	1085	2 LY TIO-540-J2BD	3175	Y8		lsf CLB Corp.
☐ N199GL	Beech 99 Airliner	U-15	C-GJEZ	0068	1090	2 PWC PT6A-27	4717	Freighter		lsf CLB Corp.
☐ N326CA	Beech 99A Airliner	U-135	N10RA	0070	0898	2 PWC PT6A-27	4717	Freighter		lsf CLB Corp.
☐ N4381Y	Beech 99 Airliner	U-71	N216BH	0069	0698	2 PWC PT6A-27	4717	Freighter		lsf CLB Corp.
☐ N899CA	Beech B99 Airliner	U-104	N1922T	0070	0195	2 PWC PT6A-27	4944	Freighter		lsf CLB Corp.
☐ N950AA	Beech B99 Airliner	U-159	C-FCBU	0074	1091	2 PWC PT6A-27	4944	Freighter		lsf CLB Corp.
☐ N955AA	Beech 99A Airliner	U-128	J6-AAE	0070	0897	2 PWC PT6A-27	4717	Freighter		lsf CLB Corp.
☐ N95WA	Beech 99 Airliner	U-6	N19RA	0068	0390	2 PWC PT6A-27	4717	Freighter		lsf CLB Corp.
☐ N99CA	Beech 99A Airliner	U-127	N22AT	0069	0198	2 PWC PT6A-27	4717	Freighter		lsf CLB Corp.
☐ N99GH	Beech 99A Airliner	U-112	C-GXAZ	0070	1192	2 PWC PT6A-27	4717	Freighter		lsf CLB Corp.
☐ N99TH	Beech B99 Airliner	U-155		0074	0392	2 PWC PT6A-27	4944	Freighter		lsf CLB Corp.
☐ N175AA	Piper PA-42 Cheyenne III	42-8001017	N342TW	0081	0693	2 PWC PT6A-41	5080	Y9		lsf CLB Corp.
☐ N395DR	Piper PA-42 Cheyenne III	42-8001065	N742RB	0082	0296	2 PWC PT6A-41	5080	Y9		lsf CLB Corp.

ALPINE AIR, Inc. (formerly Alpine Air Guides)

Girdwood, AK

PO Box 1047, Girdwood, AK 99587, USA ☎ (907) 783-2360 Tx: none Fax: (907) 754-1504 SITA: n/a
F: 1991 ⁂ n/a Head: Donna S. Jefferson Net: n/a

☐ N76185	Cessna A185F Skywagon	18503013		0076	1291	1 CO IO-520-D	1520			Floats / Wheel-Skis
☐ N80359	Cessna A185F Skywagon	18503116		0076	0896	1 CO IO-520-D	1520			Floats / Wheel-Skis

ALPINE AIR SERVICE, Inc.

Flagstaff-Pulliam, AZ

PO Box 252, Flagstaff, AZ 86002, USA ☎ (520) 779-5178 Tx: none Fax: (520) 779-0508 SITA: n/a
F: 1987 ⁂ n/a Head: Michael Kavanagh Net: n/a Aircraft below MTOW 1361kg: Cessna 182P

☐ N737MN	Cessna TR182RG Skylane II	R18200853		0079	0387	1 LY O-540-L3C5D	1406			

ALPINE HELICOPTERS (Air & Auto, Inc. dba)

Salt Lake City-Municipal, UT

PO Box 441, West Jordan, UT 84084, USA ☎ (801) 978-1988 Tx: none Fax: (801) 280-8560 SITA: n/a
F: 1994 ⁂ n/a Head: Gary W. Ostler Net: n/a

☐ N206GH	Bell 206L-4 LongRanger IV	52112		0094	1194	1 AN 250-C30P	2018			

ALPINE HELICOPTERS, Inc.

Ward Cove, AK

PO Box 1478, Ward Cove, AK 99928, USA ☎ (907) 225-9190 Tx: none Fax: (907) 247-6602 SITA: n/a
F: 1996 ⁂ n/a Head: Butch Durette Net: n/a

☐ N1091W	MD Helicopters MD 500D (Hughes 369D)	300700D		0080	1196	1 AN 250-C20B	1361			lsf C&I Corp.
☐ N60PH	Bell 206B JetRanger	304	N206E	0068	1196	1 AN 250-C20	1451			lsf Timberline Helicopters / cvtd 206A

ALYESKA AIR SERVICE, Inc.

Girdwood, AK

Box 914, Girdwood, AK 99587, USA ☎ (907) 783-2163 Tx: none Fax: (907) 783-1294 SITA: n/a
F: 1992 ⁂ n/a Head: Boyce J. Bingham Net: n/a

☐ N107TA	Piper PA-32-300 Cherokee SIX	32-7540099		0075	0794	1 LY IO-540-K1A5	1542			
☐ N5782Y	Piper PA-23-250 Aztec C	27-2912		0065	0197	2 LY IO-540-C4B5	2359			

AM AIR

Hazleton-Municipal, PA

225 West Diamond Avenue, Hazleton, PA 18201, USA ☎ (717) 459-2536 Tx: none Fax: (717) 454-1861 SITA: n/a
F: 1990 ⁂ n/a Head: Mark Frumkin Net: n/a

☐ N23MF	Beech Baron B55 (95-B55)	TC-1684		0074	0296	2 CO IO-470-L	2313			

AMBLER AIR SERVICE (David Rue dba)

Ambler, AK

Box 7, Ambler, AK 99786, USA ☎ (907) 445-2121 Tx: none Fax: none SITA: n/a
F: 1976 ⁂ 1 Head: David Rue Net: n/a

☐ N1583H	Cessna A185F Skywagon	18503311		0077	0481	1 CO IO-520-D	1520			
☐ N6230J	Piper PA-32R-300 Lance	32R-7680337		0076	0692	1 LY IO-540-K1G5D	1633			
☐ N6426H	Cessna 207A Stationair 7 II	20700521		0079	0181	1 CO IO-520-F	1724			

262 registration type of aircraft cn/fn ex/ex* mfd del powered by mtow kg configuration selcal name/fln/specialitites/remarks

AMBROSE AIR CHARTER — Estherville-Municipal, IA

1108 North 6th Street, Estherville, IA 51334, USA ☎ (712) 362-3126 Tx: none Fax: none SITA: n/a
F: 1996 ⁂ n/a Head: William D. Ambrose Net: n/a

☐ N60LD	Cessna 402B II	402B1323		0078	0996	2 CO TSIO-520-E	2858			

AMBROSINI HELICOPTERS, Inc. — Fresno-Heliport, CA

4497 West Madison Avenue, Fresno, CA 93706, USA ☎ (209) 486-4069 Tx: none Fax: (209) 486-1020 SITA: n/a
F: 1988 ⁂ n/a Head: Richard Ambrosini Net: n/a

☐ N59427	Bell 206B JetRanger	1132		0073	0688	1 AN 250-C20	1451			
☐ N806SB	Bell UH-1B (204)	1147	64-14023	0064	1194	1 LY T53-L-11	3856			

AMELIA AIRWAYS, Inc. — Fort Lauderdale-Executive, FL

2500 NW 62nd Street, Hangar A, Fort Lauderdale, FL 33309, USA ☎ (954) 771-3151 Tx: none Fax: (954) 771-8053 SITA: n/a
F: 1993 ⁂ n/a Head: David M. Lippman Net: n/a

☐ N2QW	Piper PA-23-250 Aztec F	27-7754126		0077		2 LY IO-540-C4B5	2359			lsf Microlamp Inc.
☐ N116PM	Piper PA-31-350 Navajo Chieftain	31-8052127		0080	0594	2 LY TIO-540-J2BD	3175			
☐ N132MF	Piper PA-31-350 Navajo Chieftain	31-7752072		0077	0595	2 LY TIO-540-J2BD	3175			
☐ N27478	Piper PA-31-350 Navajo Chieftain	31-7852026		0078	1194	2 LY TIO-540-J2BD	3175			

AMERICAN AIR CHARTER (American Aviation, Inc. dba) — Salt Lake City-Int'l, UT

337 N.2370 W., Suite 231E, Salt Lake City, UT 84116, USA ☎ (801) 537-1537 Tx: none Fax: (801) 537-1539 SITA: n/a
F: 1990 ⁂ n/a Head: Larry D. Wright Net: n/a Aircraft below MTOW 1361kg: Cessna 152/172 & Piper PA-28

☐ N2237U	Piper PA-44-180 Seminole	44-7995257		0079	0690	2 LY O-360-E1A6D	1724			lsf Executive Aircraft Int'l Inc.
☐ N2119D	Piper PA-34-200T Seneca II	34-7970026		0079	1191	2 CO TSIO-360-EB	2073			lsf Executive Aircraft Int'l Inc.
☐ N82GB	Cessna 340A II	340A0463		0078	0896	2 CO TSIO-520-NB	2717			

AMERICAN AIRLINES, Inc. = AA / AAL (Subsidiary of AMR, Corp. / Member of Oneworld Alliance) — Dallas-Fort Worth Int'l, TX

PO Box 619616, DFW International Airport, TX 75261-9616, USA ☎ (817) 967-1234 Tx: 791651 Fax: (817) 967-4318 SITA: HDQPRAA
F: 1934 ⁂ 90000 Head: Donald J. Carty IATA: 001 ICAO: AMERICAN Net: http://www.americanair.com

A commuter system to provide feeder connection at AA major hubs is operated by sister company AMERICAN EAGLE AIRLINES (using AA flight number) for details – see under that company.

All Boeing 727-223 (A) are scheduled to be hush-kitted (HK3) until 1199. AMR Corp. has bought RENO AIR Inc. and its fleet of MD-82/83/87 & MD-90-30 aircraft will be integrated into AMERICAN AIRLINES late 1999.

☐ N1400H	Fokker 100 (F28 Mk0100)	11340	PH-EZY*	0091	0791	2 RR Tay 650-15	44452	F8Y89	AK-BQ	2AA
☐ N1401G	Fokker 100 (F28 Mk0100)	11352	PH-EZZ*	0891	0891	2 RR Tay 650-15	44452	F8Y89	AK-CQ	2AB
☐ N1402K	Fokker 100 (F28 Mk0100)	11353	PH-EZA*	0891	0891	2 RR Tay 650-15	44452	F8Y89	AK-DQ	2AC
☐ N1403M	Fokker 100 (F28 Mk0100)	11354	PH-EZC*	0991	0991	2 RR Tay 650-15	44452	F8Y89	AK-EQ	2AD
☐ N1404D	Fokker 100 (F28 Mk0100)	11355	PH-EZI*	0991	0991	2 RR Tay 650-15	44452	F8Y89	AK-FQ	2AE
☐ N1405J	Fokker 100 (F28 Mk0100)	11356	PH-EZJ*	0991	1091	2 RR Tay 650-15	44452	F8Y89	AK-GQ	2AF
☐ N1406A	Fokker 100 (F28 Mk0100)	11359	PH-EZG*	0991	1091	2 RR Tay 650-15	44452	F8Y89	AK-HQ	2AG
☐ N1407D	Fokker 100 (F28 Mk0100)	11360	PH-EZO*	1091	1091	2 RR Tay 650-15	44452	F8Y89	AK-JQ	2AH
☐ N1408B	Fokker 100 (F28 Mk0100)	11361	PH-EZS*	1091	1091	2 RR Tay 650-15	44452	F8Y89	AK-LQ	2AJ
☐ N1409B	Fokker 100 (F28 Mk0100)	11367	PH-EZI*	1191	1191	2 RR Tay 650-15	44452	F8Y89	AK-MQ	2AK
☐ N1410E	Fokker 100 (F28 Mk0100)	11368	PH-EZJ*	1291	1291	2 RR Tay 650-15	44452	F8Y89	AK-PQ	2AL
☐ N1411G	Fokker 100 (F28 Mk0100)	11369	PH-EZB*	1291	1291	2 RR Tay 650-15	44452	F8Y89	AL-BQ	2AM
☐ N1412A	Fokker 100 (F28 Mk0100)	11370	PH-EZD*	1291	1291	2 RR Tay 650-15	44452	F8Y89	AL-CQ	2AN
☐ N1413A	Fokker 100 (F28 Mk0100)	11376	PH-EZO*	0192	0292	2 RR Tay 650-15	44452	F8Y89	AL-DQ	2AP
☐ N1414D	Fokker 100 (F28 Mk0100)	11377	PH-EZS*	0292	0292	2 RR Tay 650-15	44452	F8Y89	AL-EQ	2AR
☐ N1415K	Fokker 100 (F28 Mk0100)	11385	PH-EZY*	0392	0392	2 RR Tay 650-15	44452	F8Y89	AL-FQ	2AS
☐ N1416A	Fokker 100 (F28 Mk0100)	11395	PH-EZC*	0592	0592	2 RR Tay 650-15	44452	F8Y89	AL-GQ	2AT
☐ N1417D	Fokker 100 (F28 Mk0100)	11396	PH-EZE*	0592	0592	2 RR Tay 650-15	44452	F8Y89	AL-HQ	2AU
☐ N1418A	Fokker 100 (F28 Mk0100)	11397	PH-EZI*	0592	0692	2 RR Tay 650-15	44452	F8Y89	AL-JQ	2AV
☐ N1419D	Fokker 100 (F28 Mk0100)	11402	PH-EZM*	0692	0692	2 RR Tay 650-15	44452	F8Y89	AL-KQ	2AW
☐ N1420D	Fokker 100 (F28 Mk0100)	11403	PH-EZO*	0692	0792	2 RR Tay 650-15	44452	F8Y89	GK-MR	2AX
☐ N1421K	Fokker 100 (F28 Mk0100)	11404	PH-EZD*	0692	0792	2 RR Tay 650-15	44452	F8Y89	GK-MS	2AY
☐ N1422J	Fokker 100 (F28 Mk0100)	11405	PH-EZG*	0792	0792	2 RR Tay 650-15	44452	F8Y89	GK-PR	2BA
☐ N1423A	Fokker 100 (F28 Mk0100)	11406	PH-EZP*	0792	0892	2 RR Tay 650-15	44452	F8Y89	GK-PS	2BB
☐ N1424M	Fokker 100 (F28 Mk0100)	11407	PH-EZS*	0792	0892	2 RR Tay 650-15	44452	F8Y89	GK-QR	2BC
☐ N1425A	Fokker 100 (F28 Mk0100)	11408	PH-EZE*	0792	0892	2 RR Tay 650-15	44452	F8Y89	GK-QS	2BD
☐ N1426A	Fokker 100 (F28 Mk0100)	11411	PH-EZB*	0892	0992	2 RR Tay 650-15	44452	F8Y89	GK-RS	2BE
☐ N1427A	Fokker 100 (F28 Mk0100)	11412	PH-EZC*	0892	0992	2 RR Tay 650-15	44452	F8Y89	GL-MR	2BF
☐ N1428D	Fokker 100 (F28 Mk0100)	11413	PH-EZI*	0892	0992	2 RR Tay 650-15	44452	F8Y89	GL-MS	2BG
☐ N1429G	Fokker 100 (F28 Mk0100)	11414	PH-EZJ*	0892	0992	2 RR Tay 650-15	44452	F8Y89	GL-PR	2BH
☐ N1430D	Fokker 100 (F28 Mk0100)	11415	PH-EZL*	0992	1092	2 RR Tay 650-15	44452	F8Y89	GL-PS	2BJ
☐ N1431B	Fokker 100 (F28 Mk0100)	11416	PH-EZY*	0992	1092	2 RR Tay 650-15	44452	F8Y89	GL-QR	2BK
☐ N1432A	Fokker 100 (F28 Mk0100)	11417	PH-EZZ*	0992	1092	2 RR Tay 650-15	44452	F8Y89	GL-QS	2BL
☐ N1433B	Fokker 100 (F28 Mk0100)	11418	PH-EZO*	0992	1092	2 RR Tay 650-15	44452	F8Y89	GL-RS	2BM
☐ N1434A	Fokker 100 (F28 Mk0100)	11419	PH-EZM*	0992	1092	2 RR Tay 650-15	44452	F8Y89	GM-PR	2BN
☐ N1435D	Fokker 100 (F28 Mk0100)	11425	PH-EZD*	1192	1192	2 RR Tay 650-15	44452	F8Y89	GM-PS	2BP
☐ N1436A	Fokker 100 (F28 Mk0100)	11426	PH-EZE*	1192	1192	2 RR Tay 650-15	44452	F8Y89	GM-QR	2BR
☐ N1437B	Fokker 100 (F28 Mk0100)	11427	PH-EZG*	1192	1292	2 RR Tay 650-15	44452	F8Y89	GM-QS	2BS
☐ N1438H	Fokker 100 (F28 Mk0100)	11428	PH-EZP*	1192	1292	2 RR Tay 650-15	44452	F8Y89	GM-RS	2BT
☐ N1439A	Fokker 100 (F28 Mk0100)	11434	PH-EZA*	1292	0193	2 RR Tay 650-15	44452	F8Y89	GP-QR	2BU
☐ N1440A	Fokker 100 (F28 Mk0100)	11435	PH-EZB*	1292	0193	2 RR Tay 650-15	44452	F8Y89	GP-QS	2BV
☐ N1441A	Fokker 100 (F28 Mk0100)	11436	PH-EZC*	0193	0293	2 RR Tay 650-15	44452	F8Y89	GP-RS	2BW
☐ N1442E	Fokker 100 (F28 Mk0100)	11437	PH-EZI*	0193	0293	2 RR Tay 650-15	44452	F8Y89	GQ-RS	2BX
☐ N1443A	Fokker 100 (F28 Mk0100)	11446	PH-EZN*	0393	0393	2 RR Tay 650-15	45813	F8Y89	HJ-KR	2BY
☐ N1444N	Fokker 100 (F28 Mk0100)	11447	PH-EZO*	0393	0393	2 RR Tay 650-15	45813	F8Y89	HJ-KS	2CA
☐ N1445B	Fokker 100 (F28 Mk0100)	11448	PH-EZP*	0393	0393	2 RR Tay 650-15	45813	F8Y89	HJ-LR	2CB
☐ N1446A	Fokker 100 (F28 Mk0100)	11449	PH-EZS*	0393	0493	2 RR Tay 650-15	45813	F8Y89	HJ-LS	2CC
☐ N1447L	Fokker 100 (F28 Mk0100)	11456	PH-EZA*	0593	0593	2 RR Tay 650-15	45813	F8Y89	HJ-MR	2CD
☐ N1448A	Fokker 100 (F28 Mk0100)	11457	PH-EZB*	0593	0693	2 RR Tay 650-15	45813	F8Y89	HJ-MS	2CE
☐ N1449D	Fokker 100 (F28 Mk0100)	11458	PH-EZC*	0593	0693	2 RR Tay 650-15	45813	F8Y89	HJ-PR	2CF
☐ N1450A	Fokker 100 (F28 Mk0100)	11459	PH-EZD*	0693	0693	2 RR Tay 650-15	45413	F8Y89	HJ-PS	2CG
☐ N1451N	Fokker 100 (F28 Mk0100)	11460	PH-EZE*	0693	0693	2 RR Tay 650-15	45413	F8Y89	HJ-QR	2CH
☐ N1452B	Fokker 100 (F28 Mk0100)	11464	PH-EZI*	0693	0793	2 RR Tay 650-15	45813	F8Y89	HJ-QS	2CJ
☐ N1453D	Fokker 100 (F28 Mk0100)	11465	PH-EZJ*	0693	0793	2 RR Tay 650-15	45813	F8Y89	HJ-RS	2CK
☐ N1454D	Fokker 100 (F28 Mk0100)	11466	PH-EZK*	0793	0793	2 RR Tay 650-15	45813	F8Y89	HK-LR	2CL
☐ N1455K	Fokker 100 (F28 Mk0100)	11467	PH-EZL*	0793	0793	2 RR Tay 650-15	45813	F8Y89	HK-LS	2CM
☐ N1456D	Fokker 100 (F28 Mk0100)	11468	PH-EZM*	0793	0893	2 RR Tay 650-15	45813	F8Y89	HK-MR	2CN
☐ N1457B	Fokker 100 (F28 Mk0100)	11469	PH-EZN*	0893	0893	2 RR Tay 650-15	45813	F8Y89	HK-MS	2CP
☐ N1458H	Fokker 100 (F28 Mk0100)	11478	PH-EZA*	0993	1093	2 RR Tay 650-15	45813	F8Y89	HK-PR	2CR
☐ N1459A	Fokker 100 (F28 Mk0100)	11479	PH-EZB*	1093	1093	2 RR Tay 650-15	45813	F8Y89	HK-PS	2CS
☐ N1460A	Fokker 100 (F28 Mk0100)	11480	PH-JCA*	1193	1293	2 RR Tay 650-15	45813	F8Y89	HK-QR	2CT
☐ N1461C	Fokker 100 (F28 Mk0100)	11481	PH-JCB*	1193	1293	2 RR Tay 650-15	45813	F8Y89	HK-QS	2CU
☐ N1462C	Fokker 100 (F28 Mk0100)	11482	PH-JCC*	1193	0194	2 RR Tay 650-15	45813	F8Y89	HK-RS	2CV
☐ N1463A	Fokker 100 (F28 Mk0100)	11483	PH-JCD*	1293	0194	2 RR Tay 650-15	45813	F8Y89	HL-MR	2CW
☐ N1464A	Fokker 100 (F28 Mk0100)	11490	PH-EZU*	0194	0294	2 RR Tay 650-15	45813	F8Y89	HL-MS	2CX
☐ N1465K	Fokker 100 (F28 Mk0100)	11491	PH-EZV*	0194	0294	2 RR Tay 650-15	45813	F8Y89	HL-PR	2CY
☐ N1466A	Fokker 100 (F28 Mk0100)	11498	PH-EZK*	0194	0294	2 RR Tay 650-15	45813	F8Y89	HL-PS	2DA
☐ N1467A	Fokker 100 (F28 Mk0100)	11499	PH-EZL*	0294	0294	2 RR Tay 650-15	45813	F8Y89	HL-QR	2DB
☐ N1468A	Fokker 100 (F28 Mk0100)	11501	PH-EZM*	0294	0394	2 RR Tay 650-15	45813	F8Y89	HL-QS	2DC
☐ N1469D	Fokker 100 (F28 Mk0100)	11502	PH-EZN*	0294	0394	2 RR Tay 650-15	45813	F8Y89	HL-RS	2DD
☐ N1470K	Fokker 100 (F28 Mk0100)	11506	PH-EZF*	0394	0394	2 RR Tay 650-15	45813	F8Y89	HM-PR	2DE
☐ N1471G	Fokker 100 (F28 Mk0100)	11507	PH-EZG*	0394	0494	2 RR Tay 650-15	45813	F8Y89	HM-PS	2DF
☐ N1472B	Fokker 100 (F28 Mk0100)	11514	PH-EZZ*	0494	0594	2 RR Tay 650-15	45813	F8Y89	HM-QR	2DG
☐ N1473K	Fokker 100 (F28 Mk0100)	11515	PH-EZY*	0594	0594	2 RR Tay 650-15	45813	F8Y89	HM-QS	2DH
☐ N1474D	Fokker 100 (F28 Mk0100)	11520	PH-EZV*	0594	0694	2 RR Tay 650-15	45813	F8Y89	HM-RS	2DJ
☐ N677AA	Boeing 737-3A4	23289 / 1182	N735MA	1285	0787	2 CFMI CFM56-3B2	61235	F10Y119	AB-GJ	lsf N.E.Merchants Lsng-0101/sub-lst SWA
☐ N678AA	Boeing 737-3A4	23290 / 1205	N304AC	0386	0787	2 CFMI CFM56-3B2	61235	F10Y119	AB-GK	lsf AARL -0101 / sub-lst SWA
☐ N680AA	Boeing 737-3A4	23505 / 1318	N310AC	1286	0787	2 CFMI CFM56-3B2	61235	F10Y119	BL-AJ	lsf GECA -0101 / sub-lst SWA
☐ N76200	Boeing (Douglas) MD-83 (DC-9-83)	53290 / 2013		0792	0792	2 PW JT8D-219	72575	F20Y113	GH-PS	200
☐ N76201	Boeing (Douglas) MD-83 (DC-9-83)	53291 / 2019		0892	0892	2 PW JT8D-219	72575	F20Y113	GH-QR	201
☐ N76202	Boeing (Douglas) MD-83 (DC-9-83)	53292 / 2020		0892	0892	2 PW JT8D-219	72575	F20Y113	GH-QS	202
☐ N203AA	Boeing (Douglas) MD-82 (DC-9-82)	49145 / 1097		0583	0583	2 PW JT8D-217A	67812	F14Y125	KL-BJ	203
☐ N205AA	Boeing (Douglas) MD-82 (DC-9-82)	49155 / 1103		0683	0683	2 PW JT8D-217A	67812	F14Y125	KL-CD	205
☐ N207AA	Boeing (Douglas) MD-82 (DC-9-82)	49158 / 1106		0683	0683	2 PW JT8D-217A	67812	F14Y125	KL-CE	207
☐ N208AA	Boeing (Douglas) MD-82 (DC-9-82)	49159 / 1107		0683	0683	2 PW JT8D-217A	67812	F14Y125	KL-CF	208
☐ N210AA	Boeing (Douglas) MD-82 (DC-9-82)	49161 / 1109		0683	0683	2 PW JT8D-217A	67812	F14Y125	KL-CG	210
☐ N214AA	Boeing (Douglas) MD-82 (DC-9-82)	49162 / 1110		0783	0783	2 PW JT8D-217A	67812	F14Y125	KL-CH	214
☐ N215AA	Boeing (Douglas) MD-82 (DC-9-82)	49163 / 1111		0883	0883	2 PW JT8D-217A	67812	F14Y125	KL-CJ	215
☐ N216AA	Boeing (Douglas) MD-82 (DC-9-82)	49167 / 1099		0583	0583	2 PW JT8D-217A	67812	F14Y125	KL-CM	216
☐ N218AA	Boeing (Douglas) MD-82 (DC-9-82)	49168 / 1100		0583	0583	2 PW JT8D-217A	67812	F14Y125	KL-DE	218

263 registration type of aircraft cn/fn ex/ex* mfd del powered by mtow kg configuration selcal name/fln/specialitites/remarks

	registration	type of aircraft	cn/fn	ex/εx*	mfd	del	powered by	mtow kg	configuration	selcal	name/fln/specialitites/remarks
☐	N219AA	Boeing (Douglas) MD-82 (DC-9-82)	49171 / 1112		0883	0883	2 PW JT8D-217A	67812	F14Y125	KL-DF	219
☐	N221AA	Boeing (Douglas) MD-82 (DC-9-82)	49172 / 1113		0883	0883	2 PW JT8D-217A	67812	F14Y125	KL-DH	221
☐	N223AA	Boeing (Douglas) MD-82 (DC-9-82)	49173 / 1114		0983	0983	2 PW JT8D-217A	67812	F14Y125	KL-DM	223
☐	N224AA	Boeing (Douglas) MD-82 (DC-9-82)	49174 / 1115		0883	0883	2 PW JT8D-217A	67812	F14Y125	KL-EG	224
☐	N225AA	Boeing (Douglas) MD-82 (DC-9-82)	49175 / 1116		0983	0983	2 PW JT8D-217A	67812	F14Y125	KL-EH	225
☐	N226AA	Boeing (Douglas) MD-82 (DC-9-82)	49176 / 1120		1083	1083	2 PW JT8D-217A	67812	F14Y125	KL-EJ	226
☐	N227AA	Boeing (Douglas) MD-82 (DC-9-82)	49177 / 1121		1083	1083	2 PW JT8D-217A	67812	F14Y125	KL-EM	227
☐	N228AA	Boeing (Douglas) MD-82 (DC-9-82)	49178 / 1122		1183	1183	2 PW JT8D-217A	67812	F14Y125	KL-FG	228
☐	N232AA	Boeing (Douglas) MD-82 (DC-9-82)	49179 / 1123		1183	1183	2 PW JT8D-217A	67812	F14Y125	KL-FH	232
☐	N233AA	Boeing (Douglas) MD-82 (DC-9-82)	49180 / 1124		1183	1183	2 PW JT8D-217A	67812	F14Y125	KL-FM	233
☐	N234AA	Boeing (Douglas) MD-82 (DC-9-82)	49181 / 1125		1283	1283	2 PW JT8D-217A	67812	F14Y125	KL-GJ	234
☐	N236AA	Boeing (Douglas) MD-82 (DC-9-82)	49251 / 1154		0984	0984	2 PW JT8D-217A	67812	F14Y125	KL-GH	236
☐	N237AA	Boeing (Douglas) MD-82 (DC-9-82)	49253 / 1155		0984	0984	2 PW JT8D-217A	67812	F14Y125	KL-HJ	237
☐	N241AA	Boeing (Douglas) MD-82 (DC-9-82)	49254 / 1156		0984	0984	2 PW JT8D-217A	67812	F14Y125	KL-JM	241
☐	N242AA	Boeing (Douglas) MD-82 (DC-9-82)	49255 / 1157		0984	0984	2 PW JT8D-217A	67812	F14Y125	KM-BE	242
☐	N244AA	Boeing (Douglas) MD-82 (DC-9-82)	49256 / 1158		0984	0984	2 PW JT8D-217A	67812	F14Y125	KM-BF	244
☐	N245AA	Boeing (Douglas) MD-82 (DC-9-82)	49257 / 1160		1084	1084	2 PW JT8D-217A	67812	F14Y125	JK-FH	245
☐	N246AA	Boeing (Douglas) MD-82 (DC-9-82)	49258 / 1161		1084	1084	2 PW JT8D-217A	67812	F14Y125	JK-FL	246
☐	N248AA	Boeing (Douglas) MD-82 (DC-9-82)	49259 / 1162		1084	1084	2 PW JT8D-217A	67812	F14Y125	JK-FM	248
☐	N249AA	Boeing (Douglas) MD-82 (DC-9-82)	49269 / 1164		1084	1084	2 PW JT8D-217A	67812	F14Y125	JK-GM	249
☐	N251AA	Boeing (Douglas) MD-82 (DC-9-82)	49270 / 1165		1084	1084	2 PW JT8D-217A	67812	F14Y125	KL-EF	251
☐	N253AA	Boeing (Douglas) MD-82 (DC-9-82)	49286 / 1175		0185	0185	2 PW JT8D-217A	67812	F14Y125	BE-AK	253
☐	N255AA	Boeing (Douglas) MD-82 (DC-9-82)	49287 / 1176		0185	0185	2 PW JT8D-217A	67812	F14Y125	BE-GM	255
☐	N258AA	Boeing (Douglas) MD-82 (DC-9-82)	49288 / 1187		0385	0385	2 PW JT8D-217A	67812	F14Y125	BJ-AC	258
☐	N259AA	Boeing (Douglas) MD-82 (DC-9-82)	49289 / 1193		0485	0485	2 PW JT8D-217A	67812	F14Y125	BK-AC	259
☐	N262AA	Boeing (Douglas) MD-82 (DC-9-82)	49290 / 1195		0485	0485	2 PW JT8D-217A	67812	F14Y125	DE-FH	262
☐	N266AA	Boeing (Douglas) MD-82 (DC-9-82)	49291 / 1210		0485	0485	2 PW JT8D-217A	67812	F14Y125	DE-JM	266
☐	N269AA	Boeing (Douglas) MD-82 (DC-9-82)	49292 / 1211		0785	0785	2 PW JT8D-217A	67812	F14Y125	BE-CH	269
☐	N271AA	Boeing (Douglas) MD-82 (DC-9-82)	49293 / 1212		0785	0785	2 PW JT8D-217A	67812	F14Y125	BG-FM	271
☐	N274AA	Boeing (Douglas) MD-82 (DC-9-82)	49271 / 1166		1184	1184	2 PW JT8D-217A	67812	F14Y125	JL-AH	274
☐	N275AA	Boeing (Douglas) MD-82 (DC-9-82)	49272 / 1167		1184	1184	2 PW JT8D-217A	67812	F14Y125	JL-BG	275
☐	N276AA	Boeing (Douglas) MD-82 (DC-9-82)	49273 / 1168		1184	1184	2 PW JT8D-217A	67812	F14Y125	JL-DG	276
☐	N278AA	Boeing (Douglas) MD-82 (DC-9-82)	49294 / 1213		0785	0785	2 PW JT8D-217A	67812	F14Y125	BJ-AD	278
☐	N279AA	Boeing (Douglas) MD-82 (DC-9-82)	49295 / 1214		0785	0785	2 PW JT8D-217A	67812	F14Y125	BK-AD	279
☐	N283AA	Boeing (Douglas) MD-82 (DC-9-82)	49296 / 1215		0785	0785	2 PW JT8D-217A	67812	F14Y125	DE-FJ	283
☐	N285AA	Boeing (Douglas) MD-82 (DC-9-82)	49297 / 1216		0885	0885	2 PW JT8D-217A	67812	F20Y113	DE-KM	285
☐	N286AA	Boeing (Douglas) MD-82 (DC-9-82)	49298 / 1217		0885	0885	2 PW JT8D-217A	67812	F20Y113	DF-AK	286
☐	N287AA	Boeing (Douglas) MD-82 (DC-9-82)	49299 / 1218		0885	0885	2 PW JT8D-217A	67812	F20Y113	DG-AF	287
☐	N288AA	Boeing (Douglas) MD-82 (DC-9-82)	49300 / 1219		0885	0885	2 PW JT8D-217A	67812	F20Y113	FK-BD	288
☐	N289AA	Boeing (Douglas) MD-82 (DC-9-82)	49301 / 1220		0885	0885	2 PW JT8D-217A	67812	F20Y113	KL-GM	289
☐	N290AA	Boeing (Douglas) MD-82 (DC-9-82)	49302 / 1221		0885	0885	2 PW JT8D-217A	67812	F20Y113	BE-DF	290
☐	N291AA	Boeing (Douglas) MD-82 (DC-9-82)	49303 / 1222		0985	0985	2 PW JT8D-217A	67812	F20Y113	BG-HL	291
☐	N292AA	Boeing (Douglas) MD-82 (DC-9-82)	49304 / 1223		0985	0985	2 PW JT8D-217A	67812	F20Y113	BJ-AF	292
☐	N293AA	Boeing (Douglas) MD-82 (DC-9-82)	49305 / 1226		0985	0985	2 PW JT8D-217A	67812	F20Y113	BK-AJ	293
☐	N294AA	Boeing (Douglas) MD-82 (DC-9-82)	49306 / 1227		0985	0985	2 PW JT8D-217A	67812	F20Y113	DE-FL	294
☐	N295AA	Boeing (Douglas) MD-82 (DC-9-82)	49307 / 1228		1085	1085	2 PW JT8D-217A	67812	F20Y113	DF-AC	295
☐	N296AA	Boeing (Douglas) MD-82 (DC-9-82)	49308 / 1229		1085	1085	2 PW JT8D-217A	67812	F20Y113	BE-DM	296
☐	N297AA	Boeing (Douglas) MD-82 (DC-9-82)	49309 / 1246		0186	0186	2 PW JT8D-217A	67812	F20Y113	BH-CM	297
☐	N298AA	Boeing (Douglas) MD-82 (DC-9-82)	49310 / 1247		0186	0186	2 PW JT8D-217A	67812	F20Y113	BJ-AL	298
☐	N400AA	Boeing (Douglas) MD-82 (DC-9-82)	49311 / 1248		0186	0186	2 PW JT8D-217A	67812	F20Y113	AC-BG	400
☐	N70401	Boeing (Douglas) MD-82 (DC-9-82)	49312 / 1249		0186	0186	2 PW JT8D-217A	67812	F20Y113	BD-JM	401
☐	N402A	Boeing (Douglas) MD-82 (DC-9-82)	49313 / 1255		0286	0286	2 PW JT8D-217A	67812	F20Y113	BD-LM	402
☐	N403A	Boeing (Douglas) MD-82 (DC-9-82)	49314 / 1256		0286	0286	2 PW JT8D-217A	67812	F20Y113	BE-AF	403
☐	N70404	Boeing (Douglas) MD-82 (DC-9-82)	49315 / 1257		0386	0386	2 PW JT8D-217A	67812	F20Y113	BE-AL	404
☐	N405A	Boeing (Douglas) MD-82 (DC-9-82)	49316 / 1258		0386	0386	2 PW JT8D-217A	67812	F20Y113	BE-DL	405
☐	N406A	Boeing (Douglas) MD-82 (DC-9-82)	49317 / 1259		0386	0386	2 PW JT8D-217A	67812	F20Y113	BE-FH	406
☐	N407AA	Boeing (Douglas) MD-82 (DC-9-82)	49318 / 1265		0486	0486	2 PW JT8D-217A	67812	F20Y113	BG-CL	407
☐	N408AA	Boeing (Douglas) MD-82 (DC-9-82)	49319 / 1266		0486	0486	2 PW JT8D-217A	67812	F20Y113	BG-JL	408
☐	N409AA	Boeing (Douglas) MD-82 (DC-9-82)	49320 / 1267		0486	0486	2 PW JT8D-217A	67812	F20Y113	BG-LM	409
☐	N410AA	Boeing (Douglas) MD-82 (DC-9-82)	49321 / 1273		0586	0586	2 PW JT8D-217A	67812	F20Y113	BH-AL	410
☐	N411AA	Boeing (Douglas) MD-82 (DC-9-82)	49322 / 1280		0686	0686	2 PW JT8D-217A	67812	F20Y113	BH-CJ	411
☐	N412AA	Boeing (Douglas) MD-82 (DC-9-82)	49323 / 1281		0586	0686	2 PW JT8D-217A	67812	F20Y113	BH-DG	412
☐	N413AA	Boeing (Douglas) MD-82 (DC-9-82)	49324 / 1289		0786	0786	2 PW JT8D-217A	67812	F20Y113	BH-EG	413
☐	N33414	Boeing (Douglas) MD-82 (DC-9-82)	49325 / 1290		0786	0786	2 PW JT8D-217A	67812	F20Y113	BH-EM	414
☐	N415AA	Boeing (Douglas) MD-82 (DC-9-82)	49326 / 1295		0886	0886	2 PW JT8D-217A	67812	F20Y113	BH-GM	415
☐	N416AA	Boeing (Douglas) MD-82 (DC-9-82)	49327 / 1296		0886	0886	2 PW JT8D-217A	67812	F20Y113	BH-JM	416
☐	N417AA	Boeing (Douglas) MD-82 (DC-9-82)	49328 / 1301		0886	0886	2 PW JT8D-217A	67812	F20Y113	FK-AG	417
☐	N418AA	Boeing (Douglas) MD-82 (DC-9-82)	49329 / 1302		0886	0886	2 PW JT8D-217A	67812	F20Y113	BJ-DM	418
☐	N419AA	Boeing (Douglas) MD-82 (DC-9-82)	49331 / 1306		0986	0986	2 PW JT8D-217A	67812	F20Y113	FK-AH	419
☐	N420AA	Boeing (Douglas) MD-82 (DC-9-82)	49332 / 1307		0986	0986	2 PW JT8D-217A	67812	F20Y113	DE-FK	420
☐	N77421	Boeing (Douglas) MD-82 (DC-9-82)	49333 / 1311		1086	1086	2 PW JT8D-217A	67812	F20Y113	DE-JL	421
☐	N422AA	Boeing (Douglas) MD-82 (DC-9-82)	49334 / 1312		1086	1086	2 PW JT8D-217A	67812	F20Y113	DF-AL	422
☐	N423AA	Boeing (Douglas) MD-82 (DC-9-82)	49335 / 1320		1186	1186	2 PW JT8D-217A	67812	F20Y113	DF-AM	423
☐	N424AA	Boeing (Douglas) MD-82 (DC-9-82)	49336 / 1321		1186	1186	2 PW JT8D-217A	67812	F20Y113	DG-AJ	424
☐	N70425	Boeing (Douglas) MD-82 (DC-9-82)	49337 / 1325		1186	1186	2 PW JT8D-217A	67812	F20Y113	DG-AK	425
☐	N426AA	Boeing (Douglas) MD-82 (DC-9-82)	49338 / 1327		1186	1186	2 PW JT8D-217A	67812	F20Y113	FJ-KM	426
☐	N427AA	Boeing (Douglas) MD-82 (DC-9-82)	49339 / 1328		1286	1286	2 PW JT8D-217A	67812	F20Y113	FK-BC	427
☐	N428AA	Boeing (Douglas) MD-82 (DC-9-82)	49340 / 1329		1286	1286	2 PW JT8D-217A	67812	F20Y113	FK-BE	428
☐	N429AA	Boeing (Douglas) MD-82 (DC-9-82)	49341 / 1336		1286	1286	2 PW JT8D-217A	67812	F20Y113	KL-BE	429
☐	N430AA	Boeing (Douglas) MD-82 (DC-9-82)	49342 / 1337		0187	0187	2 PW JT8D-217A	67812	F20Y113	KL-BF	430
☐	N431AA	Boeing (Douglas) MD-82 (DC-9-82)	49343 / 1339		0587	0587	2 PW JT8D-217A	67812	F20Y113	KL-BG	431
☐	N432AA	Boeing (Douglas) MD-82 (DC-9-82)	49350 / 1376		0687	0687	2 PW JT8D-217A	67812	F20Y113	KM-BD	432
☐	N433AA	Boeing (Douglas) MD-83 (DC-9-83)	49451 / 1388		0787	0787	2 PW JT8D-219	72575	F20Y113	CP-AF	433 / cvtd MD-82 (DC-9-82)
☐	N434AA	Boeing (Douglas) MD-83 (DC-9-83)	49452 / 1389		0787	0787	2 PW JT8D-219	72575	F20Y113	CP-AG	434 / cvtd MD-82 (DC-9-82)
☐	N435AA	Boeing (Douglas) MD-83 (DC-9-83)	49453 / 1390		0787	0787	2 PW JT8D-219	72575	F20Y113	CP-AH	435 / cvtd MD-82 (DC-9-82)
☐	N436AA	Boeing (Douglas) MD-83 (DC-9-83)	49454 / 1391		0787	0787	2 PW JT8D-219	72575	F20Y113	CP-AJ	436 / cvtd MD-82 (DC-9-82)
☐	N437AA	Boeing (Douglas) MD-83 (DC-9-83)	49455 / 1392		0887	0887	2 PW JT8D-219	72575	F20Y113	CP-AK	437 / cvtd MD-82 (DC-9-82)
☐	N438AA	Boeing (Douglas) MD-83 (DC-9-83)	49456 / 1393		0887	0887	2 PW JT8D-219	72575	F20Y113	CP-AL	438 / cvtd MD-82 (DC-9-82)
☐	N439AA	Boeing (Douglas) MD-83 (DC-9-83)	49457 / 1398		0887	0887	2 PW JT8D-219	72575	F20Y113	CP-AM	439 / cvtd MD-82 (DC-9-82)
☐	N440AA	Boeing (Douglas) MD-82 (DC-9-82)	49459 / 1407		0987	0987	2 PW JT8D-217C	67812	F20Y113	CP-BE	440
☐	N441AA	Boeing (Douglas) MD-82 (DC-9-82)	49460 / 1408		0987	0987	2 PW JT8D-217C	67812	F20Y113	CP-BF	441
☐	N442AA	Boeing (Douglas) MD-82 (DC-9-82)	49468 / 1409		0987	0987	2 PW JT8D-217C	67812	F20Y113	CP-BG	442
☐	N443AA	Boeing (Douglas) MD-82 (DC-9-82)	49469 / 1410		0987	0987	2 PW JT8D-217C	67812	F20Y113	CP-BH	443
☐	N73444	Boeing (Douglas) MD-82 (DC-9-82)	49470 / 1417		1087	1087	2 PW JT8D-217C	67812	F20Y113	CP-BJ	444
☐	N445AA	Boeing (Douglas) MD-82 (DC-9-82)	49471 / 1418		1087	1087	2 PW JT8D-217C	67812	F20Y113	CP-BK	445
☐	N446AA	Boeing (Douglas) MD-82 (DC-9-82)	49472 / 1426		1187	1187	2 PW JT8D-217C	67812	F20Y113	CP-BL	446
☐	N447AA	Boeing (Douglas) MD-82 (DC-9-82)	49473 / 1427		1187	1187	2 PW JT8D-217C	67812	F20Y113	CP-BM	447
☐	N448AA	Boeing (Douglas) MD-82 (DC-9-82)	49474 / 1431		1287	1287	2 PW JT8D-217C	67812	F20Y113	CP-DE	448
☐	N449AA	Boeing (Douglas) MD-82 (DC-9-82)	49475 / 1432		1287	1287	2 PW JT8D-217C	67812	F20Y113	CP-DF	449
☐	N450AA	Boeing (Douglas) MD-82 (DC-9-82)	49476 / 1439		0288	0288	2 PW JT8D-217C	67812	F20Y113	CP-DG	450
☐	N451AA	Boeing (Douglas) MD-82 (DC-9-82)	49477 / 1441		0288	0288	2 PW JT8D-217C	67812	F20Y113	CP-DH	451
☐	N452AA	Boeing (Douglas) MD-82 (DC-9-82)	49553 / 1450		0288	0288	2 PW JT8D-217C	67812	F20Y113	CP-DJ	452
☐	N453AA	Boeing (Douglas) MD-82 (DC-9-82)	49558 / 1451		0388	0388	2 PW JT8D-217C	67812	F20Y113	CP-DK	453
☐	N454AA	Boeing (Douglas) MD-82 (DC-9-82)	49559 / 1460		0388	0388	2 PW JT8D-217C	67812	F20Y113	CP-DL	454
☐	N455AA	Boeing (Douglas) MD-82 (DC-9-82)	49560 / 1462		0488	0488	2 PW JT8D-217C	67812	F20Y113	CP-DM	455
☐	N456AA	Boeing (Douglas) MD-82 (DC-9-82)	49561 / 1474		0588	0588	2 PW JT8D-217C	67812	F20Y113	CP-EF	456
☐	N457AA	Boeing (Douglas) MD-82 (DC-9-82)	49562 / 1475		0588	0588	2 PW JT8D-217C	67812	F20Y113	CP-EG	457
☐	N458AA	Boeing (Douglas) MD-82 (DC-9-82)	49563 / 1485		0688	0688	2 PW JT8D-217C	67812	F20Y113	CP-EH	458
☐	N459AA	Boeing (Douglas) MD-82 (DC-9-82)	49564 / 1486		0688	0688	2 PW JT8D-217C	67812	F20Y113	CP-EJ	459
☐	N460AA	Boeing (Douglas) MD-82 (DC-9-82)	49565 / 1496		0788	0788	2 PW JT8D-217C	67812	F20Y113	CP-EK	460
☐	N461AA	Boeing (Douglas) MD-82 (DC-9-82)	49566 / 1497		0888	0888	2 PW JT8D-217C	67812	F20Y113	CP-EL	461
☐	N462AA	Boeing (Douglas) MD-82 (DC-9-82)	49592 / 1505		0888	0888	2 PW JT8D-217C	67812	F20Y113	CP-EM	462
☐	N463AA	Boeing (Douglas) MD-82 (DC-9-82)	49593 / 1506		0888	0888	2 PW JT8D-217C	67812	F20Y113	CP-FG	463
☐	N464AA	Boeing (Douglas) MD-82 (DC-9-82)	49594 / 1507		0988	0988	2 PW JT8D-217C	67812	F20Y113	CP-FH	464
☐	N465A	Boeing (Douglas) MD-82 (DC-9-82)	49595 / 1509		0988	0988	2 PW JT8D-217C	67812	F20Y113	CP-FJ	465
☐	N466AA	Boeing (Douglas) MD-82 (DC-9-82)	49596 / 1510		0988	0988	2 PW JT8D-217C	67812	F14Y125	CP-FK	466
☐	N467AA	Boeing (Douglas) MD-82 (DC-9-82)	49597 / 1511		0988	0988	2 PW JT8D-217C	67812	F14Y125	CP-FL	467
☐	N468AA	Boeing (Douglas) MD-82 (DC-9-82)	49598 / 1513		0988	0988	2 PW JT8D-217C	67812	F14Y125	CP-FM	468
☐	N469AA	Boeing (Douglas) MD-82 (DC-9-82)	49599 / 1515		0988	0988	2 PW JT8D-217C	67812	F14Y125	FH-GP	469
☐	N470AA	Boeing (Douglas) MD-82 (DC-9-82)	49600 / 1516		1088	1088	2 PW JT8D-217C	67812	F14Y125	FH-JP	470

☐ N471AA	Boeing (Douglas) MD-82 (DC-9-82)	49601 / 1518		1088	1088	2 PW JT8D-217C	67812	F14Y125	FH-KP	471
☐ N472AA	Boeing (Douglas) MD-82 (DC-9-82)	49647 / 1520		1088	1088	2 PW JT8D-217C	67812	F14Y125	FH-LP	472
☐ N473AA	Boeing (Douglas) MD-82 (DC-9-82)	49648 / 1521		1088	1088	2 PW JT8D-217C	67812	F14Y125	FH-MP	473
☐ N474	Boeing (Douglas) MD-82 (DC-9-82)	49649 / 1526		1088	1088	2 PW JT8D-217C	67812	F14Y125	FJ-AP	474
☐ N475AA	Boeing (Douglas) MD-82 (DC-9-82)	49650 / 1527		1188	1188	2 PW JT8D-217C	67812	F14Y125	FJ-BP	475
☐ N476AA	Boeing (Douglas) MD-82 (DC-9-82)	49651 / 1528		1088	1088	2 PW JT8D-217C	67812	F14Y125	FJ-CP	476
☐ N477AA	Boeing (Douglas) MD-82 (DC-9-82)	49652 / 1529		1188	1188	2 PW JT8D-217C	67812	F14Y125	FJ-DP	477
☐ N478AA	Boeing (Douglas) MD-82 (DC-9-82)	49653 / 1534		1188	1188	2 PW JT8D-217C	67812	F14Y125	FJ-EP	478
☐ N479AA	Boeing (Douglas) MD-82 (DC-9-82)	49654 / 1535		1188	1188	2 PW JT8D-217C	67812	F14Y125	FJ-GP	479
☐ N480AA	Boeing (Douglas) MD-82 (DC-9-82)	49655 / 1536		1188	1188	2 PW JT8D-217C	67812	F14Y125	FJ-HP	480
☐ N481AA	Boeing (Douglas) MD-82 (DC-9-82)	49656 / 1545		1288	1288	2 PW JT8D-217C	67812	F14Y125	FJ-KP	481
☐ N482AA	Boeing (Douglas) MD-82 (DC-9-82)	49675 / 1546		1288	1288	2 PW JT8D-217C	67812	F14Y125	FJ-LP	482
☐ N483A	Boeing (Douglas) MD-82 (DC-9-82)	49676 / 1550		1288	1288	2 PW JT8D-217C	67812	F14Y125	FJ-MP	483
☐ N484AA	Boeing (Douglas) MD-82 (DC-9-82)	49677 / 1551		1288	1288	2 PW JT8D-217C	67812	F14Y125	FK-AP	484
☐ N485AA	Boeing (Douglas) MD-82 (DC-9-82)	49678 / 1555		0189	0189	2 PW JT8D-217C	67812	F14Y125	FK-BP	485
☐ N486AA	Boeing (Douglas) MD-82 (DC-9-82)	49679 / 1557		0189	0189	2 PW JT8D-217C	67812	F14Y125	FK-CP	486
☐ N487AA	Boeing (Douglas) MD-82 (DC-9-82)	49680 / 1558		0189	0189	2 PW JT8D-217C	67812	F14Y125	FK-DP	487
☐ N488AA	Boeing (Douglas) MD-82 (DC-9-82)	49681 / 1560		0189	0189	2 PW JT8D-217C	67812	F14Y125	FK-EP	488
☐ N489AA	Boeing (Douglas) MD-82 (DC-9-82)	49682 / 1562		0289	0289	2 PW JT8D-217C	67812	F14Y125	FK-GP	489
☐ N490AA	Boeing (Douglas) MD-82 (DC-9-82)	49683 / 1563		0289	0289	2 PW JT8D-217C	67812	F14Y125	FK-HP	490
☐ N491AA	Boeing (Douglas) MD-82 (DC-9-82)	49684 / 1564		0289	0289	2 PW JT8D-217C	67812	F14Y125	FK-JP	491
☐ N492AA	Boeing (Douglas) MD-82 (DC-9-82)	49730 / 1565		0289	0289	2 PW JT8D-217C	67812	F14Y125	FK-LP	492
☐ N493AA	Boeing (Douglas) MD-82 (DC-9-82)	49731 / 1566		0289	0289	2 PW JT8D-217C	67812	F14Y125	FK-MP	493
☐ N494AA	Boeing (Douglas) MD-82 (DC-9-82)	49732 / 1567		0289	0289	2 PW JT8D-217C	67812	F14Y125	FL-BP	494
☐ N495AA	Boeing (Douglas) MD-82 (DC-9-82)	49733 / 1607		0789	0789	2 PW JT8D-217C	67812	F14Y125	FL-CP	495
☐ N496AA	Boeing (Douglas) MD-82 (DC-9-82)	49734 / 1619		0889	0889	2 PW JT8D-217C	67812	F14Y125	FL-DP	496
☐ N497AA	Boeing (Douglas) MD-82 (DC-9-82)	49735 / 1635		0989	0989	2 PW JT8D-217C	67812	F14Y125	FL-EP	497
☐ N498AA	Boeing (Douglas) MD-82 (DC-9-82)	49736 / 1640		1089	1089	2 PW JT8D-217C	67812	F14Y125	FL-GP	498
☐ N499AA	Boeing (Douglas) MD-82 (DC-9-82)	49737 / 1641		1089	1089	2 PW JT8D-217C	67812	F14Y125	FL-HP	499
☐ N501AA	Boeing (Douglas) MD-82 (DC-9-82)	49738 / 1648		1089	1089	2 PW JT8D-217C	67812	F14Y125	FL-JP	501
☐ N33502	Boeing (Douglas) MD-82 (DC-9-82)	49739 / 1649		1089	1089	2 PW JT8D-217C	67812	F14Y125	FL-KP	502
☐ N44503	Boeing (Douglas) MD-82 (DC-9-82)	49797 / 1650		1189	1189	2 PW JT8D-217C	67812	F14Y125	FL-MP	503
☐ N70504	Boeing (Douglas) MD-82 (DC-9-82)	49798 / 1651		1089	1089	2 PW JT8D-217C	67812	F14Y125	FM-AP	504
☐ N505AA	Boeing (Douglas) MD-82 (DC-9-82)	49799 / 1652		1189	1189	2 PW JT8D-217C	67812	F14Y125	FM-BP	505
☐ N7506	Boeing (Douglas) MD-82 (DC-9-82)	49800 / 1660		1289	1289	2 PW JT8D-217C	67812	F14Y125	FM-CP	506
☐ N3507A	Boeing (Douglas) MD-82 (DC-9-82)	49801 / 1661		1289	1289	2 PW JT8D-217C	67812	F14Y125	FM-DP	507
☐ N7508	Boeing (Douglas) MD-82 (DC-9-82)	49802 / 1662		1289	1289	2 PW JT8D-217C	67812	F14Y125	FM-EP	508
☐ N7509	Boeing (Douglas) MD-82 (DC-9-82)	49803 / 1663		1289	1289	2 PW JT8D-217C	67812	F14Y125	FM-GP	509
☐ N510AM	Boeing (Douglas) MD-82 (DC-9-82)	49804 / 1669		1289	1289	2 PW JT8D-217C	67812	F14Y125	FM-HP	510
☐ N90511	Boeing (Douglas) MD-82 (DC-9-82)	49805 / 1672		1289	1289	2 PW JT8D-217C	67812	F14Y125	FM-JP	511
☐ N7512A	Boeing (Douglas) MD-82 (DC-9-82)	49806 / 1673		1289	1289	2 PW JT8D-217C	67812	F14Y125	FM-KP	512
☐ N513AA	Boeing (Douglas) MD-82 (DC-9-82)	49890 / 1686		0390	0390	2 PW JT8D-217C	67812	F14Y125	FP-AB	513
☐ N7514A	Boeing (Douglas) MD-82 (DC-9-82)	49891 / 1694		0390	0390	2 PW JT8D-217C	67812	F14Y125	FP-AC	514
☐ N3515	Boeing (Douglas) MD-82 (DC-9-82)	49892 / 1695		0390	0390	2 PW JT8D-217C	67812	F14Y125	FP-AD	515
☐ N516AM	Boeing (Douglas) MD-82 (DC-9-82)	49893 / 1696		0390	0390	2 PW JT8D-217C	67812	F14Y125	FP-AE	516
☐ N7517A	Boeing (Douglas) MD-82 (DC-9-82)	49894 / 1697		0390	0390	2 PW JT8D-217C	67812	F14Y125	FP-AG	517
☐ N7518A	Boeing (Douglas) MD-82 (DC-9-82)	49895 / 1698		0390	0390	2 PW JT8D-217C	67812	F14Y125	FP-AH	518
☐ N7519A	Boeing (Douglas) MD-82 (DC-9-82)	49896 / 1707		0590	0590	2 PW JT8D-217C	67812	F14Y125	FP-AJ	519
☐ N7520A	Boeing (Douglas) MD-82 (DC-9-82)	49897 / 1708		0590	0590	2 PW JT8D-217C	67812	F14Y125	FP-AK	520
☐ N7521A	Boeing (Douglas) MD-82 (DC-9-82)	49898 / 1709		0490	0590	2 PW JT8D-217C	67812	F14Y125	FP-AL	521
☐ N7522A	Boeing (Douglas) MD-82 (DC-9-82)	49899 / 1722		0690	0690	2 PW JT8D-217C	67812	F14Y125	FP-AM	522
☐ N59523	Boeing (Douglas) MD-82 (DC-9-82)	49915 / 1723		0690	0690	2 PW JT8D-217C	67812	F14Y125	FP-BC	523
☐ N70524	Boeing (Douglas) MD-82 (DC-9-82)	49916 / 1729		0690	0690	2 PW JT8D-217C	67812	F14Y125	FP-BD	524
☐ N7525A	Boeing (Douglas) MD-82 (DC-9-82)	49917 / 1735		0790	0790	2 PW JT8D-217C	67812	F14Y125	FP-BE	525
☐ N7526A	Boeing (Douglas) MD-82 (DC-9-82)	49918 / 1743		0890	0890	2 PW JT8D-217C	67812	F14Y125	FP-BG	526
☐ N7527A	Boeing (Douglas) MD-82 (DC-9-82)	49919 / 1744		0890	0890	2 PW JT8D-217C	67812	F14Y125	FP-BH	527
☐ N7528A	Boeing (Douglas) MD-82 (DC-9-82)	49920 / 1750		0990	0990	2 PW JT8D-217C	67812	F14Y125	FP-BJ	528
☐ N70529	Boeing (Douglas) MD-82 (DC-9-82)	49921 / 1752		0990	0990	2 PW JT8D-217C	67812	F14Y125	FP-BK	529
☐ N7530	Boeing (Douglas) MD-82 (DC-9-82)	49922 / 1753		0990	0990	2 PW JT8D-217C	67812	F14Y125	FP-BL	530
☐ N7531A	Boeing (Douglas) MD-82 (DC-9-82)	49923 / 1758		0990	0990	2 PW JT8D-217C	67812	F14Y125	FP-CD	531
☐ N7532A	Boeing (Douglas) MD-82 (DC-9-82)	49924 / 1759		0990	0990	2 PW JT8D-217C	67812	F14Y125	FP-CE	532
☐ N7533A	Boeing (Douglas) MD-82 (DC-9-82)	49987 / 1760		0990	0990	2 PW JT8D-217C	67812	F14Y125	DQ-AB	533
☐ N7534A	Boeing (Douglas) MD-82 (DC-9-82)	49988 / 1768		0990	0990	2 PW JT8D-217C	67812	F14Y125	DQ-AC	534
☐ N7535A	Boeing (Douglas) MD-82 (DC-9-82)	49989 / 1769		1090	1090	2 PW JT8D-217C	67812	F14Y125	DQ-AE	535
☐ N7536A	Boeing (Douglas) MD-82 (DC-9-82)	49990 / 1770		1090	1090	2 PW JT8D-217C	67812	F14Y125	DQ-AF	536
☐ N7537A	Boeing (Douglas) MD-82 (DC-9-82)	49991 / 1780		1090	1090	2 PW JT8D-217C	67812	F14Y125	DQ-AG	537
☐ N7538A	Boeing (Douglas) MD-82 (DC-9-82)	49992 / 1781		1190	1190	2 PW JT8D-217C	67812	F14Y125	DQ-AH	538
☐ N7539A	Boeing (Douglas) MD-82 (DC-9-82)	49993 / 1782		1190	1190	2 PW JT8D-217C	67812	F14Y125	DQ-AJ	539
☐ N7540A	Boeing (Douglas) MD-82 (DC-9-82)	49994 / 1790		1290	1290	2 PW JT8D-217C	67812	F14Y125	DQ-AK	540
☐ N7541A	Boeing (Douglas) MD-82 (DC-9-82)	49995 / 1791		1290	1290	2 PW JT8D-217C	67812	F14Y125	DQ-AL	541
☐ N7542A	Boeing (Douglas) MD-82 (DC-9-82)	49996 / 1792		1290	1290	2 PW JT8D-217C	67812	F14Y125	DQ-AM	542
☐ N7543A	Boeing (Douglas) MD-82 (DC-9-82)	53025 / 1802		1290	1290	2 PW JT8D-217C	67812	F14Y125	DQ-AP	543
☐ N7544A	Boeing (Douglas) MD-82 (DC-9-82)	53026 / 1804		1290	1290	2 PW JT8D-217C	67812	F14Y125	DQ-BC	544
☐ N16545	Boeing (Douglas) MD-82 (DC-9-82)	53027 / 1805		1290	1290	2 PW JT8D-217C	67812	F14Y125	DQ-BE	545
☐ N7546A	Boeing (Douglas) MD-82 (DC-9-82)	53028 / 1813		0191	0191	2 PW JT8D-217C	67812	F14Y125	DQ-BF	546
☐ N7547A	Boeing (Douglas) MD-82 (DC-9-82)	53029 / 1814		0191	0191	2 PW JT8D-217C	67812	F14Y125	DQ-BG	547
☐ N7548A	Boeing (Douglas) MD-82 (DC-9-82)	53030 / 1816		0291	0291	2 PW JT8D-217C	67812	F14Y125	DQ-BH	548
☐ N7549A	Boeing (Douglas) MD-82 (DC-9-82)	53031 / 1819		0291	0291	2 PW JT8D-217C	67812	F14Y125	DQ-BJ	549
☐ N7550	Boeing (Douglas) MD-82 (DC-9-82)	53032 / 1820		0291	0291	2 PW JT8D-217C	67812	F14Y125	DQ-BK	550
☐ N14551	Boeing (Douglas) MD-82 (DC-9-82)	53033 / 1822		0291	0291	2 PW JT8D-217C	67812	F14Y125	DQ-BL	551
☐ N552AA	Boeing (Douglas) MD-82 (DC-9-82)	53034 / 1826		0291	0291	2 PW JT8D-217C	67812	F14Y125	DQ-BM	552
☐ N553AA	Boeing (Douglas) MD-82 (DC-9-82)	53083 / 1828		0391	0391	2 PW JT8D-217C	67812	F14Y125	KQ-AC	553
☐ N554AA	Boeing (Douglas) MD-82 (DC-9-82)	53084 / 1830		0391	0391	2 PW JT8D-217C	67812	F14Y125	KQ-AD	554
☐ N555AN	Boeing (Douglas) MD-82 (DC-9-82)	53085 / 1839		0391	0391	2 PW JT8D-217C	67812	F14Y125	KQ-AE	555
☐ N556AA	Boeing (Douglas) MD-82 (DC-9-82)	53086 / 1840		0391	0391	2 PW JT8D-217C	67812	F14Y125	KQ-AF	556
☐ N557AN	Boeing (Douglas) MD-82 (DC-9-82)	53087 / 1841		0491	0491	2 PW JT8D-217C	67812	F14Y125	KQ-AG	557
☐ N558AA	Boeing (Douglas) MD-82 (DC-9-82)	53088 / 1852		0591	0591	2 PW JT8D-217C	67812	F14Y125	KQ-AH	558
☐ N559AA	Boeing (Douglas) MD-82 (DC-9-82)	53089 / 1853		0591	0591	2 PW JT8D-217C	67812	F14Y125	KQ-AJ	559
☐ N560AA	Boeing (Douglas) MD-82 (DC-9-82)	53090 / 1858		0591	0591	2 PW JT8D-217C	67812	F14Y125	KQ-AL	560
☐ N561AA	Boeing (Douglas) MD-82 (DC-9-82)	53091 / 1863		0591	0591	2 PW JT8D-217C	67812	F14Y125	BD-AQ	561
☐ N562AA	Boeing (Douglas) MD-83 (DC-9-83)	49344 / 1370		0687	0687	2 PW JT8D-219	72575	F20Y113	KL-BH	562
☐ N563AA	Boeing (Douglas) MD-83 (DC-9-83)	49345 / 1371		0687	0687	2 PW JT8D-219	72575	F20Y113	KL-BM	563
☐ N564AA	Boeing (Douglas) MD-83 (DC-9-83)	49346 / 1372		0687	0687	2 PW JT8D-219	72575	F20Y113	KL-DG	564
☐ N565AA	Boeing (Douglas) MD-83 (DC-9-83)	49347 / 1373		0687	0687	2 PW JT8D-219	72575	F20Y113	KL-DJ	565
☐ N566AA	Boeing (Douglas) MD-83 (DC-9-83)	49348 / 1374		0687	0687	2 PW JT8D-219	72575	F20Y113	KL-HM	566
☐ N567AM	Boeing (Douglas) MD-83 (DC-9-83)	53293 / 2021		0892	0992	2 PW JT8D-219	72575	F20Y113	GH-RS	567
☐ N568AA	Boeing (Douglas) MD-83 (DC-9-83)	49349 / 1375		0687	0687	2 PW JT8D-219	72575	F20Y113	KM-BC	568
☐ N569AA	Boeing (Douglas) MD-83 (DC-9-83)	49351 / 1385		0787	0787	2 PW JT8D-219	72575	F20Y113	CP-AB	569
☐ N570AA	Boeing (Douglas) MD-83 (DC-9-83)	49352 / 1386		0787	0787	2 PW JT8D-219	72575	F20Y113	CP-AD	570
☐ N571AA	Boeing (Douglas) MD-83 (DC-9-83)	49353 / 1387		0787	0787	2 PW JT8D-219	72575	F20Y113	CP-AE	571
☐ N572AA	Boeing (Douglas) MD-83 (DC-9-83)	49458 / 1406		0987	0987	2 PW JT8D-219	72575	F20Y113	CP-BD	572
☐ N573AA	Boeing (Douglas) MD-82 (DC-9-82)	53092 / 1864		0591	0591	2 PW JT8D-217C	67812	F14Y125	KQ-AM	573
☐ N574AA	Boeing (Douglas) MD-82 (DC-9-82)	53151 / 1866		0691	0691	2 PW JT8D-217C	67812	F14Y125	KQ-AP	574
☐ N575AM	Boeing (Douglas) MD-82 (DC-9-82)	53152 / 1875		0691	0691	2 PW JT8D-217C	67812	F14Y125	KQ-BC	575
☐ N576AA	Boeing (Douglas) MD-82 (DC-9-82)	53153 / 1876		0691	0691	2 PW JT8D-217C	67812	F14Y125	KQ-BD	576
☐ N577AA	Boeing (Douglas) MD-82 (DC-9-82)	53154 / 1878		0691	0691	2 PW JT8D-217C	67812	F14Y125	KQ-BE	577
☐ N578AA	Boeing (Douglas) MD-82 (DC-9-82)	53155 / 1883		0791	0791	2 PW JT8D-217C	67812	F14Y125	KQ-BF	578
☐ N579AA	Boeing (Douglas) MD-82 (DC-9-82)	53156 / 1884		0791	0791	2 PW JT8D-217C	67812	F14Y125	KQ-BG	579
☐ N580AA	Boeing (Douglas) MD-82 (DC-9-82)	53157 / 1885		0791	0791	2 PW JT8D-217C	67812	F14Y125	KQ-BH	580
☐ N581AA	Boeing (Douglas) MD-82 (DC-9-82)	53158 / 1891		0791	0791	2 PW JT8D-217C	67812	F14Y125	KQ-BJ	581
☐ N582AA	Boeing (Douglas) MD-82 (DC-9-82)	53159 / 1892		0791	0791	2 PW JT8D-217C	67812	F14Y125	KQ-BL	582
☐ N583AA	Boeing (Douglas) MD-82 (DC-9-82)	53160 / 1893		0891	0891	2 PW JT8D-217C	67812	F14Y125	KQ-BM	583
☐ N584AA	Boeing (Douglas) MD-82 (DC-9-82)	53247 / 1902		0891	0891	2 PW JT8D-217C	67812	F14Y125	BC-DQ	584
☐ N585AA	Boeing (Douglas) MD-82 (DC-9-82)	53248 / 1903		0891	0891	2 PW JT8D-217C	67812	F14Y125	BC-EQ	585
☐ N586AA	Boeing (Douglas) MD-82 (DC-9-82)	53249 / 1904		0891	0891	2 PW JT8D-217C	67812	F14Y125	BC-FQ	586
☐ N587AA	Boeing (Douglas) MD-82 (DC-9-82)	53250 / 1907		0991	0991	2 PW JT8D-217C	67812	F14Y125	BC-GQ	587
☐ N588AA	Boeing (Douglas) MD-83 (DC-9-83)	53251 / 1909		0991	0991	2 PW JT8D-219	72575	F20Y113	BC-HQ	588
☐ N589AA	Boeing (Douglas) MD-83 (DC-9-83)	53252 / 1910		0991	0991	2 PW JT8D-219	72575	F20Y113	BC-JQ	589
☐ N590AA	Boeing (Douglas) MD-83 (DC-9-83)	53253 / 1919		0991	0991	2 PW JT8D-219	72575	F20Y113	BC-KQ	590
☐ N591AA	Boeing (Douglas) MD-83 (DC-9-83)	53254 / 1920		0991	1091	2 PW JT8D-219	72575	F20Y113	BC-LQ	591

265 registration type of aircraft cn/fn ex/ex* mfd del powered by mtow kg configuration selcal name/fln/specialitites/remarks

registration	type of aircraft	cn/fn	ex/ex*	mfd	del	powered by	mtow kg	configuration	selcal	name/fln/specialitites/remarks
☐ N592AA	Boeing (Douglas) MD-83 (DC-9-83)	53255 / 1932		1091	1191	2 PW JT8D-219	72575	F20Y113	BC-MQ	592
☐ N593AA	Boeing (Douglas) MD-83 (DC-9-83)	53256 / 1933		1091	1191	2 PW JT8D-219	72575	F20Y113	BC-PQ	593
☐ N594AA	Boeing (Douglas) MD-83 (DC-9-83)	53284 / 1966		0192	0292	2 PW JT8D-219	72575	F20Y113	GH-KS	594
☐ N595AA	Boeing (Douglas) MD-83 (DC-9-83)	53285 / 1989		0392	0492	2 PW JT8D-219	72575	F20Y113	GH-LR	595
☐ N596AA	Boeing (Douglas) MD-83 (DC-9-83)	53286 / 2000		0692	0692	2 PW JT8D-219	72575	F20Y113	GH-LS	596
☐ N597AA	Boeing (Douglas) MD-83 (DC-9-83)	53287 / 2006		0692	0692	2 PW JT8D-219	72575	F20Y113	GH-MR	597
☐ N598AA	Boeing (Douglas) MD-83 (DC-9-83)	53288 / 2011		0792	0792	2 PW JT8D-219	72575	F20Y113	GH-MS	598
☐ N599AA	Boeing (Douglas) MD-83 (DC-9-83)	53289 / 2012		0792	0792	2 PW JT8D-219	72575	F20Y113	GH-PR	599
☐ N901AN	Boeing 737-823	29503 / 184		1298	0299	2 CFMI CFM56-7B26	79016	F20Y126	AC-BJ	3AA
☐ N902AN	Boeing 737-823	29504 / 190		1298	0299	2 CFMI CFM56-7B26	79016	F20Y126	BE-CD	3AB
☐ N903AN	Boeing 737-823	29505 / 196		0199	0299	2 CFMI CFM56-7B26	79016	F20Y126	BG-CH	3AC
☐ N904AN	Boeing 737-823	29506 / 207		0199	0399	2 CFMI CFM56-7B26	79016	F20Y126	BH-FM	3AD
☐ N905AN	Boeing 737-823	29507 / 231		0299	0399	2 CFMI CFM56-7B26	79016	F20Y126	BH-AD	3AE
☐ N906AN	Boeing 737-823	29508 / 240		0399	0499	2 CFMI CFM56-7B26	79016	F20Y126	BH-AG	3AF
☐ N907AN	Boeing 737-823	29509 / 254		0399	0499	2 CFMI CFM56-7B26	79016	F20Y126	BH-AL	3AG
☐ N908AN	Boeing 737-823	29510				2 CFMI CFM56-7B26	79016	F20Y126	BH-DJ	3AH / oo-delivery 0599
☐ N909AM	Boeing 737-823	29511				2 CFMI CFM56-7B26	79016	F20Y126	BH-DK	3AJ / oo-delivery 0599
☐ N910AN	Boeing 737-823	29512				2 CFMI CFM56-7B26	79016	F20Y126	BH-DL	3AK / oo-delivery 0599
☐ N912AN	Boeing 737-823	29513				2 CFMI CFM56-7B26	79016	F20Y126	BH-EK	3AL / oo-delivery 0599
☐ N913AN	Boeing 737-823	29514				2 CFMI CFM56-7B26	79016	F20Y126	BH-FK	3AM / oo-delivery 0699
☐ N914AN	Boeing 737-823					2 CFMI CFM56-7B26	79016	F20Y126		3AN / oo-delivery 0699
☐ N915AN	Boeing 737-823					2 CFMI CFM56-7B26	79016	F20Y126		3AP / oo-delivery 0799
☐ N916AN	Boeing 737-823					2 CFMI CFM56-7B26	79016	F20Y126		3AR / oo-delivery 0899
☐ N917AN	Boeing 737-823					2 CFMI CFM56-7B26	79016	F20Y126		3AS / oo-delivery 0899
☐ N918AN	Boeing 737-823					2 CFMI CFM56-7B26	79016	F20Y126		3AT / oo-delivery 0999
☐ N919AN	Boeing 737-823					2 CFMI CFM56-7B26	79016	F20Y126		3AU / oo-delivery 0999
☐ N920AN	Boeing 737-823					2 CFMI CFM56-7B26	79016	F20Y126		3AV / oo-delivery 1099
☐ N921AN	Boeing 737-823					2 CFMI CFM56-7B26	79016	F20Y126		3AW / oo-delivery 1099
☐ N922AN	Boeing 737-823					2 CFMI CFM56-7B26	79016	F20Y126		3AX / oo-delivery 1199
☐ N923AN	Boeing 737-823					2 CFMI CFM56-7B26	79016	F20Y126		3AY / oo-delivery 1199
☐ N924AN	Boeing 737-823					2 CFMI CFM56-7B26	79016	F20Y126		3BA / oo-delivery 1299
☐ N925AN	Boeing 737-823					2 CFMI CFM56-7B26	79016	F20Y126		3BB / oo-delivery 1299
☐ N926AN	Boeing 737-823					2 CFMI CFM56-7B26	79016	F20Y126		oo-delivery 0100
☐ N927AN	Boeing 737-823					2 CFMI CFM56-7B26	79016	F20Y126		oo-delivery 0100
☐ N928AN	Boeing 737-823					2 CFMI CFM56-7B26	79016	F20Y126		oo-delivery 0200
☐ N929AN	Boeing 737-823					2 CFMI CFM56-7B26	79016	F20Y126		oo-delivery 0200
☐ N930AN	Boeing 737-823					2 CFMI CFM56-7B26	79016	F20Y126		oo-delivery 0300
☐ N931AN	Boeing 737-823					2 CFMI CFM56-7B26	79016	F20Y126		oo-delivery 0300
☐ N932AN	Boeing 737-823					2 CFMI CFM56-7B26	79016	F20Y126		oo-delivery 0400
☐ N933AN	Boeing 737-823					2 CFMI CFM56-7B26	79016	F20Y126		oo-delivery 0400
☐ N934AN	Boeing 737-823					2 CFMI CFM56-7B26	79016	F20Y126		oo-delivery 0500
☐ N935AN	Boeing 737-823					2 CFMI CFM56-7B26	79016	F20Y126		oo-delivery 0500
☐ N936AN	Boeing 737-823					2 CFMI CFM56-7B26	79016	F20Y126		oo-delivery 0600
☐ N937AN	Boeing 737-823					2 CFMI CFM56-7B26	79016	F20Y126		oo-delivery 0600
☐ N938AN	Boeing 737-823					2 CFMI CFM56-7B26	79016	F20Y126		oo-delivery 0700
☐ N939AN	Boeing 737-823					2 CFMI CFM56-7B26	79016	F20Y126		oo-delivery 0800
☐ N940AN	Boeing 737-823					2 CFMI CFM56-7B26	79016	F20Y126		oo-delivery 0800
☐ N941AN	Boeing 737-823					2 CFMI CFM56-7B26	79016	F20Y126		oo-delivery 0900
☐ N942AN	Boeing 737-823					2 CFMI CFM56-7B26	79016	F20Y126		oo-delivery 0900
☐ N943AN	Boeing 737-823					2 CFMI CFM56-7B26	79016	F20Y126		oo-delivery 0900
☐ N944AN	Boeing 737-823					2 CFMI CFM56-7B26	79016	F20Y126		oo-delivery 1000
☐ N945AN	Boeing 737-823					2 CFMI CFM56-7B26	79016	F20Y126		oo-delivery 1000
☐ N946AN	Boeing 737-823					2 CFMI CFM56-7B26	79016	F20Y126		oo-delivery 1100
☐ N947AN	Boeing 737-823					2 CFMI CFM56-7B26	79016	F20Y126		oo-delivery 1100
☐ N948AN	Boeing 737-823					2 CFMI CFM56-7B26	79016	F20Y126		oo-delivery 1200
☐ N949AN	Boeing 737-823					2 CFMI CFM56-7B26	79016	F20Y126		oo-delivery 1200
☐ N950AN	Boeing 737-823					2 CFMI CFM56-7B26	79016	F20Y126		oo-delivery 0101
☐ N951AA	Boeing 737-823					2 CFMI CFM56-7B26	79016	F20Y126		oo-delivery 0101
☐ N952AA	Boeing 737-823					2 CFMI CFM56-7B26	79016	F20Y126		oo-delivery 0201
☐ N953AN	Boeing 737-823					2 CFMI CFM56-7B26	79016	F20Y126		oo-delivery 0201
☐ N954AN	Boeing 737-823					2 CFMI CFM56-7B26	79016	F20Y126		oo-delivery 0301
☐ N955AN	Boeing 737-823					2 CFMI CFM56-7B26	79016	F20Y126		oo-delivery 0301
☐ N956AN	Boeing 737-823					2 CFMI CFM56-7B26	79016	F20Y126		oo-delivery 0401
☐ N957AN	Boeing 737-823					2 CFMI CFM56-7B26	79016	F20Y126		oo-delivery 0401
☐ N958AN	Boeing 737-823					2 CFMI CFM56-7B26	79016	F20Y126		oo-delivery 0501
☐ N959AN	Boeing 737-823					2 CFMI CFM56-7B26	79016	F20Y126		oo-delivery 0501
☐ N960AN	Boeing 737-823					2 CFMI CFM56-7B26	79016	F20Y126		oo-delivery 0601
☐ N961AN	Boeing 737-823					2 CFMI CFM56-7B26	79016	F20Y126		oo-delivery 0601
☐ N962AN	Boeing 737-823					2 CFMI CFM56-7B26	79016	F20Y126		oo-delivery 0701
☐ N963AN	Boeing 737-823					2 CFMI CFM56-7B26	79016	F20Y126		oo-delivery 0701
☐ N964AN	Boeing 737-823					2 CFMI CFM56-7B26	79016	F20Y126		oo-delivery 0801
☐ N965AN	Boeing 737-823					2 CFMI CFM56-7B26	79016	F20Y126		oo-delivery 0801
☐ N966AN	Boeing 737-823					2 CFMI CFM56-7B26	79016	F20Y126		oo-delivery 0901
☐ N967AN	Boeing 737-823					2 CFMI CFM56-7B26	79016	F20Y126		oo-delivery 0901
☐ N968AN	Boeing 737-823					2 CFMI CFM56-7B26	79016	F20Y26		oo-delivery 1001
☐ N969AN	Boeing 737-823					2 CFMI CFM56-7B26	79016	F20Y126		oo-delivery 1001
☐ N970AN	Boeing 737-823					2 CFMI CFM56-7B26	79016	F20Y126		oo-delivery 1101
☐ N971AN	Boeing 737-823					2 CFMI CFM56-7B26	79016	F20Y126		oo-delivery 1101
☐ N972AN	Boeing 737-823					2 CFMI CFM56-7B26	79016	F20Y126		oo-delivery 1201
☐ N973AN	Boeing 737-823					2 CFMI CFM56-7B26	79016	F20Y126		oo-delivery 1201
☐ N974AN	Boeing 737-823					2 CFMI CFM56-7B26	79016	F20Y126		oo-delivery 0102
☐ N975AN	Boeing 737-823					2 CFMI CFM56-7B26	79016	F20Y126		oo-delivery 0102
☐ N976AN	Boeing 737-823					2 CFMI CFM56-7B26	79016	F20Y126		oo-delivery 0202
☐ N977AN	Boeing 737-823					2 CFMI CFM56-7B26	79016	F20Y126		oo-delivery 0302
☐ N978AN	Boeing 737-823					2 CFMI CFM56-7B26	79016	F20Y126		oo-delivery 0402
☐ N979AN	Boeing 737-823					2 CFMI CFM56-7B26	79016	F20Y126		oo-delivery 0502
☐ N980AN	Boeing 737-823					2 CFMI CFM56-7B26	79016	F20Y126		oo-delivery 0602
☐ N981AN	Boeing 737-823					2 CFMI CFM56-7B26	79016	F20Y126		oo-delivery 0702
☐ N982AN	Boeing 737-823					2 CFMI CFM56-7B26	79016	F20Y126		oo-delivery 0802
☐ N983AN	Boeing 737-823					2 CFMI CFM56-7B26	79016	F20Y126		oo-delivery 0902
☐ N984AM	Boeing 737-823					2 CFMI CFM56-7B26	79016	F20Y126		oo-delivery 1002
☐ N985AM	Boeing 737-823					2 CFMI CFM56-7B26	79016	F20Y126		oo-delivery 1102
☐ N986AM	Boeing 737-823					2 CFMI CFM56-7B26	79016	F20Y126		oo-delivery 1202
☐ N987AM	Boeing 737-823					2 CFMI CFM56-7B26	79016	F20Y126		oo-delivery 0103
☐ N988AM	Boeing 737-823					2 CFMI CFM56-7B26	79016	F20Y126		oo-delivery 0203
☐ N989AM	Boeing 737-823					2 CFMI CFM56-7B26	79016	F20Y126		oo-delivery 0303
☐ N990AN	Boeing 737-823					2 CFMI CFM56-7B26	79016	F20Y126		oo-delivery 0403
☐ N991AN	Boeing 737-823					2 CFMI CFM56-7B26	79016	F20Y126		oo-delivery 0503
☐ N992AN	Boeing 737-823					2 CFMI CFM56-7B26	79016	F20Y126		oo-delivery 0603
☐ N993AN	Boeing 737-823					2 CFMI CFM56-7B26	79016	F20Y126		oo-delivery 0703
☐ N994AN	Boeing 737-823					2 CFMI CFM56-7B26	79016	F20Y126		oo-delivery 0803
☐ N995AN	Boeing 737-823					2 CFMI CFM56-7B26	79016	F20Y126		oo-delivery 0903
☐ N996AN	Boeing 737-823					2 CFMI CFM56-7B26	79016	F20Y126		oo-delivery 1003
☐ N997AN	Boeing 737-823					2 CFMI CFM56-7B26	79016	F20Y126		oo-delivery 1103
☐ N998AN	Boeing 737-823					2 CFMI CFM56-7B26	79016	F20Y126		oo-delivery 1203
☐ N	Boeing 737-823					2 CFMI CFM56-7B26	79016	F20Y126		oo-delivery 0104
☐ N	Boeing 737-823					2 CFMI CFM56-7B26	79016	F20Y126		oo-delivery 0204
☐ N	Boeing 737-823					2 CFMI CFM56-7B26	79016	F20Y126		oo-delivery 0304
☐ N701AA	Boeing 727-223 (A)	22459 / 1742		0481	0481	3 PW JT8D-15 (HK3/FDX)	86409	F12Y138	FM-JK	701
☐ N702AA	Boeing 727-223 (A)	22460 / 1746		0581	0581	3 PW JT8D-15 (HK3/FDX)	86409	F12Y138	GH-AF	702
☐ N703AA	Boeing 727-223 (A)	22461 / 1750		0581	0581	3 PW JT8D-15 (HK3/FDX)	86409	F12Y138	GH-BC	703
☐ N705AA	Boeing 727-223 (A)	22462 / 1751		0681	0681	3 PW JT8D-15 (HK3/FDX)	86409	F12Y138	GH-BK	705
☐ N706AA	Boeing 727-223 (A)	22463 / 1755		0681	0681	3 PW JT8D-15 (HK3/FDX)	86409	F12Y138	GK-BC	706
☐ N707AA	Boeing 727-223 (A)	22464 / 1758		0681	0681	3 PW JT8D-15 (HK3/FDX)	86409	F12Y138	GH-AJ	707
☐ N708AA	Boeing 727-223 (A)	22465 / 1761		0681	0681	3 PW JT8D-15 (HK3/FDX)	86409	F12Y138	GH-BD	708
☐ N709AA	Boeing 727-223 (A)	22466 / 1763		0781	0781	3 PW JT8D-15 (HK3/FDX)	86409	F12Y138	GH-BL	709
☐ N710AA	Boeing 727-223 (A)	22467 / 1765		0781	0781	3 PW JT8D-15 (HK3/FDX)	86409	F12Y138	GH-AC	710
☐ N712AA	Boeing 727-223 (A)	22468 / 1766		0781	0781	3 PW JT8D-15 (HK3/FDX)	86409	F12Y138	GH-AK	712
☐ N713AA	Boeing 727-223 (A)	22469 / 1769		0881	0881	3 PW JT8D-15 (HK3/FDX)	86409	F12Y138	GH-BE	713
☐ N715AA	Boeing 727-223 (A)	22470 / 1771		0981	0981	3 PW JT8D-15 (HK3/FDX)	86409	F12Y138	GH-BM	715

registration	type of aircraft	cn/fn	ex/ex*	mfd	del	powered by	mtow kg	configuration	selcal	name/fln/specialitites/remarks
☐ N716AA	Boeing 727-227 (A)	20608 / 891	N410BN	0772	0381	3 PW JT8D-9A	81148	F12Y138	GH-AD	716
☐ N717AA	Boeing 727-227 (A)	20610 / 893	N412BN	0772	1280	3 PW JT8D-9A	81148	F12Y138	GH-AL	717
☐ N718AA	Boeing 727-227 (A)	20611 / 894	N413BN	0872	0181	3 PW JT8D-9A	81148	F12Y138	GH-BF	718
☐ N719AA	Boeing 727-227 (A)	20612 / 928	N414BN	0373	0281	3 PW JT8D-9A (HK3/RAI)	81148	F12Y138	GH-CD	719
☐ N720AA	Boeing 727-227 (A)	20613 / 929	N415BN	0373	0381	3 PW JT8D-9A (HK3/RAI)	81148	F12Y138	GH-AE	720
☐ N721AA	Boeing 727-227 (A)	20729 / 955	N416BN	0773	1280	3 PW JT8D-9A (HK3/RAI)	81148	F12Y138	GK-DH	721
☐ N722AA	Boeing 727-227 (A)	20730 / 956	N417BN	0773	0381	3 PW JT8D-9A (HK3/RAI)	81148	F12Y138	GH-AM	722
☐ N723AA	Boeing 727-227 (A)	20731 / 957	N418BN	0773	0181	3 PW JT8D-9A (HK3/RAI)	81148	F12Y138	GH-BJ	723
☐ N725AA	Boeing 727-227 (A)	20732 / 963	N419BN	0873	1180	3 PW JT8D-9A (HK3/RAI)	81148	F12Y138	GH-CE	725
☐ N726AA	Boeing 727-227 (A)	20733 / 964	N420BN	0873	1180	3 PW JT8D-9A (HK3/RAI)	81148	F12Y138	BK-AF	726
☐ N727AA	Boeing 727-227 (A)	20734 / 965	N421BN	0873	0181	3 PW JT8D-9A (HK3/RAI)	81148	F12Y138	BK-AG	727
☐ N728AA	Boeing 727-227 (A)	20735 / 973	N422BN	0973	0281	3 PW JT8D-9A	81148	F12Y138	BK-AL	728
☐ N729AA	Boeing 727-227 (A)	20736 / 974	N423BN	0973	0281	3 PW JT8D-9A	81148	F12Y138	HK-BM	729
☐ N730AA	Boeing 727-227 (A)	20737 / 976	N424BN	0973	0381	3 PW JT8D-9A (HK3/RAI)	81148	F12Y138	HL-BF	730
☐ N731AA	Boeing 727-227 (A)	20738 / 977	N425BN	1073	0181	3 PW JT8D-9A	81148	F12Y138	HL-BG	731
☐ N6818	Boeing 727-223 (A)	19493 / 657		1168	1168	3 PW JT8D-9A	81148	F12Y138	CE-FJ	818 / cvtd -223 / to be wfu 0999
☐ N6822	Boeing 727-223 (A)	19700 / 673		0169	0169	3 PW JT8D-9A	81148	F12Y138	BG-EJ	822 / cvtd -223 / to be wfu 0999
☐ N6823	Boeing 727-223 (A)	19701 / 677		0169	0169	3 PW JT8D-9A	81148	F12Y138	BH-EJ	823 / cvtd -223 / to be wfu 0999
☐ N6835	Boeing 727-223 (A)	20188 / 730		0669	0669	3 PW JT8D-9A	81148	F12Y138	BH-AC	835 / cvtd -223 / to be wfu 0999
☐ N843AA	Boeing 727-223 (A)	20984 / 1121		0575	0575	3 PW JT8D-9A (HK3/RAI)	81148	F12Y138	CJ-GK	843
☐ N844AA	Boeing 727-223 (A)	20985 / 1123		0575	0575	3 PW JT8D-9A	81148	F12Y138	CK-EF	844
☐ N846AA	Boeing 727-223 (A)	20987 / 1126		0575	0575	3 PW JT8D-9A	81148	F12Y138	DE-HJ	846
☐ N847AA	Boeing 727-223 (A)	20988 / 1141		0675	0675	3 PW JT8D-9A	81148	F12Y138	CK-BD	847
☐ N848AA	Boeing 727-223 (A)	20989 / 1144		0675	0675	3 PW JT8D-9A	81148	F12Y138	DH-BL	848
☐ N849AA	Boeing 727-223 (A)	20990 / 1184		0576	0576	3 PW JT8D-9A	81148	F12Y138	DH-BM	849
☐ N850AA	Boeing 727-223 (A)	20991 / 1185		0576	0576	3 PW JT8D-9A	81148	F12Y138	DF-EK	850
☐ N859AA	Boeing 727-223 (A)	21086 / 1248		0377	0377	3 PW JT8D-9A (HK3/RAI)	81148	F12Y138	CK-AF	859
☐ N860AA	Boeing 727-223 (A)	21087 / 1250		0377	0377	3 PW JT8D-9A	81148	F12Y138	CK-BH	860
☐ N861AA	Boeing 727-223 (A)	21088 / 1255		0477	0477	3 PW JT8D-9A (HK3/RAI)	81148	F12Y138	CK-BJ	861
☐ N862AA	Boeing 727-223 (A)	21089 / 1263		0577	0577	3 PW JT8D-9A	81148	F12Y138	BD-GM	862
☐ N863AA	Boeing 727-223 (A)	21090 / 1267		0677	0677	3 PW JT8D-9A (HK3/RAI)	81148	F12Y138	BD-JL	863
☐ N864AA	Boeing 727-223 (A)	21369 / 1275		0677	0677	3 PW JT8D-9A (HK3/RAI)	81148	F12Y138	JL-AE	864
☐ N865AA	Boeing 727-223 (A)	21370 / 1276		0777	0777	3 PW JT8D-9A (HK3/RAI)	81148	F12Y138	JL-AF	865
☐ N866AA	Boeing 727-223 (A)	21371 / 1277		0777	0777	3 PW JT8D-9A	81148	F12Y138	CK-FG	866
☐ N867AA	Boeing 727-223 (A)	21372 / 1278		0777	0777	3 PW JT8D-9A	81148	F12Y138	DE-GJ	867
☐ N868AA	Boeing 727-223 (A)	21373 / 1279		0777	0777	3 PW JT8D-9A	81148	F12Y138	KL-FJ	868
☐ N869AA	Boeing 727-223 (A)	21374 / 1280		0877	0877	3 PW JT8D-9A	81148	F12Y138	CK-AB	869
☐ N870AA	Boeing 727-223 (A)	21382 / 1304		1177	1177	3 PW JT8D-9A	81148	F12Y138	BG-AJ	870
☐ N871AA	Boeing 727-223 (A)	21383 / 1324		0378	0378	3 PW JT8D-9A	81148	F12Y138	BH-CL	871
☐ N872AA	Boeing 727-223 (A)	21384 / 1328		0378	0378	3 PW JT8D-9A (HK3/RAI)	81148	F12Y138	FG-AL	872
☐ N873AA	Boeing 727-223 (A)	21385 / 1331		0478	0478	3 PW JT8D-9A	81148	F12Y138	BH-LM	873
☐ N874AA	Boeing 727-223 (A)	21386 / 1333		0478	0478	3 PW JT8D-9A	81148	F12Y138	BG-DH	874
☐ N875AA	Boeing 727-223 (A)	21387 / 1335		0478	0478	3 PW JT8D-9A	81148	F12Y138	BG-AF	875
☐ N876AA	Boeing 727-223 (A)	21388 / 1345		0578	0578	3 PW JT8D-9A	81148	F12Y138	BG-FK	876
☐ N877AA	Boeing 727-223 (A)	21389 / 1349		0578	0578	3 PW JT8D-9A	81148	F12Y138	CK-AL	877
☐ N878AA	Boeing 727-223 (A)	21390 / 1361		0778	0778	3 PW JT8D-9A	81148	F12Y138	BG-AK	878
☐ N879AA	Boeing 727-223 (A)	21391 / 1367		0778	0778	3 PW JT8D-9A	81148	F12Y138	DE-GK	879
☐ N880AA	Boeing 727-223 (A)	21519 / 1459		0379	0379	3 PW JT8D-9A	81148	F12Y138	DE-GM	880
☐ N881AA	Boeing 727-223 (A)	21520 / 1461		0379	0379	3 PW JT8D-9A	81148	F12Y138	BE-CJ	881
☐ N882AA	Boeing 727-223 (A)	21521 / 1463		0479	0479	3 PW JT8D-9A	81148	F12Y138	BE-JL	882
☐ N883AA	Boeing 727-223 (A)	21522 / 1465		0479	0479	3 PW JT8D-9A	81148	F12Y138	BE-HL	883
☐ N884AA	Boeing 727-223 (A)	21523 / 1467		0479	0479	3 PW JT8D-9A	81148	F12Y138	BE-AG	884
☐ N885AA	Boeing 727-223 (A)	21524 / 1473		0479	0479	3 PW JT8D-9A	81148	F12Y138	BJ-HL	885
☐ N886AA	Boeing 727-223 (A)	21525 / 1475		0579	0579	3 PW JT8D-9A	81148	F12Y138	CK-BF	886
☐ N887AA	Boeing 727-223 (A)	21526 / 1476		0579	0579	3 PW JT8D-9A	81148	F12Y138	BM-DE	887
☐ N889AA	Boeing 727-223 (A)	21527 / 1477		0579	0579	3 PW JT8D-9A	81148	F12Y138	BG-DJ	889
☐ N890AA	Boeing 727-223 (A)	22006 / 1636		0780	0780	3 PW JT8D-15 (HK3/FDX)	86409	F12Y138	BE-CM	890
☐ N891AA	Boeing 727-223 (A)	22007 / 1643		0780	0780	3 PW JT8D-15 (HK3/FDX)	86409	F12Y138	BG-CE	891
☐ N892AA	Boeing 727-223 (A)	22008 / 1646		0780	0780	3 PW JT8D-15 (HK3/FDX)	86409	F12Y138	BM-EF	892
☐ N893AA	Boeing 727-223 (A)	22009 / 1649		0880	0880	3 PW JT8D-15 (HK3/FDX)	86409	F12Y138	BG-DK	893
☐ N894AA	Boeing 727-223 (A)	22010 / 1650		0880	0880	3 PW JT8D-15 (HK3/FDX)	86409	F12Y138	BJ-GM	894
☐ N895AA	Boeing 727-223 (A)	22011 / 1653		0880	0880	3 PW JT8D-15 (HK3/FDX)	86409	F12Y138	BH-FL	895
☐ N896AA	Boeing 727-223 (A)	22012 / 1655		0980	0980	3 PW JT8D-15 (HK3/FDX)	86409	F12Y138	CJ-KM	896
☐ N897AA	Boeing 727-223 (A)	22013 / 1659		0980	0980	3 PW JT8D-15 (HK3/FDX)	86409	F12Y138	BE-FK	897
☐ N899AA	Boeing 727-223 (A)	22015 / 1666		1080	1080	3 PW JT8D-15 (HK3/FDX)	86409	F12Y138	BE-DJ	899
☐ N673AN	Boeing 757-223	29423 / 812		0798	0898	2 RR RB211-535E4-B	113852	F22Y166	KM-BH	5EE
☐ N674AN	Boeing 757-223	29424 / 816		0898	0898	2 RR RB211-535E4-B	113852	F22Y166	KM-PR	5EF
☐ N675AN	Boeing 757-223	29425 / 817		0898	0898	2 RR RB211-535E4-B	113852	F22Y166	KM-PS	5EG
☐ N676AN	Boeing 757-223	29426 / 827	N1798B*	1098	1098	2 RR RB211-535E4-B	113852	F22Y166	KM-QR	5EH
☐ N677AN	Boeing 757-223	29427 / 828		1098	1198	2 RR RB211-535E4-B	113852	F22Y166	KM-QS	5EJ
☐ N678AN	Boeing 757-223	29428 / 837		1098	1198	2 RR RB211-535E4-B	113852	F22Y166	KM-RS	5EK
☐ N181AN	Boeing 757-223	29591 / 852		0299	0299	2 RR RB211-535E4-B	113852	F22Y166	AL-PQ	5EN
☐ N182AN	Boeing 757-223	29592 / 853		0299	0299	2 RR RB211-535E4-B	113852	F22Y166	BJ-FH	5EP
☐ N183AN	Boeing 757-223 (ET)	29593 / 862		0499	0499	2 RR RB211-535E4-B	113852	F22Y166	BJ-FK	5ER
☐ N184AN	Boeing 757-223 (ET)	29594				2 RR RB211-535E4-B	113852	F22Y166	BJ-FL	5ES / oo-delivery 0599
☐ N601AN	Boeing 757-223	27052 / 661		0295	0295	2 RR RB211-535E4-B	113852	F22Y166	CQ-LP	5DU
☐ N602AN	Boeing 757-223	27053 / 664		0295	0395	2 RR RB211-535E4-B	113852	F22Y166	CQ-MP	5DV
☐ N603AA	Boeing 757-223	27054 / 670		0495	0495	2 RR RB211-535E4-B	113852	F22Y166	CR-EF	5DW
☐ N604AA	Boeing 757-223	27055 / 677		0695	0695	2 RR RB211-535E4-B	113852	F22Y166	CR-FQ	5DX
☐ N605AA	Boeing 757-223	27056 / 680		0695	0695	2 RR RB211-535E4-B	113852	F22Y166	CR-FS	5DY
☐ N606AA	Boeing 757-223	27057 / 707		0496	0496	2 RR RB211-535E4-B	113852	F22Y166	JS-FG	5EA
☐ N607AM	Boeing 757-223	27058 / 712		0596	0596	2 RR RB211-535E4-B	113852	F22Y166	JS-FH	5EB
☐ N608AA	Boeing 757-223 (ET)	27446 / 720		0796	0796	2 RR RB211-535E4-B	113852	C22Y166	JM-PR	5EC
☐ N609AA	Boeing 757-223 (ET)	27447 / 722		0796	0796	2 RR RB211-535E4-B	113852	C22Y166	JM-PS	5ED
☐ N610AA	Boeing 757-223	24486 / 234		0589	0789	2 RR RB211-535E4-B	108862	F22Y166	KM-FQ	610
☐ N611AM	Boeing 757-223	24487 / 236		0589	0789	2 RR RB211-535E4-B	108862	F22Y166	KM-GQ	611
☐ N612AA	Boeing 757-223	24488 / 240		0689	0889	2 RR RB211-535E4-B	108862	F22Y166	KM-HQ	612
☐ N613AA	Boeing 757-223	24489 / 242		0689	0889	2 RR RB211-535E4-B	113852	F22Y166	KM-JQ	613
☐ N614AA	Boeing 757-223	24490 / 243		0789	0889	2 RR RB211-535E4-B	113852	F22Y166	KM-LQ	614
☐ N615AM	Boeing 757-223	24491 / 245		0789	0989	2 RR RB211-535E4-B	113852	F22Y166	KM-PQ	615
☐ N616AA	Boeing 757-223	24524 / 248		0889	0989	2 RR RB211-535E4-B	113852	F22Y166	KP-AQ	616
☐ N617AM	Boeing 757-223	24525 / 253		0989	1189	2 RR RB211-535E4-B	108862	F22Y166	KP-BQ	617
☐ N618AA	Boeing 757-223	24526 / 260		1289	0290	2 RR RB211-535E4-B	108862	F22Y166	KP-CQ	618
☐ N619AA	Boeing 757-223	24577 / 269		0290	0390	2 RR RB211-535E4-B	108862	F22Y166	KP-DQ	619
☐ N620AA	Boeing 757-223	24578 / 276		0390	0490	2 RR RB211-535E4-B	108862	F22Y166	KP-EQ	620
☐ N621AM	Boeing 757-223	24579 / 283		0490	0590	2 RR RB211-535E4-B	113852	F22Y166	KP-FQ	621
☐ N622AA	Boeing 757-223	24580 / 289		0590	0690	2 RR RB211-535E4-B	113852	F22Y166	KP-GQ	622
☐ N623AA	Boeing 757-223	24581 / 296		0590	0790	2 RR RB211-535E4-B	108862	F22Y166	KP-HQ	623
☐ N624AA	Boeing 757-223	24582 / 297		0690	0790	2 RR RB211-535E4-B	108862	F22Y166	KP-JQ	624
☐ N625AA	Boeing 757-223	24583 / 303		0690	0890	2 RR RB211-535E4-B	108862	F22Y166	KP-LQ	625
☐ N626AA	Boeing 757-223	24584 / 304		0790	0890	2 RR RB211-535E4-B	108862	F22Y166	KP-MQ	626
☐ N627AA	Boeing 757-223	24585 / 308		0790	0990	2 RR RB211-535E4-B	108862	F22Y166	LM-AQ	627
☐ N628AA	Boeing 757-223	24586 / 309		0790	0890	2 RR RB211-535E4-B	108862	F22Y166	LM-BQ	628
☐ N629AA	Boeing 757-223	24587 / 315		0890	0990	2 RR RB211-535E4-B	108862	F22Y166	LM-CQ	629
☐ N630AA	Boeing 757-223	24588 / 316		0890	1090	2 RR RB211-535E4-B	108862	F22Y166	LM-DQ	630
☐ N631AA	Boeing 757-223	24589 / 317		0890	1090	2 RR RB211-535E4-B	108862	F22Y166	LM-EQ	631
☐ N632AA	Boeing 757-223	24590 / 321		0990	1090	2 RR RB211-535E4-B	108862	F22Y166	LM-FQ	632
☐ N633AA	Boeing 757-223	24591 / 324		0990	1190	2 RR RB211-535E4-B	108862	F22Y166	LM-GQ	633
☐ N634AA	Boeing 757-223	24592 / 327		1090	1190	2 RR RB211-535E4-B	108862	F22Y166	LM-HQ	634
☐ N635AA	Boeing 757-223	24593 / 328		1090	1190	2 RR RB211-535E4-B	108862	F22Y166	LM-JQ	635
☐ N636AM	Boeing 757-223	24594 / 336		1190	0191	2 RR RB211-535E4-B	108862	F22Y166	LM-KQ	636
☐ N637AM	Boeing 757-223	24595 / 337		1190	0191	2 RR RB211-535E4-B	108862	F22Y166	LM-PQ	637
☐ N638AA	Boeing 757-223	24596 / 344		0191	0291	2 RR RB211-535E4-B	108862	F22Y166	LP-AQ	638
☐ N639AA	Boeing 757-223	24597 / 345		0191	0291	2 RR RB211-535E4-B	108862	F22Y166	LP-BQ	639
☐ N640A	Boeing 757-223	24598 / 350		0191	0391	2 RR RB211-535E4-B	108862	F22Y166	LP-CQ	640
☐ N641AA	Boeing 757-223	24599 / 351		0191	0391	2 RR RB211-535E4-B	108862	F22Y166	LP-DQ	641
☐ N642AA	Boeing 757-223	24600 / 357		0291	0491	2 RR RB211-535E4-B	108862	F22Y166	LP-EQ	642
☐ N643AA	Boeing 757-223	24601 / 360		0391	0491	2 RR RB211-535E4-B	108862	F22Y166	LP-FQ	643
☐ N644AA	Boeing 757-223	24602 / 365		0491	0591	2 RR RB211-535E4-B	108862	F22Y166	LP-GQ	5BP
☐ N645AA	Boeing 757-223	24603 / 370		0491	0591	2 RR RB211-535E4-B	113852	F22Y166	LP-HQ	5BR

registration	type of aircraft	cn/fn	ex/ex*	mfd	del	powered by	mtow kg	configuration	selcal	name/fln/specialitites/remarks
☐ N646AA	Boeing 757-223	24604 / 375		0591	0691	2 RR RB211-535E4-B	113852	F22Y166	LP-JQ	5BS
☐ N647AM	Boeing 757-223	24605 / 378		0591	0791	2 RR RB211-535E4-B	113852	F22Y166	LP-KQ	5BT
☐ N648AA	Boeing 757-223	24606 / 379		0591	0791	2 RR RB211-535E4-B	113852	F22Y166	LP-MQ	5BU
☐ N649AA	Boeing 757-223	24607 / 383		0691	0791	2 RR RB211-535E4-B	113852	F22Y166	MP-AQ	5BV
☐ N650AA	Boeing 757-223	24608 / 384		0691	0791	2 RR RB211-535E4-B	113852	F22Y166	MP-BQ	5BW
☐ N652AA	Boeing 757-223	24610 / 391		0791	0891	2 RR RB211-535E4-B	113852	F22Y166	MP-DQ	5BY
☐ N653A	Boeing 757-223	24611 / 397		0891	1091	2 RR RB211-535E4-B	113852	F22Y166	MP-EQ	5CA
☐ N654A	Boeing 757-223	24612 / 398		0991	1091	2 RR RB211-535E4-B	113852	F22Y166	MP-FQ	5CB
☐ N655AA	Boeing 757-223	24613 / 402		0991	1091	2 RR RB211-535E4-B	113852	F22Y166	MP-GQ	5CC
☐ N656AA	Boeing 757-223	24614 / 404		1091	1191	2 RR RB211-535E4-B	113852	F22Y166	MP-HQ	5CD
☐ N657AM	Boeing 757-223	24615 / 409		1191	1291	2 RR RB211-535E4-B	113852	F22Y166	MP-JQ	5CE
☐ N658AA	Boeing 757-223	24616 / 410		1191	1191	2 RR RB211-535E4-B	113852	F22Y166	MP-KQ	5CF
☐ N659AA	Boeing 757-223	24617 / 417		1291	0192	2 RR RB211-535E4-B	113852	F22Y166	MP-LQ	5CG / Pride of American
☐ N660AM	Boeing 757-223	25294 / 418		1291	0192	2 RR RB211-535E4-B	113852	F22Y166	FL-RS	5CH
☐ N661AA	Boeing 757-223	25295 / 423		0192	0192	2 RR RB211-535E4-B	113852	F22Y166	FM-PR	5CJ
☐ N662AA	Boeing 757-223	25296 / 425		0192	0292	2 RR RB211-535E4-B	113852	F22Y166	FM-PS	5CK
☐ N663AM	Boeing 757-223	25297 / 432		0292	0392	2 RR RB211-535E4-B	113852	F22Y166	FM-QR	5CL
☐ N664AA	Boeing 757-223	25298 / 433		0292	0392	2 RR RB211-535E4-B	113852	F22Y166	FM-QS	5CM
☐ N665AA	Boeing 757-223	25299 / 436		0392	0392	2 RR RB211-535E4-B	108862	F22Y166	FM-RS	5CN
☐ N666A	Boeing 757-223	25300 / 451		0492	0592	2 RR RB211-535E4-B	108862	F22Y166	FP-QR	5CP
☐ N7667A	Boeing 757-223	25301 / 459		0592	0692	2 RR RB211-535E4-B	108862	F22Y166	FP-QS	5CR
☐ N668AA	Boeing 757-223	25333 / 460		0592	0692	2 RR RB211-535E4-B	108862	F22Y166	FP-RS	5CS
☐ N669AA	Boeing 757-223	25334 / 463		0692	0692	2 RR RB211-535E4-B	108862	F22Y166	FQ-RS	5CT
☐ N670AA	Boeing 757-223	25335 / 468		0692	0792	2 RR RB211-535E4-B	108862	F22Y166	GH-JR	5CU
☐ N671AA	Boeing 757-223	25336 / 473		0792	0792	2 RR RB211-535E4-B	108862	F22Y166	GH-JS	5CV
☐ N672AA	Boeing 757-223	25337 / 474		0792	0792	2 RR RB211-535E4-B	108862	F22Y166	GH-KR	5CW
☐ N679AN	Boeing 757-223	29589 / 842	N1800B*	1198	0199	2 RR RB211-535E4-B	113852	F22Y166	AM-KQ	5EL / *special 1959 Astrojet-colors*
☐ N680AN	Boeing 757-223	29590 / 847	N1787B*	1298	0199	2 RR RB211-535E4-B	113852	F22Y166	AM-LQ	5EM
☐ N681AA	Boeing 757-223	25338 / 483		0892	0892	2 RR RB211-535E4-B	108862	F22Y166	GJ-KR	5CX
☐ N682AA	Boeing 757-223	25339 / 484		0892	0992	2 RR RB211-535E4-B	108862	F22Y166	GJ-KS	5CY
☐ N683A	Boeing 757-223	25340 / 491		0992	1092	2 RR RB211-535E4-B	108862	F22Y166	GJ-LR	5DA
☐ N684AA	Boeing 757-223	25341 / 504		1192	1292	2 RR RB211-535E4-B	108862	F22Y166	GJ-LS	5DB
☐ N685AA	Boeing 757-223	25342 / 507		1192	1292	2 RR RB211-535E4-B	108862	F22Y166	GJ-MR	5DC
☐ N686AA	Boeing 757-223	25343 / 509		1292	1292	2 RR RB211-535E4-B	108862	F22Y166	GJ-MS	5DD
☐ N687AA	Boeing 757-223 (ET)	25695 / 536		0393	0393	2 RR RB211-535E4-B	113852	C22Y166	GJ-PR	5DE
☐ N688AA	Boeing 757-223 (ET)	25730 / 548		0493	0593	2 RR RB211-535E4-B	113852	C22Y166	GJ-PS	5DF
☐ N689AA	Boeing 757-223 (ET)	25731 / 562		0693	0793	2 RR RB211-535E4-B	113852	C22Y166	GJ-QR	5DG
☐ N690AA	Boeing 757-223 (ET)	25696 / 566		0793	0793	2 RR RB211-535E4-B	113852	C22Y166	GJ-QS	5DH
☐ N691AA	Boeing 757-223 (ET)	25697 / 568		0793	0893	2 RR RB211-535E4-B	113852	C22Y166	GJ-RS	5DJ
☐ N692AA	Boeing 757-223 (ET)	26972 / 578		0993	1093	2 RR RB211-535E4-B	113852	C22Y166	GK-LR	5DK
☐ N693AA	Boeing 757-223	26973 / 580		1093	0194	2 RR RB211-535E4-B	113852	F22Y166	GK-LS	5DL
☐ N694AN	Boeing 757-223	26974 / 582		1293	0194	2 RR RB211-535E4-B	113852	F22Y166	MP-QR	5DM
☐ N695AN	Boeing 757-223	26975 / 621		0694	0694	2 RR RB211-535E4-B	113852	F22Y166	MP-QS	5DN
☐ N696AN	Boeing 757-223	26976 / 627		0794	0794	2 RR RB211-535E4-B	113852	F22Y166	MP-RS	5DP
☐ N697AN	Boeing 757-223	26977 / 633		0894	0894	2 RR RB211-535E4-B	113852	F22Y166	MQ-RS	5DR
☐ N698AN	Boeing 757-223	26980 / 635		0894	0894	2 RR RB211-535E4-B	113852	F22Y166	PQ-RS	5DS
☐ N699AN	Boeing 757-223	27051 / 660		0195	0295	2 RR RB211-535E4-B	113852	F22Y166	LQ-RS	5DT
☐ N301AA	Boeing 767-223	22307 / 8		1182	1182	2 GE CF6-80A	141974	F14C30Y128	DL-EH	301
☐ N302AA	Boeing 767-223	22308 / 19		1182	1182	2 GE CF6-80A	141974	F14C30Y128	DM-FH	302
☐ N303AA	Boeing 767-223	22309 / 23		1282	1282	2 GE CF6-80A	141974	F14C30Y128	EH-FM	303
☐ N304AA	Boeing 767-223	22310 / 25		0383	0383	2 GE CF6-80A	141974	F14C30Y128	EL-BK	304
☐ N305AA	Boeing 767-223	22311 / 34		0583	0583	2 GE CF6-80A	141974	F14C30Y128	JK-DL	305
☐ N306AA	Boeing 767-223	22312 / 44		0483	0483	2 GE CF6-80A	141974	F14C30Y128	DL-EJ	306
☐ N307AA	Boeing 767-223	22313 / 72		1183	1183	2 GE CF6-80A	141974	F14C30Y128	EF-KM	307
☐ N308AA	Boeing 767-223	22314 / 73		1183	1183	2 GE CF6-80A	141974	F14C30Y128	EJ-CM	308
☐ N312AA	Boeing 767-223 (ER)	22315 / 94		0684	0684	2 GE CF6-80A2	159211	F9C30Y126	EL-BM	312 / *cvtd -223*
☐ N313AA	Boeing 767-223 (ER)	22316 / 95		0684	0684	2 GE CF6-80A2	159211	F9C30Y126	JK-EF	313 / *cvtd -223*
☐ N315AA	Boeing 767-223 (ER)	22317 / 109		0285	0285	2 GE CF6-80A2	159211	F9C30Y126	DL-FH	315 / *cvtd -223*
☐ N316AA	Boeing 767-223 (ER)	22318 / 111		0485	0485	2 GE CF6-80A2	159211	F9C30Y126	EG-CM	316 / *cvtd -223*
☐ N317AA	Boeing 767-223 (ER)	22319 / 112		0485	0485	2 GE CF6-80A2	159211	F9C30Y126	EJ-GL	317 / *cvtd -223*
☐ N319AA	Boeing 767-223 (ER)	22320 / 128		1185	1185	2 GE CF6-80A2	159211	F9C30Y126	FG-EM	319
☐ N320AA	Boeing 767-223 (ER)	22321 / 130		1285	1285	2 GE CF6-80A2	159211	F9C30Y126	KL-AC	320
☐ N321AA	Boeing 767-223 (ER)	22322 / 139		0486	0486	2 GE CF6-80A2	159211	F9C30Y126	DL-KM	321
☐ N322AA	Boeing 767-223 (ER)	22323 / 140		0586	0586	2 GE CF6-80A2	159211	F9C30Y126	EG-DJ	322
☐ N323AA	Boeing 767-223 (ER)	22324 / 146		0786	0786	2 GE CF6-80A2	159211	F9C30Y126	EJ-KM	323
☐ N324AA	Boeing 767-223 (ER)	22325 / 147		0886	0886	2 GE CF6-80A2	159211	F9C30Y126	FH-CJ	324
☐ N325AA	Boeing 767-223 (ER)	22326 / 157		1186	1186	2 GE CF6-80A2	159211	F9C30Y126	JM-HK	325
☐ N327AA	Boeing 767-223 (ER)	22327 / 159		1286	1286	2 GE CF6-80A2	159211	F9C30Y126	DM-FG	327
☐ N328AA	Boeing 767-223 (ER)	22328 / 160		1286	1286	2 GE CF6-80A2	159211	F9C30Y126	EG-HL	328
☐ N329AA	Boeing 767-223 (ER)	22329 / 164		0287	0287	2 GE CF6-80A2	159211	F9C30Y126	EQ-DJ	329
☐ N330AA	Boeing 767-223 (ER)	22330 / 166		0387	0387	2 GE CF6-80A2	159211	F9C30Y126	JK-HM	330
☐ N332AA	Boeing 767-223 (ER)	22331 / 168		0387	0387	2 GE CF6-80A2	159211	F9C30Y126	JK-HL	332
☐ N334AA	Boeing 767-223 (ER)	22332 / 169		0487	0487	2 GE CF6-80A2	159211	F9C30Y126	BG-AD	334
☐ N335AA	Boeing 767-223 (ER)	22333 / 194		1187	1187	2 GE CF6-80A2	159211	F9C30Y126	BM-GK	335
☐ N336AA	Boeing 767-223 (ER)	22334 / 195		1287	1287	2 GE CF6-80A2	159211	F9C30Y126	BE-FM	336
☐ N338AA	Boeing 767-223 (ER)	22335 / 196		1287	1287	2 GE CF6-80A2	159211	F9C30Y126	BE-LM	338
☐ N339AA	Boeing 767-223 (ER)	22336 / 198		0188	0188	2 GE CF6-80A2	159211	F9C30Y126	BJ-GL	339
☐ N91050	Airbus Industrie A300-605R (A300B4-605R)	423	F-WWAV*	0288	0488	2 GE CF6-80C2A5	171700	F16Y251	BP-DE	050
☐ N50051	Airbus Industrie A300-605R (A300B4-605R)	459	F-WWAX*	0388	0588	2 GE CF6-80C2A5	171700	F16Y251	BP-DF	051
☐ N80052	Airbus Industrie A300-605R (A300B4-605R)	460	F-WWAY*	0388	0588	2 GE CF6-80C2A5	171700	F16Y251	BP-DG	052
☐ N14053	Airbus Industrie A300-605R (A300B4-605R)	420	F-WWAU*	1286	0788	2 GE CF6-80C2A5	171700	F16Y251	BP-DH	053
☐ N70054	Airbus Industrie A300-605R (A300B4-605R)	461	F-WWAZ*	0488	0688	2 GE CF6-80C2A5	171700	F16Y251	BP-DJ	054
☐ N7055A	Airbus Industrie A300-605R (A300B4-605R)	462	F-WWAC*	0388	0688	2 GE CF6-80C2A5	171700	F16Y251	BP-DK	055
☐ N14056	Airbus Industrie A300-605R (A300B4-605R)	463	F-WWAD*	0488	0688	2 GE CF6-80C2A5	171700	F16Y251	BP-DL	056
☐ N80057	Airbus Industrie A300-605R (A300B4-605R)	465	F-WWAM*	0588	0888	2 GE CF6-80C2A5	171700	F16Y251	BP-DM	057
☐ N80058	Airbus Industrie A300-605R (A300B4-605R)	466	F-WWAE*	0688	0988	2 GE CF6-80C2A5	171700	F16Y251	BP-EF	058
☐ N19059	Airbus Industrie A300-605R (A300B4-605R)	469	F-WWAF*	0688	0988	2 GE CF6-80C2A5	171700	F16Y251	BP-EG	059
☐ N11060	Airbus Industrie A300-605R (A300B4-605R)	470	F-WWAA*	0788	1088	2 GE CF6-80C2A5	171700	F16Y251	BP-EH	060
☐ N14061	Airbus Industrie A300-605R (A300B4-605R)	471	F-WWAH*	0888	1088	2 GE CF6-80C2A5	171700	F16Y251	BP-EJ	061
☐ N7062A	Airbus Industrie A300-605R (A300B4-605R)	474	F-WWAK*	0988	1188	2 GE CF6-80C2A5	171700	F16Y251	BP-EK	062
☐ N41063	Airbus Industrie A300-605R (A300B4-605R)	506	F-WWAP*	1188	0289	2 GE CF6-80C2A5	171700	F16Y251	BP-EL	063
☐ N40064	Airbus Industrie A300-605R (A300B4-605R)	507	F-WWAQ*	1188	0289	2 GE CF6-80C2A5	171700	F16Y251	BP-EM	064
☐ N14065	Airbus Industrie A300-605R (A300B4-605R)	508	F-WWAR*	1288	0289	2 GE CF6-80C2A5	171700	F10C34Y148	BP-FG	065
☐ N18066	Airbus Industrie A300-605R (A300B4-605R)	509	F-WWAS*	1288	0289	2 GE CF6-80C2A5	171700	F10C34Y148	BP-FH	066
☐ N8067A	Airbus Industrie A300-605R (A300B4-605R)	510	F-WWAU*	0189	0389	2 GE CF6-80C2A5	171700	F10C34Y148	BP-FJ	067
☐ N14068	Airbus Industrie A300-605R (A300B4-605R)	511	F-WWAV*	0189	0489	2 GE CF6-80C2A5	171700	F10C34Y148	BP-FK	068
☐ N33069	Airbus Industrie A300-605R (A300B4-605R)	512	F-WWAC*	0289	0489	2 GE CF6-80C2A5	171700	F10C34Y148	BP-FL	069
☐ N90070	Airbus Industrie A300-605R (A300B4-605R)	513	F-WWAX*	0389	0489	2 GE CF6-80C2A5	171700	F10C34Y148	BP-FM	070
☐ N25071	Airbus Industrie A300-605R (A300B4-605R)	514	F-WWAY*	0389	0589	2 GE CF6-80C2A5	171700	F10C34Y148	BP-GH	071
☐ N70072	Airbus Industrie A300-605R (A300B4-605R)	515	F-WWAZ*	0389	0689	2 GE CF6-80C2A5	171700	F10C34Y148	BP-GJ	072
☐ N70073	Airbus Industrie A300-605R (A300B4-605R)	516	F-WWAA*	0489	0689	2 GE CF6-80C2A5	171700	F10C34Y148	BP-GK	073
☐ N70074	Airbus Industrie A300-605R (A300B4-605R)	517	F-WWAD*	0589	0689	2 GE CF6-80C2A5	171700	F10C34Y148	BP-GL	074
☐ N3075A	Airbus Industrie A300-605R (A300B4-605R)	606	F-WWAA*	0391	0591	2 GE CF6-80C2A5	171700	F16Y250	AL-MQ	075
☐ N7076A	Airbus Industrie A300-605R (A300B4-605R)	610	F-WWAF*	0591	0791	2 GE CF6-80C2A5	171700	F16Y250	AL-PQ	076
☐ N14077	Airbus Industrie A300-605R (A300B4-605R)	612	F-WWAH*	0691	0891	2 GE CF6-80C2A5	171700	F16Y250	AM-BQ	077
☐ N34078	Airbus Industrie A300-605R (A300B4-605R)	615	F-WWAO*	0791	0991	2 GE CF6-80C2A5	171700	F16Y250	AM-CQ	078
☐ N70079	Airbus Industrie A300-605R (A300B4-605R)	619	F-WWAU*	0991	1291	2 GE CF6-80C2A5	171700	F16Y250	AM-DQ	079
☐ N77080	Airbus Industrie A300-605R (A300B4-605R)	626	F-WWAR*	1291	0492	2 GE CF6-80C2A5	171700	F16Y251	AM-EQ	080
☐ N59081	Airbus Industrie A300-605R (A300B4-605R)	639	F-WWAV*	0592	0792	2 GE CF6-80C2A5	171700	F16Y251	AM-FQ	081
☐ N7082A	Airbus Industrie A300-605R (A300B4-605R)	643	F-WWAN*	0692	0992	2 GE CF6-80C2A5	171700	F16Y251	AM-GQ	082
☐ N7083A	Airbus Industrie A300-605R (A300B4-605R)	645	F-WWAO*	0692	1092	2 GE CF6-80C2A5	171700	F16Y251	AM-HQ	083
☐ N80084	Airbus Industrie A300-605R (A300B4-605R)	675	F-WWAE*	1192	0293	2 GE CF6-80C2A5	171700	F16Y251	AM-JQ	084
☐ N351AA	Boeing 767-323 (ER)	24032 / 202		0288	0288	2 GE CF6-80C2B6	185066	F14C30Y163	CL-GP	351
☐ N352AA	Boeing 767-323 (ER)	24033 / 205		0388	0388	2 GE CF6-80C2B6	185066	F14C30Y163	CL-HP	352
☐ N353AA	Boeing 767-323 (ER)	24034 / 206		0388	0388	2 GE CF6-80C2B6	185066	F14C30Y163	CL-JP	353
☐ N354AA	Boeing 767-323 (ER)	24035 / 211		0488	0488	2 GE CF6-80C2B6	185066	F14C30Y163	CL-KP	354
☐ N355AA	Boeing 767-323 (ER)	24036 / 221		0588	0588	2 GE CF6-80C2B6	185066	F14C30Y163	CL-MP	355
☐ N39356	Boeing 767-323 (ER)	24037 / 226		0688	0688	2 GE CF6-80C2B6	185066	F14C30Y163	CM-AP	356
☐ N357AA	Boeing 767-323 (ER)	24038 / 227		0688	0688	2 GE CF6-80C2B6	185066	F14C30Y163	CM-BP	357
☐ N358AA	Boeing 767-323 (ER)	24039 / 228		0788	0788	2 GE CF6-80C2B6	185066	F14C30Y163	CM-DP	358

☐ N359AA	Boeing 767-323 (ER)	24040 / 230		0788	0788	2 GE CF6-80C2B6	185066	F14C30Y163	CM-EP	359
☐ N360AA	Boeing 767-323 (ER)	24041 / 232		0788	0788	2 GE CF6-80C2B6	185066	F14C30Y163	CM-FP	360
☐ N361AA	Boeing 767-323 (ER)	24042 / 235		0888	0888	2 GE CF6-80C2B6	185066	F14C30Y163	CM-GP	361
☐ N362AA	Boeing 767-323 (ER)	24043 / 237		0988	0988	2 GE CF6-80C2B6	185066	F14C30Y163	CM-HP	362
☐ N363AA	Boeing 767-323 (ER)	24044 / 238		0988	0988	2 GE CF6-80C2B6	185066	F14C30Y163	CM-JP	363
☐ N39364	Boeing 767-323 (ER)	24045 / 240		0988	0988	2 GE CF6-80C2B6	185066	F14C30Y163	CM-KP	364
☐ N39365	Boeing 767-323 (ER)	24046 / 241		1088	1088	2 GE CF6-80C2B6	185066	F14C30Y163	CM-LP	365
☐ N366AA	Boeing 767-323 (ER)	25193 / 388		0891	0991	2 GE CF6-80C2B6	185066	F14C30Y163	AP-BQ	366
☐ N39367	Boeing 767-323 (ER)	25194 / 394		0991	1091	2 GE CF6-80C2B6	185066	F14C30Y163	AP-CQ	367
☐ N368AA	Boeing 767-323 (ER)	25195 / 404		1191	1291	2 GE CF6-80C2B6	185066	F14C30Y163	AP-DQ	368
☐ N369AA	Boeing 767-323 (ER)	25196 / 422		0392	0392	2 GE CF6-80C2B6	185066	F14C30Y163	AP-EQ	369
☐ N370AA	Boeing 767-323 (ER)	25197 / 425		0392	0492	2 GE CF6-80C2B6	185066	F14C30Y163	AP-FQ	370
☐ N371AA	Boeing 767-323 (ER)	25198 / 431		0592	0592	2 GE CF6-80C2B6	185066	F14C30Y163	AP-GQ	371
☐ N372AA	Boeing 767-323 (ER)	25199 / 433		0592	0592	2 GE CF6-80C2B6	185066	F14C30Y163	AP-HQ	372
☐ N373AA	Boeing 767-323 (ER)	25200 / 435		0592	0692	2 GE CF6-80C2B6	185066	F14C30Y163	AP-JQ	373
☐ N374AA	Boeing 767-323 (ER)	25201 / 437		0692	0692	2 GE CF6-80C2B6	185066	F14C30Y163	AP-KQ	374
☐ N7375A	Boeing 767-323 (ER)	25202 / 441		0692	0792	2 GE CF6-80C2B6	185066	F14C30Y163	AP-LQ	375
☐ N376AN	Boeing 767-323 (ER)	25445 / 447		0792	0892	2 GE CF6-80C2B6	185066	F14C30Y163	HP-QS	376
☐ N377AN	Boeing 767-323 (ER)	25446 / 453		0992	0992	2 GE CF6-80C2B6	185066	F14C30Y163	HP-RS	377
☐ N378AN	Boeing 767-323 (ER)	25447 / 469		1292	1292	2 GE CF6-80C2B6	185066	F14C30Y163	HQ-RS	378
☐ N379AA	Boeing 767-323 (ER)	25448 / 481		0293	0393	2 GE CF6-80C2B6	185066	F14C30Y163	JK-LR	379
☐ N380AN	Boeing 767-323 (ER)	25449 / 489		0093	0493	2 GE CF6-80C2B6	185066	F14C30Y163	JK-LS	380
☐ N381AN	Boeing 767-323 (ER)	25450 / 495		0493	0593	2 GE CF6-80C2B6	185066	F14C30Y163	JK-MR	381
☐ N382AN	Boeing 767-323 (ER)	25451 / 498		0593	0593	2 GE CF6-80C2B6	185066	F14C30Y163	JK-MS	382
☐ N383AN	Boeing 767-323 (ER)	26995 / 500		0693	0693	2 GE CF6-80C2B6	185066	F14C30Y163	JK-PR	383
☐ N384AA	Boeing 767-323 (ER)	26996 / 512		0893	0893	2 GE CF6-80C2B6	185066	F14C30Y163	JK-PS	384
☐ N385AM	Boeing 767-323 (ER)	27059 / 536		0394	0394	2 GE CF6-80C2B6	185066	F14C30Y163	JK-QR	385
☐ N386AA	Boeing 767-323 (ER)	27060 / 540		0594	0594	2 GE CF6-80C2B6	185066	F14C30Y163	JK-QS	386
☐ N387AM	Boeing 767-323 (ER)	27184 / 541		0594	0594	2 GE CF6-80C2B6	185066	F14C30Y163	JK-RS	387
☐ N388AA	Boeing 767-323 (ER)	27448 / 563		1294	0195	2 GE CF6-80C2B6	185066	F14C30Y163	JL-MR	388
☐ N389AA	Boeing 767-323 (ER)	27449 / 564		1294	0195	2 GE CF6-80C2B6	185066	F14C30Y163	JL-MS	389
☐ N390AA	Boeing 767-323 (ER)	27450 / 565		0195	0295	2 GE CF6-80C2B6	185066	F14C30Y163	JL-PR	390
☐ N391AA	Boeing 767-323 (ER)	27451 / 566		0195	0295	2 GE CF6-80C2B6	185066	F14C30Y163	JL-PS	391
☐ N392AN	Boeing 767-323 (ER)	29429 / 700		0498	0498	2 GE CF6-80C2B6	185066	F14C30Y163	LM-PR	392
☐ N393AN	Boeing 767-323 (ER)	29430 / 701		0498	0598	2 GE CF6-80C2B6	185066	F14C30Y163	LM-PS	393
☐ N394AN	Boeing 767-323 (ER)	29431 / 703		0098	0698	2 GE CF6-80C2B6	185066	F14C30Y163	LM-QR	394
☐ N395AN	Boeing 767-323 (ER)	29432 / 709		0098	0798	2 GE CF6-80C2B6	185066	F14C30Y163	LM-QS	395
☐ N396AN	Boeing 767-323 (ER)	29603 / 739		0299	0299	2 GE CF6-80C2B6	185066	F14C30Y163	KL-PS	396
☐ N397AN	Boeing 767-323 (ER)	29604 / 744		0299	0499	2 GE CF6-80C2B6	185066	F14C30Y163	KL-QR	397
☐ N398AN	Boeing 767-323 (ER)	29605 / 748		0399	0499	2 GE CF6-80C2B6	185066	F14C30Y163	KL-QS	398
☐ N399AN	Boeing 767-323 (ER)	29606 / 752		0099	0399	2 GE CF6-80C2B6	185066	F14C30Y163	KL-RS	399
☐ N116AA	Boeing (Douglas) DC-10-10	46516 / 48		0772	0772	3 GE CF6-6K	195045	F34Y270	GK-EJ	116 / std TUL / to be sold to FDX 0099
☐ N119AA	Boeing (Douglas) DC-10-10	46519 / 52		0872	0872	3 GE CF6-6K	195045	F34Y270	GK-FH	119 / lst HAL
☐ N122AA	Boeing (Douglas) DC-10-10	46522 / 56		0972	0972	3 GE CF6-6K	195045	F34Y270	GK-FM	122 / lst HAL
☐ N123AA	Boeing (Douglas) DC-10-10	46523 / 58		1072	1072	3 GE CF6-6K	195045	F28C62Y157	GK-HJ	123 / std AMA / to be sold to FDX 0099
☐ N125AA	Boeing (Douglas) DC-10-10	46525 / 72		1272	1272	3 GE CF6-6K	195045	F34Y270	GK-HM	125 / lst HAL
☐ N126AA	Boeing (Douglas) DC-10-10	46947 / 247		0278	0278	3 GE CF6-6K	195045	F28C52Y157	DG-FL	126
☐ N127AA	Boeing (Douglas) DC-10-10	46948 / 249		0378	0378	3 GE CF6-6K	195045	F28C52Y157	CK-AH	127
☐ N128AA	Boeing (Douglas) DC-10-10	46984 / 250		0578	0578	3 GE CF6-6K	195045	F34Y270	CK-AG	128 / lst HAL
☐ N129AA	Boeing (Douglas) DC-10-10	46996 / 270		0279	0279	3 GE CF6-6K	195045	F28C52Y157	JL-AB	129 / to be wfu 0999
☐ N130AA	Boeing (Douglas) DC-10-10	46989 / 271		0279	0279	3 GE CF6-6K	195045	F36Y261	JL-AC	130 / to be wfu 0999
☐ N131AA	Boeing (Douglas) DC-10-10	46994 / 273		0479	0479	3 GE CF6-6K	195045	F36Y261	JL-AG	131
☐ N132AA	Boeing (Douglas) DC-10-10	47827 / 294		1179	1179	3 GE CF6-6K	195045	F28C52Y157	BE-CL	132 / to be wfu 0599
☐ N133AA	Boeing (Douglas) DC-10-10	47828 / 319		0580	0580	3 GE CF6-6K	195045	F36Y261	BE-DH	133
☐ N134AA	Boeing (Douglas) DC-10-10	47829 / 321		0580	0580	3 GE CF6-6K	195045	F28C52Y157	BG-AC	134 / to be wfu 0599
☐ N135AA	Boeing (Douglas) DC-10-10	47830 / 323		0680	0680	3 GE CF6-6K	195045	F36Y261	BJ-FM	135 / to be wfu 1299
☐ N148AA	Boeing (Douglas) DC-10-10	46703 / 19	N63NA	0172	0584	3 GE CF6-6K	195045	F34Y270	FJ-GH	148 / lst HAL
☐ N152AA	Boeing (Douglas) DC-10-10	46707 / 61	N65NA	1072	0684	3 GE CF6-6K	195045	F34Y270	FJ-GM	152 / lst HAL
☐ N153AA	Boeing (Douglas) DC-10-10	46708 / 62	N66NA	1072	0784	3 GE CF6-6K	195045	F34Y270	EJ-FM	153 / lst HAL
☐ N160AA	Boeing (Douglas) DC-10-10	46710 / 70	N68NA	1273	1183	3 GE CF6-6K	195045	F34Y270	EJ-GK	160 / lst HAL
☐ N162AA	Boeing (Douglas) DC-10-10	46943 / 163	N70NA	0675	0784	3 GE CF6-6K	195045	F34Y270	EJ-HK	162 / lst HAL -0999 / to be wfu 0999
☐ N166AA	Boeing (Douglas) DC-10-10	46908 / 95	N901WA	0473	0485	3 GE CF6-6K	195045	F28C52Y157	DF-AG	166 / to be wfu 0699
☐ N167AA	Boeing (Douglas) DC-10-10	46930 / 112	N904WA	0773	1086	3 GE CF6-6K	195045	F28C52Y157	KM-AJ	167 / to be wfu 0799
☐ N168AA	Boeing (Douglas) DC-10-10	46938 / 153	N905WA	0574	1086	3 GE CF6-6K	195045	F36Y261	CH-JK	168 / to be wfu 1199
☐ N171AA	Boeing (Douglas) DC-10-10	46906 / 50	N916JW	1172	0187	3 GE CF6-6K	195045	F34Y270	KM-CD	171 / lst HAL
☐ N750AN	Boeing 777-223 (ER)					2 RR Trent 892-17	297562	F18C56Y163		7BJ / oo-delivery 0501
☐ N751AN	Boeing 777-223 (ER)					2 RR Trent 892-17	297562	F18C56Y163		7BK / oo-delivery 0601
☐ N752AN	Boeing 777-223 (ER)					2 RR Trent 892-17	297562	F18C56Y163		7BL / oo-delivery 0701
☐ N753AN	Boeing 777-223 (ER)					2 RR Trent 892-17	297562	F18C56Y163		7BM / oo-delivery 0801
☐ N770AN	Boeing 777-223 (ER)	29578 / 185		1298	0199	2 RR Trent 892-17	293928	F18C56Y163	LP-RS	7AA
☐ N771AN	Boeing 777-223 (ER)	29579 / 190		0199	0199	2 RR Trent 892-17	293928	F18C56Y163	LP-QS	7AB
☐ N772AN	Boeing 777-223 (ER)	29580 / 198		0299	0399	2 RR Trent 892-17	293928	F18C56Y163	LP-QR	7AC
☐ N773AN	Boeing 777-223 (ER)	29583 / 199		0399	0399	2 RR Trent 892-17	293928	F18C56Y163	LM-RS	7AD
☐ N774AN	Boeing 777-223 (ER)	29581 / 208		0499	0499	2 RR Trent 892-17	293928	F18C56Y163	KQ-RS	7AE
☐ N775AN	Boeing 777-223 (ER)	29584 / 209		0499	0499	2 RR Trent 892-17	293928	F18C56Y163	KP-RS	7AF
☐ N776AN	Boeing 777-223 (ER)	29582				2 RR Trent 892-17	297562	F18C56Y163	KP-QS	7AG / oo-delivery 0599
☐ N777AN	Boeing 777-223 (ER)	29585				2 RR Trent 892-17	297562	F18C56Y163	KP-QR	7AH / oo-delivery 0599
☐ N778AN	Boeing 777-223 (ER)	29587				2 RR Trent 892-17	297562	F18C56Y163	KL-PR	7AJ / oo-delivery 0699
☐ N779AN	Boeing 777-223 (ER)	29955				2 RR Trent 892-17	297562	F18C56Y163	KL-MS	7AK / oo-delivery 0699
☐ N780AN	Boeing 777-223 (ER)	29956				2 RR Trent 892-17	297562	F18C56Y163	KL-MR	7AL / oo-delivery 0999
☐ N781AN	Boeing 777-223 (ER)	29586				2 RR Trent 892-17	297562	F18C56Y163	JL-QR	7AM / oo-delivery 0100
☐ N782AN	Boeing 777-223 (ER)	30003				2 RR Trent 892-17	297562	F18C56Y163	JL-QS	7AN / oo-delivery 0200
☐ N783AN	Boeing 777-223 (ER)	30004				2 RR Trent 892-17	297562	F18C56Y163	JL-RS	7AP / oo-delivery 0200
☐ N784AN	Boeing 777-223 (ER)	29588				2 RR Trent 892-17	297562	F18C56Y163	JM-QR	7AR / oo-delivery 0300
☐ N785AN	Boeing 777-223 (ER)	30005				2 RR Trent 892-17	297562	F18C56Y163	JM-QS	7AS / oo-delivery 0300
☐ N786AN	Boeing 777-223 (ER)	30250				2 RR Trent 892-17	297562	F18C56Y163	JM-RS	7AT / oo-delivery 0300
☐ N787AL	Boeing 777-223 (ER)	30010				2 RR Trent 892-17	297562	F18C56Y163	JP-QR	7AU / oo-delivery 0400
☐ N788AN	Boeing 777-223 (ER)					2 RR Trent 892-17	297562	F18C56Y163		7AV / oo-delivery 0500
☐ N789AN	Boeing 777-223 (ER)					2 RR Trent 892-17	297562	F18C56Y163		7AW / oo-delivery 0500
☐ N790AN	Boeing 777-223 (ER)					2 RR Trent 892-17	297562	F18C56Y163		7AX / oo-delivery 0600
☐ N791AN	Boeing 777-223 (ER)					2 RR Trent 892-17	297562	F18C56Y163		7AY / oo-delivery 0600
☐ N792AN	Boeing 777-223 (ER)					2 RR Trent 892-17	297562	F18C56Y163		7BA / oo-delivery 0700
☐ N793AN	Boeing 777-223 (ER)					2 RR Trent 892-17	297562	F18C56Y163		7BB / oo-delivery 1000
☐ N794AN	Boeing 777-223 (ER)					2 RR Trent 892-17	297562	F18C56Y163		7BC / oo-delivery 1200
☐ N795AN	Boeing 777-223 (ER)					2 RR Trent 892-17	297562	F18C56Y163		7BD / oo-delivery 0101
☐ N796AN	Boeing 777-223 (ER)					2 RR Trent 892-17	297562	F18C56Y163		7BE / oo-delivery 0201
☐ N797AN	Boeing 777-223 (ER)					2 RR Trent 892-17	297562	F18C56Y163		7BF / oo-delivery 0301
☐ N798AN	Boeing 777-223 (ER)					2 RR Trent 892-17	297562	F18C56Y163		7BG / oo-delivery 0401
☐ N799AN	Boeing 777-223 (ER)					2 RR Trent 892-17	297562	F18C56Y163		7BH / oo-delivery 0501
☐ N137AA	Boeing (Douglas) DC-10-30	47847 / 116	ZK-NZM	0873	0782	3 GE CF6-50C2	256280	F36Y246	HK-BJ	137
☐ N143AA	Boeing (Douglas) DC-10-30	46555 / 91	YV-133C	0473	0684	3 GE CF6-50C2	256280	F36Y246	CJ-HK	143
☐ N144AA	Boeing (Douglas) DC-10-30	47848 / 136	N821L	1273	0185	3 GE CF6-50C2	256280	F36Y246	CM-AL	144
☐ N163AA	Boeing (Douglas) DC-10-30	46914 / 195	PH-DTK	0375	0485	3 GE CF6-50C2	256280	F36Y246	BE-GL	163
☐ N164AA	Boeing (Douglas) DC-10-30	46950 / 242	CC-CJT	1177	0686	3 GE CF6-50C2	256280	F36Y246	HK-BG	164
☐ N1755	Boeing (Douglas) MD-11	48490 / 499		0592	0592	3 GE CF6-80C2D1F	280320	F19C56Y163	AH-KQ	1AF / for FDX 0600
☐ N1756	Boeing (Douglas) MD-11	48491 / 503		0592	0592	3 GE CF6-80C2D1F	280320	F19C56Y163	AH-LQ	1AG / for FDX 1200
☐ N1758B	Boeing (Douglas) MD-11	48527 / 504		0692	0792	3 GE CF6-80C2D1F	280320	F19C56Y163	AH-PQ	1AJ / for FDX 0301
☐ N1760A	Boeing (Douglas) MD-11	48550 / 526		1292	0293	3 GE CF6-80C2D1F	280320	F19C56Y163	AJ-CQ	1AM / for FDX 0200
☐ N1761R	Boeing (Douglas) MD-11	48551 / 527		1292	0193	3 GE CF6-80C2D1F	280320	F19C56Y163	AJ-DQ	1AN / for FDX 0901
☐ N1762B	Boeing (Douglas) MD-11	48552 / 530		1292	0293	3 GE CF6-80C2D1F	280320	F19C56Y163	AJ-EQ	1AP / for FDX 1200
☐ N1763	Boeing (Douglas) MD-11	48553 / 531		0193	0393	3 GE CF6-80C2D1F	280320	F19C56Y163	AJ-FQ	1AR / for FDX 0601
☐ N1764B	Boeing (Douglas) MD-11	48554 / 535		0193	0393	3 GE CF6-80C2D1F	280320	F19C56Y163	AJ-GQ	1AS / for FDX 0900
☐ N1765B	Boeing (Douglas) MD-11	48596 / 537		0193	0393	3 GE CF6-80C2D1F	280320	F19C56Y163	AJ-HQ	1AT / for FDX 0602
☐ N1766A	Boeing (Douglas) MD-11	48597 / 540		0493	0593	3 GE CF6-80C2D1F	280320	F19C56Y163	AJ-KQ	1AU / for FDX 0502
☐ N1767A	Boeing (Douglas) MD-11	48598 / 550		0893	0993	3 GE CF6-80C2D1F	280320	F19C56Y163	AJ-LQ	1AV / for FDX 0502

AMERICAN AVIATION, Llc — **Lafayette-Regional, LA**

301 Shepard Drive, Lafayette, LA 70508, USA ☎ (318) 896-6664 Tx: none Fax: (318) 266-5837 SITA: n/a
F: 1995 n/a Head: David A. Jeansonne Net: n/a

☐ N113HT	MD Helicopters MD 500D (Hughes 369D)	780314D	N6612C	0078	1097	1 AN 250-C20B	1361			
☐ N500DX	MD Helicopters MD 500E (Hughes 369E)	0121E	N222TL	0085	1297	1 AN 250-C20B	1361			

269 registration type of aircraft cn/fn ex/8x* mfd del powered by mtow kg configuration selcal name/fln/specialitites/remarks

registration	type of aircraft	cn/fn	ex/ex*	mfd	del	powered by	mtow kg	configuration	selcal	name/fln/specialitites/remarks
☐ N842LA	MD Helicopters MD 500E (Hughes 369E)	0020E		0084	1197	1 AN 250-C20B	1361			
☐ N86ST	MD Helicopters MD 500D (Hughes 369D)	711012D	N58BH	0081	0897	1 AN 250-C20B	1361			
☐ N133RT	Bell 206B JetRanger III	3262	XC-KAN	0081	0996	1 AN 250-C20B	1451			
☐ N181AA	Bell 206B JetRanger III	3277	N39088	0081	1096	1 AN 250-C20B	1451			
☐ N182AA	Bell 206B JetRanger III	2752	N206WP	0079	0596	1 AN 250-C20B	1451			
☐ N187AA	Bell 206B JetRanger III	3969	XC-HIF	0087	0497	1 AN 250-C20J	1451			
☐ N5009G	Bell 206B JetRanger III	2517		0078	0697	1 AN 250-C20B	1451			
☐ N9667Q	Cessna A185F Skywagon II	18503785		0078	0797	1 CO IO-520-D	1520			
☐ N973AA	Bell 407	53167		0097	0797	1 AN 250-C47B	2268			
☐ N3AH	Beech King Air 300	FA-130	N9UP	0087	0397	2 PWC PT6A-60A	6350			

AMERICAN AVIATION SERVICES, Inc.

Jackson-McKellar Sipes Regional, TN

2358 Westover Road, Jackson, TN 38301, USA ☎ (901) 427-6020 Tx: none Fax: (901) 427-6755 SITA: n/a
F: 1989 ✦✦✦ n/a Head: Billy F. Douglas Net: n/a

registration	type of aircraft	cn/fn	ex/ex*	mfd	del	powered by	mtow kg	configuration	selcal	name/fln/specialitites/remarks
☐ N474SA	Piper PA-31-350 Navajo Chieftain	31-8052036		0079	0390	2 LY TIO-540-J2BD	3175			

AMERICAN EAGLE AIRLINES, Inc. = EGF (Subs.of AMR Corp./formerly consisted of Executive/Flagship/Simmons & Wings West Airlines, Inc.)

Dallas-DFW, TX **American** *Eagle*

PO Box 612527, DFW International Airport, TX 75261-2527, USA ☎ (972) 425-1520 Tx: 791651 Fax: (972) 425-1518 SITA: HDQREAA
F: 1984 ✦✦✦ 9500 Head: Peter Bowler ICAO: EAGLE FLIGHT Net: http://www.aa.com AMERICAN EAGLE is a commuter system to provide feeder connection at American Airlines major hubs, using AA flight numbers.
AMR Corp. has bought BUSINESS EXPRESS AIRLINES. Its fleet of Saab 340A/B will be intergrated into American Eagle later in 1999. For details – see under that company.
16 ATR42 & 6 ATR72 (registrations varies) are operated by subsidiary EXECUTIVE AIRLINES, San Juan but is expected to be integrated into American Eagle later in 1999.

registration	type of aircraft	cn/fn	ex/ex*	mfd	del	powered by	mtow kg	configuration	selcal	name/fln/specialitites/remarks
☐ N174AE	Saab 340B	340B-174	SE-F74*	0090	0290	2 GE CT7-9B	13155	Y34		std / for sale
☐ N177AE	Saab 340B	340B-177	SE-F77*	0090	0390	2 GE CT7-9B	13155	Y34		std / for sale
☐ N180AE	Saab 340B	340B-180	SE-F80*	0090	0390	2 GE CT7-9B	13155	Y34		std / for sale
☐ N184AE	Saab 340B	340B-184	SE-F84*	0090	0490	2 GE CT7-9B	13155	Y34		std be std / for sale 0699
☐ N191AE	Saab 340B	340B-191	SE-F91*	0090	0590	2 GE CT7-9B	13155	Y34		to be std / for sale 0799
☐ N193AE	Saab 340B	340B-193	SE-F93*	0090	0690	2 GE CT7-9B	13155	Y34		to be std / for sale 0599
☐ N194AE	Saab 340B	340B-194	SE-F94*	0090	0690	2 GE CT7-9B	13155	Y34		std / for sale
☐ N198AE	Saab 340B	340B-198	SE-F98*	0090	0790	2 GE CT7-9B	13155	Y34		to be std / for sale 0999
☐ N201AE	Saab 340B	340B-201	SE-G01*	0090	0890	2 GE CT7-9B	13155	Y34		
☐ N202KD	Saab 340B	340B-202	SE-G02*	0090	0890	2 GE CT7-9B	13155	Y34		
☐ N203NE	Saab 340B	340B-203	SE-G03*	0090	0990	2 GE CT7-9B	13155	Y34		
☐ N204NE	Saab 340B	340B-204	SE-G04*	0090	0990	2 GE CT7-9B	13155	Y34		
☐ N210AE	Saab 340B	340B-210	SE-G10*	0090	1090	2 GE CT7-9B	13155	Y34		std / for sale
☐ N211NE	Saab 340B	340B-211	SE-G11*	0090	1090	2 GE CT7-9B	13155	Y34		
☐ N214DA	Saab 340B	340B-214	SE-G14*	0090	1190	2 GE CT7-9B	13155	Y34		
☐ N218AE	Saab 340B	340B-218	SE-G18*	0090	1290	2 GE CT7-9B	13155	Y34		
☐ N219AE	Saab 340B	340B-219	SE-G19*	0090	1290	2 GE CT7-9B	13155	Y34		
☐ N222NE	Saab 340B	340B-222	SE-G22*	0090	0191	2 GE CT7-9B	13155	Y34		
☐ N227AE	Saab 340B	340B-227	SE-G27*	0091	0291	2 GE CT7-9B	13155	Y34		
☐ N231LN	Saab 340B	340B-231	SE-G31*	0091	0391	2 GE CT7-9B	13155	Y34		
☐ N232AE	Saab 340B	340B-232	SE-G32*	0091	0491	2 GE CT7-9B	13155	Y34		
☐ N234AE	Saab 340B	340B-234	SE-G34*	0091	0391	2 GE CT7-9B	13155	Y34		
☐ N235AE	Saab 340B	340B-235	SE-G35*	0091	0391	2 GE CT7-9B	13155	Y34		
☐ N236AE	Saab 340B	340B-236	SE-G36*	0091	0591	2 GE CT7-9B	13155	Y34		
☐ N238AE	Saab 340B	340B-238	SE-G38*	0091	0591	2 GE CT7-9B	13155	Y34		
☐ N240DS	Saab 340B	340B-240	SE-G40*	0091	0591	2 GE CT7-9B	13155	Y34		
☐ N241AE	Saab 340B	340B-241	SE-G41*	0091	0591	2 GE CT7-9B	13155	Y34		
☐ N243AE	Saab 340B	340B-243	SE-G43*	0091	0591	2 GE CT7-9B	13155	Y34		
☐ N244AE	Saab 340B	340B-244	SE-G44*	0091	0691	2 GE CT7-9B	13155	Y34		
☐ N245AE	Saab 340B	340B-245	SE-G45*	0091	0691	2 GE CT7-9B	13155	Y34		
☐ N247AE	Saab 340B	340B-247	SE-G47*	0091	0691	2 GE CT7-9B	13155	Y34		
☐ N250AE	Saab 340B	340B-250	SE-G50*	0091	0891	2 GE CT7-9B	13155	Y34		
☐ N253AE	Saab 340B	340B-253	SE-G53*	0091	0891	2 GE CT7-9B	13155	Y34		
☐ N254AE	Saab 340B	340B-254	SE-G54*	0091	0891	2 GE CT7-9B	13155	Y34		
☐ N256AE	Saab 340B	340B-256	SE-G56*	0091	0991	2 GE CT7-9B	13155	Y34		
☐ N259AE	Saab 340B	340B-259	SE-G59*	0091	0991	2 GE CT7-9B	13155	Y34		
☐ N261AE	Saab 340B	340B-261	SE-G61*	0091	1091	2 GE CT7-9B	13155	Y34		
☐ N263AE	Saab 340B	340B-263	SE-G63*	0091	1091	2 GE CT7-9B	13155	Y34		
☐ N264AE	Saab 340B	340B-264	SE-G64*	0091	1091	2 GE CT7-9B	13155	Y34		
☐ N266AE	Saab 340B	340B-266	SE-G66*	0091	1191	2 GE CT7-9B	13155	Y34		
☐ N268AE	Saab 340B	340B-268	SE-G68*	0091	1191	2 GE CT7-9B	13155	Y34		
☐ N272AE	Saab 340B	340B-272	SE-G72*	1191	1291	2 GE CT7-9B	13155	Y34		
☐ N273AE	Saab 340B	340B-273	SE-G73*	1191	1291	2 GE CT7-9B	13155	Y34		
☐ N278AE	Saab 340B	340B-278	SE-G78*	1291	0192	2 GE CT7-9B	13155	Y34		
☐ N280AE	Saab 340B	340B-280	SE-G80*	1291	0192	2 GE CT7-9B	13155	Y34		
☐ N283AE	Saab 340B	340B-283	SE-G83*	0092	0292	2 GE CT7-9B	13155	Y34		
☐ N284AE	Saab 340B	340B-284	SE-G84*	0092	0392	2 GE CT7-9B	13155	Y34		
☐ N286AE	Saab 340B	340B-286	SE-G86*	0092	0392	2 GE CT7-9B	13155	Y34		
☐ N297AE	Saab 340B	340B-297	SE-G97*	0092	0592	2 GE CT7-9B	13155	Y34		
☐ N298AE	Saab 340B	340B-298	SE-G98*	0092	0592	2 GE CT7-9B	13155	Y34		
☐ N301AE	Saab 340B	340B-301	SE-C01*	0092	0692	2 GE CT7-9B	13155	Y34		
☐ N304AE	Saab 340B	340B-304	SE-C04*	0092	0692	2 GE CT7-9B	13155	Y34		
☐ N305AE	Saab 340B	340B-305	SE-C05*	0092	0692	2 GE CT7-9B	13155	Y34		
☐ N306AE	Saab 340B	340B-306	SE-C06*	0092	0892	2 GE CT7-9B	13155	Y34		
☐ N307AE	Saab 340B	340B-307	SE-C07*	0092	0892	2 GE CT7-9B	13155	Y34		
☐ N309AE	Saab 340B	340B-309	SE-C09*	0092	0892	2 GE CT7-9B	13155	Y34		
☐ N312AE	Saab 340B	340B-312	SE-C12*	0092	0992	2 GE CT7-9B	13155	Y34		
☐ N313AE	Saab 340B	340B-313	SE-C13*	0092	0992	2 GE CT7-9B	13155	Y34		
☐ N317AE	Saab 340B	340B-317	SE-C17*	0092	1092	2 GE CT7-9B	13155	Y34		
☐ N320AE	Saab 340B	340B-320	SE-C20*	0092	1192	2 GE CT7-9B	13155	Y34		
☐ N323AE	Saab 340B	340B-323	SE-C23*	0092	1192	2 GE CT7-9B	13155	Y34		
☐ N324AE	Saab 340B	340B-324	SE-C24*	0092	1292	2 GE CT7-9B	13155	Y34		
☐ N326AE	Saab 340B	340B-326	SE-C26*	0092	1292	2 GE CT7-9B	13155	Y34		
☐ N329AE	Saab 340B	340B-329	SE-C29*	0092	0193	2 GE CT7-9B	13155	Y34		
☐ N330AE	Saab 340B	340B-330	SE-C30*	0092	0193	2 GE CT7-9B	13155	Y34		
☐ N332AE	Saab 340B	340B-332	SE-C32*	0093	0293	2 GE CT7-9B	13155	Y34		
☐ N334AE	Saab 340B	340B-334	SE-C34*	0093	0493	2 GE CT7-9B	13155	Y34		
☐ N335AE	Saab 340B	340B-335	SE-C35*	0093	0493	2 GE CT7-9B	13155	Y34		
☐ N338SB	Saab 340B	340B-338	SE-C38*	0093	0593	2 GE CT7-9B	13155	Y34		
☐ N339SB	Saab 340B	340B-339	SE-C39*	0093	0593	2 GE CT7-9B	13155	Y34		
☐ N340RC	Saab 340B	340B-340	SE-C40*	0093	0693	2 GE CT7-9B	13155	Y34		
☐ N341SB	Saab 340B	340B-341	SE-C41*	0093	0693	2 GE CT7-9B	13155	Y34		
☐ N343SB	Saab 340B	340B-343	SE-C43*	0093	0893	2 GE CT7-9B	13155	Y34		
☐ N344SB	Saab 340B	340B-344	SE-C44*	0093	0893	2 GE CT7-9B	13155	Y34		
☐ N345SB	Saab 340B	340B-345	SE-C45*	0093	0993	2 GE CT7-9B	13155	Y34		
☐ N346SB	Saab 340B	340B-346	SE-C46*	0093	0993	2 GE CT7-9B	13155	Y34		
☐ N347SB	Saab 340B	340B-347	SE-C47*	0093	1093	2 GE CT7-9B	13155	Y34		
☐ N349SB	Saab 340B	340B-349	SE-C49*	0093	1193	2 GE CT7-9B	13155	Y34		
☐ N350CF	Saab 340B	340B-350	SE-C50*	0093	1193	2 GE CT7-9B	13155	Y34		
☐ N352SB	Saab 340B	340B-352	SE-C52*	0093	1293	2 GE CT7-9B	13155	Y34		
☐ N353SB	Saab 340B	340B-353	SE-C53*	0093	1293	2 GE CT7-9B	13155	Y34		
☐ N354SB	Saab 340B	340B-354	SE-C54*	0093	1293	2 GE CT7-9B	13155	Y34		
☐ N356SB	Saab 340B	340B-356	SE-C56*	0093	0194	2 GE CT7-9B	13155	Y34		
☐ N358RZ	Saab 340B	340B-358	SE-C58*	0094	0294	2 GE CT7-9B	13155	Y34		
☐ N359SB	Saab 340B	340B-359	SE-C59*	0094	0494	2 GE CT7-9B	13155	Y34		
☐ N371AE	Saab 340B (Plus)	340B-371	SE-C71*	0095	0995	2 GE CT7-9B	13155	Y34		
☐ N373AE	Saab 340B (Plus)	340B-373	SE-C73*	0095	1195	2 GE CT7-9B	13155	Y34		
☐ N374AE	Saab 340B (Plus)	340B-374	SE-C74*	0095	1195	2 GE CT7-9B	13155	Y34		
☐ N375AE	Saab 340B (Plus)	340B-375	SE-C75*	0095	1195	2 GE CT7-9B	13155	Y34		
☐ N376AE	Saab 340B (Plus)	340B-376	SE-C76*	0095	1295	2 GE CT7-9B	13155	Y34		
☐ N380AE	Saab 340B (Plus)	340B-380	SE-C80*	0095	0196	2 GE CT7-9B	13155	Y34		for Saab 0099
☐ N381AE	Saab 340B (Plus)	340B-381	SE-C81*	0095	0196	2 GE CT7-9B	13155	Y34		
☐ N382AE	Saab 340B (Plus)	340B-382	SE-C82*	0096	0296	2 GE CT7-9B	13155	Y34		
☐ N383AE	Saab 340B (Plus)	340B-383	SE-C83*	0096	0296	2 GE CT7-9B	13155	Y34		
☐ N384AE	Saab 340B (Plus)	340B-384	SE-C84*	0096	0396	2 GE CT7-9B	13155	Y34		
☐ N386AE	Saab 340B (Plus)	340B-386	SE-C86*	0096	0396	2 GE CT7-9B	13155	Y34		
☐ N387AE	Saab 340B (Plus)	340B-387	SE-C87*	0096	0396	2 GE CT7-9B	13155	Y34		
☐ N388AE	Saab 340B (Plus)	340B-388	SE-C88*	0096	0396	2 GE CT7-9B	13155	Y34		
☐ N389AE	Saab 340B (Plus)	340B-389	SE-C89*	0096	0496	2 GE CT7-9B	13155	Y34		

	registration	type of aircraft	cn/fn	ex/ex*	mfd	del	powered by	mtow kg	configuration	selcal	name/fln/specialitites/remarks
☐	N390AE	Saab 340B (Plus)	340B-390	SE-C90*	0096	0496	2 GE CT7-9B	13155	Y34		
☐	N391AE	Saab 340B (Plus)	340B-391	SE-C91*	0096	0596	2 GE CT7-9B	13155	Y34		
☐	N392AE	Saab 340B (Plus)	340B-392	SE-C92*	0096	0596	2 GE CT7-9B	13155	Y34		
☐	N393AE	Saab 340B (Plus)	340B-393	SE-C93*	0096	0596	2 GE CT7-9B	13155	Y34		
☐	N394AE	Saab 340B (Plus)	340B-394	SE-C94*	0096	0696	2 GE CT7-9B	13155	Y34		
☐	N396AE	Saab 340B (Plus)	340B-396	SE-C96*	0096	0696	2 GE CT7-9B	13155	Y34		
☐	N397AE	Saab 340B (Plus)	340B-397	SE-C97*	0096	0696	2 GE CT7-9B	13155	Y34		
☐	N398AM	Saab 340B (Plus)	340B-398	SE-C98*	0096	0796	2 GE CT7-9B	13155	Y34		
☐	N400BR	Saab 340B (Plus)	340B-400	SE-400*	0096	0896	2 GE CT7-9B	13155	Y34		
☐	N901AE	Saab 340B (Plus)	340B-401	SE-B01*	0096	0896	2 GE CT7-9B	13155	Y34		
☐	N902AE	Saab 340B	340B-269	N269AE	0091	1191	2 GE CT7-9B	13155	Y34		Spirit of Nashville
☐	N903AE	Saab 340B	340B-282	N282AE	0192	0292	2 GE CT7-9B	13155	Y34		
☐	N904AE	Saab 340B	340B-314	N314AE	0092	0992	2 GE CT7-9B	13155	Y34		
☐	N905AE	Saab 340B	340B-319	N319AE	0092	1092	2 GE CT7-9B	13155	Y34		
☐	N906AE	Saab 340B	340B-348	N348SB	0093	1093	2 GE CT7-9B	13155	Y34		
☐	N135MQ	ATR 42-300	135	N429MQ	0089	0489	2 PWC PW120	16700	Y46		
☐	N141AE	ATR 42-300	141	N431MQ	0089	0689	2 PWC PW120	16700	Y46		
☐	N142DD	ATR 42-300	040	F-WWEV*	0087	0687	2 PWC PW120	16700	Y46		
☐	N144DD	ATR 42-300	074	F-WWEX*	0087	1287	2 PWC PW120	16700	Y46		
☐	N209AT	ATR 42-300	209	F-WWEA*	0091	0491	2 PWC PW120	16700	Y46		lsf GECA
☐	N213AT	ATR 42-300	211	N211AM	0091	0491	2 PWC PW120	16700	Y46		lsf GECA
☐	N216AT	ATR 42-300	216	F-WWEI*	0091	0491	2 PWC PW120	16700	Y46		lsf GECA
☐	N223AT	ATR 42-300	223	F-WWEL*	0091	0591	2 PWC PW120	16700	Y46		lsf GECA
☐	N233RM	ATR 42-300	235	N235RM	0091	0691	2 PWC PW120	16700	Y46		lsf GECA
☐	N242AT	ATR 42-300	242	F-WWEW*	0091	0691	2 PWC PW120	16700	Y46		lsf GECA
☐	N246AE	ATR 42-300	243	N243AT	0091	0891	2 PWC PW120	16700	Y46		
☐	N249AT	ATR 42-300	249	F-WWEB*	0091	0691	2 PWC PW120	16700	Y46		lsf GECA
☐	N251AE	ATR 42-300	250	N250AA	0091	1091	2 PWC PW120	16700	Y46		
☐	N255AE	ATR 42-300	254	N254AT	0091	0791	2 PWC PW120	16700	Y46		lsf GECA
☐	N262AT	ATR 42-300	262	F-WWEL*	0091	0991	2 PWC PW120	16700	Y46		
☐	N265AE	ATR 42-300	266	N266AT	0091	1091	2 PWC PW120	16700	Y46		
☐	N269AT	ATR 42-300	269	F-WWEA*	0091	1191	2 PWC PW120	16700	Y46		
☐	N271AT	ATR 42-300	273	N273AT	0091	1191	2 PWC PW120	16700	Y46		
☐	N275BC	ATR 42-300	275	F-WWEG*	0091	1191	2 PWC PW120	16700	Y46		
☐	N277AT	ATR 42-300	277	F-WWLA*	0091	1291	2 PWC PW120	16700	Y46		
☐	N282AT	ATR 42-300	282	F-WWLI*	0091	0192	2 PWC PW120	16700	Y46		
☐	N293AT	ATR 42-300	293	F-WWLR*	0092	0492	2 PWC PW120	16700	Y46		
☐	N310DK	ATR 42-300	310	F-WWEC*	0092	0692	2 PWC PW120	16700	Y46		
☐	N314AM	ATR 42-300	314	F-WWEK*	0092	0892	2 PWC PW120	16700	Y46		
☐	N319AM	ATR 42-300	319	F-WWER*	0092	0992	2 PWC PW120	16700	Y46		
☐	N325AT	ATR 42-300	325	F-WWLK*	0092	1092	2 PWC PW120	16700	Y46		
☐	N327AT	ATR 42-300	327	F-WWLM*	0092	1192	2 PWC PW120	16700	Y46		
☐	N351AT	ATR 42-300	354	N354AT	0093	0393	2 PWC PW120	16700	Y46		
☐	N37AE	ATR 42-300	037	N426MQ	0087	0687	2 PWC PW120	16700	Y46		
☐	N423MQ	ATR 42-300	030		0086	1286	2 PWC PW120	16700	Y46		lsf CITG
☐	N424MQ	ATR 42-300	045		0087	0487	2 PWC PW120	16700	Y46		
☐	N47AE	ATR 42-300	047	N425MQ	0087	0587	2 PWC PW120	16700	Y46		
☐	N971NA	ATR 42-300	017	F-WWER*	0086	0986	2 PWC PW120	16700	Y46		
☐	N972NA	ATR 42-300	023	F-WWEA*	0086	1086	2 PWC PW120	16700	Y46		
☐	N973NA	ATR 42-300	065	F-WWEQ*	0087	1187	2 PWC PW120	16700	Y46		
☐	N500LE	Embraer RJ135 (EMB-135)					2 AN AE3007A3	19000	Y37		oo-delivery 0799
☐	N501MR	Embraer RJ135 (EMB-135)					2 AN AE3007A3	19000	Y37		oo-delivery 0899
☐	N502AE	Embraer RJ135 (EMB-135)					2 AN AE3007A3	19000	Y37		oo-delivery 0999
☐	N503AE	Embraer RJ135 (EMB-135)					2 AN AE3007A3	19000	Y37		oo-delivery 1099
☐	N504AE	Embraer RJ135 (EMB-135)					2 AN AE3007A3	19000	Y37		oo-delivery 1199
☐	N505AE	Embraer RJ135 (EMB-135)					2 AN AE3007A3	19000	Y37		oo-delivery 1299
☐	N506AE	Embraer RJ135 (EMB-135)					2 AN AE3007A3	19000	Y37		oo-delivery 0100
☐	N507AE	Embraer RJ135 (EMB-135)					2 AN AE3007A3	19000	Y37		oo-delivery 0200
☐	N508AE	Embraer RJ135 (EMB-135)					2 AN AE3007A3	19000	Y37		oo-delivery 0300
☐	N509AE	Embraer RJ135 (EMB-135)					2 AN AE3007A3	19000	Y37		oo-delivery 0400
☐	N510RG	Embraer RJ135 (EMB-135)					2 AN AE3007A3	19000	Y37		oo-delivery 0500
☐	N511AE	Embraer RJ135 (EMB-135)					2 AN AE3007A3	19000	Y37		oo-delivery 0500
☐	N512AE	Embraer RJ135 (EMB-135)					2 AN AE3007A3	19000	Y37		oo-delivery 0600
☐	N513AE	Embraer RJ135 (EMB-135)					2 AN AE3007A3	19000	Y37		oo-delivery 0600
☐	N514AE	Embraer RJ135 (EMB-135)					2 AN AE3007A3	19000	Y37		oo-delivery 0700
☐	N515AE	Embraer RJ135 (EMB-135)					2 AN AE3007A3	19000	Y37		oo-delivery 0700
☐	N516AE	Embraer RJ135 (EMB-135)					2 AN AE3007A3	19000	Y37		oo-delivery 0800
☐	N517AE	Embraer RJ135 (EMB-135)					2 AN AE3007A3	19000	Y37		oo-delivery 0800
☐	N518AE	Embraer RJ135 (EMB-135)					2 AN AE3007A3	19000	Y37		oo-delivery 0800
☐	N519AE	Embraer RJ135 (EMB-135)					2 AN AE3007A3	19000	Y37		oo-delivery 0900
☐	N520AE	Embraer RJ135 (EMB-135)					2 AN AE3007A3	19000	Y37		oo-delivery 0900
☐	N521AE	Embraer RJ135 (EMB-135)					2 AN AE3007A3	19000	Y37		oo-delivery 0900
☐	N522AE	Embraer RJ135 (EMB-135)					2 AN AE3007A3	19000	Y37		oo-delivery 1000
☐	N523AE	Embraer RJ135 (EMB-135)					2 AN AE3007A3	19000	Y37		oo-delivery 1000
☐	N524AE	Embraer RJ135 (EMB-135)					2 AN AE3007A3	19000	Y37		oo-delivery 1000
☐	N525MR	Embraer RJ135 (EMB-135)					2 AN AE3007A3	19000	Y37		oo-delivery 1100
☐	N526AE	Embraer RJ135 (EMB-135)					2 AN AE3007A3	19000	Y37		oo-delivery 1100
☐	N527AE	Embraer RJ135 (EMB-135)					2 AN AE3007A3	19000	Y37		oo-delivery 1100
☐	N528AE	Embraer RJ135 (EMB-135)					2 AN AE3007A3	19000	Y37		oo-delivery 1200
☐	N529AE	Embraer RJ135 (EMB-135)					2 AN AE3007A3	19000	Y37		oo-delivery 1200
☐	N530AE	Embraer RJ135 (EMB-135)					2 AN AE3007A3	19000	Y37		oo-delivery 1200
☐	N531AE	Embraer RJ135 (EMB-135)					2 AN AE3007A3	19000	Y37		oo-delivery 1100
☐	N532AE	Embraer RJ135 (EMB-135)					2 AN AE3007A3	19000	Y37		oo-delivery 1100
☐	N533AE	Embraer RJ135 (EMB-135)					2 AN AE3007A3	19000	Y37		oo-delivery 1200
☐	N534AE	Embraer RJ135 (EMB-135)					2 AN AE3007A3	19000	Y37		oo-delivery 1200
☐	N535AE	Embraer RJ135 (EMB-135)					2 AN AE3007A3	19000	Y37		oo-delivery 0001
☐	N536AE	Embraer RJ135 (EMB-135)					2 AN AE3007A3	19000	Y37		oo-delivery 0001
☐	N537AE	Embraer RJ135 (EMB-135)					2 AN AE3007A3	19000	Y37		oo-delivery 0001
☐	N538AE	Embraer RJ135 (EMB-135)					2 AN AE3007A3	19000	Y37		oo-delivery 0001
☐	N539AE	Embraer RJ135 (EMB-135)					2 AN AE3007A3	19000	Y37		oo-delivery 0001
☐	N540MR	Embraer RJ135 (EMB-135)					2 AN AE3007A3	19000	Y37		oo-delivery 0001
☐	N541MR	Embraer RJ135 (EMB-135)					2 AN AE3007A3	19000	Y37		oo-delivery 0001
☐	N542AE	Embraer RJ135 (EMB-135)					2 AN AE3007A3	19000	Y37		oo-delivery 0001
☐	N543AE	Embraer RJ135 (EMB-135)					2 AN AE3007A3	19000	Y37		oo-delivery 0001
☐	N544AE	Embraer RJ135 (EMB-135)					2 AN AE3007A3	19000	Y37		oo-delivery 0001
☐	N545AE	Embraer RJ135 (EMB-135)					2 AN AE3007A3	19000	Y37		oo-delivery 0001
☐	N546AE	Embraer RJ135 (EMB-135)					2 AN AE3007A3	19000	Y37		oo-delivery 0001
☐	N547AE	Embraer RJ135 (EMB-135)					2 AN AE3007A3	19000	Y37		oo-delivery 0001
☐	N548AE	Embraer RJ135 (EMB-135)					2 AN AE3007A3	19000	Y37		oo-delivery 0001
☐	N549AE	Embraer RJ135 (EMB-135)					2 AN AE3007A3	19000	Y37		oo-delivery 0001
☐	N550AE	Embraer RJ135 (EMB-135)					2 AN AE3007A3	19000	Y37		oo-delivery 0001
☐	N551AE	Embraer RJ135 (EMB-135)					2 AN AE3007A3	19000	Y37		oo-delivery 0001
☐	N552AE	Embraer RJ135 (EMB-135)					2 AN AE3007A3	19000	Y37		oo-delivery 0001
☐	N553AE	Embraer RJ135 (EMB-135)					2 AN AE3007A3	19000	Y37		oo-delivery 0001
☐	N554AE	Embraer RJ135 (EMB-135)					2 AN AE3007A3	19000	Y37		oo-delivery 0001
☐	N555AE	Embraer RJ135 (EMB-135)					2 AN AE3007A3	19000	Y37		oo-delivery 0001
☐	N556AE	Embraer RJ135 (EMB-135)					2 AN AE3007A3	19000	Y37		oo-delivery 0001
☐	N557AE	Embraer RJ135 (EMB-135)					2 AN AE3007A3	19000	Y37		oo-delivery 0001
☐	N558AE	Embraer RJ135 (EMB-135)					2 AN AE3007A3	19000	Y37		oo-delivery 0001
☐	N559AE	Embraer RJ135 (EMB-135)					2 AN AE3007A3	19000	Y37		oo-delivery 0001
☐	N560AE	Embraer RJ135 (EMB-135)					2 AN AE3007A3	19000	Y37		oo-delivery 0001
☐	N561AE	Embraer RJ135 (EMB-135)					2 AN AE3007A3	19000	Y37		oo-delivery 0001
☐	N562AE	Embraer RJ135 (EMB-135)					2 AN AE3007A3	19000	Y37		oo-delivery 0001
☐	N563AE	Embraer RJ135 (EMB-135)					2 AN AE3007A3	19000	Y37		oo-delivery 0001
☐	N564AE	Embraer RJ135 (EMB-135)					2 AN AE3007A3	19000	Y37		oo-delivery 0002
☐	N565AE	Embraer RJ135 (EMB-135)					2 AN AE3007A3	19000	Y37		oo-delivery 0002
☐	N566AE	Embraer RJ135 (EMB-135)					2 AN AE3007A3	19000	Y37		oo-delivery 0002
☐	N567AE	Embraer RJ135 (EMB-135)					2 AN AE3007A3	19000	Y37		oo-delivery 0002
☐	N568AE	Embraer RJ135 (EMB-135)					2 AN AE3007A3	19000	Y37		oo-delivery 0002
☐	N569AE	Embraer RJ135 (EMB-135)					2 AN AE3007A3	19000	Y37		oo-delivery 0002

registration	type of aircraft	cn/fn	ex/ex*	mfd	del	powered by	mtow kg	configuration	selcal	name/fln/specialitites/remarks
☐ N570AE	Embraer RJ135 (EMB-135)					2 AN AE3007A3	19000	Y37		oo-delivery 0002
☐ N571AE	Embraer RJ135 (EMB-135)					2 AN AE3007A3	19000	Y37		oo-delivery 0002
☐ N572AE	Embraer RJ135 (EMB-135)					2 AN AE3007A3	19000	Y37		oo-delivery 0002
☐ N573AE	Embraer RJ135 (EMB-135)					2 AN AE3007A3	19000	Y37		oo-delivery 0002
☐ N574AE	Embraer RJ135 (EMB-135)					2 AN AE3007A3	19000	Y37		oo-delivery 0002
☐ N575AE	Embraer RJ135 (EMB-135)					2 AN AE3007A3	19000	Y37		oo-delivery 0002
☐ N576AE	Embraer RJ135 (EMB-135)					2 AN AE3007A3	19000	Y37		oo-delivery 0002
☐ N577AE	Embraer RJ135 (EMB-135)					2 AN AE3007A3	19000	Y37		oo-delivery 0002
☐ N578AE	Embraer RJ135 (EMB-135)					2 AN AE3007A3	19000	Y37		oo-delivery 0002
☐ N579AE	Embraer RJ135 (EMB-135)					2 AN AE3007A3	19000	Y37		oo-delivery 0002
☐ N580AE	Embraer RJ135 (EMB-135)					2 AN AE3007A3	19000	Y37		oo-delivery 0002
☐ N581AE	Embraer RJ135 (EMB-135)					2 AN AE3007A3	19000	Y37		oo-delivery 0002
☐ N582AE	Embraer RJ135 (EMB-135)					2 AN AE3007A3	19000	Y37		oo-delivery 0002
☐ N583AE	Embraer RJ135 (EMB-135)					2 AN AE3007A3	19000	Y37		oo-delivery 0002
☐ N584AE	Embraer RJ135 (EMB-135)					2 AN AE3007A3	19000	Y37		oo-delivery 0002
☐ N585AE	Embraer RJ135 (EMB-135)					2 AN AE3007A3	19000	Y37		oo-delivery 0002
☐ N586AE	Embraer RJ135 (EMB-135)					2 AN AE3007A3	19000	Y37		oo-delivery 0002
☐ N587AE	Embraer RJ135 (EMB-135)					2 AN AE3007A3	19000	Y37		oo-delivery 0002
☐ N588AE	Embraer RJ135 (EMB-135)					2 AN AE3007A3	19000	Y37		oo-delivery 0002
☐ N589AE	Embraer RJ135 (EMB-135)					2 AN AE3007A3	19000	Y37		oo-delivery 0002
☐ N590AE	Embraer RJ135 (EMB-135)					2 AN AE3007A3	19000	Y37		oo-delivery 0002
☐ N591AE	Embraer RJ135 (EMB-135)					2 AN AE3007A3	19000	Y37		oo-delivery 0002
☐ N592AE	Embraer RJ135 (EMB-135)					2 AN AE3007A3	19000	Y37		oo-delivery 0002
☐ N593AE	Embraer RJ135 (EMB-135)					2 AN AE3007A3	19000	Y37		oo-delivery 0002
☐ N594AE	Embraer RJ135 (EMB-135)					2 AN AE3007A3	19000	Y37		oo-delivery 0002
☐ N600BK	Embraer RJ145MR (EMB-145MR)	145044	PT-SZJ*	0098	0298	2 AN AE3007A1/2	22000	Y50		cvtd 145ER
☐ N601GH	Embraer RJ145MR (EMB-145MR)	145046	PT-SZL*	0098	0398	2 AN AE3007A1/2	22000	Y50		
☐ N602AE	Embraer RJ145LR (EMB-145LR)	145048	PT-SZN*	0098	0598	2 AN AE3007A1/2	22000	Y50		
☐ N603AE	Embraer RJ145LR (EMB-145LR)	145055		0098	0598	2 AN AE3007A1/2	22000	Y50		
☐ N604DG	Embraer RJ145LR (EMB-145LR)	145058		0098	0598	2 AN AE3007A1/2	22000	Y50		
☐ N605RR	Embraer RJ145LR (EMB-145LR)	145059		0098	0598	2 AN AE3007A1/2	22000	Y50		
☐ N606AE	Embraer RJ145LR (EMB-145LR)	145062		0098	0598	2 AN AE3007A1/2	22000	Y50		
☐ N607AE	Embraer RJ145LR (EMB-145LR)	145064		0098	0698	2 AN AE3007A1/2	22000	Y50		
☐ N608AE	Embraer RJ145LR (EMB-145LR)	145068		0098	0798	2 AN AE3007A1/2	22000	Y50		
☐ N609AE	Embraer RJ145LR (EMB-145LR)	145069		0098	0798	2 AN AE3007A1/2	22000	Y50		
☐ N610AE	Embraer RJ145LR (EMB-145LR)	145073		0098	0898	2 AN AE3007A1/2	22000	Y50		
☐ N611AE	Embraer RJ145LR (EMB-145LR)	145074		0098	0898	2 AN AE3007A1/2	22000	Y50		
☐ N612AE	Embraer RJ145LR (EMB-145LR)	145079		0098	0998	2 AN AE3007A1/2	22000	Y50		
☐ N613AE	Embraer RJ145LR (EMB-145LR)	145081		0098	0998	2 AN AE3007A1/2	22000	Y50		
☐ N614AE	Embraer RJ145LR (EMB-145LR)	145086		0098	1098	2 AN AE3007A1/2	22000	Y50		
☐ N615AE	Embraer RJ145LR (EMB-145LR)	145087		0098	1098	2 AN AE3007A1/2	22000	Y50		
☐ N616AE	Embraer RJ145LR (EMB-145LR)	145092		0098	1198	2 AN AE3007A1/2	22000	Y50		
☐ N617AE	Embraer RJ145LR (EMB-145LR)	145093	PT-SBP*	0098	1198	2 AN AE3007A1/2	22000	Y50		
☐ N618AE	Embraer RJ145LR (EMB-145LR)	145097	PT-SBT*	0098	1298	2 AN AE3007A1/2	22000	Y50		
☐ N619AE	Embraer RJ145LR (EMB-145LR)	145101		0098	1298	2 AN AE3007A1/2	22000	Y50		
☐ N620AE	Embraer RJ145LR (EMB-145LR)	145102		0098	0199	2 AN AE3007A1/2	22000	Y50		
☐ N621AE	Embraer RJ145LR (EMB-145LR)	145105		0099	0199	2 AN AE3007A1/2	22000	Y50		
☐ N622AE	Embraer RJ145LR (EMB-145LR)	145108		0099	0299	2 AN AE3007A1/2	22000	Y50		
☐ N623AE	Embraer RJ145LR (EMB-145LR)	145109		0099	0299	2 AN AE3007A1/2	22000	Y50		
☐ N624AE	Embraer RJ145LR (EMB-145LR)	145111		0099	0299	2 AN AE3007A1/2	22000	Y50		
☐ N625AE	Embraer RJ145LR (EMB-145LR)	145115		0099	0399	2 AN AE3007A1/2	22000	Y50		
☐ N626AE	Embraer RJ145LR (EMB-145LR)	145117		0099	0399	2 AN AE3007A1/2	22000	Y50		
☐ N627AE	Embraer RJ145LR (EMB-145LR)	145121		0099	0499	2 AN AE3007A1/2	22000	Y50		
☐ N628AE	Embraer RJ145LR (EMB-145LR)	145124		0099	0499	2 AN AE3007A1/2	22000	Y50		
☐ N629AE	Embraer RJ145LR (EMB-145LR)	145130				2 AN AE3007A1/2	22000	Y50		oo-delivery 0599
☐ N630AE	Embraer RJ145LR (EMB-145LR)	145132				2 AN AE3007A1/2	22000	Y50		oo-delivery 0599
☐ N631AE	Embraer RJ145LR (EMB-145LR)					2 AN AE3007A1/2	22000	Y50		oo-delivery 0699
☐ N632AE	Embraer RJ145LR (EMB-145LR)					2 AN AE3007A1/2	22000	Y50		oo-delivery 0699
☐ N633AE	Embraer RJ145LR (EMB-145LR)					2 AN AE3007A1/2	22000	Y50		oo-delivery 0799
☐ N634AE	Embraer RJ145LR (EMB-145LR)					2 AN AE3007A1/2	22000	Y50		oo-delivery 0799
☐ N635AE	Embraer RJ145LR (EMB-145LR)					2 AN AE3007A1/2	22000	Y50		oo-delivery 0899
☐ N636AE	Embraer RJ145LR (EMB-145LR)					2 AN AE3007A1/2	22000	Y50		oo-delivery 0899
☐ N637AE	Embraer RJ145LR (EMB-145LR)					2 AN AE3007A1/2	22000	Y50		oo-delivery 0999
☐ N638AE	Embraer RJ145LR (EMB-145LR)					2 AN AE3007A1/2	22000	Y50		oo-delivery 0999
☐ N639AE	Embraer RJ145LR (EMB-145LR)					2 AN AE3007A1/2	22000	Y50		oo-delivery 1099
☐ N640AE	Embraer RJ145LR (EMB-145LR)					2 AN AE3007A1/2	22000	Y50		oo-delivery 1099
☐ N641AE	Embraer RJ145LR (EMB-145LR)					2 AN AE3007A1/2	22000	Y50		oo-delivery 1199
☐ N642AE	Embraer RJ145LR (EMB-145LR)					2 AN AE3007A1/2	22000	Y50		oo-delivery 1199
☐ N643AE	Embraer RJ145LR (EMB-145LR)					2 AN AE3007A1/2	22000	Y50		oo-delivery 1299
☐ N644AE	Embraer RJ145LR (EMB-145LR)					2 AN AE3007A1/2	22000	Y50		oo-delivery 0100
☐ N645AE	Embraer RJ145LR (EMB-145LR)					2 AN AE3007A1/2	22000	Y50		oo-delivery 0200
☐ N646AE	Embraer RJ145LR (EMB-145LR)					2 AN AE3007A1/2	22000	Y50		oo-delivery 0300
☐ N647AE	Embraer RJ145LR (EMB-145LR)					2 AN AE3007A1/2	22000	Y50		oo-delivery 0500
☐ N648AE	Embraer RJ145LR (EMB-145LR)					2 AN AE3007A1/2	22000	Y50		oo-delivery 0600
☐ N649AE	Embraer RJ145LR (EMB-145LR)					2 AN AE3007A1/2	22000	Y50		oo-delivery 0700
☐ N248AT	ATR 72-202	248	F-WWEN*	0091	0991	2 PWC PW124B	21500	Y64		lsf GECA
☐ N252AM	ATR 72-202	253	N253AT	0091	1091	2 PWC PW124B	21500	Y64		lsf GECA
☐ N260AE	ATR 72-202	263	N263AT	0091	1191	2 PWC PW124B	21500	Y64		lsf GECA
☐ N270AT	ATR 72-202	270	F-WWEL*	0091	1291	2 PWC PW124B	21500	Y64		
☐ N274AT	ATR 72-202	274	F-WWLC*	0091	0192	2 PWC PW124B	21500	Y64		lsf GECA
☐ N288AM	ATR 72-202	288	F-WWLP*	0092	0392	2 PWC PW124B	21500	Y64		
☐ N308AE	ATR 72-202	309	N309AM	0092	0692	2 PWC PW124B	21500	Y64		
☐ N322AC	ATR 72-212	320	N320AT	0092	1292	2 PWC PW127	21500	Y64		
☐ N342AT	ATR 72-212	345	N345AT	0092	0193	2 PWC PW127	21500	Y64		
☐ N348AE	ATR 72-212	349	N349AT	0092	0293	2 PWC PW127	21500	Y64		
☐ N355AT	ATR 72-212	355	F-WWEQ*	0093	0393	2 PWC PW127	21500	Y64		
☐ N369AT	ATR 72-212	369	F-WWEC*	0093	1293	2 PWC PW127	21500	Y64		
☐ N377AT	ATR 72-212	377	F-WWLA*	0094	0194	2 PWC PW127	21500	Y64		
☐ N399AT	ATR 72-212	399	F-WWLK*	0094	0294	2 PWC PW127	21500	Y64		
☐ N407AT	ATR 72-212	407	F-WWEL*	0094	0494	2 PWC PW127	21500	Y64		
☐ N408AT	ATR 72-212	408	F-WWEM*	0094	0494	2 PWC PW127	21500	Y64		
☐ N410AT	ATR 72-212	410	F-WWLS*	0094	0594	2 PWC PW127	21500	Y64		
☐ N414WF	ATR 72-212	414	F-WWLD*	0094	0694	2 PWC PW127	21500	Y64		
☐ N417AT	ATR 72-212	417	F-WWIT*	0094	0694	2 PWC PW127	21500	Y64		
☐ N420AT	ATR 72-212	420	F-WWLY*	0094	0794	2 PWC PW127	21500	Y64		
☐ N425MJ	ATR 72-212	425	F-WWEC*	0094	0994	2 PWC PW127	21500	Y64		
☐ N426AT	ATR 72-212	426	F-WWED*	0094	1094	2 PWC PW127	21500	Y64		
☐ N429AT	ATR 72-212	429	F-WWEH*	0094	1194	2 PWC PW127	21500	Y64		
☐ N431AT	ATR 72-212	431	F-WWEI*	0094	1194	2 PWC PW127	21500	Y64		
☐ N434AT	ATR 72-212	434	F-WWFM*	0094	1194	2 PWC PW127	21500	Y64		
☐ N438AT	ATR 72-212	438	F-WWEO*	0095	0395	2 PWC PW127	21500	Y64		
☐ N440AM	ATR 72-212	440	F-WWEP*	0095	0395	2 PWC PW127	21500	Y64		
☐ N447AM	ATR 72-212	447	F-WWEC*	0095	0495	2 PWC PW127	21500	Y64		
☐ N448AM	ATR 72-212	448	F-WWED*	0095	0495	2 PWC PW127	21500	Y64		
☐ N451AT	ATR 72-212	451	F-WWES*	0095	0495	2 PWC PW127	21500	Y64		
☐ N494AE	ATR 72-500 (72-212A)	494	F-WWLS*	0097	0797	2 PWC PW127F	22500	Y64		
☐ N498AT	ATR 72-500 (72-212A)	498	F-WWLW*	0097	0897	2 PWC PW127F	22500	Y64		
☐ N499AT	ATR 72-500 (72-212A)	499	F-WWLY*	0097	0997	2 PWC PW127F	22500	Y64		500th-sticker
☐ N4AE	ATR 72-202	244	N244AT	0091	0791	2 PWC PW124B	21500	Y64		
☐ N529AM	ATR 72-500 (72-212A)	529	F-WWLR*	0097	1097	2 PWC PW127F	22500	Y64		
☐ N533AT	ATR 72-500 (72-212A)	533	F-WWLO*	0097	1197	2 PWC PW127F	22500	Y64		
☐ N536AT	ATR 72-500 (72-212A)	536	F-WWLZ*	0097	1297	2 PWC PW127F	22500	Y64		
☐ N538AT	ATR 72-500 (72-212A)	538	F-WWEA*	0097	1297	2 PWC PW127F	22500	Y64		
☐ N540AM	ATR 72-500 (72-212A)	540	F-WWLJ*	0098	0198	2 PWC PW127F	22500	Y64		
☐ N541AT	ATR 72-500 (72-212A)	541	F-WWLA*	0098	0298	2 PWC PW127F	22500	Y64		
☐ N545AT	ATR 72-500 (72-212A)	545	F-WWLE*	0098	0398	2 PWC PW127F	22500	Y64		
☐ N548AT	ATR 72-500 (72-212A)	548	F-WWLI*	0098	0498	2 PWC PW127F	22500	Y64		
☐ N550LL	ATR 72-500 (72-212A)	550	F-WWLK*	0098	0498	2 PWC PW127F	22500	Y64		
☐ N700AE	Canadair Regional Jet 700					2 GE CF34-8C1	32885	Y70		oo-delivery 0201
☐ N701AE	Canadair Regional Jet 700					2 GE CF34-8C1	32885	Y70		oo-delivery 0301

☐ N702AE	Canadair Regional Jet 700					2 GE CF34-8C1	32885	Y70		oo-delivery 0401
☐ N703AE	Canadair Regional Jet 700					2 GE CF34-8C1	32885	Y70		oo-delivery 0501
☐ N704AE	Canadair Regional Jet 700					2 GE CF34-8C1	32885	Y70		oo-delivery 0601
☐ N705AE	Canadair Regional Jet 700					2 GE CF34-8C1	32885	Y70		oo-delivery 0801
☐ N706AM	Canadair Regional Jet 700					2 GE CF34-8C1	32885	Y70		oo-delivery 1001
☐ N707MR	Canadair Regional Jet 700					2 GE CF34-8C1	32885	Y70		oo-delivery 1201
☐ N708AE	Canadair Regional Jet 700					2 GE CF34-8C1	32885	Y70		oo-delivery 0002
☐ N709AE	Canadair Regional Jet 700					2 GE CF34-8C1	32885	Y70		oo-delivery 0002
☐ N710AE	Canadair Regional Jet 700					2 GE CF34-8C1	32885	Y70		oo-delivery 0002
☐ N711AE	Canadair Regional Jet 700					2 GE CF34-8C1	32885	Y70		oo-delivery 0002
☐ N712AE	Canadair Regional Jet 700					2 GE CF34-8C1	32885	Y70		oo-delivery 0002
☐ N713AE	Canadair Regional Jet 700					2 GE CF34-8C1	32885	Y70		oo-delivery 0002
☐ N714MR	Canadair Regional Jet 700					2 GE CF34-8C1	32885	Y70		oo-delivery 0002
☐ N715AE	Canadair Regional Jet 700					2 GE CF34-8C1	32885	Y70		oo-delivery 0002
☐ N716AE	Canadair Regional Jet 700					2 GE CF34-8C1	32885	Y70		oo-delivery 0002
☐ N717AE	Canadair Regional Jet 700					2 GE CF34-8C1	32885	Y70		oo-delivery 0003
☐ N718AE	Canadair Regional Jet 700					2 GE CF34-8C1	32885	Y70		oo-delivery 0003
☐ N719AE	Canadair Regional Jet 700					2 GE CF34-8C1	32885	Y70		oo-delivery 0003
☐ N720AE	Canadair Regional Jet 700					2 GE CF34-8C1	32885	Y70		oo-delivery 0003
☐ N721MR	Canadair Regional Jet 700					2 GE CF34-8C1	32885	Y70		oo-delivery 0003
☐ N722AE	Canadair Regional Jet 700					2 GE CF34-8C1	32885	Y70		oo-delivery 0003
☐ N723AE	Canadair Regional Jet 700					2 GE CF34-8C1	32885	Y70		oo-delivery 0003
☐ N724AE	Canadair Regional Jet 700					2 GE CF34-8C1	32885	Y70		oo-delivery 0003

AMERICAN EXECUTIVE AIR CHARTER, Inc.

Charleston-Yeager, WV

707 Virginia Street E, Bank 1 Ceter, S1113, Charleston, WV 25301, USA ☎ (304) 343-4181 Tx: none Fax: (304) 347-5055 SITA: n/a
F: 1995 ⁂ n/a Head: James F. Humphreys Net: n/a

☐ N87SA	Beech King Air B200	BB-1089	D-INKA	0082	1195	2 PWC PT6A-42	5670			to be re-reg. N69JH

AMERICAN HEALTH AVIATION, Inc.

Parsons-Scott Field, TN

PO Box 10, Parsons, TN 38363, USA ☎ (901) 847-4962 Tx: none Fax: (901) 847-4973 SITA: n/a
F: 1991 ⁂ n/a Head: James W. Ayers Net: n/a

☐ N769MB	Beech King Air 200	BB-571	N702AS	0079	0491	2 PWC PT6A-41	5670	EMS		lsf American Health Centers Inc.

AMERICAN HELICOPTERS, Inc.

Galveston-Scholes Field, TX

6610 Stewart Road, No. 154, Galveston, TX 77551, USA ☎ (409) 744-7179 Tx: none Fax: (409) 744-4453 SITA: n/a
F: 1995 ⁂ n/a Head: Ronald L. Diggins Net: n/a

☐ N202AL	Bell 206B JetRanger	1324		0074	0597	1 AN 250-C20	1451			
☐ N222LM	Bell 206B JetRanger II	1916		0076	0297	1 AN 250-C20	1451			

AMERICAN JET INTERNATIONAL, Corp.

Houston-William P. Hobby, TX

8402 Nelms, Suite 201, Houston, TX 77061-4134, USA ☎ (713) 641-9700 Tx: none Fax: (713) 641-6788 SITA: n/a
F: 1990 ⁂ n/a Head: Roger E. Woolsey Net: n/a

☐ N6037U	Beech Baron 58	TH-1021		0079	0397	2 CO IO-520-CB	2449			
☐ N690G	Beech King Air E90	LW-34	N214K	0073	0797	2 PWC PT6A-28	4581			
☐ N438BM	Beech King Air 200	BB-438		0078	0798	2 PWC PT6A-41	5670	EMS CareFilte		opf CareFlite / based Dallas-Love Field
☐ N777XS	Beech King Air 200	BB-126	N208AJ	0076	1196	2 PWC PT6A-41	5670			lsf Grand Casino Coushatta
☐ N273M	Learjet 25D	25D-315	N273KH	0080	0894	2 GE CJ610-8A	6804			
☐ N715MH	Learjet 25B	25B-132	N715JF	0073	0392	2 GE CJ610-6	6804			
☐ N135FA	Learjet 35A	35A-067	N32FN	0076	0598	2 GA TFE731-2-2B	8301	EMS CareFlite		opf CareFlite / based Dallas-Love Field
☐ N18LH	Learjet 35A	35A-379	N23VG	0081	0896	2 GA TFE731-2-2B	8301			
☐ N203RW	Learjet 35A	35A-203	VR-CUC	0079	0397	2 GA TFE731-2-2B	8301			
☐ N500DS	Learjet 35A	35A-079	N7777B	0076	0997	2 GA TFE731-2-2B	8301			
☐ N575GH	Learjet 55	55-042	D-CMTM	0082	1097	2 GA TFE731-3A-2B	8845			
☐ N313QS	Cessna 650 Citation III	650-0013	N119EL	0083	0396	2 GA TFE731-3-100S	9752			lsf Excellent Aviation Rentals Inc.

AMERICAN JET SAN ANTONIO (Aerostar Executive Aviation Corporation dba)

San Antonio-Int'l, TX

4415 Piedras West, Suite 100, San Antonio, TX 78228-1213, USA ☎ (210) 733-5213 Tx: none Fax: (210) 733-6268 SITA: n/a
F: 1994 ⁂ n/a Head: Joseph H. Clayburne Net: n/a

☐ N1855Y	Beech Baron 58P	TJ-388		0081	0297	2 CO TSIO-520-WB	2812			lsf Renegade Inc.
☐ N321DM	Beech King Air E90	LW-250	N600EF	0078	0097	2 PWC PT6A-28	4581			lsf Air Charter Express Inc.

AMERICAN MEDFLIGHT, Inc. (Associated with Reno Flying Service, Inc.)

Reno-Tahoe Int'l, NV

PO Box 7813, Reno, NV 89510, USA ☎ (702) 856-2003 Tx: none Fax: (702) 856-5801 SITA: n/a
F: 1990 ⁂ n/a Head: John R. Carstarphen Net: n/a

☐ N111KV	Piper PA-31T Cheyenne II	31T-7920035	N110MP	0079	0495	2 PWC PT6A-28	4082	EMS		
☐ N789CH	Piper PA-31T Cheyenne II	31T-7920079	N555RC	0079	0097	2 PWC PT6A-28	4082	EMS		lsf Lincoln Computer Center Inc.

AMERICAN TRANS AIR, Inc. – ATA = TZ / AMT (Subsidiary of Amtran, Inc.)

Indianapolis-Int'l, IN

PO Box 51609, Indianapolis, IN 46251-0609, USA ☎ (317) 247-4000 Tx: 797518 ata ind ud Fax: (317) 243-4165 SITA: HDQSSTZ
F: 1973 ⁂ 3690 Head: John P. Tague IATA: 366 ICAO: AMTRAN Net: http://www.ata.com
Feeder connection-flights in a code-share agreement are operated as ATA CONNECTION by CHICAGO EXPRESS AIRLINES (using TZ-flight numbers). For details – see under that company.

☐ N760AT	Boeing 727-2B7 (A)	21954 / 1525	N760US	0079	1294	3 PW JT8D-17A (HK3/FDX)	89358	Y168	CK-FM	lsf Finova Capital Corp.
☐ N762AT	Boeing 727-2B7 (A)	22162 / 1717	N762US	0281	0193	3 PW JT8D-17A (HK3/FDX)	89358	Y168	JM-BE	
☐ N763AT	Boeing 727-264 (A)	22983 / 1806	N763US	0482	0293	3 PW JT8D-17A	88360	Y168	BH-CM	
☐ N764AT	Boeing 727-264 (A)	22984 / 1813	N764US	1282	0293	3 PW JT8D-17A	88360	Y168	AH-BG	lsf GECA
☐ N765AT	Boeing 727-264 (A)	23014 / 1816	N765US	0283	0193	3 PW JT8D-17A (HK3/FDX)	88360	Y168	DM-AH	
☐ N766AT	Boeing 727-227 (A)	21999 / 1581	N766US	0280	0293	3 PW JT8D-17A (HK3/FDX)	88360	Y168	HM-BC	
☐ N767AT	Boeing 727-227 (A)	22001 / 1585	N767US	0280	0293	3 PW JT8D-17A (HK3/FDX)	88360	Y168	JM-BG	
☐ N768AT	Boeing 727-227 (A)	21996 / 1571	N768US	0180	0293	3 PW JT8D-17A (HK3/FDX)	88360	Y168	BH-CL	
☐ N769AT	Boeing 727-227 (A)	21998 / 1577	N769US	0280	0293	3 PW JT8D-17A (HK3/FDX)	88360	Y168	JM-BF	
☐ N770AT	Boeing 727-2B7 (A)	21953 / 1516	N755US	0079	1294	3 PW JT8D-17A (HK3/FDX)	89358	Y168	EH-DK	lsf Finova Capital Corp.
☐ N772AT	Boeing 727-227 (A)	22003 / 1629	N288AS	0080	0394	3 PW JT8D-17R (HK3/FDX)	86409	Y168	AH-BM	lsf TX Nationalease Corp.
☐ N773AT	Boeing 727-227 (A)	22004 / 1631	N289AS	0080	0394	3 PW JT8D-17R (HK3/FDX)	86409	Y168	BC-DE	lsf Texas Nationalease Corp.
☐ N774AT	Boeing 727-290 (A)	21510 / 1359	N290AS	0078	1193	3 PW JT8D-17 (HK3/FDX)	89358	Y168	CH-EL	lsf Finova Capital Corp.
☐ N775AT	Boeing 727-290 (A)	21511 / 1439	N291AS	0079	1193	3 PW JT8D-17 (HK3/FDX)	89448	Y168	CH-KM	lsf John Hancock Leasing Corp.
☐ N776AT	Boeing 727-2Q8 (A)	21608 / 1426	N297AS	0078	1293	3 PW JT8D-17 (HK3/FDX)	89358	Y168	CJ-EK	lsf PEGA
☐ N778AT	Boeing 727-227 (A)	22005 / 1651	N304AS	0080	1193	3 PW JT8D-17R (HK3/FDX)	86409	Y168	DG-EL	lsf GECA
☐ N779AT	Boeing 727-227 (A)	22091 / 1706	N305AS	0081	1193	3 PW JT8D-17R (HK3/FDX)	86409	Y168	FH-AE	lsf GECA
☐ N780AT	Boeing 727-208 (A)	22295 / 1622	N329AS	0080	0194	3 PW JT8D-15 (HK3/FDX)	87409	Y168	FM-AJ	
☐ N782AT	Boeing 727-2Q6 (A)	21972 / 1637	N1280E	0680	1294	3 PW JT8D-17	86409	Y168	EH-BJ	
☐ N783AT	Boeing 727-227 (A)	22000 / 1583	N307AS	0280	1095	3 PW JT8D-17R (HK3/FDX)	79605	Y168	EH-CF	lsf BTM Capital
☐ N784AT	Boeing 727-247 (A)	21393 / 1307	N749US	0077	0196	3 PW JT8D-15 (HK3/FDX)	86409	Y168	EM-CJ	lsf National City Leasing Corp.
☐ N785AT	Boeing 727-214 (A)	21691 / 1480	N752US	0079	0296	3 PW JT8D-7B (HK3/FDX)	78245	Y168	FK-JM	lsf CMCA Lease Inc.
☐ N786AT	Boeing 727-214 (A)	21692 / 1482	N753US	0079	0296	3 PW JT8D-7B (HK3/FDX)	78245	Y168	DF-EH	lsf Suntrust Bank
☐ N788AT	Boeing 727-214 (A)	21958 / 1533	N754US	0079	0296	3 PW JT8D-7B (HK3/FDX)	78245	Y168	DM-BG	lsf FSBU Trustee
☐ N514AT	Boeing 757-23N	27971 / 690		0095	0995	2 RR RB211-535E4	115666	Y216	JM-HR	lsf GATX
☐ N515AT	Boeing 757-23N	27598 / 692		0095	1095	2 PW PW2040	115666	Y216	JM-HS	lsf ILFC
☐ N516AT	Boeing 757-23N	27972 / 694		0095	1295	2 RR RB211-535E4	115666	Y216	JQ-CH	lsf Finova Capital Corp.
☐ N517AT	Boeing 757-23N	27973 / 735		0096	1196	2 RR RB211-535E4	115666	Y216	LS-FK	lsf Finova Capital Corp.
☐ N518AT	Boeing 757-23N	27974 / 737		0096	1296	2 RR RB211-535E4	115666	Y216	KQ-DF	lsf GECA
☐ N519AT	Boeing 757-23N	27975 / 779		0097	1197	2 RR RB211-535E4	115666	Y216	FQ-DE	lsf GECA
☐ N520AT	Boeing 757-23N	27976 / 814		0798	0798	2 RR RB211-535E4	115666	Y216		lsf FANB Lease
☐ N521AT	Boeing 757-28A	24368 / 213	G-MCKE	0089	1196	2 RR RB211-535E4	113398	Y218	KQ-DG	lsf ACG Acquisition XX Llc
☐ N522AT	Boeing 757-23N	29330 / 843		1298	1298	2 RR RB211-535E4	115666	Y216		lsf Debis AirFinance
☐ N523AT	Boeing 757-23N					2 RR RB211-535E4	115666	Y216		oo-delivery 0999
☐ N524AT	Boeing 757-23N					2 RR RB211-535E4	115666	Y216		oo-delivery 1099
☐ N525AT	Boeing 757-23N					2 RR RB211-535E4	115666	Y216		oo-delivery 0600
☐ N185AT	Lockheed L-1011-385-1 TriStar 50	193C-1052	N703DA	0073	0385	3 RR RB211-22B	204117	Y362	FK-BE	cvtd TriStar 1
☐ N186AT	Lockheed L-1011-385-1 TriStar 50	193C-1074	N706DA	0074	0185	3 RR RB211-22B	204117	Y362	FK-BD	cvtd TriStar 1
☐ N187AT	Lockheed L-1011-385-1 TriStar 50	193C-1077	N707DA	0074	0185	3 RR RB211-22B	204117	Y362	FK-BC	cvtd Tri 1
☐ N188AT	Lockheed L-1011-385-1 TriStar 50	193C-1078	N708DA	0074	0285	3 RR RB211-22B	204117	Y362	HL-JK	cvtd TriStar 1
☐ N189AT	Lockheed L-1011-385-1 TriStar 50	193C-1081	N709DA	0074	0585	3 RR RB211-22B	204117	Y362	BJ-HK	cvtd TriStar 1
☐ N190AT	Lockheed L-1011-385-1 TriStar 50	193C-1086	N711DA	0074	0585	3 RR RB211-22B	204117	Y362	JM-BL	cvtd Tri.1
☐ N191AT	Lockheed L-1011-385-1 TriStar 50	193C-1084	N710DA	0074	0685	3 RR RB211-22B	204117	Y362	JM-BK	cvtd TriStar 1
☐ N192AT	Lockheed L-1011-385-1 TriStar 50	193C-1057	N704DA	0073	1185	3 RR RB211-22B	204117	Y362	JM-CD	cvtd TriStar 1
☐ N193AT	Lockheed L-1011-385-1 TriStar 50	193C-1071	N705DA	0074	1285	3 RR RB211-22B	204117	Y362	JM-CE	cvtd TriStar 1
☐ N194AT	Lockheed L-1011-385-1-15 TriStar 100	193B-1230	N8034T	0082	0994	3 RR RB211-22B	211374	Y362	DF-EG	lsf Shawmut Bank CT Trustee

273 registration type of aircraft cn/fn ex/ex* mfd del powered by mtow kg configuration selcal name/fln/specialitites/remarks

☐ N195AT	Lockheed L-1011-385-1-14 TriStar 150	193C-1041	N701TT	0073	0587	3 RR RB211-22B	215003	Y362	BH-CJ	cvtd TriStar 1
☐ N196AT	Lockheed L-1011-385-1 TriStar 50	193B-1076	N31022	0074	0790	3 RR RB211-22B	204117	Y362	HK-AM	cvtd TriStar 1
☐ N197AT	Lockheed L-1011-385-1 TriStar 50	193P-1082	N763BE	0074	0691	3 RR RB211-22B	204117	Y362	GH-KQ	cvtd TriStar 1
☐ N198AT	Lockheed L-1011-385-1-15 TriStar 100	193B-1111	N31030	0075	0398	3 RR RB211-22B	211374	Y362		cvtd TriStar 1
☐ N162AT	Lockheed L-1011-385-3 TriStar 500	293A-1220	JY-AGC	0382	1198	3 RR RB211-524B4	231332	Y307		
☐ N163AT	Lockheed L-1011-385-3 TriStar 500	293A-1229	JY-AGD	0682	0798	3 RR RB211-524B4	231332	Y307		
☐ N164AT	Lockheed L-1011-385-3 TriStar 500	293A-1238	JY-AGE	1082	0299	3 RR RB211-524B4	231332	Y307		
☐ N	Lockheed L-1011-385-3 TriStar 500	293A-1217	JY-AGA	0981		3 RR RB211-524B4	231332	Y307		oo-delivery 0000 / ex RJA
☐ N	Lockheed L-1011-385-3 TriStar 500	293A-1219	JY-AGB	1081		3 RR RB211-524B4	231332	Y307		oo-delivery 0000 / ex AMT

AMERICAN TRANS AIR EXECUJET, Inc. (Affiliated with American Trans Air, Inc.)

Indianapolis-Int'l, IN

PO Box 51609, Indianapolis, IN 46251-0609, USA ☎ (765) 240-7081 Tx: 797518 ata ind ud Fax: (765) 240-7091 SITA: n/a
F: 1986 ☃ n/a Head: J. George Mikelsons Net: n/a

☐ N13AT	Bell 206B JetRanger III	3267	N39085	0081	0989	1 AN 250-C20B	1451			lsf Betaco Inc.
☐ N42AT	Eurocopter (Aerosp.) AS355F2 Ecureuil 2	5462	N70PB	0091	0995	2 AN 250-C20F	2540			lsf Betaco Inc.
☐ N308AT	Cessna 501 Citation I/SP	501-0159	N666JJ	0080	1087	2 PWC JT15D-1A	5375			lsf Betaco Inc.

AMERICA WEST AIRLINES, Inc. = HP / AWE

Phoenix, AZ

4000 East Sky Harbor Blvd, Phoenix, AZ 85034, USA ☎ (520) 693-0800 Tx: 755139 amerwest phx Fax: (520) 693-5546 SITA: n/a
F: 1981 ☃ 11000 Head: William A. Franke IATA: 401 ICAO: CACTUS Net: http://www.americawest.com

A commuter system to provide feeder connection at HP hubs is operated under the marketing name AMERICA WEST EXPRESS by MESA AIRLINES (Beech 1900D & CRJ200. For details– see under that co.

☐ N708AW	Boeing 737-112	19771 / 212	HP-1038	0069	1085	2 PW JT8D-9A	50349	F8Y82		Phoenix Suns-special colors
☐ N138AW	Boeing 737-2E3 (A)	22792 / 887	CC-CIY	0082	0384	2 PW JT8D-15	53070	F8Y105		lsf CITG
☐ N141AW	Boeing 737-2M8 (A)	21955 / 659	OO-TEN	0080	0484	2 PW JT8D-9A	53070	F8Y105	CH-EM	lsf CITG
☐ N145AW	Boeing 737-2A6	20194 / 196	N3333M	0069	0685	2 PW JT8D-9A	51936	F8Y105		
☐ N147AW	Boeing 737-297 (A)	22630 / 860	N729AL	0082	0885	2 PW JT8D-9A	53070	F8Y105		lsf ACG Aquisition VIII Llc
☐ N149AW	Boeing 737-2U9 (A)	22575 / 749	ZK-NEF	0081	0587	2 PW JT8D-15 (HK3/NOR)	53070	F8Y105		
☐ N178AW	Boeing 737-277 (A)	22645 / 768	VH-CZM	0081	1086	2 PW JT8D-15 (HK3/NOR)	53070	F8Y105		lsf IBM
☐ N179AW	Boeing 737-277 (A)	22646 / 778	VH-CZN	0081	0187	2 PW JT8D-15 (HK3/NOR)	53070	F8Y105		
☐ N180AW	Boeing 737-277 (A)	22647 / 785	VH-CZO	0081	1186	2 PW JT8D-15 (HK3/NOR)	53070	F8Y105		lsf Pacificorp
☐ N181AW	Boeing 737-277 (A)	22648 / 789	VH-CZP	0081	1086	2 PW JT8D-15 (HK3/NOR)	53070	F8Y105		lsf Pacificorp
☐ N182AW	Boeing 737-277 (A)	22649 / 801	VH-CZQ	0081	1186	2 PW JT8D-15 (HK3/NOR)	53070	F8Y105		lsf Pacificorp
☐ N183AW	Boeing 737-277 (A)	22650 / 806	VH-CZR	0081	0287	2 PW JT8D-15	53070	F8Y105		
☐ N184AW	Boeing 737-277 (A)	22651 / 819	VH-CZS	0081	0187	2 PW JT8D-15	53070	F8Y105		
☐ N185AW	Boeing 737-277 (A)	22652 / 831	VH-CZT	0082	1286	2 PW JT8D-15 (HK3/NOR)	53070	F8Y105		lsf Pacificorp
☐ N186AW	Boeing 737-277 (A)	22653 / 832	VH-CZU	0082	0187	2 PW JT8D-15	53070	F8Y105		lsf EDS Leasing Co.
☐ N187AW	Boeing 737-277 (A)	22654 / 862	VH-CZV	0082	0287	2 PW JT8D-15	53070	F8Y105		lsf EDS Leasing Co.
☐ N188AW	Boeing 737-277 (A)	22655 / 872	VH-CZW	0082	1186	2 PW JT8D-15	53070	F8Y105		lsf IBM
☐ N189AW	Boeing 737-277 (A)	22656 / 876	VH-CZX	0082	0986	2 PW JT8D-15 (HK3/NOR)	53070	F8Y105		lsf CITG
☐ N150AW	Boeing 737-3G7	23218 / 1076		0085	0285	2 CFMI CFM56-3B2	56472	F8Y124		lsf IBM
☐ N151AW	Boeing 737-3G7	23219 / 1090		0085	0385	2 CFMI CFM56-3B2	56472	F8Y124		lsf IBM
☐ N154AW	Boeing 737-3G7	23776 / 1417		0087	0787	2 CFMI CFM56-3B1	56472	F8Y124		
☐ N155AW	Boeing 737-3G7	23777 / 1419		0087	0787	2 CFMI CFM56-3B1	56472	F8Y124		
☐ N156AW	Boeing 737-3G7	23778 / 1455		0087	1087	2 CFMI CFM56-3B1	56472	F8Y124		
☐ N157AW	Boeing 737-3G7	23779 / 1457		0087	1087	2 CFMI CFM56-3B1	56472	F8Y124		
☐ N158AW	Boeing 737-3G7	23780 / 1459		0087	1087	2 CFMI CFM56-3B1	56472	F8Y124		
☐ N160AW	Boeing 737-3G7	23782 / 1496		0088	0188	2 CFMI CFM56-3B2	56472	F8Y124		
☐ N164AW	Boeing 737-33A	23625 / 1283	N3281V*	0086	1086	2 CFMI CFM56-3B1	61235	F8Y124		lsf AWAS
☐ N165AW	Boeing 737-33A	23626 / 1284	N3281W*	0086	1086	2 CFMI CFM56-3B1	61235	F8Y124		lsf AWAS
☐ N166AW	Boeing 737-33A	23627 / 1302		0086	1186	2 CFMI CFM56-3B1	61235	F8Y124		lsf AWAS
☐ N167AW	Boeing 737-33A	23628 / 1304		0086	1186	2 CFMI CFM56-3B1	61235	F8Y124		lsf AWAS
☐ N168AW	Boeing 737-33A	23629 / 1311		0086	1286	2 CFMI CFM56-3B1	61235	F8Y124		lsf AWAS
☐ N169AW	Boeing 737-33A	23630 / 1312		0086	1286	2 CFMI CFM56-3B1	61235	F8Y124		lsf AWAS
☐ N172AW	Boeing 737-33A	23631 / 1337		0087	0287	2 CFMI CFM56-3B1	61235	F8Y124		lsf AWAS
☐ N173AW	Boeing 737-33A	23632 / 1344		0087	0287	2 CFMI CFM56-3B1	61235	F8Y124		lsf AWAS
☐ N174AW	Boeing 737-33A	23633 / 1421		0087	0887	2 CFMI CFM56-3B1	61235	F8Y124		lsf AWAS
☐ N175AW	Boeing 737-33A	23634 / 1423		0087	0887	2 CFMI CFM56-3B1	61235	F8Y124		lsf AWAS
☐ N302AW	Boeing 737-3G7	24009 / 1578		0088	0788	2 CFMI CFM56-3B1	56472	F8Y124		
☐ N303AW	Boeing 737-3G7	24010 / 1606		0088	0988	2 CFMI CFM56-3B1	56472	F8Y124		lsf Marcap
☐ N304AW	Boeing 737-3G7	24011 / 1608		0088	1088	2 CFMI CFM56-3B1	56472	F8Y124		lsf CIT Leasing
☐ N305AW	Boeing 737-3G7	24012 / 1612		0088	1088	2 CFMI CFM56-3B1	56472	F8Y124		lsf P.S. Group
☐ N306AW	Boeing 737-3G7	24633 / 1809		0090	0190	2 CFMI CFM56-3B2	56472	F8Y124		
☐ N307AW	Boeing 737-3G7	24634 / 1823		0090	0290	2 CFMI CFM56-3B2	56472	F8Y124		
☐ N308AW	Boeing 737-3G7	24710 / 1825		0090	0390	2 CFMI CFM56-3B2	56472	F8Y124		
☐ N309AW	Boeing 737-3G7	24711 / 1843		0090	0390	2 CFMI CFM56-3B2	56472	F8Y124		
☐ N311AW	Boeing 737-3G7	24712 / 1869		0090	0690	2 CFMI CFM56-3B2	56472	F8Y124		
☐ N312AW	Boeing 737-3S3	24060 / 1519	N200KG	0090	1297	2 CFMI CFM56-3B2	62142	F8Y118		lsf KG Aircraft Leasing Co. Ltd
☐ N313AW	Boeing 737-3S3	23712 / 1336	EC-EBZ	0087	1190	2 CFMI CFM56-3B2	62142	F8Y118	AF-EL	lsf BOUL
☐ N314AW	Boeing 737-3S3	23733 / 1345	G-BMTG	0087	1190	2 CFMI CFM56-3B2	62142	F8Y118	AK-FG	lsf BOUL
☐ N315AW	Boeing 737-3S3	23734 / 1359	G-BMTH	0087	1290	2 CFMI CFM56-3B2	62142	F8Y118		lsf BOUL
☐ N316AW	Boeing 737-3S3	23713 / 1341	G-BMTF	0087	0191	2 CFMI CFM56-3B2	62142	F8Y118		lsf BOUL
☐ N322AW	Boeing 737-3G7	25400 / 2112		0091	0991	2 CFMI CFM56-3B1	56472	F8Y118		lsf GECA
☐ N323AW	Boeing 737-3Y0	23684 / 1353	EC-FQB	0087	0295	2 CFMI CFM56-3B2	62822	F8Y124		lsf GECA
☐ N324AW	Boeing 737-301	23261 / 1157	N583US	0085	0695	2 CFMI CFM56-3B2	62823	F8Y118		lsf GECA
☐ N325AW	Boeing 737-301	23260 / 1146	N582US	0085	0695	2 CFMI CFM56-3B2	62823	F8Y118		lsf GECA
☐ N326AW	Boeing 737-301	23258 / 1126	N579US	0085	0889	2 CFMI CFM56-3B2	62823	F8Y120		lsf GECA
☐ N327AW	Boeing 737-3Q8	23507 / 1252	N398US	0086	1295	2 CFMI CFM56-3B1	61235	F8Y120		lsf GECA
☐ N328AW	Boeing 737-3B7	23377 / 1320	N502AU	0086	1295	2 CFMI CFM56-3B2	62823	F8Y120		lsf GECA
☐ N329AW	Boeing 737-3Y0 (QC)	23500 / 1243	N304AL	0086	0997	2 CFMI CFM56-3B1	61235	F8Y124		lsf GECA / cvtd -3Y0
☐ N330AW	Boeing 737-3Y0 (QC)	23499 / 1242	N303AL	0086	0797	2 CFMI CFM56-3B1	61235	F8Y124		lsf GECA / cvtd -3Y0
☐ N331AW	Boeing 737-3Y0	23747 / 1363	EI-CKV	0087	1294	2 CFMI CFM56-3B2	62822	F8Y124	HP-GJ	lsf GECA
☐ N332AW	Boeing 737-3B7	23384 / 1427	N953WP	0087	0598	2 CFMI CFM56-3B2	62823	F8Y124		lsf GECA
☐ N334AW	Boeing 737-3Y0	23748 / 1381	N962WP	0087	0898	2 CFMI CFM56-3B2	62823	F8Y124		lsf ACG Acquisition XX Llc
☐ N335AW	Boeing 737-3U3	28740 / 3003	N1790B*	0098	0998	2 CFMI CFM56-3C1	63276	F8Y124		lsf GECA
☐ N509DC	Boeing 737-33A	23636 / 1438	EC-EHJ	0087	0989	2 CFMI CFM56-3B2	62142	F8Y124		lsf AWAS
☐ N801AW	Airbus Industrie A319-132	889	D-AVYM*	0098	1098	2 IAE V2524-A5	64000	F12Y112		
☐ N802AW	Airbus Industrie A319-132	924	D-AVYR*	0098	1298	2 IAE V2524-A5	64000	F12Y112		
☐ N803AW	Airbus Industrie A319-132	931	D-AVYK*	0098	1298	2 IAE V2524-A5	64000	F12Y112		
☐ N804AW	Airbus Industrie A319-132					2 IAE V2524-A5	64000	F12Y112		oo-delivery 0799
☐ N805AW	Airbus Industrie A319-132					2 IAE V2524-A5	64000	F12Y112		oo-delivery 0799
☐ N806AW	Airbus Industrie A319-132					2 IAE V2524-A5	64000	F12Y112		oo-delivery 0899
☐ N807AW	Airbus Industrie A319-132					2 IAE V2524-A5	64000	F12Y112		oo-delivery 0999
☐ N808AW	Airbus Industrie A319-132					2 IAE V2524-A5	64000	F12Y112		oo-delivery 1199
☐ N809AW	Airbus Industrie A319-132					2 IAE V2524-A5	64000	F12Y112		oo-delivery 1199
☐ N810AW	Airbus Industrie A319-132					2 IAE V2524-A5	64000	F12Y112		oo-delivery 0000
☐ N812AW	Airbus Industrie A319-132					2 IAE V2524-A5	64000	F12Y112		oo-delivery 0000
☐ N814AW	Airbus Industrie A319-132					2 IAE V2524-A5	64000	F12Y112		oo-delivery 0000
☐ N815AW	Airbus Industrie A319-132					2 IAE V2524-A5	64000	F12Y112		oo-delivery 0000
☐ N816AW	Airbus Industrie A319-132					2 IAE V2524-A5	64000	F12Y112		oo-delivery 0000
☐ N817AW	Airbus Industrie A319-132					2 IAE V2524-A5	64000	F12Y112		oo-delivery 0000
☐ N819AW	Airbus Industrie A319-132					2 IAE V2524-A5	64000	F12Y112		oo-delivery 0001
☐ N820AW	Airbus Industrie A319-132					2 IAE V2524-A5	64000	F12Y112		oo-delivery 0001
☐ N821AW	Airbus Industrie A319-132					2 IAE V2524-A5	64000	F12Y112		oo-delivery 0001
☐ N822AW	Airbus Industrie A319-132					2 IAE V2524-A5	64000	F12Y112		oo-delivery 0001
☐ N823AW	Airbus Industrie A319-132					2 IAE V2524-A5	64000	F12Y112		oo-delivery 0001
☐ N824AW	Airbus Industrie A319-132					2 IAE V2524-A5	64000	F12Y112		oo-delivery 0001
☐ N825AW	Airbus Industrie A319-132					2 IAE V2524-A5	64000	F12Y112		oo-delivery 0001
☐ N618AW	Airbus Industrie A320-231	304	N303ML	0092	0596	2 IAE V2500-A1	73500	F12Y138		lsf ORIX
☐ N620AW	Airbus Industrie A320-231	052	N901BN	0089	0291	2 IAE V2500-A1	73500	F12Y138		lsf GECA
☐ N621AW	Airbus Industrie A320-231	053	N902BN	0089	0291	2 IAE V2500-A1	73500	F12Y138	EQ-JL	lsf GECA
☐ N622AW	Airbus Industrie A320-231	054	N903BN	0089	0291	2 IAE V2500-A1	73500	F12Y138	EQ-JM	lsf GECA
☐ N624AW	Airbus Industrie A320-231	055	N904BN	0089	0291	2 IAE V2500-A1	73500	F12Y138	EQ-JP	lsf GECA
☐ N625AW	Airbus Industrie A320-231	064	N905BN	0089	0391	2 IAE V2500-A1	73500	F12Y138	EQ-KL	lsf GECA
☐ N626AW	Airbus Industrie A320-231	065	N906BN	0089	0591	2 IAE V2500-A1	73500	F12Y138	EQ-KM	lsf GECA
☐ N627AW	Airbus Industrie A320-231	066	N907GP	0089	0591	2 IAE V2500-A1	73500	F12Y138	EQ-KP	lsf GECA
☐ N628AW	Airbus Industrie A320-231	067	N908GP	0089	0591	2 IAE V2500-A1	73500	F12Y138	EQ-LM	lsf GECA
☐ N629AW	Airbus Industrie A320-231	076	N910GP	0089	0691	2 IAE V2500-A1	73500	F12Y138		lsf GECA
☐ N631AW	Airbus Industrie A320-231	077	N911GP	0089	0791	2 IAE V2500-A1	73500	F12Y138		lsf GECA
☐ N632AW	Airbus Industrie A320-231	081	N912GP	0089	0791	2 IAE V2500-A1	73500	F12Y138		lsf GECA
☐ N633AW	Airbus Industrie A320-231	082	N913GP	0089	0891	2 IAE V2500-A1	73500	F12Y138	AC-PQ	lsf GECA

274 registration type of aircraft cn/fn ex/ex* mfd del powered by mtow kg configuration selcal name/fln/specialitites/remarks

☐ N634AW	Airbus Industrie A320-231	091	N914GP	0090	0991	2 IAE V2500-A1	73500	F12Y138		lsf GECA
☐ N635AW	Airbus Industrie A320-231	092	N915GP	0090	1091	2 IAE V2500-A1	73500	F12Y138	AD-CQ	lsf GECA
☐ N636AW	Airbus Industrie A320-231	098	N916GP	0090	1191	2 IAE V2500-A1	73500	F12Y138	AD-EQ	lsf GECA
☐ N637AW	Airbus Industrie A320-231	099	N917GP	0090	1291	2 IAE V2500-A1	73500	F12Y138	AC-PQ	lsf GECA
☐ N638AW	Airbus Industrie A320-232	455	F-WWBK*	0093	0495	2 IAE V2527-A5	73500	F12Y138		lsf GECA
☐ N639AW	Airbus Industrie A320-232	471	F-WWIR*	0095	0495	2 IAE V2527-A5	73500	F12Y138		lsf GECA
☐ N640AW	Airbus Industrie A320-232	448	N931LF	0094	0196	2 IAE V2527-A5	77000	F12Y138		lsf ILFC
☐ N641AW	Airbus Industrie A320-232	453	N961LF	0094	0196	2 IAE V2527-A5	77000	F12Y138		lsf ILFC
☐ N642AW	Airbus Industrie A320-232	584	F-WWDZ*	0096	0696	2 IAE V2527-A5	73500	F12Y138		lsf GECA
☐ N643AW	Airbus Industrie A320-231	315	N301ML	0092	0896	2 IAE V2500-A1	73500	F12Y138		lsf ORIX
☐ N644AW	Airbus Industrie A320-231	317	N300ML	0092	0596	2 IAE V2500-A1	73500	F12Y138		lsf ORIX
☐ N645AW	Airbus Industrie A320-231	238	N238RX	0091	1096	2 IAE V2500-A1	73500	F12Y138	CF-JS	lsf ORIX
☐ N646AW	Airbus Industrie A320-231	271	N271RX	0091	0297	2 IAE V2500-A1	73500	F12Y138		lsf ORIX
☐ N647AW	Airbus Industrie A320-232	762	F-WWDE*	0098	0298	2 IAE V2527-A5	73500	F12Y138	HP-JS	lsf SALE
☐ N648AW	Airbus Industrie A320-232	770	F-WWDJ*	0098	0298	2 IAE V2527-A5	73500	F12Y138	HP-LR	lsf SALE
☐ N649AW	Airbus Industrie A320-232	803	F-WWDZ*	0098	0498	2 IAE V2527-A5	73500	F12Y138	HP-LS	lsf SALE
☐ N650AW	Airbus Industrie A320-232	856	F-WWBM*	0098	0998	2 IAE V2527-A5	73500	F12Y138		lsf SALE
☐ N651AW	Airbus Industrie A320-232	866	F-WWBS*	0098	0998	2 IAE V2527-A5	73500	F12Y138	HP-MS	lsf SALE
☐ N652AW	Airbus Industrie A320-232	953	F-WWDR*			2 IAE V2527-A5	73500	F12Y138		oo-delivery 0499
☐ N653AW	Airbus Industrie A320-232	1003				2 IAE V2527-A5	73500	F12Y138		oo-delivery 0599
☐ N654AW	Airbus Industrie A320-232	1050				2 IAE V2527-A5	73500	F12Y138		oo-delivery 0799
☐ N655AW	Airbus Industrie A320-232	1114				2 IAE V2527-A5	73500	F12Y138		oo-delivery 1199
☐ N656AW	Airbus Industrie A320-232					2 IAE V2527-A5	73500	F12Y138		oo-delivery 0000
☐ N657AW	Airbus Industrie A320-232					2 IAE V2527-A5	73500	F12Y138		oo-delivery 0000
☐ N658AW	Airbus Industrie A320-232					2 IAE V2527-A5	73500	F12Y138		oo-delivery 0000
☐ N659AW	Airbus Industrie A320-232					2 IAE V2527-A5	73500	F12Y138		oo-delivery 0000
☐ N660AW	Airbus Industrie A320-232					2 IAE V2527-A5	73500	F12Y138		oo-delivery 0000
☐ N661AW	Airbus Industrie A320-232					2 IAE V2527-A5	73500	F12Y138		oo-delivery 0000
☐ N662AW	Airbus Industrie A320-232					2 IAE V2527-A5	73500	F12Y138		oo-delivery 0000
☐ N663AW	Airbus Industrie A320-232					2 IAE V2527-A5	73500	F12Y138		oo-delivery 0000
☐ N664AW	Airbus Industrie A320-232					2 IAE V2527-A5	73500	F12Y138		oo-delivery 0000
☐ N665AW	Airbus Industrie A320-232					2 IAE V2527-A5	73500	F12Y138		oo-delivery 0000
☐ N667AW	Airbus Industrie A320-232					2 IAE V2527-A5	73500	F12Y138		oo-delivery 0000
☐ N668AW	Airbus Industrie A320-232					2 IAE V2527-A5	73500	F12Y138		oo-delivery 0000
☐ N669AW	Airbus Industrie A320-232					2 IAE V2527-A5	73500	F12Y138		oo-delivery 0000
☐ N670AW	Airbus Industrie A320-232					2 IAE V2527-A5	73500	F12Y138		oo-delivery 0001
☐ N672AW	Airbus Industrie A320-232					2 IAE V2527-A5	73500	F12Y138		oo-delivery 0001
☐ N901AW	Boeing 757-2S7	23321 / 76	N601RC	0085	0687	2 RR RB211-535E4	108862	F16Y176		City of PHX/TUS / lsf Boeing/Arizona cs
☐ N902AW	Boeing 757-2S7	23322 / 79	N602RC	0085	0587	2 RR RB211-535E4	108862	F14Y176		lsf Boeing / special "Teamwork" colors
☐ N903AW	Boeing 757-2S7	23323 / 80	N603RC	0085	0687	2 RR RB211-535E4	108862	F16Y176		lsf Boeing
☐ N904AW	Boeing 757-2S7	23566 / 96	N604RC	0086	0587	2 RR RB211-535E4	108862	F14Y176		lsf Boeing / special AZ Diamondbacks cs
☐ N905AW	Boeing 757-2S7	23567 / 97	N605RC	0086	0587	2 RR RB211-535E4	108862	F14Y176		City of Columbus / lsf Boeing / Ohio cs
☐ N906AW	Boeing 757-2S7	23568 / 99	N606RC	0086	0587	2 RR RB211-535E4	108862	F16Y176		lsf Boeing
☐ N907AW	Boeing 757-225	22691 / 155	XA-TCD	0087	0494	2 RR RB211-535E4	108862	F14Y175		lsf CITG / Phoenix Suns colours
☐ N908AW	Boeing 757-2G7	24233 / 244		0089	0889	2 RR RB211-535E4	108862	F16Y176		Arizona Cardinals-colors
☐ N909AW	Boeing 757-2G7	24522 / 252		0089	1189	2 RR RB211-535E4	108862	F16Y176		
☐ N910AW	Boeing 757-2G7	24523 / 256		0089	1189	2 RR RB211-535E4	108862	F16Y176		lsf PLC Leasing Corp.
☐ N913AW	Boeing 757-225	22207 / 35	N517EA	0084	0692	2 RR RB211-535E4	104326	F16Y175		lsf WTC Trustee
☐ N914AW	Boeing 757-225	22208 / 38	N518EA	0084	0692	2 RR RB211-535E4	104326	F16Y175		lsf WTC Trustee
☐ N915AW	Boeing 757-225	22209 / 40	N747BJ	0084	1294	2 RR RB211-535E4	104326	F12Y175		City of LAS & Reno / lsf WTC/Nevada-cs

AMERICOPTER AVIATION SERVICES

La Grande-Union County, OR

60272 Pierce Road, La Grande, OR 97850, USA ☎ (541) 962-6276 Tx: none Fax: (541) 962-6276 SITA: n/a

F: 1996 staff n/a Head: Kemit W. Knight Net: n/a

☐ N37488	Bell 206B JetRanger II	2188		0077	0197	1 AN 250-C20	1451			lsf Knight Leasing Inc.
☐ N58003	Bell 206B JetRanger	1020	VH-HRZ	0073	0197	1 AN 250-C20	1451			lsf Knight Leasing Inc.

AMERIFLIGHT, Inc. = AMF (Subs.of Armoured Transport Industries/formerly California Air Charter Inc.)

Burbank, CA & APA/BFI/BIL/CVG/DAL/DEN/PDX/PHX/SAT/SLC

4700 Empire Avenue, Hangar 1, Burbank, CA 91505-1098, USA ☎ (818) 980-5005 Tx: none Fax: (818) 980-5101 SITA: n/a

F: 1968 staff 600 Head: Gary Richards ICAO: AMFLIGHT Net: n/a

☐ N123KC	Piper PA-32R-300 Lance	32R-7680431		0076	0884	1 LY IO-540-K1G5D	1633	Freighter		
☐ N1333H	Piper PA-32R-300 Lance	32R-7780154		0077	0179	1 LY IO-540-K1G5D	1633	Freighter		
☐ N1512X	Piper PA-32R-300 Lance	32R-7680002		0075	0788	1 LY IO-540-K1G5D	1633	Freighter		
☐ N188SP	Piper PA-32R-300 Lance	32R-7780309		0077	0493	1 LY IO-540-K1G5D	1633	Freighter		
☐ N2165M	Piper PA-32R-300 Lance	32R-7880053		0078	0983	1 LY IO-540-K1G5D	1633	Freighter		
☐ N3609Q	Piper PA-32R-300 Lance	32R-7780319		0077	0493	1 LY IO-540-K1G5D	1633	Freighter		
☐ N4085F	Piper PA-32R-300 Lance	32R-7680427		0076	0378	1 LY IO-540-K1G5D	1633	Freighter		
☐ N4342F	Piper PA-32R-300 Lance	32R-7680440		0076	1288	1 LY IO-540-K1G5D	1633	Freighter		
☐ N4588F	Piper PA-32R-300 Lance	32R-7680462		0076	0179	1 LY IO-540-K1G5D	1633	Freighter		
☐ N5363F	Piper PA-32R-300 Lance	32R-7680510		0076	0879	1 LY IO-540-K1G5D	1633	Freighter		
☐ N6812J	Piper PA-32R-300 Lance	32R-7680352		0076	0977	1 LY IO-540-K1G5D	1633	Freighter		
☐ N6851J	Piper PA-32R-300 Lance	32R-7680370		0076	0979	1 LY IO-540-K1G5D	1633	Freighter		
☐ N75195	Piper PA-32R-300 Lance	32R-7680277		0076	0190	1 LY IO-540-K1G5D	1633	Freighter		
☐ N75397	Piper PA-32R-300 Lance	32R-7680301		0076	0785	1 LY IO-540-K1G5D	1633	Freighter		
☐ N7612F	Piper PA-32R-300 Lance	32R-7780063		0076	0184	1 LY IO-540-K1G5D	1633	Freighter		
☐ N7838C	Piper PA-32R-300 Lance	32R-7680064		0076	0493	1 LY IO-540-K1G5D	1633	Freighter		
☐ N8456F	Piper PA-32R-300 Lance	32R-7780100		0077	0884	1 LY IO-540-K1G5D	1633	Freighter		
☐ N8701E	Piper PA-32R-300 Lance	32R-7680160		0076	0493	1 LY IO-540-K1G5D	1633	Freighter		
☐ N8929C	Piper PA-32R-300 Lance	32R-7680144		0076	1283	1 LY IO-540-K1G5D	1633	Freighter		
☐ N9226K	Piper PA-32R-300 Lance	32R-7680199		0076	0493	1 LY IO-540-K1G5D	1633	Freighter		
☐ N1024B	Piper PA-31-350 Navajo Chieftain	31-7652107	N554CF	0076	1284	2 LY TIO-540-J2BD	3175	Freighter		
☐ N199DS	Piper PA-31-310 Navajo B	31-7400980		0073	0481	2 LY TIO-540-A2C	2948	Freighter		
☐ N27275	Piper PA-31-310 Navajo C	31-7712066		0077	0781	2 LY TIO-540-A2C	2948	Freighter		
☐ N27426	Piper PA-31-350 Navajo Chieftain	31-7752175		0077	0785	2 LY TIO-540-J2BD	3175	Freighter		
☐ N27579	Piper PA-31-350 Navajo Chieftain	31-7852063		0078	0585	2 LY TIO-540-J2BD	3175	Freighter		
☐ N27677	Piper PA-31-350 Navajo Chieftain	31-7852101		0078	0092	2 LY TIO-540-J2BD	3175	Freighter		
☐ N27996	Piper PA-31-350 Navajo Chieftain	31-7952083		0079	1087	2 LY TIO-540-J2BD	3175	Freighter		
☐ N29UM	Piper PA-31-350 Navajo Chieftain	31-7652127	N29JM	0076	1279	2 LY TIO-540-J2BD	3175	Freighter		
☐ N3525G	Piper PA-31-350 Navajo Chieftain	31-7952123		0079	0092	2 LY TIO-540-J2BD	3175	Freighter		lsf Quebec Enterprises Inc.
☐ N3527D	Piper PA-31-350 Navajo Chieftain	31-7952137		0079	0586	2 LY TIO-540-J2BD	3175	Freighter		
☐ N35336	Piper PA-31-350 Navajo Chieftain	31-7952189		0079	0485	2 LY TIO-540-J2BD	3175	Freighter		
☐ N3540N	Piper PA-31-350 Navajo Chieftain	31-7952214		0079	0785	2 LY TIO-540-J2BD	3175	Freighter		
☐ N3548B	Piper PA-31-350 Navajo Chieftain	31-8052025		0080	1087	2 LY TIO-540-J2BD	3175	Freighter		
☐ N3553F	Piper PA-31-350 Navajo Chieftain	31-8052044		0080	1087	2 LY TIO-540-J2BD	3175	Freighter		
☐ N3555D	Piper PA-31-350 Navajo Chieftain	31-8052059		0080	1087	2 LY TIO-540-J2BD	3175	Freighter		lsf Quebec Enterprises Inc.
☐ N35805	Piper PA-31-350 Navajo Chieftain	31-8052090		0080	1087	2 LY TIO-540-J2BD	3175	Freighter		
☐ N3BT	Piper PA-31-350 Navajo Chieftain	31-7752172	N27422	0077	0984	2 LY TIO-540-J2BD	3175	Freighter		
☐ N4044P	Piper PA-31-350 Navajo Chieftain	31-8152004		0081	1187	2 LY TIO-540-J2BD	3175	Freighter		
☐ N4078B	Piper PA-31-350 Navajo Chieftain	31-8152055		0081	0390	2 LY TIO-540-J2BD	3175	Freighter		
☐ N4087J	Piper PA-31-350 Navajo Chieftain	31-8152128		0081	1087	2 LY TIO-540-J2BD	3175	Freighter		
☐ N4098A	Piper PA-31-350 Navajo Chieftain	31-8152200		0081	0785	2 LY TIO-540-J2BD	3175	Freighter		
☐ N42076	Piper PA-31-350 Navajo Chieftain	31-7405209	N54362	0074	1283	2 LY TIO-540-J2BD	3175	Freighter		
☐ N42079	Piper PA-31-350 Navajo Chieftain	31-7405488	G-BCOD	0074	0781	2 LY TIO-540-J2BD	3175	Freighter		
☐ N45004	Piper PA-31-350 Navajo Chieftain	31-8052163		0080	1288	2 LY TIO-540-J2BD	3175	Freighter		
☐ N45014	Piper PA-31-350 Navajo Chieftain	31-8052171		0080	1087	2 LY TIO-540-J2BD	3175	Freighter		
☐ N4502Y	Piper PA-31-350 Navajo Chieftain	31-8052189		0080	1087	2 LY TIO-540-J2BD	3175	Freighter		
☐ N500CF	Piper PA-31-310 Navajo	31-425		0069	1075	2 LY TIO-540-A1A	2948	Freighter		
☐ N555RG	Piper PA-31-350 Navajo Chieftain	31-7305103	N555RC	0073	1283	2 LY TIO-540-J2BD	3175	Freighter		
☐ N59820	Piper PA-31-350 Navajo Chieftain	31-7652073		0076	0493	2 LY TIO-540-J2BD	3175	Freighter		
☐ N59973	Piper PA-31-350 Navajo Chieftain	31-7552079		0075	0484	2 LY TIO-540-J2BD	3175	Freighter		
☐ N600TS	Piper PA-31-350 Navajo Chieftain	31-7305047		0073	0493	2 LY TIO-540-J2BD	3175	Freighter		
☐ N62858	Piper PA-31-350 Navajo Chieftain	31-7652115		0076	0379	2 LY TIO-540-J2BD	3175	Freighter		
☐ N62959	Piper PA-31-350 Navajo Chieftain	31-7752008		0077	0493	2 LY TIO-540-J2BD	3175	Freighter		
☐ N6480L	Piper PA-31-310 Navajo	31-443		0069	1273	2 LY TIO-540-A1A	2948	Freighter		
☐ N66859	Piper PA-31-350 Navajo Chieftain	31-7405168		0074	0493	2 LY TIO-540-J2BD	3175	Freighter		
☐ N6733L	Piper PA-31-310 Navajo	31-636		0070	0978	2 LY TIO-540-A1A	2948	Freighter		
☐ N6759L	Piper PA-31-310 Navajo	31-661		0070	0777	2 LY TIO-540-A1A	2948	Freighter		
☐ N7434L	Piper PA-31-310 Navajo B	31-822		0072	0878	2 LY TIO-540-A2C	2948	Freighter		
☐ N7441L	Piper PA-31-310 Navajo B	31-844		0072	1078	2 LY TIO-540-A2C	2948	Freighter		
☐ N777MP	Piper PA-31-350 Navajo Chieftain	31-7552072	N59983	0075	0480	2 LY TIO-540-J2BD	3175	Freighter		
☐ N9132Y	Piper PA-31-310 Navajo	31-178		0068	0375	2 LY TIO-540-A1A	2948	Freighter		

275 registration type of aircraft cn/fn ex/ex* mfd del powered by mtow kg configuration selcal name/fln/specialitites/remarks

☐	N961CA	Piper PA-31-350 Navajo Chieftain	31-7652014	N961PS	0076	0484	2 LY TIO-540-J2BD	3175	Freighter		
☐	N106GP	Cessna 402B II	402B1235		0077	0097	2 CO TSIO-520-E	2858	Freighter		lsf Sports Air Travel Inc.
☐	N1399G	Cessna 402B	402B0573		0074	0097	2 CO TSIO-520-E	2858	Freighter		lsf Sport Air Travel Inc.
☐	N141MC	Cessna 402B	402B0547		0073	0097	2 CO TSIO-520-E	2858	Freighter		lsf Sports Air Travel Inc.
☐	N1532T	Cessna 402B	402B0307		0072	0097	2 CO TSIO-520-E	2858	Freighter		lsf Sports Air Travel Inc.
☐	N2713X	Cessna 402C II	402C0207		0079	0097	2 CO TSIO-520-VB	3107	Freighter		lsf Sports Air Travel Inc.
☐	N29854	Cessna 402B	402B0878		0075	0097	2 CO TSIO-520-E	2858	Freighter		lsf Sports Air Travel Inc.
☐	N305AT	Cessna 402C II	402C0030	C-GZVM	0079	0097	2 CO TSIO-520-VB	3107	Freighter		lsf Sports Air Travel Inc.
☐	N3826C	Cessna 402B	402B0814		0075	0097	2 CO TSIO-520-E	2858	Freighter		lsf Sports Air Travel Inc.
☐	N3997C	Cessna 402B	402B0864		0075	0097	2 CO TSIO-520-E	2858	Freighter		lsf Sports Air Travel Inc.
☐	N4188G	Cessna 402B II	402B1234		0077	0097	2 CO TSIO-520-E	2858	Freighter		lsf Sports Air Travel Inc.
☐	N49PB	Cessna 402B II	402B1361		0078	0097	2 CO TSIO-520-E	2858	Freighter		lsf Sports Air Travel Inc.
☐	N5550K	Cessna 402B II	402B1226		0077	0097	2 CO TSIO-520-E	2858	Freighter		lsf Sports Air Travel Inc.
☐	N6384X	Cessna 402B II	402B1347		0078	0097	2 CO TSIO-520-E	2858	Freighter		lsf Sports Air Travel Inc.
☐	N7162J	Cessna 402B II	402B1229		0077	0097	2 CO TSIO-520-E	2858	Freighter		lsf Sports Air Travel Inc.
☐	N7162K	Cessna 402B II	402B1208		0077	0097	2 CO TSIO-520-E	2858	Freighter		lsf Sports Air Travel Inc.
☐	N8FB	Cessna 402B II	402B1372		0078	0097	2 CO TSIO-520-E	2858	Freighter		lsf Sports Air Travel Inc.
☐	N98635	Cessna 402B II	402B1024		0075	0097	2 CO TSIO-520-E	2858	Freighter		lsf Sports Air Travel Inc.
☐	N98702	Cessna 402B II	402B1054		0076	0097	2 CO TSIO-520-E	2858	Freighter		lsf Sports Air Travel Inc.
☐	N98764	Cessna 402B II	402B1069		0076	0097	2 CO TSIO-520-E	2858	Freighter		lsf Sports Air Travel Inc.
☐	N1049C	Beech B99 Airliner	U-9		0068	0485	2 PWC PT6A-27/28	4944	Freighter		cvtd 99
☐	N104BE	Beech C99 Airliner	U-221	N7203L	0084	0992	2 PWC PT6A-36	5126	Freighter		lsf Fleet Capital Corp.
☐	N106SX	Beech C99 Airliner	U-166		0081	1093	2 PWC PT6A-36	5126	Freighter		
☐	N107SX	Beech C99 Airliner	U-176		0081	0289	2 PWC PT6A-36	5126	Freighter		
☐	N108SX	Beech C99 Airliner	U-184		0082	0289	2 PWC PT6A-36	5126	Freighter		
☐	N130GP	Beech C99 Airliner	U-222	N818FL	0084	0497	2 PWC PT6A-36	5126	Freighter		lsf Fleet Capital Corp.
☐	N134PM	Beech B99 Airliner	U-34	N852SA	0068	0387	2 PWC PT6A-27/28	4944	Freighter		cvtd 99
☐	N164HA	Beech B99 Airliner	U-60	N72TC	0068	0488	2 PWC PT6A-27/28	4944	Freighter		
☐	N1924T	Beech B99 Airliner	U-115	N24AT	0069	0384	2 PWC PT6A-27/28	4944	Freighter		cvtd A99
☐	N193SU	Beech C99 Airliner	U-193	C-GFAT	0082	0998	2 PWC PT6A-36	5126	Freighter		lsf Raytheon Aircraft Credit Corp.
☐	N199AF	Beech B99 Airliner	U-161	N12AK	0074	0288	2 PWC PT6A-27/28	4944	Freighter		
☐	N20FW	Beech B99 Airliner	U-111		0069	0486	2 PWC PT6A-27/28	4944	Freighter		lsf Nationwide Leasing Corp./cvtd A99
☐	N21FW	Beech B99 Airliner	U-117		0069	0286	2 PWC PT6A-27/28	4944	Freighter		cvtd A99
☐	N221BH	Beech C99 Airliner	U-168	N18AK	0081	1194	2 PWC PT6A-36	5126	Freighter		
☐	N223BH	Beech C99 Airliner	U-173	N6460D	0081	0192	2 PWC PT6A-36	5126	Freighter		
☐	N225BH	Beech C99 Airliner	U-181	N62936	0081	0192	2 PWC PT6A-36	5126	Freighter		
☐	N226BH	Beech C99 Airliner	U-182	N6263D	0081	0192	2 PWC PT6A-36	5126	Freighter		
☐	N261SW	Beech C99 Airliner	U-202		0083	0190	2 PWC PT6A-36	5126	Freighter		
☐	N34AK	Beech B99 Airliner	U-105	N4099A	0069	0288	2 PWC PT6A-27/28	4944	Freighter		cvtd A99
☐	N4199C	Beech C99 Airliner	U-50	N7940	0069	0485	2 PWC PT6A-36	5126	Freighter		cvtd B99/Prototype C99
☐	N4299A	Beech B99 Airliner	U-146		0071	1287	2 PWC PT6A-27/28	4944	Freighter		Prototype B99
☐	N51RP	Beech C99 Airliner	U-212		0083	0189	2 PWC PT6A-36	5126	Freighter		
☐	N52RP	Beech C99 Airliner	U-210		0083	0289	2 PWC PT6A-36	5126	Freighter		
☐	N53RP	Beech C99 Airliner	U-195	N64997	0082	0489	2 PWC PT6A-36	5126	Freighter		
☐	N54RP	Beech C99 Airliner	U-218		0083	0289	2 PWC PT6A-36	5126	Freighter		
☐	N55RP	Beech C99 Airliner	U-198	N64002	0082	0289	2 PWC PT6A-36	5126	Freighter		
☐	N6199D	Beech C99 Airliner	U-169		0081	0791	2 PWC PT6A-36	5126	Freighter		lsf Nationwide Leasing Corp.
☐	N62989	Beech C99 Airliner	U-183		0082	0192	2 PWC PT6A-36	5126	Freighter		lsf Nationwide Leasing Corp.
☐	N63978	Beech C99 Airliner	U-171		0081	0791	2 PWC PT6A-36	5126	Freighter		lsf Nationwide Leasing Corp.
☐	N6724D	Beech C99 Airliner	U-215		0084	1094	2 PWC PT6A-36	5126	Freighter		
☐	N7200Z	Beech C99 Airliner	U-219		0084	0395	2 PWC PT6A-36	5126	Freighter		
☐	N7209W	Beech C99 Airliner	U-224		0084	0497	2 PWC PT6A-36	5126	Freighter		lsf Fleet Capital Corp.
☐	N7862R	Beech B99 Airliner	U-85		0069	1283	2 PWC PT6A-27/28	4944	Freighter		cvtd A99
☐	N802BA	Beech B99 Airliner	U-29	N800BE	0068	1094	2 PWC PT6A-27/28	4944	Freighter		lsf Raytheon Aircraft Credit / cvtd 99
☐	N805BA	Beech B99 Airliner	U-147	N803BE	0071	1194	2 PWC PT6A-27/28	4944	Freighter		lsf Raytheon Aircraft Credit / cvtd A99
☐	N8226Z	Beech C99 Airliner	U-190	6Y-JVB	0082	0898	2 PWC PT6A-36	5126	Freighter		lsf Raytheon Aircraft Credit Corp.
☐	N8227P	Beech C99 Airliner	U-194	6Y-JVA	0082	0898	2 PWC PT6A-36	5126	Freighter		lsf Raytheon Aircraft Credit Corp.
☐	N949K	Beech B99 Airliner	U-36		0068	1184	2 PWC PT6A-27/28	4944	Freighter		cvtd Prototype A99
☐	N96AV	Beech C99 Airliner	U-201		0083	0092	2 PWC PT6A-36	5126	Freighter		lsf Fleet Capital Corp.
☐	N990AF	Beech C99 Airliner	U-211	N113GP	0083	1195	2 PWC PT6A-36	5126	Freighter		lsf Fleet Capital Corp.
☐	N991AF	Beech C99 Airliner	U-214	N112GP	0083	1195	2 PWC PT6A-36	5126	Freighter		lsf Fleet Capital Corp.
☐	N992AF	Beech C99 Airliner	U-203	N541JC	0083	1095	2 PWC PT6A-36	5126	Freighter		lsf Fleet Capital Corp.
☐	N997SB	Beech C99 Airliner	U-192	N6534A	0082	0190	2 PWC PT6A-36	5126	Freighter		
☐	N439AF	Fairchild (Swearingen) SA227AT Merlin IVC	AT-439B	N555GB	0081	0298	2 GA TPE331-11U-611G	7257	Freighter		
☐	N573G	Fairchild (Swearingen) SA227AT Merlin IVC	AT-446B	N3008L	0081	0997	2 GA TPE331-11U-611G	7257	Freighter		lsf Banc Boston Leasing Corp.
☐	N807M	Fairchild (Swearingen) SA227AT Merlin IVC	AT-454B	N3013T	0081	1297	2 GA TPE331-11U-611G	7257	Freighter		lsf Banc One Leasing Corp.
☐	N200AF	Beech King Air 200	BB-102	N997MA	0076	0194	2 PWC PT6A-41	5670	9 Pax		lsf Quebec Enterprises Inc.
☐	N155AF	Fairchild (Swearingen) SA227AC Metro III	AC-455	N356AE	0081	0394	2 GA TPE331-11U-611G	6577	Freighter		lsf Textron Financial Corp.
☐	N191AF	Fairchild (Swearingen) SA227AC Metro III	AC-491	N209CA	0081	0994	2 GA TPE331-11U-611G	6577	Freighter		
☐	N240DH	Fairchild (Swearingen) SA227AT Expediter	AT-602B	N3117P*	0085	0992	2 GA TPE331-11U-611G	7257	Freighter		lsf Banc One Leasing Corp.
☐	N241DH	Fairchild (Swearingen) SA227AT Expediter	AT-607B	N3118A*	0085	0992	2 GA TPE331-11U-611G	7257	Freighter		lsf Banc One Leasing Corp.
☐	N242DH	Fairchild (Swearingen) SA227AT Expediter	AT-608B	N3118G*	0085	0992	2 GA TPE331-11U-611G	7257	Freighter		lsf Banc One Leasing Corp.
☐	N243DH	Fairchild (Swearingen) SA227AT Expediter	AT-609B	N3118H*	0085	0992	2 GA TPE331-11U-611G	7257	Freighter		lsf Banc One Leasing Corp.
☐	N244DH	Fairchild (Swearingen) SA227AT Expediter	AT-618B		0085	0393	2 GA TPE331-11U-611G	7257	Freighter		lsf MCC Financial Corp.
☐	N245DH	Fairchild (Swearingen) SA227AT Expediter	AT-624B		0085	0393	2 GA TPE331-11U-611G	7257	Freighter		lsf MCC Financial Corp.
☐	N246DH	Fairchild (Swearingen) SA227AT Expediter	AT-625B		0085	0693	2 GA TPE331-11U-611G	7257	Freighter		lsf MCC Financial Corp.
☐	N247DH	Fairchild (Swearingen) SA227AT Expediter	AT-626B		0085	0693	2 GA TPE331-11U-611G	7257	Freighter		lsf MCC Financial Corp.
☐	N248DH	Fairchild (Swearingen) SA227AT Expediter	AT-630B		0085	0693	2 GA TPE331-11U-611G	7257	Freighter		lsf MCC Financial Corp.
☐	N249DH	Fairchild (Swearingen) SA227AT Expediter	AT-631B		0085	0693	2 GA TPE331-11U-611G	7257	Freighter		lsf MCC Financial Corp.
☐	N377PH	Fairchild (Swearingen) SA227AC Metro III	AC-574		0083	0295	2 GA TPE331-11U-611G	6577	Freighter		
☐	N421MA	Fairchild (Swearingen) SA227AC Metro III	AC-634	N3119Q*	0086	0797	2 GA TPE331-11U-611G	6577	Freighter		lsf BancBoston Leasing Inc.
☐	N422MA	Fairchild (Swearingen) SA227AC Metro III	AC-635	N3119T*	0086	0797	2 GA TPE331-11U-611G	6577	Freighter		lsf BancBoston Leasing Inc.
☐	N423MA	Fairchild (Swearingen) SA227AC Metro III	AC-636	N26823*	0086	0797	2 GA TPE331-11U-611G	6577	Freighter		lsf BancBoston Leasing Inc.
☐	N424MA	Fairchild (Swearingen) SA227AC Metro III	AC-639		0086	0298	2 GA TPE331-11U-611G	6577	Freighter		
☐	N426MA	Fairchild (Swearingen) SA227AC Metro III	AC-645		0086	0298	2 GA TPE331-11U-611G	6577	Freighter		
☐	N428MA	Fairchild (Swearingen) SA227AC Metro III	AC-646		0086	0298	2 GA TPE331-11U-611G	6577	Freighter		
☐	N443AF	Fairchild (Swearingen) SA227AC Metro III	AC-443	N443NE	0081	0693	2 GA TPE331-11U-611G	6577	Freighter		lsf Nationwide Leasing Corp.
☐	N473AF	Fairchild (Swearingen) SA227AC Metro III	AC-473	N473NE	0081	0393	2 GA TPE331-11U-611G	6577	Freighter		lsf Nationwide Leasing Corp.
☐	N475AF	Fairchild (Swearingen) SA227AC Metro III	AC-475	N475NE	0081	0793	2 GA TPE331-11U-611G	6577	Freighter		lsf Nationwide Leasing Corp.
☐	N476AF	Fairchild (Swearingen) SA227AC Metro III	AC-476	N476NE	0081	0493	2 GA TPE331-11U-611G	6577	Freighter		lsf Nationwide Leasing Corp.
☐	N488AF	Fairchild (Swearingen) SA227AC Metro III	AC-488	N488NE	0081	0393	2 GA TPE331-11U-611G	6577	Freighter		lsf Nationwide Leasing Corp.
☐	N544UP	Fairchild (Swearingen) SA227AT Expediter	AT-544	N68TA	0083	1296	2 GA TPE331-11U-611G	6577	Freighter		lsf BancBoston Leasing Inc.
☐	N548UP	Fairchild (Swearingen) SA227AT Expediter	AT-548	N548SA	0083	1296	2 GA TPE331-11U-611G	6577	Freighter		lsf BancBoston Leasing Inc.
☐	N556UP	Fairchild (Swearingen) SA227AT Expediter	AT-556	N3113B*	0083	0497	2 GA TPE331-11U-601G	6577	Freighter		
☐	N560UP	Fairchild (Swearingen) SA227AT Expediter	AT-560	N3113A*	0083	0497	2 GA TPE331-11U-611G	6577	Freighter		
☐	N561UP	Fairchild (Swearingen) SA227AT Expediter	AT-561	N3113F*	0083	0497	2 GA TPE331-11U-601G	6577	Freighter		
☐	N566UP	Fairchild (Swearingen) SA227AT Expediter	AT-566	N3113N*	0083	0497	2 GA TPE331-11U-601G	6577	Freighter		
☐	N569UP	Fairchild (Swearingen) SA227AT Expediter	AT-569	N31134*	0083	0497	2 GA TPE331-11U-601G	6577	Freighter		
☐	N578AF	Fairchild (Swearingen) SA227AC Metro III	AC-578	C-FJLE	0083	0794	2 GA TPE331-11U-611G	6577	Freighter		
☐	N3052K	Beech 1900C Airliner	UB-70		0087	0595	2 PWC PT6A-65B	7530	Freighter		
☐	N3071A	Beech 1900C Airliner	UB-46		0085	0695	2 PWC PT6A-65B	7530	Freighter		lsf Banc One Leasing Corp.
☐	N31701	Beech 1900C Airliner	UB-2	N121CZ	0083	0595	2 PWC PT6A-65B	7530	Freighter		lsf Banc One Leasing Corp.
☐	N31702	Beech 1900C Airliner	UB-3	N122CZ	0083	0595	2 PWC PT6A-65B	7530	Freighter		lsf NationsBanc Leasing Corp.
☐	N31703	Beech 1900C Airliner	UB-10	N123CZ	0084	0295	2 PWC PT6A-65B	7530	Freighter		
☐	N31704	Beech 1900C Airliner	UB-12	N124CZ	0084	0595	2 PWC PT6A-65B	7530	Freighter		lsf NationsBanc Leasing Corp.
☐	N31705	Beech 1900C Airliner	UB-60		0086	0395	2 PWC PT6A-65B	7530	Freighter		
☐	N3229A	Beech 1900C Airliner	UB-51		0086	0195	2 PWC PT6A-65B	7530	Freighter		
☐	N330AF	Beech 1900C Airliner	UB-38	N805BE	0085	0196	2 PWC PT6A-65B	7530	Freighter		
☐	N331AF	Beech 1900C Airliner	UB-44	N807BE	0085	1295	2 PWC PT6A-65B	7530	Freighter		
☐	N7203C	Beech 1900C Airliner	UB-28		0084	0297	2 PWC PT6A-65B	7530	Freighter		lsf Banc One Leasing Corp.
☐	N128CA	Learjet 35A	35A-248	C-GBFA	0079	1086	2 GA TFE731-2-2B	8165	Freighter		
☐	N237AF	Learjet 35A	35A-262	N237GA	0079	1287	2 GA TFE731-2-2B	8165	Freighter		
☐	N535AF	Learjet 35A	35A-191	N35SE	0078	0996	2 GA TFE731-2-2B	8165	Freighter		
☐	N754GL	Learjet 35A	35A-197		0078	0781	2 GA TFE731-2-2B	8165	Freighter		
☐	N94AF	Learjet 35A	35A-094	N94GP	0077	1195	2 GA TFE731-2-2B	8165	Freighter		

AMERIJET INTERNATIONAL, Inc. = M6 / AJT **Fort Lauderdale-Hollywood Int'l & Miami-Int'l, FL**

498 SW 34th Street, Fort Lauderdale, FL 33315, USA ☎ (954) 359-0077 Tx: 529213 amerijet intl Fax: (954) 359-7899 SITA: FLLHQJH
F: 1974 390 Head: David G. Bassett IATA: 810 ICAO: AMERIJET Net: http://www.amerijet.com

☐	N196AJ	Boeing 727-227 (F) (A)	20838 / 1017	N556PE	0074	0795	3 PW JT8D-9A (HK3/FDX)	79605	Freighter	AH-GK	cvtd -227
☐	N296AJ	Boeing 727-251 (F) (A)	21156 / 1170	N277US	1075	0196	3 PW JT8D-15 (HK3/FDX)	80286	Freighter	DK-CG	cvtd -251

276 registration type of aircraft cn/fn ex/ex* mfd del powered by mtow kg configuration selcal name/fln/specialitites/remarks

registration	type of aircraft	cn/fn	ex/ex*	mfd	del	powered by	mtow kg	configuration	selcal	name/fin/specialitites/remarks
☐ N395AJ	Boeing 727-233 (F) (A)	21100 / 1148	N727SN	0075	1294	3 PW JT8D-15	89358	Freighter	HK-DL	
☐ N397AJ	Boeing 727-2X3 (F) (A)	22608 / 1727	OO-LLS	0081	1296	3 PW JT8D-15 (HK3/FDX)	88451	Freighter	AK-FH	Isf IPID / cvtd -2X3
☐ N495AJ	Boeing 727-233 (F) (A)	20937 / 1103	C-GAAD	0075	1294	3 PW JT8D-15 (HK3/FDX)	89358	Freighter	HK-CL	
☐ N598AJ	Boeing 727-212 (F) (A) (QWS / winglets)	21947 / 1506	N86430	0079	0598	3 PW JT8D-17 (HK3/DUG)	89358	Freighter		cvtd -212
☐ N794AJ	Boeing 727-227 (F) (A) (QWS / winglets)	21243 / 1197	N567PE	0076	0794	3 PW JT8D-15 (HK3/DUG)	79651	Freighter	EK-AG	cvtd -227
☐ N797AJ	Boeing 727-2X3 (F) (A)	22609 / 1731	OO-CAH	0081	0497	3 PW JT8D-15 (HK3/FDX)	88451	Freighter		Isf IPID / cvtd -2X3
☐ N895AJ	Boeing 727-224 (F) (A)	20660 / 985	N66731	0073	1295	3 PW JT8D-9A (HK3/FDX)	78245	Freighter	FG-KM	cvtd -224
☐ N994AJ	Boeing 727-233 (F) (A)	20942 / 1130	N727JH	0475	1194	3 PW JT8D-15	89358	Freighter	HK-DJ	cvtd -233

AMERISTAR JET CHARTER, Inc. = AJI (Associated with Chaparral, Inc.)   Dallas-Addison, TX

AMERISTAR JET CHARTER

PO Box 700548, Dallas, TX 75370-0548, USA   ☎ (972) 248-2478   Tx: none   Fax: (972) 931-6011   SITA: n/a
F: 1982   ✦✦✦ 155   Head: Tom Wachendorfer, Jr.   ICAO: AMERISTAR   Net: http://www.ameristarjet.com

☐ N206TW	Bell 206B JetRanger III	2403	N123KH	0078	1298	1 AN 250-C20B	1451	Utility		Isf Sierra American Corp.
☐ N176TW	Beech King Air E90	LW-76	ZS-LJF	0074	0297	2 PWC PT6A-28	4581	Freighter		Isf Sierra American Corp.
☐ N237TW	Learjet 24D	24D-237	N825DM	0071	1195	2 GE CJ610-6	6123	Freighter		Isf Sierra American Corp.
☐ N266TW	Learjet 24D	24D-266	N266BS	0073	0397	2 GE CJ610-6	6123	Freighter		Isf Sierra American Corp.
☐ N277TW	Learjet 24D	24D-277	N57BC	0073	0196	2 GE CJ610-6	6123	Freighter		Isf Sierra American Corp.
☐ N299TW	Learjet 24D	24D-299	XB-GJS	0074	1296	2 GE CJ610-6	6123	Freighter		Isf Chaparral Leasing Inc.
☐ N324TW	Learjet 24D	24D-324	XA-SCY	0076	0595	2 GE CJ610-6	6123	Freighter		Isf Chaparral Leasing Inc.
☐ N330TW	Learjet 24F	24E-330	N511AT	0076	1297	2 GE CJ610-6	6123	Freighter		Isf Sierra American Corp. / cvtd 24E
☐ N444TW	Learjet 24F	24F-348	N8BG	0077	0394	2 GE CJ610-6	6123	Freighter		Isf Sierra American Corp.
☐ N888TW	Learjet 24D	24D-292	N800PC	0074	0493	2 GE CJ610-6	6123	Freighter		Isf Sierra American Corp.
☐ N157TW	Learjet 24	24-157	N659AT	0068	1298	2 GE CJ610-4	5897	Freighter		Isf Sierra American Corp.
☐ N222TW	Learjet 24	24-161	N24KF	0068	0890	2 GE CJ610-4	5897	Freighter		Isf Sierra American Corp.
☐ N233TW	Learjet 24B	24B-221	N59JG	0070	1296	2 GE CJ610-6	6123	Freighter		Isf Sierra American Corp.
☐ N333TW	Learjet 24	24-168	N155BT	0068	1291	2 GE CJ610-4	5897	Freighter		Isf Sierra American Corp.
☐ N147TW	Learjet 25	25-023	N767SC	0069	1197	2 GE CJ610-6	6804	Freighter		Isf Sierra American Corp.
☐ N153TW	Learjet 25	25-053	N37GB	0070	1197	2 GE CJ610-6	6804	Freighter		Isf Sierra American Corp.
☐ N265TW	Learjet 25D	25D-265	N69GF	0079	1097	2 GE CJ610-8A	6804	Freighter		Isf Chaparral Leasing Inc.
☐ N525TW	Learjet 25	25-011	N108GA	0068	0796	2 GE CJ610-6	6804	Freighter		Isf Sierra American Corp.
☐ N666TW	Learjet 25B	25B-116	N819GY	0073	0396	2 GE CJ610-6	6804	Freighter		Isf Sierra American Corp.
☐ N165TW	Dassault Falcon 20C (C)	65	C-GSKN	0066	0198	2 GE CF700-2D2	13000	Freighter		Isf Sierra American Corp. / cvtd 20C
☐ N204TW	Dassault Falcon 20D (C)	204	EC-EGM	0070	0896	2 GE CF700-2D2	13000	Freighter		Isf Sierra American Corp. / cvtd 20D
☐ N221TW	Dassault Falcon 20D (C)	221	EC-EIV	0070	0796	2 GE CF700-2D2	13000	Freighter		Isf Sierra American Corp. / cvtd 20D
☐ N232TW	Dassault Falcon 20C (C)	32	F-GIVT	0066	0298	2 GE CF700-2D2	13000	Freighter		Isf Sierra American Corp. / cvtd 20C
☐ N240TW	Dassault Falcon 20C (C)	40	C-GSKQ	0066	0198	2 GE CF700-2D2	13000	Freighter		Isf Sierra American Corp. / cvtd 20C
☐ N285TW	Dassault Falcon 20E (C)	285	N285AP	0073	0794	2 GE CF700-2D2	13000	Freighter		Isf Sierra American Corp. / cvtd 20E
☐ N295TW	Dassault Falcon 20C (C)	5	F-GJPR	0065	1298	2 GE CF700-2D2	13000	Freighter		Isf Sierra American Corp. / cvtd 20C
☐ N314TW	Dassault Falcon 20E (C)	314	F-GDLU	0074	1298	2 GE CF700-2D2	13000	Freighter		Isf Sierra American Corp. / cvtd 20E
☐ N699TW	Dassault Falcon 20D (C)	50	EC-EDO	0066	0796	2 GE CF700-2D2	13000	Freighter		Isf Sierra American Corp. / cvtd 20D
☐ N977TW	Dassault Falcon 20C (C)	13	F-BTCY	0065	1097	2 GE CF700-2D2	13000	Freighter		Isf Sierra American Corp. / cvtd 20C

AMP Air = MMP (Flight division of AMP, Inc.)   Harrisburg-Int'l, PA

PO Box 3608, M-S 207-01, Harrisburg, PA 17105-3608, USA   ☎ (717) 986-7188   Tx: none   Fax: (717) 985-2927   SITA: n/a
F: 1980   ✦✦✦ n/a   Head: William E. Burgerhoff   ICAO: AMP-INC   Net: n/a   Private, non-commercial company conducting corporate flights for itself only.

☐ N77CV	Beech King Air B200	BB-1625		0098	0898	2 PWC PT6A-42	5670	Corporate		
☐ N77W	Hawker 800A (BAe 125-800A)	258150 / NA0434	N588BA	0089	0489	2 GA TFE731-5R-1H	12428	Corporate		
☐ N77M	Saab SF340A	340A-036	N260PM	0085	0591	2 GE CT7-5A2	12372	Corporate		
☐ N77A	Dassault Falcon 2000	17	N2035	0095	1195	2 CFE CFE738-1-1B	16556	Corporate		

AMWAY Corporation   Grand Rapids-Kent County Int'l, MI

Flight Dept, 5410 44th Street S.E., Grand Rapids, MI 49512, USA   ☎ (616) 949-0790   Tx: none   Fax: (616) 949-0876   SITA: n/a
F: 1982   ✦✦✦ n/a   Head: Paul E. Landers   Net: http://www.amway.com   Conducting commerical flight operations under contract for various executive customers.

☐ N520AC	Sikorsky S-76B	760380		0091	1092	2 PWC PT6B-36A	5307	Executive		
☐ N521AC	Sikorsky S-76A	760261	N84SM	0084	1086	2 AN 250-C30S	4672	Executive		
☐ N526AC	Hawker 800A (BAe 125-800A)	258169 / NA0443	N47CG	0089	1194	2 GA TFE731-5R-1H	12428	Executive		
☐ N527AC	Hawker 800A (BAe 125-800A)	258104 / NA0405	N542BA	0087	0488	2 GA TFE731-5R-1H	12428	Executive	FP-AC	
☐ N528AC	Hawker 800A (BAe 125-800A)	258070	N520BA	0086	1186	2 GA TFE731-5R-1H	12428	Executive	BH-AP	
☐ N254DV	Dassault Falcon 50	85	N40TH	0081	0695	3 GA TFE731-3-1C	17600	Executive		Isf RDV Properties Inc.
☐ N522AC	Dassault Falcon 900B	148	N148FJ	0094	0695	3 GA TFE731-5BR-1C	21099	Executive	JS-KQ	
☐ N523AC	Dassault Falcon 900B	139	N140FJ	0094	1194	3 GA TFE731-5BR-1C	21099	Executive	HP-DE	
☐ N529AC	Boeing 727-17 (RE) (Super 27/winglets)	20328 / 806	G-BKCG	0070	1182	3 PW JT8D-217C/7B (BFG)	76884	Executive 29Pax	GJ-AK	cvtd -17

AMY AIR (Gold Coast Airways Corporation dba)   San Juan-Luis Munoz Marin Int'l, PR

Laguna Gardens III, Apt. 7B, Carolina, PR 00979, USA   ☎ (787) 791-0686   Tx: none   Fax: none   SITA: n/a
F: 1995   ✦✦✦ n/a   Head: Ulpiano L. Amy   Net: n/a

☐ N8498C	Twin (Aero) Commander 500	500-848		0059	0195	2 LY O-540-A2B	2722			

ANDERSON AVIATION, Inc. = ADX   Anderson-Municipal, IN

282 Airport Road, Anderson, IN 46017, USA   ☎ (765) 644-1238   Tx: none   Fax: (765) 378-3443   SITA: n/a
F: 1938   ✦✦✦ n/a   Head: Steve W. Darlington   ICAO: ANDAX   Net: n/a   Aircraft below MTOW 1361 kg: Cessna 172

☐ N333BS	Cessna 310R II	310R0865		0077	1294	2 CO IO-520-M	2495			
☐ N12852	Cessna 208B Grand Caravan	208B0469		0095	0696	1 PWC PT6A-114A	3969			
☐ N208SD	Cessna 208B Grand Caravan	208B0491		0095	0196	1 PWC PT6A-114A	3969			Isf Cessna Finance Corp.
☐ N64MD	Mitsubishi MU-2B-60 Marquise	1561SA	N486MA	0082	1194	2 GA TPE331-10-501M	5250			

ANDERSON AVIATION, Inc.   Anderson-County, SC

PO Box 380, Anderson, SC 29622, USA   ☎ (864) 225-3171   Tx: none   Fax: (864) 225-3172   SITA: n/a
F: 1975   ✦✦✦ n/a   Head: Reid J. Garrison   Net: n/a

☐ N32TF	Cessna 402B	402B0932		0075	0191	2 CO TSIO-520-E	2858			

ANDREW AIRWAYS, Inc.   Kodiak, AK

PO Box 1037, Kodiak, AK 99617, USA   ☎ (907) 487-2566   Tx: none   Fax: (907) 487-2578   SITA: n/a
F: 1995   ✦✦✦ n/a   Head: Dean T. Andrew   Net: n/a

☐ N5303X	Cessna U206G Stationair 6 II	U20605622		0080	0395	1 CO IO-520-F	1633			Wheel-Skis
☐ N67686	De Havilland DHC-2 Beaver I	1230	N1018T	0058	0097	1 PW R-985	2309			Ist Northwest Seaplanes / Wheel-Skis

ANGEL FIRE HELICOPTERS, Inc.   Taos-Municipal, NM

PO Box 456, Angel Fire, NM 87710, USA   ☎ (505) 377-6898   Tx: none   Fax: (505) 377-6898   SITA: n/a
F: 1994   ✦✦✦ n/a   Head: Carl D. Shelton   Net: n/a

☐ N302PD	Bell 206B JetRanger III	3801		0084	0697	1 AN 250-C20J	1451			

ANIAK AIR GUIDES (Richard A. Townsend dba)   Aniak, AK

Box 93, Aniak, AK 99557, USA   ☎ (907) 675-4540   Tx: none   Fax: (907) 675-4540   SITA: n/a
F: 1995   ✦✦✦ n/a   Head: Richard A. Townsend   Net: n/a

☐ N5343G	De Havilland DHC-2 Beaver I	862	54-1716	0055	1296	1 PW R-985	2313			Floats / Wheel-Skis

ANTELOPE AIR, Inc.   Red Wing-Municipal, MN

N5695 1245th Street, Prescott, WI 54021, USA   ☎ (715) 262-3919   Tx: none   Fax: (715) 262-3963   SITA: n/a
F: 1997   ✦✦✦ n/a   Head: Gordon L. Stangl   Net: n/a

☐ N3641W	Piper PA-32-260 Cherokee SIX	32-544		0066	0197	1 LY O-540-E4B5	1542			

APOLLO AVIATION, Co. Inc.   Gulfport-Biloxi Regional, MS

4455 Hewes, Gulfport, MS 39506, USA   ☎ (228) 863-8563   Tx: none   Fax: (228) 863-8515   SITA: n/a
F: 1984   ✦✦✦ n/a   Head: Christopher V. Loepke   Net: n/a   Aircraft below MTOW 1361kg: Cessna 172

☐ N943V	Beech Baron 58	TH-659		0075	1288	2 CO IO-520-C	2449			
☐ N955RA	Beech King Air F90	LA-201	N653LP	0082	0993	2 PWC PT6A-135	4967			Isf Apollo Leasing Co. Inc.

AQUILA AIR, Inc. = CNH   Endicott-Tri Cities, NY

Tri-Cities Airport, Endicott, NY 13760, USA   ☎ (402) 894-2917   Tx: none   Fax: none   SITA: n/a
F: 1980   ✦✦✦ n/a   Head: George H. Richmond, Jr.   ICAO: CHENANGO   Net: n/a

☐ N415HP	Piper PA-30-160 Twin Comanche	30-181		0063	1293	2 LY IO-320-B1A	1633			
☐ N74CE	Piper PA-31-350 Navajo Chieftain	31-7305041		0073	1193	2 LY TIO-540-J2BD	3175			

ARAWAK AVIATION, Inc.   Fort Lauderdale-Executive, FL

➤ ARAWAK AVIATION ✦

5330 N.W. 21st Ave, Hangar 59, Fort Lauderdale, FL 33309, USA   ☎ (954) 491-5800   Tx: none   Fax: (954) 491-6002   SITA: n/a
F: 1987   ✦✦✦ n/a   Head: C. Scott Albury   Net: n/a

☐ N500AD	Cessna 500 Citation	500-0091	C-FCHJ	0073	1298	2 PWC JT15D-1	5216			Isf Diversified Professional Enterpr.
☐ N990AL	Cessna 500 Citation	500-0033	N20RF	0072	0292	2 PWC JT15D-1	5216			Isf Opercorp.

registration	type of aircraft	cn/fn	ex/ex*	mfd	del	powered by	mtow kg	configuration	selcal	name/fln/specialitites/remarks
☐ N50AZ	Cessna 550 Citation II	550-0261	N261SS	0081	0197	2 PWC JT15D-4	6033			lsf HPZ Investments Inc.
☐ N773AA	Hawker F400A (HS 125-F400A)	25175 / NA713	N272B	0068	0295	2 GA TFE731-3R-1H	10568			lsf Zebra Investment / cvtd -400A

ARCHER AVIATION, Inc.
Prescott-Helipad, WA

PO Box 86, Prescott, WA 99348, USA ☎ (509) 849-2650 Tx: none Fax: none SITA: n/a
F: 1988 ♦♦♦ n/a Head: Janet K. Archer Net: n/a

registration	type of aircraft	cn/fn	ex/ex*	mfd	del	powered by	mtow kg	configuration	selcal	name/fln/specialitites/remarks
☐ N2060N	Bell 206B JetRanger III	3327		0081	0191	1 AN 250-C20B	1451			lsf pvt

ARCO Flight Operations = NRS (Aviation Dept. of ARCO-Atlantic Richfield Company)
Anchorage-Int'l, AK

6601 South Airpark Place, Anchorage, AK 99502, USA ☎ (907) 263-3586 Tx: none Fax: (907) 263-3576 SITA: n/a
F: 1979 ♦♦♦ n/a Head: Daniel B. Ahern ICAO: NORTH SLOPE Net: n/a Operates non-commercial corporate flights for its parent company only.

registration	type of aircraft	cn/fn	ex/ex*	mfd	del	powered by	mtow kg	configuration	selcal	name/fln/specialitites/remarks
☐ N842AR	De Havilland DHC-6 Twin Otter 300	842	C-FDHA	0088	0689	2 PWC PT6A-27	5670	Corporate		
☐ N733AR	Boeing 737-205 (A)	23466 / 1236	LN-SUZ	0586	0993	2 PW JT8D-17A (HK3/NOR)	56472	Corporate		lsf Sanwa Business Credit Corp.

ARCTIC AIR ALASKA, Inc.
Fairbanks-Int'l, AK

6655 Johnson Road, Salcha, AK 99714, USA ☎ (907) 488-6115 Tx: none Fax: (907) 488-5668 SITA: n/a
F: 1994 ♦♦♦ n/a Head: James I. Hamilton Net: n/a Aircraft below MTOW 1361kg: Piper PA-18 (on Floats/Wheel-Skis)

registration	type of aircraft	cn/fn	ex/ex*	mfd	del	powered by	mtow kg	configuration	selcal	name/fln/specialitites/remarks
☐ N1074F	Cessna A185F Skywagon	18502730		0075	0794	1 CO IO-520-D	1520			Floats / Wheel-Skis

ARCTIC AIR GUIDES (Lawrence E. Maxson dba / Seasonal May-October ops only)
Kotzebue-Ralph Wien Memorial, AK

PO Box 94, Kotzebue, AK 99752, USA ☎ (907) 442-3030 Tx: none Fax: none SITA: n/a
F: 1983 ♦♦♦ n/a Head: Lawrence E. Maxson Net: n/a Aircraft below MTOW 1361kg: Maule M6-235 & M7-235

registration	type of aircraft	cn/fn	ex/ex*	mfd	del	powered by	mtow kg	configuration	selcal	name/fln/specialitites/remarks
☐ N2233T	Cessna A185E Skywagon	185-1386		0068	0383	1 CO IO-520-D	1520			Floats
☐ N7691D	Cessna U206C Super Skywagon	U206-1015		0068	0197	1 CO IO-520-F	1633			

ARCTIC AIR SERVICE, Inc.
Lompoc, CA

1801-A North H Street, Lompoc, CA 93436-2827, USA ☎ (805) 735-3717 Tx: none Fax: (805) 735-3790 SITA: n/a
F: 1966 ♦♦♦ 13 Head: Walter N. Attebery Net: n/a

registration	type of aircraft	cn/fn	ex/ex*	mfd	del	powered by	mtow kg	configuration	selcal	name/fln/specialitites/remarks
☐ N349AA	Eurocopter (Aerosp.) AS355F1 TwinStar	5189	N5800E	0082	1092	2 AN 250-C20F	2400			
☐ N347AA	Sikorsky S-76A	760006	C-GIMY	0079	0199	2 AN 250-C30	4763			
☐ N348AA	Sikorsky S-76A	760043	C-GIMG	0080	1085	2 AN 250-C30	4763			

ARCTIC CIRCLE AIR SERVICE, Inc. = CIR
Aniak, Bethel, Dillingham & Fairbanks-Int'l, AK

PO Box 190228, Anchorage, AK 99519, USA ☎ (907) 243-1380 Tx: none Fax: (907) 248-0042 SITA: n/a
F: 1973 ♦♦♦ 40 Head: Steve Anderson ICAO: AIR ARCTIC Net: n/a

registration	type of aircraft	cn/fn	ex/ex*	mfd	del	powered by	mtow kg	configuration	selcal	name/fln/specialitites/remarks
☐ N7721C	Piper PA-32R-300 Lance	32R-7680060		0076	0893	1 LY IO-540-K1G5D	1633			lsf Arctic Air Group Inc.
☐ N456TA	Cessna U206G Stationair 6 II	U20605034		0079	0192	1 CO IO-520-F	1633			lsf Arctic Air Group Inc.
☐ N7305U	Cessna 207A Skywagon	20700392		0077	0596	1 CO IO-520-F	1724			lsf Arctic Air Group Inc.
☐ N73467	Cessna 207A Stationair 8 II	20700594		0080	0294	1 CO IO-520-F	1724			lsf Arctic Air Group Inc.
☐ N73533	Cessna 207A Stationair 8 II	20700602		0080	0692	1 CO IO-520-F	1724			lsf Arctic Air Group Inc.
☐ N9936M	Cessna 207A Stationair 8 II	20700752		0082	0997	1 CO IO-520-F	1724			lsf Arctic Air Group Inc.
☐ N9965M	Cessna 207A Stationair 8 II	20700767		0083	0693	1 CO IO-520-F	1724			lsf Arctic Air Group Inc.
☐ N402ET	Cessna 402C II	402C0054	C-GTKJ	0079	0792	2 CO TSIO-520-VB	3107			lsf Arctic Air Group Inc.
☐ N6790B	Cessna 402C II	402C0442		0081	1092	2 CO TSIO-520-VB	3107			lsf Arctic Air Group Inc.
☐ N5187B	Cessna 208B Grand Caravan	208B0270	F-OGRO	0091	0397	1 PWC PT6A-114A	3969			lsf Arctic Air Group Inc.
☐ N101WA	Shorts Skyvan 3 Variant 200 (SC-7)	SH1859	C-GHBQ	0069	0091	2 GA TPE331-2-201A	5670	Freighter		lsf Arctic Air Group Inc.
☐ N1906	Shorts Skyvan 3A Variant 100 (SC-7)	SH1906	HS-DCC	0072	0398	2 GA TPE331-2-201A	5670	Freighter		lsf Arctic Air Group Inc.
☐ N2088Z	Shorts Skyvan 3 Variant 100 (SC-7)	SH1963	9M-PIF	0091	0394	2 GA TPE331-2-201A	5670	Freighter		

ARCTIC TRANSPORTATION SERVICES, Inc. = 7S / RCT (formerly Ryan Air Service, Inc.)
Aniak/Bethel/Emmonak/Kotzebue/Nome/St.Mary's/Unalakleet, AK

5701 Silverado Way, Unit L, Anchorage, AK 99518-1656, USA ☎ (907) 562-2227 Tx: none Fax: (907) 563-8177 SITA: n/a
F: 1957 ♦♦♦ 65 Head: John Eckels ICAO: ARCTIC TRANSPORT Net: n/a

registration	type of aircraft	cn/fn	ex/ex*	mfd	del	powered by	mtow kg	configuration	selcal	name/fln/specialitites/remarks
☐ N19TA	Cessna 207A Stationair 7 II	20700468	N6289H	0078	1190	1 CO IO-520-F	1724	Freighter		
☐ N26TA	Cessna 207A Stationair 8 II	20700725		0081	0391	1 CO IO-520-F	1724	Freighter		
☐ N73217	Cessna 207A Stationair 8 II	20700572		0080	1081	1 CO IO-520-F	1724	Freighter		
☐ N73503	Cessna 207A Stationair 8 II	20700599		0080	0984	1 CO IO-520-F	1724	Freighter		
☐ N73789	Cessna 207A Stationair 8 II	20700629		0080	0691	1 CO IO-520-F	1724	Freighter		
☐ N7605U	Cessna 207A Stationair 7 II	20700443		0078	0787	1 CO IO-520-F	1724	Freighter		
☐ N9475M	Cessna 207A Stationair 8 II	20700695		0081	0985	1 CO IO-520-F	1724	Freighter		
☐ N9736M	Cessna 207A Stationair 8 II	20700722		0081	0182	1 CO IO-520-F	1724	Freighter		
☐ N9829M	Cessna 207A Stationair 8 II	20700741		0081	0793	1 CO IO-520-F	1724	Freighter		
☐ N9956M	Cessna 207A Stationair 8 II	20700763		0083	0985	1 CO IO-520-F	1724	Freighter		
☐ N2719A	Cessna 402C II	402C0233		0079	0180	2 CO TSIO-520-VB	3107	Freighter		
☐ N151H	Beech G18S	BA-476		0059	0495	2 PW R-985-AN14B	4400	Freighter		
☐ N62TP	Beech E18S	BA-45		0055	0395	2 PW R-985-AN14B	4400	Freighter		
☐ N424CA	CASA 212 Aviocar Srs 200	242		0082	0398	2 GA TPE331-10-501C	7450	Freighter		lsf pvt
☐ N437CA	CASA 212 Aviocar Srs 200	166	TI-SAC	0080	0897	2 GA TPE331-10-501C	7450	Freighter		

ARCTIC WILDERNESS LODGE & FLYING SERVICE (Archery Outfitters, Inc. dba / Seasonal May-October ops only)
Wasilla-Anderson Lake Strip, AK

PO Box 870350, Wasilla, AK 99687, USA ☎ (907) 376-7955 Tx: none Fax: (907) 373-5252 SITA: n/a
F: 1993 ♦♦♦ n/a Head: David F. Neel Net: n/a Aircraft below MTOW 1361kg: Piper PA-18

registration	type of aircraft	cn/fn	ex/ex*	mfd	del	powered by	mtow kg	configuration	selcal	name/fln/specialitites/remarks
☐ N72412	Cessna TU206D Turbo Skywagon	U206-1396		0069	0991	1 CO TSIO-520-C	1633			

ARCTIC WINGS (Donald E. Glaser dba / Seasonal April-November ops only)
McKinley National Park & Fairbanks-Int'l, AK

PO Box 1085, Palmer, AK 99645, USA ☎ (907) 373-3475 Tx: none Fax: (907) 373-3475 SITA: n/a
F: 1990 ♦♦♦ n/a Head: Donald E. Glaser Net: n/a Aircraft below MTOW 1361kg: Piper PA-18

registration	type of aircraft	cn/fn	ex/ex*	mfd	del	powered by	mtow kg	configuration	selcal	name/fln/specialitites/remarks
☐ N3308S	Cessna A185F Skywagon	18502267		0073	0991	1 CO IO-520-D	1520			Floats / Wheels
☐ N75773	Cessna T207A Turbo Stationair 8 II	20700643		0080	0390	1 CO TSIO-520-M	1724			lst Denali Air
☐ N3307S	De Havilland DHC-2 Beaver I	1092	C-FZNA	0055	0397	1 PW R-985	2313			Floats / Wheels

ARDCO, Inc. (Aerial Retardant Delivery Company dba)
Tucson-Ryan Field, AZ

PO Box 23450, Tucson, AZ 85734, USA ☎ (520) 883-4119 Tx: none Fax: (520) 883-5878 SITA: n/a
F: 1976 ♦♦♦ 15 Head: Garrold Garrett Net: n/a

registration	type of aircraft	cn/fn	ex/ex*	mfd	del	powered by	mtow kg	configuration	selcal	name/fln/specialitites/remarks
☐ N406WA	Boeing (Douglas) DC-4 (C-54G-1-DO)	35944 / DO 338	45-491	0045	0182	4 WR R-2600	32205	Tanker		119
☐ N460WA	Boeing (Douglas) DC-4 (C-54E-15-DO)	27359 / DO 305	44-9133	0045	1181	4 PW R-2000	32205	Tanker		151
☐ N9015Q	Boeing (Douglas) DC-4 (C-54D-15-DC)	22178 / DC 630	43-17228	0045	0482	4 PW R-2000	32205	Tanker		152 / lsf pvt

ARGOSY AIRWAYS = ARY (The Argosy Group, Inc. dba)
Burbank-Glendale/Pasadena, CA

4409 Empire Avenue, Burbank, CA 91505, USA ☎ (626) 559-5500 Tx: none Fax: (626) 559-5523 SITA: n/a
F: 1987 ♦♦♦ 10 Head: Gail P. Black ICAO: GOSEY Net: http://www.argosyair.com

registration	type of aircraft	cn/fn	ex/ex*	mfd	del	powered by	mtow kg	configuration	selcal	name/fln/specialitites/remarks
☐ N352AC	Piper PA-31-350 Navajo Chieftain	31-7852171		0078		2 LY TIO-540-J2BD	3175			lsf Rohuff Corp.
☐ N3546B	Piper PA-31-350 Navajo Chieftain	31-8052007		0080		2 LY TIO-540-J2BD	3175			lsf Black Inc.
☐ N59826	Piper PA-31-350 Navajo Chieftain	31-7652077		0076		2 LY TIO-540-J2BD	3175			lsf Rohuff Corp.

ARGUS AIR CHARTER (Grand Rapids Charter, Inc. dba)
Grand Rapids-Kent County Int'l, MI

2741 Mulford Drive SE, Grand Rapids, MI 49546, USA ☎ (616) 956-7600 Tx: none Fax: none SITA: n/a
F: 1995 ♦♦♦ n/a Head: Daniel J. Dunn Net: n/a

registration	type of aircraft	cn/fn	ex/ex*	mfd	del	powered by	mtow kg	configuration	selcal	name/fln/specialitites/remarks
☐ N7EF	Piper PA-34-200T Seneca II	34-7970457		0079	0895	2 CO TSIO-360-EB	2073			

ARIS HELICOPTERS, Ltd
San Jose-Int'l & Hawthorne-Municipal, CA

1138 Coleman Avenue, San Jose, CA 95110, USA ☎ (408) 998-3266 Tx: none Fax: (408) 998-4061 SITA: n/a
F: 1972 ♦♦♦ 60 Head: Stephen R. Sullivan Net: n/a

registration	type of aircraft	cn/fn	ex/ex*	mfd	del	powered by	mtow kg	configuration	selcal	name/fln/specialitites/remarks
☐ N56SM	MD Helicopters MD 500D (Hughes 369D)	380287D	N7424F	0078	0491	1 AN 250-C20B	1361			lsf Acme Rocket Sleds Inc.
☐ N549W	Bell 206B JetRanger III	2604	N484Z	0079	0592	1 AN 250-C20B	1451			
☐ N5770F	Eurocopter (Aerosp.) SA315B Lama	2593		0080	0787	1 TU Artouste IIIB1	1950			
☐ N3597T	Eurocopter (Aerosp.) AS350B AStar	1126		0079	0380	1 TU Arriel 1B	1950			cvtd AS350D
☐ N3609N	Eurocopter (Aerosp.) AS350B AStar	1248		0080	0181	1 TU Arriel 1B	1950			
☐ N1168U	Sikorsky S-58ET	58-1070		0059	0685	1 PWC PT6T-6 TwinPac	5897			cvtd S-58E
☐ N15AH	Sikorsky S-58ET	58-1563	D-HBWR	0062	0986	1 PWC PT6T-6 TwinPac	5897			lst Hi-Lift Helicopters / cvtd S-58E
☐ N58AH	Sikorsky S-58ET	58-328	N39790	0056	0584	1 PWC PT6T-3 TwinPac	5897			cvtd S-58E

ARIZONA HELICOPTER ADVENTURES (Diamondback Aviation Services, Inc. dba)
Sedona, AZ

PO Box 1729, Sedona, AZ 86339, USA ☎ (520) 282-0904 Tx: none Fax: (520) 282-1045 SITA: n/a
F: 1994 ♦♦♦ n/a Head: Patricia J. Burroughs Net: n/a

registration	type of aircraft	cn/fn	ex/ex*	mfd	del	powered by	mtow kg	configuration	selcal	name/fln/specialitites/remarks
☐ N59506	Bell 206B JetRanger	1347		0074	0496	1 AN 250-C20	1451			

registration type of aircraft   cn/fn   ex/ex*   mfd del powered by   mtow kg configuration   selcal   name/fln/specialitites/remarks

ARIZONA PUBLIC SERVICE, Company — Scottsdale, AZ

PO Box 53933, Mail STN3350, Phoenix, AZ 85072-3933, USA ☎ (602) 371-6749 Tx: none Fax: (602) 371-6172 SITA: n/a
F: 1982 ⁂ n/a Head: O. Mark Demichele Net: n/a

☐ N303PS	Bell 230	23016		0093	1293	2 AN 250C-30G2	3810			

ARKANSAS AIRCRAFT, Inc. – Aircharter — Jonesboro-Municipal, AR

3901 Lindberg Drive, Suite C, Jonesboro, AR 72401, USA ☎ (870) 935-0142 Tx: none Fax: (870) 935-4595 SITA: n/a
F: 1992 ⁂ n/a Head: Mark Haggenmacher Net: n/a Beside aircharter flights, company also trades with aircraft, mainly Beechcraft, Cessna & Piper types.

☐ N3748C	Cessna 402B	402B0606		0074	0896	2 CO TSIO-520-E	2858			
☐ N776L	Beech King Air 100	B-54		0070	0397	2 PWC PT6A-28	4808			
☐ N39ML	Cessna 551 Citation II/SP	551-0002	XA-SLD	0079	0597	2 PWC JT15D-4	5670			

ARKANSAS AIR TRANSPORT, Inc. — Springdale-Municipal, AR

2433 Cardinal Drive, Springdale, AR 72764, USA ☎ (501) 957-8618 Tx: none Fax: none SITA: n/a
F: 1996 ⁂ n/a Head: James S. Tate, Jr. Net: n/a

☐ N53JK	AAC (Ted Smith) Aerostar 601P	61P-0303-078	N90514	0076	0996	2 LY IO-540-S1A5	2722			

ARLINGTON JET (Arlington Jet Center, Inc. dba) — Arlington-Municipal, TX

5070 South Collins, Suite 101, Arlington, TX 76018, USA ☎ (817) 467-4571 Tx: none Fax: (817) 472-9725 SITA: n/a
F: 1990 ⁂ n/a Head: Sam J. Binion Net: n/a

☐ N300AJ	Beech King Air B200	BB-965	N184MQ	0081	0297	2 PWC PT6A-42	5670			lsf SI Aircraft & Sales Inc.
☐ N25MD	Learjet 25	25-054	N509G	0070	0295	2 GE CJ610-6	6804			lsf SI Aircraft & Sales Inc.

ARNER FLYING SERVICE, Inc. — Lehighton-Jake Arner Memorial, PA

1001 Coal Street, Lehighton, PA 18235, USA ☎ (717) 386-2330 Tx: none Fax: (717) 386-2330 SITA: n/a
F: 1935 ⁂ n/a Head: Byron J. Arner Net: n/a Aircraft below MTOW 1361kg: Piper PA-28

☐ N118BL	Piper PA-30-160 Twin Comanche B	30-913		0066	0693	2 LY IO-320-B1A	1633			

ARNOLD AVIATION (Arnold Aviation & Thunder Mountain Express, Inc. dba) — Cascade, ID

Box 1094, Cascade, ID 83611, USA ☎ (208) 382-4336 Tx: none Fax: (208) 382-3941 SITA: n/a
F: 1972 ⁂ n/a Head: Ray E. Arnold Net: n/a

☐ N411A	Cessna A185F Skywagon II	18503748	C-GQDR	0079	0594	1 CO IO-520-D	1520			
☐ N206RA	Cessna TU206G Turbo Stationair 6 II	U20605329		0080	0581	1 CO TSIO-520-M	1633			
☐ N756AV	Cessna TU206G Turbo Stationair	U20603944		0077	1077	1 CO TSIO-520-M	1633			
☐ N6328C	Cessna T210N Turbo Centurion II	21063865		0080	0783	1 CO TSIO-520-R	1814			

AROOSTOOK AVIATION, Inc. = PXX (formerly dba Pine State Airlines) — Frenchville-Northern Aroostook Regional, ME

74 Airport Avenue, Frenchville, ME 04745, USA ☎ (207) 543-6334 Tx: none Fax: (207) 543-6038 SITA: n/a
F: 1991 ⁂ n/a Head: Roland M. Martin ICAO: PINE STATE Net: http://www.sjv.com/psa/psa.htm Aircraft below MTOW 1361kg: Cessna 172

☐ N87397	Cessna 310R II	310R0545		0076	1288	2 CO IO-520-M	2495			lsf pvt
☐ N3249M	Cessna 402C II	402C0296		0080	0595	2 CO TSIO-520-VB	3107			

ARROW AIR, Inc. = JW / APW — Miami-Int'l, FL

PO Box 026062, Miami, FL 33102-6062, USA ☎ (305) 526-0900 Tx: 525000 arrow air mia Fax: (305) 526-0933 SITA: n/a
F: 1946 ⁂ 335 Head: Guillermo Cabeca IATA: 404 ICAO: BIG A Net: http://www.arrowair.com

☐ N1803	Boeing (Douglas) DC-8-62F	45895 / 299	EC-EQI	0067	1193	4 PW JT3D-3B (HK3/BAC)	151953	Freighter	KM-CL	lsf IALI / cvtd -62
☐ N1804	Boeing (Douglas) DC-8-62F	45896 / 303		0067	0092	4 PW JT3D-7 (HK3/BAC)	151953	Freighter	KM-DE	Dayton Express / lsf IALI / cvtd -62
☐ N1808E	Boeing (Douglas) DC-8-62F	46105 / 494	EC-GCY	0069	1096	4 PW JT3D-7 (HK3/BAC)	151953	Freighter	KM-CJ	lsf IALI / cvtd -62
☐ N791AL	Boeing (Douglas) DC-8-62F (AF)	46150 / 539	RTAF 60-109	0070	0796	4 PW JT3D-7 (HK3/BAC)	151953	Freighter	KM-DH	Pride of Miami / lsf IALI
☐ N802BN	Boeing (Douglas) DC-8-62F	45909 / 307	XA-AMT	0067	0489	4 PW JT3D-7 (HK3/BAC)	151953	Freighter	KM-DJ	lsf IALI / cvtd -62
☐ N810BN	Boeing (Douglas) DC-8-62F	45905 / 298	EC-ELM	0067	1295	4 PW JT3D-7 (HK3/BAC)	151953	Freighter	KM-DF	lsf IALI / cvtd -62
☐ N441J	Boeing (Douglas) DC-8-63F	45988 / 416	N941JW	0068	1283	4 PW JT3D-7 (HK3/BAC)	161025	Freighter	HK-AF	Andrew / lsf IALI / cvtd (CF)
☐ N661AV	Boeing (Douglas) DC-8-63F	45969 / 396	N6161A	0068	0882	4 PW JT3D-7 (HK3/BAC)	161025	Freighter	HK-AD	lsf IALI / cvtd (CF)
☐ N306GB	Lockheed L-1011-385-1-15 TriStar 200 (F)	193U-1138	A4O-TY	0076	0196	3 RR RB211-524B-02	215003	Freighter	KR-HP	lsf IALI / cvtd TriStar 100
☐ N307GB	Lockheed L-1011-385-1-15 TriStar 200 (F)	193U-1131	A4O-TW	0075	1196	3 RR RB211-524B-02	215003	Freighter	MS-EP	San Juan / lsf IALI / cvtd TriStar 100
☐ N308GB	Lockheed L-1011-385-1-15 TriStar 200 (F)	193U-1133	A4O-TX	0076	0996	3 RR RB211-524B-02	215003	Freighter	KR-HQ	lsf IALI / cvtd TriStar 100

ARROWSMITH, Inc. — Dunkirk-Chautauqua County, NY

9952 Tice Road, Eden, NY 14057, USA ☎ (716) 337-2732 Tx: none Fax: (716) 337-2732 SITA: n/a
F: 1992 ⁂ n/a Head: John W. Henrich Net: n/a

☐ N1274G	Cessna 310R II	310R0001		0075	0692	2 CO IO-520-M	2495			

ASA – Atlantic Southeast Airlines, Inc. = EV / ASE (Delta Connection) (Subsidiary of ASA Holdings) — Atlanta, GA

100 Hartsfield Central Parkway, Suite 800, Atlanta, GA 30354-1356, USA ☎ (770) 766-1400 Tx: n/a Fax: (770) 209-0162 SITA: n/a
F: 1979 ⁂ 2270 Head: George F. Pickett, Jr. IATA: 862 ICAO: ASEA Net: http://www.irinfo.com/asai
All aircraft are operated as ASA/Delta Connection (in own colours & titles), a commuter system to provide feeder connection at DL major hubs, using DL flight numbers. On option: further 60 Canadair Regional Jet 200

☐ N126AM	Embraer 120RT Brasilia (EMB-120RT)	120102	PT-SMU*	0088	1095	2 PWC PW118	11500	Y30		
☐ N127AM	Embraer 120RT Brasilia (EMB-120RT)	120103	PT-SMV*	0088	1195	2 PWC PW118	11500	Y30		
☐ N130AM	Embraer 120RT Brasilia (EMB-120RT)	120134	PT-SPA*	0089	0895	2 PWC PW118	11500	Y30		
☐ N131AM	Embraer 120RT Brasilia (EMB-120RT)	120158	PT-SPX*	0089	0895	2 PWC PW118	11500	Y30		
☐ N210AS	Embraer 120RT Brasilia (EMB-120RT)	120006	PT-SIA*	0085	0885	2 PWC PW118	11500	Y30		
☐ N214AS	Embraer 120RT Brasilia (EMB-120RT)	120009	PT-SID*	0085	1185	2 PWC PW118	11500	Y30		
☐ N215AS	Embraer 120RT Brasilia (EMB-120RT)	120010	PT-SIE*	0085	1285	2 PWC PW118	11500	Y30		
☐ N217AS	Embraer 120RT Brasilia (EMB-120RT)	120011	PT-SIF*	0085	1285	2 PWC PW118	11500	Y30		
☐ N218AS	Embraer 120RT Brasilia (EMB-120RT)	120015	PT-SIK*	0086	0686	2 PWC PW118	11500	Y30		
☐ N221AS	Embraer 120RT Brasilia (EMB-120RT)	120020	PT-SIP*	0086	0986	2 PWC PW118	11500	Y30		
☐ N223AS	Embraer 120RT Brasilia (EMB-120RT)	120021	PT-SIQ*	0086	1186	2 PWC PW118	11500	Y30		
☐ N225AS	Embraer 120RT Brasilia (EMB-120RT)	120022	PT-SIR*	0086	1286	2 PWC PW118	11500	Y30		
☐ N228AS	Embraer 120RT Brasilia (EMB-120RT)	120025	PT-SIU*	0086	0287	2 PWC PW118	11500	Y30		
☐ N229AS	Embraer 120RT Brasilia (EMB-120RT)	120042	PT-SJK*	0087	0687	2 PWC PW118	11500	Y30		
☐ N230AS	Embraer 120RT Brasilia (EMB-120RT)	120032	PT-SJB*	0087	0587	2 PWC PW118	11500	Y30		
☐ N232AS	Embraer 120RT Brasilia (EMB-120RT)	120036	PT-SJF*	0087	0687	2 PWC PW118	11500	Y30		
☐ N233AS	Embraer 120RT Brasilia (EMB-120RT)	120031	PT-SJA*	0087	0487	2 PWC PW118	11500	Y30		
☐ N235AS	Embraer 120RT Brasilia (EMB-120RT)	120047	PT-SJQ*	0087	0787	2 PWC PW118	11500	Y30		
☐ N236AS	Embraer 120RT Brasilia (EMB-120RT)	120049	PT-SJS*	0087	0787	2 PWC PW118	11500	Y30		
☐ N237AS	Embraer 120RT Brasilia (EMB-120RT)	120051	PT-SJU*	0087	0887	2 PWC PW118	11500	Y30		
☐ N238AS	Embraer 120RT Brasilia (EMB-120RT)	120053	PT-SJW*	0087	0987	2 PWC PW118	11500	Y30		
☐ N239AS	Embraer 120RT Brasilia (EMB-120RT)	120057	PT-SKA*	0087	0987	2 PWC PW118	11500	Y30		
☐ N240AS	Embraer 120RT Brasilia (EMB-120RT)	120060	PT-SKD*	0087	1087	2 PWC PW118	11500	Y30		
☐ N241AS	Embraer 120RT Brasilia (EMB-120RT)	120065	PT-SKI*	0087	1187	2 PWC PW118	11500	Y30		
☐ N242AS	Embraer 120RT Brasilia (EMB-120RT)	120069	PT-SKM*	0087	0488	2 PWC PW118	11500	Y30		
☐ N243AS	Embraer 120RT Brasilia (EMB-120RT)	120072	PT-SKP*	0087	0488	2 PWC PW118	11500	Y30		
☐ N244AS	Embraer 120RT Brasilia (EMB-120RT)	120073	PT-SKQ*	0088	0488	2 PWC PW118	11500	Y30		
☐ N245AS	Embraer 120RT Brasilia (EMB-120RT)	120075	PT-SKS*	0088	0488	2 PWC PW118	11500	Y30		
☐ N246AS	Embraer 120RT Brasilia (EMB-120RT)	120100	PT-SMS*	0088	1288	2 PWC PW118	11500	Y30		
☐ N247AS	Embraer 120RT Brasilia (EMB-120RT)	120113	PT-SNF*	0088	0189	2 PWC PW118	11500	Y30		
☐ N257AS	Embraer 120RT Brasilia (EMB-120RT)	120126	PT-SNS*	0089	0489	2 PWC PW118	11500	Y30		
☐ N258AS	Embraer 120RT Brasilia (EMB-120RT)	120131	PT-SNX*	0089	0589	2 PWC PW118	11500	Y30		
☐ N260AS	Embraer 120RT Brasilia (EMB-120RT)	120132	PT-SNY*	0089	0589	2 PWC PW118	11500	Y30		
☐ N261AS	Embraer 120RT Brasilia (EMB-120RT)	120141	PT-SPH*	0089	0889	2 PWC PW118	11500	Y30		
☐ N262AS	Embraer 120RT Brasilia (EMB-120RT)	120146	PT-SPM*	0089	0989	2 PWC PW118	11500	Y30		
☐ N263AS	Embraer 120RT Brasilia (EMB-120RT)	120157	PT-SPW*	0089	1189	2 PWC PW118	11500	Y30		
☐ N264AS	Embraer 120RT Brasilia (EMB-120RT)	120165	PT-SQD*	0089	0190	2 PWC PW118	11500	Y30		
☐ N265AS	Embraer 120RT Brasilia (EMB-120RT)	120170	PT-SQI*	0089	0190	2 PWC PW118	11500	Y30		
☐ N266AS	Embraer 120RT Brasilia (EMB-120RT)	120188	PT-SRB*	0090	0690	2 PWC PW118	11500	Y30		
☐ N267AS	Embraer 120RT Brasilia (EMB-120RT)	120198	PT-SRO*	0090	0890	2 PWC PW118	11500	Y30		
☐ N268AS	Embraer 120RT Brasilia (EMB-120RT)	120202	PT-SRS*	0090	0990	2 PWC PW118	11500	Y30		
☐ N269AS	Embraer 120RT Brasilia (EMB-120RT)	120210	PT-SSE*	0090	1290	2 PWC PW118	11500	Y30		
☐ N273AS	Embraer 120RT Brasilia (EMB-120RT)	120222	PT-SSR*	0091	0291	2 PWC PW118	11500	Y30		
☐ N274AS	Embraer 120RT Brasilia (EMB-120RT)	120229	PT-STB*	0091	0291	2 PWC PW118	11500	Y30		
☐ N275AS	Embraer 120RT Brasilia (EMB-120RT)	120234	PT-STG*	0091	0391	2 PWC PW118	11500	Y30		
☐ N280AS	Embraer 120RT Brasilia (EMB-120RT)	120231	PT-STD*	0091	0391	2 PWC PW118	11500	Y30		
☐ N281AS	Embraer 120RT Brasilia (EMB-120RT)	120224	PT-SST*	0091	0491	2 PWC PW118	11500	Y30		
☐ N282AS	Embraer 120RT Brasilia (EMB-120RT)	120226	PT-SSV*	0091	0491	2 PWC PW118	11500	Y30		
☐ N283AS	Embraer 120RT Brasilia (EMB-120RT)	120236	PT-STI*	0091	0491	2 PWC PW118	11500	Y30		
☐ N284AS	Embraer 120RT Brasilia (EMB-120RT)	120249	PT-STV*	0091	0392	2 PWC PW118	11500	Y30		
☐ N285AS	Embraer 120RT Brasilia (EMB-120RT)	120265	PT-SUL*	0092	0692	2 PWC PW118	11500	Y30		

279 registration type of aircraft cn/fn ex/ex* mfd del powered by mtow kg configuration selcal name/fln/specialitites/remarks

☐ N286AS	Embraer 120RT Brasilia (EMB-120RT)	120268	PT-SUO*	0092	0692	2 PWC PW118	11500	Y30		
☐ N500AS	Embraer 120RT Brasilia (EMB-120RT)	120272	PT-SUS*	0092	0692	2 PWC PW118	11500	Y30		
☐ N501AS	Embraer 120RT Brasilia (EMB-120RT)	120273	PT-SUT*	0092	1092	2 PWC PW118	11500	Y30		
☐ N502AS	Embraer 120RT Brasilia (EMB-120RT)	120274	PT-SUU*	0092	1192	2 PWC PW118	11500	Y30		
☐ N503AS	Embraer 120RT Brasilia (EMB-120RT)	120275	PT-SUV*	0092	1292	2 PWC PW118	11500	Y30		
☐ N504AS	Embraer 120RT Brasilia (EMB-120RT)	120278	PT-SUY*	0092	1292	2 PWC PW118	11500	Y30		
☐ N505AS	Embraer 120RT Brasilia (EMB-120RT)	120279	PT-SUZ*	0092	0293	2 PWC PW118	11500	Y30		
☐ N638AS	Embraer 120ER Brasilia (EMB-120ER)	120282	PT-SVC*	0093	0793	2 PWC PW118	11990	Y30		
☐ N639AS	Embraer 120ER Brasilia (EMB-120ER)	120283	PT-SVD*	0093	0893	2 PWC PW118	11990	Y30		
☐ N630AS	ATR 72-212	336	F-WWLS*	0093	0593	2 PWC PW127	21500	Y66		
☐ N631AS	ATR 72-212	362	F-WWEZ*	0093	0593	2 PWC PW127	21500	Y66		
☐ N632AS	ATR 72-212	338	F-WWLT*	0093	0693	2 PWC PW127	21500	Y66		
☐ N633AS	ATR 72-212	344	F-WWLC*	0093	0693	2 PWC PW127	21500	Y66		
☐ N634AS	ATR 72-212	370	F-WWEF*	0093	0793	2 PWC PW127	21500	Y66		
☐ N635AS	ATR 72-212	372	F-WWEP*	0093	0893	2 PWC PW127	21500	Y66		
☐ N636AS	ATR 72-212	375	F-WWLW*	0093	0993	2 PWC PW127	21500	Y66		
☐ N637AS	ATR 72-212	383	F-WWEB*	0093	0993	2 PWC PW127	21500	Y66		
☐ N640AS	ATR 72-212	405	F-WWLP*	0094	0494	2 PWC PW127	21500	Y66		
☐ N641AS	ATR 72-212	387	F-WWLG*	0094	0594	2 PWC PW127	21500	Y66		
☐ N642AS	ATR 72-212	395	F-WWLJ*	0094	0694	2 PWC PW127	21500	Y66		
☐ N643AS	ATR 72-212	413	F-WWLC*	0094	0694	2 PWC PW127	21500	Y66		
☐ N820AS	Canadair Regional Jet 200ER (CL-600-2B19)	7188		0097	0897	2 GE CF34-3B1	23133	Y50		
☐ N821AS	Canadair Regional Jet 200ER (CL-600-2B19)	7194		0097	0997	2 GE CF34-3B1	23133	Y50		
☐ N823AS	Canadair Regional Jet 200ER (CL-600-2B19)	7196		0097	1097	2 GE CF34-3B1	23133	Y50		
☐ N824AS	Canadair Regional Jet 200ER (CL-600-2B19)	7203		0097	1197	2 GE CF34-3B1	23133	Y50		
☐ N825AS	Canadair Regional Jet 200ER (CL-600-2B19)	7207		0097	1297	2 GE CF34-3B1	23133	Y50		
☐ N826AS	Canadair Regional Jet 200ER (CL-600-2B19)	7210	C-FMOW*	0098	0198	2 GE CF34-3B1	23133	Y50		
☐ N827AS	Canadair Regional Jet 200ER (CL-600-2B19)	7212	C-FMND*	0098	0198	2 GE CF34-3B1	23133	Y50		
☐ N828AS	Canadair Regional Jet 200ER (CL-600-2B19)	7213	C-FMNQ*	0098	0198	2 GE CF34-3B1	23133	Y50		
☐ N829AS	Canadair Regional Jet 200ER (CL-600-2B19)	7232		0098	0498	2 GE CF34-3B1	23133	Y50		
☐ N830AS	Canadair Regional Jet 200ER (CL-600-2B19)	7236		0098	0598	2 GE CF34-3B1	23133	Y50		
☐ N832AS	Canadair Regional Jet 200ER (CL-600-2B19)	7243		0098	0698	2 GE CF34-3B1	23133	Y50		
☐ N833AS	Canadair Regional Jet 200ER (CL-600-2B19)	7246	C-FMMB*	0098	0798	2 GE CF34-3B1	23133	Y50		
☐ N834AS	Canadair Regional Jet 200ER (CL-600-2B19)	7254		0098	0898	2 GE CF34-3B1	23133	Y50		
☐ N835AS	Canadair Regional Jet 200ER (CL-600-2B19)	7258	C-FMLF*	0098	1098	2 GE CF34-3B1	23133	Y50		
☐ N836AS	Canadair Regional Jet 200ER (CL-600-2B19)	7263	C-FMLU*	0098	1098	2 GE CF34-3B1	23133	Y50		
☐ N837AS	Canadair Regional Jet 200ER (CL-600-2B19)	7271	C-FVAZ*	0098	1198	2 GE CF34-3B1	23133	Y50		
☐ N838AS	Canadair Regional Jet 200ER (CL-600-2B19)	7276	C-FMMB*	0098	1298	2 GE CF34-3B1	23133	Y50		
☐ N839AS	Canadair Regional Jet 200ER (CL-600-2B19)	7290		0099	0199	2 GE CF34-3B1	23133	Y50		
☐ N840AS	Canadair Regional Jet 200ER (CL-600-2B19)	7295		0099	0199	2 GE CF34-3B1	23133	Y50		
☐ N841AS	Canadair Regional Jet 200ER (CL-600-2B19)					2 GE CF34-3B1	23133	Y50		oo-delivery 0499
☐ N842AS	Canadair Regional Jet 200ER (CL-600-2B19)					2 GE CF34-3B1	23133	Y50		oo-delivery 0499
☐ N843AS	Canadair Regional Jet 200ER (CL-600-2B19)					2 GE CF34-3B1	23133	Y50		oo-delivery 0599
☐ N844AS	Canadair Regional Jet 200ER (CL-600-2B19)					2 GE CF34-3B1	23133	Y50		oo-delivery 0699
☐ N845AS	Canadair Regional Jet 200ER (CL-600-2B19)					2 GE CF34-3B1	23133	Y50		oo-delivery 0799
☐ N846AS	Canadair Regional Jet 200ER (CL-600-2B19)					2 GE CF34-3B1	23133	Y50		oo-delivery 0899
☐ N847AS	Canadair Regional Jet 200ER (CL-600-2B19)					2 GE CF34-3B1	23133	Y50		oo-delivery 0999
☐ N848AS	Canadair Regional Jet 200ER (CL-600-2B19)					2 GE CF34-3B1	23133	Y50		oo-delivery 1099
☐ N849AS	Canadair Regional Jet 200ER (CL-600-2B19)					2 GE CF34-3B1	23133	Y50		oo-delivery 1199
☐ N850AS	Canadair Regional Jet 200ER (CL-600-2B19)					2 GE CF34-3B1	23133	Y50		oo-delivery 1299
☐ N851AS	Canadair Regional Jet 200ER (CL-600-2B19)					2 GE CF34-3B1	23133	Y50		oo-delivery 0100
☐ N852AS	Canadair Regional Jet 200ER (CL-600-2B19)					2 GE CF34-3B1	23133	Y50		oo-delivery 0200
☐ N853AS	Canadair Regional Jet 200ER (CL-600-2B19)					2 GE CF34-3B1	23133	Y50		oo-delivery 0300
☐ N854AS	Canadair Regional Jet 200ER (CL-600-2B19)					2 GE CF34-3B1	23133	Y50		oo-delivery 0400
☐ N855AS	Canadair Regional Jet 200ER (CL-600-2B19)					2 GE CF34-3B1	23133	Y50		oo-delivery 0500
☐ N856AS	Canadair Regional Jet 200ER (CL-600-2B19)					2 GE CF34-3B1	23133	Y50		oo-delivery 0600
☐ N857AS	Canadair Regional Jet 200ER (CL-600-2B19)					2 GE CF34-3B1	23133	Y50		oo-delivery 0700
☐ N858AS	Canadair Regional Jet 200ER (CL-600-2B19)					2 GE CF34-3B1	23133	Y50		oo-delivery 0800
☐ N859AS	Canadair Regional Jet 200ER (CL-600-2B19)					2 GE CF34-3B1	23133	Y50		oo-delivery 0900
☐ N860AS	Canadair Regional Jet 200ER (CL-600-2B19)					2 GE CF34-3B1	23133	Y50		oo-delivery 1000
☐ N861AS	Canadair Regional Jet 200ER (CL-600-2B19)					2 GE CF34-3B1	23133	Y50		oo-delivery 1100
☐ N862AS	Canadair Regional Jet 200ER (CL-600-2B19)					2 GE CF34-3B1	23133	Y50		oo-delivery 1200
☐ N863AS	Canadair Regional Jet 200ER (CL-600-2B19)					2 GE CF34-3B1	23133	Y50		oo-delivery 0001
☐ N864AS	Canadair Regional Jet 200ER (CL-600-2B19)					2 GE CF34-3B1	23133	Y50		oo-delivery 0001
☐ N865AS	Canadair Regional Jet 200ER (CL-600-2B19)					2 GE CF34-3B1	23133	Y50		oo-delivery 0001
☐ N866AS	Canadair Regional Jet 200ER (CL-600-2B19)					2 GE CF34-3B1	23133	Y50		oo-delivery 0001
☐ N	Canadair Regional Jet 700					2 GE CF34-8C1	32885	Y70		oo-delivery 0001
☐ N	Canadair Regional Jet 700					2 GE CF34-8C1	32885	Y70		oo-delivery 0001
☐ N	Canadair Regional Jet 700					2 GE CF34-8C1	32885	Y70		oo-delivery 0001
☐ N	Canadair Regional Jet 700					2 GE CF34-8C1	32885	Y70		oo-delivery 0002
☐ N	Canadair Regional Jet 700					2 GE CF34-8C1	32885	Y70		oo-delivery 0002
☐ N	Canadair Regional Jet 700					2 GE CF34-8C1	32885	Y70		oo-delivery 0002
☐ N	Canadair Regional Jet 700					2 GE CF34-8C1	32885	Y70		oo-delivery 0002
☐ N	Canadair Regional Jet 700					2 GE CF34-8C1	32885	Y70		oo-delivery 0002
☐ N	Canadair Regional Jet 700					2 GE CF34-8C1	32885	Y70		oo-delivery 0002
☐ N	Canadair Regional Jet 700					2 GE CF34-8C1	32885	Y70		oo-delivery 0002
☐ N	Canadair Regional Jet 700					2 GE CF34-8C1	32885	Y70		oo-delivery 0002
☐ N	Canadair Regional Jet 700					2 GE CF34-8C1	32885	Y70		oo-delivery 0003

ASAP AVIATION INTERNATIONAL, Inc. — Cincinnati-Municipal/Lunken Field, OH

358 Walmer Avenue, Cincinnati, OH 45226, USA ☎ (513) 533-0808 Tx: none Fax: (606) 344-8869 SITA: n/a
F: 1995 ⁂ n/a Head: Michael Schmitt Net: n/a

☐ N555V	Piper PA-23-250 Aztec E	27-7405394		0074	1095	2 LY IO-540-C4B5	2359			

ASI CHARTER, Inc. (Aircraft Specialists, Inc. dba) — Jeffersonville-Clark County, IN

6005 Propeller Lane, Sellersburg, IN 47172, USA ☎ (812) 246-4696 Tx: none Fax: (812) 246-4365 SITA: n/a
F: 1990 ⁂ n/a Head: Eric H. Taylor Net: http://www.aircraft-specialists.com

☐ N540ME	Cessna 208B Grand Caravan	208B0540		0096	0596	1 PWC PT6A-114A	3969			lsf Textron Financial Corp.
☐ N292ME	Learjet 35A	35A-292	N634H	0080	0196	2 GA TFE731-2-2B	8301			
☐ N8280	Learjet 35A	35A-310	N13HB	0080	0797	2 GA TFE731-2-2B	8301			to be re-reg. N310ME

ASPEN AVIATION, Inc. — Aspen-Pitkin County/Sardy Field, CO

ASPEN Aviation

69 East Airport Road, Suite B, Aspen, CO 81611, USA ☎ (970) 925-2522ext.2 Tx: none Fax: (970) 920-9841 SITA: n/a
F: 1981 ⁂ n/a Head: Clifford R. Runge Net: http://www.aspen.com/aspenaviation

☐ N5393U	Cessna TU206G Turbo Stationair 6 II	U20605274		0079	0289	1 CO TSIO-520-M	1633			lsf Aspen Base Operation Inc.
☐ N900DS	Twin (Aero) Jetprop Commander 900 (690D)	15035	OE-FGS	0083	0197	2 GA TPE331-5-254K	4853			lsf Aspen Base Operation Inc.
☐ N200TP	Beech King Air 200	BB-191	N1PC	0076	0295	2 PWC PT6A-21	5670			lsf The November Group Llc
☐ N351AM	Learjet 35A	35A-409	N35FE	0081	0198	2 GA TFE731-2-2B	8301			lsf Aspen Base Operation Inc.
☐ N37FA	Learjet 35A	35A-091	D-CIRS	0076	1196	2 GA TFE731-2-2B	8301			lsf Aspen Base Operation Inc.
☐ N58MM	Learjet 35A	35A-261	N63DH	0079	0694	2 GA TFE731-2-2B	8301			lsf Aspen Base Operation Inc.

ASPEN HELICOPTERS, Inc. = AHF — Oxnard, CA

2899 West 5th Street, Oxnard, CA 93030, USA ☎ (805) 985-5416 Tx: none Fax: (805) 985-7327 SITA: n/a
F: 1980 ⁂ 21 Head: Charles W. McLaughlin ICAO: ASPEN Net: n/a

☐ N39049	Bell 206B JetRanger III	3101		0080	0488	1 AN 250-C20B	1451			
☐ N49643	Bell 206B JetRanger	1813		0075	0390	1 AN 250-C20	1451			
☐ N5006Y	Bell 206B JetRanger III	2485		0078	0688	1 AN 250-C20B	1451			lsf pvt
☐ N5012F	Bell 206B JetRanger III	2559		0079	0885	1 AN 250-C20B	1451			
☐ N90214	Bell 206B JetRanger	1662		0075	0588	1 AN 250-C20	1451			
☐ N1085T	Bell 206L-1 LongRanger III	45376		0080	0784	1 AN 250-C30P	1882			cvtd LongRanger II
☐ N383SH	Bell 206L-3 LongRanger III	51073		0083	0594	1 AN 250-C30P	1882			
☐ N5736N	Bell 206L-1 LongRanger II	45418		0080	1091	1 AN 250-C28B	1882			
☐ N8057B	Bell 206L LongRanger	45045		0076	0984	1 AN 250-C20B	1814			
☐ N999AH	Bell 206L-3 LongRanger III	51046	C-GALM	0082	0594	1 AN 250-C30P	1882			
☐ N300LF	Partenavia P.68C	295		0084	0988	2 LY IO-360-A1B6	1990			lsf Partenavia
☐ N3832K	Partenavia P.68C	272		0083	0385	2 LY IO-360-A1B6	1990			lsf Partenavia
☐ N6602L	Partenavia P.68 Observer	326-19-OB		0084	1193	2 LY IO-360-A1B6	1990	Surveyer		lsf Partenavia
☐ N4107Q	Piper PA-31-350 T1020	31-8253008		0082	0596	2 LY TIO-540-J2B	3175			lsf Partenavia
☐ N8131	Piper PA-31-350 Navajo Chieftain	31-8152032		0081	0396	2 LY TIO-540-J2BD	3175			
☐ N422RM	Bell 222UT	47530	N222DU	0084	0597	2 LY LTS101-750C.1	3742	EMS MercyAir		

280 registration type of aircraft cn/fn ex/ex* mfd del powered by mtow kg configuration selcal name/fln/specialitites/remarks

ASPEN MOUNTAIN AIR = LSS (Exec Express II, Inc.dba/Subsidiary of Peak Int'l/formerly Lone Star Airlines) **Denver-Int'l, CO & Dallas-Fort Worth, TX**

2100 North Highway 360, Suite 1807, Grande Prairie, TX 75050, USA ☎ (972) 641-7337 Tx: none Fax: (972) 606-2713 SITA: n/a
F: 1995 ♟♟♟ n/a Head: Ronald P. Stone IATA: 504 ICAO: LONE STAR Net: n/a Filed for Chapter 11 bankruptcy protection 0898 & suspended operations 1298 (with Dornier 328 & SA227AC Metro III aircraft). Intends to re-start.

ASSOCIATED AIR ACTIVITIES, Inc. **Chicago-Lansing Municipal, IL**

PO Box 158, Lansing, IL 60438, USA ☎ (708) 474-6073 Tx: none Fax: (708) 895-1656 SITA: n/a
F: 1978 ♟♟♟ n/a Head: Wade Palmer Net: n/a Aircraft below MTOW 1361kg: Piper PA-28

☐ N210MS	Cessna T210N Turbo Centurion II	21063411		0079	0596	1 CO TSIO-520-R	1814			

ASSOCIATED AIRCRAFT (Associated Aircraft Group, Inc. dba / Subsidiary of Sikorsky) **Danbury-Municipal, CT & Poughkeepsie-Dutchess County, NY**

49 Miry Brook Road, Danbury, CT 06810, USA ☎ (203) 790-6800 Tx: none Fax: (203) 797-8647 SITA: n/a
F: 1989 ♟♟♟ n/a Head: John C. Agor Net: http://www.aag-inc.com

☐ N206SH	Bell 206B JetRanger	1666	N384EH	0075	0294	1 AN 250-C20	1451			lsf Candler Travel Inc.
☐ N468AG	Bell 206L-3 LongRanger III	51155	N468KC	0085	0198	1 AN 250-C30P	1882			
☐ N176SH	Sikorsky S-76A+	760182	N94WW	0081	0390	2 TU Arriel 1S	4899			lsf Wings Venture Ltd / cvtd S-76A
☐ N595ST	Sikorsky S-76B	760330	N5AY	0086	0398	2 PWC PT6B-36A	5307			lsf Steiner Air Llc
☐ N63AG	Sikorsky S-76B	760314	N361G	0086	1196	2 PWC PT6B-36A	5307			lsf General Electric Capital Corp.
☐ N85PS	Sikorsky S-76A+	760265	N169BJ	0084	1296	2 TU Arriel 1S	4899			lsf TBG Aviation Inc. / cvtd S-76A

ASTRO STAR AVIATION, Inc. **Niles-Jerry Tyler Memorial, MI**

2018 Lake Street, Niles, MI 49120, USA ☎ (616) 684-7030 Tx: none Fax: (616) 684-7033 SITA: n/a
F: 1984 ♟♟♟ n/a Head: M. Keith Mosher Net: n/a

☐ N8371Y	Piper PA-30-160 Twin Comanche B	30-1522		0067	1092	2 LY IO-320-B1A	1633			
☐ N40597	Piper PA-23-250 Aztec E	27-7405344		0074		2 LY IO-540-C4B5	2359			lsf Kendallville Aviation Inc.
☐ N54828	Piper PA-23-250 Aztec E	27-7554125		0075	0289	2 LY IO-540-C4B5	2359			
☐ N9215Y	Piper PA-31-310 Navajo	31-279		0068	0289	2 LY TIO-540-A1A	2948			

ATHENS AIR **Dallas-Addison, TX**

16250 North Dallas Pkwy, Ste 111, Dallas, TX 75248, USA ☎ (972) 250-2990 Tx: none Fax: (972) 247-5026 SITA: n/a
F: 1993 ♟♟♟ n/a Head: Neill P. Clayton Net: http://www.athensair.com/

☐ N27L	Cessna 500 Citation	500-0038	N777FC	0072	1093	2 PWC JT15D-1	5216			

ATKIN AIR CHARTER SERVICE (Willard K. Atkin dba) **Lincoln-Regional, CA**

1420 Flightline Drive, Suite F, Lincoln, CA 95648, USA ☎ (530) 645-6242 Tx: none Fax: (530) 645-7132 SITA: n/a
F: 1990 ♟♟♟ n/a Head: Willard K. Atkin Net: http://www.atkinair.com

☐ N1661R	Cessna R182 Skylane RG II	R18200502		0078	0595	1 LY O-540-J3C5D	1406			lsf CKMPS
☐ N9075C	Cessna R182 Skylane RG II	R18200386		0078	0890	1 LY O-540-J3C5D	1406			lsf SC Harms Corp.
☐ N5340Y	Cessna T210N Turbo Centurion II	21064173		0080	0391	2 CO TSIO-520-R	1814			
☐ N3038P	Piper PA-34-200T Seneca II	34-7970136		0079	1196	2 CO TSIO-360-E	2073			lsf T&C Enterprises Inc.
☐ N32936	Piper PA-34-200T Seneca II	34-7570067		0075	0494	2 CO TSIO-360-E	2073			
☐ N351MC	Piper PA-34-200 Seneca	34-7350314		0073	0597	2 LY IO-360-C1E6	1905			lsf American & European Aircraft
☐ N20DC	Cessna 414A Chancellor III	414A0257		0079	0197	2 CO TSIO-52O-N	3062			lsf pvt

ATLANTIC AERO, Inc. **Greensboro-Piedmont Triad Int'l, NC**

PO Box 35408, Greensboro, NC 27425-5408, USA ☎ (910) 722-1396 Tx: none Fax: (910) 668-4435 SITA: n/a
F: 1971 ♟♟♟ n/a Head: Don S. Godwin Net: http://www.atlantic-aero.com

☐ N99PA	Beech Baron 58P	TJ-179		0078	0386	2 CO TSIO-520-L	2767			lsf Southeastern Mechanical Contr.
☐ N464WF	Pilatus PC-12/45	149	HB-FRK*	0096	0996	1 PWC PT6A-67B	4500			
☐ N62300	Beech King Air C90	LJ-989		0081	0596	2 PWC PT6A-21	4377			lsf Sunland Fire Protection Inc.
☐ N46SC	Cessna 501 Citation I/SP	501-0137	N26503	0079	1094	2 PWC JT15D-1A	5375			lsf Southeastern Mechanical Contr.
☐ N1217V	Cessna 560 Citation V	560-0001		0088	0696	2 PWC JT15D-5A	7212			lsf Philipps-Slick Llc

ATLANTIC AIR CARGO, Inc. **Miami-Int'l, FL**

1840 N.W. 93rd Avenue, Miami, FL 33172, USA ☎ (305) 594-2251 Tx: none Fax: (305) 594-6674 SITA: n/a
F: 1994 ♟♟♟ n/a Head: Ernesto Castrillo Net: n/a

☐ N705GB	Boeing (Douglas) DC-3C (C-47A-DL)	13854	CF-HBX	0043		2 PW R-1830	12202	Freighter		lsf J & E Aviation Leasing Inc.

ATLANTIC AIRCRAFT, Inc. **St. Croix-Alexander Hamilton, VI**

PO Box 3028, Kingshill, St. Croix, VI 00851, USA ☎ (340) 778-3999 Tx: none Fax: (340) 778-5757 SITA: n/a
F: 1992 ♟♟♟ n/a Head: John Leonard Net: n/a Operates non-commercial corporate flights for its partent company, EmCOM Emerging Communications, only.

☐ N88TN	Cessna 402C II	402C0621	N59FA	0081	0193	2 CO TSIO-520-VB	3107	Corporate		
☐ N1093Z	Beech King Air B200	BB-1593		0097	0998	2 PWC PT6A-42	5670	Corporate		lsf Group B-200 Inc.
☐ N727EC	Boeing 727-30 (winglets)	18365 / 52	N700TE	0064	0598	3 PW JT8D-9A (HK3/FDX)	74162	Corporate		

ATLANTIC AIRWAYS, Inc. **Orlando-Central Florida Regional/Sanford, FL**

8702 Catbrair Lane, Suite 202, Orlando, FL 32829, USA ☎ (561) 324-1111 Tx: none Fax: none SITA: n/a
F: 1992 ♟♟♟ n/a Head: David G. Tracey Net: n/a

☐ N225DM	Piper PA-31-350 Navajo Chieftain	31-7652001		0076	0596	2 LY TIO-540-J2BD	3175			
☐ N236BC	Piper PA-31-310 Navajo	31-373		0069	0394	2 LY TIO-540-A1A	2948			

ATLANTIC COAST AIRLINES, Inc. = DH / BLR (United Express) **Washington-Dulles, DC**

515A Shaw Road, Sterling, VA 20166, USA ☎ (540) 925-6000 Tx: none Fax: (540) 925-6299 SITA: n/a
F: 1989 ♟♟♟ 1350 Head: C. Edward Acker IATA: 480 ICAO: BLUE RIDGE Net: http://www.atlanticcoast.com
All aircraft are operated as UNITED EXPRESS (in full such colours & titles), a commuter system to provide feeder connection at United Airlines major hubs, using UA flight numbers.

☐ N470UE	BAe 3201 Jetstream 32	814	N332QB	0088	1091	2 GA TPE331-12UAR-701H	7350	Y19		op in United Express-colors
☐ N471UE	BAe 3201 Jetstream 32	821	N332QE	0088	1091	2 GA TPE331-12UAR-701H	7350	Y19		op in United Express-colors
☐ N472UE	BAe 3201 Jetstream 32	823	N332QF	0088	1091	2 GA TPE331-12UAR-701H	7350	Y19		op in United Express-colors
☐ N473UE	BAe 3201 Jetstream 32	828	N332QH	0088	1091	2 GA TPE331-12UAR-701H	7350	Y19		op in United Express-colors
☐ N474UE	BAe 3201 Jetstream 32	849	N332QQ	0089	1091	2 GA TPE331-12UAR-701H	7350	Y19		op in United Express-colors
☐ N475UE	BAe 3201 Jetstream 32	850	G-31-850*	0089	1091	2 GA TPE331-12UAR-701H	7350	Y19		op in United Express-colors
☐ N476UE	BAe 3201 Jetstream 32	884	G-31-884*	0090	1091	2 GA TPE331-12UAR-701H	7350	Y19		op in United Express-colors
☐ N477UE	BAe 3201 Jetstream 32	890	G-31-890*	0090	1091	2 GA TPE331-12UAR-701H	7350	Y19		op in United Express-colors
☐ N478UE	BAe 3201 Jetstream 32	892	G-31-892*	0090	0790	2 GA TPE331-12UAR-701H	7350	Y19		op in United Express-colors
☐ N479UE	BAe 3201 Jetstream 32	893	G-31-893*	0090	1091	2 GA TPE331-12UAR-701H	7350	Y19		op in United Express-colors
☐ N480UE	BAe 3201 Jetstream 32	894	G-31-894*	0090	1091	2 GA TPE331-12UAR-701H	7350	Y19		op in United Express-colors
☐ N481UE	BAe 3201 Jetstream 32	895	G-31-895*	0090	1091	2 GA TPE331-12UAR-701H	7350	Y19		op in United Express-colors
☐ N482UE	BAe 3201 Jetstream 32	897	G-31-897*	0090	1091	2 GA TPE331-12UAR-701H	7350	Y19		op in United Express-colors
☐ N483UE	BAe 3201 Jetstream 32	898	G-31-898*	0090	1091	2 GA TPE331-12UAR-701H	7350	Y19		op in United Express-colors
☐ N484UE	BAe 3201 Jetstream 32	899	G-31-899*	0090	1091	2 GA TPE331-12UAR-701H	7350	Y19		op in United Express-colors
☐ N485UE	BAe 3201 Jetstream 32	901	G-31-901*	0090	1091	2 GA TPE331-12UAR-701H	7350	Y19		op in United Express-colors
☐ N486UE	BAe 3201 Jetstream 32	905	G-31-905*	0090	1091	2 GA TPE331-12UAR-701H	7350	Y19		op in United Express-colors
☐ N487UE	BAe 3201 Jetstream 32	906	G-31-906*	0090	1091	2 GA TPE331-12UAR-701H	7350	Y19		op in United Express-colors
☐ N488UE	BAe 3201 Jetstream 32	907	G-31-907*	0090	1091	2 GA TPE331-12UAR-701H	7350	Y19		op in United Express-colors
☐ N489UE	BAe 3201 Jetstream 32	908	G-31-908*	0090	1091	2 GA TPE331-12UAR-701H	7350	Y19		op in United Express-colors
☐ N490UE	BAe 3201 Jetstream 32	909	G-31-909*	0090	1091	2 GA TPE331-12UAR-701H	7350	Y19		op in United Express-colors
☐ N491UE	BAe 3201 Jetstream 32	911	G-31-911*	0090	1091	2 GA TPE331-12UAR-701H	7350	Y19		op in United Express-colors
☐ N492UE	BAe 3201 Jetstream 32	790	N332QA	0088	0193	2 GA TPE331-12UAR-701H	7350	Y19		op in United Express-colors
☐ N493UE	BAe 3201 Jetstream 32	805	N371MT	0088	0293	2 GA TPE331-12UAR-701H	7350	Y19		op in United Express-colors
☐ N494UE	BAe 3201 Jetstream 32	810	N372MT	0088	0293	2 GA TPE331-12UAR-701H	7350	Y19		op in United Express-colors
☐ N495UE	BAe 3201 Jetstream 32	818	N332QC	0088	0193	2 GA TPE331-12UAR-701H	7350	Y19		op in United Express-colors
☐ N496UE	BAe 3201 Jetstream 32	900	N3142	0090	0493	2 GA TPE331-12UAR-701H	7350	Y19		op in United Express-colors
☐ N497UE	BAe 3201 Jetstream 32	904	N3157	0090	0493	2 GA TPE331-12UAR-701H	7350	Y19		op in United Express-colors
☐ N301UE	BAe 4101 Jetstream 41	41012	G-4-012*	0093	0593	2 GA TPE331-14HR-802H	10433	Y29		Blue Ridge Highlander / op in UA Ex.-cs
☐ N302UE	BAe 4101 Jetstream 41	41013	G-4-013*	0093	0593	2 GA TPE331-14HR-802H	10433	Y29		op in United Express-colors
☐ N303UE	BAe 4101 Jetstream 41	41015	G-4-015*	0093	0693	2 GA TPE331-14HR-802H	10433	Y29		op in United Express-colors
☐ N305UE	BAe 4101 Jetstream 41	41019	G-4-019*	0093	0893	2 GA TPE331-14HR-802H	10433	Y29		op in United Express-colors
☐ N306UE	BAe 4101 Jetstream 41	41020	G-4-020*	0093	0993	2 GA TPE331-14HR-802H	10433	Y29		op in United Express-colors
☐ N307UE	BAe 4101 Jetstream 41	41021	G-4-021*	0093	0194	2 GA TPE331-14HR-802H	10433	Y29		op in United Express-colors
☐ N308UE	BAe 4101 Jetstream 41	41023	G-4-023*	0093	1093	2 GA TPE331-14HR-802H	10433	Y29		op in United Express-colors
☐ N309UE	BAe 4101 Jetstream 41	41022	G-4-022*	0093	1293	2 GA TPE331-14HR-802H	10433	Y29		op in United Express-colors
☐ N310UE	BAe 4101 Jetstream 41	41028	G-4-028*	0094	0294	2 GA TPE331-14HR-802H	10433	Y29		op in United Express-colors
☐ N311UE	BAe 4101 Jetstream 41	41029	G-4-029*	0094	0394	2 GA TPE331-14HR-802H	10433	Y29		op in United Express-colors
☐ N312UE	BAe 4101 Jetstream 41	41025	G-4-025*	0094	0494	2 GA TPE331-14HR-802H	10433	Y29		op in United Express-colors
☐ N313UE	BAe 4101 Jetstream 41	41026	G-4-026*	0094	0594	2 GA TPE331-14HR-802H	10433	Y29		op in United Express-colors
☐ N314UE	BAe 4101 Jetstream 41	41027	G-4-027*	0094	0694	2 GA TPE331-14HR-802H	10433	Y29		op in United Express-colors
☐ N315UE	BAe 4101 Jetstream 41	41033	G-4-033*	0094	0794	2 GA TPE331-14HR-802H	10433	Y29		op in United Express-colors
☐ N316UE	BAe 4101 Jetstream 41	41055	G-4-055*	0095	0595	2 GA TPE331-14HR-805H	10886	Y29		op in United Express-colors
☐ N317UE	BAe 4101 Jetstream 41	41031	G-4-031*	0094	0195	2 GA TPE331-14HR-805H	10886	Y29		op in United Express-colors
☐ N318UE	BAe 4101 Jetstream 41	41041	G-4-041*	0094	0195	2 GA TPE331-14HR-805H	10886	Y29		op in United Express-colors
☐ N319UE	BAe 4101 Jetstream 41	41042	G-4-042*	0095	0295	2 GA TPE331-14HR-805H	10886	Y29		op in United Express-colors

281 registration type of aircraft cn/fn ex/ex* mfd del powered by mtow kg configuration selcal name/fln/specialitites/remarks

☐ N320UE	BAe 4101 Jetstream 41	41043	G-4-043*	0095	0295	2 GA TPE331-14HR-805H	10886	Y29		op in United Express-colors
☐ N321UE	BAe 4101 Jetstream 41	41045	G-4-045*	0095	0395	2 GA TPE331-14HR-805H	10886	Y29		op in United Express-colors
☐ N322UE	BAe 4101 Jetstream 41	41058	G-4-058*	0095	0695	2 GA TPE331-14HR-805H	10886	Y29		op in United Express-colors
☐ N323UE	BAe 4101 Jetstream 41	41059	G-4-059*	0095	0695	2 GA TPE331-14HR-805H	10886	Y29		op in United Express-colors
☐ N324UE	BAe 4101 Jetstream 41	41017	N304UE	0093	1294	2 GA TPE331-14HR-801H	10433	Y29		op in United Express-colors
☐ N325UE	BAe 4101 Jetstream 41	41063	G-4-063*	0095	0695	2 GA TPE331-14HR-805H	10886	Y29		op in United Express-colors
☐ N326UE	BAe 4101 Jetstream 41	41064	G-4-064*	0095	0795	2 GA TPE331-14HR-805H	10886	Y29		op in United Express-colors
☐ N327UE	BAe 4101 Jetstream 41	41080	G-4-080*	0096	0396	2 GA TPE331-14HR-805H	10886	Y29		op in United Express-colors
☐ N328UE	BAe 4101 Jetstream 41	41083	G-4-083*	0096	0396	2 GA TPE331-14HR-805H	10886	Y29		op in United Express-colors
☐ N329UE	BAe 4101 Jetstream 41	41097	G-4-097*	0096	0397	2 GA TPE331-14HR-805H	10886	Y29		op in United Express-colors
☐ N330UE	BAe 4101 Jetstream 41	41098	G-4-098*	0096	0397	2 GA TPE331-14HR-805H	10886	Y29		op in United Express-colors
☐ N331UE	BAe 4101 Jetstream 41	41099	G-4-099*	0097	0497	2 GA TPE331-14HR-805H	10886	Y29		op in United Express-colors
☐ N332UE	BAe 4101 Jetstream 41	41100	G-4-100*	0097	0497	2 GA TPE331-14HR-805H	10886	Y29		op in United Express-colors
☐ N333UE	BAe 4101 Jetstream 41	41101	G-4-101*	0097	1297	2 GA TPE331-14HR-805H	10886	Y29		op in United Express-colors
☐ N620BR	Canadair Regional Jet 200ER (CL-600-2B19)	7179		0097	0997	2 GE CF34-3B1	23133	Y50		op in United Express-colors
☐ N621BR	Canadair Regional Jet 200ER (CL-600-2B19)	7186	C-FMML*	0097	1097	2 GE CF34-3B1	23133	Y50		op in United Express-colors
☐ N622BR	Canadair Regional Jet 200ER (CL-600-2B19)	7187		0097	0997	2 GE CF34-3B1	23133	Y50		op in United Express-colors
☐ N623BR	Canadair Regional Jet 200ER (CL-600-2B19)	7192		0097	0997	2 GE CF34-3B1	23133	Y50		op in United Express-colors
☐ N624BR	Canadair Regional Jet 200ER (CL-600-2B19)	7211		0097	1297	2 GE CF34-3B1	23133	Y50		op in United Express-colors
☐ N625BR	Canadair Regional Jet 200ER (CL-600-2B19)	7214	C-FMLU*	0098	0198	2 GE CF34-3B1	23133	Y50		op in United Express-colors
☐ N626BR	Canadair Regional Jet 200ER (CL-600-2B19)	7225	C-FMKW*	0098	0398	2 GE CF34-3B1	23133	Y50		op in United Express-colors
☐ N627BR	Canadair Regional Jet 200ER (CL-600-2B19)	7233		0098	0498	2 GE CF34-3B1	23133	Y50		op in United Express-colors
☐ N628BR	Canadair Regional Jet 200ER (CL-600-2B19)	7240		0098	0598	2 GE CF34-3B1	23133	Y50		op in United Express-colors
☐ N629BR	Canadair Regional Jet 200ER (CL-600-2B19)	7251		0098	0798	2 GE CF34-3B1	23133	Y50		op in United Express-colors
☐ N630BR	Canadair Regional Jet 200ER (CL-600-2B19)	7255		0098	0898	2 GE CF34-3B1	23133	Y50		op in United Express-colors
☐ N631BR	Canadair Regional Jet 200ER (CL-600-2B19)	7261	C-FMLS*	0098	0998	2 GE CF34-3B1	23133	Y50		op in United Express-colors
☐ N632BR	Canadair Regional Jet 200ER (CL-600-2B19)	7268	C-FMNY*	0098	1098	2 GE CF34-3B1	23133	Y50		op in United Express-colors
☐ N633BR	Canadair Regional Jet 200ER (CL-600-2B19)	7274	C-FMLU*	0098	1198	2 GE CF34-3B1	23133	Y50		op in United Express-colors
☐ N634BR	Canadair Regional Jet 200ER (CL-600-2B19)	7284	C-FMKV*	0099	0199	2 GE CF34-3B1	23133	Y50		op in United Express-colors
☐ N635BR	Canadair Regional Jet 200ER (CL-600-2B19)	7294		0099	0199	2 GE CF34-3B1	23133	Y50		op in United Express-colors
☐ N636BR	Canadair Regional Jet 200ER (CL-600-2B19)	7300		0099	0299	2 GE CF34-3B1	23133	Y50		op in UA Express-colors
☐ N637BR	Canadair Regional Jet 200ER (CL-600-2B19)					2 GE CF34-3B1	23133	Y50		oo-delivery 0499/tb op in UA Exp.-cs
☐ N638BR	Canadair Regional Jet 200ER (CL-600-2B19)					2 GE CF34-3B1	23133	Y50		oo-delivery 0499/tb op in UA Exp.-cs
☐ N639BR	Canadair Regional Jet 200ER (CL-600-2B19)					2 GE CF34-3B1	23133	Y50		oo-delivery 0599/tb op in UA Exp.-cs
☐ N640BR	Canadair Regional Jet 200ER (CL-600-2B19)					2 GE CF34-3B1	23133	Y50		oo-delivery 0599/tb op in UA Exp.-cs
☐ N641BR	Canadair Regional Jet 200ER (CL-600-2B19)					2 GE CF34-3B1	23133	Y50		oo-delivery 0699/tb op in UA Exp.-cs
☐ N642BR	Canadair Regional Jet 200ER (CL-600-2B19)					2 GE CF34-3B1	23133	Y50		oo-delivery 0799/tb op in UA Exp.-cs
☐ N643BR	Canadair Regional Jet 200ER (CL-600-2B19)					2 GE CF34-3B1	23133	Y50		oo-delivery 0999/tb op in UA Exp.-cs
☐ N644BR	Canadair Regional Jet 200ER (CL-600-2B19)					2 GE CF34-3B1	23133	Y50		oo-delivery 0100/tb op in UA Exp.-cs
☐ N645BR	Canadair Regional Jet 200ER (CL-600-2B19)					2 GE CF34-3B1	23133	Y50		oo-delivery 0300/tb op in UA Exp.-cs
☐ N646BR	Canadair Regional Jet 200ER (CL-600-2B19)					2 GE CF34-3B1	23133	Y50		oo-delivery 0500/tb op in UA Exp.-cs
☐ N647BR	Canadair Regional Jet 200ER (CL-600-2B19)					2 GE CF34-3B1	23133	Y50		oo-delivery 0600/tb op in UA Exp.-cs
☐ N648BR	Canadair Regional Jet 200ER (CL-600-2B19)					2 GE CF34-3B1	23133	Y50		oo-delivery 0700/tb op in UA Exp.-cs
☐ N649BR	Canadair Regional Jet 200ER (CL-600-2B19)					2 GE CF34-3B1	23133	Y50		oo-delivery 0800/tb op in UA Exp.-cs
☐ N650BR	Canadair Regional Jet 200ER (CL-600-2B19)					2 GE CF34-3B1	23133	Y50		oo-delivery 0900/tb op in UA Exp.-cs
☐ N651BR	Canadair Regional Jet 200ER (CL-600-2B19)					2 GE CF34-3B1	23133	Y50		oo-delivery 0900/tb op in UA Exp.-cs
☐ N652BR	Canadair Regional Jet 200ER (CL-600-2B19)					2 GE CF34-3B1	23133	Y50		oo-delivery 1000/tb op in UA Exp.-cs
☐ N653BR	Canadair Regional Jet 200ER (CL-600-2B19)					2 GE CF34-3B1	23133	Y50		oo-delivery 1100/tb op in UA Exp.-cs
☐ N654BR	Canadair Regional Jet 200ER (CL-600-2B19)					2 GE CF34-3B1	23133	Y50		oo-delivery 1200/tb op in UA Exp.-cs
☐ N655BR	Canadair Regional Jet 200ER (CL-600-2B19)					2 GE CF34-3B1	23133	Y50		oo-delivery 1200/tb op in UA Exp.-cs
☐ N656BR	Canadair Regional Jet 200ER (CL-600-2B19)					2 GE CF34-3B1	23133	Y50		oo-delivery 0101/tb op in UA Exp.-cs
☐ N657BR	Canadair Regional Jet 200ER (CL-600-2B19)					2 GE CF34-3B1	23133	Y50		oo-delivery 0201/tb op in UA Exp.-cs
☐ N658BR	Canadair Regional Jet 200ER (CL-600-2B19)					2 GE CF34-3B1	23133	Y50		oo-delivery 0401/tb op in UA Exp.-cs
☐ N659BR	Canadair Regional Jet 200ER (CL-600-2B19)					2 GE CF34-3B1	23133	Y50		oo-delivery 0501/tb op in UA Exp.-cs
☐ N660BR	Canadair Regional Jet 200ER (CL-600-2B19)					2 GE CF34-3B1	23133	Y50		oo-delivery 0701/tb op in UA Exp.-cs
☐ N661BR	Canadair Regional Jet 200ER (CL-600-2B19)					2 GE CF34-3B1	23133	Y50		oo-delivery 0701/tb op in UA Exp.-cs
☐ N662BR	Canadair Regional Jet 200ER (CL-600-2B19)					2 GE CF34-3B1	23133	Y50		oo-delivery 0901/tb op in UA Exp.-cs

ATLAS AIR, Inc. = 5Y / GTI (Subsidiary of Atlas Holdings / Sister company of Aeronautics Leasing, Inc.)

New York-JFK, NY

538 Commons Drive, Golden, CO 80401, USA ☎ (303) 526-5050 Tx: none Fax: (303) 526-5051 SITA: n/a
F: 1992 ☨☨☨ 300 Head: Michael A. Chowdry ICAO: GIANT Net: n/a

☐ N505MC	Boeing 747-2D3B (SF)	21251 / 296	F-GFUK	0477	1292	4 GE CF6-50E2	377842	Freighter	FL-KM	cvtd -2D3B (M)
☐ N506MC	Boeing 747-2D3B (SF)	21252 / 297	LX-ZCV	0577	0394	4 GE CF6-50E2	371946	Freighter	AG-EL	lsf POTO / cvtd -2D3B (M)
☐ N507MC	Boeing 747-230B (SF)	21380 / 320	D-ABYL	0378	1194	4 GE CF6-50E2	377842	Freighter	DK-FG	cvtd -230B (M)
☐ N508MC	Boeing 747-230B (SF)	21644 / 356	D-ABYS	0279	1194	4 GE CF6-50E2	377842	Freighter	GL-FM	cvtd -230B (M)
☐ N509MC	Boeing 747-230B (SF)	21221 / 299	D-ABYK	1276	0495	4 GE CF6-50E2	377842	Freighter	FH-CE	cvtd -230B (M)
☐ N512MC	Boeing 747-230B (SF)	21220 / 294	D-ABYJ	1176	0396	4 GE CF6-50E2	377842	Freighter	CG-EJ	cvtd -230B (M)
☐ N516MC	Boeing 747-243B (SF)	22507 / 497	I-DEMD	1280	0695	4 GE CF6-50E2	377842	Freighter	CK-GL	cvtd -243B (M)
☐ N517MC	Boeing 747-243B (SF)	23300 / 613	I-DEMT	0585	1295	4 GE CF6-50E2	377842	Freighter	BM-EK	op in partial Iberia-cs/cvtd -243B (M)
☐ N518MC	Boeing 747-243B (SF)	23476 / 647	I-DEMW	0686	0196	4 GE CF6-50E2	377842	Freighter	BM-FK	op in China Airlines-cs/cvtd -243B (M)
☐ N522MC	Boeing 747-2D7B (SF)	21783 / 417	HS-TGB	1279	0996	4 GE CF6-50E2	371946	Freighter	MR-EJ	op in Thai Airways-colors / cvtd -2D7B
☐ N523MC	Boeing 747-2D7B (SF)	21782 / 402	ZK-TGA	1179	0596	4 GE CF6-50E2	371946	Freighter	MR-EK	cvtd -2D7B
☐ N524MC	Boeing 747-2D7B (SF)	21784 / 424	HS-TGC	0280	0996	4 GE CF6-50E2	371946	Freighter	MR-EL	cvtd -2D7B
☐ N526MC	Boeing 747-2D7B (SF)	22337 / 479	HS-TGF	0980	1196	4 GE CF6-50E2	371946	Freighter	MR-EP	cvtd -2D7B
☐ N527MC	Boeing 747-2D7B (SF)	22471 / 504	HS-TGG	0381	0497	4 GE CF6-50E2	371946	Freighter	MR-EQ	cvtd -2D7B
☐ N528MC	Boeing 747-2D7B (SF)	22472 / 597	HS-TGS	0684	0597	4 GE CF6-50E2	371946	Freighter	MR-ES	op in China Airlines-cs / cvtd -2D7B
☐ N534MC	Boeing 747-2F6B (SF)	21832 / 421	N741PR	0079	0597	4 GE CF6-50E2	371946	Freighter		cvtd -2F6B
☐ N535MC	Boeing 747-2F6B (SF)	21833 / 423	N742PR	0080	0197	4 GE CF6-50E2	371946	Freighter	AS-DH	op in partial Alitalia-colors/cvtd-2F6B
☐ N536MC	Boeing 747-228F (SCD)	21576 / 334	F-BPVV	0078	0299	4 GE CF6-50E2	371946	Freighter		
☐ N537MC	Boeing 747-271C (SCD)	22403 / 524	LX-BCV	0081	1098	4 GE CF6-50E2	377842	Freighter		op in Cargolux-colors
☐ N538MC	Boeing 747-271C (SCD)	21964 / 416	LX-ACV	0079	1198	4 GE CF6-50E2	377842	Freighter		
☐ N539MC	Boeing 747-271C (SCD)	21965 / 438	LX-ECV	0080	0299	4 GE CF6-50E2	377842	Freighter		
☐ N808MC	Boeing 747-212B (SF)	21048 / 253	N726PA	0275	0493	4 GE CF6-50E2	371946	Freighter	FJ-BG	cvtd -212B / re-engined PW JT9D-7J
☐ N809MC	Boeing 747-228F (SCD)	20887 / 245	LX-DCV	0874	0995	4 GE CF6-50E2	371946	Freighter	CK-AB	re-engined PW JT9D-7J
☐ N408MC	Boeing 747-47UF (SCD)	29261 / 1192		1298	1298	4 GE CF6-80C2B1F	396893	Freighter	RS-PQ	
☐ N409MC	Boeing 747-47UF (SCD)					4 GE CF6-80C2B1F	396893	Freighter		oo-delivery 0300
☐ N412MC	Boeing 747-47UF (SCD)					4 GE CF6-80C2B1F	396893	Freighter		oo-delivery 0400
☐ N491MC	Boeing 747-47UF (SCD)	29252 / 1165		0098	0798	4 GE CF6-80C2B1F	396893	Freighter		
☐ N492MC	Boeing 747-47UF (SCD)	29253 / 1169		0898	0898	4 GE CF6-80C2B1F	396893	Freighter		
☐ N493MC	Boeing 747-47UF (SCD)	29254 / 1179		1098	1098	4 GE CF6-80C2B1F	396893	Freighter		
☐ N494MC	Boeing 747-47UF (SCD)	29255 / 1184		0098	1298	4 GE CF6-80C2B1F	396893	Freighter		
☐ N495MC	Boeing 747-47UF (SCD)	29256		0099	0399	4 GE CF6-80C2B1F	396893	Freighter		
☐ N496MC	Boeing 747-47UF (SCD)	29257				4 GE CF6-80C2B1F	396893	Freighter		oo-delivery 0599
☐ N497MC	Boeing 747-47UF (SCD)	29258				4 GE CF6-80C2B1F	396893	Freighter		oo-delivery 0899
☐ N498MC	Boeing 747-47UF (SCD)	29259				4 GE CF6-80C2B1F	396893	Freighter		oo-delivery 1299
☐ N499MC	Boeing 747-47UF (SCD)	29260				4 GE CF6-80C2B1F	396893	Freighter		oo-delivery 0100

AUBURN FLIGHT SERVICE, Inc.

Auburn-Municipal, WA

506 23rd Ave NE, Auburn, WA 98002, USA ☎ (206) 939-3456 Tx: none Fax: (206) 931-0768 SITA: n/a
F: 1969 ☨☨☨ n/a Head: Jamelle R. Garcia Net: n/a Aircraft below MTOW 1361kg: Piper PA-28

☐ N3047B	Piper PA-44-180 Seminole	44-7995113		0079	1087	2 LY O-360-E1A6D	1724			
☐ N2157K	Piper PA-34-200T Seneca II	34-7970092		0079	0195	2 CO TSIO-360-EB	2073			lsf Franken Flight Service Inc.

AUBURN FLYING SERVICE (Aviation & Transportation Properties dba)

Auburn-Municipal, WA

13622 New Airport Road, Auburn, CA 95602, USA ☎ (530) 823-5610 Tx: none Fax: (530) 823-5376 SITA: n/a
F: 1978 ☨☨☨ n/a Head: Dennis K. Denham Net: n/a

☐ N5378V	Cessna T210L Turbo Centurion II	21060923		0075	0595	1 CO TSIO-520-H	1724			
☐ N6266Q	Cessna 401A	401A0066		0069	0487	2 CO TSIO-520-E	2858			
☐ N207AC	Twin (Aero) Commander 500A	500A-1266-89		0063	0890	2 CO IO-470-M	2835			
☐ N538LJ	Cessna 402B	402B0538		0074	1096	2 CO TSIO-520-E	2858			

AUGUSTA AVIATION, Inc.

Augusta-Daniel Field, GA

Daniel Field, Augusta, GA 30904-5302, USA ☎ (706) 733-8970 Tx: none Fax: (706) 738-9746 SITA: n/a
F: 1947 ☨☨☨ n/a Head: Steven R. Gay Net: n/a

☐ N2604Z	Piper PA-23-250 Aztec F	27-8154012		0081	0691	2 LY IO-540-C4B5	2359			
☐ N27693	Piper PA-31-325 Navajo C/R	31-7812091		0078	0195	2 LY TIO-540-F2BD	2948			
☐ N61454	Piper PA-31-350 Navajo Chieftain	31-7405479		0074	0592	2 LY TIO-540-J2BD	3175			
☐ N8KT	Fairchild (Swearingen) SA26AT Merlin IIB	T26-158E	N256WC	0069	0893	2 GA TPE331-1-151G	4536			

282 registration type of aircraft cn/fn ex/ex* mfd del powered by mtow kg configuration selcal name/fln/specialitites/remarks

AUSTIN EXPRESS, Inc. = 7V / TXX — Austin-Robert Mueller Municipal, TX

1901 East 51st Street, Suite 210, Austin, TX 78723, USA ☎ (512) 236-1110 Tx: none Fax: (512) 236-1112 SITA: n/a
F: 1997 ⁂ n/a Head: James Echols IATA: 342 ICAO: COWBOY Net: n/a

☐ N446MA	Fairchild (Swearingen) SA227AC Metro III	AC-693	N456AM	0087	1197	2 GA TPE331-11U-612G	6577	Y19		lsf MEI
☐ N730C	Fairchild (Swearingen) SA227AC Metro III	AC-697	N369AE	0087	1197	2 GA TPE331-11U-611G	6577	Y19		lsf MEI

AUTEC AVIATION SERVICES (Flight Dept.of Range Systems Engineering, a Raytheon Company) — West Palm Beach-Int'l,FL & N.Andros-Heliport (Bahamas)

PO Box 24619, West Palm Beach, FL 33416-4619, USA ☎ (561) 832-8566 Tx: none Fax: (561) 655-7188 SITA: n/a
F: 1966 ⁂ 22 Head: James C. Peterson Net: n/a AUTEC (Atlantic Underwater Test & Evaluation Center) AVIATION SERVICES operates under contract for the US Navy, conducting transport/support flights with the Sikorsky S-61N and passenger (personnel-transfer) flights with the Beech 1900D Airliner.

☐ N45AR	Beech 1900D Airliner	UE-12	N138MA	0092	0892	2 PWC PT6A-67D	7688	Y19		opf US Navy
☐ N46AR	Beech 1900D Airliner	UE-27		0092	1192	2 PWC PT6A-67D	7688	Y19		opf US Navy
☐ N138AR	Sikorsky S-61N	61767	C-GOKH	0077	0195	2 GE CT58-140-1	9979	Utility		opf US Navy
☐ N232AC	Sikorsky S-61N	61470	ZS-HXX	0069	0294	2 GE CT58-140-1	9979	Utility		opf US Navy

AVAG, Inc. — Richvale-AVAG, CA

PO Box 156, Richvale, CA 95974, USA ☎ (530) 882-4286 Tx: none Fax: (530) 882-4543 SITA: n/a
F: 1975 ⁂ n/a Head: Craig S. Compton Net: n/a Ag-aircraft below MTOW 5000kg: Grumman G-164A/B/D

☐ N843M	Garlick-Bell UH-1B (204)	901	63-8676	0062	0194	1 LY T53-L-13	3856			cvtd Bell UH-1B
☐ N91320	Garlick-Bell UH-1B (204)	407	887	0062	1291	1 LY T53-L-13	3856			cvtd Bell UH-1B
☐ N6258Z	Bell UH-1H (205)	10748	68-16089	0068	0396	1 LY T53-L-13	4309			

AVATLANTIC = KYC (HCL Aviation, Inc. dba) — St. Petersburg/Clearwater Int'l, FL

PO Box 17728, Clearwater, FL 33762, USA ☎ (727) 531-7575 Tx: none Fax: (727) 531-3664 SITA: n/a
F: 1989 ⁂ n/a Head: n/a ICAO: DOLPHIN Net: n/a Suspended operations 0397 (with Boeing 727 aircraft). Intends to restart 1999 with Boeing 737-200.

AVBASE AVIATION, Llc — Cleveland-Hopkins Int'l, OH

6200 Riverside Drive, I-X Jet Center, Cleveland, OH 44135, USA ☎ (216) 265-9500 Tx: none Fax: (216) 265-9501 SITA: n/a
F: 1993 ⁂ n/a Head: John V. DePalma Net: n/a

☐ N17KD	Cessna 500 Citation I	500-0337	N22MB	0076	0998	2 PWC JT15D-1A	5375			lsf Bika Air Inc.
☐ N1904S	Learjet 31A	31A-149		0097	0498	2 GA TFE731-2-3B	7711			lsf Spitzer Management Inc.
☐ N211BR	Sabreliner 60 (Rockwell NA265-60)	306-85	N855CD	0074	0297	2 PW JT12A-8	9150			lsf BR Wings Inc.
☐ N92FE	IAI 1124 Westwind I	286	N4447T	0080	1298	2 GA TFE731-3-1G	10365			lsf Pivot Aviation Llc
☐ N795A	Hawker 700A (HS 125-700A)	257127	HB-VLC	0081	0199	2 GA TFE731-3R-1H	11567			lsf W.W. Aircraft / cvtd 700B

AVCENTER, Inc. (formerly Pocatello Avcenter, Inc.) — Pocatello-Regional & Idaho Falls-Fanning Field, ID

1428 West Cessna Avenue, Pocatello, ID 83204, USA ☎ (208) 234-2141 Tx: none Fax: (208) 233-3979 SITA: n/a
F: 1978 ⁂ n/a Head: Allan C. Gliege, Jr. Net: n/a Aircraft below MTOW 1361kg: Cessna 182

☐ N3408Q	Piper PA-34-200T Seneca II	34-7770228		0077	0678	2 CO TSIO-360-E	2073			lsf PIH Leasing Inc.
☐ N73MJ	Piper PA-34-200T Seneca II	34-7670114		0076	0496	2 CO TSIO-360-E	2073			
☐ N821GS	Piper PA-34-200T Seneca II	34-7770419		0077	0896	2 CO TSIO-360-E	2073			
☐ N8514C	Piper PA-34-200T Seneca II	34-7670147		0076	0695	2 CO TSIO-360-E	2073			
☐ N911AG	Cessna 414A Chancellor III	414A0438		0079	0397	2 CO TSIO-520-NB	3062			
☐ N299RJ	Beech King Air B200	BB-1613		0098	0498	2 PWC PT6A-42	5670			lsf Raytheon Aircraft Co.

AVENGAIR, Inc. = (AVEG) (Associated with Ansett Worldwide Aviation Services, Australia) — Bellevue, WA

110-110th Ave NE No. 410, Bellevue, WA 98004, USA ☎ (206) 455-0952 Tx: n/a Fax: (206) 451-9439 SITA: n/a
F: 1988 ⁂ 10 Head: Leslie Hong Net: n/a Used aircraft leasing and sales company.
Some leasing & sales business is done under the name CORSAIR Inc. = (CORS) & TRANSPACIFIC ENTERPRISES Inc. = (TPEI), (subsidiaries, same headquarters).
Owner / lessor of the following (main) aircraft types: Boeing 707C, 727-100, 737-200 & Fokker F27-500. Aircraft leased from AVEG are listed and mentioned as such under the leasing carriers.

AVIA FLIGHT SERVICES, Inc. — Corvallis-Municipal, OR

5671 Plumley Street, Corvallis, OR 97333, USA ☎ (541) 757-2842 Tx: none Fax: (541) 757-1403 SITA: n/a
F: 1990 ⁂ n/a Head: William Gleaves Net: n/a Aircraft below MTOW 1361kg: Robinson R22

☐ N3596G	Eurocopter (Aerosp.) AS350D AStar	1110		0079	0497	1 LY LTS101-600A.2	1950			lsf Danielson Aviation Llc

AVIATION CHARTER, Inc. (Wings of Care) — Minneapolis-Flying Cloud, MN

9960 Flying Cloud Drive, Minneapolis, MN 55347, USA ☎ (612) 943-1519 Tx: none Fax: (612) 942-9264 SITA: n/a
F: 1982 ⁂ n/a Head: Shirley Wikner Net: http://www.aviationcharter.com EMS/Air Ambulance-services are operated under the marketing name WINGS OF CARE (same headquarters).

☐ N979SP	Piper PA-31-325 Navajo C/R	31-7812015		0078	0693	2 LY TIO-540-F2BD	2948			lsf Beech Transportation Inc.
☐ N12ED	Cessna 414	414-0521		0074	0793	2 CO TSIO-520-J	2880			lsf Beech Transportation Inc.
☐ N14CF	Beech King Air A100	B-209	N100AN	0075	0392	2 PWC PT6A-28	5216	EMS WingsofCare		lsf Beech Transportation Inc.
☐ N2050A	Beech King Air C90	LJ-813	N517PC	0079	0488	2 PWC PT6A-21	4377	EMS WingsofCare		lsf Beech Transportation Inc.
☐ N3741M	Beech King Air E90	LW-342		0081	1093	2 PWC PT6A-28	4581	EMS WingsofCare		lsf Beech Transportation Inc.
☐ N41BE	Beech King Air A100	B-245	N41BP	0079	0295	2 PWC PT6A-28	5216	EMS WingsofCare		lsf Beech Transportation Inc.
☐ N41WC	Beech King Air B90	LJ-430	N551SS	0068	0793	2 PWC PT6A-20	4377	EMS WingsofCare		lsf Beech Transportation Inc.
☐ N46BE	Beech King Air A100	B-214	HZ-AFC	0075	0197	2 PWC PT6A-28	5216	EMS WingsofCare		lsf Beech Transportation Inc.
☐ N6280E	Beech King Air C90-1	LJ-1015		0082	0387	2 PWC PT6A-21	4377	EMS WingsofCare		lsf Beech Transportation Inc.
☐ N851KA	Beech King Air C90	LJ-851	N4B	0079	0892	2 PWC PT6A-21	4377	EMS WingsofCare		lsf Beech Transportation Inc.
☐ N49KC	Beech King Air 200	BB-318		0078	0398	2 PWC PT6A-41	5670	EMS WingsofCare		lsf Beech Transportation Inc.
☐ N83GA	Beech King Air 200	BB-518	VH-MKR	0079	0495	2 PWC PT6A-41	5670	EMS WingsofCare		lsf Beech Transportation Inc.
☐ N30JD	Cessna 550 Citation II	550-0205		0080	0696	2 PWC JT15D-4	6033			lsf WWB Llc
☐ N66MC	Cessna 550 Citation II	550-0239	N4720T	0081	1295	2 PWC JT15D-4	6033			lsf Cashman Holdings Llc
☐ N212FJ	Dassault Falcon 10	147	N125GA	0079	0896	2 GA TFE731-2-1C	8500			lsf Mobek Aviation Llc

AVIATION CHARTERS, Inc. — Robbinsville-Trenton, NJ

106A Sharon Road, Robbinsville, NJ 08691, USA ☎ (609) 259-0700 Tx: none Fax: (609) 259-6404 SITA: n/a
F: 1981 ⁂ n/a Head: Theodore Pichel Net: n/a

☐ N18TP	Piper PA-34-200T Seneca II	34-7970431		0079	1181	2 CO TSIO-360-EB	2073			
☐ N19TP	Piper PA-34-200T Seneca II	34-7870383	N88AF	0078	1193	2 CO TSIO-360-E	2073			

AVIATION CHARTER SERVICES (Kokomo Aviation, Inc. dba) — Indianapolis-Int'l, IN

6551 Pierson Drive, Indianapolis, IN 46241-4220, USA ☎ (765) 244-7200 Tx: none Fax: (765) 241-8091 SITA: n/a
F: 1977 ⁂ n/a Head: Michael J. Pittard Net: n/a

☐ N247B	Beech King Air A100	B-139		0072	0289	2 PWC PT6A-28	5216			
☐ N819MH	Beech King Air C90	LJ-735	N190TT	0077	0994	2 PWC PT6A-21	4377			lsf Windward Charter Ltd
☐ N402KA	Beech King Air 200	BB-296	N402CJ	0077	0792	2 PWC PT6A-41	5670			
☐ N261PG	Learjet 35A	35A-329	N261PC	0080	0496	2 GA TFE731-2-2B	8301			
☐ N620JM	Learjet 35A	35A-207	N3PW	0079	0289	2 GA TFE731-2-2B	8301			lsf M-S Air Inc.
☐ N77LA	Hawker 800A (BAe 125-800A)	258029	N600HS	0085	0696	2 GA TFE731-5R-1H	12428			lsf L2 Aviation Group Llc

AVIATION ENTERPRISES UNLIMITED, Inc. — Fort Lauderdale-Executive, FL

1020 NW 62nd Street, Hangar 10, Fort Lauderdale, FL 33309, USA ☎ (954) 772-1717 Tx: none Fax: (954) 772-0363 SITA: n/a
F: 1990 ⁂ n/a Head: Andres Barcenas Net: n/a

☐ N55322	Piper PA-34-200 Seneca	34-7350201		0073	0394	2 LY IO-360-C1E6	1905			
☐ N3548J	Piper PA-31-350 Navajo Chieftain	31-8052027		0080	1294	2 LY TIO-540-J2BD	3175			

AVIATION INVESTORS INTERNATIONAL, Inc. = (AVII) — Hackensack, NJ

Two University Plaza, Suite 411, Hackensack, NJ 07601, USA ☎ (201) 488-0600 Tx: none Fax: (201) 488-5980 SITA: n/a
F: 1993 ⁂ 9 Head: Carl D. Simoni Net: n/a New and used aircraft leasing, sales and financing company.
Owner / lessor of the following (main) aircraft types: Boeing 737-400/757/767-300ER, Fokker 50, McDonnell Douglas DC-10-30 & MD-83. Aircraft leased from AVII are listed and mentioned as such under the leasing carriers.

AVIATION LEASING GROUP, Inc. = (ALGI) — Kansas City, MO

4600 Madison, Suite 800, Kansas City, MO 64112-2765, USA ☎ (816) 931-7300 Tx: n/a Fax: (816) 931-8200 SITA: n/a
F: n/a ⁂ n/a Head: Farhad Azima Net: n/a Used aircraft leasing, sales and financing company.
Owner / lessor of following (main) aircraft types : BAe 111-200, Boeing 707-320C, 727-100, DC-8F & DC-8-61. Aircraft leased from ALGI are listed and mentioned as such under the leasing carriers .

AVIATION RESOURCES, Ltd — Fargo-Hector Int'l, ND

3801 20th Street North, Fargo, ND 58102-0909, USA ☎ (701) 237-0123 Tx: none Fax: (701) 237-6887 SITA: n/a
F: 1960 ⁂ n/a Head: Clif S. Hamilton, Jr. Net: http://www.valleyaviation.com

☐ N9798C	Piper PA-34-200T Seneca II	34-7870222		0078	0295	2 CO TSIO-360-E	2073			
☐ N65315	Piper PA-23-250 Aztec C	27-2866		0065	0990	2 LY IO-540-C4B5	2359			
☐ N6588Y	Piper PA-23-250 Aztec C	27-3891		0068	0592	2 LY IO-540-C4B5	2359			
☐ N325YH	Piper PA-31-325 Navajo C/R	31-7812007	N27380	0078	0187	2 LY TIO-540-F2BD	2948			
☐ N502SE	Beech King Air C90	LJ-740		0077	0893	2 PWC PT6A-21	4377	EMS LifeFlight		opf St. Lukes LifeFlight Meritcare
☐ N911ND	Beech King Air C90	LJ-774	N4742M	0078	0487	2 PWC PT6A-21	4377	EMS LifeFlight		opf St. Lukes LifeFlight Meritcare

283 registration type of aircraft cn/fn ex/ex* mfd del powered by mtow kg configuration selcal name/fln/specialitites/remarks

AVIATION SALES, Inc. — Dayton-Int'l, OH

501 North Dixie Drive, Vandalia, OH 45377, USA ☎ (937) 898-3927 Tx: none Fax: (937) 898-1846 SITA: n/a
F: 1965 ⁂ n/a Head: Richard Penwell Net: n/a

☐ N9922Y	Cessna T210N Turbo Centurion II	*21064640*		*0082*	*0597*	*1 CO TSIO-520-R*	*1814*		
☐ N6186X	Cessna 310R II	*310R1325*		*0078*	*0293*	*2 CO IO-520-M*	*2495*		
☐ N4630G	Cessna 402B II	*402B1307*		*0077*	*0693*	*2 CO TSIO-520-E*	*2858*		
☐ N57KA	Beech King Air C90	*LJ-577*		*0073*	*0495*	*2 PWC PT6A-20*	*4377*		

AVIATION SERVICES, Inc. — Marshfield-Municipal, WI

400 West 29th Street, Marshfield, WI 54449, USA ☎ (715) 384-3149 Tx: none Fax: (715) 387-1831 SITA: n/a
F: 1988 ⁂ n/a Head: Lynn A. Eberl Net: n/a

☐ N627KM	Piper PA-23-250 Aztec F	*27-7754006*		*0077*	*0290*	*2 LY IO-540-C4B5*	*2359*		*lsf pvt*
☐ N7248R	Beech Baron 58	*TH-578*		*0075*	*0791*	*2 CO IO-520-C*	*2449*		
☐ N57D	Piper PA-31-310 Navajo	*31-260*		*0068*	*0391*	*2 LY TIO-540-A1A*	*2948*		
☐ N93BC	Beech King Air 100	*B-41*	*N502CW*	*0070*	*0396*	*2 PWC PT6A-28*	*4808*		*lsf Badger Aircraft Leasing Inc.*

AVIATION SERVICES UNLIMITED, Inc. — Utica-Oneida County, NY

PO Box 629, Oriskany, NY 13424, USA ☎ (315) 736-4842 Tx: none Fax: (315) 736-4872 SITA: n/a
F: 1975 ⁂ n/a Head: Paul C. Rayhill Net: n/a

☐ N134VG	Bell 206B JetRanger	*1512*		*0074*	*0981*	*1 AN 250-C20*	*1451*		
☐ N206GR	Bell 206A JetRanger	*615*	*N717SH*	*0071*	*0189*	*1 AN 250-C20*	*1361*		
☐ N9984K	Bell 206L LongRanger	*45054*		*0076*	*0098*	*1 AN 250-C20B*	*1814*		

AVIEX JET, Inc. — Houston-William P. Hobby, TX

8430 Larson Street, Houston, TX 77061, USA ☎ (281) 641-1576 Tx: none Fax: (281) 641-5326 SITA: n/a
F: 1979 ⁂ n/a Head: David D. Trigg Net: http://www.aviex.com

☐ N200AJ	Beech King Air 200	*BB-378*	*N482SW*	*0078*	*0691*	*2 PWC PT6A-41*	*5670*		
☐ N308AJ	Learjet 25	*25-039*	*N66NJ*	*0069*	*0294*	*2 GE CJ610-6*	*6804*		
☐ N303AJ	IAI 1121B Jet Commander	*1121-149*	*N343DA*	*0069*	*0788*	*2 GE CJ610-5*	*8391*		

AVIOR AIRCRAFT CHARTERS ((AvTech Executive Flight Services dba / Subsidiary of Avior Technologies, Inc.) — Marietta-Cobb County McCollum Field, GA

1800 Airport Road, Kennesaw, GA 30144, USA ☎ (770) 422-2345 Tx: none Fax: (770) 423-1544 SITA: n/a
F: 1987 ⁂ n/a Head: Robert W. Freeman Net: http://www.avior.com

☐ N58JC	Beech Baron 58P	*TJ-20*		*0076*	*0796*	*2 CO TSIO-520-L*	*2767*		*lsf Gem City Aviation Inc. / tbr N313AV*
☐ N312AV	Piper PA-31-350 Navajo Chieftain	*31-7752033*	*N63685*	*0077*	*1296*	*2 LY TIO-540-J2BD*	*3175*		*lsf Gem City Aviation Inc.*
☐ N30JN	Cessna 500 Citation	*500-0272*	*N30SB*	*0075*	*0196*	*2 PWC JT15D-1*	*5216*		*lsf Automotive Consultants Inc.*
☐ N311AV	Beech King Air 200	*BB-336*	*N50TW*	*0078*	*0793*	*2 PWC PT6A-41*	*5670*		
☐ N310AV	Cessna 550 Citation II	*550-0028*	*5Y-HAB*	*0079*	*1093*	*2 PWC JT15D-4*	*6033*		

AVJET, Corp. — Burbank-Glendale/Pasadena, CA

4531 Empire Avenue, Burbank, CA 91505, USA ☎ (818) 841-6190 Tx: none Fax: (818) 841-6209 SITA: n/a
F: 1979 ⁂ n/a Head: Marc A. Foulkrod Net: n/a

☐ N62BR	Cessna 500 Citation	*500-0093*	*G-OCPI*	*0073*	*0997*	*2 PWC JT15D-1*	*5216*		
☐ N3AV	IAI 1124A Westwind II	*361*	*N610HC*	*0081*	*1090*	*2 GA TFE731-3-1G*	*10659*		
☐ N60AV	IAI 1124 Westwind I	*254*	*N72HB*	*0079*	*0594*	*2 GA TFE731-3-1G*	*10659*		
☐ N53DF	Canadair CL-601-3A (CL-600-2B16) Challen.	*5078*	*N601MD*	*0090*	*0694*	*2 GE CF34-3A*	*19550*		*lsf Sierra Land Group Inc.*
☐ N451CS	GAC (Grumman) G-1159B Gulfstream IIB	*070*	*N165A*	*0069*	*0196*	*2 RR Spey 511-8*	*31615*		*lsf 5161 Corp. / cvtd G-1159*
☐ N62K	GAC (Grumman) G-1159 Gulfstream II	*093*	*N215GA*	*0070*	*0897*	*2 RR Spey 511-8*	*29393*		*lsf Boxing Cat Prod. Inc. / tbr N484TL*
☐ N663PD	GAC (Grumman) G-1159B Gulfstream IIB	*139*	*N2UJ*	*0073*	*0393*	*2 RR Spey 511-8*	*31615*		*lsf Paul Davril Inc. / cvtd G-1159*
☐ N812RS	GAC (Grumman) G-1159B Gulfstream IIB	*098*	*N198AV*	*0071*	*1195*	*2 RR Spey 511-8*	*31615*		*lsf Rastar Holdings Llc / cvtd G-1159*
☐ N500WW	GAC G-1159A Gulfstream III	*318*	*N150RK*	*0080*	*0595*	*2 RR Spey 511-8*	*30935*		*lsf Winged Wolf Inc.*
☐ N555KC	GAC G-1159A Gulfstream III	*366*	*N333KC*	*0082*	*0891*	*2 RR Spey 511-8*	*30935*		*lsf Odin Aviation Inc.*

AVLINE LEASING, Corp. = (AVLI) — Sarasota, FL

806 Sarasota Quay, Sarasota, FL 34236, USA ☎ (941) 366-9171 Tx: none Fax: (941) 955-1889 SITA: n/a
F: 1986 ⁂ 7 Head: John A. Timmins Net: n/a New and used aircraft leasing, sales and financing company.
Owner / lessor of following (main) aircraft types: DHC-8-100 & Metro II & Metro III. Aircraft leased from AVLI are listed and mentioned as such under the leasing carriers.

BAAN AIRE (Cheryl Baanhofman dba) — Lamar-Municipal, CO

3652 County Road, GG.2, Lamar, CO 81052, USA ☎ (719) 336-7701 Tx: none Fax: (719) 336-7702 SITA: n/a
F: 1965 ⁂ n/a Head: Cheryl Baanhofman Net: n/a Aircraft below MTOW 1361kg: Cessna 172

☐ N71516	Cessna TU206F Turbo Stationair	*U20602150*		*0073*	*0791*	*1 CO TSIO-520-C*	*1633*		
☐ N3030K	Piper PA-34-200T Seneca II	*34-7970103*		*0079*	*0891*	*2 CO TSIO-360-EB*	*2073*		

BABCOCK & BROWN AIRCRAFT MANAGEMENT, Inc. = (BBAM) (Subsidiary of Babcock & Brown, Inc.) — San Francisco, CA

2 Harrison Street, San Francisco, CA 94105, USA ☎ (650) 512-1515 Tx: none Fax: (650) 267-1500 SITA: n/a
F: n/a ⁂ n/a Head: Steve Zissis Net: n/a New and used aircraft leasing, sales and financing company.
Owner / lessor of following (main) aircraft types: Airbus Ind. A300B4, Boeing 737-300/400/500, 747-200, 757 & 767-300. Aircraft leased from BBAM are listed and mentioned as such under the leasing carriers.

BAJ AIRCRAFT (Baj Aircraft Management Group, Inc. dba) — Jackson-County/Reynolds Field, MI

850 Airport Road, Hangar 104, Jackson, MI 49202, USA ☎ (734) 783-1028 Tx: none Fax: (734) 782-9355 SITA: n/a
F: 1995 ⁂ n/a Head: Michael F. Layton Net: n/a

☐ N234L	Beech C-45G (18)	*AF-447*	*N9632C*	*0052*	*1295*	*2 PW R-985-AN14B*	*3969*	*Freighter*	

BAKER AVIATION, Inc. = 8Q / BAJ — Kotzebue-Ralph Wien Memorial, AK

PO Box 708, Kotzebue, AK 99752, USA ☎ (907) 442-3108 Tx: none Fax: (907) 442-2745 SITA: n/a
F: 1964 ⁂ 12 Head: Marjorie Baker ICAO: BAKER AVIATION Net: n/a

☐ N5293X	Cessna U206G Stationair 6 II	*U20605612*		*0080*	*0590*	*1 CO IO-520-F*	*1633*		*lsf pvt*
☐ N6908M	Cessna 207A Stationair 8 II	*20700672*		*0080*	*0681*	*1 CO IO-520-F*	*1724*		
☐ N9942M	Cessna 207A Stationair 8 II	*20700756*		*0082*	*0982*	*1 CO IO-520-F*	*1724*		
☐ N3246M	Cessna 402C II	*402C0294*		*0080*	*0494*	*2 CO TSIO-520-VB*	*3107*		
☐ N9642F	Cessna 208 Caravan I	*20800110*		*0086*	*0596*	*1 PWC PT6A-114*	*3629*		*lsf Avion Capital Corp.*
☐ N9820F	Cessna 208B Grand Caravan	*208B0410*		*0093*	*0396*	*1 PWC PT6A-114A*	*3969*		*lsf Richeson Eugene Trustee*
☐ N380M	Beech King Air A90 (65-A90)	*LJ-218*	*N360M*	*0067*	*0895*	*2 PWC PT6A-20*	*4218*		
☐ N45PE	Beech King Air C90	*LJ-830*	*N45PK*	*0079*	*0497*	*2 PWC PT6A-21*	*4377*		*lsf pvt*

BALD MOUNTAIN AVIATION (Gary D. Porter dba / Seasonal May-October ops only) — Homer-Belgua Lake SPB, AK

PO Box 3134, Homer, AK 99603, USA ☎ (907) 235-7969 Tx: none Fax: (907) 235-6602 SITA: n/a
F: 1993 ⁂ n/a Head: Gary D. Porter Net: n/a

☐ N102SY	De Havilland DHC-2 Beaver I	*1367*	*58-2035*	*0052*	*0494*	*1 PW R-985*	*2309*		*Floats*
☐ N103SY	De Havilland DHC-3 Otter	*296*	*C-FFIJ*	*0058*	*0697*	*1 PW R-1340*	*3629*		*Floats*

BA LEASING & Capital, Corp. = (BALG) (managed by Bank of America Leasing & Capital Group) — San Francisco, CA

555 California Street, 4th Floor, San Francisco, CA 94104, USA ☎ (415) 765-7300 Tx: none Fax: (415) 765-7343 SITA: n/a
F: 1992 ⁂ n/a Head: Richard V. Harris Net: n/a New and used aircraft leasing, sales and financing company.
Owner / Lessor of following (main) aircraft types: Airbus Industrie A300/310/320/340, ATR 42, BAe 146-200 & Jetstream, Boeing 727-200/737-200,-300,-400,-500/747-200F,-300,-400/757/767-200,-300/777, DC-8-73F, DC-10-30, MD-11/-11F, MD-82/83/87/77, Canadair RJ, Dornier 328, Embraer 120, Saab 340, Short 360 & an assortment of corporate aircraft. Aircraft leased from BA Leasing are listed and mentioned as lsf BALG under the leasing carriers.

BALLARDS FLYING SERVICE = EMD (Eaglemed) (Ballard Aviation, Inc. dba) — Wichita-Mid Continent, KS

2120 South Airport Road, Wichita, KS 67209, USA ☎ (316) 946-4855 Tx: none Fax: (316) 946-4853 SITA: n/a
F: 1977 ⁂ n/a Head: Jimmy E. Ballard ICAO: EAGLEMED Net: n/a EMS flights are operated under the marketing name EAGLEMED (same headquarters).

☐ N116HA	Cessna 414A Chancellor III	*414A0501*		*0080*	*1195*	*2 CO TSIO-520-NB*	*3062*	*EMS*	
☐ N777KU	Beech King Air B90	*LJ-377*	*N8473N*	*0068*	*0895*	*2 PWC PT6A-20*	*4377*	*EMS*	
☐ N887KU	Beech King Air B90	*LJ-357*	*N887K*	*0068*	*0786*	*2 PWC PT6A-20*	*4377*	*EMS*	

BALTIA AIR LINES, Inc. = BTL — New York-JFK, NY

63-25 Saunders Street, Suite 7-1, Rego Park, NY 11374, USA ☎ (718) 553-6636 Tx: none Fax: (718) 275-4731 SITA: n/a
F: 1989 ⁂ n/a Head: Igor Dmitrowsky ICAO: BALTIA FLIGHT Net: n/a Presently being set-up. Intends to start operations during 1999 with 1 Boeing 747 aircraft.

BALTIMORE AIR TRANSPORT, Inc. - BAT — Baltimore-Martin State, MD

201 Ballard Avenue, Baltimore, MD 21220, USA ☎ (443) 687-3801 Tx: none Fax: (443) 687-0263 SITA: n/a
F: 1995 ⁂ n/a Head: Govind Madhiraju Net: n/a

☐ N208BA	Cessna 208B Grand Caravan	*208B0494*		*0095*	*0196*	*1 PWC PT6A-114A*	*3969*	*Freighter*	

BANC ONE SERVICES, Corp. = BNS (formerly Bancstar) — Phoenix-Deer Valley Municipal, AZ

PO Box 71, Phoenix, AZ 85001, USA ☎ (520) 589-3977 Tx: none Fax: (520) 589-3365 SITA: n/a
F: 1984 ⁂ n/a Head: Thomas D. Janes ICAO: BANCSTAR Net: n/a

☐ N170VB	Cessna 402C III	*402C0808*	*N1235B*	*0084*	*1184*	*2 CO TSIO-520-VB*	*3107*		
☐ N171VB	Cessna 402C III	*402C1001*	*N1235F*	*0085*	*1186*	*2 CO TSIO-520-VB*	*3107*		
☐ N172VB	Cessna 402C III	*402C1014*		*0085*	*1085*	*2 CO TSIO-520-VB*	*3107*		
☐ N173VB	Cessna 402C III	*402C1003*		*0085*	*0386*	*2 CO TSIO-520-VB*	*3107*		

284 registration type of aircraft *cn/fn ex/ex* mfd del powered by mtow kg configuration selcal name/fln/specialitites/remarks*

☐ N174VB	Cessna 402C III	402C0809	N1235C	0084	1090	2 CO TSIO-520-VB	3107			
☐ N175VB	Cessna 550 Citation II	550-0202	N10CF	0080	0393	2 PWC JT15D-4	6033			

B & C AVIATION, Co. Inc. (Aviation Services Corporation dba) **Nashville-Int'l, TN**

Hangar 7, Hangar Lane, Nashville, TN 37217, USA ☎ (931) 361-3000 Tx: none Fax: (931) 360-7174 SITA: n/a
F: 1973 n/a Head: Thomas F. Cone Net: n/a

☐ N207SB	Beech King Air 100	B-69	N2SC	0071	0390	2 PWC PT6A-28	4808			
☐ N117AE	Learjet 24E	24E-346	N117AJ	0077	0996	2 GE CJ610-6	5851			lsf Averitt Inc.
☐ N124MA	Learjet 25B	25B-118	N118SE	0073	1190	2 GE CJ610-6	6804			
☐ N41TC	Learjet 25D	25D-346	N300WG	0081	1294	2 GE CJ610-8A	6804			

BANKAIR, Inc. = B4 / BKA **Columbia-Metropolitan, SC**

2406 Edmund Road, West Columbia, SC 29169, USA ☎ (843) 822-8832 Tx: none Fax: (843) 822-8775 SITA: n/a
F: 1973 75 Head: John E. Dickerson ICAO: BANKAIR Net: n/a

☐ N8564E	Piper PA-32-300 Cherokee SIX	32-7640072		0076	0984	1 LY IO-540-K1A5	1542	Freighter		
☐ N204CB	Piper PA-34-200 Seneca	34-7450078		0074	0589	2 LY IO-360-C1E6	1905	Freighter		
☐ N345AC	Piper PA-34-200T Seneca II	34-7870087		0078	0595	2 CO TSIO-360-E	2073	Freighter		lsf Dickerson Associates
☐ N55443	Piper PA-34-200 Seneca	34-7350216		0073	0486	2 LY IO-360-C1E6	1905	Freighter		
☐ N8076N	Piper PA-34-200T Seneca II	34-7970487		0079	1095	2 CO TSIO-360-EB	2073	Freighter		lsf Dickerson Associates
☐ N8313C	Piper PA-34-200T Seneca II	34-7570226		0075	1294	2 CO TSIO-360-E	2073	Freighter		lsf Dickerson Associates
☐ N402NQ	Cessna 402C II	402C0093		0079	1185	2 CO TSIO-520-VB	3107	Freighter		
☐ N4630N	Cessna 402C II	402C0001		0078	1281	2 CO TSIO-520-VB	3107	Freighter		lsf Dickerson Associates
☐ N5073Q	Cessna 402B	402B0348		0073	0388	2 CO TSIO-520-E	2858	Freighter		
☐ N67909	Cessna 402C II	402C0449		0081	0783	2 CO TSIO-520-VB	3107	Freighter		
☐ N401EX	Cessna 404 Titan II	404-0403		0079	0685	2 CO GTSIO-520-M	3810	Freighter		
☐ N102BG	Mitsubishi MU-2B-60 Marquise	748SA	N945MA	0080	0889	2 GA TPE331-10-501M	5250	Freighter		
☐ N174MA	Mitsubishi MU-2B-60 Marquise	753SA	N100BY	0079	1192	2 GA TPE331-10-501M	5250	Freighter		lsf Dickerson Associates
☐ N1VY	Mitsubishi MU-2J (MU-2B-35)	567	N1VN	0072	0991	2 GA TPE331-6-251M	4899	Freighter		lsf Dickerson Associates
☐ N21CJ	Mitsubishi MU-2B-60 Marquise	789SA	N278MA	0080	0891	2 GA TPE331-10-501M	5250	Freighter		
☐ N44KU	Mitsubishi MU-2J (MU-2B-35)	647	N44KS	0074	0189	2 GA TPE331-6-251M	4899	Freighter		
☐ N610CA	Mitsubishi MU-2B-60 Marquise	788SA	N277MA	0080	0396	2 GA TPE331-10-501M	5250	Freighter		lsf Dickerson Associates
☐ N637WG	Mitsubishi MU-2J (MU-2B-35)	637	N951MS	0074	0294	2 GA TPE331-6-251M	4899	Freighter		lsf Dickerson Associates
☐ N823MA	Mitsubishi MU-2L (MU-2B-36)	663	YV-409P	0075	1286	2 GA TPE331-6-251M	5250	Freighter		lsf Dickerson Associates
☐ N856JC	Mitsubishi MU-2B-40 Soltaire	430SA	N170MA	0080	0788	2 GA TPE331-10-501M	4749	Freighter		
☐ N920S	Mitsubishi MU-2G (MU-2B-30)	534	N882MA	0070	0285	2 GA TPE331-1-151A	4900	Freighter		
☐ N942ST	Mitsubishi MU-2B-60 Marquise	745SA	N942MA	0079	0293	2 GA TPE331-10-501M	5250	Freighter		
☐ N33PT	Learjet 25D	25D-240	N83EA	0078	1296	2 GE CJ610-8A	6804	Freighter		
☐ N58HC	Learjet 25D	25D-341	XA-SAE	0078	1296	2 GE CJ610-8A	6804	Freighter		
☐ N88BY	Learjet 25B	25B-168	N88BT	0074	0191	2 GE CJ610-6	6804	Freighter		lsf Dickerson Associates
☐ N135AG	Learjet 35A	35A-132	N37TJ	0077	1196	2 GA TFE731-2-2B	8301	Freighter		lsf Dickerson Associates
☐ N369BA	Learjet 35A	35A-312	LV-OFV	0080	0996	2 GA TFE731-2-2B	8301	Freighter		lsf Dickerson Associates
☐ N399BA	Learjet 35A	35A-371	LV-ALF	0081	0896	2 GA TFE731-2-2B	8301	Freighter		
☐ N465NW	Learjet 35A	35A-465		0082	0591	2 GA TFE731-2-2B	8301	Freighter		lsf Dickerson Associates
☐ N500ED	Learjet 35A	35A-241	N500EX	0079	1296	2 GA TFE731-2-2B	8301	Freighter		lsf Dickerson Associates
☐ N67PA	Learjet 35A	35A-208	N39DK	0079	0896	2 GA TFE731-2-2B	8301	Freighter		lsf Dickerson Associates
☐ N86BE	Learjet 35A	35A-194	N86BL	0078	0392	2 GA TFE731-2-2B	8301	Freighter		lsf Dickerson Associates

BANNOCK LIFE FLIGHT (Bannock Regional Medical Center dba) **Pocatello-Bannock Medical Center Heliport, ID**

651 Memorial Drive, Pocatello, ID 83201, USA ☎ (208) 239-1000 Tx: none Fax: (208) 239-1938 SITA: n/a
F: 1986 n/a Head: Fred Eaton Net: n/a

☐ N93LF	Eurocopter (MBB) BO105LS-A3	2038	N3108K	0091	0394	2 AN 250-C28C	2600	EMS		

BARKEN INTERNATIONAL, Inc. = BKJ **Salt Lake City-Int'l, UT**

PO Box 22360 AMF, Salt Lake City, UT 84122, USA ☎ (801) 539-7700 Tx: none Fax: (801) 596-8741 SITA: n/a
F: 1974 48 Head: Barbara W. Hepner ICAO: BARKEN JET Net: n/a Aircraft below MTOW 1361 kg: Cessna 182.

☐ N2030D	Piper PA-31-350 Navajo Chieftain	31-7952045		0079	0296	2 LY TIO-540-J2BD	3175			lsf Barken Int'l of NC Inc.
☐ N4089Y	Piper PA-31-350 Navajo Chieftain	31-8152101		0081	1193	2 LY TIO-540-J2BD	3175			lsf pvt
☐ N132BK	Mitsubishi MU-2B-60 Marquise	1529SA	N818R	0081	1188	2 GA TPE331-10-501M	5250	EMS		
☐ N152BK	Mitsubishi MU-2B-60 Marquise	1537SA	OY-BHY	0082	0590	2 GA TPE331-10-501M	5250	EMS		
☐ N290SJ	Beech King Air 200	BB-290		0077	0297	2 PWC PT6A-41	5670			lsf Legacy Leasing of NC
☐ N8534W	Beech King Air 200	BB-225	I-PIAO	0077	0291	2 PWC PT6A-41	5670			
☐ N252BK	Learjet 25B	25B-107	N25NB	0073	0986	2 GE CJ610-6	6804			lsf pvt
☐ N45BK	Learjet 25	25-036	N15M	0069	0289	2 GE CJ610-6	6804			
☐ N77NR	Learjet 35A	35A-503	N8567A	0084	1096	2 GA TFE731-2-2B	8301			lsf pvt
☐ N1124G	IAI 1124 Westwind	216	N216SC	0077	0496	2 GA TFE731-3-1G	10659			lsf Barken Int'l of NC Inc.
☐ N46BK	IAI 1124 Westwind	214	N24RH	0077	1296	2 GA TFE731-3-1G	10659			lsf Barken Int'l of NC Inc.
☐ N277T	GAC (Grumman) G-1159 Gulfstream II (SP)	209	N806GA	0077	1095	2 RR Spey 511-8	29710			lsf Arrow Plane / cvtd II

BARON AVIATION SERVICES, Inc. = BVN **Rolla-Vichy, MO**

PO Box 518, Vichy, MO 65580, USA ☎ (573) 299-4744 Tx: none Fax: (573) 299-4272 SITA: n/a
F: 1973 n/a Head: Charles E. Schmidt ICAO: SHOW-ME Net: n/a

☐ N832FE	Cessna 208A Caravan I Cargomaster	20800081		0086	0286	1 PWC PT6A-114	3629	Freighter		lsf/opf FDX in FedEx Feeder-colors
☐ N702FX	Cessna 208B Caravan I Super Cargomaster	208B0422		0095	0295	1 PWC PT6A-114A	3969	Freighter		lsf/opf FDX in FedEx Feeder-colors
☐ N718FX	Cessna 208B Caravan I Super Cargomaster	208B0448		0095	0695	1 PWC PT6A-114A	3969	Freighter		lsf/opf FDX in FedEx Feeder colors
☐ N719FX	Cessna 208B Caravan I Super Cargomaster	208B0450		0095	0695	1 PWC PT6A-114A	3969	Freighter		lsf/opf FDX in FedEx Feeder-colors
☐ N723FX	Cessna 208B Caravan I Super Cargomaster	208B0456		0095	0895	1 PWC PT6A-114A	3969	Freighter		lsf/opf FDX in FedEx Feeder-colors
☐ N738FX	Cessna 208B Caravan I Super Cargomaster	208B0482		0095	1195	1 PWC PT6A-114A	3969	Freighter		lsf/opf FDX in FedEx Feeder-colors
☐ N741FX	Cessna 208B Caravan I Super Cargomaster	208B0486		0095	1195	1 PWC PT6A-114A	3969	Freighter		lsf/opf FDX in FedEx Feeder-colors
☐ N745FX	Cessna 208B Caravan I Super Cargomaster	208B0495		0095	1295	1 PWC PT6A-114A	3969	Freighter		lsf/opf FDX in FedEx Feeder-colors
☐ N749FE	Cessna 208B Caravan I Super Cargomaster	208B0242		0090	1290	1 PWC PT6A-114A	3969	Freighter		lsf/opf FDX in FedEx Feeder-colors
☐ N751FX	Cessna 208B Caravan I Super Cargomaster	208B0514		0096	0296	1 PWC PT6A-114A	3969	Freighter		lsf/opf FDX in FedEx Feeder-colors
☐ N753FX	Cessna 208B Caravan I Super Cargomaster	208B0520		0096	0396	1 PWC PT6A-114A	3969	Freighter		lsf/opf FDX in FedEx Feeder-colors
☐ N756FE	Cessna 208B Caravan I Super Cargomaster	208B0251		0091	0191	1 PWC PT6A-114A	3969	Freighter		lsf/opf FDX in FedEx Feeder-colors
☐ N765FE	Cessna 208B Caravan I Super Cargomaster	208B0259		0091	0391	1 PWC PT6A-114A	3969	Freighter		lsf/opf FDX in FedEx Feeder-colors
☐ N770FE	Cessna 208B Caravan I Super Cargomaster	208B0265		0091	0591	1 PWC PT6A-114A	3969	Freighter		lsf/opf FDX in FedEx Feeder-colors
☐ N773FE	Cessna 208B Caravan I Super Cargomaster	208B0269		0091	0691	1 PWC PT6A-114A	3969	Freighter		lsf/opf FDX in FedEx Feeder-colors
☐ N774FE	Cessna 208B Caravan I Super Cargomaster	208B0271		0091	0691	1 PWC PT6A-114A	3969	Freighter		lsf/opf FDX in FedEx Feeder-colors
☐ N786FE	Cessna 208B Caravan I Super Cargomaster	208B0284		0091	1091	1 PWC PT6A-114A	3969	Freighter		lsf/opf FDX in FedEx Feeder-colors
☐ N793FE	Cessna 208B Caravan I Super Cargomaster	208B0291		0091	1291	1 PWC PT6A-114A	3969	Freighter		lsf/opf FDX in FedEx Feeder-colors
☐ N841FE	Cessna 208B Caravan I Super Cargomaster	208B0144		0089	0189	1 PWC PT6A-114	3969	Freighter		lsf/opf FDX in FedEx Feeder-colors
☐ N845FE	Cessna 208B Caravan I Super Cargomaster	208B0152		0089	0289	1 PWC PT6A-114	3969	Freighter		lsf/opf FDX in FedEx Feeder-colors
☐ N861FE	Cessna 208B Caravan I Super Cargomaster	208B0183		0089	0889	1 PWC PT6A-114	3969	Freighter		lsf/opf FDX in FedEx Feeder-colors
☐ N866FE	Cessna 208B Caravan I Super Cargomaster	208B0189		0089	0989	1 PWC PT6A-114	3969	Freighter		lsf/opf FDX in FedEx Feeder-colors
☐ N889FE	Cessna 208B Caravan I Super Cargomaster	208B0218		0090	0590	1 PWC PT6A-114	3969	Freighter		lsf/opf FDX in FedEx Feeder-colors
☐ N894FE	Cessna 208B Caravan I Super Cargomaster	208B0224		0090	0790	1 PWC PT6A-114	3969	Freighter		lsf/opf FDX in FedEx Feeder-colors
☐ N900FE	Cessna 208B Caravan I Super Cargomaster	208B0054	SE-KLX	0087	1187	1 PWC PT6A-114	3969	Freighter		lsf/opf FDX in FedEx Feeder-colors
☐ N902FE	Cessna 208B Caravan I Super Cargomaster	208B0002		0086	1086	1 PWC PT6A-114	3969	Freighter		lsf/opf FDX in FedEx Feeder-colors
☐ N912FE	Cessna 208B Caravan I Super Cargomaster	208B0012		0087	0187	1 PWC PT6A-114	3969	Freighter		lsf/opf FDX in FedEx Feeder-colors
☐ N922FE	Cessna 208B Caravan I Super Cargomaster	208B0022		0087	0487	1 PWC PT6A-114	3969	Freighter		lsf/opf FDX in FedEx Feeder-colors
☐ N927FE	Cessna 208B Caravan I Super Cargomaster	208B0027		0087	0587	1 PWC PT6A-114	3969	Freighter		lsf/opf FDX in FedEx Feeder-colors
☐ N928FE	Cessna 208B Caravan I Super Cargomaster	208B0028		0087	0687	1 PWC PT6A-114	3969	Freighter		lsf/opf FDX in FedEx Feeder-colors
☐ N929FE	Cessna 208B Caravan I Super Cargomaster	208B0029		0087	0687	1 PWC PT6A-114	3969	Freighter		lsf/opf FDX in FedEx Feeder-colors
☐ N934FE	Cessna 208B Caravan I Super Cargomaster	208B0034		0087	0787	1 PWC PT6A-114	3969	Freighter		lsf/opf FDX in FedEx Feeder-colors
☐ N939FE	Cessna 208B Caravan I Super Cargomaster	208B0180		0089	0689	1 PWC PT6A-114	3969	Freighter		lsf/opf FDX in FedEx Feeder-colors
☐ N944FE	Cessna 208B Caravan I Super Cargomaster	208B0044		0087	1087	1 PWC PT6A-114	3969	Freighter		lsf/opf FDX in FedEx Feeder-colors
☐ N950FE	Cessna 208B Caravan I Super Cargomaster	208B0056		0087	1187	1 PWC PT6A-114	3969	Freighter		lsf/opf FDX in FedEx Feeder-colors
☐ N957FE	Cessna 208B Caravan I Super Cargomaster	208B0070		0087	0188	1 PWC PT6A-114	3969	Freighter		lsf/opf FDX in FedEx Feeder-colors
☐ N961FE	Cessna 208B Caravan I Super Cargomaster	208B0077		0088	0388	1 PWC PT6A-114	3969	Freighter		lsf/opf FDX in FedEx Feeder-colors
☐ N970FE	Cessna 208B Caravan I Super Cargomaster	208B0093		0088	0588	1 PWC PT6A-114	3969	Freighter		lsf/opf FDX in FedEx Feeder-colors
☐ N978FE	Cessna 208B Caravan I Super Cargomaster	208B0105		0088	0788	1 PWC PT6A-114	3969	Freighter		lsf/opf FDX in FedEx Feeder-colors
☐ N994FE	Cessna 208B Caravan I Super Cargomaster	208B0132		0088	1188	1 PWC PT6A-114	3969	Freighter		lsf/opf FDX in FedEx Feeder-colors

BASIN AVIATION (West Texas Gas, Inc. dba) **Midland-Airpark, TX**

PO Box 50547, Midland, TX 79710, USA ☎ (915) 685-7000 Tx: none Fax: (915) 683-8851 SITA: n/a
F: 1977 n/a Head: David L. Davis Net: n/a

☐ N340BA	Cessna 340A II	340A0283	N4110G	0077	0688	2 CO TSIO-520-N	2717			
☐ N421WT	Cessna 421C Golden Eagle III	421C0620	N88633	0078	0790	2 CO GTSIO-520-L	3379			
☐ N9RZ	Cessna 421C Golden Eagle II	421C0236		0076	0696	2 CO GTSIO-520-L	3379			lsf pvt
☐ N48CR	Beech King Air 200	BB-599		0080	0495	2 PWC PT6A-41	5670			

285 registration type of aircraft cn/fn ex/EX* mfd del powered by mtow kg configuration selcal name/fln/specialitites/remarks

BASLER AIRLINES = BFC (Basler Turbo Conversions, Llc dba) — **Oshkosh-Wittman Regional, WI**

PO Box 2305, Oshkosh, WI 54903-2305, USA ☎ (920) 236-7827 Tx: none Fax: (920) 236-7833 SITA: n/a
F: 1956 ⁂ 35 Head: Roderick L. McNeal ICAO: BASLER Net: n/a

☐ N11EC	Beech Baron 58	TH-128		0071	0779	2 CO IO-520-C	2449	5 Pax		
☐ N21BF	Boeing (Douglas) DC-3C (C-47A-40-DL)	9832	CAF 12938	0043	0192	2 PW R-1830	12202	Freighter		
☐ N400BF	Boeing (Douglas) DC-3C (C-47A-25-DL)	9415	CAF 12937	0043	0392	2 PW R-1830	12202	Freighter		
☐ N300BF	USAC Turbo Express DC-3C	26744	N300TX	0044	1087	2 PWC PT6A-45R	12202	Freighter		cvtd Douglas C-47B-15-DK

BATES AVIATION (Bates & Associates, Inc. dba) — **Bainbridge-Decatur County Industrial Airpark, GA**

210 Airport Road, Bainbridge, GA 31717, USA ☎ (912) 246-6338 Tx: none Fax: (912) 246-8596 SITA: n/a
F: 1993 ⁂ n/a Head: Karl P. Young Net: n/a

☐ N851MK	Beech King Air 200	BB-674	N351MK	0080	0696	2 PWC PT6A-41	5670			

BATTLE CREEK AVIATION, Inc. — **Battle Creek-W.K. Kellogg, MI**

3300 6th Avenue, Battle Creek, MI 49015, USA ☎ (616) 963-9363 Tx: none Fax: (616) 962-3883 SITA: n/a
F: 1991 ⁂ n/a Head: Gilbert A. Collver Net: n/a

☐ N27FN	Piper PA-44-180 Seminole	44-7995110	N270FN	0079		2 LY 0-360-E1AD	1724			lsf Flying N Inc.
☐ N93DC	Piper PA-31-310 Navajo C	31-7712017		0077	0396	2 LY TIO-540-A2C	2948			

BATTLES AVIATION (Richard Battles dba) — **Paris-Henry County, TN**

1949 Diggs Road, Paris, TN 38242, USA ☎ (901) 642-7676 Tx: none Fax: (901) 641-0368 SITA: n/a
F: 1988 ⁂ n/a Head: Richard Battles Net: n/a Aircraft below MTOW 1361kg: Cessna 172

☐ N6792Y	Piper PA-23-250 Aztec D	27-4130		0069	0290	2 LY IO-540-C4B5	2359			

BAUDETTE FLYING SERVICE, Inc. (formerly Bernhardt Flying Service) — **Baudette-Bernhardt SPB, MN**

Route 1, Box 171, Baudette, MN 56623, USA ☎ (218) 634-1040 Tx: none Fax: (218) 634-1216 SITA: n/a
F: 1965 ⁂ n/a Head: Kirk Erickson Net: n/a

☐ N714MX	Cessna A185F Skywagon II	18504404		0083	0984	1 CO IO-520-D	1520			Floats / Wheel-Skis
☐ N9028	De Havilland DHC-2 Beaver I	803	54-1672	0054	1286	1 PW R-985	2313			Floats / Wheel-Skis

BAX GLOBAL, Inc. – Transportation and Logistics Worldwide = 8W (Subsidiary of Pittston Co./formerly Burlington Air Express, Inc.) — **Toledo-Express, OH**

Air Operations, 1 Aircargo Parkway East, Swanton, OH 43558, USA ☎ (419) 867-9911 Tx: none Fax: (419) 867-0138 SITA: n/a
F: 1972 ⁂ 5100 Head: Joseph Farrell Net: http://www.baxworld.com/
Airfreight forwarder with own aircraft, which are all contracted out and operated on behalf of BAX Global (in such colours & titles) by: Air Transport International, Amerijet & American International.

☐ N6806	Boeing 727-223 (F)	19481 / 548	N719CK	0468	0898	3 PW JT8D-9 (HK3/FDX)	80966	Freighter		lsf/opb KHA / cvtd -223
☐ N6816	Boeing 727-223 (F)	19491 / 611		0768	0396	3 PW JT8D-9 (HK3/FDX)	80966	Freighter		lsf/opb KHA / cvtd -223
☐ N6831	Boeing 727-223 (F)	20184 / 707		0469	0995	3 PW JT8D-9	80966	Freighter		lsf/opb KHA / cvtd -223
☐ N858AA	Boeing 727-223 (F) (A)	21085 / 1200		0476	0498	3 PW JT8D-9A (HK3/FDX)	80966	Freighter		lsf/opb KHA / cvtd -223
☐ N820BX	Boeing (Douglas) DC-8-71F	46065 / 460	N8098U	0069	0293	4 CFMI CFM56-2C	147418	Freighter		lsf GECA/sub-lst/opb ATN/cvtd -61/-71
☐ N821BX	Boeing (Douglas) DC-8-71F	45811 / 262	N8071U	0067	0293	4 CFMI CFM56-2C	147418	Freighter		lsf GECA/sub-lst/opb ATN/cvtd -61/-71
☐ N822BX	Boeing (Douglas) DC-8-71F	45813 / 284	N8073U	0067	0293	4 CFMI CFM56-2C	147418	Freighter	EF-DM	lsf GECA/sub-lst/opb ATN/cvtd -61/-71
☐ N823BX	Boeing (Douglas) DC-8-71F	46064 / 459	N8097U	0069	0293	4 CFMI CFM56-2C	147418	Freighter		lsf GECA/sub-lst/opb ATN/cvtd -61/-71
☐ N824BX	Boeing (Douglas) DC-8-71F	45946 / 339	N8078U	0068	0293	4 CFMI CFM56-2C	147418	Freighter		lsf GECA/sub-lst/opb ATN/cvtd -61/-71
☐ N825BX	Boeing (Douglas) DC-8-71F	45978 / 381	N8088U	0068	0693	4 CFMI CFM56-2C	147418	Freighter		lsf GECA/sub-lst/opb ATN/cvtd -61/-71
☐ N826BX	Boeing (Douglas) DC-8-71F	45998 / 399	N8094U	0068	0793	4 CFMI CFM56-2C	147418	Freighter		lsf GECA/sub-lst/opb ATN/cvtd -61/-71
☐ N827BX	Boeing (Douglas) DC-8-71F	45971 / 356	SE-DLM	0068	1193	4 CFMI CFM56-2C	148900	Freighter		lsf GECA/sub-lst/opb ATN/cvtd -61/-71
☐ N828BX	Boeing (Douglas) DC-8-71F	45993 / 382	N8089U	0068	1193	4 CFMI CFM56-2C	147418	Freighter		lsf GECA/sub-lst/opb ATN/cvtd -61/-71
☐ N829BX	Boeing (Douglas) DC-8-71F	45994 / 387	N501SR	0068	1194	4 CFMI CFM56-2C	147418	Freighter		lsf GECA/sub-lst/opb ATN/cvtd -61/-71
☐ N830BX	Boeing (Douglas) DC-8-71F	45973 / 358	N783UP	0068	0796	4 CFMI CFM56-2C	147418	Freighter		lsf GECA/sub-lst/opb ATN/cvtd -61/-71
☐ N799AL	Boeing (Douglas) DC-8-62F	45922 / 335	RTAF 60-112	0068	0798	4 PW JT3D-7 (HK3/BAC)	151953	Freighter		lsf/opb ATN / cvtd (CF)
☐ N781AL	Boeing (Douglas) DC-8-63F	45926 / 323	C-FCPO	0067	0495	4 PW JT3D-7 (HK3/BAC)	161025	Freighter		lsf/opb CKS/cvtd -63
☐ N784AL	Boeing (Douglas) DC-8-63F	46135 / 531	TU-TCF	0070	1197	4 PW JT3D-7 (HK3/BAC)	161025	Freighter		lsf/opb CKX / cvtd (CF)
☐ N867BX	Boeing (Douglas) DC-8-63F	46049 / 479	TF-FLC	0069	0787	4 PW JT3D-7 (HK3/BAC)	161025	Freighter		lst/opb ATN / cvtd (CF)
☐ N868BX	Boeing (Douglas) DC-8-63F	46034 / 434	C-FTIL	0069	0186	4 PW JT3D-7 (HK3/BAC)	161025	Freighter		lst/opb ATN/cvtd -63
☐ N869BX	Boeing (Douglas) DC-8-63F	46035 / 438	C-FTIM	0069	0186	4 PW JT3D-7 (HK3/BAC)	161025	Freighter		lst/opb ATN/cvtd -63
☐ N870BX	Boeing (Douglas) DC-8-63F	46036 / 445	C-FTIN	0069	1285	4 PW JT3D-7 (HK3/BAC)	161025	Freighter		Carl Taccini / lst/opb ATN/cvtd -63

BAY AIR (Tom Schlagel dba) — **Dillingham & Shannons Pond SPB, AK**

PO Box 714, Dillingham, AK 99576, USA ☎ (907) 842-2570 Tx: none Fax: (907) 842-2470 SITA: n/a
F: 1991 ⁂ n/a Head: Tom Schlagel Net: n/a Aircraft below MTOW 1361kg: Piper PA-18

☐ N1701U	Cessna 207 Skywagon	20700301		0075	0396	1 CO IO-520-F	1724			
☐ N364RA	De Havilland DHC-2 Beaver I	364	N62300	0052	0794	1 PW R-985	2309			Floats

BAYER – Flight Dept. (Flight Dept. of Bayer Corporation) — **Elkhart-Municipal, IN**

PO Box 40, Elkhart, IN 46515, USA ☎ (219) 264-8866 Tx: none Fax: (219) 262-7095 SITA: n/a
F: 1995 ⁂ n/a Head: Michael Galen Net: n/a Operates non-commercial corporate flights for its parent company ((medicine producer) only.

☐ N1128M	Beech 1900C-1 Airliner	UC-139		0090	0795	2 PWC PT6A-65B	7530	Corporate		to be re-reg. N9331M
☐ N1125M	Learjet 55	55-065	N555GL	0082	0595	2 GA TFE731-3AR-2B	9752	Corporate		

BEAR AIR (Sherman W. Bear dba) — **Wasilla, AK**

PO Box 875493, Wasilla, AK 99687, USA ☎ (907) 373-3373 Tx: none Fax: none SITA: n/a
F: 1991 ⁂ n/a Head: Sherman W. Bear Net: n/a

☐ N8366Q	Cessna U206F Stationair II	U20603227		0076	0191	1 CO IO-520-F	1633			Floats / Wheel-Skis

BEAR AVIATION & HELICOPTERS (Charles Bella dba) — **El Paso-Int'l, TX**

4711 Atlas, El Paso, TX 79904, USA ☎ (915) 755-9667 Tx: none Fax: (915) 751-4711 SITA: n/a
F: 1975 ⁂ n/a Head: Charles Bella Net: n/a

☐ N341G	Eurocopter (Aerosp.) SA341G Gazelle	1056		0073	0892	1 TU Astazou IIIA	1800			
☐ N505KH	Eurocopter (Aerosp.) SA341G Gazelle	1239		0075	0386	1 TU Astazou IIIA	1800			
☐ N544PP	AAC (Ted Smith) Aerostar 601	61-0058-107	N7495S	0070	0788	2 LY IO-540-P1A5	2585			
☐ N410TH	Twin (Aero) Turbo Commander 680W	680W-1790-20	N5061E	0068	0391	2 GA TPE331-43BL	4264			

BEAR LAKE AIR SERVICE (Manufactured Homes of Alaska, Inc. dba) — **Seward, AK**

HCR64, Box 386, Seward, AK 99664, USA ☎ (907) 224-5725 Tx: none Fax: (907) 224-2283 SITA: n/a
F: 1990 ⁂ n/a Head: Joseph D. Stanton Net: n/a

☐ N70021	Cessna A185E Skywagon	18501896		0071	0192	1 CO IO-520-D	1520			Floats / Wheels

BEAVER AVIATION SERVICE, Inc. — **Beaver Falls-County, PA**

Beaver County Airport, Beaver Falls, PA 15010, USA ☎ (724) 843-8600 Tx: none Fax: (724) 843-6021 SITA: n/a
F: 1972 ⁂ n/a Head: Dale G. Rabassi Net: n/a

☐ N30101	Piper PA-44-180 Seminole	44-7995069		0079	1087	2 LY O-360-E1A6D	1724			
☐ N6026H	Piper PA-34-200T Seneca II	34-7870047		0078	0387	2 CO TSIO-360-E	2073			
☐ N59718	Piper PA-31-310 Navajo C	31-7612003		0076	1095	2 LY TIO-540-A2C	2948			
☐ N61410	Piper PA-31-310 Navajo B	31-7401233		0074	1196	2 LY TIO-540-A2C	2948			lsf Falcon Air Leasing Llp

BECKAIR, Co. Inc. — **Elkhart-Municipal, IN**

PO Box 1905, Elkhart, IN 46515, USA ☎ (219) 293-8805 Tx: none Fax: (219) 294-5628 SITA: n/a
F: 1978 ⁂ n/a Head: Roy L. Beck Net: n/a

☐ N68PC	Beech King Air C90	LJ-1007	N61254	0082	0286	2 PWC PT6A-21	4581			
☐ N218NB	Learjet 25D	25D-361		0083	0983	2 GE CJ610-8A	6804			

BELLAIR, Inc. = 7G — **Fairbanks-Int'l, AK**

PO Box 60311, Fairbanks, AK 99707, USA ☎ (907) 457-8359 Tx: none Fax: (907) 479-2239 SITA: n/a
F: 1980 ⁂ 10 Head: Karl M. Braun Net: n/a Aircraft below MTOW 1361kg: Cessna 172

☐ N1392H	Piper PA-32R-300 Lance	32R-7780156		0077	0996	1 LY IO-540-K1G5D	1633			

BELL ATLANTIC TRICON LEASING, Inc. = (BATL) (formerly National Funding, Corp. / Subsidiary of Bell Atlantic Capital, Inc.) — **Paramus, NJ**

95N Route 17 South, Paramus, NJ 07652, USA ☎ (973) 712-3300 Tx: n/a Fax: (973) 368-0491 SITA: n/a
F: n/a ⁂ n/a Head: Michael Foster Net: n/a New & used aircraft leasing, sales & financing company.
Owner / lessor of following (main) aircraft types: DC-8-73F, DHC-7, Dornier 228, MBB BK117, Saab SF340A & Swearingen SA227AC Metro III. Aircraft leased from BATL are listed and mentioned as such under the leasing carriers.

BELLSOUTH CORPORATE AVIATION & TRAVEL SERVICES, Inc. (Subsidiary/Flight Dept. of BellSouth Telecommunications, Inc.) — **Atlanta-Fulton County, GA**

Flight Dept., 4005 Fulton Industrial Blvd SW, Atlanta, GA 30336, USA ☎ (404) 699-8300 Tx: none Fax: (404) 699-8315 SITA: n/a
F: 1980 ⁂ n/a Head: James C. Lott Net: n/a Operates non-commerical corporate flights exclusively for the BellSouth-group of companies.

☐ N205SC	Cessna 550 Citation II	550-0156	N205SG	0080	1180	2 PWC JT15D-4	6033	Corporate		
☐ N404SB	Cessna 550 Citation II	550-0426	N1218F	0082	1282	2 PWC JT15D-4	6033			
☐ N404BS	Hawker 800XP	258294	N682H	0096	1196	2 GA TFE731-5BR-1H	12701	Corporate		
☐ N404CE	Hawker 800XP	258293	N670H	0096	1096	2 GA TFE731-5BR-1H	12701	Corporate		
☐ N404SS	Dornier 328-110	3090	D-CDYY*	0097	1097	2 PWC PW119B	13990	Corporate		
☐ N404R	Dassault Falcon 900	55	N495GA	0088	1193	3 GA TFE731-5AR-1C	20638	Corporate		

286 registration type of aircraft cn/fn ex/ex* mfd del powered by mtow kg configuration selcal name/fln/specialitites/remarks

BELUGA LAKE FLOATPLANE SERVICE (Jon M. Berryman dba / Seasonal April-October ops only) — Homer-Beluga Lake, AK

Box 2072, Homer, AK 99603, USA ☎ (907) 235-8256 Tx: none Fax: none SITA: n/a
F: 1980 ♁♁♁ n/a Head: Jon M. Berryman Net: n/a

	registration	type of aircraft	cn/fn	ex/ex*	mfd	del	powered by	mtow kg	configuration	name/fln/remarks
☐	N70212	Cessna A185E Skywagon	18502059		0072	0880	1 CO IO-520-D	1520		Floats
☐	N77BA	De Havilland DHC-2 Beaver I	1549	CF-WCA	0064	0684	1 PW R-985	2313		Floats

BEMIDJI AIRLINES = CH / BMJ (Air Direct Charter) (Bemidji Aviation Services, Inc. dba) — Bemidji-Beltrami County & Minneapolis-St.Paul Int'l, MN

Bemidji Airlines

PO Box 624, Bemidji, MN 56619-0624, USA ☎ (218) 751-1880 Tx: none Fax: (218) 759-3552 SITA: n/a
F: 1946 ♁♁♁ 50 Head: Larry A. Diffley IATA: 872 ICAO: BEMIDJI Net: n/a Aircraft below MTOW 1361 kg: Cessna 172
AIR DIRECT CHARTER is the trading name used for charter-services out of the Minneapolis-St. Paul Int'l-base (same fleet & headquarters).

	registration	type of aircraft	cn/fn	ex/ex*	mfd	del	powered by	mtow kg	configuration	name/fln/remarks
☐	N204RD	Piper PA-23-250 Aztec D	27-3994		0069	0685	2 LY IO-540-C4B5	2359	5 Pax	
☐	N6513Y	Piper PA-23-250 Aztec C	27-3804		0067	0985	2 LY IO-540-C4B5	2359	5 Pax	
☐	N6881Y	Piper PA-23-250 Aztec D	27-4230		0069	0885	2 LY IO-540-C4B5	2359	5 Pax	
☐	N4016A	Beech Baron 58	TH-9		0070	0484	2 CO IO-520-C	2449	5 Pax	
☐	N70DD	Beech Baron 58	TH-370		0073	0785	2 CO IO-520-C	2449	5 Pax	
☐	N5078E	Beech Queen Air 65	LF-76		0063	0696	2 LY IGSO-480-A1B6	3493	Freighter	cvtd U-8F
☐	N5078N	Beech Queen Air 65	LF-16		0060	0696	2 LY IGSO-480-A1B6	3493	Freighter	cvtd U-8F
☐	N5078U	Beech Queen Air 65	LF-32	62-3834	0062	0696	2 LY IGSO-480-A1B6	3493	Freighter	cvtd U-8F
☐	N5079E	Beech Queen Air 65	LF-52		0062	0696	2 LY IGSO-480-A1B6	3493	Freighter	cvtd U-8F
☐	N5080H	Beech Queen Air 65	LF-27		0061	0696	2 LY IGSO-480-A1B6	3493	Freighter	cvtd U-8F
☐	N5080L	Beech Queen Air 65	LF-59	62-3861	0062	0696	2 LY IGSO-480-A1B6	3493	Freighter	cvtd U-8F
☐	N103BA	Beech Excalibur Queenaire 8800	LD-435	N103EE	0071	1081	2 LY IO-720-A1B	3992	Freighter	cvtd Queen Air 65-B80
☐	N106BA	Beech Excalibur Queenaire 8800	LD-409	N1338T	0069	0184	2 LY IO-720-A1B	3992	Freighter	cvtd Queen Air 65-B80
☐	N107BA	Beech Excalibur Queenaire 8800	LD-358	N7838L	0067	0283	2 LY IO-720-A1B	3992	Freighter	cvtd Queen Air 65-B80
☐	N110BA	Beech Excalibur Queenaire 8800	LD-279	N102KK	0066	0287	2 LY IO-720-A1B	3992	Freighter	cvtd Queen Air 65-B80
☐	N131BA	Beech Excalibur Queenaire 8800	LD-297	N1555M	0066	1285	2 LY IO-720-A1B	3992	Freighter	cvtd Queen Air 65-B80
☐	N132BA	Beech Excalibur Queenaire 8800	LD-331	C-GRID	0067	0388	2 LY IO-720-A1B	3992	Freighter	cvtd Queen Air 65-B80
☐	N134BA	Beech Excalibur Queenaire 8800	LD-202	N848S	0064	1189	2 LY IO-720-A1B	3992	Freighter	cvtd Queen Air 65-A80
☐	N135BA	Beech Excalibur Queenaire 8800	LD-68	N29RG	0063	0890	2 LY IO-720-A1B	3992	Frtr / 9 Pax	cvtd Queen Air 65-80
☐	N55SA	Beech Excalibur Queenaire 8800	LD-243		0065	0887	2 LY IO-720-A1B	3992	Freighter	cvtd Queen Air 65-A80
☐	N95LL	Beech Excalibur Queenaire 8800	LD-235		0065	1192	2 LY IO-720-A1B	3992	Freighter	cvtd Queen Air 65-A80
☐	N108BA	Beech 99 Airliner	U-40	C-GQFD	0068	0586	2 PWC PT6A-27	4717	Freighter	
☐	N130BA	Beech 99A Airliner	U-80	N51PA	0069	0395	2 PWC PT6A-27	4717	Freighter	
☐	N139BA	Beech 99 Airliner	U-76	N983MA	0069	1189	2 PWC PT6A-27	4717	Freighter	
☐	N7207E	Beech C99 Airliner	U-223		0084	1193	2 PWC PT6A-36	5126	Freighter	
☐	N60BA	Beech King Air E90	LW-79	N12AK	0073	0793	2 PWC PT6A-28	4581	7 Pax	

BERING AIR, Inc. = 8E / BRG — Nome & Kotzebue-Ralph Wien Memorial, AK

BERING AIR

PO Box 1650, Nome, AK 99762, USA ☎ (907) 443-5464 Tx: none Fax: (907) 443-5919 SITA: n/a
F: 1979 ♁♁♁ 65 Head: James D. Rowe ICAO: BERING AIR Net: http://www.spectrav.com/20075.html

	registration	type of aircraft	cn/fn	ex/ex*	mfd	del	powered by	mtow kg	configuration	name/fln/remarks
☐	N75682	Cessna T207A Turbo Stationair 8 II	20700638		0080	0781	1 CO TSIO-520-M	1724	Y6	
☐	N75738	Cessna T207A Turbo Stationair 8 II	20700641		0080	0781	1 CO TSIO-520-M	1724	Y6	lsf Gustavus Dray Inc.
☐	N9964M	Cessna 207A Stationair 8 II	20700766		0083	0488	1 CO IO-520-F	1724	Y7	
☐	N9988M	Cessna 207A Stationair 8 II	20700776		0084	0388	1 CO IO-520-F	1724	Y7	
☐	N141ME	Piper PA-31-350 Navajo Chieftain	31-8152117		0081	0593	2 LY TIO-540-J2BD	3295	Y9	lsf Metlife Capital Corp.
☐	N4112D	Piper PA-31-350 T1020	31-8353004		0083	0783	2 LY TIO-540-J2B	3295	Y9	
☐	N4112E	Piper PA-31-350 T1020	31-8353005		0083	0783	2 LY TIO-540-J2B	3295	Y9	
☐	N4118G	Piper PA-31-350 T1020	31-8453001		0084	0690	2 LY TIO-540-J2B	3295	Y9	
☐	N45052	Piper PA-31-350 Navajo Chieftain	31-8152063		0081	1087	2 LY TIO-540-J2BD	3295	Y9	
☐	N1123R	Cessna 208B Grand Caravan	208B0395		0094	0694	1 PWC PT6A-114A	3969	Y9	lsf Textron Financial Corp.
☐	N1128L	Cessna 208B Grand Caravan	208B0536		0096	0796	1 PWC PT6A-114A	3969	Y9	lsf Cessna Finance Corp.
☐	N135W	Beech H18	BA-643		0063	1188	2 PW R-985	4763	Freighter	lsf pvt
☐	N228A	Beech H18	BA-629		0063	1188	2 PW R-985	4763	Freighter	lsf pvt
☐	N340K	Beech G18S	BA-605		0062	0392	2 PW R-985	4763	Freighter	
☐	N93CA	Beech G18S	BA-604	N8087	0062	0290	2 PW R-985	4763	Freighter	
☐	N79CF	Beech Catpass 250	BB-441		0078	0794	2 PWC PT6A-41	5670	Y13	cvtd King Air 200
☐	N349TA	CASA 212 Aviocar Srs 200	349	N316CA	0085	0997	2 GA TPE331-10-501C	7450	Freighter	

BERLIN AIRLIFT Historical Foundation — Toms River-Robert J. Miller Air Park, NJ

PO Box 782, Farmingdale, NJ 07727, USA ☎ (732) 818-0034 Tx: none Fax: (732) 818-0456 SITA: n/a
F: 1991 ♁♁♁ 3 Head: Timothy A. Chopp Net: http://www.berlin-airlift.org Volunteer organisation dedicated to the restoration & preservation of airworthy aircraft used during the Berlin Airlift, 1948-49.

	registration	type of aircraft	cn/fn	ex/ex*	mfd	del	powered by	mtow kg	configuration	name/fln/remarks
☐	N500EJ	Boeing (Douglas) DC-4 (C-54E-15-DO)	27370 / DO 316	C-GQIB	0045	1294	4 PW R-2000	31752	Flying Museum	Spirit of Freedom
☐	N117GA	Boeing C-97G Stratofreighter	16749	N1175K	0054	0197	4 PW R-4360	69400	Flying Museum	Deliverance / being made op.at Greybull

BERRY AVIATION, Inc. = BYA — San Marcos-Municipal, TX

BERRY AVIATION

1807 Airport Drive, San Marcos, TX 78666, USA ☎ (512) 353-2379 Tx: none Fax: (512) 353-2593 SITA: n/a
F: 1983 ♁♁♁ 10 Head: Harry M. Berry, III ICAO: BERRY Net: n/a

	registration	type of aircraft	cn/fn	ex/ex*	mfd	del	powered by	mtow kg	configuration	name/fln/remarks
☐	N255AM	Fairchild (Swearingen) SA226TC Metro II	TC-331E	N1006U	0081	0092	2 GA TPE331-10UA-511G	5670	Y19 / Freighter	
☐	N27442	Fairchild (Swearingen) SA227AC Metro III	AC-750		0089	0998	2 GA TPE331-11U-611G	6577	Y19 / Freighter	
☐	N373PH	Fairchild (Swearingen) SA227AC Metro III	AC-538	N3110T	0083	0198	2 GA TPE331-11U-611G	6577	Y19 / Freighter	
☐	N442BA	Fairchild (Swearingen) SA227AC Metro III	AC-442	N3005J	0081	0194	2 GA TPE331-11U-611G	6577	Y19 / Freighter	
☐	N558BA	Fairchild (Swearingen) SA227AC Metro III	AC-558	N169SW	0083	0797	2 GA TPE331-11U-611G	6577	Y19 / Freighter	
☐	N589BA	Fairchild (Swearingen) SA227AC Metro III	AC-589	N382PH	0084	0496	2 GA TPE331-11U-611G	6577	Y19 / Freighter	
☐	N590BA	Fairchild (Swearingen) SA227AC Metro III	AC-590	N383PH	0084	0496	2 GA TPE331-11U-611G	6577	Y19 / Freighter	
☐	N685BA	Fairchild (Swearingen) SA227AC Metro III	AC-685	N685AV	0087	0797	2 GA TPE331-11U-611G	6577	Y19 / Freighter	
☐	N729C	Fairchild (Swearingen) SA227AC Metro III	AC-571	N374PH	0082	0598	2 GA TPE331-11U-611G	6577	Y19 / Freighter	
☐	N789C	Fairchild (Swearingen) SA227AC Metro III	AC-540	N389PH	0082	0797	2 GA TPE331-11U-611G	6577	Y19 / Freighter	

BETTLES AIR SERVICE (Dan Klaes dba / Affiliated with Bettles Lodge / Seasonal May-October ops only) — Bettles, AK

PO Box 27, Bettles, AK 99726, USA ☎ (907) 692-5111 Tx: none Fax: (907) 692-5655 SITA: n/a
F: 1991 ♁♁♁ n/a Head: Dan Klaes Net: http://www.akcache.com/bettleslodge/

	registration	type of aircraft	cn/fn	ex/ex*	mfd	del	powered by	mtow kg	configuration	name/fln/remarks
☐	N1931Q	Cessna A185F Skywagon II	18503504		0078	0691	1 CO IO-520-D	1520		Floats / Wheels
☐	N2248T	Cessna A185E Skywagon	185-1406		0068	0691	1 CO IO-520-D	1520		lsf pvt / Floats / Wheels
☐	N109SW	Cessna U206G Stationair	U20603799		0078	0895	1 CO IO-520-F	1633		Floats / Wheels
☐	N46DG	De Havilland DHC-2 Beaver I	340	N765	0051	0692	1 PW R-985	2309		lsf D&D Aviation Inc. / Floats / Wheels

BEVINS AIR SERVICE, Inc. — St. Thomas-Cyril E. King, VI

PO Box 3542, St. Thomas, VI 00803, USA ☎ (340) 776-2197 Tx: none Fax: (340) 776-2197 SITA: n/a
F: 1994 ♁♁♁ n/a Head: Bevin Romain Net: n/a

	registration	type of aircraft	cn/fn	ex/ex*	mfd	del	powered by	mtow kg	configuration	name/fln/remarks
☐	N78336	Twin (Aero) Commander 500B	500B-1187-94		0062	0594	2 LY IO-540-B1A5	3062		

BF AVIATION, Corp. — Farmingdale-Republic, NY

Route 109, Farmingdale, NY 11735, USA ☎ (516) 752-7034 Tx: none Fax: (516) 752-9028 SITA: n/a
F: 1995 ♁♁♁ 6 Head: Lisa M. Scaffa Net: http://www.bfac.com

	registration	type of aircraft	cn/fn	ex/ex*	mfd	del	powered by	mtow kg	configuration	name/fln/remarks
☐	N22BF	Sikorsky S-76A	760216	N357JS	0082	1095	2 AN 250-C30	4672		

BIGHORN AIRWAYS, Inc. = BHR — Sheridan County, WY

PO Box 4037, Sheridan, WY 82801, USA ☎ (307) 672-3421 Tx: none Fax: (307) 674-4468 SITA: n/a
F: 1947 ♁♁♁ 21 Head: Robert D. Eisele IATA: 405 ICAO: BIGHORN AIR Net: n/a Ag-Aircraft below MTOW 5000kg: AT-301 & Hiller UH-12E

	registration	type of aircraft	cn/fn	ex/ex*	mfd	del	powered by	mtow kg	configuration	name/fln/remarks
☐	N2669C	Cessna R182 Skylane RG II	R18200203		0078	1188	1 LY O-540-J3C5D	1406	Utility	
☐	N543CC	Bell 206B JetRanger III	3593	N2295W	0082	1296	1 AN 250-C20B	1451	Utility	
☐	N6266C	Cessna T210N Turbo Centurion II	21063849		0079	0484	1 CO TSIO-520-R	1814	Utility	
☐	N114BH	Cessna 340A II	340A1230	N6228X	0081	1297	2 CO TSIO-520-NB	2717	5 Pax	
☐	N115BH	Cessna 340A II	340A1531	N2688Q	0082	1297	2 CO TSIO-520-NB	2717	5 Pax	
☐	N118BH	Cessna 340A II	340A0003	N5168J	0072	0186	2 CO TSIO-520-N	2717	5 Pax	
☐	N27956	Piper PA-31-350 Navajo Chieftain	31-7952064		0079	0794	2 LY TIO-540-J2BD	3175	Freighter	
☐	N4091D	Piper PA-31-350 Navajo Chieftain	31-8152154		0081	0289	2 LY TIO-540-J2BD	3175	Freighter	
☐	N700WJ	Cessna 425 Conquest I	425-0036	F-GCQN	0081	0996	2 PWC PT6A-112	3719	7 Pax	
☐	N257MC	Dornier 228-202	8102	YV-648C	0086	1198	2 GA TPE331-5-252D	6200	9 Pax & Cargo	cvtd -201
☐	N263MC	Dornier 228-202	8141	N116DN	0087	1198	2 GA TPE331-5-252D	6200	9 Pax & Cargo	
☐	N266MC	Dornier 228-202	8150		0088	1198	2 GA TPE331-5-252D	6200	9 Pax & Cargo	
☐	N276MC	Dornier 228-202	8109	YV-649C	0086	1198	2 GA TPE331-5-252D	6200	9 Pax & Cargo	cvtd -201
☐	N107BH	CASA 212 Aviocar Srs 200	165	N212TH	0080	0489	2 GA TPE331-10-501C	7450	9 Pax & Cargo	
☐	N117BH	CASA 212 Aviocar Srs 200	171	N349CA	0080	0489	2 GA TPE331-10-501C	7450	9 Pax & Cargo	

BIG ISLAND AIR, Inc. - BIA = BIG — Kailua-Keahole Kona Int'l, HI

BIG ISLAND AIR

PO Box 1476, Kailua-Kona, HI 96745-1476, USA ☎ (808) 329-0991 Tx: none Fax: (808) 329-0855 SITA: n/a
F: 1985 ♁♁♁ 6 Head: Guerry A. Buehman ICAO: BIG ISLE Net: http://www.ilhawaii.net:80/pt/bigair.html

	registration	type of aircraft	cn/fn	ex/ex*	mfd	del	powered by	mtow kg	configuration	name/fln/remarks
☐	N41073	Piper PA-31-350 T1020	31-8253007		0082	0194	2 LY TIO-540-J2B	3175		lsf GECC Financial Corp.
☐	N683ML	Piper PA-31-350 Navajo Chieftain	31-7552124		0075	0593	2 LY TIO-540-J2BD	3175		lsf pvt

BIG SKY AIR, Inc. Terrell-Municipal, TX

8324 Lake June Road, Dallas, TX 75217, USA ☎ (972) 398-2360 Tx: none Fax: (972) 398-2360 SITA: n/a
F: 1992 n/a Head: Richard M. Linden, Jr. Net: n/a

☐ N408D	Boeing (Douglas) DC-3-201D	2247	N15596	0040	0592	2 WR R-1820	12202	Para	

BIG SKY AIRLINES = GQ / BSY (Big Sky Transportation Company dba) Billings-Logan Int'l, MT & Dallas-DFW, TX

1601 Aviation Place, Billings, MT 59105, USA ☎ (406) 245-9449 Tx: none Fax: (406) 259-8750 SITA: n/a
F: 1978 75 Head: Kim B. Champney IATA: 387 ICAO: BIG SKY Net: http://www.bigskyair.com

☐ N158MC	Fairchild (Swearingen) SA227AC Metro III	AC-726B		0089	0997	2 GA TPE331-11U-612G	7257	Y19	lsf CCD Air Twenty Inc.
☐ N159MC	Fairchild (Swearingen) SA227AC Metro III	AC-728B		0088	0797	2 GA TPE331-11U-612G	7257	Y19	lsf CCD Air Twenty One Inc.
☐ N160MC	Fairchild (Swearingen) SA227AC Metro III	AC-733B		0089	1097	2 GA TPE331-11U-612G	7257	Y19	lsf CCD Air Twenty Two Inc.
☐ N27465	Fairchild (Swearingen) SA227AC Metro III	AC-755B		0089	0897	2 GA TPE331-11U-612G	7257	Y19	lsf CCD Air Thirty Inc.
☐ N425MA	Fairchild (Swearingen) SA227AC Metro III	AC-640		0086	0398	2 GA TPE331-11U-611G	6577	Y19	lsf State Street Boston Leasing Corp.
☐ N430MA	Fairchild (Swearingen) SA227AC Metro III	AC-710	N2710T*	0088	1098	2 GA TPE331-11U-612G	6577	Y19	
☐ N60NE	Fairchild (Swearingen) SA227AC Metro III	AC-760B	N307NE	0090	0897	2 GA TPE331-11U-612G	7257	Y19	lsf CCD Air Thirty-Eight Inc.
☐ N850LS	Fairchild (Swearingen) SA227DC Metro 23	DC-850B	N3025B	0094	0299	2 GA TPE331-12U-701G	7484	Y19	lsf CITG
☐ N853LS	Fairchild (Swearingen) SA227DC Metro 23	DC-853B	N3025Y	0094	0299	2 GA TPE331-12U-701G	7484	Y19	lsf CITG
☐ N854LS	Fairchild (Swearingen) SA227DC Metro 23	DC-854B	N3026R	0094	0299	2 GA TPE331-12U-701G	7484	Y19	lsf CITG

BIJAN AIR, Inc. Ann Arbor-Municipal, MI

747 Airport Drive, Ann Arbor, MI 48108, USA ☎ (734) 769-8400 Tx: none Fax: (734) 769-6555 SITA: n/a
F: 1988 6 Head: Bijan Moazami Net: http://www.bijanair.com Aircraft below MTOW 1361kg: Schweizer 269C/CB (300C/CB)

☐ N90TJ	MD Helicopters MD 500E (Hughes 369E)	0016E	N5146N	0087	0493	1 AN 250-C20B	1361	lsf Rotorall Corp.
☐ N727BB	Bell 206B JetRanger	735	N57EA	0071	0898	1 AN 250-C20	1451	cvtd 206A
☐ N57843	Eurocopter (Aerosp.) AS350BA AStar	1430		0281	0098	1 TU Arriel 1B	2100	lsf Roberts Ac./cvtd 350B/opf WDIV TV 4

BILLINGS FLYING SERVICE Billings-Logan Int'l, MT

153 Jack Street, Billings, MT 59101, USA ☎ (406) 259-3731 Tx: none Fax: none SITA: n/a
F: 1995 n/a Head: Gary Blain Net: n/a

☐ N453CC	Bell UH-1E (204)	6208	155352	0068	0996	1 LY T53-L-11	3856	lst Withrotor Aviation
☐ N454CC	Bell UH-1E (204)	6200	155344	0068	0996	1 LY T53-L-11	3856	
☐ N455CC	Bell UH-1L (204)	6002	151267	0067	1195	1 LY T53-L-13	3856	

BILL LAW AVIATION, Inc. Rochester-Greater Int'l, NY

1313 Scottsville Road, Rochester, NY 14624, USA ☎ (716) 328-8830 Tx: none Fax: (716) 328-5332 SITA: n/a
F: 1981 n/a Head: William Law Net: n/a

☐ N2656Z	Piper PA-23-250 Aztec F	27-8054048		0080	1189	2 LY IO-540-C4B5	2359	
☐ N27CY	Piper PA-23-250 Aztec F	27-7654118		0076	0197	2 LY IO-540-C4B5	2359	
☐ N3234L	Piper PA-23-250 Aztec C	27-3626		0067	1286	2 LY IO-540-C4B5	2359	
☐ N510WA	Piper PA-23-250 Aztec E	27-7405436		0074	0693	2 LY IO-540-C4B5	2359	
☐ N711WE	Piper PA-31-350 Navajo Chieftain	31-7752190		0077	0193	2 LY TIO-540-J2BD	3175	lsf pvt

BIRCHWOOD AIR SERVICE (Michael J. Osolnik dba) Anchorage-Merrill Field, AK

PO Box 140813, Anchorage, AK 99514, USA ☎ (907) 276-0402 Tx: none Fax: (907) 276-5400 SITA: n/a
F: 1976 n/a Head: Michael J. Osolnik Net: n/a

☐ N555FS	Piper PA-31-350 Navajo Chieftain	31-7952046	N27914	0079	0694	2 LY TIO-540-J2BD	3175

BIRD AIR FLEET, Inc. = BIR (formerly Bird Leasing, Inc.) Lawrence-Municipal, MA & Manchester, NH

PO Box 373, Atkinson, NH 03811-0373, USA ☎ (978) 372-6566 Tx: none Fax: (978) 382-6256 SITA: n/a
F: 1972 11 Head: Peter E. Torosian ICAO: BIRD AIR Net: http://www.flybirdair.com

☐ N40571	Piper PA-23-250 Aztec E	27-7405313		0074	0293	2 LY IO-540-C4B5	2359	
☐ N4464S	Beech Baron B55 (95-B55)	TC-1878		0075		2 CO IO-470-L	2313	lsf The Cruising Group Inc.
☐ N30DF	Piper PA-31-310 Navajo B	31-7401263		0074		2 LY TIO-540-A2C	2948	lsf Aircraft Leasing & Management Co.
☐ N61RT	Piper PA-31-350 Navajo Chieftain	31-7952222		0079		2 LY TIO-540-J2BD	3175	
☐ N628HA	Piper PA-31-350 Navajo Chieftain	31-7952085		0079	1191	2 LY TIO-540-J2BD	3175	

BIRD SPACE (Forrest M. Bird dba) Sandpoint-Dave Wall Field, ID

PO Box 817, Sandpoint, ID 83864, USA ☎ (208) 263-2549 Tx: none Fax: (208) 263-0577 SITA: n/a
F: 1978 n/a Head: Forrest M. Bird Net: n/a Aircraft below MTOW 1361kg: Bell 47G3-B2

☐ N381RD	Bell 212	30850	N16735	0077	1078	2 PWC PT6T-3 TwinPac	5080

BISCAYNE HELICOPTERS, Inc. Miami-Kendall Tamiami Executive, FL

13955 SW 127th Street, Bldg 121, Miami, FL 33186, USA ☎ (305) 252-3883 Tx: none Fax: (305) 378-4407 SITA: n/a
F: 1987 n/a Head: Daryl R. Martin Net: n/a

☐ N161BH	Bell 206B JetRanger	1675	N90212	0075	0294	1 AN 250-C20	1451	
☐ N163BH	Bell 206B JetRanger III	3027	N57380	0080	1290	1 AN 250-C20B	1451	
☐ N167BH	Bell 206B JetRanger II	1961	N9911K	0076	0187	1 AN 250-C20	1451	opf WSVN Channel 7 Television
☐ N261BH	Bell 206B JetRanger III	2817	N2779T	0079	0995	1 AN 250-C20B	1451	
☐ N262BH	Bell 206B JetRanger III	3563	N2234W	0081	0595	1 AN 250-C20B	1451	
☐ N263BH	Bell 206B JetRanger	753	N8127J	0072	0995	1 AN 250-C20	1451	
☐ N5016M	Bell 206B JetRanger III	2636		0079	0995	1 AN 250-C20B	1451	lsf L'Eagle Air II Inc.
☐ N165BH	Bell 206L-1 LongRanger II	45249		0079	0591	1 AN 250-C28B	1882	opf Channel 10 Television
☐ N166BH	Bell 206L-1 LongRanger II	45661	N206ML	0081	0995	1 AN 250-C28B	1882	
☐ N162BH	Eurocopter (Aerosp.) AS350B AStar	1362	N29SG	0080	0995	1 TU Arriel 1B	1950	cvtd AS350D
☐ N264BH	Eurocopter (Aerosp.) AS350B AStar	1370	N34WH	0080	0995	1 TU Arriel 1B	1950	cvtd AS350D
☐ N169BH	Agusta A109A II	7302	N109TJ	0083	0397	2 AN 250-C20B	2600	lsf Thunderbird Helicopters
☐ N18BH	Agusta A109A II	7256	N8WH	0082	0386	2 AN 250-C20B	2600	

BLUE BIRD HELICOPTERS (Kenneth G. Guthrie dba) Cougar-Heliport, WA

PO Box 14, Cougar, WA 98616-0014, USA ☎ (360) 238-5326 Tx: none Fax: none SITA: n/a
F: 1980 5 Head: Kenneth G. Guthrie Net: n/a

☐ N678KG	Bell 206B JetRanger III	603		0070	0680	1 AN 250-C20B	1451	cvtd 206A
☐ N5363G	Bell UH-1E (204)	6060	Bu 151866	0069	0588	1 LY T53-L-13	3856	
☐ N664Y	Sikorsky S-61R	61501		0063	1295	2 GE CT58-100-1	10002	
☐ N467KG	Sikorsky CH-54B (S-64 Skycrane)	64074		0069	0992	2 PW T-73-P-700	19051	
☐ N470KG	Sikorsky CH-54B (S-64 Skycrane)		69-18470	0069	0693	2 PW T-73-P-700	19051	
☐ N484KG	Sikorsky CH-54B (S-64 Skycrane)	64092	70-18484	0070	0992	2 PW T-73-P-700	19051	

BLUE HAWAIIAN HELICOPTERS (Helicopter Consultants of Maui, Inc. dba) Kahului-Heliport & Hilo-Int'l, HI

Kahului Heliport, Hangar 105, Kahului, HI.96732, USA ☎ (808) 871-8844 Tx: none Fax: (808) 871-6971 SITA: n/a
F: 1981 n/a Head: David J. Chevalier Net: http://www.bluehawaiian.com

☐ N193BH	Eurocopter (Aerosp.) AS350B2 AStar	2894	N4025S	0096	0996	1 TU Arriel 1D1	2250
☐ N194BH	Eurocopter (Aerosp.) AS350B2 AStar	2903	N4027K	0096	0996	1 TU Arriel 1D1	2250
☐ N196BH	Eurocopter (Aerosp.) AS350B2 AStar	3036		0097	1197	1 TU Arriel 1D1	2250
☐ N197BH	Eurocopter (Aerosp.) AS350B2 AStar	2666	N6343Z	0092	0498	1 TU Arriel 1D1	2250
☐ N198BH	Eurocopter (Aerosp.) AS350B2 AStar	3126		0098	1198	1 TU Arriel 1D1	2250
☐ N312B	Eurocopter (Aerosp.) AS350BA AStar	2243		0089	1089	1 TU Arriel 1B	2100
☐ N422B	Eurocopter (Aerosp.) AS350BA AStar	2391	N31AS	0090	0297	1 TU Arriel 1B	2100
☐ N532BH	Eurocopter (Aerosp.) AS350BA AStar	2494		0091	1191	1 TU Arriel 1B	2100
☐ N642BH	Eurocopter (Aerosp.) AS350BA AStar	2495		0091	1291	1 TU Arriel 1B	2100
☐ N752BH	Eurocopter (Aerosp.) AS350BA AStar	2510		0091	0692	1 TU Arriel 1B	2100
☐ N862BH	Eurocopter (Aerosp.) AS350BA AStar	2713		0093	0194	1 TU Arriel 1B	2100
☐ N972BH	Eurocopter (Aerosp.) AS350B2 AStar	2804		0094	1194	1 TU Arriel 1D1	2250
☐ N982BH	Eurocopter (Aerosp.) AS350B2 AStar	2876		0095	0895	1 TU Arriel 1D1	2250
☐ N992BH	Eurocopter (Aerosp.) AS350B2 AStar	2889		0095	0196	1 TU Arriel 1D1	2250
☐ N995BH	Eurocopter (Aerosp.) AS350B2 AStar	2987		0097	0997	1 TU Arriel 1D1	2250

BLUE MOUNTAIN HELICOPTERS, Inc. Milton-Freewater Private Heliport, OR

1820 South Main Street, Milton-Freewater, OR 97862, USA ☎ (541) 938-4275 Tx: none Fax: (541) 938-4297 SITA: n/a
F: 1984 n/a Head: R. Gary Knight Net: n/a Aircraft below MTOW 1361kg: Bell 47G-3B-1

☐ N4086B	Bell UH-1F (204)	7305	66-1229	0066	1094	1 GE T58-GE-3	3856
☐ N32800	Bell UH-1H (205)	9048	66-16854	0066	0395	1 LY T53-L-13	4309

BLUFFTON FLYING SERVICE, Co. (Subsidiary of Amalgamated Leasing, Inc.) Bluffton, OH

1080 Navajo Drive, Bluffton, OH 45817, USA ☎ (419) 358-7045 Tx: none Fax: (419) 358-6851 SITA: n/a
F: 1947 n/a Head: Calvin E. Roeder Net: n/a

☐ N8597Q	Cessna U206F Stationair II	U20603452		0076	1093	1 CO IO-520-F	1633
☐ N2117V	Piper PA-34-200T Seneca II	34-7970160		0079	1183	2 CO TSIO-360-EB	2073
☐ N16WC	Piper PA-31-350 Navajo Chieftain	31-7552039		0075	0584	2 LY TIO-540-J2BD	3175
☐ N43BM	Cessna 421C Golden Eagle III	421C1224		0082	1196	2 CO GTSIO-520-N	3379
☐ N98487	Cessna 421C Golden Eagle II	421C0065		0076	0294	2 CO GTSIO-520-L	3379

288 registration type of aircraft cn/fn ex/ex* mfd del powered by mtow kg configuration selcal name/fln/specialitites/remarks

BOHLKE INTERNATIONAL AIRWAYS, Inc. – BIA (formerly Eastern Caribbean Airways)

St. Croix-Alexander Hamilton, VI

PO Box 599, Kingshill, St. Croix, VI 00850, USA ☎ (340) 778-9177 Tx: none Fax: (340) 772-5932 SITA: n/a
F: 1959 ✦✦✦ 20 Head: William Bohlke, Jr. Net: http://www.bohlke.com

registration	type of aircraft	cn/fn	ex/ex*	mfd	del	powered by	mtow kg	configuration	name/fln/specialitites/remarks
☐ N3045R	Piper PA-34-200T Seneca II	34-7970142		0079	0694	2 CO TSIO-360-EB	2073		
☐ N4076T	Piper PA-31-350 Navajo Chieftain	31-8152046		0081	0294	2 LY TIO-540-J2BD	3175		lsf Tropical Aircraft Co. Inc.
☐ N113CT	Twin (Aero) Hawk Commander 681	681-6006	N2725B	0069	1289	2 GA TPE331-1-151K	4264		
☐ N550K	IAI 1121 Jet Commander	1121-127	N100SR	0068	0688	2 GE CJ610-5	8391		
☐ N1125E	IAI 1125 Astra SP	058		0092	1292	2 GA TFE731-3A-200G	10659		lsf Atlantic Aircraft Inc.

BOMBARDIER BUSINESS JET SOLUTIONS, Inc. (FlexJet) (Subs. of Bombardier Aerospace/formerly part of Business Jet Solutions)

Dallas-Love Field, TX

14651 Dallas Parkway, Suite 600, Dallas, TX 75240, USA ☎ (972) 720-2800 Tx: none Fax: (972) 720-2434 SITA: n/a
F: 1995 ✦✦✦ n/a Head: Bruce D. McNeely Net: n/a Aircraft are operated under the FLEXJET fractional shared-ownership program, in which an owner purchases a portion of the flight hours annually & contract BBJS to manage it. FAR135 operations are conducted under the licence of BUSINESS JET SOLUTIONS (sister company.)

registration	type of aircraft	cn/fn	ex/ex*	mfd	del	powered by	mtow kg	configuration	name/fln/specialitites/remarks
☐ N105FX	Learjet 31A	31A-086	N867JS	0093	0795	2 GA TFE731-2-3B	7484	Executive	
☐ N106FX	Learjet 31A	31A-087	N868JS	0093	0795	2 GA TFE731-2-3B	7484	Executive	
☐ N107FX	Learjet 31A	31A-102	N5002D	0095	0995	2 GA TFE731-2-3B	7484	Executive	
☐ N108FX	Learjet 31A	31A-104	N4010N	0095	0995	2 GA TFE731-2-3B	7484	Executive	
☐ N109FX	Learjet 31A	31A-105	N5005K	0095	0995	2 GA TFE731-2-3B	7484	Executive	
☐ N110FX	Learjet 31A	31A-108		0095	1095	2 GA TFE731-2-3B	7484	Executive	
☐ N112FX	Learjet 31A	31A-116	N113FX	0096	0396	2 GA TFE731-2-3B	7484	Executive	
☐ N114FX	Learjet 31A	31A-119		0096	0996	2 GA TFE731-2-3B	7484	Executive	
☐ N115FX	Learjet 31A	31A-129	N8079Q	0096	0197	2 GA TFE731-2-3B	7484	Executive	
☐ N116FX	Learjet 31A	31A-132		0097	0597	2 GA TFE731-2-3B	7484	Executive	
☐ N117FX	Learjet 31A	31A-133	N8073Y	0097	0597	2 GA TFE731-2-3B	7484	Executive	
☐ N118FX	Learjet 31A	31A-134		0097	0897	2 GA TFE731-2-3B	7484	Executive	
☐ N119FX	Learjet 31A	31A-136		0097	1297	2 GA TFE731-2-3B	7484	Executive	
☐ N120FX	Learjet 31A	31A-137		0097	0397	2 GA TFE731-2-3B	7484	Executive	
☐ N121FX	Learjet 31A	31A-141		0097	0997	2 GA TFE731-2-3B	7484	Executive	
☐ N122FX	Learjet 31A	31A-143		0098	0398	2 GA TFE731-2-3B	7484	Executive	
☐ N124FX	Learjet 31A	31A-156		0098	0798	2 GA TFE731-2-3B	7484	Executive	
☐ N125FX	Learjet 31A	31A-157		0098	0898	2 GA TFE731-2-3B	7484	Executive	
☐ N126FX	Learjet 31A	31A-158		0098	0898	2 GA TFE731-2-3B	7484	Executive	
☐ N127FX	Learjet 31A	31A-159		0098	0898	2 GA TFE731-2-3B	7484	Executive	
☐ N128FX	Learjet 31A	31A-163		0098	0998	2 GA TFE731-2-3B	7484	Executive	
☐ N	Learjet 45	45-				2 GA TFE731-20	9163	Executive	oo-delivery 0099
☐ N	Learjet 45	45-				2 GA TFE731-20	9163	Executive	oo-delivery 0099
☐ N	Learjet 45	45-				2 GA TFE731-20	9163	Executive	oo-delivery 0099
☐ N	Learjet 45	45-				2 GA TFE731-20	9163	Executive	oo-delivery 0099
☐ N	Learjet 45	45-				2 GA TFE731-20	9163	Executive	oo-delivery 0099
☐ N	Learjet 45	45-				2 GA TFE731-20	9163	Executive	oo-delivery 0099
☐ N	Learjet 45	45-				2 GA TFE731-20	9163	Executive	oo-delivery 0099
☐ N	Learjet 45	45-				2 GA TFE731-20	9163	Executive	oo-delivery 0099
☐ N	Learjet 45	45-				2 GA TFE731-20	9163	Executive	oo-delivery 0099
☐ N	Learjet 45	45-				2 GA TFE731-20	9163	Executive	oo-delivery 0099
☐ N	Learjet 45	45-				2 GA TFE731-20	9163	Executive	oo-delivery 0099
☐ N	Learjet 45	45-				2 GA TFE731-20	9163	Executive	oo-delivery 0099
☐ N	Learjet 45	45-				2 GA TFE731-20	9163	Executive	oo-delivery 0099
☐ N	Learjet 45	45-				2 GA TFE731-20	9163	Executive	oo-delivery 0099
☐ N	Learjet 45	45-				2 GA TFE731-20	9163	Executive	oo-delivery 0000
☐ N	Learjet 45	45-				2 GA TFE731-20	9163	Executive	oo-delivery 0000
☐ N	Learjet 45	45-				2 GA TFE731-20	9163	Executive	oo-delivery 0000
☐ N	Learjet 45	45-				2 GA TFE731-20	9163	Executive	oo-delivery 0000
☐ N	Learjet 45	45-				2 GA TFE731-20	9163	Executive	oo-delivery 0000
☐ N	Learjet 45	45-				2 GA TFE731-20	9163	Executive	oo-delivery 0000
☐ N	Learjet 45	45-				2 GA TFE731-20	9163	Executive	oo-delivery 0000
☐ N	Learjet 45	45-				2 GA TFE731-20	9163	Executive	oo-delivery 0000
☐ N	Learjet 45	45-				2 GA TFE731-20	9163	Executive	oo-delivery 0000
☐ N	Learjet 45	45-				2 GA TFE731-20	9163	Executive	oo-delivery 0000
☐ N	Learjet 45	45-				2 GA TFE731-20	9163	Executive	oo-delivery 0000
☐ N	Learjet 45	45-				2 GA TFE731-20	9163	Executive	oo-delivery 0000
☐ N	Learjet 45	45-				2 GA TFE731-20	9163	Executive	oo-delivery 0000
☐ N	Learjet 45	45-				2 GA TFE731-20	9163	Executive	oo-delivery 0000
☐ N139XX	Learjet 60	60-139	N233FX	0098	1298	2 PWC PW305A	10659	Executive	based Glasgow-Prestwick
☐ N205FX	Learjet 60	60-005	N869JS	0093	0795	2 PWC PW305A	10659	Executive	
☐ N206FX	Learjet 60	60-028	N870JS	0094	0795	2 PWC PW305A	10659	Executive	
☐ N207FX	Learjet 60	60-050	N50450	0095	0595	2 PWC PW305A	10659	Executive	
☐ N208FX	Learjet 60	60-059	N5059J	0095	1195	2 PWC PW305A	10659	Executive	
☐ N209FX	Learjet 60	60-060	N50602	0095	0895	2 PWC PW305A	10659	Executive	
☐ N210FX	Learjet 60	60-064		0095	1095	2 PWC PW305A	10659	Executive	
☐ N211FX	Learjet 60	60-076		0096	0796	2 PWC PW305A	10659	Executive	
☐ N212FX	Learjet 60	60-099		0097	0597	2 PWC PW305A	10659	Executive	
☐ N214FX	Learjet 60	60-046	N5006G	0094	0496	2 PWC PW305A	10659	Executive	
☐ N215FX	Learjet 60	60-101		0097	0198	2 PWC PW305A	10659	Executive	
☐ N216FX	Learjet 60	60-103		0097	0997	2 PWC PW305A	10659	Executive	
☐ N217FX	Learjet 60	60-105		0097	1097	2 PWC PW305A	10659	Executive	
☐ N218FX	Learjet 60	60-098	N50758	0097	0897	2 PWC PW305A	10659	Executive	
☐ N219FX	Learjet 60	60-007	N448HM	0093	1096	2 PWC PW305A	10659	Executive	
☐ N220FX	Learjet 60	60-108		0097	1297	2 PWC PW305A	10659	Executive	
☐ N221FX	Learjet 60	60-111		0097	1297	2 PWC PW305A	10659	Executive	
☐ N222FX	Learjet 60	60-008	N608LJ	0093	0198	2 PWC PW305A	10659	Executive	
☐ N223FX	Learjet 60	60-124		0098	0398	2 PWC PW305A	10659	Executive	
☐ N224FX	Learjet 60	60-126		0098	0498	2 PWC PW305A	10659	Executive	
☐ N225FX	Learjet 60	60-127		0098	0798	2 PWC PW305A	10659	Executive	
☐ N226FX	Learjet 60	60-128		0098	0898	2 PWC PW305A	10659	Executive	
☐ N227FX	Learjet 60	60-077	C-GLRS	0096	0498	2 PWC PW305A	10659	Executive	
☐ N228FX	Learjet 60	60-132		0098	0998	2 PWC PW305A	10659	Executive	
☐ N229FX	Learjet 60	60-137		0098	1098	2 PWC PW305A	10659	Executive	
☐ N230FX	Learjet 60	60-138		0098	1198	2 PWC PW305A	10659	Executive	
☐ N234FX	Learjet 60	60-141		0098	1098	2 PWC PW305A	10659	Executive	
☐ N235FX	Learjet 60	60-143		0098	1098	2 PWC PW305A	10659	Executive	
☐ N304FX	Canadair CL-601-3A (CL-600-2B16) Challen.	5063	N801FL	0090	1098	2 GE CF34-3A	19550	Executive	
☐ N305FX	Canadair CL-601-3A (CL-600-2B16) Challen.	5070	N780HC	0090	1195	2 GE CF34-3A	19550	Executive	
☐ N306FX	Canadair CL-601-3R (CL-600-2B16) Challen.	5175	N601FR	0095	1095	2 GE CF34-3A1	20457	Executive	
☐ N307FX	Canadair CL-601-3R (CL-600-2B16) Challen.	5179	N608CC	0095	1195	2 GE CF34-3A1	20457	Executive	
☐ N308FX	Canadair CL-601-3A (CL-600-2B16) Challen.	5110	N392PT	0096	0396	2 GE CF34-3A	19550	Executive	
☐ N309FX	Canadair CL-604 (CL-600-2B16) Challen.	5306		0096	0396	2 GE CF34-3B	21863	Executive	
F: ☐ N310FX	Canadair CL-604 (CL-600-2B16) Challen.	5336		0097	0397	2 GE CF34-3B	21863	Executive	
☐ N311FX	Canadair CL-604 (CL-600-2B16) Challen.	5342		0097	0597	2 GE CF34-3B	21863	Executive	
☐ N312FX	Canadair CL-604 (CL-600-2B16) Challen.	5349		0097	0997	2 GE CF34-3B	21863	Executive	
☐ N314FX	Canadair CL-604 (CL-600-2B16) Challen.	5372		0098	1298	2 GE CF34-3B	21863	Executive	
☐ N315FX	Canadair CL-604 (CL-600-2B16) Challen.	5377		0098	0598	2 GE CF34-3B	21863	Executive	
☐ N316FX	Canadair CL-604 (CL-600-2B16) Challen.	5387		0098	0998	2 GE CF34-3B	21863	Executive	
☐ N	Bombardier BD-700-1A10 Global Express					2 BR BR710A2-20	42411	Executive	oo-delivery 0099
☐ N	Bombardier BD-700-1A10 Global Express					2 BR BR710A2-20	42411	Executive	oo-delivery 0099

BONNEVILLE AIRCRAFT SERVICES (Bonneville Power Administration dba / Part of U.S. Department of Energy)

Portland-Int'l, OR

PO Box 3621, Portland, OR 97208-3621, USA ☎ (503) 230-4100 Tx: none Fax: (503) 230-7359 SITA: n/a
F: 1948 ✦✦✦ 18 Head: Ashton T. Ardis, Jr. Net: http://www.bpa.gov Operates exclusively for the U.S. Department of Energy.

registration	type of aircraft	cn/fn	ex/ex*	mfd	del	powered by	mtow kg	configuration	name/fln/specialitites/remarks
☐ N3209H	Bell 206B JetRanger III	4212		0092	0692	1 AN 250-C20J	1451		lsf / opf US Department of Energy

289 registration | type of aircraft | cn/fn | ex/ex* | mfd del | powered by | mtow kg | configuration | selcal | name/fln/specialitites/remarks

☐ N34698	Bell 206B JetRanger III	4324		0095	0695	1 AN 250-C20J	1451			lsf / opf US Department of Energy
☐ N5015H	Bell 206B JetRanger III	2610		0079	0479	1 AN 250-C20B	1451			lsf / opf US Department of Energy
☐ N6181A	Bell 206B JetRanger III	4277		0093	0793	1 AN 250-C20J	1451			lsf / opf US Department of Energy
☐ N6181K	Bell 206B JetRanger III	4276		0093	0793	1 AN 250-C20J	1451			lsf / opf US Department of Energy
☐ N3209G	Bell 206L-3 LongRanger III	51567		0092	0692	1 AN 250-C20P	1882			lsf / opf US Department of Energy
☐ N2748X	Beech King Air B200	BB-1258		0086	0786	2 PWC PT6A-42	5670			lsf / opf US Department of Energy
☐ N63791	Beech King Air B200	BB-1100		0083	0283	2 PWC PT6A-42	5670			lsf / opf US Department of Energy

BORINQUEN AIR – Air Puerto Rico (Diaz Aviation, Corp. dba) — **San Juan-Luis Munoz Marin Int'l, PR**

PO Box 37309, Airport Station, San Juan, PR 00937-7309, USA ☎ (787) 791-5060 Tx: none Fax: (787) 791-8600 SITA: n/a
F: 1961 ⁂ 15 Head: Sixto Diaz-Saldana Net: n/a

☐ N1019B	Beech E18S	BA-254		0056	1189	2 PW R-985-AN14B	4581	Freighter		lsf Del Caribbean Corp.
☐ N398B	Beech E18S	BA-329		0058	0892	2 PW R-985-AN14B	4581	Freighter		lsf Del Caribbean Corp.
☐ N28PR	Boeing (Douglas) DC-3-454	6323	N18916	0043	0382	2 PW R-1830	12202	Freighter		lsf Del Caribbean Corp.
☐ N86553	Boeing (Douglas) DC-3C (C-47-DL)	4715	41-18590	0043	0393	2 PW R-1830	12202	Freighter		lsf Del Caribbean Corp.

BOSTON-MAINE AIRWAYS (Division of Guilford Transportation Industries, Inc.) — **Portsmouth-Pease Int'l Tradeport, NH**

14 Aviation Ave., Portsmouth, NH 03801, USA ☎ (603) 766-2002 Tx: none Fax: (603) 766-2094 SITA: n/a
F: 1998 ⁂ n/a Head: Gordon Lang Net: n/a Flights are operated in conjunction with sister company PAN AM in full such colors & both titles.

☐ N203PA	CASA 212 Aviocar Series 200	304	N72405	0083	1098	2 GA TPE331-10R-512/3C	7700	Freighter		Clipper Casablanca / op in Pan Am-cs
☐ N204PA	CASA 212 Aviocar Series 200	309	N72408	0083	1098	2 GA TPE331-10R-512/3C	7700	Freighter		op in Pan Am-colors

BOULLIOUN AVIATION SERVICES, Inc. = (BOUL) (Subsidiary of Deutsche Bank-Structured Finance division) — **Bellevue, WA & London (UK) & Singapore**

BOULLIOUN AVIATION SERVICES

500-108TH Avenue NE, 25th Floor, Bellevue, WA 98004, USA ☎ (425) 454-3106 Tx: none Fax: (425) 454-1913 SITA: n/a
F: 1986 ⁂ 52 Head: Robert J. Genise Net: n/a New & used aircraft leasing & sales company.
Owner / lessor of following (main) aircraft types: Airbus Industrie A319 (on order) & A320 (on order) & Boeing 737 / 747 / 757 / 767. Aircraft leased from BOUL are listed & mentioned as such under the leasing carriers.
European business is handled by: Bouillon Aviation Services (Int'l) Inc, 10 Magellan Terrace, Gatwick Road, Crawley, West Sussex RH10 2PJ, UK, Phone:(1293) 84 46 00, Fax:(1293) 52 23 30.
Singapore office: 5 Shenton Way, No.32-05, UIC Building, Singapore 068808. Phone: 323 55 59, Fax: 323 69 62.

BOWMAN AVIATION, Inc. = BMN — **Fort Wayne-Smith Field, IN**

426 West Ludwig Road, Fort Wayne, IN 46825, USA ☎ (219) 489-5517 Tx: none Fax: (219) 489-8056 SITA: n/a
F: 1976 ⁂ n/a Head: Marcia Nix ICAO: BOWMAN Net: n/a

☐ N101TL	Cessna 310K	310K0225		0066	0893	2 CO IO-470-V	2359			lsf pvt
☐ N3284M	Cessna 310R II	310R1892		0080	0695	2 CO IO-520-MB	2495			lsf Lan Aircraft Leasing Llc
☐ N5033J	Cessna 310R II	310R0153		0080	0596	2 CO IO-520-M	2495			lsf Carma Leasing Llc
☐ N5119J	Cessna 310R II	310R0996		0077	0188	2 CO IO-520-M	2495			
☐ N87403	Cessna 310R II	310R0547		0076	0396	2 CO IO-520-M	2495			
☐ N67850	Cessna 402C II	402C0410		0080	0989	2 CO TSIO-520-VB	3107			
☐ N6787V	Cessna 402C II	402C0421		0081	0196	2 CO TSIO-520-VB	3107			
☐ N25SC	Cessna 414A Chancellor II	414A0114		0078	0596	2 CO TSIO-520-NB	3062			lsf Abby Aircraft Leasing Llc
☐ N37167	Cessna 404 Titan II	404-0129		0077	0495	2 CO GTSIO-520-M	3810			
☐ N120JP	Cessna 550 Citation II	550-0468	N123FH	0083	0596	2 PWC JT15D-4	6033			lsf AAA Aircraft Leasing Llc

BP EXPLORATION ALASKA – Charter Flight Dept. (Aviation Dept. of BP Exploration Alaska, Inc.) — **Anchorage-Int'l, AK**

6601 South Airpark Place, Anchorage, AK 99502, USA ☎ (907) 263-3520 Tx: none Fax: (907) 263-3576 SITA: n/a
F: 1981 ⁂ n/a Head: Daniel B. Ahern Net: n/a Operates non-commercial flights to transfer personnel of its parent company only.

☐ N736BP	Boeing 737-205 (A)	23465 / 1226	LN-SUU	0586	0693	2 PW JT8D-17A (HK3/NOR)	56472	Y111	GL-BE	lsf Sanwa Business Credit Corp.

BRAINERD HELICOPTERS (Brainerd Helicopter Service, Inc. dba) — **Brainerd-Crow Wing County Regional, MN**

Box 482, Brainerd, MN 56401, USA ☎ (218) 829-5484 Tx: none Fax: (218) 829-2862 SITA: n/a
F: 1973 ⁂ 10 Head: Leland T. Andrew Net: n/a

☐ N52BH	Bell 206B JetRanger III	1652	VH-FHB	0075	0293	1 AN 250-C20B	1451			cvtd JetRanger
☐ N56BH	Bell 206B JetRanger III	1018	N83139	0073	1293	1 AN 250-C20B	1451			cvtd JetRanger
☐ N79BH	Bell 206B JetRanger III	2788	N444EB	0079	0795	1 AN 250-C20B	1451			
☐ N85BH	Bell 206B JetRanger III	3792	JA9377	0084	1294	1 AN 250-C20J	1451			

BRAN AIR (CDM, Inc. dba / Affiliated with Branham Adventures) — **Anchorage-Lake Hood SPB, AK**

PO Box 190184, Anchorage, AK 99519-0184, USA ☎ (907) 243-4901 Tx: none Fax: (907) 243-4907 SITA: n/a
F: 1949 ⁂ 6 Head: Christopher R. Branham Net: n/a

☐ N4195D	Helio H-395 Super Courier	1008		0062	0862	1 LY GO-480-G1D6	1361			lsf BranhamAdventures/Floats/Wheel-Skis
☐ N47055	Helio H-395 Super Courier	570		0062	0880	1 LY GO-480-G1D6	1361			lsf BranhamAdventures/Floats/Wheel-Skis
☐ N295BA	Helio H-295 Super Courier	1409	N295TA	0069	0788	1 LY GO-480-G1D6	1542			lsf BranhamAdventures/Floats/Wheel-Skis

BRANCH RIVER AIR SERVICE (Hartley, Inc. dba / Seasonal May-October ops only) — **King Salmon, AK**

4540 Edinburgh Drive, Anchorage, AK 99515, USA ☎ (907) 248-3539 Tx: none Fax: (902) 248-3539 SITA: n/a
F: 1984 ⁂ 5 Head: Van G. Hartley Net: n/a

☐ N4773U	Cessna U206G Stationair 6 II	U20605094		0079	0898	1 CO IO-520-F	1633			Floats
☐ N9608G	Cessna U206F Stationair	U20601808		0072	0498	1 CO IO-520-F	1633			Floats
☐ N24BR	De Havilland DHC-2 Beaver I	644	N90410	0054	0889	1 PW R-985	2313			Floats
☐ N5217G	De Havilland DHC-2 Beaver I	738	N5463	0053	0797	1 PW R-985	2309			Floats
☐ N9313Z	De Havilland DHC-2 Beaver I	441	52-6078	0052	0592	1 PW R-985	2313			Floats

BRAVO HELICOPTERS & WING (Benbow Helicopters, Inc. dba) — **Torrance-Zamperini Field, CA**

3401 Airport Drive, Torrance, CA 90595, USA ☎ (310) 325-9565 Tx: none Fax: (310) 325-9856 SITA: n/a
F: 1991 ⁂ n/a Head: Robin Petgrave Net: n/a Aircraft below MTOW 1361kg: Hughes 269C (300C) & Robinson R22

☐ N70SP	Bell 206B JetRanger	238		0068	0497	1 AN 250-C20	1451			cvtd 206A
☐ N522RS	Bell 206L-1 LongRanger II	45653	N6620C	0081	0191	1 AN 250-C28B	1882			lsf Ashley Aviation Inc.
☐ N317LT	Eurocopter (Aerosp.) AS350D AStar	1403	N138EH	0081	0596	1 LY LTS101-600A.2	1950			lsf pvt

BRILES WING & HELICOPTER, Inc. — **Van Nuys, CA**

16303 Waterman Drive, Van Nuys, CA 91406, USA ☎ (818) 994-1445 Tx: none Fax: (818) 994-1447 SITA: n/a
F: 1958 ⁂ n/a Head: Greg W. Briles Net: http://www.briles.rotor.com

☐ N47122	Bell 206B JetRanger	971		0073	0381	1 AN 250-C20	1451			lsf Stalokt Inc.
☐ N58129	Bell 206B JetRanger	1136		0074	0774	1 AN 250-C20	1451			
☐ N919FS	Bell 206B JetRanger	1847		0075	1295	1 AN 250-C20	1451			
☐ N3178B	Bell 206L-3 LongRanger III	51033		0083	0186	1 AN 250-C30P	1882			
☐ N3178L	Bell 206L-3 LongRanger III	51054		0083	0395	1 AN 250-C30P	1882			
☐ N4389S	Sikorsky S-58ET	58-1552		0062	0473	1 PWC PT6T-3 TwinPac	5897			lst Tundra Copters / cvtd S-58E

BRISTOL BAY AIR SERVICE, Inc. — **Dillingham, AK**

PO Box 241, Dillingham, AK 99576, USA ☎ (907) 842-4583 Tx: none Fax: none SITA: n/a
F: 1994 ⁂ n/a Head: John P. Bouker Net: n/a

☐ N7331U	Cessna 207A Stationair 7 II	20700402		0077	0596	1 CO IO-520-F	1724			

BRITISH AEROSPACE ASSET MANAGEMENT, Inc. – Turboprops = (BAMT) (Division of British Aerospace / formerly JSX Capital Corp.) — **Chantilly, VA**

15000 Conference Center Drive, Suite 200, Chantilly, VA 20151-3819, USA ☎ (540) 802-0080 Tx: n/a Fax: (540) 277-1610 SITA: n/a
F: n/a ⁂ n/a Head: Stephen Sullivan Net: n/a Specializes in the sale & lease of the Jetstream family of products, including Jetstream 31/32EP/41 & ATP. The portofolio consists of regional airliners, corporate business shuttles, air ambulances & cargo/freight variants. Aircraft leased from BAe Asset Management-Turboprops are listed and mentioned as lsf BAMT under the leasing carriers.
Aircraft leased from BAe Asset Management-Turboprops are listed and mentioned as lsf BAMT under the leasing carriers.

BROOKS AIR TRANSPORT, Inc. (Sister company of Brooks Fuel, Inc.) — **Fairbanks-Int'l, AK**

PO Box 61143, Fairbanks, AK 99706-1143, USA ☎ (907) 479-8330 Tx: none Fax: (907) 479-0578 SITA: n/a
F: 1995 ⁂ n/a Head: Roger W. Brooks Net: n/a Operates FAR125 contract cargo flights within Alaska.

☐ N9551Z	Beech C-45G (18)	AF-217	51-11660	0052	0196	2 PW R-985-AN14B	3969	Freighter		
☐ N67018	Boeing (Douglas) DC-4 (C-54D-15-DC)	22196 / DC 648	BU56544	0045	1196	4 PW R-2000	30241	Freighter		
☐ N9027K	Fairchild C-119G-FA Flying Boxcar	176	53-8073	0053	0698	2 PW R-4360	34927	Freighter		
☐ N90251	Boeing (Douglas) DC-7C	45367 / 918	F-ZBCB	0058	0295	4 WR R-3350	64864	Freighter		std FAI / to be made operational

BROOKS AVIATION (Brooks Auto Parts, Inc. dba) — **Douglas-Municipal, GA**

PO Box 610, Douglas, GA 31533, USA ☎ (912) 384-4011 Tx: none Fax: (912) 384-1849 SITA: n/a
F: 1988 ⁂ n/a Head: Don Brooks Net: n/a Operates cargo flights for its parent company only.

☐ N99FS	Boeing (Douglas) DC-3C (C-47A-10-DK)	12425	C-GZCR	0043	0389	2 PW R-1830	12202	Freighter		

BROOKS FUEL Inc. — **Fairbanks-Int'l, AK**

Brooks Fuel

PO Box 61143, Fairbanks, AK 99706-1143, USA ☎ (907) 479-8330 Tx: none Fax: (907) 479-0578 SITA: n/a
F: 1986 ⁂ n/a Head: Roger W. Brooks Net: n/a Operates FAR91 contract fuel-delivery flights within Alaska.

☐ N44906	Boeing (Douglas) DC-4 (C-54B-15-DO)	18388 / DO 162	N44SB	0044	1098	4 PW R-2000-4	30241	Fuel Tanker		
☐ N44908	Boeing (Douglas) DC-4 (C-54B-20-DO)	27246 / DO 192	USN90393	0044	1297	4 PW R-2000	30241	Fuel Tanker		lsf Brooks Fuel Inc.
☐ N44910	Boeing (Douglas) DC-4 (C-54D-1-DC)	10601 / DC 332	USN56493	0045	1297	4 PW R-2000	30241	Fuel Tanker		lsf Brooks Fuel Inc.
☐ N44911	Boeing (Douglas) DC-4 (C-54B-1-DC)	10461 / DC 192	USN50857	0044	1096	4 PW R-2000	30241	Fuel Tanker		lsf Brooks Fuel Inc.
☐ N90201	Boeing (Douglas) DC-4 (C-54D-10-DC)	10828 / DC 559	42-72723	0045	0294	4 PW R-2000	30241	Fuel Tanker		lsf Brooks Fuel Inc.

290 registration type of aircraft cn/fn ex/ex* mfd del powered by mtow kg configuration selcal name/fln/specialitites/remarks

BROOKS RANGE AVIATION (Sourdough Air Service, Inc. dba / Subsidiary of Jespersen Aircraft Services / Seasonal April-October ops only) **Bettles, AK**

PO Box 10, Bettles, AK 99726, USA ☎ (907) 692-5444 Tx: none Fax: (907) 692-2185 SITA: n/a
F: 1979 n/a Head: Jay & Judy Jespersen Net: n/a Winter address: 18140 West Carol Ave., Casa Grande, AZ 85222. Phone & Fax: (520) 426-1275.

☐ N58316	Cessna A185F Skywagon	*18503284*		*0077*	*0296*	*1 CO IO-520-D*	*1520*			
☐ N93769	Cessna A185F Skywagon	*18503241*		*0077*	*0991*	*1 CO IO-520-D*	*1520*			*Floats*
☐ N42013	Helio H-295 Super Courier	*1256*		*0067*	*0295*	*1 LY GO-480-G1A6*	*1542*			
☐ N1954J	De Havilland DHC-2 Beaver I	*740*	*C-GAEA*	*0054*	*0294*	*1 PW R-985*	*2313*			*Floats*
☐ N4040W	De Havilland DHC-2 Beaver I	*1147*	*N90793*	*0057*	*0491*	*1 PW R-985*	*2313*			*lsf pvt / Floats*

BROOKS SEAPLANE SERVICE, Inc. (Seasonal March-November ops only) **Coeur d'Alene-Brooks SPB, ID**

PO Box 1028, Coeur d'Alene, ID 83814, USA ☎ (208) 664-2842 Tx: none Fax: none SITA: n/a
F: 1946 n/a Head: William R. Brooks Net: n/a

☐ N9752Z	Cessna U206G Stationair 6 II	*U20606644*		*0082*	*1293*	*1 CO IO-520-F*	*1633*			*Floats*
☐ N2106K	De Havilland DHC-2 Beaver I	*1131*	*LN-KCQ*	*0056*	*0790*	*1 PW R-985*	*2313*			*Floats*

BULLDOG AIRLINES, Inc. (Affiliated with Downtown Heliport Corp. / formerly The Phoenix Corp.) **Orlando-Sanford, FL & Savannah-Int'l, GA**

PO Box 951899, Lake Mary, FL 32795-1899, USA ☎ (561) 324-4110 Tx: none Fax: (561) 324-4113 SITA: n/a
F: 1985 10 Head: Robert R. Uttal Net: http://www.film-orlando.org/.bulldog/

☐ N222TV	Eurocopter (Aerosp.) AS350B AStar	*1313*	*N909BA*	*0080*	*0395*	*1 TU Arriel 1B*	*1950*			*cvtd AS350D*
☐ N5802X	Eurocopter (Aerosp.) AS355F1 TwinStar	*5225*		*0082*	*0295*	*2 AN 250-C20F*	*2400*			*lsf Heliproperties Inc.*

BULLOCK CHARTER, Inc. **Fitchburg-Municipal, MA**

72 Goodnow Road, Princeton, MA 01541, USA ☎ (978) 464-2706 Tx: none Fax: (978) 464-5310 SITA: n/a
F: 1974 n/a Head: Richard B. Bullock Net: n/a

☐ N860S	Learjet 35A	*35A-086*	*N86CS*	*0076*	*1197*	*2 GA TFE731-2-2B*	*8301*			

BURLINGTON AIR (Bernard Gilding dba) **Memphis-Int'l, TN**

4112 Elkgrove Cove, Memphis, TN 38115, USA ☎ (901) 365-4699 Tx: none Fax: none SITA: n/a
F: 1983 n/a Head: Bernard Gilding Net: n/a

☐ N390V	Beech E18S	*BA-419*		*0059*	*0186*	*2 PW R-985-AN14B*	*4400*	*Freighter*		

BUSINESS AIR, Inc. = BEN (formerly Bennington Aviation, Inc.) **Bennington-William H. Morse State, VT**

RR 1 Box 1104, Airport Drive, Bennington, VT 05201-9711, USA ☎ (802) 447-2111 Tx: none Fax: (802) 442-3582 SITA: n/a
F: 1972 25 Head: Robert K. Corey ICAO: SKY COURIER Net: n/a

☐ N4025C	Cessna 310R II	*310R1350*		*0078*	*1096*	*2 CO IO-520-M*	*2495*	*Freighter*		
☐ N402ME	Cessna 402C II	*402C0010*		*0079*	*1291*	*2 CO TSIO-520-VB*	*3107*	*Freighter*		
☐ N404BA	Cessna 404 Titan II	*404-0237*	*EI-BVA*	*0078*	*0993*	*2 CO GTSIO-520-M*	*3810*	*Freighter*		
☐ N101TN	Embraer 110P1 Bandeirante (EMB-110P1)	*110271*	*PT-SBI**	*0080*	*0497*	*2 PWC PT6A-34*	*5670*	*Freighter*		
☐ N121GA	Embraer 110P1 Bandeirante (EMB-110P1)	*110209*	*F-GBME*	*0079*	*1196*	*2 PWC PT6A-34*	*5670*	*Freighter*		*lsf General Aviation Svcs / cvtd 110P2*
☐ N49BA	Embraer 110P1 Bandeirante (EMB-110P1)	*110301*	*N401AS*	*0080*	*0496*	*2 PWC PT6A-34*	*5670*	*Freighter*		*lsf FSBU Trustee*
☐ N51BA	Embraer 110P1 Bandeirante (EMB-110P1)	*110404*	*N903FB*	*0082*	*0496*	*2 PWC PT6A-34*	*5900*	*Freighter*		*lsf FSBU Trustee*
☐ N59BA	Embraer 110P1 Bandeirante (EMB-110P1)	*110396*	*N900FB*	*0082*	*0496*	*2 PWC PT6A-34*	*5900*	*Freighter*		*lsf FSBU Trustee*
☐ N621KC	Embraer 110P1 Bandeirante (EMB-110P1)	*110335*	*PT-SDL**	*0081*	*1295*	*2 PWC PT6A-34*	*5670*	*Freighter*		
☐ N710NH	Embraer 110P1 Bandeirante (EMB-110P1)	*110250*	*PT-SAQ*	*0080*	*0394*	*2 PWC PT6A-34*	*5670*	*Freighter*		
☐ N790RA	Embraer 110P1 Bandeirante (EMB-110P1)	*110278*	*G-SWAG*	*0080*	*0693*	*2 PWC PT6A-34*	*5670*	*Freighter*		
☐ N830AC	Embraer 110P1 Bandeirante (EMB-110P1)	*110205*	*N524MW*	*0079*	*0295*	*2 PWC PT6A-34*	*5670*	*Freighter*		
☐ N83BA	Embraer 110P1 Bandeirante (EMB-110P1)	*110351*	*N405AS*	*0081*	*0496*	*2 PWC PT6A-34*	*5670*	*Freighter*		*lsf FSBU Trustee*
☐ N97BA	Embraer 110P1 Bandeirante (EMB-110P1)	*110322*	*N403AS*	*0081*	*0496*	*2 PWC PT6A-34*	*5670*	*Freighter*		*lsf FSBU Trustee*

BUSINESS AVIATION (Daedalus, Inc. dba) **Sioux Falls-Joe Foss Field, SD**

3501 Aviation Avenue, Sioux Falls, SD 57104-0197, USA ☎ (605) 336-7791 Tx: none Fax: (605) 336-8009 SITA: n/a
F: 1957 n/a Head: Dale E. Froehlich Net: http://www.busav.com

☐ N36VG	Beech Bonanza A36	*E-309*		*0072*	*0393*	*1 CO IO-520-BA*	*1633*			*lsf Viking Aircraft Owners Llc*
☐ N340PL	Cessna 340 II	*340-0546*		*0075*	*0393*	*2 CO TSIO-520-K*	*2710*			*lsf Viking Aircraft Owners Llc*
☐ N721YG	Cessna 340 II	*340-0342*		*0073*	*0195*	*2 CO TSIO-520-K*	*2710*			
☐ N7914Q	Cessna 414A Chancellor III	*414A0305*	*N666PM*	*0079*	*1090*	*2 CO TSIO-520-NB*	*3062*			
☐ N100DG	Cessna 421B Golden Eagle	*421B0903*		*0075*	*0393*	*2 CO GTSIO-520-H*	*3379*			*lsf Viking Aircraft Owners Llc*
☐ N616GB	Beech King Air 200	*BB-752*	*N300QW*	*0081*	*0296*	*2 PWC PT6A-41*	*5670*			*lsf King Air Llc*

BUSINESS EXPRESS AIRLINES, Inc. - BEX = HQ / GAA (Subs.of AMR Corp. / formerly Business Express, Inc. & Atlantic Air) **Portsmouth-Pease Int'l, NH**

55 Washington Street, Suite 300, Dover, NH 03820, USA ☎ (603) 740-3000 Tx: none Fax: (603) 740-3058 SITA: n/a
F: 1981 1500 Head: Robert E. Martens IATA: 357 ICAO: BIZEX Net: n/a Expected to be integrated into AMERICAN EAGLE AIRLINES later in 1999.
Aircraft are operated in code-sharing agreements with AA as AMERICAN CONNECTION, DL as DELTA CONNECTION & Northwest Airlines as NORTHWEST AIRLINK (in own colors) using the IATA-codes of the mentioned airlines.

☐ N334BE	Saab SF340A	*340A-158*	*N158CA*	*0089*	*0398*	*2 GE CT7-5A2*	*12372*	*Y34*		
☐ N335BE	Saab SF340A	*340A-146*	*N146CA*	*0089*	*0298*	*2 GE CT7-5A2*	*12372*	*Y34*		
☐ N336BE	Saab SF340A	*340A-028*	*N347CA*	*0085*	*0498*	*2 GE CT7-5A2*	*12372*	*Y34*		
☐ N337BE	Saab SF340A	*340A-047*	*N358CA*	*0085*	*0398*	*2 GE CT7-5A2*	*12372*	*Y34*		
☐ N338BE	Saab SF340A	*340A-034*	*N356CA*	*0085*	*0697*	*2 GE CT7-5A2*	*12372*	*Y34*		
☐ N339BE	Saab SF340A	*340A-044*	*N357CA*	*0085*	*0697*	*2 GE CT7-5A2*	*12372*	*Y34*		
☐ N340BE	Saab SF340A	*340A-062*	*SE-E62**	*0086*	*0986*	*2 GE CT7-5A2*	*12372*	*Y34*		
☐ N341BE	Saab SF340A	*340A-063*	*SE-E63**	*0086*	*0986*	*2 GE CT7-5A2*	*12372*	*Y34*		
☐ N342BE	Saab SF340A	*340A-096*	*SE-E96**	*0087*	*0787*	*2 GE CT7-5A2*	*12372*	*Y34*		
☐ N343BE	Saab SF340A	*340A-101*	*SE-F01**	*0087*	*0987*	*2 GE CT7-5A2*	*12372*	*Y34*		
☐ N344BE	Saab SF340A	*340A-104*	*SE-F04**	*0087*	*1087*	*2 GE CT7-5A2*	*12372*	*Y34*		
☐ N345BE	Saab SF340A	*340A-108*	*SE-F08**	*0087*	*1287*	*2 GE CT7-5A2*	*12372*	*Y34*		
☐ N346BE	Saab SF340A	*340A-150*	*SE-F50**	*0089*	*0689*	*2 GE CT7-5A2*	*12372*	*Y34*		
☐ N347BE	Saab 340B	*340B-187*	*SE-F87**	*0090*	*0490*	*2 GE CT7-9B*	*12927*	*Y34*		
☐ N348BE	Saab 340B	*340B-190*	*SE-F90**	*0090*	*0590*	*2 GE CT7-9B*	*12927*	*Y34*		
☐ N349BE	Saab 340B	*340B-196*	*SE-F96**	*0090*	*0690*	*2 GE CT7-9B*	*12927*	*Y34*		
☐ N350BE	Saab 340B	*340B-197*	*SE-F97**	*0090*	*0690*	*2 GE CT7-9B*	*12927*	*Y34*		
☐ N351BE	Saab 340B	*340B-237*	*SE-G37**	*0091*	*0591*	*2 GE CT7-9B*	*12927*	*Y34*		
☐ N352BE	Saab 340B	*340B-239*	*SE-G39**	*0091*	*0591*	*2 GE CT7-9B*	*12927*	*Y34*		
☐ N353BE	Saab 340B	*340B-242*	*SE-G42**	*0091*	*0591*	*2 GE CT7-9B*	*12927*	*Y34*		
☐ N354BE	Saab 340B	*340B-246*	*SE-G46**	*0091*	*0691*	*2 GE CT7-9B*	*12927*	*Y34*		
☐ N355BE	Saab 340B	*340B-209*	*SE-G09**	*0091*	*1291*	*2 GE CT7-9B*	*12927*	*Y34*		
☐ N356BE	Saab 340B	*340B-275*	*SE-G75**	*0091*	*1291*	*2 GE CT7-9B*	*12927*	*Y34*		
☐ N357BE	Saab 340B	*340B-277*	*SE-G77**	*0091*	*1291*	*2 GE CT7-9B*	*12927*	*Y34*		
☐ N358BE	Saab 340B	*340B-279*	*SE-G79**	*0091*	*0192*	*2 GE CT7-9B*	*12927*	*Y34*		
☐ N359BE	Saab 340B	*340B-285*	*SE-G85**	*0092*	*0292*	*2 GE CT7-9B*	*12927*	*Y34*		
☐ N360BE	Saab 340B	*340B-287*	*SE-G87**	*0092*	*0392*	*2 GE CT7-9B*	*12927*	*Y34*		
☐ N361BE	Saab 340B	*340B-290*	*SE-G90**	*0092*	*0392*	*2 GE CT7-9B*	*12927*	*Y34*		
☐ N362BE	Saab 340B	*340B-291*	*SE-G91**	*0092*	*0392*	*2 GE CT7-9B*	*12927*	*Y34*		
☐ N363BE	Saab 340B	*340B-293*	*SE-G93**	*0092*	*0492*	*2 GE CT7-9B*	*12927*	*Y34*		
☐ N364BE	Saab 340B	*340B-294*	*SE-G94**	*0092*	*0492*	*2 GE CT7-9B*	*12927*	*Y34*		
☐ N365BE	Saab 340B	*340B-299*	*SE-G99**	*0092*	*0592*	*2 GE CT7-9B*	*12927*	*Y34*		
☐ N366BE	Saab 340B	*340B-303*	*SE-C03**	*0092*	*0692*	*2 GE CT7-9B*	*12927*	*Y34*		
☐ N741BA	Saab SF340A	*340A-090*	*SE-E90**	*0087*	*0491*	*2 GE CT7-5A2*	*12372*	*Y34*		
☐ N742BA	Saab SF340A	*340A-092*	*SE-E92**	*0087*	*0691*	*2 GE CT7-5A2*	*12372*	*Y34*		
☐ N743BA	Saab SF340A	*340A-093*	*SE-E93**	*0087*	*0491*	*2 GE CT7-5A2*	*12372*	*Y34*		
☐ N744BA	Saab SF340A	*340A-105*	*SE-F05**	*0087*	*0691*	*2 GE CT7-5A2*	*12372*	*Y34*		
☐ N745BA	Saab SF340A	*340A-111*	*SE-F11**	*0087*	*0691*	*2 GE CT7-5A2*	*12372*	*Y34*		
☐ N746BA	Saab SF340A	*340A-138*	*SE-F38**	*0088*	*0691*	*2 GE CT7-5A2*	*12372*	*Y34*		
☐ N747BA	Saab SF340A	*340A-148*	*SE-F48**	*0089*	*0691*	*2 GE CT7-5A2*	*12372*	*Y34*		
☐ N748BA	Saab SF340A	*340A-149*	*SE-F49**	*0089*	*0691*	*2 GE CT7-5A2*	*12372*	*Y34*		
☐ N749BA	Saab SF340A	*340A-152*	*SE-F52**	*0089*	*0591*	*2 GE CT7-5A2*	*12372*	*Y34*		
☐ N751BA	Saab SF340A	*340A-157*	*SE-F57**	*0089*	*0491*	*2 GE CT7-5A2*	*12372*	*Y34*		

BUSINESS HELICOPTERS (New Hampshire Helicopters, Inc. dba) **Hampton, NH**

PO Box 5000, Hampton, NH 03842-5000, USA ☎ (603) 929-6060 Tx: none Fax: (603) 929-6061 SITA: n/a
F: 1984 12 Head: Stephen W. Foss Net: n/a

☐ N87TV	Bell 206L-1 LongRanger II	*45572*	*N57NH*	*0080*	*1085*	*1 AN 250-C28B*	*1882*			*lsf pvt*
☐ N4NH	Agusta A109A II	*7383*	*N109NH*	*0087*	*1096*	*2 AN 250-C20B*	*2600*			*lsf pvt*

BUSINESS JET SOLUTIONS (Jet Solutions Llc dba/Subs.of Bombardier Business Jet Solutions Inc./formerly AMR Combs Worldwide Flight Operations) **Dallas-Love Field, TX**

8001 Lemmon Ave., Suite 402, Dallas, TX 75209, USA ☎ (214) 956-1413 Tx: none Fax: (214) 956-1452 SITA: n/a
F: 1971 n/a Head: Dale Niederhauser Net: n/a Operates executive air charters (from 30 US bases) in connection with ALLIANCE-program, offering commercial air carrier certificate FAR135 to companies without own certificate.
Companies using the Alliance-management program: BOMBARDIER BUSINESS JET SOLUTIONS, CHANTILLY AIR, I.C. JET, JET RESOURCE & SPECIALIZED TRANSPORT – for details see under each company.
Additional, non-commerical executive aircraft are operated under management contract on behalf of private companies.

291 registration type of aircraft *cn/fn* *ex/ex** *mfd* *del* *powered by* *mtow kg* *configuration* *selcal* *name/fln/specialitites/remarks*

BUTLER AIR, Inc.
Butler-County/K.W. Scholter Field, PA

485 Airport Road, Butler, PA 16002, USA ☎ (724) 586-6023 Tx: none Fax: (724) 586-6554 SITA: n/a
F: 1989 ⁂ n/a Head: Richard M. Ryan Net: n/a

☐ N1707G	Cessna 340 II	*340-0514*		*0075*	*0894*	*2 CO TSIO-520-K*	*2710*			
☐ N74RR	Beech King Air B100	*BE-122*	*XB-ESH*	*0081*	*0597*	*2 GA TPE331-6-252B*	*5352*			
☐ N673LR	Cessna 550 Citation II	*550-0179*	*N673LP*	*0080*	*0994*	*2 PWC JT15D-4*	*6033*			

BUTLER AIRCRAFT, Company
Redmond, OR

1050 East Sisters Avenue, Redmond, OR 97756, USA ☎ (541) 548-8166 Tx: none Fax: (541) 548-0863 SITA: n/a
F: 1946 ⁂ 25 Head: Calvin J. Butler Net: n/a Aircraft below MTOW 1361 kg: Cessna 150 & 182.

☐ N60018	Cessna TU206F Turbo Stationair	*U20602002*		*0073*	*1088*	*1 CO TSIO-520-C*	*1633*			
☐ N401US	Boeing (Douglas) DC-7	*45145 / 767*	*N6331C*	*0057*	*0376*	*4 WR R-3350*	*51619*	*Tanker*		62
☐ N6318C	Boeing (Douglas) DC-7	*44282 / 520*		*0054*	*0373*	*4 WR R-3350*	*51619*	*Tanker*		167
☐ N6353C	Boeing (Douglas) DC-7	*45486 / 964*		*0058*	*0882*	*4 WR R-3350*	*51619*	*Tanker*		66
☐ N531BA	Lockheed L-182 (C-130A) Hercules	*1A-3139*	*56-0531*	*0057*	*0291*	*4 AN T56-A*	*56336*	*Tanker / Frtr*		67

BUTTE AVIATION, Inc. = PPS
Butte-Bert Mooney, MT

PO Box 4183, Butte, MT 59701, USA ☎ (406) 494-6694 Tx: none Fax: (406) 494-4498 SITA: n/a
F: 1988 ⁂ n/a Head: Eugene F. Hughes, Jr. ICAO: PIPESTONE Net: n/a Aircraft below MTOW 1361kg: Cessna 172/182 & Mooney M20K

☐ N36026	Piper PA-32RT-300 Lance II	*32R-7885152*		*0078*	*0995*	*1 LY IO-540-K1G5D*	*1633*			
☐ N30252	Cessna T210L Turbo Centurion II	*21059896*		*0073*	*0990*	*1 CO TSIO-520-H*	*1724*			
☐ N24CT	Piper PA-34-200T Seneca II	*34-7670248*		*0076*	*0894*	*2 CO TSIO-360-E*	*2073*			
☐ N47537	Piper PA-34-200T Seneca II	*34-7770413*		*0077*	*0994*	*2 CO TSIO-360-E*	*2073*			
☐ N81070	Piper PA-34-200T Seneca II	*34-8070013*		*0080*	*0392*	*2 CO TSIO-360-EB*	*2073*			
☐ N2637Y	Cessna 340	*340-0013*		*0072*	*0394*	*2 CO TSIO-520-K*	*2710*			
☐ N50CB	Cessna 414A Chancellor III	*414A0228*		*0079*	*0588*	*2 CO TSIO-520-NB*	*3062*			
☐ N27319	Piper PA-31-350 Navajo Chieftain	*31-7852137*		*0078*	*0794*	*2 LY TIO-540-J2BD*	*3175*			
☐ N59982	Piper PA-31-350 Navajo Chieftain	*31-7552071*		*0075*	*0794*	*2 LY TIO-540-J2BD*	*3175*			
☐ N7694L	Piper PA-31-350 Navajo Chieftain	*31-7305024*		*0073*	*0794*	*2 LY TIO-540-J2BD*	*3175*			

BYERLY AVIATION, Inc.
Peoria-Greater Peoria Regional, IL

Greater Peoria Airport, Peoria, IL 61607, USA ☎ (309) 697-6300 Tx: none Fax: (309) 697-2779 SITA: n/a
F: 1955 ⁂ n/a Head: Larry Byerly Net: n/a Aircraft below MTOW 1361kg: Mooney M20J.

☐ N50BA	Twin (Aero) Shrike Commander 500S	*500S-1860-39*	*N708M*	*0069*	*1086*	*2 LY IO-540-E1B5*	*3062*			
☐ N48BA	Twin (Aero) Jetprop Commander 840 (690C)	*11665*	*D-IWKW*	*0081*	*0597*	*2 GA TPE331-5-254K*	*4683*			
☐ N811EC	Twin (Aero) Jetprop Commander 840 (690C)	*11615*	*N811LC*	*0080*	*1196*	*2 GA TPE331-5-254K*	*4683*			
☐ N700BA	Beech King Air B100	*BE-84*	*N300TN*	*0080*	*0391*	*2 GA TPE331-6-252B*	*5352*			

C-AIR (Cecil R. Shuman dba / Seasonal April-October ops only)
King Salmon, AK

PO Box 82, King Salmon, AK 99613, USA ☎ (907) 246-6318 Tx: none Fax: (907) 688-3969 SITA: n/a
F: 1993 ⁂ n/a Head: Cecil R. Shuman Net: n/a

☐ N8388Z	Cessna 205 (210-5)	*205-0388*		*0063*	*0197*	*1 CO IO-470-S*	*1497*			*Floats / Wheels*
☐ N3969Q	Cessna A185F Skywagon	*18502216*		*0073*	*0293*	*1 CO IO-520-D*	*1520*			*Floats / Wheels*

CALALASKA HELICOPTERS, Inc. (formerly Calalaska Air Transport)
Santa Maria-Capt.G.Allan Hancock Field, CA & Homer, AK

3123 Liberator Street, Santa Maria, CA 93455, USA ☎ (805) 922-1199 Tx: none Fax: (805) 928-7395 SITA: n/a
F: 1982 ⁂ 4 Head: Cy L. Asta Net: n/a

☐ N22EA	Bell 206B JetRanger III	*1783*		*0075*	*0782*	*1 AN 250-C20B*	*1451*			*lsf pvt / cvtd JetRanger*
☐ N5006R	Bell 206B JetRanger III	*2532*		*0078*	*0584*	*1 AN 250-C20B*	*1451*			*lsf pvt*

CALSTAR (California Shock-Trauma Air Rescue dba)
Hayward-Air Terminal, CA

20876 Corsair Blvd, Suite B, Hayward, CA 94545, USA ☎ (510) 887-3063 Tx: none Fax: (510) 887-3185 SITA: n/a
F: 1986 ⁂ 85 Head: Joseph F. Cook Net: http://www.calstar.org

☐ N105LS	Eurocopter (MBB) BO105LS-A3	*2012*	*C-FMCL*	*0087*	*0494*	*2 AN 250-C28C*	*2600*	*EMS*		
☐ N105SM	Eurocopter (MBB) BO105CBS	*S-549*	*N105LF*	*0081*	*0194*	*2 AN 250-C20B*	*2500*	*EMS*		
☐ N477CS	Eurocopter (MBB) BO105LS-A3	*2045*	*N3073D*	*0091*	*0795*	*2 AN 250-C28C*	*2600*	*EMS*		
☐ N623MB	Eurocopter (MBB) BO105CBS	*S-750*	*D-HDXL**	*0086*	*0993*	*2 AN 250-C20B*	*2500*	*EMS*		
☐ N7HG	Cessna 421B Golden Eagle	*421B0869*		*0075*	*0498*	*2 CO GTSIO-520-H*	*3379*	*EMS*		
☐ N222RX	Bell 222UT	*47561*	*CS-MHC*	*0088*	*0898*	*2 LY LTS101-750C.1*	*3560*	*EMS*		
☐ N222UT	Bell 222UT	*47559*	*CS-MHA*	*0087*	*0898*	*2 LY LTS101-750C.1*	*3560*	*EMS*		

CAMAI AIR = R9 / CAM (Village Aviation, Inc. dba)
Bethel, AK

PO Box 221188, Bethel, AK 99522-1188, USA ☎ (907) 543-4040 Tx: none Fax: (907) 543-2369 SITA: n/a
F: 1977 ⁂ 25 Head: Don R. King IATA: 451 ICAO: AIR CAMAI Net: n/a Aircraft below MTOW 1361kg: Cessna 172 & Piper PA-28

☐ N76RL	Piper PA-32-300 Cherokee SIX	*32-7540024*		*0075*	*0190*	*1 LY IO-540-K1A5*	*1542*			
☐ N7353Q	Cessna U206F Stationair	*U20602180*		*0073*	*0784*	*1 CO IO-520-F*	*1633*			
☐ N1668U	Cessna 207 Skywagon	*20700268*		*0075*	*0289*	*1 CO IO-520-F*	*1724*			*lsf Tununrmuit Rinit Corp.*
☐ N6314H	Cessna 207A Stationair 7 II	*20700478*		*0078*	*0893*	*1 CO IO-520-F*	*1724*			
☐ N707FY	Cessna 207 Skywagon	*20700063*		*0069*	*0791*	*1 CO IO-520-F*	*1724*			
☐ N73188	Cessna 207A Stationair 8 II	*20700568*		*0079*	*1096*	*1 CO IO-520-F*	*1724*			
☐ N7389U	Cessna 207A Stationair 7 II	*20700432*		*0078*	*1296*	*1 CO IO-520-F*	*1724*			

C & D – Flight Dept. (Flight Dept. of C & D Interiors / Member of C & D Plastics, Inc.)
Santa Ana-John Wayne/Orange County, CA

19401 Campus Drive, Hangar 10, Santa Ana, CA 92707, USA ☎ (714) 757-1214 Tx: none Fax: (714) 757-1215 SITA: n/a
F: 1991 ⁂ n/a Head: Joseph Moran Net: n/a Operates non-commercial VIP flights for its own group of companies only.

☐ N87NW	Beech King Air B100	*BE-42*	*N700SB*	*0078*	*0992*	*2 GA TPE331-6-252B*	*5352*	*VIP*		
☐ N73CD	Boeing (Douglas) DC-3C (C-47B-27-DK)	*32529*	*N87664*	*0045*	*1091*	*2 PW R-1830*	*12202*	*VIP*		

C & M AIRCRAFT, Inc.
Sacramento-Executive, CA

5963 Freeport Blvd, Suite 102, Sacramento, CA 95822, USA ☎ (916) 428-2250 Tx: none Fax: (916) 428-2277 SITA: n/a
F: 1995 ⁂ n/a Head: Byron H. McCluskey Net: n/a

☐ N1010F	Twin (Aero) Commander 500B	*500B-1403-145*		*0064*	*0995*	*2 LY IO-540-B1A5*	*3062*			

C & M AIRWAYS, Inc.
El Paso-Int'l, TX

7335 Boeing Drive, El Paso, TX 79925, USA ☎ (915) 779-3097 Tx: none Fax: (915) 779-0479 SITA: n/a
F: 1993 ⁂ n/a Head: Bradley A. Cryderman Net: n/a

☐ N3410	Convair 640 (F) (SCD)	*27*		*0052*	*1098*	*2 RR Dart 542-4*	*24948*	*Freighter*		*lsf Century Airlines Inc./cvtd CV340-32*
☐ N3417	Convair 640 (F) (SCD)	*48*		*0053*	*1197*	*2 RR Dart 542-4*	*24948*	*Freighter*		*lsf Century Airlines Inc./cvtd CV340-32*
☐ N3420	Convair 640 (F) (SCD)	*64*		*0053*	*1197*	*2 RR Dart 542-4*	*24948*	*Freighter*		*lsf Century Airlines Inc./cvtd CV340-32*
☐ N640CM	Convair 640 (F) (SCD)	*104*	*C-GCWY*	*0053*	*0993*	*2 RR Dart 542-4*	*24948*	*Freighter*		*lsf Century Airlines Inc./cvtd CV340-48*
☐ N640R	Convair 640 (F) (SCD)	*332*	*PH-MAL*	*0056*	*0397*	*2 RR Dart 542-4*	*24948*	*Freighter*		*lsf Century Airlines Inc./cvtd CV440-11*
☐ N73137	Convair 640 (F) (SCD)	*88*		*0053*	*1098*	*2 RR Dart 542-4*	*24948*	*Freighter*		*lsf Century Airlines Inc./cvtd CV340-31*

CAPE AIR = 9K / KAP (Key West Express / Nantucket Airlines) (Hyannis Air Service, Inc. dba)
Hyannis-Barnstable Municipal, MA

660 Barnstable Road, Hyannis, MA 02601, USA ☎ (978) 771-6944 Tx: none Fax: (978) 775-8815 SITA: n/a
F: 1956 ⁂ 50 Head: Daniel A. Wolf IATA: 306 ICAO: CAIR Net: n/a
Operations between Hyannis & Nantucket are conducted under the name NANTUCKET AIRLINES & out of Naples, FL under the name of KEY WEST EXPRESS (same headquarters & fleet).

☐ N120PC	Cessna 402C II	*402C0079*		*0079*	*1195*	*2 CO TSIO-520-VB*	*3107*	*Y9*		*lsf Hyannis Air Leasing Inc.*
☐ N121PB	Cessna 402C II	*402C0507*	*N6874X*	*0081*	*1291*	*2 CO TSIO-520-VB*	*3107*	*Y9*		*lsf Hyannis Air Leasing Inc.*
☐ N1361G	Cessna 402C II	*402C0270*		*0080*	*0196*	*2 CO TSIO-520-VB*	*3107*	*Y9*		
☐ N1376G	Cessna 402C II	*402C0271*		*0080*	*0889*	*2 CO TSIO-520-VB*	*3107*	*Y9*		*lsf Hyannis Air Leasing Inc.*
☐ N161TA	Cessna 402C II	*402C0070*		*0079*	*0598*	*2 CO TSIO-520-VB*	*3107*	*Y9*		
☐ N223PB	Cessna 402C II	*402C0105*	*N261PB*	*0079*	*0796*	*2 CO TSIO-520-VB*	*3107*	*Y9*		
☐ N2611X	Cessna 402C II	*402C0072*		*0079*	*0194*	*2 CO TSIO-520-VB*	*3107*	*Y9*		
☐ N2615G	Cessna 402C II	*402C0101*		*0079*	*0495*	*2 CO TSIO-520-VB*	*3107*	*Y9*		
☐ N26514	Cessna 402C II	*402C0344*		*0080*	*0497*	*2 CO TSIO-520-VB*	*3107*	*Y9*		*lsf Ocean Air Inc.*
☐ N26632	Cessna 402C II	*402C0404*		*0080*	*0894*	*2 CO TSIO-520-VB*	*3107*	*Y9*		
☐ N2714M	Cessna 402C II	*402C0211*		*0079*	*0698*	*2 CO TSIO-520-VB*	*3107*	*Y9*		
☐ N36911	Cessna 402C II	*402C0314*		*0080*	*0196*	*2 CO TSIO-520-VB*	*3107*	*Y9*		
☐ N402VN	Cessna 402C II	*402C0488*		*0081*	*0396*	*2 CO TSIO-520-VB*	*3107*	*Y9*		
☐ N406GA	Cessna 402C II	*402C0329*	*N2642D*	*0080*	*0987*	*2 CO TSIO-520-VB*	*3107*	*Y9*		*lsf Charles R. Harris Inc.*
☐ N4652N	Cessna 402C II	*402C0011*		*0078*	*0498*	*2 CO TSIO-520-VB*	*3107*	*Y9*		
☐ N524CA	Cessna 402C II	*402C0522*	*C-GSKG*	*0081*	*0596*	*2 CO TSIO-520-VB*	*3107*	*Y9*		
☐ N548GA	Cessna 402C II	*402C0653*		*0082*	*1291*	*2 CO TSIO-520-VB*	*3107*	*Y9*		*lsf Charles R. Harris Inc.*
☐ N618CA	Cessna 402C II	*402C0620*		*0081*	*0598*	*2 CO TSIO-520-VB*	*3107*	*Y9*		
☐ N660CA	Cessna 402C II	*402C0406*		*0081*	*0493*	*2 CO TSIO-520-VB*	*3107*	*Y9*		
☐ N67786	Cessna 402C II	*402C0631*		*0082*	*0296*	*2 CO TSIO-520-VB*	*3107*	*Y9*		*Key West Express-colors*
☐ N67886	Cessna 402C II	*402C0435*		*0081*	*0294*	*2 CO TSIO-520-VB*	*3107*	*Y9*		
☐ N6813J	Cessna 402C II	*402C0641*		*0081*	*1294*	*2 CO TSIO-520-VB*	*3107*	*Y9*		

292 registration type of aircraft cn/fn ex/ex* mfd del powered by mtow kg configuration selcal name/fln/specialitites/remarks

☐ N6837Y	Cessna 402C II	402C0467		0081	0491	2 CO TSIO-520-VB	3107	Y9		lsf Hyannis Air Leasing Inc.
☐ N68391	Cessna 402C II	402C0483		0081	0694	2 CO TSIO-520-VB	3107	Y9		
☐ N6875D	Cessna 402C II	402C0511		0081	0588	2 CO TSIO-520-VB	3107	Y9		lsf Charles R. Harris Inc.
☐ N6879R	Cessna 402C II	402C0611		0082	0493	2 CO TSIO-520-VB	3107	Y9		lsf Ocean Air Inc.
☐ N69SC	Cessna 402C II	402C0041		0078	0896	2 CO TSIO-520-VB	3107	Y9		
☐ N7037E	Cessna 402C II	402C0471	C-GGXH	0081	0395	2 CO TSIO-520-VB	3107	Y9		
☐ N770CA	Cessna 402C II	402C0432	C-GIBL	0081	0593	2 CO TSIO-520-VB	3107	Y9		
☐ N818AN	Cessna 402C II	402C0501	N6842Q	0081	0398	2 CO TSIO-520-VB	3107	Y9		
☐ N83PB	Cessna 402C II	402C0350	N26627	0080	0490	2 CO TSIO-520-VB	3107	Y9		lsf Hyannis Air Leasing Inc.
☐ N88833	Cessna 402C II	402C0265		0080	0290	2 CO TSIO-520-VB	3107	Y9		lsf Charles R. Harris Inc.
☐ N991AA	Cessna 402C II	402C0317	N36916	0080	0294	2 CO TSIO-520-VB	3107	Y9		lsf Ocean Air Inc.

CAPE SMYTHE AIR SERVICE, Inc. = 6C / CMY (formerly Fel Air, Inc.) — **Barrow-Wiley Post/Will Rogers Memorial, AK**

Cape Smythe Air

PO Box 549, Barrow, AK 99723, USA ☎ (907) 852-8333 Tx: none Fax: (907) 852-8332 SITA: n/a
F: 1975 👥 45 Head: Grant B. Thompson IATA: 879 ICAO: CAPE SMYTHE AIR Net: n/a

☐ N20752	Cessna A185F Skywagon	18503041		0076	0886	1 CO IO-520-D	1520	4 Pax		
☐ N61500	Cessna A185F Skywagon II	18504217		0081	0583	1 CO IO-520-D	1520	4 Pax		
☐ N207DH	Cessna 207 Skywagon	20700345		0076	1288	1 CO IO-520-F	1724	7 Pax		
☐ N6295H	Cessna 207A Stationair 7 II	20700471		0078	0385	1 CO IO-520-F	1724	7 Pax		
☐ N73100	Cessna 207A Stationair 7 II	20700559		0079	0380	1 CO IO-520-F	1724	7 Pax		
☐ N7396U	Cessna 207A Stationair 7 II	20700438		0078	0690	1 CO IO-520-F	1724	7 Pax		
☐ N9620M	Cessna 207A Stationair 8 II	20700711		0081	0284	1 CO IO-520-F	1724	8 Pax		
☐ N9641M	Cessna 207A Stationair 8 II	20700714		0081	0482	1 CO IO-520-F	1724			
☐ N9950M	Cessna 207A Stationair 8 II	20700760		0082	1182	1 CO IO-520-F	1724	8 Pax		
☐ N3542H	Piper PA-31-350 Navajo Chieftain	31-7952233		0079	0986	2 LY TIO-540-J2BD	3175	9 Pax		
☐ N4585U	Piper PA-31-350 Navajo Chieftain	31-8052198		0080	0985	2 LY TIO-540-J2BD	3175	9 Pax		
☐ N110JK	Piper PA-31T3-T1040	31T-8375005		0083	0389	2 PWC PT6A-11	4082	9 Pax		
☐ N217CS	Piper PA-31T3-T1040	31T-8275014		0082	1295	2 PWC PT6A-11	4082	9 Pax		
☐ N218CS	Piper PA-31T3-T1040	31T-8275016		0082	1295	2 PWC PT6A-11	4082	9 Pax		
☐ N219CS	Piper PA-31T3-T1040	31T-8275005	C-GPBC	0082	0796	2 PWC PT6A-11	4082	9 Pax		
☐ N315SC	Piper PA-31T3-T1040	31T-8275008	N308SC	0082	1198	2 PWC PT6A-11	4082	9 Pax		
☐ N207CS	Beech C99 Airliner	U-207	C-GGLE	0083	1092	2 PWC PT6A-36	5126	15 Pax		
☐ N216CS	Beech C99 Airliner	U-216	C-GGPP	0083	1291	2 PWC PT6A-36	5126	15 Pax		
☐ N995SB	Beech C99 Airliner	U-179		0081	0591	2 PWC PT6A-36	5126	15 Pax		

CAPITAL AIRLINES, Inc. = CAP — **Oxford-Waterbury, CT**

288 Christian Street, Oxford, CT 06478, USA ☎ (203) 264-3727 Tx: none Fax: (203) 264-0522 SITA: n/a
F: 1986 👥 n/a Head: Milton F. Marshall ICAO: CAPITAL Net: n/a

☐ N421KW	Cessna 421B Golden Eagle	421B0222		0072	0297	2 CO GTSIO-520-H	3379			lsf Royer Aviation Inc.

CAPITAL CARGO INTERNATIONAL AIRLINES, Inc. = PT / CCI — **Orlando-Int'l, FL**

6200 Hazeltine National Drive, Suite 100, Orlando, FL 32822, USA ☎ (407) 855-2004 Tx: none Fax: (407) 855-6620 SITA: n/a
F: 1995 👥 n/a Head: Peter F. Fox ICAO: CAPPY Net: http://www.capitalcargo.com

☐ N1279E	Boeing 727-2Q6 (F) (A)	21971 / 1540		1079	0497	3 PW JT8D-17 (HK)	86487	Freighter		lsf PACA / cvtd -2Q6
☐ N128NA	Boeing 727-2J7 (F) (A)	20879 / 1033		0074	0396	3 PW JT8D-15 (HK3/FDX)	86409	Freighter		Lady Jean / lsf PEGA
☐ N227JL	Boeing 727-214 (F) (A)	20875 / 1020	N375PA	0074	1096	3 PW JT8D-15 (HK3/FDX)	78245	Freighter		lsf PACA
☐ N308AS	Boeing 727-227 (F) (A)	22002 / 1627	N479BN	0080	1198	3 PW JT8D-17R (HK3/FDX)	86409	Freighter		cvtd -227
☐ N357KP	Boeing 727-230 (F) (A)	20675 / 924	G-BPNY	0073	0797	3 PW JT8D-15 (HK3/FDX)	86409	Freighter		Princess Kendall / lsf PEGA / cvtd -230
☐ N808EA	Boeing 727-225 (F) (A)	22439 / 1689	TC-DEL	0080	0398	3 PW JT8D-15A	86409	Freighter		cvtd -225 / Aeromarine, Cargo Broker-TL

CAPITAL CITY AIR CARRIER, Inc. (formerly Dakota Aviation Service, Inc.) — **Pierre-Regional, SD**

4000 Airport Road, Pierre, SD 57501, USA ☎ (605) 224-9000 Tx: none Fax: (605) 224-4876 SITA: n/a
F: 1989 👥 n/a Head: James R. Peitz Net: n/a Aircraft below MTOW 1361kg: Piper PA-28

☐ N75156	Piper PA-32R-300 Lance	32R-7680272		0076	0290	1 LY IO-540-K1A5D	1633			lsf Aircraft Unlimited Inc.
☐ N8745E	Piper PA-32-300 Cherokee SIX	32-7640073		0076	0191	1 LY IO-540-K1A5	1542			lsf pvt
☐ N36369	Piper PA-34-200T Seneca II	34-7870323		0078	0290	2 CO TSIO-360-E	2073			lsf Aircraft Unlimited Ltd
☐ N8180G	Piper PA-34-200T Seneca II	34-8070174		0080	0192	2 CO TSIO-360-EB	2073			lsf pvt
☐ N9638K	Piper PA-34-200T Seneca II	34-7670212		0076	0290	2 CO TSIO-360-E	2073			lsf Aircraft Unlimited Ltd
☐ N300VF	Piper PA-31-350 Navajo Chieftain	31-7852050		0078	0297	2 LY TIO-540-J2BD	3175			lsf Aircraft Unlimited Inc.
☐ N305SK	Piper PA-31-350 Navajo Chieftain	31-7652039		0076	0696	2 LY TIO-540-J2BD	3175			lsf Aircraft Unlimited Inc.
☐ N777ZM	Piper PA-31-350 Navajo Chieftain	31-8052193		0080	0290	2 LY TIO-540-J2BD	3175			lsf Aircraft Unlimited Inc.
☐ N126BP	Cessna 414A Chancellor III	414A0214		0079	0295	2 CO TSIO-520-NB	3062			lsf Aircraft Unlimited Inc.

CARDINAL AIRLINES, Inc. — **Melbourne-Int'l, FL**

1380 Sarno Road, Melbourne, FL 32935, USA ☎ (407) 757-7388 Tx: none Fax: (407) 757-7390 SITA: n/a
F: 1999 👥 n/a Head: Vince Paris Net: n/a Presently being set-up. Intends to start operations during 1999 with Boeing (Douglas) MD-80 aircraft.

CARE FLIGHT AIR AMBULANCE (Air Ambulance Care Flight International, Inc. dba) — **St. Petersburg-Clearwater Int'l, FL**

St. Petersburg-Clearwater Airport, Clearwater, FL 33762, USA ☎ (941) 530-7972 Tx: none Fax: (941) 531-9136 SITA: n/a
F: 1990 👥 n/a Head: Kenneth G. Kreye Net: http://www.careflight.com

☐ N4838A	Cessna 414A Chancellor III	414A0102		0078	1090	2 CO TSIO-520-N	3062	EMS		lst Mercy Medical Airlift
☐ N196CF	Learjet 24B	24B-186	N73PS	0069	0796	2 GE CJ610-6	6123	EMS		
☐ N197CF	Learjet 25B	25B-197	N197WC	0076	1295	2 GE CJ610-6	6804	EMS		
☐ N279LE	Learjet 25B	25B-112	N173J	0073	0897	2 GE CJ610-6	6804			

CAREFLITE (North Central Texas Services, Inc. dba) — **Grand Prairie-Municipal, TX**

3110 South Great Southwest Parkway, Grand Prairie, TX 75052, USA ☎ (972) 988-3353 Tx: none Fax: (972) 988-3144 SITA: n/a
F: 1979 👥 n/a Head: Lura Donnely Net: n/a

☐ N1083G	Bell 206L-3 LongRanger III	51001		0082	1182	1 AN 250-C30P	1882	EMS		
☐ N145CF	Bell 206L-3 LongRanger III	51032	N2017N	0082	1082	1 AN 250-C30P	1882	EMS		
☐ N141CF	Bell 222UT	47507	N146EH	0083	0491	2 LY LTS101-750C.1	3742	EMS		
☐ N142CF	Bell 222UT	47531	N3190K	0085	0491	2 LY LTS101-750C.1	3742	EMS		
☐ N143CF	Bell 222UT	47506	N145EH	0083	0491	2 LY LTS101-750C.1	3742	EMS		
☐ N144CF	Bell 222U	47535	N3217E	0085	0491	2 LY LTS101-750C.1	3742	EMS		

CARGOMASTER Corporation — **Anchorage-Int'l, AK**

2401 Chilligan Drive, Anchorage, AK 99503, USA ☎ (907) 243-1628 Tx: none Fax: (907) 243-4947 SITA: n/a
F: 1981 👥 n/a Head: Maurice L. Carlson Net: n/a Operates FAR91 contract cargo flights for US Government-agencies.

☐ N133B	Boeing (Douglas) C-133B-DL Cargomaster	45584	N77152	0060	1182	4 PW T34-P-9W	129727	Freighter		all silver cs

CARIB-AIR CARGO, Ltd — **West Palm Beach-County Park/Lantana, FL**

PO 6319, Lake Worth, FL 33461, USA ☎ (561) 434-2774 Tx: none Fax: (561) 434-4479 SITA: n/a
F: 1990 👥 n/a Head: Michael L. O'Farrell Net: n/a

☐ N6259Y	Piper PA-23-250 Aztec C	27-3499		0066	1194	2 LY IO-540-C4B5	2359			lsf Idle Time Inc.
☐ N3824C	Twin (Aero) Commander 500	500-697		0059	1095	2 LY O-540-A2B	2722			lsf Candy Yellow Apple Inc.
☐ N6256B	Twin (Aero) Commander 500	500-808		0059	0098	2 LY O-540-A2B	2722			lsf Hartford Holding Corp.
☐ N38BW	Beech H18 Tri-gear	BA-725		0065	0098	2 PW R-985-AN14B	4491	Freighter		lsf Greentree Financial
☐ N486JB	Beech C-45H (18) Tri-gear	AF-858	N9833Z	0056	0497	2 PW R-985-AN14B	3969	Freighter		lsf Hartford Holding Corp./std Lantana
☐ N697Q	Beech G18S	BA-468		0059	0897	2 PW R-985-AN14B	4581	Freighter		lsf Hartford Holding Corp.
☐ N45861	Beech C-45H (18) Tri-gear		46-7236	0046	0398	2 PW R-985-AN14B	3969	Freighter		lsf Hartford Holding Corp.
☐ N838MA	De Havilland DHC-6 Twin Otter 200	188	HH-AIY	0068	1098	2 PWC PT6A-20	5250			lsf Aero Toys Inc.

CARISCH HELICOPTERS, Inc. — **Bozeman-Gallatin Field, MT**

897 Cobb Hill Road., Bozeman, MT 59718, USA ☎ (406) 586-4300 Tx: none Fax: none SITA: n/a
F: 1993 👥 n/a Head: Michael G. Carisch Net: n/a

☐ N2277T	Bell 206B JetRanger III	3631		0482	0696	1 AN 250-C20J	1451			

CAROLINAS HISTORIC AVIATION — **Charlotte-Douglas Int'l, NC**

4108 Airport Road, Charlotte, NC 29219, USA ☎ (704) 359-8442 Tx: none Fax: (704) 359-8442 SITA: n/a
F: 1996 👥 n/a Head: Jim Taylor Net: n/a Non-commerical organisation conducting historic demonstration flights at airshows.

☐ N44V	Boeing (Douglas) DC-3C (C-47-DL)	4545	N46BF	0042	0896	2 PW R-1830	12202	22 Pax/Demo flts		old Piedmont Airlines-colors

CAROLINA SHUTTLE (Division of Airborne Marketing, Inc.) — **Greensboro-Piedmont Triad Int'l, NC**

c/o Airborne Marketing, 7716 Airline Drive, Greensboro, NC 27409, USA ☎ (336) 851-5040 Tx: none Fax: (336) 851-5088 SITA: n/a
F: 1994 👥 n/a Head: Hooman Bahrani Net: n/a

☐ N124WA	Piper PA-31-350 Navajo Chieftain	31-7405242		0074	1194	2 LY TIO-540-J2BD	3175			
☐ N74589	Boeing (Douglas) DC-3C (C-47A-40-DL)	9926	42-24064	0043	0198	2 PW R-1830	12202	Freighter		lsf pvt
☐ N154RH	GAC (Grumman) G-159 Gulfstream I	132	N54NS	0064	0797	2 RR Dart 529-8X	16329			lsf BJ Management Inc.

293 registration type of aircraft cn/fn ex/ex* mfd del powered by mtow kg configuration selcal name/fln/specialitites/remarks

CAROLINA SKY SPORTS (Fayard Enterprises, Inc. dba) — North Raleigh-CSS, NC

PO Box 703, Louisburg, NC 27549, USA ☎ (919) 496-2224 Tx: none Fax: (919) 496-7000 SITA: n/a
F: 1965 ⁂ n/a Head: Paul D. Fayard Net: n/a Operates skydiving flights only for all sort of customers.

☐ N100UE	Beech King Air A90 (65-A90)	LJ-138	N100UF	0066	0591	2 PWC PT6A-20	4218	Para		
☐ N1999G	Beech King Air B90	LJ-319	N845K	0068	0992	2 PWC PT6A-20	4377	Para		
☐ N525JK	Beech King Air A90 (65-A90)	LJ-305	N732NM	0067	0694	2 PWC PT6A-20	4218	Para		
☐ N587M	Beech King Air B90	LJ-361	N530M	0068	1292	2 PWC PT6A-20	4377	Para		
☐ N798K	Beech King Air A90 (65-A90)	LJ-178A		0066	0693	2 PWC PT6A-20	4218	Para		
☐ N81PG	Beech King Air B90	LJ-395	N81PA	0068	0992	2 PWC PT6A-20	4377	Para		
☐ N866A	Beech King Air A90 (65-A90)	LJ-201		0067	0192	2 PWC PT6A-20	4218	Para		
☐ N100AP	De Havilland DHC-6 Twin Otter 100	22	HP-772	0067	1295	2 PWC PT6A-20	5252	Para		
☐ N1022S	De Havilland DHC-6 Twin Otter 100	79	C-GHYH	0067	0396	2 PWC PT6A-20	5252	Para		
☐ N227CS	De Havilland DHC-6 Twin Otter 100	27	ZK-FQK	0067	0698	2 PWC PT6A-20	5252	Para		
☐ N669JW	De Havilland DHC-6 Twin Otter 200	88	P2-RDB	0067	0597	2 PWC PT6A-20	5252	Para		cvtd -100
☐ N932MA	De Havilland DHC-6 Twin Otter 200	211	V3-HTD	0069	0397	2 PWC PT6A-27	5252	Para		
☐ N433CA	CASA 212 Aviocar Srs 200	272	TI-AVV	0082	1196	2 GA TPE331-10-501C	7450	Para		
☐ N434CA	CASA 212 Aviocar Srs 200	286		0082	0395	2 GA TPE331-10-501C	7450	Para		
☐ N439CA	CASA 212 Aviocar Srs 200	290	YN-BYY	0083	1196	2 GA TPE331-10-501C	7450	Para		

CARSON HELICOPTERS, Inc. (Carson Services, Inc. dba) — Perkasie-Heliport, PA & Jacksonville-Heliport, OR

32-H Blooming Glen Road, Perkasie, PA 18944, USA ☎ (215) 249-3535 Tx: none Fax: (215) 249-0726 SITA: n/a
F: 1957 ⁂ 105 Head: Franklin Carson Net: n/a

☐ N239Z	De Havilland DHC-6 Twin Otter 300	239	N15239	0069	0486	2 PWC PT6A-27	5670	Surveyer		lsf Air Associates / tail magnetometer
☐ N920R	De Havilland DHC-6 Twin Otter 100	45	HC-BYK	0067	0388	2 PWC PT6A-20	5252			lsf JMF Aircraft
☐ N116AZ	Sikorsky S-61N	61242	VH-BHO	0064	0488	2 GE CT58-140-1	9979			
☐ N13491	Sikorsky S-61A	61129		0061	0182	2 GE CT58-140-1	9752			
☐ N42626	Sikorsky S-61R	61522		0066	1194	2 GE CT58-140-1	10002			cvtd H-3E
☐ N4263A	Sikorsky S-61R	61551	65-5700	0066	1094	2 GE CT58-140-1	10002			cvtd H-3E
☐ N4263F	Sikorsky S-61R	61533		0066	1194	2 GE CT58-140-1	10002			cvtd H-3E
☐ N4503E	Sikorsky S-61N	61220	G-ASNL	0062	1183	2 GE CT58-140-1	9979			
☐ N612RM	Sikorsky S-61N	61744	C-FSYH	0075	0395	2 GE CT58-140-1	9979			
☐ N7011M	Sikorsky S-61N	61216	G-AWFX	0062	0788	2 GE CT58-140-1	9979			
☐ N81661	Sikorsky S-61A	61272		0064	0395	2 GE CT58-140-1	9752			cvtd SH-3H
☐ N81664	Sikorsky S-61A	61063		0062	0395	2 GE CT58-140-1	9752			cvtd SH-3H
☐ N8167B	Sikorsky S-61A	61137		0062	0395	2 GE CT58-140-1	9752			cvtd SH-3H
☐ N81692	Sikorsky S-61A	61074		0062	0395	2 GE CT58-140-1	9752			cvtd SH-3H
☐ N81697	Sikorsky S-61A	61147		0062	0395	2 GE CT58-140-1	9752			cvtd SH-3H
☐ N81701	Sikorsky S-61A	61529		0066	0395	2 GE CT58-140-1	9752			cvtd SH-3H/std/to be made operational
☐ N81702	Sikorsky S-61A	61608		0067	0395	2 GE CT58-140-1	9752			cvtd SH-3H/std/to be made operational
☐ N8170V	Sikorsky S-61A	61232		0064	0395	2 GE CT58-140-1	9752			cvtd SH-3H
☐ N81743	Sikorsky S-61R	61575		0066	0495	2 GE CT58-140-1	10002			cvtd H-3E/std/to be made operational
☐ N8174J	Sikorsky S-61R	61584		0066	0495	2 GE CT58-140-1	10002			cvtd H-3E/std/to be made operational
☐ N92590	Sikorsky S-61A	61351	152696	0067	0995	2 GE CT58-140-1	9752			cvtd SH-3H
☐ N92592	Sikorsky S-61A	61432	156486	0068	0995	2 GE CT58-140-1	9752			cvtd SH-3H
☐ N9260A	Sikorsky S-61A	61442	156496	0068	0995	2 GE CT58-140-1	9752			cvtd SH-3H
☐ N9271A	Sikorsky S-61A	61449	156503	0068	0995	2 GE CT58-140-1	9752			cvtd SH-3H

CARTERS COUNTRY AVIATION (Carters Shooting Center, Inc. dba) — Houston-David Wayne Hooks Memorial, TX

6231 Treschwig Road, Spring, TX 77373-7698, USA ☎ (281) 443-8393 Tx: none Fax: (281) 443-7672 SITA: n/a
F: 1991 ⁂ n/a Head: William O. Carter Net: n/a

☐ N80BC	Beech King Air B200	BB-1571		0097	1097	2 PWC PT6A-42	5670			

CASCADE HELICOPTERS, Inc. — Cashmere-Heliport, WA

Box 596, Cashmere, WA 98815-0596, USA ☎ (509) 782-2915 Tx: none Fax: (509) 782-3737 SITA: n/a
F: 1960 ⁂ 30 Head: William H. Wells, Jr. Net: http://www.cascade.helicopters.com Aircraft below MTOW 1361 kg: Bell 47G.

☐ N1219W	Bell 206B JetRanger III	1843		0075	0788	1 AN 250-C20B	1451			lsf pvt / cvtd JetRanger
☐ N206CH	Bell 206B JetRanger III	1735		0075	0775	1 AN 250-C20B	1451			cvtd JetRanger
☐ N49573	Bell 206B JetRanger III	1665		0075	0687	1 AN 250-C20B	1451			cvtd JetRanger
☐ N49589	Bell 206B JetRanger III	1912		0076	0581	1 AN 250-C20B	1451			cvtd JetRanger II

CASINO AIRLINES, Inc. = CSO — Shreveport-Downtown/Municipal, LA

1550 Airport Drive, Suite 155, Shreveport, LA 71107, USA ☎ (318) 227-2121 Tx: none Fax: (318) 424-0000 SITA: n/a
F: 1996 ⁂ 42 Head: Lewis McPherson ICAO: CASAIR Net: n/a

☐ N650JX	BAe 3101 Jetstream 31	650	N405AE	0085	0497	2 GA TPE331-10UR-513H	6900	Y19		
☐ N653JX	BAe 3101 Jetstream 31	653	N407AE	0085	0896	2 GA TPE331-10UR-513H	6900	Y19		

CASINO EXPRESS = XP / CXP (T.E.M. Enterprises, Inc. dba) — Elko-Municipal J.C. Harris Field, NV

976 Mountain City Highway, Elko, NV 89801-2728, USA ☎ (702) 738-6040 Tx: none Fax: (702) 738-1881 SITA: n/a
F: 1987 ⁂ 108 Head: Norval Nelson ICAO: CASINO EXPRESS Net: n/a

☐ N233TM	Boeing 737-282 (A)	23043 / 972	CS-TEM	0083	0299	2 PW JT8D-17A	56472	Y119		
☐ N344TM	Boeing 737-282 (A)	23044 / 973	CS-TEN	0083	0299	2 PW JT8D-17A	56472	Y119		
☐ N456TM	Boeing 737-2H4	20336 / 239	N709ML	0670	0987	2 PW JT8D-15 (HK3/AVA)	53070	Y124		
☐ N457TM	Boeing 737-214	20156 / 181	N323XV	0669	0692	2 PW JT8D-15 (HK3/AVA)	49442	Y124		
☐ N789TM	Boeing 737-282 (A)	23046 / 981	CS-TEP	0083	0299	2 PW JT8D-17A	56472	Y119		

CASPER AIR SERVICE, Inc. = CSP — Casper-Natrona County Int'l, WY

7956 Fuller Road, Casper, WY 82604-1696, USA ☎ (307) 472-3400 Tx: none Fax: (307) 237-8534 SITA: n/a
F: 1956 ⁂ 72 Head: Chuck R. Fredrickson ICAO: CASPER AIR Net: n/a

☐ N122MW	Cessna R182 Skylane RG II	R18201276		0079	0296	1 LY O-540-J3C5D	1406			
☐ N4095V	Cessna T303 Crusader	T30300275		0084	0385	2 CO TSIO-520-AE	2336			
☐ N5ER	Cessna T303 Crusader	T30300137		0082	0796	2 CO TSIO-520-AE	2336			
☐ N9272S	Cessna 402C II	402C0252	C-FHDN	0080	0895	2 CO TSIO-520-VB	3107			

CASTLE AVIATION, Inc. = CSJ — Ravenna-Portage County, OH

8101 State Route 44, Ravenna, OH 44266, USA ☎ (330) 296-5563 Tx: none Fax: (330) 296-2265 SITA: n/a
F: 1984 ⁂ n/a Head: Michael H. Grossmann ICAO: CASTLE Net: http://www.castleair.com

☐ N3543A	Piper PA-31-350 Navajo Chieftain	31-7952242		0079	0595	2 LY TIO-540-J2BD	3175			
☐ N35WT	Piper PA-31-310 Navajo B	31-817		0072	0193	2 LY TIO-540-A2C	2948			
☐ N45VT	Twin (Aero) Turbo Commander 690A	11134	N7RB	0073	0395	2 GA TPE331-5-251K	4683			lsf Kolar Aviation Inc.

CATALINA AIR, Inc. — Knoxville-McGhee Tyson, TN

2297 Alcoa Highway, Alcoa, TN 37701, USA ☎ (423) 984-4092 Tx: none Fax: (423) 984-5010 SITA: n/a
F: 1995 ⁂ n/a Head: Linda Lane Net: n/a

☐ N28AA	Boeing (Douglas) DC-3A	2239	N139PB	0040	0197	2 PW R-1830	12202	19 Pax		lsf N28AA Inc.
☐ N62CC	Boeing (Douglas) DC-3C (C-47A-DL)	13798	N625SL	0043	1194	2 PW R-1830	12202	16 Pax		

CATALINA FLYING BOATS, Inc. = CBT (Sister company of Aeronautical Services, Inc.) — Long Beach-Daugherty Field, CA

3215 East Spring Street, Long Beach, CA 90806, USA ☎ (562) 595-5026 Tx: none Fax: (562) 490-0777 SITA: n/a
F: 1989 ⁂ n/a Head: Steve D. Franklin ICAO: CATALINA AIR Net: n/a

☐ N18R	Beech E18S	BA-312		0057		2 PW R-985-AN14B	4218	Freighter		lsf Aeronautical Services Inc.
☐ N9375Y	Beech G18S	BA-564		0060		2 PW R-985-AN14B	4400	Freighter		lsf Aeronautical Services Inc.
☐ N2298C	Boeing (Douglas) DC-3C (TC-47B-35-DK)	33201	N211GB	0045	0896	2 PW R-1830-90D	12202	Freighter		
☐ N403JB	Boeing (Douglas) DC-3C (C-47B-45-DK)	34202	N17778	0045		2 PW R-1830-90D	12202	Freighter		lsf Aeronautical Services Inc.

CAUSEY AVIATION CHARTERS (Causey Aviation Service, Inc. dba) — Liberty-Causey, NC

6120 Smithwood Road, Liberty, NC 27298, USA ☎ (910) 685-4423 Tx: none Fax: (910) 685-4419 SITA: n/a
F: 1967 ⁂ n/a Head: B. Winfield Causey, Jr. Net: n/a

☐ N27272	Piper PA-31-310 Navajo C	31-7712063		0077	0484	2 LY TIO-540-A2C	2948			
☐ N214CK	Beech King Air A100	B-191	N4391W	0074	1189	2 PWC PT6A-28	5216			
☐ N38P	Beech King Air A100	B-231	N3EP	0077	0893	2 PWC PT6A-28	5216			
☐ N53CK	Beech King Air 200	BB-329	N311GA	0078	0397	2 PWC PT6A-41	5670			
☐ N52CK	Cessna S550 Citation S/II	S550-0124	N1867W	0087	1296	2 PWC JT15D-4B	6849			lsf Koury Aviation Inc.
☐ N61CK	Cessna 550 Citation II	550-0195	N60JD	0080	0395	2 PWC JT15D-4	6033			
☐ N48CK	Beech Beechjet 400	RJ-22	N724AA	0087	0198	2 PWC JT15D-5	7158			

CCAIR, Inc. = ED / CDL (US Airways Express) (formerly Sunbird Airlines, Inc.) — Charlotte-Douglas Int'l, NC

PO Box 19929, Charlotte, NC 28219-9929, USA ☎ (704) 359-8990 Tx: none Fax: (704) 359-8997 SITA: n/a
F: 1979 ⁂ 600 Head: Kenneth W. Gann IATA: 354 ICAO: CAROLINA Net: n/a
All aircraft are operated as US AIRWAYS EXPRESS (in full such colours & both titles), a commuter system to provide feeder connection at US Airways major hubs, using US flight numbers.

☐ N159PC	BAe 3101 Jetstream 31	768	G-31-768*	0087	1087	2 GA TPE331-10UGR-514H	6900	Y19		lsf BAMT / op in US Airways Express-cs

294 registration type of aircraft cn/fn ex/ex* mfd del powered by mtow kg configuration selcal name/fln/specialitites/remarks

☐ N913AE	BAe 3201 Jetstream 32EP	913	G-31-913*	0090	1197	2 GA TPE331-12UAR-704H	7350	Y19		lsf BAMT/cvtd 32/op in US Airw.Exp.-cs
☐ N914AE	BAe 3201 Jetstream 32EP	914	G-31-914*	0090	0398	2 GA TPE331-12UAR-704H	7350	Y19		lsf BAMT/cvtd 32/op in US Airw.Exp.-cs
☐ N919AE	BAe 3201 Jetstream 32EP	919	G-31-919*	0090	0398	2 GA TPE331-12UAR-704H	7350	Y19		lsf BAMT/cvtd 32/op in US Airw.Exp.-cs
☐ N920AE	BAe 3201 Jetstream 32EP	920	G-31-920*	0090	1197	2 GA TPE331-12UAR-704H	7350	Y19		lsf BAMT/cvtd 32/op in US Airw.Exp.-cs
☐ N927AE	BAe 3201 Jetstream 32EP	927	G-31-927*	0091	1197	2 GA TPE331-12UAR-704H	7350	Y19		lsf BAMT/cvtd 32/op in US Airw.Exp.-cs
☐ N928AE	BAe 3201 Jetstream 32EP	928	G-31-928*	0091	1197	2 GA TPE331-12UAR-704H	7350	Y19		lsf BAMT/cvtd 32/op in US Airw.Exp.-cs
☐ N930AE	BAe 3201 Jetstream 32EP	930	G-31-930*	0091	1297	2 GA TPE331-12UAR-704H	7350	Y19		lsf BAMT/cvtd 32/op in US Airw.Exp.-cs
☐ N942AE	BAe 3201 Jetstream 32EP	942	G-31-942*	0091	1197	2 GA TPE331-12UAR-704H	7350	Y19		lsf BAMT/cvtd 32/op in US Airw.Exp.-cs
☐ N943AE	BAe 3201 Jetstream 32EP	943	G-31-943*	0091	1197	2 GA TPE331-12UAR-704H	7350	Y19		lsf BAMT/cvtd 32/op in US Airw.Exp.-cs
☐ N952AE	BAe 3201 Jetstream 32EP	952	G-31-952*	0091	0798	2 GA TPE331-12UAR-704H	7350	Y19		lsf BAMT/cvtd 32/op in US Airw.Exp.-cs
☐ N957AE	BAe 3201 Jetstream 32EP	957	G-31-957*	0092	1197	2 GA TPE331-12UAR-704H	7350	Y19		lsf BAMT/cvtd 32/op in US Airw.Exp.-cs
☐ N958AE	BAe 3201 Jetstream 32EP	958	G-31-958*	0092	1197	2 GA TPE331-12UAR-704H	7350	Y19		lsf BAMT/cvtd 32/op in US Airw.Exp.-cs
☐ N959AE	BAe 3201 Jetstream 32EP	959	G-31-959*	0092	1197	2 GA TPE331-12UAR-704H	7350	Y19		lsf BAMT/cvtd 32/op in US Airw.Exp.-cs
☐ N961AE	BAe 3201 Jetstream 32EP	961	G-31-961*	0092	1197	2 GA TPE331-12UAR-704H	7350	Y19		lsf BAMT/cvtd 32/op in US Airw.Exp.-cs
☐ N962AE	BAe 3201 Jetstream 32EP	962	G-31-962*	0092	1297	2 GA TPE331-12UAR-704H	7350	Y19		lsf BAMT/cvtd 32/op in US Airw.Exp.-cs
☐ N963AE	BAe 3201 Jetstream 32EP	963	G-31-963*	0092	1197	2 GA TPE331-12UAR-704H	7350	Y19		lsf BAMT/cvtd 32/op in US Airw.Exp.-cs
☐ N964AE	BAe 3201 Jetstream 32EP	964	G-31-964*	0092	1297	2 GA TPE331-12UAR-704H	7350	Y19		lsf BAMT/cvtd 32/op in US Airw.Exp.-cs
☐ N965AE	BAe 3201 Jetstream 32EP	965	G-31-965*	0092	1197	2 GA TPE331-12UAR-704H	7350	Y19		lsf BAMT/cvtd 32/op in US Airw.Exp.-cs
☐ N966AE	BAe 3201 Jetstream 32EP	966	G-31-966*	0092	1197	2 GA TPE331-12UAR-704H	7350	Y19		lsf BAMT/cvtd 32/op in US Airw.Exp.-cs
☐ N801WP	De Havilland DHC-8-102 Dash 8	086	C-GTBU	0087	1098	2 PWC PW120A	15649	Y37		lsf CBL Capital / op in US Airw.Exp.-cs
☐ N812PH	De Havilland DHC-8-102 Dash 8	026	C-GESR*	0086	0399	2 PWC PW120A	15649	Y37		lsf DHC / op in US Airways Express-cs
☐ N817MA	De Havilland DHC-8-102 Dash 8	249	N803YW	0090	1198	2 PWC PW120A	15649	Y37		lsf DHC / op in US Airways Express-cs
☐ N817PH	De Havilland DHC-8-102 Dash 8	056	C-GFUM*	0086	0698	2 PWC PW120A	15649	Y37		lsf DHC / op in US Airways Express-cs
☐ N818PH	De Havilland DHC-8-102 Dash 8	058	C-GFYI*	0086	0798	2 PWC PW120A	15649	Y37		lsf DHC / op in US Airways Express-cs
☐ N820PH	De Havilland DHC-8-102 Dash 8	063	C-GLOT*	0086	0798	2 PWC PW120A	15649	Y37		lsf DHC / op in US Airways Express-cs
☐ N841PH	De Havilland DHC-8-102 Dash 8	082	N804AW	0087	1098	2 PWC PW120A	15649	Y37		lsf FBS Business/op in US Airw.Exp.-cs
☐ N880CC	De Havilland DHC-8-102 Dash 8	277	C-GLOT*	0091	0592	2 PWC PW120A	15649	Y37		op in US Airways Express-colors
☐ N881CC	De Havilland DHC-8-102 Dash 8	294	C-GEVB*	0091	0592	2 PWC PW120A	15649	Y37		Martin M.Hutton / op in US Airw.Exp.-cs
☐ N882CC	De Havilland DHC-8-102 Dash 8	168	C-FDNH	0089	0692	2 PWC PW120A	15649	Y37		op in US Airways Express-colors
☐ N883CC	De Havilland DHC-8-102 Dash 8	162	C-FCJI	0089	0692	2 PWC PW120A	15649	Y37		op in US Airways Express-colors

CENTRAL AIR SERVICE, Inc. — Tucson, AZ / East Wenatchee, WA & Rantoul, KS

1662 North Painted Hills Road, Tucson, AZ 85745, USA ☎ (520) 743-3403 Tx: none Fax: (520) 743-3403 SITA: n/a
F: 1970 ⁂ 25 Head: William A. Dempsay Net: n/a

☐ N216D	Piper PA-23-250 Aztec A	27-292	N4753P	0060	0180	2 LY O-540-A1D5	2177			
☐ N31356	Boeing (Douglas) DC-4-1009	42914 / D4 26	CF-TAW	0045	0982	4 PW R-2000	30241	Tanker		117
☐ N67034	Boeing (Douglas) DC-4 (C-54D-15-DC)	22202 / DC 654	56548	0045	1076	4 PW R-2000	30241	Tanker		150
☐ N67040	Boeing (Douglas) DC-4 (C-54B-20-DO)	27232 / DO 178	90392	0044	1076	4 PW R-2000	30241	Tanker		147
☐ N67061	Boeing (Douglas) DC-4 (C-54D-1-DC)	10560 / DC 291	50875	0045	1076	4 PW R-2000	30241	Tanker		146 / lsf Maricopa Aircraft Service Inc.
☐ N67062	Boeing (Douglas) DC-4 (C-54D-5-DC)	10741 / DC 472	56514	0045	1076	4 PW R-2000	30241	Tanker		148
☐ N6816D	Boeing (Douglas) DC-4 (C-54E-15-DO)	27368 / DO 314	N96361	0045	1084	4 PW R-2000	30241	Tanker		109
☐ N816D	Boeing (Douglas) DC-4 (C-54E-20-DO)	27376 / DO 322	N8049H	0045	0781	4 PW R-2000	30241	Tanker		102 / lsf Maricopa Aircraft Service Inc.
☐ N96451	Boeing (Douglas) DC-4 (C-54D-1-DC)	10592 / DC 323	56489	0045	1080	4 PW R-2000	30241	Tanker		111 / lsf Maricopa Aircraft Service Inc.
☐ N96454	Boeing (Douglas) DC-4 (C-54D-15-DC)	10864 / DC 595	56431	0045	0781	4 PW R-2000	30241	Tanker		105 / lsf Maricopa Aircraft Service Inc.

CENTRAL AIR SERVICE, Inc. — Lewistown-Municipal, MT

PO Box 895, Lewistown, MT 59457, USA ☎ (406) 538-3767 Tx: none Fax: none SITA: n/a
F: 1946 ⁂ 3 Head: John W. Rogers Net: n/a Aircraft below 1361kg: Cessna 172, Piper PA-18 & PA-24

☐ N5001K	Bell 206B JetRanger III	2408		0078	0379	1 AN 250-C20B	1451			

CENTRAL AIR SOUTHWEST, Inc. = CTL (formerly Central Airlines, Inc. dba Central Air Charter) — Kansas City-Downtown, MO & Cushing-Municipal, OK

411 Lou Holland Drive, Kansas City, MO 64116, USA ☎ (816) 472-7711 Tx: none Fax: (816) 472-1682 SITA: n/a
F: 1974 ⁂ 50 Head: Dewey E. Towner ICAO: CENTRAL COMMUTER Net: n/a

☐ N106CA	Twin (Aero) Commander 500B	500B-1235-106	N2403Z	0062	0785	2 LY IO-540-B1A5	3062	Freighter		
☐ N107DF	Twin (Aero) Commander 500B	500B-1191-97	N88PC	0062	1191	2 LY IO-540-B1A5	3062	Freighter		
☐ N1153C	Twin (Aero) Commander 500B	500B-1474-169		0064	0876	2 LY IO-540-B1A5	3062	Freighter		
☐ N127KH	Twin (Aero) Commander 500B	500B-1027-38	N801TC	0061	0796	2 LY IO-540-B1A5	3062	Freighter		
☐ N159BM	Twin (Aero) Commander 500B	500B-1523-185	N1159Z	0065	0685	2 LY IO-540-B1A5	3062	Freighter		
☐ N30MB	Twin (Aero) Commander 500B	500B-1453-160	N6376U	0064	0679	2 LY IO-540-B1A5	3062	Freighter		
☐ N315TG	Twin (Aero) Commander 500B	500B-1460-163	N9260N	0064	0785	2 LY IO-540-B1A5	3062	Freighter		
☐ N411ET	Twin (Aero) Commander 500B	500B-1621-214	N445CA	0065	0885	2 LY IO-540-B1A5	3062	Freighter		
☐ N411JF	Twin (Aero) Commander 500B	500B-1014-35	N6178X	0061	0479	2 LY IO-540-B1A5	3062	Freighter		
☐ N411JT	Twin (Aero) Shrike Commander 500S	3097	N9134N	0071	0282	2 LY IO-540-E1B5	3062	Freighter		
☐ N411PT	Twin (Aero) Commander 500B	500B-1207-99	N291CA	0062	1184	2 LY IO-540-B1A5	3062	Freighter		
☐ N415BH	Twin (Aero) Commander 500B	500B-918-5	N6129X	0060	0381	2 LY IO-540-B1A5	3062	Freighter		
☐ N444CA	Twin (Aero) Commander 500B	500B-1458-162	N6362U	0064	1076	2 LY IO-540-B1A5	3062	Freighter		
☐ N471A	Twin (Aero) Commander 500B	500B-1386-139		0064	1278	2 LY IO-540-B1A5	3062	Freighter		
☐ N477CC	Twin (Aero) Commander 500B	500B-1480-172	N477CA	0064	0479	2 LY IO-540-B1A5	3062	Freighter		
☐ N516DT	Twin (Aero) Commander 500B	500B-1574-200	N134X	0065	1085	2 LY IO-540-B1A5	3062	Freighter		
☐ N524HW	Twin (Aero) Commander 500B	500B-1533-191	N324MA	0065	0977	2 LY IO-540-B1A5	3062	Freighter		
☐ N553RA	Twin (Aero) Commander 500B	500B-1315-124	N153K	0063	1280	2 LY IO-540-B1A5	3062	Freighter		lsf pvt
☐ N607MM	Twin (Aero) Commander 500U	500B-1712-25		0067	0692	2 LY IO-540-E1B5	3062	Freighter		
☐ N615MT	Twin (Aero) Commander 500B	500B-911-2	N193CA	0060	0785	2 LY IO-540-B1A5	3062	Freighter		
☐ N6196X	Twin (Aero) Commander 500B	500B-1065-46		0061	0279	2 LY IO-540-B1A5	3062	Freighter		
☐ N630KC	Twin (Aero) Commander 500B	500B-997-28		0060	1087	2 LY IO-540-B1A5	3062	Freighter		
☐ N667CA	Twin (Aero) Commander 500B	500B-1468-166	C-FRJU	0064	0797	2 LY IO-540-B1C	3062	Freighter		
☐ N712AC	Twin (Aero) Commander 500B	500B-1100-61	N414CA	0061	0986	2 LY IO-540-B1A5	3062	Freighter		
☐ N712AT	Twin (Aero) Commander 500B	500B-1118-68	N6213X	0061	0785	2 LY IO-540-B1A5	3062	Freighter		
☐ N716TC	Twin (Aero) Commander 500B	500B-1225-102	N192CA	0062	0885	2 LY IO-540-B1A5	3062	Freighter		
☐ N724LH	Twin (Aero) Commander 500B	500B-1613-211	N13M	0065	0679	2 LY IO-540-B1A5	3062	Freighter		
☐ N777CM	Twin (Aero) Commander 500B	500B-1412-147	N120EL	0064	0290	2 LY IO-540-B1A5	3062	Freighter		
☐ N780SP	Twin (Aero) Commander 500B	500B-1362-133	N510SP	0063	0986	2 LY IO-540-B1A5	3062	Freighter		lsf pvt
☐ N888CA	Twin (Aero) Commander 500B	500B-1318-127	N621RM	0063	0377	2 LY IO-540-B1A5	3062	Freighter		
☐ N917GT	Twin (Aero) Commander 500B	500B-1137-77	N177CA	0061	0779	2 LY IO-540-B1A5	3062	Freighter		
☐ N922BS	Twin (Aero) Commander 500B	500B-1598-207	N1193Z	0065	0785	2 LY IO-540-B1A5	3062	Freighter		lsf pvt
☐ N690AT	Twin (Aero) Turbo Commander 690A	11202	N600PB	0074	0883	2 GA TPE331-5-251K	4649	Freighter		

CENTRAL AMERICAN AIRWAYS, Inc. (formerly Central American Air Taxi, Inc.) — Louisville-Bowman Field, KY

Bowman Field, Louisville, KY 40205, USA ☎ (502) 458-3211 Tx: none Fax: (502) 458-1109 SITA: n/a
F: 1946 ⁂ n/a Head: Wilbur L. Paris, II Net: n/a

☐ N23WL	Beech Baron 58	TH-806	N17645	0077	0896	2 CO IO-520-C	2449			lsf W.L. Paris Enterprises Inc.
☐ N26WL	Beech Baron 58	TH-406	N58CR	0074	1086	2 CO IO-520-C	2449			lsf W.L. Paris Enterprises Inc.
☐ N27WL	Beech Baron 58	TH-485	N7352R	0074	0286	2 CO IO-520-C	2449			lsf W.L. Paris Enterprises Inc.
☐ N28WL	Beech Baron 58P	TJ-124	N300AR	0078	0191	2 CO TSIO-520-WB	2812			lsf W.L. Paris Enterprises Inc.
☐ N901WL	Beech King Air B90	LJ-410	N33CS	0068	0994	2 PWC PT6A-20	4377			lsf W.L. Paris Enterprises Inc.
☐ N90WL	Beech King Air B90	LJ-461	N453SR	0069	0294	2 PWC PT6A-20	4377			lsf W.L. Paris Enterprises Inc.
☐ N560HP	Cessna 560 Citation V	560-0081	OE-GID	0090	0394	2 PWC JT15D-5A	7212			lsf Hesco Paris Corp.

CENTRAL COPTERS, Inc. — Bozeman-Gallatin Field, MT

PO Box 777, Bozeman, MT 59715, USA ☎ (406) 586-9185 Tx: none Fax: (406) 586-4152 SITA: n/a
F: 1964 ⁂ n/a Head: Mark Duffy Net: n/a

☐ N777CX	Bell 206B JetRanger III	4264		0092	0493	1 AN 250-C20J	1451			
☐ N5803X	Eurocopter (Aerosp.) SA315B Lama	2649		0083	0786	1 TU Artouste IIIB	1950			
☐ N21MX	Kaman K-1200 K-Max	A94-0021		0097	0797	1 LY T5317A-1	2722			

CENTRAL FLYING SERVICE, Inc. — Little Rock-Adams Field, AR

1501 Bond Street, Little Rock, AR 72202, USA ☎ (501) 375-3245 Tx: none Fax: (501) 375-7274 SITA: n/a
F: 1939 ⁂ n/a Head: Donald L. Holbert Net: n/a

☐ N3734K	Beech Duchess 76	ME-365		0080	0989	2 LY O-360-A1G6D	1769			
☐ N6015Q	Beech Duchess 76	ME-141		0079	0279	2 LY O-360-A1G6D	1769			
☐ N3711Y	Beech Baron 58	TH-828		0077	1091	2 CO IO-520-C	2449			
☐ N37GN	Beech Baron 58	TH-1195		0080	1097	2 CO IO-520-CB	2449			
☐ N4613S	Beech Baron 58	TH-682		0075	0178	2 CO IO-520-C	2451			
☐ N640LS	Beech Baron 58	TH-1107		0080	0896	2 CO IO-520-CB	2449			
☐ N94HB	Beech King Air C90	LJ-904	N90HB	0080	0993	2 PWC PT6A-21	4377			
☐ N921S	Beech King Air 200	BB-307	N23687	0078	0296	2 PWC PT6A-41	5670			

CHALK'S INTERNATIONAL AIRLINES = OP (Flying Boat, Inc. dba/Subs. of Air Alaska/formerly dba Pan Am Air Bridge) — Miami-Watson Island SPB, FL

1000 McArthur Causeway, Miami Beach, FL 33132, USA ☎ (305) 373-1120 Tx: none Fax: (305) 371-7968 SITA: n/a
F: 1919 ⁂ n/a Head: William Jones IATA: 370 Net: n/a

☐ N1208	Grumman G-73 Turbo Mallard	J-44	N2977	0049	1281	2 PWC PT6A-34	6350	Y17		Amphibian / cvtd Mallard

295 registration type of aircraft cn/fn ex/ex* mfd del powered by mtow kg configuration selcal name/fln/specialitites/remarks

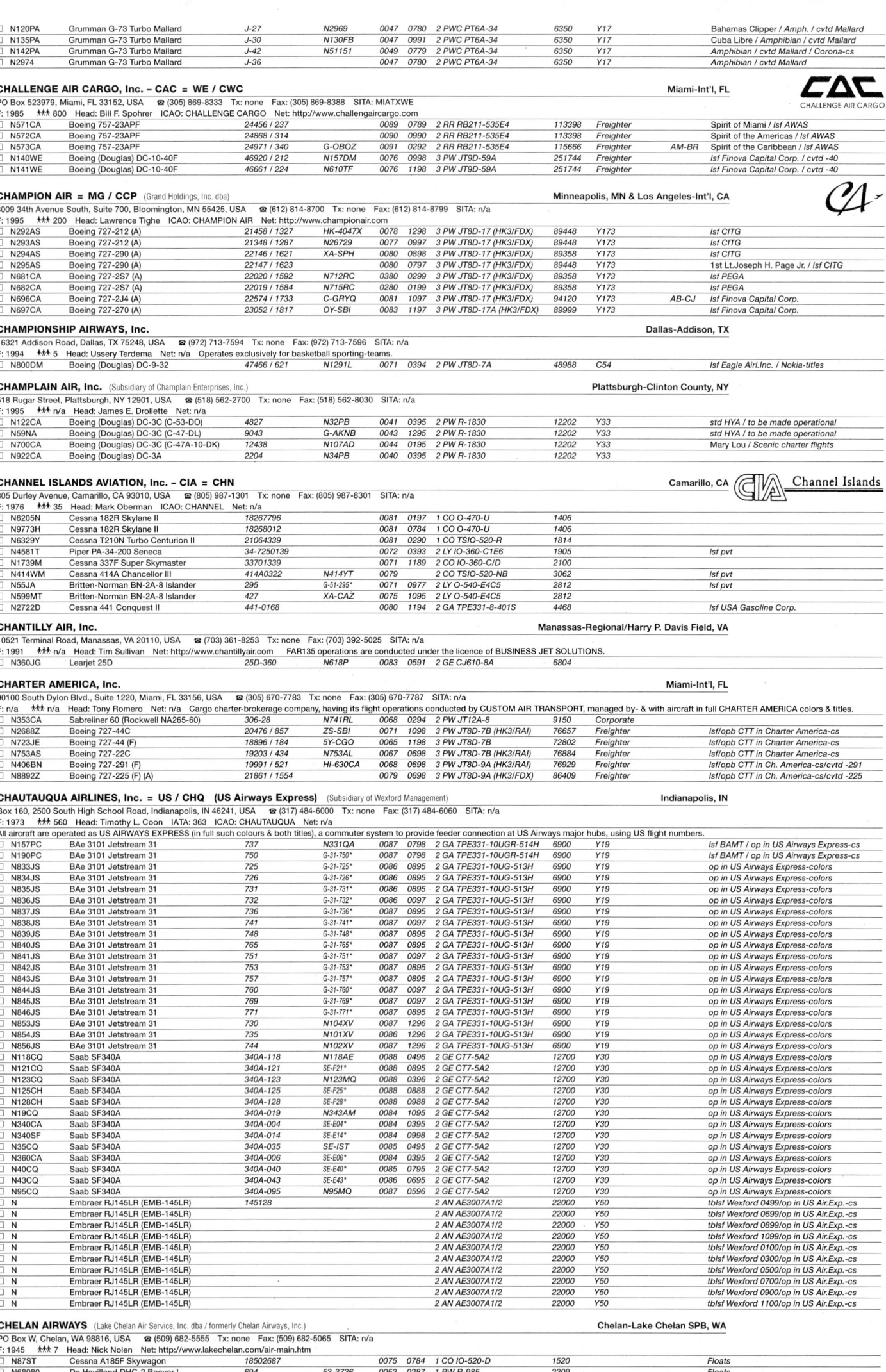

☐ N120PA	Grumman G-73 Turbo Mallard	J-27	N2969	0047	0780	2 PWC PT6A-34	6350	Y17		Bahamas Clipper / Amph. / cvtd Mallard
☐ N135PA	Grumman G-73 Turbo Mallard	J-30	N130FB	0047	0991	2 PWC PT6A-34	6350	Y17		Cuba Libre / Amphibian / cvtd Mallard
☐ N142PA	Grumman G-73 Turbo Mallard	J-42	N51151	0049	0779	2 PWC PT6A-34	6350	Y17		Amphibian / cvtd Mallard / Corona-cs
☐ N2974	Grumman G-73 Turbo Mallard	J-36		0047	0780	2 PWC PT6A-34	6350	Y17		Amphibian / cvtd Mallard

CHALLENGE AIR CARGO, Inc. - CAC = WE / CWC — Miami-Int'l, FL

CHALLENGE AIR CARGO

PO Box 523979, Miami, FL 33152, USA ☎ (305) 869-8333 Tx: none Fax: (305) 869-8388 SITA: MIATXWE
F: 1985 ⁂ 800 Head: Bill F. Spohrer ICAO: CHALLENGE CARGO Net: http://www.challengaircargo.com

☐ N571CA	Boeing 757-23APF	24456 / 237		0089	0789	2 RR RB211-535E4	113398	Freighter		Spirit of Miami / lsf AWAS
☐ N572CA	Boeing 757-23APF	24868 / 314		0090	0990	2 RR RB211-535E4	113398	Freighter		Spirit of the Americas / lsf AWAS
☐ N573CA	Boeing 757-23APF	24971 / 340	G-OBOZ	0091	0292	2 RR RB211-535E4	115666	Freighter	AM-BR	Spirit of the Caribbean / lsf AWAS
☐ N140WE	Boeing (Douglas) DC-10-40F	46920 / 212	N157DM	0076	0998	3 PW JT9D-59A	251744	Freighter		lsf Finova Capital Corp. / cvtd -40
☐ N141WE	Boeing (Douglas) DC-10-40F	46661 / 224	N610TF	0076	1198	3 PW JT9D-59A	251744	Freighter		lsf Finova Capital Corp. / cvtd -40

CHAMPION AIR = MG / CCP (Grand Holdings, Inc. dba) — Minneapolis, MN & Los Angeles-Int'l, CA

8009 34th Avenue South, Suite 700, Bloomington, MN 55425, USA ☎ (612) 814-8700 Tx: none Fax: (612) 814-8799 SITA: n/a
F: 1995 ⁂ 200 Head: Lawrence Tighe ICAO: CHAMPION AIR Net: http://www.championair.com

☐ N292AS	Boeing 727-212 (A)	21458 / 1327	HK-4047X	0078	1298	3 PW JT8D-17 (HK3/FDX)	89448	Y173		lsf CITG
☐ N293AS	Boeing 727-212 (A)	21348 / 1287	N26729	0077	0997	3 PW JT8D-17 (HK3/FDX)	89448	Y173		lsf CITG
☐ N294AS	Boeing 727-290 (A)	22146 / 1621	XA-SPH	0080	0898	3 PW JT8D-17 (HK3/FDX)	89358	Y173		lsf CITG
☐ N295AS	Boeing 727-290 (A)	22147 / 1623		0080	0797	3 PW JT8D-17 (HK3/FDX)	89448	Y173		1st Lt.Joseph H. Page Jr. / lsf CITG
☐ N681CA	Boeing 727-2S7 (A)	22020 / 1592	N712RC	0380	0299	3 PW JT8D-17 (HK3/FDX)	89358	Y173		lsf PEGA
☐ N682CA	Boeing 727-2S7 (A)	22019 / 1584	N715RC	0280	0199	3 PW JT8D-17 (HK3/FDX)	89358	Y173		lsf PEGA
☐ N696CA	Boeing 727-2J4 (A)	22574 / 1733	C-GRYQ	0081	1097	3 PW JT8D-17 (HK3/FDX)	94120	Y173	AB-CJ	lsf Finova Capital Corp.
☐ N697CA	Boeing 727-270 (A)	23052 / 1817	OY-SBI	0083	1197	3 PW JT8D-17A (HK3/FDX)	89999	Y173		lsf Finova Capital Corp.

CHAMPIONSHIP AIRWAYS, Inc. — Dallas-Addison, TX

16321 Addison Road, Dallas, TX 75248, USA ☎ (972) 713-7594 Tx: none Fax: (972) 713-7596 SITA: n/a
F: 1994 ⁂ 5 Head: Ussery Terdema Net: n/a Operates exclusively for basketball sporting-teams.

☐ N800DM	Boeing (Douglas) DC-9-32	47466 / 621	N1291L	0071	0394	2 PW JT8D-7A	48988	C54		lsf Eagle Airl.Inc. / Nokia-titles

CHAMPLAIN AIR, Inc. (Subsidiary of Champlain Enterprises, Inc.) — Plattsburgh-Clinton County, NY

518 Rugar Street, Plattsburgh, NY 12901, USA ☎ (518) 562-2700 Tx: none Fax: (518) 562-8030 SITA: n/a
F: 1995 ⁂ n/a Head: James E. Drollette Net: n/a

☐ N122CA	Boeing (Douglas) DC-3C (C-53-DO)	4827	N32PB	0041	0395	2 PW R-1830	12202	Y33		std HYA / to be made operational
☐ N59NA	Boeing (Douglas) DC-3C (C-47-DL)	9043	G-AKNB	0043	1295	2 PW R-1830	12202	Y33		std HYA / to be made operational
☐ N700CA	Boeing (Douglas) DC-3C (C-47A-10-DK)	12438	N107AD	0044	0195	2 PW R-1830	12202	Y33		Mary Lou / Scenic charter flights
☐ N922CA	Boeing (Douglas) DC-3A	2204	N34PB	0040	0395	2 PW R-1830	12202	Y33		

CHANNEL ISLANDS AVIATION, Inc. - CIA = CHN — Camarillo, CA

Channel Islands

305 Durley Avenue, Camarillo, CA 93010, USA ☎ (805) 987-1301 Tx: none Fax: (805) 987-8301 SITA: n/a
F: 1976 ⁂ 35 Head: Mark Oberman ICAO: CHANNEL Net: n/a

☐ N6205N	Cessna 182R Skylane II	18267796		0081	0197	1 CO O-470-U	1406			
☐ N9773H	Cessna 182R Skylane II	18268012		0081	0784	1 CO O-470-U	1406			
☐ N6329Y	Cessna T210N Turbo Centurion II	21064339		0081	0290	1 CO TSIO-520-R	1814			
☐ N4581T	Piper PA-34-200 Seneca	34-7250139		0072	0393	2 LY IO-360-C1E6	1905			lsf pvt
☐ N1739M	Cessna 337F Super Skymaster	33701339		0071	1189	2 CO IO-360-C/D	2100			
☐ N414WM	Cessna 414A Chancellor III	414A0322	N414YT	0079		2 CO TSIO-520-NB	3062			lsf pvt
☐ N55JA	Britten-Norman BN-2A-8 Islander	295	G-51-295*	0071	0977	2 LY O-540-E4C5	2812			lsf pvt
☐ N599MT	Britten-Norman BN-2A-8 Islander	427	XA-CAZ	0075	1095	2 LY O-540-E4C5	2812			
☐ N2722D	Cessna 441 Conquest II	441-0168		0080	1194	2 GA TPE331-8-401S	4468			lsf USA Gasoline Corp.

CHANTILLY AIR, Inc. — Manassas-Regional/Harry P. Davis Field, VA

10521 Terminal Road, Manassas, VA 20110, USA ☎ (703) 361-8253 Tx: none Fax: (703) 392-5025 SITA: n/a
F: 1991 ⁂ n/a Head: Tim Sullivan Net: http://www.chantillyair.com FAR135 operations are conducted under the licence of BUSINESS JET SOLUTIONS.

☐ N360JG	Learjet 25D	25D-360	N618P	0083	0591	2 GE CJ610-8A	6804			

CHARTER AMERICA, Inc. — Miami-Int'l, FL

90100 South Dylon Blvd., Suite 1220, Miami, FL 33156, USA ☎ (305) 670-7783 Tx: none Fax: (305) 670-7787 SITA: n/a
F: n/a ⁂ n/a Head: Tony Romero Net: n/a Cargo charter-brokerage company, having its flight operations conducted by CUSTOM AIR TRANSPORT, managed by- & with aircraft in full CHARTER AMERICA colors & titles.

☐ N353CA	Sabreliner 60 (Rockwell NA265-60)	306-28	N741RL	0068	0294	2 PW JT12A-8	9150	Corporate		
☐ N2688Z	Boeing 727-44C	20476 / 857	ZS-SBI	0071	1098	3 PW JT8D-7B (HK3/RAI)	76657	Freighter		lsf/opb CTT in Charter America-cs
☐ N723JE	Boeing 727-44 (F)	18896 / 184	5Y-CGO	0065	1198	3 PW JT8D-7B	72802	Freighter		lsf/opb CTT in Charter America-cs
☐ N753AS	Boeing 727-22C	19203 / 434	N753AL	0067	0698	3 PW JT8D-7B (HK3/RAI)	76884	Freighter		lsf/opb CTT in Charter America-cs
☐ N406BN	Boeing 727-291 (F)	19991 / 521	HI-630CA	0068	0698	3 PW JT8D-9A (HK3/RAI)	76929	Freighter		lsf/opb CTT in Ch. America-cs/cvtd -291
☐ N8892Z	Boeing 727-225 (F) (A)	21861 / 1554		0079	0698	3 PW JT8D-9A (HK3/FDX)	86409	Freighter		lsf/opb CTT in Ch. America-cs/cvtd -225

CHAUTAUQUA AIRLINES, Inc. = US / CHQ (US Airways Express) (Subsidiary of Wexford Management) — Indianapolis, IN

Box 160, 2500 South High School Road, Indianapolis, IN 46241, USA ☎ (317) 484-6000 Tx: none Fax: (317) 484-6060 SITA: n/a
F: 1973 ⁂ 560 Head: Timothy L. Coon IATA: 363 ICAO: CHAUTAUQUA Net: n/a
All aircraft are operated as US AIRWAYS EXPRESS (in full such colours & both titles), a commuter system to provide feeder connection at US Airways major hubs, using US flight numbers.

☐ N157PC	BAe 3101 Jetstream 31	737	N331QA	0087	0798	2 GA TPE331-10UGR-514H	6900	Y19		lsf BAMT / op in US Airways Express-cs
☐ N190PC	BAe 3101 Jetstream 31	750	G-31-750*	0087	0798	2 GA TPE331-10UGR-514H	6900	Y19		lsf BAMT / op in US Airways Express-cs
☐ N833JS	BAe 3101 Jetstream 31	725	G-31-725*	0086	0895	2 GA TPE331-10UG-513H	6900	Y19		op in US Airways Express-colors
☐ N834JS	BAe 3101 Jetstream 31	726	G-31-726*	0086	0895	2 GA TPE331-10UG-513H	6900	Y19		op in US Airways Express-colors
☐ N835JS	BAe 3101 Jetstream 31	731	G-31-731*	0086	0895	2 GA TPE331-10UG-513H	6900	Y19		op in US Airways Express-colors
☐ N836JS	BAe 3101 Jetstream 31	732	G-31-732*	0086	0097	2 GA TPE331-10UG-513H	6900	Y19		op in US Airways Express-colors
☐ N837JS	BAe 3101 Jetstream 31	736	G-31-736*	0087	0895	2 GA TPE331-10UG-513H	6900	Y19		op in US Airways Express-colors
☐ N838JS	BAe 3101 Jetstream 31	741	G-31-741*	0087	0097	2 GA TPE331-10UG-513H	6900	Y19		op in US Airways Express-colors
☐ N839JS	BAe 3101 Jetstream 31	748	G-31-748*	0087	0895	2 GA TPE331-10UG-513H	6900	Y19		op in US Airways Express-colors
☐ N840JS	BAe 3101 Jetstream 31	765	G-31-765*	0087	0895	2 GA TPE331-10UG-513H	6900	Y19		op in US Airways Express-colors
☐ N841JS	BAe 3101 Jetstream 31	751	G-31-751*	0087	0097	2 GA TPE331-10UG-513H	6900	Y19		op in US Airways Express-colors
☐ N842JS	BAe 3101 Jetstream 31	753	G-31-753*	0087	0895	2 GA TPE331-10UG-513H	6900	Y19		op in US Airways Express-colors
☐ N843JS	BAe 3101 Jetstream 31	757	G-31-757*	0087	0895	2 GA TPE331-10UG-513H	6900	Y19		op in US Airways Express-colors
☐ N844JS	BAe 3101 Jetstream 31	760	G-31-760*	0087	0097	2 GA TPE331-10UG-513H	6900	Y19		op in US Airways Express-colors
☐ N845JS	BAe 3101 Jetstream 31	769	G-31-769*	0087	0097	2 GA TPE331-10UG-513H	6900	Y19		op in US Airways Express-colors
☐ N846JS	BAe 3101 Jetstream 31	771	G-31-771*	0087	0895	2 GA TPE331-10UG-513H	6900	Y19		op in US Airways Express-colors
☐ N853JS	BAe 3101 Jetstream 31	730	N104XV	0087	1296	2 GA TPE331-10UG-513H	6900	Y19		op in US Airways Express-colors
☐ N854JS	BAe 3101 Jetstream 31	735	N101XV	0086	1296	2 GA TPE331-10UG-513H	6900	Y19		op in US Airways Express-colors
☐ N856JS	BAe 3101 Jetstream 31	744	N102XV	0087	1296	2 GA TPE331-10UG-513H	6900	Y19		op in US Airways Express-colors
☐ N118CQ	Saab SF340A	340A-118	N118AE	0088	0496	2 GE CT7-5A2	12700	Y30		op in US Airways Express-colors
☐ N121CQ	Saab SF340A	340A-121	SE-F21*	0088	0895	2 GE CT7-5A2	12700	Y30		op in US Airways Express-colors
☐ N123CQ	Saab SF340A	340A-123	N123MQ	0088	0396	2 GE CT7-5A2	12700	Y30		op in US Airways Express-colors
☐ N125CH	Saab SF340A	340A-125	SE-F25*	0088	0888	2 GE CT7-5A2	12700	Y30		op in US Airways Express-colors
☐ N128CH	Saab SF340A	340A-128	SE-F28*	0088	0988	2 GE CT7-5A2	12700	Y30		op in US Airways Express-colors
☐ N19CQ	Saab SF340A	340A-019	N343AM	0084	1095	2 GE CT7-5A2	12700	Y30		op in US Airways Express-colors
☐ N340CA	Saab SF340A	340A-004	SE-E04*	0084	0395	2 GE CT7-5A2	12700	Y30		op in US Airways Express-colors
☐ N340SF	Saab SF340A	340A-014	SE-E14*	0084	0998	2 GE CT7-5A2	12700	Y30		op in US Airways Express-colors
☐ N35CQ	Saab SF340A	340A-035	SE-IST	0085	0495	2 GE CT7-5A2	12700	Y30		op in US Airways Express-colors
☐ N360CA	Saab SF340A	340A-006	SE-E06*	0084	0395	2 GE CT7-5A2	12700	Y30		op in US Airways Express-colors
☐ N40CQ	Saab SF340A	340A-040	SE-E40*	0085	0795	2 GE CT7-5A2	12700	Y30		op in US Airways Express-colors
☐ N43CQ	Saab SF340A	340A-043	SE-E43*	0086	0695	2 GE CT7-5A2	12700	Y30		op in US Airways Express-colors
☐ N95CQ	Saab SF340A	340A-095	N95MQ	0087	0596	2 GE CT7-5A2	12700	Y30		op in US Airways Express-colors
☐ N	Embraer RJ145LR (EMB-145LR)	145128				2 AN AE3007A1/2	22000	Y50		tblsf Wexford 0499/op in US Air.Exp.-cs
☐ N	Embraer RJ145LR (EMB-145LR)					2 AN AE3007A1/2	22000	Y50		tblsf Wexford 0699/op in US Air.Exp.-cs
☐ N	Embraer RJ145LR (EMB-145LR)					2 AN AE3007A1/2	22000	Y50		tblsf Wexford 0899/op in US Air.Exp.-cs
☐ N	Embraer RJ145LR (EMB-145LR)					2 AN AE3007A1/2	22000	Y50		tblsf Wexford 1099/op in US Air.Exp.-cs
☐ N	Embraer RJ145LR (EMB-145LR)					2 AN AE3007A1/2	22000	Y50		tblsf Wexford 0100/op in US Air.Exp.-cs
☐ N	Embraer RJ145LR (EMB-145LR)					2 AN AE3007A1/2	22000	Y50		tblsf Wexford 0300/op in US Air.Exp.-cs
☐ N	Embraer RJ145LR (EMB-145LR)					2 AN AE3007A1/2	22000	Y50		tblsf Wexford 0500/op in US Air.Exp.-cs
☐ N	Embraer RJ145LR (EMB-145LR)					2 AN AE3007A1/2	22000	Y50		tblsf Wexford 0700/op in US Air.Exp.-cs
☐ N	Embraer RJ145LR (EMB-145LR)					2 AN AE3007A1/2	22000	Y50		tblsf Wexford 0900/op in US Air.Exp.-cs
☐ N	Embraer RJ145LR (EMB-145LR)					2 AN AE3007A1/2	22000	Y50		tblsf Wexford 1100/op in US Air.Exp.-cs

CHELAN AIRWAYS (Lake Chelan Air Service, Inc. dba / formerly Chelan Airways, Inc.) — Chelan-Lake Chelan SPB, WA

PO Box W, Chelan, WA 98816, USA ☎ (509) 682-5555 Tx: none Fax: (509) 682-5065 SITA: n/a
F: 1945 ⁂ 7 Head: Nick Nolen Net: http://www.lakechelan.com/air-main.htm

☐ N87ST	Cessna A185F Skywagon	18502687		0075	0784	1 CO IO-520-D	1520			Floats
☐ N68080	De Havilland DHC-2 Beaver I	694	53-3736	0053	0287	1 PW R-985	2309			Floats

296 registration type of aircraft cn/fn ex/ex* mfd del powered by mtow kg configuration selcal name/fln/specialitites/remarks

CHEM-AIR, Inc.

Shreveport-Downtown/Municipal, LA

PO Box 7241, Shreveport, LA 71137-7241, USA ☎ (318) 425-5944 Tx: none Fax: (318) 424-6562 SITA: n/a
F: 1986 ⁂ n/a Head: Bill Alexander Net: n/a Aircraft below MTOW 1361 kg: Bell 47G.

□ N16916	Bell 206B JetRanger III	2342		0078	0593	1 AN 250-C20B	1451			
□ N206DS	Bell 206B JetRanger III	3037		0080	0597	1 AN 250-C20B	1451			
□ N59612	Bell 206B JetRanger	1500		0074	0293	1 AN 250-C20	1451			
□ N75CW	Bell 206B JetRanger	1762		0075	0788	1 AN 250-C20	1451			
□ N90330	Bell 206B JetRanger	1785		0075	0586	1 AN 250-C20	1451			
□ N3928B	Bell 206L-1 LongRanger III	45214		0078	0796	1 AN 250-C30P	1882			cvtd LongRanger II

CHEROKEE HELICOPTER SERVICE

Ford City-Heliport, PA

RD 2, Brickchurch, Ford City, PA 16226, USA ☎ (724) 845-9132 Tx: none Fax: none SITA: n/a
F: 1990 ⁂ n/a Head: Kenneth E. Walker Net: n/a

□ N511TV	Eurocopter (Aerosp.) AS350B AStar	2306	N757KR	0089	0394	1 TU Arriel 1B	1950			

CHERRY-AIR, Inc.

Dallas-Addison, TX

4584 Claire Chennault Road, Dallas, TX 75248, USA ☎ (972) 248-1707 Tx: none Fax: (972) 380-0046 SITA: n/a
F: 1988 ⁂ n/a Head: Kenneth C. Donaldson Net: n/a

□ N151WW	Learjet 24	24-170	N200DH	0068	0690	2 GE CJ610-4	5897			lsf Addison Aviation Services Inc.
□ N213CA	Learjet 25D	25D-241	N713LJ	0078		2 GE CJ610-8A	6804			lsf Delaware di Properties LLC
□ N233CA	Learjet 25B	25B-133	XA-RZY	0073	1096	2 GE CJ610-6	6804			lsf Addison Aviation Services Inc.
□ N238CA	Learjet 25	25-040	N23FN	0069	0292	2 GE CJ610-6	6804			lsf Delaware di Properties LLC
□ N8005Y	Learjet 25B	25B-121	XA-SID	0073	0895	2 GE CJ610-6	6804			lsf Delaware di Properties Llc
□ N216CA	Dassault Falcon 20C (C)	11	N983AJ	0065	1194	2 GE CF700-2D2	13000	Freighter		lsf Delaware di Properties Llc / cvtd C
□ N218CA	Dassault Falcon 20D (C)	218	EC-EEU	0069	0194	2 GE CF700-2D2	13000	Freighter		lsf Delaware di Properties / cvtd 20D
□ N219CA	Dassault Falcon 20D (C)	193	9Q-CTT	0069	1095	2 GE CF700-2D2	13000	Freighter		lsf Delaware di Properties Llc / cvtd D
□ N220CA	Dassault Falcon 20D (C)	220	EC-EDL	0070	1096	2 GE CF700-2D	13000	Freighter		lsf Addison Aviation Services / cvtd D

CHERRY HELICOPTERS, Inc.

Kahuku-Hilton Helipad, HI

PO Box 399, Kahuku, HI 96731, USA ☎ (808) 293-2570 Tx: none Fax: (808) 293-7588 SITA: n/a
F: 1985 ⁂ n/a Head: Gregory C. Mattson Net: n/a

□ N220AL	MD Helicopters MD 500D (Hughes 369D)	1090606D	C-FGGL	0079	0995	1 AN 250-C20B	1361			

CHESTER COUNTY AVIATION, Inc.

Coatesville-Chester County G.O. Carlson, PA

1 Earhart Drive, Coatesville, PA 19320, USA ☎ (610) 384-9003 Tx: none Fax: (610) 384-9238 SITA: n/a
F: 1964 ⁂ 38 Head: Alexander Sheves IATA: 491 Net: n/a Aircraft below MTOW 1361kg: Piper PA-28

□ N2343Z	Piper PA-23-250 Aztec F	27-8054018		0080	0480	2 LY IO-540-C4B5	2359			
□ N9EQ	Piper PA-23-250 Aztec E	27-7405412	N9EC	0074	0393	2 LY IO-540-C4B5	2359			
□ N3555U	Piper PA-31-350 Navajo Chieftain	31-8052061		0080	0590	2 LY TIO-540-J2BD	3175			

CHEVRON AIRCRAFT OPERATIONS (Helicopter Department of Chevron USA Production Company / Subsidiary of Chevron USA, Inc.)

New Orleans-Lakefront, LA

PO Box 26845, New Orleans, LA 70186, USA ☎ (504) 244-4115 Tx: none Fax: (504) 244-4121 SITA: n/a
F: 1945 ⁂ n/a Head: John S. Sabree Net: n/a Operates (with Helicopters) gas exploration flights for the Chevron group of companies & its customers as well as corporate flight. Beside listed helicopters, also operates a fixed-wing department with Beechcraft King Air 200, BAe 125-700A, Cessna 550 & Gulfstream III/IV aircraft for corporate purposes only.

□ N2033J	Bell 206B JetRanger III	3337		0081	0781	1 AN 250-C20B	1451			
□ N21460	Bell 206B JetRanger III	4075		0089	1289	1 AN 250-C20J	1451			
□ N2146F	Bell 206B JetRanger III	4073		0089	1189	1 AN 250-C20J	1451			
□ N2148A	Bell 206B JetRanger III	4080	C-FHCY	0089	0190	1 AN 250-C20J	1451			
□ N3181B	Bell 206B JetRanger III	3770		0083	0484	1 AN 250-C20J	1451			
□ N57499	Bell 206B JetRanger III	3086		0080	0281	1 AN 250-C20J	1451			
□ N71319	Bell 206B JetRanger III	4112		0090	0790	1 AN 250-C20J	1451			
□ N7131U	Bell 206B JetRanger III	4111		0090	0790	1 AN 250-C20J	1451			
□ N83109	Bell 206B JetRanger	938		0073	1276	1 AN 250-C20	1451			
□ N17237	Bell 206L-3 LongRanger III	51478		0091	0691	1 AN 250-C30P	1882			
□ N17238	Bell 206L-3 LongRanger III	51492		0091	0891	1 AN 250-C30P	1882			
□ N17592	Bell 206L-3 LongRanger III	51535		0091	1291	1 AN 250-C30P	1882			
□ N31079	Bell 206L-3 LongRanger III	51526		0091	1191	1 AN 250-C30P	1882			
□ N53702	Bell 206L-3 LongRanger III	51249		0088	0688	1 AN 250-C30P	1882			
□ N6533U	Bell 206L-3 LongRanger III	51439		0091	0291	1 AN 250-C30P	1882			
□ N6533Y	Bell 206L-3 LongRanger III	51457		0091	0491	1 AN 250-C30P	1882			
□ N7159H	Bell 206L-3 LongRanger III	51397		0090	1090	1 AN 250-C30P	1882			
□ N7159J	Bell 206L-3 LongRanger III	51408		0090	1190	1 AN 250-C30P	1882			
□ N715CC	Bell 206L-3 LongRanger III	51380	N7159C	0090	0890	1 AN 250-C30P	1882			
□ N50588	Eurocopter (MBB) BO105CBS-2	S-780	D-HDYP*	0088	0788	2 AN 250-C20B	2500			
□ N5059C	Eurocopter (MBB) BO105CBS-2	S-779	D-HDYO*	0088	0788	2 AN 250-C20B	2500			
□ N5352Y	Eurocopter (MBB) BO105CBS	S-781	D-HDYQ*	0088	1288	2 AN 250-C20B	2500			
□ N5366Y	Eurocopter (MBB) BO105CBS	S-782	D-HDYR*	0088	0988	2 AN 250-C20B	2500			
□ N826MB	Eurocopter (MBB) BO105CBS-4	S-771	D-HDYG*	0087	0188	2 AN 250-C20B	2500			
□ N8775	Eurocopter (MBB) BO105CBS-2	S-775	N828MB	0087	0488	2 AN 250-C20B	2500			
□ N8776	Eurocopter (MBB) BO105CBS-2	S-776	N829MB	0088	0488	2 AN 250-C20B	2500			
□ N5401G	Sikorsky S-76A	760137		0081	0381	2 AN 250-C30S	4763			
□ N5402T	Sikorsky S-76A	760140		0081	0381	2 AN 250-C30S	4763			
□ N5403C	Sikorsky S-76A	760141		0081	0381	2 AN 250-C30S	4763			
□ N5414X	Sikorsky S-76A	760152		0081	0581	2 AN 250-C30S	4763			
□ N5447C	Sikorsky S-76A	760180		0082	0482	2 AN 250-C30S	4763			
□ N72649	Sikorsky S-76A	760292		0084	0188	2 AN 250-C30S	4763			
□ N7266F	Sikorsky S-76A	760273		0084	1284	2 AN 250-C30S	4763			
□ N7266K	Sikorsky S-76A	760283		0084	0186	2 AN 250-C30S	4763			

CHICAGO EXPRESS AIRLINES, Inc. = C8 / WDY (Associated with Phoenix Airline Services, Inc.)

Chicago-Midway, IL

5575 South Archer Avenue, Chicago, IL 60638, USA ☎ (773) 585-0585 Tx: none Fax: (773) 585-4877 SITA: n/a
F: 1993 ⁂ n/a Head: Carol Brady IATA: 488 ICAO: WINDYCITY Net: http://home.earthlink.net/%7Ephlerb/CEX.html
All flights are operated in code sharing-agreement with AMERICAN TRANS AIR as ATA CONNECTION (in Chicago Express-colors) using TZ-flight numbers.

□ N309PX	BAe 3101 Jetstream 31	676	G-31-676*	0085	0298	2 GA TPE331-10UG-513H	6900	Y19		lsf BAMT
□ N460CE	BAe 3101 Jetstream 31	680	N312PX	0085	0793	2 GA TPE331-10UG-513H	6900	Y19		lsf Saab Aircraft of America Inc.
□ N827JS	BAe 3101 Jetstream 31	697	N331BL	0086	1195	2 GA TPE331-10UG-513H	6900	Y19		lsf BAMT
□ N828JS	BAe 3101 Jetstream 31	708	N331BN	0086	0993	2 GA TPE331-10UG-513H	6900	Y19		lsf BAMT
□ N829JS	BAe 3101 Jetstream 31	713	G-31-713*	0086	0097	2 GA TPE331-10UG-513H	6900	Y19		lsf BAMT
□ N830JS	BAe 3101 Jetstream 31	722	N331BP	0086	0097	2 GA TPE331-10UG-513H	6900	Y19		lsf BAMT
□ N831JS	BAe 3101 Jetstream 31	716	G-31-716*	0086	0097	2 GA TPE331-10UG-513H	6900	Y19		lsf BAMT
□ N832JS	BAe 3101 Jetstream 31	721	G-31-721*	0086	0993	2 GA TPE331-10UG-513H	6900	Y19		lsf BAMT

CHIGNIK AIRWAYS, Inc.

Chignik, AK

202 Alec Street, Chignik Lagoon, AK 99565, USA ☎ (907) 840-2212 Tx: none Fax: (907) 840-2333 SITA: n/a
F: 1997 ⁂ n/a Head: A. Moore Jeffery Net: n/a

□ N8076Z	Cessna U206A Super Skywagon	U206-0476		0066	0897	1 CO IO-520-A	1633			lsf pvt

CHIPOLA AVIATION, Inc.

Marianna-Municipal, FL

PO Box 875, Marianna, FL 32446, USA ☎ (352) 482-8480 Tx: none Fax: (352) 482-7991 SITA: n/a
F: 1970 ⁂ n/a Head: James H. Foran Net: n/a Aircraft below MTOW 1361kg: Cessna 172

□ N107HF	Learjet 25 (XR)	25-029	N28LA	0069	0289	2 GE CJ610-6	6804			mod. 25

CHRYSLER AVIATION, Inc. (Sister company of International Jet Aviation, Inc.)

Van Nuys, CA

7120 Hayvenhurst Ave., Suite 309, Van Nuys, CA 91406-3836, USA ☎ (818) 989-7900 Tx: none Fax: (818) 989-0116 SITA: n/a
F: 1976 ⁂ 16 Head: Stergios D. Rapis Net: http://www.chrysleraviation.base.org

□ N501JC	Cessna 500 Citation	500-0252	N244JW	0075	1183	2 PWC JT15D-1	5216			lsf International Jet Aviation Inc.
□ N298DR	Learjet 25D	25D-298	XA-ABH	0080	0797	2 GE CJ610-8A	6804			lsf International Jet Aviation Inc.
□ N831LH	Learjet 25D	25D-244	N24EP	0077	0797	2 GE CJ610-8A	6804			
□ N54DD	Cessna 560 Citation V	560-0089	ZS-MPT	0090	0898	2 PWC JT15D-5A	7212			lsf 54 DD Llc
□ N32AJ	Learjet 36A	36A-048	PT-WGM	0081	1198	2 GA TFE731-2-2B	8301			lsf Pacific Coast Lease Corp.
□ N978E	Learjet 36A	36A-024	N38D	0077	0792	2 GA TFE731-2-2B	8301			lsf International Jet Aviation Inc.

CHRYSLER PENTASTAR AVIATION, Inc. = CYL (Subsidiary of DaimlerChrysler Corporation)

Pontiac-Oakland, MI

7310 Highland Road, Waterford, MI 48327-1503, USA ☎ (248) 666-3630 Tx: none Fax: (248) 666-9667 SITA: n/a
F: 1974 ⁂ n/a Head: Thomas E. Davis ICAO: CHRYSLER Net: n/a

□ N811CC	Hawker 800	258267	N294H	0095	0695	2 GA TFE731-5R-1H	12428	Executive		
□ N815CC	Hawker 800A (BAe 125-800A)	258100 / NA0401	N108CF	0087	1087	2 GA TFE731-5R-1H	12428	Executive		lsf NBD Transportation Co.
□ N802CC	GAC (Grumman) G-1159 Gulfstream II	187	N202GA	0076	0389	2 RR Spey 511-8	29393	Executive		
□ N807CC	GAC (Grumman) G-1159 Gulfstream II (TT)	212	N551MD	0077	0185	2 RR Spey 511-8	29710	Executive		
□ N803CC	GAC G-1159A Gulfstream III	378	N378HC	0083	0495	2 RR Spey 511-8	30935	Executive		
□ N800CC	GAC G-IV Gulfstream IV	1052	N419GA	0089	0889	2 RR Tay 611-8	33203	Executive		lsf Pitney Bowes Credit Corp.
□ N801CC	GAC G-IV Gulfstream IV (SP)	1254	N436GA	0095	0895	2 RR Tay 611-8	33838	Executive		

297 registration type of aircraft cn/fn ex/ex* mfd del powered by mtow kg configuration selcal name/fln/specialitites/remarks

CIMARRON AIRE = CMN (Eckles Aircraft, Co. dba) — Holdenville-Municipal, OK

PO Box 305, Holdenville, OK 74848, USA ☎ (405) 379-9044 Tx: none Fax: (405) 379-7120 SITA: n/a
F: 1993 n/a Head: William Ph. Eckles ICAO: CIMARRON AIRE Net: n/a

☐ N737SW	Beech E18S	BA-402		0058	0793	2 PW R-985-AN14B	4218	Freighter		

CIN-AIR, Lp — Cincinnati-Municipal/Lunken Field, OH

212 East Third Street, Suite 300, Cincinnati, OH 45202, USA ☎ (513) 321-7142 Tx: none Fax: (513) 321-4955 SITA: n/a
F: 1979 n/a Head: William J. Williams Net: n/a

☐ N511WS	Cessna 550 Citation II	550-0439	N550RS	0082	0390	2 PWC JT15D-4	6033			lsf B & J Jet Corp.
☐ N511WV	Cessna 560 Citation V	560-0138	OY-FFV	0091	1194	2 PWC JT15D-5A	7212			lsf Cin-Jet Inc.
☐ N511WA	IAI 1125 Astra	034	VR-CMG	0089	0596	2 GA TFE731-3A-200G	10659			lsf B & J Jet Corp.

CIRCLE AIR (Dawn E. Foster dba) — Central, AK

PO Box 35, Central, AK 99730, USA ☎ (907) 520-5223 Tx: none Fax: (907) 520-5332 SITA: n/a
F: 1995 n/a Head: Dawn E. Foster Net: n/a

☐ N710MH	Cessna U206F Stationair	U20602383		0074	0694	1 CO IO-520-F	1633			Wheel-Skis

CIRCLE RAINBOW AIR, Inc. — Honolulu-Int'l, HI

155 Kapalulu Place, Honolulu, HI 96819, USA ☎ (808) 833-3507 Tx: none Fax: (808) 839-6054 SITA: n/a
F: 1979 32 Head: Douglas Ledet Net: n/a

☐ N26MR	Britten-Norman BN-2A-26 Islander	882	XC-DUL	0080		2 LY O-540-E4C5	2722	Y9		
☐ N27MR	Britten-Norman BN-2A-26 Islander	884	XC-DUN	0080		2 LY O-540-E4C5	2722	Y9		
☐ N29MR	Britten-Norman BN-2A-26 Islander	885	XC-DUO	0080		2 LY O-540-E4C5	2722	Y9		
☐ N32MR	Britten-Norman BN-2A-26 Islander	891	XC-DUR	0080	0493	2 LY O-540-E4C5	2722	Y9		
☐ N38MR	Britten-Norman BN-2A-26 Islander	893	XC-DUM	0080		2 LY O-540-E4C5	2722	Y9		
☐ N7136K	Britten-Norman BN-2A-26 Islander	900	XC-DUT	0080	0295	2 LY O-540-E4C5	2722	Y9		

CIRRUSAIR = NTS (Agamemnon Operating, Inc. dba) — Dallas-Love Field, TX

8605 Lemmon Avenue, Dallas, TX 75209, USA ☎ (972) 358-3174 Tx: none Fax: (972) 358-0430 SITA: n/a
F: 1993 100 Head: Jon R. Tinkle ICAO: NITE STAR Net: n/a

☐ N17520	Beech Bonanza A36	E-974		0077	1093	1 CO IO-520-BA	1633	Freighter		
☐ N17545	Beech Bonanza A36	E-978		0078	1093	1 CO IO-520-BA	1633	Freighter		
☐ N1804L	Beech Bonanza A36	E-835		0076	1093	1 CO IO-520-BA	1633	Freighter		
☐ N23746	Beech Bonanza A36	E-1288		0078	1093	1 CO IO-520-BA	1633	Freighter		
☐ N7455N	Beech Bonanza 36	E-33		0068	1093	1 CO IO-520-B	1633	Freighter		
☐ N246L	Beech Baron B55 (95-B55)	TC-502		0064	1093	2 CO IO-470-L	2313	Freighter		
☐ N95KC	Beech Baron C55 (95-C55)	TE-203	N95BJ	0066	1093	2 CO IO-520-C	2404	Freighter		
☐ N96NL	Beech Baron B55 (95-B55)	TC-721		0064	1093	2 CO IO-470-L	2313	Freighter		
☐ N17915	Beech Baron 58	TH-78	N179WP	0070	1093	2 CO IO-520-C	2449	Freighter		
☐ N18447	Beech Baron 58	TH-883		0077	1093	2 CO IO-520-C	2449	Freighter		
☐ N1888W	Beech Baron 58	TH-340		0073	1093	2 CO IO-520-C	2449	Freighter		
☐ N8195R	Beech Baron 58	TH-529		0074	1093	2 CO IO-520-C	2449	Freighter		
☐ N950JP	Beech Baron 58	TH-432		0074	1093	2 CO IO-520-C	2449	Freighter		
☐ N8409F	Cessna 401	401-0257		0068	1093	2 CO TSIO-520-E	2858	Freighter		
☐ N4153G	Cessna 402B II	402B1203		0076	1093	2 CO TSIO-520-E	2858	Freighter		
☐ N68TN	Mitsubishi MU-2L (MU-2B-36) Cargoliner	675	N835MA	0075	0795	2 GA TPE331-6-251M	5250	Freighter		Cavenaugh SCD conversion
☐ N741FN	Mitsubishi MU-2L (MU-2B-36) Cargoliner	658	N741DM	0074	0795	2 GA TPE331-6-251M	5250	Freighter		Cavenaugh SCD conversion

CIS AIR, Corp. = (CISA) (Division of CIS Corporation) — Syracuse, NY

PO Box 4785, Syracuse, NY 13221, USA ☎ (315) 455-1900 Tx: none Fax: (315) 455-4713 SITA: n/a
F: 1980 6 Head: Thomas J. Prinzing Net: n/a Used aircraft leasing, sales and financing company.
Owner / Lessor of following (main) aircraft types: Boeing 727-200, 737-200, Fairchild Metro III, Learjet 35A, Lockheed TriStar, McDonnell Douglas DC-9 & MD-80.
Aircraft leased from CISL are listed and mentioned as such under the leasing carriers.

CIT GROUP – Capital Equipment Financing = (CITG) (Division of The CIT Group, a company of Dai-Ichi Kangyo Bank & Chemical Bank) — New York, NY

1211 Avenue of the Americas, New York, NY 10036, USA ☎ (212) 536-9400 Tx: n/a Fax: (212) 536-9401 SITA: n/a
F: 1908 2500 Head: Nikita Zdanow Net: n/a New and used aircraft leasing, sales and financing company.
Owner / lessor of following (main) aircraft types: Airbus A320, Boeing 727-200, 737-200/-300, 747, Douglas DC-9, DC-10, MD-11 & MD-80. Aircraft leased from CITG are listed and mentioned as such under the leasing carriers.

CLASSIC CARGO (Air Classic Cargo, Inc. dba / formerly Leading Edge Air Charter, Inc.) — Tampa-Int'l, FL

12140 Pilot Country Drive, Spring Hill, FL 34610, USA ☎ (813) 995-9110 Tx: none Fax: none SITA: n/a
F: 1991 n/a Head: J. Tuggle Brooks Net: n/a

☐ N40JT	Beech 3T (18)	CA-128	CF-SIJ	0052	0792	2 PW R-985-AN14B	3969	Freighter		

CLASSIC EXPRESS AIRWAYS, Inc. — Santa Ana-John Wayne/Orange County, CA

8191 Sandcove Circle, Apt. 201, Huntington Beach, CA 92646, USA ☎ (949) 832-7312 Tx: none Fax: (949) 730-6221 SITA: n/a
F: 1995 n/a Head: Thomas L. Brown Net: n/a

☐ N103NA	Boeing (Douglas) DC-3C (C-47B-40-DK)	33569	C-FIKD	0045	0195	2 PW R-1830	12202	28 Pax		

CLASSIC HELICOPTER, Corp. — Seattle-Boeing Field/King County Int'l, WA

6505 Perimeter Road, Seattle, WA 98108, USA ☎ (206) 767-0515 Tx: none Fax: (206) 767-4018 SITA: n/a
F: 1982 16 Head: Karen Walling Net: http://www.home.sprynet.com/sprynet/classich Aircraft below MTOW 1361 kg: Robinson R22 & R44

☐ N1076G	Bell 206B JetRanger III	2831		0079		1 AN 250-C20B	1451			lsf Novastar Enterprises Inc.
☐ N206CS	Bell 206B JetRanger III	3521	N2202F	0081		1 AN 250-C20B	1451			
☐ N101FW	Eurocopter (Aerosp.) AS350B AStar	1018	C-GRGC	0078	0698	1 TU Arriel 1B	1950			

CLASSIC HELICOPTERS, Ltd — Salt Lake City-Int'l, UT

9151 South 255 West, Sandy, UT 84070, USA ☎ (801) 580-1694 Tx: none Fax: (801) 539-0223 SITA: n/a
F: 1982 n/a Head: Mark R. Henderson Net: n/a

☐ N5736B	Bell 206B JetRanger III	3033		0080	0387	1 AN 250-C20B	1451			
☐ N5739V	Bell 206B JetRanger III	3025		0080	0196	1 AN 250-C20B	1451			
☐ N206AH	Bell 206L-1 LongRanger III	45562	N22HU	0080	0694	1 AN 250-C30P	1882			cvtd LongRanger II
☐ N2233F	Bell 206L-1 LongRanger III	45739		0081	1189	1 AN 250-C30P	1882			cvtd LongRanger II
☐ N2752U	Bell 206L-1 LongRanger III	45258		0079	0488	1 AN 250-C30P	1882			cvtd LongRanger II
☐ N560P	Bell 206L-3 LongRanger III	51013		0082	0494	1 AN 250-C30P	1882			
☐ N5746N	Bell 206L-1 LongRanger III	45461		0080	0893	1 AN 250-C30P	1882			cvtd LongRanger II
☐ N6122	Bell 206L-3 LongRanger III	51114		0084	0596	1 AN 250-C30P	1882			
☐ N902EH	Bell 206L-1 LongRanger III	45769	N902FH	0083	0495	1 AN 250-C30P	1882			cvtd LongRanger II

CLASSIC WINGS, Corp. — Vero Beach-Municipal, FL

144 Royale Square, Vero Beach, FL 32962, USA ☎ (800) 580-7631 Tx: none Fax: (561) 569-2489 SITA: n/a
F: 1996 n/a Head: Barry Holm Net: n/a Conducting airshow (flying museum) flights only.

☐ N131CW	Convair 340-67 (VC-131D)	205	N6288Y	0754	0197	2 PW R-2800	21772	Flying Museum		US Air Force 42809-colors

CLAY LACY AVIATION, Inc. — Van Nuys, CA

7435 Valjean Avenue, Van Nuys, CA 91406, USA ☎ (818) 989-2900 Tx: n/a Fax: (818) 904-3450 SITA: n/a
F: 1968 n/a Head: H. Clay Lacy Net: http://www.claylacy.com

☐ N764CL	Bell 206B JetRanger III	2811		0079	0280	1 AN 250-C20B	1451	Corporate		lsf Kestel Enterprises Inc.
☐ N464CL	Learjet 24A	24A-096	N1972L	0065	1275	2 GE CJ610-4	5897	Exec / Photo		lsf pvt
☐ N664CL	Learjet 24	24-167	N888B	0068	0378	2 GE CJ610-4	5897	Exec / Photo		lsf pvt
☐ N254CL	Learjet 25D	25D-275	N211CD	0079	0595	2 GE CJ610-8A	6804	Exec / Photo		
☐ N564CL	Learjet 25	25-060	N695LJ	0070	0384	2 GE CJ610-6	6804	Exec / Photo		lsf pvt
☐ N364CL	Learjet 35A	35A-383	N66FE	0081	0790	2 GA TFE731-2-2B	8301	Exec / Photo		lsf pvt
☐ N541GA	Boeing (Douglas) DC-3C (C-47B-50-DK)	34370	N541Q	0045	0685	2 PW R-1830	12202	Corporate		
☐ N264CL	GAC (Grumman) G-1159 Gulfstream II (SP)	227	N200LS	0076	0992	2 RR Spey 511-8	29710	Executive		lsf pvt
☐ N724CL	Boeing 727-51	19121 / 264	N299LA	0066	1195	3 PW JT8D-7B (HK)	72802	VIP		
☐ N727HC	Boeing 727-35	19835 / 501	N900CH	0067	0690	3 PW JT8D-7B (HK3/FDX)	72802	VIP		lsf pvt

CLEAR CREEK COPTERS, Inc. — Redding-Municipal, CA

PO Box 994346, Redding, CA 96099, USA ☎ (530) 241-1133 Tx: none Fax: none SITA: n/a
F: 1996 n/a Head: William Borelli Net: n/a

☐ N99478	Garlick-Bell UH-1B (204)	858	63-8636	0063	0697	1 LY T53-L-13	3856			cvtd Bell UH-1B

CLEARWATER AIR, Inc. — Soldotna, AK

PO Box 1915, Soldotna, AK 99669, USA ☎ (907) 262-5022 Tx: none Fax: (907) 262-9375 SITA: n/a
F: 1984 3 Head: Will J. Satathite Net: n/a Aircraft below MTOW 1361 kg: Cessna 180 & Piper PA-18

☐ N800DF	Cessna 207A Stationair 8 II	20700621		0080	0285	1 CO IO-520-F	1724			
☐ N900DF	Cessna 207 Skywagon	20700234	N40CF	0074	0593	1 CO IO-520-F	1724			

298 registration type of aircraft cn/fn ex/ex* mfd del powered by mtow kg configuration selcal name/fln/specialitites/remarks

CLINT AERO, Inc. (Clinton K. Shillingford dba) — St. Thomas-Cyril E. King, VI

PO Box 2402, St. Thomas, VI 00803, USA ☎ (340) 776-3958 Tx: none Fax: (340) 776-0020 SITA: n/a
F: 1979 ⛹ n/a Head: Clinton K. Shillingford Net: n/a

☐ N17CK	Reims/Cessna F406 Caravan II	F406-0001	PH-ALO	0086	1195	2 PWC PT6A-112	4468			

COASTAL AIR TRANSPORT, Inc. = TCL — Mobile-Downtown, AL

2495 Michigan Avenue, Mobile, AL 36615, USA ☎ (334) 438-5576 Tx: none Fax: (334) 433-2857 SITA: n/a
F: 1985 ⛹ n/a Head: Ernest H. Douglas ICAO: TRANS COASTAL Net: n/a

☐ N7201L	Piper PA-31-310 Navajo	31-712		0071	0295	2 LY TIO-540-A2C	2948			
☐ N154JR	Convair 340-32	47	N454GA	0053	0996	2 PW R-2800	21772	Freighter		

COASTAL AIR TRANSPORT, Inc. = DQ / CXT — St. Croix-Alexander Hamilton, VI

PO Box 3985, Christiansted, St. Croix, VI 00822, USA ☎ (340) 773-6862 Tx: none Fax: none SITA: n/a
F: 1976 ⛹ 6 Head: Michael W. Foster IATA: 457 ICAO: COASTAL Net: n/a

☐ N676MF	Cessna 402B	402B0106	N7856Q	0071	0684	2 CO TSIO-520-E	2858	Y9		Cruzan Queen / lsf Coastal Resource

COASTAL HELICOPTERS, Inc. — Juneau-Int'l, AK

8995 Yandukin Drive, Juneau, AK 99801, USA ☎ (907) 789-5600 Tx: none Fax: (907) 789-7076 SITA: n/a
F: 1987 ⛹ 10 Head: James M. Wilson Net: http://www.alaskaone.com/coastal

☐ N371AH	Bell 206B JetRanger	1660	N450AS	0075	0596	1 AN 250-C20	1451			
☐ N49686	Bell 206B JetRanger II	1905		0076	0290	1 AN 250-C20	1451			
☐ N3607S	Eurocopter (Aerosp.) AS350D AllStar	1254		0080	0390	1 AN 250-C30	1950			cvtd AStar
☐ N6080D	Eurocopter (Aerosp.) AS350B1 AStar	2054		0088	0693	1 TU Arriel 1D	2200			
☐ N6099S	Eurocopter (Aerosp.) AS350BA AStar	2810		0094	0695	1 TU Arriel 1B	2100			
☐ N	Eurocopter (Aerosp.) AS350B1 AStar	2027	C-FUAM	0087	0398	1 TU Arriel 1D	2200			

COCKRELL AIR (Cockrell Resources, Inc. dba) — Houston-William P. Hobby, TX

8703 Telephone Road, Houston, TX 77061, USA ☎ (713) 649-8616 Tx: none Fax: (713) 649-6742 SITA: n/a
F: 1992 ⛹ n/a Head: Ernest H. Cockrell Net: n/a

☐ N711R	Learjet 35	35-035		0075	0992	2 GA TFE731-2-2B	8301			

COLEMILL ENTERPRISES, Inc. — Nashville-Cornelia Fort Airpark, TN

PO Box 60627, Nashville, TN 37206, USA ☎ (615) 226-4256 Tx: none Fax: (615) 226-4702 SITA: n/a
F: 1944 ⛹ n/a Head: Ernest W. Colbert Net: http://www.colemill.com Aircraft below MTOW 1361kg: Cessna 172

☐ N40731	Piper PA-31-350 Navajo Chieftain	31-8152003		0081	0497	2 LY TIO-540-J2BD	3175			
☐ N7485L	Piper PA-31-310 Navajo B	31-7300907		0073	0191	2 LY TIO-540-A2C	2948			
☐ N3076W	Beech King Air A100	B-176	YV-O-CVG-4	0073	0698	2 PWC PT6A-28	5216			
☐ N43WS	Beech King Air E90	LW-16	N80NC	0072	0696	2 PWC PT6A-28	4581			
☐ N715WA	Beech King Air A100	B-168	F-GFVM	0073	1196	2 PWC PT6A-28	5216			

COLGAN AIR, Inc. = 9L (Continental Connection) (formerly National Capital Airways) — Manassas-Regional/Harry P. Davis Field, VA

PO Box 1650, Manassas, VA 22110, USA ☎ (540) 368-8880 Tx: none Fax: (540) 368-5968 SITA: n/a
F: 1991 ⛹ 137 Head: Charles J. Colgan IATA: 426 Net: http://www.colganair.com All scheduled flights are operated in conjunction with CO as Continental Connection (in own Colgan-colors) using CO-flight numbers.

☐ N119CJ	Beech 1900C-1 Airliner	UC-19	N1552C	0088	0493	2 PWC PT6A-65B	7530	Y19		lsf Raytheon Aircraft Credit Corp.
☐ N129CJ	Beech 1900C-1 Airliner	UC-129	N15615	0090	0195	2 PWC PT6A-65B	7530	Y19		
☐ N15031	Beech 1900C-1 Airliner	UC-103		0090	0794	2 PWC PT6A-65B	7530	Y19		
☐ N207CJ	Beech 1900C-1 Airliner	UC-107	N15539	0090	1194	2 PWC PT6A-65B	7530	Y19		
☐ N210CJ	Beech 1900C-1 Airliner	UC-110	N132GP	0090	0498	2 PWC PT6A-65B	7530	Y19		lsf Raytheon Aircraft Credit Corp.
☐ N550CJ	Beech 1900C-1 Airliner	UC-50	N1568C	0088	0892	2 PWC PT6A-65B	7530	Y19		lsf Raytheon Aircraft Credit Corp.
☐ N215CJ	Beech 1900D Airliner	UE-215		0096	0696	2 PWC PT6A-67D	7688	Y19		
☐ N221CJ	Beech 1900D Airliner	UE-221		0096	0696	2 PWC PT6A-67D	7688	Y19		

COLONY HELICOPTERS (Colony Services, Inc. dba) — Labelle-Helipad, FL

Box 1589, Labelle, FL 33935, USA ☎ (941) 675-2047 Tx: none Fax: (941) 675-4716 SITA: n/a
F: n/a ⛹ n/a Head: Robert W. Smith Net: n/a Aircraft below MTOW 1361kg: Bell 47G3-B2 & FH1100

☐ N70696	Bell UH-1B (204)	608	62-2088	0062	0794	1 LY T53-L-11	3856			lsf Helicop Inc.
☐ N9846F	Bell UH-1B (204)	366	61-786	0062	0791	1 LY T53-L-11	3856			

COLORADO HELICOPTERS, Inc. — Colorado Springs-Private Heliport, CO

10970 Hardy Road, Colorado Springs, CO 80908, USA ☎ (719) 495-2165 Tx: none Fax: (719) 495-2165 SITA: n/a
F: 1994 ⛹ n/a Head: Ronald R. Magnus Net: n/a

☐ N5190C	MD Helicopters MD 500D (Hughes 369D)	1145D	N5189G	0082	1195	1 AN 250-C20B	1361			lsf pvt

COLUMBIA HELICOPTERS, Inc. = WCO — Aurora-State, OR

PO Box 3500, Portland, OR 97208-9952, USA ☎ (503) 678-1222 Tx: 360307 Fax: (503) 678-5841 SITA: n/a
F: 1957 ⛹ 350 Head: Roy Simmons ICAO: COLUMBIA HELI Net: n/a Aircraft below MTOW 1361 kg: Hiller UH-12.

☐ N501CH	MD Helicopters MD 500D (Hughes 369D)	170050D	N8360F	0077	0688	1 AN 250-C20B	1361			lsf Columbia Helicopters Leasing Inc.
☐ N502CH	MD Helicopters MD 500D (Hughes 369D)	180252D	N8693F	0077	0289	1 AN 250-C20B	1361			lsf Columbia Helicopters Leasing Inc.
☐ N832AH	Bell 206L-1 LongRanger III	45560		0080	0296	1 AN 250-C30P	1882			lsf Columbia Hel.Leasing/cvtd LongR. II
☐ N111NS	Beech King Air 200C	BL-36		0081	0894	2 PWC PT6A-41	5670	Corporate		
☐ N3697F	Beech King Air 200C	BL-14		0080	0381	2 PWC PT6A-41	5670	Corporate		
☐ N184CH	Kawasaki (B.V.) KV-107-II	4001	Thai 4001	0062	0976	2 GE CT58-140-2	9752			
☐ N185CH	Kawasaki (B.V.) KV-107-II	4003	Thai 4003	0063	0976	2 GE CT58-140-2	9752			
☐ N186CH	Kawasaki (B.V.) KV-107-II	4005	P2-CHA	0063	0976	2 GE CT58-140-2	9752			lsf Columbia Helicopters Leasing Inc.
☐ N187CH	Kawasaki (B.V.) KV-107-II	4012	Thai 4012	0063	0976	2 GE CT58-140-2	9752			lsf Columbia Helicopters Leasing Inc.
☐ N188CH	Boeing Vertol 107-II	107	P2-CHB	0064	0976	2 GE CT58-140-2	9752			lst Helifor as C-FHFW
☐ N190CH	Boeing Vertol 107-II	2002	C-GHFY	0062	0480	2 GE CT58-140-2	9752			
☐ N191CH	Boeing Vertol 107-II	2003	P2-CHD	0062	0480	2 GE CT58-140-2	9752			lst MBA as P2-CHD
☐ N192CH	Kawasaki (B.V.) KV-107-II	4011	JA9505	0063	0283	2 GE CT58-140-2	9752			lsf Columbia Helicopters Leasing Inc.
☐ N193CH	Boeing Vertol 107-II (HKP-4A)	402	04452	0062	1093	2 GE CT58-140-2	9752			lst Helifor as C-GHFT
☐ N194CH	Boeing Vertol 107-II (HKP-4A)	404	04454	0062	1093	2 GE CT58-140-2	9752			lsf Columbia Helicopters Leasing Inc.
☐ N195CH	Boeing Vertol 107-II (HKP-4A)	406	04456	0062	1093	2 GE CT58-140-2	9752			lst Helifor as C-GHFF
☐ N6672D	Boeing Vertol 107-II	2		0062	0172	2 GE CT58-140-2	9752			
☐ N6674D	Boeing Vertol 107-II	4		0062	0172	2 GE CT58-140-2	9752			
☐ N6675D	Boeing Vertol 107-II	5	C-GHFI	0062	0172	2 GE CT58-140-2	9752			
☐ N6682D	Boeing Vertol 107-II	101	JA9500	0064	0372	2 GE CT58-140-2	9752			
☐ N2270B	Sikorsky CH-54A (S-64 Skycrane)	64052	68-18450	0068	1094	2 PW T-73-P-700	19051			std / to be made operational
☐ N4410K	Sikorsky CH-54A (S-64 Skycrane)	64027	67-18425	0067	0296	2 PW T-73-P-700	19051			std / to be made operational
☐ N544CH	Sikorsky CH-54A (S-64 Skycrane)	64022	N22696	0067	0197	2 PW T-73-P-700	19051			std / to be made operational
☐ N548CH	Sikorsky CH-54A (S-64 Skycrane)		N4410N	0068	0194	2 PW T-73-P-700	19051			lsf Columbia Helicopters Leasing Inc.
☐ N7073C	Sikorsky CH-54A (S-64 Skycrane)	64042	68-18440	0068	0296	2 PW T-73-P-700	19051			std / to be made operational
☐ N235CH	Boeing Vertol 234UT Chinook	MJ-002	G-BISO	0081	1185	2 LY 5512	19278			cvtd 234LR
☐ N237CH	Boeing Vertol 234UT Chinook	MJ-003	G-BISR	0081	0389	2 LY 5512	19278			lst MBA as P2-CHI / cvtd 234LR
☐ N238CH	Boeing Vertol 234UT Chinook	MJ-005	P2-CHY	0081	0589	2 LY 5512	19278			cvtd 234LR
☐ N239CH	Boeing Vertol 234UT Chinook	MJ-006	C-GHFP	0081	0789	2 LY 5512	19278			lsf Columbia Hel. Leasing / cvtd 234LR
☐ N241CH	Boeing Vertol 234UT Chinook	MJ-016	N224TA	0083	0191	2 LY 5512	19278			lsf Col.Hel.Lsng/lst Heli-U.Peru/cvtdLR
☐ N242CH	Boeing Vertol 234UT Chinook	MJ-023	N225RA	0082	0191	2 LY 5512	19278			lsf Columbia Hel. Leasing / cvtd 234LR
☐ N245CH	Boeing Vertol 234UT Chinook	MJ-022	LN-OMA	0082	1095	2 LY 5512	19278			cvtd 234LR
☐ N246CH	Boeing Vertol 234UT Chinook	MJ-017	LN-OMK	0082	1195	2 LY 5512	19278			cvtd 234LR

COLUMBIA PACIFIC AIRLINES = 7C (Thomas G. Packard dba) — Everett-Snohomish County/Paine Field, WA

7005-150th Place Southwest, Edmonds, WA 98026, USA ☎ (425) 742-8720 Tx: none Fax: (425) 776-5255 SITA: n/a
F: 1989 ⛹ n/a Head: Thomas G. Packard Net: n/a Aircraft below MTOW 1361kg: Cessna 172

☐ N40036	Piper PA-34-200T Seneca II	34-7770369		0077	0189	2 CO TSIO-360-E	2073			

COLUMBUS BUSINESS CHARTER, Inc. — Columbus-Port Columbus Int'l, OH

4700 East 5th Avenue, Columbus, OH 43219, USA ☎ (614) 237-2120 Tx: none Fax: (614) 237-1156 SITA: n/a
F: 1986 ⛹ n/a Head: Alexis A. Jacobs Net: n/a

☐ N328AJ	Fairchild (Swear.) SA227TT Merlin 300	TT-483	N300CV	0084	0794	2 GA TPE331-10U-503G	5670			lsf Columbus Fair Auto Auction/cvtdIIIC

COLVIN AVIATION, Inc. = GHP — Athens-Ben Epps, GA

1080 Ben Epps Drive, Athens, GA 30605, USA ☎ (706) 548-0717 Tx: none Fax: (706) 549-2038 SITA: n/a
F: 1980 ⛹ n/a Head: John B. Colvin ICAO: GRASSHOPPER EX Net: http://www.colvinair.com

☐ N212GA	Learjet 35A	35A-354	D-CART	0080	0397	2 GA TFE731-2-2B	8301			lsf Apple Jet Inc.
☐ N386CM	Learjet 35A	35A-283	N205FL	0080	1197	2 GA TFE731-2-2B	8301			lsf Apple Jet Inc.
☐ N508GP	Learjet 35A	35A-424	N2844	0081	1096	2 GA TFE731-2-2B	8301			lsf Colvin Air Charter Inc.

299 registration type of aircraft cn/fn ex/ex* mfd del powered by mtow kg configuration selcal name/fln/specialitites/remarks

COMAIR AIRLINES = OH / COM (Delta Connection) (Comair, Inc. dba / Subsidiary of Comair Holdings, Inc.) Cincinnati-Northern Kentucky Int'l, OH & Orlando-Int'l, FL

ComAir

PO Box 75021, Cincinnati, OH 45275, USA ☎ (606) 767-2550 Tx: none Fax: (606) 767-2969 SITA: n/a
F: 1976 ⁂ 2500 Head: David A. Siebenburgen IATA: 886 ICAO: COMAIR Net: http://www.fly-comair.com
All aircraft are operated as COMAIR/Delta Connection (in own colours & titles), a commuter system to provide feeder connection at DL major hubs, using DL flight numbers.

registration	type of aircraft	cn/fn	ex/ex*	mfd	del	powered by	mtow kg	configuration	selcal	name/fln/specialitites/remarks
N152CA	Embraer 120RT Brasilia (EMB-120RT)	120152	PT-SPR*	0089	1089	2 PWC PW118	11500	Y30		
N159A	Embraer 120RT Brasilia (EMB-120RT)	120159	PT-SPY*	0089	1289	2 PWC PW118	11500	Y30		
N164D	Embraer 120RT Brasilia (EMB-120RT)	120164	PT-SQC*	0089	1289	2 PWC PW118	11500	Y30		
N168CA	Embraer 120RT Brasilia (EMB-120RT)	120168	PT-SQG*	0089	1289	2 PWC PW118	11500	Y30		
N179CA	Embraer 120RT Brasilia (EMB-120RT)	120179	PT-SQR*	0090	0490	2 PWC PW118	11500	Y30		
N189CA	Embraer 120RT Brasilia (EMB-120RT)	120189	PT-SRC*	0090	0790	2 PWC PW118	11500	Y30		
N205CA	Embraer 120RT Brasilia (EMB-120RT)	120205	PT-SRX*	0090	1090	2 PWC PW118	11500	Y30		
N241CA	Embraer 120RT Brasilia (EMB-120RT)	120211	PT-SSF*	0090	1190	2 PWC PW118	11500	Y30		
N243CA	Embraer 120RT Brasilia (EMB-120RT)	120212	PT-SSG*	0090	1190	2 PWC PW118	11500	Y30		
N244CA	Embraer 120RT Brasilia (EMB-120RT)	120217	PT-SSL*	0090	1290	2 PWC PW118	11500	Y30		
N246CA	Embraer 120RT Brasilia (EMB-120RT)	120223	PT-SSS*	0090	1290	2 PWC PW118	11500	Y30		
N247CA	Embraer 120RT Brasilia (EMB-120RT)	120225	PT-SSU*	0090	0191	2 PWC PW118	11500	Y30		
N248CA	Embraer 120RT Brasilia (EMB-120RT)	120228	PT-SSX*	0091	0391	2 PWC PW118	11500	Y30		
N249CA	Embraer 120RT Brasilia (EMB-120RT)	120230	PT-STC*	0091	0391	2 PWC PW118	11500	Y30		
N254CA	Embraer 120RT Brasilia (EMB-120RT)	120233	PT-STF*	0091	0491	2 PWC PW118	11500	Y30		
N255CA	Embraer 120RT Brasilia (EMB-120RT)	120238	PT-STK*	0091	0591	2 PWC PW118	11500	Y30		
N256CA	Embraer 120RT Brasilia (EMB-120RT)	120245	PT-STR*	0091	0691	2 PWC PW118	11500	Y30		
N257CA	Embraer 120RT Brasilia (EMB-120RT)	120248	PT-STU*	0091	1191	2 PWC PW118	11500	Y30		
N258CA	Embraer 120RT Brasilia (EMB-120RT)	120247	PT-STT*	0091	1091	2 PWC PW118	11500	Y30		
N259CA	Embraer 120RT Brasilia (EMB-120RT)	120252	PT-STY*	0091	1091	2 PWC PW118	11500	Y30		
N261CA	Embraer 120RT Brasilia (EMB-120RT)	120254	PT-SUA*	0091	1291	2 PWC PW118	11500	Y30		
N263CA	Embraer 120RT Brasilia (EMB-120RT)	120255	PT-SUB*	0091	1291	2 PWC PW118	11500	Y30		
N264CA	Embraer 120RT Brasilia (EMB-120RT)	120256	PT-SUC*	0092	0292	2 PWC PW118	11500	Y30		
N266CA	Embraer 120RT Brasilia (EMB-120RT)	120258	PT-SUE*	0092	0392	2 PWC PW118	11500	Y30		
N267CA	Embraer 120RT Brasilia (EMB-120RT)	120259	PT-SUF*	0092	0392	2 PWC PW118	11500	Y30		
N268CA	Embraer 120RT Brasilia (EMB-120RT)	120262	PT-SUI*	0092	0392	2 PWC PW118	11500	Y30		
N269CA	Embraer 120RT Brasilia (EMB-120RT)	120263	PT-SUJ*	0092	0392	2 PWC PW118	11500	Y30		
N462CA	Embraer 120RT Brasilia (EMB-120RT)	120264	PT-SUK*	0092	0792	2 PWC PW118	11500	Y30		
N463CA	Embraer 120RT Brasilia (EMB-120RT)	120267	PT-SUN*	0092	0892	2 PWC PW118	11500	Y30		
N708CA	Canadair Regional Jet 100ER (CL-600-2B19)	7235		0098	0498	2 GE CF34-3A1	23133	Y50		7235
N709CA	Canadair Regional Jet 100ER (CL-600-2B19)	7238		0098	0598	2 GE CF34-3A1	23133	Y50		7238
N710CA	Canadair Regional Jet 100ER (CL-600-2B19)	7241		0098	0698	2 GE CF34-3A1	23133	Y50		7241
N712CA	Canadair Regional Jet 100ER (CL-600-2B19)	7244		0098	0698	2 GE CF34-3A1	23133	Y50		7244
N713CA	Canadair Regional Jet 100ER (CL-600-2B19)	7245		0098	0798	2 GE CF34-3A1	23133	Y50		7245
N716CA	Canadair Regional Jet 100ER (CL-600-2B19)	7250	C-FMMW*	0098	0798	2 GE CF34-3A1	23133	Y50		7250
N719CA	Canadair Regional Jet 100ER (CL-600-2B19)	7253		0098	0898	2 GE CF34-3A1	23133	Y50		
N721CA	Canadair Regional Jet 100ER (CL-600-2B19)	7259	C-FMLI*	0098	0998	2 GE CF34-3A1	23133	Y50		
N729CA	Canadair Regional Jet 100ER (CL-600-2B19)	7265		0098	1098	2 GE CF34-3A1	23133	Y50		special Cincinnati The Jet Hub-colors
N735CA	Canadair Regional Jet 100ER (CL-600-2B19)	7267		0098	1098	2 GE CF34-3A1	23133	Y50		
N739CA	Canadair Regional Jet 100ER (CL-600-2B19)	7273	C-FMNQ*	0098	1198	2 GE CF34-3A1	23133	Y50		
N759CA	Canadair Regional Jet 100ER (CL-600-2B19)	7279	C-FMMQ*	0099	1298	2 GE CF34-3A1	23133	Y50		
N767CA	Canadair Regional Jet 100ER (CL-600-2B19)	7285	C-FMKW*	0099	0199	2 GE CF34-3A1	23133	Y50		
N769CA	Canadair Regional Jet 100ER (CL-600-2B19)	7292		0099	0299	2 GE CF34-3A1	23133	Y50		
N776CA	Canadair Regional Jet 100ER (CL-600-2B19)	7293		0099	0299	2 GE CF34-3A1	23133	Y50		
N778CA	Canadair Regional Jet 100ER (CL-600-2B19)	7297		0099	0299	2 GE CF34-3A1	23133	Y50		
N779CA	Canadair Regional Jet 100ER (CL-600-2B19)					2 GE CF34-3A1	23133	Y50		oo-delivery 0499
N781CA	Canadair Regional Jet 100ER (CL-600-2B19)					2 GE CF34-3A1	23133	Y50		oo-delivery 0499
N783CA	Canadair Regional Jet 100ER (CL-600-2B19)					2 GE CF34-3A1	23133	Y50		oo-delivery 0499
N784CA	Canadair Regional Jet 100ER (CL-600-2B19)					2 GE CF34-3A1	23133	Y50		oo-delivery 0499
N785CA	Canadair Regional Jet 100ER (CL-600-2B19)					2 GE CF34-3A1	23133	Y50		oo-delivery 0599
N786CA	Canadair Regional Jet 100ER (CL-600-2B19)					2 GE CF34-3A1	23133	Y50		oo-delivery 0999
N796CA	Canadair Regional Jet 100ER (CL-600-2B19)					2 GE CF34-3A1	23133	Y50		oo-delivery 1099
N797CA	Canadair Regional Jet 100ER (CL-600-2B19)					2 GE CF34-3A1	23133	Y50		oo-delivery 1199
N798CA	Canadair Regional Jet 100ER (CL-600-2B19)					2 GE CF34-3A1	23133	Y50		oo-delivery 1299
N804CA	Canadair Regional Jet 100ER (CL-600-2B19)					2 GE CF34-3A1	23133	Y50		oo-delivery 0000
N805CA	Canadair Regional Jet 100ER (CL-600-2B19)					2 GE CF34-3A1	23133	Y50		oo-delivery 0000
N806CA	Canadair Regional Jet 100ER (CL-600-2B19)					2 GE CF34-3A1	23133	Y50		oo-delivery 0000
N807CA	Canadair Regional Jet 100ER (CL-600-2B19)					2 GE CF34-3A1	23133	Y50		oo-delivery 0000
N809CA	Canadair Regional Jet 100ER (CL-600-2B19)					2 GE CF34-3A1	23133	Y50		oo-delivery 0000
N810CA	Canadair Regional Jet 100ER (CL-600-2B19)					2 GE CF34-3A1	23133	Y50		oo-delivery 0000
N811CA	Canadair Regional Jet 100ER (CL-600-2B19)					2 GE CF34-3A1	23133	Y50		oo-delivery 0000
N812CA	Canadair Regional Jet 100ER (CL-600-2B19)					2 GE CF34-3A1	23133	Y50		oo-delivery 0000
N814CA	Canadair Regional Jet 100ER (CL-600-2B19)					2 GE CF34-3A1	23133	Y50		oo-delivery 0000
N815CA	Canadair Regional Jet 100ER (CL-600-2B19)					2 GE CF34-3A1	23133	Y50		oo-delivery 0000
N816CA	Canadair Regional Jet 100ER (CL-600-2B19)					2 GE CF34-3A1	23133	Y50		oo-delivery 0000
N818CA	Canadair Regional Jet 100ER (CL-600-2B19)					2 GE CF34-3A1	23133	Y50		oo-delivery 0000
N819CA	Canadair Regional Jet 100ER (CL-600-2B19)					2 GE CF34-3A1	23133	Y50		oo-delivery 0000
N821CA	Canadair Regional Jet 100ER (CL-600-2B19)					2 GE CF34-3A1	23133	Y50		oo-delivery 0000
N912CA	Canadair Regional Jet 100ER (CL-600-2B19)	7011	C-FMKZ*	0093	0493	2 GE CF34-3A1	23133	Y50		7011
N914CA	Canadair Regional Jet 100ER (CL-600-2B19)	7012	C-FMLB*	0093	0493	2 GE CF34-3A1	23133	Y50		7012
N915CA	Canadair Regional Jet 100ER (CL-600-2B19)	7013	C-FMLQ*	0093	0693	2 GE CF34-3A1	23133	Y50		7013
N916CA	Canadair Regional Jet 100ER (CL-600-2B19)	7014	C-FMLI*	0093	0693	2 GE CF34-3A1	23133	Y50		7014
N917CA	Canadair Regional Jet 100ER (CL-600-2B19)	7017	C-FMLT*	0093	0793	2 GE CF34-3A1	23133	Y50		7017
N918CA	Canadair Regional Jet 100ER (CL-600-2B19)	7018	C-FMLU*	0093	0993	2 GE CF34-3A1	23133	Y50		7018
N920CA	Canadair Regional Jet 100ER (CL-600-2B19)	7022	C-FMMN*	0093	0993	2 GE CF34-3A1	23133	Y50		7022
N924CA	Canadair Regional Jet 100ER (CL-600-2B19)	7026	C-FMMX*	0093	1093	2 GE CF34-3A1	23133	Y50		7026
N926CA	Canadair Regional Jet 100ER (CL-600-2B19)	7027	C-FMMY*	0093	1193	2 GE CF34-3A1	23133	Y50		7027
N927CA	Canadair Regional Jet 100ER (CL-600-2B19)	7031	C-FMNQ*	0093	0194	2 GE CF34-3A1	23133	Y50		7031
N929CA	Canadair Regional Jet 100ER (CL-600-2B19)	7035	C-FMOI*	0094	0294	2 GE CF34-3A1	23133	Y50		7035
N931CA	Canadair Regional Jet 100ER (CL-600-2B19)	7037	C-FMOS*	0094	0394	2 GE CF34-3A1	23133	Y50		7037
N932CA	Canadair Regional Jet 100ER (CL-600-2B19)	7038	C-FMOW*	0094	0494	2 GE CF34-3A1	23133	Y50		7038
N933CA	Canadair Regional Jet 100ER (CL-600-2B19)	7040		0094	0694	2 GE CF34-3A1	23133	Y50		7040
N934CA	Canadair Regional Jet 100ER (CL-600-2B19)	7042		0094	0794	2 GE CF34-3A1	23133	Y50		7042
N936CA	Canadair Regional Jet 100ER (CL-600-2B19)	7043		0094	0994	2 GE CF34-3A1	23133	Y50		7043
N937CA	Canadair Regional Jet 100ER (CL-600-2B19)	7044		0094	0994	2 GE CF34-3A1	23133	Y50		7044
N938CA	Canadair Regional Jet 100ER (CL-600-2B19)	7046		0094	0994	2 GE CF34-3A1	23133	Y50		7046
N940CA	Canadair Regional Jet 100ER (CL-600-2B19)	7048		0094	1094	2 GE CF34-3A1	23133	Y50		7048
N941CA	Canadair Regional Jet 100ER (CL-600-2B19)	7050		0094	1194	2 GE CF34-3A1	23133	Y50		7050
N943CA	Canadair Regional Jet 100ER (CL-600-2B19)	7062	C-FMNW*	0095	0395	2 GE CF34-3A1	23133	Y50		7062
N945CA	Canadair Regional Jet 100ER (CL-600-2B19)	7069	C-FMKV*	0095	0595	2 GE CF34-3A1	23133	Y50		7069
N946CA	Canadair Regional Jet 100ER (CL-600-2B19)	7072	C-FMLB*	0095	0695	2 GE CF34-3A1	23133	Y50		7072
N947CA	Canadair Regional Jet 100ER (CL-600-2B19)	7077	C-FMLT*	0095	0895	2 GE CF34-3A1	23133	Y50		7077
N948CA	Canadair Regional Jet 100ER (CL-600-2B19)	7079	C-FMLV*	0095	0995	2 GE CF34-3A1	23133	Y50		7079
N949CA	Canadair Regional Jet 100ER (CL-600-2B19)	7080	C-FMMB*	0095	0995	2 GE CF34-3A1	23133	Y50		7080
N951CA	Canadair Regional Jet 100ER (CL-600-2B19)	7091		0095	1195	2 GE CF34-3A1	23133	Y50		7091
N952CA	Canadair Regional Jet 100ER (CL-600-2B19)	7092		0095	1295	2 GE CF34-3A1	23133	Y50		7092
N954CA	Canadair Regional Jet 100ER (CL-600-2B19)	7100		0095	0196	2 GE CF34-3A1	23133	Y50		7100 / 100th RJ spec. cs
N956CA	Canadair Regional Jet 100ER (CL-600-2B19)	7105		0096	0296	2 GE CF34-3A1	23133	Y50		7105
N957CA	Canadair Regional Jet 100ER (CL-600-2B19)	7109	C-FMLV*	0096	0496	2 GE CF34-3A1	23133	Y50		7109
N958CA	Canadair Regional Jet 100ER (CL-600-2B19)	7111	C-FMML*	0096	0496	2 GE CF34-3A1	23133	Y50		7111
N959CA	Canadair Regional Jet 100ER (CL-600-2B19)	7116	C-FMMX*	0096	0596	2 GE CF34-3A1	23133	Y50		7116
N960CA	Canadair Regional Jet 100ER (CL-600-2B19)	7117	C-FMMY*	0096	0596	2 GE CF34-3A1	23133	Y50		7117
N962CA	Canadair Regional Jet 100ER (CL-600-2B19)	7123	C-FMLU*	0096	0696	2 GE CF34-3A1	23133	Y50		7123
N963CA	Canadair Regional Jet 100ER (CL-600-2B19)	7127	C-FMMN*	0096	0796	2 GE CF34-3A1	23133	Y50		7127
N964CA	Canadair Regional Jet 100ER (CL-600-2B19)	7129	C-FMMT*	0096	0796	2 GE CF34-3A1	23133	Y50		7129
N965CA	Canadair Regional Jet 100ER (CL-600-2B19)	7131	C-FMMX*	0096	0896	2 GE CF34-3A1	23133	Y50		7131
N966CA	Canadair Regional Jet 100ER (CL-600-2B19)	7132	C-FMMY*	0096	0996	2 GE CF34-3A1	23133	Y50		7132
N967CA	Canadair Regional Jet 100ER (CL-600-2B19)	7134	C-FMND*	0096	0996	2 GE CF34-3A1	23133	Y50		7134
N969CA	Canadair Regional Jet 100ER (CL-600-2B19)	7141	C-FMML*	0096	1096	2 GE CF34-3A1	23133	Y50		7141
N971CA	Canadair Regional Jet 100ER (CL-600-2B19)	7145	C-FMMW*	0096	1196	2 GE CF34-3A1	23133	Y50		7145
N973CA	Canadair Regional Jet 100ER (CL-600-2B19)	7146		0096	1196	2 GE CF34-3A1	23133	Y50		7146
N975CA	Canadair Regional Jet 100ER (CL-600-2B19)	7150	C-FMNH*	0096	1296	2 GE CF34-3A1	23133	Y50		7150
N976CA	Canadair Regional Jet 100ER (CL-600-2B19)	7151	C-FMNQ*	0096	1296	2 GE CF34-3A1	23133	Y50		7151
N977CA	Canadair Regional Jet 100ER (CL-600-2B19)	7157		0097	0197	2 GE CF34-3A1	23133	Y50		7157
N978CA	Canadair Regional Jet 100ER (CL-600-2B19)	7158		0097	0197	2 GE CF34-3A1	23133	Y50		7158
N979CA	Canadair Regional Jet 100ER (CL-600-2B19)	7159		0097	0197	2 GE CF34-3A1	23133	Y50		7159 / 20 years in flight-special colors

☐ N981CA	Canadair Regional Jet 100ER (CL-600-2B19)	7163	C-FMOS*	0097	0497	2 GE CF34-3A1	23133	Y50		7163
☐ N982CA	Canadair Regional Jet 100ER (CL-600-2B19)	7168	C-FMLU*	0097	0497	2 GE CF34-3A1	23133	Y50		7168
☐ N983CA	Canadair Regional Jet 100ER (CL-600-2B19)	7169		0097	0697	2 GE CF34-3A1	23133	Y50		7169
☐ N984CA	Canadair Regional Jet 100ER (CL-600-2B19)	7171		0097	0697	2 GE CF34-3A1	23133	Y50		7171
☐ N986CA	Canadair Regional Jet 100ER (CL-600-2B19)	7174		0097	0697	2 GE CF34-3A1	23133	Y50		7174
☐ N987CA	Canadair Regional Jet 100ER (CL-600-2B19)	7199		0097	1097	2 GE CF34-3A1	23133	Y50		7199
☐ N988CA	Canadair Regional Jet 100ER (CL-600-2B19)	7204		0097	1297	2 GE CF34-3A1	23133	Y50		7204
☐ N989CA	Canadair Regional Jet 100ER (CL-600-2B19)	7215	C-FMOI*	0098	0198	2 GE CF34-3A1	23133	Y50		7215
☐ N991CA	Canadair Regional Jet 100ER (CL-600-2B19)	7216		0098	0298	2 GE CF34-3A1	23133	Y50		7216
☐ N995CA	Canadair Regional Jet 100ER (CL-600-2B19)	7229		0098	0398	2 GE CF34-3A1	23133	Y50		7229
☐ N999CA	Canadair Regional Jet 100ER (CL-600-2B19)	7230		0098	0498	2 GE CF34-3A1	23133	Y50		7230
☐ N	Canadair Regional Jet 100ER (CL-600-2B19)					2 GE CF34-3A1	23133	Y50		oo-delivery 0001
☐ N	Canadair Regional Jet 100ER (CL-600-2B19)					2 GE CF34-3A1	23133	Y50		oo-delivery 0001
☐ N	Canadair Regional Jet 100ER (CL-600-2B19)					2 GE CF34-3A1	23133	Y50		oo-delivery 0001
☐ N	Canadair Regional Jet 100ER (CL-600-2B19)					2 GE CF34-3A1	23133	Y50		oo-delivery 0001
☐ N	Canadair Regional Jet 100ER (CL-600-2B19)					2 GE CF34-3A1	23133	Y50		oo-delivery 0001
☐ N	Canadair Regional Jet 100ER (CL-600-2B19)					2 GE CF34-3A1	23133	Y50		oo-delivery 0001
☐ N	Canadair Regional Jet 100ER (CL-600-2B19)					2 GE CF34-3A1	23133	Y50		oo-delivery 0001
☐ N	Canadair Regional Jet 100ER (CL-600-2B19)					2 GE CF34-3A1	23133	Y50		oo-delivery 0001
☐ N	Canadair Regional Jet 100ER (CL-600-2B19)					2 GE CF34-3A1	23133	Y50		oo-delivery 0001
☐ N	Canadair Regional Jet 100ER (CL-600-2B19)					2 GE CF34-3A1	23133	Y50		oo-delivery 0001
☐ N	Canadair Regional Jet 100ER (CL-600-2B19)					2 GE CF34-3A1	23133	Y50		oo-delivery 0001
☐ N	Canadair Regional Jet 100ER (CL-600-2B19)					2 GE CF34-3A1	23133	Y50		oo-delivery 0001
☐ N	Canadair Regional Jet 700					2 GE CF34-8C1	32885	Y70		oo-delivery 1101
☐ N	Canadair Regional Jet 700					2 GE CF34-8C1	32885	Y70		oo-delivery 1201
☐ N	Canadair Regional Jet 700					2 GE CF34-8C1	32885	Y70		oo-delivery 0002
☐ N	Canadair Regional Jet 700					2 GE CF34-8C1	32885	Y70		oo-delivery 0002
☐ N	Canadair Regional Jet 700					2 GE CF34-8C1	32885	Y70		oo-delivery 0002
☐ N	Canadair Regional Jet 700					2 GE CF34-8C1	32885	Y70		oo-delivery 0002
☐ N	Canadair Regional Jet 700					2 GE CF34-8C1	32885	Y70		oo-delivery 0002
☐ N	Canadair Regional Jet 700					2 GE CF34-8C1	32885	Y70		oo-delivery 0002
☐ N	Canadair Regional Jet 700					2 GE CF34-8C1	32885	Y70		oo-delivery 0002
☐ N	Canadair Regional Jet 700					2 GE CF34-8C1	32885	Y70		oo-delivery 0002
☐ N	Canadair Regional Jet 700					2 GE CF34-8C1	32885	Y70		oo-delivery 0002
☐ N	Canadair Regional Jet 700					2 GE CF34-8C1	32885	Y70		oo-delivery 0002
☐ N	Canadair Regional Jet 700					2 GE CF34-8C1	32885	Y70		oo-delivery 0003
☐ N	Canadair Regional Jet 700					2 GE CF34-8C1	32885	Y70		oo-delivery 0003
☐ N	Canadair Regional Jet 700					2 GE CF34-8C1	32885	Y70		oo-delivery 0003
☐ N	Canadair Regional Jet 700					2 GE CF34-8C1	32885	Y70		oo-delivery 0003
☐ N	Canadair Regional Jet 700					2 GE CF34-8C1	32885	Y70		oo-delivery 0003
☐ N	Canadair Regional Jet 700					2 GE CF34-8C1	32885	Y70		oo-delivery 0003
☐ N	Canadair Regional Jet 700					2 GE CF34-8C1	32885	Y70		oo-delivery 0003
☐ N	Canadair Regional Jet 700					2 GE CF34-8C1	32885	Y70		oo-delivery 0003

COMAIR JET EXPRESS – JETEX (CVG Aviation, Inc. dba / formerly CVG CorpFlite / Subsidiary of Comair, Inc.) — Cincinnati-Northern Kentucky Int'l, OH

PO Box 75021, Cincinnati, OH 45275, USA ☎ (606) 767-3500 Tx: none Fax: (606) 283-5043 SITA: n/a
F: 1977 n/a Head: David R. Mueller Net: n/a

☐ N552DM	Bell 206L-3 LongRanger III	51212	N187TW	0087	0194	1 AN 250-C30P	1882			
☐ N436DM	Learjet 35A	35A-389	VR-BLU	0081	0493	2 GA TFE731-2-2B	8165			
☐ N442DM	Learjet 35A	35A-405	N35FS	0081	0490	2 GA TFE731-2-2B	8165			
☐ N440DM	Learjet 55	55-005	N550CS	0081	0597	2 GA TFE731-3AR-2B	9752			
☐ N477DM	Canadair CL-601-3R (CL-600-2B16) Challen.	5174	N605CC	0095	1295	2 GE CF34-3A1	20457			
☐ N497DM	Canadair CL-604 (CL-600-2B16) Challen.	5359		0098	0598	2 GE CF34-3B	21591			
☐ N80BF	Canadair CL-601-3A (CL-600-2B16) Challen.	5117	N606CC	0092	0994	2 GE CF34-3A	20457			lsf NWT Aircraft Co.

COMMANDER NORTHWEST, Ltd — Wenatchee-Pangborn Mem.,WA/Anchorage-Int'l & Palmer-Mun.,AK

PO Box 3281, Wenatchee, WA 98807, USA ☎ (509) 662-7906 Tx: none Fax: (509) 662-7191 SITA: n/a
F: 1980 n/a Head: Thomas R. Blaesing Net: n/a

☐ N210HD	Twin (Aero) Shrike Commander 500S	500S-1841-33		0069	1287	2 LY IO-540-E1B5	3062			
☐ N900RA	Twin (Aero) Shrike Commander 500S	3070		0070	1287	2 LY IO-540-E1B5	3062			
☐ N7UP	Twin (Aero) Grand Commander 680FL	680FL-1349-29		0063	0191	2 LY IGSO-540-B1A	3856			

COMMERCIAL AVIATION ENTERPRISES, Inc. — Fort Lauderdale-Executive, FL

16082 Rio del Sol, Delray Beach, FL 33446, USA ☎ (561) 637-8646 Tx: none Fax: (561) 637-8725 SITA: n/a
F: 1974 n/a Head: Gus Maestrales Net: http://www.commercialaviation.com

☐ N333GM	Sabreliner 40A (Rockwell NA265-40A)	282-106	XA-RKG	0072	0297	2 PW JT12A-8	8896	Freighter		
☐ N333NM	Sabreliner 40 (Rockwell NA265-40)	282-45	N333GM	0065	0789	2 PW JT12A-8	8459	Freighter		
☐ N40LB	Sabreliner 40 (Rockwell NA265-40)	282-36	N200MP	0065	0490	2 PW JT12A-8	8459	Freighter		

COMMERCIAL FLYER — Honolulu-Int'l, HI

2330 Makanani Drive, Honolulu, HI 96817, USA ☎ (888) 842-5761 Tx: none Fax: (808) 833-8014 SITA: n/a
F: 1995 n/a Head: Wallace K. Suenaga Net: n/a Aircraft below MTOW 1361kg: Cessna 150

☐ N4576Q	Cessna 402A	402A0076		0069	0195	2 CO TSIO-520-E	2858	Para		
☐ N300EE	Piper PA-31-350 Navajo Chieftain	31-8052112		0080	0097	2 LY TIO-540-J2BD	3175	9 Pax		lsf Bernhart Aircraft Equipment
☐ N500EE	Piper PA-31-350 Navajo Chieftain	31-8052131		0080	0098	2 LY TIO-540-J2BD	3175	9 Pax		lsf Bernhart Aircraft Equipment

COMMODORE SEAPLANES, Inc. — Homewood-SPB, CA

PO Box 207, Kings Beach, CA 95719, USA ☎ (530) 546-3958 Tx: none Fax: none SITA: n/a
F: 1945 n/a Head: Michael A. Brown Net: n/a Flights are operated in conjunction with SAN FRANCISCO SEAPLANE TOURS at Sausalito-SPB.

☐ N9279Z	De Havilland DHC-2 Beaver I	345	51-16821	0051	0384	1 PW R-985	2309			lsf pvt / Floats

COMMUNITY AIR, Inc. — Ukiah-Municipal, CA

1100 Hastings Road, Suite A, Ukiah, CA 95482, USA ☎ (707) 463-1245 Tx: none Fax: (707) 463-5888 SITA: n/a
F: 1998 n/a Head: John Mayginness Net: http://www.communityair.com Presently being set-up. Intends to start operations during 1999.

☐ N	Pilatus PC-12/45					1 PWC PT6A-67B	4500	Y10 / Freighter		oo-delivery 0099
☐ N	Pilatus PC-12/45					1 PWC PT6A-67B	4500	Y10 / Freighter		oo-delivery 0099
☐ N	Pilatus PC-12/45					1 PWC PT6A-67B	4500	Y10 / Freighter		oo-delivery 0099
☐ N	Pilatus PC-12/45					1 PWC PT6A-67B	4500	Y10 / Freighter		oo-delivery 0099
☐ N	Pilatus PC-12/45					1 PWC PT6A-67B	4500	Y10 / Freighter		oo-delivery 0000
☐ N	Pilatus PC-12/45					1 PWC PT6A-67B	4500	Y10 / Freighter		oo-delivery 0000
☐ N	Pilatus PC-12/45					1 PWC PT6A-67B	4500	Y10 / Freighter		oo-delivery 0000
☐ N	Pilatus PC-12/45					1 PWC PT6A-67B	4500	Y10 / Freighter		oo-delivery 0000
☐ N	Pilatus PC-12/45					1 PWC PT6A-67B	4500	Y10 / Freighter		oo-delivery 0000
☐ N	Pilatus PC-12/45					1 PWC PT6A-67B	4500	Y10 / Freighter		oo-delivery 0000
☐ N	Pilatus PC-12/45					1 PWC PT6A-67B	4500	Y10 / Freighter		oo-delivery 0000

COMMUTAIR = UCA (US Airways Express) (Division of Champlain Enterprises, Inc.) — Plattsburgh-Clinton County, NY

518 Rugar Street, Plattsburgh, NY 12901, USA ☎ (518) 562-2700 Tx: none Fax: (518) 562-8030 SITA: n/a
F: 1989 350 Head: Antony von Elbe IATA: 841 ICAO: COMMUTAIR Net: n/a
All aircraft are operated as US AIRWAYS EXPRESS (in full such colour & both titles), a commuter system to provide feeder connection at US Airways major hubs, using US flight numbers.

☐ N830CA	Beech 1900D Airliner	UE-19		0092	0892	2 PWC PT6A-67D	7688	Y19		op in US Airways Express-colors
☐ N831CA	Beech 1900D Airliner	UE-20		0092	0992	2 PWC PT6A-67D	7688	Y19		op in US Airways Express-colors
☐ N832CA	Beech 1900D Airliner	UE-22		0092	0992	2 PWC PT6A-67D	7688	Y19		op in US Airways Express-colors
☐ N833CA	Beech 1900D Airliner	UE-24		0092	1092	2 PWC PT6A-67D	7688	Y19		op in US Airways Express-colors
☐ N834CA	Beech 1900D Airliner	UE-25		0092	1092	2 PWC PT6A-67D	7688	Y19		op in US Airways Express-colors
☐ N835CA	Beech 1900D Airliner	UE-30		0092	1292	2 PWC PT6A-67D	7688	Y19		op in US Airways Express-colors
☐ N836CA	Beech 1900D Airliner	UE-32		0092	0193	2 PWC PT6A-67D	7688	Y19		op in US Airways Express-colors
☐ N837CA	Beech 1900D Airliner	UE-16	N140MA	0092	0792	2 PWC PT6A-67D	7688	Y19		op in US Airways Express-colors
☐ N838CA	Beech 1900D Airliner	UE-34		0093	0193	2 PWC PT6A-67D	7688	Y19		op in US Airways Express-colors
☐ N839CA	Beech 1900D Airliner	UE-36		0093	0193	2 PWC PT6A-67D	7688	Y19		op in US Airways Express-colors
☐ N840CA	Beech 1900D Airliner	UE-38		0093	0393	2 PWC PT6A-67D	7688	Y19		op in US Airways Express-colors
☐ N841CA	Beech 1900D Airliner	UE-40		0093	0493	2 PWC PT6A-67D	7688	Y19		op in US Airways Express-colors
☐ N842CA	Beech 1900D Airliner	UE-41		0093	0493	2 PWC PT6A-67D	7688	Y19		op in US Airways Express-colors
☐ N843CA	Beech 1900D Airliner	UE-43		0093	0593	2 PWC PT6A-67D	7688	Y19		op in US Airways Express-colors
☐ N844CA	Beech 1900D Airliner	UE-45		0093	0593	2 PWC PT6A-67D	7688	Y19		op in US Airways Express-colors
☐ N845CA	Beech 1900D Airliner	UE-47		0093	0693	2 PWC PT6A-67D	7688	Y19		op in US Airways Express-colors
☐ N846CA	Beech 1900D Airliner	UE-49		0093	0693	2 PWC PT6A-67D	7688	Y19		op in US Airways Express-colors
☐ N847CA	Beech 1900D Airliner	UE-52		0093	0793	2 PWC PT6A-67D	7688	Y19		op in US Airways Express-colors
☐ N848CA	Beech 1900D Airliner	UE-53		0093	0793	2 PWC PT6A-67D	7688	Y19		op in US Airways Express-colors
☐ N852CA	Beech 1900D Airliner	UE-55		0093	0793	2 PWC PT6A-67D	7688	Y19		op in US Airways Express-colors
☐ N853CA	Beech 1900D Airliner	UE-56		0093	0893	2 PWC PT6A-67D	7688	Y19		op in US Airways Express-colors

301 registration type of aircraft cn/fn ex/ex* mfd del powered by mtow kg configuration selcal name/fln/specialitites/remarks

☐ N854CA	Beech 1900D Airliner	UE-60		0093	0993	2 PWC PT6A-67D	7688	Y19		op in US Airways Express-colors
☐ N855CA	Beech 1900D Airliner	UE-61		0093	1093	2 PWC PT6A-67D	7688	Y19		op in US Airways Express-colors
☐ N856CA	Beech 1900D Airliner	UE-66		0093	1093	2 PWC PT6A-67D	7688	Y19		op in US Airways Express-colors
☐ N857CA	Beech 1900D Airliner	UE-71		0093	1193	2 PWC PT6A-67D	7688	Y19		op in US Airways Express-colors
☐ N858CA	Beech 1900D Airliner	UE-72		0093	1293	2 PWC PT6A-67D	7688	Y19		op in US Airways Express-colors
☐ N859CA	Beech 1900D Airliner	UE-128		0094	1294	2 PWC PT6A-67D	7688	Y19		op in US Airways Express-colors
☐ N860CA	Beech 1900D Airliner	UE-134	N134ZV	0094	0595	2 PWC PT6A-67D	7688	Y19		op in US Airways Express-colors
☐ N861CA	Beech 1900D Airliner	UE-164	N81538	0095	0995	2 PWC PT6A-67D	7688	Y19		op in US Airways Express-colors
☐ N862CA	Beech 1900D Airliner	UE-180		0095	1195	2 PWC PT6A-67D	7688	Y19		op in US Airways Express-colors

COMSTOCK AIR (Comstock Air Services, Inc. dba) — **Sacramento-Executive, CA**

PO Box 22849, Sacramento, CA 95822, USA ☎ (530) 422-7577 Tx: none Fax: (530) 424-1512 SITA: n/a
F: 1978 , ⁂ n/a Head: Orin B. Koukol Net: n/a Aircraft below MTOW 1361kg: Cessna 182P

☐ N1680R	Cessna R182 Skylane RG II	R18200512		0078	0584	1 LY O-540-J3C5D	1406			
☐ N35840	Cessna TU206F Turbo Stationair II	U20602750		0075	0889	1 CO TSIO-520-C	1633			
☐ N35964	Cessna TU206F Turbo Stationair II	U20602835		0075	0688	1 CO TSIO-520-C	1633			
☐ N6285H	Cessna T207A Turbo Stationair 7 II	20700466		0078	0881	1 CO TSIO-520-M	1724			
☐ N5357A	Cessna T210N Turbo Centurion II	21063386		0079	0784	1 CO TSIO-520-R	1814			
☐ N1360L	Cessna 337H Super Skymaster II	33701852		0078	0687	2 CO IO-360-GB	2100			
☐ N4949A	Cessna T310R II	310R1505		0078	0696	2 CO TSIO-520-B	2495			
☐ N6193X	Cessna 310R II	310R1330		0078	0486	2 CO IO-520-M	2495			

CONCORD JET SERVICE, Inc. — **Concord-Buchanan Field, CA**

530 Sally Ride Drive, Concord, CA 94520, USA ☎ (925) 825-2980 Tx: none Fax: none SITA: n/a
F: 1983 ⁂ n/a Head: Goy F. Fuller Net: n/a

☐ N890AK	Eurocopter (Aerosp.) AS350B AStar	2138	N907SH	0088	0489	1 TU Arriel 1B	1950			

CONDOR EXPRESS, Corp. — **Danbury-Municipal, CT**

81 Kenosia Avenue, Danbury, CT 06810, USA ☎ (203) 730-8436 Tx: none Fax: (203) 798-8899 SITA: n/a
F: 1989 ⁂ n/a Head: Ronald O'Neil Net: n/a

☐ N840SB	Beech King Air F90-1	LA-202	N777AS	0082	0694	2 PWC PT6A-135A	4967			lsf Finova Capital Corp.
☐ N202CE	Cessna 550 Citation II	550-0097	N404E	0079	0592	2 PWC JT15D-4	6033			

CONSTELLATION HISTORICAL SOCIETY — **Camarillo, CA**

7701 Woodley Avenue, Van Nuys, CA 91406, USA ☎ (818) 785-2743 Tx: none Fax: (818) 785-2753 SITA: n/a
F: 1992 ⁂ n/a Head: Benny D. Younesi Net: n/a Non-profit organisation conducting historical flying presentations.

☐ N73544	Lockh. L-1049F (C-121C) S. Constellation	4175	54-0156	0055	0292	4 WR R-3350	58967	8 seats		Queen of The Skies

CONSTRUCTION HELICOPTER, Inc. — **Ukiah-Municipal, CA**

PO Box 58, Potter Valley, CA 95469, USA ☎ (707) 743-1958 Tx: none Fax: (707) 743-2732 SITA: n/a
F: 1996 ⁂ n/a Head: Martin P. Smith Net: n/a

☐ N38EA	Bell 206B JetRanger III	2555	N201PS	0078	0796	1 AN 250-C20B	1451			
☐ N375AV	Bell UH-1H (205)	10320	68-15390	0068	0397	1 LY T53-L-13	4309			

CONSTRUCTION HELICOPTER, Inc. — **Detroit-Willow Run, MI**

807 Willow Run Airport, Ypsilanti, MI 48198-0807, USA ☎ (734) 483-6362 Tx: none Fax: (734) 483-3656 SITA: n/a
F: 1983 ⁂ 6 Head: Christopher G. Turner Net: n/a

☐ N438DS	Sikorsky S-58HT	58-738		0057	0683	1 PWC PT6T-6 TwinPac	5897			cvtd S-58H
☐ N901CH	Sikorsky S-58HT	58-1464	LV-OCN	0062	0585	1 PWC PT6T-6 TwinPac	5897			cvtd S-58H

CONTINENTAL AERIAL SURVEYS, Inc. — **Knoxville-McGhee Tyson, TN**

PO Box 300, Alcoa, TN 37701, USA ☎ (423) 970-3115 Tx: none Fax: (423) 984-7367 SITA: n/a
F: 1968 ⁂ 32 Head: Kenneth H. Howard, III Net: n/a

☐ N206TF	Cessna P206A Super Skylane	P206-0289		0066	0296	1 CO IO-520-A	1633	Photo / Survey		
☐ N7HE	Cessna T310P	310P0153		0069	0394	2 CO TSIO-520-B	2449	Photo / Survey		

CONTINENTAL AIRLINES, Inc. = CO / COA (Subs.of Continental Airlines Holdings, Inc. / Associated with Northwest Airlines) — **Houston-George Bush Intercontinental, TX** **Continental**

2929 Allen Parkway, Suite 1157, Houston, TX 77019, USA ☎ (713) 324-5000 Tx: 790275 Fax: (713) 324-8540 SITA: n/a
F: 1934 ⁂ 40000 Head: Gordon M. Bethune IATA: 005 ICAO: CONTINENTAL Net: http://www.flycontinental.com
A commuter system to provide feeder connection at CO major hubs is operated by subsidiary CONTINENTAL EXPRESS & as Continental Connection by COLGAN AIR, GULFSTREAM INTERNATIONAL & & SKYWEST AIRLINES (Continenal Connection carriers in their own colors). For details – see under each company.

☐ N33506	Boeing (Douglas) DC-9-32	47765 / 900	N3506T	0079	1082	2 PW JT8D-15	49895	F8Y95		506
☐ N12507	Boeing (Douglas) DC-9-32	47788 / 901	N3507T	0079	1082	2 PW JT8D-15	49895	F8Y95		507
☐ N12508	Boeing (Douglas) DC-9-32	47797 / 913	N3508T	0079	1082	2 PW JT8D-15	49895	F8Y95		508
☐ N27509	Boeing (Douglas) DC-9-32	47798 / 914	N3509T	0079	1082	2 PW JT8D-15	49895	F8Y95		509
☐ N12510	Boeing (Douglas) DC-9-32	47799 / 918	N3510T	0079	1082	2 PW JT8D-15	49895	F8Y95		510
☐ N18513	Boeing (Douglas) DC-9-32	48112 / 926	N3513T	0079	1082	2 PW JT8D-15	49895	F8Y95		513
☐ N14524	Boeing (Douglas) DC-9-32	47539 / 637	N524TX	0071	1082	2 PW JT8D-9A	49895	F8Y95	CG-HK	524
☐ N15525	Boeing (Douglas) DC-9-32	47531 / 638	N525NY	0871	0287	2 PW JT8D-9A	49895	F8Y95	CG-FH	525
☐ N17531	Boeing (Douglas) DC-9-32	45847 / 394	N531TX	0068	1082	2 PW JT8D-9A	49895	F8Y95		531
☐ N12532	Boeing (Douglas) DC-9-32	45791 / 349	N532TX	0068	1082	2 PW JT8D-9A	49895	F8Y95		532 / lsf PACA
☐ N17533	Boeing (Douglas) DC-9-32	47281 / 427	N533TX	0068	1082	2 PW JT8D-9A	49895	F8Y95		533 / lsf PACA
☐ N14534	Boeing (Douglas) DC-9-32	47110 / 167	N534TX	0067	1082	2 PW JT8D-9A	49895	F8Y95	CM-DG	534
☐ N43537	Boeing (Douglas) DC-9-32	47112 / 199	N537TX	0067	1082	2 PW JT8D-9A	49895	F8Y95	AE-HJ	537 / lsf POLA
☐ N12538	Boeing (Douglas) DC-9-32	47218 / 312	N538TX	0068	1082	2 PW JT8D-9A	49895	F8Y95		538
☐ N12539	Boeing (Douglas) DC-9-32	45792 / 372	N539NY	0068	0287	2 PW JT8D-9A	49895	F8Y95	CG-FJ	539
☐ N70542	Boeing (Douglas) DC-9-32	47535 / 610	N542TX	0070	1082	2 PW JT8D-9A	49895	F8Y95		542
☐ N17543	Boeing (Douglas) DC-9-32	45789 / 217	N543NY	0067	0287	2 PW JT8D-9A	49895	F8Y95	CH-BJ	543
☐ N18544	Boeing (Douglas) DC-9-32	47219 / 325	N544TX	0068	1082	2 PW JT8D-9A	49895	F8Y95	AE-HK	544 / lsf PACA
☐ N58545	Boeing (Douglas) DC-9-32	47094 / 149	N545NY	0067	0287	2 PW JT8D-9A	49895	F8Y95	CH-BK	545
☐ N17557	Boeing (Douglas) DC-9-32	47424 / 582	N557NY	0070	0287	2 PW JT8D-9A	49895	F8Y95	CH-AM	557
☐ N18563	Boeing (Douglas) DC-9-31	47487 / 553	N1310T	1169	0287	2 PW JT8D-9A	48988	F8Y95	CH-AJ	563
☐ N14564	Boeing (Douglas) DC-9-31	47490 / 560	N1311T	0069	1082	2 PW JT8D-9A	48988	F8Y95	CH-AK	564
☐ N14601	Boeing 737-524	27314 / 2566		0094	0294	2 CFMI CFM56-3C1	52390	F10Y94		601
☐ N69602	Boeing 737-524	27315 / 2571		0094	0294	2 CFMI CFM56-3C1	52390	F10Y94		602
☐ N69603	Boeing 737-524	27316 / 2573		0094	0294	2 CFMI CFM56-3C1	52390	F10Y94		603
☐ N14604	Boeing 737-524	27317 / 2576		0094	0294	2 CFMI CFM56-3C1	52390	F10Y94		604
☐ N14605	Boeing 737-524	27318 / 2582		0094	0394	2 CFMI CFM56-3C1	52390	F10Y94		605
☐ N58606	Boeing 737-524	27319 / 2590		0094	0394	2 CFMI CFM56-3C1	52390	F10Y94		606
☐ N16607	Boeing 737-524	27320 / 2596		0094	0494	2 CFMI CFM56-3C1	52390	F10Y94		607
☐ N33608	Boeing 737-524	27321 / 2597		0094	0494	2 CFMI CFM56-3C1	52390	F10Y94		608
☐ N14609	Boeing 737-524	27322 / 2607		0094	0594	2 CFMI CFM56-3C1	52390	F10Y94		609
☐ N27610	Boeing 737-524	27323 / 2616		0094	0594	2 CFMI CFM56-3C1	52390	F10Y94		610
☐ N18611	Boeing 737-524	27324 / 2621		0094	0694	2 CFMI CFM56-3C1	52390	F10Y94		611
☐ N11612	Boeing 737-524	27325 / 2630		0094	0794	2 CFMI CFM56-3C1	52390	F10Y94		612
☐ N14613	Boeing 737-524	27326 / 2633		0094	0794	2 CFMI CFM56-3C1	52390	F10Y94		613
☐ N17614	Boeing 737-524	27327 / 2634		0094	0894	2 CFMI CFM56-3C1	52390	F10Y94		614 / lsf Castle Harbour Leasing Inc.
☐ N37615	Boeing 737-524	27328 / 2640		0094	0894	2 CFMI CFM56-3C1	52390	F10Y94		615
☐ N52616	Boeing 737-524	27329 / 2641		0094	0894	2 CFMI CFM56-3C1	52390	F10Y94		616
☐ N16617	Boeing 737-524	27330 / 2648		0094	0994	2 CFMI CFM56-3C1	52390	F10Y94		617 / lsf Castle Harbour Leasing Inc.
☐ N16618	Boeing 737-524	27331 / 2652		0094	0994	2 CFMI CFM56-3C1	52390	F10Y94		618
☐ N17619	Boeing 737-524	27332 / 2659		0094	1094	2 CFMI CFM56-3C1	52390	F10Y94		619
☐ N17620	Boeing 737-524	27333 / 2660	N1790B*	0094	0295	2 CFMI CFM56-3C1	52390	F10Y94		620 / lsf GECA
☐ N19621	Boeing 737-524	27334 / 2661		0094	1294	2 CFMI CFM56-3C1	52390	F10Y94		621
☐ N18622	Boeing 737-524	27526 / 2669		0094	1294	2 CFMI CFM56-3C1	52390	F10Y94		622
☐ N19623	Boeing 737-524	27527 / 2672		0094	0195	2 CFMI CFM56-3C1	52390	F10Y94		623 / lsf GECA
☐ N13624	Boeing 737-524	27528 / 2675		0094	0295	2 CFMI CFM56-3C1	52390	F10Y94		624 / lsf GECA
☐ N46625	Boeing 737-524	27529 / 2683		0094	0195	2 CFMI CFM56-3C1	52390	F10Y94		625 / lsf GECA
☐ N32626	Boeing 737-524	27530 / 2686		0095	0495	2 CFMI CFM56-3C1	52390	F10Y94		626 / lsf GECA
☐ N17627	Boeing 737-524	27531 / 2700		0095	0495	2 CFMI CFM56-3C1	52390	F10Y94		627 / lsf GECA
☐ N14628	Boeing 737-524	27532 / 2712		0095	0495	2 CFMI CFM56-3C1	52390	F10Y94		628
☐ N14629	Boeing 737-524	27533 / 2725		0095	0595	2 CFMI CFM56-3C1	52390	F10Y94		629
☐ N59630	Boeing 737-524	27534 / 2726		0095	0595	2 CFMI CFM56-3C1	52390	F10Y94		630
☐ N62631	Boeing 737-524	27535 / 2728		0095	0695	2 CFMI CFM56-3C1	52390	F10Y94		631 / lsf GECA
☐ N16632	Boeing 737-524	27900 / 2736		0095	0795	2 CFMI CFM56-3C1	52390	F10Y94		632 / lsf GECA
☐ N24633	Boeing 737-524	27901 / 2743		0095	0895	2 CFMI CFM56-3C1	52390	F10Y94		633 / lsf GECA
☐ N19634	Boeing 737-524	26319 / 2748		0095	0895	2 CFMI CFM56-3C1	52390	F10Y94		634 / lsf ILFC
☐ N33635	Boeing 737-524	26339 / 2771		0096	0296	2 CFMI CFM56-3C1	52390	F10Y94		635 / lsf ILFC
☐ N19636	Boeing 737-524	26340 / 2777		0096	0496	2 CFMI CFM56-3C1	52390	F10Y94		636 / lsf ILFC
☐ N33637	Boeing 737-524	27540 / 2776		0096	0496	2 CFMI CFM56-3C1	52390	F10Y94		637
☐ N19638	Boeing 737-524	28899 / 2912		0797	0797	2 CFMI CFM56-3C1	52390	F10Y94		638
☐ N14639	Boeing 737-524	28900 / 2913		0797	0797	2 CFMI CFM56-3C1	52390	F10Y94		639

302 registration type of aircraft cn/fn ex/ex* mfd del powered by mtow kg configuration selcal name/fln/specialitites/remarks

registration	type of aircraft	cn/fn	ex/ex*	mfd	del	powered by	mtow kg	configuration	selcal	name/fln/specialitites/remarks
☐ N17640	Boeing 737-524	28901 / 2924		0897	0897	2 CFMI CFM56-3C1	52390	F10Y94		640
☐ N11641	Boeing 737-524	28902 / 2926		0897	0897	2 CFMI CFM56-3C1	52390	F10Y94		641
☐ N16642	Boeing 737-524	28903 / 2927		0097	0997	2 CFMI CFM56-3C1	52390	F10Y94		642
☐ N20643	Boeing 737-524	28904 / 2933		0997	0997	2 CFMI CFM56-3C1	52390	F10Y94		643
☐ N17644	Boeing 737-524	28905 / 2934	N1786B*	0997	0997	2 CFMI CFM56-3C1	52390	F10Y94		644
☐ N14645	Boeing 737-524	28906 / 2935	N1786B*	0997	0997	2 CFMI CFM56-3C1	52390	F10Y94		645
☐ N16646	Boeing 737-524	28907 / 2956	N1786B*	0097	1297	2 CFMI CFM56-3C1	52390	F10Y94		646
☐ N16647	Boeing 737-524	28908 / 2958		0097	1197	2 CFMI CFM56-3C1	52390	F10Y94		647
☐ N16648	Boeing 737-524	28909 / 2960		0097	1297	2 CFMI CFM56-3C1	52390	F10Y94		648
☐ N16649	Boeing 737-524	28910 / 2972		0097	1297	2 CFMI CFM56-3C1	52390	F10Y94		649
☐ N16650	Boeing 737-524	28911 / 2973		1297	1297	2 CFMI CFM56-3C1	52390	F10Y94		650
☐ N11651	Boeing 737-524	28912 / 2980		1297	1297	2 CFMI CFM56-3C1	52390	F10Y94		651
☐ N14652	Boeing 737-524	28913 / 2985		0198	0198	2 CFMI CFM56-3C1	52390	F10Y94		652
☐ N14653	Boeing 737-524	28914 / 2986		0198	0198	2 CFMI CFM56-3C1	52390	F10Y94		653
☐ N14654	Boeing 737-524	28915 / 2993		0098	0298	2 CFMI CFM56-3C1	52390	F10Y94		654
☐ N14655	Boeing 737-524	28916 / 2994		0098	0298	2 CFMI CFM56-3C1	52390	F10Y94		655
☐ N11656	Boeing 737-524	28917 / 3019		0098	0498	2 CFMI CFM56-3C1	52390	F10Y94		656
☐ N23657	Boeing 737-524	28918 / 3026	N1787B*	0098	0598	2 CFMI CFM56-3C1	52390	F10Y94		657
☐ N18658	Boeing 737-524	28919 / 3045		0098	0698	2 CFMI CFM56-3C1	52390	F10Y94		658
☐ N15659	Boeing 737-524	28920 / 3048		0098	0698	2 CFMI CFM56-3C1	52390	F10Y94		659
☐ N14660	Boeing 737-524	28921 / 3052		0098	0798	2 CFMI CFM56-3C1	52390	F10Y94		660
☐ N23661	Boeing 737-524	28922 / 3055		0098	0798	2 CFMI CFM56-3C1	52390	F10Y94		661
☐ N14662	Boeing 737-524	28923 / 3060		0098	0898	2 CFMI CFM56-3C1	52390	F10Y94		662
☐ N17663	Boeing 737-524	28924 / 3063		0098	0898	2 CFMI CFM56-3C1	52390	F10Y94		663
☐ N14664	Boeing 737-524	28925 / 3066	N1787B*	0898	0898	2 CFMI CFM56-3C1	52390	F10Y94		664
☐ N13665	Boeing 737-524	28926 / 3069	N1786B*	0898	0898	2 CFMI CFM56-3C1	52390	F10Y94		665
☐ N14667	Boeing 737-524	28927 / 3074	N1786B*	0998	0998	2 CFMI CFM56-3C1	52390	F10Y94		667
☐ N14668	Boeing 737-524	28928 / 3077	N1786B*	0098	1098	2 CFMI CFM56-3C1	52390	F10Y94		668
☐ N16301	Boeing 737-3T0	23352 / 1119		0085	0685	2 CFMI CFM56-3B1	61235	F10Y120		301
☐ N59302	Boeing 737-3T0	23353 / 1129		0085	0785	2 CFMI CFM56-3B1	61235	F10Y120		302
☐ N77303	Boeing 737-3T0	23354 / 1130		0085	0785	2 CFMI CFM56-3B1	61235	F10Y120		303
☐ N61304	Boeing 737-3T0	23355 / 1131		0085	0785	2 CFMI CFM56-3B1	61235	F10Y120		304
☐ N63305	Boeing 737-3T0	23356 / 1133		0085	0287	2 CFMI CFM56-3B1	61235	F10Y120	AE-KL	305
☐ N17306	Boeing 737-3T0	23357 / 1141		0085	0586	2 CFMI CFM56-3B1	61235	F10Y120		306
☐ N14307	Boeing 737-3T0	23358 / 1142		0085	0885	2 CFMI CFM56-3B1	61235	F10Y120		307
☐ N14308	Boeing 737-3T0	23359 / 1144		0085	0287	2 CFMI CFM56-3B1	61235	F10Y120	AE-KM	308
☐ N17309	Boeing 737-3T0	23360 / 1147		0085	0586	2 CFMI CFM56-3B1	61235	F10Y120		309
☐ N16310	Boeing 737-3T0	23361 / 1150		0085	0287	2 CFMI CFM56-3B1	61235	F10Y120	AE-LM	310
☐ N69311	Boeing 737-3T0	23362 / 1152		0085	0287	2 CFMI CFM56-3B1	61235	F10Y120		311
☐ N60312	Boeing 737-3T0	23363 / 1153		0085	1085	2 CFMI CFM56-3B1	61235	F10Y120		312
☐ N12313	Boeing 737-3T0	23364 / 1158		0085	1085	2 CFMI CFM56-3B1	61235	F10Y120		313
☐ N71314	Boeing 737-3T0	23365 / 1159		0085	1085	2 CFMI CFM56-3B1	61235	F10Y120		314
☐ N34315	Boeing 737-3T0	23366 / 1174		0085	1185	2 CFMI CFM56-3B1	61235	F10Y120		315
☐ N17316	Boeing 737-3T0	23367 / 1180		0086	0287	2 CFMI CFM56-3B1	61235	F10Y120	AE-GH	316
☐ N17317	Boeing 737-3T0	23368 / 1181		0086	0287	2 CFMI CFM56-3B1	61235	F10Y120	AE-GL	317
☐ N12318	Boeing 737-3T0	23369 / 1188		0086	0186	2 CFMI CFM56-3B1	61235	F10Y120		318 / lsf CITG
☐ N12319	Boeing 737-3T0	23370 / 1190		0086	0186	2 CFMI CFM56-3B1	61235	F10Y120		319 / lsf CITG
☐ N14320	Boeing 737-3T0	23371 / 1191		0086	0186	2 CFMI CFM56-3B1	61235	F10Y120		320
☐ N17321	Boeing 737-3T0	23372 / 1192		0086	0286	2 CFMI CFM56-3B1	61235	F10Y120		321
☐ N12322	Boeing 737-3T0	23373 / 1202		0086	0286	2 CFMI CFM56-3B1	61235	F10Y120		322
☐ N10323	Boeing 737-3T0	23374 / 1204		0086	0386	2 CFMI CFM56-3B1	61235	F10Y120		323
☐ N14324	Boeing 737-3T0	23375 / 1207		0086	0386	2 CFMI CFM56-3B1	61235	F10Y120		324
☐ N14325	Boeing 737-3T0	23455 / 1228		0086	0287	2 CFMI CFM56-3B1	61235	F10Y120	AE-HL	325
☐ N17326	Boeing 737-3T0	23456 / 1230		0086	0287	2 CFMI CFM56-3B1	61235	F10Y120	AE-JK	326
☐ N12327	Boeing 737-3T0	23457 / 1238		0086	0686	2 CFMI CFM56-3B1	61235	F10Y120		327
☐ N17328	Boeing 737-3T0	23458 / 1244		0086	0786	2 CFMI CFM56-3B1	61235	F10Y120		328
☐ N17329	Boeing 737-3T0	23459 / 1247		0086	0786	2 CFMI CFM56-3B1	61235	F10Y120		329
☐ N70330	Boeing 737-3T0	23460 / 1253		0086	0786	2 CFMI CFM56-3B1	61235	F10Y120		330
☐ N13331	Boeing 737-3T0	23569 / 1258		0086	0886	2 CFMI CFM56-3B1	61235	F10Y120	CG-JL	331
☐ N47332	Boeing 737-3T0	23570 / 1263		0086	0686	2 CFMI CFM56-3B1	61235	F10Y120		332
☐ N69333	Boeing 737-3T0	23571 / 1276		0086	1086	2 CFMI CFM56-3B1	61235	F10Y120		333
☐ N14334	Boeing 737-3T0	23572 / 1296		0086	1086	2 CFMI CFM56-3B1	61235	F10Y120		334
☐ N14335	Boeing 737-3T0	23573 / 1298		0086	1186	2 CFMI CFM56-3B1	61235	F10Y120		335
☐ N14336	Boeing 737-3T0	23574 / 1328		0087	0187	2 CFMI CFM56-3B1	61235	F10Y120		336
☐ N14337	Boeing 737-3T0	23575 / 1333		0087	0187	2 CFMI CFM56-3B1	61235	F10Y120		337
☐ N59338	Boeing 737-3T0	23576 / 1338		0087	0287	2 CFMI CFM56-3B1	61235	F10Y120		338
☐ N16339	Boeing 737-3T0	23577 / 1340		0087	0287	2 CFMI CFM56-3B1	61235	F10Y120		339 / lsf GECA
☐ N39340	Boeing 737-3T0	23578 / 1358		0087	0387	2 CFMI CFM56-3B1	61235	F10Y120		340 / lsf GECA
☐ N14341	Boeing 737-3T0	23579 / 1368		0087	0487	2 CFMI CFM56-3B1	61235	F10Y120		341
☐ N14342	Boeing 737-3T0	23580 / 1373		0087	0487	2 CFMI CFM56-3B1	61235	F10Y120		342
☐ N39343	Boeing 737-3T0	23581 / 1376		0087	0487	2 CFMI CFM56-3B1	61235	F10Y120		343
☐ N17344	Boeing 737-3T0	23582 / 1383		0087	0587	2 CFMI CFM56-3B1	61235	F10Y120		344
☐ N17345	Boeing 737-3T0	23583 / 1385		0087	0587	2 CFMI CFM56-3B1	61235	F10Y120		345
☐ N14346	Boeing 737-3T0	23584 / 1396		0087	0687	2 CFMI CFM56-3B1	61235	F10Y120		346
☐ N14347	Boeing 737-3T0	23585 / 1404		0087	0687	2 CFMI CFM56-3B1	61235	F10Y120		347
☐ N69348	Boeing 737-3T0	23586 / 1411		0087	0787	2 CFMI CFM56-3B1	61235	F10Y120		348
☐ N12349	Boeing 737-3T0	23587 / 1413		0087	0787	2 CFMI CFM56-3B1	61235	F10Y120		349
☐ N18350	Boeing 737-3T0	23588 / 1448		0087	0687	2 CFMI CFM56-3B1	61235	F10Y120		350
☐ N69351	Boeing 737-3T0	23589 / 1466		0087	1187	2 CFMI CFM56-3B1	61235	F10Y120		351
☐ N70352	Boeing 737-3T0	23590 / 1468		0087	1187	2 CFMI CFM56-3B1	61235	F10Y120		352
☐ N70353	Boeing 737-3T0	23591 / 1472		0087	1187	2 CFMI CFM56-3B1	61235	F10Y120		353
☐ N76354	Boeing 737-3T0	23592 / 1476		0087	1287	2 CFMI CFM56-3B1	61235	F10Y120		354
☐ N76355	Boeing 737-3T0	23593 / 1478		0087	1287	2 CFMI CFM56-3B1	61235	F10Y120		355
☐ N17356	Boeing 737-3T0	23942 / 1522	N320AW	0088	0393	2 CFMI CFM56-3B1	61235	F10Y120	CK-DM	356 / lsf ICX Corp.
☐ N19357	Boeing 737-3T0	23841 / 1518	N301AL	0088	0593	2 CFMI CFM56-3B1	61235	F10Y120		357 / lsf GECA
☐ N14358	Boeing 737-3T0	23943 / 1558	N302AL	0088	0593	2 CFMI CFM56-3B1	61235	F10Y120		358 / lsf GECA
☐ N73380	Boeing 737-3Q8	26309 / 2674		0094	1294	2 CFMI CFM56-3B1	61235	F10Y120		380 / lsf ILFC
☐ N14381	Boeing 737-3Q8	26310 / 2680		0095	0195	2 CFMI CFM56-3B1	61235	F10Y120		381 / lsf ILFC
☐ N19382	Boeing 737-3Q8	26311 / 2681		0095	0195	2 CFMI CFM56-3B1	61235	F10Y120		382 / lsf ILFC
☐ N14383	Boeing 737-3Q8	26312 / 2693		0095	0295	2 CFMI CFM56-3B1	61235	F10Y120		383 / lsf ILFC
☐ N14384	Boeing 737-3Q8	26313 / 2704		0095	0395	2 CFMI CFM56-3B1	61235	F10Y120		384 / lsf ILFC
☐ N73385	Boeing 737-3Q8	26314 / 2707		0095	0395	2 CFMI CFM56-3B1	61235	F10Y120		385 / lsf ILFC
☐ N17386	Boeing 737-3Q8	26321 / 2764		0095	1295	2 CFMI CFM56-3B1	61235	F10Y120		386 / lsf ILFC
☐ N16701	Boeing 737-724	28762 / 29	N1786B*	0098	0398	2 CFMI CFM56-7B24	69400	F12Y112		
☐ N24702	Boeing 737-724	28763 / 32		0098	0398	2 CFMI CFM56-7B24	69400	F12Y112		702
☐ N16703	Boeing 737-724	28764 / 37		0098	0498	2 CFMI CFM56-7B24	69400	F12Y112		703
☐ N14704	Boeing 737-724	28765 / 43		0098	0498	2 CFMI CFM56-7B24	69400	F12Y112		704
☐ N25705	Boeing 737-724	28766 / 46		0098	0598	2 CFMI CFM56-7B24	69400	F12Y112		705
☐ N24706	Boeing 737-724	28767 / 47		0098	0598	2 CFMI CFM56-7B24	69400	F12Y112		706
☐ N23707	Boeing 737-724	28768 / 48	N1787B*	0098	0598	2 CFMI CFM56-7B24	69400	F12Y112		707
☐ N23708	Boeing 737-724	28769 / 52		0098	0698	2 CFMI CFM56-7B24	69400	F12Y112		708
☐ N16709	Boeing 737-724	28779 / 93		0898	0898	2 CFMI CFM56-7B24	69400	F12Y112		709
☐ N15710	Boeing 737-724	28780 / 94		0898	0898	2 CFMI CFM56-7B24	69400	F12Y112		710
☐ N54711	Boeing 737-724	28782 / 97	N1786B*	0098	0998	2 CFMI CFM56-7B24	69400	F12Y112		711
☐ N15712	Boeing 737-724	28783 / 105	N1786B*	0998	0998	2 CFMI CFM56-7B24	69400	F12Y112		712
☐ N16713	Boeing 737-724	28784 / 107	N1786B*	0998	0998	2 CFMI CFM56-7B24	69400	F12Y112		713
☐ N33714	Boeing 737-724	28785 / 119	N1786B*	0998	0998	2 CFMI CFM56-7B24	69400	F12Y112		714
☐ N24715	Boeing 737-724	28786 / 125	N1795B*	0098	1098	2 CFMI CFM56-7B24	69400	F12Y112		715
☐ N13716	Boeing 737-724	28787 / 156	N1782B*	0098	1298	2 CFMI CFM56-7B24	69400	F12Y112		716
☐ N29717	Boeing 737-724	28936 / 182	N1786B*	1298	0199	2 CFMI CFM56-7B24	69400	F12Y112		717
☐ N13718	Boeing 737-724	28937 / 185	N1786B*	0199	0199	2 CFMI CFM56-7B24	69400	F12Y112		718
☐ N17719	Boeing 737-724	28938 / 195	N1786B*	0099	0299	2 CFMI CFM56-7B24	69400	F12Y112		719
☐ N13720	Boeing 737-724	28939 / 214		0299	0299	2 CFMI CFM56-7B24	69400	F12Y112		720
☐ N23721	Boeing 737-724	28940		0099	0399	2 CFMI CFM56-7B24	69400	F12Y112		721
☐ N27722	Boeing 737-724	28789		0099	0399	2 CFMI CFM56-7B24	69400	F12Y112		722
☐ N21723	Boeing 737-724	28790				2 CFMI CFM56-7B24	69400	F12Y112		723 / oo-delivery 0499
☐ N27724	Boeing 737-724	28791				2 CFMI CFM56-7B24	69400	F12Y112		724 / oo-delivery 0499
☐ N49725	Boeing 737-724					2 CFMI CFM56-7B24	69400	F12Y112		725 / oo-delivery 0499
☐ N39726	Boeing 737-724					2 CFMI CFM56-7B24	69400	F12Y112		726 / oo-delivery 0499
☐ N38727	Boeing 737-724	28797				2 CFMI CFM56-7B24	69400	F12Y112		727 / oo-delivery 0599

☐ N39728	Boeing 737-724	28944				2 CFMI CFM56-7B24	69400	F12Y112		728 / oo-delivery 0599
☐ N24729	Boeing 737-724	28945				2 CFMI CFM56-7B24	69400	F12Y112		729 / oo-delivery 0599
☐ N17730	Boeing 737-724	28798				2 CFMI CFM56-7B24	69400	F12Y112		730 / oo-delivery 0599
☐ N14731	Boeing 737-724	28799				2 CFMI CFM56-7B24	69400	F12Y112		731 / oo-delivery 0599
☐ N16732	Boeing 737-724	28948				2 CFMI CFM56-7B24	69400	F12Y112		732 / oo-delivery 0599
☐ N27733	Boeing 737-724	28800				2 CFMI CFM56-7B24	69400	F12Y112		733 / oo-delivery 0699
☐ N27734	Boeing 737-724	28949				2 CFMI CFM56-7B24	69400	F12Y112		734 / oo-delivery 0699
☐ N14735	Boeing 737-724	28950				2 CFMI CFM56-7B24	69400	F12Y112		735 / oo-delivery 0699
☐ N24736	Boeing 737-724					2 CFMI CFM56-7B24	69400	F12Y112		736 / oo-delivery 0799
☐ N16737	Boeing 737-724					2 CFMI CFM56-7B24	69400	F12Y112		737 / oo-delivery 0799
☐ N13738	Boeing 737-724					2 CFMI CFM56-7B24	69400	F12Y112		738 / oo-delivery 0799
☐ N17739	Boeing 737-724					2 CFMI CFM56-7B24	69400	F12Y112		739 / oo-delivery 0899
☐ N15740	Boeing 737-724	28796				2 CFMI CFM56-7B24	69400	F12Y112		740 / oo-delivery 0899
☐ N14741	Boeing 737-724					2 CFMI CFM56-7B24	69400	F12Y112		741 / oo-delivery 0899
☐ N15742	Boeing 737-724					2 CFMI CFM56-7B24	69400	F12Y112		742 / oo-delivery 0999
☐ N19743	Boeing 737-724					2 CFMI CFM56-7B24	69400	F12Y112		743 / oo-delivery 0999
☐ N13744	Boeing 737-724					2 CFMI CFM56-7B24	69400	F12Y112		744 / oo-delivery 1099
☐ N19745	Boeing 737-724					2 CFMI CFM56-7B24	69400	F12Y112		745 / oo-delivery 1099
☐ N12746	Boeing 737-724					2 CFMI CFM56-7B24	69400	F12Y112		746 / oo-delivery 1099
☐ N15747	Boeing 737-724					2 CFMI CFM56-7B24	69400	F12Y112		747 / oo-delivery 1199
☐ N23748	Boeing 737-724					2 CFMI CFM56-7B24	69400	F12Y112		748 / oo-delivery 1199
☐ N15749	Boeing 737-724					2 CFMI CFM56-7B24	69400	F12Y112		749 / oo-delivery 1299
☐ N13750	Boeing 737-724	28941				2 CFMI CFM56-7B24	69400	F12Y112		750 / oo-delivery 1299
☐ N10801	Boeing (Douglas) MD-82 (DC-9-82)	49127 / 1082	N801NY	0083	0287	2 PW JT8D-217	66678	F14Y130	CG-FM	801 / lsf Kuta-Two Aircraft Corp.
☐ N16802	Boeing (Douglas) MD-82 (DC-9-82)	49222 / 1139	N802NY	0084	0684	2 PW JT8D-217A	67812	F14Y130		802 / lsf PEGA
☐ N69803	Boeing (Douglas) MD-82 (DC-9-82)	49229 / 1140	N803NY	0084	0684	2 PW JT8D-217A	67812	F14Y130		803
☐ N16804	Boeing (Douglas) MD-82 (DC-9-82)	49246 / 1146	N804NY	0084	0884	2 PW JT8D-217A	67812	F14Y130		804
☐ N33805	Boeing (Douglas) MD-82 (DC-9-82)	49249 / 1149	N805NY	0084	0287	2 PW JT8D-217A	67812	F14Y130	AE-GJ	805
☐ N16806	Boeing (Douglas) MD-82 (DC-9-82)	49260 / 1150	N806NY	0084	0287	2 PW JT8D-217A	67812	F14Y130	AE-GK	806 / lsf BALG
☐ N16807	Boeing (Douglas) MD-82 (DC-9-82)	49261 / 1153	N807NY	0084	0984	2 PW JT8D-217A	67812	F14Y130		807
☐ N16808	Boeing (Douglas) MD-82 (DC-9-82)	49262 / 1159	N808NY	0084	1184	2 PW JT8D-217A	67812	F14Y130		808
☐ N809NY	Boeing (Douglas) MD-82 (DC-9-82)	49263 / 1163		0084	1184	2 PW JT8D-217A	67812	F14Y130		809 / to be re-reg. N13809
☐ N14810	Boeing (Douglas) MD-82 (DC-9-82)	49264 / 1171	N810NY	0084	0287	2 PW JT8D-217A	67812	F14Y130		810
☐ N12811	Boeing (Douglas) MD-82 (DC-9-82)	49265 / 1185	N811NY	0085	0287	2 PW JT8D-217A	67812	F14Y130		811
☐ N17812	Boeing (Douglas) MD-82 (DC-9-82)	49250 / 1186	N812NY	0085	0485	2 PW JT8D-217A	67812	F14Y130		812 / lsf Kuta-Two Aircraft Corp.
☐ N16813	Boeing (Douglas) MD-82 (DC-9-82)	48066 / 1019	N813NY	0081	1186	2 PW JT8D-217	66678	F14Y130	CG-HJ	813 / lsf INGL
☐ N14814	Boeing (Douglas) MD-82 (DC-9-82)	49112 / 1068	N814NY	0082	1186	2 PW JT8D-217	66678	F14Y130	AE-JL	814 / lsf INGL
☐ N16815	Boeing (Douglas) MD-82 (DC-9-82)	49113 / 1069	N815NY	0082	1186	2 PW JT8D-217	66678	F14Y130	AE-JM	815 / lsf INGL
☐ N14816	Boeing (Douglas) MD-82 (DC-9-82)	49370 / 1206	N816NY	0085	0685	2 PW JT8D-217A	67812	F14Y130		816 / lsf PEGA
☐ N33817	Boeing (Douglas) MD-82 (DC-9-82)	49371 / 1207	N817NY	0085	0685	2 PW JT8D-217A	67812	F14Y130		817
☐ N14818	Boeing (Douglas) MD-82 (DC-9-82)	49478 / 1293	N818NY	0086	0886	2 PW JT8D-217A	67812	F14Y130		818
☐ N819NY	Boeing (Douglas) MD-82 (DC-9-82)	49479 / 1297		0086	0686	2 PW JT8D-217A	67812	F14Y130		819 / to be re-reg. N38819
☐ N15820	Boeing (Douglas) MD-82 (DC-9-82)	49480 / 1298	N820NY	0086	0886	2 PW JT8D-217A	67812	F14Y130	EM-BD	820
☐ N72821	Boeing (Douglas) MD-82 (DC-9-82)	49481 / 1308		0086	0986	2 PW JT8D-217A	67812	F14Y130		821
☐ N72822	Boeing (Douglas) MD-82 (DC-9-82)	49482 / 1309		0086	1086	2 PW JT8D-217A	67812	F14Y130		822 / lsf PACA
☐ N76823	Boeing (Douglas) MD-82 (DC-9-82)	49483 / 1314	N6200N*	0086	1086	2 PW JT8D-217A	67812	F14Y130		823
☐ N72824	Boeing (Douglas) MD-82 (DC-9-82)	49484 / 1315		0086	1186	2 PW JT8D-217A	67812	F14Y130		824
☐ N69826	Boeing (Douglas) MD-82 (DC-9-82)	49486 / 1317		0086	1186	2 PW JT8D-217A	67812	F14Y130		826
☐ N72825	Boeing (Douglas) MD-82 (DC-9-82)	49485 / 1316		0086	1186	2 PW JT8D-217A	67812	F14Y130		825
☐ N77827	Boeing (Douglas) MD-82 (DC-9-82)	49487 / 1335		0086	1286	2 PW JT8D-217A	67812	F14Y130		827
☐ N71828	Boeing (Douglas) MD-82 (DC-9-82)	49488 / 1350		0087	0487	2 PW JT8D-217A	67812	F14Y130		828 / lsf POTO
☐ N72829	Boeing (Douglas) MD-82 (DC-9-82)	49489 / 1351		0087	0487	2 PW JT8D-217A	67812	F14Y130		829
☐ N72830	Boeing (Douglas) MD-82 (DC-9-82)	49490 / 1352		0087	0487	2 PW JT8D-217A	67812	F14Y130		830
☐ N14831	Boeing (Douglas) MD-82 (DC-9-82)	49491 / 1360		0087	0587	2 PW JT8D-217A	67812	F14Y130		831 / lsf POTO
☐ N35832	Boeing (Douglas) MD-82 (DC-9-82)	49492 / 1361		0087	0587	2 PW JT8D-217A	67812	F14Y130		832
☐ N18833	Boeing (Douglas) MD-82 (DC-9-82)	49493 / 1364		0087	0587	2 PW JT8D-217A	67812	F14Y130		833
☐ N10834	Boeing (Douglas) MD-82 (DC-9-82)	49494 / 1368		0087	0587	2 PW JT8D-217A	67812	F14Y130		834
☐ N18835	Boeing (Douglas) MD-82 (DC-9-82)	49439 / 1318	N6200N*	0086	1286	2 PW JT8D-217A	67812	F14Y130		835 / lsf Kuta-Two Aircraft Corp.
☐ N35836	Boeing (Douglas) MD-82 (DC-9-82)	49441 / 1322	N6202D*	0086	1286	2 PW JT8D-217A	67812	F14Y130		836 / Colorado Express
☐ N57837	Boeing (Douglas) MD-82 (DC-9-82)	49582 / 1411		0087	1087	2 PW JT8D-217A	67812	F14Y130		837 / Colorado Express
☐ N34838	Boeing (Douglas) MD-82 (DC-9-82)	49634 / 1419		0087	1287	2 PW JT8D-217A	67812	F14Y130		838 / Colorado Express
☐ N14839	Boeing (Douglas) MD-82 (DC-9-82)	49635 / 1420		0087	1187	2 PW JT8D-217A	67812	F14Y130		839
☐ N14840	Boeing (Douglas) MD-82 (DC-9-82)	49580 / 1369		0087	0687	2 PW JT8D-217A	67812	F14Y130		840
☐ N15841	Boeing (Douglas) MD-82 (DC-9-82)	49581 / 1384		0087	0787	2 PW JT8D-217A	67812	F14Y130		841
☐ N936AS	Boeing (Douglas) MD-83 (DC-9-83)	49363 / 1275		0086	1096	2 PW JT8D-219	72575	F14Y130		842 / to be re-reg. N23842
☐ N938AS	Boeing (Douglas) MD-83 (DC-9-83)	49365 / 1277		0086	1096	2 PW JT8D-219	72575	F14Y130		843 / to be re-reg. N17843
☐ N83870	Boeing (Douglas) MD-82 (DC-9-82)	48056 / 1012	N930MC	0082	0887	2 PW JT8D-217	66678	F14Y130		870
☐ N14871	Boeing (Douglas) MD-82 (DC-9-82)	48022 / 1079	N80UA	0982	0493	2 PW JT8D-217	67812	F14Y130	AE-HL	871 / cvtd MD-81
☐ N83872	Boeing (Douglas) MD-82 (DC-9-82)	49120 / 1071	N932MC	0082	0887	2 PW JT8D-217	67812	F14Y130		872 / cvtd MD-81
☐ N83873	Boeing (Douglas) MD-82 (DC-9-82)	49121 / 1072	N933MC	0082	0887	2 PW JT8D-217	67812	F14Y130		873 / cvtd MD-81
☐ N92874	Boeing (Douglas) MD-82 (DC-9-82)	49122 / 1073	N934MC	0082	0887	2 PW JT8D-217	67812	F14Y130		874 / cvtd MD-81
☐ N93875	Boeing (Douglas) MD-82 (DC-9-82)	49125 / 1074	N935MC	0082	0887	2 PW JT8D-217	67812	F14Y130		875 / cvtd MD-81
☐ N98876	Boeing (Douglas) MD-82 (DC-9-82)	49444 / 1323	N936MC	0086	0987	2 PW JT8D-217	66678	F14Y130	FG-CD	876 / lsf PACA
☐ N937MC	Boeing (Douglas) MD-82 (DC-9-82)	49450 / 1324	N9807F	0086	0987	2 PW JT8D-217	66678	F14Y130	FG-CL	877 / lsf Forsun Leasing/tbr N85877
☐ N938MC	Boeing (Douglas) MD-83 (DC-9-83)	49525 / 1340		0087	0887	2 PW JT8D-219	72575	F14Y130	EK-BF	878 / lsf AWAS
☐ N14879	Boeing (Douglas) MD-83 (DC-9-83)	49526 / 1342	N939MC	0087	0987	2 PW JT8D-219	72575	F14Y130	EK-BG	879 / lsf AWAS
☐ N14880	Boeing (Douglas) MD-81 (DC-9-81)	48044 / 967	N809HA	0081	1186	2 PW JT8D-217	63503	F14Y130		880
☐ N13881	Boeing (Douglas) MD-81 (DC-9-81)	48045 / 970	N819HA	0081	1186	2 PW JT8D-217	63503	F14Y130		881
☐ N37882	Boeing (Douglas) MD-81 (DC-9-81)	48027 / 973	N475AC	0081	1186	2 PW JT8D-217	63503	F14Y130	EM-CH	882 / lsf ILFC
☐ N16883	Boeing (Douglas) MD-81 (DC-9-81)	48073 / 1018	N849HA	0081	1186	2 PW JT8D-217	63503	F14Y130	EM-AC	883
☐ N16884	Boeing (Douglas) MD-81 (DC-9-81)	48074 / 1026	N859HA	0081	1186	2 PW JT8D-217	63503	F14Y130	EM-AF	884
☐ N477AC	Boeing (Douglas) MD-82 (DC-9-82)	48062 / 1015		0081	1186	2 PW JT8D-217	66678	F14Y130	EM-CL	885 / to be re-reg. N16885
☐ N478AC	Boeing (Douglas) MD-82 (DC-9-82)	48063 / 1020		0081	1186	2 PW JT8D-217	66678	F14Y130	FG-AC	886 / to be re-reg. N14886
☐ N16887	Boeing (Douglas) MD-82 (DC-9-82)	49116 / 1061	N9801F	0082	1186	2 PW JT8D-217	66678	F14Y130	FG-CJ	887 / lsf POLA
☐ N35888	Boeing (Douglas) MD-82 (DC-9-82)	49117 / 1063	N9802F	0082	1186	2 PW JT8D-217	66678	F14Y130	EM-CF	888 / Spirit of Newark / lsf POLA
☐ N14889	Boeing (Douglas) MD-82 (DC-9-82)	49118 / 1065	N9803F	0082	1186	2 PW JT8D-217	66678	F14Y130	EM-CJ	889 / lsf POLA
☐ N14890	Boeing (Douglas) MD-82 (DC-9-82)	49114 / 1066	N9804F	0082	1186	2 PW JT8D-217	66678	F14Y130	EM-AD	890 / lsf POLA
☐ N13891	Boeing (Douglas) MD-82 (DC-9-82)	49102 / 1076	N9805F	0082	1186	2 PW JT8D-217	66678	F14Y130	EM-BL	891 / lsf POLA
☐ N16892	Boeing (Douglas) MD-82 (DC-9-82)	49391 / 1270	EI-BTA	0086	0294	2 PW JT8D-219	67812	F14Y130	FG-AK	892 / lsf CISA
☐ N16893	Boeing (Douglas) MD-82 (DC-9-82)	49392 / 1272	EI-BTB	0086	0194	2 PW JT8D-219	67812	F14Y130	FG-AL	893 / lsf CISA
☐ N16894	Boeing (Douglas) MD-82 (DC-9-82)	49393 / 1279	EI-BTC	0086	1186	2 PW JT8D-219	67812	F14Y130	FG-BC	894 / lsf BALG
☐ N16895	Boeing (Douglas) MD-82 (DC-9-82)	49394 / 1285	EI-BTD	0086	1186	2 PW JT8D-219	67812	F14Y130	FG-BD	895 / lsf BALG
☐ N26210	Boeing 737-824	28770 / 56		0098	0698	2 CFMI CFM56-7B26	78245	F14Y141		210
☐ N24211	Boeing 737-824	28771 / 58		0098	0698	2 CFMI CFM56-7B26	78245	F14Y141		211
☐ N24212	Boeing 737-824	28772 / 63		0098	0698	2 CFMI CFM56-7B26	78245	F14Y141		212
☐ N27213	Boeing 737-824	28773 / 65		0098	0798	2 CFMI CFM56-7B26	78245	F14Y141		213
☐ N14214	Boeing 737-824	28774 / 74		0098	0798	2 CFMI CFM56-7B26	78245	F14Y141		214
☐ N26215	Boeing 737-824	28775 / 76		0098	0898	2 CFMI CFM56-7B26	78245	F14Y141		215
☐ N12216	Boeing 737-824	28776 / 79		0098	0898	2 CFMI CFM56-7B26	78245	F14Y141		216
☐ N16217	Boeing 737-824	28777 / 81		0098	0798	2 CFMI CFM56-7B26	78245	F14Y141		217
☐ N12218	Boeing 737-824	28778 / 84		0098	0898	2 CFMI CFM56-7B26	78245	F14Y141		218
☐ N14219	Boeing 737-824	28781 / 88		0898	0898	2 CFMI CFM56-7B26	78245	F14Y141		219
☐ N18220	Boeing 737-824	28929 / 134	N60436*	0098	1198	2 CFMI CFM56-7B26	78245	F14Y141		220
☐ N12221	Boeing 737-824	28930 / 153	N1796B*	0098	1298	2 CFMI CFM56-7B26	78245	F14Y141		221
☐ N34222	Boeing 737-824	28931 / 159		0098	1298	2 CFMI CFM56-7B26	78245	F14Y141		222
☐ N18223	Boeing 737-824	28932 / 162	N1786B*	0098	1298	2 CFMI CFM56-7B26	78245	F14Y141		223
☐ N24224	Boeing 737-824	28933 / 165	N1782B*	0098	1298	2 CFMI CFM56-7B26	78245	F14Y141		224
☐ N12225	Boeing 737-824	28934 / 168	N1782B*	1298	1298	2 CFMI CFM56-7B26	78245	F14Y141		225
☐ N26226	Boeing 737-824	28935 / 171	N1787B*	1298	1298	2 CFMI CFM56-7B26	78245	F14Y141		226
☐ N13227	Boeing 737-824	28788				2 CFMI CFM56-7B26	78245	F14Y141		227 / oo-delivery 0499
☐ N14228	Boeing 737-824	28792				2 CFMI CFM56-7B26	78245	F14Y141		228 / oo-delivery 0599
☐ N17229	Boeing 737-824	28793				2 CFMI CFM56-7B26	78245	F14Y141		229 / oo-delivery 0599
☐ N14230	Boeing 737-824	28794				2 CFMI CFM56-7B26	78245	F14Y141		230 / oo-delivery 0599
☐ N14231	Boeing 737-824	28795				2 CFMI CFM56-7B26	78245	F14Y141		231 / oo-delivery 0699
☐ N26232	Boeing 737-824	28942				2 CFMI CFM56-7B26	78245	F14Y141		232 / oo-delivery 0799
☐ N17233	Boeing 737-824	28943				2 CFMI CFM56-7B26	78245	F14Y141		233 / oo-delivery 0899
☐ N16234	Boeing 737-824	28946				2 CFMI CFM56-7B26	78245	F14Y141		234 / oo-delivery 0999
☐ N14235	Boeing 737-824	28947				2 CFMI CFM56-7B26	78245	F14Y141		235 / oo-delivery 1099
☐ N35236	Boeing 737-824	28801				2 CFMI CFM56-7B26	78245	F14Y141		236 / oo-delivery 1199
☐ N14237	Boeing 737-824	28802				2 CFMI CFM56-7B26	78245	F14Y141		237 / oo-delivery 1299

304 registration type of aircraft cn/fn ex/ex* mfd del powered by mtow kg configuration selcal name/fln/specialitites/remarks

	registration	type of aircraft	cn/fn	ex/ex*	mfd	del	powered by	mtow kg	configuration	selcal	name/fln/specialitites/remarks
☐	N	Boeing 737-924					2 CFMI CFM56-7B26	79016			oo-delivery 0501
☐	N	Boeing 737-924					2 CFMI CFM56-7B26	79016			oo-delivery 0601
☐	N	Boeing 737-924					2 CFMI CFM56-7B26	79016			oo-delivery 0701
☐	N	Boeing 737-924					2 CFMI CFM56-7B26	79016			oo-delivery 0801
☐	N	Boeing 737-924					2 CFMI CFM56-7B26	79016			oo-delivery 0901
☐	N	Boeing 737-924					2 CFMI CFM56-7B26	79016			oo-delivery 1001
☐	N	Boeing 737-924					2 CFMI CFM56-7B26	79016			oo-delivery 1101
☐	N	Boeing 737-924					2 CFMI CFM56-7B26	79016			oo-delivery 1201
☐	N	Boeing 737-924					2 CFMI CFM56-7B26	79016			oo-delivery 0002
☐	N	Boeing 737-924					2 CFMI CFM56-7B26	79016			oo-delivery 0002
☐	N	Boeing 737-924					2 CFMI CFM56-7B26	79016			oo-delivery 0002
☐	N	Boeing 737-924					2 CFMI CFM56-7B26	79016			oo-delivery 0002
☐	N	Boeing 737-924					2 CFMI CFM56-7B26	79016			oo-delivery 0002
☐	N	Boeing 737-924					2 CFMI CFM56-7B26	79016			oo-delivery 0002
☐	N	Boeing 737-924					2 CFMI CFM56-7B26	79016			oo-delivery 0002
☐	N17402	Boeing 727-243 (A)	21265 / 1226	N572PE	0076	0287	3 PW JT8D-9A	79651	F14Y137	BF-AM	402
☐	N17407	Boeing 727-243 (A)	21270 / 1231	N577PE	0076	0287	3 PW JT8D-9A	79651	F14Y137	BF-DJ	407
☐	N579PE	Boeing 727-243 (A)	21662 / 1421	I-DIRF	0078	0287	3 PW JT8D-9A	79651	F14Y137	BF-DL	409 / to be re-reg. N10409
☐	N17410	Boeing 727-243 (A)	21663 / 1438	N580PE	0078	0287	3 PW JT8D-9A	79651	F14Y137	BF-DM	410
☐	N86425	Boeing 727-212 (A)	21459 / 1329	N296AS	0078	0193	3 PW JT8D-17	89358	C10Y143	AD-BG	425 / lst CMI
☐	N86426	Boeing 727-227 (A)	21364 / 1261	N322AS	0077	0193	3 PW JT8D-17R	86409	C10Y143	CM-DF	426 / lst CMI
☐	N89427	Boeing 727-227 (A)	21365 / 1273	N323AS	0077	0193	3 PW JT8D-17R	86409	C10Y143		427 / lst CMI
☐	N83428	Boeing 727-2F9 (A)	21426 / 1285	N298AS	0077	0393	3 PW JT8D-17	89358	C10Y143		428 / lsf IPID/sub-lst CMI
☐	N75429	Boeing 727-2F9 (A)	21427 / 1291	N299AS	0077	0393	3 PW JT8D-17	89358	C10Y143		429 / lsf IPID/sub-lst CMI
☐	N32725	Boeing 727-224 (A)	20655 / 934		0073	0473	3 PW JT8D-9A	78245	F14Y137	FG-DJ	725 / lsf IAC Aviation Resources
☐	N66734	Boeing 727-224 (A)	20663 / 1073		0074	1074	3 PW JT8D-9A	78245	F14Y137	HL-AM	734
☐	N93738	Boeing 727-224 (A)	20666 / 1151		0075	0975	3 PW JT8D-9A	78245	F14Y137	HL-BE	738
☐	N69741	Boeing 727-224 (A)	22250 / 1684		0080	1180	3 PW JT8D-15	86409	F14Y137	DK-EJ	741
☐	N79743	Boeing 727-224 (A)	22252 / 1697		0081	0281	3 PW JT8D-15	86409	C10Y143	DK-EM	743 / lsf Pacific AirCorp/sub-lst CMI
☐	N79744	Boeing 727-224 (A)	22253 / 1702		0081	0281	3 PW JT8D-15 (HK3/FDX)	86409	C10Y143	DK-FH	744 / lsf Pacific AirCorp/sub-lst CMI
☐	N79745	Boeing 727-224 (A)	22448 / 1740		0081	0581	3 PW JT8D-15	86409	C10Y143	DK-FM	745 / lst CMI
☐	N79748	Boeing 727-224 (A)	22450 / 1760		0081	0681	3 PW JT8D-15	86409	F14Y137	DK-HL	748 / lsf PACA
☐	N79749	Boeing 727-224 (A)	22451 / 1767		0081	0781	3 PW JT8D-15	86409	F14Y137	DK-JL	749
☐	N73751	Boeing 727-227 (A)	21247 / 1217	N446BN	0076	0585	3 PW JT8D-9A	79651	F14Y137	BM-HK	751 / lsf IPID
☐	N17773	Boeing 727-227 (A)	21045 / 1133	N563PE	0075	0287	3 PW JT8D-9A	79651	F14Y137	CG-EL	773
☐	N15774	Boeing 727-227 (A)	21242 / 1196	N566PE	0076	0287	3 PW JT8D-9A	79651	F14Y137	BM-AC	774
☐	N511PE	Boeing 727-232 (A)	20634 / 917	N452DA	0073	0287	3 PW JT8D-15	83552	F14Y137	DG-FH	779 / to be re-reg. N17779
☐	N77780	Boeing 727-232 (A)	20635 / 918	N13780	0073	0287	3 PW JT8D-15	83552	F14Y137	BK-DM	780
☐	N15781	Boeing 727-232 (A)	20636 / 919	N513PE	0073	0287	3 PW JT8D-15	83552	F10Y143	BK-GJ	781
☐	N27783	Boeing 727-232 (A)	20638 / 926	N515PE	0073	0287	3 PW JT8D-15	83552	F14Y137	CF-AK	783
☐	N33785	Boeing 727-232 (A)	20640 / 935	N517PE	0073	0287	3 PW JT8D-15	83552	F14Y137	CF-AM	785 / lsf PACA
☐	N14788	Boeing 727-232 (A)	20642 / 944	N519PE	0073	0287	3 PW JT8D-15	83552	F14Y137	CF-JM	788
☐	N15790	Boeing 727-232 (A)	20644 / 959	N521PE	0073	0287	3 PW JT8D-15	83552	F10Y143	CG-AF	790 / lsf CMI
☐	N10791	Boeing 727-232 (A)	20645 / 961	N522PE	0073	0287	3 PW JT8D-15	83552	F14Y137	CG-AH	791 / lsf PACA
☐	N59792	Boeing 727-232 (A)	20646 / 967	N523PE	0073	0287	3 PW JT8D-15	83552	F14Y137	CG-AJ	792
☐	N45793	Boeing 727-232 (A)	20647 / 968	N524PE	0073	0287	3 PW JT8D-15	83552	F14Y137	CG-AK	793 / lsf PACA
☐	N58101	Boeing 757-224	27291 / 614		0094	0594	2 RR RB211-535E4-B	108862	F24Y159	ER-HP	101
☐	N14102	Boeing 757-224	27292 / 619		0094	0694	2 RR RB211-535E4-B	108862	F24Y159	ER-HQ	102
☐	N33103	Boeing 757-224	27293 / 623		0094	0694	2 RR RB211-535E4-B	108862	F24Y159	ER-HS	103
☐	N17104	Boeing 757-224	27294 / 629		0094	0794	2 RR RB211-535E4-B	108862	F24Y159	ER-JK	104 / lsf GECA
☐	N17105	Boeing 757-224	27295 / 632		0094	0894	2 RR RB211-535E4-B	108862	F24Y159	ER-JL	105 / lsf GECA
☐	N14106	Boeing 757-224	27296 / 637		0094	0994	2 RR RB211-535E4-B	108862	F24Y159	ER-JM	106 / Sam E. Ashmore / lsf GECA
☐	N14107	Boeing 757-224	27297 / 641		0094	1094	2 RR RB211-535E4-B	108862	F24Y159	ER-JP	107 / lsf GECA
☐	N21108	Boeing 757-224	27298 / 645		0094	1194	2 RR RB211-535E4-B	108862	F24Y159	ER-JQ	108 / lsf GECA
☐	N12109	Boeing 757-224	27299 / 648		0094	1294	2 RR RB211-535E4-B	108862	F24Y159	ER-JS	109 / lsf GECA
☐	N13110	Boeing 757-224	27300 / 650		0094	1294	2 RR RB211-535E4-B	108862	F24Y159	ER-KL	110 / lsf GECA
☐	N57111	Boeing 757-224	27301 / 652		0094	1294	2 RR RB211-535E4-B	108862	F24Y159	ER-KM	111
☐	N18112	Boeing 757-224	27302 / 653		0095	0295	2 RR RB211-535E4-B	108862	F24Y159	ER-KP	112 / lsf GECA
☐	N13113	Boeing 757-224	27555 / 668		0095	0495	2 RR RB211-535E4-B	108862	F24Y159	BL-AC	113 / lsf GECA
☐	N12114	Boeing 757-224	27556 / 682		0095	0795	2 RR RB211-535E4-B	108862	F24Y159	CG-DF	114
☐	N14115	Boeing 757-224	27557 / 686		0095	0895	2 RR RB211-535E4-B	108862	F24Y159	CM-BG	115
☐	N12116	Boeing 757-224	27558 / 702		0096	0396	2 RR RB211-535E4-B	108862	F24Y159	CM-FG	116
☐	N19117	Boeing 757-224	27559 / 706		0096	0496	2 RR RB211-535E4-B	108862	F24Y159		117
☐	N14118	Boeing 757-224	27560 / 748		0097	0397	2 RR RB211-535E4-B	108862	F24Y159		118
☐	N18119	Boeing 757-224	27561 / 753		0597	0597	2 RR RB211-535E4-B	108862	F24Y159		119
☐	N14120	Boeing 757-224	27562 / 761		0697	0697	2 RR RB211-535E4-B	108862	F24Y159		120
☐	N14121	Boeing 757-224	27563 / 766		0797	0797	2 RR RB211-535E4-B	108862	F24Y159		121
☐	N17122	Boeing 757-224	27564 / 768		0897	0897	2 RR RB211-535E4-B	108862	F24Y159		122
☐	N26123	Boeing 757-224	28966 / 781		0097	1297	2 RR RB211-535E4-B	108862	F24Y159		123
☐	N29124	Boeing 757-224	27565 / 786		0098	0198	2 RR RB211-535E4-B	108862	F24Y159		124
☐	N12125	Boeing 757-224	28967 / 788	N1787B*	0198	0298	2 RR RB211-535E4-B	108862	F24Y159		125
☐	N17126	Boeing 757-224 (ET)	27566 / 790		0098	0298	2 RR RB211-535E4-B	113398	C12Y210		126 / lst / opf CMI
☐	N48127	Boeing 757-224 (ET)	28968 / 791		0098	0298	2 RR RB211-535E4-B	113398	C12Y210		127 / lst / opf CMI
☐	N17128	Boeing 757-224 (ET)	27567 / 795		0098	0398	2 RR RB211-535E4-B	113398	C12Y210		128 / lst / opf CMI
☐	N29129	Boeing 757-224 (ET)	28969 / 796		0398	0398	2 RR RB211-535E4-B	113398	C12Y210		129 / lst / opf CMI
☐	N19130	Boeing 757-224 (ET)	28970 / 799		0098	0598	2 RR RB211-535E4-B	113398	C12Y210		130 / lst / opf CMI
☐	N34131	Boeing 757-224	28971 / 806		0098	0698	2 RR RB211-535E4-B	108862	F24Y159		131
☐	N33132	Boeing 757-224	29281 / 809		0698	0698	2 RR RB211-535E4-B	108862	F24Y159		132
☐	N17133	Boeing 757-224	29282 / 840	N1795B*	1298	1298	2 RR RB211-535E4-B	108862	F24Y159		133
☐	N67134	Boeing 757-224	29283 / 848	N1800B*	0099	0299	2 RR RB211-535E4-B	108862	F24Y159		134
☐	N41135	Boeing 757-224	29284 / 851		0299	0299	2 RR RB211-535E4-B	108862	F24Y159		135
☐	N19136	Boeing 757-224					2 RR RB211-535E4-B	108862	F24Y159		136 / oo-delivery 0699
☐	N34137	Boeing 757-224					2 RR RB211-535E4-B	108862	F24Y159		137 / oo-delivery 0999
☐	N13138	Boeing 757-224					2 RR RB211-535E4-B	108862	F24Y159		138 / oo-delivery 1199
☐	N17139	Boeing 757-224					2 RR RB211-535E4-B	108862	F24Y159		139 / oo-delivery 0300
☐	N41140	Boeing 757-224					2 RR RB211-535E4-B	108862	F24Y159		140 / oo-delivery 0500
☐	N19141	Boeing 757-224					2 RR RB211-535E4-B	108862	F24Y159		141 / oo-delivery 0600
☐	N	Boeing 767-224 (ER)					2 GE CF6-80C2B4F	175540	CY176		oo-delivery 0300
☐	N	Boeing 767-224 (ER)					2 GE CF6-80C2B4F	175540	CY176		oo-delivery 0600
☐	N	Boeing 767-224 (ER)					2 GE CF6-80C2B4F	175540	CY176		oo-delivery 0101
☐	N	Boeing 767-224 (ER)					2 GE CF6-80C2B4F	175540	CY176		oo-delivery 0701
☐	N	Boeing 767-224 (ER)					2 GE CF6-80C2B4F	175540	CY176		oo-delivery 0002
☐	N	Boeing 767-224 (ER)					2 GE CF6-80C2B4F	175540	CY176		oo-delivery 0002
☐	N	Boeing 767-224 (ER)					2 GE CF6-80C2B4F	175540	CY176		oo-delivery 0003
☐	N	Boeing 767-224 (ER)					2 GE CF6-80C2B4F	175540	CY176		oo-delivery 0003
☐	N	Boeing 767-224 (ER)					2 GE CF6-80C2B4F	175540	CY176		oo-delivery 0004
☐	N	Boeing 767-224 (ER)					2 GE CF6-80C2B4F	175540	CY176		oo-delivery 0004
☐	N68041	Boeing (Douglas) DC-10-10	46900 / 34		0072	0572	3 GE CF6-6D	195045	C28Y254	FJ-CM	041
☐	N68043	Boeing (Douglas) DC-10-10	46902 / 41		0072	0572	3 GE CF6-6D	195045	C28Y254	FJ-DL	043
☐	N68044	Boeing (Douglas) DC-10-10	46903 / 43		0072	0672	3 GE CF6-6D	195045	C28Y254	FJ-DM	044
☐	N68046	Boeing (Douglas) DC-10-10	47800 / 92		0073	0473	3 GE CF6-6D	195045	C28Y254	FJ-EH	046
☐	N68047	Boeing (Douglas) DC-10-10	47801 / 98		0073	0573	3 GE CF6-6D	195045	C28Y254	FJ-EK	047
☐	N	Boeing 767-424 (ER)					2 GE CF6-80C2B7F	204117	CY235		oo-delivery 0500
☐	N	Boeing 767-424 (ER)					2 GE CF6-80C2B7F	204117	CY235		oo-delivery 0700
☐	N	Boeing 767-424 (ER)					2 GE CF6-80C2B7F	204117	CY235		oo-delivery 0800
☐	N	Boeing 767-424 (ER)					2 GE CF6-80C2B7F	204117	CY235		oo-delivery 1000
☐	N	Boeing 767-424 (ER)					2 GE CF6-80C2B7F	204117	CY235		oo-delivery 1200
☐	N	Boeing 767-424 (ER)					2 GE CF6-80C2B7F	204117	CY235		oo-delivery 0101
☐	N	Boeing 767-424 (ER)					2 GE CF6-80C2B7F	204117	CY235		oo-delivery 0301
☐	N	Boeing 767-424 (ER)					2 GE CF6-80C2B7F	204117	CY235		oo-delivery 0501
☐	N	Boeing 767-424 (ER)					2 GE CF6-80C2B7F	204117	CY235		oo-delivery 0601
☐	N	Boeing 767-424 (ER)					2 GE CF6-80C2B7F	204117	CY235		oo-delivery 0801
☐	N	Boeing 767-424 (ER)					2 GE CF6-80C2B7F	204117	CY235		oo-delivery 1001
☐	N	Boeing 767-424 (ER)					2 GE CF6-80C2B7F	204117	CY235		oo-delivery 1101
☐	N	Boeing 767-424 (ER)					2 GE CF6-80C2B7F	204117	CY235		oo-delivery 0002
☐	N	Boeing 767-424 (ER)					2 GE CF6-80C2B7F	204117	CY235		oo-delivery 0002
☐	N	Boeing 767-424 (ER)					2 GE CF6-80C2B7F	204117	CY235		oo-delivery 0002
☐	N	Boeing 767-424 (ER)					2 GE CF6-80C2B7F	204117	CY235		oo-delivery 0002
☐	N	Boeing 767-424 (ER)					2 GE CF6-80C2B7F	204117	CY235		oo-delivery 0002
☐	N	Boeing 767-424 (ER)					2 GE CF6-80C2B7F	204117	CY235		oo-delivery 0002

registration	type of aircraft	cn/fn	ex/ex*	mfd	del	powered by	mtow kg	configuration	selcal	name/fln/specialitites/remarks
☐ N	Boeing 767-424 (ER)					2 GE CF6-80C2B7F	204117	CY235		oo-delivery 0002
☐ N	Boeing 767-424 (ER)					2 GE CF6-80C2B7F	204117	CY235		oo-delivery 0003
☐ N	Boeing 767-424 (ER)					2 GE CF6-80C2B7F	204117	CY235		oo-delivery 0003
☐ N	Boeing 767-424 (ER)					2 GE CF6-80C2B7F	204117	CY235		oo-delivery 0003
☐ N	Boeing 767-424 (ER)					2 GE CF6-80C2B7F	204117	CY235		oo-delivery 0003
☐ N	Boeing 767-424 (ER)					2 GE CF6-80C2B7F	204117	CY235		oo-delivery 0003
☐ N	Boeing 767-424 (ER)					2 GE CF6-80C2B7F	204117	CY235		oo-delivery 0003
☐ N78001	Boeing 777-224 (ER)	27577 / 161		0998	0998	2 GE GE90-92B	294200	C50Y235		001
☐ N78002	Boeing 777-224 (ER)	27578 / 165		0998	0998	2 GE GE90-92B	294200	C50Y235		002
☐ N78003	Boeing 777-224 (ER)	27579 / 167		0098	1198	2 GE GE90-92B	294200	C50Y235		003
☐ N78004	Boeing 777-224 (ER)	27580 / 169		0098	1198	2 GE GE90-92B	294200	C50Y235		004
☐ N78005	Boeing 777-224 (ER)	27581 / 177		0098	1298	2 GE GE90-92B	294200	C50Y235		005
☐ N77006	Boeing 777-224 (ER)	29476 / 183		0098	1298	2 GE GE90-92B	294200	C50Y235		006
☐ N74007	Boeing 777-224 (ER)	29477 / 197		0299	0299	2 GE GE90-92B	294200	C50Y235		007
☐ N78008	Boeing 777-224 (ER)					2 GE GE90-92B	294200	C50Y235		008 / oo-delivery 0499
☐ N78009	Boeing 777-224 (ER)					2 GE GE90-92B	294200	C50Y235		009 / oo-delivery 0599
☐ N76010	Boeing 777-224 (ER)					2 GE GE90-92B	294200	C50Y235		010 / oo-delivery 0699
☐ N79011	Boeing 777-224 (ER)	29859				2 GE GE90-92B	294200	C50Y235		011 / oo-delivery 0799
☐ N77012	Boeing 777-224 (ER)					2 GE GE90-92B	294200	C50Y235		012 / oo-delivery 0899
☐ N78013	Boeing 777-224 (ER)					2 GE GE90-92B	294200	C50Y235		013 / oo-delivery 1099
☐ N74014	Boeing 777-224 (ER)					2 GE GE90-92B	294200	C50Y235		014 / oo-delivery 1199
☐ N68060	Boeing (Douglas) DC-10-30	47850 / 331		0080	0880	3 GE CF6-50C2	263084	C38Y204	DL-GM	060 / Robert F.Six
☐ N12061	Boeing (Douglas) DC-10-30	47851 / 334		0080	0980	3 GE CF6-50C2	263084	C38Y204	DL-JM	061 / Richard M. Adams
☐ N14062	Boeing (Douglas) DC-10-30	47863 / 94	N3878M	0073	0484	3 GE CF6-50C2	256280	C38Y204	EF-AB	062 / lsf POTO
☐ N14063	Boeing (Douglas) DC-10-30	47864 / 121	N3878F	0073	0684	3 GE CF6-50C2	256280	C38Y204	EF-AC	063 / lsf POTO
☐ N12064	Boeing (Douglas) DC-10-30	47862 / 88	N390EA	0073	1086	3 GE CF6-50C2	256280	C38Y204	GH-AC	064 / lsf POTO
☐ N68065	Boeing (Douglas) DC-10-30	46590 / 266	G-BFGI	0079	0587	3 GE CF6-50C2	259455	C38Y204	BH-KM	065 / Robert D. Gallaway
☐ N13066	Boeing (Douglas) DC-10-30	46591 / 287	G-BGAT	0079	0687	3 GE CF6-50C2	259455	C38Y204	AG-FJ	066 / VASP-colors on right hand side
☐ N13067	Boeing (Douglas) DC-10-30	47866 / 149	N391EA	0073	0990	3 GE CF6-50C2	256280	C38Y204	HM-DG	067
☐ N41068	Boeing (Douglas) DC-10-30	47867 / 178	N392EA	0073	0995	3 GE CF6-50C2	256280	C38Y204	GH-AE	068 / lsf PACA
☐ N15069	Boeing (Douglas) DC-10-30	46584 / 293	N610PH	0079	0892	3 GE CF6-50C2B	259455	C38Y204	CM-HK	069 / lsf POLA
☐ N87070	Boeing (Douglas) DC-10-30	48292 / 368	HB-IHN	0082	0492	3 GE CF6-50C2B	263084	C38Y204	CM-BE	070 / lsf POLA
☐ N83071	Boeing (Douglas) DC-10-30	48293 / 371	HB-IHO	0082	0692	3 GE CF6-50C2B	263084	C38Y204	CM-BF	071 / lsf POLA
☐ N19072	Boeing (Douglas) DC-10-30	46576 / 73	EC-DUG	0073	1086	3 GE CF6-50C2	256280	C38Y204	EG-CJ	072 / lsf POTO
☐ N76073	Boeing (Douglas) DC-10-30	46940 / 141	N234DC	0074	0493	3 GE CF6-50C2	256280	C38Y204	FG-KL	073 / lsf POTO
☐ N14074	Boeing (Douglas) DC-10-30	46911 / 189	N138AA	0275	0196	3 GE CF6-50C2	256280	C38Y204	AE-HJ	074
☐ N14075	Boeing (Douglas) DC-10-30	46922 / 221	EC-CSJ	0076	0496	3 GE CF6-50C2	259455	C38Y204	BL-AD	075
☐ N37077	Boeing (Douglas) DC-10-30	46981 / 259	F-GPVE	0078	0496	3 GE CF6-50C1	259455	C38Y204	BM-AG	077 / lsf AVIS
☐ N37078	Boeing (Douglas) DC-10-30	46926 / 99	EC-CBO	0073	1096	3 GE CF6-50C	259455	C38Y204	CG-FM	078
☐ N14079	Boeing (Douglas) DC-10-30	46927 / 100	EC-CBP	0073	0397	3 GE CF6-50C	251744	C38Y204	CG-HK	079
☐ N12080	Boeing (Douglas) DC-10-30	47981 / 186	EC-CLB	0075	1296	3 GE CF6-50C	256280	C38Y204	AG-BL	080
☐ N39081	Boeing (Douglas) DC-10-30	47861 / 75	XA-TFM	0473	0397	3 GE CF6-50C2R	256280	C38Y204	GJ-AF	081 / lsf CITG
☐ N49082	Boeing (Douglas) DC-10-30	47927 / 190	D-ADHO	0075	1196	3 GE CF6-50C2	259455	C38Y204	AG-DF	082 / lsf AVII
☐ N59083	Boeing (Douglas) DC-10-30	47926 / 170	D-ADGO	0075	0597	3 GE CF6-50C2	251744	C38Y204	FG-AL	083 / lsf AVII
☐ N35084	Boeing (Douglas) DC-10-30	46991 / 261	N6857X	0078	0297	3 GE CF6-50C2	259455	C38Y204	FL-BD	084
☐ N17085	Boeing (Douglas) DC-10-30	47957 / 201	F-GPVB	0475	0597	3 GE CF6-50C2	259455	C38Y204	CE-HK	085
☐ N13086	Boeing (Douglas) DC-10-30	46917 / 211	D-ADLO	0075	1197	3 GE CF6-50C2	256280	C38Y204	CM-DG	086 / lsf AVII
☐ N17087	Boeing (Douglas) DC-10-30	47928 / 192	D-ADJO	0075	0198	3 GE CF6-50C2	259455	C38Y204	DG-EH	087 / lsf AVII
☐ N13088	Boeing (Douglas) DC-10-30	46850 / 63	OO-JOT	0072	1097	3 GE CF6-50C2R	256280	C38Y204	HJ-AB	088 / lsf PACA
☐ N12089	Boeing (Douglas) DC-10-30	46550 / 46	N525MD	0072	0897	3 GE CF6-50C	256280	C38Y204	DH-JM	089
☐ N14090	Boeing (Douglas) DC-10-30	46553 / 82	N533MD	0073	0797	3 GE CF6-50C	256280	C38Y204	DK-BF	090
☐ EI-DLA	Boeing (Douglas) DC-10-30	46958 / 232	RP-C2003	0076	0796	3 GE CF6-50C2R	259455	C38Y204	AM-BK	076 / lsf POLA

CONTINENTAL AIRLINES HISTORICAL Society

Dallas-Love Field, TX

15 Point Vista Drive, Hickory Creek, TX 76205-3955, USA   ☎ (940) 321-5949 Tx: none Fax: (940) 321-5949 SITA: n/a
F: 1989 ♦♦♦ 200 Head: James F. Minor Net: n/a Operates promotional & demonstration-flights at airshows, and historical scenic charter flights.

registration	type of aircraft	cn/fn	ex/ex*	mfd	del	powered by	mtow kg	configuration	selcal	name/fln/specialitites/remarks
☐ N25673	Boeing (Douglas) DC-3A	2213	N130PB	0040	1294	2 PW R-1830	11884	Y24		old Continental-colors

CONTINENTAL AVIATION SERVICES, Inc.

Naples-Municipal, FL

4820 Bayshore Drive, Suite D, Naples, FL 33962, USA   ☎ (941) 435-0600 Tx: none Fax: (941) 435-0333 SITA: n/a
F: 1990 ♦♦♦ n/a Head: James P. Lennane Net: n/a

registration	type of aircraft	cn/fn	ex/ex*	mfd	del	powered by	mtow kg	configuration	selcal	name/fln/specialitites/remarks
☐ N776BE	De Havilland DHC-6 Twin Otter 300	672	C-GBOX	0080	0697	2 PWC PT6A-27	5670	Y19		

CONTINENTAL EXPRESS, Inc. = CO / BTA (Subsidiary of Continental Airlines, Inc. / formerly Britt Airways, Inc.)

Cleveland, OH / Houston-Int'l, TX / Denver, CO

Continental Express

15333 JFK Blvd, Gateway 2, Suite 600, Houston, TX 77032, USA   ☎ (281) 985-2700 Tx: none Fax: (281) 590-3820 SITA: n/a
F: 1956 ♦♦♦ 2200 Head: David N. Siegel IATA: 565 ICAO: JET LINK Net: http://www.flycontinental.com

registration	type of aircraft	cn/fn	ex/ex*	mfd	del	powered by	mtow kg	configuration	selcal	name/fln/specialitites/remarks
☐ N81533	Beech 1900D Airliner	UE-137	N137ZV	0095	0495	2 PWC PT6A-67D	7688	Y19		533
☐ N17534	Beech 1900D Airliner	UE-141		0095	0495	2 PWC PT6A-67D	7688	Y19		534
☐ N81535	Beech 1900D Airliner	UE-147		0095	0595	2 PWC PT6A-67D	7688	Y19		535
☐ N81536	Beech 1900D Airliner	UE-152		0095	0895	2 PWC PT6A-67D	7688	Y19		536
☐ N38537	Beech 1900D Airliner	UE-158		0095	0895	2 PWC PT6A-67D	7688	Y19		537
☐ N81538	Beech 1900D Airliner	UE-199		0096	0296	2 PWC PT6A-67D	7688	Y19		538
☐ N82539	Beech 1900D Airliner	UE-168		0095	0995	2 PWC PT6A-67D	7688	Y19		539
☐ N16540	Beech 1900D Airliner	UE-172		0095	0995	2 PWC PT6A-67D	7688	Y19		540
☐ N17541	Beech 1900D Airliner	UE-203		0096	0396	2 PWC PT6A-67D	7688	Y19		541
☐ N47542	Beech 1900D Airliner	UE-198		0096	0296	2 PWC PT6A-67D	7688	Y19		542
☐ N49543	Beech 1900D Airliner	UE-181		0095	1195	2 PWC PT6A-67D	7688	Y19		543
☐ N48544	Beech 1900D Airliner	UE-183		0095	1195	2 PWC PT6A-67D	7688	Y19		544
☐ N53545	Beech 1900D Airliner	UE-185		0095	1195	2 PWC PT6A-67D	7688	Y19		545
☐ N81546	Beech 1900D Airliner	UE-187		0095	1295	2 PWC PT6A-67D	7688	Y19		546
☐ N69547	Beech 1900D Airliner	UE-189		0095	1295	2 PWC PT6A-67D	7688	Y19		547
☐ N69548	Beech 1900D Airliner	UE-193		0095	1295	2 PWC PT6A-67D	7688	Y19		548
☐ N69549	Beech 1900D Airliner	UE-194		0096	0296	2 PWC PT6A-67D	7688	Y19		549
☐ N87550	Beech 1900D Airliner	UE-205		0096	0396	2 PWC PT6A-67D	7688	Y19		550
☐ N87551	Beech 1900D Airliner	UE-206		0096	0396	2 PWC PT6A-67D	7688	Y19		551
☐ N87552	Beech 1900D Airliner	UE-216		0096	0596	2 PWC PT6A-67D	7688	Y19		552
☐ N81553	Beech 1900D Airliner	UE-222		0096	0696	2 PWC PT6A-67D	7688	Y19		553
☐ N87554	Beech 1900D Airliner	UE-227		0096	0796	2 PWC PT6A-67D	7688	Y19		554
☐ N87555	Beech 1900D Airliner	UE-234		0096	0996	2 PWC PT6A-67D	7688	Y19		555
☐ N81556	Beech 1900D Airliner	UE-239		0096	0996	2 PWC PT6A-67D	7688	Y19		556
☐ N87557	Beech 1900D Airliner	UE-246		0096	1096	2 PWC PT6A-67D	7688	Y19		557
☐ N16718	Embraer 120ER Brasilia (EMB-120ER)	120136	PT-SPC*	0089	0889	2 PWC PW118	11990	Y30		718 / cvtd 120RT
☐ N40717	Embraer 120ER Brasilia (EMB-120ER)	120133	PT-SNZ*	0089	0689	2 PWC PW118	11990	Y30		717 / cvtd 120RT
☐ N16702	Embraer 120ER Brasilia (EMB-120ER)	120078	PT-SKV*	0088	0488	2 PWC PW118	11990	Y30		702 / cvtd 120RT
☐ N12703	Embraer 120ER Brasilia (EMB-120ER)	120084	PT-SMB*	0088	0688	2 PWC PW118	11990	Y30		703 / cvtd 120RT
☐ N19704	Embraer 120ER Brasilia (EMB-120ER)	120086	PT-SMD*	0088	0788	2 PWC PW118	11990	Y30		704 / cvtd 120RT
☐ N12705	Embraer 120ER Brasilia (EMB-120ER)	120089	PT-SMG*	0088	0888	2 PWC PW118	11990	Y30		705 / cvtd 120RT
☐ N27707	Embraer 120ER Brasilia (EMB-120ER)	120095	PT-SMM*	0088	0989	2 PWC PW118	11990	Y30		707 / cvtd 120RT
☐ N59708	Embraer 120ER Brasilia (EMB-120ER)	120098	PT-SMQ*	0088	1088	2 PWC PW118	11990	Y30		708 / cvtd 120RT
☐ N12709	Embraer 120ER Brasilia (EMB-120ER)	120101	PT-SMT*	0088	1188	2 PWC PW118	11990	Y30		709 / cvtd 120RT
☐ N16710	Embraer 120ER Brasilia (EMB-120ER)	120106	PT-SMY*	0088	1188	2 PWC PW118	11990	Y30		710 / cvtd 120RT
☐ N31711	Embraer 120ER Brasilia (EMB-120ER)	120107	PT-SMZ*	0088	1288	2 PWC PW118	11990	Y30		711 / cvtd 120RT
☐ N34712	Embraer 120ER Brasilia (EMB-120ER)	120111	PT-SND*	0088	1288	2 PWC PW118	11990	Y30		712 / cvtd 120RT
☐ N15713	Embraer 120ER Brasilia (EMB-120ER)	120114	PT-SNG*	0088	0189	2 PWC PW118	11990	Y30		713 / cvtd 120RT
☐ N26714	Embraer 120ER Brasilia (EMB-120ER)	120118	PT-SNK*	0088	0289	2 PWC PW118	11990	Y30		714 / cvtd 120RT
☐ N12715	Embraer 120ER Brasilia (EMB-120ER)	120125	PT-SNR*	0089	0389	2 PWC PW118	11990	Y30		715 / cvtd 120RT
☐ N27716	Embraer 120ER Brasilia (EMB-120ER)	120128	PT-SNU*	0089	0489	2 PWC PW118	11990	Y30		716 / cvtd 120RT
☐ N16719	Embraer 120ER Brasilia (EMB-120ER)	120138	PT-SPE*	0089	0889	2 PWC PW118	11990	Y30		719 / cvtd 120RT
☐ N17720	Embraer 120ER Brasilia (EMB-120ER)	120142	PT-SPI*	0089	0889	2 PWC PW118	11990	Y30		720 / cvtd 120RT
☐ N15721	Embraer 120ER Brasilia (EMB-120ER)	120160	PT-SPZ*	0090	0290	2 PWC PW118	11990	Y30		721 / cvtd 120RT
☐ N47722	Embraer 120ER Brasilia (EMB-120ER)	120166	PT-SQE*	0090	0290	2 PWC PW118	11990	Y30		722 / cvtd 120RT
☐ N16723	Embraer 120ER Brasilia (EMB-120ER)	120169	PT-SQH*	0090	0290	2 PWC PW118	11990	Y30		723 / cvtd 120RT
☐ N16724	Embraer 120ER Brasilia (EMB-120ER)	120171	PT-SQJ*	0090	0290	2 PWC PW118	11990	Y30		724 / cvtd 120RT
☐ N15725	Embraer 120ER Brasilia (EMB-120ER)	120173	PT-SQL*	0090	0390	2 PWC PW118	11990	Y30		725 / cvtd 120RT
☐ N51726	Embraer 120ER Brasilia (EMB-120ER)	120174	PT-SQM*	0090	0390	2 PWC PW118	11990	Y30		726 / cvtd 120RT
☐ N22727	Embraer 120ER Brasilia (EMB-120ER)	120177	PT-SQP*	0090	0590	2 PWC PW118	11990	Y30		727 / cvtd 120RT
☐ N17728	Embraer 120ER Brasilia (EMB-120ER)	120182	PT-SQU*	0090	0590	2 PWC PW118	11990	Y30		728 / cvtd 120RT
☐ N16729	Embraer 120ER Brasilia (EMB-120ER)	120185	PT-SQX*	0090	0690	2 PWC PW118	11990	Y30		729 / cvtd 120RT
☐ N15730	Embraer 120ER Brasilia (EMB-120ER)	120187	PT-SQZ*	0090	0790	2 PWC PW118	11990	Y30		730 / cvtd 120RT
☐ N16731	Embraer 120ER Brasilia (EMB-120ER)	120190	PT-SRD*	0090	0990	2 PWC PW118	11990	Y30		731 / cvtd 120RT

registration	type of aircraft	cn/fn	ex/ex*	mfd	del	powered by	mtow kg	configuration	selcal	name/fln/specialitites/remarks
☐ N15732	Embraer 120ER Brasilia (EMB-120ER)	120195	PT-SRK*	0090	0990	2 PWC PW118	11990	Y30		732 / cvtd 120RT
☐ N58733	Embraer 120ER Brasilia (EMB-120ER)	120197	PT-SRN*	0090	0990	2 PWC PW118	11990	Y30		733 / cvtd 120RT
☐ N57734	Embraer 120ER Brasilia (EMB-120ER)	120199	PT-SRP*	0090	0990	2 PWC PW118	11990	Y30		734 / cvtd 120RT
☐ N14445	ATR 42-500	503	F-WWEN*	0096	0596	2 PWC PW127E	18600	Y46		445
☐ N19446	ATR 42-500	504	F-WWEO*	0096	0596	2 PWC PW127E	18600	Y46		446
☐ N15447	ATR 42-500	505	F-WWEP*	0096	0796	2 PWC PW127E	18600	Y46		447
☐ N17448	ATR 42-500	506	F-WWER*	0096	1296	2 PWC PW127E	18600	Y46		448
☐ N33449	ATR 42-500	507	F-WWEU*	0096	1096	2 PWC PW127E	18600	Y46		449
☐ N16450	ATR 42-500	510	F-WWLB*	0096	1196	2 PWC PW127E	18600	Y46		450
☐ N14451	ATR 42-500	512	F-WWLH*	0096	0996	2 PWC PW127E	18600	Y46		451
☐ N19452	ATR 42-500	511	F-WWLF*	0096	0896	2 PWC PW127E	18600	Y46		452
☐ N25811	ATR 42-320	094	F-WWET*	0088	0688	2 PWC PW121	16150	Y46		811
☐ N19812	ATR 42-320	099	F-WWEV*	0088	0788	2 PWC PW121	16150	Y46		812
☐ N14813	ATR 42-320	100	F-WWEX*	0088	0788	2 PWC PW121	16150	Y46		813
☐ N18814	ATR 42-320	103	F-WWEA*	0088	0988	2 PWC PW121	16150	Y46		814
☐ N14815	ATR 42-320	104	F-WWEB*	0088	0988	2 PWC PW121	16150	Y46		815
☐ N15816	ATR 42-320	105	F-WWEC*	0088	0988	2 PWC PW121	16700	Y46		816
☐ N34817	ATR 42-320	152	F-WWEX*	0089	0989	2 PWC PW121	16700	Y46		817
☐ N15818	ATR 42-320	153	F-WWEA*	0089	0989	2 PWC PW121	16700	Y46		818
☐ N14819	ATR 42-320	156	F-WWED*	0089	1089	2 PWC PW121	16700	Y46		819
☐ N34820	ATR 42-320	159	F-WWEF*	0089	1089	2 PWC PW121	16700	Y46		820
☐ N14821	ATR 42-320	160	F-WWEG*	0089	1189	2 PWC PW121	16700	Y46		821
☐ N14822	ATR 42-320	163	F-WWEN*	0089	1189	2 PWC PW121	16700	Y46		822
☐ N15823	ATR 42-320	165	F-WWEP*	0089	1289	2 PWC PW121	16700	Y46		823
☐ N16824	ATR 42-320	166	F-WWEQ*	0089	1289	2 PWC PW121	16700	Y46		824
☐ N14825	ATR 42-320	170	F-WWEX*	0090	0190	2 PWC PW121	16700	Y46		825
☐ N26826	ATR 42-320	172	F-WWEC*	0090	0290	2 PWC PW121	16700	Y46		826
☐ N15827	ATR 42-320	175	F-WWEF*	0090	0290	2 PWC PW121	16700	Y46		827
☐ N14828	ATR 42-320	179	F-WWEN*	0090	0390	2 PWC PW121	16700	Y46		828
☐ N14829	ATR 42-320	181	F-WWEQ*	0090	0390	2 PWC PW121	16700	Y46		829
☐ N14830	ATR 42-320	184	F-WWET*	0090	0590	2 PWC PW121	16700	Y46		830
☐ N17831	ATR 42-320	185	F-WWEV*	0090	0590	2 PWC PW121	16700	Y46		831
☐ N14832	ATR 42-320	187	F-WWEJ*	0090	0590	2 PWC PW121	16700	Y46		832
☐ N14833	ATR 42-320	188	F-WWEC*	0090	0590	2 PWC PW121	16700	Y46		833
☐ N14834	ATR 42-320	193	F-WWEG*	0090	0690	2 PWC PW121	16700	Y46		834
☐ N11835	ATR 42-320	194	F-WWEH*	0090	0690	2 PWC PW121	16700	Y46		835
☐ N42836	ATR 42-320	200	F-WWEN*	0090	0890	2 PWC PW121	16700	Y46		836
☐ N21837	ATR 42-320	202	N11737	0090	0890	2 PWC PW121	16700	Y46		837
☐ N99838	ATR 42-320	259	F-WWEP*	0092	1292	2 PWC PW121	16700	Y46		838 / lst AES as HK-4035X
☐ N93840	ATR 42-320	271	F-WWLH*	0092	1192	2 PWC PW121	16700	Y46		840
☐ N97841	ATR 42-320	280	F-WWLF*	0092	1292	2 PWC PW121	16700	Y46		841
☐ N86842	ATR 42-320	286	F-WWLY*	0092	1292	2 PWC PW121	16700	Y46		842
☐ N	Embraer RJ135 (EMB-135)					2 AN AE3007A3	19000	Y37		oo-delivery 0799
☐ N	Embraer RJ135 (EMB-135)					2 AN AE3007A3	19000	Y37		oo-delivery 0999
☐ N	Embraer RJ135 (EMB-135)					2 AN AE3007A3	19000	Y37		oo-delivery 1199
☐ N	Embraer RJ135 (EMB-135)					2 AN AE3007A3	19000	Y37		oo-delivery 0200
☐ N	Embraer RJ135 (EMB-135)					2 AN AE3007A3	19000	Y37		oo-delivery 0400
☐ N	Embraer RJ135 (EMB-135)					2 AN AE3007A3	19000	Y37		oo-delivery 0700
☐ N	Embraer RJ135 (EMB-135)					2 AN AE3007A3	19000	Y37		oo-delivery 0900
☐ N	Embraer RJ135 (EMB-135)					2 AN AE3007A3	19000	Y37		oo-delivery 1200
☐ N	Embraer RJ135 (EMB-135)					2 AN AE3007A3	19000	Y37		oo-delivery 0201
☐ N	Embraer RJ135 (EMB-135)					2 AN AE3007A3	19000	Y37		oo-delivery 0501
☐ N	Embraer RJ135 (EMB-135)					2 AN AE3007A3	19000	Y37		oo-delivery 0701
☐ N	Embraer RJ135 (EMB-135)					2 AN AE3007A3	19000	Y37		oo-delivery 1001
☐ N	Embraer RJ135 (EMB-135)					2 AN AE3007A3	19000	Y37		oo-delivery 1201
☐ N	Embraer RJ135 (EMB-135)					2 AN AE3007A3	19000	Y37		oo-delivery 0002
☐ N	Embraer RJ135 (EMB-135)					2 AN AE3007A3	19000	Y37		oo-delivery 0002
☐ N	Embraer RJ135 (EMB-135)					2 AN AE3007A3	19000	Y37		oo-delivery 0002
☐ N	Embraer RJ135 (EMB-135)					2 AN AE3007A3	19000	Y37		oo-delivery 0002
☐ N	Embraer RJ135 (EMB-135)					2 AN AE3007A3	19000	Y37		oo-delivery 0003
☐ N	Embraer RJ135 (EMB-135)					2 AN AE3007A3	19000	Y37		oo-delivery 0003
☐ N	Embraer RJ135 (EMB-135)					2 AN AE3007A3	19000	Y37		oo-delivery 0003
☐ N	Embraer RJ135 (EMB-135)					2 AN AE3007A3	19000	Y37		oo-delivery 0003
☐ N	Embraer RJ135 (EMB-135)					2 AN AE3007A3	19000	Y37		oo-delivery 0003
☐ N	Embraer RJ135 (EMB-135)					2 AN AE3007A3	19000	Y37		oo-delivery 0004
☐ N	Embraer RJ135 (EMB-135)					2 AN AE3007A3	19000	Y37		oo-delivery 0004
☐ N	Embraer RJ135 (EMB-135)					2 AN AE3007A3	19000	Y37		oo-delivery 0004
☐ N14925	Embraer RJ145ER (EMB-145ER)	145004	PT-SYA*	0096	1296	2 AN AE3007A	20600	Y50		925
☐ N15926	Embraer RJ145ER (EMB-145ER)	145005	PT-SYB*	0096	1296	2 AN AE3007A	20600	Y50		926
☐ N16927	Embraer RJ145ER (EMB-145ER)	145006	PT-SYC*	0096	0197	2 AN AE3007A	20600	Y50		927
☐ N17928	Embraer RJ145ER (EMB-145ER)	145007	PT-SYD*	0096	0197	2 AN AE3007A	20600	Y50		928
☐ N13929	Embraer RJ145ER (EMB-145ER)	145009	PT-SYF*	0097	0297	2 AN AE3007A	20600	Y50		929
☐ N14930	Embraer RJ145ER (EMB-145ER)	145011	PT-SYH*	0097	0497	2 AN AE3007A	20600	Y50		930
☐ N15932	Embraer RJ145ER (EMB-145ER)	145015	PT-SYL*	0097	0597	2 AN AE3007A	20600	Y50		932
☐ N14933	Embraer RJ145ER (EMB-145ER)	145018	PT-SYO*	0097	0797	2 AN AE3007A	20600	Y50		933
☐ N12934	Embraer RJ145ER (EMB-145ER)	145019	PT-SYP*	0097	0797	2 AN AE3007A	20600	Y50		934
☐ N13935	Embraer RJ145ER (EMB-145ER)	145022	PT-SYS*	0097	0897	2 AN AE3007A	20600	Y50		935
☐ N13936	Embraer RJ145ER (EMB-145ER)	145025	PT-SYV*	0097	0997	2 AN AE3007A	20600	Y50		936
☐ N14937	Embraer RJ145ER (EMB-145ER)	145026	PT-SYW*	0097	0997	2 AN AE3007A	20600	Y50		937
☐ N14938	Embraer RJ145ER (EMB-145ER)	145029	PT-SYZ*	0097	1097	2 AN AE3007A	20600	Y50		938
☐ N14939	Embraer RJ145ER (EMB-145ER)	145030		0097	1197	2 AN AE3007A	20600	Y50		939
☐ N14940	Embraer RJ145ER (EMB-145ER)	145033		0097	1197	2 AN AE3007A	20600	Y50		940
☐ N15941	Embraer RJ145ER (EMB-145ER)	145035		0097	1297	2 AN AE3007A	20600	Y50		941
☐ N14942	Embraer RJ145ER (EMB-145ER)	145037		0097	1297	2 AN AE3007A	20600	Y50		942
☐ N14943	Embraer RJ145ER (EMB-145ER)	145040		0098	0198	2 AN AE3007A	20600	Y50		943
☐ N16944	Embraer RJ145ER (EMB-145ER)	145045	PT-SZK*	0098	0298	2 AN AE3007A	20600	Y50		944
☐ N14945	Embraer RJ145ER (EMB-145ER)	145049	PT-SZO*	0098	0398	2 AN AE3007A	20600	Y50		945
☐ N12946	Embraer RJ145ER (EMB-145ER)	145052	PT-SZR*	0098	0498	2 AN AE3007A	20600	Y50		946
☐ N14947	Embraer RJ145ER (EMB-145ER)	145054		0098	0498	2 AN AE3007A	20600	Y50		947
☐ N15948	Embraer RJ145ER (EMB-145ER)	145056		0098	0598	2 AN AE3007A	20600	Y50		948
☐ N13949	Embraer RJ145LR (EMB-145LR)	145057		0098	0598	2 AN AE3007A1/2	22000	Y50		949
☐ N14950	Embraer RJ145LR (EMB-145LR)	145061		0098	0698	2 AN AE3007A1/2	22000	Y50		950
☐ N16951	Embraer RJ145LR (EMB-145LR)	145063		0098	0698	2 AN AE3007A1/2	22000	Y50		951
☐ N14952	Embraer RJ145LR (EMB-145LR)	145067	PT-SAK*	0098	0798	2 AN AE3007A1/2	22000	Y50		952
☐ N14953	Embraer RJ145LR (EMB-145LR)	145071		0098	0798	2 AN AE3007A1/2	22000	Y50		953
☐ N16954	Embraer RJ145LR (EMB-145LR)	145072		0098	0898	2 AN AE3007A1/2	22000	Y50		954
☐ N13955	Embraer RJ145LR (EMB-145LR)	145075		0098	0898	2 AN AE3007A1/2	22000	Y50		955
☐ N13956	Embraer RJ145LR (EMB-145LR)	145078		0098	0998	2 AN AE3007A1/2	22000	Y50		956
☐ N12957	Embraer RJ145LR (EMB-145LR)	145080		0098	0998	2 AN AE3007A1/2	22000	Y50		957
☐ N13958	Embraer RJ145LR (EMB-145LR)	145085		0098	0998	2 AN AE3007A1/2	22000	Y50		958
☐ N14959	Embraer RJ145LR (EMB-145LR)	145091		0098	1198	2 AN AE3007A1/2	22000	Y50		959
☐ N14960	Embraer RJ145LR (EMB-145LR)	145100		0098	1298	2 AN AE3007A1/2	22000	Y50		960
☐ N16961	Embraer RJ145LR (EMB-145LR)					2 AN AE3007A1/2	22000	Y50		961 / oo-delivery 0499
☐ N27962	Embraer RJ145LR (EMB-145LR)					2 AN AE3007A1/2	22000	Y50		962 / oo-delivery 0499
☐ N16963	Embraer RJ145LR (EMB-145LR)					2 AN AE3007A1/2	22000	Y50		963 / oo-delivery 0499
☐ N13964	Embraer RJ145LR (EMB-145LR)					2 AN AE3007A1/2	22000	Y50		964 / oo-delivery 0499
☐ N13965	Embraer RJ145LR (EMB-145LR)					2 AN AE3007A1/2	22000	Y50		965 / oo-delivery 0599
☐ N19966	Embraer RJ145LR (EMB-145LR)					2 AN AE3007A1/2	22000	Y50		966 / oo-delivery 0599
☐ N12967	Embraer RJ145LR (EMB-145LR)					2 AN AE3007A1/2	22000	Y50		967 / oo-delivery 0699
☐ N13968	Embraer RJ145LR (EMB-145LR)					2 AN AE3007A1/2	22000	Y50		968 / oo-delivery 0799
☐ N13969	Embraer RJ145LR (EMB-145LR)					2 AN AE3007A1/2	22000	Y50		969 / oo-delivery 0899
☐ N13970	Embraer RJ145LR (EMB-145LR)					2 AN AE3007A1/2	22000	Y50		970 / oo-delivery 0899
☐ N22971	Embraer RJ145LR (EMB-145LR)					2 AN AE3007A1/2	22000	Y50		971 / oo-delivery 0999
☐ N14972	Embraer RJ145LR (EMB-145LR)					2 AN AE3007A1/2	22000	Y50		972 / oo-delivery 0999
☐ N15973	Embraer RJ145LR (EMB-145LR)					2 AN AE3007A1/2	22000	Y50		973 / oo-delivery 1099
☐ N14974	Embraer RJ145LR (EMB-145LR)					2 AN AE3007A1/2	22000	Y50		974 / oo-delivery 1199
☐ N12975	Embraer RJ145LR (EMB-145LR)					2 AN AE3007A1/2	22000	Y50		975 / oo-delivery 1199
☐ N	Embraer RJ145LR (EMB-145LR)					2 AN AE3007A1/2	22000	Y50		oo-delivery 1299
☐ N	Embraer RJ145LR (EMB-145LR)					2 AN AE3007A1/2	22000	Y50		oo-delivery 0100
☐ N	Embraer RJ145LR (EMB-145LR)					2 AN AE3007A1/2	22000	Y50		oo-delivery 0200

registration	type of aircraft	cn/fn	ex/ex*	mfd	del	powered by	mtow kg	configuration	selcal	name/fln/specialitites/remarks
☐ N	Embraer RJ145LR (EMB-145LR)					2 AN AE3007A1/2	22000	Y50		oo-delivery 0200
☐ N	Embraer RJ145LR (EMB-145LR)					2 AN AE3007A1/2	22000	Y50		oo-delivery 0300
☐ N	Embraer RJ145LR (EMB-145LR)					2 AN AE3007A1/2	22000	Y50		oo-delivery 0400
☐ N	Embraer RJ145LR (EMB-145LR)					2 AN AE3007A1/2	22000	Y50		oo-delivery 0400
☐ N	Embraer RJ145LR (EMB-145LR)					2 AN AE3007A1/2	22000	Y50		oo-delivery 0500
☐ N	Embraer RJ145LR (EMB-145LR)					2 AN AE3007A1/2	22000	Y50		oo-delivery 0500
☐ N	Embraer RJ145LR (EMB-145LR)					2 AN AE3007A1/2	22000	Y50		oo-delivery 0600
☐ N	Embraer RJ145LR (EMB-145LR)					2 AN AE3007A1/2	22000	Y50		oo-delivery 0700
☐ N	Embraer RJ145LR (EMB-145LR)					2 AN AE3007A1/2	22000	Y50		oo-delivery 0800
☐ N	Embraer RJ145LR (EMB-145LR)					2 AN AE3007A1/2	22000	Y50		oo-delivery 0800
☐ N	Embraer RJ145LR (EMB-145LR)					2 AN AE3007A1/2	22000	Y50		oo-delivery 0900
☐ N	Embraer RJ145LR (EMB-145LR)					2 AN AE3007A1/2	22000	Y50		oo-delivery 0900
☐ N	Embraer RJ145LR (EMB-145LR)					2 AN AE3007A1/2	22000	Y50		oo-delivery 1000
☐ N	Embraer RJ145LR (EMB-145LR)					2 AN AE3007A1/2	22000	Y50		oo-delivery 1100
☐ N	Embraer RJ145LR (EMB-145LR)					2 AN AE3007A1/2	22000	Y50		oo-delivery 1100
☐ N	Embraer RJ145LR (EMB-145LR)					2 AN AE3007A1/2	22000	Y50		oo-delivery 1200
☐ N	Embraer RJ145LR (EMB-145LR)					2 AN AE3007A1/2	22000	Y50		oo-delivery 0101
☐ N	Embraer RJ145LR (EMB-145LR)					2 AN AE3007A1/2	22000	Y50		oo-delivery 0201
☐ N	Embraer RJ145LR (EMB-145LR)					2 AN AE3007A1/2	22000	Y50		oo-delivery 0201
☐ N	Embraer RJ145LR (EMB-145LR)					2 AN AE3007A1/2	22000	Y50		oo-delivery 0301
☐ N	Embraer RJ145LR (EMB-145LR)					2 AN AE3007A1/2	22000	Y50		oo-delivery 0401
☐ N69901	ATR 72-212	379	F-WWLD*	0093	1193	2 PWC PW127	21500	Y64		901
☐ N69902	ATR 72-212	385	F-WWLF*	0093	1293	2 PWC PW127	21500	Y64		902
☐ N12903	ATR 72-212	459	F-WWLE*	0095	1195	2 PWC PW127	21500	Y64		903

CONTINENTAL MICRONESIA, Inc. = CS / CMI (Subs.of Continental Airl.& United Micron.Develop.Ass./formerly Air Micronesia Inc.) **Honolulu-Int'l, HI & Guam-Ab Won Pat Int'l, GU**

PO Box 8778, Tamuning, GU 96931, USA ☎ 647-6453 Tx: none Fax: 646-9219 SITA: n/a

F: 1966 n/a Head: James B. Ream IATA: 596 ICAO: AIR MIKE Net: n/a Beside aircraft listed, also uses 1-3 Boeing (Douglas) DC-10-30 (registrations varies) lsf/opb Continental Airlines, when required.

registration	type of aircraft	cn/fn	ex/ex*	mfd	del	powered by	mtow kg	configuration	selcal	name/fln/specialitites/remarks
☐ N622DH	Boeing 727-264 (F) (A)	20896 / 1051	XA-DUK	0074	0196	3 PW JT8D-17R (HK3/FDX)	83552	Freighter		lsf / opf DHL / cvtd -264
☐ N623DH	Boeing 727-264 (F) (A)	20895 / 1049	XA-DUJ	0074	0296	3 PW JT8D-17R (HK3/FDX)	83552	Freighter		lsf / opf DHL / cvtd -264
☐ N624DH	Boeing 727-264 (F) (A)	20709 / 950	XA-CUB	0073	0396	3 PW JT8D-17R (HK3/FDX)	83779	Freighter		lsf / opf DHL / cvtd -264
☐ N625DH	Boeing 727-264 (F) (A)	20780 / 986	XA-CUN	0073	0496	3 PW JT8D-17R (HK3/FDX)	83552	Freighter		lsf / opf DHL / cvtd -264
☐ N626DH	Boeing 727-277 (F) (A)	22644 / 1768	N72381	0081	1097	3 PW JT8D-15 (HK3/FDX)	89358	Freighter		lsf / opf DHL / cvtd -277
☐ N627DH	Boeing 727-277 (F) (A)	22641 / 1753	N6393X	0081	1297	3 PW JT8D-15 (HK3/FDX)	89358	Freighter		lsf / opf DHL / cvtd -277
☐ N86425	Boeing 727-212 (A)	21459 / 1329	N296AS	0078	0193	3 PW JT8D-17	89358	C10Y143	AD-BG	425 / lsf COA
☐ N86426	Boeing 727-227 (A)	21364 / 1261	N322AS	0077	0193	3 PW JT8D-17R	86409	C10Y143	CM-DF	426 / lsf COA
☐ N89427	Boeing 727-227 (A)	21365 / 1273	N323AS	0077	0193	3 PW JT8D-17R	86409	C10Y143		427 / lsf COA
☐ N83428	Boeing 727-2F9 (A)	21426 / 1285	N298AS	0077	0393	3 PW JT8D-17	89358	C10Y143		428 / lsf COA
☐ N75429	Boeing 727-2F9 (A)	21427 / 1291	N299AS	0077	0393	3 PW JT8D-17	89358	C10Y143		429 / lsf COA
☐ N79743	Boeing 727-224 (A)	22252 / 1697		0081	0789	3 PW JT8D-15	86409	C10Y143	DK-EM	743 / lsf COA
☐ N79744	Boeing 727-224 (A)	22253 / 1702		0081	0089	3 PW JT8D-15 (HK3/FDX)	86409	C10Y143	DK-FH	744 / lsf COA
☐ N79745	Boeing 727-224 (A)	22448 / 1740		0081	1296	3 PW JT8D-15	86409	C10Y143	DK-FM	745 / lsf COA
☐ N15790	Boeing 727-232 (A)	20644 / 959	N521PE	0073	1190	3 PW JT8D-15	83552	C10Y143	CG-AF	790 / lst COA
☐ N17126	Boeing 757-224 (ET)	27566 / 790		0098	0298	2 RR RB211-535E4-B	113398	C12Y210		126 / lsf / opb COA
☐ N48127	Boeing 757-224 (ET)	28968 / 791		0098	0298	2 RR RB211-535E4-B	113398	C12Y210		127 / lsf / opb COA
☐ N17128	Boeing 757-224 (ET)	27567 / 795		0098	0398	2 RR RB211-535E4-B	113398	C12Y210		128 / lsf / opb COA
☐ N29129	Boeing 757-224 (ET)	28969 / 796		0398	0398	2 RR RB211-535E4-B	113398	C12Y210		129 / lsf / opb COA
☐ N19130	Boeing 757-224 (ET)	28970 / 799		0098	0598	2 RR RB211-535E4-B	113398	C12Y210		130 / lsf / opb COA

CONTRACT AIR CARGO = TSU (Division of IFL Group, Inc.) **Pontiac-Oakland, MI**

6860 South Service Drive, Waterford, MI 48327, USA ☎ (248) 666-9630 Tx: none Fax: (248) 666-9614 SITA: n/a

F: 1992 60 Head: Alan C. Ross ICAO: TRANS-AUTO Net: n/a

registration	type of aircraft	cn/fn	ex/ex*	mfd	del	powered by	mtow kg	configuration	selcal	name/fln/specialitites/remarks
☐ N3427	Convair 340-32 (F) (SCD)	90		0053	0594	2 PW R-2800	21772	Freighter		cvtd CV340-32
☐ N7813B	Convair 340 (C-131B)	265	53-7813	0055	1294	2 PW R-2800	21772	Freighter		
☐ N141FL	Convair 580 (F) (SCD)	111	N302K	0853	0396	2 AN 501-D13	24766	Freighter		cvtd CV340-32
☐ N161FL	Convair 580 (F) (SCD)	430	N303K	0557	0396	2 AN 501-D13	24766	Freighter		cvtd CV440-95
☐ N171FL	Convair 580 (F) (SCD)	318	N300K	0256	1294	2 AN 501-D13	24766	Freighter		cvtd CV440-35
☐ N181FL	Convair 580 (F) (SCD)	387	N301K	1256	0695	2 AN 501-D13	24766	Freighter		cvtd CV440-24
☐ N5804	Convair 580	155	N130B	0254	1198	2 AN 501-D13	24766	Freighter		cvtd 340-42/440
☐ N723ES	Convair 580	217	N7146X	0054	0998	2 AN 501-D13	24766	Freighter		cvtd 340-67/VC-131D
☐ N923DR	Convair 580	326	N4276C	0456	0998	2 AN 501-D13	24766	Freighter		cvtd 440-79/C-131D
☐ N381FL	Convair 5800 (F) (SCD) (Super Stretch)	276	C-FKFS	0055	0698	2 AN 501-D22G	28576	Freighter		cvtd CV 340-71 (C-131F)
☐ N391FL	Convair 5800 (F) (SCD) (Super Stretch)	278	C-GKFD	0055	0598	2 AN 501-D22G	28576	Freighter		cvtd CV 340-71 (C-131F)

CONTRACT CARGO AIRLINES, Inc. (Subsidiary of Traffic Management Corporation) **Detroit-Ypsilanti, MI**

836 Willow Run Yirport, Ypsilanti, MI 48198-0836, USA ☎ (734) 485-8907 Tx: none Fax: (734) 481-9182 SITA: n/a

F: 1996 n/a Head: James H. Loree Net: n/a

registration	type of aircraft	cn/fn	ex/ex*	mfd	del	powered by	mtow kg	configuration	selcal	name/fln/specialitites/remarks
☐ N811TC	Boeing (Douglas) DC-8-55F (JT)	45883 / 308	N52958	0067	1296	4 PW JT3D-3B (HK2/BAC)	147418	Freighter		lsf TMC Airlines

COOK AIRCRAFT LEASING, Inc. (formerly Calcutta Aircraft Leasing, Inc.) **Bloomington-Monroe County, IN**

971 South Kirby Road, Bloomington, IN 47403, USA ☎ (812) 333-1037 Tx: none Fax: (812) 333-1058 SITA: n/a

F: 1989 n/a Head: Robert Harbstreit Net: n/a Conducting commercial flight operations under contract for various executive customers.

registration	type of aircraft	cn/fn	ex/ex*	mfd	del	powered by	mtow kg	configuration	selcal	name/fln/specialitites/remarks
☐ N502MG	Boeing 727-191	19391 / 309	N502RA	0666	0597	3 PW JT8D-7B (HK3/FDX)	72802	Exec 45 Pax	CG-AE	std OSC
☐ N503MG	Boeing 727-191	19392 / 317	N503RA	0066	1195	3 PW JT8D-7B (HK3/FDX)	72802	Exec 45 Pax		
☐ N504MG	Boeing 727-191	19395 / 431	N801SC	0667	0698	3 PW JT8D-7B (HK3/FDX)	72802	Exec 45 Pax		

COOK INLET AIR SERVICE (Priewe Air Service, Inc. dba) **Anchorage-Int'l, AK**

3600 International Airport Road, Suite 100, Anchorage, AK 99502, USA ☎ (907) 248-6220 Tx: none Fax: (907) 248-6220 SITA: n/a

F: 1993 n/a Head: Robert J. Priewe Net: n/a

registration	type of aircraft	cn/fn	ex/ex*	mfd	del	powered by	mtow kg	configuration	selcal	name/fln/specialitites/remarks
☐ N9515G	Cessna U206F Stationair	U20601715		0072	1194	1 CO IO-520-F	1633			

COPTERS, Corp. (Sister co. of Icarus Caribbean, Corp.) **San Juan-Isla Grande/Fernando Luis Ribas Dominicci, PR**

PO Box 41268, San Juan, PR 00940-1268, USA ☎ (787) 729-0000 Tx: none Fax: (787) 729-0003 SITA: n/a

F: 1992 n/a Head: Luis A. Alvarez Net: http://www.coptco.com Aircraft below MTOW 1361kg: Fairchild Ind. FH-1100 & Robinson R22

registration	type of aircraft	cn/fn	ex/ex*	mfd	del	powered by	mtow kg	configuration	selcal	name/fln/specialitites/remarks
☐ N915B	Bell 206B JetRanger	720		0071	0398	1 AN 250-C20	1451			
☐ N335WC	Eurocopter (Aerosp.) AS350B AStar	2061	N51191	0087	0795	1 TU Arriel 1B	1950			
☐ N611TC	Eurocopter (Aerosp.) AS350B AStar	2123	ZK-HJZ	0088	1094	1 TU Arriel 1B	1950			

CORDOVA AIR SERVICE, Inc. **Cordova-City Airstrip Eyak Lake, AK**

PO Box 528, Cordova, AK 99574, USA ☎ (907) 424-3289 Tx: none Fax: (907) 424-3495 SITA: n/a

F: 1987 5 Head: Davis G. Erbey Net: n/a

registration	type of aircraft	cn/fn	ex/ex*	mfd	del	powered by	mtow kg	configuration	selcal	name/fln/specialitites/remarks
☐ N1983U	Cessna A185E Skywagon	18501731		0070	0488	1 CO IO-520-D	1520			Floats / Wheel-Skis
☐ N5428U	Cessna U206G Stationair 6 II	U20605290		0079	0889	1 CO IO-520-F	1633			Floats / Wheel-Skis
☐ N756VC	Cessna U206G Stationair 6 II	U20604382		0078	0390	1 CO IO-520-F	1633			Floats / Wheel-Skis
☐ N218GB	De Havilland DHC-2 Beaver I	1160	56-4426	0057	0191	1 PW R-985	2313			Floats / Wheel-Skis

CORNING AVIATION (Division of Corning, Inc.) **Elmira-Corning Regional, NY**

348 Sing Sing Road, Horseheads, NY 14845, USA ☎ (607) 796-9560 Tx: none Fax: (607) 796-0147 SITA: n/a

F: 1950 n/a Head: William J. Schultz Net: n/a Operates non-commercial corporate flights for its parent company, a producer of scientific equipment.

registration	type of aircraft	cn/fn	ex/ex*	mfd	del	powered by	mtow kg	configuration	selcal	name/fln/specialitites/remarks
☐ N58CG	Learjet 55	55-124		0086	1186	2 GA TFE731-3AR-2B	9752	Corporate		
☐ N28CG	Dornier 328-110	3024	N95CG	0094	0994	2 PWC PW119B	13990	Corporate		lsf Fleet National Bank Trustee
☐ N38CG	Dornier 328-110	3034	D-CDXA*	0095	0395	2 PWC PW119B	13990	Corporate		lsf Fleet National Bank Trustee
☐ N18CG	Dassault Falcon 2000	57	N2132	0098	0698	2 CFE CFE738-1-1B	16556	Corporate		lsf Wachovia Leasing Corp.
☐ N48CG	Dassault Falcon 2000	41	N2073	0096	0597	2 CFE CFE738-1-1B	16556	Corporate		lsf Wachovia Leasing Corp.

CORPORATE AIR = CPT **Billings-Logan Int'l, MT**

PO Box 30998, Billings, MT 59107-0998, USA ☎ (406) 248-1541 Tx: none Fax: (406) 248-7670 SITA: n/a

F: 1981 250 Head: Linda K. Overstreet ICAO: AIR SPUR Net: n/a

registration	type of aircraft	cn/fn	ex/ex*	mfd	del	powered by	mtow kg	configuration	selcal	name/fln/specialitites/remarks
☐ N1933G	Cessna 414 II	414-0832		0076	0790	2 CO TSIO-520-N	2880	Y5 / Freighter		
☐ N6154X	Twin (Aero) Commander 500B	500B-983-24		0060	1297	2 LY IO-540-B1A5	3062	Freighter		
☐ N9382R	Twin (Aero) Commander 500A	500A-899-8		0060	0189	2 CO IO-470-M	2835	Freighter		
☐ N799FE	Cessna 208A Caravan I Cargomaster	20800065	C-FEXF	0085	1185	1 PWC PT6A-114	3629	Freighter		lsf/opf FDX in FedEx Feeder-colors
☐ N800FE	Cessna 208A Caravan I Cargomaster	20800007		0085	0285	1 PWC PT6A-114	3629	Freighter		lsf/opf FDX in FedEx Feeder-colors
☐ N812FE	Cessna 208A Caravan I Cargomaster	20800040		0085	0785	1 PWC PT6A-114	3629	Freighter		lsf/opf FDX in FedEx Feeder-colors
☐ N827FE	Cessna 208A Caravan I Cargomaster	20800072		0085	1185	1 PWC PT6A-114	3629	Freighter		lsf/opf FDX in FedEx Feeder-colors
☐ N113NA	Twin (Aero) RPM Commander 800L	680FL-1794-149		0069		2 LY IO-720-B1A	3856	Freighter		cvtd Courser 680FL
☐ N30321	Twin (Aero) RPM Commander 800L	680FLP-1475-4		0064		2 LY IO-720-B1A	3856	Freighter		cvtd Grand 680FLP
☐ N4704E	Twin (Aero) RPM Commander 800L	680FL-1441-76		0064		2 LY IO-720-B1A	3856	Freighter		cvtd Grand 680FL
☐ N6344U	Twin (Aero) RPM Commander 800L	680FL-1430-72		0064		2 LY IO-720-B1A	3856	Freighter		cvtd Grand 680FL
☐ N710FX	Cessna 208B Caravan I Super Cargomaster	208B0431		0095	0495	1 PWC PT6A-114A	3969	Freighter		lsf/opf FDX in FedEx Feeder-colors
☐ N716FX	Cessna 208B Caravan I Super Cargomaster	208B0442		0095	0595	1 PWC PT6A-114A	3969	Freighter		lsf/opf FDX in FedEx Feeder-colors

☐ N724FX	Cessna 208B Caravan I Super Cargomaster	208B0458		0095	0895	1 PWC PT6A-114A	3969	Freighter		lsf/opf FDX in FedEx Feeder-colors
☐ N730FX	Cessna 208B Caravan I Super Cargomaster	208B0477		0095	1095	1 PWC PT6A-114A	3969	Freighter		lsf/opf FDX in FedEx Feeder-colors
☐ N751FE	Cessna 208B Caravan I Super Cargomaster	208B0245		0090	1290	1 PWC PT6A-114A	3969	Freighter		lsf/opf FDX in FedEx Feeder-colors
☐ N791FE	Cessna 208B Caravan I Super Cargomaster	208B0289		0091	1191	1 PWC PT6A-114A	3969	Freighter		lsf/opf FDX in FedEx Feeder-colros
☐ N794FE	Cessna 208B Caravan I Super Cargomaster	208B0292		0092	0192	1 PWC PT6A-114A	3969	Freighter		lsf/opf FDX in FedEx Feeder-colors
☐ N796FE	Cessna 208B Caravan I Super Cargomaster	208B0212	C-FEXY	0090	0490	1 PWC PT6A-114	3969	Freighter		lsf/opf FDX in FedEx Feeder-colors
☐ N797FE	Cessna 208B Caravan I Super Cargomaster	208B0042	C-FEXH	0087	0987	1 PWC PT6A-114	3969	Freighter		lsf/opf FDX in FedEx Feeder-colors
☐ N798FE	Cessna 208B Caravan I Super Cargomaster	208B0174	C-FEDY	0089	0589	1 PWC PT6A-114	3969	Freighter		lsf/opf FDX in FedEx Feeder-colors
☐ N846FE	Cessna 208B Caravan I Super Cargomaster	208B0154		0089	0289	1 PWC PT6A-114	3969	Freighter		lsf/opf FDX in FedEx Feeder-colors
☐ N851FE	Cessna 208B Caravan I Super Cargomaster	208B0166		0089	0489	1 PWC PT6A-114	3969	Freighter		lsf/opf FDX in FedEx Feeder-colors
☐ N860FE	Cessna 208B Caravan I Super Cargomaster	208B0182		0089	0789	1 PWC PT6A-114	3969	Freighter		lsf/opf FDX in FedEx Feeder-colors
☐ N863FE	Cessna 208B Caravan I Super Cargomaster	208B0186		0089	0889	1 PWC PT6A-114	3969	Freighter		lsf/opf FDX in FedEx Feeder-colors
☐ N864FE	Cessna 208B Caravan I Super Cargomaster	208B0187		0089	0889	1 PWC PT6A-114	3969	Freighter		lsf/opf FDX in FedEx Feeder-colors
☐ N867FE	Cessna 208B Caravan I Super Cargomaster	208B0191		0089	0989	1 PWC PT6A-114	3969	Freighter		lsf/opf FDX in FedEx Feeder-colors
☐ N877FE	Cessna 208B Caravan I Super Cargomaster	208B0232		0090	0990	1 PWC PT6A-114A	3969	Freighter		lsf/opf FDX in FedEx Feeder-colors
☐ N885FE	Cessna 208B Caravan I Super Cargomaster	208B0185		0089	0889	1 PWC PT6A-114	3969	Freighter		lsf/opf FDX in FedEx Feeder-colors
☐ N890FE	Cessna 208B Caravan I Super Cargomaster	208B0219		0090	0690	1 PWC PT6A-114	3969	Freighter		lsf/opf FDX in FedEx Feeder-colors
☐ N903FE	Cessna 208B Caravan I Super Cargomaster	208B0003		0086	1186	1 PWC PT6A-114	3969	Freighter		lsf/opf FDX in FedEx Feeder-colors
☐ N904FE	Cessna 208B Caravan I Super Cargomaster	208B0004		0086	1186	1 PWC PT6A-114	3969	Freighter		lsf/opf FDX in FedEx Feeder-colors
☐ N910FE	Cessna 208B Caravan I Super Cargomaster	208B0010		0086	1286	1 PWC PT6A-114	3969	Freighter		lsf/opf FDX in FedEx Feeder-colors
☐ N916FE	Cessna 208B Caravan I Super Cargomaster	208B0016		0087	0387	1 PWC PT6A-114	3969	Freighter		lsf/opf FDX in FedEx Feeder-colors
☐ N924FE	Cessna 208B Caravan I Super Cargomaster	208B0024		0087	0587	1 PWC PT6A-114	3969	Freighter		lsf/opf FDX in FedEx Feeder-colors
☐ N926FE	Cessna 208B Caravan I Super Cargomaster	208B0026		0087	0587	1 PWC PT6A-114	3969	Freighter		lsf/opf FDX in FedEx Feeder-colors
☐ N933FE	Cessna 208B Caravan I Super Cargomaster	208B0033		0087	0787	1 PWC PT6A-114	3969	Freighter		lsf/opf FDX in FedEx Feeder-colors
☐ N936FE	Cessna 208B Caravan I Super Cargomaster	208B0036		0087	0887	1 PWC PT6A-114	3969	Freighter		lsf/opf FDX in FedEx Feeder-colors
☐ N948FE	Cessna 208B Caravan I Super Cargomaster	208B0052		0087	1187	1 PWC PT6A-114A	3969	Freighter		lsf/opf FDX in FedEx Feeder-colors
☐ N952FE	Cessna 208B Caravan I Super Cargomaster	208B0060		0087	1287	1 PWC PT6A-114	3969	Freighter		lsf/opf FDX in FedEx Feeder-colors
☐ N964FE	Cessna 208B Caravan I Super Cargomaster	208B0083		0088	0488	1 PWC PT6A-114	3969	Freighter		lsf/opf FDX in FedEx Feeder-colors
☐ N971FE	Cessna 208B Caravan I Super Cargomaster	208B0094		0088	0588	1 PWC PT6A-114	3969	Freighter		lsf/opf FDX in FedEx Feeder-colors
☐ N972FE	Cessna 208B Caravan I Super Cargomaster	208B0096		0088	0688	1 PWC PT6A-114	3969	Freighter		lsf/opf FDX in FedEx Feeder-colors
☐ N977FE	Cessna 208B Caravan I Super Cargomaster	208B0104		0088	0788	1 PWC PT6A-114	3969	Freighter		lsf/opf FDX in FedEx Feeder-colors
☐ N980FE	Cessna 208B Caravan I Super Cargomaster	208B0108		0088	0888	1 PWC PT6A-114	3969	Freighter		lsf/opf FDX in FedEx Feeder-colors
☐ N990FE	Cessna 208B Caravan I Super Cargomaster	208B0125		0088	1088	1 PWC PT6A-114	3969	Freighter		lsf/opf FDX in FedEx Feeder-colors
☐ N991FE	Cessna 208B Caravan I Super Cargomaster	208B0127		0088	1188	1 PWC PT6A-114	3969	Freighter		lsf/opf FDX in FedEx Feeder-colors
☐ N997FE	Cessna 208B Caravan I Super Cargomaster	208B0197		0089	1189	1 PWC PT6A-114	3969	Freighter		lsf/opf FDX in FedEx Feeder-colors
☐ N199CA	Beech 99A Airliner	U-96	N503TF	0069	0091	2 PWC PT6A-27	4717	Freighter		lsf Molo Leasing Inc.
☐ N223CA	Beech C99 Airliner	U-200	SE-IZX	0083	0598	2 PWC PT6A-36	5126	Freighter		lsf Molo Lesing Inc.
☐ N27AL	Beech 99A Airliner	U-133	N803BA	0069	1194	2 PWC PT6A-27	4717	Freighter		lsf Molo Leasing Inc.
☐ N7212P	Beech C99 Airliner	U-220		0084	1292	2 PWC PT6A-36	5126	Freighter		lsf Molo Leasing Inc.
☐ N38535	De Havilland DHC-6 Twin Otter 300	414	G-BDHC	0074	0894	2 PWC PT6A-27	5670	Y19 / Freighter		lsf LOPS Partnership
☐ N533SW	De Havilland DHC-6 Twin Otter 300	533	4X-AHZ	0077	0597	2 PWC PT6A-27	5670	Y19 / Freighter		lsf LOPS Llc
☐ N702PV	De Havilland DHC-6 Twin Otter 300	702		0080	0596	2 PWC PT6A-27	5670	Freighter		lsf LOPS Llc/sublst Corporate Air,Phil.
☐ N972SW	De Havilland DHC-6 Twin Otter 300	356	JA8790	0073	0797	2 PWC PT6A-27	5670	Y19 / Freighter		lsf Molo Leasing Inc.
☐ N974SW	De Havilland DHC-6 Twin Otter 300	410	JA8796	0074	1197	2 PWC PT6A-27	5670	Y19 / Freighter		lsf Molo Leasing Inc.
☐ N4298S	Beech King Air 200	BB-198		0077	0596	2 PWC PT6A-21	5670	Y9 / Freighter		
☐ N319BH	Beech 1900C Airliner	UB-36	N19RA	0085	1296	2 PWC PT6A-65B	7530	Freighter		lsf Skywalker International Inc.
☐ N715GL	Beech 1900C Airliner	UB-15	N309BH	0084	0197	2 PWC PT6A-65B	7530	Freighter		lsf Molo Leasing Inc.
☐ N7254R	Beech 1900C Airliner	UB-22		0084	1291	2 PWC PT6A-65B	7530	Freighter		lsf Molo Leasing Inc.
☐ N820BE	Beech 1900C Airliner	UB-64	N3039X	0086	0197	2 PWC PT6A-65B	7530	Freighter		lsf Molo Leasing Inc.
☐ N	Ayres LM200 Loadmaster					1 AN CTP800-4T TwinPac	8618	Freighter		oo-delivery 0000
☐ N	Ayres LM200 Loadmaster					1 AN CTP800-4T TwinPac	8618	Freighter		oo-delivery 0000
☐ N	Ayres LM200 Loadmaster					1 AN CTP800-4T TwinPac	8618	Freighter		oo-delivery 0001
☐ N	Ayres LM200 Loadmaster					1 AN CTP800-4T TwinPac	8618	Freighter		oo-delivery 0001
☐ N	Ayres LM200 Loadmaster					1 AN CTP800-4T TwinPac	8618	Freighter		oo-delivery 0001
☐ N	Ayres LM200 Loadmaster					1 AN CTP800-4T TwinPac	8618	Freighter		oo-delivery 0001
☐ N	Ayres LM200 Loadmaster					1 AN CTP800-4T TwinPac	8618	Freighter		oo-delivery 0001
☐ N	Ayres LM200 Loadmaster					1 AN CTP800-4T TwinPac	8618	Freighter		oo-delivery 0001
☐ N	Ayres LM200 Loadmaster					1 AN CTP800-4T TwinPac	8618	Freighter		oo-delivery 0001
☐ N	Ayres LM200 Loadmaster					1 AN CTP800-4T TwinPac	8618	Freighter		oo-delivery 0001
☐ N330SB	Shorts 330-200 (SD3-30)	SH3013	N241CA	0077	0793	2 PWC PT6A-45R	10387	Freighter		lsf Molo Leasing Inc.
☐ N331SB	Shorts 330-200 (SD3-30)	SH3015	N331CA	0078	0294	2 PWC PT6A-45R	10387	Freighter		
☐ N334AC	Shorts 330-200 (SD3-30)	SH3029	VH-LSI	0079	0498	2 PWC PT6A-45R	10387	Freighter		
☐ N789US	Shorts 330-200 (SD3-30)	SH3002	N335GW	0075	0793	2 PWC PT6A-45R	10387	Freighter		lsf Molo Leasing Inc.
☐ N125AM	Embraer 120RT Brasilia (EMB-120RT)	120017	PT-SIM*	0086	0898	2 PWC PW118	11500	Freighter		
☐ N617FB	Shorts 360-200 (SD3-60)	SH3617	G-BKUF*	0083	1296	2 PWC PT6A-65AR	11999	Freighter		
☐ N701A	Shorts 360-200 (SD3-60)	SH3627	G-BKZP*	0083	0198	2 PWC PT6A-65AR	11999	Freighter		

CORPORATE AIR CHARTERS, Inc. — Miami-Int'l, FL

20251 SW 272 Street, Homestead, FL 33031, USA ☎ (954) 248-0098 Tx: none Fax: (954) 248-0970 SITA: n/a
F: 1995 ⅲ n/a Head: Jeffrey D. Losner Net: n/a

☐ N774MA	Mitsubishi MU-2P (MU-2B-26A)	384SA		0078		2 GA TPE331-5-252M	4749	6 Pax		lsf R.M. Equipment Inc.
☐ N122V	Beech D18S	A-828		0052		2 PW R-985-AN14B	3969	Freighter		lsf South Florida Aircraft Leasing

CORPORATE AIR FLEET, Inc. = CTX (formerly Carolina Air Transit, Inc.) — Lincolnton-Lincoln County, NC

724 Airport Road, Iron Station, NC 28080, USA ☎ (704) 732-8821 Tx: none Fax: (704) 735-2325 SITA: n/a
F: 1993 ⅲ 14 Head: Norbert Steinwedel ICAO: CATBIRD Net: n/a

☐ N165R	Piper PA-32RT-300 Lance II	32R-7885217	D-EOTM	0078	1298	1 LY IO-540-K1G5D	1633			lsf Ridge Aire Inc.
☐ N6YB	Piper PA-32-260B Cherokee SIX	32-1179		0069	0595	1 LY O-540-E4B5	1542			
☐ N94206	Cessna 210L Centurion II	21060539		0074	0897	1 CO IO-520-L	1724			
☐ N40259	Piper PA-23-250 Aztec E	27-7305069		0073	0996	2 LY IO-540-C4B5	2359			
☐ N6975Y	Piper PA-23-250 Aztec D	27-4342		0069	0694	2 LY IO-540-C4B5	2359			
☐ N999PF	Cessna 310R II	310R0682		0076	0697	2 CO IO-520-M	2495			
☐ N657WM	Cessna 421C Golden Eagle III	421C0474		0078	0796	2 CO GTSIO-520-L	3379			lsf Truck Transfer Service Inc.

CORPORATE AIRLINES = 3C (Division of Corporate Flight Management, Inc. / formerly Corporate Express Airlines) — Nashville-Int'l, TN

PO Box 270487, Nashville, TN 37227-0487, USA ☎ (615) 223-5644 Tx: none Fax: (615) 223-8631 SITA: n/a
F: 1996 ⅲ n/a Head: Charles R. Howell, IV IATA: 310 Net: n/a

☐ N917AE	BAe 3201 Jetstream 32EP	917	G-31-917*	0090	1096	2 GA TPE331-12UAR-704H	7350	Y19		lsf BAMT / cvtd 32 / tbr N917CX
☐ N922CX	BAe 3201 Jetstream 32EP	922	N922AE	0091	0597	2 GA TPE331-12UAR-704H	7350	Y19		lsf BAMT / cvtd 32
☐ N924AE	BAe 3201 Jetstream 32EP	924	G-31-924*	0091	0697	2 GA TPE331-12UAR-704H	7350	Y19		lsf BAMT / cvtd 32 / tbr N924CX
☐ N933CX	BAe 3201 Jetstream 32EP	933	N933AE	0091	0597	2 GA TPE331-12UAR-704H	7350	Y19		lsf BAMT / cvtd 32
☐ N936AE	BAe 3201 Jetstream 32EP	936	G-31-936*	0091	1296	2 GA TPE331-12UAR-704H	7350	Y19		lsf BAMT / cvtd 32 / tbr N936CX
☐ N937AE	BAe 3201 Jetstream 32EP	937	G-31-937*	0091	1096	2 GA TPE331-12UAR-704H	7350	Y19		lsf BAMT / cvtd 32 / tbr N937CX
☐ N938AE	BAe 3201 Jetstream 32EP	938	G-31-938*	0091	1196	2 GA TPE331-12UAR-704H	7350	Y19		lsf BAMT / cvtd 32 / tbr N938CX
☐ N940AE	BAe 3201 Jetstream 32EP	940	G-31-940*	0091	1096	2 GA TPE331-12UAR-704H	7350	Y19		lsf BAMT / cvtd 32 / tbr N940CX
☐ N944AE	BAe 3201 Jetstream 32EP	944	G-31-944*	0091	1296	2 GA TPE331-12UAR-704H	7350	Y19		lsf BAMT / cvtd 32 / tbr N944CX

CORPORATE AVIATION SERVICES, Inc. – CASI = CKE — Tulsa-Int'l, OK

Corporate Aviation Services

7303 East Apache Road, Hangar 1, Tulsa, OK 74115-2237, USA ☎ (918) 834-8348 Tx: none Fax: (918) 836-3626 SITA: n/a
F: 1980 ⅲ 35 Head: Larry M. Wilk ICAO: CHECKMATE Net: n/a

☐ N142BK	Mitsubishi MU-2B-60 Marquise	733SA	N533MA	0079	0495	2 GA TPE331-10-501M	5250			
☐ N155BA	Mitsubishi MU-2J (MU-2B-35)	582	N286MA	0073	0791	2 GA TPE331-6-251M	4899			
☐ N175CA	Mitsubishi MU-2B-60 Marquise	736SA	N711PD	0080	0394	2 GA TPE331-10-501M	5250			
☐ N1790M	Mitsubishi MU-2B-60 Marquise	756SA	N179CM	0079	1189	2 GA TPE331-10-501M	5250			
☐ N183MA	Mitsubishi MU-2F (MU-2B-20) Cargoliner	217		0072	1091	2 GA TPE331-1-151A	4500			Cavenaugh SCD conversion
☐ N26AP	Mitsubishi MU-2B-60 Marquise	763SA	N95BE	0080	0493	2 GA TPE331-10-501M	5250			
☐ N34AL	Mitsubishi MU-2B-60 Marquise	792SA	N66LA	0080	1092	2 GA TPE331-10-501M	5250			
☐ N35RR	Mitsubishi MU-2B-60 Marquise	1525SA	N442MA	0081	0394	2 GA TPE331-10-501M	5250			
☐ N37AL	Mitsubishi MU-2B-60 Marquise	752SA	N11WQ	0079	1189	2 GA TPE331-10-501M	5250			
☐ N400TR	Mitsubishi MU-2F (MU-2B-20)	161	N11LQ	0069	0496	2 GA TPE331-1-151A	4500			
☐ N500PS	Mitsubishi MU-2F (MU-2B-20) Cargoliner	224	N190MA	0072	0992	2 GA TPE331-1-151A	4500			Cavenaugh SCD conversion
☐ N538EA	Mitsubishi MU-2B-60 Marquise	1538SA	N538MC	0081	0292	2 GA TPE331-10-501M	5250			
☐ N5PQ	Mitsubishi MU-2B-60 Marquise	1558SA	N12WF	0082	0895	2 GA TPE331-10-501M	5250			
☐ N89CR	Mitsubishi MU-2F (MU-2B-20)	233	N5NE	0072	0394	2 GA TPE331-1-151A	4500			
☐ N61EW	Learjet 25B	25B-161	N4VC	0074	0590	2 GE CJ610-6	6804			
☐ N13VG	Learjet 35A	35A-386		0081	1089	2 GA TFE731-2-2B	8301			
☐ N163A	Learjet 35A	35A-073		0076	0192	2 GA TFE731-2-2B	8301			
☐ N727GL	Learjet 35A	35A-127		0077	0592	2 GA TFE731-2-2B	8301			

309 registration type of aircraft cn/fn ex/ex* mfd del powered by mtow kg configuration selcal name/fln/specialitites/remarks

CORPORATE EXPRESS = IFL (Division of IFL Group, Inc.)

Pontiac-Oakland, MI

6860 South Service Drive, Waterford, MI 48327, USA ☎ (248) 666-1961 Tx: none Fax: (248) 666-9618 SITA: n/a
F: 1983 👥 45 Head: Michael N. Church ICAO: EIFEL Net: n/a

☐ N514AC	Boeing (Douglas) DC-3C (C-47B-15-DK)	26558	N235GB	0044	0991	2 PW R-1830	12202	Freighter		

CORPORATE EXPRESS DELIVERY SYSTEM = CSD (formerly Courier Services)

Phoenix-Int'l, AZ

3402 East Wier Avenue, Phoenix, AZ 85040, USA ☎ (520) 243-9810 Tx: none Fax: (520) 243-9584 SITA: n/a
F: 1988 👥 35 Head: David G. Seymour ICAO: DELIVERY Net: n/a

☐ N15316	Piper PA-32-300 Cherokee SIX	32-7340036		0072	0589	1 LY IO-540-K1A5	1542	Freighter		
☐ N1942H	Piper PA-32R-300 Lance	32R-7780206		0077	0789	1 LY IO-540-K1G5D	1633	Freighter		
☐ N3393D	Piper PA-32-300C Cherokee SIX	32-40656		0069	0590	1 LY IO-540-K1A5	1542	Freighter		
☐ N43331	Piper PA-32-300 Cherokee SIX	32-7440122		0074	0291	1 LY IO-540-K1A5	1542	Freighter		
☐ N43551	Piper PA-32-300 Cherokee SIX	32-7440133		0074	0495	1 LY IO-540-K1A5	1542	Freighter		
☐ N49SF	Piper PA-32-300 Cherokee SIX	32-7940019		0079	0593	1 LY IO-540-K1G5	1542	Freighter		
☐ N8160A	Piper PA-32-300 Cherokee SIX	32-7940285		0079	0392	1 LY IO-540-K1G5	1542	Freighter		
☐ N9166K	Piper PA-32R-300 Lance	32R-7680194		0076	0591	1 LY IO-540-K1G5D	1633	Freighter		
☐ N5317X	Cessna TU206G Turbo Stationair 6 II	U20605636		0080	0188	1 CO TSIO-520-M	1633	Freighter		
☐ N6347H	Cessna T207A Turbo Stationair 7 II	20700488		0078	0389	1 CO TSIO-520-M	1724	Freighter		
☐ N6480H	Cessna 207A Stationair 7 II	20700540		0079	1193	1 CO IO-520-F	1724	Freighter		
☐ N75870	Cessna T207A Turbo Stationair 8 II	20700648		0080	0489	1 CO TSIO-520-M	1724	Freighter		
☐ N3589X	Piper PA-31-350 Navajo Chieftain	31-8052138		0080	0789	2 LY TIO-540-J2BD	3175	Freighter		

CORPORATE FLIGHT (Division of Corporate Flight Management, Inc.)

Smyrna, TN

Hangar 625, Smyrna Airport, Smyrna, TN 37167, USA ☎ (615) 459-8883 Tx: none Fax: (615) 459-8155 SITA: n/a
F: 1982 👥 n/a Head: Charles R. Howell, IV Net: n/a

☐ N193AA	Mitsubishi MU-2B-60 Cargoliner	741SA	N31480	0079	0497	2 GA TPE331-10-511M	5250			lsf FMS Flight Mngt/Cavenaugh SCD-conv.
☐ N38MH	Cessna 500 Citation	500-0265	XA-VYF	0075	0696	2 PWC JT15D-1A	5216			lsf Sawyer Brown Inc.
☐ N186EB	Beech King Air B200	BB-1186	ZS-NBA	0084	0696	2 PWC PT6A-42	5670			lsf Executive Business Aviation Inc.
☐ N200BT	Beech King Air 200	BB-293	N500CP	0077	0197	2 PWC PT6A-41	5670			lsf pvt
☐ N21DE	Beech King Air 200	BB-117	N1DE	0075	0595	2 PWC PT6A-41	5670			lsf Sky King Aviation Llc
☐ N281JH	Beech King Air 200	BB-516	N231JH	0079	0797	2 PWC PT6A-41	5670			lsf Hermitage Aviation Inc.
☐ N56KA	Beech King Air 200	BB-763	N50PM	0081	0697	2 PWC PT6A-41	5670			lsf Raytheon Aircraft Co.
☐ N510TP	Learjet 25D	25D-353	XA-RLI	0082	0496	2 GE CJ610-8A	6804			lsf pvt
☐ N643JX	BAe 3101 Jetstream 31	643	N421MX	0084	0297	2 GA TPE331-10UG-513H	6900	C10		lsf CT Flight Management Llc
☐ N32PE	Learjet 35A	35A-327	N32PF	0080	0695	2 GA TFE731-2-2B	8301			lsf Blue Canyon Inc.
☐ N35AZ	Learjet 35A	35A-201	XA-PIN	0078	1096	2 GA TFE731-2-2B	8301			lsf Comm Aviation Llc

CORPORATE HELICOPTERS OF SAN DIEGO (Shier Aviation Corporation dba)

San Diego-Montgomery Field, CA

3753 John J. Montgomery Drive, Suite 2, San Diego, CA 92123, USA ☎ (760) 505-5650 Tx: none Fax: (760) 874-3038 SITA: n/a
F: 1989 👥 n/a Head: Ivor Shier Net: n/a

☐ N191RH	Bell 206B JetRanger III	3177		0080	0898	1 AN 250-C20B	1451			
☐ N2750F	Bell 206B JetRanger III	2674		0079	0693	1 AN 250-C20B	1451			
☐ N9916K	Bell 206B JetRanger II	1939		0076	0695	1 AN 250-C20	1451			
☐ N49HU	Bell 206L-3 LongRanger III	51411		0090	0395	1 AN 250-C30P	1882			
☐ N5806B	Eurocopter (Aerosp.) AS350BA AStar	1924		0086	0096	1 TU Arriel 1B	2100			

CORPORATE JETS, Inc.

Pittsburgh-Allegheny County, PA & Scottsdale, AZ

Allegheny County Airport, West Mifflin, PA 15122, USA ☎ (412) 466-2500 Tx: none Fax: (412) 466-1978 SITA: n/a
F: 1969 👥 n/a Head: Thomas M. Ramirez Net: n/a

☐ N206CJ	Bell 206L-3 LongRanger III	51579	N5090Y	0092	0792	1 AN 250-C30P	1882	EMS		lsf General Electric Capital Corp.
☐ N101UC	Eurocopter (Aerosp.) AS355F1 TwinStar	5186	N5801J	0082	0497	2 AN 250-C20F	2400	EMS		lsf RTS Helicopter Services Corp.
☐ N355DU	Eurocopter (Aerosp.) AS355F2 TwinStar	5489	N6065B	0091	0892	2 AN 250-C20F	2540	EMS		lsf Duke University Hospital
☐ N356DU	Eurocopter (Aerosp.) AS355F1 TwinStar	5179	N355DU	0082	1084	2 AN 250-C20F	2400	EMS		lsf Debis Financial Services Inc.
☐ N135ME	Eurocopter EC135P1	0009		0096	0996	2 PWC PW206B	2720	EMS STAT MedEvac		lsf Center for Emergency Medicine
☐ N1174U	Eurocopter (MBB) BK117A-4	7086	N9745N	0086	1286	2 LY LTS101-650B.1	3200	EMS		lsf Deutsche Financial Services Inc.
☐ N117CJ	Eurocopter (MBB) BK117A-3	7051	N44932	0084	0284	2 LY LTS101-650B.1	3200	EMS STAT MedEvac		lsf Debis Financial Services Inc.
☐ N117LG	Eurocopter (MBB) BK117A-3	7032	N4493U	0084	0284	2 LY LTS101-650B.1	2850	EMS STAT MedEvac		lsf General Electric Capital Corp.
☐ N117TX	Eurocopter (MBB) BK117B-1	7177	N7067R	0089	0189	2 LY LTS101-750B.1	3200	EMS		lsf Mother Frances Hospital
☐ N117UB	Eurocopter (MBB) BK117A-3	7062	N117UP	0085	1185	2 LY LTS101-650B.1	3200	EMS		lsf General Electric Capital Corp.
☐ N117US	Eurocopter (MBB) BK117B-1	7175	N7060P	0089	0189	2 LY LTS101-750B.1	3200	EMS		lsf MDFC Equipment Leasing Corp.
☐ N39181	Eurocopter (MBB) BK117A-3	7003	N921US	0083	0783	2 LY LTS101-650B.1	3200	EMS		lsf Banc One Leasing Corp.
☐ N39188	Eurocopter (MBB) BK117A-3	7011	D-HBKM*	0083	1283	2 LY LTS101-650B.1	3200	EMS		lsf Banc One Leasing Corp.
☐ N39257	Eurocopter (MBB) BK117A-3	7027	D-HBMB*	0084	0185	2 LY LTS101-650B.1	2850	EMS STAT MedEvac		lsf Debis Financial Services / cvtd A-1
☐ N5405G	Eurocopter (MBB) BK117B-1	7179	D-HBHV*	0089	0189	2 LY LTS101-750B.1	3200	EMS STAT MedEvac		lsf Center Emergency Medicine West
☐ N601FH	Eurocopter (MBB) BK117B-1	7181	N5404Q	0089	0189	2 LY LTS101-750B.1	3200	EMS		lsf MDFC Equipment Leasing Corp.
☐ N626MB	Eurocopter (MBB) BK117A-3	7109	D-HBCD*	0086	0886	2 LY LTS101-650B.1	3200	EMS		lsf Scientific Leasing Inc.
☐ N911BK	Eurocopter (MBB) BK117A-4	7099	N540H	0086	0686	2 LY LTS101-650B.1	3200	EMS		lsf Rockford Memorial Hospital
☐ N911TG	Eurocopter (MBB) BK117C-1	7506	N60953	0092	0494	2 TU Arriel 1E2	3350	EMS		lsf Hillsborough County Hospital
☐ N912TG	Eurocopter (MBB) BK117B-1	7174	N7060N	0089	0189	2 LY LTS101-750B.1	3200	EMS		lsf MDFC Equipment Leasing Corp.
☐ N922CJ	Eurocopter (MBB) BK117A-3	7030	N922US	0083	0684	2 LY LTS101-650B.1	3200	EMS		lsf Debis Financial Services Inc.
☐ N932CJ	Eurocopter (MBB) BK117A-3	7024	N117US	0083	0684	2 LY LTS101-650B.1	3200	EMS		lsf Debis Financial Services Inc.
☐ N945ME	Eurocopter (MBB) BK117B-1	7235	N4293T	0091	0891	2 LY LTS101-750B.1	3200	EMS STAT MedEvac		lsf Debis Financial Services Inc.
☐ N952CJ	Eurocopter (MBB) BK117A-3	7052	N952US	0084	0284	2 LY LTS101-650B.1	3200	EMS		lsf General Electric Capital Corp.
☐ N955ME	Eurocopter (MBB) BK117B-1	7243	N3202V	0091	1191	2 LY LTS101-750B.1	3200	EMS STAT MedEvac		lsf Debis Financial Services Inc.
☐ N967LS	Eurocopter (MBB) BK117A-3	7067	N967US	0085	1285	2 LY LTS101-650B.1	2850	EMS		lsf Tri-State Emergency System Inc.
☐ N1UW	Eurocopter (Aerosp.) SA365N Dauphin 2	6089	N5192E	0083	0992	2 TU Arriel 1C	4000	EMS		lsf Senstar Finance Co.
☐ N2XJ	Eurocopter (Aerosp.) AS365N2 Dauphin 2	6396	N60391	0091	0391	2 TU Arriel 1C2	4250	EMS		lsf Pitney Credit Corp.
☐ N89SM	Eurocopter (Aerosp.) SA365N1 Dauphin 2	6282	N6010Y	0087	1187	2 TU Arriel 1C1	4100	EMS		lsf Wilmington Trust Co.
☐ N911UF	Eurocopter (Aerosp.) SA365N1 Dauphin 2	6338	JA6600	0089	0896	2 TU Arriel 1C1	4100	EMS		lsf Metlife Capital Corp.
☐ N915ME	Eurocopter (Aerosp.) AS365N2 Dauphin 2	6417	N161BC	0091	0495	2 TU Arriel 1C2	4250	EMS STAT MedEvac		lsf Debis Financial Services Inc.
☐ N222LF	Bell 222UT	47528	N444DE	0084	0292	2 LY LTS101-750C.1	3742	EMS		lsf General Electric Capital Corp.
☐ N587MC	Bell 222U	47566	N3209D	0087	0893	2 LY LTS101-750C.1	3742	EMS		lsf First Security Bank NA Trustee
☐ N231UM	Bell 230	23012		0093	1193	2 AN 250C-30G2	3810	EMS		lsf First Security Bank NA Trustee
☐ N232UM	Bell 230	23013		0093	0993	2 AN 250C-30G2	3810	EMS		lsf First Security Bank NA Trustee
☐ N777GS	Beech King Air A100	B-241	N777GF	0079	0493	2 PWC PT6A-28	5216	EMS STAT MedEvac		lsf PNC Leasing Corp.
☐ N90806	Beech King Air 200	BB-33	ZS-AAA	0075	0482	2 PWC PT6A-41	5670	EMS STAT MedEvac		
☐ N199CJ	Learjet 35A	35A-071	N82GA	0076	0995	2 GA TFE731-2-2B	8301			
☐ N20DK	Learjet 35A	35A-143	OE-GER	0078	0494	2 GA TFE731-2-2B	8301	EMS STAT MedEvac		lsf PNC Leasing Corp.
☐ N30DK	Learjet 35A	35A-345	N345LJ	0080	0194	2 GA TFE731-2-2B	8301	EMS STAT MedEvac		lsf BA Leasing & Capital Corp.
☐ N40DK	Learjet 35A	35A-171	N455RM	0078	1189	2 GA TFE731-2-2B	8301			

CORPORATE WINGS SERVICES, Corp.

Cleveland-Cuyahoga County,OH & Binghamton-E.A. Link, NY

36180 Curtiss-Wright Parkway, Cleveland, OH 44143, USA ☎ (216) 261-3500 Tx: none Fax: (216) 261-3595 SITA: n/a
F: 1981 👥 500 Head: James R. Dauterman Net: n/a

☐ N410MA	Cessna 441 Conquest II	441-0254	SE-IPB	0082	0998	2 GA TPE331-8-403S	4468			
☐ N441FC	Cessna 441 Conquest II	441-0078	G-HOSP	0079	0998	2 GA TPE331-10N-515S	4468			lsf Thunderskies Inc.
☐ N536MA	Cessna 441 Conquest II	441-0322	D-IEWA	0084	0998	2 GA TPE331-10N-515S	4468			lsf Universal Instruments Corp.
☐ N101BX	Cessna 550 Citation II	550-0157	N550K	0080	0998	2 PWC JT15D-4	6033			lsf Rose Aviation Llc
☐ N341CW	Cessna 550 Citation II	550-0306	N550MT	0081	0798	2 PWC JT15D-4	6033			lsf Alta Leasing/cvtd Ce551 cn 551-0341
☐ N792MA	Cessna 550 Citation II	550-0302	N133BC	0081	0998	2 PWC JT15D-4	6033			lsf Mattco Electric Corp.
☐ N425AS	Learjet 35A	35A-281	N425M	0080	0998	2 GA TFE731-2-2B	8301			
☐ N7117	Learjet 35A	35A-462	N147K	0082	0998	2 GA TFE731-2-2B	8301			lsf Business Jet Inc.
☐ N95WK	Learjet 55	55-099	N17GL	0084	0998	2 GA TFE731-3AR-2B	9752			lsf Cole/TDI Aviation Llc
☐ N648WW	Hawker 700A (HS 125-700A)	257004 / NA0218	N746BC	0078	0998	2 GA TFE731-3R-1H	11567			
☐ N701NW	Hawker 700A (HS 125-700A)	257009 / NA0206	XA-SNN	0077	0998	2 GA TFE731-3R-1H	11567			lsf Cole Aeronautics Inc.

COURTNEY AVIATION (Hart B. Drobish dba)

Columbia, CA

PO Box 1196, Columbia, CA 95310, USA ☎ (209) 532-2345 Tx: none Fax: (209) 532-3865 SITA: n/a
F: 1967 👥 n/a Head: Hart B. Drobish Net: http://www.flyosemite.com Aircraft below MTOW 1361kg: Cessna 182

☐ N2522S	Cessna T337C Turbo Skymaster	337-0822		0068	0894	2 CO TSIO-360-A/B	2041			lsf Skystar Inc.

COYOTE AIR, Llc

Talkeetna, AK

PO Box 70, Talkeetna, AK 99676, USA ☎ (907) 733-1765 Tx: none Fax: (907) 733-1965 SITA: n/a
F: 1996 👥 n/a Head: Dirk D. Nickisch Net: n/a

☐ N60844	Cessna A185F Skywagon II	18504062		0080	0197	1 CO IO-520-D	1520			Floats / Wheel-Skis

CRAIG AIR (Craig A. Emery dba)

Bethel, AK

PO Box 2018, Bethel, AK 99559, USA ☎ (907) 543-2575 Tx: none Fax: (907) 543-3602 SITA: n/a
F: 1989 👥 n/a Head: Craig A. Emery Net: n/a Aircraft below MTOW 1361kg: Cessna 182

☐ N90193	Cessna T207 Turbo Skywagon	20700007	N520SA	0069	1095	1 CO TSIO-520-M	1724			
☐ N91170	Cessna 207 Skywagon	20700101		0069	0291	1 CO IO-520-F	1724			
☐ N91190	Cessna 207 Skywagon	20700109		0069	0989	1 CO IO-520-F	1724			

310 registration type of aircraft cn/fn ex/ex* mfd del powered by mtow kg configuration selcal name/fln/specialitites/remarks

CRANE HELICOPTERS (Crane Helicopter Services, Inc. dba) — **Alamo, CA**

938 Forest Lane, Alamo, CA 94507, USA ☎ (925) 820-0174 Tx: none Fax: (925) 831-9507 SITA: n/a
F: 1979 n/a Head: Linda J. Lotspeich Net: n/a

☐ N109CH	Bell 204B	2030	N8514F	0065	0290	1 LY T5313B	3856			

CRESCENT HELICOPTERS (Shasta Aviation Corporation dba) — **Hollywood-North Perry, FL**

7750 Pines Blvd, Pembroke Pines, FL 33024, USA ☎ (954) 987-1900 Tx: none Fax: (954) 987-1912 SITA: n/a
F: 1996 n/a Head: Dean H. Shealy Net: http://www.crescentair.com

☐ N284CA	Bell 206B JetRanger	1578	N13WK	0075	0896	1 AN 250-C20	1451			
☐ N48SV	Bell 206B JetRanger	1365	N207AL	0074	0498	1 AN 250-C20	1451			
☐ N5370Y	Bell 206L-3 LongRanger III	51252		0088	0498	1 AN 250-C30P	1882			

CRITICAL AIR MEDICINE, Inc. — **San Diego-Montgomery Field, CA & San Antonio-Int'l, TX**

1403 Northern Boulevard, San Antonio, TX 78216, USA ☎ (210) 829-8720 Tx: none Fax: (210) 829-0444 SITA: n/a
F: 1981 n/a Head: Harry R. Metz Net: n/a

☐ N288JB	Bell 206L-3 LongRanger III	51288		0089	0897	1 AN 250-C30P	1882	EMS		
☐ N911KP	Bell 206L-3 LongRanger III	51455	N66435	0091	0597	1 AN 250-C30P	1882			
☐ N19MH	Cessna 421C Golden Eagle III	421C1008		0081	1194	2 CO GTSIO-520-N	3379	EMS		
☐ N411MZ	Cessna 421C Golden Eagle III	421C1002		0081	0693	2 CO GTSIO-520-N	3379	EMS		
☐ N6793V	Cessna 421C Golden Eagle III	421C1022		0081	0896	2 CO GTSIO-520-N	3379	EMS		
☐ N6796R	Cessna 421C Golden Eagle III	421C1044		0081	0494	2 CO GTSIO-520-N	3379	EMS		
☐ N745CA	Cessna 421C Golden Eagle III	421C1043	N6796L	0081	0991	2 CO GTSIO-520-N	3379	EMS		
☐ N746CA	Cessna 421C Golden Eagle III	421C1049	N6797C	0081	0394	2 CO GTSIO-520-N	3379	EMS		
☐ N747CA	Cessna 421C Golden Eagle III	421C0850	N42AJ	0080	1192	2 CO GTSIO-520-L	3379	EMS		
☐ N748CA	Cessna 421C Golden Eagle III	421C0905	N6251X	0080	0992	2 CO GTSIO-520-L	3379	EMS		
☐ N749CA	Cessna 421C Golden Eagle III	421C1239	N2725Q	0082	0192	2 CO GTSIO-520-N	3379	EMS		
☐ N763CA	Cessna 421C Golden Eagle III	421C1019	D-IWOS	0081	0796	2 CO GTSIO-520-N	3379	EMS		
☐ N751CA	Learjet 25B	25B-122	N122WC	0073	0592	2 GE CJ610-6	6804	EMS		

CROMAN, Corp. — **Medford-Jackson County, OR**

801 Ave C, White City, OR 97503, USA ☎ (541) 826-4455 Tx: 5106009448 croman co Fax: (541) 826-4730 SITA: n/a
F: 1975 n/a Head: Bill L. Kaufman Net: n/a Aircraft below MTOW 1361kg: Soloy-Hiller UH-12ET.

☐ N59584	Bell 206B JetRanger III	1463		0074	0488	1 AN 250-C20B	1451			cvtd JetRanger
☐ N100ZG	Cessna 340 II	340-0528		0075	0796	2 CO TSIO-520-K	2710			lst Pacific Flights
☐ N1043T	Sikorsky S-61A	61083		0062	1081	2 GE CT58-140-1	8618			
☐ N1048Y	Sikorsky S-61A	61161		0062	0287	2 GE CT58-140-1	8618			
☐ N318Y	Sikorsky S-61A	61094	N299BC	0062	0780	2 GE CT58-140-1	8618			
☐ N692CC	Sikorsky SH-3A (S-61A)	61439		0068	1194	2 GE CT58-140-1	8618			
☐ N693CC	Sikorsky SH-3A (S-61A)	61215		0063	1194	2 GE CT58-140-1	8618			
☐ N694CC	Sikorsky SH-3A (S-61A)	61088		0061	1194	2 GE CT58-140-1	8618			std Medford
☐ N9119S	Sikorsky S-61N	61703	C-FHCH	0072	0987	2 GE CT58-140-1	9979			

CROTTS AIRCRAFT (Crotts Aircraft Service, Inc. dba) — **Dodge City-Regional, KS**

102 Airport Road, Dodge City, KS 67801, USA ☎ (316) 227-3553 Tx: none Fax: (316) 227-3411 SITA: n/a
F: 1985 n/a Head: Leigh O. Crotts Net: n/a

☐ N6174J	Piper PA-32R-300 Lance	32R-7680325		0076	1285	1 LY IO-540-K1G5D	1633			
☐ N66863	Beech Bonanza A36	E-2086		0084	0493	1 CO IO-520-BB	1633			
☐ N77HT	Beech Bonanza A36	E-1324		0078	0286	1 CO IO-520-BA	1633			
☐ N818GW	Beech Baron C55 (95-C55)	TE-118		0066	0191	2 CO IO-520-C	2404			
☐ N726RT	Cessna 421C Golden Eagle II	421C0087		0076	0597	2 CO GTSIO-520-L	3379			

CROW EXECUTIVE AIR, Inc. = CWX (formerly Crow Executive Air Charter, Inc.) — **Toledo-Metcalf Field, OH**

28331 Lemoyne Road, Millbury, OH 43447, USA ☎ (419) 838-6921 Tx: none Fax: (419) 838-6911 SITA: n/a
F: 1947 56 Head: Eric E. Barnum ICAO: CROW EXPRESS Net: http://www.crowair.com Aircraft below MTOW 1361kg: Piper PA-28.

☐ N2591Z	Piper PA-23-250 Aztec F	27-8154005		0081	0282	2 LY IO-540-C4B5	2359			
☐ N4078L	Piper PA-31-350 Navajo Chieftain	31-8152060		0081	0784	2 LY TIO-540-J2BD	3175			
☐ N444FA	Cessna 208B Grand Caravan	208B0490		0095	1097	1 PWC PT6A-114A	3969			lsf Textron Financial Corp.
☐ N333FA	Fairchild (Swearingen) SA226TC Metro II	TC-214	N26836	0074	1291	2 GA TPE331-3UW-303G	5670			
☐ N119MA	Learjet 24B	24B-200	N246CM	0069	1295	2 GE CJ610-6	6123			lsf Tango Juliet Llc
☐ N740EJ	Learjet 24B	24B-222	N740F	0070	0395	2 GE CJ610-6	6123			lsf Tango Juliet Llc
☐ N57FL	Learjet 24D (XR)	24D-243	N56WS	0072	0996	2 GE CJ610-6	6804			lsf Flight Operations Leasing Inc.
☐ N59FL	Learjet 25B	25B-169	N893WA	0074	1197	2 GE CJ610-6	6804			lsf Flight Operations Leasing Inc.
☐ N43TJ	Learjet 35A	35A-121		0077	1093	2 GA TFE731-2-2B	8301			lsf Foxtrot Alpha Inc.

CSA AIR, Inc. = IRO — **Iron Mountain/Kingsford-Ford, MI**

Ford Airport, Iron Mountain, MI 49801, USA ☎ (906) 774-3101 Tx: none Fax: (906) 779-1304 SITA: n/a
F: 1988 n/a Head: Harald W. Ross ICAO: IRON AIR Net: n/a

☐ N830FE	Cessna 208A Caravan I Cargomaster	20800075		0085	1285	1 PWC PT6A-114	3629	Freighter		lsf/opf FDX in FedEx Feeder-colors
☐ N703FX	Cessna 208B Caravan I Super Cargomaster	208B0423		0095	0295	1 PWC PT6A-114A	3969	Freighter		lsf/opf FDX in FedEx Feeder-colors
☐ N706FX	Cessna 208B Caravan I Super Cargomaster	208B0426		0095	0395	1 PWC PT6A-114A	3969	Freighter		lsf/opf FDX in FedEx Feeder-colors
☐ N712FX	Cessna 208B Caravan I Super Cargomaster	208B0435		0095	0595	1 PWC PT6A-114A	3969	Freighter		lsf/opf FDX in FedEx Feeder-colors
☐ N717FX	Cessna 208B Caravan I Super Cargomaster	208B0445		0095	0695	1 PWC PT6A-114A	3969	Freighter		lsf/opf FDX in FedEx Feeder-colors
☐ N727FX	Cessna 208B Caravan I Super Cargomaster	208B0468		0095	0995	1 PWC PT6A-114A	3969	Freighter		lsf/opf FDX in FedEx Feeder-colors
☐ N752FE	Cessna 208B Caravan I Super Cargomaster	208B0247		0090	1290	1 PWC PT6A-114A	3969	Freighter		lsf/opf FDX in FedEx Feeder-colors
☐ N761FE	Cessna 208B Caravan I Super Cargomaster	208B0254		0091	0291	1 PWC PT6A-114A	3969	Freighter		lsf/opf FDX in FedEx Feeder-colors
☐ N767FE	Cessna 208B Caravan I Super Cargomaster	208B0262		0091	0491	1 PWC PT6A-114A	3969	Freighter		lsf/opf FDX in FedEx Feeder-colors
☐ N784FE	Cessna 208B Caravan I Super Cargomaster	208B0282		0091	0991	1 PWC PT6A-114A	3969	Freighter		lsf/opf FDX in FedEx Feeder-colors
☐ N795FE	Cessna 208B Caravan I Super Cargomaster	208B0293		0092	0192	1 PWC PT6A-114A	3969	Freighter		lsf/opf FDX in FedEx Feeder-colors
☐ N828FE	Cessna 208B Caravan I Super Cargomaster	208B0122	F-GHHD	0088	1088	1 PWC PT6A-114	3969	Freighter		lsf/opf FDX in FedEx Feeder-colors
☐ N843FE	Cessna 208B Caravan I Super Cargomaster	208B0147		0089	0189	1 PWC PT6A-114	3969	Freighter		lsf/opf FDX in FedEx Feeder-colors
☐ N858FE	Cessna 208B Caravan I Super Cargomaster	208B0178		0089	0689	1 PWC PT6A-114	3969	Freighter		lsf/opf FDX in FedEx Feeder-colors
☐ N871FE	Cessna 208B Caravan I Super Cargomaster	208B0198		0089	1189	1 PWC PT6A-114	3969	Freighter		lsf/opf FDX in FedEx Feeder-colors
☐ N883FE	Cessna 208B Caravan I Super Cargomaster	208B0210		0090	0390	1 PWC PT6A-114	3969	Freighter		lsf/opf FDX in FedEx Feeder-colors
☐ N884FE	Cessna 208B Caravan I Super Cargomaster	208B0233		0090	1090	1 PWC PT6A-114	3969	Freighter		lsf/opf FDX in FedEx Feeder-colors
☐ N893FE	Cessna 208B Caravan I Super Cargomaster	208B0223		0090	0790	1 PWC PT6A-114	3969	Freighter		lsf/opf FDX in FedEx Feeder-colors
☐ N906FE	Cessna 208B Caravan I Super Cargomaster	208B0006		0086	1286	1 PWC PT6A-114	3969	Freighter		lsf/opf FDX in FedEx Feeder-colors
☐ N907FE	Cessna 208B Caravan I Super Cargomaster	208B0007		0086	1286	1 PWC PT6A-114	3969	Freighter		lsf/opf FDX in FedEx Feeder-colors
☐ N914FE	Cessna 208B Caravan I Super Cargomaster	208B0014		0087	0287	1 PWC PT6A-114	3969	Freighter		lsf/opf FDX in FedEx Feeder-colors
☐ N923FE	Cessna 208B Caravan I Super Cargomaster	208B0023		0087	0587	1 PWC PT6A-114	3969	Freighter		lsf/opf FDX in FedEx Feeder-colors
☐ N925FE	Cessna 208B Caravan I Super Cargomaster	208B0025		0087	0587	1 PWC PT6A-114	3969	Freighter		lsf/opf FDX in FedEx Feeder-colors
☐ N946FE	Cessna 208B Caravan I Super Cargomaster	208B0048		0087	1087	1 PWC PT6A-114	3969	Freighter		lsf/opf FDX in FedEx Feeder-colors
☐ N954FE	Cessna 208B Caravan I Super Cargomaster	208B0064		0087	1287	1 PWC PT6A-114	3969	Freighter		lsf/opf FDX in FedEx Feeder-colors
☐ N986FE	Cessna 208B Caravan I Super Cargomaster	208B0194		0089	1089	1 PWC PT6A-114	3969	Freighter		lsf/opf FDX in FedEx Feeder-colors
☐ N993FE	Cessna 208B Caravan I Super Cargomaster	208B0130		0088	1188	1 PWC PT6A-114	3969	Freighter		lsf/opf FDX in FedEx Feeder-colors

C-S AVIATION SERVICES, Inc. = (CSAV) (managing company for S-C Aircraft Holding, Llc) — **New York, NY**

888 7th Ave., Ste 2901, New York, NY 10106, USA ☎ (212) 333-9898 Tx: n/a Fax: (212) 246-0102 SITA: n/a
F: n/a n/a Head: Bharat Bhise Net: n/a Used aircraft operating leasing & financing company.
Owner / lessor of following (main) aircraft types: Airbus Industrie A300F, Boeing 727-100 & McDonnell Douglas MD-82. Aircraft leased from C-S Aviation Services are listed and mentioned as lsf CSAV under the leasing carriers.

CURRIER'S FLYING SERVICE, Inc. (Seasonal May-October ops only) — **Greenville-SPB, ME**

Box 351, Greenville, ME 04442, USA ☎ (207) 695-2778 Tx: none Fax: none SITA: n/a
F: 1981 4 Head: Roger L. Currier Net: n/a Aircraft below MTOW 1361kg: Cessna 180 & Piper PA-12 (on Floats)

☐ N145V	Cessna 195	7135		0048	0686	1 JA R-755-A2	1633			Floats
☐ N3488V	Cessna 195	7192		0048	0794	1 JA R-755-A2	1633			lsf Edmaier Chesna Inc. / Floats
☐ N91549	De Havilland DHC-2 Beaver I	628	C-FHNM	0053	1187	1 PW R-985	2313			Floats

CUSTOM AIR CHARTER (Buxmont Aviation Services, Inc. dba) — **Philadelphia-Northeast, PA**

1607 Eastern Road, Warrington, PA 18976, USA ☎ (215) 343-1480 Tx: none Fax: (215) 343-0352 SITA: n/a
F: 1978 11 Head: Mark Timmerman Net: n/a

☐ N469CA	Piper PA-31-350 Navajo Chieftain	31-7952248	N469PT	0079	0790	2 LY TIO-540-J2BD	3175			
☐ N728CA	Piper PA-31-350 Navajo Chieftain	31-7752035	N727VM	0077	1291	2 LY TIO-540-J2BD	3175			
☐ N570AB	Piper PA-31T Cheyenne II	31T-7820026	N36JM	0078	0396	2 PWC PT6A-28	4082			lsf JB Air Corp.

CUSTOM AIR SERVICE, Inc. — **Hampton-Clayton County Tara Field, GA**

PO Box 72, Griffin, GA 30223, USA ☎ (770) 412-6999 Tx: none Fax: (770) 229-8991 SITA: n/a
F: 1996 n/a Head: Robert D. McSwiggan Net: n/a

☐ N89FA	ATL-98 Carvair	27249 / DO 195	G-ASHZ	0045	0096	4 PW R-2000	33475	Freighter		cvtd Douglas C-54B-20-DO / conv. no. 9

311 registration type of aircraft cn/fn ex/ex* mfd del powered by mtow kg configuration selcal name/fln/specialitites/remarks

registration	type of aircraft	cn/fn	ex/ex*	mfd	del	powered by	mtow kg	configuration	selcal	name/fln/specialitites/remarks
☐ N753AS	Boeing 727-22C	19203 / 434.	N753AL	0067	0698	3 PW JT8D-7B (HK3/RAI)	76884	Freighter		lsf New Quick Co/lst/opf CharterAmerica
☐ N406BN	Boeing 727-291 (F)	19991 / 521	HI-630CA	0068	1197	3 PW JT8D-9A (HK3/RAI)	76929	Freighter		lsfArrivaAl/lst/opf Ch.America/cvtd-291
☐ N8887Z	Boeing 727-225 (F) (A)	21856 / 1537		0079	0496	3 PW JT8D-15	86409	Freighter		lsf PEGA / cvtd -225 / white-cs
☐ N8892Z	Boeing 727-225 (F) (A)	21861 / 1554		0079	0698	3 PW JT8D-9A (HK3/FDX)	86409	Freighter		lsfNewQuick/lst/opf Ch.America/cvtd-225

DAIRY AIRE (Contract Aviation Services, Inc. dba) — Detroit-Grosse Ile Municipal, MI

PO Box 391, Grosse Ile, MI 48138, USA ☎ (734) 692-7850 Tx: none Fax: (734) 692-4901 SITA: n/a
F: 1995 ⁂ n/a Head: Robert A. Wernecke Net: n/a

registration	type of aircraft	cn/fn	ex/ex*	mfd	del	powered by	mtow kg	configuration	selcal	name/fln/specialitites/remarks
☐ N200MU	Britten-Norman BN-2A-27 Islander	78	C-FYZT	0069	0397	2 LY O-540-E4C5	2885			lsf Dairy Air Llc

D & E (D&E Storage dba) — Brewster-Anderson Field, WA

PO Box 735, Brewster, WA 98812, USA ☎ (509) 689-2521 Tx: none Fax: (509) 689-2033 SITA: n/a
F: 1982 ⁂ n/a Head: Danny Pariseau Net: n/a

registration	type of aircraft	cn/fn	ex/ex*	mfd	del	powered by	mtow kg	configuration	selcal	name/fln/specialitites/remarks
☐ N90307	Bell 206B JetRanger	1747		0075	0689	1 AN 250-C20	1451			

DAVISAIR, Inc. — Pittsburgh-Allegheny County, PA

Hangar, Box 56, West Mifflin, PA 15122, USA ☎ (724) 469-1700 Tx: none Fax: (724) 469-3156 SITA: n/a
F: 1989 ⁂ n/a Head: Gary I. Davis Net: http://www.davisair.com

registration	type of aircraft	cn/fn	ex/ex*	mfd	del	powered by	mtow kg	configuration	selcal	name/fln/specialitites/remarks
☐ N55EZ	Beech Baron E55	TE-785		0070	0194	2 CO IO-520-C	2404			
☐ N27990	Piper PA-31-350 Navajo Chieftain	31-7952079		0079	0397	2 LY TIO-540-J2BD	3175			
☐ N1565L	Beech King Air C90	LJ-704		0077	0491	2 PWC PT6A-21	4377			
☐ N52SF	Beech King Air 200	BB-106	N383AS	0076	0794	2 PWC PT6A-41	5670			lsf SAK Aviation Inc.
☐ N700DA	Learjet 25D	25D-302	N740K	0080	0994	2 GE CJ610-8A	6804			
☐ N190DA	Learjet 35A	35A-156	N190EB	0078	1289	2 GA TFE731-2-2B	8301			

DAVIS OIL – Flight Dept. (Flight Dept. of Davis Oil Company) — Los Angeles-Int'l, CA

2121 Ave of the Stars, Los Angeles, CA 90067-5000, USA ☎ (562) 551-1470 Tx: none Fax: (562) 551-2214 SITA: n/a
F: 1988 ⁂ n/a Head: Marvin Davis Net: n/a Operates non-commerical executive flights exclusively for its parent company only.

registration	type of aircraft	cn/fn	ex/ex*	mfd	del	powered by	mtow kg	configuration	selcal	name/fln/specialitites/remarks
☐ N44MD	Boeing 727-44	19318 / 348	N727EC	0066	0588	3 PW JT8D-7	72802	Executive	EF-JM	

DB AVIATION, Inc. — Chicago-Waukegan Regional, IL

3800 North McAree Road, Waukegan, IL 60087, USA ☎ (847) 263-5600 Tx: none Fax: (847) 263-6486 SITA: n/a
F: 1989 ⁂ n/a Head: Daniel A. Bitton Net: http://www.dbaviation.com

registration	type of aircraft	cn/fn	ex/ex*	mfd	del	powered by	mtow kg	configuration	selcal	name/fln/specialitites/remarks
☐ N858MA	Cessna 208 Caravan I	20800262		0097	0497	1 PWC PT6A-114	3629			lsf Spence Enterprises 1 Inc.
☐ N690SM	Twin (Aero) Turbo Commander 690A	11337	N1547A	0076		2 GA TPE331-5-251K	4650			lsf Pascomar Inc.
☐ N55WL	Cessna 550 Citation II	550-0140	N2646Z	0080	0995	2 PWC JT15D-4	6033			lsf Trebuchet Transport Llc
☐ N232FX	Learjet 35A	35A-620	VR-BNI	0087	0694	2 GA TFE731-2-2B	8301			lsf Aviation Properties Inc.
☐ N83SD	Learjet 55	55-032	N11TS	0082	0996	2 GA TFE731-3A-2B	9752			lsf Wesdix Corp.
☐ N65WL	Cessna 650 Citation III	650-0122	N650TT	0087	0395	2 GA TFE731-3B-100S	9072			lsf Lane Industries
☐ N711GF	Cessna 650 Citation VII	650-7075		0096	0197	2 GA TFE731-4R-2S	10180			lsf IPO II Llc
☐ N26SC	Hawker 700A (HS 125-700A)	257117 / NA0283	N93GR	0080	0794	2 GA TFE731-3R-1H	11567			lsf Swiss Colony Inc.
☐ N24TW	Dassault Falcon 20C	80	N76MB	0067	1194	2 GE CF700-2C	12000			lsf Tailwind Aviation Corp.
☐ N255RK	Dassault Falcon 20D	196	N79AE	0069	1296	2 GE CF700-2D2	13000			lsf Purdy Aviation Corp.

DBS HELICOPTERS (DBS Air, Inc. dba / Subsidiary of The Delta Bravo Sierra Corporation) — Leadville-Lake County, CO

PO Box 1770, Aspen, CO 81612, USA ☎ (970) 920-4472 Tx: none Fax: (970) 625-2997 SITA: n/a
F: 1993 ⁂ n/a Head: Doug Sheffer Net: n/a

registration	type of aircraft	cn/fn	ex/ex*	mfd	del	powered by	mtow kg	configuration	selcal	name/fln/specialitites/remarks
☐ N207DS	Bell 206L-3 LongRanger III	51546	N46EA	0091	1197	1 AN 250-C30P	1882			

DC-3 FLIGHTS, Inc. — Minden-Douglas County, NV

23987 North Highway 99, Acampo, CA 95220, USA ☎ (209) 369-9126 Tx: none Fax: (209) 369-9143 SITA: n/a
F: 1992 ⁂ n/a Head: Robert Kupka Net: n/a

registration	type of aircraft	cn/fn	ex/ex*	mfd	del	powered by	mtow kg	configuration	selcal	name/fln/specialitites/remarks
☐ N45366	Boeing (Douglas) DC-3A (C-53D-DO)	11757	42-68830	0043	0592	2 PW R-1830	12202	Para		

DELIVERY SERVICE, Inc. – DSI (formerly Fast Delivery Service, Inc. & Federal Armored Services, Inc.) — Grand Rapids-Kent County Int'l, MI

PO Box 888284, Grand Rapids, MI 49588-8284, USA ☎ (616) 956-0202 Tx: none Fax: (616) 956-0824 SITA: n/a
F: 1949 ⁂ 22 Head: Terry Larkin Net: n/a

registration	type of aircraft	cn/fn	ex/ex*	mfd	del	powered by	mtow kg	configuration	selcal	name/fln/specialitites/remarks
☐ N36ZX	Beech Bonanza A36	E-1087		0077	0187	1 CO IO-520-BA	1633	Freighter		
☐ N4182S	Beech Bonanza A36	E-668		0075	0278	1 CO IO-520-BA	1633	Freighter		
☐ N222AY	AAC (Piper) Aerostar 600A	60-0595-7961191	N222AZ	0079	0886	2 LY IO-540-K1J5	2495	Freighter		
☐ N300SK	AAC (Ted Smith) Aerostar 600A	60-0355-127	N9532Q	0076	0387	2 LY IO-540-K1F5	2495	Freighter		
☐ N8051J	AAC (Piper) Aerostar 600A	60-0659-7961208		0079	0191	2 LY IO-540-K1F5	2495	Freighter		
☐ N8234J	AAC (Piper) Aerostar 600A	60-0638-7961202		0079	1286	2 LY IO-540-K1J5	2495	Freighter		
☐ N9823Q	AAC (Ted Smith) Aerostar 600A	60-0466-154		0077	0481	2 LY IO-540-K1F5	2495	Freighter		

DELTA AIR LINES, Inc. = DL / DAL (Delta Express) — Atlanta-Hartsfield Int'l, GA

Hartsfield Atlanta Int'l Airport, Atlanta, GA 30320, USA ☎ (770) 715-2600 Tx: 542316 Fax: (770) 767-8499 SITA: n/a
F: 1928 ⁂ 63440 Head: Leo F. Mullin IATA: 006 ICAO: DELTA Net: http://www.deltaair.com/index.html   A commuter system to provide feeder connection at DL major hubs is operated
under the marketing name DELTA CONNECTION by: ASA-Atlantic Southeast, BUSINESS EXPRESS AIRLINES, COMAIR & SKYWEST AIRLINES – for details see under each company.
DELTA EXPRESS is a low-cost internal-division operating in dedicated markets with Boeing 737-200 & carrying such titles (same HQ). Aircraft marked as such in the fleet-list.

registration	type of aircraft	cn/fn	ex/ex*	mfd	del	powered by	mtow kg	configuration	selcal	name/fln/specialitites/remarks
☐ N235WA	Boeing 737-2J8 (A)	22859 / 890	N4562N*	0082	0487	2 PW JT8D-15 (HK3/NOR)	52390	F12Y95		359
☐ N236WA	Boeing 737-247 (A)	23184 / 1061		0084	0487	2 PW JT8D-15 (HK3/NOR)	52390	F12Y95	LM-GH	360 / lsf Finova
☐ N237WA	Boeing 737-247 (A)	23185 / 1065		0084	0487	2 PW JT8D-15 (HK3/NOR)	52390	Y119	LM-GJ	361 / lsf Finova / Delta Express-div.
☐ N238WA	Boeing 737-247 (A)	23186 / 1066		0084	0487	2 PW JT8D-15 (HK3/NOR)	52390	Y119	LM-GK	362 / lsf Finova / Delta Express-div. / 362
☐ N239WA	Boeing 737-247 (A)	23187 / 1070		0084	0487	2 PW JT8D-15 (HK3/NOR)	52390	Y119	LM-HJ	363 / lsf Finova / Delta Express-div.
☐ N242WA	Boeing 737-247 (A)	23516 / 1257		0086	0487	2 PW JT8D-15A (HK3/NOR)	52390	Y119		364 / Delta Express-division
☐ N243WA	Boeing 737-247 (A)	23517 / 1261		0086	0487	2 PW JT8D-15A (HK3/NOR)	52390	Y119		365 / Delta Express-division
☐ N244WA	Boeing 737-247 (A)	23518 / 1265		0086	0487	2 PW JT8D-15A (HK3/NOR)	52390	F12Y95		366
☐ N245WA	Boeing 737-247 (A)	23519 / 1299		0086	0487	2 PW JT8D-15A (HK3/NOR)	52390	F12Y95		372
☐ N301DL	Boeing 737-232 (A)	23073 / 991		0083	1083	2 PW JT8D-15A (HK3/NOR)	52390	Y119	BE-KL	301 / Delta Express-division
☐ N302DL	Boeing 737-232 (A)	23074 / 993		0083	1183	2 PW JT8D-15A (HK3/NOR)	52390	Y119	BE-KM	302 / Delta Express-division
☐ N303DL	Boeing 737-232 (A)	23075 / 994		0083	1183	2 PW JT8D-15A (HK3/NOR)	52390	Y119	BF-AC	303 / Delta Express-division
☐ N304DL	Boeing 737-232 (A)	23076 / 995		0083	1283	2 PW JT8D-15A (HK3/NOR)	52390	Y119	BF-AE	304 / Delta Express-division
☐ N305DL	Boeing 737-232 (A)	23077 / 996		0083	1283	2 PW JT8D-15A (HK3/NOR)	52390	Y119	BF-AH	305 / Delta Express-division
☐ N306DL	Boeing 737-232 (A)	23078 / 1000		0083	1283	2 PW JT8D-15A (HK3/NOR)	52390	Y119	BF-AJ	306 / Delta Express-division
☐ N307DL	Boeing 737-232 (A)	23079 / 1003		0084	0584	2 PW JT8D-15A (HK3/NOR)	52390	Y119	BF-AK	307 / Delta Express-division
☐ N308DL	Boeing 737-232 (A)	23080 / 1004		0084	0184	2 PW JT8D-15A (HK3/NOR)	52390	Y119	BF-AL	308 / Delta Express-division
☐ N309DL	Boeing 737-232 (A)	23081 / 1005		0084	0284	2 PW JT8D-15A (HK3/NOR)	52390	Y119	BF-AM	309 / Delta Express-division
☐ N310DA	Boeing 737-232 (A)	23082 / 1006		0084	0284	2 PW JT8D-15A (HK3/NOR)	52390	Y119	BF-CE	310 / Delta Express-division
☐ N311DL	Boeing 737-232 (A)	23083 / 1008		0084	0284	2 PW JT8D-15A (HK3/NOR)	52390	Y119	BF-CG	311 / Delta Express-division
☐ N312DL	Boeing 737-232 (A)	23084 / 1009		0084	0384	2 PW JT8D-15A (HK3/NOR)	52390	Y119	BF-CH	312 / Delta Express-division
☐ N313DL	Boeing 737-232 (A)	23085 / 1011		0084	0384	2 PW JT8D-15A (HK3/NOR)	52390	Y119	BF-CJ	313 / Delta Express-division
☐ N314DA	Boeing 737-232 (A)	23086 / 1012		0084	0384	2 PW JT8D-15A (HK3/NOR)	52390	Y119	BF-CK	314 / Delta Express-division
☐ N315DL	Boeing 737-232 (A)	23087 / 1013		0084	0484	2 PW JT8D-15A (HK3/NOR)	52390	Y119	BF-CL	315 / Delta Express-division
☐ N316DL	Boeing 737-232 (A)	23088 / 1018		0084	0484	2 PW JT8D-15A (HK3/NOR)	52390	Y119	BF-CM	316 / Delta Express-division
☐ N317DL	Boeing 737-232 (A)	23089 / 1019		0084	0584	2 PW JT8D-15A (HK3/NOR)	52390	Y119	BF-DE	317 / Delta Express-division
☐ N318DL	Boeing 737-232 (A)	23090 / 1020		0084	0584	2 PW JT8D-15A (HK3/NOR)	52390	Y119	BF-DG	318 / Delta Express-division
☐ N319DL	Boeing 737-232 (A)	23091 / 1021		0084	1184	2 PW JT8D-15A (HK3/NOR)	52390	Y119	BF-DH	319 / Delta Express-division
☐ N320DL	Boeing 737-232 (A)	23092 / 1023		0084	0684	2 PW JT8D-15A (HK3/NOR)	52390	Y119	BF-DJ	320 / Delta Express-division
☐ N321DL	Boeing 737-232 (A)	23093 / 1024		0084	0984	2 PW JT8D-15A (HK3/NOR)	52390	Y119	BF-DK	321 / Delta Express-division
☐ N322DL	Boeing 737-232 (A)	23094 / 1026		0084	0884	2 PW JT8D-15A (HK3/NOR)	52390	Y119	BF-DL	322 / Delta Express-division
☐ N323DL	Boeing 737-232 (A)	23095 / 1027		0084	0684	2 PW JT8D-15A (HK3/NOR)	52390	F12Y95	BF-DM	323
☐ N324DL	Boeing 737-232 (A)	23096 / 1028		0084	0784	2 PW JT8D-15A (HK3/NOR)	52390	Y119	BF-EG	324 / Delta Express-division
☐ N325DL	Boeing 737-232 (A)	23097 / 1029		0084	0784	2 PW JT8D-15A (HK3/NOR)	52390	Y119	BF-EH	325 / Delta Express-division
☐ N326DL	Boeing 737-232 (A)	23098 / 1031		0084	1084	2 PW JT8D-15A (HK3/NOR)	52390	Y119	BF-EJ	326 / Delta Express-division
☐ N327DL	Boeing 737-232 (A)	23099 / 1035		0084	0884	2 PW JT8D-15A (HK3/NOR)	52390	Y119	BF-KL	327 / Delta Express-division
☐ N328DL	Boeing 737-232 (A)	23100 / 1038		0084	0984	2 PW JT8D-15A (HK3/NOR)	52390	Y119	HK-CD	328 / Delta Express-division
☐ N329DL	Boeing 737-232 (A)	23101 / 1041		0084	1184	2 PW JT8D-15A (HK3/NOR)	52390	Y119	HK-CE	329 / Delta Express-division
☐ N330DL	Boeing 737-232 (A)	23102 / 1045		0084	1084	3 PW JT8D-15A (HK3/NOR)	52390	Y119	HK-CF	330 / Delta Express-division
☐ N331DL	Boeing 737-232 (A)	23103 / 1051		0084	1184	2 PW JT8D-15A (HK3/NOR)	52390	Y119	HK-CG	331 / Delta Express-division
☐ N332DL	Boeing 737-232 (A)	23104 / 1062		0084	1284	2 PW JT8D-15A (HK3/NOR)	52390	Y119	HK-CJ	332 / Delta Express-division
☐ N334DL	Boeing 737-232 (A)	23105 / 1068		0084	1284	2 PW JT8D-15A (HK3/NOR)	52390	Y119	HK-CL	333 / Delta Express-division
☐ N367DL	Boeing 737-2S3 (A)	21774 / 563	EI-BPY	0079	0487	2 PW JT8D-15 (HK3/NOR)	52390	F12Y95		367 / lsf GECA
☐ N369DL	Boeing 737-2S3 (A)	21776 / 577	N368DL	0079	0487	2 PW JT8D-15A (HK3/NOR)	52390	F12Y95		369 / lsf GECA
☐ N373DL	Boeing 737-247 (A)	23520 / 1329		0086	0287	2 PW JT8D-15A (HK3/NOR)	52390	F12Y95		373
☐ N374DL	Boeing 737-247 (A)	23521 / 1342		0087	0287	2 PW JT8D-15A (HK3/NOR)	52390	F12Y95		374
☐ N375DL	Boeing 737-247 (A)	23602 / 1347		0087	0287	2 PW JT8D-15A (HK3/NOR)	52390	F12Y95		375
☐ N376DL	Boeing 737-247 (A)	23603 / 1361		0087	0387	2 PW JT8D-15A (HK3/NOR)	52390	F12Y95		376
☐ N377DL	Boeing 737-247 (A)	23604 / 1369		0087	0487	2 PW JT8D-15A (HK3/NOR)	52390	F12Y95		377
☐ N378DL	Boeing 737-247 (A)	23605 / 1371		0087	0487	2 PW JT8D-15A (HK3/NOR)	52390	F12Y95		378
☐ N379DL	Boeing 737-247 (A)	23606 / 1379		0087	0587	2 PW JT8D-15A	52390	F12Y95		379

	registration	type of aircraft	cn/fn	ex/ex*	mfd	del	powered by	mtow kg	configuration	selcal	name/fln/specialitites/remarks
☐	N380DL	Boeing 737-247 (A)	23607 / 1387		0087	0587	2 PW JT8D-15A	52390	F12Y95		380
☐	N381DL	Boeing 737-247 (A)	23608 / 1399		0087	0687	2 PW JT8D-15A	52390	F12Y95		381
☐	N382DL	Boeing 737-247 (A)	23609 / 1403		0087	0687	2 PW JT8D-15A	52390	F12Y95		382
☐	N221DL	Boeing 737-35B	23970 / 1467	D-AGEA	0087	0298	2 CFMI CFM56-3B2	62822	F8Y120		221 / lsf PEMB
☐	N222DZ	Boeing 737-35B	23971 / 1482	D-AGEB	0087	0798	2 CFMI CFM56-3B2	62822	F8Y120		222 / lsf PEMB
☐	N223DZ	Boeing 737-35B	23972 / 1537	D-AGEC	0088	0998	2 CFMI CFM56-3B2	62822	F8Y120		223 / lsf PEMB
☐	N224DA	Boeing 737-35B	24269 / 1628	D-AGED	0088	0698	2 CFMI CFM56-3B2	62822	F8Y120		224 / lsf PEMB
☐	N225DL	Boeing 737-35B	25069 / 2053	D-AGEF	0091	0498	2 CFMI CFM56-3B2	62822	F8Y120	EL-GQ	225 / lsf PEMB
☐	N2310	Boeing 737-347	23596 / 1269		0086	0487	2 CFMI CFM56-3B1	58967	F8Y120		210
☐	N231DN	Boeing 737-3L9	23717 / 1365	D-AGEH	0087	0398	2 CFMI CFM56-3B2	62822	F8Y120		231 / lsf PEMB
☐	N232DZ	Boeing 737-3L9	24220 / 1602	D-AGEI	0088	0398	2 CFMI CFM56-3B2	62822	F8Y120		232 / lsf PEMB
☐	N241DL	Boeing 737-330	23833 / 1439	D-ABWA	0087	0798	2 CFMI CFM56-3B2	62822	F8Y120		241 / lsf PEMB
☐	N242DL	Boeing 737-330	23834 / 1454	D-ABWB	0087	0798	2 CFMI CFM56-3B2	62822	F8Y120		242 / lsf PEMB
☐	N302WA	Boeing 737-347	23182 / 1106		0085	0487	2 CFMI CFM56-3B1	58967	F8Y120	LM-EJ	202 / Wally Bird
☐	N303WA	Boeing 737-347	23183 / 1108		0085	0487	2 CFMI CFM56-3B1	58967	F8Y120	LM-EK	203 / Salt Lake City
☐	N304WA	Boeing 737-347	23345 / 1170		0085	0487	2 CFMI CFM56-3B1	58967	F8Y120	HK-CF	204
☐	N305WA	Boeing 737-347	23346 / 1172		0085	0487	2 CFMI CFM56-3B1	58967	F8Y120	HK-CG	205
☐	N306WA	Boeing 737-347	23347 / 1173		0085	0487	2 CFMI CFM56-3B1	58967	F8Y120	HK-CJ	206
☐	N307WA	Boeing 737-347	23440 / 1218		0086	0487	2 CFMI CFM56-3B1	58967	F8Y120	HK-CL	207
☐	N308WA	Boeing 737-347	23441 / 1220		0086	0487	2 CFMI CFM56-3B1	58967	F8Y120	HK-CM	208
☐	N309WA	Boeing 737-347	23442 / 1239		0086	0487	2 CFMI CFM56-3B1	58967	F8Y120	HK-DE	209
☐	N311WA	Boeing 737-347	23597 / 1287		0086	0487	2 CFMI CFM56-3B1	58967	F8Y120	KM-DJ	211
☐	N312WA	Boeing 737-347	23598 / 1289		0086	0487	2 CFMI CFM56-3B1	58967	F8Y120		212
☐	N313WA	Boeing 737-347	23599 / 1324		0086	0487	2 CFMI CFM56-3B1	58967	F8Y120	KM-FH	213
☐	N3301	Boeing 737-347	23181 / 1087		0085	0487	2 CFMI CFM56-3B1	58967	F8Y120	LM-EH	201 / Larry Lee
☐	N947WP	Boeing 737-3B7	23376 / 1308	N501AU	0086	0698	2 CFMI CFM56-3B2	62823	F8Y120		253 / lsf GECA
☐	N948WP	Boeing 737-301	23259 / 1132	N581US	0085	0898	2 CFMI CFM56-3B2	62823	F8Y120		252 / lsf GECA
☐	N951WP	Boeing 737-3B7	22951 / 1007	N372US	0084	0698	2 CFMI CFM56-3B1	61235	F8Y120		251 / lsf GECA
☐	N952WP	Boeing 737-3B7	23378 / 1339	N503AU	0087	0698	2 CFMI CFM56-3B2	62823	F8Y120		254 / lsf GECA
☐	N900DE	Boeing (Douglas) MD-88 (DC-9-88)	53372 / 1970		0092	0392	2 PW JT8D-219	67812	F14Y128		9000
☐	N901DE	Boeing (Douglas) MD-88 (DC-9-88)	53378 / 1980		0292	0492	2 PW JT8D-219	67812	F14Y128		9001
☐	N901DL	Boeing (Douglas) MD-88 (DC-9-88)	49532 / 1338		0087	0387	2 PW JT8D-219	67812	F14Y128		901 / cvtd MD-82
☐	N902DE	Boeing (Douglas) MD-88 (DC-9-88)	53379 / 1983		0292	0492	2 PW JT8D-219	67812	F14Y128		9002
☐	N902DL	Boeing (Douglas) MD-88 (DC-9-88)	49533 / 1341		0087	0387	2 PW JT8D-219	67812	F14Y128		902 / cvtd MD-82
☐	N903DE	Boeing (Douglas) MD-88 (DC-9-88)	53380 / 1986		0392	0492	2 PW JT8D-219	67812	F14Y128		9003
☐	N903DL	Boeing (Douglas) MD-88 (DC-9-88)	49534 / 1344		0087	0387	2 PW JT8D-219	67812	F14Y128		903 / cvtd MD-82
☐	N904DE	Boeing (Douglas) MD-88 (DC-9-88)	53409 / 1990		0092	0592	2 PW JT8D-219	67812	F14Y128		9004
☐	N904DL	Boeing (Douglas) MD-88 (DC-9-88)	49535 / 1347		0287	0387	2 PW JT8D-219	67812	F14Y128		904 / cvtd MD-82
☐	N905DE	Boeing (Douglas) MD-88 (DC-9-88)	53410 / 1992		0092	0592	2 PW JT8D-219	67812	F14Y128		9005
☐	N905DL	Boeing (Douglas) MD-88 (DC-9-88)	49536 / 1348		0087	0487	2 PW JT8D-219	67812	F14Y128		905 / cvtd MD-82
☐	N906DE	Boeing (Douglas) MD-88 (DC-9-88)	53415 / 2027		0092	1092	2 PW JT8D-219	67812	F14Y128		9006
☐	N906DL	Boeing (Douglas) MD-88 (DC-9-88)	49537 / 1355		0087	0487	2 PW JT8D-219	67812	F14Y128		906 / cvtd MD-82
☐	N907DE	Boeing (Douglas) MD-88 (DC-9-88)	53416 / 2029		0092	1092	2 PW JT8D-219	67812	F14Y128		9007
☐	N907DL	Boeing (Douglas) MD-88 (DC-9-88)	49538 / 1365		0087	0587	2 PW JT8D-219	67812	F14Y128		907 / cvtd MD-82
☐	N908DE	Boeing (Douglas) MD-88 (DC-9-88)	53417 / 2032		0092	1192	2 PW JT8D-219	67812	F14Y128		9008
☐	N908DL	Boeing (Douglas) MD-88 (DC-9-88)	49539 / 1366		0087	0587	2 PW JT8D-219	67812	F14Y128		908 / cvtd MD-82
☐	N909DE	Boeing (Douglas) MD-88 (DC-9-88)	53418 / 2033		0092	1192	2 PW JT8D-219	67812	F14Y128		9009
☐	N909DL	Boeing (Douglas) MD-88 (DC-9-88)	49540 / 1395		0087	1287	2 PW JT8D-219	67812	F14Y128		909
☐	N910DE	Boeing (Douglas) MD-88 (DC-9-88)	53419 / 2036		0092	1292	2 PW JT8D-219	67812	F14Y128		9010
☐	N910DL	Boeing (Douglas) MD-88 (DC-9-88)	49541 / 1416		0087	1287	2 PW JT8D-219	67812	F14Y128		910
☐	N911DE	Boeing (Douglas) MD-88 (DC-9-88)	49967 / 2037		0092	0193	2 PW JT8D-219	67812	F14Y128		9011
☐	N911DL	Boeing (Douglas) MD-88 (DC-9-88)	49542 / 1433		1187	1287	2 PW JT8D-219	67812	F14Y128		911
☐	N912DE	Boeing (Douglas) MD-88 (DC-9-88)	49997 / 2038		0092	0193	2 PW JT8D-219	67812	F14Y128		9012
☐	N912DL	Boeing (Douglas) MD-88 (DC-9-88)	49543 / 1434		0087	1287	2 PW JT8D-219	67812	F14Y128		912
☐	N913DE	Boeing (Douglas) MD-88 (DC-9-88)	49956 / 2039		0093	0293	2 PW JT8D-219	67812	F14Y128		9013
☐	N913DL	Boeing (Douglas) MD-88 (DC-9-88)	49544 / 1443		0188	0288	2 PW JT8D-219	67812	F14Y128		913
☐	N914DE	Boeing (Douglas) MD-88 (DC-9-88)	49957 / 2049		0193	0293	2 PW JT8D-219	67812	F14Y128		9014
☐	N914DL	Boeing (Douglas) MD-88 (DC-9-88)	49545 / 1444		0088	0288	2 PW JT8D-219	67812	F14Y128		914
☐	N915DE	Boeing (Douglas) MD-88 (DC-9-88)	53420 / 2050		0093	0393	2 PW JT8D-219	67812	F14Y128		9015
☐	N915DL	Boeing (Douglas) MD-88 (DC-9-88)	49546 / 1447		0088	0388	2 PW JT8D-219	67812	F14Y128		915
☐	N916DE	Boeing (Douglas) MD-88 (DC-9-88)	53421 / 2051		0093	0593	2 PW JT8D-219	67812	F14Y128		9016
☐	N916DL	Boeing (Douglas) MD-88 (DC-9-88)	49591 / 1448		0288	0388	2 PW JT8D-219	67812	F14Y128		916
☐	N917DE	Boeing (Douglas) MD-88 (DC-9-88)	49958 / 2054		0093	0993	2 PW JT8D-219	67812	F14Y128		9017
☐	N917DL	Boeing (Douglas) MD-88 (DC-9-88)	49573 / 1469		0088	0588	2 PW JT8D-219	67812	F14Y128		917
☐	N918DE	Boeing (Douglas) MD-88 (DC-9-88)	49959 / 2055		0093	0993	2 PW JT8D-219	67812	F14Y128		9018
☐	N918DL	Boeing (Douglas) MD-88 (DC-9-88)	49583 / 1470		0088	0588	2 PW JT8D-219	67812	F14Y128		918
☐	N919DE	Boeing (Douglas) MD-88 (DC-9-88)	53422 / 2058		0093	1193	2 PW JT8D-219	67812	F14Y128		9019
☐	N919DL	Boeing (Douglas) MD-88 (DC-9-88)	49584 / 1471		0488	0588	2 PW JT8D-219	67812	F14Y128		919
☐	N920DE	Boeing (Douglas) MD-88 (DC-9-88)	53423 / 2059		0093	1293	2 PW JT8D-219	67812	F14Y128		9020
☐	N920DL	Boeing (Douglas) MD-88 (DC-9-88)	49644 / 1473		0488	0688	2 PW JT8D-219	67812	F14Y128		920
☐	N921DL	Boeing (Douglas) MD-88 (DC-9-88)	49645 / 1480		0088	0688	2 PW JT8D-219	67812	F14Y128		921
☐	N922DL	Boeing (Douglas) MD-88 (DC-9-88)	49646 / 1481		0088	0688	2 PW JT8D-219	67812	F14Y128		922
☐	N923DL	Boeing (Douglas) MD-88 (DC-9-88)	49705 / 1491		0688	0788	2 PW JT8D-219	67812	F14Y128		923
☐	N924DL	Boeing (Douglas) MD-88 (DC-9-88)	49711 / 1492		0088	0788	2 PW JT8D-219	67812	F14Y128		924
☐	N925DL	Boeing (Douglas) MD-88 (DC-9-88)	49712 / 1500		0088	0888	2 PW JT8D-219	67812	F14Y128		925
☐	N926DL	Boeing (Douglas) MD-88 (DC-9-88)	49713 / 1523		0088	1088	2 PW JT8D-219	67812	F14Y128		926
☐	N927DA	Boeing (Douglas) MD-88 (DC-9-88)	49714 / 1524		0088	1188	2 PW JT8D-219	67812	F14Y128		927
☐	N928DL	Boeing (Douglas) MD-88 (DC-9-88)	49715 / 1530		0088	1188	2 PW JT8D-219	67812	F14Y128		928
☐	N929DL	Boeing (Douglas) MD-88 (DC-9-88)	49716 / 1531		0088	1188	2 PW JT8D-219	67812	F14Y128		929
☐	N930DL	Boeing (Douglas) MD-88 (DC-9-88)	49717 / 1532		1088	1188	2 PW JT8D-219	67812	F14Y128		930
☐	N931DL	Boeing (Douglas) MD-88 (DC-9-88)	49718 / 1533		1088	1288	2 PW JT8D-219	67812	F14Y128		931
☐	N932DL	Boeing (Douglas) MD-88 (DC-9-88)	49719 / 1570		0089	0389	2 PW JT8D-219	67812	F14Y128		932
☐	N933DL	Boeing (Douglas) MD-88 (DC-9-88)	49720 / 1571		0089	0389	2 PW JT8D-219	67812	F14Y128		933
☐	N934DL	Boeing (Douglas) MD-88 (DC-9-88)	49721 / 1574		0089	0389	2 PW JT8D-219	67812	F14Y128		934
☐	N935DL	Boeing (Douglas) MD-88 (DC-9-88)	49722 / 1575		0089	0389	2 PW JT8D-219	67812	F14Y128		935
☐	N936DL	Boeing (Douglas) MD-88 (DC-9-88)	49723 / 1576		0289	0489	2 PW JT8D-219	67812	F14Y128		936
☐	N937DL	Boeing (Douglas) MD-88 (DC-9-88)	49810 / 1588		0489	0589	2 PW JT8D-219	67812	F14Y128		937
☐	N938DL	Boeing (Douglas) MD-88 (DC-9-88)	49811 / 1590		0089	0589	2 PW JT8D-219	67812	F14Y128		938
☐	N939DL	Boeing (Douglas) MD-88 (DC-9-88)	49812 / 1593		0089	0589	2 PW JT8D-219	67812	F14Y128		939
☐	N940DL	Boeing (Douglas) MD-88 (DC-9-88)	49813 / 1599		0089	0689	2 PW JT8D-219	67812	F14Y128		940
☐	N941DL	Boeing (Douglas) MD-88 (DC-9-88)	49814 / 1602		0689	0789	2 PW JT8D-219	67812	F14Y128		941
☐	N942DL	Boeing (Douglas) MD-88 (DC-9-88)	49815 / 1605		0689	0789	2 PW JT8D-219	67812	F14Y128		942
☐	N943DL	Boeing (Douglas) MD-88 (DC-9-88)	49816 / 1608		0689	0889	2 PW JT8D-219	67812	F14Y128		943
☐	N944DL	Boeing (Douglas) MD-88 (DC-9-88)	49817 / 1612		0089	0889	2 PW JT8D-219	67812	F14Y128		944
☐	N945DL	Boeing (Douglas) MD-88 (DC-9-88)	49818 / 1613		0789	0889	2 PW JT8D-219	67812	F14Y128		945
☐	N946DL	Boeing (Douglas) MD-88 (DC-9-88)	49819 / 1629		0889	0989	2 PW JT8D-219	67812	F14Y128		946
☐	N947DL	Boeing (Douglas) MD-88 (DC-9-88)	49878 / 1664		0089	1289	2 PW JT8D-219	67812	F14Y128		947
☐	N948DL	Boeing (Douglas) MD-88 (DC-9-88)	49879 / 1666		0089	1289	2 PW JT8D-219	67812	F14Y128		948
☐	N949DL	Boeing (Douglas) MD-88 (DC-9-88)	49880 / 1676		0090	0290	2 PW JT8D-219	67812	F14Y128		949
☐	N950DL	Boeing (Douglas) MD-88 (DC-9-88)	49881 / 1677		0090	0290	2 PW JT8D-219	67812	F14Y128		950
☐	N951DL	Boeing (Douglas) MD-88 (DC-9-88)	49882 / 1679		0190	0290	2 PW JT8D-219	67812	F14Y128		951
☐	N952DL	Boeing (Douglas) MD-88 (DC-9-88)	49883 / 1683		0290	0390	2 PW JT8D-219	67812	F14Y128		952
☐	N953DL	Boeing (Douglas) MD-88 (DC-9-88)	49884 / 1685		0090	0390	2 PW JT8D-219	67812	F14Y128		953
☐	N954DL	Boeing (Douglas) MD-88 (DC-9-88)	49885 / 1689		0090	0390	2 PW JT8D-219	67812	F14Y128		954
☐	N955DL	Boeing (Douglas) MD-88 (DC-9-88)	49886 / 1691		0090	0390	2 PW JT8D-219	67812	F14Y128		955
☐	N956DL	Boeing (Douglas) MD-88 (DC-9-88)	49887 / 1699		0090	0490	2 PW JT8D-219	67812	F14Y128		956
☐	N957DL	Boeing (Douglas) MD-88 (DC-9-88)	49976 / 1700		0090	0490	2 PW JT8D-219	67812	F14Y128		957
☐	N958DL	Boeing (Douglas) MD-88 (DC-9-88)	49977 / 1701		0390	0590	2 PW JT8D-219	67812	F14Y128		958
☐	N959DL	Boeing (Douglas) MD-88 (DC-9-88)	49978 / 1710		0090	0590	2 PW JT8D-219	67812	F14Y128		959
☐	N960DL	Boeing (Douglas) MD-88 (DC-9-88)	49979 / 1711		0090	0590	2 PW JT8D-219	67812	F14Y128		960
☐	N961DL	Boeing (Douglas) MD-88 (DC-9-88)	49980 / 1712		0090	0690	2 PW JT8D-219	67812	F14Y128		961
☐	N962DL	Boeing (Douglas) MD-88 (DC-9-88)	49981 / 1725		0090	0690	2 PW JT8D-219	67812	F14Y128		962
☐	N963DL	Boeing (Douglas) MD-88 (DC-9-88)	49982 / 1726		0090	0690	2 PW JT8D-219	67812	F14Y128		963
☐	N964DL	Boeing (Douglas) MD-88 (DC-9-88)	49983 / 1747		0090	0990	2 PW JT8D-219	67812	F14Y128		964
☐	N965DL	Boeing (Douglas) MD-88 (DC-9-88)	49984 / 1748		0090	0890	2 PW JT8D-219	67812	F14Y128		965
☐	N966DL	Boeing (Douglas) MD-88 (DC-9-88)	53115 / 1795		0090	1290	2 PW JT8D-219	67812	F14Y128		966
☐	N967DL	Boeing (Douglas) MD-88 (DC-9-88)	53116 / 1796		1190	1290	2 PW JT8D-219	67812	F14Y128		967
☐	N968DL	Boeing (Douglas) MD-88 (DC-9-88)	53161 / 1808		0090	0191	2 PW JT8D-219	67812	F14Y128		968
☐	N969DL	Boeing (Douglas) MD-88 (DC-9-88)	53172 / 1810		1290	0191	2 PW JT8D-219	67812	F14Y128		969
☐	N970DL	Boeing (Douglas) MD-88 (DC-9-88)	53173 / 1811		0090	0191	2 PW JT8D-219	67812	F14Y128		970

	registration	type of aircraft	cn/fn	ex/ex*	mfd	del	powered by	mtow kg	configuration	selcal	name/fln/specialitites/remarks
☐	N971DL	Boeing (Douglas) MD-88 (DC-9-88)	53214 / 1823		0091	0291	2 PW JT8D-219	67812	F14Y128		971
☐	N972DL	Boeing (Douglas) MD-88 (DC-9-88)	53215 / 1824		0091	0391	2 PW JT8D-219	67812	F14Y128		972
☐	N973DL	Boeing (Douglas) MD-88 (DC-9-88)	53241 / 1832		0091	0391	2 PW JT8D-219	67812	F14Y128		973
☐	N974DL	Boeing (Douglas) MD-88 (DC-9-88)	53242 / 1833		0091	0391	2 PW JT8D-219	67812	F14Y128		974
☐	N975DL	Boeing (Douglas) MD-88 (DC-9-88)	53243 / 1834		0091	0391	2 PW JT8D-219	67812	F14Y128		975
☐	N976DL	Boeing (Douglas) MD-88 (DC-9-88)	53257 / 1845		0391	0491	2 PW JT8D-219	67812	F14Y128		976
☐	N977DL	Boeing (Douglas) MD-88 (DC-9-88)	53258 / 1848		0091	0491	2 PW JT8D-219	67812	F14Y128		977
☐	N978DL	Boeing (Douglas) MD-88 (DC-9-88)	53259 / 1849		0391	0491	2 PW JT8D-219	67812	F14Y128		978
☐	N979DL	Boeing (Douglas) MD-88 (DC-9-88)	53266 / 1859		0091	0591	2 PW JT8D-219	67812	F14Y128		979
☐	N980DL	Boeing (Douglas) MD-88 (DC-9-88)	53267 / 1860		0091	0591	2 PW JT8D-219	67812	F14Y128		980
☐	N981DL	Boeing (Douglas) MD-88 (DC-9-88)	53268 / 1861		0491	0591	2 PW JT8D-219	67812	F14Y128		981
☐	N982DL	Boeing (Douglas) MD-88 (DC-9-88)	53273 / 1870		0091	0691	2 PW JT8D-219	67812	F14Y128		982
☐	N983DL	Boeing (Douglas) MD-88 (DC-9-88)	53274 / 1873		0091	0691	2 PW JT8D-219	67812	F14Y128		983
☐	N984DL	Boeing (Douglas) MD-88 (DC-9-88)	53311 / 1912		0891	0991	2 PW JT8D-219	67812	F14Y128		984
☐	N985DL	Boeing (Douglas) MD-88 (DC-9-88)	53312 / 1914		0091	0991	2 PW JT8D-219	67812	F14Y128		985
☐	N986DL	Boeing (Douglas) MD-88 (DC-9-88)	53313 / 1924		0091	1191	2 PW JT8D-219	67812	F14Y128		986
☐	N987DL	Boeing (Douglas) MD-88 (DC-9-88)	53338 / 1926		0091	1191	2 PW JT8D-219	67812	F14Y128		987
☐	N988DL	Boeing (Douglas) MD-88 (DC-9-88)	53339 / 1928		0991	1191	2 PW JT8D-219	67812	F14Y128		988
☐	N989DL	Boeing (Douglas) MD-88 (DC-9-88)	53341 / 1936		0091	1291	2 PW JT8D-219	67812	F14Y128		989
☐	N990DL	Boeing (Douglas) MD-88 (DC-9-88)	53342 / 1939		1091	1291	2 PW JT8D-219	67812	F14Y128		990
☐	N991DL	Boeing (Douglas) MD-88 (DC-9-88)	53343 / 1941		0091	1291	2 PW JT8D-219	67812	F14Y128		991
☐	N992DL	Boeing (Douglas) MD-88 (DC-9-88)	53344 / 1943		0091	1291	2 PW JT8D-219	67812	F14Y128		992
☐	N993DL	Boeing (Douglas) MD-88 (DC-9-88)	53345 / 1950		0092	0192	2 PW JT8D-219	67812	F14Y128		993
☐	N994DL	Boeing (Douglas) MD-88 (DC-9-88)	53346 / 1952		0092	0192	2 PW JT8D-219	67812	F14Y128		994
☐	N995DL	Boeing (Douglas) MD-88 (DC-9-88)	53362 / 1955		0092	0292	2 PW JT8D-219	67812	F14Y128		995
☐	N996DL	Boeing (Douglas) MD-88 (DC-9-88)	53363 / 1958		0092	0292	2 PW JT8D-219	67812	F14Y128		996
☐	N997DL	Boeing (Douglas) MD-88 (DC-9-88)	53364 / 1961		0092	0292	2 PW JT8D-219	67812	F14Y128		997
☐	N998DL	Boeing (Douglas) MD-88 (DC-9-88)	53370 / 1963		0092	0392	2 PW JT8D-219	67812	F14Y128		998
☐	N999DN	Boeing (Douglas) MD-88 (DC-9-88)	53371 / 1965		0092	0392	2 PW JT8D-219	67812	F14Y128		999
☐	N901DA	Boeing (Douglas) MD-90-30	53381 / 2100	N902DC*	0094	0695	2 IAE V2525-D5	70760	F12Y138		9201
☐	N902DA	Boeing (Douglas) MD-90-30	53382 / 2094		0095	0295	2 IAE V2525-D5	70760	F12Y138		9202
☐	N903DA	Boeing (Douglas) MD-90-30	53383 / 2095		0095	0395	2 IAE V2525-D5	70760	F12Y138		9203
☐	N904DA	Boeing (Douglas) MD-90-30	53384 / 2096		0095	0395	2 IAE V2525-D5	70760	F12Y138		9204
☐	N905DA	Boeing (Douglas) MD-90-30	53385 / 2097		0095	0495	2 IAE V2525-D5	70760	F12Y138		9205
☐	N906DA	Boeing (Douglas) MD-90-30	53386 / 2099		0095	0795	2 IAE V2525-D5	70760	F12Y138		9206
☐	N907DA	Boeing (Douglas) MD-90-30	53387 / 2115		0095	1095	2 IAE V2525-D5	70760	F12Y138		9207
☐	N908DA	Boeing (Douglas) MD-90-30	53388 / 2117		0095	0995	2 IAE V2525-D5	70760	F12Y138		9208
☐	N909DA	Boeing (Douglas) MD-90-30	53389 / 2122		0095	1095	2 IAE V2525-D5	70760	F12Y138		9209
☐	N910DN	Boeing (Douglas) MD-90-30	53390 / 2123		0095	1195	2 IAE V2525-D5	70760	F12Y138		9210
☐	N911DA	Boeing (Douglas) MD-90-30	53391 / 2126		0096	1295	2 IAE V2525-D5	70760	F12Y138		9211
☐	N912DN	Boeing (Douglas) MD-90-30	53392 / 2136		0096	0796	2 IAE V2525-D5	70760	F12Y138		9212
☐	N913DN	Boeing (Douglas) MD-90-30	53393 / 2154		0096	1096	2 IAE V2525-D5	70760	F12Y138		9213
☐	N914DN	Boeing (Douglas) MD-90-30	53394 / 2156		0096	1196	2 IAE V2525-D5	70760	F12Y138		9214
☐	N915DN	Boeing (Douglas) MD-90-30	53395 / 2159		0096	1196	2 IAE V2525-D5	70760	F12Y138		9215
☐	N916DN	Boeing (Douglas) MD-90-30	53396 / 2161		0096	1296	2 IAE V2525-D5	70760	F12Y138		9216
☐	N371DA	Boeing 737-832	29619 / 115	N1787B*	0098	1098	2 CFMI CFM56-7B26	78245			3701
☐	N372DA	Boeing 737-832	29620 / 118	N1782B*	0098	1098	2 CFMI CFM56-7B26	78245			3702
☐	N373DA	Boeing 737-832	29621 / 123	N1800B*	0098	1098	2 CFMI CFM56-7B26	78245			3703
☐	N374DA	Boeing 737-832	29622 / 128	N1787B*	0098	1198	2 CFMI CFM56-7B26	78245			3704
☐	N375DA	Boeing 737-832	29623 / 145		1198	1198	2 CFMI CFM56-7B26	78245			3705
☐	N376DA	Boeing 737-832	29624 / 176	N1786B*	0199	0199	2 CFMI CFM56-7B26	78245			3706
☐	N377DA	Boeing 737-832	29625				2 CFMI CFM56-7B26	78245			3707 / oo-delivery 0599
☐	N378DA	Boeing 737-832	30265				2 CFMI CFM56-7B26	78245			3708 / oo-delivery 0699
☐	N379DA	Boeing 737-832	30349				2 CFMI CFM56-7B26	78245			3709 / oo-delivery 0899
☐	N380DA	Boeing 737-832	30266				2 CFMI CFM56-7B26	78245			3710 / oo-delivery 0999
☐	N	Boeing 737-832					2 CFMI CFM56-7B26	78245	F16Y138		3711 / oo-delivery 0999
☐	N	Boeing 737-832					2 CFMI CFM56-7B26	78245	F16Y138		3712 / oo-delivery 1099
☐	N	Boeing 737-832					2 CFMI CFM56-7B26	78245	F16Y138		3713 / oo-delivery 1099
☐	N	Boeing 737-832					2 CFMI CFM56-7B26	78245	F16Y138		3714 / oo-delivery 1199
☐	N	Boeing 737-832					2 CFMI CFM56-7B26	78245	F16Y138		3715 / oo-delivery 1199
☐	N	Boeing 737-832					2 CFMI CFM56-7B26	78245	F16Y138		3716 / oo-delivery 1299
☐	N	Boeing 737-832					2 CFMI CFM56-7B26	78245	F16Y138		3717 / oo-delivery 0100
☐	N	Boeing 737-832					2 CFMI CFM56-7B26	78245	F16Y138		3718 / oo-delivery 0200
☐	N	Boeing 737-832					2 CFMI CFM56-7B26	78245	F16Y138		3719 / oo-delivery 0300
☐	N	Boeing 737-832					2 CFMI CFM56-7B26	78245	F16Y138		3720 / oo-delivery 0300
☐	N	Boeing 737-832					2 CFMI CFM56-7B26	78245	F16Y138		3721 / oo-delivery 0400
☐	N	Boeing 737-832					2 CFMI CFM56-7B26	78245	F16Y138		3722 / oo-delivery 0600
☐	N	Boeing 737-832					2 CFMI CFM56-7B26	78245	F16Y138		3723 / oo-delivery 0800
☐	N	Boeing 737-832					2 CFMI CFM56-7B26	78245	F16Y138		3724 / oo-delivery 0800
☐	N	Boeing 737-832					2 CFMI CFM56-7B26	78245	F16Y138		3725 / oo-delivery 0900
☐	N	Boeing 737-832					2 CFMI CFM56-7B26	78245	F16Y138		3726 / oo-delivery 0900
☐	N	Boeing 737-832					2 CFMI CFM56-7B26	78245	F16Y138		3727 / oo-delivery 1000
☐	N	Boeing 737-832					2 CFMI CFM56-7B26	78245	F16Y138		3728 / oo-delivery 1000
☐	N	Boeing 737-832					2 CFMI CFM56-7B26	78245	F16Y138		3729 / oo-delivery 1100
☐	N	Boeing 737-832					2 CFMI CFM56-7B26	78245	F16Y138		3730 / oo-delivery 1100
☐	N	Boeing 737-832					2 CFMI CFM56-7B26	78245	F16Y138		3731 / oo-delivery 1200
☐	N	Boeing 737-832					2 CFMI CFM56-7B26	78245	F16Y138		3732 / oo-delivery 1200
☐	N	Boeing 737-832					2 CFMI CFM56-7B26	78245	F16Y138		3733 / oo-delivery 0101
☐	N	Boeing 737-832					2 CFMI CFM56-7B26	78245	F16Y138		3734 / oo-delivery 0601
☐	N	Boeing 737-832					2 CFMI CFM56-7B26	78245	F16Y138		3735 / oo-delivery 0601
☐	N	Boeing 737-832					2 CFMI CFM56-7B26	78245	F16Y138		3736 / oo-delivery 0701
☐	N	Boeing 737-832					2 CFMI CFM56-7B26	78245	F16Y138		3737 / oo-delivery 0701
☐	N	Boeing 737-832					2 CFMI CFM56-7B26	78245	F16Y138		3738 / oo-delivery 0801
☐	N	Boeing 737-832					2 CFMI CFM56-7B26	78245	F16Y138		3739 / oo-delivery 0801
☐	N	Boeing 737-832					2 CFMI CFM56-7B26	78245	F16Y138		3740 / oo-delivery 0801
☐	N	Boeing 737-832					2 CFMI CFM56-7B26	78245	F16Y138		3741 / oo-delivery 1001
☐	N	Boeing 737-832					2 CFMI CFM56-7B26	78245	F16Y138		3742 / oo-delivery 1201
☐	N	Boeing 737-832					2 CFMI CFM56-7B26	78245	F16Y138		3743 / oo-delivery 0003
☐	N	Boeing 737-832					2 CFMI CFM56-7B26	78245	F16Y138		3744 / oo-delivery 0003
☐	N	Boeing 737-832					2 CFMI CFM56-7B26	78245	F16Y138		3745 / oo-delivery 0003
☐	N	Boeing 737-832					2 CFMI CFM56-7B26	78245	F16Y138		3746 / oo-delivery 0004
☐	N	Boeing 737-832					2 CFMI CFM56-7B26	78245	F16Y138		3747 / oo-delivery 0004
☐	N	Boeing 737-832					2 CFMI CFM56-7B26	78245	F16Y138		3748 / oo-delivery 0004
☐	N	Boeing 737-832					2 CFMI CFM56-7B26	78245	F16Y138		3749 / oo-delivery 0004
☐	N	Boeing 737-832					2 CFMI CFM56-7B26	78245	F16Y138		3750 / oo-delivery 0004
☐	N	Boeing 737-832					2 CFMI CFM56-7B26	78245	F16Y138		3751 / oo-delivery 0004
☐	N	Boeing 737-832					2 CFMI CFM56-7B26	78245	F16Y138		3752 / oo-delivery 0004
☐	N	Boeing 737-832					2 CFMI CFM56-7B26	78245	F16Y138		3753 / oo-delivery 0004
☐	N	Boeing 737-832					2 CFMI CFM56-7B26	78245	F16Y138		3754 / oo-delivery 0004
☐	N	Boeing 737-832					2 CFMI CFM56-7B26	78245	F16Y138		3755 / oo-delivery 0005
☐	N	Boeing 737-832					2 CFMI CFM56-7B26	78245	F16Y138		3756 / oo-delivery 0005
☐	N	Boeing 737-832					2 CFMI CFM56-7B26	78245	F16Y138		3757 / oo-delivery 0005
☐	N	Boeing 737-832					2 CFMI CFM56-7B26	78245	F16Y138		3758 / oo-delivery 0005
☐	N	Boeing 737-832					2 CFMI CFM56-7B26	78245	F16Y138		3759 / oo-delivery 0005
☐	N	Boeing 737-832					2 CFMI CFM56-7B26	78245	F16Y138		3760 / oo-delivery 0005
☐	N	Boeing 737-832					2 CFMI CFM56-7B26	78245	F16Y138		3761 / oo-delivery 0005
☐	N	Boeing 737-832					2 CFMI CFM56-7B26	78245	F16Y138		3762 / oo-delivery 0005
☐	N	Boeing 737-832					2 CFMI CFM56-7B26	78245	F16Y138		3763 / oo-delivery 0006
☐	N	Boeing 737-832					2 CFMI CFM56-7B26	78245	F16Y138		3764 / oo-delivery 0006
☐	N	Boeing 737-832					2 CFMI CFM56-7B26	78245	F16Y138		3765 / oo-delivery 0006
☐	N	Boeing 737-832					2 CFMI CFM56-7B26	78245	F16Y138		3766 / oo-delivery 0006
☐	N	Boeing 737-832					2 CFMI CFM56-7B26	78245	F16Y138		3767 / oo-delivery 0006
☐	N	Boeing 737-832					2 CFMI CFM56-7B26	78245	F16Y138		3768 / oo-delivery 0006
☐	N	Boeing 737-832					2 CFMI CFM56-7B26	78245	F16Y138		3769 / oo-delivery 0006
☐	N	Boeing 737-832					2 CFMI CFM56-7B26	78245	F16Y138		3770 / oo-delivery 0006
☐	N	Boeing 737-832					2 CFMI CFM56-7B26	78245	F16Y138		3771 / oo-delivery 0006
☐	N	Boeing 737-832					2 CFMI CFM56-7B26	78245	F16Y138		3772 / oo-delivery 0007
☐	N	Boeing 737-832					2 CFMI CFM56-7B26	78245	F16Y138		3773 / oo-delivery 0007
☐	N	Boeing 737-832					2 CFMI CFM56-7B26	78245	F16Y138		3774 / oo-delivery 0007
☐	N	Boeing 737-832					2 CFMI CFM56-7B26	78245	F16Y138		3775 / oo-delivery 0007

	registration	type of aircraft	cn/fn	ex/ex*	mfd	del	powered by	mtow kg	configuration	selcal	name/fln/specialitites/remarks
☐	N	Boeing 737-832					2 CFMI CFM56-7B26	78245	F16Y138		3776 / oo-delivery 0007
☐	N	Boeing 737-832					2 CFMI CFM56-7B26	78245	F16Y138		3777 / oo-delivery 0007
☐	N	Boeing 737-832					2 CFMI CFM56-7B26	78245	F16Y138		3778 / oo-delivery 0007
☐	N	Boeing 737-832					2 CFMI CFM56-7B26	78245	F16Y138		3779 / oo-delivery 0007
☐	N	Boeing 737-832					2 CFMI CFM56-7B26	78245	F16Y138		3780 / oo-delivery 0007
☐	N	Boeing 737-832					2 CFMI CFM56-7B26	78245	F16Y138		3781 / oo-delivery 0007
☐	N	Boeing 737-832					2 CFMI CFM56-7B26	78245	F16Y138		3782 / oo-delivery 0007
☐	N	Boeing 737-832					2 CFMI CFM56-7B26	78245	F16Y138		3783 / oo-delivery 0007
☐	N	Boeing 737-832					2 CFMI CFM56-7B26	78245	F16Y138		3784 / oo-delivery 0007
☐	N	Boeing 737-832					2 CFMI CFM56-7B26	78245	F16Y138		3785 / oo-delivery 0007
☐	N	Boeing 737-832					2 CFMI CFM56-7B26	78245	F16Y138		3786 / oo-delivery 0007
☐	N	Boeing 737-832					2 CFMI CFM56-7B26	78245	F16Y138		3787 / oo-delivery 0007
☐	N	Boeing 737-832					2 CFMI CFM56-7B26	78245	F16Y138		3788 / oo-delivery 0007
☐	N	Boeing 737-832					2 CFMI CFM56-7B26	78245	F16Y138		3789 / oo-delivery 0007
☐	N	Boeing 737-832					2 CFMI CFM56-7B26	78245	F16Y138		3790 / oo-delivery 0007
☐	N	Boeing 737-832					2 CFMI CFM56-7B26	78245	F16Y138		3791 / oo-delivery 0007
☐	N	Boeing 737-832					2 CFMI CFM56-7B26	78245	F16Y138		3792 / oo-delivery 0007
☐	N	Boeing 737-832					2 CFMI CFM56-7B26	78245	F16Y138		3793 / oo-delivery 0007
☐	N	Boeing 737-832					2 CFMI CFM56-7B26	78245	F16Y138		3794 / oo-delivery 0007
☐	N	Boeing 737-832					2 CFMI CFM56-7B26	78245	F16Y138		3795 / oo-delivery 0007
☐	N	Boeing 737-832					2 CFMI CFM56-7B26	78245	F16Y138		3796 / oo-delivery 0007
☐	N	Boeing 737-832					2 CFMI CFM56-7B26	78245	F16Y138		3797 / oo-delivery 0007
☐	N	Boeing 737-832					2 CFMI CFM56-7B26	78245	F16Y138		3798 / oo-delivery 0007
☐	N	Boeing 737-832					2 CFMI CFM56-7B26	78245	F16Y138		3799 / oo-delivery 0007
☐	N	Boeing 737-832					2 CFMI CFM56-7B26	78245	F16Y138		3800 / oo-delivery 0007
☐	N	Boeing 737-832					2 CFMI CFM56-7B26	78245	F16Y138		3801 / oo-delivery 0008
☐	N2807W	Boeing 727-247 (A)	20579 / 886		0072	0487	3 PW JT8D-9A	78290	F12Y137	CH-FJ	557
☐	N2809W	Boeing 727-247 (A)	20581 / 890		0072	0487	3 PW JT8D-9A	78290	F12Y137	CH-FM	559
☐	N2810W	Boeing 727-247 (A)	20648 / 895		0072	0487	3 PW JT8D-9A	78290	F12Y137	CH-GJ	560
☐	N2811W	Boeing 727-247 (A)	20649 / 896		0072	0487	3 PW JT8D-9A	78290	F12Y137	CH-KL	561
☐	N2812W	Boeing 727-247 (A)	20868 / 1024		0074	0487	3 PW JT8D-15	86409	F12Y137	JL-DK	562
☐	N2813W	Boeing 727-247 (A)	20869 / 1025		0074	0487	3 PW JT8D-15	86409	F12Y137	JL-DM	563
☐	N2814W	Boeing 727-247 (A)	20870 / 1032		0074	0487	3 PW JT8D-15	86409	F12Y137	JL-EF	564
☐	N2815W	Boeing 727-247 (A)	20871 / 1039		0074	0487	3 PW JT8D-15	86409	F12Y137	JL-EG	565
☐	N2816W	Boeing 727-247 (A)	20872 / 1040		0074	0487	3 PW JT8D-15 (HK3/FDX)	86409	F12Y137	JL-EH	566
☐	N2817W	Boeing 727-247 (A)	20873 / 1043		0074	0487	3 PW JT8D-15 (HK3/FDX)	86409	F12Y137	JL-GH	567
☐	N2819W	Boeing 727-247 (A)	21057 / 1135		0075	0487	3 PW JT8D-15 (HK3/FDX)	86409	F12Y137	HL-AB	568
☐	N2820W	Boeing 727-247 (A)	21058 / 1136		0075	0487	3 PW JT8D-15	86409	F12Y137	HL-AC	569
☐	N2821W	Boeing 727-247 (A)	21059 / 1137		0075	0487	3 PW JT8D-15 (HK3/FDX)	86409	F12Y137	HL-AD	570
☐	N2829W	Boeing 727-247 (A)	21481 / 1338		0078	0487	3 PW JT8D-15 (HK3/FDX)	86409	F12Y137	FG-DK	576
☐	N282WA	Boeing 727-247 (A)	21484 / 1362		0078	0487	3 PW JT8D-15 (HK3/FDX)	86409	F12Y137		579
☐	N283WA	Boeing 727-247 (A)	21485 / 1364		0078	0487	3 PW JT8D-15 (HK3/FDX)	86409	F12Y137		580
☐	N290WA	Boeing 727-247 (A)	22108 / 1587		0080	0487	3 PW JT8D-15 (HK3/FDX)	86409	F12Y137		582
☐	N291WA	Boeing 727-247 (A)	22109 / 1589		0080	0487	3 PW JT8D-15 (HK3/FDX)	86409	F12Y137		583
☐	N292WA	Boeing 727-247 (A)	22110 / 1613		0080	0487	3 PW JT8D-15 (HK3/FDX)	86409	F12Y137		584
☐	N293WA	Boeing 727-247 (A)	22111 / 1615		0080	0487	3 PW JT8D-15 (HK3/FDX)	86409	F12Y137		585
☐	N294WA	Boeing 727-247 (A)	22112 / 1618		0080	0487	3 PW JT8D-15 (HK3/FDX)	86409	F12Y137		586
☐	N295WA	Boeing 727-247 (A)	22532 / 1730		0081	0487	3 PW JT8D-15 (HK3/FDX)	86409	F12Y137		587
☐	N296WA	Boeing 727-247 (A)	22533 / 1736		0081	0487	3 PW JT8D-15 (HK3/FDX)	86409	F12Y137		588
☐	N297WA	Boeing 727-247 (A)	22534 / 1738		0081	0487	3 PW JT8D-15 (HK3/FDX)	86409	F12Y137		589
☐	N400DA	Boeing 727-232 (A)	21144 / 1157		0075	0975	3 PW JT8D-15 (HK3/FDX)	83552	F12Y137	DG-AJ	400
☐	N401DA	Boeing 727-232 (A)	21145 / 1159		0075	0975	3 PW JT8D-15 (HK3/FDX)	83552	F12Y137	DG-AK	401
☐	N402DA	Boeing 727-232 (A)	21146 / 1161		0075	1075	3 PW JT8D-15 (HK3/FDX)	83552	F12Y137	DG-FJ	402
☐	N403DA	Boeing 727-232 (A)	21147 / 1162		0075	1075	3 PW JT8D-15 (HK3/FDX)	83552	F12Y137	BH-GM	403
☐	N404DA	Boeing 727-232 (A)	21148 / 1163		0075	1175	3 PW JT8D-15 (HK3/FDX)	83552	F12Y137	BH-JL	404
☐	N405DA	Boeing 727-232 (A)	21149 / 1164		0075	1175	3 PW JT8D-15 (HK3/FDX)	83552	F12Y137	BH-JM	405
☐	N406DA	Boeing 727-232 (A)	21150 / 1165		0075	1275	3 PW JT8D-15	83552	F12Y137	BH-FM	406
☐	N407DA	Boeing 727-232 (A)	21151 / 1166		0075	1275	3 PW JT8D-15 (HK3/FDX)	83552	F12Y137	BH-GL	407
☐	N408DA	Boeing 727-232 (A)	21152 / 1182		0076	0176	3 PW JT8D-15 (HK3/FDX)	83552	F12Y137		408
☐	N409DA	Boeing 727-232 (A)	21153 / 1183		0076	0176	3 PW JT8D-15 (HK3/FDX)	83552	F12Y137		409
☐	N410DA	Boeing 727-232 (A)	21222 / 1205		0076	0776	3 PW JT8D-15	83552	F12Y137		410
☐	N411DA	Boeing 727-232 (A)	21223 / 1207		0076	0776	3 PW JT8D-15	83552	F12Y137		411
☐	N412DA	Boeing 727-232 (A)	21232 / 1208		0076	0876	3 PW JT8D-9A (HK3/FDX)	83552	Y157/Shuttle		412
☐	N413DA	Boeing 727-232 (A)	21233 / 1211		0076	0876	3 PW JT8D-9A (HK3/FDX)	83552	Y157/Shuttle		413
☐	N414DA	Boeing 727-232 (A)	21256 / 1212		0076	1076	3 PW JT8D-15 (HK3/FDX)	83552	Y157/Shuttle		414
☐	N415DA	Boeing 727-232 (A)	21257 / 1214		0076	1076	3 PW JT8D-9A (HK3/FDX)	83552	Y157/Shuttle		415
☐	N416DA	Boeing 727-232 (A)	21258 / 1223		0076	1276	3 PW JT8D-15 (HK3/FDX)	83552	F12Y137		416
☐	N417DA	Boeing 727-232 (A)	21259 / 1224		0076	1276	3 PW JT8D-9A (HK3/FDX)	83552	Y157/Shuttle		417
☐	N418DA	Boeing 727-232 (A)	21271 / 1242		0076	0177	3 PW JT8D-15 (HK3/FDX)	83552	F12Y137		418
☐	N419DA	Boeing 727-232 (A)	21272 / 1243		0076	0177	3 PW JT8D-15 (HK3/FDX)	83552	F12Y137		419
☐	N420DA	Boeing 727-232 (A)	21273 / 1244		0076	0277	3 PW JT8D-15	83552	F12Y137		420
☐	N421DA	Boeing 727-232 (A)	21274 / 1245		0077	0277	3 PW JT8D-15 (HK3/FDX)	83552	F12Y137		421
☐	N466DA	Boeing 727-232 (A)	20743 / 971		0073	0973	3 PW JT8D-15	83552	F12Y137	AE-DJ	466
☐	N476DA	Boeing 727-232 (A)	20753 / 1012	N1785B*	0074	0474	3 PW JT8D-15	83552	F12Y137	AE-HM	476 / to be wfu 0699
☐	N477DA	Boeing 727-232 (A)	20754 / 1013		0074	0274	3 PW JT8D-15	83552	F12Y137	EF-GH	477 / to be wfu 0699
☐	N478DA	Boeing 727-232 (A)	20755 / 1014		0074	0274	3 PW JT8D-15	83552	F12Y137	EF-GK	478 / to be wfu 0699
☐	N480DA	Boeing 727-232 (A)	20860 / 1038		0074	0574	3 PW JT8D-9A (HK3/FDX)	83552	Y157/Shuttle	AE-DG	480
☐	N481DA	Boeing 727-232 (A)	20861 / 1041		0074	0574	3 PW JT8D-15	83552	Y157/Shuttle	BE-CL	481
☐	N482DA	Boeing 727-232 (A)	20862 / 1042		0074	0674	3 PW JT8D-15	83552	F12Y137	BJ-FG	482
☐	N483DA	Boeing 727-232 (A)	20863 / 1053		0074	0774	3 PW JT8D-15	83552	F12Y137	BJ-FH	483
☐	N484DA	Boeing 727-232 (A)	20864 / 1060		0074	0874	3 PW JT8D-15	83552	F12Y137	BK-AD	484
☐	N485DA	Boeing 727-232 (A)	20865 / 1062		0074	0874	3 PW JT8D-15	83552	F12Y137	DM-FG	485
☐	N489DA	Boeing 727-232 (A)	21019 / 1097		0075	0375	3 PW JT8D-15	83552	F12Y137	BE-CF	489
☐	N490DA	Boeing 727-232 (A)	21020 / 1102		0075	0475	3 PW JT8D-15	83552	F12Y137		490
☐	N491DA	Boeing 727-232 (A)	21060 / 1115		0075	0475	3 PW JT8D-9A (HK3/FDX)	83552	Y157/Shuttle		491
☐	N492DA	Boeing 727-232 (A)	21061 / 1116		0075	0375	3 PW JT8D-15	83552	F12Y137		492
☐	N493DA	Boeing 727-232 (A)	21062 / 1127		0075	0575	3 PW JT8D-15	83552	F12Y137	BE-DF	493
☐	N494DA	Boeing 727-232 (A)	21074 / 1138		0075	0675	3 PW JT8D-15 (HK3/FDX)	83552	F12Y137	DG-KM	494
☐	N495DA	Boeing 727-232 (A)	21075 / 1139		0075	0675	3 PW JT8D-15 (HK3/FDX)	83552	F12Y137	DG-LM	495
☐	N496DA	Boeing 727-232 (A)	21076 / 1140		0075	0775	3 PW JT8D-15 (HK3/FDX)	83552	F12Y137	DF-AC	496
☐	N497DA	Boeing 727-232 (A)	21077 / 1147		0075	0775	3 PW JT8D-15 (HK3/FDX)	83552	F12Y137	DF-AJ	497
☐	N498DA	Boeing 727-232 (A)	21142 / 1155		0075	0875	3 PW JT8D-15 (HK3/FDX)	83552	F12Y137	DG-AC	498
☐	N499DA	Boeing 727-232 (A)	21143 / 1156		0075	0975	3 PW JT8D-15 (HK3/FDX)	83552	F12Y137	DG-AF	499
☐	N501DA	Boeing 727-232 (A)	21303 / 1262		0077	0577	3 PW JT8D-15	86409	F12Y137		501
☐	N502DA	Boeing 727-232 (A)	21304 / 1264		0077	0577	3 PW JT8D-15	86409	F12Y137		502
☐	N503DA	Boeing 727-232 (A)	21305 / 1268		0077	0677	3 PW JT8D-15	86409	F12Y137		503
☐	N504DA	Boeing 727-232 (A)	21306 / 1270		0077	0677	3 PW JT8D-15 (HK3/FDX)	86409	F12Y137		504
☐	N505DA	Boeing 727-232 (A)	21307 / 1272		0077	0677	3 PW JT8D-15 (HK3/FDX)	86409	F12Y137		505
☐	N506DA	Boeing 727-232 (A)	21308 / 1292		0077	0977	3 PW JT8D-15 (HK3/FDX)	86409	F12Y137		506
☐	N507DA	Boeing 727-232 (A)	21309 / 1294		0077	1077	3 PW JT8D-15 (HK3/FDX)	86409	F12Y137		507
☐	N508DA	Boeing 727-232 (A)	21310 / 1298		0077	1077	3 PW JT8D-15 (HK3/FDX)	86409	F12Y137		508
☐	N509DA	Boeing 727-232 (A)	21311 / 1300		0077	1077	3 PW JT8D-15 (HK3/FDX)	86409	F12Y137		509
☐	N510DA	Boeing 727-232 (A)	21312 / 1330		0078	0378	3 PW JT8D-15 (HK3/FDX)	86409	F12Y137	HJ-FG	510
☐	N511DA	Boeing 727-232 (A)	21313 / 1347		0078	0678	3 PW JT8D-15 (HK3/FDX)	86409	F12Y137	HJ-FK	511
☐	N512DA	Boeing 727-232 (A)	21314 / 1358		0078	0678	3 PW JT8D-15 (HK3/FDX)	86409	F12Y137	HJ-FL	512
☐	N513DA	Boeing 727-232 (A)	21315 / 1360		0078	0678	3 PW JT8D-15 (HK3/FDX)	86409	F12Y137	HJ-FM	513
☐	N514DA	Boeing 727-232 (A)	21430 / 1374		0078	0878	3 PW JT8D-15 (HK3/FDX)	86409	F12Y137	HJ-GK	514
☐	N515DA	Boeing 727-232 (A)	21431 / 1376		0078	0878	3 PW JT8D-15 (HK3/FDX)	83552	F12Y137	HJ-GL	515
☐	N516DA	Boeing 727-232 (A)	21432 / 1381		0078	0878	3 PW JT8D-15 (HK3/FDX)	83552	F12Y137	HJ-GM	516
☐	N517DA	Boeing 727-232 (A)	21433 / 1384		0078	0978	3 PW JT8D-15 (HK3/FDX)	83552	F12Y137	BE-FM	517
☐	N518DA	Boeing 727-232 (A)	21469 / 1398		0078	1078	3 PW JT8D-15 (HK3/FDX)	83552	F12Y137	BE-JM	518
☐	N519DA	Boeing 727-232 (A)	21470 / 1400		0078	1078	3 PW JT8D-15 (HK3/FDX)	83552	F12Y137	BJ-CK	519
☐	N520DA	Boeing 727-232 (A)	21471 / 1411		0078	1178	3 PW JT8D-15 (HK3/FDX)	83552	F12Y137	BJ-CM	520
☐	N521DA	Boeing 727-232 (A)	21472 / 1413		0078	1178	3 PW JT8D-15 (HK3/FDX)	83552	F12Y137	BJ-DF	521
☐	N522DA	Boeing 727-232 (A)	21582 / 1422		0078	1278	3 PW JT8D-15 (HK3/FDX)	83552	F12Y137	BE-GL	522
☐	N523DA	Boeing 727-232 (A)	21583 / 1423		0078	1278	3 PW JT8D-15 (HK3/FDX)	83552	F12Y137	BE-GM	523
☐	N524DA	Boeing 727-232 (A)	21584 / 1478		0079	0579	3 PW JT8D-15 (HK3/FDX)	83552	Y157/Shuttle	HL-FJ	524
☐	N525DA	Boeing 727-232 (A)	21585 / 1479		0079	0579	3 PW JT8D-15 (HK3/FDX)	83552	Y157/Shuttle	BE-JL	525
☐	N526DA	Boeing 727-232 (A)	21586 / 1488		0079	0679	3 PW JT8D-15 (HK3/FDX)	83552	Y157/Shuttle	BE-HL	526
☐	N527DA	Boeing 727-232 (A)	21587 / 1492		0079	0679	3 PW JT8D-15 (HK3/FDX)	83552	F12Y137	HL-FG	527

registration	type of aircraft	cn/fn	ex/ex*	mfd	del	powered by	mtow kg	configuration	selcal	name/fln/specialitites/remarks
☐ N528DA	Boeing 727-232 (A)	21702 / 1522		0079	1079	3 PW JT8D-15 (HK3/FDX)	83552	F12Y137	HL-GK	528
☐ N529DA	Boeing 727-232 (A)	21703 / 1550		0079	1179	3 PW JT8D-15 (HK3/FDX)	83552	Y157/Shuttle	EG-AC	529
☐ N531DA	Boeing 727-232 (A)	21814 / 1556		0079	1279	3 PW JT8D-15 (HK3/FDX)	83552	F12Y137		531
☐ N532DA	Boeing 727-232 (A)	22045 / 1602		0080	0480	3 PW JT8D-15 (HK3/FDX)	83552	F12Y137		532
☐ N533DA	Boeing 727-232 (A)	22046 / 1604		0080	0480	3 PW JT8D-15 (HK3/FDX)	83552	F12Y137		533
☐ N534DA	Boeing 727-232 (A)	22047 / 1606		0080	0480	3 PW JT8D-15 (HK3/FDX)	83552	F12Y137		534
☐ N535DA	Boeing 727-232 (A)	22048 / 1608		0080	0580	3 PW JT8D-15 (HK3/FDX)	83552	F12Y137		535
☐ N536DA	Boeing 727-232 (A)	22049 / 1610		0080	0580	3 PW JT8D-15 (HK3/FDX)	83552	F12Y137		536
☐ N537DA	Boeing 727-232 (A)	22073 / 1624		0080	0580	3 PW JT8D-15 (HK3/FDX)	83552	F12Y137		537
☐ N538DA	Boeing 727-232 (A)	22076 / 1656	N1786B*	0080	1080	3 PW JT8D-15 (HK3/FDX)	83552	F12Y137		538
☐ N539DA	Boeing 727-232 (A)	22385 / 1667		0080	1080	3 PW JT8D-15 (HK3/FDX)	83552	F12Y137		539
☐ N540DA	Boeing 727-232 (A)	22386 / 1669		0080	1080	3 PW JT8D-15 (HK3/FDX)	83552	F12Y137		540
☐ N541DA	Boeing 727-232 (A)	22387 / 1672		0080	1080	3 PW JT8D-15 (HK3/FDX)	83552	F12Y137		541
☐ N542DA	Boeing 727-232 (A)	22391 / 1705		0081	0181	3 PW JT8D-15 (HK3/FDX)	83552	F12Y137		542
☐ N543DA	Boeing 727-232 (A)	22392 / 1707		0081	0181	3 PW JT8D-15 (HK3/FDX)	83552	F12Y137		543
☐ N544DA	Boeing 727-232 (A)	22493 / 1741		0081	0581	3 PW JT8D-15 (HK3/FDX)	83552	F12Y137		544
☐ N545DA	Boeing 727-232 (A)	22494 / 1749		0081	0581	3 PW JT8D-15 (HK3/FDX)	83552	F12Y137		545
☐ N546DA	Boeing 727-232 (A)	22677 / 1785		0081	1181	3 PW JT8D-15 (HK3/FDX)	83552	F12Y137		546
☐ N805EA	Boeing 727-225 (A)	22436 / 1677		1180	0997	3 PW JT8D-15 (HK3/FDX)	86409	F12Y137		590
☐ N830WA	Boeing 727-247 (A)	21482 / 1341		0078	0487	3 PW JT8D-15 (HK3/FDX)	86409	F12Y137		577
☐ N831L	Boeing 727-2Q8 (A)	21826 / 1509		0079	0487	3 PW JT8D-15 (HK3/FDX)	86409	F12Y137		581 / lsf Int'l Aircraft Investors Inc.
☐ N831WA	Boeing 727-247 (A)	21483 / 1350		0078	0487	3 PW JT8D-15 (HK3/FDX)	86409	F12Y137		578
☐ N8873Z	Boeing 727-225 (A)	21291 / 1239		0076	0991	3 PW JT8D-15	86409	F12Y137		445 / lsf Finova Capital Corp.
☐ N8875Z	Boeing 727-225 (A)	21293 / 1241		0076	0991	3 PW JT8D-15	86409	F12Y137	BL-EM	441 / lsf Finova Capital Corp.
☐ N8882Z	Boeing 727-225 (A)	21579 / 1412		1178	0897	3 PW JT8D-15 (HK3/FDX)	86409	F12Y137		591
☐ N8889Z	Boeing 727-225 (A)	21858 / 1542		0079	0991	3 PW JT8D-15 (HK3/FDX)	86409	F12Y137	GJ-CE	440
☐ N8890Z	Boeing 727-225 (A)	21859 / 1544		0079	0991	3 PW JT8D-15 (HK3/FDX)	86409	F12Y137	GJ-CF	438
☐ N8891Z	Boeing 727-225 (A)	21860 / 1546		0079	0991	3 PW JT8D-15 (HK3/FDX)	86409	F12Y137	AL-DK	439
☐ N601DL	Boeing 757-232	22808 / 37		0084	0285	2 PW PW2037	108862	F24Y159		601
☐ N602DL	Boeing 757-232	22809 / 39		0084	1184	2 PW PW2037	108862	F24Y159		602
☐ N603DL	Boeing 757-232	22810 / 41		0084	1184	2 PW PW2037	108862	F24Y159		603
☐ N604DL	Boeing 757-232	22811 / 43		0084	1284	2 PW PW2037	108862	F24Y159		604
☐ N605DL	Boeing 757-232	22812 / 46		0084	1284	2 PW PW2037	108862	F24Y159		605
☐ N606DL	Boeing 757-232	22813 / 49		0084	0185	2 PW PW2037	108862	F24Y159		606
☐ N607DL	Boeing 757-232	22814 / 61		0085	0585	2 PW PW2037	108862	F24Y159		607
☐ N608DA	Boeing 757-232	22815 / 64		0085	0585	2 PW PW2037	108862	F24Y159		608
☐ N609DL	Boeing 757-232	22816 / 65		0085	0685	2 PW PW2037	108862	F24Y159		609
☐ N610DL	Boeing 757-232	22817 / 66		0085	0685	2 PW PW2037	108862	F24Y159		610
☐ N611DL	Boeing 757-232	22818 / 71		0085	0885	2 PW PW2037	108862	F24Y159		611
☐ N612DL	Boeing 757-232	22819 / 73		0085	1085	2 PW PW2037	108862	F24Y159		612
☐ N613DL	Boeing 757-232	22820 / 84		0086	0186	2 PW PW2037	108862	F24Y159		613
☐ N614DL	Boeing 757-232	22821 / 85		0086	0186	2 PW PW2037	108862	F24Y159	DP-BG	614
☐ N615DL	Boeing 757-232	22822 / 87		0086	0286	2 PW PW2037	108862	F24Y159		615
☐ N616DL	Boeing 757-232	22823 / 91		0086	0486	2 PW PW2037	108862	F24Y159	DP-BJ	616
☐ N617DL	Boeing 757-232	22907 / 92		0086	0586	2 PW PW2037	108862	F24Y159		617
☐ N618DL	Boeing 757-232	22908 / 95		0086	0486	2 PW PW2037	108862	F24Y159		618
☐ N619DL	Boeing 757-232	22909 / 101		0086	0686	2 PW PW2037	108862	F24Y159		619
☐ N620DL	Boeing 757-232	22910 / 111		0086	1186	2 PW PW2037	108862	F24Y159		620
☐ N621DL	Boeing 757-232	22911 / 112		0086	1186	2 PW PW2037	108862	F24Y159		621
☐ N622DL	Boeing 757-232	22912 / 113		0086	1286	2 PW PW2037	108862	F24Y159		622
☐ N623DL	Boeing 757-232	22913 / 118		0086	0187	2 PW PW2037	108862	F24Y159		623
☐ N624DL	Boeing 757-232	22914 / 120		0087	0187	2 PW PW2037	108862	F24Y159		624
☐ N625DL	Boeing 757-232	22915 / 126		0087	0487	2 PW PW2037	108862	F24Y159		625
☐ N626DL	Boeing 757-232	22916 / 128		0087	0587	2 PW PW2037	108862	F24Y159		626
☐ N627DL	Boeing 757-232	22917 / 129		0087	0487	2 PW PW2037	108862	F24Y159		627
☐ N628DL	Boeing 757-232	22918 / 133		0087	0687	2 PW PW2037	108862	F24Y159		628
☐ N629DL	Boeing 757-232	22919 / 134		0087	1087	2 PW PW2037	108862	F24Y159		629
☐ N630DL	Boeing 757-232	22920 / 135		0087	1187	2 PW PW2037	108862	F24Y159		630
☐ N631DL	Boeing 757-232	23612 / 138		0087	1287	2 PW PW2037	108862	F24Y159		631
☐ N632DL	Boeing 757-232	23613 / 154		0087	1287	2 PW PW2037	108862	F24Y159		632
☐ N633DL	Boeing 757-232	23614 / 157		0087	1287	2 PW PW2037	108862	F24Y159		633
☐ N634DL	Boeing 757-232	23615 / 158		0088	0188	2 PW PW2037	108862	F24Y159		634
☐ N635DL	Boeing 757-232	23762 / 159		0088	0288	2 PW PW2037	108862	F24Y159		635
☐ N636DL	Boeing 757-232	23763 / 164		0088	0388	2 PW PW2037	108862	F24Y159		636
☐ N637DL	Boeing 757-232	23760 / 171		0088	0488	2 PW PW2037	108862	F24Y159		637
☐ N638DL	Boeing 757-232	23761 / 177		0088	0588	2 PW PW2037	108862	F24Y159		638
☐ N639DL	Boeing 757-232	23993 / 198		0088	1188	2 PW PW2037	108862	F24Y159		639
☐ N640DL	Boeing 757-232	23994 / 201		0088	1188	2 PW PW2037	108862	F24Y159		640
☐ N641DL	Boeing 757-232	23995 / 202		0088	1288	2 PW PW2037	108862	F24Y159		641
☐ N642DL	Boeing 757-232	23996 / 205		0088	1288	2 PW PW2037	108862	F24Y159		642
☐ N643DL	Boeing 757-232	23997 / 206		0088	0189	2 PW PW2037	108862	F24Y159		643
☐ N644DL	Boeing 757-232	23998 / 207		0088	0189	2 PW PW2037	108862	F24Y159		644
☐ N645DL	Boeing 757-232	24216 / 216		0089	0489	2 PW PW2037	108862	F24Y159		645
☐ N646DL	Boeing 757-232	24217 / 217		0089	0489	2 PW PW2037	108862	F24Y159		646
☐ N647DL	Boeing 757-232	24218 / 222		0089	0589	2 PW PW2037	108862	F24Y159		647
☐ N648DL	Boeing 757-232	24372 / 223		0089	0589	2 PW PW2037	108862	F24Y159		648
☐ N649DL	Boeing 757-232	24389 / 229		0089	0589	2 PW PW2037	108862	F24Y159		649
☐ N650DL	Boeing 757-232	24390 / 230		0089	0689	2 PW PW2037	108862	F24Y159	EK-GP	650
☐ N651DL	Boeing 757-232	24391 / 238		0089	0789	2 PW PW2037	108862	F24Y159		651
☐ N652DL	Boeing 757-232	24392 / 239		0089	0789	2 PW PW2037	108862	F24Y159		652
☐ N653DL	Boeing 757-232	24393 / 261		0090	0290	2 PW PW2037	108862	F24Y159		653
☐ N654DL	Boeing 757-232	24394 / 264		0090	0290	2 PW PW2037	108862	F24Y159		654
☐ N655DL	Boeing 757-232	24395 / 265		0090	0290	2 PW PW2037	108862	F24Y159		655
☐ N656DL	Boeing 757-232	24396 / 266		0090	0390	2 PW PW2037	108862	F24Y159		656
☐ N657DL	Boeing 757-232	24419 / 286		0090	0590	2 PW PW2037	108862	F24Y159		657
☐ N658DL	Boeing 757-232	24420 / 287		0090	0590	2 PW PW2037	108862	F24Y159		658
☐ N659DL	Boeing 757-232	24421 / 293		0090	0690	2 PW PW2037	108862	F24Y159		659
☐ N660DL	Boeing 757-232	24422 / 294		0090	0690	2 PW PW2037	108862	F24Y159		660
☐ N661DN	Boeing 757-232	24972 / 335		0090	1290	2 PW PW2037	108862	F24Y159		661
☐ N662DN	Boeing 757-232	24991 / 342		0091	0191	2 PW PW2037	108862	F24Y159		662
☐ N663DN	Boeing 757-232	24992 / 343		0091	0291	2 PW PW2037	108862	F24Y159		663
☐ N664DN	Boeing 757-232	25012 / 347		0091	0291	2 PW PW2037	108862	F24Y159		664
☐ N665DN	Boeing 757-232	25013 / 349		0091	0391	2 PW PW2037	108862	F24Y159	CQ-FL	665
☐ N666DN	Boeing 757-232	25034 / 354		0091	0391	2 PW PW2037	108862	F24Y159		666
☐ N667DN	Boeing 757-232	25035 / 355		0091	0391	2 PW PW2037	108862	F24Y159		667
☐ N668DN	Boeing 757-232	25141 / 376		0091	0691	2 PW PW2037	108862	F24Y159		668
☐ N669DN	Boeing 757-232	25142 / 377		0091	0691	2 PW PW2037	108862	F24Y159		669
☐ N670DN	Boeing 757-232	25331 / 415		1291	0192	2 PW PW2037	108862	F24Y159		670
☐ N671DN	Boeing 757-232	25332 / 416		1291	0192	2 PW PW2037	108862	F24Y159		671
☐ N672DL	Boeing 757-232	25977 / 429		0092	0292	2 PW PW2037	108862	F24Y159		672
☐ N673DL	Boeing 757-232	25978 / 430		0092	0292	2 PW PW2037	108862	F24Y159		673
☐ N674DL	Boeing 757-232	25979 / 439		0092	0392	2 PW PW2037	108862	F24Y159		674
☐ N675DL	Boeing 757-232	25980 / 448		0092	0492	2 PW PW2037	108862	F24Y159		675
☐ N676DL	Boeing 757-232	25981 / 455		0092	0592	2 PW PW2037	108862	F24Y159		676
☐ N677DL	Boeing 757-232	25982 / 456		0092	0592	2 PW PW2037	108862	F24Y159	CQ-HM	677
☐ N678DL	Boeing 757-232	25983 / 465		0092	0692	2 PW PW2037	108862	F24Y159		678
☐ N679DA	Boeing 757-232	26955 / 500		1092	1192	2 PW PW2037	108862	F24Y159		679
☐ N680DA	Boeing 757-232	26956 / 502		1192	1192	2 PW PW2037	108862	F24Y159		680
☐ N681DA	Boeing 757-232	26957 / 516		0193	0193	2 PW PW2037	108862	F24Y159		681
☐ N682DA	Boeing 757-232	26958 / 518		0193	0193	2 PW PW2037	108862	F24Y159		682
☐ N683DA	Boeing 757-232	27103 / 533		0393	0393	2 PW PW2037	108862	F24Y159		683
☐ N684DA	Boeing 757-232	27104 / 535		0393	0393	2 PW PW2037	108862	F24Y159		684
☐ N685DA	Boeing 757-232	27588 / 667		0095	0395	2 PW PW2037	108862	F24Y159		685
☐ N686DA	Boeing 757-232	27589 / 689		0095	0995	2 PW PW2037	108862	F24Y159		686
☐ N687DL	Boeing 757-232	27586 / 800		0098	0598	2 PW PW2037	108862	F24Y159		687
☐ N688DL	Boeing 757-232	27587 / 803		0098	0598	2 PW PW2037	108862	F24Y159		688
☐ N689DL	Boeing 757-232	27172 / 807		0098	0698	2 PW PW2037	108862	F24Y159		689
☐ N690DL	Boeing 757-232	27585 / 808		0098	0698	2 PW PW2037	108862	F24Y159		690
☐ N692DL	Boeing 757-232	29724 / 820	N1799B*	0098	0998	2 PW PW2037	108862	F24Y159		692
☐ N693DL	Boeing 757-232	29725 / 826	N1799B*	0098	1098	2 PW PW2037	108862	F24Y159		693

registration	type of aircraft	cn/fn	ex/ex*	mfd	del	powered by	mtow kg	configuration	selcal	name/fln/specialitites/remarks
☐ N694DL	Boeing 757-232	29726 / 831		0098	1198	2 PW PW2037	108862	F24Y159		694
☐ N695DL	Boeing 757-232	29727 / 838	N1795B*	0098	1298	2 PW PW2037	108862	F24Y159		695
☐ N696DL	Boeing 757-232	29728 / 845		0199	0199	2 PW PW2037	108862	F24Y159		696
☐ N697DL	Boeing 757-232					2 PW PW2037	108862	F24Y159		697 / oo-delivery 0799
☐ N698DL	Boeing 757-232					2 PW PW2037	108862	F24Y159		698 / oo-delivery 0899
☐ N699DL	Boeing 757-232					2 PW PW2037	108862	F24Y159		699 / oo-delivery 0999
☐ N750AT	Boeing 757-212	23126 / 45	9V-SGL	0084	0996	2 PW PW2037	108862	F24Y159		6902
☐ N751AT	Boeing 757-212	23125 / 44	9V-SGK	0084	1196	2 PW PW2037	108862	F24Y159		6901
☐ N752AT	Boeing 757-212	23128 / 48	9V-SGN	0084	1096	2 PW PW2037	108862	F24Y159		6904
☐ N757AT	Boeing 757-212	23127 / 47	9V-SGM	0084	1196	2 PW PW2037	108862	F24Y159		6903
☐ N900PC	Boeing 757-26D	28446 / 740		0197	0197	2 PW PW2037	108862	F24Y159		691
☐ N	Boeing 757-232					2 PW PW2037	108862	F24Y159		6700 / oo-delivery 0999
☐ N	Boeing 757-232					2 PW PW2037	108862	F24Y159		6701 / oo-delivery 1099
☐ N	Boeing 757-232					2 PW PW2037	108862	F24Y159		6702 / oo-delivery 1199
☐ N	Boeing 757-232					2 PW PW2037	108862	F24Y159		6703 / oo-delivery 0100
☐ N	Boeing 757-232					2 PW PW2037	108862	F24Y159		6704 / oo-delivery 0300
☐ N	Boeing 757-232					2 PW PW2037	108862	F24Y159		6705 / oo-delivery 0300
☐ N	Boeing 757-232					2 PW PW2037	108862	F24Y159		6706 / oo-delivery 0400
☐ N	Boeing 757-232					2 PW PW2037	108862	F24Y159		6707 / oo-delivery 0500
☐ N	Boeing 757-232					2 PW PW2037	108862	F24Y159		6708 / oo-delivery 0700
☐ N	Boeing 757-232					2 PW PW2037	108862	F24Y159		6709 / oo-delivery 0800
☐ N	Boeing 757-232					2 PW PW2037	108862	F24Y159		6710 / oo-delivery 0900
☐ N	Boeing 757-232					2 PW PW2037	108862	F24Y159		6711 / oo-delivery 1000
☐ N	Boeing 757-232					2 PW PW2037	108862	F24Y159		6712 / oo-delivery 1200
☐ N	Boeing 757-232					2 PW PW2037	108862	F24Y159		6713 / oo-delivery 1200
☐ N	Boeing 757-232					2 PW PW2037	108862	F24Y159		6714 / oo-delivery 0301
☐ N101DA	Boeing 767-232	22213 / 6		0082	0383	2 GE CF6-80A	140614	F18Y186	BG-DK	101
☐ N102DA	Boeing 767-232	22214 / 12		0082	1082	2 GE CF6-80A	140614	F18Y186	BG-DL	102 / Spirit of Delta
☐ N103DA	Boeing 767-232	22215 / 17		0082	1082	2 GE CF6-80A	140614	F18Y186	BG-DM	103
☐ N104DA	Boeing 767-232	22216 / 26		0082	1282	2 GE CF6-80A	140614	F18Y186	BG-EH	104
☐ N105DA	Boeing 767-232	22217 / 27		0082	0183	2 GE CF6-80A	140614	F18Y186	BG-EJ	105
☐ N106DA	Boeing 767-232	22218 / 31		0082	1282	2 GE CF6-80A	140614	F18Y186	BG-EK	106
☐ N107DL	Boeing 767-232	22219 / 37		0082	0183	2 GE CF6-80A	140614	F18Y186	EM-FG	107
☐ N108DL	Boeing 767-232	22220 / 38		0082	0183	2 GE CF6-80A	140614	F18Y186	EM-FH	108
☐ N109DL	Boeing 767-232	22221 / 53		0083	0483	2 GE CF6-80A	140614	F18Y186	EM-FJ	109
☐ N110DL	Boeing 767-232	22222 / 56		0083	0683	2 GE CF6-80A	140614	F18Y186	EM-FK	110
☐ N111DN	Boeing 767-232	22223 / 74		0083	1183	2 GE CF6-80A	140614	F18Y186	EM-FL	111
☐ N112DL	Boeing 767-232	22224 / 76		0083	1283	2 GE CF6-80A	140614	F18Y186	EM-GH	112
☐ N113DA	Boeing 767-232	22225 / 77		0083	1283	2 GE CF6-80A	140614	F18Y186	EM-GJ	113
☐ N114DL	Boeing 767-232	22226 / 78		0083	0184	2 GE CF6-80A2	140614	F18Y186	EM-GK	114
☐ N115DA	Boeing 767-232	22227 / 83		0084	0284	2 GE CF6-80A2	140614	F18Y186	EM-GL	115
☐ N116DL	Boeing 767-332	23275 / 136		0086	1186	2 GE CF6-80A2	159211	F24Y228	EM-HJ	116
☐ N117DL	Boeing 767-332	23276 / 151		0086	1286	2 GE CF6-80A2	159211	F24Y228	EM-HK	117
☐ N118DL	Boeing 767-332	23277 / 152		0086	1186	2 GE CF6-80A2	159211	F24Y228	EM-HL	118
☐ N119DL	Boeing 767-332	23278 / 153		0086	1286	2 GE CF6-80A2	159211	F24Y228		119
☐ N120DL	Boeing 767-332	23279 / 154		0086	1286	2 GE CF6-80A2	159211	F24Y228	EM-JL	120
☐ N121DE	Boeing 767-332	23435 / 162		0087	0387	2 GE CF6-80A2	159211	F24Y228		121
☐ N122DL	Boeing 767-332	23436 / 163		0087	0387	2 GE CF6-80A2	159211	F24Y228		122
☐ N123DN	Boeing 767-332	23437 / 188		0087	1187	2 GE CF6-80A2	159211	F24Y228	BJ-GM	123
☐ N124DE	Boeing 767-332	23438 / 189		0087	1187	2 GE CF6-80A2	159211	F24Y228		124
☐ N125DL	Boeing 767-332	24075 / 200		0088	0288	2 GE CF6-80A2	159211	F24Y228		125
☐ N126DL	Boeing 767-332	24076 / 201		0088	0388	2 GE CF6-80A2	159211	F24Y228		126
☐ N127DL	Boeing 767-332	24077 / 203		0088	0488	2 GE CF6-80A2	159211	F24Y228	EK-LM	127
☐ N128DL	Boeing 767-332	24078 / 207		0088	0488	2 GE CF6-80A2	159211	F24Y228	EM-BD	128
☐ N129DL	Boeing 767-332	24079 / 209		0088	0588	2 GE CF6-80A2	159211	F24Y228		129
☐ N130DL	Boeing 767-332	24080 / 216		0088	0588	2 GE CF6-80A2	159211	F24Y228		130
☐ N131DN	Boeing 767-332	24852 / 320		0090	0890	2 GE CF6-80A2	159211	F24Y228		131
☐ N132DN	Boeing 767-332	24981 / 345		0091	0191	2 GE CF6-80A2	159211	F24Y228	HQ-CK	132
☐ N133DN	Boeing 767-332	24982 / 348		0091	0191	2 GE CF6-80A2	159211	F24Y228	HQ-CD	133
☐ N134DL	Boeing 767-332	25123 / 353		0091	0291	2 GE CF6-80A2	159211	F24Y228		134
☐ N135DL	Boeing 767-332	25145 / 356		0091	0391	2 GE CF6-80A2	159211	F24Y228		135
☐ N136DL	Boeing 767-332	25146 / 374		0091	0691	2 GE CF6-80A2	159211	F24Y228		136
☐ N137DL	Boeing 767-332	25306 / 392		0091	0991	2 GE CF6-80A2	159211	F24Y228		137
☐ N138DL	Boeing 767-332	25409 / 410		1291	0192	2 GE CF6-80A2	159211	F24Y228	HQ-CL	138
☐ N139DL	Boeing 767-332	25984 / 427		0092	0592	2 GE CF6-80A2	159211	F24Y228	HQ-CM	139
☐ N140LL	Boeing 767-332	25988 / 499		0093	0693	2 PW PW4060	159211	F24Y228		1401
☐ N1402A	Boeing 767-332	25989 / 506		0093	0793	2 PW PW4060	159211	F24Y228		1402
☐ N143DA	Boeing 767-332	25991 / 721		1098	1098	2 PW PW4060	159211	F24Y228		1403
☐ N144DA	Boeing 767-332	27584				2 PW PW4060	159211	F24Y228		1404 / oo-delivery 0599
☐ N1501P	Boeing 767-3P6 (ER)	24983 / 334	A4O-GL	0090	0497	2 GE CF6-80C2B4	175540	C48Y147	MS-FQ	1501
☐ N152DL	Boeing 767-3P6 (ER)	24984 / 339	A4O-GM	0090	0297	2 GE CF6-80C2B4	175540	C48Y147	MS-GJ	1502
☐ N153DL	Boeing 767-3P6 (ER)	24985 / 340	A4O-GN	0090	0297	2 GE CF6-80C2B4	175540	C48Y147	MS-GL	1503
☐ N154DL	Boeing 767-3P6 (ER)	25241 / 389	A4O-GO	0091	0497	2 GE CF6-80C2B4	175540	C48Y147	PQ-CF	1504
☐ N155DL	Boeing 767-3P6 (ER)	25269 / 390	A4O-GP	0091	0697	2 GE CF6-80C2B4	175540	C48Y147	PQ-DJ	1505
☐ N156DL	Boeing 767-3P6 (ER)	25354 / 406	A4O-GR	0091	0797	2 GE CF6-80C2B4	175540	C48Y147	PQ-DK	1506
☐ N169DZ	Boeing 767-332 (ER)	29689 / 706		0098	0698	2 GE CF6-80C2B6F	181437	C48Y147	DF-MR	169
☐ N171DN	Boeing 767-332 (ER)	24759 / 304		0090	0690	2 PW PW4060	181437	C48Y147	EQ-AB	171
☐ N171DZ	Boeing 767-332 (ER)	29690 / 717		0998	0998	2 GE CF6-80C2B6F	181437	C48Y147		1701
☐ N172DN	Boeing 767-332 (ER)	24775 / 312		0090	0690	2 PW PW4060	181437	C48Y147	EQ-AC	172
☐ N172DZ	Boeing 767-332 (ER)	29691 / 719		0998	0998	2 GE CF6-80C2B6F	181437	C48Y147		1702
☐ N173DN	Boeing 767-332 (ER)	24800 / 313		0090	0690	2 PW PW4060	181437	C48Y147	EQ-AD	173
☐ N173DZ	Boeing 767-332 (ER)	29692 / 723		0098	1198	2 GE CF6-80C2B6F	181437	C48Y147		1703
☐ N174DN	Boeing 767-332 (ER)	24802 / 317		0090	0790	2 PW PW4060	181437	C48Y147	EQ-AF	174
☐ N174DZ	Boeing 767-332 (ER)	29693 / 725		0098	1198	2 GE CF6-80C2B6F	181437	C48Y147		1704
☐ N175DN	Boeing 767-332 (ER)	24803 / 318		0090	0790	2 PW PW4060	181437	C48Y147	EQ-AG	175
☐ N176DN	Boeing 767-332 (ER)	25061 / 341		0090	1290	2 PW PW4060	181437	C48Y147	EQ-AH	176
☐ N177DN	Boeing 767-332 (ER)	25122 / 346		0091	0191	2 PW PW4060	181437	C48Y147	EQ-AJ	177
☐ N175DZ	Boeing 767-332 (ER)	29696		0099	0399	2 GE CF6-80C2B6F	181437	C48Y147		1705
☐ N178DN	Boeing 767-332 (ER)	25143 / 349		0091	0491	2 PW PW4060	181437	C48Y147	EQ-AK	178
☐ N176DZ	Boeing 767-332 (ER)	29697		0099	0499	2 GE CF6-80C2B6F	181437	C48Y147		1706
☐ N179DN	Boeing 767-332 (ER)	25144 / 350		0091	0491	2 PW PW4060	181437	C48Y147	EQ-AL	179
☐ N177DZ	Boeing 767-332 (ER)	29698				2 GE CF6-80C2B6F	181437	C48Y147		1707 / oo-delivery 0599
☐ N180DN	Boeing 767-332 (ER)	25985 / 428		0092	0492	2 PW PW4060	181437	C48Y147	CD-AS	180
☐ N181DN	Boeing 767-332 (ER)	25986 / 446		0092	0892	2 PW PW4060	181437	C48Y147	CD-BR	181
☐ N182DN	Boeing 767-332 (ER)	25987 / 461		0092	1192	2 PW PW4060	181437	C48Y147	CD-BS	182
☐ N183DN	Boeing 767-332 (ER)	27110 / 492		0093	0493	2 PW PW4060	181437	C48Y147	CD-ER	183
☐ N184DN	Boeing 767-332 (ER)	27111 / 496		0093	0593	2 PW PW4060	181437	C48Y147	CD-ES	184
☐ N185DN	Boeing 767-332 (ER)	27961 / 576		0095	0595	2 PW PW4060	181437	C48Y147	FL-AQ	185
☐ N186DN	Boeing 767-332 (ER)	27962 / 585		0095	0795	2 PW PW4060	181437	C48Y147	FL-BQ	186
☐ N187DN	Boeing 767-332 (ER)	27582 / 617		0096	0696	2 PW PW4060	181437	C48Y147	DF-KR	187
☐ N188DN	Boeing 767-332 (ER)	27583 / 631		0096	1096	2 PW PW4060	181437	C48Y147	DF-LR	188
☐ N189DN	Boeing 767-332 (ER)	25990 / 646		0097	0297	2 PW PW4060	181437	C48Y147	DF-LS	189
☐ N190DN	Boeing 767-332 (ER)	28447 / 653		0097	0397	2 PW PW4060	181437	C48Y147	DG-PR	190
☐ N191DN	Boeing 767-332 (ER)	28448 / 654		0097	0497	2 PW PW4060	181437	C48Y147	DG-QR	191
☐ N192DN	Boeing 767-332 (ER)	28449 / 664		0697	0697	2 PW PW4060	181437	C48Y147	AF-PS	192
☐ N193DN	Boeing 767-332 (ER)	28450 / 671		0897	0897	2 PW PW4060	181437	C48Y147	AF-QS	193
☐ N194DN	Boeing 767-332 (ER)	28451 / 675		0997	0997	2 PW PW4060	181437	C48Y147	AG-BP	194
☐ N195DN	Boeing 767-332 (ER)	28452 / 676		0997	0997	2 PW PW4060	181437	C48Y147	AG-CP	195
☐ N196DN	Boeing 767-332 (ER)	28453 / 679		1097	1097	2 PW PW4060	181437	C48Y147	AG-EP	196
☐ N197DN	Boeing 767-332 (ER)	28454 / 683		1297	1297	2 PW PW4060	181437	C48Y147	AG-HP	197
☐ N198DN	Boeing 767-332 (ER)	28455 / 685		0098	0298	2 PW PW4060	181437	C48Y147	AG-PQ	198
☐ N199DN	Boeing 767-332 (ER)	28456 / 690		0098	0398	2 PW PW4060	181437	C48Y147	AH-JP	199
☐ N1200K	Boeing 767-332 (ER)	28457 / 696		0098	0498	2 PW PW4060	181437	C48Y147	AK-MR	200
☐ N1201P	Boeing 767-332 (ER)	28458 / 697		0098	0498	2 PW PW4060	181437	C48Y147	AK-PS	201
☐ N394DL	Boeing 767-324 (ER)	27394 / 572	HL7505	0095	0498	2 GE CF6-80C2B7F	181437	C48Y147		1521 / lsf GECA
☐ N1602	Boeing 767-332 (ER)	29694 / 735		0199	0199	2 GE CF6-80C2B6F	181437	C48Y147		1602
☐ N1603	Boeing 767-332 (ER)	29695 / 739		0299	0299	2 GE CF6-80C2B6F	181437	C48Y147		1603
☐ N1604	Boeing 767-332 (ER)					2 GE CF6-80C2B6F	181437	C48Y147		1604 / oo-delivery 0599
☐ N1605	Boeing 767-332 (ER)					2 GE CF6-80C2B6F	181437	C48Y147		1605 / oo-delivery 0699
☐ N1606P	Boeing 767-332 (ER)					2 GE CF6-80C2B6F	181437	C48Y147		1606 / oo-delivery 0699

☐ N1607	Boeing 767-332 (ER)					2 GE CF6-80C2B6F	181437	C48Y147		1607 / oo-delivery 0300
☐ N	Boeing 767-432 (ER)					2 GE CF6-80C2B7F	204117			1801 / oo-delivery 0500
☐ N	Boeing 767-432 (ER)					2 GE CF6-80C2B7F	204117			1802 / oo-delivery 0600
☐ N	Boeing 767-432 (ER)					2 GE CF6-80C2B7F	204117			1803 / oo-delivery 0700
☐ N	Boeing 767-432 (ER)					2 GE CF6-80C2B7F	204117			1804 / oo-delivery 0800
☐ N	Boeing 767-432 (ER)					2 GE CF6-80C2B7F	204117			1805 / oo-delivery 0900
☐ N	Boeing 767-432 (ER)					2 GE CF6-80C2B7F	204117			1806 / oo-delivery 0900
☐ N	Boeing 767-432 (ER)					2 GE CF6-80C2B7F	204117			1807 / oo-delivery 0100
☐ N	Boeing 767-432 (ER)					2 GE CF6-80C2B7F	204117			1808 / oo-delivery 1000
☐ N	Boeing 767-432 (ER)					2 GE CF6-80C2B7F	204117			1809 / oo-delivery 1100
☐ N	Boeing 767-432 (ER)					2 GE CF6-80C2B7F	204117			1810 / oo-delivery 1100
☐ N	Boeing 767-432 (ER)					2 GE CF6-80C2B7F	204117			1811 / oo-delivery 1200
☐ N	Boeing 767-432 (ER)					2 GE CF6-80C2B7F	204117			1812 / oo-delivery 1200
☐ N	Boeing 767-432 (ER)					2 GE CF6-80C2B7F	204117			1813 / oo-delivery 0101
☐ N	Boeing 767-432 (ER)					2 GE CF6-80C2B7F	204117			1814 / oo-delivery 0201
☐ N	Boeing 767-432 (ER)					2 GE CF6-80C2B7F	204117			1815 / oo-delivery 0201
☐ N	Boeing 767-432 (ER)					2 GE CF6-80C2B7F	204117			1816 / oo-delivery 0201
☐ N	Boeing 767-432 (ER)					2 GE CF6-80C2B7F	204117			1818 / oo-delivery 0301
☐ N	Boeing 767-432 (ER)					2 GE CF6-80C2B7F	204117			1819 / oo-delivery 0401
☐ N	Boeing 767-432 (ER)					2 GE CF6-80C2B7F	204117			1820 / oo-delivery 0401
☐ N	Boeing 767-432 (ER)					2 GE CF6-80C2B7F	204117			1821 / oo-delivery 0501
☐ N	Boeing 767-432 (ER)					2 GE CF6-80C2B7F	204117			1817 / oo-delivery 0901
☐ N718DA	Lockheed L-1011-385-1 TriStar 1	193C-1097		0074	1274	3 RR RB211-22B	199581	F32Y270	AB-EF	718 / to be wfu 0799
☐ N720DA	Lockheed L-1011-385-1 TriStar 1	193C-1136		0076	0576	3 RR RB211-22B	199581	F32Y270	AB-EH	720 / to be wfu 0799
☐ N721DA	Lockheed L-1011-385-1 TriStar 1	193C-1139		0076	0676	3 RR RB211-22B	199581	F32Y270	AB-EJ	721 / to be wfu 0799
☐ N723DA	Lockheed L-1011-385-1 TriStar 1	193C-1150		0077	1277	3 RR RB211-22B	199581	F32Y270		723 / to be wfu 0799
☐ N727DA	Lockheed L-1011-385-1 TriStar 1	193C-1167		0079	0679	3 RR RB211-22B	199581	F32Y270		727
☐ N728DA	Lockheed L-1011-385-1 TriStar 1	193C-1173		0079	1179	3 RR RB211-22B	199581	F32Y270		728
☐ N729DA	Lockheed L-1011-385-1 TriStar 1	193C-1180		0080	0380	3 RR RB211-22B	199581	F32Y270		729
☐ N730DA	Lockheed L-1011-385-1 TriStar 1	193C-1199		0080	1280	3 RR RB211-22B	199581	F32Y270		730
☐ N1731D	Lockheed L-1011-385-1 TriStar 1	193C-1200		0080	1280	3 RR RB211-22B	199581	F32Y270	EM-DF	731
☐ N1732D	Lockheed L-1011-385-1 TriStar 1	193C-1213		0081	0681	3 RR RB211-22B	199581	F32Y270		732
☐ N733DS	Lockheed L-1011-385-1 TriStar 1	193C-1224		0081	1281	3 RR RB211-22B	199581	F32Y270		733
☐ N1734D	Lockheed L-1011-385-1 TriStar 1	193C-1225		0081	1281	3 RR RB211-22B	199581	F32Y270		734
☐ N735D	Lockheed L-1011-385-1 TriStar 1	193C-1226		0081	0182	3 RR RB211-22B	199581	F30Y270		735
☐ N736DY	Lockheed L-1011-385-1-15 TriStar 250	193C-1227		0082	0382	3 RR RB211-524B4	224982	F32Y265	AK-CH	736 / cvtd TriStar 1
☐ N737D	Lockheed L-1011-385-1-15 TriStar 250	193C-1228		0082	0582	3 RR RB211-524B4	224982	F32Y265	AK-CH	737 / cvtd TriStar 1
☐ N1738D	Lockheed L-1011-385-1-15 TriStar 250	193C-1234		0082	0782	3 RR RB211-524B4	224982	F32Y265	BH-EM	738 / cvtd TriStar 1
☐ N1739D	Lockheed L-1011-385-1-15 TriStar 250	193C-1237		0082	1282	3 RR RB211-524B4	224982	F32Y265	BH-FK	739 / cvtd TriStar 1
☐ N740DA	Lockheed L-1011-385-1-15 TriStar 250	193C-1244		0083	0483	3 RR RB211-524B4	224982	F32Y265	AH-CM	740 / cvtd TriStar 1
☐ N741DA	Lockheed L-1011-385-1-15 TriStar 250	193C-1245		0083	0583	3 RR RB211-524B4	224982	F32Y265	DF-AK	741 / cvtd TriStar 1
☐ N786DL	Lockheed L-1011-385-1 TriStar 1	193A-1123	N332EA	0075	1291	3 RR RB211-22B	199581	F32Y270	HM-KL	786 / to be wfu 0799
☐ N790DL	Lockheed L-1011-385-1 TriStar 1	193A-1143	N336EA	0077	0991	3 RR RB211-22B	199581	F32Y270	GH-CK	790 / to be wfu 0799
☐ N753DA	Lockheed L-1011-385-3 TriStar 500	193W-1189		0080	0880	3 RR RB211-524B4	228611	F12C23Y183	AH-EK	753
☐ N754DL	Lockheed L-1011-385-3 TriStar 500	193Y-1181	N504PA	0080	0984	3 RR RB211-524B4	228611	F12C23Y183	AK-CM	754
☐ N755DL	Lockheed L-1011-385-3 TriStar 500	193Y-1184	N505PA	0080	0185	3 RR RB211-524B4	228611	F12C23Y183	AK-DF	755
☐ N756DR	Lockheed L-1011-385-3 TriStar 500	193Y-1185	N507PA	0080	0185	3 RR RB211-524B4	228611	F12C23Y183	AK-DJ	756
☐ N760DH	Lockheed L-1011-385-3 TriStar 500	193Y-1194	N510PA	0080	0688	3 RR RB211-524B4	234054	F12C23Y183	JM-DL	760 / to be wfu 0699
☐ N764DA	Lockheed L-1011-385-3 TriStar 500	193H-1202	C-GAGF	0081	0891	3 RR RB211-524B4	224982	F12C23Y183	CK-BF	764
☐ N765DA	Lockheed L-1011-385-3 TriStar 500	193H-1206	C-GAGG	0081	0891	3 RR RB211-524B4	224982	F12C23Y183	CK-BH	765
☐ N766DA	Lockheed L-1011-385-3 TriStar 500	193H-1207	C-GAGH	0081	0192	3 RR RB211-524B4	234054	F12C23Y183	CK-BJ	766
☐ N767DA	Lockheed L-1011-385-3 TriStar 500	193H-1209	C-GAGI	0081	0492	3 RR RB211-524B4	234054	F12C23Y183	CK-BL	767
☐ N768DL	Lockheed L-1011-385-3 TriStar 500	193H-1216	C-GAGJ	0081	1291	3 RR RB211-524B4	234054	F12C23Y183	CK-BM	768
☐ N769DL	Lockheed L-1011-385-3 TriStar 500	193H-1218	C-GAGK	0081	0192	3 RR RB211-524B4	234054	F12C23Y183	CK-DE	769
☐ N860DA	Boeing 777-232 (ER)	29951		0099	0399	2 RR Trent 892	294200			7001
☐ N861DA	Boeing 777-232 (ER)	29952		0099	0399	2 RR Trent 892	294200			7002
☐ N862DA	Boeing 777-232 (ER)	29734				2 RR Trent 892	294200			7003 / oo-delivery 0899
☐ N863DA	Boeing 777-232 (ER)	29735				2 RR Trent 892	294200			7004 / oo-delivery 0999
☐ N864DA	Boeing 777-232 (ER)	29736				2 RR Trent 892	294200			7005 / oo-delivery 1099
☐ N865DA	Boeing 777-232 (ER)	29737				2 RR Trent 892	294200			7006 / oo-delivery 1199
☐ N866DA	Boeing 777-232 (ER)	29738				2 RR Trent 892	294200			7007 / oo-delivery 1199
☐ N867DA	Boeing 777-232 (ER)					2 RR Trent 892	294200			7008 / oo-delivery 1299
☐ N868DA	Boeing 777-232 (ER)					2 RR Trent 892	294200			7009 / oo-delivery 1299
☐ N869DA	Boeing 777-232 (ER)					2 RR Trent 892	294200			7010 / oo-delivery 0300
☐ N870DA	Boeing 777-232 (ER)					2 RR Trent 892	294200			7011 / oo-delivery 0400
☐ N871DA	Boeing 777-232 (ER)					2 RR Trent 892	294200			7012 / oo-delivery 0600
☐ N872DA	Boeing 777-232 (ER)					2 RR Trent 892	294200			7013 / oo-delivery 0800
☐ N873DA	Boeing 777-232 (ER)					2 RR Trent 892	294200			7014 / oo-delivery 0900
☐ N801DE	Boeing (Douglas) MD-11	48472 / 480		0092	0392	3 PW PW4460	280320	C50Y219	EQ-AM	801
☐ N802DE	Boeing (Douglas) MD-11	48473 / 481		0092	0492	3 PW PW4460	280320	C50Y219	EQ-AP	802
☐ N803DE	Boeing (Douglas) MD-11	48474 / 485	N30075*	0091	0392	3 PW PW4460	280320	C50Y210	EQ-BC	803
☐ N804DE	Boeing (Douglas) MD-11	48475 / 489		0092	0592	3 PW PW4460	280320	C50Y210	EQ-BD	804
☐ N805DE	Boeing (Douglas) MD-11	48476 / 510		0092	1192	3 PW PW4460	280320	C50Y210	EQ-BF	805
☐ N806DE	Boeing (Douglas) MD-11	48477 / 511		0092	1192	3 PW PW4460	280320	C50Y210	EQ-BG	806
☐ N807DE	Boeing (Douglas) MD-11	48478 / 514		0092	1292	3 PW PW4460	280320	C50Y210	EQ-BH	807
☐ N808DE	Boeing (Douglas) MD-11	48479 / 536		0093	1093	3 PW PW4460	280320	C50Y219	EQ-BJ	808
☐ N809DE	Boeing (Douglas) MD-11	48480 / 538		0093	1193	3 PW PW4460	280320	C50Y219	EQ-BK	809
☐ N810DE	Boeing (Douglas) MD-11	48565 / 542		0093	0394	3 PW PW4460	280320	C50Y219	EQ-BL	810
☐ N811DE	Boeing (Douglas) MD-11	48566 / 543		0093	0394	3 PW PW4460	280320	C50Y219	EQ-BM	811
☐ N812DE	Boeing (Douglas) MD-11	48601 / 562	N6202S*	0094	0496	3 PW PW4460	280320	C50Y219	DH-CE	813 / The Centennial Spirit / Olympic cs
☐ N813DE	Boeing (Douglas) MD-11	48600 / 560	N9017S*	0094	1096	3 PW PW4460	280320	C50Y219	DK-CF	812
☐ N814DE	Boeing (Douglas) MD-11	48623 / 605		0096	0996	3 PW PW4460	280320	C50Y219	DL-CE	814
☐ N815DE	Boeing (Douglas) MD-11	48624 / 622		0098	0298	3 PW PW4460	280320	C50Y219	DL-CK	815

DELTA JET, Ltd — **Hartford-Brainard, CT**

PO Box 1379, Hartford, CT 06143, USA ☎ (860) 241-8891 Tx: none Fax: (860) 246-2953 SITA: n/a
F: 1980 n/a Head: Herbert S. Chambers Net: n/a

☐ N142HC	Agusta A109C	7677	N109AB	0093	0396	2 AN 250-C20R/1	2720			

DENALI AIR (Ronald D. Rosso dba / Seasonal April-September ops only) — **McKinley National Park, AK**

PO Box 82, Denali National Park, AK 99755, USA ☎ (907) 683-2261 Tx: none Fax: (907) 683-1347 SITA: n/a
F: 1986 n/a Head: Ronald D. Rosso Net: n/a

☐ N28897	Cessna U206G Stationair	U20603957		0077	0490	1 CO IO-520-F	1633			
☐ N1621U	Cessna T207 Turbo Skywagon	20700221		0073	1090	1 CO TSIO-520-G	1724			
☐ N75773	Cessna T207A Turbo Stationair 8 II	20700643		0080	0390	1 CO TSIO-520-M	1724			lsf Arctic Wings
☐ N9794M	Cessna T207A Turbo Stationair 8 II	20700730		0081	0887	1 CO TSIO-520-M	1724			
☐ N14PW	Beech C-45H (18)	AF-314	N14DA	0051	0193	2 PW R-985-AN14B	3969			
☐ N766L	Beech D18S	A-952		0053	0696	2 PW R-985-AN14B	3969			

DENALI HUNT CONSULTANTS OF ALASKA (Stanley L. Parkerson dba) — **Fairbanks-Int'l, AK**

1441 Ivans Alley, Fairbanks, AK 99709, USA ☎ (907) 455-6056 Tx: none Fax: none SITA: n/a
F: 1990 n/a Head: Stanley L. Parkerson Net: n/a

☐ N8594Q	Cessna U206F Stationair II	U20603450		0076	0492	1 CO IO-520-F	1633			Floats / Wheels

DENALI WINGS, Inc. (formerly Denali Wings Air Tours) — **Healy, AK & Carlsbad-McClellan Palomar, CA**

PO Box 254, Healy, AK 99743, USA ☎ (907) 683-2245 Tx: none Fax: (714) 240-9726 SITA: n/a
F: 1993 n/a Head: Michael C. Lauver Net: n/a Winter- & Maintenance basis: 629 Camino de Los Mares, Suite 306, San Clemente, CA 92672. Phone: (714) 240-3752.

☐ N5040U	Cessna 206 Super Skywagon	206-0040		0063	0294	1 CO IO-520-A	1588			
☐ N8499Q	Cessna U206F Stationair II	U20603357		0076	0495	1 CO IO-520-F	1633			
☐ N901KA	Piper PA-34-200 Seneca	34-7450045		0074	0397	2 LY IO-360-C1E6	1905			lsf pvt

DESERT AIRLINES (Desert Airlines & Aeromedical Transportation, Inc. dba) — **Palm Springs-Bermuda Dunes, CA**

79-880 Ave 42, Bermuda Dunes, CA 92201, USA ☎ (760) 345-1331 Tx: none Fax: (760) 345-1027 SITA: n/a
F: 1972 n/a Head: Darryl L. Silverstein Net: n/a

☐ N328JK	Learjet 24B	24B-212	N328TL	0069	0397	2 GE CJ610-6	6123			lsf 429K Corp.
☐ N251DS	Learjet 25D	25D-218	N14NA	0077	0597	2 GE CJ610-8A	6804			
☐ N377Q	Learjet 25D	25D-257	N377C	0078	1294	2 GE CJ610-8A	6804			

DESERT AIR TRANSPORT, Inc. — **Salt Lake City-Int'l, UT**

180 North 2400 West, Salt Lake City, UT 84116, USA ☎ (801) 539-8555 Tx: none Fax: (801) 539-1923 SITA: n/a
F: 1996 n/a Head: Dennis Gladwin Net: n/a

☐ N105CA	Boeing (Douglas) DC-3C (C-47B-1-DK)	25720	N85FA	0044	0498	2 PW R-1830	12202	Freighter		lsf Alta Leasing Inc.

318 registration type of aircraft cn/fn ex/ex* mfd del powered by mtow kg configuration selcal name/fln/specialitites/remarks

☐ N19906	Boeing (Douglas) DC-3C (C-47-DL)	4747	41-38644	0043	0096	2 PW R-1830	12202	Freighter		lsf Alta Leasing Inc.
☐ N44587	Boeing (Douglas) DC-3C (C-47A-DK)	12857	N353SA	0044	1297	2 PW R-1830	12202	Freighter		lsf Alta Leasing Inc.

DETROIT RED WINGS – Flight Operations Dept. (Flight Operations Dept. of the Detroit Red Wings)

Pontiac-Oakland, MI

7151 Astro Road North, Hangar 1, Waterford, MI 48327, USA ☎ (248) 666-3677 Tx: none Fax: (248) 666-8891 SITA: n/a
F: 1991 ⁂ n/a Head: Mike Ilitch Net: n/a Operates executive flights for its parent company exclusively for the transport of hockey-teams to sporting events.

☐ N682RW	BAe (BAC) One-Eleven 401AK	061	EI-BWR	0066	0790	2 RR Spey 511-14	40597	Exec 40 Pax		Red Bird One

DHL AIRWAYS, Inc. = ER / DHL (DHL WORLDWIDE EXPRESS) (Subsidiary of DHL Corporation)

Cincinnati, OH

PO Box 75122, Cincinnati, OH 45275, USA ☎ (606) 283-2232 Tx: 6842160 cvghub Fax: (606) 525-1998 SITA: n/a
F: 1982 ⁂ 42000 Head: Patrick Foley IATA: 423 ICAO: DAHL Net: http://www.dhl.com All aircraft are operated in the colors & on behalf of DHL WORLDWIDE EXPRESS.
Additional (various) aircraft are operated on behalf of DHL AIRWAYS on a contract basis by: AEROPAK (N), AIR CARGO CARRIERS (N), AIR TAHOMA (N), AIRWAVE TRANSPORT (C), ALL CANADA EXPRESS (C), AMERICAN INTERNATIONAL (N), AMERIFLIGHT (N), AVCENTER (N), CHARTER AMERICA (N), CIRRUSAIR (N), CLASSIC CARGO (N), CUSTOM AIR TRANSPORT (N), DOWNEAST CHARTER FLIGHTS (N), EVERGREEN INTERNATIONAL (N), EXPRESS ONE (N), JET-PROP EXPRESS (N), KIITY HAWK AIR CARGO (N), MARTINAIRE (N), MERLIN EXPRESS (N), MID-ATLANTIC FREIGHT (N), SUPERIOR AVIATION (N), T.D. AVIATION (N), UNION FLIGHTS (N), USA JET (Active Aero) (N) & WESTEX AIRLINES (C). For details – see under each company.

☐ N7DQ	Bell 206L-1 LongRanger II	45685	N2022G	0081	0782	1 AN 250-C28B	1882	Freighter		
☐ N701DH	Boeing 727-30C	19011 / 387	N727JE	0367	0586	3 PW JT8D-7	76884	Freighter		
☐ N702DH	Boeing 727-30C	19793 / 519	N748EV	0168	1189	3 PW JT8D-7 (HK3/FDX)	76884	Freighter		
☐ N703DH	Boeing 727-30C	19010 / 382	N750EV	0367	1189	3 PW JT8D-7B (HK3/FDX)	76884	Freighter		
☐ N705DH	Boeing 727-22C	19191 / 386	N725PL	0367	0384	3 PW JT8D-7B (HK3/FDX)	76884	Freighter		
☐ N706DH	Boeing 727-22C	19192 / 388	N726PL	0467	0484	3 PW JT8D-7B (HK3/FDX)	76884	Freighter		
☐ N707DH	Boeing 727-22 (F)	18321 / 122	N8700R	0365	0488	3 PW JT8D-7B (HK3/FDX)	75024	Freighter		cvtd -22
☐ N708DH	Boeing 727-25 (F)	18275 / 101	N238DH	1264	0784	3 PW JT8D-7	72802	Freighter		cvtd -25
☐ N709DH	Boeing 727-82C	19968 / 660	N251DH	1168	1088	3 PW JT8D-7	76884	Freighter		
☐ N712DH	Boeing 727-29 (F)	19401 / 419	N711GN	0667	0188	3 PW JT8D-7	76884	Freighter		cvtd -29
☐ N715DH	Boeing 727-155C	19618 / 461	N720JE	0967	0586	3 PW JT8D-7B (HK3/FDX)	76884	Freighter		
☐ N717DH	Boeing 727-23 (F)	19389 / 343	N514FE	0066	1191	3 PW JT8D-7B (HK3/FDX)	76884	Freighter		cvtd -23
☐ N12305	Boeing 727-231 (F)	19562 / 576		0068	0198	3 PW JT8D-9A (HK3/FDX)	76884	Freighter	AE-FJ	lsf / opb LHN in DHL colors / cvtd -231
☐ N15DF	Boeing 727-264 (F) (A) (QWS)	20710 / 975	C-GRYO	0073	0997	3 PW JT8D-17R (HK3/DUG)	86410	Freighter		lsf / opb LHN in DHL colors / cvtd -264
☐ N622DH	Boeing 727-264 (F) (A)	20896 / 1051	XA-DUK	0074	0895	3 PW JT8D-17R (HK3/FDX)	83552	Freighter		lst / opb CMI / cvtd -264
☐ N623DH	Boeing 727-264 (F) (A)	20895 / 1049	XA-DUJ	0074	0995	3 PW JT8D-17R (HK3/FDX)	83552	Freighter		lst / opb CMI / cvtd -264
☐ N624DH	Boeing 727-264 (F) (A)	20709 / 950	XA-CUB	0073	0396	3 PW JT8D-17R (HK3/FDX)	83779	Freighter		lst / opb CMI / cvtd -264
☐ N625DH	Boeing 727-264 (F) (A)	20780 / 986	XA-CUN	0073	1195	3 PW JT8D-17R (HK3/FDX)	83552	Freighter		lst / opb CMI / cvtd -264
☐ N626DH	Boeing 727-277 (F) (A)	22644 / 1768	N72381	0081	1097	3 PW JT8D-15 (HK3/FDX)	89358	Freighter		lst / opb CMI / cvtd -277
☐ N627DH	Boeing 727-277 (F) (A)	22641 / 1753	N6393X	0081	1297	3 PW JT8D-15 (HK3/FDX)	89358	Freighter		lst / opb CMI / cvtd -277
☐ N6813	Boeing 727-223 (F) (A)	19488 / 588		0668	0398	3 PW JT8D-9A (HK3/FDX)	80966	Freighter	BK-FM	lsf / opb LHN in DHL colors / cvtd -223
☐ N6819	Boeing 727-223 (F) (A)	19494 / 661		1168	0398	3 PW JT8D-9A (HK3/FDX)	80966	Freighter	CE-GH	lsf / opb LHN in DHL colors / cvtd -223
☐ N720DH	Boeing 727-228 (F)	19544 / 562	N606AR	0468	1090	3 PW JT8D-7B (HK3/FDX)	78245	Freighter		cvtd -228
☐ N721DH	Boeing 727-228 (F)	19545 / 564	N605AR	0568	0990	3 PW JT8D-7 (HK3/FDX)	78245	Freighter		The Blue Grass State / cvtd -228
☐ N724DH	Boeing 727-228 (F)	19862 / 685	N603AR	0269	0890	3 PW JT8D-7B (HK3/FDX)	78245	Freighter		cvtd -228
☐ N726DH	Boeing 727-228 (F)	20409 / 845	N604AR	1270	0890	3 PW JT8D-7B (HK3/FDX)	78245	Freighter		cvtd -228
☐ N727DH	Boeing 727-228 (F)	20204 / 778	F-BPJM	1269	0191	3 PW JT8D-7B (HK3/FDX)	78245	Freighter		cvtd -228
☐ N740DH	Boeing 727-2Q9 (F) (A)	21930 / 1508	N200AV	0079	1194	3 PW JT8D-17R (HK3/FDX)	89676	Freighter		cvtd -2Q9
☐ N741DH	Boeing 727-2Q9 (F) (A)	21931 / 1531	N202AV	0079	1194	3 PW JT8D-17R (HK3/FDX)	89676	Freighter		cvtd -2Q9
☐ N742DH	Boeing 727-225 (F) (A)	21290 / 1238	N8872Z	0076	0595	3 PW JT8D-15 (HK3/FDX)	86409	Freighter		cvtd -225
☐ N74318	Boeing 727-231 (F)	20051 / 708		0069	1297	3 PW JT8D-9A (HK3/FDX)	78245	Freighter	DM-GJ	lsf / opb LHN in DHL colors / cvtd -231
☐ N801DH	Boeing (Douglas) DC-8-73F	46033 / 431	C-FTIK	0069	1094	4 CFMI CFM56-2C	161025	Freighter	DG-CL	New York Transit / cvtd -63F
☐ N802DH	Boeing (Douglas) DC-8-73F	46076 / 451	C-FTIO	0069	1293	4 CFMI CFM56-2C	161025	Freighter	EF-HK	cvtd -63/-63F
☐ N803DH	Boeing (Douglas) DC-8-73F	46123 / 508	C-FTIQ	0070	1293	4 CFMI CFM56-2C	161025	Freighter	FG-AC	cvtd -63/-63F
☐ N804DH	Boeing (Douglas) DC-8-73F	46124 / 511	C-FTIR	0070	0794	4 CFMI CFM56-2C	161025	Freighter	FG-AK	cvtd -63/-63F
☐ N805DH	Boeing (Douglas) DC-8-73F	46125 / 515	C-FTIS	0070	1093	4 CFMI CFM56-2C	161025	Freighter	FG-AJ	cvtd -63/-63F
☐ N806DH	Boeing (Douglas) DC-8-73F	46002 / 394	N815UP	0068	0395	4 CFMI CFM56-2C	161025	Freighter	BH-CF	cvtd -63F (CF)
☐ N807DH	Boeing (Douglas) DC-8-73F	45990 / 375	N816UP	0068	0395	4 CFMI CFM56-2C	161025	Freighter	BH-FG	cvtd -63F (CF)
☐ N873SJ	Boeing (Douglas) DC-8-73F	46091 / 519	F-GESM	0070	0898	4 CFMI CFM56-2C	161025	Freighter		lsf GECA / cvtd -63F (CF)
☐ N	Airbus Industrie A300B4-103 (F)	071	HS-THN	0078		2 GE CF6-50C2	157500	Freighter		oo-del.0099/ex THA/cvtd A300B4-2C/-103
☐ N	Airbus Industrie A300B4-103 (F)	084	HS-THP	0079		2 GE CF6-50C2	157500	Freighter		oo-del.0099/ex THA/cvtd A300B4-2C/-103
☐ N	Airbus Industrie A300B4-103 (F)	085	HS-THR	0079		2 GE CF6-50C2	157500	Freighter		oo-del.0099/ex THA/cvtd A300B4-2C/-103
☐ N	Airbus Industrie A300B4-203 (F)	141	HS-THT	0081		2 GE CF6-50C2	165000	Freighter		oo-delivery 0099/ex THA/cvtd A300B4-203
☐ N	Airbus Industrie A300B4-203 (F)	149	HS-THW	0081		2 GE CF6-50C2	165000	Freighter		oo-delivery 0099/ex THA/cvtd A300B4-203
☐ N	Airbus Industrie A300B4-203 (F)	249	HS-THX	0083		2 GE CF6-50C2	165000	Freighter		oo-delivery 0099/ex THA/cvtd A300B4-203
☐ N	Airbus Industrie A300B4-203 (F)	265	HS-THY	0083		2 GE CF6-50C2	165000	Freighter		oo-delivery 0099/ex THA/cvtd A300B4-203

DIAMOND AVIATION, Inc. = SPK (formerly Diamond Airways)

Statesboro-Municipal, GA

PO Box 1240, Statesboro, GA 30458-1240, USA ☎ (912) 764-9181 Tx: none Fax: (912) 489-8978 SITA: n/a
F: 1983 ⁂ n/a Head: Joseph A. Cleland ICAO: SPARKLE Net: n/a

☐ N22522	Mitsubishi MU-2J (MU-2B-35)	625	C-GSKM	0074	1294	2 GA TPE331-6-251M	4899			
☐ N360RA	Mitsubishi MU-2B-60 Cargoliner	740SA	XA-RWP	0079	0397	2 GA TPE331-10-501M	5250	Freighter		Cavenaugh SCD conversion

DILLON AERO, Inc. (Subsidiary of Dillon Precision Products, Inc.)

Scottsdale, AZ

8009 Dillons Way, Scottsdale, AZ 85260, USA ☎ (602) 948-8009 Tx: none Fax: (602) 998-2786 SITA: n/a
F: 1988 ⁂ n/a Head: Michael J. Dillon Net: n/a

☐ N380F	MD Helicopters MD 500E (Hughes 369E)	0123E	N5254N	0085	0589	1 AN 250-C20B	1361			lsf Dillon Precision Products Inc.
☐ N205DP	Bell UH-1H (205)	10715	68-16056	0068	0697	1 LY T53-L-13	4309			lsf Dillon Precision Products Inc.

DODITA AIR CARGO, Inc.

San Juan-Luis Munoz Marin Int'l, PR

118, 4th Villamar, Isla Verde, PR 00979, USA ☎ (787) 268-2341 Tx: none Fax: (787) 791-8385 SITA: n/a
F: 1990 ⁂ n/a Head: Lisa Rosello Net: n/a

☐ N4826C	Convair 440-38 Metropolitan	391		1256	0897	2 PW R-2800	21772	Freighter		
☐ N912AL	Convair 440-78 (SCD)	353	PZ-TGA	0056	0897	2 PW R-2800	21772	Freighter		cvtd CV440-78

DODSON INTERNATIONAL AIR – DIA (Dodson International Corp. dba)

Covington-Municipal, GA

PO Box 1447, Oxford, GA 30054-1447, USA ☎ (770) 489-2272 Tx: none Fax: (770) 489-2275 SITA: n/a
F: 1987 ⁂ 26 Head: Donald R. Dodson Net: n/a

☐ N27371	Piper PA-31-310 Navajo C	31-7712100		0077	0595	2 LY TIO-540-J2BD	2948	Freighter		lsf pvt
☐ N2805J	Boeing (Douglas) DC-3C (C-47B-1-DL)	20835	43-16369	0044	1195	2 PW R-1830	12202	Freighter		
☐ N303SF	Boeing (Douglas) DC-3C (C-47A-45-DL)	9967	N103CA	0042	0298	2 PW R-1830	12202	Freighter		
☐ N308SF	Boeing (Douglas) DC-3C (C-47A-65-DL)	18984	84	0043	0792	2 PW R-1830	12202	Freighter		
☐ N4550J	Boeing (Douglas) DC-3C (C-47-DL)	6055	F-OGFJ	0042	0593	2 PW R-1830	12202	Freighter		lsf R & R Partnership
☐ N683LS	Boeing (Douglas) DC-3C	43084	N121L	0046	0289	2 PW R-1830	12202	Freighter		
☐ N9382	Boeing (Douglas) DC-3C (C-47A-10-DK)	12331	42-92521	0043	0298	2 PW R-1830	12202	Freighter		

DOMTRAVE AIRWAYS, Inc.

St. Croix-Alexander Hamilton, VI

PO Box 1438, Kingshill, St. Croix, VI 00850, USA ☎ (340) 778-9555 Tx: none Fax: (340) 692-2877 SITA: n/a
F: 1981 ⁂ 4 Head: Bernadette Pringle Net: n/a

☐ N84DT	Twin (Aero) Turbo Commander 690	11031	N1SS	0072	0491	2 GA TPE331-5-251K	4649			lsf pvt

DON DAVIS AVIATION, Inc.

Henderson-City County, KY

2154 Highway, 136W, Henderson, KY 42420, USA ☎ (502) 826-6000 Tx: none Fax: (502) 826-6040 SITA: n/a
F: 1957 ⁂ n/a Head: Donald C. Davis Net: n/a

☐ N2766L	Bell 206B JetRanger III	2776		0079	0187	1 AN 250-C20B	1451			
☐ N310DB	Cessna 310R II	310R0891		0077	0281	2 CO IO-520-M	2495			
☐ N371JD	Cessna 402B II	402B1322		0078	0193	2 CO TSIO-520-E	2858			

DOTHAN AIR CHARTER, Inc. = NAP (Sister company of Dothan Jet Charter / formerly Napier Air Service, Inc.)

Dothan, AL

300 Flight Line Drive, Suite 100, Dothan, AL 36303, USA ☎ (334) 983-4541 Tx: none Fax: (334) 983-4814 SITA: n/a
F: 1948 ⁂ n/a Head: George A. Dezso ICAO: NAPIER Net: n/a

☐ N7554Q	Cessna 310Q	310Q0054		0070		2 CO IO-470-VO	2404			lsf Lower Alabama Air Inc.

DOUG GEETING AVIATION (Douglas E. Geeting dba)

Talkeetna, AK

Box 42, Talkeetna, AK 99676, USA ☎ (907) 733-2366 Tx: none Fax: (907) 733-1000 SITA: n/a
F: 1984 ⁂ n/a Head: Douglas E. Geeting Net: http://www.alaska.net/nairtours/ Aircraft below MTOW 1361kg: Piper PA-18 (on Wheel-Skis)

☐ N1473F	Cessna A185F Skywagon	18502851		0075	1095	1 CO IO-520-D	1520			Wheel-Skis
☐ N185DG	Cessna A185F Skywagon II	18503802	N8848D	0079	0287	1 CO IO-520-D	1520			Wheel-Skis
☐ N333DG	Cessna A185F Skywagon	18503234	N93430	0077	0889	1 CO IO-520-D	1520			Wheel-Skis

DOWNTOWN AIRCHARTER (Downtown Airpark, Inc. dba)

Oklahoma City-Downtown Airpark, OK

1701 South Western Avenue, Oklahoma City, OK 73109, USA ☎ (405) 634-6472 Tx: none Fax: (405) 634-4942 SITA: n/a
F: 1973 ⁂ n/a Head: Jim Johnson Net: http://www.downtownairpark.com Aircraft below MTOW 1361kg: Cessna 172

☐ N15690	Beech Baron 58	TH-1544		0088	0596	2 CO IO-550-C	2495			
☐ N340MP	Cessna 340A II	340A0359		0077	1196	2 CO TSIO-520-N	2717			lsf Brett Aviation Llc

319 registration type of aircraft cn/fn ex/ex* mfd del powered by mtow kg configuration selcal name/fln/specialitites/remarks

☐ N31AW	Cessna 414 II	414-0803		0075	0897	2 CO TSIO-520-N	2880		lsf Natcat Airline Inc.
☐ N1553N	Beech King Air C90A	LJ-1238		0090	0297	2 PWC PT6A-21	4581		lsf Quick Way Aviation of Nevada

DRAKE & DRAKE, Inc.

Kennett-Memorial, MO

Route 4, Box 4136, Gravois Mills, MO 65037, USA ☎ (573) 374-5321 Tx: none Fax: (573) 374-9141 SITA: n/a
F: 1991 n/a Head: Donald D. Drake Net: n/a

☐ N862DD	Beech King Air 200	BB-298	N5110	0077	0493	2 PWC PT6A-41	5670		

DUNCAN AVIATION, Inc. = PHD

Lincoln-Municipal, NE

PO Box 81887, Lincoln, NE 68501, USA ☎ (402) 475-2611 Tx: none Fax: (402) 475-5541 SITA: n/a
F: 1964 n/a Head: John R. Duncan ICAO: PANHANDLE Net: http://www.duncanav.com

☐ N811DA	Piper PA-42 Cheyenne III	42-8001029	N40PT	0081	0895	2 PWC PT6A-41	5080		
☐ N824LJ	Learjet 23	23-083		0066	1289	2 GE CJ610-4	5670		
☐ N72DA	Learjet 35A	35A-098	N44UC	0077	0887	2 GA TFE731-2-2B	8301		
☐ N85DA	Cessna 650 Citation III	650-0073	N673JS	0085	0295	2 GA TFE731-3B-100S	9752		

DWYAIR AIR CHARTER = DFS (Dwyer Aircraft Sales, Inc. dba)

Mason City-Municipal, IA

PO Box 239, Mason City, IA 50401, USA ☎ (515) 423-6453 Tx: none Fax: (515) 357-5087 SITA: n/a
F: 1952 n/a Head: Hubert J. Dwyer ICAO: DWYAIR Net: n/a Aircraft below MTOW 1361kg: Cessna 172

☐ N732TN	Cessna 210M Centurion II	21061763		0077	0377	1 CO IO-520-L	1724		
☐ N55425	Piper PA-34-200 Seneca	34-7350213		0073	0480	2 LY IO-360-C1E6	1905		
☐ N55643	Piper PA-34-200 Seneca	34-7350234		0073	0480	2 LY IO-360-C1E6	1905		
☐ N9053K	Piper PA-34-200T Seneca II	34-7870035		0078	0784	2 CO TSIO-360-E	2073		
☐ N108RS	Cessna 402B	402B0440		0073	0684	2 CO TSIO-520-E	2858		
☐ N22NC	Cessna 402B	402B0227		0072	0181	2 CO TSIO-520-E	2858		
☐ N50BR	Cessna 402B	402B0812		0075	0489	2 CO TSIO-520-E	2858		
☐ N20GL	Beech E18S	BA-174	N423W	0057	1091	2 PW R-985-AN14B	4218	Freighter	
☐ N5600D	Beech E18S	BA-296		0057	1283	2 PW R-985-AN14B	4218	Freighter	

EAGLE AIR HELICOPTER, Inc.

Forks, WA

PO Box 1555, Forks, WA 98331, USA ☎ (360) 374-9276 Tx: none Fax: (360) 374-9286 SITA: n/a
F: 1976 n/a Head: James D. Mott Net: n/a

☐ N1096L	MD Helicopters MD 500D (Hughes 369D)	800789D		0080	0691	1 AN 250-C20B	1361		
☐ N1109P	MD Helicopters MD 500D (Hughes 369D)	1100849D		0080	0389	1 AN 250-C20B	1361		
☐ N5225C	MD Helicopters MD 500D (Hughes 369D)	590497D		0079	0488	1 AN 250-C20B	1361		
☐ N9163F	MD Helicopters MD 500D (Hughes 369D)	690540D		0079	0382	1 AN 250-C20B	1361		

EAGLE AIR = EGJ (Eagle Jet Charter Inc. dba/Member of Eagle Scienic Aviation Group/formerly part of Lang Aire)

Las Vegas-McCarran Int'l, NV

275 East Tropicana Ave, Suite 220, Las Vegas, NV 89109-7313, USA ☎ (702) 736-3333 Tx: none Fax: (702) 895-7824 SITA: n/a
F: 1975 n/a Head: Clifford P. Evarts ICAO: EAGLE JET Net: n/a

☐ N819GY	Sabreliner 75A (Rockwell NA265-80)	380-66	N943CC	0078	0495	2 GE CF700-2D2	10433	Exec 8 Pax	lsf Lear 25 Inc.
☐ N278MA	Fokker F27 Friendship 200 (F27 Mk200)	10280	LX-LGK	0066	1295	2 RR Dart 532-7R	19051	Y44	lsf Canyon Leasing Inc.
☐ N279MA	Fokker F27 Friendship 200 (F27 Mk200)	10297	LX-LGJ	0066	0695	2 RR Dart 532-7R	19051	Y44	lsf Canyon Leasing Inc.
☐ N280EA	Fokker F27 Friendship 600 (F27 Mk600)	10394	OY-SRB	0069	0295	2 RR Dart 532-7R	20412	Y44	
☐ N283EA	Fokker F27 Friendship 500F (F27 Mk500F)	10522	N280MA	0075	0396	2 RR Dart 532-7R	20412	Y48	lsf Canyon Leasing Inc.
☐ N284MA	Fokker F27 Friendship 500F (F27 Mk500F)	10560	VH-FCF	0077	1296	2 RR Dart 532-7R	20412	Y48	lsf Canyon Leasing Inc.

EAGLE AIR TRANSPORT, Inc.

Ottawa, IL

PO Box 458, Sheridan, IL 60551, USA ☎ (815) 433-0000 Tx: none Fax: (815) 433-6806 SITA: n/a
F: 1993 n/a Head: Roger Nelson Net: n/a Aircraft below MTOW 1361kg: Cessna 182

☐ N10EA	De Havilland DHC-6 Twin Otter 200	199	TF-JME	0068	0394	2 PWC PT6A-20	5252	Para	lsf Alberta Ac.Lsng/opf Skydive Chicago
☐ N30EA	De Havilland DHC-6 Twin Otter 200	191	SE-KOK	0068	0598	2 PWC PT6A-20	5252	Para	lsf Alberta Aircraft Inc.

EAGLE AIR (Scenic Aviation, Inc. dba)

Blanding-Municipal, UT

PO Box 67, Blanding, UT 84511, USA ☎ (801) 678-3222 Tx: none Fax: (801) 678-3425 SITA: n/a
F: 1968 n/a Head: Jon L. Hunt Net: n/a

☐ N395JJ	Piper PA-34-200T Seneca II	34-7870393		0078	0496	2 CO TSIO-360-E	2073	EMS	opf Blanding Air Ambulance
☐ N47744	Piper PA-34-200T Seneca II	34-7870026		0078	0996	2 CO TSIO-360-E	2073	EMS	opf Blanding Air Ambulance
☐ N47830	Piper PA-34-200T Seneca II	34-7870006		0078	0289	2 CO TSIO-360-E	2073	EMS	opf Blanding Air Ambulance
☐ N6935C	Piper PA-34-200T Seneca II	34-7870167		0078	0294	2 CO TSIO-360-E	2073	EMS	opf Blanding Air Ambulance

EAGLE AVIATION, Inc.

Detroit-Grosse Ile Municipal, MI

PO Box 211, Grosse Ile, MI 48138, USA ☎ (734) 676-8880 Tx: none Fax: (734) 676-6501 SITA: n/a
F: 1989 n/a Head: Robert R. Johnston Net: n/a

☐ N40EA	Bell 222	47061	SE-HTN	0081	0291	2 LY LTS101-650C.3	3561		

EAGLE CANYON AIRLINES, Inc. = FE / TLO (Member of Eagle Scienic Aviation Group/formerly Lang Aire)

Las Vegas-McCarran Int'l & -North, NV

275 East Tropicana Ave, Suite 220, Las Vegas, NV 89109-7313, USA ☎ (702) 736-3333 Tx: none Fax: (702) 895-7824 SITA: n/a
F: 1975 n/a Head: Grant G. Murray IATA: 328 ICAO: TALON AIR Net: http://www.eagleair.com/

☐ N774EA	Cessna T207A Turbo Stationair 8 II	20700666	N101EN	0080	0789	1 CO TSIO-520-M	1724	Y6	lsf Canyon Leasing Inc.
☐ N775EA	Cessna T207 Turbo Skywagon	20700162	N1562U	0070	0791	1 CO TSIO-520-G	1724	Y6	lsf Canyon Leasing Inc.
☐ N776EA	Cessna T207A Turbo Stationair 7 II	20700499	N6372H	0079	0789	1 CO TSIO-520-M	1724	Y6	lsf Canyon Leasing Inc.
☐ N2714B	Cessna 402C II	402C0210		0079	0895	2 CO TSIO-520-VB	3107	Y9	lsf Canyon Leasing Inc.
☐ N760EA	Cessna 402C II	402C0056	PZ-TAE	0079	0593	2 CO TSIO-520-VB	3107	Y9	lsf Canyon Leasing Inc.
☐ N762EA	Cessna 402C II	402C0061	N5872C	0079	0887	2 CO TSIO-520-VB	3107	Y9	lsf Canyon Leasing Inc.
☐ N763EA	Cessna 402C II	402C0497	N3208G	0081	0493	2 CO TSIO-520-VB	3107	Y9	lsf Canyon Leasing Inc.
☐ N764EA	Cessna 402C II	402C0237	N2719T	0079	0888	2 CO TSIO-520-VB	3107	Y9	lsf Canyon Leasing Inc.
☐ N765EA	Cessna 402B	402B0314	N1547T	0072	0192	2 CO TSIO-520-E	2858	Y9	lsf Canyon Leasing Inc.
☐ N766EA	Cessna 402B II	402B0401	N8049Q	0073	0490	2 CO TSIO-520-E	2858	Y9	lsf Canyon Leasing Inc.
☐ N767EA	Cessna 402B II	402B1244	N4616G	0077	0589	2 CO TSIO-520-E	2858	Y9	lsf Canyon Leasing Inc.
☐ N768EA	Cessna 402C II	402C0290	N3189M	0080	0288	2 CO TSIO-520-VB	3107	Y9	lsf Canyon Leasing Inc.
☐ N769EA	Cessna 402C II	402C0303	N3283M	0080	0986	2 CO TSIO-520-VB	3107	Y9	lsf Canyon Leasing Inc.
☐ N771EA	Cessna 402C II	402C0046	N5809C	0078	0995	2 CO TSIO-520-VB	3107	Y9	lsf Canyon Leasing Inc.
☐ N772EA	Cessna 402	402-0113	N3500T	0067	1091	2 CO TSIO-520-E	2858	Y9	lsf Canyon Leasing Inc.
☐ N773EA	Cessna 402B	402B0544	N97158	0074	0690	2 CO TSIO-520-E	2858	Y9	lsf Canyon Leasing Inc.
☐ N780EA	Cessna 402C II	402C0257	N821AN	0079	0298	2 CO TSIO-520-VB	3107	Y9	lsf Canyon Leasing Inc.
☐ N781EA	Cessna 402C II	402C0310	N822AN	0080	0298	2 CO TSIO-520-VB	3107	Y9	lsf Canyon Leasing Inc.
☐ N122SA	De Havilland DHC-6 Vista Liner 300	515	N75482	0076	1298	2 PWC PT6A-27	5670	Y19	lsf TWIN / cvtd Twin Otter
☐ N140SA	De Havilland DHC-6 Vista Liner 300	267	N387EX	0069	1298	2 PWC PT6A-27	5670	Y19	cvtd Twin Otter
☐ N142SA	De Havilland DHC-6 Vista Liner 300	241	N385EX	0069	1298	2 PWC PT6A-27	5670	Y19	cvtd Twin Otter
☐ N144SA	De Havilland DHC-6 Vista Liner 300	365	N544N	0073	1298	2 PWC PT6A-27	5670	Y19	lsf TWIN / cvtd Twin Otter
☐ N146SA	De Havilland DHC-6 Vista Liner 300	514	N27RA	0076	1298	2 PWC PT6A-27	5670	Y19	cvtd Twin Otter
☐ N147SA	De Havilland DHC-6 Vista Liner 300	537	N19RA	0077	1298	2 PWC PT6A-27	5670	Y19	lsf TWIN / cvtd Twin Otter
☐ N148SA	De Havilland DHC-6 Vista Liner 300	409	N548N	0074	1298	2 PWC PT6A-27	5670	Y19	cvtd Twin Otter
☐ N149SA	De Havilland DHC-6 Vista Liner 300	359	N410LP	0072	1298	2 PWC PT6A-27	5670	Y19	lsf TWIN / cvtd Twin Otter
☐ N227SA	De Havilland DHC-6 Vista Liner 300	517	N43SP	0076	1298	2 PWC PT6A-27	5670	Y19	cvtd Twin Otter
☐ N228SA	De Havilland DHC-6 Vista Liner 300	253	N103AC	0070	1298	2 PWC PT6A-27	5670	Y19	cvtd Twin Otter
☐ N230SA	De Havilland DHC-6 Vista Liner 300	692	N549N	0080	1298	2 PWC PT6A-27	5670	Y19	lsf TWIN / cvtd Twin Otter
☐ N232SA	De Havilland DHC-6 Vista Liner 300	421	N545N	0074	1298	2 PWC PT6A-27	5670	Y19	lsf TWIN / cvtd Twin Otter
☐ N233SA	De Havilland DHC-6 Vista Liner 300	440	N547N	0074	1298	2 PWC PT6A-27	5670	Y19	lsf TWIN / cvtd Twin Otter
☐ N237SA	De Havilland DHC-6 Vista Liner 300	683	N7020G	0080	1298	2 PWC PT6A-27	5670	Y19	lsf TWIN / cvtd Twin Otter
☐ N241SA	De Havilland DHC-6 Vista Liner 300	556	N97RA	0077	1298	2 PWC PT6A-27	5670	Y19	cvtd Twin Otter
☐ N245SA	De Havilland DHC-6 Vista Liner 300	388	N529N	0073	1298	2 PWC PT6A-27	5670	Y19	lsf TWIN / cvtd Twin Otter
☐ N253SA	De Havilland DHC-6 Vista Liner 300	350	N305EH	0075	1298	2 PWC PT6A-27	5670	Y19	lsf TWIN / cvtd Twin Otter
☐ N297SA	De Havilland DHC-6 Vista Liner 300	297	N852TB	0071	1298	2 PWC PT6A-27	5670	Y19	cvtd Twin Otter
☐ N331SA	De Havilland DHC-6 Vista Liner 300	337	N2886Z	0071	1298	2 PWC PT6A-27	5670	Y19	lsf TWIN / cvtd Twin Otter

EAGLE EXECUTIVE CHARTER (Eagle Aviation, Inc. dba)

Columbia-Metropolitan, SC

2861 Aviation Way, West Columbia, SC 29170, USA ☎ (803) 822-5555 Tx: none Fax: (803) 822-5592 SITA: n/a
F: 1970 n/a Head: David A. Lipski Net: n/a

☐ N218DM	Beech Baron 58	TH-925		0078	0196	2 CO IO-520-C	2449		
☐ N101PM	Piper PA-31-350 Navajo Chieftain	31-7952202		0079	0996	2 LY TIO-540-J2BD	3175		
☐ N800LA	Cessna 550 Citation II	550-0295	N483G	0081	1091	2 PWC JT15D-4	6033		
☐ N920EA	Learjet 25	25-057	C-FTXT	0070	1094	2 GE CJ610-6	6804		
☐ N238RC	Learjet 35	35-061	N4246N	0076	1089	2 GA TFE731-2-2B	8301		

EAGLE HELICOPTERS, Inc.

Spokane-Felts Field, WA

East 5311 Rutter Avenue, Spokane, WA 99212-1368, USA ☎ (509) 534-1285 Tx: none Fax: (509) 534-9772 SITA: n/a
F: 1982 n/a Head: Dennis Hanson Net: n/a

☐ N1102	Eurocopter (Aerosp.) SA315B Lama	1918 / 19		0076	1196	1 TU Artouste IIIB	1950		cvtd Alouette II

320 registration type of aircraft cn/fn ex/ex* mfd del powered by mtow kg configuration selcal name/fln/specialitites/remarks

registration	type of aircraft	cn/fn	ex/ex*	mfd	del	powered by	mtow kg	configuration	selcal	name/fln/specialities/remarks
☐ N1109	Eurocopter (Aerosp.) SA315B Lama	2570	C-FKIA	0079	1197	1 TU Artouste IIIB	1950			
☐ N32079	Eurocopter (Aerosp.) SA315B Lama	2572		0079	1291	1 TU Artouste IIIB	1950			
☐ N112SH	Eurocopter (Aerosp.) AS350D AStar	1334	N57717	0080	0287	1 LY LTS101-600A.2	1950			
☐ N13HF	Eurocopter (Aerosp.) AS350B1 AStar	2267		0089	0290	1 TU Arriel 1D	2200			
☐ N3598D	Eurocopter (Aerosp.) AS350D AStar	1152		0079	0688	1 LY LTS101-600A.2	1950			
☐ N32075	Eurocopter (Aerosp.) SA316B Alouette III	1888		0071	1291	1 TU Artouste IIIB	2200			
☐ N3207Y	Eurocopter (Aerosp.) SA316B Alouette III	2375		0079	1291	1 TU Artouste IIIB	2200			
☐ N911HF	Fairchild (Swearingen) SA226TC Metro II	TC-215	N62SA	0074	0590	2 GA TPE331-10UA-511G	5670			
☐ N550PG	Cessna 550 Citation II	550-0216	N240AR	0081	0192	2 PWC JT15D-4	6033			

EASTERN AIR CHARTER (Eastern Air Center, Inc. dba)
Norwood-Memorial, MA

209 Access Road, Norwood, MA 02062, USA ☎ (781) 769-8680 Tx: none Fax: (781) 769-7743 SITA: n/a
F: 1981 ⋔⋔⋔ n/a Head: Sidney Fagelman Net: n/a

registration	type of aircraft	cn/fn	ex/ex*	mfd	del	powered by	mtow kg	configuration	selcal	name/fln/specialities/remarks
☐ N109TT	Piper PA-31T Cheyenne II	31T-7920082	N56HF	0079	0594	2 PWC PT6A-28	4082			
☐ N10MC	Piper PA-31T Cheyenne II	31T-7920028	N94TW	0079	0287	2 PWC PT6A-28	4082			
☐ N51RD	Piper PA-31T Cheyenne II	31T-7820056	N4NH	0078	1094	2 PWC PT6A-28	4082			lsf Weston Air Service Inc.
☐ N70MG	Cessna 500 Citation	500-0063	OO-RST	0073	0195	2 PWC JT15D-1	5216			lsf AGG Aircraft Sales & Leasing Inc.
☐ N245CC	Cessna 550 Citation II	550-0212		0081	1194	2 PWC JT15D-4	6033			

EAST HAMPTON AIRLINES (Aviation Resources, Inc. dba)
East Hampton, NY

East Hampton Airlines

PO Box 398, Wainscott, NY 11975, USA ☎ (516) 537-4272 Tx: none Fax: (516) 537-3755 SITA: n/a
F: 1992 ⋔⋔⋔ n/a Head: Bennard Krupinski Net: n/a

registration	type of aircraft	cn/fn	ex/ex*	mfd	del	powered by	mtow kg	configuration	selcal	name/fln/specialities/remarks
☐ N7248W	Beech Bonanza A36	E-2275		0085	0187	1 CO IO-550-B	1656			
☐ N41142	Piper PA-31-350 Navajo Chieftain	31-8352034		0083	0492	2 LY TIO-540-J2BD	3175			
☐ N520D	Beech King Air B200	BB-989		0082	1293	2 PWC PT6A-42	5670			

EASTON AVIATION (Associated Aerial Applicators, Inc. dba)
Greeley-Easton, CO

PO Box 787, Evens, CO 80620, USA ☎ (970) 284-6701 Tx: none Fax: (970) 284-5215 SITA: n/a
F: 1978 ⋔⋔⋔ n/a Head: Robert Easton Net: n/a

registration	type of aircraft	cn/fn	ex/ex*	mfd	del	powered by	mtow kg	configuration	selcal	name/fln/specialities/remarks
☐ N3889W	Bell 206B JetRanger III	3570		0082	0192	1 AN 250-C20B	1451			lsf pvt

EASTWAY AVIATION, Inc.
Islip-Long Island Mac Arthur, NY

Long Island Mac Arthur Airport, Ronkonkoma, NY 11779, USA ☎ (516) 737-9911 Tx: none Fax: (516) 737-4926 SITA: n/a
F: 1979 ⋔⋔⋔ n/a Head: Dale Lang Net: n/a

registration	type of aircraft	cn/fn	ex/ex*	mfd	del	powered by	mtow kg	configuration	selcal	name/fln/specialities/remarks
☐ N369GA	Beech King Air C90	LJ-934	F-GCTA	0081	0893	2 PWC PT6A-21	4377			
☐ N44SR	Beech King Air 200	BB-853	N3832B	0081	0387	2 PWC PT6A-41	5670			
☐ N5UN	Beech King Air 200	BB-697	N50N	0080	0296	2 PWC PT6A-41	5670			

EASTWIND AIRLINES, Inc. – The Bee Line = W9 / BBE
Greensboro-Piedmont Triad Int'l

6415 Bryan Blvd., Box 14, Terminal Bldg, PTI Airport, Greensboro, NC 27409, USA ☎ (336) 393-0111 Tx: none Fax: (336) 393-0277 SITA: n/a
F: 1993 ⋔⋔⋔ 250 Head: John Aglialoro IATA: 175 ICAO: STINGER Net: n/a

registration	type of aircraft	cn/fn	ex/ex*	mfd	del	powered by	mtow kg	configuration	selcal	name/fln/specialities/remarks
☐ N220US	Boeing 737-2H5	20453 / 246	N753N	0070	0795	2 PW JT8D-9A	49442	Y120		lsf PLMI / cvtd 737-201
☐ N221US	Boeing 737-2H5	20454 / 247	N754N	0070	0795	2 PW JT8D-9A (HK3/NOR)	49442	Y120		lsf PLMI / cvtd 737-201
☐ N309VA	Boeing 737-247	19614 / 105	N473AC	1268	0298	2 PW JT8D-9A (HK3/NOR)	49442	Y120		lsf CISA
☐ N700EW	Boeing 737-7AD	28436 / 41		0098	0598	2 CFMI CFM56-7B24	69400	Y132		
☐ N701EW	Boeing 737-7AD	28437 / 72		0098	0798	2 CFMI CFM56-7B24	69400	Y132		

ECO AIR Tours-Hawaii (Call Air, Inc. dba)
Honolulu-Int'l, HI

99 Mokuea Place, Honolulu, HI 96819, USA ☎ (808) 839-1499 Tx: none Fax: (808) 839-1499 SITA: n/a
F: 1994 ⋔⋔⋔ n/a Head: John Callahan Net: n/a

registration	type of aircraft	cn/fn	ex/ex*	mfd	del	powered by	mtow kg	configuration	selcal	name/fln/specialities/remarks
☐ N351CA	Piper PA-31-350 Navajo Chieftain	31-7852075		0078	0197	2 LY TIO-540-J2BD	3175			

EDELWEISS AIR (Edelweiss Holdings, Inc. dba)
Taos-Municipal, NM

PO Box 2219, El Prado, NM 87526, USA ☎ (505) 758-4995 Tx: none Fax: (505) 751-4038 SITA: n/a
F: 1995 ⋔⋔⋔ n/a Head: Timothy G. Wooldridge Net: n/a

registration	type of aircraft	cn/fn	ex/ex*	mfd	del	powered by	mtow kg	configuration	selcal	name/fln/specialities/remarks
☐ N803AN	Cessna T207A Turbo Stationair 8 II	20700570		0079	0195	1 CO TSIO-520-M	1724			

ED'S FLYING SERVICE, Inc. (Air Ambulance East)
Walnut Cove-Meadow Brook Field, NC

Meadow Brook Field, Route 4, Box 86, Walnut Cove, NC 27052, USA ☎ (910) 591-7881 Tx: none Fax: none SITA: n/a
F: 1971 ⋔⋔⋔ n/a Head: Charles E. Lasley Net: n/a   AIR AMBULANCE EAST is the service-name for EMS-flights (same headquarters & fleet).

registration	type of aircraft	cn/fn	ex/ex*	mfd	del	powered by	mtow kg	configuration	selcal	name/fln/specialities/remarks
☐ N206EL	Cessna U206G Stationair	U20604037		0077	1077	1 CO IO-520-F	1633			
☐ N19WM	Beech Baron 58	TH-393		0074	1185	2 CO IO-520-C	2449			
☐ N6658C	Cessna 414A Chancellor III	414A0051		0078	0487	2 CO TSIO-520-N	3062			
☐ N1975G	Beech King Air E90	LW-252	N505RG	0078	0393	2 PWC PT6A-28	4581			

ED'S FLYING SERVICE, Inc.
Alamogordo-White Sands Regional, NM

PO Box 966, Alamogordo, NM 88310, USA ☎ (505) 437-4330 Tx: none Fax: (505) 439-0195 SITA: n/a
F: 1960 ⋔⋔⋔ n/a Head: Edward J. Pavelka Net: n/a   Aircraft below MTOW 1361kg: Cessna 182

registration	type of aircraft	cn/fn	ex/ex*	mfd	del	powered by	mtow kg	configuration	selcal	name/fln/specialities/remarks
☐ N732RU	Cessna U206G Stationair 6 II	U20604713		0079	1178	1 CO IO-520-F	1633			
☐ N3137A	Cessna 310R II	310R0284		0075	0291	2 CO IO-520-M	2495			
☐ N87256	Cessna T310R II	310R0502		0076	1294	2 CO TSIO-520-B	2495			
☐ N71CZ	Piper PA-31-350 Navajo Chieftain	31-7952235		0079	1195	2 LY TIO-540-J2BD	3175			

EG&G Special Projects, Inc. (Member of EG&G Group)
Las Vegas-McCarran Int'l, NV

PO Box 93747, Las Vegas, NV 89193-3747, USA ☎ (702) 736-3538 Tx: none Fax: (702) 736-1821 SITA: n/a
F: 1988 ⋔⋔⋔ n/a Head: John Hall Net: n/a   Private company conducting corporate & contract project air operations for federal organisations.

registration	type of aircraft	cn/fn	ex/ex*	mfd	del	powered by	mtow kg	configuration	selcal	name/fln/specialities/remarks
☐ N654BA	Beech King Air B200C	BL-54	N6563C	0082	0589	2 PWC PT6A-42	5670	Y9 / Freighter		lsf Dept of the Air Force
☐ N661BA	Beech King Air B200C	BL-61	N6564C	0083	0589	2 PWC PT6A-42	5670	Y9 / Freighter		lsf Dept of the Air Force
☐ N662BA	Beech King Air B200C	BL-62	N6566C	0083	0589	2 PWC PT6A-42	5670	Y9 / Freighter		lsf Dept of the Air Force
☐ N20RA	Beech 1900C Airliner	UB-42		0085	0788	2 PWC PT6A-65B	7530	Y19 / Freighter		lsf Dept of the Air Force
☐ N27RA	Beech 1900C Airliner	UB-37	N7214K	0085	0788	2 PWC PT6A-65B	7530	Y19 / Freighter		lsf Dept of the Air Force
☐ N4529W	Boeing 737-275 (A)	20785 / 335	C-FPWB	0073	0283	2 PW JT8D-9A (HK3/NOR)	53070	Y126		lsf Dept of the Air Force
☐ N5175U	Boeing 737-200 (A)	20689 / 334	72-0282	1273	0992	2 PW JT8D-9A (HK3/NOR)	52390	Y126		lsf Dept of the Air Force / cvtd T43A
☐ N5176Y	Boeing 737-200 (A)	20692 / 337	72-0285	0274	0992	2 PW JT8D-9A (HK3/NOR)	52390	Y126		lsf Dept of the Air Force / cvtd T43A
☐ N5177C	Boeing 737-200 (A)	20693 / 340	72-0286	0274	0992	2 PW JT8D-9A (HK3/NOR)	52390	Y126		lsf Dept of the Air Force / cvtd T43A
☐ N5294E	Boeing 737-200 (A)	20691 / 337	72-0284	0174	0494	2 PW JT8D-9A (HK3/NOR)	52390	Y126		lsf Dept of the Air Force / cvtd T43A
☐ N5294M	Boeing 737-200 (A)	20694 / 343	72-0287	0274	0494	2 PW JT8D-9A (HK3/NOR)	52390	Y126		lsf Dept of the Air Force / cvtd T43A

EGLI AIR HAUL, Inc.
King Salmon, AK

egli air Haul

Box 169, King Salmon, AK 99613, USA ☎ (907) 246-3554 Tx: none Fax: (907) 246-3654 SITA: n/a
F: 1979 ⋔⋔⋔ 5 Head: Harold S. Egli Net: n/a   Aircraft below MTOW 1361kg: Cessna 172

registration	type of aircraft	cn/fn	ex/ex*	mfd	del	powered by	mtow kg	configuration	selcal	name/fln/specialities/remarks
☐ N83193	Bell 206B JetRanger III	943		0073	0397	1 AN 250-C20B	1451			cvtd JetRanger
☐ N756CL	Cessna U206G Stationair	U20603983		0077	0590	1 CO IO-520-F	1633			lsf pvt

EL AERO SERVICES, Inc.
Elko-Municipal J.C. Harris Field / Ely & Carson City, NV

PO Box 159, Elko, NV 89803, USA ☎ (702) 738-7123 Tx: none Fax: (702) 738-5699 SITA: n/a
F: 1966 ⋔⋔⋔ 25 Head: Kathy J. Gilbert Net: n/a   Aircraft below MTOW 1361 kg: Cessna 172

registration	type of aircraft	cn/fn	ex/ex*	mfd	del	powered by	mtow kg	configuration	selcal	name/fln/specialities/remarks
☐ N20620	Bell 206B JetRanger III	3369		0081	0881	1 AN 250-C20B	1451			
☐ N51698	Bell 206B JetRanger III	4010		0088	0588	1 AN 250-C20J	1451			
☐ N8052G	Bell 206B JetRanger III	4050		0089	0589	1 AN 250-C20J	1451			
☐ N756MX	Cessna U206G Stationair 6	U20604210		0077	0778	1 CO IO-520-F	1633			
☐ N9690G	Cessna U206F Stationair	U20601890		0072	0787	1 CO IO-520-F	1633			
☐ N9718Z	Cessna U206G Stationair 6 II	U20606623		0082	1187	1 CO IO-520-F	1633			
☐ N9878M	Cessna 210M Centurion II	21062084		0077	0478	1 CO IO-520-L	1724			
☐ N3185A	Bell 206L-3 LongRanger III	51093		0084	0784	1 AN 250-C30P	1882			
☐ N414RM	Cessna 414A Chancellor III	414A0306		0079	0693	2 CO TSIO-520-NB	3062			
☐ N6646R	Beech King Air C90	LJ-836		0079	1287	2 PWC PT6A-21	4377			

ELLIOTT AVIATION = ELT (Elliott Aviation Flight Services, Inc. dba)
Des Moines/IA, Omaha-Eppley/NE, Minneapolis-FC/MN, Moline/IL

Box 35250, Des Moines, IA 50315-0303, USA ☎ (515) 285-6551 Tx: none Fax: (515) 285-7251 SITA: n/a
F: 1936 ⋔⋔⋔ n/a Head: Donald H. Jay ICAO: ELLIOTT Net: http://www.elliottaviation.com

registration	type of aircraft	cn/fn	ex/ex*	mfd	del	powered by	mtow kg	configuration	selcal	name/fln/specialities/remarks
☐ N66363	Beech Duchess 76	ME-254		0079	1182	2 LY O-360-A1G6D	1769			
☐ N1817S	Beech Baron 58	TH-1271		0081	1095	2 CO IO-520-CB	2449			
☐ N557CE	Beech Baron 58	TH-864		0077	1194	2 CO IO-520-C	2449			
☐ N580EA	Beech Baron 58	TH-316	N91MF	0073	0595	2 CO IO-520-C	2449			
☐ N8140R	Beech Baron 58	TH-505		0074	0388	2 CO IO-520-C	2449			
☐ N1089L	Beech King Air C90B	LJ-1439		0096	0596	2 PWC PT6A-21	4581			lsf The Outback Llc
☐ N3242L	Beech King Air C90B	LJ-1413		0095	0196	2 PWC PT6A-21	4581			lsf Norfolk Iron & Metal Co.
☐ N363EA	Beech King Air B100	BE-134	N888RK	0082	0995	2 GA TPE331-6-252B	5352			
☐ N3690F	Beech King Air C90	LJ-921		0080	0996	2 PWC PT6A-21	4377			

registration   type of aircraft   cn/fn   ex/ex*   mfd   del   powered by   mtow kg   configuration   selcal   name/fln/specialities/remarks

☐ N400RK	Beech King Air B100	BE-49	N98D	0078	0690	2 GA TPE331-6-252B	5352			
☐ N44HP	Beech King Air C90	LJ-702		0077	0991	2 PWC PT6A-21	4377			lsf Professional Office Services Inc.
☐ N90MV	Beech King Air C90	LJ-701	N90LJ	0077	0788	2 PWC PT6A-21	4377			lsf Holmes Leasing Inc.
☐ N187MQ	Beech King Air 200	BB-689	N187MC	0080	0997	2 PWC PT6A-41	5670			lsf Elliott Aviation Aircr. Sales Inc.
☐ N200WZ	Beech King Air 200	BB-89	N16BF	0075	0997	2 PWC PT6A-41	5670			lsf Elliott Aviation Aircr. Sales Inc.
☐ N28CN	Beech King Air 200	BB-959	N2SC	0082	0198	2 PWC PT6A-41	5670			lsf Elliott Aviation Aircr. Sales Inc.
☐ N824TT	Beech King Air 200	BB-824	F-GJCF	0080	1097	2 PWC PT6A-41	5670			lsf Elliott Aviation Aircr. Sales Inc.
☐ N8186S	Beech Starship 2000	NC-20		0091	0891	2 PWC PT6A-67A	6627			lsf Raytheon Aircraft Credit Corp.
☐ N866BB	Beech Beechjet 400A	RK-98	N400A	0094	0396	2 PWC JT15D-5	7303			lsf Shamrock Aviation Charters Inc.

ELLIS AIR TAXI, Inc. — Gulkana, AK

PO Box 106, Glennallen, AK 99588, USA ☎ (907) 822-3368 Tx: none Fax: (907) 822-3368 SITA: n/a
F: 1953 ✈✈✈ n/a Head: Darry L. Ellis Net: n/a Aircraft below MTOW 1361 kg: Piper PA-18

☐ N6978H	Cessna A185F Skywagon	18503347		0077	0678	1 CO IO-520-D	1520			lsf pvt / Wheel-Skis
☐ N29137	Cessna U206C Super Skywagon	U206-1107		0068	0697	1 CO IO-520-F	1633			Wheel-Skis
☐ N27529	Piper PA-31-350 Navajo Chieftain	31-7852046		0078	0593	2 LY TIO-540-J2BD	3175			

ELLISON AIR, Inc. (Seasonal May-October ops only) — Anchorage-Lake Hood SPB, AK

PO Box 190505, Anchorage, AK 99519, USA ☎ (907) 243-1959 Tx: none Fax: (907) 243-5218 SITA: n/a
F: 1990 ✈✈✈ 4 Head: John P. Ellison, Jr. Net: http://alaskan.com/vendors/ellisonair.html

☐ N59352	Cessna U206F Stationair II	U20603221		0076	0792	1 CO IO-520-F	1633			Floats
☐ N7375N	Cessna U206G Stationair	U20603641		0077	0489	1 CO IO-520-F	1633			Floats

EMERY WORLDWIDE Airlines, Inc. = EB / EWW (A CNF Company) (Aff.Emery Worldwide/Subs.of Consolidated Freightways) — Dayton-Int'l, OH / Indianapolis, IN / San Jose, CA

1 Lagoon Drive, Suite 400, Redford City, CA 94065, USA ☎ (650) 596-9600 Tx: none Fax: (650) 596-7901 SITA: n/a
F: 1980 ✈✈✈ 900 Head: David I. Beatson IATA: 591 ICAO: EMERY Net: http://www.emeryworld.com
Emery also manages the air-operation for United States Postal Service – USPS. Those aircraft (22 Boeing 727-100/200) are contracted to/opb EXPRESS ONE & RYAN INTERNATIONAL for USPS.
Beside aircraft listed, also uses a DC-10-30F, lsf/opb GEMINI AIR CARGO & an MD-11F, lsf/opb WORLD AIRWAYS – for details see under that companies.

☐ N210NE	Boeing 727-31 (F)	18903 / 147	N833TW	0065	0394	3 PW JT8D-7B	72802	Freighter	AC-EF	lsf IASG/sub-lst/opb RYN / cvtd -31
☐ N220NE	Boeing 727-31 (F)	18905 / 160	N840TW	0065	0394	3 PW JT8D-7B	72802	Freighter		lsf IASG/sub-lst/opb RYN / cvtd -31
☐ N329QS	Boeing 727-21 (F)	19038 / 285	N329PA	0066	0185	3 PW JT8D-7B (HK3/FDX)	72802	Freighter		lst/opb RYN in Emery colors / cvtd -21
☐ N355QS	Boeing 727-21 (F)	19257 / 385	N355PA	0067	0185	3 PW JT8D-7B (HK3/FDX)	72802	Freighter		lst/opb RYN in Emery colors / cvtd -21
☐ N356QS	Boeing 727-21 (F)	19258 / 397	N356PA	0067	0185	3 PW JT8D-7B	72802	Freighter		lst/opb RYN in Emery colors / cvtd -21
☐ N357QS	Boeing 727-21 (F)	19259 / 408	N357PA	0067	0185	3 PW JT8D-7B (HK3/FDX)	72802	Freighter		lst/opb RYN in Emery colors / cvtd -21
☐ N359QS	Boeing 727-21 (F)	19007 / 269	HK-2846X	0066	0985	3 PW JT8D-7B (HK3/FDX)	72802	Freighter		lst/opb RYN in Emery colors / cvtd -21
☐ N413EX	Boeing 727-51C	19206 / 294	N495US	0066	0281	3 PW JT8D-7B (HK3/FDX)	76884	Freighter		lst RYN in USPS colors
☐ N416EX	Boeing 727-51C	19287 / 383	N496US	0067	0681	3 PW JT8D-7B (HK3/FDX)	76884	Freighter		lst RYN in USPS colors
☐ N417EX	Boeing 727-51C	19290 / 417	N499US	0067	0781	3 PW JT8D-7B (HK3/FDX)	76884	Freighter		lst RYN in USPS colors
☐ N421EX	Boeing 727-22C	19099 / 322	HK-2474	0066	1181	3 PW JT8D-7B (HK3/FDX)	76884	Freighter		lst RYN in USPS colors
☐ N424EX	Boeing 727-134C	20042 / 626	SE-DDC	0068	0981	3 PW JT8D-7B (HK3/FDX)	76884	Freighter		
☐ N426EX	Boeing 727-22C	19089 / 250	N7401U	0066	0881	3 PW JT8D-7B (HK3/FDX)	76884	Freighter		lst RYN in USPS colors
☐ N427EX	Boeing 727-22C	19090 / 277	N7402U	0066	0881	3 PW JT8D-7B (HK3/FDX)	76884	Freighter		lst RYN in USPS colors
☐ N428EX	Boeing 727-22C	19097 / 307	N7409U	0066	0881	3 PW JT8D-7B (HK3/FDX)	76884	Freighter		lst RYN in USPS colors
☐ N429EX	Boeing 727-22C	19100 / 324	N7412U	0066	1081	3 PW JT8D-7B (HK3/FDX)	76884	Freighter		lst RYN in USPS colors
☐ N432EX	Boeing 727-151C	19867 / 514	N488US	0068	0182	3 PW JT8D-7B (HK3/FDX)	76884	Freighter		Judy Carmine / lst RYN in USPS colors
☐ N433EX	Boeing 727-151C	19868 / 529	N489US	0068	0582	3 PW JT8D-7B (Hk3/FDX)	76884	Freighter		lst RYN in USPS colors
☐ N435EX	Boeing 727-51C	19288 / 389	N497US	0067	1082	3 PW JT8D-7B (HK3/FDX)	76884	Freighter		lst RYN in USPS colors
☐ N436EX	Boeing 727-51C	19289 / 403	N498US	0067	1082	3 PW JT8D-7B (HK3/FDX)	76884	Freighter		lst RYN in USPS colors
☐ N526PC	Boeing 727-77C	20370 / 821	N555BN	0070	0987	3 PW JT8D-7B (HK3/FDX)	76884	Freighter		lst RYN in USPS colors
☐ N527PC	Boeing 727-172C	19665 / 476	N45498	0067	0987	3 PW JT8D-7B (HK3/FDX)	76884	Freighter		lst RYN in USPS colors
☐ N528PC	Boeing 727-82C	19597 / 524	N4564U	0068	0987	3 PW JT8D-7B (HK3/FDX)	76884	Freighter		lst RYN in USPS colors
☐ N721JE	Boeing 727-76 (F)	18843 / 170	N4602D	0065	0987	3 PW JT8D-7B (HK3/FDX)	72802	Freighter		lst RYN in USPS colors
☐ N94GS	Boeing 727-44 (F)	18892 / 148	N92GS	0065	0394	3 PW JT8D-7B	72802	Freighter		lsf IASG/sub-lst/opb RYN / cvtd -44
☐ N311NE	Boeing 727-223 (F)	19703 / 684	N6825	0169	0493	3 PW JT8D-9A (HK3/FDX)	80966	Freighter	CE-DJ	lst LHN in USPS colors / cvtd -223
☐ N312NE	Boeing 727-223 (F)	20193 / 755	N6841	0969	0593	3 PW JT8D-9A (HK3/FDX)	80966	Freighter	BH-AL	lst LHN in USPS colors / cvtd -223
☐ N313NE	Boeing 727-223 (F)	19702 / 680	N6824	0169	0593	3 PW JT8D-9A (HK3/FDX)	80966	Freighter	CE-FK	lst LHN in USPS colors / cvtd -223
☐ N7635U	Boeing 727-222 (F)	19908 / 653		0068	1294	3 PW JT8D-7B (HK3/FDX)	78018	Freighter		cvtd -222
☐ N7638U	Boeing 727-222 (F)	19911 / 668		0068	1194	3 PW JT8D-7B (HK3/FDX)	78018	Freighter		cvtd -222
☐ N7639U	Boeing 727-222 (F)	19912 / 670		0068	0295	3 PW JT8D-7B (HK3/FDX)	78018	Freighter		cvtd -222
☐ N7640U	Boeing 727-222 (F)	19913 / 672		0068	1294	3 PW JT8D-7B (HK3/FDX)	78018	Freighter		cvtd -222
☐ N7642U	Boeing 727-222 (F)	19915 / 681		0069	0295	3 PW JT8D-7B (HK3/FDX)	78018	Freighter		cvtd -222
☐ N7643U	Boeing 727-222 (F)	20037 / 701		0069	1294	3 PW JT8D-7B (HK3/FDX)	78018	Freighter		cvtd -222
☐ N7644U	Boeing 727-222 (F)	20038 / 716		0069	1194	3 PW JT8D-7B (HK3/FDX)	78018	Freighter		cvtd -222
☐ N7645U	Boeing 727-222 (F)	20039 / 720		0069	1194	3 PW JT8D-7B (HK3/FDX)	78018	Freighter		cvtd -222
☐ N991CF	Boeing (Douglas) DC-8-54F (JT)	45801 / 235	N45UA	0065	1287	4 PW JT3D-3B (HK2/QNC)	140523	Freighter		
☐ N992CF	Boeing (Douglas) DC-8-54F (JT)	45884 / 340	N50UA	0068	0687	4 PW JT3D-3B (HK2/QNC)	140523	Freighter		
☐ N500MH	Boeing (Douglas) DC-8-71F	45812 / 277	EI-TLD	0268	0394	4 CFMI CFM56-2C	147418	Freighter	GH-LM	lsf GPAG / cvtd -61/-71
☐ N801GP	Boeing (Douglas) DC-8-71F	46039 / 448	N870SJ	0069	1194	4 CFMI CFM56-2C	147418	Freighter	GM-FK	cvtd -61/-71
☐ N8076U	Boeing (Douglas) DC-8-71F	45941 / 317	C-FQPM	1267	0594	4 CFMI CFM56-2C	148780	Freighter	GM-EL	cvtd -61/-71
☐ N8079U	Boeing (Douglas) DC-8-71F	45947 / 341		0068	0394	4 CFMI CFM56-2C	147418	Freighter	GL-DJ	cvtd -61/-71
☐ N8084U	Boeing (Douglas) DC-8-71F	45974 / 368	C-FQPL	0068	0494	4 CFMI CFM56-2C	147418	Freighter	GM-EK	lsf GECA / cvtd -61/-71
☐ N8085U	Boeing (Douglas) DC-8-71F	45975 / 369	Z-WZL	0068	0694	4 CFMI CFM56-2C	147418	Freighter	GM-HJ	cvtd -61/-71
☐ N8087U	Boeing (Douglas) DC-8-71F	45977 / 373	N871SJ	0068	0494	4 CFMI CFM56-2C	147418	Freighter	GM-DK	cvtd -61/-71
☐ N8091U	Boeing (Douglas) DC-8-71F	45995 / 388	EI-TLC	0268	0295	4 CFMI CFM56-2C	147418	Freighter	BJ-AM	lsf GECA / cvtd -61/-71
☐ N811AL	Boeing (Douglas) DC-8-71F	46099 / 507	9J-AFL	0069	1095	4 CFMI CFM56-2C	147418	Freighter		lsf AERO / cvtd -61/-71
☐ N8177U	Boeing (Douglas) DC-8-71F	45983 / 350	JA8057	0068	0394	4 CFMI CFM56-2C	147418	Freighter	GL-DK	cvtd -61/-71
☐ N990CF	Boeing (Douglas) DC-8-62F	46068 / 463	N816ZA	0069	0588	4 PW JT3D-3B (HK3/BAC)	158757	Freighter	AK-CE	cvtd -62
☐ N993CF	Boeing (Douglas) DC-8-62F	46028 / 461	N812ZA	0069	0588	4 PW JT3D-3B (HK3/BAC)	151953	Freighter	AJ-HL	cvtd -62
☐ N994CF	Boeing (Douglas) DC-8-62F	45956 / 376	N814ZA	0068	0688	4 PW JT3D-3B (HK3/BAC)	151953	Freighter	AD-CE	cvtd -62
☐ N995CF	Boeing (Douglas) DC-8-62F	46024 / 428	N815ZA	0069	0688	4 PW JT3D-3B (HK3/BAC)	151953	Freighter	AD-BH	cvtd -62
☐ N996CF	Boeing (Douglas) DC-8-62F (AF)	46162 / 555	N810ZA	0072	0888	4 PW JT3D-3B (HK3/BAC)	158757	Freighter	AC-LM	
☐ N997CF	Boeing (Douglas) DC-8-62F (AF)	46154 / 554	N811ZA	0072	0988	4 PW JT3D-3B (HK3/BAC)	158757	Freighter	AC-GK	
☐ N998CF	Boeing (Douglas) DC-8-62F (AF)	46139 / 537	N813ZA	0070	0488	4 PW JT3D-3B (HK3/BAC)	151953	Freighter	AD-BE	
☐ N796AL	Boeing (Douglas) DC-8-63F	46054 / 453	OY-SBL	0069	0989	4 PW JT3D-7 (HK3/BAC)	161025	Freighter	AK-BG	cvtd -63
☐ N797AL	Boeing (Douglas) DC-8-63F	46163 / 556	SE-DBL	0072	0889	4 PW JT3D-7 (HK3/BAC)	161025	Freighter	AK-BH	cvtd -63
☐ N865F	Boeing (Douglas) DC-8-63F	46088 / 464	TF-FLC	0069	0784	4 PW JT3D-7 (HK3/BAC)	161025	Freighter	BM-DH	cvtd (CF)
☐ N921R	Boeing (Douglas) DC-8-63F	46145 / 548	N806WA	0071	0885	4 PW JT3D-7 (HK3/BAC)	161025	Freighter	DE-AG	cvtd (CF)
☐ N950R	Boeing (Douglas) DC-8-63F	45903 / 286	N908CL	0067	1084	4 PW JT3D-7 (HK3/BAC)	158757	Freighter	FM-EG	cvtd -63
☐ N951R	Boeing (Douglas) DC-8-63F	46092 / 505	N926CL	0069	1084	4 PW JT3D-7 (HK3/BAC)	161025	Freighter	FM-DL	cvtd -63
☐ N957R	Boeing (Douglas) DC-8-63F	46137 / 527	N804WA	0070	0185	4 PW JT3D-7 (HK3/BAC)	161025	Freighter	FK-AL	cvtd (CF)
☐ N959R	Boeing (Douglas) DC-8-63F	46143 / 547	N805WA	0071	0785	4 PW JT3D-7 (HK3/BAC)	161025	Freighter	BL-GM	cvtd (CF)
☐ N964R	Boeing (Douglas) DC-8-63F	46000 / 386	N904R	0068	1184	4 PW JT3D-7 (HK3/BAC)	161025	Freighter	EH-BC	cvtd -63
☐ N105WP	Boeing (Douglas) DC-8-73F	46095 / 497	N809CK	0069	0793	4 CFMI CFM56-2C	161025	Freighter	CK-AD	cvtd -63 (PF)
☐ N2674U	Boeing (Douglas) DC-8-73F	46062 / 486	N6163A	0069	1284	4 CFMI CFM56-2C	158757	Freighter	FG-BK	lsf GECC / cvtd -63F (CF)
☐ N602AL	Boeing (Douglas) DC-8-73F	45991 / 380	D-ADUI	0768	0996	4 CFMI CFM56-2C	161025	Freighter	CD-BM	lsf AERO / cvtd -63F (CF)
☐ N603AL	Boeing (Douglas) DC-8-73F	46003 / 401	D-ADUA	0068	0996	4 CFMI CFM56-2C	161025	Freighter	FG-AM	lsf AERO / cvtd -63F (AF)
☐ N604AL	Boeing (Douglas) DC-8-73F	46047 / 447	D-ADUO	0069	0597	4 CFMI CFM56-2C	161025	Freighter	FL-HK	lsf AERO / cvtd -63F (CF)
☐ N605AL	Boeing (Douglas) DC-8-73F	46106 / 490	D-ADUC	0069	1196	4 CFMI CFM56-2C	161025	Freighter	GM-JK	lsf AERO / cvtd -63F (CF)
☐ N606AL	Boeing (Douglas) DC-8-73F	46044 / 432	D-ADUE	0069	0697	4 CFMI CFM56-2C	161025	Freighter	CL-BM	lsf AERO / cvtd -63F (AF)
☐ N791FT	Boeing (Douglas) DC-8-73F	46045 / 441		0069	0484	4 CFMI CFM56-2C	161025	Freighter	CF-DE	lsf GECC/cvtd -63F (CF)
☐ N792FT	Boeing (Douglas) DC-8-73F	46046 / 444		0069	0184	4 CFMI CFM56-2C	161025	Freighter	BL-HJ	J.C.Emery, Jr / cvtd -63F (CF)
☐ N795FT	Boeing (Douglas) DC-8-73F	46103 / 483		0069	0684	4 CFMI CFM56-2C	161025	Freighter	CF-DM	cvtd -63F (CF)
☐ N796FT	Boeing (Douglas) DC-8-73F	46104 / 488		0869	0584	4 CFMI CFM56-2C	161025	Freighter	BL-GH	cvtd -63F (CF)
☐ N832AL	Boeing (Douglas) DC-8-73F	46063 / 457	N875SJ	0069	1298	4 CFMI CFM56-2C	161025	Freighter		lsf AERO / cvtd DC-8-63
☐ N870TV	Boeing (Douglas) DC-8-73F	46086 / 478	N794FT	0069	0784	4 CFMI CFM56-2C	161025	Freighter	JK-DH	cvtd -63F (CF)
☐ N961R	Boeing (Douglas) DC-8-73F	46133 / 545	N801WA	0070	0884	4 CFMI CFM56-2C	161025	Freighter	FG-AL	cvtd -63F (CF)
☐ N68042	Boeing (Douglas) DC-10-10F	46901 / 40		0072		3 GE CF6-6D	195045	Freighter		to be lsf PEGA 0099 / cvtd -10
☐ N	Boeing (Douglas) DC-10-10F			0072		3 GE CF6-6D	195045	Freighter		to be lsf PEGA 0099 / ex COA / cvtd -10
☐ N	Boeing (Douglas) DC-10-10F			0072		3 GE CF6-6D	195045	Freighter		to be lsf PEGA 0099 / ex COA / cvtd -10
☐ N	Boeing (Douglas) DC-10-10F			0072		3 GE CF6-6D	195045	Freighter		to be lsf PEGA 0099 / ex COA / cvtd -10
☐ N	Boeing (Douglas) DC-10-10F			0072		3 GE CF6-6D	195045	Freighter		to be lsf PEGA 0099 / ex COA / cvtd -10

EMPIRE AIRLINES, Inc. = EM / CFS (formerly Empire Airways) — Coeur d'Alene, ID

2115 Government Way, Coeur d'Alene, ID 83814, USA ☎ (208) 667-5400 Tx: none Fax: (208) 667-8787 SITA: n/a
F: 1977 ✈✈✈ 140 Head: Melvin E. Spelde IATA: 464 ICAO: EMPIRE AIR Net: http://www.empirecoe.com/

☐ N819FE	Cessna 208A Caravan I Cargomaster	20800056		0085	0985	1 PWC PT6A-114	3629	Freighter		lsf/opf FDX in FedEx Feeder-colors
☐ N833FE	Cessna 208A Caravan I Cargomaster	20800084	EI-FDX	0086	0386	1 PWC PT6A-114	3629	Freighter		lsf/opf FDX in FedEx Feeder-colors
☐ N835FE	Cessna 208A Caravan I Cargomaster	20800016	EI-FEX	0085	0485	1 PWC PT6A-114	3629	Freighter		lsf/opf FDX in FedEx Feeder-colors
☐ N700FX	Cessna 208B Caravan I Super Cargomaster	208B0419		0095	0195	1 PWC PT6A-114A	3969	Freighter		lsf/opf FDX in FedEx Feeder-colors
☐ N705FX	Cessna 208B Caravan I Super Cargomaster	208B0425		0095	0295	1 PWC PT6A-114A	3969	Freighter		lsf/opf FDX in FedEx Feeder-colors

322 registration type of aircraft cn/fn ex/ex* mfd del powered by mtow kg configuration selcal name/fln/specialitites/remarks

registration	type of aircraft	cn/fn	ex/ex*	mfd	del	powered by	mtow kg	configuration	selcal	name/fln/specialtites/remarks
☐ N709FX	Cessna 208B Caravan I Super Cargomaster	208B0430		0095	0395	1 PWC PT6A-114A	3969	Freighter		lsf/opf FDX in FedEx Feeder-colors
☐ N711FX	Cessna 208B Caravan I Super Cargomaster	208B0433		0095	0495	1 PWC PT6A-114A	3969	Freighter		lsf/opf FDX in FedEx Feeder-colors
☐ N720FX	Cessna 208B Caravan I Super Cargomaster	208B0452		0095	0795	1 PWC PT6A-114A	3969	Freighter		lsf/opf FDX in FedEx Feeder-colors
☐ N728FX	Cessna 208B Caravan I Super Cargomaster	208B0471		0095	1095	1 PWC PT6A-114A	3969	Freighter		lsf/opf FDX in FedEx Feeder-colors
☐ N746FX	Cessna 208B Caravan I Super Cargomaster	208B0498		0096	0196	1 PWC PT6A-114A	3969	Freighter		lsf/opf FDX in FedEx Feeder-colors
☐ N752FX	Cessna 208B Caravan I Super Cargomaster	208B0517		0096	0396	1 PWC PT6A-114A	3969	Freighter		lsf/opf FDX in FedEx Feeder-colors
☐ N753FE	Cessna 208B Caravan I Super Cargomaster	208B0248		0091	0191	1 PWC PT6A-114A	3969	Freighter		lsf/opf FDX in FedEx Feeder-colors
☐ N756FX	Cessna 208B Caravan I Super Cargomaster	208B0532		0096	0496	1 PWC PT6A-114A	3969	Freighter		lsf/opf FDX in FedEx Feeder-colors
☐ N775FE	Cessna 208B Caravan I Super Cargomaster	208B0272		0091	0791	1 PWC PT6A-114A	3969	Freighter		lsf/opf FDX in FedEx Feeder-colors
☐ N778FE	Cessna 208B Caravan I Super Cargomaster	208B0275		0091	0891	1 PWC PT6A-114A	3969	Freighter		lsf/opf FDX in FedEx Feeder-colors
☐ N779FE	Cessna 208B Caravan I Super Cargomaster	208B0276		0091	0891	1 PWC PT6A-114A	3969	Freighter		lsf/opf FDX in FedEx Feeder-colors
☐ N788FE	Cessna 208B Caravan I Super Cargomaster	208B0286		0091	1091	1 PWC PT6A-114A	3969	Freighter		lsf/opf FDX in FedEx Feeder-colors
☐ N850FE	Cessna 208B Caravan I Super Cargomaster	208B0164		0089	0489	1 PWC PT6A-114	3969	Freighter		lsf/opf FDX in FedEx Feeder-colors
☐ N856FE	Cessna 208B Caravan I Super Cargomaster	208B0176		0089	0689	1 PWC PT6A-114	3969	Freighter		lsf/opf FDX in FedEx Feeder-colors
☐ N859FE	Cessna 208B Caravan I Super Cargomaster	208B0181		0089	0789	1 PWC PT6A-114	3969	Freighter		lsf/opf FDX in FedEx Feeder-colors
☐ N873FE	Cessna 208B Caravan I Super Cargomaster	208B0202		0089	1289	1 PWC PT6A-114	3969	Freighter		lsf/opf FDX in FedEx Feeder-colors
☐ N875FE	Cessna 208B Caravan I Super Cargomaster	208B0206		0090	0290	1 PWC PT6A-114	3969	Freighter		lsf/opf FDX in FedEx Feeder-colors
☐ N876FE	Cessna 208B Caravan I Super Cargomaster	208B0207		0090	0290	1 PWC PT6A-114	3969	Freighter		lsf/opf FDX in FedEx Feeder-colors
☐ N880FE	Cessna 208B Caravan I Super Cargomaster	208B0215		0090	0490	1 PWC PT6A-114	3969	Freighter		lsf/opb FDX in FedEx Feeder-colors
☐ N882FE	Cessna 208B Caravan I Super Cargomaster	208B0208		0090	0290	1 PWC PT6A-114	3969	Freighter		lsf/opf FDX in FedEx Feeder-colors
☐ N895FE	Cessna 208B Caravan I Super Cargomaster	208B0015	C-FEXG	0087	0387	1 PWC PT6A-114	3969	Freighter		lsf/opf FDX in FedEx Feeder-colors
☐ N896FE	Cessna 208B Caravan I Super Cargomaster	208B0226		0090	0890	1 PWC PT6A-114	3969	Freighter		lsf/opf FDX in FedEx Feeder-colors
☐ N897FE	Cessna 208B Caravan I Super Cargomaster	208B0227		0090	0890	1 PWC PT6A-114	3969	Freighter		lsf/opf FDX in FedEx Feeder-colors
☐ N899FE	Cessna 208B Caravan I Super Cargomaster	208B0235		0090	1090	1 PWC PT6A-114A	3969	Freighter		lsf/opf FDX in FedEx Feeder-colors
☐ N918FE	Cessna 208B Caravan I Super Cargomaster	208B0018		0087	0387	1 PWC PT6A-114	3969	Freighter		lsf/opf FDX in FedEx Feeder-colors
☐ N940FE	Cessna 208B Caravan I Super Cargomaster	208B0040		0087	0987	1 PWC PT6A-114	3969	Freighter		lsf/opf FDX in FedEx Feeder-colors
☐ N941FE	Cessna 208B Caravan I Super Cargomaster	208B0192		0089	1089	1 PWC PT6A-114	3969	Freighter		lsf/opf FDX in FedEx Feeder-colors
☐ N953FE	Cessna 208B Caravan I Super Cargomaster	208B0062		0087	1287	1 PWC PT6A-114	3969	Freighter		lsf/opf FDX in FedEx Feeder-colors
☐ N956FE	Cessna 208B Caravan I Super Cargomaster	208B0068		0087	0188	1 PWC PT6A-114	3969	Freighter		lsf/opf FDX in FedEx Feeder-colors
☐ N960FE	Cessna 208B Caravan I Super Cargomaster	208B0075		0088	0388	1 PWC PT6A-114	3969	Freighter		lsf/opf FDX in FedEx Feeder-colors
☐ N965FE	Cessna 208B Caravan I Super Cargomaster	208B0084		0088	0488	1 PWC PT6A-114	3969	Freighter		lsf/opf FDX in FedEx Feeder-colors
☐ N976FE	Cessna 208B Caravan I Super Cargomaster	208B0103		0088	0788	1 PWC PT6A-114	3969	Freighter		lsf/opf FDX in FedEx Feeder-colors
☐ N983FE	Cessna 208B Caravan I Super Cargomaster	208B0113		0088	0888	1 PWC PT6A-114	3969	Freighter		lsf/opf FDX in FedEx Feeder-colors
☐ N992FE	Cessna 208B Caravan I Super Cargomaster	208B0128		0088	1188	1 PWC PT6A-114	3969	Freighter		lsf/opf FDX in FedEx Feeder-colors
☐ N995FE	Cessna 208B Caravan I Super Cargomaster	208B0133		0088	1188	1 PWC PT6A-114	3969	Freighter		lsf/opf FDX in FedEx Feeder-colors
☐ N153CC	Shorts 360-300 (SD3-60)	SH3753	N753CN	0089	1298	2 PWC PT6A-67R	12292	Freighter		lsf/opf FDX in FedEx Feeder-colors
☐ N262GA	Shorts 360-300 (SD3-60)	SH3749	N828BE	0089	1298	2 PWC PT6A-67R	12292	Freighter		lsf/opf FDX in FedEx Feeder-colors
☐ N748CC	Shorts 360-300 (SD3-60)	SH3748	N748SA	0088	1298	2 PWC PT6A-67R	12292	Freighter		lsf/opf FDX in FedEx Feeder-colors
☐ N701FE	Fokker F27 Friendship 600 (F27 Mk600)	10419	OO-FEF	0069	0690	2 RR Dart 532-7R	20412	Freighter		lsf/opf FDX in FedEx Feeder-colors
☐ N702FE	Fokker F27 Friendship 600 (F27 Mk600)	10350	OO-FEG	0067	0790	2 RR Dart 532-7R	20412	Freighter		lsf/opf FDX in FedEx Feeder-colors
☐ N703FE	Fokker F27 Friendship 600 (F27 Mk600)	10420	D-AFEH	0069	0790	2 RR Dart 532-7R	20412	Freighter		lsf/opf FDX in FedEx Feeder-colors
☐ N729FE	Fokker F27 Friendship 600 (F27 Mk600)	10385	EI-FEA	0068	0989	2 RR Dart 532-7R	20412	Freighter		lsf/opf FDX in FedEx Feeder-colors
☐ N730FE	Fokker F27 Friendship 600 (F27 Mk600)	10386	I-FEAB	0068	1089	2 RR Dart 532-7R	20412	Freighter		lsf/opf FDX in FedEx Feeder-colors
☐ N740FE	Fokker F27 Friendship 600 (F27 Mk600)	10329	HB-ISJ	0067	1189	2 RR Dart 532-7R	20412	Freighter		lsf/opf FDX in FedEx Feeder-colors
☐ N741FE	Fokker F27 Friendship 600 (F27 Mk600)	10387	G-FEAD	0068	1289	2 RR Dart 532-7R	20412	Freighter		lsf/opf FDX in FedEx Feeder-colors
☐ N742FE	Fokker F27 Friendship 600 (F27 Mk600)	10349	G-FEAE	0068	0190	2 RR Dart 532-7R	20412	Freighter		lsf/opf FDX in FedEx Feeder-colors
☐ N222DG	Fairchild Ind. F-27F (SCD)	31	C-GJON	0058	0290	2 RR Dart 529-7E	19051	Freighter		cvtd F-27A
☐ N711FE	Fokker F27 Friendship 500 (F27 Mk500)	10383	F-BPNI	0069	0389	2 RR Dart 532-7R	20412	Freighter		lsf/opf FDX in FedEx Feeder-colors
☐ N720FE	Fokker F27 Friendship 500 (F27 Mk500)	10464	9M-MCE	0071	0690	2 RR Dart 532-7R	20412	Freighter		lsf/opf FDX in FedEx Feeder-colors

ENGLAND JET, Inc.   Alexandria-Int'l, LA

1037 Billy Mitchell Blvd, 2502, Alexandria, LA 71311, USA   ☎ (318) 443-5566   Tx: none   Fax: (318) 487-6576   SITA: n/a
F: 1995   ✦✦✦ n/a   Head: Roger C. Black   Net: http://www.englandjet.com

☐ N55476	Piper PA-32-300 Cherokee SIX	32-7340120		0073	0895	1 LY IO-540-K1A5	1542			lsf pvt
☐ N310MH	Cessna 310R II	310R2132		0081	1196	2 CO IO-520-M	2495			

ENTERPRISE FLYING, Inc.   McGrath, AK

PO Box 185, McGrath, AK 99627, USA   ☎ (907) 524-3550   Tx: none   Fax: (907) 524-3163   SITA: n/a
F: 1997   ✦✦✦ n/a   Head: James F. Ellis   Net: n/a   Aircraft below MTOW 1361kg: Piper PA-12

☐ N2750J	Cessna A185E Skywagon	185-1500		0069	1297	1 CO IO-520-D	1520			lsf pvt / Floats / Wheel-Skis

EPPS AIR SERVICE, Inc. = EPS   Atlanta-DeKalb Peachtree, GA   *EPPS*

1 Aviation Way, Atlanta, GA 30341, USA   ☎ (770) 458-9851   Tx: none   Fax: (770) 458-0320   SITA: n/a
F: 1965   ✦✦✦ 140   Head: E. Patrick Epps   ICAO: EPPS AIR   Net: http://www.eppsaviation.com

☐ N6666X	Beech Baron 58	TH-1093	N666X	0079	0198	2 CO IO-520-CB	2449			
☐ N10HT	Mitsubishi MU-2B-60 Cargoliner	778SA	N264MA	0080	1092	2 GA TPE331-10-501M	5250	Freighter		Cavenaugh SCD conversion
☐ N1164F	Mitsubishi MU-2B-60 Cargoliner	1562SA	D-ICDG	0082	1096	2 GA TPE331-10-501M	5250	Freighter		Cavenaugh SCD conversion
☐ N42AF	Mitsubishi MU-2B-60 Cargoliner	1539SA	ZS-MRJ	0081	0197	2 GA TPE331-10-501M	5250	Freighter		Cavenaugh SCD conversion
☐ N46AK	Mitsubishi MU-2B-60 Cargoliner	754SA	XB-FBY	0079	0198	2 GA TPE331-10-501M	5250	Freighter		Cavenaugh SCD conversion
☐ N772DA	Mitsubishi MU-2B-60 Cargoliner	772SA	I-MPLT	0080	0192	2 GA TPE331-10-501M	5250	Freighter		Cavenaugh SCD conversion
☐ N8083A	Mitsubishi MU-2B-60 Cargoliner	739SA	N707EZ	0079	0392	2 GA TPE331-10-501M	5250	Freighter		Cavenaugh SCD conversion
☐ N888RH	Mitsubishi MU-2B-60 Cargoliner	737SA	N315MA	0079	0498	2 GA TPE331-10-501M	5250	Freighter		Cavenaugh SCD conversion
☐ N888SE	Mitsubishi MU-2B-60 Cargoliner	1549SA	N475MA	0082	0292	2 GA TPE331-10-501M	5250	Freighter		Cavenaugh SCD conversion
☐ N941MA	Mitsubishi MU-2B-60 Cargoliner	744SA		0079	0192	2 GA TPE331-10-501M	5250	Freighter		Cavenaugh SCD conversion
☐ N984RE	Mitsubishi MU-2B-60 Cargoliner	787SA	N267PC	0080	1096	2 GA TPE331-10-501M	5250	Freighter		Cavenaugh SCD conversion
☐ N102AD	Cessna 500 Citation	500-0280	N100HP	0075	1293	2 PWC JT15D-1	5216			
☐ N601CF	Beech King Air 200	BB-25	N1555N	0074	0289	2 PWC PT6A-41	5670			
☐ N178CP	Learjet 35	35-005	N175J	0075	1183	2 GA TFE731-2-2B	8165			

EQUATOR LEASING, Inc. = (EQUA) (Division of Equator Aviation Services, Equator Bank,Ltd & Equator Holdings, Ltd)   Hartford, CT & London   *EQUATOR*

45 Glastonbury Blvd, Glastonbury, CT 06033-6033, USA   ☎ (860) 633-9999   Tx: none   Fax: (860) 633-6799   SITA: n/a
F: 1975   ✦✦✦ 98   Head: Frank Kennedy   Net: n/a   New and used aircraft leasing, sales and financing company.
Owner / lessor of the following (main) aircraft types: Boeing 707-320C & DC-10-30.   Aircraft leased from EQUA are listed and mentioned as such under the leasing carriers.

ERA Aviation, Inc. = 7H / ERH (ERA Classic Airlines) (Subs of Rowan Co./formerly ERA Helicopters & ERA Jet Alaska)   Anchorage-Int'l South, AK & Lake Charles-Regional, LA   *Era Aviation*

6160 Carl Brady Drive, Anchorage, AK 99502-1801, USA   ☎ (907) 248-4422   Tx: 090253244 eraincahg   Fax: (907) 266-8383   SITA: n/a
F: 1948   ✦✦✦ 350   Head: Charles W. Johnson   IATA: 808   ICAO: ERAH   Net: http://www.era-aviation.com
Scheduled services in Alaska are operated in conjunction with Alaska Airlines as an ALASKA AIRLINES COMMUTER but in own colors & titles, using AS flight numbers.
DC-3 aircraft are operated under the marketing name ERA CLASSIC AIRLINES (same headquarters).

☐ N207EH	Bell 206B JetRanger III	3296		0081	0981	1 AN 250-C20B	1451			
☐ N265AH	Bell 206B JetRanger	369	N4770R	0069	0196	1 AN 250-C20	1451			cvtd 206A
☐ N400EH	Bell 206L LongRanger	45108		0077	0977	1 AN 250-C20B	1814			
☐ N402EH	Bell 206L LongRanger	45109		0077	0977	1 AN 250-C20B	1814			
☐ N403EH	Bell 206L LongRanger	45113		0077	1077	1 AN 250-C20B	1814			
☐ N404EH	Bell 206L LongRanger	45114		0077	1077	1 AN 250-C20B	1814			
☐ N405EH	Bell 206L LongRanger	45115		0077	1077	1 AN 250-C20B	1814			
☐ N161EH	Eurocopter (Aerosp.) AS350B2 AStar	2144		0089	0389	1 TU Arriel 1D1	2100			cvtd AS350B1
☐ N162EH	Eurocopter (Aerosp.) AS350B2 AStar	2147		0089	0489	1 TU Arriel 1D1	2100			cvtd AS350B1
☐ N165EH	Eurocopter (Aerosp.) AS350B2 AStar	2185		0089	0689	1 TU Arriel 1D1	2100			cvtd AS350B1
☐ N166EH	Eurocopter (Aerosp.) AS350B2 AStar	2194		0089	0689	1 TU Arriel 1D1	2100			cvtd AS350B1
☐ N178EH	Eurocopter (Aerosp.) AS350B2 AStar	2264		0090	0490	1 TU Arriel 1D1	2100			cvtd AS350B1
☐ N181EH	Eurocopter (Aerosp.) AS350B2 AStar	2680		0092	0693	1 TU Arriel 1D1	2250			
☐ N182EH	Eurocopter (Aerosp.) AS350B2 AStar	2681		0092	0693	1 TU Arriel 1D1	2250			
☐ N183EH	Eurocopter (Aerosp.) AS350B2 AStar	2752		0093	0694	1 TU Arriel 1D1	2250			
☐ N185EH	Eurocopter (Aerosp.) AS350B2 AStar	2823		0094	0695	1 TU Arriel 1D1	2250			
☐ N186EH	Eurocopter (Aerosp.) AS350B2 AStar	2844		0095	0695	1 TU Arriel 1D1	2250			
☐ N187EH	Eurocopter (Aerosp.) AS350B2 AStar	2839		0095	0695	1 TU Arriel 1D1	2250			
☐ N188EH	Eurocopter (Aerosp.) AS350B2 AStar	2954		0097	0597	1 TU Arriel 1D1	2250			
☐ N189EH	Eurocopter (Aerosp.) AS350B2 AStar	2956		0097	0497	1 TU Arriel 1D1	2250			
☐ N190EH	Eurocopter (Aerosp.) AS350B2 AStar	2974		0097	0797	1 TU Arriel 1D1	2250			
☐ N191EH	Eurocopter (Aerosp.) AS350B2 AStar	2505		0091	0192	1 TU Arriel 1D1	2250			
☐ N192EH	Eurocopter (Aerosp.) AS350B2 AStar	2582		0091	0192	1 TU Arriel 1D1	2250			
☐ N193EH	Eurocopter (Aerosp.) AS350B2 AStar	2599		0091	0392	1 TU Arriel 1D1	2250			
☐ N194EH	Eurocopter (Aerosp.) AS350B2 AStar	2608		0092	0392	1 TU Arriel 1D1	2250			
☐ N195EH	Eurocopter (Aerosp.) AS350B2 AStar	2615		0092	0392	1 TU Arriel 1D1	2250			
☐ N196EH	Eurocopter (Aerosp.) AS350B2 AStar	2976		0097	0797	1 TU Arriel 1D1	2250			
☐ N197EH	Eurocopter (Aerosp.) AS350B2 AStar	2983		0097	1297	1 TU Arriel 1D1	2250			
☐ N212EH	Eurocopter (Aerosp.) AS350B2 AStar	3151		0099	0399	1 TU Arriel 1D1	2250			
☐ N	Eurocopter (Aerosp.) AS350B2 AStar					1 TU Arriel 1D1	2250			oo-delivery 0099
☐ N	Eurocopter (Aerosp.) AS350B2 AStar					1 TU Arriel 1D1	2250			oo-delivery 0099

☐ N	Eurocopter (Aerosp.) AS350B2 AStar					1 TU Arriel 1D1	2250			oo-delivery 0099
☐ N	Eurocopter (Aerosp.) AS350B2 AStar					1 TU Arriel 1D1	2250			oo-delivery 0099
☐ N124EH	Eurocopter (MBB) BO105CBS	S-559	N9373H	0082	0382	2 AN 250-C20B	2300			
☐ N125EH	Eurocopter (MBB) BO105CBS	S-562	N9376Y	0082	0482	2 AN 250-C20B	2300			
☐ N127EH	Eurocopter (MBB) BO105CBS	S-571	D-HDPT*	0082	0882	2 AN 250-C20B	2300			
☐ N128EH	Eurocopter (MBB) BO105CBS	S-572	D-HDPU*	0082	0782	2 AN 250-C20B	2300			
☐ N129EH	Eurocopter (MBB) BO105CBS	S-580	N29077	0082	1082	2 AN 250-C20B	2300			
☐ N130EH	Eurocopter (MBB) BO105CBS	S-588	N2910H	0082	0982	2 AN 250-C20B	2300			
☐ N131EH	Eurocopter (MBB) BO105CBS	S-595	N3129U	0082	0283	2 AN 250-C20B	2300			
☐ N133EH	Eurocopter (MBB) BO105CBS	S-598	N29128	0082	0383	2 AN 250-C20B	2300			
☐ N134EH	Eurocopter (MBB) BO105CBS	S-635	N2785A	0083	0485	2 AN 250-C20B	2300			
☐ N135EH	Eurocopter (MBB) BO105CBS	S-675	N4573D	0085	0485	2 AN 250-C20B	2300			
☐ N141LG	Eurocopter (MBB) BO105CBS	S-704	N154EH	0085	0286	2 AN 250-C20B	2300			
☐ N148EH	Eurocopter (MBB) BO105CBS	S-703	PH-NZX	0085	0885	2 AN 250-C20B	2500			
☐ N149EH	Eurocopter (MBB) BO105CBS	S-705	N968MB	0085	0985	2 AN 250-C20B	2300			
☐ N151EH	Eurocopter (MBB) BO105CBS	S-706	N955MB	0085	0885	2 AN 250-C20B	2300			
☐ N152EH	Eurocopter (MBB) BO105CBS	S-701	N954MB	0085	0286	2 AN 250-C20B	2300			
☐ N153EH	Eurocopter (MBB) BO105CBS	S-702	PH-NZY	0085	0186	2 AN 250-C20B	2500			
☐ N290EH	Eurocopter (MBB) BO105CBS	S-850	N6554Y	0090	0191	2 AN 250-C20B	2300			
☐ N291EH	Eurocopter (MBB) BO105CBS	S-842	N65962	0090	0291	2 AN 250-C20B	2300			
☐ N292EH	Eurocopter (MBB) BO105CBS	S-843	N7170C	0090	0291	2 AN 250-C20B	2300			
☐ N293EH	Eurocopter (MBB) BO105CBS	S-844	N6612K	0090	0391	2 AN 250-C20B	2300			
☐ N294EH	Eurocopter (MBB) BO105CBS	S-846	N6595A	0090	0491	2 AN 250-C20B	2300			
☐ N296EH	Eurocopter (MBB) BO105CBS	S-849	N65385	0090	0491	2 AN 250-C20B	2300			
☐ N297EH	Eurocopter (MBB) BO105CBS	S-835	N41854	0090	0591	2 AN 250-C20B	2300			
☐ N298EH	Eurocopter (MBB) BO105CBS	S-845	N4186F	0090	0691	2 AN 250-C20B	2300			
☐ N423EH	Eurocopter (MBB) BO105CBS	S-543	N42018	0081	0182	2 AN 250-C20B	2300			
☐ N424EH	Eurocopter (MBB) BO105CBS	S-548	N42001	0081	1281	2 AN 250-C20B	2300			
☐ N426EH	Eurocopter (MBB) BO105CBS	S-552	N93173	0081	0282	2 AN 250-C20B	2300			
☐ N427EH	Eurocopter (MBB) BO105CBS	S-554	N93205	0081	0282	2 AN 250-C20B	2300			
☐ N576EH	Sikorsky S-76A+	760212	N15458	1082	1198	2 TU Arriel 1S	4763			cvtd S-76A
☐ N577EH	Sikorsky S-76A+	760222	N15459	1282	1298	2 TU Arriel 1S	4763			cvtd S-76A
☐ N357EH	Bell 212	31209		0082	0382	2 PWC PT6T-3B TwinPac	5080			
☐ N358EH	Bell 212	31211		0082	0482	2 PWC PT6T-3B TwinPac	5080			
☐ N359EH	Bell 212	31212	C-GRVN	0082	0682	2 PWC PT6T-3B TwinPac	5080			
☐ N360EH	Bell 212	31213		0082	0482	2 PWC PT6T-3B TwinPac	5080			
☐ N361EH	Bell 212	30554	N213AH	0073	0196	2 PWC PT6T-3 TwinPac	5080			
☐ N362EH	Bell 212	30853	N212AH	0077	0196	2 PWC PT6T-3 TwinPac	5080			
☐ N370EH	Bell 212	30624		0074	0574	2 PWC PT6T-3 TwinPac	5080			
☐ N399EH	Bell 212	30810		0077	0177	2 PWC PT6T-3 TwinPac	5080			
☐ N500EH	Bell 212	30945		0079	0979	2 PWC PT6T-3 TwinPac	5080			
☐ N507EH	Bell 212	30950		0079	0380	2 PWC PT6T-3 TwinPac	5080			
☐ N508EH	Bell 212	30908		0079	0379	2 PWC PT6T-3 TwinPac	5080			
☐ N509EH	Bell 212	30925		0079	0779	2 PWC PT6T-3 TwinPac	5080			
☐ N510EH	Bell 212	31113		0080	0780	2 PWC PT6T-3 TwinPac	5080			
☐ N511EH	Bell 212	31118		0080	0780	2 PWC PT6T-3 TwinPac	5080			
☐ N522EH	Bell 212	31199		0081	1281	2 PWC PT6T-3 TwinPac	5080			
☐ N523EH	Bell 212	31214	C-GRWX	0082	0482	2 PWC PT6T-3 TwinPac	5080			
☐ N163EH	Bell 412	33008	C-GKHS	0081	0489	2 PWC PT6T-3B TwinPac	5398			
☐ N164EH	Bell 412	33004	N58RC	0081	0186	2 PWC PT6T-3B TwinPac	5398			
☐ N167EH	Bell 412	33089	VH-NSO	0083	0689	2 PWC PT6T-3B TwinPac	5398			
☐ N168EH	Bell 412	33058	N9104F	0082	0689	2 PWC PT6T-3B TwinPac	5398			
☐ N169EH	Bell 412	33064	C-GBHH	0082	1189	2 PWC PT6T-3B TwinPac	5398			
☐ N174EH	Bell 412	33085	JA9583	0082	0490	2 PWC PT6T-3B TwinPac	5398			
☐ N177EH	Bell 412	33037	N412S	0081	0390	2 PWC PT6T-3B TwinPac	5398			
☐ N412EH	Bell 412	33001		0081	0381	2 PWC PT6T-3B TwinPac	5398			
☐ N414EH	Bell 412	33007		0081	0581	2 PWC PT6T-3B TwinPac	5398			
☐ N415EH	Bell 412	33009		0081	0681	2 PWC PT6T-3B TwinPac	5398			
☐ N416EH	Bell 412	33011		0081	0781	2 PWC PT6T-3B TwinPac	5398			
☐ N417EH	Bell 412	33031	N3911E	0081	0182	2 PWC PT6T-3B TwinPac	5398			
☐ N418EH	Bell 412	33032	N3911J	0081	0182	2 PWC PT6T-3B TwinPac	5398			
☐ N419EH	Bell 412	33043		0082	0382	2 PWC PT6T-3B TwinPac	5398			
☐ N421EH	Bell 412	33067	N57413	0082	0282	2 PWC PT6T-3B TwinPac	5398			
☐ N422EH	Bell 412	33068		0082	0782	2 PWC PT6T-3B TwinPac	5398			
☐ N201EH	De Havilland DHC-6 Twin Otter 200	217	N4901W	0069	1277	2 PWC PT6A-20	5252	Y19		
☐ N202EH	De Havilland DHC-6 Twin Otter 100	48	N4914	0067	1277	2 PWC PT6A-20	5252	Y19		
☐ N203EH	De Havilland DHC-6 Twin Otter 100	97	N2715R	0068	1177	2 PWC PT6A-20	5252	Y19		
☐ N204EH	De Havilland DHC-6 Twin Otter 100	61	N8082N	0067	0675	2 PWC PT6A-20	5252	Y19		
☐ N206EH	De Havilland DHC-6 Twin Otter 200	194	N995SA	0069	0871	2 PWC PT6A-20	5252	Y19		
☐ N302EH	De Havilland DHC-6 Twin Otter 300	576	N57AN	0078	0890	2 PWC PT6A-27	5670	Y19		
☐ N320EA	De Havilland DHC-6 Twin Otter 300	625	C-GCVI	0079	0491	2 PWC PT6A-27	5670	Y19		
☐ N321EA	De Havilland DHC-6 Twin Otter 300	299	C-GNTH	0071	0798	2 PWC PT6A-27	5670	Y19		
☐ N885EA	De Havilland DHC-6 Twin Otter 300	454	N454MG	0075	0194	2 PWC PT6A-27	5670	Y19		
☐ N886EA	De Havilland DHC-6 Twin Otter 300	756	N126AS	0081	0594	2 PWC PT6A-27	5670	Y19		
☐ N887EA	De Havilland DHC-6 Twin Otter 300	467	N404X	0076	0696	2 PWC PT6A-27	5670	Y19		
☐ N143LG	Beech King Air 200C	BL-5	N390AC	0080	0193	2 PWC PT6A-41	5670			
☐ N335RD	Learjet 35A	35A-216	N142LG	0078	0293	2 GA TFE731-2-2B	8301	Executive		lst RDC Marine
☐ N170EH	Eurocopter (Aerosp.) AS332L Super Puma	2016	C-GSLB	0082	0489	2 TU Makila 1A	8600			
☐ N171EH	Eurocopter (Aerosp.) AS332L Super Puma	2058	C-GSLA	0082	0589	2 TU Makila 1A	8600			
☐ N561EH	Sikorsky S-61N	61471	ZS-RAX	0069	0997	2 GE CT58-140-1	9299	Y19		
☐ N562EH	Sikorsky S-61N	61257	PH-NZA	0067	0398	2 GE CT58-140-1	9298	Y19		
☐ N563EH	Sikorsky S-61N	61808	PH-NZR	0078	0398	2 GE CT58-140-1	9298	Y19		
☐ N1944H	Boeing (Douglas) DC-3C (C-47B-50-DK)	34378	N54542	0044	0495	2 PW R-1830-90	12202	Y21		ERA Classic Airlines-colors
☐ N1944M	Boeing (Douglas) DC-3C (C-47A-75-DL)	19394	N394CA	0044	1094	2 PW R-1830-90	12202	Y21		ERA Classic Airlines-colors
☐ N881EA	De Havilland DHC-8-102 Dash 8	233	C-GFOD*	0090	1190	2 PWC PW120A	15649	Y37		
☐ N882EA	De Havilland DHC-8-103 Dash 8	098	D-BERT	0088	0494	2 PWC PW121	15649	Y37		
☐ N538JA	Convair 580	34	N73120	0052	1180	2 AN 501-D13H	24766	Y48		cvtd CV 340-31
☐ N565EA	Convair 580	399	N57RD	0057	0496	2 AN 501-D13H	24766	Y48		cvtd CV 440-83
☐ N566EA	Convair 580	381	N73167	0056	0589	2 AN 501-D13H	24766	Y48		cvtd CV 440-12
☐ N568JA	Convair 580	57	N73129	0053	1281	2 AN 501-D13H	24766	Y48		cvtd CV 340-31
☐ N569JA	Convair 580	69	N73132	0053	0980	2 AN 501-D13H	24766	Y48		cvtd CV 340-31
☐ N57RD	Convair 580	509	N12FV	0059	0296	2 AN 501-D13H	24766	Executive		lst RDC Marine / cvtd CV 440-61

ERICKSON AIR CRANE Company, Llc (Subsidiary of Erickson Air Group, Ltd) **Central Point, OR**

PO Box 3247, Central Point, OR 97502, USA ☎ (541) 664-5544 Tx: 15-1673 Fax: (541) 664-7613 SITA: n/a
F: 1971 ⁂ 400 Head: Brian F. Haig Net: http://www.erickson-aircrane.com

☐ N114AC	Bell UH-1H (205)	9464	67-17266	0067	0595	1 LY T53-L-13	4309			
☐ N126AC	Bell UH-1H (205)	5645	66-1162	0066	0595	1 LY T53-L-13	4309			cvtd UH-1D
☐ N149AC	Bell UH-1H (205)	5229	66-746	0066	1195	1 LY T53-L-13	4309			cvtd UH-1D
☐ N92349	Bell UH-1H (205)	12360	70-15750	0070	0397	1 LY T53-L-13	4309			
☐ N999BE	Cessna 441 Conquest II	441-0147	N999PP	0080	1191	2 GA TPE331-8-401S	4468			
☐ N154AC	Sikorsky S-64E Skycrane	64037	68-18435	0068	0392	2 PW JFTD12-4A	19051			cvtd CH-54A
☐ N157AC	Sikorsky S-64E Skycrane	64065		0068	0792	2 PW JFTD12-4A	19051			lst Canadian Air-Crane as C-GESG
☐ N158AC	Sikorsky S-64F Skycrane	64081	HL9260	0068	0792	2 PW JFTD12-4A	21319			cvtd CH-54B
☐ N159AC	Sikorsky S-64F Skycrane	64084	69-18476	0069	0892	2 PW JFTD12-4A	21319			cvtd CH-54B
☐ N163AC	Sikorsky S-64F Skycrane	64093	70-18485	0069	0892	2 PW JFTD12-4A	21319			cvtd CH-54B
☐ N164AC	Sikorsky S-64E Skycrane	64034	C-FCRN	0067	1281	2 PW JFTD12-4A	19051			Incredible Hulk
☐ N165AC	Sikorsky S-64F Skycrane	64085	69-18477	0069	0892	2 PW JFTD12-4A	21319			cvtd CH-54B/std/to be made operational
☐ N171AC	Sikorsky S-64F Skycrane	64090	69-18482	0069	0892	2 PW JFTD12-4A	21319			cvtd CH-54B/std/to be made operational
☐ N172AC	Sikorsky S-64E Skycrane	64061		0068	1294	2 PW JFTD12-4A	19051			lst Canadian Air-Crane as C-FCRN
☐ N173AC	Sikorsky S-64E Skycrane	64015	66-18413	0068	0494	2 PW JFTD12-4A	19051			cvtd CH-54A
☐ N174AC	Sikorsky S-64F Skycrane		N7094X	0069	0594	2 PW JFTD12-4A	21319			cvtd CH-54B/std/to be made operational
☐ N176AC	Sikorsky S-64E Skycrane	64003	C-GJZK	0062	0683	2 PW JFTD12-4A	19051			
☐ N178AC	Sikorsky S-64F Skycrane	64097	70-18489	0070	0594	2 PW JFTD12-4A	21319			cvtd CH-54B
☐ N179AC	Sikorsky S-64F Skycrane	64091	C-GFAH	0070	0994	2 PW JFTD12-4A	21319			
☐ N189AC	Erickson (Sikorsky) S-64E Skycrane	641001		0697	0697	2 PW JFTD12-4A	19051			46
☐ N194AC	Sikorsky S-64E Skycrane	64017	C-GFLH	0068	0596	2 PW JFTD12-4A	19051			cvtd CH-54A
☐ N197AC	Sikorsky S-64F Skycrane		N7028U	0069	1294	2 PW JFTD12-4A	21319			cvtd CH-54B/std/to be made operational
☐ N198AC	Sikorsky S-64F Skycrane	64098	N70280	0070	1294	2 PW JFTD12-4A	21319			cvtd CH-54B/std/to be made operational
☐ N213AC	Sikorsky S-64F Skycrane	64088	69-18480	0069	0795	2 PW JFTD12-4A	21319			cvtd CH-54B/std/to be made operational
☐ N223AC	Sikorsky S-64F Skycrane	64086	69-18478	0069	1294	2 PW JFTD12-4A	21319			cvtd CH-54B

324 registration type of aircraft cn/fn ex/ex* mfd del powered by mtow kg configuration selcal name/fln/specialitites/remarks

☐ N227AC	Sikorsky S-64F Skycrane		69-18471	0069	1294	2 PW JFTD12-4A	21319			cvtd CH-54B/std/to be made operational
☐ N236AC	Sikorsky S-64F Skycrane	64089	69-18481	0069	1095	2 PW JFTD12-4A	21319			cvtd CH-54B/std/to be made operational
☐ N237AC	Sikorsky S-64F Skycrane	64095	70-18487	0069	1095	2 PW JFTD12-4A	21319			cvtd CH-54B/std/to be made operational
☐ N6959R	Sikorsky S-64E Skycrane	64002		0062	0173	2 PW JFTD12-4A	19051			std/to be made operational
☐ N6962R	Sikorsky S-64E Skycrane	64058	C-GFBH	0068	0375	2 PW JFTD12-4A	19051			
☐ N23AC	Curtiss C-46F-1-CU Commando	22451	N18AC	0045	0795	2 PW R-2800	21772	Freighter		

ERIE AIRWAYS, Inc. = ERE (Subsidiary of Connor Holding, Inc.) **Erie-Int'l, PA**

1603 Asbury Road, Erie Int' Airport, Erie, PA 16505, USA ☎ (814) 833-1188 Tx: none Fax: (814) 838-9305 SITA: n/a
F: 1957 57 Head: William B. Conners ICAO: AIR ERIE Net: n/a

☐ N67720	Cessna 402C II	402C0651		0082	0483	2 CO TSIO-520-VB	3107			
☐ N602BC	Cessna 500 Citation	500-0190	N500HK	0074	1295	2 PWC JT15D-1	5216			lsf pvt
☐ N80AW	Cessna 550 Citation II	550-0186	YV-187CP	0080	1196	2 PWC JT15D-4	6577			lsf EZ Partnership

ERIM International, Inc. (Environmental Research Institute Michigan dba) **Detroit-Ypsilanti**

Flight Dept, 813 Willow Run Airport, Hangar 1, Ypsilanti, MI 48198, USA ☎ (734) 483-0500 Tx: none Fax: (734) 483-1280 SITA: n/a
F: 1977 n/a Head: Terry Lewis Net: http://www.erim-int.com Non-commercial State of Michigan organisation conducting scientific research flights.

☐ N51211	Convair 580	489	N5121	1257	0478	2 AN 501-D13	24766	Research+13 Pax		cvtd CV440-0
☐ N51255	Convair 580	383	N45LC	1156	0387	2 AN 501-D13	24766	Research+11 Pax		cvtd CV440-85

ERIN AIR (Michael J. Malone dba) **Seattle-Boeing Field/King County Int'l, CA**

900 East Pine Drive, Seattle, WA 98122, USA ☎ (206) 329-4664 Tx: none Fax: (206) 329-9952 SITA: n/a
F: 1980 n/a Head: Michael J. Malone Net: n/a

☐ N1MM	Beech King Air 200	BB-274	N18243	0077	1083	2 PWC PT6A-41	5670			

EVERGREEN HELICOPTERS (Evergreen Helic.Inc. & Evergreen Helic.of Alaska Inc.dba/Subs.of Evergreen Int'l Aviation Inc.) **McMinnville/OR, ANC-Merrill/AK,Galveston/TX**

3850 Three Mile Lane, McMinnville, OR 97128-9496, USA ☎ (503) 472-9361 Tx: 151306 evergreen mcm Fax: (503) 434-6484 SITA: n/a
F: 1958 n/a Head: Delford M. Smith Net: http://www.evergreen.rotor.com Aircraft below MTOW 1361 kg: Hiller UH12ET

☐ N11035	MD Helicopters MD 500D (Hughes 369D)	900810D		0080	0484	1 AN 250-C20B	1361			
☐ N1103L	MD Helicopters MD 500D (Hughes 369D)	1000812D		0080	0484	1 AN 250-C20B	1361			
☐ N1106K	MD Helicopters MD 500D (Hughes 369D)	410950D		0081	0484	1 AN 250-C20B	1361			
☐ N1106V	MD Helicopters MD 500D (Hughes 369D)	410944D		0081	0682	1 AN 250-C20B	1361			
☐ N1601K	MD Helicopters MD 500E (Hughes 369E)	0202E		0086	0187	1 AN 250-C20B	1361			lsf Evergreen Equity Inc.
☐ N1622X	MD Helicopters MD 500E (Hughes 369E)	0220E	N1601X	0087	0487	1 AN 250-C20B	1361			lsf Evergreen Equity Inc.
☐ N369TH	MD Helicopters MD 500D (Hughes 369D)	1000830D		0080	0789	1 AN 250-C20B	1361			lsf Evergreen Equity Inc.
☐ N5264Q	MD Helicopters MD 500E (Hughes 369E)	0126E		0086	0487	1 AN 250-C20B	1361			lsf Evergreen Equity Inc.
☐ N5291X	MD Helicopters MD 500D (Hughes 369D)	911062D		0081	0289	1 AN 250-C20B	1361			lsf Evergreen Equity Inc.
☐ N58424	MD Helicopters MD 500D (Hughes 369D)	1090593D		0079	0693	1 AN 250-C20B	1361			lsf Evergreen Ventures Inc.
☐ N10729	Bell 206B JetRanger III	2876		0079	0984	1 AN 250-C20B	1451			lsf Evergreen Equity Inc.
☐ N108FH	Bell 206B JetRanger III	2770	N301GP	0079	0588	1 AN 250-C20B	1451			lsf Evergreen Equity Inc.
☐ N2777Q	Bell 206B JetRanger III	2805		0079	0388	1 AN 250-C20B	1451			lsf Evergreen Equity Inc.
☐ N3889Y	Bell 206B JetRanger III	3099		0080	1280	1 AN 250-C20B	1451			lsf Evergreen Equity Inc.
☐ N59558	Bell 206B JetRanger	1413		0074	0774	1 AN 250-C20	1451			lsf Evergreen Equity Inc.
☐ N70DB	Bell 206B JetRanger	1730		0075	1283	1 AN 250-C20	1451			lsf Evergreen Equity Inc.
☐ N3599D	Eurocopter (Aerosp.) SA315B Lama	2579		0079	0395	1 TU Artouste IIIB	1950			lsf Evergreen Equity Inc.
☐ N48087	Eurocopter (Aerosp.) SA315B Lama	2396		0074	0290	1 TU Artouste IIIB	1950			lsf Evergreen Equity Inc.
☐ N55963	Eurocopter (Aerosp.) SA315B Lama	2428		0075	0775	1 TU Artouste IIIB	1950			lsf Evergreen Equity Inc.
☐ N9688G	Cessna U206F Stationair	U20601888		0072	1172	1 CO IO-520-F	1633			lsf Evergreen Equity Inc.
☐ N255EV	Bell 206L-3 LongRanger III	51488		0091	0791	1 AN 250-C30P	1882			lsf Evergreen Equity Inc.
☐ N5000G	Bell 206L-1 LongRanger III	45163		0078	0290	1 AN 250-C30P	1882			lsf Everg.Equity/sublst MOBIL/cvtd LRII
☐ N5007F	Bell 206L-1 LongRanger III	45186		0078	0886	1 AN 250-C30P	1882			lst MOBIL Global Aircraft / cvtd LR II
☐ N5748H	Bell 206L-1 LongRanger II	45490		0080	0696	1 AN 250-C28B	1882			lsf Evergreen Equity Inc.
☐ N600CK	Bell 206L-1 LongRanger II	45787	N3181F	0083	0288	1 AN 250-C28B	1882			lsf Evergreen Equity Inc.
☐ N350EV	Eurocopter (Aerosp.) AS350B2 AStar	2961	C-FZWB	0096	0498	1 TU Arriel 1D1	2250			lsf pvt
☐ N49552	Eurocopter (Aerosp.) SA316B Alouette III	2275		0075	0580	1 TU Artouste IIIB	2200			lsf Evergreen Equity Inc.
☐ N49968	Eurocopter (Aerosp.) SA316B Alouette III	1311		0065	0180	1 TU Artouste IIIB	2200			lsf Evergreen Equity Inc.
☐ N4996G	Eurocopter (Aerosp.) SA316B Alouette III	1233		0065	0180	1 TU Artouste IIIB	2200			lsf Evergreen Equity Inc.
☐ N4997J	Eurocopter (Aerosp.) SA316B Alouette III	1316		0065	0180	1 TU Artouste IIIB	2200			lsf Evergreen Equity Inc.
☐ N67092	Eurocopter (Aerosp.) SA316B Alouette III	2190		0074	0580	1 TU Artouste IIIB	2200			lsf Evergreen Equity Inc.
☐ N204BB	Eurocopter (MBB) BO105C	S-57	D-HDBH*	0072	0688	2 AN 250-C20	2300			lsf Evergreen Equity Inc.
☐ N500KM	Eurocopter (MBB) BO105C	S-76		0073	0281	2 AN 250-C20	2300			lsf Evergreen Equity Inc.
☐ N911MH	Eurocopter (MBB) BO105CBS	S-148	N400MB	0074	0880	2 AN 250-C20	2300	EMS		
☐ N4750R	Bell 205A-1	30009		0068	1268	1 LY T5313B	4309			lsf Evergreen Equity Inc.
☐ N16973	Bell 212	30882	VH-CRO	0078	0884	2 PWC PT6T-3 TwinPac	5080			lsf Evergreen Equity Inc.
☐ N16974	Bell 212	30886		0078	0778	2 PWC PT6T-3 TwinPac	5080			lsf Evergreen Equity Inc.
☐ N212EV	Bell 212	30881	HK-4064X	0078	0594	2 PWC PT6T-3 TwinPac	5080			lsf Evergreen Equity Inc.
☐ N398EH	Bell 212	30766	HK-4059X	0074	0477	2 PWC PT6T-3 TwinPac	5080			lsf Evergreen Equity Inc.
☐ N5017H	Bell 212	30930		0079	0679	2 PWC PT6T-3 TwinPac	5080			lsf Evergreen Equity Inc.
☐ N59633	Bell 212	30676		0075	0375	2 PWC PT6T-3 TwinPac	5080			lsf Evergreen Ventures Inc.
☐ N711EV	Bell 212	31205	N2462V	0081	0383	2 PWC PT6T-3 TwinPac	5080			lsf Evergreen Equity Inc.
☐ N348CA	CASA 212 Aviocar Srs 200	175		0081	0389	2 GA TPE331-10R-511C	7450			lsf Evergreen Equity Inc.
☐ N422CA	CASA 212 Aviocar Srs 200	238		0082	0389	2 GA TPE331-10R-511C	7450			lsf Evergreen Equity Inc.
☐ N423CA	CASA 212 Aviocar Srs 200	240		0082	0389	2 GA TPE331-10R-511C	7450			lsf Evergreen Equity Inc.
☐ N22MS	Learjet 35A	35A-209	N711DS	0078	0786	2 GA TFE731-2-2B	8165			lsf Evergreen Int'l Aviation Inc.
☐ N61EV	Sikorsky S-61R	61566	65-12791	0065	1195	2 GE CT58-140-1	10002			lsf Evergreen Ventures Inc. / cvtd H-3E
☐ N62EV	Sikorsky S-61R	61670	1493	0067	1195	2 GE CT58-140-1	10002			lsf Evergreen Ventures Inc. / cvtd H-3E
☐ N63EV	Sikorsky S-61R	61674	1497	0067	0196	2 GE CT58-140-1	10002			lsf Ventures Holdings Inc. / cvtd H-3E
☐ N6979R	Sikorsky S-64E Skycrane	64079	68-18471	0068	0173	2 PW JFTD12-4A	19051			lsf Evergreen Equity Inc.
☐ N202EV	Lockheed P-2E Neptune	5387	131502	0054	0779	2 WR R-3350	36240	Tanker		141 / lsf Evergreen Equity Inc.

EVERGREEN INTERNATIONAL AIRLINES, Inc. = EZ / EIA (Subsidiary of Evergreen International Aviation, Inc.) **Marana, AZ**

3850 Three Mile Lane, McMinnville, OR 97128-9409, USA ☎ (503) 472-0011 Tx: 151576 evergreen mcm Fax: (503) 434-6492 SITA: n/a
F: 1975 500 Head: Delford M. Smith IATA: 494 ICAO: EVERGREEN Net: http://www.evergreenaviation.com

☐ N915F	Boeing (Douglas) DC-9-15F (MC)	47061 / 207	EC-EYS	0067	0988	2 PW JT8D-7B	41141	Freighter		
☐ N916F	Boeing (Douglas) DC-9-15F (MC)	47044 / 165	OH-LYH	0067	1088	2 PW JT8D-7A	41141	Freighter		
☐ N932F	Boeing (Douglas) DC-9-32F	47355 / 452	I-DIBK	0069	1280	2 PW JT8D-9 (HK3/ABS)	47627	Freighter		
☐ N933F	Boeing (Douglas) DC-9-33F (RC)	47191 / 280	N33UA	0068	1287	2 PW JT8D-9	51710	Freighter		
☐ N935F	Boeing (Douglas) DC-9-32F	47220 / 296	I-DIKF	0068	1081	2 PW JT8D-9 (HK3/ABS)	47627	Freighter		
☐ N940F	Boeing (Douglas) DC-9-33F	47414 / 536	LN-RLW	0069	0588	2 PW JT8D-9 (HK3/ABS)	47627	Freighter		
☐ N944F	Boeing (Douglas) DC-9-33F (RC)	47194 / 324	PH-DNP	0068	0189	2 PW JT8D-9	51710	Freighter		
☐ N945F	Boeing (Douglas) DC-9-33F (RC)	47279 / 337	PH-DNR	0068	0289	2 PW JT8D-9	51710	Freighter		
☐ N3203Y	Boeing 747-128 (SF)	19751 / 39	F-BPVC	0570	1198	4 PW JT9D-7A	332936	Freighter		lsf Arkia Leasing / cvtd -128
☐ N470EV	Boeing 747-273C	20653 / 237	N749WA	0074	0587	4 PW JT9D-7J	362874	Freighter	DE-KM	
☐ N471EV	Boeing 747-273C	20651 / 209	N747WR	0073	0386	4 PW JT9D-7J	362874	Freighter	LM-AF	std MZJ
☐ N472EV	Boeing 747-131 (SF)	20320 / 98	N93115	0070	0588	4 PW JT9D-7AH	332937	Freighter	DG-JL	cvtd -131 / std MZJ
☐ N474EV	Boeing 747-121 (SF)	19637 / 4	N731PA	0069	0289	4 PW JT9D-7A	332937	Freighter	AJ-HL	cvtd -121 / std MZJ
☐ N477EV	Boeing 747SR-46 (SF)	20784 / 231	N688UP	0074	0490	4 PW JT9D-7A	332937	Freighter	AJ-GL	cvtd -46
☐ N478EV	Boeing 747SR-46 (SF)	21033 / 254	N689UP	0075	1290	4 PW JT9D-7A	332937	Freighter	FM-AH	cvtd -46
☐ N479EV	Boeing 747-132 (SF)	19898 / 94	N725PA	0070	0290	4 PW JT9D-7A	342916	Freighter	CG-AK	cvtd -132
☐ N480EV	Boeing 747-121 (SF)	20348 / 106	N690UP	0071	0390	4 PW JT9D-7A	342916	Freighter	CJ-LM	cvtd -121
☐ N481EV	Boeing 747-132 (SF)	19896 / 72	N902PA	0070	0290	4 PW JT9D-7A	342916	Freighter	DK-AB	cvtd -132
☐ N482EV	Boeing 747-212B (SF)	20713 / 219	N729PA	0073	1289	4 PW JT9D-7J	362874	Freighter	FG-AH	lst / opf TFS / cvtd -212B
☐ N485EV	Boeing 747-212B (SF)	20712 / 218	N728PA	0073	1289	4 PW JT9D-7J	362874	Freighter	AJ-GM	lst / opb TFS / cvtd -212B

EVERTS AIR FUEL **Fairbanks-Int'l, AK**

PO Box 60908, Fairbanks, AK 99706, USA ☎ (907) 474-0802 Tx: none Fax: (907) 479-3826 SITA: n/a
F: n/a 44 Head: Clifford R. Everts Net: n/a Operates FAR125 contract fuel-delivery flights within Alaska.

☐ N1419Z	Curtiss C-46A-45-CU Commando	30228	N808Z	0044	1176	2 PW R-2800	21772	Fuel Tanker		
☐ N1651M	Curtiss C-46F-1-CU Commando	22399	44-78576	0045	1198	2 PW R-2800	21772	Freighter		
☐ N1822M	Curtiss C-46F-1-CU Commando	22521	44-78698	0045	0786	2 PW R-2800	21772	Fuel Tanker		Salmon Ella
☐ N1837M	Curtiss C-46F-1-CU Commando	22388	CF-FNC	0045	0990	2 PW R-2800	21772	Fuel Tanker		Hot Stuff
☐ N7848B	Curtiss C-46R Commando	273	HP-238	0045	1176	2 PW R-2800	21772	Fuel Tanker		Dumbo / cvtd C-46A
☐ N4390F	Boeing (Douglas) DC-6B	44898 / 674	F-ZBAC	0056	0792	4 PW R-2800-CB16	45534	Fuel Tanker		Joker's Wild
☐ N4390X	Boeing (Douglas) DC-6B	45066 / 696	F-ZBAD	0056	0792	4 PW R-2800-CB16	45534	Fuel Tanker		std FAI / to be made operational
☐ N451CE	Boeing (Douglas) DC-6A (C-118B)	43712 / 358	N840CS	0053	0191	4 PW R-2800-CB16	47083	Fuel Tanker		

EXCEL AIR CHARTER, Llc **Baton Rouge-Metropolitan/Ryan Field, LA**

4411 Chuck Yeager Ave, Baton Rouge, LA 70807-5255, USA ☎ (504) 357-3366 Tx: none Fax: (504) 357-3366 SITA: n/a
F: 1997 n/a Head: Thomas Allain Net: n/a

☐ N385CG	Twin (Aero) RPM Commander 800L	680FLP-1495-14		0065	0298	2 LY IO-720-B1B	3856			cvtd Grand 680FLP

EXCELSIOR AIR CHARTER, Inc. — San Francisco-Int'l, CA

172 Golden Gate Ave, San Francisco, CA 94102, USA ☎ (415) 928-3200 Tx: none Fax: (415) 673-3329 SITA: n/a
F: 1991 n/a Head: John Sherwood Net: n/a

registration	type of aircraft	cn/fn	ex/ex*	mfd	del	powered by	mtow kg	configuration	selcal	name/fln/specialitites/remarks
☐ N1YS	Beech King Air 200	BB-430	N1BS	0078	0391	2 PWC PT6A-41	5670			

EXECUTIVE AIR CHARTER (HHR Corporation dba) — Houston-William P. Hobby, TX

2040 West Sam Houston Parkway, Houston, TX 77043, USA ☎ (713) 641-1393 Tx: none Fax: (713) 641-1328 SITA: n/a
F: 1996 n/a Head: Albert J. Smith Net: n/a

registration	type of aircraft	cn/fn	ex/ex*	mfd	del	powered by	mtow kg	configuration	selcal	name/fln/specialitites/remarks
☐ N57096	Twin (Aero) Turbo Commander 690A	11120		0073	1196	2 GA TPE331-5-251K	4679			

EXECUTIVE AIR CHARTER OF BOCA RATON, Inc. — Boca Raton, FL

4710 NW Second Avenue, Suite 400, Boca Raton, FL 33431, USA ☎ (561)994-3900ext149 Tx: none Fax: (561) 994-3969 SITA: n/a
F: 1980 n/a Head: Randall T. Rogers Net: n/a

registration	type of aircraft	cn/fn	ex/ex*	mfd	del	powered by	mtow kg	configuration	selcal	name/fln/specialitites/remarks
☐ N792JM	Beech King Air 300	FA-140	N117DR	0088	0792	2 PWC PT6A-60A	6350			lsf Jamestown Metal Marine Sales

EXECUTIVE AIR CHARTERS OF NEW ORLEANS, Inc. — New Orelans-Lakefront, LA

1 Wren Street, New Orleans, LA 70124, USA ☎ (504) 246-6543 Tx: none Fax: (504) 488-4070 SITA: n/a
F: 1993 n/a Head: Kelvin J. Contreary Net: n/a

registration	type of aircraft	cn/fn	ex/ex*	mfd	del	powered by	mtow kg	configuration	selcal	name/fln/specialitites/remarks
☐ N111JA	Beech King Air E90	LW-84	TF-DCA	0073	0298	2 PWC PT6A-28	4581			
☐ N6177Y	Learjet 24	24-151	N53GH	0067	0694	2 GE CJ610-4	5897			
☐ N33JW	Sabreliner 60 (Rockwell NA265-60)	306-92	N74AB	0074	0297	2 PW JT12A-8	9150			lsf Starflight Llc

EXECUTIVE AIRLINES = YL / ORA (East Coast Aviation Services, Ltd dba / formerly Long Island Airlines) — Farmingdale-Republic, NY

1300 New Highway, Farmingdale, NY 11735-1526, USA ☎ (516) 694-0600 Tx: none Fax: (516) 694-0172 SITA: n/a
F: 1960 n/a Head: Michael S. Peragine ICAO: LONG ISLAND Net: n/a

registration	type of aircraft	cn/fn	ex/ex*	mfd	del	powered by	mtow kg	configuration	selcal	name/fln/specialitites/remarks
☐ N350SL	Eurocopter (Aerosp.) AS350BA AStar	2782		0094	1194	1 TU Arriel 1B	2100	Y4		lsf Executive Aircraft & Heli Holdings
☐ N25EC	Learjet 25	25-026	N281R	0069	0284	2 GE CJ610-6	6804	Y8		lsf M&M Executive Aircraft Holdings
☐ N16EJ	BAe 3101 Jetstream 31	834	N851JS	0088	1296	2 GA TPE331-10UG-513H	6900	Y19		
☐ N850JS	BAe 3101 Jetstream 31	826	G-31-826*	0088	1296	2 GA TPE331-10UG-513H	6900	Y19		
☐ N801SM	IAI 1124 Westwind I	297	N51PD	0080	0994	2 GA TFE731-3-1G	10365	Y7		lsf Diversified Aircraft Holdings

EXECUTIVE AIRLINES, Inc. (American Eagle) (Subsidiary of AMR Corp.) — San Juan-LMM Int'l

PO Box 38082, Airport Station, San Juan, PR 00937-0082, USA ☎ (787) 253-6401 Tx: none Fax: (787) 253-6568 SITA: SJUSSNA
F: 1979 1600 Head: George G. Hazy Net: http://www.aa.com Operates 16 ATR42 & 6 ATR72 aircraft as AMERICAN EAGLE (in full such colors & titles), a commuter system to provide feeder connection at American Airlines major hubs, using AA flight numbers. Aircraft registrations varies and are lsf AMR/American Eagle Airlines. Company is expected to be integrated into AMERICAN EAGLE AIRLINES later in 1999.
For aircraft details – see under American Eagle Airlines.

EXECUTIVE AIR TAXI, Corp. — Bismarck-Municipal, ND

Box 2273, Bismarck, ND 58502, USA ☎ (701) 258-5024 Tx: none Fax: (701) 258-2693 SITA: n/a
F: 1973 n/a Head: Dennis D. Rohlfs Net: n/a Aircraft below MTOW 1361kg: Cessna 152 & 172

registration	type of aircraft	cn/fn	ex/ex*	mfd	del	powered by	mtow kg	configuration	selcal	name/fln/specialitites/remarks
☐ N4873S	Cessna R182 Skylane RG II	R18201440		0080	0787	1 LY O-540-J3C5D	1406			
☐ N2025V	Bell 206L-1 LongRanger II	45691		0082	0287	1 AN 250-C28B	1882	EMS Air Care		lst Med-Trans Corp.
☐ N3183T	Bell 206L-1 LongRanger II	45785		0083	1289	1 AN 250-C28B	1882	EMS Air Care		lst Med-Trans Corp.
☐ N911NE	Bell 206L-3 LongRanger III	51160	N160LE	0085	0995	1 AN 250-C30P	1882	EMS Air Care		lsf FBS Business Fin./sub-lst Med-Trans
☐ N911WA	Bell 206L-1 LongRanger II	45621	N3904B	0082	1087	1 AN 250-C28B	1882	EMS Air Care		lst Med-Trans Corp.
☐ N47611	Piper PA-34-200T Seneca II	34-7770418		0077	0992	2 CO TSIO-360-E	2073			
☐ N7693F	Piper PA-34-200T Seneca II	34-7770068		0077	0697	2 CO TSIO-360-E	2073			
☐ N812JA	Piper PA-34-200T Seneca II	34-7970422		0079	0487	2 CO TSIO-360-EB	2073			
☐ N911TM	Eurocopter (Aerosp.) AS355F1 TwinStar	5059	N5779U	0081	1195	2 AN 250-C20F	2400	EMS Air Care		lst Med-Trans Corp.
☐ N35497	Piper PA-31-350 Navajo Chieftain	31-8052039		0079	0180	2 LY TIO-540-J2BD	3175			
☐ N112EF	Twin (Aero) Turbo Commander 690A	11123	N122PG	0073	0693	2 GA TPE331-5-251K	4679			

EXECUTIVE BEECHCRAFT, Inc. (Sister company of Executive Beechcraft STL, Inc.) — Kansas City-Downtown, MO

10 Richards Road, Kansas City, MO 64116, USA ☎ (816) 842-8484 Tx: none Fax: (816) 842-6133 SITA: n/a
F: 1938 n/a Head: Dan L. Meisinger, Jr. Net: n/a

registration	type of aircraft	cn/fn	ex/ex*	mfd	del	powered by	mtow kg	configuration	selcal	name/fln/specialitites/remarks
☐ N38023	Beech Baron 58	TH-1209		0081	0294	2 CO IO-520-CB	2449			
☐ N7758B	Beech Baron 58P	TJ-394		0081	1197	2 CO TSIO-520-WB	2812			
☐ N211GA	Mitsubishi MU-300 Diamond IA	A011SA	N307DM	0081	0498	2 PWC JT15D-4	6636			
☐ N711EC	Beech Beechjet 400	RJ-53	N195KA	0088	0298	2 PWC JT15D-5	7158			
☐ N750T	Beech Beechjet 400A	RK-70	C-FOPC	0093	0898	2 PWC JT15D-5	7303			
☐ N995SA	Hawker 700A (HS 125-700A)	257035 / NA0225	N995SK	0078	0798	2 GA TFE731-3R-1H	11567			

EXECUTIVE BEECHCRAFT STL, Inc. (Sister company of Executive Beechcraft, Inc.) — Chesterfield-Spirit of St. Louis, MO

532 Beechcraft Drive, Chesterfield, MO 63005, USA ☎ (314) 532-4800 Tx: none Fax: (314) 532-8320 SITA: n/a
F: 1972 n/a Head: Mark Meisinger Net: n/a

registration	type of aircraft	cn/fn	ex/ex*	mfd	del	powered by	mtow kg	configuration	selcal	name/fln/specialitites/remarks
☐ N158TT	Beech Baron 58P	TJ-333		0081	0498	2 CO TSIO-520-WB	2812			
☐ N331GB	Beech King Air B100	BE-16		0076	0698	2 GA TPE331-6-252B	5352			
☐ N601DM	Beech King Air C90	LJ-825	N11LS	0079	1297	2 PWC PT6A-21	4377			
☐ N112EB	Cessna 501 Citation I/SP	501-0112	N74PM	0079	0698	2 PWC JT15D-1A	5375			
☐ N266EB	Beech King Air 200	BB-266	ZS-NNS	0077	0498	2 PWC PT6A-41	5670			
☐ N444EB	Beech King Air 200	BB-444	ZS-LZU	0079	0698	2 PWC PT6A-41	5670			
☐ N30HD	Mitsubishi MU-300 Diamond IA	A005SA	N700LP	0080	0298	2 PWC JT15D-4	6636			

EXECUTIVE FLIGHT SERVICES (The Plane Broker, Inc. dba) — Oxford-Waterbury, CT

288 Christian Street, Oxford, CT 06478, USA ☎ (203) 264-8800 Tx: none Fax: (203) 264-8765 SITA: n/a
F: 1985 n/a Head: Joseph Tringali Net: n/a

registration	type of aircraft	cn/fn	ex/ex*	mfd	del	powered by	mtow kg	configuration	selcal	name/fln/specialitites/remarks
☐ N28DF	Piper PA-31-325 Navajo C/R	31-7812121		0078	0195	2 LY TIO-540-F2BD	2948			lsf Miken Corp.
☐ N33MV	Piper PA-31-350 Navajo Chieftain	31-8252035		0082	0797	2 LY TIO-540-J2BD	3175			lsf MV Aviation Corp.

EXECUTIVE JET AVIATION, Inc. = EJA (NetJets) (Subsidiary of Berkshire Hathaway) — Columbus-Port Columbus Int'l, OH

Box 369099, Columbus, OH 43236-9099, USA ☎ (614) 239-5500 Tx: 245495 execjet col Fax: (604) 239-5589 SITA: n/a
F: 1964 n/a Head: Richard T. Santulli ICAO: EXECJET Net: n/a On order (Letter of intent): 50 Cessna 580 Sovereign for delivery starting 2002.
Most aircraft are operated under the NETJETS Quarter-Share ownership program, in which an owner purchases a portion of the shares in a individual aircraft & contract EJA to manage it.
Gulfstream IV/V are jointly marked with Gulfstream Aerospace through GULFSTREAM SHARES-program.Boeing 737BBJ are jointly marked through BBJ joint venture co.with Boeing & General Electric.
NETJETS Europe, a joint-venture company between Executive Jet Aviation, Air Luxor (CS) & Zimex Aviation (HB) is operated by AIR LUXOR (CS). For details see under that company.

registration	type of aircraft	cn/fn	ex/ex*	mfd	del	powered by	mtow kg	configuration	selcal	name/fln/specialitites/remarks
☐ N101QS	Cessna S550 Citation S/II	S550-0101		0086	1286	2 PWC JT15D-4B	6849	7 Pax		
☐ N103QS	Cessna S550 Citation S/II	S550-0103	N12900	0086	0488	2 PWC JT15D-4B	6849	7 Pax		
☐ N106QS	Cessna S550 Citation S/II	S550-0106		0086	1286	2 PWC JT15D-4B	6849	7 Pax		
☐ N111QS	Cessna S550 Citation S/II	S550-0111		0086	0187	2 PWC JT15D-4B	6849	7 Pax		
☐ N112QS	Cessna S550 Citation S/II	S550-0112		0086	0187	2 PWC JT15D-4B	6849	7 Pax		
☐ N126QS	Cessna S550 Citation S/II	S550-0126	N1293K	0087	0588	2 PWC JT15D-4B	6849	7 Pax		
☐ N157QS	Cessna S550 Citation S/II	S550-0157	N2639N	0088	0195	2 PWC JT15D-4B	6849	7 Pax		
☐ N211QS	Cessna S550 Citation S/II	S550-0011	N68SK	0084	0589	2 PWC JT15D-4B	6849	7 Pax		
☐ N214QS	Cessna S550 Citation S/II	S550-0014	N32TJ	0084	0490	2 PWC JT15D-4B	6849	7 Pax		
☐ N232QS	Cessna S550 Citation S/II	S550-0032	N532CF	0084	1289	2 PWC JT15D-4B	6849	7 Pax		lst LXR as CS-DNA
☐ N251QS	Cessna S550 Citation S/II	S550-0051	N1270Y	0085	0489	2 PWC JT15D-4B	6849	7 Pax		lst LXR as CS-DNB
☐ N260QS	Cessna S550 Citation S/II	S550-0060	N314G	0085	0394	2 PWC JT15D-4B	6849	7 Pax		
☐ N274QS	Cessna S550 Citation S/II	S550-0074	N22EH	0085	0395	2 PWC JT15D-4B	6849	7 Pax		
☐ N277QS	Cessna S550 Citation S/II	S550-0077	N747CP	0085	0589	2 PWC JT15D-4B	6849	7 Pax		lst LXR as CS-DNC
☐ N282QS	Cessna S550 Citation S/II	S550-0082	N9KH	0085	0694	2 PWC JT15D-4B	6849	7 Pax		
☐ N288QS	Cessna S550 Citation S/II	S550-0088	N825HL	0086	0190	2 PWC JT15D-4B	6849	7 Pax		
☐ N299QS	Cessna S550 Citation S/II	S550-0099	N44GT	0086	0194	2 PWC JT15D-4B	6849	7 Pax		
☐ N86QS	Cessna S550 Citation S/II	S550-0086	N900RB	0086	0290	2 PWC JT15D-4B	6849	7 Pax		
☐ N92QS	Cessna S550 Citation S/II	S550-0092		0086	0986	2 PWC JT15D-4B	6849	7 Pax		
☐ N93QS	Cessna S550 Citation S/II	S550-0093	N33DS	0086	0492	2 PWC JT15D-4B	6849	7 Pax		
☐ N98QS	Cessna S550 Citation S/II	S550-0098		0086	1186	2 PWC JT15D-4B	6849	7 Pax		
☐ N293QS	Cessna 560 Citation V Ultra	560-0293	N51575	0095	0895	2 PWC JT15D-5D	7394	7 Pax		
☐ N301QS	Cessna 560 Citation V Ultra	560-0038		0089	1289	2 PWC JT15D-5D	7394	7 Pax		
☐ N302QS	Cessna 560 Citation V Ultra	560-0402		0097	0397	2 PWC JT15D-5D	7394	7 Pax		
☐ N307QS	Cessna 560 Citation V Ultra	560-0307	N5233J	0095	0895	2 PWC JT15D-5D	7394	7 Pax		
☐ N309QS	Cessna 560 Citation V Ultra	560-0509				2 PWC JT15D-5D	7394	7 Pax		oo-delivery 0099
☐ N311QS	Cessna 560 Citation V Ultra	560-0311		0095	0895	2 PWC JT15D-5D	7394	7 Pax		
☐ N312QS	Cessna 560 Citation V Ultra	560-0312		0095	0995	2 PWC JT15D-5D	7394	7 Pax		
☐ N314QS	Cessna 560 Citation V Ultra	560-0441		0098	0198	2 PWC JT15D-5D	7394	7 Pax		
☐ N315QS	Cessna 560 Citation V Ultra	560-0315		0095	1095	2 PWC JT15D-5D	7394	7 Pax		
☐ N316QS	Cessna 560 Citation V Ultra	560-0516				2 PWC JT15D-5D	7394	7 Pax		oo-delivery 0099
☐ N317QS	Cessna 560 Citation V Ultra	560-0317		0095	1095	2 PWC JT15D-5D	7394	7 Pax		
☐ N318QS	Cessna 560 Citation V Ultra	560-0418		0097	0797	2 PWC JT15D-5D	7394	7 Pax		
☐ N319QS	Cessna 560 Citation V Ultra	560-0519				2 PWC JT15D-5D	7394	7 Pax		oo-delivery 0099
☐ N320QS	Cessna 560 Citation V Ultra	560-0321	N5262W	0095	1195	2 PWC JT15D-5D	7394	7 Pax		
☐ N322QS	Cessna 560 Citation V Ultra	560-0421		0097	0997	2 PWC JT15D-5D	7394	7 Pax		
☐ N323QS	Cessna 560 Citation V Ultra	560-0323	N5097H	0095	1195	2 PWC JT15D-5D	7394	7 Pax		
☐ N324QS	Cessna 560 Citation V Ultra	560-0423		0097	0797	2 PWC JT15D-5D	7394	7 Pax		
☐ N325QS	Cessna 560 Citation V Ultra	560-0425		0097	1097	2 PWC JT15D-5D	7394	7 Pax		

registration	type of aircraft	cn/fn	ex/ex*	mfd	del	powered by	mtow kg	configuration	selcal	name/fln/specialitites/remarks
☐ N326QS	Cessna 560 Citation V Ultra	560-0526				2 PWC JT15D-5D	7394	7 Pax		oo-delivery 0099
☐ N327QS	Cessna 560 Citation V Ultra	560-0327		0095	1295	2 PWC JT15D-5D	7394	7 Pax		
☐ N328QS	Cessna 560 Citation V Ultra	560-0428		0097	1197	2 PWC JT15D-5D	7394	7 Pax		
☐ N330QS	Cessna 560 Citation V Ultra	560-0329	N5105F	0095	1295	2 PWC JT15D-5D	7394	7 Pax		
☐ N331QS	Cessna 560 Citation V Ultra	560-0331	N51072	0095	0196	2 PWC JT15D-5D	7394	7 Pax		
☐ N332QS	Cessna 560 Citation V Ultra	560-0523				2 PWC JT15D-5D	7394	7 Pax		oo-delivery 0099
☐ N333QS	Cessna 560 Citation V Ultra	560-0333		0095	0196	2 PWC JT15D-5D	7394	7 Pax		
☐ N334QS	Cessna 560 Citation V Ultra	560-0434		0097	1097	2 PWC JT15D-5D	7394	7 Pax		
☐ N335QS	Cessna 560 Citation V Ultra	560-0335		0095	0296	2 PWC JT15D-5D	7394	7 Pax		
☐ N336QS	Cessna 560 Citation V Ultra	560-0336	N5265B	0095	0296	2 PWC JT15D-5D	7394	7 Pax		
☐ N337QS	Cessna 560 Citation V Ultra	560-0437		0097	1097	2 PWC JT15D-5D	7394	7 Pax		
☐ N339QS	Cessna 560 Citation V Ultra	560-0339		0095	0196	2 PWC JT15D-5D	7394	7 Pax		
☐ N340QS	Cessna 560 Citation V Ultra	560-0514				2 PWC JT15D-5D	7394	7 Pax		oo-delivery 0099
☐ N341QS	Cessna 560 Citation V Ultra	560-0341		0096	0396	2 PWC JT15D-5D	7394	7 Pax		
☐ N343QS	Cessna 560 Citation V Ultra	560-0444		0098	0298	2 PWC JT15D-5D	7394	7 Pax		
☐ N344QS	Cessna 560 Citation V Ultra	560-0344		0096	0396	2 PWC JT15D-5D	7394	7 Pax		
☐ N345QS	Cessna 560 Citation V Ultra	560-0445		0098	0298	2 PWC JT15D-5D	7394	7 Pax		
☐ N348QS	Cessna 560 Citation V Ultra	560-0348		0096	0396	2 PWC JT15D-5D	7394	7 Pax		
☐ N351QS	Cessna 560 Citation V Ultra	560-0451		0098	0298	2 PWC JT15D-5D	7394	7 Pax		
☐ N352QS	Cessna 560 Citation V Ultra	560-0352		0096	0496	2 PWC JT15D-5D	7394	7 Pax		
☐ N353QS	Cessna 560 Citation V Ultra	560-0530				2 PWC JT15D-5D	7394	7 Pax		oo-delivery 0099
☐ N354QS	Cessna 560 Citation V Ultra	560-0356		0096	0596	2 PWC JT15D-5D	7394	7 Pax		
☐ N358QS	Cessna 560 Citation V Ultra	560-0455		0098	0498	2 PWC JT15D-5D	7394	7 Pax		
☐ N360QS	Cessna 560 Citation V Ultra	560-0460		0098	0498	2 PWC JT15D-5D	7394	7 Pax		
☐ N361QS	Cessna 560 Citation V Ultra	560-0361		0096	0696	2 PWC JT15D-5D	7394	7 Pax		
☐ N363QS	Cessna 560 Citation V Ultra	560-0536				2 PWC JT15D-5D	7394	7 Pax		oo-delivery 0099
☐ N366QS	Cessna 560 Citation V Ultra	560-0466		0098	0598	2 PWC JT15D-5D	7394	7 Pax		
☐ N367QS	Cessna 560 Citation V Ultra	560-0367		0096	0796	2 PWC JT15D-5D	7394	7 Pax		
☐ N371QS	Cessna 560 Citation V Ultra	560-0471		0098	0698	2 PWC JT15D-5D	7394	7 Pax		
☐ N373QS	Cessna 560 Citation V Ultra	560-0373		0096	0896	2 PWC JT15D-5D	7394	7 Pax		
☐ N374QS	Cessna 560 Citation V Ultra	560-0475		0098	0398	2 PWC JT15D-5D	7394	7 Pax		
☐ N375QS	Cessna 560 Citation V Ultra	560-0375		0096	0996	2 PWC JT15D-5D	7394	7 Pax		
☐ N376QS	Cessna 560 Citation V Ultra	560-0276	N183AJ	0095	0295	2 PWC JT15D-5D	7394	7 Pax		
☐ N377QS	Cessna 560 Citation V Ultra	560-0377	N450RA	0096	0896	2 PWC JT15D-5D	7394	7 Pax		
☐ N379QS	Cessna 560 Citation V Ultra	560-0479		0098	0998	2 PWC JT15D-5D	7394	7 Pax		
☐ N382QS	Cessna 560 Citation V Ultra	560-0382		0096	1096	2 PWC JT15D-5D	7394	7 Pax		
☐ N383QS	Cessna 560 Citation V Ultra	560-0483		0098	0998	2 PWC JT15D-5D	7394	7 Pax		
☐ N386QS	Cessna 560 Citation V Ultra	560-0486		0098	1098	2 PWC JT15D-5D	7394	7 Pax		
☐ N390QS	Cessna 560 Citation V Ultra	560-0490		0098	1098	2 PWC JT15D-5D	7394	7 Pax		
☐ N391QS	Cessna 560 Citation V Ultra	560-0493		0098	1298	2 PWC JT15D-5D	7394	7 Pax		
☐ N392QS	Cessna 560 Citation V Ultra	560-0429		0097	1297	2 PWC JT15D-5D	7394	7 Pax		
☐ N393QS	Cessna 560 Citation V Ultra	560-0393		0096	1196	2 PWC JT15D-5D	7394	7 Pax		
☐ N394QS	Cessna 560 Citation V Ultra	560-0394		0096	1196	2 PWC JT15D-5D	7394	7 Pax		
☐ N395QS	Cessna 560 Citation V Ultra	560-0496		0098	1298	2 PWC JT15D-5D	7394	7 Pax		
☐ N396QS	Cessna 560 Citation V Ultra	560-0396		0096	1196	2 PWC JT15D-5D	7394	7 Pax		
☐ N397QS	Cessna 560 Citation V Ultra	560-0531				2 PWC JT15D-5D	7394	7 Pax		oo-delivery 0099
☐ N398QS	Cessna 560 Citation V Ultra	560-0522				2 PWC JT15D-5D	7394	7 Pax		oo-delivery 0099
☐ N399QS	Cessna 560 Citation V Ultra	560-0510				2 PWC JT15D-5D	7394	7 Pax		oo-delivery 0099
☐ N501QS	Cessna 560 Citation V Ultra	560-0024		0089	1089	2 PWC JT15D-5D	7394	7 Pax		
☐ N	Cessna 560XL Citation Excel	560-				2 PWC PW545A	8709	7 Pax		oo-delivery 0000
☐ N	Cessna 560XL Citation Excel	560-				2 PWC PW545A	8709	7 Pax		oo-delivery 0000
☐ N	Cessna 560XL Citation Excel	560-				2 PWC PW545A	8709	7 Pax		oo-delivery 0000
☐ N	Cessna 560XL Citation Excel	560-				2 PWC PW545A	8709	7 Pax		oo-delivery 0000
☐ N	Cessna 560XL Citation Excel	560-				2 PWC PW545A	8709	7 Pax		oo-delivery 0000
☐ N	Cessna 560XL Citation Excel	560-				2 PWC PW545A	8709	7 Pax		oo-delivery 0000
☐ N	Cessna 560XL Citation Excel	560-				2 PWC PW545A	8709	7 Pax		oo-delivery 0000
☐ N	Cessna 560XL Citation Excel	560-				2 PWC PW545A	8709	7 Pax		oo-delivery 0000
☐ N	Cessna 560XL Citation Excel	560-				2 PWC PW545A	8709	7 Pax		oo-delivery 0000
☐ N	Cessna 560XL Citation Excel	560-				2 PWC PW545A	8709	7 Pax		oo-delivery 0000
☐ N	Cessna 560XL Citation Excel	560-				2 PWC PW545A	8709	7 Pax		oo-delivery 0000
☐ N	Cessna 560XL Citation Excel	560-				2 PWC PW545A	8709	7 Pax		oo-delivery 0000
☐ N	Cessna 560XL Citation Excel	560-				2 PWC PW545A	8709	7 Pax		oo-delivery 0000
☐ N	Cessna 560XL Citation Excel	560-				2 PWC PW545A	8709	7 Pax		oo-delivery 0000
☐ N	Cessna 560XL Citation Excel	560-				2 PWC PW545A	8709	7 Pax		oo-delivery 0000
☐ N	Cessna 560XL Citation Excel	560-				2 PWC PW545A	8709	7 Pax		oo-delivery 0001
☐ N	Cessna 560XL Citation Excel	560-				2 PWC PW545A	8709	7 Pax		oo-delivery 0001
☐ N	Cessna 560XL Citation Excel	560-				2 PWC PW545A	8709	7 Pax		oo-delivery 0001
☐ N	Cessna 560XL Citation Excel	560-				2 PWC PW545A	8709	7 Pax		oo-delivery 0001
☐ N	Cessna 560XL Citation Excel	560-				2 PWC PW545A	8709	7 Pax		oo-delivery 0001
☐ N	Cessna 560XL Citation Excel	560-				2 PWC PW545A	8709	7 Pax		oo-delivery 0001
☐ N	Cessna 560XL Citation Excel	560-				2 PWC PW545A	8709	7 Pax		oo-delivery 0001
☐ N	Cessna 560XL Citation Excel	560-				2 PWC PW545A	8709	7 Pax		oo-delivery 0001
☐ N	Cessna 560XL Citation Excel	560-				2 PWC PW545A	8709	7 Pax		oo-delivery 0001
☐ N	Cessna 560XL Citation Excel	560-				2 PWC PW545A	8709	7 Pax		oo-delivery 0001
☐ N	Cessna 560XL Citation Excel	560-				2 PWC PW545A	8709	7 Pax		oo-delivery 0001
☐ N	Cessna 560XL Citation Excel	560-				2 PWC PW545A	8709	7 Pax		oo-delivery 0001
☐ N	Cessna 560XL Citation Excel	560-				2 PWC PW545A	8709	7 Pax		oo-delivery 0001
☐ N	Cessna 560XL Citation Excel	560-				2 PWC PW545A	8709	7 Pax		oo-delivery 0002
☐ N	Cessna 560XL Citation Excel	560-				2 PWC PW545A	8709	7 Pax		oo-delivery 0002
☐ N	Cessna 560XL Citation Excel	560-				2 PWC PW545A	8709	7 Pax		oo-delivery 0002
☐ N	Cessna 560XL Citation Excel	560-				2 PWC PW545A	8709	7 Pax		oo-delivery 0002
☐ N	Cessna 560XL Citation Excel	560-				2 PWC PW545A	8709	7 Pax		oo-delivery 0002
☐ N	Cessna 560XL Citation Excel	560-				2 PWC PW545A	8709	7 Pax		oo-delivery 0002
☐ N	Cessna 560XL Citation Excel	560-				2 PWC PW545A	8709	7 Pax		oo-delivery 0002
☐ N	Cessna 560XL Citation Excel	560-				2 PWC PW545A	8709	7 Pax		oo-delivery 0002
☐ N	Cessna 560XL Citation Excel	560-				2 PWC PW545A	8709	7 Pax		oo-delivery 0002
☐ N	Cessna 560XL Citation Excel	560-				2 PWC PW545A	8709	7 Pax		oo-delivery 0002
☐ N	Cessna 560XL Citation Excel	560-				2 PWC PW545A	8709	7 Pax		oo-delivery 0002
☐ N139N	Cessna 650 Citation III	650-0149	N139M	0085	0597	2 GA TFE731-3B-100S	9979	7 Pax		
☐ N222GT	Cessna 650 Citation III	650-0093	N93VP	0085	0997	2 GA TFE731-3B-100S	9979	7 Pax		lst LXR as CS-DND
☐ N709QS	Cessna 650 Citation VII	650-7109				2 GA TFE731-4R-2S	10180	7 Pax		oo-delivery 0099
☐ N710QS	Cessna 650 Citation VII	650-7100				2 GA TFE731-4R-2S	10180	7 Pax		oo-delivery 0099
☐ N713QS	Cessna 650 Citation VII	650-7103				2 GA TFE731-4R-2S	10180	7 Pax		oo-delivery 0099
☐ N715QS	Cessna 650 Citation VII	650-7105				2 GA TFE731-4R-2S	10180	7 Pax		oo-delivery 0099
☐ N716QS	Cessna 650 Citation VII	650-7106				2 GA TFE731-4R-2S	10180	7 Pax		oo-delivery 0099
☐ N779QS	Cessna 650 Citation VII	650-7079		0097	1097	2 GA TFE731-4R-2S	10180	7 Pax		
☐ N780QS	Cessna 650 Citation VII	650-7080		0097	1297	2 GA TFE731-4R-2S	10180	7 Pax		lst LXR as CS-DNF
☐ N781QS	Cessna 650 Citation VII	650-7081		0097	0198	2 GA TFE731-4R-2S	10180	7 Pax		lst LXR as CS-DNG
☐ N782QS	Cessna 650 Citation VII	650-7082		0097	1097	2 GA TFE731-4R-2S	10180	7 Pax		
☐ N785QS	Cessna 650 Citation VII	650-7085		0098	0598	2 GA TFE731-4R-2S	10180	7 Pax		
☐ N787QS	Cessna 650 Citation VII	650-7087	N5163C*	0098	0698	2 GA TFE731-4R-2S	10180	7 Pax		
☐ N789QS	Cessna 650 Citation VII	650-7089	N5117U*	0098	0998	2 GA TFE731-4R-2S	10180	7 Pax		
☐ N790QS	Cessna 650 Citation VII	650-7090		0098	1098	2 GA TFE731-4R-2S	10180	7 Pax		
☐ N791QS	Cessna 650 Citation VII	650-7091		0098	1098	2 GA TFE731-4R-2S	10180	7 Pax		
☐ N792QS	Cessna 650 Citation VII	650-7092		0098	1298	2 GA TFE731-4R-2S	10180	7 Pax		
☐ N793QS	Cessna 650 Citation VII	650-7093				2 GA TFE731-4R-2S	10180	7 Pax		oo-delivery 0099
☐ N794QS	Cessna 650 Citation VII	650-7094				2 GA TFE731-4R-2S	10180	7 Pax		oo-delivery 0099
☐ N796QS	Cessna 650 Citation VII	650-7096				2 GA TFE731-4R-2S	10180	7 Pax		oo-delivery 0099
☐ N797QS	Cessna 650 Citation VII	650-7097				2 GA TFE731-4R-2S	10180	7 Pax		oo-delivery 0099

registration	type of aircraft	cn/fn	ex/ex*	mfd	del	powered by	mtow kg	configuration	selcal	name/fln/specialtities/remarks
N599EC	Hawker 800A (BAe 125-800A)	258183 / NA0451	N63PM	0090	1198	2 GA TFE731-5R-1H	12428	8 Pax		to be lst LXR CS-DNI 0499
N699EC	Hawker 800A (BAe 125-800A)	258193 / NA0457	N300PM	0091	1198	2 GA TFE731-5R-1H	12428	8 Pax		to be lst LXR as CS-DNH 0499
N838QS	Hawker 800XP	258338		0097	1197	2 GA TFE731-5BR-1H	12701	8 Pax		
N840QS	Hawker 800XP	258340		0097	1297	2 GA TFE731-5BR-1H	12701	8 Pax		
N855QS	Hawker 800XP	258355		0098	0698	2 GA TFE731-5BR-1H	12701	8 Pax		
N861QS	Hawker 800XP	258361		0098	0998	2 GA TFE731-5BR-1H	12701	8 Pax		
N862QS	Hawker 800XP	258362		0098	0998	2 GA TFE731-5BR-1H	12701	8 Pax		
N875QS	Hawker 800XP	258375		0098	1198	2 GA TFE731-5BR-1H	12701	8 Pax		
N879QS	Hawker 800XP	258379		0098	1298	2 GA TFE731-5BR-1H	12701	8 Pax		
N887QS	Hawker 800XP	258387		0099	0199	2 GA TFE731-5BR-1H	12701	8 Pax		
N893QS	Hawker 800XP	258393		0099	0299	2 GA TFE731-5BR-1H	12701	8 Pax		
N899QS	Hawker 800XP	258399		0099	0399	2 GA TFE731-5BR-1H	12701	8 Pax		to be lst LXR as CS-DNJ 0599
N	Hawker 800XP					2 GA TFE731-5BR-1H	12701	8 Pax		oo-delivery 0099
N	Hawker 800XP					2 GA TFE731-5BR-1H	12701	8 Pax		oo-delivery 0099
N	Hawker 800XP					2 GA TFE731-5BR-1H	12701	8 Pax		oo-delivery 0000
N	Hawker 800XP					2 GA TFE731-5BR-1H	12701	8 Pax		oo-delivery 0000
N	Hawker 800XP					2 GA TFE731-5BR-1H	12701	8 Pax		oo-delivery 0000
N	Hawker 800XP					2 GA TFE731-5BR-1H	12701	8 Pax		oo-delivery 0000
N	Hawker 800XP					2 GA TFE731-5BR-1H	12701	8 Pax		oo-delivery 0000
N	Hawker 800XP					2 GA TFE731-5BR-1H	12701	8 Pax		oo-delivery 0001
N	Hawker 800XP					2 GA TFE731-5BR-1H	12701	8 Pax		oo-delivery 0001
N	Hawker 800XP					2 GA TFE731-5BR-1H	12701	8 Pax		oo-delivery 0001
N	Hawker 800XP					2 GA TFE731-5BR-1H	12701	8 Pax		oo-delivery 0001
N	Hawker 800XP					2 GA TFE731-5BR-1H	12701	8 Pax		oo-delivery 0001
N	Hawker 800XP					2 GA TFE731-5BR-1H	12701	8 Pax		oo-delivery 0002
N	Hawker 800XP					2 GA TFE731-5BR-1H	12701	8 Pax		oo-delivery 0002
N	Hawker 800XP					2 GA TFE731-5BR-1H	12701	8 Pax		oo-delivery 0002
N	Hawker 800XP					2 GA TFE731-5BR-1H	12701	8 Pax		oo-delivery 0002
N	Hawker 800XP					2 GA TFE731-5BR-1H	12701	8 Pax		oo-delivery 0002
N	Hawker 800XP					2 GA TFE731-5BR-1H	12701	8 Pax		oo-delivery 0003
N	Hawker 800XP					2 GA TFE731-5BR-1H	12701	8 Pax		oo-delivery 0003
N	Hawker 800XP					2 GA TFE731-5BR-1H	12701	8 Pax		oo-delivery 0003
N	Hawker 800XP					2 GA TFE731-5BR-1H	12701	8 Pax		oo-delivery 0003
N	Hawker 800XP					2 GA TFE731-5BR-1H	12701	8 Pax		oo-delivery 0003
N	Hawker 800XP					2 GA TFE731-5BR-1H	12701	8 Pax		oo-delivery 0004
N	Hawker 800XP					2 GA TFE731-5BR-1H	12701	8 Pax		oo-delivery 0004
N	Hawker 800XP					2 GA TFE731-5BR-1H	12701	8 Pax		oo-delivery 0004
N503QS	Hawker 1000A (BAe 125-1000A)	259003	G-ELRA	0093	1098	2 PWC PW305	14061	9 Pax		cvtd 1000B
N505QS	Hawker 1000A (BAe 125-1000A)	259005 / NA1000	N410US	0093	1198	2 PWC PW305	14061	9 Pax		
N512QS	Hawker 1000A (BAe 125-1000A)	259012	HZ-SJP2	0092	0198	2 PWC PW305	14061	9 Pax		cvtd 1000B
N513QS	Hawker 1000A (BAe 125-1000A)	259013 / NA1004	N125BA	0093	0793	2 PWC PW305	14061	9 Pax	ES-HJ	
N514QS	Hawker 1000A (BAe 125-1000A)	259014 / NA1005	N125CJ	0093	0993	2 PWC PW305	14061	9 Pax	ES-PQ	
N515QS	Hawker 1000A (BAe 125-1000A)	259015 / NA1006	N1000E	0093	0893	2 PWC PW305	14061	9 Pax		
N520QS	Hawker 1000A (BAe 125-1000A)	259020 / NA1008	N676BA	0093	0893	2 PWC PW305	14061	9 Pax		
N523QS	Hawker 1000A (BAe 125-1000A)	259023 / NA1010	N679BA	0093	1193	2 PWC PW305	14061	9 Pax		
N525QS	Hawker 1000A (BAe 125-1000A)	259025	N292H	0092	0895	2 PWC PW305	14061	9 Pax		
N530QS	Hawker 1000A (BAe 125-1000A)	259030	G-5-753*	0093	0496	2 PWC PW305	14061	9 Pax	MS-DP	
N533QS	Hawker 1000A (BAe 125-1000A)	259033	N850BL	0093	0394	2 PWC PW305	14061	9 Pax		
N535QS	Hawker 1000A (BAe 125-1000A)	259035	N160BA	0093	1293	2 PWC PW305	14061	9 Pax		
N539QS	Hawker 1000A (BAe 125-1000A)	259039	N169BA	0094	0294	2 PWC PW305	14061	9 Pax	JR-HQ	
N540QS	Hawker 1000A (BAe 125-1000A)	259040	N22UP	0094	0394	2 PWC PW305	14061	9 Pax		
N541QS	Hawker 1000A (BAe 125-1000A)	259041	N936H	0094	0394	2 PWC PW305	14061	9 Pax		
N542QS	Hawker 1000A (BAe 125-1000A)	259042	N941H	0094	0794	2 PWC PW305	14061	9 Pax		
N544QS	Hawker 1000A (BAe 125-1000A)	259044	N956H	0094	0394	2 PWC PW305	14061	9 Pax		
N545QS	Hawker 1000A (BAe 125-1000A)	259045	G-5-801*	0094	0594	2 PWC PW305	14061	9 Pax		
N546QS	Hawker 1000A (BAe 125-1000A)	259046	N962H	0094	0196	2 PWC PW305	14061	9 Pax		
N547QS	Hawker 1000A (BAe 125-1000A)	259047	N296H	0094	1095	2 PWC PW305	14061	9 Pax		
N548QS	Hawker 1000A (BAe 125-1000A)	259048	N802H	0095	1295	2 PWC PW305	14061	9 Pax	LS-EF	
N549QS	Hawker 1000A (BAe 125-1000A)	259049	G-5-837*	0095	0196	2 PWC PW305	14061	9 Pax		
N550QS	Hawker 1000A (BAe 125-1000A)	259050	G-5-846*	0095	0196	2 PWC PW305	14061	9 Pax		
N551QS	Hawker 1000A (BAe 125-1000A)	259051	G-5-859*	0096	1096	2 PWC PW305	14061	9 Pax		
N552QS	Hawker 1000A (BAe 125-1000A)	259052	G-5-863*	0096	1096	2 PWC PW305	14061	9 Pax		
N270QS	Dassault Falcon 2000	70	N2168	0099	0199	2 CFE CFE738-1-1B	16238	10 Pax		
N275QS	Dassault Falcon 2000	75	F-WWMJ*	0099	0299	2 CFE CFE738-1-1B	16238	10 Pax		
N278QS	Dassault Falcon 2000	77		0099	0299	2 CFE CFE738-1-1B	16238	10 Pax		
N	Dassault Falcon 2000					2 CFE CFE738-1-1B	16238	10 Pax		oo-delivery 0099
N	Dassault Falcon 2000					2 CFE CFE738-1-1B	16238	10 Pax		oo-delivery 0099
N	Dassault Falcon 2000					2 CFE CFE738-1-1B	16238	10 Pax		oo-delivery 0099
N	Dassault Falcon 2000					2 CFE CFE738-1-1B	16238	10 Pax		oo-delivery 0099
N	Dassault Falcon 2000					2 CFE CFE738-1-1B	16238	10 Pax		oo-delivery 0000
N	Dassault Falcon 2000					2 CFE CFE738-1-1B	16238	10 Pax		oo-delivery 0000
N	Dassault Falcon 2000					2 CFE CFE738-1-1B	16238	10 Pax		oo-delivery 0000
N	Dassault Falcon 2000					2 CFE CFE738-1-1B	16238	10 Pax		oo-delivery 0000
N	Dassault Falcon 2000					2 CFE CFE738-1-1B	16238	10 Pax		oo-delivery 0000
N	Dassault Falcon 2000					2 CFE CFE738-1-1B	16238	10 Pax		oo-delivery 0001
N	Dassault Falcon 2000					2 CFE CFE738-1-1B	16238	10 Pax		oo-delivery 0001
N	Dassault Falcon 2000					2 CFE CFE738-1-1B	16238	10 Pax		oo-delivery 0001
N	Dassault Falcon 2000					2 CFE CFE738-1-1B	16238	10 Pax		oo-delivery 0001
N	Dassault Falcon 2000					2 CFE CFE738-1-1B	16238	10 Pax		oo-delivery 0001
N	Dassault Falcon 2000					2 CFE CFE738-1-1B	16238	10 Pax		oo-delivery 0002
N	Dassault Falcon 2000					2 CFE CFE738-1-1B	16238	10 Pax		oo-delivery 0002
N	Dassault Falcon 2000					2 CFE CFE738-1-1B	16238	10 Pax		oo-delivery 0002
N	Dassault Falcon 2000					2 CFE CFE738-1-1B	16238	10 Pax		oo-delivery 0002
N	Dassault Falcon 2000					2 CFE CFE738-1-1B	16238	10 Pax		oo-delivery 0003
N	Dassault Falcon 2000					2 CFE CFE738-1-1B	16238	10 Pax		oo-delivery 0003
N	Dassault Falcon 2000					2 CFE CFE738-1-1B	16238	10 Pax		oo-delivery 0003
N	Dassault Falcon 2000					2 CFE CFE738-1-1B	16238	10 Pax		oo-delivery 0003
N	Dassault Falcon 2000					2 CFE CFE738-1-1B	16238	10 Pax		oo-delivery 0003
N	Dassault Falcon 2000					2 CFE CFE738-1-1B	16238	10 Pax		oo-delivery 0004
N	Dassault Falcon 2000					2 CFE CFE738-1-1B	16238	10 Pax		oo-delivery 0004
N901QS	Cessna 750 Citation X	750-0101				2 AN AE3007C	16193	8 Pax		oo-delivery 0099
N902QS	Cessna 750 Citation X	750-0002	N752CX	0097	1097	2 AN AE3007C	16193	8 Pax		
N905QS	Cessna 750 Citation X	750-0105				2 AN AE3007C	16193	8 Pax		oo-delivery 0099
N909QS	Cessna 750 Citation X	750-0009	N96TX	0097	0697	2 AN AE3007C	16193	8 Pax		
N910QS	Cessna 750 Citation X	750-0110				2 AN AE3007C	16193	8 Pax		oo-delivery 0099
N913QS	Cessna 750 Citation X	750-0113				2 AN AE3007C	16193	8 Pax		oo-delivery 0099
N916QS	Cessna 750 Citation X	750-0116				2 AN AE3007C	16193	8 Pax		oo-delivery 0099
N920QS	Cessna 750 Citation X	750-0120				2 AN AE3007C	16193	8 Pax		oo-delivery 0099
N923QS	Cessna 750 Citation X	750-0023		0097	0897	2 AN AE3007C	16193	8 Pax		
N924QS	Cessna 750 Citation X	750-0124				2 AN AE3007C	16193	8 Pax		oo-delivery 0099
N926QS	Cessna 750 Citation X	750-0026		0097	1097	2 AN AE3007C	16193	8 Pax		
N930QS	Cessna 750 Citation X	750-0130				2 AN AE3007C	16193	8 Pax		oo-delivery 0099
N932QS	Cessna 750 Citation X	750-0032		0097	0198	2 AN AE3007C	16193	8 Pax		
N934QS	Cessna 750 Citation X	750-0034		0097	0198	2 AN AE3007C	16193	8 Pax		
N936QS	Cessna 750 Citation X	750-0036		0098	0298	2 AN AE3007C	16193	8 Pax		

registration	type of aircraft	cn/fn	ex/ex*	mfd	del	powered by	mtow kg	configuration	selcal	name/fln/specialitites/remarks
☐ N937QS	Cessna 750 Citation X	750-0137				2 AN AE3007C	16193	8 Pax		oo-delivery 0099
☐ N941QS	Cessna 750 Citation X	750-0141				2 AN AE3007C	16193	8 Pax		oo-delivery 0099
☐ N943QS	Cessna 750 Citation X	750-0043		0098	0598	2 AN AE3007C	16193	8 Pax		
☐ N944QS	Cessna 750 Citation X	750-0144				2 AN AE3007C	16193	8 Pax		oo-delivery 0099
☐ N947QS	Cessna 750 Citation X	750-0047		0098	0698	2 AN AE3007C	16193	8 Pax		
☐ N948QS	Cessna 750 Citation X	750-0149				2 AN AE3007C	16193	8 Pax		oo-delivery 0099
☐ N949QS	Cessna 750 Citation X	750-0049		0098	0798	2 AN AE3007C	16193	8 Pax		
☐ N950QS	Cessna 750 Citation X	750-0050		0098	0898	2 AN AE3007C	16193	8 Pax		
☐ N951QS	Cessna 750 Citation X	750-0151				2 AN AE3007C	16193	8 Pax		oo-delivery 0099
☐ N955QS	Cessna 750 Citation X	750-0055	N5068R*	0098	1098	2 AN AE3007C	16193	8 Pax		
☐ N956QS	Cessna 750 Citation X	750-0156				2 AN AE3007C	16193	8 Pax		oo-delivery 0099
☐ N961QS	Cessna 750 Citation X	750-0061		0098	1298	2 AN AE3007C	16193	8 Pax		
☐ N967QS	Cessna 750 Citation X	750-0067		0098	0398	2 AN AE3007C	16193	8 Pax		
☐ N970QS	Cessna 750 Citation X	750-0070		0098	0398	2 AN AE3007C	16193	8 Pax		
☐ N971QS	Cessna 750 Citation X	750-0071		0098	0298	2 AN AE3007C	16193	8 Pax		
☐ N977QS	Cessna 750 Citation X	750-0077		0098	0298	2 AN AE3007C	16193	8 Pax		
☐ N979QS	Cessna 750 Citation X	750-0079		0098	0298	2 AN AE3007C	16193	8 Pax		
☐ N983QS	Cessna 750 Citation X	750-0083		0098	0398	2 AN AE3007C	16193	8 Pax		
☐ N984QS	Cessna 750 Citation X	750-0084		0098	0398	2 AN AE3007C	16193	8 Pax		
☐ N985QS	Cessna 750 Citation X	750-0085		0098	0498	2 AN AE3007C	16193	8 Pax		
☐ N987QS	Cessna 750 Citation X	750-0087		0098	0398	2 AN AE3007C	16193	8 Pax		
☐ N989QS	Cessna 750 Citation X	750-0089		0098	0398	2 AN AE3007C	16193	8 Pax		
☐ N993QS	Cessna 750 Citation X	750-0093		0098	0398	2 AN AE3007C	16193	8 Pax		
☐ N404QS	GAC G-IV Gulfstream IV (SP)	1304	N436GA*	0097	0797	2 RR Tay 611-8	33838	13 Pax	AQ-CD	
☐ N408QS	GAC G-IV Gulfstream IV (SP)	1308	N446GA*	0097	0997	2 RR Tay 611-8	33838	13 Pax	AQ-CS	
☐ N410QS	GAC G-IV Gulfstream IV (SP)	1210	N9PC	0093	0396	2 RR Tay 611-8	33838	13 Pax	LS-FM	lsf Gulfstream Aerospace Corp.
☐ N411QS	GAC G-IV Gulfstream IV (SP)	1311	N449GA*	0097	1297	2 RR Tay 611-8	33838	13 Pax	AQ-GJ	
☐ N416QS	GAC G-IV Gulfstream IV (SP)	1316	N427GA*	0097	0198	2 RR Tay 611-8	33838	13 Pax		
☐ N420QS	GAC G-IV Gulfstream IV (SP)	1320	N437GA*	0098	0498	2 RR Tay 611-8	33838	13 Pax		
☐ N422QS	GAC G-IV Gulfstream IV (SP)	1322	N445GA*	0098	0598	2 RR Tay 611-8	33838	13 Pax		
☐ N424QS	GAC G-IV Gulfstream IV (SP)	1324	N457GA*	0098	0898	2 RR Tay 611-8	33838	13 Pax		
☐ N428QS	GAC G-IV Gulfstream IV (SP)	1328	N328GA*	0098	0998	2 RR Tay 611-8	33838	13 Pax		
☐ N432QS	GAC G-IV Gulfstream IV	1032	N888UE	0087	1096	2 RR Tay 611-8	33203	13 Pax		lsf Gulfstream Aerospace Corp.
☐ N434QS	GAC G-IV Gulfstream IV (SP)	1334	N334GA*	0098	1198	2 RR Tay 611-8	33838	13 Pax		
☐ N441QS	GAC G-IV Gulfstream IV (SP)	1341	N341GA*	0098	1298	2 RR Tay 611-8	33838	13 Pax		
☐ N451QS	GAC G-IV Gulfstream IV (SP)	1351	N351GA*	0098	1298	2 RR Tay 611-8	33838	13 Pax		
☐ N452QS	GAC G-IV Gulfstream IV (SP)	1352	N352GA*	0098	1298	2 RR Tay 611-8	33838	13 Pax		
☐ N462QS	GAC G-IV Gulfstream IV (SP)	1262	N496GA*	0095	1295	2 RR Tay 611-8	33838	13 Pax	KR-EJ	
☐ N464QS	GAC G-IV Gulfstream IV (SP)	1264	N499GA*	0096	0396	2 RR Tay 611-8	33838	13 Pax	KS-EF	
☐ N475QS	GAC G-IV Gulfstream IV (SP)	1275	N459GA*	0096	0696	2 RR Tay 611-8	33838	13 Pax	LS-FG	
☐ N481QS	GAC G-IV Gulfstream IV (SP)	1281	N470GA*	0096	0796	2 RR Tay 611-8	33838	13 Pax	LS-FH	
☐ N487QS	GAC G-IV Gulfstream IV (SP)	1287	N484GA*	0096	0796	2 RR Tay 611-8	33838	13 Pax	LS-FJ	
☐ N493QS	GAC G-IV Gulfstream IV (SP)	1293	N415GA*	0096	0696	2 RR Tay 611-8	33838	13 Pax	LS-FK	
☐ N495QS	GAC G-IV Gulfstream IV (SP)	1295	N417GA*	0096	0796	2 RR Tay 611-8	33838	13 Pax	HS-AD	
☐ N499QS	GAC G-IV Gulfstream IV (SP)	1299	N423GA*	0097	0297	2 RR Tay 611-8	33838	13 Pax	AQ-BP	
☐ N	GAC G-IV Gulfstream IV (SP)					2 RR Tay 611-8	33838	13 Pax		oo-delivery 0099
☐ N	GAC G-IV Gulfstream IV (SP)					2 RR Tay 611-8	33838	13 Pax		oo-delivery 0000
☐ N	GAC G-IV Gulfstream IV (SP)					2 RR Tay 611-8	33838	13 Pax		oo-delivery 0000
☐ N	GAC G-IV Gulfstream IV (SP)					2 RR Tay 611-8	33838	13 Pax		oo-delivery 0000
☐ N	GAC G-IV Gulfstream IV (SP)					2 RR Tay 611-8	33838	13 Pax		oo-delivery 0000
☐ N	GAC G-IV Gulfstream IV (SP)					2 RR Tay 611-8	33838	13 Pax		oo-delivery 0000
☐ N	GAC G-IV Gulfstream IV (SP)					2 RR Tay 611-8	33838	13 Pax		oo-delivery 0000
☐ N	GAC G-IV Gulfstream IV (SP)					2 RR Tay 611-8	33838	13 Pax		oo-delivery 0001
☐ N	GAC G-IV Gulfstream IV (SP)					2 RR Tay 611-8	33838	13 Pax		oo-delivery 0001
☐ N	GAC G-IV Gulfstream IV (SP)					2 RR Tay 611-8	33838	13 Pax		oo-delivery 0001
☐ N	GAC G-IV Gulfstream IV (SP)					2 RR Tay 611-8	33838	13 Pax		oo-delivery 0001
☐ N	GAC G-IV Gulfstream IV (SP)					2 RR Tay 611-8	33838	13 Pax		oo-delivery 0001
☐ N	GAC G-IV Gulfstream IV (SP)					2 RR Tay 611-8	33838	13 Pax		oo-delivery 0001
☐ N	GAC G-IV Gulfstream IV (SP)					2 RR Tay 611-8	33838	13 Pax		oo-delivery 0002
☐ N	GAC G-IV Gulfstream IV (SP)					2 RR Tay 611-8	33838	13 Pax		oo-delivery 0002
☐ N	GAC G-IV Gulfstream IV (SP)					2 RR Tay 611-8	33838	13 Pax		oo-delivery 0002
☐ N	GAC G-IV Gulfstream IV (SP)					2 RR Tay 611-8	33838	13 Pax		oo-delivery 0002
☐ N	GAC G-IV Gulfstream IV (SP)					2 RR Tay 611-8	33838	13 Pax		oo-delivery 0002
☐ N	GAC G-IV Gulfstream IV (SP)					2 RR Tay 611-8	33838	13 Pax		oo-delivery 0002
☐ N	GAC G-IV Gulfstream IV (SP)					2 RR Tay 611-8	33838	13 Pax		oo-delivery 0003
☐ N	GAC G-IV Gulfstream IV (SP)					2 RR Tay 611-8	33838	13 Pax		oo-delivery 0003
☐ N	GAC G-IV Gulfstream IV (SP)					2 RR Tay 611-8	33838	13 Pax		oo-delivery 0003
☐ N	GAC G-IV Gulfstream IV (SP)					2 RR Tay 611-8	33838	13 Pax		oo-delivery 0003
☐ N	GAC G-IV Gulfstream IV (SP)					2 RR Tay 611-8	33838	13 Pax		oo-delivery 0003
☐ N	GAC G-V Gulfstream V					2 BR BR710A1-10	41050	15 Pax		oo-delivery 1299
☐ N	GAC G-V Gulfstream V					2 BR BR710A1-10	41050	15 Pax		oo-delivery 0000
☐ N	GAC G-V Gulfstream V					2 BR BR710A1-10	41050	15 Pax		oo-delivery 0000
☐ N	GAC G-V Gulfstream V					2 BR BR710A1-10	41050	15 Pax		oo-delivery 0000
☐ N	GAC G-V Gulfstream V					2 BR BR710A1-10	41050	15 Pax		oo-delivery 0001
☐ N	GAC G-V Gulfstream V					2 BR BR710A1-10	41050	15 Pax		oo-delivery 0001
☐ N	GAC G-V Gulfstream V					2 BR BR710A1-10	41050	15 Pax		oo-delivery 0002
☐ N	GAC G-V Gulfstream V					2 BR BR710A1-10	41050	15 Pax		oo-delivery 0002
☐ N	GAC G-V Gulfstream V					2 BR BR710A1-10	41050	15 Pax		oo-delivery 0003
☐ N	GAC G-V Gulfstream V					2 BR BR710A1-10	41050	15 Pax		oo-delivery 0003
☐ N	GAC G-V Gulfstream V					2 BR BR710A1-10	41050	15 Pax		oo-delivery 0004
☐ N	GAC G-V Gulfstream V					2 BR BR710A1-10	41050	15 Pax		oo-delivery 0004
☐ N	Boeing 737-700 (BBJ)					2 CFMI CFM56-7B26	77564	Executive		oo-delivery 0599
☐ N	Boeing 737-700 (BBJ)					2 CFMI CFM56-7B26	77564	Executive		oo-delivery 0899
☐ N	Boeing 737-700 (BBJ)					2 CFMI CFM56-7B26	77564	Executive		oo-delivery 1199
☐ N	Boeing 737-700 (BBJ)					2 CFMI CFM56-7B26	77564	Executive		oo-delivery 0200
☐ N	Boeing 737-700 (BBJ)					2 CFMI CFM56-7B26	77564	Executive		oo-delivery 0400
☐ N	Boeing 737-700 (BBJ)					2 CFMI CFM56-7B26	77564	Executive		oo-delivery 0700
☐ N	Boeing 737-700 (BBJ)					2 CFMI CFM56-7B26	77564	Executive		oo-delivery 1000
☐ N	Boeing 737-700 (BBJ)					2 CFMI CFM56-7B26	77564	Executive		oo-delivery 0101
☐ N	Boeing 737-700 (BBJ)					2 CFMI CFM56-7B26	77564	Executive		oo-delivery 0401

EXECUTIVE JET INTERNATIONAL, Inc. (Subsidiary of Berkshire Hathaway/Sister company of Executive Jet Aviation, Inc.) — Windsor Locks-Bradley Int'l, CT

130 Signature Way, East Granby, CT 06026, USA ☎ (860) 292-1191 Tx: none Fax: (860) 292-6886 SITA: n/a
F: 1995 ⁂ n/a Head: Richard T. Santulli Net: n/a

registration	type of aircraft	cn/fn	ex/ex*	mfd	del	powered by	mtow kg	configuration	selcal	name/fln/specialitites/remarks
☐ N200QS	Beech King Air B200	BB-1130	N16KK	0083	0496	2 PWC PT6A-42	5670	Executive		
☐ N199QS	GAC G-IV Gulfstream IV	1099	N299FB	0089	0995	2 RR Tay 611-8	33203	Executive	LS-FG	lsf Gulfstream Aerospace Corp.

EXECUTIVE JET MANAGEMENT, Inc. = EJM (Subsidiary of Berkshire Hathaway/Sister company of Executive Jet Aviation Inc.) — Cincinnati-Municipal/Lunken Field, OH

4536 Airport Road, Cincinnati, OH 45226, USA ☎ (513) 871-2004 Tx: none Fax: (513) 871-7310 SITA: n/a
F: 1977 ⁂ n/a Head: Richard T. Santulli ICAO: JET SPEED Net: http://www.lunken.com/ejm Operates airtaxi/charter flights mainly with BAe 125-700/1000, Cessna 501/550/S550/560, Falcon 50, IAI 1124 & Learjet 35,leased from private owners (it has under management), when required.

EXPRESS AIRLINES I, Inc. = 9E / FLG (Northwest Airlink) (Subsidiary of Northwest Airlines, Inc.) — Memphis-Int'l, TN

1689 Nonconnah Blvd., Suite 111, Memphis, TN 38132-2111, USA ☎ (901) 348-4100 Tx: none Fax: (901) 348-4130 SITA: MEMTBNW
F: 1985 ⁂ 1500 Head: Phillip H. Trenary IATA: 430 ICAO: FLAGSHIP Net: http://www.nwairlink.com
All aircraft are operated as NORTHWEST AIRLINK (in full such colours & titles), a commuter system to provide feeder connection at NW major hubs, using NW flight numbers.

registration	type of aircraft	cn/fn	ex/ex*	mfd	del	powered by	mtow kg	configuration	selcal	name/fln/specialitites/remarks
☐ N107PX	Saab SF340A	340A-010	N370CA	0086	0095	2 GE CT7-5A2	12372	Y33		3107 / op in Northwest Airlink-colors
☐ N108PX	Saab SF340A	340A-012	N380CA	0085	0197	2 GE CT7-5A2	12372	Y33		3108 / op in Northwest Airlink-colors
☐ N109PX	Saab SF340A	340A-021	N341CA	0085	0197	2 GE CT7-5A2	12372	Y33		3109/Spirit of Gulfport / NW Airlink-cs
☐ N110PX	Saab SF340A	340A-023	N342CA	0085	0197	2 GE CT7-5A2	12372	Y33		3110/Spirit of Alexandria / NW Airl.-cs
☐ N111PX	Saab SF340A	340A-024	N343CA	0085	0197	2 GE CT7-5A2	12372	Y33		3111 / op in Northwest Airlink-colors
☐ N112PX	Saab SF340A	340A-025	N344CA	0085	0197	2 GE CT7-5A2	12372	Y33		3112/Spirit of Panama City / NW Air.-cs
☐ N325PX	Saab SF340A	340A-051	SE-E51*	0086	0486	2 GE CT7-5A2	12372	Y33		3325 / op in Northwest Airlink-colors
☐ N326PX	Saab SF340A	340A-054	SE-E54*	0086	0586	2 GE CT7-5A2	12372	Y33		3326 / op in Northwest Airlink-colors
☐ N327PX	Saab SF340A	340A-059	SE-E59*	0086	0686	2 GE CT7-5A2	12372	Y33		3327 / op in Northwest Airlink-colors
☐ N344AM	Saab SF340A	340A-030	SE-E30*	0085	0291	2 GE CT7-5A2	12372	Y33		3344 / op in Northwest Airlink-colors
☐ N346AM	Saab SF340A	340A-032	SE-E32*	0085	0291	2 GE CT7-5A2	12372	Y33		3346 / op in Northwest Airlink-colors
☐ N347AM	Saab SF340A	340A-039	SE-E39*	0085	0291	2 GE CT7-5A2	12372	Y33		3347 / op in Northwest Airlink-colors
☐ N360PX	Saab 340B	340B-220	SE-G20*	0090	0291	2 GE CT7-9B	12927	Y33		3360/Spirit of Pensacola / NW Airl.-cs
☐ N361PX	Saab 340B	340B-249	SE-G49*	0091	0691	2 GE CT7-9B	12927	Y33		3361 / op in Northwest Airlink-colors
☐ N362PX	Saab 340B	340B-258	SE-G58*	0091	0991	2 GE CT7-9B	12927	Y33		3362 / op in Northwest Airlink-colors
☐ N363PX	Saab 340B	340B-260	SE-G60*	0091	0991	2 GE CT7-9B	12927	Y33		3363 / op in Northwest Airlink-colors

registration	type of aircraft	cn/fn	ex/ex*	mfd	del	powered by	mtow kg	configuration	selcal	name/fln/specialitites/remarks
N364PX	Saab 340B	340B-262	SE-G62*	0091	0991	2 GE CT7-9B	12927	Y33		3364 / op in Northwest Airlink-colors
N365PX	Saab 340B	340B-265	SE-G65*	0091	1091	2 GE CT7-9B	12927	Y33		3365 / op in Northwest Airlink-colors
N366PX	Saab 340B	340B-267	SE-G67*	0091	1091	2 GE CT7-9B	12927	Y33		3366 / op in Northwest Airlink-colors
N367PX	Saab 340B	340B-271	SE-G71*	0091	1291	2 GE CT7-9B	12927	Y33		3367/Spirit of Montgomery / NW Airl.-cs
N368PX	Saab 340B	340B-274	SE-G74*	0091	1291	2 GE CT7-9B	12927	Y33		3368 / op in Northwest Airlink-colors
N369PX	Saab 340B	340B-295	SE-G95*	0092	0492	2 GE CT7-9B	12927	Y33		3369/Spirit of Lafayette / NW Airl.-cs
N370PX	Saab 340B	340B-300	SE-E03*	0092	0692	2 GE CT7-9B	12927	Y33		3370/Spirit of Monroe / NW Airlink-cs
N401BH	Saab SF340A	340A-057	SE-E57*	0086	0591	2 GE CT7-5A2	12372	Y33		3401 / op in Northwest Airlink-colors
N402BH	Saab SF340A	340A-058	SE-E58*	0086	0591	2 GE CT7-5A2	12372	Y33		3402 / op in Northwest Airlink-colors
N403BH	Saab SF340A	340A-060	SE-E60*	0086	0591	2 GE CT7-5A2	12372	Y33		3403 / op in Northwest Airlink-colors
N404BH	Saab SF340A	340A-061	SE-E61*	0086	0591	2 GE CT7-5A2	12372	Y33		3404 / op in Northwest Airlink-colors
N406BH	Saab SF340A	340A-074	SE-E74*	0086	0591	2 GE CT7-5A2	12372	Y33		3406 / op in Northwest Airlink-colors
N407BH	Saab SF340A	340A-078	SE-E78*	0086	0591	2 GE CT7-5A2	12372	Y33		3407 / op in Northwest Airlink-colors
N922MA	Saab SF340A	340A-077	SE-E77*	0086	0190	2 GE CT7-5A2	12372	Y33		3922 / op in Northwest Airlink-colors
N935MA	Saab SF340A	340A-073	SE-E73*	0086	0190	2 GE CT7-5A2	12372	Y33		3935/Spirit of Springfield / NWAirl.-cs

EXPRESS ONE International, Inc. = EO / LHN (formerly Jet East Int. Airlines, Inc. / Associated with Air Corp, Inc.) — Dallas-Love Field, TX

3890 West Northwest Hwy, Suite 700, Dallas, TX 75220, USA ☎ (214) 902-2501 Tx: none Fax: (214) 350-1399 SITA: n/a
F: 1980 500 Head: Alinda H. Wikert ICAO: LONGHORN Net: n/a

registration	type of aircraft	cn/fn	ex/ex*	mfd	del	powered by	mtow kg	configuration	selcal	name/fln/specialitites/remarks
N943VJ	Boeing (Douglas) DC-9-31	47058 / 123	N973NE	0067	0398	2 PW JT8D-7B	47627	Y115		
N945VJ	Boeing (Douglas) DC-9-31	47066 / 150	N974NE	0067	0398	2 PW JT8D-7B	47627	Y115		
N950VJ	Boeing (Douglas) DC-9-31	47564 / 681		0072	0398	2 PW JT8D-7B	47627	Y115		
N969VJ	Boeing (Douglas) DC-9-31	47421 / 558		0070	1198	2 PW JT8D-7B	47627	Y115		
N977ML	Boeing (Douglas) DC-9-31	47329 / 406	N8980E	0068	0497	2 PW JT8D-7B	47627	Y115		Harrah's City Expr. / lsf Twin Jet Lsng
N240NE	Boeing 727-31 (F)	18906 / 176	N841TW	0065	0189	3 PW JT8D-7B (HK3/FDX)	72802	Freighter	AC-GH	cvtd -31
N290NE	Boeing 727-25 (F)	18972 / 242	N8148N	0066	0889	3 PW JT8D-7B (HK3/FDX)	72802	Freighter	FM-HJ	cvtd -25
N300NE	Boeing 727-25 (F)	18974 / 252	C-FACW	0066	0889	3 PW JT8D-7B (HK3/FDX)	72802	Freighter		cvtd -25
N12305	Boeing 727-231 (F)	19562 / 576		0068	0897	3 PW JT8D-9A (HK3/FDX)	76884	Freighter	AE-FJ	lsf Prewitt Lsng/cvtd-231/sublst/opfDHL
N15DF	Boeing 727-264 (F) (A)	20710 / 975	C-GRYO	0073	0997	3 PW JT8D-17R (HK3/FDX)	86410	Freighter		lsf Prewitt Lsng/cvtd-264/sublst/opfDHL
N275WC	Boeing 727-277 (F) (A)	20549 / 989	YU-AKR	0073	0290	3 PW JT8D-15 (HK3/FDX)	86409	Freighter		lsf Aviation Enterprises Inc./cvtd -277
N310NE	Boeing 727-2A7 (F)	20241 / 726	N6842	0469	0593	3 PW JT8D-9A (HK3/FDX)	80966	Freighter	AC-BJ	opf USPS in USPS colors / cvtd -2A7
N311NE	Boeing 727-223 (F)	19703 / 684	N6825	0169	0194	3 PW JT8D-9A (HK3/FDX)	80966	Freighter	CE-DJ	lsf EWW/opf USPS in USPS cs/cvtd -223
N312NE	Boeing 727-223 (F)	20193 / 755	N6841	0969	0194	3 PW JT8D-9A (HK3/FDX)	80966	Freighter	BH-AL	lsf EWW/opf USPS in USPS cs/cvtd -223
N313NE	Boeing 727-223 (F)	19702 / 680	N6824	0169	0194	3 PW JT8D-9A (HK3/FDX)	80966	Freighter	CE-FK	lsf EWW/opf USPS in USPS cs/cvtd -223
N314NE	Boeing 727-223 (F)	19495 / 664	N6820	1268	0793	3 PW JT8D-9A (HK3/FDX)	80966	Freighter	CE-GJ	opf USPS in USPS colors / cvtd -223
N315NE	Boeing 727-223 (F)	20190 / 738	N6837	0769	0793	3 PW JT8D-9A (HK3/FDX)	80966	Freighter	BH-AG	opf USPS in USPS colors / cvtd -223
N316NE	Boeing 727-223 (F)	19475 / 511	N6800	0268	0893	3 PW JT8D-9A (HK3/FDX)	80966	Freighter	BE-CD	opf USPS in USPS colors / cvtd -223
N317NE	Boeing 727-212 (F) (A)	21945 / 1502	OY-SCC	0079	0199	3 PW JT8D-17A (HK3/FDX)	90039	Freighter		lsf Prewitt Leasing Inc. / cvtd -212
N352PA	Boeing 727-225 (F) (A)	20616 / 899	N8853E	0072	0998	3 PW JT8D-15 (HK3/FDX)	80104	Freighter		lsf Aircorp Inc. / cvtd -225
N6813	Boeing 727-223 (F) (A)	19488 / 588		0668	1297	3 PW JT8D-9A (HK3/FDX)	80966	Freighter	BK-FM	lsf Prewitt Lsng/cvtd-223/sublst/opfDHL
N6815	Boeing 727-223 (F)	19490 / 602		0768	0993	3 PW JT8D-9A (HK3/FDX)	80966	Freighter	CE-BF	lsf Aircorp Inc. / cvtd -223
N6819	Boeing 727-223 (F) (A)	19494 / 661		1168	1297	3 PW JT8D-9A (HK3/FDX)	80966	Freighter	CE-GH	lsf Prewitt Lsng/cvtd-223/sublst/opfDHL
N6826	Boeing 727-223 (F)	19704 / 689		0269	1094	3 PW JT8D-9A (HK3/FDX)	80966	Freighter	CE-DL	lsf Prewitt Leasing Inc. / cvtd -223
N6839	Boeing 727-223 (F)	20192 / 752		0969	0195	3 PW JT8D-9 (HK3/FDX)	80966	Freighter	BH-AK	lsf Aircorp Inc. / cvtd -223
N721RW	Boeing 727-2M7 (F) (A)	21200 / 1206		0876	0797	3 PW JT8D-17R (HK3/FDX)	88360	Freighter	FM-BL	cvtd -2M7
N742RW	Boeing 727-2M7 (F) (A)	21952 / 1693		1280	0497	3 PW JT8D-17R (HK3/FDX)	88360	Freighter	EH-BG	cvtd -2M7
N74318	Boeing 727-231 (F)	20051 / 708		0069	0897	3 PW JT8D-9A (HK3/FDX)	78245	Freighter	DM-GJ	lsf Prewitt Lsng/cvtd-231/sublst/opfDHL

EXTRAORDINAIR (Extraordinaire, Inc. dba) — Washington-Dulles Int'l, DC

PO Box 20314, Dulles Int'l Airport, Washington, DC 20041-2314, USA ☎ (703) 435-9872 Tx: none Fax: (703) 435-9873 SITA: n/a
F: 1993 n/a Head: John M. Hinerman, Jr. Net: n/a

registration	type of aircraft	cn/fn	ex/ex*	mfd	del	powered by	mtow kg	configuration	selcal	name/fln/specialitites/remarks
N690HT	Twin (Aero) Turbo Commander 690B	11467	N690PG	0078	1093	2 GA TPE331-5-251K	4683			

FALCON AIR EXPRESS, Inc. = F2 / FAO — Miami-Int'l, FL

7270 NW 12th Street, Suite 600, Miami, FL 33126, USA ☎ (305) 592-5672 Tx: none Fax: (305) 592-7298 SITA: MIADDF2
F: 1995 100 Head: Emilio J. Dirube ICAO: PANTHER Net: n/a

registration	type of aircraft	cn/fn	ex/ex*	mfd	del	powered by	mtow kg	configuration	selcal	name/fln/specialitites/remarks
N203AV	Boeing 727-259 (A)	22474 / 1688		0080	1298	3 PW JT8D-17R (HK3/FDX)	86637	Y170		lsf PEGA / sub-lst / opf ROM
N266US	Boeing 727-251	19985 / 745		0869	0496	3 PW JT8D-9A	82780	Y170		Lillian / lsf PACA / sub-lst / opf ROM
N32719	Boeing 727-224	20388 / 805		0070	0397	3 PW JT8D-9A (HK3/FDX)	78245	Y170		Carolina / lsf PEGA
N369FA	Boeing 727-2K5 (A)	21851 / 1551	ZS-OAZ	0079	0598	3 PW JT8D-17 (HK3/FDX)	86409	Y170		lsf Airfl.Credit/occlst/opf Air D'Ayiti
N79750	Boeing 727-224 (A)	22452 / 1772		0081	0299	3 PW JT8D-15	86409	Y170		lsf FSBU Trustee

FALCON AVIATION, Inc. — Yankton-Chan Gurney Municipal, SD

702 East 31st Street, Yankton, SD 57078, USA ☎ (605) 665-3473 Tx: none Fax: none SITA: n/a
F: 1977 n/a Head: Myron D. Van Gerpen Net: n/a Aircraft below MTOW 1361kg: Cessna 172.

registration	type of aircraft	cn/fn	ex/ex*	mfd	del	powered by	mtow kg	configuration	selcal	name/fln/specialitites/remarks
N6960N	Cessna T210N Turbo Centurion II	21063170		0079	1179	1 CO TSIO-520-R	1814			
N7849Y	Piper PA-30-160 Twin Comanche B	30-929		0065	0387	2 LY IO-320-B1A	1633			
N7986Y	Piper PA-30-160 Twin Comanche B	30-1089		0066	0377	2 LY IO-320-B1A	1633			
N5MG	Cessna T303 Crusader	T30300212		0083	0290	2 CO TSIO-520-AE	2336			
N9846C	Cessna T303 Crusader	T30300217		0083	0287	2 CO TSIO-520-AE	2336			

FALWELL AVIATION, Inc. = FAW — Lynchburg-Falwell, VA

4332 Richmond Hwy, Lynchburg, VA 24501, USA ☎ (757) 845-8769 Tx: none Fax: (757) 528-1992 SITA: n/a
F: 1948 20 Head: Calvin W. Falwell ICAO: FALWELL Net: n/a Aircraft below MTOW 1361 kg: Cessna 172

registration	type of aircraft	cn/fn	ex/ex*	mfd	del	powered by	mtow kg	configuration	selcal	name/fln/specialitites/remarks
N55FA	Cessna 414	414-0058		0070	0274	2 CO TSIO-520-J	2880			
N330V	Beech King Air C90	LJ-811		0079	0895	2 PWC PT6A-21	4377			lsf Truck Body Aviation Inc.
N3FA	Cessna 550 Citation II	550-0112	N550PS	0080	0193	2 PWC JT15D-4	6033			lsf Truck Body Aviation Inc.

FARWEST AIRLINES, Llc (formerly Biegert Aviation, Inc.) — Chandler-Memorial, AZ

22022 South Price Road, Chandler, AZ 85248, USA ☎ (520) 796-2400 Tx: none Fax: (520) 796-5895 SITA: n/a
F: 1957 n/a Head: James C. Jefferies Net: n/a

registration	type of aircraft	cn/fn	ex/ex*	mfd	del	powered by	mtow kg	configuration	selcal	name/fln/specialitites/remarks
N701AC	De Havilland DHC-7-102 Dash 7	018	N895S	0079	0698	4 PWC PT6A-50	19958	Y50		

FEDERAL AVIATION ADMINISTRATION – FAA = NHK (US Department of Transportation) — Oklahoma City, OK

Flight Program Oversight Staff (AFP-100), PO Box 25082, Oklahoma City, OK 73125, USA ☎ (405) 954-6269 Tx: none Fax: (405) 954-9187 SITA: n/a
F: 1946 48 Head: Edgar C. Fell Net: n/a Aircraft below MTOW 1361kg: 1 GlaStar.
Non-commercial Federal Governmental Agency conducting flight inspection, training, support, research & development missions from main bases at Anchorage-Intl/AK, Atlantic City/NJ, Fort Worth/TX & Washington-National/DC.

registration	type of aircraft	cn/fn	ex/ex*	mfd	del	powered by	mtow kg	configuration	selcal	name/fln/specialitites/remarks
N50	Twin (Aero) Commander 680E	818-62		0058	0260	2 LY GSO-480-B1A6	3402	R & D		
N38	Sikorsky S-76A	760087		0081	0983	2 AN 250-C30	4672	R & D		
N15	Beech King Air F90	LA-138		0081	0681	2 PWC PT6A-135	4967	SUP		
N16	Beech King Air C90	LJ-893		0080	0480	2 PWC PT6A-21	4377	Trainer		
N17	Beech King Air C90	LJ-896		0080	0380	2 PWC PT6A-21	4377	Trainer		
N18	Beech King Air F90	LA-145		0081	0781	2 PWC PT6A-135	4967	Flight Insp		
N19	Beech King Air C90	LJ-909		0080	0580	2 PWC PT6A-21	4377	Trainer		
N20	Beech King Air C90	LJ-912		0080	0680	2 PWC PT6A-21	4377	Trainer		
N21	Beech King Air C90	LJ-902	N5	0080	0480	2 PWC PT6A-21	4377	Trainer		
N35	Beech King Air 200	BB-88	N4	0075	1176	2 PWC PT6A-41	5670	R & D		
N66	Beech King Air 300	FF-1		0088	0888	2 PWC PT6A-60A	6350	Flight Insp		
N67	Beech King Air 300	FF-2		0088	0488	2 PWC PT6A-60A	6350	Flight Insp		
N68	Beech King Air 300	FF-3		0088	0488	2 PWC PT6A-60A	6350	Flight Insp		
N69	Beech King Air 300	FF-4		0088	0588	2 PWC PT6A-60A	6350	Flight Insp		
N70	Beech King Air 300	FF-5		0088	0588	2 PWC PT6A-60A	6350	Flight Insp		
N71	Beech King Air 300	FF-6		0088	0888	2 PWC PT6A-60A	6350	Flight Insp		
N72	Beech King Air 300	FF-7		0088	0688	2 PWC PT6A-60A	6350	Flight Insp		
N73	Beech King Air 300	FF-8		0088	0888	2 PWC PT6A-60A	6350	Flight Insp		
N74	Beech King Air 300	FF-9		0088	1288	2 PWC PT6A-60A	6350	Flight Insp		
N75	Beech King Air 300	FF-10		0088	0988	2 PWC PT6A-60A	6350	Flight Insp		
N76	Beech King Air 300	FF-11		0088	0988	2 PWC PT6A-60A	6350	Flight Insp		
N77	Beech King Air 300	FF-12		0088	0988	2 PWC PT6A-60A	6350	Flight Insp		
N78	Beech King Air 300	FF-13		0088	0988	2 PWC PT6A-60A	6350	Flight Insp		
N79	Beech King Air 300	FF-14		0088	1088	2 PWC PT6A-60A	6350	Flight Insp		
N80	Beech King Air 300	FF-15		0088	1088	2 PWC PT6A-60A	6350	Flight Insp		
N81	Beech King Air 300	FF-16		0088	1088	2 PWC PT6A-60A	6350	Flight Insp		
N83	Beech King Air 300	FF-18		0088	1188	2 PWC PT6A-60A	6350	Flight Insp		
N84	Beech King Air 300	FF-19		0088	1288	2 PWC PT6A-60A	6350	Flight Insp		
N4	Cessna 560 Citation V	560-0113	N26	0091	0692	2 PWC JT15D-5A	7212	Support		lsf Cessna Finance Corp.
N2	Learjet 31A	31A-063	N27	0092	0892	2 GA TFE731-2-3B	7484	SUP		lsf CITG
N54	Learjet 60	60-009	N26029	0093	1296	2 PWC PW305A	10478	Flight Insp		
N55	Learjet 60	60-013	N26011	0093	0196	2 PWC PW305A	10478	Flight Insp		

registration	type of aircraft	cn/fn	ex/EX*	mfd	del	powered by	mtow kg	configuration	selcal	name/fln/specialities/remarks
□ N56	Learjet 60	60-033	N4031A	0094	0896	2 PWC PW305A	10478	Flight Insp		
□ N57	Learjet 60	60-039	N5003X	0094	0297	2 PWC PW305A	10478	Flight Insp		
□ N58	Learjet 60	60-057	N50050	0095	0697	2 PWC PW305A	10478	Flight Insp		
□ N94	Hawker 800A (BAe 125-800A)	258129	N269X	0089	1091	2 GA TFE731-5R-1H	12428	Flight Insp		
□ N95	Hawker 800A (BAe 125-800A)	258131	N270X	0089	1091	2 GA TFE731-5R-1H	12428	Flight Insp		
□ N96	Hawker 800A (BAe 125-800A)	258134	N271X	0089	1091	2 GA TFE731-5R-1H	12428	Flight Insp		
□ N97	Hawker 800A (BAe 125-800A)	258154	N272X	0089	1091	2 GA TFE731-5R-1H	12428	Flight Insp		
□ N98	Hawker 800A (BAe 125-800A)	258156	N273X	0090	1091	2 GA TFE731-5R-1H	12428	Flight Insp		
□ N99	Hawker 800A (BAe 125-800A)	258158	N274X	0090	1091	2 GA TFE731-5R-1H	12428	Flight Insp		
□ N3	GAC (Grumman) G-159 Gulfstream I	160	N752G	0065	0566	2 RR Dart 529-8X	16329	SUP		
□ N85	Canadair CL-601-3A (CL-600-2B16) Challen.	5138	N138CC	0093	0897	2 GE CF34-3A1	20457	Flight Insp		
□ N39	Convair 580	480	N74	0057	0158	2 AN 501-D13D	24766	R & D		cvtd CV440-72
□ N49	Convair 580	479	N103	0057	0159	2 AN 501-D13D	24766	R & D		cvtd CV440-61
□ N1	GAC G-IV Gulfstream IV	1071	N410GA*	0088	0589	2 RR Tay 611-8	31615	Support	FL-AK	Spirit of America
□ N40	Boeing 727-25C	19854 / 628	N8171G	0068	1077	3 PW JT8D-7	76929	R & D		

FEDERICO HELICOPTERS, Inc. = FDE

Fresno-Air Terminal & Mariposa-Yosemite, CA

4955 East Anderson, Suite 115, Fresno, CA 93727-1521, USA ☎ (209) 454-7680 Tx: n/a Fax: (209) 454-7683 SITA: n/a
F: 1981 ⁂ n/a Head: Leonard A. Federico Net: n/a

registration	type of aircraft	cn/fn	ex/EX*	mfd	del	powered by	mtow kg	configuration	selcal	name/fln/specialities/remarks
□ N111VF	Cessna T210N Turbo Centurion II	21064005	N7067N	0080	0693	1 CO TSIO-520-R	1814			lsf pvt
□ N747A	Sikorsky S-55T	55910		0055	0383	1 GA TPE331-3U-303N	3266			lsf pvt / cvtd S-55
□ N752A	Sikorsky S-55T	55981	C-GRXA	0055	1185	1 GA TPE331-3U-303N	3266			lsf pvt / cvtd S-55
□ N1386L	Bell UH-1B (204)	652	62-4592	0062	0384	1 LY T5311	3856			lsf pvt
□ N7936C	Sikorsky UH-34D (S-58C)	58-996		0058	1287	1 WR R-1820	5897			

FEDEX – Federal Express Corporation = FX / FDX

Memphis, TN / Indianapolis, IN & Anchorage-Int'l, AK

PO Box 727, Memphis, TN 38194-2424, USA ☎ (901) 369-3600 Tx: 4621053 Fax: (901) 332-3772 SITA: n/a
F: 1972 ⁂ 94000 Head: Frederick W. Smith IATA: 023 ICAO: FEDEX Net: http://www.fedex.com FEDEX FEEDER operations (in USA/Asia/Canada) of Cessna 208A/B, F27 & Shorts 360 are contracted out. They are operated on behalf of FEDEX - Federal Express (in full colours and titles) by: Baron Aviation, Corporate Air, Corporate Air Inc., CSA Air, Empire Airlines, Morningstar Air Express, Mountain Air Cargo, West Air & Wiggins Airways. Beside aircraft listed, also uses a DC-10-30F, lsf/opb GEMINI AIR CARGO (N) & 2 Boeing 747-400F lsf/opb ATLAS AIR (N), when required.

registration	type of aircraft	cn/fn	ex/EX*	mfd	del	powered by	mtow kg	configuration	selcal	name/fln/specialities/remarks
□ N799FE	Cessna 208A Caravan I Cargomaster	20800065	C-FEXF	0085	1185	1 PWC PT6A-114	3629	Freighter		lst/opb Corporate Air
□ N800FE	Cessna 208A Caravan I Cargomaster	20800007		0085	0285	1 PWC PT6A-114	3629	Freighter		lst/opb Corporate Air
□ N801FE	Cessna 208A Caravan I Cargomaster	20800009		0085	0385	1 PWC PT6A-114	3629	Freighter		lst/opb Mountain Air Cargo
□ N812FE	Cessna 208A Caravan I Cargomaster	20800040		0085	0785	1 PWC PT6A-114	3629	Freighter		lst/opb Corporate Air
□ N819FE	Cessna 208A Caravan I Cargomaster	20800056		0085	0985	1 PWC PT6A-114	3629	Freighter		lst/opb Empire Airlines
□ N827FE	Cessna 208A Caravan I Cargomaster	20800072		0085	1185	1 PWC PT6A-114	3629	Freighter		lst/opb Corporate Air
□ N830FE	Cessna 208A Caravan I Cargomaster	20800075		0085	1285	1 PWC PT6A-114	3629	Freighter		lst/opb CSA Air
□ N832FE	Cessna 208A Caravan I Cargomaster	20800081		0086	0286	1 PWC PT6A-114	3629	Freighter		lst/opb Baron Aviation
□ N833FE	Cessna 208A Caravan I Cargomaster	20800084	EI-FDX	0086	0386	1 PWC PT6A-114	3629	Freighter		lst/opb Empire Airlines
□ N835FE	Cessna 208A Caravan I Cargomaster	20800016	EI-FEX	0085	0485	1 PWC PT6A-114	3629	Freighter		lst/opb Empire Airlines
□ N700FX	Cessna 208B Caravan I Super Cargomaster	208B0419		0095	0195	1 PWC PT6A-114A	3969	Freighter		lst/opb Empire Airlines
□ N701FX	Cessna 208B Caravan I Super Cargomaster	208B0420		0095	0195	1 PWC PT6A-114A	3969	Freighter		lst/opb Wiggins Airways
□ N702FX	Cessna 208B Caravan I Super Cargomaster	208B0422		0095	0295	1 PWC PT6A-114A	3969	Freighter		lst/opb Baron Aviation
□ N703FX	Cessna 208B Caravan I Super Cargomaster	208B0423		0095	0295	1 PWC PT6A-114A	3969	Freighter		lst/opb CSA Air
□ N705FX	Cessna 208B Caravan I Super Cargomaster	208B0425		0095	0295	1 PWC PT6A-114A	3969	Freighter		lst/opb Empire Airlines
□ N706FX	Cessna 208B Caravan I Super Cargomaster	208B0426		0095	0395	1 PWC PT6A-114A	3969	Freighter		lst/opb CSA Air
□ N707FX	Cessna 208B Caravan I Super Cargomaster	208B0427		0095	0395	1 PWC PT6A-114A	3969	Freighter		lst/opb West Air
□ N708FX	Cessna 208B Caravan I Super Cargomaster	208B0429		0095	0395	1 PWC PT6A-114A	3969	Freighter		lst/opb Mountain Air Cargo
□ N709FX	Cessna 208B Caravan I Super Cargomaster	208B0430		0095	0395	1 PWC PT6A-114A	3969	Freighter		lst/opb Empire Airlines
□ N710FX	Cessna 208B Caravan I Super Cargomaster	208B0431		0095	0495	1 PWC PT6A-114A	3969	Freighter		lst/opb Corporate Air
□ N711FX	Cessna 208B Caravan I Super Cargomaster	208B0433		0095	0495	1 PWC PT6A-114A	3969	Freighter		lst/opb Empire Airlines
□ N712FX	Cessna 208B Caravan I Super Cargomaster	208B0435		0095	0595	1 PWC PT6A-114A	3969	Freighter		lst/opb CSA Air
□ N713FX	Cessna 208B Caravan I Super Cargomaster	208B0438		0095	0595	1 PWC PT6A-114A	3969	Freighter		lst/opb West Air
□ N715FX	Cessna 208B Caravan I Super Cargomaster	208B0440		0095	0595	1 PWC PT6A-114A	3969	Freighter		lst/opb Mountain Air Cargo
□ N716FX	Cessna 208B Caravan I Super Cargomaster	208B0442		0095	0595	1 PWC PT6A-114A	3969	Freighter		lst/opb Corporate Air
□ N717FX	Cessna 208B Caravan I Super Cargomaster	208B0445		0095	0695	1 PWC PT6A-114A	3969	Freighter		lst/opb CSA Air
□ N718FX	Cessna 208B Caravan I Super Cargomaster	208B0448		0095	0695	1 PWC PT6A-114A	3969	Freighter		lst/opb Baron Aviation
□ N719FX	Cessna 208B Caravan I Super Cargomaster	208B0450		0095	0695	1 PWC PT6A-114A	3969	Freighter		lst/opb Baron Aviation
□ N720FX	Cessna 208B Caravan I Super Cargomaster	208B0452		0055	0795	1 PWC PT6A-114A	3969	Freighter		lst/opb Empire Airlines
□ N721FX	Cessna 208B Caravan I Super Cargomaster	208B0453		0095	0795	1 PWC PT6A-114A	3969	Freighter		lst/opb Mountain Air Cargo
□ N722FX	Cessna 208B Caravan I Super Cargomaster	208B0454		0095	0895	1 PWC PT6A-114A	3969	Freighter		lst/opb West Air
□ N723FX	Cessna 208B Caravan I Super Cargomaster	208B0456		0095	0895	1 PWC PT6A-114A	3969	Freighter		lst/opb Baron Aviation
□ N724FX	Cessna 208B Caravan I Super Cargomaster	208B0458		0095	0895	1 PWC PT6A-114A	3969	Freighter		lst/opb Corporate Air
□ N725FX	Cessna 208B Caravan I Super Cargomaster	208B0460		0095	0895	1 PWC PT6A-114A	3969	Freighter		lst/opb Wiggins Airways
□ N726FX	Cessna 208B Caravan I Super Cargomaster	208B0465		0095	0995	1 PWC PT6A-114A	3969	Freighter		lst/opb West Air
□ N727FX	Cessna 208B Caravan I Super Cargomaster	208B0468		0095	0995	1 PWC PT6A-114A	3969	Freighter		lst/opb CSA Air
□ N728FX	Cessna 208B Caravan I Super Cargomaster	208B0471		0095	1095	1 PWC PT6A-114A	3969	Freighter		lst/opb Empire Airlines
□ N729FX	Cessna 208B Caravan I Super Cargomaster	208B0474		0095	1095	1 PWC PT6A-114A	3969	Freighter		lst/opb Mountain Air Cargo
□ N730FX	Cessna 208B Caravan I Super Cargomaster	208B0477		0095	1095	1 PWC PT6A-114A	3969	Freighter		lst/opb Corporate Air
□ N731FX	Cessna 208B Caravan I Super Cargomaster	208B0480		0095	1195	1 PWC PT6A-114A	3969	Freighter		lst/opb Wiggins Airways
□ N738FX	Cessna 208B Caravan I Super Cargomaster	208B0482		0095	1195	1 PWC PT6A-114A	3969	Freighter		lst/opb Baron Aviation
□ N740FX	Cessna 208B Caravan I Super Cargomaster	208B0484		0095	1195	1 PWC PT6A-114A	3969	Freighter		lst/opb Mountain Air Cargo
□ N741FX	Cessna 208B Caravan I Super Cargomaster	208B0486		0095	1195	1 PWC PT6A-114A	3969	Freighter		lst/opb Baron Aviation
□ N742FX	Cessna 208B Caravan I Super Cargomaster	208B0489		0095	1295	1 PWC PT6A-114A	3969	Freighter		lst/opb Mountain Air Cargo
□ N744FX	Cessna 208B Caravan I Super Cargomaster	208B0492		0095	1295	1 PWC PT6A-114A	3969	Freighter		lst/opb West Air
□ N745FX	Cessna 208B Caravan I Super Cargomaster	208B0495		0095	1295	1 PWC PT6A-114A	3969	Freighter		lst/opb Baron Aviation
□ N746FX	Cessna 208B Caravan I Super Cargomaster	208B0498		0096	0196	1 PWC PT6A-114A	3969	Freighter		lst/opb Empire Airlines
□ N747FE	Cessna 208B Caravan I Super Cargomaster	208B0238		0090	1190	1 PWC PT6A-114A	3969	Freighter		lst/opb Mountain Air Cargo
□ N747FX	Cessna 208B Caravan I Super Cargomaster	208B0501		0096	0196	1 PWC PT6A-114A	3969	Freighter		lst/opb Mountain Air Cargo
□ N748FE	Cessna 208B Caravan I Super Cargomaster	208B0241		0090	1190	1 PWC PT6A-114A	3969	Freighter		lst/opb Wiggins Airways
□ N748FX	Cessna 208B Caravan I Super Cargomaster	208B0503		0096	0196	1 PWC PT6A-114A	3969	Freighter		lst/opb West Air
□ N749FE	Cessna 208B Caravan I Super Cargomaster	208B0242		0090	1290	1 PWC PT6A-114A	3969	Freighter		lst/opb Baron Aviation
□ N749FX	Cessna 208B Caravan I Super Cargomaster	208B0508		0096	0296	1 PWC PT6A-114A	3969	Freighter		lst/opb Mountain Air Cargo
□ N750FX	Cessna 208B Caravan I Super Cargomaster	208B0511		0096	0296	1 PWC PT6A-114A	3969	Freighter		lst/opb West Air
□ N751FE	Cessna 208B Caravan I Super Cargomaster	208B0245		0090	1290	1 PWC PT6A-114A	3969	Freighter		lst/opb Corporate Air
□ N751FX	Cessna 208B Caravan I Super Cargomaster	208B0514		0096	0296	1 PWC PT6A-114A	3969	Freighter		lst/opb Baron Aviation
□ N752FE	Cessna 208B Caravan I Super Cargomaster	208B0247		0090	1290	1 PWC PT6A-114A	3969	Freighter		lst/opb CSA Air
□ N752FX	Cessna 208B Caravan I Super Cargomaster	208B0517		0096	0396	1 PWC PT6A-114A	3969	Freighter		lst/opb Empire Airlines
□ N753FE	Cessna 208B Caravan I Super Cargomaster	208B0248		0091	0191	1 PWC PT6A-114A	3969	Freighter		lst/opb Empire Airlines
□ N753FX	Cessna 208B Caravan I Super Cargomaster	208B0520		0096	0396	1 PWC PT6A-114A	3969	Freighter		lst/opb Baron Aviation
□ N754FX	Cessna 208B Caravan I Super Cargomaster	208B0526		0096	0396	1 PWC PT6A-114A	3969	Freighter		lst/opb West Air
□ N755FE	Cessna 208B Caravan I Super Cargomaster	208B0250		0091	0191	1 PWC PT6A-114A	3969	Freighter		lst/opb Mountain Air Cargo
□ N755FX	Cessna 208B Caravan I Super Cargomaster	208B0529		0096	0496	1 PWC PT6A-114A	3969	Freighter		lst/opb Wiggins Airways
□ N756FE	Cessna 208B Caravan I Super Cargomaster	208B0251		0091	0191	1 PWC PT6A-114A	3969	Freighter		lst/opb Baron Aviation
□ N756FX	Cessna 208B Caravan I Super Cargomaster	208B0532		0096	0496	1 PWC PT6A-114A	3969	Freighter		lst/opb Empire Airlines
□ N757FX	Cessna 208B Caravan I Super Cargomaster	208B0535		0096	0496	1 PWC PT6A-114A	3969	Freighter		lst/opb Wiggins Airlines
□ N758FX	Cessna 208B Caravan I Super Cargomaster	208B0539		0096	0596	1 PWC PT6A-114A	3969	Freighter		lst/opb West Air
□ N759FX	Cessna 208B Caravan I Super Cargomaster	208B0542		0096	0696	1 PWC PT6A-114A	3969	Freighter		lst/opb West Air
□ N760FE	Cessna 208B Caravan I Super Cargomaster	208B0252		0091	0291	1 PWC PT6A-114A	3969	Freighter		lst/opb Corporate Air, Philippines
□ N761FE	Cessna 208B Caravan I Super Cargomaster	208B0254		0091	0291	1 PWC PT6A-114A	3969	Freighter		lst/opb CSA Air
□ N762FE	Cessna 208B Caravan I Super Cargomaster	208B0255		0091	0291	1 PWC PT6A-114A	3969	Freighter		lst/opb West Air
□ N763FE	Cessna 208B Caravan I Super Cargomaster	208B0256		0091	0391	1 PWC PT6A-114A	3969	Freighter		lst/opb West Air
□ N764FE	Cessna 208B Caravan I Super Cargomaster	208B0258		0091	0391	1 PWC PT6A-114A	3969	Freighter		lst/opb Mountain Air Cargo
□ N765FE	Cessna 208B Caravan I Super Cargomaster	208B0259		0091	0391	1 PWC PT6A-114A	3969	Freighter		lst/opb Baron Aviation
□ N766FE	Cessna 208B Caravan I Super Cargomaster	208B0260		0091	0491	1 PWC PT6A-114A	3969	Freighter		lst/opb Corporate Air, Philippines
□ N767FE	Cessna 208B Caravan I Super Cargomaster	208B0262		0091	0491	1 PWC PT6A-114A	3969	Freighter		lst/opb CSA Air
□ N768FE	Cessna 208B Caravan I Super Cargomaster	208B0263		0091	0491	1 PWC PT6A-114A	3969	Freighter		lst/opb West Air
□ N769FE	Cessna 208B Caravan I Super Cargomaster	208B0264		0091	0591	1 PWC PT6A-114A	3969	Freighter		lst/opb Mountain Air Cargo
□ N770FE	Cessna 208B Caravan I Super Cargomaster	208B0265		0091	0591	1 PWC PT6A-114A	3969	Freighter		lst/opb Baron Aviation
□ N771FE	Cessna 208B Caravan I Super Cargomaster	208B0267		0091	0691	1 PWC PT6A-114A	3969	Freighter		lst/opb West Air
□ N772FE	Cessna 208B Caravan I Super Cargomaster	208B0268		0091	0691	1 PWC PT6A-114A	3969	Freighter		lst/opb West Air
□ N773FE	Cessna 208B Caravan I Super Cargomaster	208B0269		0091	0691	1 PWC PT6A-114A	3969	Freighter		lst/opb Baron Aviation
□ N774FE	Cessna 208B Caravan I Super Cargomaster	208B0271		0091	0691	1 PWC PT6A-114A	3969	Freighter		lst/opb Baron Aviation
□ N775FE	Cessna 208B Caravan I Super Cargomaster	208B0272		0091	0791	1 PWC PT6A-114A	3969	Freighter		lst/opb Empire Airlines
□ N776FE	Cessna 208B Caravan I Super Cargomaster	208B0273		0091	0791	1 PWC PT6A-114A	3969	Freighter		lst/opb Mountain Air Cargo
□ N778FE	Cessna 208B Caravan I Super Cargomaster	208B0275		0091	0891	1 PWC PT6A-114A	3969	Freighter		lst/opb Empire Airlines
□ N779FE	Cessna 208B Caravan I Super Cargomaster	208B0276		0091	0891	1 PWC PT6A-114A	3969	Freighter		lst/opb Empire Airlines
□ N780FE	Cessna 208B Caravan I Super Cargomaster	208B0277		0091	0891	1 PWC PT6A-114A	3969	Freighter		lst/opb Wiggins Airways
□ N781FE	Cessna 208B Caravan I Super Cargomaster	208B0278		0091	0891	1 PWC PT6A-114A	3969	Freighter		lst/opb West Air
□ N782FE	Cessna 208B Caravan I Super Cargomaster	208B0280		0091	0991	1 PWC PT6A-114A	3969	Freighter		lst/opb West Air

registration	type of aircraft	cn/fn	ex/ex*	mfd	del	powered by	mtow kg	configuration	selcal	name/fln/specialitites/remarks
N783FE	Cessna 208B Caravan I Super Cargomaster	208B0281		0091	0991	1 PWC PT6A-114A	3969	Freighter		lst/opb Wiggins Airways
N784FE	Cessna 208B Caravan I Super Cargomaster	208B0282		0091	0991	1 PWC PT6A-114A	3969	Freighter		lst/opb CSA Air
N785FE	Cessna 208B Caravan I Super Cargomaster	208B0283		0091	1091	1 PWC PT6A-114A	3969	Freighter		lst/opb West Air
N786FE	Cessna 208B Caravan I Super Cargomaster	208B0284		0091	1091	1 PWC PT6A-114A	3969	Freighter		lst/opb Baron Aviation
N787FE	Cessna 208B Caravan I Super Cargomaster	208B0285		0091	1091	1 PWC PT6A-114A	3969	Freighter		lst/opb Mountain Air Cargo
N788FE	Cessna 208B Caravan I Super Cargomaster	208B0286		0091	1091	1 PWC PT6A-114A	3969	Freighter		lst/opb Empire Airlines
N789FE	Cessna 208B Caravan I Super Cargomaster	208B0287		0091	1191	1 PWC PT6A-114A	3969	Freighter		lst/opb Wiggins Airways
N790FE	Cessna 208B Caravan I Super Cargomaster	208B0288		0091	1191	1 PWC PT6A-114A	3969	Freighter		lst/opb West Air
N791FE	Cessna 208B Caravan I Super Cargomaster	208B0289		0091	1191	1 PWC PT6A-114A	3969	Freighter		lst/opb Corporate Air
N792FE	Cessna 208B Caravan I Super Cargomaster	208B0290		0091	1291	1 PWC PT6A-114A	3969	Freighter		lst/opb Mountain Air Cargo
N793FE	Cessna 208B Caravan I Super Cargomaster	208B0291		0091	1291	1 PWC PT6A-114A	3969	Freighter		lst/opb Baron Aviation
N794FE	Cessna 208B Caravan I Super Cargomaster	208B0292		0092	0192	1 PWC PT6A-114A	3969	Freighter		lst/opb Corporate Air
N795FE	Cessna 208B Caravan I Super Cargomaster	208B0293		0092	0192	1 PWC PT6A-114A	3969	Freighter		lst/opb CSA Air
N796FE	Cessna 208B Caravan I Super Cargomaster	208B0212	C-FEXY	0090	0490	1 PWC PT6A-114	3969	Freighter		lst/opb Corporate Air
N797FE	Cessna 208B Caravan I Super Cargomaster	208B0042	C-FEXH	0087	0987	1 PWC PT6A-114	3969	Freighter		lst/opb Corporate Air
N798FE	Cessna 208B Caravan I Super Cargomaster	208B0174	C-FEDY	0089	0589	1 PWC PT6A-114	3969	Freighter		lst/opb Corporate Air
N804FE	Cessna 208B Caravan I Super Cargomaster	208B0039	F-GETN	0087	0987	1 PWC PT6A-114	3969	Freighter		lst/opb Wiggins Airways
N807FE	Cessna 208B Caravan I Super Cargomaster	208B0041	F-GETO	0087	0987	1 PWC PT6A-114	3969	Freighter		lst/opb Wiggins Airways
N820FE	Cessna 208B Caravan I Super Cargomaster	208B0111	F-GHHC	0088	0888	1 PWC PT6A-114	3969	Freighter		lst/opb Mountain Air Cargo
N828FE	Cessna 208B Caravan I Super Cargomaster	208B0122	F-GHHD	0088	1088	1 PWC PT6A-114	3969	Freighter		lst/opb CSA Air
N831FE	Cessna 208B Caravan I Super Cargomaster	208B0225	F-GHHE	0090	0890	1 PWC PT6A-114	3969	Freighter		lst/opb Mountain Air Cargo
N841FE	Cessna 208B Caravan I Super Cargomaster	208B0144		0089	0189	1 PWC PT6A-114	3969	Freighter		lst/opb Baron Aviation
N842FE	Cessna 208B Caravan I Super Cargomaster	208B0146		0089	0189	1 PWC PT6A-114	3969	Freighter		lst/opb Mountain Air Cargo
N843FE	Cessna 208B Caravan I Super Cargomaster	208B0147		0089	0189	1 PWC PT6A-114	3969	Freighter		lst/opb CSA Air
N844FE	Cessna 208B Caravan I Super Cargomaster	208B0149		0089	0289	1 PWC PT6A-114	3969	Freighter		lst/opb West Air
N845FE	Cessna 208B Caravan I Super Cargomaster	208B0152		0089	0289	1 PWC PT6A-114	3969	Freighter		lst/opb Baron Aviation
N846FE	Cessna 208B Caravan I Super Cargomaster	208B0154		0089	0289	1 PWC PT6A-114	3969	Freighter		lst/opb Corporate Air
N847FE	Cessna 208B Caravan I Super Cargomaster	208B0156		0089	0389	1 PWC PT6A-114	3969	Freighter		lst/opb Mountain Air Cargo
N848FE	Cessna 208B Caravan I Super Cargomaster	208B0158		0089	0389	1 PWC PT6A-114	3969	Freighter		lst/opb Mountain Air Cargo
N849FE	Cessna 208B Caravan I Super Cargomaster	208B0162		0089	0389	1 PWC PT6A-114	3969	Freighter		lst/opb Mountain Air Cargo
N850FE	Cessna 208B Caravan I Super Cargomaster	208B0164		0089	0489	1 PWC PT6A-114	3969	Freighter		lst/opb Empire Airlines
N851FE	Cessna 208B Caravan I Super Cargomaster	208B0166		0089	0489	1 PWC PT6A-114	3969	Freighter		lst/opb Corporate Air
N852FE	Cessna 208B Caravan I Super Cargomaster	208B0168		0089	0489	1 PWC PT6A-114	3969	Freighter		lst/opb Mountain Air Cargo
N853FE	Cessna 208B Caravan I Super Cargomaster	208B0170		0089	0589	1 PWC PT6A-114	3969	Freighter		lst/opb Mountain Air Cargo
N855FE	Cessna 208B Caravan I Super Cargomaster	208B0203		0090	0190	1 PWC PT6A-114	3969	Freighter		lst/opb Mountain Air Cargo
N856FE	Cessna 208B Caravan I Super Cargomaster	208B0176		0089	0689	1 PWC PT6A-114	3969	Freighter		lst/opb Empire Airlines
N857FE	Cessna 208B Caravan I Super Cargomaster	208B0177		0089	0689	1 PWC PT6A-114	3969	Freighter		lst/opb West Air
N858FE	Cessna 208B Caravan I Super Cargomaster	208B0178		0089	0689	1 PWC PT6A-114	3969	Freighter		lst/opb CSA Air
N859FE	Cessna 208B Caravan I Super Cargomaster	208B0181		0089	0789	1 PWC PT6A-114	3969	Freighter		lst/opb Empire Airlines
N860FE	Cessna 208B Caravan I Super Cargomaster	208B0182		0089	0789	1 PWC PT6A-114	3969	Freighter		lst/opb Corporate Air
N861FE	Cessna 208B Caravan I Super Cargomaster	208B0183		0089	0889	1 PWC PT6A-114	3969	Freighter		lst/opb Baron Aviation
N862FE	Cessna 208B Caravan I Super Cargomaster	208B0184		0089	0889	1 PWC PT6A-114	3969	Freighter		lst/opb Mountain Air Cargo
N863FE	Cessna 208B Caravan I Super Cargomaster	208B0186		0089	0889	1 PWC PT6A-114	3969	Freighter		lst/opb Corporate Air
N864FE	Cessna 208B Caravan I Super Cargomaster	208B0187		0089	0889	1 PWC PT6A-114	3969	Freighter		lst/opb Corporate Air
N865FE	Cessna 208B Caravan I Super Cargomaster	208B0188		0089	0989	1 PWC PT6A-114	3969	Freighter		lst/opb Wiggins Airways
N866FE	Cessna 208B Caravan I Super Cargomaster	208B0189		0089	0989	1 PWC PT6A-114	3969	Freighter		lst/opb Baron Aviation
N867FE	Cessna 208B Caravan I Super Cargomaster	208B0191		0089	0989	1 PWC PT6A-114	3969	Freighter		lst/opb Corporate Air
N869FE	Cessna 208B Caravan I Super Cargomaster	208B0195		0089	1089	1 PWC PT6A-114	3969	Freighter		lst/opb Mountain Air Cargo
N870FE	Cessna 208B Caravan I Super Cargomaster	208B0196		0089	1189	1 PWC PT6A-114	3969	Freighter		lst/opb Wiggins Airways
N871FE	Cessna 208B Caravan I Super Cargomaster	208B0198		0089	1189	1 PWC PT6A-114	3969	Freighter		lst/opb CSA Air
N872FE	Cessna 208B Caravan I Super Cargomaster	208B0200		0089	1289	1 PWC PT6A-114	3969	Freighter		lst/opb West Air
N873FE	Cessna 208B Caravan I Super Cargomaster	208B0202		0089	1289	1 PWC PT6A-114	3969	Freighter		lst/opb Empire Airlines
N874FE	Cessna 208B Caravan I Super Cargomaster	208B0205		0090	0190	1 PWC PT6A-114	3969	Freighter		lst/opb Mountain Air Cargo
N875FE	Cessna 208B Caravan I Super Cargomaster	208B0206		0090	0290	1 PWC PT6A-114	3969	Freighter		lst/opb Empire Airlines
N876FE	Cessna 208B Caravan I Super Cargomaster	208B0207		0090	0290	1 PWC PT6A-114	3969	Freighter		lst/opb Empire Airlines
N877FE	Cessna 208B Caravan I Super Cargomaster	208B0232		0090	0990	1 PWC PT6A-114A	3969	Freighter		lst/opb Corporate Air
N878FE	Cessna 208B Caravan I Super Cargomaster	208B0211		0090	0390	1 PWC PT6A-114	3969	Freighter		lst/opb Mountain Air Cargo
N879FE	Cessna 208B Caravan I Super Cargomaster	208B0213		0090	0490	1 PWC PT6A-114	3969	Freighter		lst/opb West Air
N880FE	Cessna 208B Caravan I Super Cargomaster	208B0215		0090	0490	1 PWC PT6A-114	3969	Freighter		lst/opb Empire Airlines
N881FE	Cessna 208B Caravan I Super Cargomaster	208B0204		0090	0190	1 PWC PT6A-114	3969	Freighter		lst/opb Mountain Air Cargo
N882FE	Cessna 208B Caravan I Super Cargomaster	208B0208		0090	0290	1 PWC PT6A-114	3969	Freighter		lst/opb Empire Airlines
N883FE	Cessna 208B Caravan I Super Cargomaster	208B0210		0090	0390	1 PWC PT6A-114	3969	Freighter		lst/opb CSA Air
N884FE	Cessna 208B Caravan I Super Cargomaster	208B0233		0090	1090	1 PWC PT6A-114	3969	Freighter		lst/opb CSA Air
N885FE	Cessna 208B Caravan I Super Cargomaster	208B0185		0089	0889	1 PWC PT6A-114	3969	Freighter		lst/opb Corporate Air
N886FE	Cessna 208B Caravan I Super Cargomaster	208B0190		0089	0989	1 PWC PT6A-114	3969	Freighter		lst/opb West Air
N887FE	Cessna 208B Caravan I Super Cargomaster	208B0216		0090	0590	1 PWC PT6A-114	3969	Freighter		lst/opb Mountain Air Cargo
N888FE	Cessna 208B Caravan I Super Cargomaster	208B0217		0090	0590	1 PWC PT6A-114	3969	Freighter		lst/opb Wiggins Airways
N889FE	Cessna 208B Caravan I Super Cargomaster	208B0218		0090	0590	1 PWC PT6A-114	3969	Freighter		lst/opb Baron Aviation
N890FE	Cessna 208B Caravan I Super Cargomaster	208B0219		0090	0690	1 PWC PT6A-114	3969	Freighter		lst/opb Corporate Air
N891FE	Cessna 208B Caravan I Super Cargomaster	208B0221		0090	0690	1 PWC PT6A-114	3969	Freighter		lst/opb West Air
N892FE	Cessna 208B Caravan I Super Cargomaster	208B0222		0090	0690	1 PWC PT6A-114	3969	Freighter		lst/opb West Air
N893FE	Cessna 208B Caravan I Super Cargomaster	208B0223		0090	0790	1 PWC PT6A-114	3969	Freighter		lst/opb CSA Air
N894FE	Cessna 208B Caravan I Super Cargomaster	208B0224		0090	0790	1 PWC PT6A-114	3969	Freighter		lst/opb Baron Aviation
N895FE	Cessna 208B Caravan I Super Cargomaster	208B0015	C-FEXG	0087	0387	1 PWC PT6A-114	3969	Freighter		lst/opb Empire Airlines
N896FE	Cessna 208B Caravan I Super Cargomaster	208B0226		0090	0890	1 PWC PT6A-114	3969	Freighter		lst/opb Empire Airlines
N897FE	Cessna 208B Caravan I Super Cargomaster	208B0227		0090	0890	1 PWC PT6A-114	3969	Freighter		lst/opb Empire Airlines
N898FE	Cessna 208B Caravan I Super Cargomaster	208B0228		0090	0990	1 PWC PT6A-114	3969	Freighter		lst/opb Wiggins Airways
N899FE	Cessna 208B Caravan I Super Cargomaster	208B0235		0090	1090	1 PWC PT6A-114A	3969	Freighter		lst/opb Empire Airlines
N900FE	Cessna 208B Caravan I Super Cargomaster	208B0054	SE-KLX	0087	1187	1 PWC PT6A-114	3969	Freighter		lst/opb Baron Aviation
N901FE	Cessna 208B Caravan I Super Cargomaster	208B0001	N9767F*	0086	1186	1 PWC PT6A-114	3969	Freighter		lst/opb Wiggins Airways
N902FE	Cessna 208B Caravan I Super Cargomaster	208B0002		0086	1086	1 PWC PT6A-114	3969	Freighter		lst/opb Baron Aviation
N903FE	Cessna 208B Caravan I Super Cargomaster	208B0003		0086	1186	1 PWC PT6A-114	3969	Freighter		lst/opb Corporate Air
N904FE	Cessna 208B Caravan I Super Cargomaster	208B0004		0086	1186	1 PWC PT6A-114	3969	Freighter		lst/opb Corporate Air
N905FE	Cessna 208B Caravan I Super Cargomaster	208B0005		0086	1286	1 PWC PT6A-114	3969	Freighter		lst/opb Mountain Air Cargo
N906FE	Cessna 208B Caravan I Super Cargomaster	208B0006		0086	1286	1 PWC PT6A-114	3969	Freighter		lst/opb CSA Air
N907FE	Cessna 208B Caravan I Super Cargomaster	208B0007		0086	1286	1 PWC PT6A-114	3969	Freighter		lst/opb CSA Air
N908FE	Cessna 208B Caravan I Super Cargomaster	208B0008		0086	1286	1 PWC PT6A-114	3969	Freighter		lst/opb West Air
N909FE	Cessna 208B Caravan I Super Cargomaster	208B0009		0086	1286	1 PWC PT6A-114	3969	Freighter		lst/opb Wiggins Airways
N910FE	Cessna 208B Caravan I Super Cargomaster	208B0010		0086	1286	1 PWC PT6A-114	3969	Freighter		lst/opb Corporate Air
N911FE	Cessna 208B Caravan I Super Cargomaster	208B0011		0087	0187	1 PWC PT6A-114	3969	Freighter		lst/opb Wiggins Airways
N912FE	Cessna 208B Caravan I Super Cargomaster	208B0012		0087	0187	1 PWC PT6A-114	3969	Freighter		lst/opb Baron Aviation
N914FE	Cessna 208B Caravan I Super Cargomaster	208B0014		0087	0287	1 PWC PT6A-114	3969	Freighter		lst/opb CSA Air
N916FE	Cessna 208B Caravan I Super Cargomaster	208B0016		0087	0387	1 PWC PT6A-114	3969	Freighter		lst/opb Corporate Air
N917FE	Cessna 208B Caravan I Super Cargomaster	208B0017		0087	0387	1 PWC PT6A-114	3969	Freighter		lst/opb Mountain Air Cargo
N918FE	Cessna 208B Caravan I Super Cargomaster	208B0018		0087	0387	1 PWC PT6A-114	3969	Freighter		lst/opb Empire Airlines
N919FE	Cessna 208B Caravan I Super Cargomaster	208B0019		0087	0387	1 PWC PT6A-114	3969	Freighter		lst/opb Wiggins Airways
N920FE	Cessna 208B Caravan I Super Cargomaster	208B0020		0087	0487	1 PWC PT6A-114	3969	Freighter		lst/opb West Air
N921FE	Cessna 208B Caravan I Super Cargomaster	208B0021		0087	0487	1 PWC PT6A-114	3969	Freighter		lst/opb Mountain Air Cargo
N922FE	Cessna 208B Caravan I Super Cargomaster	208B0022		0087	0487	1 PWC PT6A-114	3969	Freighter		lst/opb Baron Aviation
N923FE	Cessna 208B Caravan I Super Cargomaster	208B0023		0087	0587	1 PWC PT6A-114	3969	Freighter		lst/opb CSA Air
N924FE	Cessna 208B Caravan I Super Cargomaster	208B0024		0087	0587	1 PWC PT6A-114	3969	Freighter		lst/opb Corporate Air
N925FE	Cessna 208B Caravan I Super Cargomaster	208B0025		0087	0587	1 PWC PT6A-114	3969	Freighter		lst/opb CSA Air
N926FE	Cessna 208B Caravan I Super Cargomaster	208B0026		0087	0587	1 PWC PT6A-114	3969	Freighter		lst/opb Corporate Air
N927FE	Cessna 208B Caravan I Super Cargomaster	208B0027		0087	0587	1 PWC PT6A-114	3969	Freighter		lst/opb Baron Aviation
N928FE	Cessna 208B Caravan I Super Cargomaster	208B0028		0087	0687	1 PWC PT6A-114	3969	Freighter		lst/opb Baron Aviation
N929FE	Cessna 208B Caravan I Super Cargomaster	208B0029		0087	0687	1 PWC PT6A-114	3969	Freighter		lst/opb Baron Aviation
N930FE	Cessna 208B Caravan I Super Cargomaster	208B0030		0087	0687	1 PWC PT6A-114	3969	Freighter		lst/opb West Air
N931FE	Cessna 208B Caravan I Super Cargomaster	208B0031		0087	0687	1 PWC PT6A-114	3969	Freighter		lst/opb Wiggins Airways
N933FE	Cessna 208B Caravan I Super Cargomaster	208B0033		0087	0787	1 PWC PT6A-114	3969	Freighter		lst/opb Corporate Air
N934FE	Cessna 208B Caravan I Super Cargomaster	208B0034		0087	0787	1 PWC PT6A-114	3969	Freighter		lst/opb Baron Aviation
N935FE	Cessna 208B Caravan I Super Cargomaster	208B0035		0087	0787	1 PWC PT6A-114	3969	Freighter		lst/opb Wiggins Airways
N936FE	Cessna 208B Caravan I Super Cargomaster	208B0036		0087	0887	1 PWC PT6A-114	3969	Freighter		lst/opb Corporate Air
N937FE	Cessna 208B Caravan I Super Cargomaster	208B0037		0087	0887	1 PWC PT6A-114	3969	Freighter		lst/opb Wiggins Airways
N938FE	Cessna 208B Caravan I Super Cargomaster	208B0038		0087	0887	1 PWC PT6A-114	3969	Freighter		lst/opb Mountain Air Cargo
N939FE	Cessna 208B Caravan I Super Cargomaster	208B0180		0089	0689	1 PWC PT6A-114	3969	Freighter		lst/opb Baron Aviation
N940FE	Cessna 208B Caravan I Super Cargomaster	208B0040		0087	0987	1 PWC PT6A-114	3969	Freighter		lst/opb Empire Airlines
N941FE	Cessna 208B Caravan I Super Cargomaster	208B0192		0089	1089	1 PWC PT6A-114	3969	Freighter		lst/opb Empire Airlines
N943FE	Cessna 208B Caravan I Super Cargomaster	208B0043		0087	0987	1 PWC PT6A-114	3969	Freighter		lst/opb Mountain Air Cargo
N944FE	Cessna 208B Caravan I Super Cargomaster	208B0044		0087	1087	1 PWC PT6A-114	3969	Freighter		lst/opb Baron Aviation
N946FE	Cessna 208B Caravan I Super Cargomaster	208B0048		0087	1087	1 PWC PT6A-114	3969	Freighter		lst/opb CSA Air

registration	type of aircraft	cn/fn	ex/ex*	mfd	del	powered by	mtow kg	configuration	selcal	name/fln/specialitites/remarks
☐ N947FE	Cessna 208B Caravan I Super Cargomaster	208B0050		0087	1087	1 PWC PT6A-114	3969	Freighter		lst/opb Wiggins Airways
☐ N948FE	Cessna 208B Caravan I Super Cargomaster	208B0052		0087	1187	1 PWC PT6A-114A	3969	Freighter		lst/opb Baron Aviation
☐ N950FE	Cessna 208B Caravan I Super Cargomaster	208B0056		0087	1187	1 PWC PT6A-114	3969	Freighter		lst/opb Corporate Air
☐ N952FE	Cessna 208B Caravan I Super Cargomaster	208B0060		0087	1287	1 PWC PT6A-114	3969	Freighter		lst/opb Corporate Air
☐ N953FE	Cessna 208B Caravan I Super Cargomaster	208B0062		0087	1287	1 PWC PT6A-114	3969	Freighter		lst/opb Empire Airlines
☐ N954FE	Cessna 208B Caravan I Super Cargomaster	208B0064		0087	1287	1 PWC PT6A-114	3969	Freighter		lst/opb CSA Air
☐ N955FE	Cessna 208B Caravan I Super Cargomaster	208B0066		0087	1287	1 PWC PT6A-114	3969	Freighter		lst/opb Mountain Air Cargo
☐ N956FE	Cessna 208B Caravan I Super Cargomaster	208B0068		0087	0188	1 PWC PT6A-114	3969	Freighter		lst/opb Empire Airlines
☐ N957FE	Cessna 208B Caravan I Super Cargomaster	208B0070		0087	0188	1 PWC PT6A-114	3969	Freighter		lst/opb Baron Aviation
☐ N958FE	Cessna 208B Caravan I Super Cargomaster	208B0071		0088	0288	1 PWC PT6A-114	3969	Freighter		lst/opb Wiggins Airways
☐ N959FE	Cessna 208B Caravan I Super Cargomaster	208B0073		0088	0288	1 PWC PT6A-114	3969	Freighter		lst/opb Wiggins Airways
☐ N960FE	Cessna 208B Caravan I Super Cargomaster	208B0075		0088	0388	1 PWC PT6A-114	3969	Freighter		lst/opb Empire Airlines
☐ N961FE	Cessna 208B Caravan I Super Cargomaster	208B0077		0088	0388	1 PWC PT6A-114	3969	Freighter		lst/opb Baron Aviation
☐ N962FE	Cessna 208B Caravan I Super Cargomaster	208B0078		0088	0388	1 PWC PT6A-114	3969	Freighter		lst/opb Mountain Air Cargo
☐ N963FE	Cessna 208B Caravan I Super Cargomaster	208B0080		0088	0388	1 PWC PT6A-114	3969	Freighter		lst/opb Wiggins Airways
☐ N964FE	Cessna 208B Caravan I Super Cargomaster	208B0083		0088	0488	1 PWC PT6A-114	3969	Freighter		lst/opb Corporate Air
☐ N965FE	Cessna 208B Caravan I Super Cargomaster	208B0084		0088	0488	1 PWC PT6A-114	3969	Freighter		lst/opb Empire Airlines
☐ N966FE	Cessna 208B Caravan I Super Cargomaster	208B0086		0088	0488	1 PWC PT6A-114	3969	Freighter		lst/opb Wiggins Airways
☐ N967FE	Cessna 208B Caravan I Super Cargomaster	208B0088		0088	0488	1 PWC PT6A-114	3969	Freighter		lst/opb Mountain Air Cargo
☐ N968FE	Cessna 208B Caravan I Super Cargomaster	208B0090		0088	0588	1 PWC PT6A-114	3969	Freighter		lst/opb West Air
☐ N969FE	Cessna 208B Caravan I Super Cargomaster	208B0092		0088	0588	1 PWC PT6A-114	3969	Freighter		lst/opb West Air
☐ N970FE	Cessna 208B Caravan I Super Cargomaster	208B0093		0088	0588	1 PWC PT6A-114	3969	Freighter		lst/opb Baron Aviation
☐ N971FE	Cessna 208B Caravan I Super Cargomaster	208B0094		0088	0588	1 PWC PT6A-114	3969	Freighter		lst/opb Corporate Air
☐ N972FE	Cessna 208B Caravan I Super Cargomaster	208B0096		0088	0688	1 PWC PT6A-114	3969	Freighter		lst/opb Corporate Air
☐ N973FE	Cessna 208B Caravan I Super Cargomaster	208B0098		0088	0688	1 PWC PT6A-114	3969	Freighter		lst/opb Mountain Air Cargo
☐ N974FE	Cessna 208B Caravan I Super Cargomaster	208B0099		0088	0688	1 PWC PT6A-114	3969	Freighter		lst/opb Wiggins Airways
☐ N975FE	Cessna 208B Caravan I Super Cargomaster	208B0101		0088	0688	1 PWC PT6A-114	3969	Freighter		lst/opb Mountain Air Cargo
☐ N976FE	Cessna 208B Caravan I Super Cargomaster	208B0103		0088	0788	1 PWC PT6A-114	3969	Freighter		lst/opb Empire Airlines
☐ N977FE	Cessna 208B Caravan I Super Cargomaster	208B0104		0088	0788	1 PWC PT6A-114	3969	Freighter		lst/opb Corporate Air
☐ N978FE	Cessna 208B Caravan I Super Cargomaster	208B0105		0088	0788	1 PWC PT6A-114	3969	Freighter		lst/opb Baron Aviation
☐ N979FE	Cessna 208B Caravan I Super Cargomaster	208B0106		0088	0788	1 PWC PT6A-114	3969	Freighter		lst/opb Mountain Air Cargo
☐ N980FE	Cessna 208B Caravan I Super Cargomaster	208B0108		0088	0888	1 PWC PT6A-114	3969	Freighter		lst/opb Corporate Air
☐ N981FE	Cessna 208B Caravan I Super Cargomaster	208B0110		0088	0888	1 PWC PT6A-114	3969	Freighter		lst/opb Wiggins Airways
☐ N983FE	Cessna 208B Caravan I Super Cargomaster	208B0113		0088	0888	1 PWC PT6A-114	3969	Freighter		lst/opb Empire Airlines
☐ N984FE	Cessna 208B Caravan I Super Cargomaster	208B0115		0088	0988	1 PWC PT6A-114	3969	Freighter		lst/opb West Air
☐ N985FE	Cessna 208B Caravan I Super Cargomaster	208B0117		0088	0988	1 PWC PT6A-114	3969	Freighter		lst/opb West Air
☐ N986FE	Cessna 208B Caravan I Super Cargomaster	208B0194		0089	1089	1 PWC PT6A-114	3969	Freighter		lst/opb CSA Air
☐ N987FE	Cessna 208B Caravan I Super Cargomaster	208B0201		0089	1289	1 PWC PT6A-114	3969	Freighter		lst/opb West Air
☐ N989FE	Cessna 208B Caravan I Super Cargomaster	208B0124		0088	1088	1 PWC PT6A-114	3969	Freighter		lst/opb Wiggins Airways
☐ N990FE	Cessna 208B Caravan I Super Cargomaster	208B0125		0088	1088	1 PWC PT6A-114	3969	Freighter		lst/opb Corporate Air
☐ N991FE	Cessna 208B Caravan I Super Cargomaster	208B0127		0088	1188	1 PWC PT6A-114	3969	Freighter		lst/opb Corporate Air
☐ N992FE	Cessna 208B Caravan I Super Cargomaster	208B0128		0088	1088	1 PWC PT6A-114	3969	Freighter		lst/opb Empire Airlines
☐ N993FE	Cessna 208B Caravan I Super Cargomaster	208B0130		0088	1188	1 PWC PT6A-114	3969	Freighter		lst/opb CSA Air
☐ N994FE	Cessna 208B Caravan I Super Cargomaster	208B0132		0088	1188	1 PWC PT6A-114	3969	Freighter		lst/opb Baron Aviation
☐ N995FE	Cessna 208B Caravan I Super Cargomaster	208B0133		0088	1188	1 PWC PT6A-114	3969	Freighter		lst/opb Empire Airlines
☐ N996FE	Cessna 208B Caravan I Super Cargomaster	208B0135		0088	1288	1 PWC PT6A-114	3969	Freighter		lst/opb Wiggins Airways
☐ N997FE	Cessna 208B Caravan I Super Cargomaster	208B0197		0089	1189	1 PWC PT6A-114	3969	Freighter		lst/opb Corporate Air
☐ N998FE	Cessna 208B Caravan I Super Cargomaster	208B0139		0088	1288	1 PWC PT6A-114	3969	Freighter		lst/opb Wiggins Airways
☐ N999FE	Cessna 208B Caravan I Super Cargomaster	208B0231		0090	0990	1 PWC PT6A-114A	3969	Freighter		lst/opb Mountain Air Cargo
☐ C-FEXE	Cessna 208B Caravan I Super Cargomaster	208B0244		0090	1290	1 PWC PT6A-114A	3969	Freighter		lst/opb Morningstar Air Express
☐ C-FEXX	Cessna 208B Caravan I Super Cargomaster	208B0209		0090	0390	1 PWC PT6A-114	3969	Freighter		lst/opb Morningstar Air Express
☐ N6FE	Cessna 560 Citation V	560-0028		0089	1189	2 PWC JT15D-5A	7212	Executive		
☐ N	Ayres LM200 Loadmaster					1 AN CTP800-4T TwinPac	8618	Freighter		oo-delivery 1100
☐ N	Ayres LM200 Loadmaster					1 AN CTP800-4T TwinPac	8618	Freighter		oo-delivery 1100
☐ N	Ayres LM200 Loadmaster					1 AN CTP800-4T TwinPac	8618	Freighter		oo-delivery 1200
☐ N	Ayres LM200 Loadmaster					1 AN CTP800-4T TwinPac	8618	Freighter		oo-delivery 1200
☐ N	Ayres LM200 Loadmaster					1 AN CTP800-4T TwinPac	8618	Freighter		oo-delivery 0001
☐ N	Ayres LM200 Loadmaster					1 AN CTP800-4T TwinPac	8618	Freighter		oo-delivery 0001
☐ N	Ayres LM200 Loadmaster					1 AN CTP800-4T TwinPac	8618	Freighter		oo-delivery 0001
☐ N	Ayres LM200 Loadmaster					1 AN CTP800-4T TwinPac	8618	Freighter		oo-delivery 0001
☐ N	Ayres LM200 Loadmaster					1 AN CTP800-4T TwinPac	8618	Freighter		oo-delivery 0001
☐ N	Ayres LM200 Loadmaster					1 AN CTP800-4T TwinPac	8618	Freighter		oo-delivery 0001
☐ N	Ayres LM200 Loadmaster					1 AN CTP800-4T TwinPac	8618	Freighter		oo-delivery 0001
☐ N	Ayres LM200 Loadmaster					1 AN CTP800-4T TwinPac	8618	Freighter		oo-delivery 0001
☐ N	Ayres LM200 Loadmaster					1 AN CTP800-4T TwinPac	8618	Freighter		oo-delivery 0001
☐ N	Ayres LM200 Loadmaster					1 AN CTP800-4T TwinPac	8618	Freighter		oo-delivery 0001
☐ N	Ayres LM200 Loadmaster					1 AN CTP800-4T TwinPac	8618	Freighter		oo-delivery 0001
☐ N	Ayres LM200 Loadmaster					1 AN CTP800-4T TwinPac	8618	Freighter		oo-delivery 0001
☐ N	Ayres LM200 Loadmaster					1 AN CTP800-4T TwinPac	8618	Freighter		oo-delivery 0001
☐ N	Ayres LM200 Loadmaster					1 AN CTP800-4T TwinPac	8618	Freighter		oo-delivery 0001
☐ N	Ayres LM200 Loadmaster					1 AN CTP800-4T TwinPac	8618	Freighter		oo-delivery 0001
☐ N	Ayres LM200 Loadmaster					1 AN CTP800-4T TwinPac	8618	Freighter		oo-delivery 0001
☐ N	Ayres LM200 Loadmaster					1 AN CTP800-4T TwinPac	8618	Freighter		oo-delivery 0001
☐ N	Ayres LM200 Loadmaster					1 AN CTP800-4T TwinPac	8618	Freighter		oo-delivery 0001
☐ N	Ayres LM200 Loadmaster					1 AN CTP800-4T TwinPac	8618	Freighter		oo-delivery 0001
☐ N	Ayres LM200 Loadmaster					1 AN CTP800-4T TwinPac	8618	Freighter		oo-delivery 0001
☐ N	Ayres LM200 Loadmaster					1 AN CTP800-4T TwinPac	8618	Freighter		oo-delivery 0001
☐ N	Ayres LM200 Loadmaster					1 AN CTP800-4T TwinPac	8618	Freighter		oo-delivery 0002
☐ N	Ayres LM200 Loadmaster					1 AN CTP800-4T TwinPac	8618	Freighter		oo-delivery 0002
☐ N	Ayres LM200 Loadmaster					1 AN CTP800-4T TwinPac	8618	Freighter		oo-delivery 0002
☐ N	Ayres LM200 Loadmaster					1 AN CTP800-4T TwinPac	8618	Freighter		oo-delivery 0002
☐ N	Ayres LM200 Loadmaster					1 AN CTP800-4T TwinPac	8618	Freighter		oo-delivery 0002
☐ N	Ayres LM200 Loadmaster					1 AN CTP800-4T TwinPac	8618	Freighter		oo-delivery 0002
☐ N	Ayres LM200 Loadmaster					1 AN CTP800-4T TwinPac	8618	Freighter		oo-delivery 0002
☐ N	Ayres LM200 Loadmaster					1 AN CTP800-4T TwinPac	8618	Freighter		oo-delivery 0002
☐ N	Ayres LM200 Loadmaster					1 AN CTP800-4T TwinPac	8618	Freighter		oo-delivery 0002
☐ N	Ayres LM200 Loadmaster					1 AN CTP800-4T TwinPac	8618	Freighter		oo-delivery 0002
☐ N	Ayres LM200 Loadmaster					1 AN CTP800-4T TwinPac	8618	Freighter		oo-delivery 0002
☐ N	Ayres LM200 Loadmaster					1 AN CTP800-4T TwinPac	8618	Freighter		oo-delivery 0002
☐ N	Ayres LM200 Loadmaster					1 AN CTP800-4T TwinPac	8618	Freighter		oo-delivery 0002
☐ N	Ayres LM200 Loadmaster					1 AN CTP800-4T TwinPac	8618	Freighter		oo-delivery 0002
☐ N153CC	Shorts 360-300 (SD3-60)	SH3753	N753CN	0089	1298	2 PWC PT6A-67R	12292	Freighter		lsf Lynrise Air Lease/sub-lst/opb CFS
☐ N262GA	Shorts 360-300 (SD3-60)	SH3749	N828BE	0089	1298	2 PWC PT6A-67R	12292	Freighter		lsf Lynrise Air Lease/sub-lst/opb CFS
☐ N748CC	Shorts 360-300 (SD3-60)	SH3748	N748SA	0088	1298	2 PWC PT6A-67R	12292	Freighter		lsf Lynrise Air Lease/sub-lst/opb CFS
☐ N2FE	Canadair CL-601-3A (CL-600-2B16) Challen.	5095	N95FE	0091	0791	2 GE CF34-3A	19550	Executive	FK-CL	
☐ N3FE	Canadair CL-601-3A (CL-600-2B16) Challen.	5054	N619FE	0089	1189	2 GE CF34-3A	19550	Executive	FK-CJ	
☐ N701FE	Fokker F27 Friendship 600 (F27 Mk600)	10419	OO-FEF	0069	0690	2 RR Dart 532-7R	20412	Freighter		lst/opb Empire Airlines
☐ N702FE	Fokker F27 Friendship 600 (F27 Mk600)	10350	OO-FEG	0067	0790	2 RR Dart 532-7R	20412	Freighter		lst/opb Empire Airlines
☐ N703FE	Fokker F27 Friendship 600 (F27 Mk600)	10420	D-AFEH	0069	0790	2 RR Dart 532-7R	20412	Freighter		lst/opb Empire Airlines
☐ N729FE	Fokker F27 Friendship 600 (F27 Mk600)	10385	EI-FEA	0068	0989	2 RR Dart 532-7R	20412	Freighter		lst/opb Empire Airlines
☐ N730FE	Fokker F27 Friendship 600 (F27 Mk600)	10386	I-FEAB	0068	1089	2 RR Dart 532-7R	20412	Freighter		lst/opb Empire Airlines
☐ N740FE	Fokker F27 Friendship 600 (F27 Mk600)	10329	HB-ISJ	0067	1189	2 RR Dart 532-7R	20412	Freighter		lst/opb Empire Airlines
☐ N741FE	Fokker F27 Friendship 600 (F27 Mk600)	10387	G-FEAD	0068	1289	2 RR Dart 532-7R	20412	Freighter		lst/opb Empire Airlines
☐ N742FE	Fokker F27 Friendship 600 (F27 Mk600)	10349	G-FEAE	0068	0190	2 RR Dart 532-7R	20412	Freighter		lst/opb Mountain Air Cargo
☐ N705FE	Fokker F27 Friendship 500 (F27 Mk500)	10367	G-FEDX	0068	1287	2 RR Dart 532-7R	20412	Freighter		lst/opb Mountain Air Cargo
☐ N706FE	Fokker F27 Friendship 500 (F27 Mk500)	10384	G-OFEC	0069	1287	2 RR Dart 532-7R	20412	Freighter		lst/opb Mountain Air Cargo
☐ N707FE	Fokker F27 Friendship 500 (F27 Mk500)	10371	G-FEBZ	0068	0388	2 RR Dart 532-7R	20412	Freighter		lst/opb Mountain Air Cargo
☐ N708FE	Fokker F27 Friendship 500 (F27 Mk500)	10372	G-BOMV	0068	0488	2 RR Dart 532-7R	20412	Freighter		lst/opb Mountain Air Cargo
☐ N709FE	Fokker F27 Friendship 500 (F27 Mk500)	10375	F-BPNE	0068	0488	2 RR Dart 532-7R	20412	Freighter		lst/opb Mountain Air Cargo
☐ N710FE	Fokker F27 Friendship 500 (F27 Mk500)	10380	F-BPNG	0068	0389	2 RR Dart 532-7R	20412	Freighter		lst/opb Empire Airlines
☐ N711FE	Fokker F27 Friendship 500 (F27 Mk500)	10383	F-BPNI	0069	0389	2 RR Dart 532-7R	20412	Freighter		lst/opb Empire Airlines

registration	type of aircraft	cn/fn	ex/ex*	mfd	del	powered by	mtow kg	configuration	selcal	name/fln/specialitites/remarks
☐ N712FE	Fokker F27 Friendship 500RF (F27 Mk500RF)	10613	9M-MCK	0081	1189	2 RR Dart 532-7R	20412	Freighter		lst/opb Mountain Air Cargo
☐ N713FE	Fokker F27 Friendship 500RF (F27 Mk500RF)	10615	9M-MCL	0081	1189	2 RR Dart 532-7R	20412	Freighter		lst/opb Mountain Air Cargo
☐ N714FE	Fokker F27 Friendship 500 (F27 Mk500)	10461	9M-MCD	0071	1289	2 RR Dart 532-7R	20412	Freighter		lst/opb Mountain Air Cargo
☐ N715FE	Fokker F27 Friendship 500 (F27 Mk500)	10468	9M-MCG	0071	1289	2 RR Dart 532-7R	20412	Freighter		lst/opb Mountain Air Cargo
☐ N716FE	Fokker F27 Friendship 500 (F27 Mk500)	10471	9M-MCI	0071	0690	2 RR Dart 532-7R	20412	Freighter		lst/opb Mountain Air Cargo
☐ N717FE	Fokker F27 Friendship 500 (F27 Mk500)	10455	9M-MCA	0071	0390	2 RR Dart 532-7R	20412	Freighter		lst/opb Mountain Air Cargo
☐ N718FE	Fokker F27 Friendship 500 (F27 Mk500)	10470	9M-MCH	0071	0390	2 RR Dart 532-7R	20412	Freighter		lst/opb Mountain Air Cargo
☐ N719FE	Fokker F27 Friendship 500 (F27 Mk500)	10467	9M-MCF	0071	0690	2 RR Dart 532-7R	20412	Freighter		lst/opb Mountain Air Cargo
☐ N720FE	Fokker F27 Friendship 500 (F27 Mk500)	10464	9M-MCE	0071	0690	2 RR Dart 532-7R	20412	Freighter		lst/opb Empire Airlines
☐ N721FE	Fokker F27 Friendship 500 (F27 Mk500)	10460	9M-MCC	0071	0290	2 RR Dart 532-7R	20412	Freighter		lst/opb Mountain Air Cargo
☐ N722FE	Fokker F27 Friendship 500 (F27 Mk500)	10472	9M-MCJ	0071	0690	2 RR Dart 532-7R	20412	Freighter		lst/opb Mountain Air Cargo
☐ N723FE	Fokker F27 Friendship 500 (F27 Mk500)	10682	OO-FEI	0085	1091	2 RR Dart 552-7R	20412	Freighter		lst/opb Mountain Air Cargo
☐ N724FE	Fokker F27 Friendship 500 (F27 Mk500)	10677	OO-FEK	0084	1091	2 RR Dart 552-7R	20412	Freighter		lst/opb Mountain Air Cargo
☐ N725FE	Fokker F27 Friendship 500 (F27 Mk500)	10658	N514AW	0083	0592	2 RR Dart 552-7R	20412	Freighter		lst/opb Mountain Air Cargo
☐ N726FE	Fokker F27 Friendship 500 (F27 Mk500)	10683	N508AW	0085	1291	2 RR Dart 552-7R	20412	Freighter		lst/opb Mountain Air Cargo
☐ N727FE	Fokker F27 Friendship 500 (F27 Mk500)	10661	N502AW	0083	1291	2 RR Dart 552-7R	20412	Freighter		lst/opb Mountain Air Cargo
☐ N728FE	Fokker F27 Friendship 500 (F27 Mk500)	10657	OO-FEL	0083	1291	2 RR Dart 552-7R	20412	Freighter		lst/opb Mountain Air Cargo
☐ N101FE	Boeing 727-22C	19197 / 410	N7422U	0567	0178	3 PW JT8D-7B (HK3/FDX)	76884	Freighter	EJ-AH	Nicole / lsf GECA
☐ N102FE	Boeing 727-22C	19193 / 392	N7418U	0467	0378	3 PW JT8D-7B (HK3/FDX)	76884	Freighter	EJ-AK	Laura Lane
☐ N103FE	Boeing 727-22C	19199 / 414	N7424U	1267	0478	3 PW JT8D-7B (HK3/FDX)	76884	Freighter	EJ-AL	Jennifer
☐ N104FE	Boeing 727-22C	19198 / 413	N7423U	0667	0478	3 PW JT8D-7B (HK3/FDX)	76884	Freighter	EJ-AM	Catherine Anne
☐ N105FE	Boeing 727-22C	19194 / 394	N7419U	0467	0678	3 PW JT8D-7B (HK3/FDX)	76884	Freighter	EJ-BC	Danielle Marie
☐ N106FE	Boeing 727-22C	19201 / 421	N7426U	0667	0778	3 PW JT8D-7B (HK3/FDX)	76884	Freighter	EJ-BD	Melissa / lsf RFC N106FE/8 Inc.
☐ N107FE	Boeing 727-22C	19202 / 424	N7427U	0667	0878	3 PW JT8D-7B (HK3/FDX)	76884	Freighter	EJ-BF	Kira
☐ N112FE	Boeing 727-22C	19890 / 630	N7433U	0868	0879	3 PW JT8D-7B (HK3/FDX)	76884	Freighter	AH-CF	Alicia
☐ N113FE	Boeing 727-22C	19894 / 647	N7437U	1068	0979	3 PW JT8D-7B (HK3/FDX)	76884	Freighter	AH-CL	Jarrod
☐ N114FE	Boeing 727-24C	19527 / 460	CC-CAN	0967	0779	3 PW JT8D-7B (HK3/FDX)	76884	Freighter	CF-AH	Rollin III
☐ N116FE	Boeing 727-25C	19298 / 335	N8151G	1266	0582	3 PW JT8D-7B (HK3/FDX)	76884	Freighter	FK-DL	Vanessa / lsf RFC N116FE/15 Inc.
☐ N117FE	Boeing 727-25C	19299 / 344	N8152G	1266	0482	3 PW JT8D-7B (HK3/FDX)	76884	Freighter	BK-AH	Cassy
☐ N118FE	Boeing 727-25C	19300 / 346	N8153G	1266	0581	3 PW JT8D-7B (HK3/FDX)	76884	Freighter	FK-DM	Taryn Michelle
☐ N119FE	Boeing 727-25C	19301 / 352	N8154G	0167	0781	3 PW JT8D-7	76884	Freighter	FK-GH	Stefani Lynn
☐ N120FE	Boeing 727-25C	19356 / 356	N8156G	0267	1081	3 PW JT8D-7B (HK3/FDX)	76884	Freighter	FK-EG	April Dawn / lsf RFC N120FE/9 Inc.
☐ N124FE	Boeing 727-25C	19360 / 371	N8160G	0367	1181	3 PW JT8D-7B (HK3/FDX)	76884	Freighter	HK-FG	Marcella
☐ N127FE	Boeing 727-25C	19719 / 478	N8163G	1067	1182	3 PW JT8D-7B (HK3/FDX)	76884	Freighter	HM-DG	Sidney Lewis
☐ N128FE	Boeing 727-25C	19720 / 482	N8164G	1167	0982	3 PW JT8D-7B (HK3/FDX)	76884	Freighter	HK-FJ	Stuart Shawn
☐ N133FE	Boeing 727-25C	19851 / 510	N8168G	0168	0580	3 PW JT8D-7	76884	Freighter		Kimberley Ann
☐ N134FE	Boeing 727-25C	19852 / 517	N8169G	0168	0780	3 PW JT8D-7	76884	Freighter		Theresa LeAnn
☐ N135FE	Boeing 727-25C	19853 / 522	N8170G	0268	0580	3 PW JT8D-7B (HK3/FDX)	76884	Freighter		Annie
☐ N136FE	Boeing 727-25C	19855 / 632	N8172G	0168	0982	3 PW JT8D-7B (HK3/FDX)	76884	Freighter		Christopher
☐ N143FE	Boeing 727-21C	19136 / 314	N722EV	0866	0287	3 PW JT8D-7B (HK3/FDX)	76884	Freighter		Patrick / lsf RFC Aircraft N143FE Inc.
☐ N144FE	Boeing 727-21C	19137 / 316	N723EV	0866	0287	3 PW JT8D-7B (HK3/FDX)	76884	Freighter		Spencer
☐ N145FE	Boeing 727-27C	19109 / 271	N724EV	0466	0287	3 PW JT8D-7 (HK3/FDX)	76884	Freighter		Ashley
☐ N146FE	Boeing 727-27C	19110 / 283	N730EV	0666	1087	3 PW JT8D-7 (HK3/FDX)	76884	Freighter		Heather
☐ N147FE	Boeing 727-22 (F)	19080 / 270	N7067U	0566	0787	3 PW JT8D-7B (HK3/FDX)	72802	Freighter		Landon / cvtd -22
☐ N148FE	Boeing 727-22 (F)	19086 / 353	N7073U	0167	0287	3 PW JT8D-7B	72802	Freighter		Rosemary / cvtd -22
☐ N149FE	Boeing 727-22 (F)	19087 / 359	N7074U	0167	0787	3 PW JT8D-7B (HK3/FDX)	72802	Freighter	GL-EH	Holly / cvtd -22
☐ N150FE	Boeing 727-22 (F)	19141 / 370	N7077U	0267	0887	3 PW JT8D-7B	72802	Freighter		Amber / cvtd -22
☐ N151FE	Boeing 727-22 (F)	19147 / 472	N7083U	0267	0887	3 PW JT8D-7B	72802	Freighter		Rob / cvtd -22
☐ N152FE	Boeing 727-25 (F)	18285 / 172	N8134N	0765	0488	3 PW JT8D-7B (HK3/FDX)	72802	Freighter	FM-DG	Michelle / cvtd -25
☐ N154FE	Boeing 727-25 (F)	18287 / 190	N8136N	0865	0888	3 PW JT8D-7B (HK3/FDX)	72802	Freighter		Kenny / cvtd -25
☐ N155FE	Boeing 727-25 (F)	18288 / 192	N8137N	0965	0988	3 PW JT8D-7B (HK3/FDX)	72802	Freighter	FM-DK	Shannon / cvtd -25
☐ N156FE	Boeing 727-25 (F)	18289 / 194	N8138N	0965	1088	3 PW JT8D-7B (HK3/FDX)	72802	Freighter	FM-DL	Darryl / cvtd -25
☐ N166FE	Boeing 727-22 (F)	18863 / 227	N7056U	0066	0689	3 PW JT8D-7B (HK3/FDX)	72575	Freighter	AK-CH	Katy / cvtd -22
☐ N167FE	Boeing 727-22 (F)	18864 / 231	N7057U	0166	0189	3 PW JT8D-7B (HK3/FDX)	72802	Freighter	AK-CJ	George / cvtd -22
☐ N168FE	Boeing 727-22 (F)	18865 / 232	N7058U	0166	1288	3 PW JT8D-7B (HK3/FDX)	72802	Freighter	AK-CM	William / cvtd -22
☐ N169FE	Boeing 727-22 (F)	18866 / 241	N7059U	0266	0688	3 PW JT8D-7B (HK3/FDX)	72802	Freighter	AK-DG	Darius / cvtd -22
☐ N181FE	Boeing 727-22 (F)	18868 / 248	N7061U	0266	1188	3 PW JT8D-7B (HK3/FDX)	72802	Freighter	AK-DM	Jeanine / cvtd -22
☐ N184FE	Boeing 727-22 (F)	18870 / 258	N7063U	0366	0789	3 PW JT8D-7B (HK3/FDX)	72575	Freighter	AK-FL	Jimasha / cvtd -22
☐ N185FE	Boeing 727-22 (F)	18871 / 259	N7064U	0366	0689	3 PW JT8D-7B (HK3/FDX)	72575	Freighter	AK-FM	Casey / cvtd -22
☐ N186FE	Boeing 727-22 (F)	18872 / 261	N7065U	0366	0889	3 PW JT8D-7B (HK3/FDX)	72575	Freighter	AK-GM	Clayton / cvtd -22
☐ N187FE	Boeing 727-22 (F)	19079 / 268	N7066U	0466	0988	3 PW JT8D-7B (HK3/FDX)	72802	Freighter	AG-EK	Aaron / cvtd -22
☐ N188FE	Boeing 727-22 (F)	19081 / 275	N7068U	0566	0989	3 PW JT8D-7B (HK3/FDX)	72802	Freighter	AJ-CF	Austin / cvtd -22
☐ N189FE	Boeing 727-22 (F)	19082 / 279	N7069U	0566	1089	3 PW JT8D-7B (HK3/FDX)	73802	Freighter	AJ-FL	Micah / cvtd -22
☐ N190FE	Boeing 727-22 (F)	19083 / 281	N7070U	0666	1189	3 PW JT8D-7B (HK3/FDX)	72802	Freighter	AK-EM	Curtis / cvtd -22
☐ N191FE	Boeing 727-22 (F)	19084 / 337	N7071U	0966	0790	3 PW JT8D-7B (HK3/FDX)	72802	Freighter	AL-BD	Thomas / cvtd -22
☐ N193FE	Boeing 727-22 (F)	19142 / 440	N7078U	0667	1090	3 PW JT8D-7B (HK3/FDX)	72802	Freighter	BM-HJ	Anna / cvtd -22
☐ N194FE	Boeing 727-22 (F)	19143 / 446	N7079U	0767	1090	3 PW JT8D-7B (HK3/FDX)	72802	Freighter		Lindsay / cvtd -22
☐ N195FE	Boeing 727-22 (F)	19144 / 450	N7080U	0767	0390	3 PW JT8D-7B (HK3/FDX)	72802	Freighter	HK-BM	Kittie / cvtd -22
☐ N196FE	Boeing 727-22 (F)	19145 / 451	N7081U	0767	1190	3 PW JT8D-7B	72802	Freighter		Jane / cvtd -22
☐ N198FE	Boeing 727-22 (F)	19154 / 512	N7090U	1167	1088	3 PW JT8D-7B	72802	Freighter	AF-GL	Faye / cvtd -22
☐ N199FE	Boeing 727-173C	19509 / 459	TZ-ADR	0967	0788	3 PW JT8D-7B (HK3/FDX)	72802	Freighter		Ms. Mali
☐ N502FE	Boeing 727-25 (F)	18271 / 82	N8120N	1064	0289	3 PW JT8D-7B	72802	Freighter	FL-JK	Ricky / cvtd -25
☐ N503FE	Boeing 727-25 (F)	18273 / 91	N8122N	1164	0589	3 PW JT8D-7B (HK3/FDX)	72802	Freighter	FM-BC	JoJo / cvtd -25
☐ N504FE	Boeing 727-25 (F)	18274 / 96	N8123N	1264	0689	3 PW JT8D-7B (HK3/FDX)	72802	Freighter	FM-BD	cvtd -25
☐ N505FE	Boeing 727-25 (F)	18276 / 103	N8125N	0165	0988	3 PW JT8D-7B (HK3/FDX)	72802	Freighter		Sirvontes / cvtd -25
☐ N506FE	Boeing 727-25 (F)	18277 / 107	N8126N	0165	1188	3 PW JT8D-7B (HK3/FDX)	72802	Freighter		Deidre Shea / cvtd -25
☐ N507FE	Boeing 727-25 (F)	18278 / 113	N8127N	0265	0489	3 PW JT8D-7B (HK3/FDX)	72802	Freighter	FM-BJ	Adrienne / cvtd -25
☐ N508FE	Boeing 727-25 (F)	18279 / 121	N8128N	0365	1188	3 PW JT8D-7B (HK3/FDX)	72802	Freighter	FM-BK	Annalise / cvtd -25
☐ N509FE	Boeing 727-25 (F)	18280 / 129	N8129N	0465	0289	3 PW JT8D-7B (HK3/FDX)	72802	Freighter	FM-BL	Autumn / cvtd -25
☐ N510FE	Boeing 727-25 (F)	18282 / 149	N8131N	0665	1288	3 PW JT8D-7B (HK3/FDX)	72802	Freighter	FM-AK	Carissa / cvtd -25
☐ N511FE	Boeing 727-25 (F)	18283 / 155	N8132N	0765	0189	3 PW JT8D-7B (HK3/FDX)	72802	Freighter	FM-CL	Arjun / cvtd -25
☐ C-FBWX	Boeing 727-25 (F)	18286 / 182	N153FE	0865	0688	3 PW JT8D-7B (HK3/FDX)	72802	Freighter	FM-DH	Chase / lst/opb MEI / cvtd -25
☐ C-FBWY	Boeing 727-22 (F)	19085 / 349	N192FE	1066	1189	3 PW JT8D-7B	72802	Freighter	AJ-FM	Kellye / lst/opb MEI / cvtd -22
☐ C-GBWH	Boeing 727-116C	19814 / 600	N115FE	0768	0879	3 PW JT8D-7B (HK3/FDX)	76884	Freighter		Tracy / lst/opb MEI
☐ C-GBWS	Boeing 727-22 (F)	18867 / 247	N180FE	0266	0688	3 PW JT8D-7B (HK3/FDX)	72802	Freighter	AK-DH	Alayna / lst/opb MEI / cvtd -22
☐ N201FE	Boeing 727-2S2F (A/RE) (Super 27)	22924 / 1818		0683	0683	3 PW JT8D-217C/17A(BFG)	92125	Freighter	BD-HJ	Bridgette Patrice / cvtd -2S2F
☐ N203FE	Boeing 727-2S2F (A)	22925 / 1819		0883	0883	3 PW JT8D-17A	92125	Freighter	BD-HK	Jonathan Richard
☐ N204FE	Boeing 727-2S2F (A)	22926 / 1820		0883	0883	3 PW JT8D-17A	92125	Freighter	BD-HM	Rebecca Rose
☐ N205FE	Boeing 727-2S2F (A/RE) (Super 27)	22927 / 1821		0983	0983	3 PW JT8D-217C/17A(BFG)	92125	Freighter	BD-JK	Robert Christopher / cvtd -2S2F
☐ N206FE	Boeing 727-2S2F (A/RE) (Super 27)	22928 / 1822		0983	0983	3 PW JT8D-217C/17A(BFG)	92125	Freighter	BD-KL	Joshua Gene / cvtd -2S2F
☐ N207FE	Boeing 727-2S2F (A/RE) (Super 27)	22929 / 1823		1083	1083	3 PW JT8D-217C/17A(BFG)	92125	Freighter	BD-KM	Matthew David / cvtd -2S2F
☐ N208FE	Boeing 727-2S2F (A/RE) (Super 27)	22930 / 1824		1183	1183	3 PW JT8D-217C/17A(BFG)	92125	Freighter	BE-AH	Audrey / cvtd -2S2F
☐ N209FE	Boeing 727-2S2F (A/RE) (Super 27)	22931 / 1825		0184	0184	3 PW JT8D-217C/17A(BFG)	92125	Freighter	BE-AJ	Kasey Sue-Ellen / cvtd -2S2F
☐ N210FE	Boeing 727-2S2F (A/RE) (Super 27)	22932 / 1826		0184	0184	3 PW JT8D-217C/17A(BFG)	92125	Freighter	DE-GH	Missy / cvtd -2S2F
☐ N211FE	Boeing 727-2S2F (A)	22933 / 1827		0284	0284	3 PW JT8D-17A	92125	Freighter	DE-HM	Adam Bradley
☐ N212FE	Boeing 727-2S2F (A/RE) (Super 27)	22934 / 1828		0484	0484	3 PW JT8D-217C/17A(BFG)	92125	Freighter	DE-LM	Jeremy David / cvtd -2S2F
☐ N213FE	Boeing 727-2S2F (A)	22935 / 1829		0584	0584	3 PW JT8D-17A	92125	Freighter	DF-AH	Christine
☐ N215FE	Boeing 727-2S2F (A/RE) (Super 27)	22936 / 1830		0684	0684	3 PW JT8D-217C/17A(BFG)	92125	Freighter	EK-BC	Billy / cvtd -2S2F
☐ N216FE	Boeing 727-2S2F (A/RE) (Super 27)	22937 / 1831		0884	0884	3 PW JT8D-217C/17A(BFG)	92125	Freighter	EK-FJ	Wade / cvtd -2S2F
☐ N217FE	Boeing 727-2S2F (A/RE) (Super 27)	22938 / 1832		0984	0984	3 PW JT8D-217C/17A(BFG)	92125	Freighter	EK-FH	Sonja / cvtd -2S2F
☐ N218FE	Boeing 727-233 (F) (A)	21101 / 1150	C-GAAM	0875	0485	3 PW JT8D-15	88360	Freighter	BG-AM	Christin Leigh / cvtd -233
☐ N219FE	Boeing 727-233 (F) (A)	21102 / 1152	C-GAAN	0975	0485	3 PW JT8D-15	88360	Freighter	BG-EF	Jakob / cvtd -233
☐ N220FE	Boeing 727-233 (F) (A)	20934 / 1074	C-GAAC	1074	0885	3 PW JT8D-15	88360	Freighter	CM-FL	Emily Rose / cvtd -233
☐ N221FE	Boeing 727-233 (F) (A)	20932 / 1069	C-GAAA	0974	1086	3 PW JT8D-15	88360	Freighter	HK-CD	Megan Nicole / cvtd -233
☐ N222FE	Boeing 727-233 (F) (A)	20933 / 1071	C-GAAB	0974	1286	3 PW JT8D-15	88360	Freighter	HK-CE	Michael / cvtd -233
☐ N223FE	Boeing 727-233 (F) (A)	20935 / 1076	C-GAAD	1074	0187	3 PW JT8D-15	88360	Freighter	HK-CG	Dustin / cvtd -233
☐ N233FE	Boeing 727-247 (F) (A)	21327 / 1249	N2822W	0077	0196	3 PW JT8D-15 (HK3/FDX)	86409	Freighter		Monika / cvtd -247
☐ N234FE	Boeing 727-247 (F) (A)	21328 / 1251	N2823W	0077	0496	3 PW JT8D-15 (HK3/FDX)	86409	Freighter		cvtd -247
☐ N235FE	Boeing 727-247 (F) (A)	21329 / 1254	N2824W	0077	0496	3 PW JT8D-15 (HK3/FDX)	86409	Freighter		Stephanie / cvtd -247
☐ N236FE	Boeing 727-247 (F) (A)	21330 / 1260	N2825W	0077	0196	3 PW JT8D-15 (HK3/FDX)	86409	Freighter		Stephanie / cvtd -247
☐ N237FE	Boeing 727-247 (F) (A)	21331 / 1266	N2826W	0077	0496	3 PW JT8D-15 (HK3/FDX)	86409	Freighter		cvtd -247
☐ N240FE	Boeing 727-277 (F) (A)	20978 / 1083	VH-RMY	1174	0189	3 PW JT8D-15 (HK3/FDX)	86409	Freighter		Baron / cvtd -277
☐ N241FE	Boeing 727-277 (F) (A)	20979 / 1086	VH-RMZ	0475	0289	3 PW JT8D-15	86409	Freighter		Jill / cvtd -277
☐ N242FE	Boeing 727-277 (F) (A)	21178 / 1237	VH-RMK	1276	1188	3 PW JT8D-15	86409	Freighter		Brittney / cvtd -277
☐ N243FE	Boeing 727-277 (F) (A)	21480 / 1352	VH-RML	0678	0389	3 PW JT8D-15 (HK3/FDX)	86409	Freighter	FM-BC	Braden / cvtd -277
☐ N244FE	Boeing 727-277 (F) (A)	21647 / 1436	VH-RMM	0179	0589	3 PW JT8D-15 (HK3/FDX)	86409	Freighter		Crystal / cvtd -277
☐ N245FE	Boeing 727-277 (F) (A)	22016 / 1566	VH-RMO	0579	0889	3 PW JT8D-15 (HK3/FDX)	86409	Freighter		Kelsey / cvtd -277
☐ N246FE	Boeing 727-277 (F) (A)	22068 / 1660	VH-RMP	0980	1288	3 PW JT8D-15 (HK3/FDX)	86409	Freighter		Daisy / cvtd -277
☐ N254FE	Boeing 727-233 (F) (A)	20936 / 1078	C-GAAE	0074	1092	3 PW JT8D-15	88360	Freighter	HK-CJ	Courtney / cvtd -233
☐ N257FE	Boeing 727-233 (F) (A)	20939 / 1112	C-GAAH	0075	0191	3 PW JT8D-15	88360	Freighter	HK-DE	Kurt / cvtd -233

N258FE	Boeing 727-233 (F) (A)	20940 / 1120	C-GAAI	0075	0791	3 PW JT8D-15 (HK3/FDX)	88360	Freighter	HK-DF	Ivie / cvtd -233
N262FE	Boeing 727-233 (F) (A)	21624 / 1468	C-GAAO	0079	1192	3 PW JT8D-15 (HK3/FDX)	88360	Freighter	FG-CD	Betsy / cvtd -233
N263FE	Boeing 727-233 (F) (A)	21625 / 1470	C-GAAP	0079	1292	3 PW JT8D-15 (HK3/FDX)	88360	Freighter	FG-CE	Marc / cvtd -233
N264FE	Boeing 727-233 (F) (A)	21626 / 1472	C-GAAQ	0079	0992	3 PW JT8D-15 (HK3/FDX)	88360	Freighter	FG-CH	Chastity / cvtd -233
N265FE	Boeing 727-233 (F) (A)	21671 / 1523	C-GAAR	0079	0293	3 PW JT8D-15 (HK3/FDX)	88360	Freighter	FG-CJ	Paul / cvtd -233
N266FE	Boeing 727-233 (F) (A)	21672 / 1538	C-GAAS	0079	0593	3 PW JT8D-15 (HK3/FDX)	88360	Freighter	FG-CK	Steven / cvtd -233
N267FE	Boeing 727-233 (F) (A)	21673 / 1541	C-GAAT	0079	0393	3 PW JT8D-15 (HK3/FDX)	88360	Freighter	FG-CL	cvtd -233
N268FE	Boeing 727-233 (F) (A)	21674 / 1543	C-GAAU	0079	1292	3 PW JT8D-15 (HK3/FDX)	88360	Freighter	FG-CM	cvtd -233
N269FE	Boeing 727-233 (F) (A)	21675 / 1555	C-GAAV	0079	0793	3 PW JT8D-15 (HK3/FDX)	88360	Freighter	FG-DE	cvtd -233
N270FE	Boeing 727-233 (F) (A)	22035 / 1578	C-GAAW	0080	0693	3 PW JT8D-15 (HK3/FDX)	88360	Freighter	EH-AB	Harrison / cvtd -233
N271FE	Boeing 727-233 (F) (A)	22036 / 1596	C-GAAX	0080	0790	3 PW JT8D-15 (HK3/FDX)	88360	Freighter	EH-AC	cvtd -233
N272FE	Boeing 727-233 (F) (A)	22037 / 1600	C-GAAY	0080	0892	3 PW JT8D-15 (HK3/FDX)	88360	Freighter	EH-AD	Logan / cvtd -233
N273FE	Boeing 727-233 (F) (A)	22038 / 1612	C-GAAZ	0080	0890	3 PW JT8D-15 (HK3/FDX)	88360	Freighter	EH-AK	Samantha / cvtd -233
N274FE	Boeing 727-233 (F) (A)	22039 / 1614	C-GYNA	0080	1290	3 PW JT8D-15 (HK3/FDX)	88360	Freighter	EH-BD	Jessica / cvtd -233
N275FE	Boeing 727-233 (F) (A)	22040 / 1626	C-GYNB	0080	1090	3 PW JT8D-15 (HK3/FDX)	88360	Freighter	EH-BG	Skylar / cvtd -233
N276FE	Boeing 727-233 (F) (A)	22041 / 1628	C-GYNC	0080	0291	3 PW JT8D-17 (HK3/FDX)	89358	Freighter	EH-BJ	Devon / cvtd -233
N277FE	Boeing 727-233 (F) (A)	22042 / 1630	C-GYND	0080	0691	3 PW JT8D-17 (HK3/FDX)	89358	Freighter	EH-BK	Tineka / cvtd -233
N278FE	Boeing 727-233 (F) (A)	22345 / 1699	C-GYNE	0080	0592	3 PW JT8D-17 (HK3/FDX)	89358	Freighter	EH-BL	Jeffrey / cvtd -233
N279FE	Boeing 727-233 (F) (A)	22346 / 1704	C-GYNF	0081	1291	3 PW JT8D-17 (HK3/FDX)	89358	Freighter	EH-BM	Ryan / cvtd -233
N280FE	Boeing 727-233 (F) (A)	22347 / 1708	C-GYNG	0081	0891	3 PW JT8D-17 (HK3/FDX)	89358	Freighter	EH-CD	Quinesia / cvtd -233
N281FE	Boeing 727-233 (F) (A)	22348 / 1714	C-GYNH	0081	1091	3 PW JT8D-17 (HK3/FDX)	89358	Freighter	EH-CG	Lacey / cvtd -233
N282FE	Boeing 727-233 (F) (A)	22349 / 1722	C-GYNI	0081	0192	3 PW JT8D-17 (HK3/FDX)	89358	Freighter	EH-FJ	Dominique / cvtd -233
N283FE	Boeing 727-233 (F) (A)	22350 / 1745	C-GYNJ	0081	0392	3 PW JT8D-17 (HK3/FDX)	89358	Freighter	HK-DM	Randall / cvtd -233
N284FE	Boeing 727-233 (F) (A)	22621 / 1791	C-GYNK	0082	0792	3 PW JT8D-17 (HK3/FDX)	89358	Freighter	BG-CK	Victoria / cvtd -233
N285FE	Boeing 727-233 (F) (A)	22622 / 1792	C-GYNL	0082	0292	3 PW JT8D-17 (HK3/FDX)	89358	Freighter	BG-CL	Miranda / cvtd -233
N286FE	Boeing 727-233 (F) (A)	22623 / 1803	C-GYNM	0082	0892	3 PW JT8D-15	89358	Freighter	BG-CM	Charlsi / cvtd -233
N287FE	Boeing 727-2D4 (F) (A)	21849 / 1527	N361PA	0079	1093	3 PW JT8D-15 (HK3/FDX)	88360	Freighter	CE-FH	lsf BALG / cvtd -2D4
N288FE	Boeing 727-2D4 (F) (A)	21850 / 1536	N362PA	0079	1093	3 PW JT8D-15 (HK3/FDX)	88360	Freighter	CE-FK	cvtd -2D4
N461FE	Boeing 727-225 (F) (A)	22548 / 1734	N811EA	0081	0892	3 PW JT8D-15 (HK3/FDX)	86409	Freighter	GJ-AH	cvtd -225
N462FE	Boeing 727-225 (F) (A)	22550 / 1739	N813EA	0081	0792	3 PW JT8D-15 (HK3/FDX)	86409	Freighter	GJ-AL	cvtd -225
N463FE	Boeing 727-225 (F) (A)	22551 / 1744	N814EA	0081	0892	3 PW JT8D-15 (HK3/FDX)	86409	Freighter	GJ-AM	cvtd -225
N464FE	Boeing 727-225 (F) (A)	21288 / 1234	N8870Z	0076	0992	3 PW JT8D-15	86409	Freighter	GH-CE	cvtd -225
N465FE	Boeing 727-225 (F) (A)	21289 / 1235	N8871Z	0076	0992	3 PW JT8D-15	86409	Freighter	GH-CF	cvtd -225
N466FE	Boeing 727-225 (F) (A)	21292 / 1240	N8874Z	0076	1092	3 PW JT8D-15 (HK3/FDX)	86409	Freighter	CJ-AG	cvtd -225
N467FE	Boeing 727-225 (F) (A)	21449 / 1306	N8876Z	0077	0593	3 PW JT8D-15 (HK3/FDX)	86409	Freighter	FK-EM	cvtd -225
N468FE	Boeing 727-225 (F) (A)	21452 / 1312	N8879Z	0077	0693	3 PW JT8D-15 (HK3/FDX)	86409	Freighter	GJ-EL	cvtd -225
N469FE	Boeing 727-225 (F) (A)	21581 / 1437	N8884Z	0079	0593	3 PW JT8D-15 (HK3/FDX)	86409	Freighter	FM-JK	cvtd -225
N477FE	Boeing 727-227 (F) (A)	21394 / 1281	N453BN	0077	0490	3 PW JT8D-9A (HK3/FDX)	83824	Freighter		Walter / cvtd -227
N478FE	Boeing 727-227 (F) (A)	21395 / 1283	N454BN	0077	0490	3 PW JT8D-9A (HK3/FDX)	83824	Freighter		Nikki / cvtd -227
N479FE	Boeing 727-227 (F) (A)	21461 / 1337	N455BN	0078	0390	3 PW JT8D-17 (HK3/FDX)	86409	Freighter		Norah / cvtd -227
N480FE	Boeing 727-227 (F) (A)	21462 / 1342	N456BN	0078	0490	3 PW JT8D-9A (HK3/FDX)	83824	Freighter		Warren / cvtd -227
N481FE	Boeing 727-227 (F) (A)	21463 / 1353	N457BN	0078	0390	3 PW JT8D-17 (HK3/FDX)	86409	Freighter		Tiffany / cvtd -227
N482FE	Boeing 727-227 (F) (A)	21464 / 1355	N458BN	0078	0390	3 PW JT8D-17 (HK3/FDX)	86409	Freighter		Natalie / cvtd -227
N483FE	Boeing 727-227 (F) (A)	21465 / 1363	N459BN	0078	0590	3 PW JT8D-15 (HK3/FDX)	83824	Freighter		David / cvtd -227
N484FE	Boeing 727-227 (F) (A)	21466 / 1372	N460BN	0078	0590	3 PW JT8D-9A (HK3/FDX)	83824	Freighter		Hallie / cvtd -227
N485FE	Boeing 727-227 (F) (A)	21488 / 1388	N461BN	0078	0690	3 PW JT8D-9A (HK3/FDX)	83824	Freighter		Kirsten / cvtd -227
N486FE	Boeing 727-227 (F) (A)	21489 / 1390	N462BN	0078	0690	3 PW JT8D-9A (HK3/FDX)	83824	Freighter		Hunter / cvtd -227
N487FE	Boeing 727-227 (F) (A)	21490 / 1396	N463BN	0078	0790	3 PW JT8D-15 (HK3/FDX)	83824	Freighter		Britney / cvtd -227
N488FE	Boeing 727-227 (F) (A)	21491 / 1402	N464BN	0078	0890	3 PW JT8D-15 (HK3/FDX)	83824	Freighter		Olivia / cvtd -227
N489FE	Boeing 727-227 (F) (A)	21492 / 1440	N465BN	0079	0390	3 PW JT8D-15 (HK3/FDX)	86409	Freighter		Timothy / cvtd -227
N490FE	Boeing 727-227 (F) (A)	21493 / 1442	N466BN	0079	0390	3 PW JT8D-15 (HK3/FDX)	86409	Freighter		Chase / cvtd -227
N491FE	Boeing 727-227 (F) (A)	21529 / 1444	N467BN	0079	0890	3 PW JT8D-9A (HK3/FDX)	83824	Freighter		Tobias / cvtd -227
N492FE	Boeing 727-227 (F) (A)	21530 / 1446	N468BN	0079	0990	3 PW JT8D-15 (HK3/FDX)	83824	Freighter		cvtd -227
N493FE	Boeing 727-227 (F) (A)	21531 / 1450	N469BN	0079	1090	3 PW JT8D-15 (HK3/FDX)	83824	Freighter		Maxx / cvtd -227
N494FE	Boeing 727-227 (F) (A)	21532 / 1453	N470BN	0079	1090	3 PW JT8D-15 (HK3/FDX)	83824	Freighter		Ian / cvtd -227
N495FE	Boeing 727-227 (F) (A)	21669 / 1484	N471BN	0079	1190	3 PW JT8D-15 (HK3/FDX)	83824	Freighter		Leslie / cvtd -227
N496FE	Boeing 727-227 (F) (A)	21670 / 1486	N472BN	0079	0790	3 PW JT8D-15 (HK3/FDX)	83824	Freighter		Zachary / cvtd -227
N497FE	Boeing 727-232 (F) (A)	20866 / 1067	CS-TCH	0074	1289	3 PW JT8D-15	86409	Freighter	FG-AD	cvtd -232
N498FE	Boeing 727-232 (F) (A)	20867 / 1068	CS-TCI	0074	1289	3 PW JT8D-15 (HK3/FDX)	86409	Freighter	FG-AH	Aidan / cvtd -232
N499FE	Boeing 727-232 (F) (A)	21018 / 1095	CS-TCJ	0075	1289	3 PW JT8D-15	86409	Freighter	FG-BE	cvtd -232
N401FE	Airbus Industrie A310-203 (F)	191	D-AICA	0082	0195	2 GE CF6-80A3	142000	Freighter	FG-BR	Mickey / cvtd -203
N402FE	Airbus Industrie A310-203 (F)	201	D-AICB	0083	0395	2 GE CF6-80A3	142000	Freighter	FG-BS	Carlye / cvtd -203
N403FE	Airbus Industrie A310-203 (F)	230	D-AICC	0083	0495	2 GE CF6-80A3	142000	Freighter	FG-CR	Lindsey / cvtd -203
N404FE	Airbus Industrie A310-203 (F)	233	D-AICD	0083	0595	2 GE CF6-80A3	142000	Freighter	FG-CS	Sarah / cvtd -203
N405FE	Airbus Industrie A310-203 (F)	237	D-AICF	0083	0795	2 GE CF6-80A3	142000	Freighter	FG-DR	Mariah / cvtd -203
N407FE	Airbus Industrie A310-203 (F)	254	D-AICH	0083	0794	2 GE CF6-80A3	142000	Freighter	FG-DS	Stacey Denise / cvtd -203
N408FE	Airbus Industrie A310-203 (F)	257	D-AICK	0083	0795	2 GE CF6-80A3	142000	Freighter	FG-ER	Patrice / cvtd -203
N409FE	Airbus Industrie A310-203 (F)	273	D-AICL	0084	0994	2 GE CF6-80A3	142000	Freighter	FG-ES	Sheena / cvtd -203
N410FE	Airbus Industrie A310-203 (F)	356	D-AICM	0085	0695	2 GE CF6-80A3	142000	Freighter	FG-HR	Jerel / cvtd -203
N411FE	Airbus Industrie A310-203 (F)	359	D-AICN	0085	0195	2 GE CF6-80A3	142000	Freighter	FG-HS	cvtd -293
N412FE	Airbus Industrie A310-203 (F)	360	D-AICP	0085	1194	2 GE CF6-80A3	142000	Freighter	FG-JR	Corina / cvtd -203
N413FE	Airbus Industrie A310-203 (F)	397	D-AICR	0086	0894	2 GE CF6-80A3	142000	Freighter	FG-JS	Skip Mayer / cvtd -203
N414FE	Airbus Industrie A310-203 (F)	400	D-AICS	0086	1094	2 GE CF6-80A3	142000	Freighter	FG-KR	Tanner / cvtd -203
N415FE	Airbus Industrie A310-203C	349	PH-MCB	0084	1195	2 GE CF6-80A3	142000	Freighter	JS-PR	Jacquelyn
N416FE	Airbus Industrie A310-222 (F)	288	N801PA	0083	0695	2 PW JT9D-7R4E1	142000	Freighter		Patrick / cvtd -221
N417FE	Airbus Industrie A310-222 (F)	333	N802PA	0085	0495	2 PW JT9D-7R4E1	142000	Freighter		Kyle / cvtd -221
N418FE	Airbus Industrie A310-222 (F)	343	N803PA	0085	0795	2 PW JT9D-7R4E1	142000	Freighter	HR-EG	Rachel / cvtd -221
N419FE	Airbus Industrie A310-222 (F)	345	N804PA	0085	0595	2 PW JT9D-7R4E1	142000	Freighter	HR-EJ	Krystle / cvtd -221
N420FE	Airbus Industrie A310-222 (F)	339	N805PA	0084	0295	2 PW JT9D-7R4E1	142000	Freighter	HR-EK	Molly / cvtd -222
N421FE	Airbus Industrie A310-222 (F)	342	N806PA	0084	0495	2 PW JT9D-7R4E1	142000	Freighter	HR-EL	Caitlin / cvtd -222
N422FE	Airbus Industrie A310-222 (F)	346	N807PA	0084	0495	2 PW JT9D-7R4E1	142000	Freighter	HR-EM	Joseph / cvtd -222
N423FE	Airbus Industrie A310-203 (F)	281	PH-MCA	0084	1195	2 GE CF6-80A3	142000	Freighter	JS-QR	Trey / cvtd -203
N424FE	Airbus Industrie A310-203 (F)	241	PH-AGA	0083	0696	2 GE CF6-80A3	142000	Freighter		Kendall / cvtd -203
N425FE	Airbus Industrie A310-203 (F)	264	PH-AGD	0083	0796	2 GE CF6-80A3	142000	Freighter	LR-BG	Jerome / cvtd -203
N426FE	Airbus Industrie A310-203 (F)	245	PH-AGB	0083	0796	2 GE CF6-80A3	142000	Freighter	LR-BH	Shana / cvtd -203
N427FE	Airbus Industrie A310-203 (F)	362	PH-AGH	0085	1196	2 GE CF6-80A3	142000	Freighter	LR-BJ	Zackary / cvtd -203
N428FE	Airbus Industrie A310-203 (F)	248	PH-AGC	0083	0397	2 GE CF6-80A3	142000	Freighter	LR-BK	Kristina / cvtd -203
N429FE	Airbus Industrie A310-203 (F)	364	PH-AGI	0085	1296	2 GE CF6-80A3	142000	Freighter	LR-BM	Conner / cvtd -203
N430FE	Airbus Industrie A310-203 (F)	394	PH-AGK	0085	0996	2 GE CF6-80A3	142000	Freighter	LR-BP	cvtd -203
N442FE	Airbus Industrie A310-203 (F)	353	PH-AGG	0084	1096	2 GE CF6-80A3	142000	Freighter		Breanna / cvtd -203
N443FE	Airbus Industrie A310-203 (F)	283	PH-AGE	0083	1297	2 GE CF6-80A3	142000	Freighter		cvtd -203
N445FE	Airbus Industrie A310-203 (F)	297	PH-AGF	0083	0498	2 GE CF6-80A3	142000	Freighter		Catalina / cvtd -203
N446FE	Airbus Industrie A310-222 (F)	224	HB-IPA	0083	1295	2 PW JT9D-7R4E1	142000	Freighter		Kyler / lsf ILFC / cvtd -221
N447FE	Airbus Industrie A310-222 (F)	251	HB-IPB	0083	0396	2 PW JT9D-7R4E1	142000	Freighter		Shaunna / cvtd -221
N448FE	Airbus Industrie A310-222 (F)	260	HB-IPD	0083	0596	2 PW JT9D-7R4E1	142000	Freighter	LR-CG	Augustine / cvtd -221
N449FE	Airbus Industrie A310-222 (F)	217	F-GOCJ	0083	0197	2 PW JT9D-7R4E1	142000	Freighter		Treydn / cvtd -221
N450FE	Airbus Industrie A310-222 (F)	162	F-GPDJ	0082	0297	2 PW JT9D-7R4E1	142000	Freighter		Selna / cvtd -221
N451FE	Airbus Industrie A310-222 (F)	303	OO-SCA	0084	0498	2 PW JT9D-7R4E1	144000	Freighter		cvtd -222
N452FE	Airbus Industrie A310-222 (F)	313	OO-SCB	0084	0498	2 PW JT9D-7R4E1	144000	Freighter		Ashley / cvtd -222
N650FE	Airbus Industrie A300-605F (A300F4-605R)	726	F-WWAP*	0094	0594	2 GE CF6-80C2A5	171700	Freighter	DF-RS	Molly Mickler
N651FE	Airbus Industrie A300-605F (A300F4-605R)	728	F-WWAJ*	0094	0494	2 GE CF6-80C2A5	171700	Freighter	DF-PS	Diane Kathleen
N652FE	Airbus Industrie A300-605F (A300F4-605R)	735	F-WWAN*	0094	0794	2 GE CF6-80C2A5	171700	Freighter	DG-BR	Rachel Patricia
N653FE	Airbus Industrie A300-605F (A300F4-605R)	736	F-WWAD*	0094	0794	2 GE CF6-80C2A5	171700	Freighter	DG-BS	Samantha Massey
N654FE	Airbus Industrie A300-605F (A300F4-605R)	738	F-WWAX*	0094	0994	2 GE CF6-80C2A5	171700	Freighter	DG-CR	Kartherine Warner
N655FE	Airbus Industrie A300-605F (A300F4-605R)	742	F-WWAJ*	0094	1194	2 GE CF6-80C2A5	171700	Freighter	DG-CS	Dion
N656FE	Airbus Industrie A300-605F (A300F4-605R)	745	F-WWAP*	0095	0295	2 GE CF6-80C2A5	171700	Freighter	DG-ER	Devin
N657FE	Airbus Industrie A300-605F (A300F4-605R)	748	F-WWAM*	0095	0395	2 GE CF6-80C2A5	171700	Freighter	DG-ES	Lizzie
N658FE	Airbus Industrie A300-605F (A300F4-605R)	752	F-WWAE*	0095	0595	2 GE CF6-80C2A5	171700	Freighter	DG-FR	Rudy
N659FE	Airbus Industrie A300-605F (A300F4-605R)	757	F-WWAF*	0095	0795	2 GE CF6-80C2A5	171700	Freighter	DG-FS	Calvin
N660FE	Airbus Industrie A300-605F (A300F4-605R)	759	F-WWAG*	0095	0995	2 GE CF6-80C2A5	171700	Freighter	FG-KQ	Michaela
N661FE	Airbus Industrie A300-605F (A300F4-605R)	760	F-WWAL*	0095	1095	2 GE CF6-80C2A5	171700	Freighter	FG-KS	Whitney
N662FE	Airbus Industrie A300-605F (A300F4-605R)	761	F-WWAK*	0096	0996	2 GE CF6-80C2A5	171700	Freighter		Tessa
N663FE	Airbus Industrie A300-605F (A300F4-605R)	766	F-WWAO*	0095	1195	2 GE CF6-80C2A5	171700	Freighter		Domenick
N664FE	Airbus Industrie A300-605F (A300F4-605R)	768	F-WWAA*	0096	0296	2 GE CF6-80C2A5	171700	Freighter	FG-MR	Amanda
N665FE	Airbus Industrie A300-605F (A300F4-605R)	769	F-WWAM*	0096	0396	2 GE CF6-80C2A5	171700	Freighter	FG-MS	Ethan
N667FE	Airbus Industrie A300-605F (A300F4-605R)	771	F-WWAF*	0096	0896	2 GE CF6-80C2A5	171700	Freighter	FG-PR	Sean
N668FE	Airbus Industrie A300-605F (A300F4-605R)	772	F-WWAP*	0096	0596	2 GE CF6-80C2A5	171700	Freighter	FG-QR	Tianna
N669FE	Airbus Industrie A300-605F (A300F4-605R)	774	F-WWAE*	0096	0696	2 GE CF6-80C2A5	171700	Freighter		Kaitlyn
N670FE	Airbus Industrie A300-605F (A300F4-605R)	777	F-WWAQ*	0097	0697	2 GE CF6-80C2A5	171700	Freighter		Amrit
N671FE	Airbus Industrie A300-605F (A300F4-605R)	778	F-WWAV*	0097	0797	2 GE CF6-80C2A5	171700	Freighter		Drew

335 registration type of aircraft cn/fn ex/ex* mfd del powered by mtow kg configuration selcal name/fln/specialitites/remarks

☐ N672FE	Airbus Industrie A300-605F (A300F4-605R)	779	F-WWAZ*	0097	0897	2 GE CF6-80C2A5	171700	Freighter		
☐ N673FE	Airbus Industrie A300-605F (A300F4-605R)	780	F-WWAU*	0097	0897	2 GE CF6-80C2A5	171700	Freighter		
☐ N674FE	Airbus Industrie A300-605F (A300F4-605R)	781	F-WWAN*	0097	0997	2 GE CF6-80C2A5	171700	Freighter		Thea
☐ N675FE	Airbus Industrie A300-605F (A300F4-605R)	789	F-WWAZ*	0098	0698	2 GE CF6-80C2A5	171700	Freighter		
☐ N676FE	Airbus Industrie A300-605F (A300F4-605R)	790	F-WWAV*	0098	0798	2 GE CF6-80C2A5	171700	Freighter		Jade
☐ N677FE	Airbus Industrie A300-605F (A300F4-605R)	791	F-WWAD*	0098	0898	2 GE CF6-80C2A5	171700	Freighter		Clifford
☐ N678FE	Airbus Industrie A300-605F (A300F4-605R)	792	F-WWAF*	0098	0998	2 GE CF6-80C2A5	171700	Freighter		Allison
☐ N679FE	Airbus Industrie A300-605F (A300F4-605R)	793	F-WWAG*	0098	1098	2 GE CF6-80C2A5	171700	Freighter		Ty
☐ N680FE	Airbus Industrie A300-605F (A300F4-605R)	794	F-WWAH*	0098	1198	2 GE CF6-80C2A5	171700	Freighter		Tierney
☐ N681FE	Airbus Industrie A300-605F (A300F4-605R)	799				2 GE CF6-80C2A5	171700	Freighter		oo-delivery 0599
☐ N682FE	Airbus Industrie A300-605F (A300F4-605R)	800				2 GE CF6-80C2A5	171700	Freighter		oo-delivery 0699
☐ N683FE	Airbus Industrie A300-605F (A300F4-605R)	801				2 GE CF6-80C2A5	171700	Freighter		oo-delivery 1199
☐ N684FE	Airbus Industrie A300-605F (A300F4-605R)	802				2 GE CF6-80C2A5	171700	Freighter		oo-delivery 0400
☐ N685FE	Airbus Industrie A300-605F (A300F4-605R)	803				2 GE CF6-80C2A5	171700	Freighter		oo-delivery 0700
☐ N686FE	Airbus Industrie A300-605F (A300F4-605R)	804				2 GE CF6-80C2A5	171700	Freighter		oo-delivery 1100
☐ N101AA	Boeing (Douglas) DC-10-10	46500 / 1	N10DC*	1272	0297	3 GE CF6-6K	202302	Freighter		std GYR / to be cvtd to -10F & MD-10F
☐ N102AA	Boeing (Douglas) DC-10-10	46502 / 3		0572	0297	3 GE CF6-6K	202302	Freighter		std GYR / to be cvtd to -10F & MD-10F
☐ N103AA	Boeing (Douglas) DC-10-10	46503 / 5		0771	1296	3 GE CF6-6K	202302	Freighter		std GYR / to be cvtd to -10F & MD-10F
☐ N105AA	Boeing (Douglas) DC-10-10	46505 / 9		1171	1297	3 GE CF6-6K	202302	Freighter		std GYR / to be cvtd to -10F & MD-10F
☐ N106AA	Boeing (Douglas) DC-10-10	46506 / 12		1271	1197	3 GE CF6-6K	202302	Freighter		std GYR / to be cvtd to -10F & MD-10F
☐ N107AA	Boeing (Douglas) DC-10-10	46507 / 13		1271	0397	3 GE CF6-6K	202302	Freighter		std GYR / to be cvtd to -10F & MD-10F
☐ N108AA	Boeing (Douglas) DC-10-10	46508 / 20		0172	0497	3 GE CF6-6K	202302	Freighter		std GYR / to be cvtd to -10F & MD-10F
☐ N112AA	Boeing (Douglas) DC-10-10	46512 / 24		0372	0597	3 GE CF6-6K	202302	Freighter		std GYR / to be cvtd to -10F & MD-10F
☐ N115AA	Boeing (Douglas) DC-10-10	46515 / 37		0572	0697	3 GE CF6-6K	202302	Freighter		std GYR / to be cvtd to -10F & MD-10F
☐ N116AA	Boeing (Douglas) DC-10-10	46516 / 48		0772	0294	3 GE CF6-6K	202302	Freighter		oo-delivery 0099/ex AAL/tb cvtd to -10F
☐ N117AA	Boeing (Douglas) DC-10-10	46517 / 49		0772	1097	3 GE CF6-6K	202302	Freighter		std GYR / to be cvtd to -10F & MD-10F
☐ N118AA	Boeing (Douglas) DC-10-10	46518 / 51		0772	0897	3 GE CF6-6K	202302	Freighter		std GYR / to be cvtd to -10F & MD-10F
☐ N120AA	Boeing (Douglas) DC-10-10	46520 / 54		0872	0997	3 GE CF6-6K	202302	Freighter		std GYR / to be cvtd to -10F & MD-10F
☐ N121AA	Boeing (Douglas) DC-10-10	46521 / 55		0972	0797	3 GE CF6-6K	202302	Freighter		std GYR / to be cvtd to -10F & MD-10F
☐ N123AA	Boeing (Douglas) DC-10-10	46523 / 58		1072	0298	3 GE CF6-6K	202302	Freighter		oo-delivery 0099/ex FDX/tb cvtd to -10F
☐ N146AA	Boeing (Douglas) DC-10-10	46701 / 16	N61NA	1171	1296	3 GE CF6-6K	202302	Freighter		std GYR / to be cvtd to -10F & MD-10F
☐ N154AA	Boeing (Douglas) DC-10-10	46709 / 68	N67NA	1172	0298	3 GE CF6-6K	202302	Freighter		std GYR / to be cvtd to -10F & MD-10F
☐ N364FE	Boeing (Douglas) DC-10-10F	46600 / 4	N1801U	0070	0798	3 GE CF6-6D	202302	Freighter		cvtd -10 / to be cvtd to MD-10F
☐ N365FE	Boeing (Douglas) DC-10-10F	46601 / 6	N1802U	0071	1197	3 GE CF6-6D	202302	Freighter		Joey / cvtd -10 / to be cvtd to MD-10F
☐ N366FE	Boeing (Douglas) DC-10-10F	46602 / 8	N1803U	0071	0997	3 GE CF6-6D	202302	Freighter		cvtd -10 / to be cvtd to MD-10F
☐ N367FE	Boeing (Douglas) DC-10-10F	46605 / 15	N1806U	0071	0897	3 GE CF6-6D	202302	Freighter		cvtd -10 / to be cvtd to MD-10F
☐ N368FE	Boeing (Douglas) DC-10-10F	46606 / 17	N1807U	0071	0897	3 GE CF6-6D	202302	Freighter		cvtd -10 / to be cvtd to MD-10F
☐ N369FE	Boeing (Douglas) DC-10-10F	46607 / 25	N1808U	0071	0897	3 GE CF6-6D	202302	Freighter		cvtd -10 / to be cvtd to MD-10F
☐ N370FE	Boeing (Douglas) DC-10-10F	46608 / 26	N1809U	0072	0897	3 GE CF6-6D	202302	Freighter		cvtd -10 / to be cvtd to MD-10F
☐ N371FE	Boeing (Douglas) DC-10-10F	46609 / 27	N1810U	0072	0198	3 GE CF6-6D	202302	Freighter		cvtd -10 / to be cvtd to MD-10F
☐ N372FE	Boeing (Douglas) DC-10-10F	46610 / 32	N1811U	0072	0998	3 GE CF6-6D	202302	Freighter		cvtd -10 / to be cvtd to MD-10F
☐ N373FE	Boeing (Douglas) DC-10-10F	46611 / 35	N1812U	0072	1297	3 GE CF6-6D	202302	Freighter		cvtd -10 / to be cvtd to MD-10F
☐ N374FE	Boeing (Douglas) DC-10-10F	46612 / 39	N1813U	0072	0598	3 GE CF6-6D	202302	Freighter		cvtd -10 / to be cvtd to MD-10F
☐ N375FE	Boeing (Douglas) DC-10-10F	46613 / 42	N1814U	0072	0398	3 GE CF6-6D	202302	Freighter		cvtd -10 / to be cvtd to MD-10F
☐ N377FE	Boeing (Douglas) DC-10-10F	47965 / 59	N1833U	0072	0897	3 GE CF6-6D	202302	Freighter		Shelby / cvtd -10/to be cvtd to MD-10F
☐ N384FE	Boeing (Douglas) DC-10-10F	46617 / 89	N1818U	0073	0798	3 GE CF6-6D	202302	Freighter		cvtd -10 / to be cvtd to MD-10F
☐ N385FE	Boeing (Douglas) DC-10-10F	46619 / 119	N1820U	0074	0797	3 GE CF6-6D	202302	Freighter		Lindsay / cvtd -10/to be cvtd to MD-10F
☐ N386FE	Boeing (Douglas) DC-10-10F	46620 / 138	N1821U	0074	0497	3 GE CF6-6D	202302	Freighter		cvtd -10 / to be cvtd to MD-10F
☐ N387FE	Boeing (Douglas) DC-10-10F	46621 / 140	N1822U	0074	0497	3 GE CF6-6D	202302	Freighter		cvtd -10 / to be cvtd to MD-10F
☐ N388FE	Boeing (Douglas) DC-10-10F	46622 / 144	N1823U	0074	0197	3 GE CF6-6D	202302	Freighter		Izzul / cvtd -10 / to be cvtd to MD-10F
☐ N389FE	Boeing (Douglas) DC-10-10F	46623 / 154	N1824U	0074	1198	3 GE CF6-6D	202302	Freighter		cvtd -10 / to be cvtd to MD-10F
☐ N390FE	Boeing (Douglas) DC-10-10F	46624 / 155	N1825U	0074	0197	3 GE CF6-6D	202302	Freighter		Rasik / cvtd -10 / to be cvtd to MD-10F
☐ N391FE	Boeing (Douglas) DC-10-10F	46625 / 169	N1826U	0074	0597	3 GE CF6-6D	202302	Freighter	DE-BM	Chandra / cvtd -10/to be cvtd to MD-10F
☐ N392FE	Boeing (Douglas) DC-10-10F	46626 / 198	N1827U	0075	0197	3 GE CF6-6D	202302	Freighter		Axton / cvtd -10 / to be cvtd to MD-10F
☐ N395FE	Boeing (Douglas) DC-10-10F	46629 / 208	N1830U	0075	0199	3 GE CF6-6D	202302	Freighter		cvtd -10 / to be cvtd to MD-10F
☐ N397FE	Boeing (Douglas) DC-10-10F	46631 / 210	N1832U	0075	0197	3 GE CF6-6D	202302	Freighter		Stefani / cvtd -10/to be cvtd to MD-10F
☐ N68048	Boeing (Douglas) DC-10-10	47802 / 101		0073	0897	3 GE CF6-6D	199581	Freighter		std GYR / to be cvtd to -10F
☐ N68049	Boeing (Douglas) DC-10-10F	47803 / 139		0174	0781	3 GE CF6-6D	199581	Freighter	HM-DE	Dusty / cvtd (CF)/to be cvtd to MD-10F
☐ N68050	Boeing (Douglas) DC-10-10F	47804 / 142		0174	0980	3 GE CF6-6D	199581	Freighter	HL-BK	Merideth Allison / cvtd(CF)tbcvtd MD-10F
☐ N68051	Boeing (Douglas) DC-10-10F	47805 / 145		0474	1186	3 GE CF6-6D	199581	Freighter	EK-AC	Todd / cvtd (CF)/to be cvtd to MD-10F
☐ N68052	Boeing (Douglas) DC-10-10F	47806 / 148		0374	0583	3 GE CF6-6D	199581	Freighter	EK-FL	Janette Louise / cvtd (CF)/tbcvtd to MD-10F
☐ N68053	Boeing (Douglas) DC-10-10F	47807 / 173		0974	1083	3 GE CF6-6D	199581	Freighter	EK-BL	Chayne / cvtd (CF)/to be cvtd to MD-10F
☐ N68054	Boeing (Douglas) DC-10-10F	47808 / 177		1074	0380	3 GE CF6-6D	199581	Freighter	JK-AF	Dani Elena / cvtd (CF)/tbcvtd to MD-10F
☐ N68056	Boeing (Douglas) DC-10-10F	47810 / 194		0375	1086	3 GE CF6-6D	199581	Freighter	EK-AH	Valerie Ann / cvtd (CF)/tb cvtd to MD-10F
☐ N68057	Boeing (Douglas) DC-10-10F	48264 / 379	N1848U	0081	0990	3 GE CF6-6D	195045	Freighter	FK-CM	cvtd (CF) / to be cvtd to MD-10F
☐ N68058	Boeing (Douglas) DC-10-10F	46705 / 33	TC-JAU	0071	1189	3 GE CF6-6D	195045	Freighter	AK-BD	cvtd -10 / to be cvtd to MD-10F
☐ N68059	Boeing (Douglas) DC-10-10F	46907 / 78	TC-JAY	0072	0190	3 GE CF6-6D	195045	Freighter	AK-BE	cvtd -10 / to be cvtd to MD-10F
☐ N10060	Boeing (Douglas) DC-10-10F	46970 / 269	N581LF	0079	1194	3 GE CF6-6D1A	206385	Freighter	DH-CK	Haylee / lsf CITG / cvtd -10
☐ N40061	Boeing (Douglas) DC-10-10F	46973 / 272	N591LF	0079	1194	3 GE CF6-6D1A	206385	Freighter	AM-DJ	lsf CITG / cvtd -10
☐ N301FE	Boeing (Douglas) DC-10-30F	46800 / 96	N101TV	0473	0484	3 GE CF6-50C2	256280	Freighter	HK-DG	Tara Lynn / cvtd (CF)
☐ N302FE	Boeing (Douglas) DC-10-30F	46801 / 103	N102TV	0673	0384	3 GE CF6-50C2	256280	Freighter	HK-DJ	Brian jr. / cvtd (CF)
☐ N303FE	Boeing (Douglas) DC-10-30F	46802 / 110	N103TV	0773	0284	3 GE CF6-50C2	256280	Freighter	HK-DL	Amanda Marie / cvtd (CF)
☐ N304FE	Boeing (Douglas) DC-10-30F	46992 / 257	EC-DSF	0978	0584	3 GE CF6-50C2	259455	Freighter	HK-DM	Alison / cvtd (CF)
☐ N305FE	Boeing (Douglas) DC-10-30F	47870 / 339		0684	0984	3 GE CF6-50C2	263084	Freighter	HK-EF	Lamar / cvtd (CF)
☐ N306FE	Boeing (Douglas) DC-10-30F	48287 / 409		0186	0186	3 GE CF6-50C2	263084	Freighter	HK-EJ	John Peter jr.
☐ N307FE	Boeing (Douglas) DC-10-30F	48291 / 412		0386	0386	3 GE CF6-50C2	263084	Freighter	HK-EL	Erin Lee
☐ N308FE	Boeing (Douglas) DC-10-30F	48297 / 416		0586	0586	3 GE CF6-50C2	263084	Freighter	HK-EM	Ann
☐ N309FE	Boeing (Douglas) DC-10-30F	48298 / 419		0786	0786	3 GE CF6-50C2	263084	Freighter	HK-EG	Stacey
☐ N310FE	Boeing (Douglas) DC-10-30F	48299 / 422		0986	0986	3 GE CF6-50C2	263084	Freighter	BG-AH	John Shelby
☐ N311FE	Boeing (Douglas) DC-10-30F	46871 / 219	LN-RKB	1285	1285	3 GE CF6-50C2	256280	Freighter	CM-DK	Abe / cvtd -30
☐ N312FE	Boeing (Douglas) DC-10-30F	48300 / 433		0087	0387	3 GE CF6-50C2	263084	Freighter	CM-DL	Angela
☐ N313FE	Boeing (Douglas) DC-10-30F	48311 / 440		0088	0688	3 GE CF6-50C2	263084	Freighter	CM-GL	Brandon Parks
☐ N314FE	Boeing (Douglas) DC-10-30F	48312 / 442		0088	0788	3 GE CF6-50C2	263084	Freighter	CM-EG	Caitlin Ann
☐ N315FE	Boeing (Douglas) DC-10-30F	48313 / 443		0088	0888	3 GE CF6-50C2	263084	Freighter	FK-CE	Kevin
☐ N316FE	Boeing (Douglas) DC-10-30F	48314 / 444		0088	0988	3 GE CF6-50C2	263084	Freighter	FK-CH	Brandon
☐ N317FE	Boeing (Douglas) DC-10-30F	46835 / 277	N106WA	0079	1189	3 GE CF6-50C2	259455	Freighter	BK-CL	Madison / lsf Mitsui & Co.Ltd/cvtd (CF)
☐ N318FE	Boeing (Douglas) DC-10-30F	46837 / 282	N108WA	0079	1189	3 GE CF6-50C2	259455	Freighter	BK-DH	lsf Mitsui & Co. Ltd / cvtd (CF)
☐ N319FE	Boeing (Douglas) DC-10-30F	47820 / 317	N112WA	0080	1189	3 GE CF6-50C2	259455	Freighter	BK-HJ	lsf Mitsui & Co. Ltd / cvtd (CF)
☐ N320FE	Boeing (Douglas) DC-10-30F	47835 / 326	OO-SLD	0080	0292	3 GE CF6-50C2	251744	Freighter	DE-CG	Maura / lsf POTO / cvtd (CF)
☐ N321FE	Boeing (Douglas) DC-10-30F	47836 / 330	OO-SLE	0080	0692	3 GE CF6-50C2	251744	Freighter	HJ-BK	lsf POTO / cvtd (CF)
☐ N322FE	Boeing (Douglas) DC-10-30F	47908 / 215	OO-SLC	0075	1092	3 GE CF6-50C2	251744	Freighter	CH-FL	Gerald / lsf CITG / cvtd (CF)
☐ N1755	Boeing (Douglas) MD-11	48490 / 499		0592		3 GE CF6-80C2D1F	280320	Freighter		oo-delivery 0600/ex AAL/to be cvtd to F
☐ N1756	Boeing (Douglas) MD-11	48491 / 503		0592		3 GE CF6-80C2D1F	280320	Freighter		oo-delivery 1200/ex AAL/to be cvtd to F
☐ N1758B	Boeing (Douglas) MD-11	48527 / 504		0692		3 GE CF6-80C2D1F	280320	Freighter		oo-delivery 0301/ex AAL/to be cvtd to F
☐ N1760A	Boeing (Douglas) MD-11	48550 / 526		1292		3 GE CF6-80C2D1F	280320	Freighter		oo-delivery 0200/ex AAL/to be cvtd to F
☐ N1761R	Boeing (Douglas) MD-11	48551 / 527		1292		3 GE CF6-80C2D1F	280320	Freighter		oo-delivery 0901/ex AAL/to be cvtd to F
☐ N1762B	Boeing (Douglas) MD-11	48552 / 530		1292		3 GE CF6-80C2D1F	280320	Freighter		oo-delivery 1200/ex AAL/to be cvtd to F
☐ N1763	Boeing (Douglas) MD-11	48553 / 531		0193		3 GE CF6-80C2D1F	280320	Freighter		oo-delivery 0601/ex AAL/to be cvtd to F
☐ N1764B	Boeing (Douglas) MD-11	48554 / 535		0193		3 GE CF6-80C2D1F	280320	Freighter		oo-delivery 0900/ex AAL/to be cvtd to F
☐ N1765B	Boeing (Douglas) MD-11	48596 / 537		0193		3 GE CF6-80C2D1F	280320	Freighter		oo-delivery 0602/ex AAL/to be cvtd to F
☐ N1766A	Boeing (Douglas) MD-11	48597 / 540		0493		3 GE CF6-80C2D1F	280320	Freighter		oo-delivery 0502/ex AAL/to be cvtd to F
☐ N1767A	Boeing (Douglas) MD-11	48598 / 550		0893		3 GE CF6-80C2D1F	280320	Freighter		oo-delivery 0502/ex AAL/to be cvtd to F
☐ N581FE	Boeing (Douglas) MD-11F	48419 / 450	N1750B	0090	0297	3 GE CF6-80C2D1F	280320	Freighter	KL-AR	Joshua / cvtd -11
☐ N582FE	Boeing (Douglas) MD-11F	48420 / 451	N1751A	0090	0196	3 GE CF6-80C2D1F	280320	Freighter	KL-AS	cvtd -11
☐ N583FE	Boeing (Douglas) MD-11F	48421 / 452	N1752K	0090	0697	3 GE CF6-80C2D1F	280320	Freighter		Nancy / cvtd -11
☐ N584FE	Boeing (Douglas) MD-11F	48436 / 483	N1768D	0492	1097	3 GE CF6-80C2D1F	280320	Freighter		cvtd -11
☐ N585FE	Boeing (Douglas) MD-11F	48481 / 482	N1759	0492	0698	3 GE CF6-80C2D1F	280320	Freighter		cvtd -11
☐ N586FE	Boeing (Douglas) MD-11F	48487 / 469	N1753	0891	0596	3 GE CF6-80C2D1F	280320	Freighter	KL-CS	cvtd -11
☐ N587FE	Boeing (Douglas) MD-11F	48489 / 492	N1754	0392	0996	3 GE CF6-80C2D1F	280320	Freighter	KL-DR	cvtd -11
☐ N590FE	Boeing (Douglas) MD-11F	48505 / 462	N1757A	0891	0198	3 GE CF6-80C2D1F	280320	Freighter		cvtd -11
☐ N601FE	Boeing (Douglas) MD-11F	48401 / 447	N111MD*	0090	0691	3 GE CF6-80C2D1F	280320	Freighter	GP-EM	Jim Riedmeyer
☐ N602FE	Boeing (Douglas) MD-11F	48402 / 448	N211MD*	0090	0591	3 GE CF6-80C2D1F	280320	Freighter	GP-FH	Malcolm Baldrige 1990
☐ N603FE	Boeing (Douglas) MD-11F	48459 / 470		0091	0991	3 GE CF6-80C2D1F	280320	Freighter	GP-FJ	Elizabeth
☐ N604FE	Boeing (Douglas) MD-11F	48460 / 497		0092	0592	3 GE CF6-80C2D1F	280320	Freighter	GP-FK	Hollis
☐ N605FE	Boeing (Douglas) MD-11F	48514 / 515		0092	0992	3 GE CF6-80C2D1F	280320	Freighter	GP-FL	April Star
☐ N606FE	Boeing (Douglas) MD-11F	48602 / 549		0093	0793	3 GE CF6-80C2D1F	280320	Freighter	AB-ES	
☐ N607FE	Boeing (Douglas) MD-11F	48547 / 517		0092	1092	3 GE CF6-80C2D1F	280320	Freighter	GP-FM	Louis III
☐ N608FE	Boeing (Douglas) MD-11F	48548 / 521		0092	1192	3 GE CF6-80C2D1F	280320	Freighter	AB-DS	Betsey
☐ N609FE	Boeing (Douglas) MD-11F	48549 / 545		0093	0693	3 GE CF6-80C2D1F	280320	Freighter	AB-ER	Scott
☐ N610FE	Boeing (Douglas) MD-11F	48603 / 551		0093	0893	3 GE CF6-80C2D1F	280320	Freighter	BL-CS	

336 registration type of aircraft cn/fn ex/ex* mfd del powered by mtow kg configuration selcal name/fln/specialitites/remarks

☐ N612FE	Boeing (Douglas) MD-11F	48605 / 555		0093	0993	3 GE CF6-80C2D1F	280320	Freighter	BM-DS	
☐ N613FE	Boeing (Douglas) MD-11F	48749 / 598		0096	0496	3 GE CF6-80C2D1F	280320	Freighter	KM-AR	Krista / lsf MD Federal Holding Co.
☐ N614FE	Boeing (Douglas) MD-11F	48528 / 507		0692	1192	3 GE CF6-80C2D1F	280320	Freighter	BM-ER	
☐ N615FE	Boeing (Douglas) MD-11F	48767 / 602		0096	0696	3 GE CF6-80C2D1F	280320	Freighter	KM-AS	Max / lsf McDonnell Dougl. Express Inc.
☐ N616FE	Boeing (Douglas) MD-11F	48747 / 594		0095	1195	3 GE CF6-80C2D1F	280320	Freighter	FH-CR	Shanita / lsf MDFC Aircraft Leasing Co.
☐ N617FE	Boeing (Douglas) MD-11F	48748 / 595		0095	1295	3 GE CF6-80C2D1F	280320	Freighter	FH-CS	Travis / lsf MDFC Express Leasing Co.
☐ N618FE	Boeing (Douglas) MD-11F	48754 / 604		0096	0896	3 GE CF6-80C2D1F	280320	Freighter	KM-BR	Justin / lsf Douglas Leasing Inc.
☐ N619FE	Boeing (Douglas) MD-11F	48770 / 607		0096	1196	3 GE CF6-80C2D1F	280320	Freighter	KM-PS	lsf MDAFC-Nashville Co.
☐ N620FE	Boeing (Douglas) MD-11F					3 PW PW4462	280320	Freighter		oo-delivery 0499
☐ N621FE	Boeing (Douglas) MD-11F					3 PW PW4462	280320	Freighter		oo-delivery 0699
☐ N623FE	Boeing (Douglas) MD-11F					3 PW PW4462	280320	Freighter		oo-delivery 0699
☐ N	Boeing (Douglas) MD-11	48443 / 458	HB-IWA	0291		3 PW PW4462	285990	Freighter		oo-del. 0002-4/ex GATX/SWR/tb cvtd to F
☐ N	Boeing (Douglas) MD-11	48444 / 459	HB-IWB	0391		3 PW PW4462	285990	Freighter		oo-del. 0002-4/ex GATX/SWR/tb cvtd to F
☐ N	Boeing (Douglas) MD-11	48445 / 460	HB-IWC	0491		3 PW PW4462	285990	Freighter		oo-del. 0002-4/ex GATX/SWR/tb cvtd to F
☐ N	Boeing (Douglas) MD-11	48446 / 463	HB-IWD	0591		3 PW PW4462	285990	Freighter		oo-del. 0002-4/ex GATX/SWR/tb cvtd to F
☐ N	Boeing (Douglas) MD-11	48447 / 464	HB-IWE	0691		3 PW PW4462	285990	Freighter		oo-del. 0002-4/ex GATX/SWR/tb cvtd to F
☐ N	Boeing (Douglas) MD-11	48452 / 472	HB-IWG	0991		3 PW PW4462	285990	Freighter		oo-del. 0002-4/ex GATX/SWR/tb cvtd to F
☐ N	Boeing (Douglas) MD-11	48453 / 473	HB-IWH	0991		3 PW PW4462	285990	Freighter		oo-del. 0002-4/ex GATX/SWR/tb cvtd to F
☐ N	Boeing (Douglas) MD-11	48454 / 477	HB-IWI	1091		3 PW PW4462	285990	Freighter		oo-del. 0002-4/ex GATX/SWR/tb cvtd to F
☐ N	Boeing (Douglas) MD-11	48455 / 487	HB-IWK	0192		3 PW PW4462	283722	Freighter		oo-del. 0002-4/ex GATX/SWR/tb cvtd to F
☐ N	Boeing (Douglas) MD-11	48456 / 494	HB-IWL	0392		3 PW PW4462	285990	Freighter		oo-del. 0002-4/ex GATX/SWR/tb cvtd to F
☐ N	Boeing (Douglas) MD-11	48457 / 498	HB-IWM	0492		3 PW PW4462	283722	Freighter		oo-del. 0002-4/ex GATX/SWR/tb cvtd to F
☐ N	Boeing (Douglas) MD-11	48539 / 571	HB-IWN	0694		3 PW PW4462	285990	Freighter		oo-del. 0002-4/ex GATX/SWR/tb cvtd to F
☐ N	Boeing (Douglas) MD-11	48540 / 611	HB-IWO	0097		3 PW PW4462	285990	Freighter		oo-del. 0002-4/ex GATX/SWR/tb cvtd to F
☐ N	Boeing (Douglas) MD-11	48634 / 614	HB-IWP	0097		3 PW PW4462	285990	Freighter		oo-del. 0002-4/ex GATX/SWR/tb cvtd to F
☐ N	Boeing (Douglas) MD-11	48541 / 621	HB-IWQ	1197		3 PW PW4462	285990	Freighter		oo-del. 0002-4/ex GATX/SWR/tb cvtd to F
☐ N	Boeing (Douglas) MD-11	48484 / 484	HB-IWR	1291		3 PW PW4462	283722	Freighter		oo-del. 0002-4/ex GATX/SWR/tb cvtd to F
☐ N	Boeing (Douglas) MD-11	48485 / 502	HB-IWS	0592		3 PW PW4462	283722	Freighter		oo-del. 0002-4/ex GATX/SWR/tb cvtd to F
☐ N	Boeing (Douglas) MD-11	48486 / 509	HB-IWT	0092		3 PW PW4462	283722	Freighter		oo-del. 0002-4/ex GATX/SWR/tb cvtd to F
☐ N	Boeing (Douglas) MD-11	48538 / 533	HB-IWU	0193		3 PW PW4462	283722	Freighter		oo-del. 0002-4/ex GATX/SWR/tb cvtd to F

FELTS FIELD AVIATION, Inc.

Spokane-Felts Field, WA

PO Box 11877, Spokane, WA 99211, USA ☎ (509) 535-9011 Tx: none Fax: (509) 535-9014 SITA: n/a
F: 1976 n/a Head: David A. Klaue Net: n/a Aircraft below MTOW 1361kg: Cessna 172 & 182P

☐ N5949E	Cessna 182R Skylane II	18268340		0082	1188	1 CO O-470-U	1406			
☐ N2131F	Cessna U206 Super Skywagon	U206-0331		0065	1287	1 CO IO-520-A	1588			
☐ N8694Z	Cessna P206C Super Skylane	P206-0494		0068	1091	1 CO IO-520-A	1633			
☐ N1974U	Cessna T210N Turbo Centurion II	21064760		0082	1083	1 CO TSIO-520-R	1814			
☐ N2AK	Cessna T210N Turbo Centurion II	21064861		0084	0786	1 CO TSIO-520-R	1814			
☐ N761TK	Cessna T210M Turbo Centurion II	21062503		0078	0887	1 CO TSIO-520-R	1724			
☐ N313G	Cessna 421C Golden Eagle III	421C0430		0078	0488	2 CO GTSIO-520-L	3379			
☐ N441DK	Cessna 441 Conquest II	441-0176	N139ML	0080	1095	2 GA TPE331-8-403S	4468			
☐ N55MS	Cessna 441 Conquest II	441-0061	N111MP	0078	0590	2 GA TPE331-8-403S	4468			lsf Hanger One Inc.
☐ N56MS	Cessna 441 Conquest II	441-0057	N441AK	0078	0978	2 GA TPE331-8-403S	4468			

FINE AIR = FB / FBF (Fine Air Services, Inc. dba / Associated with Agro Air Associates, Inc.)

Miami-Int'l, FL

PO Box 523726, Miami, FL 33152, USA ☎ (305) 871-6606 Tx: none Fax: (305) 871-4232 SITA: MIAAGFB
F: 1992 800 Head: Frank J. Fine IATA: 340 ICAO: FINE AIR Net: http://www.finair.com

☐ N85HS	Sabreliner 60 (Rockwell NA265-60)	306-23	N68MA	0068	0894	2 PW JT12A-8	9150	Corporate		
☐ N426FB	Boeing (Douglas) DC-8-54F (JT)	45667 / 185	HI-426CA	0063	1192	4 PW JT3D-3B (HK2/BAC)	142882	Freighter	DK-GJ	lsf Agro Air Associates Inc.
☐ N427FB	Boeing (Douglas) DC-8-54F (JT)	45684 / 195	YV-447C	0063	0493	4 PW JT3D-3B (HK2/BAC)	142882	Freighter	DK-HJ	lsf Agro Air Associates Inc.
☐ N44UA	Boeing (Douglas) DC-8-54F (JT)	45800 / 234	N8044U	0065	0293	4 PW JT3D-3B (HK2/QNC)	140523	Freighter	AK-HL	lsf Agro Air Associates Inc.
☐ N507DC	Boeing (Douglas) DC-8-51F	45855 / 281	C-FFQI	0066	0794	4 PW JT3D-3B (HK2/BAC)	125191	Freighter	JK-DE	lsf Agro Air Assoc./sub-lst TCO/cvtd-51
☐ N508DC	Boeing (Douglas) DC-8-51F	45935 / 330	C-FFSB	0066	1294	4 PW JT3D-3B (HK2/BAC)	125191	Freighter	JK-DF	lsf Agro Air Assoc./sub-lst TCO/cvtd-51
☐ N54FA	Boeing (Douglas) DC-8-54F (FM)	45637 / 157	N53AF	0062	1192	4 PW JT3D-3B (HK2/BAC)	142882	Freighter	EK-JM	lsf Agro Air Associates Inc. / cvtd -43
☐ N55FB	Boeing (Douglas) DC-8-55F (JT)	45678 / 218	HP-950	0065	1192	4 PW JT3D-3B (HK2/BAC)	147418	Freighter	DK-BG	lsf Agro Air Associates Inc.
☐ N56FA	Boeing (Douglas) DC-8-54F (JT)	45663 / 189	YV-445C	0063	1296	4 PW JT3D-3B (HK2/BAC)	142882	Freighter		lsf Agro Air Associates Inc.
☐ N57FB	Boeing (Douglas) DC-8-54F (JT)	45669 / 182	N141RD	0063	1192	4 PW JT3D-3B (HK3/QNC)	142882	Freighter	CD-BF	lsf Agro Air Associates Inc.
☐ N7046H	Boeing (Douglas) DC-8-54F (JT)	46011 / 408	EC-DYB	0068	0994	4 PW JT3D-3B	142884	Freighter	BL-CH	lsf Agro Air Associates Inc.
☐ N29UA	Boeing (Douglas) DC-8-61F	46159 / 544	F-GFCN	0071	0593	4 PW JT3D-3B (HK2/QNC)	145286	Freighter	AD-CG	lsf Agro Air Assoc./cvtd -61/tbr N61FB
☐ N30UA	Boeing (Douglas) DC-8-61F	45888 / 290	EC-DYY	0067	1193	4 PW JT3D-3B (HK2/QNC)	145286	Freighter	LM-BD	Pat Thompson / lsf Agro Air / cvtd -61
☐ N260FA	Lockheed L-1011-385-1-14 TriStar 200 (F)	193A-1158	N851MA	0078	0697	3 RR RB211-524B-02	215003	Freighter		cvtd TriStar 1

FIREFLY AVIATION (Joseph Berto dba)

Shady Cove, OR

6539 Rogue River Drive, Shady Cove, OR 97539-9704, USA ☎ (541) 878-3112 Tx: none Fax: (541) 878-4386 SITA: n/a
F: 1995 n/a Head: Joseph Berto Net: n/a

☐ N242F	Bell UH-1F (204)	7309	N504AH	0066	0495	1 GE T58-GE-3	3856			
☐ N243F	Bell UH-1F (204)	7059	N212AC	0065	0895	1 GE T58-GE-3	3856			
☐ N244F	Bell UH-1F (204)	7116	N204AC	0066	0697	1 GE T58-GE-3	3856			
☐ N246F	Bell UH-1F (204)	7021	N204FF	0063	0695	1 GE T58-GE-3	3856			

FIREHAWK HELICOPTERS, Inc. (Subsidiary of Brainerd Helicopters, Inc.)

Leesburg, FL

8850 Airport Road, Leesburg, FL 34788, USA ☎ (352) 365-9077 Tx: none Fax: (352) 365-0077 SITA: n/a
F: 1978 n/a Head: Charles M. Brainerd Net: n/a

☐ N70C	Sikorsky S-70C	70583	N60FH	0083	1295	2 GE T700-GE-T6A	9185			

FISHING and FLYING (Gayle & Steve Ranney dba)

Cordova-City Airstrip Eyak Lake, AK

PO Box 2349, Cordova, AK 99574, USA ☎ (907) 424-3324 Tx: none Fax: (907) 424-3764 SITA: n/a
F: 1983 n/a Head: Gayle Ranney Net: n/a Aircraft below MTOW 1361 kg: Cessna 180 (on Floats / Wheel-Skis)

☐ N771X	Cessna A185E Skywagon	185-1336		0067	0892	1 CO IO-520-D	1520			Floats / Wheel-Skis
☐ N756DU	Cessna U206G Stationair	U20604015		0077	0893	1 CO IO-520-F	1633			Floats / Wheel-Skis
☐ N723DR	De Havilland DHC-2 Beaver I	1546	N4294K	0064	0691	1 PW R-985	2313			Floats / Wheel-Skis

FISKEHAUK AIRWAYS (Lori L. Egge dba / Affiliated with Sky Trekking Alaska / Seasonal May-October ops only)

Wasilla, AK

485 Pioneer Drive, Wasilla, AK 99654, USA ☎ (907) 373-4966 Tx: none Fax: (907) 373-4966 SITA: n/a
F: 1987 n/a Head: Lori L. Egge Net: n/a

☐ N70341	Cessna A185F Skywagon	18502119		0073	0587	1 CO IO-520-D	1520			Floats / Wheel-Skis
☐ N79906	Grumman G-44 Widgeon	1327		0045	0897	2 CO IO-470	2359			Amphibian

FIVESTAR AIRCRAFT = (FACE) (TriStar-aircraft leasing division of Interface Group-Nevada, Inc.)

Boston, MA

300 First Avenue, Needham Heights, MA 02194, USA ☎ (781) 444-1800 Tx: 6817504 Fax: (781) 449-6617 SITA: n/a
F: 1984 4 Head: Irvin Chafetz Net: n/a Used aircraft leasing and financing company.
Owner / lessor of following (main) aircraft types: Lockheed L-1011 TriStar 1/100. Aircraft leased from FACE are listed and mentioned as such under the leasing carriers.

5-STATE HELICOPTERS, Inc.

Rockwall-5-State Heliport, TX

PO Box 1357, Wylie, TX 75098, USA ☎ (972) 442-4009 Tx: none Fax: (972) 772-4048 SITA: n/a
F: 1989 n/a Head: Brad Ladue Net: n/a

☐ N6BL	Sikorsky S-58ET	58-1567	C-GPTP	0062	0798	1 PWC PT6T-6 TwinPac	5897			cvtd S-58E
☐ N75BL	Sikorsky S-58BT	58-700	C-GPTQ	0057	1298	1 PWC PT6T-6 TwinPac	5897			cvtd S-58B
☐ N506	Sikorsky S-58H	58-1193	N6BL	0059	0889	1 WR R-1820	5897			cvtd UH-34D
☐ N508	Sikorsky S-58E	58-189	N8043V	0056	0797	1 WR R-1820	5897			
☐ N865	Sikorsky S-58C	58-462		0057	0895	1 WR R-1820	5897			

FLAMINGO AIR, Inc. = FMR

Cincinnati-Municipal/Lunken Field, OH

358 Wilmer Avenue, Cincinnati, OH 45226, USA ☎ (513) 871-8600 Tx: none Fax: (513) 871-8619 SITA: n/a
F: 1993 n/a Head: David P. Macdonald ICAO: FLAMINGO AIR Net: n/a

☐ N6868D	Piper PA-32-300C Cherokee SIX	32-40608		0069	1093	1 LY IO-540-K1A5	1542			

FLIGHTCRAFT, Inc. = CSK

Portland-Int'l, OR

7505 N.E. Airport Way, Portland, Oregon 97218, USA ☎ (503) 331-4244 Tx: none Fax: (503) 331-4247 SITA: n/a
F: 1948 n/a Head: Ernie Sturm ICAO: CASCADE Net: n/a

☐ N4128W	Piper PA-32R-301 Saratoga IIHP	3246109		0098	0598	1 LY IO-540-K1G5	1633			
☐ N92877	Piper PA-32R-301 Saratoga IIHP	3246078		0097	0897	1 LY IO-540-K1G5	1633			
☐ N20321	Beech Baron 58	TH-975		0078	0989	2 CO IO-520-C	2449			
☐ N8002N	Beech Baron 58	TH-1599		0089	0696	2 CO IO-550-C	2495			
☐ N4600K	Beech King Air 300	FA-21	N4000K	0084	0196	2 PWC PT6A-60A	6350			lsf Blue Sky Aviation Inc.
☐ N270CS	Beech King Air 200	BB-911	N73LX	0081	0398	2 PWC PT6A-41	5670			lsf Sunshine Aviation Llc
☐ N600AM	Beech King Air 200	BB-337		0078	1193	2 PWC PT6A-41	5670			
☐ N533MA	Cessna 550 Citation II	550-0078	C-GPTR	0079	0396	2 PWC JT15D-4	6033			lsf 533MA Llc

337 registration type of aircraft cn/fn ex/ex* mfd del powered by mtow kg configuration selcal name/fln/specialitites/remarks

FLIGHT EXPRESS, Inc. = EXR

Orlando-Executive, FL

PO Box 1823, Orlando, FL 32802, USA ☎ (561) 896-9358 Tx: none Fax: (561) 894-2944 SITA: n/a
F: 1985 👥 n/a Head: John D. Kirchhoefer ICAO: FLIGHT EXPRESS Net: n/a Aircraft below MTOW 1361 kg: Cessna 172 & Mooney M20J

☐ N2268S	Cessna TR182 Skylane RG II	R18201317		0079	1285	1 LY O-540-L3C5D	1406	Freighter		
☐ N115WL	Cessna 210L Centurion II	21060949		0075	0690	1 CO IO-520-L	1724	Freighter		
☐ N2013S	Cessna 210L Centurion II	21060981		0075	0190	1 CO IO-520-L	1724	Freighter		
☐ N2110S	Cessna 210L Centurion II	21061074		0075	1285	1 CO IO-520-L	1724	Freighter		
☐ N2137S	Cessna 210L Centurion II	21061098		0075	0497	1 CO IO-520-L	1724	Freighter		
☐ N221AT	Cessna T210N Turbo Centurion II	21064567		0081	0797	1 CO TSIO-520-R	1814	Freighter		
☐ N2255S	Cessna 210L Centurion II	21061199		0076	0597	1 CO IO-520-L	1724	Freighter		
☐ N2263S	Cessna 210L Centurion II	21061207		0076	0897	1 CO IO-520-L	1724	Freighter		
☐ N2280S	Cessna 210L Centurion II	21061223		0076	0194	1 CO IO-520-L	1724	Freighter		
☐ N2437S	Cessna 210L Centurion II	21061281		0076	0792	1 CO IO-520-L	1724	Freighter		
☐ N2495S	Cessna 210L Centurion II	21061304		0076	0391	1 CO IO-520-L	1724	Freighter		
☐ N2667S	Cessna 210L Centurion II	21061347		0076	1194	1 CO IO-520-L	1724	Freighter		
☐ N274CS	Cessna 210L Centurion II	21060148		0073	1289	1 CO IO-520-L	1724	Freighter		
☐ N30326	Cessna 210L Centurion II	21059914		0073	0194	1 CO IO-520-L	1724	Freighter		
☐ N318JP	Cessna 210L Centurion II	21060770		0075	1287	1 CO IO-520-L	1724	Freighter		
☐ N4672Y	Cessna T210N Turbo Centurion II	21063977		0080	0897	1 CO TSIO-520-R	1814	Freighter		
☐ N4673C	Cessna T210N Turbo Centurion II	21063586		0079	0897	1 CO TSIO-520-R	1814	Freighter		
☐ N4781C	Cessna T210N Turbo Centurion II	21063624		0080	0997	1 CO TSIO-520-R	1814	Freighter		
☐ N5171V	Cessna 210L Centurion II	21060846		0075	0393	1 CO IO-520-L	1724	Freighter		
☐ N5229A	Cessna 210N Centurion II	21063320		0079	0389	1 CO IO-520-L	1724	Freighter		
☐ N5307A	Cessna 210N Centurion II	21063360		0079	1285	1 CO IO-520-L	1724	Freighter		
☐ N5489V	Cessna 210L Centurion II	21060961		0075	1288	1 CO IO-520-L	1724	Freighter		
☐ N59240	Cessna 210L Centurion II	21060174		0074	0494	1 CO IO-520-L	1724	Freighter		
☐ N59299	Cessna 210L Centurion II	21060199		0074	1285	1 CO IO-520-L	1724	Freighter		
☐ N6149B	Cessna T210M Turbo Centurion II	21062694		0078	0897	1 CO TSIO-520-R	1724	Freighter		
☐ N6195N	Cessna 210N Centurion II	21062966		0078	1285	1 CO IO-520-L	1724	Freighter		
☐ N640AJ	Cessna 210L Centurion II	21060758		0075	0888	1 CO IO-520-L	1724	Freighter		
☐ N6490N	Cessna 210N Centurion II	21063064		0078	0886	1 CO IO-520-L	1724	Freighter		
☐ N6622N	Cessna T210N Turbo Centurion II	21063125		0079	0997	1 CO TSIO-520-R	1814	Freighter		
☐ N70TC	Cessna 210M Centurion II	21061707		0077	0194	1 CO IO-520-L	1724	Freighter		
☐ N732CQ	Cessna 210L Centurion II	21061413		0076	0393	1 CO IO-520-L	1724	Freighter		
☐ N732LW	Cessna 210M Centurion II	21061606		0076	0391	1 CO IO-520-L	1724	Freighter		
☐ N732ST	Cessna 210M Centurion II	21061744		0077	0889	1 CO IO-520-L	1724	Freighter		
☐ N732YA	Cessna 210M Centurion II	21061870		0077	0697	1 CO IO-520-L	1724	Freighter		
☐ N7398M	Cessna T210M Turbo Centurion II	21062018		0077	0797	1 CO TSIO-520-R	1724	Freighter		
☐ N761AT	Cessna 210M Centurion II	21062108		0077	0490	1 CO IO-520-L	1724	Freighter		
☐ N777BK	Cessna 210L Centurion II	21060560		0075	0889	1 CO IO-520-L	1724	Freighter		
☐ N778VK	Cessna 210M Centurion II	21062895		0078	0588	1 CO IO-520-L	1724	Freighter		
☐ N8134L	Cessna 210L Centurion II	21060621		0075	1093	1 CO IO-520-L	1724	Freighter		
☐ N8427M	Cessna 210M Centurion II	21062043		0077	0193	1 CO IO-520-L	1724	Freighter		
☐ N93111	Cessna 210L Centurion II	21060266		0074	1193	1 CO IO-520-L	1724	Freighter		
☐ N93887	Cessna 210L Centurion II	21060445		0074	0889	1 CO IO-520-L	1724	Freighter		
☐ N9489M	Cessna 210M Centurion II	21062081		0077	0493	1 CO IO-520-L	1724	Freighter		
☐ N965B	Cessna 210L Centurion II	21061580		0076	1196	1 CO IO-520-L	1724	Freighter		
☐ N4099S	Beech Baron E55	TE-1037		0075	0691	2 CO IO-520-C	2404	Freighter		
☐ N4492F	Beech Baron E55	TE-1097		0075	0694	2 CO IO-520-C	2404	Freighter		
☐ N703MC	Beech Baron E55	TE-974		0074	0390	2 CO IO-520-C	2404	Freighter		
☐ N9313Y	Beech Baron B55 (95-B55)	TC-9		0060	0190	2 CO IO-470-L	2214	Freighter		
☐ N31T	Beech Baron 58	TH-121		0071	1088	2 CO IO-520-C	2449	Freighter		
☐ N329H	Beech Baron 58	TH-219		0072	1293	2 CO IO-520-C	2404	Freighter		
☐ N4626A	Beech Baron 58	TH-39		0070	0393	2 CO IO-520-C	2404	Freighter		
☐ N752P	Beech Baron 58	TH-422		0074	0194	2 CO IO-520-C	2449	Freighter		
☐ N796Q	Beech Baron 58	TH-43		0070	0390	2 CO IO-520-C	2449	Freighter		
☐ N9098Q	Beech Baron 58	TH-109		0070	0293	2 CO IO-520-C	2449	Freighter		

FLIGHT INTERNATIONAL, Inc. = IVJ (Subs.of The Flight International Group, Inc.)

Newport News/VA, China Lake & Miramar/CA & Yuma/AZ

FLIGHT INTERNATIONAL

Newport News/Williamsburg Int'l Airport, Newport News, VA 23602, USA ☎ (757) 886-5500 Tx: none Fax: (757) 874-7481 SITA: n/a
F: 1976 👥 150 Head: David E. Sandlin ICAO: INVADER JACK Net: http://www.fltintl.com

☐ N18SC	Beech Baron 58P	TJ-111		0078	1097	2 CO TSIO-520-WB	2812			lsf Maritime Sales & Leasing Inc.
☐ N707ML	Piper PA-31T Cheyenne II	31T-7520017	N502RH	0075	0796	2 PWC PT6A-28	4082			lsf Maritime Sales & Leasing Inc.
☐ N58FN	Learjet 24B	24B-184	N58DM	0069	0181	2 GE CJ610-6	6123			lsf Maritime Sales & Leasing Inc.
☐ N814JR	Learjet 24B	24B-202	N814HH	0069	0097	2 GE CJ610-6	6123			lsf J&R Investment Inc.
☐ N48FN	Learjet 24D	24D-238	N49DM	0071	1293	2 GE CJ610-6	6123			lsf Maritime Sales & Leasing Inc.
☐ N202FN	CASA 212 Aviocar Srs 200	248	N248MA	0082	0796	2 GA TPE331-10-511C	7700	Freighter		lsf Maritime Sales & Leasing Inc.
☐ N203FN	CASA 212 Aviocar Srs 200	231	N699MA	0082	0796	2 GA TPE331-10-511C	7700	Freighter		lsf Maritime Sales & Leasing Inc.
☐ N766C	Fairchild (Swearingen) SA227AC Metro III	AC-559	N170SW	0083	0295	2 GA TPE331-11U-611G	6577			lsf Maritime Sales & Leasing Inc.
☐ N781C	Fairchild (Swearingen) SA227AC Metro III	AC-535	N3110J	0083	0295	2 GA TPE331-11U-611G	6577			lsf Maritime Sales & Leasing Inc.
☐ N782C	Fairchild (Swearingen) SA227AC Metro III	AC-525	N31078	0083	0295	2 GA TPE331-11U-611G	6577			lsf Maritime Sales & Leasing Inc.
☐ N784C	Fairchild (Swearingen) SA227AC Metro III	AC-482	N482SA	0082	0295	2 GA TPE331-11U-611G	6577			lsf Maritime Sales & Leasing Inc.
☐ N14FN	Learjet 25C	25C-126	N114CC	0073	0792	2 GE CJ610-6	6804			lsf Maritime Sales & Leasing Inc.
☐ N25ME	Learjet 25	25-062	N27FN	0070	1087	2 GE CJ610-6	6804			lsf pvt
☐ N54FN	Learjet 25C	25C-083	N200MH	0072	0589	2 GE CJ610-6	6804			
☐ N97FN	Learjet 25	25-003	N97DM	0067	1293	2 GE CJ610-6	6804			lsf Maritime Sales & Leasing Inc.
☐ N10FN	Learjet 36	36-015	N14CF	0075	1286	2 GA TFE731-2-2B	8301			lsf Maritime Sales & Leasing Inc.
☐ N12FN	Learjet 36	36-016	F-GBGD	0075	0887	2 GA TFE731-2-2B	8301			lsf Maritime Sales & Leasing Inc.
☐ N39FN	Learjet 35	35-006	N39DM	0074	0487	2 GA TFE731-2-2B	8301			lsf pvt
☐ N83FN	Learjet 36	36-007	N83DM	0075	0186	2 GA TFE731-2-2B	8301			
☐ N84FN	Learjet 36	36-002	N84DM	0074	1086	2 GA TFE731-2-2B	8301			lsf Maritime Sales & Leasing Inc.
☐ N96FN	Learjet 35A	35A-186	N96DM	0078	0286	2 GA TFE731-2-2B	8301			

FLIGHT SERVICES GROUP, Inc. – FSG

Bridgeport-Igor I. Sikorsky Memorial, CT

FLIGHT SERVICES GROUP FSG

1000 Great Meadow Road, Sikorsky Memorial Airport, Stratford, CT 06497, USA ☎ (203) 380-4009 Tx: none Fax: (203) 380-4017 SITA: n/a
F: 1984 👥 60 Head: David C. Hurley Net: http://www.fsg-inc.com Aircraft below MTOW 1361kg: Piper PA-28

☐ N508DF	Beech Bonanza A36	E-2541	N5538N	0090	0196	1 CO IO-550-B	1656	Executive		lsf Ziff Air Services Inc.
☐ N423AB	Beech Baron 58	TH-1754	N1TP	0095	1297	2 CO IO-550-C	2495	Executive		lsf Ziff Air Services Inc.
☐ N121RF	Pilatus PC-12/45	114	N114SV	0095	1195	1 PWC PT6A-67B	4500	Executive		lsf Richard A. Foreman Associates
☐ N399G	Cessna 525 CitationJet	525-0183	N97CJ	0097	0497	2 WRR FJ44-1A	4717	Executive		lsf Dineair Corp.
☐ N472SW	Cessna 525 CitationJet	525-0033	N526CA	0093	0796	2 WRR FJ44-1A	4717	Executive		lsf Jen Linz Ltd
☐ N525AL	Cessna 525 CitationJet	525-0011		0093	0593	2 WRR FJ44-1A	4717	Executive		lsf Elmair Inc.
☐ N776DF	Cessna 525 CitationJet	525-0111	N52136	0095	0895	2 WRR FJ44-1A	4717	Executive		lsf Delta Fox Inc.
☐ N124MB	Beech King Air C90A	LJ-1088	N71WW	0085	1094	2 PWC PT6A-21	4377	Executive		lsf AND Inc.
☐ N178RC	Beech King Air C90	LJ-762	N24176	0078	0897	2 PWC PT6A-21	4377	Executive		lsf Beech Travel Air Services Inc.
☐ N2057N	Beech King Air C90	LJ-815		0079	1196	2 PWC PT6A-21	4377	Executive		lsf McClinch Aviation Corp.
☐ N15CQ	Cessna 500 Citation	500-0101	N15CC	0073	1296	2 PWC JT15D-1	5216	Executive		lsf NY Central Mutual Fire Insurance Co
☐ N23YZ	Cessna 501 Citation I/SP	501-0088	N86MT	0079	1293	2 PWC JT15D-1	5375	Executive		lsf YZ Corp.
☐ N508MV	Beech King Air B200	BB-877	N711BU	0081	1095	2 PWC PT6A-42	5670	Executive		lsf Ziff Air Services Inc.
☐ N1249P	Cessna 550 Citation II	550-0451		0083	1294	2 PWC JT15D-4	6033	Executive		lsf Greyhound Financial Corp.
☐ N830KE	Cessna 550 Citation Bravo	550-0830		0098	0498	2 PWC PW530A	6713	Executive		lsf Conquest One Inc.
☐ N3197Q	Beech Beechjet 400A	RK-97		0094	0595	2 PWC JT15D-5	7303	Executive		lsf Skyland Leasing Corp.
☐ N54HP	Beech Beechjet 400A	RK-160	N2360F	0097	0198	2 PWC JT15D-5	7303	Executive		lsf Ampco Inc.
☐ N120MB	Learjet 35A	35A-307		0081	0494	2 GA TFE731-2-2B	8301	Executive		lsf AND Inc.
☐ N286WL	Learjet 35A	35A-286	PT-LSW	0080	0396	2 GA TFE731-2-2B	8301	Executive		lsf Norwalk Aircraft Corp.
☐ N20AE	Dassault Falcon 20F	258	N544X	0071	1284	2 GE CF700-2D2	13000	Executive		lsf Double Wharf Corp.
☐ N68TS	Dassault Falcon 20C	129	N666DA	0068	0597	2 GE CF700-2C	12000	Executive		lsf New Valley Corp.
☐ N450KP	Dassault Falcon 50	82	N511GG	0082	1297	3 GA TFE731-3-1C	17600	Executive		lsf Rock Island Air Inc.
☐ N397BE	Canadair CL-600S (CL-600-1A11) Challenger	1053	N32BQ	0082	0797	2 LY ALF502L-2C	18711	Executive		lsf BE Aerospace
☐ N315SL	Canadair CL-601-1A (CL-600-2A12) Challen.	3054	N375PK	0086	0897	2 GE CF34-1A	19550	Executive		lsf LPL Management Group Inc.
☐ N298W	Dassault Falcon 900	45	N64BE	0088	0092	3 GA TFE731-5AR-1C	21092	Executive		lsf Abex Inc.
☐ N540EA	GAC (Grumman) G-1159 Gulfstream II (SP)	174	N900ES	0075	0297	2 RR Spey 511-8	29710	Executive		lsf Jetmark Aviation Llc / cvtd II
☐ N624BP	GAC G-1159A Gulfstream III	320	N320WE	0081	0195	2 RR Spey 511-8	30935	Executive		lsf Ziff Air Services Inc.
☐ N765B	BAe (BAC) One-Eleven 401AK	067	N109TH	0066	1192	2 RR Spey 511-14	40597	Corporate 19Pax		lsf Calumet Inc.

FLIGHT TRAILS HELICOPTERS (Civic Helicopters, Inc. dba)

Carlsbad-McClellan, CA

2192H Palomar Airport Road, Carlsbad, CA 92008, USA ☎ (760) 438-8424 Tx: none Fax: (760) 438-0451 SITA: n/a
F: 1988 👥 n/a Head: Chin Yi Tu Net: http://www.civichelicopters.com Aircraft below MTOW 1361kg: Hughes 269C (300C) & Robinson R22

☐ N268ST	MD Helicopters MD 500D (Hughes 369D)	470122D	N14BC	0077	0692	1 AN 250-C20B	1361			lsf pvt
☐ N2183Y	Bell 206B JetRanger III	3519		0081	0896	1 AN 250-C20B	1451			lsf pvt

338 registration type of aircraft cn/fn ex/ex* mfd del powered by mtow kg configuration selcal name/fln/specialitites/remarks

FLINT AIR SERVICE = FAZ (Flint Aviation Services, Inc. dba) — Flint-Bishop Int'l, MI

3375 West Bristol Road, Flint, MI 48507, USA ☎ (248) 235-0681 Tx: none Fax: (248) 235-9778 SITA: n/a
F: 1979 n/a Head: Walter Duncan ICAO: FLINT AIR Net: n/a

registration	type of aircraft	cn/fn	ex/ex*	mfd	del	powered by	mtow kg	configuration	selcal	name/fln/specialitites/remarks
☐ N1761G	Cessna 310R II	310R1223		0078	0293	2 CO IO-520-M	2495			lsf Duncan Air Service Inc.
☐ N197WS	Cessna 402B II	402B1384		0078	0197	2 CO TSIO-520-E	2858			lsf Duncan Air Service Inc.
☐ N103FA	Cessna 404 Titan II	404-0220	G-BKTW	0078	0394	2 CO GTSIO-520-M	3810			
☐ N104FA	Cessna 404 Titan II	404-0128	N37165	0077	0395	2 CO GTSIO-520-M	3810			

FLORIDA AIR CARGO, Inc. — Miami-Opa Locka, FL

3921 NW 144th Street, Bldg. 66, Opa Locka, FL 33054, USA ☎ (954) 687-1080 Tx: none Fax: (954) 681-2168 SITA: n/a
F: 1995 n/a Head: Paul G. Kupke Net: n/a

registration	type of aircraft	cn/fn	ex/ex*	mfd	del	powered by	mtow kg	configuration	selcal	name/fln/specialitites/remarks
☐ N123DZ	Boeing (Douglas) DC-3C (C-47A-1-DK)	12004	N337AF	0043	0995	2 PW R-1830	12202	Freighter		lsf South Florida Aircraft Leasing Inc.
☐ N15MA	Boeing (Douglas) DC-3C (C-47A-70-DL)	19286	F-WSGV	0043	0496	2 PW R-1830	12202	Freighter		lsf South Florida Aircraft Leasing Inc.

FLORIDA AIR TRANSPORT, Inc. (Subsidiary of Florida Aircraft Leasing, Corp.) — Fort Lauderdale-Executive, FL

5601 NW 15th Avenue, Fort Lauderdale, FL 33309, USA ☎ (954) 938-9709 Tx: none Fax: (954) 351-9779 SITA: n/a
F: 1997 n/a Head: Rafael Cur Net: n/a

registration	type of aircraft	cn/fn	ex/ex*	mfd	del	powered by	mtow kg	configuration	selcal	name/fln/specialitites/remarks
☐ N766WC	Boeing (Douglas) DC-6A (C-118A-DO)	44597 / 501	USN 153691	0054	0597	4 PW R-2800	47083	Freighter		lsf Aztec Capital Corp.

FLORIDA JET SERVICE, Inc. — Fort Lauderdale-Executive, FL

2665 NW 56th Street, Hangar 54, Fort Lauderdale, FL 33309, USA ☎ (954) 772-0778 Tx: none Fax: (954) 491-4537 SITA: n/a
F: 1993 n/a Head: Terry N. Robertson Net: n/a

registration	type of aircraft	cn/fn	ex/ex*	mfd	del	powered by	mtow kg	configuration	selcal	name/fln/specialitites/remarks
☐ N517AM	Learjet 55	55-108	N220VE	0084	1094	2 GA TFE731-3AR-2B	9752			

FLORIDA WEST INTERNATIONAL AIRWAYS, Inc. = RF / FWL (formerly Florida West Airlines, Inc. & Pan Aero Int'l Corp.) — Miami-Int'l, FL

PO Box 025752, Miami, FL 33102-5752, USA ☎ (305) 341-9000 Tx: none Fax: (305) 591-8580 SITA: n/a
F: 1981 20 Head: Richard Haberly Net: n/a

registration	type of aircraft	cn/fn	ex/ex*	mfd	del	powered by	mtow kg	configuration	selcal	name/fln/specialitites/remarks
☐ N161DB	Boeing (Douglas) DC-8-61F	45980 / 374	N48UA	0068	0992	4 PW JT3D-3B (HK2)	147418	Freighter	CG-DJ	lsf ALGI / cvtd DC-8-61

FLORIDA WINGS, Inc. — Fort Lauderdale-Executive, FL

2211 NW 55th Court, Hangar 12, Fort Lauderdale, FL 33309, USA ☎ (954) 491-1890 Tx: none Fax: (954) 491-3642 SITA: n/a
F: 1977 n/a Head: Paul Warsaw Net: n/a

registration	type of aircraft	cn/fn	ex/ex*	mfd	del	powered by	mtow kg	configuration	selcal	name/fln/specialitites/remarks
☐ N54EW	Britten-Norman BN-2T Turbine Islander	2145	G-BOBC	0082	1298	2 AN 250-B17C	3175			cvtd BN-2B-26
☐ N99KW	Learjet 60	60-085	N685LJ	0096	1296	2 PWC PW305A	10478			

FLYING A FLIGHT SERVICE, Inc. — Silver City-Whiskey Creek, NM

PO Box 5049, Silver City, NM 88062, USA ☎ (505) 538-5508 Tx: none Fax: (505) 538-3432 SITA: n/a
F: 1975 n/a Head: Robert T. Alexander Net: n/a

registration	type of aircraft	cn/fn	ex/ex*	mfd	del	powered by	mtow kg	configuration	selcal	name/fln/specialitites/remarks
☐ N1596G	Cessna 340 II	340-0507		0075	0486	2 CO TSIO-520-K	2710			
☐ N3LN	Cessna 340 II	340-0301		0073	0290	2 CO TSIO-520-K	2710			
☐ N44SV	Cessna 340	340-0032		0072	0990	2 CO TSIO-520-K	2710			
☐ N8652K	Cessna 340A II	340A0606		0079	1286	2 CO TSIO-520-NB	2717			
☐ N7938Q	Cessna 401B	401B0038		0070	0893	2 CO TSIO-520-E	2858			
☐ N1234W	Cessna 414	414-0043		0070	0189	2 CO TSIO-520-J	2880			
☐ N28LH	Cessna 414A Chancellor III	414A0614	C-GJON	0081	0696	2 CO TSIO-520-NB	3062			
☐ N4693N	Cessna 414A Chancellor III	414A0079		0078	1284	2 CO TSIO-520-N	3062			

FLYING DOLLAR AIR, Inc. — Wisconsin Rapids-Alexander Field South Wood County, WI

170 Third Street North, Wisconsin Rapids, WI 54495-0997, USA ☎ (715) 423-8200 Tx: none Fax: (715) 424-4401 SITA: n/a
F: 1990 n/a Head: Francis J. Podvin Net: n/a

registration	type of aircraft	cn/fn	ex/ex*	mfd	del	powered by	mtow kg	configuration	selcal	name/fln/specialitites/remarks
☐ N690FD	Twin (Aero) Turbo Commander 690B	11393	N699GN	0077	0690	2 GA TPE331-5-251K	4683			

FLYING FIREMAN, Inc. — Spanaway, WA

26117 35th Ave. East, Spanaway, WA 98387, USA ☎ (253) 847-2967 Tx: none Fax: (253) 847-3269 SITA: n/a
F: 1986 n/a Head: Bud Rude Net: n/a

registration	type of aircraft	cn/fn	ex/ex*	mfd	del	powered by	mtow kg	configuration	selcal	name/fln/specialitites/remarks
☐ N85U	Consolidated PBY-5A Super Catalina	Bu64041	C-GFFI	0040	0386	2 WR R-2600	13835	Tanker		85

FLY ONE, Llc — El Paso-Int'l, TX

6775 Convair Road, El Paso, TX 79925, USA ☎ (915) 772-3273 Tx: none Fax: (915) 772-9243 SITA: n/a
F: 1998 n/a Head: Terry Herbert Net: n/a

registration	type of aircraft	cn/fn	ex/ex*	mfd	del	powered by	mtow kg	configuration	selcal	name/fln/specialitites/remarks
☐ N844TH	Boeing (Douglas) DC-3C (C-47A-20-DK)	13070	N582LA	0044	0498	2 PW R-1830	12202	Freighter		

FM AVIATION SERVICES, Llc (Subsidiary of Freeport-McMoran, Inc. / formerly Freeport McMoran-Aviation Dept.) — New Orleans-Int'l, LA

PO Box 20109, New Orleans, LA 70141-0109, USA ☎ (504) 582-4000 Tx: none Fax: (504) 582-5321 SITA: n/a
F: 1987 n/a Head: Mickey L. Bull Net: n/a Operates non-commercial corporate flights for its parent, an internationally active mining company, only.

registration	type of aircraft	cn/fn	ex/ex*	mfd	del	powered by	mtow kg	configuration	selcal	name/fln/specialitites/remarks
☐ N681FM	GAC G-1159A Gulfstream III	371	N680FM	0082	0689	2 RR Spey 511-8	30935	Corporate VIP	FM-LP	
☐ N680FM	Boeing 757-23A	24923 / 332	N680EM	0090	0591	2 RR RB211-535E4	113398	Corporate VIP		

FOLSOMS AIR SERVICE, Inc. — Greenville-Municipal & Moosehead Lake, ME

PO Box 507, Greenville, ME 04441, USA ☎ (207) 695-2821 Tx: none Fax: (207) 695-2317 SITA: n/a
F: 1946 n/a Head: Malcolm R. Folsom Net: n/a

registration	type of aircraft	cn/fn	ex/ex*	mfd	del	powered by	mtow kg	configuration	selcal	name/fln/specialitites/remarks
☐ N1344Q	Cessna A185F Skywagon II	18503477		0078	1292	1 CO IO-520-D	1520			lsf Romeo Papa Alpha/Floats/Wheel-Skis
☐ N430RC	Cessna A185E Skywagon	185-1592		0069	0596	1 CO IO-520-D	1520			Floats / Wheel-Skis
☐ N97FA	Cessna A185F Skywagon II	18504373	N9937N	0082	0397	1 CO IO-520-D	1520			Floats / Wheel-Skis
☐ N59024	Cessna T210L Turbo Centurion II	21060030		0073	0395	1 CO TSIO-520-H	1724			lsf Romeo Papa Alpha
☐ N1537V	De Havilland DHC-2 Beaver I	494	ZK-CLP	0053	1278	1 PW R-985	2313			lsf pvt / Floats / Wheel-Skis
☐ N130Q	Boeing (Douglas) DC-3A (C-53D-DO)	11761	N20W	0043	0186	2 PW R-1830	12202	Freighter		lsf HBF Inc. / Amphibian

FORD MOTOR Company – Air Transportation division = FRD (Air Transportation division of Ford Motor Company) — Detroit-Metro, MI

Metro Airport, Bldg 359, Detroit, MI 48242, USA ☎ (734) 322-5500 Tx: none Fax: (734) 845-4926 SITA: n/a
F: 1981 n/a Head: Philip A. Roberts ICAO: FORD Net: n/a Private, non-commercial company conducting corporate flights for itself only.

registration	type of aircraft	cn/fn	ex/ex*	mfd	del	powered by	mtow kg	configuration	selcal	name/fln/specialitites/remarks
☐ N329K	Dassault Falcon 900	46	N434FJ	0088	1088	3 GA TFE731-5A-1C	20638	Corporate C12	AQ-JM	
☐ N330K	Dassault Falcon 900	50	N436FJ	0088	1188	3 GA TFE731-5A-1C	20638	Corporate C12	AQ-JP	
☐ N300K	GAC G-IV Gulfstream IV (SP)	1266	N412GA	0095	1295	2 RR Tay 611-8	33838	Corporate C12		
☐ N301K	GAC G-IV Gulfstream IV (SP)	1267	N417GA	0095	1295	2 RR Tay 611-8	33838	Corporate C12		
☐ N322K	Fokker 70 (F28 Mk0070)	11521	PH-MKS*	0094	1094	2 RR Tay 620-15	36740	Corporate C48		lsf Ford Holdings Financing Inc.
☐ N324K	Fokker 70 (F28 Mk0070)	11545	PH-EZH*	0095	0795	2 RR Tay 620-15	36740	Corporate C48		lsf Ford Holdings Financing Inc.

FORT WAYNE AIR SERVICE, Inc. — Fort Wayne-Int'l, IN

4021 Air Street, Fort Wayne, IN 46809, USA ☎ (219) 747-1565 Tx: none Fax: (219) 747-6758 SITA: n/a
F: 1956 n/a Head: Thomas W. Kelley Net: n/a

registration	type of aircraft	cn/fn	ex/ex*	mfd	del	powered by	mtow kg	configuration	selcal	name/fln/specialitites/remarks
☐ N131DF	Piper PA-31T1 Cheyenne I	31T-7904015	N23235	0079	0790	2 PWC PT6A-11	3946			lsf KIF Aviation Inc.

40-MILE AIR, Ltd = Q5 / MLA (Forty-Mile Air) — Tok-Junction, AK

PO Box 61116, Fairbanks, AK 99706, USA ☎ (907) 883-5191 Tx: none Fax: (907) 883-5194 SITA: n/a
F: 1981 n/a Head: Charles M. Warbelow ICAO: MILE-AIR Net: n/a Aircraft below MTOW 1361kg: Piper PA-18

registration	type of aircraft	cn/fn	ex/ex*	mfd	del	powered by	mtow kg	configuration	selcal	name/fln/specialitites/remarks
☐ N1541F	Cessna 185D Skywagon	185-0896		0065	1292	1 CO IO-470-F	1451			lsf Charlie Inc. / Wheel-Skis
☐ N5200X	Cessna U206G Stationair 6 II	U20605591		0080	0790	1 CO IO-520-F	1633			lsf Charlie Inc. / Floats / Wheels
☐ N734GW	Cessna U206G Stationair 6 II	U20604832		0079	0882	1 CO IO-520-F	1633			lsf Charlie Inc. / Floats / Wheels
☐ N8515Q	Cessna U206F Stationair II	U20603372		0076	0894	1 CO IO-520-F	1633			lsf Charlie Inc. / Floats / Wheels
☐ N207DG	Cessna T207 Turbo Skywagon	20700070		0069	0397	1 CO TSIO-520-M	1724			lsf Charlie Inc.
☐ N9935M	Cessna 207A Stationair 8 II	20700751		0082	0885	1 CO IO-520-F	1724			lsf Charlie Inc.
☐ N87TS	Piper PA-31-310 Navajo B	31-7300969		0073	0593	2 LY TIO-540-A2C	2948			
☐ N3125N	De Havilland DHC-3 Otter	394	C-FAXD	0060	0588	1 PW R-1340	3629			lsf Charlie Inc. / Wheel-Skis

FORWARD AIR INTERNATIONAL AIRLINES, Inc. — Greeneville-Municipal, TN

PO Box 1058, Greeneville, TN 37744, USA ☎ (423) 639-7196 Tx: none Fax: (423) 636-7274 SITA: n/a
F: 1993 n/a Head: Bruce A. Campbell Net: http://www.landair.co.uk

registration	type of aircraft	cn/fn	ex/ex*	mfd	del	powered by	mtow kg	configuration	selcal	name/fln/specialitites/remarks
☐ N1SN	Cessna 560 Citation V	560-0153	N502F	0091	0796	2 PWC JT15D-5A	7212	Freighter		lsf Sky Night Llc

FOSTAIRE HELICOPTERS (D H Helicopter, Inc. dba) — Cahokia/St. Louis-Downtown Parks, IL

2 Omega Drive, Sauget, IL 62206-1448, USA ☎ (618) 337-4440 Tx: none Fax: (618) 337-8509 SITA: n/a
F: 1967 7 Head: Clarke M. Thomas Net: n/a Aircraft below MTOW 1361kg: Bell 47G-2

registration	type of aircraft	cn/fn	ex/ex*	mfd	del	powered by	mtow kg	configuration	selcal	name/fln/specialitites/remarks
☐ N1069Z	Bell 206B JetRanger III	2855		0079	0384	1 AN 250-C20B	1451			
☐ N27758	Bell 206B JetRanger III	2791		0079	0386	1 AN 250-C20B	1451			
☐ N5001N	Bell 206B JetRanger III	2410		0078	0484	1 AN 250-C20B	1451			
☐ N206FH	Bell 206L-1 LongRanger II	45322	C-GLGF	0079	0487	1 AN 250-C28B	1882			

FOUR CORNERS AVIATION, Inc. – FCA (Member of Mesa Air Group, Inc.)

Farmington-Four Corners Regional, NM

1260 West Navajo, Farmington, NM 87401, USA ☎ (505) 325-2867 Tx: none Fax: (505) 326-4728 SITA: n/a
F: 1959 👥 43 Head: James T. Dean Net: n/a

☐ N9205C	Cessna R182 Skylane RG II	R18200444		0078	1093	1 LY O-540-J3C5D	1406			
☐ N6420Z	Cessna TU206G Turbo Stationair 6 II	U20606274		0081	0984	1 CO TSIO-520-M	1633			
☐ N6185N	Cessna T210N Turbo Centurion II	21062956		0079	0385	1 CO TSIO-520-R	1814			
☐ N9786Y	Cessna T210N Turbo Centurion II	21064598		0081	1282	1 CO TSIO-520-R	1814			
☐ N2690T	Cessna 414A Chancellor III	414A0408		0079	0486	2 CO TSIO-520-NB	3062			
☐ N11692	Beech King Air C90	LJ-772	F-GFBO	0078	0697	2 PWC PT6A-21	4377			
☐ N4954S	Beech King Air E90	LW-231	YV-27P	0077	0992	2 PWC PT6A-28	4581			
☐ N130PA	Beech King Air 200	BB-330	N200CE	0078	1192	2 PWC PT6A-41	5670			lsf Mesa Air Group Inc.
☐ N131PA	Beech King Air 200	BB-161	C-GTIM	0076	0494	2 PWC PT6A-41	5670			lsf Mesa Air Group Inc.
☐ N240S	Beech King Air 300	FA-116	N2998X	0087	0595	2 PWC PT6A-60A	6350			
☐ N510WR	Beech King Air 300	FA-111	N510WP	0086	1295	2 PWC PT6A-60A	6350			lsf pvt

FOUR STAR AVIATION, Inc. = HK / FSC (formerly Four Star Air Cargo)

St. Thomas-Cyril E. King, VI

One Air Cargo Center, Cyril E. King Airport, St. Thomas, VI 00802, USA ☎ (340) 776-8847 Tx: 3470156 Fax: (340) 776-5536 SITA: n/a
F: 1982 👥 42 Head: F.J. McCarthy IATA: 861 ICAO: FOUR STAR Net: n/a

☐ N7HW	Piper PA-23-250 Aztec C	27-3718		0067	0395	2 LY IO-540-C4B5	2359	Freighter		
☐ N131FS	Boeing (Douglas) DC-3C (TC-47B-30-DK)	32920	N67PA	0044	0986	2 PW R-1830	12202	Freighter		
☐ N132FS	Boeing (Douglas) DC-3C (C-47B-1-DK)	25778	N333EF	0044	0986	2 PW R-1830	12202	Freighter		
☐ N133FS	Boeing (Douglas) DC-3C (C-47B-20-DK)	27202	N53NA	0044	0986	2 PW R-1830	12202	Freighter		
☐ N135FS	Boeing (Douglas) DC-3C (C-47A-85-DL)	20063	N63107	0044	0988	2 PW R-1830	12202	Freighter		
☐ N136FS	Boeing (Douglas) DC-3C (C-47A-60-DL)	10267	N58296	0043	1287	2 PW R-1830	12202	Freighter		
☐ N153JR	Convair 440 Metropolitan	117	N453GA	0053	0896	2 PW R-2800	21772	Freighter		cvtd CV340-38
☐ N155JR	Convair 440-86 Metropolitan	433	N455GA	0057	0596	2 PW R-2800	21772	Freighter		
☐ N323CF	Convair 440-75 Metropolitan	323	SE-CCU	0056	0595	2 PW R-2800	21772	Freighter		

4W AIR (William H. Woodin dba / Seasonal May-October ops only)

Soldotna, AK

PO Box 4401, Soldotna, AK 99669, USA ☎ (907) 776-5370 Tx: none Fax: (907) 776-5370 SITA: n/a
F: 1985 👥 n/a Head: William H. Woodin Net: n/a Aircraft below MTOW 1361kg: Piper PA-18 (on Floats)

☐ N68073	De Havilland DHC-2 Beaver I	1005	55-4607	0056	0592	1 PW R-985	2313			Floats

FRANCE FLYING SERVICE, Inc.

Rawlins-Municipal, WY

PO Box 606, Rawlins, WY 82301, USA ☎ (307) 324-2361 Tx: none Fax: (307) 324-2726 SITA: n/a
F: 1975 👥 n/a Head: Dwight H. France Net: n/a Aircraft below MTOW 1361kg: Cessna 180 & Piper PA-18

☐ N7610C	Cessna TU206G Turbo Stationair	U20603924		0077	0881	1 CO TSIO-520-M	1633			
☐ N6364C	Cessna T210N Turbo Centurion II	21063875		0080	0781	1 CO TSIO-520-R	1814			
☐ N5169J	Cessna 340A II	340A0004		0072	0389	2 CO TSIO-520-N	2717			
☐ N519SC	Cessna 340A II	340A0720		0079	0297	2 CO TSIO-520-NB	2717			

FREEDOM AIR = FRE (Aviation Services (CNMI), Ltd dba)

Guam-Ab Won Pat Int'l, GU

PO Box 1578, Agana, GU 96910, USA ☎ 472-8010 Tx: 3388110 mci uw Fax: 649-0729 SITA: n/a
F: 1974 👥 34 Head: Joaquin L. Flores, Jr. ICAO: FREEDOM Net: n/a Aircraft below MTOW 1361 kg: Cessna 172

☐ N4168R	Piper PA-32-300 Cherokee SIX	32-40484		0068	0190	1 LY IO-540-K1A5	1542	Y5		
☐ N4171R	Piper PA-32-300 Cherokee SIX	32-40504		0068	0987	1 LY IO-540-K1A5	1542	Y5		
☐ N8628N	Piper PA-32-300 Cherokee SIX	32-7140021		0071	1085	1 LY IO-540-K1A5	1542	Y5		
☐ N8938N	Piper PA-32-300C Cherokee SIX	32-40736		0069	0577	1 LY IO-540-K1A5	1542	Y5		
☐ N8969N	Piper PA-32-300C Cherokee SIX	32-40769		0069	0891	1 LY IO-540-K1A5	1542	Y5		
☐ N44FA	Cessna 207A Stationair 8 II	20700659	N75975	0080	0389	1 CO IO-520-F	1724	Y7		
☐ N72FA	Piper PA-31-310 Navajo C	31-7812023	JA5278	0078	0293	2 LY TIO-540-A2C	2948	Y7		
☐ N76NF	Shorts 330-200 (SD3-30)	SH3044	N344SB*	0080	0193	2 PWC PT6A-45R	10387	Y30		

FREEFALL EXPRESS, Inc.

Deland-Municipal, FL

1600 Flightline Blvd, Deland, FL 32724, USA ☎ (352) 738-0120 Tx: none Fax: (352) 822-4227 SITA: n/a
F: 1986 👥 n/a Head: William Richards Net: n/a

☐ N355AG	Eurocopter (Aerosp.) AS355F1 TwinStar	5109	N182EA	0082	0797	2 AN 250-C20F	2300	Para		
☐ N2185M	Pilatus PC-6/B1-H2 Turbo Porter	687	A14-687	0068	0494	1 PWC PT6A-27	2200	Para		
☐ N122PM	De Havilland DHC-6 Twin Otter 100	15	N346MA	0066	0787	2 PWC PT6A-20	5252	Para		
☐ N123FX	De Havilland DHC-6 Twin Otter 210	200	G-BUOM	0068	0293	2 PWC PT6A-20	5252	Para		Blue Sky Express
☐ N40269	De Havilland DHC-6 Twin Otter 200	152	F-GHXY	0068	1293	2 PWC PT6A-20	5252	Para		
☐ N716NC	De Havilland DHC-6 Twin Otter 100	110	N925SM	0068	0690	2 PWC PT6A-20	5252	Para		

FRESH AIR, Inc. (Sister company of Four Star Aviation, Inc.)

St. Thomas-Cyril E. King, VI

One Air Cargo Center, Cyril E. King, St. Thomas, VI 00802, USA ☎ (340) 776-4702 Tx: none Fax: (340) 776-5536 SITA: n/a
F: 1996 👥 n/a Head: Curtis R. White Net: n/a Operates cargo flights with Convair 440 aircraft leased from FOUR STAR AVIATION when required.

FRESH WATER ADVENTURES, Inc. (Seasonal May-October ops only)

Dillingham, AK

PO Box 126, Cheshire, OR 97419, USA ☎ (541) 998-3284 Tx: none Fax: (541) 998-1285 SITA: n/a
F: 1991 👥 3 Head: Lester L. Bingman Net: http://www.fresh-h20.com

☐ N139F	Grumman G-44 Widgeon	1375	N101KB	0045	0492	2 CO IO-470-M	2449			lsf pvt / Amphibian
☐ N4763C	Grumman G-21A Goose	B-86		0044	0095	2 PW R-985	4082			lsf pvt / Amphibian
☐ N7F	Grumman G-21A Goose	B-55		0044	1093	2 PW R-985	4082			lsf pvt / Amphibian

FRONTIER AIR (Arthur D. Hayes dba)

Gustavus, AK

PO Box 1, Gustavus, AK 99826, USA ☎ (907) 697-2386 Tx: none Fax: (907) 697-2342 SITA: n/a
F: 1997 👥 n/a Head: Arthur D. Hayes Net: n/a

☐ N6621X	Cessna U206G Stationair 6 II	U20605970		0080	0297	1 CO IO-520-F	1633			

FRONTIER AIRLINES, Inc. = F9 / FFT ("The Spirit of the West")

Denver-Int'l, CO

12015 East 46th Ave, Denver, CO 80239-3116, USA ☎ (303) 371-7400 Tx: none Fax: (303) 371-7007 SITA: n/a
F: 1994 👥 725 Head: Samuel Addoms IATA: 422 ICAO: FRONTIER FLIGHT Net: http://www.flyfrontier.com

☐ N1PC	Boeing 737-2P6 (A)	21613 / 530	A6-AAA	0078	1198	2 PW JT8D-15 (HK3/NOR)	53070	Y108		lsf INTL
☐ N205AU	Boeing 737-201	19421 / 53	N737N	0068	0994	2 PW JT8D-9A	49442	Y108		lsf FSBU Trustee/Fox & Raccoon-motif cs
☐ N207AU	Boeing 737-201	19423 / 67	N740N	0068	0694	2 PW JT8D-9A	49442	Y108		lsf FSBU Trustee/Bear & Coyote-motif cs
☐ N212US	Boeing 737-201	20212 / 159	N743N	0069	0794	2 PW JT8D-9A	49442	Y108		lsf FSBU Trustee/Buffalo & Ram-motif cs
☐ N214AU	Boeing 737-201	20214 / 172	N745N	0069	0794	2 PW JT8D-9A	49442	Y108		lsf FSBU Trustee/Fawn&Mtn.Goat-motif cs
☐ N217US	Boeing 737-201	20215 / 207	N746N	0069	1094	2 PW JT8D-9A	49442	Y108		lsf FSBUTrustee/Eagle&Mtn.Lion-motif cs
☐ N270FL	Boeing 737-2L9 (A)	22733 / 812	N170PL	0081	0696	2 PW JT8D-17 (HK3/NOR)	58105	Y108		lsf POLA / Mule Deer & Owl-motif colors
☐ N271FL	Boeing 737-2L9 (A)	22734 / 818	N171PL	1181	0696	2 PW JT8D-17 (HK3/NOR)	58105	Y108		lsf POLA / Goose & Heron-motif colors
☐ N303FL	Boeing 737-3M8	25039 / 2007	OO-LTJ	0391	1296	2 CFMI CFM56-3B2	61235	Y138		303 / lsf Sanwa/Bear Cub&Hawk-motif cs
☐ N304FL	Boeing 737-3Q8	27633 / 2878		0097	0597	2 CFMI CFM56-3C1	62823	Y138		304 / lsf ILFC / Moose & Wolf-motif cs
☐ N305FA	Boeing 737-36Q	28662 / 2914		0097	0897	2 CFMI CFM56-3C1	62823	Y138		305 / lsf BOUL / Papa Lynx&Baby Lynx-cs
☐ N306FL	Boeing 737-36N	28563 / 2921		0897	0897	2 CFMI CFM56-3C1	62823	Y138		306 / lsf GECA/Snow Hark & Pelican-cs
☐ N307FL	Boeing 737-36Q	28760 / 2989		0098	0298	2 CFMI CFM56-3C1	62823	Y138		307 / lsf BOUL/Dolphin sunset&water-cs
☐ N308FL	Boeing 737-3U3	28738 / 2988	N6069R*	0098	1198	2 CFMI CFM56-3C1	63276	Y138		lsf Heller Financial Inc.
☐ N309FL	Boeing 737-3U3	28734 / 2974	N6067E*	1297	0299	2 CFMI CFM56-3C1	63276	Y138		lsf ANZ
☐ N578US	Boeing 737-301	23257 / 1124	N305P	0085	1095	2 CFMI CFM56-3B1	62823	Y138		301 / lsfGECA/FoxPups&PolarBears-mot.cs
☐ EI-CHH	Boeing 737-317	23177 / 1216	PT-WBG	0086	1095	2 CFMI CFM56-3B1	61235	Y136		302 / lsf GECA/Mallard&Mustang-motif cs

FRONTIER FLYING SERVICE, Inc. = 2F / FTA

Fairbanks-Int'l, AK

3820 University Avenue, Fairbanks, AK 99709, USA ☎ (907) 474-0014 Tx: none Fax: (907) 474-0774 SITA: n/a
F: 1959 👥 60 Head: John Hajdukovich IATA: 517 ICAO: FRONTIER-AIR Net: http://www.frontierflying.com

☐ N1785U	Cessna 207A Skywagon	20700385		0077	0877	1 CO IO-520-F	1724	Y5		lsf pvt
☐ N200AK	Piper PA-31-350 Navajo Chieftain	31-8052180		0080	0983	2 LY TIO-540-J2BD	3175	Y9		
☐ N3536B	Piper PA-31-350 Navajo Chieftain	31-7952205		0079	0388	2 LY TIO-540-J2BD	3175	Y9		
☐ N4112K	Piper PA-31-350 T1020	31-8353006		0083	0994	2 LY TIO-540-J2B	3175	Y9		
☐ N4301C	Piper PA-31-350 T1020	31-8353001		0083	0395	2 LY TIO-540-J2B	3175	Y9		
☐ N59870	Piper PA-31-310 Navajo C	31-7612071		0076	0690	2 LY TIO-540-A2C	2948	Y7		lsf pvt
☐ N7164D	Piper PA-31-350 Navajo Chieftain	31-8052013	C-GBGI	0080	0090	2 LY TIO-540-J2BD	3175	Y9		lsf Society of Jesus Alaska
☐ N575W	Beech C99 Airliner	U-204	N199ME	0083	0792	2 PWC PT6A-36	5126	Y15		
☐ N4277C	Beech 1300 Airliner	BB-1309	N309YV	0088	0796	2 PWC PT6A-42	5670	Y13		cvtd Super King Air B200
☐ N575T	Beech 1300 Airliner	BB-1384	N912YW	0090	0396	2 PWC PT6A-42	5670	Y13		cvtd Super King Air B200
☐ N575A	Beech 1900C-1 Airliner	UC-83	N80334	0089	0598	2 PWC PT6A-65B	7530	Y19		lsf Raytheon Aircraft Credit Corp.
☐ N575Q	Beech 1900C-1 Airliner	UC-160	N160AM	0591	0598	2 PWC PT6A-65B	7530	Y19		lsf Raytheon Aircraft Credit Corp.
☐ N59314	Boeing (Douglas) DC-3C (C-47A-10-DK)	12363	C-GABE	0044	0782	2 PW R-1830	12202	Freighter		lsf pvt

340 registration type of aircraft cn/fn ex/ex* mfd del powered by mtow kg configuration selcal name/fln/specialitites/remarks

F.S. AIR SERVICE, Inc.

Anchorage-Int'l, AK

6121 South Airpark Place, Anchorage, AK 99502, USA ☎ (907) 248-9595 Tx: none Fax: (907) 243-1247 SITA: n/a
F: 1986 ⁂ n/a Head: Sandra Saltz Net: http://www.micronet.net/fsair

registration	type of aircraft	cn/fn	ex/ex*	mfd	del	powered by	mtow kg	configuration	selcal	name/fln/specialitites/remarks
N503FS	Piper PA-34-220T Seneca III	34-8133098	N8SN	0081	0494	2 CO TSIO-360-KB	2155			
N509FS	Piper PA-31-350 Navajo Chieftain	31-7952162	N35249	0079	1289	2 LY TIO-540-J2BD	3175			
N74923	Piper PA-31-350 Navajo Chieftain	31-7305066		0073	0896	2 LY TIO-540-J2BD	3175			
N508FS	Volpar Turboliner	BA-688	N800TH	0064	0690	2 GA TPE331-1-101B	5216	Freighter		lsf KFS / cvtd Beech H18
N700WA	Volpar Turboliner	BA-28	N3626B	0054	0690	2 GA TPE331-1-101B	5216	Freighter		lsf KFS / cvtd Beech E18S
N504FS	Shorts Skyvan 3 Variant 100 (SC-7)	SH1953	N38314	0077	0789	2 GA TPE331-2-201A	5670			
N502FS	CASA 212 Aviocar Srs 200	294	N31BR	0083	0392	2 GA TPE331-10-501C	7450			
N505FS	Fairchild (Swearingen) SA227AC Metro III	AC-591	N176SW	0084	0996	2 GA TPE331-11U-611G	6577			cvtd SA227AT
N90WR	Learjet 35	35-022	OY-BLG	0075	1095	2 GA TFE731-2-2B	8301	Freighter		lsf Pacific Coast Lease Corp.

FUN AIR, Corporation

Miami-Int'l, FL

3655 NW 87th Avenue, MSAC-401S, Miami, FL 33178-2428, USA ☎ (305) 599-2600 Tx: none Fax: (305) 471-4758 SITA: n/a
F: 1984 ⁂ n/a Head: Ted Arison Net: n/a Operates executive flights for contract-clients only.

registration	type of aircraft	cn/fn	ex/ex*	mfd	del	powered by	mtow kg	configuration	selcal	name/fln/specialitites/remarks
N727LA	Boeing 727-21	19260 / 412	N727SG	0067	0584	3 PW JT8D-7B (HK3/FDX)	72802	Executive		

GAI AIRCRAFT CHARTER (Airwest, Inc. dba)

Worcester-Municipal, MA

PO Box 174, New Braintree, MA 01531, USA ☎ (508) 755-2801 Tx: none Fax: (508) 867-8942 SITA: n/a
F: 1993 ⁂ n/a Head: Steve Grady Net: n/a

registration	type of aircraft	cn/fn	ex/ex*	mfd	del	powered by	mtow kg	configuration	selcal	name/fln/specialitites/remarks
N756AR	Cessna R182 Skylane RG II	R18201024		0079	1293	1 LY O-540-J3C5D	1406			
N411JL	Piper PA-32R-301 Saratoga SP	32R-8213047		0082	0497	1 LY IO-540-K1G5D	1633			

GAIL FORCE, Corporation

Janesville-Rock County, WI

4746 South Columbia Drive, Janesville, WI 53546, USA ☎ (608) 756-1000 Tx: none Fax: (608) 756-5719 SITA: n/a
F: 1993 ⁂ n/a Head: Mark T. Jacobson Net: n/a Aircraft below MTOW 1361kg: Cessna 172 & Piper PA-28

registration	type of aircraft	cn/fn	ex/ex*	mfd	del	powered by	mtow kg	configuration	selcal	name/fln/specialitites/remarks
N9446Q	Beech Baron 58	TH-236		0072	0197	2 CO IO-520-C	2404			
N4833A	Cessna 340A II	340A1026		0080	0795	2 CO TSIO-520-NB	2717			lsf Thor Enterprises Inc.
N27299	Piper PA-31-350 Navajo Chieftain	31-7752128		0077	0197	2 LY TIO-540-J2BD	3175			
N103AF	Beech G18S	BA-526	N277S	0060	0197	2 PW R-985-AN14B	4581	Freighter		
N166H	Beech E18S	BA-253		0056	0197	2 PW R-985-AN14B	4581	Freighter		
N200RX	Mitsubishi MU-2J (MU-2B-35) Cargoliner	548	N68DA	0072	1095	2 GA TPE331-6-251M	4899	Freighter		lsf Internet Jet/Cavenaugh SCD convers.
N298MA	Mitsubishi MU-2J (MU-2B-35) Cargoliner	594		0073	0896	2 GA TPE331-6-251M	4899	Freighter		lsf ExecutiveCashSvcs/Cavenaugh SCD cv.
N680CA	Mitsubishi MU-2J (MU-2B-35) Cargoliner	642	N492MA	0074	0195	2 GA TPE331-6-251M	4899	Freighter		lsf Thor Enterpr./Cavenaugh SCD conver.
N81601	Mitsubishi MU-2J (MU-2B-35) Cargoliner	577	C-FBAN	0073	1295	2 GA TPE331-6-251M	4899	Freighter		lsf Air Lease Inc./Cavenaugh SCD conv.
N915RF	Mitsubishi MU-2L (MU-2B-36) Cargoliner	677	N2ND	0075	0596	2 GA TPE331-6-251M	5250	Freighter		lsf Thor Enterpr./Cavenaugh SCD conver.

GALLUP FLYING SERVICES, Inc.

Gallup-Municipal, NM

West Highway 66, Gallup, NM 87301, USA ☎ (505) 863-6606 Tx: none Fax: (505) 863-4381 SITA: n/a
F: 1976 ⁂ n/a Head: Thomas J. Sheppard Net: n/a Aircraft below MTOW 1361kg: Cessna 172

registration	type of aircraft	cn/fn	ex/ex*	mfd	del	powered by	mtow kg	configuration	selcal	name/fln/specialitites/remarks
N9700M	Cessna U206G Stationair 6 II	U20604557		0078	0878	1 CO IO-520-F	1633			
N29359	Cessna 210L Centurion II	21059858		0073	0681	1 CO IO-520-L	1724			
N7909Q	Cessna T310Q	310Q0620		0073	1278	2 CO TSIO-520-B	2495			
N41BG	Cessna 340A II	340A0305		0077	0186	2 CO TSIO-520-N	2717			
N6640C	Cessna 414A Chancellor III	414A0044		0078	0590	2 CO TSIO-520-N	3062			
N68149	Cessna 414A Chancellor III	414A0642		0081	0591	2 CO TSIO-520-NB	3062			
N8840K	Cessna 414A Chancellor III	414A0236		0079	0992	2 CO TSIO-520-NB	3062			
N986GM	Cessna 414A Chancellor III	414A0089		0078	1092	2 CO TSIO-520-N	3062			

G & L AIRSERVICE (George E. Walters dba)

Bethel, AK

PO Box 1612, Bethel, AK 99559-1612, USA ☎ (907) 543-5323 Tx: none Fax: (907) 543-3820 SITA: n/a
F: 1984 ⁂ n/a Head: George E. Walters Net: n/a

registration	type of aircraft	cn/fn	ex/ex*	mfd	del	powered by	mtow kg	configuration	selcal	name/fln/specialitites/remarks
N1576H	Cessna A185F Skywagon	18503309		0077	0884	1 CO IO-520-D	1520			Floats / Wheels

G & S AVIATION

Donnelly, ID

PO Box 280, Donnelly, ID 83615, USA ☎ (208) 325-4432 Tx: none Fax: (208) 325-5020 SITA: n/a
F: 1995 ⁂ n/a Head: George W. Dorris Net: n/a Aircraft below MTOW 1361kg: Cessna 182

registration	type of aircraft	cn/fn	ex/ex*	mfd	del	powered by	mtow kg	configuration	selcal	name/fln/specialitites/remarks
N2119V	Britten-Norman BN-2B-26 Islander	2105	XA-MAP	0081	0895	2 LY O-540-E4C5	2994			

GE Corporate Air Operations (GE Air Transport Services, Inc. dba / Subsidiary of General Electric Co.)

White Plains-Westchester County, NY

73 Tower Road, White Plains, NY 10604, USA ☎ (914) 287-6600 Tx: none Fax: (914) 287-6641 SITA: n/a
F: 1980 ⁂ n/a Head: Richard Sismour Net: n/a Operates non-commercial corporate flights exclusively for the GE group of companies.

registration	type of aircraft	cn/fn	ex/ex*	mfd	del	powered by	mtow kg	configuration	selcal	name/fln/specialitites/remarks
N362G	Sikorsky S-76C	760441		0096	0796	2 TU Arriel 1S1	5307	Corporate		
N363G	Sikorsky S-76C	760442		0096	0796	2 TU Arriel 1S1	5307	Corporate		
N372G	Canadair CL-604 (CL-600-2B16) Challen.	5351	N374G	0097	1097	2 GE CF34-3B	21591	Corporate		
N374G	Canadair CL-604 (CL-600-2B16) Challen.	5368	N368G	0098	0298	2 GE CF34-3B	21591	Corporate		
N364G	GAC G-IV Gulfstream IV	1091	N467GA	0089	0389	2 RR Tay 611-8	33203	Corporate		
N365G	GAC G-IV Gulfstream IV	1101	N404GA	0089	0889	2 RR Tay 611-8	33203	Corporate		
N366G	Boeing 737-75V (BBJ)	28581 / 126	N1787B*	0098	1198	2 CFMI CFM56-7B26	69400	Corporate		

GEMINI AIR CARGO, Llc = GR / GCO

Minneapolis/St. Paul, MN

44965 Aviation Drive, Dulles, VA 20166, USA ☎ (703) 260-8100 Tx: none Fax: (703) 260-8102 SITA: IADGCXH
F: 1995 ⁂ 350 Head: William D. Stockbridge IATA: 358 ICAO: GEMINI Net: n/a Operates all-cargo services on behalf of several airlines.

registration	type of aircraft	cn/fn	ex/ex*	mfd	del	powered by	mtow kg	configuration	selcal	name/fln/specialitites/remarks
N600GC	Boeing (Douglas) DC-10-30F	46965 / 245	D-ADMO	0077	0995	3 GE CF6-50C2	260000	Freighter	AL-CJ	Christopher / lsf GeminiLeasing/cvtd-30
N601GC	Boeing (Douglas) DC-10-30F	47921 / 117	D-ADAO	0073	1295	3 GE CF6-50C2	260000	Freighter	CH-AG	Molly / lsf Gemini Leasing Inc./cvtd-30
N602GC	Boeing (Douglas) DC-10-30F	47923 / 123	D-ADCO	0074	0396	3 GE CF6-50C2	260000	Freighter	CL-BK	Doris / lsf Gemini Leasing Inc./cvtd-30
N603GC	Boeing (Douglas) DC-10-30F	47922 / 122	D-ADBO	0074	0596	3 GE CF6-50C2	260000	Freighter	CG-EM	Leslie / lsf Gemini Leasing / cvtd -30
N604GC	Boeing (Douglas) DC-10-30F	47924 / 129	D-ADDO	0074	0196	3 GE CF6-50C2	260000	Freighter	CK-FH	Edward / lsf Gemini Leasing / cvtd -30
N605GC	Boeing (Douglas) DC-10-30F	47925 / 166	D-ADFO	0074	0296	3 GE CF6-50C2	260000	Freighter	CL-FH	Ryan / lsf Gemini Leasing Inc./cvtd -30
N606GC	Boeing (Douglas) DC-10-30F	47929 / 196	PP-AJM	0375	1296	3 GE CF6-50C2	260000	Freighter	CM-BL	Naomi / lsf Gemini Leasing Inc./cvtd-30
N607GC	Boeing (Douglas) DC-10-30F	46978 / 256	N777SJ	0078	1197	3 GE CF6-50C2	260000	Freighter		lsf Gemini Leasing Inc. / cvtd -30
N	Boeing (Douglas) DC-10-30F	46921 / 214	G-BEBM*	0076		3 GE CF6-50C2	260000	Freighter		tblsf Gemini Lsng 0999/cvtd -30/ex BAW
N	Boeing (Douglas) DC-10-30F	47840 / 337	G-BHDJ*	0080		3 GE CF6-50C2	260000	Freighter		tblsf Gemini Lsng 0999/cvtd -30/ex BAW
N	Boeing (Douglas) DC-10-30F	46932 / 158	G-NIUK	0074		3 GE CF6-50C2	260000	Freighter		tblsf Gemini Lsng 0200/cvtd -30/ex BAW

GENAVCO AIR CARGO (Genavco Corporation dba)

Honolulu-Int'l, HI

38 Lagoon Drive, Honolulu, HI 96819, USA ☎ (808) 836-3467 Tx: none Fax: (808) 836-3467 SITA: n/a
F: 1982 ⁂ n/a Head: Harry J. Clark Net: n/a

registration	type of aircraft	cn/fn	ex/ex*	mfd	del	powered by	mtow kg	configuration	selcal	name/fln/specialitites/remarks
N99131	Boeing (Douglas) DC-3C (C-47A-65-DL)	18949	VH-ANX	0043	0378	2 PW R-1830	12202	Freighter		Tyranna
N9796N	Boeing (Douglas) Super DC-3S (C-117D)	43375	C-FLED	0044	0695	2 WR R-1820	13301	Freighter		cvtd R4D-5 cn 12879

GENE HARNED, Inc.

Chico-Municipal, CA

4185 Sanders Road, Live Oak, CA 95953, USA ☎ (530) 674-5082 Tx: none Fax: (530) 695-3030 SITA: n/a
F: 1980 ⁂ n/a Head: Gene Harned Net: n/a

registration	type of aircraft	cn/fn	ex/ex*	mfd	del	powered by	mtow kg	configuration	selcal	name/fln/specialitites/remarks
N3880J	Sikorsky UH-34D (S-58)	58-1410	148821	0061	0984	1 WR R-1820	5897			

GENERAL AIRCRAFT SERVICES (Carl D. Hagglund dba)

Pendleton-Eastern Oregon Regional, OR

5101 NWA Avenue, Pendleton, OR 97801, USA ☎ (541) 276-3554 Tx: none Fax: (514) 278-9934 SITA: n/a
F: 1982 ⁂ n/a Head: Carl D. Hagglund Net: n/a Aircraft below MTOW 1361kg: Cessna 182 & Enstrom F28C/F

registration	type of aircraft	cn/fn	ex/ex*	mfd	del	powered by	mtow kg	configuration	selcal	name/fln/specialitites/remarks
N3463L	Cessna TU206B Super Skywagon	U206-0763		0067	0198	1 CO TSIO-520-C	1633			
N1219T	Piper PA-34-200 Seneca	34-7250265		0072	1296	2 LY IO-360-C1E6	1905			

GENERAL MOTORS - Worldwide Travel Services = GMC (Worldwide Travel Services division of General Motors Corporation)

Detroit-Metro, MI

Metro Airport, Building 530, E. Services Dr., Detroit, MI 48242, USA ☎ (734) 942-5650 Tx: none Fax: (734) 942-5601 SITA: n/a
F: 1960 ⁂ n/a Head: Kenneth Emerick ICAO: GENERAL MOTORS Net: n/a Operates non-commercial corporate flights for its parent company only.

registration	type of aircraft	cn/fn	ex/ex*	mfd	del	powered by	mtow kg	configuration	selcal	name/fln/specialitites/remarks
N5113	Cessna 750 Citation X	750-0013		0097	0297	2 AN AE3007C	16193	Corporate C8		
N5114	Cessna 750 Citation X	750-0017		0097	0597	2 AN AE3007C	16193	Corporate C8		
N5115	Cessna 750 Citation X	750-0018		0097	0697	2 AN AE3007C	16193	Corporate C8		
N5116	Cessna 750 Citation X	750-0019		0097	0697	2 AN AE3007C	16193	Corporate C8		
N5123	Saab 2000	2000-020	N5123L	0095	0196	2 AN AE2100A	22800	Corporate C37		
N5124	Saab 2000	2000-027	SE-027*	0095	1295	2 AN AE2100A	22800	Corporate C37		
N5125	Saab 2000	2000-030	SE-030*	0095	1295	2 AN AE2100A	22800	Corporate C37		
N5104	GAC G-1159A Gulfstream III	443	N315GA*	0084	1184	2 RR Spey 511-8	31615	Corporate C12		
N5105	GAC G-1159A Gulfstream III	445	N316GA*	0084	1284	2 RR Spey 511-8	31615	Corporate C12		

GENESIS AVIATION, Inc. — Van Nuys, CA

7435 Valjean Avenue, Van Nuys, CA 91506, USA ☎ (818) 988-2440 Tx: none Fax: (818) 988-2548 SITA: n/a
F: 1997 ⁂ n/a Head: Ramy El-Batrawi Net: n/a Operates executive flights exclusively for contract-customers.

registration	type of aircraft	cn/fn	ex/ex*	mfd	del	powered by	mtow kg	configuration	selcal	name/fln/specialitites/remarks
☐ N120NE	Boeing (Douglas) DC-9-15	45731 / 34	HB-IFA	0066	0997	2 PW JT8D-7A (HK3/ABS)	41141	Executive		
☐ N13FE	Boeing (Douglas) DC-9-14	45706 / 61	N5NE	0066	1297	2 PW JT8D-7B	41141	Executive		

GENI AIRCRAFT, Corp. (Georgetown Aircraft Services, Inc., a Helmsley Company dba) — Georgetown-Sussex County, DE

15 Nanticoke Avenue, Georgetown, DE 19947, USA ☎ (302) 855-2440 Tx: none Fax: (302) 855-2444 SITA: n/a
F: 1988 ⁂ 10 Head: Ronald Hoskins Net: n/a Operates non-commercial VIP flights for its owners only.

registration	type of aircraft	cn/fn	ex/ex*	mfd	del	powered by	mtow kg	configuration	selcal	name/fln/specialitites/remarks
☐ N18HH	Boeing 727-30 (RE) (Super 27)	18936 / 249	N5073L	0066	0388	3 PW JT8D-217C/9A (BFG)	72802	VIP	FJ-CL	cvtd -30

GEO AIR (RPG Airlift, Inc. dba / Associated with One by Air, Inc.) — Boca Raton, FL

2424 North Federal Highway, Suite 151, Boca Raton, FL 33431, USA ☎ (954) 394-4322 Tx: none Fax: (954) 394-4304 SITA: n/a
F: 1995 ⁂ 9 Head: John M. Gerbas, Jr. Net: n/a

registration	type of aircraft	cn/fn	ex/ex*	mfd	del	powered by	mtow kg	configuration	selcal	name/fln/specialitites/remarks
☐ N41527	Convair 440-72 (C-131E) Metropolitan	346	C-FPUM	0056	1195	2 PW R-2800	21772	Freighter		lsf Air Safaris Inc.
☐ N905GA	Convair 580 (F) (SCD)	121	C-FMGC	0053	0698	2 AN 501-D13	26379	Freighter		cvtd CV 440

GEORGIA-PACIFIC – Flight Operations Dept. (Flight Operations Dept. of Georgia-Pacific Corporation) — Atlanta-Fulton County/Brown Field & -Hartsfield Int'l, GA

3905 Aero Road, Suite 8R-8, Atlanta, GA 30336, USA ☎ (770) 652-4000 Tx: none Fax: (770) 691-4805 SITA: n/a
F: 1968 ⁂ n/a Head: Dewey L. Mobley Net: n/a Operates non-commercial corporate flights exclusively for its parent company which is mainly active in forestry products, construction material & rail-transportation.

registration	type of aircraft	cn/fn	ex/ex*	mfd	del	powered by	mtow kg	configuration	selcal	name/fln/specialitites/remarks
☐ N225GP	Bell 206L-4 LongRanger IV	52143	N88EA	0095	0296	1 AN 250-C30P	2018	Corporate		
☐ N510GP	Cessna 550 Citation II	550-0421	N67HW	0082	1295	2 PWC JT15D-4	6033	Corporate		
☐ N514GP	BAe 4107 Jetstream 41	41038	N438JX	0094	0796	2 GA TPE331-14HR-805H	10886	Corporate		
☐ N509GP	Hawker 800A (BAe 125-800A)	258077	N523BA	0086	0187	2 GA TFE731-5R-1H	12428	Corporate		
☐ N515GP	Hawker 800XP	258289	N669H	0096	0896	2 GA TFE731-5BR-1H	12701	Corporate		

GEO-SEIS HELICOPTERS, Inc. — Fort Collins-Downtown, CO

116 North Raquette, Fort Collins, CO 80524-2575, USA ☎ (970) 484-3600 Tx: none Fax: (970) 482-8463 SITA: n/a
F: 1982 ⁂ n/a Head: William T. Browder Net: n/a

registration	type of aircraft	cn/fn	ex/ex*	mfd	del	powered by	mtow kg	configuration	selcal	name/fln/specialitites/remarks
☐ N180US	Eurocopter (Aerosp.) SA315B Lama	2631		0082	1193	1 TU Artouste IIIB	1950			lsf Roberts Aircraft Co.
☐ N230US	Eurocopter (Aerosp.) SA315B Lama	2638	C-GPHQ	0082	0195	1 TU Artouste IIIB	1950			lsf Roberts Aircraft Co.
☐ N27443	Eurocopter (Aerosp.) SA315B Lama	2426		0075	0788	1 TU Artouste IIIB	1950			lsf Roberts Aircraft Co.
☐ N3128G	Eurocopter (Aerosp.) SA315B Lama	2488		0075	0589	1 TU Artouste IIIB	1950			lsf Roberts Aircraft Co.
☐ N345RA	Eurocopter (Aerosp.) SA315B Lama	2591	G-BNNF	0080	1296	1 TU Artouste IIIB	1950			lsf Roberts Aircraft Co.
☐ N348RA	Eurocopter (Aerosp.) SA315B Lama	2569	VR-HIP	0079	0497	1 TU Artouste IIIB	1950			lsf Roberts Aircraft Co.
☐ N37903	Eurocopter (Aerosp.) SA315B Lama	2565	LN-ORX	0079	0491	1 TU Artouste IIIB	1950			lsf Roberts Aircraft Co.
☐ N402AH	Eurocopter (Aerosp.) SA315B Lama	2484	C-FZXZ	0876	0898	1 TU Artouste IIIB	1950			lsf Roberts Aircraft Co.
☐ N42PL	Eurocopter (Aerosp.) SA315B Lama	2438		0076	1290	1 TU Artouste IIIB	1950			lsf Roberts Aircraft Co.
☐ N47273	Eurocopter (Aerosp.) SA315B Lama	2446		0075	0984	1 TU Artouste IIIB	1950			lsf Roberts Aircraft Co.
☐ N47294	Eurocopter (Aerosp.) SA315B Lama	2448		0075	0981	1 TU Artouste IIIB	1950			lsf Roberts Aircraft Co.
☐ N49511	Eurocopter (Aerosp.) SA315B Lama	2485		0077	0795	1 TU Artouste IIIB	1950			lsf Roberts Aircraft Co.
☐ N57948	Eurocopter (Aerosp.) SA315B Lama	2628		0082	0993	1 TU Artouste IIIB	1950			lsf Trans Aero Ltd
☐ N58000	Eurocopter (Aerosp.) SA315B Lama	2639	C-FSWN	0080	0397	1 TU Artouste IIIB	1950			lsf Roberts Aircraft Co.
☐ N607CD	Eurocopter (Aerosp.) SA315B Lama	2601	VR-HJG	0081	0596	1 TU Artouste IIIB	1950			lsf Roberts Aircraft Co.
☐ N6272Z	Eurocopter (Aerosp.) SA315B Lama	2502	N351RM	0077	0496	1 TU Artouste IIIB	1950			lsf Roberts Aircraft Co.
☐ N65185	Eurocopter (Aerosp.) SA315B Lama	2288	B-HJM	0072	0597	1 TU Artouste IIIB	1950			lsf Trans Aero Ltd
☐ N707EX	Eurocopter (Aerosp.) SA315B Lama	2430	N16297	0076	0190	1 TU Artouste IIIB	1950			lsf Roberts Aircraft Co.
☐ N85356	Eurocopter (Aerosp.) SA315B Lama	2383		0074	0288	1 TU Artouste IIIB	1950			lsf Roberts Aircraft Co.
☐ N9005E	Eurocopter (Aerosp.) SA315B Lama	2538	VR-HHZ	0078	1290	1 TU Artouste IIIB	1950			lsf Roberts Aircraft Co.
☐ N12NT	Eurocopter (Aerosp.) AS350BA AStar	1670	C-FSWI	0083	1296	1 TU Arriel 1B	2100			lsf Roberts Aircraft Co. / cvtd AS350B
☐ N156EH	Eurocopter (Aerosp.) AS350D AStar	1185	N3600B	0079	0695	1 LY LTS101-600A.2	1950			lsf Roberts Aircraft Co.
☐ N20840	Eurocopter (Aerosp.) AS350B AStar	1070	C-FIOC	0079	0796	1 TU Arriel 1B	1950			lsf Roberts Aircraft Co. / cvtd AS350D
☐ N333SA	Eurocopter (Aerosp.) AS350D AStar	1140		0079	0196	1 LY LTS101-600A.2	1950			lsf Roberts Aircraft Co.
☐ N3609R	Eurocopter (Aerosp.) AS350B AStar	1250		0080	0795	1 TU Arriel 1B	1950			lsf Roberts Aircraft Co. / cvtd AS350D
☐ N453NW	Eurocopter (Aerosp.) AS350B2 AStar	2475	HB-XYC	0091	0593	1 TU Arriel 1D1	2250			lsf Roberts Aircraft Co.
☐ N494AM	Eurocopter (Aerosp.) AS350D AStar	1125		0079	0196	1 LY LTS101-600A.2	1950			lsf Roberts Aircraft Co.
☐ N5771L	Eurocopter (Aerosp.) AS350D AStar	1343		0080	0795	1 LY LTS101-600A.2	1950			lsf Roberts Aircraft Co.
☐ N6093R	Eurocopter (Aerosp.) AS350B2 AStar	2415		0090	0491	1 TU Arriel 1D1	2250			lsf Roberts Aircraft Co.
☐ N6096R	Eurocopter (Aerosp.) AS350B2 AStar	2417		0090	0491	1 TU Arriel 1D1	2250			lsf Roberts Aircraft Co.
☐ N9004G	Eurocopter (Aerosp.) AS350B AStar	1031	F-WZFS	0078	0894	1 TU Arriel 1B	1950			lsf Trans Aero Ltd / cvtd AS350D
☐ N10361	Eurocopter (Aerosp.) SA316B Alouette III	1657		0070	0288	1 TU Artouste IIIB	2200			lsf Roberts Aircraft Co.
☐ N10364	Eurocopter (Aerosp.) SA316B Alouette III	1773		0071	0892	1 TU Artouste IIIB	2200			lsf Roberts Aircraft Co.
☐ N227RA	Eurocopter (Aerosp.) SA316B Alouette III	1227	A-227	0064	1196	1 TU Artouste IIIB	2200			lsf Roberts Aircraft Co. / cvtd SE3160
☐ N3153R	Eurocopter (Aerosp.) SA316B Alouette III	1484		0067	0891	1 TU Artouste IIIB	2200			lsf Roberts Aircraft Co.
☐ N31660	Eurocopter (Aerosp.) SA316B Alouette III	1481		0067	0891	1 TU Artouste IIIB	2200			lsf Roberts Aircraft Co.
☐ N48184	Eurocopter (Aerosp.) SA316B Alouette III	1906		0071	0592	1 TU Artouste IIIB	2200			lsf Roberts Aircraft Co.
☐ N482RA	Eurocopter (Aerosp.) SA316B Alouette III	1482	SE-JCM	0068	0497	1 TU Artouste IIIB	2200			lsf Roberts Aircraft Co.
☐ N49550	Eurocopter (Aerosp.) SA316B Alouette III	2271		0075	0494	1 TU Artouste IIIB	2200			lsf Roberts Aircraft Co.
☐ N49913	Eurocopter (Aerosp.) SA316B Alouette III	1091	FAP9252	0063	1192	1 TU Artouste IIIB	2200			lsf Roberts Aircraft Co. / cvtd SE3160
☐ N499RA	Eurocopter (Aerosp.) SA316B Alouette III	1499	A-499	0068	1196	1 TU Artouste IIIB	2200			lsf Roberts Aircraft Co.
☐ N5109C	Eurocopter (Aerosp.) SA316B Alouette III	2201		0075	0288	1 TU Artouste IIIB	2200			lsf Roberts Aircraft Co.
☐ N5170B	Eurocopter (Aerosp.) SA316B Alouette III	2206		0075	0590	1 TU Artouste IIIB	2200			lsf Roberts Aircraft Co.
☐ N528RA	Eurocopter (Aerosp.) SA316B Alouette III	1528	SE-JCN	0069	1096	1 TU Artouste IIIB	2200			lsf Roberts Aircraft Co.
☐ N529RA	Eurocopter (Aerosp.) SA316B Alouette III	1529	SE-JCO	0069	1096	1 TU Artouste IIIB	2200			lsf Roberts Aircraft Co.
☐ N607RM	Eurocopter (Aerosp.) SA316B Alouette III	1167		0064	0495	1 TU Artouste IIIB	2200			lsf Roberts Aircraft Co. / cvtd SE3160
☐ N72036	Eurocopter (Aerosp.) SA316B Alouette III	1488	A-488	0068	0797	1 TU Artouste IIIB	2200			lsf Roberts Aircraft Co.
☐ N7208L	Eurocopter (Aerosp.) SA316B Alouette III	1483	A-483	0068	0797	1 TU Artouste IIIB	2200			lsf Roberts Aircraft Co.
☐ N7251P	Eurocopter (Aerosp.) SA316B Alouette III	1398	SE-JCT	0072	0597	1 TU Artouste IIIB	2200			lsf Roberts Aircraft Co.
☐ N8099R	Eurocopter (Aerosp.) SA316B Alouette III	1761		0070	0490	1 TU Artouste IIIB	2200			lsf Roberts Aircraft Co.
☐ N8656	Eurocopter (Aerosp.) SA316B Alouette III	1729		0071	1181	1 TU Artouste IIIB	2200			lsf Roberts Aircraft Co.
☐ N91213	Eurocopter (Aerosp.) SA316B Alouette III	2159		0074	0590	1 TU Artouste IIIB	2200			lsf Roberts Aircraft Co.
☐ N9829C	Eurocopter (Aerosp.) SA316B Alouette III	1242	HKG-1	0065	1181	1 TU Artouste IIIB	2200			lsf Roberts Aircraft Co.
☐ N98325	Eurocopter (Aerosp.) SA316B Alouette III	1243	HKG-2	0065	1181	1 TU Artouste IIIB	2200			lsf Roberts Aircraft Co.
☐ N510TG	Eurocopter (Aerosp.) AS355F1 TwinStar	5168	P4-PLH	0082	0696	2 AN 250-C20F	2400			lsf Roberts Aircraft Co.
☐ N57927	Eurocopter (Aerosp.) AS355F1 TwinStar	5122		0082	1197	2 AN 250-C20F	2400			lsf Roberts Aircraft Co.
☐ N117FF	Eurocopter (MBB) BK117A-4	7085	C-GOFJ	0086	0595	2 LY LTS101-650B.1	3200			lsf American Eurocopter Corp./cvtd A-3
☐ N49678	Bell 212	30743	C-FADZ	0075	0297	2 PWC PT6T-3 TwinPac	5080			lsf Trans Aero Ltd

GIBSON AVIATION, Inc. — Pompano Beach-Airpark, FL & Westminster-Carroll County, MD

2731 NE 14th Street, Causeway 206A, Pompano Beach, FL 33062, USA ☎ (956) 946-9231 Tx: none Fax: none SITA: n/a
F: 1977 ⁂ n/a Head: Joseph W.M. Gibson, III Net: n/a Aircraft below MTOW 1361kg: Cessna 172

registration	type of aircraft	cn/fn	ex/ex*	mfd	del	powered by	mtow kg	configuration	selcal	name/fln/specialitites/remarks
☐ N102GA	Beech Baron E55	TE-771		0070	0877	2 CO IO-520-C	2404			lsf pvt
☐ N106GA	Beech Baron 58	TH-437	N4379W	0074	0587	2 CO IO-520-C	2449			lsf pvt
☐ N4445W	Beech Duke A60	P-245		0073	0198	2 LY TIO-541-E1B4	3073			lsf pvt
☐ N107GA	Piper PA-31-350 Navajo Chieftain	31-7405446		0074	0392	2 LY TIO-540-J2BD	3175			lsf pvt
☐ N203GA	Mitsubishi MU-2J (MU-2B-35) Cargoliner	573	N3929L	0072	0396	2 GA TPE331-6-251M	4899			lsf pvt / Cavenaugh SCD conversion

GILA-COPTERS, Llc — Mesa-Falcon Field, AZ

4251 East Edgewood Avenue, Mesa, AZ 85206-2645, USA ☎ (520) 641-8488 Tx: none Fax: (520) 832-6253 SITA: n/a
F: 1992 ⁂ n/a Head: John E. Boyles Net: n/a

registration	type of aircraft	cn/fn	ex/ex*	mfd	del	powered by	mtow kg	configuration	selcal	name/fln/specialitites/remarks
☐ N1255T	Sikorsky S-55BT	55607		0053	1292	1 GA TPE331-3U-303N	3266			cvtd S-55B
☐ N2738	Sikorsky S-55BT	551273		0058	1292	1 GA TPE331-3U-303N	3266			cvtd S-55B

GLIKO AVIATION, Inc. (formerly Dan Gliko Helicopters) — Lewistown-Municipal, MT

579 Belt Creek Road, Belt, MT 59412, USA ☎ (406) 277-3255 Tx: none Fax: (406) 277-3255 SITA: n/a
F: 1964 ⁂ n/a Head: Daniel A. Gliko Net: http://www.aviation.net Aircraft below MTOW 1361kg: Cessna 182

registration	type of aircraft	cn/fn	ex/ex*	mfd	del	powered by	mtow kg	configuration	selcal	name/fln/specialitites/remarks
☐ N1604Z	MD Helicopters MD 500E (Hughes 369E)	0341E		0089	0192	1 AN 250-C20R	1361			

GLOBAL AERONAUTICAL FOUNDATION (Waynes Aviation, Inc. dba) — Camarillo, CA

PO Box 27, Moorpark, CA 93020, USA ☎ (805) 529-1748 Tx: none Fax: (805) 523-1805 SITA: n/a
F: 1994 ⁂ n/a Head: Waynes L. Jones Net: n/a
Non-profit organisation (a tax exempt education foundation) conducting historical flying presentations.

registration	type of aircraft	cn/fn	ex/ex*	mfd	del	powered by	mtow kg	configuration	selcal	name/fln/specialitites/remarks
☐ N548GF	Lockh.L-1049E (EC-121T) S.Const.(tip tks)	4363	53-0548	0055	0495	4 WR R-3350	69173	fly.presentation		

GO HELICOPTERS, Inc. — Alvin-Heliport, TX

PO Box 850, Alvin, TX 77512, USA ☎ (409) 864-3888 Tx: none Fax: (409) 864-4404 SITA: n/a
F: 1994 ⁂ n/a Head: Gregory M. Obert Net: n/a

registration	type of aircraft	cn/fn	ex/ex*	mfd	del	powered by	mtow kg	configuration	selcal	name/fln/specialitites/remarks
☐ N2963W	Bell 206B JetRanger III	817		0072	0397	1 AN 250-C20B	1451			cvtd JetRanger

GO JET, Inc. (Subsidiary of Jet Place, Inc.) — Dallas-Love Field, TX

c/o Business Jet Svcs, 8629 Lemmon Ave, Hangar H, Dallas, TX 75209, USA ☎ (214) 357-7477 Tx: none Fax: (214) 352-3066 SITA: n/a
F: 1998 ⁂ n/a Head: Mrs Stephanie Jordan Net: n/a Operates VIP flights for its parent company only.

registration	type of aircraft	cn/fn	ex/ex*	mfd	del	powered by	mtow kg	configuration	selcal	name/fln/specialitites/remarks
☐ N17MK	BAe (BAC) One-Eleven 410AQ	054	N17VK	0065	0698	2 RR Spey 511-14	40597	VIP		

GOLDEN NUGGET AVIATION, Corp.

Las Vegas-McCarran, NV

3400 Las Vegas Blvd. SO, Las Vegas, NV 89109, USA ☎ (702) 791-7193 Tx: none Fax: (702) 736-6356 SITA: n/a
F: 1991 👥 n/a Head: Stephan A. Wynn Net: n/a Operates executive flights exclusively for the Golden Nugget Hotel & Casino.

☐	N721RB	GAC G-1159A Gulfstream III	311	N311GA	0080	0894	2 RR Spey 511-8	30935	Executive		
☐	N711SW	GAC G-IV Gulfstream IV	1170	N464GA	0091	1091	2 RR Tay 611-8	33203	Executive		
☐	N721EW	Boeing (Douglas) MD-87 (DC-9-87)	49767 / 1587	D-ALLI	0489	1195	2 PW JT8D-219	67812	Executive		

GOLDEN PLOVER AIR (James W. Helmericks dba)

Colville Delta-Helmericks, AK

Colville Village, via Pouch 340109, Prudhoe Bay, AK 99734, USA ☎ (907) 659-3991 Tx: none Fax: none SITA: n/a
F: 1975 👥 3 Head: James W. Helmericks Net: n/a Aircraft below MTOW 1361 kg: Piper PA-18

☐	N8273Q	Cessna U206F Stationair II	U20603134		0076	0677	1 CO IO-520-F	1633			Floats / Wheel-Skis

GOLDEN WEST AIRLINES, Inc. = GW

La Verne-Brackett Field, CA

1615 McKinley Ave., La Verne, CA 91750, USA ☎ (909) 593-3626 Tx: none Fax: (909) 593-1883 SITA: n/a
F: 1994 👥 n/a Head: Andrew A. Pike Net: n/a

☐	N93141	Cessna 210L Centurion II	21060281		0074	0194	1 CO IO-520-L	1724	Freighter		lsf pvt

GRAN-AIRE, Inc.

Milwaukee-Lawrence J. Timmerman, WI

9305 West Appleton Avenue, Milwaukee, WI 53225, USA ☎ (414) 461-3222 Tx: none Fax: (414) 461-8207 SITA: n/a
F: 1950 👥 n/a Head: John W. Lotzer Net: n/a Aircraft below MTOW 1361kg: Cessna 172

☐	N1914G	Cessna 310R II	310R0059		0074	0686	2 CO IO-520-M	2495			
☐	N6209X	Cessna 310R II	310R1339		0078	1093	2 CO IO-520-M	2495			lsf pvt
☐	N3247M	Cessna 414A Chancellor III	414A0828		0081	0888	2 CO TSIO-520-NB	3062			
☐	N5601C	Cessna 414A Chancellor III	414A0113		0078	0694	2 CO TSIO-520-N	3062			lsf Purtell Aviation Inc.
☐	N63JH	Cessna 414A Chancellor III	414A0036		0078	0192	2 CO TSIO-520-N	3062			lsf Morrill Lewis Trustee
☐	N999GA	Beech King Air B200	BB-929	N81AJ	0081	0194	2 PWC PT6A-42	5670			lsf Badger Airlines Inc.

GRAND AIRE EXPRESS, Inc. = GAE

Monroe-Custer, MI

PO Box 721, Monroe, MI 48161, USA ☎ (734) 457-1730 Tx: none Fax: (734) 457-1733 SITA: n/a
F: 1985 👥 170 Head: Tahir S. Cheema ICAO: GRAND EXPRESS Net: http://www.grandaire.com/

☐	N158GA	AAC (Piper) Aerostar 600A	60-0608-7961195	N8208J	0079	0297	2 LY IO-540-K1F5	2495	Pax / Freighter		
☐	N159GA	AAC (Ted Smith) Aerostar 601P	61P-0437-163	N9763Q	0077	0394	2 LY IO-540-S1A5	2722	Pax / Freighter		
☐	N160GA	AAC (Ted Smith) Aerostar 601	61-0021-50	N7436S	0069	0792	2 LY IO-540-P1A5	2585	Pax / Freighter		
☐	N161GA	AAC (Piper) Aerostar 601P	61P-0629-7963287	N321GB	0079	0387	2 LY IO-540-S1A5	2722	Pax / Freighter		
☐	N162GA	AAC (Ted Smith) Aerostar 601	61-0050-95	N7483S	0070	0788	2 LY IO-540-P1A5	2585	Pax / Freighter		
☐	N601GA	AAC (Ted Smith) Aerostar 601P	61P-0282-064	N76AC	0075	0795	2 LY IO-540-S1A5	2722	Pax / Freighter		
☐	N168GA	Fairchild (Swearingen) SA226TC Metro	TC-207	N501AB	0073	0594	2 GA TPE331-10UA-511G	5670	Freighter		lsf Czars Inc.
☐	N164GA	Fairchild (Swearingen) SA226TC Metro II	TC-281	N5473M	0079	1191	2 GA TPE331-10UA-511G	5670	Freighter		
☐	N165GA	Fairchild (Swearingen) SA226TC Metro II	TC-396	N396AV	0081	0491	2 GA TPE331-10UA-511G	5670	Freighter		
☐	N166GA	Fairchild (Swearingen) SA226TC Metro II	TC-337	N256AM	0080	0691	2 GA TPE331-10UA-511G	5670	Freighter		
☐	N167GA	Fairchild (Swearingen) SA226TC Metro II	TC-219	N538S	0075	0390	2 GA TPE331-10UA-511G	5670	Freighter		
☐	N169GA	Fairchild (Swearingen) SA226TC Metro II	TC-376	N251AM	0080	0794	2 GA TPE331-10UA-511G	5670	Freighter		lsf Czars Inc.
☐	N615GA	Fairchild (Swearingen) SA226AT Merlin IV	AT-009	C-FJTC	0073	0197	2 GA TPE331-10UA-511G	5670	Freighter		lsf Arrow Trading Inc.
☐	N616GA	Fairchild (Swearingen) SA226TC Metro II	TC-377	C-FJTD	0080	0197	2 GA TPE331-3UW-303G	5670	Freighter		lsf Arrow Trading Inc.
☐	N171GA	HFB 320 Hansa Jet	1039	N208MM	0069	0691	2 GE CJ610-5	8800	Freighter		
☐	N173GA	HFB 320 Hansa Jet	1052	PT-IDW	0071	0793	2 GE CJ610-5	8800	Freighter		
☐	N176GA	HFB 320 Hansa Jet	1053	PT-IOB	0071	0194	2 GE CJ610-5	8800	Freighter		
☐	N605GA	HFB 320 Hansa Jet	1038	N301AT	0069	0396	2 GE CJ610-5	8800	Freighter		
☐	N777PQ	HFB 320 Hansa Jet	1050	N777PZ	0070	0696	2 GE CJ610-5	8800	Freighter		
☐	N174GA	Dassault Falcon 20C (C)	27	N33TP	0066	0792	2 GE CF700-2C	13000	Freighter		cvtd Falcon 20C
☐	N175GA	Dassault Falcon 20C (C)	45	N202KH	0066	1192	2 GE CF700-2C	13000	Freighter		cvtd Falcon 20C
☐	N179GA	Dassault Falcon 20C (C)	100	I-VEPA	0067	0594	2 GE CF700-2C	13000	Freighter		lsf Czars Inc. / cvtd Falcon 20C
☐	N182GA	Dassault Falcon 20C (C)	146	C-FCDS	0068	0794	2 GE CF700-2C	13000	Freighter		lsf Czars Inc. / cvtd Falcon 20C
☐	N183GA	Dassault Falcon 20C (C)	147	N41154	0068	0994	2 GE CF700-2C	13000	Freighter		lsf Czars Inc. / cvtd Falcon 20C
☐	N184GA	Dassault Falcon 20E (C)	266	N4115B	0072	0894	2 GE CF700-2D2	13000	Freighter		lsf Czars Inc. / cvtd Falcon 20E
☐	N613GA	Dassault Falcon 20C (C)	77	F-GHSG	0067	0495	2 GE CF700-2C	13000	Freighter		lsf TKC Inc. / cvtd Falcon 20C
☐	N614GA	Dassault Falcon 20C	8	N190BD	0065	0597	2 GE CF700-2C	13000	Executive		lsf N190BD Llc
☐	N617GA	Dassault Falcon 20C (C)	88	N41CD	0066	0496	2 GE CF700-2C	13000	Freighter		cvtd Falcon 20C
☐	N618GA	Dassault Falcon 20D (C)	211	8101	0069	1194	2 GE CF700-2D	13000	Freighter		lsf Czars Inc. / cvtd Falcon 20D
☐	N619GA	Dassault Falcon 20D (C)	215	8102	0069	1194	2 GE CF700-2D	13000	Freighter		lsf Czars Inc. / cvtd Falcon 20D

GRAND CANYON AIRLINES, Inc. - GCA = CVU

Grand Canyon-National Park, AZ

PO Box 3038, Grand Canyon, AZ 86023, USA ☎ (520) 638-2463 Tx: none Fax: (520) 638-9461 SITA: n/a
F: 1927 👥 50 Head: John R. Seibold ICAO: CANYON VIEW Net: http://www.travelpos.com/gca/gcahome.htm

☐	N171GC	De Havilland DHC-6 Vista Liner 300	406	N101AC	0074	1089	2 PWC PT6A-27	5670	Y19		cvtd Twin Otter
☐	N173GC	De Havilland DHC-6 Vista Liner 300	295	C-GLAZ	0071	0287	2 PWC PT6A-27	5670	Y19		cvtd Twin Otter
☐	N177GC	De Havilland DHC-6 Vista Liner 300	263	N102AC	0070	1289	2 PWC PT6A-27	5670	Y19		cvtd Twin Otter
☐	N178GC	De Havilland DHC-6 Vista Liner 300	697	N226SA	0080	0294	2 PWC PT6A-27	5670	Y19		cvtd Twin Otter
☐	N72GC	De Havilland DHC-6 Vista Liner 300	264	N264Z	0069	0689	2 PWC PT6A-27	5670	Y19		cvtd Twin Otter
☐	N74GC	De Havilland DHC-6 Vista Liner 300	559	J8-SVD	0077	0284	2 PWC PT6A-27	5670	Y19		cvtd Twin Otter

GRANT AVIATION, Inc. = GS (formerly Delta Air Service, Inc.)

Emmonak, AK

PO Box 89, Emmonak, AK 99581, USA ☎ (907) 949-1715 Tx: none Fax: (907) 949-1848 SITA: n/a
F: 1969 👥 8 Head: Mark W. Hiekel Net: n/a Aircraft below MTOW 1361kg: Cessna 172

☐	N1581U	Cessna 207 Skywagon	20700181		0070	0996	1 CO IO-520-F	1724			
☐	N1864	Cessna 207A Stationair 7 II	20700526		0079	0392	1 CO IO-520-F	1724			
☐	N48CF	Cessna T207A Turbo Skywagon	20700366		0076	0897	1 CO TSIO-520-M	1724			
☐	N562CT	Cessna 207A Stationair 7 II	20700487	HI-562CT	0078	0798	1 CO IO-520-F	1724			
☐	N91090	Cessna 207 Skywagon	20700069		0069	1096	1 CO IO-520-F	1724			
☐	N9728M	Cessna 207A Stationair 8 II	20700721		0081	0897	1 CO IO-520-F	1724			
☐	N9973M	Cessna 207A Stationair 8 II	20700771		0084	0884	1 CO IO-520-F	1724			
☐	N27472	Piper PA-31-350 Navajo Chieftain	31-7852019		0078	0291	2 LY TIO-540-J2BD	3175			lsf pvt
☐	N4105D	Piper PA-31-350 Navajo Chieftain	31-8252027		0082	0396	2 LY TIO-540-J2BD	3175			
☐	N77HV	Piper PA-31-350 Navajo Chieftain	31-8152193	C-GLCN	0081	1096	2 LY TIO-540-J2BD	3175			
☐	N555CG	Beech G18S	BA-539	N321	0060	1094	2 PW R-985-AN14B	4400			
☐	N90PB	Beech King Air 200	BB-125	TG-UGA	0076	0797	2 PWC PT6A-41	5670			

GRAYBACK AVIATION, Inc.

Glendale-Heliport, OR

303 Mehlwood Lane, Glendale, OR 97442, USA ☎ (541) 832-3265 Tx: none Fax: (541) 832-3272 SITA: n/a
F: 1992 👥 n/a Head: Mike Wheelock Net: n/a

☐	N5207C	MD Helicopters MD 500E (Hughes 369E)	0118E		0085	0292	1 AN 250-C20B	1361			

GREAT LAKES AIRLINES = ZK / GLA (United Express) (Great Lakes Aviation, Ltd dba)

Spencer-Municipal, IA

1965 330th Street, Spencer, IA 51301, USA ☎ (712) 262-1000 Tx: none Fax: (712) 262-7215 SITA: n/a
F: 1977 👥 1250 Head: Douglas G. Voss IATA: 846 ICAO: LAKES AIR Net: http://www.greatlakesav.com
All aircraft are operated as UNITED EXPRESS (in full such colours & titles), a commuter system to provide feeder connection at United Airlines major hubs, using UA flight numbers.

☐	N104GL	Beech 1900C-1 Airliner	UC-104	N198GL	0090	0491	2 PWC PT6A-65B	7530	Y19		lsf Raytheon / op in United Express-cs
☐	N105GL	Beech 1900C-1 Airliner	UC-105	N191GL	0090	0590	2 PWC PT6A-65B	7530	Y19		lsf M&G Air Travel Inc./sub-lst GFT
☐	N119GL	Beech 1900C-1 Airliner	UC-119	N119YV	0090	0798	2 PWC PT6A-65B	7530	Y19		op in United Express-colors
☐	N122GL	Beech 1900C-1 Airliner	UC-122	N195GL	0090	0990	2 PWC PT6A-65B	7530	Y19		lsf Raytheon/sub-lst Air Cargo Masters
☐	N123UE	Beech 1900C-1 Airliner	UC-123	N193GL	0090	0990	2 PWC PT6A-65B	7530	Y19		lsf Raytheon / op in United Express-cs
☐	N125GL	Beech 1900C-1 Airliner	UC-125	N196GL	0090	1290	2 PWC PT6A-65B	7530	Y19		lsf Raytheon / op in United Express-cs
☐	N126UE	Beech 1900C-1 Airliner	UC-126	N194GL	0090	1090	2 PWC PT6A-65B	7530	Y19		lsf Raytheon Ac.Receivables/sub-lst GLT
☐	N130UE	Beech 1900C-1 Airliner	UC-130	N197GL	0090	1290	2 PWC PT6A-65B	7530	Y19		lsf Raytheon / op in United Express-cs
☐	N138GL	Beech 1900C-1 Airliner	UC-138	N55668	0090	1093	2 PWC PT6A-65B	7530	Y19		lsf Raytheon Aircraft Credit/sub-lstGLT
☐	N141UE	Beech 1900C-1 Airliner	UC-141	N55132	0090	0993	2 PWC PT6A-65B	7530	Y19		op in United Express-colors
☐	N145GL	Beech 1900C-1 Airliner	UC-145	N55594	0091	1093	2 PWC PT6A-65B	7530	Y19		lsf Raytheon Aircraft Credit/sub-lstGLT
☐	N150UE	Beech 1900C-1 Airliner	UC-150	N55872	0091	1293	2 PWC PT6A-65B	7530	Y19		lst GLT
☐	N159GL	Beech 1900C-1 Airliner	UC-159		0091	0591	2 PWC PT6A-65B	7530	Y19		lsf Iowa Great Lakes Flyers/UA Exp.-cs
☐	N167GL	Beech 1900C-1 Airliner	UC-167		0091	0691	2 PWC PT6A-65B	7530	Y19		lsf Raytheon / op in United Express-cs
☐	N168GL	Beech 1900C-1 Airliner	UC-168	N55782	0091	1193	2 PWC PT6A-65B	7530	Y19		lsf Raytheon / op in United Express-cs
☐	N171GL	Beech 1900C-1 Airliner	UC-171	N55522	0091	1193	2 PWC PT6A-65B	7530	Y19		lst GLT
☐	N86UE	Beech 1900C-1 Airliner	UC-86	N15547	0089	0293	2 PWC PT6A-65B	7530	Y19		lsf Raytheon Ac.Receivables/sub-lst GLT
☐	N89UE	Beech 1900C-1 Airliner	UC-89	N15536	0089	0293	2 PWC PT6A-65B	7530	Y19		lsf Raytheon Ac.Receivables/sub-lst GLT
☐	N96UE	Beech 1900C-1 Airliner	UC-96	N15680	0090	0993	2 PWC PT6A-65B	7530	Y19		op in United Express-colors
☐	N98GL	Beech 1900C-1 Airliner	UC-98	N192GL	0090	0390	2 PWC PT6A-65B	7530	Y19		lsf Raytheon / op in United Express-cs
☐	N100UX	Beech 1900D Airliner	UE-100		0094	0694	2 PWC PT6A-67D	7688	Y19		lsf Raytheon / op in United Express-cs
☐	N101UX	Beech 1900D Airliner	UE-101		0094	0694	2 PWC PT6A-67D	7688	Y19		lsf Raytheon / op in United Express-cs
☐	N118UX	Beech 1900D Airliner	UE-118		0094	1194	2 PWC PT6A-67D	7688	Y19		lsf Raytheon / op in United Express-cs
☐	N122YV	Beech 1900D Airliner	UE-122		1194	0498	2 PWC PT6A-67D	7688	Y19		op in United Express-cs / tbr N122UX

registration	type of aircraft	cn/fn	ex/ex*	mfd	del	powered by	mtow kg	configuration	selcal	name/fln/specialities/remarks
☐ N150YV	Beech 1900D Airliner	UE-150		0595	0498	2 PWC PT6A-67D	7688	Y19		op in United Express-cs / tbr N150UX
☐ N151ZV	Beech 1900D Airliner	UE-151		0595	0498	2 PWC PT6A-67D	7688	Y19		op in United Express-cs / tbr N151UX
☐ N153ZV	Beech 1900D Airliner	UE-153		0695	0498	2 PWC PT6A-67D	7688	Y19		op in United Express-cs / tbr N153GL
☐ N154ZV	Beech 1900D Airliner	UE-154		0595	0498	2 PWC PT6A-67D	7688	Y19		op in United Express-cs / tbr N154GL
☐ N169GL	Beech 1900D Airliner	UE-169		0095	0995	2 PWC PT6A-67D	7688	Y19		lsf Raytheon / op in United Express-cs
☐ N170GL	Beech 1900D Airliner	UE-170	N170YV	1294	0995	2 PWC PT6A-67D	7688	Y19		lsf Raytheon / op in United Express-cs
☐ N179YV	Beech 1900D Airliner	UE-179		1195	0498	2 PWC PT6A-67D	7688	Y19		op in United Express-cs / tbr N179GL
☐ N184YV	Beech 1900D Airliner	UE-184		1195	0498	2 PWC PT6A-67D	7688	Y19		op in United Express-cs / tbr N184UX
☐ N192YV	Beech 1900D Airliner	UE-192		1295	0498	2 PWC PT6A-67D	7688	Y19		op in United Express-cs / tbr N192GL
☐ N195YV	Beech 1900D Airliner	UE-195		0296	0498	2 PWC PT6A-67D	7688	Y19		op in United Express-cs / tbr N195GL
☐ N201YQ	Beech 1900D Airliner	UE-201		0096	0396	2 PWC PT6A-67D	7688	Y19		lsf Raytheon / op in United Express-cs
☐ N202UX	Beech 1900D Airliner	UE-202	N202ZK	0096	0396	2 PWC PT6A-67D	7688	Y19		lsf Raytheon / op in United Express-cs
☐ N204GL	Beech 1900D Airliner	UE-204	N204YV	0096	0396	2 PWC PT6A-67D	7688	Y19		lsf Raytheon / op in United Express-cs
☐ N208GL	Beech 1900D Airliner	UE-208	N208YV	0096	0396	2 PWC PT6A-67D	7688	Y19		lsf Raytheon / op in United Express-cs
☐ N210UX	Beech 1900D Airliner	UE-210		0096	0796	2 PWC PT6A-67D	7688	Y19		lsf Raytheon / op in United Express-cs
☐ N211UX	Beech 1900D Airliner	UE-211		0096	0496	2 PWC PT6A-67D	7688	Y19		lsf Raytheon / op in United Express-cs
☐ N219YV	Beech 1900D Airliner	UE-219		0696	0498	2 PWC PT6A-67D	7688	Y19		op in United Express-cs / tbr N219GL
☐ N220YV	Beech 1900D Airliner	UE-220		0696	0498	2 PWC PT6A-67D	7688	Y19		op in United Express-cs / tbr N220GL
☐ N225GL	Beech 1900D Airliner	UE-225	N3229G*	0096	0696	2 PWC PT6A-67D	7688	Y19		lsf Raytheon / op in United Express-cs
☐ N226YV	Beech 1900D Airliner	UE-226		0796	0498	2 PWC PT6A-67D	7688	Y19		op in United Express-cs / tbr N226GL
☐ N228YV	Beech 1900D Airliner	UE-228		0896	0498	2 PWC PT6A-67D	7688	Y19		op in United Express-cs / tbr N228GL
☐ N240YV	Beech 1900D Airliner	UE-240		0996	0498	2 PWC PT6A-67D	7688	Y19		op in United Express-cs / tbr N240GL
☐ N245YV	Beech 1900D Airliner	UE-245		1096	0498	2 PWC PT6A-67D	7688	Y19		op in United Express-cs / tbr N245GL
☐ N247YV	Beech 1900D Airliner	UE-247		1196	0498	2 PWC PT6A-67D	7688	Y19		op in United Express-colors
☐ N249YV	Beech 1900D Airliner	UE-249		1196	0498	2 PWC PT6A-67D	7688	Y19		lsf ASH / op in United Express-colors
☐ N251ZV	Beech 1900D Airliner	UE-251		1196	0498	2 PWC PT6A-67D	7688	Y19		op in United Express-cs / tbr N251GL
☐ N253YV	Beech 1900D Airliner	UE-253		1296	0498	2 PWC PT6A-67D	7688	Y19		op in United Express-cs / tbr N253GL
☐ N254GL	Beech 1900D Airliner	UE-254	N10840	0096	1296	2 PWC PT6A-67D	7688	Y19		lsf Raytheon / op in United Express-cs
☐ N255GL	Beech 1900D Airliner	UE-255	N10860	0096	1296	2 PWC PT6A-67D	7688	Y19		lsf Raytheon / op in United Express-cs
☐ N257YV	Beech 1900D Airliner	UE-257		1296	0498	2 PWC PT6A-67D	7688	Y19		op in United Express-cs / tbr N257GL
☐ N260YV	Beech 1900D Airliner	UE-260		1296	0498	2 PWC PT6A-67D	7688	Y19		op in United Express-cs / tbr N260GL
☐ N261YV	Beech 1900D Airliner	UE-261		1296	0498	2 PWC PT6A-67D	7688	Y19		op in United Express-cs / tbr N261GL
☐ N262GL	Beech 1900D Airliner	UE-262	N10746	0096	0197	2 PWC PT6A-67D	7688	Y19		lsf Raytheon / op in United Express-cs
☐ N26YV	Beech 1900D Airliner	UE-26		1092	0498	2 PWC PT6A-67D	7688	Y19		lsf ASH / op in United Express-colors
☐ N94UX	Beech 1900D Airliner	UE-94		0094	0694	2 PWC PT6A-67D	7688	Y19		lsf Raytheon / op in United Express-cs
☐ N96UX	Beech 1900D Airliner	UE-96		0094	0594	2 PWC PT6A-67D	7688	Y19		lsf Raytheon / op in United Express-cs
☐ N97UX	Beech 1900D Airliner	UE-97		0094	0594	2 PWC PT6A-67D	7688	Y19		lsf Raytheon / op in United Express-cs
☐ N267UE	Embraer 120ER Brasilia (EMB-120ER)	120071	PT-LUS	0087	0694	2 PWC PW118A	11990	Y30		op in United Express-colors/cvtd 120RT
☐ N281UE	Embraer 120RT Brasilia (EMB-120RT)	120092	PT-SMJ*	0088	0695	2 PWC PW118	11500	Y30		lsf Finova Capital / op in UA Exp.-cs
☐ N293UX	Embraer 120ER Brasilia (EMB-120ER)	120293	PT-SVN*	0094	1294	2 PWC PW118A	11990	Y30		lsf McDonnell Douglas Finance/UA Exp.cs
☐ N297UX	Embraer 120ER Brasilia (EMB-120ER)	120297	PT-SVR*	0095	0495	2 PWC PW118A	11990	Y30		lsf McDonnell Douglas Finance/UA Exp.cs
☐ N299UX	Embraer 120ER Brasilia (EMB-120ER)	120299	PT-SVT*	0095	0795	2 PWC PW118A	11990	Y30		op in United Express-colors
☐ N451UE	Embraer 120RT Brasilia (EMB-120RT)	120108	PT-SNA*	1188	0995	2 PWC PW118A	11500	Y30		op in United Express-colors
☐ N452UE	Embraer 120RT Brasilia (EMB-120RT)	120096	PT-SMN*	1288	1195	2 PWC PW118A	11500	Y30		op in United Express-colors

GREAT LAKES HELICOPTERS, Inc.
West Chicago-Private Heliport, IL

PO Box 860, West Chicago, IL 60185, USA ☎ (630) 293-3600 Tx: none Fax: (630) 293-4401 SITA: n/a
F: 1987 ✈✈✈ n/a Head: James B. Panoff Net: n/a

☐ N302SH	Bell 206B JetRanger	1315	N374EH	0074	0395	1 AN 250-C20	1451			lsf Rotorcraft Partnerships Ltd
☐ N317CA	Bell 206B JetRanger III	4320		0094	1294	1 AN 250-C20J	1451			lsf Rotorcraft Partnerships Ltd
☐ N125RP	Bell 206L-1 LongRanger II	45542	N199MA	0080	0290	1 AN 250-C28B	1882			lsf Rotorcraft Partnerships Ltd
☐ N700EA	Bell 206L-3 LongRanger III	51497	N42928	0091	0394	1 AN 250-C30P	1882			lsf Rotorcraft Partnerships Ltd
☐ N109TS	Agusta A109A II	7276	N102TJ	0085	0396	2 AN 250-C20B	2600			lsf Rotorcraft Partnerships Ltd
☐ N109WS	Agusta A109A II	7324	D-HOOC	0085	0296	2 AN 250-C20B	2600			lsf Rotorcraft Partnerships Ltd

GREATLAND AIR CARGO, Inc.
Anchorage-Int'l, AK

3600 West Int'l Airport Road, Suite 2, Anchorage, AK 99502, USA ☎ (907) 243-4476 Tx: none Fax: (907) 243-1783 SITA: n/a
F: 1995 ✈✈✈ 7 Head: Kimberley W. O'Meara Net: n/a

☐ N2225C	De Havilland DHC-4A Caribou	215	63-9754	0063	0397	2 PW R-2000	12927	Freighter		
☐ N800NC	De Havilland DHC-4A Caribou	98	62-4160	0062	0895	2 PW R-2000	12927	Freighter		

GREAT NORTHERN AIR GUIDES (Gee Bee, Inc. dba / Seasonal May-October ops only)
Anchorage-Lake Hood SPB, AK

4131 Float Plane Drive, Anchorage, AK 99502, USA ☎ (907) 243-1968 Tx: none Fax: (907) 243-1907 SITA: n/a
F: 1994 ✈✈✈ n/a Head: Gene K. Zerkel Net: n/a

☐ N49GB	De Havilland DHC-2 Beaver I	1181	N3355F	0056	1094	1 PW R-985	2309			Floats

GREAT SMOKY MOUNTAIN HELICOPTERS, Inc.
Sevierville-Private Heliport, TN

1101 Winfield Dunn Parkway, Sevierville, TN 37862, USA ☎ (423) 429-2426 Tx: none Fax: (423) 908-4777 SITA: n/a
F: 1995 ✈✈✈ n/a Head: Bobby W. Riggs Net: n/a

☐ N44BC	Bell 206B JetRanger II	1904		0076	0395	1 AN 250-C20	1451			lsf pvt

GRECOAIR, Inc.
El Paso-Int'l, TX & Africa

PO Box 12988, El Paso, TX 79912, USA ☎ (915) 772-0005 Tx: none Fax: (915) 775-0298 SITA: n/a
F: 1985 ✈✈✈ n/a Head: David P. Tokoph Net: n/a Leasing company & contract VIP flights (with Boeing 727-30) for private companies.

☐ N63119	De Havilland DHC-6 Twin Otter 200	119		0068	0186	2 PWC PT6A-20	5252	Combi		lst RZL
☐ N25AZ	Boeing 727-30	18370 / 134	Z-WYY	0065	1195	3 PW JT8D-7	72802	VIP		lsf Aviation Consultants / opf pvt
☐ N77AZ	Boeing 727-116C	19813 / 594	D2-TJA	0068	0194	3 PW JT8D-9A	77111	Freighter		lsf Avn Consultants/stdJNB/for sublease
☐ N14AZ	Boeing 707-336C	19498 / 645	9G-ACX	0067	0288	4 PW JT3D-3B (HK2/COM)	150850	Freighter		lst RZL
☐ N21AZ	Boeing 707-351C	18747 / 369	Z-WST	0064	0890	4 PW JT3D-3B (HK2/COM)	150850	Freighter	AH-BG	lst RZL
☐ N29AZ	Boeing 707-323C	19517 / 614	CC-CDI	0067	0990	4 PW JT3D-3B (HK2/COM)	150850	Freighter	KL-CF	lst RZL
☐ N80AZ	Boeing 707-351C	18748 / 379	D2-TOR	0064	0786	4 PW JT3D-3B (HK2/COM)	150850	Freighter	CJ-BK	lsf Aviation Consultants / for sublease

GREENWOOD HELICOPTERS, Inc.
Washington-Warren Field, NC

PO Box 280, Washington, NC 27889, USA ☎ (919) 975-2194 Tx: none Fax: (919) 975-1373 SITA: n/a
F: 1989 ✈✈✈ n/a Head: Charles G. Lewis Net: n/a

☐ N50141	Bell 206B JetRanger III	2603		0079	0489	1 AN 250-C20B	1451			
☐ N204DS	Bell UH-1B (204)	240	M508SC	0060	1195	1 LY T53-L-11	3856			

GRIFFING FLYING SERVICE, Inc. (Affiliated with Griffing Sandusky Airport, Inc.)
Sandusky-Griffing & Port Clinton-C.R.Keller Field, OH

3115 Cleveland Road, Sandusky, OH 44870, USA ☎ (419) 626-5161 Tx: none Fax: (419) 626-8775 SITA: n/a
F: 1937 ✈✈✈ n/a Head: Harry T. Griffing, Sr. Net: n/a Aircraft below MTOW 1361 kg: Piper PA-28

☐ N428S	Piper PA-32-301 Saratoga	32-8106021		0081	0781	1 LY IO-540-K1G5	1633			lsf Griffing Sandusky Airport Inc.
☐ N429S	Piper PA-32-300 Cherokee SIX	32-7940136		0079	0879	1 LY IO-540-K1G5	1542			lsf Griffing Sandusky Airport Inc.
☐ N430S	Piper PA-32-300 Cherokee SIX	32-7940168	N2872F	0079	0789	1 LY IO-540-K1G5	1542			lsf Griffing Sandusky Airport Inc.
☐ N1382V	Cessna U206F Stationair II	U20602594		0075	0194	1 CO IO-520-F	1633			lsf Griffing Sandusky Airport/tbr N436S
☐ N425S	Cessna U206E Stationair	U20601692	N9492G	0071	1291	1 CO IO-520-F	1633			lsf Griffing Sandusky Airport Inc.
☐ N423S	Piper PA-34-220T Seneca III	34-8233071		0082	0483	2 CO TSIO-360-KB	2155			lsf Griffing Sandusky Airport Inc.
☐ N3586W	Piper PA-31-325 Navajo C/R	31-8112016		0081	0996	2 LY TIO-540-F2BD	2948			lsf Tromi Corp.
☐ N426S	Piper PA-31-350 Navajo Chieftain	31-8152190	N426SC	0081	0386	2 LY TIO-540-J2BD	3175			lsf Griffing Sandusky Airport Inc.
☐ N427S	Piper PA-31-350 Navajo Chieftain	31-8152173	N776WS	0081	0187	2 LY TIO-540-J2BD	3175			lsf Griffing Sandusky Airport Inc.
☐ N88AJ	Piper PA-31-350 Navajo Chieftain	31-8252048		0082	0596	2 LY TIO-540-J2BD	3175			lsf Specchio Cablevision Co.
☐ N6863G	Britten-Norman BN-2A-20 Islander	770	C-GTOP	0076	0797	2 LY IO-540-K1B5	2976			

GRIM LOGGING, Inc.
Portland-Troutdale, OR

PO Box 5930, Salem, OR 97304, USA ☎ (503) 581-7890 Tx: none Fax: (503) 581-7926 SITA: n/a
F: 1993 ✈✈✈ n/a Head: Donald H. Grim Net: n/a

☐ N46969	Bell UH-1B (204)	770	63-8548	0063	0594	1 LY T53-L-11	3856			
☐ N205GL	Bell UH-1H (205)	13680	74-22356	0074	0396	1 LY T53-L-13	4309			
☐ N894GL	Bell UH-1H (205)	12894	71-20070	0071	0696	1 LY T53-L-13	4309			

GRIZZLY MOUNTAIN AVIATION, Inc.
Prineville-Heliport, OR

1110 East Laughlin Road, Prineville, OR 97754, USA ☎ (541) 447-8600 Tx: none Fax: (541) 447-7141 SITA: n/a
F: 1996 ✈✈✈ n/a Head: Bob P. Gatlin Net: n/a

☐ N22753	Bell UH-1B (204)	1109	64-13985	0064	0496	1 LY T53-L-11	3856			
☐ N224GM	Kaman K-1200 K-Max	A94-0022		0097	0597	1 LY T5317A-1	2722			

GULF AIR TAXI, Inc.
Yakutat, AK

PO Box 367, Yakutat, AK 99689, USA ☎ (907) 784-3240 Tx: none Fax: (907) 784-3380 SITA: n/a
F: 1959 ✈✈✈ n/a Head: Marie Ivers Net: n/a

☐ N3347L	Cessna A185E Skywagon	185-1275		0067	0583	1 CO IO-520-D	1520			Floats / Wheel-Skis
☐ N4611E	Cessna A185F Skywagon II	18503813		0079	0788	1 CO IO-520-D	1520			Floats / Wheel-Skis

registration	type of aircraft	cn/fn	ex/ex*	mfd	del	powered by	mtow kg	configuration	selcal	name/fln/specialitites/remarks
☐ N85CG	Cessna A185E Skywagon	18501927		0072	0293	1 CO IO-520-D	1520			Floats / Wheel-Skis
☐ N2102F	Cessna U206 Super Skywagon	U206-0302		0065	1095	1 CO IO-520-A	1497			Floats / Wheel-Skis
☐ N8063S	Cessna U206A Super Skywagon	U206-0463		0066	0491	1 CO IO-520-A	1633			Floats / Wheel-Skis
☐ N8316Q	Cessna U206F Stationair II	U20603177		0076	0989	1 CO IO-520-F	1633			Floats / Wheel-Skis
☐ N1748U	Cessna 207 Skywagon	20700348		0076	0694	1 CO IO-520-F	1724			

GULF & CARIBBEAN AIR (Gulf & Caribbean Cargo, Inc. dba)   Fort Lauderdale-Hollywood Int'l, FL

1100 Lee Wagener Blvd, Suite 317, Fort Lauderdale, FL 33315, USA ☎ (954) 359-7776 Tx: none Fax: (954) 359-7656 SITA: n/a
F: 1992 ♠♠♠ n/a Head: Fedrick L. Mason Net: n/a

☐ N4753B	Convair 440-72 (C-131E) Metropolitan	340	55-4753	0056	0095	2 PW R-2800	21319	Freighter		lsf Leaseair Ltd

GULF COAST HELICOPTERS, Inc. (Edward Acuna, Sr. dba)   Pearland-Heliport, TX

4810 Comal, 13601 Max Road, Pearland, TX 77581, USA ☎ (281) 485-7345 Tx: none Fax: none SITA: n/a
F: 1979 ♠♠♠ n/a Head: Edward Acuna, Sr. Net: n/a

☐ N2927W	Bell 206B JetRanger	750		0071	1180	1 AN 250-C20	1451			cvtd 206A
☐ N4068G	Bell 206B JetRanger	230		0068	1087	1 AN 250-C20	1451			cvtd 206A

GULFSTREAM INTERNATIONAL AIRLINES, Inc. = 3M / GFT (Continental Connection) (Subsidiary of G-Air Holdings Corp.)   Miami-Int'l, FL

GG GULFSTREAM international airlines

PO Box 777, Miami Springs, FL 33266, USA ☎ (305) 871-0727 Tx: none Fax: (305) 871-4800 SITA: n/a
F: 1990 ♠♠♠ 480 Head: Thomas L. Cooper IATA: 449 ICAO: GULF FLIGHT Net: http://www.gulfstreamair.com
All scheduled flights are operated in conjunction with Continental Connection as Continental Connection (in own Gulfstream-colors) using CO-flight numbers.

☐ N105GL	Beech 1900C-1 Airliner	UC-105	N191GL	0090	1297	2 PWC PT6A-65B	7530	Y19		lsf GLA
☐ N11ZR	Beech 1900C Airliner	UB-11	N306BH	0084	1095	2 PWC PT6A-65B	7530	Y19		lsf Raytheon Aircraft Receivables Corp.
☐ N126UE	Beech 1900C-1 Airliner	UC-126	N194GL	0090	0997	2 PWC PT6A-65B	7530	Y19		lsf GLA
☐ N138GL	Beech 1900C-1 Airliner	UC-138	N55668	0090	0997	2 PWC PT6A-65B	7530	Y19		lsf GLA
☐ N145GL	Beech 1900C-1 Airliner	UC-145	N55594	0091	0997	2 PWC PT6A-65B	7530	Y19		lsf GLA
☐ N150UE	Beech 1900C-1 Airliner	UC-150	N55872	0091	0298	2 PWC PT6A-65B	7530	Y19		lsf GLA
☐ N153GA	Beech 1900C Airliner	UB-34	N734GL	0085	1295	2 PWC PT6A-65B	7530	Y19		lsf Raytheon Aircraft Receivables Corp.
☐ N154GA	Beech 1900C Airliner	UB-25	N315RL	0084	1295	2 PWC PT6A-65B	7530	Y19		lsf Raytheon Aircraft Receivables Corp.
☐ N155GA	Beech 1900C Airliner	UB-55	N259AF	0086	0196	2 PWC PT6A-65B	7530	Y19		lsf Raytheon Rec. / Grand Bahama Isl.cs
☐ N171GL	Beech 1900C-1 Airliner	UC-171	N55522	0091	0298	2 PWC PT6A-65B	7530	Y19		lsf GLA
☐ N181GA	Beech 1900C Airliner	UB-24	N7243R	0084	1095	2 PWC PT6A-65B	7530	Y19		lsf Raytheon Aircraft Receivables Corp.
☐ N187GA	Beech 1900C-1 Airliner	UC-31	C-FCMV	0088	1195	2 PWC PT6A-65B	7530	Y19		lsf Raytheon Aircraft Receivables Corp.
☐ N188GA	Beech 1900C Airliner	UB-14	N14ZR	0084	0995	2 PWC PT6A-65B	7530	Y19		lsf Raytheon Aircraft Receivables Corp.
☐ N189GA	Beech 1900C Airliner	UB-9	N9ZR	0084	0895	2 PWC PT6A-65B	7530	Y19		lsf Raytheon Aircraft Receivables Corp.
☐ N190GA	Beech 1900C Airliner	UB-1	N1YW	0083	0895	2 PWC PT6A-65B	7530	Y19		lsf Raytheon Aircraft Credit Corp.
☐ N192GA	Beech 1900C Airliner	UB-17	N17ZR	0084	0695	2 PWC PT6A-65B	7530	Y19		lsf Raytheon Aircraft Credit Corp.
☐ N194GA	Beech 1900C Airliner	UB-8	N8ZR	0084	0695	2 PWC PT6A-65B	7530	Y19		lsf Raytheon Aircraft Credit Corp.
☐ N195GA	Beech 1900C Airliner	UB-65	N65CJ	0086	1294	2 PWC PT6A-65B	7530	Y19		lsf Raytheon Aircraft Receivables Corp.
☐ N196GA	Beech 1900C Airliner	UB-31	N331CJ	0085	1194	2 PWC PT6A-65B	7530	Y19		lsf Raytheon Aircraft Receivables Corp.
☐ N197GA	Beech 1900C Airliner	UB-16	N16ZR	0084	0494	2 PWC PT6A-65B	7530	Y19		lsf Raytheon Aircraft Receivables Corp.
☐ N198GA	Beech 1900C Airliner	UB-5	N5ZR	0084	0194	2 PWC PT6A-65B	7530	Y19		lsf Raytheon Aircraft Receivables Corp.
☐ N199GA	Beech 1900C Airliner	UB-13	N13ZR	0084	0294	2 PWC PT6A-65B	7530	Y19		lsf Raytheon Aircraft Receivables Corp.
☐ N86UE	Beech 1900C-1 Airliner	UC-86	N15547	0089	0697	2 PWC PT6A-65B	7530	Y19		lsf GLA
☐ N89UE	Beech 1900C-1 Airliner	UC-89	N15536	0089	0697	2 PWC PT6A-65B	7530	Y19		lsf GLA
☐ N173RA	De Havilland DHC-7-102 Dash 7	038		0081	0499	4 PWC PT6A-50	19958	Y50		
☐ N174RA	De Havilland DHC-7-102 Dash 7	053		0081	0499	4 PWC PT6A-50	19958	Y50		
☐ N234SL	De Havilland DHC-7-102 Dash 7	024	C-FDNR	0080	0499	4 PWC PT6A-50	19958	Y50		
☐ N4860J	De Havilland DHC-7-102 Dash 7	019		0080	0499	4 PWC PT6A-50	19958	Y50		
☐ N67DA	De Havilland DHC-7-102 Dash 7	079	RP-C1382	0082	0499	4 PWC PT6A-50	19958	Y50		lsf DGV Inc.
☐ N703MG	De Havilland DHC-7-102 Dash 7	103	N773BE	0085	0499	4 PWC PT6A-50	19958	Y50		lsf AGES

GUND BUSINESS ENTERPRISES, Inc. – Air Operations   Cleveland-Hopkins Int'l & -Burke Lakefront, OH

1228 Euclid Ave, Halle Bldg, 6th Floor, Cleveland, OH 44115, USA ☎ (216) 579-0300 Tx: none Fax: (216) 687-6115 SITA: n/a
F: 1990 ♠♠♠ n/a Head: Gordon Gund Net: n/a Operates non-commercial executive flights exclusively for itself & its subsidiaries in the advertising & P.R. business.

☐ N583CC	BAe (BAC) One-Eleven 203AE	015	N523AC	0065	0991	2 RR Spey 511-14D	35834	Executive		lsf Nationwide Advertising Services
☐ N15255	Boeing 737-291 (A)	21069 / 415	N7385F	0075	1198	2 PW JT8D-9A	49442	Executive		op in Cleveland Cavaliers-colors

HAGELAND AVIATION SERVICES, Inc. = H6   St. Mary's, Bethel & Unalakleet, AK

PO Box 195, St. Mary's, AK 99658, USA ☎ (907) 438-2246 Tx: none Fax: (907) 438-2435 SITA: n/a
F: 1981 ♠♠♠ n/a Head: Ron J. Tweto Net: n/a Aircraft below MTOW 1361 kg: Cessna 172 & 180

☐ N185FK	Cessna A185F Skywagon	18502513		0074	0792	1 CO IO-520-D	1520			
☐ N9575G	Cessna U206F Stationair	U20601775		0072	0795	1 CO IO-520-F	1633			lsf Gussic Ventures
☐ N104K	Cessna 207 Skywagon	20700122		0069	0395	1 CO IO-520-F	1724			lsf Gussic Ventures
☐ N17GN	Cessna 207A Stationair 8 II	20700693		0081	0895	1 CO IO-520-F	1724			lsf Gussic Ventures
☐ N207SE	Cessna 207 Skywagon	20700237		0073	0885	1 CO IO-520-F	1724			
☐ N23CF	Cessna 207 Skywagon	20700276		0074	0790	1 CO IO-520-F	1724			
☐ N327CT	Cessna 207A Stationair 7 II	20700535		0079	0995	1 CO IO-520-F	1724			
☐ N5277J	Cessna 207A Stationair 8 II	20700772		0084	0994	1 CO IO-520-F	1724			lsf Gussic Ventures
☐ N6439H	Cessna 207A Stationair 7 II	20700525		0079	1291	1 CO IO-520-F	1724			lsf Gussic Ventures
☐ N6874M	Cessna 207A Stationair 8 II	20700671		0080	0493	1 CO IO-520-F	1724			lsf Gussic Ventures
☐ N73067	Cessna 207A Stationair 7 II	20700558		0079	0294	1 CO IO-520-F	1724			
☐ N7326U	Cessna 207A Skywagon	20700399		0077	0289	1 CO IO-520-F	1724			
☐ N7340U	Cessna T207A Turbo Stationair 7 II	20700407		0077	0192	1 CO TSIO-520-M	1724			lsf Gussic Ventures
☐ N7373U	Cessna 207A Stationair 7 II	20700423		0078	1290	1 CO IO-520-F	1724			lsf Gussic Ventures
☐ N75703	Cessna 207A Stationair 8 II	20700639		0080	0994	1 CO IO-520-F	1724			
☐ N9400M	Cessna 207A Stationair 8 II	20700687		0081	0885	1 CO IO-520-F	1724			
☐ N9869M	Cessna 207A Stationair 8 II	20700744		0081	0296	1 CO IO-520-F	1724			lsf Gussic Ventures
☐ N9970M	Cessna 207A Stationair 8 II	20700769		0084	0186	1 CO IO-520-F	1724			lsf Gussic Ventures
☐ N1233T	Cessna 402C III	402C0805		0084	0696	2 CO TSIO-520-VB	3107			lsf Bear Aircraft Sales & Leasing
☐ N402QA	Cessna 402C II	402C0338		0080	1296	2 CO TSIO-520-VB	3107			lsf Gussic Ventures
☐ N303GV	Cessna 208B Grand Caravan	208B0581		0096	1196	1 PWC PT6A-114A	3969			lsf Gussic Ventures
☐ N407GV	Cessna 208B Grand Caravan	208B0616		0097	0697	1 PWC PT6A-114A	3969			lsf Gussic Ventures
☐ N410GV	Cessna 208B Grand Caravan	208B0632		0097	0897	1 PWC PT6A-114A	3969			lsf Gussic Ventures
☐ N411GV	Cessna 208B Grand Caravan	208B0672		0098	0698	1 PWC PT6A-114A	3969			lsf Gussic Ventures
☐ N16U	Beech E18S	BA-394		0058	0894	2 PW R-985-AN14B	4218	Freighter		
☐ N855MA	Twin (Aero) Turbo Commander 690A	11299	N856MA	0076	0597	2 GA TPE331-5-251K	4649			lsf Joda Partnership

HAINES AIRWAYS, Inc. = 7A   Haines & Sitka, AK

PO Box 470, Haines, AK 99827, USA ☎ (907) 766-2646 Tx: none Fax: (907) 766-2780 SITA: n/a
F: 1985 ♠♠♠ 12 Head: Ken Brewer Net: http://www.haines.ak.us/hainesair Aircraft below MTOW 1361 kg: Piper PA-28

☐ N4136R	Piper PA-32-300 Cherokee SIX	32-40492		0068	0389	1 LY IO-540-K1A5	1542			lsf pvt
☐ N56143	Piper PA-32-300 Cherokee SIX	32-7340163		0073	0693	1 LY IO-540-K1A5	1542			
☐ N56728	Piper PA-32-300 Cherokee SIX	32-7440021		0074	0597	1 LY IO-540-K1A5	1542			
☐ N8991N	Piper PA-32-300C Cherokee SIX	32-40874		0069	0294	1 LY IO-540-K1A5	1542			
☐ N234CE	Piper PA-31-350 Navajo Chieftain	31-8052203		0080	0098	2 LY TIO-540-J2BD	3175			lsf pvt
☐ N27726	Piper PA-31-350 Navajo Chieftain	31-7852125		0078	0690	2 LY TIO-540-J2BD	3175			
☐ N31PR	Piper PA-31-350 Navajo Chieftain	31-7952049		0079	0897	2 LY TIO-540-J2BD	3175			
☐ N693MA	Piper PA-31-350 Navajo Chieftain	31-7852005		0078	0897	2 LY TIO-540-J2BD	3175			

HALLIBURTON AVIATION (Halliburton Company dba / Subsidiary of Halliburton Industries, Corp.)   Dallas-Love Field, TX

7515 Lemmon Ave, Hangar F, Dallas, TX 75209, USA ☎ (214) 358-1661 Tx: none Fax: (214) 358-2132 SITA: n/a
F: 1979 ♠♠♠ n/a Head: Charles R. McConnell Net: n/a Operates non-commercial executive & personnel-transfer flights exclusively for its parent company which is active in the oil industry.

☐ N228H	De Havilland DHC-8-102 Dash 8	265	N41873	0091	0391	2 PWC PW120A	15649	Executive		
☐ N335H	GAC (Grumman) G-1159 Gulfstream II (TT)	238	N831GA	0079	0279	2 RR Spey 511-8	29710	Executive		
☐ N339H	GAC (Grumman) G-1159 Gulfstream II	145	N871E	0074	0984	2 RR Spey 511-8	29393	Executive		
☐ N437H	GAC (Grumman) G-1159 Gulfstream II	258	N929GV	0079	0497	2 RR Spey 511-8	29393	Executive		

HAMMONDS AIR SERVICE = HMD (Charlie Hammonds Flying Service, Inc. dba)   Houma-Terrebonne & Houma-SPB, LA

PO Box 966, Houma, LA 70361, USA ☎ (504) 876-0584 Tx: none Fax: (504) 851-4681 SITA: n/a
F: 1964 ♠♠♠ 20 Head: Charles L. Hammonds ICAO: HAMMOND Net: n/a

☐ N1867Q	Cessna A185F Skywagon II	18503497		0077	0179	1 CO IO-520-D	1520			Floats
☐ N2906Q	Cessna A185F Skywagon II	18503542		0078	0279	1 CO IO-520-D	1520			Floats
☐ N4603E	Cessna A185F Skywagon II	18503811		0079	0679	1 CO IO-520-D	1520			Floats
☐ N4691E	Cessna A185F Skywagon II	18503842		0079	0180	1 CO IO-520-D	1520			Floats
☐ N4836Q	Cessna A185F Skywagon II	18503561		0078	1178	1 CO IO-520-D	1520			Floats
☐ N9866Q	Cessna A185F Skywagon II	18503794		0079	0679	1 CO IO-520-D	1520			Floats

HANGAR 10, Inc. (Affiliated with Atkins Aviation, Inc., air cargo forwarder) — McAllen-Miller Int'l, TX

PO Box 3363, McAllen, TX 78502, USA ☎ (956) 682-7573 Tx: none Fax: (956) 686-5116 SITA: n/a
F: 1968 ⁂ 14 Head: Patti M. Atkins Net: n/a

registration	type of aircraft	cn/fn	ex/ex*	mfd	del	powered by	mtow kg	configuration	selcal	name/fln/specialities/remarks
☐ N12BA	Boeing (Douglas) DC-3C (C-47A-50-DL)	10035	N55LT	0043	0198	2 PW R-1830	12202	Freighter		lsf Avlease Inc.
☐ N3906J	Boeing (Douglas) Super DC-3S (C-117D)	43344	N90628	0043	0996	2 WR R-1820-80	13301	Freighter		lsf Avlease Inc. / cvtd R4D-5 cn 9859

HANGER ONE AIR, Inc. (A Faulkner Company) — Bethel, AK

PO Box 7010, Bethel, AK 99559, USA ☎ (907) 543-4001 Tx: none Fax: (907) 543-3010 SITA: n/a
F: 1992 ⁂ n/a Head: Harry E. Faulkner, Jr. Net: n/a

registration	type of aircraft	cn/fn	ex/ex*	mfd	del	powered by	mtow kg	configuration	selcal	name/fln/specialities/remarks
☐ N9422K	Cessna U206G Stationair 6 II	U20604395		0078	1092	1 CO IO-520-F	1633			

HAPS AIR SERVICE, Inc. — Ames-Municipal, IA

2501 Airport Drive, Ames, IA 50010-8297, USA ☎ (515) 232-4310 Tx: none Fax: (515) 232-4325 SITA: n/a
F: 1953 ⁂ 16 Head: Hartley A. Westbrook Net: http://www.global-reach.com/has Aircraft below MTOW 1361kg: Cessna 172

registration	type of aircraft	cn/fn	ex/ex*	mfd	del	powered by	mtow kg	configuration	selcal	name/fln/specialities/remarks
☐ N3172E	Cessna 182R Skylane II	18268237		0082	1182	1 CO O-470-U	1406			
☐ N6227Y	Cessna T210N Turbo Centurion II	21064301		0081	0690	1 CO TSIO-520-R	1814			
☐ N111SC	Cessna 340A II	340A0335		0077	0885	2 CO TSIO-520-N	2717			
☐ N135BG	Cessna 414A Chancellor III	414A0419		0079	0994	2 CO TSIO-520-NB	3062			
☐ N6764C	Cessna 402C II	402C0628	N153PB	0081	0386	2 CO TSIO-520-VB	3107			

HARBOR AIRLINES, Inc. = HB / HAR (Subsidiary of Crossings Aviation, Inc.) — Oak Harbor-Air Park/Wes Lupien, WA

1302 26th Avenue NW, Gig Harbor, WA 98335, USA ☎ (253) 851-2381 Tx: none Fax: (253) 851-2365 SITA: n/a
F: 1971 ⁂ 50 Head: Richard W. Boehlke IATA: 495 ICAO: HARBOR Net: http://www.harborair.com

registration	type of aircraft	cn/fn	ex/ex*	mfd	del	powered by	mtow kg	configuration	selcal	name/fln/specialities/remarks
☐ N335WB	Piper PA-31-350 Navajo Chieftain	31-7952135	N35268	0079	1087	2 LY TIO-540-J2BD	3175	Y9		
☐ N3516A	Piper PA-31-350 Navajo Chieftain	31-7952106		0079	0797	2 LY TIO-540-J2BD	3175	Y9		lsf CXA Financial Inc.
☐ N3525Y	Piper PA-31-350 Navajo Chieftain	31-7952127		0079	0997	2 LY TIO-540-J2BD	3175	Y9		lsf CXA Financial Inc.
☐ N3534Y	Piper PA-31-350 Navajo Chieftain	31-7952195		0079	0797	2 LY TIO-540-J2BD	3175	Y9		lsf CXA Financial Inc.
☐ N3535F	Piper PA-31-350 Navajo Chieftain	31-7952200		0079	0984	2 LY TIO-540-J2BD	3175	Y9		
☐ N3590L	Piper PA-31-350 Navajo Chieftain	31-8052146		0080	0686	2 LY TIO-540-J2BD	3175	Y9		
☐ N417PM	Piper PA-31-350 Navajo Chieftain	31-8052051		0080	0298	2 LY TIO-540-J2BD	3175	Y9		lsf CXA Financial Inc.
☐ N601DA	Piper PA-31-350 T1020	31-8453002		0084	0390	2 LY TIO-540-J2B	3175	Y9		
☐ N86VA	Piper PA-31-350 Navajo Chieftain	31-7952020		0079	0298	2 LY TIO-540-J2BD	3175	Y9		lsf CXA Financial Inc.
☐ N919C	Cessna 208B Grand Caravan	208B0561	ZK-VAN	0096	1198	1 PWC PT6A-114A	3969	Y9		lsf CXA Financial Inc.

HAWAII AIR AMBULANCE, Inc. (Subsidiary of Air Ambulance, Inc., California) — Honolulu-Int'l, HI

PO Box 30242, Honolulu, HI 96820, USA ☎ (808) 833-2270 Tx: none Fax: (808) 836-2809 SITA: n/a
F: 1979 ⁂ n/a Head: Sandra Apter Net: n/a

registration	type of aircraft	cn/fn	ex/ex*	mfd	del	powered by	mtow kg	configuration	selcal	name/fln/specialities/remarks
☐ N4573V	Cessna 414A Chancellor III	414A0300		0079	0693	2 CO TSIO-520-NB	3062	EMS		
☐ N4686N	Cessna 414A Chancellor III	414A0075		0078	0381	2 CO TSIO-520-N	3062	EMS		lsf Air Ambulance
☐ N5614C	Cessna 414A Chancellor III	414A0203		0078	0779	2 CO TSIO-520-NB	3062	EMS		lsf Air Ambulance
☐ N5637C	Cessna 414A Chancellor III	414A0118		0078	0481	2 CO TSIO-520-N	3062	EMS		lsf Air Ambulance
☐ N6604C	Cessna 414A Chancellor III	414A0030		0078	0989	2 CO TSIO-520-N	3062	EMS		

HAWAIIAN AIR = HA / HAL (Hawaiian Airlines, Inc. dba / Subsidiary of Airline Investor Partnership) — Honolulu-Int'l, HI

PO Box 30008, Honolulu, HI 96820, USA ☎ (808) 835-3700 Tx: none Fax: (808) 835-3690 SITA: n/a
F: 1929 ⁂ 2140 Head: Paul J. Casey IATA: 173 ICAO: HAWAIIAN Net: http://www.hawaiianair.com

registration	type of aircraft	cn/fn	ex/ex*	mfd	del	powered by	mtow kg	configuration	selcal	name/fln/specialities/remarks
☐ N420EA	Boeing (Douglas) DC-9-51	47689 / 802	N639HA	0075	1091	2 PW JT8D-17	54885	Y139	JM-FH	71 / Kahului
☐ N601AP	Boeing (Douglas) DC-9-51	47658 / 790	OY-CTD	0075	1090	2 PW JT8D-17	54885	Y139	BF-DK	59 / Hana
☐ N603DC	Boeing (Douglas) DC-9-51	47784 / 902	YV-41C	0079	0792	2 PW JT8D-17	54885	Y139	DG-BE	57 / Lanai City / lsf GECA/tbr N957HA
☐ N649HA	Boeing (Douglas) DC-9-51	47715 / 825	I-SMEU	0076	1298	2 PW JT8D-17	52163	Y139		
☐ N650HA	Boeing (Douglas) DC-9-51	47714 / 824	I-SMEI	0076	0199	2 PW JT8D-17	52163	Y139		
☐ N660HA	Boeing (Douglas) DC-9-51	48122 / 972	EI-CBI	0080	1190	2 PW JT8D-17	55429	Y139	FG-AE	60 / Kamuela / lsf GECA
☐ N661HA	Boeing (Douglas) DC-9-51	47796 / 903	EI-CBH	0079	0490	2 PW JT8D-17	55429	Y139	AD-HK	61 / Kaunakakai / lsf GECA
☐ N662HA	Boeing (Douglas) DC-9-51	47742 / 857	EI-CBG	0077	0490	2 PW JT8D-17	55429	Y139	AD-HJ	62 / Lihue / lsf GECA
☐ N669HA	Boeing (Douglas) DC-9-51	47654 / 757	HB-ISK	0075	1086	2 PW JT8D-17	54885	Y139	BD-CM	66
☐ N672MC	Boeing (Douglas) DC-9-51	47661 / 812	HB-ISS	0276	0688	2 PW JT8D-17A	54885	Y139	BD-EH	65 / Kailua-Kona / lsf BEF Corp.
☐ N673MC	Boeing (Douglas) DC-9-51	47726 / 849	OE-LDM	0076	0688	2 PW JT8D-17A	55429	Y139	AD-HL	64 / Honolulu
☐ N674MC	Boeing (Douglas) DC-9-51	47735 / 869	OE-LDN	0077	0988	2 PW JT8D-17A	55429	Y139	BD-GM	63 / Hilo
☐ N679HA	Boeing (Douglas) DC-9-51	47662 / 850	HB-IST	0077	0494	2 PW JT8D-17	54885	Y139	BD-CF	67
☐ N699HA	Boeing (Douglas) DC-9-51	47763 / 879		0078	0778	2 PW JT8D-17	52163	Y139	BD-CM	66
☐ N709HA	Boeing (Douglas) DC-9-51	47764 / 882		0078	0878	2 PW JT8D-17	52163	Y139	BC-DJ	70 / Awapuhi
☐ N119AA	Boeing (Douglas) DC-10-10	46519 / 52		0872	0994	3 GE CF6-6K	195045	F34Y270	GK-FH	Oahu - the gathering place / lsf AAL
☐ N122AA	Boeing (Douglas) DC-10-10	46522 / 56		0972	0395	3 GE CF6-6K	195045	F34Y270	GK-FM	Kauai - the garden island / lsf AAL
☐ N125AA	Boeing (Douglas) DC-10-10	46525 / 72		1272	0697	3 GE CF6-6K	195045	F34Y270	GK-HM	lsf AAL
☐ N128AA	Boeing (Douglas) DC-10-10	46984 / 250		0578	0299	3 GE CF6-6K	195045	F34Y270	CK-AG	lsf AAL
☐ N148AA	Boeing (Douglas) DC-10-10	46703 / 19	N63NA	0172	0294	3 GE CF6-6K	195045	F34Y270	FJ-GH	19 / lsf AAL
☐ N152AA	Boeing (Douglas) DC-10-10	46707 / 61	N65NA	1072	0894	3 GE CF6-6K	195045	F34Y270	FJ-GM	Hawaii - the orchid island / lsf AAL
☐ N153AA	Boeing (Douglas) DC-10-10	46708 / 62	N66NA	1072	0894	3 GE CF6-6K	195045	F34Y270	EJ-FM	Maui-The Valley Isle / lsf AAL
☐ N160AA	Boeing (Douglas) DC-10-10	46710 / 70	N68NA	1273	0197	3 GE CF6-6K	195045	F34Y270	EJ-GK	lsf AAL
☐ N162AA	Boeing (Douglas) DC-10-10	46943 / 163	N70NA	0675	1297	3 GE CF6-6K	195045	F34Y270	EJ-HK	lsf AAL -0999
☐ N171AA	Boeing (Douglas) DC-10-10	46906 / 16	N916JW	1172	0696	3 GE CF6-6K	195045	F34Y270	KM-CD	lsf AAL
☐ N140AA	Boeing (Douglas) DC-10-30	46712 / 106	N81NA	0673	1198	3 GE CF6-50C2	256280	F34Y270		
☐ N141AA	Boeing (Douglas) DC-10-30	46713 / 165	N82NA	0675	1298	3 GE CF6-50C2	256280	F34Y270		lsf FIN 3 Ltd
☐ N142AA	Boeing (Douglas) DC-10-30	46714 / 167	N83NA	0675		3 GE CF6-50C2	256280	F34Y270		to be lsf FIN 3 Ltd 0899 / ex TSO

HAWAII COUNTY FIRE DEPARTMENT – Helicopter Flight Dept. (Division of County of Hawaii Police Department) — Kamuela-Heliport, HI

Queen Kaahumanu Highway, Kamuela, HI 96743, USA ☎ (808) 885-5799 Tx: none Fax: none SITA: n/a
F: 1983 ⁂ n/a Head: Nelson M. Tsuji Net: n/a

registration	type of aircraft	cn/fn	ex/ex*	mfd	del	powered by	mtow kg	configuration	selcal	name/fln/specialities/remarks
☐ N5132Y	MD Helicopters MD 500D (Hughes 369D)	1108D		0082	0883	1 AN 250-C20B	1361			
☐ N911FF	Bell 206L-3 LongRanger III	51581		0092	0992	1 AN 250-C30P	1882			

HAWAII HELICOPTERS, Inc. — Kahului-Heliport, HI

Kahului Heliport, Hangar 106, Kahului, HI 96732, USA ☎ (808) 877-3900 Tx: none Fax: (808) 877-4724 SITA: n/a
F: 1985 ⁂ n/a Head: Donald P. Ballard Net: http://www.hawaiiheli.com/

registration	type of aircraft	cn/fn	ex/ex*	mfd	del	powered by	mtow kg	configuration	selcal	name/fln/specialities/remarks
☐ N350SB	Eurocopter (Aerosp.) AS350BA AStar	2196		0089	0889	1 TU Arriel 1B	2100			
☐ N351HH	Eurocopter (Aerosp.) AS350BA AStar	2695		0093	0693	1 TU Arriel 1B	2100			
☐ N352HH	Eurocopter (Aerosp.) AS350BA AStar	2714		0093	0893	1 TU Arriel 1B	2100			
☐ N353HH	Eurocopter (Aerosp.) AS350BA AStar	2707		0093	0194	1 TU Arriel 1B	2100			
☐ N354HH	Eurocopter (Aerosp.) AS350BA AStar	2774		0094	0794	1 TU Arriel 1B	2100			
☐ N57936	Eurocopter (Aerosp.) AS355F1 TwinStar	5129		0082	0197	2 AN 250-C20F	2400			
☐ N5799Z	Eurocopter (Aerosp.) AS355F1 TwinStar	5188	C-FPHS	0082	0197	2 AN 250-C20F	2400			
☐ N811DB	Eurocopter (Aerosp.) AS355F1 TwinStar	5143		0082	0896	2 AN 250-C20F	2400			

HAWKINS & POWERS AVIATION, Inc. – H & P — Greybull, WY & Fairbanks-Ft. Wainright, AK

PO Box 391, Greybull, WY 82426, USA ☎ (307) 765-4482 Tx: 551599 Fax: (307) 765-2535 SITA: n/a
F: 1969 ⁂ 60 Head: Daniel J. Hawkins Net: n/a Aircraft below MTOW 1361 kg: Hiller UH-12 & PA-18

registration	type of aircraft	cn/fn	ex/ex*	mfd	del	powered by	mtow kg	configuration	selcal	name/fln/specialities/remarks
☐ N5013P	MD Helicopters MD 500D (Hughes 369D)	610984D		0081	0881	1 AN 250-C20B	1361			
☐ N8353F	MD Helicopters MD 500D (Hughes 369D)	1260062D		0076	1077	1 AN 250-C20B	1361			
☐ N2751U	Bell 206B JetRanger III	2689		0079	0679	1 AN 250-C20B	1451			
☐ N401HP	Bell 206B JetRanger III	3314	N401AH	0081	0396	1 AN 250-C20B	1451			
☐ N123HP	Bell 206L-1 LongRanger II	45394	N93ZT	0080	0289	1 AN 250-C28B	1882			
☐ N2751X	Bell 206L-1 LongRanger II	45252		0079	0592	1 AN 250-C28B	1882			
☐ N112HP	Cessna 310I	310I0104	N199W	0064	0791	2 CO IO-470-U	2313			
☐ N4748C	North American SNJ-5 (AT-6D) Texan	8816640		0043	1093	1 PW R-1340	2548	Trainer		
☐ N6292N	Cessna 340A II	340A0465		0078	0684	2 CO TSIO-520-NB	2717			
☐ N8043Z	Bell UH-1B (204)	198	60-3552	0060	0286	1 LY T53-L-11	4173			
☐ N88976	Bell UH-1B (204)	1203	64-14009	0064	0978	1 LY T53-L-11	4173			
☐ N141ZA	Beech E18S	BA-178	N141Z	0057	0686	2 PW R-985-AN14B	4218			
☐ N126HP	Boeing (Douglas) B-26B-61-DL Invader	27799	N94207	0044	1188	2 PW R-2800-59	15876			
☐ N127HP	Fairchild Ind. F-27F	33	N1004	0059	0888	2 RR Dart 529-7	19051			
☐ N9701F	Fairchild C-82A-FA Jet Packet	10184	ET-T-12	0047	0992	2 PW R-2800 + 1 J34 jet	24494	Freighter		
☐ N2871G	Consolidated PB4Y-2 Super Privateer		66302	0045	0769	4 WR R-2600	27216	Tanker		121
☐ N2872G	Consolidated PB4Y-2 Super Privateer		66300	0045	0370	4 WR R-2600	27216	Tanker		124
☐ N6884C	Consolidated PB4Y-2 Super Privateer		59701	0044	0970	4 WR R-2600	27216	Tanker		127
☐ N7620C	Consolidated PB4Y-2 Super Privateer		66260	0045	0669	4 WR R-2600	27216	Tanker		123
☐ N7962C	Consolidated PB4Y-2 Super Privateer		59882	0044	0771	4 WR R-2600	27216	Tanker		126
☐ N138HP	Lockheed P2V-7 (P-2H) Neptune	726-7223	N22166	0058	0290	2 WR R-3350	34246	Tanker		138
☐ N139HP	Lockheed P2V-7 (P-2H) Neptune	726-7168	N8064A	0058	0589	2 WR R-3350	34246	Tanker		139
☐ N140HP	Lockheed P2V-7 (P-2H) Neptune	726-7102	N8063S	0057	0589	2 WR R-3350	34246	Tanker		140
☐ N173AM	Lockheed P2V-7 (P-2H) Neptune	726-7129	143173	0058	0591	2 WR R-3350	34246	Tanker		std Greybull / to be made operational

☐ N22154	Lockheed P2V-7 (P-2H) Neptune	726-7200	147950	0058	0290	2 WR R-3350	34246	Tanker		std Greybull / to be made operational
☐ N2215G	Lockheed P2V-7 (P-2H) Neptune	726-7073	140972	0058	0290	2 WR R-3350	34246	Tanker		std Greybull / to be made operational
☐ N2216K	Lockheed P2V-7 (P-2H) Neptune	726-7226	148341	0058	0290	2 WR R-3350	34246	Tanker		std Greybull / to be made operational
☐ N2216S	Lockheed P2V-7 (P-2H) Neptune	726-7231	148346	0058	0290	2 WR R-3350	34246	Tanker		std Greybull / to be made operational
☐ N2218A	Lockheed P2V-7 (P-2H) Neptune	726-7243	148355	0058	0290	2 WR R-3350	34246	Tanker		std Greybull / to be made operational
☐ N2218E	Lockheed P2V-7 (P-2H) Neptune	726-7246	148356	0058	0290	2 WR R-3350	34246	Tanker		std Greybull / to be made operational
☐ N2218Q	Lockheed P2V-7 (P-2H) Neptune	726-7255	148359	0058	0290	2 WR R-3350	34246	Tanker		std Greybull / to be made operational
☐ N7060X	Lockheed P2V-7 (P-2H) Neptune	726-7207	147957	0058	0189	2 WR R-3350	34246	Tanker		std Greybull / to be made operational
☐ N7060Y	Lockheed P2V-7 (P-2H) Neptune	726-7167	145905	0058	0189	2 WR R-3350	34246	Tanker		std Greybull / to be made operational
☐ N90203	Boeing (Douglas) DC-4 (C-54G-1-DO)	35934 / DO 328	45-481	0045	1292	4 PW R-2000	30241	Tanker / Frtr		166
☐ N130HP	Lockheed L-182 (C-130A) Hercules	1A-3146	N134FF	0056	1288	4 AN T56-A	56336	Tanker/Freighter		130
☐ N131HP	Lockheed L-182 (C-130A) Hercules	1A-3142	N132FF	0056	0189	4 AN T56-A	56336	Tanker/Freighter		131
☐ N133FF	Lockheed L-182 (C-130A) Hercules	1A-3143	56-0535	0056	0189	4 AN T56-A	56336	Tanker/Freighter		
☐ N133HP	Lockheed L-182 (C-130A) Hercules	1A-3189	N8026J	0058	0389	4 AN T56-A	56336	Tanker/Freighter		133
☐ N134HP	Lockheed L-182A (C-130A) Hercules	2A-3218	57-0511	0059	0290	4 AN T56-A	56336	Tanker/Freighter		std Greybull / camo cs
☐ N135HP	Lockheed L-182 (C-130A) Hercules	1A-3166	57-0459	0058	0290	4 AN T56-A	56336	Tanker/Freighter		std Greybull / camo cs
☐ N4172Q	Lockheed L-182 (C-130A) Hercules	1A-3115	N45S	0057	1190	4 AN T56-A	56336	Tanker/Freighter		std Greybull / camo cs / tbr N132HP
☐ N8230H	Lockheed L-182A (C-130A) Hercules	2A-3220	57-0513	0059	0798	4 AN T56-A	56336	Tanker/Freighter		std Greybull / camo cs
☐ N1365N	Boeing C-97G Stratofreighter	16729	52-2698	0052	0491	4 PW R-4360	69400	Tanker		97
☐ N97HP	Boeing C-97G Stratofreighter	16612	N8516T	0052	0281	4 PW R-4360	69400	Freighter		
☐ N97KC	Boeing C-97G Stratofreighter	17700	53-218	0053	1290	4 PW R-4360	69400	Freighter		

HEARTLAND AVIATION, Inc. = NTC (formerly Gibson Aviation, Inc.) — **Eau Claire-Chippewa Valley Regional, WI**

3800 Starr Avenue, Eau Claire, WI 54703, USA ☎ (715) 835-3181 Tx: none Fax: (715) 835-7150 SITA: n/a
F: 1960 👥 27 Head: Lawrence W. Husby ICAO: NIGHT CHASE Net: http://www.heartland-travel.com

☐ N1448Z	Cessna 310R II	310R1527		0079	0589	2 CO IO-520-MB	2495			
☐ N3286M	Cessna 310R II	310R1894		0080	0586	2 CO IO-520-MB	2495			
☐ N1551G	Cessna 402B II	402B1072		0076	0596	2 CO TSIO-520-E	2858			
☐ N26635	Cessna 414A Chancellor III	414A0531		0080	0791	2 CO TSIO-520-NB	3062			
☐ N550LH	Cessna 550 Citation II	550-0105	N105BA	0079	0395	2 PWC JT15D-4	6033			

HEAVY LIFT HELICOPTERS, Inc. (Sister company of A.I.R., Inc.) — **Apple Valley & Fresno, CA**

19378 Central Road, Apple Valley, CA 92307, USA ☎ (760) 240-1074 Tx: none Fax: (760) 240-1202 SITA: n/a
F: 1995 👥 n/a Head: Chester C. Rasberry Net: n/a

☐ N428RR	Sikorsky CH-54A (S-64E) Skycrane	64030	N428CR	0067	0695	2 PW T-73-P-700	19051			
☐ N44094	Sikorsky CH-54A (S-64E Skycrane)	64023	67-18421	0067	0196	2 PW T-73-P-700	19051			194

HEETCO JET CENTER, Inc. — **Quincy-Municipal Baldwin Field, IL**

Quincy Municipal Airport, Quincy, IL 62301, USA ☎ (217) 885-3627 Tx: none Fax: (217) 885-3628 SITA: n/a
F: 1982 👥 n/a Head: Dean Phillips Net: n/a

☐ N340CE	Cessna 340A II	340A0430		0077	0291	2 CO TSIO-520-N	2717			lsf Great River Finance Co.
☐ N241VW	Piper PA-31-325 Navajo C/R	31-7612101		0076	0296	2 LY TIO-540-F2BD	2948			lsf Equipment Enterprises Inc.
☐ N756Q	Mitsubishi MU-2F (MU-2B-20)	132		0068	0187	2 GA TPE331-1-151A	4500			lst Interair, Australia

HELICAIR (Helicair AG, Inc. dba) — **Salinas-Municipal, CA**

37 Mortensen Avenue, Salinas, CA 93905, USA ☎ (408) 422-2188 Tx: none Fax: (408) 757-2069 SITA: n/a
F: 1984 👥 n/a Head: Niels C. Andrews Net: n/a

☐ N6251G	Bell OH-58A (206 JetRanger)	40995	70-15444	0070	1096	1 AN T63-A-700	1361			

HELICOPTER APPLICATORS, Inc. — **Frederick-Municipal, MD**

PO Box 810, Frederick, MD 21705, USA ☎ (240) 663-1330 Tx: none Fax: (240) 846-4643 SITA: n/a
F: 1974 👥 n/a Head: Glenn A. Martin Net: n/a Aircraft below MTOW 1361kg: Bell 47G

☐ N121HD	Bell 206B JetRanger	1166		0073	0490	1 AN 250-C20	1451			lsf pvt
☐ N3917G	Bell 206B JetRanger	1364	C-GOKF	0074	0493	1 AN 250-C20	1451			
☐ N503W	Bell 206B JetRanger	823		0072	0391	1 AN 250-C20	1451			
☐ N94WF	Bell 206B JetRanger III	2622	N28W	0079	0496	1 AN 250-C20B	1451			
☐ N417NP	Bell UH-1M (204)	1590	N417NA	0066	0296	1 LY T53-L-11	3856			cvtd UH-1C
☐ N4692Z	Bell UH-1L (204)	6173	154951	0068	0488	1 LY T53-L-11	3856			cvtd UH-1E

HELICOPTER FLITE SERVICES, Inc. — **Charleston-Yeager, WV**

290 Eagle Mountain Road, Charleston, WV 25311, USA ☎ (304) 344-3627 Tx: none Fax: (304) 344-3628 SITA: n/a
F: 1978 👥 n/a Head: Ammon A. Webster Net: n/a

☐ N137VG	Bell 206B JetRanger III	3445		0081	0287	1 AN 250-C20B	1451			
☐ N35HF	Bell 206B JetRanger II	2046	N331HC	0076	0694	1 AN 250-C20	1451			
☐ N36HF	Bell 206B JetRanger	1886	N136VG	0075	0885	1 AN 250-C20	1451			
☐ N3176L	Bell 206L-1 LongRanger II	45648		0081	0390	1 AN 250-C28B	1882			lsf Ford Coal Co.

HELICOPTER MINIT-MEN, Inc. — **Columbus-Heliport, OH**

PO Box 21758, Columbus, OH 43221, USA ☎ (614) 486-9309 Tx: none Fax: (614) 486-7531 SITA: n/a
F: 1990 👥 n/a Head: Charles W. Thomas Net: n/a Aircraft below MTOW 1361kg: Hughes 369HS (500C)

☐ N5119N	MD Helicopters MD 500D (Hughes 369D)	1097D	N500TP	0081	0498	1 AN 250-C20B	1361			
☐ N7168F	MD Helicopters MD 500D (Hughes 369D)	570131D	N560SM	0077	0790	1 AN 250-C20B	1361			
☐ N9159F	MD Helicopters MD 500D (Hughes 369D)	1090605D		0079	0288	1 AN 250-C20B	1361			
☐ N9413F	MD Helicopters MD 500D (Hughes 369D)	1180379D	N58236	0078	0588	1 AN 250-C20B	1361			

HELICOPTERS, Inc. — **Scottsdale, AZ**

7507 East San Miguel, Scottsdale, AZ 85250, USA ☎ (602) 990-0669 Tx: none Fax: (602) 990-2550 SITA: n/a
F: 1995 👥 n/a Head: Michelle Monzo Net: n/a

☐ N818MM	Bell 206B JetRanger III	3149	N38878	0080	0995	1 AN 250-C20B	1451			

HELICOPTERS, Inc. (Corporate Air Charter) (Affiliated with Lieber Enterprises, Inc.) — **Cahokia/St. Louis-Downtown Parks, IL**

14 Omega Drive, Cahokia, IL 62206, USA ☎ (618) 337-2903 Tx: none Fax: (618) 337-7107 SITA: n/a
F: 1979 👥 50 Head: Stephen C. Lieber Net: n/a Fixed-wing charter flights are operated under the marketing name CORPORATE AIR CHARTER (same headquarters).

☐ N118W	Bell 206B JetRanger III	4247		0092	0297	1 AN 250-C20J	1451			
☐ N15L	Bell 206B JetRanger III	2315	N16928	0077	0588	1 AN 250-C20B	1451			
☐ N15Q	Bell 206B JetRanger III	2235	N15CT	0077	0884	1 AN 250-C20B	1451			
☐ N177TV	Bell 206B JetRanger III	3074	N90Q	0080	1180	1 AN 250-C20B	1451			
☐ N23L	Bell 206B JetRanger III	3582	N22366	0082	0588	1 AN 250-C20B	1451			
☐ N23Q	Bell 206B JetRanger III	3111	N5753U	0080	0685	1 AN 250-C20B	1451			
☐ N26S	Bell 206B JetRanger III	2316	N7NJ	0077	0595	1 AN 250-C20B	1451			
☐ N28Z	Bell 206B JetRanger III	2875	N406HC	0079	0193	1 AN 250-C20B	1451			
☐ N35Q	Bell 206B JetRanger III	3073	N80WS	0080	0188	1 AN 250-C20B	1451			
☐ N411TV	Bell 206B JetRanger III	4034	N75SJ	0088	0894	1 AN 250-C20J	1451			
☐ N50Q	Bell 206B JetRanger III	3419	N700TU	0081	0786	1 AN 250-C20B	1451			
☐ N52L	Bell 206B JetRanger III	3150	N5757Q	0080	0887	1 AN 250-C20B	1451			
☐ N52Q	Bell 206B JetRanger III	2558	N48335	0078	0689	1 AN 250-C20B	1451			
☐ N52Z	Bell 206B JetRanger III	2251	N751H	0077	0792	1 AN 250-C20B	1451			
☐ N53Q	Bell 206B JetRanger III	4035	N75VJ	0088	0794	1 AN 250-C20J	1451			
☐ N57Z	Bell 206B JetRanger III	3016	N5736Y	0080	0190	1 AN 250-C20B	1451			
☐ N59Z	Bell 206B JetRanger III	4039	N7036J	0088	1093	1 AN 250-C20J	1451			
☐ N62158	Bell 206B JetRanger III	4378		0096	0297	1 AN 250-C20J	1451			to be re-reg. N29S
☐ N63Q	Bell 206B JetRanger II	2063	N16596	0076	0387	1 AN 250-C20	1451			
☐ N70Q	Bell 206B JetRanger III	3160	N13Q	0080	0484	1 AN 250-C20B	1451			
☐ N71TV	Bell 206B JetRanger III	3145		0080	0992	1 AN 250-C20B	1451			
☐ N86N	Bell 206B JetRanger III	3204	N102BP	0080	1088	1 AN 250-C20B	1451			
☐ N91L	Bell 206B JetRanger	788	N591Q	0072	0782	1 AN 250-C20	1451			
☐ N20Z	Bell 206L-1 LongRanger II	45334	N98HH	0079	0891	1 AN 250-C28B	1882			
☐ N27M	Bell 206L-4 LongRanger IV	52045	D-HHSK	0093	0297	1 AN 250-C30P	2018			
☐ N38Q	Bell 206L-1 LongRanger II	45364	N515EH	0080	0686	1 AN 250-C28B	1882			
☐ N63L	Bell 206L-3 LongRanger III	51399	N252EV	0090	0894	1 AN 250-C30P	1882			
☐ N73FA	Bell 206L-1 LongRanger II	45204	N16970	0078	0197	1 AN 250-C28B	1882			
☐ N90U	Bell 206L-3 LongRanger III	51298	JA9816	0089	0996	1 AN 250-C30P	1882			Skyeye / opf ABC 13 Witness News
☐ N97N	Bell 206L-1 LongRanger II	45771	N3177L	0083	0488	1 AN 250-C28B	1882			
☐ N9CN	Bell 206L-4 LongRanger IV	52020	C-GMEX	0093	0897	1 AN 250-C30P	2018			
☐ N90Q	Eurocopter (Aerosp.) AS350D AllStar	2324	N89065	0090	1092	1 AN 250-C30	1950			cvtd AStar
☐ N92N	Bell 407	53093		0096	0197	1 AN 250-C47B	2268			
☐ N48Q	Beech King Air 200	BB-263	F-GCTP	0077	0494	2 PWC PT6A-41	5670			
☐ N49U	Cessna 550 Citation II	550-0082	N21DA	0079	0195	2 PWC JT15D-4	6033			

347 registration type of aircraft cn/fn ex/ex* mfd del powered by mtow kg configuration selcal name/fln/specialitites/remarks

HELICOPTER TRANSPORT SERVICES, Inc.
Baltimore-Martin State, MD

701 Wilson Point Road, Martin State Airport, Baltimore, MD 21220, USA ☎ (410) 391-7722 Tx: none Fax: (410) 686-4507 SITA: n/a
F: 1993 ꕔꕔꕔ n/a Head: Michael L. Aslaksen Net: http://www.hts.rotor.com/

registration	type of aircraft	cn/fn	ex/ex*	mfd	del	powered by	mtow kg	name/fln/specialities/remarks
☐ N16917	Bell 206B JetRanger III	2303		0077	0893	1 AN 250-C20B	1451	lsf Fleetwind Int'l
☐ N206YP	Bell 206B JetRanger II	1981	C-GLLA	0076	0996	1 AN 250-C20	1451	
☐ N2168S	Bell 206B JetRanger III	3490		0081	0893	1 AN 250-C20B	1451	lsf US Leaseco Inc.
☐ N70523	Bell 206B JetRanger III	3162	C-GDKN	0080	1093	1 AN 250-C20B	1451	
☐ N89FB	Bell 206B JetRanger II	1980		0076	0893	1 AN 250-C20	1451	lsf US Leaseco Inc.
☐ N208WB	Bell 206L-1 LongRanger II	45550	C-GBHZ	0080	1293	1 AN 250-C28B	1882	
☐ N2097K	Bell 206L-1 LongRanger II	45732		0081	0893	1 AN 250-C28B	1882	lsf Fleetwind Int'l
☐ N3193U	Bell 206L-3 LongRanger III	51146	C-FFTZ	0085	1093	1 AN 250-C30P	1882	
☐ N219AC	Sikorsky S-61N	61755	G-BDKI	0076	0297	2 GE CT58-140-1	9979	
☐ N91158	Sikorsky S-61N Helipro Short	61424	G-AZDC	0068	0297	2 GE CT58-140-1	8618	cvtd S-61N

HELICORP, Inc.
Las Piedras-Heliport, PR

PO Box 2025, Las Piedras, PR 07771, USA ☎ (787) 733-6121 Tx: none Fax: (787) 733-4808 SITA: n/a
F: 1984 ꕔꕔꕔ n/a Head: Pedro F. Benitez Net: n/a

registration	type of aircraft	cn/fn	ex/ex*	mfd	del	powered by	mtow kg	name/fln/specialities/remarks
☐ N213LP	Eurocopter (Aerosp.) AS350B2 AStar	2828	N355HH	0094	0595	1 TU Arriel 1D1	2250	
☐ N113LP	Eurocopter (Aerosp.) AS355N TwinStar	5535		0092	0693	2 TU Arrius 1A	2540	
☐ N313LP	Eurocopter EC135T1	0022		0097	0997	2 TU Arrius 2B	2720	

HELI-EAST, Inc.
Mount Pleasant-East Cooper, SC

PO Box 30399, Charleston, SC 29417, USA ☎ (843) 856-4600 Tx: none Fax: (843) 762-2226 SITA: n/a
F: 1991 ꕔꕔꕔ n/a Head: Donald E. Mullis Net: n/a

registration	type of aircraft	cn/fn	ex/ex*	mfd	del	powered by	mtow kg	name/fln/specialities/remarks
☐ N206E	Bell 206B JetRanger	469	JA9037	0069	0098	1 AN 250-C20	1451	lsf Park Meridien Bank / cvtd 206A
☐ N316JP	Bell 206B JetRanger III	2880	N1073K	0079	0695	1 AN 250-C20B	1451	
☐ N868	Bell 206B JetRanger III	4249	N860	0092	1297	1 AN 250-C20J	1451	lsf PWB Leasing Corp.

HELIFLIGHT, Inc.
Fort Lauderdale-Executive, FL

2675 NW 56th Street, Hangar 51, Fort Lauderdale, FL 33309, USA ☎ (954) 771-6969 Tx: none Fax: (954) 938-9317 SITA: n/a
F: 1983 ꕔꕔꕔ n/a Head: Keith J. Mackey Net: http://www.heliflight.com Aircraft below MTOW 1361kg: Robinson R44

registration	type of aircraft	cn/fn	ex/ex*	mfd	del	powered by	mtow kg	name/fln/specialities/remarks
☐ N3198C	Bell 206B JetRanger III	3813		0084	0995	1 AN 250-C20J	1451	lsf 3198C Inc.
☐ N33HF	Bell 206B JetRanger II	2192	N16732	0077		1 AN 250-C20	1451	lsf Prospect Leasing Inc.
☐ N58HF	Sikorsky S-58J (H-34A)	57-1692		0058	0289	1 WR R-1820	5670	lsf Helicrane Inc.

HELI-FLITE, Inc.
Corona-Municipal, CA

1969 Aviation Drive, Suite C, Corona, CA 91720, USA ☎ (909) 340-1969 Tx: none Fax: (909) 340-1970 SITA: n/a
F: 1994 ꕔꕔꕔ n/a Head: Scott A. Donley Net: n/a

registration	type of aircraft	cn/fn	ex/ex*	mfd	del	powered by	mtow kg	name/fln/specialities/remarks
☐ N9276F	MD Helicopters MD 500D (Hughes 369D)	180254D		0078	0296	1 AN 250-C20B	1361	lsf Sunwest Inc.
☐ N1078Q	Bell 206B JetRanger III	2425	N5002X	0078	0096	1 AN 250-C20B	1451	lsf Sunwest Inc.
☐ N87717	Sikorsky S-58 (SH-34G)	58-1269	148011	0060	0596	1 WR R-1820	5897	
☐ N9043N	Sikorsky S-58 (SH-34G)	58-761	143957	0057	0597	1 WR R-1820	5897	

HELI-JET, Corporation (Associated with Heli Trade, Corp.)
Eugene-Private Heliport, OR

3830 Cross Street, Eugene, OR 97402, USA ☎ (541) 461-0310 Tx: 364419 heli eug Fax: (541) 461-0395 SITA: n/a
F: 1976 ꕔꕔꕔ 30 Head: Rod Kvamme Net: http://www.heli-jet.com

registration	type of aircraft	cn/fn	ex/ex*	mfd	del	powered by	mtow kg	name/fln/specialities/remarks
☐ N181HJ	Bell 206B JetRanger	1649	N90181	0075	0888	1 AN 250-C20	1451	
☐ N58HJ	Bell 205A-1	30314		0080	0680	1 LY T5317A	4309	
☐ N66HJ	Bell 205A-1	30239	N49766	0076	0587	1 LY T5317A	4309	
☐ N97HJ	Bell 205A-1	30173	C-GFHG	0075	0797	1 LY T5317A	4309	
☐ N73HJ	Bell 212	30552		0072	0890	2 PWC PT6T-3 TwinPac	5080	

HELIMAX AVIATION (Brad J. & Chantal Hasse dba)
Sacramento-Mather, CA

12370 Airport Road, Hanger 156, Martell, CA 95654, USA ☎ (209) 223-7901 Tx: none Fax: (209) 223-7902 SITA: n/a
F: 1995 ꕔꕔꕔ n/a Head: Brad J. Hasse Net: n/a

registration	type of aircraft	cn/fn	ex/ex*	mfd	del	powered by	mtow kg	name/fln/specialities/remarks
☐ N198HM	Bell UH-1B (204)	516	62-1996	0062	0397	1 LY T53-L-11	3856	
☐ N97HM	Bell UH-1B (204)	554	N93NW	0062	1295	1 LY T53-L-11	3856	

HELINET AVIATION SERVICES (HeliNet, Corp. dba)
Van Nuys, CA

16425 Hart Street, Van Nuys, CA 91406, USA ☎ (818) 902-0229 Tx: none Fax: (818) 902-9278 SITA: n/a
F: 1986 ꕔꕔꕔ n/a Head: Alan D. Purwin Net: http://travelassist.com/tcd/helinet.html Aircraft below MTOW 1361kg: Hughes 369HS (500C)

registration	type of aircraft	cn/fn	ex/ex*	mfd	del	powered by	mtow kg	name/fln/specialities/remarks
☐ N134TV	Bell 206B JetRanger	1801	N830RC	0078	0198	1 AN 250-C20	1451	lsf pvt
☐ N169JR	Bell 206B JetRanger III	3502	N2169X	0081	0198	1 AN 250-C20B	1451	lsf pvt
☐ N2044C	Bell 206B JetRanger III	3363		0081	0788	1 AN 250-C20B	1451	
☐ N50PE	Bell 206B JetRanger II	1992	N48US	0076	1297	1 AN 250-C20	1451	
☐ N6FX	Bell 206B JetRanger III	3434	N901WC	0081	0198	1 AN 250-C20B	1451	lsf pvt
☐ N3486H	Bell 206L-3 LongRanger III	51430	N779WC	0090	0897	1 AN 250-C30P	1882	
☐ N87WC	Bell 206L-1 LongRanger II	45201	N2181K	0078	0198	1 AN 250-C28B	1882	lsf pvt
☐ N102FX	Eurocopter (Aerosp.) AS350B AStar	1059	N114DR	0079	0198	1 TU Arriel 1B	1950	
☐ N111FN	Eurocopter (Aerosp.) AS350B AStar	2060	JA9713	0088	0198	1 TU Arriel 1B	1950	
☐ N213WC	Eurocopter (Aerosp.) AS350B AStar	2180	JA9811	0089	0198	1 TU Arriel 1B	1950	lsf pvt
☐ N29FX	Eurocopter (Aerosp.) AS350B AStar	2085	N510TK	0088	0198	1 TU Arriel 1B	1950	lsf pvt
☐ N315TV	Eurocopter (Aerosp.) AS350B AStar	2269	N350EL	0089	0598	1 TU Arriel 1B	1950	
☐ N32FX	Eurocopter (Aerosp.) AS350BA AStar	2791	N500XP	0094	0198	1 TU Arriel 1B	2100	
☐ N410TV	Eurocopter (Aerosp.) AS350B2 AStar	2408	N6371P	0091	1097	1 TU Arriel 1D1	2250	lsf pvt
☐ N500WC	Eurocopter (Aerosp.) AS350B AStar	1509	N514WW	0082	0198	1 TU Arriel 1B	1950	lsf pvt
☐ N5FX	Eurocopter (Aerosp.) AS350B AStar	1714	N669WG	0083	0198	1 TU Arriel 1B	1950	lsf pvt
☐ N5NY	Eurocopter (Aerosp.) AS350BA AStar	2822	N60992	0094	0198	1 TU Arriel 1B	2100	lsf pvt
☐ N67TV	Eurocopter (Aerosp.) AS350BA AStar	2859	N4024P	0095	0198	1 TU Arriel 1B	2100	lsf pvt
☐ N794WC	Eurocopter (Aerosp.) AS350B AStar	2122	N8693Z	0088	0198	1 TU Arriel 1B	1950	lsf pvt
☐ N795WC	Eurocopter (Aerosp.) AS350B AStar	2376	JA6030	0090	0198	1 TU Arriel 1B	1950	lsf pvt
☐ N989WC	Eurocopter (Aerosp.) AS350B AStar	1923	N58058	0086	0198	1 TU Arriel 1B	1950	lsf pvt
☐ N253WC	Eurocopter (Aerosp.) AS355F1 TwinStar	5206	N355H	0082	0198	2 AN 250-C20F	2400	lsf pvt
☐ N255BB	Eurocopter (Aerosp.) AS355F2 TwinStar	5413		0089	0198	2 AN 250-C20F	2540	lsf pvt
☐ N96WC	Agusta A109C	7661	N1NQ	0092	0198	2 AN 250-C20R/1	2720	lsf pvt
☐ N313CF	Bell UH-1H (205)	5657	66-1174	0066	1296	1 LY T53-L-13B	4309	

HELITAC AVIATION, Inc.
Los Angeles-Heliport, CA

1910 West Sunset Blvd, Suite 900, Los Angeles, CA 90026, USA ☎ (213) 483-6898 Tx: none Fax: (213) 483-4185 SITA: n/a
F: 1978 ꕔꕔꕔ n/a Head: Michael V. Dreesman Net: n/a Aircraft below MTOW 1361kg: Hughes 369HS (500C)

registration	type of aircraft	cn/fn	ex/ex*	mfd	del	powered by	mtow kg	name/fln/specialities/remarks
☐ N17TV	Bell 206B JetRanger	1751	N15BG	0075	0381	1 AN 250-C20	1451	
☐ N16728	Bell 206L LongRanger	45073		0077	0483	1 AN 250-C20B	1814	

HELITRADEWINDS, Inc.
Portland-Private Heliport, OR

2244 SE 28th Place, Portland, OR 97214, USA ☎ (503) 829-4354 Tx: none Fax: none SITA: n/a
F: 1988 ꕔꕔꕔ n/a Head: John M. Solvay Net: n/a

registration	type of aircraft	cn/fn	ex/ex*	mfd	del	powered by	mtow kg	name/fln/specialities/remarks
☐ N214PC	MD Helicopters MD 500D (Hughes 369D)	1100851D	N214FA	0080	0892	1 AN 250-C20B	1361	
☐ N5205G	MD Helicopters MD 530F (Hughes 369FF)	0011F		0084	0593	1 AN 250-C30	1406	

HELITRANS, Co. Inc. (Sister company of Heli Tech, Inc.)
Manvel-Heliport, TX

22015 S. Freeway, Manvel, TX 77578, USA ☎ (281) 431-0531 Tx: NONE Fax: (281) 431-1354 SITA: n/a
F: 1980 ꕔꕔꕔ n/a Head: Gene E. Allen Net: n/a

registration	type of aircraft	cn/fn	ex/ex*	mfd	del	powered by	mtow kg	name/fln/specialities/remarks
☐ N12HT	Bell 206B JetRanger III	3064	N5744L	0080	1089	1 AN 250-C20B	1451	lsf Heli Tech Inc.
☐ N18HT	Bell 206B JetRanger II	2210	N16789	0077	0286	1 AN 250-C20	1451	lsf Heli Tech Inc.
☐ N28HT	Bell 206B JetRanger III	2840	N1068A	0079	0488	1 AN 250-C20B	1451	lsf Heli Tech Inc.
☐ N31HT	Bell 206B JetRanger III	3193	N3896N	0080	0489	1 AN 250-C20B	1451	lsf Heli Tech Inc.

HELIVISION, Llc
Concord-Regional, NC

9000 Aviation Blvd, Suite 220, Concord, NC 28027, USA ☎ (704) 792-1807 Tx: none Fax: (704) 792-1907 SITA: n/a
F: 1996 ꕔꕔꕔ n/a Head: John Porter Net: n/a

registration	type of aircraft	cn/fn	ex/ex*	mfd	del	powered by	mtow kg	name/fln/specialities/remarks
☐ N1086G	Bell 206B JetRanger III	2981		0080	0296	1 AN 250-C20B	1451	

HENDERSON AVIATION, Company
Junction City-Meadowview Heliport, OR

29484 Meadowview Road, Junction City, OR 97448, USA ☎ (541) 688-4777 Tx: none Fax: none SITA: n/a
F: 1946 ꕔꕔꕔ n/a Head: John P. Henderson Net: n/a Aircraft below MTOW 1361 kg: Bell 47G.

registration	type of aircraft	cn/fn	ex/ex*	mfd	del	powered by	mtow kg	name/fln/specialities/remarks
☐ N3896Y	Bell 206B JetRanger III	3199		0080	0281	1 AN 250-C20B	1451	
☐ N90326	Bell 206B JetRanger	1764		0075	0775	1 AN 250-C20	1451	
☐ N3913N	Bell 206L-1 LongRanger III	45664		0081	0284	1 AN 250-C30P	1882	cvtd LongRanger II
☐ N972JG	Bell 206L-3 LongRanger III	51293		0089	0593	1 AN 250-C30P	1882	

HENDRICK MOTORSPORTS – Flight Dept. (Flight Dept. of Hendrick Motorsports, Inc.)

Concord-Regional, NC

PO Box 9, Harrisburg, NC 28075, USA ☎ (704) 455-3400 Tx: none Fax: (704) 455-0346 SITA: n/a
F: n/a ⁂ n/a Head: Jay Lockwall Net: n/a Operates non-commercial corporate flights exclusively for itself and its motor-racing-teams.

registration	type of aircraft	cn/fn	ex	mfd	del	powered by	mtow kg	configuration	selcal	remarks
☐ N501RH	Beech King Air 200	BB-805	N3812S	0081	0190	2 PWC PT6A-41	5670	Corporate		
☐ N502RH	Beech King Air 200	BB-673	N673YV	0080	0992	2 PWC PT6A-41	5670	Corporate		
☐ N504RH	Beech 1900C Airliner	UB-72	OY-JRS	0087	0897	2 PWC PT6A-65B	7530	Corporate		
☐ N505RH	Beech 1900C Airliner	UB-56	OY-JRP	0086	1096	2 PWC PT6A-65B	7530	Corporate		
☐ N500RH	GAC (Grumman) G-1159 Gulfstream II	080	N85VT	0070	0896	2 RR Spey 511-8	29393	Corporate		

HERMANN HOSPITAL LIFEFLIGHT (The Hermann Trust dba)

Houston-Hermann Hospital Helipad, TX

6411 Fannin Street, Houston, TX 77030, USA ☎ (281) 704-4747 Tx: none Fax: (281) 704-2789 SITA: n/a
F: 1981 ⁂ n/a Head: R. Page David Net: n/a

registration	type of aircraft	cn/fn	ex	mfd	del	powered by	mtow kg	configuration	selcal	remarks
☐ N110HH	Eurocopter (MBB) BK117A-4	7122	D-HBCQ	0087	0394	2 LY LTS101-650B.1	3200	EMS LifeFlight		
☐ N117UT	Eurocopter (MBB) BK117A-4	7133	N9024R	0087	0394	2 LY LTS101-650B.1	3200	EMS LifeFlight		
☐ N220HH	Eurocopter (MBB) BK117B-1	7215	N33038	0090	0394	2 LY LTS101-750B.1	3200	EMS LifeFlight		

HIGH ADVENTURE AIR CHARTER Guides & Outfitters, Inc.

Soldotna, AK

PO Box 486, Soldotna, AK 99669, USA ☎ (907) 262-5237 Tx: none Fax: (907) 262-6566 SITA: n/a
F: 1982 ⁂ 5 Head: Sandra J. Bell Net: http://www.highadventureair.com Aircraft below MTOW 1361 kg: Piper PA-18 (on Floats / Wheel-Skis)

registration	type of aircraft	cn/fn	ex	mfd	del	powered by	mtow kg	configuration	selcal	remarks
☐ N9676H	Cessna A185F Skywagon II	18503459		0077	0983	1 CO IO-520-D	1520			lsf Soldotna Aircraft/Floats/Wheel-Skis
☐ N500HA	Cessna U206F Stationair II	U20603446	N8590Q	0076	0690	1 CO IO-520-F	1633			lsf Soldotna Aircraft / Floats/Wheels
☐ N338JM	De Havilland DHC-2 Beaver I	456	CF-EYP	0052	0588	1 PW R-985	2313			lsf Soldotna Aircraft/Floats/Wheel-Skis
☐ N4982U	De Havilland DHC-2 Beaver I	904	C-GJAK	0055	0885	1 PW R-985	2313			lsf Soldotna Aircraft/Floats/Wheel-Skis
☐ N104KH	Piper PA-31-350 Navajo Chieftain	31-7752131		0077	0491	2 LY TIO-540-J2BD	3175			lsf Soldotna Aircraft & Equipment

HIGH COUNTRY HELICOPTERS, Inc.

Montrose-Regional, CO

1551 Road 6450, Montrose, CO 81401, USA ☎ (970) 249-6569 Tx: none Fax: (970) 249-6743 SITA: n/a
F: 1980 ⁂ n/a Head: Richard A. Dick Net: n/a Aircraft below MTOW 1361kg: Bell 47G

registration	type of aircraft	cn/fn	ex	mfd	del	powered by	mtow kg	configuration	selcal	remarks
☐ N213HC	Bell 206L-1 LongRanger III	45354	N222AC	0079	0597	1 AN 250-C30P	1882			cvtd LongRanger II
☐ N209HC	Bell UH-1H (205)	12199	N6195C	0069	0497	1 LY T53-L-13	4309			

HI-LIFT HELICOPTERS International, Ltd

Orlando-Kissimmee Municipal, FL

51 North Airport Road, Kissimmee, FL 34741, USA ☎ (561) 846-2229 Tx: none Fax: (561) 846-8690 SITA: n/a
F: 1988 ⁂ n/a Head: Burnell O. Stutesman Net: n/a

registration	type of aircraft	cn/fn	ex	mfd	del	powered by	mtow kg	configuration	selcal	remarks
☐ N15AH	Sikorsky S-58ET	58-1563	D-HBWR	0062		1 PWC PT6T-6 TwinPac	5897			lsf Aris Helicopters / cvtd S-58E

HILINE HELICOPTERS, Inc.

Darrington-Municipal, WA

47225 Sauk Prairie Road, Darrington, WA 98241, USA ☎ (206) 436-1302 Tx: none Fax: none SITA: n/a
F: 1978 ⁂ 2 Head: Anthony B. Reece Net: n/a

registration	type of aircraft	cn/fn	ex	mfd	del	powered by	mtow kg	configuration	selcal	remarks
☐ N1088G	MD Helicopters MD 500D (Hughes 369D)	700736D		0080	0393	1 AN 250-C20B	1361			lsf pvt
☐ N8612F	MD Helicopters MD 500D (Hughes 369D)	570142D		0077	0782	1 AN 250-C20B	1361			
☐ N5517N	Bell UH-1H (205)	9589	67-17391	0067	0996	1 LY T53-L-13	4309			

HILLCREST AIRCRAFT, Company Inc.

Lewiston-Nez Perce County, ID

PO Box 504, Lewiston, ID 83501, USA ☎ (208) 746-8271 Tx: none Fax: (208) 743-6872 SITA: n/a
F: 1945 ⁂ 10 Head: Gale E. Wilson Net: n/a

registration	type of aircraft	cn/fn	ex	mfd	del	powered by	mtow kg	configuration	selcal	remarks
☐ N1087N	Bell 206B JetRanger III	3019		0080	0880	1 AN 250-C20B	1451			
☐ N2061J	Bell 206B JetRanger III	3333		0081	0881	1 AN 250-C20B	1451			lsf pvt
☐ N27637	Bell 206B JetRanger III	2740		0079	0298	1 AN 250-C20B	1451			
☐ N39102	Bell 206B JetRanger III	3291		0081	0581	1 AN 250-C20B	1451			
☐ N5373U	Bell 206B JetRanger III	4011		0088	0888	1 AN 250-C20J	1451			lsf pvt
☐ N618PC	Bell 206B JetRanger III	4222		0092	0492	1 AN 250-C20J	1451			
☐ N124H	Bell 206L-3 LongRanger III	51333		0090	0290	1 AN 250-C30P	1882			
☐ N7061E	Bell 206L-3 LongRanger III	51277		0089	0389	1 AN 250-C30P	1882			
☐ N868H	Bell 206L-3 LongRanger III	51318	C-GHHZ	0089	0195	1 AN 250-C30P	1882			
☐ N669H	Bell 205A-1	30171	C-GMHC	0074	0597	1 LY T5313B	4309			

HILLSBORO AVIATION & HELICOPTERS (Hillsboro Aviation, Inc. dba)

Portland-Hillsboro, OR

3565 NE Cornell Road, Hillsboro, OR 97124, USA ☎ (541) 648-2831 Tx: none Fax: (541) 648-1886 SITA: n/a
F: 1980 ⁂ n/a Head: Edward Cooley Net: http://www.hillsboro-aviation.com Aircraft below MTOW 1361kg: Cessna 172/182 & Robinson R22

registration	type of aircraft	cn/fn	ex	mfd	del	powered by	mtow kg	configuration	selcal	remarks
☐ N58251	MD Helicopters MD 500D (Hughes 369D)	880317D		0078	0893	1 AN 250-C20B	1361			
☐ N106TV	Bell 206B JetRanger III	2783	N102LP	0079	0497	1 AN 250-C20B	1451			
☐ N12AT	Bell 206B JetRanger	1329	N358ST	0074	1090	1 AN 250-C20	1451			
☐ N636ES	Bell 206B JetRanger III	4117		0090	0890	1 AN 250-C20J	1451			lsf pvt
☐ N8NU	Bell 206B JetRanger III	3346		0081	0893	1 AN 250-C20B	1451			
☐ N9993K	Bell 206B JetRanger II	2054		0076	1197	1 AN 250-C20	1451			
☐ N1186Q	Cessna TU206F Turbo Stationair	U20601941	HL1045	0073	0297	1 CO TSIO-520-F	1633			
☐ N2163N	Piper PA-44-180 Seminole	44-7995222		0079	0696	2 LY O-360-E1A6D	1724			
☐ N39523	Piper PA-44-180 Seminole	44-7995011		0079	0593	2 LY O-360-E1A6D	1724			
☐ N81EA	Bell 206L-3 LongRanger III	51094	N22433	0084	0395	1 AN 250-C30P	1882			lsf GST America Inc.
☐ N27279	Piper PA-31-325 Navajo C/R	31-7712070		0077	1094	2 LY TIO-540-F2BD	2948			

HILTON AVIATION (BAC 1-11 Corp. dba / Subsidiary of Hilton Hotel Corporation)

Las Vegas-McCarran Int'l, NV

6005 Las Vegas Blvd. South, Suite 157, Las Vegas, NV 89119, USA ☎ (702) 739-8732 Tx: none Fax: (702) 739-6827 SITA: n/a
F: 1985 ⁂ n/a Head: Tom Hartmann Net: n/a Operates non-commercial corporate flights exclusively for the Hilton Hotel group.

registration	type of aircraft	cn/fn	ex	mfd	del	powered by	mtow kg	configuration	selcal	remarks
☐ N700HH	Hawker 700A (HS 125-700A)	257045 / NA0240	N130BA	0078	0679	2 GA TFE731-3R-1H	11567	Corporate		
☐ N354TC	Canadair CL-601-3R (CL-600-2B16) Challen.	5192		0096	0197	2 GE CF34-3A1	20457	Corporate		lsf Benco Inc.
☐ N700BH	GAC (Grumman) G-1159 Gulfstream II (SP)	115	N200BP	0072	1192	2 RR Spey 511-8	29710	Corporate		lsf Benco Inc. / cvtd II

HIRTH AIR TANKERS – H.A.T. (Constance C. Hirth dba)

Buffalo-Johnson County, WY

160 Airport Road, Buffalo, WY 82834, USA ☎ (307) 684-7160 Tx: none Fax: (307) 684-7160 SITA: n/a
F: 1987 ⁂ 5 Head: Constance C. Hirth Net: n/a

registration	type of aircraft	cn/fn	ex	mfd	del	powered by	mtow kg	configuration	selcal	remarks
☐ N7080C	Lockheed PV-2 (Model 15) Harpoon	15-1465	37499	0044	1189	2 PW R-2800	14969	Sprayer/Tanker		39
☐ N7272C	Lockheed PV-2 (Model 15) Harpoon	15-1242	37276	0044	0588	2 PW R-2800	14969	Sprayer		40
☐ N7458C	Lockheed PV-2 (Model 15) Harpoon	15-1200	37234	0044	0588	2 PW R-2800	14969	Sprayer/Tanker		37
☐ N7459C	Lockheed PV-2 (Model 15) Harpoon	15-1196	37230	0044	0889	2 PW R-2800	14969	Sprayer		
☐ N7670C	Lockheed PV-2 (Model 15) Harpoon	15-1438	37472	0044	1287	2 PW R-2800	14969	Sprayer		36

HMC HELICOPTER SERVICE, Inc.

Homestead-General Aviation, FL

28790 SW 217 Avenue, Homestead, FL 33030, USA ☎ (305) 233-8788 Tx: none Fax: (305) 248-1507 SITA: n/a
F: 1989 ⁂ n/a Head: James P. Hunter Net: n/a

registration	type of aircraft	cn/fn	ex	mfd	del	powered by	mtow kg	configuration	selcal	remarks
☐ N900HH	Bell 206B JetRanger III	3139	N5758N	0080	0497	1 AN 250-C20B	1451			
☐ N911HH	Bell 206B JetRanger III	3571	N2249B	0082	0794	1 AN 250-C20B	1451			
☐ N914HH	Bell 206B JetRanger III	2297	N16914	0077	0295	1 AN 250-C20B	1451			

HOLMAN AVIATION (Holman Enterprises dba)

Kalispell-Glacier Park Int'l, MT

PO Box 218, Kalispell, MT 59901, USA ☎ (406) 755-5362 Tx: none Fax: (406) 755-5900 SITA: n/a
F: 1972 ⁂ n/a Head: Robert C. Holman Net: n/a Aircraft below MTOW 1361kg: Cessna 172

registration	type of aircraft	cn/fn	ex	mfd	del	powered by	mtow kg	configuration	selcal	remarks
☐ N61902	Cessna A185F Skywagon II	18504271		0081	0794	1 CO IO-520-D	1520			lsf Tern
☐ N21BE	Cessna P210N Pressurized Centurion II	P21000456		0079	0689	1 CO TSIO-520-P	1814			lsf Centurions
☐ N1920E	Cessna 340A II	340A0669		0079	1090	2 CO TSIO-520-NB	2717			
☐ N160NA	Piper PA-31T Cheyenne II	31T-7720060	XB-JIC	0077	1096	2 PWC PT6A-28	4082			

HOLMAN'S MED WING (Holman Funeral Home, Inc. dba)

Ozark-Blackwell Field, AL

905 South Union Avenue, Ozark, AL 36360, USA ☎ (334) 774-5348 Tx: none Fax: (334) 774-7272 SITA: n/a
F: 1977 ⁂ n/a Head: William A. Holman Net: n/a

registration	type of aircraft	cn/fn	ex	mfd	del	powered by	mtow kg	configuration	selcal	remarks
☐ N800MW	Piper PA-31-350 Navajo Chieftain	31-8252011		0082	0792	2 LY TIO-540-J2BD	3175	EMS/Air Hearse		

HOMER AIR (C & L, Inc. dba)

Homer, AK

PO Box 302, Homer, AK 99603, USA ☎ (907) 235-4767 Tx: none Fax: (907) 235-2301 SITA: n/a
F: 1973 ⁂ n/a Head: Larry T. Thompson Net: n/a

registration	type of aircraft	cn/fn	ex	mfd	del	powered by	mtow kg	configuration	selcal	remarks
☐ N7138Q	Cessna U206F Stationair II	U20603074		0076	1095	1 CO IO-520-F	1633			
☐ N8337Q	Cessna U206F Stationair II	U20603198		0076	0376	1 CO IO-520-F	1633			lsf pvt
☐ N9815M	Cessna U206G Stationair 6 II	U20604572		0078	0789	1 CO IO-520-F	1633			
☐ N5742Y	Piper PA-23-250 Aztec C	27-2867		0065	0584	2 LY IO-540-C4B5	2359			lsf pvt
☐ N104PC	Britten-Norman BN-2A-6 Islander	198	N31JA	0070	1288	2 LY O-540-E4C5	2812			lsf pvt
☐ N6522T	Britten-Norman BN-2A-8 Islander	136	F-OCOZ	0069	1296	2 LY O-540-E4C5	2858			

HOP-A-JET, Inc. (Associate with Air Castle & Global Aviation/Member of The Winfair Aviation Alliance)

Fort Lauderdale-Executive, FL

5500 NW 21st Terrace, Building 17, Fort Lauderdale, FL 33309, USA ☎ (954) 565-6633 Tx: none Fax: (954) 772-6981 SITA: n/a
F: 1976 ⁂ 6 Head: Jack Tse Net: http://www.hopajet.com

registration	type of aircraft	cn/fn	ex/ex*	mfd	del	powered by	mtow kg	configuration	selcal	name/fln/specialitites/remarks
☐ N20HJ	Learjet 25	25-024	N137BC	0069	0194	2 GE CJ610-6	6804	Executive		lsf Winfair Aviation Ltd
☐ N70HJ	Learjet 25	25-049	N900Q	0069	1194	2 GE CJ610-6	6804	Executive		lsf Winfair Aviation Ltd
☐ N30HJ	Learjet 35A	35A-226	N1127M	0079	1193	2 GA TFE731-2-2B	8301	Executive		
☐ N32HJ	Learjet 35A	35A-463	N68LL	0082	0997	2 GA TFE731-2-2B	8301	Executive		
☐ N358AC	Learjet 35A	35A-427	N42LL	0081	0997	2 GA TFE731-2-2B	7711	Executive		lst Air Castle
☐ N53HJ	Learjet 55	55-037	PT-OBR	0082	1097	2 GA TFE731-3AR-2B	9752	Executive		
☐ N556GA	Learjet 55	55-028	N7244W	0082	0897	2 GA TFE731-3AR-2B	9752	Executive		lst Air Castle
☐ N60HJ	Canadair CL-600S (CL-600-1A11) Challenger	1058	N4000X	0082	0995	2 LY ALF502L-2C	18711	Executive		
☐ N63HJ	Canadair CL-600S (CL-600-1A11) Challenger	1021	N914XA	0081	0796	2 LY ALF502L-2C	18711	Executive		lsf Chaljet 1021 Holdings Inc.
☐ N65HJ	Canadair CL-600S (CL-600-1A11) Challenger	1038	N1045X	0082	0796	2 LY ALF502L-2C	18711	Executive		lsf Chaljet 1038 Holdings Inc.
☐ N651AC	Canadair CL-601-1A (CL-600-2A12) Challen.	3009	N873G	0083	1298	2 GE CF34-1A	19550	Executive		lst Air Castle

HORIZON AIR = QX / QXE (Horizon Air Industries, Inc. dba / Member of Alaska Air Group, Inc.)

Seattle-Boeing Field, WA

PO Box 48309, Seattle, WA 98148, USA ☎ (206) 241-6757 Tx: none Fax: (206) 431-4696 SITA: n/a
F: 1981 ⁂ 2900 Head: George Bagley IATA: 481 ICAO: HORIZON AIR Net: http://www.horizonair.com

Scheduled services are operated as an Alaska Airlines Commuter (in own colours & titles), a commuter system to provide feeder connection at AS major hubs, using AS flight numbers.

registration	type of aircraft	cn/fn	ex/ex*	mfd	del	powered by	mtow kg	configuration	selcal	name/fln/specialitites/remarks
☐ N102AV	De Havilland DHC-8-102 Dash 8	091	OE-LLO	0087	0693	2 PWC PW120A	15649	Y37		lsf AVLI
☐ N345PH	De Havilland DHC-8-202 Dash 8Q	476	C-GFYI*	0097	0397	2 PWC PW123D	16465	Y37		The Great City of Wenatchee
☐ N346PH	De Havilland DHC-8-202 Dash 8Q	477		0097	0497	2 PWC PW123D	16465	Y37		The Great City of Redmond/Bend
☐ N347PH	De Havilland DHC-8-202 Dash 8Q	480	C-FWBB*	0097	0597	2 PWC PW123D	16465	Y37		The Great City of Moses Lake
☐ N348PH	De Havilland DHC-8-202 Dash 8Q	484	C-FWBB*	0097	0697	2 PWC PW123D	16465	Y37		
☐ N349PH	De Havilland DHC-8-202 Dash 8Q	486	C-GEOA*	0097	0697	2 PWC PW123D	16465	Y37		
☐ N350PH	De Havilland DHC-8-202 Dash 8Q	488	C-GFQL*	0097	0797	2 PWC PW123D	16465	Y37		The Great City of Pendleton
☐ N351PH	De Havilland DHC-8-202 Dash 8Q	490	C-GFUM*	0097	1297	2 PWC PW123D	16465	Y37		The Great City of Eugene
☐ N352PH	De Havilland DHC-8-202 Dash 8Q	494	C-GHRI*	0097	0897	2 PWC PW123D	16465	Y37		
☐ N353PH	De Havilland DHC-8-202 Dash 8Q	496	C-GFRP*	0097	0997	2 PWC PW123D	16465	Y37		
☐ N354PH	De Havilland DHC-8-202 Dash 8Q	498	C-FCSG*	0097	1097	2 PWC PW123D	16465	Y37		The Great City of North Bend/Coos Bay
☐ N355PH	De Havilland DHC-8-202 Dash 8Q	500	C-GEMU*	0097	1097	2 PWC PW123D	16465	Y37		
☐ N356PH	De Havilland DHC-8-202 Dash 8Q	502	C-GEOZ*	0097	1097	2 PWC PW123D	16465	Y37		
☐ N357PH	De Havilland DHC-8-202 Dash 8Q	504	C-GFRP*	0097	1297	2 PWC PW123D	16465	Y37		The Great City of Portland
☐ N358PH	De Havilland DHC-8-202 Dash 8Q	506	C-FWBB*	0098	0198	2 PWC PW123D	16465	Y37		
☐ N359PH	De Havilland DHC-8-202 Dash 8Q	514	C-GEOA*	0098	0398	2 PWC PW123D	16465	Y37		The Great City of Kelowna
☐ N360PH	De Havilland DHC-8-202 Dash 8Q	515	C-GEWI*	0098	0498	2 PWC PW123D	16465	Y37		The Great City of Medford
☐ N361PH	De Havilland DHC-8-202 Dash 8Q	516	C-GFOD*	0098	0498	2 PWC PW123D	16465	Y37		The Great City of Sun Valley
☐ N362PH	De Havilland DHC-8-202 Dash 8Q	518	C-FDHI*	0098	0698	2 PWC PW123D	16465	Y37		
☐ N363PH	De Havilland DHC-8-202 Dash 8Q	520		0098	0798	2 PWC PW123D	16465	Y37		The Great City of Boise
☐ N364PH	De Havilland DHC-8-202 Dash 8Q	524		0098	1098	2 PWC PW123D	16465	Y37		
☐ N365PH	De Havilland DHC-8-202 Dash 8Q	526		0098	1298	2 PWC PW123D	16465	Y37		
☐ N366PH	De Havilland DHC-8-202 Dash 8Q	510	C-GELN*	0098	0998	2 PWC PW123D	16465	Y37		The Great Cities of Seattle/Tacoma
☐ N367PH	De Havilland DHC-8-202 Dash 8Q	511	C-GDLD*	0098	1298	2 PWC PW123D	16465	Y37		
☐ N368PH	De Havilland DHC-8-202 Dash 8Q	512	C-GDFT*	0098	0898	2 PWC PW123D	16465	Y37		The Great City of Idaho Falls
☐ N369PH	De Havilland DHC-8-202 Dash 8Q	513	C-FWBB*	0098	1198	2 PWC PW123D	16465	Y37		
☐ N370PH	De Havilland DHC-8-202 Dash 8Q	528		0099	0199	2 PWC PW123D	16465	Y37		
☐ N811PH	De Havilland DHC-8-102 Dash 8	023	C-GEOA*	0085	1285	2 PWC PW120A	15649	Y37		The Great Cities of Seattle/Tacoma
☐ N814PH	De Havilland DHC-8-102 Dash 8	043	C-GETI*	0086	0786	2 PWC PW120A	15649	Y37		The Great City of Spokane
☐ N815PH	De Havilland DHC-8-102 Dash 8	050	C-GESR*	0086	1086	2 PWC PW120A	15649	Y37		The Great City of Yakima
☐ N816PH	De Havilland DHC-8-102 Dash 8	054	C-GFOD*	0086	1186	2 PWC PW120A	15649	Y37		The Great Tri-Cities
☐ N821PH	De Havilland DHC-8-102 Dash 8	104	C-GEVP*	0088	0688	2 PWC PW120A	15649	Y37		The Great City of Walla Walla
☐ N822PH	De Havilland DHC-8-102 Dash 8	106	C-GFQL*	0088	0688	2 PWC PW120A	15649	Y37		The Great City of Klamath Falls
☐ N823PH	De Havilland DHC-8-102 Dash 8	110	C-GFUM*	0088	0888	2 PWC PW120A	15649	Y37		The Great City of Bellingham
☐ N824PH	De Havilland DHC-8-102 Dash 8	157	C-GEOA*	0089	0789	2 PWC PW120A	15649	Y37		The Great Cities of Pullman/Moscow
☐ N825PH	De Havilland DHC-8-102 Dash 8	213	C-GEOA*	0090	0590	2 PWC PW120A	15649	Y37		The Great Cities of Lewiston/Clarkston
☐ N826PH	De Havilland DHC-8-102 Dash 8	214	C-GFUM*	0090	0590	2 PWC PW120A	15649	Y37		The Great City of Vancouver BC
☐ N827PH	De Havilland DHC-8-102 Dash 8	275	C-GDNG*	0091	0591	2 PWC PW120A	15649	Y37		The Great City of Missoula
☐ N828PH	De Havilland DHC-8-102 Dash 8	287	C-GFYI*	0091	0791	2 PWC PW120A	15649	Y37		The Great Flathead Valley
☐ N829PH	De Havilland DHC-8-102 Dash 8	304	C-GEVP*	0091	1191	2 PWC PW120A	15649	Y37		The Great City of Victoria BC
☐ N830PH	De Havilland DHC-8-102 Dash 8	314	C-GFYI*	0092	0392	2 PWC PW120A	15649	Y37		The Great City of Calgary
☐ N831PH	De Havilland DHC-8-102 Dash 8	328	C-FWBB*	0092	0592	2 PWC PW120A	15649	Y37		The Great City of Billings
☐ N840PH	De Havilland DHC-8-102 Dash 8	074	N802AW	0087	0192	2 PWC PW120A	15649	Y37		The Great City of Pocattelo
☐ N	De Havilland DHC-8-202 Dash 8Q					2 PWC PW123D	16465	Y37		oo-delivery 0499
☐ N	De Havilland DHC-8-202 Dash 8Q					2 PWC PW123D	16465	Y37		oo-delivery 0499
☐ N	De Havilland DHC-8-202 Dash 8Q					2 PWC PW123D	16465	Y37		oo-delivery 0499
☐ N	De Havilland DHC-8-202 Dash 8Q					2 PWC PW123D	16465	Y37		oo-delivery 0599
☐ N	De Havilland DHC-8-202 Dash 8Q					2 PWC PW123D	16465	Y37		oo-delivery 0599
☐ N	De Havilland DHC-8-202 Dash 8Q					2 PWC PW123D	16465	Y37		oo-delivery 0599
☐ N	De Havilland DHC-8-202 Dash 8Q					2 PWC PW123D	16465	Y37		oo-delivery 0699
☐ N	De Havilland DHC-8-202 Dash 8Q					2 PWC PW123D	16465	Y37		oo-delivery 0699
☐ N	De Havilland DHC-8-202 Dash 8Q					2 PWC PW123D	16465	Y37		oo-delivery 0699
☐ N475AU	Fokker F28 Fellowship 4000 (F28 Mk4000)	11222	N117UR	0085	0897	2 RR Spey 555-15P	33112	Y69		lsf Capital Airline Leasing Co.
☐ N476US	Fokker F28 Fellowship 4000 (F28 Mk4000)	11224	N118UR	0085	0897	2 RR Spey 555-15P	33112	Y69		lsf Capital Airline Leasing Co.
☐ N477AU	Fokker F28 Fellowship 4000 (F28 Mk4000)	11226	N119UR	0085	1097	2 RR Spey 555-15P	33112	Y69		lsf USAL
☐ N478US	Fokker F28 Fellowship 4000 (F28 Mk4000)	11227	N204P	0085	0197	2 RR Spey 555-15P	33112	Y69		lsf USAL
☐ N479AU	Fokker F28 Fellowship 4000 (F28 Mk4000)	11228	N205P	0085	1197	2 RR Spey 555-15P	33112	Y69		lsf USAL
☐ N480AU	Fokker F28 Fellowship 4000 (F28 Mk4000)	11229	N206P	0085	0197	2 RR Spey 555-15P	33112	Y69		lsf USAL
☐ N481US	Fokker F28 Fellowship 4000 (F28 Mk4000)	11230	N207P	0086	1097	2 RR Spey 555-15P	33112	Y69		lsf USAL
☐ N482US	Fokker F28 Fellowship 4000 (F28 Mk4000)	11231	N120UR	0086	1197	2 RR Spey 555-15P	33112	Y69		lsf USAL
☐ N483US	Fokker F28 Fellowship 4000 (F28 Mk4000)	11233	N208P	0086	1197	2 RR Spey 555-15P	33112	Y69		lsf USAL
☐ N484US	Fokker F28 Fellowship 4000 (F28 Mk4000)	11234	N209P	0086	0197	2 RR Spey 555-15P	33112	Y69		lsf USAL
☐ N486US	Fokker F28 Fellowship 4000 (F28 Mk4000)	11237	N121UR	0086	0997	2 RR Spey 555-15P	33112	Y69		lsf USAL
☐ N487US	Fokker F28 Fellowship 4000 (F28 Mk4000)	11238	N122UR	0086	0596	2 RR Spey 555-15P	33112	Y69		lsf USAL
☐ N488US	Fokker F28 Fellowship 4000 (F28 Mk4000)	11240	N215P	0086	1297	2 RR Spey 555-15P	33112	Y69		lsf USAL
☐ N490US	Fokker F28 Fellowship 4000 (F28 Mk4000)	11152	N504	0079	0197	2 RR Spey 555-15P	33112	Y69		
☐ N491US	Fokker F28 Fellowship 4000 (F28 Mk4000)	11156	N505	0080	0696	2 RR Spey 555-15P	33112	Y69		
☐ N492US	Fokker F28 Fellowship 4000 (F28 Mk4000)	11159	N107UR	0080	1098	2 RR Spey 555-15P	33112	Y69		
☐ N493US	Fokker F28 Fellowship 4000 (F28 Mk4000)	11161	N509	0080	0796	2 RR Spey 555-15P	33112	Y69		
☐ N494US	Fokker F28 Fellowship 4000 (F28 Mk4000)	11167	N510	0081	0798	2 RR Spey 555-15P	33112	Y69		
☐ N496US	Fokker F28 Fellowship 4000 (F28 Mk4000)	11169	N513	0081	0998	2 RR Spey 555-15P	33112	Y69		
☐ N497US	Fokker F28 Fellowship 4000 (F28 Mk4000)	11173	N108UR	0081	1098	2 RR Spey 555-15P	33112	Y69		
☐ N498US	Fokker F28 Fellowship 4000 (F28 Mk4000)	11181	N109UR	0082	0998	2 RR Spey 555-15P	33112	Y69		
☐ N499US	Fokker F28 Fellowship 4000 (F28 Mk4000)	11182	N110UR	0082	0998	2 RR Spey 555-15P	33112	Y69		
☐ N803PH	Fokker F28 Fellowship 1000 (F28 Mk1000)	11031	VH-FKG	0071	1189	2 RR Spey 555-15	29484	Y62		
☐ N	Canadair Regional Jet 700					2 GE CF34-8C1	32885	Y70		oo-delivery 0002
☐ N	Canadair Regional Jet 700					2 GE CF34-8C1	32885	Y70		oo-delivery 0002
☐ N	Canadair Regional Jet 700					2 GE CF34-8C1	32885	Y70		oo-delivery 0002
☐ N	Canadair Regional Jet 700					2 GE CF34-8C1	32885	Y70		oo-delivery 0002
☐ N	Canadair Regional Jet 700					2 GE CF34-8C1	32885	Y70		oo-delivery 0002
☐ N	Canadair Regional Jet 700					2 GE CF34-8C1	32885	Y70		oo-delivery 0003
☐ N	Canadair Regional Jet 700					2 GE CF34-8C1	32885	Y70		oo-delivery 0003
☐ N	Canadair Regional Jet 700					2 GE CF34-8C1	32885	Y70		oo-delivery 0003
☐ N	Canadair Regional Jet 700					2 GE CF34-8C1	32885	Y70		oo-delivery 0003
☐ N	Canadair Regional Jet 700					2 GE CF34-8C1	32885	Y70		oo-delivery 0003
☐ N	Canadair Regional Jet 700					2 GE CF34-8C1	32885	Y70		oo-delivery 0003
☐ N	Canadair Regional Jet 700					2 GE CF34-8C1	32885	Y70		oo-delivery 0003
☐ N	Canadair Regional Jet 700					2 GE CF34-8C1	32885	Y70		oo-delivery 0003
☐ N	Canadair Regional Jet 700					2 GE CF34-8C1	32885	Y70		oo-delivery 0003
☐ N	Canadair Regional Jet 700					2 GE CF34-8C1	32885	Y70		oo-delivery 0003
☐ N	Canadair Regional Jet 700					2 GE CF34-8C1	32885	Y70		oo-delivery 0004
☐ N	Canadair Regional Jet 700					2 GE CF34-8C1	32885	Y70		oo-delivery 0004
☐ N	Canadair Regional Jet 700					2 GE CF34-8C1	32885	Y70		oo-delivery 0004
☐ N	Canadair Regional Jet 700					2 GE CF34-8C1	32885	Y70		oo-delivery 0004
☐ N	Canadair Regional Jet 700					2 GE CF34-8C1	32885	Y70		oo-delivery 0004
☐ N	Canadair Regional Jet 700					2 GE CF34-8C1	32885	Y70		oo-delivery 0004
☐ N	Canadair Regional Jet 700					2 GE CF34-8C1	32885	Y70		oo-delivery 0004
☐ N	Canadair Regional Jet 700					2 GE CF34-8C1	32885	Y70		oo-delivery 0004
☐ N	Canadair Regional Jet 700					2 GE CF34-8C1	32885	Y70		oo-delivery 0004
☐ N	Canadair Regional Jet 700					2 GE CF34-8C1	32885	Y70		oo-delivery 0004

jp airline-fleets international *99/2000*

PHOTO-SECTION

78 postcardsized colour photographs

(current airliner, commuter and helicopter photos of all major aircraft types
in present use, sorted according manufacturers and types)

(they will become available as postcards in autumn 1999 – see advertisement)

Aerospatiale/BAe Concorde 101
F-BVFB (cn 207)
of Air France
at Zurich (8/98)
Photo by Ulrich Klee

Also available as postcard

BUCHairCARD 9901

Airbus Ind. A300-608ST Beluga
(A300-600ST) F-GSTD (cn 776 / fn 4)
of Airbus Transport International
at Zurich (11/98)
Photo by Ulrich Klee

Also available as postcard

BUCHairCARD 9902

Airbus Industrie A310-322
PP-PSD (cn 437)
of Passaredo Transportes Aéreos – PAZ
at Sao Paulo-Guarulhos Int'l (SP) (5/98)
Photo by Alexandre Polati de Carvalho

Also available as postcard

BUCHairCARD 9903

Airbus Industrie A319-112
9A-CTG (cn 767)
of Croatia Airlines «Zadar»
at Zurich (8/98)
Photo by Ulrich Klee

BUCH*air*CARD 9904

Also available as postcard

Airbus Industrie A320-214
HB-IHX (cn 942)
of Edelweiss Air
at Zurich (2/99)
Photo by Martin E. Siegrist

BUCH*air*CARD 9905

Also available as postcard

Airbus Industrie A321-231
G-MIDA (cn 806)
of British Midland
at London-Heathrow (5/98)
Photo by S.P.A.

BUCH*air*CARD 9906

Also available as postcard

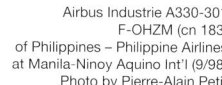

Airbus Industrie A330-301
F-OHZM (cn 183)
of Philippines – Philippine Airlines
at Manila-Ninoy Aquino Int'l (9/98)
Photo by Pierre-Alain Petit

BUCH*air*CARD 9907

Airbus Industrie A340-313
EC-GPB (cn 193)
of Iberia «Teresa de Avila»
at Santiago-Arturo Merino Benitez (11/98)
Photo by Stéphane Mutzenberg

BUCH*air*CARD 9908

Antonov 12BP
LZ-BAE (cn 402001)
of Balkan Bulgarian Airlines
at Zurich (7/98)
Photo by Ulrich Klee

BUCH*air*CARD 9909

Boeing 737-505
LN-BRJ (cn 24273 / fn 2018)
of Braathens «Magnus Barfot»
at Amsterdam-Schiphol (10/98)
Photo by Rob Hemelrijk

BUCHairCARD 9928

Boeing 737-683
SE-DNM (cn 28288 / fn 49)
of Scandinavian Airlines SAS
«Bernt Viking»
at Zurich (1/99)
Photo by Pierre-Alain Petit

BUCHairCARD 9929

Boeing 737-7Q8
LV-YYC (cn 28210 / fn 22)
of LAPA – Lineas Aéreas Privadas Argentinas
at Buenos Aires-Aeroparque J. Newbery (11/98)
Photo by Stéphane Mutzenberg

BUCHairCARD 9930

Boeing 737-8Q8
OY-SEB (cn 28214 / fn 78)
of Sterling European Airlines
at Palma de Mallorca (10/98)
Photo by Rolf Keller

BUCH**air**CARD 9931

Boeing 747-2J9F
EP-ICC (cn 21514 / fn 343)
of Iran Air
at Zurich (8/98)
Photo by Ulrich Klee

BUCH**air**CARD 9932

Boeing 747-4D7
HS-TGO (cn 26609 / fn 1001)
of Thai Airways International
«Bowonrangsi»
at Zurich (12/98)
Photo by Ulrich Klee

BUCH**air**CARD 9933

Boeing 757-2Q8
N713TW (cn 28173 / fn 764)
of Trans World Airlines «fln 7513»
at Las Vegas-McCarran Int'l (NV) (11/98)
Photo by Manfred Turek

BUCH**air**CARD 9934

Boeing 767-259 (ER)
N985AN (cn 24618 / fn 292)
of Avianca Colombia «Cristobal Colon»
at Bogota-Eldorado (2/98)
Photo by Michel Saint-Felix

BUCH**air**CARD 9935

Boeing 767-36D
B-2567 (cn 27685 / fn 686)
of Shanghai Airlines
at Beijing-Capital (11/98)
Photo by Guido E. Bühlmann

BUCH**air**CARD 9936

365

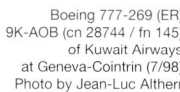

Boeing 777-269 (ER)
9K-AOB (cn 28744 / fn 145)
of Kuwait Airways
at Geneva-Cointrin (7/98)
Photo by Jean-Luc Altherr

BUCHairCARD 9937

Boeing 777-346
JA8941 (cn 28393 / fn 152)
of Japan Airlines – JAL
at Tokyo-Haneda (11/98))
Photo by Ian Bowley

BUCHairCARD 9938

Boeing (Douglas) DC-3A (C-53D-DO)
CU-T127 (cn 11645)
of Aerotaxi
at Havana-Jose Marti Int'l (11/98)
Photo by Daniel Dufner

BUCHairCARD 9939

Boeing (Douglas) DC-4-1009
ZS-BMH (cn 43157 / D4 79)
of South African Airways – SAA «Lebombo»
(op by Historic-Flight division)
at Zurich (7/98)
Photo by Ulrich Klee

Also available as postcard

BUCHairCARD 9940

Boeing (Douglas) DC-8-71F
HK-3786X (cn 45849 / fn 289)
of Tampa Colombia
at Miami-International (FL) (2/99)
Photo by Peter Weder

Also available as postcard

BUCHairCARD 9941

Boeing (Douglas) DC-9-51
N420EA (cn 47689 / fn 802)
of Hawaiian Air «fln 71 / Kahului»
at Kahului (HI) (2/98)
Photo by Rolf Keller

Also available as postcard

BUCHairCARD 9942

367

Boeing (Douglas) DC-10-30
JA8550 (cn 48315 / fn 436)
of Harlequin Air
at Kathmandu-Tribhuvan (11/98)
Photo by Guido E. Bühlmann

BUCHairCARD 9943

Boeing (Douglas) MD-88 (DC-9-88)
LV-VBZ (cn 53049 / fn 2031)
of Aerolineas Argentinas «Parque Baritu»
at San Carlos de Bariloche (2/98)
(Cerro Otto Mountain in background)
Photo by Guido E. Bühlmann

BUCHairCARD 9944

Boeing (Douglas) MD-90-30
HZ-APB (cn 53492 / fn 2205)
of Saudi Arabian Airlines
at Nice-Côte D'Azur (7/98)
Photo by Christian Laugier

BUCHairCARD 9945

Canadair Regional Jet 200LR (CL-600-2B19)
G-MSKL (cn 7247)
of Maersk Air
(op in British Airways Ndebele Emmly-cs.)
at Amsterdam-Schiphol (8/98)
Photo by Rob Hemelrijk

BUCHairCARD 9946

De Havilland DHC-3 Otter
C-FBEP (cn 118)
of Air-Dale Flying Services
at Hawk Junction SPB (Ont.) (7/98)
Photo by Philip M. Kitchen

BUCHairCARD 9947

De Havilland DHC-6 Twin Otter 300
9N-AEQ (cn 708)
of Lumbini Airways
at Lukla (Kwangde Mountain, peak 6187 m,
in background)
Photo by Guido E. Bühlmann

BUCHairCARD 9948

De Havilland DHC-8-311 Dash 8
C-FACV (cn 278)
of AirBC «fln 855 / Campbell River»
at Kelowna (BC) (6/98)
Photo by Damiano Gualdoni

BUCH**air**CARD 9949

Also available as postcard

Dornier 228-202
CS-TGO (cn 8119)
of SATA Air Açores
at Horta (4/98)
Photo by Ralf Kurz

BUCH**air**CARD 9950

Also available as postcard

Dornier 328-110
LN-ASL (cn 3069)
of Air Stord «Macody Lund»
at Chambery (1/99)
Photo by Daniel Heritier

370

BUCH**air**CARD 9951

Also available as postcard

Embraer 110P1 Bandeirante
ZK-LBC (cn 110345)
of Eagle Airways
(op in Air New Zealand Link-colors)
at Auckland-International (11/98)
Photo by Peter Weder

BUCH*air*CARD 9952

Embraer 120ER Brasilia
PH-BRK (cn 120253)
of BASE Airlines
at Ostend (6/98)
Photo by Nik Deblauwe

BUCH*air*CARD 9953

Embraer RJ145ER (EMB-145ER)
N15926 (cn 145005)
of Continental Express «fln 926»
(ExpressJet)
at Minneapolis-St. Paul-Int'l (MN) (4/98)
Photo by Marcus Kolskog

BUCH*air*CARD 9954

371

Eurocopter (Aerosp.) AS350B2 Ecureuil
OE-XHB (cn 2536)
of Helicopter Wucher
at Zürs (Austrian Alps) (2/98)
Photo by Bruno Siegfried

Also available as postcard

BUCHairCARD 9955

Fairchild (Swearingen) SA226TC Metro II
LV-WDU (cn TC-310)
of Kaiken Lineas Aéreas
at Ushuaia-Islas Malvinas (2/98) (Mountain
range Isla Hoste, peak 1533 m, in backgr.)
Photo by Guido E. Bühlmann

Also available as postcard

BUCHairCARD 9956

Fokker F27 Friendship 500F
N284MA (cn 10560)
of Eagle Air
at Las Vegas-McCarran Int'l (NV) (11/98)
Photo by Peter Weder

Also available as postcard

BUCHairCARD 9957

Fokker 50 (F27-050)
B-1272 (cn 20286)
of Formosa Airlines
at Taipei-Sung Shan (4/98)
Photo by Bernhard Baur

BUCH**air**CARD 9958

Fokker 70 (F28-0070)
PH-WXC (cn 11574)
of KLM cityhopper
at Munich-Franz Josef Strauss (7/98)
Photo by S.P.A.

BUCH**air**CARD 9959

Fokker 100 (F28-0100)
F-GPXD (cn 11494)
of Air France
at Basel/Mulhouse-EuroAirport (8/98)
Photo by Lukas Lusser

BUCH**air**CARD 9960

Also available as postcard

Ilyushin 18D
YR-IMM (cn 187009904)
of Romavia
at Malta-Luqa (6/98)
Photo by Daniel Dufner

Also available as postcard

BUCHairCARD 9961

Ilyushin 76TD
UK-76811 (cn 1013407223)
of Uzbekistan Airways
at Zurich (5/98)
Photo by Ulrich Klee

Also available as postcard

BUCHairCARD 9962

Ilyushin 86
RA-86140 (cn 51483211102)
of AJT Air International
at Rimini-Miramare (10/98)
Photo by Claudio Bruschi

Also available as postcard

374

BUCHairCARD 9963

Ilyushin 114T
UK-91004
of Tashkent Aircraft Production
at Bangalore-Yelahanka AFB (12/98)
Photo by Guido E. Bühlmann

BUCHairCARD 9964

Lockheed L-188PF Electra
G-FIJR (cn 1138)
of Atlantic Airlines
at Stockholm-Arlanda (4/98)
Photo by Ola Carlsson

BUCHairCARD 9965

Lockheed L-382G (L-100-30) Hercules
5X-UCF (cn 34C-4610)
of Uganda Air Cargo «The Silver Lady»
at Zurich (8/98)
Photo by Ulrich Klee

BUCHairCARD 9966

Also available as postcard

Also available as postcard

Also available as postcard

Lockheed L-1011-385-3 TriStar 500
SE-DVF (cn 293B-1241)
of Novair
at Stockholm-Arlanda (3/98)
Photo by Ola Carlsson

BUCHairCARD 9967

Mil Mi-26
HL9261 (cn 071217)
of Samsung Aerospace – Transport division
at Seoul-Sungnam AB (10/98)
Photo by Guido E. Bühlmann

BUCHairCARD 9968

Saab 340A
LV-AXV (cn 340A-094)
of TAN – Transportes Aéreos Neuquen
at Neuquen (2/98)
Photo by Guido E. Bühlmann

BUCHairCARD 9969

Saab 2000
SE-LSH (cn 2000-052)
of Med Airlines
at Verona (8/98)
Photo by Marco Ceschi

BUCH*air*CARD 9970

Shorts 360-200 (SD3-60)
SE-LDA (cn SH3688)
of Flying Enterprise
at Stockholm-Bromma (9/98)
Photo by Marcus Kolskog

BUCH*air*CARD 9971

Tupolev 134A-3
RA-65093 (cn 60215)
of Pulkovo Aviation Enterprise
at Rimini-Miramare (10/98)
Photo by Claudio Bruschi

BUCH*air*CARD 9972   377

Tupolev 154B-2
RA-85457 (cn 457)
of KMV – Kavkazskie Mineralnye Vody
at Sharjah (12/98)
Photo by S.P.A.

BUCHairCARD 9973

Yakovlev 40
RA-87966 (cn 9820958)
of Tulpar Aviation Company
at Geneva-Cointrin (1/99)
Photo by Jean-Luc Altherr

BUCHairCARD 9974

Yakovlev 42D
RA-42417 (cn 4520423219110)
of East Line Airlines
at Moscow-Domodedovo (7/98)
Photo by Guido E. Bühlmann

BUCHairCARD 9975

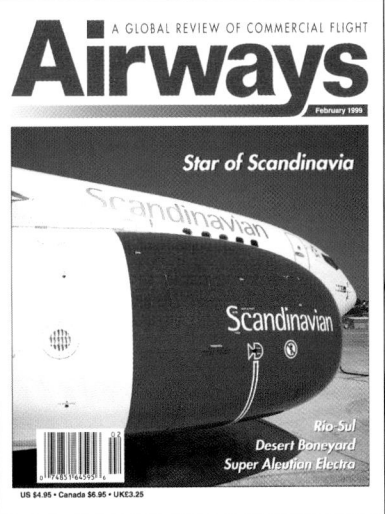

"*Airways* is, by far, the best aviation magazine I have seen!"

—Flight Engineer, US Major Airline

Airways—the exciting international monthly magazine devoted to airlines and commercial aircraft. Featuring superb color photography, *Airways* focuses on the present-day airline industry and commercial aircraft: flying them, operating them, traveling in them, and supporting them. The magazine's worldwide editorial contributors cover the airlines, the manufacturers, the people, the new technologies, the airports, and the airways. Plus, *Airways* takes a nostalgic look at the past.

Written for airline and air travel industry professionals and aficionados, *Airways* features quality editorial written by those with a genuine and comprehensive background in the airline and air transport industry.

The CD-ROM jp 99 / 2000
is an identical electronic
version of the yearbook

(no database)

800
pages packed
with data

78 color
pictures

With
indexed
fast
search

jp **airline-
fleets**
international

The Origi...

including
specialit...
governme...
plus 78 co...

With
Option
for
Printing

...ince 1966,

The «Bible» of Airline Aviation

Edition 99 / 2000

Windows
Macintosh
Unix

Minimum System Requirements:

Windows
 – 486- or Pentium-PC
 – Microsoft Windows 3.x, 95 / 98, NT
 – 8 MB system RAM, 4 MB hard disk space (Acrobat Reader Software)

Macintosh
 – Macintosh computer with 68020 (Macintosh II series) or greater processor
 – MacOS 7.0 or greater
 – 4 MB application RAM, 4 MB hard disk space (Acrobat Reader Software)

TAKE OFF !

ORDER NOW WITH THE COLOURED CARD
IN THE FRONT SECTION OF THIS BOOK

OR CONTACT OUR REPRESENTATIVE IN YOUR COUNTRY   (SEE PAGE 2)

380

HORIZON HELICOPTERS (Dennis N. Westerberg dba) — Rancho Murieta, CA

7443 Murieta Drive, Rancho Murieta, CA 95683, USA ☎ (530) 966-8181 Tx: none Fax: (530) 354-0911 SITA: n/a
F: 1984 7 Head: Dennis N. Westerberg Net: http://www.hhcopters.com

☐ N969W	Bell 206B JetRanger III	2320	N131VG	0078	0887	1 AN 250-C20B	1451			
☐ N869W	Bell UH-1H (205)	10460	68-15530	0068	0497	1 LY T53-L-13	4309			

HORIZON HELICOPTERS, Inc. — Matagorda-Private Heliport, TX

PO Box 150, Matagorda, TX 77457, USA ☎ (409) 863-7241 Tx: none Fax: (403) 863-2282 SITA: n/a
F: 1991 n/a Head: Mark R. Lancaster Net: n/a Aircraft below MTOW 1361kg: Hughes 369HS (500C)

☐ N158H	Bell 206B JetRanger III	2974	N10857	0080	0394	1 AN 250-C20B	1451			
☐ N167H	Bell 206B JetRanger III	2968	N227EH	0080	0496	1 AN 250-C20B	1451			
☐ N2201W	Bell 206B JetRanger III	3477		0081	0697	1 AN 250-C20B	1451			
☐ N35WH	Bell 206B JetRanger III	2736		0079	0498	1 AN 250-C20B	1451			
☐ N45SH	Bell 206B JetRanger III	3453	N711NM	0081	0398	1 AN 250-C20B	1451			
☐ N605RD	Bell 206B JetRanger III	3216	N605PD	0080	0898	1 AN 250-C20B	1451			
☐ N907CA	Bell 206B JetRanger III	4130		0090	1296	1 AN 250-C20B	1451			to be re-reg. N168H

HORIZONS UNLIMITED, Inc. = HUD — Portland-Hillsboro, OR

PO Box 1778, Hillsboro, OR 97123, USA ☎ (541) 640-1134 Tx: none Fax: (541) 681-9199 SITA: n/a
F: 1990 n/a Head: Kevin R. McCullough ICAO: HUD Net: n/a

☐ N222LE	Twin (Aero) Commander 500B	500B-1525-187		0065	0795	2 LY IO-540-B1A5 Rajay	3062	Freighter		
☐ N23KM	Twin (Aero) Commander 500B	500B-1436-153	N6364U	0064	0590	2 LY IO-540-B1A5	3062	Freighter		
☐ N24KM	Twin (Aero) Commander 500B	500B-1296-111	N3114X	0063	0793	2 LY IO-540-B1A5	3062	Freighter		
☐ N353CC	Twin (Aero) Commander 500B	500B-1230-105		0062	0796	2 LY IO-540-B1A5 Rajay	3062	Freighter		
☐ N78384	Twin (Aero) Commander 500B	500B-1297-112		0063	1096	2 LY IO-540-B1A5 Rajay	3062	Freighter		
☐ N349AC	Twin (Aero) Turbo Commander 690	11032	N8LD	0072	0498	2 GA TPE331-5-251K	4649	Freighter		

HOSPITAL AIRTRANSPORT, Inc. — Seattle-Boeing Field/King County Int'l, WA

PO Box 2520, Portland, OR 97208, USA ☎ (503) 249-2145 Tx: none Fax: (503) 249-2064 SITA: n/a
F: 1982 n/a Head: Thomas Hutson, Sr. Net: n/a

☐ N1VH	Agusta A109A II	7273	N109AZ	0083	0392	2 AN 250-C20B	2600	EMS		
☐ N1YH	Agusta A109A II	7264	N109AH	0083	0392	2 AN 250-C20B	2600	EMS		
☐ N2MF	Agusta A109A II	7277	N1EQ	0083	0185	2 AN 250-C20B	2600	EMS		lsf Agusta Aerospace Corp.
☐ N55NW	Agusta A109A II	7267	N72520	0083	0882	2 AN 250-C20B	2600	EMS		lsf MK II Inc.

HOUSTON HELICOPTERS, Inc. - HHI = HHO — Pearland-Heliport, TX

3506 Lockheed, Pearland, TX 77581, USA ☎ (281) 485-1777 Tx: none Fax: (281) 485-3701 SITA: n/a
F: 1962 25 Head: R. Lee Grimes ICAO: HOUSTON HELI Net: n/a

☐ N107CC	Bell 206B JetRanger III	2374		0078	0690	1 AN 250-C20J	1451			
☐ N16770	Bell 206B JetRanger II	2147		0077	0377	1 AN 250-C20	1451			
☐ N16814	Bell 206B JetRanger III	2229		0077	0977	1 AN 250-C20J	1451			
☐ N2949W	Bell 206B JetRanger	824		0072	0774	1 AN 250-C20	1451			
☐ N49742	Bell 206B JetRanger II	1972		0076	0676	1 AN 250-C20	1451			
☐ N5007E	Bell 206B JetRanger III	2484		0078	0978	1 AN 250-C20J	1451			
☐ N59518	Bell 206B JetRanger	1322		0074	0474	1 AN 250-C20	1451			
☐ N59531	Bell 206B JetRanger	1352		0074	0578	1 AN 250-C20	1451			
☐ N59589	Bell 206B JetRanger	1482		0074	1074	1 AN 250-C20	1451			
☐ N59604	Bell 206B JetRanger	1490		0074	1274	1 AN 250-C20	1451			
☐ N6139Q	Bell 206B JetRanger	1276		0074	0578	1 AN 250-C20	1451			
☐ N1071A	Bell 206L-1 LongRanger II	45340		0079	0180	1 AN 250-C28B	1882			
☐ N2135Y	Bell 206L-1 LongRanger II	45640		0081	0189	1 AN 250-C28B	1882			
☐ N2774V	Bell 206L-1 LongRanger II	45308		0079	1179	1 AN 250-C28B	1882			
☐ N4246Z	Bell 206L-3 LongRanger III	51475		0091	0591	1 AN 250-C30P	1882			
☐ N42489	Bell 206L-3 LongRanger III	51474		0091	0591	1 AN 250-C30P	1882			
☐ N57377	Bell 206L-1 LongRanger II	45458		0080	0880	1 AN 250-C28B	1882			
☐ N5737V	Bell 206L-1 LongRanger II	45457		0080	0880	1 AN 250-C28B	1882			
☐ N57400	Bell 206L-1 LongRanger II	45464		0080	0880	1 AN 250-C28B	1882			
☐ N5755N	Bell 206L-1 LongRanger II	45535		0080	1280	1 AN 250-C28B	1882			
☐ N5009M	Sikorsky S-76A	760041		0080	0380	2 AN 250-C30	4672			
☐ N90421	Sikorsky S-76A	760039	C-GMQD	0080	0587	2 AN 250-C30	4672			
☐ N8144M	Bell 212	30706	C-FSAI	0075	0795	2 PWC PT6T-3 TwinPac	5080			
☐ N8145Y	Bell 212	30795	C-FSAU	0076	0795	2 PWC PT6T-3 TwinPac	5080			
☐ N8223V	Bell 212	30728	C-FRUQ	0075	0795	2 PWC PT6T-3 TwinPac	5080			
☐ N8224V	Bell 212	30808	C-FRUP	0076	0795	2 PWC PT6T-3 TwinPac	5080			
☐ N9937K	Bell 212	30778		0076	0679	2 PWC PT6T-3 TwinPac	5080			

HUDSON AIR SERVICE, Inc. — Talkeetna, AK

PO Box 648, Talkeetna, AK 99676, USA ☎ (907) 733-2321 Tx: none Fax: (907) 733-2333 SITA: n/a
F: 1948 7 Head: Clifford L. Hudson Net: http://www.alaskan.com/hudsonair Aircraft below MTOW 1361 kg: Cessna 172 & Piper PA-18 (Wheel-Skis)

☐ N1589F	Cessna 185E Skywagon	185-0971		0066	1280	1 CO IO-470-F	1497			lsf pvt / Floats
☐ N9855X	Cessna 185 Skywagon	1850055		0061	0675	1 CO IO-470-F	1451			lsf pvt / Wheel-Skis
☐ N9890X	Cessna 185 Skywagon	1850090		0061	0168	1 CO IO-470-F	1451			lsf pvt / Wheel-Skis
☐ N7396C	Cessna TU206G Turbo Stationair	U20603920		0077	0885	1 CO TSIO-520-M	1633			Wheel-Skis

IBC AIRWAYS, Inc. (Subsidiary of International Bonded Couriers) — Miami-Int'l, FL

8401 NW 17th Street, Miami, FL 33126, USA ☎ (305) 594-9304 Tx: none Fax: (305) 591-2056 SITA: n/a
F: 1991 n/a Head: Joseph Costigan Net: n/a

☐ N248AM	Fairchild (Swearingen) SA226TC Metro II	TC-282	N45RA	0078	1295	2 GA TPE331-10UA-511G	5670	Freighter		lsf Worldwide Aircraft Services Inc.
☐ N355AE	Fairchild (Swearingen) SA227AC Metro III	AC-642	N2684S	0086	1298	2 GA TPE331-11U-611G	6577	Freighter		lsf Int'l Bonded Couriers Inc.
☐ N811BC	Fairchild (Swearingen) SA227AC Metro III	AC-463	N630PA	0081	1196	2 GA TPE331-11U-611G	6577	Freighter		lsf Int'l Bonded Couriers Inc.

ICARUS CARIBBEAN, Corp. (Sister co. of Copters, Corp. & associated with Avitech, Inc.) — San Juan-Isla Grande/Fernando Luis Ribas Dominicci, PR

ICARUS CARIBBEAN

PO Box 41268, San Juan, PR 00940-1268, USA ☎ (787) 729-0007 Tx: none Fax: (787) 729-0003 SITA: n/a
F: 1996 n/a Head: Luis S. Sierra Net: n/a

☐ N278CC	Piper PA-31-325 Navajo C/R	31-7812100		0078	0188	2 LY TIO-540-F2BD	2948			
☐ N279CC	Piper PA-31-310 Navajo	31-402	N360BR	0068	0797	2 LY TIO-540-A1A	2948			

I.C. JET (Investment Capital Group, Llc dba) — Sacramento-Mather, CA

1209 Orange Street, Wilmington, DE 19801, USA ☎ (916) 852-9838 Tx: none Fax: (916) 852-9822 SITA: n/a
F: 1990 n/a Head: Dean Ingemanson Net: http://www.icjet.com
FAR135 operations are conducted under the licence of BUSINESS JET SOLUTIONS.

☐ N48SE	Beech Beechjet 400A	RK-48	N94HT	0092	0496	2 PWC JT15D-5	7303			

ICN - Flight Dept. (Flight Dept. of ICN Pharmaceuticals, Inc.) — Long Beach-Daugherty Field, CA

3300 Hyland Avenue, Costa Mesa, CA 92626, USA ☎ (714) 545-0100 Tx: none Fax: (714) 641-7206 SITA: n/a
F: 1998 n/a Head: David Watts Net: n/a Operates non-commercial corporate flights for its owners only.

☐ N30MP	Boeing 727-21	18998 / 239	N111JL	0066	0398	2/1 PW JT8D-7	72802	Corporate		lsf Mike Plueger Construction

IDAHO HELICOPTERS, Inc. — Boise-Air Terminal/Gowen Field, ID

2471 Commerce Ave, Boise, ID 83705, USA ☎ (208) 344-4361 Tx: n/a Fax: (208) 343-7135 SITA: n/a
F: 1970 30 Head: Larry D. Kelley Net: n/a

☐ N1882	Bell 206B JetRanger III	3960		0086	0988	1 AN 250-C20J	1451			lsf Allen Noble Farms Inc.
☐ N206JH	Bell 206B JetRanger III	2918		0080	0683	1 AN 250-C20B	1451			lsf Farm Development Corp.
☐ N4783P	Cessna P210N Pressurized Centurion II	P21000105		0078	1178	1 CO TSIO-520-P	1814			lsf Allen Noble Farms Inc.
☐ N3186F	Bell 206L-3 LongRanger III	51091		0084	0884	1 AN 250-C30P	1882			lsf Allen Noble Farms Inc.
☐ N377LF	Bell 206L-3 LongRanger III	51281	N7061L	0089	0489	1 AN 250-C30P	1882			lsf Farm Development Corp.
☐ N70606	Bell 206L-3 LongRanger III	51282		0089	0489	1 AN 250-C30P	1882			lsf Farm Development Corp.
☐ N977LF	MD Helicopters MD 900 Explorer	900-00027	N9100L	0096	0896	2 PWC PW206A	2720	EMS LifeFlight		lsf Alvac Inc/opf Saint Alphonsus Boise
☐ N41699	Bell 204B	2040	N204AH	0065	1290	1 LY T5313B	3856			lsf Farm Development Corp.
☐ N10RF	Bell UH-1H (205)	13403	73-21715	0073	0597	1 LY T53-L-13	4309			lsf Farm Development Corp.
☐ N133	Bell UH-1H (205)	4891	65-9847	0065	0395	1 LY T53-L-13	4309			lsf Farm Development Corp.
☐ N23Y	Bell UH-1H (205)	4243	64-13536	0064	0395	1 LY T53-L-13	4309			lsf Farm Development Corp.

IDEAL HELICOPTER SERVICE (McDermott Enterprises, Inc. dba) — Sullivan-McDermott, WI

200 Main Street, Sullivan, WI 53178, USA ☎ (920) 593-8612 Tx: none Fax: (920) 593-2111 SITA: n/a
F: 1976 n/a Head: Wayne E. McDermott Net: n/a Aircraft below MTOW 1361kg: Bell 47G

☐ N8155J	Bell 206B JetRanger	547		0070	0189	1 AN 250-C20	1451			cvtd 206A

381 registration type of aircraft cn/fn ex/ex* mfd del powered by mtow kg configuration selcal name/fln/specialitites/remarks

ILIAMNA AIR TAXI, Inc. = LS / IAR
Iliamna, AK

PO Box 109, Iliamna, AK 99606, USA ☎ (907) 571-1248 Tx: none Fax: (907) 571-1244 SITA: n/a
F: 1967 ⁂ 8 Head: Timothy J. LaPorte ICAO: ILIAMNA AIR Net: n/a

registration	type of aircraft	cn/fn	ex/ex*	mfd	del	powered by	mtow kg	configuration	name/fln/specialitites/remarks
☐ N1577H	Cessna A185F Skywagon	18503310		0077	0194	1 CO IO-520-D	1520		Floats
☐ N756HG	Cessna U206G Stationair 6 II	U20604099		0077	0290	1 CO IO-520-D	1633		
☐ N4495S	Beech Bonanza A36	E-712		0075	0588	1 CO IO-520-B	1633		
☐ N7379U	Cessna 207A Stationair 7 II	20700427		0078	0578	1 CO IO-520-F	1724		
☐ N9720M	Cessna 207A Stationair 8 II	20700720		0081	0583	1 CO IO-520-F	1724		
☐ N121AK	De Havilland DHC-2 Beaver I	121	C-FDJO	0051	0589	1 PW R-985	2313		Floats
☐ N62230	De Havilland DHC-2 Beaver I	707	53-7899	0053	0685	1 PW R-985	2313		Floats
☐ N68088	De Havilland DHC-2 Beaver I	1197		0056	0794	1 PW R-985	2313		Floats
☐ N76SU	De Havilland DHC-2 Beaver I	483	52-6107	0053	0487	1 PW R-985	2313		Floats / Wheel-Skis
☐ N3682Z	Beech Baron 58	TH-1159		0081	1294	2 CO IO-520-CB	2450		
☐ N214TL	Britten-Norman BN-2A-21 Islander	214	N6661A*	0070	0291	2 LY IO-540-K1B5	2994		
☐ N38KC	Piper PA-31-350 Navajo Chieftain	31-8352033		0083	0298	2 LY TIO-540-J2BD	3175		
☐ N715HL	Cessna 208B Grand Caravan	208B0603		0097	0397	1 PWC PT6A-114A	3969		

IMPERIAL PALACE AIR, Ltd
Las Vegas-McCarran Int'l, NV

PO Box 97979, Las Vegas, NV 89193-7979, USA ☎ (702) 794-3394 Tx: none Fax: (702) 794-3375 SITA: n/a
F: 1990 ⁂ n/a Head: Ralph L. Engelstad Net: n/a Operates private executive flights exclusively for the owners (in the Antique Auto Collection-business) only.

☐ N331P	GAC (Grumman) G-1159 Gulfstream II	020	N4SP	0068	1193	2 RR Spey 511-8	29393	Executive	
☐ N7271P	Boeing 727-30 (QWS / winglets)	18933 / 185	N727BE	0965	0790	3 PW JT8D-7 (HK3/DUG)	72802	Executive	
☐ N727RE	Boeing 727-282 (A) (QWS / winglets)	22430 / 1715	N6167D	0381	0598	3 PW JT8D-217C/17 (DUG)	86409	Executive	

INDEPENDENCE AIR CHARTER, Inc.
Kansas City-Downtown, MO

3823 South Noland Road, Independence, MO 64055, USA ☎ (816) 252-7039 Tx: none Fax: (816) 252-1601 SITA: n/a
F: 1986 ⁂ n/a Head: Floyd D. Castle Net: n/a

☐ N21407	Piper PA-34-200T Seneca II	34-7870435		0078	0596	2 CO TSIO-360-E	2073		

INDIANAERO, Inc.
Indianapolis-Int'l, IN **INDIANAERO**

PO Box 51016, Indianapolis, IN 46251-0016, USA ☎ (765) 487-5936 Tx: none Fax: none SITA: n/a
F: 1977 ⁂ 6 Head: James W. Doyle Net: n/a

☐ N4939P	Piper PA-23-235 Apache	27-534		0063	0787	2 LY O-540-B1A5	2177		
☐ N556RT	Cessna 310P	310P0077		0069	0596	2 CO IO-470-VO	2359		lsf Gazelle Air Transport Ltd
☐ N87334	Cessna 310R II	310R0517		0075	0897	2 CO IO-520-M	2495		lsf Gazelle Air Transport Ltd

INDIANA FLIGHT CENTER (DSTS, Inc. dba / Associated with Hilton Corporation)
Las Vegas-McCarran Int'l, NV

6005 Las Vegas Blvd. South, Suite 157, Las Vegas, NV 89119, USA ☎ (219) 262-4422 Tx: none Fax: (219) 262-4433 SITA: n/a
F: 1996 ⁂ n/a Head: Joe Harnish Net: n/a Operates non-commercial corporate flights for itself and for the members of the Hilton group of companies.

☐ N727X	Boeing 727-191	19394 / 418	N3946A	0067	0896	3 PW JT8D-7B (HK3/FDX)	76884	Corporate	

INDIANAPOLIS AVIATION, Inc.
Indianapolis-Metropolitan, IN

9913 Willowview Road, Fishers, IN 46038, USA ☎ (317) 849-0840 Tx: none Fax: (317) 849-0912 SITA: n/a
F: 1970 ⁂ n/a Head: Thomas J. Auda Net: n/a

☐ N70TB	Beech Bonanza A36	E-1289		0078	0489	1 CO IO-520-BA	1633		
☐ N18273	Beech Baron B55 (95-B55)	TC-2065		0078	1095	2 CO IO-470-L	2313		
☐ N16BE	Beech Baron 58	TH-946		0078	1092	2 CO IO-520-C	2449		
☐ N550S	Cessna 340A II	340A0086		0076	0888	2 CO TSIO-520-N	2717		lsf Burd & Kimmel Aviation Inc.
☐ N6290N	Cessna 340A II	340A0464		0078	0190	2 CO TSIO-520-NB	2717		
☐ N421RB	Cessna 421B Golden Eagle	421B0330		0073	0597	2 CO GTSIO-520-H	3379		
☐ N535LR	Cessna 525 CitationJet	525-0128	N5092D	0095	0296	2 WRR FJ44-1A	4717		lsf L.R. Green Co. Inc.
☐ N42PC	Beech King Air E90	LW-85	N20RF	0073	0794	2 PWC PT6A-28	4581		lsf Schroeder Aircraft Leasing Inc.
☐ N6571S	Beech King Air E90	LW-171		0075	0895	2 PWC PT6A-28	4581		

INDUSTRIAL HELICOPTERS, Inc.
Lafayette-Regional, LA *Industrial Helicopters*

PO Box 90210, Lafayette, LA 70509, USA ☎ (318) 233-3356 Tx: none Fax: (318) 233-4573 SITA: n/a
F: 1973 ⁂ n/a Head: Joseph O. Richard Net: n/a Aircraft below MTOW 1361 kg: Bell & Soloy-Bell 47G.

☐ N2069L	Bell 206B JetRanger III	3405		0081	1287	1 AN 250-C20B	1451		
☐ N21466	Bell 206B JetRanger III	3459		0081	1181	1 AN 250-C20B	1451		
☐ N21470	Bell 206B JetRanger III	3467		0081	0182	1 AN 250-C20B	1451		
☐ N2187L	Bell 206B JetRanger III	3497		0081	0282	1 AN 250-C20B	1451		
☐ N2187P	Bell 206B JetRanger III	3499		0081	0282	1 AN 250-C20B	1451		
☐ N2193X	Bell 206B JetRanger III	3506		0081	0790	1 AN 250-C20B	1451		
☐ N23JH	Bell 206B JetRanger II	2047		0076	0679	1 AN 250-C20	1451		
☐ N374M	Bell 206B JetRanger III	4161		0091	0591	1 AN 250-C20B	1451		
☐ N375M	Bell 206B JetRanger III	4162		0091	0591	1 AN 250-C20B	1451		
☐ N376M	Bell 206B JetRanger III	4170		0091	0691	1 AN 250-C20B	1451		
☐ N2150M	Bell 206L-1 LongRanger II	45703		0081	1081	1 AN 250-C28B	1882		
☐ N3777M	Bell 206L-3 LongRanger III	51485		0091	0691	1 AN 250-C30P	1882		
☐ N57441	Bell 206L-1 LongRanger II	45438		0080	0880	1 AN 250-C28B	1882		
☐ N6560K	Bell 206L-3 LongRanger III	51426		0091	0191	1 AN 250-C30P	1882		

INLAND AVIATION SERVICES, Inc.
Aniak, AK

PO Box 244, Aniak, AK 99557, USA ☎ (907) 675-4335 Tx: none Fax: (907) 675-4335 SITA: n/a
F: 1985 ⁂ 3 Head: Stephen Hill Net: n/a

☐ N910SP	Helio H-395 Super Courier	627		0065	0997	1 LY GO-480-G2D6	1361		
☐ N1673U	Cessna 207 Skywagon	20700273		0074	0186	1 CO IO-520-F	1724		

INLET AIR (Daniel A. Hill dba)
Soldotna, AK

330 West Corral, Soldotna, AK 99669, USA ☎ (907) 262-4457 Tx: none Fax: (907) 262-3215 SITA: n/a
F: 1993 ⁂ n/a Head: Daniel A. Hill Net: n/a

☐ N996PK	Piper PA-32-260 Cherokee SIX	32-168		0065	0793	1 LY O-540-E4B5	1542		

INTER ISLAND EXPRESS = IIE (Air Borinquen, Inc. dba)
San Juan-Isla Grande/Fernando Luis Ribas Dominicci, PR

Garden Hills Plaza, MSC 373, 1353 Road 19, Guaynabo, PR 00966, USA ☎ (787) 648-8077 Tx: none Fax: (787) 792-4257 SITA: n/a
F: 1998 ⁂ 6 Head: Eric J. Stubbe Net: n/a

☐ N1253K	Cessna 208B Grand Caravan	208B0648		0097	0498	1 PWC PT6A-114A	3969		Y9 / Freighter
☐ N1253Y	Cessna 208B Grand Caravan	208B0649		0097	0498	1 PWC PT6A-114A	3969		Y9 / Freighter

INTER-ISLAND HELICOPTERS (Smoky Mountain Helicopters, Inc. dba)
Hanapepe-Port Allen/Burns Field, HI

PO Box 156, Hanapepe, HI 96716, USA ☎ (808) 335-5009 Tx: none Fax: (808) 335-5567 SITA: n/a
F: 1981 ⁂ 10 Head: Kenneth J. D'Attilio Net: http://www.hawaiian.net

☐ N1109V	MD Helicopters MD 500D (Hughes 369D)	1100858D		0080	1198	1 AN 250-C20B	1361		
☐ N115HD	MD Helicopters MD 500D (Hughes 369D)	711020D		0081	0193	1 AN 250-C20B	1361		
☐ N5119V	MD Helicopters MD 500D (Hughes 369D)	1000800D	N8387F	0080	0891	1 AN 250-C20B	1361		
☐ N530R	MD Helicopters MD 530F (Hughes 369FF)	0005F		0084	0594	1 AN 250-C30	1406		

INTERLEASE AVIATION Corporation = (INTL) (formerly Cadmus Corporation)
Northfield, IL

Suite 525, One Northfield Plaza, Northfield, IL 60093, USA ☎ (847) 446-2644 Tx: none Fax: (847) 446-2749 SITA: n/a
F: 1989 ⁂ n/a Head: Monica Carroll Net: n/a Used aircraft leasing & sales company. Some leasing business is done by subsidiary company MIMI LEASING Corporation (same address).
Owner / lessor of following (main) aircraft types: Boeing 737-200, Lockheed 1011 TriStar & executive aircraft. Aircraft leased from Interlease & Mimi are listed and mentioned as lsf INTL under the leasing carriers.

INTERMOUNTAIN HELICOPTER, Inc.
Columbia, CA

22361 South Airport Road, Sonora, CA 95370, USA ☎ (209) 533-4374 Tx: none Fax: (209) 533-0420 SITA: n/a
F: 1986 ⁂ n/a Head: Richard Livingston Net: n/a

☐ N1107T	MD Helicopters MD 500D (Hughes 369D)	210898D		0081	0189	1 AN 250-C20B	1361		

INTERNATIONAL AIR LEASES, Inc. = (IALI)
Hialeah, FL International Air Leases, Inc.

950 SE 12th Street, Hialeah, FL 33010, USA ☎ (954) 889-6000 Tx: 3728093 interair mia Fax: (954) 887-9831 SITA: MIAXCJW
F: 1971 ⁂ 140 Head: Anthony C. Tirri Net: n/a Some leasing business is done under the name Compania Inter-Americana Export/Import, SA Panama = (CIEI) (subsidiary, contact thru same headquarters).
Used aircraft leasing, sales and financing company. Owner / Lessor of following (main) aircraft types: Boeing 707-320C, 727-100/200, 737-100/200, 747, Lockheed L-1011, McDonnell DC-8-62/63 & DC-9-10.
Aircraft leased from IALI are listed and mentioned as such under the leasing carriers.

INTERNATIONAL AIRLINE SUPPORT GROUP, Inc. = (IASG)
Atlanta, GA

1954 Airport Road, Suite 200, Atlanta, GA 30341, USA ☎ (770) 455-7575 Tx: none Fax: (770) 455-7550 SITA: n/a
F: 1982 ⁂ 30 Head: Alexis A. Dyer Net: http://www.iasgroup.com Used aircraft leasing, sales & suppliers of aircraft spare parts & engines company.
Owner / lessor of following (main) aircraft types: Boeing 727-100 & DC-9-41. Aircraft leased from International Airline Support Group are listed and mentioned as lsf IASG under leasing carriers.

INTERNATIONAL AIR RESPONSE, Inc. (formerly T & G Aviation, Inc.) — Chandler-Memorial, AZ

22000 South Price Road, Chandler, AZ 85248, USA ☎ (520) 796-5188 Tx: none Fax: (520) 796-1064 SITA: n/a
F: 1975 ⁂ 22 Head: William W. Grantham Net: n/a

☐ N4887C	Boeing (Douglas) DC-7B	*45351 / 903*	*N4887D*	*0057*	*0580*	*4 WR R-3350*	*53025*	*Tanker/Sprayer*		*33*
☐ N116TG	Lockheed L-182 (C-130A) Hercules	*1A-3086*	*56-0478*	*0057*	*1089*	*4 AN T56-A-9D*	*56336*	*Tanker/Freighter*		*30*
☐ N117TG	Lockheed L-182 (C-130A) Hercules	*1A-3018*	*54-1631*	*0057*	*1089*	*4 AN T56-A-9D*	*56336*	*Tanker/Freighter*		*31*
☐ N118TG	Lockheed L-182 (C-130A) Hercules	*1A-3219*	*57-0512*	*0059*	*1089*	*4 AN T56-A-9D*	*56336*	*Tanker/Freighter*		*32 / std Chandler*

INTERNATIONAL BUSINESS AIRCRAFT, Inc. – IBA = IBY — Tulsa-Int'l, OK

PO Box 581870, Tulsa, OK 74158, USA ☎ (918) 836-8895 Tx: none Fax: (918) 834-6098 SITA: n/a
F: 1975 ⁂ n/a Head: R. George Mall ICAO: CENTRAL STAGE Net: n/a

☐ N36343	Piper PA-34-200T Seneca II	*34-7870320*		*0078*	*0791*	*2 CO TSIO-360-E*	*2073*	*Pax/Cargo*		
☐ N291MB	Mitsubishi MU-2K (MU-2B-25) Cargoliner	*291*	*CP-1147*	*0074*	*0496*	*2 GA TPE331-6-251M*	*4500*	*Pax/Cargo/EMS*		*Cavenaugh SCD conversion*
☐ N349MA	Mitsubishi MU-2J (MU-2B-35) Cargoliner	*615*	*YV-108CP*	*0074*	*1093*	*2 GA TPE331-6-251M*	*4899*	*Pax/Cargo/EMS*		*Cavenaugh SCD conversion*
☐ N390K	Mitsubishi MU-2K (MU-2B-25) Cargoliner	*277*	*C-GMUK*	*0073*	*1094*	*2 GA TPE331-6-251M*	*4500*	*Pax/Cargo/EMS*		*Cavenaugh SCD conversion*
☐ N4065D	Mitsubishi MU-2J (MU-2B-35) Cargoliner	*660*	*TF-FHL*	*0075*	*1196*	*2 GA TPE331-6-251M*	*4899*	*Pax/Cargo/EMS*		*Cavenaugh SCD conversion*
☐ N45CE	Mitsubishi MU-2J (MU-2B-35) Cargoliner	*653*	*N350HE*	*0074*	*0496*	*2 GA TPE331-6-251M*	*4899*	*Pax/Cargo/EMS*		*Cavenaugh SCD conversion*
☐ N490MA	Mitsubishi MU-2J (MU-2B-35) Cargoliner	*640*		*0074*	*0796*	*2 GA TPE331-6-251M*	*4899*	*Pax/Cargo/EMS*		*Cavenaugh SCD conversion*
☐ N539MA	Mitsubishi MU-2J (MU-2B-35) Cargoliner	*552*	*N246W*	*0072*	*0593*	*2 GA TPE331-6-251M*	*4899*	*Pax/Cargo/EMS*		*Cavenaugh SCD conversion*
☐ N755MA	Mitsubishi MU-2J (MU-2B-35) Cargoliner	*553*	*N7034K*	*0072*	*0793*	*2 GA TPE331-6-251M*	*4899*	*Pax/Cargo/EMS*		*Cavenaugh SCD conversion*

INTERNATIONAL JET AVIATION SERVICES (Milam International, Inc. dba) — Denver-Centennial, CO

12830 East Control Tower Road, Englewood, CO 80112, USA ☎ (303) 790-0414 Tx: none Fax: (303) 790-4144 SITA: n/a
F: 1979 ⁂ 30 Head: H. William W. Milam, III Net: http://www.internationaljet.com

☐ N241JA	Learjet 24	*24-131*	*N11FH*	*0066*	*0884*	*2 GE CJ610-6*	*5897*			
☐ N251JA	Learjet 25B	*25B-150*	*N888RB*	*0074*	*0384*	*2 GE CJ610-6*	*6804*			
☐ N600GM	Learjet 25D	*25D-290*	*N321RB*	*0079*	*0196*	*2 GE CJ610-6*	*6804*			*lsf Learjet 25D-290 Llc*
☐ N727CS	Learjet 25D	*25D-313*	*N631CW*	*0080*	*0295*	*2 GE CJ610-8A*	*6804*			
☐ N110FT	Learjet 35A	*35A-471*	*N95AP*	*0082*	*0894*	*2 GA TFE731-2-2B*	*8300*			
☐ N925DM	Learjet 35A	*35A-486*	*N810CC*	*0082*	*0196*	*2 GA TFE731-2-2B*	*8301*			

INTERNATIONAL JET CHARTER, Inc. — Norfolk-Int'l, VA

PO Box 41005, Norfolk, VA 23541, USA ☎ (757) 857-6481 Tx: none Fax: (757) 857-1684 SITA: n/a
F: 1993 ⁂ n/a Head: Robert W. Lake Net: http://www.intljetcharter.com

☐ N475DJ	GAC G-1159A Gulfstream III	*358*	*N200DE*	*0082*	*0996*	*2 RR Spey 511-8*	*30935*	*Executive*		*lsf Baymark Development Corp.*
☐ N787M	Lockheed L-1011-385-1 TriStar 50	*193L-1064*	*C-GIES*	*0074*	*0696*	*3 RR RB211-22B*	*204117*	*Flying Hospital*		*lsf/opf Operation Blessing / cvtd 1*

INTERNATIONAL LEASE FINANCE, Corp. = (ILFC) (Member of American International Group) — Los Angeles, CA

1999 Avenue of the Stars, 39th Fl., Los Angeles, CA 90067-4605, USA ☎ (310) 788-1999 Tx: 691400 interleas bvh Fax: (310) 788-1990 SITA: n/a
F: 1973 ⁂ 75 Head: Steven F. Udvar-Hazy Net: n/a New and used aircraft leasing, sales and financing company.
Owner / lessor of following (main) aircraft types: A300-600R, A310-300, A319, A320, A321-200, A330-200/-300, A340-300/-500/-600, Boeing 737-300/400/500/600/700/800,747-200/300/400, 757, 767-200/300/400, 777-200, McDonnell Douglas MD-11, MD-83 & MD-87. Aircraft leased from ILFC are listed and mentioned as such under the leasing carriers .

INTERSTATE HELICOPTERS (Jim P. Johnson dba) — Oklahoma City-Downtown Airpark, OK

941 SW 22nd, Oklahoma City, OK 73109, USA ☎ (405) 632-5683 Tx: none Fax: (405) 632-3683 SITA: n/a
F: 1978 ⁂ 3 Head: Jim P. Johnson Net: n/a Aircraft below MTOW 1361kg: Robinson R22

☐ N213TV	Bell 206B JetRanger III	*2844*	*N555TV*	*0079*	*0293*	*1 AN 250-C20B*	*1451*			
☐ N27TV	Bell 206B JetRanger III	*3764*	*N31798*	*0083*	*0890*	*1 AN 250-C20J*	*1451*			
☐ N67JJ	Bell 206B JetRanger III	*4062*	*N44TV*	*0089*	*0493*	*1 AN 250-C20J*	*1451*			

INTREPID AVIATION PARTNERS, Llc = (IPID) — Cordova, TN

1894 Woodchase Glen Drive, Cordova, TN 38018, USA ☎ (901) 755-1247 Tx: none Fax: (901) 759-9965 SITA: n/a
F: 1997 ⁂ n/a Head: Ron Anderson Net: n/a Used aircraft leasing & sales company.
Owner / lessor of following (main) aircraft types: Boeing 727-200F Aircraft leased from Intrepid are listed and mentioned as lsf IPID under the leasing carriers.

IOWA CITY FLYING SERVICE, Inc. (Cedar Rapids Flying Service) — Iowa City-Municipal & Cedar Rapids-Municipal, IA

1801 South Riverside Drive, Iowa City, IA 52240, USA ☎ (319) 338-7543 Tx: none Fax: (319) 338-6632 SITA: n/a
F: 1960 ⁂ n/a Head: Gordon Ch. Peterson Net: n/a CEDAR RAPIDS FLYING SERVICE is the operational name for flights out of the Cedar Rapids-base (same headquarters & fleet).

☐ N71CF	Piper PA-23-250 Aztec F	*27-7954092*		*0079*	*0180*	*2 LY IO-540-C4B5*	*2359*			
☐ N111CF	Piper PA-31-350 Navajo Chieftain	*31-7652105*	*N171MD*	*0076*	*0284*	*2 LY TIO-540-J2BD*	*3175*			
☐ N91CF	Piper PA-31-310 Navajo	*31-174*		*0068*	*0179*	*2 LY TIO-540-A1A*	*2948*			

ISLAND AIR = ISC (Island Air Charter, Inc. dba) — Fort Lauderdale-Hollywood Int'l, FL

1050 Lee Wagener Blvd, Suite 410, Fort Lauderdale, FL 33335, USA ☎ (954) 359-9942 Tx: none Fax: (954) 359-5870 SITA: n/a
F: 1986 ⁂ 10 Head: James D. Birmingham ICAO: BARRACUDA Net: n/a

☐ N238LW	Piper PA-23-250 Aztec D	*27-4361*	*N222NH*	*0069*	*0498*	*2 LY IO-540-C4B5*	*2359*	*5 Pax*		*lsf Jafco Leasing Inc.*
☐ N101NE	Britten-Norman BN-2A-8 Islander	*201*	*N12JC*	*0070*	*0791*	*2 LY O-540-E4C5*	*2858*	*9 Pax*		*lsf Professional Anesthesia Consulting*
☐ N138LW	Britten-Norman BN-2A-27 Islander	*138*	*YR-BNF*	*0070*	*0795*	*2 LY O-540-E4C5*	*2994*	*9 Pax*		
☐ N779KS	Britten-Norman BN-2A-27 Islander	*779*	*YR-BNE*	*0076*	*0795*	*2 LY O-540-E4C5*	*2994*	*9 Pax*		

ISLAND AIR = WP / MKU (Aloha Island Air, Inc. dba / Subsidiary of Aloha Air Group, Inc. / formerly Princeville Airways, Inc.) — Honolulu-Int'l, HI

99 Kapalulu Place, Int'l Airport, Honolulu, HI 96819-1843, USA ☎ (808) 833-0077 Tx: 7431375 pvhnl Fax: (808) 833-5498 SITA: n/a
F: 1980 ⁂ 270 Head: Han H. Ching IATA: 347 ICAO: MOKU Net: http://www.alohaair.com/aloha Scheduled commuter services are operated in conjunction with Aloha Airlines using AQ flight numbers.

☐ N709PV	De Havilland DHC-6 Twin Otter 300	*640*	*N664MA*	*0079*	*0489*	*2 PWC PT6A-27*	*5670*	*Y18*		*lsf JetFleet III*
☐ N710PV	De Havilland DHC-6 Twin Otter 300	*751*	*HZ-PL6*	*0081*	*0489*	*2 PWC PT6A-27*	*5670*	*Y18*		*lsf JetFleet III*
☐ N712PV	De Havilland DHC-6 Twin Otter 300	*696*	*N696WJ*	*0080*	*0491*	*2 PWC PT6A-27*	*5670*	*Y18*		*lsf JetFleet III*
☐ N803WP	De Havilland DHC-8-102 Dash 8	*141*	*C-FDNE*	*0089*	*0396*	*2 PWC PW120A*	*15649*	*Y37*		*lsf McDonnell Douglas Finance Corp.*
☐ N805WP	De Havilland DHC-8-102 Dash 8	*353*	*N853MA*	*0093*	*0398*	*2 PWC PW120A*	*15649*	*Y37*		*lsf Willis Lease Finance Corp.*
☐ N806WP	De Havilland DHC-8-102 Dash 8	*357*	*N854MA*	*0093*	*0698*	*2 PWC PW120A*	*15649*	*Y37*		*lsf Willis Lease Finance Corp.*

ISLAND AIR (Air Charter Services, Inc. dba) — Hilton Head Island, SC

PO Box 23601, Hilton Head Island, SC 29925, USA ☎ (843) 689-5014 Tx: none Fax: (843) 689-5755 SITA: n/a
F: 1994 ⁂ 2 Head: John F. Durbin Net: n/a

☐ N1234Q	Beech Bonanza A36	*E-165*		*0070*	*1091*	*1 CO IO-520-B*	*1633*			

ISLAND AIRLINES, Inc. = IS / ISA — Nantucket-Memorial, MA

PO Box 2640, Nantucket, MA 02584, USA ☎ (978) 228-7575 Tx: none Fax: (978) 775-6645 SITA: n/a
F: 1991 ⁂ 25 Head: William F. McGrath, Jr. ICAO: ISLAND Net: n/a

☐ N401BK	Cessna 402C II	*402C0297*	*N3252M*	*0080*	*1091*	*2 CO TSIO-520-VB*	*3107*	*Y9*		*lsf B & K Leasing Inc.*
☐ N403BK	Cessna 402C II	*402C0330*	*N26436*	*0080*	*1192*	*2 CO TSIO-520-VB*	*3107*	*Y9*		*lsf B & K Leasing Inc.*
☐ N404BK	Cessna 402C II	*402C0637*	*N10LJ*	*0082*	*0694*	*2 CO TSIO-520-VB*	*3107*	*Y9*		
☐ N405BK	Cessna 402C II	*402C0459*	*N459RC*	*0081*	*0996*	*2 CO TSIO-520-VB*	*3107*	*Y9*		*lsf B & K Leasing Inc.*
☐ N406BK	Cessna 402C III	*402C0807*	*N1235A*	*0084*	*0296*	*2 CO TSIO-520-VB*	*3107*	*Y9*		*lsf B & K Leasing Inc.*
☐ N408BK	Beech H18	*BA-653*	*N8451*	*0064*	*1193*	*2 PW R-985*	*4491*	*Y9*		*lsf pvt*

ISLAND AIR SERVICE (Redemption, Inc. dba) — Kodiak-Municipal, AK

PO Box 125, Kodiak, AK 99615, USA ☎ (907) 486-6196 Tx: none Fax: (907) 486-5529 SITA: n/a
F: 1972 ⁂ n/a Head: Robert G. Stanford Net: n/a

☐ N8152Z	Piper PA-32-301 Saratoga	*32-8006004*		*0080*	*0296*	*1 LY IO-540-K1G5*	*1633*			
☐ N8385G	Piper PA-32-301 Saratoga	*32-8106063*		*0081*	*1181*	*1 LY IO-540-K1G5*	*1633*			*lsf pvt*
☐ N5891V	Britten-Norman BN-2A-26 Islander	*3011*	*J8-VAN*	*0084*	*0597*	*2 LY O-540-E4C5*	*2994*			

ISLAND AIRWAYS (McPhillips Flying Service, Inc. dba / formerly Gemini Air Service, Inc.) — Charlevoix-Municipal, MI

PO Box 80, Saint James, MI 49782, USA ☎ (616) 547-2141 Tx: none Fax: (616) 547-5277 SITA: n/a
F: 1975 ⁂ n/a Head: Paul R. Welke Net: n/a

☐ N4334P	Piper PA-23-160 Apache	*23-1835*		*0059*		*2 LY O-320-B*	*1724*			
☐ N4490P	Piper PA-23-160 Apache	*23-2012*		*0062*		*2 LY O-320-B*	*1724*			
☐ N19WA	Britten-Norman BN-2A-8 Islander	*524*	*N64JA*	*0076*	*1285*	*2 LY O-540-E4C5*	*2812*			
☐ N866JA	Britten-Norman BN-2A-6 Islander	*185*	*G-51-185**	*0070*	*1280*	*2 LY O-540-E4C5*	*2812*			
☐ N95BN	Britten-Norman BN-2A-8 Islander	*95*	*G-AXKB*	*0069*	*1180*	*2 LY O-540-E4C5*	*2812*			

ISLAND EXPRESS = 2S / SDY (Safe Air International, Inc. dba) — Fort Lauderdale-Hollywood Int'l, FL

750 SW 34th Street, Fort Lauderdale, FL 33315, USA ☎ (954) 359-0380 Tx: none Fax: (954) 359-7944 SITA: n/a
F: 1989 ⁂ n/a Head: Ruben Acrich IATA: 579 ICAO: SANDY ISLE Net: n/a

☐ N108GP	Cessna 402C II	*402C0058*		*0079*	*1095*	*2 CO TSIO-520-VB*	*3107*	*Y9*		*lsf pvt*
☐ N2651Y	Cessna 402C II	*402C0343*		*0080*	*0189*	*2 CO TSIO-520-VB*	*3107*	*Y9*		*lsf Broward Avionics Services Inc.*
☐ N5736C	Cessna 402C II	*402C0031*		*0079*	*0392*	*2 CO TSIO-520-VB*	*3107*	*Y9*		*lsf Broward Avionics Services Inc.*

383 registration type of aircraft *cn/fn* *ex/ex** *mfd* *del* *powered by* *mtow kg* *configuration* *selcal* *name/fln/specialitites/remarks*

ISLAND EXPRESS HELICOPTERS, Inc.
Long Beach-Daugherty Field, CA

1175 Queens Highway South, Long Beach, CA 90802, USA ☎ (562) 510-2525 Tx: none Fax: (562) 510-9761 SITA: n/a
F: 1981 21 Head: John E. Moore Net: http://www.catalina.com/helicopter.html

☐ N3593S	Eurocopter (Aerosp.) AS350D AStar	*1063*		*0079*	*1094*	*1 LY LTS101-600A.3*	*1950*			
☐ N3604T	Eurocopter (Aerosp.) AS350D AStar	*1158*		*0079*	*0995*	*1 LY LTS101-600A.3*	*1950*			
☐ N57708	Eurocopter (Aerosp.) AS350D AStar	*1358*		*0080*	*0491*	*1 LY LTS101-600A.3*	*1950*			

ISLAND HELICOPTERS (Island Helicopters Kauai, Inc. dba)
Lihue, HI

PO Box 831, Lihue, HI 96766, USA ☎ (808) 245-8588 Tx: none Fax: (808) 245-6258 SITA: n/a
F: 1980 n/a Head: Curtis W. Lofstedt Net: http://www.planet-hawaii.com/island

☐ N801H	Bell 206B JetRanger III	*3186*	*N206SA*	*0080*	*1292*	*1 AN 250-C20B*	*1451*			
☐ N971H	Eurocopter (Aerosp.) AS350BA AStar	*2955*		*0096*	*0397*	*1 TU Arriel 1B*	*2100*			

ISLAND WINGS AIR SERVICE (Michelle L. Masden dba)
Ketchikan-Harbor SPB, AK

PO Box 7432, Ketchikan, AK 99901, USA ☎ (907) 225-2444 Tx: none Fax: (907) 225-2444 SITA: n/a
F: 1994 n/a Head: Michelle L. Masden Net: n/a

☐ N4573F	Cessna A185E Skywagon	*185-1080*		*0066*	*0895*	*1 CO IO-520-D*	*1520*			*Floats*

ISLA NENA AIR SERVICE, Inc.
Vieques, PR

PO Box 259, Vieques, PR 00765, USA ☎ (787) 741-1577 Tx: none Fax: (787) 791-5110 SITA: n/a
F: 1993 n/a Head: Manuel A. Ortiz Net: n/a

☐ N5376Y	Piper PA-23-250 Aztec B	*27-2449*		*0063*	*0895*	*2 LY O-540-A1D5*	*2177*			
☐ N1202S	Britten-Norman BN-2A-26 Islander	*193*	*J6-SLV*	*0070*	*0996*	*2 LY O-540-E4C5*	*2994*			*lsf pvt*
☐ N555DM	Britten-Norman BN-2A-26 Islander	*129*	*C-GGYY*	*0069*	*0695*	*2 LY O-540-E4C5*	*2858*			*to be re-reg. N724JP*
☐ N678TA	Britten-Norman BN-2A-26 Islander	*77*	*J6-SLZ*	*0069*	*0896*	*2 LY O-540-E4C5*	*2994*			
☐ N7049T	Britten-Norman BN-2A-21 Islander	*643*	*C-GPAB*	*0071*	*0696*	*2 LY IO-540-K1B5*	*2994*			

ISLE ROYALE SEAPLANE SERVICE, Inc. (formerly Grognet Flying Service / Seasonal summer ops only)
Houghton-SPB, MI

PO Box 371, Houghton, MI 49931, USA ☎ (715) 526-2465 Tx: none Fax: none SITA: n/a
F: 1971 6 Head: Tom Wunderlich Net: n/a

☐ N841RS	Dornier DO 28A-1	*3012*		*0061*	*1283*	*2 LY O-540-A1D5*	*2450*			*Floats*

ISO AERO SERVICE, Inc.
Kinston-Regional Jetport, NC

PO Box 1294, Kinston, NC 28503, USA ☎ (919) 522-1156 Tx: none Fax: (919) 522-4571 SITA: n/a
F: 1961 n/a Head: Kenneth A. Vojta Net: n/a Aircraft below MTOW 1361kg: Cessna 172

☐ N11999	Beech Baron 58	*TH-563*		*0075*	*1084*	*2 CO IO-520-C*	*2449*			
☐ N402G	Beech King Air 100	*B-14*	*N40TG*	*0070*	*1087*	*2 PWC PT6A-28*	*4808*			

ITOCHU AirLease, Inc. = (ITOH)
Seattle, WA, Dublin (Ireland) & Tokyo (Japan)

18000 Pacific Hy, Tower 1, Suite 415, Seattle, WA 98188, USA ☎ (206) 242-2323 Tx: none Fax: (206) 242-2626 SITA: n/a
F: 1988 n/a Head: Tetsuya Nozaki Net: n/a New & used aircraft leasing management (including technical inspection), sales & financing company.
New & used aircraft leasing is done by affiliated companies: ITOCHU AirLease (Europe) Ltd, AIB Int'l Centre - I.F.S.C., Dublin 1, Ireland. Phone: (1) 829 03 01, Fax: (1) 874 30 50 &
ITOCHU AirLease Corp., Kita-Aoyama Yoshikawa Bldg. 9F, 2-12-16, Kita-Aoyama, Minato-Ku, Tokyo 107-0061, Japan. Phone; (3) 54 13 23 61 Fax: (3) 54 11 72 26.
Owner / lessor of following (main) aircraft types: Boeing 737/757/767. Aircraft leased from Itochu are listed and mentioned as lsf ITOH under the leasing carriers.

JAARS Aviation (JAARS, Inc. dba / Subsidiary of Summer Institute of Linguistics)
Waxhaw-JAARS Townsend, NC & South America

Box 248, Waxhaw, NC 28173, USA ☎ (704) 843-6141 Tx: none Fax: (704) 843-6630 SITA: n/a
F: 1946 n/a Head: James Akovenko Net: http://www.jaars.org Aircraft below MTOW 1361kg: Hiller UH-12D/E.
Non-commercial missionary organisation (serving Wycliffe Bible Translators), conducting charter flights in remote areas.

☐ N242B	Helio H-391B Courier	*001*		*0052*	*0671*	*1 LY GO-435-C2B2*	*1361*			
☐ N87763	Helio H-395 Super Courier	*558*		*0062*	*0877*	*1 LY GO-480-G1D6*	*1361*			
☐ N22AC	Helio H-295 Super Courier	*1443*		*0072*	*1174*	*1 LY GO-480-G1D6*	*1542*			
☐ N269L	Helio H-295 Super Courier	*1286*		*0067*	*0185*	*1 LY GO-480-G1A6*	*1542*			
☐ N60JA	Helio H-295 Super Courier	*1240*	*HK-3120W*	*0067*	*0498*	*1 LY GO-480-G1A6*	*1542*			
☐ N6490V	Helio H-295 Super Courier	*1444*	*HK-1361W*	*0072*	*1297*	*1 LY GO-480-G1A6*	*1542*			
☐ N7211Q	Helio H-295 Super Courier	*1243*	*EL-LBT*	*0067*	*0897*	*1 LY GO-480-G1A6*	*1542*			
☐ N8208J	Helio H-295 Super Courier	*1287*	*OB-951*	*0068*	*0998*	*1 LY GO-480-G1A6*	*1542*			
☐ N123TM	Cessna U206F Stationair	*U20601768*		*0072*	*0785*	*1 CO IO-520-F*	*1633*			
☐ N39269	Cessna U206G Stationair 6 II	*U20605781*		*0080*	*0596*	*1 CO IO-520-F*	*1633*			
☐ N4292P	Cessna U206F Stationair II	*U20603207*		*0076*	*0198*	*1 CO IO-520-F*	*1633*			
☐ N4691U	Cessna TU206G Turbo Stationair 6 II	*U20605060*	*P2-SIE*	*0079*	*1197*	*1 CO TSIO-520-M*	*1633*			
☐ N6620Z	Cessna TU206G Turbo Stationair 6 II	*U20606347*		*0081*	*0298*	*1 CO TSIO-520-M*	*1633*			
☐ N9419G	Cessna U206E Stationair	*U20601619*		*0070*	*1078*	*1 CO IO-520-F*	*1633*			
☐ N13919	Piper PA-23-250 Aztec D	*27-4555*		*0070*	*0490*	*2 LY IO-540-C4B5*	*2359*			
☐ N401A	Piper PA-23-250 Aztec C	*27-3023*		*0065*	*0198*	*2 LY IO-540-C4B5*	*2359*			
☐ N6239P	Piper PA-31-310 Navajo	*31-474*	*HK-3567X*	*0069*	*1297*	*2 LY TIO-540-A1A*	*2948*			

JAAX FLYING SERVICE (Gerhard J. Jaax dba)
Calexico-Int'l, CA

702 Calle de Oro, Calexico, CA 92231, USA ☎ (760) 357-4647 Tx: none Fax: (760) 357-4647 SITA: n/a
F: 1970 n/a Head: Gerhard J. Jaax Net: n/a

☐ N333WF	Mitsubishi MU-2P (MU-2B-26A)	*387SA*	*N8TB*	*0078*	*0792*	*2 GA TPE331-5-252M*	*4749*			
☐ N71DP	Mitsubishi MU-2B-60 Marquise	*1502SA*	*VH-MVU*	*0081*	*0598*	*2 GA TPE331-10-511M*	*5250*			
☐ N868MA	Mitsubishi MU-2N (MU-2B-36A)	*708SA*	*N15UD*	*0078*	*0395*	*2 GA TPE331-5-252M*	*5250*			

JACK HARTER HELICOPTERS, Inc.
Lihue, HI

PO Box 306, Lihue, HI 96766, USA ☎ (808) 245-3774 Tx: none Fax: (808) 245-4661 SITA: n/a
F: 1971 n/a Head: Jack Harter Net: http://www.helicopters-kauai.com/

☐ N37741	Bell 206B JetRanger	*1695*	*N389EH*	*0075*	*0590*	*1 AN 250-C20*	*1451*			
☐ N83181	Bell 206B JetRanger	*1095*		*0073*	*0176*	*1 AN 250-C20*	*1451*			
☐ N798JH	Eurocopter (Aerosp.) AS350BA AStar	*1548*	*C-GHAS*	*0082*	*0798*	*1 TU Arriel 1B*	*2100*			*cvtd AS350D*

JACKSON AIR (Jackson Air Center, Inc. dba)
Jackson-Int'l, MS

110 South Hangar Drive, Jackson, MS 39208, USA ☎ (228) 939-9366 Tx: none Fax: (228) 939-8119 SITA: n/a
F: 1995 n/a Head: William Walker Net: n/a

☐ N9340Q	Beech Baron B55 (95-B55)	*TC-1412*		*0072*	*0397*	*2 CO IO-470-L*	*2313*			
☐ N123US	Beech Baron 58	*TH-1335*		*0082*	*0397*	*2 CO IO-520-CB*	*2449*			
☐ N4950C	Beech King Air C90	*LJ-629*	*YV-39CP*	*0074*	*0397*	*2 PWC PT6A-20*	*4377*			

JACKSON HOLE AVIATION, Llc
Jackson-Hole, WY

PO Box 3829, Jackson, WY 83001, USA ☎ (307) 799-1999 Tx: none Fax: (307) 739-1996 SITA: n/a
F: 1983 n/a Head: Jeffrey Brown Net: n/a

☐ N2457E	Cessna T182R Turbo Skylane II	*18268205*		*0081*	*0884*	*1 LY O-540-L3C5D*	*1406*			*lsf JH Aircraft Management Inc.*
☐ N206AM	Cessna TU206F Turbo Stationair II	*U20602598*		*0074*	*0697*	*1 CO TSIO-520-C*	*1633*			
☐ N5454X	Cessna 340A II	*340A1512*		*0082*	*0994*	*2 CO TSIO-520-NB*	*2717*			*lsf JH Aircraft Management Inc.*
☐ N441VH	Cessna 441 Conquest II	*441-0225*	*N6854D*	*0081*	*0697*	*2 GA TPE331-8-403S*	*4468*			*lsf Satellite Aero Inc.*

JAYHAWK AIR (ACE Flyers, Inc. dba)
Anchorage-Merrill Field, AK

1842 Merrill Field Drive, Anchorage, AK 99501, USA ☎ (907) 276-4404 Tx: none Fax: (907) 276-0883 SITA: n/a
F: 1983 n/a Head: Tim J. Karlovich Net: n/a

☐ N7311N	Cessna U206G Stationair	*U20603609*		*0077*	*0497*	*1 CO IO-520-F*	*1633*			*lsf pvt*
☐ N8491Q	Cessna U206F Stationair II	*U20603349*		*0076*	*0898*	*1 CO IO-520-F*	*1633*			*Amphibian*
☐ N27179	Piper PA-31-350 Navajo Chieftain	*31-7752091*		*0077*	*0397*	*2 LY TIO-540-J2BD*	*3175*			

JEM INVESTMENTS - Flight Dept. (Flight Dept. of JEM Investments, Inc.)
Seattle-Boeing Field/King County Int'l, WA

7777 Perimeter Road South, Suite 103-125, Seattle, WA 98108, USA ☎ (206) 763-7678 Tx: none Fax: (206) 763-7761 SITA: n/a
F: 1997 n/a Head: Lockie Christler Net: n/a Operates non-commercial executive flights for its parent company only.

☐ N4H	Eurocopter (Aerosp.) AS355N TwinStar	*5533*	*N355M*	*0092*	*1097*	*2 TU Arrius 1A*	*2540*	*Executive*		*lsf Otter Corp.*
☐ N422DV	GAC (Grumman) G-1159 Gulfstream II	*017*	*N1PR*	*0068*	*1097*	*2 RR Spey 511-8*	*29393*	*Executive*		*lsf Otter Corp.*
☐ N3H	Boeing (Douglas) MD-87 (DC-9-87)	*49670 / 1453*	*N14708*	*0088*	*1097*	*2 PW JT8D-219*	*67812*	*Executive*		*lsf 422 Holdings Inc.*

JET AIRWAYS, Inc. = QJ
Boston-Int'l, MA

PO Box 6432, Chelsea, MA 02150-0008, USA ☎ (781) 887-3300 Tx: none Fax: (781) 887-3310 SITA: n/a
F: 1988 n/a Head: Harvey E. Cohen IATA: 508 Net: n/a

☐ N43304	Piper PA-28-180 Cherokee Archer	*28-7405188*		*0074*	*0188*	*1 LY O-360-A4A*	*1111*	*Frtr/Courier*		*lsf pvt*

384 registration type of aircraft *cn/fn* *ex/ex** *mfd* *del* *powered by* *mtow kg* *configuration* *selcal* *name/fln/specialitites/remarks*

JETCOPTERS, Inc.
Van Nuys, CA

16233 Van Owen Street, Suite 200, Van Nuys, CA 91406, USA ☎ (818) 902-0800 Tx: none Fax: (818) 902-1168 SITA: n/a
F: 1979 ⭐⭐⭐ n/a Head: Kevin N. Larosa Net: n/a

	registration	type of aircraft	cn/fn	ex/ex*	mfd	del	powered by	mtow kg	configuration	selcal	name/fln/remarks
☐	N123KY	Bell 206B JetRanger III	2806	N21MW	0079	0197	1 AN 250-C20B	1451			
☐	N25AJ	Bell 206B JetRanger III	2842	N969YD	0079	0495	1 AN 250-C20B	1451			
☐	N570P	Bell 206B JetRanger III	3671		0082	0998	1 AN 250-C20R	1451			
☐	N572TV	Bell 206B JetRanger III	2642	N2757M	0079	0585	1 AN 250-C20B	1451			
☐	N388JC	Bell 206L-1 LongRanger II	45568	N3388H	0081	0584	1 AN 250-C28B	1882			
☐	N410JC	Eurocopter (Aerosp.) AS350BA AStar	2130	N31621	0088	0598	1 TU Arriel 1B	2100			cvtd AS350B

JET EAST, Inc. (Sister company of Alpha Century Aviation)
Dallas-Love Field, TX

7515 Lemmon Avenue, Hangar P, Dallas, TX 75209, USA ☎ (972) 350-8523 Tx: none Fax: (972) 358-7641 SITA: n/a
F: 1987 ⭐⭐⭐ n/a Head: Aubry Von Rodman Net: http://www.jeteast.com Operates executive flights with aircraft used from its sister company ALPHA CENTURY AVIATION when required.

JET EXPRESS, Inc.
Myrtle Beach-Jetport Int'l, SC

1100 Jetport Road, Myrtle Beach, SC 29577, USA ☎ (843) 626-3097 Tx: none Fax: (843) 626-3471 SITA: n/a
F: 1996 ⭐⭐⭐ n/a Head: Steve Gillig Net: http://www.jetexp.com/index.html Operates passenger flights with McDonnell Douglas DC-9-30 aircraft, lsf/opb SPIRIT AIRLINES when required.

JETPROP, Inc.
Tulsa-Int'l, OK

11367 Depew Way, Westminster, CO 80020, USA ☎ (303) 466-6724 Tx: none Fax: (303) 469-2577 SITA: n/a
F: 1988 ⭐⭐⭐ n/a Head: Ralph J. Hemmer Net: n/a Operates in conjunction with AIR CHARTER EXPRESS, Inc. (San Diego, CA).

☐	N772MA	Mitsubishi MU-2P (MU-2B-26A)	382SA		0078	0988	2 GA TPE331-5-252M	4749			

JET-PROP EXPRESS, Inc.
Dallas-Addison, TX

4651 Airport Pky, Dallas, TX 75248, USA ☎ (972) 980-4822 Tx: none Fax: (972) 702-8383 SITA: n/a
F: 1994 ⭐⭐⭐ n/a Head: Michael E. Cohen Net: n/a

☐	N31DB	Cessna 401	401-0202		0068	1097	2 CO TSIO-520-E	2858			
☐	N3260Q	Cessna 401	401-0060		0067	1097	2 CO TSIO-520-E	2858			
☐	N4046Q	Cessna 401	401-0146		0067	1097	2 CO TSIO-520-E	2858			
☐	N110TW	Piper PA-31-310 Navajo	31-715		0070	0496	2 LY TIO-540-A2C	2948			lsf Ari Ben Aviator Inc.
☐	N112AG	Piper PA-31-310 Navajo	31-698		0070	0892	2 LY TIO-540-A2C	2948			lsf Ari Ben Aviator Inc.
☐	N620WF	Piper PA-31-310 Navajo	31-17		0067	0197	2 LY TIO-540-A1A	2948			lsf Ari Ben Aviator Inc.
☐	N71PC	Piper PA-31-310 Navajo	31-430		0069	0697	2 LY TIO-540-A1A	2948			
☐	N777TN	Piper PA-31-310 Navajo B	31-7401261	N61466	0074	0396	2 LY TIO-540-A2C	2948			lsf Ari Ben Aviator Inc.

JET RESOURCE, Inc. (a Chemed Company)
Cincinnati-Municipal/Lunken Field, OH

455 Wilmer Ave., Cinicnnati, OH 45226-1833, USA ☎ (513) 762-6909 Tx: none Fax: (513) 871-4181 SITA: n/a
F: 1972 ⭐⭐⭐ n/a Head: George Diehl Net: http://www.jetresource.com FAR 135 operations are conducted under the licence of BUSINESS JET SOLUTIONS.

☐	N571CH	Hawker 700A (HS 125-700A)	257078 / NA0256	N125AK	0079	1279	2 GA TFE731-3R-1H	11567			lsf Chemed Corp.
☐	N810CR	Hawker 700A (HS 125-700A)	257071 / NA0251	N396U	0079	0488	2 GA TFE731-3R-1H	11567			lsf Chemed Corp.

JET SYSTEMS (41 North 73 West, Inc. dba)
White Plains-Westchester County, NY

Hangar E, Westchester County Airport, White Plains, NY 10604, USA ☎ (914) 421-9100 Tx: none Fax: (914) 428-6309 SITA: n/a
F: 1993 ⭐⭐⭐ n/a Head: Michael W. Dolphin Net: n/a

☐	N1940	Learjet 60	60-002	N190AS	0092	0697	2 PWC PW305A	10478			lsf Astro Air Inc.

JETWAYS, Inc. (formerly Wheel-Air Charter, Inc.)
St. Paul-Downtown Holman Field, MN

644 Bayfield Street, St. Paul, MN 55107, USA ☎ (612) 224-3678 Tx: none Fax: (612) 224-3590 SITA: n/a
F: 1978 ⭐⭐⭐ n/a Head: Bill Waterman Net: http://www.jetways.com

☐	N193CS	Fairchild (Swearingen) SA226T Merlin IIIB	T-300	N210SW	0070	0897	2 GA TPE331-10U-501G	5670			lsf Jetways of Iowa Lc
☐	N221NC	Beech King Air B90	LJ-393	N800CT	0068	0393	2 PWC PT6A-20	4377			lsf Wheel Air Inc.
☐	N821CT	Beech King Air C90	LJ-821	C-GKCA	0079	0197	2 PWC PT6A-21	4377			lsf Wheel Air Inc.
☐	N73WC	Cessna 500 Citation I	500-0338	N97LA	0076	0792	2 PWC JT15D-1A	5375			lsf Jetways Llc
☐	N43JG	Sabreliner 60 (Rockwell NA265-60)	306-79	N768DV	0074	1193	2 PW JT12A-8	9150			lsf Wheel Air Inc.
☐	N401JW	Dassault Falcon 10	46	N908RF	0075	0196	2 GA TFE731-2-1C	8500			lsf Wheel Air Inc.
☐	N402JW	Dassault Falcon 10	120	N100WG	0078	0896	2 GA TFE731-2-1C	8500			lsf Jetways of Iowa Lc
☐	N403JW	Dassault Falcon 20C	102	N710WB	0067	1096	2 GE CF700-2D2	12400			lsf General Aviation Inc.

JETZ = (JETZ) (Joint venture of Cauff Lippman Aviation & NSJ Corp.)
Miami, FL

9420 SW 77th Ave, Miami, FL 33156, USA ☎ (305) 274-7277 Tx: none Fax: (305) 271-1339 SITA: n/a
F: 1996 ⭐⭐⭐ n/a Head: n/a Net: n/a Used aircraft leasing and financing company.
Owner / lessor of following (main) aircraft types: Boeing 737-200 Aircraft leased from JETZ are listed and mentioned as such under the leasing carriers.

JIM AIR, Inc.
Anchorage-Lake Hood SPB, AK

PO Box 190989, Anchorage, AK 99519-0989, USA ☎ (907) 243-5161 Tx: none Fax: (907) 243-1711 SITA: n/a
F: 1954 ⭐⭐⭐ n/a Head: James H. Bern Net: n/a

☐	N4672U	Cessna U206G Stationair 6 II	U20605046		0079	0193	1 CO IO-520-F	1633			
☐	N4975U	Cessna U206G Stationair 6 II	U20605179		0079	0193	1 CO IO-520-F	1633			Floats
☐	N756TV	Cessna U206G Stationair 6 II	U20604352		0078	1096	1 CO IO-520-F	1633			
☐	N6GR	Piper PA-31-350 Navajo Chieftain	31-7752130		0077	0597	2 LY TIO-540-J2BD	3175			

JIM HANKINS AIR SERVICE, Inc. = HKN
Jackson-Hawkins Field, MS

PO Box 10652, Jackson, MS 39209, USA ☎ (228) 354-2789 Tx: none Fax: (228) 352-8984 SITA: n/a
F: 1958 ⭐⭐⭐ 10 Head: James A. Hankins ICAO: HANKINS Net: n/a

☐	N3106W	Beech Baron 58	TH-408		0074	1183	2 CO IO-520-C	2449			
☐	N40XL	Beech Baron 58	TH-400		0074	0290	2 CO IO-520-C	2449			
☐	N6652A	Beech Baron 58	TH-1045		0079	1095	2 CO IO-520-CB	2449			
☐	N123MD	Beech H18	BA-701		0064	0790	2 PW R-985-AN14B	4491			Freighter
☐	N22BR	Beech H18	BA-729		0065	1190	2 PW R-985-AN14B	4491			Freighter
☐	N495DM	Beech C-45H (18)	AF-225	N495D	0051	0195	2 PW R-985-AN14B	3969			Freighter
☐	N797SB	Beech E18S	BA-172	N797S	0057	0596	2 PW R-985-AN14B	4218			Freighter
☐	N8476H	Beech H18	BA-749		0066	1194	2 PW R-985-AN14B	4491			Freighter
☐	N8495A	Beech H18	BA-668		0064	0396	2 PW R-985-AN14B	4491			Freighter
☐	N92756	Beech H18	BA-728	JA5133	0065	1094	2 PW R-985-AN14B	4491			Freighter
☐	N933T	Beech H18	BA-665		0064	1191	2 PW R-985-AN14B	4491			Freighter
☐	N958B	Beech H18	BA-651		0063	0392	2 PW R-985-AN14B	4491			Freighter
☐	N781G	Lockheed 18-56 (C-60A) Lodestar	18-2430	42-55969	0043	0596	2 WR R-1820	9525			Freighter
☐	N8061A	Boeing (Douglas) DC-3C (C-47-DL)	6085	CF-CPX	0043	1196	2 PW R-1830-90D	12202			Freighter

J.L. AVIATION (Jeffrey R. Linscott dba)
Portland-Int'l, OR

PO Box 97, Troutdale, OR 97060, USA ☎ (503) 249-2770 Tx: none Fax: (503) 249-2773 SITA: n/a
F: 1997 ⭐⭐⭐ n/a Head: Jeffrey R. Linscott Net: n/a

☐	N2268X	Bell 206B JetRanger III	3607		0382	0897	1 AN 250-C20J	1451			

JOE BRIGHAM, Inc.
Brigham-Heliport, NH & Double A-Heliport, MA

720 Clough Mill Road, Pembroke, NH 03275, USA ☎ (603) 225-3134 Tx: none Fax: (605) 224-9050 SITA: n/a
F: 1983 ⭐⭐⭐ n/a Head: Raymond G. Newcomb Net: http://www.jbi.rotor.com

☐	N444JB	Bell OH-58A (206 JetRanger)	41223	N58EA	0072	0497	1 AN T63-A-720	1361			lsf Air First Llc
☐	N445JB	Bell OH-58A (206 JetRanger)	41712	N337SP	0072	0497	1 AN T63-A-720	1361			lsf Finish Line Aviation Inc.
☐	N64JB	Bell 206B JetRanger III	2437	N49CH	0078	0488	1 AN 250-C20B	1451			lsf NC Transportation Inc.
☐	N800JB	Bell 206B JetRanger III	2832	N47CT	0079	0384	1 AN 250-C20B	1451			lsf C&A Transportation Inc.
☐	N204JB	Bell UH-1B (204)	1016	088	0063	0192	1 LY T53-L-11	3856			lsf Lift Inc.

JPATS - Justice Prisoner & Alien Transportation System = JUD (Branch of the U.S. Dept of Justice / formerly U.S.Marshal's NPTS & INS)
Oklahoma City-Will Rogers World, OK

Air Ops Branch c/o U.S. Dept. of Justice, 5900 Air Cargo Road, Oklahoma City, OK 73159-1198, USA ☎ (405) 680-3400 Tx: none Fax: (405) 680-3429 SITA: n/a
F: 1980 ⭐⭐⭐ n/a Head: Tom Little ICAO: JUSTICE Net: n/a Non-commercial government organisation conducting prisoner & alien transportation by aircraft both within the continental United States &
to select foreign countries. Beside aircraft listed, additional government or commercial aircraft may be leased from time to time depending upon demand.

☐	N2213T	Learjet 25D	25D-369	N369MJ	0084	1193	2 GE CJ610-8A	6804			Gvmt transport
☐	N12659	Sabreliner 75A (Rockwell NA265-80)	380-16	N126MS	0074	0888	2 GE CF700-2D2	10433			Gvmt transport
☐	N2200A	Sabreliner 75A (Rockwell NA265-80)	380-26	N128MS	0075	0888	2 GE CF700-2D2	10433			Gvmt transport
☐	N71460	Sabreliner 75A (Rockwell NA265-80)	380-5	N223LP	0074	0888	2 GE CF700-2D2	10433			Gvmt transport
☐	N7148J	Sabreliner 75A (Rockwell NA265-80)	380-33	N129MS	0075	0888	2 GE CF700-2D2	10433			Gvmt transport
☐	N713M	De Havilland DHC-8-102 Dash 8	030	N444T	0086	0297	2 PWC PW120A	15649			cvtd -101 Gvmt transport
☐	N813TL	Boeing (Douglas) DC-9-15	45732 / 41	N29	0066	0694	2 PW JT8D-7 (HK3/ABS)	41141			Gvmt transport
☐	N113	Boeing 727-30	18935 / 234	N18G	0066	0388	3 PW JT8D-7 (HK3/FDX)	72802			Gvmt transport
☐	N530KF	Boeing 727-61	19176 / 290	N2777	0066	0685	3 PW JT8D-7 (HK3/FDX)	73028			Gvmt transport
☐	N109KM	Boeing 727-251 (A)	21155 / 1169	N276US	1075	1196	3 PW JT8D-15 (HK3/FDX)	80059			Gvmt transport

registration type of aircraft   cn/fn   ex/ex*   mfd del   powered by   mtow kg   configuration   selcal   name/fln/specialitites/remarks

KACHEMAK AIR SERVICE, Inc. (Seasonal May-October ops only)

PO Box 1769, Homer, AK 99603, USA ☎ (907) 235-8924 Tx: none Fax: (907) 235-5699 SITA: n/a
F: 1967 ⋔⋔⋔ 4 Head: William J. DeCreeft Net: n/a

		cn/fn	ex/ex*	mfd	del	powered by	mtow kg	configuration	selcal	name/fln/specialtites/remarks
☐ N3904	De Havilland DHC-3 Otter	54	CF-NTR	0054	1276	1 PW R-1340	3629	9 Pax		Floats

KACHEMAK BAY FLYING SERVICE, Inc. (Sister company of Kachemak Air Service, Inc. / Seasonal May-October ops only)

Homer-Belgua Lake SPB, AK

PO Box 1769, Homer, AK 99603, USA ☎ (907) 235-8924 Tx: none Fax: (907) 235-5699 SITA: n/a
F: 1991 ⋔⋔⋔ n/a Head: William J. DeCreeft Net: n/a

☐ N9084	Curtiss Travel Air S-6000B	865		0029	0191	1 WR R-975	2109	6 Pax		Floats

KACHINA AVIATION (Eagle Helicopter, Inc. & Kachina Forest Products Holding, Inc. dba)

Boise-Air Terminal/Gowen Field, ID

4300 Kennedy Street, Boise, ID 83705, USA ☎ (208) 343-8749 Tx: none Fax: (208) 343-8874 SITA: n/a
F: 1983 ⋔⋔⋔ n/a Head: Keith A. Watson Net: n/a Beside helicopters listed, additional (Bell 212) are lsf ALPINE HELICOPTERS (C-) when required.

☐ N104HC	Bell 206L-1 LongRanger III	45500	N5759B	0080	0694	1 AN 250-C30P	1882			cvtd LongRanger II
☐ N171KA	Bell 206L-1 LongRanger III	45607	C-GZPZ	0081	0495	1 AN 250-C30P	1882			cvtd LongRanger II
☐ N161KA	Kaman K-1200 K-Max	A94-0016		0096	0796	1 LY T5317A-1	2722			

KAISERAIR, Inc.

Oakland-Int'l, CA

PO Box 2626, Oakland, CA 94614, USA ☎ (925) 569-9622 Tx: none Fax: (925) 635-3173 SITA: n/a
F: 1946 ⋔⋔⋔ n/a Head: Ronald J. Guerra Net: http://www.kaiserair.com Beside aircraft listed, additional non-commercial executive aircraft are operated under fleet management-contract for private companies.

☐ N116K	Cessna 550 Citation II	550-0149		0080	0880	2 PWC JT15D-4	6033			
☐ N112K	Hawker 800A (BAe 125-800A)	258042	N20S	0085	0388	2 GA TFE731-5R-1H	12429			lsf Wells Fargo & Co.
☐ N119K	GAC G-IV Gulfstream IV	1046	HB-ITP	0088	1296	2 RR Tay 611-8	33203			lsf Wells Fargo & Co.
☐ N232K	GAC G-IV Gulfstream IV (SP)	1232	N471GA	0094	0794	2 RR Tay 611-8	33838			lsf Robert Dickson Co. Trustee

KALAIR USA, Corp.

Basel-Mulhouse/EuroAirport (Switzerland)

Operations office; c/o Jet Aviation AG, CH-4030 Basel-Flughafen, Switzerland ☎ (61) 325 20 85 Tx: none Fax: (61) 325 20 55 SITA: n/a
F: 1989 ⋔⋔⋔ n/a Head: Fredrick J. Peyton Net: n/a Operates executive flights (in conjunction with Jet Aviation AG) exclusively for itself & its owners.

☐ N707KS	Boeing 707-321B	20025 / 780	N728Q	0169	0889	4 PW JT3D-3B (HK2/COM)	147418	Executive	EL-JK	
☐ VP-BKS	Boeing 767-3P6 (ER)	27254 / 522	A4O-GW	0093	0498	2 GE CF6-80C2B4	175540	Executive		

KAMAKA AIR, Inc.

Honolulu-Int'l, HI

109 Mokuea Place, Honolulu, HI 96819, USA ☎ (808) 839-0946 Tx: none Fax: (808) 839-0946 SITA: n/a
F: 1993 ⋔⋔⋔ n/a Head: Jerry H. Jackson Net: n/a

☐ N231H	Beech E18S	BA-281		0057	1195	2 PW R-985-AN14B	4218	Freighter		
☐ N9881Z	Beech C-45H (18)	AF-851	52-10921	0056	0996	2 PW R-985-AN14B	3969	Freighter		

K&K AIRCRAFT, Inc.

Bridgewater-Air Park, VA — K&K AIRCRAFT

PO Box 7, Bridgewater, VA 22812, USA ☎ (540) 828-6070 Tx: none Fax: (540) 828-4031 SITA: n/a
F: 1967 ⋔⋔⋔ 70 Head: Karl D. Stoltzfus Net: n/a

☐ N202GW	Hamilton Westwind III	BA-321	N63E	0057	0491	2 PWC PT6A-20	5094	Freighter		cvtd Beech E18S
☐ N38L	Hamilton Westwind III	51132		0053	0989	2 PWC PT6A-20	5094	Freighter		cvtd Beech TC-45J (18)
☐ N5653D	Hamilton Westwind III	BA-385		0058	0491	2 PWC PT6A-20	5094	Freighter		cvtd Beech E18S
☐ N909GP	Hamilton Westwind III	BA-236		0057	1289	2 PWC PT6A-20	5094	Sprayer / Frtr		cvtd Beech E18S
☐ N961GP	Hamilton Westwind III	BA-559		0060	0491	2 PWC PT6A-20	5094	Sprayer / Frtr		cvtd Beech G18S
☐ N1400E	Beech E18S	BA-227		0056	1271	2 PW R-985-AN14B	4218	Sprayer		
☐ N117CP	Beech King Air A90-1	LM-68	67-18067	0068	0195	2 PWC PT6A-20	4377	Freighter		cvtd U-21A
☐ N48A	Beech King Air B90	LJ-381	N91DT	0068	0894	2 PWC PT6A-20	4377	Pax		
☐ N500NA	Beech King Air B90	LJ-401	N8NM	0068	0995	2 PWC PT6A-20	4377	Pax		
☐ N5WG	Beech King Air A90 (65-A90)	LJ-289	N35P	0067	0696	2 PWC PT6A-20	4377	Pax		
☐ N611ND	Beech King Air A90-1	LM-11	66-18010	0068	1294	2 PWC PT6A-20	4377	Freighter		cvtd U-21A
☐ N7644R	Beech King Air B90	LJ-335		0068	0294	2 PWC PT6A-20	4377	Pax		lsf Turbine Power Inc.
☐ N77SS	Beech King Air A90 (65-A90)	LJ-230	N93BA	0067	0696	2 PWC PT6A-20	4218	Pax		
☐ N9838Z	Beech King Air B90	LJ-435	D-IHCH	0068	0795	2 PWC PT6A-20	4377	Pax		
☐ N17334	Boeing (Douglas) DC-3-178	1920	N177H	0037	0285	2 WR R-1820	12202	Sprayer		
☐ N47E	Boeing (Douglas) DC-3C (C-47A-DL)	13816	N7043N	0044	0590	2 PW R-1830	12202	Freighter / Pax		
☐ N56KS	Boeing (Douglas) DC-3C (C-47B-1-DK)	25769	N2566B	0044	0490	2 WR R-1820	12202	Sprayer / Frtr		
☐ N321L	Boeing (Douglas) Super DC-3S (C-117D)	43345	N307SF	0043	1191	2 WR R-1820	13301	Freighter		cvtd R4D-5 cn 12343

KAPOWSIN AIR SPORTS, Ltd

Kapowsin, WA

PO Box 8, Kapowsin, WA 98344, USA ☎ (360) 893-3483 Tx: n/a Fax: (360) 893-6907 SITA: n/a
F: 1979 ⋔⋔⋔ n/a Head: Leonard A. Aikins Net: n/a Aircraft below MTOW 1361kg: Cessna 182

☐ N21SC	Cessna U206G Turbine Stationair 6 II	U20605278		0079	0589	1 AN 250-C20S	1633	Para		Soloy cvtd
☐ N9438F	Cessna 208 Caravan I	20800053		0085	0495	1 PWC PT6A-114	3629	Para		
☐ N9641F	Cessna 208 Caravan I	20800122		0087	0798	1 PWC PT6A-114	3629	Para		
☐ N9652F	Cessna 208 Caravan I	20800113		0087	0797	1 PWC PT6A-114	3629	Para		
☐ N52FW	De Havilland DHC-6 Twin Otter 100	52	N952	0067	0892	2 PWC PT6A-20	5252	Para		

KATMAI AIR (Katmailand, Inc. dba / affiliated with Anglers Paradise Lodges / Seasonal May-October ops only)

King Salmon & Anchorage-Lake Hood, AK — *Katmai*

4550 Aircraft Drive, Suite 2, Anchorage, AK 99502, USA ☎ (907) 243-5448 Tx: none Fax: (907) 243-0649 SITA: n/a
F: 1974 ⋔⋔⋔ 10 Head: Raymond F. Petersen Net: n/a

☐ N35851	Cessna U206F Stationair II	U20602757		0075	1192	1 CO IO-520-F	1633			Floats
☐ N495K	Cessna U206G Stationair II	U20602730	N35566	0075	0593	1 CO IO-520-F	1633			Floats
☐ N496K	Cessna U206G Stationair	U20603953	N756BE	0077	0696	1 CO IO-520-F	1633			Floats
☐ N9644G	Cessna U206F Stationair	U20601844		0072	0575	1 CO IO-520-F	1633			Floats
☐ N498K	Cessna T207A Turbine Stationair 8 II	20700624	N73762	0080	1285	1 AN 250-C20S	1724			cvtd Soloy / Floats
☐ N499K	Cessna T207A Turbine Stationair 8 II	20700632	N73835	0080	1285	1 AN 250-C20S	1724			cvtd Soloy / Floats
☐ N492K	Piper PA-31-350 Navajo Chieftain	31-8052176	C-GAWL	0080	0393	2 LY TIO-540-J2BD	3175			
☐ N491K	De Havilland DHC-3 Otter	434	N49KA	0062	0390	1 PW R-1340	3629			Floats

KATMAI PRO SHOP, Inc. (Affiliated with Katmai Lodge, Ltd / Seasonal May-October ops only)

King Salmon-SPB, AK

PO Box 421, King Salmon, AK 99613, USA ☎ (800) 330-0326 Tx: none Fax: (907) 439-3082 SITA: n/a
F: 1994 ⋔⋔⋔ 4 Head: Tony Sarpe Net: n/a

☐ N444EF	De Havilland DHC-2 Beaver I	926	N5231G	0056	0794	1 PW R-985	2309			Floats
☐ N17689	De Havilland DHC-3 Otter	431	C-GHYA	0063	0896	1 PW R-1340	3629	Corporate		Floats

KEB AIRCRAFT (KEB Aircraft Sales, Inc. dba / formerly Seattle Seahawks)

Oakland-Int'l, CA

849 East Stanley Blvd, Suite 283, Livermore, CA 94550, USA ☎ (925) 371-0378 Tx: none Fax: (925) 371-0379 SITA: n/a
F: 1989 ⋔⋔⋔ n/a Head: Tom H. Baker Net: n/a Company operates exclusively non-commercial Corporate flights for the owner of the company only.

☐ N287KB	Boeing (Douglas) MD-87 (DC-9-87)	49768 / 1595	D-ALLJ	0589	0197	2 PW JT8D-219	67812	Corporate		

KENAI AIR ALASKA, Inc. (formerly Kenai Air Service, Inc.)

Kenai-Municipal, AK — KENAI AIR

155 Granite Point Court, Kenai, AK 99611, USA ☎ (907) 283-7561 Tx: none Fax: (907) 283-3287 SITA: n/a
F: 1953 ⋔⋔⋔ 20 Head: Craig R. Lofstedt Net: n/a

☐ N277KA	Bell 206B JetRanger II	2177		0077	0777	1 AN 250-C20	1451			
☐ N377KA	Bell 206B JetRanger II	2187		0077	0777	1 AN 250-C20	1451			
☐ N476KA	Bell 206B JetRanger II	1953		0076	0976	1 AN 250-C20	1451			
☐ N576KA	Bell 206B JetRanger II	1971		0076	0776	1 AN 250-C20	1451			
☐ N802KA	Bell 206B JetRanger	1664	N90186	0075	0575	1 AN 250-C20	1451			
☐ N803KA	Bell 206B JetRanger III	2393	N5004P	0078	0678	1 AN 250-C20B	1451			
☐ N804KA	Bell 206B JetRanger III	3315		0081	0781	1 AN 250-C20B	1451			
☐ N806KA	Bell 206B JetRanger II	2179	N9931K	0077	0281	1 AN 250-C20	1451			
☐ N678KA	Bell 206L-1 LongRanger II	45185		0078	0979	1 AN 250-C28B	1882			
☐ N80KA	Bell 206L-1 LongRanger II	45688	N2024Z	0081	0493	1 AN 250-C28B	1882			lsf pvt
☐ N82KA	Bell 206L-1 LongRanger II	45694	N44TV	0081	0493	1 AN 250-C28B	1882			lsf pvt
☐ N801KA	Bell 212	30621	N59572	0074	0780	2 PWC PT6T-3 TwinPac	5080			
☐ N811KA	Bell 212	30656	N59630	0074	0283	2 PWC PT6T-3 TwinPac	5080			

KENAI AVIATION (Robert T. Bielefeld dba)

Kenai-Municipal, AK

PO Box 46, Kenai, AK 99611, USA ☎ (907) 283-4124 Tx: none SITA: n/a
F: 1961 ⋔⋔⋔ 2 Head: Robert T. Bielefeld Net: n/a

☐ N4988F	Cessna U206B Super Skywagon	U206-0688		0066	0871	1 CO IO-520-F	1633			
☐ N9563G	Cessna TU206F Turbo Stationair	U20601763		0072	0491	1 CO TSIO-520-F	1633			
☐ N17529	Beech Baron 58	TH-796		0077	1287	2 CO IO-520-C	2449			

KENAI FJORD AIR SERVICES (Kenai Fjord Outfitters, Inc. dba / Seasonal May-October ops only)

Homer-Beluga Lake SPB, AK

PO Box 72, Homer, AK 99603, USA ☎ (907) 235-6066 Tx: none Fax: (907) 235-6049 SITA: n/a
F: 1993 ⋔⋔⋔ n/a Head: Billy R. Smith Net: n/a

☐ N4447Z	Cessna U206E Super Skywagon	U20601479		0070	0595	1 CO IO-520-F	1633			Floats
☐ N14BP	Piper PA-23-250 Aztec D	27-4279		0069	0796	2 LY IO-540-C4B5	2359			lsf Ballentine Ltd Liability / Floats

KENAI FLOAT PLANE SERVICE, Inc.
Port Moller, AK

PO Box 152, Kenai, AK 99611, USA ☎ (907) 283-4761 Tx: none Fax: none SITA: n/a
F: 1957 ♦♦♦ 3 Head: Warren E. Johnson Net: n/a Aircraft below MTOW 1361 kg: Cessna 180 & Piper PA-18

registration	type of aircraft	cn/fn	ex/ex*	mfd	del	powered by	mtow kg	configuration	name/fln/specialities/remarks
☐ N9992Z	Cessna U206G Stationair 6 II	U20606800		0084	0693	1 CO IO-520-F	1633		Floats
☐ N75551	Cessna 207A Stationair 8 II	20700633		0080	0585	1 CO IO-520-F	1724		lsf pvt

KENAI HELICOPTERS (Kenai Air of Hawaii Inc. dba/affiliated with Kenai Air Alaska Inc.)
Grand Canyon-National Park, AZ & Honolulu-Int'l, HI

PO Box 1153, Chino Valley, AZ 86323-1153, USA ☎ (520) 636-0558 Tx: none Fax: (520) 636-0834 SITA: n/a
F: 1968 ♦♦♦ 100 Head: Christy K. Johnson Net: http://www.arizonaguide.com/kenai/

registration	type of aircraft	cn/fn	ex/ex*	mfd	del	powered by	mtow kg	configuration	name/fln/specialities/remarks
☐ N2760K	Bell 206B JetRanger III	2733		0079	1288	1 AN 250-C20B	1451		
☐ N2777R	Bell 206B JetRanger III	2813		0079	0486	1 AN 250-C20B	1451		
☐ N3179X	Bell 206B JetRanger III	3756		0083	1183	1 AN 250-C20J	1451		
☐ N5015E	Bell 206B JetRanger III	2583		0079	1188	1 AN 250-C20B	1451		
☐ N678LD	Bell 206B JetRanger III	3171		0080	0885	1 AN 250-C20B	1451		
☐ N90194	Bell 206B JetRanger	1697		0075	0486	1 AN 250-C20	1451		
☐ N9902K	Bell 206B JetRanger II	1923		0076	0586	1 AN 250-C20	1451		
☐ N2267N	Bell 206L-3 LongRanger III	51021		0082	0685	1 AN 250-C30P	1882		Heavenly
☐ N2758C	Bell 206L-1 LongRanger II	45261		0079	0791	1 AN 250-C28B	1882		
☐ N278KA	Bell 206L LongRanger	46613		0078	0785	1 AN 250-C20B	1814		
☐ N3174P	Bell 206L-1 LongRanger III	45741		0082	0183	1 AN 250-C30P	1882		cvtd LongRanger II
☐ N3905Z	Bell 206L-1 LongRanger II	45624		0082	0681	1 AN 250-C28B	1882		Kaanapali
☐ N805KA	Bell 206L-1 LongRanger II	45578	N3889V	0080	1084	1 AN 250-C20B	1882		

KENAI LAKE AIR SERVICE (Kenneth E. Bethe dba / Seasonal May-October ops only)
Cooper Landing, AK

PO Box 830, Cooper Landing, AK 99572, USA ☎ (907) 595-1363 Tx: none Fax: (907) 595-1363 SITA: n/a
F: 1966 ♦♦♦ n/a Head: Kenneth E. Bethe Net: n/a

registration	type of aircraft	cn/fn	ex/ex*	mfd	del	powered by	mtow kg	configuration	name/fln/specialities/remarks
☐ N5978	De Havilland DHC-2 Beaver I	308	N51516	0051	0190	1 PW R-985	2313		lsf pvt / Floats

KENMORE AIR = M5 (Kenmore Air Harbor, Inc. dba)
Kenmore-SPB, WA

PO Box 82064, Kenmore, WA 98028-0064, USA ☎ (425) 486-1257 Tx: none Fax: (425) 486-5471 SITA: n/a
F: 1946 ♦♦♦ 72 Head: Robert B. Munro Net: http://www.kenmoreair.com Aircraft below MTOW 1361 kg: Cessna 180 (on Floats)

registration	type of aircraft	cn/fn	ex/ex*	mfd	del	powered by	mtow kg	configuration	name/fln/specialities/remarks
☐ N1018U	De Havilland DHC-2 Beaver I	1381	58-2049	0059	0590	1 PW R-985	2313		Floats
☐ N17598	De Havilland DHC-2 Beaver I	1129	VP-FAH	0058	0468	1 PW R-985	2313		Floats
☐ N62SJ	De Havilland DHC-2 Beaver I	710	N1018G	0053	0496	1 PW R-985	2313		Floats
☐ N6781L	De Havilland DHC-2 Beaver I	788	N10LU	0053	0293	1 PW R-985	2313		Floats
☐ N6782L	De Havilland DHC-2 Beaver I	820	N23LU	0054	0293	1 PW R-985	2313		Floats
☐ N6783L	De Havilland DHC-2 Beaver I	1369	N26LU	0058	0293	1 PW R-985	2313		Floats
☐ N72355	De Havilland DHC-2 Beaver I	1164	N1453Z	0056	1086	1 PW R-985	2313		Floats
☐ N900KA	De Havilland DHC-2 Beaver I	1676	LN-BFH	0067	1184	1 PW R-985	2313		Floats
☐ N9766Z	De Havilland DHC-2 Beaver I	504	N13454	0053	0585	1 PW R-985	2313		Floats
☐ N1455T	De Havilland DHC-2 Turbo Beaver III	1647TB26	C-FOEI	0066	1286	1 PWC PT6A-135	2436		Floats
☐ N9744T	De Havilland DHC-2 Turbo Beaver III	1692TB60	N1944	0068	0289	1 PWC PT6A-135A	2436		Floats
☐ N234KA	De Havilland DHC-3 Turbo Otter	42	C-FMPP	0054	0293	1 PWC PT6A-135	3629		Floats / cvtd Otter
☐ N3125S	De Havilland DHC-3 Turbo Otter	407	CAF 9424	0060	1088	1 PWC PT6A-135	3629		Amphibian / cvtd Otter
☐ N90422	De Havilland DHC-3 Turbo Otter	152	55-3296	0056	1092	1 PWC PT6A-135	3629		Floats / cvtd Otter
☐ N50KA	De Havilland DHC-3 Turbo Otter	221	IM 1720	0058	0595	1 PWC PT6A-135	3629		Floats / cvtd Otter
☐ N58JH	De Havilland DHC-3 Turbo Otter	131	N8510Q	0056	0197	1 PWC PT6A-135	3629		Floats / cvtd Otter
☐ N87KA	De Havilland DHC-3 Turbo Otter	11	N8262V	0053	0595	1 PWC PT6A-135	3629		Floats / cvtd Otter

KENNICOTT WILDERNESS AIR, Inc. (Sister company of McCarthy Air)
McCarthy, AK

c/o McCarthy Air, 101 Shushana Avenue, McCarthy, AK 99588, USA ☎ (907) 554-4440 Tx: none Fax: none SITA: n/a
F: 1996 ♦♦♦ n/a Head: David C. Flets Net: n/a Aircraft below MTOW 1361kg: Piper PA-18

registration	type of aircraft	cn/fn	ex/ex*	mfd	del	powered by	mtow kg	configuration	name/fln/specialities/remarks
☐ N3853W	Piper PA-32-260 Cherokee SIX	32-794		0066	0696	1 LY O-540-E4B5	1542		lsf pvt

KETCHUM AIR SERVICE, Inc.
Anchorage-Lake Hood SPB, AK

PO Box 190588, Anchorage, AK 99519, USA ☎ (907) 243-5525 Tx: none Fax: (907) 243-8311 SITA: n/a
F: 1968 ♦♦♦ 15 Head: Craig L. Ketchum Net: n/a

registration	type of aircraft	cn/fn	ex/ex*	mfd	del	powered by	mtow kg	configuration	name/fln/specialities/remarks
☐ N4875X	Cessna U206G Stationair 6 II	U20605559		0080	0792	1 CO IO-520-F	1633		lsf Ketchum&Ketchum Inc./Floats/Wh-Skis
☐ N756QG	Cessna U206G Stationair 6 II	U20604267		0078	0582	1 CO IO-520-F	1633		lsf Ketchum Airc.Lsng/Floats/Wheel-Skis
☐ N8340Q	Cessna U206F Stationair II	U20603201		0076	0776	1 CO IO-520-F	1633		lsf Ketchum Airc.Lsng/Floats/Wheel-Skis
☐ N340KA	De Havilland DHC-2 Beaver I	1127	N1018N	0056	0293	1 PW R-985	2313		lsf Ketchum Airc.Lsng/Floats/Wheel-Skis
☐ N345KA	De Havilland DHC-2 Beaver I	1306	N67678	0058	0293	1 PW R-985	2313		lsf Ketchum Airc.Lsng/Floats/Wheel-Skis
☐ N62469	De Havilland DHC-2 Beaver I	1237	57-6147	0057	0776	1 PW R-985	2313		lsf Ketchum Airc.Lsng/Floats/Wheel-Skis
☐ N836KA	De Havilland DHC-2 Beaver I	604	N727KA	0053	0589	1 PW R-985	2313		lsf Ketchum Airc.Lsng/Floats/Wheel-Skis
☐ N342KA	De Havilland DHC-3 Turbo Otter	465	N32910	0067	0397	1 PWC PT6A-135A	3629		lsf Ketchum Ac.Lsng/cvtd Otter/Fl./Wh-S
☐ N888KA	De Havilland DHC-3 Turbo Otter	106	N888XX	0056	0689	1 PWC PT6A-135A	3629		lsf Ketchum Ac.Lsng/cvtd Otter/Fl./Wh-S

KEY LARGO AIR SERVICE, Inc.
Homestead-General Aviation, FL

PO Box 90-1789, Homestead, FL 33090-1789, USA ☎ (954) 248-1100 Tx: none Fax: (954) 248-1100 SITA: n/a
F: 1958 ♦♦♦ 10 Head: Patricia L. Barnes Net: n/a

registration	type of aircraft	cn/fn	ex/ex*	mfd	del	powered by	mtow kg	configuration	name/fln/specialities/remarks
☐ N530JB	Piper PA-31-350 Navajo Chieftain	31-7952156	N3529M	0079	1294	2 LY TIO-540-J2BD	3175		

KEY LIME AIR = LYM
Denver-Centennial, CO

7625 South Peoria Street, Suite D-15, Englewood, CO 80112, USA ☎ (303) 619-6667 Tx: none Fax: (303) 768-8144 SITA: n/a
F: 1997 ♦♦♦ n/a Head: Clifford D. Honeycutt ICAO: KEY LIME Net: n/a

registration	type of aircraft	cn/fn	ex/ex*	mfd	del	powered by	mtow kg	configuration	name/fln/specialities/remarks
☐ N411BJ	Piper PA-31-350 Navajo Chieftain	31-7952043		0079	0997	2 LY TIO-540-J2BD	3175	Y9 / Freighter	lsf Western Aero Llc
☐ N67BJ	Piper PA-31-350 Navajo Chieftain	31-7952250		0079	0797	2 LY TIO-540-J2BD	3175	Y9 / Freighter	lsf Western Aero Llc
☐ N74952	Piper PA-31-350 Navajo Chieftain	31-7305100		0073	0597	2 LY TIO-540-J2BD	3175	Y9 / Freighter	lsf Western Aero Llc
☐ N9247L	Piper PA-31-350 Navajo Chieftain	31-8152160		0081	0597	2 LY TIO-540-J2BD	3175	Y9 / Freighter	lsf Western Aero Llc
☐ N404MG	Cessna 404 Titan II	404-0813		0081	0198	2 CO GTSIO-520-M	3810	Y9 / Freighter	lsf Western Aero Llc
☐ N509SS	Fairchild (Swearingen) SA226TC Metro II	TC-206	N261S	0073	1098	2 GA TPE331-3UW-303G	5670	Freighter	lsf Byrds Nest 1 Corp.
☐ N323GW	Fairchild (Swearingen) SA226TC Metro II	TC-323	SE-IVU	0080	1098	2 GA TPE331-3UW-303G	5670	Freighter	lsf EDB Air Inc.
☐ N60U	Fairchild (Swearingen) SA226TC Metro II	TC-237	N5389M	0077	1098	2 GA TPE331-3UW-303G	5670	Freighter	lsf Truman Arnold Companies
☐ N62Z	Fairchild (Swearingen) SA226TC Metro II	TC-237	N5437M	0077	0798	2 GA TPE331-10UA-511G	5670	Freighter	lsf Truman Arnold Companies
☐ N770S	Fairchild (Swearingen) SA226TC Metro II	TC-248		0078	0798	2 GA TPE331-10UA-511G	5670	Freighter	
☐ N27BJ	Learjet 24B	24B-227	N28AT	0071	0197	2 GE CJ610-6	6123	Y5 / Freighter	

KEYSTONE FLIGHT SERVICES (Division of Keystone Helicopter, Corporation)
West Chester-Keystone Heliport, PA

1420 Phoenixville Pike, West Chester, PA 19380, USA ☎ (610) 644-4430 Tx: 510-668-5061 khc-wch Fax: (610) 644-7681 SITA: n/a
F: 1953 ♦♦♦ 180 Head: Peter Wright, Jr. Net: http://www.keystone-helicopter.com

registration	type of aircraft	cn/fn	ex/ex*	mfd	del	powered by	mtow kg	configuration	name/fln/specialities/remarks
☐ N901CM	Agusta A109C MAX	7652	N652DH	0091	1098	2 AN 250-C20R/1	2720	EMS LifeFlight	lsf Agusta / opf LifeFlight of Maine
☐ N900LF	MD Helicopters MD 900 Explorer	900-00022	N9118A	0096	0296	2 PWC PW206A	2722	EMS LifeFlight	lsf GECC/opf Allegheny General Hospital
☐ N903LF	MD Helicopters MD 900 Explorer	900-00030		0096	1096	2 PWC PW206A	2722	EMS LifeFlight	lsf GECC/opf Allegheny General Hospital
☐ N904LF	MD Helicopters MD 900 Explorer	900-00031		0096	1296	2 PWC PW206A	2722	EMS LifeFlight	lsf GECC/opf Allegheny General Hospital
☐ N905LF	MD Helicopters MD 900 Explorer	900-00011	N92011	0095	0797	2 PWC PW206A	2722	EMS LifeFlight	lsf GECC/opf Allegheny General Hospital
☐ N116MB	Eurocopter (MBB) BK117A-3	7095		0086	0187	2 LY LTS101-650B.1	3200		lsf/opf Geisinger Medical Center
☐ N121LF	Eurocopter (MBB) BK117B-1	7226	N71709	0090	0191	2 LY LTS101-750B.1	3200	EMS	lsf General Electric Capital Corp.
☐ N271	Eurocopter (MBB) BK117A-3	7059	N159BK	0085	0186	2 LY LTS101-650B.1	3200		
☐ N526MB	Eurocopter (MBB) BK117A-3	7102		0086	0187	2 LY LTS101-650B.1	3200	EMS Med Star	opf Conemaugh Memorial Medical Center
☐ N532KH	Eurocopter (MBB) BK117A-3	7069	N912WS	0085	0893	2 LY LTS101-650B.1	3200	EMS	
☐ N7062J	Eurocopter (MBB) BK117B-1	7178		0088	0189	2 LY LTS101-750B.1	3200		lsf MDFC Equipment Leasing Corp.
☐ N911CH	Eurocopter (MBB) BK117B-1	7223	N65377	0090	0590	2 LY LTS101-750B.1	3200	EMS Med Star	lsf Debis/opf Conemaugh Memorial MedCtr
☐ N272NE	Eurocopter (Aerosp.) AS365N2 Dauphin 2	6435	N365NZ	0091	0395	2 TU Arriel 1C2	4250	EMS LifeFlight	lsf/opf New England Life Flight Inc.
☐ N4238S	Sikorsky S-76A+	760013		0079	0895	2 TU Arriel 1S	4899		cvtd S-76A
☐ N886AH	Sikorsky S-76A++	760153	N986AH	0081	1196	2 TU Arriel 1S1	4899	EMS	cvtd 76A/opf Allegheny University Hosp.
☐ N911GH	Sikorsky S-76A	760108	N300JW	0080	0595	2 AN 250-C30S	4763	EMS	lsf/opf Robert Packer Hospital

KING AIRLINES, Inc.
Las Vegas-Henderson Executive, NV

1400 Executive Airport Drive, Suite K, Henderson, NV 89012, USA ☎ (702) 361-7811 Tx: none Fax: (702) 361-1442 SITA: n/a
F: 1988 ♦♦♦ n/a Head: David R. King Net: n/a

registration	type of aircraft	cn/fn	ex/ex*	mfd	del	powered by	mtow kg	configuration	name/fln/specialities/remarks
☐ N8467Q	Cessna U206F Stationair II	U20603325		0076	1094	1 CO IO-520-F	1633		
☐ N8564Q	Cessna U206F Stationair II	U20603420		0076	1094	1 CO IO-520-F	1633		
☐ N8785Q	Cessna TU206G Turbo Stationair	U20603537		0076	0195	1 CO TSIO-520-M	1633		
☐ N1570U	Cessna 207 Skywagon	20700170		0070	0195	1 CO IO-520-F	1724		
☐ N1783U	Cessna T207A Turbo Skywagon	20700383		0076	1094	1 CO TSIO-520-M	1724		
☐ N3156X	Cessna T207 Turbo Skywagon	20700376		0076	0796	1 CO TSIO-520-G	1724		
☐ N3728B	Cessna T207 Turbo Skywagon	20700298		0074	0196	1 CO TSIO-520-G	1724		
☐ N73320	Cessna T207A Turbo Stationair 8 II	20700577		0079	0597	1 CO TSIO-520-M	1724		
☐ N2966Q	Cessna 402B	402B0321		0073	0594	2 CO TSIO-520-E	2858		
☐ N3278Q	Cessna 402	402-0078		0067	1293	2 CO TSIO-520-E	2858		

	registration	type of aircraft	cn/fn	ex/ex*	mfd	del	powered by	mtow kg	configuration	selcal	name/fln/specialitites/remarks
☐	N4010Q	Cessna 402	402-0110		0067	0594	2 CO TSIO-520-E	2858			
☐	N402SW	Cessna 402	402-0036		0067	1293	2 CO TSIO-520-E	2858			
☐	N5098G	Cessna 402A	402A0056		0069	1093	2 CO TSIO-520-E	2858			
☐	N5210J	Cessna 402B	402B0897		0075	0193	2 CO TSIO-520-E	2858			
☐	N57SA	Cessna 402A	402A0101		0069	0494	2 CO TSIO-520-E	2858			
☐	N69341	Cessna 402B	402B0449		0073	1093	2 CO TSIO-520-E	2858			
☐	N69PB	Cessna 402B II	402B1248		0077	0491	2 CO TSIO-520-E	2858			
☐	N82TA	Cessna 402	402-0156		0067	1294	2 CO TSIO-520-E	2858			
☐	N9901F	Cessna 402B	402B0402		0073	1293	2 CO TSIO-520-E	2858			
☐	N99AT	Cessna 402A	402A0022		0069	0494	2 CO TSIO-520-E	2858			

KING FLYING SERVICE (King Air, Inc. dba) — **Naknek, AK**

PO Box 26, Naknek, AK 99633, USA ☎ (907) 246-4414 Tx: none Fax: (907) 246-7426 SITA: n/a
F: 1959 ⁂ n/a Head: Ellen M. King Net: n/a Aircraft below MTOW 1361 kg: Piper PA-18 & PA-28

	registration	type of aircraft	cn/fn	ex/ex*	mfd	del	powered by	mtow kg	configuration	selcal	name/fln/specialitites/remarks
☐	N38186	Piper PA-32-300 Cherokee SIX	32-7740077		0077	0977	1 LY IO-540-K1G5	1542			
☐	N44851	Piper PA-32-300 Cherokee SIX	32-7740107		0077	0791	1 LY IO-540-K1G5	1542			lsf pvt

KITTY HAWK AIR CARGO, Inc. = KR / KHA (Subsidiary of Kitty Hawk Group, Inc.) — **Dallas-DFW & Fort Worth-Meacham, TX**

PO Box 612787, DFW Int'l Airport, TX 75261, USA ☎ (972) 456-6000 Tx: none Fax: (972) 456-2277 SITA: n/a
F: 1976 ⁂ 3600 Head: M. Tom Christopher ICAO: AIR KITTYHAWK Net: http://www.kha.com

	registration	type of aircraft	cn/fn	ex/ex*	mfd	del	powered by	mtow kg	configuration	selcal	name/fln/specialitites/remarks
☐	N74850	Convair 600 (F) (SCD)	74	N94237	0048	0291	2 RR Dart 542-4	20956	Freighter		lsf Aircraft Leasing Inc./cvtd CV240-0
☐	N94205	Convair 600 (F) (SCD)	10		0048	0394	2 RR Dart 542-4	20956	Freighter		lsf Aircraft Leasing Inc./cvtd CV240-0
☐	N94226	Convair 600 (F) (SCD)	48		0048	1091	2 RR Dart 542-4	20956	Freighter		lsf Aircraft Leasing Inc./cvtd CV240-0
☐	N94246	Convair 600 (F) (SCD)	102		0048	1091	2 RR Dart 542-4	20956	Freighter		lsf Aircraft Leasing Inc./cvtd CV240-0
☐	N94258	Convair 600 (F) (SCD)	119		0048	1091	2 RR Dart 542-4	20956	Freighter		lsf Aircraft Leasing Inc./cvtd CV240-0
☐	N94279	Convair 600 (F) (SCD)	101	N90860	0049	1091	2 RR Dart 542-4	20956	Freighter		lsf Aircraft Leasing Inc./cvtd CV240-0
☐	N3412	Convair 640 (F) (SCD)	32		0052	1091	2 RR Dart 542-4	24948	Freighter		lsf Aircraft Leasing Inc./cvtd CV340-32
☐	N587CA	Convair 640 (F) (SCD)	463	C-FPWO	0057	0894	2 RR Dart 542-4	24948	Freighter		lsf Aircraft Leasing Inc./cvtd CV440-75
☐	N860FW	Convair 640 (F) (SCD)	10	N2569D	0052	0494	2 RR Dart 542-4	24948	Freighter		lsf Aircraft Leasing Inc./cvtd CV340-33
☐	N866TA	Convair 640 (F) (SCD)	283	141000	0055	0291	2 RR Dart 542-4	24948	Freighter		lsf AcLsg/cvtdC-131F/rebuilt with cn409
☐	N112PS	Boeing (Douglas) DC-9-15F (RC)	47013 / 129	N557AS	0067	0392	2 PW JT8D-7B (HK3/ABS)	41141	Freighter		lsf Aircraft Leasing Inc.
☐	N561PC	Boeing (Douglas) DC-9-15F (RC)	47014 / 141	N70AF	0067	0495	2 PW JT8D-7B (HK3/ABS)	41141	Freighter		lsf Aircraft Leasing Inc.
☐	N562PC	Boeing (Douglas) DC-9-15F (RC)	47012 / 115	N75AF	0567	1093	2 PW JT8D-7B (HK3/ABS)	41141	Freighter		lsf Aircraft Leasing Inc.
☐	N563PC	Boeing (Douglas) DC-9-15F (MC)	47055 / 194	N1305T	1167	0295	2 PW JT8D-7B (HK3/ABS)	41141	Freighter		lsf Aircraft Leasing Inc.
☐	N564PC	Boeing (Douglas) DC-9-15F (MC)	47062 / 223	N1307T	0068	1093	2 PW JT8D-7B	41141	Freighter		lsf Aircraft Leasing Inc.
☐	N270AX	Boeing 727-90C	19170 / 332	N798AS	0066	0898	3 PW JT8D-7B (HK3/FDX)	76884	Freighter		
☐	N727CK	Boeing 727-22C	19195 / 406	N727PL	0067	0997	3 PW JT8D-7B	76884	Freighter		
☐	N180AX	Boeing 727-222 (F)	20041 / 732	N7647U	0069	0898	3 PW JT8D-7B	78018	Freighter		cvtd -222
☐	N252US	Boeing 727-251 (F)	19971 / 655		1168	1296	3 PW JT8D-7B (HK3/FDX)	78245	Freighter		lsf Aircraft Leasing Inc. / cvtd -251
☐	N255US	Boeing 727-251 (F)	19974 / 667		1268	0997	3 PW JT8D-7B (HK3/FDX)	78245	Freighter		cvtd -251
☐	N264US	Boeing 727-251 (F)	19983 / 741		0869	1296	3 PW JT8D-7B	78018	Freighter		lsf PEGA / cvtd -251
☐	N278US	Boeing 727-251 (F) (A)	21157 / 1173		1175	1295	3 PW JT8D-15 (HK3/FDX)	80059	Freighter		lsf Aircraft Leasing Inc. / cvtd -251
☐	N279US	Boeing 727-251 (F) (A)	21158 / 1177		1275	1095	3 PW JT8D-15 (HK3/FDX)	80059	Freighter		lsf Aircraft Leasing Inc. / cvtd -251
☐	N281KH	Boeing 727-2J0 (F) (A)	21105 / 1158	6Y-JMM	0075	0197	3 PW JT8D-15 (HK3/FDX)	88360	Freighter		cvtd -2J0
☐	N284KH	Boeing 727-2J0 (A)	21108 / 1174	6Y-JMP	0075	0497	3 PW JT8D-15 (HK3/FDX)	88360	Y170		lst Sky Trek Int'l / cvtd -2J0
☐	N6806	Boeing 727-223 (F)	19481 / 548	N719CK	0468	0997	3 PW JT8D-9 (HK3/FDX)	80966	Freighter		lst / opf BAX Global / cvtd -223
☐	N6807	Boeing 727-223 (F)	19482 / 557	N729CK	0468	0997	3 PW JT8D-9 (HK3/FDX)	80966	Freighter		cvtd -223
☐	N6808	Boeing 727-223 (F)	19483 / 558		0468	0997	3 PW JT8D-9 (HK3/FDX)	80966	Freighter		cvtd -223
☐	N6809	Boeing 727-223 (F)	19484 / 560		0468	0894	3 PW JT8D-9 (HK3/FDX)	80966	Freighter	BK-EL	lsf Ac.Lsng/sub-lst TNT Int'l/cvtd -223
☐	N6810	Boeing 727-223 (F)	19485 / 571	N722CK	0568	0997	3 PW JT8D-9 (HK3/FDX)	80966	Freighter		cvtd -223
☐	N6811	Boeing 727-223 (F)	19486 / 578		0568	0997	3 PW JT8D-9 (HK3/FDX)	80966	Freighter		cvtd -223
☐	N6812	Boeing 727-223 (F)	19487 / 579	N720CK	0568	0997	3 PW JT8D-9 (HK3/FDX)	80966	Freighter		cvtd -223
☐	N6816	Boeing 727-223 (F)	19491 / 611		0768	0997	3 PW JT8D-9 (HK3/FDX)	80966	Freighter		lst / opf BAX Global / cvtd -223
☐	N6821	Boeing 727-223 (F)	19496 / 669	N706CA	1268	0997	3 PW JT8D-9A (HK3/FDX)	80966	Freighter		cvtd -223
☐	N6827	Boeing 727-223 (F)	20180 / 698		0369	0794	3 PW JT8D-9	80966	Freighter		lsf Aircraft Leasing Inc. / cvtd -223
☐	N6831	Boeing 727-223 (F)	20184 / 707		0469	0997	3 PW JT8D-9	80966	Freighter		lst / opf BAX Global / cvtd -223
☐	N6833	Boeing 727-223 (F)	20186 / 721		0569	0594	3 PW JT8D-9 (HK3/FDX)	80966	Freighter		lsf Ac.Lsng/sublst Ansett A.F./cvtd-223
☐	N6834	Boeing 727-223 (F)	20187 / 722		0569	0997	3 PW JT8D-9 (HK3/FDX)	80966	Freighter		cvtd -223
☐	N6838	Boeing 727-223 (F)	20191 / 739	N723CK	0769	0997	3 PW JT8D-9 (HK3/FDX)	80966	Freighter		cvtd -223
☐	N69739	Boeing 727-224 (F) (A)	20667 / 1153		0075	0197	3 PW JT8D-9A (HK3/FDX)	78245	Freighter		lsf Aircraft Leasing Inc. / cvtd -224
☐	N69740	Boeing 727-224 (F) (A)	20668 / 1154		0075	0596	3 PW JT8D-9A (HK3/FDX)	78245	Freighter		lsf Aircraft Leasing Inc. / cvtd -224
☐	N705CA	Boeing 727-223 (F)	19479 / 544	N6804	0368	0997	3 PW JT8D-9A	80966	Freighter		cvtd -223
☐	N750US	Boeing 727-214 (F) (A)	21512 / 1343	N555PS	0078	0796	3 PW JT8D-7B (HK3/FDX)	88360	Freighter		lsf TA Air IX Corp. / cvtd -214
☐	N751US	Boeing 727-214 (F) (A)	21513 / 1365	N556PS	0078	0796	3 PW JT8D-7B (HK3/FDX)	88360	Freighter		lsf TA Air IX Corp. / cvtd -214
☐	N79746	Boeing 727-224 (F) (A)	22449 / 1756		0081	0797	3 PW JT8D-15	86409	Freighter		lsf Aircraft Leasing Inc.
☐	N854AA	Boeing 727-223 (F) (A)	20995 / 1192		0676	0195	3 PW JT8D-9A (HK3/FDX)	80966	Freighter		lsf Aircraft Leasing Inc. / cvtd -223
☐	N855AA	Boeing 727-223 (F) (A)	20996 / 1193		0676	0195	3 PW JT8D-9A (HK3/FDX)	80966	Freighter		lsf Aircraft Leasing Inc. / cvtd -223
☐	N856AA	Boeing 727-223 (F) (A)	20997 / 1195		0676	0997	3 PW JT8D-9A (HK3/FDX)	80966	Freighter		cvtd -223
☐	N858AA	Boeing 727-223 (F) (A)	21085 / 1200		0476	0997	3 PW JT8D-9A (HK3/FDX)	80966	Freighter		lst / opf BAX Global / cvtd -223
☐	N90AX	Boeing 727-222 (F)	20040 / 729	N7646U	0069	0898	3 PW JT8D-7B	78018	Freighter		cvtd -222

KITTY HAWK CHARTERS = CB / KFS (Connie Kalitta Services) (Kalitta Flying Service Inc. dba/Subs.of Kitty Hawk Group Inc.) — **Detroit-Willow Run, MI & Morristown, TN**

842 Willow Run Airport, Ypsilanti, MI 48197, USA ☎ (734) 484-0088 Tx: none Fax: (734) 484-9812 SITA: n/a
F: 1973 ⁂ 100 Head: Louis B. Birurakis ICAO: KALITTA Net: http://www.mjoseph.kalitta.com CONNIE KALITTA SERVICES titles are used on some aircraft as a marketing name to remember older times.

	registration	type of aircraft	cn/fn	ex/ex*	mfd	del	powered by	mtow kg	configuration	selcal	name/fln/specialitites/remarks
☐	N4147R	Piper PA-32-300 Cherokee SIX	32-40347		0068	1286	1 LY IO-540-K1A5	1542	5 Pax / Frtr		
☐	N311JB	Mitsubishi MU-2K (MU-2B-25) Cargoliner	311	N501MA	0074	0894	2 GA TPE331-6-251M	4500	Freighter		Cavenaugh SCD conversion
☐	N32CK	Mitsubishi MU-2J (MU-2B-35) Cargoliner	588	N292MA	0073	1091	2 GA TPE331-6-251M	4899	Freighter		Cavenaugh SCD conversion
☐	N66CL	Mitsubishi MU-2F (MU-2B-20) Cargoliner	135	N44MA	0068	0589	2 GA TPE331-1-151A	4500	Freighter		Cavenaugh SCD conversion
☐	N16SL	Volpar Turboliner	BA-65	N114PA	0055	0981	2 GA TPE331-1-101B	5216	Freighter		cvtd Beech E18S
☐	N16TM	Volpar Turboliner	AF-350	N9518Z	0051	1089	2 GA TPE331-1-101B	5216	Freighter		cvtd Beech C-45H (18)
☐	N231LJ	Hamilton Westwind IISTD		N8539	0045	1176	2 GA TPE331-1-101B	5216	Freighter		cvtd Beech TC-45J (18)
☐	N231SK	Volpar Turboliner	AF-856	N346V	0056	0780	2 GA TPE331-1-101B	5216	Freighter		cvtd Beech C-45H (18)
☐	N331FD	Volpar Turboliner	AF-280	HB-GFU	0052	0883	2 GA TPE331-1-101B	5216	Freighter		cvtd Beech C-45H (18)
☐	N346V	Volpar Turboliner	AF-186	HB-GGH	0052	0381	2 GA TPE331-1-101B	5216	Freighter		cvtd Beech C-45H (18)
☐	N400WA	Volpar Turboliner	AF-764	52-10834	0054	0690	2 GA TPE331-1-101B	5216	Freighter		cvtd Beech C-45H (18)
☐	N401CK	Volpar Turboliner	AF-60	N401TH	0052	0690	2 GA TPE331-1-101B	5216	Freighter		cvtd Beech C-45G (18)
☐	N404CK	Volpar Turboliner	AF-297	N404TH	0053	0389	2 GA TPE331-1-101B	5216	Freighter		cvtd Beech C-45H (18)
☐	N407TH	Volpar Turboliner	AF-897	N8SL	0055	0690	2 GA TPE331-1-101B	5216	Freighter		cvtd Beech C-45H (18)
☐	N408TH	Volpar Turboliner	BA-110	N17SL	0055	0584	2 GA TPE331-1-101B	5216	Freighter		cvtd Beech E18S (18)
☐	N4209V	Volpar Turboliner	AF-884	HB-GFX	0056	0984	2 GA TPE331-1-101B	5216	Freighter		cvtd Beech C-45H (18)
☐	N431DK	Volpar Turboliner	AF-458	HB-GGF	0053	0883	2 GA TPE331-1-101B	5216	Freighter		cvtd Beech C-45H (18)
☐	N502CK	Volpar Turboliner	A-366	N4234A	0054	0492	2 GA TPE331-1-101B	5216	Freighter		cvtd Beech D18S
☐	N508FS	Volpar Turboliner	BA-688	N800TH	0064	0690	2 GA TPE331-1-101B	5216	Freighter		lst F.S. Air Svc / cvtd Beech H18
☐	N531CK	Volpar Turboliner	AF-171	HB-GFT	0051	0991	2 GA TPE331-1-101B	5216	Freighter		cvtd Beech C-45H (18)
☐	N700WA	Volpar Turboliner	BA-28	N3626B	0054	0690	2 GA TPE331-1-101B	5216	Freighter		lst F.S. Air Svc / cvtd Beech E18S
☐	N81CK	Volpar Turboliner	BA-509	F-ODHJ	0060	0491	2 GA TPE331-1-101B	5216	Freighter		cvtd Beech G18S
☐	N8487A	Volpar Turboliner	AF-65		0051	0587	2 GA TPE331-1-101B	5216	Freighter		cvtd Beech C-45H (18)
☐	N900TH	Volpar Turboliner	BA-106	N900WA	0055	0690	2 GA TPE331-1-101B	5216	Freighter		cvtd Beech E18S
☐	N20TA	Learjet 23	23-062	N670MF	0065	0885	2 GE CJ610-4	5670	Freighter		
☐	N49CK	Learjet 23	23-009	N13SN	0065	0690	2 GE CJ610-4	5670	Freighter		
☐	N555LB	Learjet 24	24-177	N555LA	0068	0589	2 GE CJ610-4	5897	6 Pax / Frtr		
☐	N63CK	Learjet 24	24-119	N61CK	0067	0384	2 GE CJ610-4	5897	6 Pax / Frtr		
☐	N825AA	Learjet 24	24-147	N33NJ	0067	0295	2 GE CJ610-6	5897	Freighter		
☐	N93BP	Learjet 24	24-169	N927AA	0068	0594	2 GE CJ610-6	5897	Freighter		
☐	N96AA	Learjet 24	24-139	N481EZ	0067	0494	2 GE CJ610-6	5897	Freighter		
☐	N96CK	Learjet 23	23-016	N7GF	0065	0395	2 GE CJ610-4	5670	Freighter		
☐	N588CG	Learjet 24D	24D-304	N500CG	0075	0798	2 GE CJ610-6	6123	Freighter		
☐	N789AA	Learjet 24D	24D-309	N45AJ	0075	0295	2 GE CJ610-6	6123	Freighter		
☐	N222B	Learjet 25	25-047		0069	1293	2 GE CJ610-6	6804	8 Pax / Frtr		
☐	N28CK	Learjet 25	25-045	N24FN	0069	0392	2 GE CJ610-6	6804	8 Pax / Frtr		
☐	N39CK	Learjet 25	25-005	XA-SDQ	0068	0994	2 GE CJ610-6	6804	8 Pax / Frtr		
☐	N50CK	Learjet 25B	25B-157	N57CK	0074	0585	2 GE CJ610-6	6804	8 Pax / Frtr		
☐	N6LL	Learjet 25D	25D-256		0078	0187	2 GE CJ610-8A	6804	8 Pax / Frtr		
☐	N813JW	Learjet 25	25-038	N400AJ	0069	0498	2 GE CJ610-6	6804	8 Pax / Frtr		
☐	N83CK	Learjet 25B	25B-183	N5LL	0074	1086	2 GE CJ610-6	6804	8 Pax / Frtr		
☐	N95CK	Learjet 25D	25D-248	N900WA	0078	0595	2 GE CJ610-8A	6804	8 Pax / Frtr		
☐	N71CK	Learjet 36A	36A-035	VH-BIB	0077	0391	2 GA TFE731-2-2B	8165	8 Pax / Frtr	KM-GH	
☐	N72CK	Learjet 35A	35A-165	N16BJ	0078	1191	2 GA TFE731-2-2B	8165	8 Pax / Frtr		
☐	N228CK	Dassault Falcon 20C (C)	128	EC-FAM	0068	0197	2 GE CF700-2D	13000	Freighter		cvtd Falcon 20C
☐	N125CK	Hawker F400A (HS 125-F400A)	25266	N135CK	0071	0195	2 GA TFE731-3R-1H	10705	Exec / Frtr	AH-CG	cvtd 400A
☐	N197JS	Lockheed L-1329 JetStar 731	5069 / 6	XA-PGO	0066	0196	4 GA TFE731-3E	19845	Exec / Frtr		cvtd JetStar 6

KITTY HAWK INTERNATIONAL = CB / CKS (Div. of Kitty Hawk Group, Inc./formerly American Int'l Airways, Inc.) — Detroit-Willow Run, MI

842 Willow Run Airport, Ypsilanti, MI 48198, USA ☎ (734) 484-0088 Tx: none Fax: (734) 484-9812 SITA: n/a
F: 1973 ✈✈✈ 3000 Head: Charles C. Carson IATA: 571 ICAO: CONNIE Net: http://www.kalitta.com

registration	type of aircraft	cn/fn	ex/ex*	mfd	del	powered by	mtow kg	configuration	selcal	name/fln/specialitites/remarks
☐ N6161C	Boeing (Douglas) DC-8-55F (JT)	45856 / 269	C-FDWW	0066	0193	4 PW JT3D-3B (HK2/QNC)	147418	Freighter	JK-PQ	
☐ N6161M	Boeing (Douglas) DC-8-55F (JT)	45762 / 232	C-FCWW	0065	1292	4 PW JT3D-3B (HK2/QNC)	147418	Freighter		
☐ N801CK	Boeing (Douglas) DC-8-55F (JT)	45816 / 236	N804SW	0065	0287	4 PW JT3D-3B (HK2/QNC)	140523	Freighter	CK-GH	
☐ N804CK	Boeing (Douglas) DC-8-51F	45689 / 212	8Q-CA005	0064	0587	4 PW JT3D-3B (HK2/QNC)	125191	Freighter		cvtd -51 / std OSC
☐ N8052U	Boeing (Douglas) DC-8-54F (JT)	46009 / 404	N5094Q	0068	1296	4 PW JT3D-3B (HK2/BAC)	142882	Freighter	BC-EL	
☐ N805CK	Boeing (Douglas) DC-8-51F	45649 / 170	8Q-PNB	0062	0587	4 PW JT3D-3B (HK2/QNC)	125191	Freighter		cvtd -51 / std OSC
☐ N806CK	Boeing (Douglas) DC-8-54F (FM)	45932 / 328	ZK-NZD	0067	0889	4 PW JT3D-3B (HK2/QNC)	142882	Freighter	CK-AH	cvtd -52
☐ N807CK	Boeing (Douglas) DC-8-55F	45767 / 250	N902R	0066	0288	4 PW JT3D-3B (HK2/QNC)	144152	Freighter	CK-AE	cvtd -55
☐ N809CK	Boeing (Douglas) DC-8-55F (JT)	45803 / 229	N29549	0065	1194	4 PW JT3D-3B (HK2/QNC)	147418	Freighter	BK-HM	
☐ N810CK	Boeing (Douglas) DC-8-52F	45814 / 258	T15-1	0066	1189	4 PW JT3D-3B (HK2/QNC)	136078	Freighter	BK-FJ	cvtd -52
☐ N24UA	Boeing (Douglas) DC-8-61F	45963 / 355	C-FTJX	0068	1096	4 PW JT3D-3B (HK2/QNC)	145286	Freighter	EM-AG	cvtd DC-8-61
☐ N812CK	Boeing (Douglas) DC-8-61F	45890 / 301	N20UA	0967	0291	4 PW JT3D-3B (HK2/QNC)	145286	Freighter	BH-CG	cvtd DC-8-61
☐ N813CK	Boeing (Douglas) DC-8-61F	45893 / 310	N23UA	1167	1290	4 PW JT3D-3B (HK2/QNC)	145286	Freighter	EM-AF	cvtd DC-8-61
☐ N816CK	Boeing (Douglas) DC-8-61F	45892 / 306	N22UA	0067	0693	4 PW JT3D-3B (HK2/BAC)	145286	Freighter	EM-AD	cvtd DC-8-61
☐ N817CK	Boeing (Douglas) DC-8-61F	45887 / 287	N26UA	0067	0993	4 PW JT3D-3B (HK2/QNC)	145286	Freighter	LM-BD	cvtd DC-8-61
☐ N801MG	Boeing (Douglas) DC-8-62F	45986 / 379	N3931G	0068	0695	4 PW JT3D-3B (HK3/BAC)	158757	Freighter	JL-AQ	cvtd DC-8-62
☐ N802MG	Boeing (Douglas) DC-8-62F	46098 / 516	N39305	0170	1294	4 PW JT3D-3B (HK3/BAC)	158757	Freighter	BC-JK	cvtd DC-8-62
☐ N803CK	Boeing (Douglas) DC-8-62F	46085 / 481	N8973U	0069	0994	4 PW JT3D-7 (HK3/BAC)	158757	Freighter	BM-GJ	cvtd DC-8-62
☐ N818CK	Boeing (Douglas) DC-8-62F	45961 / 361	N3931A	0068	1195	4 PW JT3D-3B (HK3/BAC)	158757	Freighter	BC-FM	cvtd (CF)
☐ N781AL	Boeing (Douglas) DC-8-63F	45926 / 323	C-FCPO	0067	1197	4 PW JT3D-7 (HK3/BAC)	161025	Freighter		lsf AERO/sub-lst/opf BAX Global/cvtd-63
☐ N784AL	Boeing (Douglas) DC-8-63F	46135 / 531	TU-TCF	0070	1197	4 PW JT3D-7 (HK3/BAC)	161025	Freighter	DK-FH	lsf AERO/sub-lst/opf BAX Gl./cvtd (CF)
☐ N811CK	Boeing (Douglas) DC-8-63F	46147 / 547	9Q-CLH	0071	0190	4 PW JT3D-7 (HK3/BAC)	161025	Freighter	CK-DG	cvtd (CF)
☐ N815CK	Boeing (Douglas) DC-8-63F	46151 / 540	9Q-CLG	0070	0292	4 PW JT3D-7 (HK3/BAC)	161025	Freighter	CK-BG	cvtd (CF)
☐ N102CK	Lockheed L-1011-385-1-15 TriStar 200 (F)	193N-1198	G-BHBM	0080	0794	3 RR RB211-524B-02	215003	Freighter	DH-AE	cvtd TriStar 200
☐ N103CK	Lockheed L-1011-385-1-15 TriStar 200 (F)	293C-1212	G-BHBR	0081	0794	3 RR RB211-524B-02	215003	Freighter	DF-KM	cvtd TriStar 200
☐ N104CK	Lockheed L-1011-385-1-15 TriStar 200 (F)	193N-1193	G-BHBL	0080	0994	3 RR RB211-524B-02	215003	Freighter	DF-LM	cvtd TriStar 200
☐ N105CK	Lockheed L-1011-385-1-15 TriStar 200 (F)	193N-1178	G-BGBB	0079	1294	3 RR RB211-524B-02	215003	Freighter	DF-BM	cvtd TriStar 200
☐ N106CK	Lockheed L-1011-385-1-15 TriStar 200 (F)	293C-1211	G-BHBP	0081	0795	3 RR RB211-524B-02	215003	Freighter	DG-BM	cvtd TriStar 200
☐ N107CK	Lockheed L-1011-385-1-15 TriStar 200 (F)	193N-1182	G-BGBC	0080	0896	3 RR RB211-524B-02	215003	Freighter	AD-JK	cvtd TriStar 200
☐ N108CK	Lockheed L-1011-385-1-15 TriStar 200	193N-1204	G-BHBN	0081	1296	3 RR RB211-524B-02	215003	Y362	DG-EF	to be wfu 0099
☐ N109CK	Lockheed L-1011-385-1-15 TriStar 200	193N-1205	G-BHBO	0081	1296	3 RR RB211-524B-02	215003	Y362	JK-GS	to be wfu 0099
☐ N701CK	Boeing 747-146 (SF)	19725 / 31	JA8101	0070	0892	4 PW JT9D-7A	340194	Freighter	AL-FG	cvtd -146 / std OSC
☐ N702CK	Boeing 747-146 (SF)	20332 / 161	JA8107	0071	0892	4 PW JT9D-7A	340194	Freighter	AL-HK	cvtd -146A
☐ N703CK	Boeing 747-146	19727 / 54	JA8103	0070	1292	4 PW JT9D-7A	333390	Y476	DM-JL	to be wfu 0099
☐ N704CK	Boeing 747-146	20528 / 191	JA8112	0072	0693	4 PW JT9D-7A	332937	Y476	BM-CF	to be wfu 0099
☐ N706CK	Boeing 747-238B (SF)	20010 / 149	VH-EBB	0071	0594	4 PW JT9D-7F	356070	Freighter	EJ-HK	cvtd -238 / std OSC
☐ N707CK	Boeing 747-269B (SF)	21541 / 332	9K-ADA	0078	0895	4 PW JT9D-7J	356070	Freighter	LM-AB	cvtd -269B (M)
☐ N708CK	Boeing 747-269B (SF)	21543 / 359	9K-ADC	0079	0695	4 PW JT9D-7J	356070	Freighter	CK-DH	cvtd -269B (M)
☐ N709CK	Boeing 747-132 (SF)	20247 / 159	N625PL	0071	0394	4 PW JT9D-7A	340194	Freighter	AD-EG	cvtd -132
☐ N710CK	Boeing 747-2B4B (SF)	21097 / 262	OD-AGH	0075	0997	4 PW JT9D-7FW	362874	Freighter		lst/opf North Atl.Aw / cvtd -2B4B (M)
☐ N712CK	Boeing 747-2B4B (SF)	21098 / 263	N203AE	0075	0298	4 PW JT9D-7FW	362874	Freighter		cvtd -2B4B (M)
☐ N713CK	Boeing 747-2B4B (SF)	21099 / 264	N204AE	0075	0298	4 PW JT9D-7FW	362874	Freighter		lst/opf North Atl.Aw / cvtd-2B4B (M)

KIWI INTERNATIONAL AIR LINES = KP / KIA (Kiwi International Holdings, Inc. dba) — Newark-Int'l, NJ

Hemisphere Centre, Suite 624, R1&9, Newark, NJ 07114-0006, USA ☎ (973) 645-1133 Tx: none Fax: (973) 645-1161 SITA: n/a
F: 1992 ✈✈✈ 1000 Head: Charles Edwards IATA: 538 ICAO: KIWI AIR Net: http://www.jetkiwi.com Filed for Chapter 11 bankruptcy protection 300996. Charter operations continue.

registration	type of aircraft	cn/fn	ex/ex*	mfd	del	powered by	mtow kg	configuration	selcal	name/fln/specialitites/remarks
☐ N353PA	Boeing 727-225 (A)	20622 / 933	N8860E	0073	1194	3 PW JT8D-15 (HK3/FDX)	79923	Y150	GJ-AC	lsf Aircraft 23456 Inc.
☐ N354PA	Boeing 727-225 (A)	20624 / 940	N8862E	0473	1294	3 PW JT8D-15 (HK3/FDX)	79923	Y150		lsf Aircraft 20624/20626 Inc.
☐ N356PA	Boeing 727-225 (A)	20626 / 946	N8864E	0073	1294	3 PW JT8D-15 (HK3/FDX)	79923	Y150		lsf Aircraft 20624/20626 Inc.
☐ N361KP	Boeing 727-225 (A)	20627 / 947	N357PA	0073	0995	3 PW JT8D-15 (HK3/FDX)	79923	Y150		lsf Aircraft 20627 Inc.
☐ N8880Z	Boeing 727-225 (A)	21453 / 1314		0078	0793	3 PW JT8D-15	86409	Y150	FJ-DK	lsf FSBU Trustee
☐ N8881Z	Boeing 727-225 (A)	21578 / 1409		0078	0793	3 PW JT8D-15	86409	Y150		lsf FSBU Trustee
☐ N8883Z	Boeing 727-225 (A)	21580 / 1435		0079	0793	3 PW JT8D-15	86409	Y150		lsf FSBU Trustee

K-MAX, Corp. (Subsidiary of Kaman Corporation) — Bloomfield, CT

1332 Blue Hills Avenue, Bloomfield, CT 06002, USA ☎ (860) 286-4161 Tx: none Fax: (860) 243-7099 SITA: n/a
F: 1997 ✈✈✈ n/a Head: Charles H. Kaman Net: http://www.kaman.com

registration	type of aircraft	cn/fn	ex/ex*	mfd	del	powered by	mtow kg	configuration	selcal	name/fln/specialitites/remarks
☐ N162KA	Kaman K-1200 K-Max	A94-0010		0095	0597	1 LY T5317A-1	2722	Crane/Tanker		lsf Kaman Aerospace Corp.
☐ N163KA	Kaman K-1200 K-Max	A94-0013		0095	0597	1 LY T5317A-1	2722	Crane/Tanker		lsf Kaman Aerospace Corp.

KNIGHTHAWK EXPRESS = KHX (Rizzuto, Inc. dba) — Boston-Logan Int'l, MA

231 American Legion Highway, Revere, MA 02151, USA ☎ (781) 284-1955 Tx: none Fax: (781) 284-2779 SITA: n/a
F: 1983 ✈✈✈ 5 Head: Hugo Rizzuto ICAO: RIZZ Net: n/a

registration	type of aircraft	cn/fn	ex/ex*	mfd	del	powered by	mtow kg	configuration	selcal	name/fln/specialitites/remarks
☐ N63TT	Piper PA-31-350 Navajo Chieftain	31-8152026		0081	0595	2 LY TIO-540-J2BD	3175			lsf pvt

KODIAK AIR SERVICE (William E. Hall dba / Seasonal May-October ops only) — Kodiak-SPB, AK

415 Mill Bay Road, Kodiak, AK 99615, USA ☎ (907) 486-4446 Tx: none Fax: (907) 486-2422 SITA: n/a
F: 1987 ✈✈✈ n/a Head: William E. Hall Net: n/a

registration	type of aircraft	cn/fn	ex/ex*	mfd	del	powered by	mtow kg	configuration	selcal	name/fln/specialitites/remarks
☐ N22306	Cessna U206G Stationair 6 II	U20606570		0082	0287	1 CO IO-520-F	1633			Floats

KORO AVIATION, Inc. — Hazleton-Municipal, PA

PO Box 538, Hazleton, PA 18201, USA ☎ (717) 459-2670 Tx: none Fax: (717) 459-2678 SITA: n/a
F: 1990 ✈✈✈ n/a Head: Seymour Graham Net: n/a

registration	type of aircraft	cn/fn	ex/ex*	mfd	del	powered by	mtow kg	configuration	selcal	name/fln/specialitites/remarks
☐ N1545W	Beech Baron 58	TH-1545		0089	0589	2 CO IO-550-C	2495			lsf Kola Aviation Inc.
☐ N32BG	Beech King Air F90	LA-168	N6128P	0082	0285	2 PWC PT6A-135	4967			lsf Kola Aviation Inc.
☐ N21EG	Cessna S550 Citation S/II	S550-0087	N1274Z	0086	0690	2 PWC JT15D-4B	6849			lsf Kola Air Inc.
☐ N91ML	Cessna S550 Citation S/II	S550-0132	N91ME	0087	0194	2 PWC JT15D-4B	6849			

KRUGER HELICOPTER SERVICE (James W. Kruger dba) — Lakeside-Private Heliport, MT

Box 235, Lakeside, MT 59922, USA ☎ (406) 387-4565 Tx: none Fax: (406) 387-5615 SITA: n/a
F: 1987 ✈✈✈ n/a Head: James W. Kruger Net: n/a

registration	type of aircraft	cn/fn	ex/ex*	mfd	del	powered by	mtow kg	configuration	selcal	name/fln/specialitites/remarks
☐ N165JK	Bell 206B JetRanger III	2930	G-BRHI	0080	0693	1 AN 250-C20B	1451			

K2 AVIATION (K2 Adventures, Inc. dba / Subsidiary of Rustair, Inc.) — Talkeetna, AK

PO Box 545, Talkeetna, AK 99676, USA ☎ (907) 733-2291 Tx: none Fax: (907) 733-1221 SITA: n/a
F: 1980 ✈✈✈ 12 Head: Todd S. Rust Net: http://www.alaska.net/flyk2 Aircraft below MTOW 1361 kg: Piper PA-18 (Floats / Wheel-Skis)

registration	type of aircraft	cn/fn	ex/ex*	mfd	del	powered by	mtow kg	configuration	selcal	name/fln/specialitites/remarks
☐ N124KT	Cessna A185F Skywagon II	18503765	N8747Q	0079	0683	1 CO IO-520-D	1520			lsf Rustair Inc. / Floats / Wheel-Skis
☐ N125KT	Cessna A185F Skywagon II	18503494	N1855Q	0077	0185	1 CO IO-520-D	1520			lsf Rustair Inc. / Floats / Wheel-Skis
☐ N1292F	Cessna A185F Skywagon	18502668	N3263C	0075	1189	1 CO IO-520-D	1520			lsf Rustair Inc. / Floats / Wheel-Skis
☐ N129KT	Cessna A185F Skywagon	18502812	N1292F	0075	0582	1 CO IO-520-D	1520			lsf Rustair Inc. / Floats / Wheel-Skis
☐ N122KT	Piper PA-32-300 Cherokee SIX	32-7940190	N2898W	0079	0591	1 LY IO-540-K1G5	1542			lsf Rustair Inc.
☐ N126KT	Cessna TU206G Turbo Stationair 6 II	U20604967	N735UN	0079	0888	1 CO TSIO-520-M	1633			lsf Rustair Inc. / Floats / Wheels
☐ N127KT	Cessna T207A Turbo Stationair 8 II	20700709	N9594M	0081	0792	1 CO TSIO-520-M	1724			lsf Rustair Inc.

KUMULANI AIR, Inc. — Lihue, HI

PO Box 3778, Lihue, HI 96766, USA ☎ (808) 246-9123 Tx: none Fax: (808) 246-4556 SITA: n/a
F: 1992 ✈✈✈ n/a Head: Kevin V. Britt Net: n/a

registration	type of aircraft	cn/fn	ex/ex*	mfd	del	powered by	mtow kg	configuration	selcal	name/fln/specialitites/remarks
☐ N749RV	Cessna U206F Stationair II	U20603480	N8727Q	0076	0192	1 CO IO-520-F	1633			
☐ N500SA	Piper PA-31-350 Navajo Chieftain	31-7552056		0075	0496	2 LY TIO-540-J2BD	3175			
☐ N7816Q	Cessna 402A	402A0116		0069	1292	2 CO TSIO-520-E	2858			

KUSKO AVIATION, Inc. — Bethel, AK

PO Box 1425, Bethel, AK 99559, USA ☎ (907) 556-8811 Tx: none Fax: (907) 478-8822 SITA: n/a
F: 1985 ✈✈✈ n/a Head: Julian F. LePage Net: n/a

registration	type of aircraft	cn/fn	ex/ex*	mfd	del	powered by	mtow kg	configuration	selcal	name/fln/specialitites/remarks
☐ N4025W	Piper PA-32-300 Cherokee SIX	32-40039		0066	0188	1 LY IO-540-K1A5	1542			
☐ N4170R	Piper PA-32-300 Cherokee SIX	32-40502		0068	0694	1 LY IO-540-K1A5	1542			
☐ N9000N	Piper PA-32-300C Cherokee SIX	32-40883		0069	1195	1 LY IO-540-K1A5	1542			
☐ N2162C	Cessna 207A Stationair 8 II	20700575		0080	0796	1 CO IO-520-F	1724			
☐ N800JS	Piper PA-31-350 Navajo Chieftain	31-7852077		0078	0596	2 LY TIO-540-J2BD	3175			

LAB Flying Service, Inc. = JF / LAB — Haines, AK

PO Box 272, Haines, AK 99827, USA ☎ (907) 766-2222 Tx: none Fax: (907) 766-2734 SITA: n/a
F: 1956 ✈✈✈ 100 Head: Layton A. Bennett IATA: 510 ICAO: LAB Net: http://www.haines.ak.vs/lab/ Aircraft below MTOW 1361kg: Enstrom F28A & Piper PA-28-180/1.

registration	type of aircraft	cn/fn	ex/ex*	mfd	del	powered by	mtow kg	configuration	selcal	name/fln/specialitites/remarks
☐ N8548Y	Lake LA-250 Renegade	107		0090	0790	1 LY IO-540-C4B5	1383	Ambulance		Amphibian
☐ N2181Z	Piper PA-32-300 Cherokee SIX	32-7940104		0079	0685	1 LY IO-540-K1G5	1542	5 Pax		
☐ N23LA	Piper PA-32-300 Cherokee SIX	32-7840045		0078	1095	1 LY IO-540-K1G5	1542	5 Pax		

registration	type of aircraft	cn/fn	ex/ex*	mfd	del	powered by	mtow kg	configuration	selcal	name/fln/specialitites/remarks
☐ N2897X	Piper PA-32-300 Cherokee SIX	32-7940187		0079	0879	1 LY IO-540-K1G5	1542	5 Pax		
☐ N2930Q	Piper PA-32R-300 Lance	32R-7780269		0077	0979	1 LY IO-540-K1G5D	1633	6 Pax		
☐ N2947N	Piper PA-32-300 Cherokee SIX	32-7940225		0079	0180	1 LY IO-540-K1G5	1542	6 Pax		lsf pvt
☐ N30505	Piper PA-32-300 Cherokee SIX	32-7840199		0078	1092	1 LY IO-540-K1G5	1542	5 Pax		
☐ N3957X	Piper PA-32-300 Cherokee SIX	32-7640003		0076	1195	1 LY IO-540-K1A5	1542	6 Pax		
☐ N39586	Piper PA-32-300 Cherokee SIX	32-7840168		0078	0690	1 LY IO-540-K1G5	1542	5 Pax		
☐ N39636	Piper PA-32-300 Cherokee SIX	32-7840172		0078	1187	1 LY IO-540-K1G5	1542	5 Pax		
☐ N44560	Piper PA-32-300 Cherokee SIX	32-7440160		0074	0591	1 LY IO-540-K1A5	1542	6 Pax		
☐ N4485X	Piper PA-32-300 Cherokee SIX	32-7640026		0076	0981	1 LY IO-540-K1A5	1542	6 Pax		
☐ N54KA	Piper PA-32-300 Cherokee SIX	32-7840197		0078	1096	1 LY IO-540-K1G5	1542	5 Pax		
☐ N5686V	Piper PA-32R-300 Lance	32R-7780361		0077	1277	1 LY IO-540-K1G5D	1633	6 Pax		
☐ N6117J	Piper PA-32-300 Cherokee SIX	32-7640095		0076	0191	1 LY IO-540-K1G5	1542	6 Pax		
☐ N666EB	Piper PA-32-300 Cherokee SIX	32-7940115		0079	0590	1 LY IO-540-K1G5	1542	6 Pax		
☐ N6968J	Piper PA-32R-300 Lance	32R-7680397		0076	0791	1 LY IO-540-K1G5D	1633	6 Pax		
☐ N7718C	Piper PA-32-300 Cherokee SIX	32-7640049		0076	0491	1 LY IO-540-K1A5	1542	6 Pax		
☐ N8127Q	Piper PA-32-300 Cherokee SIX	32-7940269		0079	1084	1 LY IO-540-K1G5	1542	5 Pax		
☐ N82300	Piper PA-32-301T Turbo Saratoga	32-8024028		0080	0294	1 LY TIO-540-S1AD	1633	6 Pax		
☐ N8359M	Piper PA-32-301T Turbo Saratoga	32-8124019		0081	0393	1 LY TIO-540-S1AD	1633	6 Pax		
☐ N8493C	Piper PA-32R-300 Lance	32R-7680118		0076	1095	1 LY IO-540-K1G5D	1633	6 Pax		
☐ N9795C	Piper PA-32-300 Cherokee SIX	32-7840118		0078	1088	1 LY IO-540-K1G5	1542	6 Pax		
☐ N5462E	Helio H-295 Super Courier	1203		0066	0872	1 LY GO-480-G1A6	1542	5 Pax		
☐ N6314V	Helio H-250 Courier II	2534		0067	0273	1 LY O-540-A1A5	1542	5 Pax		
☐ N44617	Piper PA-28-235 Pathfinder	28-7410100		0074	0590	1 LY O-540-B4B5	1361	4 Pax		
☐ N1362T	Piper PA-34-200 Seneca	34-7250300		0074	0191	2 LY IO-360-C1E6	1905	5 Pax		
☐ N55363	Piper PA-34-200 Seneca	34-7350206		0073	0795	2 LY IO-360-C1E6	1910	5 Pax		
☐ N57019	Piper PA-34-200 Seneca	34-7450047		0074	0685	2 LY IO-360-C1E6	1905	5 Pax		
☐ N7333L	Piper PA-34-200T Seneca II	34-7670099		0076	1286	2 CO TSIO-360-E	2073	5 Pax		
☐ N9828Q	AAC (Ted Smith) Aerostar 601P	61P-0477-191		0078	1285	2 LY IO-540-S1A5	2722	5 Pax		lsf pvt
☐ N29884	Britten-Norman BN-2A-26 Islander	847	G-BESH	0079	0482	2 LY O-540-E4C5	2994	9 Pax		
☐ N3835Z	Britten-Norman BN-2A-26 Islander	2010	G-BEJW	0077	0383	2 LY O-540-E4C5	2994	9 Pax		
☐ N27513	Piper PA-31-350 Navajo Chieftain	31-7852033		0078	0478	2 LY TIO-540-J2BD	3175	9 Pax		
☐ N3523Y	Piper PA-31-350 Navajo Chieftain	31-7952115		0079	0695	2 LY TIO-540-J2BD	3175	9 Pax		
☐ N54732	Piper PA-31-350 Navajo Chieftain	31-7405254		0074	0793	2 LY TIO-540-J2BD	3175	9 Pax		

LAHAIE ALASKA AIR SERVICE (Gregory S. Lahaie dba) — Anchorage-Merrill Field & McKinley Park, AK

1841 Merrill Field Drive, Hangar 1, Anchorage, AK 99501, USA ☎ (907) 278-1223 Tx: none Fax: (907) 278-1223 SITA: n/a
F: 1993 n/a Head: Gregory S. Lahaie Net: n/a

☐ N619CH	Cessna U206D Super Skywagon	U206-1276		0069	0395	1 CO IO-520-F	1633			Wheel-Skis
☐ N72395	Cessna U206D Super Skywagon	U206-1393		0069	0295	1 CO IO-520-F	1633			Wheel-Skis

LAKE & PENINSULA AIRLINES (David J. Wilder dba) — Port Alsworth, AK

3323 Dry Creek, Port Alsworth, AK 99653, USA ☎ (907) 781-2228 Tx: none Fax: (907) 781-2280 SITA: n/a
F: 1992 n/a Head: David J. Wilder Net: n/a Aircraft below MTOW 1361kg: Cessna 180 (Floats / Wheel-Skis)

☐ N9909Z	Cessna U206G Stationair 6 II	U20606740		0083	0294	1 CO IO-520-F	1633			Floats / Wheel-Skis

LAKE CLARK AIR, Inc. — Port Alsworth, AK

The Farm Lodge, Box 1, Port Alsworth, AK 99653, USA ☎ (907) 781-2211 Tx: none Fax: (907) 781-2215 SITA: n/a
F: 1978 6 Head: Glen R. Alsworth, Sr. Net: n/a Aircraft below MTOW 1361 kg: Cessna 180.

☐ N733KD	Cessna U206G Stationair 6 II	U20604772		0078	0886	1 CO IO-520-D	1633			lsf pvt / Floats
☐ N8300Q	Cessna U206F Stationair II	U20603161		0076	0197	1 CO IO-520-F	1633			Floats
☐ N70076	Cessna 207A Stationair 7 II	20700547		0079	1196	1 CO IO-520-F	1724			
☐ N91028	Cessna 207 Skywagon	20700019		0069	0791	1 CO IO-520-F	1724			
☐ N200VF	Piper PA-31-350 Navajo Chieftain	31-7405445		0074	0187	2 LY TIO-540-J2BD	3175			lsf pvt
☐ N27231	Piper PA-31-350 Navajo Chieftain	31-7752106		0077	0690	2 LY TIO-540-J2BD	3175			
☐ N76RA	Piper PA-31-350 Navajo Chieftain	31-7752089		0077	1291	2 LY TIO-540-J2BD	3175			
☐ N90574	De Havilland DHC-3 Otter	174	55-3312	0056	1187	1 PW R-1340	3629			Floats

LAKE MEAD AIR, Inc. — Boulder City-Municipal, NV

PO Box 60035, Boulder City, NV 89006, USA ☎ (702) 293-1848 Tx: none Fax: (702) 294-0232 SITA: n/a
F: 1965 23 Head: Mark Leseberg Net: n/a Aircraft below MTOW 1361 kg: Cessna 172 & Piper PA-18

☐ N2082U	Cessna U206F Stationair	U20602327		0074	1285	1 CO IO-520-F	1633			
☐ N3259R	Cessna U206F Stationair	U20602215		0073	0191	1 CO IO-520-F	1633			
☐ N3467L	Cessna U206B Super Skywagon	U206-0767		0066	1280	1 CO IO-520-F	1633			
☐ N4769U	Cessna TU206G Turbo Stationair 6 II	U20605093		0079	0285	1 CO TSIO-520-M	1633			
☐ N5337U	Cessna TU206G Turbo Stationair 6 II	U20605218		0079	0487	1 CO TSIO-520-M	1633			
☐ N70Y	Cessna U206B Super Skywagon	U206-0828		0067	1191	1 CO IO-520-F	1633			
☐ N72218	Cessna U206D Super Skywagon	U206-1328		0069	1280	1 CO IO-520-F	1633			
☐ N9681G	Cessna U206F Stationair	U20601881		0072	1189	1 CO IO-520-F	1633			
☐ N2138S	Cessna T210L Turbo Centurion II	21061099		0075	0486	1 CO TSIO-520-H	1724			
☐ N1653U	Cessna 207 Super Skywagon	20700253		0074	1280	1 CO IO-520-F	1724			
☐ N1675U	Cessna T207 Turbo Skywagon	20700275		0074	0797	1 CO TSIO-520-G	1724			
☐ N6328H	Cessna T207A Turbo Stationair 7 II	20700485		0078	0481	1 CO TSIO-520-M	1724			
☐ N6427H	Cessna T207A Turbo Stationair 7 II	20700522		0079	0283	1 CO TSIO-520-M	1724			
☐ N6460H	Cessna T207A Turbo Stationair 7 II	20700530		0079	0683	1 CO TSIO-520-M	1724			
☐ N73445	Cessna 207A Stationair 8 II	20700591		0080	0890	1 CO IO-520-F	1724			
☐ N73612	Cessna T207A Turbo Stationair 8 II	20700608		0080	1186	1 CO TSIO-520-M	1724			
☐ N801AN	Cessna 207A Stationair 8 II	20700640	N111LS	0080	0694	1 CO IO-520-F	1724			
☐ N9100D	Cessna 207 Skywagon	20700001		0069	0585	1 CO IO-520-F	1724			
☐ N91038	Cessna 207 Super Skywagon	20700027		0069	0182	1 CO IO-520-F	1724			

LAKER AIRWAYS, Inc. = 6F / LKR (Sister company of Princess Vacations, Bahamas / Subs. of Smith Management) — Fort Lauderdale-Hollywood Int'l, FL

6261 NW 61th Way, Suite 201, Fort Lauderdale, FL 33309, USA ☎ (954) 202-0444 Tx: none Fax: (954) 772-7153 SITA: n/a
F: 1995 n/a Head: James B. Kenney ICAO: LAKER Net: n/a

☐ N511DB	Boeing 727-89	19139 / 255	VR-CDB	0066	1298	3 PW JT8D-7B (HK3/FDX)	72802	E53		lsf Riverhorse Invest./opf MVP AirTours
☐ N946LL	Boeing (Douglas) DC-10-10	46946 / 222	N907WA	0076	0497	3 GE CF6-6D	199405	Y353	JK-LM	Atlantis / lsf Midair S.A. / tbr N834LA
☐ N831LA	Boeing (Douglas) DC-10-30	46936 / 147	G-BWIN	0074	0796	3 GE CF6-50C2	251744	Y353	EJ-CH	lsf POLA
☐ N832LA	Boeing (Douglas) DC-10-30	46931 / 137	XA-AMR	0074	0496	3 GE CF6-50C2	251744	Y353	FJ-DG	Endeavour / lsf POLA
☐ N833LA	Boeing (Douglas) DC-10-30	46937 / 152	N8228P	0074	0496	3 GE CF6-50C2	251744	Y353	FL-CJ	Discovery / lsf POLA

LAKESIDE AVIATION, Inc. — Oakland-Garrett County, MD

PO Box 81, Mchenry, MD 21541, USA ☎ (240) 387-0331 Tx: none Fax: (240) 387-0331 SITA: n/a
F: 1983 n/a Head: Thomas E. Glotfelty Net: n/a

☐ N4871U	Cessna 205A (210-5A)	205-0571		0064	0585	1 CO IO-470-S	1497			
☐ N334EB	Mitsubishi MU-2J (MU-2B-35)	568	N99SL	0073	0995	2 GA TPE331-6-251M	4899			

LANDELLS AVIATION (Palm Springs Aviation, Inc. dba) — Desert Hot Springs-Heliport, CA

69873 Silver Moon Trail, Desert Hot Springs, CA 92241, USA ☎ (760) 329-6468 Tx: none Fax: (760) 329-7907 SITA: n/a
F: 1964 6 Head: Elaine Landells Net: n/a

☐ N185BC	Bell 206B JetRanger III	3826		0084	1291	1 AN 250-C20B	1451			
☐ N5016U	Bell 206B JetRanger III	2634		0079	0983	1 AN 250-C20B	1451			
☐ N31LA	Bell 206L-1 LongRanger II	45448		0080	0785	1 AN 250-C30P	1882			
☐ N613LH	Bell 206L-3 LongRanger III	51594	9M-BAO	0092	0898	1 AN 250-C30P	1882			

LARRY'S FLYING SERVICE, Inc. = J6 — Fairbanks-Int'l, AK

PO Box 2348, Fairbanks, AK 99707, USA ☎ (907) 474-9169 Tx: none Fax: (907) 474-8815 SITA: n/a
F: 1977 35 Head: Lawrence A. Chenaille Net: n/a Aircraft below MTOW 1361kg: Cessna 172

☐ N31657	Piper PA-32-300 Cherokee SIX	32-7840139		0078	0291	1 LY IO-540-K1G5	1542			
☐ N4375B	Piper PA-32R-301 Saratoga SP	32R-8413023		0084	0185	1 LY IO-540-K1G5D	1633			lsf pvt
☐ N8147A	Piper PA-32R-301 Saratoga SP	32R-8013047		0080	0592	1 LY IO-540-K1G5D	1633			lsf Chartercraft Leasing
☐ N84023	Piper PA-32R-301 Saratoga SP	32R-8113081		0081	0592	1 LY IO-540-K1G5D	1633			lsf Chartercraft Leasing
☐ N9243K	Piper PA-32R-300 Lance	32R-7680201		0076	0489	1 LY IO-540-K1G5D	1633			
☐ N734CM	Cessna U206G Stationair 6 II	U20604821		0079	0796	1 CO IO-520-F	1633			lsf pvt
☐ N1824Q	Cessna 207A Stationair 8 II	20700788		0084	1284	1 CO IO-520-F	1724			
☐ N9996M	Cessna 207A Stationair 8 II	20700779		0084	0984	1 CO IO-520-F	1724			
☐ N21406	Piper PA-31-350 Navajo Chieftain	31-7752117		0077	0690	2 LY TIO-540-J2BD	3175			lsf pvt
☐ N59722	Piper PA-31-350 Navajo Chieftain	31-7652002		0076	1284	2 LY TIO-540-J2BD	3175			lsf pvt
☐ N7678L	Piper PA-31-350 Navajo Chieftain	31-7305005		0073	0290	2 LY TIO-540-J2BD	3175			
☐ N414JA	Britten-Norman BN-2B-21 Islander	2107	YV-2174P	0081	1096	2 LY IO-540-K1B5	2994			

LAS VEGAS AIRLINES, Inc. = 6G (Subsidiary of The Hermaton Co.) — Las Vegas-North Air Terminal, NV — Las Vegas Airlines

PO Box 15105, Las Vegas, NV 89114, USA ☎ (702) 647-3056 Tx: 684526 Fax: (702) 647-1846 SITA: n/a
F: 1973 ♦♦♦ 32 Head: Jehu Hand IATA: 540 Net: n/a

registration	type of aircraft	cn/fn	ex/ex*	mfd	del	powered by	mtow kg	configuration	selcal	name/fln/specialitites/remarks
☐ N27196	Piper PA-31-350 Navajo Chieftain	31-7752095		0077	0495	2 LY TIO-540-J2BD	3175			lsf Capitol Express Airlines Inc.
☐ N27917	Piper PA-31-350 Navajo Chieftain	31-7952007		0078	0786	2 LY TIO-540-J2BD	3175			
☐ N27989	Piper PA-31-350 Navajo Chieftain	31-7952077		0079	0592	2 LY TIO-540-J2BD	3175			
☐ N51EM	Piper PA-31-350 Navajo Chieftain	31-7952099		0079	0396	2 LY TIO-540-J2BD	3175			lsf G&L Airlines Properties Inc.
☐ N62971	Piper PA-31-350 Navajo Chieftain	31-7752013		0079	0396	2 LY TIO-540-J2BD	3175			lsf G&L Airlines Properties Inc.
☐ N777LV	Piper PA-31-350 Navajo Chieftain	31-7752125		0077	0295	2 LY TIO-540-J2BD	3175			lsf pvt

LAS VEGAS HELICOPTERS, Inc. — Las Vegas-McCarren Int'l, NV

5112 Winston Street, Las Vegas, NV 89103, USA ☎ (702) 876-0340 Tx: none Fax: none SITA: n/a
F: 1993 ♦♦♦ n/a Head: Gerald J. Shlesinger Net: http://www.lvhelicopters.com

registration	type of aircraft	cn/fn	ex/ex*	mfd	del	powered by	mtow kg	configuration	selcal	name/fln/specialitites/remarks
☐ N113ML	Bell 206L-1 LongRanger II	45777	N713ML	0083	1096	1 AN 250-C28B	1882			
☐ N383T	Bell 206L-4 LongRanger IV	52046	D-HSFJ	0093	0297	1 AN 250-C30P	2018			

LC'S FLYING SERVICE (formerly American Air Transport, Inc.) — Roanoke-Regional/Woodrum Field, VA

Building 3, Woodrum Field, Roanoke, VA 24012, USA ☎ (540) 362-2501 Tx: none Fax: none SITA: n/a
F: 1972 ♦♦♦ n/a Head: Lee C. Marshall Net: n/a

registration	type of aircraft	cn/fn	ex/ex*	mfd	del	powered by	mtow kg	configuration	selcal	name/fln/specialitites/remarks
☐ N83612	Piper PA-32R-301 Saratoga SP	32R-8113059		0081	0789	1 LY IO-540-K1G5D	1633			lsf Browning Cooper Inc.
☐ N2516R	Piper PA-23-250 Aztec F	27-8154029		0081	0693	2 LY IO-540-C4B5	2359			lsf Vaero Inc.
☐ N939C	Fairchild (Swearingen) SA26AT Merlin IIB	T26-152	N4ER	0069	1192	2 GA TPE331-1-151G	4536			lsf Vaero Inc.

LEADING EDGE AVIATION SERVICES, Inc. — Missoula-Int'l, MT

5225 Highway 10 West, Box 4, Missoula, MT 59802, USA ☎ (406) 542-7740 Tx: none Fax: (406) 542-0024 SITA: n/a
F: 1992 ♦♦♦ n/a Head: Joseph L. Degen Net: n/a Operates DHC-6 Twin Otter & Embraer 110P1 Bandeirante aircraft, leased from KENN BOREK AIR (C-) when required.

LEE's GUIDE SERVICE (Alfred M. Lee dba) — Palmer & Glennallen, AK

HCO-1, Box 2260, Glenallen, AK 99588, USA ☎ (907) 822-3343 Tx: none Fax: (907) 822-3403 SITA: n/a
F: 1960 ♦♦♦ n/a Head: Alfred M. Lee Net: n/a Aircraft below MTOW 1361 kg: Cessna 180 Piper PA-18 (on Floats/Wheel-Skis)

registration	type of aircraft	cn/fn	ex/ex*	mfd	del	powered by	mtow kg	configuration	selcal	name/fln/specialitites/remarks
☐ N5147G	De Havilland DHC-2 Beaver I	350	51-16550	0051	0386	1 PW R-985	2313			Floats / Wheel-Skis
☐ N5381U	De Havilland DHC-2 Beaver I	915	N5377G	0055	0392	1 PW R-985	2313			Floats / Wheel-Skis

LEE's SEA AIR (Lee A. Staheli dba) — Kiana-Bob Baker Memorial, AK

PO Box 75, Kiana, AK 99749, USA ☎ (907) 475-2101 Tx: none Fax: (907) 475-2101 SITA: n/a
F: 1950 ♦♦♦ n/a Head: Lee A. Staheli Net: n/a Aircraft below MTOW 1361 kg: Cessna 172

registration	type of aircraft	cn/fn	ex/ex*	mfd	del	powered by	mtow kg	configuration	selcal	name/fln/specialitites/remarks
☐ N31736	Piper PA-32-300 Cherokee SIX	32-7840145		0078	1178	1 LY IO-540-K1G5D	1542			

LEGEND AIRLINES, Inc. — Dallas-Love Field, TX

7555 Lemmon Ave, Dallas, TX 75209, USA ☎ (214) 358-8200 Tx: none Fax: (214) 358-8282 SITA: n/a
F: 1997 ♦♦♦ n/a Head: T. Allan McArtor Net: n/a Presently being set-up. Intends to start operations during 1999 with Boeing (Douglas) DC-9-30 aircraft (C56 configuration).

LEGEND AIRWAYS, Inc. — Nashua-Boire Field, NH

99 Pine Hill Road, Nashua, NH 03063, USA ☎ (603) 881-9691 Tx: none Fax: (603) 881-9691 SITA: n/a
F: 1996 ♦♦♦ n/a Head: Bill Brian Net: n/a

registration	type of aircraft	cn/fn	ex/ex*	mfd	del	powered by	mtow kg	configuration	selcal	name/fln/specialitites/remarks
☐ N25641	Boeing (Douglas) DC-3C (C-47-DL)	9059	42-32833	0043	0096	2 PW R-1830	12202	Pax / Freighter		lsf Fleming Corporation

LESEA GLOBAL, Inc. (Feed the Hungry) (Lester Sumrall Evangelistic Assocation dba) — South Bend-Michiana Regional, IN — LESEA GLOBAL FEED THE HUNGRY

PO Box 12, South Bend, IN 46624, USA ☎ (219) 291-3292 Tx: none Fax: (219) 299-4248 SITA: n/a
F: 1957 ♦♦♦ 250 Head: Dr. Lester Sumrall Net: n/a Non-profit charity organisation conducting relief flight missions.

registration	type of aircraft	cn/fn	ex/ex*	mfd	del	powered by	mtow kg	configuration	selcal	name/fln/specialitites/remarks
☐ N213LS	Dassault Falcon 20C	107	N330PC	0067	0785	2 GE CF700-2C	12000	Corporate		
☐ N226LS	Lockheed L-182 (C-130A) Hercules	1A-3052	OB-1394	1256	1190	4 AN T56-A-9D	56336	Freighter		Feed The Hungry

LIBERTY AIR (Liberty Air Management, Inc. dba) — Hagerstown-Washington County Regional, MD

18515-7A Henson Blvd, Hagerstown, MD 21742, USA ☎ (240) 739-4401 Tx: none Fax: (240) 739-2718 SITA: n/a
F: 1996 ♦♦♦ n/a Head: Neal A. Samonte Net: n/a

registration	type of aircraft	cn/fn	ex/ex*	mfd	del	powered by	mtow kg	configuration	selcal	name/fln/specialitites/remarks
☐ N121LA	Cessna 310Q II	310Q0973	N69779	0073	0396	2 CO IO-470-VO	2404			
☐ N340DM	Cessna 340A II	340A0462		0078	1096	2 CO TSIO-520-NB	2717			lsf Hi Tail Inc.

LIBERTY HELICOPTERS, Inc. — Linden & Teterboro, NJ & New York-West 30th St.Heliport, NY

Linden Municipal Airport, Box 1338, Rt 1N, Linden, NJ 07036, USA ☎ (908) 474-9700 Tx: none Fax: (908) 474-0488 SITA: n/a
F: 1986 ♦♦♦ n/a Head: Albert Trenk Net: http://www.libertyhelicopters.com

registration	type of aircraft	cn/fn	ex/ex*	mfd	del	powered by	mtow kg	configuration	selcal	name/fln/specialitites/remarks
☐ N401LH	Eurocopter (Aerosp.) AS350BA AStar	3059		0098	0298	1 TU Arriel 1B	2100			lsf Meridien Consulting Co. Inc.
☐ N402LH	Eurocopter (Aerosp.) AS350BA AStar	3060		0098	0298	1 TU Arriel 1B	2100			lsf Meridien Consulting Co. Inc.
☐ N444LH	Eurocopter (Aerosp.) AS350BA AStar	3001	N40495	0097	0398	1 TU Arriel 1B	2100			lsf Meridien Consulting Co. Inc.
☐ N555LD	Eurocopter (Aerosp.) AS350BA AStar	2588	N555LH	0092	0198	1 TU Arriel 1B	2100			lsf American Eurocopter Corp.
☐ N555LH	Eurocopter (Aerosp.) AS350BA AStar	3018	N40480	0098	0398	1 TU Arriel 1B	2100			lsf Meridien Consulting Co. Inc.
☐ N666LH	Eurocopter (Aerosp.) AS350BA AStar	3009		0098	0198	1 TU Arriel 1B	2100			lsf Meridien Consulting Co. Inc.
☐ N87BH	Eurocopter (Aerosp.) AS350BA AStar	2708	N350BA	0093	0694	1 TU Arriel 1B	2100			lsf Broadcast Helicopter Corp.
☐ N106KF	Eurocopter (Aerosp.) AS355F1 TwinStar	5111	N5801S	0082	0495	2 AN 250-C20F	2400			lsf American Eurocopter Corp.

LIFE FORCE AIR MEDICAL (Division of Chattanooga-Hamilton County Hospital, a Erlanger Health System) — Chattanooga-CHC Heliport, TN

975 East 3rd Street, Chattanooga, TN 37403, USA ☎ (423) 778-5433 Tx: none Fax: (423) 778-5431 SITA: n/a
F: 1982 ♦♦♦ n/a Head: Dennis A. Pettigrew Net: n/a

registration	type of aircraft	cn/fn	ex/ex*	mfd	del	powered by	mtow kg	configuration	selcal	name/fln/specialitites/remarks
☐ N412BE	Bell 412	33036	N2181K	0081	0888	2 PWC PT6T-3B TwinPac	5398	EMS		
☐ N911BE	Bell 412SP	36018	N412GH*	0090	0795	2 PWC PT6T-3B TwinPac	5398	EMS		

LIFE LION Air Medical Program (Division of Milton S. Hershey Medical Center) — Hershey-Pennsylvania University Helipad, PA

500 University Drive, Hershey, PA 17033, USA ☎ (717) 531-7365 Tx: none Fax: (717) 531-6604 SITA: n/a
F: 1991 ♦♦♦ n/a Head: Ted Townsend Net: n/a

registration	type of aircraft	cn/fn	ex/ex*	mfd	del	powered by	mtow kg	configuration	selcal	name/fln/specialitites/remarks
☐ N291LL	Eurocopter (Aerosp.) AS365N2 Dauphin 2	6402		0091	1091	2 TU Arriel 1C2	4250	EMS		
☐ N896LL	Eurocopter (Aerosp.) SA365N1 Dauphin 2	6294	N588FA	0088	0197	2 TU Arriel 1C1	4100	EMS		

LIFESTAR (Division of University of Tennessee-Medical Center) — Knoxville-University of TN Hospital Heliport, TN

University of TN, Drawer 103, 1924 Alcoa Highway, Medical Center, Knoxville, TN 37920, USA ☎ (423) 544-9112 Tx: none Fax: (423) 544-8868 SITA: n/a
F: 1984 ♦♦♦ n/a Head: Norman Majors Net: n/a

registration	type of aircraft	cn/fn	ex/ex*	mfd	del	powered by	mtow kg	configuration	selcal	name/fln/specialitites/remarks
☐ N411UT	Bell 412SP	33125	N412CF	0086	1294	2 PWC PT6T-3B TwinPac	5398	EMS		
☐ N412UT	Bell 412	33025	N9106D	0081	1187	2 PWC PT6T-3B TwinPac	5398	EMS		

LINDSAY AVIATION, Inc. = LSY (Affiliated with L J P Leasing, Corp.) — Buffalo-Int'l, NY — Lindsay

3806 Union Road, Cheektowaga, NY 14225-4248, USA ☎ (716) 683-4523 Tx: none Fax: (716) 683-4525 SITA: n/a
F: 1985 ♦♦♦ 10 Head: Larry J. Pezzanite ICAO: LINDSAY AIR Net: n/a

registration	type of aircraft	cn/fn	ex/ex*	mfd	del	powered by	mtow kg	configuration	selcal	name/fln/specialitites/remarks
☐ N6161V	Beech Travel Air D95A	TD-614		0065	0796	2 LY IO-360-B1B	1905			
☐ N1852E	Cessna 310R II	310R1587		0079	0995	2 CO IO-520-MB	2495			
☐ N2640F	Cessna 310R II	310R1676		0079	0995	2 CO IO-520-MB	2495			
☐ N310SA	Cessna 310R II	310R1565		0078	1196	2 CO IO-520-M	2495			
☐ N3376G	Cessna 310R II	310R0818		0077	1196	2 CO IO-520-M	2495			
☐ N37289	Cessna 310R II	310R1203		0078	1196	2 CO IO-520-M	2495			
☐ N5009J	Cessna 310R II	310R0730		0076	1294	2 CO IO-520-M	2495			
☐ N85DS	Cessna 310Q	310Q0080		0070	1290	2 CO IO-470-VO	2404			
☐ N8669G	Cessna 310R II	310R0948		0077	0894	2 CO IO-520-M	2495			

LONG BEACH HELICOPTERS, Inc. — Long Beach-Daugherty Field, CA

4137 Donald Douglas Drive, Long Beach, CA 90808, USA ☎ (562) 496-1166 Tx: none Fax: (562) 496-1166 SITA: n/a
F: 1987 ♦♦♦ n/a Head: Caesar Wackeen Net: n/a

registration	type of aircraft	cn/fn	ex/ex*	mfd	del	powered by	mtow kg	configuration	selcal	name/fln/specialitites/remarks
☐ N9KC	Bell 206L-3 LongRanger III	51061	N303JG	0083	0794	1 AN 250-C30P	1882			

LORAIR, Ltd — Tucson-Int'l, AZ

1002 East Valencia Road, Tucson, AZ 85706, USA ☎ (520) 294-3136 Tx: none Fax: (520) 294-3145 SITA: n/a
F: 1995 ♦♦♦ 30 Head: Walter L. Cole Net: n/a

registration	type of aircraft	cn/fn	ex/ex*	mfd	del	powered by	mtow kg	configuration	selcal	name/fln/specialitites/remarks
☐ N902WC	Boeing 737-247	19613 / 104	N308VA	1268	0796	2 PW JT8D-9A (HK3/NOR)	49442	Y122		lsf 9 Lives Holdings Inc.
☐ N903RC	Boeing 737-247	19598 / 33	C-GVJC	0668	0797	2 PW JT8D-9	52388	Y122		lsf 9 Lives Holdings Inc. / opf Tracor

LOST NATION AVIATION (Air Z Flying Service, Inc. dba) — Willoughby-Lost Nation Municipal, OH

1885 Lost Nation Road, Willoughby, OH 44094, USA ☎ (440) 953-2992 Tx: none Fax: (440) 953-2993 SITA: n/a
F: 1986 ♦♦♦ n/a Head: Laurence E. Rohl Net: n/a

registration	type of aircraft	cn/fn	ex/ex*	mfd	del	powered by	mtow kg	configuration	selcal	name/fln/specialitites/remarks
☐ N8188J	Piper PA-32R-301 Saratoga SP	32R-8213041		0082	1089	1 LY IO-540-K1G5D	1633			lsf pvt
☐ N5359U	Cessna U206G Stationair 6 II	U20605240		0079	0186	1 CO IO-520-F	1633			lsf pvt
☐ N62368	Cessna 310R II	310R0131	OH-CHH	0075	0693	2 CO IO-520-M	2495			lsf IPCF Aviation Inc.
☐ N4520S	Beech Baron 58	TH-660		0075	0490	2 CO IO-520-C	2449			lsf pvt

LOUISIANA AIRCRAFT, Inc. (Louisiana Aircraft Companies, Inc. dba) — Baton Rouge Metro, LA

4225 Chuck Yeager Avenue, Baton Rouge, LA 70807, USA ☎ (504) 356-1401 Tx: none Fax: (504) 359-3919 SITA: n/a
F: 1941 n/a Head: James Davison, Jr. Net: n/a

☐ N2434W	Piper PA-31T1A Cheyenne IA	31T-1104006		0084	0591	2 PWC PT6A-11	3946			lsf Davison Terminal Service Inc.
☐ N68TW	Beech King Air C90A	LJ-1200	N1546U	0089	0192	2 PWC PT6A-21	4581			lsf Mathews Trucking Co. Inc.
☐ N777PR	Beech King Air 200	BB-404	N921DT	0078	1192	2 PWC PT6A-41	5670			lsf Mathews Trucking Co. Inc.
☐ N999DT	Beech King Air 200	BB-138	N925BQ	0076	0677	2 PWC PT6A-41	5670			lsf Davison Transport Inc.
☐ N40NB	Beech King Air 300	FA-55	N40NE	0085	0492	2 PWC PT6A-60A	6350			lsf Davison Transport Inc.
☐ N437SJ	IAI 1124A Westwind II	437	N437WW	0086	1095	2 GA TFE731-3-1G	10659			lsf Davison Transport Inc.

LOWA, Ltd — Basel/Mulhouse-EuroAirport (Switzerland)

Flight ops: c/o Jet Aviation Business Jets AG, Postfach, CH-4030 Basel-Flughafen, Switzerland ☎ (61) 325 20 20 Tx: none Fax: (61) 352 22 42 SITA: n/a
F: 1979 n/a Head: Ray G. Hanna Net: n/a Operates non-commercial flights (in conjunction with Jet Aviation Business Jets AG, Switzerland) for itself only.

☐ N88ZL	Boeing 707-330B	18928 / 457	N5381X	0065	0784	4 PW JT3D-3B (HK3/BAC)	146500	VIP	DK-HM	

LYNCH FLYING SERVICE, Inc. = LCH — Billings-Logan Int'l, MT

Billings Logan International Airport, Billings, MT 59105, USA ☎ (406) 252-0508 Tx: none Fax: (406) 245-9491 SITA: n/a
F: 1939 41 Head: John D. Lynch ICAO: LYNCH AIR Net: n/a Aircraft below MTOW 1361 kg: Cessna 172 & 182

☐ N2563S	Cessna 210L Centurion II	21061330		0076	0485	1 CO IO-520-L	1724			
☐ N5152Y	Cessna T210N Turbo Centurion II	21064097		0080	1096	2 CO TSIO-520-R	1814			
☐ N9605Y	Cessna 210N Centurion II	21064558		0081	0682	1 CO IO-520-L	1724			
☐ N277JD	Cessna 310R II	310R0581		0076	0790	2 CO IO-520-M	2495			
☐ N289WB	Cessna T310R II	310R0817		0077	0191	2 CO TSIO-520-B	2495			
☐ N5043J	Cessna 310R II	310R0163		0075	1192	2 CO IO-520-M	2495			
☐ N2703U	Cessna 340A II	340A0914		0080	0193	2 CO TSIO-520-N	2717			
☐ N6316X	Cessna 340A II	340A0487		0078	0678	2 CO TSIO-520-N	2717			
☐ N5113G	Cessna 414 II	414-0952		0077	0886	2 CO TSIO-520-N	2880			
☐ N9781S	Cessna 414A Chancellor III	414A0515		0080	0790	2 CO TSIO-520-NB	3062			
☐ N401NA	Cessna 402B	402B0035		0070	0794	2 CO TSIO-520-E	2858			
☐ N5774C	Cessna 402C II	402C0039		0079	0894	2 CO TSIO-520-VB	3107			
☐ N6839Y	Cessna 402C II	402C0481		0081	0387	2 CO TSIO-520-VB	3107			
☐ N69316	Cessna 402B	402B0433		0073	0398	2 CO TSIO-520-E	2858			
☐ N6858C	Cessna 421C Golden Eagle III	421C0481		0078	0485	2 CO GTSIO-520-L	3379			
☐ N102LF	Beech King Air 100	B-65	N102RS	0070	0787	2 PWC PT6A-28	4808			
☐ N53MD	Beech King Air 100	B-86	N500Y	0071	0190	2 PWC PT6A-28	4808			
☐ N552R	Beech King Air C90	LJ-749	N93BA	0077	0891	2 PWC PT6A-21	4377			
☐ N900DN	Beech King Air A100	B-170	N900DH	0073	0894	2 PWC PT6A-28	5216			
☐ N911SR	Beech King Air B200	BB-898	N98GA	0081	0792	2 PWC PT6A-42	5670			

LYNDEN AIR CARGO, Llc = L2 / LYC (Affiliated with Lynden Air Freight, Inc.) — Anchorage-Int'l, AK

6441 South Airpark Place, Anchorage, AK 99502-1809, USA ☎ (907) 245-1544 Tx: none Fax: (907) 245-0213 SITA: ANCLYCR
F: 1995 n/a Head: Michael T. Hart IATA: 344 ICAO: LYNDEN Net: http://www.lac.lynden.com

☐ N401LC	Lockheed L-382G (L-100-30) Hercules	31C-4606	ZS-RSJ	0775	0397	4 AN 501-D22A	70307	Freighter		
☐ N402LC	Lockheed L-382G (L-100-30) Hercules	35C-4698	ZS-JJA	0076	0397	4 AN 501-D22A	70307	Freighter		
☐ N403LC	Lockheed L-382G (L-100-30) Hercules	31C-4590	N903SJ	0075	0997	4 AN 501-D22A	70307	Freighter		
☐ N404LC	Lockheed L-382G (L-100-30) Hercules	38C-4763	N909SJ	1177	1198	4 AN 501-D22A	70307	Freighter		

LYNSTAR AVIATION, Inc. (Member of The Lynton Group) — Morristown-Municipal, NJ

9 Airport Road, Morristown, NJ 07960, USA ☎ (973) 292-2829 Tx: none Fax: (973) 292-9284 SITA: n/a
F: 1987 n/a Head: Richard G. Eimert Net: n/a

☐ N111EH	Eurocopter (Aerosp.) AS355F1 TwinStar	5153	N57949	0082	0097	2 AN 250-C20F	2400			lsf Public Service Electric & Gas
☐ N188S	Agusta A109A II	7349	N100S	0085	0092	2 AN 250-C20B	2600			lsf Agusta Aerospace Corp.

LYNX AIR INTERNATIONAL — Fort Lauderdale-Executive, FL

2525 NW 55th Court, Fort Lauderdale, FL 33309, USA ☎ (954) 772-9808 Tx: none Fax: (954) 772-9808 SITA: n/a
F: 1992 n/a Head: Linda G. Tonks Net: n/a

☐ N5441F	Fairchild (Swearingen) SA227AC Metro III	AC-528		0082	0696	2 GA TPE331-11U-611G	6577	Y19		lsf LAI Leasing Inc.
☐ N61NE	Fairchild (Swearingen) SA227AC Metro III	AC-761B		0090	0896	2 GA TPE331-11U-612G	7257	Y19		lsf LAI Leasing Inc.
☐ N63NE	Fairchild (Swearingen) SA227AC Metro III	AC-763B		0090	1197	2 GA TPE331-11U-612G	7257	Y19		lsf Textron Financial Corp.

LYON AVIATION, Inc. — Pittsfield-Municipal, MA

Tamarack Road, Pittsfield Municipal Airport, Pittsfield, MA 01201, USA ☎ (413) 443-6700 Tx: none Fax: (413) 499-4335 SITA: n/a
F: 1979 n/a Head: Shirley A. Lyon Net: n/a Aircraft below MTOW 1361kg: Cessna 172

☐ N1339G	Cessna 310R II	310R0023		0074	0983	2 CO IO-520-M	2495			
☐ N3LA	Piper PA-31-350 Navajo Chieftain	31-8052064		0080	0386	2 LY TIO-540-J2BD	3175			
☐ N456CG	Learjet 25D	25D-343	N3797L	0081	0395	2 GE CJ610-8A	6804			lsf L & W Leasing Inc.

MAC AIR Corporation — McPherson, KS

PO Box 189, McPherson, KS 67460, USA ☎ (316) 241-0684 Tx: none Fax: (316) 241-3188 SITA: n/a
F: 1984 30 Head: John M. Britting Net: http://www.halcyon.com/wpowers/mac_air.html

☐ N2268T	Cessna R182 Skylane RG II	R18200015		0077	0590	1 LY O-540-J3C5D	1406			
☐ N1656H	Piper PA-34-200T Seneca II	34-7770131		0077	0595	2 CO TSIO-360-E	2073			
☐ N4088Q	Cessna 401	401-0188		0068	0793	2 CO TSIO-520-E	2858			
☐ N701CJ	Cessna 401A	401A0022		0069	0694	2 CO TSIO-520-E	2858			
☐ N124EA	Piper PA-31-350 Navajo Chieftain	31-7652159	N17CA	0076	0198	2 LY TIO-540-J2BD	3175			
☐ N444TS	Piper PA-31-350 Navajo Chieftain	31-8152195		0081	0396	2 LY TIO-540-J2BD	3175			
☐ N54269	Piper PA-31-350 Navajo Chieftain	31-7405217		0074	0796	2 LY TIO-540-J2BD	3175			

MACAW HELICOPTERS (Micronesian Aviation, Corp. dba) — Saipan

PO Box 1160, Saipan, Mariana Islands 96950, Commonwealth of Northern Mariana Islands ☎ (670) 234-1304 Tx: none Fax: (670) 288-5099 SITA: n/a
F: 1989 n/a Head: Kenneth R. Crowe Net: n/a

☐ N192PB	Bell 206B JetRanger	825	N192P	0072	1297	1 AN 250-C20	1451			

MAC DAN AVIATION, Corp. = MCN — Caldwell-Essex County, NJ

Hangar C, Essex-County-Airport, Fairfield, NJ 07004, USA ☎ (973) 244-9400 Tx: none Fax: (973) 227-8339 SITA: n/a
F: 1971 50 Head: Charles McKenna, Jr. ICAO: MAC DAN Net: http://www.macdan.com

☐ N1312G	Cessna 310Q II	310Q1153		0074	1090	2 CO IO-520-M	2495			
☐ N3237W	Cessna 310R II	310R0070		0075	0992	2 CO IO-520-M	2495			
☐ N69610	Cessna 310R II	310R0102		0074	0495	2 CO IO-520-M	2495			lsf Susan G. Aviation Services Inc.

MAF USA – Mission Aviation Fellowship (Affiliated with MAF Indonesia, MAF Lesotho, MAF Suriname & MAF Congo) — Latin America & Africa

PO Box 3202, Redlands, CA 92373-0998, USA ☎ (909) 794-1151 Tx: none Fax: (909) 794-3016 SITA: n/a
F: 1945 n/a Head: Gary Bishop Net: n/a Non-commercial multinational ecclesiastical consortium conducting flights for relief & development agencies & missions in remote areas of third world countries.
Program / bases are in: Albania, Congo, Ecuador, Haiti, Honduras, Indonesia, Kenya, Lesotho, Nicaragua, Venezuela, Zambia & Zimbabwe.

☐ N1084F	Cessna A185F Skywagon	18502739		0075	0978	1 CO IO-520-D	1520			
☐ N1003V	Cessna U206F Stationair	U20602388		0074	1187	1 CO IO-520-F	1633			lsf Pactec / based Haiti
☐ N206CE	Cessna U206G Stationair II	U20606629	ZS-LDX	0082	0185	1 CO IO-520-F	1633			lsf Pactec / based Zimbabwe
☐ N5119X	Cessna TU206G Turbo Stationair 6 II	U20605571		0080	0198	1 CO TSIO-520-M	1633			
☐ N5437X	Cessna TU206G Turbo Stationair II	U20605753		0080	0698	1 CO TSIO-520-M	1633			
☐ N54620	Cessna U206F Stationair	U20601708		0072	0578	1 CO IO-520-F	1633			lsf Pactec / based Zimbabwe
☐ N5494X	Cessna TU206G Turbo Stationair 6 II	U20605808		0080	0895	1 CO TSIO-520-M	1633			lsf Pactec / based Mozambique
☐ N6233Z	Cessna TU206G Turbo Stationair 6 II	U20606195		0081	1182	1 CO TSIO-520-M	1633			
☐ N9933R	Cessna U206G Stationair 6 II	U20606987		0086	1297	1 CO IO-520-F	1633			
☐ N1802Q	Cessna 207A Stationair 8 II	20700786		0084	0792	1 CO IO-520-F	1724			lsf Pactec / based Haiti
☐ N677BC	Beech Catpass 250	BB-86	5Y-BKM	0075	0698	2 PWC PT6A-41	5670			lsf Pactec/cvtd King Air 200/based Mali

MAGIC CARPET AVIATION, Inc. (Subsidiary of Amway Corporation) — Orlando-Int'l, FL

4225 Execuair Street, Orlando, FL 32827, USA ☎ (407) 859-9393 Tx: none Fax: (407) 859-7186 SITA: n/a
F: 1996 n/a Head: James J. Rosloniec Net: n/a Operates exclusively non-commercial VIP flights for the NBA Orlando Magic-basketball club, an affiliate of Amway Corporation.

☐ N253DV	Boeing 737-39A	23800 / 1409	N117DF	0087	0096	2 CFMI CFM56-3B2	61235	Executive 21Pax	CH-MP	lsf Aviation Inc./opf NBA Orlando Magic

MAINE AVIATION, Corp. = MAT (Sister company of Maine Aviation Sales, Inc.) — Portland-Int'l Jetport, ME

1127 Westbrook Street, Portland, ME 04102, USA ☎ (207) 780-1811 Tx: none Fax: (207) 775-3359 SITA: n/a
F: 1959 n/a Head: Allyn J. Caruso ICAO: MAINE-AV Net: http://www.maineaviation.com

☐ N87508	Cessna 310R II	310R0597		0076	0198	2 CO IO-520-M	2495			lsf BHA Leasing Inc.
☐ N414ME	Cessna 414	414-0512		0074	0694	2 CO TSIO-520-J	2880			lsf Horizon Charters Inc.
☐ N567JS	Cessna 402B II	402B1090		0076	0195	2 CO TSIO-520-E	2858			lsf BHA Leasing Inc.
☐ N208BH	Beech 99 Airliner	U-2	N201TC	0068	0889	2 PWC PT6A-27	4717			lsf BHA Leasing Inc.
☐ N186SC	Cessna 500 Citation	500-0186	N186MW	0074	1196	2 PWC JT15D-1	5216			lsf Cumberland Aircraft Leasing

392 registration type of aircraft cn/fn ex/ex* mfd del powered by mtow kg configuration selcal name/fln/specialitites/remarks

MAINE FLIGHT (Maine Flight Center, Ltd dba)

Pittsfield-Municipal, ME

Pittsfield Municipal Airport, Harrison Avenue, Pittsfield, ME 04967, USA ☎ (207) 487-6000 Tx: none Fax: (207) 487-6655 SITA: n/a
F: 1991 n/a Head: Robert L. Hart Net: n/a Aircraft below MTOW 1361kg: Cessna 172 & 182

N6365Y	Piper PA-23-250 Aztec C	27-3638		0067	1291	2 LY IO-540-C4B5	2359			
N7527S	AAC (Ted Smith) Aerostar 600A	60-0188-084		0074	0795	2 LY IO-540-K1F5	2495			

MAINE HELICOPTERS, Inc.

Whitefield-Private Heliport, ME

Box 110, Route 218, Whitefield, ME 04353, USA ☎ (207) 549-3400 Tx: none Fax: (207) 549-3400 SITA: n/a
F: 1960 n/a Head: Andrew B. Berry Net: n/a Aircraft below MTOW 1361kg: Bell 47G

N9913K	Bell 206B JetRanger II	2055		0076	0688	1 AN 250-C20	1451			
N99021	Bell UH-1B (204)	1073	64-13949	0064	0889	1 LY T53-L-11	3856			

MAJESTIC AIR CARGO (Galaxy Air Cargo, Inc. dba)

Anchorage-Int'l, AK

3105 Lakeshore Drive, Suite B-101, Anchorage, AK 99517, USA ☎ (907) 245-0444 Tx: none Fax: (907) 266-4251 SITA: n/a
F: 1997 n/a Head: Jody R. Pond Net: n/a

N305SF	Boeing (Douglas) DC-3C (C-47-DL)	6208	N4BA	0043	0897	2 PW R-1830	12202	Freighter		lsf Majestic Leasing Inc.
N67588	Boeing (Douglas) DC-3C (C-47A-90-DL)	20536	43-16070	0044	0897	2 PW R-1830	12202	Freighter		lsf Majestic Leasing Inc.

MAKANI KAI HELICOPTERS

Honolulu-Int'l, HI

120 Kapalulu Place, Suite 302, Honolulu, HI 96819, USA ☎ (808) 834-5813 Tx: none Fax: (808) 837-7867 SITA: n/a
F: 1991 n/a Head: Gustav R. Schuman Net: n/a Aircraft below MTOW 1361kg: Bell 47G-4A

N968YC	Bell 206B JetRanger	1427		0074		1 AN 250-C20	1451			lsf pvt

M & N AVIATION, Inc. = W4

San Juan-Isla Grande/Fernando Luis Ribas Dominicci, PR

Hangar 1, North Side, Isla Grande Airport, San Juan, PR 00906-6566, USA ☎ (787) 722-5980 Tx: none Fax: (787) 723-0465 SITA: n/a
F: 1992 n/a Head: José Maldonado Net: http://www.guides.com/acg/mnaviation

N2717B	Cessna 402C II	402C0221		0079	1097	2 CO TSIO-520-VB	3107			
N402DD	Cessna 402C II	402C0485	N94MM	0081	0493	2 CO TSIO-520-VB	3107			
N403GC	Cessna 402B	402B0305	N1530T	0072	0394	2 CO TSIO-520-E	2858			
N404MN	Cessna 402C II	402C0640	N640RC	0081	0597	2 CO TSIO-520-VB	3107			
N560ME	Cessna 560 Citation V	560-0012	N1217N	0089	0897	2 PWC JT15D-5A	7212			lsf General Electric Capital Corp.

MARIO'S AIR, Inc. = M2

Miami-Int'l, FL

8209 NW 30th Terrace, Miami, FL 33122, USA ☎ (305) 477-7213 Tx: none Fax: (305) 477-6481 SITA: n/a
F: 1997 n/a Head: Mario F. Mimbella Net: n/a

N1293E	Cessna 208B Grand Caravan	208B0537		0096	1098	1 PWC PT6A-114A	3969	Freighter		lsf Southeast Air Freight Inc.
N701SE	Cessna 208B Grand Caravan	208B0701		0098	1098	1 PWC PT6A-114A	3969	Freighter		lsf Southeast Air Freight Inc.

MARITIME HELICOPTERS, Inc.

Homer, AK

3520 F.A.A. Road, Homer, AK 99603, USA ☎ (907) 235-7771 Tx: n/a Fax: (907) 235-7773 SITA: n/a
F: 1973 9 Head: Donald M. Fell Net: n/a Aircraft below MTOW 1361 kg: Piper PA-18.

N301MH	Bell 206B JetRanger III	2371	N16964	0078	0878	1 AN 250-C20B	1451	5 Pax		Floats
N302MH	Bell 206B JetRanger III	2958	N1075G	0080	0080	1 AN 250-C20B	1451	5 Pax		Hi-Skids / Pop-out Floats
N303MH	Bell 206L-3 LongRanger III	51340	N2245P	0090	0590	1 AN 250-C30P	1882	7 Pax		Hi-Skids / Pop-out Floats

MARLIN AIR, Inc.

Detroit-Willow Run, MI

48162 "F" Street, Willow Run Airport, Belleville, MI 48111, USA ☎ (734) 485-9181 Tx: none Fax: (734) 485-9187 SITA: n/a
F: 1985 n/a Head: Stuart W. Dingman Net: n/a

N234UM	Cessna 500 Citation	500-0105	N32W	0073	0390	2 PWC JT15D-1	5216			
N111F	Sabreliner 60 (Rockwell NA265-60)	306-126	HC-BUN	0077	0199	2 PW JT12A-8	9150			lsf pvt
N510SD	Cessna 650 Citation III	650-0161	N500AE	0088	0596	2 GA TFE731-3B-100S	9072			lsf MDFC Equipment Leasing Corp.

MARTINAIRE, Inc. = MRA (Member of The Kitty Hawk Group)

Dallas-Love Field & -DFW, TX

2550 Midway Road, Suite 190, Carrollton, TX 75006-2366, USA ☎ (214) 358-5858 Tx: none Fax: (214) 350-7979 SITA: n/a
F: 1978 140 Head: Edward C. Acker ICAO: MARTINAIRE US Net: n/a

N761UJ	Cessna 210M Centurion II	21062526		0078	0788	1 CO IO-520-L	1724	Freighter		
N4591B	Cessna 208B Caravan I Super Cargomaster	208B0137	N997FE	0088	0389	1 PWC PT6A-114	3969	Freighter		lsf Cessna Finance Corp.
N4602B	Cessna 208B Caravan I Super Cargomaster	208B0140	N999FE	0088	0289	1 PWC PT6A-114	3969	Freighter		lsf Cessna Finance Corp.
N4625B	Cessna 208B Caravan I Super Cargomaster	208B0159		0089	1289	1 PWC PT6A-114	3969	Freighter		lsf Cessna Finance Corp.
N4655B	Cessna 208B Caravan I Super Cargomaster	208B0160		0089	0589	1 PWC PT6A-114	3969	Freighter		lsf Cessna Finance Corp.
N4662B	Cessna 208B Caravan I Super Cargomaster	208B0161		0089	1289	1 PWC PT6A-114	3969	Freighter		lsf Cessna Finance Corp.
N4674B	Cessna 208B Caravan I Super Cargomaster	208B0165		0089	0689	1 PWC PT6A-114	3969	Freighter		lsf Cessna Finance Corp.
N4687B	Cessna 208B Caravan I Super Cargomaster	208B0167		0089	1289	1 PWC PT6A-114	3969	Freighter		lsf Cessna Finance Corp.
N9331B	Cessna 208B Caravan I Super Cargomaster	208B0055		0087	0188	1 PWC PT6A-114	3969	Freighter		lsf Cessna Finance Corp.
N9469B	Cessna 208B Caravan I Super Cargomaster	208B0079		0088	0488	1 PWC PT6A-114	3969	Freighter		lsf Cessna Finance Corp.
N9471B	Cessna 208B Caravan I Super Cargomaster	208B0081		0088	0588	1 PWC PT6A-114	3969	Freighter		lsf Cessna Finance Corp.
N9505B	Cessna 208B Caravan I Super Cargomaster	208B0085		0088	0588	1 PWC PT6A-114	3969	Freighter		lsf Cessna Finance Corp.
N9546B	Cessna 208B Caravan I Super Cargomaster	208B0126		0088	1188	1 PWC PT6A-114	3969	Freighter		lsf Cessna Finance Corp.
N9623B	Cessna 208B Caravan I Super Cargomaster	208B0138		0088	0189	1 PWC PT6A-114	3969	Freighter		lsf Cessna Finance Corp.
N9714B	Cessna 208B Caravan I Super Cargomaster	208B0153		0089	1289	1 PWC PT6A-114	3969	Freighter		lsf Cessna Finance Corp.
N9738B	Cessna 208B Caravan I Super Cargomaster	208B0097		0088	0788	1 PWC PT6A-114	3969	Freighter		lsf Cessna Finance Corp.
N9760B	Cessna 208B Caravan I Super Cargomaster	208B0102		0088	0788	1 PWC PT6A-114	3969	Freighter		lsf Cessna Finance Corp.
N9761B	Cessna 208B Caravan I Super Cargomaster	208B0107		0088	0888	1 PWC PT6A-114	3969	Freighter		lsf Cessna Finance Corp.
N9762B	Cessna 208B Caravan I Super Cargomaster	208B0109		0088	0888	1 PWC PT6A-114	3969	Freighter		lsf Cessna Finance Corp.
N9766B	Cessna 208B Caravan I Super Cargomaster	208B0112		0088	0988	1 PWC PT6A-114	3969	Freighter		lsf Cessna Finance Corp.
N9956B	Cessna 208B Caravan I Super Cargomaster	208B0119		0088	1088	1 PWC PT6A-114	3969	Freighter		lsf Cessna Finance Corp.
N110DN	Dornier 228-202 (F)	8110	D-CAAB*	0086	1291	2 GA TPE331-5-252D	6200	Freighter		lsf Deutsche Financial Svcs / cvtd -202
N117DN	Dornier 228-202 (F)	8117	D-CIMB*	0087	1195	2 GA TPE331-5-252D	6200	Freighter		lsf Deutsche Financial Svcs / cvtd -202
N228ME	Dornier 228-202 (F)	8097	D-COCO*	0086	0490	2 GA TPE331-5-252D	6200	Freighter		lsf Deutsche Financial Svcs / cvtd -202
N260MC	Dornier 228-202 (F)	8121	D-CBDA	0087	1195	2 GA TPE331-5-252D	6200	Freighter		lsf Deutsche Financial Svcs / cvtd -201
N264MC	Dornier 228-202 (F)	8144		0087	0195	2 GA TPE331-5-252D	6200	Freighter		lsf State Street Boston Lsng / cvtd-202
N265MC	Dornier 228-202 (F)	8149		0088	0195	2 GA TPE331-5-252D	6200	Freighter		lsf State Street Boston Lsng / cvtd-202
N269MC	Dornier 228-202 (F)	8135	N229PT*	0087	0795	2 GA TPE331-5-252D	6200	Freighter		lsf Deutsche Financial Svcs / cvtd -202
N279MC	Dornier 228-202 (F)	8120	N228RM	0087	0195	2 GA TPE331-5-252D	6200	Freighter		lsf State Street Boston Lsng / cvtd-202
N354AE	Fairchild (Swearingen) SA227AC Metro III	AC-633	N3113C	0085	1096	2 GA TPE331-11U-611G	6577	Freighter		
N360AE	Fairchild (Swearingen) SA227AC Metro III	AC-675		0087	1195	2 GA TPE331-11U-611G	6577	Freighter		lsf Textron Financial Corp.
N367AE	Fairchild (Swearingen) SA227AC Metro III	AC-691	N27060	0087	1195	2 GA TPE331-11U-611G	6577	Freighter		lsf US Bancorp Leasing & Finance
N672AV	Fairchild (Swearingen) SA227AC Metro III	AC-672		0087	1195	2 GA TPE331-11U-611G	6577	Freighter		lsf Textron Financial Corp.

MARYLAND AIRLINES, Inc.

Easton-Municipal, MD

PO Box 2405, Easton, MD 21601, USA ☎ (443) 451-5693 Tx: none Fax: (443) 451-5693 SITA: n/a
F: 1946 24 Head: Gary Ambler Net: n/a

N38305	Piper PA-32R-300 Lance	32R-7780413		0077	1188	1 LY IO-540-K1G5D	1633			
N6116X	Cessna 310R II	310R1284		0078	0990	2 CO IO-520-M	2495			
N4091Y	Piper PA-31-350 Navajo Chieftain	31-8152161		0081	0788	2 LY TIO-540-J2BD	3175			
N4504J	Piper PA-31-350 Navajo Chieftain	31-8052204		0080	1193	2 LY TIO-540-J2BD	3175			lsf Maryland Jet Center Inc.

MAUNA KEA HELICOPTERS, Inc.

Kamuela-Waimea Kohala, HI

Box 1713, Kamuela, HI 96743, USA ☎ (808) 885-7596 Tx: none Fax: (808) 885-2104 SITA: n/a
F: 1987 n/a Head: Scott M. Shupe Net: n/a

N58295	MD Helicopters MD 500D (Hughes 369D)	490494D		0079	0393	1 AN 250-C20B	1361			
N591RB	Eurocopter (Aerosp.) AS350B AStar	1389	N5773V	0080	0197	1 TU Arriel 1B	1950			
N905BA	Eurocopter (Aerosp.) AS350B AStar	1189	N142BH	0079	0197	1 TU Arriel 1B	1950			cvtd AS350D

MAVERICK HELICOPTER, Inc.

Las Vegas-McCarren Int'l, NV

105 East Reno Avenue, Suite 4, Las Vegas, NV 89119, USA ☎ (702) 261-0007 Tx: none Fax: (702) 262-9610 SITA: n/a
F: 1996 n/a Head: Gregory D. Rochna Net: n/a

N43MH	Eurocopter (Aerosp.) AS350B2 AStar	2856	C-FXAP	0095	1297	1 TU Arriel 1D1	2250			
N64MH	Eurocopter (Aerosp.) AS350BA AStar	1206	C-FHNC	0079	0698	1 TU Arriel 1B	2100			cvtd AS350D
N91MH	Eurocopter (Aerosp.) AS350BA AStar	2786	C-FYNI	0094	0697	1 TU Arriel 1B	2100			
N92MH	Eurocopter (Aerosp.) AS350BA AStar	2898	C-FZHN	0095	0297	1 TU Arriel 1B	2100			

MAXAIR, Inc.

Appleton-Outgamie County, WI

W6381 Columbia Drive, Appleton, WI 54915, USA ☎ (920) 738-3020 Tx: none Fax: (920) 738-3026 SITA: n/a
F: 1959 50 Head: Steven R. Kalmanson Net: n/a Aircraft below MTOW 1361 kg: Cessna 172

N1670W	Beech Baron 58	TH-259		0072	1294	2 CO IO-520-C	2449			lsf pvt
N3664N	Beech Baron 58	TH-1139		0080	0888	2 CO IO-520-CB	2449			
N6025Y	Beech Baron 58	TH-1010		0079	0887	2 CO IO-520-CB	2449			
N7239R	Beech Baron 58	TH-565		0075	0387	2 CO IO-520-C	2449			
N7313R	Beech Baron 58	TH-456		0074	0389	2 CO IO-520-C	2449			

393 registration type of aircraft cn/fn ex/ex* mfd del powered by mtow kg configuration selcal name/fln/specialitites/remarks

☐ N8565R	Beech Baron 58	TH-532		0074	0685	2 CO IO-520-C	2449			
☐ N376NC	Piper PA-31-350 Navajo Chieftain	31-7852048		0078	0590	2 LY TIO-540-J2BD	3175			
☐ N5494R	Piper PA-31-350 Navajo Chieftain	31-7405410		0074	0794	2 LY TIO-540-J2BD	3175			lsf Rock Aviation Inc.
☐ N4677N	Cessna 414A Chancellor III	414A0068		0078	0192	2 CO TSIO-520-N	3062			
☐ N2883	Beech King Air 200	BB-144	N28S	0076	0589	2 PWC PT6A-41	5670			
☐ N44UF	Beech King Air 200	BB-36	N816RB	0075	0196	2 PWC PT6A-41	5670			

MAY AIR X-PRESS = MXP

Dallas-DFW, TX & Shreveport-Regional, LA

Rt 3, Box 236, New Boston, TX 75570, USA ☎ (903) 628-6446 Tx: none Fax: (903) 628-5044 SITA: n/a
F: 1986 n/a Head: Thomas W. May ICAO: BEECHNUT Net: n/a

☐ N1291N	Beech G18S	BA-586		0061	0889	2 PW R-985-AN14B	4400	Freighter		
☐ N3038C	Beech E18S	BA-374		0058	0694	2 PW R-985-AN14B	4218	Freighter		
☐ N48M	Beech E18S	BA-155		0056	0989	2 PW R-985-AN14B	4218	Freighter		
☐ N621KE	Beech G18S	BA-556		0060	1087	2 PW R-985-AN14B	4400	Freighter		
☐ N7765N	Beech E18S	BA-413		0059	0395	2 PW R-985-AN14B	4218	Freighter		
☐ N79LA	Beech G18S	BA-543	N331Z	0060	0888	2 PW R-985-AN14B	4400	Freighter		
☐ N931GM	Beech G18S	BA-568	N5798	0060	0389	2 PW R-985-AN14B	4400	Freighter		
☐ N114CA	Lockheed 18-56 (C-60A) Lodestar	18-2560	42-56067	0043	0397	2 WR R-1820	9525	Freighter		
☐ N339	Lockheed 18-56 (C-60A) Lodestar	18-2548	42-56055	0043	0796	2 WR R-1820	9525	Freighter		
☐ N25646	Boeing (Douglas) DC-3A	2234	NC25646	0040	0995	2 PW R-1830	12202	Freighter		

MAYO AVIATION, Inc.

Denver-Centennial, CO

Box F-16, 7765 South Peoria Street, Englewood, CO 80112, USA ☎ (303) 790-9777 Tx: none Fax: (303) 790-4909 SITA: n/a
F: 1978 n/a Head: Gwendolyn O. Mayo Net: n/a

☐ N3922C	Cessna 421C Golden Eagle III	421C0419		0078	0795	2 CO GTSIO-520-L	3379			lsf pvt
☐ N4948W	Beech King Air 90 (65-90)	LJ-31	N7009	0065	0381	2 PWC PT6A-6	4218			lsf pvt
☐ N5911P	Beech King Air E90	LW-70	N133K	0073	1286	2 PWC PT6A-28	4581			
☐ N63BV	Beech King Air E90	LW-256	N63BW	0078	0384	2 PWC PT6A-28	4581			lsf pvt
☐ N74MA	Beech King Air B90	LJ-479	N11LA	0069	0778	2 PWC PT6A-20	4377			lsf pvt
☐ N87CH	Beech King Air E90	LW-20	N84LS	0072	0484	2 PWC PT6A-28	4581			lsf pvt
☐ N520MC	Beech King Air 200	BB-43	N500UR	0075	0994	2 PWC PT6A-41	5670			lsf pvt
☐ N60PD	Beech King Air 200	BB-58	N60PC	0075	1092	2 PWC PT6A-41	5670			lsf CWW Inc.
☐ N103CL	Learjet 35A	35A-273	N103C	0079	1196	2 GA TFE731-2-2B	8301			lsf AOX Technologies Co.
☐ N222BE	Learjet 35A	35A-489		0082	0793	2 GA TFE731-2-2B	8301			lsf pvt
☐ N49BE	Learjet 35A	35A-192	N49PE	0078	1087	2 GA TFE731-2-2B	8301			lsf CWW Inc.
☐ N553V	Learjet 35A	35A-141	N553M	0077	1293	2 GA TFE731-2-2B	8301			lsf CWW Inc.
☐ N55G	Hawker 3A/731 (HS 125-3A/731)	25163 / NA709	N208H	0068	0395	2 GA TFE731-3R-1H	10568			cvtd 125-3A/RA

MBD AIR (MBD Corporation dba / Sister company of TOLAIR Services, Inc.)

San Juan-Luis Munoz Marin Int'l, PR

PO Box 37840, Airport Station, San Juan, PR 00937-0840, USA ☎ (787) 791-5235 Tx: none Fax: (787) 791-8385 SITA: n/a
F: 1981 n/a Head: Jorge A. Toledo Operates charter flights with Beechcraft E18S/H-18 & MDC Douglas DC-3 aircraft, leased from TOLAIR when required.

MCCALL & WILDERNESS AIR (McCall Air Taxi, Inc. dba)

McCall & Salmon, ID

PO Box 771, McCall Airport, ID 83638, USA ☎ (208) 634-7137 Tx: none Fax: (208) 634-3917 SITA: n/a
F: 1976 n/a Head: Michael R. Dorris Net: n/a Aircraft below MTOW 1361kg: Cessna 170

☐ N93039	Cessna A185F Skywagon	18503169		0077	0881	1 CO IO-520-D	1520			lsf pvt
☐ N1488M	Cessna TU206E Turbo Skywagon	U20601488		0070	0691	1 CO TSIO-520-C	1633			lsf pvt
☐ N33179	Cessna U206F Stationair II	U20602655		0075	1091	1 CO IO-520-F	1633			lsf pvt
☐ N3985G	Cessna U206C Super Skywagon	U206-0985		0067	0987	1 CO IO-520-F	1633			lsf pvt
☐ N58441	Cessna U206F Stationair II	U20602604		0075	0687	1 CO IO-520-F	1633			lsf NFL Aircraft
☐ N7372Q	Cessna TU206F Turbo Stationair	U20602186		0073	0495	1 CO TSIO-520-C	1633			
☐ N7520N	Cessna TU206G Turbo Stationair	U20603663		0077	0487	1 CO TSIO-520-M	1633			lsf pvt
☐ N8455Q	Cessna U206F Stationair II	U20603313		0076	0490	1 CO IO-520-F	1633			lsf pvt
☐ N1599U	Cessna T207 Turbo Skywagon	20700199		0071	0292	1 CO TSIO-520-G	1724			
☐ N555JA	Britten-Norman BN-2A Islander	20	N585JA	0068	0493	2 LY O-540-E4C5	2722			lsf pvt

MCCARTHY AIR (D & P Transportation, Inc. dba)

McCarthy, AK

101 Shushana Avenue, McCarthy, AK 99588, USA ☎ (907) 554-4440 Tx: none Fax: none SITA: n/a
F: 1996 n/a Head: David C. Flets Net: n/a

☐ N15268	Piper PA-32-300 Cherokee SIX	32-7340029		0073	0696	1 LY IO-540-K1A5	1542			lsf pvt

MCCAUSLAND AVIATION, Inc.

Carlsbad-Cavern City Air Terminal, NM

PO Box 2294, Carlsbad, NM 88220, USA ☎ (505) 887-1500 Tx: none Fax: (505) 885-1645 SITA: n/a
F: 1946 n/a Head: Phillip H. Carrell Net: n/a Aircraft below MTOW 1361kg: Cessna 172

☐ N1660T	Cessna 414	414-0453		0073	0293	2 CO TSIO-520-N	2880			lsf pvt

MCI TRANSCON, Corp. - Flight Operations (Sister company of MCI Communications, Corp.)

Washington-Dulles Int'l, DC

Complex ABC, Hangar B, Washington, DC 20041, USA ☎ (703) 661-8821 Tx: none Fax: (703) 661-3154 SITA: n/a
F: 1984 n/a Head: Lee Buell Net: n/a Operates non-commercial corporate flights exclusively for the MCI group of companies.

☐ N330MC	Dassault Falcon 900EX	21	F-WWFH*	0097	0198	3 GA TFE731-60-1C	22226	Corporate		
☐ N331MC	Dassault Falcon 900EX	22	F-WWFQ*	0097	0298	3 GA TFE731-60-1C	22226	Corporate		
☐ N334MC	Dassault Falcon 900B	108	N471FJ	0091	0292	3 GA TFE731-5BR-1C	21099	Corporate		
☐ N335MC	Dassault Falcon 900B	150	N150FJ	0095	0995	3 GA TFE731-5BR-1C	21099	Corporate		
☐ N337MC	Dassault Falcon 900B	152	F-WWFJ*	0095	0196	3 GA TFE731-5BR-1C	21099	Corporate		
☐ N374MC	Boeing 737-7BJ (BBJ)	30076 / 179	N1784B*	0199	0199	2 CFMI CFM56-7B26	69400	Corporate		

MCKINLEY AIR SERVICE (Keli A. Mahoney dba)

Talkeetna, AK

PO Box 544, Talkeetna, AK 99676, USA ☎ (907) 733-1765 Tx: none Fax: (907) 733-1965 SITA: n/a
F: 1995 n/a Head: Keli A. Mahoney Net: n/a

☐ N70176	Cessna A185E Skywagon	18502037		0072	0296	1 CO IO-520-D	1520			Floats / Wheel-Skis

MCMAHAN AVIATION, Inc.

Monroe-Regional, LA

5106 Operations Road, Monroe, LA 71203, USA ☎ (318) 325-7558 Tx: none Fax: (318) 323-2290 SITA: n/a
F: 1992 n/a Head: Michael P. McMahan Net: n/a

☐ N2110J	Piper PA-44-180 Seminole	44-7995197		0079	1194	2 LY O-360-E1A6D	1724			
☐ N4HG	Twin (Aero) Commander 500B	500B-999-30		0060	1195	2 LY IO-540-B1A5	3062			

MCMAHON HELICOPTERS (McMahon Helicopter Services, Inc. dba)

Plymouth-Canton Executive Heliport, MI

8351 Ronda Drive, Canton, MI 48187, USA ☎ (734) 459-5980 Tx: none Fax: (734) 459-6315 SITA: n/a
F: 1980 n/a Head: Brian P. McMahon Net: n/a

☐ N59623	Bell 206B JetRanger	1525		0074	0896	1 AN 250-C20	1451			
☐ N76DC	Bell 206L-1 LongRanger II	45471	N185KC	0080	0392	1 AN 250-C28B	1882			lsf LongRanger II Corp.
☐ N911EC	Bell 222U	47505	N12GH	0083	1194	2 LY LTS101-750C.1	3742			lsf pvt
☐ N58S	Sikorsky S-58T	58-1502	N903CH	0062	0995	1 PWC PT6T TwinPac	5897			cvtd S-58E

MCNEELY CHARTER SERVICE, Inc.

Memphis-Int'l, TN

PO Box 1057, West Memphis, AR 72303, USA ☎ (870) 735-0207 Tx: none Fax: (870) 735-0855 SITA: n/a
F: 1966 13 Head: Reggie S. Hopwood Net: n/a

☐ N103RC	Mitsubishi MU-2L (MU-2B-36) Cargoliner	673	N4565E	0075	1089	2 GA TPE331-6-251M	5250	Freighter		Cavenaugh SCD conversion
☐ N32EC	Mitsubishi MU-2N (MU-2B-36A) Cargoliner	699SA	N859MA	0077	0796	2 GA TPE331-5-252M	5250	Freighter		lsf River City Avn/Cavenaugh SCD conv.
☐ N117ME	Beech H18	BA-638	N2009H	0064	0197	2 PW R-985-AN14B	4491	Freighter		
☐ N445DM	Beech TC-45G (18) Dumod Liner	AF-152	N9485Z	0054	0197	2 PW R-985-AN14B	3969	Freighter		cvtd TC-45G
☐ N811BF	Beech H18	BA-659	N13AW	0064	1096	2 PW R-985-AN14B	4491	Freighter		lsf River City Aviation Inc.
☐ N24320	Boeing (Douglas) DC-3C (C-47A-90-DL)	20197	43-15731	0044	0785	2 PW R-1830	12202	Freighter		
☐ N5831B	Boeing (Douglas) DC-3C (C-47A-75-DL)	19345	C-FKAZ	0043	0195	2 PW R-1830	12202	Freighter		

MEDFORD AIR SERVICE, Inc.

Medford-Rogue Valley Int'l, OR

PO Box 699, Medford, OR 97501, USA ☎ (541) 779-5451 Tx: none Fax: (541) 779-8213 SITA: n/a
F: 1980 n/a Head: Michael D. Owen Net: n/a Aircraft below MTOW 1361kg: Cessna 172 & 177

☐ N40GV	Cessna U206F Stationair II	U20603438		0076	0688	1 CO IO-520-F	1633			lsf DSM Inc.

MEDIC AIR, Inc. (Premier Aviation)

Reno-Tahoe Int'l, NV

659 South Rock Blvd., Reno, NV 89502, USA ☎ (702) 856-2350 Tx: none Fax: (702) 856-2354 SITA: n/a
F: 1979 n/a Head: Gary D. Brenner Net: n/a PREMIER AVIATION is the marketing name used for executive flights (same headquarters).

☐ N520CS	Twin (Aero) TurboCommander 681B (Century)	681-6061	N22EE	0071	0589	2 GA TPE331-1-151K	4264	EMS		lsf BRS Services Inc. / cvtd 681B
☐ N236CP	Beech King Air B100	BE-9	YV-36CP	0076	0296	2 GA TPE331-6-252B	5352	Executive/EMS		
☐ N811CU	Beech King Air A100	B-165	C-GTLA	0073	0998	2 PWC PT6A-28	5216	Executive/EMS		
☐ N911CU	IAI 1124 Westwind I	246	N101SV	0078	0694	2 GA TFE731-3-1G	10365	Executive/EMS		

394 registration type of aircraft cn/fn ex/ex* mfd del powered by mtow kg configuration selcal name/fln/specialitites/remarks

MEDICAL AIR RESCUE (Dale Aviation, Inc. dba) — Rapid City-Regional, SD

4025 Lacroix Court, Rapid City, SD 57701-8702, USA ☎ (605) 393-0300 Tx: none Fax: (605) 393-0306 SITA: n/a
F: 1987 ⁂ n/a Head: Jerry Dale Net: n/a

☐ N2930V	Piper PA-34-200T Seneca II	34-7970384		0079	1193	2 CO TSIO-360-EB1	2073	EMS		
☐ N414YH	Cessna 414A Chancellor III	414A0514		0080	1093	2 CO TSIO-520-NB	3062	EMS		
☐ N4680N	Cessna 414A Chancellor III	414A0070		0078	0490	2 CO TSIO-520-N	3062	EMS		
☐ N323HA	Beech King Air E90	LW-323	N323KA	0079	0997	2 PWC PT6A-28	4581	EMS		
☐ N911RL	Beech King Air 100	B-55	N4167P	0070	0591	2 PWC PT6A-28	4808	EMS		

MEDICAL AIR SERVICES ASSOCIATION – MASA — Dallas-DFW, TX & Charlotte Amalie-Cyril E. King, VI

9 Village Circle, Suite 540, Roanoke, TX 76262, USA ☎ (817) 430-4655 Tx: none Fax: (817) 491-1368 SITA: n/a
F: 1975 ⁂ n/a Head: Frank M. Halley, Jr. Net: n/a Medical-organisation conducting its flight operations in conjunction with and under the operating licence of several contract partners.

☐ N642JX	BAe 3101 Jetstream 31	642	N402AE	0084	0197	2 GA TPE331-10UR-513H	6900	EMS		
☐ N664JX	BAe 3101 Jetstream 31	664	N408AE	0085	0697	2 GA TPE331-10UR-513H	6900	EMS		

MEDICAL TRANSPORTATION (North Memorial Medical Center dba) — Minneapolis-Crystal, MN

3300 North Oakdale, Robbinsdale, MN 55422, USA ☎ (320) 520-5859 Tx: none Fax: (320) 520-7567 SITA: n/a
F: 1995 ⁂ n/a Head: Scott R. Anderson Net: n/a

☐ N1PJ	Agusta A109A II	7262	N109AW	0082	0695	2 AN 250-C20B	2600	EMS		lsf Agusta Aerospace Corp.
☐ N911D	Agusta A109C MAX	7637	N1PU	0091	0695	2 AN 250-C20R/1	2720	EMS		lsf pvt

MEDJET INTERNATIONAL, Inc. = MEJ — Birmingham-Int'l, AL

MEDJet

4900 69th Street North, Birmingham, AL 35206, USA ☎ (205) 592-4460 Tx: none Fax: (205) 592-4556 SITA: n/a
F: 1946 ⁂ n/a Head: Jeffrey T. Tolbert ICAO: MEDJET Net: n/a

☐ N28MJ	Learjet 35A	35A-224	N40RW	0079	0497	2 GA TFE731-2-2B	8301	EMS		

MED-TRANS, Corp. (Subsidiary of Executive Air Taxi, Corp.) — Tucson-St. Mary's Hospital Heliport, AZ

525 West Plata Street, Suite 400, Tucson, AZ 85705-6401, USA ☎ (520) 628-8088 Tx: none Fax: (520) 628-8092 SITA: n/a
F: 1995 ⁂ n/a Head: Dennis Rohlfs Net: n/a

☐ N2025V	Bell 206L-1 LongRanger II	45691		0082	0895	1 AN 250-C28B	1882	EMS Air Care		lsf Executive Air Taxi Corp.
☐ N3183T	Bell 206L-1 LongRanger II	45785		0083	0895	1 AN 250-C28B	1882	EMS Air Care		lsf Executive Air Taxi Corp.
☐ N911NE	Bell 206L-3 LongRanger III	51160	N160LE	0085	0995	1 AN 250-C30P	1882	EMS Air Care		lsf Executive Air Taxi Corp.
☐ N911WA	Bell 206L-1 LongRanger II	45621	N3904B	0082	0895	1 AN 250-C28B	1882	EMS Air Care		lsf Executive Air Taxi Corp.
☐ N911TM	Eurocopter (Aerosp.) AS355F1 TwinStar	5059	N5779U	0081	1195	2 AN 250-C20F	2400	EMS Air Care		lsf Executive Air Taxi Corp.

MEMPHIS JET SERVICE, L.P. (Air Path, Inc. dba) — Memphis-Int'l, TN

2540 Winchester Road, Memphis, TN 38116, USA ☎ (901) 346-7111 Tx: none Fax: (901) 346-6622 SITA: n/a
F: 1985 ⁂ n/a Head: Cecil L. Jernigan Net: http://www.memphisjet.com

☐ N32KJ	Learjet 55	55-093	N725K	0084	0396	2 GA TFE731-3AR-2B	9752			

MENARD – Flight Dept. (Flight Dept. of Menard, Inc.) — Eau Claire-Chippewa Regional, WI

4777 Menard Drive, Eau Claire, WI 54703, USA ☎ (715) 834-0457 Tx: none Fax: (715) 831-1091 SITA: n/a
F: 1978 ⁂ n/a Head: Gary McConnell Net: n/a Operates non-commercial corporate flights for its parent company only.

☐ N514M	Piper PA-31T1 Cheyenne I	31T-8104045	N150BC	0081	0190	2 PWC PT6A-11	3946	Corporate		
☐ N578M	Cessna 550 Citation II	550-0612	N380AK	0089	0697	2 PWC JT15D-4	6033	Corporate		
☐ N583M	Cessna 560 Citation V Ultra	560-0326	N5103J	0095	1295	2 PWC JT15D-5D	7394	Corporate		
☐ N521M	Beech 1900C Airliner	UB-68	N30CY	0087	0294	2 PWC PT6A-65B	7530	Corporate		
☐ N565M	Beech 1900C Airliner	UB-43	N34GT	0087	1195	2 PWC PT6A-65B	7530	Corporate		
☐ N534M	Beech 1900D Airliner	UE-333	N23235*	0098	0998	2 PWC PT6A-67D	7688	Corporate		
☐ N535M	Beech 1900D Airliner	UE-332		0098	0998	2 PWC PT6A-67D	7688	Corporate		
☐ N536M	Beech 1900D Airliner	UE-334		0098	1198	2 PWC PT6A-67D	7688	Corporate		

MENASHA AIR (Menasha Corporation dba) — North Bend-Municipal, OR

PO Box 588, North Bend, OR 97459, USA ☎ (541) 756-1193 Tx: none Fax: (541) 756-7833 SITA: n/a
F: 1975 ⁂ n/a Head: William Lansing Net: n/a

☐ N1611W	MD Helicopters MD 500E (Hughes 369E)	0319E		0089	0590	1 AN 250-C20R	1361			

MERCHANT CHARTERS (Clifford R. Merchant dba / Seasonal April-October ops only) — Anchorage-Lake Hood SPB, AK

12100 Galena Circle, Anchorage, AK 99516, USA ☎ (907) 345-4481 Tx: none Fax: (907) 345-4411 SITA: n/a
F: 1992 ⁂ 1 Head: Clifford R. Merchant Net: n/a

☐ N692F	De Havilland DHC-2 Beaver I	1407	N67692	0058	0592	1 PW R-985	2313			Floats

MERCY AIR (Mercy Air Service, Inc. dba / Subsidiary of Air Methods Corporation) — Rialto-Municipal, CA

PO Box 2532, Fontana, CA 92334-2532, USA ☎ (909) 357-9006 Tx: none Fax: (909) 357-1009 SITA: n/a
F: 1989 ⁂ n/a Head: David L. Dolstein Net: n/a

☐ N402MA	Bell 222U	47540	C-FVVB	0085	0598	2 LY LTS101-750C.1	3742	EMS		lsf General Electric Capital Corp.
☐ N403MA	Bell 222U	47516	N3180K	0084	0194	2 LY LTS101-750C.1	3742	EMS		
☐ N406MA	Bell 222B	47134	N3179K	0083	1190	2 LY LTS101-750C.1	3742	EMS		lsf FC Corp.
☐ N408MA	Bell 222B	47135	N67WT	0083	0194	2 LY LTS101-750C.1	3742	EMS		
☐ N415MA	Bell 222UT	47568	N270AM	0088	1293	2 LY LTS101-750C.1	3742	EMS		
☐ N416MA	Bell 222UT	47526	N79SP	0085	1293	2 LY LTS101-750C.1	3742	EMS		
☐ N429MA	Bell 222UT	47523	C-GVUT	0084	0194	2 LY LTS101-750C.1	3742	EMS		lsf FSBU Trustee
☐ N401MA	Bell 412	33060	N5313J	0082	0289	2 PWC PT6T-3B TwinPac	5262	EMS ClarkAirLife		based Las Vegas-Henderson, NV
☐ N586AC	Bell 412SP	36009	N402MA	0090	0191	2 PWC PT6T-3B TwinPac	5398	EMS		lst Air Methods

MERCY AIR AMBULANCE (Mercy Healthcare North dba / Division of Mercy Hospital of Redding, Inc.) — Redding-Municipal, CA

PO Box 496009, Redding, CA 96049, USA ☎ (530) 225-6290 Tx: none Fax: (530) 225-6295 SITA: n/a
F: 1982 ⁂ n/a Head: George A. Govier Net: n/a

☐ N61CU	Eurocopter (Aerosp.) AS350B AStar	1636	N351SM	0082	0697	1 TU Arriel 1B	1950	EMS		lst/opb Redding Air Service
☐ N31CU	Cessna 421C Golden Eagle II	421C0341	N37408	0077	0687	2 CO GTSIO-520-L	3379	EMS		
☐ N41CU	Cessna 421C Golden Eagle II	421C0318	N69PL	0077	0887	2 CO GTSIO-520-L	3379	EMS		
☐ N51CU	Cessna 425 Conquest I	425-0171	D-IBBP	0083	1296	2 PWC PT6A-112	3901	EMS		

MERCY FLIGHTS, Inc. — Medford-Rogue Valley Int'l, OR

914 W. Main Road, Medford, OR 97501, USA ☎ (541) 779-1019 Tx: none Fax: (541) 779-0259 SITA: n/a
F: 1949 ⁂ 66 Head: Ken Parsons Net: n/a

☐ N8181Q	Cessna 414	414-0081		0070	0786	2 CO TSIO-520-J	2880	EMS		
☐ N117MF	Beech King Air C90	LJ-779	N216KA	0078	1189	2 PWC PT6A-21	4377	EMS		

MERCY MEDICAL AIRLIFT — Manassas-Regional-HPD Field, VA & Redlands-Municipal, CA

PO Box 1940, Manassas, VA 20108-0804, USA ☎ (540) 361-1191 Tx: none Fax: (540) 361-1792 SITA: n/a
F: 1985 ⁂ n/a Head: Edward R. Borer Net: n/a Operates non-commercial non-profit, charitably financed EMS/air-ambulance flights.

☐ N7709R	Beech Bonanza 36	E-102		0068	0293	1 CO IO-520-B	1633	EMS Support		
☐ N4838A	Cessna 414A Chancellor III	414A0102		0078	0096	2 CO TSIO-520-N	3062	EMS		lsf Care Flight Air Ambulance

MERCY WINGS (Living Water Teaching International dba) — Caddo Mills-Municipal, TX

PO Box 1190, Caddo Mills, TX 75135, USA ☎ (903) 527-4160 Tx: none Fax: (903) 527-2134 SITA: n/a
F: 1993 ⁂ n/a Head: Jay Dunlap Net: n/a Non-commercial charity organisation conducting support flights in Central America for missionaries, development aid agencies and disaster relief campaigns.

☐ N421LP	Cessna 421B Golden Eagle	421B0323		0073	0996	2 CO GTSIO-520-H	3379	Utility		

MERLIN EXPRESS, Inc. = MEI (Subsidiary of Fairchild Aircraft Service, Inc. / formerly SAT-Air, Inc.) — San Antonio, TX

MERLIN EXPRESS

9623 West Terminal Drive, San Antonio, TX 78216, USA ☎ (210) 824-9421 Tx: none Fax: (210) 824-9476 SITA: n/a
F: 1983 ⁂ 150 Head: Ronald Stotz ICAO: AVALON Net: n/a

☐ N162MA	Fairchild (Swearingen) SA226TC Metro II	TC-234E		0077	0494	2 GA TPE331-10UA-511G	5670	Freighter		lsf Fairchild Aircraft Inc.
☐ N163MA	Fairchild (Swearingen) SA226TC Metro II	TC-236		0077	0394	2 GA TPE331-10UA-511G	5670	Freighter		lsf Fairchild Aircraft Inc.
☐ N5448M	Fairchild (Swearingen) SA226TC Metro II	TC-247	HZ-SN9	0076	0796	2 GA TPE331-3U-303G	5670	Freighter		lsf Leland Leasing Inc.
☐ N26863	Fairchild (Swearingen) SA227AC Metro III	AC-650B		0086	1296	2 GA TPE331-11U-612G	7257	Freighter		lsf BAMT
☐ N26906	Fairchild (Swearingen) SA227AC Metro III	AC-654B		0086	1196	2 GA TPE331-11U-612G	7257	Y19		lsf BAMT
☐ N2691W	Fairchild (Swearingen) SA227AC Metro III	AC-655B		0086	0395	2 GA TPE331-11U-612G	7257	Freighter		lsf BAMT
☐ N2692P	Fairchild (Swearingen) SA227AC Metro III	AC-658B		0086	0197	2 GA TPE331-11U-612G	7257	Freighter		lsf BAMT
☐ N2693C	Fairchild (Swearingen) SA227AC Metro III	AC-659B		0086	0197	2 GA TPE331-11U-612G	7257	Y19		lsf BAMT
☐ N27188	Fairchild (Swearingen) SA227AC Metro III	AC-708B		0088	0097	2 GA TPE331-11U-612G	7257	Y19		lsf Textron
☐ N3108B	Fairchild (Swearingen) SA227AC Metro III	AC-509	XA-TAK	0082	0796	2 GA TPE331-11U-612G	6577	Freighter		lsf GAS Wilson Inc.
☐ N3114G	Fairchild (Swearingen) SA227AC Metro III	AC-583		0084	1094	2 GA TPE331-11U-612G	6577	Freighter		lsf GAS Wilson Inc.
☐ N357AE	Fairchild (Swearingen) SA227AC Metro III	AC-667		0087	0395	2 GA TPE331-11U-611G	6577	Freighter		lsf BAMT
☐ N358AE	Fairchild (Swearingen) SA227AC Metro III	AC-668		0087	1296	2 GA TPE331-11U-611G	6577	Freighter		lsf BAMT
☐ N359AE	Fairchild (Swearingen) SA227AC Metro III	AC-674		0087	1296	2 GA TPE331-11U-611G	6577	Y19		lsf BAMT
☐ N361AE	Fairchild (Swearingen) SA227AC Metro III	AC-676		0087	1296	2 GA TPE331-11U-611G	6577	Freighter		lsf BAMT
☐ N362AE	Fairchild (Swearingen) SA227AC Metro III	AC-677		0087	0297	2 GA TPE331-11U-611G	6577	Y19		lsf BAMT
☐ N363AE	Fairchild (Swearingen) SA227AC Metro III	AC-678		0087	1196	2 GA TPE331-11U-612G	6577	Freighter		lsf BAMT
☐ N364AE	Fairchild (Swearingen) SA227AC Metro III	AC-679		0087	1098	2 GA TPE331-11U-611G	6577	Freighter		lsf BAMT

395 registration type of aircraft cn/fn ex/ex* mfd del powered by mtow kg configuration selcal name/fln/specialitites/remarks

☐	N365AE	Fairchild (Swearingen) SA227AC Metro III	AC-680		0087	0397	2 GA TPE331-11U-611G	6577	Freighter		lsf BAMT
☐	N366AE	Fairchild (Swearingen) SA227AC Metro III	AC-681B		0087	0795	2 GA TPE331-11U-611G	6577	Y19		lsf BAMT
☐	N368AE	Fairchild (Swearingen) SA227AC Metro III	AC-696		0087	0998	2 GA TPE331-11U-611G	6577	Freighter		lsf BAMT
☐	N370AE	Fairchild (Swearingen) SA227AC Metro III	AC-506	N87FM	0087	0497	2 GA TPE331-11U-611G	6577	Freighter		lsf BAMT / cvtd SA227AT
☐	N372PH	Fairchild (Swearingen) SA227AC Metro III	AC-532	N3110B	0082	0598	2 GA TPE331-11U-611G	6577	Freighter		lsf GAS Wilson Inc.
☐	N376PH	Fairchild (Swearingen) SA227AC Metro III	AC-573		0083	1097	2 GA TPE331-11U-611G	6577	Freighter		lsf GAS Wilson Inc.
☐	N378PH	Fairchild (Swearingen) SA227AC Metro III	AC-575	N3114X*	0083	0898	2 GA TPE331-11U-611G	6577	Freighter		lsf Air Metro Leasing Inc.
☐	N445MA	Fairchild (Swearingen) SA227AC Metro III	AC-687	N455AM	0087	1196	2 GA TPE331-11U-612G	6577	Freighter		lsf BAMT
☐	N446MA	Fairchild (Swearingen) SA227AC Metro III	AC-693	N456AM	0087	1296	2 GA TPE331-11U-612G	6577	Y19		lsf BAMT / sub-lst TXX
☐	N550TD	Fairchild (Swearingen) SA227AC Metro III	AC-487B	XA-SYW	0081	0796	2 GA TPE331-11U-612G	7257	Freighter		lsf IMAC Aviation/cvtd 227AT cn AT-487
☐	N671AV	Fairchild (Swearingen) SA227AC Metro III	AC-671		0087	0195	2 GA TPE331-11U-611G	6577	Freighter		lsf BAMT
☐	N673AV	Fairchild (Swearingen) SA227AC Metro III	AC-673		0087	0195	2 GA TPE331-11U-611G	6577	Freighter		lsf BAMT
☐	N682AV	Fairchild (Swearingen) SA227AC Metro III	AC-682		0087	0395	2 GA TPE331-11U-611G	6577	Freighter		lsf BAMT
☐	N730C	Fairchild (Swearingen) SA227AC Metro III	AC-697	N369AE	0087	1296	2 GA TPE331-11U-611G	6577	Y19		lsf BAMT / sub-lst TXX

MESA AIRLINES = YV / ASH (America West Express / US Airways Express) (Subs.of Mesa Air Group Inc.) **Phoenix-Int'l, AZ & Albuquerque-Int'l, NM**

410 North 44th Street, Phoenix, AZ 85008, USA ☎ (602) 685-4000 Tx: none Fax: (602) 685-4350 SITA: n/a

F: 1980 ✝✝✝ 4100 Head: Jonathan Ornstein IATA: 533 ICAO: AIR SHUTTLE Net: http://www.mesa-air.com Beside independent flights, also operates in conjunction/on behalf of AMERICA WEST as AMERICA WEST EXPRESS (mainly from Phoenix-Int'l, AZ) & US AIRWAYS as US AIRWAYS EXPRESS (mainly from Dubois-County & Reading-Regional, PA & Jacksonville-Int'l, FL. Such aircraft are operated in full such colors & titles (marked as such in fleet-list) & under AW & US-flight no's.

☐	N104YV	Beech 1900D Airliner	UE-104		0894	0894	2 PWC PT6A-67D	7688	Y19		
☐	N105YV	Beech 1900D Airliner	UE-105		0894	0894	2 PWC PT6A-67D	7688	Y19		
☐	N10675	Beech 1900D Airliner	UE-229		0896	0896	2 PWC PT6A-67D	7688	Y19		op in US Airways Express-colors
☐	N107YV	Beech 1900D Airliner	UE-107		0894	0894	2 PWC PT6A-67D	7688	Y19		op in US Airways Express-colors
☐	N109ZV	Beech 1900D Airliner	UE-109		1094	1094	2 PWC PT6A-67D	7688	Y19		op in US Airways Express-colors
☐	N110YV	Beech 1900D Airliner	UE-110		0994	0994	2 PWC PT6A-67D	7688	Y19		op in US Airways Express-colors
☐	N112ZV	Beech 1900D Airliner	UE-112		0994	0994	2 PWC PT6A-67D	7688	Y19		
☐	N113YV	Beech 1900D Airliner	UE-113		0994	1094	2 PWC PT6A-67D	7688	Y19		std ROW in United Express-colors
☐	N114YV	Beech 1900D Airliner	UE-114		0994	1094	2 PWC PT6A-67D	7688	Y19		
☐	N116YV	Beech 1900D Airliner	UE-116		0994	1094	2 PWC PT6A-67D	7688	Y19		std ROW in United Express-colors
☐	N11ZV	Beech 1900D Airliner	UE-11		0492	0492	2 PWC PT6A-67D	7688	Y19		op in US Airways Express-colors
☐	N120YV	Beech 1900D Airliner	UE-120		1194	1194	2 PWC PT6A-67D	7688	Y19		op in US Airways Express-colors
☐	N123YV	Beech 1900D Airliner	UE-123		1194	1294	2 PWC PT6A-67D	7688	Y19		op in US Airways Express-colors
☐	N124YV	Beech 1900D Airliner	UE-124		1194	1294	2 PWC PT6A-67D	7688	Y19		op in US Airways Express-colors
☐	N125YV	Beech 1900D Airliner	UE-125		1294	1294	2 PWC PT6A-67D	7688	Y19		op in US Airways Express-colors
☐	N126YV	Beech 1900D Airliner	UE-126		1294	1294	2 PWC PT6A-67D	7688	Y19		op in US Airways Express-colors
☐	N127ZV	Beech 1900D Airliner	UE-127		1294	1294	2 PWC PT6A-67D	7688	Y19		op in US Airways Express-colors
☐	N131YV	Beech 1900D Airliner	UE-131		0195	0195	2 PWC PT6A-67D	7688	Y19		op in US Airways Express-colors
☐	N132YV	Beech 1900D Airliner	UE-132		0195	0195	2 PWC PT6A-67D	7688	Y19		op in America West Express-colors
☐	N133YV	Beech 1900D Airliner	UE-133		0195	0195	2 PWC PT6A-67D	7688	Y19		op in US Airways Express-colors
☐	N135YV	Beech 1900D Airliner	UE-135		0295	0295	2 PWC PT6A-67D	7688	Y19		op in US Airways Express-colors
☐	N138YV	Beech 1900D Airliner	UE-138		0295	0295	2 PWC PT6A-67D	7688	Y19		op in US Airways Express-colors
☐	N139ZV	Beech 1900D Airliner	UE-139		0395	0395	2 PWC PT6A-67D	7688	Y19		lst AMW
☐	N13ZV	Beech 1900D Airliner	UE-13		0592	0692	2 PWC PT6A-67D	7688	Y19		op in US Airways Express-colors
☐	N140ZV	Beech 1900D Airliner	UE-140		0395	0395	2 PWC PT6A-67D	7688	Y19		op in US Airways Express-colors
☐	N142ZV	Beech 1900D Airliner	UE-142		0395	0395	2 PWC PT6A-67D	7688	Y19		op in US Airways Express-colors
☐	N143YV	Beech 1900D Airliner	UE-143		0395	0395	2 PWC PT6A-67D	7688	Y19		op in US Airways Express-colors
☐	N144ZV	Beech 1900D Airliner	UE-144		0395	0395	2 PWC PT6A-67D	7688	Y19		op in US Airways Express-colors
☐	N146ZV	Beech 1900D Airliner	UE-146		0495	0595	2 PWC PT6A-67D	7688	Y19		
☐	N14YV	Beech 1900D Airliner	UE-14		0692	0692	2 PWC PT6A-67D	7688	Y19		op in US Airways Express-colors
☐	N155ZV	Beech 1900D Airliner	UE-155		0695	0695	2 PWC PT6A-67D	7688	Y19		op in US Airways Express-colors
☐	N159YV	Beech 1900D Airliner	UE-159		0695	0695	2 PWC PT6A-67D	7688	Y19		op in US Airways Express-colors
☐	N15YV	Beech 1900D Airliner	UE-15		0692	0692	2 PWC PT6A-67D	7688	Y19		op in US Airways Express-colors
☐	N161YV	Beech 1900D Airliner	UE-161		0795	0795	2 PWC PT6A-67D	7688	Y19		op in US Airways Express-colors
☐	N162ZV	Beech 1900D Airliner	UE-162		0895	0895	2 PWC PT6A-67D	7688	Y19		op in US Airways Express-colors
☐	N163YV	Beech 1900D Airliner	UE-163		0895	0895	2 PWC PT6A-67D	7688	Y19		lst AMW
☐	N165YV	Beech 1900D Airliner	UE-165		0895	0895	2 PWC PT6A-67D	7688	Y19		op in US Airways Express-colors
☐	N166YV	Beech 1900D Airliner	UE-166		0895	0895	2 PWC PT6A-67D	7688	Y19		lst AMW
☐	N167YV	Beech 1900D Airliner	UE-167		0895	0895	2 PWC PT6A-67D	7688	Y19		op in US Airways Express-colors
☐	N171ZV	Beech 1900D Airliner	UE-171		1095	1095	2 PWC PT6A-67D	7688	Y19		lst AMW
☐	N173YV	Beech 1900D Airliner	UE-173		0995	0995	2 PWC PT6A-67D	7688	Y19		op in US Airways Express-colors
☐	N174YV	Beech 1900D Airliner	UE-174		1095	1095	2 PWC PT6A-67D	7688	Y19		lst AMW
☐	N176YV	Beech 1900D Airliner	UE-176		1095	1095	2 PWC PT6A-67D	7688	Y19		lst AMW
☐	N178YV	Beech 1900D Airliner	UE-178		1195	1195	2 PWC PT6A-67D	7688	Y19		lst AMW
☐	N17YV	Beech 1900D Airliner	UE-17		0792	0792	2 PWC PT6A-67D	7688	Y19		op in US Airways Express-colors
☐	N182YV	Beech 1900D Airliner	UE-182		1195	1195	2 PWC PT6A-67D	7688	Y19		lst AMW
☐	N18YV	Beech 1900D Airliner	UE-18		0892	0892	2 PWC PT6A-67D	7688	Y19		lst AMW
☐	N190YV	Beech 1900D Airliner	UE-190		1295	1295	2 PWC PT6A-67D	7688	Y19		op in US Airways Express-colors
☐	N218YV	Beech 1900D Airliner	UE-218		0696	0696	2 PWC PT6A-67D	7688	Y19		op in US Airways Express-colors
☐	N21YV	Beech 1900D Airliner	UE-21		0992	0992	2 PWC PT6A-67D	7688	Y19		op in US Airways Express-colors
☐	N224YV	Beech 1900D Airliner	UE-224		0696	0696	2 PWC PT6A-67D	7688	Y19		op in US Airways Express-colors
☐	N231YV	Beech 1900D Airliner	UE-231		0896	0896	2 PWC PT6A-67D	7688	Y19		lst AMW
☐	N233YV	Beech 1900D Airliner	UE-233		0896	0896	2 PWC PT6A-67D	7688	Y19		lst AMW
☐	N237YV	Beech 1900D Airliner	UE-237		0996	0996	2 PWC PT6A-67D	7688	Y19		lst AMW
☐	N23YV	Beech 1900D Airliner	UE-23		0992	1092	2 PWC PT6A-67D	7688	Y19		op in US Airways Express-colors
☐	N242YV	Beech 1900D Airliner	UE-242		0996	0996	2 PWC PT6A-67D	7688	Y19		lst AMW
☐	N244YV	Beech 1900D Airliner	UE-244		1096	1096	2 PWC PT6A-67D	7688	Y19		lst AMW
☐	N249YV	Beech 1900D Airliner	UE-249		1196	1196	2 PWC PT6A-67D	7688	Y19		lst GLA
☐	N26YV	Beech 1900D Airliner	UE-26		1092	1192	2 PWC PT6A-67D	7688	Y19		lst GLA
☐	N28YV	Beech 1900D Airliner	UE-28		1192	1192	2 PWC PT6A-67D	7688	Y19		op in US Airways Express-colors
☐	N29YV	Beech 1900D Airliner	UE-29		1192	1192	2 PWC PT6A-67D	7688	Y19		std ROW in United Express-colors
☐	N2YV	Beech 1900D Airliner	UE-2		0891	0891	2 PWC PT6A-67D	7688	Y19		
☐	N3199Q	Beech 1900D Airliner	UE-213		0896	0896	2 PWC PT6A-67D	7688	Y19		op in US Airways Express-colors
☐	N31YV	Beech 1900D Airliner	UE-31		1292	1292	2 PWC PT6A-67D	7688	Y19		std ROW in United Express-colors
☐	N33YV	Beech 1900D Airliner	UE-33		1292	0193	2 PWC PT6A-67D	7688	Y19		
☐	N35YV	Beech 1900D Airliner	UE-35		0293	0293	2 PWC PT6A-67D	7688	Y19		
☐	N37YV	Beech 1900D Airliner	UE-37		0293	0293	2 PWC PT6A-67D	7688	Y19		
☐	N39ZV	Beech 1900D Airliner	UE-39		0393	0493	2 PWC PT6A-67D	7688	Y19		op in US Airways Express-colors
☐	N3YV	Beech 1900D Airliner	UE-3		1291	1291	2 PWC PT6A-67D	7688	Y19		
☐	N42YV	Beech 1900D Airliner	UE-42		0493	0493	2 PWC PT6A-67D	7688	Y19		
☐	N46YV	Beech 1900D Airliner	UE-46		0593	0593	2 PWC PT6A-67D	7688	Y19		op in US Airways Express-colors
☐	N48YV	Beech 1900D Airliner	UE-48		0593	0693	2 PWC PT6A-67D	7688	Y19		
☐	N4ZV	Beech 1900D Airliner	UE-4	N304YV	1291	1291	2 PWC PT6A-67D	7688	Y19		op in US Airways Express-colors
☐	N51YV	Beech 1900D Airliner	UE-51		0793	0793	2 PWC PT6A-67D	7688	Y19		
☐	N57ZV	Beech 1900D Airliner	UE-57		0893	0893	2 PWC PT6A-67D	7688	Y19		op in US Airways Express-colors
☐	N59YV	Beech 1900D Airliner	UE-59		0993	0993	2 PWC PT6A-67D	7688	Y19		op in US Airways Express-colors
☐	N5YV	Beech 1900D Airliner	UE-5		0192	0192	2 PWC PT6A-67D	7688	Y19		op in US Airways Express-colors
☐	N62ZV	Beech 1900D Airliner	UE-62		0993	0993	2 PWC PT6A-67D	7688	Y19		op in US Airways Express-colors
☐	N64YV	Beech 1900D Airliner	UE-64		0993	1093	2 PWC PT6A-67D	7688	Y19		op in US Airways Express-colors
☐	N65YV	Beech 1900D Airliner	UE-65		1093	1093	2 PWC PT6A-67D	7688	Y19		op in US Airways Express-colors
☐	N67YV	Beech 1900D Airliner	UE-67		1093	1093	2 PWC PT6A-67D	7688	Y19		op in US Airways Express-colors
☐	N68ZV	Beech 1900D Airliner	UE-68		1093	1193	2 PWC PT6A-67D	7688	Y19		op in US Airways Express-colors
☐	N6YV	Beech 1900D Airliner	UE-6		1292	1292	2 PWC PT6A-67D	7688	Y19		op in US Airways Express-colors
☐	N70ZV	Beech 1900D Airliner	UE-70		1093	1193	2 PWC PT6A-67D	7688	Y19		op in US Airways Express-colors
☐	N74YV	Beech 1900D Airliner	UE-74		1293	1293	2 PWC PT6A-67D	7688	Y19		std ROW in United Express-colors
☐	N75ZV	Beech 1900D Airliner	UE-75		1293	1293	2 PWC PT6A-67D	7688	Y19		std ROW in United Express-colors
☐	N76ZV	Beech 1900D Airliner	UE-76		1293	1293	2 PWC PT6A-67D	7688	Y19		op in America West Express-colors
☐	N78YV	Beech 1900D Airliner	UE-78		1293	1293	2 PWC PT6A-67D	7688	Y19		op in America West Express-colors
☐	N82YV	Beech 1900D Airliner	UE-82		0294	0294	2 PWC PT6A-67D	7688	Y19		op in America West Express-colors
☐	N86YV	Beech 1900D Airliner	UE-86		0394	0394	2 PWC PT6A-67D	7688	Y19		op in America West Express-colors
☐	N93ZV	Beech 1900D Airliner	UE-93		0494	0594	2 PWC PT6A-67D	7688	Y19		op in America West Express-colors
☐	N95YV	Beech 1900D Airliner	UE-95		0594	0594	2 PWC PT6A-67D	7688	Y19		
☐	N98YV	Beech 1900D Airliner	UE-98		0594	0594	2 PWC PT6A-67D	7688	Y19		op in US Airways Express-colors
☐	N99YV	Beech 1900D Airliner	UE-99		0694	0694	2 PWC PT6A-67D	7688	Y19		
☐	N9YV	Beech 1900D Airliner	UE-9		0392	0392	2 PWC PT6A-67D	7688	Y19		op in US Airways Express-colors
☐	N434YV	De Havilland DHC-8-202 Dash 8	434		0596	0596	2 PWC PW123D	16465	Y37	PR-LQ	op in America West Express-colors
☐	N436YV	De Havilland DHC-8-202 Dash 8	436		0696	0696	2 PWC PW123D	16465	Y37	QR-MP	op in America West Express-colors
☐	N437YV	De Havilland DHC-8-202 Dash 8	437		0696	0696	2 PWC PW123D	16465	Y37	QR-MS	op in America West Express-colors
☐	N444YV	De Havilland DHC-8-202 Dash 8Q	444	C-GFRP*	0996	0996	2 PWC PW123D	16465	Y37	BD-FR	op in America West Express-colors
☐	N445YV	De Havilland DHC-8-202 Dash 8Q	445	C-GFEN*	0896	0896	2 PWC PW123D	16465	Y37	AE-BS	op in America West Express-colors

396 registration type of aircraft cn/fn ex/ex* mfd del powered by mtow kg configuration selcal name/fln/specialitites/remarks

☐ N446YV	De Havilland DHC-8-202 Dash 8Q	446	C-GEOA*	1096	1096	2 PWC PW123D	16465	Y37	BE-MR	op in America West Express-colors
☐ N447YV	De Havilland DHC-8-202 Dash 8Q	447	C-GFYI*	1096	1096	2 PWC PW123D	16465	Y37	CQ-EG	op in America West Express-colors
☐ N448YV	De Havilland DHC-8-202 Dash 8Q	448	C-GLOT*	1296	1296	2 PWC PW123D	16465	Y37	CQ-EH	op in America West Express-colors
☐ N449YV	De Havilland DHC-8-202 Dash 8Q	449	C-GFHZ*	1296	1296	2 PWC PW123D	16465	Y37	CQ-EJ	op in America West Express-colors
☐ N454YV	De Havilland DHC-8-202 Dash 8Q	454		0197	0197	2 PWC PW123D	16465	Y37	PR-EJ	op in America West Express-colors
☐ N455YV	De Havilland DHC-8-202 Dash 8Q	455		0197	0197	2 PWC PW123D	16465	Y37	HS-BJ	op in America West Express-colors
☐ N456YV	De Havilland DHC-8-202 Dash 8Q	456	C-GFOD*	0397	0397	2 PWC PW123D	16465	Y37	LR-FP	op in America West Express-colors
☐ N17156	Canadair Regional Jet 200ER (CL-600-2B19)	7156	C-FZSC*	0397	0397	2 GE CF34-3B1	23133	Y50	HS-AC	op in US Airways Express-colors
☐ N17175	Canadair Regional Jet 200ER (CL-600-2B19)	7175	LV-WXB	0097	0198	2 GE CF34-3B1	23133	Y50		op in US Airways Express-colors
☐ N17217	Canadair Regional Jet 200ER (CL-600-2B19)	7217		0098	0198	2 GE CF34-3B1	23133	Y50		op in US Airways Express-colors
☐ N17231	Canadair Regional Jet 200ER (CL-600-2B19)	7231		0098	0498	2 GE CF34-3B1	23133	Y50		
☐ N17275	Canadair Regional Jet 200ER (CL-600-2B19)	7275	C-FMOI*	0098	1198	2 GE CF34-3B1	23133	Y50		op in America West Express-colors
☐ N27172	Canadair Regional Jet 200ER (CL-600-2B19)	7172		0097	0497	2 GE CF34-3B1	23133	Y50	HS-AD	op in US Airways Express-colors
☐ N27173	Canadair Regional Jet 200ER (CL-600-2B19)	7173		0097	0497	2 GE CF34-3B1	23133	Y50	HS-AE	
☐ N27185	Canadair Regional Jet 200ER (CL-600-2B19)	7185		0097	0797	2 GE CF34-3B1	23133	Y50		op in America West Express-colors
☐ N27191	Canadair Regional Jet 200ER (CL-600-2B19)	7191		0097	0997	2 GE CF34-3B1	23133	Y50		op in US Airways Express-colors
☐ N37178	Canadair Regional Jet 200ER (CL-600-2B19)	7178	C-GAVO*	0097	0697	2 GE CF34-3B1	23133	Y50		op in America West Express-colors
☐ N37208	Canadair Regional Jet 200ER (CL-600-2B19)	7208	C-FMNY*	0097	1297	2 GE CF34-3B1	23133	Y50		op in US Airways Express-colors
☐ N37218	Canadair Regional Jet 200ER (CL-600-2B19)	7218		0098	0198	2 GE CF34-3B1	23133	Y50		op in US Airways Express-colors
☐ N37228	Canadair Regional Jet 200ER (CL-600-2B19)	7228	C-FMLF*	0098	0398	2 GE CF34-3B1	23133	Y50		op in US Airways Express-colors
☐ N47202	Canadair Regional Jet 200ER (CL-600-2B19)	7202		0097	1297	2 GE CF34-3B1	23133	Y50		op in US Airways Express-colors
☐ N47239	Canadair Regional Jet 200ER (CL-600-2B19)	7239		0098	0598	2 GE CF34-3B1	23133	Y50		
☐ N7264V	Canadair Regional Jet 200ER (CL-600-2B19)	7264		0098	1098	2 GE CF34-3B1	23133	Y50		op in America West Express-colors
☐ N7291Z	Canadair Regional Jet 200ER (CL-600-2B19)	7291		0099	0199	2 GE CF34-3B1	23133	Y50		
☐ N77181	Canadair Regional Jet 200ER (CL-600-2B19)	7181		0097	0797	2 GE CF34-3B1	23133	Y50		op in America West Express-colors
☐ N77195	Canadair Regional Jet 200ER (CL-600-2B19)	7195		0097	1297	2 GE CF34-3B1	23133	Y50		
☐ N77260	Canadair Regional Jet 200ER (CL-600-2B19)	7260	C-FMLQ*	0098	0998	2 GE CF34-3B1	23133	Y50		op in America West Express-colors
☐ N77278	Canadair Regional Jet 200ER (CL-600-2B19)	7278	C-FMMN*	0098	1298	2 GE CF34-3B1	23133	Y50		op in America West Express-colors
☐ N77286	Canadair Regional Jet 200ER (CL-600-2B19)	7286		0099	0199	2 GE CF34-3B1	23133	Y50		
☐ N	Canadair Regional Jet 200ER (CL-600-2B19)					2 GE CF34-3B1	23133	Y50		oo-delivery 0099
☐ N	Canadair Regional Jet 200ER (CL-600-2B19)					2 GE CF34-3B1	23133	Y50		oo-delivery 0099
☐ N	Canadair Regional Jet 200ER (CL-600-2B19)					2 GE CF34-3B1	23133	Y50		oo-delivery 0099
☐ N	Canadair Regional Jet 200ER (CL-600-2B19)					2 GE CF34-3B1	23133	Y50		oo-delivery 0099
☐ N	Canadair Regional Jet 200ER (CL-600-2B19)					2 GE CF34-3B1	23133	Y50		oo-delivery 0099
☐ N	Canadair Regional Jet 200ER (CL-600-2B19)					2 GE CF34-3B1	23133	Y50		oo-delivery 0099
☐ N	Canadair Regional Jet 200ER (CL-600-2B19)					2 GE CF34-3B1	23133	Y50		oo-delivery 0099
☐ N	Canadair Regional Jet 200ER (CL-600-2B19)					2 GE CF34-3B1	23133	Y50		oo-delivery 0099
☐ N	Canadair Regional Jet 200ER (CL-600-2B19)					2 GE CF34-3B1	23133	Y50		oo-delivery 0099
☐ N	Canadair Regional Jet 200ER (CL-600-2B19)					2 GE CF34-3B1	23133	Y50		oo-delivery 0099

MESABA AIRLINES = XJ / MES (Northwest Airlink & Jet Airlink) (Mesaba Aviation, Inc. dba / Subsidiary of Mesaba Holdings, Inc.) **Minneapolis-St. Paul Int'l, MN**

7501 26th Avenue South, Minneapolis, MN 55450, USA ☎ (612) 726-5151 Tx: 5101002441 mesaba ai Fax: (612) 726-5151 SITA: n/a
F: 1944 ✱✱✱ 1700 Head: Carl Pohlad IATA: 582 ICAO: MESABA Net: http://www.mesaba.com

Aircraft are operated as NORTHWEST AIRLINK (Saab 340) and NORTHWEST JET AIRLINK (Avro RJ85), in full such colors & both titles, a commuter system to provide feeder connection at major NW hubs, using NW-flight numbers.

☐ N102XJ	Saab SF340A	340A-102	N102AE	0087	0696	2 GE CT7-5A2	12700	Y34		op in Northwest Airlink-colors
☐ N103XJ	Saab SF340A	340A-103	N103AE	0087	0796	2 GE CT7-5A2	12700	Y34		op in Northwest Airlink-colors
☐ N106XJ	Saab SF340A	340A-106	N106PX	0087	0498	2 GE CT7-5A2	12700	Y33		op in Northwest Airlink-colors
☐ N107XJ	Saab SF340A	340A-107	N107AE	0087	0896	2 GE CT7-5A2	12700	Y34		op in Northwest Airlink-colors
☐ N109XJ	Saab SF340A	340A-109	N109AE	0087	0996	2 GE CT7-5A2	12700	Y34		op in Northwest Airlink-colors
☐ N110XJ	Saab SF340A	340A-110	N110MQ	0087	0596	2 GE CT7-5A2	12700	Y34		op in Northwest Airlink-colors
☐ N112XJ	Saab SF340A	340A-112	N112AE	0087	0896	2 GE CT7-5A2	12700	Y34		op in Northwest Airlink-colors
☐ N114XJ	Saab SF340A	340A-114	N114SB	0087	1096	2 GE CT7-5A2	12700	Y34		op in Northwest Airlink-colors
☐ N115XJ	Saab SF340A	340A-115	N115SB	0088	0297	2 GE CT7-5A2	12700	Y34		op in Northwest Airlink-colors
☐ N119XJ	Saab SF340A	340A-119	N119AE	0088	0796	2 GE CT7-5A2	12700	Y34		op in Northwest Airlink-colors
☐ N142XJ	Saab SF340A	340A-142	N341PX	0089	0498	2 GE CT7-5A2	12700	Y33		op in Northwest Airlink-colors
☐ N233CH	Saab 340B	340B-233	SE-G33*	0091	0498	2 GE CT7-9B	12927	Y34		op in Northwest Airlink-colors
☐ N252CH	Saab 340B	340B-252	SE-G52*	0091	0498	2 GE CT7-9B	12927	Y34		op in Northwest Airlink-colors
☐ N27XJ	Saab SF340A	340A-027	N320PX	0085	1097	2 GE CT7-5A2	12700	Y33		op in Northwest Airlink-colors
☐ N31XJ	Saab SF340A	340A-031	N321PX	0085	0398	2 GE CT7-5A2	12700	Y33		op in Northwest Airlink-colors
☐ N402XJ	Saab 340B (Plus)	340B-402	SE-B02*	0096	1096	2 GE CT7-9B	13155	Y34		op in Northwest Airlink-colors
☐ N403XJ	Saab 340B (Plus)	340B-403	SE-B03*	0096	1196	2 GE CT7-9B	13155	Y34		op in Northwest Airlink-colors
☐ N404XJ	Saab 340B (Plus)	340B-404	SE-B04*	0096	1096	2 GE CT7-9B	13155	Y34		op in Northwest Airlink-colors
☐ N406XJ	Saab 340B (Plus)	340B-406	SE-B06*	0096	1196	2 GE CT7-9B	13155	Y34		op in Northwest Airlink-colors
☐ N407XJ	Saab 340B (Plus)	340B-407	SE-B07*	0096	1196	2 GE CT7-9B	13155	Y34		op in Northwest Airlink-colors
☐ N408XJ	Saab 340B (Plus)	340B-408	SE-B08*	0096	1196	2 GE CT7-9B	13155	Y34		op in Northwest Airlink-colors
☐ N410XJ	Saab 340B (Plus)	340B-410	SE-B10*	0097	0297	2 GE CT7-9B	13155	Y34		op in Northwest Airlink-colors
☐ N411XJ	Saab 340B (Plus)	340B-411	SE-B11*	0097	0297	2 GE CT7-9B	13155	Y34		op in Northwest Airlink-colors
☐ N412XJ	Saab 340B (Plus)	340B-412	SE-B12*	0097	0397	2 GE CT7-9B	13155	Y34		op in Northwest Airlink-colors
☐ N413XJ	Saab 340B (Plus)	340B-413	SE-B13*	0097	0397	2 GE CT7-9B	13155	Y34		op in Northwest Airlink-colors
☐ N414XJ	Saab 340B (Plus)	340B-414	SE-B14*	0097	0397	2 GE CT7-9B	13155	Y34		op in Northwest Airlink-colors
☐ N415XJ	Saab 340B (Plus)	340B-415	SE-B15*	0097	0497	2 GE CT7-9B	13155	Y34		op in Northwest Airlink-colors
☐ N416XJ	Saab 340B (Plus)	340B-416	SE-B16*	0097	0797	2 GE CT7-9B	13155	Y34		op in Northwest Airlink-colors
☐ N417XJ	Saab 340B (Plus)	340B-417	SE-B17*	0097	0597	2 GE CT7-9B	13155	Y34		op in Northwest Airlink-colors
☐ N418XJ	Saab 340B (Plus)	340B-418	SE-B18*	0097	0697	2 GE CT7-9B	13155	Y34		op in Northwest Airlink-colors
☐ N41XJ	Saab SF340A	340A-041	N322PX	0085	0298	2 GE CT7-5A2	12700	Y33		op in Northwest Airlink-colors
☐ N420XJ	Saab 340B (Plus)	340B-420	SE-B20*	0097	0697	2 GE CT7-9B	13155	Y34		op in Northwest Airlink-colors
☐ N421XJ	Saab 340B (Plus)	340B-421	SE-B21*	0097	0697	2 GE CT7-9B	13155	Y34		op in Northwest Airlink-colors
☐ N422XJ	Saab 340B (Plus)	340B-422	SE-B22*	0097	0897	2 GE CT7-9B	13155	Y34		op in Northwest Airlink-colors
☐ N423XJ	Saab 340B (Plus)	340B-423	SE-B23*	0097	0897	2 GE CT7-9B	13155	Y34		op in Northwest Airlink-colors
☐ N424XJ	Saab 340B (Plus)	340B-424	SE-B24*	0097	0997	2 GE CT7-9B	13155	Y34		op in Northwest Airlink-colors
☐ N425XJ	Saab 340B (Plus)	340B-425	SE-B25*	0097	0997	2 GE CT7-9B	13155	Y34		op in Northwest Airlink-colors
☐ N426XJ	Saab 340B (Plus)	340B-426	SE-B26*	0097	0997	2 GE CT7-9B	13155	Y34		op in Northwest Airlink-colors
☐ N427XJ	Saab 340B (Plus)	340B-427	SE-B27*	0097	1097	2 GE CT7-9B	13155	Y34		op in Northwest Airlink-colors
☐ N428XJ	Saab 340B (Plus)	340B-428	SE-B28*	0097	1197	2 GE CT7-9B	13155	Y34		op in Northwest Airlink-colors
☐ N429XJ	Saab 340B (Plus)	340B-429	SE-B29*	0097	1197	2 GE CT7-9B	13155	Y34		op in Northwest Airlink-colors
☐ N430XJ	Saab 340B (Plus)	340B-430	SE-B30*	0097	1297	2 GE CT7-9B	13155	Y34		op in Northwest Airlink-colors
☐ N433XJ	Saab 340B (Plus)	340B-433	SE-B33*	0097	1297	2 GE CT7-9B	13155	Y34		op in Northwest Airlink-colors
☐ N434XJ	Saab 340B (Plus)	340B-434	SE-B34*	0098	0198	2 GE CT7-9B	13155	Y34		op in Northwest Airlink-colors
☐ N435XJ	Saab 340B (Plus)	340B-435	SE-B35*	0098	0198	2 GE CT7-9B	13155	Y34		op in Northwest Airlink-colors
☐ N436XJ	Saab 340B (Plus)	340B-436	SE-B36*	0098	0298	2 GE CT7-9B	13155	Y34		op in Northwest Airlink-colors
☐ N437XJ	Saab 340B (Plus)	340B-437	SE-B37*	0098	0398	2 GE CT7-9B	13155	Y34		op in Northwest Airlink-colors
☐ N438XJ	Saab 340B (Plus)	340B-438	SE-B38*	0098	0498	2 GE CT7-9B	13155	Y34		op in Northwest Airlink-colors
☐ N439XJ	Saab 340B (Plus)	340B-439	SE-B39*	0098	0498	2 GE CT7-9B	13155	Y34		op in Northwest Airlink-colors
☐ N441XJ	Saab 340B (Plus)	340B-441	SE-B41*	0098	0698	2 GE CT7-9B	13155	Y34		op in Northwest/special anniversary-cs
☐ N442XJ	Saab 340B (Plus)	340B-442	SE-B42*	0098	0698	2 GE CT7-9B	13155	Y34		op in Northwest Airlink-colors
☐ N443XJ	Saab 340B (Plus)	340B-443	SE-B43*	0098	0698	2 GE CT7-9B	13155	Y34		op in Northwest Airlink-colors
☐ N444XJ	Saab 340B (Plus)	340B-444	SE-B44*	0098	0898	2 GE CT7-9B	13155	Y34		op in Northwest Airlink-colors
☐ N445XJ	Saab 340B (Plus)	340B-445	SE-B45*	0098	0898	2 GE CT7-9B	13155	Y34		op in Northwest Airlink-colors
☐ N446XJ	Saab 340B (Plus)	340B-446	SE-B46*	0098	0898	2 GE CT7-9B	13155	Y34		op in Northwest Airlink-colors
☐ N447XJ	Saab 340B (Plus)	340B-447	SE-B47*	0098	0998	2 GE CT7-9B	13155	Y34		op in Northwest Airlink-colors
☐ N448XJ	Saab 340B (Plus)	340B-448	SE-B48*	0098	0998	2 GE CT7-9B	13155	Y34		op in Northwest Airlink-colors
☐ N449XJ	Saab 340B (Plus)	340B-449	SE-B49*	0098	0998	2 GE CT7-9B	13155	Y34		op in Northwest Airlink-colors
☐ N450XJ	Saab 340B (Plus)	340B-450	SE-B50*	0098	1098	2 GE CT7-9B	13155	Y34		op in Northwest Airlink-colors
☐ N451XJ	Saab 340B (Plus)	340B-451	SE-B51*	0098	0998	2 GE CT7-9B	13155	Y34		op in Northwest Airlink-colors
☐ N452XJ	Saab 340B (Plus)	340B-452	SE-B52*	0098	1098	2 GE CT7-9B	13155	Y34		op in Northwest Airlink-colors
☐ N453XJ	Saab 340B (Plus)	340B-453	SE-B53*	0098	1098	2 GE CT7-9B	13155	Y34		op in Northwest Airlink-colors
☐ N454XJ	Saab 340B (Plus)	340B-454	SE-B54*	0098	1198	2 GE CT7-9B	13155	Y34		op in Northwest Airlink-colors
☐ N456XJ	Saab 340B (Plus)	340B-456	SE-B56*	0098	1198	2 GE CT7-9B	13155	Y34		op in Northwest Airlink-colors
☐ N457XJ	Saab 340B (Plus)	340B-457	SE-B57*	0098	1298	2 GE CT7-9B	13155	Y34		op in Northwest Airlink-colors
☐ N46XJ	Saab SF340A	340A-046	N323PX	0086	0897	2 GE CT7-5A2	12700	Y33		op in Northwest Airlink-colors
☐ N48XJ	Saab SF340A	340A-048	N324PX	0086	1097	2 GE CT7-5A2	12700	Y33		op in Northwest Airlink-colors
☐ N586MA	Saab 340B	340B-165	SE-F65*	0089	0697	2 GE CT7-9B	13155	Y34		op in Northwest Airlink-colors
☐ N590MA	Saab 340B	340B-181	SE-F81*	0090	0697	2 GE CT7-9B	13155	Y34		op in Northwest Airlink-colors
☐ N592MA	Saab 340B	340B-199	SE-F99*	0090	0597	2 GE CT7-9B	13155	Y34		op in Northwest Airlink-colors
☐ N595MA	Saab 340B	340B-216	SE-G16*	0090	0597	2 GE CT7-9B	13155	Y34		op in Northwest Airlink-colors
☐ N68XJ	Saab SF340A	340A-068	N328PX	0086	1297	2 GE CT7-5A2	12700	Y33		op in Northwest Airlink-colors
☐ N76XJ	Saab SF340A	340A-076	N329PX	0086	0997	2 GE CT7-5A2	12700	Y33		op in Northwest Airlink-colors
☐ N79XJ	Saab SF340A	340A-079	N340PX	0087	0298	2 GE CT7-5A2	12700	Y33		op in Northwest Airlink-colors
☐ N89XJ	Saab SF340A	340A-089	N89MQ	0087	0996	2 GE CT7-5A2	12700	Y34		op in Northwest Airlink-colors
☐ N98XJ	Saab SF340A	340A-098	N98MQ	0087	0796	2 GE CT7-5A2	12700	Y34		op in Northwest Airlink-colors
☐ N991XJ	Saab SF340A	340A-091	N91MQ	0087	1296	2 GE CT7-5A2	12700	Y34		op in Northwest Airlink-colors

397 registration type of aircraft cn/fn ex/ex* mfd del powered by mtow kg configuration selcal name/fln/specialitites/remarks

registration	type of aircraft	cn/fn	ex/ex*	mfd	del	powered by	mtow kg	configuration	selcal	name/fln/specialitites/remarks
N99XJ	Saab SF340A	340A-099	N99RZ	0087	0596	2 GE CT7-5A2	12700	Y34		op in Northwest Airlink-colors
N9CJ	Saab 340B	340B-224	N224TH*	0091	0598	2 GE CT7-9B	12927	Y34		op in Northwest Airlink-colors
N501XJ	Avro RJ85A (Avro 146-RJ85A)	E2208	G-6-208*	0092	0497	4 LY LF507-1F	43998	CY69		cvtd BAe 146-200/op in NW Jet Airl.-cs
N502XJ	Avro RJ85A (Avro 146-RJ85A)	E2307	G-6-307*	0097	0597	4 LY LF507-1F	43998	CY69		op in Northwest Jet Airlink-colors
N503XJ	Avro RJ85A (Avro 146-RJ85A)	E2310	G-6-310*	0097	0697	4 LY LF507-1F	43998	CY69		op in Northwest Jet Airlink-colors
N504XJ	Avro RJ85A (Avro 146-RJ85A)	E2311	G-4-311*	0097	0797	4 LY LF507-1F	43998	CY69		op in Northwest Jet Airlink-colors
N505XJ	Avro RJ85A (Avro 146-RJ85A)	E2314	G-6-313*	0097	0897	4 LY LF507-1F	43998	CY69		op in Northwest Jet Airlink-colors
N506XJ	Avro RJ85A (Avro 146-RJ85A)	E2314	G-6-314*	0097	0997	4 LY LF507-1F	43998	CY69		op in Northwest Jet Airlink-colors
N507XJ	Avro RJ85A (Avro 146-RJ85A)	E2316	G-6-316*	0097	1097	4 LY LF507-1F	43998	CY69		op in Northwest Jet Airlink-colors
N508XJ	Avro RJ85A (Avro 146-RJ85A)	E2318	G-6-318*	0097	1297	4 LY LF507-1F	43998	CY69		op in Northwest Jet Airlink-colors
N509XJ	Avro RJ85A (Avro 146-RJ85A)	E2321	G-6-321*	0098	0198	4 LY LF507-1F	43998	CY69		op in Northwest Jet Airlink-colors
N510XJ	Avro RJ85A (Avro 146-RJ85A)	E2323	G-6-323*	0098	0398	4 LY LF507-1F	43998	CY69		op in Northwest Jet Airlink-colors
N511XJ	Avro RJ85A (Avro 146-RJ85A)	E2325	G-6-325*	0098	0498	4 LY LF507-1F	43998	CY69		op in Northwest Jet Airlink-colors
N512XJ	Avro RJ85A (Avro 146-RJ85A)	E2326	G-6-326*	0098	0498	4 LY LF507-1F	43998	CY69		op in Northwest Jet Airlink-colors
N513XJ	Avro RJ85A (Avro 146-RJ85A)	E2329	G-6-329*	0098	0698	4 LY LF507-1F	43998	CY69		op in Northwest Jet Airlink-colors
N514XJ	Avro RJ85A (Avro 146-RJ85A)	E2330	G-6-330*	0098	0698	4 LY LF507-1F	43998	CY69		op in Northwest Jet Airlink-colors
N515XJ	Avro RJ85A (Avro 146-RJ85A)	E2333	G-6-333*	0098	0898	4 LY LF507-1F	43998	CY69		op in Northwest Jet Airlink-colors
N516XJ	Avro RJ85A (Avro 146-RJ85A)	E2334	G-6-334*	0098	0998	4 LY LF507-1F	43998	CY69		op in Northwest Jet Airlink-colors
N517XJ	Avro RJ85A (Avro 146-RJ85A)	E2335	G-6-335*	0098	1098	4 LY LF507-1F	43998	CY69		op in Northwest Jet Airlink-colors
N518XJ	Avro RJ85A (Avro 146-RJ85A)	E2337	G-6-337*	0098	1098	4 LY LF507-1F	43998	CY69		op in Northwest Jet Airlink-colors
N519XJ	Avro RJ85A (Avro 146-RJ85A)	E2344	G-6-344*	0099	0299	4 LY LF507-1F	43998	CY69		op in Northwest Jet Airlink-colors
N520XJ	Avro RJ85A (Avro 146-RJ85A)	E2345	G-6-345*	0099	0299	4 LY LF507-1F	43998	CY69		op in Northwest Jet Airlink-colors
N521XJ	Avro RJ85A (Avro 146-RJ85A)	E2346	G-6-346*	0099	0399	4 LY LF507-1F	43998	CY69		op in Northwest Jet Airlink-colors
N522XJ	Avro RJ85A (Avro 146-RJ85A)	E2347	G-6-347*	0099	0399	4 LY LF507-1F	43998	CY69		op in Northwest Jet Airlink-colors
N523XJ	Avro RJ85A (Avro 146-RJ85A)	E2348	G-6-348*	0099	0399	4 LY LF507-1F	43998	CY69		op in Northwest Jet Airlink-colors
N524XJ	Avro RJ85A (Avro 146-RJ85A)	E2349	G-6-349*	0099	0499	4 LY LF507-1F	43998	CY69		op in Northwest Jet Airlink-colors
N525XJ	Avro RJ85A (Avro 146-RJ85A)	E2350	G-6-350*	0099	0499	4 LY LF507-1F	43998	CY69		op in Northwest Jet Airlink-colors
N526XJ	Avro RJ85A (Avro 146-RJ85A)	E2351				4 LY LF507-1F	43998	CY69		oo-del. 0499/tb op in NW Jet Airlink-cs
N527XJ	Avro RJ85A (Avro 146-RJ85A)	E2352				4 LY LF507-1F	43998	CY69		oo-del. 0599/tb op in NW Jet Airlink-cs
N528XJ	Avro RJ85A (Avro 146-RJ85A)	E2353				4 LY LF507-1F	43998	CY69		oo-del. 0599/tb op in NW Jet Airlink-cs
N529XJ	Avro RJ85A (Avro 146-RJ85A)					4 LY LF507-1F	43998	CY69		oo-del. 0001/tb op in NW Jet Airlink-cs
N530XJ	Avro RJ85A (Avro 146-RJ85A)					4 LY LF507-1F	43998	CY69		oo-del. 0001/tb op in NW Jet Airlink-cs
N531XJ	Avro RJ85A (Avro 146-RJ85A)					4 LY LF507-1F	43998	CY69		oo-del. 0001/tb op in NW Jet Airlink-cs
N532XJ	Avro RJ85A (Avro 146-RJ85A)					4 LY LF507-1F	43998	CY69		oo-del. 0001/tb op in NW Jet Airlink-cs
N533XJ	Avro RJ85A (Avro 146-RJ85A)					4 LY LF507-1F	43998	CY69		oo-del. 0001/tb op in NW Jet Airlink-cs
N534XJ	Avro RJ85A (Avro 146-RJ85A)					4 LY LF507-1F	43998	CY69		oo-del. 0001/tb op in NW Jet Airlink-cs
N535XJ	Avro RJ85A (Avro 146-RJ85A)					4 LY LF507-1F	43998	CY69		oo-del. 0202/tb op in NW Jet Airlink-cs
N536XJ	Avro RJ85A (Avro 146-RJ85A)					4 LY LF507-1F	43998	CY69		oo-del. 0402/tb op in NW Jet Airlink-cs

METHOW AVIATION, Inc. = MER

Everett-Snohomish County/Paine Field, WA

3311 109th Street SW, No. 221, Everett, WA 98204, USA ☎ (206) 355-2055 Tx: none Fax: (206) 742-6868 SITA: n/a
F: 1975 21 Head: Hugh Glassburn ICAO: METHOW Net: n/a

registration	type of aircraft	cn/fn	ex/ex*	mfd	del	powered by	mtow kg	configuration	selcal	name/fln/specialitites/remarks
N1827M	Beech D18S	A-394		0047	0384	2 PW R-985	3969	Freighter		
N250RP	Beech E18S	BA-47		0055	1191	2 PW R-985	4400	Freighter		
N42D	Beech E18S	BA-117		0055	0781	2 PW R-985	4400	Freighter		
N9001	Beech E18S	BA-460		0059	0292	2 PW R-985	4400	Freighter		
N9210	Beech G18S	BA-472	N92D	0059	0283	2 PW R-985	4400	Freighter		
N432U	Hamilton Westwind III	BA-161		0056	0184	2 PWC PT6A-27	5216	Freighter		cvtd Beech E18S
N926T	Hamilton Westwind III	BA-711		0064	0286	2 PWC PT6A-27	5216	Freighter		cvtd Beech H18
N91314	Boeing (Douglas) DC-3C (C-47-DL)	4538	NC17884	0042	0685	2 PW R-1830	12202	Freighter		lsf Comanche Air Inc.

METRO AVIATION, Inc.

Shreveport-Downtown, LA

PO Box 7008, Shreveport, LA 71137, USA ☎ (318) 222-5529 Tx: none Fax: (318) 222-0503 SITA: n/a
F: 1982 n/a Head: Thomas M. Stanberry Net: n/a

registration	type of aircraft	cn/fn	ex/ex*	mfd	del	powered by	mtow kg	configuration	selcal	name/fln/specialitites/remarks
N130FH	Eurocopter (Aerosp.) AS350B AStar	1016	G-GINA	0078	1096	1 TU Arriel 1B	1950			
N390MA	Eurocopter (Aerosp.) AS350B AStar	1549	N512WW	0082	1091	1 TU Arriel 1B	1950			
N391MA	Eurocopter (Aerosp.) AS350BA AStar	2277	C-GHMS	0090	0192	1 TU Arriel 1B	2100			
N398MA	Eurocopter (Aerosp.) AS350BA AStar	1856	C-GMWX	0086	1096	1 TU Arriel 1B	2100			
N105SJ	Eurocopter (MBB) BO105C	S-104	N8570W	0073	1284	2 AN 250-C20B	2400	EMS		
N25SE	Eurocopter (MBB) BO105CBS	S-455	N455BH	0080	1286	2 AN 250-C20B	2400	EMS		
N2783X	Eurocopter (MBB) BO105CBS	S-584	D-HDQF	0082	1095	2 AN 250-C20B	2400	EMS		
N3130E	Eurocopter (MBB) BO105CBS	S-601	D-HDQX	0082	0989	2 AN 250-C20B	2400	EMS		
N911ET	Eurocopter (MBB) BO105CS	S-187	N83HJ	0077	0186	2 AN 250-C20B	2400	EMS		
N911HR	Eurocopter (MBB) BO105CBS	S-646	N83LF	0083	1087	2 AN 250-C20B	2400	EMS		
N912ET	Eurocopter (MBB) BO105CBS	S-340	N340WA	0077	0589	2 AN 250-C20B	2400	EMS		
N913ET	Eurocopter (MBB) BO105CBS	S-583	N2783V	0082	1095	2 AN 250-C20B	2400	EMS		
N941MS	Eurocopter (Aerosp.) AS355F2 TwinStar	5495		0091	1194	2 AN 250-C20F	2540			lsf Debis Financial Services Inc.
N942MS	Eurocopter (Aerosp.) AS355F2 TwinStar	5498		0091	1194	2 AN 250-C20F	2540			lsf Debis Financial Services Inc.
N943MS	Eurocopter (Aerosp.) AS355F2 TwinStar	5500		0091	1194	2 AN 250-C20F	2540			lsf Debis Financial Services Inc.
N944MS	Eurocopter (Aerosp.) AS355F1 TwinStar	5118	N5791X	0082	1094	2 AN 250-C20F	2400			lsf RTS Helicopter Services Corp.
N109MM	Agusta A109A II	7279	N1QH	0083	1190	2 AN 250-C20B	2600			lsf Agusta Aerospace Corp.
N217MM	Agusta A109A II	7271	N4NM	0083	1190	2 AN 250-C20B	2600			lsf Agusta Aerospace Corp.
N135DH	Eurocopter EC135P1	0064		0098	1298	2 PWC PW206B	2720	EMS		lsf/opf Mary Hitchock Memorial Hospital
N911KB	Eurocopter EC135P1	0013	N4053H	0097	0398	2 PWC PW206B	2720	EMSLifeAirRescue		opf Schumpert&Willis Knighton-HealthSy.
N914ET	Eurocopter EC135P1	0018	N40467	0097	0298	2 PWC PW206B	2720	EMS		opf East Texas Medical Center
N399MA	Eurocopter (MBB) BK117A-4	7123	N117SM	0087	0288	2 LY LTS101-650B.1	3200	EMS		

MIAMI AIR = GL / BSK (Miami Air International, Inc. dba)

Miami-Int'l, FL

PO Box 660880, Miami Springs, FL 33266-0880, USA ☎ (305) 876-3600 Tx: none Fax: (305) 871-4222 SITA: n/a
F: 1991 350 Head: Douglas R. Fischer ICAO: BISCAYNE Net: http://www.miamiair.com

registration	type of aircraft	cn/fn	ex/ex*	mfd	del	powered by	mtow kg	configuration	selcal	name/fln/specialitites/remarks
N803MA	Boeing 727-225 (A)	22434 / 1671	N803EA	0080	1191	3 PW JT8D-15 (HK3/FDX)	83461	Y173		Kim
N804MA	Boeing 727-225 (A)	22435 / 1674	N804EA	0080	1091	3 PW JT8D-15 (HK3/FDX)	83461	Y173	JL-CH	Lois
N806MA	Boeing 727-225 (A)	22437 / 1682	N806EA	0080	0492	3 PW JT8D-15 (HK3/FDX)	83461	Y173	JL-CM	Ely
N808MA	Boeing 727-231 (A)	21988 / 1586	F-WKPZ	0280	0992	3 PW JT8D-15A (HK3/FDX)	86409	Y173	DJ-FM	Loisita / lsf Aviation Investments
N886MA	Boeing 727-225 (A)	21855 / 1535	N8886Z	0079	1295	3 PW JT8D-15	86409	Y173	JK-AL	Diane / lsf Aero-MA Leasing 1 Corp.
N887MA	Boeing 727-225 (A)	21857 / 1539	N8888Z	0079	1194	3 PW JT8D-15 (HK3/FDX)	86409	Y173		Carolyn / lsf FSBU Trustee
N889MA	Boeing 727-225 (A)	21854 / 1532	N8885Z	0079	1095	3 PW JT8D-15	86409	Y173	AK-DE	Billie / lsf Aero-MA Leasing 1 Corp.

MIAMI AIR LEASE, Inc.

Miami-Int'l, FL

7905 NW 66th Street, Miami, FL 33166, USA ☎ (305) 477-1185 Tx: none Fax: (305) 477-7375 SITA: n/a
F: 1994 n/a Head: Evelio Alpizar Net: n/a

registration	type of aircraft	cn/fn	ex/ex*	mfd	del	powered by	mtow kg	configuration	selcal	name/fln/specialitites/remarks
N41626	Convair 340-70 (C-131B)	274	53-7822	0955	1293	2 PW R-2800	21772	Freighter		

MIAMI CITY FLIGHTS, Inc. (Airswiss)

Miami-Opa Locka, FL

9309 Collins Avenue, PH.2, Surfside, FL 33154, USA ☎ (305) 861-0077 Tx: none Fax: (305) 861-4979 SITA: n/a
F: 1991 n/a Head: Markus K. Walliser Net: n/a AIRSWISS is the marketing name used for charter flights outside the Great Miami Area.

registration	type of aircraft	cn/fn	ex/ex*	mfd	del	powered by	mtow kg	configuration	selcal	name/fln/specialitites/remarks
N3269Q	Cessna 402	402-0069		0067	0193	2 CO TSIO-520-E	2858			
N9873F	Cessna 402	402-0303		0068	0398	2 CO TSIO-520-E	2858			

MIAMI VALLEY AVIATION, Inc. - MVA

Middletown-Hook Field Municipal, OH

1707 Run Way, Middletown, OH 45042, USA ☎ (513) 422-5050 Tx: none Fax: (513) 422-1494 SITA: n/a
F: 1979 40 Head: Terrence T. Hogan Net: n/a

registration	type of aircraft	cn/fn	ex/ex*	mfd	del	powered by	mtow kg	configuration	selcal	name/fln/specialitites/remarks
N62498	Piper PA-23-250 Aztec F	27-7654023		0076	1094	2 LY IO-540-C4B5	2359			lsf The Eagle & The Hawks Inc.
N62650	Piper PA-23-250 Aztec F	27-7654115		0076	0287	2 LY IO-540-C4B5	2359			lsf The Eagle & The Hawks Inc.
N63911	Piper PA-23-250 Aztec F	27-7854053		0078	0294	2 LY IO-540-C4B5	2359			lsf The Eagle & The Hawks Inc.
N8627A	Beech E18S	BA-283	N86HA	0057	1288	2 PW R-985	4218	Freighter		lsf The Eagle & The Hawks Inc.
N8711H	Beech E18S	BA-87	N87HA	0055	0480	2 PW R-985	4218	Freighter		lsf The Eagle & The Hawks Inc.
N9669N	Beech E18S	BA-382	N96HA	0058	1283	2 PW R-985	4218	Freighter		lsf The Eagle & The Hawks Inc.
N25FM	Learjet 25	25-063	N24LT	0070	0792	2 GE CJ610-6	6804			lsf Jets Inc.
N294NW	Learjet 25	25-031		0069	1194	2 GE CJ610-6	6804			lsf Southern Management Services Inc.
N108RB	Learjet 35A	35A-097	N135J	0077	0197	2 GA TFE731-2-2B	8301			lsf Labrador Leasing Corp.
N36AP	Boeing (Douglas) DC-3C (C-47A-25-DK)	13439	N11VU	0044	1091	2 PW R-1830	12202	Freighter		lsf The Eagle & The Hawks Inc.
N8187E	Boeing (Douglas) DC-3C (C-47A-DL)	13840	N81HA	0043	1091	2 PW R-1830	12202	Freighter		lsf The Eagle & The Hawks Inc.
N907Z	Boeing (Douglas) DC-3C (C-47A-5-DK)	12300	N90HA	0042	0892	2 PW R-1830	12202	Freighter		lsf The Eagle & The Hawks Inc.
N932H	Boeing (Douglas) DC-3C (C-47B-50-DK)	34368	N93HA	0045	0187	2 PW R-1830	12202	Freighter		lsf The Eagle & The Hawks Inc.
N982Z	Boeing (Douglas) DC-3C (C-47A-30-DK)	25485	N98HA	0043	0187	2 PW R-1830	12202	Freighter		lsf pvt
N9923S	Boeing (Douglas) DC-3C (C-47B-5-DK)	25964	N99HA	0044	1091	2 PW R-1830	12202	Freighter		lsf The Eagle & The Hawks Inc.
N131MV	Dassault Falcon 20C (C)	31	N828AA	0466	0697	2 GE CF700-2D2	13000	Freighter		lsf The Eagle & The Hawks Inc. / cvtd C

MICHAUDS AVIATION (Frank H. Michaud, Jr. dba)
Willows-Gelnn County, CA

PO Box 1279, Willows, CA 95988, USA ☎ (530) 934-3113 Tx: none Fax: (530) 934-2060 SITA: n/a
F: 1966 ☃ n/a Head: Frank H. Michaud, Jr. Net: n/a Ag-aircraft below MTOW 5000kg: Air Tractor AT-400, AT-502, Bell 47G, Cessna 205 & Grumman G-164

☐ N17285	Eurocopter (Aerosp.) SA315B Lama	2333		0073	0182	1 TU Artouste IIIB	1950			

MID ATLANTIC AIR MUSEUM
Reading-Regional/Carl A. Spaatz Field, PA

11 Museum Drive, Reading, PA 19605, USA ☎ (610) 372-7333 Tx: none Fax: (610) 372-1702 SITA: n/a
F: 1981 ☃ n/a Head: Russell A. Strine Net: n/a Museum conducting show-flights without passengers at airshows. Beside the airliner type-aircraft listed, also has many military and smaller types in its Museum-fleet.

☐ N229GB	Boeing (Douglas) DC-3C (C-47B-20-DK)	26874	N68AH	0044	0681	2 PW R-1830	12202	fly.presentation		US Navy 50819-colors
☐ N450A	Martin 404	14141	N149S	0052	0891	2 PW R-2800	19051	fly.presentation		Fly-Eastern Air Lines-colors
☐ N30EG	Convair 580	202	N8500	0754	0296	2 AN 501-D13	24766	fly.presentation		cvtd340-71 / being rest.in Allegheny-cs
☐ N7471	BAe (Vickers) Viscount 798D	233	N555SL	0057	0592	4 RR Dart 510	29257	fly.presentation		Capital Airlines-colors / cvtd 745D

MID-ATLANTIC FREIGHT, Inc. = MDC (Sister company of Atlantic Aero, Inc.)
Greensboro-High Point / Winston Salem Regional, NC

PO Box 35409, Greensboro, NC 27425-5409, USA ☎ (910) 722-1396 Tx: 574356 atlan aero gb Fax: (910) 668-4434 SITA: n/a
F: 1972 ☃ 42 Head: Lawson L. Josey ICAO: NIGHT SHIP Net: n/a

☐ N9653F	Cessna 208 Caravan I	20800114		0087	0687	1 PWC PT6A-114	3629	Freighter		
☐ N1041L	Cessna 208B Grand Caravan	208B0337		0093	0693	1 PWC PT6A-114A	3969	Freighter		
☐ N1058N	Cessna 208B Grand Caravan	208B0347		0093	1093	1 PWC PT6A-114A	3969	Freighter		
☐ N1114N	Cessna 208B Grand Caravan	208B0406		0094	1194	1 PWC PT6A-114A	3969	Freighter		
☐ N1116Y	Cessna 208B Grand Caravan	208B0368		0093	1193	1 PWC PT6A-114A	3969	Freighter		
☐ N1209X	Cessna 208B Grand Caravan	208B0443		0095	0895	1 PWC PT6A-114A	3969	Freighter		
☐ N1229A	Cessna 208B Grand Caravan	208B0663		0098	0498	1 PWC PT6A-114A	3969	Freighter		
☐ N398A	Cessna 208B Grand Caravan	208B0390	LN-TWE	0094	0199	1 PWC PT6A-114A	3969	Freighter		
☐ N430A	Cessna 208B Grand Caravan	208B0415	LN-TWF	0095	0199	1 PWC PT6A-114A	3969	Freighter		
☐ N4667B	Cessna 208B Caravan I Super Cargomaster	208B0163		0089	1189	1 PWC PT6A-114	3969	Freighter		
☐ N4698B	Cessna 208B Caravan I Super Cargomaster	208B0175		0089	1189	1 PWC PT6A-114	3969	Freighter		
☐ N9452B	Cessna 208B Caravan I Super Cargomaster	208B0123		0088	1288	1 PWC PT6A-114	3969	Freighter		
☐ N9479B	Cessna 208B Caravan I Super Cargomaster	208B0082		0088	0488	1 PWC PT6A-114	3969	Freighter		
☐ N9525B	Cessna 208B Caravan I Super Cargomaster	208B0087		0088	0588	1 PWC PT6A-114	3969	Freighter		
☐ N9594B	Cessna 208B Caravan I Super Cargomaster	208B0131		0088	1288	1 PWC PT6A-114	3969	Freighter		
☐ N9662B	Cessna 208B Caravan I Super Cargomaster	208B0095		0088	0788	1 PWC PT6A-114	3969	Freighter		
☐ N9793B	Cessna 208B Caravan I Super Cargomaster	208B0114		0088	0988	1 PWC PT6A-114	3969	Freighter		
☐ N9829B	Cessna 208B Caravan I Super Cargomaster	208B0116		0088	1088	1 PWC PT6A-114	3969	Freighter		

MID-COAST AIR CHARTER, Inc.
Houston-Willam P. Hobby, TX

4107 Rice Blvd, Houston, TX 77005, USA ☎ (281) 644-6470 Tx: none Fax: (281) 660-6615 SITA: n/a
F: 1978 ☃ n/a Head: Earle P. Martin, III Net: n/a

☐ N115AP	Mitsubishi MU-2F (MU-2B-20)	136	N75RJ	0068	1192	2 GA TPE331-1-151A	4500			

MIDLANTIC JET CHARTERS, Inc.
Atlantic City-Int'l, NJ

Suite 112, Atlantic City Int'l Airport, Egg Harbor, NJ 08234, USA ☎ (609) 383-1555 Tx: none Fax: (609) 383-0051 SITA: n/a
F: 1968 ☃ n/a Head: Michael Hodel Net: n/a

☐ N62980	Piper PA-31-325 Navajo C/R	31-7712002		0077	0389	2 LY TIO-540-F2BD	2948			
☐ N400AC	Beech King Air B100	BE-12		0076	0289	2 GA TPE331-6-252B	5352			
☐ N225JL	Learjet 25B	25B-182	F-GFMZ	0074	0197	2 GE CJ610-6	6804			
☐ N78MC	Learjet 35A	35A-117	N3155B	0077	1194	2 GA TFE731-2-2B	8301			

MIDLINE AIR FREIGHT
Elizabethtown-Addington, KY

1828 Kitty Hawk Drive, Elizabethtown, KY 42701, USA ☎ (502) 862-5312 Tx: none Fax: (502) 769-9100 SITA: n/a
F: 1995 ☃ n/a Head: Nickolas H. Disselkamp Net: n/a

☐ N1480K	Beech G18S	BA-601		0062	0995	2 PW R-985-AN14B	4400	Freighter		

MID-OHIO AVIATION, Inc.
Wooster-Wayne County, OH

6020 N Honeytown Road, Smithville, OH 44677-9720, USA ☎ (330) 669-2671 Tx: none Fax: (330) 669-2402 SITA: n/a
F: 1991 ☃ n/a Head: Richard N. Seaman Net: n/a

☐ N84643	Piper PA-34-220T Seneca III	34-8233033		0082	0391	2 CO TSIO-360-KB	2155			lsf Prentke Ronich Co.
☐ N45NS	Cessna 550 Citation II	550-0479	PT-OOM	0084	0597	2 PWC JT15D-4	6033			lsf Seacorp Leasing Co.

MID VALLEY HELICOPTERS, Inc.
Jefferson-Heliport, OR

397 Talbot Road SE, Jefferson, OR 97352, USA ☎ (541) 327-1169 Tx: none Fax: (541) 327-2910 SITA: n/a
F: 1965 ☃ 8 Head: Frank Gilmour Net: n/a Aircraft below MTOW 1361 kg: Hiller UH-12.

☐ N16MV	Bell 206B JetRanger III	4040	N7036H	0089	0493	1 AN 250-C20J	1451			lsf Pioneer Helicopters
☐ N26MV	Bell 206B JetRanger III	4052		0089	0589	1 AN 250-C20J	1451			
☐ N747UT	Bell 206L-1 LongRanger II	45636	N3901A	0080	0298	1 AN 250-C28B	1882			

MIDWAY AIRLINES, Corp. = JI / MDW (formerly Jet Express, Inc.)
Raleigh-Durham, NC

300W Morgan Street, Suite 1200, Durham, NC 27701-2162, USA ☎ (919) 956-4800 Tx: n/a Fax: (919) 956-4801 SITA: n/a
F: 1993 ☃ 1000 Head: Robert Ferguson IATA: 878 ICAO: MIDWAY Net: http://www.midwayair.com

☐ N570ML	Canadair Regional Jet 200ER (CL-600-2B19)	7206	C-GBNO*	0097	1197	2 GE CF34-3B1	23133	Y50		
☐ N571ML	Canadair Regional Jet 200ER (CL-600-2B19)	7209	C-GBNW*	0097	1297	2 GE CF34-3B1	23133	Y50		
☐ N572ML	Canadair Regional Jet 200ER (CL-600-2B19)	7224	C-GBNX*	0098	0398	2 GE CF34-3B1	23133	Y50		
☐ N573ML	Canadair Regional Jet 200ER (CL-600-2B19)	7227	C-GBOD*	0098	0398	2 GE CF34-3B1	23133	Y50		
☐ N574ML	Canadair Regional Jet 200ER (CL-600-2B19)	7242		0098	0698	2 GE CF34-3B1	23133	Y50		
☐ N575ML	Canadair Regional Jet 200ER (CL-600-2B19)	7256		0098	0998	2 GE CF34-3B1	23133	Y50		
☐ N576ML	Canadair Regional Jet 200ER (CL-600-2B19)	7257		0098	0998	2 GE CF34-3B1	23133	Y50		
☐ N577ML	Canadair Regional Jet 200ER (CL-600-2B19)	7269		0098	1098	2 GE CF34-3B1	23133	Y50		
☐ N578ML	Canadair Regional Jet 200ER (CL-600-2B19)	7270	C-FMOW*	0098	1198	2 GE CF34-3B1	23133	Y50		
☐ N579ML	Canadair Regional Jet 200ER (CL-600-2B19)	7277	C-FMML*	0098	1298	2 GE CF34-3B1	23133	Y50		
☐ N580ML	Canadair Regional Jet 200ER (CL-600-2B19)	7289		0099	0199	2 GE CF34-3B1	23133	Y50		
☐ N581ML	Canadair Regional Jet 200ER (CL-600-2B19)					2 GE CF34-3B1	23133	Y50		oo-delivery 0499
☐ N582ML	Canadair Regional Jet 200ER (CL-600-2B19)					2 GE CF34-3B1	23133	Y50		oo-delivery 0699
☐ N583ML	Canadair Regional Jet 200ER (CL-600-2B19)					2 GE CF34-3B1	23133	Y50		oo-delivery 0799
☐ N584ML	Canadair Regional Jet 200ER (CL-600-2B19)					2 GE CF34-3B1	23133	Y50		oo-delivery 0899
☐ N585ML	Canadair Regional Jet 200ER (CL-600-2B19)					2 GE CF34-3B1	23133	Y50		oo-delivery 0999
☐ N586ML	Canadair Regional Jet 200ER (CL-600-2B19)					2 GE CF34-3B1	23133	Y50		oo-delivery 0999
☐ N587ML	Canadair Regional Jet 200ER (CL-600-2B19)					2 GE CF34-3B1	23133	Y50		oo-delivery 1099
☐ N588ML	Canadair Regional Jet 200ER (CL-600-2B19)					2 GE CF34-3B1	23133	Y50		oo-delivery 1199
☐ N589ML	Canadair Regional Jet 200ER (CL-600-2B19)					2 GE CF34-3B1	23133	Y50		oo-delivery 1299
☐ N590ML	Canadair Regional Jet 200ER (CL-600-2B19)					2 GE CF34-3B1	23133	Y50		oo-delivery 1299
☐ N591ML	Canadair Regional Jet 200ER (CL-600-2B19)					2 GE CF34-3B1	23133	Y50		oo-delivery 0200
☐ N592ML	Canadair Regional Jet 200ER (CL-600-2B19)					2 GE CF34-3B1	23133	Y50		oo-delivery 0300
☐ N103ML	Fokker 100 (F28 Mk0100)	11444	PH-MXC*	0093	1093	2 RR Tay 650-15	44452	F8Y90		
☐ N104ML	Fokker 100 (F28 Mk0100)	11445	PH-MXD*	0093	1193	2 RR Tay 650-15	44452	F8Y90		
☐ N105ML	Fokker 100 (F28 Mk0100)	11475	PH-EZX*	0093	1293	2 RR Tay 650-15	44452	F8Y90		
☐ N106ML	Fokker 100 (F28 Mk0100)	11477	PH-EZZ*	0093	0194	2 RR Tay 650-15	44452	F8Y90		
☐ N107ML	Fokker 100 (F28 Mk0100)	11450	PH-MXL*	0093	0794	2 RR Tay 650-15	44452	F8Y90		
☐ N108ML	Fokker 100 (F28 Mk0100)	11484	PH-EZA*	0094	1194	2 RR Tay 650-15	44452	F8Y90		
☐ N109ML	Fokker 100 (F28 Mk0100)	11485	PH-EZB*	0094	0195	2 RR Tay 650-15	44452	F8Y90		
☐ N110ML	Fokker 100 (F28 Mk0100)	11486	PH-EZC*	0095	0695	2 RR Tay 650-15	44452	F8Y90		
☐ N133ML	Fokker 100 (F28 Mk0100)	11330	SE-DUG	0091	1295	2 RR Tay 650-15	44452	F8Y90		lsf Debis AirFinance
☐ N304ML	Airbus Industrie A320-231	373	N373KA	0092	0695	2 IAE V2500-A1	73500	F12Y138		lsf KAWA
☐ N	Airbus Industrie A320-232					2 IAE V2527-A5	73500	F12Y138		oo-delivery 00XX
☐ N	Airbus Industrie A320-232					2 IAE V2527-A5	73500	F12Y138		oo-delivery 00XX
☐ N	Airbus Industrie A320-232					2 IAE V2527-A5	73500	F12Y138		oo-delivery 00XX
☐ N	Airbus Industrie A320-232					2 IAE V2527-A5	73500	F12Y138		oo-delivery 00XX

MIDWEST AVIATION = MWT (Division of Southwest Aviation, Inc.)
Marshall-Ryan Field, MN

RR 4, Box 16C, Marshall, MN 56258-9739, USA ☎ (507) 532-3164 Tx: none Fax: (507) 532-5881 SITA: n/a
F: 1961 ☃ 10 Head: Raymond C. Johnson ICAO: MIDWEST Net: n/a

☐ N43305	Piper PA-32R-301 Saratoga SP	32R-8413002		0084	0690	1 LY IO-540-K1G5D	1633			
☐ N6184Y	Piper PA-23-250 Aztec C	27-3410		0066	1174	2 LY IO-540-C4B5	2359			
☐ N3558X	Piper PA-31-350 Navajo Chieftain	31-8052073		0080	1085	2 LY TIO-540-J2BD	3175			
☐ N711HG	Piper PA-31-350 Navajo Chieftain	31-8052110		0080	0495	2 LY TIO-540-J2BD	3175			
☐ N727SC	Piper PA-31-350 Navajo Chieftain	31-7305110		0073	0787	2 LY TIO-540-J2BD	3175			
☐ N185MV	Beech King Air 200	BB-1034	N185MC	0082	0197	2 PWC PT6A-42	5670			

399 registration type of aircraft cn/fn ex/ex* mfd del powered by mtow kg configuration selcal name/fln/specialitites/remarks

MIDWEST CORPORATE AVIATION, Inc. — Wichita-Colonel James Jabara, KS

PO Box 8067, Wichita, KS 67208-0067, USA ☎ (316) 636-9700 Tx: none Fax: (316) 636-9718 SITA: n/a
F: 1975 n/a Head: Marvin E. Autry Net: http://www.midwestaviation.com

N51CH	Cessna A185E Skywagon	18501899		0071	0896	1 CO IO-520-D	1520			
N301CT	Beech Baron 58	TH-1166		0080	0297	2 CO IO-520-CB	2449			
N6493S	Beech Baron 58	TH-710		0076	1284	2 CO IO-520-C	2449			
N55LH	Beech King Air A90 (65-A90)	LJ-266	N55GM	0067	0881	2 PWC PT6A-20	4218			
N77HE	Beech King Air C90	LJ-969	9Q-CHE	0081	0397	2 PWC PT6A-21	4377			lsf Weaver Aero Int'l Inc.
N91LW	Beech King Air C90	LJ-1001	N88EL	0082	1090	2 PWC PT6A-21	4581	EMS LifeWatch		opf Columbia Wesley Medical Center
N701SC	Learjet 24D (XR)	24D-235	N51VL	0071	0390	2 GE CJ610-6	6804			lsf MCA Lear 24 Ltd Partnership/cvtd24D
N417BA	Learjet 35A	35A-257	N275DJ	0079	0695	2 GA TFE731-2-2B	8301			lsf MCA Lear 24 Ltd Partnership

MIDWEST EXPRESS AIRLINES, Inc. = YX / MEP — Milwaukee-General Mitchell Int'l, WI

6744 South Howell Avenue, HO-7, Oak Creek, WI 53154-1402, USA ☎ (920) 570-4000 Tx: n/a Fax: (920) 570-0102 SITA: n/a
F: 1983 2150 Head: Timothy E. Hoeksema IATA: 453 ICAO: MIDEX Net: http://www.midwestexpress.com
A commuter system to provide feeder connection at YX major hubs is operated under the marketing name Midwest Express Connection by SKYWAY AIRLINES – see under that company.

N300ME	Boeing (Douglas) DC-9-15	45718 / 17	N928AX	0166	0384	2 PW JT8D-7B (HK3/ABS)	41141	F60		
N400ME	Boeing (Douglas) DC-9-14	45727 / 43	N628TX	0766	0484	2 PW JT8D-7B	41141	F60		
N500ME	Boeing (Douglas) DC-9-14	45711 / 4	N85AS	0665	1185	2 PW JT8D-7B (HK3/ABS)	41141	F60		
N600ME	Boeing (Douglas) DC-9-14	45725 / 19	N25AS	0266	1085	2 PW JT8D-7B (HK3/ABS)	41141	F60		
N700ME	Boeing (Douglas) DC-9-14	45696 / 2	N3301L	0766	0986	2 PW JT8D-7B (HK3/ABS)	41141	F60		
N800ME	Boeing (Douglas) DC-9-14	45842 / 23	N8961	0266	1187	2 PW JT8D-7B	41141	F60		
N80ME	Boeing (Douglas) DC-9-14	45795 / 65	N9102	1066	1288	2 PW JT8D-7B	41141	F52		
N900ME	Boeing (Douglas) DC-9-15	45841 / 46	N2892Q	0866	0188	2 PW JT8D-7B	41141	F60		
N202ME	Boeing (Douglas) DC-9-32	47672 / 778	D-ALLC	0675	0294	2 PW JT8D-9A (HK3/ABS)	48534	F84	LM-EH	lsf Fifth Third Leasing Co.
N203ME	Boeing (Douglas) DC-9-32	47673 / 779	D-ALLA	0075	1093	2 PW JT8D-9A (HK3/ABS)	48534	F84	LM-EF	lsf Nationsbanc Leasing Corp.
N204ME	Boeing (Douglas) DC-9-32	47680 / 781	D-ALLB	0775	0194	2 PW JT8D-9A (HK3/ABS)	48534	F84		lsf Nationsbanc Leasing Corp.
N205ME	Boeing (Douglas) DC-9-32	47601 / 715	PK-GNG	0073	0496	2 PW JT8D-9A (HK3/ABS)	48534	F84		lsf M&I First National Leasing Co.
N206ME	Boeing (Douglas) DC-9-32	47791 / 908	PK-GNU	0079	1295	2 PW JT8D-9A (HK3/ABS)	48534	F84		lsf Nationsbanc Leasing Corp.
N207ME	Boeing (Douglas) DC-9-32	47794 / 915	PK-GNX	0079	1295	2 PW JT8D-9A (HK3/ABS)	48534	F84		lsf Nationsbanc Leasing Corp.
N209ME	Boeing (Douglas) DC-9-32	47730 / 828	PK-GNO	0676	0296	2 PW JT8D-9A (HK3/ABS)	48534	F84		lsf M&I First National Leasing Co.
N212ME	Boeing (Douglas) DC-9-32	47701 / 822	PK-GNM	0076	0796	2 PW JT8D-9A (HK3/ABS)	48534	F84		lsf M&I First National Leasing Co.
N215ME	Boeing (Douglas) DC-9-32	47744 / 837	PK-GNR	0076	0796	2 PW JT8D-9A (HK3/ABS)	48534	F84		lsf M&I First National Leasing Co.
N216ME	Boeing (Douglas) DC-9-32	47740 / 835	PK-GNP	0076	0896	2 PW JT8D-9A (HK3/ABS)	48534	F84		lsf Nationsbanc Leasing Corp.
N301ME	Boeing (Douglas) DC-9-32	47190 / 240	N942ML	0168	0888	2 PW JT8D-7B	49895	F84		
N302ME	Boeing (Douglas) DC-9-32	47102 / 198	N940ML	0067	0991	2 PW JT8D-7B	49895	F84		
N401ME	Boeing (Douglas) DC-9-32	47133 / 230	N943ML	0168	0888	2 PW JT8D-7B (HK3/ABS)	49895	F84		
N501ME	Boeing (Douglas) DC-9-32	47132 / 229	N944ML	1267	0988	2 PW JT8D-7B	49895	F84		
N502ME	Boeing (Douglas) DC-9-32	48132 / 956	N943U	0580	1092	2 PW JT8D-9A (HK3/ABS)	48534	F84		
N602ME	Boeing (Douglas) DC-9-32	48133 / 959	N944U	0080	1192	2 PW JT8D-9A (HK3/ABS)	48534	F84	AB-CE	
N601ME	Boeing (Douglas) MD-88 (DC-9-88)	49762 / 1624	N159PL	0989	1189	2 PW JT8D-219	72575	F112		lsf POLA
N701ME	Boeing (Douglas) MD-88 (DC-9-88)	49760 / 1620	N157PL	0889	1289	2 PW JT8D-219	72575	F112		lsf POLA
N803ME	Boeing (Douglas) MD-81 (DC-9-81)	48029 / 953	JA8458	0080	0199	2 PW JT8D-217C	67812	F116		
N804ME	Boeing (Douglas) MD-81 (DC-9-81)	48030 / 962	JA8459	0081	0998	2 PW JT8D-217C	67812	F116		
N808ME	Boeing (Douglas) MD-81 (DC-9-81)	48070 / 999	JA8468	0081	0698	2 PW JT8D-217C	67812	F116		
N809ME	Boeing (Douglas) MD-82 (DC-9-82)	48071 / 1004	JA8469	0081	0198	2 PW JT8D-217C	67812	F116		cvtd MD-81 (DC-9-81)
N810ME	Boeing (Douglas) MD-81 (DC-9-81)	48072 / 1011	JA8470	0081	0498	2 PW JT8D-217C	67812	F116		

MIDWEST FLYING SERVICE, Inc. — Sheldon-Municipal, IA

3040A Hwy 60 Blvd, Sheldon, IA 51201-7508, USA ☎ (712) 324-4005 Tx: none Fax: (712) 324-4507 SITA: n/a
F: 1993 n/a Head: Lyle A. Vust Net: n/a Aircraft below MTOW 1361kg: Beech Bonanza E35 & Mooney M20F

N63851	Piper PA-23-250 Aztec F	27-7854003		0078	0794	2 LY IO-540-C4B5	2359			
N900TS	Piper PA-23-250 Aztec E	27-7405429		0074	0497	2 LY IO-540-C4B5	2359			lsf pvt
N9007Y	Piper PA-31-310 Navajo	31-11		0067	0396	2 LY TIO-540-A1A	2948			
N9085Y	Piper PA-31-310 Navajo	31-119		0068	1196	2 LY TIO-540-A1A	2948			

MIDWEST HELICOPTER AIRWAYS, Inc. — Hinsdale-Midwest Heliport, IL

6225 Garfield Avenue, Burr Ridge, IL 60521, USA ☎ (630) 325-7860 Tx: none Fax: (630) 325-3313 SITA: n/a
F: 1962 15 Head: Richard J. Smith Net: n/a

N4247V	Sikorsky S-58ET	58-1547		0062	1283	1 PWC PT6T-6 TwinPac	5897			lsf Midwest Truxton Int'l / cvtd S-58E
N580US	Sikorsky S-58ET	58-1673		0063	0889	1 PWC PT6T-6 TwinPac	5897			lsf Midwest Truxton Int'l / cvtd S-58E
N2256Z	Sikorsky S-58J	58-867	57-1707	0058	0581	1 WR R-1820	5670			cvtd H-34A
N4388S	Sikorsky S-58J	58-1551		0062	0174	1 WR R-1820	5670			
N90561	Sikorsky S-58J	58-1332		0060	0777	1 WR R-1820	5579			

MILLION AIR CHARTER TETERBORO (General Aviation Flying Service, Inc. dba / Franchisee of the Million Air Charter chain) — Teterboro, NJ

485 Industrial Avenue, Teterboro, NJ 07608, USA ☎ (201) 288-5459 Tx: none Fax: (201) 288-1229 SITA: n/a
F: 1958 95 Head: Kenneth C. Forester Net: n/a

N122G	Cessna 550 Citation II	550-0110	N222SG	0079	0897	2 PWC JT15D-4	6033			lsf Dakota Investment Corp.
N232DM	Cessna 550 Citation II	550-0079	N33RH	0079	0791	2 PWC JT15D-4	6033			lsf Teterboro Aviation Inc.
N550KM	Cessna S550 Citation S/II	S550-0081	N168HC	0085	1189	2 PWC JT15D-4B	6849			lsf TEB Charter Services Inc.
N19MK	Cessna 560 Citation V Ultra	560-0395	N5093Y	0096	0197	2 PWC JT15D-5D	7394			lsf Moki Corp.
N50MJ	Learjet 35A	35A-164	N248HM	0078	0896	2 GA TFE731-2-2B	8301			lsf K & K Jets Llc
N200GH	GAC (Grumman) G-1159 Gulfstream II (SP)	108	N801GA	0071	0797	2 RR Spey 511-8	29710			lsf Meridian Service Inc. / cvtd II

MILLION AIR DALLAS (RR Investments, Inc. dba / Franchisee of the Million Air Charter chain) — Dallas-Love Field, TX

4300 Westgrove, Dallas, TX 75248, USA ☎ (972) 248-1600 Tx: none Fax: (972) 733-5857 SITA: n/a
F: 1983 n/a Head: Louis T. Pepper Net: http://www.millionair.com
Beside aircraft listed, additional executive aircraft (Beech King Air C90/200, Falcon 20, Gulfstream II, Learjet 25/31/35) are leased from private lessors when required.

N999F	Dassault Falcon 10	29	N332J	0074	0398	2 GA TFE731-2-1C	8500			

MILLION AIR OKLAHOMA CITY (Sierra Aviation, Inc. / Franchisee of the Million Air Charter chain) — Oklahoma City-Wiley Post, OK

Wiley Post Airport, Hangar 14, Bethany, OK 73008, USA ☎ (405) 787-3300 Tx: none Fax: (405) 787-4040 SITA: n/a
F: 1997 n/a Head: Randy R. Warren Net: n/a

N1000E	Cessna 525 CitationJet	525-0077		0094	0497	2 WRR FJ44-1A	4717			lsf UTE Management Corp.

MILLION AIR OWENSBORO (MidAmerica Jet, Inc, dba / Franchisee of the Million Air Charter chain) — Owensboro-Daviess County, KY

PO Box 21949, Owensboro, KY 42302-1949, USA ☎ (502) 926-6700 Tx: NONE Fax: (502) 684-6695 SITA: n/a
F: 1981 n/a Head: James T. Hines, Jr. Net: n/a

N84568	Piper PA-34-220T Seneca III	34-8133014		0081	0192	2 CO TSIO-360-KB	2155			
N137JH	Piper PA-31-350 Navajo Chieftain	31-8252025		0082	0682	2 LY TIO-540-J2BD	3175			
N136JH	Beech King Air 100	B-25	N352NR	0069	0187	2 PWC PT6A-28	4808			
N700WP	Beech King Air B200	BB-1313	8P-BAR	0088	0395	2 PWC PT6A-42	5670			
N93ME	Beech King Air B200	BB-1345		0089	0895	2 PWC PT6A-42	5670			
N702JH	Mitsubishi MU-300 Diamond IA	A035SA	N135GA	0083	0987	2 PWC JT15D-4	6636			
N703JH	Mitsubishi MU-300 Diamond IA	A010SA	N300DH	0081	0190	2 PWC JT15D-4	6636			
N149JH	BAe 3201 Jetstream 32EP	947	N947AE	0091	0399	2 GA TPE331-12UAR-704H	7350	Y19		cvtd 32 / opf Nascar Racing Team Brewco
N701JH	Lockheed L-1329 JetStar II	5230	N901EH	0078	0894	4 GA TFE731-3	20185			

MILLION AIR READING (Marc Fruchter Aviation, Inc. dba / Franchisee of the Million Air Charter chain) — Reading-Regional/Carl A. Spaatz Field, PA

2365 Bareville Road, Reading, PA 19605, USA ☎ (610) 374-0100 Tx: none Fax: (610) 374-7580 SITA: n/a
F: 1978 n/a Head: Marc A. Fruchter Net: n/a

N67511	Beech King Air C90	LJ-888		0080	0485	2 PWC PT6A-21	4377			
N6051C	Beech King Air 200	BB-499	N302PC	0079	0988	2 PWC PT6A-41	5670			lsf Arrow Int'l Inc.
N811FA	Beech King Air 200	BB-678	N811VG	0080	0196	2 PWC PT6A-41	5670			
N295FA	Beech Beechjet 400A	RK-68	N8280J	0093	1294	2 PWC JT15D-5	7303			lsf Raytheon Aircraft Receivables
N296FA	Beech Beechjet 400A	RK-91	N1545N	0094	1295	2 PWC JT15D-5	7303			lsf Raytheon Aircraft Receivables

MILLION AIR RICHMOND (Commonwealth Aviation Service, Inc. dba / Franchisee of the Million Air Charter chain) — Richmond-Int'l, VA

400 Portugee Road, Sandston, VA 23250-2417, USA ☎ (757) 222-3700 Tx: n/a Fax: (757) 222-4044 SITA: n/a
F: 1992 n/a Head: Eugene A. McDonough Net: n/a

N22823	Bell 206B JetRanger III	3635		0082	0493	1 AN 250-C20J	1451			lsf CAS Leasing LLC
N18UG	Bell 206L-1 LongRanger II	45368	N18UC	0080	0597	1 AN 250-C28B	1882			
N3054W	Beech Baron 58	TH-398		0074	0294	2 CO IO-520-C	2449			lsf CAS Leasing LLC
N58WC	Beech Baron 58	TH-766		0076	1295	2 CO IO-520-C	2449			lsf Jay & Studie Aviation Inc.
N70FS	Piper PA-31-350 Navajo Chieftain	31-7652129		0076	0493	2 LY TIO-540-J2BD	3175			lsf CAS Leasing LLC
N934DC	Beech King Air E90	LW-202	N127	0077	1294	2 PWC PT6A-28	4581			lsf Dixie Capital Corp.
N12CF	Beech King Air 200	BB-534		0079	0493	2 PWC PT6A-41	5670			lsf CAS Leasing LLC
N33TP	Learjet 24D	24D-321	C-FRNR	0075	0996	2 GE CJ610-6	6123			lsf Mundet Inc.
N217SA	Cessna 550 Citation II	550-0217		0081	1193	2 PWC JT15D-4	6033			lsf CAS Leasing LLC
N92EC	Learjet 31	31-024	N90PB	0090	0097	2 GA TFE731-2-3B	7484			lsf Virginia Air Corp.

400 registration type of aircraft cn/fn ex/ex* mfd del powered by mtow kg configuration selcal name/fln/specialitites/remarks

MILLION AIR SALT LAKE CITY (Business Aviation Management, Inc. dba / Franchisee of the Million Air Charter chain) — Salt Lake City-Int'l, UT

303 North 2370 West, Salt Lake City, UT 84116, USA ☎ (801) 359-2085 Tx: none Fax: (801) 539-0223 SITA: n/a
F: 1996 ⁂ n/a Head: Leon Christensen Net: n/a

registration	type of aircraft	cn/fn	ex/ex*	mfd	del	powered by	mtow kg	configuration	selcal	name/fln/specialitites/remarks
☐ N830VL	Cessna 550 Citation II	550-0412	N410CC	0082	0698	2 PWC JT15D-4	6033			lsf SC Leasing Corp.
☐ N911AE	Learjet 35A	35A-109	N506GP	0077	0497	2 GA TFE731-2-2B	8301			lsf Keystone Group Llc

MINDEN AIR, Corp. — Tucson-Avra Valley, AZ

9991 Desert Aire Drive, Tucson, AZ 85730, USA ☎ (520) 574-2400 Tx: none Fax: (520) 886-3546 SITA: n/a
F: 1991 ⁂ 5 Head: Leonard K. Parker Net: n/a

registration	type of aircraft	cn/fn	ex/ex*	mfd	del	powered by	mtow kg	configuration	selcal	name/fln/specialitites/remarks
☐ N299MA	Lockheed P2V-7 (P-2H) Neptune	726-7211	147961	0058	0491	2 WR R-3350	34246	Tanker		99
☐ N355MA	Lockheed P2V-7 (P-2H) Neptune	726-7229	148344	0058	0495	2 WR R-3350	34246	Tanker		55

MINUTEMAN AVIATION, Inc. – MAI — Missoula-Int'l & Conrad, MT

5225 Hwy 10 West, Box 16, Missoula, MT 59808, USA ☎ (406) 728-9363 Tx: none Fax: (406) 728-6981 SITA: n/a
F: 1964 ⁂ 40 Head: Kenneth G. Mamuzich Net: n/a Aircraft below MTOW 1361 kg: Cessna 182P

registration	type of aircraft	cn/fn	ex/ex*	mfd	del	powered by	mtow kg	configuration	selcal	name/fln/specialitites/remarks
☐ N5523T	Cessna R182 Skylane RG II	R18201884		0082	0682	1 LY O-540-J3C5D	1406			
☐ N38MA	Bell 206B JetRanger III	2893		0080	0280	1 AN 250-C20B	1451			
☐ N43MA	Bell 206B JetRanger III	4156		0091	0491	1 AN 250-C20J	1451			
☐ N47MA	Bell 206B JetRanger III	2647	N2754A	0079	0679	1 AN 250-C20B	1451			
☐ N9538Y	Cessna T210N Turbo Centurion II	21064542		0081	1084	1 CO TSIO-520-R	1814			lsf Turbo Air Llc
☐ N48MA	Bell 206L-3 LongRanger III	51537		0091	1291	1 AN 250-C30P	1882			
☐ N49MA	Bell 206L-4 LongRanger IV	52001		0092	0393	1 AN 250-C30P	2018			
☐ N142MA	Bell 407	53123		0097	0397	1 AN 250-C47B	2268			
☐ N56MA	Cessna 340A II	340A0067	N20FB	0076	1291	2 CO TSIO-520-N	2717			
☐ N52TT	Piper PA-31T Cheyenne II	31T-7920057	N102E	0079	0591	2 PWC PT6A-28	4082			
☐ N109MA	Bell UH-1H (205)	10264	68-15334	0068	0596	1 LY T53-L-13B	4309			
☐ N144MA	Bell UH-1H (205)	13122	71-20298	0071	0697	1 LY T53-L-13B	4309			

MIRABELLA YACHTS, Inc. – Amphibian operations — Fort Lauderdale-Executive, FL

2600 NW 62nd Street, Hangar I-3, Fort Lauderdale, FL 33309, USA ☎ (954) 938-7907 Tx: none Fax: (954) 938-8327 SITA: n/a
F: 1994 ⁂ n/a Head: Joseph V. Vittoria Net: n/a Company is conducting on-demand charters, flights for the customers of its yachting operations & executive flights for itself.

registration	type of aircraft	cn/fn	ex/ex*	mfd	del	powered by	mtow kg	configuration	selcal	name/fln/specialitites/remarks
☐ N26PR	Grumman G-111 Albatross	464	PK-PAM	0061	0694	2 WR R-1820-C9HE3	14129	19 Pax		cvtd HU-16B / Amphibian

MISSIONAIR, Inc. — Orlando-Kissimmee Municipal, FL

150 South Roma Way, Kissimmee, FL 34746, USA ☎ (407) 922-3482 Tx: none Fax: (407) 397-1913 SITA: n/a
F: 1990 ⁂ n/a Head: Dr. Robert M. Helmer Net: n/a

registration	type of aircraft	cn/fn	ex/ex*	mfd	del	powered by	mtow kg	configuration	selcal	name/fln/specialitites/remarks
☐ N25BA	Helio H-391B Courier	011		0055	0498	1 LY GO-435-C2B2	1361			
☐ N4654F	Cessna P206A Super Skylane	P206-0254		0066	0498	1 CO IO-520-A	1633			
☐ N213MA	Boeing (Douglas) DC-3A (C-53-DO)	7320	N123BA	0042	1090	2 PW R-1830	12202	Y20		
☐ N79MA	Boeing (Douglas) DC-3-201F	4089	N168LG	0041	0691	2 WR R-1820	12202	Y20		

MISSION LODGE (Bristol Aviation, Inc. dba / Seasonal May-October ops only) — Aleknagek, AK

PO Box 165, Aleknagek, AK 99555, USA ☎ (907) 842-2250 Tx: none Fax: (907) 842-5776 SITA: n/a
F: 1994 ⁂ n/a Head: Dale Depriest Net: n/a

registration	type of aircraft	cn/fn	ex/ex*	mfd	del	powered by	mtow kg	configuration	selcal	name/fln/specialitites/remarks
☐ N331NJ	Cessna U206G Stationair	U20603864		0077	0596	1 CO IO-520-F	1633			Floats
☐ N5333G	De Havilland DHC-2 Beaver I	772	53-7952	0056	0786	1 PW R-985	2309			lsf Aleknagek Mission Lodge Inc./Floats
☐ N7333N	De Havilland DHC-2 Beaver I	1172	N66KZ	0056	1088	1 PW R-985	2309			lsf Aleknagek Mission Lodge Inc./Floats

MISTY FJORD'S AIR & OUTFITTING (David P. Doyon dba) — Ketchikan-Harbor SPB, AK

1285 Tongass Avenue, Ketchikan, AK 99901, USA ☎ (907) 225-5155 Tx: none Fax: (907) 225-5155 SITA: n/a
F: 1981 ⁂ n/a Head: David P. Doyon Net: n/a

registration	type of aircraft	cn/fn	ex/ex*	mfd	del	powered by	mtow kg	configuration	selcal	name/fln/specialitites/remarks
☐ N9204H	Cessna A185F Skywagon	18503421		0077	0582	1 CO IO-520-D	1520			Floats

MOBIL Global Aircraft Services – Helicopter Dept. (Mobil Business Resources Corp. dba/Subsidiary of Mobil Oil Corp.) — Morgan City-Heliport, LA

1200 Youngs Road, Morgan City, LA 70380, USA ☎ (504) 380-5556 Tx: none Fax: (504) 380-5575 SITA: n/a
F: 1980 ⁂ n/a Head: Lonnie J. Welch Net: n/a

registration	type of aircraft	cn/fn	ex/ex*	mfd	del	powered by	mtow kg	configuration	selcal	name/fln/specialitites/remarks
☐ N104RT	Bell 206L-3 LongRanger III	51364	LV-WCF	0090	0198	1 AN 250-C30P	1882			lsf Rotorcraft Leasing Co. Llc
☐ N2611	Bell 206L-1 LongRanger III	45417		0080	0780	1 AN 250-C30P	1882			cvtd LongRanger II
☐ N2616	Bell 206L-3 LongRanger III	51418		0090	1290	1 AN 250-C30P	1882			
☐ N2618	Bell 206L-1 LongRanger III	45503		0080	1280	1 AN 250-C28B	1882			cvtd LongRanger II
☐ N2619	Bell 206L-3 LongRanger III	51375		0090	0790	1 AN 250-C30P	1882			
☐ N2621	Bell 206L-1 LongRanger III	45400	C-GBSD	0080	1296	1 AN 250-C30P	1882			lsf ATEL Financial / cvtd LongRanger II
☐ N2629	Bell 206L-1 LongRanger III	45419	C-GBHQ	0080	1296	1 AN 250-C30P	1882			lsf ATEL Financial / cvtd LongRanger II
☐ N2630	Bell 206L-1 LongRanger III	45643	C-GQZT	0081	1296	1 AN 250-C30P	1882			lsf ATEL Financial / cvtd LongRanger II
☐ N2654	Bell 206L-1 LongRanger III	45482		0080	1080	1 AN 250-C28B	1882			cvtd LongRanger II
☐ N3899C	Bell 206L-1 LongRanger III	45596		0080	0195	1 AN 250-C28B	1882			cvtd LongRanger II
☐ N405RL	Bell 206L-3 LongRanger III	51405	N253EV	0090	0198	1 AN 250-C30P	1882			lsf Rotorcraft Leasing Co. Llc
☐ N40LP	Bell 206L-1 LongRanger III	45233	N289JH	0079	0294	1 AN 250-C30P	1882			cvtd LongRanger II
☐ N5000G	Bell 206L-1 LongRanger III	45163		0078	0098	1 AN 250-C30P	1882			lsf Evergreen Helicopters / cvtd LR II
☐ N5007F	Bell 206L-1 LongRanger III	45186		0078	0098	1 AN 250-C30P	1882			lsf Evergreen Helicopters / cvtd LR II
☐ N5759M	Bell 206L-1 LongRanger III	45555		0080	0294	1 AN 250-C30P	1882			cvtd LongRanger II
☐ N577E	Bell 206L-1 LongRanger III	45577	ZS-HJR	0080	0195	1 AN 250-C30P	1882			cvtd LongRanger II
☐ N202SR	Sikorsky S-76A	760236	N202SK	0083	0395	2 AN 250-C30S	4763			
☐ N2634	Sikorsky S-76A	76007	VH-HRT	0079	1197	2 AN 250-C30S	4763			
☐ N31211	Sikorsky S-76A	760225		0082	0395	2 AN 250-C30S	4763			
☐ N917QS	Sikorsky S-76A	760217	N3122E	0082	0295	2 AN 250-C30S	4763			

MOBLEY AVIATION (Flight division of Norton Cattle Company) — Madras-City County, OR

2028 NW Airport Way, Madras, OR 97741, USA ☎ (541) 475-6483 Tx: none Fax: (541) 475-6792 SITA: n/a
F: 1986 ⁂ 5 Head: Thomas A. Norton Net: n/a

registration	type of aircraft	cn/fn	ex/ex*	mfd	del	powered by	mtow kg	configuration	selcal	name/fln/specialitites/remarks
☐ N695NC	Twin (Aero) Jetprop Commander 1000 (695A)	96032	VH-GAB	0082	0796	2 GA TPE331-10-511K	5080	9 Pax		

MOLOKAI AIR SHUTTLE (Molokai Lanai Air Shuttle, Inc. dba) — Honolulu, HI

99 Mokuea Place, Honolulu, HI 96819, USA ☎ (808) 545-4988 Tx: none Fax: none SITA: n/a
F: 1990 ⁂ n/a Head: Henry A. Younge, III Net: n/a

registration	type of aircraft	cn/fn	ex/ex*	mfd	del	powered by	mtow kg	configuration	selcal	name/fln/specialitites/remarks
☐ N17512	Piper PA-23-250 Aztec D	27-4265		0069	0393	2 LY IO-540-C4B5	2359			lsf pvt
☐ N4DR	Piper PA-23-250 Aztec C	27-3175		0065	0592	2 LY IO-540-C4B5	2359			lsf pvt
☐ N5971Y	Piper PA-23-250 Aztec C	27-3142		0065	0292	2 LY IO-540-C4B5	2359			lsf pvt

MONTEX DRILLING – Aviation Dept. (Aviation Dept. of Montex Drilling, Co.) — Fort Worth-Meacham Int'l, TX

Moncrief Bldg, Ninth at Commerce, Fort Worth, TX 76102, USA ☎ (817) 624-7650 Tx: none Fax: (817) 624-1988 SITA: n/a
F: 1951 ⁂ n/a Head: Edwin W. Word Net: n/a Operates non-commercial executive flight exclusively for its parent company which is active in the oil industry.

registration	type of aircraft	cn/fn	ex/ex*	mfd	del	powered by	mtow kg	configuration	selcal	name/fln/specialitites/remarks
☐ N114M	BAe 146-100	E1068	N861MC	0086	1297	4 LY ALF502R-5	38102	Exec 25 Pax		Lucky Liz
☐ N114MX	BAe (BAC) One-Eleven 422EQ	119	N114M	0067	1276	2 RR Spey 511-14	39463	Exec 25 Pax		lsf pvt

MORIAN AVIATION, Inc. (Sister co. of DX Service, Co. Inc.) — Houston-William P. Hobby, TX

300 Jackson Hill, Houston, TX 77007, USA ☎ (713) 641-0558 Tx: none Fax: (713) 643-0732 SITA: n/a
F: 1990 ⁂ n/a Head: William L. Hixon, Jr. Net: n/a

registration	type of aircraft	cn/fn	ex/ex*	mfd	del	powered by	mtow kg	configuration	selcal	name/fln/specialitites/remarks
☐ N147X	Dassault Falcon 20D-5B	185	N3WN	0069	0390	2 GA TFE731-5BR-2C	13200			lsf DX Service Co. Inc. / cvtd 20D

MOSELEY AVIATION, Inc. — Phoenix-Moseley Heliport, AZ

PO Bio 70, Litchfield, AZ 85340, USA ☎ (602) 853-9560 Tx: none Fax: (602) 853-1185 SITA: n/a
F: 1972 ⁂ n/a Head: Ernest E. Moseley Net: n/a Ag-aircraft below MTOW 5000kg: Ayres S2R

registration	type of aircraft	cn/fn	ex/ex*	mfd	del	powered by	mtow kg	configuration	selcal	name/fln/specialitites/remarks
☐ N140EH	Eurocopter (Aerosp.) AS350B AStar	1456	N5791R	0082	0198	1 TU Arriel 1B	1950			lsf Evro Llc / cvtd AS350D
☐ N100PL	Kaman HH-43F (K600) Huskie	64	59-1583	0059	0694	1 LY T53-L-11A	4150			lst Pro-Lift Helicopters / cvtd HH-43B
☐ N323WN	Kaman HH-43F (K600) Huskie	62	59-1581	0059	0984	1 LY T53-L-11A	4150			cvtd HH-43B
☐ N325WN	Kaman HH-43F (K600) Huskie	110	60-0286	0060	1090	1 LY T53-L-11A	4150			cvtd HH-43B
☐ N3268D	Kaman HH-43F (K600) Huskie	60	59-1579	0059	1082	1 LY T53-L-11A	4150			cvtd HH-43B
☐ N62387	Kaman HH-43F (K600) Huskie	28	59-1547	0059	1082	1 LY T53-L-11A	4150			cvtd HH-43B
☐ N90944	Kaman HH-43F (K600) Huskie	140	62-4514	0062	1182	1 LY T53-L-11A	4150			lst Pro-Lift Helicopters / cvtd HH-43B

MOUNTAIN AIR CARGO, Inc. – MAC = MTN — Denver, NC

PO Box 488, Denver, NC 28037, USA ☎ (704) 464-8741 Tx: n/a Fax: (704) 465-5281 SITA: n/a
F: 1975 ⁂ 300 Head: David Clark ICAO: MOUNTAIN Net: n/a

registration	type of aircraft	cn/fn	ex/ex*	mfd	del	powered by	mtow kg	configuration	selcal	name/fln/specialitites/remarks
☐ N801FE	Cessna 208A Caravan I Cargomaster	20800009		0085	0385	1 PWC PT6A-114	3629	Freighter		lsf/opf FDX in FedEx Feeder-colors
☐ N708FX	Cessna 208B Caravan I Super Cargomaster	208B0429		0095	0395	1 PWC PT6A-114A	3969	Freighter		lsf/opf FDX in FedEx Feeder-colors
☐ N715FX	Cessna 208B Caravan I Super Cargomaster	208B0440		0095	0595	1 PWC PT6A-114A	3969	Freighter		lsf/opf FDX in FedEx Feeder-colors
☐ N721FX	Cessna 208B Caravan I Super Cargomaster	208B0453		0095	0795	1 PWC PT6A-114A	3969	Freighter		lsf/opf FDX in FedEx Feeder-colors
☐ N729FX	Cessna 208B Caravan I Super Cargomaster	208B0474		0095	1095	1 PWC PT6A-114A	3969	Freighter		lsf/opf FDX in FedEx Feeder-colors
☐ N740FX	Cessna 208B Caravan I Super Cargomaster	208B0484		0095	1195	1 PWC PT6A-114A	3969	Freighter		lsf/opf FDX in FedEx Feeder-colors
☐ N742FX	Cessna 208B Caravan I Super Cargomaster	208B0489		0095	1295	1 PWC PT6A-114A	3969	Freighter		lsf/opf FDX in FedEx Feeder-colors

N747FE	Cessna 208B Caravan I Super Cargomaster	208B0238		0090	1190	1 PWC PT6A-114A	3969	Freighter		lsf/opf FDX in FedEx Feeder-colors
N747FX	Cessna 208B Caravan I Super Cargomaster	208B0501		0096	0196	1 PWC PT6A-114A	3969	Freighter		lsf/opf FDX in FedEx Feeder-colors
N749FX	Cessna 208B Caravan I Super Cargomaster	208B0508		0096	0296	1 PWC PT6A-114A	3969	Freighter		lsf/opf FDX in FedEx Feeder-colors
N755FE	Cessna 208B Caravan I Super Cargomaster	208B0250		0091	0191	1 PWC PT6A-114A	3969	Freighter		lsf/opf FDX in FedEx Feeder-colors
N764FE	Cessna 208B Caravan I Super Cargomaster	208B0258		0091	0391	1 PWC PT6A-114A	3969	Freighter		lsf/opf FDX in FedEx Feeder-colors
N769FE	Cessna 208B Caravan I Super Cargomaster	208B0264		0091	0591	1 PWC PT6A-114A	3969	Freighter		lsf/opf FDX in FedEx Feeder-colors
N776FE	Cessna 208B Caravan I Super Cargomaster	208B0273		0091	0791	1 PWC PT6A-114A	3969	Freighter		lsf/opf FDX in FedEx Feeder-colors
N787FE	Cessna 208B Caravan I Super Cargomaster	208B0285		0091	1091	1 PWC PT6A-114A	3969	Freighter		lsf/opf FDX in FedEx Feeder-colors
N792FE	Cessna 208B Caravan I Super Cargomaster	208B0290		0091	1291	1 PWC PT6A-114A	3969	Freighter		lsf/opf FDX in FedEx Feeder-colors
N820FE	Cessna 208B Caravan I Super Cargomaster	208B0111	F-GHHC	0088	0888	1 PWC PT6A-114	3969	Freighter		lsf/opf FDX in FedEx Feeder-colors
N831FE	Cessna 208B Caravan I Super Cargomaster	208B0225	F-GHHE	0090	0890	1 PWC PT6A-114	3969	Freighter		lsf/opf FDX in FedEx Feeder-colors
N842FE	Cessna 208B Caravan I Super Cargomaster	208B0146		0089	0189	1 PWC PT6A-114	3969	Freighter		lsf/opf FDX in FedEx Feeder-colors
N847FE	Cessna 208B Caravan I Super Cargomaster	208B0156		0089	0389	1 PWC PT6A-114	3969	Freighter		lsf/opf FDX in FedEx Feeder-colors
N848FE	Cessna 208B Caravan I Super Cargomaster	208B0158		0089	0389	1 PWC PT6A-114	3969	Freighter		lsf/opf FDX in FedEx Feeder-colors
N849FE	Cessna 208B Caravan I Super Cargomaster	208B0162		0089	0389	1 PWC PT6A-114	3969	Freighter		lsf/opf FDX in FedEx Feeder-colors
N852FE	Cessna 208B Caravan I Super Cargomaster	208B0168		0089	0489	1 PWC PT6A-114	3969	Freighter		lsf/opf FDX in FedEx Feeder-colors
N853FE	Cessna 208B Caravan I Super Cargomaster	208B0170		0089	0589	1 PWC PT6A-114	3969	Freighter		lsf/opf FDX in FedEx Feeder-colors
N855FE	Cessna 208B Caravan I Super Cargomaster	208B0203		0090	0190	1 PWC PT6A-114	3969	Freighter		lsf/opf FDX in FedEx Feeder-colors
N862FE	Cessna 208B Caravan I Super Cargomaster	208B0184		0089	0889	1 PWC PT6A-114	3969	Freighter		lsf/opf FDX in FedEx Feeder-colors
N869FE	Cessna 208B Caravan I Super Cargomaster	208B0195		0089	1089	1 PWC PT6A-114	3969	Freighter		lsf/opf FDX in FedEx Feeder-colors
N874FE	Cessna 208B Caravan I Super Cargomaster	208B0205		0090	0190	1 PWC PT6A-114	3969	Freighter		lsf/opf FDX in FedEx Feeder-colors
N878FE	Cessna 208B Caravan I Super Cargomaster	208B0211		0090	0390	1 PWC PT6A-114	3969	Freighter		lsf/opf FDX in FedEx Feeder-colors
N881FE	Cessna 208B Caravan I Super Cargomaster	208B0204		0090	0190	1 PWC PT6A-114	3969	Freighter		lsf/opf FDX in FedEx Feeder-colors
N887FE	Cessna 208B Caravan I Super Cargomaster	208B0216		0090	0590	1 PWC PT6A-114	3969	Freighter		lsf/opf FDX in FedEx Feeder-colors
N905FE	Cessna 208B Caravan I Super Cargomaster	208B0005		0086	1286	1 PWC PT6A-114	3969	Freighter		lsf/opf FDX in FedEx Feeder-colors
N917FE	Cessna 208B Caravan I Super Cargomaster	208B0017		0087	0387	1 PWC PT6A-114	3969	Freighter		lsf/opf FDX in FedEx Feeder-colors
N921FE	Cessna 208B Caravan I Super Cargomaster	208B0021		0087	0487	1 PWC PT6A-114	3969	Freighter		lsf/opf FDX in FedEx Feeder-colors
N938FE	Cessna 208B Caravan I Super Cargomaster	208B0038		0087	0887	1 PWC PT6A-114	3969	Freighter		lsf/opf FDX in FedEx Feeder-colors
N943FE	Cessna 208B Caravan I Super Cargomaster	208B0043		0087	0987	1 PWC PT6A-114	3969	Freighter		lsf/opf FDX in FedEx Feeder-colors
N955FE	Cessna 208B Caravan I Super Cargomaster	208B0066		0087	1287	1 PWC PT6A-114	3969	Freighter		lsf/opf FDX in FedEx Feeder-colors
N962FE	Cessna 208B Caravan I Super Cargomaster	208B0078		0088	0388	1 PWC PT6A-114	3969	Freighter		lsf/opf FDX in FedEx Feeder-colors
N967FE	Cessna 208B Caravan I Super Cargomaster	208B0088		0088	0488	1 PWC PT6A-114	3969	Freighter		lsf/opf FDX in FedEx Feeder-colors
N973FE	Cessna 208B Caravan I Super Cargomaster	208B0098		0088	0688	1 PWC PT6A-114	3969	Freighter		lsf/opf FDX in FedEx Feeder-colors
N975FE	Cessna 208B Caravan I Super Cargomaster	208B0101		0088	0688	1 PWC PT6A-114	3969	Freighter		lsf/opf FDX in FedEx Feeder-colors
N979FE	Cessna 208B Caravan I Super Cargomaster	208B0106		0088	0788	1 PWC PT6A-114	3969	Freighter		lsf/opf FDX in FedEx Feeder-colors
N999FE	Cessna 208B Caravan I Super Cargomaster	208B0231		0090	0990	1 PWC PT6A-114A	3969	Freighter		lsf/opf FDX in FedEx Feeder-colors
N169FB	CASA 212 Aviocar Srs 200	169	N37838	0080	0288	2 GA TPE331-10R-511C	7450	Freighter		
N26288	Shorts 330-200 (SD3-30)	SH3074	G-BIYF*	0081	0887	2 PWC PT6A-45R	10387	Freighter		
N2679U	Shorts 330-200 (SD3-30)	SH3071	N330AE	0081	0887	2 PWC PT6A-45R	10387	Freighter		
N705FE	Fokker F27 Friendship 500 (F27 Mk500)	10367	G-FEDX	0068	1287	2 RR Dart 532-7R	20412	Freighter		lsf/opf FDX in FedEx Feeder-colors
N706FE	Fokker F27 Friendship 500 (F27 Mk500)	10384	G-OFEC	0069	1287	2 RR Dart 532-7R	20412	Freighter		lsf/opf FDX in FedEx Feeder-colors
N707FE	Fokker F27 Friendship 500 (F27 Mk500)	10371	G-FEBZ	0068	0388	2 RR Dart 532-7R	20412	Freighter		lsf/opf FDX in FedEx Feeder-colors
N708FE	Fokker F27 Friendship 500 (F27 Mk500)	10372	G-BOMV	0068	0488	2 RR Dart 532-7R	20412	Freighter		lsf/opf FDX in FedEx Feeder-colors
N709FE	Fokker F27 Friendship 500 (F27 Mk500)	10375	F-BPNE	0068	0488	2 RR Dart 532-7R	20412	Freighter		lsf/opf FDX in FedEx Feeder-colors
N710FE	Fokker F27 Friendship 500 (F27 Mk500)	10380	F-BPNG	0068	0389	2 RR Dart 532-7R	20412	Freighter		lsf/opf FDX in FedEx Feeder-colors
N712FE	Fokker F27 Friendship 500RF (F27 Mk500RF)	10613	9M-MCK	0081	1189	2 RR Dart 532-7R	20412	Freighter		lsf/opf FDX in FedEx Feeder-colors
N713FE	Fokker F27 Friendship 500RF (F27 Mk500RF)	10615	9M-MCL	0081	1189	2 RR Dart 532-7R	20412	Freighter		lsf/opf FDX in FedEx Feeder-colors
N714FE	Fokker F27 Friendship 500 (F27 Mk500)	10461	9M-MCD	0071	1289	2 RR Dart 532-7R	20412	Freighter		lsf/opf FDX in FedEx Feeder-colors
N715FE	Fokker F27 Friendship 500 (F27 Mk500)	10468	9M-MCG	0071	1289	2 RR Dart 532-7R	20412	Freighter		lsf/opf FDX in FedEx Feeder-colors
N716FE	Fokker F27 Friendship 500 (F27 Mk500)	10471	9M-MCI	0071	0690	2 RR Dart 532-7R	20412	Freighter		lsf/opf FDX in FedEx Feeder-colors
N717FE	Fokker F27 Friendship 500 (F27 Mk500)	10455	9M-MCA	0071	0390	2 RR Dart 532-7R	20412	Freighter		lsf/opf FDX in FedEx Feeder-colors
N718FE	Fokker F27 Friendship 500 (F27 Mk500)	10470	9M-MCH	0071	0390	2 RR Dart 532-7R	20412	Freighter		lsf/opf FDX in FedEx Feeder-colors
N719FE	Fokker F27 Friendship 500 (F27 Mk500)	10467	9M-MCF	0071	0690	2 RR Dart 532-7R	20412	Freighter		lsf/opf FDX in FedEx Feeder-colors
N721FE	Fokker F27 Friendship 500 (F27 Mk500)	10460	9M-MCC	0071	0290	2 RR Dart 532-7R	20412	Freighter		lsf/opf FDX in FedEx Feeder-colors
N722FE	Fokker F27 Friendship 500 (F27 Mk500)	10472	9M-MCJ	0071	0690	2 RR Dart 532-7R	20412	Freighter		lsf/opf FDX in FedEx Feeder-colors
N723FE	Fokker F27 Friendship 500 (F27 Mk500)	10682	OO-FEI	0085	1091	2 RR Dart 552-7R	20412	Freighter		lsf/opf FDX in FedEx Feeder-colors
N724FE	Fokker F27 Friendship 500 (F27 Mk500)	10677	OO-FEK	0084	1091	2 RR Dart 552-7R	20412	Freighter		lsf/opf FDX in FedEx Feeder-colors
N725FE	Fokker F27 Friendship 500 (F27 Mk500)	10658	N514AW	0083	0592	2 RR Dart 552-7R	20412	Freighter		lsf/opf FDX in FedEx Feeder-colors
N726FE	Fokker F27 Friendship 500 (F27 Mk500)	10683	N508AW	0085	1291	2 RR Dart 552-7R	20412	Freighter		lsf/opf FDX in FedEx Feeder-colors
N727FE	Fokker F27 Friendship 500 (F27 Mk500)	10661	N502AW	0083	1291	2 RR Dart 552-7R	20412	Freighter		lsf/opf FDX in FedEx Feeder-colors
N728FE	Fokker F27 Friendship 500 (F27 Mk500)	10657	OO-FEL	0083	1291	2 RR Dart 552-7R	20412	Freighter		lsf/opf FDX in FedEx Feeder-colors

MOUNTAIN EMPIRE FLYING SERVICE (Air Taxi of Southwest Virginia, Inc. dba) — Asheville-Regional, VA

Box 390, Marion, VA 24354, USA ☎ (910) 982-4273 Tx: none Fax: none SITA: n/a
F: 1965 n/a Head: John D. Greear Net: n/a

N5157U	Cessna 206 Super Skywagon	206-0157		0064	1070	1 CO IO-520-A	1588			

MOUNTAIN HIGH AVIATION = MHA (Richard E. & Cheryl L. Roth dba) — Walla Walla-Regional, WA

Rt 4, Box 177A, Walla Walla, WA 99362, USA ☎ (509) 525-2175 Tx: none Fax: (509) 525-8610 SITA: n/a
F: 1982 4 Head: Richard E. Roth ICAO: MOUNTAIN HIGH Net: n/a

N411WA	Britten-Norman BN-2A Mk.III-2 Trislander	1023	G-BDOM	0076	0194	3 LY O-540-E4C5	4241	Freighter		

MOUNTAIN WEST HELICOPTERS, Llc — Provo-Municipal, UT

73 West 620 South, Orem, UT 84058, USA ☎ (801) 222-9814 Tx: none Fax: (801) 222-0290 SITA: n/a
F: 1995 n/a Head: Bryan J. Burr Net: n/a

N132KA	Kaman K-1200 K-Max	A94-0004		0094	0296	1 LY T5317A-1	2722			lsf pvt
N164KA	Kaman K-1200 K-Max	A94-0014		0096	0697	1 LY T5317A-1	2722			lsf Long Line Leasing Llc

MOYER AVIATION, Inc. — Mount Pocono-Municipal, PA

Box 275, Rt 611, Mount Pocono, PA 18344, USA ☎ (717) 839-6080 Tx: none Fax: (717) 839-7163 SITA: n/a
F: 1981 n/a Head: Laverne S. Moyer Net: n/a Aircraft below MTOW 1361kg: Piper PA-28

N2932M	Piper PA-32-300 Cherokee SIX	32-7840060		0077	1296	1 LY IO-540-K1G5	1542			lsf Herfurth Brothers Inc.
N101MA	Piper PA-31-350 Navajo Chieftain	31-7752186	N287PC	0077	0687	2 LY TIO-540-J2BD	3175			
N326D	Cessna 421C Golden Eagle III	421C0493		0078	0794	2 CO GTSIO-520-L	3379			to be re-reg. N103MA

MUHL AIR (Wayne C. Muhler dba / Sister company of Sunwest Aviation, Inc.) — Erie-Tri County, CO

185 East Piper Drive, Erie, CO 80516, USA ☎ (303) 665-5989 Tx: none Fax: (303) 399-9510 SITA: n/a
F: 1997 n/a Head: Wayne C. Muhler Net: n/a

N78GH	Piper PA-31-350 Navajo Chieftain	31-7852121		0078	0296	2 LY TIO-540-J2BD	3175	Freighter		lst Sunrise Airlines
N80MA	Piper PA-31T Cheyenne II	31T-7720043	F-GEBH	0077	0498	2 PWC PT6A-28	4082	Executive		
N336PL	Beech 99 Airliner	U-35		0068	0497	2 PWC PT6A-27	4717	Freighter		
N7899R	Beech 99 Airliner	U-88		0069	0497	2 PWC PT6A-27	4717	Freighter		
N9FH	Beech 99 Airliner	U-94	F-OGKF	0069	0497	2 PWC PT6A-27	4717	Freighter		

MULCHATNA AIR SERVICE (Leon C. Braswell dba) — Dillingham, AK

PO Box 990, Dillingham, AK 99576, USA ☎ (907) 842-7166 Tx: none Fax: (907) 842-3877 SITA: n/a
F: 1991 n/a Head: Leon C. Braswell Net: n/a

N6124Z	Cessna U206G Stationair 6 II	U20606150		0081	0891	1 CO IO-520-F	1633			
N88PB	Cessna 207A Stationair 7 II	20700458		0079	1194	1 CO IO-520-F	1724			

MULTI-AERO, Inc. — Chesterfield-Spirit of St. Louis, MO

900 Airport Road, Festus, MO 63028, USA ☎ (573) 296-1911 Tx: none Fax: (573) 931-0124 SITA: n/a
F: 1979 n/a Head: H. Ivan Storz Net: n/a

N388SQ	Beech Baron 58	TH-114		0071	1296	2 CO IO-520-C	2449			
N86SJ	Beech Baron 58	TH-656		0075	1093	2 CO IO-520-C	2449			
N22PB	Cessna 402B	402B0243		0072	1294	2 CO TSIO-520-EB	2858			
N744MA	Cessna 402B	402B0592	N3734C	0074	0393	2 CO TSIO-520-EB	2858			
N112RL	Cessna 421C Golden Eagle II	421C0012		0075	0596	2 CO GTSIO-520-L	3379			lsf RJ Aviation Inc.
N6166Y	Beech Queen Air B80 (65-B80)	LD-388		0068	0297	2 LY IGSO-540-A1D	3992			
N80JF	Beech Queen Air B80 (65-B80)	LD-376		0068	0695	2 LY IGSO-540-A1D	3992			

MURRAY AVIATION, Inc. = MUA — Detroit-Willow Run, MI

835 Willow Run Airport, Ypsilanti, MI 48198-0835, USA ☎ (734) 484-4800 Tx: none Fax: (734) 484-4875 SITA: n/a
F: 1985 70 Head: Mark A. Murray ICAO: MURRAY AIR Net: http://www.murray-aviation.com

N305CW	Mitsubishi MU-2L (MU-2B-36) Cargoliner	667	N300CW	0075	0686	2 GA TPE331-6-252M	5250	Freighter		Cavenaugh SCD conversion
N412MA	Beech King Air A90 (65-A90)	LJ-214	N985AA	0067	1197	2 PWC PT6A-20	4218	6 Pax/Freighter		
N70UA	Beech King Air A90 (65-A90)	LJ-130	N70TG	0066	0495	2 PWC PT6A-20	4218	6 Pax/Freighter		
N992MA	Beech King Air E90	LW-59	VR-CGK	0073	0198	2 PWC PT6A-28	4581	8 Pax/Freighter		to be re-reg. N290KA
N262MA	CASA 212 Aviocar Srs 200	262	N429CA	0082	0493	2 GA TPE331-10-511C	7700	Freighter		
N263MA	CASA 212 Aviocar Srs 200	263	LV-WCV	0082	0896	2 GA TPE331-10R-511C	7700	Freighter		
N287MA	CASA 212 Aviocar Srs 200	287	N436CA	0082	0194	2 GA TPE331-10-511C	7700	Freighter		
N687MA	CASA 212 Aviocar Srs 200	174	N174FB	0080	0289	2 GA TPE331-10-511C	7700	Freighter		

402 registration type of aircraft cn/fn ex/ex* mfd del powered by mtow kg configuration selcal name/fln/specialitites/remarks

NAC AIRLINE, Inc.

Chicago-Midway, IL

PO Box 388-440, Chicago, IL 60638, USA ☎ (773) 471-3420 Tx: none Fax: (773) 471-3429 SITA: n/a

F: 1975 n/a Head: Emmett L. Stovall Net: n/a

☐ N127ML	Beech D18S	A-212	N127M	0046	0475	2 PW R-985	3969	Freighter		lsf National Air Service Inc.

NASA – National Aeronautics & Space Administration

Washington, DC

300 E Street SW, Washington, DC 20546, USA ☎ (202) 358-0000 Tx: none Fax: (202) 358-3151 SITA: n/a

F: 1958 n/a Head: Daniel S. Goldin ICAO: NASA Net: n/a Non-commercial Federal organisation, conducting calibration, research, test and transport-flights for scientific purposes.

Operations are from the HQ=Headquartes, Washington/DC & 9 centers: ARC=Ames Research Center, Moffett Field/CA, DFRC=Dryden Flight Research Center, Edwards AFB/CA, JSC=Johnson Space Center, Ellington ANGB/TX, KSC=Kennedy Space Center,Cape Canaveral/FL, LaRC=Langley Research Center, Langley AFB/VA, LeRC=Lewis Research Center, Cleveland-Hopkins Int'l/OH,MSFC=Marshall Space Flight Center, Huntsville-Int'l/AL, SSC=Stennis Space Center,Bay St.Louis-Stennis Intl/MS & WFF=Goddard Space Flight Center, Wallops Island/VA.Some aircraft carry only the 3-digit number together with NASA instead the full civil-registration.

☐ N808NA	Piper PA-30-160 Twin Comanche B	30-1498		0067	0669	2 LY IO-320-B1A	1633	Program Support		808 / opb DFRC, Edwards AFB/CA
☐ N718NA	Lockheed YO-3A Q-Star	011	69-18010	0070	1077	1 CO IO-360-D	1724	Research&Develop		718 / opb DFRC, Edwards AFB/CA
☐ N509NA	Beech Mentor T-34C	GL-180	161053	0078	1194	1 PWC PT6A-25	1939	Research&Develop		509 / opb LaRC, Langley AFB/VA
☐ N619NA	Beech Mentor T-34C	GL-131	160945	0078	1194	1 PWC PT6A-25	1939	Research&Develop		619 / opb DFRC, Edwards AFB/CA
☐ N417NA	Bell UH-1H (205)	4335	64-13628	0064	1293	1 LY T53-L-11	3856	Support/Training		417 / opb KSC, Cape Canaveral/FL
☐ N418NA	Bell UH-1H (205)	5209	65-12876	0065	0993	1 LY T53-L-11	3856	Program Support		418 / opb KSC, Cape Canaveral/FL
☐ N419NA	Bell UH-1H (205)	4752	65-9708	0065	1090	1 LY T53-L-11	3856	Program Support		419 / opb KSC, Cape Canaveral/FL
☐ N420NA	Bell UH-1H (205)	5148	65-10104	0065	1090	1 LY T53-L-11	3856	Program Support		420 / opb KSC, Cape Canaveral/FL
☐ N535NA	Bell UH-1H (205)	5036	65-9992	0065	0793	1 LY T53-L-11	3856	Program Support		535 / opb LaRC, Langley AFB/VA
☐ N511NA	Northrop T-38A Talon	N.5748	65-10329	0065	0869	2 GE J85-GE-5	5485	Program Support		511 / opb JSC, Ellington ANGB/TX
☐ N901NA	Northrop T-38A Talon	N.5951	66-8381	0066	0969	2 GE J85-GE-5	5485	Support/Training		901 / opb JSC, Ellington ANGB/TX
☐ N902NA	Northrop T-38A Talon	N.5540	63-8193	0063	0969	2 GE J85-GE-5	5485	Support/Training		902 / opb JSC, Ellington ANGB/TX
☐ N903NA	Northrop T-38A Talon	N.5547	63-8200	0063	0969	2 GE J85-GE-5	5485	Support/Training		903 / opb JSC, Ellington ANGB/TX
☐ N904NA	Northrop T-38A Talon	N.5551	63-8204	0063	1078	2 GE J85-GE-5	5485	Support/Training		904 / opb JSC, Ellington ANGB/TX
☐ N906NA	Northrop T-38A Talon	N.5745	65-10326	0065	1078	2 GE J85-GE-5	5485	Support/Training		906 / opb JSC, Ellington ANGB/TX
☐ N907NA	Northrop T-38A Talon	N.5278	61-0912	0061	1078	2 GE J85-GE-5	5485	Support/Training		907 / opb JSC, Ellington ANGB/TX
☐ N908NA	Northrop T-38A Talon	N.5747	65-10328	0065	0969	2 GE J85-GE-5	5485	Support/Training		908 / opb JSC, Ellington ANGB/TX
☐ N909NA	Northrop T-38A Talon	N.5770	65-10351	0065	0969	2 GE J85-GE-5	5485	Support/Training		909 / opb JSC, Ellington ANGB/TX
☐ N910NA	Northrop T-38A Talon	N.5771	65-10352	0065	1078	2 GE J85-GE-5	5485	Support/Training		910 / opb JSC, Ellington ANGB/TX
☐ N912NA	Northrop T-38A Talon	N.5773	65-10354	0065	1078	2 GE J85-GE-5	5485	Support/Training		912 / opb JSC, Ellington ANGB/TX
☐ N913NA	Northrop T-38A Talon	N.5774	65-10355	0065	0969	2 GE J85-GE-5	5485	Support/Training		913 / opb JSC, Ellington ANGB/TX
☐ N914NA	Northrop T-38A Talon	N.5775	65-10356	0065	0969	2 GE J85-GE-5	5485	Support/Training		914 / opb JSC, Ellington ANGB/TX
☐ N915NA	Northrop T-38A Talon	N.5158	60-0585	0060	1089	2 GE J85-GE-5	5485	Support/Training		915 / opb JSC, Ellington ANGB/TX
☐ N916NA	Northrop T-38A Talon	N.5952	66-8382	0066	0969	2 GE J85-GE-5	5485	Support/Training		916 / opb JSC, Ellington ANGB/TX
☐ N917NA	Northrop T-38A Talon	N.5953	66-8383	0066	0969	2 GE J85-GE-5	5485	Support/Training		917 / opb JSC, Ellington ANGB/TX
☐ N918NA	Northrop T-38A Talon	N.5954	66-8384	0066	0969	2 GE J85-GE-5	5485	Support/Training		918 / opb JSC, Ellington ANGB/TX
☐ N919NA	Northrop T-38A Talon	N.5955	66-8385	0066	0969	2 GE J85-GE-5	5485	Support/Training		919 / opb JSC, Ellington ANGB/TX
☐ N920NA	Northrop T-38A Talon	N.5956	66-8386	0066	0969	2 GE J85-GE-5	5485	Support/Training		920 / opb JSC, Ellington ANGB/TX
☐ N921NA	Northrop T-38A Talon	N.5957	66-8387	0066	0969	2 GE J85-GE-5	5485	Support/Training		921 / opb JSC, Ellington ANGB/TX
☐ N923NA	Northrop T-38A Talon	N.5971	66-8355	0066	0969	2 GE J85-GE-5	5485	Support/Training		923 / opb JSC, Ellington ANGB/TX
☐ N924NA	Northrop T-38A Talon	T.6027	67-14825	0067	0969	2 GE J85-GE-5	5485	Support/Training		924 / opb JSC, Ellington ANGB/TX
☐ N955NA	Northrop T-38A Talon	T.6232	69-7082	0069	0472	2 GE J85-GE-5	5485	Support/Training		955 / opb JSC, Ellington ANGB/TX
☐ N956NA	Northrop T-38A Talon	T.6234	69-7084	0069	0472	2 GE J85-GE-5	5485	Support/Training		956 / opb JSC, Ellington ANGB/TX
☐ N959NA	Northrop T-38A Talon	T.6240	70-1550	0070	0472	2 GE J85-GE-5	5485	Support/Training		959 / opb JSC, Ellington ANGB/TX
☐ N960NA	Northrop T-38A Talon	T.6242	70-1552	0070	0472	2 GE J85-GE-5	5485	Support/Training		960 / opb JSC, Ellington ANGB/TX
☐ N961NA	Northrop T-38A Talon	T.6245	70-1555	0070	0472	2 GE J85-GE-5	5485	Support/Training		961 / opb JSC, Ellington ANGB/TX
☐ N962NA	Northrop T-38A Talon	T.6246	70-1556	0070	0472	2 GE J85-GE-5	5485	Support/Training		962 / opb JSC, Ellington ANGB/TX
☐ N963NA	Northrop T-38A Talon	N.5116	59-1603	0059	1090	2 GE J85-GE-5	5485	Support/Training		963 / opb JSC, Ellington ANGB/TX
☐ N964NA	Northrop T-38A Talon	T.6118	68-8113	0068	1296	2 GE J85-GE-5	5485	Training		964 / opb LaRC, Langley AFB/VA
☐ N965NA	Northrop T-38A Talon	T.6121	68-8116	0068	1196	2 GE J85-GE-5	5485	Support/Training		965 / opb JSC, Ellington ANGB/TX
☐ N966NA	Northrop T-38A Talon	N.5776	65-10357	0065	0373	2 GE J85-GE-5	5485	Support/Training		966 / opb JSC, Ellington ANGB/TX
☐ N967NA	Northrop T-38A Talon	N.5772	65-10353	0065	0969	2 GE J85-GE-5	5485	Support/Training		967 / opb JSC, Ellington ANGB/TX
☐ 63-8117	Northrop T-38A Talon	N.5464		0063	0097	2 GE J85-GE-5	5485	Program Support		117 / opb LaRC, Langley AFB/VA
☐ 68-8133	Northrop T-38A Talon	T.6138		0068	0097	2 GE J85-GE-5	5485	Support/Training		133 / opb JSC, Ellington ANGB/TX
☐ N607NA	De Havilland DHC-6 Twin Otter 100	4	N508NA	0066	0772	2 PWC PT6A-20	5252	Research&Develop		607 / opb LeRC, Cleveland-Hopkins/OH
☐ N529NA	Beech King Air B200	BB-1091	N9NA	0082	0183	2 PWC PT6A-42	5670	Program Support		529 / opb LaRC, Langley AFB/VA
☐ N701NA	Beech King Air B200	BB-1164		0083	0288	2 PWC PT6A-42	5670	Program Support		701 / opb DFRC, Edwards AFB/CA
☐ N7NA	Beech King Air B200	BB-997		0082	0282	2 PWC PT6A-42	5670	Mission Mgmt		7 / opb DFRC, Edwards AFB/CA
☐ N8NA	Beech King Air B200	BB-950		0081	1281	2 PWC PT6A-42	5670	Mission Mgmt		8 / opb WFF, Wallops Island/VA
☐ N705NA	Learjet 24A	24A-102	N365EJ	0066	0974	2 GE CJ610-4	5897	Program Support		705/opb DFRC,Edwards/CA/tbrN805NA
☐ N933NA	Learjet 23	23-049	N701NA	0065	0681	2 GE CJ610-4	5670	Nat.SpaceTechLab		933 / opb SSC, Bay St.Louis-Stennis, MS
☐ N524NA	Rockwell (N.A.) OV-10A Bronco	305A-95	67-14687	0067	1193	2 AN T76-G-416/417	6562	Research&Develop		524 / opb LaRC, Langley AFB/VA
☐ N615NA	Rockwell (N.A.) OV-10A Bronco	305-46	155436	0067	0494	2 AN T76-G-416/417	6562	Research&Develop		615 / opb LeRC, Cleveland-Hopkins/OH
☐ N616NA	Learjet 25	25-035	N33TR	0069	0679	2 GE CJ610-6	6804	Program Support		616 / opb LeRC, Cleveland-Hopkins/OH
☐ N703NA	Bell 301 (XV-15)	0002		0077	0181	2 LY LTC1K-4K	6804	Research&Develop		703 / opb ARC, Moffett Field/CA
☐ N425NA	Sabreliner CT-39E (Rockwell NA265-40)	282-95	158380	0068	0891	2 PW JT12A-8	8459	Program Support		425 / opb WFF, Wallops Island/VA
☐ N516NA	General Dynamics F-16A Falcon	61-569	82-0976	0082	1093	1 PW F100-PW-100	14969	Program Support		516 / opb DFRC, Edwards AFB/CA
☐ N848NA	General Dynamics F-16XL Falcon	61-3	75-0747	0075	0090	1 PW F100-PW-100	14969	Research&Develop		848 / opb DFRC, Edwards AFB/CA
☐ N849NA	General Dynamics F-16XL Falcon	61-5	75-0749	0075	0090	1 PW F100-PW-100	14969	Research&Develop		849 / opb DFRC, Edwards AFB/CA
☐ 75-0750	General Dynamics F-16AFTI Falcon	61-6		0075	0097	1 PW F100-PW-100	14969	Research&Develop		750 / opb DFRC, Edwards AFB/CA
☐ N2NA	GAC (Grumman) G-159 Gulfstream I	096	N1NA	0062	1262	2 RR Dart 529-8X	16329	Mission Mgmt		2 / opb JSC, Ellington ANGB/TX
☐ N3NA	GAC (Grumman) G-159 Gulfstream I	092	N710G	0062	1262	2 RR Dart 529-8X	16329	Mission Mgmt		3 / opb MSFC, Huntsville-Int'l/AL
☐ N4NA	GAC (Grumman) G-159 Gulfstream I	151	N776G	0065	0265	2 RR Dart 529-8X	16329	Mission Mgmt		4 / opb KSC, Cape Canaveral/FL
☐ N706NA	Lockheed ER-2	1-063	80-1063	0081	0684	1 PW J75-P-13B	18733	Research&Develop		706 / opb DFRC,Edwards AFB/CA/cvtdTR-1A
☐ N709NA	Lockheed ER-2	7-097	80-1097	0081	0689	1 PW J75-P-13B	18733	Research&Develop		709 / opb DFRC,Edwards AFB/CA/cvtdTR-1A
☐ N836NA	Boeing (McDonnell Aircraft) F-15B Eagle	86	74-0141	0074	0095	1 PW F100-PW-100	18824	Research&Develop		836 / opb DFRC, Edwards AFB/CA
☐ N837NA	Boeing (McDonnell Aircraft) NF-15B Eagle	8	71-0290	0071	0095	1 PW F100-PW-100	18824	Research&Develop		837 / opb DFRC, Edwards AFB/CA
☐ N432NA	Fairchild Ind. F-27F	35	N768RL	0059	1294	2 RR Dart 529-7E	19051	Research&Develop		432 / opb WFF,Wallops Island/VA,cvtd-27
☐ N840NA	Boeing (McDonnell Aircraft) F-18A Hornet	6	160780	0082	0087	2 GE F404-GE-400	25401	Research&Develop		840 / opb DFRC, Edwards AFB/CA
☐ N843NA	Boeing (McDonnell Aircraft) F-18A Hornet	36	161519	0083	0087	2 GE F404-GE-400	25401	Program Support		843 / opb DFRC, Edwards AFB/CA
☐ N845NA	Boeing (McDonnell Aircraft) TF-18A Hornet	7	160781	0082	0087	2 GE F404-GE-400	25401	Research&Develop		845 / opb DFRC, Edwards AFB/CA
☐ N846NA	Boeing (McDonnell Aircraft) F-18A Hornet	23	161355	0083	0087	2 GE F404-GE-400	25401	Program Support		846 / opb DFRC, Edwards AFB/CA
☐ N847NA	Boeing (McDonnell Aircraft) F-18A Hornet	37	161520	0083	0087	2 GE F404-GE-400	25401	Program Support		847 / opb DFRC, Edwards AFB/CA
☐ N850NA	Boeing (McDonnell Aircraft) F-18A Hornet	48	161703	0083	0096	2 GE F404-GE-400	25401	Program Support		850 / opb DFRC, Edwards AFB/CA
☐ N851NA	Boeing (McDonnell Aircraft) F-18A Hornet	50	161705	0083	0096	2 GE F404-GE-400	25401	Program Support		851 / opb DFRC, Edwards AFB/CA
☐ N928NA	Martin/General Dynamics WB-57F		63-13298	0064	0074	2 PW TF33-P-11	24948	Program Support		928 / opb JSC, Ellington ANGB/TX
☐ N944NA	GAC (Grumman) G-1159 Gulfstream II	144		0074	0583	2 RR Spey 511-8	29393	Shuttle Training		944 / opb JSC, Ellington ANGB/TX
☐ N945NA	GAC (Grumman) G-1159 Gulfstream II	118	N650PF	0072	0289	2 RR Spey 511-8	29393	Shuttle Training		945 / opb JSC, Ellington ANGB/TX
☐ N946NA	GAC (Grumman) G-1159 Gulfstream II	146	N897GA	0074	0975	2 RR Spey 511-8	29393	Shuttle Training		946 / opb JSC, Ellington ANGB/TX
☐ N947NA	GAC (Grumman) G-1159 Gulfstream II	147	N898GA	0074	0674	2 RR Spey 511-8	29393	Shuttle Training		947 / opb JSC, Ellington ANGB/TX
☐ N948NA	GAC (Grumman) G-1159 Gulfstream II	222	N5253A	0078	0591	2 RR Spey 511-8	29393	Shuttle Training		948 / opb JSC, Ellington ANGB/TX
☐ N1NA	GAC G-1159A Gulfstream III	309	N18LB	0080	1089	2 RR Spey 511-8	30935	Mission Mgmt/VIP		1 / opb HQ, based Langley AFB/VA
☐ N426NA	Lockheed P-3B Orion	185-5175	152735	0063	0291	4 AN T56-A	64410	Program Support		426 / opb WFF, Wallops Island/VA
☐ N707NA	Lockheed L-282 (NC-130B) Hercules	1B-3507	N929NA	0060	0969	4 AN T56-A-7	70307	Research&Develop		707 / opb DFRC, Edwards AFB/CA
☐ N427NA	Lockheed L-382C (C-130Q) Hercules	85D-4901	161495	0081	1291	4 AN T56-A-15	70307	Freighter		427 / opb WFF, Wallops Island/VA
☐ N941NA	Airbus Industrie Super Guppy 377SGT-201F	004	F-GEAI	0083	1097	4 AN 501-D22C	77110	Freighter		941 / opb JSC, Ellington ANGB/TX
☐ N831NA	Lockheed SR-71B	2007	61-7956	0062	0090	2 PW JT11D-20B	77111	Research&Develop		831 / opb DFRC, Edwards AFB/CA
☐ N844NA	Lockheed SR-71B	2031	61-7980	0062	0091	2 PW JT11D-20B	77111	Research&Develop		844 / opb DFRC, Edwards AFB/CA/cvtd-71A
☐ N557NA	Boeing 757-225	22191 / 2	N501EA	0082	1294	2 RR RB211-535E4	104326	Research&Develop		557 / opb LaRC, Langley AFB/VA
☐ N931NA	Boeing KC-135A	18615	63-7998	0064	0094	4 PW J57-P-59W	134717	Research&Develop		931 / opb JSC, Ellington ANGB/TX
☐ N817NA	Boeing (Douglas) DC-8-72	46082 / 458	N717NA	0069	0286	4 CFMI CFM56-2C	158757	Research&Develop	JM-AB	717 / opb DFRC,Edwards AFB/CA, cvtd -62
☐ 0008	Boeing B-52G Stratofortress	16498	52-0008	0052	0057	8 PW J57-P-43WB	221353	Research&Develop		008 / opb DFRC,Edw.AFB/CA / cvtd NB-52A
☐ N145UA	Boeing 747SP-21	21441 / 306	N536PA	0077	0497	4 PW JT9D-7A	315700	Telescope SOFIA		145 / being cvtd/tbopb Ames RC eff.0301
☐ N905NA	Boeing 747-123	20107 / 86	N9668	0070	0774	4 PW JT9D-3A	332937	Shuttle Carrier		905 / opb JSC, Ellington ANGB/TX
☐ N911NA	Boeing 747SR-46	20781 / 221	N747BL	0073	1088	4 PW JT9D-7A	258548	Shuttle Carrier		911 / opb JSC, Ellington ANGB/TX

NATIONAL AIRLINES, Inc.

Las Vegas-McCarren Int'l, NV

PO Box 97916, Las Vegas, NV 89193-7916, USA ☎ (702) 260-8300 Tx: none Fax: none SITA: n/a

F: 1998 n/a Head: Michael Conway Net: http://www.nationalairlines.com

☐ N506NA	Boeing 757-236	24771 / 272	TC-AJA	0090	0299	2 RR RB211-535E4	113398			lsf SUNR
☐ N507NA	Boeing 757-256	26244 / 616	EC-FYL	0094	0299	2 RR RB211-535E4	113398			lsf SUNR
☐ N757NA	Boeing 757-23A	24567 / 257	N1791B*	0090		2 RR RB211-535E4	113398			to be lsf AWAS 0599
☐ N	Boeing 757-204	26962 / 440	TC-ARA	0092		2 RR RB211-535E4	113398			to be lsf BOUL 0499

NATIONAL HELICOPTER SERVICE (National Helicopter Service & Engineering, Co. Inc. dba)

Van Nuys, CA

16800 Roscoe Blvd, Van Nuys, CA 91406, USA ☎ (818) 345-5222 Tx: none Fax: (818) 782-0466 SITA: n/a

F: 1957 n/a Head: Richard H. Hart Net: http://www.nationalhelicopter.com

☐ N111JG	Bell 206B JetRanger	1115		0073	0781	1 AN 250-C20	1451			
☐ N555NH	Bell 206B JetRanger	1738	N90296	0075	0977	1 AN 250-C20	1451			

403 registration type of aircraft cn/fn ex/ex* mfd del powered by mtow kg configuration selcal name/fln/specialitites/remarks

☐ N555TH	Bell 206B JetRanger	1173	N59398	0073	1089	1 AN 250-C20	1451			
☐ N55WT	Bell 206B JetRanger	1683	N90210	0075	0396	1 AN 250-C20	1451			

NATIONAL JETS, Inc. (National Air Ambulance) (Affiliated with Florida Aircraft Leasing, Corp.)

Fort Lauderdale-Int'l, FL

National Jets

PO Box 22460, Fort Lauderdale, FL 33335-2460, USA ☎ (954) 359-9900 Tx: none Fax: (954) 359-0039 SITA: n/a
F: 1972 30 Head: Thomas E. Boy Net: http://www.nationaljets.com EMS/Ambulance flights are operated under the marketing name NATIONAL AIR AMBULANCE (same headquarters & fleet).

☐ N711NJ	Cessna 402B	402B0342	N4187Q	0072	0378	2 CO TSIO-520-E	2858			
☐ N555NJ	Volpar Turboliner	AF-236	N90EG	0052	0794	2 GA TPE331-1-101B	5216	Freighter		cvtd Beech C-45H (18)
☐ N77NJ	Learjet 25	25-033	YV-88CP	0069	1279	2 GE CJ610-6	6804			
☐ N88NJ	Learjet 25D	25D-294	N161RB	0080	0696	2 GE CJ610-8A	6804			
☐ N99NJ	Learjet 25D (XR)	25D-220	N220NJ	0077	0687	2 GE CJ610-6	6804			mod. 25D
☐ N33NJ	Learjet 35A	35A-305	N3VG	0080	0392	2 GA TFE731-2-2B	8301			
☐ N66NJ	Learjet 35A	35A-296	N51JA	0080	0296	2 GA TFE731-2-2B	8301			

NATIONS AIR = N5 / NAE (Nations Air Express, Inc. dba)

Atlanta-WBH Int'l, GA

5275 Triangle Parkway, Suite 100, Norcross, GA 30092, USA ☎ (770) 453-9977 Tx: none Fax: (770) 446-1545 SITA: n/a
F: 1994 n/a Head: Mark W. McDonald ICAO: NATIONS EXPRESS Net: n/a

☐ N7375F	Boeing 737-291	20363 / 218	SE-DTV	0069	0598	2 PW JT8D-9A (HK3/AVA)	53297	Y125		lsf IALI

NATIVE AMERICAN AIR AMBULANCE, Inc.

Chandler-Gateway, AZ

6001 South Power Road, Bldg 19, Mesa, AZ 85208, USA ☎ (602) 988-3840 Tx: none Fax: (602) 988-3843 SITA: n/a
F: 1994 n/a Head: Richard H. Heape Net: n/a

☐ N206MH	Bell 206L-1 LongRanger III	45426	N518EH	0080	0098	1 AN 250-C30P	1882	EMS		lsf/opb Omniflight Helic. / cvtd LR II
☐ N2210H	Bell 206L-3 LongRanger III	51006		0082	0098	1 AN 250-C30P	1882	EMS		lsf/opb Omniflight Helicopters
☐ N224LF	Bell 206L-1 LongRanger II	45199	N5013Y	0079	0098	1 AN 250-C28B	1882	EMS		lsf/opb Omniflight Helicopters
☐ N95NA	Cessna 208B Grand Caravan	208B0666		0098	1098	1 PWC PT6A-114A	3969	EMS		lsf Textron Financial Corp.
☐ N174PC	Pilatus PC-12/45	174	HB-FSJ*	0098	1298	1 PWC PT6A-67B	4500	EMS		
☐ N308NA	Pilatus PC-12/45	226	N226PC	0098	0998	1 PWC PT6A-67B	4500	EMS		
☐ N317NA	Pilatus PC-12/45	223	N223PD	0098	0898	1 PWC PT6A-67B	4500	EMS		
☐ N613NA	Pilatus PC-12/45	197	N197PC	0098	0798	1 PWC PT6A-67B	4500	EMS		
☐ N608JX	BAe 3101 Jetstream 31	608	N331BJ	0083	0997	2 GA TPE331-10UG-513H	6900	EMS		lsf BAMT
☐ N752JX	BAe 3101 Jetstream 31	752	N711PN	0087	0095	2 GA TPE331-10UR-513H	6900	EMS		lsf BAMT
☐ N754JX	BAe 3101 Jetstream 31	754	N711HH	0087	0096	2 GA TPE331-10UR-513H	6900	EMS		lsf BAMT

NCAR - National Center for Atmospheric Research

Denver-Jeffco, CO & Houston-Johnson Space Center, TX

PO Box 3000, Boulder, CO 80307, USA ☎ (970) 497-1032 Tx: n/a Fax: (970) 497-1091 SITA: n/a
F: 1962 n/a Head: Lawrence F. Ratke Net: n/a Non-profit national research-organisation (finanzed through National Science Foundation).

☐ N357AR	Martin/General Dynamics WB-57F		63-13503A	0064	0294	2 PW TF33-P-11	24948	Survey/Research		
☐ N308D	Lockheed L-188C Electra	1130	N595KR	0060	0573	4 AN 501-D13A	52617	Survey/Research		lsf National Science Foundation
☐ N130AR	Lockheed L-382C (C-130H) Hercules	85D-4984	162312	0083	1093	4 AN T56-A-15	70307	Survey/Research		lsf National Science Foundation

NEPTUNE AVIATION (Neptune, Inc. dba)

Missoula-Int'l, MT

5225 Hwy 10 West, Box 17, Missoula, MT 59808, USA ☎ (406) 542-0606 Tx: none Fax: (406) 542-3222 SITA: n/a
F: 1993 n/a Head: Mark Timmons Net: n/a

☐ N13852	Lockheed P2V-5 (P-2E) Neptune	426-5387	131506	0054	0993	2 WR R-3350	33339	Tanker		std
☐ N13859	Lockheed P2V-5 (P-2E) Neptune	426-5344	131463	0054	0993	2 WR R-3350	33339	Tanker		std
☐ N1386C	Lockheed P2V-5 (P-2E) Neptune	426-5268	128422	0054	0993	2 WR R-3350	33339	Tanker		std
☐ N1386K	Lockheed P2V-5 (P-2E) Neptune	426-5305	131424	0054	0993	2 WR R-3350	33339	Tanker		07
☐ N14447	Lockheed P2V-7 (P-2H) Neptune	826-8010	RCAF24110	0059	0993	2 WR R-3350	34246	Tanker		11
☐ N4235N	Lockheed P2V-7 (P-2H) Neptune	726-7158	144681	0058	0993	2 WR R-3350	34246	Tanker		10
☐ N4235T	Lockheed P2V-7 (P-2H) Neptune	726-7285	150282	0058	0993	2 WR R-3350	34246	Tanker		09
☐ N96264	Lockheed P2V-5 (P-2E) Neptune	426-5192	128346	0054	0993	2 WR R-3350	33339	Tanker		12
☐ N96278	Lockheed P2V-5 (P-2E) Neptune	426-5340	131459	0054	0993	2 WR R-3350	33339	Tanker		05
☐ N9855F	Lockheed P2V-5 (P-2E) Neptune	426-5326	131445	0054	0993	2 WR R-3350	33339	Tanker		06

NEVADA HELICOPTERS (Moore Helicopter Services, Inc. dba)

Des Moines-Int'l, IA

5321 Brookview Drive, West Des Moines, IA 50266, USA ☎ (515) 223-6618 Tx: none Fax: (515) 223-6618 SITA: n/a
F: 1989 n/a Head: John D. Moore Net: n/a

☐ N16733	Bell 206B JetRanger II	2138		0077	0789	1 AN 250-C20	1451			

NEW AIR HELICOPTERS (Thomas R. Edison dba)

Durango-Animas Air Park, CO

PO Box 3268, Durango, CO 81302, USA ☎ (970) 259-6247 Tx: none Fax: (970) 382-9221 SITA: n/a
F: 1983 n/a Head: Thomas R. Edison Net: n/a

☐ N5754K	Bell 206B JetRanger III	3126		0080	0883	1 AN 250-C20B	1451			

NEW ENGLAND AIRLINES, Inc. = EJ / NEA (Block Island Airlines & Air Charter)

Westerly-State, RI

NEW ENGLAND AIRLINES

State Airport, Westerly, RI 02891, USA ☎ (401) 596-2460 Tx: none Fax: (401) 596-7366 SITA: n/a
F: 1970 25 Head: William G. Bendokas ICAO: NEW ENGLAND Net: http://www.block-island.com/nea Aircraft below MTOW 1361kg: Piper PA-28
Some flights are operated under the marketing name BLOCK ISLAND AIRLINE & AIR CHARTER (same fleet & headquarters).

☐ N345CS	Piper PA-32-300 Cherokee SIX	32-7640043		0076	0888	1 LY IO-540-K1A5	1542			
☐ N4830S	Piper PA-32-260 Cherokee SIX	32-1261		0069	0986	1 LY O-540-E4B5	1542			
☐ N4885T	Piper PA-32-300E Cherokee SIX	32-7240092		0072	0984	1 LY IO-540-K1A5	1542			
☐ N5035Y	Piper PA-23-250 Aztec B	27-2041		0062	1174	2 LY O-540-A1D5	2177			
☐ N304SK	Britten-Norman BN-2A-26 Islander	564	N80PA	0076	0884	2 LY O-540-E4C5	2812			
☐ N598JA	Britten-Norman BN-2A Islander	66		0069	1171	2 LY O-540-E4C5	2722			

NEW ENGLAND HELICOPTER, Inc.

Poughkeepsie-Dutchess County, NY

17 Round Hill Road, Washingtonville, NY 10992, USA ☎ (914) 496-7928 Tx: none Fax: none SITA: n/a
F: 1985 3 Head: Robert R. Warfield Net: n/a

☐ N206NE	Bell 206B JetRanger	441	N1484W	0069	1087	1 AN 250-C20	1451			cvtd 206A

NEWHALEN LODGE FLYING SERVICE (Newhalen Lodge, Inc. dba)

Anchorage-Lake Hood SPB, AK

3851 Chiniak Bay Drive, Anchorage, AK 99515, USA ☎ (907) 522-3355 Tx: none Fax: none SITA: n/a
F: 1991 n/a Head: William E. Sims Net: n/a

☐ N600NL	Cessna U206G Stationair	U20603976	N756CD	0077	0294	1 CO IO-520-F	1633			Floats / Wheel-Skis
☐ N800NL	Cessna U206G Stationair 6 II	U20604860	N734QK	0079	0294	1 CO IO-520-F	1633			Floats / Wheel-Skis
☐ N900NL	Cessna U206G Stationair 6 II	U20606180	N4950R	0081	0294	1 CO IO-520-F	1633			Floats / Wheel-Skis
☐ N5359J	De Havilland DHC-2 Beaver I	1063	CF-ZVQ	0057	1097	1 PW R-985	2313			Floats / Wheel-Skis
☐ N700NL	De Havilland DHC-2 Beaver I	1232	N700RM	0058	0294	1 PW R-985	2313			Floats / Wheel-Skis

NEW MEXICO FLYING SERVICE (B & M Enterprises, Inc. dba)

Albuquerque-Int'l, NM

PO Box 9185, Albuquerque, NM 87119, USA ☎ (505) 842-4000 Tx: none Fax: (506) 842-4002 SITA: n/a
F: 1983 n/a Head: Billy J. Ware Net: n/a

☐ N310DC	Cessna 210L Centurion II	21060555		0074	1092	1 CO IO-520-L	1724			lsf pvt
☐ N59217	Cessna 210L Centurion II	21060167		0074	0291	1 CO IO-520-L	1724			lsf pvt
☐ N613CW	Cessna T210L Turbo Centurion II	21059920		0073	0791	1 CO TSIO-520-H	1724			lsf pvt
☐ N6687B	Cessna T210M Turbo Centurion II	21062819		0078	0596	1 CO TSIO-520-R	1724			lsf pvt
☐ N732RD	Cessna 210M Centurion II	21061706		0077	1294	1 CO IO-520-L	1724			lsf pvt
☐ N761EC	Cessna 210M Centurion II	21062189		0077	0184	1 CO IO-520-L	1724			
☐ N761GB	Cessna T210M Turbo Centurion II	21062236		0077	1195	1 CO TSIO-520-R	1724			lsf pvt
☐ N761MU	Cessna T210M Turbo Centurion II	21062371		0077	0487	1 CO TSIO-520-R	1724			lsf pvt
☐ N761PE	Cessna T210M Turbo Centurion II	21062403		0077	0497	1 CO TSIO-520-R	1724			lsf pvt
☐ N761PF	Cessna 210M Centurion II	21062404		0077	0990	1 CO IO-520-L	1724			lsf pvt
☐ N94032	Cessna T210L Turbo Centurion II	21060485		0074	1294	1 CO TSIO-520-H	1724			lsf pvt
☐ N25BH	Cessna 402B II	402B1228		0077	0797	2 CO TSIO-520-E	2858			lsf Distribution Management Corp.
☐ N38CJ	Cessna 402C II	402C0023		0079	1194	2 CO TSIO-520-VB	3107			lsf Distribution Management Corp.
☐ N1648T	Cessna 414	414-0428		0073	0385	2 CO TSIO-520-J	2880			lsf pvt

NICKLAS FOUNDATION

Arlington-Municipal, TX

516 Estate Drive, Grande Prairie, TX 75052, USA ☎ (972) 263-0407 Tx: none Fax: (972) 263-0407 SITA: n/a
F: 1996 n/a Head: Isabelle Debaun Net: n/a Non-commercial organisation conducting promotional flights & semi-commerical sightseeing-flights at airshows.
The Foundation is trying to popularize the idea of authorizing the transplantation of organs.

☐ N5106X	Boeing (Douglas) DC-3C (C-47-DL)	9058	N5106	0043	0896	2 PW R-1830	12202	18 seats		Heart of America-titles

NIEDERHAUSER AIRWAYS, Inc.

Waterloo-Municipal, IA

2814 Airport Blvd., Waterloo, IA 50703, USA ☎ (319) 234-1783 Tx: none Fax: (319) 234-7763 SITA: n/a
F: 1952 n/a Head: Russell Knock Net: n/a

☐ N31KA	Piper PA-31-350 Navajo Chieftain	31-7552026		0075	0098	2 LY TIO-540-J2BD	3175			
☐ N40992	Piper PA-31-350 Navajo Chieftain	31-8252045		0082	0098	2 LY TIO-540-J2BD	3175			

404 registration type of aircraft cn/fn ex/ex* mfd del powered by mtow kg configuration selcal name/fln/specialitites/remarks

NIEMEYER AVIATION (Donald C. & Yvonne Niemeyer dba) — Hobart-Sky Ranch, IN

3600 North Lake Park Ave, Hobart, IN 46342, USA ☎ (219) 962-3020 Tx: none Fax: (219) 962-3698 SITA: n/a
F: 1972 n/a Head: Donald C. Niemeyer Net: n/a

☐ N2087A	Piper PA-32RT-300T Turbo Lance II	32R-7987001		0079	0695	1 LY TIO-540-S1AD	1633			
☐ N18BS	Piper PA-23-250 Aztec E	27-4590		0071	0597	2 LY IO-540-C4B5	2359			
☐ N6092Y	Piper PA-23-250 Aztec C	27-3298		0066	0696	2 LY IO-540-C4B5	2359			

NIIHAU HELICOPTERS, Inc. — Makaweli-Heliport, HI

PO Box 370, Makaweli (Kauai), HI 96769, USA ☎ (808) 338-9869 Tx: none Fax: (808) 338-1463 SITA: n/a
F: 1986 n/a Head: Helen M. Robinson Net: n/a

☐ N293G	Agusta A109A	7133		0078	0187	2 AN 250-C20B	2600			

NMB Air Operations Corp. (Joint vent.of NMB Nippon Miniature Ballbearing,Co.& NHBB New Hampshire Ball Bearings,Inc./Member of MINEBEA Group of Companies) — Singapore-Changi

Operations office: 1 Loyang Crescent, Unit 2, Offshore Supply Base, Singapore 508988, Republic of Singapore ☎ 545 18 38 Tx: none Fax: 542 16 62 SITA: n/a
F: 1988 n/a Head: Peng Hock D. Puar Net: n/a Operates non-commercial corporate flights exclusively for itself & other members of the Minebea Group of Companies.

☐ N10MB	Boeing (Douglas) DC-10-30F (CF)	47907 / 157	OO-SLB	0074	0894	3 GE CF6-50C2	251744	Corp.50Pax/Plts	FG-AL	

NOAA Aircraft Operations = NAA (Aeronautical Dept. of National Oceanic & Atmospheric Administration, a part of U.S. Dept. of Commerce) — Tampa-MacDill AFB, FL

Aircraft Operations Center, PO Box 6829, Tampa-MacDill AFB, FL 33608-0829, USA ☎ (813) 828-3310 Tx: none Fax: (813) 828-3266 SITA: n/a
F: 1983 80 Head: Capt. Donald D. Winter ICAO: NOAA Net: n/a Non-commercial state-organisation conducting charting, scientific & weather research flights.

☐ N59RF	MD Helicopters MD 500D (Hughes 369D)	590510D	N241CR	0079	0288	1 AN 250-C20B	1361	3 Pax/Survey		
☐ N64RF	Lake LA-250 Turbo Renegade	126	N8551G	0091	0595	1 LY TIO-540-AA1AB	1424	Observation		Amphibian
☐ N65RF	Lake LA-250 Turbo Renegade	127	N8551K	0091	0495	1 LY TIO-540-AA1AB	1424	Observation		Amphibian
☐ N47RF	Twin (Aero) Shrike Commander 500S	3261	N500FC	0075	1087	2 LY IO-540-E1B5	3062	Airfield Survey		
☐ N51RF	Twin (Aero) Shrike Commander 500S	3298	N766	0077	1187	2 LY IO-540-E1B5	3062	Snow Survey		
☐ N53RF	Twin (Aero) Turbo Commander 690A	11153	N57074	0074	1189	2 GA TPE331-5-251K	4649	Aerial Photo		
☐ N60RF	Bell 212	30964	N2766K	0079	0686	2 PWC PT6T-3 TwinPac	5080	11 Pax/Survey		
☐ N61RF	Bell 212	30941	N58RF	0079	0786	2 PWC PT6T-3 TwinPac	5080	11 Pax/Survey		
☐ N48RF	De Havilland DHC-6 Twin Otter 300	740	N600LJ	0081	0986	2 PWC PT6A-27	5670	6 Pax/Survey		
☐ N57RF	De Havilland DHC-6 Twin Otter 300	688	N485RF	0080	0694	2 PWC PT6A-27	5670	6 Pax/Survey		
☐ N52RF	Cessna 550 Citation II	550-0021	N900LJ	0078	0188	2 PWC JT15D-4	6033	Aerial Photo		
☐ N49RF	GAC G-IV Gulfstream IV (SP)	1246	N407GA*	0095	0495	2 RR Tay 611-8	33838	Weather Research		
☐ N42RF	Lockheed WP-3D Orion	285A-5622	Bu159773	0075	0083	4 AN T56-A-14	61235	FlyingLaboratory		
☐ N43RF	Lockheed WP-3D Orion	285A-5633	Bu159875	0075	0083	4 AN T56-A-14	61235	FlyingLaboratory		

NOMADS, Inc. — Detroit-Metro, MI

Nomads World Terminal, Detroit Metro Airport, Detroit, MI 48242, USA ☎ (734) 941-8000 Tx: none Fax: (734) 941-4043 SITA: n/a
F: 1965 12 Head: Jack Kozma Net: n/a Non-profit Michigan AIR TRAVEL CLUB corporation guided by a member-elected Board of Directors who serve without pay.

☐ N727M	Boeing 727-221 (A/RE) (Super 27)	22541 / 1797	N369PA	0082	0193	3 PW JT8D-217C/17 (BFG)	88360	Y146		cvtd -221

NORD AVIATION, Inc. (Sister company of Nord Star Airlines, Inc.) — Santa Teresa-Dona Ana County, NM

PO Box 1641, Santa Teresa, NM 88008, USA ☎ (505) 589-1718 Tx: none Fax: (505) 589-1721 SITA: n/a
F: 1955 8 Head: Terence L. Nord Net: n/a

☐ N738WB	Beech Twin Bonanza D50C	DH-286		0060	0890	2 LY GO-480-G2D6	2858	Freighter		
☐ N57626	Boeing (Douglas) DC-3C (C-47-DL)	4564	41-18472	0042	0379	2 PW R-1830	12202	Freighter		

NORDIC AIR (Douglas D. Reimer dba) — Petersburg-James A. Johnson, AK

PO Box 1752, Petersburg, AK 99833, USA ☎ (907) 772-3535 Tx: none Fax: (907) 772-3505 SITA: n/a
F: 1990 n/a Head: Douglas D. Reimer Net: n/a

☐ N815V	Cessna A185F Skywagon	18502331	N53038	0073	0192	1 CO IO-520-D	1520			Amphibian

NORD STAR AIRLINES, Inc. (Sister company of Nord Aviation, Inc.) — Santa Teresa-Dona Ana County, NM

PO Box 1641, Santa Teresa, NM 88008, USA ☎ (505) 589-1718 Tx: none Fax: (505) 589-1721 SITA: n/a
F: 1986 4 Head: Terence L. Nord Net: n/a

☐ N620NA	Boeing (Douglas) DC-6A	44677 / 527	N32RU	0054	0986	4 PW R-2800	47083	Freighter		

NORTH AMERICAN AIRLINES, Inc. = XG / NAO — New York-JFK, NY

Bldg 75, Suite 250, JFK Int'l Airport, Jamaica, NY 11430, USA ☎ (718) 656-2650 Tx: none Fax: (718) 995-3372 SITA: JFKOZXG
F: 1989 200 Head: Dan McKinnon IATA: 455 ICAO: NORTH AMERICAN Net: n/a

☐ N800NA	Boeing 737-8Q8	28215 / 75		0098	0898	2 CFMI CFM56-7B26	78245	Y169		Janice M. / lsf ILFC
☐ N802NA	Boeing 737-86N	28587 / 192	N1795B*	0099	0299	2 CFMI CFM56-7B26	78245	Y169		lsf GECA
☐ N750NA	Boeing 757-28A	26277 / 658		0095	0195	2 RR RB211-535E4	113398	Y213		Lisa Caroline / lsf ILFC
☐ N	Boeing 757-2Q8	28174				2 RR RB211-535E4	113398	Y213		to be lsf ILFC 0699

NORTH AMERICAN JET, Inc. (Sister company of Air America Jet Charter, Inc.) — Banning-Municipal, CA

Box 1334, Banning, CA 92220, USA ☎ (909) 849-1776 Tx: none Fax: (909) 849-8222 SITA: n/a
F: 1997 n/a Head: William B. McCarter, Jr. Net: n/a

☐ N900GG	Learjet 24B	24B-216	N217AT	0070	0997	2 GE CJ610-6	6123			lsf VEC Corp. of Delaware
☐ N800GG	Learjet 25	25-008	N88NJ	0068	0198	2 GE CJ610-6	6804			lsf VEC Corp. of Delaware

NORTHEAST AIRLINES = NEE (Downeast Flying Service, Inc. dba) — Portland-Int'l Jetport, ME

1001 Westbrook Street, Portland, ME 04102, USA ☎ (207) 772-0943 Tx: none Fax: (207) 772-6363 SITA: n/a
F: 1983 n/a Head: Wayne D. Hazard ICAO: NORTHEAST Net: n/a

☐ N913YW	Beech 1300 Airliner	BB-1383	N383YV	0090	0995	2 PWC PT6A-42	5670	Y13		cvtd Super King Air B200
☐ N152GL	Beech 1900C-1 Airliner	UC-152		0091	0797	2 PWC PT6A-65B	7530	Y19		

NORTHEASTERN AVIATION, Corp. (SMC Aviation, Inc. dba) — Farmingdale-Republic, NY

65-07 Fresh Meadow Lane, Fresh Meadows, NY 11365, USA ☎ (718) 961-4600 Tx: none Fax: (718) 961-2820 SITA: n/a
F: 1977 n/a Head: Michael J. Russo Net: n/a

☐ N16671	Bell 206B JetRanger II	2087		0076	1189	1 AN 250-C20	1451			lsf Air North Helicopters LP
☐ N8282P	Piper PA-34-200T Seneca II	34-8170022		0081	1081	2 CO TSIO-360-EB1	2073			
☐ N47MM	Piper PA-31-310 Navajo C	31-7812036		0078	0179	2 LY TIO-540-A2C	2948			
☐ N72MM	Beech King Air 200	BB-497	N73CA	0079	0490	2 PWC PT6A-41	5670			
☐ N56MM	Learjet 24F	24F-332	N13KL	0076	0982	2 GE CJ610-8A	6123			
☐ N35PF	Learjet 55	55-020	N123LC	0082	0797	2 GA TFE731-3AR-2B	9752			lsf Air New York Llc

NORTHEAST HELICOPTER SERVICES, Inc. — Plymouth-Municipal, MA

246 South Meadow Road, Plymouth, MA 02360, USA ☎ (508) 746-8744 Tx: none Fax: (508) 746-8721 SITA: n/a
F: 1992 4 Head: David B. Jansen Net: n/a

☐ N11NE	Bell UH-1B (204)	1014	N8769D	0063	1092	1 LY T53-L-11	3856			
☐ N12NE	Bell UH-1B (204)	270	N2298E	0061	0492	1 LY T53-L-11	3856			

NORTHERN AIR CARGO, Inc. = NC / NAC (formerly Sholton & Carlson, Inc.) — Anchorage-Int'l, AK

3900 West International Airport Road, Anchorage, AK 99502-1097, USA ☎ (907) 243-3331 Tx: none Fax: (907) 249-5193 SITA: n/a
F: 1956 220 Head: Mary A. Sholton IATA: 345 ICAO: NORTHERN AIR CARGO Net: http://www.nacargo.com

☐ N1027N	Boeing (Douglas) DC-6A (C-118A-DO)	43580 / 294	51-3833	0052	0576	4 PW R-2800	47083	Freighter		
☐ N1036F	Boeing (Douglas) DC-6A (C-118A-DO)	43581 / 295	51-3834	0052	0576	4 PW R-2800	45359	Freighter		
☐ N1377K	Boeing (Douglas) DC-6A (C-118A-DO)	44596 / 499	53-3225	0053	0482	4 PW R-2800	47083	Freighter		
☐ N2907F	Boeing (Douglas) DC-6A (C-118A-DO)	44636 / 574	53-3265	0055	0391	4 PW R-2800	45359	Freighter		
☐ N4206L	Boeing (Douglas) DC-6A (C-118B)	43709 / 355	131606	0059	0681	4 PW R-2800	45359	Freighter		
☐ N4213X	Boeing (Douglas) DC-6A (C-118A-DO)	44605 / 518	53-3234	0054	0581	4 PW R-2800	47083	Freighter		
☐ N434TA	Boeing (Douglas) DC-6BF (Swingtail)	44434 / 515	EC-BBK	0054	0387	4 PW R-2800	47083	Freighter		cvtd DC-6B
☐ N43872	Boeing (Douglas) DC-6A (C-118A-DO)	44665 / 632	53-3294	0055	1189	4 PW R-2800	47083	Freighter		
☐ N7780B	Boeing (Douglas) DC-6A	45372 / 875		0057	0374	4 PW R-2800	47083	Freighter		lst Northern Air Fuel
☐ N779TA	Boeing (Douglas) DC-6A/C	45529 / 1035	PP-LFC	0058	0889	4 PW R-2800	47083	Freighter		
☐ N7919C	Boeing (Douglas) DC-6B	43554 / 247	PH-DFM	0052	0678	4 PW R-2800	47083	Fuel Tanker		
☐ N867TA	Boeing (Douglas) DC-6BF (Swingtail)	45202 / 880	OH-KDA	0057	0586	4 PW R-2800	47083	Freighter		cvtd DC-6B
☐ N99330	Boeing (Douglas) DC-6A (C-118A-DO)	43576 / 275	C-GPEG	0052	0587	4 PW R-2800	47083	Freighter		
☐ N190AJ	Boeing 727-46 (F)	18878 / 236	G-BAJW	0066	0498	3 PW JT8D-7B (HK3/FDX)	76657	Freighter		cvtd -46
☐ N930FT	Boeing 727-23 (F)	19387 / 329	N1929	0066	0895	3 PW JT8D-7B (HK3/FDX)	76657	Freighter		cvtd -23
☐ N992AJ	Boeing 727-23 (F)	19428 / 358	N515FE	0067	0398	3 PW JT8D-7B (HK3/FDX)	76884	Freighter		cvtd -23

NORTHERN AIR FUEL (Subsidiary of Northern Air Cargo, Inc.) — Fairbanks-Int'l, AK

5385 Airport Industrial Road, Fairbanks, AK 99709, USA ☎ (907) 474-3835 Tx: none Fax: (907) 474-3839 SITA: n/a
F: 1997 8 Head: Kenneth L. Zachary Net: n/a Operates FAR125 contract fuel-delivery flights within Alaska.

☐ N7780B	Boeing (Douglas) DC-6A	45372 / 875		0057	0098	4 PW R-2800	47083	Fuel Tanker		lsf NAC

NORTHERN AIRMOTIVE, Corp. (formerly K-Airways, Inc.) — Hillsboro-Highland County, OH

9500 North Shore Drive, Hillsboro, OH 45133, USA ☎ (937) 393-9250 Tx: none Fax: (937) 393-0200 SITA: n/a
F: 1972 12 Head: Sue M. Soderstrom Net: n/a

☐ N2067C	Beech E18S	BA-424		0059	0689	2 PW R-985	4218	Freighter		
☐ N307B	Beech E18S	BA-457		0059	0593	2 PW R-985	4218	Freighter		

405 registration type of aircraft cn/fn ex/ex* mfd del powered by mtow kg configuration selcal name/fln/specialitites/remarks

NORTHERN PIONEER (Stephen R. Carvalho dba) — Big Lake, AK

1830 East Parks Hwy, No. 346, Wasilla, AK 99654, USA ☎ (907) 373-1303 Tx: none Fax: (907) 373-1302 SITA: n/a
F: 1995 ⁂ n/a Head: Stephen R. Carvalho Net: n/a

☐ N70NW	Bell UH-1B (204)	214	N77NW	0060	0396	1 LY T53-L-11	3856			

NORTH QUEST AVIATION (William E. Anker dba) — North Pole, AK

PO Box 61305, Fairbanks, AK 99706, USA ☎ (907) 455-4582 Tx: none Fax: none SITA: n/a
F: 1996 ⁂ n/a Head: William E. Anker Net: n/a Aircraft below MTOW 1361kg: Piper PA-18

☐ N1205F	Cessna A185F Skywagon	18502768		0075	0697	1 CO IO-520-D	1520			Floats / Wheel-Skis
☐ N4913F	Cessna U206A Super Skywagon	U206-0613		0066	0197	1 CO IO-520-A	1633			

NORTHROP GRUMMAN AVIATION, Inc. (Subsidiary of Northrop Grumman Corporation) — Hawthorne-Municipal, CA

1 Northrop Ave. 9X00/65, Hawthorne, CA 90250-3277, USA ☎ (562) 332-5151 Tx: none Fax: (562) 332-3016 SITA: n/a
F: 1945 ⁂ n/a Head: Raymond B. Pollok Net: http://www.interjet-osi.com

☐ N8898Q	Cessna TU206G Turbo Stationair	U20603561		0076	0495	1 CO TSIO-520-M	1633	EquipmentTestbed		
☐ N89G	Beech Baron 58	TH-616		0075	0597	2 CO IO-520-C	2449	5 Pax		
☐ N360TL	Britten-Norman BN-2T-4R Turbine Islander	2143	G-MSSA	0083	0396	2 AN 250-B17F/1	3856	Radar Testbed		cvtd BN-2B-26
☐ N12NG	Beech King Air 200	BB-581	N14NA	0079	1079	2 PWC PT6A-41	5670	9 Pax		
☐ N15NG	Beech King Air 200	BB-666	N15NA	0080	0580	2 PWC PT6A-41	5670	9 Pax		
☐ N16NG	De Havilland DHC-6 Twin Otter 300	596	N16NA	0078	0386	2 PWC PT6A-27	5670	Freighter		
☐ N19NG	Beech 1900C-1 Airliner	UC-2	N19NA	0087	0188	2 PWC PT6A-65B	7530	Corporate		
☐ N21NG	Learjet 35A	35A-343	N80BT	0080	0585	2 GA TFE731-2-2B	8301	8 Pax		
☐ N115CR	Sabreliner 60 (Rockwell NA265-60)	306-43	N10UM	0069	0293	2 PW JT12A-8	9072	Testbed		
☐ N160W	Sabreliner 40A (Rockwell NA265-40A)	282-101	N101RR	0072	0696	2 PW JT12A-8	8896	Testbed		
☐ N168W	Sabreliner 40 (Rockwell NA265-40)	282-33	N903KB	0065	0696	2 PW JT12A-8A	8459	Testbed		
☐ N162W	BAe (BAC) One-Eleven 401AK	087	N173FE	0066	0396	2 RR Spey 511-14	40597	Testbed		
☐ N164W	BAe (BAC) One-Eleven 401AK	090	G-AXCK	0066	0696	2 RR Spey 511-14	40597	Testbed		
☐ N165W	Boeing 737-247	19605 / 57	N4508W	0068	0696	2 PW JT8D-9A	49442	Testbed		

NORTH STAR AIR CARGO, Inc. = SBX (Associated with Air Cargo Carriers, Inc.) — Milwaukee-GM Int'l, WI & Anchorage-Merrill Field, AK

4984 South Howell Avenue, Milwaukee, WI 53207, USA ☎ (920) 482-1711 Tx: none Fax: (920) 482-2038 SITA: n/a
F: 1984 ⁂ n/a Head: Baxter F. Snider ICAO: SKY BOX Net: n/a

☐ N86080	Cessna 337D Super Skymaster	337-1069		0069	1184	2 CO IO-360-C/D	1996	Freighter		lsf pvt
☐ N47CK	Twin (Aero) Turbo Commander 681B	681-6058	N4ME	0071	0796	2 GA TPE331-43BL	4264	Freighter		
☐ N50NS	Shorts Skyvan 3 Variant 200 (SC-7)	SH1856	N50GA	0069	0392	2 GA TPE331-2-201A	5670	Freighter		
☐ N51NS	Shorts Skyvan 3 Variant 200 (SC-7)	SH1843	N20DA	0067	0889	2 GA TPE331-2-201A	5670	Freighter		
☐ N52NS	Shorts Skyvan 3 Variant 100 (SC-7)	SH1905	C-GKOA	0071	1098	2 GA TPE331-2-201A	5670	Freighter		
☐ N53NS	Shorts Skyvan 3 Variant 100 (SC-7)	SH1920	C-FPSQ	0073	0990	2 GA TPE331-2-201A	5670	Freighter		

NORTHSTAR AIR EXPRESS, Inc. — Missoula-Int'l, MT

5225 Highway 10 West, Box 7, Missoula, MT 59802, USA ☎ (406) 721-8886 Tx: none Fax: (406) 721-8828 SITA: n/a
F: 1987 ⁂ n/a Head: Mark W. Timmons Net: n/a

☐ N15SF	Twin (Aero) Turbo Commander 690B II	11528	N690SH	0079	0892	2 GA TPE331-5-251K	4649			

NORTHWEST AERO SERVICES, Inc. — Enid-Woodring Municipal, OK

Rt 5, Box 41, Enid, OK 73701, USA ☎ (405) 233-4531 Tx: none Fax: (405) 249-4939 SITA: n/a
F: 1972 ⁂ n/a Head: Laverne Friesen Net: n/a Aircraft below MTOW 1361kg: Cessna 172

☐ N760PS	Piper PA-32R-300 Lance	32R-7680342		0076	0992	1 LY IO-540-K1G5D	1633			
☐ N777W	Piper PA-32R-300 Lance	32R-7780297		0077	0593	1 LY IO-540-K1G5D	1633			lsf Reesers Inc.

NORTHWEST AIRLINES, Inc. = NW / NWA (Subsidiary of Northwest Airlines, Corp. / formerly Northwest Orient) — Minneapolis/St. Paul, MN

5101 Northwest Drive, Int'l Airport, St. Paul, MN 55111, USA ☎ (320) 726-2111 Tx: 297024 nwair stp a Fax: (320) 726-6599 SITA: n/a
F: 1926 ⁂ 47000 Head: Gary L. Wilson IATA: 012 ICAO: NORTHWEST Net: http://www.nwa.com

A commuter system to provide feeder connection at NW major hubs is operated under the marketing name NORTHWEST AIRLINK or JET AIRLINK by: EXPRESS AIRLINES I (BAe Jetstream 31 & 340) & MESABA AIRLINES (Saab 340 & Avro RJ85). All aircraft are operated in full NORTHWEST AIRLINK or JETLINK-colors & both titles. For details – see under each company.

On order: 54 Canadair Regional Jet 200LR for delivery starting April 2000. Aircraft will be operated by Northwest Airlink companies but distribution not yet finalised.

☐ N9348	Boeing (Douglas) DC-9-15	45787 / 127	N1793U	0667	1086	2 PW JT8D-7B (HK3/ABS)	41141	F8Y70	EF-CH	9138
☐ N948L	Boeing (Douglas) DC-9-14	47049 / 42	N6140A	0766	1086	2 PW JT8D-7B (HK3/ABS)	41141	F8Y70	FM-CG	9139
☐ N930RC	Boeing (Douglas) DC-9-14	45729 / 16	OH-LYE	0166	1086	2 PW JT8D-7B (HK3/ABS)	41141	F8Y70	JL-GM	9140 / cvtd -11
☐ N8908E	Boeing (Douglas) DC-9-14	45749 / 50		0966	1086	2 PW JT8D-7B (HK3/ABS)	41141	F8Y70	DK-AC	9150
☐ N8909E	Boeing (Douglas) DC-9-14	45770 / 57		1166	1086	2 PW JT8D-7B (HK3/ABS)	41141	F8Y70	DK-AF	9151
☐ N8911E	Boeing (Douglas) DC-9-14	45825 / 67		1166	1086	2 PW JT8D-7B (HK3/ABS)	41141	F8Y70	DK-AG	9152
☐ N8912E	Boeing (Douglas) DC-9-14	45829 / 68		1166	1086	2 PW JT8D-7B (HK3/ABS)	41141	F8Y70	DK-AL	9153
☐ N8913E	Boeing (Douglas) DC-9-14	45830 / 75		1266	1086	2 PW JT8D-7B (HK3/ABS)	41141	F8Y70	DK-BE	9154
☐ N8914E	Boeing (Douglas) DC-9-14	45831 / 76		1266	1086	2 PW JT8D-7B	41141	F8Y70	DK-BG	9155
☐ N8915E	Boeing (Douglas) DC-9-14	45832 / 84		0267	1086	2 PW JT8D-7B (HK3/ABS)	41141	F8Y70	DK-BL	9156
☐ N601NW	Boeing (Douglas) DC-9-32	47038 / 136	I-DIBA	0867	0395	2 PW JT8D-9A (HK3/ABS)	48534	F16Y84		9601
☐ N602NW	Boeing (Douglas) DC-9-32	47046 / 168	I-DIBE	0967	0995	2 PW JT8D-9A (HK3/ABS)	48534	F16Y84		9602
☐ N603NW	Boeing (Douglas) DC-9-32	47101 / 195	I-DIBL	1167	0595	2 PW JT8D-7B (HK3/ABS)	48534	F16Y84		9603
☐ N604NW	Boeing (Douglas) DC-9-32	47222 / 299	I-DIBP	0568	0195	2 PW JT8D-9A (HK3/ABS)	48534	F16Y84		9604
☐ N605NW	Boeing (Douglas) DC-9-32	47223 / 300	I-DIBM	0468	0895	2 PW JT8D-9A (HK3/ABS)	48534	F16Y84		9605
☐ N606NW	Boeing (Douglas) DC-9-32	47225 / 317	I-RIFG	0568	0995	2 PW JT8D-9A (HK3/ABS)	48534	F16Y84		9606
☐ N607NW	Boeing (Douglas) DC-9-32	47232 / 428	I-RIFY	1268	1294	2 PW JT8D-7B (HK3/ABS)	48534	F16Y84		9607
☐ N608NW	Boeing (Douglas) DC-9-32	47233 / 429	I-RIFC	1268	1194	2 PW JT8D-7B (HK3/ABS)	48534	F16Y84		9608
☐ N609NW	Boeing (Douglas) DC-9-32	47234 / 435	I-RIFD	0169	0195	2 PW JT8D-7B (HK3/ABS)	48534	F16Y84		9609
☐ N610NW	Boeing (Douglas) DC-9-32	47432 / 525	I-RIFB	0869	0795	2 PW JT8D-9A (HK3/ABS)	48534	F16Y84		9610
☐ N611NA	Boeing (Douglas) DC-9-32	47435 / 540	I-RIFL	1069	1095	2 PW JT8D-9A (HK3/ABS)	48534	F16Y84		9611
☐ N612NW	Boeing (Douglas) DC-9-32	47436 / 541	I-RIFZ	1069	0195	2 PW JT8D-7B (HK3/ABS)	48534	F16Y84		9612
☐ N613NW	Boeing (Douglas) DC-9-32	47438 / 545	I-RIFP	1169	0395	2 PW JT8D-9A (HK3/ABS)	48534	F16Y84		9613
☐ N614NW	Boeing (Douglas) DC-9-32	47128 / 210	I-RIFH	1267	0496	2 PW JT8D-9A (HK3/ABS)	48534	F16Y84		9614
☐ N615NW	Boeing (Douglas) DC-9-32	47129 / 225	I-DIBI	1267	0996	2 PW JT8D-9A (HK3/ABS)	48534	F16Y84		9615
☐ N616NW	Boeing (Douglas) DC-9-32	47229 / 356	I-RIFS	0868	0597	2 PW JT8D-9A (HK3/ABS)	48534	F16Y84		9616
☐ N617NW	Boeing (Douglas) DC-9-32	47235 / 436	I-RIFJ	0169	0597	2 PW JT8D-9A (HK3/ABS)	48534	F16Y84		9617
☐ N618NW	Boeing (Douglas) DC-9-32	47433 / 526	I-RIFU	0869	0496	2 PW JT8D-9A (HK3/ABS)	48534	F16Y84		9618
☐ N619NW	Boeing (Douglas) DC-9-32	47518 / 614	I-RIFE	0271	1096	2 PW JT8D-9A (HK3/ABS)	48534	F16Y84		9619
☐ N620NW	Boeing (Douglas) DC-9-32	47533 / 641	I-RIFV	1271	0797	2 PW JT8D-9A (HK3/ABS)	48534	F16Y84		9620
☐ N621NW	Boeing (Douglas) DC-9-32	47544 / 676	I-RIFM	1072	0696	2 PW JT8D-9A (HK3/ABS)	48534	F16Y84		9621
☐ N622NW	Boeing (Douglas) DC-9-32	47575 / 680	I-RIFW	1272	1296	2 PW JT8D-9A (HK3/ABS)	48534	F16Y84		9622
☐ N623NW	Boeing (Douglas) DC-9-32	47591 / 706	I-RIFT	0973	1196	2 PW JT8D-9A (HK3/ABS)	48534	F16Y84		9623
☐ N952N	Boeing (Douglas) DC-9-31	47073 / 161		0967	1086	2 PW JT8D-7B (HK3/ABS)	48988	F16Y84	BC-AF	9902
☐ N953N	Boeing (Douglas) DC-9-31	47083 / 177		1067	1086	2 PW JT8D-7B (HK3/ABS)	48988	F16Y84		9903
☐ N955N	Boeing (Douglas) DC-9-31	47160 / 241		0168	1086	2 PW JT8D-7B (HK3/ABS)	48988	F16Y84	BC-AJ	9905
☐ N956N	Boeing (Douglas) DC-9-31	47252 / 294		0468	1086	2 PW JT8D-7B (HK3/ABS)	48988	F16Y84	BC-AK	9906
☐ N957N	Boeing (Douglas) DC-9-31	47253 / 295		0468	1086	2 PW JT8D-7B (HK3/ABS)	48988	F16Y84	BC-AL	9907
☐ N958N	Boeing (Douglas) DC-9-31	47254 / 301		0468	1086	2 PW JT8D-7B (HK3/ABS)	48988	F16Y84	BC-AM	9908
☐ N959N	Boeing (Douglas) DC-9-31	47255 / 310		0568	1086	2 PW JT8D-7B (HK3/ABS)	48988	F16Y84	BC-DJ	9909
☐ N960N	Boeing (Douglas) DC-9-31	47256 / 326		0668	1086	2 PW JT8D-7B (HK3/ABS)	48988	F16Y84	BC-DK	9910
☐ N961N	Boeing (Douglas) DC-9-31	47405 / 487		0569	1086	2 PW JT8D-9A (HK3/ABS)	48988	F16Y84	BC-DL	9911
☐ N962N	Boeing (Douglas) DC-9-31	47406 / 499		0569	1086	2 PW JT8D-9A (HK3/ABS)	48988	F16Y84	BC-DM	9912
☐ N963N	Boeing (Douglas) DC-9-31	47415 / 511		0669	1086	2 PW JT8D-9A (HK3/ABS)	48988	F16Y84	BC-EF	9913
☐ N964N	Boeing (Douglas) DC-9-31	47416 / 512		0770	1086	2 PW JT8D-9A (HK3/ABS)	48988	F16Y84	BC-EG	9914
☐ N965N	Boeing (Douglas) DC-9-31	47417 / 518		0770	1086	2 PW JT8D-9A (HK3/ABS)	48988	F16Y84	BC-EH	9915
☐ N949N	Boeing (Douglas) DC-9-32	47566 / 691		0473	1086	2 PW JT8D-9A (HK3/ABS)	49895	F16Y84	BC-EJ	9916 / cvtd -31
☐ N967N	Boeing (Douglas) DC-9-32	47573 / 694		0573	1086	2 PW JT8D-15 (HK3/ABS)	49895	F16Y84	BC-EK	9917 / cvtd -31
☐ N940N	Boeing (Douglas) DC-9-32	47572 / 708		1073	1086	2 PW JT8D-15 (HK3/ABS)	49895	F16Y84	BC-EL	9918 / cvtd -31
☐ N941N	Boeing (Douglas) DC-9-32	47450 / 535	D-ADIT	0270	1086	2 PW JT8D-15 (HK3/ABS)	49895	F16Y84	BC-EM	9919
☐ N942N	Boeing (Douglas) DC-9-32	47459 / 549	D-ADIS	0170	1086	2 PW JT8D-15 (HK3/ABS)	49895	F16Y84	BC-AD	9920
☐ N943N	Boeing (Douglas) DC-9-32	47647 / 773		0575	1086	2 PW JT8D-15 (HK3/ABS)	49895	F16Y84	AM-CF	9921 / cvtd -31
☐ N945N	Boeing (Douglas) DC-9-32	47664 / 775		0575	1086	2 PW JT8D-15 (HK3/ABS)	49895	F16Y84	AM-CG	9922 / cvtd -31
☐ N927RC	Boeing (Douglas) DC-9-32	47469 / 590	YU-AHM	0570	1086	2 PW JT8D-9A (HK3/ABS)	48988	F16Y84	JK-EM	9923
☐ N926RC	Boeing (Douglas) DC-9-32	47473 / 598	YU-AHP	0670	1086	2 PW JT8D-9A (HK3/ABS)	48988	F16Y84	JK-GH	9924
☐ N925US	Boeing (Douglas) DC-9-32	47472 / 596	YU-AHO	0670	1087	2 PW JT8D-9A (HK3/ABS)	48988	F16Y84	HJ-AL	9925
☐ N926NW	Boeing (Douglas) DC-9-32	47425 / 589	YU-AHL	0570	0988	2 PW JT8D-9A (HK3/ABS)	48988	F16Y84	HJ-AK	9926
☐ N8920E	Boeing (Douglas) DC-9-31	45835 / 95		0367	0694	2 PW JT8D-7B (HK3/ABS)	48534	F16Y84	GJ-EH	9927
☐ N8921E	Boeing (Douglas) DC-9-31	45836 / 96		0367	0694	2 PW JT8D-9A (HK3/ABS)	48534	F16Y84	GJ-FK	9928
☐ N8923E	Boeing (Douglas) DC-9-31	45838 / 104		0467	0694	2 PW JT8D-7B (HK3/ABS)	48534	F16Y84	GJ-FM	9929
☐ N89S	Boeing (Douglas) DC-9-31	47042 / 486		0469	1086	2 PW JT8D-7B (HK3/ABS)	48988	F16Y84	HJ-DG	9930
☐ N90S	Boeing (Douglas) DC-9-31	47244 / 498		0569	1086	2 PW JT8D-7B (HK3/ABS)	48534	F16Y84	GL-DJ	9931
☐ N1334U	Boeing (Douglas) DC-9-31	47280 / 597		0671	1086	2 PW JT8D-7B (HK3/ABS)	48534	F16Y84	GL-EJ	9933
☐ N1332U	Boeing (Douglas) DC-9-31	47404 / 554		1171	1086	2 PW JT8D-7B (HK3/ABS)	48534	F16Y84	GL-DM	9935
☐ N1799U	Boeing (Douglas) DC-9-31	47370 / 551		0971	1086	2 PW JT8D-7B (HK3/ABS)	48988	F16Y84	GL-HJ	9936

406 registration type of aircraft cn/fn ex/ex* mfd del powered by mtow kg configuration selcal name/fln/specialitites/remarks

registration	type of aircraft	cn/fn	ex/ex*	mfd	del	powered by	mtow kg	configuration	selcal	name/fln/specialitites/remarks
☐ N908H	Boeing (Douglas) DC-9-31	47517 / 583		0470	1086	2 PW JT8D-7B (HK3/ABS)	48988	F16Y84	HJ-CG	9937
☐ N1798U	Boeing (Douglas) DC-9-31	47369 / 529		1069	1086	2 PW JT8D-7B (HK3/ABS)	48988	F16Y84	HJ-DF	9938
☐ N3322L	Boeing (Douglas) DC-9-32	47031 / 187	YV-68C	1167	1086	2 PW JT8D-9A (HK3/ABS)	48988	F16Y84	FM-DH	9940
☐ N3324L	Boeing (Douglas) DC-9-32	47103 / 205	YV-70C	1167	1086	2 PW JT8D-9A (HK3/ABS)	48988	F16Y84	FM-DL	9941
☐ N3991C	Boeing (Douglas) DC-9-32	47175 / 298	PJ-SNE	0468	1086	2 PW JT8D-15 (HK3/ABS)	48988	F16Y84	EL-DK	9942
☐ N1308T	Boeing (Douglas) DC-9-31	47315 / 433		0169	1086	2 PW JT8D-9A (HK3/ABS)	48988	F16Y84	JK-EH	9943
☐ N1309T	Boeing (Douglas) DC-9-31	47316 / 439		0169	1086	2 PW JT8D-9A (HK3/ABS)	48988	F16Y84	HJ-BC	9944
☐ N8925E	Boeing (Douglas) DC-9-31	45840 / 117		0567	0794	2 PW JT8D-7B (HK3/ABS)	48534	F16Y84	AL-CK	9945
☐ N8926E	Boeing (Douglas) DC-9-31	45863 / 124		0667	0794	2 PW JT8D-7B (HK3/ABS)	48534	F16Y84	AL-CM	9946
☐ N8938E	Boeing (Douglas) DC-9-31	47161 / 249	5N-GIN	0268	0594	2 PW JT8D-7B (HK3/ABS)	48534	F16Y84	AL-FK	9947
☐ N8929E	Boeing (Douglas) DC-9-31	45866 / 138		0767	0794	2 PW JT8D-7B (HK3/ABS)	48534	F16Y84	AL-DJ	9948
☐ N8928E	Boeing (Douglas) DC-9-31	45865 / 137		0767	0794	2 PW JT8D-7B (HK3/ABS)	48534	F16Y84	AL-DH	9949
☐ N9346	Boeing (Douglas) DC-9-32	47376 / 517	N394PA	0769	1086	2 PW JT8D-9A (HK3/ABS)	48988	F16Y84	FM-BK	9950
☐ N9347	Boeing (Douglas) DC-9-32	45827 / 135	HL7201	0767	1086	2 PW JT8D-9A (HK3/ABS)	48988	F16Y84	EF-CJ	9951
☐ N916RW	Boeing (Douglas) DC-9-31	47144 / 239	N8935E	0168	1086	2 PW JT8D-9A (HK3/ABS)	48988	F16Y84	EH-AD	9952
☐ N918RW	Boeing (Douglas) DC-9-31	47158 / 248	N8937E	0168	1086	2 PW JT8D-15 (HK3/ABS)	48988	F16Y84	FM-AJ	9953
☐ N921RW	Boeing (Douglas) DC-9-31	47164 / 259	N8941E	0268	1086	2 PW JT8D-15 (HK3/ABS)	48988	F16Y84	FM-AL	9954
☐ N922RW	Boeing (Douglas) DC-9-31	47182 / 271	N8946E	0368	1086	2 PW JT8D-9A (HK3/ABS)	48988	F16Y84	FM-BC	9955
☐ N923RW	Boeing (Douglas) DC-9-31	47183 / 272	N8947E	0368	1086	2 PW JT8D-15 (HK3/ABS)	48988	F16Y84	FM-BD	9956
☐ N915RW	Boeing (Douglas) DC-9-31	47139 / 169	N8930E	1067	1086	2 PW JT8D-15 (HK3/ABS)	48988	F16Y84	HM-BE	9957
☐ N917RW	Boeing (Douglas) DC-9-31	47145 / 247	N8936E	0168	1086	2 PW JT8D-9A (HK3/ABS)	48988	F16Y84	HM-AG	9958
☐ N919RW	Boeing (Douglas) DC-9-31	47162 / 255	N8939E	0268	1086	2 PW JT8D-9A (HK3/ABS)	48988	F16Y84	FM-AK	9959
☐ N920RW	Boeing (Douglas) DC-9-31	47163 / 256	N8940E	0268	1086	2 PW JT8D-9A (HK3/ABS)	48988	F16Y84	EH-BL	9960
☐ N924RW	Boeing (Douglas) DC-9-31	47185 / 275	N8949E	0368	1086	2 PW JT8D-9A (HK3/ABS)	48534	F16Y84	FM-DK	9961
☐ N914RW	Boeing (Douglas) DC-9-31	47362 / 492	N907H	0569	1086	2 PW JT8D-9A (HK3/ABS)	48534	F16Y84	EL-FG	9962
☐ N913RW	Boeing (Douglas) DC-9-31	47171 / 473	N906H	0369	1086	2 PW JT8D-9A (HK3/ABS)	48988	F16Y84	EH-CG	9963
☐ N912RW	Boeing (Douglas) DC-9-31	47150 / 284	N905H	0468	1086	2 PW JT8D-9A (HK3/ABS)	48988	F16Y84	EH-CD	9964
☐ N911RW	Boeing (Douglas) DC-9-31	47149 / 202	N903H	1167	1086	2 PW JT8D-9A (HK3/ABS)	48988	F16Y84	EH-BM	9965
☐ N9330	Boeing (Douglas) DC-9-31	47138 / 318		0568	1086	2 PW JT8D-9A (HK3/ABS)	48988	F16Y84	DM-BC	9966
☐ N9331	Boeing (Douglas) DC-9-31	47263 / 320	N9106	0668	1086	2 PW JT8D-9A (HK3/ABS)	48988	F16Y84	DM-BF	9967
☐ N9332	Boeing (Douglas) DC-9-31	47264 / 329		0668	1086	2 PW JT8D-9A (HK3/ABS)	48988	F16Y84	EF-CK	9968
☐ N9333	Boeing (Douglas) DC-9-31	47246 / 292		0668	1086	2 PW JT8D-9A (HK3/ABS)	48988	F16Y84	FM-DE	9969
☐ N9334	Boeing (Douglas) DC-9-31	47247 / 342		0768	1086	2 PW JT8D-9A (HK3/ABS)	48988	F16Y84	FM-DG	9970
☐ N9335	Boeing (Douglas) DC-9-31	47337 / 415		1168	1086	2 PW JT8D-9A (HK3/ABS)	48534	F16Y84	DM-KL	9971
☐ N9336	Boeing (Douglas) DC-9-31	47338 / 416		1168	1086	2 PW JT8D-7B (HK3/ABS)	48988	F16Y84	EF-CD	9972
☐ N9337	Boeing (Douglas) DC-9-31	47346 / 464		0369	1086	2 PW JT8D-9A (HK3/ABS)	48988	F16Y84	EF-CG	9973
☐ N9338	Boeing (Douglas) DC-9-31	47347 / 478		0469	1086	2 PW JT8D-7B (HK3/ABS)	48534	F16Y84	EF-CL	9974
☐ N9339	Boeing (Douglas) DC-9-31	47382 / 479		0469	1086	2 PW JT8D-7B (HK3/ABS)	48988	F16Y84	HM-AD	9975
☐ N9340	Boeing (Douglas) DC-9-31	47389 / 489		0569	1086	2 PW JT8D-7B (HK3/ABS)	48988	F16Y84	EL-CD	9976
☐ N9341	Boeing (Douglas) DC-9-31	47390 / 490		0569	1086	2 PW JT8D-7B (HK3/ABS)	48988	F16Y84	EL-CG	9977
☐ N9342	Boeing (Douglas) DC-9-31	47391 / 491		0569	1086	2 PW JT8D-7B (HK3/ABS)	48988	F16Y84	EL-DG	9978
☐ N9343	Boeing (Douglas) DC-9-31	47439 / 501		0669	1086	2 PW JT8D-7B (HK3/ABS)	48988	F16Y84	EL-DH	9979
☐ N9344	Boeing (Douglas) DC-9-31	47440 / 502		0669	1086	2 PW JT8D-7B (HK3/ABS)	48534	F16Y84	EL-DJ	9980
☐ N994Z	Boeing (Douglas) DC-9-31	47097 / 193	N979NE	1167	1086	2 PW JT8D-7B (HK3/ABS)	48534	F16Y84	FM-BE	9981
☐ N982US	Boeing (Douglas) DC-9-32	45790 / 264	HB-IFH	0268	1188	2 PW JT8D-15 (HK3/ABS)	49895	F16Y84	FM-HK	9982
☐ N983US	Boeing (Douglas) DC-9-32	47282 / 446	HB-IFU	0169	0788	2 PW JT8D-15 (HK3/ABS)	48988	F16Y84	FM-GJ	9983
☐ N984US	Boeing (Douglas) DC-9-32	47383 / 538	HB-IFV	1069	1088	2 PW JT8D-15 (HK3/ABS)	48988	F16Y84	FM-GL	9984
☐ N985US	Boeing (Douglas) DC-9-32	47479 / 605	HB-IFZ	0970	0688	2 PW JT8D-15 (HK3/ABS)	49895	F16Y84	FM-HJ	9985
☐ N986US	Boeing (Douglas) DC-9-32	47480 / 607	N988US	1070	0188	2 PW JT8D-15 (HK3/ABS)	48988	F16Y84	JL-BM	9986
☐ N987US	Boeing (Douglas) DC-9-32	47458 / 646	OE-LDF	1271	1287	2 PW JT8D-15 (HK3/ABS)	49895	F16Y84	JL-FK	9987
☐ N8944E	Boeing (Douglas) DC-9-31	47167 / 266		0268	0694	2 PW JT8D-9A (HK3/ABS)	48534	F16Y84	AM-BG	9988
☐ N8945E	Boeing (Douglas) DC-9-31	47181 / 267		0268	0694	2 PW JT8D-7B (HK3/ABS)	48534	F16Y84	AM-BH	9989
☐ N8950E	Boeing (Douglas) DC-9-31	47186 / 276	C-FBKT	0368	0694	2 PW JT8D-9A (HK3/ABS)	48534	F16Y84	CE-AL	9990
☐ N8957E	Boeing (Douglas) DC-9-31	47215 / 313		0568	0694	2 PW JT8D-7B (HK3/ABS)	48534	F16Y84	CH-AD	9991
☐ N8960E	Boeing (Douglas) DC-9-31	45869 / 331		0668	0694	2 PW JT8D-9A (HK3/ABS)	48534	F16Y84	CH-AJ	9992
☐ N8986E	Boeing (Douglas) DC-9-31	47402 / 482	5N-INZ	0569	0594	2 PW JT8D-9A (HK3/ABS)	48534	F16Y84	CJ-BD	9993
☐ N8979E	Boeing (Douglas) DC-9-31	47328 / 392		1068	0694	2 PW JT8D-9A (HK3/ABS)	48534	F16Y84	BL-DH	9994
☐ N8978E	Boeing (Douglas) DC-9-31	47327 / 391		1068	0694	2 PW JT8D-9A (HK3/ABS)	48534	F16Y84	BL-DG	9995
☐ N8932E	Boeing (Douglas) DC-9-31	47141 / 227		1267	0188	2 PW JT8D-7B (HK3/ABS)	47627	F16Y84	EH-BF	9996
☐ N8933E	Boeing (Douglas) DC-9-31	47142 / 232		1267	0288	2 PW JT8D-7B (HK3/ABS)	47627	F16Y84	EH-BK	9997
☐ N8934E	Boeing (Douglas) DC-9-31	47143 / 238		0168	0688	2 PW JT8D-9A (HK3/ABS)	47627	F16Y84	EH-AB	9998
☐ N750NW	Boeing (Douglas) DC-9-41	47114 / 218	SE-DBX	1067	0891	2 PW JT8D-11 (HK3/ABS)	51710	F12Y100	BC-EF	9750
☐ N751NW	Boeing (Douglas) DC-9-41	47115 / 261	OY-KGA	0268	0991	2 PW JT8D-11 (HK3/ABS)	51710	F12Y100	BC-AH	9751
☐ N752NW	Boeing (Douglas) DC-9-41	47116 / 308	LN-RLK	0568	0491	2 PW JT8D-11 (HK3/ABS)	51710	F12Y100	BC-AJ	9752
☐ N753NW	Boeing (Douglas) DC-9-41	47117 / 319	SE-DBW	0568	0191	2 PW JT8D-11 (HK3/ABS)	51710	F12Y100	BC-DE	9753
☐ N754NW	Boeing (Douglas) DC-9-41	47178 / 323	OY-KGB	0668	0591	2 PW JT8D-11 (HK3/ABS)	51710	F12Y100	BC-DF	9754
☐ N755NW	Boeing (Douglas) DC-9-41	47179 / 335	LN-RLC	0668	0291	2 PW JT8D-11 (HK3/ABS)	51710	F12Y100	BF-CH	9755
☐ N756NW	Boeing (Douglas) DC-9-41	47180 / 354	SE-DBU	0768	0691	2 PW JT8D-11 (HK3/ABS)	51710	F12Y100	BC-EM	9756
☐ N758NW	Boeing (Douglas) DC-9-41	47286 / 359	OY-KGC	0868	1191	2 PW JT8D-11 (HK3/ABS)	51710	F12Y100	FL-CG	9758
☐ N759NW	Boeing (Douglas) DC-9-41	47287 / 364	LN-RLJ	0868	1189	2 PW JT8D-11 (HK3/ABS)	51710	F12Y100	FL-EG	9759
☐ N760NW	Boeing (Douglas) DC-9-41	47288 / 369	SE-DBT	0868	1291	2 PW JT8D-11 (HK3/ABS)	51710	F12Y100	FL-EJ	9760
☐ N762NW	Boeing (Douglas) DC-9-41	47395 / 555	OY-KGG	1169	0591	2 PW JT8D-11 (HK3/ABS)	51710	F12Y100	BF-EH	9762
☐ N763NW	Boeing (Douglas) DC-9-41	47396 / 557	LN-RLD	1269	0791	2 PW JT8D-11 (HK3/ABS)	51710	F12Y100	BF-AC	9763
☐ N760NC	Boeing (Douglas) DC-9-51	47708 / 813		0476	1086	2 PW JT8D-17 (HK3/ABS)	54885	F12Y110	AM-CH	9851
☐ N761NC	Boeing (Douglas) DC-9-51	47709 / 814		0476	1086	2 PW JT8D-17 (HK3/ABS)	54885	F12Y110	AM-CJ	9852
☐ N762NC	Boeing (Douglas) DC-9-51	47710 / 818		0476	1086	2 PW JT8D-17 (HK3/ABS)	54885	F12Y110	BF-EH	9853
☐ N763NC	Boeing (Douglas) DC-9-51	47716 / 832		0976	1086	2 PW JT8D-17 (HK3/ABS)	54885	F12Y110	BC-DE	9854
☐ N764NC	Boeing (Douglas) DC-9-51	47717 / 833		1276	1086	2 PW JT8D-17 (HK3/ABS)	54885	F12Y110	BC-DF	9855
☐ N765NC	Boeing (Douglas) DC-9-51	47718 / 834		1176	1086	2 PW JT8D-17 (HK3/ABS)	54885	F12Y110	BC-DG	9856
☐ N766NC	Boeing (Douglas) DC-9-51	47739 / 852		0377	1086	2 PW JT8D-17 (HK3/ABS)	54885	F12Y110	BC-DH	9857
☐ N767NC	Boeing (Douglas) DC-9-51	47724 / 853		0477	1086	2 PW JT8D-17 (HK3/ABS)	54885	F12Y110	BC-FG	9858
☐ N768NC	Boeing (Douglas) DC-9-51	47729 / 854		0577	1086	2 PW JT8D-17 (HK3/ABS)	54885	F12Y110	BC-FH	9859
☐ N769NC	Boeing (Douglas) DC-9-51	47757 / 877		0578	1086	2 PW JT8D-17 (HK3/ABS)	54885	F12Y110	BC-AE	9860
☐ N770NC	Boeing (Douglas) DC-9-51	47758 / 880		0778	1086	2 PW JT8D-17 (HK3/ABS)	54885	F12Y110	BC-AH	9861
☐ N771NC	Boeing (Douglas) DC-9-51	47769 / 881		0878	1086	2 PW JT8D-17 (HK3/ABS)	54885	F12Y110	BC-FJ	9862
☐ N772NC	Boeing (Douglas) DC-9-51	47774 / 884		0978	1086	2 PW JT8D-17 (HK3/ABS)	54885	F12Y110	BC-FK	9863
☐ N773NC	Boeing (Douglas) DC-9-51	47775 / 888		1078	1086	2 PW JT8D-17 (HK3/ABS)	54885	F12Y110	BC-FL	9864
☐ N774NC	Boeing (Douglas) DC-9-51	47776 / 889		1178	1086	2 PW JT8D-17 (HK3/ABS)	54885	F12Y110	BC-FM	9865
☐ N775NC	Boeing (Douglas) DC-9-51	47785 / 904		0479	1086	2 PW JT8D-17	54885	F12Y110	BC-GH	9866
☐ N776NC	Boeing (Douglas) DC-9-51	47786 / 905		0479	1086	2 PW JT8D-17	54885	F12Y110	BC-GM	9867
☐ N777NC	Boeing (Douglas) DC-9-51	47787 / 912		0679	1086	2 PW JT8D-17 (HK3/ABS)	54885	F12Y110	BC-HK	9868
☐ N778NC	Boeing (Douglas) DC-9-51	48100 / 927		1179	1086	2 PW JT8D-17	54885	F12Y110	BC-JK	9869
☐ N779NC	Boeing (Douglas) DC-9-51	48101 / 931		1279	1086	2 PW JT8D-17	54885	F12Y110	BC-JL	9870
☐ N780NC	Boeing (Douglas) DC-9-51	48102 / 932		1279	1086	2 PW JT8D-17	54885	F12Y110	BC-JM	9871
☐ N781NC	Boeing (Douglas) DC-9-51	48121 / 935		1279	1086	2 PW JT8D-17	54885	F12Y110	HJ-CM	9872
☐ N782NC	Boeing (Douglas) DC-9-51	48107 / 936		0180	1086	2 PW JT8D-17 (HK3/ABS)	54885	F12Y110	AM-BF	9873
☐ N783NC	Boeing (Douglas) DC-9-51	48108 / 937		0180	1086	2 PW JT8D-17	54885	F12Y110	AM-GH	9874
☐ N784NC	Boeing (Douglas) DC-9-51	48109 / 939		0280	1086	2 PW JT8D-17	54885	F12Y110	AM-BL	9875
☐ N785NC	Boeing (Douglas) DC-9-51	48110 / 945		0480	1086	2 PW JT8D-17	54885	F12Y110	AM-GJ	9876
☐ N786NC	Boeing (Douglas) DC-9-51	48148 / 984		1280	1086	2 PW JT8D-17 (HK3/ABS)	54885	F12Y110	HJ-DL	9877
☐ N787NC	Boeing (Douglas) DC-9-51	48149 / 990		0481	1086	2 PW JT8D-17 (HK3/ABS)	54885	F12Y110	HJ-DM	9878
☐ N675MC	Boeing (Douglas) DC-9-51	47651 / 780	OE-LDK	0875	0392	2 PW JT8D-17 (HK3/ABS)	54885	F12Y107	GH-AF	9880
☐ N676MC	Boeing (Douglas) DC-9-51	47652 / 798	OE-LDL	1275	0392	2 PW JT8D-17 (HK3/ABS)	54885	F12Y107	GH-AJ	9881
☐ N670MC	Boeing (Douglas) DC-9-51	47659 / 807	HB-ISP	0276	0392	2 PW JT8D-17 (HK3/ABS)	54885	F12Y107	FL-HM	9882
☐ N671MC	Boeing (Douglas) DC-9-51	47660 / 810	HB-ISR	0276	0392	2 PW JT8D-17 (HK3/ABS)	54885	F12Y107	FL-HM	9883
☐ N677MC	Boeing (Douglas) DC-9-51	47756 / 873	OE-LDO	0178	0392	2 PW JT8D-17 (HK3/ABS)	54885	F12Y107		9884
☐ N401EA	Boeing (Douglas) DC-9-51	47682 / 788	N920VJ	1075	0394	2 PW JT8D-17 (HK3/ABS)	54885	F12Y107	HM-FL	9885
☐ N600TR	Boeing (Douglas) DC-9-51	47783 / 899	YV-40C	0379	0295	2 PW JT8D-17 (HK3/ABS)	54885	F12Y107		9886
☐ N301NB	Airbus Industrie A319-113					2 CFMI CFM56-5A4	64000	F16Y108		oo-delivery 0799
☐ N302NB	Airbus Industrie A319-113					2 CFMI CFM56-5A4	64000	F16Y108		oo-delivery 0799
☐ N303NB	Airbus Industrie A319-113					2 CFMI CFM56-5A4	64000	F16Y108		oo-delivery 0899
☐ N304NB	Airbus Industrie A319-113					2 CFMI CFM56-5A4	64000	F16Y108		oo-delivery 0999
☐ N305NB	Airbus Industrie A319-113					2 CFMI CFM56-5A4	64000	F16Y108		oo-delivery 0999
☐ N306NB	Airbus Industrie A319-113					2 CFMI CFM56-5A4	64000	F16Y108		oo-delivery 0999
☐ N307NB	Airbus Industrie A319-113					2 CFMI CFM56-5A4	64000	F16Y108		oo-delivery 1199
☐ N308NB	Airbus Industrie A319-113					2 CFMI CFM56-5A4	64000	F16Y108		oo-delivery 1199
☐ N309NB	Airbus Industrie A319-113					2 CFMI CFM56-5A4	64000	F16Y108		oo-delivery 1299
☐ N310NB	Airbus Industrie A319-113					2 CFMI CFM56-5A4	64000	F16Y108		oo-delivery 0200
☐ N311NB	Airbus Industrie A319-113					2 CFMI CFM56-5A4	64000	F16Y108		oo-delivery 0300
☐ N312NB	Airbus Industrie A319-113					2 CFMI CFM56-5A4	64000	F16Y108		oo-delivery 0400

☐	N313NB	Airbus Industrie A319-113					2 CFMI CFM56-5A4	64000	F16Y108		oo-delivery 0500
☐	N314NB	Airbus Industrie A319-113					2 CFMI CFM56-5A4	64000	F16Y108		oo-delivery 0600
☐	N315NB	Airbus Industrie A319-113					2 CFMI CFM56-5A4	64000	F16Y108		oo-delivery 0700
☐	N316NB	Airbus Industrie A319-113					2 CFMI CFM56-5A4	64000	F16Y108		oo-delivery 0800
☐	N317NB	Airbus Industrie A319-113					2 CFMI CFM56-5A4	64000	F16Y108		oo-delivery 0900
☐	N318NB	Airbus Industrie A319-113					2 CFMI CFM56-5A4	64000	F16Y108		oo-delivery 1000
☐	N319NB	Airbus Industrie A319-113					2 CFMI CFM56-5A4	64000	F16Y108		oo-delivery 1100
☐	N320NB	Airbus Industrie A319-113					2 CFMI CFM56-5A4	64000	F16Y108		oo-delivery 1200
☐	N321NB	Airbus Industrie A319-113					2 CFMI CFM56-5A4	64000	F16Y108		oo-delivery 0101
☐	N322NB	Airbus Industrie A319-113					2 CFMI CFM56-5A4	64000	F16Y108		oo-delivery 0201
☐	N323NB	Airbus Industrie A319-113					2 CFMI CFM56-5A4	64000	F16Y108		oo-delivery 0301
☐	N324NB	Airbus Industrie A319-113					2 CFMI CFM56-5A4	64000	F16Y108		oo-delivery 0401
☐	N325NB	Airbus Industrie A319-113					2 CFMI CFM56-5A4	64000	F16Y108		oo-delivery 0501
☐	N326NB	Airbus Industrie A319-113					2 CFMI CFM56-5A4	64000	F16Y108		oo-delivery 0601
☐	N327NB	Airbus Industrie A319-113					2 CFMI CFM56-5A4	64000	F16Y108		oo-delivery 0701
☐	N328NB	Airbus Industrie A319-113					2 CFMI CFM56-5A4	64000	F16Y108		oo-delivery 0801
☐	N329NB	Airbus Industrie A319-113					2 CFMI CFM56-5A4	64000	F16Y108		oo-delivery 0901
☐	N330NB	Airbus Industrie A319-113					2 CFMI CFM56-5A4	64000	F16Y108		oo-delivery 1001
☐	N331NB	Airbus Industrie A319-113					2 CFMI CFM56-5A4	64000	F16Y108		oo-delivery 1101
☐	N332NB	Airbus Industrie A319-113					2 CFMI CFM56-5A4	64000	F16Y108		oo-delivery 1201
☐	N333NB	Airbus Industrie A319-113					2 CFMI CFM56-5A4	64000	F16Y108		oo-delivery 0002
☐	N334NB	Airbus Industrie A319-113					2 CFMI CFM56-5A4	64000	F16Y108		oo-delivery 0002
☐	N335NB	Airbus Industrie A319-113					2 CFMI CFM56-5A4	64000	F16Y108		oo-delivery 0002
☐	N336NB	Airbus Industrie A319-113					2 CFMI CFM56-5A4	64000	F16Y108		oo-delivery 0002
☐	N337NB	Airbus Industrie A319-113					2 CFMI CFM56-5A4	64000	F16Y108		oo-delivery 0002
☐	N338NB	Airbus Industrie A319-113					2 CFMI CFM56-5A4	64000	F16Y108		oo-delivery 0002
☐	N339NB	Airbus Industrie A319-113					2 CFMI CFM56-5A4	64000	F16Y108		oo-delivery 0002
☐	N340NB	Airbus Industrie A319-113					2 CFMI CFM56-5A4	64000	F16Y108		oo-delivery 0002
☐	N341NB	Airbus Industrie A319-113					2 CFMI CFM56-5A4	64000	F16Y108		oo-delivery 0002
☐	N342NB	Airbus Industrie A319-113					2 CFMI CFM56-5A4	64000	F16Y108		oo-delivery 0002
☐	N343NB	Airbus Industrie A319-113					2 CFMI CFM56-5A4	64000	F16Y108		oo-delivery 0002
☐	N344NB	Airbus Industrie A319-113					2 CFMI CFM56-5A4	64000	F16Y108		oo-delivery 0003
☐	N345NB	Airbus Industrie A319-113					2 CFMI CFM56-5A4	64000	F16Y108		oo-delivery 0003
☐	N346NB	Airbus Industrie A319-113					2 CFMI CFM56-5A4	64000	F16Y108		oo-delivery 0003
☐	N347NB	Airbus Industrie A319-113					2 CFMI CFM56-5A4	64000	F16Y108		oo-delivery 0003
☐	N348NB	Airbus Industrie A319-113					2 CFMI CFM56-5A4	64000	F16Y108		oo-delivery 0003
☐	N349NB	Airbus Industrie A319-113					2 CFMI CFM56-5A4	64000	F16Y108		oo-delivery 0003
☐	N350NB	Airbus Industrie A319-113					2 CFMI CFM56-5A4	64000	F16Y108		oo-delivery 0003
☐	N301RC	Boeing (Douglas) MD-82 (DC-9-82)	48054 / 996		0881	1086	2 PW JT8D-217	67812	F12Y134	AM-HK	9301
☐	N302RC	Boeing (Douglas) MD-82 (DC-9-82)	48055 / 1007		0981	1086	2 PW JT8D-217	67812	F12Y134	AM-DL	9302
☐	N931MC	Boeing (Douglas) MD-82 (DC-9-82)	48057 / 1023	N10035	0582	1287	2 PW JT8D-217	66678	F12Y134	GM-AE	9304
☐	N307RC	Boeing (Douglas) MD-82 (DC-9-82)	48086 / 1029		1281	1086	2 PW JT8D-217	67812	F12Y134	GL-KM	9305
☐	N309RC	Boeing (Douglas) MD-82 (DC-9-82)	48088 / 1037	N1004S	1282	1086	2 PW JT8D-217	67812	F12Y134	GM-AC	9307
☐	N311RC	Boeing (Douglas) MD-82 (DC-9-82)	48089 / 1038	N1004D	1282	1086	2 PW JT8D-217	67812	F12Y134	GM-AD	9308
☐	N313RC	Boeing (Douglas) MD-82 (DC-9-82)	48091 / 1041	N1004G	0483	1086	2 PW JT8D-217	67812	F12Y134	GM-AF	9310
☐	N314RC	Boeing (Douglas) MD-82 (DC-9-82)	49110 / 1062	N1004L	0883	1086	2 PW JT8D-217	67812	F12Y134	EH-BJ	9311
☐	N301US	Airbus Industrie A320-211	031	F-WWDJ*	0689	0689	2 CFMI CFM56-5A1	75500	F12Y138	JK-EL	3201
☐	N302US	Airbus Industrie A320-211	032	F-WWDK*	0789	0789	2 CFMI CFM56-5A1	75500	F12Y138	JK-FG	3202
☐	N303US	Airbus Industrie A320-211	034	F-WWDL*	0689	0689	2 CFMI CFM56-5A1	75500	F12Y138	BC-LM	3203
☐	N304US	Airbus Industrie A320-211	040	F-WWDD*	0889	0889	2 CFMI CFM56-5A1	75500	F12Y138	AM-GK	3204
☐	N305US	Airbus Industrie A320-211	041	F-WWDS*	0789	0789	2 CFMI CFM56-5A1	75500	F12Y138	FM-CD	3205
☐	N306US	Airbus Industrie A320-211	060	F-WWIE*	0989	0989	2 CFMI CFM56-5A1	75500	F12Y138	FM-BJ	3206
☐	N307US	Airbus Industrie A320-211	106	F-WWIA*	0490	0490	2 CFMI CFM56-5A1	75500	F12Y138	EH-GP	3207
☐	N308US	Airbus Industrie A320-211	107	F-WWIB*	0490	0490	2 CFMI CFM56-5A1	75500	F12Y138	BC-FG	3208
☐	N309US	Airbus Industrie A320-211	118	F-WWIM*	1090	1090	2 CFMI CFM56-5A1	75500	F12Y138	BF-GM	3209
☐	N310NW	Airbus Industrie A320-211	121	F-WWIO*	1090	1090	2 CFMI CFM56-5A1	75500	F12Y138	BC-FM	3210
☐	N311US	Airbus Industrie A320-211	125	F-WWIT*	1190	1190	2 CFMI CFM56-5A1	75500	F12Y138	BC-GH	3211
☐	N312US	Airbus Industrie A320-211	152	F-WWDT*	0291	0291	2 CFMI CFM56-5A1	75500	F12Y138	BC-JL	3212
☐	N313US	Airbus Industrie A320-211	153	F-WWDX*	0391	0391	2 CFMI CFM56-5A1	75500	F12Y138	BC-KL	3213
☐	N314US	Airbus Industrie A320-211	160	F-WWDZ*	0391	0391	2 CFMI CFM56-5A1	75500	F12Y138	DK-AF	3214
☐	N315US	Airbus Industrie A320-211	171	F-WWIJ*	0491	0491	2 CFMI CFM56-5A1	75500	F12Y138	DK-AG	3215
☐	N316US	Airbus Industrie A320-211	192	F-WWIY*	0691	0691	2 CFMI CFM56-5A1	75500	F12Y138	HJ-BC	3216
☐	N317US	Airbus Industrie A320-211	197	F-WWDF*	0691	0691	2 CFMI CFM56-5A1	75500	F12Y138	JL-GM	3217
☐	N318US	Airbus Industrie A320-211	206	F-WWDK*	0791	0791	2 CFMI CFM56-5A1	75500	F12Y138	FM-BC	3218
☐	N319US	Airbus Industrie A320-211	208	F-WWDT*	0791	0791	2 CFMI CFM56-5A1	75500	F12Y138	EL-FG	3219
☐	N320US	Airbus Industrie A320-211	213	F-WWIB*	0791	0791	2 CFMI CFM56-5A1	75500	F12Y138	BC-EK	3220
☐	N321US	Airbus Industrie A320-211	262	F-WWID*	0192	0192	2 CFMI CFM56-5A1	75500	F12Y138	HJ-CF	3221
☐	N322US	Airbus Industrie A320-211	263	F-WWDQ*	0192	0192	2 CFMI CFM56-5A1	75500	F12Y138	GM-AE	3222
☐	N323US	Airbus Industrie A320-211	272	F-WWBP*	0292	0292	2 CFMI CFM56-5A1	75500	F12Y138	BC-JK	3223
☐	N324US	Airbus Industrie A320-211	273	F-WWDS*	0292	0292	2 CFMI CFM56-5A1	75500	F12Y138	BC-AF	3224
☐	N325US	Airbus Industrie A320-211	281	F-WWBS*	0392	0392	2 CFMI CFM56-5A1	75500	F12Y138	BC-AL	3225
☐	N326US	Airbus Industrie A320-211	282	F-WWIA*	0392	0392	2 CFMI CFM56-5A1	75500	F12Y138	GL-JM	3226
☐	N327NW	Airbus Industrie A320-211	297	F-WWIO*	0492	0492	2 CFMI CFM56-5A1	75500	F12Y138	HJ-CG	3227
☐	N328NW	Airbus Industrie A320-211	298	F-WWIP*	0492	0492	2 CFMI CFM56-5A1	75500	F12Y138	AF-BH	3228
☐	N329NW	Airbus Industrie A320-211	306	F-WWDG*	0592	0592	2 CFMI CFM56-5A1	75500	F12Y138	AL-JK	3229
☐	N330NW	Airbus Industrie A320-211	307	F-WWDJ*	0592	0592	2 CFMI CFM56-5A1	75500	F12Y138	DL-GK	3230
☐	N331NW	Airbus Industrie A320-211	318	F-WWBF*	0692	0692	2 CFMI CFM56-5A1	75500	F12Y138	EF-BJ	3231
☐	N332NW	Airbus Industrie A320-211	319	F-WWBG*	0692	0692	2 CFMI CFM56-5A1	75500	F12Y138	GL-AB	3232
☐	N333NW	Airbus Industrie A320-211	329	F-WWDY*	0792	0792	2 CFMI CFM56-5A1	75500	F12Y138	AL-BC	3233
☐	N334NW	Airbus Industrie A320-212	339	F-WWBP*	0892	0892	2 CFMI CFM56-5A3	75500	F12Y138	AL-CD	3234
☐	N335NW	Airbus Industrie A320-212	340	F-WWBQ*	1292	1292	2 CFMI CFM56-5A3	75500	F12Y138	AL-CG	3235
☐	N336NW	Airbus Industrie A320-212	355	F-WWIE*	1292	1292	2 CFMI CFM56-5A3	75500	F12Y138	AJ-KL	3236
☐	N337NW	Airbus Industrie A320-212	358	F-WWIO*	1292	1292	2 CFMI CFM56-5A3	75500	F12Y138	BK-DG	3237
☐	N338NW	Airbus Industrie A320-212	360	F-WWBY*	1292	1292	2 CFMI CFM56-5A3	75500	F12Y138	CE-DG	3238
☐	N339NW	Airbus Industrie A320-212	367	F-WWDG*	1292	1292	2 CFMI CFM56-5A3	75500	F12Y138	CE-DH	3239
☐	N340NW	Airbus Industrie A320-212	372	F-WWIX*	1292	1292	2 CFMI CFM56-5A3	75500	F12Y138	CE-DJ	3240
☐	N341NW	Airbus Industrie A320-212	380	F-WWIS*	0193	0193	2 CFMI CFM56-5A3	75500	F12Y138	CE-FH	3241
☐	N342NW	Airbus Industrie A320-212	381	F-WWIJ*	0193	0193	2 CFMI CFM56-5A3	75500	F12Y138	CE-FK	3242
☐	N343NW	Airbus Industrie A320-212	387	F-WWBV*	0293	0293	2 CFMI CFM56-5A3	75500	F12Y138	CE-FM	3243
☐	N344NW	Airbus Industrie A320-212	388	F-WWDC*	0293	0293	2 CFMI CFM56-5A3	75500	F12Y138	CE-GL	3244
☐	N345NW	Airbus Industrie A320-212	399	F-WWIG*	0393	0393	2 CFMI CFM56-5A3	75500	F12Y138	CE-GM	3245
☐	N346NW	Airbus Industrie A320-212	400	F-WWII*	0393	0393	2 CFMI CFM56-5A3	75500	F12Y138	CE-HJ	3246
☐	N347NW	Airbus Industrie A320-212	408	F-WWDN*	0493	0493	2 CFMI CFM56-5A3	75500	F12Y138	CE-HL	3247
☐	N348NW	Airbus Industrie A320-212	410	F-WWDV*	0493	0493	2 CFMI CFM56-5A3	75500	F12Y138	CE-JM	3248
☐	N349NW	Airbus Industrie A320-212	417	F-WWBR*	0593	0593	2 CFMI CFM56-5A3	75500	F12Y138	CE-KM	3249
☐	N350NA	Airbus Industrie A320-212	418	F-WWDG*	0593	0593	2 CFMI CFM56-5A3	75500	F12Y138	CF-AD	3250
☐	N351NW	Airbus Industrie A320-212	766	F-WWDG*	0198	0198	2 CFMI CFM56-5A3	75500	F12Y138		3251
☐	N352NW	Airbus Industrie A320-212	778	F-WWDO*	0298	0298	2 CFMI CFM56-5A3	75500	F12Y138		3252
☐	N353NW	Airbus Industrie A320-212	786	F-WWDP*	0398	0398	2 CFMI CFM56-5A3	75500	F12Y138		3253
☐	N354NW	Airbus Industrie A320-212	801	F-WWDY*	0498	0498	2 CFMI CFM56-5A3	75500	F12Y138	AK-EM	3254
☐	N355NW	Airbus Industrie A320-212	807	F-WWIC*	0498	0498	2 CFMI CFM56-5A3	75500	F12Y138	BE-GK	3255
☐	N356NW	Airbus Industrie A320-212	818	F-WWBD*	0598	0598	2 CFMI CFM56-5A3	75500	F12Y138	BG-EM	3256
☐	N357NW	Airbus Industrie A320-212	830	F-WWIN*	0098	0698	2 CFMI CFM56-5A3	75500	F12Y138	BH-DJ	3257
☐	N358NW	Airbus Industrie A320-212	832	F-WWIO*	0098	0698	2 CFMI CFM56-5A3	75500	F12Y138	BH-DL	3258
☐	N359NW	Airbus Industrie A320-212	846	F-WWBH*	0098	0798	2 CFMI CFM56-5A3	75500	F12Y138		3259
☐	N360NW	Airbus Industrie A320-212	903	F-WWDO*	0098	1198	2 CFMI CFM56-5A3	75500	F12Y138		3260
☐	N361NW	Airbus Industrie A320-212	907	F-WWDQ*	0098	1198	2 CFMI CFM56-5A3	75500	F12Y138		3261
☐	N362NW	Airbus Industrie A320-212	911	F-WWDT*	0098	1198	2 CFMI CFM56-5A3	75500	F12Y138		3262
☐	N363NW	Airbus Industrie A320-212	923	F-WWDZ*	0098	1298	2 CFMI CFM56-5A3	75500	F12Y138		3263
☐	N364NW	Airbus Industrie A320-212	962	F-WWBF*	0099	0399	2 CFMI CFM56-5A3	75500	F12Y138		3264
☐	N365NW	Airbus Industrie A320-212	964	F-WWBJ*	0099	0399	2 CFMI CFM56-5A3	75500	F12Y138		3265
☐	N366NW	Airbus Industrie A320-212	981				2 CFMI CFM56-5A3	75500	F12Y138		3266 / oo-delivery 0499
☐	N367NW	Airbus Industrie A320-212	996				2 CFMI CFM56-5A3	75500	F12Y138		3267 / oo-delivery 0599
☐	N368NW	Airbus Industrie A320-212	1011				2 CFMI CFM56-5A3	75500	F12Y138		3268 / oo-delivery 0699
☐	N369NW	Airbus Industrie A320-212	1037				2 CFMI CFM56-5A3	75500	F12Y138		3269 / oo-delivery 0799
☐	N370NW	Airbus Industrie A320-212					2 CFMI CFM56-5A3	75500	F12Y138		3270 / oo-delivery 0799
☐	N201US	Boeing 727-251 (A)	22154 / 1645		0780	0780	3 PW JT8D-7B (HK3/FDX)	80059	F12Y137		2201
☐	N202US	Boeing 727-251 (A)	22155 / 1648		0880	0880	3 PW JT8D-15 (HK3/FDX)	80059	F12Y137		2202
☐	N203US	Boeing 727-251 (A)	22543 / 1700		0181	0181	3 PW JT8D-15 (HK3/FDX)	80059	F12Y137		2203
☐	N204US	Boeing 727-251 (A)	22544 / 1703		0181	0181	3 PW JT8D-15 (HK3/FDX)	80059	F12Y137		2204

408 registration type of aircraft cn/fn ex/ex* mfd del powered by mtow kg configuration selcal name/fln/specialitites/remarks

registration	type of aircraft	cn/fn	ex/ex*	mfd	del	powered by	mtow kg	configuration	selcal	name/fln/specialitites/remarks
N275US	Boeing 727-251 (A)	21154 / 1168		1075	1075	3 PW JT8D-15 (HK3/FDX)	80059	F12Y137		2275
N284US	Boeing 727-251 (A)	21323 / 1284		0877	0877	3 PW JT8D-15/-15A	80059	F12Y137		2284
N285US	Boeing 727-251 (A)	21324 / 1286		0877	0877	3 PW JT8D-15/-15A	80059	F12Y137		2285
N286US	Boeing 727-251 (A)	21325 / 1288		0877	0877	3 PW JT8D-7B (HK3/FDX)	80059	F12Y137		2286
N287US	Boeing 727-251 (A)	21375 / 1290		0977	0977	3 PW JT8D-15 (HK3/FDX)	80059	F12Y137		2287
N288US	Boeing 727-251 (A)	21376 / 1293		0977	0977	3 PW JT8D-15 (HK3/FDX)	80059	F12Y137		2288
N289US	Boeing 727-251 (A)	21377 / 1295		1177	1177	3 PW JT8D-15 (HK3/FDX)	80059	F12Y137		2289
N290US	Boeing 727-251 (A)	21378 / 1297		1077	1077	3 PW JT8D-15 (HK3/FDX)	80059	F12Y137		2290
N291US	Boeing 727-251 (A)	21379 / 1299		1077	1077	3 PW JT8D-15 (HK3/FDX)	80059	F12Y137		2291
N292US	Boeing 727-251 (A)	21503 / 1317		0278	0278	3 PW JT8D-15 (HK3/FDX)	86409	F12Y137		2292
N293US	Boeing 727-251 (A)	21504 / 1319		0278	0278	3 PW JT8D-15 (HK3/FDX)	86409	F12Y137		2293
N295US	Boeing 727-251 (A)	21506 / 1392		0978	0978	3 PW JT8D-15 (HK3/FDX)	80059	F12Y137		2295
N296US	Boeing 727-251 (A)	21788 / 1495		0679	0679	3 PW JT8D-15 (HK3/FDX)	80059	F12Y137		2296
N297US	Boeing 727-251 (A)	21789 / 1496		0679	0679	3 PW JT8D-15 (HK3/FDX)	80059	F12Y137		2297
N298US	Boeing 727-251 (A)	22152 / 1599		0480	0480	3 PW JT8D-15 (HK3/FDX)	80059	F12Y137		2298
N299US	Boeing 727-251 (A)	22153 / 1601		0480	0480	3 PW JT8D-15 (HK3/FDX)	80059	F12Y137		2299
N8877Z	Boeing 727-225 (A)	21450 / 1308		1277	0392	3 PW JT8D-15 (HK3/FDX)	83461	F12Y137	HJ-CK	2702
N8878Z	Boeing 727-225 (A)	21451 / 1310		0178	0392	3 PW JT8D-15/-15A	83461	F12Y137	GJ-EK	2703
N801EA	Boeing 727-225 (A)	22432 / 1658		0180	0392	3 PW JT8D-15/-15A	83461	F12Y137	JL-CE	2704
N802EA	Boeing 727-225 (A)	22433 / 1668		0280	0392	3 PW JT8D-15/-15A	83461	F12Y137	JL-CF	2705
N815EA	Boeing 727-225 (A)	22552 / 1773		0181	0392	3 PW JT8D-15/-15A	83461	F12Y137	FL-CD	2706
N816EA	Boeing 727-225 (A)	22553 / 1775		0181	0392	3 PW JT8D-15 (HK3/FDX)	83461	F12Y137	HJ-CK	2707
N817EA	Boeing 727-225 (A)	22554 / 1781		0281	0392	3 PW JT8D-15 (HK3/FDX)	83461	F12Y137	GJ-DH	2708
N818EA	Boeing 727-225 (A)	22555 / 1783		0381	0392	3 PW JT8D-15 (HK3/FDX)	83461	F12Y137	JL-CE	2709
N820EA	Boeing 727-225 (A)	22557 / 1795		0182	0392	3 PW JT8D-15 (HK3/FDX)	86183	F12Y137	KL-AJ	2710
N716RC	Boeing 727-2S7 (A)	22021 / 1617		0680	1086	3 PW JT8D-17 (HK3/FDX)	89358	F12Y137	BD-AC	2713
N718RC	Boeing 727-2S7 (A)	22344 / 1654		0980	1086	3 PW JT8D-17 (HK3/FDX)	89358	F12Y137	BC-KL	2714
N719RC	Boeing 727-2S7 (A)	22490 / 1721		0281	1086	3 PW JT8D-17 (HK3/FDX)	89358	F12Y137	AM-CL	2715
N720RC	Boeing 727-2S7 (A)	22491 / 1726		0381	1086	3 PW JT8D-17 (HK3/FDX)	89358	F12Y137	AM-GK	2716
N721RC	Boeing 727-2S7 (A)	22492 / 1729		0381	1086	3 PW JT8D-17 (HK3/FDX)	89358	F12Y137	AM-DG	2717
N722RW	Boeing 727-2M7 (A)	21201 / 1220		1176	1086	3 PW JT8D-17R (HK3/FDX)	88360	F12Y137	FM-CD	2762
N727RW	Boeing 727-2M7 (A)	21656 / 1455		0379	1086	3 PW JT8D-17R (HK3/FDX)	88360	F12Y137	FM-BG	2767
N728RW	Boeing 727-2M7 (A)	21741 / 1491		0779	1086	3 PW JT8D-17R (HK3/FDX)	88360	F12Y137	FM-BH	2768
N729RW	Boeing 727-2M7 (A)	21742 / 1514		0879	1086	3 PW JT8D-17R (HK3/FDX)	88360	F12Y137	FM-BJ	2769
N501US	Boeing 757-251	23190 / 53		0285	0285	2 PW PW2037	103192	F14Y176		5501 / City of St. Paul
N502US	Boeing 757-251	23191 / 55		0385	0385	2 PW PW2037	103192	F14Y176		5502 / City of Minneapolis
N503US	Boeing 757-251	23192 / 59		0485	0485	2 PW PW2037	103192	F14Y176		5503 / City of Detroit
N504US	Boeing 757-251	23193 / 60		0485	0485	2 PW PW2037	103192	F14Y176		5504 / City of Los Angeles
N505US	Boeing 757-251	23194 / 62		0585	0585	2 PW PW2037	103192	F14Y176		5505 / City of Boston
N506US	Boeing 757-251	23195 / 67		0785	0785	2 PW PW2037	103192	F14Y176		5506 / City of New York
N507US	Boeing 757-251	23196 / 68		0785	0785	2 PW PW2037	103192	F14Y176		5507 / City of Seattle
N508US	Boeing 757-251	23197 / 69		0885	0885	2 PW PW2037	103192	F14Y176		5508 / City of Washington D.C.
N509US	Boeing 757-251	23198 / 70		1085	1085	2 PW PW2037	103192	F14Y176		5509 / City of Anchorage
N511US	Boeing 757-251	23199 / 72		1085	1085	2 PW PW2037	103192	F14Y176		5511 / Cities of Tampa Bay
N512US	Boeing 757-251	23200 / 82		1285	1285	2 PW PW2037	103192	F14Y176		5512 / City of Chicago
N513US	Boeing 757-251	23201 / 83		0286	0286	2 PW PW2037	103192	F14Y176		5513 / City of Orlando
N514US	Boeing 757-251	23202 / 86		0286	0286	2 PW PW2037	103192	F14Y176		5514 / City of San Francisco
N515US	Boeing 757-251	23203 / 88		0586	0586	2 PW PW2037	103192	F14Y176		5515 / City of Phoenix
N516US	Boeing 757-251	23204 / 104		0786	0786	2 PW PW2037	103192	F14Y176		5516 / City of San Diego
N517US	Boeing 757-251	23205 / 105		0886	0886	2 PW PW2037	103192	F14Y176		5517 / City of Portland
N518US	Boeing 757-251	23206 / 107		0886	0886	2 PW PW2037	103192	F14Y176		5518 / City of Milwaukee
N519US	Boeing 757-251	23207 / 108		1086	1086	2 PW PW2037	103192	F14Y176		5519 / City of Cleveland
N520US	Boeing 757-251	23208 / 109		1086	1086	2 PW PW2037	103192	F14Y176		5520 / City of Philadelphia
N521US	Boeing 757-251	23209 / 110		1286	1286	2 PW PW2037	103192	F14Y176		5521 / City of Denver
N522US	Boeing 757-251	23616 / 119		0187	0187	2 PW PW2037	103192	F14Y176		5522 / City of Spokane
N523US	Boeing 757-251	23617 / 121		0187	0187	2 PW PW2037	103192	F14Y176		5523 / City of Dallas
N524US	Boeing 757-251	23618 / 122		0287	0287	2 PW PW2037	103192	F14Y176		5524 / City of Houston
N525US	Boeing 757-251	23619 / 124		0487	0487	2 PW PW2037	103192	F14Y176		5525 / City of Miami
N526US	Boeing 757-251	23620 / 131		0587	0587	2 PW PW2037	103192	F14Y176		5526 / City of Memphis
N527US	Boeing 757-251	23842 / 136		0787	0787	2 PW PW2037	103192	F14Y176		5527 / City of Fargo
N528US	Boeing 757-251	23843 / 137		0987	0987	2 PW PW2037	103192	F14Y176		5528 / City of Toronto
N529US	Boeing 757-251	23844 / 140		0987	0987	2 PW PW2037	103192	F14Y176		5529 / City of New Orleans
N530US	Boeing 757-251	23845 / 188		0888	0888	2 PW PW2037	103192	F14Y176		5530 / City of Omaha
N531US	Boeing 757-251	23846 / 190		0888	0888	2 PW PW2037	103192	F14Y176		5531 / City of Newark
N532US	Boeing 757-251	24263 / 192		0988	0988	2 PW PW2037	103192	F14Y176		5532 / City of Fort Myers
N533US	Boeing 757-251	24264 / 194		0988	0988	2 PW PW2037	103192	F14Y176		5533 / City of Orange County
N534US	Boeing 757-251	24265 / 196		1088	1088	2 PW PW2037	103192	F14Y176		5534 / City of Winnipeg
N535US	Boeing 757-251	26482 / 693		1195	1195	2 PW PW2037	103192	F14Y180		5635
N536US	Boeing 757-251	26483 / 695		1295	1295	2 PW PW2037	103192	F14Y180		5636
N537US	Boeing 757-251	26484 / 697		0296	0296	2 PW PW2037	103192	F14Y180		5637
N538US	Boeing 757-251	26485 / 699		0396	0396	2 PW PW2037	103192	F14Y180		5638
N539US	Boeing 757-251	26486 / 700		0396	0396	2 PW PW2037	103192	F14Y180		5639
N540US	Boeing 757-251	26487 / 701		0096	0496	2 PW PW2037	103192	F14Y180		5640
N541US	Boeing 757-251	26488 / 703		0096	0496	2 PW PW2037	103192	F14Y180		5641
N542US	Boeing 757-251	26489 / 705		0096	0596	2 PW PW2037	103192	F14Y180		5642
N543US	Boeing 757-251	26490 / 709		0096	0596	2 PW PW2037	103192	F14Y180		5643
N544US	Boeing 757-251	26491 / 710		0096	0596	2 PW PW2037	103192	F14Y180		5644
N545US	Boeing 757-251	26492 / 711		0096	0696	2 PW PW2037	103192	F14Y180		5645
N546US	Boeing 757-251	26493 / 713		0096	0796	2 PW PW2037	103192	F14Y180		5646
N547US	Boeing 757-251	26494 / 714		0096	0896	2 PW PW2037	103192	F14Y180		5647
N548US	Boeing 757-251	26495 / 715		0096	0896	2 PW PW2037	103192	F14Y180		5648
N549US	Boeing 757-251	26496 / 716		0096	0996	2 PW PW2037	103192	F14Y180		5649
N550NA	Boeing 757-251					2 PW PW2037	103192	F14Y180		5550 / oo-delivery 0000
N551US	Boeing 757-251					2 PW PW2037	103192	F14Y180		5551 / oo-delivery 0000
N552US	Boeing 757-251					2 PW PW2037	103192	F14Y180		5552 / oo-delivery 0000
N553US	Boeing 757-251					2 PW PW2037	103192	F14Y180		5553 / oo-delivery 0000
N554US	Boeing 757-251					2 PW PW2037	103192	F14Y180		5554 / oo-delivery 0000
N555ND	Boeing 757-251					2 PW PW2037	103192	F14Y180		5555 / oo-delivery 0000
N556US	Boeing 757-251					2 PW PW2037	103192	F14Y180		5556 / oo-delivery 0000
N557US	Boeing 757-251					2 PW PW2037	103192	F14Y180		5557 / oo-delivery 0000
N558US	Boeing 757-251					2 PW PW2037	103192	F14Y180		5558 / oo-delivery 0000
N559US	Boeing 757-251					2 PW PW2037	103192	F14Y180		5559 / oo-delivery 0000
N560US	Boeing 757-251					2 PW PW2037	103192	F14Y180		5560 / oo-delivery 0001
N561US	Boeing 757-251					2 PW PW2037	103192	F14Y180		5561 / oo-delivery 0001
N562US	Boeing 757-251					2 PW PW2037	103192	F14Y180		5562 / oo-delivery 0001
N563US	Boeing 757-251					2 PW PW2037	103192	F14Y180		5563 / oo-delivery 0001
N564NW	Boeing 757-251					2 PW PW2037	103192	F14Y180		5564 / oo-delivery 0001
N565NW	Boeing 757-251					2 PW PW2037	103192	F14Y180		5565 / oo-delivery 0001
N566NW	Boeing 757-251					2 PW PW2037	103192	F14Y180		5566 / oo-delivery 0001
N567NW	Boeing 757-251					2 PW PW2037	103192	F14Y180		5567 / oo-delivery 0001
N568NW	Boeing 757-251					2 PW PW2037	103192	F14Y180		5568 / oo-delivery 0001
N569NW	Boeing 757-251					2 PW PW2037	103192	F14Y180		5569 / oo-delivery 0001
N570NW	Boeing 757-251					2 PW PW2037	103192	F14Y180		5570 / oo-delivery 0002
N571NW	Boeing 757-251					2 PW PW2037	103192	F14Y180		5571 / oo-delivery 0002
N572NW	Boeing 757-251					2 PW PW2037	103192	F14Y180		5572 / oo-delivery 0002
N573NW	Boeing 757-251					2 PW PW2037	103192	F14Y180		5573 / oo-delivery 0002
N574NW	Boeing 757-251					2 PW PW2037	103192	F14Y180		5574 / oo-delivery 0002
N3301C	Airbus Industrie A330-321					2 PW PW4164	212000			3301 / oo-delivery 0004
N3302B	Airbus Industrie A330-321					2 PW PW4164	212000			3302 / oo-delivery 0004
N3303B	Airbus Industrie A330-321					2 PW PW4164	212000			3303 / oo-delivery 0004
N3304N	Airbus Industrie A330-321					2 PW PW4164	212000			3304 / oo-delivery 0004
N3305N	Airbus Industrie A330-321					2 PW PW4164	212000			3305 / oo-delivery 0004
N3306N	Airbus Industrie A330-321					2 PW PW4164	212000			3306 / oo-delivery 0004
N3307N	Airbus Industrie A330-321					2 PW PW4164	212000			3307 / oo-delivery 0004
N3308B	Airbus Industrie A330-321					2 PW PW4164	212000			3308 / oo-delivery 0004
N3309N	Airbus Industrie A330-321					2 PW PW4164	212000			3309 / oo-delivery 0005
N3310D	Airbus Industrie A330-321					2 PW PW4164	212000			3310 / oo-delivery 0005
N3311G	Airbus Industrie A330-321					2 PW PW4164	212000			3311 / oo-delivery 0005
N3312D	Airbus Industrie A330-321					2 PW PW4164	212000			3312 / oo-delivery 0005
N3313A	Airbus Industrie A330-321					2 PW PW4164	212000			3313 / oo-delivery 0005

registration	type of aircraft	cn/fn	ex/ex*	mfd	del	powered by	mtow kg	configuration	selcal	name/fln/specialitites/remarks
☐ N3314B	Airbus Industrie A330-321					2 PW PW4164	212000			3314 / oo-delivery 0005
☐ N3315D	Airbus Industrie A330-321					2 PW PW4164	212000			3315 / oo-delivery 0005
☐ N3316G	Airbus Industrie A330-321					2 PW PW4164	212000			3316 / oo-delivery 0005
☐ N141US	Boeing (Douglas) DC-10-40	46750 / 28		0172	0673	3 PW JT9D-20J	240404	C34Y247	CJ-AL	1141
☐ N133JC	Boeing (Douglas) DC-10-40	46752 / 53	N143US	0772	0586	3 PW JT9D-20	240404	C32Y256	CJ-BD	1143 / lsf AFGR
☐ N144JC	Boeing (Douglas) DC-10-40	46753 / 66	N144US	0072	0791	3 PW JT9D-20J	240404	C34Y247	CJ-AM	1144 / lsf AFGR
☐ N145US	Boeing (Douglas) DC-10-40	46754 / 79		0173	0173	3 PW JT9D-20	240404	C32Y256	CJ-BH	1145
☐ N146US	Boeing (Douglas) DC-10-40	46755 / 97		0573	0573	3 PW JT9D-20J	240404	C34Y247	CJ-BK	1146
☐ N147US	Boeing (Douglas) DC-10-40	46756 / 102		0673	0673	3 PW JT9D-20J	240404	C34Y247	CJ-AD	1147
☐ N148US	Boeing (Douglas) DC-10-40	46757 / 108		0773	0773	3 PW JT9D-20J	240404	C34Y247	AH-FK	1148
☐ N149US	Boeing (Douglas) DC-10-40	46758 / 111		0773	0773	3 PW JT9D-20J	240404	C34Y247	CJ-AG	1149
☐ N150US	Boeing (Douglas) DC-10-40	46759 / 113		0773	0773	3 PW JT9D-20	240404	C32Y256	CJ-AK	1150
☐ N151US	Boeing (Douglas) DC-10-40	46760 / 120		1073	1073	3 PW JT9D-20	240404	C32Y256	CE-BK	1151
☐ N152US	Boeing (Douglas) DC-10-40	46761 / 124		1173	1173	3 PW JT9D-20	240404	C32Y256	CE-BL	1152
☐ N153US	Boeing (Douglas) DC-10-40	46762 / 126		1173	1173	3 PW JT9D-20	240404	C32Y256	CJ-BE	1153
☐ N154US	Boeing (Douglas) DC-10-40	46763 / 128		1173	1173	3 PW JT9D-20	240404	C32Y256	CE-BH	1154
☐ N155US	Boeing (Douglas) DC-10-40	46764 / 130		1273	1273	3 PW JT9D-20	240404	C32Y256	CE-BD	1155
☐ N156US	Boeing (Douglas) DC-10-40	46765 / 143		0374	0374	3 PW JT9D-20J	240404	C34Y247	CH-BM	1156 / City of Amsterdam
☐ N157US	Boeing (Douglas) DC-10-40	46766 / 151		0574	0574	3 PW JT9D-20	240404	C32Y256	AL-FK	1157
☐ N158US	Boeing (Douglas) DC-10-40	46767 / 161		0774	0774	3 PW JT9D-20J	240404	C34Y247	AL-FM	1158
☐ N159US	Boeing (Douglas) DC-10-40	46768 / 164		0874	0874	3 PW JT9D-20	240404	C32Y256	AL-GM	1159
☐ N160US	Boeing (Douglas) DC-10-40	46769 / 168		0974	0974	3 PW JT9D-20J	240404	C34Y247	AL-JM	1160
☐ N161US	Boeing (Douglas) DC-10-40	46770 / 175		1174	1174	3 PW JT9D-20J	240404	C34Y247	CH-AL	1161
☐ N162US	Boeing (Douglas) DC-10-40	46771 / 180		1274	1274	3 PW JT9D-20	240404	C32Y256	CH-AD	1162
☐ N238NW	Boeing (Douglas) DC-10-30 (ER)	48267 / 434	HS-TMA	0087	0498	3 GE CF6-50C2B	267200	C34Y247		1238
☐ N239NW	Boeing (Douglas) DC-10-30 (ER)	48290 / 435	HS-TMB	0087	0498	3 GE CF6-50C2B	267200	C34Y247		1239
☐ N240NW	Boeing (Douglas) DC-10-30 (ER)	48319 / 438	HS-TMC	0088	0498	3 GE CF6-50C2B	267200	C34Y247		1240
☐ N211NW	Boeing (Douglas) DC-10-30	46868 / 171	HB-IHP	1074	0191	3 GE CF6-50C	256280	C34Y247	FM-GL	1211 / City of Amsterdam / lsf INGL
☐ N220NW	Boeing (Douglas) DC-10-30	46577 / 114	HB-IHC	1173	0991	3 GE CF6-50C	256280	C34Y247	FM-HK	1220
☐ N221NW	Boeing (Douglas) DC-10-30	46579 / 132	HB-IHE	0274	0591	3 GE CF6-50C	256280	C34Y247	GL-EM	1221 / lsf PK AirFinance
☐ N223NW	Boeing (Douglas) DC-10-30	46580 / 183	HB-IHF	0174	1091	3 GE CF6-50C	256280	C34Y247	GL-FH	1223
☐ N224NW	Boeing (Douglas) DC-10-30	46581 / 184	HB-IHG	0275	0591	3 GE CF6-50C	256280	C34Y247	FK-GJ	1224
☐ N225NW	Boeing (Douglas) DC-10-30	46582 / 187	HB-IHH	0275	0292	3 GE CF6-50C	256280	C34Y247	GL-FK	1225
☐ N226NW	Boeing (Douglas) DC-10-30	46583 / 292	HB-IHL	0380	0292	3 GE CF6-50C2B	263084	C34Y247	GL-HK	1226
☐ N227NW	Boeing (Douglas) DC-10-30	46969 / 241	HB-IHI	1077	0692	3 GE CF6-50C	251744	C34Y247	GL-HM	1227
☐ N228NW	Boeing (Douglas) DC-10-30	46578 / 131	VR-BMP	1273	0795	3 GE CF6-50C	256280	C34Y247	DK-BE	1228
☐ N229NW	Boeing (Douglas) DC-10-30	46551 / 60	N4655Y	1272	0795	3 GE CF6-50C	251744	C34Y247	CF-BD	1229 / lsf CITG
☐ N230NW	Boeing (Douglas) DC-10-30	46552 / 71	N4655Z	0273	0795	3 GE CF6-50C	251744	C34Y247	DM-KL	1230 / lsf CITG
☐ N232NW	Boeing (Douglas) DC-10-30	46961 / 236	N961GF	0577	1195	3 GE CF6-50C2	251744	C34Y247	FL-KM	1232 / lsf Nationscredit Commerc.Corp.
☐ N233NW	Boeing (Douglas) DC-10-30	46640 / 240	N962GF	0077	0296	3 GE CF6-50C2	251744	C34Y247	GL-JK	1233 / lsf Nationscredit Comm. Corp.
☐ N234NW	Boeing (Douglas) DC-10-30	46912 / 188	HL7316	0074	0796	3 GE CF6-50C	251744	C34Y247	HK-JL	1234
☐ N235NW	Boeing (Douglas) DC-10-30	46915 / 199	HL7317	0075	0796	3 GE CF6-50C	251744	C34Y247	HL-AE	1235
☐ N236NW	Boeing (Douglas) DC-10-30	46934 / 160	HL7315	0074	0896	3 GE CF6-50C	251744	C34Y247	JL-DF	1236
☐ N237NW	Boeing (Douglas) DC-10-30	47844 / 336	PP-VMW	0080	1297	3 GE CF6-50C2	263084	C34Y247		1237 / l/side KL tail&r/side KL fus.cs
☐ N601US	Boeing 747-151	19778 / 27		0470	0470	4 PW JT9D-7A	332937	C34Y416	AL-CH	6601
☐ N608US	Boeing 747-151	19785 / 75		0970	0970	4 PW JT9D-7A	332937	C34Y416	AL-DK	6608
☐ N611US	Boeing 747-251B	20356 / 88		0371	0371	4 PW JT9D-7F	351534	F8C66Y296	AL-EH	6611
☐ N612US	Boeing 747-251B	20357 / 135		0571	0571	4 PW JT9D-7F	351534	F8C66Y296	AL-EJ	6612
☐ N613US	Boeing 747-251B	20358 / 141		0671	0671	4 PW JT9D-7F	351534	F8C66Y296	AL-EK	6613
☐ N614US	Boeing 747-251B	20359 / 163		1071	1071	4 PW JT9D-7F	351534	F8C66Y296	AL-EM	6614
☐ N615US	Boeing 747-251B	20360 / 165		1171	1171	4 PW JT9D-7Q	362874	F10C63Y296	AL-FH	6615
☐ N616US	Boeing 747-251F (SCD)	21120 / 258		0775	0775	4 PW JT9D-7F	362874	Freighter	AM-BD	6716
☐ N617US	Boeing 747-251F (SCD)	21121 / 261		0775	0775	4 PW JT9D-7F	362874	Freighter	AM-BE	6717
☐ N618US	Boeing 747-251F (SCD)	21122 / 269		0875	0875	4 PW JT9D-7F	362874	Freighter	AM-BJ	6718
☐ N619US	Boeing 747-251F (SCD)	21321 / 308		0677	0677	4 PW JT9D-7F	362874	Freighter	AM-BG	6719
☐ N622US	Boeing 747-251B	21704 / 357		0979	0979	4 PW JT9D-7Q	362874	F10C63Y296	CE-AK	6622
☐ N623US	Boeing 747-251B	21705 / 374		0579	0579	4 PW JT9D-7Q	362874	F10C63Y296	CE-AL	6623
☐ N624US	Boeing 747-251B	21706 / 377		0679	0679	4 PW JT9D-7Q	362874	F10C63Y296	CE-AM	6624
☐ N625US	Boeing 747-251B	21707 / 378		0679	0679	4 PW JT9D-7Q	362874	F10C63Y296	CE-BJ	6625
☐ N626US	Boeing 747-251B	21708 / 379		0679	0679	4 PW JT9D-7Q	362874	F10C63Y296	CF-AG	6626
☐ N627US	Boeing 747-251B	21709 / 412		0180	0180	4 PW JT9D-7Q	362874	F10C63Y296	CF-AJ	6627
☐ N628US	Boeing 747-251B	22389 / 442		0480	0480	4 PW JT9D-7Q	362874	F10C63Y296	CF-AM	6628
☐ N629US	Boeing 747-251F (SCD)	22388 / 444		0480	0480	4 PW JT9D-7F	362874	Freighter	AM-BK	6729
☐ N630US	Boeing 747-2J9F	21668 / 400	N1288E*	0983	0983	4 PW JT9D-7F	362874	Freighter	CF-BM	6730
☐ N631US	Boeing 747-251B	23111 / 594		0484	0484	4 PW JT9D-7R4G2	362874	F10C63Y296	CF-AL	6631
☐ N632US	Boeing 747-251B	23112 / 595		0584	0584	4 PW JT9D-7R4G2	362874	F10C63Y296	CF-AK	6632
☐ N633US	Boeing 747-227B	21991 / 437	N8284V*	0484	0484	4 PW JT9D-7Q	362874	F10C63Y296	CE-BG	6633
☐ N634US	Boeing 747-227B	22234 / 465	N8285V*	0584	0584	4 PW JT9D-7Q	362874	F10C63Y296	CH-BG	6634
☐ N635US	Boeing 747-227B	21682 / 375	N602PE	0579	1284	4 PW JT9D-7Q	362874	F10C63Y296	CH-AF	6635
☐ N636US	Boeing 747-251B	23547 / 642		0586	0586	4 PW JT9D-7R4G2	369224	F10C63Y296	CH-AM	6636
☐ N637US	Boeing 747-251B	23548 / 644		0586	0586	4 PW JT9D-7R4G2	369224	F10C63Y296	CH-BE	6637
☐ N638US	Boeing 747-251B	23549 / 651		0786	0786	4 PW JT9D-7R4G2	369224	F10C63Y296	CJ-BG	6638
☐ N639US	Boeing 747-251F (SCD)	23887 / 680		0687	0687	4 PW JT9D-7Q	377842	Freighter	CH-AK	6739
☐ N640US	Boeing 747-251F (SCD)	23888 / 682		0787	0787	4 PW JT9D-7Q	377842	Freighter	FM-GK	6740
☐ N641NW	Boeing 747-212B	21941 / 470	9V-SQP	0080	0796	4 PW JT9D-7Q	371946	F10C63Y296	CD-HM	6641
☐ N642NW	Boeing 747-212B	21942 / 471	9V-SQQ	0080	0796	4 PW JT9D-7Q	371946	F10C63Y296	CM-AD	6642
☐ N661US	Boeing 747-451	23719 / 696	N401PW*	1289	1289	4 PW PW4056	394625	F18C62Y338	EG-JP	6301
☐ N662US	Boeing 747-451	23720 / 708		0389	0389	4 PW PW4056	394625	F18C62Y338	EG-KP	6302
☐ N663US	Boeing 747-451	23818 / 715		0189	0189	4 PW PW4056	394625	F18C62Y338	EG-LP	6303
☐ N664US	Boeing 747-451	23819 / 721		0489	0489	4 PW PW4056	394625	F18C62Y338	EG-MP	6304 / The Spirit of Beijing
☐ N665US	Boeing 747-451	23820 / 726		0989	0989	4 PW PW4056	394625	F18C62Y338	EH-AP	6305
☐ N666US	Boeing 747-451	23821 / 742		0889	0889	4 PW PW4056	394625	F18C62Y338	EH-BP	6306
☐ N667US	Boeing 747-451	24222 / 799		0790	0790	4 PW PW4056	394625	F18C62Y338	EH-CP	6307
☐ N668US	Boeing 747-451	24223 / 800		0790	0790	4 PW PW4056	394625	F18C62Y338	EH-DP	6308
☐ N669US	Boeing 747-451	24224 / 803		0890	0890	4 PW PW4056	394625	F18C62Y338	EH-FP	6309
☐ N670US	Boeing 747-451	24225 / 804		0890	0890	4 PW PW4056	394625	F18C62Y338	EH-GP	6310
☐ N671US	Boeing 747-451	26477 / 1206		0099	0399	4 PW PW4056	394625	F18C62Y338		6311
☐ N672US	Boeing 747-451	30267 / 1223				4 PW PW4056	394625	F18C62Y338		6312 / oo-delivery 0799
☐ N673US	Boeing 747-451	30268 / 1226				4 PW PW4056	394625	F18C62Y338		6313 / oo-delivery 0899
☐ N674US	Boeing 747-451	30269				4 PW PW4056	394625	F18C62Y338		6314 / oo-delivery 1099
☐ N675US	Boeing 747-451					4 PW PW4056	394625	F18C62Y338		6315 / oo-delivery 0002
☐ N676US	Boeing 747-451					4 PW PW4056	394625	F18C62Y338		6316 / oo-delivery 0002

NORTHWESTERN AVIATION (James D. Rood dba / formerly Aircraft Services)

Kotzebue-Ralph Wien Memorial, AK

PO Box 741, Kotzebue, AK 99752, USA ☎ (907) 442-3525 Tx: none Fax: (907) 442-2145 SITA: n/a
F: 1978 ☃ 1 Head: James D. Rood Net: n/a Aircraft below MTOW 1361 kg: Piper PA-18

registration	type of aircraft	cn/fn	ex/ex*	mfd	del	powered by	mtow kg	configuration	selcal	name/fln/specialitites/remarks
☐ N60768	Cessna U206F Stationair	U20602045		0073	0395	1 CO IO-520-F	1633			
☐ N756AH	Cessna U206G Stationair	U20603932		0077	0885	1 CO IO-520-F	1633			Floats / Wheels

NORTHWEST HELICOPTERS, Inc.

Olympia, WA

7822 Old Highway 99 S.E., Olympia, WA 98501, USA ☎ (360) 754-7200 Tx: none Fax: (360) 754-1761 SITA: n/a
F: 1986 ☃ n/a Head: Brian A. Reynolds Net: n/a Aircraft below MTOW 1361kg: Hiller UH-12E

registration	type of aircraft	cn/fn	ex/ex*	mfd	del	powered by	mtow kg	configuration	selcal	name/fln/specialitites/remarks
☐ N408H	Bell 206B JetRanger III	4390	C-GFNR	0096	0796	1 AN 250-C20J	1451			
☐ N96NW	Bell 206B JetRanger III	4389	N144H	0096	0796	1 AN 250-C20J	1451			
☐ N1MX	Bell UH-1B (204)	515	N96NW	0062	0295	1 LY T53-L-11	3856			
☐ N61650	Bell UH-1H (205)	6308	157184	0065	1294	1 LY T53-L-13	4309			
☐ N61654	Bell UH-1H (205)	6314	157190	0065	1294	1 LY T53-L-13	4309			
☐ N6165X	Bell UH-1H (205)	6307	157183	0065	1294	1 LY T53-L-13	4309			
☐ N6166R	Bell UH-1H (205)	6323	157199	0065	1294	1 LY T53-L-13	4309			lsf Reynold Aviation Inc.
☐ N6166V	Bell UH-1H (205)	6318	157194	0065	1294	1 LY T53-L-13	4309			
☐ N78NW	Bell UH-1H (205)	9266	66-17072	0066	0397	1 LY T53-L-13	4309			
☐ N79NW	Bell UH-1H (205)	4417	64-13710	0064	0197	1 LY T53-L-13	4309			
☐ N83NW	Bell UH-1H (205)	4406	64-13699	0064	1195	1 LY T53-L-13	4309			
☐ N84NW	Bell UH-1H (205)	5386	66-903	0066	0695	1 LY T53-L-13	4309			
☐ N85NW	Bell UH-1H (205)	5275	66-792	0066	0595	1 LY T53-L-13	4309			lsf Reynolds Aviation Inc.
☐ N86NW	Bell UH-1H (205)	9143	66-16949	0066	0595	1 LY T53-L-13	4309			lsf Reynolds Aviation Inc.
☐ N95NW	Bell UH-1H (205)	5204	N15NH	0065	1294	1 LY T53-L-13	4309			lsf Reynolds Aviation Inc.
☐ N98NW	Bell UH-1H (205)	4529	N2290F	0064	0694	1 LY T53-L-13	4309			lsf Reynolds Aviation Inc.
☐ N7239L	Bell AH-1P (209) Cobra Lifter	24035	76-22601	0076	0897	1 LY T53-L-703	4763	ENG		
☐ N7239T	Bell AH-1P (209) Cobra Lifter	24079	77-22741	0077	0897	1 LY T53-L-703	4763	ENG		
☐ N7239Y	Bell AH-1P (209) Cobra Lifter	24096	77-22758	0077	0897	1 LY T53-L-703	4763	ENG		

NORTHWEST JET, Inc.
Chino, CA

7000 Merrill Avenue, Hangar 31, Chino, CA 91710, USA ☎ (909) 597-9999 Tx: none Fax: (909) 597-6569 SITA: n/a
F: 1987 ♦♦♦ n/a Head: Jack R. Urich Net: n/a

registration	type of aircraft	cn/fn	ex/ex*	mfd	del	powered by	mtow kg	configuration	selcal	name/fln/specialtites/remarks
☐ N3UX	Twin (Aero) Shrike Commander 500S	3146	N9141N	0073	1189	2 LY IO-540-E1B5	3062			lsf Aero General Llc
☐ N8U	Learjet 36A	36A-026	N6617B	0077	0892	2 GA TFE731-2-2B	8301			lsf Learstar Llc

NORTHWEST SEAPLANES, Inc.
Renton-SPB, WA

PO Box 1845, Renton, WA 98057, USA ☎ (425) 277-1590 Tx: none Fax: (425) 277-8831 SITA: n/a
F: 1988 ♦♦♦ n/a Head: Clyde E. Carlson Net: n/a

registration	type of aircraft	cn/fn	ex/ex*	mfd	del	powered by	mtow kg	configuration	selcal	name/fln/specialtites/remarks
☐ N67681	De Havilland DHC-2 Beaver I	1158	N215LU	0057	0893	1 PW R-985	2309			lst Air Rainbow as C-GCYN / Floats
☐ N67683	De Havilland DHC-2 Beaver I	6617	N21LU	0089	0393	1 PW R-985	2309			Floats / rebuilt 1989
☐ N67684	De Havilland DHC-2 Beaver I	1667	C-FQQF	0067	0492	1 PW R-985	2309			lst Air Rainbow as C-GCZA / Floats
☐ N67685	De Havilland DHC-2 Beaver I	1250	N128WA	0058	0289	1 PW R-985	2309			lst Air Rainbow as C-GCZC / Floats
☐ N67686	De Havilland DHC-2 Beaver I	1230	N1018T	0058	0589	1 PW R-985	2309			lsf pvt/sub-lst Andrew Airways / Floats
☐ N67687	De Havilland DHC-2 Beaver I	1359	N301GT	0058	0589	1 PW R-985	2309			lsf pvt / Floats
☐ N67689	De Havilland DHC-2 Beaver I	1242	N127WA	0058	1193	1 PW R-985	2309			lst Air Rainbow as C-GCYX / Floats
☐ N90YC	De Havilland DHC-2 Beaver I	1338	N67675	0059	0596	1 PW R-985	2309			lst Adirondack Air / Floats

NOVELL – Flight Dept. (Flight Dept. of Novell, Inc.)
San Jose-International, CA

2211 North First Street, San Jose, CA 95131, USA ☎ (408) 967-5000 Tx: none Fax: (408) 967-5001 SITA: n/a
F: 1996 ♦♦♦ n/a Head: Dana Butcher Net: http://www.novell.com Operates non-commercial corporate flights for itself only.

registration	type of aircraft	cn/fn	ex/ex*	mfd	del	powered by	mtow kg	configuration	selcal	name/fln/specialtites/remarks
☐ N801WB	Hawker 800XP	258287	N668H	0095	1096	2 GA TFE731-5BR-1H	12701	Corporate		
☐ N383DT	Canadair CL-604 (CL-600-2B16) Challen.	5383	C-GLYK*	0098	0798	2 GE CF34-3B	21909	Corporate		
☐ N43AE	Fokker F28 Fellowship 1000 (F28 Mk1000)	11016	C-FHFP	0069	0698	2 RR Spey 555-15	30164	Corporate		

NUSHAGAK AIR (Mickey D. Foster dba)
Dillingham, AK

PO Box 976, Dillingham, AK 99576, USA ☎ (907) 842-1656 Tx: none Fax: (907) 842-3259 SITA: n/a
F: 1995 ♦♦♦ n/a Head: Mickey D. Foster Net: n/a

registration	type of aircraft	cn/fn	ex/ex*	mfd	del	powered by	mtow kg	configuration	selcal	name/fln/specialtites/remarks
☐ N7320U	Cessna 207A Skywagon	20700397		0077	0897	1 CO IO-520-F	1724			

OASIS AIRLINES, Inc.
Boulder City-Municipal, NV

1201 Airport Road, Boulder City, NV 89006, USA ☎ (702) 524-2829 Tx: none Fax: (702) 293-7310 SITA: n/a
F: 1996 ♦♦♦ n/a Head: Jason Yu Net: n/a

registration	type of aircraft	cn/fn	ex/ex*	mfd	del	powered by	mtow kg	configuration	selcal	name/fln/specialtites/remarks
☐ N2614L	Cessna 402C II	402C0092		0079	0497	2 CO TSIO-520-VB	3107			
☐ N402CT	Cessna 402C II	402C0441		0081	0197	2 CO TSIO-520-VB	3107			
☐ N6838Y	Cessna 402C II	402C0477		0081	0497	2 CO TSIO-520-VB	3107			

OCCIDENTAL PETROLEUM – Flight Operations (Flight Operations of Occidental Petroleum Corporation)
Los Angeles-Int'l, CA   OXY OCCIDENTAL PETROLEUM

7000 World Way West, Los Angeles, CA 90045, USA ☎ (562) 649-0885 Tx: none Fax: (562) 641-8105 SITA: n/a
F: 1966 ♦♦♦ n/a Head: Ray Irani Net: n/a Operates non-commercial executive flights for its parent company only.

registration	type of aircraft	cn/fn	ex/ex*	mfd	del	powered by	mtow kg	configuration	selcal	name/fln/specialtites/remarks
☐ N682G	Boeing 727-76 (RE) (Super 27/winglets)	19254 / 298	N10XY	0066	0780	3 PW JT8D-217C/7B (BFG)	72802	Executive	EL-BF	cvtd -76

OCEAN WINGS AIR CHARTER (Coastal Wings, Inc. dba)
Nantucket-Memorial, MA

PO Box 2825, Nantucket, MA 02584, USA ☎ (508) 325-5548 Tx: none Fax: (508) 228-3962 SITA: n/a
F: 1990 ♦♦♦ n/a Head: Herbert C. Cabral, Jr. Net: n/a

registration	type of aircraft	cn/fn	ex/ex*	mfd	del	powered by	mtow kg	configuration	selcal	name/fln/specialtites/remarks
☐ N2900S	Piper PA-34-200T Seneca II	34-7970344		0079	1297	2 CO TSIO-360-EB	2073			lsf Island Aviation Inc. / tbr N670W
☐ N8394A	Piper PA-34-220T Seneca III	34-8133114		0081	0497	2 CO TSIO-360-KB	2155			lsf Emily Air Llc
☐ N119PA	Cessna 402B	402B0610		0074	0498	2 CO TSIO-520-E	2858			lsf pvt
☐ N660W	Cessna 402B	402B0828		0074	0594	2 CO TSIO-520-E	2858			lsf Connecting Wings

OHANA HELICOPTERS (Ohana Aviation, Inc. & Ohana Helicopter Tours dba)
Lihue, HI

PO Box 471, Lihue, HI 96766, USA ☎ (808) 245-3996 Tx: none Fax: (808) 245-5041 SITA: n/a
F: 1986 ♦♦♦ n/a Head: Bogart L. Kealoha Net: n/a

registration	type of aircraft	cn/fn	ex/ex*	mfd	del	powered by	mtow kg	configuration	selcal	name/fln/specialtites/remarks
☐ N392BK	Eurocopter (Aerosp.) AS350BA AStar	2539		0091	0292	1 TU Arriel 1B	2100			
☐ N493BK	Eurocopter (Aerosp.) AS350BA AStar	2734		0093	0694	1 TU Arriel 1B	2100			

OKLAHOMA EXECUTIVE JET CHARTER, Inc.
Oklahoma City-Will Rogers World, OK   OKLAHOMA EXECUTIVE JET CHARTER

Box 59150, Oklahoma City, OK 73159, USA ☎ (405) 681-4466 Tx: none Fax: (405) 681-1661 SITA: n/a
F: 1987 ♦♦♦ 6 Head: Happy H. Wells Net: n/a

registration	type of aircraft	cn/fn	ex/ex*	mfd	del	powered by	mtow kg	configuration	selcal	name/fln/specialtites/remarks
☐ N4847C	Cessna T210N Turbo Centurion II	21063644		0080	1287	1 CO TSIO-520-R	1814			lsf pvt
☐ N3141L	Cessna 310J	310J0141		0065	0995	2 CO IO-470-U	2313			lsf Embassy Freight Co.
☐ N5790M	Cessna 340	340-0044		0072	0795	2 CO TSIO-520-K	2710			lsf DC Frame
☐ N17TU	Piper PA-31T Cheyenne II	31T-7520035	N66LD	0075	1197	2 PWC PT6A-28	4082			lsf Private Jets I Llc
☐ N74RD	Learjet 25D	25D-260	N43783	0079	0097	2 GE CJ610-8A	6804			lsf Professional Flight Crew Services

OLSON AIR SERVICE, Inc. = 4B (Subsidiary of Donald Olson Enterprises, Inc. / Sister company of Polar Express Airways, Inc.)
Nome, AK

PO Box 142, Nome, AK 99762, USA ☎ (907) 443-2229 Tx: none Fax: (907) 443-5017 SITA: n/a
F: 1955 ♦♦♦ 16 Head: Donald C. Olson Net: n/a

registration	type of aircraft	cn/fn	ex/ex*	mfd	del	powered by	mtow kg	configuration	selcal	name/fln/specialtites/remarks
☐ N6299H	Cessna 207A Stationair 7 II	20700474		0078	0889	1 CO IO-520-F	1724			
☐ N747SQ	Cessna 207A Skywagon	20700387		0077	1281	1 CO IO-520-F	1724			lsf pvt
☐ N341FX	Cessna 402C II	402C0480	C-GJVS	0081	0193	2 CO TSIO-520-VB	3107			
☐ N7011X	Cessna 402C II	402C0255	OH-CIH	0080	1093	2 CO TSIO-520-VB	3107			lsf Olson & Sons Inc.

OLYMPIC AIR, Inc.
Shelton-Sanderson Field, WA

11771 Highway 101, Shelton, WA 98584, USA ☎ (360) 426-1477 Tx: none Fax: (360) 426-1993 SITA: n/a
F: 1978 ♦♦♦ n/a Head: Curtis S. Cousins Net: n/a Aircraft below MTOW 1361kg: Cessna 172 & Hughes 269C (300C)

registration	type of aircraft	cn/fn	ex/ex*	mfd	del	powered by	mtow kg	configuration	selcal	name/fln/specialtites/remarks
☐ N1089Y	MD Helicopters MD 500D (Hughes 369D)	510962D	N58400	0081	0585	1 AN 250-C20B	1361			
☐ N5063G	MD Helicopters MD 500D (Hughes 369D)	711021D		0081	0585	1 AN 250-C20B	1361			
☐ N75299	Piper PA-32R-300 Lance	32R-7680289		0076	0792	1 LY IO-540-K1A5D	1633			
☐ N564RA	AAC (Ted Smith) Aerostar 601P	61P-0365-115	N325MA	0077	0698	2 LY IO-540-S1A5	2722			

OMNI AIR EXPRESS (Chris Finkbeiner dba)
Little Rock-Adams Field, AR

2008 Beckenham Cove, Little Rock, AR 72212, USA ☎ (870) 374-5022 Tx: none Fax: (870) 374-8573 SITA: n/a
F: 1975 ♦♦♦ n/a Head: Chris Finkbeiner Net: n/a

registration	type of aircraft	cn/fn	ex/ex*	mfd	del	powered by	mtow kg	configuration	selcal	name/fln/specialtites/remarks
☐ N2012C	Beech Travel Air B95	TD-430		0060	1293	2 LY O-360-A1A	1860			
☐ N800CW	Beech Travel Air D95A	TD-602		0065	0794	2 LY IO-360-B1B	1905			
☐ N2852W	Beech Baron 58	TH-349		0073	0785	2 CO IO-520-C	2449			
☐ N6040R	Beech Baron 58	TH-1026		0079	0496	2 CO IO-520-CB	2449			
☐ N799DD	Beech King Air A100	B-102		0072	0190	2 PWC PT6A-28	5216			

OMNI AIR INTERNATIONAL, Inc. – OAI = X9 / OAE (Affiliated with GATX-Airlog, Co. / formerly Continental Air Transport, Co.)
Tulsa-Int'l, OK

PO Box 582527, Tulsa, OK 74158, USA ☎ (918) 836-5393 Tx: none Fax: (918) 836-1038 SITA: n/a
F: 1984 ♦♦♦ 150 Head: Sanford P. Burnstein ICAO: OMNI-EXPRESS Net: http://www.omniairintl.com

registration	type of aircraft	cn/fn	ex/ex*	mfd	del	powered by	mtow kg	configuration	selcal	name/fln/specialtites/remarks
☐ N360AX	Boeing (Douglas) DC-10-10	46706 / 38	N151AA	0572	0997	3 GE CF6-6K	195045	Y380		lsf Omni DC-10 Leasing Llc
☐ N450AX	Boeing (Douglas) DC-10-10	46942 / 162	N161AA	0675	0797	3 GE CF6-6K	195045	Y380	DL-BC	lsf Omni DC-10 Leasing Llc
☐ N540AX	Boeing (Douglas) DC-10-30	46595 / 299	D-ADPO	0079	1298	3 GE CF6-50C2	263100	Y370		lsf Omni Aircraft Leasing Corp.
☐ N630AX	Boeing (Douglas) DC-10-30	46596 / 301	D-ADQO	0079		3 GE CF6-50C2	263100	Y370		oo-delivery 0699 / ex CFG

OMNI AIR TRANSPORT, Corp. (Sister company of Omni Air International, Inc. – OAI)
Tulsa-Int'l, OK

PO Box 582527, Tulsa, OK 74158, USA ☎ (918) 836-5393 Tx: none Fax: (918) 836-1038 SITA: n/a
F: 1994 ♦♦♦ n/a Head: Sanford P. Burnstein Net: n/a

registration	type of aircraft	cn/fn	ex/ex*	mfd	del	powered by	mtow kg	configuration	selcal	name/fln/specialtites/remarks
☐ N453	Learjet 24D	24D-323	N104MC	0075	0694	2 GE CJ610-6	6123	6 Pax		

OMNIFLIGHT HELICOPTERS, Inc. (Subsidiary of Omniflight, Inc. / Affiliated with Omniflight Aircraft, Corp.)
Dallas-Addison, TX   OMNIFLIGHT

4650 Airport Parkway, Dallas, TX 75248-3206, USA ☎ (972) 776-0130 Tx: none Fax: (972) 776-0133 SITA: n/a
F: 1962 ♦♦♦ 300 Head: Joann Parker Net: n/a

registration	type of aircraft	cn/fn	ex/ex*	mfd	del	powered by	mtow kg	configuration	selcal	name/fln/specialtites/remarks
☐ N206AZ	Bell 206L-3 LongRanger III	51007	N725RE	0082	0492	1 AN 250-C30P	1882			
☐ N206MH	Bell 206L-1 LongRanger III	45426	N518EH	0080	0592	1 AN 250-C30P	1882	EMS		lst / opf Native American / cvtd LR II
☐ N2210H	Bell 206L-3 LongRanger III	51006		0082	0492	1 AN 250-C30P	1882	EMS		lst / opf Native American
☐ N224LF	Bell 206L-1 LongRanger III	45199	N5013Y	0079	0893	1 AN 250-C28B	1882	EMS		lst / opf Native American
☐ N39112	Bell 206L-1 LongRanger III	45652		0081	0592	1 AN 250-C30P	1882			cvtd LongRanger II
☐ N400SL	Bell 206L-1 LongRanger II	45235	N400CE	0079	0983	1 AN 250-C28B	1882			
☐ N519EH	Bell 206L-1 LongRanger III	45429		0080	0592	1 AN 250-C30P	1882			cvtd LongRanger II
☐ N721SP	Bell 206L-1 LongRanger III	45486	N77SU	0080	0788	1 AN 250-C30P	1882			cvtd LongRanger II
☐ N105MH	Eurocopter (MBB) BO105CBS	S-419	N400MF	0080	0185	2 AN 250-C20B	2500			
☐ N105NG	Eurocopter (MBB) BO105CBS	S-632	N2784L	0083	0684	2 AN 250-C20B	2500			
☐ N2907T	Eurocopter (MBB) BO105CBS	S-577	D-HDPZ*	0082	1287	2 AN 250-C20B	2500			
☐ N495LF	Eurocopter (MBB) BO105CBS	S-645	N27854*	0083	0185	2 AN 250-C20B	2500			
☐ N911LF	Eurocopter (MBB) BO105CBS	S-663	N4572R	0083	0185	2 AN 250-C20B	2500			
☐ N911SV	Eurocopter (MBB) BO105LS-A3	2033	N911MB	0089	0192	2 AN 250-C28C	2600			lsf Debis Financial Services Inc.
☐ N4066P	Eurocopter EC135P1	0070		0098	1198	2 PWC PW206B	2720			lsf General Electric Capital Corp.
☐ N1140H	Eurocopter (MBB) BK117A-3	7078	N212AE	0086	1086	2 LY LTS101-650B.1	3200			lsf Nations Credit Commercial Corp.

☐ N117CH	Eurocopter (MBB) BK117A-3	7061	N950MB*	0085	0186	2 LY LTS101-650B.1	3200			lsf General Electric Capital Corp.
☐ N117LF	Eurocopter (MBB) BK117A-4	7013	N3919A	0083	0184	2 LY LTS101-650B.1	3200			cvtd 117A-1
☐ N117LS	Eurocopter (MBB) BK117A-3	7113	N628MB	0086	0187	2 LY LTS101-650B.1	3200			lsf State Street Bank & Trust
☐ N117LU	Eurocopter (MBB) BK117B-1	7144	N9027Z	0087	0188	2 LY LTS101-750B.1	3200			lsf Banc One Equipment Fin./cvtd 117A-4
☐ N117M	Eurocopter (MBB) BK117A-3	7023	N39251	0083	1084	2 LY LTS101-650B.1	3200	EMS		cvtd 117A-1
☐ N117MH	Eurocopter (MBB) BK117A-3	7112	N627MB	0086	1286	2 LY LTS101-650B.1	3200	EMS LifeLine		lsf State Street Bank/opf Meth.Hospital
☐ N117NC	Eurocopter (MBB) BK117C-1	7509	N4042H	0092	0197	2 TU Arriel 1E2	3350			lsf Debis Financial Services Inc.
☐ N117NG	Eurocopter (MBB) BK117A-4	7083	N312LF	0086	1086	2 LY LTS101-650B.1	3200			lsf Heller Financial Leasing Inc.
☐ N117VU	Eurocopter (MBB) BK117B-1	7211	N8194S	0089	0190	2 LY LTS101-750B.1	3200			lsf Heller Financial Leasing Inc.
☐ N118LL	Eurocopter (MBB) BK117A-3	7097	N117SJ	0087	0187	2 LY LTS101-650B.1	3200			lsf Heller Financial Leasing Inc.
☐ N170MC	Eurocopter (MBB) BK117B-1	7217	N7161S	0090	1290	2 LY LTS101-750B.1	3200			lsf Debis Financial Services Inc.
☐ N214AE	Eurocopter (MBB) BK117B-1	7206	N8193Y	0089	0190	2 LY LTS101-750B.1	3200	EMS		lsf Heller Financial Leasing Inc.
☐ N217MC	Eurocopter (MBB) BK117B-1	7195	N54113	0089	1289	2 LY LTS101-750B.1	3200	EMS Mayo One		lsf / opf Mayo Foundation
☐ N313LF	Eurocopter (MBB) BK117A-4	7138	N290H	0087	0188	2 LY LTS101-650B.1	3200			lsf Banc One Equipment Finance Inc.
☐ N317MC	Eurocopter (MBB) BK117C-1	7505	N117AE	0092	0294	2 TU Arriel 1E2	3350	EMS Mayo One		lsf / opf Mayo Foundation
☐ N4493X	Eurocopter (MBB) BK117A-3	7038	D-HBMM*	0084	1285	2 LY LTS101-650B.1	3200			lsf General Electric Capital Corp.
☐ N460H	Eurocopter (MBB) BK117B-1	7142	N90266	0087	0188	2 LY LTS101-750B.1	3200	EMS		lsf Banc One Equipment Finance Inc.
☐ N527MB	Eurocopter (MBB) BK117A-3	7103	D-HBPX*	0086	0187	2 LY LTS101-650B.1	3200			lsf State Street Bank & Trust
☐ N711FC	Eurocopter (MBB) BK117A-4	7070	N311LF	0086	1086	2 LY LTS101-650B.1	3200	EMS		lsf Metlife Cap Corp. / cvtd 117A-3
☐ N8765J	Eurocopter (MBB) BK117A-4	7054		0184	0097	2 LY LTS101-650B.1	3200			lsf Petroleum Helicopters
☐ N911MZ	Eurocopter (MBB) BK117A-3	7098	N117UC	0086	0187	2 LY LTS101-650B.1	3200			lsf State Street Bank & Trust
☐ N219HM	Bell 222UT	47573	C-FTIU	0086	1194	2 LY LTS101-750C.1	3742			lsf Mitsui Canada
☐ N222HX	Bell 222UT	47533	N3201W	0085	0393	2 LY LTS101-750C.1	3742			lsf Mitsui Busan
☐ N911LW	Bell 222UT	47520		0085	0395	2 LY LTS101-750C.1	3742	EMS		lsf HCA Health Services of KS Inc.
☐ N911MK	Bell 222UT	47515	N4072G	0084	0392	2 LY LTS101-750C.1	3742			lsf Mitsui & Co. USA Inc.
☐ N4UV	Bell 230	23019	N230JP	0094	0294	2 AN 250C-30G2	3810			lsf Bell Helicopter Textron Inc.
☐ N417MC	Beech King Air B200	BB-1526	N3258P	0096	0297	2 PWC PT6A-42	5670	EMS Mayo MedAir		lsf / opf Mayo Foundation
☐ N75LV	Beech King Air B200	BB-1075	C-GTDY	0082	0493	2 PWC PT6A-42	5670	EMS		lsf Cook-Ft. Worth Childrens Med.Cent.

OPERATION BLESSING International Relief & Development — Norfolk-Int'l, VA

977 Centerville Turnpike, Virginia Beach, VA 23463, USA ☎ (757) 579-7000 Tx: none Fax: (757) 579-3411 SITA: n/a
F: 1978 ⁂ n/a Head: Pat Robertson Net: n/a Non-commercial organisation conducting humanitarian aid missions worldwide.

☐ N787M	Lockheed L-1011-385-1 TriStar 50	193L-1064	C-GIES	0074	1094	3 RR RB211-22B	204117	Flying Hospital		lst/opb International Jet Charter/cvtd1

ORBIS (Project Orbis, Inc. dba) — Macau

330 West 42nd Street, Suite 1900, New York, NY 10036, USA ☎ (212) 244-2525 Tx: 669109 orbs uw Fax: (212) 244-2744 SITA: n/a
F: 1973 ⁂ 29 Head: Albert Ueltschi Net: n/a Non-profit humanitarian organization conducting worldwide medical education programs. The DC-10 aircraft contains a fully-equipped ophthalmological teaching hospital.

☐ N220AU	Boeing (Douglas) DC-10-10	46501 / 2	G-GCAL	0071	1191	3 GE CF6-6D1A	206385	Flying Hospital		

ORBITAL SCIENCES Pegasus ALB – OSC (Orbital Sciences Corp. dba) — Bakersfield-Meadows Field, CA

21700 Atlantic Blvd, Dulles, VA 20166, USA ☎ (703) 406-5000 Tx: none Fax: (703) 406-3412 SITA: n/a
F: 1982 ⁂ 1300 Head: David W. Thompson Net: n/a Privately owned commercial company conducting rocket/satellite air launched booster (ALB) flights for the space industry.

☐ N140SC	Lockheed L-1011-385-1-15 TriStar 100	193E-1067	C-FTNJ	0074	0592	3 RR RB211-22B	215003	Pegasus ALB/R&D		cvtd TriStar 1

ORCA BAY AVIATION, Llc (Sister company of Sportco Investments II, Inc.) — Seattle-Boeing Field, WA

7777 Perimeter Road South, Suite 201, Seattle, WA 98108, USA ☎ (206) 764-9827 Tx: none Fax: (206) 764-9831 SITA: n/a
F: 1996 ⁂ n/a Head: Stanley B. McCammon Net: n/a Company operates VIP flights exclusively for the Vancouver Canucks-Land Hockey & Vancouver Grizzlies-Basketball sport-teams.

☐ N7270B	Boeing 727-232 (A)	20641 / 936	N18786	0073	1295	3 PW JT8D-15 (HK3/FDX)	83552	VIP		opf Vancouver Canucks & Grizzlies

ORION HELICOPTERS, Inc. — Fort Collins-Downtown, CO

PO Box 2211, Fort Collins, CO 80522, USA ☎ (970) 221-5552 Tx: none Fax: (970) 482-6139 SITA: n/a
F: 1982 ⁂ 4 Head: Paul S. Bennett Net: n/a

☐ N39101	Bell 206B JetRanger III	3289		0081	0284	1 AN 250-C20B	1451			lsf pvt

OTIS SPUNKMEYER AIR (Subsidiary of Otis Spunkmeyer Cookie Company / formerly Sentimental Journey Aviation) — Oakland-Int'l, CA

14490 Catalina Street, San Leandro, CA 94577, USA ☎ (800) 938-1900 Tx: none Fax: (510) 667-3841 SITA: n/a
F: 1987 ⁂ 20 Head: Geoff Macfee Net: n/a Operates sightsseing-charter flights.

☐ N41HQ	Boeing (Douglas) DC-3-253	2053	N54595	0038	0489	2 PW R-1830-75	12202	18 Pax		
☐ N97H	Boeing (Douglas) DC-3C (C-47B-40-DK)	33613	N63288	0045	0688	2 PW R-1830-75	12202	18 Pax		Skytrain

PACE – Pinnacle Air Cargo Enterprises, Inc. = (PACE) (Associated with Bristol Associates, Inc. — Washington, DC

1023 15th Street NW, Suite 1100, Washington, DC 20005, USA ☎ (202) 682-4000 Tx: none Fax: (202) 682-1809 SITA: n/a
F: 1997 ⁂ n/a Head: James Bryan Net: n/a Used aircraft leasing, sales and financing company.
Owner / lessor of following (main) aircraft types: Airbus Industrie A300B4 & A310 freighters. Aircraft leased from PACE are listed and mentioned as lsf PACE under the leasing carriers.

PACE AIRLINES (Div.of Piedmont Aviation Services, Inc.) — Atlanta-ATL/GA, Baltimore-BWI/MD & Charlotte-CLT/NC,

PO Box 525, Winston Salem, NC 27102-0525, USA ☎ (336) 776-6103 Tx: none Fax: (336) 776-6101 SITA: n/a
F: 1995 ⁂ n/a Head: Jim McPhail Net: http://www.flypiedmont.com

☐ N159PL	Boeing 737-242 (A)	21186 / 438	C-GNDL	0075	0598	2 PW JT8D-9A (HK3/NOR)	53070	Exec 46 Pax		lsf C.R. Acquisition Co.
☐ N487GS	Boeing 737-247	19600 / 44	N307VA	0768	0196	2 PW JT8D-9A	49442	Exec 44 Pax		lsf G.S.Sports / opf Charlotte Hornets
☐ N737AP	Boeing 737-222	19956 / 211	N9075U	0069	1297	2 PW JT8D-7B (HK3/NOR)	49442	Exec 44 Pax		lsf WS Aircr.Llc/opf Washington Wizards

PACIFIC AVIATION Holding Company = (PACA) (Sister company of Pegasus Capital Corp.) — San Francisco, CA

4 Embarcadero Center, 35th Fl., Suite 3550, San Francisco, CA 94111, USA ☎ (650) 434-3900 Tx: none Fax: (650) 434-3917 SITA: n/a
F: 1988 ⁂ n/a Head: Richard S. Wiley Net: n/a New and used aircraft leasing, sales and financing company.
Owner / lessor of following (main) aircraft types: Boeing 727-200, De Havilland DHC-7 & McDonnell Douglas DC-9-30. Aircraft leased from PACA are listed and mentioned as such under the leasing carriers.

PACIFIC FLIGHTS, Inc. (Subsidiary of Croman, Corp.) — Medford-Jackson County, OR

5000 Cirrus Drive, Medford, OR 97504-4182, USA ☎ (541) 779-5445 Tx: none Fax: (541) 772-2759 SITA: n/a
F: 1977 ⁂ n/a Head: Bud L. Kaufman Net: n/a

☐ N100ZG	Cessna 340 II	340-0528		0075	0596	2 CO TSIO-520-K	2710			lsf Croman Corp.
☐ N36885	Cessna 340A II	340A0681		0079	0883	2 CO TSIO-520-NB	2717			
☐ N290PF	Twin (Aero) Turbo Commander 690A	11290	N100JJ	0076	1097	2 GA TPE331-5-251K	4649			
☐ N143CK	Learjet 25B	25B-143	N113RF	0073	0188	2 GE CJ610-6	6804			

PACIFIC GAS & ELECTRIC – Flight Dept. (Flight Dept. of Pacific Gas & Electric Company) — Oakland-Int'l, CA

PO Box 2641 Airport Station, Oakland, CA 94614, USA ☎ (415) 973-8463 Tx: none Fax: none SITA: n/a
F: 1986 ⁂ n/a Head: Willim E. Craft Net: n/a Operates non-commercial corporate flights for its parent (Gas & Electric) company only.

☐ N328DC	Dornier 328-110	3019	D-CDHD*	0094	1194	2 PWC PW119B	13990	Corporate 27Pax		cvtd -100
☐ N71CJ	GAC (Grumman) G-159 Gulfstream I	107	N7ZB	0063	0186	2 RR Dart 529-8X	16329	Corporate 16Pax		

PACIFIC HELICOPTER SERVICES, Llc (Pacific Helicopter Tours, Inc. dba / formerly Pacific Helicopters, Inc. — Kahului-Heliport, HI

Hangar 109, Kahului Heliport, Kahului, HI 96732, USA ☎ (808) 871-9771 Tx: n/a Fax: (808) 871-5806 SITA: n/a
F: 1974 ⁂ n/a Head: Thomas L. Hauptman Net: n/a Aircraft below MTOW 1361kg: Hughes 369HS (500C)

☐ N1113L	MD Helicopters MD 500D (Hughes 369D)	1100837D	N1112Z	0080	0386	1 AN 250-C20B	1451			
☐ N503AH	Bell 206B JetRanger	686	C-FAOL	0071	1193	1 AN 250-C20	1451			cvtd 206A
☐ N38993	Bell 206L-1 LongRanger III	45601		0081	0598	1 AN 250-C30P	1882			cvtd LongRanger II
☐ N6651H	Bell 206L-1 LongRanger II	45211		0079	0196	1 AN 250-C28B	1882			
☐ N866JH	AAC (Ted Smith) Aerostar 601	61-0042-83	N7471S	0069	0691	2 LY IO-540-P1A5	2585			
☐ N1076C	Bell TH-1F (204)	6436	N64F	0067	1092	1 GE T58-GE-3	3856			
☐ N4963F	Bell TH-1L (204)	6404	BU157809	0069	0190	1 LY T53-L-11	3856			
☐ N64F	Bell 204B	2027	N103CR	0065	0196	1 LY T5311A	3856			
☐ N3280U	Bell UH-1H (205)	9098	66-16904	0066	1096	1 LY T53-L-13	4309			lsf pvt
☐ N261F	Sikorsky S-61N	61771	G-BEOO	0077	1098	2 GE CT58-140-1	9299	26 Pax		

PACIFIC ISLAND AVIATION, Inc. = 9J / PSA — Saipan

PPP 318, Box 10000, Saipan, Mariana Islands 96950, Commonwealth of Northern Mariana Islands ☎ (670) 234-3600 Tx: none Fax: (670) 234-3604 SITA: n/a
F: 1988 ⁂ 67 Head: Robert F. Christian IATA: 321 ICAO: PACIFIC ISLE Net: n/a Aircraft below MTOW 1361kg: Cessna 172

☐ N1256H	Piper PA-32-300 Cherokee SIX	32-7740033		0077	0494	1 LY IO-540-K1G5	1542	Y6		
☐ N4509T	Piper PA-32-300E Cherokee SIX	32-7240083		0072	1294	1 LY IO-540-K1A5	1542	Y6		lsf CCI Inc.
☐ N711HJ	Shorts 360-200 (SD3-60)	SH3697	G-BMUW*	0086	0995	2 PWC PT6A-65AR	11999	Y30		lsf FSBU Trustee
☐ N711MP	Shorts 360-200 (SD3-60)	SH3698	G-BMUX*	0086	0795	2 PWC PT6A-65AR	11999	Y30		lsf FSBU Trustee
☐ N711PK	Shorts 360-200 (SD3-60)	SH3696	G-BMUV*	0086	1294	2 PWC PT6A-65AR	11999	Y30		lsf FSBU Trustee
☐ N711PM	Shorts 360-200 (SD3-60)	SH3715	G-BNDL*	0087	0994	2 PWC PT6A-65AR	11999	Y30		lsf Morrison Stephen Trustee

PACIFIC JET CHARTER (Pacific Coast Building Products, Inc. dba) — Rancho Murieta, CA

14670 Cantova Way, Suite 200, Rancho Murieta, CA 95683, USA ☎ (530) 354-3222 Tx: none Fax: (530) 354-0144 SITA: n/a
F: 1988 ⁂ n/a Head: David J. Lucchetti Net: http://www.pacificjet.com

☐ N4761K	Cessna P210N Pressurized Centurion II	P21000292		0078	0893	1 CO TSIO-520-P	1814			lsf pvt
☐ N674PC	Cessna 340A II	340A0544	N4552N	0078	0190	2 CO TSIO-520-NB	2717			
☐ N675PC	Beech King Air 200	BB-680	N6750Y	0080	0780	2 PWC PT6A-41	5670			
☐ N676PC	Hawker 3A/731 (HS 125-3A/731)	25153	N336MB	0067	0794	2 GA TFE731-3R-1H	10568			cvtd 125-3A/RA

412 registration type of aircraft cn/fn ex/ex* mfd del powered by mtow kg configuration selcal name/fln/specialitites/remarks

PACIFIC MISSIONARY AVIATION – PMA (Member of ECFA-Evangelical Council for Financial Accountability) — Ponape, E.C.I. & Yap, W.C.I.

PO Box 3209, Agana, GU 96910, USA ☎ 646-6464 Tx: 6803 fm attn: pma Fax: 649-6066 SITA: n/a
F: 1975 ⁂ 20 Head: Rev. Edmund Kalau Net: http://www.pmafms.orgl

☐ N337LA	Cessna 337 Super Skymaster	337-0134	N2234X	0065	0995	2 CO IO-360-C/D	1905	5 Pax		
☐ N799MT	Britten-Norman BN-2A-21 Islander	449	C-GMND	0075	0391	2 LY IO-540-K1B5	2994	9 Pax		
☐ N44MA	Beech Excalibur Queenaire 8800	LD-412		0069	1187	2 LY IO-720-A1B	3992	9 Pax		cvtd Queen Air 65-B80
☐ N46MA	Beech Excalibur Queenaire 8800	LD-413	N37615	0069	0285	2 LY IO-720-A1B	3992	9 Pax		cvtd Queen Air 65-B80
☐ N5611D	Beech E18S	BA-316		0057	0978	2 PW R-985-AN14B	4218	9 Pax		

PACIFIC WING, Inc. — Petersburg-SPB, AK

PO Box 1560, Petersburg, AK 99833, USA ☎ (907) 772-9258 Tx: none Fax: (907) 772-9282 SITA: n/a
F: 1985 ⁂ 7 Head: Rodney H. Judy Net: n/a

☐ N4891Q	Cessna A185F Skywagon II	18503572		0078	0587	1 CO IO-520-D	1520	4 Pax		lsf pvt / Amphibian
☐ N9863Q	Cessna A185F Skywagon II	18503793		0079	0786	1 CO IO-520-D	1520	4 Pax		Amphibian
☐ N616W	De Havilland DHC-2 Beaver I	1290		0058	0691	1 PW R-985	2313	6 Pax		Floats

PACIFIC WINGS = LW / NMI (Air Nevada Airlines, Inc. dba) — Kahului, HI

PO Box 19, Paia, HI 96779, USA ☎ (808) 873-0877 Tx: none Fax: (808) 873-7920 SITA: OGGRRLW
F: 1998 ⁂ n/a Head: Myron L. Caplan IATA: 568 ICAO: TSUNAMI Net: http://www.pacificwings.com Aircraft below MTOW 1361kg: Cessna 172

☐ N811AN	Cessna 402C II	402C0078	N2612D	0079	0698	2 CO TSIO-520-VB	3107	Y9		lsf pvt
☐ N814AN	Cessna 402C II	402C0277	N2841A	0080	0698	2 CO TSIO-520-VB	3107	Y9		
☐ N815AN	Cessna 402C II	402C0098	N2615B	0079	0698	2 CO TSIO-520-VB	3107	Y9		lsf pvt
☐ N816AN	Cessna 402C II	402C0261	N88615	0080	0598	2 CO TSIO-520-VB	3107	Y9		
☐ N817AN	Cessna 402C II	402C0353	N2663F	0080	0298	2 CO TSIO-520-VB	3107	Y9		lsf pvt

PALM BEACH COUNTY TRAUMA HAWK (Division of Palm Beach County Health Care District) — West Palm Beach-Int'l, FL

324 Datura Street, Suite 401, West Palm Beach, FL 33401, USA ☎ (561) 659-1270 Tx: none Fax: (561) 659-1628 SITA: n/a
F: 1990 ⁂ n/a Head: Cecil W. Bennett Net: n/a

☐ N	Sikorsky S-76C+					2 TU Arriel 2S1	5307	EMS		oo-delivery 0899
☐ N	Sikorsky S-76C+					2 TU Arriel 2S1	5307	EMS		oo-delivery 1099
☐ N911PB	Bell 412SP	33186	N3214H	0089	0790	2 PWC PT6T-3B TwinPac	5398	EMS		

PANAGRA AIRWAYS, Inc. = 7E — Fort Lauderdale-Hollywood Int'l, FL

750 SW 34th Street, Suite 201A, Fort Lauderdale, FL 33315, USA ☎ (954) 359-9944 Tx: none Fax: (954) 359-3075 SITA: n/a
F: 1996 ⁂ n/a Head: James Peabody Net: http://www.panagra.com

☐ C-GKKF	Boeing 727-227 (A)	21043 / 1113	N16758	0075	1197	3 PW JT8D-9A (HK3/FDX)	79606	Y170	CG-EH	lsf KFA

PAN AIR, Inc. = PAX — Houston-George Bush Intercontinental, TX

PO Box 60872 AMF, Houston, TX 77205, USA ☎ (281) 443-4848 Tx: none Fax: (281) 443-0858 SITA: n/a
F: 1992 ⁂ 10 Head: Michael J. Orrson ICAO: PANNEX Net: http://www.panairinc.com

☐ N40358	Piper PA-23-250 Aztec E	27-7305117		0073	1195	2 LY TIO-540-C1A	2359	Freighter		Jupiter Rex / lsf Aeromaritime Inc.

PAN AM = PAA (Pan American Airways, Corp. dba / Subsidiary of Guilford Transportation Industries, Inc.) — Fort Lauderdale-Hollywood Int'l, FL

1401 SW 39th Street, Fort Lauderdale, FL 33315, USA ☎ (954) 359-3101 Tx: none Fax: (954) 923-3350 SITA: n/a
F: 1996 ⁂ 125 Head: Timothy Mellon ICAO: CLIPPER Net: http://www.panamairlines.com/
Cargo flights on behalf of Pan Am are operated by sister company BOSTON-MAINE AIRWAYS (with CASA 212 aircraft) in PanAm colors & both titles. For details – see under that company.

☐ N362PA	Boeing 727-2J0 (A)	21106 / 1160	6Y-JMN	0075	0199	3 PW JT8D-15	88360	F8Y140		lsf Guilford Transportation Industries
☐ N363PA	Boeing 727-221 (A)	22535 / 1764		0081	1198	3 PW JT8D-17R	88360	Y173	HJ-DG	lsf Guilford Transportation Industries
☐ N364PA	Boeing 727-2J0 (A)	21107 / 1172	6Y-JMO	0075	1298	3 PW JT8D-15	88360	Y173		lsf Guilford Transportation Industries
☐ N367PA	Boeing 727-221 (A)	22539 / 1794		0082	1298	3 PW JT8D-17R (HK3/FDX)	88360	Y173		Clipper Egil / lsf ARON
☐ N609KW	Boeing 727-282 (A)	21950 / 1579	CS-TBX	0180	0597	3 PW JT8D-17	86409	Y173	BE-DH	Cl.Pathfinder / lsf Guilford/tbr N369PA
☐ N8861E	Boeing 727-225 (A) (QWS)	20623 / 939		0473	1097	3 PW JT8D-15 (HK3/DUG)	86409	Y173	CM-AG	
☐ N8866E	Boeing 727-225 (A) (QWS)	20628 / 948		0573	0497	3 PW JT8D-15 (HK3/DUG)	86409	Y173		to be re-reg. N365PA

PANAMA AVIATION, Inc. — Panama City-Bay County Int'l, FL

1000 Jackson Way, Panama City, FL 32405, USA ☎ (352) 785-1234 Tx: none Fax: (352) 872-8684 SITA: n/a
F: 1972 ⁂ n/a Head: Jonathan B. McMinis IATA: 421 Net: n/a

☐ N43PA	Lake LA-250 Renegade	055	N8403H	0088	1194	1 LY IO-540-C4B5	1383			lsf Aero Consulting Corp. / Amphibian
☐ N39PA	Piper PA-44-180T Turbo Seminole	44-8107010	N8244L	0080	0886	2 LY TO-360-E1A6D	1780			lsf pvt
☐ N515RM	Piper PA-31-350 Navajo Chieftain	31-7405159		0074	0797	2 LY TIO-540-J2BD	3175			lsf Eastern Shipbuilding Group Inc.

PANHANDLE HELICOPTER, Inc. — Coeur d'Alene-Air Terminal, ID

West 1005 Prairie Avenue, Post Falls, ID 83854, USA ☎ (208) 772-1785 Tx: none Fax: none SITA: n/a
F: 1987 ⁂ n/a Head: Jon M. Hubof Net: n/a Aircraft below MTOW 1361kg: Hughes 369HS (500C)

☐ N622PB	MD Helicopters MD 500D (Hughes 369D)	880318D	N58214	0078	0790	1 AN 250-C20B	1361			
☐ N69PF	MD Helicopters MD 500D (Hughes 369D)	1060012D	N64EC	0076	0796	1 AN 250-C20B	1361			

PANORAMA FLIGHT SERVICE, Inc. – PFS = AFD — White Plains, NY

Hangar F, Westchester County Airport, White Plains, NY 10604, USA ☎ (914) 328-9800 Tx: none Fax: (914) 328-9684 SITA: n/a
F: 1958 ⁂ 60 Head: Eugene J. Condreras ICAO: AIRFED Net: n/a

☐ N414RS	Cessna 414A Chancellor III	414A0821		0081		2 CO TSIO-520-NB	3062			lsf Sky High Wings Inc.
☐ N50AF	Learjet 55	55-038	N551HB	0082	1092	2 GA TFE731-3A-2B	9752			lsf Polygon Air Corp.
☐ N555CJ	Learjet 55	55-089	N170VE	0083	0795	2 GA TFE731-3AR-2B	9752			lsf King Aircraft Ltd

PAPILLON GRAND CANYON HELICOPTERS = HI (Papillon Airways, Inc. dba / formerly Grand Canyon Helicopters) — Grand Canyon-National Park, AZ

PO Box 455, Grand Canyon, AZ 86023, USA ☎ (520) 638-9330 Tx: none Fax: (520) 638-9349 SITA: n/a
F: 1965 ⁂ 55 Head: Elling B. Halvorson IATA: 563 Net: http://www.papillon.com/

☐ N16869	Bell 206B JetRanger III	2264		0077	0794	1 AN 250-C20B	1451			14 / lsf Monarch Enterprises Inc.
☐ N21507	Bell 206B JetRanger III	3464		0081	0694	1 AN 250-C20B	1451			lsf Monarch Enterprises Inc.
☐ N83037	Bell 206B JetRanger III	1128		0073	0279	1 AN 250-C20B	1451			7 / lsf Monarch Enterpr./cvtd JetRanger
☐ N8533F	Bell 206B JetRanger III	254		0068	1079	1 AN 250-C20B	1451			lsf pvt / cvtd 206A
☐ N90065	Bell 206B JetRanger III	1572		0075	0578	1 AN 250-C20B	1451			lsf Monarch Enterprises/cvtd JetRanger
☐ N992UC	Bell 206B JetRanger III	421		0069	0992	1 AN 250-C20B	1451			16 / lsf Monarch Enterprises/cvtd 206A
☐ N1075S	Bell 206L-1 LongRanger III	45366		0080	0586	1 AN 250-C30P	1882			10 / lsf Monarch Enterprises/cvtd LR II
☐ N177PA	Bell 206L-1 LongRanger III	45194	N77PA	0078	0293	1 AN 250-C30P	1882			17 / lsf pvt / cvtd LongRanger II
☐ N178PA	Bell 206L-1 LongRanger III	45319	F-ODUB	0079	0794	1 AN 250-C30P	1882			18 / lsf Monarch Enterprises/cvtd LR II
☐ N2072M	Bell 206L-1 LongRanger II	45720		0082	0283	1 AN 250-C28B	1882			lsf Monarch Enterprises Inc.
☐ N27694	Bell 206L-1 LongRanger II	45282		0779	0294	1 AN 250-C28B	1882			4 / lsf Monarch Enterprises Inc.
☐ N333ER	Bell 206L-1 LongRanger III	45203		0079	0988	1 AN 250-C30P	1882			12 / lsf Monarch Enterprises/cvtd LR II
☐ N3893U	Bell 206L-3 LongRanger III	51020		0082	0882	1 AN 250-C30P	1882			9 / lsf Monarch Enterprises Inc.
☐ N3895D	Bell 206L-1 LongRanger III	45590		0080	0683	1 AN 250-C30P	1882			1 / lsf Monarch Enterprises/cvtd LR II
☐ N4227E	Bell 206L-1 LongRanger III	45702	N725RE	0081	0294	1 AN 250-C30P	1882			lsf Monarch Enterprises / cvtd LR II
☐ N5745Y	Bell 206L-1 LongRanger III	45531		0080	1086	1 AN 250-C30P	1882			11 / lsf Monarch Enterprises/cvtd LR II
☐ N57491	Bell 206L-1 LongRanger III	45505		0080	0492	1 AN 250-C30P	1882			15 / lsf Monarch Enterprises/cvtd LR II
☐ N7VG	Bell 206L-1 LongRanger III	45463		0080	0586	1 AN 250-C30P	1882			5 / lsf Monarch Enterprises/cvtd LR II
☐ N811CM	MD Helicopters MD 900 Explorer	900-00021	N9021T	0096	1297	2 PWC PW206A	2722			opf NPS-National Park Service
☐ N17758	Sikorsky (Vertical Avn Techn.) S-55QT	V55396T		0058	0596	1 GA TSE331-10	3270			19 / lsf Monarch Enterprises/cvtd S-55

PARAGON AIR, Inc. — Kahului, HI

PO Box 575, Kahului, HI 96732, USA ☎ (808) 244-3356 Tx: none Fax: (808) 871-8300 SITA: n/a
F: 1980 ⁂ n/a Head: Eric Barto Net: n/a

☐ N4234L	Partenavia P.68C	225		0080	0185	2 LY IO-360-A1B6	1990			
☐ N27659	Piper PA-31-350 Navajo Chieftain	31-7852090		0078	0593	2 LY TIO-540-J2BD	3175			

PARAGON AIR EXPRESS, Inc. = PGX — Nashville, TN

PO Box 270185, Nashville, TN 37227, USA ☎ (931) 361-3044 Tx: none Fax: (931) 361-3076 SITA: n/a
F: 1993 ⁂ n/a Head: Jimmy L. Rhodes ICAO: PARAGON EXPRESS Net: n/a

☐ N103GA	Beech Baron 58	TH-213		0072	0894	2 CO IO-520-C	2449			
☐ N159TH	Beech Baron 58	TH-159		0071	1094	2 CO IO-520-C	2449			
☐ N31CE	Beech Baron 58	TH-220		0072	0996	2 CO IO-520-C	2449			
☐ N38CL	Beech Baron 58	TH-829		0077	0794	2 CO IO-520-C	2449			
☐ N4174S	Beech Baron 58	TH-621		0075	0894	2 CO IO-520-C	2449			
☐ N80UL	Beech Baron 58	TH-1118		0080	0694	2 CO IO-520-C	2449			
☐ N93DF	Beech Baron 58	TH-61		0070	1293	2 CO IO-520-C	2449			
☐ N102GP	Beech C99 Airliner	U-208	N6628K	0083	1295	2 PWC PT6A-36	5126			

PARALIFT, Inc. — Lake Elsinore-Skylark, CA

PO Box 332, Perris, CA 92572, USA ☎ (909) 657-7216 Tx: none Fax: (909) 657-9435 SITA: n/a
F: 1981 ⁂ n/a Head: Dick G.S. Evans Net: n/a

☐ N7129	Beech 3NM (18)	CA-217	RCAF2338	0052	0787	2 PW R-985	3969	Para		
☐ N20TW	Boeing (Douglas) DC-3-201C	2236	N25648	0040	0288	2 WR R-1820	12202	Para		

413 registration type of aircraft cn/fn ex/ex* mfd del powered by mtow kg configuration selcal name/fln/specialitites/remarks

registration	type of aircraft	cn/fn	ex/ex*	mfd	del	powered by	mtow kg	configuration	selcal	name/fln/specialitites/remarks
☐ N26MA	Boeing (Douglas) DC-3-313	2169	N180WK	0039	0587	2 WR R-1820	12202	Para		

PARK – Flight Department (Flight Department of Park Corporation)
Cleveland-Hopkins Int'l, OH

6200 Riverside Drive, Cleveland, OH 44135, USA ☎ (216) 362-1500 Tx: none Fax: (216) 362-1908 SITA: n/a
F: 1994 ♦♦♦ n/a Head: Raymond P. Park Net: n/a Operates non-commercial VIP flights exclusively the Park Corporation, a holding company with diverse interests, and its partners.

registration	type of aircraft	cn/fn	ex/ex*	mfd	del	powered by	mtow kg	configuration	selcal	name/fln/specialitites/remarks
☐ N317PC	MD Helicopters MD 520N (Hughes 500N)	LN014	N16113	0092	1294	1 AN 250-C20R	1520	VIP		
☐ N261PC	Learjet 60	60-146	N50776*	0098	0199	2 PWC PW305A	10659	VIP		
☐ N263PC	BAe (BAC) One-Eleven 401AK	068	N111LP	0066	1195	2 RR Spey 511-14	40597	VIP F21		for sale

PATCO = ETL (Patterson Aviation Company dba)
Sacramento-Executive, CA

6133 Freeport Blvd, Sacramento, CA 95822, USA ☎ (916) 428-8292 Tx: none Fax: (916) 428-3032 SITA: n/a
F: 1946 ♦♦♦ n/a Head: John J. Gudebski ICAO: ENTEL Net: n/a

registration	type of aircraft	cn/fn	ex/ex*	mfd	del	powered by	mtow kg	configuration	selcal	name/fln/specialitites/remarks
☐ N421YP	Cessna 421B Golden Eagle	421B0511		0073	0892	2 CO GTSIO-520-H	3379			lsf pvt

PATHFINDER HELICOPTER, Inc.
Spokane-Heliport, WA

North 11310 Judkins Road, Spokane, WA 99207, USA ☎ (509) 927-2224 Tx: none Fax: (509) 926-0244 SITA: n/a
F: 1983 ♦♦♦ n/a Head: Steven R. Tolle Net: n/a

registration	type of aircraft	cn/fn	ex/ex*	mfd	del	powered by	mtow kg	configuration	selcal	name/fln/specialitites/remarks
☐ N570CA	MD Helicopters MD 500E (Hughes 369E)	0182E	N5258C	0086	1095	1 AN 250-C20B	1361			

PATUXENT AIRWAYS (Airpark Sales & Service, Inc. dba)
Leonardtown-St. Marys County, MD

PO Box 40, Hollywood, MD 20636, USA ☎ (240) 373-2101 Tx: none Fax: (240) 373-2154 SITA: n/a
F: 1987 ♦♦♦ n/a Head: Steven J. Bildman Net: n/a Aircraft below MTOW 1361kg: Piper PA-28

registration	type of aircraft	cn/fn	ex/ex*	mfd	del	powered by	mtow kg	configuration	selcal	name/fln/specialitites/remarks
☐ N202HF	Piper PA-31-350 Navajo Chieftain	31-7405437		0074	0595	2 LY TIO-540-J2BD	3175			lsf N202HF Inc.

PAXSON COMMUNICATIONS – Flight Dept. (Flight Dept. of Paxson Communications Management Corporation)
West Palm Beach-Int'l, FL

601 Clearwater Park Road, West Palm Beach, FL 33401, USA ☎ (561) 659-4122 Tx: none Fax: (561) 659-4252 SITA: n/a
F: 1995 ♦♦♦ n/a Head: Bud Paxson Net: n/a Operates non-commercial corporate flights for its parent company (in the Communications, incl. Internet & Television-business) only.

registration	type of aircraft	cn/fn	ex/ex*	mfd	del	powered by	mtow kg	configuration	selcal	name/fln/specialitites/remarks
☐ N176PC	Sikorsky S-76A+	760092	N117WB	0080	0696	2 TU Arriel 1S	4899	Corporate		cvtd S-76A
☐ N729PX	Cessna 501 Citation I/SP	501-0284	N284PC	0083	0996	2 PWC JT15D-1A	5375	Corporate		
☐ N728PX	Lockheed L-1329 JetStar 731	5112 / 7	N499PC	0068	0195	4 GA TFE731-3-1E	20071	Corporate		cvtd JetStar 8
☐ N727PX	Boeing 727-21	19261 / 422	N260GS	0067	0897	3 PW JT8D-7	72802	Corporate		PAX NET-titles

PEARL PACIFIC ENTERPRISES
Honolulu-Int'l, HI

98-1022 Kaamilo Street, Aiea, HI 96701, USA ☎ (808) 486-6657 Tx: none Fax: none SITA: n/a
F: 1993 ♦♦♦ n/a Head: Robert Justman Net: n/a

registration	type of aircraft	cn/fn	ex/ex*	mfd	del	powered by	mtow kg	configuration	selcal	name/fln/specialitites/remarks
☐ N40370	Piper PA-23-250 Aztec E	27-7305133		0073	0793	2 LY IO-540-C4B5	2359			

PEGASUS CAPITAL, Corp. = (PEGA) (Sister company of Pacific Aviation Holding Company)
San Francisco, CA

4 Embarcadero Center, 35th Fl., Suite 3550, San Francisco, CA 94111, USA ☎ (650) 434-3900 Tx: none Fax: (650) 434-3917 SITA: n/a
F: 1988 ♦♦♦ 15 Head: R.S. Wiley Net: n/a New and used aircraft leasing, sales and financing company.
Owner / lessor of following (main) aircraft types: Boeing 727-200 / 747-200 & McDonnell Douglas DC-10-30. Aircraft leased from PEGA are listed and mentioned as such under the leasing carriers.

PEGASUS EXECUTIVE LINE CHARTERS (Haps Aerial Enterprises, Inc. dba)
Jeffersonville-Clark County, IN

7001 Airport Drive, Sellersburg, IN 47172, USA ☎ (812) 246-5491 Tx: none Fax: (812) 246-3819 SITA: n/a
F: 1953 ♦♦♦ n/a Head: William E. Happel, Sr. Net: n/a

registration	type of aircraft	cn/fn	ex/ex*	mfd	del	powered by	mtow kg	configuration	selcal	name/fln/specialitites/remarks
☐ N6334S	Beech Baron 58	TH-702		0076	0496	2 CO IO-520-C	2449			
☐ N8590R	Beech Baron 58	TH-645		0075	1296	2 CO IO-520-C	2449			
☐ N2427W	Piper PA-31T1A Cheyenne IA	31T-1104005		0084	0993	2 PWC PT6A-11	3946			
☐ N60DR	Piper PA-31T Cheyenne II	31T-7720064	N45LS	0077	0690	2 PWC PT6A-28	4082			
☐ N52WA	Piper PA-42 Cheyenne III	42-8001028		0081	0694	2 PWC PT6A-41	5080			

PENAIR = KS / PEN (Peninsula Airways, Inc. dba)
Anchorage-Int'l, AK

6100 Boeing Ave., Anchorage, AK 99502, USA ☎ (907) 243-2485 Tx: none Fax: (907) 243-6848 SITA: n/a
F: 1956 ♦♦♦ 350 Head: Orin D. Seybert IATA: 339 ICAO: PENINSULA Net: http://www.penair.com
Some scheduled services are operated as an Alaska Airlines Commuter (in own titles/titles), a commuter system to provide feeder connection at AS major hubs, using AS flight numbers.
Beside Anchorage head office-base, also operates from 6 sub-bases: Bethel, Cold Bay, Dillingham, Dutch Harbor, Kodiak & King Salmon, AK.

registration	type of aircraft	cn/fn	ex/ex*	mfd	del	powered by	mtow kg	configuration	selcal	name/fln/specialitites/remarks
☐ N4327P	Piper PA-32-301 Saratoga	32-8406002		0083	0789	1 LY IO-540-K1G5	1633	Y5		
☐ N8004N	Piper PA-32-301 Saratoga	32-8206014		0082	0497	1 LY IO-540-K1G5	1633	Y5		
☐ N81052	Piper PA-32-301 Saratoga	32-8206023		0082	0097	1 LY IO-540-K1G5	1633	Y5		
☐ N81844	Piper PA-32-301 Saratoga	32-8006012		0080	1090	1 LY IO-540-K1G5	1633	Y5		
☐ N8212H	Piper PA-32-301 Saratoga	32-8006046		0080	0794	1 LY IO-540-K1G5	1633	Y5		
☐ N82455	Piper PA-32-301 Saratoga	32-8006079		0080	0197	1 LY IO-540-K1G5	1633	Y5		
☐ N8259V	Piper PA-32-301 Saratoga	32-8006097		0080	0681	1 LY IO-540-K1G5	1633	Y5		
☐ N8305H	Piper PA-32-301 Saratoga	32-8106017		0081	0794	1 LY IO-540-K1G5	1633	Y5		
☐ N8327S	Piper PA-32-301 Saratoga	32-8106039		0081	1192	1 LY IO-540-K1G5	1633	Y5		
☐ N8361Q	Piper PA-32-301 Saratoga	32-8106055		0081	0881	1 LY IO-540-K1G5	1633	Y5		
☐ N8402S	Piper PA-32-301 Saratoga	32-8106075		0081	0782	1 LY IO-540-K1G5	1633	Y5		
☐ N8429N	Piper PA-32-301 Saratoga	32-8106089		0081	0197	1 LY IO-540-K1G5	1633	Y5		
☐ N8470Y	Piper PA-32-301 Saratoga	32-8206012		0081	0398	1 LY IO-540-K1G5	1633	Y5		
☐ N141R	Grumman G-44 Widgeon	1378	N199VC	0045	1174	2 LY GO-480-B1D	2495	Y5		Amphibian
☐ N17481	Grumman G-44 Widgeon	1360		0045	0481	2 LY GO-480-B1D	2495	Y5		Steve Harvey / lsf pvt / Amphibian
☐ N15PR	Piper PA-31-350 Navajo Chieftain	31-8352011		0083	0696	2 LY TIO-540-J2BD	3175	Y9		
☐ N27663	Piper PA-31-350 Navajo Chieftain	31-7852094		0078	0986	2 LY TIO-540-J2BD	3175	Y9		
☐ N27801	Piper PA-31-350 Navajo Chieftain	31-7852157		0078	0589	2 LY TIO-540-J2BD	3175	Y9		
☐ N27987	Piper PA-31-310 Navajo C	31-7912054		0079	0685	2 LY TIO-540-A2C	2948	Y7		
☐ N28KE	Piper PA-31-350 Navajo Chieftain	31-8152049		0081	0391	2 LY TIO-540-J2BD	3175	Y9		
☐ N3588Z	Piper PA-31-350 Navajo Chieftain	31-8052130		0080	0491	2 LY TIO-540-J2BD	3175	Y9		
☐ N9304F	Cessna 208 Caravan I	20800008		0085	0489	1 PWC PT6A-114	3311	Y9		lsf Avion Capital Corp.
☐ N9481F	Cessna 208 Caravan I	20800070		0086	0593	1 PWC PT6A-114	3629	Y9		lsf Avion Capital Corp.
☐ N9530F	Cessna 208 Caravan I	20800088		0086	0096	1 PWC PT6A-114	3629	Y9		lsf Avion Capital Corp.
☐ N9536F	Cessna 208 Caravan I	20800090		0086	0098	1 PWC PT6A-114	3629	Y9		lsf Avion Capital Corp.
☐ N9602F	Cessna 208 Caravan I	20800103		0086	0593	1 PWC PT6A-114	3629	Y9		lsf Avion Capital Corp.
☐ N22932	Grumman G-21A Goose	B-139		0045	0986	2 PW R-985	4082	Y6		Amphibian
☐ N641	Grumman G-21A Goose	B-115	87721	0051	0482	2 PW R-985	4082	Y6		Amphibian
☐ N741	Grumman G-21A Goose	B-97		0044	1296	2 PW R-985	4082	Y6		Amphibian
☐ N7811	Grumman G-21A Goose	B-122		0045	1296	2 PW R-985	4082	Y6		Amphibian
☐ N750PA	Cessna 208B Grand Caravan	208B0628		0097	0498	1 PWC PT6A-114A	3969	Y9		
☐ N700RD	Piper PA-31T3-T1040	31T-5575001	HP-1101P	0085	1096	2 PWC PT6A-11	4082	Y9		
☐ N441LL	Cessna 441 Conquest II	441-0139	N10CC	0080	0697	2 GA TPE331-8-401S	4468	Y10		
☐ N544AL	Cessna 441 Conquest II	441-0120	N441DM	0079	0585	2 GA TPE331-8-401S	4468	Y10		
☐ N2708D	Fairchild (Swearingen) SA227AC Metro III	AC-709B		0088	0295	2 GA TPE331-11U-612G	7257	Y19		lsf General Electric Capital Corp.
☐ N2719H	Fairchild (Swearingen) SA227AC Metro III	AC-713B		0088	1295	2 GA TPE331-11U-612G	7257	Y19		lsf Chrysler Asset Management Corp.
☐ N41NE	Fairchild (Swearingen) SA227AC Metro III	AC-741B	N301NE	0089	0396	2 GA TPE331-11U-612G	7257	Y19		lsf Chrysler Asset Managment Corp.
☐ N640PA	Fairchild (Swearingen) SA227AC Metro III	AC-759B	N306NE	0090	0990	2 GA TPE331-11U-612G	7257	Y19		lsf IMH Aircraft Leasing Corp.
☐ N650PA	Fairchild (Swearingen) SA227AC Metro III	AC-775B		0091	0591	2 GA TPE331-11U-612G	7257	Y19		
☐ N675PA	Saab 340B	340B-206	N593MA	0090	0297	2 GE CT7-9B	13155	Y30		Spirit of Bristol Bay / lsfFairbrookLsg
☐ N685PA	Saab 340B	340B-212	N594MA	0090	0397	2 GE CT7-9B	13155	Y30		Spirit of the Alaskas / lsfFairbrookLsg

PENN AIR, Inc.
Altoona-Blair County, PA

Altoona Blair County Airport, Martinsburg, PA 16662, USA ☎ (814) 793-2164 Tx: none Fax: (814) 793-2445 SITA: n/a
F: 1963 ♦♦♦ n/a Head: Leland R. McQuaide Net: n/a

registration	type of aircraft	cn/fn	ex/ex*	mfd	del	powered by	mtow kg	configuration	selcal	name/fln/specialitites/remarks
☐ N107MC	Piper PA-31T2 Cheyenne II XL	31T-8166032	N48CP	0081	0586	2 PWC PT6A-135	4297			lsf WC McQuaide Inc.

PENSACOLA AVIATION (Pensacola Aviation Center, Inc. dba)
Pensacola-Regional, FL

PO Box 2781, Pensacola, FL 32513, USA ☎ (352) 434-0636 Tx: none Fax: (352) 434-3984 SITA: n/a
F: 1977 ♦♦♦ n/a Head: J. Richard Bennett Net: http://www.home.onestop.net/paci Aircraft below MTOW 1361kg: Mooney M20J

registration	type of aircraft	cn/fn	ex/ex*	mfd	del	powered by	mtow kg	configuration	selcal	name/fln/specialitites/remarks
☐ N4299C	Piper PA-34-220T Seneca III	34-8333086		0083	0483	2 CO TSIO-360-KB	2155			
☐ N27467	Piper PA-31-350 Navajo Chieftain	31-7852016		0078	0989	2 LY TIO-540-J2BD	3175			

PEN TURBO AVIATION (Pen Turbo, Inc. dba)
Wildwood-Cape May County, NJ

1340 East Road, Rio Grande, NJ 08242, USA ☎ (609) 886-7631 Tx: none Fax: (609) 886-7411 SITA: n/a
F: 1994 ♦♦♦ n/a Head: Rubin Gobalian Net: n/a Maintenance/overhaul-company conducting, beside testing & delivery flights, some on-demand-charter operations on a limited basis.

PERE AIR (Guy A. Pere dba)
Healy, AK

PO Box 496, Healy, AK 99743, USA ☎ (907) 683-6033 Tx: none Fax: (907) 683-2247 SITA: n/a
F: 1991 ♦♦♦ n/a Head: Guy A. Pere Net: n/a

registration	type of aircraft	cn/fn	ex/ex*	mfd	del	powered by	mtow kg	configuration	selcal	name/fln/specialitites/remarks
☐ N8796Q	Cessna U206G Stationair	U20603548		0076	0693	1 CO IO-520-F	1633			lsf pvt

PERRIS VALLEY AVIATION SERVICE (PM Leasing, Inc. dba)

2091 Goetz Road, Perris, CA 92570, USA ☎ (909) 657-3904 Tx: none Fax: (909) 657-6178 SITA: n/a
F: 1983 ♦♦♦ n/a Head: Jerry Brown Net: n/a Operates Para-flights exclusively for the Perris-Valley Skydiving club.

registration	type of aircraft	cn/fn	ex/ex*	mfd	del	powered by	mtow kg	configuration	name/fln/specialitites/remarks
☐ N125SA	De Havilland DHC-6 Twin Otter 100	104		0068	0390	2 PWC PT6A-20	5252	Para	The Shark / Shark colors
☐ N64150	De Havilland DHC-6 Twin Otter 200	150		0068	1194	2 PWC PT6A-20	5252	Para	Gypsy Rose / Skydive the Golden West cs
☐ N708PV	De Havilland DHC-6 Twin Otter 300	489	C-GDMP	0076	0296	2 PWC PT6A-27	5670	Para	The Ultimate Otter / Island Air colors
☐ N4NE	Shorts Skyvan 3 Variant 100 (SC-7)	SH1885	N4280Y	0070	0794	2 GA TPE331-2-201A	5670	Para	

PETERSEN AVIATION

7155 Valjean Ave, Van Nuys, CA 91406, USA ☎ (818) 989-2300 Tx: none Fax: (818) 902-9386 SITA: n/a
F: 1982 ♦♦♦ n/a Head: Robert E. Petersen Net: http://www.petersenaviation.com

registration	type of aircraft	cn/fn	ex/ex*	mfd	del	powered by	mtow kg	name/fln/specialitites/remarks
☐ N8DX	Cessna 500 Citation Eagle	500-0303	C-GDWS	0076	0693	2 PWC JT15D-1A	5670	lsf Abiquin Development / cvtd Citation
☐ N50KH	Beech Beechjet 400A	RK-59	N80544	0093	1195	2 PWC JT15D-5	7303	lsf Kayhall Corp.
☐ N92RP	Hawker 700A (HS 125-700A)	257022	N34RE	0078	0992	2 GA TFE731-3R-1H	11567	
☐ N4QB	Hawker F400A (HS 125-F400A)	25255	N102AB	0071	1194	2 GA TFE731-3R-1H	10569	lsf Wilmington Trust Co. / cvtd -CC1
☐ N303GA	GAC G-1159A Gulfstream III	303	N1761W	0080	0196	2 RR Spey 511-8	30935	lsf Airborne Charter Inc.
☐ N98RP	GAC G-1159A Gulfstream III	328	N78RP	0081	0594	2 RR Spey 511-8	30935	
☐ N277RP	GAC G-IV Gulfstream IV	1026	N151A	0087	0697	2 RR Tay 610-8	33203	
☐ N7RP	GAC G-IV Gulfstream IV	1064	HB-ITT	0088	0996	2 RR Tay 611-8	33203	

PETROLEUM HELICOPTERS, Inc. – PHI = PHM

PO Box 90808, Lafayette, LA 70509, USA ☎ (318) 235-2452 Tx: 460302 phi ui Fax: (318) 235-1351 SITA: n/a
F: 1949 ♦♦♦ 1700 Head: Carroll W. Suggs ICAO: PETROLEUM Net: http://www.phihelico.com

registration	type of aircraft	cn/fn	ex/ex*	mfd	del	powered by	mtow kg	name/fln/specialitites/remarks
☐ N103PH	Bell 206B JetRanger III	3000	F-GHRS	0480	0795	1 AN 250-C20B	1451	
☐ N104PH	Bell 206B JetRanger III	3622	YV-898C	0482	0882	1 AN 250-C20J	1451	
☐ N21431	Bell 206B JetRanger III	3452		0981	1081	1 AN 250-C20B	1451	
☐ N2145C	Bell 206B JetRanger III	3456		0981	1181	1 AN 250-C20B	1451	
☐ N2268G	Bell 206B JetRanger III	3603		0382	0582	1 AN 250-C20J	1451	
☐ N2268V	Bell 206B JetRanger III	3605		0382	0682	1 AN 250-C20J	1451	
☐ N2269A	Bell 206B JetRanger III	3608		0482	0882	1 AN 250-C20J	1451	
☐ N2270G	Bell 206B JetRanger III	3610		0482	0882	1 AN 250-C20J	1451	
☐ N22718	Bell 206B JetRanger III	3618		0482	0882	1 AN 250-C20J	1451	
☐ N2271Z	Bell 206B JetRanger III	3616		0482	0882	1 AN 250-C20J	1451	lst AAOP Helicopters as RP-C1156
☐ N2272J	Bell 206B JetRanger III	3620		0382	0882	1 AN 250-C20J	1451	
☐ N2272V	Bell 206B JetRanger III	3621		0482	0882	1 AN 250-C20J	1451	
☐ N22743	Bell 206B JetRanger III	3624		0482	0882	1 AN 250-C20J	1451	
☐ N22751	Bell 206B JetRanger III	3627		0482	0882	1 AN 250-C20J	1451	
☐ N2275Q	Bell 206B JetRanger III	3625		0482	0882	1 AN 250-C20J	1451	
☐ N2275Y	Bell 206B JetRanger III	3626		0482	0882	1 AN 250-C20J	1451	
☐ N2276B	Bell 206B JetRanger III	3628		0482	0882	1 AN 250-C20J	1451	
☐ N2277A	Bell 206B JetRanger III	3630		0482	0882	1 AN 250-C20J	1451	
☐ N2278V	Bell 206B JetRanger III	3632		0482	0882	1 AN 250-C20J	1451	
☐ N2285B	Bell 206B JetRanger III	3642		1182	0384	1 AN 250-C20J	1451	
☐ N2753F	Bell 206B JetRanger III	2729		0579	0879	1 AN 250-C20B	1451	
☐ N3181J	Bell 206B JetRanger III	3771		1183	0384	1 AN 250-C20J	1451	
☐ N3181Y	Bell 206B JetRanger III	3772		1183	0384	1 AN 250-C20J	1451	
☐ N39122	Bell 206B JetRanger III	3312		0481	0681	1 AN 250-C20B	1451	
☐ N32074	Eurocopter (Aerosp.) SA315B Lama	2442	YS-1001N	1176	1195	1 TU Artouste IIIB	1950	
☐ N3207T	Eurocopter (Aerosp.) SA315B Lama	2441		1175	1195	1 TU Artouste IIIB	1950	
☐ N10072T	Bell 206L-1 LongRanger II	45385		0280	0480	1 AN 250-C28B	1882	
☐ N1073W	Bell 206L-1 LongRanger II	45386		0280	0480	1 AN 250-C28B	1882	
☐ N10761	Bell 206L-1 LongRanger II	45381		0280	0480	1 AN 250-C28B	1882	
☐ N1076T	Bell 206L-1 LongRanger II	45373		0280	0380	1 AN 250-C28B	1882	
☐ N1076Y	Bell 206L-1 LongRanger II	45380		0280	0480	1 AN 250-C28B	1882	
☐ N10778	Bell 206L-1 LongRanger II	45391		0280	0480	1 AN 250-C28B	1882	
☐ N1077A	Bell 206L-1 LongRanger II	45382		0280	0480	1 AN 250-C28B	1882	
☐ N1078C	Bell 206L-1 LongRanger II	45392		0380	0480	1 AN 250-C28B	1882	
☐ N1078D	Bell 206L-1 LongRanger II	45397		0380	0580	1 AN 250-C28B	1882	
☐ N1078G	Bell 206L-1 LongRanger II	45398		0380	0580	1 AN 250-C28B	1882	
☐ N10814	Bell 206L-1 LongRanger II	45415		0480	0680	1 AN 250-C28B	1882	
☐ N108PH	Bell 206L-3 LongRanger III	51334	C-FPUB	0090	0596	1 AN 250-C30P	1882	
☐ N11027	Bell 206L-1 LongRanger II	45411	YV-908C	0480	0580	1 AN 250-C28B	1882	
☐ N129MR	Bell 206L-3 LongRanger III	51129		0085	0596	1 AN 250-C30P	1882	
☐ N141BH	Bell 206L-3 LongRanger III	51303	N996PT	0089	1095	1 AN 250-C30P	1882	
☐ N16938	Bell 206L-1 LongRanger II	45157		0678	0878	1 AN 250-C28B	1882	lsf Fifth Third Leasing Co.
☐ N205FC	Bell 206L-3 LongRanger III	51130		0385	1292	1 AN 250-C30P	1882	
☐ N206FS	Bell 206L-3 LongRanger III	51506		0991	0991	1 AN 250-C30P	1882	lsf CIT Leasing Corp.
☐ N206LS	Bell 206L-3 LongRanger III	51070		1283	1090	1 AN 250-C30P	1882	
☐ N20898	Bell 206L-1 LongRanger II	45721		1182	0187	1 AN 250-C28B	1882	
☐ N210PH	Bell 206L-3 LongRanger III	51541	OM-WIO	0091	1096	1 AN 250-C30P	1882	
☐ N21240	Bell 206L-1 LongRanger II	45647		0781	0981	1 AN 250-C28B	1882	
☐ N2124Z	Bell 206L-1 LongRanger II	45646		0781	0981	1 AN 250-C28B	1882	
☐ N2125M	Bell 206L-1 LongRanger II	45649		0781	0981	1 AN 250-C28B	1882	
☐ N2133X	Bell 206L-1 LongRanger II	45634		0781	0981	1 AN 250-C28B	1882	
☐ N21497	Bell 206L-3 LongRanger III	51518		1091	1191	1 AN 250-C30P	1882	lsf CIT Leasing Corp.
☐ N22425	Bell 206L-1 LongRanger II	45743		0382	0482	1 AN 250-C28B	1882	
☐ N2245Y	Bell 206L-1 LongRanger II	45751		0382	0582	1 AN 250-C28B	1882	
☐ N2249Z	Bell 206L-1 LongRanger II	45753		0482	0882	1 AN 250-C28B	1882	
☐ N2250U	Bell 206L-1 LongRanger II	45754		0482	0882	1 AN 250-C28B	1882	
☐ N2251A	Bell 206L-1 LongRanger II	45755		0482	0882	1 AN 250-C28B	1882	
☐ N2251Z	Bell 206L-1 LongRanger II	45756		0482	0682	1 AN 250-C28B	1882	
☐ N2253E	Bell 206L-1 LongRanger II	45758		0482	0882	1 AN 250-C28B	1882	
☐ N2758N	Bell 206L-1 LongRanger II	45267		0679	0779	1 AN 250-C28B	1882	
☐ N2759U	Bell 206L-1 LongRanger II	45272		0679	0779	1 AN 250-C28B	1882	
☐ N2761N	Bell 206L-1 LongRanger II	45277		0679	0879	1 AN 250-C28B	1882	
☐ N2761X	Bell 206L-1 LongRanger II	45283		0779	0879	1 AN 250-C28B	1882	
☐ N2764F	Bell 206L-1 LongRanger II	45279		0779	0879	1 AN 250-C28B	1882	
☐ N27702	Bell 206L-1 LongRanger II	45300		0879	1079	1 AN 250-C28B	1882	
☐ N2770Y	Bell 206L-1 LongRanger II	45291		0879	1079	1 AN 250-C28B	1882	
☐ N2772A	Bell 206L-1 LongRanger II	45311		0979	1179	1 AN 250-C28B	1882	
☐ N2775A	Bell 206L-1 LongRanger II	45297		0879	1079	1 AN 250-C28B	1882	
☐ N27766	Bell 206L-1 LongRanger II	45312		1079	0887	1 AN 250-C28B	1882	
☐ N2777D	Bell 206L-1 LongRanger II	45299		0879	1179	1 AN 250-C28B	1882	
☐ N31073	Bell 206L-3 LongRanger III	51519		1091	1191	1 AN 250-C30P	1882	lsf CIT Leasing Corp.
☐ N31077	Bell 206L-3 LongRanger III	51520		1091	1191	1 AN 250-C30P	1882	lsf CIT Leasing Corp.
☐ N3107N	Bell 206L-3 LongRanger III	51512		0091	0996	1 AN 250-C30P	1882	
☐ N3108E	Bell 206L-3 LongRanger III	51498		0891	1091	1 AN 250-C30P	1882	lsf CIT Leasing Corp.
☐ N3116L	Bell 206L-3 LongRanger III	51529		1191	1291	1 AN 250-C30P	1882	lsf CIT Leasing Corp.
☐ N3116P	Bell 206L-3 LongRanger III	51530		1191	1291	1 AN 250-C30P	1882	lsf CIT Leasing Corp.
☐ N3178K	Bell 206L-1 LongRanger II	45765		0683	0888	1 AN 250-C28B	1882	
☐ N31801	Bell 206L-3 LongRanger III	51074		1283	0384	1 AN 250-C30P	1882	
☐ N31821	Bell 206L-3 LongRanger III	51076		1283	0384	1 AN 250-C30P	1882	
☐ N3193E	Bell 206L-3 LongRanger III	51042		1182	0383	1 AN 250-C30P	1882	lsf Exxon Co.
☐ N32041	Bell 206L-3 LongRanger III	51539		1191	1291	1 AN 250-C30P	1882	lsf Fleet Capital Corp.
☐ N3207Q	Bell 206L-3 LongRanger III	51540		1291	1291	1 AN 250-C30P	1882	lsf Fleet Capital Corp.
☐ N363BH	Bell 206L-3 LongRanger III	51345	N997PT	0590	1295	1 AN 250-C30P	1882	
☐ N3892R	Bell 206L-1 LongRanger II	45594		0181	0781	1 AN 250-C28B	1882	
☐ N3904L	Bell 206L-1 LongRanger II	45597		0181	0781	1 AN 250-C28B	1882	
☐ N3905B	Bell 206L-1 LongRanger II	45598		0281	0781	1 AN 250-C28B	1882	
☐ N406EH	Bell 206L-1 LongRanger II	45183		1178	1090	1 AN 250-C28B	1882	lsf Fifth Third Leasing Co.
☐ N41128	Bell 206L-3 LongRanger III	51134		0485	0296	1 AN 250-C30P	1882	
☐ N41791	Bell 206L-3 LongRanger III	51465		0591	0591	1 AN 250-C30P	1882	
☐ N4180F	Bell 206L-3 LongRanger III	51469		0591	0691	1 AN 250-C30P	1882	
☐ N4282Z	Bell 206L-3 LongRanger III	51499		0891	1091	1 AN 250-C30P	1882	lsf CIT Leasing Corp.
☐ N42EA	Bell 206L-3 LongRanger III	51542	OM-WIP	0091	0996	1 AN 250-C30P	1882	
☐ N45RP	Bell 206L-1 LongRanger II	45521	HC-BXS	0080	0498	1 AN 250-C28B	1882	
☐ N49EA	Bell 206L-3 LongRanger III	51507	D-HHSG	0091	1096	1 AN 250-C30P	1882	
☐ N50034	Bell 206L-1 LongRanger II	45169		0878	0878	1 AN 250-C28B	1882	
☐ N50046	Bell 206L-1 LongRanger II	45173		1078	1178	1 AN 250-C28B	1882	
☐ N5005B	Bell 206L-1 LongRanger II	45175		1078	1178	1 AN 250-C28B	1882	

registration	type of aircraft	cn/fn	ex/ex*	mfd	del	powered by	mtow kg	configuration	selcal	name/fln/specialitites/remarks
☐ N5005F	Bell 206L-1 LongRanger II	45176		1078	1178	1 AN 250-C28B	1882			
☐ N5006F	Bell 206L-1 LongRanger II	45181		1178	1278	1 AN 250-C28B	1882			
☐ N5007N	Bell 206L-1 LongRanger II	45184		1178	1278	1 AN 250-C28B	1882			
☐ N5007Q	Bell 206L-1 LongRanger II	45187		1278	0179	1 AN 250-C28B	1882			
☐ N5007Y	Bell 206L-1 LongRanger II	45192		1278	0179	1 AN 250-C28B	1882			
☐ N5012V	Bell 206L-1 LongRanger II	45200		0179	0279	1 AN 250-C28B	1882			
☐ N5014V	Bell 206L-1 LongRanger II	45217		0379	0379	1 AN 250-C28B	1882			
☐ N5014Y	Bell 206L-1 LongRanger II	45219	HC-BXL	0379		1 AN 250-C28B	1882			
☐ N5017G	Bell 206L-1 LongRanger II	45228		0379	0479	1 AN 250-C28B	1882			
☐ N50182	Bell 206L-1 LongRanger II	45242		0479	0579	1 AN 250-C28B	1882			
☐ N513EH	Bell 206L-1 LongRanger II	45421		0280	1090	1 AN 250-C28B	1882			lsf Fifth Third Leasing Co.
☐ N515KA	Bell 206L-3 LongRanger III	51048		0082	0797	1 AN 250-C30P	1882			
☐ N53119	Bell 206L-3 LongRanger III	51575	XA-SFW	0092	0696	1 AN 250-C30P	1882			
☐ N54641	Bell 206L-3 LongRanger III	51184	JA9471	0086	1096	1 AN 250-C30P	1882			
☐ N5737T	Bell 206L-1 LongRanger II	45454		0680	0880	1 AN 250-C28B	1882			
☐ N5742H	Bell 206L-1 LongRanger II	45476		0880	0880	1 AN 250-C28B	1882			lsf Fifth Third Leasing Co.
☐ N5742N	Bell 206L-1 LongRanger II	45477		0880	0880	1 AN 250-C28B	1882			
☐ N5745N	Bell 206L-1 LongRanger II	45489		0880	1080	1 AN 250-C28B	1882			lsf Fifth Third Leasing Co.
☐ N5745S	Bell 206L-1 LongRanger II	45491		0880	1080	1 AN 250-C28B	1882			
☐ N5748Q	Bell 206L-1 LongRanger II	45499		0880	1180	1 AN 250-C28B	1882			
☐ N6160Y	Bell 206L-3 LongRanger III	51609		1192	1292	1 AN 250-C30P	1882			
☐ N6160Z	Bell 206L-3 LongRanger III	51610		1292	1292	1 AN 250-C30P	1882			
☐ N6161A	Bell 206L-3 LongRanger III	51611		1292	1292	1 AN 250-C30P	1882			
☐ N62127	Bell 206L-4 LongRanger IV	52023		0193	0693	1 AN 250-C30P	2018			
☐ N6251V	Bell 206L-3 LongRanger III	51404	C-FLYD	0092	0796	1 AN 250-C30P	1882			
☐ N6251X	Bell 206L-3 LongRanger III	51552	C-FLYF	0092	0796	1 AN 250-C30P	1882			
☐ N6251Y	Bell 206L-3 LongRanger III	51556	C-FLYG	0092	0796	1 AN 250-C30P	1882			
☐ N6603X	Bell 206L-3 LongRanger III	51412		1190	1190	1 AN 250-C30P	1882			
☐ N6610C	Bell 206L-3 LongRanger III	51425		0191	0291	1 AN 250-C30P	1882			
☐ N6610E	Bell 206L-3 LongRanger III	51424		0191	0291	1 AN 250-C30P	1882			
☐ N6610Y	Bell 206L-3 LongRanger III	51419		1290	1290	1 AN 250-C30P	1882			
☐ N6748D	Bell 206L-3 LongRanger III	51106	HC-BVB	0084	0596	1 AN 250-C30P	1882			lst Helica del Peru
☐ N7074W	Bell 206L-4 LongRanger IV	52033		0693	0693	1 AN 250-C30P	2018			
☐ N7077B	Bell 206L-4 LongRanger IV	52037		0693	0693	1 AN 250-C30P	2018			
☐ N7077F	Bell 206L-4 LongRanger IV	52038		0693	0693	1 AN 250-C30P	2018			
☐ N8094L	Bell 206L-4 LongRanger IV	52125		0495	0695	1 AN 250-C30P	2018			lsf Bell Helicopter Textron Inc.
☐ N81671	Bell 206L-3 LongRanger III	51301		0889	1090	1 AN 250-C30P	1882			lsf Fifth Third Leasing Co.
☐ N81SP	Bell 206L-3 LongRanger III	51029	N82AW	0082	0197	1 AN 250-C30P	1882			
☐ N83MT	Bell 206L-1 LongRanger II	45492	N7063E	0080	0496	1 AN 250-C28C	1882			
☐ N8587X	Bell 206L-3 LongRanger III	51464		0591	0591	1 AN 250-C30P	1882			
☐ N8588X	Bell 206L-3 LongRanger III	51486		0691	0791	1 AN 250-C30P	1882			
☐ N8589X	Bell 206L-3 LongRanger III	51487		0691	0791	1 AN 250-C30P	1882			lsf CIT Leasing Corp.
☐ N8590X	Bell 206L-3 LongRanger III	51494		0791	0891	1 AN 250-C30P	1882			lsf CIT Leasing Corp.
☐ N8591X	Bell 206L-3 LongRanger III	51495		0891	0891	1 AN 250-C30P	1882			lsf CIT Leasing Corp.
☐ N8592X	Bell 206L-3 LongRanger III	51508		0991	0991	1 AN 250-C30P	1882			lsf CIT Leasing Corp.
☐ N8593X	Bell 206L-3 LongRanger III	51509		0991	1091	1 AN 250-C30P	1882			lsf CIT Leasing Corp.
☐ N8594X	Bell 206L-3 LongRanger III	51531		1191	1291	1 AN 250-C30P	1882			lsf CIT Leasing Corp.
☐ N92MT	Bell 206L-3 LongRanger III	51175	CC-CTY	0086	0496	1 AN 250-C30P	1882			
☐ N979BH	Bell 206L-3 LongRanger III	51403	N998PT	1190	1295	1 AN 250-C30P	1882			
☐ N350BZ	Eurocopter (Aerosp.) AS350B2 AStar	2653		0992	1094	1 TU Arriel 1D1	2250			
☐ N4000L	Eurocopter (Aerosp.) AS350B2 AStar	2873		0795	1095	1 TU Arriel 1D1	2250			
☐ N4031L	Eurocopter (Aerosp.) AS350B2 AStar	2907		0096	0996	1 TU Arriel 1D1	2250			opf Nat. Science Foundation, Antarctica
☐ N4034Q	Eurocopter (Aerosp.) AS350B2 AStar	2918		0096	0996	1 TU Arriel 1D1	2250			opf Nat. Science Foundation, Antarctica
☐ N4036H	Eurocopter (Aerosp.) AS350B2 AStar	2919		0096	0996	1 TU Arriel 1D1	2250			opf Nat. Science Foundation, Antarctica
☐ N60951	Eurocopter (Aerosp.) AS350B2 AStar	2771		1293	1094	1 TU Arriel 1D1	2250			
☐ N6095S	Eurocopter (Aerosp.) AS350B2 AStar	2777		1293	1094	1 TU Arriel 1D1	2250			
☐ N6097Z	Eurocopter (Aerosp.) AS350B2 AStar	2820		0694	0195	1 TU Arriel 1D1	2250			lsf CIT Leasing Corp.
☐ N6100R	Eurocopter (Aerosp.) AS350B2 AStar	2862		0595	0995	1 TU Arriel 1D1	2250			lsf Banc One Leasing Corp.
☐ N141MA	Bell 407	53016		0096	0896	1 AN 250-C47B	2268			
☐ N407PH	Bell 407	53003	C-FWRD*	0095	0396	1 AN 250-C47B	2268			lsf General Electric Capital Corp.
☐ N417PH	Bell 407	53038		0096	0896	1 AN 250-C47B	2268			
☐ N427PH	Bell 407	53059		0096	1096	1 AN 250-C47B	2268			lsf Fifth Third Leasing Co.
☐ N437PH	Bell 407	53072		0096	1196	1 AN 250-C47B	2268			lsf Fifth Third Leasing Co.
☐ N447PH	Bell 407	53114		0097	0397	1 AN 250-C47B	2268			
☐ N457PH	Bell 407	53147		0097	0597	1 AN 250-C47B	2268			lsf General Electric Capital Corp.
☐ N467PH	Bell 407	53142		0097	0597	1 AN 250-C47B	2268			lsf General Electric Capital Corp.
☐ N131AE	Eurocopter (MBB) BO105CBS-4	S-787	N4391S	0488	1292	2 AN 250-C20B	2500	EMS		lst/opf SMR
☐ N133AE	Eurocopter (MBB) BO105CBS-4	S-800	N5418A	0988	0190	2 AN 250-C20B	2500	EMS		lsf Deutsche Financial/sub-lst/opf SMR
☐ N135AE	Eurocopter (MBB) BO105CBS-4	S-838	N7171A	0790	0191	2 AN 250-C20B	2500	EMS		lsf Deutsche Financial/sub-lst/opf SMR
☐ N137AE	Eurocopter (MBB) BO105CBS-4	S-851	N4193R	0191	1091	2 AN 250-C20B	2500	EMS		lst/opf SMR
☐ N205UC	Eurocopter (MBB) BO105CB	S-668	N9190F	0787	1091	2 AN 250-C20B	2500			
☐ N3071K	Eurocopter (MBB) BO105CBS-4	S-859		0591	1091	2 AN 250-C20B	2500			
☐ N3520T	Eurocopter (MBB) BO105CBS	S-539		0081	1297	2 AN 250-C20B	2500			
☐ N4294R	Eurocopter (MBB) BO105CBS-4	S-860		0691	1091	2 AN 250-C20B	2500			
☐ N4302G	Eurocopter (MBB) BO105CBS-4	S-853		0291	1091	2 AN 250-C20B	2500			
☐ N50293	Eurocopter (MBB) BO105CB	S-677		1087	1091	2 AN 250-C20B	2500			
☐ N5029H	Eurocopter (MBB) BO105CB	S-670		1087	1091	2 AN 250-C20B	2500			
☐ N5031U	Eurocopter (MBB) BO105CB	S-678		0188	1091	2 AN 250-C20B	2500			
☐ N54191	Eurocopter (MBB) BO105CBS-4	S-804		0289	0190	2 AN 250-C20B	2500			lsf Deutsche Financial Services Holding
☐ N54197	Eurocopter (MBB) BO105CBS-4	S-805		1288	0190	2 AN 250-C20B	2500			lsf Deutsche Financial Services Holding
☐ N5421E	Eurocopter (MBB) BO105CBS-4	S-806		0389	0190	2 AN 250-C20B	2500			lsf Deutsche Financial Services Holding
☐ N624MB	Eurocopter (MBB) BO105CBS	S-751		0586	0187	2 AN 250-C20B	2500			lsf American Eurocopter Corp.
☐ N6607K	Eurocopter (MBB) BO105CBS-4	S-841		0890	0191	2 AN 250-C20B	2500			lsf Deutsche Financial Services Holding
☐ N7062X	Eurocopter (MBB) BO105CBS-4	S-793		0188	0189	2 AN 250-C20B	2500			lsf MDFC Equipment Leasing Corp.
☐ N7136H	Eurocopter (MBB) BO105CBS-4	S-833		0390	0191	2 AN 250-C20B	2500			lsf Deutsche Financial Services Holding
☐ N7170D	Eurocopter (MBB) BO105CBS-4	S-840		0790	0191	2 AN 250-C20B	2500			lsf Deutsche Financial Services Holding
☐ N721MB	Eurocopter (MBB) BO105CBS	S-752		0586	0187	2 AN 250-C20B	2500			lsf American Eurocopter Corp.
☐ N724MB	Eurocopter (MBB) BO105CBS-4	S-756		0986	0991	2 AN 250-C20B	2500			
☐ N81832	Eurocopter (MBB) BO105CBS-4	S-828		1089	0790	2 AN 250-C20B	2500			lsf Deutsche Financial Services Holding
☐ N8197X	Eurocopter (MBB) BO105CBS-4	S-808		0389	0190	2 AN 250-C20B	2500			lsf Deutsche Financial Services Holding
☐ N81982	Eurocopter (MBB) BO105CBS-4	S-818		0689	0190	2 AN 250-C20B	2500			lsf Deutsche Financial Services Holding
☐ N81992	Eurocopter (MBB) BO105CBS-4	S-827		0989	0790	2 AN 250-C20B	2500			lsf Deutsche Financial Services Holding
☐ N86CH	Eurocopter (MBB) BO105CBS	S-557		1181	0588	2 AN 250-C20B	2500	EMS		lsf Arkansas Childrens Hospital
☐ N90752	Eurocopter (MBB) BO105CS	S-156		1074	0777	2 AN 250-C20B	2400	EMS		lsf RTS Aircraft Services Corp.
☐ N91070	Eurocopter (MBB) BO105C	S-145		0474	1091	2 AN 250-C20B	2400			
☐ N911BR	Eurocopter (MBB) BO105CB	S-719	N10034	0688	1091	2 AN 250-C20B	2500	EMS		
☐ N911DD	Eurocopter (MBB) BO105CBS-4	S-830	N7136J	0390	0191	2 AN 250-C20B	2500			lsf Deutsche Financial Services Holding
☐ N911EB	Eurocopter (MBB) BO105CBS-4	S-812	N105WK	0489	0190	2 AN 250-C20B	2500			lsf Deutsche Financial Services Holding
☐ N911FL	Eurocopter (MBB) BO105CB-4	S-717	N5352H	0788	0991	2 AN 250-C20B	2500	EMS AirMed		opf Acadian Ambulance Service Inc.
☐ N911HM	Eurocopter (MBB) BO105CBS-2	S-683	N4573L	0884	1290	2 AN 250-C20B	2500			
☐ N911PF	Eurocopter (MBB) BO105CB-4	S-718	N5368F	0788	0991	2 AN 250-C20B	2500			
☐ N9190Y	Eurocopter (MBB) BO105CB	S-669		0787	1091	2 AN 250-C20B	2500			
☐ N967MB	Eurocopter (MBB) BO105CBS-4	S-737		1085	1185	2 AN 250-C20B	2500			lsf American Eurocopter Corp.
☐ N9213P	MD Helicopters MD 900 Explorer	900-00013		0195	0395	2 PWC PW206A	2722			lsf General Electric Capital Corp.
☐ N9214U	MD Helicopters MD 900 Explorer	900-00014		0495	0495	2 PWC PW206A	2722			lsf General Electric Capital Corp.
☐ N132AE	Eurocopter (MBB) BK117B-2	7238	N31502	1091	0792	2 LY LTS101-750B.1	3350	EMS		lst/opf SMR / cvtd B-1
☐ N134AE	Eurocopter (MBB) BK117B-2	7237	N3152E	0991	0792	2 LY LTS101-750B.1	3350	EMS		lst/opf SMR / cvtd B-1
☐ N136AE	Eurocopter (MBB) BK117B-2	7234	N4280V	0991	0792	2 LY LTS101-750B.1	3350	EMS		lst/opf SMR / cvtd B-1
☐ N191BK	Eurocopter (MBB) BK117B-2	7146		0188	0189	2 LY LTS101-750B.1	3350			lsf MDFC Equipment Lsng Corp./cvtd B-1
☐ N217UC	Eurocopter (MBB) BK117B-2	7152		0189	0189	2 LY LTS101-750B.1	3350			lsf MDFC Equipment Lsng Corp./cvtd B-1
☐ N401PH	Eurocopter (MBB) BK117A-4	7050	N507AL	0485	0495	2 LY LTS101-650B.1	3200	EMS		lsf Debis Financial / sub-lst/opf SMR
☐ N7040U	Eurocopter (MBB) BK117B-1	7180	D-HBHW*	0088	0297	2 LY LTS101-750B.1	3200			
☐ N7059J	Eurocopter (MBB) BK117B-1	7151	D-HBDT*	0088	1096	2 LY LTS101-750B.1	3200			
☐ N8765J	Eurocopter (MBB) BK117A-4	7054		0184	0194	2 LY LTS101-650B.1	3200			lst Omniflight Helicopters
☐ N911LK	Eurocopter (MBB) BK117B-2	7168		0188	0788	2 LY LTS101-750B.1	3350			lsf MDFC Equipment Lsng Corp./cvtd B-1
☐ N911NC	Eurocopter (MBB) BK117A-4	7026	N720H	0183	0185	2 LY LTS101-650B.1	3200	EMS		
☐ N911RZ	Eurocopter (MBB) BK117A-4	7092	N520WJ	1086	0189	2 LY LTS101-650B.1	3200	EMS		lsf MDFC Equipment Leasing Corp.
☐ N911TL	Eurocopter (MBB) BK117B-2	7198	N911AF	1189	1193	2 LY LTS101-750B.1	3350	EMS		cvtd B-1
☐ N230UN	Bell 230	23009		0593	1093	2 AN 250C-30G2	3810			lsf Textron Financial Corp.
☐ N236X	Bell 230	23015		0294	0195	2 AN 250C-30G2	3810			lsf Exxon Co.

☐ N1545K	Sikorsky S-76A	760047		0380	0883	2 AN 250-C30S	4763			
☐ N1545X	Sikorsky S-76A	760050		0380	0480	2 AN 250-C30S	4763			
☐ N15460	Sikorsky S-76A+	760223		1282	0483	2 TU Arriel 1S	4763	EMS		lsf Variety Childrens Hospital/cvtd-76A
☐ N1546G	Sikorsky S-76A	760076		0780	0980	2 AN 250-C30S	4763			
☐ N1546K	Sikorsky S-76A	760082		0580	1080	2 AN 250-C30S	4763			
☐ N1547D	Sikorsky S-76A	760077		0980	0581	2 AN 250-C30S	4763			
☐ N22342	Sikorsky S-76A	760096		0980	0291	2 AN 250-C30S	4763			
☐ N2743E	Sikorsky S-76A	760155	C-GSLE	0381	1182	2 AN 250-C30S	4763	EMS		
☐ N276X	Sikorsky S-76C	760405		1194	0295	2 TU Arriel 1S1	5307			lsf Exxon Co.
☐ N278X	Sikorsky S-76C	760440		1195	0196	2 TU Arriel 1S1	5307			lsf Exxon Co.
☐ N31217	Sikorsky S-76A	760229		0283	0883	2 AN 250-C30S	4763			
☐ N31219	Sikorsky S-76A	760230		0283	0883	2 AN 250-C30S	4763	EMS MetroLifeFlt		lsf / opf The Metro Health System
☐ N3122G	Sikorsky S-76A	760232		0282	0983	2 AN 250-C30S	4763	EMS MetroLifeFlt		lsf / opf The Metro Health System
☐ N3122H	Sikorsky S-76A	760233		0382	1083	2 AN 250-C30S	4763	EMS MetroLifeFlt		lsf / opf The Metro Health System
☐ N4253S	Sikorsky S-76A	760035		1179	0883	2 AN 250-C30S	4763			
☐ N476X	Sikorsky S-76C	760436		0895	1095	2 TU Arriel 1S1	5307			lsf Exxon Co.
☐ N5128	Sikorsky S-76A	760181	N5448G	0284	0284	2 AN 250-C30S	4763	EMS MetroLifeFlt		lsf / opf Metro Health System
☐ N5426U	Sikorsky S-76A	760167		0481	0681	2 AN 250-C30S	4763	EMS		
☐ N5435V	Sikorsky S-76A	760158		0481	0981	2 AN 250-C30S	4763	EMS		
☐ N706AE	Sikorsky S-76A	760275	N706AL	0784	0784	2 AN 250-C30S	4763	EMS		
☐ N707AE	Sikorsky S-76A	760276	N707AL	0784	0784	2 AN 250-C30S	4763	EMS		
☐ N792CH	Sikorsky S-76A	760193	N28PL	1181	0387	2 AN 250-C30S	4763	EMS		lsf Arkansas Childrens Hospital
☐ N89H	Sikorsky S-76C	760406		1294	0395	2 TU Arriel 1S1	5307			lsf Exxon Co.
☐ N911MJ	Sikorsky S-76A	760231	N3122D	0282	0983	2 AN 250-C30S	4763	EMS		
☐ N102PH	Bell 212	30899	C-FSKS	1078	0495	2 PWC PT6T-3 TwinPac	5080			
☐ N1074C	Bell 212	30989		0280	0380	2 PWC PT6T-3 TwinPac	5080			lst Helicol Colombia as HK-3900X
☐ N1079U	Bell 212	31122		0280	0880	2 PWC PT6T-3 TwinPac	5080			
☐ N1082G	Bell 212	31109		0080	0898	2 PWC PT6T-3 TwinPac	5080			
☐ N27805	Bell 212	31106		0380	0480	2 PWC PT6T-3 TwinPac	5080			
☐ N3131S	Bell 212	30953	SU-BCU	0979	0284	2 PWC PT6T-3 TwinPac	5080			
☐ N3208H	Bell 212	31304		0088	0896	2 PWC PT6T-3B TwinPac	5080			opf Nat. Science Foundation, Antarctica
☐ N5009N	Bell 212	30915		0179	0279	2 PWC PT6T-3 TwinPac	5080			lst Helicol Colombia as HK-3899X
☐ N5010F	Bell 212	30936		0679	0679	2 PWC PT6T-3 TwinPac	5080			
☐ N5736J	Bell 212	31140		0980	0288	2 PWC PT6T-3 TwinPac	5080			
☐ N107X	Bell 412	33113		0685	0985	2 PWC PT6T-3B TwinPac	5398			lsf General Electric Capital Corp.
☐ N108X	Bell 412	33115		0685	0985	2 PWC PT6T-3B TwinPac	5398			lsf General Electric Capital Corp.
☐ N141PH	Bell 412SP	33197	HL9241	0089	0697	2 PWC PT6T-3B TwinPac	5398			
☐ N142PH	Bell 412SP	33150	HL9236	0087	0697	2 PWC PT6T-3B TwinPac	5398			
☐ N2014K	Bell 412	33020		0681	0881	2 PWC PT6T-3B TwinPac	5398			lst Aeroservicios Ranger as YV-922C
☐ N2148K	Bell 412	36001		1089	1189	2 PWC PT6T-3B TwinPac	5398			lsf Fleet Capital Corp.
☐ N21498	Bell 412	36003		1189	1189	2 PWC PT6T-3B TwinPac	5398			lsf Fleet Capital Corp.
☐ N2149S	Bell 412	36002		1189	1189	2 PWC PT6T-3B TwinPac	5398			lsf CIT Leasing Corp.
☐ N22347	Bell 412	36005	XA-RSL	0590	0694	2 PWC PT6T-3B TwinPac	5398			lsf Signet Leasing & Financial Co.
☐ N22608	Bell 412	33075		0482	0682	2 PWC PT6T-3B TwinPac	5398			
☐ N2261D	Bell 412	33076		0482	0882	2 PWC PT6T-3B TwinPac	5398			
☐ N2298Z	Bell 412	33077		0482	0882	2 PWC PT6T-3B TwinPac	5398			
☐ N23023	Bell 412	33080		0482	0882	2 PWC PT6T-3B TwinPac	5398			
☐ N33008	Bell 412	36004		0290	0790	2 PWC PT6T-3B TwinPac	5398			lsf Signet Leasing & Financial Co.
☐ N3893N	Bell 412	33010		0581	0681	2 PWC PT6T-3B TwinPac	5398			lsf General Electric Capital Corp.
☐ N3893P	Bell 412	33012		0581	0781	2 PWC PT6T-3B TwinPac	5398			
☐ N3893S	Bell 412	33022		0681	0881	2 PWC PT6T-3B TwinPac	5398			
☐ N3911L	Bell 412	33023		0681	0881	2 PWC PT6T-3B TwinPac	5398			
☐ N6559Z	Bell 412	36019		1190	0691	2 PWC PT6T-3B TwinPac	5398			lsf Fleet Capital Corp.
☐ N7128R	Bell 412	36007		0490	0490	2 PWC PT6T-3B TwinPac	5398			lsf Signet Leasing & Financial Co.
☐ N30PH	Beech King Air 200	BB-635	N30PM	0280	1184	2 PWC PT6A-41	5670			
☐ N39PH	Beech King Air 200C	BL-3	N141GS	0879	0388	2 PWC PT6A-41	5670			
☐ N500PH	Beech King Air 200C	BL-29	N3847H	0381	0582	2 PWC PT6A-41	5670			
☐ N789DS	Beech King Air 200	BB-478	N789BT	0079	0997	2 PWC PT6A-41	5670			
☐ N3897N	Bell 214ST	28106		0482	1294	2 GE CT7-2A	7938			lsf General Electric Capital Corp.
☐ N8045T	Bell 214ST	28101	VH-LHQ	0082	0295	2 GE CT7-2A	7938			lsf Fleet Capital Corp.
☐ N125CS	Hawker 700A (HS 125-700A)	257018 / NA0212	N662JB	1177	1294	2 GA TFE731-3R-1H	11567			

PETTY ENTERPRISES - Flight Dept. (Flight Dept. of Petty Enterprises, Inc.) **Greensboro-Piedmont Triad Int'l & Concord-Regional, NC**

311 Branson Mill Road, Randleman, NC 27317-8008, USA ☎ (336) 498-2156 Tx: none Fax: (336) 498-4334 SITA: n/a

F: 1996 ✈ n/a Head: Richard Petty Net: n/a Operates non-commercial corporate flights exclusively for itself and its NASCAR stockcar-racing-teams.

☐ N43PE	Beech King Air 200	BB-585	N438P	0080	0596	2 PWC PT6A-41	5670	Corp. 11 Pax		lsf Richard Petty Transportation Llc
☐ N443PE	BAe 3101 Jetstream 31	777	N777JX	0087	1097	2 GA TPE331-10UR-513H	6900	Y19		lsf Southern Pride

PHOENIX AIR = PHA (Phoenix Air Group, Inc. dba) **Cartersville, GA**

100 Phoenix Air Drive, S.W., Cartersville, GA 30120, USA ☎ (770) 387-2000 Tx: 6713076 phxa uw Fax: (770) 386-3053 SITA: n/a

F: 1978 ✈ 110 Head: Mark H. Thompson ICAO: GRAY BIRD Net: n/a Most Learjet 35/36 are leased to/operated under contract for the US Dept of Defence as Special Mission-aircraft.

☐ N52PY	Twin (Aero) Turbo Commander 690A	11196	N52PB	0074	1092	2 GA TPE331-5-251K	4649			
☐ N510PA	Learjet 24D	24D-305	N43DM	0075	0192	2 GE CJ610-6	6123			
☐ N611DB	Learjet 24D	24D-318	N114JT	0075	0988	2 GE CJ610-6	6123			
☐ N32PA	Learjet 36A	36A-025	N800BL	0077	0288	2 GA TFE731-2-2B	8301			
☐ N520PA	Learjet 35	35-037	N600WT	0075	0892	2 GA TFE731-2-2B	8301			
☐ N522PA	Learjet 35A	35A-254	N34FN	0079	0892	2 GA TFE731-2-2B	8301			
☐ N524PA	Learjet 35	35-033	N31FN	0075	0595	2 GA TFE731-2-2B	8301			
☐ N527PA	Learjet 36A	36A-019	N540PA	0076	0890	2 GA TFE731-2-2B	8301			
☐ N541PA	Learjet 35	35-053	N53FN	0076	1191	2 GA TFE731-2-2B	8301			
☐ N542PA	Learjet 35	35-030	N16FN	0075	0792	2 GA TFE731-2-2B	8301			
☐ N543PA	Learjet 35A	35A-070	N50FN	0076	1191	2 GA TFE731-2-2B	8301			
☐ N544PA	Learjet 35A	35A-247	N523PA	0079	0592	2 GA TFE731-2-2B	8301			
☐ N545PA	Learjet 36A	36A-028	N75TD	0076	0887	2 GA TFE731-2-2B	8301			
☐ N547PA	Learjet 36	36-012	N712JE	0075	0690	2 GA TFE731-2-2B	8301			
☐ N548PA	Learjet 36A	36A-038	N15FN	0075	0193	2 GA TFE731-2-2B	8301			lsf Cff Air Inc.
☐ N549PA	Learjet 35A	35A-119		0077	0593	2 GA TFE731-2-2B	8301			lsf Cff Air Inc.
☐ N56PA	Learjet 36A	36A-023	N6YY	0077	1291	2 GA TFE731-2-2B	8301			
☐ N62PG	Learjet 36A	36A-031	N20UG	0077	0992	2 GA TFE731-2-2B	8301			
☐ N71PG	Learjet 36	36-013	D-CBRD	0075	1092	2 GA TFE731-2-2B	8301			
☐ N80PG	Learjet 35	35-063	N663CA	0076	0296	2 GA TFE731-2-2B	8301			
☐ N109P	GAC (Grumman) G-159 Gulfstream I	109	N307AT	0063	1195	2 RR Dart 529-8X	16329			
☐ N190PA	GAC (Grumman) G-159 (F/SCD) Gulfstream I	195	N1900W	0069	0989	2 RR Dart 529-8X	16329	Freighter		cvtd G-159
☐ N192PA	GAC (Grumman) G-159 (F/SCD) Gulfstream I	149	N684FM	0065	0794	2 RR Dart 529-8X	16329	Freighter		cvtd G-159
☐ N193PA	GAC (Grumman) G-159 Gulfstream I	023	OE-HAZ	0059	1098	2 RR Dart 529-8X	16329			
☐ N196PA	GAC (Grumman) G-159 Gulfstream I	139	C-FRTU	0064	0795	2 RR Dart 529-8X	16329			
☐ N198PA	GAC (Grumman) G-159C Gulfstream IC	027	N415CA	0059	0596	2 RR Dart 529-8X	16329			cvtd G-159

PIEDMONT AIRLINES, Inc. = US / PDT (US Airways Express) (Subsidiary of US Airways Group/formerly Henson Aviation, Inc.) **Salisbury, MD / WAS, DC & FLL, FL**

5443 Airport Terminal Road, Salisbury, MD 21801-9432, USA ☎ (410) 742-2996 Tx: 710-864-0011 Fax: (410) 742-1728 SITA: n/a

F: 1931 ✈ 1640 Head: John F. Leonard IATA: 531 ICAO: PIEDMONT Net: n/a

All aircraft are operated as US AIRWAYS EXPRESS (in full such colours & both titles), a commuter system to provide feeder connection at US Airways major hubs, using US flight numbers.

☐ N816MA	De Havilland DHC-8-102 Dash 8	231	N801RM	0090	0698	2 PWC PW120A	15649	Y37		956 / lsf DHC / op in US Airways Ex.-cs
☐ N906HA	De Havilland DHC-8-102 Dash 8	009	C-GHRI*	0085	0485	2 PWC PW120A	15649	Y37		cvtd -101 / op in US Airways Express-cs
☐ N907HA	De Havilland DHC-8-102 Dash 8	011	C-GESR*	0085	0585	2 PWC PW120A	15649	Y37		cvtd -101 / op in US Airways Express-cs
☐ N908HA	De Havilland DHC-8-102 Dash 8	015	C-GIBQ*	0085	0885	2 PWC PW120A	15649	Y37		cvtd -101 / op in US Airways Express-cs
☐ N909HA	De Havilland DHC-8-102 Dash 8	018	C-GESR*	0085	1085	2 PWC PW120A	15649	Y37		cvtd -101 / op in US Airways Express-cs
☐ N910HA	De Havilland DHC-8-102 Dash 8	022	C-GEVP*	0085	1285	2 PWC PW120A	15649	Y37		cvtd -101 / op in US Airways Express-cs
☐ N911HA	De Havilland DHC-8-102 Dash 8	034	C-GEOA*	0086	0486	2 PWC PW120A	15649	Y37		cvtd -101 / op in US Airways Express-cs
☐ N912HA	De Havilland DHC-8-102 Dash 8	040	C-GEOA*	0086	0686	2 PWC PW120A	15649	Y37		cvtd -101 / op in US Airways Express-cs
☐ N914HA	De Havilland DHC-8-102 Dash 8	053	C-GETI*	0086	1186	2 PWC PW120A	15649	Y37		op in US Airways Express-colors
☐ N915HA	De Havilland DHC-8-102 Dash 8	069	C-GFUM*	0087	0387	2 PWC PW120A	15649	Y37		op in US Airways Express-colors
☐ N916HA	De Havilland DHC-8-102 Dash 8	072	C-GEOA*	0087	0487	2 PWC PW120A	15649	Y37		op in US Airways Express-colors
☐ N917HA	De Havilland DHC-8-102 Dash 8	075	C-GEVP*	0087	0587	2 PWC PW120A	15649	Y37		op in US Airways Express-colors
☐ N920HA	De Havilland DHC-8-102 Dash 8	084	C-GFRP*	0087	0787	2 PWC PW120A	15649	Y37		op in US Airways Express-colors
☐ N921HA	De Havilland DHC-8-102 Dash 8	089	C-GLOT*	0087	1287	2 PWC PW120A	15649	Y37		op in US Airways Express-colors
☐ N922HA	De Havilland DHC-8-102 Dash 8	094	C-GETI*	0088	0388	2 PWC PW120A	15649	Y37		op in US Airways Express-colors
☐ N923HA	De Havilland DHC-8-102 Dash 8	099	C-GEOA*	0088	0488	2 PWC PW120A	15649	Y37		op in US Airways Express-colors
☐ N924HA	De Havilland DHC-8-102 Dash 8	105	C-GFOD*	0088	0688	2 PWC PW120A	15649	Y37		op in US Airways Express-colors
☐ N925HA	De Havilland DHC-8-102 Dash 8	111	C-GFYI*	0088	0888	2 PWC PW120A	15649	Y37		op in US Airways Express-colors
☐ N926HA	De Havilland DHC-8-102 Dash 8	114	C-GETI*	0088	0988	2 PWC PW120A	15649	Y37		op in US Airways Express-colors

417 registration type of aircraft cn/fn ex/ex* mfd del powered by mtow kg configuration selcal name/fln/specialitites/remarks

N927HA	De Havilland DHC-8-102 Dash 8	117	C-GEOA*	0088	0988	2 PWC PW120A	15649	Y37		op in US Airways Express-colors
N928HA	De Havilland DHC-8-102 Dash 8	120	C-GFOD*	0088	1088	2 PWC PW120A	15649	Y37		op in US Airways Express-colors
N930HA	De Havilland DHC-8-102 Dash 8	126	C-GFQL*	0088	1288	2 PWC PW120A	15649	Y37		op in US Airways Express-colors
N931HA	De Havilland DHC-8-102 Dash 8	132	C-GFOD*	0089	0189	2 PWC PW120A	15649	Y37		op in US Airways Express-colors
N933HA	De Havilland DHC-8-102 Dash 8	134	C-GFUM*	0089	0189	2 PWC PW120A	15649	Y37		op in US Airways Express-colors
N934HA	De Havilland DHC-8-102 Dash 8	139	C-GETI*	0089	0389	2 PWC PW120A	15649	Y37		op in US Airways Express-colors
N935HA	De Havilland DHC-8-102 Dash 8	142	C-GLOT*	0089	0389	2 PWC PW120A	15649	Y37		op in US Airways Express-colors
N936HA	De Havilland DHC-8-102 Dash 8	145	C-GFQL*	0089	0389	2 PWC PW120A	15649	Y37		op in US Airways Express-colors
N937HA	De Havilland DHC-8-102 Dash 8	148	C-GLOT*	0089	0489	2 PWC PW120A	15649	Y37		op in US Airways Express-colors
N938HA	De Havilland DHC-8-102 Dash 8	152	C-GFUM*	0089	0589	2 PWC PW120A	15649	Y37		op in US Airways Express-colors
N940HA	De Havilland DHC-8-102 Dash 8	156	C-GLOT*	0089	0689	2 PWC PW120A	15649	Y37		op in US Airways Express-colors
N941HA	De Havilland DHC-8-102 Dash 8	161	C-GETI*	0089	0789	2 PWC PW120A	15649	Y37		op in US Airways Express-colors
N942HA	De Havilland DHC-8-102 Dash 8	163	C-GFUM*	0089	0789	2 PWC PW120A	15649	Y37		op in US Airways Express-colors
N943HA	De Havilland DHC-8-102 Dash 8	167	C-GFQL*	0089	0889	2 PWC PW120A	15649	Y37		op in US Airways Express-colors
N960HA	De Havilland DHC-8-102 Dash 8	326	N822MA	0092	1298	2 PWC PW120A	15649	Y37		lsf DHC / op in US Airways Express-cs
N963HA	De Havilland DHC-8-102 Dash 8	337	N830MA	0092	1298	2 PWC PW120A	15649	Y37		lsf DHC / op in US Airways Express-cs
N975HA	De Havilland DHC-8-102 Dash 8	176	C-GEWQ*	0089	1089	2 PWC PW120A	15649	Y37		op in US Airways Express-colors
N979HA	De Havilland DHC-8-102 Dash 8	373	C-GFQL*	0094	0194	2 PWC PW120A	15649	Y37		op in US Airways Express-colors
N980HA	De Havilland DHC-8-102 Dash 8	376	C-GFBW*	0094	0394	2 PWC PW120A	15649	Y37		op in US Airways Express-colors
N981HA	De Havilland DHC-8-102 Dash 8	378	C-GDNG*	0094	0494	2 PWC PW120A	15649	Y37		op in US Airways Express-colors
N982HA	De Havilland DHC-8-102 Dash 8	380	C-FWBB*	0094	0594	2 PWC PW120A	15649	Y37		op in US Airways Express-colors
N984HA	De Havilland DHC-8-102 Dash 8	377	N823EX	0094	1195	2 PWC PW120A	15649	Y37		op in US Airways Express-colors
N986HA	De Havilland DHC-8-202 Dash 8	421	C-GFYI*	0096	0496	2 PWC PW123D	16465	Y37		op in US Airways Express-colors
N987HA	De Havilland DHC-8-202 Dash 8	425	C-GFHZ*	0096	0296	2 PWC PW123D	16465	Y37		op in US Airways Express-colors
N988HA	De Havilland DHC-8-202 Dash 8	426	C-FDHD*	0096	0296	2 PWC PW123D	16465	Y37		op in US Airways Express-colors
N989HA	De Havilland DHC-8-202 Dash 8	427	C-GFEN*	0096	0296	2 PWC PW123D	16465	Y37		op in US Airways Express-colors
N990HA	De Havilland DHC-8-202 Dash 8	428		0096	0396	2 PWC PW123D	16465	Y37		op in US Airways Express-colors
N991HA	De Havilland DHC-8-202 Dash 8	431		0096	0496	2 PWC PW123D	16465	Y37		op in US Airways Express-colors
N992HA	De Havilland DHC-8-202 Dash 8	432		0096	0696	2 PWC PW123D	16465	Y37		op in US Airways Express-colors
N993HA	De Havilland DHC-8-202 Dash 8Q	457	C-GDIU*	0096	1296	2 PWC PW123D	16465	Y37		op in US Airways Express-colors
N994HA	De Havilland DHC-8-202 Dash 8Q	459	C-GFYI*	0096	1296	2 PWC PW123D	16465	Y37		op in US Airways Express-colors
N995HA	De Havilland DHC-8-202 Dash 8Q	460	C-GFBW*	0096	1296	2 PWC PW123D	16465	Y37		op in US Airways Express-colors

PIEDMONT AVIATION (Division of Piedmont Aviation Services, Inc. / Subsidiary of USAir Group, Inc.)

Winston-Salem & Raleigh, NC & Norfolk & Roanoke, VA

PIEDMONT

PO Box 525, Winston Salem, NC 27102-0525, USA ☎ (910) 776-6060 Tx: none Fax: (910) 776-6061 SITA: n/a
F: 1966 n/a Head: Jim A. Taylor Net: http://www.flypiedmont.com

N208P	Beech Baron 58	TH-1626		0091	0691	2 CO IO-550-C	2495			lsf pvt
N206P	Beech King Air 200	BB-466	N200TW	0079	0991	2 PWC PT6A-41	5670			
N697P	Beech Catpass 200	BB-217	C-FCGM	0076	0797	2 PWC PT6A-41	5670			cvtd King Air 200, cvn 9
N303P	Mitsubishi MU-300 Diamond I	A034SA	N318DM	0083	0590	2 PWC JT15D-4	6636			lsf Motion Industries Inc.
N306P	Mitsubishi MU-300 Diamond I	A009SA	N909GA	0080	0190	2 PWC JT15D-4	6636			lsf Chattem Inc.

PIONEER AIR SERVICE

Du Bois-Jefferson County, PA

PO Box 219, West Point, PA 19486, USA ☎ (215) 699-6300 Tx: none Fax: (215) 699-6050 SITA: n/a
F: 1994 n/a Head: Robert Marsh Net: n/a

N501SB	Cessna 310R II	310R0166		0075	0798	2 CO IO-520-M	2495			
N50DA	Shorts Skyvan 3 Variant 200 (SC-7)	SH1852	G-AWVM	0068	0697	2 GA TPE331-2-201A	5670	Para		

PIONEER AVIATION, Inc.

McCall-Municipal, ID

PO Box 962, McCall, ID 83638, USA ☎ (208) 634-7127 Tx: none Fax: (208) 634-7117 SITA: n/a
F: 1979 n/a Head: Kirk F. Braun Net: n/a

N5421X	Cessna TU206G Turbo Stationair II	U20605737		0081	0392	1 CO TSIO-520-M	1633			
N944JD	Cessna TU206G Turbo Stationair	U20603536		0076	1296	1 CO TSIO-520-M	1633			lsf pvt
N732PE	Cessna T210M Turbo Centurion II	21061659		0076	0593	1 CO TSIO-520-R	1724			lsf pvt

PIONEER HELICOPTERS (Thermal Graphics, Inc. dba)

Mill City-Heliport, OR

PO Box 1219, Mill City, OR 97360, USA ☎ (541) 897-4627 Tx: none Fax: (541) 897-2097 SITA: n/a
F: 1994 n/a Head: Jill M. Johnson Net: n/a

N16MV	Bell 206B JetRanger III	4040	N7036H	0089	0195	1 AN 250-C20J	1451			lst Mid Valley Helicopters

P.J. HELICOPTERS, Inc.

Red Bluff-Municipal, CA

1495 Vista Avenue, Red Bluff, CA 96080, USA ☎ (530) 527-5059 Tx: none Fax: (530) 527-1730 SITA: n/a
F: 1973 n/a Head: Mark Gunsauls Net: n/a

N61PJ	MD Helicopters MD 500D (Hughes 369D)	770162D	N6SX	0077	0993	1 AN 250-C20B	1361			
N60PJ	Bell 206B JetRanger III	2349	N216GP	0078	0593	1 AN 250-C20B	1451			
N67PJ	Bell 206B JetRanger III	3966	N345RS	0087	0597	1 AN 250-C20J	1451			
N68PJ	Bell 206B JetRanger III	3384	N2068B	0081	0788	1 AN 250-C20B	1451			
N64PJ	Bell 206L-3 LongRanger III	51100	N3205M	0084	0593	1 AN 250-C30P	1882			
N65PJ	Bell 206L-3 LongRanger III	51127	N256SN	0085	1295	1 AN 250-C30P	1882			
N204PJ	Bell UH-1B (204)	413	62-1893	0062	0191	1 LY T53-L-11	3856			

PLANEMASTERS, Ltd = PMS

Chicago-DuPage, IL

PLANEMASTER AIR CHARTERS

32W515 West Tower Road, DuPage Airport, West Chicago, IL 60185, USA ☎ (630) 513-2100 Tx: none Fax: (630) 377-3283 SITA: n/a
F: 1969 n/a Head: John McHugh ICAO: PLANEMASTER Net: http://www.planemasters.com

N9635F	Cessna 208 Caravan I	20800119		0087	0987	1 PWC PT6A-114	3629			
N1114A	Cessna 208B Caravan I Super Cargomaster	208B0309		0092	0193	1 PWC PT6A-114	3969	Freighter		
N1256P	Cessna 208B Grand Caravan	208B0564		0096	1296	1 PWC PT6A-114A	3969			
N278PM	Cessna 208B Caravan I Super Cargomaster	208B0171	N4694B	0089	1189	1 PWC PT6A-114	3969	Freighter		
N286PM	Cessna 208B Grand Caravan	208B0631		0097	1297	1 PWC PT6A-114A	3969			
N9457B	Cessna 208B Caravan I Super Cargomaster	208B0074		0088	0388	1 PWC PT6A-114	3969	Freighter		
N9648B	Cessna 208B Caravan I Super Cargomaster	208B0143		0088	0789	1 PWC PT6A-114	3969	Freighter		
N401LG	Cessna 525 CitationJet	525-0154	N51246	0096	0996	2 WRR FJ44-1A	4717			lsf A. Lakin & Sons Inc.
N283PM	Beech King Air 100	B-46	N678RM	0070	0989	2 PWC PT6A-28	4808			
N284PM	Beech King Air C90	LJ-734	N928JR	0077	0993	2 PWC PT6A-21	4377			
N200CG	Cessna 500 Citation	500-0230	N299TB	0075	0997	2 PWC JT15D-1	5216			lsf Illinois Data Mart Inc.
N270PM	Cessna 500 Citation	500-0196	N499BA	0074	0996	2 PWC JT15D-1	5216			
N280PM	Cessna 550 Citation II	550-0188	N38NA	0080	0898	2 PWC JT15D-4	6033			
N550RP	Cessna 550 Citation II	550-0219	YV-606CP	0081	0796	2 PWC JT15D-4	6033			lsf RDD Leasing Inc.

PLANET AIRWAYS, Inc. (formerly Airship Airways)

Orlando-Int'l, FL

7380 Sand Lake Road, Suite 350, Orlando, FL 32819, USA ☎ (407) 363-1800 Tx: none Fax: (407) 363-4410 SITA: n/a
F: 1997 n/a Head: Jerry Bushnell Net: n/a

N1910	Boeing 727-23	19385 / 311		0966	0698	3 PW JT8D-7B	72847	Y128		

PLM Transportation Equipment, Corp. = (PLMI) (Subsidiary of PLM International, Inc.)

San Francisco, CA

One Market, Steuart Street Tower, Suite 800, San Francisco, CA 94105, USA ☎ (415) 974-1399 Tx: 34430 Fax: (415) 882-0862 SITA: n/a
F: 1972 150 Head: Steven Layne Net: http://www.plm.com New and used aircraft leasing, sales and financing company.
Owner/lessor of following (main) aircraft types: Boeing 727 / 737, Douglas DC-9 & De Havilland DHC-8. Aircraft leased from PLMI are listed and mentioned as such under the leasing carriers.

POLAR AIR CARGO, Inc. = PO / PAC

New York-JFK, NY

100 Oceangate, 15th Floor, Long Beach, CA 90802, USA ☎ (562) 436-7471 Tx: none Fax: (562) 436-9333 SITA: n/a
F: 1993 470 Head: Louis Valerio IATA: 403 ICAO: POLAR TIGER Net: http://www.polaraircargo.com

N806FT	Boeing 747-249F (SCD)	21827 / 406	N888KH	0079	0298	4 PW JT9D-7Q	371946	Freighter	CM-EJ	lsf UT Capital Corp.
N830FT	Boeing 747-121 (SF)	19642 / 10	N735SJ	0069	0593	4 PW JT9D-7A	340194	Freighter	HK-DE	lsf POLA / cvtd -121
N831FT	Boeing 747-121 (SF)	19648 / 17	N741SJ	0070	0493	4 PW JT9D-7A	340194	Freighter	HL-CF	lsf POLA / cvtd -121
N832FT	Boeing 747-121 (SF)	20347 / 103	N652SJ	0070	0693	4 PW JT9D-7A	340194	Freighter	LM-FG	lsf POLA / cvtd -121
N850FT	Boeing 747-122 (SF)	19755 / 61	N4710U	0070	0794	4 PW JT9D-7A	340194	Freighter	GK-DJ	lsf POLA / cvtd -122
N851FT	Boeing 747-122 (SF)	19756 / 66	N4711U	0070	0594	4 PW JT9D-7A	340194	Freighter	GK-EL	Kevin Milan / lsf POLA / cvtd -122
N852FT	Boeing 747-122 (SF)	19757 / 67	N4712U	0070	0594	4 PW JT9D-7A	340194	Freighter	BK-GL	Martin Moore / lsf POLA / cvtd -122
N853FT	Boeing 747-122 (SF)	19753 / 52	N4703U	0070	1194	4 PW JT9D-7A	340194	Freighter	GK-DF	lsf POLA / cvtd -122
N854FT	Boeing 747-122 (SF)	19754 / 60	N4704U	0070	0894	4 PW JT9D-7A	340194	Freighter	GK-DH	Mike Redmond / lsf POLA / cvtd -122
N855FT	Boeing 747-124 (SF)	19733 / 42	N630SJ	0070	0693	4 PW JT9D-7A	340194	Freighter	BL-GH	Peter Beckett / lsf TRIT / cvtd -124
N856FT	Boeing 747-132 (SF)	19897 / 82	VR-HKN	0070	0796	4 PW JT9D-7A	340194	Freighter	HK-AL	Ernest W. Bell Jr. / lsf POLA/cvtd -132
N857FT	Boeing 747-132 (SF)	20246 / 155	N624PL	0071	0195	4 PW JT9D-7A	340194	Freighter	HK-LM	Charles Barnes / lsf POLA / cvtd -132
N858FT	Boeing 747-123 (SF)	20109 / 90	N9670	1270	0895	4 PW JT9D-7A	340194	Freighter	EM-CK	R.David Hill,Jr. / lsf PSGroup/cvtd-123
N859FT	Boeing 747-123 (SF)	20326 / 133	N9674	0071	0895	4 PW JT9D-7AH	340194	Freighter	CK-EM	lsf PS Group Inc. / cvtd -123
N920FT	Boeing 747-249F (SCD)	22237 / 460	VR-HKO	0080	1196	4 PW JT9D-7Q	371946	Freighter	BF-AG	Brent C. Ogden / lsf POLA
N921FT	Boeing 747-283B (SF)	21575 / 358	N9727N	0079	0397	4 PW JT9D-70A	371946	Freighter	CG-DL	Grant Ledford / cvtd -283B (M)

418 registration type of aircraft cn/fn ex/ex* mfd del powered by mtow kg configuration selcal name/fln/specialitites/remarks

POLAR EXPRESS AIRWAYS, Inc. (Subsidiary of Donald Olson Enterprises, Inc. / Sister company of Olson Air Service)

Anchorage-Int'l & Nome, AK

2421 West 69th Court, Anchorage, AK 99502-2272, USA ☎ (907) 248-3848 Tx: none Fax: none SITA: n/a
F: 1994 n/a Head: Donald C. Olson Net: n/a Aircraft below MTOW 1361kg: Cessna 182 & Robinson R22

registration	type of aircraft	cn/fn	ex/ex*	mfd	del	powered by	mtow kg	configuration	selcal	name/fln/specialitites/remarks
☐ N4501L	Evangel Air 4500-300 II	001		0068	0894	2 LY IO-540-K1B5	2494			lsf pvt

POLARIS AIRCRAFT LEASING, Corp. = (POLA) (Subsidiary of General Electric Capital, Corp.)

San Francisco, CA

POLARIS

201 Mission Street, San Francisco, CA 94105, USA ☎ (650) 284-7400 Tx: n/a Fax: (650) 284-7466 SITA: n/a
F: 1974 n/a Head: Peter G. Pfendler Net: n/a New and used aircraft leasing, sales and financing company.
Owner / Lessor of the following (main) aircraft types: Airbus Ind. A300-600R (on order), Boeing 727-100 / 200, 737-200 / 300, 747-100 / 200, 767-300, DC-9-10 / 30 / 40 / 50, DC-10-10 / 30, L1011 & MD-80.
Aircraft leased from POLA are listed and mentioned as such under the leasing carriers.

POLYNESIAN AIRWAYS, Inc. = PLA

Honolulu-Int'l, HI

471 Aowena Place, Honolulu, HI 96819, USA ☎ (808) 836-3838 Tx: none Fax: none SITA: n/a
F: 1946 n/a Head: Robert S. Whittinghill ICAO: POLYAIR Net: n/a

registration	type of aircraft	cn/fn	ex/ex*	mfd	del	powered by	mtow kg	configuration	selcal	name/fln/specialitites/remarks
☐ N4342D	Beech Twin Bonanza D50	DH-95		0056	0467	2 LY GO-480-G2D6	2858	Freighter		
☐ N187R	Beech D18S	A-136	N44647	0046	1278	2 PW R-985-AN14B	3969	Freighter		
☐ N3785A	Beech SNB-5 (18)	12361		0042	0585	2 PW R-985-AN14B	3969	Freighter		lsf pvt
☐ N7969K	Beech H18	BA-702		0064	0794	2 PW R-985-AN14B	4491	Freighter		
☐ N954RJ	Beech C-45G (18)	AF-5	N9939Z	0051	0897	2 PW R-985-AN14B	3969	Freighter		

POND AIR EXPRESS, Inc. = PND

Madison-Dane County Regional/Truax Field, WI

3430 Miller Street, Office 1, Madison, WI 53704, USA ☎ (608) 249-5860 Tx: none Fax: (608) 249-6299 SITA: n/a
F: 1996 n/a Head: Guy B. Comer ICAO: POND AIR Net: http://www.pondair.com

registration	type of aircraft	cn/fn	ex/ex*	mfd	del	powered by	mtow kg	configuration	selcal	name/fln/specialitites/remarks
☐ N200LE	Cessna 310R II	310R1842		0079	1096	2 CO IO-520-M	2495	Y5		lsf Cleo Wisconsin Inc.
☐ N954PA	Cessna 208B Grand Caravan	208B0556		0096	0996	1 PWC PT6A-114A	3969	Y9		lsf Cleo Wisconsin Inc.
☐ N955PA	Cessna 208B Grand Caravan	208B0687		0098	0898	1 PWC PT6A-114A	3969	Y9		lsf Cleo Wisconsin Inc.

PONDEROSA AVIATION, Inc.

Taylor, AZ

PO Box 269, Taylor, AZ 85939, USA ☎ (520) 536-7771 Tx: none Fax: (520) 536-7655 SITA: n/a
F: 1976 n/a Head: Jay L. Perry Net: n/a

registration	type of aircraft	cn/fn	ex/ex*	mfd	del	powered by	mtow kg	configuration	selcal	name/fln/specialitites/remarks
☐ N1165Z	Twin (Aero) Commander 500B	500B-1555-198		0065	1088	2 LY IO-540-B1A5	3062			
☐ N40TC	Twin (Aero) Shrike Commander 500S	3091	SE-EWH	0070	0377	2 LY IO-540-E1B5	3062			
☐ N4664E	Twin (Aero) Shrike Commander 500S	500S-1786-9		0068	0980	2 LY IO-540-E1B5	3062			
☐ N4QS	Twin (Aero) Shrike Commander 500S	500S-1755-1	N5007E	0068	0378	2 LY IO-540-E1B5	3062			
☐ N8485P	Twin (Aero) Shrike Commander 500S	500S-1816-22		0068	1086	2 LY IO-540-E1B5	3062			
☐ N9027N	Twin (Aero) Shrike Commander 500S	3059		0069	0183	2 LY IO-540-E1B5	3062			
☐ N89PK	Twin (Aero) Commander 680F	680F-1192-99		0062	0694	2 LY IGSO-540-B1A	3629			

PORTERVILLE AVIATION, Inc.

Porterville-Municipal, GA

PO Box 8251, Porterville, CA 93257, USA ☎ (209) 784-9460 Tx: none Fax: (209) 784-2011 SITA: n/a
F: 1969 n/a Head: Eddie G. Wood Net: n/a

registration	type of aircraft	cn/fn	ex/ex*	mfd	del	powered by	mtow kg	configuration	selcal	name/fln/specialitites/remarks
☐ N4494F	Piper PA-23-160 Apache	23-1815		0059	0895	2 LY O-320-B	1724			
☐ N2028W	Beech Baron C55 (95-C55)	TE-87		0066	1296	2 CO IO-520-C	2404			
☐ N25647	Beech Baron 58	TH-301		0073	0493	2 CO IO-520-C	2449			
☐ N711RX	Beech Baron 58	TH-611		0075	0789	2 CO IO-520-C	2449			
☐ N1176Z	Twin (Aero) Commander 500B	500B-1549-196		0065	1182	2 LY IO-540-E1A5	3062			
☐ N828JB	Beech King Air 200	BB-795	N502EB	0081	0594	2 PWC PT6A-41	5670			lsf Walco International Inc.

POTOMAC Capital Investment, Corp. = (POTO)

Washington, DC

1801 K Street NW, Suite 900, Washington, DC 20006, USA ☎ (202) 775-4620 Tx: 284224 pcic ur Fax: (202) 857-5759 SITA: n/a
F: 1983 43 Head: Don McCallum Net: n/a Used aircraft leasing, sales and financing company.
Owner / Lessor of following (main) aircraft types: Boeing 737-300/747-200B/747-300, McDonnell Douglas DC-10-30, MD-11F & MD-82. Aircraft leased from POTO are listed and mentioned as such under the leasing carriers.

PRAIRIE AVIATION MUSEUM

Bloomington-Normal, IL

PO Box 856, Bloomington, IL 61702, USA ☎ (309) 663-7632 Tx: none Fax: (309) 663-8411 SITA: n/a
F: 1984 n/a Head: Norm Wingler Net: http://www.pamusa.com Aviation Museum conduction passenger flights with its DC-3 (beside other smaller aircraft in the Museum) for the members of the Museum-club.

registration	type of aircraft	cn/fn	ex/ex*	mfd	del	powered by	mtow kg	configuration	selcal	name/fln/specialitites/remarks
☐ N763A	Boeing (Douglas) DC-3C (C-53-DO)	4894	N70SA	0042	0784	2 PW R-1830	12202	Y26		Ozark Air Lines-colors

PRECISION AIR SERVICES, Inc.

Selma-Craig Field, AL

Craig Field, Hangar 209, Selma, AL 36701, USA ☎ (334) 872-6001 Tx: none Fax: (334) 874-3948 SITA: n/a
F: 1990 n/a Head: Benton J. Oliver Net: n/a

registration	type of aircraft	cn/fn	ex/ex*	mfd	del	powered by	mtow kg	configuration	selcal	name/fln/specialitites/remarks
☐ N204GP	Bell UH-1B (204)	1197	N3880A	0064	0397	1 LY T53-L-11	3856			
☐ N46942	Bell UH-1B (204)	743	63-8521	0063	0296	1 LY T53-L-11	3856			
☐ N63CD	Bell UH-1B (204)	500	62-1980	0062	0494	1 LY T53-L-11	3856			

PRECISION HELICOPTERS, Inc.

Newberg-Chehalem Airpark, OR

17770 NE Aviation Way, Newberg, OR 97132, USA ☎ (503) 537-0108 Tx: none Fax: (503) 538-2414 SITA: n/a
F: 1983 n/a Head: Nancy N. Sturdevant Net: n/a Aircraft below MTOW 1361kg: Hiller UH-12E & Hughes 269C (300C)

registration	type of aircraft	cn/fn	ex/ex*	mfd	del	powered by	mtow kg	configuration	selcal	name/fln/specialitites/remarks
☐ N84PH	Bell 206B JetRanger III	2253	N16853	0077	0196	1 AN 250-C20B	1451			

PREMIER JETS, Inc.

Portland-Hillsboro, OR

PO Box 91430, Portland, OR 97291, USA ☎ (541) 640-2927 Tx: none Fax: (541) 681-3064 SITA: n/a
F: 1985 n/a Head: Roger B. Kelsay Net: n/a

registration	type of aircraft	cn/fn	ex/ex*	mfd	del	powered by	mtow kg	configuration	selcal	name/fln/specialitites/remarks
☐ N340PJ	Cessna 340 II	340-0539	N5149J	0075	0789	2 CO TSIO-520-K	2710			
☐ N421PJ	Cessna 421C Golden Eagle III	421C0860	N35PM	0080	0190	2 CO GTSIO-520-L	3379			
☐ N500PJ	Mitsubishi MU-2L (MU-2B-36) Cargoliner	668	N500RM	0075	0790	2 GA TPE331-6-251M	5250			Cavenaugh SCD conversion
☐ N869P	Mitsubishi MU-2L (MU-2B-36) Cargoliner	692	N623DC	0077	1290	2 GA TPE331-6-251M	5250			Cavenaugh SCD conversion
☐ N652ND	Cessna 500 Citation	500-0277	N67MA	0075	0691	2 PWC JT15D-1	5216			lsf Electrical Distributing Inc.
☐ N711CW	Learjet 24	24-055	N511WH	0065	0590	2 GE CJ610-4	5897			
☐ N198T	Learjet 35A	35A-074	N100T	0076	0593	2 GA TFE731-2-2B	8301			
☐ N55CJ	Learjet 36	36-003	N36TA	0074	1093	2 GA TFE731-2-2B	8301			

PREMIER TRANS AIRE, Inc. = P3

San Jose-Int'l, CA

PO Box 240867, Honolulu, HI 96824-0867, USA ☎ (808) 833-5151 Tx: none Fax: (808) 833-4899 SITA: n/a
F: 1993 n/a Head: Wendrick K. Yee IATA: 435 Net: n/a

registration	type of aircraft	cn/fn	ex/ex*	mfd	del	powered by	mtow kg	configuration	selcal	name/fln/specialitites/remarks
☐ N6918L	Cessna 310K	310K0018		1265	0393	2 CO IO-470-VO	2359	Freighter		lsf Three Ten Air Inc.

PRIESTER CHARTER (Pal-Waukee Aviation, Inc. dba / Charter division of George J. Priester Aviation Service)

Chicago-Wheeling, IL

Pal-Waukee Airport, Wheeling, IL 60090, USA ☎ (847) 537-1200 Tx: none Fax: (847) 459-0778 SITA: n/a
F: 1979 n/a Head: Charles E. Priester Net: http://www.priesterav.com

registration	type of aircraft	cn/fn	ex/ex*	mfd	del	powered by	mtow kg	configuration	selcal	name/fln/specialitites/remarks
☐ N414GN	Beech King Air E90	LW-156		0075	1294	2 PWC PT6A-28	4581			lsf Newberg Flying Enterprise Inc.
☐ N429DM	Beech King Air C90	LJ-804	HK-3276	0078	1195	2 PWC PT6A-21	4377			lsf 310 Enterprises Inc.
☐ N100GP	Learjet 35	35-064	N291BC	0076	0185	2 GA TFE731-2-2B	8301			
☐ N600GP	Learjet 35A	35A-236	N900EC	0079	1194	2 GA TFE731-2-2B	8301			lsf Rubloff Aviation Llc
☐ N800GP	Learjet 35A	35A-158	N158NE	0078	0888	2 GA TFE731-2-2B	8301			
☐ N802JW	Learjet 35A	35A-453	N124MC	0082	0896	2 GA TFE731-2-2B	8301			lsf EAC Leasing Corp.
☐ N654E	Dassault Falcon 20C	164	N4367F	0068	0290	2 GE CF700-2C	12000			lsf MTI Vacations Inc.
☐ N865VP	Dassault Falcon 20F	360	N165PA	0077	0795	2 GE CF700-2D2	13000			lsf Volare Aviation Inc.
☐ N48PA	GAC (Grumman) G-159 Gulfstream I	018	N3UP	0859	0291	2 RR Dart 529-8X	16329			
☐ N999TF	Canadair CL-600S (CL-600-1A11) Challenger	1042	N999SR	0082	1190	2 LY ALF502L-2C	18779			lsf US Bancorp Leasing
☐ N7789	GAC (Grumman) G-1159 Gulfstream II	090	N883GA	0070	0293	2 RR Spey 511-8	29393			lsf Rynes Aviation Inc.

PRIMAC AIR = PMC (Primac Courier, Inc. dba)

Teterboro, NJ

PRIMAC AIR

333 Sylvan Avenue, Englewood Cliffs, NJ 07632, USA ☎ (201) 871-1800 Tx: none Fax: (201) 871-2324 SITA: n/a
F: 1989 n/a Head: Mary J. McLaughlin ICAO: PRIMAC Net: n/a

registration	type of aircraft	cn/fn	ex/ex*	mfd	del	powered by	mtow kg	configuration	selcal	name/fln/specialitites/remarks
☐ N87365	Cessna 310R II	310R0532		0076	0590	2 CO IO-520-M	2495	Freighter		
☐ N87464	Cessna 310R II	310R0576		0076	0589	2 CO IO-520-M	2495	Freighter		
☐ N30LT	Cessna 402C II	402C0259		0080	0197	2 CO TSIO-520-VB	3107	Freighter		
☐ N401SX	Cessna 402C II	402C0447		0081	0795	2 CO TSIO-520-VB	3107	Freighter		

PRINAIR (City Wings, Inc. dba)

Aguadilla-Rafael Hernandez, PR

PO Box 250319, Aguadilla, PR 00604, USA ☎ (787) 890-0697 Tx: none Fax: (787) 890-2333 SITA: n/a
F: 1990 n/a Head: Victor M. Villafane Net: n/a

registration	type of aircraft	cn/fn	ex/ex*	mfd	del	powered by	mtow kg	configuration	selcal	name/fln/specialitites/remarks
☐ N411CW	Twin (Aero) Commander 560	560-191	N2691B	0055	0597	2 LY GO-480-B	2722			
☐ N37098	Cessna 404 Titan II	404-0106	D-IORA	0077	0098	2 CO GTSIO-520-M	3810			

PRIOR AVIATION SERVICE, Inc. Buffalo-Greater Buffalo Int'l, NY

50 North Airport Drive, Buffalo, NY 14225-1437, USA ☎ (716) 633-1000 Tx: none Fax: (716) 633-1543 SITA: n/a
F: 1961 ☘ n/a Head: Jack B. Prior Net: n/a

☐ N137JP	Beech Baron 58	TH-1322	N6377M	0082	0691	2 CO IO-520-CB	2449			lsf Archer Aero & Marine Inc.
☐ N117JP	Piper PA-31-325 Navajo C/R	31-7612086	N769M	0076	1090	2 LY TIO-540-F2BD	2948			lsf Archer Aero & Marine Inc.
☐ N64JP	Piper PA-31-350 Navajo Chieftain	31-7652156		0076	0181	2 LY TIO-540-J2BD	3175			
☐ N75JP	Beech King Air E90	LW-158	N940SR	0076	0189	2 PWC PT6A-28	4581			
☐ N288JE	Learjet 35A	35A-288	N288NE	0080	0495	2 GA TFE731-2-2B	8301			

PRIORITY AIR, Inc. New Orleans-Lakefront, LA

PO Box 6379, New Orleans, LA 70174, USA ☎ (504) 366-2992 Tx: none Fax: (504) 365-2170 SITA: n/a
F: 1990 ☘ n/a Head: Michael E. Boatright Net: n/a

☐ N46SA	Fairchild (Swearingen) SA226T Merlin III	T-231	N20QN	0073	1098	2 GA TPE331-3U-303G	5670	EMS		
☐ N121BA	Mitsubishi MU-2J (MU-2B-35)	599	N304MA	0073	0493	2 GA TPE331-6-251M	4899	EMS		

PRIORITY AIR CHARTER (Jilco Industries, Inc. dba) Kidron-Stoltzfus Airfield, OH

PO Box 12, Kidron, OH 44636, USA ☎ (330) 698-4604 Tx: none Fax: (330) 698-3165 SITA: n/a
F: 1982 ☘ 30 Head: Ken L. Stoltzfus, Jr. Net: n/a

☐ N283PT	Cessna 421C Golden Eagle III	421C0852		0080	0398	2 CO GTSIO-520-L	3379	Y6		
☐ N1194F	Cessna 208B Grand Caravan	208B0593		0097	1097	1 PWC PT6A-114A	3969	Y9 / Freighter		
☐ N208JL	Cessna 208B Caravan I Super Cargomaster	208B0134	N9608B	0088	0397	1 PWC PT6A-114	3969	Freighter		
☐ N208PA	Cessna 208B Grand Caravan	208B0312	N208PF	0092	1297	1 PWC PT6A-114A	3969	Y9 / Freighter		
☐ N218PA	Cessna 208B Grand Caravan	208B0306	N218PF	0092	1297	1 PWC PT6A-114A	3969	Y9 / Freighter		

PRO AIR, Inc. = P9 / PRH Detroit-City, MI

101 Elliott Avenue West, Suite 500, Seattle, WA 98119-4220, USA ☎ (206) 623-2000 Tx: none Fax: (206) 623-6612 SITA: n/a
F: 1996 ☘ 275 Head: Kevin Stamper ICAO: PROHAWK Net: http://www.proair.com

☐ N360PR	Boeing 737-3U3	28742 / 2992	N60436*	0098	1198	2 CFMI CFM56-3C1	63276	F20Y88		lsf Heller Financial Inc.
☐ N460PR	Boeing 737-49R	28881 / 2833	N1790B*	1296	0697	2 CFMI CFM56-3C1	65091	F8Y138	CK-JR	lsf GECA
☐ N461PR	Boeing 737-49R	28882 / 2845	N35050*	1296	0697	2 CFMI CFM56-3C1	65091	F8Y138	CL-AP	
☐ N462PR	Boeing 737-43Q	28494 / 2839	B-18677	0096	1298	2 CFMI CFM56-3C1	65091	F8Y138		lsf BOUL

PROFESSIONAL FLIGHT CREW SERVICES, Inc. (Cirrus Air International, Inc.) Melbourne-Int'l, FL

1371 General Aviation Drive, Hangar 19, Melbourne, FL 32935, USA ☎ (407) 254-8490 Tx: none Fax: (407) 254-2763 SITA: n/a
F: 1987 ☘ 65 Head: Gary L. Flaugher Net: n/a International flights are operated under the name CIRRUS AIR INTERNATIONAL Inc., a sister company (same headquarters & fleet).

☐ N206BZ	Bell 206B JetRanger III	2851	C-GAVK	0079	0996	1 AN 250-C20B	1451	4 Pax		lsf Flaugher Aviation Service
☐ N10UH	Cessna 500 Citation	500-0304	N70U	0076	0483	2 PWC JT15D-1	5216	5 Pax / EMS		lsf University of AL Critical Care Trsp
☐ N105GA	Learjet 24	24-116	N51B	0066	1096	2 GE CJ610-4	5897	5 Pax / Frtr		lsf W & M Co.
☐ N39KM	Learjet 24B	24B-198	N21XB	0069	0494	2 GE CJ610-6	6123	5 Pax / Frtr		lsf Cirrus Air Int'l Inc.
☐ N289SA	Learjet 24D	24D-289	N131MA	0074	1095	2 GE CJ610-6	6123	5 Pax / Frtr		lsf BL Bennett Aviation
☐ N972H	Learjet 24D	24D-322	N105GL	0076	1094	2 GE CJ610-6	6123	5 Pax / Frtr		lsf Cita Aviation Leasing Inc.
☐ N125JL	Learjet 25B	25B-088	N42FE	0072	0297	2 GE CJ610-6	6804	8 Pax / Frtr		lsf Universal Jet Aviation Inc.
☐ N17AH	Learjet 25D	25D-316	N1AH	0080	0495	2 GE CJ610-8A	6804	8 Pax / Frtr		lsf Astec Industries Inc.
☐ N207JC	Learjet 25D	25D-207	I-LEAR	0076	0896	2 GE CJ610-6	6804	8 Pax / Frtr		lsf BL Bennett Aviation Llc
☐ N225DS	Learjet 25	25-025	N242AG	0069	1195	2 GE CJ610-6	6804	8 Pax / Frtr		lsf Sagittarius Leasing Inc./tbr N111LM
☐ N325JL	Learjet 25D	25D-215	N44FE	0077	0297	2 GE CJ610-8A	6804	8 Pax / Frtr		lsf Universal Jet Aviation Inc.
☐ N425JL	Learjet 25B	25B-127	N222AK	0073	0297	2 GE CJ610-6	6804	8 Pax / Frtr		lsf Dolphin Aviation Inc.
☐ N711NM	Learjet 25D	25D-224	N50B	0077	0197	2 GE CJ610-8A	6804	8 Pax / Frtr		lsf Aero Charters Nashville Inc.
☐ N717EP	Learjet 25D	25D-255	N25GJ	0078	0497	2 GE CJ610-8A	6804	8 Pax / Frtr		lsf Apple 10 Aero Llc
☐ N74RD	Learjet 25D	25D-260	N43783	0079	0796	2 GE CJ610-8A	6804	8 Pax / Frtr		lsf Private Jets/sub-lst Oklahoma Exec
☐ N185BA	Learjet 35	35-025	N510LJ	0075	0995	2 GA TFE731-2-2B	8301	8 Pax / Frtr		lsf N185BA Lear Inc.
☐ N450KK	Learjet 35A	35A-450		0081	1096	2 GA TFE731-2-2B	8301	8 Pax / Frtr		lsf BYR737
☐ N50AK	Learjet 35A	35A-172	SX-BFJ	0078	0397	2 GA TFE731-2-2B	8301	8 Pax / Frtr		lsf Anker Inc.
☐ N110ET	Learjet 55	55-023	N7784	0082	0494	2 GA TFE731-3AR-2B	9752	9 Pax / Frtr		lsf Morse Operations Inc.

PRO-LIFT HELICOPTERS (Evan E. Moseley dba) Litchfield-Private Heliport, AZ

202 West Sonoma Drive, Litchfield Park, AZ 85340, USA ☎ (602) 935-3703 Tx: none Fax: none SITA: n/a
F: 1992 ☘ n/a Head: Evan E. Moseley Net: n/a

☐ N100PL	Kaman HH-43F (K600) Huskie	64	59-1583	0059	0694	1 LY T53-L-11A	4150			lsf Moseley Aviation / cvtd HH-43B
☐ N90944	Kaman HH-43F (K600) Huskie	140	62-4514	0062	0792	1 LY T53-L-11A	4150			lsf Moseley Aviation / cvtd HH-43B

PRO MECH AIR, Inc. = Z3 Ketchikan-Harbor SPB, AK

1515 Tongass Avenue, Ketchikan, AK 99901, USA ☎ (907) 225-3845 Tx: none Fax: (907) 247-3875 SITA: n/a
F: 1977 ☘ 15 Head: Kevin M. Hack Net: n/a

☐ N44309	Cessna A185F Skywagon II	18503486		0078	0284	1 CO IO-550-D	1520			lsf pvt / Floats
☐ N444BA	Cessna A185E Skywagon	185-1433		0068	0793	1 CO IO-520-D	1520			Floats
☐ N531H	Cessna A185E Skywagon	185-1348		0068	1190	1 CO IO-520-D	1520			lsf pvt / Floats
☐ N471PM	De Havilland DHC-2 Beaver I	1366	N55235	0052	0292	1 PW R-985	2313			lsf pvt / Floats
☐ N4787C	De Havilland DHC-2 Beaver I	1330	C-FGMK	0058	0489	1 PW R-985	2313			Floats
☐ N64393	De Havilland DHC-2 Beaver I	845	54-1701	0054	0595	1 PW R-985	2313			lsf Mink Bay Partners / Floats
☐ N64397	De Havilland DHC-2 Beaver I	760	53-7943	0055	0692	1 PW R-985	2313			Floats
☐ N995WA	De Havilland DHC-2 Beaver I	1100	C-GAEG	0056	0895	1 PW R-985	2313			lsf pvt / Floats

PROTO FLIGHT (Minta, Inc. dba) Wasilla, AK

PO Box 872734, Wasilla, AK 99687, USA ☎ (907) 746-4009 Tx: none Fax: (907) 746-4020 SITA: n/a
F: 1996 ☘ n/a Head: William R. Russell Net: n/a

☐ N16SC	Piper PA-31-310 Navajo	31-639		0070	0696	2 LY TIO-540-A1A	2948			

PROVIMI Puerto Rico (Provimentos, Inc. dba) San Juan-Isla Grande/Fernando Luis Ribas Dominicci, PR

Box 248, Vega Baja, PR 00694, USA ☎ (787) 726-1287 Tx: none Fax: (787) 858-0218 SITA: n/a
F: 1990 ☘ n/a Head: Eliott O. Reyes Net: n/a

☐ N9697B	Cessna 208B Caravan I Super Cargomaster	208B0151		0089	1189	1 PWC PT6A-114	3969	Freighter		
☐ N9697C	Cessna 208B Grand Caravan	208B0355		0093	0393	1 PWC PT6A-114A	3969	Freighter / Pax		

PSA AIRLINES, Inc. = JIA (US Airways Express) (Subsidiary of US Airways/formerly Jetstream Int'l Airlines, Inc. & Vee Neal, Inc.) Dayton-Int'l, OH

3400 Terminal Drive, Vandalia, OH 45377, USA ☎ (513) 454-1116 Tx: none Fax: (513) 454-5828 SITA: n/a
F: 1969 ☘ 770 Head: Richard E. Pfennig IATA: 320 ICAO: BLUE STREAK Net: http://www.flypsa.com
All aircraft are operated as US AIRWAYS EXPRESS (in full such colours & both titles), a commuter system to provide feeder connection at US Airways major hubs, using US flight numbers.

☐ N328JS	Dornier 328-110	3030	D-CDHP*	0094	0495	2 PWC PW119B	13990	Y31		op in US Airways Express-colors
☐ N422JS	Dornier 328-110	3018	D-CDHC*	0094	0795	2 PWC PW119B	13990	Y32		cvtd -100 / op in US Airways Express-cs
☐ N423JS	Dornier 328-110	3032	D-CDHR*	0095	0795	2 PWC PW119B	13990	Y31		op in US Airways Express-colors
☐ N424JS	Dornier 328-110	3033	D-CDHS*	0095	0795	2 PWC PW119B	13990	Y31		op in US Airways Express-colors
☐ N425JS	Dornier 328-110	3037	D-CDXC*	0095	0795	2 PWC PW119B	13990	Y31		op in US Airways Express-colors
☐ N426JS	Dornier 328-110	3038	D-CDXD*	0095	0795	2 PWC PW119B	13990	Y31		op in US Airways Express-colors
☐ N427JS	Dornier 328-110	3039	D-CDXE*	0095	0795	2 PWC PW119B	13990	Y31		op in US Airways Express-colors
☐ N429JS	Dornier 328-110	3043	D-CDXJ*	0095	0795	2 PWC PW119B	13990	Y31		op in US Airways Express-colors
☐ N430JS	Dornier 328-110	3044	D-CDXK*	0095	0795	2 PWC PW119B	13990	Y31		op in US Airways Express-colors
☐ N431JS	Dornier 328-110	3028	D-CDHN*	0095	0795	2 PWC PW119B	13990	Y32		op in US Airways Express-colors
☐ N432JS	Dornier 328-110	3045	D-CDXL*	0095	0795	2 PWC PW119B	13990	Y31		op in US Airways Express-colors
☐ N433JS	Dornier 328-110	3047	D-CDXN*	0095	0795	2 PWC PW119B	13990	Y32		op in US Airways Express-colors
☐ N434JS	Dornier 328-110	3051	D-CDXS*	0095	0895	2 PWC PW119B	13990	Y32		op in US Airways Express-colors
☐ N436JS	Dornier 328-110	3052	D-CDXT*	0095	0895	2 PWC PW119B	13990	Y32		op in US Airways Express-colors
☐ N437JS	Dornier 328-110	3055	D-CDXW*	0095	0995	2 PWC PW119B	13990	Y32		op in US Airways Express-colors
☐ N438JS	Dornier 328-110	3056	D-CDXX*	0095	0995	2 PWC PW119B	13990	Y32		op in US Airways Express-colors
☐ N439JS	Dornier 328-110	3057	D-CDXY*	0095	1095	2 PWC PW119B	13990	Y32		op in US Airways Express-colors
☐ N440JS	Dornier 328-110	3058	D-CDXZ*	0095	1095	2 PWC PW119B	13990	Y32		op in US Airways Express-colors
☐ N441JS	Dornier 328-110	3059	D-CDXA*	0095	1195	2 PWC PW119B	13990	Y32		op in US Airways Express-colors
☐ N442JS	Dornier 328-110	3060	D-CDXC*	0095	1195	2 PWC PW119B	13990	Y32		op in US Airways Express-colors
☐ N457PS	Dornier 328-110	3048	D-CDXP*	0096	0596	2 PWC PW119B	13990	Y32		op in US Airways Express-colors
☐ N458PS	Dornier 328-110	3068	D-CDXS*	0096	0596	2 PWC PW119B	13990	Y32		op in US Airways Express-colors
☐ N459PS	Dornier 328-110	3070	D-CDXW*	0096	0696	2 PWC PW119B	13990	Y32		op in US Airways Express-colors
☐ N460PS	Dornier 328-110	3061	D-CDXD*	0096	0796	2 PWC PW119B	13990	Y32		op in US Airways Express-colors
☐ N461PS	Dornier 328-110	3075	D-CDXC*	0096	0796	2 PWC PW119B	13990	Y32		op in US Airways Express-colors

PS AIR, Inc. (Affiliated with PS Sales, Inc.) Cedar Rapids-Municipal, IA

3411 Wright Brothers Blvd, Cedar Rapids, IA 52404, USA ☎ (319) 846-3600 Tx: none Fax: (319) 846-3605 SITA: n/a
F: 1993 ☘ n/a Head: Gordon Ch. Peterson Net: n/a

☐ N8123N	Beech Baron 58	TH-1671		0092	0398	2 CO IO-520-CB	2449			lsf PS Sales Inc.
☐ N93KA	Beech King Air F90	LA-24		0080	0293	2 PWC PT6A-135	4967			

420 registration type of aircraft cn/fn ex/ex* mfd del powered by mtow kg configuration selcal name/fln/specialitites/remarks

PTARMIGAN AIR (Steven C. Williams) — **Anchorage-Lake Hood SPB, AK**

PO Box 190834, Anchorage, AK 99519-0834, USA ☎ (907) 248-4421 Tx: none Fax: (907) 243-1996 SITA: n/a
F: 1992 n/a Head: Steven C. Williams Net: n/a

☐ N2658S	Cessna A185F Skywagon	18502260		0073	0398	1 CO IO-520-D	1520			Floats / Wheel-Skis
☐ N144Q	De Havilland DHC-2 Beaver I	1465		0061	0496	1 PW R-985	2313			Floats / Wheel-Skis

PUERTO RICO AIRWAYS, Corp. — **New York-JFK**

PO Box 300688, JFK Airport Station, Jamaica, NY 11430-0688, USA ☎ (718) 342-7965 Tx: none Fax: (718) 922-9256 SITA: n/a
F: 1998 n/a Head: Guillermo Ortiz-Osorio Net: n/a Presently being set-up. Intends to start operations with 2 Boeing 727-200 aircraft during 1999.

PUGET SOUND SEAPLANES (American Lake Marina, Inc. dba) — **Tacoma-American Lake SPB, WA**

9306 Veterans Drive S.W., Tacoma, WA 98498, USA ☎ (206) 582-3777 Tx: none Fax: (206) 582-0391 SITA: n/a
F: 1983 n/a Head: Robert D. McMahon Net: n/a

☐ N41PS	De Havilland DHC-2 Beaver I	746	N746DB	0054	0291	1 PW R-985	2313			Floats
☐ N460DB	De Havilland DHC-2 Beaver I	914	C-GTER	0055	0594	1 PW R-985	2313			Floats

QUEEN BEE AIR SPECIALTIES, Inc. — **Rigby-Jefferson County, ID**

PO Box 245, Rigby, ID 83442, USA ☎ (208) 745-7654 Tx: none Fax: (208) 745-6672 SITA: n/a
F: 1978 n/a Head: Charles A. Kemper Net: n/a Ag-aircraft below MTOW 5000kg: Air Tractor AT-402/502 & Piper PA-36

☐ N5035K	Air Tractor AT-802 (F)	802-0048		0097	0997	1 PWC PT6A-65AG	7257	Tanker/Sprayer		181
☐ N91092	Air Tractor AT-802A (F)	802A-0005		0093	0494	1 PWC PT6A-65AG	7257	Tanker/Sprayer		182

QUICK AIR (Quick Air Freight, Inc. dba) — **Danville-Vermilion County, IL**

22655 North Bowman, Danville, IL 61832, USA ☎ (217) 442-4674 Tx: none Fax: (217) 442-4882 SITA: n/a
F: 1982 n/a Head: William Ingram Net: n/a

☐ N1031W	Beech Bonanza A36	E-403		0073	0582	1 CO IO-520-BA	1633			
☐ N4941A	Cessna 310R II	310R1407		0078	1094	2 CO IO-520-M	2495			
☐ N6126	Beech 3N (18)	CA-73		0051	0694	2 PW R-985-AN14B	3969	Freighter		

RACO HELICOPTERS, Corp. — **Belmar/Farmingdale-Allaire, NJ**

PO Box 555, Farmingdale, NJ 07727, USA ☎ (732) 938-5335 Tx: none Fax: (732) 938-4462 SITA: n/a
F: 1974 n/a Head: John Ford Net: n/a

☐ N2297G	Bell 206B JetRanger III	3613		0082	0687	1 AN 250-C20J	1451			

RADER AVIATION, Inc. = GBR (formerly Rader's Greenbrier Airlines) — **Lewisburg-Greenbrier Valley, WV**

602 Lincoln Street, Summersville, WV 26651, USA ☎ (304) 872-3660 Tx: none Fax: (304) 872-2136 SITA: n/a
F: 1939 8 Head: Gerald L. Rader, II ICAO: GREENBRIER AIR Net: n/a Aircraft below MTOW 1361 kg: Cessna 172

☐ N123RA	Cessna 310R II	310R0221	N5101J	0075	1079	2 CO IO-520-M	2495			
☐ N60RR	Cessna 421C Golden Eagle III	421C0885		0080	0195	2 CO GTSIO-520-L	3379			
☐ N62SK	Beech King Air C90	LJ-784	YV-254CP	0078	0296	2 PWC PT6A-21	4377			lsf Little Laurel Leasing Inc.
☐ N200BE	Beech King Air 200	BB-832	N45BR	0081	1193	2 PWC PT6A-41	5670			lsf Land Use Corp.
☐ N500UB	Cessna 560 Citation V	560-0052	N500LE	0090	0194	2 PWC JT15D-5A	7212			lsf Pomeroy Transport Inc.

RAINBOW HELICOPTERS, Inc. — **Redmond-Roberts Field, OR**

PO Box 863, Redmond, OR 97756, USA ☎ (541) 548-3255 Tx: none Fax: none SITA: n/a
F: 1992 n/a Head: David W. Evans Net: n/a

☐ N5016G	Bell 206B JetRanger III	2624		0079	0497	1 AN 250-C20B	1451			
☐ N921RB	Bell 206B JetRanger III	2742	N2760X	0079	0595	1 AN 250-C20B	1451			

RAINIER HELICOPTERS (Rainier Helicopter Logging, Inc. dba) — **Everett-Snohomish County/Paine Field, WA**

12515 Willows Road NE, Suite 125, Kirkland, WA 98034-8795, USA ☎ (425) 825-8411 Tx: none Fax: (425) 825-8511 SITA: n/a
F: 1991 n/a Head: Lon A. Halvorson Net: n/a

☐ N50330	Bell UH-1B (204)	598	62-2078	0062	0897	1 LY T53-L-11	3856			lsf Delta III Inc.
☐ N88992	Bell UH-1B (204)	298	61-718	0061	0091	1 LY T53-L-11	3856			lsf pvt
☐ N6257P	Bell UH-1H (205)	4099	63-8807	0063	0596	1 LY T53-L-13	4309			lsf Charlie I Inc.
☐ N313KA	Kaman K-1200 K-Max	A94-0019		0096	0597	1 LY T5317A-1	2722			

RAM AIR, Inc. — **Anchorage-Int'l, AK**

PO Box 221363, Anchorage, AK 99522, USA ☎ (907) 345-4559 Tx: none Fax: (907) 345-4559 SITA: n/a
F: 1988 n/a Head: Douglas A. Burts Net: n/a

☐ N17DL	Twin (Aero) Shrike Commander 500S	500S-1866-42		0069	0593	2 LY IO-540-B1A	3062			
☐ N6114X	Twin (Aero) Commander 500B	500B-924-9		0060	0191	2 LY IO-540-B1A5	3062			
☐ N999GB	Twin (Aero) Commander 500U	500U-1717-27		0067	0890	2 LY IO-540-E1B5	3062			

RAM AIR FREIGHT, Inc. = REX — **Raleigh-Durham Int'l, NC**

PO Box 80123, Raleigh, NC 27623-0123, USA ☎ (919) 840-0448 Tx: none Fax: none SITA: n/a
F: 1982 15 Head: James G. McClure ICAO: RAM EXPRESS Net: n/a Aircraft below MTOW 1361 kg: AA-5A

☐ N7748J	Piper PA-32-260B Cherokee SIX	32-1152		0069	1096	1 LY O-540-E4B5	1542	Freighter		lsf Bellefonte Inc.
☐ N44RA	Beech Baron B55 (95-B55)	TC-916		0065	0386	2 CO IO-470-L	2313	Freighter		lsf Bellefonte Inc.
☐ N6WF	Beech Baron B55 (95-B55)	TC-794		0064	0490	2 CO IO-470-L	2313	Freighter		lsf Bellefonte Inc.
☐ N11HW	Beech Baron 58	TH-271		0073	0495	2 CO IO-520-C	2449	Freighter		lsf Bellefonte Inc.
☐ N707RA	Beech Baron 58	TH-257		0072	0593	2 CO IO-520-C	2449	Freighter		lsf Bellefonte Inc.
☐ N7351R	Beech Baron 58	TH-481		0074	0490	2 CO IO-520-C	2449	Freighter		lsf Bellefonte Inc.

RAMP 66 = PPK (Grand Strand Aviation, Inc. dba) — **North Myrtle Beach-Grand Strand, SC**

PO Box 1499, North Myrtle Beach, SC 29598, USA ☎ (843) 272-5337 Tx: none Fax: (843) 272-5822 SITA: n/a
F: 1970 n/a Head: Edward S. Bauer ICAO: PELICAN Net: n/a Aircraft below MTOW 1361kg: Cessna 172 & Piper PA-28

☐ N36575	Piper PA-32RT-300 Lance II	32R-7885195		0078	0187	1 LY IO-540-K1G5D	1633			
☐ N136B	Beech Bonanza A36	E-390		0073	0495	1 CO IO-520-BA	1633			
☐ N1763W	Beech Bonanza A36	E-406		0072	1195	1 CO IO-520-BA	1633			
☐ N72GP	Beech Bonanza 36	E-59		0068	0188	1 CO IO-520-B	1633			
☐ N31BW	Beech Baron 58	TH-490		0074	0283	2 CO IO-520-C	2449			
☐ N8121R	Beech Baron 58	TH-690		0075	0689	2 CO IO-520-C	2449			
☐ N1436G	Cessna 402B	402B0581		0074	0294	2 CO TSIO-520-E	2858			
☐ N1577T	Cessna 402B	402B0546		0073	0592	2 CO TSIO-520-E	2858			
☐ N4165G	Cessna 402B II	402B1212		0076	0390	2 CO TSIO-520-E	2858			
☐ N5205J	Cessna 402B	402B0892		0075	1193	2 CO TSIO-520-E	2858			
☐ N87CG	Cessna 402B	402B0883		0075	0191	2 CO TSIO-520-E	2858			
☐ N885GP	Cessna 402B	402B0894		0075	0991	2 CO TSIO-520-E	2858			

RAPID AIR (Sparta Aviation Service, Inc. dba) — **Grand Rapids-Kent County Int'l, MI**

5500 44th Street, S.E., Grand Rapids, MI 49508, USA ☎ (616) 957-5050 Tx: none Fax: (616) 957-2151 SITA: n/a
F: 1965 n/a Head: Loretta A. Vantine Net: n/a

☐ N1240G	Cessna 310Q II	310Q1091		0074	1076	2 CO IO-470-VO	2404			
☐ N1249G	Cessna 310Q II	310Q1100		0074	0379	2 CO IO-470-VO	2404			
☐ N4084L	Cessna 310Q	310Q0493		0072	0376	2 CO IO-470-VO	2404			
☐ N69811	Cessna 310Q II	310Q0992		0073	1077	2 CO IO-470-VO	2404			
☐ N36934	Cessna 414A Chancellor III	414A0486		0080	0988	2 CO TSIO-520-NB	3062			
☐ N6362X	Cessna 402B II	402B1325		0078	1278	2 CO TSIO-520-E	2858			
☐ N707BA	Boeing (Douglas) DC-3C (C-47B-30-DK)	33046	C-GWUH	0045	0993	2 PW R-1830	12202	Freighter		std GRR

RAS, Inc. = RAS — **Columbus/West Point/Starkville-Golden Triangle Regional, MS**

1900 Airport Road, Columbus, MS 39701-9574, USA ☎ (228) 328-9312 Tx: none Fax: (228) 328-1981 SITA: n/a
F: 1985 9 Head: Michael J. Ratliff ICAO: SHANHIL Net: n/a Aircraft below MTOW 1361 kg: Cessna 152

☐ N25TT	Beech Bonanza A36	E-1072		0077	1293	1 CO IO-520-BA	1633			
☐ N98709	Cessna 402B II	402B1059		0076	0395	2 CO TSIO-520-E	2858			

RASMARK JET CHARTER, Inc. — **El Paso-Int'l, TX**

6915 Boeing Drive, El Paso, TX 79925, USA ☎ (915) 772-4616 Tx: none Fax: (915) 779-5387 SITA: n/a
F: 1982 25 Head: Mark B. Rasmusson Net: http://www.rasmark.com

☐ N98MR	Twin (Aero) Turbo Commander 690	11022	N14BH	0072	0695	2 GA TPE331-5-251K	4649			
☐ N44CP	Learjet 24B	24B-185	N754M	0069	0689	2 GE CJ610-6	6123			
☐ N25MR	Learjet 25C	25C-129	N71DM	0073	0394	2 GE CJ610-6	6804			
☐ N25TK	Learjet 25B	25B-100		0073	1291	2 GE CJ610-6	6804			
☐ N47MR	Learjet 25B	25B-101	N821AW	0073	0689	2 GE CJ610-6	6804			
☐ N45MR	Dassault Falcon 20C	123	N513T	0067	0592	2 GE CF700-2C	12000			

421 registration type of aircraft cn/fn ex/ex* mfd del powered by mtow kg configuration selcal name/fln/specialitites/remarks

RAYTHEON AIRCRAFT SERVICES, Inc. (Subsidiary of Raytheon Aircraft, Co. / formerly United Beechcraft, Inc.)

Birmingham-Int'l, AL

Flight Ops, Charter Dept, 1 Perimeter Park S, S100N, Birmingham, AL 35243, USA ☎ (205) 591-6830 Tx: none Fax: (205) 599-7643 SITA: n/a

F: 1991 👥 n/a Head: David Patterson Net: n/a In addition to the listed commercially operated aircraft also offers turnkey management services (for additional executive aircraft) to private corporate aircraft owners.

registration	type of aircraft	cn/fn	ex/ex*	mfd	del	powered by	mtow kg	configuration	selcal	name/fln/specialitites/remarks
☐ N333W	Beech Baron E55	TE-1172	N333T	0079	0293	2 CO IO-520-CB	2404			
☐ N1135G	Beech King Air C90B	LJ-1488		0097	0897	2 PWC PT6A-21	4581			lsf Executive Air Llc
☐ N3083K	Beech King Air C90B	LJ-1378		0094	1194	2 PWC PT6A-21	4581			lsf Special Devices Inc.
☐ N3237K	Beech King Air C90B	LJ-1390		0095	1095	2 PWC PT6A-21	4581			lsf City Transportation Llc
☐ N4488L	Beech King Air C90B	LJ-1423	N3253Q	0095	0196	2 PWC PT6A-21	4581			lsf Kidenfair Management Systems
☐ N500EQ	Beech King Air C90B	LJ-1387	N500ED	0094	0195	2 PWC PT6A-21	4581			lsf Dearborn Associates
☐ N862CC	Beech King Air C90B	LJ-1499		0098	0398	2 PWC PT6A-21	4581			
☐ N24CV	Beech King Air B200	BB-1524	N1024A	0096	0896	2 PWC PT6A-42	5670			lsf Calico Ventures Llc
☐ N345WK	Beech King Air B200	BB-1580	N200KA	0097	1097	2 PWC PT6A-42	5670			lsf AviaServ Llc
☐ N50PM	Beech King Air B200	BB-1570	N1120Z	0097	1097	2 PWC PT6A-42	5670			lsf Mallen Industries Inc.
☐ N833BK	Beech King Air B200	BB-1239	N7250V	0085	0291	2 PWC PT6A-42	5670			lsf Jamm Aviation Inc.
☐ N860CC	Beech King Air 300	FA-147	N3085Z	0088	0295	2 PWC PT6A-60A	6350			lsf Citation Corp.
☐ N14VR	Beech Starship 2000	NC-22	N14VP	0091	0595	2 PWC PT6A-67A	6627			
☐ N515JS	Beech Starship 2000A	NC-52	N1564Q	0095	0196	2 PWC PT6A-67A	6627			lsf Osborn Energy Llc
☐ N5549B	Beech Starship 2000	NC-15		0091	0993	2 PWC PT6A-67A	6627			
☐ N8300S	Beech Starship 2000A	NC-40		0093	0696	2 PWC PT6A-67A	6627			lsf PMB Aviation Inc.
☐ N999RF	Beech Starship 2000	NC-9	N2009W	0091	1295	2 PWC PT6A-67A	6627			
☐ N1083N	Beech King Air 350 (B300)	FL-153		0097	0197	2 PWC PT6A-60A	6804			lsf Calabasas BCD Inc.
☐ N220CL	Beech King Air 350 (B300)	FL-28	N203HG	0091	0498	2 PWC PT6A-60A	6804			lsf Blackrock Mountain Inc.
☐ N2298B	Beech King Air 350 (B300)	FL-198		0098	0698	2 PWC PT6A-60A	6804			lsf Executive Air Llc
☐ N350LL	Beech King Air 350 (B300)	FL-157	N1093Q	0097	0297	2 PWC PT6A-60A	6804			lsf Leavitt Leasing Co.
☐ N861CC	Beech King Air 350 (B300)	FL-94	N8194Q	0093	0296	2 PWC PT6A-60A	6350			lsf Citation Corp.
☐ N100AG	Beech Beechjet 400A	RK-150	N1135U	0097	0198	2 PWC JT15D-5	7303			lsf Richard S. Allen Aviation Inc.
☐ N197SD	Beech Beechjet 400A	RK-126	N3226B	0096	0497	2 PWC JT15D-5	7303			lsf Bur-Con Llc
☐ N53MS	Beech Beechjet 400A	RK-64	N8164M	0093	1193	2 PWC JT15D-5	7303			lsf Image Air Llc
☐ N57B	Beech Beechjet 400A	RK-36	N56327	0092	0997	2 PWC JT15D-5	7303			lsf General Electric Capital Corp.
☐ N58AU	Beech Beechjet 400	RJ-45	N3145F	0088	0694	2 PWC JT15D-5	7158			lsf Highland Aviation Llc
☐ N127YV	Beech 1900C-1 Airliner	UC-127	N530LX	1090	0596	2 PWC PT6A-65B	7530			lsf Raytheon Aircraft Credit Corp.
☐ N154YV	Beech 1900C-1 Airliner	UC-154		0491	0596	2 PWC PT6A-65B	7530			lsf Raytheon Aircraft Credit Corp.
☐ N155YV	Beech 1900C-1 Airliner	UC-155		0491	0797	2 PWC PT6A-65B	7530			lsf Raytheon Aircraft Credit Corp.
☐ N1562C	Beech 1900C-1 Airliner	UC-26	N31228	0088	0896	2 PWC PT6A-65B	7530			lsf Raytheon Aircraft Credit Corp.
☐ N31134	Beech 1900C-1 Airliner	UC-42		0088	0895	2 PWC PT6A-65B	7530	Y19		lsf Raytheon Aircraft Credit Corp.
☐ N34010	Beech 1900C-1 Airliner	UC-3	N917RM	0087	0295	2 PWC PT6A-65B	7530			lsf Raytheon Aircraft Credit Corp.
☐ N23SK	Hawker 700A (HS 125-700A)	257016 / NA0216	N23SB	0077	0495	2 GA TFE731-3R-1H	11567			lsf PNC Leasing Corp.

RAYTHEON TRAVEL AIR, Company (Subsidiary of Raytheon Aircraft, Co.)

Wichita-Mid Continent, KS

PO Box 2902, Wichita, KS 67201, USA ☎ (316) 676-8000 Tx: none Fax: (316) 676-8600 SITA: n/a

F: 1997 👥 180 Head: Gary E. Hart Net: n/a Aircraft are operated under the TravelAir fractional ownership program in which an owner purchases a portion of the shares in a individual aircraft & contract Raytheon to manage it.

registration	type of aircraft	cn/fn	ex/ex*	mfd	del	powered by	mtow kg	configuration	selcal	name/fln/specialitites/remarks
☐ N702TA	Beech King Air B200	BB-1573		0097	0597	2 PWC PT6A-42	5670	Executive		
☐ N703TA	Beech King Air B200	BB-1574		0097	0597	2 PWC PT6A-42	5670	Executive		
☐ N705TA	Beech King Air B200	BB-1575		0097	0597	2 PWC PT6A-42	5670	Executive		
☐ N706TA	Beech King Air B200	BB-1656		0099	0299	2 PWC PT6A-42	5670	Executive		
☐ N713TA	Beech King Air B200	BB-1610		0097	1297	2 PWC PT6A-42	5670	Executive		
☐ N716TA	Beech King Air B200	BB-1509	N109NB	0095	0198	2 PWC PT6A-42	5670	Executive		
☐ N719TA	Beech King Air B200	BB-1619		0098	0698	2 PWC PT6A-42	5670	Executive		
☐ N724TA	Beech King Air B200	BB-1607		0098	0398	2 PWC PT6A-42	5670	Executive		
☐ N743TA	Beech King Air B200	BB-1623		0098	1198	2 PWC PT6A-42	5670	Executive		
☐ N744TA	Beech King Air B200	BB-1627		0098	1298	2 PWC PT6A-42	5670	Executive		
☐ N788TA	Beech King Air B200	BB-1648		0098	0199	2 PWC PT6A-42	5670	Executive		
☐ N110TG	Beech Beechjet 400A	RK-123	N1123Z	0096	0797	2 PWC JT15D-5	7303	Executive		
☐ N708TA	Beech Beechjet 400A	RK-178		0097	0198	2 PWC JT15D-5	7303	Executive		
☐ N709TA	Beech Beechjet 400A	RK-180		0097	0498	2 PWC JT15D-5	7303	Executive		
☐ N710TA	Beech Beechjet 400A	RK-183		0097	1297	2 PWC JT15D-5	7303	Executive		
☐ N712TA	Beech Beechjet 400A	RK-186		0097	0698	2 PWC JT15D-5	7303	Executive		
☐ N715TA	Beech Beechjet 400A	RK-189		0097	1297	2 PWC JT15D-5	7303	Executive		
☐ N718TA	Beech Beechjet 400A	RK-195		0098	0898	2 PWC JT15D-5	7303	Executive		
☐ N741TA	Beech Beechjet 400A	RK-201		0098	1198	2 PWC JT15D-5	7303	Executive		
☐ N742TA	Beech Beechjet 400A	RK-202		0098	1098	2 PWC JT15D-5	7303	Executive		
☐ N745TA	Beech Beechjet 400A	RK-145		0097	0897	2 PWC JT15D-5	7303	Executive		
☐ N746TA	Beech Beechjet 400A	RK-146		0097	0897	2 PWC JT15D-5	7303	Executive		
☐ N748TA	Beech Beechjet 400A	RK-222		0099	0299	2 PWC JT15D-5	7303	Executive		
☐ N749TA	Beech Beechjet 400A	RK-149	N149TA	0097	0897	2 PWC JT15D-5	7303	Executive		
☐ N751TA	Beech Beechjet 400A	RK-225		0099	0299	2 PWC JT15D-5	7303	Executive		
☐ N753TA	Beech Beechjet 400A	RK-230		0099	0399	2 PWC JT15D-5	7303	Executive		
☐ N761TA	Beech Beechjet 400A	RK-161		0097	1297	2 PWC JT15D-5	7303	Executive		
☐ N768TA	Beech Beechjet 400A	RK-168		0097	1197	2 PWC JT15D-5	7303	Executive		
☐ N798TA	Beech Beechjet 400A	RK-198		0098	0898	2 PWC JT15D-5	7303	Executive		
☐ N799TA	Beech Beechjet 400A	RK-209		0098	1298	2 PWC JT15D-5	7303	Executive		
☐ N707TA	Hawker 800XP	258296	N801JT	0096	0797	2 GA TFE731-5BR-1H	12701	Executive		
☐ N720TA	Hawker 800XP	258320		0097	0897	2 GA TFE731-5BR-1H	12701	Executive		
☐ N722TA	Hawker 800XP	258322		0097	0997	2 GA TFE731-5BR-1H	12701	Executive		
☐ N725TA	Hawker 800XP	258297	N297XP	0096	0198	2 GA TFE731-5BR-1H	12701	Executive		
☐ N726TA	Hawker 800XP	258363		0098	0498	2 GA TFE731-5BR-1H	12701	Executive		
☐ N728TA	Hawker 800XP	258364		0098	0498	2 GA TFE731-5BR-1H	12701	Executive		
☐ N729TA	Hawker 800XP	258374		0098	0498	2 GA TFE731-5BR-1H	12701	Executive		
☐ N730TA	Hawker 800XP	258383		0098	0498	2 GA TFE731-5BR-1H	12701	Executive		
☐ N752TA	Hawker 800XP	258397		0099	0299	2 GA TFE731-5BR-1H	12701	Executive		
☐ N782TA	Hawker 800XP	258282	PT-WHH	0095	0998	2 GA TFE731-5BR-1H	12701	Executive		
☐ N791TA	Hawker 800XP	258291	N291SJ	0095	0298	2 GA TFE731-5BR-1H	12701	Executive		

RDC MARINE – Flight Operations (Flight Operations of RDC Marine, Inc. / Subsidiary of Rowan Drilling Company)

Houston-William P. Hobby, TX

8802 Travelair, Houston, TX 77061, USA ☎ (713) 649-7777 Tx: none Fax: (713) 649-8136 SITA: n/a

F: 1970 👥 n/a Head: Richard Sharp Net: n/a Operates executive flights exclusively for the Rowan Drilling Company and its subsidiaries.

registration	type of aircraft	cn/fn	ex/ex*	mfd	del	powered by	mtow kg	configuration	selcal	name/fln/specialitites/remarks
☐ N85RD	Piper PA-31-350 Navajo Chieftain	31-7752113	N27239	0077	1282	2 LY TIO-540-J2BD	3175	Executive		
☐ N58RC	Bell 222B	47141	N3187H	0083	0586	2 LY LTS101-750C.1	3742	Executive		
☐ N56RD	Learjet 24D (XR)	24D-286	N86GC	0074	0180	2 GE CJ610-6	6804	Executive		cvtd 24D
☐ N335RD	Learjet 35A	35A-216	N142LG	0078	1098	2 GA TFE731-2-2B	8301	Executive		lsf ERH
☐ N14RD	Boeing (Douglas) DC-3A-253	2145	N132BP	0039	0695	2 PW R-1830	12202	Executive		
☐ N57RD	Convair 580	509	N12FV	0059	0296	2 AN 501-D13H	24766	Executive		lsf ERH / cvtd CV 440-61
☐ N5RD	GAC (Grumman) G-1159 Gulfstream II	142	N60CC	0074	0281	2 RR Spey 511-8	28123	Executive		

RED BARON AVIATION, Inc. = RBN

Tampa-Pilot Field, FL

8488 West Hillsborough Ave, Suite 224, Tampa, FL 33615, USA ☎ (941) 873-1446 Tx: none Fax: (941) 873-1443 SITA: n/a

F: 1987 👥 n/a Head: Myrle B. Gallops ICAO: RED BARON Net: n/a

registration	type of aircraft	cn/fn	ex/ex*	mfd	del	powered by	mtow kg	configuration	selcal	name/fln/specialitites/remarks
☐ N72074	Cessna U206D Super Skywagon	U206-1275		0069	0494	1 CO IO-520-F	1633	Freighter		lsf Gallops Inc.
☐ N4345X	Cessna 210B	21058033		0062	0494	1 CO IO-470-S	1361	Freighter		lsf Gallops Inc.
☐ N5874F	Cessna 210G Centurion	21058874		0068	0390	1 CO IO-520-A	1542	Freighter		lsf Gallops Inc.
☐ N8280M	Cessna 210K Centurion	21059280		0070	0295	1 CO IO-520-L	1724	Freighter		lsf Gallops Inc.
☐ N93100	Cessna 210L Centurion II	21060264		0074	1188	1 CO IO-520-L	1724			lsf Gallops Inc.
☐ N7425S	AAC (Ted Smith) Aerostar 601	61-0010		0069	0790	2 LY IO-540-P1A5	2585	Freighter		lsf Gallops Inc.
☐ N8064J	AAC (Ted Smith) Aerostar 600A	60-0547-177		0078	0689	2 LY IO-540-K1F5	2495	Freighter		lsf Gallops Inc.

REDDING AERO ENTERPRISES, Inc. = BXR

Redding-Municipal, CA

3775 Flight Avenue, Redding, CA 96002, USA ☎ (530) 224-2300 Tx: none Fax: (530) 224-2315 SITA: n/a

F: 1989 👥 n/a Head: John N. Kilpatrick ICAO: BOXER Net: n/a Aircraft below MTOW 1361kg: Piper PA-28

registration	type of aircraft	cn/fn	ex/ex*	mfd	del	powered by	mtow kg	configuration	selcal	name/fln/specialitites/remarks
☐ N20TP	Piper PA-34-200T Seneca II	34-7870306		0078	0286	2 CO TSIO-360-EB	2073			lsf pvt
☐ N6072V	AAC (Piper) Aerostar 601P	61P-0696-7963332		0079	0596	2 LY IO-540-S1A5	2722			lsf pvt
☐ N2613B	Cessna 402C II	402C0083		0079	0893	2 CO TSIO-520-VB	3107			lsf pvt
☐ N36908	Cessna 402C II	402C0313		0080	1093	2 CO TSIO-520-VB	3107			
☐ N5826C	Cessna 402C II	402C0050		0079	1093	2 CO TSIO-520-VB	3107			
☐ N5849C	Cessna 402C II	402C0052		0079	0596	2 CO TSIO-520-VB	3107			
☐ N6814A	Cessna 402C II	402C0645		0082	0596	2 CO TSIO-520-VB	3107			
☐ N209BH	Beech 99 Airliner	U-73	N796A	0069	0596	2 PWC PT6A-20	4717			

REDDING AIR SERVICE, Inc.

Redding-Municipal, CA

6831 Airway Ave, Redding, CA 96002, USA ☎ (530) 221-2851 Tx: none Fax: (530) 221-3728 SITA: n/a

F: 1956 👥 8 Head: J. Burt Train Net: n/a

registration	type of aircraft	cn/fn	ex/ex*	mfd	del	powered by	mtow kg	configuration	selcal	name/fln/specialitites/remarks
☐ N5738Y	Bell 206B JetRanger III	3061		0080	1280	1 AN 250-C20B	1451			

☐ N90301	Bell 206B JetRanger III	1740		0075	0775	1 AN 250-C20B	1451			cvtd JetRanger
☐ N801HM	Bell 206L-3 LongRanger III	51218		0087	0895	1 AN 250-C30P	1882			
☐ N61CU	Eurocopter (Aerosp.) AS350B AStar	1636	N351SM	0082	0386	1 TU Arriel 1B	1950	EMS		lsf/opf Mercy Air Ambulance

REDISKE AIR, Inc. — Anchorage-Int'l, AK

Box 7079, Nikiski, AK 99635, USA ☎ (907) 776-8985 Tx: none Fax: (907) 776-8985 SITA: n/a
F: 1991 👥 n/a Head: Charles E. Rediske Net: n/a

☐ N100PC	Cessna T207A Turbo Stationair 7 II	20700467		0078	0893	1 CO TSIO-520-M	1724			

REDLINE AIR CHARTERS (Mike F. Stewart dba) — McGrath, AK

Box 271, McGrath, AK 99627, USA ☎ (907) 524-3008 Tx: none Fax: (907) 524-3125 SITA: n/a
F: 1996 👥 n/a Head: Mike F. Stewart Net: n/a

☐ N4140R	Piper PA-32-300 Cherokee SIX	32-40459		0068	0796	1 LY IO-540-K1A5	1542			

REDTAIL AVIATION, Inc. — Green River-Municipal & Moab-Canyonlands Field, UT

PO Box 606, Green River, UT 84525, USA ☎ (801) 564-3412 Tx: none Fax: (801) 564-8157 SITA: n/a
F: 1976 👥 n/a Head: Robert Lindgren Net: n/a Aircraft below MTOW 1361kg: Cessna 172 & 182

☐ N54110	Cessna U206G Stationair 6 II	U20604509		0078	0194	1 CO IO-520-F	1633			
☐ N71001	Cessna U206F Stationair	U20602115		0073	0194	1 CO IO-520-F	1633			
☐ N71234	Cessna U206F Stationair	U20602131		0073	0194	1 CO IO-520-F	1633			
☐ N7389Q	Cessna U206F Stationair	U20602189		0073	0194	1 CO IO-520-F	1633			
☐ N1758U	Cessna T207 Turbo Skywagon	20700358		0076	0194	1 CO TSIO-520-G	1724			
☐ N91096	Cessna 207 Skywagon	20700071		0069	0594	1 CO IO-520-F	1724			
☐ N91116	Cessna 207 Skywagon	20700079		0069	0194	1 CO IO-520-F	1724			
☐ N9264K	Piper PA-34-200T Seneca II	34-7670195		0076	0097	2 CO TSIO-360-E	2073			lsf pvt
☐ N60GP	Cessna 402B	402B0848		0075	0097	2 CO TSIO-520-E	2858			lsf Legion Express Inc.

REDWING AIRWAYS, Inc. = RX / RWG — Kirksville, MO

RR 6, Box 64, Kirksville Regional Airport, Kirksville, MO 63501, USA ☎ (660) 665-6607 Tx: none Fax: (660) 665-6061 SITA: n/a
F: 1979 👥 n/a Head: James R. Kelsey ICAO: REDWING AIR Net: n/a

☐ N401RW	Cessna 401	401-0118	N13361	0067	1189	2 CO TSIO-520-E	2858			
☐ N412RW	Cessna 402	402-0127	N4027Q	0067	0794	2 CO TSIO-520-E	2858			
☐ N65RW	Beech Queen Air B80 (65-B80)	LD-404	N5124X	0069	0492	2 LY IGSO-540-A1D	3992			

REDWOOD EMPIRE AIR CARE HELICOPTER (Mediplane, Inc. dba) — Santa Rosa-Heliport, CA

5010 Flightline Drive, Santa Rosa, CA 95403, USA ☎ (707) 575-6886 Tx: none Fax: (707) 571-2369 SITA: n/a
F: 1990 👥 n/a Head: Ken Stults Net: n/a

☐ N1MR	Agusta A109A	7185	XC-FUJ	0080	1294	2 AN 250-C20B	2600	EMS		lsf Agusta Aerospace Corp.
☐ N4999B	Agusta A109A	7155		0079	0192	2 AN 250-C20B	2600	EMS		
☐ N613AC	Agusta A109A	7205	N109LE	0081	0794	2 AN 250-C20B	2600	EMS		
☐ N7CR	Agusta A109A	7131	N880J	0078	0990	2 AN 250-C20B	2600	EMS		

REEDER FLYING SERVICE, Inc. — Twin Falls, ID

Reeder Flying Service

644 Airport Loop, Twin Falls, ID 83301-9617, USA ☎ (208) 733-5920 Tx: none Fax: (208)733-1561 SITA: n/a
F: 1941 👥 13 Head: John W. Reeder Net: n/a Aircraft / Ag-Aircraft below MTOW 1361 / 5000 kg: Air Tractor AT-400A, Bell 47G & Grumman G-164A.

☐ N59556	Bell 206B JetRanger III	1372		0074	0774	1 AN 250-C20B	1451			cvtd JetRanger
☐ N9944K	Bell 206B JetRanger III	2001		0076	0776	1 AN 250-C20B	1451			cvtd JetRanger II
☐ N29100	Cessna U206C Super Skywagon	U206-1072		0068	0689	1 CO IO-520-F	1633			
☐ N761QP	Cessna T210M Turbo Centurion II	21062436		0077	0678	1 CO TSIO-520-R	1724			
☐ N350CR	Eurocopter (Aerosp.) AS350BA Ecureuil	2328	JA9889	0090	0697	1 TU Arriel 1B	2100			
☐ N917JT	Eurocopter (Aerosp.) AS350B2 AStar	2759	N6096P	0093	0498	1 TU Arriel 1D1	2250			
☐ N316RF	Eurocopter (Aerosp.) SE3160 Alouette III	1539	JA9031	0069	0395	1 TU Artouste IIIB	2100			cargo hook / Skis

REEVE ALEUTIAN AIRWAYS, Inc. – RAA = RV / RVV — Anchorage-Int'l, AK

RAA

4700 West Int'l Airport Road, Anchorage, AK 99502-1091, USA ☎ (907) 243-1112 Tx: none Fax: (907) 249-2317 SITA: n/a
F: 1932 👥 320 Head: Richard D. Reeve IATA: 338 ICAO: REEVE Net: http://www.alaskan.com/promos/raa.html

☐ N178RV	Lockheed L-188PF Electra	2010	C-GNWC	0059	0478	4 AN 501-D13A	52617	Combi/Y84/Frtr		cvtd L-188C
☐ N1968R	Lockheed L-188C Electra	2007	ZK-CLX	0059	0268	4 AN 501-D13A	52617	Y84		
☐ N9744C	Lockheed L-188PF Electra	1140		0061	0970	4 AN 501-D13A	51256	Combi/Y84/Frtr		cvtd L-188A
☐ N831RV	Boeing 727-22C	19093 / 293	N498WC	0066	1283	3 PW JT8D-7B	76657	Combi/Y110/Frtr		
☐ N832RV	Boeing 727-22C	19098 / 318	N496WC	0066	1283	3 PW JT8D-7B	76657	Combi/Y110/Frtr		

REFORESTATION SERVICES, Inc. — Salem-McNary Field, OR

PO Box 3197, Salem, OR 97302, USA ☎ (541) 362-8322 Tx: none Fax: (541) 363-6101 SITA: n/a
F: 1959 👥 n/a Head: Gilbert E. Liming Net: n/a Aircraft below MTOW 1361kg: Hiller UH-12E

☐ N220GP	Bell 206B JetRanger III	4196		0091	1096	1 AN 250-C20B	1451			
☐ N92CA	Bell 206B JetRanger III	2016	N9983K	0076	0490	1 AN 250-C20B	1451			cvtd JetRanger II

REGAL AIR (Alaska Skyways, Inc. dba) — Anchorage-Lake Hood SPB, AK

REGAL AIR

PO Box 190702, Anchorage, AK 99519-0702, USA ☎ (907) 243-8535 Tx: none Fax: (907) 248-5791 SITA: n/a
F: 1978 👥 3 Head: Craig M. Elg Net: n/a

☐ N1780R	Cessna A185F Skywagon	18502498		0074	1280	1 CO IO-520-D	1520			lsf C&S Leasing Inc./Floats/Wheel-Skis
☐ N1779R	Cessna U206G Stationair 6 II	U20604379	N756UZ	0078	0492	1 CO IO-520-F	1633			Floats/Wheel-Skis
☐ N9877R	De Havilland DHC-2 Beaver I	1180	N98JT	0056	0298	1 PW R-985	2313			lsf C&S Leasing Inc./Floats/Wheels-Skis
☐ N9878R	De Havilland DHC-2 Beaver I	1135	N88788	0056	0790	1 PW R-985	2313			lsf C&S Leasing Inc./Floats/Wheel-Skis

RELIANCE INSURANCE – Aviation Dept. (Aviation Dept. of Reliance Insurance Company / Subsidiary of Reliance Group Holdings, Inc.) — Morristown-Municipal & Newark-Int'l, NJ

55 East 52nd Street, Park Avenue Plaza, New York, NY 10055, USA ☎ (212) 909-1783 Tx: none Fax: (212) 909-1377 SITA: n/a
F: 1989 👥 n/a Head: Eilene S. Bloom Net: n/a Operates executive flights exclusively for its parent group of companies only.

☐ N800RG	Sikorsky S-76B	760315	N103ME	0085	0889	2 PWC PT6B-36A	5307	Executive		
☐ N400RG	Boeing 727-22 (RE) (Super 27)	19149 / 481	N7085U	0067	0581	3 PW JT8D-217C/7B (BFG)	72802	Executive	FH-AL	cvtd -22

RELIANT AIRLINES, Inc. = RLT — Detroit-Willow Run, MI

Willow Run Airport, Box 827, Ypsilanti, MI 48198-0899, USA ☎ (734) 483-3266 Tx: none Fax: (734) 483-5544 SITA: n/a
F: 1984 👥 100 Head: Reese C. Zantop ICAO: RELIANT Net: http://www.reliantairlines.com

☐ N8GA	Dassault Falcon 10	127	I-CALC	0079	0695	2 GA TFE731-2-1C	8500	7 Pax		lsf RCL Leasing Inc.
☐ N108R	Dassault Falcon 20D (C)	108	N101ZE	0067	0993	2 GE CF700-2D2	13000	Freighter		cvtd D
☐ N126R	Dassault Falcon 20C (C)	126	N102ZE	0068	0993	2 GE CF700-2D2	13000	Freighter		cvtd C
☐ N212R	Dassault Falcon 20D (C)	212	N31FE	0070	0188	2 GE CF700-2D2	13000	Freighter		cvtd D
☐ N226R	Dassault Falcon 20D (C)	226	N21FE	0070	0188	2 GE CF700-2D2	13000	Freighter		cvtd D
☐ N227R	Dassault Falcon 20D (C)	227	N24EV	0070	1286	2 GE CF700-2D2	13000	Freighter		cvtd D
☐ N229R	Dassault Falcon 20D (C)	229	N25EV	0070	0186	2 GE CF700-2D2	13000	Freighter		cvtd D
☐ N230RA	Dassault Falcon 20D (C)	230	N26EV	0070	1286	2 GE CF700-2D2	13000	Freighter		cvtd D
☐ N301R	Dassault Falcon 20C (C)	3	N92MH	0065	0688	2 GE CF700-2D2	13000	Freighter		cvtd C
☐ N388AJ	Dassault Falcon 20C (C)	56	OO-OOO	0066	0195	2 GE CF700-2D2	13000	Freighter		cvtd C / to be re-reg. N560RA
☐ N810RA	Dassault Falcon 20C (C)	81	N93RS	0067	0192	2 GE CF700-2D2	13000	Freighter		cvtd C
☐ N950RA	Dassault Falcon 20C (C)	95	N664B	0067	1189	2 GE CF700-2D2	13000	Freighter		cvtd C
☐ N980R	Dassault Falcon 20C (C)	98	N781AJ	0067	0794	2 GE CF700-2D2	13000	Freighter		cvtd C
☐ N568PC	Boeing (Douglas) DC-9-15F (RC)	47086 / 219	N9356	0067	0398	2 PW JT8D-7B	41141	Freighter		

RENO AIR, Inc. = QQ / ROA (Subsidiary of AMR, Corp.) — Reno-Tahoe Int'l, NV

RENO Air®

PO Box 30059, Reno, NV 89520-3059, USA ☎ (702) 954-5000 Tx: none Fax: (702) 858-7960 SITA: n/a
F: 1990 👥 1700 Head: Don O'Hare IATA: 384 ICAO: RENO AIR Net: http://www.renoair.com Expected to be merged into AMERICAN AIRLINES late 1999.

☐ N751RA	Boeing (Douglas) MD-87 (DC-9-87)	49779 / 1670	EC-FXX	0089	0295	2 PW JT8D-219	63503	F12Y105		lsf CITG
☐ N752RA	Boeing (Douglas) MD-87 (DC-9-87)	49780 / 1674	N780EG	0090	0595	2 PW JT8D-219	63503	F12Y105		
☐ N753RA	Boeing (Douglas) MD-87 (DC-9-87)	49587 / 1541	HB-IUC	0088	1195	2 PW JT8D-217C	66905	F12Y105		lsf Investors Asset Holding Corp.
☐ N754RA	Boeing (Douglas) MD-87 (DC-9-87)	49641 / 1617	HB-IUD	0089	1195	2 PW JT8D-217C	66905	F12Y105		lsf Boxen Corp.
☐ N755RA	Boeing (Douglas) MD-87 (DC-9-87)	49727 / 1621	N1074T	0089	0397	2 PW JT8D-219	63503	F12Y105		lsf Marubeni America Corp.
☐ N821RA	Boeing (Douglas) MD-82 (DC-9-82)	49931 / 1754	N809ML	0090	0692	2 PW JT8D-219	67812	F20Y120		lsf EDS Financial Corp.
☐ N822RA	Boeing (Douglas) MD-82 (DC-9-82)	49932 / 1756	N810ML	0090	0692	2 PW JT8D-219	67812	F20Y120		lsf EDS Financial Corp.
☐ N823RA	Boeing (Douglas) MD-82 (DC-9-82)	49889 / 1761	N811ML	0090	0595	2 PW JT8D-217C	66678	F20Y120		lsf Boeing Capital Corp.
☐ N824RA	Boeing (Douglas) MD-82 (DC-9-82)	53017 / 1797	N812ML	0090	0595	2 PW JT8D-217C	66678	F20Y120		lsf Boeing Capital Corp.
☐ N832RA	Boeing (Douglas) MD-83 (DC-9-83)	53044 / 1776	N905ML	0090	0792	2 PW JT8D-219	72575	F20Y120		lsf POLA
☐ N833RA	Boeing (Douglas) MD-83 (DC-9-83)	53045 / 1777	P4-MDB	1090	0892	2 PW JT8D-219	72575	F20Y120		lsf POLA
☐ N834RA	Boeing (Douglas) MD-83 (DC-9-83)	53124 / 1991	N9017P	0091	1092	2 PW JT8D-219	72575	F20Y120		lsf Boeing Capital Corp.
☐ N836RA	Boeing (Douglas) MD-83 (DC-9-83)	53046 / 1794	YV-44C	0090	0393	2 PW JT8D-219	72575	F20Y120		lsf POLA
☐ N871RA	Boeing (Douglas) MD-83 (DC-9-83)	49788 / 1637	YV-43C	0089	0593	2 PW JT8D-219	72575	F20Y120		Patty Sheehan / Hall of Fame
☐ N872RA	Boeing (Douglas) MD-83 (DC-9-83)	49793 / 1656	N793DG	0090	0793	2 PW JT8D-219	72575	F20Y120		lsf Finova Capital Corp.
☐ N878RA	Boeing (Douglas) MD-83 (DC-9-83)	53184 / 2088		0094	0994	2 PW JT8D-219	72575	F20Y120		lsf AWAS
☐ N879RA	Boeing (Douglas) MD-83 (DC-9-83)	53185 / 2090		0094	0994	2 PW JT8D-219	72575	F20Y120		lsf AWAS

423 registration type of aircraft cn/fn ex/ex* mfd del powered by mtow kg configuration selcal name/fln/specialitites/remarks

registration	type of aircraft	cn/fn	ex/ex*	mfd	del	powered by	mtow kg	configuration	name/fln/specialitites/remarks
☐ N880RA	Boeing (Douglas) MD-83 (DC-9-83)	53186 / 2092		0094	1094	2 PW JT8D-219	72575	F20Y120	lsf AWAS
☐ N881RA	Boeing (Douglas) MD-83 (DC-9-83)	49941 / 1793	G-DEVR	1190	0496	2 PW JT8D-219	72575	F20Y120	lsf GECA
☐ N882RA	Boeing (Douglas) MD-83 (DC-9-83)	49949 / 1906	G-RJER	0091	0596	2 PW JT8D-219	72575	F20Y120	lsf GECA
☐ N901RA	Boeing (Douglas) MD-90-30	53489 / 2129		0096	0396	2 IAE V2525-D5	70760	F20Y128	lsf MDFC Reno Co.
☐ N902RA	Boeing (Douglas) MD-90-30	53490 / 2133		0096	0596	2 IAE V2525-D5	70760	F20Y128	lsf MDFC Tahoe Co.
☐ N903RA	Boeing (Douglas) MD-90-30	53551 / 2144		0096	0896	2 IAE V2525-D5	70760	F20Y128	lsf MDFC Sierra Co.
☐ N904RA	Boeing (Douglas) MD-90-30	53570 / 2181		0097	1297	2 IAE V2525-D5	70760	F20Y128	lsf Boeing Capital Corp.
☐ N905RA	Boeing (Douglas) MD-90-30	53573 / 2182		0097	1297	2 IAE V2525-D5	70760	F20Y128	lsf Boeing Capital Corp.

RENO FLYING SERVICE, Inc. (Associated with American Medflight, Inc.)   Reno-Tahoe Int'l, NV
PO Box 7813, Reno, NV 89510, USA ☎ (702) 856-5800 Tx: none Fax: (702) 856-5801 SITA: n/a
F: 1986 ♦♦♦ n/a Head: John A. Dawson Net: n/a Aircraft below MTOW 1361kg: Cessna 172

registration	type of aircraft	cn/fn	ex/ex*	mfd	del	powered by	mtow kg	configuration	name/fln/specialitites/remarks
☐ N9371Y	Cessna T210N Turbo Centurion II	21064490		0081	1091	1 CO TSIO-520-R	1814		
☐ N224BD	Piper PA-34-220T Seneca III	34-8133186	N229JC	0081		2 CO TSIO-360-KB	2155		lsf Bardic Airlines Corp.
☐ N2788M	Piper PA-34-200T Seneca III	34-7870094		0078	0991	2 CO TSIO-360-E	2073		
☐ N155CA	Piper PA-31T Cheyenne II	31T-7820024	YV-762CP	0078	1295	2 PWC PT6A-28	4082		
☐ N419R	Piper PA-31T Cheyenne II	31T-7820034	N82249	0078	0592	2 PWC PT6A-28	4082		

RENOWN AVIATION, Inc. = RGS (Sister company of JBQ Aviation Corp.)   Santa Maria, CA & Fort Lauderdale-Executive, FL
3940 Mitchell Road, Santa Maria, CA 93455, USA ☎ (805) 937-8484 Tx: none Fax: (805) 934-2007 SITA: n/a
F: 1975 ♦♦♦ 100 Head: Capt. Terry Cedar ICAO: RENOWN Net: n/a

registration	type of aircraft	cn/fn	ex/ex*	mfd	del	powered by	mtow kg	configuration	name/fln/specialitites/remarks
☐ N153PA	Convair 240-27 (T-29B)	304	51-7892	0053	0291	2 PW R-2800	18956	Freighter	lsf Cool Air Inc.
☐ N156PA	Convair 240-27 (T-29B)	324	N9016L	0052	0991	2 PW R-2800	18956	Freighter	lsf Cool Air Inc.
☐ N99380	Convair 240-27 (T-29B)	249	51-5118	0052	1287	2 PW R-2800	18956	Freighter	lsf Cool Air Inc.
☐ N1360D	Convair 340-70 (C-131B)	241	53-7789	0054	0596	2 PW R-2800	21772	Freighter	lsf JBQ Aviation Corp.
☐ N202RA	Convair 440-98 Metropolitan	497	C-GRNB	0058	1186	2 PW R-2800	21772	Y48	lsf JBQ Aviation Corp.
☐ N204RA	Convair 440-62 Metropolitan	504	C-GKFC	0058	0487	2 PW R-2800	21772	Y43	lsf JBQ Aviation Corp.
☐ N3HH	Convair 440 Metropolitan	173	C-GTVU	0054	1286	2 PW R-2800	21772	Y49	lsf JBQ Aviation Corp. / cvtd CV340-48
☐ N203RA	Convair 580	89	C-GDTC	0053	0893	2 AN 501-D13	24766	Y50	lsf JBQ Aviation Corp. / cvtd CV340-31
☐ N73104	Convair 580	4		0052	0391	2 AN 501-D13	24766	Y50	lsf R&R Holdings Inc./cvtd CV340-31
☐ N73126	Convair 580	53		0053	0391	2 AN 501-D13	24766	Y50	lsf R&R Holdings Inc. / cvtd CV340-31
☐ N73163	Convair 580	366	OO-SCO	0056	0888	2 AN 501-D13	24766	Y50	cvtd CV440-12
☐ N968N	Convair 580	462	11163	0057	0996	2 AN 501-D13	24766	Y48	lsf R&R Holdings / cvtd CV 540/CL-66C
☐ N285F	Lockheed L-188A (F) Electra	1107	N5012K	0059	0798	4 AN 501-D13A	51256	Freighter	lst EXS / cvtd L-188A
☐ N351Q	Lockheed L-188A Electra	1036	VH-IOB	0059	0095	4 AN 501-D13A	51257	Y99	San Clemente Lady / lsf JBQ Aviation
☐ N360Q	Lockheed L-188C (F) Electra	1112	N360WS	0059	0297	4 AN 501-D13A	52617	Freighter	lsf JBQ Aviation/sub-lst EXS/cvtdL-188C

REPP AIR FREIGHT, Inc.   Columbus-Municipal, IN
16094 Cottage Ave., Columbus, IN 47201, USA ☎ (812) 373-0788 Tx: none Fax: (812) 376-6833 SITA: n/a
F: 1997 ♦♦♦ n/a Head: John Repp Net: n/a

registration	type of aircraft	cn/fn	ex/ex*	mfd	del	powered by	mtow kg	configuration	name/fln/specialitites/remarks
☐ N140JR	Boeing (Douglas) DC-3C (C-47B-15-DK)	26815	C-GABI	0044	0497	2 PW R-1830	12202	Freighter	

RHINO AVIATION (J & A Properties, Inc. dba)   Greenville-Downtown, SC
100 Tower Drive, Box 4, Greenville, SC 29607, USA ☎ (864) 232-9566 Tx: none Fax: (864) 370-2496 SITA: n/a
F: 1979 ♦♦♦ n/a Head: Tim McConnell Net: n/a

registration	type of aircraft	cn/fn	ex/ex*	mfd	del	powered by	mtow kg	configuration	name/fln/specialitites/remarks
☐ N4837A	Cessna 414A Chancellor III	414A0101	N412MA	0078	0496	2 CO TSIO-520-N	3062		
☐ N10LY	Cessna 550 Citation II	550-0466		0083	1096	2 PWC JT15D-4	6033		lsf Aircraft Leasing Group Llc

RHOADES INTERNATIONAL = RDS (Rhoades Aviation, Inc. dba)   Columbus-Municipal, IN   *RHOADES*
4770 Ray Boll Boulevard, Columbus, IN 47203, USA ☎ (812) 372-1819 Tx: none Fax: (812) 378-2708 SITA: n/a
F: 1965 ♦♦♦ 40 Head: Jack L. Rhoades ICAO: RHOADES EXPRESS Net: n/a Operates additional Cessna aircraft for short periods as company is also sales agent.

registration	type of aircraft	cn/fn	ex/ex*	mfd	del	powered by	mtow kg	configuration	name/fln/specialitites/remarks
☐ N134JR	Cessna 310R II	310R2117	N6831X	0080	0385	2 CO IO-520-M	2495		
☐ N132JR	Cessna 402B II	402B1363	N4606N	0078	0789	2 CO TSIO-520-E	2858		
☐ N421SM	Cessna 421B Golden Eagle	421B0889		0075	0298	2 CO GTSIO-520-H	3379		lsf Fox Flite Inc.
☐ N70CP	Cessna 421B Golden Eagle	421B0950		0075	0996	2 CO GTSIO-520-H	3379		lsf RGB Aircraft Inc.
☐ N36CC	Learjet 25B (XR)	25B-079	N50DH	0071	0598	2 GE CJ610-6	6804		lsf Johnson Aviation Corp.
☐ N731CW	Learjet 25B	25B-117	C-FMGM	0073	0996	2 GE CJ610-6	6804		lsf Johnson Aviation Corp.
☐ N139JR	Boeing (Douglas) DC-3C (C-47A-90-DL)	20550	N16475	0043	0379	2 PW R-1830	12202	Freighter	std CLU
☐ N141JR	Boeing (Douglas) DC-3C (C-47A-75-DL)	19366	CF-CUC	0044	0985	2 PW R-1830	12202	Freighter	std CLU
☐ N142JR	Boeing (Douglas) DC-3C (C-47B-25-DK)	32843	C-FCTA	0045	0387	2 PW R-1830	12202	Freighter	
☐ N148JR	Convair 240 (T-29B-CO)	232	N351JD	0052		2 PW R-2800	18956	Freighter	lsf Air Cargo Express Int'l Inc.
☐ N151JR	Convair 240-52 (T-29D)	52-31	N451GA	0054	0091	2 PW R-2800	18915	Freighter	std CLU
☐ N152JR	Convair 240-27 (T-29B)	283	N452GA	0051	0091	2 PW R-2800	18915	Freighter	
☐ N157JR	Convair 340-71 (C-131F)	284	N820TA	0055	0195	2 PW R-2800	21772	Freighter	
☐ N156JR	Convair 440 Metropolitan	200	N440CF	0054	0091	2 PW R-2800	21772	Freighter	cvtd CV340-62

RICHARDS AVIATION, Inc. = RVC   Memphis-Int'l, TN   *ra richards aviation*
PO Box 30079, Memphis, TN 38130, USA ☎ (901) 332-7239 Tx: none Fax: (901) 332-7243 SITA: n/a
F: 1981 ♦♦♦ 18 Head: Michie T. Hill ICAO: RIVER CITY Net: http://www.raijets.com

registration	type of aircraft	cn/fn	ex/ex*	mfd	del	powered by	mtow kg	configuration	name/fln/specialitites/remarks
☐ N249WM	Beech King Air E90	LW-139	N345KA	0075	0596	2 PWC PT6A-28	4581		
☐ N2690M	Cessna 501 Citation I/SP	501-0151	N269CM	0080	0297	2 PWC JT15D-1A	5375		
☐ N323LJ	Learjet 31A	31A-123		0096	1196	2 GA TFE731-2-3B	7484		
☐ N337RB	Learjet 31A	31A-154		0098	0898	2 GA TFE731-2-3B	7484		

RICHLAND AVIATION = RCA (Philip O. Petrik dba)   Sidney-Richland Municipal, MT
PO Box 701, Sidney, MT 59270, USA ☎ (406) 482-1832 Tx: none Fax: (406) 482-1834 SITA: n/a
F: 1971 ♦♦♦ n/a Head: Philip O. Petrik ICAO: RICHLAND Net: n/a Aircraft/Ag-aircraft below MTOW 1361/5000kg: Cessna 172, Piper PA-11, PA-18 & Weatherly 620B

registration	type of aircraft	cn/fn	ex/ex*	mfd	del	powered by	mtow kg	configuration	name/fln/specialitites/remarks
☐ N398LT	Beech Bonanza S35	D-7406		0064	0294	1 CO IO-520-B	1497		
☐ N444TC	Beech Bonanza V35B	D-9783		0075	0197	1 CO IO-520-BA	1542		
☐ N1772W	Beech Bonanza A36	E-377		0072	0576	1 CO IO-520-BA	1633		
☐ N119D	Beech Baron B55 (95-B55)	TC-1941		0076	0294	2 CO IO-470-L	2313		
☐ N30RA	Cessna 310R II	310R0079		0074	0796	2 CO IO-520-M	2495		
☐ N6131X	Cessna T310R II	310R1296		0078	1189	2 CO TSIO-520-B	2495		
☐ N87221	Cessna T310R II	310R0306		0075	0285	2 CO TSIO-520-B	2495		
☐ N687CA	Cessna 402C II	402C0609		0081	0794	2 CO TSIO-520-VB	3107		
☐ N502RA	Cessna 404 Titan II	404-0066	C-GJMP	0077	0497	2 CO GTSIO-520-M	3810		

RICHMOR AVIATION, Inc. (Subsidiary of Kamyr, Inc.)   Hudson-Columbia County, NY   *Richmor Aviation*
PO Box 423, Hudson, NY 12534, USA ☎ (518) 828-9461 Tx: none Fax: (518) 828-1303 SITA: n/a
F: 1967 ♦♦♦ n/a Head: Mahlon W. Richards Net: http://www.aero.com/fbo/richmor/index.html

registration	type of aircraft	cn/fn	ex/ex*	mfd	del	powered by	mtow kg	configuration	name/fln/specialitites/remarks
☐ N2738B	Cessna 310R II	310R1828		0079	0181	2 CO IO-520-M	2495		
☐ N300FL	Beech King Air C90A	LJ-1066	N6727M	0084	0186	2 PWC PT6A-21	4377		lsf Fleet Financial Group Inc.
☐ N600FL	Beech King Air C90	LJ-935	N3709W	0080	0883	2 PWC PT6A-21	4377		lsf Fleet Financial Group Inc.
☐ N88SD	Beech King Air C90	LJ-661	N969BH	0075	0185	2 PWC PT6A-21	4377		
☐ N98PC	Beech King Air E90	LW-131	N9031R	0075	0488	2 PWC PT6A-28	4581		lsf Alistar Beverages Corp.
☐ N689BV	Beech King Air 200	BB-338	VR-BGN	0078	0190	2 PWC PT6A-41	5670		
☐ N255DG	Mitsubishi MU-300 Diamond IA	A056SA	I-FRTT	0083	0498	2 PWC JT15D-4D	6636		
☐ N600CG	Mitsubishi MU-300 Diamond IA	A055SA	N600MS	0083	1196	2 PWC JT15D-4D	6636		lsf CGT Ltd
☐ N357PR	Learjet 55	55-073	N73WE	0083	0397	2 GA TFE731-3AR-2B	9752		lsf Full Gospel Ame Zion Church
☐ N57MH	Learjet 55	55-113	N236HR	0085	0193	2 GA TFE731-3AR-2B	9752		lsf Marriott Int'l Inc.
☐ N900FL	Cessna 650 Citation VII	650-7049	N749CM	0095	0496	2 GA TFE731-4R-2S	10183		lsf Fleet Financial Group Inc.
☐ N50TG	IAI 1125 Astra	065	N75TT	0093	0797	2 GA TFE731-3A-200G	10659		lsf Lake Creek Research Llc
☐ N60AJ	IAI 1125 Astra	071	4X-CUW*	0090	0597	2 GA TFE731-3A-200G	10659		lsf Durandal Inc.
☐ N816HB	IAI 1125 Astra	028	N11MZ	0089	0497	2 GA TFE731-3A-200G	10659		lsf HPB Aviation Inc.
☐ N357RT	Canadair CL-600S (CL-600-1A11) Challenger	1033	N101ST	0081	0996	2 LY ALF502L-2C	18711		lsf Reading Jet Service Inc.
☐ N722HP	Canadair CL-600S (CL-600-1A11) Challenger	1039	N1868S	0082	0693	2 LY ALF502L-2C	18711		lsf HSP Transportation Inc.
☐ N74JA	Canadair CL-600S (CL-600-1A11) Challenger	1060	N22AZ	0082	0996	2 LY ALF502L-2C	18711		lsf JA Interests Inc.
☐ N58JF	GAC (Grumman) G-1159 Gulfstream II	065	N500PC	0069	0489	2 RR Spey 511-8	29393		lsf Sterling Jet Ltd
☐ N900DH	GAC (Grumman) G-1159 Gulfstream II	111	N900BR	0072	1193	2 RR Spey 511-8	29393		lsf D&H Flying Corp.
☐ N6513X	GAC G-1159A Gulfstream III	310	C-FYAG	0080	0495	2 RR Spey 511-8	30935		lsf Assembly Pointe Aviation inc.

RITEL COPTER SERVICE, Inc.   Waterloo-Private Heliport, IA
2838 West Tama Road, Hudson, IA 50643, USA ☎ (319) 988-3598 Tx: none Fax: (319) 988-4095 SITA: n/a
F: 1970 ♦♦♦ n/a Head: Richard Green Net: n/a Aircraft below MTOW 1361kg: Bell 47G-5

registration	type of aircraft	cn/fn	ex/ex*	mfd	del	powered by	mtow kg	configuration	name/fln/specialitites/remarks
☐ N2877F	Bell 206B JetRanger III	2971	N10851	0080	0885	1 AN 250-C20B	1451		

RIVER CITY HELICOPTERS (John T. Scanlon dba)   Coeur d'Alene & Hayden Lake, ID
6995 West Riverview Drive, Post Falls, ID 83854, USA ☎ (208) 772-2117 Tx: none Fax: (208) 772-2548 SITA: n/a
F: 1985 ♦♦♦ 10 Head: John T. Scanlon Net: n/a

registration	type of aircraft	cn/fn	ex/ex*	mfd	del	powered by	mtow kg	configuration	name/fln/specialitites/remarks
☐ N540GH	Bell UH-1L (204 Super)	6001	151266	0067	0498	1 LY T53-L-13	3856		lsf Aviation Investments of NV/cvtd 204

☐ N600MA	Bell UH-1B (204 Super)	1094	64-13970	0064	0098	1 LY T53-L-13	3856			lsf Garlick Helicopters Inc./cvtd 204
☐ N842M	Bell UH-1B (204 Super)	343	61-763	0061	0098	1 LY T53-L-13	3856			lsf pvt / cvtd 204
☐ N209AH	Bell AH-1Q (209) Cobra Lifter	20401	67-15737	0067	0098	1 LY T53-L-703	4763			lsf Garlick Helicopters Inc.

RIVERSIDE AIR SERVICE – RAS (Orco Aviation, Inc. dba) **Riverside-Municipal, CA & Houston-William P.Hobby, TX**

6741 Gemende Road, Riverside, CA 92504, USA ☎ (909) 689-1160 Tx: none Fax: (909) 689-1380 SITA: n/a
F: 1959 👥 25 Head: Joseph Pagan Net: n/a Aircraft below MTOW 1361 kg: Beech 23/24 & Bell 47G

☐ N2066A	Beech Bonanza A36	E-1431		0079	1284	1 CO IO-520-BB	1633	5 Pax		
☐ N747PE	Piper PA-34-200T Seneca II	34-7770217		0077	0295	2 CO TSIO-360-E	2073	5 Pax		
☐ N5782D	Eurocopter (Aerosp.) AS355F1 TwinStar	5076		0082	1085	2 AN 250-C20F	2400	6 Pax		lsf MC SPI Inc.
☐ N717JP	GAC (Grumman) G-159 Gulfstream I	127	XA-TDJ	0063	0691	2 RR Dart 529-8X	16329	19 Pax		
☐ N717RA	GAC (Grumman) G-159 Gulfstream I	167	C-GDWM	0065	0589	2 RR Dart 529-8X	16329	14 - 17 Pax		
☐ N717RS	GAC (Grumman) G-159 Gulfstream I	038	N333AH	0060	0292	2 RR Dart 529-8X	16329	16 Pax		

ROCKY MOUNTAIN HELICOPTERS – RMH = RMA (Rocky Mountain Holdings, Llc dba) **Provo-Municipal, UT**

Box 1337, Provo, UT 84603-1337, USA ☎ (801) 375-1124 Tx: none Fax: (801) 375-6712 SITA: n/a
F: 1969 👥 425 Head: Russell. J. Spray ICAO: ROCKY MOUNTAIN Net: http://www.rmhllc.com

☐ N1184H	Eurocopter (Aerosp.) AS350B AStar	1124		0079	0781	1 TU Arriel 1B	1950			lsf Pitt Helicopters Inc.
☐ N147BH	Eurocopter (Aerosp.) AS350B AStar	1273		0080	0383	1 TU Arriel 1B	1950			lsf Pafford Ambulance Svc / cvtd AS350D
☐ N151AC	Eurocopter (Aerosp.) AS350D AStar	1173	N141BH	0079	0483	1 LY LTS101-600A.2	1950			
☐ N152AC	Eurocopter (Aerosp.) AS350D AStar	1101	N139BH	0079	0383	1 LY LTS101-600A.2	1950			
☐ N21UM	Eurocopter (Aerosp.) AS350B AStar	1674	N5801B	0082	0284	1 TU Arriel 1B	1950			
☐ N350RM	Eurocopter (Aerosp.) AS350D AStar	1024		0078	0579	1 LY LTS101-600A.2	1950			
☐ N3593X	Eurocopter (Aerosp.) AS350B AStar	1081		0079	0383	1 TU Arriel 1B	1950			cvtd AS350D
☐ N5771C	Eurocopter (Aerosp.) AS350B AStar	1369		0081	0983	1 TU Arriel 1B	1950			lsf General Electric Capital Corp.
☐ N57731	Eurocopter (Aerosp.) AS350D AllStar	1434		0081	0182	1 AN 250-C30	1950			cvtd AStar
☐ N5797T	Eurocopter (Aerosp.) AS350D AStar	1472	N3944S	0082	0483	1 LY LTS101-600A.2	1950			
☐ N58045	Eurocopter (Aerosp.) AS350B AStar	1602		0082	0785	1 TU Arriel 1B	1950			
☐ N779LF	Eurocopter (Aerosp.) AS350 AllStar	1621		0082	0492	1 AN 250-C30	1950			cvtd AS350B
☐ N781LF	Eurocopter (Aerosp.) AS350B AStar	1178	N1113H	0079	0482	1 TU Arriel 1B	1950			
☐ N792LF	Eurocopter (Aerosp.) AS350B AStar	1035	N9004M	0078	0483	1 TU Arriel 1B	1950			cvtd AS350D
☐ N92LG	Eurocopter (Aerosp.) AS350B AStar	2575		0091	1291	1 TU Arriel 1B	1950			
☐ N93LG	Eurocopter (Aerosp.) AS350B2 AStar	2654	N60662	0092	0293	1 TU Arriel 1D1	2250			
☐ N94LG	Eurocopter (Aerosp.) AS350BA AStar	2728	N60928	0093	0693	1 TU Arriel 1B	2100			
☐ N	Eurocopter (Aerosp.) AS350B3 AStar					1 TU Arriel 2B	2250	EMS LifeNet		oo-delivery 0099
☐ N	Eurocopter (Aerosp.) AS350B3 AStar					1 TU Arriel 2B	2250	EMS LifeNet		oo-delivery 0099
☐ N	Eurocopter (Aerosp.) AS350B3 AStar					1 TU Arriel 2B	2250	EMS LifeNet		oo-delivery 0099
☐ N	Eurocopter (Aerosp.) AS350B3 AStar					1 TU Arriel 2B	2250	EMS LifeNet		oo-delivery 0099
☐ N	Eurocopter (Aerosp.) AS350B3 AStar					1 TU Arriel 2B	2250	EMS LifeNet		oo-delivery 0099
☐ N	Eurocopter (Aerosp.) AS350B3 AStar					1 TU Arriel 2B	2250	EMS LifeNet		oo-delivery 0099
☐ N	Eurocopter (Aerosp.) AS350B2 AStar					1 TU Arriel 1D1	2250	EMS LifeNet		oo-delivery 0099
☐ N	Eurocopter (Aerosp.) AS350B2 AStar					1 TU Arriel 1D1	2250	EMS LifeNet		oo-delivery 0099
☐ N11HB	Eurocopter (Aerosp.) SA316B Alouette III	1826		0070	1278	1 TU Artouste IIIB	2200			lsf Nampa Valley Helicopters Inc.
☐ N4679	Eurocopter (Aerosp.) SA316B Alouette III	1902		0071	0983	1 TU Artouste IIIB	2200			lsf Nampa Valley Helicopters Inc.
☐ N67081	Eurocopter (Aerosp.) SA316B Alouette III	2184		0074	0584	1 TU Artouste IIIB	2200			
☐ N105MM	Eurocopter (MBB) BO105CBS	S-739		0086	1290	2 AN 250-C20B	2400			lsf Southeast Missouri Hospital
☐ N105NC	Eurocopter (MBB) BO105CBS-4	S-790	N301LG	0088	0189	2 AN 250-C20B	2400			lsf MDFC Equipment Leasing Corp.
☐ N485EC	Eurocopter (MBB) BO105CBS-4	S-754	N722MB	0086	0187	2 AN 250-C20B	2400			lsf State Street Bank Trustee
☐ N825LF	Eurocopter (MBB) BO105CBS-4	S-796	N5417E	0088	0190	2 AN 250-C20B	2400			lsf Deutsche Financial Services
☐ N911BH	Eurocopter (MBB) BO105CBS	S-685		0084	0395	2 AN 250-C20B	2400			
☐ N30LG	Eurocopter (Aerosp.) AS355F1 TwinStar	5065		0081	0591	2 AN 250-C20F	2400			lsf General Electric Capital Corp.
☐ N53LH	Eurocopter (Aerosp.) AS355F1 TwinStar	5093	N57898	0081	0696	2 AN 250-C20F	2400			
☐ N5787M	Eurocopter (Aerosp.) AS355F1 TwinStar	5067		0081	0591	2 AN 250-C20F	2400			lsf General Electric Capital Corp.
☐ N109RX	Agusta A109K2	10016		0093	0893	2 TU Arriel 1K1	2850	EMS		lsf/opf IHC-Intermountain Health Care
☐ N123RX	Agusta A109K2	10018		0093	0494	2 TU Arriel 1K1	2850	EMS		lsf/opf IHC-Intermountain Health Care
☐ N901CF	MD Helicopters MD 900 Explorer	900-00012	N9212Z	0095	0295	2 PWC PW206A	2722	EMS Care Flight		lsf Regional Emergency Medical Service
☐ N10UM	Eurocopter (MBB) BK117B-1	7231	N65541	0090	0693	2 LY LTS101-750B.1	3200			lsf Debis Financial Services Inc.
☐ N117CW	Eurocopter (MBB) BK117A-4	7125	N9021D	0087	1087	2 LY LTS101-650B.1	3200			lsf State Street Bank Trustee
☐ N117MA	Eurocopter (MBB) BK117A-3	7107	N529MB	0086	1186	2 LY LTS101-650B.1	3200			lsf DRL Enterprises Inc.
☐ N117MV	Eurocopter (MBB) BK117A-3	7089	N429MB	0086	0986	2 LY LTS101-650B.1	3200			lsf General Electric Capital Corp.
☐ N117NY	Eurocopter (MBB) BK117A-3	7110	N9017Z	0086	0987	2 LY LTS101-650B.1	3200			lsf S.S.Bank Trustee / opf Aeromed NYH
☐ N118HH	Eurocopter (MBB) BK117A-1	7036	N4493W	0084	1185	2 LY LTS101-650B.1	2850	EMS Life Star		lsf Debis Financ./opf Hartford Hospital
☐ N118LF	Eurocopter (MBB) BK117A-4	7137	N9025N	0087	0188	2 LY LTS101-650B.1	3200	EMS		lsf MDFC Equipment Leasing Corp.
☐ N127HH	Eurocopter (MBB) BK117A-3	7060	N160BK	0086	0186	2 LY LTS101-650B.1	3200			
☐ N155SC	Eurocopter (MBB) BK117A-3	7065	N155BK	0085	1290	2 LY LTS101-650B.1	3200			lsf Debis Financial Services Inc.
☐ N158BK	Eurocopter (MBB) BK117A-3	7058		0085	0186	2 LY LTS101-650B.1	3200			lsf Deutsche Financial Services
☐ N17SJ	Eurocopter (MBB) BK117B-1	7230	N6593M	0090	0191	2 LY LTS101-750B.1	3200			lsf Debis Financial Services Inc.
☐ N202HN	Eurocopter (MBB) BK117A-4	7115	N90184	0086	0787	2 LY LTS101-650B.1	3200			lsf State Street Bank Trustee
☐ N417BK	Eurocopter (MBB) BK117B-1	7143		0087	0188	2 LY LTS101-750B.1	3200			lsf MDFC Equipment Leasing Corp.
☐ N420MB	Eurocopter (MBB) BK117A-3	7077		0086	0986	2 LY LTS101-650B.1	3200			lsf General Electric Capital Corp.
☐ N424MB	Eurocopter (MBB) BK117A-3	7082		0086	0986	2 LY LTS101-650B.1	3200			lsf General Electric Capital Corp.
☐ N428MB	Eurocopter (MBB) BK117A-3	7088		0086	0986	2 LY LTS101-650B.1	3200			lsf General Electric Capital Corp.
☐ N5188B	Eurocopter (MBB) BK117B-1	7163		0089	0189	2 LY LTS101-750B.1	3200			lsf MDFC Equipment Leasing Corp.
☐ N5194C	Eurocopter (MBB) BK117B-1	7169		0089	0189	2 LY LTS101-750B.1	3200			lsf MDFC Equipment Leasing Corp.
☐ N527RM	Eurocopter (MBB) BK117A-4	7111	N527SF	0086	0787	2 LY LTS101-650B.1	3200			lsf State Street Bank Trustee
☐ N528SF	Eurocopter (MBB) BK117A-3	7104	N528MB	0086	1186	2 LY LTS101-650B.1	3200			lsf DRL Enterprises Inc.
☐ N586BH	Eurocopter (MBB) BK117A-4	7129	N9022E	0087	1087	2 LY LTS101-650B.1	3200			lsf State Street Bank Trustee
☐ N625MB	Eurocopter (MBB) BK117A-3	7108		0086	1186	2 LY LTS101-650B.1	3200			lsf DRL Enterprises Inc.
☐ N7059N	Eurocopter (MBB) BK117B-1	7154		0088	0189	2 LY LTS101-750B.1	3200			lsf MDFC Equipment Leasing Corp.
☐ N7060G	Eurocopter (MBB) BK117B-1	7173		0089	0189	2 LY LTS101-750B.1	3200			lsf MDFC Equipment Leasing Corp.
☐ N71703	Eurocopter (MBB) BK117B-1	7227		0090	0191	2 LY LTS101-750B.1	3200			lsf Debis Financial Services Inc.
☐ N90260	Eurocopter (MBB) BK117B-1	7140		0087	0188	2 LY LTS101-750B.1	3200			lsf MDFC Equipment Leasing Corp.
☐ N911BY	Eurocopter (MBB) BK117A-4	7127	N11UM	0087	1087	2 LY LTS101-650B.1	3200			lsf State Street Bank Trustee
☐ N911VU	Eurocopter (MBB) BK117B-1	7141	N90263	0087	0188	2 LY LTS101-750B.1	3200			lsf MDFC Equipment Leasing Corp.
☐ N951AM	Eurocopter (MBB) BK117A-3	7017	N317RM	0084	0495	2 LY LTS101-650B.1	3200			
☐ N185GA	Cessna 441 Conquest II	441-0066	D-INKA	0078	0889	2 GA TPE331-8-403S	4468			
☐ N26PK	Cessna 441 Conquest II	441-0143	N2627K	0080	0389	2 GA TPE331-8-403S	4468			
☐ N441RC	Cessna 441 Conquest II	441-0076		0078	0289	2 GA TPE331-8-403S	4468			
☐ N8970N	Cessna 441 Conquest II	441-0092		0079	0289	2 GA TPE331-8-403S	4468			lsf General Electric Capital Corp.
☐ N454MA	Mitsubishi MU-2B-60 Marquise	1535SA		0081	0289	2 GA TPE331-10-501M	5250			
☐ N479MA	Mitsubishi MU-2B-60 Marquise	1553SA		0082	0289	2 GA TPE331-10-501M	5250			
☐ N28MS	Beech King Air E90	LW-100	N31FN	0074	0198	2 PWC PT6A-28	4581			
☐ N220TB	Beech King Air B200	BB-1057	F-GILY	0083	0697	2 PWC PT6A-42	5670			

RODGERS HELICOPTER SERVICES, Llc **Kearney, NE**

Rt 1, Box 121, Kearney, NE 68847, USA ☎ (308) 234-3948 Tx: none Fax: (308) 234-6090 SITA: n/a
F: 1992 👥 n/a Head: Merle D. Fratzke Net: n/a

☐ N42BJ	Cessna 421B Golden Eagle	421B0342		0073	0392	2 CO GTSIO-520-H	3379			
☐ N5445J	Sikorsky S-76A	760178		0081	0295	2 AN 250-C30	4672	EMS		opf Good Samaritan Hospital

ROGERS HELICOPTERS, Inc. (Rogers Aviation / TGR Helicopters) **Clovis-Rogers Heliport, CA**

PO Box 4, Clovis, CA 93613, USA ☎ (209) 299-4903 Tx: none Fax: (209) 299-2003 SITA: n/a
F: 1962 👥 30 Head: Wanda L. Rogers Net: n/a EMS/ambulance services are operated under the marketing names AIR LIFE, ROAM, SKY LIFE & WINGS AIR RESCUE. All same headquarters & fleet.
Fixed wing flights are operated under the marketing names AIR AVIATION. TGR HELICOPTERS-name (a sub. of Rogers Helicopters & Whirlwide Inc.) is used for some activities.

☐ N16832	Bell 206B JetRanger III	2243		0077	0380	1 AN 250-C20B	1451			
☐ N20395	Bell 206B JetRanger III	3301		0081	0783	1 AN 250-C20B	1451			
☐ N2292W	Bell 206B JetRanger III	505		0067	0488	1 AN 250-C20B	1451			cvtd 206A
☐ N2762P	Bell 206B JetRanger III	2711		0079	0890	1 AN 250-C20B	1451			
☐ N2763M	Bell 206B JetRanger III	2646		0079	1284	1 AN 250-C20B	1451			
☐ N58140	Bell 206B JetRanger III	1108		0073	0880	1 AN 250-C20B	1451			cvtd JetRanger
☐ N59564	Bell 206B JetRanger III	1389		0074	1189	1 AN 250-C20B	1451			cvtd JetRanger
☐ N59571	Bell 206B JetRanger III	1433		0074	0588	1 AN 250-C20B	1451			cvtd JetRanger
☐ N29176	Cessna T210L Turbo Centurion II	21059828		0073	0389	1 CO TSIO-520-H	1724			
☐ N10864	Bell 206L-1 LongRanger III	45434		0080	0286	1 AN 250-C30P	1882			cvtd LongRanger II
☐ N712M	Bell 206L-3 LongRanger III	51072		0083	0891	1 AN 250-C30P	1882			
☐ N3609J	Eurocopter (Aerosp.) AS350D AStar	1245		0080	0883	1 LY LTS101-600A.2	1950			
☐ N505WW	Eurocopter (Aerosp.) AS350B2 AStar	2442	JA6046	0091	0298	1 TU Arriel 1D1	2250			
☐ N911EW	Eurocopter (Aerosp.) AS350B2 AStar	2657	I-MUSY	0092	0698	1 TU Arriel 1D1	2250			
☐ N105RH	Eurocopter (MBB) BO105C	S-55	N99896	0072	0687	2 AN 250-C20	2300			
☐ N101MZ	Eurocopter (Aerosp.) AS355F1 TwinStar	5045		0081	0285	2 AN 250-C20F	2400			
☐ N102UM	Eurocopter (Aerosp.) AS355F1 TwinStar	5075	N130US	0081	1095	2 AN 250-C20F	2400			

425 registration type of aircraft cn/fn ex/ex* mfd del powered by mtow kg configuration selcal name/fln/specialitites/remarks

☐ N5013H	Bell 222	47010		0080	0391	2 LY LTS101-650C.2	3561	EMS Air Life		
☐ N911WL	Bell 222U	47557		0086	0493	2 LY LTS101-750C.1	3742	EMS Air Life		
☐ N45731	Bell UH-1B (204)	330	61-0750	0062	0884	1 LY T5311D	3856			
☐ N896SB	Beech King Air A100	B-160	OY-CCS	0073	0695	2 PWC PT6A-28	5216			
☐ N911HW	Bell 212	31101	N703H	0080	0596	2 PWC PT6T-3 TwinPac	5080			
☐ N911KW	Bell 212	30592	N50EW	0073	0796	2 PWC PT6T-3 TwinPac	5080			
☐ N911VR	Bell 212	30998	N701H	0080	0693	2 PWC PT6T-3 TwinPac	5080			
☐ N91AL	Bell 212	30821		0077	0693	2 PWC PT6T-3 TwinPac	5080			

RONSON AVIATION, Inc. (Subsidiary of Ronson, Corp.) — **Trenton-Mercer County, NJ**

Trenton-Mercer Airport, Trenton, NJ 08628, USA ☎ (609) 771-9500 Tx: none Fax: (609) 771-4366 SITA: n/a
F: 1962 ⁂ 70 Head: Gary Hilton Net: n/a

☐ N6645K	Beech C99 Airliner	U-209		0083	0384	2 PWC PT6A-36	5126	Y15		
☐ N6656N	Beech C99 Airliner	U-213		0083	0484	2 PWC PT6A-36	5126	Y15		

ROSS AVIATION, Inc. = NRG — **Albuquerque-Kirkland AFB, NM**

PO Box 9124, Albuquerque, NM 87119, USA ☎ (505) 845-6042 Tx: none Fax: (505) 845-5023 SITA: n/a
F: 1971 ⁂ n/a Head: Lewis A. Pierce ICAO: ENERGY Net: n/a All operations are conducted in conjunction with the Albuquerque operations office of the US Department of Energy.

☐ N7232R	Beech King Air B200C	BL-69	N2811B	0083	0186	2 PWC PT6A-42	5670	Y9 / Freighter		lsf / opf US Department of Energy
☐ N148DE	De Havilland DHC-6 Twin Otter 300	493	N72348	0076	0676	2 PWC PT6A-27	5670	Y19		lsf / opf US Department of Energy
☐ N162DE	De Havilland DHC-6 Twin Otter 300	429	N35062	0074	0974	2 PWC PT6A-27	5670	Y19		lsf / opf US Department of Energy
☐ N135DE	Learjet 35A	35A-667	N91566	0091	0891	2 GA TFE731-2-2B	8301	Y8		lsf / opf US Department of Energy
☐ N166DE	Boeing (Douglas) DC-9-15F (RC)	47152 / 170	N66AF	0067	0684	2 PW JT8D-7A (HK3/ABS)	41141	Y80 / Freighter		lsf / opf US Department of Energy
☐ N179DE	Boeing (Douglas) DC-9-15F (RC)	47011 / 102	N79SL	0067	1179	2 PW JT8D-7 (HK3/ABS)	41141	Y80 / Freighter		lsf / opf US Department of Energy
☐ N229DE	Boeing (Douglas) DC-9-15F (RC)	45826 / 79	N29AF	0067	0779	2 PW JT8D-7A (HK3/ABS)	41141	Y80 / Freighter		lsf / opf US Department of Energy

ROTEC INDUSTRIES – Flight Department (Flight Dept. of Rotec Industries, Inc.) — **Rockford-Greater Rockford , IL**

333 West Lake Street, Elmhurst, IL 60126, USA ☎ (630) 279-3300 Tx: none Fax: (630) 279-3317 SITA: n/a
F: 1997 ⁂ n/a Head: Robert F. Oury Net: n/a Operates non-commercial corporate flights for its parent (manufacturing of concrete components) company only.

☐ N111RZ	BAe (BAC) One-Eleven 401AK	056	N491ST	0065	0797	2 RR Spey 511-14	40597	Corporate 29Pax		

ROTOR AIR ALASKA, Inc. — **Soldotna, AK**

HC 1, Box 1290, Soldotna, AK 99669, USA ☎ (907) 262-4718 Tx: n/a Fax: (907) 262-6620 SITA: n/a
F: 1994 ⁂ n/a Head: Linda R. Alsworth Net: n/a Aircraft below MTOW 1361kg: Hughes 369HS (500C)

☐ N158EH	Eurocopter (Aerosp.) AS350BA AStar	2055		0087	1197	1 TU Arriel 1B	2100			cvtd AS350B
☐ N58ET	Sikorsky S-58ET	58-1090		0059	1097	1 PWC PT6T-3 TwinPac	5897			cvtd S-58E

ROTORS IN MOTION, Corp. — **Chicago-Waukegan Regional, IL**

PO Box 229, Gurnee, IL 60031-0229, USA ☎ (847) 662-2900 Tx: none Fax: (847) 662-4020 SITA: n/a
F: 1993 ⁂ n/a Head: James Terra Net: http://www.flyrotors.com

☐ N45EA	Bell 206L-3 LongRanger III	51104	N6NJ	0084	0896	1 AN 250-C30P	1882			
☐ N109SL	Agusta A109A II	7299	JA9677	0083	1195	2 AN 250-C20B	2600			
☐ N6FF	Agusta A109A	7153	N39P	0078	1095	2 AN 250-C20B	2600			

ROTOR WING, Inc. — **Mount Olive-Rotor Wing Heliport, AL**

PO Box 130, Mount Olive, AL 35117, USA ☎ (205) 631-6531 Tx: none Fax: (205) 631-6552 SITA: n/a
F: 1979 ⁂ 5 Head: Peter L. Basler Net: n/a Aircraft below MTOW 1361 kg: Hughes 269C (300C)

☐ N369RW	MD Helicopters MD 500E (Hughes 369E)	0253E		0088	0388	1 AN 250-C20B	1361			lsf Blue Ridge Helicopters Inc.
☐ N2175J	Bell 206L-3 LongRanger III	51515		0091	1094	1 AN 250-C30P	1882			

ROUNDBALL ONE – Flight operations (Roundball One, Corp. dba / Associated with the "Detroit Pistons") — **Detroit-Metropolitan, MI**

29840 Northline Road, Romulus, MI 48174, USA ☎ (734) 941-5822 Tx: none Fax: (734) 941-8888 SITA: n/a
F: 1987 ⁂ n/a Head: William Davidson Net: n/a Non-commercial flights, exclusively sports-teams of the "Detroit Pistons" to and from their matches.

☐ N880DP	BAe (BAC) One-Eleven 401AK	079	N800DM	0066	0687	2 RR Spey 511-14	40597	C24		opf "Detroit Pistons"
☐ N880RB	Boeing (Douglas) DC-9-32	47635 / 754	PK-GNH	0074	0695	2 PW JT8D-9 (HK3/ABS)	48988	C80		std DTT / to be opf "Detroit Pistons"

ROVER AIRWAYS INTERNATIONAL, Inc. = 5R / ROV (formerly Air Express) — **Pagosa Springs-Stevens Field, CO**

PO Box 850, Pagosa Springs, CO 81147, USA ☎ (970) 731-2190 Tx: 168214 Fax: (970) 731-2194 SITA: DROHQ5R
F: 1987 ⁂ 12 Head: Roger M. Wickham IATA: 376 ICAO: ROVERAIR Net: n/a

☐ N4447R	Cessna R182 Skylane RG II	R18200601		0078	0188	1 LY O-540-J3C5D	1406	Freighter		

ROYAL AIR FREIGHT, Inc. = RAX (Royal Air Charter) — **Pontiac-Oakland, MI**

2141 Airport Road, Waterford, MI 48327, USA ☎ (248) 666-3070 Tx: none Fax: (248) 666-4719 SITA: n/a
F: 1961 ⁂ n/a Head: William Kostich ICAO: AIR ROYAL Net: n/a Passenger flight are operated under the marketing name ROYAL AIR CHARTER (same fleet & headquarters).

☐ N1591T	Cessna 310R II	310R0112		0074	0789	2 CO IO-520-M	2495	Freighter/Pax		
☐ N22DM	Cessna 310R II	310R0069		0074	1287	2 CO IO-520-M	2495	Freighter/Pax		
☐ N22LE	Cessna 310R II	310R0033		0074	1186	2 CO IO-520-M	2495	Freighter/Pax		
☐ N2643D	Cessna 310R II	310R1686		0079	0198	2 CO IO-520-MB	2495	Freighter/Pax		
☐ N87309	Cessna 310R II	310R0510		0075	0788	2 CO IO-520-M	2495	Freighter/Pax		
☐ N87341	Cessna 310R II	310R0520		0075	0987	2 CO IO-520-M	2495	Freighter/Pax		
☐ N160PB	Cessna 402C II	402C0493	N6841M	0081	0692	2 CO TSIO-520-VB	3107	Freighter/Pax		
☐ N5279J	Cessna 402B II	402B1202		0076	0297	2 CO TSIO-520-E	2858	Freighter/Pax		
☐ N54307	Piper PA-31-350 Navajo Chieftain	31-7405233		0074	0385	2 LY TIO-540-J2BD	3175	Freighter		
☐ N201UV	Mitsubishi MU-2L (MU-2B-36) Cargoliner	680	N201U	0075	0893	2 GA TPE331-6-251M	5250	Freighter		Cavenaugh SCD conversion
☐ N688RA	Mitsubishi MU-2L (MU-2B-36) Cargoliner	688	N688MA	0075	0397	2 GA TPE331-6-252M	5250	Freighter		Cavenaugh SCD conversion
☐ N717PS	Mitsubishi MU-2L (MU-2B-36) Cargoliner	686	N23RA	0075	0593	2 GA TPE331-6-251M	5250	Freighter		Cavenaugh SCD conversion
☐ N34A	Embraer 110P1 Bandeirante (EMB-110P1)	110350	N4361Q	0081	0292	2 PWC PT6A-34	5670	Freighter		
☐ N49RA	Embraer 110P1 Bandeirante (EMB-110P1)	110424	C-GPRV	0083	0494	2 PWC PT6A-34	5670	Freighter		
☐ N64DA	Embraer 110P1 Bandeirante (EMB-110P1)	110385	PT-SFC*	0081	0593	2 PWC PT6A-34	5670	Freighter		
☐ N72RA	Embraer 110P1 Bandeirante (EMB-110P1)	110377	C-GHOV	0081	0494	2 PWC PT6A-34	5670	Freighter		
☐ N73RA	Embraer 110P1 Bandeirante (EMB-110P1)	110413	C-GPNW	0082	0494	2 PWC PT6A-34	5670	Freighter		
☐ N120RA	Learjet 24	24-153	N153BR	0068	1293	2 GE CJ610-4	5897	Freighter		
☐ N48L	Learjet 24A	24A-107		0066	0190	2 GE CJ610-4	5897	Freighter		
☐ N64CE	Learjet 24B	24B-205	N64CF	0069	0886	2 GE CJ610-6	6123	Freighter		
☐ N710TV	Learjet 24	24-159	N66MR	0068	0198	2 GE CJ610-4	5897	Freighter		
☐ N9RA	Learjet 23	23-095	N5D	0066	0396	2 GE CJ610-4	5670	Freighter		
☐ N16KK	Learjet 25B	25B-174	N412SP	0074	0798	2 GE CJ610-6	6804	Freighter		
☐ N2094L	Learjet 25B	25B-095	C-GRCO	0072	0497	2 GE CJ610-6	6804	Freighter		

RUSTS FLYING SERVICE, Inc. (Subsidiary of Rustair, Inc.) — **Anchorage-Lake Hood SPB, AK**

PO Box 190325, Anchorage, AK 99502, USA ☎ (907) 243-1595 Tx: none Fax: (907) 248-0552 SITA: n/a
F: 1963 ⁂ 8 Head: Henry B. Rust Net: http://www.alaskanet.com/rusts

☐ N4596U	Cessna U206G Stationair 6 II	U20604990		0079	0579	1 CO IO-520-F	1633			lsf Rustair Inc. / Floats / Wheel-Skis
☐ N4661Z	Cessna U206G Stationair 6 II	U20605998		0080	0982	1 CO IO-520-F	1633			lsf Rustair Inc. / Floats / Wheel-Skis
☐ N4891Z	Cessna U206G Stationair 6 II	U20606044		0080	0589	1 CO IO-520-F	1633			lsf Rustair Inc. / Floats / Wheel-Skis
☐ N756WY	Cessna U206G Stationair 6 II	U20604426		0078	0691	1 CO IO-520-F	1633			lsf Rustair Inc. / Floats / Wheel-Skis
☐ N2740X	De Havilland DHC-2 Beaver I	579		0053	0883	1 PW R-985	2313			lsf Rustair Inc. / Floats / Wheel-Skis
☐ N4444Z	De Havilland DHC-2 Beaver I	1307	N123PG	0058	0789	1 PW R-985	2313			lsf Rustair Inc. / Floats / Wheel-Skis
☐ N68083	De Havilland DHC-2 Beaver I	1254	57-2580	0057	0778	1 PW R-985	2313			lsf Rustair Inc. / Floats / Wheel-Skis
☐ N2899J	De Havilland DHC-3 Otter	425	C-GLCR	0061	0689	1 PW R-1340	3629			lsf Rustair Inc. / Floats / Wheel-Skis

RYAN INTERNATIONAL AIRLINES, Inc. = RYN (formerly Ryan Aviation Corporation) — **Wichita-Mid Continent, KS**

266 North Main, Wichita, KS 67202, USA ☎ (316) 942-0141 Tx: none Fax: (316) 942-7949 SITA: n/a
F: 1972 ⁂ 650 Head: Ronald D. Ryan ICAO: RYAN INTERNATIONAL Net: n/a

☐ EI-BXK	Boeing 737-448	25736 / 2269		0092	1298	2 CFMI CFM56-3B2	65000	Y170	BD-HR	lsf EIN/opf TransGlobal Tours in winter
☐ EI-CRC	Boeing 737-46B	24124 / 1679	EC-GNC	0089	1198	2 CFMI CFM56-3C1	65770	Y170	JM-KR	lsf EIN/opf TransGlobal Tours in winter
☐ N714AW	Airbus Industrie A320-214	714	G-BXKA*	0097	1098	2 CFMI CFM56-5B4	77000	Y180	RS-EF	lsf FCL in winter / opf Apple Vacations
☐ N716AW	Airbus Industrie A320-214	716	G-BXKB*	0097	1298	2 CFMI CFM56-5B4	77000	Y180	RS-EG	lsf FCL in winter / opf Apple Vacations
☐ C-GVXB	Airbus Industrie A320-212	409	F-WWDU*	0093	1298	2 CFMI CFM56-5A3	77000	Y168	EQ-AR	lsf CMM / cvtd -231
☐ G-BXKC	Airbus Industrie A320-214	730	F-WWBQ*	0097	1298	2 CFMI CFM56-5B4	77000	Y180	RS-EH	lsf FCL in winter / opf Apple Vacations
☐ G-BXKD	Airbus Industrie A320-214	735	F-WWBV*	0097	1298	2 CFMI CFM56-5B4	77000	Y180	RS-EJ	lsf FCL in winter / opf Apple Vacations
☐ G-CRPH	Airbus Industrie A320-231	424	F-WQBB	0093	0598	2 IAE V2500-A1	75500	Y180	JM-AS	lsf/opf Skyservice USA in Skyservice-cs
☐ N210NE	Boeing 727-31 (F)	18903 / 147	N833TW	0065	0394	3 PW JT8D-7B	72802	Freighter	AC-EF	lsf/opf EWW / cvtd -31
☐ N220NE	Boeing 727-31 (F)	18905 / 160	N840TW	0065	0394	3 PW JT8D-7B	72802	Freighter		lsf/opf EWW / cvtd -31
☐ N329QS	Boeing 727-21 (F)	19038 / 285	N329PA	0066		3 PW JT8D-7B (HK3/FDX)	72802	Freighter		lsf/opf EWW in Emery colors / cvtd -21
☐ N355QS	Boeing 727-21 (F)	19257 / 385	N355PA	0067		3 PW JT8D-7B (HK3/FDX)	72802	Freighter		lsf/opf EWW in Emery colors / cvtd -21
☐ N356QS	Boeing 727-21 (F)	19258 / 397	N356PA	0067		3 PW JT8D-7B (HK3/FDX)	72802	Freighter		lsf/opf EWW in Emery colors / cvtd -21
☐ N357QS	Boeing 727-21 (F)	19259 / 408	N357PA	0067		3 PW JT8D-7B (HK3/FDX)	72802	Freighter		lsf/opf EWW in Emery colors / cvtd -21
☐ N359QS	Boeing 727-21 (F)	19007 / 269	HK-2846X	0066		3 PW JT8D-7B (HK3/FDX)	72802	Freighter		lsf/opf EWW in Emery colors / cvtd -21
☐ N413EX	Boeing 727-51C	19206 / 294	N495US	0066		3 PW JT8D-7B (HK3/FDX)	76884	Freighter		lsf EWW / opf USPS in USPS colors

426 registration type of aircraft cn/fn ex/ex* mfd del powered by mtow kg configuration selcal name/fln/specialitites/remarks

registration	type of aircraft	cn/fn	ex/ex*	mfd	del	powered by	mtow kg	configuration	selcal	name/fln/specialitites/remarks
☐ N416EX	Boeing 727-51C	19287 / 383	N496US	0067		3 PW JT8D-7B (HK3/FDX)	76884	Freighter		lsf EWW / opf USPS in USPS colors
☐ N417EX	Boeing 727-51C	19290 / 417	N499US	0067		3 PW JT8D-7B (HK3/FDX)	76884	Freighter		lsf EWW / opf USPS in USPS colors
☐ N421EX	Boeing 727-22C	19099 / 322	HK-2474	0066		3 PW JT8D-7B (HK3/FDX)	76884	Freighter		lsf EWW / opf USPS in USPS colors
☐ N426EX	Boeing 727-22C	19089 / 250	N7401U	0066		3 PW JT8D-7B (HK3/FDX)	76884	Freighter		lsf EWW / opf USPS in USPS colors
☐ N427EX	Boeing 727-22C	19090 / 277	N7402U	0066		3 PW JT8D-7B (HK3/FDX)	76884	Freighter		lsf EWW / opf USPS in USPS colors
☐ N428EX	Boeing 727-22C	19097 / 307	N7409U	0066		3 PW JT8D-7B (HK3/FDX)	76884	Freighter		lsf EWW / opf USPS in USPS colors
☐ N429EX	Boeing 727-22C	19100 / 324	N7412U	0066		3 PW JT8D-7B (HK3/FDX)	76884	Freighter		lsf EWW / opf USPS in USPS colors
☐ N432EX	Boeing 727-151C	19867 / 514	N488US	0068		3 PW JT8D-7B (HK3/FDX)	76884	Freighter		lsf EWW / opf USPS in USPS colors
☐ N433EX	Boeing 727-151C	19868 / 529	N489US	0068		3 PW JT8D-7B (HK3/FDX)	76884	Freighter		lsf EWW / opf USPS in USPS colors
☐ N435EX	Boeing 727-51C	19288 / 389	N497US	0067		3 PW JT8D-7B (HK3/FDX)	76884	Freighter		lsf EWW / opf USPS in USPS colors
☐ N436EX	Boeing 727-51C	19289 / 403	N498US	0067		3 PW JT8D-7B (HK3/FDX)	76884	Freighter		lsf EWW / opf USPS in USPS colors
☐ N526PC	Boeing 727-77C	20370 / 821	N555BN	0070		3 PW JT8D-7B (HK3/FDX)	76884	Freighter		lsf EWW / opf USPS in USPS colors
☐ N527PC	Boeing 727-172C	19665 / 476	N45498	0067		3 PW JT8D-7B (HK3/FDX)	76884	Freighter		lsf EWW / opf USPS in USPS colors
☐ N528PC	Boeing 727-82C	19597 / 524	N4564U	0068		3 PW JT8D-7B (HK3/FDX)	76884	Freighter		lsf EWW / opf USPS in USPS colors
☐ N721JE	Boeing 727-76 (F)	18843 / 170	N4602D	0065		3 PW JT8D-7B (HK3/FDX)	72802	Freighter		lsf EWW / opf USPS in USPS colors
☐ N94GS	Boeing 727-44 (F)	18892 / 148	N92GS	0065	0394	3 PW JT8D-7B	72802	Freighter		lsf/opf EWW / cvtd -44
☐ N17789	Boeing 727-232 (F) (A)	20643 / 951	N520PE	0073	0696	3 PW JT8D-15	83552	Freighter		lsf TPLsng./cvtd-232/opf Nat'lFisheries
☐ N521DB	Boeing 727-243 (A)	21266 / 1227	N573PE	0076	0797	3 PW JT8D-9A (HK3/FDX)	79832	E59	JM-EG	lsf Riverhorse Inv./opf Star Air Tours
☐ C-GIKF	Boeing 727-227 (A)	20772 / 982	N99763	0073	1197	3 PW JT8D-7B (HK3/FDX)	79606	Y170	EH-DK	lsf KFA
☐ C-GMKF	Boeing 727-227 (A)	21119 / 1175	N16761	0075	1197	3 PW JT8D-9A (HK3/FDX)	79606	Y170	DG-BF	lsf KFA
☐ N571SC	Boeing (Douglas) DC-10-10	46645 / 283	SE-DHX	0079	0798	3 GE CF6-6D1A	206385	Y380		lsf/opf Skyservice USA in Skyservice-cs
☐ N572SC	Boeing (Douglas) DC-10-10	46977 / 251	SE-DHZ	0078	0798	3 GE CF6-6D1A	206385	Y380		lsf/opf Skyservice USA in Skyservice-cs

SABER CARGO AIRLINES, Inc. = SBR   (Saber Executive Helicopters)   (formerly Saber Aviation, Inc.)   Charlotte-Douglas Int'l, NC   *Saber* CARGO AIRLINES

PO Box 19049, Charlotte, NC 28219-0049, USA   ☎ (704) 359-8456   Tx: none   Fax: (704) 359-8275   SITA: n/a
F: 1978   ♔♔♔ n/a   Head: Michael W. Dockery   IATA: 854   ICAO: FREIGHTER   Net: n/a   Helicopter-services are operated under the name SABER EXECUTIVE HELICOPTERS (same headquarters).

☐ N8104J	Bell 206B JetRanger	501		0070	0397	1 AN 250-C20	1451	Executive		cvtd 206A
☐ N402NA	Cessna 402A	402A0033		0069	1283	2 CO TSIO-520-E	2858	Freighter		lsf First Charlotte Leasing Co.
☐ N204AA	Beech C-45G (18)	AF-79	N204A	0054	0481	2 PW R-985-AN14B	3969	Freighter		lsf First Charlotte Leasing Co.
☐ N115SA	Boeing (Douglas) DC-3C (C-47A-25-DK)	13310	C-GRTM	0044	1285	2 PW R-1830	12202	Freighter		lsf First Charlotte Leasing Co.
☐ N116SA	Boeing (Douglas) DC-3C (C-47B-25-DK)	32855	C-FTVL	0045	0493	2 PW R-1830	12202	Freighter		lsf JAT Aviation Inc.
☐ N12907	Boeing (Douglas) DC-3C (C-47B-20-DK)	27187	N92BF	0045	0495	2 PW R-1830	12202	Freighter		
☐ N58NA	Boeing (Douglas) DC-3C (C-47A-5-DK)	12970	FinAF DO-12	0044	0795	2 PW R-1830	12202	Freighter		
☐ N79017	Boeing (Douglas) DC-3C (C-47A-70-DL)	19227	42-100764	0043	0795	2 PW R-1830	12202	Freighter		

SABER HELICOPTERS, Inc.   San Antonio-Int'l, TX

Tower Life Building, Suite 500, San Antonio, TX 78205, USA   ☎ (210) 226-1657   Tx: none   Fax: (210) 554-4401   SITA: n/a
F: 1973   ♔♔♔ n/a   Head: James P. Zachry   Net: n/a

☐ N5743W	Bell 206B JetRanger III	3050		0080	0890	1 AN 250-C20B	1451			

SABRE AERO CHARTER   (National Flight Services)   (Sabre Leasing Associates, Inc. dba)   Toledo-Express, OH

10971 East Airport Service Road, Swanton, OH 43558, USA   ☎ (419) 865-2311   Tx: none   Fax: (419) 867-4230   SITA: n/a
F: 1992   ♔♔♔ n/a   Head: Bill Kessell   Net: n/a   Operates in conjunction/under the licence of AERO CHARTER, Inc. (MO). Marketing is done under the name NATIONAL FLIGHT SERVICES.

☐ N15HF	Sabreliner 60 (Rockwell NA265-60)	306-60	N15H	0070	0294	2 PW JT12A-8	9150			
☐ N306CF	Sabreliner 60 (Rockwell NA265-60)	306-13	N60EL	0067	0793	2 PW JT12A-8	9150			

SACRAMENTO EXECUTIVE HELICOPTERS, Inc.   Sacramento-Executive, CA

6107 Freeport Blvd., Sacramento, CA 95822, USA   ☎ (916) 424-9691   Tx: none   Fax: (916) 424-0304   SITA: n/a
F: 1988   ♔♔♔ n/a   Head: John E. Hamilton   Net: n/a   Aircraft below MTOW 1361kg: Robinson R22

☐ N802EH	Bell 206B JetRanger III	2835	N73LM	0079	0396	1 AN 250-C20B	1451			

SAFARI HELICOPTERS   (Safari Aviation, Inc. / Safari Helicopter Tours & Hilo Safari Air, Inc. dba)   Lihue & Hilo, HI

PO Box 1941, Lihue, HI 96766, USA   ☎ (808) 246-0136   Tx: none   Fax: (808) 246-0670   SITA: n/a
F: 1991   ♔♔♔ n/a   Head: Preston S. Myers   Net: http://safariair.com

☐ N891SA	Eurocopter (Aerosp.) AS350BA AStar	2201		0089	0592	1 TU Arriel 1B	2100			lsf SAF Ltd
☐ N963SA	Eurocopter (Aerosp.) AS350BA AStar	2855		0095	1196	1 TU Arriel 1B	2100			lsf SAF Ltd
☐ N964SA	Eurocopter (Aerosp.) AS350BA AStar	2931		0096	0197	1 TU Arriel 1B	2100			lsf SAF Ltd
☐ N985SA	Eurocopter (Aerosp.) AS350B2 AStar	3111		0098	1198	1 TU Arriel 1D1	2250			lsf SAF Ltd

SAFEWING AVIATION, Co. Inc. = SFF   Kansas City-Downtown, MO

1025 Lou Holland Drive, Suite 211, Kansas City, MO 64116, USA   ☎ (816) 421-7737   Tx: none   Fax: (816) 421-8009   SITA: n/a
F: 1979   ♔♔♔ n/a   Head: Donnie J. Dorothy   ICAO: SWIFTWING   Net: n/a

☐ N31SW	Piper PA-32R-300 Lance	32R-7680311		0076	1292	1 LY IO-540-K1G5D	1633			lsf Delta Sales Co.
☐ N47977	Piper PA-32R-300 Lance	32R-7880031		0078	0396	1 LY IO-540-K1G5D	1633			lsf Delta Sales Co.
☐ N6249J	Piper PA-32R-300 Lance	32R-7680340		0076	1292	1 LY IO-540-K1G5D	1633			lsf Delta Sales Co.
☐ N7197F	Piper PA-32R-300 Lance	32R-7780058		0077	1292	1 LY IO-540-K1G5D	1633			lsf Delta Sales Co.
☐ N8304C	Piper PA-32R-300 Lance	32R-7680091		0076	0396	1 LY IO-540-K1G5D	1633			lsf Delta Sales Co.
☐ N88RH	Piper PA-32R-300 Lance	32R-7680065		0076	1292	1 LY IO-540-K1G5D	1633			lsf Delta Sales Co.
☐ N2883Q	Piper PA-34-200T Seneca II	34-7970326		0079	0398	2 CO TSIO-360-EB	2073			lsf Delta Sales Co.
☐ N3065J	Piper PA-34-200T Seneca II	34-7970066		0079	0295	2 CO TSIO-360-EB	2073			lsf Delta Sales Co.

SAFFORD AVIATION SERVICE, Inc.   Safford-Municipal/Regional, AZ

4550 East Aviation Way, Safford, AZ 85546, USA   ☎ (520) 428-7670   Tx: none   Fax: (520) 428-5368   SITA: n/a
F: 1954   ♔♔♔ n/a   Head: Andrea R. Benson   Net: n/a

☐ N113AB	Beech Baron B55 (95-B55)	TC-1622	N3089W	0074	0489	2 CO IO-470-L	2313			
☐ N119AB	Beech Baron C55 (95-C55)	TE-145	N237WM	0066	0495	2 CO IO-520-C	2404			
☐ N732	Twin (Aero) Shrike Commander 500S	500S-1800-15		0068	0595	2 LY IO-540-E1B5	3062			

SAFFORD SPRAYERS   (John Hunt dba)   Safford-Municipal, AZ

PO Box 815, Thatcher, AZ 85552, USA   ☎ (520) 428-2741   Tx: none   Fax: (520) 428-2741   SITA: n/a
F: 1977   ♔♔♔ n/a   Head: John Hunt   Net: n/a

☐ N9190G	Air Tractor AT-802A (F)	802A-0006		0093	0595	1 PWC PT6A-65AG	7257	Tanker/Sprayer		400 / lsf First National Bank West TX

SAINT CHARLES FLYING SERVICES, Inc.   St. Charles, MO

3001 Airport Road, St. Charles, MO 63301, USA   ☎ (573) 946-6066   Tx: none   Fax: (573) 946-6245   SITA: n/a
F: 1972   ♔♔♔ n/a   Head: Dennis Bampton   Net: n/a

☐ N2623C	Cessna R182 Skylane RG II	R18200179		0078	0782	1 LY O-540-J3C5D	1406			lsf pvt
☐ N2056S	Cessna T210L Turbo Centurion II	21061023		0075	0492	1 CO TSIO-520-H	1724			
☐ N50DB	Cessna 210L Centurion II	21060107		0073	0992	1 CO IO-520-L	1724			
☐ N6864C	Cessna T210L Turbo Centurion II	21061317	C-GMIF	0076	0494	1 CO TSIO-520-H	1724			
☐ N7235F	Cessna T210N Turbo Centurion II	21063038	C-GSYS	0079	1296	1 CO TSIO-520-R	1814			
☐ N732GH	Cessna 210L Centurion II	21061498		0076	0692	1 CO IO-520-L	1724			lsf pvt
☐ N3733D	Beech Duchess 76	ME-362		0080	0493	2 LY O-360-A1G6D	1769			lsf pvt
☐ N6015Z	Beech Duchess 76	ME-145		0079	1292	2 LY O-360-A1G6D	1769			lsf pvt
☐ N4264J	Cessna 310R II	310R0201		0075	1093	2 CO IO-520-M	2495			

SAINT LOUIS HELICOPTER AIRWAYS, Inc.   Chesterfield-Spirit of St. Louis, MO

PO Box 809, Chesterfield, MO 63006-0809, USA   ☎ (314) 532-1177   Tx: none   Fax: (314) 536-1714   SITA: n/a
F: 1970   ♔♔♔ 72   Head: John R. Murphy   Net: n/a

☐ N1075P	Bell 206L-1 LongRanger II	45348		0079	0384	1 AN 250-C28B	1882			
☐ N2070Z	Bell 206L-1 LongRanger II	45730		0081	1095	1 AN 250-C28B	1882			
☐ N5741Y	Bell 206L-1 LongRanger II	45467		0080	0895	1 AN 250-C28B	1882			
☐ N5751M	Bell 206L-1 LongRanger II	45522	N911WB	0080	0686	1 AN 250-C28B	1882			
☐ N810F	Bell 206L LongRanger	46603		0078	0784	1 AN 250-C20B	1814			
☐ N205LF	Eurocopter (MBB) BO105CBS	S-146	N770H	0074	0993	2 AN 250-C20B	2400			
☐ N233SL	Eurocopter (MBB) BO105CBS	S-387	I-EHBB	0077	0191	2 AN 250-C20B	2400			
☐ N26SE	Eurocopter (MBB) BO105CBS-2	S-587	N2909L	0082	0294	2 AN 250-C20B	2400			
☐ N2784F	Eurocopter (MBB) BO105CBS-2	S-621		0084	0784	2 AN 250-C20B	2400			lsf St. John's Regional Health Centre
☐ N692DD	Eurocopter (MBB) BO105CS	S-149	N21SE	0074	1288	2 AN 250-C20B	2400			
☐ N9107R	Eurocopter (MBB) BO105C	S-129		0073	0994	2 AN 250-C20B	2400			
☐ N230H	Eurocopter (MBB) BK117A-4	7136	N90241	0087	0396	2 LY LTS101-650B.1	3200	EMS LifeStar		lsf Debis / opf Topeka Air Ambulance
☐ N45726	Sikorsky S-58 (H-34A)	58-675	56-4307	0056	0495	1 WR R-1820	5897			
☐ N6488	Sikorsky S-58D	58-1573		0064	0572	1 WR R-1820	5897			
☐ N6488C	Sikorsky S-58E	58-269		0056	0474	1 WR R-1820	5897			
☐ N887	Sikorsky S-58B	58-482		0057	0279	1 WR R-1820	5897			
☐ N97AR	Sikorsky S-58 (H-34A)	58-531	55-4497	0057	0484	1 WR R-1820	5897			
☐ N99275	Sikorsky S-58E	58-245		0058	0178	1 WR R-1820	5897			
☐ N1078T	Sikorsky S-58DT	58-1016	C-FOHA	0059	0897	1 PWC PT6T-3 TwinPac	5897			cvtd S-58D

SAINT MARYS LIFE FLIGHT (Saint Marys Medical Center dba) **Duluth-St. Marys Hospital Heliport, MN**

407 East 3rd Street, Duluth, MN 55805, USA ☎ (218) 726-4134 Tx: none Fax: (218) 720-2470 SITA: n/a
F: 1991 n/a Head: Stephen Durst Net: n/a

☐ N911SM	Eurocopter (MBB) BK117B-2	*7150*	*N7059H*	*0088*	*0391*	*2 LY LTS101-750B.1*	*3350*			

SAIR AVIATION = SRA (Empire Aero Services, Inc. dba) **Syracuse-Hanock Int'l Airport, NY**

PO Box 216, Syracuse, NY 13211-0216, USA ☎ (315) 455-7951 Tx: 937244 sair pts syr Fax: (315) 455-0147 SITA: n/a
F: 1961 80 Head: James H. Messenger ICAO: SAIR Net: n/a Aircraft below MTOW 1361 kg: Piper PA-28 & PA-38.

☐ N161SA	Piper PA-31-350 Navajo Chieftain	*31-8052029*	*N3548V*	*0080*	*0495*	*2 LY TIO-540-J2BD*	*3175*	*Freighter*		
☐ N555SA	Cessna 208B Grand Caravan	*208B0562*	*N12155*	*0096*	*1296*	*1 PWC PT6A-114A*	*3969*	*Freighter*		*lsf Textron Financial Corp.*
☐ N3699B	Beech King Air B100	*BE-107*		*0081*	*1086*	*2 GA TPE331-6-252B*	*5352*	*Freighter/8 Pax*		

SALMON AIR TAXI (Challis Aviation) (Mountain Bird, Inc. dba) **Salmon-Lemhi County & Challis, ID**

PO Box 698, Salmon, ID 83467, USA ☎ (208) 756-6211 Tx: none Fax: (208) 756-6219 SITA: n/a
F: 1968 6 Head: Joann E. Wolters Net: n/a Aircraft below MTOW 1361kg: Cessna 150 & 182. CHALLIS AVIATION is the marketing name used for operations out of Challis, ID (same fleet/headquarters).

☐ N4759U	Cessna TU206G Turbo Stationair 6	*U20605086*		*0079*	*1186*	*1 CO TSIO-520-M*	*1633*			
☐ N7537N	Cessna TU206G Turbo Stationair	*U20603665*		*0077*	*0590*	*1 CO TSIO-520-M*	*1633*			
☐ N25SA	Britten-Norman BN-2A-20 Islander	*766*	*C-GTWI*	*0076*	*0285*	*2 LY IO-540-K1B5*	*2976*			
☐ N6561B	Britten-Norman BN-2A-20 Islander	*520*	*YV-1073P*	*0076*	*1191*	*2 LY IO-540-K1B5*	*2976*			
☐ N3528Y	Piper PA-31-350 Navajo Chieftain	*31-7952149*		*0079*	*0894*	*2 LY TIO-540-J2BD*	*3175*			
☐ N4237D	Piper PA-31-350 Navajo Chieftain	*31-7305055*		*0073*	*1297*	*2 LY TIO-540-J2BD*	*3175*			
☐ N84859	Piper PA-31-350 Navajo Chieftain	*31-7305043*		*0073*	*0190*	*2 LY TIO-540-J2BD*	*3175*			

SALMON RIVER HELICOPTERS, Inc. **Riggins-Private Heliport, ID**

PO Box 1293, Riggins, ID 83549, USA ☎ (208) 628-3133 Tx: none Fax: (208) 628-3038 SITA: n/a
F: 1994 20 Head: Cindy Carlson Net: n/a

☐ N4582D	Bell UH-1F (204 Super)	*7023*	*63-13163*	*0063*	*0394*	*1 LY T5343B*	*3856*			*cvtd 204*

SAMOA AIR, Inc. = SE (Samoa Aviation, Inc. dba / formerly Maui Airlines, Inc.) **Pago Pago, AM Samoa**

PO Box 280, Pago Pago, American Samoa 96799, USA ☎ (684) 699-9106 Tx: none Fax: (684) 699-9751 SITA: n/a
F: 1986 60 Head: James A. Porter Net: n/a

☐ N710AS	Beech King Air A100	*B-127*	*C-GJVK*	*0072*	*0795*	*2 PWC PT6A-28*	*5216*	*Y9*		
☐ N28SP	De Havilland DHC-6 Twin Otter 300	*601*		*0078*	*0793*	*2 PWC PT6A-27*	*5670*	*Y18*		*lsf Ashley Marshall Trustee*
☐ N711AS	De Havilland DHC-6 Twin Otter 200	*202*		*0069*	*0892*	*2 PWC PT6A-20*	*5252*	*Y15*		*lsf Ashley Marshall Trustee*
☐ N719AS	De Havilland DHC-6 Twin Otter 200	*139*	*N711SD*	*0068*	*0398*	*2 PWC PT6A-20*	*5252*	*Y19*		

S & B AVIATION (Aircraft Management Group, Inc. dba) **Wabash-Municipal, IN**

8925 Greenleaf Drive, Fort Wayne, IN 46819, USA ☎ (219) 478-9084 Tx: none Fax: (219) 563-1587 SITA: n/a
F: 1995 n/a Head: Loren C. Bunnell Net: n/a

☐ N217SB	Mitsubishi MU-2J (MU-2B-35) Cargoliner	*586*	*N21AU*	*0073*	*0297*	*2 GA TPE331-6-251M*	*4899*			*lsf Geiger Avn Lsng/Cavenaugh SCD conv.*

SANDSTONE AERIAL SERVICE **Honolulu-Int'l, HI**

90 Nakolo Place, Room 2, Honolulu, HI 96819, USA ☎ (808) 833-5678 Tx: none Fax: (808) 839-1504 SITA: n/a
F: 1991 n/a Head: James R. Stone Net: n/a

☐ N1610N	MD Helicopters MD 500E (Hughes 369E)	*0485E*		*0091*	*0693*	*1 AN 250-C20B*	*1361*			

SAN FRANCISCO – Flight Operations (Flight Ops of Ferreteria & Implementos San Francisco/San Francisco Iron goods & tools trade) **Laredo-Int'l, TX**

211 Esperanza, Laredo, TX 78041, USA ☎ (956) 724-7897 Tx: none Fax: (956) 726-0685 SITA: n/a
F: 1982 n/a Head: Douglas R. Taylor Net: n/a Operates FAR125 contract cargo flights for itself & its customers only.

☐ N6362Y	Piper PA-23-250 Aztec C	*27-3632*	*XB-DUC*	*0067*	*0197*	*2 LY IO-540-C4B5*	*2359*	*Freighter*		*lsf pvt*
☐ N1663M	Curtiss C-46F-1-CU Commando	*22548*	*44-78725*	*0045*	*0085*	*2 PW R-2800*	*21772*	*Freighter*		*lsf La Mesa Leasing Inc.*
☐ N24DR	Convair 440-75 Metropolitan	*393*	*CF-GLM*	*0157*	*0095*	*2 PW R-2800*	*21772*	*Freighter*		*lsf pvt*

SAN FRANCISCO SEAPLANE TOURS, Inc. **Sausalito-SPB, CA**

242 Redwood Highway, Mill Valley, CA 94941, USA ☎ (650) 332-4843 Tx: none Fax: (650) 332-4851 SITA: n/a
F: 1945 n/a Head: Amber Byassee Net: n/a Flights are operated in conjuntion with COMMODORE SEAPLANES at Homewood-SPB.

☐ N5220G	De Havilland DHC-2 Beaver I	*833*	*54-1693*	*0054*	*0794*	*1 PW R-985*	*2309*			*Floats*

SAN JOAQUIN HELICOPTERS, Inc. **Delano-Municipal & Rancho Cordova, CA**

1407 South Lexington, Delano, CA 93215, USA ☎ (805) 725-1898 Tx: 682411 Fax: (805) 725-5401 SITA: n/a
F: 1975 75 Head: James C. Josephson Net: n/a Aircraft below MTOW 1361 kg: Hiller-Soloy UH-12ET.

☐ N175SJ	Bell OH-58A (206 JetRanger)	*41080*	*N582MP*	*0070*	*0796*	*1 AN T63-A-700*	*1361*			
☐ N176SJ	Bell OH-58A (206 JetRanger)	*41107*	*N586MP*	*0070*	*0796*	*1 AN T63-A-700*	*1361*			
☐ N177SJ	Bell OH-58A (206 JetRanger)	*42097*	*N587MP*	*0072*	*0796*	*1 AN T63-A-700*	*1361*			
☐ N2944W	Bell 206B JetRanger III	*748*		*0071*	*0684*	*1 AN 250-C20B*	*1451*			*lsf B&J Land Company / cvtd 206A*
☐ N460DF	Cessna 337C Super Skymaster	*337-0841*		*0068*	*0196*	*2 CO IO-360-C/D*	*1950*	*Surveyer*		*lsf/opf CA Dept of Forestry*
☐ N465DF	Cessna O-2A (337B) Super Skymaster	*M3370266*	*68-10990*	*0068*	*0196*	*2 CO IO-360-C/D*	*1950*	*Surveyer*		*A14 / lsf/opf CA Dept of Forestry*
☐ N467DF	Cessna O-2A (337B) Super Skymaster	*M3370290*	*68-11014*	*0068*	*0196*	*2 CO IO-360-C/D*	*1950*	*Surveyer*		*lsf/opf CA Dept of Forestry*
☐ N469DF	Cessna O-2A (337B) Super Skymaster	*M3370323*	*68-11047*	*0068*	*0196*	*2 CO IO-360-C/D*	*1950*	*Surveyer*		*A63 / lsf/opf CA Dept of Forestry*
☐ N470DF	Cessna O-2A (337B) Super Skymaster	*M3370254*	*68-10978*	*0068*	*0196*	*2 CO IO-360-C/D*	*1950*	*Surveyer*		*lsf/opf CA Dept of Forestry*
☐ N471DF	Cessna O-2A (337B) Super Skymaster	*M3370246*	*68-10970*	*0068*	*0196*	*2 CO IO-360-C/D*	*1950*	*Surveyer*		*A24 / lsf/opf CA Dept of Forestry*
☐ N472DF	Cessna O-2A (337B) Super Skymaster	*M3370321*	*68-11045*	*0068*	*0196*	*2 CO IO-360-C/D*	*1950*	*Surveyer*		*A23 / lsf/opf CA Dept of Forestry*
☐ N473DF	Cessna O-2A (337B) Super Skymaster	*M3370296*	*68-11020*	*0068*	*0196*	*2 CO IO-360-C/D*	*1950*	*Surveyer*		*A11 / lsf/opf CA Dept of Forestry*
☐ N474DF	Cessna O-2A (337B) Super Skymaster	*M3370318*	*68-11042*	*0068*	*0196*	*2 CO IO-360-C/D*	*1950*	*Surveyer*		*lsf/opf CA Dept of Forestry*
☐ N475DF	Cessna O-2A (337B) Super Skymaster	*M3370343*	*68-11067*	*0068*	*0196*	*2 CO IO-360-C/D*	*1950*	*Surveyer*		*A12 / lsf/opf CA Dept of Forestry*
☐ N123SJ	Bell UH-1B (204)	*716*		*0062*	*0290*	*1 LY T53-L-13B*	*3856*			
☐ N15FC	Bell UH-1B (204)	*358*	*61-778*	*0061*	*0382*	*1 LY T53-L-11*	*3856*			
☐ N234SJ	Bell UH-1B (204)	*388*		*0062*	*0290*	*1 LY T53-L-11*	*3856*			
☐ N2721X	Bell UH-1B (204)	*377*	*61-797*	*0061*	*0882*	*1 LY T53-L-11*	*3856*			
☐ N345SJ	Bell UH-1B (204)	*390*		*0062*	*0290*	*1 LY T53-L-11*	*3856*			
☐ N444SJ	Bell UH-1B (204)	*391*		*0061*	*0190*	*1 LY T53-L-11*	*3856*			
☐ N456SJ	Bell UH-1B (204)	*720*		*0063*	*0490*	*1 LY T53-L-11*	*3856*			
☐ N46928	Bell UH-1B (204)	*292*	*61-712*	*0061*	*0882*	*1 LY T53-L-11*	*3856*			
☐ N567SJ	Bell UH-1B (204)	*763*	*63-8541*	*0063*	*0695*	*1 LY T53-L-11*	*3856*			
☐ N59368	Bell UH-1B (204)	*448*	*62-1928*	*0062*	*0382*	*1 LY T53-L-11*	*3856*			
☐ N64CC	Bell UH-1B (204)	*414*	*62-1894*	*0062*	*0888*	*1 LY T53-L-11*	*3856*			
☐ N98F	Bell UH-1B (204)	*488*	*62-1968*	*0062*	*0582*	*1 LY T53-L-11*	*3856*			
☐ N999SJ	Bell UH-1B (204)	*1025*	*63-13593*	*0063*	*0190*	*1 LY T53-L-11*	*3856*			
☐ N409DF	Rockwell (N.A.) OV-10A Bronco	*305A-11*	*155401*	*0067*	*0996*	*2 AN T76-G-416/417*	*6562*	*Tanker*		*lsf/opf CA Dept of Forestry*
☐ N404DF	Grumman TS-2A Tracker	*455*	*136546*	*0056*	*0196*	*2 WR R-1820-82B*	*11793*	*Tanker*		*80 / lsf/opf CA Dept of Forestry*
☐ N405DF	Grumman TS-2A Tracker	*266*	*133295*	*0055*	*0196*	*2 WR R-1820-82B*	*11793*	*Tanker*		*72 / lsf/opf CA Dept of Forestry*
☐ N406DF	Grumman TS-2A Tracker	*293*	*133322*	*0055*	*0196*	*2 WR R-1820-82B*	*11793*	*Tanker*		*73 / lsf/opf CA Dept of Forestry*
☐ N411DF	Grumman TS-2A Tracker	*476*	*136567*	*0056*	*0196*	*2 WR R-1820-82B*	*11793*	*Tanker*		*74 / lsf/opf CA Dept of Forestry*
☐ N412DF	Grumman TS-2A Tracker	*222*	*133251*	*0054*	*0196*	*2 WR R-1820-82B*	*11793*	*Tanker*		*78 / lsf/opf CA Dept of Forestry*
☐ N417DF	Grumman TS-2A Tracker	*061*	*133090*	*0054*	*0196*	*2 WR R-1820-82B*	*11793*	*Tanker*		*76 / lsf/opf CA Dept of Forestry*
☐ N420DF	Grumman TS-2A Tracker	*388*	*136479*	*0056*	*0196*	*2 WR R-1820-82B*	*11793*	*Tanker*		*75 / lsf/opf CA Dept of Forestry*
☐ N422DF	Marsh (Grumman) TS-2F Turbo Tracker	*212*	*133241*	*0054*	*0199*	*2 GA TPE331-14GR*	*11793*	*Tanker*		*82 / lsf/opf CDF / cvtd Tracker*
☐ N423DF	Grumman TS-2A Tracker	*246*	*133275*	*0055*	*0196*	*2 WR R-1820-82B*	*11793*	*Tanker*		*77 / lsf/opf CA Dept of Forestry*
☐ N436DF	Grumman TS-2A Tracker	*445*	*136536*	*0056*	*0196*	*2 WR R-1820-82B*	*11793*	*Tanker*		*100 / lsf/opf CA Dept of Forestry*
☐ N446DF	Grumman S-2F Tracker	*175*	*133204*	*0054*	*0196*	*2 WR R-1820-82B*	*11793*	*Tanker*		*94 / lsf/opf CA Dept of Forestry*
☐ N447DF	Grumman TS-2A Tracker	*417*	*136508*	*0056*	*0196*	*2 WR R-1820-82B*	*11793*	*Tanker*		*93 / lsf/opf CA Dept of Forestry*
☐ N448DF	Grumman TS-2A Tracker	*584*	*144723*	*0056*	*0196*	*2 WR R-1820-82B*	*11793*	*Tanker*		*95 / lsf/opf CA Dept of Forestry*
☐ N450DF	Grumman S-2F Tracker	*421*	*136512*	*0055*	*0196*	*2 WR R-1820-82B*	*11793*	*Tanker*		*90 / lsf/opf CA Dept of Forestry*
☐ N453DF	Grumman TS-2A Tracker	*572*	*136663*	*0056*	*0196*	*2 WR R-1820-82B*	*11793*	*Tanker*		*91 / lsf/opf CA Dept of Forestry*

SAS EXECUTIVE AVIATION, Ltd (Division of Superstition Air Service, Inc.) **Mesa-Falcon Field, AZ**

4766 Falcon Drive, Mesa, AZ 85205, USA ☎ (520) 832-0704 Tx: none Fax: (520) 981-3609 SITA: n/a
F: 1967 n/a Head: Bob G. Figgins Net: n/a

☐ N33PV	Partenavia P.68C-TC	*347-33-TC*		*0085*	*0197*	*2 LY TIO-360-C1A6D*	*1990*			
☐ N20SS	Cessna 310Q	*310Q0521*		*0072*	*0696*	*2 CO IO-470-VO*	*2404*			
☐ N1167T	Beech Baron B55 (95-B55)	*TC-1864*		*0075*	*0694*	*2 CO IO-470-L*	*2313*			
☐ N650PV	Beech Baron C55 (95-C55)	*TE-427*		*0067*	*0896*	*2 CO IO-520-C*	*2404*			
☐ N812D	Beech Baron B55 (95-B55)	*TC-1839*		*0075*	*0395*	*2 CO IO-470-L*	*2313*			

SAVE A CONNIE, Inc. – SAC **Kansas City-Downtown, MO**

480 NW Richards Road, Kansas City, MO 64116-4234, USA ☎ (816) 421-3401 Tx: none Fax: (816) 421-3421 SITA: n/a
F: 1986 n/a Head: Richard C. McMahon Net: n/a Non-profit organisation (a tax exempt education foundation) conducting historical flying presentations. All employees are volunteers. SAC has 566 members.

☐ N1945	Boeing (Douglas) DC-3-G202A	*3294*	*NC1945*	*0041*	*0995*	*2 WR R-1820*	*11884*	*fly.presentation*		*being restored to flying condition*
☐ N145S	Martin 404	*14142*	*N451A*	*0052*	*1090*	*2 PW R-2800*	*19051*	*fly.presentation*		Skyliner Kansas City
☐ N472M	Martin 404	*14234*	*N486A*	*0052*	*0694*	*2 PW R-2800*	*19051*	*fly.presentation*		*std Douglas Bisbee, AZ*
☐ N6937C	Lockheed L-1049H Super Const. (tip tanks)	*4830*		*0059*	*0287*	*4 WR R-3350*	*64637*	*fly.presentation*		Star ofAm./Capt.JackDavenport / *oldTWcs*

428 registration type of aircraft *cn/fn* *ex/ex** *mfd* *del* *powered by* *mtow kg* *configuration* *selcal* *name/fln/specialitites/remarks*

SCAIFE FLIGHT OPERATIONS — Latrobe-Westmoreland County, PA

1 Oxford Ctr, 301 Grant Street, Ste 30900, Pittsburgh, PA 15219, USA ☎ (724) 392-2915 Tx: none Fax: (724) 392-2917 SITA: n/a
F: 1971 n/a Head: Richard M. Scaife Net: n/a Operates non-commercial executive flights for itself only.

☐ N8860	Boeing (Douglas) DC-9-15	45797 / 51	N8953U	0066	1071	2 PW JT8D-7	41141	Executive		

SCENIC AIR, Inc. = 3L — Oakland-Int'l, CA

PO Box 471287, San Francisco, CA 94147-1287, USA ☎ (650) 922-2386 Tx: none Fax: (650) 346-6940 SITA: n/a
F: 1994 n/a Head: Jacques Sinoncelli Net: n/a

☐ N207VA	Cessna 207 Skywagon	20700291		0075	0896	1 CO IO-520-F	1724			lsf Las Vegas Aircraft Leasing
☐ N9177M	Cessna 207A Stationair 8 II	20700677		0080	0694	1 CO IO-520-F	1724			lsf pvt
☐ N97AK	Cessna 207A Stationair 8 II	20700736	N93AK	0081	0796	1 CO IO-520-F	1724			lsf S&S Aircraft Leasing Inc.

SCENIC AIRLINES, Inc. = YR / YRR (Member of Eagle Scenic Aviation Group) — Las Vegas-McCarran Int'l & -North, NV & Page-Municipal, AZ

2705 Airport Drive, North Las Vegas Airport, Las Vegas, NV 89030, USA ☎ (702) 739-1900 Tx: none Fax: (702) 739-8065 SITA: n/a
F: 1967 340 Head: David Young IATA: 398 ICAO: SCENIC Net: http://www.scenic.com

☐ N4673Y	Cessna T210N Turbo Centurion II	21063978		0080	0389	1 CO TSIO-520-R	1814	Y5		
☐ N4689Y	Cessna T210N Turbo Centurion II	21063987		0080	1189	1 CO TSIO-520-R	1814	Y5		
☐ N5416A	Cessna T210N Turbo Centurion II	21063423		0079	0790	1 CO TSIO-520-R	1814	Y5		
☐ N6348A	Cessna T210N Turbo Centurion II	21063522		0079	1089	1 CO TSIO-520-R	1814	Y5		
☐ N761JE	Cessna T210M Turbo Centurion II	21062287		0078	0587	1 CO TSIO-520-R	1724	Y5		
☐ N51SA	Cessna T207A Turbo Stationair 8 II	20700699		0081	0588	1 CO TSIO-520-M	1724	Y6		
☐ N6449H	Cessna T207A Turbo Stationair 7 II	20700529		0079	0186	1 CO TSIO-520-M	1724	Y6		
☐ N73727	Cessna T207A Turbo Stationair 8 II	20700617		0080	0792	1 CO TSIO-520-M	1724	Y6		
☐ N7608U	Cessna T207A Turbo Stationair 7 II	20700446		0078	0186	1 CO TSIO-520-M	1724	Y6		
☐ N9317M	Cessna T207A Turbo Stationair 8 II	20700680		0080	0388	1 CO TSIO-520-M	1724	Y6		
☐ N9436M	Cessna T207A Turbo Stationair 8 II	20700689		0081	0186	1 CO TSIO-520-M	1724	Y6		
☐ N9482M	Cessna T207A Turbo Stationair 8 II	20700698		0081	0389	1 CO TSIO-520-M	1724	Y6		
☐ N9825M	Cessna T207A Turbo Stationair 8 II	20700739		0081	0386	1 CO TSIO-520-M	1724	Y6		
☐ N1203S	Cessna 208B Grand Caravan	208B0439		0095	0895	1 PWC PT6A-114A	3969	Y9		
☐ N5512B	Cessna 208B Grand Caravan	208B0299		0092	0493	1 PWC PT6A-114A	3969	Y9		
☐ N120GP	Beech 1900C-1 Airliner	UC-59	N1568K	0090	1297	2 PWC PT6A-65B	7530	Y19		Spirit of Page-Lake Powell / lsf Rayth.

SCENIC MOUNTAIN AIR, Inc. (Seasonal May-October ops only) — Moose Pass, AK

PO Box 4, Moose Pass, AK 99631, USA ☎ (907) 288-3646 Tx: none Fax: (907) 288-3647 SITA: n/a
F: 1993 n/a Head: Lura A. Kingsford Net: n/a Aircraft below MTOW 1361kg: Cessna 172 & Piper PA-18

☐ N8030Z	Cessna U206 Super Skywagon	U206-0430		0065	0793	1 CO IO-520-A	1497			Floats
☐ N3275X	Cessna 310L	310L0125		0067	0686	2 CO IO-470-V	2359			

SCHAEFER'S AIR SERVICES (Schaefer Ambulance Service, Inc. dba) — Van Nuys, CA

16425 Vanowen Street, Van Nuys, CA 91406, USA ☎ (818) 786-8713 Tx: none Fax: (818) 786-7536 SITA: n/a
F: 1947 n/a Head: James H. McNeal Net: n/a

☐ N1500G	Cessna 414 II	414-0814		0075	1087	2 CO TSIO-520-N	2880	EMS		
☐ N4820A	Cessna 414A Chancellor III	414A0201		0078	0596	2 CO TSIO-520-NB	3062	EMS		
☐ N876WB	Cessna 500 Citation I	500-0347	N500XY	0077	0188	2 PWC JT15D-1A	5375	EMS		

SCHIAVONE AIR CHARTER SERVICE (Schiavone Construction, Co. dba) — Teterboro, NJ

1600 Paterson Plank Road, Secaucus, NJ 07094, USA ☎ (973) 440-5555 Tx: none Fax: (973) 440-3979 SITA: n/a
F: 1975 3 Head: Ronald A. Schiavone Net: n/a

☐ N201SC	Bell 206B JetRanger III	3427		0081	0686	1 AN 250-C20B	1451			
☐ N202SC	Eurocopter (Aerosp.) AS355F TwinStar	5204	N202SE	0084	0686	1 AN 250-C20F	2300			

SCOTT AVIATION, Inc. — Chicago-DuPage, IL

32W751 Tower Road, West Chicago, IL 60185, USA ☎ (630) 513-2222 Tx: none Fax: (630) 513-2227 SITA: n/a
F: 1989 n/a Head: Anthony Aiello Net: n/a

☐ N90J	Learjet 24	24-060	N899WF	0065	0388	2 GE CJ610-4	5897			lsf Sunward Corp.
☐ N33PF	Learjet 25	25-028	N277LE	0069	0995	2 GE CJ610-6	6804			lsf E&J Partnership
☐ N777FH	Cessna 560 Citation V	560-0076	N777FE	0090	0396	2 PWC JT15D-5A	7212			lsf Kittyhawk Enterprises Llc
☐ N105HS	Hawker 1A (HS 125-1A)	25031	N79AE	0065	0297	2 RR Viper 522	9616			lsf pvt

SCOTT PAPER, Company – Helicopter Dept. (Subsidiary of Kimberley Clark, Corp.) — Mount Vernon-Private Heliport, AL

PO Box 1090, Mount Vernon, AL 36560, USA ☎ (334) 829-9025/ext6 Tx: none Fax: (334) 829-5533 SITA: n/a
F: 1989 n/a Head: Daniel L. Stollee Net: n/a Conducting aerial work flights both for the Kimberley Clark Group & outside customers.

☐ N5197W	Kaman HH-43F (K600) Huskie	45	59-1564	0059	0294	1 LY T53-L-11A	4150			cvtd HH-43B
☐ N55714	Kaman HH-43F (K600) Huskie	154	62-4528	0059	0290	1 LY T53-L-11A	4150			cvtd HH-43B
☐ N133KA	Kaman K-1200 K-Max	A94-0005		0094	0694	1 LY T5317A-1	2722			lsf Kaman Aerospace Corp.

SCOTTS HELICOPTERS (Scotts Helicopter Service, Inc. dba) — Le Sueur-Municipal, MN

PO Box 92, Le Sueur, MN 56058, USA ☎ (507) 665-4064 Tx: none Fax: (507) 665-3680 SITA: n/a
F: 1993 n/a Head: Scott Churchill Net: n/a

☐ N2995W	Bell 206B JetRanger	1192		0073	0593	1 AN 250-C20	1451			

SCOTTY'S FLYING SERVICE (Richard S. Skinner dba / Seasonal, summer ops only) — Patten-Shin Pond SPB, ME

RR 1, Box 256, Shin Pond Road, Patten, ME 04765, USA ☎ (207) 528-2626 Tx: none Fax: none SITA: n/a
F: 1973 2 Head: Richard S. Skinner Net: n/a Seasonal (summer) operations only.

☐ N5217E	Cessna A185F Skywagon II	18503941		0079	0581	1 CO IO-520-D	1520			Floats

SEABORNE AVIATION, Inc. = BB — Ketchikan-Harbor SPB, AK & St. Thomas-SPB, VI

PO Box 6440, Ketchikan, AK 99901, USA ☎ (907) 225-3424 Tx: none Fax: (907) 225-8530 SITA: n/a
F: 1992 n/a Head: Charles F. Slagle Net: n/a Alaska (Ketchikan) base is operated seasonal (April-October), Virgin Islands (St. Thomas) is operated all year-round.

☐ N224SA	De Havilland DHC-6 Vista Liner 300	247	C-GOES	0069	0893	2 PWC PT6A-27	5670	Y19		lsf Twin Otter Intl/cvtd T.O./Amphibian
☐ N229SA	De Havilland DHC-6 Vista Liner 300	468	C-FWCA	0075	0297	2 PWC PT6A-27	5670	Y19		lsf Twin Otter Intl/cvtd T.O./Amphibian
☐ N251SA	De Havilland DHC-6 Vista Liner 300	524	N81708	0077	0395	2 PWC PT6A-27	5670	Y19		lsf Twin Otter Intl/cvtd T.O./Amphibian

SEA HAWK AIR, Inc. — Kodiak-SPB, AK

PO Box 3561, Kodiak, AK 99615, USA ☎ (907) 486-8282 Tx: none Fax: (907) 487-4350 SITA: n/a
F: 1983 8 Head: Roland B. Ruoss Net: n/a

☐ N38938	De Havilland DHC-2 Beaver I	424	52-6069	0058		1 PW R-985	2309			Floats
☐ N4756T	De Havilland DHC-2 Beaver I	499	52-6118	0053		1 PW R-985	2309			Floats

SEAPLANES OF KEY WEST (Island City Flying Service, Inc. dba) — Key West-Int'l, FL

3471 South Roosevelt Boulevard, Key West, FL 33040, USA ☎ (954) 294-0709 Tx: none Fax: (954) 296-5691 SITA: n/a
F: 1972 9 Head: Paul J. Depoo Net: n/a Aircraft below MTOW 1361 kg: Cessna 172

☐ N111KW	Cessna U206F Stationair	U20602460	N779A	0074	0397	1 CO IO-520-F	1633			Amphibian
☐ N200KW	Cessna U206F Stationair II	U20602785	N108SMA	0075	0297	1 CO IO-520-F	1633			Amphibian
☐ N208KW	Cessna 208 Caravan I	20800292		0098	1198	1 PWC PT6A-114	3629			Amphibian

SEATTLE SEAPLANES (James W. Chrysler dba / formerly Chrysler Air) — Seattle-Lake Union SPB, WA

1325 Fairview Ave East, Seattle, WA 98102, USA ☎ (206) 329-9638 Tx: none Fax: (206) 329-1284 SITA: n/a
F: 1981 n/a Head: James W. Chrysler Net: n/a

☐ N185CD	Cessna A185F Skywagon	18502428		0074	0895	1 CO IO-520-D	1520			lsf Charlie Tango Corp. / Floats
☐ N14C	Cessna U206F Stationair II	U20602803		0075	0897	1 CO IO-520-F	1633			Floats
☐ N6243Z	Cessna U206G Stationair 6 II	U20606199		0081	1287	1 CO IO-520-F	1633			Floats
☐ N8397Q	Cessna U206F Stationair II	U20603258		0076	0484	1 CO IO-520-F	1633			lsf pvt / Floats

SEBASTIAN AERO SERVICES, Inc. — Sebastian-Municipal, FL

300 West Airport Drive, Sebastian, FL 32958, USA ☎ (561) 589-0800 Tx: none Fax: (561) 388-0800 SITA: n/a
F: 1992 n/a Head: Robert A. Vanwyck Net: n/a

☐ N132SA	Piper PA-34-200 Seneca	34-7450174	C-FAFC	0074	0796	2 LY IO-360-C1E6	1905			
☐ N1508G	Piper PA-34-200 Seneca	34-7250352		0072	0397	2 LY IO-360-C1E6	1905			
☐ N15156	Piper PA-34-200 Seneca	34-7350028		0073	1196	2 LY IO-360-C1E6	1905			
☐ N15242	Piper PA-34-200 Seneca	34-7350040		0073	0796	2 LY IO-360-C1E6	1905			
☐ N16499	Piper PA-34-200 Seneca	34-7350132		0073	1296	2 LY IO-360-C1E6	1905			

SECURITY AVIATION, Inc. = SVX — Anchorage-Int'l, AK

3600 West Int'l Airport Road, Anchorage, AK 99502, USA ☎ (907) 248-2677 Tx: none Fax: (907) 248-6911 SITA: n/a
F: 1984 16 Head: Michael O'Neill Net: n/a

☐ N5037J	Cessna T310R II	310R0733		0076	1188	2 CO TSIO-520-B	2495			
☐ N888PS	Piper PA-31-350 Navajo Chieftain	31-8052162		0080	0492	2 LY TIO-540-J2BD	3175			
☐ N12099	Cessna 441 Conquest II	441-0329		0083	0190	2 GA TPE331-8-403S	4468			lsf pvt
☐ N441SA	Cessna 441 Conquest II	441-0172	N441VP	0080	0186	2 GA TPE331-8-401S	4468			lsf pvt
☐ N550SA	Cessna 550 Citation II	550-0248	N6804C	0081	0487	2 PWC JT15D-4	6033			

429 registration type of aircraft cn/fn ex/ex* mfd del powered by mtow kg configuration selcal name/fln/specialitites/remarks

SELDOM HELICOPTERS LOGGING, Inc. — Fort Benton, MT

SR Box 55, Fort Benton, MT 59442, USA ☎ (406) 734-5222 Tx: none Fax: (406) 734-5222 SITA: n/a
F: 1997 n/a Head: Dallas B. Romaine Net: n/a Aircraft below MTOW 1361kg: Hiller UH-12E

registration	type of aircraft	cn/fn	ex/ex*	mfd	del	powered by	mtow kg	configuration	selcal	name/fln/specialitites/remarks
N1215F	Bell UH-1H (205)	4395	64-13688	0064	0797	1 LY T53-L-13	4309			

SELECT AVIATION (Select Leasing, Inc. dba) — Waukesha-County, WI

528 Northview Road, Waukesha, WI 53188, USA ☎ (414) 544-4619 Tx: none Fax: none SITA: n/a
F: 1998 n/a Head: John Safro Net: n/a Operates non-commercial VIP/corporate flights for its owners only.

registration	type of aircraft	cn/fn	ex/ex*	mfd	del	powered by	mtow kg	configuration	selcal	name/fln/specialitites/remarks
N123H	BAe (BAC) One-Eleven 414EG	163	D-AILY	0069	0998	2 RR Spey 511-14	40143	VIP/Corporate		
N490ST	BAe (BAC) One-Eleven 212AR	083	N70611	0066	0199	2 RR Spey 511-14	35834	VIP/Corporate		

SEVEN BAR FLYING SERVICE, Inc. = SBF — Albuquerque-Int'l, NM

2505 Clark Carr Loop S.E., Albuquerque, NM 87106, USA ☎ (505) 842-4949 Tx: none Fax: (505) 842-4987 SITA: n/a
F: 1947 n/a Head: A. Wade Black ICAO: S-BAR Net: n/a

registration	type of aircraft	cn/fn	ex/ex*	mfd	del	powered by	mtow kg	configuration	selcal	name/fln/specialitites/remarks
N17NM	Piper PA-31T Cheyenne II	31T-7820035	N6NB	0078	0189	2 PWC PT6A-28	4082			
N19NM	Piper PA-31T Cheyenne II	31T-7520006	N33DT	0075	0389	2 PWC PT6A-28	4082			
N112SB	Beech King Air E90	LW-232	N232CL	0077	1096	2 PWC PT6A-28	4581			
N14NM	Beech King Air E90	LW-35	N811JB	0073	0891	2 PWC PT6A-28	4581			
N16NM	Beech King Air E90	LW-62	N96DA	0073	0390	2 PWC PT6A-28	4581			
N5NM	Beech King Air E90	LW-123	N158D	0074	0293	2 PWC PT6A-28	4581			
N714F	Beech King Air E90	LW-237	N23707	0077	1296	2 PWC PT6A-28	4581			

SHAMROCK AVIATION, Inc. — Teterboro, NJ

233 Industrial Ave, Teterboro, NJ 07608-1021, USA ☎ (973) 288-2329 Tx: none Fax: (973) 288-5771 SITA: n/a
F: 1994 n/a Head: William P. Stewart Net: n/a

registration	type of aircraft	cn/fn	ex/ex*	mfd	del	powered by	mtow kg	configuration	selcal	name/fln/specialitites/remarks
N253S	Learjet 55	55-053	N205EL	0083	0994	2 GA TFE731-3AR-2B	9752			
N263S	GAC G-IV Gulfstream IV (SP)	1263	N830CB	0095	1096	2 RR Tay 611-8	33838			

SHANAIR, Inc. — Visalia-Municipal, CA

9509 Airport Drive, No. 9, Visalia, CA 93277, USA ☎ (209) 651-1215 Tx: none Fax: (209) 651-1740 SITA: n/a
F: 1973 n/a Head: Clarence J. Ritchie Net: n/a

registration	type of aircraft	cn/fn	ex/ex*	mfd	del	powered by	mtow kg	configuration	selcal	name/fln/specialitites/remarks
N222T	Beech Baron 58	TH-1224		0081	0197	2 CO IO-520-CB	2449			
N170S	Beech King Air B200	BB-1527	N1027Y	0096	0896	2 PWC PT6A-42	5670			
N102CS	Beech King Air 350 (B300)	FL-126	N3164C	0095	0695	2 PWC PT6A-60A	6350			lsf King Aire Inc.

SHANNONS AIR (Eric L. Shade & Thomas Johnston dba / Joint-venture co. of Shannons Air Service & Shannons Air Taxi) — Dillingham, AK

PO Box 214, Dillingham, AK 99576, USA ☎ (907) 842-5609 Tx: none Fax: 907) 842-4609 SITA: n/a
F: 1996 n/a Head: Eric L. Shade Net: n/a

registration	type of aircraft	cn/fn	ex/ex*	mfd	del	powered by	mtow kg	configuration	selcal	name/fln/specialitites/remarks
N32139	Piper PA-32-300 Cherokee SIX	32-7540017		0075	0897	1 LY IO-540-K1A5	1542			
N32979	Piper PA-32-300 Cherokee SIX	32-7540077		0074	1196	1 LY IO-540-K1A5	1542			
N507FS	Cessna 207A Stationair 8 II	20700757		0082	0997	1 CO IO-520-F	1724			

SHEENJEK AIR SERVICE (Sheenjek River Air, Inc. dba) — Fort Yukon, AK

PO Box 353, Fort Yukon, AK 99740, USA ☎ (907) 662-2563 Tx: none Fax: (907) 662-2563 SITA: n/a
F: 1991 n/a Head: Woody W. Salmon Net: n/a

registration	type of aircraft	cn/fn	ex/ex*	mfd	del	powered by	mtow kg	configuration	selcal	name/fln/specialitites/remarks
N2564Z	Cessna 185B Skywagon	185-0564		0063	0891	1 CO IO-470-F	1451			Floats / Wheel-Skis
N1587U	Cessna 207 Skywagon	20700187		0070	0793	1 CO IO-520-F	1724			

SHORELINE AVIATION, Inc. — New Haven-Tweed, CT

PO Box 120187, East Haven, CT 06512, USA ☎ (203) 468-8639 Tx: none Fax: (203) 468-1864 SITA: n/a
F: 1980 n/a Head: John D. Kelly Net: http://www.shorelineaviation.com Aircraft below MTOW 1361kg: Cessna 172 & Piper PA-28

registration	type of aircraft	cn/fn	ex/ex*	mfd	del	powered by	mtow kg	configuration	selcal	name/fln/specialitites/remarks
N5168E	Cessna A185F Skywagon II	18503937		0079	0895	1 CO IO-520-D	1520			Amphibian
N6955N	Cessna A185F Skywagon II	18504315		0081	0593	1 CO IO-520-D	1520			Amphibian
N8137D	Piper PA-32-300 Cherokee SIX	32-7940273		0079	0294	1 LY IO-540-K1G5	1542			
N9630G	Cessna U206F Stationair	U20601830		0072	0196	1 CO IO-520-F	1633			lsf Seaplanes Int'l / Amphibian
N88AG	Piper PA-34-200 Seneca	34-7450093		0074	0797	2 LY IO-360-C1E6	1905			lsf Professional Flight Training
N63858	Beech Baron 58	TH-1360		0082	0394	2 CO IO-520-CB	2449			
N799CA	Piper PA-31-350 Navajo Chieftain	31-7952187	N999JT	0079	0698	2 LY TIO-540-J2BD	3175			
N923BA	Piper PA-31-350 Navajo Chieftain	31-8252024		0082	0197	2 LY TIO-540-J2BD	3175			
N208RD	Cessna 208 Caravan I	20800054	N347TC	0085	0995	1 PWC PT6A-114	3629			lsf LB Aviation Inc. / Amphibian
N89RD	Cessna 208 Caravan I	20800096	N242SS	0086	1295	1 PWC PT6A-114	3629			Amphibian
N9670F	Cessna 208 Caravan I	20800117		0087	0995	1 PWC PT6A-114	3629			Amphibian
N495CA	Piper PA-42-1000 Cheyenne 400LS	42-5527044	HL5205	0091	0396	2 GA TPE331-114	5466			lsf LB Aviation Inc.
N728LB	Dassault Falcon 50	46	N725LB	0081	0895	3 GA TFE731-3-1C	17600			lsf LB Aviation Inc.
N725LB	GAC G-IV Gulfstream IV (SP)	1296	N419GA	0096	0896	2 RR Tay 611-8	33838			lsf General Electric Capital Corp.

SHUTTLE AMERICA, Corp. = S5 / TCF — Windsor Locks-Bradley Int'l, CT

334 Ella Grasso Turnpike, Windsor Locks, CT 06096, USA ☎ (860) 623-4114 Tx: none Fax: (860) 292-6266 SITA: n/a
F: 1998 n/a Head: David F. Hackett ICAO: SHUTTLECRAFT Net: n/a

registration	type of aircraft	cn/fn	ex/ex*	mfd	del	powered by	mtow kg	configuration	selcal	name/fln/specialitites/remarks
N801SA	De Havilland DHC-8-315 Dash 8	393	ZS-NMF	0095	1198	2 PWC PW123B	19505	Y50		lsf De Havilland Corp.
N802SA	De Havilland DHC-8-314 Dash 8	250	OE-LTB	0090	1198	2 PWC PW123B	19505	Y50		lsf De Havilland Corp. / cvtd -311
N803SA	De Havilland DHC-8-314 Dash 8	221	OE-LTC	0090	1298	2 PWC PW123B	19505	Y50		lsf De Havilland Corp. / cvtd -311
N804SA	De Havilland DHC-8-315 Dash 8	375	ZS-NMD	0094	0199	2 PWC PW123B	19505	Y50		lsf De Havilland Corp. / cvtd -314

SIERRA PACIFIC AIRLINES, Inc. = SI / SPA — Tucson-Int'l & -Avra Valley, AZ

7700 North Business Park Drive, Tucson, AZ 85743-9622, USA ☎ (520) 744-1144 Tx: none Fax: (520) 744-0138 SITA: n/a
F: 1976 40 Head: Garfield M. Thorsrud ICAO: SIERRA PACIFIC Net: n/a

registration	type of aircraft	cn/fn	ex/ex*	mfd	del	powered by	mtow kg	configuration	selcal	name/fln/specialitites/remarks
N73153	Convair 580	179		0054	1178	2 AN 501-D13H	24766	Y50		cvtd 340-31
N73166	Convair 580	374	OO-SCS	0056	0385	2 AN 501-D13H	24766	Y50/Q.C. Frtr		cvtd 440-12
N73301	Convair 580	80	N3425	0053	1174	2 AN 501-D13H	24766	Freighter		cvtd 340-32
N703S	Boeing 737-2T4 (A)	22529 / 750	N703ML	0081	0591	2 PW JT8D-17	54204	Y122		

SIERRA WEST AIRLINES = PKW (Pak West Airlines, Inc. dba) — Oakdale, CA

642 Hi-Tech Parkway, Suite A, Oakdale, CA 95361, USA ☎ (209) 848-0290 Tx: none Fax: (209) 848-0299 SITA: n/a
F: 1992 n/a Head: Deborah Robinson ICAO: PLATINUM WEST Net: n/a

registration	type of aircraft	cn/fn	ex/ex*	mfd	del	powered by	mtow kg	configuration	selcal	name/fln/specialitites/remarks
N332BA	Fairchild (Swearingen) SA226TC Metro II	TC-222E	N639S	0076	0892	2 GA TPE331-3UW-303G	5670	Freighter		lsf Career Aviation Academy Inc.
N4019	Fairchild (Swearingen) SA226AT Merlin IV	AT-014	C-GSDR	0073	0292	2 GA TPE331-3U-303G	5670	Freighter		lsf Career Aviation Academy Inc.
N71Z	Fairchild (Swearingen) SA226TC Metro II	TC-245		0077	0892	2 GA TPE331-3UW-303G	5670	Freighter		lsf Career Aviation Academy Inc.
N81418	Fairchild (Swearingen) SA226TC Metro II	TC-223	EC-GNM	0076	0199	2 GA TPE331-10UA-511G	5670	Freighter		lsf Carrier Aviation Academy Inc.
N8897Y	Fairchild (Swearingen) SA227AT Merlin IVC	AT-492	C-FJTA	0081	0997	2 GA TPE331-11U-611G	6577	Freighter		lsf Career Aviation Academy Inc.
N37BL	Learjet 23	23-069	N6GJ	0065	0691	2 GE CJ610-4	5670	Freighter		lsf CG Aviation / to be re-reg. N34TR
N2728G	Fairchild (Swearingen) SA227AC Metro III	AC-731		0089	1096	2 GA TPE331-11U-611G	6577	Freighter		lsf Career Aviation Academy Inc.
N3109B	Fairchild (Swearingen) SA227AC Metro III	AC-522		0082	0594	2 GA TPE331-11U-611G	6577	Freighter		lsf Career Aviation Academy Inc.
N3116N	Fairchild (Swearingen) SA227AC Metro III	AC-596		0084	0995	2 GA TPE331-11U-611G	6577	Freighter		lsf Career Aviation Academy Inc.
N343AE	Fairchild (Swearingen) SA227AC Metro III	AC-554	N3112K	0083	1096	2 GA TPE331-11U-611G	6577	Freighter		lsf Career Aviation Academy Inc.
N620PA	Fairchild (Swearingen) SA227AC Metro III	AC-533	N3110H	0083	0795	2 GA TPE331-11U-611G	6577	Freighter		lsf Career Aviation Academy Inc.
N70JF	Learjet 25D	25D-278		0079	0793	2 GE CJ610-8A	6804	Freighter		lsf Career Aviation / op in DHL-colors
N221TR	Learjet 35A	35A-221	VH-FSY	0079	1196	2 GA TFE731-2-2B	8165	Freighter		lsf Career Aviation Academy Inc.
N242DR	Learjet 35A	35A-242	VH-FSZ	0079	1196	2 GA TFE731-2-2B	8165	Freighter		lsf Career Aviation Academy Inc.
N315TR	IAI 1124A Westwind II	315	VH-NJW	0081	0597	2 GA TFE731-3-1G	10659	Freighter		

SILLER AVIATION (Siller Brothers, Inc. dba / formerly Tri Eagle, Company) — Yuba City-Sutter County, CA

PO Box 1585, Yuba City, CA 95992, USA ☎ (530) 674-9460 Tx: none Fax: (530) 673-5872 SITA: n/a
F: 1958 45 Head: Andy Siller Net: n/a

registration	type of aircraft	cn/fn	ex/ex*	mfd	del	powered by	mtow kg	configuration	selcal	name/fln/specialitites/remarks
N15456	Sikorsky S-61N	61826		0080	1080	2 GE CT58-140-1	9979			
N4196Z	Sikorsky S-61R	61567	65-12792	0065	1294	2 GE T58-100	10002			lsf pvt / cvtd H-3E
N4197R	Sikorsky S-61R	61571	65-12796	0068	1294	2 GE T58-100	10002			lsf pvt / cvtd H-3E
N45917	Sikorsky S-61V	61271		0065	0778	2 GE CT58-140-1	9979			
N5193J	Sikorsky S-61A	61014	148036	0060	0497	2 GE T58-100-5	8618			cvtd SH-3A
N51953	Sikorsky S-61A	61172	149903	0062	0596	2 GE T58-100-5	8618			cvtd SH-3A
N2268L	Sikorsky CH-54A (S-64 Skycrane)	64013	66-18411	0066	0694	2 PW T-73-P-700	19051			lsf pvt
N4035S	Sikorsky S-64E Skycrane	64099	70-18491	0070	0680	2 PW JFTD12-4A	19051			
N4037S	Sikorsky S-64E Skycrane	64101	70-18493	0070	0680	2 PW JFTD12-4A	19051			
N429C	Sikorsky CH-54A (S-64 Skycrane)	64031	67-18429	0067	0397	2 PW T-73-P-700	19051			
N7095B	Sikorsky CH-54A (S-64 Skycrane)	64032	67-18430	0067	1193	2 PW T-73-P-700	19051			lsf pvt
N9125M	Sikorsky CH-54A (S-64 Skycrane)		68-18455	0068	1095	2 PW T-73-P-700	19051			

SILVER BAY LOGGING – Helicopter division (Helicopter division of Silver Bay Logging, Inc.) — Juneau-Int'l, AK

Cube Cove 2, Juneau, AK 99850-0360, USA ☎ (907) 789-9033 Tx: none Fax: (907) 789-9516 SITA: n/a
F: 1987 n/a Head: Richard Buhler, Jr. Net: n/a

registration	type of aircraft	cn/fn	ex/ex*	mfd	del	powered by	mtow kg	configuration	selcal	name/fln/specialitites/remarks
N511SB	MD Helicopters MD 500D (Hughes 369D)	1090592D	N58402	0079	1094	1 AN 250-C20B	1361			
N512SB	MD Helicopters MD 500D (Hughes 369D)	1180390D	N58259	0078	0487	1 AN 250-C20B	1361			

☐ N513SB	MD Helicopters MD 500D (Hughes 369D)	1120D	N5168X	0082	0896	1 AN 250-C20B	1361			
☐ N515SB	MD Helicopters MD 500D (Hughes 369D)	711029D	N5069E	0081	0796	1 AN 250-C20B	1361			
☐ N730SB	Eurocopter (Aerosp.) AS350B AStar	1378	N57720	0080	0493	1 TU Arriel 1B	1950			
☐ N3173U	Sikorsky S-61N	61186		0062	0597	2 GE CT58-140-1	9299			
☐ N4240S	Sikorsky S-61N	61818	C-GOKV	0079	0993	2 GE CT58-140-1	9979			to be re-reg. N611SB
☐ N5193Y	Sikorsky S-61A	61186	149914	0062	0597	2 GE CT58-140-1	9752			cvtd SH-3H
☐ N542SB	Sikorsky CH-54B (S-64 Skycrane)		N20098	0068	0395	2 PW T-73-P-700	19051			
☐ N545SB	Sikorsky CH-54A (S-64 Skycrane)	64033	N5297V	0067	0394	2 PW T-73-P-700	19051			

SILVERHAWK AVIATION, Inc. = SLH (Silverhawk Security Specialists / Star Care V) — Lincoln-Municipal, NE

4221 North Park Road, Lincoln, NE 68524, USA ☎ (402) 475-8600 Tx: none Fax: (402) 475-1442 SITA: n/a
F: 1991 ☗☗☗ n/a Head: Anthony W. Mateer ICAO: SILVERHAWK Net: n/a Uses the service-name STAR CARE V for its EMS-operation & SILVERHAWK SECURITY SPECIALISTS for its VAL/cargo-operation.

☐ N52BA	Beech Baron 58	TH-52	N318P	0070	1196	2 CO IO-520-C	2404	Pax/EMS/Frtr		
☐ N76WD	Cessna 340A II	340A0099		0076	0293	2 CO TSIO-520-N	2717	Pax/EMS/Frtr		
☐ N900CG	Piper PA-31-325 Navajo C/R	31-7612002		0076	0895	2 LY TIO-540-F2BD	2948	Pax/EMS/Frtr		
☐ N816CM	Piper PA-31T1 Cheyenne I	31T-8104009		0081	0192	2 PWC PT6A-11	3946	Pax/EMS/Frtr		lsf Municipal Energy Agency of NE
☐ N22BJ	Beech King Air A100	B-133	N1200Z	0072	0196	2 PWC PT6A-28	5216	Pax/EMS/Frtr		
☐ N75GR	Beech King Air A100	B-210	N75ZZ	0074	0997	2 PWC PT6A-28	5216	Pax/EMS/Frtr		
☐ N86BM	Beech King Air A100	B-206	N86PA	0075	1196	2 PWC PT6A-28	5216	Pax/EMS/Frtr		

SINTON HELICOPTERS (Jack Sinton dba) — Paso Robles-Municipal, CA

PO Box 337, Paso Robles, CA 93447, USA ☎ (805) 238-4037 Tx: none Fax: (805) 238-3370 SITA: n/a
F: 1983 ☗☗☗ n/a Head: Jack Sinton Net: n/a

☐ N59553	Bell 206B JetRanger	1451		0074	0185	1 AN 250-C20	1451			lsf Sycan Corp.

SIOUX FALLS AVIATION - SFA (Business Aviation Courier Inc. dba/Subs.of Daedalus Inc./Air Cargo division of Business Aviation) — Sioux Falls-Joe Foss Field, SD

3501 Aviation Avenue, Sioux Falls, SD 57104-0197, USA ☎ (605) 336-7791 Tx: none Fax: (605) 336-8009 SITA: n/a
F: 1970 ☗☗☗ n/a Head: Linda K. Barker Net: n/a

☐ N9453Q	Beech Bonanza V35B	D-9321		0071	0597	1 CO IO-520-BA	1542	Freighter		
☐ N1533T	Cessna 310R II	310R0111		0074	0195	2 CO IO-520-M	2495	Freighter		
☐ N5771M	Cessna 310P	310P0071		0069	0197	2 CO IO-470-VO	2359	Freighter		
☐ N5937M	Cessna 310P	310P0237		0069	0197	2 CO IO-470-VO	2359	Freighter		
☐ N6268Q	Cessna 310Q	310Q0526		0072	1296	2 CO IO-470-VO	2404	Freighter		
☐ N69827	Cessna 310Q II	310Q1002		0074	0197	2 CO IO-470-VO	2404	Freighter		
☐ N1048	Cessna 402B	402B0628		0074	0197	2 CO TSIO-520-E	2858	Freighter		
☐ N306	Cessna 402B	402B0435	C-GTAV	0073	1096	2 CO TSIO-520-E	2858	Freighter		
☐ N3729C	Cessna 402B	402B0589		0074	0597	2 CO TSIO-520-E	2858	Freighter		
☐ N3796C	Cessna 402B	402B0803		0075	0397	2 CO TSIO-520-E	2858	Freighter		
☐ N3813	Cessna 402B	402B0807		0075	0996	2 CO TSIO-520-E	2858	Freighter		
☐ N402BP	Cessna 402B	402B0353		0073	1196	2 CO TSIO-520-E	2858	Freighter		
☐ N402SS	Cessna 402B	402B0562		0074	0996	2 CO TSIO-520-E	2858	Freighter		
☐ N5087Q	Cessna 402B	402B0565		0074	0596	2 CO TSIO-520-E	2858	Freighter		
☐ N76MD	Cessna 402B II	402B1055		0076	0891	2 CO TSIO-520-E	2858	Freighter		
☐ N780MB	Cessna 402B	402B0249		0072	0697	2 CO TSIO-520-E	2858	Freighter		
☐ N80BS	Cessna 404 Titan II	404-0048		0077	0597	2 CO GTSIO-520-M	3810	Freighter		
☐ N387PH	Fairchild (Swearingen) SA227AC Metro III	AC-531	N31094	0083	0298	2 GA TPE331-11U-611G	6577	Freighter		lsf GAS Wilson Inc.

SKAGWAY AIR SERVICE, Inc. = 7J / SGY — Skagway, AK

PO Box 357, Skagway, AK 99840, USA ☎ (907) 983-2218 Tx: none Fax: (907) 983-2948 SITA: n/a
F: 1964 ☗☗☗ 10 Head: Ben L. Lingle ICAO: SKAGWAY AIR Net: n/a Aircraft below MTOW 1361kg: Piper PA-28

☐ N1132Q	Piper PA-32-300 Cherokee SIX	32-7740046		0077	0591	1 LY IO-540-K1G5	1542			
☐ N2884M	Piper PA-32-300 Cherokee SIX	32-7840058		0078	0388	1 LY IO-540-K1G5	1542			
☐ N30004	Piper PA-32-300 Cherokee SIX	32-7840120		0078	0590	1 LY IO-540-K1G5	1542			
☐ N31589	Piper PA-32-300 Cherokee SIX	32-7840135		0078	1084	1 LY IO-540-K1G5	1542			
☐ N40698	Piper PA-32-300 Cherokee SIX	32-7440056		0074	0880	1 LY IO-540-K1A5	1542			
☐ N8127K	Piper PA-32-300 Cherokee SIX	32-7940268		0079	0690	1 LY IO-540-K1G5	1542			
☐ N8216T	Piper PA-32-301 Saratoga	32-8206037		0082	0782	1 LY IO-540-K1G5D	1633			
☐ N9540K	Piper PA-34-200T Seneca II	34-7670208		0076	0984	2 CO TSIO-360-E	2073			
☐ N4109D	Piper PA-31-350 T1020	31-8253012	N260SW	0082	0595	2 LY TIO-540-J2B	3175			
☐ N999SA	Britten-Norman BN-2A-26 Islander	897	C-GVKE	0080	0789	2 LY O-540-E4C5	2812			

SKYBIRD AVIATION, Inc. — Van Nuys, CA

7401 Valjean, Suite 100, Van Nuys, CA 91406, USA ☎ (818) 988-7210 Tx: none Fax: (818) 988-4086 SITA: n/a
F: 1976 ☗☗☗ n/a Head: Norman Anderson Net: n/a

☐ N234DB	GAC G-IV Gulfstream IV	1000	N404GA	0085	1285	2 RR Tay 610-8	32205	18 Pax		

SKY CASTLE AVIATION (Clifford A. Marlatt dba) — New Castle-Henry Co Municipal, IN

2912 East County Road 400S, New Castle, IN 47362, USA ☎ (765) 529-7903 Tx: none Fax: (765) 529-7903 SITA: n/a
F: 1965 ☗☗☗ n/a Head: Clifford A. Marlatt Net: n/a Aircraft below MTOW 1361 kg: Cessna 172

☐ N6685S	Beech Baron 58	TH-718		0076	0692	2 CO IO-520-C	2449			
☐ N4231V	Piper PA-31-350 Navajo Chieftain	31-7652162		0076	0484	2 LY TIO-540-J2BD	3175			
☐ N38W	Beech H18	BA-580		0060	0579	2 PW R-985	4491	Freighter		

SKYDANCE HELICOPTERS (Skydance Operations, Inc. dba) — Minden-Douglas County, NV & Sedona, AZ

2207 Bellanca Street, Minden, NV 89423, USA ☎ (702) 782-4040 Tx: none Fax: (702) 588-1896 SITA: n/a
F: 1986 ☗☗☗ n/a Head: Jeffrey K. Cain Net: http://www.skydanceheli.com

☐ N38CP	MD Helicopters MD 500D (Hughes 369D)	470125D		0077	0495	1 AN 250-C20B	1361			
☐ N219SH	Bell 206B JetRanger III	1532	N59624	0074	0797	1 AN 250-C20B	1451			cvtd JetRanger
☐ N83148	Bell 206B JetRanger	1040		0073	0889	1 AN 250-C20	1451			
☐ N220SH	Eurocopter (Aerosp.) SA315B Lama	2466	N220RM	0076	1195	1 TU Artouste IIIB	1950			

SKY DIVE, Inc. — Baldwin, WI

2235 Oakgreen Ave N, Stillwater, MN 55082, USA ☎ (320) 436-5225 Tx: none Fax: none SITA: n/a
F: 1984 ☗☗☗ 10 Head: David Mills & Mike Hayden Net: n/a Aircraft below MTOW 1361kg: Cessna 180 & 182

☐ N17393	De Havilland DHC-2 Beaver I	388	51-16568	0052	0586	1 PW R-985	2313	Para		

SKYDIVE ARIZONA, Inc. — Coolidge-Municipal, AZ

4900 North Tumbleweed Road, Eloy, AZ 85231, USA ☎ (520) 466-3753 Tx: none Fax: (520) 466-4720 SITA: n/a
F: 1984 ☗☗☗ n/a Head: Mohammed Khalil Net: n/a

☐ N101UV	Shorts Skyvan 3 Variant 100 (SC-7)	SH1842	N3126W	0068	1295	2 GA TPE331-2-201A	5670	Para		

SKYDIVE ELSINORE, Inc. — Lake Elsinore-Skylark, CA

20701 Cereal Road, Lake Elsinore, CA 92530, USA ☎ (909) 245-9939 Tx: none Fax: (909) 245-3661 SITA: n/a
F: 1997 ☗☗☗ n/a Head: Karl Gulledge Net: n/a

☐ N923MA	De Havilland DHC-6 Twin Otter 200	168	N923HM	0068	1297	2 PWC PT6A-27	5252	Para		lsf Alberta Aircraft Leasing Inc.
☐ N926MA	De Havilland DHC-6 Twin Otter 200	133	N953SM	0068	1297	2 PWC PT6A-20	5252	Para		lsf Speed Star Express Llc

SKY HARBOR AIR SERVICE, Inc. = SHC — Cheyenne, WY

3913 Evans Avenue, Cheyenne, WY 82001, USA ☎ (307) 634-4417 Tx: none Fax: (307) 635-7316 SITA: n/a
F: 1988 ☗☗☗ n/a Head: Charles R. Porter ICAO: SKY HARBOR CHEYENNE Net: n/a Aircraft below MTOW 1361kg: Cessna 172 & Piper PA-28.

☐ N2935M	Piper PA-34-200T Seneca II	34-7870100		0078	0088	2 CO TSIO-360-EB	2073			
☐ N83864	Piper PA-34-220T Seneca III	34-8133091		0081	0190	2 CO TSIO-360-KB	2155			lsf pvt
☐ N6631C	Cessna 414A Chancellor III	414A0038		0078	1091	2 CO TSIO-520-N	3062			lsf pvt

SKY KING, Inc. (Lukenbill Enterprises dba) — Sacramento-Metropolitan, CA

3600 Power Inn Road, Sacramento, CA 95826, USA ☎ (916) 736-6821 Tx: none Fax: (916) 454-9151 SITA: n/a
F: 1990 ☗☗☗ 6 Head: Greg Lukenbill Net: n/a Operates VIP flights exclusively for Basketball sport-teams (Sacramento Kings) & Entertainment-groups.

☐ N401SK	BAe (BAC) One-Eleven 401AK	073	N5LC	0066	0790	2 RR Spey 511-14	40597	VIP 30 Pax		
☐ N135TA	Boeing 737-222	19940 / 171	N135AW	0569	0998	2 PW JT8D-9A (HK3/NOR)	49442	VIP 36 Pax		

SKYLIFE AVIATION (Area Rescue Consortium of Hospitals dba) — St. Louis-Heliport & Chesterfield-Spirit of St. Louis, MO

2207 Scott Avenue, St. Louis, MO 63103, USA ☎ (573) 621-7007 Tx: none Fax: (573) 621-6530 SITA: n/a
F: 1990 ☗☗☗ n/a Head: Cyril C. Woodrome Net: n/a

☐ N204LF	Eurocopter (MBB) BO105LS-A3	2016	N7035P	0088	0895	2 AN 250-C28C	2600			lsf American Eurocopter Corp.
☐ N122SL	Eurocopter (MBB) BK117B-1	7207	N81932	0089	0890	2 LY LTS101-750B.1	3200	EMS		
☐ N211SL	Eurocopter (MBB) BK117B-1	7201	N8196Q	0089	0890	2 LY LTS101-750B.1	3200	EMS		
☐ N215AE	Eurocopter (MBB) BK117B-1	7216	N7138Y	0090	0297	2 LY LTS101-750B.1	3200	EMS		
☐ N250GP	Mitsubishi MU-300 Diamond IA	A069SA	N56MC*	0084	1296	2 PWC JT15D-4D	6636	EMS		

SKYLINE AVIATION (Aviation Management, Corp. dba) — Chicago-Lansing Municipal, IL

PO Box 553, Lansing, IL 60438, USA ☎ (708) 895-2666 Tx: none Fax: (708) 895-2683 SITA: n/a
F: 1980 ☗☗☗ n/a Head: Michael R. Sices Net: http://www.skylineair.com

☐ N8377C	Piper PA-34-200T Seneca II	34-7670133		0076	0993	2 CO TSIO-360-E	2073			

431 registration type of aircraft cn/fn ex/ex* mfd del powered by mtow kg configuration selcal name/fln/specialitites/remarks

SKYMASTER AVIATION (James R. Blumenthal dba) — Kingman, AZ

4650 Flightline Drive, Kingman, AZ 86401, USA ☎ (520) 757-4980 Tx: none Fax: (520) 757-4980 SITA: n/a
F: 1975 n/a Head: James R. Blumenthal Net: n/a

☐ N546S	Blumenthal (Fairchild) C-123K Provider	*20064*	*54-615*	*0054*	*0291*	*2 PW R-2800-99W +2 J85*	*27215*	*Freighter*		*cvtd Fairchild C-123B*
☐ N51802	Boeing (Douglas) DC-4 (C-54G-1-DO)	*35930 / DO 324*	*45-0477*	*0045*	*1077*	*4 PW R-2000*	*30241*	*Freighter*		

SKYNET AIRWAYS (Rolling Hills Aviation, Inc. dba) — Torrance-Municipal, CA

3115 Airport Drive, Torrance, CA 90505, USA ☎ (562) 326-3213 Tx: none Fax: (562) 534-9628 SITA: n/a
F: 1965 n/a Head: William H. Sherwood Net: n/a Aircraft below MTOW 1361kg: Cessna 152/172/182 & Piper PA-28

☐ N6636P	Beech Duchess 76	*ME-258*		*0079*	*0794*	*2 LY O-360-A1G6D*	*1769*			

SKYSERVICE USA, Inc. (Sister company of Skyservice, Canada) — Denver-Int'l, CO & San Francisco-Int'l, CA

266 North Main, Wichita, KS 67202, USA ☎ (650) 876-1739 Tx: none Fax: (650) 877-0789 SITA: n/a
F: 1997 n/a Head: Christopher Stewart Net: n/a

☐ G-CRPH	Airbus Industrie A320-231	*424*	*F-WQBB*	*0093*	*0598*	*2 IAE V2500-A1*	*75500*	*Y180*	*JM-AS*	*lsf AIH/sublst/opb RYN in Skyservice-cs*
☐ N571SC	Boeing (Douglas) DC-10-10	*46645 / 283*	*SE-DHX*	*0079*	*0798*	*3 GE CF6-6D1A*	*206385*	*Y380*		*lst / opb RYN in Skyservice-cs*
☐ N572SC	Boeing (Douglas) DC-10-10	*46977 / 251*	*SE-DHZ*	*0078*	*0798*	*3 GE CF6-6D1A*	*206385*	*Y380*		*lst / opb RYN in Skyservice-cs*

SKYTRAIN, Inc. — Wakeman, OH

9620 North Route 60, Wakeman, OH 44889, USA ☎ (440) 967-8010 Tx: none Fax: (440) 967-8036 SITA: n/a
F: 1994 n/a Head: Jack L. Harmon Net: n/a

☐ N510Q	Beech E18S	*BA-164*		*0056*	*0796*	*2 PW R-985-AN14B*	*4218*	*Frtr / Pax*		*lsf pvt*
☐ N59E	Beech E18S	*BA-206*		*0056*	*0294*	*2 PW R-985-AN14B*	*4218*	*Frtr / Pax*		

SKY TREK INTERNATIONAL AIRLINES, Inc. = PZR — Newark-Int'l, NJ

67 Scotch Road, Ewing, NJ 08628, USA ☎ (609) 671-0200 Tx: none Fax: (609) 671-0300 SITA: n/a
F: 1996 n/a Head: Robert W. Iverson, II ICAO: PHAZER Net: n/a

☐ N259US	Boeing 727-251	*19978 / 692*		*0269*	*1097*	*3 PW JT8D-7B*	*78245*	*Y171*		*lsf PACA*
☐ N267US	Boeing 727-251	*20289 / 746*		*0869*	*0397*	*3 PW JT8D-7B (HK3/FDX)*	*78245*	*Y168*		*lsf PEGA*
☐ N284KH	Boeing 727-2J0 (A)	*21108 / 1174*	*6Y-JMP*	*0075*	*1297*	*3 PW JT8D-15 (HK3/FDX)*	*88360*	*Y170*		*lsf KHA / cvtd -2J0*
☐ N901PG	Boeing 727-260 (A)	*21978 / 1520*	*ZS-OAO*	*0079*	*0398*	*3 PW JT8D-17R (HK3/FDX)*	*86409*	*Y173*		*lsf PACA*
☐ N908PG	Boeing 727-276 (A)	*20951 / 1101*	*TF-AIA*	*0475*	*0397*	*3 PW JT8D-15*	*86409*	*Y172*		*lsf PACA*

SKYWAY AIRLINES = AL / SYX (Midwest Express Connection) (Astral Aviation, Inc. dba/Subs. of Midwest Express) — Milwaukee-General Mitchell Int'l, WI

1190 West Rawson Ave., Oak Creek, WI 53154-1453, USA ☎ (920) 570-2300 Tx: none Fax: (920) 570-1441 SITA: HDQSKYX
F: 1993 240 Head: Dennis Crabtree ICAO: SKYWAY-EX Net: n/a
All aircraft are operated as a Midwest Express Connection (in own colours & titles), a commuter system to provide feeder connection at major Midwest Express hubs, using YX flight nos.

☐ N118SK	Beech 1900D Airliner	*UE-108*		*0094*	*0994*	*2 PWC PT6A-67D*	*7688*	*Y19*		*lsf TBCC Funding Trust I*
☐ N145SK	Beech 1900D Airliner	*UE-145*		*0095*	*0495*	*2 PWC PT6A-67D*	*7688*	*Y19*		*lsf Provident Commercial Group Inc.*
☐ N148SK	Beech 1900D Airliner	*UE-148*		*0095*	*0595*	*2 PWC PT6A-67D*	*7688*	*Y19*		*lsf Provident Commercial Group Inc.*
☐ N79SK	Beech 1900D Airliner	*UE-79*		*0094*	*0194*	*2 PWC PT6A-67D*	*7688*	*Y19*		
☐ N801SK	Beech 1900D Airliner	*UE-80*		*0094*	*0294*	*2 PWC PT6A-67D*	*7688*	*Y19*		
☐ N81SK	Beech 1900D Airliner	*UE-81*		*0094*	*0294*	*2 PWC PT6A-67D*	*7688*	*Y19*		
☐ N831SK	Beech 1900D Airliner	*UE-83*		*0094*	*0394*	*2 PWC PT6A-67D*	*7688*	*Y19*		
☐ N841SK	Beech 1900D Airliner	*UE-84*		*0094*	*0394*	*2 PWC PT6A-67D*	*7688*	*Y19*		
☐ N85SK	Beech 1900D Airliner	*UE-85*		*0094*	*0394*	*2 PWC PT6A-67D*	*7688*	*Y19*		*lsf FSBU Trustee*
☐ N87SK	Beech 1900D Airliner	*UE-87*		*0094*	*0494*	*2 PWC PT6A-67D*	*7688*	*Y19*		*lsf FSBU Trustee*
☐ N881SK	Beech 1900D Airliner	*UE-88*		*0094*	*0494*	*2 PWC PT6A-67D*	*7688*	*Y19*		*lsf FSBU Trustee*
☐ N891SK	Beech 1900D Airliner	*UE-89*		*0094*	*0594*	*2 PWC PT6A-67D*	*7688*	*Y19*		*lsf Boatmens Equipment Finance Inc.*
☐ N901SK	Beech 1900D Airliner	*UE-90*		*0094*	*0594*	*2 PWC PT6A-67D*	*7688*	*Y19*		*lsf Firstar Equipment Finance Corp.*
☐ N91SK	Beech 1900D Airliner	*UE-91*		*0094*	*0694*	*2 PWC PT6A-67D*	*7688*	*Y19*		*lsf Firstar Equipment Finance Corp.*
☐ N92SK	Beech 1900D Airliner	*UE-92*		*0094*	*0694*	*2 PWC PT6A-67D*	*7688*	*Y19*		*lsf Boatmens Equipment Finance Inc.*
☐ N351SK	Dornier 328JET (328-300)	*3108*				*2 PWC PW306B*	*14990*	*Y32*		*oo-delivery 0499*
☐ N352SK	Dornier 328JET (328-300)	*3111*				*2 PWC PW306B*	*14990*	*Y32*		*oo-delivery 0699*
☐ N353SK	Dornier 328JET (328-300)	*3121*				*2 PWC PW306B*	*14990*	*Y32*		*oo-delivery 0899*
☐ N354SK	Dornier 328JET (328-300)	*3126*				*2 PWC PW306B*	*14990*	*Y32*		*oo-delivery 0200*
☐ N355SK	Dornier 328JET (328-300)	*3134*				*2 PWC PW306B*	*14990*	*Y32*		*oo-delivery 0600*

SKYWAY Enterprises, Inc. = SKZ — Kissimmee, FL & Detroit-Willow Run, MI

3031 West Patrick, Kissimmee, FL 34741, USA ☎ (407) 932-0600 Tx: none Fax: (407) 932-0600 SITA: n/a
F: 1981 n/a Head: Thomas Loumankin ICAO: SKYWAY-INC Net: n/a

☐ N806LJ	Learjet 23	*23-073*		*0065*	*1085*	*2 GE CJ610-4*	*5670*	*Freighter/Exec*		*lsf A-Liner 8 Aviation*
☐ N856JB	Learjet 23	*23-052*	*N360EJ*	*0065*	*0284*	*2 GE CJ610-4*	*5670*	*Freighter/Exec*		
☐ N106SW	Shorts 330 (SD3-30)	*SH3072*	*C-GLAT*	*0081*	*1198*	*2 PWC PT6A-45R*	*10387*	*Freighter*		
☐ N805SW	Shorts 330-200 (SD3-30)	*SH3055*	*C-FLAC*	*0080*	*0998*	*2 PWC PT6A-45B*	*10160*	*Freighter*		
☐ N366MQ	Shorts 360-200 (SD3-60)	*SH3639*	*G-14-3639**	*0084*	*0498*	*2 PWC PT6A-65AR*	*11999*	*Freighter*		
☐ N367MQ	Shorts 360-200 (SD3-60)	*SH3640*	*G-14-3640**	*0084*	*0498*	*2 PWC PT6A-65AR*	*11999*	*Freighter*		

SKYWEST AIRLINES, Inc. = OO / SKW (Delta Connection / United Express) (Subs. of SkyWest, Inc.) — Salt Lake City-Int'l, UT & Los Angeles-Int'l, CA

444 South River Road, St. George, UT 84790, USA ☎ (435) 634-3000 Tx: none Fax: (435) 634-3305 SITA: n/a
F: 1972 2550 Head: Jerry C. Atkin IATA: 302 ICAO: SKYWEST Net: http://www.skywest.com All aircraft are operated in conjunction with Delta Air Lines as DELTA CONNECTION (in Skywest/Delta Connection-colors, some of them code-shared with Continental Airlines as Continental Connection) & United Airlines as UNITED EXPRESS (in full such colors & both titles) using their flight numbers.

☐ N1105G	Embraer 120RT Brasilia (EMB-120RT)	*120105*	*PT-SMX**	*0088*	*0498*	*2 PWC PW118*	*11500*	*Y30*		*op in United Express-colors*
☐ N1110J	Embraer 120RT Brasilia (EMB-120RT)	*120110*	*PT-SNC**	*0088*	*0498*	*2 PWC PW118*	*11500*	*Y30*		
☐ N1117H	Embraer 120RT Brasilia (EMB-120RT)	*120117*	*PT-SNJ**	*0089*	*0498*	*2 PWC PW118*	*11500*	*Y30*		*op in United Express-colors*
☐ N128AM	Embraer 120RT Brasilia (EMB-120RT)	*120109*	*PT-SNB**	*0088*	*0398*	*2 PWC PW118*	*11500*	*Y30*		
☐ N129AM	Embraer 120RT Brasilia (EMB-120RT)	*120119*	*PT-SNL**	*0089*	*0498*	*2 PWC PW118*	*11500*	*Y30*		
☐ N130G	Embraer 120RT Brasilia (EMB-120RT)	*120130*	*PT-SNW**	*0089*	*0598*	*2 PWC PW118*	*11500*	*Y30*		
☐ N137H	Embraer 120RT Brasilia (EMB-120RT)	*120137*	*PT-SPD**	*0089*	*0698*	*2 PWC PW118*	*11500*	*Y30*		
☐ N156CA	Embraer 120RT Brasilia (EMB-120RT)	*120156*	*PT-SPV**	*0089*	*0898*	*2 PWC PW118*	*11500*	*Y30*		
☐ N161CA	Embraer 120RT Brasilia (EMB-120RT)	*120143*	*PT-SPJ**	*0089*	*0798*	*2 PWC PW118*	*11500*	*Y30*		
☐ N162CA	Embraer 120RT Brasilia (EMB-120RT)	*120150*	*PT-SPP**	*0089*	*0898*	*2 PWC PW118*	*11500*	*Y30*		
☐ N186SW	Embraer 120ER Brasilia (EMB-120ER)	*120034*	*PT-SJD**	*0086*	*1286*	*2 PWC PW118A*	*11990*	*Y30*		*cvtd 120RT*
☐ N187SW	Embraer 120ER Brasilia (EMB-120ER)	*120037*	*PT-SJG**	*0086*	*1186*	*2 PWC PW118A*	*11990*	*Y30*		*cvtd 120RT*
☐ N188SW	Embraer 120ER Brasilia (EMB-120ER)	*120039*	*PT-SJI**	*0086*	*1286*	*2 PWC PW118A*	*11990*	*Y30*		*cvtd 120RT*
☐ N189SW	Embraer 120ER Brasilia (EMB-120ER)	*120048*	*PT-SJR**	*0087*	*0387*	*2 PWC PW118A*	*11990*	*Y30*		*cvtd 120RT*
☐ N190SW	Embraer 120ER Brasilia (EMB-120ER)	*120050*	*PT-SJT**	*0087*	*0587*	*2 PWC PW118A*	*11990*	*Y30*		*cvtd 120RT*
☐ N193SW	Embraer 120ER Brasilia (EMB-120ER)	*120088*	*PT-SMF**	*0088*	*0888*	*2 PWC PW118A*	*11990*	*Y30*		*cvtd 120RT*
☐ N194SW	Embraer 120ER Brasilia (EMB-120ER)	*120120*	*PT-SNM**	*0089*	*0289*	*2 PWC PW118A*	*11990*	*Y30*		*cvtd 120RT*
☐ N195SW	Embraer 120ER Brasilia (EMB-120ER)	*120127*	*PT-SNT**	*0089*	*0489*	*2 PWC PW118A*	*11990*	*Y30*		*cvtd 120RT*
☐ N196CA	Embraer 120RT Brasilia (EMB-120RT)	*120196*	*PT-SRL**	*0090*	*0998*	*2 PWC PW118*	*11500*	*Y30*		
☐ N196SW	Embraer 120ER Brasilia (EMB-120ER)	*120151*	*PT-SPQ**	*0089*	*0989*	*2 PWC PW118A*	*11990*	*Y30*		*cvtd 120RT*
☐ N197SW	Embraer 120ER Brasilia (EMB-120ER)	*120186*	*PT-SQY**	*0090*	*0690*	*2 PWC PW118A*	*11990*	*Y30*		*cvtd 120RT*
☐ N198SW	Embraer 120ER Brasilia (EMB-120ER)	*120227*	*PT-SSW**	*0091*	*0191*	*2 PWC PW118A*	*11990*	*Y30*		*cvtd 120RT*
☐ N199SW	Embraer 120ER Brasilia (EMB-120ER)	*120237*	*PT-STJ**	*0091*	*0591*	*2 PWC PW118A*	*11990*	*Y30*		*cvtd 120RT*
☐ N200CD	Embraer 120RT Brasilia (EMB-120RT)	*120200*	*PT-SRQ**	*0090*	*0798*	*2 PWC PW118*	*11500*	*Y30*		
☐ N203SW	Embraer 120ER Brasilia (EMB-120ER)	*120240*	*PT-STM**	*0091*	*0591*	*2 PWC PW118A*	*11990*	*Y30*		*cvtd 120RT*
☐ N204SW	Embraer 120ER Brasilia (EMB-120ER)	*120243*	*PT-STP**	*0091*	*0591*	*2 PWC PW118A*	*11990*	*Y30*		*cvtd 120RT*
☐ N205SW	Embraer 120ER Brasilia (EMB-120ER)	*120260*	*PT-SUG**	*0091*	*1291*	*2 PWC PW118A*	*11990*	*Y30*		*cvtd 120RT*
☐ N207SW	Embraer 120ER Brasilia (EMB-120ER)	*120266*	*PT-SUM**	*0092*	*0292*	*2 PWC PW118A*	*11990*	*Y30*		*cvtd 120RT*
☐ N209SW	Embraer 120ER Brasilia (EMB-120ER)	*120269*	*PT-SUP**	*0092*	*0292*	*2 PWC PW118A*	*11990*	*Y30*		*cvtd 120RT*
☐ N212SW	Embraer 120ER Brasilia (EMB-120ER)	*120276*	*PT-SUW**	*0092*	*0892*	*2 PWC PW118A*	*11990*	*Y30*		*cvtd 120RT*
☐ N213SW	Embraer 120ER Brasilia (EMB-120ER)	*120277*	*PT-SUX**	*0092*	*1092*	*2 PWC PW118A*	*11990*	*Y30*		*cvtd 120RT*
☐ N214SW	Embraer 120ER Brasilia (EMB-120ER)	*120280*	*PT-SVA**	*0093*	*0593*	*2 PWC PW118A*	*11990*	*Y30*		
☐ N215SW	Embraer 120ER Brasilia (EMB-120ER)	*120281*	*PT-SVB**	*0093*	*0593*	*2 PWC PW118A*	*11990*	*Y30*		
☐ N216SW	Embraer 120ER Brasilia (EMB-120ER)	*120285*	*PT-SVF**	*0093*	*0993*	*2 PWC PW118A*	*11990*	*Y30*		
☐ N217SW	Embraer 120ER Brasilia (EMB-120ER)	*120286*	*PT-SVG**	*0093*	*1093*	*2 PWC PW118A*	*11990*	*Y30*		
☐ N218SW	Embraer 120ER Brasilia (EMB-120ER)	*120287*	*PT-SVH**	*0094*	*0494*	*2 PWC PW118A*	*11990*	*Y30*		
☐ N220SW	Embraer 120ER Brasilia (EMB-120ER)	*120288*	*PT-SVI**	*0094*	*0494*	*2 PWC PW118A*	*11990*	*Y30*		
☐ N221SW	Embraer 120ER Brasilia (EMB-120ER)	*120290*	*PT-SVK**	*0094*	*0794*	*2 PWC PW118A*	*11990*	*Y30*		
☐ N223SW	Embraer 120ER Brasilia (EMB-120ER)	*120291*	*PT-SVL**	*0095*	*0395*	*2 PWC PW118A*	*11990*	*Y30*		
☐ N224SW	Embraer 120ER Brasilia (EMB-120ER)	*120294*	*PT-SVO**	*0095*	*0395*	*2 PWC PW118A*	*11990*	*Y30*		
☐ N226SW	Embraer 120ER Brasilia (EMB-120ER)	*120296*	*PT-SVQ**	*0095*	*0595*	*2 PWC PW118A*	*11990*	*Y30*		
☐ N227SW	Embraer 120ER Brasilia (EMB-120ER)	*120304*	*PT-SVW**	*0095*	*1095*	*2 PWC PW118A*	*11990*	*Y30*		
☐ N229SW	Embraer 120ER Brasilia (EMB-120ER)	*120305*	*PT-SVX**	*0095*	*1195*	*2 PWC PW118A*	*11990*	*Y30*		
☐ N232SW	Embraer 120ER Brasilia (EMB-120ER)	*120306*	*PT-SVY**	*0095*	*1295*	*2 PWC PW118A*	*11990*	*Y30*		
☐ N233SW	Embraer 120ER Brasilia (EMB-120ER)	*120307*	*PT-SVZ**	*0095*	*1295*	*2 PWC PW118A*	*11990*	*Y30*		
☐ N234SW	Embraer 120ER Brasilia (EMB-120ER)	*120308*	*PT-SXA**	*0096*	*0296*	*2 PWC PW118A*	*11990*	*Y30*		
☐ N235SW	Embraer 120ER Brasilia (EMB-120ER)	*120310*	*PT-SXC**	*0096*	*0396*	*2 PWC PW118A*	*11990*	*Y30*		
☐ N236SW	Embraer 120ER Brasilia (EMB-120ER)	*120312*	*PT-SXE**	*0096*	*0496*	*2 PWC PW118B*	*11990*	*Y30*		
☐ N237SW	Embraer 120ER Brasilia (EMB-120ER)	*120314*	*PT-SXG**	*0096*	*0596*	*2 PWC PW118B*	*11990*	*Y30*		
☐ N250YV	Embraer 120RT Brasilia (EMB-120RT)	*120250*	*PT-STW**	*0693*	*0598*	*2 PWC PW118A*	*11500*	*Y30*		
☐ N251YV	Embraer 120RT Brasilia (EMB-120RT)	*120251*	*PT-STX**	*0693*	*0598*	*2 PWC PW118A*	*11500*	*Y30*		

registration	type of aircraft	cn/fn	ex/ex*	mfd	del	powered by	mtow kg	configuration	name/fln/specialitites/remarks
☐ N268UE	Embraer 120RT Brasilia (EMB-120RT)	120207	PT-SRZ*	1090	0698	2 PWC PW118A	11500	Y30	
☐ N269UE	Embraer 120RT Brasilia (EMB-120RT)	120194	PT-SRJ*	0690	0898	2 PWC PW118	11500	Y30	
☐ N270YV	Embraer 120RT Brasilia (EMB-120RT)	120270	PT-SUQ*	0893	0698	2 PWC PW118A	11500	Y30	
☐ N271YV	Embraer 120RT Brasilia (EMB-120RT)	120271	PT-SUR*	0893	0498	2 PWC PW118A	11500	Y30	
☐ N284YV	Embraer 120RT Brasilia (EMB-120RT)	120284	PT-SVE*	0394	0498	2 PWC PW118A	11500	Y30	
☐ N288SW	Embraer 120ER Brasilia (EMB-120ER)	120316	PT-SXI*	0096	0696	2 PWC PW118A	11990	Y30	
☐ N289UE	Embraer 120RT Brasilia (EMB-120RT)	120191	PT-SRE*	0690	0898	2 PWC PW118	11500	Y30	
☐ N289YV	Embraer 120RT Brasilia (EMB-120RT)	120289	PT-SVJ*	0594	0598	2 PWC PW118A	11500	Y30	
☐ N290SW	Embraer 120ER Brasilia (EMB-120ER)	120317	PT-SXJ*	0096	0796	2 PWC PW118B	11990	Y30	
☐ N291SW	Embraer 120ER Brasilia (EMB-120ER)	120318	PT-SXK*	0096	0796	2 PWC PW118B	11990	Y30	
☐ N292SW	Embraer 120ER Brasilia (EMB-120ER)	120319	PT-SXL*	0096	0896	2 PWC PW118B	11990	Y30	
☐ N292UX	Embraer 120ER Brasilia (EMB-120ER)	120292	PT-SVM*	0094	0498	2 PWC PW118A	11990	Y30	
☐ N293SW	Embraer 120ER Brasilia (EMB-120ER)	120320	PT-SXM*	0096	0996	2 PWC PW118B	11990	Y30	
☐ N294SW	Embraer 120ER Brasilia (EMB-120ER)	120321	PT-SXN*	0096	0996	2 PWC PW118B	11990	Y30	
☐ N295SW	Embraer 120ER Brasilia (EMB-120ER)	120322	PT-SXO*	0096	1196	2 PWC PW118B	11990	Y30	
☐ N295UX	Embraer 120ER Brasilia (EMB-120ER)	120295	PT-SVP*	0095	0498	2 PWC PW118A	11990	Y30	
☐ N296SW	Embraer 120ER Brasilia (EMB-120ER)	120325	PT-SXR*	0096	1196	2 PWC PW118B	11990	Y30	
☐ N297SW	Embraer 120ER Brasilia (EMB-120ER)	120327	PT-SXT*	0096	1296	2 PWC PW118B	11990	Y30	op in United Express-colors
☐ N298SW	Embraer 120ER Brasilia (EMB-120ER)	120328	PT-SXU*	0096	1296	2 PWC PW118B	11990	Y30	
☐ N299SW	Embraer 120ER Brasilia (EMB-120ER)	120329	PT-SXV*	0096	0197	2 PWC PW118B	11990	Y30	op in United Express-colors
☐ N301YV	Embraer 120ER Brasilia (EMB-120ER)	120301	PT-SVV*	1295	0598	2 PWC PW118A	11990	Y30	
☐ N308SW	Embraer 120ER Brasilia (EMB-120ER)	120326	PT-SXS*	0096	0197	2 PWC PW118B	11990	Y30	
☐ N393SW	Embraer 120ER Brasilia (EMB-120ER)	120330	PT-SXW*	0096	0297	2 PWC PW118B	11990	Y30	25th anniversary colors
☐ N560SW	Embraer 120ER Brasilia (EMB-120ER)	120334		0098	0398	2 PWC PW118B	11990	Y30	op in United Express-colors
☐ N561SW	Embraer 120ER Brasilia (EMB-120ER)	120335		0098	0398	2 PWC PW118B	11990	Y30	op in United Express-colors
☐ N562SW	Embraer 120ER Brasilia (EMB-120ER)	120336		0098	0498	2 PWC PW118B	11990	Y30	op in United Express-colors
☐ N563SW	Embraer 120ER Brasilia (EMB-120ER)	120338		0098	0598	2 PWC PW118B	11990	Y30	op in United Express-colors
☐ N564SW	Embraer 120ER Brasilia (EMB-120ER)	120339		0098	0698	2 PWC PW118B	11990	Y30	op in United Express-colors
☐ N565SW	Embraer 120ER Brasilia (EMB-120ER)	120340		0098	0698	2 PWC PW118B	11990	Y30	
☐ N566SW	Embraer 120ER Brasilia (EMB-120ER)	120341	PT-SAF*	0098	0798	2 PWC PW118B	11990	Y30	op in United Express-colors
☐ N567SW	Embraer 120ER Brasilia (EMB-120ER)	120342		0098	0798	2 PWC PW118B	11990	Y30	op in United Express-colors
☐ N568SW	Embraer 120ER Brasilia (EMB-120ER)	120343		0098	1098	2 PWC PW118B	11990	Y30	
☐ N569SW	Embraer 120ER Brasilia (EMB-120ER)	120344		0098	0998	2 PWC PW118B	11990	Y30	
☐ N576SW	Embraer 120ER Brasilia (EMB-120ER)	120345		0098	1098	2 PWC PW118B	11990	Y30	
☐ N578SW	Embraer 120ER Brasilia (EMB-120ER)	120346		0098	1298	2 PWC PW118B	11990	Y30	
☐ N579SW	Embraer 120ER Brasilia (EMB-120ER)	120347		0098	1298	2 PWC PW118B	11990	Y30	
☐ N580SW	Embraer 120ER Brasilia (EMB-120ER)					2 PWC PW118B	11990	Y30	oo-delivery 0499
☐ N581SW	Embraer 120ER Brasilia (EMB-120ER)					2 PWC PW118B	11990	Y30	oo-delivery 0499
☐ N582SW	Embraer 120ER Brasilia (EMB-120ER)					2 PWC PW118B	11990	Y30	oo-delivery 0599
☐ N583SW	Embraer 120ER Brasilia (EMB-120ER)					2 PWC PW118B	11990	Y30	oo-delivery 0599
☐ N584SW	Embraer 120ER Brasilia (EMB-120ER)					2 PWC PW118B	11990	Y30	oo-delivery 0699
☐ N585SW	Embraer 120ER Brasilia (EMB-120ER)					2 PWC PW118B	11990	Y30	oo-delivery 0799
☐ N586SW	Embraer 120ER Brasilia (EMB-120ER)					2 PWC PW118B	11990	Y30	oo-delivery 0899
☐ N403SW	Canadair Regional Jet 100LR (CL-600-2B19)	7028	C-FMNB*	0093	0194	2 GE CF34-3A1	23995	Y50	cvtd 100ER
☐ N405SW	Canadair Regional Jet 100LR (CL-600-2B19)	7029	C-FMND*	0093	0194	2 GE CF34-3A1	23995	Y50	cvtd 100ER
☐ N406SW	Canadair Regional Jet 100LR (CL-600-2B19)	7030	C-FMNH*	0093	0194	2 GE CF34-3A1	23995	Y50	cvtd 100ER
☐ N407SW	Canadair Regional Jet 100LR (CL-600-2B19)	7034	C-FMNY*	0094	0394	2 GE CF34-3A1	23995	Y50	cvtd 100ER
☐ N408SW	Canadair Regional Jet 100LR (CL-600-2B19)	7055	C-FMMW*	0094	1294	2 GE CF34-3A1	23995	Y50	cvtd 100ER
☐ N409SW	Canadair Regional Jet 100LR (CL-600-2B19)	7056	C-FMMX*	0094	0195	2 GE CF34-3A1	23995	Y50	cvtd 100ER
☐ N410SW	Canadair Regional Jet 100LR (CL-600-2B19)	7066	C-FMOL*	0095	0595	2 GE CF34-3A1	23995	Y50	cvtd 100ER
☐ N411SW	Canadair Regional Jet 100LR (CL-600-2B19)	7067	C-FMOS*	0095	0595	2 GE CF34-3A1	23995	Y50	cvtd 100ER
☐ N412SW	Canadair Regional Jet 100LR (CL-600-2B19)	7101		0095	0196	2 GE CF34-3A1	23995	Y50	cvtd 100ER
☐ N413SW	Canadair Regional Jet 100LR (CL-600-2B19)	7102		0095	0196	2 GE CF34-3A1	23995	Y50	cvtd 100ER
☐ N60SR	Canadair Regional Jet 100LR (CL-600-2B19)	7089	C-GDYX	0095	1298	2 GE CF34-3A1	23995	Y50	cvtd 100ER
☐ N	Canadair Regional Jet 200LR (CL-600-2B19)					2 GE CF34-3B1	24040	Y50	oo-delivery 0400
☐ N	Canadair Regional Jet 200LR (CL-600-2B19)					2 GE CF34-3B1	24040	Y50	oo-delivery 0500
☐ N	Canadair Regional Jet 200LR (CL-600-2B19)					2 GE CF34-3B1	24040	Y50	oo-delivery 0600
☐ N	Canadair Regional Jet 200LR (CL-600-2B19)					2 GE CF34-3B1	24040	Y50	oo-delivery 0700
☐ N	Canadair Regional Jet 200LR (CL-600-2B19)					2 GE CF34-3B1	24040	Y50	oo-delivery 0800
☐ N	Canadair Regional Jet 200LR (CL-600-2B19)					2 GE CF34-3B1	24040	Y50	oo-delivery 0900
☐ N	Canadair Regional Jet 200LR (CL-600-2B19)					2 GE CF34-3B1	24040	Y50	oo-delivery 1000
☐ N	Canadair Regional Jet 200LR (CL-600-2B19)					2 GE CF34-3B1	24040	Y50	oo-delivery 0101
☐ N	Canadair Regional Jet 200LR (CL-600-2B19)					2 GE CF34-3B1	24040	Y50	oo-delivery 0301
☐ N	Canadair Regional Jet 200LR (CL-600-2B19)					2 GE CF34-3B1	24040	Y50	oo-delivery 0501
☐ N	Canadair Regional Jet 200LR (CL-600-2B19)					2 GE CF34-3B1	24040	Y50	oo-delivery 0601
☐ N	Canadair Regional Jet 200LR (CL-600-2B19)					2 GE CF34-3B1	24040	Y50	oo-delivery 0701
☐ N	Canadair Regional Jet 200LR (CL-600-2B19)					2 GE CF34-3B1	24040	Y50	oo-delivery 0801
☐ N	Canadair Regional Jet 200LR (CL-600-2B19)					2 GE CF34-3B1	24040	Y50	oo-delivery 0901
☐ N	Canadair Regional Jet 200LR (CL-600-2B19)					2 GE CF34-3B1	24040	Y50	oo-delivery 1101
☐ N	Canadair Regional Jet 200LR (CL-600-2B19)					2 GE CF34-3B1	24040	Y50	oo-delivery 1201
☐ N	Canadair Regional Jet 200LR (CL-600-2B19)					2 GE CF34-3B1	24040	Y50	oo-delivery 0002
☐ N	Canadair Regional Jet 200LR (CL-600-2B19)					2 GE CF34-3B1	24040	Y50	oo-delivery 0002
☐ N	Canadair Regional Jet 200LR (CL-600-2B19)					2 GE CF34-3B1	24040	Y50	oo-delivery 0002
☐ N	Canadair Regional Jet 200LR (CL-600-2B19)					2 GE CF34-3B1	24040	Y50	oo-delivery 0002
☐ N	Canadair Regional Jet 200LR (CL-600-2B19)					2 GE CF34-3B1	24040	Y50	oo-delivery 0002
☐ N	Canadair Regional Jet 200LR (CL-600-2B19)					2 GE CF34-3B1	24040	Y50	oo-delivery 0002

SKYYWAY AVIATION (Skyyway, Lc dba)
Ness City-Municipal, KS

1 King Court, Suite 119, New Century, KS 66031, USA ☎ (913) 768-0444 Tx: none Fax: (913) 768-0094 SITA: n/a
F: 1996 ♦♦♦ n/a Head: Mike S. Jurkovich Net: n/a

☐ N888TR	Beech King Air 200	BB-50	N500FE	0075	1297	2 PWC PT6A-41	5670		

SMITHAIR, Inc. = SMH
Hampton-Clayton County/Tara Field, GA

510 Mt. Pleasant Road, Hampton, GA 30228, USA ☎ (770) 477-8888 Tx: none Fax: (770) 477-9165 SITA: n/a
F: 1974 ♦♦♦ n/a Head: Brenda Smith ICAO: SMITHAIR Net: n/a

☐ N5AL	Beech Baron 58	TH-356		0073	0489	2·CO IO-520-C	2449	Freighter	lsf RBS Aviation Group Inc.
☐ N400KU	Beech G18S	BA-572		0061	0480	2 PW R-985-AN14B	4400	Freighter	lsf RBS Aviation Group Inc.
☐ N140RC	Learjet 23	23-048	N48MW	0065	0688	2 GE CJ610-4	5670	Freighter	lsf RBS Aviation Group Inc.
☐ N16HC	Learjet 24	24-126	N332FP	0066	0590	2 GE CJ610-4	5897	Freighter	lsf RBS Aviation Group Inc.
☐ N351N	Learjet 23	23-054	N351NR	0065	0793	2 GE CJ610-4	5670	Freighter	lsf RBS Aviation Group Inc.
☐ N7200K	Learjet 23	23-099		0066	0787	2 GE CJ610-4	5670	Freighter	lsf RBS Aviation Group Inc.
☐ N77VJ	Learjet 23	23-041	C-GDDB	0065	0190	2 GE CJ610-4	5670	Freighter	lsf RBS Aviation Group Inc.
☐ N900NA	Learjet 24A	24A-111	N44WD	0066	0894	2 GE CJ610-4	5897	Freighter	lsf RBS Aviation Group Inc.
☐ N767SA	Learjet 25D	25D-216	N216SA	0077	0395	2 GE CJ610-8A	6804	Freighter	lsf RBS Aviation Group Inc.

SNOWY BUTTE HELICOPTERS, Inc.
White City-Sutton on the Rogue Heliport, OR

PO Box 3216, Central Point, OR 97502, USA ☎ (541) 826-1150 Tx: none Fax: (541) 826-1977 SITA: n/a
F: 1987 ♦♦♦ n/a Head: Herb Sutton Net: n/a

☐ N121HS	Bell 407	53095	N47496	0097	0497	1 AN 250-C47B	2268		
☐ N5025V	Bell UH-1E (204)	6205	Bu 155350	0068	0896	1 LY T53-L-11	3856		
☐ N212HS	Bell 212	30665	C-FJKL	0074	0298	2 PWC PT6T-3 TwinPac	5080		

SOLLEY CONSTRUCTION, Co. Inc.
Decatur-Pryor Field, AL

PO Box 1561, Decatur, AL 35602, USA ☎ (205) 350-1756 Tx: none Fax: (205) 350-1974 SITA: n/a
F: 1988 ♦♦♦ n/a Head: Ray Solley Net: n/a Operates flights for the construction business, mainly for itself but also for contract-customers.

☐ N703SC	Sikorsky S-58E	58-1607	N70666	0063	0993	1 WR R-1820	5897		

SOUND AVIATION (Daniel W. Easley dba)
Anchorage-Merrill Field, AK

4272 Chelsea Way, Anchorage, AK 99504, USA ☎ (907) 229-7173 Tx: none Fax: (907) 277-6863 SITA: n/a
F: 1993 ♦♦♦ n/a Head: Daniel W. Easley Net: n/a Aircraft below MTOW 1361kg: Piper PA-28

☐ N8631N	Piper PA-32-300 Cherokee SIX	32-7140024		0071	0894	1 LY IO-540-K1A5	1542		

SOUND FLIGHT, Inc.
Renton-SPB, WA

PO Box 812, Renton, WA 98057, USA ☎ (425) 255-6500 Tx: none Fax: (425) 255-2313 SITA: n/a
F: 1988 ♦♦♦ n/a Head: Mark W. Schoening Net: http://www.soundflight.com Aircraft below MTOW 1361kg: Cessna 180 & 182 (on Floats)

☐ N2SF	De Havilland DHC-2 Beaver I	329	N5163G	0052	0590	1 PW R-985	2313		Floats
☐ N49771	De Havilland DHC-2 Beaver I	1079	N1102N	0057		1 PW R-985	2313		lsf Airlease Inc. / Floats
☐ N82SF	De Havilland DHC-2 Beaver I	839	N44CD	0055	0790	1 PW R-985	2313		lsf Airlease Inc. / Floats
☐ N84SF	De Havilland DHC-3 Turbo Otter	284	57-6136	0058	0694	1 PWC PT6A-135	3629		lsf Airlease Inc. / Floats / cvtd Otter

SOUTH AERO, Inc.

Albuquerque-Int'l, NM

PO Box 9175, Albuquerque, NM 87119, USA ☎ (505) 873-2092 Tx: none Fax: none SITA: n/a
F: 1982 n/a Head: Wayne South Net: n/a Aircraft below MTOW 1361kg: Cessna 182

N1689X	Cessna 210L Centurion II	21060724		0075	0989	1 CO IO-520-L	1724	Freighter		
N2179S	Cessna T210L Turbo Centurion II	21061140		0076	0192	1 CO TSIO-520-H	1724	Freighter		
N6479N	Cessna T210N Turbo Centurion II	21063053		0079	0491	1 CO TSIO-520-R	1814	Freighter		
N7213N	Cessna T210N Turbo Centurion II	21063207		0079	0393	2 CO TSIO-520-R	1814	Freighter		
N732HN	Cessna T210L Turbo Centurion II	21061527		0076	1290	1 CO TSIO-520-H	1724	Freighter		
N761DW	Cessna T210M Turbo Centurion II	21062183		0077	0888	1 CO TSIO-520-R	1724	Freighter		
N26156	Cessna 402C II	402C0112		0079	0290	2 CO TSIO-520-VB	3107	Freighter		
N2711X	Cessna 402C II	402C0116		0079	0794	2 CO TSIO-520-VB	3107	Freighter		
N3292M	Cessna 402C II	402C0304		0080	0187	2 CO TSIO-520-VB	3107	Freighter		
N402KP	Cessna 402C III	402C1013		0085	1095	2 CO TSIO-520-VB	3107	Freighter		
N402MQ	Cessna 402C II	402C0095		0079	0891	2 CO TSIO-520-VB	3107	Freighter		
N402SA	Cessna 402C II	402C0623	C-GHOR	0081	0692	2 CO TSIO-520-VB	3107	Freighter		
N42MG	Cessna 402C II	402C0320		0080	1193	2 CO TSIO-520-VB	3107	Freighter		
N4643N	Cessna 402C II	402C0006		0078	0990	2 CO TSIO-520-VB	3107	Freighter		
N494BC	Cessna 402C II	402C0308	N67PB	0080	1188	2 CO TSIO-520-VB	3107	Freighter		
N525RH	Cessna 402C II	402C0525		0081	0287	2 CO TSIO-520-VB	3107	Freighter		
N57PB	Cessna 402C II	402C0300		0080	1189	2 CO TSIO-520-VB	3107	Freighter		
N5820C	Cessna 402C II	402C0047		0078	0591	2 CO TSIO-520-VB	3107	Freighter		
N6880A	Cessna 402C II	402C0616		0081	0293	2 CO TSIO-520-VB	3107	Freighter		
N747WS	Cessna 402C II	402C0080	C-GHYZ	0079	0888	2 CO TSIO-520-VB	3107	Freighter		
N36891	Cessna 414A Chancellor III	414A0243		0079	0294	2 CO TSIO-520-NB	3062	Freighter		
N5388J	Cessna 404 Titan II	404-0666		0080	1095	2 CO GTSIO-520-M	3810	Freighter		
N54ZP	Cessna 404 Titan II	404-0694		0080	1296	2 CO GTSIO-520-M	3810	Freighter		

SOUTHCENTRAL AIR, Inc. = XE / SCA

Kenai-Municipal, AK

135 Granite Point Court, Kenai, AK 99611, USA ☎ (907) 283-7676 Tx: none Fax: (907) 283-3678 SITA: n/a
F: 1975 90 Head: James A. Munson IATA: 301 ICAO: SOUTH CENTRAL Net: n/a

N4098R	Piper PA-32-300 Cherokee SIX	32-40406		0068	0791	1 LY IO-540-K1A5	1542	Y5		
N490SC	Piper PA-31-350 Navajo Chieftain	31-7305001	N7700L	0073	0381	2 LY TIO-540-J2BD	3175	Freighter		
N493SC	Piper PA-31-350 Navajo Chieftain	31-7652048	N59793	0076	0381	2 LY TIO-540-J2BD	3175	Y7		
N495SC	Piper PA-31-350 Navajo Chieftain	31-8052062	N3555Y	0080	0385	2 LY TIO-540-J2BD	3175	Y9		
N178SC	Britten-Norman BN-2A-26 Islander	599	N20875	0077	0383	2 LY O-540-E4C5	2812	Y9		
N304SC	Piper PA-31T3-T1040	31T-8275017	N9096C	0082	0783	2 PWC PT6A-11	4082	Y9		
N311SC	Piper PA-31T3-T1040	31T-8275006	N9176Y	0082	0789	2 PWC PT6A-11	4082	Y9		
N314SC	Piper PA-31T3-T1040	31T-8275007	N9180Y	0082	0490	2 PWC PT6A-11	4082	Y9		
N19454	Boeing (Douglas) DC-3C (C-47A-DL)	13863	NC19454	0043	1298	2 PW R-1830	12202	Freighter		

SOUTH COAST HELICOPTERS, Inc.

Santa-Ana John Wayne/Orange County, CA

361 Paularino, Hangar 21, Costa Mesa, CA 92626, USA ☎ (949) 751-3515 Tx: none Fax: (949) 751-4705 SITA: n/a
F: 1992 n/a Head: Clifford T. Fleming Net: n/a

N369SC	MD Helicopters MD 500D (Hughes 369D)	480295D	N66180	0078	0592	1 AN 250-C20B	1361			
N250CA	Bell 206B JetRanger III	2615		0079	0993	1 AN 250-C20B	1451			lsf pvt
N15SC	Bell 206L-3 LongRanger III	51019	HC-BVE	0082	0695	1 AN 250-C30P	1882			
N350SC	Eurocopter (Aerosp.) AS350BA AStar	1408	N5778M	0081	0997	1 TU Arriel 1B	2100			cvtd AS350D

SOUTHEAST AIR (Seaflight, Llc dba)

Manteo-Dare County Regional, NC

PO Box 1358, Manteo, NC 27954, USA ☎ (919) 473-3222 Tx: none Fax: (919) 473-1349 SITA: n/a
F: 1996 n/a Head: Betty S. Brindley Net: n/a Aircraft below MTOW 1361kg: Cessna 177 & 182

N7WK	Cessna 310Q	310Q0426		0072	0797	2 CO IO-470-VO	2404			
N323AP	Piper PA-31-350 Navajo Chieftain	31-8252031		0082	0398	2 LY TIO-540-J2BD	3175			lsf Breezy Llc

SOUTHEAST AIR CHARTER, Inc.

Southern Pines-Moore County, NC

PO Box 3333, Pinehurst, NC 28374, USA ☎ (910) 692-2095 Tx: none Fax: (910) 692-8216 SITA: n/a
F: 1993 n/a Head: Thomas Hughes Net: n/a

N128TX	Beech Baron 58	TH-1338		0082	0395	2 CO IO-520-CB	2449			lsf Air Moore Inc.
N25AP	Beech King Air E90	LW-309	N20GM	0078	0395	2 PWC PT6A-28	4581			lsf Air Moore Inc.

SOUTHEAST AIRMOTIVE, Corp. = SPU

Charlotte-Douglas Int'l, NC

PO Box 19027, Charlotte, NC 28219, USA ☎ (704) 359-8403 Tx: none Fax: (704) 359-8602 SITA: n/a
F: 1946 18 Head: Michael S. Karr ICAO: SPUTTER Net: n/a Aircraft below MTOW 1361 kg: Piper PA-28.

N1397H	Piper PA-34-200T Seneca II	34-7770124		0077	0183	2 CO TSIO-360-E	2073			
N7633C	Piper PA-34-200T Seneca II	34-7670098		0076	1179	2 CO TSIO-360-E	2073			
N8793E	Piper PA-34-200T Seneca II	34-7670180		0076	1084	2 CO TSIO-360-E	2073			
N3542D	Piper PA-31-350 Navajo Chieftain	31-7952232		0079	0985	2 LY TIO-540-J2BD	3175			
N5JX	Piper PA-31-310 Navajo	31-433		0069	1078	2 LY TIO-540-A1A	2948			
N7451L	Piper PA-31-310 Navajo B	31-847		0072	0184	2 LY TIO-540-A2C	2948			
N20WS	Beech King Air E90	LW-30	N159B	0072	0891	2 PWC PT6A-28	4581			
N303DK	Beech King Air 200	BB-578	N578G	0079	0196	2 PWC PT6A-41	5670			lsf CLG Associates Inc.

SOUTHEAST MISSISSIPPI AIR AMBULANCE

Hattiesburg-Forest County Hospital Heliport, MS

PO Box 17889, Hattiesburg, MS 39401, USA ☎ (601) 264-3405 Tx: none Fax: (601) 288-4360 SITA: n/a
F: 1979 n/a Head: Harvel R. Smith Net: n/a

N521RC	Bell 206L-3 LongRanger III	51566	N93EA	0092	0197	1 AN 250-C20P	1882	EMS		

SOUTHERN HELICOPTERS, Inc.

Sunshine-Private Heliport, LA

1127 River Road, Sunshine, LA 70780, USA ☎ (504) 642-0075 Tx: none Fax: (504) 642-0075 SITA: n/a
F: 1977 n/a Head: Benjamin C. Seal, Jr. Net: n/a

N42TV	Bell 206B JetRanger III	3040	N44TU	0080	0382	1 AN 250-C20B	1451			
N90332	Bell 206B JetRanger	1739		0075	0277	1 AN 250-C20	1451			

SOUTHERN PRIDE - Flight Dept. (Flight Dept. of Southern Pride Trucking, Inc.)

Concord-Regional, NC

Southern Pride Compound, San Diego, CA 92126, USA ☎ (619) 683-3400 Tx: none Fax: (619) 683-7478 SITA: n/a
F: 1997 n/a Head: Dave Hodgeman Net: n/a Operates non-commerical flights exclusively for itself and for NASCAR Stockcar-racing teams of Petty Enterprises.

N443PE	BAe 3101 Jetstream 31	777	N777JX	0087	1097	2 GA TPE331-10UR-513H	6900	Y19		lsf Global Resour./sublst Petty Enterp.
N755SP	BAe 3101 Jetstream 31	755	N405UE	0587	0998	2 GA TPE331-10UG-513H	6900	Y19		lsf Racing Airways Inc.

SOUTHERN SEAPLANE, Inc. = SSC

Belle Chasse-Southern Seaplane SPB, LA

No. 1 Coquille Drive, Belle Chasse, LA 70037, USA ☎ (504) 394-5633 Tx: none Fax: (504) 394-8458 SITA: n/a
F: 1954 30 Head: Lyle Panepinto ICAO: SOUTHERN SKIES Net: n/a Aircraft below MTOW 1361kg: Cessna 180 (on Floats)

N6034N	Cessna A185F Skywagon II	18504293		0081	0188	1 CO IO-520-D	1520			Amphibian
N61301	Cessna A185F Skywagon II	18504144		0080	0488	1 CO IO-520-D	1520			Floats
N61441	Cessna A185F Skywagon II	18504191		0081	0188	1 CO IO-520-D	1520			Floats
N70117	Cessna A185E Skywagon	18501997		0072	1180	1 CO IO-520-D	1520			Floats
N2272X	Cessna U206E Super Skywagon	U20601556		0070	0789	1 CO IO-520-F	1633			Floats
N227SS	Cessna U206E Super Skywagon	U20601516		0070	1190	1 CO IO-520-F	1633			Amphibian
N70822	Cessna U206F Stationair	U20602099		0073	0493	1 CO IO-520-F	1633			Amphibian
N7896S	Cessna U206B Super Skywagon	U206-0814		0067	0796	1 CO IO-520-F	1633			Amphibian
N21058	De Havilland DHC-2 Beaver I	630	CF-HOE	0053	1289	1 PW R-985	2313			Floats

SOUTH SEA HELICOPTERS, Inc. (Subsidiary of South Sea Tours, Corp.)

Lihue, HI

3901 Mokulele Loop, Box 32, Lihue, HI 96766, USA ☎ (808) 245-2222 Tx: none Fax: (808) 246-9586 SITA: n/a
F: 1981 11 Head: Dennis M. Esaki Net: n/a

N38SG	Bell 206B JetRanger III	3492		0081	1294	1 AN 250-C20B	1451			
N40SG	Bell 206B JetRanger III	3023		0080	0495	1 AN 250-C20B	1451			
N29SS	Bell 206L LongRanger	45102		0077	1294	1 AN 250-C20B	1814			

SOUTHWEST AIRLINES, Company = WN / SWA

Dallas-Love Field & Houston-Hobby, TX

PO Box 36611, Dallas, TX 75235-1611, USA ☎ (972) 904-4000 Tx: 988124 southwest air Fax: (972) 904-5097 SITA: n/a
F: 1967 23970 Head: Herbert D. Kelleher IATA: 526 ICAO: SOUTHWEST Net: http://www.southwest.com

N102SW	Boeing 737-2H4 (A)	23108 / 1014		0084	0384	2 PW JT8D-9A (HK3/AVA)	52390	Y122		
N103SW	Boeing 737-2H4 (A)	23109 / 1016		0084	0384	2 PW JT8D-9A (HK3/AVA)	52390	Y122		
N104SW	Boeing 737-2H4 (A)	23110 / 1017		0084	0384	2 PW JT8D-9A (HK3/AVA)	52390	Y122		
N105SW	Boeing 737-2H4 (A)	23249 / 1095		0085	0385	2 PW JT8D-9A (HK3/AVA)	52390	Y122		
N129SW	Boeing 737-2K6 (A)	22340 / 678	N148AW	0080	0493	2 PW JT8D-15 (HK3/AVA)	52390	Y122		lsf Citicorp
N130SW	Boeing 737-2T4 (A)	22699 / 855	N83AF	0082	0883	2 PW JT8D-15 (HK3/AVA)	54204	Y122		
N54SW	Boeing 737-2H4 (A)	21535 / 543		0078	1278	2 PW JT8D-9A	52390	Y122		
N55SW	Boeing 737-2H4 (A)	21593 / 544		0078	1278	2 PW JT8D-9A	52390	Y122		
N56SW	Boeing 737-2H4 (A)	21721 / 553		0079	0279	2 PW JT8D-9A	52390	Y122		

434 registration type of aircraft cn/fn ex/ex* mfd del powered by mtow kg configuration selcal name/fln/specialitites/remarks

	registration	type of aircraft	cn/fn	ex/ex*	mfd	del	powered by	mtow kg	configuration	selcal	name/fln/specialitites/remarks
☐	N57SW	Boeing 737-2H4 (A)	21722 / 568		0079	0479	2 PW JT8D-9A	52390	Y122		
☐	N59SW	Boeing 737-2H4 (A)	21811 / 609		0079	1079	2 PW JT8D-9A	52390	Y122		
☐	N60SW	Boeing 737-2H4 (A)	21812 / 611		0079	1179	2 PW JT8D-9A	52390	Y122		
☐	N61SW	Boeing 737-2H4 (A)	21970 / 613		0079	1179	2 PW JT8D-9A (HK3/AVA)	52390	Y122		
☐	N62SW	Boeing 737-2H4 (A)	22060 / 638		0080	0380	2 PW JT8D-9A (HK3/AVA)	52390	Y122		
☐	N63SW	Boeing 737-2H4 (A)	22061 / 639		0080	0380	2 PW JT8D-9A (HK3/AVA)	52390	Y122		
☐	N64SW	Boeing 737-2H4 (A)	22062 / 640		0080	0380	2 PW JT8D-9A (HK3/AVA)	52390	Y122		
☐	N67SW	Boeing 737-2H4 (A)	22356 / 719		0080	1280	2 PW JT8D-9A (HK3/AVA)	52390	Y122		The Rollin W. King
☐	N68SW	Boeing 737-2H4 (A)	22357 / 725		0080	1280	2 PW JT8D-9A (HK3/AVA)	52390	Y122		The Winning Spirit
☐	N702ML	Boeing 737-2T4 (A)	22054 / 624	G-BJXL	0079	0591	2 PW JT8D-15 (HK3/AVA)	54204	Y122		
☐	N71SW	Boeing 737-2H4 (A)	22358 / 732		0081	0181	2 PW JT8D-9A (HK3/AVA)	52390	Y122		The Donald G. Ogden
☐	N721WN	Boeing 737-2T4 (A)	22697 / 817	N721ML	0081	0591	2 PW JT8D-15 (HK3/AVA)	54204	Y122		
☐	N722WN	Boeing 737-2T4 (A)	22698 / 823	N722ML	0081	0591	2 PW JT8D-15 (HK3/AVA)	54204	Y122		
☐	N73SW	Boeing 737-2H4 (A)	22673 / 826		0081	1281	2 PW JT8D-9A (HK3/AVA)	52390	Y122		
☐	N74SW	Boeing 737-2H4 (A)	22674 / 827		0081	1281	2 PW JT8D-9A (HK3/AVA)	52390	Y122		
☐	N80SW	Boeing 737-2H4 (A)	22675 / 839		0082	0282	2 PW JT8D-9A (HK3/AVA)	52390	Y122		
☐	N81SW	Boeing 737-2H4 (A)	22730 / 841		0082	0282	2 PW JT8D-9A (HK3/AVA)	52390	Y122		
☐	N82SW	Boeing 737-2H4 (A)	22731 / 864		0082	0482	2 PW JT8D-9A (HK3/AVA)	52390	Y122		
☐	N83SW	Boeing 737-2H4 (A)	22732 / 877		0082	0582	2 PW JT8D-9A (HK3/AVA)	52390	Y122		
☐	N85SW	Boeing 737-2H4 (A)	22826 / 878		0082	0682	2 PW JT8D-9A (HK3/AVA)	52390	Y122		
☐	N86SW	Boeing 737-2H4 (A)	22827 / 882		0082	0682	2 PW JT8D-9A	52390	Y122		
☐	N87SW	Boeing 737-2H4 (A)	22903 / 905		0082	0982	2 PW JT8D-9A	52390	Y122		
☐	N89SW	Boeing 737-2H4 (A)	22904 / 913		0082	0982	2 PW JT8D-9A	52390	Y122		
☐	N90SW	Boeing 737-2H4 (A)	22905 / 918		0082	1082	2 PW JT8D-9A	52390	Y122		
☐	N91SW	Boeing 737-2H4 (A)	22963 / 929		0083	1282	2 PW JT8D-9A	52390	Y122		
☐	N92SW	Boeing 737-2H4 (A)	22964 / 933		0082	0183	2 PW JT8D-9A	52390	Y122		
☐	N93SW	Boeing 737-2H4 (A)	22965 / 942		0083	0483	2 PW JT8D-9A	52390	Y122		
☐	N94SW	Boeing 737-2H4 (A)	23053 / 968		0083	0583	2 PW JT8D-9A	52390	Y122		
☐	N95SW	Boeing 737-2H4 (A)	23054 / 969		0083	0583	2 PW JT8D-9A	52390	Y122		
☐	N96SW	Boeing 737-2H4 (A)	23055 / 970		0083	0683	2 PW JT8D-9A	52390	Y122		The Fred J. Jones
☐	N501SW	Boeing 737-5H4	24178 / 1718	N73700*	0089	0990	2 CFMI CFM56-3B1	54431	Y122		Shamu Three colours
☐	N502SW	Boeing 737-5H4	24179 / 1744		0090	0590	2 CFMI CFM56-3B1	54431	Y122		
☐	N503SW	Boeing 737-5H4	24180 / 1766		0090	0290	2 CFMI CFM56-3B1	54431	Y122		
☐	N504SW	Boeing 737-5H4	24181 / 1804		0090	0390	2 CFMI CFM56-3B1	54431	Y122		
☐	N506SW	Boeing 737-5H4	24183 / 1852		0090	0590	2 CFMI CFM56-3B1	54431	Y122		
☐	N507SW	Boeing 737-5H4	24184 / 1864		0090	0590	2 CFMI CFM56-3B1	54431	Y122		Shamu Two colours
☐	N508SW	Boeing 737-5H4	24185 / 1932		0090	1090	2 CFMI CFM56-3B1	54431	Y122		
☐	N509SW	Boeing 737-5H4	24186 / 1934		0090	1090	2 CFMI CFM56-3B1	54431	Y122		
☐	N510SW	Boeing 737-5H4	24187 / 1940		0090	1090	2 CFMI CFM56-3B1	54431	Y122		
☐	N511SW	Boeing 737-5H4	24188 / 2029		0091	0491	2 CFMI CFM56-3B1	54431	Y122		
☐	N512SW	Boeing 737-5H4	24189 / 2056		0091	0591	2 CFMI CFM56-3B1	54431	Y122		
☐	N513SW	Boeing 737-5H4	24190 / 2058		0091	0691	2 CFMI CFM56-3B1	54431	Y122		
☐	N514SW	Boeing 737-5H4	25153 / 2078		0091	0791	2 CFMI CFM56-3B1	54431	Y122		
☐	N515SW	Boeing 737-5H4	25154 / 2080		0091	0791	2 CFMI CFM56-3B1	54431	Y122		
☐	N519SW	Boeing 737-5H4	25318 / 2121		0091	0991	2 CFMI CFM56-3B1	54431	Y122		
☐	N520SW	Boeing 737-5H4	25319 / 2134		0091	1091	2 CFMI CFM56-3B1	54431	Y122		
☐	N521SW	Boeing 737-5H4	25320 / 2136		0091	1091	2 CFMI CFM56-3B1	54431	Y122		
☐	N522SW	Boeing 737-5H4	26564 / 2202		0092	0192	2 CFMI CFM56-3B1	54431	Y122		
☐	N523SW	Boeing 737-5H4	26565 / 2204		0092	0192	2 CFMI CFM56-3B1	54431	Y122		
☐	N524SW	Boeing 737-5H4	26566 / 2224		0092	0292	2 CFMI CFM56-3B1	54431	Y122		
☐	N525SW	Boeing 737-5H4	26567 / 2283		0092	0592	2 CFMI CFM56-3B1	54431	Y122		
☐	N526SW	Boeing 737-5H4	26568 / 2285		0092	0592	2 CFMI CFM56-3B1	54431	Y122		
☐	N527SW	Boeing 737-5H4	26569 / 2287		0092	0592	2 CFMI CFM56-3B1	54431	Y122		
☐	N528SW	Boeing 737-5H4	26570 / 2292		0092	0592	2 CFMI CFM56-3B1	54431	Y122		
☐	N300SW	Boeing 737-3H4	22940 / 1037		0084	1184	2 CFMI CFM56-3B1	58967	Y137		The Spirit of Kitty Hawk
☐	N301SW	Boeing 737-3H4	22941 / 1048		0084	1284	2 CFMI CFM56-3B1	58967	Y137		The Spirit of Kitty Hawk
☐	N302SW	Boeing 737-3H4	22942 / 1052		0084	1284	2 CFMI CFM56-3B1	58967	Y137		The Spirit of Kitty Hawk
☐	N303SW	Boeing 737-3H4	22943 / 1101		0085	0485	2 CFMI CFM56-3B1	58967	Y137		
☐	N304SW	Boeing 737-3H4	22944 / 1138		0085	0885	2 CFMI CFM56-3B1	58967	Y137		
☐	N305SW	Boeing 737-3H4	22945 / 1139		0085	0885	2 CFMI CFM56-3B1	58967	Y137		
☐	N306SW	Boeing 737-3H4	22946 / 1148		0085	0985	2 CFMI CFM56-3B1	58967	Y137		
☐	N307SW	Boeing 737-3H4	22947 / 1156		0085	1085	2 CFMI CFM56-3B1	58967	Y137		
☐	N309SW	Boeing 737-3H4	22948 / 1160		0085	1085	2 CFMI CFM56-3B1	58967	Y137		
☐	N310SW	Boeing 737-3H4	22949 / 1161		0085	1285	2 CFMI CFM56-3B1	58967	Y137		
☐	N311SW	Boeing 737-3H4	23333 / 1183		0086	0386	2 CFMI CFM56-3B1	58967	Y137		
☐	N312SW	Boeing 737-3H4	23334 / 1185		0086	0386	2 CFMI CFM56-3B1	58967	Y137		
☐	N313SW	Boeing 737-3H4	23335 / 1201		0086	0386	2 CFMI CFM56-3B1	58967	Y137		
☐	N314SW	Boeing 737-3H4	23336 / 1229		0086	0586	2 CFMI CFM56-3B1	58967	Y137		
☐	N315SW	Boeing 737-3H4	23337 / 1231		0086	0586	2 CFMI CFM56-3B1	58967	Y137		
☐	N316SW	Boeing 737-3H4	23338 / 1232		0086	0586	2 CFMI CFM56-3B1	58967	Y137		
☐	N318SW	Boeing 737-3H4	23339 / 1255		0086	0886	2 CFMI CFM56-3B1	58967	Y137		
☐	N319SW	Boeing 737-3H4	23340 / 1348		0087	0387	2 CFMI CFM56-3B1	58967	Y137		
☐	N320SW	Boeing 737-3H4	23341 / 1350		0087	0387	2 CFMI CFM56-3B1	58967	Y137		
☐	N321SW	Boeing 737-3H4	23342 / 1351		0087	0387	2 CFMI CFM56-3B1	58967	Y137		
☐	N322SW	Boeing 737-3H4	23343 / 1377		0087	0587	2 CFMI CFM56-3B1	58967	Y137		lsf Colonial Pacific Leasing Corp.
☐	N323SW	Boeing 737-3H4	23344 / 1378		0087	0587	2 CFMI CFM56-3B1	58967	Y137		
☐	N324SW	Boeing 737-3H4	23414 / 1384		0087	0587	2 CFMI CFM56-3B1	58967	Y137		
☐	N325SW	Boeing 737-3H4	23689 / 1398		0087	0687	2 CFMI CFM56-3B1	58967	Y137		
☐	N326SW	Boeing 737-3H4	23690 / 1400		0087	0687	2 CFMI CFM56-3B1	58967	Y137		
☐	N327SW	Boeing 737-3H4	23691 / 1407		0087	0687	2 CFMI CFM56-3B1	58967	Y137		
☐	N328SW	Boeing 737-3H4	23692 / 1521		0088	0388	2 CFMI CFM56-3B1	58967	Y137		
☐	N329SW	Boeing 737-3H4	23693 / 1525		0088	0388	2 CFMI CFM56-3B1	58967	Y137		
☐	N330SW	Boeing 737-3H4	23694 / 1529		0088	0388	2 CFMI CFM56-3B1	58967	Y137		
☐	N331SW	Boeing 737-3H4	23695 / 1536		0088	0488	2 CFMI CFM56-3B1	58967	Y137		lsf Colonial Pacific Leasing Corp.
☐	N332SW	Boeing 737-3H4	23696 / 1545		0088	0588	2 CFMI CFM56-3B1	58967	Y137		
☐	N333SW	Boeing 737-3H4	23697 / 1547		0088	0588	2 CFMI CFM56-3B1	58967	Y137		
☐	N334SW	Boeing 737-3H4	23938 / 1549		0088	0588	2 CFMI CFM56-3B1	58967	Y137		Shamu / Whale colours
☐	N335SW	Boeing 737-3H4	23939 / 1553		0088	0588	2 CFMI CFM56-3B1	58967	Y137		
☐	N336SW	Boeing 737-3H4	23940 / 1557		0088	0588	2 CFMI CFM56-3B1	58967	Y137		
☐	N337SW	Boeing 737-3H4	23959 / 1567		0088	0688	2 CFMI CFM56-3B1	58967	Y137		
☐	N338SW	Boeing 737-3H4	23960 / 1571		0088	0688	2 CFMI CFM56-3B1	58967	Y137		
☐	N339SW	Boeing 737-3H4	24090 / 1591		0088	0888	2 CFMI CFM56-3B1	58967	Y137		
☐	N341SW	Boeing 737-3H4	24091 / 1593		0088	0888	2 CFMI CFM56-3B1	58967	Y137		
☐	N342SW	Boeing 737-3H4	24133 / 1682		0089	0389	2 CFMI CFM56-3B1	58967	Y137		
☐	N343SW	Boeing 737-3H4	24151 / 1686		0089	0389	2 CFMI CFM56-3B1	58967	Y137		
☐	N344SW	Boeing 737-3H4	24152 / 1688		0089	0389	2 CFMI CFM56-3B1	58967	Y137		
☐	N346SW	Boeing 737-3H4	24153 / 1690		0089	0389	2 CFMI CFM56-3B1	58967	Y137		
☐	N347SW	Boeing 737-3H4	24374 / 1708		0089	0589	2 CFMI CFM56-3B1	58967	Y137		
☐	N348SW	Boeing 737-3H4	24375 / 1710		0089	0589	2 CFMI CFM56-3B1	58967	Y137		
☐	N349SW	Boeing 737-3H4	24408 / 1734		0089	0689	2 CFMI CFM56-3B1	58967	Y137		
☐	N350SW	Boeing 737-3H4	24409 / 1748		0089	0889	2 CFMI CFM56-3B1	58967	Y137		
☐	N351SW	Boeing 737-3H4	24572 / 1790		0089	1189	2 CFMI CFM56-3B1	58967	Y137		
☐	N352SW	Boeing 737-3H4	24888 / 1942		0090	1190	2 CFMI CFM56-3B1	58967	Y137		Lone Star One-colours
☐	N353SW	Boeing 737-3H4	24889 / 1947		0090	1190	2 CFMI CFM56-3B1	58967	Y137		
☐	N354SW	Boeing 737-3H4	25219 / 2092		0091	0791	2 CFMI CFM56-3B1	58967	Y137		
☐	N355SW	Boeing 737-3H4	25250 / 2103		0091	0891	2 CFMI CFM56-3B1	58967	Y137		
☐	N356SW	Boeing 737-3H4	25251 / 2105		0091	0891	2 CFMI CFM56-3B1	58967	Y137	EM-GK	
☐	N357SW	Boeing 737-3H4	26594 / 2294		0092	0592	2 CFMI CFM56-3B1	58967	Y137		
☐	N358SW	Boeing 737-3H4	26595 / 2295		0092	0692	2 CFMI CFM56-3B1	58967	Y137		
☐	N359SW	Boeing 737-3H4	26596 / 2297		0092	0692	2 CFMI CFM56-3B1	58967	Y137		
☐	N360SW	Boeing 737-3H4	26571 / 2307		0092	0692	2 CFMI CFM56-3B1	58967	Y137		
☐	N361SW	Boeing 737-3H4	26572 / 2309		0092	0692	2 CFMI CFM56-3B1	58967	Y137		
☐	N362SW	Boeing 737-3H4	26573 / 2322		0092	0792	2 CFMI CFM56-3B1	58967	Y137		
☐	N363SW	Boeing 737-3H4	26574 / 2429		0093	0293	2 CFMI CFM56-3B1	58967	Y137		Heros of the Heart-Crew Scheduling P&R
☐	N364SW	Boeing 737-3H4	26575 / 2430		0093	0293	2 CFMI CFM56-3B1	58967	Y137		
☐	N365SW	Boeing 737-3H4	26576 / 2433		0093	0293	2 CFMI CFM56-3B1	58967	Y137		The Herbert D. Kelleher
☐	N366SW	Boeing 737-3H4	26577 / 2469		0093	0593	2 CFMI CFM56-3B1	58967	Y137		
☐	N367SW	Boeing 737-3H4	26578 / 2470		0093	0593	2 CFMI CFM56-3B1	58967	Y137		
☐	N368SW	Boeing 737-3H4	26579 / 2473		0093	0593	2 CFMI CFM56-3B1	58967	Y137		
☐	N369SW	Boeing 737-3H4	26580 / 2477		0093	0593	2 CFMI CFM56-3B1	58967	Y137		

☐ N370SW	Boeing 737-3H4	26597 / 2497		0093	0793	2 CFMI CFM56-3B1	58967	Y137		
☐ N371SW	Boeing 737-3H4	26598 / 2500		0093	0793	2 CFMI CFM56-3B1	58967	Y137		
☐ N372SW	Boeing 737-3H4	26599 / 2504		0093	0793	2 CFMI CFM56-3B1	58967	Y137		
☐ N373SW	Boeing 737-3H4	26581 / 2509		0093	0893	2 CFMI CFM56-3B1	58967	Y137		
☐ N374SW	Boeing 737-3H4	26582 / 2515		0093	0893	2 CFMI CFM56-3B1	58967	Y137		
☐ N375SW	Boeing 737-3H4	26583 / 2520		0093	0993	2 CFMI CFM56-3B1	58967	Y137		
☐ N376SW	Boeing 737-3H4	26584 / 2570		0094	0194	2 CFMI CFM56-3B1	58967	Y137		
☐ N378SW	Boeing 737-3H4	26585 / 2579		0094	0294	2 CFMI CFM56-3B1	58967	Y137		
☐ N379SW	Boeing 737-3H4	26586 / 2580		0094	0294	2 CFMI CFM56-3B1	58967	Y137		
☐ N380SW	Boeing 737-3H4	26587 / 2610		0094	0594	2 CFMI CFM56-3B1	58967	Y137		
☐ N382SW	Boeing 737-3H4	26588 / 2611		0094	0594	2 CFMI CFM56-3B1	58967	Y137		
☐ N383SW	Boeing 737-3H4	26589 / 2612		0094	0594	2 CFMI CFM56-3B1	58967	Y137		Arizona One / *Arizona flag colours*
☐ N384SW	Boeing 737-3H4	26590 / 2613		0094	0594	2 CFMI CFM56-3B1	58967	Y137		
☐ N385SW	Boeing 737-3H4	26600 / 2617		0094	0594	2 CFMI CFM56-3B1	58967	Y137		
☐ N386SW	Boeing 737-3H4	26601 / 2626		0094	0694	2 CFMI CFM56-3B1	58967	Y137		
☐ N387SW	Boeing 737-3H4	26602 / 2627		0094	0694	2 CFMI CFM56-3B1	58967	Y137		
☐ N388SW	Boeing 737-3H4	26591 / 2628		0094	0794	2 CFMI CFM56-3B1	58967	Y137		
☐ N389SW	Boeing 737-3H4	26592 / 2629		0094	0794	2 CFMI CFM56-3B1	58967	Y137		
☐ N390SW	Boeing 737-3H4	26593 / 2642		0094	0894	2 CFMI CFM56-3B1	58967	Y137		
☐ N391SW	Boeing 737-3H4	27378 / 2643		0094	0994	2 CFMI CFM56-3B1	58967	Y137		
☐ N392SW	Boeing 737-3H4	27379 / 2644		0094	0994	2 CFMI CFM56-3B1	58967	Y137		
☐ N394SW	Boeing 737-3H4	27380 / 2645		0094	0994	2 CFMI CFM56-3B1	58967	Y137		
☐ N395SW	Boeing 737-3H4	27689 / 2667		0094	1194	2 CFMI CFM56-3B1	58967	Y137		
☐ N396SW	Boeing 737-3H4	27690 / 2668		0094	1194	2 CFMI CFM56-3B1	58967	Y137		
☐ N397SW	Boeing 737-3H4	27691 / 2695		0095	0295	2 CFMI CFM56-3B1	58967	Y137		
☐ N398SW	Boeing 737-3H4	27692 / 2696		0095	0295	2 CFMI CFM56-3B1	58967	Y137		
☐ N399WN	Boeing 737-3H4	27693 / 2697		0095	0295	2 CFMI CFM56-3B1	58967	Y137		
☐ N600WN	Boeing 737-3H4	27694 / 2699		0095	0295	2 CFMI CFM56-3B1	58967	Y137		
☐ N601WN	Boeing 737-3H4	27695 / 2702		0095	0395	2 CFMI CFM56-3B1	58967	Y137		Jack Vidal
☐ N602SW	Boeing 737-3H4	27953 / 2713		0095	0495	2 CFMI CFM56-3B1	58967	Y137		
☐ N603SW	Boeing 737-3H4	27954 / 2714		0095	0495	2 CFMI CFM56-3B1	58967	Y137		
☐ N604SW	Boeing 737-3H4	27955 / 2715		0095	0495	2 CFMI CFM56-3B1	58967	Y137		
☐ N605SW	Boeing 737-3H4	27956 / 2716		0095	0495	2 CFMI CFM56-3B1	58967	Y137		
☐ N606SW	Boeing 737-3H4	27926 / 2740		0095	0795	2 CFMI CFM56-3B1	58967	Y137		
☐ N607SW	Boeing 737-3H4	27927 / 2741		0095	0795	2 CFMI CFM56-3B1	58967	Y137		June M. Morris
☐ N608SW	Boeing 737-3H4	27928 / 2742		0095	0795	2 CFMI CFM56-3B1	58967	Y137		
☐ N609SW	Boeing 737-3H4	27929 / 2744		0095	0895	2 CFMI CFM56-3B1	58967	Y137		California One / *California flag colors*
☐ N610WN	Boeing 737-3H4	27696 / 2745		0095	0895	2 CFMI CFM56-3B1	58967	Y137		
☐ N611SW	Boeing 737-3H4	27697 / 2750		0095	0995	2 CFMI CFM56-3B1	58967	Y137		
☐ N612SW	Boeing 737-3H4	27930 / 2753		0095	0995	2 CFMI CFM56-3B1	58967	Y137		
☐ N613SW	Boeing 737-3H4	27931 / 2754		0095	0995	2 CFMI CFM56-3B1	58967	Y137		
☐ N614SW	Boeing 737-3H4	28033 / 2755		0095	0995	2 CFMI CFM56-3B1	58967	Y137		
☐ N615SW	Boeing 737-3H4	27698 / 2757		0095	1095	2 CFMI CFM56-3B1	58967	Y137		
☐ N616SW	Boeing 737-3H4	27699 / 2758		0095	1095	2 CFMI CFM56-3B1	58967	Y137		
☐ N617SW	Boeing 737-3H4	27700 / 2759	N1786B*	0095	1095	2 CFMI CFM56-3B1	58967	Y137		
☐ N618WN	Boeing 737-3H4	28034 / 2761		0095	1195	2 CFMI CFM56-3B1	58967	Y137		
☐ N619SW	Boeing 737-3H4	28035 / 2762		0095	1195	2 CFMI CFM56-3B1	58967	Y137		
☐ N620SW	Boeing 737-3H4	28036 / 2766		0096	0196	2 CFMI CFM56-3B1	58967	Y137		
☐ N621SW	Boeing 737-3H4	28037 / 2767		0096	0196	2 CFMI CFM56-3B1	58967	Y137		
☐ N622SW	Boeing 737-3H4	27932 / 2779		0096	0396	2 CFMI CFM56-3B1	58967	Y137		
☐ N623SW	Boeing 737-3H4	27933 / 2780		0096	0396	2 CFMI CFM56-3B1	58967	Y137		
☐ N624SW	Boeing 737-3H4	27934 / 2781		0096	0396	2 CFMI CFM56-3B1	58967	Y137		
☐ N625SW	Boeing 737-3H4	27701 / 2787		0096	0496	2 CFMI CFM56-3B1	58967	Y137		
☐ N626SW	Boeing 737-3H4	27702 / 2789		0096	0596	2 CFMI CFM56-3B1	58967	Y137		
☐ N627SW	Boeing 737-3H4	27935 / 2790		0096	0596	2 CFMI CFM56-3B1	58967	Y137		
☐ N628SW	Boeing 737-3H4	27703 / 2795		0096	0596	2 CFMI CFM56-3B1	58967	Y137		
☐ N629SW	Boeing 737-3H4	27704 / 2796		0096	0696	2 CFMI CFM56-3B1	58967	Y137		*Silver One, 25 years silver colors*
☐ N630WN	Boeing 737-3H4	27705 / 2797		0096	0696	2 CFMI CFM56-3B1	58967	Y137		
☐ N631SW	Boeing 737-3H4	27706 / 2798		0096	0696	2 CFMI CFM56-3B1	58967	Y137		
☐ N632SW	Boeing 737-3H4	27707 / 2799		0096	0696	2 CFMI CFM56-3B1	58967	Y137		
☐ N633SW	Boeing 737-3H4	27936 / 2807		0096	0796	2 CFMI CFM56-3B1	58967	Y137		
☐ N634SW	Boeing 737-3H4	27937 / 2808		0096	0896	2 CFMI CFM56-3B1	58967	Y137		
☐ N635SW	Boeing 737-3H4	27708 / 2813		0096	0996	2 CFMI CFM56-3B1	58967	Y137		
☐ N636WN	Boeing 737-3H4	27709 / 2814		0096	0996	2 CFMI CFM56-3B1	58967	Y137		
☐ N637SW	Boeing 737-3H4	27710 / 2819		0096	1096	2 CFMI CFM56-3B1	58967	Y137		
☐ N638SW	Boeing 737-3H4	27711 / 2820		0096	1096	2 CFMI CFM56-3B1	58967	Y137		
☐ N639SW	Boeing 737-3H4	27712 / 2821		0096	1096	2 CFMI CFM56-3B1	58967	Y137		
☐ N640SW	Boeing 737-3H4	27713 / 2840		0096	1296	2 CFMI CFM56-3B1	58967	Y137		
☐ N641SW	Boeing 737-3H4	27714 / 2841		0096	1296	2 CFMI CFM56-3B1	58967	Y137		
☐ N642WN	Boeing 737-3H4	27715 / 2842		0096	0197	2 CFMI CFM56-3B1	58967	Y137		
☐ N643SW	Boeing 737-3H4	27716 / 2843		0096	0197	2 CFMI CFM56-3B1	58967	Y137		
☐ N644SW	Boeing 737-3H4	28329 / 2869		0097	0397	2 CFMI CFM56-3B1	58967	Y137		
☐ N645SW	Boeing 737-3H4	28330 / 2870		0097	0497	2 CFMI CFM56-3B1	58967	Y137		
☐ N646SW	Boeing 737-3H4	28331 / 2871		0097	0497	2 CFMI CFM56-3B1	58967	Y137		
☐ N647SW	Boeing 737-3H4	27717 / 2892		0097	0697	2 CFMI CFM56-3B1	58967	Y137		*Triple Crown One-colors*
☐ N648SW	Boeing 737-3H4	27718 / 2893		0097	0697	2 CFMI CFM56-3B1	58967	Y137		
☐ N649SW	Boeing 737-3H4	27719 / 2894		0697	0697	2 CFMI CFM56-3B1	58967	Y137		
☐ N650SW	Boeing 737-3H4	27720 / 2901		0697	0697	2 CFMI CFM56-3B1	58967	Y137		
☐ N651SW	Boeing 737-3H4	27721 / 2915		0097	0897	2 CFMI CFM56-3B1	58967	Y137		
☐ N652SW	Boeing 737-3H4	27722 / 2916		0097	0897	2 CFMI CFM56-3B1	58967	Y137		
☐ N653SW	Boeing 737-3H4	28398 / 2917		0097	0897	2 CFMI CFM56-3B1	58967	Y137		
☐ N654SW	Boeing 737-3H4	28399 / 2918		0097	0897	2 CFMI CFM56-3B1	58967	Y137		
☐ N655WN	Boeing 737-3H4	28400 / 2931		0097	0997	2 CFMI CFM56-3B1	58967	Y137		
☐ N656SW	Boeing 737-3H4	28401 / 2932		0997	0997	2 CFMI CFM56-3B1	58967	Y137		
☐ N657SW	Boeing 737-3L9	23331 / 1111	N960WP	0085	0398	2 CFMI CFM56-3B2	62823	Y137		
☐ N658SW	Boeing 737-3L9	23332 / 1118	N961WP	0085	0398	2 CFMI CFM56-3B2	62823	Y137		
☐ N659SW	Boeing 737-301	23229 / 1112	N950WP	0085	0498	2 CFMI CFM56-3B1	61235	Y137		
☐ N660SW	Boeing 737-301	23230 / 1115	N949WP	0085	0398	2 CFMI CFM56-3B1	61235	Y137		lsf Aircorp Inc.
☐ N661SW	Boeing 737-317	23173 / 1098	N946WP	0085	0698	2 CFMI CFM56-3B1	61235	Y137		lsf BBAM
☐ N662SW	Boeing 737-3Q8	23255 / 1125	N327US	0085	0495	2 CFMI CFM56-3B1	61235	Y137		lsf ILFC
☐ N663SW	Boeing 737-3Q8	23256 / 1128	N329US	0085	0495	2 CFMI CFM56-3B1	61235	Y137		lsf ILFC
☐ N664WN	Boeing 737-3Y0	23495 / 1206	EC-FVT	0086	1094	2 CFMI CFM56-3B1	61235	Y137		lsf GECA
☐ N665WN	Boeing 737-3Y0	23497 / 1227	G-MONF	0086	1194	2 CFMI CFM56-3B1	61235	Y137		lsf GECA
☐ N667SW	Boeing 737-3T5	23063 / 1092	N752MA	0385	0694	2 CFMI CFM56-3B1	61235	Y137		lsf National City Leasing Corp.
☐ N668SW	Boeing 737-3T5	23060 / 1069	N753MA	1284	0694	2 CFMI CFM56-3B1	61235	Y137		lsf B&A Leasing Corp.
☐ N669SW	Boeing 737-3A4	23752 / 1484	N758MA	1287	0794	2 CFMI CFM56-3B2	61235	Y137		lsf ACG Acquisition XX Llc
☐ N670SW	Boeing 737-3G7	23784 / 1533	N779MA	0388	0794	2 CFMI CFM56-3B1	56472	Y137		lsf GECC
☐ N671SW	Boeing 737-3G7	23785 / 1535	N778MA	0388	1094	2 CFMI CFM56-3B1	56472	Y137		lsf GECC
☐ N672SW	Boeing 737-3Q8	23406 / 1215	N755MA	0486	1094	2 CFMI CFM56-3B2	61235	Y137		lsf ILFC
☐ N673AA	Boeing 737-3A4	23251 / 1063	N307AC	0285	0192	2 CFMI CFM56-3B2	61235	Y137	BM-AL	lsf PEGA
☐ N674AA	Boeing 737-3A4	23252 / 1094	N776MA	0385	1094	2 CFMI CFM56-3B2	61235	Y137		lsf Airlease Inc.
☐ N675AA	Boeing 737-3A4	23253 / 1096	N309AC	0385	0492	2 CFMI CFM56-3B2	61235	Y137	BL-CE	lsf PEGA
☐ N676SW	Boeing 737-3A4	23288 / 1100	N742MA	0485	0494	2 CFMI CFM56-3B2	61235	Y137		
☐ N677AA	Boeing 737-3A4	23289 / 1182	N735MA	1285	1094	2 CFMI CFM56-3B2	61235	Y137		lsf AAL
☐ N678AA	Boeing 737-3A4	23290 / 1205	N304AC	0386	0491	2 CFMI CFM56-3B2	61235	Y137	AB-GK	lsf AAL
☐ N679AA	Boeing 737-3A4	23291 / 1211	N306AC	0486	0491	2 CFMI CFM56-3B2	61235	Y137	AB-GL	
☐ N680AA	Boeing 737-3A4	23505 / 1318	N310AC	1286	0491	2 CFMI CFM56-3B2	61235	Y137	BL-AJ	lsf AAL
☐ N682SW	Boeing 737-3Y0	23496 / 1217	N67AB	0086	0486	2 CFMI CFM56-3B1	61235	Y137		lsf ANAU
☐ N683SW	Boeing 737-3G7	24008 / 1576	N301AW	0088	1192	2 CFMI CFM56-3B1	56472	Y137		lsf Implicit Corp.
☐ N684WN	Boeing 737-3T0	23941 / 1520	EC-EID	0388	1192	2 CFMI CFM56-3B1	61235	Y137		lsf ANAU
☐ N685SW	Boeing 737-3Q8	23401 / 1209	G-BOWR	0086	0593	2 CFMI CFM56-3B1	61235	Y137		lsf ILFC
☐ N686SW	Boeing 737-317	23175 / 1110	EI-CHU	0085	1093	2 CFMI CFM56-3B1	61235	Y137		lsf GPAG
☐ N687SW	Boeing 737-3Q8	23388 / 1187	N103GU	0086	0394	2 CFMI CFM56-3B1	61235	Y137		
☐ N688SW	Boeing 737-3Q8	23254 / 1107	N780MA	0485	1094	2 CFMI CFM56-3B1	56472	Y137		lsf ILFC
☐ N689SW	Boeing 737-3Q8	23387 / 1163	N734MA	1185	1094	2 CFMI CFM56-3B2	61235	Y137		
☐ N690SW	Boeing 737-3G7	23783 / 1531	N785MA	0088	1094	2 CFMI CFM56-3B1	56472	Y137		lsf GECC
☐ N691WN	Boeing 737-3G7	23781 / 1494	N784MA	0088	1094	2 CFMI CFM56-3B2	56472	Y137		lsf GECC
☐ N692SW	Boeing 737-3T5	23062 / 1083	N733MA	0385	1094	2 CFMI CFM56-3B1	61235	Y137		
☐ N693SW	Boeing 737-317	23174 / 1104	N775MA	0485	1094	2 CFMI CFM56-3B1	61235	Y137		lsf GECA
☐ N694SW	Boeing 737-3T5	23061 / 1080	N744MA	0385	1094	2 CFMI CFM56-3B1	61235	Y137		

436 registration type of aircraft *cn/fn* *ex/ex** *mfd* *del* *powered by* *mtow kg* *configuration* *selcal* *name/fln/specialitites/remarks*

registration	type of aircraft	cn/fn	ex/ex*	mfd	del	powered by	mtow kg	configuration	selcal	name/fln/specialitites/remarks
☐ N695SW	Boeing 737-3Q8	23506 / 1249	N730MA	0786	1094	2 CFMI CFM56-3B2	62142	Y137		lsf ILFC
☐ N696SW	Boeing 737-3T5	23064 / 1527	N748MA	0388	1094	2 CFMI CFM56-3B1	61235	Y137		
☐ N697SW	Boeing 737-3T0	23838 / 1505	N764MA	0388	1094	2 CFMI CFM56-3B1	61235	Y137		lsf CIRR
☐ N698SW	Boeing 737-317	23176 / 1213	EI-CHD	0086	1094	2 CFMI CFM56-3B1	61235	Y137		lsf GECA
☐ N699SW	Boeing 737-3Y0	23826 / 1372	EI-CHE	0087	1094	2 CFMI CFM56-3B1	61235	Y137		lsf GECA
☐ N	Boeing 737-3Y0	23498 / 1233	G-EZYA	0086		2 CFMI CFM56-3B1	60985	Y137		oo-delivery 0499 / ex EZY
☐ N	Boeing 737-3Q8	24068 / 1506	G-EZYE	0088		2 CFMI CFM56-3B2	62142	Y137		oo-delivery 0499 / ex EZY
☐ N700GS	Boeing 737-7H4	27835 / 4		0097	1297	2 CFMI CFM56-7B22	62823	Y137		
☐ N701GS	Boeing 737-7H4	27836 / 6	N35108*	0097	1297	2 CFMI CFM56-7B22	62823	Y137		
☐ N703SW	Boeing 737-7H4	27837 / 12	N1792B*	0097	1297	2 CFMI CFM56-7B22	62823	Y137		
☐ N704SW	Boeing 737-7H4	27838 / 15		0097	0198	2 CFMI CFM56-7B22	62823	Y137		
☐ N705SW	Boeing 737-7H4	27839 / 20		0098	0398	2 CFMI CFM56-7B22	62823	Y137		
☐ N706SW	Boeing 737-7H4	27840 / 24		0098	0598	2 CFMI CFM56-7B22	62823	Y137		
☐ N707SA	Boeing 737-7H4	27841 / 1	N1787B*	0297	1098	2 CFMI CFM56-7B22	62823	Y137		
☐ N708SW	Boeing 737-7H4	27842 / 2		0297	1298	2 CFMI CFM56-7B22	62823	Y137		
☐ N709SW	Boeing 737-7H4	27843 / 3		0397	1098	2 CFMI CFM56-7B22	62823	Y137		
☐ N710SW	Boeing 737-7H4	27844 / 34		0098	0398	2 CFMI CFM56-7B22	62823	Y137		
☐ N711HK	Boeing 737-7H4	27845 / 38		0098	0498	2 CFMI CFM56-7B22	62823	Y137		
☐ N712SW	Boeing 737-7H4	27846 / 53		0098	0598	2 CFMI CFM56-7B22	62823	Y137		
☐ N713SW	Boeing 737-7H4	27847 / 54		0098	0698	2 CFMI CFM56-7B22	62823	Y137		
☐ N714CB	Boeing 737-7H4	27848 / 61		0098	0698	2 CFMI CFM56-7B22	62823	Y137		
☐ N715SW	Boeing 737-7H4	27849 / 62		0098	0698	2 CFMI CFM56-7B22	62823	Y137		
☐ N716SW	Boeing 737-7H4	27850 / 64		0098	0698	2 CFMI CFM56-7B22	62823	Y137		
☐ N717SA	Boeing 737-7H4	27851 / 70	N1799B*	0098	0798	2 CFMI CFM56-7B22	62823	Y137		
☐ N718SW	Boeing 737-7H4	27852 / 71	N3134C*	0098	0798	2 CFMI CFM56-7B22	62823	Y137		
☐ N719SW	Boeing 737-7H4	27853 / 82		0098	0898	2 CFMI CFM56-7B22	62823	Y137		
☐ N720WN	Boeing 737-7H4	27854 / 121	N1787B*	0998	0998	2 CFMI CFM56-7B22	62823	Y137		
☐ N723SW	Boeing 737-7H4	27855 / 199	N1787B*	0099	0299	2 CFMI CFM56-7B22	62823	Y137		
☐ N724SW	Boeing 737-7H4	27856 / 201	N1787B*	0099	0299	2 CFMI CFM56-7B22	62823	Y137		
☐ N725SW	Boeing 737-7H4	27857 / 208		0299	0299	2 CFMI CFM56-7B22	62823	Y137		
☐ N726SW	Boeing 737-7H4	27858 / 213		0299	0299	2 CFMI CFM56-7B22	62823	Y137		
☐ N727SW	Boeing 737-7H4	27859				2 CFMI CFM56-7B22	62823	Y137		oo-delivery 0099
☐ N728SW	Boeing 737-7H4	27860				2 CFMI CFM56-7B22	62823	Y137		oo-delivery 0099
☐ N729SW	Boeing 737-7H4	27861				2 CFMI CFM56-7B22	62823	Y137		oo-delivery 0099
☐ N730SW	Boeing 737-7H4	27862				2 CFMI CFM56-7B22	62823	Y137		oo-delivery 0099
☐ N731SA	Boeing 737-7H4	27863				2 CFMI CFM56-7B22	62823	Y137		oo-delivery 0099
☐ N732SW	Boeing 737-7H4	27864				2 CFMI CFM56-7B22	62823	Y137		oo-delivery 0099
☐ N733SA	Boeing 737-7H4	27865				2 CFMI CFM56-7B22	62823	Y137		oo-delivery 0099
☐ N734SA	Boeing 737-7H4	27866				2 CFMI CFM56-7B22	62823	Y137		oo-delivery 0099
☐ N735SA	Boeing 737-7H4	27867				2 CFMI CFM56-7B22	62823	Y137		oo-delivery 0099
☐ N736SA	Boeing 737-7H4	27868				2 CFMI CFM56-7B22	62823	Y137		oo-delivery 0099
☐ N737JW	Boeing 737-7H4	27869				2 CFMI CFM56-7B22	62823	Y137		oo-delivery 0099
☐ N738CB	Boeing 737-7H4	27870				2 CFMI CFM56-7B22	62823	Y137		oo-delivery 0099
☐ N739GB	Boeing 737-7H4	29275 / 144	N1786B*	0098	1198	2 CFMI CFM56-7B22	62823	Y137		
☐ N740SW	Boeing 737-7H4	29276 / 155		1198	1198	2 CFMI CFM56-7B22	62823	Y137		
☐ N741SA	Boeing 737-7H4	29277 / 157		1198	1198	2 CFMI CFM56-7B22	62823	Y137		
☐ N742SW	Boeing 737-7H4	29278 / 172		1298	1298	2 CFMI CFM56-7B22	62823	Y137		
☐ N743SW	Boeing 737-7H4	29279 / 175	N60436*	1298	1298	2 CFMI CFM56-7B22	62823	Y137		
☐ N744SW	Boeing 737-7H4	29490				2 CFMI CFM56-7B22	62823	Y137		oo-delivery 0099
☐ N745SW	Boeing 737-7H4	29491				2 CFMI CFM56-7B22	62823	Y137		oo-delivery 0000
☐ N746SW	Boeing 737-7H4	29798				2 CFMI CFM56-7B22	62823	Y137		oo-delivery 0000
☐ N747SA	Boeing 737-7H4	29799				2 CFMI CFM56-7B22	62823	Y137		oo-delivery 0000
☐ N748SW	Boeing 737-7H4	29800				2 CFMI CFM56-7B22	62823	Y137		oo-delivery 0000
☐ N749SW	Boeing 737-7H4	29801				2 CFMI CFM56-7B22	62823	Y137		oo-delivery 0000
☐ N750SA	Boeing 737-7H4	29802				2 CFMI CFM56-7B22	62823	Y137		oo-delivery 0000
☐ N751SW	Boeing 737-7H4	29803				2 CFMI CFM56-7B22	62823	Y137		oo-delivery 0000
☐ N752SW	Boeing 737-7H4	29804				2 CFMI CFM56-7B22	62823	Y137		oo-delivery 0000
☐ N753SW	Boeing 737-7H4					2 CFMI CFM56-7B22	62823	Y137		oo-delivery 0000
☐ N754SW	Boeing 737-7H4					2 CFMI CFM56-7B22	62823	Y137		oo-delivery 0000
☐ N755SA	Boeing 737-7H4					2 CFMI CFM56-7B22	62823	Y137		oo-delivery 0000
☐ N756SA	Boeing 737-7H4					2 CFMI CFM56-7B22	62823	Y137		oo-delivery 0000
☐ N757LV	Boeing 737-7H4					2 CFMI CFM56-7B22	62823	Y137		oo-delivery 0000
☐ N758SW	Boeing 737-7H4					2 CFMI CFM56-7B22	62823	Y137		oo-delivery 0000
☐ N759GS	Boeing 737-7H4					2 CFMI CFM56-7B22	62823	Y137		oo-delivery 0000
☐ N760SW	Boeing 737-7H4					2 CFMI CFM56-7B22	62823	Y137		oo-delivery 0000
☐ N761RR	Boeing 737-7H4					2 CFMI CFM56-7B22	62823	Y137		oo-delivery 0000
☐ N762SW	Boeing 737-7H4					2 CFMI CFM56-7B22	62823	Y137		oo-delivery 0001
☐ N763SW	Boeing 737-7H4					2 CFMI CFM56-7B22	62823	Y137		oo-delivery 0001
☐ N764SW	Boeing 737-7H4					2 CFMI CFM56-7B22	62823	Y137		oo-delivery 0001
☐ N765SW	Boeing 737-7H4					2 CFMI CFM56-7B22	62823	Y137		oo-delivery 0001
☐ N766SW	Boeing 737-7H4					2 CFMI CFM56-7B22	62823	Y137		oo-delivery 0001
☐ N767SW	Boeing 737-7H4					2 CFMI CFM56-7B22	62823	Y137		oo-delivery 0001
☐ N768SW	Boeing 737-7H4					2 CFMI CFM56-7B22	62823	Y137		oo-delivery 0001
☐ N769SW	Boeing 737-7H4					2 CFMI CFM56-7B22	62823	Y137		oo-delivery 0001
☐ N770SA	Boeing 737-7H4					2 CFMI CFM56-7B22	62823	Y137		oo-delivery 0001
☐ N771SA	Boeing 737-7H4					2 CFMI CFM56-7B22	62823	Y137		oo-delivery 0001
☐ N772SW	Boeing 737-7H4					2 CFMI CFM56-7B22	62823	Y137		oo-delivery 0001
☐ N773SA	Boeing 737-7H4					2 CFMI CFM56-7B22	62823	Y137		oo-delivery 0001
☐ N774SW	Boeing 737-7H4					2 CFMI CFM56-7B22	62823	Y137		oo-delivery 0001
☐ N775SW	Boeing 737-7H4					2 CFMI CFM56-7B22	62823	Y137		oo-delivery 0001
☐ N776WN	Boeing 737-7H4					2 CFMI CFM56-7B22	62823	Y137		oo-delivery 0001
☐ N778SW	Boeing 737-7H4					2 CFMI CFM56-7B22	62823	Y137		oo-delivery 0001
☐ N779SW	Boeing 737-7H4					2 CFMI CFM56-7B22	62823	Y137		oo-delivery 0001
☐ N780SW	Boeing 737-7H4					2 CFMI CFM56-7B22	62823	Y137		oo-delivery 0002
☐ N781WN	Boeing 737-7H4					2 CFMI CFM56-7B22	62823	Y137		oo-delivery 0002
☐ N782SA	Boeing 737-7H4					2 CFMI CFM56-7B22	62823	Y137		oo-delivery 0002
☐ N783SW	Boeing 737-7H4					2 CFMI CFM56-7B22	62823	Y137		oo-delivery 0002
☐ N784SW	Boeing 737-7H4					2 CFMI CFM56-7B22	62823	Y137		oo-delivery 0002
☐ N785SW	Boeing 737-7H4					2 CFMI CFM56-7B22	62823	Y137		oo-delivery 0002
☐ N786SW	Boeing 737-7H4					2 CFMI CFM56-7B22	62823	Y137		oo-delivery 0002
☐ N787SA	Boeing 737-7H4					2 CFMI CFM56-7B22	62823	Y137		oo-delivery 0002
☐ N788SA	Boeing 737-7H4					2 CFMI CFM56-7B22	62823	Y137		oo-delivery 0002
☐ N789SW	Boeing 737-7H4					2 CFMI CFM56-7B22	62823	Y137		oo-delivery 0002
☐ N790SW	Boeing 737-7H4					2 CFMI CFM56-7B22	62823	Y137		oo-delivery 0002
☐ N791SW	Boeing 737-7H4					2 CFMI CFM56-7B22	62823	Y137		oo-delivery 0002
☐ N792SW	Boeing 737-7H4					2 CFMI CFM56-7B22	62823	Y137		oo-delivery 0002
☐ N793SA	Boeing 737-7H4					2 CFMI CFM56-7B22	62823	Y137		oo-delivery 0002
☐ N794SW	Boeing 737-7H4					2 CFMI CFM56-7B22	62823	Y137		oo-delivery 0002
☐ N795SW	Boeing 737-7H4					2 CFMI CFM56-7B22	62823	Y137		oo-delivery 0002
☐ N796SW	Boeing 737-7H4					2 CFMI CFM56-7B22	62823	Y137		oo-delivery 0002
☐ N797SW	Boeing 737-7H4					2 CFMI CFM56-7B22	62823	Y137		oo-delivery 0003
☐ N798SW	Boeing 737-7H4					2 CFMI CFM56-7B22	62823	Y137		oo-delivery 0003
☐ N799SW	Boeing 737-7H4					2 CFMI CFM56-7B22	62823	Y137		oo-delivery 0003
☐ N	Boeing 737-7H4					2 CFMI CFM56-7B22	62823	Y137		oo-delivery 0003
☐ N	Boeing 737-7H4					2 CFMI CFM56-7B22	62823	Y137		oo-delivery 0003
☐ N	Boeing 737-7H4					2 CFMI CFM56-7B22	62823	Y137		oo-delivery 0003
☐ N	Boeing 737-7H4					2 CFMI CFM56-7B22	62823	Y137		oo-delivery 0003
☐ N	Boeing 737-7H4					2 CFMI CFM56-7B22	62823	Y137		oo-delivery 0003
☐ N	Boeing 737-7H4					2 CFMI CFM56-7B22	62823	Y137		oo-delivery 0003
☐ N	Boeing 737-7H4					2 CFMI CFM56-7B22	62823	Y137		oo-delivery 0003
☐ N	Boeing 737-7H4					2 CFMI CFM56-7B22	62823	Y137		oo-delivery 0003
☐ N	Boeing 737-7H4					2 CFMI CFM56-7B22	62823	Y137		oo-delivery 0003
☐ N	Boeing 737-7H4					2 CFMI CFM56-7B22	62823	Y137		oo-delivery 0003
☐ N	Boeing 737-7H4					2 CFMI CFM56-7B22	62823	Y137		oo-delivery 0003
☐ N	Boeing 737-7H4					2 CFMI CFM56-7B22	62823	Y137		oo-delivery 0004
☐ N	Boeing 737-7H4					2 CFMI CFM56-7B22	62823	Y137		oo-delivery 0004

registration	type of aircraft	cn/fn	ex/er*	mfd	del	powered by	mtow kg	configuration	selcal	name/fln/specialitites/remarks
☐ N	Boeing 737-7H4					2 CFMI CFM56-7B22	62823	Y137		oo-delivery 0004
☐ N	Boeing 737-7H4					2 CFMI CFM56-7B22	62823	Y137		oo-delivery 0004
☐ N	Boeing 737-7H4					2 CFMI CFM56-7B22	62823	Y137		oo-delivery 0004
☐ N	Boeing 737-7H4					2 CFMI CFM56-7B22	62823	Y137		oo-delivery 0004
☐ N	Boeing 737-7H4					2 CFMI CFM56-7B22	62823	Y137		oo-delivery 0004
☐ N	Boeing 737-7H4					2 CFMI CFM56-7B22	62823	Y137		oo-delivery 0004
☐ N	Boeing 737-7H4					2 CFMI CFM56-7B22	62823	Y137		oo-delivery 0004
☐ N	Boeing 737-7H4					2 CFMI CFM56-7B22	62823	Y137		oo-delivery 0004
☐ N	Boeing 737-7H4					2 CFMI CFM56-7B22	62823	Y137		oo-delivery 0004
☐ N	Boeing 737-7H4					2 CFMI CFM56-7B22	62823	Y137		oo-delivery 0004
☐ N	Boeing 737-7H4					2 CFMI CFM56-7B22	62823	Y137		oo-delivery 0004
☐ N	Boeing 737-7H4					2 CFMI CFM56-7B22	62823	Y137		oo-delivery 0004
☐ N	Boeing 737-7H4					2 CFMI CFM56-7B22	62823	Y137		oo-delivery 0004
☐ N	Boeing 737-7H4					2 CFMI CFM56-7B22	62823	Y137		oo-delivery 0004
☐ N	Boeing 737-7H4					2 CFMI CFM56-7B22	62823	Y137		oo-delivery 0004
☐ N	Boeing 737-7H4					2 CFMI CFM56-7B22	62823	Y137		oo-delivery 0004

SOUTHWEST HELICOPTERS, Inc. (Medivac I) — Tucson-Int'l, AZ

6666 South Plumer Avenue, Tucson, AZ 85706, USA ☎ (520) 294-9090 Tx: none Fax: (520) 573-9600 SITA: n/a
F: 1981 n/a Head: Kathy Hildebrand Net: n/a Uses the service-name MEDIVAC 1 for its EMS flights.

registration	type of aircraft	cn/fn	ex/er*	mfd	del	powered by	mtow kg	configuration	selcal	remarks
☐ N90328	Bell 206B JetRanger III	1853		0075	0894	1 AN 250-C20B	1451			cvtd JetRanger
☐ N911MV	Eurocopter (Aerosp.) AS350BA AStar	2262	N7087X	0090	0496	1 TU Arriel 1B	2100	EMS		cvtd AS350B
☐ N911SW	Eurocopter (Aerosp.) AS350B AStar	1605	N911NW	0082	0693	1 TU Arriel 1B	1950	EMS		
☐ N407S	Bell 407	53036		0096	0896	1 AN 250-C47B	2268			
☐ N355MF	Eurocopter (Aerosp.) AS355F1 TwinStar	5100	N5789X	0082	0896	2 AN 250-C20F	2400	EMS		
☐ N5794B	Eurocopter (Aerosp.) AS355F1 TwinStar	5146		0082		2 AN 250-C20F	2400	EMS		lsf G.E. Johnson Construction Co.
☐ N911BB	Eurocopter (Aerosp.) AS355F1 TwinStar	5099	N911DB	0082		2 AN 250-C20F	2400	EMS		lsf RTS Helicopter Services Corp.
☐ N911NW	Eurocopter (Aerosp.) AS355F1 TwinStar	5082	N5782A	0082	0497	2 AN 250-C20F	2400	EMS		
☐ N911TX	Eurocopter (Aerosp.) AS355F1 TwinStar	5073	N101UM	0082		2 AN 250-C20F	2400	EMS		lsf RTS Aircraft Services Corp.

SOUTHWEST SAFARIS (Bruce M. Adams dba) — Santa Fe-County Municipal, NM

PO Box 945, Santa Fe, NM 87504, USA ☎ (505) 988-4246 Tx: none Fax: (505) 988-4246 SITA: n/a
F: 1974 n/a Head: Bruce M. Adams Net: n/a

registration	type of aircraft	cn/fn	ex/er*	mfd	del	powered by	mtow kg	configuration	selcal	remarks
☐ N4912E	Cessna 182R Skylane II	18268284		0082	0489	1 CO O-470-U	1406			
☐ N73742	Cessna T207A Turbo Stationair 8 II	20700619		0080	0984	1 CO TSIO-520-M	1724			

SP AIRCRAFT (Scott W. Patrick dba) — Boise-Air Terminal/Gowen Field, ID

3180 Airport Way, Boise, ID 83705, USA ☎ (208) 383-3323 Tx: none Fax: (208) 383-9969 SITA: n/a
F: 1977 n/a Head: Scott W. Patrick Net: n/a Aircraft below MTOW 1361kg: Cessna 172

registration	type of aircraft	cn/fn	ex/er*	mfd	del	powered by	mtow kg	configuration	selcal	remarks
☐ N47MB	Cessna TU206G Turbo Stationair	U20603698		0077	0988	1 CO TSIO-520-M	1633			
☐ N756WZ	Cessna TU206G Turbo Stationair 6 II	U20604427		0078	0890	1 CO TSIO-520-M	1633			
☐ N756YC	Cessna TU206G Turbo Stationair 6 II	U20604454		0078	0287	1 CO TSIO-520-M	1633			
☐ N6993N	Cessna T210N Turbo Centurion II	21063202		0079	0596	2 CO TSIO-520-R	1814			
☐ N8273M	Cessna T210K Turbo Centurion	21059273		0070	1094	1 CO TSIO-520-H	1724			
☐ N145BK	Cessna 340	340-0211		0073	1094	2 CO TSIO-520-K	2710			

SP AVIATION, Inc. – Superior Performance — Hayward-Air Terminal, CA

26220 Industrial Blvd, Hayward, CA 94545, USA ☎ (510) 783-3584 Tx: none Fax: (510) 783-3587 SITA: n/a
F: 1992 n/a Head: Jeff Perdue Net: n/a

registration	type of aircraft	cn/fn	ex/er*	mfd	del	powered by	mtow kg	configuration	selcal	remarks
☐ N35CZ	Learjet 35A	35A-352	N71A	0080	1196	2 GA TFE731-2-2B	8301			
☐ N35WR	Learjet 35A	35A-234		0079	0696	2 GA TFE731-2-2B	8301			lsf BAL Air Services Llc

SPECIAL AVIATION SYSTEMS, Inc. — Pontiac-Oakland, MI

1675 Airport Road, Waterford, MI 48327, USA ☎ (248) 666-2509 Tx: none Fax: (248) 666-7960 SITA: n/a
F: 1996 n/a Head: Eric J. Ruhe Net: n/a

registration	type of aircraft	cn/fn	ex/er*	mfd	del	powered by	mtow kg	configuration	selcal	remarks
☐ N101RA	Embraer 110P1 Bandeirante (EMB-110P1)	110220	PT-GMM*	0079	0796	2 PWC PT6A-34	5670	Freighter		lsf Ruhe Sales Inc.
☐ N127JM	Embraer 110P1 Bandeirante (EMB-110P1)	110218	N202RA	0079	0796	2 PWC PT6A-34	5670	Freighter		lsf Ruhe Sales Inc.

SPECIALIZED TRANSPORT INTERNATIONAL, Inc. – S.T.I. — Melbourne-Int'l, FL

1383 General Aviation Drive, Melbourne, FL 32935, USA ☎ (561) 253-0209 Tx: none Fax: (561) 253-0039 SITA: n/a
F: 1992 30 Head: Richard Pere Net: n/a FAR135 Freighter operations are conducted under the licence of BUSINESS JET SOLUTIONS while FAR105 Para flights are conducted under the licence of S.T.I. itself.

registration	type of aircraft	cn/fn	ex/er*	mfd	del	powered by	mtow kg	configuration	selcal	remarks
☐ N311ST	CASA 212 Aviocar Srs 200	292	N292CA	0083	1195	2 GA TPE331-10-501C	7450	Freighter/Para		
☐ N316ST	CASA 212 Aviocar Srs 200	289	N435CA	0082	0593	2 GA TPE331-10-501C	7450	Freighter/Para		lsf FSBU Trustee
☐ N393DF	CASA 212 Aviocar Srs 300	393		0090	0095	2 GA TPE331-10R-513C	7700	Freighter/Para		

SPERNAK AIRWAYS, Inc. — Anchorage-Merrill Field, AK

PO Box 102255, Anchorage, AK 99510, USA ☎ (907) 272-9475 Tx: none Fax: (907) 272-0993 SITA: n/a
F: 1955 10 Head: Michael B. Spernak Net: n/a

registration	type of aircraft	cn/fn	ex/er*	mfd	del	powered by	mtow kg	configuration	selcal	remarks
☐ N29CF	Cessna 207 Skywagon	20700353		0076	0886	1 CO IO-520-F	1724			
☐ N6492H	Cessna 207A Stationair 7 II	20700544		0079	1279	1 CO IO-520-F	1724			
☐ N73047	Cessna 207A Stationair 7 II	20700556		0079	0194	1 CO IO-520-F	1724			
☐ N7392U	Cessna 207A Stationair 7 II	20700435		0078	0191	1 CO IO-520-F	1724			

SPIRIT AIRLINES, Inc. = NK / NKS (formerly Charter One) — Detroit-Metropolitan, MI

18121 East 8 Mile Road, Suite 100, East Point, MI 48021, USA ☎ (810) 779-2700 Tx: none Fax: (810) 779-9332 SITA: n/a
F: 1990 450 Head: Edward W. Homfeld IATA: 487 ICAO: SPIRIT WINGS Net: n/a

registration	type of aircraft	cn/fn	ex/er*	mfd	del	powered by	mtow kg	configuration	selcal	remarks
☐ N12505	Boeing (Douglas) DC-9-32	45788 / 171	N3505T	0067	0994	2 PW JT8D-9A	49895	Y117	CG-FK	lsf Avteam Inc.
☐ N12536	Boeing (Douglas) DC-9-32	47113 / 213	N536TX	0067	0994	2 PW JT8D-9A (HK3/ABS)	49895	Y117	CH-BG	lsf Jonathan Capital Resources LLC
☐ N132NK	Boeing (Douglas) DC-9-31	47202 / 400	N965VV	0068	0397	2 PW JT8D-7B	46720	Y113		lsf VJA
☐ N17535	Boeing (Douglas) DC-9-32	47111 / 182	N535TX	0067	1197	2 PW JT8D-9A (HK3/ABS)	49895	Y117		lsf POLA
☐ N928ML	Boeing (Douglas) DC-9-31	47326 / 516	N731L	0069	0895	2 PW JT8D-7B	46720	Y117		lsf RTG Fulcrum Aircraft I Llc
☐ N934ML	Boeing (Douglas) DC-9-31	47526 / 603	VH-CZH	0070	0592	2 PW JT8D-7B (HK3/ABS)	46720	Y117		
☐ N941ML	Boeing (Douglas) DC-9-32	47131 / 214	PH-DNH	0067	0596	2 PW JT8D-7B (HK3/ABS)	49895	Y117		lsf Twin Jet Leasing Inc.
☐ N942ML	Boeing (Douglas) DC-9-32	47478 / 612	5Y-BBR	0070	0592	2 PW JT8D-11 (HK3/ABS)	48988	Y117		lsf Spirit Aircraft I Trust
☐ N947ML	Boeing (Douglas) DC-9-32	47514 / 619	PH-MAX	0071	0895	2 PW JT8D-9	49895	Y117		
☐ N969ML	Boeing (Douglas) DC-9-31	47268 / 370	N8970E	0068	0592	2 PW JT8D-7B (HK3/ABS)	47627	Y117		lsf Spirit Aircraft I Trust
☐ N130NK	Boeing (Douglas) DC-9-41	47604 / 722	OH-LNB	0374	0496	2 PW JT8D-17A (HK3/ABS)	51710	Y127		
☐ N131NK	Boeing (Douglas) DC-9-41	47605 / 724	OH-LNE	0374	0496	2 PW JT8D-17A (HK3/ABS)	51710	Y127		
☐ N750RA	Boeing (Douglas) MD-87 (DC-9-87)	49777 / 1634	N497PJ	0889	1298	2 PW JT8D-219	63503	Y133		lsf Finova Capital Corp.
☐ N800NK	Boeing (Douglas) MD-82 (DC-9-82)	49144 / 1096	N500TR	0183	1297	2 PW JT8D-217	67812	Y165		lsf Nichimen (UK)
☐ N802NK	Boeing (Douglas) MD-82 (DC-9-82)	53168 / 2061	B-28015	0093	0798	2 PW JT8D-217C	66678	Y165		lsf Spirit Silver Spring II Llc
☐ N804RA	Boeing (Douglas) MD-82 (DC-9-82)	48048 / 1005	N802VV	0081	0698	2 PW JT8D-219	66678	Y165		lsf Spirit Silver Spring III Llc
☐ N805RA	Boeing (Douglas) MD-82 (DC-9-82)	48087 / 1035	N803VV	1181	0998	2 PW JT8D-219	66678	Y165		
☐ N	Boeing (Douglas) MD-83 (DC-9-83)	49619 / 1483	D-ALLU	0588	0499	2 PW JT8D-219	72575	Y165		

SPOTTED DOG AVIATION (Jeffrey J. Woods dba / Seasonal April-October ops only) — Talkeetna, AK

PO Box 786, Talkeetna, AK 99676, USA ☎ (907) 522-5101 Tx: none Fax: none SITA: n/a
F: 1996 n/a Head: Jeffrey J. Woods Net: n/a

registration	type of aircraft	cn/fn	ex/er*	mfd	del	powered by	mtow kg	configuration	selcal	remarks
☐ N21709	Cessna A185F Skywagon	18503064		0076	1096	1 CO IO-520-D	1520			lsf pvt / Floats
☐ N8091Z	Cessna U206A Super Skywagon	U206-0491		0066	0498	1 CO IO-520-A	1633			lsf pvt / Floats
☐ N8190Y	De Havilland DHC-2 Beaver I	824		0055	1296	1 PW R-985	2313			lsf Kakeldey Leasing Corp. / Floats

SPRINGDALE AIR SERVICE, Inc. = SPG — Springdale Municipal, AR

PO Box 811, Springdale, AR 72764, USA ☎ (870) 751-4462 Tx: none Fax: (870) 673-4146 SITA: n/a
F: 1972 20 Head: Mark E. Courdin ICAO: SPRING AIR Net: n/a

registration	type of aircraft	cn/fn	ex/er*	mfd	del	powered by	mtow kg	configuration	selcal	remarks
☐ N5133J	Cessna 310R II	310R0253		0075	0189	2 CO IO-520-M	2495			
☐ N29MM	Cessna 402B	402B0863		0075	0289	2 CO TSIO-520-E	2858			
☐ N402BF	Cessna 402B II	402B1076		0076	0190	2 CO TSIO-520-E	2858			
☐ N5040Q	Cessna 402B	402B0347		0073	0686	2 CO TSIO-520-E	2858			
☐ N6350X	Cessna 402B II	402B1317		0078	0290	2 CO TSIO-520-E	2858			
☐ N7886Q	Cessna 402B	402B0214		0072	0382	2 CO TSIO-520-E	2858			
☐ N136JJ	Beech E18S	BA-318	N136JR	0057	1295	2 PW R-985	4400	Freighter		lsf SCS Group Ltd
☐ N2069C	Beech E18S	BA-430		0059	0387	2 PW R-985	4581	Freighter		
☐ N210Q	Beech E18S	BA-291		0057	0393	2 PW R-985	4581	Freighter		lsf SCS Group Ltd
☐ N4980V	Beech E18S	BA-156		0056	0386	2 PW R-985	4581	Freighter		
☐ N512E	Beech G18S	BA-520		0060	0686	2 PW R-985	4581	Freighter		
☐ N5BA	Beech G18S	BA-614		0062	1095	2 PW R-985	4400	Freighter		lsf SCS Group Ltd
☐ N360D	Beech King Air A90 (65-A90)	LJ-240	N36030	0067	0693	2 PWC PT6A-20	4218			lsf SCS Group Ltd
☐ N269BW	Beech King Air 200	BB-618	HB-GID	0080	0296	2 PWC PT6A-41	5670			lsf Big County Charters Llc

STANLEY AIR TAXI, Inc. — Hailey-Friedman Memorial, ID

PO Box 30, Stanley, ID 83278, USA ☎ (208) 774-2276 Tx: none Fax: none SITA: n/a
F: 1987 ☃ n/a Head: Robert Danner Net: n/a Aircraft below MTOW 1361kg: Cessna 182

☐ N20GV	Cessna U206F Stationair	U20602260		0073	0594	1 CO IO-520-F	1633			lsf pvt

STAR AVIATION (Star, Inc. dba) — Spearfish-Black Hills/Clyde Ice Field, SD

Rt 2, Box 396A, Spearfish, SD 57783, USA ☎ (605) 642-4112 Tx: none Fax: (605) 642-1838 SITA: n/a
F: 1979 ☃ n/a Head: Madaline H. Custis Net: n/a Aircraft below MTOW 1361kg: Cessna 172

☐ N4853U	Cessna T210N Turbo Centurion II	21064824		0084	1084	1 CO TSIO-520-R	1814			
☐ N723DC	Piper PA-34-200T Seneca II	34-8170074	N101GR	0081	1295	2 CO TSIO-360-EB	2073			
☐ N1872H	Piper PA-31-350 Navajo Chieftain	31-7652053		0076	0796	2 LY TIO-540-J2BD	3175			

STARFLITE, Inc. (formerly dba Manokotak Air) — Dillingham, AK

PO Box 824, Dillingham, AK 99576, USA ☎ (907) 842-2486 Tx: none Fax: (907) 842-5863 SITA: n/a
F: 1983 ☃ 14 Head: Michael U. Harder Net: n/a

☐ N94204	Cessna A185F Skywagon	18503289		0077	0791	1 CO IO-520-D	1520			
☐ N8471Q	Cessna U206F Stationair II	U20603329		0076	0889	1 CO IO-520-F	1633			lsf pvt
☐ N9311R	Grumman G-44 Widgeon	1340		0045	0686	2 CO O-470-B	2132			Amphibian

STARFLITE INTERNATIONAL, Corp. — San Antonio-International, TX

50 Oak Bluff, New Braunfels, TX 78132, USA ☎ (830) 625-3400 Tx: none Fax: (830) 625-5027 SITA: n/a
F: 1997 ☃ n/a Head: Jack Plumly Net: n/a

☐ N312SF	Boeing 757-23A (ET)	25493 / 523	N512AT	0093	1197	2 RR RB211-535E4	108862	Y213		

STEARNS AIR ALASKA, Inc. — Anchorage-Lake Hood SPB, AK

4101 Floatplane Drive, Anchorage, AK 99502, USA ☎ (907) 348-0656 Tx: none Fax: (907) 243-2551 SITA: n/a
F: 1988 ☃ n/a Head: Geoffrey J. Stearns Net: n/a

☐ N3383L	Cessna A185E Skywagon	185-1335		0068	0888	1 CO IO-520-D	1520			lsf pvt / Floats / Wheel-Skis
☐ N7312C	Cessna U206G Stationair	U20603872		0077	1196	1 CO IO-520-F	1633			Floats / Wheel-Skis

STERLING AIRWAYS, Inc. — Hornell-Municipal & Dansville-Municipal, NY

1100 Airport Road, Hornell, NY 14843, USA ☎ (607) 324-2742 Tx: none Fax: (607) 324-2707 SITA: n/a
F: 1973 ☃ n/a Head: James T. Caneen Net: n/a

☐ N30266	Cessna T210L Turbo Centurion II	21059901		0073	0189	1 CO TSIO-520-H	1724			
☐ N5797Y	Piper PA-23-250 Aztec C	27-2927		0065	1287	2 LY IO-540-C4B5	2359			
☐ N63724	Piper PA-31-350 Navajo Chieftain	31-7752040		0077	0487	2 LY TIO-540-J2BD	3175			lsf City of Hornell Indust. Development

STERLING HELICOPTERS (Sterling Corporation dba) — Philadelphia-Penn's Landing Heliport, PA

Pier 36 South, Delaware & Catherine Street, Philadelphia, PA 19147, USA ☎ (215) 271-2510 Tx: none Fax: (215) 271-7794 SITA: n/a
F: 1983 ☃ n/a Head: Jack Brown Net: http://www.libertynet.org

☐ N302MG	Bell 206B JetRanger III	2956	N302MC	0079	0789	1 AN 250-C20B	1451			
☐ N63SH	Bell 206B JetRanger III	2640	N2755P	0079	0884	1 AN 250-C20B	1451			
☐ N8NL	Bell 206B JetRanger	1561	N8NJ	0074	0891	1 AN 250-C20	1451			
☐ N36SH	Bell 206L LongRanger	45052	N9976K	0076	0187	1 AN 250-C20B	1814			

STEWART AVIATION SERVICES, Inc. = YBE (formerly Yellow Bird Express) — Little Rock-Adams Field, AR

15926 Faulkner Lake Road, North Little Rock, AR 72117, USA ☎ (870) 961-1054 Tx: none Fax: (870) 961-1054 SITA: n/a
F: 1963 ☃ n/a Head: Robert V. Stewart ICAO: YELLOW BIRD Net: n/a

☐ N7928Y	Piper PA-30-160 Twin Comanche B	30-1019		0066	1195	2 LY IO-320-B1A	1633			
☐ N6682Y	Piper PA-23-250 Aztec D	27-4003		0068	1090	2 LY IO-540-C4B5	2359			

STORM FLYING SERVICE, Inc. — Webster City-Municipal, IA

1524 240 Street, Webster City, IA 50595, USA ☎ (515) 832-3723 Tx: none Fax: (515) 832-3840 SITA: n/a
F: 1968 ☃ n/a Head: Ralph E. Storm Net: n/a Aircraft below MTOW 1361kg: Piper PA-28

☐ N75298	Piper PA-32R-300 Lance	32R-7680287		0076	0386	1 LY IO-540-K1A5D	1633			

STUART JET CENTER, Inc. — Stuart-Witham Field, FL

2501 SE Aviation Way, Stuart, FL 34996, USA ☎ (561) 288-6700 Tx: none Fax: (561) 288-3782 SITA: n/a
F: 1986 ☃ n/a Head: Scott McDonald Net: http://www.stuartjet.com

☐ N2313Z	Piper PA-23-250 Aztec F	27-8054013		0080	0398	2 LY IO-540-C4B5	2359			
☐ N27236	Piper PA-31-350 Navajo Chieftain	31-7752111		0077	0597	2 LY TIO-540-J2BD	3175			
☐ N249RL	Fairchild (Swearingen) SA226T Merlin III	T-249	D-IFWZ	0074	1197	2 GA TPE331-3U-303G	5670			lsf GFI Int'l Inc.
☐ N600SJ	Sabreliner 60 (Rockwell NA265-60)	306-15	N604MK	0067	1298	2 PW JT12A-8	9072			lsf Skymarine Inc.

SUBURBAN AIR FREIGHT, Inc. = SUB — Omaha-Eppley Airfield, NE

PO Box 19090, Omaha, NE 68119-0090, USA ☎ (402) 344-4100 Tx: none Fax: (402) 344-0415 SITA: n/a
F: 1973 ☃ n/a Head: James V. Armstrong ICAO: SUB AIR Net: n/a

☐ N7846C	Twin (Aero) Commander 500	500-724		0063	0385	2 LY O-540-A2B	2722	Freighter		
☐ N10QP	Cessna 402B	402B0831	N10GP	0074	0393	2 CO TSIO-520-E	2858	Freighter		
☐ N1575T	Cessna 402B	402B0355		0073	0393	2 CO TSIO-520-E	2858	Freighter		
☐ N402RM	Cessna 402B	402B0607		0074	0493	2 CO TSIO-520-E	2858	Freighter		
☐ N98649	Cessna 402B II	402B1030		0076	0194	2 CO TSIO-520-E	2858	Freighter		
☐ N98695	Cessna 402B II	402B1052		0076	1294	2 CO TSIO-520-E	2858	Freighter		
☐ N114MN	Twin (Aero) Grand Commander 680FL	680FL-1553-107	N2611	0065	1187	2 LY IGSO-540-B1A	3856	Freighter		
☐ N2828S	Twin (Aero) Grand Commander 680FL	680FL-1329-14		0063	0786	2 LY IGSO-540-B1A	3856	Freighter		
☐ N290MP	Twin (Aero) Grand Commander 680FL	680FL-1535-104		0065	0885	2 LY IGSO-540-B1A	3856	Freighter		
☐ N309VS	Twin (Aero) Grand Commander 680FL	680FL-1659-128		0067	0888	2 LY IGSO-540-B1A	3856	Freighter		
☐ N31P	Twin (Aero) Grand Commander 680FL	680FL-1646-123		0066	0989	2 LY IGSO-540-B1A	3856	Freighter		
☐ N4983S	Twin (Aero) Grand Commander 680FL	680FL-1427-70		0065	0289	2 LY IGSO-540-B1A	3856	Freighter		
☐ N5035E	Twin (Aero) Grand Commander 680FL	680FL-1764-147		0068	0885	2 LY IGSO-540-B1A	3856	Freighter		
☐ N6509V	Twin (Aero) Grand Commander 680FL	680FL-1640-121		0066	0192	2 LY IGSO-540-B1A	3856	Freighter		
☐ N9011N	Twin (Aero) Courser Commander 680FL	680FL-1836-153		0069	0787	2 LY IGSO-540-B1A	3856	Freighter		
☐ N118SF	Beech 99 Airliner	U-32	C-FESU	0068	1294	2 PWC PT6A-20	4717	Freighter		
☐ N128SF	Beech 99 Airliner	U-87	N59CA	0069	0896	2 PWC PT6A-27	4717	Freighter		
☐ N147SF	Beech 99 Airliner	U-47	N204BH	0068	1197	2 PWC PT6A-20	4717	Freighter		
☐ N7994R	Beech 99 Airliner	U-103		0069	0995	2 PWC PT6A-27	4717	Freighter		
☐ N124GP	Beech 1900C Airliner	UB-23	N23VK	0084	0697	2 PWC PT6A-65B	7530	Freighter		lsf Raytheon Aircraft Credit Corp.
☐ N719GL	Beech 1900C Airliner	UB-19	N314BH	0084	1096	2 PWC PT6A-65B	7530	Freighter		lsf Raytheon Aircraft Credit Corp.

SUGAR LAND JET CENTER, Inc. — Houston-Sugar Land Municipal/Hull, TX

PO Box 1887, Sugar Land, TX 77487, USA ☎ (281) 242-2292 Tx: none Fax: (281) 242-2241 SITA: n/a
F: 1987 ☃ n/a Head: George N. Tilton Net: n/a

☐ N122RF	Beech King Air 200	BB-122	N122TJ	0076	0595	2 PWC PT6A-41	5670			lsf Que' Pasa Aviation I Ltd

SUMMIT HELICOPTERS, Inc. — Cloverdale-Heliport, VA

PO Box 39, Cloverdale, VA 24077, USA ☎ (540) 992-5500 Tx: none Fax: (540) 992-5503 SITA: n/a
F: 1980 ☃ n/a Head: Carl N. Milko Net: n/a Aircraft below MTOW 1361 kg: Hiller UH-12E.

☐ N206BE	Bell 206B JetRanger III	2375		0078	0685	1 AN 250-C20B	1451			
☐ N2150K	Bell 206B JetRanger III	3462		0081	0785	1 AN 250-C20B	1451			
☐ N5013G	Bell 206L-1 LongRanger III	45254		0079	0596	1 AN 250-C30P	1882			cvtd LongRanger II
☐ N109KC	Bell 407	53101		0097	0397	1 AN 250-C47B	2268			lsf Summit Sales & Leasing Inc.
☐ N2580V	Bell UH-1B (204)	740	63-8518	0063	0795	1 LY T53-L-11	3856			
☐ N41870	Bell UH-1B (204)	3111	65-12853	0065	0892	1 LY T53-L-11	3856			lsf Summit Sales & Leasing Inc.
☐ N4389Y	Bell UH-1B (204)	1015	63-13087	0063	0892	1 LY T53-L-11	3856			lsf Summit Sales & Leasing Inc.

SUNBIRD AIR SERVICES, Inc. — Springfield-Beckley Municipal, OH

1251 West Blee Road, Springfield, OH 45502, USA ☎ (937) 322-2711 Tx: none Fax: (937) 322-6256 SITA: n/a
F: 1978 ☃ n/a Head: James C. Hupman Net: n/a

☐ N3291M	Cessna 310R II	310R1896		0080	1192	2 CO IO-520-MB	2495			lsf Tech II Inc.
☐ N663AA	Cessna 402C II	402C0123		0079	0690	2 CO TSIO-520-VB	3107			
☐ N421MP	Cessna 421C Golden Eagle II	421C0004		0075	1095	2 CO GTSIO-520-L	3379			
☐ N125AV	Fairchild (Swearingen) SA226TC Metro II	TC-370		0080	1195	2 GA TPE331-3UW-303G	5670			
☐ N392CA	Fairchild (Swearingen) SA226TC Metro II	TC-392	ZS-LAA	0080		2 GA TPE331-3UW-303G	5670			

SUN CARE AIR AMBULANCE (Sun Western Flyers, Inc. dba) — Yuma-MCAS Int'l, AZ

2095 East 32nd Street, Yuma, AZ 85365, USA ☎ (520) 726-4715 Tx: none Fax: (520) 344-5129 SITA: n/a
F: 1965 ☃ n/a Head: John L. Ewing Net: n/a

☐ N41960	Piper PA-34-200 Seneca	34-7450165		0074	0394	2 LY IO-360-C1E6	1905	EMS		
☐ N8235Q	Cessna 414	414-0165		0071	0693	2 CO TSIO-520-J	2880	EMS		
☐ N18MC	Piper PA-31P Pressurized Navajo	31P-7300143		0073	0594	2 LY TIGO-541-E1A	3538	EMS		
☐ N252MA	Piper PA-31P Pressurized Navajo	31P-33		0070	0893	2 LY TIGO-541-E1A	3538	EMS		

439 registration type of aircraft cn/fn ex/ex* mfd del powered by mtow kg configuration selcal name/fln/specialitites/remarks

registration	type of aircraft	cn/fn	ex/ex*	mfd	del	powered by	mtow kg	configuration	selcal	name/fln/specialitites/remarks
☐ N26556	Piper PA-31P Pressurized Navajo	31P-7400184		0074	0694	2 LY TIGO-541-E1A	3538	EMS		
☐ N415AC	Piper PA-31P Pressurized Navajo	31P-16		0070	0497	2 LY TIGO-541-E1A	3538	EMS		
☐ N6805L	Piper PA-31P Pressurized Navajo	31P-7		0070	0695	2 LY TIGO-541-E1A	3538	EMS		
☐ N6811L	Piper PA-31P Pressurized Navajo	31P-13		0070	1196	2 LY TIGO-541-E1A	3538	EMS		
☐ N200CH	Cessna 421A	421A0102		0069	1093	2 CO GTSIO-520-D	3105	EMS		
☐ N4050Q	Cessna 421B Golden Eagle	421B0274		0072	0993	2 CO GTSIO-520-H	3379	EMS		
☐ N421Z	Cessna 421	421-0077		0068	0196	2 CO GTSIO-520-D	3084	EMS		

SUN COUNTRY AIRLINES, Inc. = SY / SCX

Minneapolis-St. Paul Int'l, MN — Sun Country Airlines

2520 Pilot Knob Road, Suite 250, Mendota Heights, MN 55120, USA ☎ (651) 681-3900 Tx: none Fax: (651) 681-3970 SITA: MSPSSSY
F: 1982 1140 Head: William LaMacchia IATA: 337 ICAO: SUN COUNTRY Net: http://www.suncountry.com

registration	type of aircraft	cn/fn	ex/ex*	mfd	del	powered by	mtow kg	configuration	selcal	name/fln/specialitites/remarks
☐ N275AF	Boeing 727-227 (A)	22092 / 1718	N484BN	0081	0183	3 PW JT8D-17R (HK3/FDX)	86409	Y170		lsf Finova Capital Corp.
☐ N281SC	Boeing 727-282 (A)	21949 / 1494	CS-TBW	0079	1090	3 PW JT8D-17	86409	Y170	FG-BJ	lsf Mach Aircraft Leasing Llc
☐ N282SC	Boeing 727-225 (A)	22558 / 1798	N821EA	0082	0991	3 PW JT8D-17R (HK3/FDX)	86409	Y170	KL-BC	lsf Gemanco Inc.
☐ N283SC	Boeing 727-225 (A)	22559 / 1800	N822EA	0082	0991	3 PW JT8D-17R (HK3/FDX)	86409	Y170	KL-BD	lsf Gemanco Inc.
☐ N284SC	Boeing 727-2J4 (A/RE) (Super 27)	21438 / 1301	G-BHNF	0077	0292	3 PW JT8D-217C/17A(BFG)	92986	Y170	HM-KL	lsf ILFC / cvtd -2J4
☐ N285SC	Boeing 727-2J4 (A/RE) (Super 27)	21676 / 1417	G-BHNE	0078	0392	3 PW JT8D-217C/17A(BFG)	92986	Y170	HM-JL	lsf ILFC / cvtd -2J4
☐ N286SC	Boeing 727-2A1 (A)	21601 / 1694	N328AS	0080	0993	3 PW JT8D-17	86409	Y170	BD-EM	lsf IPID
☐ N287SC	Boeing 727-2A1 (A)	21345 / 1673	N327AS	0080	0194	3 PW JT8D-17	86409	Y170	BD-EJ	lsf IPID
☐ N288SC	Boeing 727-2J4 (A/RE) (Super 27)	20765 / 984	CS-TKA	0073	0494	3 PW JT8D-217C/17A(BFG)	94990	Y170	GL-BK	lsf Avalon Leasing Corp. / cvtd -2J4
☐ N289SC	Boeing 727-259 (A)	22475 / 1690	N204AV	0080	0994	3 PW JT8D-17R	86409	Y170	GL-AC	lsf Aircraft Lease Finance I Inc.
☐ N290SC	Boeing 727-2J4 (A/RE) (Super 27)	20764 / 960	OY-SAU	0073	0597	3 PW JT8D-217C/17A(BFG)	94990	Y170		lsf Finova Capital Corp. / cvtd -2J4
☐ CC-CSW	Boeing 727-2M7 (A)	21655 / 1452	VP-CDL	0079	0199	3 PW JT8D-17R	88360	Y170		lsf VAT
☐ N151SY	Boeing (Douglas) DC-10-15	48295 / 374	XA-MEX	0082	1294	3 GE CF6-50C2F	206385	Y360	EJ-CF	lsf WTC Trustee
☐ N152SY	Boeing (Douglas) DC-10-15	48289 / 365	N1003W	0081	0195	3 GE CF6-50C2F	206385	Y360	EM-CH	lsf Sanwa
☐ N153SY	Boeing (Douglas) DC-10-15	48276 / 362	N1003N	0081	0597	3 GE CF6-50C2F	206385	Y360		lsf WTC Trustee
☐ N154SY	Boeing (Douglas) DC-10-15	48259 / 357	XA-TDI	0081	1297	3 GE CF6-50C2F	206385	Y360		lsf Boeing Capital Corp.

SUNDANCE HELICOPTERS, Inc.

Las Vegas-McCarren Int'l, NV

5596 Haven Street, Las Vegas, NV 89119, USA ☎ (702) 736-0606 Tx: none Fax: (702) 736-4107 SITA: n/a
F: 1985 43 Head: James A. Granquist Net: http://www.helicoptour.com Aircraft below MTOW 1361kg: Robinson R22

registration	type of aircraft	cn/fn	ex/ex*	mfd	del	powered by	mtow kg	configuration	selcal	name/fln/specialitites/remarks
☐ N188TV	Bell 206B JetRanger III	2704	N219GP	0079	0296	1 AN 250-C20B	1451			
☐ N667JM	Bell 206B JetRanger III	3444	C-FYRR	0081	0698	1 AN 250-C20B	1451			
☐ N73DP	Bell 206B JetRanger III	2513	N49U	0078	0894	1 AN 250-C20B	1451			
☐ N668KC	Bell 206L-1 LongRanger II	45638	N2040D	0081	0688	1 AN 250-C28B	1882			
☐ N1188P	Eurocopter (Aerosp.) AS350BA AStar	2347	N401H	0090	1096	1 TU Arriel 1B	2100			
☐ N270SH	Eurocopter (Aerosp.) AS350BA AStar	1864	N1839A*	0085	1298	1 TU Arriel 1B	2100			cvtd AS350B
☐ N350SH	Eurocopter (Aerosp.) AS350BA AStar	2957		0096	0397	1 TU Arriel 1B	2100			
☐ N37SH	Eurocopter (Aerosp.) AS350BA AStar	2300	C-FZYQ	0089	0497	1 TU Arriel 1B	2100			

SUN JET INTERNATIONAL AIRLINES, Inc. = JX / SJI

Atlanta-Hartsfield Int'l, GA & St. Petersburg/Clearwater, FL

2400 Harrodian Way, Suite 330, Smyrna, GA 30080, USA ☎ (800) 449-6000 Tx: none Fax: (770) 989-5920 SITA: n/a
F: 1993 n/a Head: Thomas Kolfenbach ICAO: SUNJET Net: n/a Operates passenger flights, currently with Airbus Industrie A320 lsf/opb TRANSMERIDIAN AIRLINES (N), when required.

SUN PACIFIC INTERNATIONAL, Inc. = SNP

Tucson-Int'l, AZ

2502 East Benson Highway, Tucson, AZ 85706, USA ☎ (520) 295-0455 Tx: none Fax: (520) 295-1125 SITA: n/a
F: 1995 n/a Head: Robert P. Fleming ICAO: SUN PACIFIC Net: n/a

registration	type of aircraft	cn/fn	ex/ex*	mfd	del	powered by	mtow kg	configuration	selcal	name/fln/specialitites/remarks
☐ N13759	Boeing 727-227 (A)	21044 / 1132	N562PE	0075	1296	3 PW JT8D-9A	79651	Y173		
☐ N370PA	Boeing 727-221 (A)	22542 / 1799		0082	0496	3 PW JT8D-17R	88360	Y173		lsf ARON
☐ N64319	Boeing 727-231 (QWS)	20052 / 709		0069		3 PW JT8D-9A (HK3/DUG)	78245	Y173		to be lsf CISA 0499
☐ N64320	Boeing 727-231 (QWS)	20053 / 713		0069		3 PW JT8D-9A (HK3/DUG)	78245	Y173		to be lsf CISA 0499
☐ N79771	Boeing 727-227 (A) (QWS)	20840 / 1036	N558PE	0074	0196	3 PW JT8D-9A (HK3/DUG)	79651	Y173		
☐ C-GOKF	Boeing 727-214	20162 / 715	N409BN	0069	0298	3 PW JT8D-9A (HK3/FDX)	80650	Y170		lsf KFA

SUN QUEST EXECUTIVE AIR CHARTER, Inc.

Van Nuys, CA

7155 Valjean Avenue, Van Nuys, CA 91406, USA ☎ (818) 778-6520 Tx: none Fax: (818) 778-6526 SITA: n/a
F: 1992 7 Head: Charles M. Smith Net: n/a

registration	type of aircraft	cn/fn	ex/ex*	mfd	del	powered by	mtow kg	configuration	selcal	name/fln/specialitites/remarks
☐ N911SQ	Cessna 310Q	310Q0767	N3361Q	0073	0489	2 CO IO-470-VO	2404			lsf pvt
☐ N1872E	Piper PA-31-350 Navajo Chieftain	31-8052114		0080	0592	2 LY TIO-540-J2BD	3175			lsf pvt
☐ N27819	Piper PA-31-350 Navajo Chieftain	31-7852166		0078	0994	2 LY TIO-540-J2BD	3175			
☐ N88SQ	Piper PA-31-350 Navajo Chieftain	31-7952026	N27889	0079	0992	2 LY TIO-540-J2BD	3175			lsf pvt
☐ N280TT	Beech King Air 200	BB-280	F-GJPD	0077	0497	2 PWC PT6A-41	5670			lsf Tyler Turbine Ltd
☐ N717HT	Beech King Air 200	BB-133	N113RL	0076	0396	2 PWC PT6A-41	5670			lsf Hidalgo Trading Co. Llc

SUNRISE AIRLINES = OQ (Express Air, Inc. dba)

Phoenix-Int'l, AZ

2635 East Air Lane, Phoenix, AZ 85034, USA ☎ (602) 244-1851 Tx: none Fax: (602) 244-8308 SITA: n/a
F: 1997 n/a Head: Larry R. Stephenson Net: n/a

registration	type of aircraft	cn/fn	ex/ex*	mfd	del	powered by	mtow kg	configuration	selcal	name/fln/specialitites/remarks
☐ N160SW	Piper PA-31-350 Navajo Chieftain	31-7405176	N66871	0074	0198	2 LY TIO-540-J2BD	3175	Y9		
☐ N3529W	Piper PA-31-350 Navajo Chieftain	31-7952159		0079	0198	2 LY TIO-540-J2BD	3175	Y9		
☐ N4500Y	Piper PA-31-350 Navajo Chieftain	31-8052160		0080	0498	2 LY TIO-540-J2BD	3175	Y9		
☐ N6657Y	Piper PA-31-350 Navajo Chieftain	31-7852164		0078	0198	2 LY TIO-540-J2BD	3175	Y9		
☐ N78GH	Piper PA-31-350 Navajo Chieftain	31-7852121		0078	0098	2 LY TIO-540-J2BD	3175	Y9		lsf Muhl Air
☐ N1029Y	Cessna 208B Grand Caravan	208B0325		0092	1097	1 PWC PT6A-114A	3969	Y9		
☐ N1032G	Cessna 208B Grand Caravan	208B0329		0093	1097	1 PWC PT6A-114A	3969	Y9		

SUNRISE AVIATION, Inc.

Wrangell, AK

PO Box 432, Wrangell, AK 99929, USA ☎ (907) 874-2319 Tx: none Fax: (907) 874-2546 SITA: n/a
F: 1990 5 Head: Tyler J. Robinson Net: n/a

registration	type of aircraft	cn/fn	ex/ex*	mfd	del	powered by	mtow kg	configuration	selcal	name/fln/specialitites/remarks
☐ N50159	Cessna U206F Stationair	U20601907		0072	0493	1 CO IO-550-F	1633			Amphibian
☐ N9468Q	Beech Bonanza A36	E-314		0072	0390	1 CO IO-520-BA	1633			

SUNSHINE AERO INDUSTRIES

Crestview-Bob Sikes, FL

5545 John Givens, Hangar B, Crestview, FL 32536, USA ☎ (352) 682-6811 Tx: none Fax: (352) 729-1507 SITA: n/a
F: 1981 n/a Head: Robert L. Keller Net: n/a Aircraft below MTOW 1361kg: Piper PA-24-250

registration	type of aircraft	cn/fn	ex/ex*	mfd	del	powered by	mtow kg	configuration	selcal	name/fln/specialitites/remarks
☐ N99801	Beech H18	BA-760	JA5149	0067	1184	2 PW R-985-AN14B	4491			
☐ N3606T	Beech King Air 100	B-30	N360BT	0072	0688	2 PWC PT6A-28	4808			

SUNSHINE AIRLINES = SON (Balter Worldwide Corp. dba / Sister company of Sunshine Air Tours)

Van Nuys, CA

7045 Sophia Avenue, Van Nuys, CA 91406, USA ☎ (818) 997-4597 Tx: none Fax: (818) 997-8372 SITA: n/a
F: 1991 n/a Head: Laurence I. Balter ICAO: SUNSHINE TOURS Net: http://www.sunshineair.com

registration	type of aircraft	cn/fn	ex/ex*	mfd	del	powered by	mtow kg	configuration	selcal	name/fln/specialitites/remarks
☐ N6PK	Cessna 310I	310I0021		0064	0396	2 CO IO-470-U	2313			
☐ N100FC	Cessna 402A	402A0063		0069	0297	2 CO TSIO-520-E	2858			
☐ N168SA	Cessna 402	402-0229	N68GC	0068	0498	2 CO TSIO-520-E	2858			
☐ N170SA	Cessna 402A	402A0043		0069	0396	2 CO TSIO-520-E	2858			
☐ N18WW	Cessna 402A	402A0003		0068	0197	2 CO TSIO-520-E	2858			
☐ N300UV	Cessna 402A	402A0086	N3BL	0069	0498	2 CO TSIO-520-E	2858			
☐ N361JP	Cessna 402B	402B0361	SX-ABG	0073	0895	2 CO TSIO-520-E	2858			lsf pvt
☐ N58SA	Cessna 402	402-0315		0068	0496	2 CO TSIO-520-E	2858			
☐ N810AN	Cessna 402C II	402C0279	N82LA	0080	0698	2 CO TSIO-520-VB	3107			
☐ N812AN	Cessna 402C II	402C0229	N2718P	0079	0598	2 CO TSIO-520-VB	3107			
☐ N819AN	Cessna 402C II	402C0423	N104GP	0081	0698	2 CO TSIO-520-VB	3107			
☐ N87193	Cessna 402B II	402B1019		0076	1296	2 CO TSIO-520-E	2858			lsf pvt

SUNSHINE HELICOPTERS, Inc.

Kahului-Heliport, HI

Kahului Heliport, No. 107, Kahului, HI 96732, USA ☎ (808) 871-0722 Tx: none Fax: (808) 877-2517 SITA: n/a
F: 1986 n/a Head: Ross R. Scott Net: n/a

registration	type of aircraft	cn/fn	ex/ex*	mfd	del	powered by	mtow kg	configuration	selcal	name/fln/specialitites/remarks
☐ N59569	Bell 206B JetRanger	1425		0074	1286	1 AN 250-C20	1451			
☐ N3607P	Eurocopter (Aerosp.) AS350BA AStar	1249		0080	0197	1 TU Arriel 1B	2100			cvtd AS350D
☐ N6077H	Eurocopter (Aerosp.) AS350BA AStar	2693		0092	0193	1 TU Arriel 1B	2100			
☐ N6094H	Eurocopter (Aerosp.) AS350BA AStar	2694		0092	0693	1 TU Arriel 1B	2100			
☐ N6094S	Eurocopter (Aerosp.) AS350BA AStar	2722		0093	1293	1 TU Arriel 1B	2100			

SUNWEST AVIATION, Inc. = SWS (Sister company of Muhl Air)

Ogden-Hinckley Municipal, UT

3909 S. Airport Road, Ogden, UT 84405, USA ☎ (801) 399-1941 Tx: none Fax: (801) 399-9510 SITA: n/a
F: 1980 n/a Head: Wayne C. Muhler ICAO: SUNNY WEST Net: http://www.sunwestaviation.com

registration	type of aircraft	cn/fn	ex/ex*	mfd	del	powered by	mtow kg	configuration	selcal	name/fln/specialitites/remarks
☐ N27354	Piper PA-31-350 Navajo Chieftain	31-7752180		0077	0894	2 LY TIO-540-J2BD	3175	Freighter		lsf pvt

SUNWORLD INTERNATIONAL AIRLINES, Inc. = SM / SWI

Cincinnati-Northern Kentucky, OH

207 Grand View Drive, Fort Mitchell, KY 41017-2799, USA ☎ (606) 331-0091 Tx: none Fax: (606) 578-1178 SITA: CVGTDSM
F: 1995 65 Head: William J. Yung IATA: 375 ICAO: SUNWORLD Net: n/a

registration	type of aircraft	cn/fn	ex/ex*	mfd	del	powered by	mtow kg	configuration	selcal	name/fln/specialitites/remarks
☐ N281US	Boeing 727-251 (A)	21160 / 1180		1275	1298	3 PW JT8D-17	86863	Y170		
☐ N282US	Boeing 727-251 (A)	21161 / 1181		1275	1195	3 PW JT8D-15/-15A	86863	Y167		

SUPERIOR AIR CHARTER, Inc. — Medford-Rogue Valley Int'l, OR

3650 Biddle Road, No. 18, Medford, OR 97504, USA ☎ (541) 772-5660 Tx: none Fax: (541) 772-8980 SITA: n/a
F: 1992 ✱✱✱ n/a Head: Larry T. Brandenburg Net: n/a

☐ N441AG	Cessna 441 Conquest II	*441-0327*		*0083*	*0793*	*2 GA TPE331-8-403S*	*4468*			
☐ N251MD	Learjet 25D	*25D-356*	*N25PT*	*0082*	*0897*	*2 GE CJ610-8A*	*6804*			

SUPERIOR AVIATION, Inc. = AB / HKA — Iron Mountain-Kingsford, MI

250 Riverhills Road, Kingsford, MI 49802, USA ☎ (906) 774-0400 Tx: none Fax: (906) 774-4118 SITA: n/a
F: 1979 ✱✱✱ n/a Head: Stephen Van Beek ICAO: SPEND AIR Net: n/a

☐ N5918S	Beech Travel Air D95A	*TD-653*		*0067*	*0689*	*2 LY IO-360-B1B*	*1905*	*Freighter*		
☐ N300SN	Cessna 402C II	*402C0060*	*N5871C*	*0079*	*0987*	*2 CO TSIO-520-VB*	*3107*	*Freighter*		
☐ N33NC	Cessna 402B	*402B0825*		*0074*	*0785*	*2 CO TSIO-520-E*	*2858*	*Freighter*		
☐ N4661N	Cessna 402C II	*402C0019*		*0078*	*1096*	*2 CO TSIO-520-VB*	*3107*	*Freighter*		
☐ N98697	Cessna 402B II	*402B1053*		*0076*	*0787*	*2 CO TSIO-520-E*	*2858*	*Freighter*		
☐ N9231F	Cessna 208 Caravan I	*20800005*		*0085*	*1191*	*1 PWC PT6A-114*	*3629*	*Freighter*		
☐ N167SA	Cessna 404 Titan II	*404-0639*		*0080*	*0390*	*2 CO GTSIO-520-M*	*3810*	*Freighter*		
☐ N255CS	Cessna 404 Titan II	*404-0019*		*0077*	*0986*	*2 CO GTSIO-520-M*	*3810*	*Freighter*		
☐ N26SA	Cessna 404 Titan II	*404-0225*		*0078*	*1186*	*2 CO GTSIO-520-M*	*3810*	*Freighter*		
☐ N27SA	Cessna 404 Titan II	*404-0038*	*C-GZJQ*	*0077*	*0494*	*2 CO GTSIO-520-M*	*3810*	*Freighter*		
☐ N28SA	Cessna 404 Titan II	*404-0072*		*0077*	*1086*	*2 CO GTSIO-520-M*	*3810*	*Freighter*		
☐ N36998	Cessna 404 Titan II	*404-0101*		*0077*	*1189*	*2 CO GTSIO-520-M*	*3810*	*Freighter*		
☐ N37127	Cessna 404 Titan II	*404-0114*		*0077*	*1085*	*2 CO GTSIO-520-M*	*3810*	*Freighter*		
☐ N37144	Cessna 404 Titan II	*404-0118*		*0077*	*1087*	*2 CO GTSIO-520-M*	*3810*	*Freighter*		
☐ N41059	Cessna 404 Titan II	*404-0012*		*0077*	*0394*	*2 CO GTSIO-520-M*	*3810*	*Freighter*		
☐ N54SA	Cessna 404 Titan II	*404-0426*		*0079*	*1285*	*2 CO GTSIO-520-M*	*3810*	*Freighter*		
☐ N8754G	Cessna 404 Titan II	*404-0083*		*0077*	*0191*	*2 CO GTSIO-520-M*	*3810*	*Freighter*		
☐ N88719	Cessna 404 Titan II	*404-0235*		*0078*	*1287*	*2 CO GTSIO-520-M*	*3810*	*Freighter*		
☐ N1037N	Cessna 208B Grand Caravan	*208B0334*		*0093*	*1193*	*1 PWC PT6A-114A*	*3969*	*Freighter*		
☐ N1119V	Cessna 208B Grand Caravan	*208B0383*		*0094*	*0594*	*1 PWC PT6A-114A*	*3969*	*Freighter*		
☐ N1120N	Cessna 208B Grand Caravan	*208B0386*		*0094*	*0594*	*1 PWC PT6A-114A*	*3969*	*Freighter*		
☐ N1120W	Cessna 208B Grand Caravan	*208B0388*		*0094*	*0794*	*1 PWC PT6A-114A*	*3969*	*Freighter*		
☐ N126HA	Cessna 208B Caravan I Super Cargomaster	*208B0067*		*0087*	*0193*	*1 PWC PT6A-114*	*3969*	*Freighter*		
☐ N162SA	Cessna 208B Grand Caravan	*208B0548*		*0096*	*1096*	*1 PWC PT6A-114A*	*3969*	*Freighter*		
☐ N164SA	Cessna 208B Grand Caravan	*208B0530*	*N1248D*	*0096*	*1196*	*1 PWC PT6A-114A*	*3969*	*Freighter*		
☐ N179SA	Cessna 208B Grand Caravan	*208B0594*		*0097*	*0297*	*1 PWC PT6A-114A*	*3969*	*Freighter*		
☐ N7580B	Cessna 208B Caravan I Super Cargomaster	*208B0051*		*0087*	*0888*	*1 PWC PT6A-114*	*3969*	*Freighter*		
☐ N78SA	Cessna 208B Grand Caravan	*208B0467*		*0095*	*1195*	*1 PWC PT6A-114A*	*3969*	*Freighter*		
☐ N6851X	Cessna 441 Conquest II	*441-0212*		*0081*	*0289*	*2 GA TPE331-8-401S*	*4468*	*Freighter*		
☐ N151SA	Fairchild (Swearingen) SA226TC Metro II	*TC-302*	*C-FJTQ*	*0079*	*0496*	*2 GA TPE331-10UA-511G*	*5670*	*Freighter*		
☐ N152SA	Fairchild (Swearingen) SA226TC Metro II	*TC-306*	*C-FJTJ*	*0079*	*0496*	*2 GA TPE331-10UA-511G*	*5670*	*Freighter*		
☐ N162SW	Fairchild (Swearingen) SA226TC Metro II	*TC-325*		*0079*	*0495*	*2 GA TPE331-10UA-511G*	*5670*	*Freighter*		
☐ N220AM	Fairchild (Swearingen) SA226TC Metro II	*TC-234*	*N160MA*	*0077*	*0895*	*2 GA TPE331-10UA-511G*	*5670*	*Freighter*		
☐ N229AM	Fairchild (Swearingen) SA226TC Metro II	*TC-305*		*0079*	*0197*	*2 GA TPE331-10UA-511G*	*5670*	*Freighter*		
☐ N235BA	Fairchild (Swearingen) SA226TC Metro II	*TC-235*	*N61Z*	*0077*	*0796*	*2 GA TPE331-10UA-511G*	*5670*	*Freighter*		
☐ N245AM	Fairchild (Swearingen) SA226TC Metro II	*TC-265*	*N5471M*	*0078*	*0895*	*2 GA TPE331-10UA-511G*	*5670*	*Freighter*		
☐ N250AM	Fairchild (Swearingen) SA226TC Metro II	*TC-316*	*N505SS*	*0079*	*0895*	*2 GA TPE331-10UA-511G*	*5670*	*Freighter*		
☐ N328BA	Fairchild (Swearingen) SA226TC Metro II	*TC-253*	*N5457M*	*0078*	*0197*	*2 GA TPE331-10UA-511G*	*5670*	*Freighter*		
☐ N329BA	Fairchild (Swearingen) SA226TC Metro II	*TC-238*	*N5436M*	*0077*	*0197*	*2 GA TPE331-10UA-511G*	*5670*	*Freighter*		
☐ N731AC	Fairchild (Swearingen) SA226TC Metro II	*TC-255*	*N265AM*	*0478*	*0895*	*2 GA TPE331-10UA-511G*	*5670*	*Freighter*		
☐ N78CP	Fairchild (Swearingen) SA226AT Merlin IVA	*AT-029*	*N294A*	*0074*	*0396*	*2 GA TPE331-3U-303G*	*5670*	*Freighter*		
☐ N31171	Fairchild (Swearingen) SA227AC Metro III	*AC-605*		*0084*	*0697*	*2 GA TPE331-11U-611G*	*6577*	*Freighter*		
☐ N592BA	Fairchild (Swearingen) SA227AC Metro III	*AC-592*	*N384PH*	*0084*	*0697*	*2 GA TPE331-11U-611G*	*6577*	*Freighter*		

SUPERIOR HELICOPTER, Llc — Glendale-Heliport, OR

PO Box 250, Glendale, OR 97442, USA ☎ (541) 832-1167 Tx: none Fax: (541) 832-1139 SITA: n/a
F: 1996 ✱✱✱ 59 Head: Gary Jantzer Net: n/a

☐ N311KA	Kaman K-1200 K-Max	*A94-0017*		*0096*	*0896*	*1 LY T5317A-1*	*2722*			
☐ N312KA	Kaman K-1200 K-Max	*A94-0024*		*0098*	*0298*	*1 LY T5317A-1*	*2722*			

SUSITNA AIR SERVICE, Inc. — Big Lake, AK

HC 89, Box 133, Willow, AK 99688, USA ☎ (907) 495-6789 Tx: none Fax: (907) 495-1010 SITA: n/a
F: 1978 ✱✱✱ n/a Head: Paul M. Englund Net: n/a

☐ N942SA	Cessna TU206A Turbo Skywagon	*U206-0553*		*0066*	*0683*	*1 CO TSIO-520-C*	*1633*			*lsf Boyds Aircraft / Floats/Wheel-Skis*
☐ N1018D	De Havilland DHC-2 Beaver I	*293*	*51-16810*	*0051*	*0894*	*1 PW R-985*	*2313*			*lsf pvt / Floats / Wheel-Skis*

SUWEST AIRWAYS, Inc. — New Orleans-Lakefront, LA

5500 Lakeshore Drive, New Orleans, LA 70126, USA ☎ (504) 242-4883 Tx: none Fax: (504) 242-0096 SITA: n/a
F: 1982 ✱✱✱ 12 Head: Paul T. Westervelt, Jr. Net: n/a

☐ N116SW	Bell 206B JetRanger III	*3403*	*N2047V*	*0081*	*0184*	*1 AN 250-C20B*	*1451*			
☐ N3848Y	Beech Baron 58P	*TJ-349*		*0081*	*0887*	*2 CO TSIO-520-WB*	*2812*			*lsf Thompson Equipment Co. Inc.*

SYSTEC 2000, Inc. — Pontiac-Oakland, MI

6230 North Service Drive, Waterford, MI 48327, USA ☎ (248) 666-4473 Tx: none Fax: (248) 666-3659 SITA: n/a
F: 1994 ✱✱✱ n/a Head: Douglas A. Pachocke Net: n/a

☐ N5712M	Cessna 310P	*310P0012*		*0068*	*0196*	*2 CO IO-470-VO*	*2359*			
☐ N535WM	Mitsubishi MU-2L (MU-2B-36) Cargoliner	*655*	*N535MA*	*0074*	*0195*	*2 GA TPE331-6-251M*	*5250*	*Freighter*		*Cavenaugh SCD conversion*
☐ N740PB	Mitsubishi MU-2L (MU-2B-36) Cargoliner	*657*	*N740PC*	*0074*	*0195*	*2 GA TPE331-6-251M*	*5250*	*Freighter*		*Cavenaugh SCD conversion*

TABLE ROCK HELICOPTERS, Inc. — Branson-Helipad, MO

3309 West Highway 76, Branson, MO 65616, USA ☎ (417) 334-6102 Tx: none Fax: (417) 334-7102 SITA: n/a
F: 1971 ✱✱✱ n/a Head: Tim Steffen Net: n/a

☐ N145BH	Eurocopter (Aerosp.) AS350D AStar	*1270*	*N3610C*	*0080*	*0393*	*1 LY LTS101-600A.2*	*1950*			*lsf A & S Associates*
☐ N510HP	Eurocopter (Aerosp.) AS350D AStar	*1555*		*0084*	*0894*	*1 LY LTS101-600A.2*	*1950*			*lsf A & S Associates*

TAC AIR (Division of Truman Arnold Companies) — Texarkana-Regional/Webb Field, AR

Rt 12, Box 638B-2, Texarkana, AR 71854, USA ☎ (870) 773-6969 Tx: none Fax: (870) 773-3681 SITA: n/a
F: 1978 ✱✱✱ n/a Head: Truman Arnold Net: n/a

☐ N169RR	Beech Baron 58	*TH-999*	*N2063X*	*0079*	*0287*	*2 CO IO-520-CB*	*2449*			
☐ N269RA	Beech Baron 58	*TH-998*	*N2058Y*	*0079*	*0290*	*2 CO IO-520-CB*	*2449*			
☐ N369TA	Beech King Air 200	*BB-820*	*N935SJ*	*0080*	*0696*	*2 PWC PT6A-41*	*5670*			
☐ N600MS	Canadair CL-604 (CL-600-2B16) Challen.	*5333*	*N811BB*	*0097*	*0298*	*2 GE CF34-3B*	*21863*			*lsf Ross Investments Inc.*

TAKE FLIGHT ALASKA, Inc. — Anchorage-Merrill Field, AK

1740 East Fifth Avenue, Anchorage, AK 99501, USA ☎ (907) 274-9943 Tx: none Fax: (907) 272-3486 SITA: n/a
F: 1994 ✱✱✱ n/a Head: John Miller Net: n/a Aircraft below MTOW 1361kg: Cessna 172

☐ N6011U	Beech Duchess 76	*ME-101*		*0078*	*0195*	*2 LY O-360-A1G6D*	*1769*			

TAL AIR — Juneau, AK

PO Box 21751, Juneau, AK 99802, USA ☎ (907) 789-6968 Tx: none Fax: none SITA: n/a
F: 1996 ✱✱✱ n/a Head: Jacques M. Norvell Net: n/a

☐ N82687	Cessna U206F Stationair II	*U20603424*		*0076*	*0897*	*1 CO IO-520-F*	*1633*			*lsf Boundary Water Aire Inc / Amphibian*

TALKEETNA AIR TAXI, Inc. — Talkeetna, AK

PO Box 73, Talkeetna, AK 99676, USA ☎ (907) 733-2218 Tx: none Fax: (907) 733-1434 SITA: n/a
F: 1947 ✱✱✱ 4 Head: Paul E. Roderick Net: http://alaskan.com/vendors/flyat.html

☐ N5246E	Cessna A185F Skywagon	*18503943*		*0080*	*0985*	*1 CO IO-520-D*	*1520*			*Floats / Wheel-Skis*
☐ N80994	Cessna A185F Skywagon	*18503144*		*0076*	*1096*	*1 CO IO-520-D*	*1520*			*Floats / Wheel-Skis*

TAMARACK AIR, Ltd — Fairbanks-Int'l, AK

PO Box 81063, College, AK 99708, USA ☎ (907) 479-6751 Tx: none Fax: none SITA: n/a
F: 1978 ✱✱✱ 4 Head: William J. Lentsch Net: n/a Aircraft below MTOW 1361 kg: Piper PA-18 (on Floats / Wheel-Skis)

☐ N22901	Cessna A185F Skywagon	*18503077*		*0076*	*0880*	*1 CO IO-520-D*	*1520*			*lsf pvt / Floats / Wheel-Skis*
☐ N85LC	Cessna A185F Skywagon	*18502643*		*0075*	*0989*	*1 CO IO-520-D*	*1520*			*lsf pvt / Floats / Wheel-Skis*

TANANA AIR SERVICE = 4E / TNR (Bidzy Ta Hot'Aana, Corp. dba) — Fairbanks-Int'l, AK

PO Box 60713, Fairbanks, AK 99706, USA ☎ (907) 474-0301 Tx: none Fax: (907) 474-9314 SITA: n/a
F: 1979 ✱✱✱ n/a Head: Harold E. Esmailka ICAO: TAN AIR Net: n/a

☐ N200HM	Piper PA-32R-300 Lance	*32R-7680025*		*0076*	*0295*	*1 LY IO-540-K1G5D*	*1633*			*lsf pvt*
☐ N31606	Piper PA-32-300 Cherokee SIX	*32-7840137*		*0078*	*0580*	*1 LY IO-540-K1G5D*	*1542*			
☐ N4352F	Piper PA-32R-300 Lance	*32R-7680441*		*0076*	*1295*	*1 LY IO-540-K1G5D*	*1633*			*lsf pvt*

441 registration type of aircraft *cn/fn* *ex/ex** *mfd* *del* *powered by* *mtow kg* *configuration* *selcal* *name/fln/specialitites/remarks*

☐ N4803S	Piper PA-32-260B Cherokee SIX	32-1188		0069	0994	1 LY O-540-E4B5	1542			
☐ N4811T	Piper PA-32-300E Cherokee SIX	32-7240086		0072	0994	1 LY IO-540-K1A5	1542			
☐ N75387	Piper PA-32R-300 Lance	32R-7680298		0076	0789	1 LY IO-540-K1G5D	1633			
☐ N97CR	Piper PA-32R-300 Lance	32R-7780078		0076	0793	1 LY IO-540-K1G5D	1633			lsf pvt
☐ N101LJ	Piper PA-31-310 Navajo	31-267		0068	0397	2 LY TIO-540-A1A	2948			lsf pvt

TAQUAN AIR SERVICE, Inc. = K3 / TQN (Air One) (Subsidiary of Kootznoowoo, Inc.) — Ketchikan-Harbor SPB & -Int'l

Taquan Air Service

1007 Water Street, Ketchikan, AK 99901, USA ☎ (907) 225-2712 Tx: none Fax: (907) 225-0522 SITA: n/a

F: 1977 n/a Head: Jerry A. Scudero ICAO: TAQUAN Net: n/a Scheduled flights (with BAe Jetstream 32EP) are operated under the marketing name AIR ONE (same headquarters).

☐ N5389Z	Cessna U206G Stationair 6 II	U20606107		0081	0597	1 CO IO-520-F	1633	Y5		
☐ N9871Z	Cessna U206G Stationair 6 II	U20606716		0083	0596	1 CO IO-520-F	1633	Y5		Floats
☐ N63AK	Cessna 207A Stationair 8 II	20700731	N9799M	0081	0597	1 CO IO-520-F	1724	Y6		lsf S&S Aircraft Leasing Inc.
☐ N1018A	De Havilland DHC-2 Beaver I	178	N52409	0052	1187	1 PW R-985	2313	Y7		Floats
☐ N1018H	De Havilland DHC-2 Beaver I	732	53-7921	0053	0597	1 PW R-985	2313	Y7		Amphibian
☐ N37756	De Havilland DHC-2 Beaver I	1456	G203	0061	0390	1 PW R-985	2313	Y7		Floats
☐ N47241	De Havilland DHC-2 Beaver I	337	51-16819	0051	0597	1 PW R-985	2313	Y7		Floats / rebuilt 1981
☐ N5160G	De Havilland DHC-2 Beaver I	236	51-16483	0052	0093	1 PW R-985	2313	Y7		Floats
☐ N5595M	De Havilland DHC-2 Beaver I	1571	105	0064	0598	1 PW R-985	2313	Y7		Floats
☐ N67667	De Havilland DHC-2 Beaver I	401	51-16846	0051	1292	1 PW R-985	2313	Y7		Floats
☐ N67671	De Havilland DHC-2 Beaver I	489	52-6111	0052	0091	1 PW R-985	2313	Y7		lsf pvt / Floats
☐ N67673	De Havilland DHC-2 Beaver I	1284		0057	1183	1 PW R-985	2313	Y7		Floats
☐ N68010	De Havilland DHC-2 Beaver I	1243	57-6150	0058	0597	1 PW R-985	2313	Y7		Floats
☐ N9290Z	De Havilland DHC-2 Beaver I	1387	58-2055	0058	0696	1 PW R-985	2313	Y7		Floats
☐ N1018B	De Havilland DHC-3 Otter	392	C-FQOR	0060	0597	1 PW R-1340	3629	Y10		Amphibian
☐ N382BH	De Havilland DHC-3 Turbo Otter	382	59-2229	0060	0591	1 PWC PT6A-135	3629	Y10		Floats / cvtd Otter
☐ N472PM	De Havilland DHC-3 Otter	419	UB 6599	0061	0395	1 PW R-1340	3629	Y10		Amphibian
☐ N511BW	De Havilland DHC-3 Otter	35	C-GOFA	0054	0093	1 PW R-1340	3629	Y10		Floats
☐ N62KA	De Havilland DHC-3 Otter	144	C-FAON	0055	0597	1 PW R-1340	3629	Y10		Amphibian
☐ N68086	De Havilland DHC-3 Otter	288	C-GXYR	0058	0598	1 PW R-1340	3629	Y10		Floats
☐ N9758N	De Havilland DHC-3 Turbo Otter	440	C-FROD	0063	0592	1 PWC PT6A-135	3629	Y10		Floats / cvtd Otter
☐ N1229C	Cessna 208B Grand Caravan	208B0589		0097	0497	1 PWC PT6A-114A	3969	Y9		lsf FSBU Trustee
☐ N242BM	BAe 3201 Jetstream 32EP	902	N3155	0090	0298	2 GA TPE331-12UAR-701H	7350	Y19		Spirit of Juneau / cvtd 32/Air One-cs
☐ N242RH	BAe 3201 Jetstream 32EP	903	N3156	0090	0398	2 GA TPE331-12UAR-701H	7350	Y19		Spirit of Ketchikan / cvtd32/Air One-cs

TAR HEEL AVIATION, Inc. = THC — Jacksonville-Ellis, NC

Tar Heel Aviation

PO Box 916, Jacksonville, NC 28541, USA ☎ (910) 324-2500 Tx: none Fax: (910) 324-3323 SITA: n/a

F: 1975 30 Head: Jere W. Fountain ICAO: TARHEEL Net: n/a Aircraft below MTOW 1361 kg: Beech 24, Cessna 172/177 & Piper PA-28

☐ N528T	Beech Travel Air D95A	TD-573		0064	0591	2 LY IO-360-B1B	1905	Freighter		
☐ N66918	Beech Baron 58	TH-1104		0080	0589	2 CO IO-520-CB	2449	5 Pax		
☐ N105GC	Piper PA-31-350 Navajo Chieftain	31-7652130		0076	0295	2 LY TIO-540-J2BD	3175	7 Pax		
☐ N19LA	Piper PA-31-350 Navajo Chieftain	31-7752160	N78JF	0077	0587	2 LY TIO-540-J2BD	3175	7 Pax		
☐ N801TH	Cessna 208 Caravan I	20800123	N9680F	0087	1087	1 PWC PT6A-114	3629	Freighter		lsf THAR Inc.
☐ N803TH	Cessna 208B Grand Caravan	208B0321	N1027G	0092	0593	1 PWC PT6A-114A	3969	Freighter		lsf Cessna Finance Corp.
☐ N804TH	Cessna 208B Grand Caravan	208B0421		0094	0195	1 PWC PT6A-114A	3969	Freighter		lsf Textron Financial Corp.

TARLTON HELICOPTERS, Inc. — Houston-Private Heliport, TX

3000 Weslayan, Suite 320, Houston, TX 77027, USA ☎ (713) 871-8010 Tx: none Fax: (713) 871-8904 SITA: n/a

F: 1982 n/a Head: Benjamin D. Tarlton Net: n/a

☐ N4711R	Bell 206A JetRanger	264		0068	0384	1 AN 250-C18	1361			
☐ N83137	Bell 206B JetRanger	1015		0073	1186	1 AN 250-C20	1451			

TATONDUK FLYING SERVICE = 3K (Division of Tatonduk Outfitters, Ltd) — Fairbanks-Int'l, AK

PO Box 61680, Fairbanks, AK 99706, USA ☎ (907) 474-4697 Tx: none Fax: (907) 474-3002 SITA: n/a

F: 1977 n/a Head: Robert W. Everts Net: n/a

☐ N1063H	Piper PA-32R-300 Lance	32R-7780129		0077	1096	1 LY IO-540-K1G5D	1633			
☐ N108NS	Piper PA-32R-300 Lance	32R-7680288		0076	0394	1 LY IO-540-K1A5D	1633			
☐ N148RF	Piper PA-32R-300 Lance	32R-7680076		0076	1094	1 LY IO-540-K1G5D	1633			
☐ N6969J	Piper PA-32R-300 Lance	32R-7680398		0076	1085	1 LY IO-540-K1A5D	1633			
☐ N6207Z	Cessna TU206G Turbo Stationair 6 II	U20606188		0081	0198	1 CO TSIO-520-M	1633			lsf C&R Leasing Llc
☐ N734VB	Cessna U206G Stationair 6 II	U20604875		0079	0689	1 CO IO-520-F	1633			
☐ N8JM	Cessna 208 Caravan I	20800031	D-FLYH	0085	1098	1 PWC PT6A-114	3629			lsf pvt
☐ N208TF	Cessna 208B Grand Caravan	208B0592		0097	0297	1 PWC PT6A-114A	3969			lsf C&R Leasing Llc

TBM, Inc. — Tulare & Visalia, CA

PO Box 868, Tulare, CA 93275, USA ☎ (209) 686-3476 Tx: none Fax: (209) 686-3477 SITA: n/a

F: 1958 18 Head: Henry C. Moore Net: n/a Beside aircraft listed, frequently leases Douglas DC-7 & Lockheed L-182 Hercules from Butler Aircraft Company when required.

☐ N2612X	Cessna P206 Super Skylane	P206-0112		0065	0868	1 CO IO-520-A	1497	Trainer		
☐ N8502R	Boeing (Douglas) DC-4 (C-54E-15-DO)	27367 / DO 313	90411	0045	0287	4 PW R-2000	30241	Tanker		65
☐ N90739	Boeing (Douglas) DC-6	43044 / 84		0047	0173	4 PW R-2800	41821	Tanker		68
☐ N756Z	Boeing (Douglas) DC-7BF	45400 / 864	N347AA	0057	0580	4 WR R-3350	53025	Freighter		cvtd DC-7B / all metallic cs
☐ N838D	Boeing (Douglas) DC-7B	45347 / 936		0058	0473	4 WR R-3350	53025	Tanker		60
☐ N466TM	Lockheed L-182 (C-130A) Hercules	1A-3173	57-0466	0057	0889	4 AN T56-A	56336	Tanker / Frtr		64
☐ N473TM	Lockheed L-182 (C-130A) Hercules	1A-3081	56-0473	0057	0889	4 AN T56-A	56336	Tanker / Frtr		63
☐ N479TM	Lockheed L-182 (C-130A) Hercules	1A-3186	57-0479	0057	1291	4 AN T56-A	56336	Tanker / Frtr		

TC AVIATION, Inc. (Subsidiary of Ackerley Communication, Inc. / formerly SS Aviation, Inc.) — Seattle-Tacoma Int'l, WA

6987 Perimeter Road, Suite 220, Seattle, WA 98108, USA ☎ (206) 763-2714 Tx: none Fax: (206) 768-0483 SITA: n/a

F: 1979 n/a Head: Ronald Davis Net: n/a Operates non-commercial VIP flights exclusively for members of the Ackerley Group, including Ackerley Communications Inc. & Seattle Supersonics Inc. (basketball-club).

☐ N119GA	Boeing 727-2B6 (A)	21068 / 1107	N610AG	0075	0298	3 PW JT8D-15 (HK3/FDX)	86409	VIP		op in Seattle Supersonics-colors

T.D. AVIATION, Inc. — Farmingdale-Republic, NY

Republic Airport, Route 109, Farmingdale, NY 11735, USA ☎ (516) 753-5757 Tx: none Fax: (516) 753-0279 SITA: n/a

F: 1994 n/a Head: Timothy Decker Net: n/a

☐ N206TD	Bell 206B JetRanger III	3945	OH-HAM	0086	1094	1 AN 250-C20J	1451			lsf Vertical Flight Inc.
☐ N402TD	Bell 206L-3 LongRanger III	51383	N92EA	0090	1297	1 AN 250-C30P	1882			
☐ N355TD	Eurocopter (Aerosp.) AS355F1 TwinStar	5191	N5800F	0082	0597	2 AN 250-C20F	2400			

TELFORD AVIATION, Inc. = TEL — Waterville-Robert LaFleur & Bangor-Int'l, ME

TELFORD

100 Airport Road, Waterville, ME 04901-4954, USA ☎ (207) 872-5555 Tx: none Fax: (207) 872-6794 SITA: n/a

F: 1981 100 Head: Telford M. Allen, Jr. ICAO: TELFORD Net: http://www.telford-usa.com Aircraft below MTOW 1361kg: Cessna 172

☐ N2751A	Bell 206B JetRanger III	2623		0079	0081	1 AN 250-C20J	1451			lsf IFAW Holding Co. Inc.
☐ N6400X	Cessna U206G Stationair 6 II	U20605865		0080	1193	1 CO IO-520-F	1633			
☐ N68BS	Piper PA-46-310P Malibu	46-8608040	N69BS	0086	0894	1 CO TSIO-520-BE	1860			lsf Imperial Airways Charter Co.
☐ N969BD	Piper PA-31-350 Navajo Chieftain	31-8152109	N4085L	0081	0387	2 LY TIO-540-J2BD	3175			lsf IFAW Holding Co. Inc.
☐ N216TA	Cessna 208 Caravan I	20800099	N9551F	0086	0593	1 PWC PT6A-114	3629			
☐ N207TA	Cessna 208B Grand Caravan	208B0371		0094	0894	1 PWC PT6A-114A	3969			lsf Textron Financial Corp.
☐ N208TA	Cessna 208B Grand Caravan	208B0365	N1116R	0094	0894	1 PWC PT6A-114A	3969			lsf Cessna Finance Corp.
☐ N215TA	Cessna 208B Grand Caravan	208B0447		0095	0895	1 PWC PT6A-114A	3969			lsf Cessna Finance Corp.
☐ N590TA	Cessna 208B Grand Caravan	208B0590		0097	0397	1 PWC PT6A-114A	3969			
☐ N7392B	Cessna 208B Caravan I Super Cargomaster	208B0045		0087	1187	1 PWC PT6A-114	3969	Freighter		lsf Avion Capital Corp.
☐ N9612B	Cessna 208B Caravan I Super Cargomaster	208B0136		0088	0397	1 PWC PT6A-114	3969	Freighter		lsf Cessna Finance Corp.
☐ N214TA	Beech 99 Airliner	U-38	N202BH	0068	0495	2 PWC PT6A-20	4717			lsf BHA Leasing Inc.
☐ N99TA	Beech 99 Airliner	U-28	N4415L	0068	0796	2 PWC PT6A-20	4717			
☐ N49CH	Beech King Air F90	LA-2	N58AB	0079	0292	2 PWC PT6A-135	4967			lsf Alternative Energy Inc.
☐ N110EJ	Hawker 700A (HS 125-700A)	257104 / NA0273	N46TJ	0080	0796	2 GA TFE731-3R-1H	11567			lsf J&E Air Inc.
☐ N701TA	Hawker 700A (HS 125-700A)	257073	N7788	0079	0194	2 GA TFE731-3R-1H	11567			lsf AAI Jet Inc.

TEMSCO HELICOPTERS, Inc. = TMS — Ketchikan-Temsco Heliport, AK

PO Box 5057, Ketchikan, AK 99901, USA ☎ (907) 225-5141 Tx: n/a Fax: (907) 225-2340 SITA: n/a

F: 1958 n/a Head: Jim Taro ICAO: TEMSCO Net: http://www.alaskaone.com/temscoair/

☐ N1088N	MD Helicopters MD 500D (Hughes 369D)	300679D		0080	0780	1 AN 250-C20B	1361			
☐ N1091P	MD Helicopters MD 500D (Hughes 369D)	300683D		0080	0880	1 AN 250-C20B	1361			
☐ N1091S	MD Helicopters MD 500D (Hughes 369D)	300691D		0080	0780	1 AN 250-C20B	1361			
☐ N1107G	MD Helicopters MD 500D (Hughes 369D)	210899D		0081	0981	1 AN 250-C20B	1361			
☐ N1107P	MD Helicopters MD 500D (Hughes 369D)	210897D		0081	0981	1 AN 250-C20B	1361			
☐ N5125Q	MD Helicopters MD 500D (Hughes 369D)	1100D		0082	0882	1 AN 250-C20B	1361			
☐ N5133U	MD Helicopters MD 500D (Hughes 369D)	1102D		0082	0882	1 AN 250-C20B	1361			
☐ N5134V	MD Helicopters MD 500D (Hughes 369D)	1103D		0082	0882	1 AN 250-C20B	1361			
☐ N58191	MD Helicopters MD 500D (Hughes 369D)	1070187D		0077	0778	1 AN 250-C20B	1361			
☐ N58317	MD Helicopters MD 500D (Hughes 369D)	490498D		0079	0779	1 AN 250-C20B	1361			

442 registration type of aircraft cn/fn ex/ex* mfd del powered by mtow kg configuration selcal name/fln/specialitites/remarks

☐ N58318	MD Helicopters MD 500D (Hughes 369D)	590499D		0079	0779	1 AN 250-C20B	1361			
☐ N58337	MD Helicopters MD 500D (Hughes 369D)	1090582D		0079	0482	1 AN 250-C20B	1361			
☐ N58415	MD Helicopters MD 500D (Hughes 369D)	480312D		0078	0881	1 AN 250-C20B	1361			
☐ N8357F	MD Helicopters MD 500D (Hughes 369D)	170069D		0077	0677	1 AN 250-C20B	1361			
☐ N1964T	Bell 206B JetRanger III	2738	N6NU	0079	0688	1 AN 250-C20B	1451			
☐ N1974T	Bell 206B JetRanger III	2464	N159L	0078	0586	1 AN 250-C20B	1451			
☐ N5001U	Bell 206B JetRanger III	2415		0078	0388	1 AN 250-C20B	1451			
☐ N121TH	Eurocopter EC120B Colibri	1003		0098	0898	1 TU Arrius 2F	1680			
☐ N122TH	Eurocopter EC120B Colibri	1017		0099	0299	1 TU Arrius 2F	1680			
☐ N124TH	Eurocopter EC120B Colibri	1020		0099	0299	1 TU Arrius 2F	1680			
☐ N125TH	Eurocopter EC120B Colibri					1 TU Arrius 2F	1680			oo-delivery 0099
☐ N127TH	Eurocopter EC120B Colibri					1 TU Arrius 2F	1680			oo-delivery 0000
☐ N	Eurocopter EC120B Colibri					1 TU Arrius 2F	1680			oo-delivery 0000
☐ N	Eurocopter EC120B Colibri					1 TU Arrius 2F	1680			oo-delivery 0001
☐ N	Eurocopter EC120B Colibri					1 TU Arrius 2F	1680			oo-delivery 0001
☐ N26492	Eurocopter (Aerosp.) AS350BA AStar	1066	G-BGIF	0077	1185	1 TU Arriel 1B	2100			cvtd AS350B
☐ N4022D	Eurocopter (Aerosp.) AS350B2 AStar	2891		0096	0696	1 TU Arriel 1D1	2250			
☐ N57954	Eurocopter (Aerosp.) AS350BA AStar	1127	N35977	0077	1185	1 TU Arriel 1B	2100			cvtd AS350B
☐ N57958	Eurocopter (Aerosp.) AS350BA AStar	1512		0082	1282	1 TU Arriel 1B	2100			cvtd AS350B
☐ N6015S	Eurocopter (Aerosp.) AS350BA AStar	1884		0086	0488	1 TU Arriel 1B	2100			cvtd AS350B
☐ N6052C	Eurocopter (Aerosp.) AS350B2 AStar	2586		0092	0592	1 TU Arriel 1D1	2250			
☐ N6052F	Eurocopter (Aerosp.) AS350B2 AStar	2587		0092	0592	1 TU Arriel 1D1	2250			
☐ N60618	Eurocopter (Aerosp.) AS350B2 AStar	2565		0092	0592	1 TU Arriel 1D1	2250			
☐ N60809	Eurocopter (Aerosp.) AS350BA AStar	2696		0092	0693	1 TU Arriel 1B	2100			
☐ N6080R	Eurocopter (Aerosp.) AS350BA AStar	2685		0092	0693	1 TU Arriel 1B	2100			
☐ N6094E	Eurocopter (Aerosp.) AS350BA AStar	2750		0094	0694	1 TU Arriel 1B	2100			
☐ N6094U	Eurocopter (Aerosp.) AS350BA AStar	2751		0094	0694	1 TU Arriel 1B	2100			
☐ N6099Y	Eurocopter (Aerosp.) AS350B2 AStar	2847		0095	0995	1 TU Arriel 1D1	2250			
☐ N6180T	Eurocopter (Aerosp.) AS350BA AStar	1149	N39GT	0077	1094	1 TU Arriel 1B	2100			cvtd AS350B
☐ N94TH	Eurocopter (Aerosp.) AS350BA AStar	2548		0091	1294	1 TU Arriel 1B	2100			
☐ N135NW	Eurocopter EC135T1	0010	N4037A	0096	0797	2 TU Arrius 2B	2720	EMS Lifestar		
☐ N99675	Bell UH-1B (204)	661	62-4601	0062	0780	1 LY T5311	3856			
☐ N16920	Bell 212	30865		0077	0985	2 PWC PT6T-3 TwinPac	5080			
☐ N83230	Bell 212	30560		0073	1081	2 PWC PT6T-3 TwinPac	5080			

TEPPER AVIATION, Inc. — Crestview-Bob Sikes, FL

PO Box 100, Crestview, FL 32536, USA ☎ (352) 682-8411 Tx: none Fax: (352) 682-8416 SITA: n/a
F: 1987 n/a Head: Scott Eder Net: n/a

☐ N2189M	Lockheed L-382G (L-100-30) Hercules	30C-4582	TR-KKA	0075	0492	4 AN 501-D22A	70307	Freighter		lsf Rapid Air Trans Inc.
☐ N8183J	Lockheed L-382G (L-100-30) Hercules	39C-4796	N123GA	0078	0289	4 AN 501-D22A	70307	Freighter		lsf Rapid Air Trans Inc.

TERRA HELICOPTERS, Inc. — McMinnville-Municipal, OR

21100 SW Eagle Point Way, McMinnville, OR 97128, USA ☎ (503) 472-6053 Tx: none Fax: (503) 852-6304 SITA: n/a
F: 1981 n/a Head: Steven H. Roberts Net: n/a

☐ N5072F	MD Helicopters MD 500D (Hughes 369D)	811024D		0081	1081	1 AN 250-C20B	1361			
☐ N4069R	Kaman HH-43F (K600) Huskie	218	HR-AKJ	0059	0997	1 LY T53-L-11A	4150			

TERYJON AVIATION, Inc. — St. Peter-Private Heliport, MN

Rt 1, Box 94A, St. Peter, MN 56082, USA ☎ (507) 931-2419 Tx: none Fax: (507) 931-1025 SITA: n/a
F: 1986 n/a Head: John C. Holmberg Net: n/a Aircraft below MTOW 1361kg: Bell 47G & Hughes 369HS (500C)

☐ N8123M	Bell UH-1F (204)	7307	66-1231	0066	0396	1 GE T58-GE-3	3856			

TEX-AIR HELICOPTERS, Inc. — Houston-William P. Hobby & San Antonio-Int'l, TX

8919 Paul B. Koonce Drive, Houston, TX 77061, USA ☎ (281) 649-6300 Tx: none Fax: (281) 649-0572 SITA: n/a
F: 1988 60 Head: Edward L. Behne Net: n/a

☐ N1073Z	Bell 206B JetRanger III	2886		0079	0296	1 AN 250-C20B	1451			
☐ N297CA	Bell 206B JetRanger	1453	N117V	0074	1095	1 AN 250-C20	1451			
☐ N39114	Bell 206B JetRanger III	3293		0081	1297	1 AN 250-C20B	1451			
☐ N59582	Bell 206B JetRanger	1460		0073	1297	1 AN 250-C20	1451			lsf pvt
☐ N707HJ	Bell 206B JetRanger III	3173	N707TV	0080	0498	1 AN 250-C20R	1451			
☐ N90280	Bell 206B JetRanger	1757		0075	1297	1 AN 250-C20	1451			lsf pvt
☐ N91EA	Bell 206B JetRanger II	1999	N222TV	0076	1295	1 AN 250-C20	1451			
☐ N9953K	Bell 206B JetRanger II	2150		0077	1297	1 AN 250-C20	1451			
☐ N151TA	Eurocopter (Aerosp.) AS350B2 AStar	2601		0092	0992	1 TU Arriel 1D1	2250			
☐ N152TA	Eurocopter (Aerosp.) AS350B1 AStar	2241	N60321	0089	1190	1 TU Arriel 1D	2200			
☐ N211TV	Eurocopter (Aerosp.) AS350B AStar	1057	N350AS	0079	0193	1 TU Arriel 1B	1950			
☐ N22TV	Eurocopter (Aerosp.) AS350B AStar	1591	N43PA	0082	0195	1 TU Arriel 1B	1950			
☐ N350EX	Eurocopter (Aerosp.) AS350B2 AStar	2789		0094	0995	1 TU Arriel 1D1	2250			
☐ N906BA	Eurocopter (Aerosp.) AS350B AStar	1479	N5786Y	0081	0195	1 TU Arriel 1B	1950			
☐ N355AH	Eurocopter (Aerosp.) AS355F2 TwinStar	5473	N300LG	0091	0995	2 AN 250-C20F	2540			
☐ N57827	Eurocopter (Aerosp.) AS355F1 TwinStar	5047		0081	0195	2 AN 250-C20F	2400			
☐ N6037J	Eurocopter (Aerosp.) AS355F2 TwinStar	5438		0090	0891	2 AN 250-C20F	2540			

TEXAS AIR CHARTERS, Inc. = TXT — Denton-Municipal, TX

5007 Airport Road, Denton, TX 76207, USA ☎ (817) 898-1200 Tx: none Fax: (817) 383-8117 SITA: n/a
F: 1993 n/a Head: James W. Huff, Jr. ICAO: TEXAS CHARTER Net: n/a

☐ N12Q	Cessna 401	401-0014		0067	0695	2 CO TSIO-520-E	2858			
☐ N150GT	Cessna 401B	401B0040		0070	0396	2 CO TSIO-520-E	2858			
☐ N6241Q	Cessna 401A	401A0041		0069	0396	2 CO TSIO-520-E	2858			
☐ N7912Q	Cessna 401B	401B0012		0070	0396	2 CO TSIO-520-E	2858			
☐ N402GR	Cessna 402C II	402C0035		0079	1096	2 CO TSIO-520-VB	3107			
☐ N402WC	Cessna 402	402-0215		0068	1195	2 CO TSIO-520-E	2858			
☐ N67887	Cessna 402C II	402C0436		0081	0698	2 CO TSIO-520-VB	3107			
☐ N710WT	Cessna 402A	402A0094		0069	0297	2 CO TSIO-520-E	2858			

THE COAST AIRLINES, Inc. (formerly AirPortland) — Portland-Int'l, OR

7700 NE Ambassador Place, Suite 104, Portland, OR 97220, USA ☎ (503) 288-8855 Tx: none Fax: (503) 288-1222 SITA: n/a
F: 1998 n/a Head: David Banmiller Net: n/a Presently being set-up. Intends to start operations during 1999 with Airbus Industrie A320 (F12Y126) aircraft.

THE CONSTELLATION GROUP, Inc. — Tucson-Avra Valley, AZ

15111 North Hayden Road, Suite 160-190, Scottsdale, AZ 85260, USA ☎ (602) 443-3967 Tx: none Fax: (602) 443-0623 SITA: n/a
F: 1991 n/a Head: Vern L. Raburn Net: http://www.connie.com Operates historical flying presentations.

☐ N494TW	Lockheed L-749A-79 (C-121A) Constellation	2601	48-609	0048	0991	4 WR R-3350	48534	24 seats		MATS-Military Air Transport Svc 8609 cs

THE JEPPESEN FOUNDATION, Inc. - Flight Operations div. (Affiliated with Jeppesen Development Inc.) — Orlando-Central Florida Regional/Sanford, FL

34 Keyes Court, Sanford, FL 32773, USA ☎ (407) 323-2040 Tx: none Fax: (407) 323-5525 SITA: n/a
F: 1994 n/a Head: Richard Jeppesen Net: n/a Conducting non-commerical medical flights in third-world-countries, using its aircraft as a flying eye-clinic.

☐ N235KT	Fairchild Ind. F-27	16	N101FG	0058	0195	2 RR Dart 514-7	18370	clinic/40 seats		016 Orlando

THE LIMITED, Inc. - Flight Dept. (Subsidiary of Limited Stores, Inc.) — Columbus-Int'l, OH

3 Limited Parkway, Columbus, OH 43230, USA ☎ (614) 479-7000 Tx: none Fax: (614) 239-7040 SITA: n/a
F: 1990 n/a Head: Leslie Wexner Net: n/a Operates executive flights exclusively for its owner.

☐ N500LS	Boeing 737-73T (BBJ)	29054 / 143	N6067E*	0098	1298	2 CFMI CFM56-7B26	69400	Executive		lsf Northwest Delaware Corp.
☐ N505LS	Boeing 727-31 (RE) (Super 27/winglets)	20115 / 735	N500LS	0069	0290	3 PW JT8D-217C/7B (BFG)	76884	Executive	AC-FM	lsf Northwest Delaware Corp. / cvtd -17

THOMAS HELICOPTERS, Inc. — Godding-Municipal, ID

1553 South 1800 East, Gooding, ID 83330, USA ☎ (208) 934-8298 Tx: none Fax: (208) 934-5934 SITA: n/a
F: 1974 n/a Head: Rodney M. Thomas Net: n/a

☐ N8653F	MD Helicopters MD 500D (Hughes 369D)	180256D		0078	0286	1 AN 250-C20B	1361			
☐ N2253A	Sikorsky S-58H	58-1396	148809	0060	0689	1 WR R-1820	5897			cvtd UH-34D

THUNDERBIRD AIR (Anthony K. Oney dba) — Anchorage-Lake Hood SPB, AK

2529 Curlew Circle, Anchorage, AK 99515, USA ☎ (907) 248-9648 Tx: none Fax: (907) 344-4870 SITA: n/a
F: 1993 n/a Head: Anthony K. Oney Net: n/a

☐ N1822R	Cessna A185F Skywagon	18502537		0074	1093	1 CO IO-520-D	1520			Floats / Wheel-Skis

TIGER CONTRACT CARGO (Tejas Avionics, Inc. dba) — Georgetown-Municipal, TX

205 Corsair Drive, Georgetown, TX 78628-2308, USA ☎ (512) 863-9567 Tx: none Fax: (512) 863-6986 SITA: n/a
F: 1998 n/a Head: Rob Diver Net: n/a

☐ N973AT	Convair 340-70 (C-131B)	257	N92102	0555	0398	2 PW R-2800	21772	Freighter		lsf pvt

443 registration type of aircraft cn/fn ex/ex* mfd del powered by mtow kg configuration selcal name/fln/specialitites/remarks

TIKCHIK AIRVENTURES (Roderick M. Grant dba)　　　　　　　　　　　　　　　　　　　　　　　　　　　Dillingham, AK

Box 71, Dillingham, AK 99576, USA　☎ (907) 842-5841　Tx: none　Fax: (907) 842-3211　SITA: n/a
F: 1993　♦♦♦ n/a　Head: Roderick M. Grant　Net: n/a　Aircraft below MTOW 1361kg: Piper PA-18 (on Floats / Wheel-Skis)

registration	type of aircraft	cn/fn	ex/ex*	mfd	del	powered by	mtow kg	configuration	selcal	name/fln/specialtites/remarks
☐ N2532S	Cessna A185F Skywagon	18502246		0073	1196	1 CO IO-520-D	1520			Floats / Wheel-Skis
☐ N911W	De Havilland DHC-2 Beaver I	616	C-FDLV	0054	0694	1 PW R-985	2313			Floats / Wheel-Skis

TIMBERLAND HELICOPTER SERVICES (Timberland Logging Forest Products, Inc. dba)　　　　　　　　Ashland-Timberland Helipad, OR

PO Box 370, Ashland, OR 97520, USA　☎ (541) 488-2880　Tx: none　Fax: (541) 488-2755　SITA: n/a
F: 1981　♦♦♦ n/a　Head: Robert Ferreira　Net: n/a　Aircraft below MTOW 1361kg: Hughes 369HS (500C)

☐ N1600Q	MD Helicopters MD 500E (Hughes 369E)	0200E		0086	0997	1 AN 250-C20B	1361			
☐ N16673	Bell 206B JetRanger III	2088		0066	1196	1 AN 250-C20B	1451			cvtd JetRanger II
☐ N656TL	Bell 206B JetRanger III	656	N7908J	0071	0185	1 AN 250-C20B	1451			cvtd 206A

TIMBERLINE AIR SERVICE, Inc.　　　　　　　　　　　　　　　　　　　　　　　　　　　　　　　Alpine-Private Heliport, OR

24155 Hewett Road, Alpine, OR 97456-9428, USA　☎ (541) 847-5199　Tx: none　Fax: (541) 847-5813　SITA: n/a
F: 1983　♦♦♦ n/a　Head: James B. Crawford, Jr.　Net: n/a

☐ N154TL	Bell UH-1E (204)	6155	154770	0068	0897	1 LY T53-L-13	3856			
☐ N155TL	Bell UH-1E (204)	6164	N157RR	0068	0797	1 LY T53-L-13	3856			
☐ N157LC	Bell UH-1L (204)	6215	157856	0068	0387	1 LY T53-L-13	3856			

TMC AIRLINES = TMM (Traffic Management Corporation dba)　　　　　　　　　　　　　　　　　　Detroit-Ypsilanti, MI

836 Willow Run Airport, Ypsilanti, MI 48198-0836, USA　☎ (734) 481-9149　Tx: none　Fax: (734) 481-9182　SITA: n/a
F: 1994　♦♦♦ n/a　Head: James H. Loree　ICAO: WILLOW RUN　Net: n/a

☐ N340HA	Lockheed L-188C (F) Electra	1109	N172PS	0059	1198	4 AN 501-D13A	52617	Freighter		lsf ZAN / cvtd L-188C
☐ N344HA	Lockheed L-188A (F) Electra	1038	N5525	0059	1198	4 AN 501-D13A	51256	Freighter		lsf ZAN / cvtd L-188A
☐ N346HA	Lockheed L-188A (F) Electra	1043	N61AJ	0059	1198	4 AN 501-D13A	51256	Freighter		lsf ZAN / cvtd L-188A
☐ N811TC	Boeing (Douglas) DC-8-55F (JT)	45883 / 308	N52958	0067	1294	4 PW JT3D-3B (HK2/BAC)	147418	Freighter		lsf Chrysler Corp/sublst Contract Cargo
☐ N812TC	Boeing (Douglas) DC-8-55F (FM)	45764 / 251	N907R	0066	1294	4 PW JT3D-3B (HK2/BAC)	147418	Freighter		lsf Chrysler Corp. / cvtd -55

TODD'S FLYING SERVICE, Inc.　　　　　　　　　　　　　　　　　　　　　　　　　　　　　Long Prairie-Todd Field, MN

2699 NE 110 Ave, Ankeny, IA 50021, USA　☎ (515) 964-0380　Tx: none　Fax: (515) 964-7646　SITA: n/a
F: 1970　♦♦♦ n/a　Head: Douglas A. Todd　Net: n/a

☐ N171H	Beech Bonanza S35	D-7959		0065	1278	1 CO IO-520-B	1497			
☐ N5678K	Beech Baron B55 (95-B55)	TC-762		0064	1090	2 CO IO-470-L	2313			
☐ N7680N	Beech Baron B55 (95-B55)	TC-1154		0068	0693	2 CO IO-470-L	2313			
☐ N9683V	Beech Baron B55 (95-B55)	TC-953		0065	0191	2 CO IO-470-L	2313			
☐ N5445U	Beech Baron 58	TH-1044		0079	1087	2 CO IO-520-CB	2449			
☐ N7276R	Beech Baron 58	TH-581		0074	0890	2 CO IO-520-C	2449			
☐ N7278R	Beech Baron 58	TH-582		0074	0696	2 CO IO-520-C	2449			
☐ N122Y	Beech Queen Air A65	LC-299	C-GSND	0068	0894	2 LY IGSO-480-A1E6	3719			
☐ N128Z	Beech Queen Air B80 (65-B80)	LD-426		0070	0694	2 LY IGSO-540-A1D	3992			

TOLAIR Services, Inc. = TI / TOL　　　　　　　　　　　　　　　　　　　　San Juan-Luis Munoz Marin Int'l, PR　TOLAIR

PO Box 37670, Airport Station, San Juan, PR 00937-0670, USA　☎ (787) 791-5235　Tx: none　Fax: (787) 791-8385　SITA: n/a
F: 1983　♦♦♦ 63　Head: Jorge A. Toledo　ICAO: TOL AIR　Net: n/a

☐ N4161W	Piper PA-32-300 Cherokee SIX	32-40234		0067	1191	1 LY IO-540-K1A5	1542			
☐ N290T	Beech Baron D55	TE-558	N244UC	0068	0493	2 CO IO-520-C	2404			
☐ N722TT	AAC (Ted Smith) Aerostar 600A	60-0285-108	N122TT	0075	1195	2 LY IO-540-K1F5	2495			
☐ N138LS	Cessna 402B	402B0861		0075	0295	2 CO TSIO-520-E	2858			
☐ N69374	Cessna 402B	402B0520		0073	0594	2 CO TSIO-520-E	2858			
☐ N87280	Cessna 402B II	402B1099		0076	0790	2 CO TSIO-520-E	2858			
☐ N28V	Beech E18S	BA-130		0056	0595	2 PW R-985-AN14B	4218	Freighter		
☐ N52A	Beech E18S	BA-114		0055	0297	2 PW R-985-AN14B	4218	Freighter		
☐ N779T	Beech H18	BA-618	N220WH	0062	0590	2 PW R-985-AN14B	4491	Freighter		
☐ N780T	Boeing (Douglas) DC-3C (C-47B-1-DL)	20865	N80617	0044	0690	2 PW R-1830	12202	Freighter		
☐ N781T	Boeing (Douglas) DC-3C (R4D-1)	4306	N92HA	0042	0190	2 PW R-1830	12202	Freighter		
☐ N782T	Boeing (Douglas) DC-3C (C-47-DL)	4382	N722A	0042	0690	2 PW R-1830	12202	Freighter		
☐ N784T	Boeing (Douglas) DC-3C (C-47-DL)	6054	N5117X	0041	1290	2 PW R-1830	12202	Y30		
☐ N147JR	Convair 240 (T-29C-CO)	403	N154PA	0054	0194	2 PW R-2800	18956	Freighter		

TOMBO AVIATION Inc. = (TOMB) (Subsidiary of Mitsui & Co. Ltd, Tokyo/Japan)　　　　　　　　　　Long Beach, CA

3760 Kilroy Airport Way, Suite 260, Long Beach, CA 90806, USA　☎ (562) 988-2688　Tx: n/a　Fax: (562) 988-2694　SITA: n/a
F: 1990　♦♦♦ 8　Head: Sho Takasugi　Net: n/a　New and used aircraft leasing, sales and financing company.
Owner / lessor of following (main) aircraft types: Boeing 737-700 (on order), McDonnell Douglas DC-9-41 & MD-11.　Aircraft leased from TOMB are listed and mentioned as such under the leasing carriers.

TOP COVER FOR ALASKA (Timothy Veenstra dba)　　　　　　　　　　　　　　　　　　　　　　　Wasilla, AK

PO Box 879050, Wasilla, AK 99687, USA　☎ (907) 357-1501　Tx: none　Fax: (907) 357-1500　SITA: n/a
F: 1990　♦♦♦ n/a　Head: Timothy S. Veenstra　Net: n/a

| ☐ N72171 | Bell UH-1H (205) | 4788 | 65-9744 | 0065 | 0898 | 1 LY T53-L-13 | 4309 | | | cvtd UH-1D |

TOWER AIR, Inc. = FF / TOW　　　　　　　　　　　　　　　　　　　　　　　　　　New York-JFK, NY　TowerAir

Hangar 17, JFK Int'l Airport, Jamaica, NY 11430, USA　☎ (718) 553-4300　Tx: 645562　Fax: (718) 553-4312　SITA: n/a
F: 1982　♦♦♦ 1850　Head: Morris K. Nachtomi　IATA: 305　ICAO: TEE AIR　Net: http://www.towerair.com

☐ N104TR	Boeing 747-237B (SF)	21446 / 318	VT-EFJ	0078	1098	4 PW JT9D-7J	362874	Freighter		lsf TRIT / cvtd -237B
☐ N602FF	Boeing 747-124	19734 / 58	N747BA	0770	0584	4 PW JT9D-7A	332937	Y480	AH-DJ	
☐ N603FF	Boeing 747-130	19746 / 12	N780T	0770	0493	4 PW JT9D-7A	332937	Y480	AH-DG	
☐ N606FF	Boeing 747-136	20273 / 184	N17126	0372	0391	4 PW JT9D-7A	332937	Y480	DJ-AC	
☐ N607PE	Boeing 747-238B	20011 / 162	N747BM	1071	0493	4 PW JT9D-7J	356070	Y480	DM-EL	
☐ N608FF	Boeing 747-131	19672 / 28	N93106	0470	0392	4 PW JT9D-7A	332937	Y480	EF-AH	
☐ N609FF	Boeing 747-121	20354 / 142	N659PA	0771	0893	4 PW JT9D-7A	332937	Y480	LM-HK	std MZJ
☐ N610FF	Boeing 747-282B	20501 / 178	N301TW	0272	0493	4 PW JT9D-7A	351534	Y480	CK-DF	std JFK
☐ N611FF	Boeing 747-282B	20502 / 189	N302TW	0572	0493	4 PW JT9D-7A	351534	Y480	DH-FL	
☐ N616FF	Boeing 747-212B	21939 / 449	G-TKYO	0080	1294	4 PW JT9D-7Q	371945	Y480	GJ-DE	
☐ N617FF	Boeing 747-121 (SF)	19650 / 24	N490GX	0070	0595	4 PW JT9D-7A	332937	Freighter	HK-EJ	lsf GECA / cvtd -121
☐ N6186	Boeing 747-212B	21439 / 312	N723PA	0977	0992	4 PW JT9D-7J	351534	Y480	HJ-FK	lsf CITG
☐ N618FF	Boeing 747-212B	21937 / 419	G-VRGN	0080	0395	4 PW JT9D-7Q	371945	Y480	AC-EH	
☐ N619FF	Boeing 747-212B	21316 / 309	N504DC	0677	0196	4 PW JT9D-7J	362878	Y480	CM-GK	
☐ N620FF	Boeing 747-212B	21162 / 283	N511P	0376	0196	4 PW JT9D-7J	351534	Y480	EF-KL	
☐ N621FF	Boeing 747-259B (SF)	21730 / 372	EI-CEO	0079	0295	4 PW JT9D-7Q	352900	Freighter	CF-GK	cvtd -259B (M)
☐ N622FF	Boeing 747-283B	22496 / 540	EI-BZA	0081	0698	4 PW JT9D-7Q	371945	Y480	BE-JK	lsf GECA
☐ N623FF	Boeing 747-2F6B	22382 / 498	N744PR	0080	0398	4 GE CF6-50E2	371945	Y480		lsf GECA

TRACINDA – Flight Dept. (Flight Dept. of Tracinda, Corp.)　　　　　　　　　　　　　　　　　　　Van Nuys, CA

150 South Rodeo Drive, Suite 250, Beverly Hills, CA 90212, USA　☎ (310) 271-0638　Tx: none　Fax: (310) 271-3416　SITA: n/a
F: 1981　♦♦♦ n/a　Head: Tracy Jackson　Net: n/a　Operates executive flights exclusively for its parent company.

| ☐ N50TC | Boeing 737-72T (BBJ) | 29024 / 131 | N1786B* | 0098 | 1198 | 2 CFMI CFM56-7B26 | 69400 | Executive | | |
| ☐ N341TC | Boeing 727-22 | 19148 / 473 | N7084U | 0067 | 0781 | 3 PW JT8D-7B (HK3/FDX) | 72802 | Executive | KM-DE | |

TRADEWINDS AIRLINES, Inc. = WI / TDX (formerly Tradewinds International Airlines)　　Greensboro-Piedmont Triad Int'l, NC　TradeWinds

PO Box 35329, Greensboro, NC 27425-5329, USA　☎ (336) 668-7500　Tx: 574360 blueair gbo　Fax: (336) 668-7554　SITA: n/a
F: 1973　♦♦♦ 180　Head: Larry Scheevel　IATA: 490　ICAO: TRADEWINDS EXPRESS

☐ N104NL	Lockheed L-1011-385-1-15 TriStar 200	193U-1203	A4O-TB	0080	0598	3 RR RB211-524B4	211374	Y345		Nancy Lea / lsf INTL
☐ N310SS	Lockheed L-1011-385-1 TriStar 1	193C-1096	N717DA	0074	0398	3 RR RB211-22B	199581	Y345		Suzanne Sabina / lsf INTL
☐ N311EA	Lockheed L-1011-385-1 TriStar 1 (F)	193A-1012		0072	0191	3 RR RB211-22B	195045	Freighter		Sara Kate / lsf Arena Avn/cvtd Tri.1
☐ N75AA	Lockheed L-1011-385-1-15 TriStar 200	193U-1201	A4O-TA	0080	0398	3 RR RB211-524B4	211374	Y345		Alison Ann / lsf INTL
☐ N814SD	Lockheed L-1011-385-1 TriStar 1	193A-1006	N782DL	0072	1298	3 RR RB211-22B	195045	Y345		lsf INTL
☐ N826CR	Lockheed L-1011-385-1 TriStar 1	193A-1141	N788DL	0076	0498	3 RR RB211-22B	199581	Y345		Charlotte Rose / lsf INTL
☐ N900D	Lockheed L-1011-385-1-15 TriStar 200	193A-1056	A4O-TV	0073	1298	3 RR RB211-524B4	211374	Y345		lsf INTL / cvtd TriStar 100
☐ N913PM	Lockheed L-1011-385-1-15 TriStar 200	193U-1223	A4O-TT	0081	1298	3 RR RB211-524B4	211374	Y345		lsf INTL
☐ N926VA	Lockheed L-1011-385-1-15 TriStar 200	193U-1140	A4O-TZ	0076	1298	3 RR RB211-524B4	211374	Y345		lsf INTL / cvtd TriStar 100

TRAIL RIDGE AIR, Inc. (Seasonal May-October ops only)　　　　　　　　　　　Anchorage-Lake Hood SPB, AK　TRAIL RIDGE AIR

PO Box 111377, Anchorage, AK 99511, USA　☎ (907) 248-0838　Tx: none　Fax: (907) 248-2658　SITA: n/a
F: 1982　♦♦♦ 4　Head: James M. Jensen　Net: n/a

☐ N4649U	Cessna U206G Stationair 6 II	U20605028		0079	0298	1 CO IO-520-F	1633			lsf pvt / Floats
☐ N310NR	De Havilland DHC-2 Beaver I	396	52-6060	0052	0791	1 PW R-985	2313			lsf J.G. Edens Trustee / Floats
☐ N6LU	De Havilland DHC-2 Beaver I	908	N97T	0056	0790	1 PW R-985	2313			lsf pvt / Floats

444　registration　type of aircraft　　　cn/fn　　ex/ex*　mfd　del　powered by　　mtow kg　configuration　selcal　name/fln/specialtites/remarks

TRANS AIR = P6 / MUI (Trans Executive Airlines of Hawaii, Inc. dba)

Honolulu-Int'l, HI

PO Box 29239, Honolulu, HI 96820, USA ☎ (808) 833-5557 Tx: none Fax: (808) 833-2636 SITA: n/a
F: 1980 ⁂ 18 Head: Teimour Riahi IATA: 356 ICAO: MAUI Net: n/a

☐ N3949C	Cessna 402B	402B0826		0075	0692	2 CO TSIO-520-E	2858			lsf pvt
☐ N4544Q	Cessna 402A	402A0044		0069	0185	2 CO TSIO-520-E	2858			Touradj
☐ N770Q	Cessna 402A	402A0077		0069	0388	2 CO TSIO-520-E	2858			

TRANS-AIR-LINK, Corporation – TAL = GJB

Miami-Int'l, FL

PO Box 521298, Miami, FL 33152, USA ☎ (305) 681-0339 Tx: none Fax: (305) 681-2910 SITA: n/a
F: 1979 ⁂ 60 Head: Hernando Gutierrez, Jr. ICAO: SKY TRUCK Net: n/a

☐ N841TA	Boeing (Douglas) DC-6BF	44891 / 649	CC-PJG	0056	0882	4 PW R-2800-CB16	47083	Freighter		lsf Trans Air Supply Corp. / cvtd DC-6B
☐ N870TA	Boeing (Douglas) DC-6A	45518 / 998	YV-293C	0058	0884	4 PW R-2800-CB16	47083	Freighter		lsf Trans Air Supply Corp.
☐ N874TA	Boeing (Douglas) DC-6A (C-118A-DO)	44641 / 584	N96039	0055	1286	4 PW R-2800-CB16	47083	Freighter		lsf Trans Air Supply Corp.
☐ N869TA	Boeing (Douglas) DC-7CF	45188 / 837	N103LM	0057	0285	4 WR R-3350-93	58513	Freighter		lsf T.A.Supply/sub-lst Filair/cvtdDC-7C

TRANS-ALASKA HELICOPTERS, Inc.

Anchorage-Merrill Field, AK

819 Orca Street, Anchorage, AK 99501, USA ☎ (907) 274-7762 Tx: none Fax: (907) 264-6491 SITA: n/a
F: 1968 ⁂ 8 Head: Melvin C. Nading Net: n/a

☐ N86TA	Bell 206B JetRanger	1647		0075	0575	1 AN 250-C20	1451			
☐ N87TA	Bell 206B JetRanger III	1996		0076	0776	1 AN 250-C20B	1451			cvtd JetRanger II
☐ N88TA	Bell 206B JetRanger III	2990		0080	0680	1 AN 250-C20B	1451			
☐ N91TA	Bell 206B JetRanger III	3310		0081	0681	1 AN 250-C20B	1451			
☐ N6125U	Cessna U206G Stationair 6 II	U20605334		0079	0697	1 CO IO-520-F	1633			
☐ N93TA	Bell 206L-1 LongRanger II	45715	N2159K*	0082	0682	1 AN 250-C28B	1882			
☐ N94TA	Bell 206L-3 LongRanger III	51449		0091	0391	1 AN 250-C30P	1882			

TRANS AMERICAN CHARTER, Ltd (Executive Flight Management dba)

Chicago-Midway, IL

5923 South Central Ave, Chicago, IL 60638, USA ☎ (773) 735-6906 Tx: none Fax: (773) 735-5622 SITA: n/a
F: 1984 ⁂ n/a Head: Lincoln Francis Net: n/a

☐ N41EB	Cessna 525 CitationJet	525-0116	N52144	0095	0995	2 WRR FJ44-1A	4717			lsf Musikantow Consulting & Management
☐ N949SW	Beech King Air B100	BE-34	N203KA	0077		2 GA TPE331-6-252B	5352			lsf Truck Components Inc.

TRANS CONTINENTAL AIRLINES, Inc. = TCN (Subsidiary of Kalitta American International Airways)

Detroit-Willow Run, MI

251 Jackson Plaza, Ana Arbor, MI 48103, USA ☎ (734) 623-0500 Tx: none Fax: (734) 623-0540 SITA: n/a
F: 1972 ⁂ 80 Head: Scott D. Kalitta IATA: 837 ICAO: TRANSCON Net: n/a

☐ N1186Z	Boeing 727-21C	19134 / 289	N339PA	0066	1198	3 PW JT8D-7B (HK3/RAI)	76884	Freighter		lsf pvt
☐ N721SK	Boeing 727-2B6 (F) (A)	21298 / 1246	CN-RMP	0077	1298	3 PW JT8D-15	86409	Freighter		lsf Kalitta Equipment Llc / cvtd -2B6
☐ N182SK	Boeing (Douglas) DC-8-55F (JT)	45817 / 248	N808CK	0065	0894	4 PW JT3D-3B (HK2/QNC)	140523	Freighter	CK-DH	
☐ N802CK	Boeing (Douglas) DC-8-54F	45679 / 203	N4768G	0064	0994	4 PW JT3D-3B (HK2/QNC)	142882	Freighter	CK-EH	lsf SDK Leasing Llc
☐ N184SK	Boeing (Douglas) DC-8-61F	45981 / 352	N915BV	0068	1196	4 PW JT3D-3B (HK2/BAC)	147418	Freighter	CG-EK	cvtd DC-8-61
☐ N181SK	Boeing (Douglas) DC-8-62F	45910 / 311	N803MG	0067	0895	4 PW JT3D-3B (HK3/BAC)	158757	Freighter	BC-KM	lst/opf KAC in Kuwait Aw.-cs / cvtd -62
☐ N183SK	Boeing (Douglas) DC-8-62F	45904 / 309	N1807	1167	0696	4 PW JT3D-3B (HK3/BAC)	151953	Freighter	BC-FL	cvtd (CF)
☐ N187SK	Boeing (Douglas) DC-8-62F (AF)	46022 / 417	N817EV	0067	0298	4 JT3D-3B (HK3/BAC)	151953	Freighter		

TRANS-EXEC Air Service, Inc.

Santa Monica-Municipal, CA

2828 Donald Douglas Loop North, Santa Monica, CA 90405, USA ☎ (562) 399-9435 Tx: none Fax: (562) 392-2474 SITA: n/a
F: 1979 ⁂ n/a Head: Mischa Hausserman Net: n/a

☐ N502RP	Agusta A109A	7220	N4210W	0080	0191	2 AN 250-C20B	2600			to be re-reg. N21TE
☐ N711TE	GAC (Grumman) G-1159 Gulfstream II	105	N6060	0071	1293	2 RR Spey 511-8	29393			
☐ N716TE	GAC (Grumman) G-1159 Gulfstream II	116	N23W	0072	0297	2 RR Spey 511-8	29393			

TRANS FLORIDA AIRLINES, Inc. = TFA

Daytona Beach-Regional, FL

PO Box 10150, Daytona Beach, FL 32120-0150, USA ☎ (904) 252-3053 Tx: none Fax: (904) 252-0037 SITA: n/a
F: 1966 ⁂ 22 Head: Robert D. Willman ICAO: TRANS FLORIDA Net: n/a

☐ N1020C	Convair 240-4	144	HB-IMA	0049	0376	2 PW R-2800	18956	Y44		lsf Bahama Air Ferries Inc.
☐ N1022C	Convair 240-0	147	N2642Z	0049	1281	2 PW R-2800	18956	Y44		lsf Bahama Air Ferries Inc.
☐ N12905	Convair 240-15	29	N12903	0049	0679	2 PW R-2800	18956	Y44		lsf Bahama Air Ferries Inc. / std DAB
☐ N22913	Convair 240-27 (T-29B)	316	51-7904	0052	0187	2 PW R-2800	18956	Freighter		lsf Bahama Air Ferries Inc.
☐ N295M	Convair 240-5	64	N3338N	0048	0495	2 PW R-2800	18956	Freighter		lsf Bahama Air Ferries Inc.
☐ N7761	Convair 240-23	176	YE-ABB	0050	0987	2 PW R-2800	18956	E20		lsf Bahama Air Ferries Inc. / std DAB
☐ N87949	Convair 240-17 (T-29A)	202	49-1935	0050	0492	2 PW R-2800	18956	Freighter		lsf Bahama Air Ferries Inc.

TRANS-GULF AVIATION, Inc. (Subsidiary of Trans-Gulf Airways, Inc.)

Slidell, LA

406 Cardinal Drive, Slidell, LA 70458, USA ☎ (504) 646-0549 Tx: none Fax: (504) 646-0549 SITA: n/a
F: 1991 ⁂ n/a Head: Tony B. Russell Net: n/a

☐ N962AA	Beech E18S	BA-442	N901NC	0059	0892	2 PW R-985-AN14B	4581	Freighter		

TRANS-GULF SEAPLANE SERVICE, Inc.

New Orleans-Int'l/Moisant Field, LA

Rte 5, Box 287AC, New Orleans, LA 70129, USA ☎ (504) 254-0621 Tx: none Fax: (504) 254-0622 SITA: n/a
F: 1960 ⁂ n/a Head: Steve Littleton Net: n/a

☐ N1997U	Cessna A185E Skywagon	18501766		0070	0682	1 CO IO-520-D	1520			Amphibian

TRANS INTERNATIONAL EXPRESS – TIE = 5B (TIE Aviation, Inc. dba)

New York-JFK, NY

PO Box 300994, JFK Int'l Airport, Jamaica, NY 11430, USA ☎ (718) 244-8909 Tx: none Fax: (718) 244-8912 SITA: n/a
F: 1993 ⁂ 20 Head: Joseph Manor IATA: 336 Net: http://www.iflytie.com

☐ N63977	Piper PA-23-250 Aztec F	27-7854106		0078	0296	2 LY IO-540-C4B5	2359	Y4 / Freighter		
☐ N313RA	Piper PA-31-350 Navajo Chieftain	31-8052069	N333BM	0080	0198	2 LY TIO-540-J2BD	3175	Y7 / Freighter		
☐ N159CC	Shorts 360-300 (SD3-60)	SH3759	G-BPXM*	0089	0898	2 PWC PT6A-67R	12292	Y36		lsf Lynrise Air Lease
☐ N350TA	Shorts 360-300 (SD3-60)	SH3757	N265GA	0089	0598	2 PWC PT6A-67R	12292	Y36		lsf Lynrise Air Lease

TRANSMERIDIAN AIRLINES = T9 / TRZ (Prime Air, Inc. dba / Subsidiary of Translift Airways, Ltd)

Chicago-O'Hare Int'l, IL

680 Thornton Way, Lithia Springs, GA 30122, USA ☎ (770) 732-6901 Tx: none Fax: (770) 732-9801 SITA: n/a
F: 1995 ⁂ n/a Head: Glen D. Schaab ICAO: TRANS-MERIDIAN Net: http://www.transmeridian-airlines.com

☐ N347TM	Airbus Industrie A320-231	347	B-22306	0092	1298	2 IAE V2500-A1	73500	Y174		lsf KAWA
☐ N573DC	Airbus Industrie A320-232	573	CS-MAD	0096	0299	2 IAE V2527-A5	77000	Corporate 50Pax		lsf AMU/sub-lst/opf DaimlerChrylser Avn
☐ EI-TLG	Airbus Industrie A320-231	428	C-GMPG	0094	1198	2 IAE V2500-A1	77000	Y180	CR-EH	lsf / opb TLA in winter
☐ EI-TLI	Airbus Industrie A320-231	405	N141LF	0093	1198	2 IAE V2500-A1	75500	Y180	JQ-CR	lsf / opb TLA in winter
☐ N280US	Boeing 727-251 (A)	21159 / 1179		1275	0596	3 PW JT8D-15/-15A	80059	Y160		lsf AFGR / sub-lst/opf LAV

TRANS NORTH AVIATION, Ltd

Eagle River, WI

PO Box 1445, Eagle River, WI 54521, USA ☎ (715) 479-6777 Tx: none Fax: (715) 479-8178 SITA: n/a
F: 1980 ⁂ 22 Head: Ronald J. Schaberg Net: http://www.travel-care.com Aircraft below MTOW 1361 kg: Cessna 172.

☐ N377JS	Cessna 340A II	340A0672		0079	0896	2 CO TSIO-520-NB	2717			
☐ N4599F	Cessna 340A II	340A0652		0079	1197	2 CO TSIO-520-NB	2717			
☐ N59773	Piper PA-31-350 Navajo Chieftain	31-7652044		0075	0489	2 LY TIO-540-J2BD	3175			

TRANS STATES AIRLINES, Inc. = 9N / LOF (TW Express)) (fomly Resort Air, Inc.)

St. Louis-Lambert Int'l, MO

9275 Genaire Drive, St. Louis, MO 63134-1912, USA ☎ (573) 895-8700 Tx: none Fax: (573) 895-1040 SITA: n/a
F: 1982 ⁂ 930 Head: Hulas Kanodia IATA: 414 ICAO: WATERSKI Net: http://www.transstates.net Most aircraft are operated as TRANS WORLD EXPRESS (in such colors & & titles), a commuter system to provide feeder connection at TWA major hubs, using TW flight numbers. 10 Jetstream 31 aircraft are operated in conjunction/code-sharing with Alaska Airlines (as an Alaska Airlines Commuter), Northwest Airlines (as Northwest Airlink) & US Airways (as US Airways) using AS, NW & US flight numbers but in own Trans State Airlines-colors. On option: further 18 Embraer RJ 145

☐ N337TE	BAe 3201 Jetstream 32	929	G-31-929*	0091	0591	2 GA TPE331-12UAR-701H	7350	Y19		op in Trans World Express-colors
☐ N338TE	BAe 3201 Jetstream 32	932	G-31-932*	0091	0691	2 GA TPE331-12UAR-701H	7350	Y19		op in Trans World Express-colors
☐ N339TE	BAe 3201 Jetstream 32	935	G-31-935*	0091	0791	2 GA TPE331-12UAR-701H	7350	Y19		op in Trans World Express-colors
☐ N340TE	BAe 3201 Jetstream 32	939	G-31-939*	0091	0891	2 GA TPE331-12UAR-701H	7350	Y19		op in Trans World Express-colors
☐ N341TE	BAe 3201 Jetstream 32	950	G-31-950*	0091	1291	2 GA TPE331-12UAR-701H	7350	Y19		op in Trans World Express-colors
☐ N342TE	BAe 3201 Jetstream 32	954	G-31-955*	0091	1291	2 GA TPE331-12UAR-701H	7350	Y19		op in Trans World Express-colors
☐ N343TE	BAe 3201 Jetstream 32	955	G-31-955*	0091	0192	2 GA TPE331-12UAR-701H	7350	Y19		op in Trans World Express-colors
☐ N422AM	BAe 3201 Jetstream 32	856	G-31-856*	0089	0191	2 GA TPE331-12UAR-701H	7350	Y19		op in Trans World Express-colors
☐ N423AM	BAe 3201 Jetstream 32	858	G-31-858*	0089	0191	2 GA TPE331-12UAR-701H	7350	Y19		op in Trans World Express-colors
☐ N424AM	BAe 3201 Jetstream 32	865	G-31-865*	0089	0191	2 GA TPE331-12UAR-701H	7350	Y19		op in Trans World Express-colors
☐ N425AM	BAe 3201 Jetstream 32	870	G-31-870*	0089	0191	2 GA TPE331-12UAR-701H	7350	Y19		op in Trans World Express-colors
☐ N426AM	BAe 3201 Jetstream 32	874	G-31-874*	0089	0191	2 GA TPE331-12UAR-701H	7350	Y19		op in Trans World Express-colors
☐ N427AM	BAe 3201 Jetstream 32	876	G-31-876*	0090	0191	2 GA TPE331-12UAR-701H	7350	Y19		op in Trans World Express-colors
☐ N428AM	BAe 3201 Jetstream 32	877	G-31-877*	0090	0191	2 GA TPE331-12UAR-701H	7350	Y19		op in Trans World Express-colors
☐ N429AM	BAe 3201 Jetstream 32	879	G-31-879*	0090	0191	2 GA TPE331-12UAR-701H	7350	Y19		op in Trans World Express-colors
☐ N430AM	BAe 3201 Jetstream 32	880	G-31-880*	0090	0191	2 GA TPE331-12UAR-701H	7350	Y19		op in Trans World Express-colors
☐ N431AM	BAe 3201 Jetstream 32	881	G-31-881*	0090	0191	2 GA TPE331-12UAR-701H	7350	Y19		op in Trans World Express-colors
☐ N432AM	BAe 3201 Jetstream 32	883	G-31-883*	0090	0191	2 GA TPE331-12UAR-701H	7350	Y19		op in Trans World Express-colors
☐ N433AM	BAe 3201 Jetstream 32	885	G-31-885*	0090	0191	2 GA TPE331-12UAR-701H	7350	Y19		op in Trans World Express-colors
☐ N434AM	BAe 3201 Jetstream 32	887	G-31-887*	0090	0191	2 GA TPE331-12UAR-701H	7350	Y19		op in Trans World Express-colors

445 registration type of aircraft cn/fn ex/ex* mfd del powered by mtow kg configuration selcal name/fln/specialitites/remarks

☐ N435AM	BAe 3201 Jetstream 32	889	G-31-889*	0090	0191	2 GA TPE331-12UAR-701H	7350	Y19		op in Trans World Express-colors
☐ N436AM	BAe 3201 Jetstream 32	891	G-31-891*	0090	0191	2 GA TPE331-12UAR-701H	7350	Y19		op in Trans World Express-colors
☐ N859AE	BAe 3201 Jetstream 32	859	G-31-859*	0089	0494	2 GA TPE331-12UAR-704H	7350	Y19		
☐ N860AE	BAe 3201 Jetstream 32	860	G-31-860*	0089	0494	2 GA TPE331-12UAR-704H	7350	Y19		
☐ N862JX	BAe 3201 Jetstream 32	862	N862AE	0089	0197	2 GA TPE331-12UAR-704H	7350	Y19		
☐ N864AE	BAe 3201 Jetstream 32	864	G-31-864*	0089	0394	2 GA TPE331-12UAR-704H	7350	Y19		
☐ N866AE	BAe 3201 Jetstream 32	866	G-31-866*	0089	0794	2 GA TPE331-12UAR-704H	7350	Y19		
☐ N867AE	BAe 3201 Jetstream 32	867	G-31-867*	0089	0794	2 GA TPE331-12UAR-704H	7350	Y19		
☐ N871JX	BAe 3201 Jetstream 32	871	N871AE	0089	1194	2 GA TPE331-12UAR-704H	7350	Y19		
☐ N872AE	BAe 3201 Jetstream 32	872	G-31-872*	0089	0494	2 GA TPE331-12UAR-704H	7350	Y19		
☐ N875JX	BAe 3201 Jetstream 32	875	N875AE	0090	0197	2 GA TPE331-12UAR-704H	7350	Y19		
☐ N926AE	BAe 3201 Jetstream 32	926	G-31-926*	0091	0997	2 GA TPE331-12UAR-704H	7350	Y19		lsf BAMT
☐ N971JX	BAe 3201 Jetstream 32	971	N971AE	0092	1193	2 GA TPE331-12UAR-704H	7350	Y19		
☐ N972JX	BAe 3201 Jetstream 32	972	N972AE	0092	1293	2 GA TPE331-12UAR-704H	7350	Y19		
☐ N973JX	BAe 3201 Jetstream 32	973	N973AE	0092	1293	2 GA TPE331-12UAR-704H	7350	Y19		
☐ N550HK	BAe 4101 Jetstream 41	41039	G-4-039*	0094	0195	2 GA TPE331-14HR-805H	10886	Y29		op in Trans World Express-colors
☐ N551HK	BAe 4101 Jetstream 41	41040	G-4-040*	0094	0195	2 GA TPE331-14HR-805H	10886	Y29		op in Trans World Express-colors
☐ N552HK	BAe 4101 Jetstream 41	41057	G-4-057*	0095	0595	2 GA TPE331-14HR-805H	10886	Y29		op in Trans World Express-colors
☐ N553HK	BAe 4101 Jetstream 41	41066	G-4-066*	0095	0795	2 GA TPE331-14HR-805H	10886	Y29		op in Trans World Express-colors
☐ N554HK	BAe 4101 Jetstream 41	41067	G-4-067*	0095	0795	2 GA TPE331-14HR-805H	10886	Y29		op in Trans World Express-colors
☐ N555HK	BAe 4101 Jetstream 41	41072	G-4-072*	0095	0995	2 GA TPE331-14HR-805H	10886	Y29		op in Trans World Express-colors
☐ N556HK	BAe 4101 Jetstream 41	41073	G-4-073*	0095	0995	2 GA TPE331-14HR-805H	10886	Y29		op in Trans World Express-colors
☐ N557HK	BAe 4101 Jetstream 41	41074	G-4-074*	0095	1095	2 GA TPE331-14HR-805H	10886	Y29		op in Trans World Express-colors
☐ N558HK	BAe 4101 Jetstream 41	41071	G-4-071*	0095	1195	2 GA TPE331-14HR-805H	10886	Y29		op in Trans World Express-colors
☐ N559HK	BAe 4101 Jetstream 41	41075	G-4-075*	0095	1195	2 GA TPE331-14HR-805H	10886	Y29		op in Trans World Express-colors
☐ N560HK	BAe 4101 Jetstream 41	41076	G-4-076*	0095	1195	2 GA TPE331-14HR-805H	10886	Y29		op in Trans World Express-colors
☐ N561HK	BAe 4101 Jetstream 41	41077	G-4-077*	0095	0196	2 GA TPE331-14HR-805H	10886	Y29		op in Trans World Express-colors
☐ N562HK	BAe 4101 Jetstream 41	41078	G-4-078*	0096	0196	2 GA TPE331-14HR-805H	10886	Y29		op in Trans World Express-colors
☐ N563HK	BAe 4101 Jetstream 41	41079	G-4-079*	0096	0296	2 GA TPE331-14HR-805H	10886	Y29		op in Trans World Express-colors
☐ N564HK	BAe 4101 Jetstream 41	41081	G-4-081*	0096	0396	2 GA TPE331-14HR-805H	10886	Y29		op in Trans World Express-colors
☐ N565HK	BAe 4101 Jetstream 41	41082	G-4-082*	0096	0396	2 GA TPE331-14HR-805H	10886	Y29		op in Trans World Express-colors
☐ N566HK	BAe 4101 Jetstream 41	41084	G-4-084*	0096	0496	2 GA TPE331-14HR-805H	10886	Y29		op in Trans World Express-colors
☐ N567HK	BAe 4101 Jetstream 41	41085	G-4-085*	0096	0496	2 GA TPE331-14HR-805H	10886	Y29		op in Trans World Express-colors
☐ N568HK	BAe 4101 Jetstream 41	41086	G-4-086*	0096	0496	2 GA TPE331-14HR-805H	10886	Y29		op in Trans World Express-colors
☐ N569HK	BAe 4101 Jetstream 41	41088	G-4-088*	0096	0596	2 GA TPE331-14HR-805H	10886	Y29		op in Trans World Express-colors
☐ N570HK	BAe 4101 Jetstream 41	41089	G-4-089*	0096	0696	2 GA TPE331-14HR-805H	10886	Y29		op in Trans World Express-colors
☐ N571HK	BAe 4101 Jetstream 41	41090	G-4-090*	0096	0696	2 GA TPE331-14HR-805H	10886	Y29		op in Trans World Express-colors
☐ N572HK	BAe 4101 Jetstream 41	41091	G-4-091*	0096	0796	2 GA TPE331-14HR-805H	10886	Y29		op in Trans World Express-colors
☐ N573HK	BAe 4101 Jetstream 41	41092	G-4-092*	0096	0796	2 GA TPE331-14HR-805H	10886	Y29		op in Trans World Express-colors
☐ N574HK	BAe 4101 Jetstream 41	41093	G-4-093*	0096	0896	2 GA TPE331-14HR-805H	10886	Y29		op in Trans World Express-colors
☐ N421TE	ATR 42-300	102	F-GFTO*	0088	0888	2 PWC PW120	16700	Y48		op in Trans World Express-colors
☐ N422TE	ATR 42-300	106	F-WWED*	0088	0988	2 PWC PW120	16700	Y48		op in Trans World Express-colors
☐ N423TE	ATR 42-300	119	F-WWEP*	0088	1288	2 PWC PW120	16700	Y48		op in Trans World Express-colors
☐ N424TE	ATR 42-300	124	F-WWEU*	0089	0289	2 PWC PW120	16700	Y48		op in Trans World Express-colors
☐ N425TE	ATR 42-300	125	F-WWEV*	0089	0289	2 PWC PW120	16700	Y48		op in Trans World Express-colors
☐ N426TE	ATR 42-300	228	F-WWEJ*	0091	0191	2 PWC PW120	16700	Y48		op in Trans World Express-colors
☐ N801HK	Embraer RJ145ER (EMB-145ER)	145053	PT-SZS*	0098	0598	2 AN AE3007A	20600	Y50		op in United Express-colors
☐ N802HK	Embraer RJ145ER (EMB-145ER)	145066	PT-SAJ*	0098	0798	2 AN AE3007A	20600	Y50		op in United Express-colors
☐ N803HK	Embraer RJ145ER (EMB-145ER)	145077		0098	0998	2 AN AE3007A	20600	Y50		op in United Express-colors
☐ N804HK	Embraer RJ145ER (EMB-145ER)	145082		0098	1098	2 AN AE3007A	20600	Y50		
☐ N805HK	Embraer RJ145ER (EMB-145ER)	145096				2 AN AE3007A	20600	Y50		oo-delivery 0699
☐ N806HK	Embraer RJ145ER (EMB-145ER)					2 AN AE3007A	20600	Y50		oo-delivery 0799
☐ N807HK	Embraer RJ145ER (EMB-145ER)					2 AN AE3007A	20600	Y50		oo-delivery 0999
☐ N808HK	Embraer RJ145ER (EMB-145ER)					2 AN AE3007A	20600	Y50		oo-delivery 1199
☐ N809HK	Embraer RJ145ER (EMB-145ER)					2 AN AE3007A	20600	Y50		oo-delivery 1299
☐ N810HK	Embraer RJ145ER (EMB-145ER)					2 AN AE3007A	20600	Y50		oo-delivery 0002
☐ N811HK	Embraer RJ145ER (EMB-145ER)					2 AN AE3007A	20600	Y50		oo-delivery 0003
☐ N812HK	Embraer RJ145ER (EMB-145ER)					2 AN AE3007A	20600	Y50		oo-delivery 0003
☐ N813HK	Embraer RJ145ER (EMB-145ER)					2 AN AE3007A	20600	Y50		oo-delivery 0003
☐ N814HK	Embraer RJ145ER (EMB-145ER)					2 AN AE3007A	20600	Y50		oo-delivery 0003
☐ N815HK	Embraer RJ145ER (EMB-145ER)					2 AN AE3007A	20600	Y50		oo-delivery 0004
☐ N721TE	ATR 72-202	217	F-WWEM*	0091	0391	2 PWC PW124B	21500	Y64		op in Trans World Express-colors
☐ N722TE	ATR 72-202	220	F-OGQP	0091	0591	2 PWC PW124B	21500	Y64		op in Trans World Express-colors
☐ N723TE	ATR 72-202	283	F-WWLM*	0092	0492	2 PWC PW124B	21500	Y64		op in Trans World Express-colors

TRANS WORLD AIRLINES, Inc. = TW / TWA (formerly Transcontinental & Western Air) — Kansas City & St. Louis, MO / New York, NY

TWA

One City Centre, 515 North 6th Street, St. Louis, MO 63101, USA ☎ (573) 589-3101 Tx: n/a Fax: (573) 589-3125 SITA: n/a

F: 1930 ✲✲✲ 25000 Head: Gerald L. Gitner IATA: 015 ICAO: TWA Net: http://www.twa.com A commuter system to provide feeder connection at TW major hubs is operated under the marketing name TRANS WORLD EXPRESS by: TRANS STATES AIRLINES. For details – see under that company.On order (Letter of intent): 50 Airbus Industrie A318 (F16Y95) for delivery starting 2003.

☐ N969Z	Boeing (Douglas) DC-9-15	47001 / 94	YV-18C	0067	1086	2 PW JT8D-7B	41141	F8Y60	BL-AE	8169
☐ N970Z	Boeing (Douglas) DC-9-15	45772 / 30		0066	1086	2 PW JT8D-7B	41141	F8Y60	BJ-HM	8170
☐ N971Z	Boeing (Douglas) DC-9-15	45773 / 39		0566	1086	2 PW JT8D-7B	41141	F8Y60	BJ-KL	8171
☐ N973Z	Boeing (Douglas) DC-9-15	47033 / 147		0767	1086	2 PW JT8D-7B	41141	F8Y60	BK-AE	8173 / std MCI
☐ N975Z	Boeing (Douglas) DC-9-15	47035 / 178		1067	1086	2 PW JT8D-7B	41141	F8Y60	BK-AH	8175
☐ N490SA	Boeing (Douglas) DC-9-15	45798 / 59		1066	1086	2 PW JT8D-7B	41141	F8Y60	BK-EF	8190
☐ N491SA	Boeing (Douglas) DC-9-15	45799 / 69		0066	1086	2 PW JT8D-7B	41141	F8Y60	BK-FG	8191
☐ N920L	Boeing (Douglas) DC-9-32	47734 / 868		1077	1086	2 PW JT8D-9A	48988	F8Y90	BL-FH	8220 / lsf POLA
☐ N921L	Boeing (Douglas) DC-9-32	47107 / 236	N3328L	0067	1086	2 PW JT8D-9A (HK3/ABS)	48988	F8Y90	BL-FG	8221 / lsf POLA
☐ N922L	Boeing (Douglas) DC-9-32	47108 / 251	N3329L	0168	1086	2 PW JT8D-9A (HK3/ABS)	48988	F8Y90	BL-FJ	8222 / lsf POLA
☐ N923L	Boeing (Douglas) DC-9-32	47109 / 252	N3330L	0168	1086	2 PW JT8D-9A (HK3/ABS)	48988	F8Y90	CD-EH	8223 / lsf POLA
☐ N924L	Boeing (Douglas) DC-9-32	47324 / 469	N1276L	0369	1086	2 PW JT8D-9A (HK3/ABS)	48988	F8Y90	CD-EM	8224 / lsf POLA
☐ N925L	Boeing (Douglas) DC-9-32	47357 / 476	N1278L	0069	1086	2 PW JT8D-9A (HK3/ABS)	48988	F8Y90	CD-EJ	8225 / lsf POLA
☐ N926L	Boeing (Douglas) DC-9-32	47172 / 263	N26175	0068	1086	2 PW JT8D-9A (HK3/ABS)	48988	F8Y90	CD-FK	8226 / lsf POLA
☐ N929L	Boeing (Douglas) DC-9-32	47174 / 286	N3333L	0068	1086	2 PW JT8D-9A (HK3/ABS)	48988	F8Y90	CD-FG	8229 / lsf POLA
☐ N931L	Boeing (Douglas) DC-9-32	47173 / 273	N3332L	0268	1086	2 PW JT8D-9A (HK3/ABS)	48988	F8Y90	CD-FJ	8231 / lsf POLA
☐ N932L	Boeing (Douglas) DC-9-32	47669 / 776	PJ-SNC	0575	1086	2 PW JT8D-9A	48988	F8Y90	DL-HJ	8232
☐ N995Z	Boeing (Douglas) DC-9-32	47027 / 132	N3318L	0667	1086	2 PW JT8D-9A (HK3/ABS)	48988	F8Y90	BL-EH	8295 / lsf POLA
☐ N996Z	Boeing (Douglas) DC-9-32	47028 / 145	N3319L	0067	1086	2 PW JT8D-9A (HK3/ABS)	48988	F8Y90	BL-EJ	8296 / lsf POLA
☐ N997Z	Boeing (Douglas) DC-9-32	47029 / 157	N3320L	0867	1086	2 PW JT8D-9A (HK3/ABS)	48988	F8Y90	BL-EK	8297 / lsf TRIT
☐ N998R	Boeing (Douglas) DC-9-32	47030 / 174	N3321L	0967	1086	2 PW JT8D-9A (HK3/ABS)	48988	F8Y90	BL-EM	8298 / lsf POLA
☐ N976Z	Boeing (Douglas) DC-9-31	47248 / 257		0268	1086	2 PW JT8D-9A (HK3/ABS)	48988	F8Y90	BK-CD	8376 / lsf TRIT
☐ N977Z	Boeing (Douglas) DC-9-31	47249 / 297		0468	1086	2 PW JT8D-9A (HK3/ABS)	48988	F8Y90	BK-CG	8377 / lsf POLA
☐ N978Z	Boeing (Douglas) DC-9-31	47250 / 309		0068	1086	2 PW JT8D-9A (HK3/ABS)	48988	F8Y90	BK-DE	8378 / lsf POLA
☐ N979Z	Boeing (Douglas) DC-9-31	47343 / 460		0069	1086	2 PW JT8D-9A (HK3/ABS)	48988	F8Y90	BK-FJ	8379 / lsf POLA
☐ N980Z	Boeing (Douglas) DC-9-31	47344 / 472		0069	1086	2 PW JT8D-9A (HK3/ABS)	48988	F8Y90	BK-GH	8380 / lsf TRIT
☐ N981Z	Boeing (Douglas) DC-9-31	47345 / 485		0069	1086	2 PW JT8D-9A (HK3/ABS)	48988	F8Y90	BK-CL	8381 / lsf POLA
☐ N982PS	Boeing (Douglas) DC-9-31	47251 / 244		0168	1086	2 PW JT8D-9A (HK3/ABS)	48988	F8Y90	BJ-GH	8382 / lsf POLA
☐ N983Z	Boeing (Douglas) DC-9-31	47411 / 533		0069	1086	2 PW JT8D-9A (HK3/ABS)	48988	F8Y90	BJ-GK	8383 / lsf POLA
☐ N984Z	Boeing (Douglas) DC-9-31	47412 / 534		0069	1086	2 PW JT8D-9A (HK3/ABS)	48988	F8Y90	BJ-HK	8384 / lsf POLA
☐ N985Z	Boeing (Douglas) DC-9-31	47491 / 599		0670	1086	2 PW JT8D-9A (HK3/ABS)	48988	F8Y90	BK-CF	8385 / lsf POLA
☐ N986Z	Boeing (Douglas) DC-9-31	47589 / 711		0073	1086	2 PW JT8D-9A	48988	F8Y90	AD-BH	8386
☐ N987Z	Boeing (Douglas) DC-9-31	47137 / 258	N983NE	0068	1086	2 PW JT8D-9A (HK3/ABS)	48988	F8Y90	AD-BJ	8387 / lsf POLA
☐ N988Z	Boeing (Douglas) DC-9-31	47134 / 215	N980NE	0067	1086	2 PW JT8D-9A (HK3/ABS)	48988	F8Y90	AD-BK	8388 / lsf POLA
☐ N989Z	Boeing (Douglas) DC-9-31	47135 / 233	N981NE	0067	1086	2 PW JT8D-9A (HK3/ABS)	48988	F8Y90	AD-BL	8389 / lsf POLA
☐ N990Z	Boeing (Douglas) DC-9-31	47136 / 243	N982NE	0168	1086	2 PW JT8D-9A (HK3/ABS)	48988	F8Y90	AD-BM	8390 / lsf POLA
☐ N991Z	Boeing (Douglas) DC-9-31	47096 / 192	N978NE	1067	1086	2 PW JT8D-9A	48988	F8Y90	BJ-KM	8391 / lsf POLA
☐ N992Z	Boeing (Douglas) DC-9-31	47095 / 191	N977NE	1067	1086	2 PW JT8D-9A (HK3/ABS)	48988	F8Y90	BL-CK	8392 / lsf POLA
☐ N993Z	Boeing (Douglas) DC-9-31	47082 / 181	N976NE	1067	1086	2 PW JT8D-9A (HK3/ABS)	48988	F8Y90	BL-CM	8393 / lsf POLA
☐ N937F	Boeing (Douglas) DC-9-33F (CF)	47409 / 497		0569	1086	2 PW JT8D-9A (HK3/ABS)	51710	F8Y90	BL-EG	8537 / lsf PACA
☐ N927L	Boeing (Douglas) DC-9-34	48123 / 934		0079	1086	2 PW JT8D-15	54885	F8Y90	CD-EK	8627 / City of Berlin / lsf PACA/stdMCI
☐ N928L	Boeing (Douglas) DC-9-34	48124 / 954		0480	1086	2 PW JT8D-15	54885	F8Y90	CD-FH	8628 / lsf PACA
☐ N936L	Boeing (Douglas) DC-9-34	47711 / 844	HB-IDT	0076	1086	2 PW JT8D-15	54885	F8Y90	BL-DF	8636 / lsf POLA
☐ N933L	Boeing (Douglas) DC-9-41	47617 / 762	JA8434	0075	1086	2 PW JT8D-15	51710	F8Y90	DM-AB	8433 / lsf POLA
☐ N934L	Boeing (Douglas) DC-9-41	47618 / 764	JA8435	0175	1086	2 PW JT8D-15	51710	F8Y90	DM-AE	8434 / lsf POLA
☐ N935L	Boeing (Douglas) DC-9-41	47603 / 720	OH-LNA	0074	1086	2 PW JT8D-15	51710	F8Y90	HM-DF	8435 / lsf POLA
☐ N401TW	Boeing 717-231					2 BR BR715	51710	F16Y95		oo-delivery 0200
☐ N402TW	Boeing 717-231					2 BR BR715	51710	F16Y95		oo-delivery 0200
☐ N403TW	Boeing 717-231					2 BR BR715	51710	F16Y95		oo-delivery 0300
☐ N2404A	Boeing 717-231					2 BR BR715	51710	F16Y95		oo-delivery 0300
☐ N405TW	Boeing 717-231					2 BR BR715	51710	F16Y95		oo-delivery 0400
☐ N406TW	Boeing 717-231					2 BR BR715	51710	F16Y95		oo-delivery 0400

446 registration type of aircraft cn/fn ex/ex* mfd del powered by mtow kg configuration selcal name/fln/specialitites/remarks

☐ N407TW	Boeing 717-231					2 BR BR715	51710	F16Y95		oo-delivery 0500
☐ N408TW	Boeing 717-231					2 BR BR715	51710	F16Y95		oo-delivery 0600
☐ N409TW	Boeing 717-231					2 BR BR715	51710	F16Y95		oo-delivery 0700
☐ N2410W	Boeing 717-231					2 BR BR715	51710	F16Y95		oo-delivery 0700
☐ N411TW	Boeing 717-231					2 BR BR715	51710	F16Y95		oo-delivery 0800
☐ N412TW	Boeing 717-231					2 BR BR715	51710	F16Y95		oo-delivery 0900
☐ N413TW	Boeing 717-231					2 BR BR715	51710	F16Y95		oo-delivery 1000
☐ N2414E	Boeing 717-231					2 BR BR715	51710	F16Y95		oo-delivery 1000
☐ N415TW	Boeing 717-231					2 BR BR715	51710	F16Y95		oo-delivery 1100
☐ N416TW	Boeing 717-231					2 BR BR715	51710	F16Y95		oo-delivery 0101
☐ N2417F	Boeing 717-231					2 BR BR715	51710	F16Y95		oo-delivery 0201
☐ N420TW	Boeing 717-231					2 BR BR715	51710	F16Y95		oo-delivery 0201
☐ N2421A	Boeing 717-231					2 BR BR715	51710	F16Y95		oo-delivery 0301
☐ N422TW	Boeing 717-231					2 BR BR715	51710	F16Y95		oo-delivery 0401
☐ N423TW	Boeing 717-231					2 BR BR715	51710	F16Y95		oo-delivery 0501
☐ N424TW	Boeing 717-231					2 BR BR715	51710	F16Y95		oo-delivery 0501
☐ N2425A	Boeing 717-231					2 BR BR715	51710	F16Y95		oo-delivery 0601
☐ N426TW	Boeing 717-231					2 BR BR715	51710	F16Y95		oo-delivery 0701
☐ N2427A	Boeing 717-231					2 BR BR715	51710	F16Y95		oo-delivery 0801
☐ N428TW	Boeing 717-231					2 BR BR715	51710	F16Y95		oo-delivery 0801
☐ N429TW	Boeing 717-231					2 BR BR715	51710	F16Y95		oo-delivery 0901
☐ N430TW	Boeing 717-231					2 BR BR715	51710	F16Y95		oo-delivery 1001
☐ N431TW	Boeing 717-231					2 BR BR715	51710	F16Y95		oo-delivery 1001
☐ N432TW	Boeing 717-231					2 BR BR715	51710	F16Y95		oo-delivery 1101
☐ N433TW	Boeing 717-231					2 BR BR715	51710	F16Y95		oo-delivery 0002
☐ N2434Q	Boeing 717-231					2 BR BR715	51710	F16Y95		oo-delivery 0002
☐ N435TW	Boeing 717-231					2 BR BR715	51710	F16Y95		oo-delivery 0002
☐ N436TW	Boeing 717-231					2 BR BR715	51710	F16Y95		oo-delivery 0002
☐ N437TW	Boeing 717-231					2 BR BR715	51710	F16Y95		oo-delivery 0002
☐ N438TW	Boeing 717-231					2 BR BR715	51710	F16Y95		oo-delivery 0002
☐ N439TW	Boeing 717-231					2 BR BR715	51710	F16Y95		oo-delivery 0002
☐ N2440F	Boeing 717-231					2 BR BR715	51710	F16Y95		oo-delivery 0002
☐ N441TW	Boeing 717-231					2 BR BR715	51710	F16Y95		oo-delivery 0002
☐ N2442H	Boeing 717-231					2 BR BR715	51710	F16Y95		oo-delivery 0002
☐ N443TW	Boeing 717-231					2 BR BR715	51710	F16Y95		oo-delivery 0002
☐ N2444F	Boeing 717-231					2 BR BR715	51710	F16Y95		oo-delivery 0002
☐ N445TW	Boeing 717-231					2 BR BR715	51710	F16Y95		oo-delivery 0003
☐ N446TW	Boeing 717-231					2 BR BR715	51710	F16Y95		oo-delivery 0003
☐ N447TW	Boeing 717-231					2 BR BR715	51710	F16Y95		oo-delivery 0003
☐ N448TW	Boeing 717-231					2 BR BR715	51710	F16Y95		oo-delivery 0003
☐ N449TW	Boeing 717-231					2 BR BR715	51710	F16Y95		oo-delivery 0003
☐ N2450H	Boeing 717-231					2 BR BR715	51710	F16Y95		oo-delivery 0003
☐ N451TW	Boeing 717-231					2 BR BR715	51710	F16Y95		oo-delivery 0003
☐ N452TW	Boeing 717-231					2 BR BR715	51710	F16Y95		oo-delivery 0003
☐ N405EA	Boeing (Douglas) DC-9-51	47688 / 799	N924VJ	1175	0594	2 PW JT8D-17	54885	F12Y95	AB-DM	8905 / lsf Boeing Capital Corp.
☐ N406EA	Boeing (Douglas) DC-9-51	47686 / 800	N925VJ	0075	0694	2 PW JT8D-17	54885	F12Y95	AB-EF	8906 / lsf Boeing Capital Corp.
☐ N408EA	Boeing (Douglas) DC-9-51	47693 / 804	N927VJ	0176	0494	2 PW JT8D-17	54885	F12Y95	AB-EG	8908 / lsf Boeing Capital Corp.
☐ N409EA	Boeing (Douglas) DC-9-51	47728 / 858	N991EA	0077	0194	2 PW JT8D-17	54885	F12Y95	AB-CF	8909 / lsf Boeing Capital Corp.
☐ N410EA	Boeing (Douglas) DC-9-51	47731 / 860	N992EA	0777	1293	2 PW JT8D-17	54885	F12Y95	AB-CG	8910 / lsf Boeing Capital Corp.
☐ N411EA	Boeing (Douglas) DC-9-51	47732 / 861	N993EA	0077	0294	2 PW JT8D-17	54885	F12Y95	AB-CH	8911 / lsf Boeing Capital Corp.
☐ N412EA	Boeing (Douglas) DC-9-51	47733 / 862	N994EA	0077	0394	2 PW JT8D-17	54885	F12Y95	AB-EH	8912 / lsf Boeing Capital Corp.
☐ N414EA	Boeing (Douglas) DC-9-51	47746 / 864	N996EA	0077	1293	2 PW JT8D-17	54885	F12Y95	AB-CJ	8914 / lsf Boeing Capital Corp./std MCI
☐ N415EA	Boeing (Douglas) DC-9-51	47749 / 865	N997EA	0077	1293	2 PW JT8D-17	54885	F12Y95	AB-CK	8915 / lsf Boeing Capital Corp.
☐ N416EA	Boeing (Douglas) DC-9-51	47751 / 866	N998EA	1077	0993	2 PW JT8D-17	54885	F12Y95	AB-CL	8916 / lsf Boeing Capital Corp.
☐ N417EA	Boeing (Douglas) DC-9-51	47753 / 867	N999EA	0077	0993	2 PW JT8D-17	54885	F12Y95	AB-CM	8917 / lsf Boeing Capital Corp.
☐ N418EA	Boeing (Douglas) DC-9-51	47676 / 785	N609HA	0875	0893	2 PW JT8D-17	54885	F12Y95	AB-DE	8918 / lsf Boeing Capital Corp.
☐ N901TW	Boeing (Douglas) MD-82 (DC-9-82)	49166 / 1098		0283	0483	2 PW JT8D-217A	67812	F12Y130	AC-KL	9001 / lsf PACA
☐ N902TW	Boeing (Douglas) MD-82 (DC-9-82)	49153 / 1101		0383	0483	2 PW JT8D-217A	67812	F12Y130	AC-KM	9002 / lsf CITG
☐ N903TW	Boeing (Douglas) MD-82 (DC-9-82)	49154 / 1102		0383	0583	2 PW JT8D-217A	67812	F12Y130	AD-BF	9003 / lsf PACA
☐ N904TW	Boeing (Douglas) MD-82 (DC-9-82)	49156 / 1104		0083	0583	2 PW JT8D-217A	67812	F12Y130	AD-CG	9004
☐ N905TW	Boeing (Douglas) MD-82 (DC-9-82)	49157 / 1105		0083	0583	2 PW JT8D-217A	67812	F12Y130	AD-FG	9005 / lsf CITG
☐ N906TW	Boeing (Douglas) MD-82 (DC-9-82)	49160 / 1108		0583	0683	2 PW JT8D-217A	67812	F12Y130	AD-FJ	9006 / lsf CITG
☐ N907TW	Boeing (Douglas) MD-82 (DC-9-82)	49165 / 1117		0883	0983	2 PW JT8D-217A	67812	F12Y130	AD-GH	9007 / lsf PLMI
☐ N908TW	Boeing (Douglas) MD-82 (DC-9-82)	49169 / 1118		0883	0983	2 PW JT8D-217A	67812	F12Y130	AD-GJ	9008
☐ N909TW	Boeing (Douglas) MD-82 (DC-9-82)	49170 / 1119		0883	1083	2 PW JT8D-217A	67812	F12Y130	AF-HK	9009
☐ N911TW	Boeing (Douglas) MD-82 (DC-9-82)	49182 / 1128		1183	1283	2 PW JT8D-217A	67812	F12Y130	AF-HM	9011 / lsf PLMI
☐ N912TW	Boeing (Douglas) MD-82 (DC-9-82)	49183 / 1129		1183	1283	2 PW JT8D-217A	67812	F12Y130	AF-JK	9012 / lsf PLMI
☐ N913TW	Boeing (Douglas) MD-82 (DC-9-82)	49184 / 1131		0084	0384	2 PW JT8D-217A	67812	F12Y130	AF-KL	9013
☐ N914TW	Boeing (Douglas) MD-82 (DC-9-82)	49185 / 1132		0384	0484	2 PW JT8D-217A	67812	F12Y130	AF-KM	9014 / lsf Kuta-3 Aircraft Corp.
☐ N915TW	Boeing (Douglas) MD-82 (DC-9-82)	49186 / 1133		0384	0484	2 PW JT8D-217A	67812	F12Y130	AG-DE	9015
☐ N916TW	Boeing (Douglas) MD-82 (DC-9-82)	49187 / 1134		0084	0484	2 PW JT8D-217A	67812	F12Y130	AG-CD	9016
☐ N917TW	Boeing (Douglas) MD-82 (DC-9-82)	49366 / 1196		0385	0592	2 PW JT8D-217A	67812	F12Y130	AD-GK	9017 / lsf PEGA
☐ N918TW	Boeing (Douglas) MD-82 (DC-9-82)	49367 / 1197		0085	0592	2 PW JT8D-217A	67812	F12Y130	AD-HJ	9018
☐ N919TW	Boeing (Douglas) MD-82 (DC-9-82)	49368 / 1198		0485	0592	2 PW JT8D-217A	67812	F12Y130	AD-HK	9019 / lsf PEGA
☐ N920TW	Boeing (Douglas) MD-82 (DC-9-82)	49369 / 1199		0485	0592	2 PW JT8D-217A	67812	F12Y130	AD-JK	9020 / lsf Boeing Capital Corp.
☐ N950U	Boeing (Douglas) MD-82 (DC-9-82)	49230 / 1141		0584	1086	2 PW JT8D-217A	67812	F12Y130	HM-EL	9050 / lsf MITS
☐ N951U	Boeing (Douglas) MD-82 (DC-9-82)	49245 / 1145		0084	1086	2 PW JT8D-217A	67812	F12Y130	HM-FG	9051 / lsf Boeing Capital Corp.
☐ N952U	Boeing (Douglas) MD-82 (DC-9-82)	49266 / 1238		0085	1086	2 PW JT8D-217A	67812	F12Y130	HM-GL	9052 / lsf Boeing Capital Corp.
☐ N953U	Boeing (Douglas) MD-82 (DC-9-82)	49267 / 1239		0085	1086	2 PW JT8D-217A	67812	F12Y130	HM-JK	9053 / lsf MITS
☐ N954U	Boeing (Douglas) MD-82 (DC-9-82)	49426 / 1399	N786JA	0787	1287	2 PW JT8D-217A	67812	F12Y130	BC-HL	9054
☐ N955U	Boeing (Douglas) MD-82 (DC-9-82)	49427 / 1401	N787JA	0887	0188	2 PW JT8D-217A	67812	F12Y130	BC-HM	9055
☐ N956U	Boeing (Douglas) MD-82 (DC-9-82)	49701 / 1478		0488	0688	2 PW JT8D-217C	67812	F12Y130	GJ-BL	9056 / lsf GECA
☐ N957U	Boeing (Douglas) MD-82 (DC-9-82)	49702 / 1479		0488	0688	2 PW JT8D-217C	67812	F12Y130	GJ-CD	9057 / lsf GECA
☐ N958U	Boeing (Douglas) MD-82 (DC-9-82)	49703 / 1489		0588	0788	2 PW JT8D-217C	67812	F12Y130	GH-CE	9058 / lsf GECA
☐ N959U	Boeing (Douglas) MD-82 (DC-9-82)	49704 / 1490		0588	0788	2 PW JT8D-217C	67812	F12Y130	GJ-CF	9059 / lsf GECA
☐ N960TW	Boeing (Douglas) MD-82 (DC-9-82)	49231 / 1177	N930AS	0285	0896	2 PW JT8D-217A	67812	F12Y130		9060 / lsf ACG Acquisition
☐ N940AS	Boeing (Douglas) MD-82 (DC-9-82)	49825 / 1577		0389	0498	2 PW JT8D-219	67812	F12Y130		9061 / lsf ILFC / to be re-reg. N961TW
☐ N941AS	Boeing (Douglas) MD-82 (DC-9-82)	49925 / 1616		0789	1198	2 PW JT8D-219	67812	F12Y130		9062 / lsf ILFC / tbr N962TW
☐ N921TW	Boeing (Douglas) MD-82 (DC-9-82)	49101 / 1051	N531MD	0282	0397	2 PW JT8D-217C	67812	F12Y130		9081 / lsf Boeing Capital Corp./cvtd-81
☐ N922TW	Boeing (Douglas) MD-82 (DC-9-82)	48013 / 1000	HB-INO	0081	0697	2 PW JT8D-217C	67812	F12Y130		9082 / lsf Boeing Capital / cvtd MD-81
☐ N923TW	Boeing (Douglas) MD-82 (DC-9-82)	49379 / 1205	D-ALLS	0585	0497	2 PW JT8D-217	66678	F12Y130		9083 / lsf ACG Acquisition XX Llc
☐ N924TW	Boeing (Douglas) MD-82 (DC-9-82)	49100 / 1025	HB-INA	1081	1097	2 PW JT8D-217C	67812	F12Y130		9084 / lsf PACA / cvtd MD-81
☐ N925TW	Boeing (Douglas) MD-82 (DC-9-82)	49357 / 1251	HB-INT	0086	0897	2 PW JT8D-217C	67812	F12Y130		9085 / lsf Boeing Capital Corp./cvtd-81
☐ N926TW	Boeing (Douglas) MD-82 (DC-9-82)	49356 / 1250	HB-INS	1285	0697	2 PW JT8D-217C	67812	F12Y130		9086 / lsf Boeing Capital Corp./cvtd-81
☐ N927TW	Boeing (Douglas) MD-82 (DC-9-82)	49358 / 1294	HB-INU	0686	1297	2 PW JT8D-217C	67812	F12Y130		9087 / lsf Boeing Capital Corp./cvtd-81
☐ N928TW	Boeing (Douglas) MD-82 (DC-9-82)	48012 / 997	HB-INN	0781	1297	2 PW JT8D-217C	67812	F12Y130		9088 / lsf Boeing Capital Corp./cvtd-81
☐ N929TW	Boeing (Douglas) MD-82 (DC-9-82)	48014 / 1013	HB-INP	0981	0398	2 PW JT8D-217C	67812	F12Y130		9089 / lsf Boeing Capital Corp./cvtd-81
☐ N931TW	Boeing (Douglas) MD-83 (DC-9-83)	49527 / 1382		0687	0787	2 PW JT8D-217C	72575	F12Y132	BC-GJ	9301 / lsf TPEI
☐ N9302B	Boeing (Douglas) MD-83 (DC-9-83)	49528 / 1383		0687	0787	2 PW JT8D-217C	72575	F12Y132	BC-GK	9302 / lsf TPEI
☐ N9303K	Boeing (Douglas) MD-83 (DC-9-83)	49529 / 1396		0787	0987	2 PW JT8D-217C	72575	F12Y132	BC-GL	9303 / lsf TPEI
☐ N9304C	Boeing (Douglas) MD-83 (DC-9-83)	49530 / 1397		0787	0987	2 PW JT8D-217C	72575	F12Y132	BC-HJ	9304 / lsf TPEI
☐ N9305N	Boeing (Douglas) MD-83 (DC-9-83)	49395 / 1286	YV-36C	0686	0596	2 PW JT8D-219	72575	F12Y132		9305 / lsf PEGA
☐ N9306T	Boeing (Douglas) MD-83 (DC-9-83)	49567 / 1367	YV-38C	0487	0496	2 PW JT8D-219	72575	F12Y132		9306 / lsf PACA
☐ N9307R	Boeing (Douglas) MD-83 (DC-9-83)	49663 / 1437	SE-DPH	1287	0494	2 PW JT8D-219	72575	F12Y132	AB-EJ	9307 / lsf Lancelot Leasing Inc.
☐ N9401W	Boeing (Douglas) MD-83 (DC-9-83)	53137 / 1872	N9001L*	0692	0793	2 PW JT8D-219	72575	F12Y132	AB-DF	9401 / lsf Boeing Capital Corp.
☐ N9402W	Boeing (Douglas) MD-83 (DC-9-83)	53138 / 1886	N9001D*	0892	0693	2 PW JT8D-219	72575	F12Y132	AB-DG	9402 / lsf Boeing Capital Corp.
☐ N9403W	Boeing (Douglas) MD-83 (DC-9-83)	53139 / 1899	N9035C*	0992	0693	2 PW JT8D-219	72575	F12Y132	AB-DH	9403 / lsf Boeing Capital Corp.
☐ N9404V	Boeing (Douglas) MD-83 (DC-9-83)	53140 / 1923	N9075H*	1192	0793	2 PW JT8D-219	72575	F12Y132	AB-DJ	9404 / lsf Boeing Capital Corp.
☐ N9405T	Boeing (Douglas) MD-83 (DC-9-83)	53141 / 1935		1292	0793	2 PW JT8D-219	72575	F12Y132	AB-DK	9405 / lsf Boeing Capital Corp.
☐ N9406W	Boeing (Douglas) MD-83 (DC-9-83)	53126 / 2026	N6203U*	0992	0793	2 PW JT8D-219	72575	F12Y132	AB-DL	9406 / lsf Boeing Capital Corp.
☐ N9407R	Boeing (Douglas) MD-83 (DC-9-83)	49400 / 1356	EI-CKB	0087	0894	2 PW JT8D-219	72575	F12Y132		9407 / lsf PACA
☐ N9409F	Boeing (Douglas) MD-83 (DC-9-83)	53121 / 1971	N532MD	0292	0394	2 PW JT8D-219	72575	F12Y132		9409 / lsf Nationscredit/cvtd MD-82
☐ N110HM	Boeing (Douglas) MD-83 (DC-9-83)	49787 / 1636	HL7274	0989	0594	2 PW JT8D-219	72575	F12Y132		9411 / lsf GECA/tbr N9411W/cvtd MD-82
☐ N9412W	Boeing (Douglas) MD-83 (DC-9-83)	53187 / 2118		0895	0995	2 PW JT8D-219	72575	F12Y132		9412 / lsf AWAS
☐ N9413T	Boeing (Douglas) MD-83 (DC-9-83)	53188 / 2119		0895	0995	2 PW JT8D-219	72575	F12Y132		9413 / lsf AWAS
☐ N9414W	Boeing (Douglas) MD-83 (DC-9-83)	53189 / 2121		1095	1095	2 PW JT8D-219	72575	F12Y132		9414 / lsf AWAS
☐ N9420D	Boeing (Douglas) MD-83 (DC-9-83)	49824 / 1554	9Y-THU	0088	1296	2 PW JT8D-219	72575	F12Y132		9420 / lsf ILFC
☐ N951TW	Boeing (Douglas) MD-83 (DC-9-83)	53470 / 2135	N978AS	0096	0696	2 PW JT8D-219	72575	F12Y132		9511
☐ N939AS	Boeing (Douglas) MD-83 (DC-9-83)	49657 / 1459		0288		2 PW JT8D-219	72575	F12Y132		9513 / tblsf ILFC 0099/exASA/tbr N953TW
☐ N9615W	Boeing (Douglas) MD-83 (DC-9-83)	53562 / 2192		0697	0797	2 PW JT8D-219	72575	F12Y132		9615 / lsf Boeing Capital Corp.

447 registration type of aircraft *cn/fn* *ex/ex** *mfd* *del* *powered by* *mtow kg* *configuration* *selcal* name/fln/*specialitites/remarks*

registration	type of aircraft	cn/fn	ex/ex*	mfd	del	powered by	mtow kg	configuration	selcal	name/fln/specialitites/remarks
☐ N9616G	Boeing (Douglas) MD-83 (DC-9-83)	53563 / 2196		0097	0897	2 PW JT8D-219	72575	F12Y132		9616 / lsf Boeing Capital Corp.
☐ N9617R	Boeing (Douglas) MD-83 (DC-9-83)	53564 / 2199		0897	0997	2 PW JT8D-219	72575	F12Y132		9617 / lsf Boeing Capital Corp.
☐ N9618A	Boeing (Douglas) MD-83 (DC-9-83)	53565 / 2201		0997	1097	2 PW JT8D-219	72575	F12Y132		9618 / lsf Boeing Capital Corp.
☐ N9619V	Boeing (Douglas) MD-83 (DC-9-83)	53566 / 2206		1097	1297	2 PW JT8D-219	72575	F12Y132		9619 / lsf Boeing Capital Corp.
☐ N9620D	Boeing (Douglas) MD-83 (DC-9-83)	53591 / 2208		0097	1197	2 PW JT8D-219	72575	F12Y132		9620 / lsf Boeing Capital Corp.
☐ N9621A	Boeing (Douglas) MD-83 (DC-9-83)	53592 / 2234		0098	0698	2 PW JT8D-219	72575	F12Y132		9621 / lsf Boeing Capital Corp.
☐ N9622A	Boeing (Douglas) MD-83 (DC-9-83)	53593 / 2239		0098	0898	2 PW JT8D-219	72575	F12Y132		9622 / lsf Boeing Capital Corp.
☐ N9624T	Boeing (Douglas) MD-83 (DC-9-83)	53594 / 2241		0098	0998	2 PW JT8D-219	72575	F12Y132		9624 / lsf Boeing Capital Corp.
☐ N9625W	Boeing (Douglas) MD-83 (DC-9-83)	53595 / 2244		0098	1098	2 PW JT8D-219	72575	F12Y132	AC-BF	9625 / lsf Boeing Capital Corp.
☐ N9626F	Boeing (Douglas) MD-83 (DC-9-83)	53596 / 2247		0098	1198	2 PW JT8D-219	72575	F12Y132	AC-DE	9626 / lsf Boeing Capital Corp.
☐ N9627R	Boeing (Douglas) MD-83 (DC-9-83)	53597 / 2249		0098	1298	2 PW JT8D-219	72575	F12Y132	AC-EF	9627 / lsf Boeing Capital Corp.
☐ N9628W	Boeing (Douglas) MD-83 (DC-9-83)	53598 / 2252		0099	0199	2 PW JT8D-219	72575	F12Y132		9628 / lsf Boeing Capital Corp.
☐ N9629H	Boeing (Douglas) MD-83 (DC-9-83)	53599 / 2254		0099	0299	2 PW JT8D-219	72575	F12Y132		9629 / lsf Boeing Capital Corp.
☐ N9630A	Boeing (Douglas) MD-83 (DC-9-83)	53561 / 2174	N90126*	0097	0597	2 PW JT8D-219	72575	F12Y132		9630 / lsf Boeing Capital Corp.
☐ N963TW	Boeing (Douglas) MD-83 (DC-9-83)					2 PW JT8D-219	72575	F12Y132		9663 / to lsf Boeing Capital Corp. 0099
☐ N964TW	Boeing (Douglas) MD-83 (DC-9-83)					2 PW JT8D-219	72575	F12Y132		9664 / to lsf Boeing Capital Corp. 0099
☐ N965TW	Boeing (Douglas) MD-83 (DC-9-83)					2 PW JT8D-219	72575	F12Y132		9665 / to lsf Boeing Capital Corp. 0099
☐ N967TW	Boeing (Douglas) MD-83 (DC-9-83)					2 PW JT8D-219	72575	F12Y132		9667 / to lsf Boeing Capital Corp. 0099
☐ N968TW	Boeing (Douglas) MD-83 (DC-9-83)					2 PW JT8D-219	72575	F12Y132		9668 / to lsf Boeing Capital Corp. 0099
☐ N969TW	Boeing (Douglas) MD-83 (DC-9-83)					2 PW JT8D-219	72575	F12Y132		9669 / to lsf Boeing Capital Corp. 0099
☐ N970TW	Boeing (Douglas) MD-83 (DC-9-83)					2 PW JT8D-219	72575	F12Y132		9670 / to lsf Boeing Capital Corp. 0099
☐ N971TW	Boeing (Douglas) MD-83 (DC-9-83)					2 PW JT8D-219	72575	F12Y132		9671 / to lsf Boeing Capital Corp. 0099
☐ N972TW	Boeing (Douglas) MD-83 (DC-9-83)					2 PW JT8D-219	72575	F12Y132		9672 / to lsf Boeing Capital Corp. 0099
☐ N973TW	Boeing (Douglas) MD-83 (DC-9-83)					2 PW JT8D-219	72575	F12Y132		9673 / to lsf Boeing Capital Corp. 0099
☐ N974TW	Boeing (Douglas) MD-83 (DC-9-83)					2 PW JT8D-219	72575	F12Y132		9674 / to lsf Boeing Capital Corp. 0099
☐ N975TW	Boeing (Douglas) MD-83 (DC-9-83)					2 PW JT8D-219	72575	F12Y132		9675 / to lsf Boeing Capital Corp. 0099
☐ N976TW	Boeing (Douglas) MD-83 (DC-9-83)					2 PW JT8D-219	72575	F12Y132		9676 / to lsf Boeing Capital Corp. 0099
☐ N9677W	Boeing (Douglas) MD-83 (DC-9-83)					2 PW JT8D-219	72575	F12Y132		9677 / to lsf Boeing Capital Corp. 0099
☐ N978TW	Boeing (Douglas) MD-83 (DC-9-83)					2 PW JT8D-219	72575	F12Y132		9678 / to lsf Boeing Capital Corp. 0099
☐ N979TW	Boeing (Douglas) MD-83 (DC-9-83)					2 PW JT8D-219	72575	F12Y132		9679 / to lsf Boeing Capital Corp. 0099
☐ N980TW	Boeing (Douglas) MD-83 (DC-9-83)					2 PW JT8D-219	72575	F12Y132		9680 / to lsf Boeing Capital Corp. 0099
☐ N981TW	Boeing (Douglas) MD-83 (DC-9-83)					2 PW JT8D-219	72575	F12Y132		9681 / to lsf Boeing Capital Corp. 0099
☐ N9681B	Boeing (Douglas) MD-83 (DC-9-83)					2 PW JT8D-219	72575	F12Y132		9682 / to lsf Boeing Capital Corp. 0099
☐ N983TW	Boeing (Douglas) MD-83 (DC-9-83)					2 PW JT8D-219	72575	F12Y132		9683 / to lsf Boeing Capital Corp. 0099
☐ N984TW	Boeing (Douglas) MD-83 (DC-9-83)					2 PW JT8D-219	72575	F12Y132		9684 / to lsf Boeing Capital Corp. 0099
☐ N985TW	Boeing (Douglas) MD-83 (DC-9-83)					2 PW JT8D-219	72575	F12Y132		9685 / to lsf Boeing Capital Corp. 0099
☐ N986TW	Boeing (Douglas) MD-83 (DC-9-83)					2 PW JT8D-219	72575	F12Y132		9686 / to lsf Boeing Capital Corp. 0099
☐ N966TW	Boeing (Douglas) MD-83 (DC-9-83)					2 PW JT8D-219	72575	F12Y132		9666 / to lsf Boeing Capital Corp. 0099
☐ EI-BWD	Boeing (Douglas) MD-83 (DC-9-83)	49575 / 1414	9Y-THT	0087	0894	2 PW JT8D-219	72575	F12Y132	BJ-AL	9408/Wings of Pride / lsfGECA/tbrN9408W
☐ N844TW	Boeing 727-31	18755 / 87		0064	1164	3 PW JT8D-7B	72802	F12Y103	AB-JL	7844 / City of Frankfurt / std MCI
☐ N848TW	Boeing 727-31	18751 / 75		0064	0864	3 PW JT8D-7B	72802	F12Y103	AB-LM	7848 / City of Vienna / std MCI
☐ N856TW	Boeing 727-31	18575 / 57		0064	0764	3 PW JT8D-7B	72802	F12Y103	AB-FJ	7856 / std MCI
☐ N857TW	Boeing 727-31	18576 / 63		0064	0864	3 PW JT8D-7B	72802	F12Y103	AB-FK	7857 / std MCI
☐ N94314	Boeing 727-231	20047 / 675		0069	0269	3 PW JT8D-9A	78245	F12Y134	AG-EF	4314 / std MCI
☐ N54333	Boeing 727-231	20460 / 859		0071	0371	3 PW JT8D-9A	78245	F12Y134	DJ-CH	4333
☐ N54334	Boeing 727-231	20461 / 860		0071	0471	3 PW JT8D-9A	78245	F12Y134	LM-BG	4334
☐ N54335	Boeing 727-231	20462 / 862		0071	0571	3 PW JT8D-9A	78245	F12Y134	LM-BH	4335
☐ N54336	Boeing 727-231	20490 / 863		0071	0571	3 PW JT8D-9A	78245	F12Y134	DH-CJ	4336
☐ N54337	Boeing 727-231	20491 / 864		0071	0571	3 PW JT8D-9A	78245	F12Y134	GL-BF	4337
☐ N64339	Boeing 727-231 (A)	20844 / 1065		0074	0974	3 PW JT8D-9A	84051	F12Y134	CH-EF	4339
☐ N54340	Boeing 727-231 (A)	20845 / 1066		0074	0974	3 PW JT8D-9A	84051	F12Y134	CH-FG	4340
☐ N54341	Boeing 727-231 (A)	21628 / 1454		0079	0379	3 PW JT8D-9A	84051	F12Y134	BF-EK	4341
☐ N54342	Boeing 727-231 (A)	21629 / 1456		0079	0379	3 PW JT8D-9A	84051	F12Y134	BF-GH	4342
☐ N24343	Boeing 727-231 (A)	21630 / 1458		0079	0379	3 PW JT8D-9A	84051	F12Y134	BF-GK	4343
☐ N54344	Boeing 727-231 (A)	21631 / 1460		0079	0379	3 PW JT8D-9A	84051	F12Y134	BF-HJ	4344
☐ N54345	Boeing 727-231 (A)	21632 / 1462		0079	0479	3 PW JT8D-9A	84051	F12Y134	BF-HK	4345
☐ N64346	Boeing 727-231 (A)	21633 / 1464		0079	0479	3 PW JT8D-9A	84051	F12Y134	BF-JK	4346
☐ N64347	Boeing 727-231 (A)	21634 / 1466		0079	0479	3 PW JT8D-9A	84051	F12Y134	DH-AG	4347 / spec St.Louis Rams-football cs
☐ N54348	Boeing 727-231 (A)	21967 / 1563		0079	0380	3 PW JT8D-9A	84051	F12Y134	DJ-CM	4348 / lsf PEGA
☐ N54349	Boeing 727-231 (A)	21968 / 1565		0079	0280	3 PW JT8D-9A	84051	F12Y134	DJ-EG	4349 / lsf PEGA
☐ N54350	Boeing 727-231 (A)	21969 / 1567		0080	0280	3 PW JT8D-9A	84051	F12Y134	DJ-EH	4350
☐ N54351	Boeing 727-231 (A)	21983 / 1569		0080	0280	3 PW JT8D-9A	84051	F12Y134	DJ-EK	4351 / lsf PEGA
☐ N54352	Boeing 727-231 (A)	21984 / 1574		0080	0280	3 PW JT8D-9A	84051	F12Y134	DJ-EL	4352 / lsf PEGA
☐ N54353	Boeing 727-231 (A)	21985 / 1576		0080	0280	3 PW JT8D-15	86409	F12Y134	DJ-EM	4353
☐ N54354	Boeing 727-231 (A)	21986 / 1580		0080	0380	3 PW JT8D-15	86409	F12Y134	DJ-FK	4354
☐ N84355	Boeing 727-231 (A)	21987 / 1582		0080	0380	3 PW JT8D-15	86409	F12Y134	DJ-FL	4355
☐ N701TW	Boeing 757-2Q8	28160 / 721		0096	0796	2 PW PW2037	108862	F22Y158	GJ-CH	7501 / lsf ILFC
☐ N702TW	Boeing 757-2Q8	28162 / 732		0096	1096	2 PW PW2037	108862	F22Y158	GJ-CK	7502 / lsf ILFC
☐ N703TW	Boeing 757-2Q8 (ET)	27620 / 736		0096	1196	2 PW PW2037	108862	F22Y158	GJ-CL	7503 / lsf ILFC
☐ N704X	Boeing 757-2Q8	28163 / 741		0097	0197	2 PW PW2037	108862	F22Y158		7504 / lsf ILFC
☐ N705TW	Boeing 757-231	28479 / 742		0097	0297	2 PW PW2037	108862	F22Y158	AE-GM	7505 / lsf PEGA
☐ N706TW	Boeing 757-2Q8	28165 / 743		0097	0297	2 PW PW2037	108862	F22Y158		7506 / lsf ILFC
☐ N707TW	Boeing 757-2Q8 (ET)	27625 / 744		0097	0297	2 PW PW2037	108862	F22Y158	GL-EK	7507 / lsf ILFC
☐ N708TW	Boeing 757-231	28480 / 750		0097	0497	2 PW PW2037	108862	F22Y158		7508 / lsf IALI
☐ N709TW	Boeing 757-2Q8	28168 / 754		0597	0597	2 PW PW2037	108862	F22Y158	AE-HJ	7509 / lsf ILFC
☐ N710TW	Boeing 757-2Q8	28169 / 757		0597	0597	2 PW PW2037	108862	F22Y158	AE-HL	7510 / lsf ILFC
☐ N711ZX	Boeing 757-231	28481 / 758		0097	0697	2 PW PW2037	108862	F22Y158	AE-JM	7511 / lsf Fleet National Bank
☐ N712TW	Boeing 757-2Q8 (ET)	27624 / 760		0697	0697	2 PW PW2037	108862	F22Y158	AE-KL	7512 / lsf ILFC
☐ N713TW	Boeing 757-2Q8	28173 / 764		0797	0797	2 PW PW2037	108862	F22Y158	AE-KM	7513 / lsf ILFC
☐ N714P	Boeing 757-231	28482 / 770		0897	0897	2 PW PW2037	108862	F22Y158	AF-GJ	7514 / Wimpy / lsf PEGA
☐ N715TW	Boeing 757-231	28483 / 777		1097	1097	2 PW PW2037	108862	F22Y158		7515 / lsf PEGA
☐ N716TW	Boeing 757-231	28484 / 825	N1799B*	0098	1098	2 PW PW2037	108862	F22Y158	AF-HJ	7516
☐ N717TW	Boeing 757-231	28485				2 PW PW2037	108862	F22Y158		7517 / oo-delivery 0099
☐ N718TW	Boeing 757-231	28486				2 PW PW2037	108862	F22Y158		7518 / oo-delivery 0099
☐ N719TW	Boeing 757-231	28487				2 PW PW2037	108862	F22Y158		7519 / oo-delivery 0099
☐ N720TW	Boeing 757-231	28488				2 PW PW2037	108862	F22Y158		7520 / oo-delivery 0099
☐ N721TW	Boeing 757-231					2 PW PW2037	108862	F22Y158		7521 / oo-delivery 0099
☐ N722TW	Boeing 757-231					2 PW PW2037	108862	F22Y158		7522 / oo-delivery 0099
☐ N723TW	Boeing 757-231					2 PW PW2037	108862	F22Y158		7523 / oo-delivery 0099
☐ N724TW	Boeing 757-231					2 PW PW2037	108862	F22Y158		7524 / oo-delivery 0099
☐ N725TW	Boeing 757-231					2 PW PW2037	108862	F22Y158		7525 / oo-delivery 0099
☐ N726TW	Boeing 757-231					2 PW PW2037	108862	F22Y158		7526 / oo-delivery 0099
☐ N727TW	Boeing 757-231					2 PW PW2037	108862	F22Y158		7527 / oo-delivery 0100
☐ N601TW	Boeing 767-231 (ER)	22564 / 14		0082	1182	2 PW JT9D-7R4D	151953	F24Y159	DJ-AF	16001 / cvtd -231
☐ N602TW	Boeing 767-231 (ER)	22565 / 21		0082	1282	2 PW JT9D-7R4D	151953	F24Y159	DJ-AG	16002 / cvtd -231
☐ N603TW	Boeing 767-231 (ER)	22566 / 29		0082	0183	2 PW JT9D-7R4D	151953	F24Y159	DJ-AK	16003 / cvtd -231
☐ N604TW	Boeing 767-231 (ER)	22567 / 30		0283	1295	2 PW JT9D-7R4D	151953	F24Y159	DJ-AL	16004 / cvtd -231
☐ N605TW	Boeing 767-231 (ER)	22568 / 33		0082	1282	2 PW JT9D-7R4D	151953	F24Y159	AD-KL	16005 / cvtd -231
☐ N606TW	Boeing 767-231 (ER)	22569 / 39		0082	0493	2 PW JT9D-7R4D	151953	F24Y159	AE-GH	lsf 767-231 Holdings Inc. / cvtd -231
☐ N607TW	Boeing 767-231 (ER)	22570 / 63		0783	0783	2 PW JT9D-7R4D	151953	F24Y159	AE-GJ	16007 / cvtd -231
☐ N608TW	Boeing 767-231 (ER)	22571 / 64		0983	0983	2 PW JT9D-7R4D	151953	F24Y159	AE-GK	16008 / cvtd -231
☐ N609TW	Boeing 767-231 (ER)	22572 / 65		0983	1183	2 PW JT9D-7R4D	151953	F24Y159	DJ-CK	16009 / cvtd -231
☐ N610TW	Boeing 767-231 (ER)	22573 / 70		1183	1087	2 PW JT9D-7R4D	151953	F24Y159	DJ-CL	16010 / Star of Geneva / cvtd-231
☐ N650TW	Boeing 767-205 (ER)	23057 / 81	G-BNAX	0084	1087	2 PW JT9D-7R4D	151953	F24Y159	AE-GL	16050 / cvtd -205
☐ N651TW	Boeing 767-205 (ER)	23058 / 101	DQ-FJA	0084	1294	2 PW JT9D-7R4D	151953	F24Y159	GL-BE	16051 / cvtd -205
☐ N632TW	Boeing 767-3Y0 (ER)	24953 / 405	EI-CAM	0091	1296	2 PW PW4060	184610	F30Y178	AF-CG	16102 / lsf GECA
☐ N691LF	Boeing 767-330 (ER)	25137 / 377	D-ABUX	0091	0294	2 PW PW4060	184610	F30Y178	AF-DE	16103 / lsf ILFC
☐ N634TW	Boeing 767-3Q8 (ER)	28132 / 692		0098	0398	2 PW PW4060	184610	F30Y178	GL-BJ	16104 / lsf ILFC
☐ N635TW	Boeing 767-3Q8 (ER)	28207 / 695		0098	0498	2 PW PW4060	184610	F30Y178	LM-BD	16105 / lsf ILFC
☐ N636TW	Boeing 767-3Q8 (ER)					2 PW PW4060	184610	F30Y178		16106 / to be lsf ILFC 0899
☐ N	Airbus Industrie A330-341					2 RR Trent 768-60	212000			oo-delivery 00XX
☐ N	Airbus Industrie A330-341					2 RR Trent 768-60	212000			oo-delivery 00XX
☐ N	Airbus Industrie A330-341					2 RR Trent 768-60	212000			oo-delivery 00XX
☐ N	Airbus Industrie A330-341					2 RR Trent 768-60	212000			oo-delivery 00XX
☐ N	Airbus Industrie A330-341					2 RR Trent 768-60	212000			oo-delivery 00XX
☐ N	Airbus Industrie A330-341					2 RR Trent 768-60	212000			oo-delivery 00XX
☐ N	Airbus Industrie A330-341					2 RR Trent 768-60	212000			oo-delivery 00XX
☐ N	Airbus Industrie A330-341					2 RR Trent 768-60	212000			oo-delivery 00XX
☐ N	Airbus Industrie A330-341					2 RR Trent 768-60	212000			oo-delivery 00XX
☐ N	Airbus Industrie A330-341					2 RR Trent 768-60	212000			oo-delivery 00XX

TRAVEL LEAR CHARTER SERVICE, Inc. — Oklahoma City-Wiley Post, OK

Hangar 4, Wiley Post Airport, Bethany, OK 73008, USA ☎ (405) 495-5387 Tx: none Fax: (405) 495-8662 SITA: n/a
F: 1988 n/a Head: Marshall W. Weir Net: n/a

registration	type of aircraft	cn/fn	ex/ex*	mfd	del	powered by	mtow kg	configuration	selcal	name/fln/specialitites/remarks
☐ N280R	Learjet 24B	24B-188	N230R	0069	0692	2 GE CJ610-6	6123			
☐ N401AJ	Learjet 25B	25B-171	N42DG	0074	1290	2 GE CJ610-6	6804			

TRAVIS COUNTY STAR FLIGHT (Division of Travis County EMS) — Austin, TX

PO Box 1748, Austin, TX 78767, USA ☎ (512) 473-9367 Tx: none Fax: (512) 473-9436 SITA: n/a
F: 1985 n/a Head: Christian E. Callsen, Jr. Net: n/a

registration	type of aircraft	cn/fn	ex/ex*	mfd	del	powered by	mtow kg	configuration	selcal	name/fln/specialitites/remarks
☐ N891T	Eurocopter EC135T1	0051		0098	1198	2 TU Arrius 2B1	2720	EMS / Rescue		
☐ N892T	Eurocopter EC135T1	0052		0098	1298	2 TU Arrius 2B1	2720	EMS / Rescue		

TRIANGLE AIRCRAFT SERVICES, Corp. — White Plains-Westchester County, NY

Hangar E, Westchester Airport, White Plains, NY 10604, USA ☎ (914) 946-0749 Tx: none Fax: (914) 946-3692 SITA: n/a
F: 1989 n/a Head: John P. Emery Net: n/a Operates VIP-contract charters for its owner group of companies only.

registration	type of aircraft	cn/fn	ex/ex*	mfd	del	powered by	mtow kg	configuration	selcal	name/fln/specialitites/remarks
☐ N280TR	Sikorsky S-76B	760344	N76UP	0088	0797	2 PWC PT6B-36A	5307	VIP		
☐ N31TR	Boeing 727-212 (A/RE) (Super 27)	21948 / 1510	VR-COJ	0079	0289	3 PW JT8D-217C/17 (BFG)	90039	VIP	CH-GL	cvtd -212

TRI STATE AERO, Inc. — Evansville-Regional, IN

6101 Flightline Drive, Evansville, IN 47711, USA ☎ (812) 426-1221 Tx: none Fax: (812) 426-1382 SITA: n/a
F: 1963 n/a Head: Thomas M. Speer Net: http://www.tristate-aero.com

registration	type of aircraft	cn/fn	ex/ex*	mfd	del	powered by	mtow kg	configuration	selcal	name/fln/specialitites/remarks
☐ N1743E	Cessna 310R II	310R1559		0079	0779	2 CO IO-520-M	2495			
☐ N5162C	Cessna 310R II	310R1511		0079	0479	2 CO IO-520-M	2495			
☐ N976JT	Beech King Air C90	LJ-699		0076	0788	2 PWC PT6A-20	4377			

TRITON AVIATION SERVICES, Inc. = (TRIT) (Subsidiary of The Triton Group, Inc.) — San Francisco, CA

55 Green Street, Suite 500, San Francisco, CA 94111, USA ☎ (650) 956-9453 Tx: none Fax: (650) 398-9184 SITA: n/a
F: 1996 n/a Head: Francis A. Lawrence Net: n/a Used aircraft leasing, sales & financing company.
Owner / lessor of follwoing (main) aircraft types: Boeing 737-200, Boeing 727-200, Boeing 747-100 & McDonnell Douglas DC-9-30. Aircraft leased from Triton Aviation are listed and mentioned as lsf TRIT under the leasing carriers.

TUCKER AVIATION, Inc. — Dillingham, AK

PO Box 1109, Dillingham, AK 99576, USA ☎ (907) 842-1023 Tx: none Fax: none SITA: n/a
F: 1986 n/a Head: Thomas G. Tucker Net: n/a

registration	type of aircraft	cn/fn	ex/ex*	mfd	del	powered by	mtow kg	configuration	selcal	name/fln/specialitites/remarks
☐ N53046	Cessna A185F Skywagon	18502336		0073	0586	1 CO IO-520-D	1520			
☐ N73408	Cessna T207A Turbo Stationair 8 II	20700586		0079	0887	1 CO TSIO-520-M	1724			

TUCSON AEROSERVICE (Tucson Aeroservice Center, Inc. dba) — Tucson-Avra Valley, AZ

11700 West Avra Valley Road, Marana, AZ 85653, USA ☎ (520) 682-2999 Tx: none Fax: (520) 682-3714 SITA: n/a
F: 1986 n/a Head: Gary L. Abrams Net: http://aso.solid.com/tucsonaero Aircraft below MTOW 1361kg: Cessna 172N & 182P

registration	type of aircraft	cn/fn	ex/ex*	mfd	del	powered by	mtow kg	configuration	selcal	name/fln/specialitites/remarks
☐ N7311S	Cessna R182 Skylane RG II	R18201703		0081	1196	1 LY O-540-J3C5D	1406			
☐ N756DV	Cessna U206G Stationair	U20604016		0077	0796	1 CO IO-520-F	1633			
☐ N415JL	Beech Bonanza A36	E-1801		0081	0196	1 CO IO-520-BB	1633			
☐ N58MW	Beech Baron 58	TH-863		0077	0695	2 CO IO-520-C	2449			
☐ N5497G	Cessna 421C Golden Eagle II	421C0244		0077	0297	2 CO GTSIO-520-L	3379			
☐ N55HC	Beech King Air E90	LW-134	N663LS	0075	0794	2 PWC PT6A-28	4581			

TULSAIR CHARTER (Tulsair Beechcraft, Inc. dba) — Tulsa-Int'l, OK

Tulsair CHARTER

PO Box 582470, Tulsa, OK 74158, USA ☎ (918) 835-7651 Tx: none Fax: (918) 832-0651 SITA: n/a
F: 1945 n/a Head: Tom G. Clark, Jr. Net: http://www.tulsair.com

registration	type of aircraft	cn/fn	ex/ex*	mfd	del	powered by	mtow kg	configuration	selcal	name/fln/specialitites/remarks
☐ N15U	Beech Duchess 76	ME-160		0079	0379	2 LY O-360-A1G6D	1769			
☐ N19U	Beech Duchess 76	ME-294		0079	1279	2 LY O-360-A1G6D	1769			
☐ N18475	Beech Baron 58	TH-879		0077	1188	2 CO IO-520-C	2449			
☐ N381TC	Beech Baron 58TC	TK-83	N21TK	0078	1284	2 CO TSIO-520-LB	2767			
☐ N3710A	Beech King Air 200	BB-760		0081	0788	2 PWC PT6A-41	5670			
☐ N473TC	Learjet 25	25-043	N234ND	0069	0792	2 GE CJ610-6	6804			
☐ N55NM	Learjet 55	55-085	N58FM	0083	0992	2 GA TFE731-3AR-2B	8845			lsf HM Int'l Inc.

TUNDRA COPTERS, Inc. (Subsidiary of Briles Wing & Helicopter, Inc.) — Fairbanks-Int'l, AK

TUNDRA copters

PO Box 60670, Fairbanks, AK 99706, USA ☎ (907) 474-0429 Tx: none Fax: (907) 474-0429 SITA: n/a
F: 1961 n/a Head: Paul R. Briles Net: n/a

registration	type of aircraft	cn/fn	ex/ex*	mfd	del	powered by	mtow kg	configuration	selcal	name/fln/specialitites/remarks
☐ N54PD	MD Helicopters MD 500E (Hughes 369E)	0180E	N2163Q	0086	0696	1 AN 250-C20B	1361			
☐ N58268	MD Helicopters MD 500D (Hughes 369D)	1280420D		0079	0479	1 AN 250-C20B	1361			lsf P B Fasteners
☐ N8343F	MD Helicopters MD 500D (Hughes 369D)	1160020D		0076	0183	1 AN 250-C20B	1361			
☐ N101HX	Bell 206B JetRanger III	3264	N200NP	0081	0696	1 AN 250-C20B	1451			
☐ N205LA	Bell 206B JetRanger III	2322	N16937	0077	0696	1 AN 250-C20B	1451			
☐ N205LT	Bell 206B JetRanger	1459	N59574	0073	0696	1 AN 250-C20	1451			
☐ N59387	Bell 206B JetRanger	1548		0074	0275	1 AN 250-C20	1451			
☐ N59452	Bell 206B JetRanger	1556		0074	0275	1 AN 250-C20	1451			
☐ N59526	Bell 206B JetRanger	1651		0075	1096	1 AN 250-C20	1451			
☐ N6587Y	Bell 206B JetRanger II	1896		0075	0696	1 AN 250-C20	1451			
☐ N810AM	Bell 206B JetRanger II	1985	N710GW	0076	0696	1 AN 250-C20	1451			
☐ N206LT	Bell 206L-3 LongRanger III	51069		0083	0696	1 AN 250-C30P	1882			
☐ N22621	Bell 206L-3 LongRanger III	51009		0082	0696	1 AN 250-C30P	1882			
☐ N3898Y	Bell 206L-3 LongRanger III	51024		0082	0696	1 AN 250-C30P	1882			
☐ N5741X	Bell 206L-3 LongRanger III	51026		0082	0696	1 AN 250-C30P	1882			
☐ N5745X	Bell 206L-1 LongRanger II	45496		0080	0381	1 AN 250-C28B	1882			
☐ N407ST	Bell 407	53103		0097	0297	1 AN 250-C47B	2268			
☐ N407XS	Bell 407	53150		0097	0597	1 AN 250-C47B	2268			
☐ N1153U	Sikorsky S-58ET	58-378		0056	0696	1 PWC PT6T-3 TwinPac	5897			cvtd S-58E
☐ N4389S	Sikorsky S-58ET	58-1552		0062	0087	1 PWC PT6T-3 TwinPac	5897			lsf Briles Wing / cvtd S-58E
☐ N698	Sikorsky S-58DT	58-1519		0062	0696	1 PWC PT6T-3 TwinPac	5897			cvtd S-58D

TURNER COPTER SERVICE, Inc. — Elliott-Heliport, IA

2350, 120th Street, Elliott, IA 51532-5011, USA ☎ (712) 767-2413 Tx: none Fax: none SITA: n/a
F: 1968 n/a Head: Philip L. Turner Net: n/a

registration	type of aircraft	cn/fn	ex/ex*	mfd	del	powered by	mtow kg	configuration	selcal	name/fln/specialitites/remarks
☐ N62243	Sikorsky S-58J	58-756	56-4333	0057	0979	1 WR R-1820	5897			cvtd H-34A
☐ N79AR	Sikorsky S-58J	58-869	57-1709	0058	0988	1 WR R-1820	5897			cvtd H-34A

TWIN AIR (Twin Town Leasing, Co. Inc. dba) — Fort Lauderdale-Hollywood Int'l, FL

PO Box 22640, Fort Lauderdale, FL 33335, USA ☎ (954) 359-8266 Tx: none Fax: (954) 359-8271 SITA: n/a
F: 1978 n/a Head: Robin V. Gamber Net: n/a

registration	type of aircraft	cn/fn	ex/ex*	mfd	del	powered by	mtow kg	configuration	selcal	name/fln/specialitites/remarks
☐ N146DC	Piper PA-31-350 Navajo Chieftain	31-7305109		0073	1096	2 LY TIO-540-J2BD	3175			lsf pvt
☐ N27337	Piper PA-31-310 Navajo	31-86		0067	1096	2 LY TIO-540-A1A	2948			lsf pvt
☐ N61518	Piper PA-31-350 Navajo Chieftain	31-7552022		0075	1096	2 LY TIO-540-J2BD	3175			lsf pvt

TWIN CITIES AIR SERVICE, Inc. — Auburn-Lewiston Municipal, ME

390 Lewiston Junction Road, Auburn, ME 04210-8846, USA ☎ (207) 784-6318 Tx: none Fax: (207) 784-3819 SITA: n/a
F: 1992 n/a Head: Roger P. Leblanc Net: http://www.landings.com/sites/tca

registration	type of aircraft	cn/fn	ex/ex*	mfd	del	powered by	mtow kg	configuration	selcal	name/fln/specialitites/remarks
☐ N511AR	Cessna T303 Crusader	T30300192		0083	0196	2 CO TSIO-520-AE	2336			
☐ N402SX	Cessna 402C II	402C0606	9A-BPX	0081	1296	2 CO TSIO-520-VB	3107			
☐ N87266	Cessna 402B II	402B1097		0076	0692	2 CO TSIO-520-E	2858			
☐ N729MS	Beech King Air 100	B-2	N43KA	0070	0198	2 PWC PT6A-28	4808			

TWO RIVERS HELICOPTERS (Fred H. Guenther dba) — St. Maries-Municipal, ID

HC 0 4, Box 38, Hi Way 3, St. Maries, ID 83861, USA ☎ (208) 245-3594 Tx: none Fax: none SITA: n/a
F: 1989 n/a Head: Fred H. Guenther Net: n/a

registration	type of aircraft	cn/fn	ex/ex*	mfd	del	powered by	mtow kg	configuration	selcal	name/fln/specialitites/remarks
☐ N53MA	Bell 206B JetRanger III	2285		0077	0689	1 AN 250-C20B	1451			lsf Two Rivers Logging Inc.

UFS, Inc. = U2 / UFS (United Express) (Sister company of Trans States Airlines, Inc.) — Chicago-O'Hare Int'l, IL

9275 Genaire Drive, St. Louis, MO 63134-1912, USA ☎ (573) 895-8700 Tx: n/a Fax: (573) 895-1040 SITA: n/a
F: 1993 n/a Head: Hulas Kanodia IATA: 425 ICAO: FEEDER EXPRESS Net: n/a
All aircraft are operated as UNITED EXPRESS (in full such colours & titles), a commuter system to provide feeder connection at United Airlines major hubs, using UA flight numbers.

registration	type of aircraft	cn/fn	ex/ex*	mfd	del	powered by	mtow kg	configuration	selcal	name/fln/specialitites/remarks
☐ N851AW	BAe ATP	2020	G-WISS*	0089	0993	2 PWC PW126A	22930	Y64		op in United Express-colors
☐ N852AW	BAe ATP	2021	G-BRKM*	0090	0993	2 PWC PW126A	22930	Y64		op in United Express-colors
☐ N853AW	BAe ATP	2022	G-11-022*	0090	0993	2 PWC PW126A	22930	Y64		op in United Express-colors
☐ N854AW	BAe ATP	2028	G-11-028*	0090	0993	2 PWC PW126A	22930	Y64		op in United Express-colors
☐ N855AW	BAe ATP	2029	G-11-029*	0090	0993	2 PWC PW126A	22930	Y64		op in United Express-colors
☐ N856AW	BAe ATP	2032	G-11-032*	0090	0993	2 PWC PW126A	22930	Y64		op in United Express-colors
☐ N857AW	BAe ATP	2034	G-11-034*	0091	0993	2 PWC PW126A	22930	Y64		op in United Express-colors
☐ N858AW	BAe ATP	2035	G-11-035*	0091	0993	2 PWC PW126A	22930	Y64		op in United Express-colors
☐ N859AW	BAe ATP	2036	G-11-036*	0091	0993	2 PWC PW126A	22930	Y64		op in United Express-colors

UK-USA HELICOPTERS, Inc. — Lawrenceville-Gwinnett County/Briscoe Field, GA

500 Briscoe Blvd, Suite 5, Lawrenceville, GA 30245, USA ☎ (770) 682-8911 Tx: none Fax: (770) 682-6606 SITA: n/a
F: 1994 ☃ n/a Head: Melanie Dalton Net: n/a

☐ N143MD	Bell 206B JetRanger III	2344	N44UK	0078	1095	1 AN 250-C20B	1451			
☐ N221GP	Bell 206B JetRanger III	4309	N187H	0094	0197	1 AN 250-C20J	1451			
☐ N2757R	Bell 206B JetRanger III	2662		0079	0695	1 AN 250-C20B	1451			
☐ N16EA	Bell 206L-3 LongRanger III	51067	G-GFRY	0084	0598	1 AN 250-C30P	1882			lsf Helicopter Express Inc.
☐ N43596	Bell 407	53073	C-FTVL	0096	0498	1 AN 250-C47B	2268			lsf Helicopter Express Inc.
☐ N6HE	Bell 407	53235	N37EA	0098	0498	1 AN 250-C47B	2268			lsf Helicopter Express Inc.

ULTIMA THULE Lodge & Outfitters (Paul E. Claus dba) — Chitina, AK

PO Box 109, Chitina, AK 99566, USA ☎ (907) 258-0636 Tx: none Fax: (907) 258-0636 SITA: n/a
F: 1993 ☃ n/a Head: Paul E. Claus Net: n/a Aircraft below MTOW 1361kg: Piper PA-18 (on Floats / Wheel-Skis)

☐ N80596	Cessna A185F Skywagon	18503130		0076	0994	1 CO IO-520-D	1520			Floats / Wheel-Skis
☐ N513F	De Havilland DHC-2 Beaver I	1268	57-6165	0058	0596	1 PW R-985	2313			Floats / Wheel-Skis

UMIAT ENTERPRISES, Inc. — Fairbanks-Int'l, AK

PO Box 60569, Fairbanks, AK 99706, USA ☎ (907) 488-2366 Tx: none Fax: (907) 488-2392 SITA: n/a
F: 1975 ☃ 10 Head: Eleanor Smith Net: n/a Aircraft below MTOW 1361 kg: Piper PA-18 (on Floats / Wheel-Skis).

☐ N1847R	Cessna A185F Skywagon	18502562		0074	1088	1 CO IO-520-D	1520			Floats / Wheel-Skis

UNION FLIGHTS = UNF — Sacramento-Exec, CA & Dayton/Carson City-Valley Airpark, NV

6273 Freeport Boulevard, Sacramento, CA 95822, USA ☎ (530) 421-8531 Tx: none Fax: (530) 421-8546 SITA: n/a
F: 1957 ☃ 55 Head: Jay C. Paynter ICAO: UNION FLIGHTS Net: n/a Aircraft below MTOW 1361 kg: Piper PA-28

☐ N8139A	Piper PA-32R-301 Saratoga SP	32R-8013040		0080	0381	1 LY IO-540-K1G5D	1633			
☐ N8617Q	Beech Debonair B33 (35-B33)	CD-812		0064	1184	1 CO IO-470-K	1361			
☐ N106RE	Piper PA-31-350 Navajo Chieftain	31-7752056		0077	0185	2 LY TIO-540-J2BD	3175			
☐ N27181	Piper PA-31-350 Navajo Chieftain	31-7752068		0077	0996	2 LY TIO-540-J2BD	3175			lsf Alcohol Aviation Fuels Inc.
☐ N3580X	Piper PA-31-350 Navajo Chieftain	31-8052085		0080	1093	2 LY TIO-540-J2BD	3175			lsf Alcohol Aviation Fuels Inc.
☐ N400JM	Piper PA-31-350 Navajo Chieftain	31-8152002		0081	1193	2 LY TIO-540-J2BD	3175			lsf Alcohol Aviation Fuels Inc.
☐ N59850	Piper PA-31-325 Navajo C/R	31-7612056		0076	1276	2 LY TIO-540-F2BD	2948			
☐ N6654Z	Piper PA-31-350 Navajo Chieftain	31-7752143		0077	0793	2 LY TIO-540-J2BD	3175			lsf Alcohol Aviation Fuels Inc.
☐ N7511L	Piper PA-31-310 Navajo B	31-837		0072	0888	2 LY TIO-540-A2C	2948			
☐ N9511F	Cessna 208 Caravan I	20800077		0086	0294	1 PWC PT6A-114	3629			lsf Alcohol Aviation Fuels Inc.
☐ N9762F	Cessna 208 Caravan I	20800181		0090	1190	1 PWC PT6A-114	3629			lsf Alcohol Aviation Fuels Inc.
☐ N1116N	Cessna 208B Grand Caravan	208B0417		0094	0696	1 PWC PT6A-114A	3969			lsf Alcohol Aviation Fuels Inc.
☐ N121HA	Cessna 208B Caravan I Super Cargomaster	208B0069	N6540Q	0087	1093	1 PWC PT6A-114	3969	Freighter		lsf Alcohol Aviation Fuels Inc.
☐ N127HA	Cessna 208B Caravan I Super Cargomaster	208B0148		0089	0794	1 PWC PT6A-114	3969	Freighter		lsf Alcohol Aviation Fuels Inc.
☐ N208N	Cessna 208B Grand Caravan	208B0279	F-OGRU	0091	0798	1 PWC PT6A-114A	3969			lsf Alcohol Aviation Fuels Inc.
☐ N932C	Cessna 208B Caravan I Super Cargomaster	208B0032		0087	1090	1 PWC PT6A-114	3969	Freighter		lsf Alcohol Aviation Fuels Inc.
☐ N9634B	Cessna 208B Caravan I Super Cargomaster	208B0141		0089	1192	1 PWC PT6A-114	3969	Freighter		lsf Alcohol Aviation Fuels Inc.
☐ N9655B	Cessna 208B Caravan I Super Cargomaster	208B0145		0089	0696	1 PWC PT6A-114	3969	Freighter		lsf Alcohol Aviation Fuels Inc.
☐ N9750B	Cessna 208B Caravan I Super Cargomaster	208B0100		0088	0696	1 PWC PT6A-114	3969	Freighter		lsf Alcohol Aviation Fuels Inc.

UNITED AIRLINES, Inc. = UA / UAL (Subsidiary of UAL, Corp. / Member of Star Alliance) — Chicago-ORD, IL & San Francisco, CA

UNITED AIRLINES

PO Box 66100, Chicago, IL 60666, USA ☎ (847) 700-4000 Tx: 253759 Fax: (847) 700-7680 SITA: n/a
F: 1931 ☃ 91780 Head: Gerald Greenwald IATA: 016 ICAO: UNITED Net: http://www.ual.com A commuter system to provide feeder connection at UA major hubs is operated under the marketing name UNITED EXPRESS by: AIR WISCONSIN (BAe 146 & Dornier 328), ATLANTIC COAST (BAe Jetstream 32/41 & CRJ 200), GREAT LAKES AIRLINES (Beech 1900C/D & Embraer 120), SKYWEST (Embraer 120) & UFS (BAe ATP). All are operated in full UNITED EXPRESS-colors & both titles. For details – see under each company.
SHUTTLE BY UNITED is a low-cost, international-division operating in dedicated markets with Boeing 737-200 carrying such titles (same HQ). Aircraft are marked as such in the fleet-list.

☐ N974UA	Boeing 737-2A1 (A)	21597 / 510	N7340F	0078	1085	2 PW JT8D-17	53070	F8Y101		1274
☐ N976UA	Boeing 737-2A1 (A)	21598 / 512	N7341F	0078	1185	2 PW JT8D-17	53070	F8Y101		1276
☐ N977UA	Boeing 737-291 (A)	21508 / 518	N7391F	0078	0985	2 PW JT8D-9A	53070	F8Y101	EM-DF	1177
☐ N978UA	Boeing 737-291 (A)	21509 / 521	N7392F	0078	0985	2 PW JT8D-9A	53070	F8Y101	EM-DG	1178
☐ N979UA	Boeing 737-291 (A)	21544 / 523	N7393F	0078	0985	2 PW JT8D-9A	53070	F8Y101	EM-DH	1179
☐ N980UA	Boeing 737-291 (A)	21545 / 525	N7394F	0078	0985	2 PW JT8D-9A	53070	F8Y101	EL-FJ	1180
☐ N981UA	Boeing 737-291 (A)	21546 / 527	N7395F	0078	1085	2 PW JT8D-9A	53070	F8Y101	EL-FM	1181
☐ N982UA	Boeing 737-291 (A)	21640 / 536	N7396F	0078	1085	2 PW JT8D-9A	53070	F8Y101	FG-CL	1182
☐ N983UA	Boeing 737-291 (A)	21641 / 537	N7397F	0078	1185	2 PW JT8D-9A	53070	F8Y101	FG-CM	1183
☐ N984UA	Boeing 737-291 (A)	21642 / 540	N7398F	0078	1185	2 PW JT8D-17	53070	F8Y101	FG-DE	1284
☐ N985UA	Boeing 737-291 (A)	21747 / 555	N7342F	0079	0286	2 PW JT8D-17	53070	F8Y101	EM-CK	1285
☐ N986UA	Boeing 737-291 (A)	21748 / 558	N7343F	0079	0386	2 PW JT8D-17	53070	F8Y101	FH-AE	1286
☐ N987UA	Boeing 737-291 (A)	21749 / 569	N7344F	0079	0386	2 PW JT8D-17	53070	F8Y101	FH-AG	1287
☐ N988UA	Boeing 737-291 (A)	21750 / 574	N7345F	0079	0386	2 PW JT8D-17	53070	F8Y101	EL-CH	1288
☐ N989UA	Boeing 737-291 (A)	21751 / 575	N7346F	0079	0386	2 PW JT8D-17	53070	F8Y101	EL-CK	1289
☐ N990UA	Boeing 737-291 (A)	21980 / 596	N7347F	0079	0486	2 PW JT8D-17	53070	F8Y101	FH-AB	1290
☐ N991UA	Boeing 737-291 (A)	21981 / 601	N7348F	0079	0486	2 PW JT8D-17	53070	F8Y101	EL-FK	1291
☐ N992UA	Boeing 737-291 (A)	22089 / 632	N7349F	0080	0586	2 PW JT8D-17	53070	F8Y101	FH-AJ	1292
☐ N993UA	Boeing 737-291 (A)	22383 / 713	N7350F	0080	0586	2 PW JT8D-17	53070	F8Y101	EM-AB	1293
☐ N994UA	Boeing 737-291 (A)	22384 / 718	N7351F	0080	0486	2 PW JT8D-17	53070	F8Y101	EM-AL	1294
☐ N995UA	Boeing 737-291 (A)	22399 / 723	N7352F	0080	0586	2 PW JT8D-17 (HK3/NOR)	53070	F8Y101	EM-AJ	1295
☐ N996UA	Boeing 737-291 (A)	22456 / 740	N7353F	0081	0486	2 PW JT8D-17 (HK3/NOR)	53070	F8Y101	EM-AH	1296
☐ N997UA	Boeing 737-291 (A)	22457 / 757	N7354F	0081	0586	2 PW JT8D-17 (HK3/NOR)	53070	F8Y101	EM-BC	1297
☐ N998UA	Boeing 737-291 (A)	22741 / 871	N7355F	0082	0586	2 PW JT8D-17 (HK3/NOR)	53070	F8Y101	FG-CE	1298
☐ N901UA	Boeing 737-522	25001 / 1948		1190	1190	2 CFMI CFM56-3B1	55565	F8Y100		1701
☐ N902UA	Boeing 737-522	25002 / 1950		1190	1190	2 CFMI CFM56-3B1	55565	F8Y100		1702
☐ N903UA	Boeing 737-522	25003 / 1952		1190	1190	2 CFMI CFM56-3B1	55565	F8Y100		1703
☐ N904UA	Boeing 737-522	25004 / 1965		1290	1290	2 CFMI CFM56-3C1	55565	F8Y100		1704
☐ N905UA	Boeing 737-522	25005 / 1976		0191	0191	2 CFMI CFM56-3C1	55565	F8Y100		1705
☐ N906UA	Boeing 737-522	25006 / 1981		0191	0191	2 CFMI CFM56-3C1	55565	F8Y100		1706
☐ N907UA	Boeing 737-522	25007 / 1983		0191	0191	2 CFMI CFM56-3C1	55565	F8Y100		1707
☐ N908UA	Boeing 737-522	25008 / 1987		0291	0291	2 CFMI CFM56-3C1	55565	F8Y100		1708
☐ N909UA	Boeing 737-522	25009 / 1999		0291	0291	2 CFMI CFM56-3C1	55565	F8Y100		1709
☐ N910UA	Boeing 737-522	25254 / 2073		0691	0691	2 CFMI CFM56-3C1	55565	F8Y108		9710 / Shuttle division
☐ N911UA	Boeing 737-522	25255 / 2075		0691	0691	2 CFMI CFM56-3C1	55565	F8Y108		9711 / Shuttle division
☐ N912UA	Boeing 737-522	25290 / 2096		0791	0791	2 CFMI CFM56-3C1	55565	F8Y108		9712 / Shuttle division
☐ N913UA	Boeing 737-522	25291 / 2101		0891	0891	2 CFMI CFM56-3C1	55565	F8Y108		9713 / Shuttle division
☐ N914UA	Boeing 737-522	25381 / 2110		0991	0991	2 CFMI CFM56-3C1	55565	F8Y108		9714 / Shuttle division
☐ N915UA	Boeing 737-522	25382 / 2119		0991	0991	2 CFMI CFM56-3C1	55565	F8Y108		9715 / Shuttle division
☐ N916UA	Boeing 737-522	25383 / 2146		1091	1091	2 CFMI CFM56-3C1	55565	F8Y108		9716 / Shuttle division
☐ N917UA	Boeing 737-522	25384 / 2149		1091	1091	2 CFMI CFM56-3C1	55565	F8Y108		9717 / Shuttle division
☐ N918UA	Boeing 737-522	25385 / 2152		1091	1091	2 CFMI CFM56-3C1	55565	F8Y108		9718 / Shuttle division
☐ N919UA	Boeing 737-522	25386 / 2154		1091	1191	2 CFMI CFM56-3C1	55565	F8Y108		9719 / Shuttle division
☐ N920UA	Boeing 737-522	25387 / 2179		1191	1291	2 CFMI CFM56-3C1	55565	F8Y108		9720 / Shuttle division
☐ N921UA	Boeing 737-522	25388 / 2181		1191	1291	2 CFMI CFM56-3C1	55565	F8Y108		9721 / Shuttle division
☐ N922UA	Boeing 737-522	26642 / 2189		1191	0192	2 CFMI CFM56-3C1	55565	F8Y108		9722 / Shuttle division
☐ N923UA	Boeing 737-522	26643 / 2190		1191	0192	2 CFMI CFM56-3C1	55565	F8Y108		9723 / Shuttle division
☐ N924UA	Boeing 737-522	26645 / 2212		0192	0292	2 CFMI CFM56-3C1	55565	F8Y108		9724 / Shuttle division
☐ N925UA	Boeing 737-522	26646 / 2214		0192	0292	2 CFMI CFM56-3C1	55565	F8Y108		9725 / Shuttle division
☐ N926UA	Boeing 737-522	26648 / 2230		0292	0392	2 CFMI CFM56-3C1	55565	F8Y108		9726 / Shuttle division
☐ N927UA	Boeing 737-522	26649 / 2246		0392	0392	2 CFMI CFM56-3C1	55565	F8Y108		9727 / Shuttle division
☐ N928UA	Boeing 737-522	26651 / 2257		0392	0492	2 CFMI CFM56-3C1	55565	F8Y108		9728 / Shuttle division
☐ N929UA	Boeing 737-522	26652 / 2259		0392	0492	2 CFMI CFM56-3C1	55565	F8Y108		9729 / Shuttle division
☐ N930UA	Boeing 737-522	26655 / 2274		0492	0492	2 CFMI CFM56-3C1	55565	F8Y108		9730 / Shuttle division
☐ N931UA	Boeing 737-522	26656 / 2289		0592	0592	2 CFMI CFM56-3C1	55565	F8Y108		9731 / Shuttle division
☐ N932UA	Boeing 737-522	26658 / 2291		0592	0592	2 CFMI CFM56-3C1	55565	F8Y108		9732 / Shuttle division
☐ N933UA	Boeing 737-522	26659 / 2293		0592	0592	2 CFMI CFM56-3C1	55565	F8Y108		9733 / Shuttle division
☐ N934UA	Boeing 737-522	26662 / 2312		0692	0692	2 CFMI CFM56-3C1	55565	F8Y108		9734 / Shuttle division
☐ N935UA	Boeing 737-522	26663 / 2315		0692	0692	2 CFMI CFM56-3C1	55565	F8Y100		1735
☐ N936UA	Boeing 737-522	26667 / 2325		0792	0792	2 CFMI CFM56-3C1	55565	F8Y100		1736
☐ N937UA	Boeing 737-522	26668 / 2329		0792	0792	2 CFMI CFM56-3C1	55565	F8Y100		1737
☐ N938UA	Boeing 737-522	26671 / 2336		0792	0792	2 CFMI CFM56-3C1	55565	F8Y100		1738
☐ N939UA	Boeing 737-522	26672 / 2343		0792	0892	2 CFMI CFM56-3C1	55565	F8Y100		1739
☐ N940UA	Boeing 737-522	26675 / 2345		0792	0992	2 CFMI CFM56-3C1	55565	F8Y100		1740
☐ N941UA	Boeing 737-522	26676 / 2364		0992	1092	2 CFMI CFM56-3C1	55565	F8Y100		1741
☐ N942UA	Boeing 737-522	26679 / 2365		0992	1092	2 CFMI CFM56-3C1	55565	F8Y100		1742
☐ N943UA	Boeing 737-522	26680 / 2366		0992	1192	2 CFMI CFM56-3C1	55565	F8Y100		1743
☐ N944UA	Boeing 737-522	26683 / 2368		0992	1192	2 CFMI CFM56-3C1	55565	F8Y100		1744
☐ N945UA	Boeing 737-522	26684 / 2388		1092	1292	2 CFMI CFM56-3C1	55565	F8Y100		1745

450 registration type of aircraft cn/fn ex/ex* mfd del powered by mtow kg configuration selcal name/fln/specialitites/remarks

☐ N946UA	Boeing 737-522	26687 / 2402		1192	1292	2 CFMI CFM56-3C1	55565	F8Y100		1746
☐ N947UA	Boeing 737-522	26688 / 2404		1192	1292	2 CFMI CFM56-3C1	55565	F8Y100		1747
☐ N948UA	Boeing 737-522	26691 / 2408		1292	1292	2 CFMI CFM56-3C1	55565	F8Y100		1748
☐ N949UA	Boeing 737-522	26692 / 2421		0193	0293	2 CFMI CFM56-3C1	55565	F8Y100		1749
☐ N950UA	Boeing 737-522	26695 / 2423		0193	0293	2 CFMI CFM56-3C1	55565	F8Y100		1750
☐ N951UA	Boeing 737-522	26696 / 2440		0293	0393	2 CFMI CFM56-3C1	55565	F8Y100		1751
☐ N952UA	Boeing 737-522	26699 / 2485		0593	0693	2 CFMI CFM56-3C1	55565	F8Y100		1752
☐ N953UA	Boeing 737-522	26700 / 2490		0693	0693	2 CFMI CFM56-3C1	55565	F8Y100		1753
☐ N954UA	Boeing 737-522	26739 / 2494		0693	0793	2 CFMI CFM56-3C1	55565	F8Y100		1754
☐ N955UA	Boeing 737-522	26703 / 2498		0693	0793	2 CFMI CFM56-3C1	55565	F8Y100		1755
☐ N956UA	Boeing 737-522	26704 / 2508		0793	0893	2 CFMI CFM56-3C1	55565	F8Y100		1756
☐ N957UA	Boeing 737-522	26707 / 2512		0793	0893	2 CFMI CFM56-3C1	55565	F8Y100		1757
☐ N202UA	Boeing 737-322	24717 / 1930		0090	1090	2 CFMI CFM56-3B1	58967	F8Y118		9002
☐ N203UA	Boeing 737-322	24718 / 1937		0090	1090	2 CFMI CFM56-3B1	58967	F8Y118		9003
☐ N301UA	Boeing 737-322	23642 / 1300		0086	1186	2 CFMI CFM56-3B1	58967	F8Y118		9301
☐ N302UA	Boeing 737-322	23643 / 1315		0086	1186	2 CFMI CFM56-3B1	58967	F8Y118		9302
☐ N303UA	Boeing 737-322	23644 / 1322		0086	1186	2 CFMI CFM56-3B1	58967	F8Y118		9303
☐ N304UA	Boeing 737-322	23665 / 1330		0087	0187	2 CFMI CFM56-3B1	58967	F8Y118		9304
☐ N305UA	Boeing 737-322	23666 / 1332		0087	0187	2 CFMI CFM56-3B1	58967	F8Y118		9305
☐ N306UA	Boeing 737-322	23667 / 1334		0087	0287	2 CFMI CFM56-3B1	58967	F8Y118		9306
☐ N307UA	Boeing 737-322	23668 / 1346		0087	0387	2 CFMI CFM56-3B1	58967	F8Y118		9307
☐ N308UA	Boeing 737-322	23669 / 1354		0087	0387	2 CFMI CFM56-3B1	58967	F8Y118		9308
☐ N309UA	Boeing 737-322	23670 / 1364		0087	0487	2 CFMI CFM56-3B1	58967	F8Y118		9309
☐ N310UA	Boeing 737-322	23671 / 1370		0087	0487	2 CFMI CFM56-3B1	58967	F8Y118		9310
☐ N311UA	Boeing 737-322	23672 / 1470		0087	1187	2 CFMI CFM56-3B2	58967	F8Y118	DE-MR	9911
☐ N312UA	Boeing 737-322	23673 / 1479		0087	1287	2 CFMI CFM56-3B2	58967	F8Y118	DE-MS	9912
☐ N313UA	Boeing 737-322	23674 / 1481		0087	1287	2 CFMI CFM56-3B2	58967	F8Y118	DE-PR	9913
☐ N314UA	Boeing 737-322	23675 / 1483		0087	1287	2 CFMI CFM56-3B2	58967	F8Y118	DE-PS	9914
☐ N315UA	Boeing 737-322	23947 / 1485		0087	1287	2 CFMI CFM56-3B2	58967	F8Y118	DE-QR	9915
☐ N316UA	Boeing 737-322	23948 / 1491		0088	0188	2 CFMI CFM56-3B2	58967	F8Y118		9416
☐ N317UA	Boeing 737-322	23949 / 1493		0088	0188	2 CFMI CFM56-3B2	58967	F8Y118		9417
☐ N318UA	Boeing 737-322	23950 / 1504		0088	0288	2 CFMI CFM56-3B2	58967	F8Y118		9418
☐ N319UA	Boeing 737-322	23951 / 1532		0088	0488	2 CFMI CFM56-3B2	58967	F8Y118		9419
☐ N320UA	Boeing 737-322	23952 / 1534		0088	0488	2 CFMI CFM56-3B2	58967	F8Y118		9420
☐ N321UA	Boeing 737-322	23953 / 1546		0088	0588	2 CFMI CFM56-3B2	58967	F8Y118		9421
☐ N322UA	Boeing 737-322	23954 / 1548		0088	0588	2 CFMI CFM56-3B2	58967	F8Y118		9422
☐ N323UA	Boeing 737-322	23955 / 1550		0088	0588	2 CFMI CFM56-3B2	58967	F8Y118		9423
☐ N324UA	Boeing 737-322	23956 / 1564		0088	0688	2 CFMI CFM56-3B2	58967	F8Y118		9424
☐ N325UA	Boeing 737-322	23957 / 1566		0088	0688	2 CFMI CFM56-3B2	58967	F8Y118	KM-DP	9925
☐ N326UA	Boeing 737-322	23958 / 1568		0088	0688	2 CFMI CFM56-3B2	58967	F8Y118	KM-EP	9926
☐ N327UA	Boeing 737-322	24147 / 1570		0088	0788	2 CFMI CFM56-3B2	58967	F8Y118		9427
☐ N328UA	Boeing 737-322	24148 / 1572		0088	0788	2 CFMI CFM56-3B2	58967	F8Y118		9428
☐ N329UA	Boeing 737-322	24149 / 1574		0088	0788	2 CFMI CFM56-3B2	58967	F8Y118	DE-QS	9929
☐ N330UA	Boeing 737-322	24191 / 1588		0088	0888	2 CFMI CFM56-3B2	58967	F8Y118	DE-RS	9930
☐ N331UA	Boeing 737-322	24192 / 1590		0088	0888	2 CFMI CFM56-3B2	58967	F8Y118	DF-AR	9931
☐ N332UA	Boeing 737-322	24193 / 1592		0088	0888	2 CFMI CFM56-3B2	58967	F8Y118	DF-AS	9932
☐ N333UA	Boeing 737-322	24228 / 1594		0088	0888	2 CFMI CFM56-3B2	58967	F8Y118	DF-BR	9933
☐ N334UA	Boeing 737-322	24229 / 1605		0088	0988	2 CFMI CFM56-3B2	58967	F8Y118	KM-FP	9934
☐ N335UA	Boeing 737-322	24230 / 1607		0088	0988	2 CFMI CFM56-3B2	58967	F8Y118	KM-GP	9935
☐ N336UA	Boeing 737-322	24240 / 1609		0088	0988	2 CFMI CFM56-3B2	58967	F8Y118		9436
☐ N337UA	Boeing 737-322	24241 / 1611		0088	0988	2 CFMI CFM56-3B2	58967	F8Y118		9437
☐ N338UA	Boeing 737-322	24242 / 1613		0088	1088	2 CFMI CFM56-3B2	58967	F8Y118		9438
☐ N339UA	Boeing 737-322	24243 / 1615		0088	1088	2 CFMI CFM56-3B2	58967	F8Y118		9439
☐ N340UA	Boeing 737-322	24244 / 1617		0088	1088	2 CFMI CFM56-3B2	58967	F8Y118		9440
☐ N341UA	Boeing 737-322	24245 / 1619		0088	1088	2 CFMI CFM56-3B2	58967	F8Y118	KM-HP	9941
☐ N342UA	Boeing 737-322	24246 / 1632		0088	1188	2 CFMI CFM56-3B2	58967	F8Y118	KM-JP	9942
☐ N343UA	Boeing 737-322	24247 / 1634		0088	1188	2 CFMI CFM56-3B2	58967	F8Y118		9443
☐ N344UA	Boeing 737-322	24248 / 1636		0088	1188	2 CFMI CFM56-3B2	58967	F8Y118		9444
☐ N345UA	Boeing 737-322	24249 / 1638		0088	1188	2 CFMI CFM56-3B2	58967	F8Y118		9445
☐ N346UA	Boeing 737-322	24250 / 1644		0088	1288	2 CFMI CFM56-3B2	58967	F8Y118		9446
☐ N347UA	Boeing 737-322	24251 / 1646		0088	1288	2 CFMI CFM56-3B2	58967	F8Y118		9447
☐ N348UA	Boeing 737-322	24252 / 1648		0088	1288	2 CFMI CFM56-3B2	58967	F8Y118		9448
☐ N349UA	Boeing 737-322	24253 / 1650		0088	1288	2 CFMI CFM56-3B2	58967	F8Y118		9449
☐ N350UA	Boeing 737-322	24301 / 1652		0088	0189	2 CFMI CFM56-3B2	58967	F8Y118		9450
☐ N351UA	Boeing 737-322	24319 / 1668		0089	0289	2 CFMI CFM56-3B2	58967	F8Y118		9451
☐ N352UA	Boeing 737-322	24320 / 1670		0089	0289	2 CFMI CFM56-3B2	58967	F8Y118		9452
☐ N353UA	Boeing 737-322	24321 / 1672		0089	0289	2 CFMI CFM56-3B2	58967	F8Y118		9453
☐ N354UA	Boeing 737-322	24360 / 1692		0089	0489	2 CFMI CFM56-3B1	58967	F8Y118		9354
☐ N355UA	Boeing 737-322	24361 / 1694		0089	0489	2 CFMI CFM56-3B1	58967	F8Y118		9355
☐ N356UA	Boeing 737-322	24362 / 1696		0089	0489	2 CFMI CFM56-3B1	58967	F8Y118		9356
☐ N357UA	Boeing 737-322	24378 / 1704		0089	0589	2 CFMI CFM56-3B1	58967	F8Y118		9357
☐ N358UA	Boeing 737-322	24379 / 1724		0089	0589	2 CFMI CFM56-3B1	58967	F8Y126		1358 / Shuttle division
☐ N359UA	Boeing 737-322	24452 / 1728		0089	0689	2 CFMI CFM56-3B1	58967	F8Y118		9359
☐ N360UA	Boeing 737-322	24453 / 1730		0089	0689	2 CFMI CFM56-3B1	58967	F8Y118		9360
☐ N361UA	Boeing 737-322	24454 / 1750		0089	0789	2 CFMI CFM56-3B1	58967	F8Y118		9361
☐ N362UA	Boeing 737-322	24455 / 1752		0089	0789	2 CFMI CFM56-3B1	58967	F8Y118		9362
☐ N363UA	Boeing 737-322	24532 / 1754		0089	0889	2 CFMI CFM56-3B1	58967	F8Y118		9363
☐ N364UA	Boeing 737-322	24533 / 1756		0089	0889	2 CFMI CFM56-3B1	58967	F8Y118		9364
☐ N365UA	Boeing 737-322	24534 / 1758		0089	0889	2 CFMI CFM56-3B1	58967	F8Y118		9365
☐ N366UA	Boeing 737-322	24535 / 1760		0089	0989	2 CFMI CFM56-3B1	58967	F8Y126		1366 / Shuttle divison
☐ N367UA	Boeing 737-322	24536 / 1762		0089	0989	2 CFMI CFM56-3B1	58967	F8Y126		1367 / Shuttle division
☐ N368UA	Boeing 737-322	24537 / 1774		0089	0989	2 CFMI CFM56-3B1	58967	F8Y118		9368
☐ N369UA	Boeing 737-322	24538 / 1776		0089	1089	2 CFMI CFM56-3B1	58967	F8Y126		1369 / Shuttle division
☐ N370UA	Boeing 737-322	24539 / 1778		0089	1089	2 CFMI CFM56-3B1	58967	F8Y126		1370 / Shuttle division
☐ N371UA	Boeing 737-322	24540 / 1780		0089	1089	2 CFMI CFM56-3B1	58967	F8Y126		1371 / Shuttle division
☐ N372UA	Boeing 737-322	24637 / 1782		0089	1089	2 CFMI CFM56-3B1	58967	F8Y126		1372 / Shuttle division
☐ N373UA	Boeing 737-322	24638 / 1784		0089	1189	2 CFMI CFM56-3B1	58967	F8Y126		1373 / Shuttle division
☐ N374UA	Boeing 737-322	24639 / 1786		0089	1189	2 CFMI CFM56-3B1	58967	F8Y126		1374 / Shuttle division
☐ N375UA	Boeing 737-322	24640 / 1798		0089	1289	2 CFMI CFM56-3B1	58967	F8Y126		1375 / Shuttle division
☐ N376UA	Boeing 737-322	24641 / 1802		0090	0190	2 CFMI CFM56-3B1	58967	F8Y126		1376 / Shuttle division
☐ N377UA	Boeing 737-322	24642 / 1806		0090	0190	2 CFMI CFM56-3B1	58967	F8Y126		1377 / Shuttle division
☐ N378UA	Boeing 737-322	24653 / 1810		0090	0190	2 CFMI CFM56-3B1	58967	F8Y126		1378 / Shuttle division
☐ N379UA	Boeing 737-322	24654 / 1812		0090	0290	2 CFMI CFM56-3B1	58967	F8Y126		1379 / Shuttle division
☐ N380UA	Boeing 737-322	24655 / 1814		0090	0290	2 CFMI CFM56-3B1	58967	F8Y126		1380 / Shuttle division
☐ N381UA	Boeing 737-322	24656 / 1822		0090	0290	2 CFMI CFM56-3B1	58967	F8Y126		1381 / Shuttle division
☐ N382UA	Boeing 737-322	24657 / 1830		0090	0390	2 CFMI CFM56-3B1	58967	F8Y126		1382 / Shuttle division
☐ N383UA	Boeing 737-322	24658 / 1832		0090	0390	2 CFMI CFM56-3B1	58967	F8Y126		1383 / Shuttle division
☐ N384UA	Boeing 737-322	24659 / 1836		0090	0390	2 CFMI CFM56-3B1	58967	F8Y126		1384 / Shuttle division
☐ N385UA	Boeing 737-322	24660 / 1838		0090	0490	2 CFMI CFM56-3B1	58967	F8Y126		1385 / Shuttle division
☐ N386UA	Boeing 737-322	24661 / 1840		0090	0490	2 CFMI CFM56-3B1	58967	F8Y126		1386 / Shuttle division
☐ N387UA	Boeing 737-322	24662 / 1862		0090	0590	2 CFMI CFM56-3B1	58967	F8Y126		1387 / Shuttle division
☐ N388UA	Boeing 737-322	24663 / 1875		0090	0690	2 CFMI CFM56-3B1	58967	F8Y126		1388 / Shuttle division
☐ N389UA	Boeing 737-322	24664 / 1877		0090	0690	2 CFMI CFM56-3B1	58967	F8Y126		1389 / Shuttle division
☐ N390UA	Boeing 737-322	24665 / 1889		0090	0790	2 CFMI CFM56-3B1	58967	F8Y126		1390 / Shuttle division
☐ N391UA	Boeing 737-322	24666 / 1891		0090	0790	2 CFMI CFM56-3B1	58967	F8Y126		1391 / Shuttle division
☐ N392UA	Boeing 737-322	24667 / 1893		0090	0790	2 CFMI CFM56-3B1	58967	F8Y126		1392 / Shuttle division
☐ N393UA	Boeing 737-322	24668 / 1905		0090	0890	2 CFMI CFM56-3B1	58967	F8Y126		1393 / Shuttle division
☐ N394UA	Boeing 737-322	24669 / 1907		0090	0890	2 CFMI CFM56-3B1	58967	F8Y126		1394 / Shuttle division
☐ N395UA	Boeing 737-322	24670 / 1909		0090	0890	2 CFMI CFM56-3B1	58967	F8Y126		1395 / Shuttle division
☐ N396UA	Boeing 737-322	24671 / 1913		0090	0990	2 CFMI CFM56-3B1	58967	F8Y126		1396 / Shuttle division
☐ N397UA	Boeing 737-322	24672 / 1915		0090	0990	2 CFMI CFM56-3B1	58967	F8Y126		1397 / Shuttle division
☐ N398UA	Boeing 737-322	24673 / 1920		0090	0990	2 CFMI CFM56-3B1	58967	F8Y126		1398 / Shuttle division
☐ N399UA	Boeing 737-322	24674 / 1928		0090	1090	2 CFMI CFM56-3B1	58967	F8Y126		1399 / Shuttle division
☐ N801UA	Airbus Industrie A319-131	686	D-AVYI*	0697	0697	2 IAE V2522-A5	70000	F8Y118	LS-AB	4101
☐ N802UA	Airbus Industrie A319-131	690	D-AVYO*	0697	0697	2 IAE V2522-A5	70000	F8Y118	PR-BH	4102
☐ N803UA	Airbus Industrie A319-131	748	D-AVYL*	0097	1197	2 IAE V2522-A5	64000	F8Y118		4103
☐ N804UA	Airbus Industrie A319-131	759	D-AVYR*	0097	1297	2 IAE V2522-A5	64000	F8Y118		4104
☐ N805UA	Airbus Industrie A319-131	783	D-AVYY*	0098	0298	2 IAE V2522-A5	64000	F8Y118	HQ-PS	4105
☐ N806UA	Airbus Industrie A319-131	788	D-AVYW*	0298	0298	2 IAE V2522-A5	64000	F8Y118		4106
☐ N807UA	Airbus Industrie A319-131	798	D-AVYX*	0098	0398	2 IAE V2522-A5	64000	F8Y118	LM-GP	4107

451 registration type of aircraft cn/fn ex/ex* mfd del powered by mtow kg configuration selcal name/fln/specialitites/remarks

registration	type of aircraft	cn/fn	ex/ex*	mfd	del	powered by	mtow kg	configuration	selcal	name/fln/specialitites/remarks
☐ N808UA	Airbus Industrie A319-131	804	D-AVYF*	0098	0398	2 IAE V2522-A5	64000	F8Y118		4108
☐ N809UA	Airbus Industrie A319-131	825	D-AVYZ*	0098	0598	2 IAE V2522-A5	64000	F8Y118		4109
☐ N810UA	Airbus Industrie A319-131	843	D-AVYR*	0098	0698	2 IAE V2522-A5	64000	F8Y118	PQ-CS	4110
☐ N811UA	Airbus Industrie A319-131	847	D-AVYB*	0098	0798	2 IAE V2522-A5	64000	F8Y118		4111
☐ N812UA	Airbus Industrie A319-131	850	D-AVYK*	0098	0798	2 IAE V2522-A5	64000	F8Y118	AC-LQ	4112
☐ N813UA	Airbus Industrie A319-131	858	D-AVYP*	0098	0798	2 IAE V2522-A5	64000	F8Y118		4113
☐ N814UA	Airbus Industrie A319-131	862	D-AVYT*	0098	0898	2 IAE V2522-A5	64000	F8Y118		4114
☐ N815UA	Airbus Industrie A319-131	867	D-AVYU*	0098	0898	2 IAE V2522-A5	64000	F8Y118		4115
☐ N816UA	Airbus Industrie A319-131	871	D-AVYY*	0098	0998	2 IAE V2522-A5	64000	F8Y118		4116
☐ N817UA	Airbus Industrie A319-131	873	D-AVYX*	0098	0998	2 IAE V2522-A5	64000	F8Y118		4117
☐ N818UA	Airbus Industrie A319-131	882	D-AVYE*	0098	1098	2 IAE V2522-A5	64000	F8Y118		4118
☐ N819UA	Airbus Industrie A319-131	893	D-AVYV*	0098	1098	2 IAE V2522-A5	64000	F8Y118		4119
☐ N820UA	Airbus Industrie A319-131	898	D-AVYZ*	0098	1098	2 IAE V2522-A5	64000	F8Y118		4120
☐ N821UA	Airbus Industrie A319-131	944	D-AVYC*	0099	0199	2 IAE V2522-A5	64000	F8Y118		4121
☐ N822UA	Airbus Industrie A319-131	948	D-AVYE*	0099	0199	2 IAE V2522-A5	64000	F8Y118		4122
☐ N823UA	Airbus Industrie A319-131	952		0099	0299	2 IAE V2522-A5	64000	F8Y118		4123
☐ N824UA	Airbus Industrie A319-131	965		0099	0299	2 IAE V2522-A5	64000	F8Y118		4124
☐ N825UA	Airbus Industrie A319-131	980		0099	0399	2 IAE V2522-A5	64000	F8Y118		4125
☐ N826UA	Airbus Industrie A319-131	989		0099	0399	2 IAE V2522-A5	64000	F8Y118		4126
☐ N827UA	Airbus Industrie A319-131	1022				2 IAE V2522-A5	64000	F8Y118		4127 / oo-delivery 0599
☐ N828UA	Airbus Industrie A319-131	1031				2 IAE V2522-A5	64000	F8Y118		4128 / oo-delivery 0699
☐ N829UA	Airbus Industrie A319-131					2 IAE V2522-A5	64000	F8Y118		4129 / oo-delivery 0001
☐ N830UA	Airbus Industrie A319-131					2 IAE V2522-A5	64000	F8Y118		4130 / oo-delivery 0001
☐ N831UA	Airbus Industrie A319-131					2 IAE V2522-A5	64000	F8Y118		4131 / oo-delivery 0001
☐ N832UA	Airbus Industrie A319-131					2 IAE V2522-A5	64000	F8Y118		4132 / oo-delivery 0001
☐ N833UA	Airbus Industrie A319-131					2 IAE V2522-A5	64000	F8Y118		4133 / oo-delivery 0001
☐ N834UA	Airbus Industrie A319-131					2 IAE V2522-A5	64000	F8Y118		4134 / oo-delivery 0001
☐ N835UA	Airbus Industrie A319-131					2 IAE V2522-A5	64000	F8Y118		4135 / oo-delivery 0001
☐ N836UA	Airbus Industrie A319-131					2 IAE V2522-A5	64000	F8Y118		4136 / oo-delivery 0001
☐ N837UA	Airbus Industrie A319-131					2 IAE V2522-A5	64000	F8Y118		4137 / oo-delivery 0001
☐ N838UA	Airbus Industrie A319-131					2 IAE V2522-A5	64000	F8Y118		4138 / oo-delivery 0001
☐ N839UA	Airbus Industrie A319-131					2 IAE V2522-A5	64000	F8Y118		4139 / oo-delivery 0002
☐ N840UA	Airbus Industrie A319-131					2 IAE V2522-A5	64000	F8Y118		4140 / oo-delivery 0002
☐ N841UA	Airbus Industrie A319-131					2 IAE V2522-A5	64000	F8Y118		4141 / oo-delivery 0002
☐ N842UA	Airbus Industrie A319-131					2 IAE V2522-A5	64000	F8Y118		4142 / oo-delivery 0002
☐ N843UA	Airbus Industrie A319-131					2 IAE V2522-A5	64000	F8Y118		4143 / oo-delivery 0002
☐ N844UA	Airbus Industrie A319-131					2 IAE V2522-A5	64000	F8Y118		4144 / oo-delivery 0002
☐ N845UA	Airbus Industrie A319-131					2 IAE V2522-A5	64000	F8Y118		4145 / oo-delivery 0002
☐ N846UA	Airbus Industrie A319-131					2 IAE V2522-A5	64000	F8Y118		4146 / oo-delivery 0002
☐ N847UA	Airbus Industrie A319-131					2 IAE V2522-A5	64000	F8Y118		4147 / oo-delivery 0002
☐ N848UA	Airbus Industrie A319-131					2 IAE V2522-A5	64000	F8Y118		4148 / oo-delivery 0002
☐ N401UA	Airbus Industrie A320-232	435	F-WWDD*	0093	1193	2 IAE V2527-A5	73500	F12Y132	ES-AL	4201 / Alan Temple Employee
☐ N402UA	Airbus Industrie A320-232	439	F-WWIJ*	0093	1193	2 IAE V2527-A5	73500	F12Y132	ES-AM	4202 / Telma Aloni Employee
☐ N403UA	Airbus Industrie A320-232	442	F-WWIY*	0093	1293	2 IAE V2527-A5	73500	F12Y132	ES-AP	4203 / Hiroko Fujishima Employee
☐ N404UA	Airbus Industrie A320-232	450	F-WWII*	0093	1293	2 IAE V2527-A5	73500	F12Y132	ES-AQ	4204 / Maria Karla Gozum Employee
☐ N405UA	Airbus Industrie A320-232	452	F-WWBF*	0093	1293	2 IAE V2527-A5	73500	F12Y132	ES-AR	4205 / John P. Maori Sr. Customer
☐ N406UA	Airbus Industrie A320-232	454	F-WWBJ*	0093	0194	2 IAE V2527-A5	73500	F12Y132	ES-BC	4206 / J. Rex Pippin Customer
☐ N407UA	Airbus Industrie A320-232	456	F-WWDB*	0093	0294	2 IAE V2527-A5	73500	F12Y132	ES-BD	4207 / Jeff Mandelbaum Customer
☐ N408UA	Airbus Industrie A320-232	457	F-WWDG*	0094	0394	2 IAE V2527-A5	73500	F12Y132	ES-BF	4208 / Peter C. Bond Customer
☐ N409UA	Airbus Industrie A320-232	462	F-WWDQ*	0094	0394	2 IAE V2527-A5	73500	F12Y132	ES-BG	4209 / Bob Young Customer
☐ N410UA	Airbus Industrie A320-232	463	F-WWDV*	0094	0494	2 IAE V2527-A5	73500	F12Y132	ES-BH	4210 / C. Nicholas Keating,Jr. Customer
☐ N411UA	Airbus Industrie A320-232	464	F-WWDX*	0094	0494	2 IAE V2527-A5	73500	F12Y132	ES-BJ	4211 / Ikaz Imai Customer
☐ N412UA	Airbus Industrie A320-232	465	F-WWIM*	0094	0594	2 IAE V2527-A5	73500	F12Y132	ES-BK	4212 / Robert Thomas Customer
☐ N413UA	Airbus Industrie A320-232	470	F-WWBM*	0094	0694	2 IAE V2527-A5	73500	F12Y132	ES-BL	4213 / Geoff Wild Customer
☐ N414UA	Airbus Industrie A320-232	472	F-WWIU*	0094	0794	2 IAE V2527-A5	73500	F12Y132	ES-BM	4214 / Toshi K. Funaki Customer
☐ N415UA	Airbus Industrie A320-232	475	F-WWBP*	0094	0994	2 IAE V2527-A5	73500	F12Y132	ES-BP	4215 / Ronald A. Schy Customer
☐ N416UA	Airbus Industrie A320-232	479	F-WWDH*	0094	0994	2 IAE V2527-A5	73500	F12Y132	ES-BQ	4216 / Timothy L. Devine Customer
☐ N417UA	Airbus Industrie A320-232	483	F-WWIT*	0094	0994	2 IAE V2527-A5	73500	F12Y132	ES-BR	4217 / Rickey Wilson Customer
☐ N418UA	Airbus Industrie A320-232	485	F-WWIZ*	0094	0994	2 IAE V2527-A5	73500	F12Y132	ES-CD	4218 / Scott Setrakian Customer
☐ N419UA	Airbus Industrie A320-232	487	F-WWDJ*	0094	1094	2 IAE V2527-A5	73500	F12Y132	ES-CF	4219 / M. J. Suhanovsky Customer
☐ N420UA	Airbus Industrie A320-232	489	F-WWDM*	0094	1194	2 IAE V2527-A5	73500	F12Y132	ES-CG	4220 / Charles A. Kelley Customer
☐ N421UA	Airbus Industrie A320-232	500	F-WWDZ*	0094	1294	2 IAE V2527-A5	73500	F12Y132	ES-CH	4221 / Peter A. Dare Customer
☐ N422UA	Airbus Industrie A320-232	503	F-WWIV*	0094	0195	2 IAE V2527-A5	73500	F12Y132	HM-JR	4222 / Yale R. Brown Customer
☐ N423UA	Airbus Industrie A320-232	504	F-WWBO*	0094	0295	2 IAE V2527-A5	73500	F12Y132	HM-JS	4223 / Ron Maehl Customer
☐ N424UA	Airbus Industrie A320-232	506	F-WWBQ*	0094	0295	2 IAE V2527-A5	73500	F12Y132	HM-KP	4224 / Albert G. Brantley Customer
☐ N425UA	Airbus Industrie A320-232	508	F-WWBY*	0094	0395	2 IAE V2527-A5	73500	F12Y132	HM-KQ	4225 / Howard A. Morgan Customer
☐ N426UA	Airbus Industrie A320-232	510	F-WWBZ*	0094	0395	2 IAE V2527-A5	73500	F12Y132	HM-KR	4226 / William Yeack Customer
☐ N427UA	Airbus Industrie A320-232	512	F-WWDD*	0095	0495	2 IAE V2527-A5	73500	F12Y132	HM-KS	4227 / Dee Groberg Customer
☐ N428UA	Airbus Industrie A320-232	523	F-WWDE*	0095	0595	2 IAE V2527-A5	73500	F12Y132	HM-LQ	4228 / Albert J. Viscio Customer
☐ N429UA	Airbus Industrie A320-232	539	F-WWIX*	0095	0695	2 IAE V2527-A5	73500	F12Y132	HM-LR	4229
☐ N430UA	Airbus Industrie A320-232	568	F-WWDC*	0096	0296	2 IAE V2527-A5	73500	F12Y132	LQ-DG	4230
☐ N431UA	Airbus Industrie A320-232	571	F-WWDH*	0096	0396	2 IAE V2527-A5	73500	F12Y132	LQ-DH	4231
☐ N432UA	Airbus Industrie A320-232	587	F-WWBB*	0096	0596	2 IAE V2527-A5	73500	F12Y132	LQ-DJ	4232
☐ N433UA	Airbus Industrie A320-232	589	F-WWBD*	0096	0696	2 IAE V2527-A5	73500	F12Y132	LQ-DR	4233
☐ N434UA	Airbus Industrie A320-232	592	F-WWBF*	0096	0696	2 IAE V2527-A5	73500	F12Y132	LQ-DS	4234
☐ N435UA	Airbus Industrie A320-232	613	F-WWBQ*	0096	0996	2 IAE V2527-A5	73500	F12Y132	LQ-EG	4235
☐ N436UA	Airbus Industrie A320-232	638	F-WWDE*	0096	1296	2 IAE V2527-A5	73500	F12Y132	LQ-ER	4236
☐ N437UA	Airbus Industrie A320-232	655	F-WWIK*	0097	0297	2 IAE V2527-A5	73500	F12Y132	LR-JQ	4237
☐ N438UA	Airbus Industrie A320-232	678	F-WWBJ*	0097	0597	2 IAE V2527-A5	73500	F12Y132	LR-JS	4238
☐ N439UA	Airbus Industrie A320-232	683	F-WWDQ*	0097	0697	2 IAE V2527-A5	73500	F12Y132	LR-KQ	4239
☐ N440UA	Airbus Industrie A320-232	702	F-WWDP*	0097	0797	2 IAE V2527-A5	73500	F12Y132	LR-KS	4240
☐ N441UA	Airbus Industrie A320-232	751	F-WWIU*	0097	1297	2 IAE V2527-A5	73500	F12Y132	LR-PQ	4241
☐ N442UA	Airbus Industrie A320-232	780	F-WWDQ*	0098	0298	2 IAE V2527-A5	73500	F12Y132	EP-MR	4242
☐ N443UA	Airbus Industrie A320-232	820	F-WWBT*	0098	0598	2 IAE V2527-A5	73500	F12Y132		4243
☐ N444UA	Airbus Industrie A320-232	824	F-WWBZ*	0098	0598	2 IAE V2527-A5	73500	F12Y132		4244
☐ N445UA	Airbus Industrie A320-232	826	F-WWIL*	0098	0698	2 IAE V2527-A5	73500	F12Y132		4245
☐ N446UA	Airbus Industrie A320-232	834	F-WWIP*	0098	0698	2 IAE V2527-A5	73500	F12Y132		4246
☐ N447UA	Airbus Industrie A320-232	836	F-WWIR*	0098	0798	2 IAE V2527-A5	73500	F12Y132	FJ-PQ	4247
☐ N448UA	Airbus Industrie A320-232	842	F-WWBF*	0098	0798	2 IAE V2527-A5	73500	F12Y132	FK-PR	4248
☐ N449UA	Airbus Industrie A320-232	851	F-WWBJ*	0098	0798	2 IAE V2527-A5	73500	F12Y132	FK-PS	4249
☐ N450UA	Airbus Industrie A320-232	857	F-WWBN*	0098	0798	2 IAE V2527-A5	73500	F12Y132		4250
☐ N451UA	Airbus Industrie A320-232	865	F-WWBR*	0098	0998	2 IAE V2527-A5	73500	F12Y132		4251
☐ N452UA	Airbus Industrie A320-232	955	F-WWBD*	0099	0299	2 IAE V2527-A5	73500	F12Y132		4252
☐ N453UA	Airbus Industrie A320-232					2 IAE V2527-A5	73500	F12Y132		4253 / oo-delivery 0200
☐ N454UA	Airbus Industrie A320-232					2 IAE V2527-A5	73500	F12Y132		4254 / oo-delivery 0300
☐ N455UA	Airbus Industrie A320-232					2 IAE V2527-A5	73500	F12Y132		4255 / oo-delivery 0400
☐ N456UA	Airbus Industrie A320-232					2 IAE V2527-A5	73500	F12Y132		4256 / oo-delivery 0500
☐ N457UA	Airbus Industrie A320-232					2 IAE V2527-A5	73500	F12Y132		4257 / oo-delivery 0700
☐ N458UA	Airbus Industrie A320-232					2 IAE V2527-A5	73500	F12Y132		4258 / oo-delivery 1000
☐ N459UA	Airbus Industrie A320-232					2 IAE V2527-A5	73500	F12Y132		4259 / oo-delivery 1200
☐ N460UA	Airbus Industrie A320-232					2 IAE V2527-A5	73500	F12Y132		4260 / oo-delivery 0001
☐ N461UA	Airbus Industrie A320-232					2 IAE V2527-A5	73500	F12Y132		4261 / oo-delivery 0001
☐ N462UA	Airbus Industrie A320-232					2 IAE V2527-A5	73500	F12Y132		4262 / oo-delivery 0001
☐ N463UA	Airbus Industrie A320-232					2 IAE V2527-A5	73500	F12Y132		4263 / oo-delivery 0001
☐ N464UA	Airbus Industrie A320-232					2 IAE V2527-A5	73500	F12Y132		4264 / oo-delivery 0001
☐ N465UA	Airbus Industrie A320-232					2 IAE V2527-A5	73500	F12Y132		4265 / oo-delivery 0001
☐ N466UA	Airbus Industrie A320-232					2 IAE V2527-A5	73500	F12Y132		4266 / oo-delivery 0001
☐ N467UA	Airbus Industrie A320-232					2 IAE V2527-A5	73500	F12Y132		4267 / oo-delivery 0001
☐ N468UA	Airbus Industrie A320-232					2 IAE V2527-A5	73500	F12Y132		4268 / oo-delivery 0001
☐ N469UA	Airbus Industrie A320-232					2 IAE V2527-A5	73500	F12Y132		4269 / oo-delivery 0001
☐ N470UA	Airbus Industrie A320-232					2 IAE V2527-A5	73500	F12Y132		4270 / oo-delivery 0001
☐ N471UA	Airbus Industrie A320-232					2 IAE V2527-A5	73500	F12Y132		4271 / oo-delivery 0001
☐ N472UA	Airbus Industrie A320-232					2 IAE V2527-A5	73500	F12Y132		4272 / oo-delivery 0001
☐ N473UA	Airbus Industrie A320-232					2 IAE V2527-A5	73500	F12Y132		4273 / oo-delivery 0001
☐ N474UA	Airbus Industrie A320-232					2 IAE V2527-A5	73500	F12Y132		4274 / oo-delivery 0002
☐ N475UA	Airbus Industrie A320-232					2 IAE V2527-A5	73500	F12Y132		4275 / oo-delivery 0002
☐ N476UA	Airbus Industrie A320-232					2 IAE V2527-A5	73500	F12Y132		4276 / oo-delivery 0002
☐ N477UA	Airbus Industrie A320-232					2 IAE V2527-A5	73500	F12Y132		4277 / oo-delivery 0002
☐ N478UA	Airbus Industrie A320-232					2 IAE V2527-A5	73500	F12Y132		4278 / oo-delivery 0002
☐ N479UA	Airbus Industrie A320-232					2 IAE V2527-A5	73500	F12Y132		4279 / oo-delivery 0002

registration	type of aircraft	cn/fn	ex/ex*	mfd	del	powered by	mtow kg	configuration	selcal	name/fln/specialitites/remarks
☐ N480UA	Airbus Industrie A320-232					2 IAE V2527-A5	73500	F12Y132		4280 / oo-delivery 0003
☐ N481UA	Airbus Industrie A320-232					2 IAE V2527-A5	73500	F12Y132		4281 / oo-delivery 0003
☐ N482UA	Airbus Industrie A320-232					2 IAE V2527-A5	73500	F12Y132		4282 / oo-delivery 0003
☐ N483UA	Airbus Industrie A320-232					2 IAE V2527-A5	73500	F12Y132		4283 / oo-delivery 0003
☐ N484UA	Airbus Industrie A320-232					2 IAE V2527-A5	73500	F12Y132		4284 / oo-delivery 0003
☐ N485UA	Airbus Industrie A320-232					2 IAE V2527-A5	73500	F12Y132		4285 / oo-delivery 0003
☐ N7251U	Boeing 727-222 (A)	21398 / 1296		0077	1077	3 PW JT8D-15 (HK3/FDX)	86409	F12Y135		7751
☐ N7252U	Boeing 727-222 (A)	21399 / 1303		0077	1177	3 PW JT8D-15 (HK3/FDX)	86409	F12Y135		7752
☐ N7253U	Boeing 727-222 (A)	21400 / 1309		0077	0178	3 PW JT8D-15 (HK3/FDX)	86409	F12Y135		7653
☐ N7254U	Boeing 727-222 (A)	21401 / 1311		0077	0178	3 PW JT8D-15 (HK3/FDX)	86409	F12Y135		7654
☐ N7255U	Boeing 727-222 (A)	21402 / 1313		0077	0178	3 PW JT8D-15 (HK3/FDX)	86409	F12Y135		7655 / City of Cleveland
☐ N7256U	Boeing 727-222 (A)	21403 / 1315		0078	0278	3 PW JT8D-15 (HK3/FDX)	86409	F12Y135		7656
☐ N7257U	Boeing 727-222 (A)	21404 / 1321		0078	0378	3 PW JT8D-15 (HK3/FDX)	86409	F12Y135		7657
☐ N7258U	Boeing 727-222 (A)	21405 / 1323		0078	0378	3 PW JT8D-15 (HK3/FDX)	86409	F12Y135		7658
☐ N7259U	Boeing 727-222 (A)	21406 / 1325		0078	0378	3 PW JT8D-15 (HK3/FDX)	86409	F12Y135		7659
☐ N7260U	Boeing 727-222 (A)	21407 / 1332		0078	0478	3 PW JT8D-15 (HK3/FDX)	86409	F12Y135		7660
☐ N7261U	Boeing 727-222 (A)	21408 / 1334		0078	0478	3 PW JT8D-15 (HK3/FDX)	86409	F12Y135		7661
☐ N7262U	Boeing 727-222 (A)	21409 / 1336		0078	0478	3 PW JT8D-15 (HK3/FDX)	86409	F12Y135		7662
☐ N7263U	Boeing 727-222 (A)	21410 / 1344		0078	0578	3 PW JT8D-15 (HK3/FDX)	86409	F12Y135		7663
☐ N7264U	Boeing 727-222 (A)	21411 / 1346		0078	0578	3 PW JT8D-15 (HK3/FDX)	86409	F12Y135		7664
☐ N7265U	Boeing 727-222 (A)	21412 / 1348		0078	0578	3 PW JT8D-15 (HK3/FDX)	86409	F12Y135		7665
☐ N7266U	Boeing 727-222 (A)	21413 / 1351		0078	0678	3 PW JT8D-15 (HK3/FDX)	86409	F12Y135		7666
☐ N7267U	Boeing 727-222 (A)	21414 / 1354		0078	0678	3 PW JT8D-15 (HK3/FDX)	86409	F12Y135		7667
☐ N7268U	Boeing 727-222 (A)	21415 / 1356		0078	0678	3 PW JT8D-15 (HK3/FDX)	86409	F12Y135		7668
☐ N7269U	Boeing 727-222 (A)	21416 / 1366		0078	0778	3 PW JT8D-15 (HK3/FDX)	86409	F12Y135		7669
☐ N7270U	Boeing 727-222 (A)	21417 / 1368		0078	0778	3 PW JT8D-15 (HK3/FDX)	86409	F12Y135		7670
☐ N7271U	Boeing 727-222 (A)	21418 / 1370		0078	0878	3 PW JT8D-15 (HK3/FDX)	86409	F12Y135		7671
☐ N7272U	Boeing 727-222 (A)	21419 / 1375		0078	0878	3 PW JT8D-15 (HK3/FDX)	86409	F12Y135		7672
☐ N7273U	Boeing 727-222 (A)	21420 / 1377		0078	0878	3 PW JT8D-15 (HK3/FDX)	86409	F12Y135		7673
☐ N7274U	Boeing 727-222 (A)	21421 / 1383		0078	0978	3 PW JT8D-15 (HK3/FDX)	86409	F12Y135		7674
☐ N7275U	Boeing 727-222 (A)	21422 / 1385		0078	0678	3 PW JT8D-15 (HK3/FDX)	86409	F12Y135		7675
☐ N7276U	Boeing 727-222 (A)	21423 / 1387		0078	0978	3 PW JT8D-15 (HK3/FDX)	86409	F12Y135		7676
☐ N7277U	Boeing 727-222 (A)	21424 / 1393		0078	1078	3 PW JT8D-15 (HK3/FDX)	86409	F12Y135		7677
☐ N7278U	Boeing 727-222 (A)	21425 / 1395		0078	1078	3 PW JT8D-15 (HK3/FDX)	86409	F12Y135		7678
☐ N7279U	Boeing 727-222 (A)	21557 / 1397		0078	1078	3 PW JT8D-15 (HK3/FDX)	86409	F12Y135		7679
☐ N7280U	Boeing 727-222 (A)	21558 / 1399		0078	1078	3 PW JT8D-15 (HK3/FDX)	86409	F12Y135		7680 / Leon D. Cuddeback
☐ N7281U	Boeing 727-222 (A)	21559 / 1401		0078	1078	3 PW JT8D-15 (HK3/FDX)	86409	F12Y135		7681
☐ N7282U	Boeing 727-222 (A)	21560 / 1405		0078	1178	3 PW JT8D-15 (HK3/FDX)	86409	F12Y135		7682
☐ N7283U	Boeing 727-222 (A)	21561 / 1408		0078	1178	3 PW JT8D-15 (HK3/FDX)	86409	F12Y135		7683
☐ N7284U	Boeing 727-222 (A)	21562 / 1410		0078	1178	3 PW JT8D-15	86409	F12Y135		7684
☐ N7285U	Boeing 727-222 (A)	21563 / 1418		0078	1278	3 PW JT8D-15	86409	F12Y135		7685
☐ N7286U	Boeing 727-222 (A)	21564 / 1420		0078	1278	3 PW JT8D-15	86409	F12Y135		7686
☐ N7287U	Boeing 727-222 (A)	21565 / 1424		0078	1278	3 PW JT8D-15	86409	F12Y135		7687
☐ N7288U	Boeing 727-222 (A)	21566 / 1428		0078	0179	3 PW JT8D-15	86409	F12Y135		7688
☐ N7289U	Boeing 727-222 (A)	21567 / 1430		0078	0179	3 PW JT8D-15	86409	F12Y135		7689
☐ N7290U	Boeing 727-222 (A)	21568 / 1432		0078	0179	3 PW JT8D-15	86409	F12Y135		7690
☐ N7291U	Boeing 727-222 (A)	21569 / 1441		0079	0279	3 PW JT8D-15	86409	F12Y135		7691
☐ N7292U	Boeing 727-222 (A)	21570 / 1443		0079	0279	3 PW JT8D-15	86409	F12Y135		7692
☐ N7293U	Boeing 727-222 (A)	21571 / 1445		0079	0279	3 PW JT8D-15	86409	F12Y135		7693
☐ N7294U	Boeing 727-222 (A)	21572 / 1447		0079	0279	3 PW JT8D-15	86409	F12Y135		7694
☐ N7295U	Boeing 727-222 (A)	21573 / 1449		0079	0379	3 PW JT8D-15	86409	F12Y135		7695
☐ N7297U	Boeing 727-222 (A)	21892 / 1500		0079	0779	3 PW JT8D-15	86409	F12Y135		7997
☐ N7298U	Boeing 727-222 (A)	21893 / 1503		0079	0779	3 PW JT8D-15 (HK3/FDX)	86409	F12Y135		7998
☐ N7299U	Boeing 727-222 (A)	21894 / 1505		0079	0779	3 PW JT8D-15 (HK3/FDX)	86409	F12Y135		7999
☐ N7441U	Boeing 727-222 (A)	21895 / 1507		0079	0779	3 PW JT8D-15 (HK3/FDX)	86409	F12Y135		7941
☐ N7442U	Boeing 727-222 (A)	21896 / 1511		0079	0879	3 PW JT8D-15 (HK3/FDX)	86409	F12Y135		7942
☐ N7443U	Boeing 727-222 (A)	21897 / 1513		0079	0879	3 PW JT8D-15 (HK3/FDX)	86409	F12Y135		7943
☐ N7444U	Boeing 727-222 (A)	21898 / 1515		0079	0879	3 PW JT8D-15 (HK3/FDX)	86409	F12Y135		7944 / City of Cleveland
☐ N7445U	Boeing 727-222 (A)	21899 / 1517		0079	0879	3 PW JT8D-15 (HK3/FDX)	86409	F12Y135	AD-CF	7945
☐ N7446U	Boeing 727-222 (A)	21900 / 1519		0079	0979	3 PW JT8D-15 (HK3/FDX)	86409	F12Y135	AG-BE	7946
☐ N7447U	Boeing 727-222 (A)	21901 / 1521		0079	0979	3 PW JT8D-15 (HK3/FDX)	86409	F12Y135	AG-BK	7947
☐ N7448U	Boeing 727-222 (A)	21902 / 1524		0079	0979	3 PW JT8D-15 (HK3/FDX)	86409	F12Y135		7948
☐ N7449U	Boeing 727-222 (A)	21903 / 1526		0079	0979	3 PW JT8D-15 (HK3/FDX)	86409	F12Y135		7949
☐ N7450U	Boeing 727-222 (A)	21904 / 1528		0079	1079	3 PW JT8D-15 (HK3/FDX)	86409	F12Y135		7950
☐ N7451U	Boeing 727-222 (A)	21905 / 1530		0079	1079	3 PW JT8D-15 (HK3/FDX)	86409	F12Y135		7951
☐ N7452U	Boeing 727-222 (A)	21906 / 1548		0079	1179	3 PW JT8D-15 (HK3/FDX)	86409	F12Y135		7952
☐ N7453U	Boeing 727-222 (A)	21907 / 1558		0079	1279	3 PW JT8D-15 (HK3/FDX)	86409	F12Y135		7953
☐ N7454U	Boeing 727-222 (A)	21908 / 1560		0079	1279	3 PW JT8D-15 (HK3/FDX)	86409	F12Y135		7954
☐ N7455U	Boeing 727-222 (A)	21909 / 1562		0079	1279	3 PW JT8D-15 (HK3/FDX)	86409	F12Y135		7955
☐ N7456U	Boeing 727-222 (A)	21910 / 1570		0080	0280	3 PW JT8D-15 (HK3/FDX)	86409	F12Y135		7956
☐ N7457U	Boeing 727-222 (A)	21911 / 1572		0080	0380	3 PW JT8D-15 (HK3/FDX)	86409	F12Y135		7957
☐ N7458U	Boeing 727-222 (A)	21912 / 1575		0080	0380	3 PW JT8D-15 (HK3/FDX)	86409	F12Y135		7958
☐ N7459U	Boeing 727-222 (A)	21913 / 1593		0080	0380	3 PW JT8D-15 (HK3/FDX)	86409	F12Y135		7959
☐ N7460U	Boeing 727-222 (A)	21914 / 1597		0080	0380	3 PW JT8D-15 (HK3/FDX)	86409	F12Y135		7960
☐ N7461U	Boeing 727-222 (A)	21915 / 1609		0080	0480	3 PW JT8D-15 (HK3/FDX)	86409	F12Y135		7961
☐ N7462U	Boeing 727-222 (A)	21916 / 1611		0080	0480	3 PW JT8D-15 (HK3/FDX)	86409	F12Y135		7962
☐ N7463U	Boeing 727-222 (A)	21917 / 1616		0080	0580	3 PW JT8D-15	86409	F12Y135		7963
☐ N7464U	Boeing 727-222 (A)	21918 / 1625		0080	0680	3 PW JT8D-15	86409	F12Y135		7964
☐ N7465U	Boeing 727-222 (A)	21919 / 1632		0080	0680	3 PW JT8D-15	86409	F12Y135		7965
☐ N7466U	Boeing 727-222 (A)	21920 / 1634		0080	0680	3 PW JT8D-15	86409	F12Y135		7966
☐ N7467U	Boeing 727-222 (A)	21921 / 1639		0080	0780	3 PW JT8D-15	86409	F12Y135		7967
☐ N501UA	Boeing 757-222	24622 / 241		0889	0889	2 PW PW2037	104326	F24Y164		5001 / lsf CITG
☐ N502UA	Boeing 757-222	24623 / 246		0989	0989	2 PW PW2037	104326	F24Y164		5002
☐ N503UA	Boeing 757-222	24624 / 247		0989	0989	2 PW PW2037	104326	F24Y164		5003
☐ N504UA	Boeing 757-222	24625 / 251		1089	1089	2 PW PW2037	104326	F24Y164		5004
☐ N505UA	Boeing 757-222	24626 / 254		1189	1189	2 PW PW2037	104326	F24Y164		5005
☐ N506UA	Boeing 757-222	24627 / 263		0290	0290	2 PW PW2037	104326	F24Y164		5006
☐ N507UA	Boeing 757-222	24743 / 270		0390	0390	2 PW PW2037	104326	F24Y164		5007
☐ N508UA	Boeing 757-222	24744 / 277		0490	0490	2 PW PW2037	104326	F24Y164		5008
☐ N509UA	Boeing 757-222	24763 / 284		0590	0590	2 PW PW2037	104326	F24Y164		5009 / lsf TOMB
☐ N510UA	Boeing 757-222	24780 / 290		0690	0690	2 PW PW2037	104326	F24Y164		5010
☐ N511UA	Boeing 757-222	24799 / 291		0690	0690	2 PW PW2037	104326	F24Y164		5011
☐ N512UA	Boeing 757-222	24809 / 298		0790	0790	2 PW PW2037	104326	F24Y164		5012
☐ N513UA	Boeing 757-222	24810 / 299		0790	0790	2 PW PW2037	104326	F24Y164		5013
☐ N514UA	Boeing 757-222	24839 / 305		0890	0890	2 PW PW2037	104326	F24Y164		5014
☐ N515UA	Boeing 757-222	24840 / 306		0890	0890	2 PW PW2037	104326	F24Y164		5015
☐ N516UA	Boeing 757-222	24860 / 307		0890	0890	2 PW PW2037	104326	F24Y164		5016
☐ N517UA	Boeing 757-222	24861 / 310		0990	0990	2 PW PW2037	104326	F24Y164		5017
☐ N518UA	Boeing 757-222	24871 / 311		0990	0990	2 PW PW2037	104326	F24Y164		5018
☐ N519UA	Boeing 757-222	24872 / 312		0990	0990	2 PW PW2037	104326	F24Y164		5019
☐ N520UA	Boeing 757-222	24890 / 313		0990	0990	2 PW PW2037	104326	F24Y164		5020
☐ N521UA	Boeing 757-222	24891 / 319		1090	1090	2 PW PW2037	104326	F24Y164		5021 / lsf Cumberland Leasing Co.
☐ N522UA	Boeing 757-222	24931 / 320		1090	1090	2 PW PW2037	104326	F24Y164		5022
☐ N523UA	Boeing 757-222	24932 / 329		1190	1190	2 PW PW2037	104326	F24Y164		5023
☐ N524UA	Boeing 757-222	24977 / 331		1290	1290	2 PW PW2037	104326	F24Y164		5024
☐ N525UA	Boeing 757-222	24978 / 338		0191	0191	2 PW PW2037	104326	F24Y164		5025
☐ N526UA	Boeing 757-222	24994 / 339		0191	0191	2 PW PW2037	104326	F24Y164		5026
☐ N527UA	Boeing 757-222	24995 / 341		0291	0291	2 PW PW2037	104326	F24Y164		5027
☐ N528UA	Boeing 757-222	25018 / 346		0291	0291	2 PW PW2037	104326	F24Y164		5028
☐ N529UA	Boeing 757-222	25019 / 352		0391	0391	2 PW PW2037	104326	F24Y164		5029
☐ N530UA	Boeing 757-222	25043 / 353		0391	0391	2 PW PW2037	104326	F24Y164		5030
☐ N531UA	Boeing 757-222	25042 / 361		0491	0491	2 PW PW2037	104326	F24Y164		5031
☐ N532UA	Boeing 757-222	25072 / 366		0091	0591	2 PW PW2037	104326	F24Y164		5032
☐ N533UA	Boeing 757-222	25073 / 367		0091	0591	2 PW PW2037	104326	F24Y164		5033
☐ N534UA	Boeing 757-222	25129 / 372		0691	0691	2 PW PW2037	104326	F24Y164		5034
☐ N535UA	Boeing 757-222	25130 / 373		0691	0691	2 PW PW2037	104326	F24Y164		5035
☐ N536UA	Boeing 757-222	25156 / 380		0791	0791	2 PW PW2037	104326	F24Y164		5036
☐ N537UA	Boeing 757-222	25157 / 381		0791	0791	2 PW PW2037	104326	F24Y164		5037
☐ N538UA	Boeing 757-222	25222 / 385		0891	0891	2 PW PW2037	104326	F24Y164		5038
☐ N539UA	Boeing 757-222	25223 / 386		0891	0891	2 PW PW2037	104326	F24Y164		5039

registration	type of aircraft	cn/fn	ex/ex*	mfd	del	powered by	mtow kg	configuration	selcal	name/fln/specialitites/remarks
☐ N540UA	Boeing 757-222	25252 / 393		0991	0991	2 PW PW2037	104326	F24Y164		5040
☐ N541UA	Boeing 757-222	25253 / 394		0991	0991	2 PW PW2037	104326	F24Y164		5041
☐ N542UA	Boeing 757-222	25276 / 396		1091	1091	2 PW PW2037	104326	F24Y164		5042
☐ N543UA	Boeing 757-222 (ET)	25698 / 401		1091	1091	2 PW PW2037	104326	F24Y164	BS-JQ	5143
☐ N544UA	Boeing 757-222 (ET)	25322 / 405		1191	1191	2 PW PW2037	104326	F24Y164	BS-JR	5144
☐ N545UA	Boeing 757-222 (ET)	25323 / 406		1191	1191	2 PW PW2037	104326	F24Y164	BS-KL	5145
☐ N546UA	Boeing 757-222 (ET)	25367 / 413		1191	1291	2 PW PW2037	104326	F24Y164	BS-KM	5146
☐ N547UA	Boeing 757-222 (ET)	25368 / 414		1191	1291	2 PW PW2037	104326	F24Y164	BS-KP	5147
☐ N548UA	Boeing 757-222 (ET)	25396 / 420		1291	0192	2 PW PW2037	104326	F24Y164	BS-KQ	5148
☐ N549UA	Boeing 757-222 (ET)	25397 / 421		1291	0192	2 PW PW2037	104326	F24Y164	BS-KR	5149
☐ N550UA	Boeing 757-222 (ET)	25398 / 426		0192	0292	2 PW PW2037	104326	F24Y164	BS-LM	5150
☐ N551UA	Boeing 757-222 (ET)	25399 / 427		0192	0292	2 PW PW2037	104326	F24Y164	BS-LP	5151
☐ N552UA	Boeing 757-222 (ET)	26641 / 431		0192	0292	2 PW PW2037	104326	F24Y164	BS-LQ	5152
☐ N553UA	Boeing 757-222	25277 / 434		0292	0392	2 PW PW2037	104326	F24Y164		5053
☐ N554UA	Boeing 757-222	26644 / 435		0292	0392	2 PW PW2037	104326	F24Y164		5054
☐ N555UA	Boeing 757-222	26647 / 442		0392	0492	2 PW PW2037	104326	F24Y164		5055
☐ N556UA	Boeing 757-222	26650 / 447		0492	0492	2 PW PW2037	104326	F24Y164		5056
☐ N557UA	Boeing 757-222	26653 / 454		0592	0592	2 PW PW2037	104326	F24Y164		5057
☐ N558UA	Boeing 757-222	26654 / 462		0692	0692	2 PW PW2037	104326	F24Y164		5058
☐ N559UA	Boeing 757-222	26657 / 467		0692	0792	2 PW PW2037	104326	F24Y164		5059
☐ N560UA	Boeing 757-222	26660 / 469		0692	0792	2 PW PW2037	104326	F24Y164		5060
☐ N561UA	Boeing 757-222	26661 / 479		0892	0892	2 PW PW2037	104326	F24Y176		5061
☐ N562UA	Boeing 757-222	26664 / 487		0992	0992	2 PW PW2037	104326	F24Y164		5062
☐ N563UA	Boeing 757-222	26665 / 488		0092	0992	2 PW PW2037	104326	F24Y164		5063
☐ N564UA	Boeing 757-222	26666 / 490		0992	1092	2 PW PW2037	104326	F24Y164		5064
☐ N565UA	Boeing 757-222	26669 / 492		0992	1092	2 PW PW2037	104326	F24Y164		5065
☐ N566UA	Boeing 757-222	26670 / 494		1092	1092	2 PW PW2037	104326	F24Y164		5066
☐ N567UA	Boeing 757-222	26673 / 497		1092	1192	2 PW PW2037	104326	F24Y164		5067
☐ N568UA	Boeing 757-222	26674 / 498		1092	1192	2 PW PW2037	104326	F24Y164		5068
☐ N569UA	Boeing 757-222	26677 / 499		1092	1192	2 PW PW2037	104326	F24Y164		5069
☐ N570UA	Boeing 757-222	26678 / 501		1192	1192	2 PW PW2037	104326	F24Y164		5070
☐ N571UA	Boeing 757-222	26681 / 506		1192	1292	2 PW PW2037	104326	F24Y164		5071
☐ N572UA	Boeing 757-222	26682 / 508		1192	1292	2 PW PW2037	104326	F24Y164		5072
☐ N573UA	Boeing 757-222	26685 / 512		1292	1292	2 PW PW2037	104326	F24Y164		5073
☐ N574UA	Boeing 757-222	26686 / 513		1292	1292	2 PW PW2037	104326	F24Y164		5074
☐ N575UA	Boeing 757-222	26689 / 515		0193	0293	2 PW PW2037	104326	F24Y164		5075
☐ N576UA	Boeing 757-222	26690 / 524		0293	0293	2 PW PW2037	104326	F24Y164	EG-JR	5376
☐ N577UA	Boeing 757-222	26693 / 527		0293	0393	2 PW PW2037	104326	F24Y164	EG-JS	5377
☐ N578UA	Boeing 757-222	26694 / 531		0293	0393	2 PW PW2037	104326	F24Y164	EG-KR	5378
☐ N579UA	Boeing 757-222	26697 / 539		0393	0493	2 PW PW2037	104326	F24Y164	EG-KS	5379
☐ N580UA	Boeing 757-222	26698 / 542		0493	0493	2 PW PW2037	104326	F24Y164	EG-LR	5380
☐ N581UA	Boeing 757-222	26701 / 543		0093	0593	2 PW PW2037	104326	F24Y164	EG-LS	5381
☐ N582UA	Boeing 757-222	26702 / 550		0093	0593	2 PW PW2037	104326	F24Y164	EG-MR	5382
☐ N583UA	Boeing 757-222	26705 / 556		0593	0693	2 PW PW2037	104326	F24Y164	EG-MS	5383
☐ N584UA	Boeing 757-222	26706 / 559		0593	0693	2 PW PW2037	104326	F24Y164	EG-PR	5384
☐ N585UA	Boeing 757-222	26709 / 563		0693	0793	2 PW PW2037	104326	F24Y164	EG-PS	5385
☐ N586UA	Boeing 757-222	26710 / 567		0793	0793	2 PW PW2037	104326	F24Y164	EG-QR	5386
☐ N587UA	Boeing 757-222	26713 / 570		0793	0893	2 PW PW2037	104326	F24Y164	EG-QS	5387
☐ N588UA	Boeing 757-222	26717 / 571		0793	0893	2 PW PW2037	104326	F24Y164	EG-RS	5388
☐ N589UA	Boeing 757-222 (ET)	28707 / 773	N3509J*	0997	1197	2 PW PW2040	104326	F24Y164		5189
☐ N590UA	Boeing 757-222 (ET)	28708 / 785		1297	1297	2 PW PW2040	104326	F24Y164		5190
☐ N591UA	Boeing 757-222	28142 / 718		0696	0696	2 PW PW2037	104326	F24Y164		5091
☐ N592UA	Boeing 757-222	28143 / 719		0696	0796	2 PW PW2037	104326	F24Y164		5092
☐ N593UA	Boeing 757-222	28144 / 724		0896	0896	2 PW PW2037	104326	F24Y164		5093
☐ N594UA	Boeing 757-222	28145 / 727		0896	0996	2 PW PW2037	104326	F24Y164		5094
☐ N595UA	Boeing 757-222 (ET)	28748 / 789		0198	0298	2 PW PW2040	104326	F24Y164		5195
☐ N596UA	Boeing 757-222 (ET)	28749 / 794		0098	0398	2 PW PW2040	104326	F24Y164		5196
☐ N597UA	Boeing 757-222 (ET)	28750 / 841		0199	0199	2 PW PW2040	104326	F24Y164		5197
☐ N598UA	Boeing 757-222 (ET)	28751 / 844	N1787B*	0199	0199	2 PW PW2040	104326	F24Y164		5198
☐ N601UA	Boeing 767-222	21862 / 2		0081	0483	2 PW JT9D-7R4D	145150	F10C33Y125		6201
☐ N602UA	Boeing 767-222 (ET)	21863 / 3		0081	0183	2 PW JT9D-7R4D	145150	F10C32Y126	JP-DE	6002 / cvtd -222
☐ N603UA	Boeing 767-222	21864 / 4		0081	0483	2 PW JT9D-7R4D	145150	F10C33Y125		6203
☐ N604UA	Boeing 767-222	21865 / 5		0082	0183	2 PW JT9D-7R4D	145150	F10C33Y125		6204
☐ N605UA	Boeing 767-222 (ET)	21866 / 7		0082	1182	2 PW JT9D-7R4D	145150	F10C32Y126	JP-DF	6005 / Bob Rosseau Customer / cvtd -222
☐ N606UA	Boeing 767-222 (ET)	21867 / 9		0082	0882	2 PW JT9D-7R4D	145150	F10C32Y126	JP-DG	6006 / City of Chicago / cvtd -222
☐ N607UA	Boeing 767-222 (ET)	21868 / 10		0082	0982	2 PW JT9D-7R4D	145150	F10C32Y126	JP-DH	6007 / City of Denver / cvtd -222
☐ N608UA	Boeing 767-222 (ET)	21869 / 11		0082	0982	2 PW JT9D-7R4D	145150	F10C32Y126	JP-DK	6008 / cvtd -222
☐ N609UA	Boeing 767-222 (ET)	21870 / 13		0082	0982	2 PW JT9D-7R4D	145150	F10C32Y126	JP-DL	6009 / cvtd -222
☐ N610UA	Boeing 767-222 (ET)	21871 / 15		0082	0982	2 PW JT9D-7R4D	145150	F10C32Y126	KM-BP	6010 / cvtd -222
☐ N611UA	Boeing 767-222 (ET)	21872 / 20		0082	1182	2 PW JT9D-7R4D	145150	F10C32Y126	KM-CP	6011 / cvtd -222
☐ N612UA	Boeing 767-222	21873 / 41		0083	0283	2 PW JT9D-7R4D	145150	F10C33Y125	KM-DP	6212
☐ N613UA	Boeing 767-222	21874 / 42		0083	0283	2 PW JT9D-7R4D	145150	F10C33Y125	KM-EP	6213
☐ N614UA	Boeing 767-222	21875 / 43		0083	0383	2 PW JT9D-7R4D	145150	F10C33Y125	KM-FP	6214
☐ N615UA	Boeing 767-222	21876 / 45		0083	0383	2 PW JT9D-7R4D	145150	F10C33Y125	KM-GP	6215
☐ N617UA	Boeing 767-222	21877 / 46		0083	0383	2 PW JT9D-7R4D	145150	F10C33Y125	KM-HP	6217
☐ N618UA	Boeing 767-222	21878 / 48		0083	0483	2 PW JT9D-7R4D	145150	F10C33Y125	KM-JP	6218
☐ N619UA	Boeing 767-222	21879 / 49		0083	0483	2 PW JT9D-7R4D	145150	F10C33Y125	KM-LP	6219
☐ N620UA	Boeing 767-222	21880 / 50		0083	0483	2 PW JT9D-7R4D	145150	F10C33Y125		6220
☐ N641UA	Boeing 767-322 (ER)	25091 / 360		0091	0491	2 PW PW4060	181437	F10C38Y158	AG-BR	6541
☐ N642UA	Boeing 767-322 (ER)	25092 / 367		0091	0591	2 PW PW4060	181437	F10C38Y158	AG-BS	6542
☐ N643UA	Boeing 767-322 (ER)	25093 / 368		0091	0591	2 PW PW4060	181437	F10C38Y158	AG-CR	6543
☐ N644UA	Boeing 767-322 (ER)	25094 / 369		0091	0591	2 PW PW4060	181437	F10C38Y158	AG-CS	6544
☐ N645UA	Boeing 767-322 (ER)	25280 / 391		0991	0991	2 PW PW4060	181437	F10C38Y158	AG-DR	6545
☐ N646UA	Boeing 767-322 (ER)	25283 / 420		0292	0392	2 PW PW4060	181437	F10C38Y158	AG-DS	6546
☐ N647UA	Boeing 767-322 (ER)	25284 / 424		0392	0492	2 PW PW4060	181437	F10C38Y158	AG-ER	6547
☐ N648UA	Boeing 767-322 (ER)	25285 / 443		0792	0792	2 PW PW4060	181437	F10C38Y158	AG-ES	6548
☐ N649UA	Boeing 767-322 (ER)	25286 / 444		0792	0792	2 PW PW4060	181437	F10C38Y158	AG-FR	6549
☐ N650UA	Boeing 767-322 (ER)	25287 / 449		0892	0992	2 PW PW4060	181437	F10C38Y158	AG-FS	6550
☐ N651UA	Boeing 767-322 (ER)	25389 / 452		0892	0992	2 PW PW4060	181437	F10C38Y158	AG-HR	6551
☐ N652UA	Boeing 767-322 (ER)	25390 / 457		0992	0992	2 PW PW4060	181437	F10C38Y158	AG-HS	6552
☐ N653UA	Boeing 767-322 (ER)	25391 / 460		1092	1092	2 PW PW4060	181437	F10C38Y158	AG-JR	6553 / Star Alliance-colors
☐ N654UA	Boeing 767-322 (ER)	25392 / 462		1092	1192	2 PW PW4060	181437	F10C38Y158	AG-JS	6554
☐ N655UA	Boeing 767-322 (ER)	25393 / 468		1192	1292	2 PW PW4060	181437	F10C38Y158	AG-KR	6555
☐ N656UA	Boeing 767-322 (ER)	25394 / 472		1292	0193	2 PW PW4060	181437	F10C38Y158	AG-KS	6556
☐ N657UA	Boeing 767-322 (ER)	27112 / 479		0293	0393	2 PW PW4060	181437	F10C38Y158	CE-QR	6557 / lsf GECA
☐ N658UA	Boeing 767-322 (ER)	27113 / 480		0293	0393	2 PW PW4060	181437	F10C38Y158	CE-QS	6558 / lsf GECA
☐ N659UA	Boeing 767-322 (ER)	27114 / 485		0393	0493	2 PW PW4060	181437	F10C38Y158	CE-RS	6559 / lsf GECA
☐ N660UA	Boeing 767-322 (ER)	27115 / 494		0093	0593	2 PW PW4060	181437	F10C38Y158	CF-AR	6560 / lsf GECA
☐ N661UA	Boeing 767-322 (ER)	27158 / 507		0793	0793	2 PW PW4060	181437	F10C38Y158	CF-AS	6561
☐ N662UA	Boeing 767-322 (ER)	27159 / 513		0893	0893	2 PW PW4060	181437	F10C38Y158	CF-BR	6562
☐ N663UA	Boeing 767-322 (ER)	27160 / 514		0893	0893	2 PW PW4060	181437	F10C38Y158	CF-BS	6563
☐ N664UA	Boeing 767-322 (ER)	29236 / 707		0698	0698	2 PW PW4060	181437	F10C38Y158		6564
☐ N665UA	Boeing 767-322 (ER)	29237 / 711		0098	0798	2 PW PW4060	181437	F10C38Y158		6565
☐ N666UA	Boeing 767-322 (ER)	29238 / 715		0898	0898	2 PW PW4060	181437	F10C38Y158		6566
☐ N667UA	Boeing 767-322 (ER)	29239 / 716		0898	0898	2 PW PW4060	181437	F10C38Y158		6567
☐ N668UA	Boeing 767-322 (ER)	30024				2 PW PW4060	181437	F10C38Y158		oo-delivery 0499
☐ N669UA	Boeing 767-322 (ER)	30025				2 PW PW4060	181437	F10C38Y158		oo-delivery 0499
☐ N670UA	Boeing 767-322 (ER)	29240				2 PW PW4060	181437	F10C38Y158		oo-delivery 0899
☐ N671UA	Boeing 767-322 (ER)					2 PW PW4060	181437	F10C38Y158		oo-delivery 1299
☐ N672UA	Boeing 767-322 (ER)	30027				2 PW PW4060	181437	F10C38Y158		oo-delivery 0300
☐ N673UA	Boeing 767-322 (ER)	29241				2 PW PW4060	181437	F10C38Y158		oo-delivery 0400
☐ N674UA	Boeing 767-322 (ER)					2 PW PW4060	181437	F10C38Y158		oo-delivery 0700
☐ N675UA	Boeing 767-322 (ER)					2 PW PW4060	181437	F10C38Y158		oo-delivery 0800
☐ N676UA	Boeing 767-322 (ER)					2 PW PW4060	181437	F10C38Y158		oo-delivery 1000
☐ N677UA	Boeing 767-322 (ER)					2 PW PW4060	181437	F10C38Y158		oo-delivery 1100
☐ N1815U	Boeing (Douglas) DC-10-10	46614 / 45		0072	0772	3 GE CF6-6D	195045	F28Y259	AH-CG	3615 / std LAS
☐ N1816U	Boeing (Douglas) DC-10-10	46615 / 76		0073	0173	3 GE CF6-6D	195045	F28Y259	AH-KM	3616 / std LAS
☐ N1817U	Boeing (Douglas) DC-10-10	46616 / 86		0073	0373	3 GE CF6-6D	195045	F28Y259	AH-LM	3617 / std LAS
☐ N1828U	Boeing (Douglas) DC-10-10	46627 / 205		0075	0675	3 GE CF6-6D	195045	F28Y259	AG-DK	3128
☐ N1829U	Boeing (Douglas) DC-10-10	46628 / 207		0075	0775	3 GE CF6-6D	195045	F28Y259	AG-DM	3129

☐ N1831U	Boeing (Douglas) DC-10-10	46630 / 209		0075	0875	3 GE CF6-6D	195045	F28Y259	AK-EL	3631 / std LAS
☐ N1834U	Boeing (Douglas) DC-10-10	47966 / 64	N602DA	0072	1172	3 GE CF6-6D	195045	F28Y259	AC-BH	3134
☐ N1835U	Boeing (Douglas) DC-10-10	47967 / 67	N603DA	0072	1172	3 GE CF6-6D	195045	F28Y259	FH-GL	3135 / std MOB
☐ N1836U	Boeing (Douglas) DC-10-10	47968 / 74	N604DA	0072	0173	3 GE CF6-6D	195045	F28Y259	AC-BJ	3136
☐ N1837U	Boeing (Douglas) DC-10-10	47969 / 80	N605DA	0072	0273	3 GE CF6-6D	195045	F28Y259	AG-DJ	3137
☐ N1838U	Boeing (Douglas) DC-10-10	46632 / 296		0079	1179	3 GE CF6-6D	195045	F28Y259	CG-BK	3138
☐ N1839U	Boeing (Douglas) DC-10-10	46633 / 297		0079	0280	3 GE CF6-6D	195045	F28Y259	CG-BM	3139 / std MZJ
☐ N1841U	Boeing (Douglas) DC-10-10	46634 / 298		0079	0180	3 GE CF6-6D	195045	F28Y259	CG-DE	3141 / std MZJ
☐ N1842U	Boeing (Douglas) DC-10-10	46635 / 307		0079	0280	3 GE CF6-6D	195045	F28Y259	CG-KM	3142 / std LAS
☐ N1843U	Boeing (Douglas) DC-10-10	46636 / 309		0079	0380	3 GE CF6-6D	195045	F28Y259	CG-LM	3143 / std LAS
☐ N1844U	Boeing (Douglas) DC-10-10	48260 / 344		0080	0481	3 GE CF6-6D	195045	F28Y259	CL-AJ	3144
☐ N1845U	Boeing (Douglas) DC-10-10	48261 / 347		0080	0481	3 GE CF6-6D	195045	F28Y259	CL-KM	3145
☐ N1846U	Boeing (Douglas) DC-10-10	48262 / 351		0081	0581	3 GE CF6-6D	195045	F28Y259	CM-AE	3146
☐ N1847U	Boeing (Douglas) DC-10-10	48263 / 353		0081	0581	3 GE CF6-6D	195045	F28Y259	DE-AH	3147
☐ N1849U	Boeing (Douglas) DC-10-10	46939 / 203	N906WA	0075	0389	3 GE CF6-6D	195045	F38Y260		3449
☐ N204UA	Boeing 777-222 (ER)	28713 / 191		0099	0299	2 PW PW4090	283362	F12C49Y217	AS-FM	2304
☐ N205UA	Boeing 777-222 (ER)	28714				2 PW PW4090	283362	F12C49Y217	AS-FP	2305 / oo-delivery 1199
☐ N206UA	Boeing 777-222 (ER)					2 PW PW4090	283362	F12C49Y217		2306 / oo-delivery 1299
☐ N207UA	Boeing 777-222 (ER)					2 PW PW4090	283362	F12C49Y217		2307 / oo-delivery 0100
☐ N208UA	Boeing 777-222 (ER)	30214				2 PW PW4090	283362	F12C49Y217		2308 / oo-delivery 0300
☐ N209UA	Boeing 777-222 (ER)					2 PW PW4090	283362	F12C49Y217		2309 / oo-delivery 0500
☐ N210UA	Boeing 777-222 (ER)					2 PW PW4090	283362	F12C49Y217		2310 / oo-delivery 0700
☐ N211UA	Boeing 777-222 (ER)					2 PW PW4090	283362	F12C49Y217		2311 / oo-delivery 0900
☐ N212UA	Boeing 777-222 (ER)					2 PW PW4090	283362	F12C49Y217		2312 / oo-delivery 1100
☐ N213UA	Boeing 777-222 (ER)					2 PW PW4090	283362	F12C49Y217		2313 / oo-delivery 0001
☐ N214UA	Boeing 777-222 (ER)					2 PW PW4090	283362	F12C49Y217		2314 / oo-delivery 0001
☐ N215UA	Boeing 777-222 (ER)					2 PW PW4090	283362	F12C49Y217		2315 / oo-delivery 0001
☐ N216UA	Boeing 777-222 (ER)					2 PW PW4090	283362	F12C49Y217		2316 / oo-delivery 0001
☐ N217UA	Boeing 777-222 (ER)					2 PW PW4090	283362	F12C49Y217		2317 / oo-delivery 0001
☐ N218UA	Boeing 777-222 (ER)					2 PW PW4090	283362	F12C49Y217		2318 / oo-delivery 0001
☐ N219UA	Boeing 777-222 (ER)					2 PW PW4090	283362	F12C49Y217		2319 / oo-delivery 0002
☐ N220UA	Boeing 777-222 (ER)					2 PW PW4090	283362	F12C49Y217		2320 / oo-delivery 0002
☐ N221UA	Boeing 777-222 (ER)					2 PW PW4090	283362	F12C49Y217		2321 / oo-delivery 0002
☐ N766UA	Boeing 777-222	26917 / 8	N77776*	0595	0595	2 PW PW4084	247210	F12C49Y231	AQ-BH	2066 / Nancy J. Meyer Customer
☐ N767UA	Boeing 777-222	26918 / 9	N77774*	0595	0595	2 PW PW4084	247210	F12C49Y231	AQ-BJ	2067 / Sam Sotoodeh Customer
☐ N768UA	Boeing 777-222	26919 / 11	N77775*	0595	0695	2 PW PW4084	247210	F12C49Y231	AQ-BK	2068 / Marcelo Amodeo Customer
☐ N769UA	Boeing 777-222	26921 / 12	N77773*	0695	0695	2 PW PW4084	247210	F12C49Y231	AQ-BL	2069 / D. Timothy Tammany Customer
☐ N770UA	Boeing 777-222	26925 / 13	N77772*	0695	0795	2 PW PW4084	247210	F12C49Y231	AQ-BM	2070 / Thomas R. Stuker Customer
☐ N771UA	Boeing 777-222	26932 / 3		0894	1195	2 PW PW4084	247210	F12C49Y231	AQ-CH	2071 / Frank Griffith Customer
☐ N772UA	Boeing 777-222	26930 / 5		1194	0995	2 PW PW4084	247210	F12C49Y231	AQ-CM	2072 / Mary Beth Loesch Customer
☐ N773UA	Boeing 777-222	26929 / 4		1094	0196	2 PW PW4084	247210	F12C49Y231	AQ-EP	2073 / Richard H. Loung Customer
☐ N774UA	Boeing 777-222	26936 / 2	N7772*	0794	0396	2 PW PW4084	247210	F12C49Y231	AQ-GK	2074 / Greg Milano Customer
☐ N775UA	Boeing 777-222	26947 / 22		0196	0196	2 PW PW4084	247210	F12C49Y231	AQ-GL	2075 / Scott A. Neumayer Customer
☐ N776UA	Boeing 777-222	26937 / 27		0396	0496	2 PW PW4084	247210	F12C49Y231	AQ-JL	2076
☐ N777UA	Boeing 777-222	26916 / 7		0495	0595	2 PW PW4084	247210	F12C49Y231	AQ-BG	2077 / Working Together
☐ N778UA	Boeing 777-222	26940 / 34		0696	0796	2 PW PW4084	247210	F12C49Y231	AQ-LM	2078
☐ N779UA	Boeing 777-222	26941 / 35		0796	0796	2 PW PW4084	247210	F12C49Y231	AR-BC	2079
☐ N780UA	Boeing 777-222	26944 / 36		0796	0896	2 PW PW4084	247210	F12C49Y231	AR-BD	2080 / Spirit of Adalyn
☐ N781UA	Boeing 777-222	26945 / 40		0896	0996	2 PW PW4084	247210	F12C49Y231	AR-BE	2081
☐ N782UA	Boeing 777-222 (ER)	26948 / 57		0297	0397	2 PW PW4090	283362	F12C49Y231	AR-BF	2282
☐ N783UA	Boeing 777-222 (ER)	26950 / 60		0297	0397	2 PW PW4090	283362	F12C49Y231	AR-BP	2283
☐ N784UA	Boeing 777-222 (ER)	26951 / 69		0497	0497	2 PW PW4090	283362	F12C49Y231	AR-CS	2284
☐ N785UA	Boeing 777-222 (ER)	26954 / 73		0597	0597	2 PW PW4090	283362	F12C49Y231	AR-EM	2285
☐ N786UA	Boeing 777-222 (ER)	26938 / 52		0397	0497	2 PW PW4090	283362	F12C49Y231	AR-EP	2286
☐ N787UA	Boeing 777-222 (ER)	26939 / 43		1096	0697	2 PW PW4090	283362	F12C49Y231	AR-EQ	2287
☐ N788UA	Boeing 777-222 (ER)	26942 / 82		0797	0797	2 PW PW4090	283362	F12C49Y231	AS-CF	2288
☐ N789UA	Boeing 777-222 (ER)	26935 / 88		0797	0897	2 PW PW4090	283362	F12C49Y231	AS-CG	2289
☐ N790UA	Boeing 777-222 (ER)	26943 / 92		0897	0897	2 PW PW4090	283362	F12C49Y231	AS-CH	2290
☐ N791UA	Boeing 777-222 (ER)	26933 / 93		0897	0897	2 PW PW4090	283362	F12C49Y231	AS-CJ	2291
☐ N792UA	Boeing 777-222 (ER)	26934 / 96		0997	0997	2 PW PW4090	283362	F12C49Y231	AS-CK	2292
☐ N793UA	Boeing 777-222 (ER)	26946 / 97		0997	1097	2 PW PW4090	283362	F12C49Y231	AS-CL	2293
☐ N794UA	Boeing 777-222 (ER)	26953 / 105		1097	1197	2 PW PW4090	283362	F12C49Y231	AS-DG	2294
☐ N795UA	Boeing 777-222 (ER)	26927 / 108		1197	1297	2 PW PW4090	283362	F12C49Y231	AS-FG	2295
☐ N796UA	Boeing 777-222 (ER)	26931 / 112		0198	0198	2 PW PW4090	283362	F12C49Y217	AS-FH	2396
☐ N797UA	Boeing 777-222 (ER)	26924 / 116		0098	0298	2 PW PW4090	283362	F12C49Y217	AS-FJ	2397
☐ N798UA	Boeing 777-222 (ER)	26928 / 123		0098	0298	2 PW PW4090	283362	F12C49Y217	AS-FK	2398
☐ N799UA	Boeing 777-222 (ER)	26926 / 139		0098	0598	2 PW PW4090	283362	F12C49Y217	AS-FL	2399
☐ N1852U	Boeing (Douglas) DC-10-30F	47811 / 302	G-BGXE	0079	0984	3 GE CF6-50C2	263084	Freighter	AF-JL	3952 / cvtd DC-10-30
☐ N1853U	Boeing (Douglas) DC-10-30F	47812 / 303	G-BGXF	0080	0884	3 GE CF6-50C2	263084	Freighter	AF-JM	3953 / cvtd DC-10-30
☐ N1854U	Boeing (Douglas) DC-10-30F	47813 / 312	G-BGXG	0080	0984	3 GE CF6-50C2	263084	Freighter	AF-LM	3954 / cvtd DC-10-30
☐ N1855U	Boeing (Douglas) DC-10-30F	47837 / 328	N84NA	0080	0485	3 GE CF6-50C2	251744	Freighter	AC-GL	3955 / cvtd DC-10-30
☐ N1856U	Boeing (Douglas) DC-10-30F (CF)	46975 / 248	N103WA	0078	0386	3 GE CF6-50C2	259455	F38Y260	AC-DJ	3056 / lsf Finova Capital Corp.
☐ N1857U	Boeing (Douglas) DC-10-30F (CF)	46986 / 253	N104WA	0078	0487	3 GE CF6-50C2	259455	F38Y260	AC-DK	3057 / lsf Finova Capital Corp.
☐ N1858U	Boeing (Douglas) DC-10-30F (CF)	46987 / 255	N105WA	0078	0487	3 GE CF6-50C2	259455	F38Y260	AC-DL	3058 / lsf Finova Capital Corp.
☐ N1859U	Boeing (Douglas) DC-10-30F	47819 / 314	N109WA	0080	0286	3 GE CF6-50C2	259455	Freighter	AC-DM	3859 / cvtd (CF)
☐ N144UA	Boeing 747SP-21	21026 / 286	N534PA	0076	0286	4 PW JT9D-7A	315700	F18C62Y164	LM-CE	4544 / std LAS
☐ N146UA	Boeing 747SP-21	21547 / 325	N537PA	0078	0286	4 PW JT9D-7A	318422	F18C62Y164	LM-DK	4546 / std MZJ
☐ N147UA	Boeing 747SP-21	21548 / 331	N538PA	0078	0286	4 PW JT9D-7A	318422	F18C62Y164	AF-GM	4547 / std MZJ
☐ N151UA	Boeing 747-222B	23736 / 673		0087	0387	4 PW JT9D-7R4G2	377842	F35C109Y124	AC-EG	8751 / std LAS
☐ N152UA	Boeing 747-222B	23737 / 675		0087	0487	4 PW JT9D-7R4G2	377842	F35C109Y124	AC-EM	8752/Carolina YC Woo Customer / std LAS
☐ N153UA	Boeing 747-123	20102 / 59	LX-KCV	0070	1287	4 PW JT9D-7A	340194	F42Y408	CE-DJ	8853
☐ N156UA	Boeing 747-123	20105 / 77	LX-LCV	0070	1087	4 PW JT9D-7A	340194	F42C408	CE-GJ	8856
☐ N157UA	Boeing 747-123	20106 / 79	LX-MCV	0070	1087	4 PW JT9D-7A	340194	F42Y408	CE-GK	8857
☐ N158UA	Boeing 747-238B	21054 / 260	VH-EBJ	0075	0691	4 PW JT9D-7J	362874	F18C79Y272	AF-BK	8058/E-Ticket Team Employees / lsf POTO
☐ N159UA	Boeing 747-238B	21140 / 267	VH-EBK	0075	0191	4 PW JT9D-7J	362874	F18C79Y272	AL-BK	8059/Bobbi Phillips Customer / lsf CITG
☐ N160UA	Boeing 747-238B	21237 / 285	VH-EBL	0076	0391	4 PW JT9D-7J	362874	F18C79Y272	AL-CE	8060/Harry M.Kubetz Customer / lsfELEC
☐ N161UA	Boeing 747-238B	21352 / 310	VH-EBM	0077	0391	4 PW JT9D-7J	362874	F18C79Y272	AL-CF	8261/Michael Stears Customs / lsf POTO
☐ N163UA	Boeing 747-238B	21353 / 316	VH-EBN	0077	0491	4 PW JT9D-7J	362874	F18C79Y272	LM-EF	8263 / lsf SNNL
☐ N164UA	Boeing 747-238B	21657 / 339	VH-EBO	0078	0691	4 PW JT9D-7J	362874	F18C79Y272	EH-GK	8264 / Jhane Barnes Customer
☐ N165UA	Boeing 747-238B	21658 / 341	VH-EBP	0078	0791	4 PW JT9D-7J	362874	F18C79Y272	GH-AF	8265 / Daniel J. Terra Customer
☐ N104UA	Boeing 747-422	26902 / 1141		0198	0198	4 PW PW4056	394625	F18C84Y270	AS-EQ	8004
☐ N105UA	Boeing 747-451	26473 / 985	N60659*	0693	0694	4 PW PW4056	394625	F18C80Y320	GM-JR	8105 / Rosa Santana Employee
☐ N106UA	Boeing 747-451	26474 / 988	N60668*	0893	0794	4 PW PW4056	394625	F18C80Y320	CG-JR	8106 / Randy Weinacht Employee
☐ N107UA	Boeing 747-422	26900 / 1168		0098	0898	4 PW PW4056	394625	F18C84Y270		8007
☐ N108UA	Boeing 747-422	26903 / 1171		0898	0898	4 PW PW4056	394625	F18C84Y270		8008
☐ N109UA	Boeing 747-422	26906 / 1185		1198	1198	4 PW PW4056	394625	F18C84Y270		8009
☐ N116UA	Boeing 747-422	26908 / 1193		1298	1298	4 PW PW4056	394625	F18C84Y270		8016
☐ N117UA	Boeing 747-422	28810 / 1197		0199	0199	4 PW PW4056	394625	F18C84Y270		8017
☐ N118UA	Boeing 747-422	28811 / 1201		0299	0299	4 PW PW4056	394625	F18C84Y270		8018
☐ N119UA	Boeing 747-422	28812				4 PW PW4056	394625	F18C84Y270		8019 / oo-delivery 0499
☐ N120UA	Boeing 747-422	29166				4 PW PW4056	394625	F18C84Y270		8020 / oo-delivery 0599
☐ N121UA	Boeing 747-422	29167				4 PW PW4056	394625	F18C84Y270		8021 / oo-delivery 0699
☐ N122UA	Boeing 747-422	29168				4 PW PW4056	394625	F18C84Y270		8022 / oo-delivery 0799
☐ N127UA	Boeing 747-422	28813				4 PW PW4056	394625	F18C84Y270		8027 / oo-delivery 0999
☐ N128UA	Boeing 747-422	30023				4 PW PW4056	394625	F18C84Y270		8028 / oo-delivery 0200
☐ N129UA	Boeing 747-422	28814				4 PW PW4056	394625	F18C84Y270		8029 / oo-delivery 0300
☐ N130UA	Boeing 747-422	28815				4 PW PW4056	394625	F18C84Y270		8030 / oo-delivery 0400
☐ N131UA	Boeing 747-422	28816				4 PW PW4056	394625	F18C84Y270		8031 / oo-delivery 1000
☐ N132UA	Boeing 747-422	28817				4 PW PW4056	394625	F18C84Y270		8032 / oo-delivery 0400
☐ N133UA	Boeing 747-422	28818				4 PW PW4056	394625	F18C84Y270		8033 / oo-delivery 0001
☐ N134UA	Boeing 747-422	28819				4 PW PW4056	394625	F18C84Y270		8034 / oo-delivery 0001
☐ N135UA	Boeing 747-422	28820				4 PW PW4056	394625	F18C84Y270		8035 / oo-delivery 0001
☐ N171UA	Boeing 747-422	24322 / 733		0089	0689	4 PW PW4056	394625	F36C123Y142	FG-AP	8671 / Spirit of Seattle II
☐ N172UA	Boeing 747-422	24363 / 740		0089	0889	4 PW PW4056	394625	F36C123Y142	FG-BP	8672
☐ N173UA	Boeing 747-422	24380 / 759		0089	1289	4 PW PW4056	394625	F36C123Y142	FG-CP	8673
☐ N174UA	Boeing 747-422	24381 / 762		0090	0190	4 PW PW4056	394625	F36C123Y142	FG-DP	8674 / Mitch Lee Employee
☐ N175UA	Boeing 747-422	24382 / 806		0090	0890	4 PW PW4056	394625	F36C123Y142	FG-EP	8675 / Gary Gendreau Employee
☐ N176UA	Boeing 747-422	24383 / 811		0090	0990	4 PW PW4056	394625	F36C123Y142	FG-HP	8676 / Jan Yamamoto Employee
☐ N177UA	Boeing 747-422	24384 / 819		0090	1190	4 PW PW4056	394625	F18C80Y320	FG-JP	8177
☐ N178UA	Boeing 747-422	24385 / 820		0090	1190	4 PW PW4056	394625	F18C80Y320	FG-KP	8178 / Joan Kellen Employee

455 registration type of aircraft cn/fn ex/ex* mfd del powered by mtow kg configuration selcal name/fln/specialitites/remarks

☐ N179UA	Boeing 747-422	25158 / 866		0791	0791	4 PW PW4056	394625	F18C80Y320	FG-LP	8179
☐ N180UA	Boeing 747-422	25224 / 867		0091	0791	4 PW PW4056	394625	F18C80Y320	FG-MP	8180 / Edwin D. Fuller Customer
☐ N181UA	Boeing 747-422	25278 / 881	N6005C*	0991	1091	4 PW PW4056	394625	F18C80Y320	FH-AP	8181
☐ N182UA	Boeing 747-422	25279 / 882		0991	1091	4 PW PW4056	394625	F18C80Y320	FH-BP	8182
☐ N183UA	Boeing 747-422	25379 / 911		0492	0492	4 PW PW4056	394625	F18C80Y320	FH-CP	8183
☐ N184UA	Boeing 747-422	25380 / 913		0492	0592	4 PW PW4056	394625	F18C80Y320	FH-DP	8184
☐ N185UA	Boeing 747-422	25395 / 919		0592	0692	4 PW PW4056	394625	F18C80Y320	FH-EP	8185
☐ N186UA	Boeing 747-422	26875 / 931		0092	0892	4 PW PW4056	394625	F18C80Y320	AS-DK	8186
☐ N187UA	Boeing 747-422	26876 / 939		0092	0992	4 PW PW4056	394625	F18C80Y320	AS-DL	8187
☐ N188UA	Boeing 747-422	26877 / 944		1092	1292	4 PW PW4056	394625	F18C80Y320	AS-DM	8188
☐ N189UA	Boeing 747-422	26878 / 966		0393	0393	4 PW PW4056	394625	F18C80Y320	AS-DP	8189 / Herkea Jea Customer
☐ N190UA	Boeing 747-422	26879 / 973		0493	0493	4 PW PW4056	394625	F18C80Y320	AS-DQ	8190 / Franklin S. Young Customer
☐ N191UA	Boeing 747-422	26880 / 984		0693	0693	4 PW PW4056	394625	F18C80Y320	AS-DR	8191
☐ N192UA	Boeing 747-422	26881 / 989		0793	0893	4 PW PW4056	394625	F18C80Y320	AS-EF	8192
☐ N193UA	Boeing 747-422	26890 / 1085		0796	0896	4 PW PW4056	394625	F18C84Y270	AS-EG	8193
☐ N194UA	Boeing 747-422	26892 / 1088		0896	0996	4 PW PW4056	394625	F18C84Y270	AS-EH	8594
☐ N195UA	Boeing 747-422	26899 / 1113		0597	0597	4 PW PW4056	394625	F18C84Y270	AS-EJ	8095
☐ N196UA	Boeing 747-422	28715 / 1120		0697	0697	4 PW PW4056	394625	F18C84Y270	AS-EK	8096
☐ N197UA	Boeing 747-422	26901 / 1121		0797	0797	4 PW PW4056	394625	F18C84Y270	AS-EL	8097
☐ N198UA	Boeing 747-422	28716 / 1124		0897	0897	4 PW PW4056	394625	F18C84Y270	AS-EM	8098
☐ N199UA	Boeing 747-422	28717 / 1126		0997	0997	4 PW PW4056	394625	F18C84Y270	AS-EP	8099

UNITED WEST AIRLINES (True North, Inc. dba) — **Miami-Opa Locka, FL**

PO Box 824870, Pembroke Pines, FL 33082, USA ☎ (954) 436-0562 Tx: none Fax: (954) 431-3575 SITA: n/a

F: 1993 ⁂ n/a Head: William S. Gardner Net: n/a

☐ N500DL	Learjet 25	25-027	EC-EBM	0069	0695	2 GE CJ610-6	6804			lsf Tack I Inc.
☐ N500BG	Dassault Falcon 20C	121	N25CP	0067	0495	2 GE CF700-2C	12000			lsf Tack I Inc.

UNIVERSAL AIRLINES, Inc. — **Statesville-Municipal, NC**

238 C-Airport Road, Statesville, NC 28677, USA ☎ (704) 871-9339 Tx: none Fax: (704) 881-0771 SITA: n/a

F: 1997 ⁂ n/a Head: Mark J. Granelli Net: n/a

☐ N3BA	Boeing (Douglas) DC-3C (C-47A-5-DK)	12172	N94530	0043	0697	2 PW R-1830	12202	Freighter		lsf pvt
☐ N600UA	Boeing (Douglas) DC-6BF	44894 / 651	N37570	0056	0998	4 PW R-2800	47083	Freighter		cvtd DC-6B

UNIVERSAL AIR SERVICE OF FLORIDA, Inc. — **Orlando-Executive, FL**

359 North Crystal Lake Drive, Orlando, FL 32803, USA ☎ (407) 896-2966 Tx: none Fax: (407) 895-1503 SITA: n/a

F: 1987 ⁂ n/a Head: Roy Henley Net: n/a

☐ N62HF	Bell 206B JetRanger	1792	N60TV	0075	1094	1 AN 250-C20	1451			
☐ N160SB	Bell 206L-3 LongRanger III	51145	N1410C	0085	0497	1 AN 250-C30P	1882			
☐ N287CA	Bell 206L-1 LongRanger II	45766	N47UF	0083	1295	1 AN 250-C28B	1882			lsf General Electric Capital Corp.
☐ N60TV	Bell 206L-3 LongRanger III	51181	N1430C	0086	0298	1 AN 250-C30P	1882			
☐ N60WJ	Bell 206L-1 LongRanger II	45276	N4470K	0079	0788	1 AN 250-C28B	1882			

UNIVERSAL ASSOCIATES, Inc. — **Miami-Kendall Tamiami Executive, FL**

1013 Centre Road, Wilmington, DE 19805, USA ☎ (305) 238-5447 Tx: none Fax: (305) 238-5447 SITA: n/a

F: 1992 ⁂ n/a Head: Charles Largay Net: n/a Operates historic show flights at airshows, festivals and exhibitions.

☐ N97UC	Beech Baron 58	TH-991	N721HG	0079	1092	2 CO IO-520-CB	2449	Support		
☐ N96UC	Consolidated PBY-5A Catalina	48375	N96FP	0045	0494	2 PW R-1830-92S	13835	22 Pax		Amphibian / 1942 PBY-colors

UNIVERSITY OF FLORIDA ATHLETIC ASSOCIATION – Aviation Dept. (Aviation Dept. of the University of Florida Athletic Association, Inc.) — **Gainesville-Regional, FL**

PO Box 14485, Gainesville, FL 32604, USA ☎ (352) 373-0517 Tx: none Fax: (352) 371-9636 SITA: n/a

F: 1984 ⁂ n/a Head: Jeremy Foley Net: n/a Operates executive flights for its parent company exclusively for the transport of athletic teams to sporting events.

☐ N102FG	Beech King Air A100	B-131	N90CC	0072	1086	2 PWC PT6A-28	5216	Executive		
☐ N103FG	Beech King Air C90	LJ-631	N100VM	0074	0392	2 PWC PT6A-20	4377	Executive		
☐ N101FG	Fairchild Ind. FH-227B	542	N4716Z	0067	0693	2 RR Dart 532-7	20638	Executive		

UPS Airlines = 5X / UPS (Division of United Parcel Service Company) — **Louisville-Int'l, KY**

United Parcel Service

1400 North Hurstbourne Pkwy, Louisville, KY 40223, USA ☎ (502) 329-6500 Tx: n/a Fax: (502) 329-6550 SITA: n/a

F: 1907 ⁂ 3350 Head: Thomas H. Weidemeyer IATA: 406 ICAO: UPS Net: http://www.ups.com Beside aircraft listed, also uses additional cargo aircraft leased from and operated by various smaller carriers when required.

☐ N902UP	Boeing 727-51C (QF)	18898 / 244	N434EX	0066	0492	3 RR Tay 651-54	76884	Freighter	DK-JQ	cvtd -51C
☐ N903UP	Boeing 727-51C (QF)	18945 / 263	N415EX	0066	0492	3 RR Tay 651-54	76884	Freighter	BJ-KQ	cvtd -51C
☐ N904UP	Boeing 727-51C (QF)	18946 / 274	N418EX	0066	0492	3 RR Tay 651-54	76884	Freighter	BJ-LQ	cvtd -51C
☐ N905UP	Boeing 727-51C (QF)	18947 / 286	N419EX	0066	0492	3 RR Tay 651-54	76884	Freighter	DK-JQ	cvtd -51C
☐ N906UP	Boeing 727-30C (QF)	19314 / 437	N423EX	0067	0492	3 RR Tay 651-54	76884	Freighter	BJ-PQ	cvtd -30C
☐ N907UP	Boeing 727-27C (QF)	19118 / 379	N7279	0267	1081	3 RR Tay 651-54	76884	Freighter	BK-AQ	cvtd -27C
☐ N908UP	Boeing 727-27C (QF)	19114 / 312	N7275	0966	0382	3 RR Tay 651-54	76884	Freighter	BK-CQ	cvtd -27C
☐ N909UP	Boeing 727-27C (QF)	19115 / 328	N7276	1066	1081	3 RR Tay 651-54	76884	Freighter	BK-DQ	cvtd -27C
☐ N910UP	Boeing 727-27C (QF)	19117 / 376	N7278	0267	1081	3 RR Tay 651-54	76884	Freighter	BK-EQ	cvtd -27C
☐ N911UP	Boeing 727-27C (QF)	19119 / 393	N7280	0367	1081	3 RR Tay 651-54	76884	Freighter	BK-FQ	cvtd -27C
☐ N912UP	Boeing 727-62C (QF)	19244 / 338	N7284	1166	1081	3 RR Tay 651-54	76884	Freighter	BK-GQ	cvtd -62C
☐ N913UP	Boeing 727-62C (QF)	19245 / 342	N7286	1166	1081	3 RR Tay 651-54	76884	Freighter	BK-HQ	cvtd -62C
☐ N914UP	Boeing 727-27C (QF)	19246 / 423	N7287	0667	1081	3 RR Tay 651-54	76884	Freighter	BK-JQ	cvtd -27C
☐ N915UP	Boeing 727-27C (QF)	19533 / 475	N7296	1067	0182	3 RR Tay 651-54	76884	Freighter	BK-LQ	cvtd -27C
☐ N916UP	Boeing 727-172C (QF/QC)	19808 / 615	N309BN	0868	0682	3 RR Tay 651-54	76884	Frtr or Y113	BK-MQ	cvtd -172C
☐ N917UP	Boeing 727-30C (QF)	19310 / 395	N701EV	0467	0382	3 RR Tay 651-54	76884	Freighter	BK-PQ	cvtd -30C
☐ N918UP	Boeing 727-30C (QF)	19008 / 364	N310BN	0267	0682	3 RR Tay 651-54	76884	Freighter	BL-AQ	cvtd -30C
☐ N919UP	Boeing 727-30C (QF)	19012 / 391	N311BN	0467	0782	3 RR Tay 651-54	76884	Freighter	BL-CQ	cvtd -30C
☐ N920UP	Boeing 727-180C (QF)	19873 / 604	N9516T	0768	0782	3 RR Tay 651-54	76884	Freighter	BL-DQ	cvtd -180C
☐ N922UP	Boeing 727-31C (QF)	19231 / 404	N892TW	0567	0582	3 RR Tay 651-54	76884	Freighter	BL-FQ	cvtd -31C
☐ N924UP	Boeing 727-31C (QF)	19234 / 463	N895TW	0967	0482	3 RR Tay 651-54	76884	Freighter	BL-HQ	cvtd -31C
☐ N925UP	Boeing 727-31C (QF)	19230 / 402	N891TW	0567	0482	3 RR Tay 651-54	76884	Freighter	BL-JQ	cvtd -31C
☐ N928UP	Boeing 727-22C (QF)	19091 / 280	N490W	0766	0982	3 RR Tay 651-54	76884	Freighter	BL-PQ	cvtd -22C
☐ N929UP	Boeing 727-22C (QF)	19092 / 291	N495WC	0766	0982	3 RR Tay 651-54	76884	Freighter	BM-AQ	cvtd -22C
☐ N930UP	Boeing 727-22C (QF)	19096 / 305	N497WC	0966	0982	3 RR Tay 651-54	76884	Freighter	BM-CQ	cvtd -22C
☐ N931UP	Boeing 727-25C (QF)	19858 / 645	N8175G	1068	0185	3 RR Tay 651-54	76884	Freighter	BM-DQ	cvtd -25C
☐ N932UP	Boeing 727-25C (QF)	19856 / 635	N8173G	1068	0585	3 RR Tay 651-54	76884	Freighter	BM-EQ	cvtd -25C
☐ N933UP	Boeing 727-25C (QF)	19857 / 641	N8174G	1068	0585	3 RR Tay 651-54	76884	Freighter	BM-FQ	cvtd -25C
☐ N934UP	Boeing 727-21C (QF)	19135 / 301	N724PL	0966	0585	3 RR Tay 651-54	76884	Freighter	BM-GQ	cvtd -21C
☐ N935UP	Boeing 727-1A7C (QF)	20143 / 619	N2915	0868	1089	3 RR Tay 651-54	76884	Freighter	BM-HQ	cvtd -1A7C
☐ N936UP	Boeing 727-108C (QF)	19503 / 420	N727TG	0667	1089	3 RR Tay 651-54	76884	Freighter	BM-JQ	cvtd -108C
☐ N937UP	Boeing 727-25C (QF)	19302 / 354	TG-ALA	0267	1289	3 RR Tay 651-54	76884	Freighter	BM-KQ	cvtd -25C
☐ N938UP	Boeing 727-173C (QF)	19506 / 447	TG-AYA	0867	1289	3 RR Tay 651-54	76884	Freighter	BM-LQ	cvtd -173C
☐ N939UP	Boeing 727-27C (QF)	19532 / 469	CC-CGD	1067	1089	3 RR Tay 651-54	76884	Freighter	BM-PQ	cvtd -27C
☐ N940UP	Boeing 727-185C (QF)	19826 / 546	TF-FLG	0468	1089	3 RR Tay 651-54	76884	Freighter	BP-AQ	cvtd -185C
☐ N941UP	Boeing 727-22C (QF)	19196 / 407	CC-CLB	0567	1289	3 RR Tay 651-54	76884	Freighter	BP-CQ	cvtd -22C
☐ N942UP	Boeing 727-22C (QF)	19101 / 333	N430EX	1166	0690	3 RR Tay 651-54	76884	Freighter	BP-DQ	cvtd -22C
☐ N946UP	Boeing 727-25C (QF/QC)	19721 / 490	N130FE	1167	0194	3 RR Tay 651-54	76884	Frtr or Y113	BP-GQ	cvtd -25C
☐ N947UP	Boeing 727-25C (QF/QC)	19722 / 493	N131FE	1167	0194	3 RR Tay 651-54	76884	Frtr or Y113	BP-HQ	cvtd -25C
☐ N948UP	Boeing 727-25C (QF/QC)	19357 / 360	N121FE	0267	0194	3 RR Tay 651-54	76884	Frtr or Y113	BP-JQ	cvtd -25C
☐ N949UP	Boeing 727-25C (QF/QC)	19717 / 468	N125FE	0967	0194	3 RR Tay 651-54	76884	Frtr or Y113	BP-KQ	cvtd -25C
☐ N950UP	Boeing 727-25C (QF/QC)	19718 / 474	N126FE	1067	0194	3 RR Tay 651-54	76884	Frtr of Y113	BP-LQ	cvtd -25C
☐ N951UP	Boeing 727-25C (QF/QC)	19850 / 497	N132FE	1267	0194	3 RR Tay 651-54	76884	Frtr or Y113	BP-MQ	cvtd -25C
☐ N954UP	Boeing 727-185C (QF)	19827 / 527	N744EV	0068	0494	3 RR Tay 651-54	76884	Freighter		cvtd -185C
☐ OY-UPA	Boeing 727-31C (QF)	19233 / 458	N926UP	0967	0382	3 RR Tay 651-54	76884	Freighter	BL-KQ	lst/opb SRR / cvtd -31C
☐ OY-UPB	Boeing 727-180C (QF)	19874 / 534	N921UP	0268	0782	3 RR Tay 651-54	76884	Freighter	BL-EQ	lst/opb SRR / cvtd -180C
☐ OY-UPD	Boeing 727-22C (QF)	19103 / 341	N944UP	1166	0690	3 RR Tay 651-54	76884	Freighter	BP-FQ	lst/opb SRR / cvtd -22C
☐ OY-UPJ	Boeing 727-22C (QF)	19102 / 336	N943UP	1166	0690	3 RR Tay 651-54	76884	Freighter	BP-EQ	lst/opb SRR / cvtd -22C
☐ OY-UPM	Boeing 727-31C (QF)	19229 / 390	N923UP	0367	0582	3 RR Tay 651-54	76884	Freighter	BL-GQ	lst/opb SRR / cvtd -31C
☐ OY-UPS	Boeing 727-31C (QF)	19232 / 425	N927UP	0667	0382	3 RR Tay 651-54	76884	Freighter	BL-MQ	lst/opb SRR / cvtd -31C
☐ OY-UPT	Boeing 727-22C (QF)	19094 / 295	N945UP	0766	0690	3 RR Tay 651-54	76884	Freighter	BP-GQ	lst/opb SRR / cvtd -22C
☐ N207UP	Boeing 727-247 (F) (A)	21699 / 1485	N287WA	0579	0685	3 PW JT8D-15 (HK3/FDX)	88360	Freighter		cvtd -247
☐ N208UP	Boeing 727-247 (F) (A)	21701 / 1493	N289WA	0679	0785	3 PW JT8D-15 (HK3/FDX)	88360	Freighter		cvtd -247
☐ N209UP	Boeing 727-247 (F) (A)	21698 / 1474	N286WA	0579	0885	3 PW JT8D-15 (HK3/FDX)	88360	Freighter		cvtd -247
☐ N210UP	Boeing 727-247 (F) (A)	21697 / 1471	N284WA	0479	0985	3 PW JT8D-15 (HK3/FDX)	88360	Freighter		cvtd -247
☐ N211UP	Boeing 727-247 (F) (A)	21700 / 1489	N288WA	0679	1085	3 PW JT8D-15 (HK3/FDX)	88360	Freighter		cvtd -247
☐ N212UP	Boeing 727-247 (F) (A)	21392 / 1305	N2827W	1277	1085	3 PW JT8D-15 (HK3/FDX)	88360	Freighter		cvtd -247
☐ N213UP	Boeing 727-2A1 (F) (A)	21341 / 1253	PP-SNE	0477	0685	3 PW JT8D-17 (HK3/FDX)	88360	Freighter		cvtd -2A1
☐ N214UP	Boeing 727-2A1 (F) (A)	21342 / 1256	PP-SNF	0477	0685	3 PW JT8D-17 (HK3/FDX)	88360	Freighter		cvtd -2A1
☐ N401UP	Boeing 757-24APF	23723 / 139		0987	0987	2 PW PW2040	113398	Freighter		
☐ N402UP	Boeing 757-24APF	23724 / 141		0887	0987	2 PW PW2040	113398	Freighter		

456 registration type of aircraft cn/fn ex/ex* mfd del powered by mtow kg configuration selcal name/fln/specialitites/remarks

registration	type of aircraft	cn/fn	ex/ex*	mfd	del	powered by	mtow kg	configuration	selcal	name/fln/specialitites/remarks
☐ N403UP	Boeing 757-24APF	23725 / 143		0887	0987	2 PW PW2040	113398	Freighter		
☐ N404UP	Boeing 757-24APF	23726 / 147		1087	1087	2 PW PW2040	113398	Freighter		
☐ N405UP	Boeing 757-24APF	23727 / 149		1087	1087	2 PW PW2040	113398	Freighter		
☐ N406UP	Boeing 757-24APF	23728 / 176		0588	0688	2 PW PW2040	113398	Freighter		
☐ N407UP	Boeing 757-24APF	23729 / 181		0688	0688	2 PW PW2040	113398	Freighter		
☐ N408UP	Boeing 757-24APF	23730 / 184		0788	0788	2 PW PW2040	113398	Freighter		
☐ N409UP	Boeing 757-24APF	23731 / 186		0788	0788	2 PW PW2040	113398	Freighter		
☐ N410UP	Boeing 757-24APF	23732 / 189		0888	0888	2 PW PW2040	113398	Freighter		
☐ N411UP	Boeing 757-24APF	23851 / 191		0888	0888	2 PW PW2040	113398	Freighter		
☐ N412UP	Boeing 757-24APF	23852 / 193		0988	0988	2 PW PW2040	113398	Freighter		
☐ N413UP	Boeing 757-24APF	23853 / 195		0988	0988	2 PW PW2040	113398	Freighter		
☐ N414UP	Boeing 757-24APF	23854 / 197		1088	1088	2 PW PW2040	113398	Freighter		
☐ N415UP	Boeing 757-24APF	23855 / 199		1088	1088	2 PW PW2040	113398	Freighter		
☐ N416UP	Boeing 757-24APF	23903 / 318		1090	1090	2 PW PW2040	113398	Freighter		
☐ N417UP	Boeing 757-24APF	23904 / 322		1090	1090	2 PW PW2040	113398	Freighter		
☐ N418UP	Boeing 757-24APF	23905 / 326		1190	1190	2 PW PW2040	113398	Freighter		
☐ N419UP	Boeing 757-24APF	23906 / 330		1290	1290	2 PW PW2040	113398	Freighter		
☐ N420UP	Boeing 757-24APF	23907 / 334		1290	1290	2 PW PW2040	113398	Freighter		
☐ N421UP	Boeing 757-24APF	25281 / 395		0991	0991	2 PW PW2040	113398	Freighter		
☐ N422UP	Boeing 757-24APF	25324 / 399		1091	1091	2 PW PW2040	113398	Freighter		
☐ N423UP	Boeing 757-24APF	25325 / 403		1091	1091	2 PW PW2040	113398	Freighter		
☐ N424UP	Boeing 757-24APF	25369 / 407		1191	1191	2 PW PW2040	113398	Freighter		
☐ N425UP	Boeing 757-24APF	25370 / 411		1291	1291	2 PW PW2040	113398	Freighter		
☐ N426UP	Boeing 757-24APF	25457 / 477		0892	0892	2 PW PW2040	113398	Freighter		
☐ N427UP	Boeing 757-24APF	25458 / 481		0992	0992	2 PW PW2040	113398	Freighter		
☐ N428UP	Boeing 757-24APF	25459 / 485		0992	0992	2 PW PW2040	113398	Freighter		
☐ N429UP	Boeing 757-24APF	25460 / 489		1092	1092	2 PW PW2040	113398	Freighter		
☐ N430UP	Boeing 757-24APF	25461 / 493		1092	1092	2 PW PW2040	113398	Freighter		
☐ N431UP	Boeing 757-24APF	25462 / 569		0893	0893	2 PW PW2040	113398	Freighter		
☐ N432UP	Boeing 757-24APF	25463 / 573		0993	0993	2 PW PW2040	113398	Freighter		
☐ N433UP	Boeing 757-24APF	25464 / 577		0993	0993	2 PW PW2040	113398	Freighter		
☐ N434UP	Boeing 757-24APF	25465 / 579		1093	1093	2 PW PW2040	113398	Freighter		
☐ N435UP	Boeing 757-24APF	25466 / 581		1093	1093	2 PW PW2040	113398	Freighter		
☐ N436UP	Boeing 757-24APF	25467 / 625		0794	0794	2 RR RB211-535E4	113398	Freighter		
☐ N437UP	Boeing 757-24APF	25468 / 628		0794	0794	2 RR RB211-535E4	113398	Freighter		
☐ N438UP	Boeing 757-24APF	25469 / 631		0894	0894	2 RR RB211-535E4	113398	Freighter		
☐ N439UP	Boeing 757-24APF	25470 / 634		0894	0894	2 RR RB211-535E4	113398	Freighter		
☐ N440UP	Boeing 757-24APF	25471 / 636		0994	0994	2 RR RB211-535E4	113398	Freighter		
☐ N441UP	Boeing 757-24APF	27386 / 638		0994	0994	2 RR RB211-535E4	113398	Freighter		
☐ N442UP	Boeing 757-24APF	27387 / 640		1094	1094	2 RR RB211-535E4	113398	Freighter		
☐ N443UP	Boeing 757-24APF	27388 / 642		1094	1094	2 RR RB211-535E4	113398	Freighter		
☐ N444UP	Boeing 757-24APF	27389 / 644		1194	1194	2 RR RB211-535E4	113398	Freighter		
☐ N445UP	Boeing 757-24APF	27390 / 646		1194	1194	2 RR RB211-535E4	113398	Freighter		
☐ N446UP	Boeing 757-24APF	27735 / 649		1294	1294	2 RR RB211-535E4	113398	Freighter		
☐ N447UP	Boeing 757-24APF	27736 / 651		1294	1294	2 RR RB211-535E4	113398	Freighter		
☐ N448UP	Boeing 757-24APF	27737 / 654		0195	0195	2 RR RB211-535E4	113398	Freighter		
☐ N449UP	Boeing 757-24APF	27738 / 656		0195	0195	2 RR RB211-535E4	113398	Freighter		
☐ N450UP	Boeing 757-24APF	25472 / 659		0295	0295	2 RR RB211-535E4	113398	Freighter		
☐ N451UP	Boeing 757-24APF	27739 / 675		0695	0695	2 RR RB211-535E4	113398	Freighter		
☐ N452UP	Boeing 757-24APF	25473 / 679		0795	0795	2 RR RB211-535E4	113398	Freighter		
☐ N453UP	Boeing 757-24APF	25474 / 683		0895	0895	2 RR RB211-535E4	113398	Freighter		
☐ N454UP	Boeing 757-24APF	25475 / 687		0995	0995	2 RR RB211-535E4	113398	Freighter		
☐ N455UP	Boeing 757-24APF	25476 / 691		0995	0995	2 RR RB211-535E4	113398	Freighter		
☐ N456UP	Boeing 757-24APF	25477 / 728		0996	0996	2 RR RB211-535E4	113398	Freighter		
☐ N457UP	Boeing 757-24APF	25478 / 729		0996	0996	2 RR RB211-535E4	113398	Freighter		
☐ N458UP	Boeing 757-24APF	25479 / 730		1096	1096	2 RR RB211-535E4	113398	Freighter		
☐ N459UP	Boeing 757-24APF	25480 / 733		1096	1096	2 RR RB211-535E4	113398	Freighter		
☐ N460UP	Boeing 757-24APF	25481 / 734		1196	1196	2 RR RB211-535E4	113398	Freighter		
☐ N461UP	Boeing 757-24APF	28265 / 755		0597	0597	2 RR RB211-535E4	113398	Freighter		
☐ N462UP	Boeing 757-24APF	28266 / 759		0697	0697	2 RR RB211-535E4	113398	Freighter		
☐ N463UP	Boeing 757-24APF	28267 / 763		0797	0797	2 RR RB211-535E4	113398	Freighter		
☐ N464UP	Boeing 757-24APF	28268 / 765		0997	0997	2 RR RB211-535E4	113398	Freighter		
☐ N465UP	Boeing 757-24APF	28269 / 767		0997	0997	2 RR RB211-535E4	113398	Freighter		
☐ N466UP	Boeing 757-24APF	25482 / 769		0997	0997	2 RR RB211-535E4	113398	Freighter		
☐ N467UP	Boeing 757-24APF	25483 / 771		0997	0997	2 RR RB211-535E4	113398	Freighter		
☐ N468UP	Boeing 757-24APF	25484 / 774		1097	1097	2 RR RB211-535E4	113398	Freighter		
☐ N469UP	Boeing 757-24APF	25485 / 776		1097	1097	2 RR RB211-535E4	113398	Freighter		
☐ N470UP	Boeing 757-24APF	25486 / 778		1197	1197	2 RR RB211-535E4	113398	Freighter		
☐ N471UP	Boeing 757-24APF	28842 / 813		0798	0798	2 RR RB211-535E4	113398	Freighter		
☐ N472UP	Boeing 757-24APF	28843 / 815		0898	0898	2 RR RB211-535E4	113398	Freighter		
☐ N473UP	Boeing 757-24APF	28846 / 823	N5573L*	0998	0998	2 RR RB211-535E4	113398	Freighter		
☐ N474UP	Boeing 757-24APF	28844				2 RR RB211-535E4	113398	Freighter		oo-delivery 0699
☐ N475UP	Boeing 757-24APF	28845				2 RR RB211-535E4	113398	Freighter		oo-delivery 0799
☐ N700UP	Boeing (Douglas) DC-8-71F	45900 / 316	N861FT	1267	0685	4 CFMI CFM56-2C	148778	Freighter	CG-AQ	cvtd -61F (CF)
☐ N701UP	Boeing (Douglas) DC-8-71F	45938 / 331	N860FT	0268	0585	4 CFMI CFM56-2C	148778	Freighter	CG-BQ	cvtd -61F (CF)
☐ N702UP	Boeing (Douglas) DC-8-71F	45902 / 294	N810EV	0667	0585	4 CFMI CFM56-2C	148778	Freighter	CG-DQ	cvtd -61F (CF)
☐ N703UP	Boeing (Douglas) DC-8-71F	45939 / 351	N867FT	0468	0685	4 CFMI CFM56-2C	148778	Freighter	CG-EQ	cvtd -61F (CF)
☐ N705UP	Boeing (Douglas) DC-8-71F	45949 / 329	N863FT	0168	0585	4 CFMI CFM56-2C	148778	Freighter	CG-FQ	cvtd -61F (CF)
☐ N706UP	Boeing (Douglas) DC-8-71F	46056 / 495	N1307L	1169	1286	4 CFMI CFM56-2C	148778	Freighter	CG-HQ	cvtd -61/-71
☐ N707UP	Boeing (Douglas) DC-8-71F	45907 / 288	N822E	0467	1286	4 CFMI CFM56-2C	148778	Freighter	CG-JQ	cvtd -61/-71
☐ N708UP	Boeing (Douglas) DC-8-71F	46048 / 450	N1304L	0469	1286	4 CFMI CFM56-2C	148778	Freighter	CG-KQ	cvtd -61/-71
☐ N709UP	Boeing (Douglas) DC-8-71F	45914 / 292	N823E	0667	1286	4 CFMI CFM56-2C	148778	Freighter	CG-LQ	cvtd -61/-71
☐ N713UP	Boeing (Douglas) DC-8-71F	46014 / 400	N1300L	1068	1286	4 CFMI CFM56-2C	148778	Freighter	CG-MQ	cvtd -61/-71
☐ N715UP	Boeing (Douglas) DC-8-71F	45915 / 295	N824E	0767	1286	4 CFMI CFM56-2C	148778	Freighter	CG-PQ	cvtd -61/-71
☐ N718UP	Boeing (Douglas) DC-8-71F	46018 / 420	N1301L	1268	1286	4 CFMI CFM56-2C	148778	Freighter	CH-AQ	cvtd -61/-71
☐ N729UP	Boeing (Douglas) DC-8-71F	46029 / 425	N1302L	0169	1286	4 CFMI CFM56-2C	148778	Freighter	CH-BQ	cvtd -61/-71
☐ N730UP	Boeing (Douglas) DC-8-71F	46030 / 426	N1303L	0169	1286	4 CFMI CFM56-2C	148778	Freighter	CH-DQ	cvtd -61/-71
☐ N744UP	Boeing (Douglas) DC-8-71F	45944 / 326	N825E	0168	1286	4 CFMI CFM56-2C	148778	Freighter	CH-EQ	cvtd -61/-71
☐ N748UP	Boeing (Douglas) DC-8-71F	45948 / 321	N862FT	1267	0585	4 CFMI CFM56-2C	148778	Freighter	CH-FQ	cvtd -61F (CF)
☐ N750UP	Boeing (Douglas) DC-8-71F	45950 / 354	N868FT	0468	0785	4 CFMI CFM56-2C	148778	Freighter	CH-GQ	cvtd -61F (CF)
☐ N752UP	Boeing (Douglas) DC-8-71F	45952 / 338	N864FT	0268	0585	4 CFMI CFM56-2C	148778	Freighter	CH-JQ	cvtd -61F (CF)
☐ N755UP	Boeing (Douglas) DC-8-71F	46055 / 492	N1306L	1169	1286	4 CFMI CFM56-2C	148778	Freighter	CH-KQ	cvtd -61/-71
☐ N772UP	Boeing (Douglas) DC-8-71F	46072 / 477	N1305L	0869	1286	4 CFMI CFM56-2C	148778	Freighter	CH-LQ	cvtd -61/-71
☐ N779UP	Boeing (Douglas) DC-8-71F	45979 / 363	N826E	0568	1286	4 CFMI CFM56-2C	148778	Freighter	CH-MQ	cvtd -61/-71
☐ N797UP	Boeing (Douglas) DC-8-71F	45897 / 313	EI-BPF	1267	0485	4 CFMI CFM56-2C	148778	Freighter	CH-PQ	cvtd -61F (CF)
☐ N798UP	Boeing (Douglas) DC-8-71F	45898 / 320	EI-BPG	1267	0385	4 CFMI CFM56-2C	148778	Freighter	CJ-AQ	cvtd -61F (CF)
☐ N801UP	Boeing (Douglas) DC-8-73F	46101 / 489	TF-FLE	0969	0884	4 CFMI CFM56-2C	161025	Freighter	CE-AQ	cvtd -63F (CF)
☐ N802UP	Boeing (Douglas) DC-8-73F	46100 / 502	C-FTIP	1269	0190	4 CFMI CFM56-2C	161025	Freighter	CF-LQ	cvtd -63/-63F
☐ N803UP	Boeing (Douglas) DC-8-73F	46073 / 485	N402FE	0869	0590	4 CFMI CFM56-2C	161025	Freighter	CF-MQ	cvtd -63F (CF)
☐ N804UP	Boeing (Douglas) DC-8-73F	46004 / 403	N784FT	1068	1282	4 CFMI CFM56-2C	161025	Freighter	CE-BQ	cvtd -63F (AF)
☐ N805UP	Boeing (Douglas) DC-8-73F	46117 / 525	N401FE	0570	0590	4 CFMI CFM56-2C	161025	Freighter	CF-PQ	cvtd -63F (CF)
☐ N806UP	Boeing (Douglas) DC-8-73F	46006 / 413	N786FT	1268	1282	4 CFMI CFM56-2C	161025	Freighter	CE-DQ	cvtd -63F (AF)
☐ N807UP	Boeing (Douglas) DC-8-73F	46007 / 422	N787FT	0169	1282	4 CFMI CFM56-2C	161025	Freighter	CE-FQ	cvtd -63F (AF)
☐ N808UP	Boeing (Douglas) DC-8-73F	46008 / 423	N788FT	0169	0383	4 CFMI CFM56-2C	161025	Freighter	CE-GQ	cvtd -63F (AF)
☐ N809UP	Boeing (Douglas) DC-8-73F	46109 / 493	N772FT	1069	0284	4 CFMI CFM56-2C	161025	Freighter	CE-HQ	cvtd -63F (CF)
☐ N810UP	Boeing (Douglas) DC-8-73F	46001 / 395	N404FE	0968	0590	4 CFMI CFM56-2C	161025	Freighter	CJ-BQ	cvtd -63F (CF)
☐ N811UP	Boeing (Douglas) DC-8-73F	46089 / 501	N407FE	1269	0590	4 CFMI CFM56-2C	161025	Freighter	CJ-DQ	cvtd -63F (CF)
☐ N812UP	Boeing (Douglas) DC-8-73F	46112 / 520	N776FT	0470	1084	4 CFMI CFM56-2C	161025	Freighter	CE-JQ	cvtd -63F (CF)
☐ N813UP	Boeing (Douglas) DC-8-73F	46059 / 456	N703FT	0469	0690	4 CFMI CFM56-2C	161025	Freighter	CJ-EQ	Spirit of Manila / cvtd -63F (CF)
☐ N814UP	Boeing (Douglas) DC-8-73F	46090 / 504	N405FE	1269	0690	4 CFMI CFM56-2C	161025	Freighter	CJ-FQ	cvtd -63F (CF)
☐ N818UP	Boeing (Douglas) DC-8-73F	46108 / 522	N798FT	0470	0784	4 CFMI CFM56-2C	161025	Freighter	CE-KQ	cvtd -63F (CF)
☐ N819UP	Boeing (Douglas) DC-8-73F	46019 / 411	TF-VLY	1168	1085	4 CFMI CFM56-2C	161025	Freighter	CE-LQ	cvtd -63
☐ N836UP	Boeing (Douglas) DC-8-73F	45936 / 344	N8631	0668	1184	4 CFMI CFM56-2C	161025	Freighter	CE-MQ	cvtd -63F (CF)
☐ N840UP	Boeing (Douglas) DC-8-73F	46140 / 528	N797FT	0570	0584	4 CFMI CFM56-2C	161025	Freighter	CE-PQ	cvtd -63F (CF)
☐ N851UP	Boeing (Douglas) DC-8-73F	46051 / 440	N811EV	0269	0385	4 CFMI CFM56-2C	161025	Freighter	CF-AQ	cvtd -63F (CF)
☐ N852UP	Boeing (Douglas) DC-8-73F	46052 / 442	N31EK	0369	0585	4 CFMI CFM56-2C	161025	Freighter	CF-BQ	cvtd -63F (CF)
☐ N866UP	Boeing (Douglas) DC-8-73F	45966 / 393	N773FT	0968	0584	4 CFMI CFM56-2C	161025	Freighter	CF-DQ	cvtd -63F (CF)
☐ N867UP	Boeing (Douglas) DC-8-73F	45967 / 385	N907CL	0868	1184	4 CFMI CFM56-2C	161025	Freighter	CF-EQ	cvtd -63F (CF)
☐ N868UP	Boeing (Douglas) DC-8-73F	45968 / 389	N871TV	0868	0984	4 CFMI CFM56-2C	161025	Freighter	CF-GQ	cvtd -63F (CF)
☐ N874UP	Boeing (Douglas) DC-8-73F	46074 / 468	HB-IDZ	0669	1285	4 CFMI CFM56-2C	161025	Freighter	CF-HQ	cvtd -63 (PF)

☐ N880UP	Boeing (Douglas) DC-8-73F	46080 / 466	TF-VLZ	0669	1085	4 CFMI CFM56-2C	161025	Freighter	CF-JQ	cvtd -63
☐ N894UP	Boeing (Douglas) DC-8-73F	46094 / 482	N910CL	0869	1184	4 CFMI CFM56-2C	161025	Freighter	CF-KQ	cvtd -63F (CF)
☐ N	Airbus Industrie A300-622F (A300F4-622R)					2 PW PW4158	171700	Freighter		oo-delivery 0700
☐ N	Airbus Industrie A300-622F (A300F4-622R)					2 PW PW4158	171700	Freighter		oo-delivery 0800
☐ N	Airbus Industrie A300-622F (A300F4-622R)					2 PW PW4158	171700	Freighter		oo-delivery 0900
☐ N	Airbus Industrie A300-622F (A300F4-622R)					2 PW PW4158	171700	Freighter		oo-delivery 1000
☐ N	Airbus Industrie A300-622F (A300F4-622R)					2 PW PW4158	171700	Freighter		oo-delivery 1100
☐ N	Airbus Industrie A300-622F (A300F4-622R)					2 PW PW4158	171700	Freighter		oo-delivery 1200
☐ N	Airbus Industrie A300-622F (A300F4-622R)					2 PW PW4158	171700	Freighter		oo-delivery 0101
☐ N	Airbus Industrie A300-622F (A300F4-622R)					2 PW PW4158	171700	Freighter		oo-delivery 0201
☐ N	Airbus Industrie A300-622F (A300F4-622R)					2 PW PW4158	171700	Freighter		oo-delivery 0301
☐ N	Airbus Industrie A300-622F (A300F4-622R)					2 PW PW4158	171700	Freighter		oo-delivery 0401
☐ N	Airbus Industrie A300-622F (A300F4-622R)					2 PW PW4158	171700	Freighter		oo-delivery 0501
☐ N	Airbus Industrie A300-622F (A300F4-622R)					2 PW PW4158	171700	Freighter		oo-delivery 0601
☐ N	Airbus Industrie A300-622F (A300F4-622R)					2 PW PW4158	171700	Freighter		oo-delivery 0801
☐ N	Airbus Industrie A300-622F (A300F4-622R)					2 PW PW4158	171700	Freighter		oo-delivery 0901
☐ N	Airbus Industrie A300-622F (A300F4-622R)					2 PW PW4158	171700	Freighter		oo-delivery 1101
☐ N	Airbus Industrie A300-622F (A300F4-622R)					2 PW PW4158	171700	Freighter		oo-delivery 1201
☐ N	Airbus Industrie A300-622F (A300F4-622R)					2 PW PW4158	171700	Freighter		oo-delivery 0002
☐ N	Airbus Industrie A300-622F (A300F4-622R)					2 PW PW4158	171700	Freighter		oo-delivery 0002
☐ N	Airbus Industrie A300-622F (A300F4-622R)					2 PW PW4158	171700	Freighter		oo-delivery 0002
☐ N	Airbus Industrie A300-622F (A300F4-622R)					2 PW PW4158	171700	Freighter		oo-delivery 0002
☐ N	Airbus Industrie A300-622F (A300F4-622R)					2 PW PW4158	171700	Freighter		oo-delivery 0002
☐ N	Airbus Industrie A300-622F (A300F4-622R)					2 PW PW4158	171700	Freighter		oo-delivery 0002
☐ N	Airbus Industrie A300-622F (A300F4-622R)					2 PW PW4158	171700	Freighter		oo-delivery 0003
☐ N	Airbus Industrie A300-622F (A300F4-622R)					2 PW PW4158	171700	Freighter		oo-delivery 0003
☐ N	Airbus Industrie A300-622F (A300F4-622R)					2 PW PW4158	171700	Freighter		oo-delivery 0003
☐ N	Airbus Industrie A300-622F (A300F4-622R)					2 PW PW4158	171700	Freighter		oo-delivery 0003
☐ N	Airbus Industrie A300-622F (A300F4-622R)					2 PW PW4158	171700	Freighter		oo-delivery 0003
☐ N	Airbus Industrie A300-622F (A300F4-622R)					2 PW PW4158	171700	Freighter		oo-delivery 0003
☐ N	Airbus Industrie A300-622F (A300F4-622R)					2 PW PW4158	171700	Freighter		oo-delivery 0003
☐ N	Airbus Industrie A300-622F (A300F4-622R)					2 PW PW4158	171700	Freighter		oo-delivery 0003
☐ N301UP	Boeing 767-34AF (ER)	27239 / 580		1095	1095	2 GE CF6-80C2B7F	185066	Freighter	BP-AQ	
☐ N302UP	Boeing 767-34AF (ER)	27240 / 590		1095	1095	2 GE CF6-80C2B7F	185066	Freighter	BP-CQ	
☐ N303UP	Boeing 767-34AF (ER)	27241 / 594		1195	1195	2 GE CF6-80C2B7F	185066	Freighter	BP-DQ	
☐ N304UP	Boeing 767-34AF (ER)	27242 / 598		1195	1195	2 GE CF6-80C2B7F	185066	Freighter	BP-EQ	
☐ N305UP	Boeing 767-34AF (ER)	27243 / 600		1295	1295	2 GE CF6-80C2B7F	185066	Freighter	BP-FQ	
☐ N306UP	Boeing 767-34AF (ER)	27759 / 622		0796	0796	2 GE CF6-80C2B7F	185066	Freighter	BP-GQ	
☐ N307UP	Boeing 767-34AF (ER)	27760 / 624		0896	0896	2 GE CF6-80C2B7F	185066	Freighter	BP-HQ	
☐ N308UP	Boeing 767-34AF (ER)	27761 / 626		0996	0996	2 GE CF6-80C2B7F	185066	Freighter	DL-BQ	
☐ N309UP	Boeing 767-34AF (ER)	27740 / 628		0996	0996	2 GE CF6-80C2B7F	185066	Freighter	DL-CQ	
☐ N310UP	Boeing 767-34AF (ER)	27762 / 630		1096	1096	2 GE CF6-80C2B7F	185066	Freighter	DL-EQ	
☐ N311UP	Boeing 767-34AF (ER)	27741 / 632		1096	1096	2 GE CF6-80C2B7F	185066	Freighter	DL-FQ	
☐ N312UP	Boeing 767-34AF (ER)	27763 / 634		1196	1196	2 GE CF6-80C2B7F	185066	Freighter	DL-GQ	
☐ N313UP	Boeing 767-34AF (ER)	27764 / 636		1196	1196	2 GE CF6-80C2B7F	185066	Freighter	DL-HQ	
☐ N314UP	Boeing 767-34AF (ER)	27742 / 638		1296	1296	2 GE CF6-80C2B7F	185066	Freighter	DL-JQ	
☐ N315UP	Boeing 767-34AF (ER)	27743 / 640		1296	1296	2 GE CF6-80C2B7F	185066	Freighter	DL-KQ	
☐ N316UP	Boeing 767-34AF (ER)	27744 / 660		0597	0597	2 GE CF6-80C2B7F	185066	Freighter	DL-MQ	
☐ N317UP	Boeing 767-34AF (ER)	27745 / 666		0797	0797	2 GE CF6-80C2B7F	185066	Freighter	DL-PQ	
☐ N318UP	Boeing 767-34AF (ER)	27746 / 670		0997	0997	2 GE CF6-80C2B7F	185066	Freighter	DM-AQ	
☐ N319UP	Boeing 767-34AF (ER)	27758 / 672		0997	0997	2 GE CF6-80C2B7F	185066	Freighter	DM-BQ	
☐ N320UP	Boeing 767-34AF (ER)	27747 / 674		0997	0997	2 GE CF6-80C2B7F	185066	Freighter	DM-CQ	special Olympic sponsor-colors
☐ N322UP	Boeing 767-34AF (ER)	27748 / 678		1297	1297	2 GE CF6-80C2B7F	185066	Freighter	DM-EQ	
☐ N323UP	Boeing 767-34AF (ER)	27749 / 682		1297	1297	2 GE CF6-80C2B7F	185066	Freighter	DM-FQ	
☐ N324UP	Boeing 767-34AF (ER)	27750 / 724		1098	1098	2 GE CF6-80C2B7F	185066	Freighter		
☐ N325UP	Boeing 767-34AF (ER)	27751 / 726		1198	1198	2 GE CF6-80C2B7F	185066	Freighter		
☐ N326UP	Boeing 767-34AF (ER)	27752 / 728		1198	1198	2 GE CF6-80C2B7F	185066	Freighter		
☐ N327UP	Boeing 767-34AF (ER)	27753 / 730		1298	1298	2 GE CF6-80C2B7F	185066	Freighter		
☐ N328UP	Boeing 767-34AF (ER)	27754 / 732		1298	1298	2 GE CF6-80C2B7F	185066	Freighter		
☐ N329UP	Boeing 767-34AF (ER)	27755				2 GE CF6-80C2B7F	185066	Freighter		oo-delivery 0899
☐ N330UP	Boeing 767-34AF (ER)	27756				2 GE CF6-80C2B7F	185066	Freighter		oo-delivery 0899
☐ N331UP	Boeing 767-34AF (ER)	27757				2 GE CF6-80C2B7F	185066	Freighter		oo-delivery 0899
☐ N520UP	Boeing 747-212B (SF)	21943 / 475	9V-SQR	1080	0696	4 PW JT9D-7Q	377842	Freighter	FS-LP	cvtd -212B
☐ N521UP	Boeing 747-212B (SF)	21944 / 510	9V-SQS	0281	0896	4 PW JT9D-7Q	377842	Freighter	FS-LQ	cvtd -212B / Olympic-colors
☐ N522UP	Boeing 747-212B (SF)	21936 / 401	VT-ENQ	0979	0298	4 PW JT9D-7Q	377842	Freighter		cvtd -212B
☐ N523UP	Boeing 747-283B (SF)	22381 / 500	N155FW	1280	0598	4 PW JT9D-7Q	377842	Freighter	BC-FL	lsf BBAM / cvtd -283B (M)
☐ N671UP	Boeing 747-123 (SF)	20323 / 115	N9671	0271	1184	4 PW JT9D-7A	332937	Freighter	CD-AQ	cvtd -123
☐ N672UP	Boeing 747-123 (SF)	20324 / 119	N9672	0471	0984	4 PW JT9D-7A	332937	Freighter	CD-BQ	cvtd -123
☐ N673UP	Boeing 747-123 (SF)	20325 / 125	N9673	0471	0884	4 PW JT9D-7A	332937	Freighter	CD-EQ	cvtd -123
☐ N674UP	Boeing 747-123 (SF)	20100 / 46	N9661	0670	1284	4 PW JT9D-7A	332937	Freighter	CD-FQ	cvtd -123
☐ N675UP	Boeing 747-123 (SF)	20390 / 136	N9675	0571	1084	4 PW JT9D-7A	332937	Freighter	CD-GQ	cvtd -123
☐ N676UP	Boeing 747-123 (SF)	20101 / 57	N9676	0770	1284	4 PW JT9D-7A	332937	Freighter	CD-HQ	cvtd -123
☐ N677UP	Boeing 747-123 (SF)	20391 / 143	N629FE	0671	1290	4 PW JT9D-7A	332937	Freighter	CD-JQ	cvtd -123
☐ N680UP	Boeing 747SR-46 (SF)	20923 / 234	JA8121	0374	0590	4 PW JT9D-7A	332937	Freighter	CD-MQ	cvtd -46
☐ N681UP	Boeing 747-121 (SF)	19661 / 70	N628FE	1070	0591	4 PW JT9D-7A	332937	Freighter	CD-PQ	cvtd -121
☐ N682UP	Boeing 747-121 (SF)	20349 / 110	N626FE	0471	0891	4 PW JT9D-7A	332937	Freighter	EG-MQ	cvtd -121
☐ N683UP	Boeing 747-121 (SF)	20353 / 131	N627FE	0671	1291	4 PW JT9D-7A	332037	Freighter	EG-PQ	cvtd -121
☐ N691UP	Boeing 747-121 (SF)	19641 / 7	N491GX	1269	1093	4 PW JT9D-7A	332937	Freighter	CD-KQ	lsf GATX / cvtd -121

URSINAIR (Michael J. Ursin dba) **Stow-Digital Heliport, MA**

302 Boxborough Road, Stow, MA 01775, USA ☎ (978) 461-0161 Tx: none Fax: (978) 461-0162 SITA: n/a
F: 1994 ✝✝✝ n/a Head: Michael J. Ursin Net: n/a

☐ N36MU	Bell 206B JetRanger	1360	N205AL	0074	0893	1 AN 250-C20	1451			

US AIRWAYS, Inc. = US / USA (MetroJet) (Subsidiary of US Airways Group, Inc. / formerly USAir, Inc. & Allegheny Airlines, Inc.) **Pittsburgh, PA / Washington, DC**

2345 Crystal Drive, Arlington, VA 22227, USA ☎ (540) 872-7000 Tx: 892645 us agtn Fax: (540) 872-5437 SITA: n/a
F: 1938 ✝✝✝ 42090 Head: Stephen M. Wolf IATA: 037 ICAO: US AIR Net: http://www.usairways.com A commuter system to provide feeder connection at US major hubs is operated under the marketing name US AIRWAYS EXPRESS by: AIR MIDWEST (Beech 1900D), ALLEGHENY AIRLINES (DHC-8), CCAir (Jetstream 32/DHC-8/Shorts 360), CHAUTAUQUA AIRLINES (Jetstream 31/RJ 145/Saab 340), COMMUTAIR (Beech 1900D), MESA AIRLINES (Beech 1900D/CRJ 200), PIEDMONT AIRLINES (DHC-8) & PSA AIRLINES (Dornier 328). All are operated in full US AIRWAYS EXPRESS-colors & both titles. For details – see under each company. MetroJet is a low-cost, internal division operating in dedicated markets with Boeing 737-200 carrying such colors/titles (same HQ). Aircraft are marked as such in the fleetlist.
On order (to be reconfirmed): further 120 Airbus Industrie A319/A320/A321.

☐ N850US	Fokker 100 (F28 Mk0100)	11276	PH-ZCI*	0089	0789	2 RR Tay 650-15	44452	F12Y85		
☐ N851US	Fokker 100 (F28 Mk0100)	11278	PH-EZG*	0089	0889	2 RR Tay 650-15	44452	F12Y85		
☐ N852US	Fokker 100 (F28 Mk0100)	11280	PH-EZH*	0089	1089	2 RR Tay 650-15	44452	F12Y85		
☐ N853US	Fokker 100 (F28 Mk0100)	11281	PH-EZI*	0089	1089	2 RR Tay 650-15	44452	F12Y85		
☐ N854US	Fokker 100 (F28 Mk0100)	11282	PH-EZP*	0089	1189	2 RR Tay 650-15	44452	F12Y85		
☐ N855US	Fokker 100 (F28 Mk0100)	11283	PH-EZR*	0089	1289	2 RR Tay 650-15	44452	F12Y85		
☐ N856US	Fokker 100 (F28 Mk0100)	11286	PH-EZU*	0089	1289	2 RR Tay 650-15	44452	F12Y85		
☐ N857US	Fokker 100 (F28 Mk0100)	11289	PH-EZG*	0089	1289	2 RR Tay 650-15	44452	F12Y85		
☐ N858US	Fokker 100 (F28 Mk0100)	11291	PH-EZH*	0090	0190	2 RR Tay 650-15	44452	F12Y85		
☐ N859US	Fokker 100 (F28 Mk0100)	11293	PH-EZY*	0090	0290	2 RR Tay 650-15	44452	F12Y85		
☐ N860US	Fokker 100 (F28 Mk0100)	11295	PH-EZZ*	0090	0390	2 RR Tay 650-15	44452	F12Y85		
☐ N861US	Fokker 100 (F28 Mk0100)	11297	PH-EZB*	0090	0390	2 RR Tay 650-15	44452	F12Y85		
☐ N862US	Fokker 100 (F28 Mk0100)	11300	PH-EZC*	0090	0490	2 RR Tay 650-15	44452	F12Y85		
☐ N863US	Fokker 100 (F28 Mk0100)	11303	PH-EZD*	0090	0590	2 RR Tay 650-15	44452	F12Y85		
☐ N864US	Fokker 100 (F28 Mk0100)	11306	PH-EZF*	0090	0690	2 RR Tay 650-15	44452	F12Y85		
☐ N865US	Fokker 100 (F28 Mk0100)	11308	PH-EZI*	0090	0790	2 RR Tay 650-15	44452	F12Y85		
☐ N866US	Fokker 100 (F28 Mk0100)	11310	PH-EZJ*	0090	0790	2 RR Tay 650-15	44452	F12Y85		
☐ N867US	Fokker 100 (F28 Mk0100)	11312	PH-EZU*	0090	0890	2 RR Tay 650-15	44452	F12Y85		
☐ N868US	Fokker 100 (F28 Mk0100)	11313	PH-EZR*	0090	0990	2 RR Tay 650-15	44452	F12Y85		
☐ N869US	Fokker 100 (F28 Mk0100)	11314	PH-EZH*	0090	1190	2 RR Tay 650-15	44452	F12Y85		
☐ N880US	Fokker 100 (F28 Mk0100)	11331	PH-EZT*	0091	0391	2 RR Tay 650-15	44452	F12Y85		
☐ N881US	Fokker 100 (F28 Mk0100)	11333	PH-EZW*	0091	0491	2 RR Tay 650-15	44452	F12Y85		
☐ N882US	Fokker 100 (F28 Mk0100)	11334	PH-EZD*	0091	0591	2 RR Tay 650-15	44452	F12Y85		
☐ N883US	Fokker 100 (F28 Mk0100)	11337	PH-EZO*	0091	0591	2 RR Tay 650-15	44452	F12Y85		
☐ N884US	Fokker 100 (F28 Mk0100)	11338	PH-EZS*	0091	0691	2 RR Tay 650-15	44452	F12Y85		
☐ N885US	Fokker 100 (F28 Mk0100)	11345	PH-EZE*	0091	0791	2 RR Tay 650-15	44452	F12Y85		
☐ N886US	Fokker 100 (F28 Mk0100)	11346	PH-EZO*	0091	0791	2 RR Tay 650-15	44452	F12Y85		
☐ N887US	Fokker 100 (F28 Mk0100)	11349	PH-EZB*	0091	0891	2 RR Tay 650-15	44452	F12Y85		
☐ N888AU	Fokker 100 (F28 Mk0100)	11357	PH-EZL*	0091	1091	2 RR Tay 650-15	44452	F12Y85		
☐ N889US	Fokker 100 (F28 Mk0100)	11358	PH-EZM*	0091	1091	2 RR Tay 650-15	44452	F12Y85		

458 registration type of aircraft cn/fn ex/ex* mfd del powered by mtow kg configuration selcal name/fln/specialitites/remarks

registration	type of aircraft	cn/fn	ex/ex*	mfd	del	powered by	mtow kg	configuration	selcal	name/fln/specialitites/remarks
N890US	Fokker 100 (F28 Mk0100)	11365	PH-EZC*	0091	1291	2 RR Tay 650-15	44452	F12Y85		
N891US	Fokker 100 (F28 Mk0100)	11366	PH-EZP*	0091	1291	2 RR Tay 650-15	44452	F12Y85		
N892US	Fokker 100 (F28 Mk0100)	11372	PH-EZE*	0091	1291	2 RR Tay 650-15	44452	F12Y85		
N893US	Fokker 100 (F28 Mk0100)	11373	PH-EZL*	0092	0292	2 RR Tay 650-15	44452	F12Y85		
N894US	Fokker 100 (F28 Mk0100)	11379	PH-EZM*	0092	0392	2 RR Tay 650-15	44452	F12Y85		
N895US	Fokker 100 (F28 Mk0100)	11380	PH-EZG*	0092	0392	2 RR Tay 650-15	44452	F12Y85		
N896US	Fokker 100 (F28 Mk0100)	11391	PH-EZB*	0092	0592	2 RR Tay 650-15	44452	F12Y85		
N897US	Fokker 100 (F28 Mk0100)	11392	PH-EZD*	0092	0592	2 RR Tay 650-15	44452	F12Y85		
N898US	Fokker 100 (F28 Mk0100)	11398	PH-EZJ*	0092	0692	2 RR Tay 650-15	44452	F12Y85		
N899US	Fokker 100 (F28 Mk0100)	11399	PH-EZL*	0092	0692	2 RR Tay 650-15	44452	F12Y85		
N912VJ	Boeing (Douglas) DC-9-32	47020 / 126	N1280L	0067	0488	2 PW JT8D-7B	48988	F12Y88		
N913VJ	Boeing (Douglas) DC-9-32	45846 / 112	N705PS	0067	0488	2 PW JT8D-7B (HK3/ABS)	48988	F12Y88		
N918VJ	Boeing (Douglas) DC-9-31	48138 / 1021		0981	1081	2 PW JT8D-9A (HK3/ABS)	47627	F12Y88		
N919VJ	Boeing (Douglas) DC-9-31	48139 / 1024		0081	1081	2 PW JT8D-9A (HK3/ABS)	47627	F12Y88		
N920VJ	Boeing (Douglas) DC-9-31	48140 / 1027		0081	1181	2 PW JT8D-9A (HK3/ABS)	47627	F12Y88		
N921VJ	Boeing (Douglas) DC-9-31	48141 / 1030		1081	1281	2 PW JT8D-9A (HK3/ABS)	47627	F12Y88		
N922VJ	Boeing (Douglas) DC-9-31	48142 / 1033		0081	1281	2 PW JT8D-9A (HK3/ABS)	47627	F12Y88		
N923VJ	Boeing (Douglas) DC-9-31	48143 / 1036		0081	1281	2 PW JT8D-9A (HK3/ABS)	47627	F12Y88		
N924VJ	Boeing (Douglas) DC-9-31	48144 / 1039		1181	1281	2 PW JT8D-9A (HK3/ABS)	47627	F12Y88		
N925VJ	Boeing (Douglas) DC-9-31	48145 / 1042		0081	1281	2 PW JT8D-9A (HK3/ABS)	47627	F12Y88		
N926VJ	Boeing (Douglas) DC-9-31	48146 / 1044		0081	0182	2 PW JT8D-9A (HK3/ABS)	47627	F12Y88		
N927VJ	Boeing (Douglas) DC-9-31	48154 / 1046		0081	0182	2 PW JT8D-9A (HK3/ABS)	47627	F12Y88		
N928VJ	Boeing (Douglas) DC-9-31	48131 / 940		0080	0280	2 PW JT8D-9A (HK3/ABS)	47627	F12Y88		
N929VJ	Boeing (Douglas) DC-9-31	48118 / 942		0080	0380	2 PW JT8D-9A (HK3/ABS)	47627	F12Y88		
N931VJ	Boeing (Douglas) DC-9-31	47188 / 291	N8954E	0068	0878	2 PW JT8D-7B	47627	F12Y88		
N932VJ	Boeing (Douglas) DC-9-31	47189 / 303	N8955E	0068	0878	2 PW JT8D-7B	47627	F12Y88		
N933VJ	Boeing (Douglas) DC-9-31	47216 / 315	N8958E	0068	0678	2 PW JT8D-7B	47627	F12Y88		
N934VJ	Boeing (Douglas) DC-9-31	48114 / 919		0079	0879	2 PW JT8D-9A (HK3/ABS)	47627	F12Y88		
N935VJ	Boeing (Douglas) DC-9-31	48115 / 920		0079	0979	2 PW JT8D-9A (HK3/ABS)	47627	F12Y88		
N936VJ	Boeing (Douglas) DC-9-31	48116 / 921		0079	0979	2 PW JT8D-9A (HK3/ABS)	47627	F12Y88		
N937VJ	Boeing (Douglas) DC-9-31	48117 / 922		0079	0979	2 PW JT8D-9A (HK3/ABS)	47627	F12Y88		
N938VJ	Boeing (Douglas) DC-9-31	48119 / 943		0080	0380	2 PW JT8D-9A (HK3/ABS)	47627	F12Y88		
N939VJ	Boeing (Douglas) DC-9-31	48120 / 949		0080	0480	2 PW JT8D-9A (HK3/ABS)	47627	F12Y88		
N942VJ	Boeing (Douglas) DC-9-31	47057 / 122	N972NE	0067	0874	2 PW JT8D-7B	47627	F12Y88		
N946VJ	Boeing (Douglas) DC-9-32	47026 / 119	N3317L	0067	0976	2 PW JT8D-7B	48988	F12Y88		
N955VJ	Boeing (Douglas) DC-9-31	47593 / 705		0073	0973	2 PW JT8D-7B (HK3/ABS)	47627	F12Y88		
N956VJ	Boeing (Douglas) DC-9-31	47588 / 699	N54630*	0073	0274	2 PW JT8D-7B	47627	F12Y88		
N958VJ	Boeing (Douglas) DC-9-32	47351 / 442	6Y-JGA	0068	1180	2 PW JT8D-7B (HK3/ABS)	48988	F12Y88		
N959VJ	Boeing (Douglas) DC-9-32	47352 / 453	6Y-JGB	0068	1180	2 PW JT8D-7B (HK3/ABS)	48988	F12Y88		
N960VJ	Boeing (Douglas) DC-9-31	47505 / 586		0070	0670	2 PW JT8D-7B (HK3/ABS)	47627	F12Y88		
N963VJ	Boeing (Douglas) DC-9-31	47508 / 595		0070	0671	2 PW JT8D-7B (HK3/ABS)	47627	F12Y88		
N965VJ	Boeing (Douglas) DC-9-31	47374 / 523		0069	0969	2 PW JT8D-7B	47627	F12Y88		
N966VJ	Boeing (Douglas) DC-9-31	47420 / 556		0069	1269	2 PW JT8D-7B (HK3/ABS).	47627	F12Y88		
N967VJ	Boeing (Douglas) DC-9-31	47375 / 531		0069	0969	2 PW JT8D-7B (HK3/ABS)	47627	F12Y88		
N970VJ	Boeing (Douglas) DC-9-31	47050 / 118		0067	0667	2 PW JT8D-7B	47627	F12Y88		
N971VJ	Boeing (Douglas) DC-9-31	47051 / 131		0067	0667	2 PW JT8D-7B	47627	F12Y88		
N973VJ	Boeing (Douglas) DC-9-31	47099 / 197		0067	1167	2 PW JT8D-7B	47627	F12Y88		
N974VJ	Boeing (Douglas) DC-9-31	47130 / 211		0067	1267	2 PW JT8D-7B	47627	F12Y88		
N976VJ	Boeing (Douglas) DC-9-31	48147 / 1048		0081	0282	2 PW JT8D-9A (HK3/ABS)	47627	F12Y88		
N977VJ	Boeing (Douglas) DC-9-31	48155 / 1050		0082	0282	2 PW JT8D-9A (HK3/ABS)	47627	F12Y88		
N978VJ	Boeing (Douglas) DC-9-31	47371 / 506		0069	0669	2 PW JT8D-7B (HK3/ABS)	47627	F12Y88		
N980VJ	Boeing (Douglas) DC-9-31	48156 / 1052		0082	0382	2 PW JT8D-9A (HK3/ABS)	47627	F12Y88		
N981VJ	Boeing (Douglas) DC-9-31	48157 / 1054		0082	0382	2 PW JT8D-9A (HK3/ABS)	47627	F12Y88		
N982VJ	Boeing (Douglas) DC-9-31	48158 / 1056		0082	0382	2 PW JT8D-9A (HK3/ABS)	47627	F12Y88		
N983VJ	Boeing (Douglas) DC-9-31	48159 / 1058		0082	0482	2 PW JT8D-9A (HK3/ABS)	47627	F12Y88		
N985VJ	Boeing (Douglas) DC-9-31	47208 / 307		0068	0568	2 PW JT8D-7B	47627	F12Y88		std MZJ / for sale or lease
N987VJ	Boeing (Douglas) DC-9-31	47210 / 341		0068	0768	2 PW JT8D-7B	47627	F12Y88		std MZJ / for sale or lease
N991VJ	Boeing (Douglas) DC-9-31	47310 / 449		0069	0269	2 PW JT8D-7B	47627	F12Y88		
N993VJ	Boeing (Douglas) DC-9-31	47332 / 461		0069	0269	2 PW JT8D-7B	47627	F12Y88		
N997VJ	Boeing (Douglas) DC-9-31	47336 / 500		0069	0569	2 PW JT8D-7B (HK3/ABS)	47627	F12Y88		
N223US	Boeing 737-201 (A)	21665 / 534	N761N	0078	0889	2 PW JT8D-9A	52390	F12Y96		
N224US	Boeing 737-201 (A)	21666 / 547	N762N	0078	0889	2 PW JT8D-9A (HK3/NOR)	52390	F12Y96		
N225US	Boeing 737-201 (A)	21667 / 548	N763N	0078	0889	2 PW JT8D-9A (HK3/NOR)	52390	F12Y96		
N226US	Boeing 737-201 (A)	21815 / 589	N768N	0079	0889	2 PW JT8D-9A (HK3/NOR)	52390	F12Y96		
N227AU	Boeing 737-201 (A)	21816 / 592	N769N	0079	0889	2 PW JT8D-9A (HK3/NOR)	52390	F12Y96		
N228US	Boeing 737-201 (A)	21817 / 602	N772N	0079	0889	2 PW JT8D-9A (HK3/NOR)	52390	F12Y96		
N229US	Boeing 737-201 (A)	21818 / 606	N773N	0079	0889	2 PW JT8D-9A (HK3/NOR)	52390	F12Y96		
N230AU	Boeing 737-2Q9 (A)	21975 / 612	N774N	0079	0889	2 PW JT8D-9A	52390	F12Y96		
N231US	Boeing 737-2Q9 (A)	21976 / 625	N775N	0079	0889	2 PW JT8D-15	53070	F12Y96		
N232US	Boeing 737-201 (A)	22018 / 651	N778N	0080	0889	2 PW JT8D-9A (HK3/NOR)	52390	F12Y96		lsf CITG
N233US	Boeing 737-201 (A)	22273 / 680	N779N	0080	0889	2 PW JT8D-9A	52390	F12Y96		
N234US	Boeing 737-201 (A)	22274 / 682	N780N	0080	0889	2 PW JT8D-9A (HK3/NOR)	52390	F12Y96		
N235US	Boeing 737-201 (A)	22275 / 687	N781N	0080	0889	2 PW JT8D-9A (HK3/NOR)	52390	F12Y96		
N236US	Boeing 737-201 (A)	22352 / 728	N782N	0081	0889	2 PW JT8D-9A (HK3/NOR)	52390	F12Y96		
N237US	Boeing 737-201 (A)	22353 / 731	N783N	0081	0889	2 PW JT8D-9A (HK3/NOR)	52390	F12Y96		
N238US	Boeing 737-296 (A)	22398 / 733	N789N	0081	0889	2 PW JT8D-9A (HK3/NOR)	52390	F12Y96		
N239US	Boeing 737-201 (A)	22354 / 736	N784N	0081	0889	2 PW JT8D-9A (HK3/NOR)	52390	F12Y96		
N240AU	Boeing 737-201 (A)	22355 / 741	N785N	0081	0889	2 PW JT8D-9A (HK3/NOR)	52390	F12Y96		
N241US	Boeing 737-201 (A)	22443 / 782	N786N	0081	0889	2 PW JT8D-15 (HK3/NOR)	53070	F12Y96		
N242US	Boeing 737-201 (A)	22444 / 800	N787N	0081	0889	2 PW JT8D-15 (HK3/NOR)	53070	F12Y96		
N243US	Boeing 737-201 (A)	22445 / 837	N788N	0082	0889	2 PW JT8D-15 (HK3/NOR)	53070	F12Y96		
N244US	Boeing 737-201 (A)	22752 / 845	N791N	0082	0889	2 PW JT8D-15 (HK3/NOR)	53070	F12Y96		
N245US	Boeing 737-201 (A)	22751 / 857	N798N	0082	0889	2 PW JT8D-15 (HK3/NOR)	53070	F12Y96		
N246US	Boeing 737-201 (A)	22753 / 865	N792N	0082	0889	2 PW JT8D-15 (HK3/NOR)	53070	F12Y96		
N247US	Boeing 737-201 (A)	22754 / 870	N793N	0082	0889	2 PW JT8D-15 (HK3/NOR)	53070	Y118		MetroJet-division
N248US	Boeing 737-201 (A)	22755 / 873	N794N	0082	0889	2 PW JT8D-15 (HK3/NOR)	53070	F12Y96		
N249US	Boeing 737-201 (A)	22756 / 879	N795N	0082	0889	2 PW JT8D-15 (HK3/NOR)	53070	F12Y96		
N251AU	Boeing 737-201 (A)	22757 / 883	N796N	0082	0889	2 PW JT8D-15 (HK3/NOR)	53070	F12Y96		
N252AU	Boeing 737-201 (A)	22758 / 889	N797N	0082	0889	2 PW JT8D-15 (HK3/NOR)	53070	F12Y96		
N253AU	Boeing 737-201 (A)	22795 / 912	N799N	0082	0889	2 PW JT8D-15 (HK3/NOR)	53070	Y118		MetroJet-division
N254AU	Boeing 737-201 (A)	22796 / 914	N802N	0082	0889	2 PW JT8D-15 (HK3/NOR)	53070	Y118		MetroJet-division
N255AU	Boeing 737-201 (A)	22797 / 916	N803N	0082	0889	2 PW JT8D-15 (HK3/NOR)	53070	Y118		MetroJet-division
N256AU	Boeing 737-201 (A)	22798 / 924	N804N	0082	0889	2 PW JT8D-15 (HK3/NOR)	53070	F12Y96		
N257AU	Boeing 737-201 (A)	22799 / 932	N805N	0083	0889	2 PW JT8D-15 (HK3/NOR)	53070	F12Y96		
N259AU	Boeing 737-201 (A)	22806 / 938	N806N	0083	0889	2 PW JT8D-15 (HK3/NOR)	53070	F12Y96		
N260AU	Boeing 737-201 (A)	22866 / 940	N807N	0083	0889	2 PW JT8D-15 (HK3/NOR)	53070	F12Y96		
N261AU	Boeing 737-201 (A)	22867 / 961	N809N	0083	0889	2 PW JT8D-15 (HK3/NOR)	53070	F12Y96		
N262AU	Boeing 737-201 (A)	22868 / 963	N810N	0083	0889	2 PW JT8D-15 (HK3/NOR)	53070	F12Y96		
N263AU	Boeing 737-201 (A)	22869 / 964	N811N	0083	0889	2 PW JT8D-15	53070	F12Y96		
N264AU	Boeing 737-201 (A)	22961 / 984	N813N	0083	0889	2 PW JT8D-15 (HK3/NOR)	53070	F12Y96		
N265AU	Boeing 737-201 (A)	22962 / 987	N814N	0083	0889	2 PW JT8D-15 (HK3/NOR)	53070	F12Y96		
N266AU	Boeing 737-2B7 (A)	22878 / 921	N310AU	0082	1182	2 PW JT8D-15A (HK3/NOR)	53070	F12Y96		
N267AU	Boeing 737-2B7 (A)	22879 / 926	N311AU	0082	1182	2 PW JT8D-15A (HK3/NOR)	53070	F12Y96		
N268AU	Boeing 737-2B7 (A)	22880 / 927	N312AU	0082	1282	2 PW JT8D-15A (HK3/NOR)	53070	F12Y96		
N269AU	Boeing 737-2B7 (A)	22881 / 931	N313AU	0082	1282	2 PW JT8D-15A (HK3/NOR)	53070	F12Y96		
N270AU	Boeing 737-2B7 (A)	22882 / 934	N314AU	0082	1282	2 PW JT8D-15A (HK3/NOR)	53070	F12Y96		
N271AU	Boeing 737-2B7 (A)	22883 / 935	N315AU	0082	1282	2 PW JT8D-15A (HK3/NOR)	53070	F12Y96		
N272AU	Boeing 737-2B7 (A)	22884 / 956	N316AU	0083	0483	2 PW JT8D-15A	53070	F8Y102		
N273AU	Boeing 737-2B7 (A)	22885 / 966	N317AU	0083	0583	2 PW JT8D-15A (HK3/NOR)	53070	F12Y96		
N274US	Boeing 737-2B7 (A)	22886 / 974	N318AU	0083	0683	2 PW JT8D-15A	53070	F12Y96		
N275AU	Boeing 737-2B7 (A)	22887 / 976	N319AU	0083	0783	2 PW JT8D-15A	53070	F12Y96		
N276AU	Boeing 737-2B7 (A)	22888 / 979	N320AU	0083	0883	2 PW JT8D-15A	53070	F12Y96		
N277AU	Boeing 737-2B7 (A)	22889 / 983	N321AU	0083	0983	2 PW JT8D-15A (HK3/NOR)	53070	Y118		MetroJet-division
N278AU	Boeing 737-2B7 (A)	22890 / 986	N322AU	0083	0983	2 PW JT8D-15A (HK3/NOR)	53070	Y118		MetroJet-division
N279AU	Boeing 737-2B7 (A)	22891 / 988	N323AU	0083	1083	2 PW JT8D-15A (HK3/NOR)	53070	Y118		MetroJet-division
N280AU	Boeing 737-2B7 (A)	22892 / 990	N324AU	0083	0983	2 PW JT8D-15A (HK3/NOR)	53070	F12Y96		
N281AU	Boeing 737-2B7 (A)	23114 / 997	N325AU	0083	1283	2 PW JT8D-15A (HK3/NOR)	53070	F12Y96		
N282AU	Boeing 737-2B7 (A)	23115 / 998	N326AU	0083	1283	2 PW JT8D-15A (HK3/NOR)	53070	Y118		MetroJet-division
N283AU	Boeing 737-2B7 (A)	23116 / 999	N327AU	0083	1283	2 PW JT8D-15A (HK3/NOR)	53070	F12Y96		
N284AU	Boeing 737-2B7 (A)	23131 / 1039	N328AU	0084	0784	2 PW JT8D-15A (HK3/NOR)	53070	Y118		MetroJet-division

registration	type of aircraft	cn/fn	ex/ex*	mfd	del	powered by	mtow kg	configuration	selcal	name/fln/specialitites/remarks
☐ N285AU	Boeing 737-2B7 (A)	23132 / 1044	N329AU	0084	0884	2 PW JT8D-15A (HK3/NOR)	53070	Y118		MetroJet-division
☐ N286AU	Boeing 737-2B7 (A)	23133 / 1049	N330AU	0084	0984	2 PW JT8D-15A (HK3/NOR)	53070	Y118		MetroJet-division
☐ N287AU	Boeing 737-2B7 (A)	23134 / 1050	N331AU	0084	1084	2 PW JT8D-15A (HK3/NOR)	53070	Y118		MetroJet-division
☐ N288AU	Boeing 737-2B7 (A)	23135 / 1054	N332AU	0084	1184	2 PW JT8D-15A (HK3/NOR)	53070	F12Y96		
☐ N300AU	Boeing 737-301	23228 / 1103	N301P	0085	0889	2 CFMI CFM56-3B1	61235	F12Y114		
☐ N334US	Boeing 737-301	23231 / 1164	N313P	0085	0889	2 CFMI CFM56-3B1	61235	F12Y114		
☐ N335US	Boeing 737-301	23232 / 1169	N314P	0085	0889	2 CFMI CFM56-3B1	61235	F12Y114		
☐ N336US	Boeing 737-301	23233 / 1200	N315P	0086	0889	2 CFMI CFM56-3B1	61235	F12Y114		
☐ N337US	Boeing 737-301	23235 / 1214	N317P	0086	0889	2 CFMI CFM56-3B1	61235	F12Y114		
☐ N338US	Boeing 737-301	23234 / 1208	N316P	0086	0889	2 CFMI CFM56-3B1	61235	F12Y114		
☐ N339US	Boeing 737-301	23236 / 1219	N319P	0086	0889	2 CFMI CFM56-3B1	61235	F12Y114		
☐ N340US	Boeing 737-301	23237 / 1222	N320P	0086	0889	2 CFMI CFM56-3B1	61235	F12Y114		
☐ N341US	Boeing 737-301	23510 / 1248	N321P	0086	0889	2 CFMI CFM56-3B1	61235	F12Y114		
☐ N342US	Boeing 737-301	23511 / 1268	N322P	0086	0889	2 CFMI CFM56-3B1	61235	F12Y114		
☐ N346US	Boeing 737-301	23515 / 1355	N326P	0087	0889	2 CFMI CFM56-3B1	61235	F12Y114		
☐ N349US	Boeing 737-301	23552 / 1382	N334P	0087	0889	2 CFMI CFM56-3B1	61235	F12Y114		
☐ N350US	Boeing 737-301	23553 / 1406	N335P	0087	0889	2 CFMI CFM56-3B1	61235	F12Y114		
☐ N351US	Boeing 737-301	23554 / 1408	N336P	0087	0889	2 CFMI CFM56-3B1	61235	F12Y114		
☐ N352US	Boeing 737-301	23555 / 1428	N337P	0087	0889	2 CFMI CFM56-3B1	61235	F12Y114		
☐ N353US	Boeing 737-301	23556 / 1435	N340P	0087	0889	2 CFMI CFM56-3B1	61235	F12Y114		
☐ N354US	Boeing 737-301	23557 / 1437	N341P	0087	0889	2 CFMI CFM56-3B1	61235	F12Y114		
☐ N355US	Boeing 737-301	23558 / 1449	N342P	0087	0889	2 CFMI CFM56-3B1	61235	F12Y114		
☐ N356US	Boeing 737-301	23559 / 1451	N348P	0087	0889	2 CFMI CFM56-3B1	61235	F12Y114		
☐ N371US	Boeing 737-3B7	22950 / 1001	N350AU	0084	0485	2 CFMI CFM56-3B1	61235	F12Y114		
☐ N373US	Boeing 737-3B7	22952 / 1015	N352AU	0084	0485	2 CFMI CFM56-3B1	61235	F12Y114		BM-DG
☐ N374US	Boeing 737-3B7	22953 / 1022	N353AU	0084	1184	2 CFMI CFM56-3B1	61235	F12Y114		
☐ N375US	Boeing 737-3B7	22954 / 1030	N354AU	0084	1184	2 CFMI CFM56-3B1	61235	F12Y114		
☐ N376US	Boeing 737-3B7	22955 / 1043	N355AU	0084	1284	2 CFMI CFM56-3B1	61235	F12Y114		
☐ N383US	Boeing 737-3B7	22956 / 1057	N356AU	0084	1284	2 CFMI CFM56-3B1	61235	F12Y114		
☐ N384US	Boeing 737-3B7	22957 / 1127	N357AU	0085	0685	2 CFMI CFM56-3B1	61235	F12Y114		
☐ N385US	Boeing 737-3B7	22958 / 1137	N358AU	0085	0785	2 CFMI CFM56-3B1	61235	F12Y114		
☐ N387US	Boeing 737-3B7	22959 / 1140	N359AU	0085	0585	2 CFMI CFM56-3B1	61235	F12Y114		
☐ N389US	Boeing 737-3B7	23311 / 1149	N361AU	0085	0985	2 CFMI CFM56-3B1	61235	F12Y114		
☐ N390US	Boeing 737-3B7	23312 / 1162	N362AU	0085	1185	2 CFMI CFM56-3B1	61235	F12Y114		
☐ N391US	Boeing 737-3B7	23313 / 1177	N363AU	0085	1285	2 CFMI CFM56-3B1	61235	F12Y114		
☐ N392US	Boeing 737-3B7	23314 / 1179	N364AU	0085	1285	2 CFMI CFM56-3B1	61235	F12Y114		
☐ N393US	Boeing 737-3B7	23315 / 1210	N365AU	0086	0386	2 CFMI CFM56-3B1	61235	F12Y114		
☐ N394US	Boeing 737-3B7	23316 / 1212	N366AU	0086	0386	2 CFMI CFM56-3B1	61235	F12Y114		
☐ N395US	Boeing 737-3B7	23317 / 1221	N367AU	0086	0486	2 CFMI CFM56-3B1	61235	F12Y114		
☐ N396US	Boeing 737-3B7	23318 / 1234	N368AU	0086	0586	2 CFMI CFM56-3B1	61235	F12Y114		
☐ N397US	Boeing 737-3B7	23319 / 1250	N369AU	0086	0786	2 CFMI CFM56-3B1	61235	F12Y114		
☐ N504AU	Boeing 737-3B7	23379 / 1362	N373AU	0087	0387	2 CFMI CFM56-3B2	62823	F12Y114		
☐ N505AU	Boeing 737-3B7	23380 / 1366	N374AU	0087	0487	2 CFMI CFM56-3B2	62823	F12Y114		
☐ N506AU	Boeing 737-3B7	23381 / 1394	N375AU	0087	0687	2 CFMI CFM56-3B2	62823	F12Y114		
☐ N507AU	Boeing 737-3B7	23382 / 1410	N376AU	0087	0787	2 CFMI CFM56-3B2	62823	F12Y114		
☐ N508AU	Boeing 737-3B7	23383 / 1425	N377AU	0087	0887	2 CFMI CFM56-3B2	62823	F12Y114		
☐ N510AU	Boeing 737-3B7	23385 / 1440	N379AU	0087	0987	2 CFMI CFM56-3B2	62823	F12Y114		
☐ N511AU	Boeing 737-3B7	23594 / 1442	N380AU	0087	0987	2 CFMI CFM56-3B2	62823	F12Y114		
☐ N512AU	Boeing 737-3B7	23595 / 1450	N381AU	0087	1087	2 CFMI CFM56-3B2	62823	F12Y114		
☐ N514AU	Boeing 737-3B7	23700 / 1461	N383AU	0087	1087	2 CFMI CFM56-3B2	62823	F12Y114		
☐ N515AU	Boeing 737-3B7	23701 / 1464	N384AU	0087	1187	2 CFMI CFM56-3B2	62823	F12Y114		
☐ N516AU	Boeing 737-3B7	23702 / 1475	N385AU	0087	1187	2 CFMI CFM56-3B2	62823	F12Y114		
☐ N517AU	Boeing 737-3B7	23703 / 1480	N386AU	0087	1287	2 CFMI CFM56-3B2	62823	F12Y114		
☐ N518AU	Boeing 737-3B7	23704 / 1488	N387AU	0087	1287	2 CFMI CFM56-3B2	62823	F12Y114		
☐ N519AU	Boeing 737-3B7	23705 / 1497	N388AU	0088	0188	2 CFMI CFM56-3B2	62823	F12Y114		
☐ N520AU	Boeing 737-3B7	23706 / 1499	N389AU	0088	0288	2 CFMI CFM56-3B2	62823	F12Y114		
☐ N521AU	Boeing 737-3B7	23856 / 1501	N390AU	0088	0288	2 CFMI CFM56-3B2	62823	F12Y114		
☐ N522AU	Boeing 737-3B7	23857 / 1503	N391AU	0088	0388	2 CFMI CFM56-3B2	62823	F12Y114		
☐ N523AU	Boeing 737-3B7	23858 / 1509	N392AU	0088	0488	2 CFMI CFM56-3B2	62823	F12Y114		
☐ N524AU	Boeing 737-3B7	23859 / 1551	N393AU	0088	0588	2 CFMI CFM56-3B2	62823	F12Y114		
☐ N525AU	Boeing 737-3B7	23860 / 1560	N394AU	0088	0688	2 CFMI CFM56-3B2	62823	F12Y114		
☐ N526AU	Boeing 737-3B7	23861 / 1584	N395AU	0088	0788	2 CFMI CFM56-3B2	62823	F12Y114		
☐ N527AU	Boeing 737-3B7	23862 / 1586	N396AU	0088	0888	2 CFMI CFM56-3B2	62823	F12Y114		
☐ N528AU	Boeing 737-3B7	24410 / 1703		0089	0489	2 CFMI CFM56-3B2	62823	F12Y114		
☐ N529AU	Boeing 737-3B7	24411 / 1713		0089	0589	2 CFMI CFM56-3B2	62823	F12Y114		
☐ N530AU	Boeing 737-3B7	24412 / 1735		0089	0689	2 CFMI CFM56-3B2	62823	F12Y114		
☐ N531AU	Boeing 737-3B7	24478 / 1743		0089	0789	2 CFMI CFM56-3B2	62823	F12Y114		
☐ N532AU	Boeing 737-3B7	24479 / 1745		0089	0789	2 CFMI CFM56-3B2	62823	F12Y114		
☐ N533AU	Boeing 737-3B7	24515 / 1767		0089	0989	2 CFMI CFM56-3B2	62823	F12Y114		
☐ N534AU	Boeing 737-3B7	24516 / 1769		0089	0989	2 CFMI CFM56-3B2	62823	F12Y114		
☐ N558AU	Boeing 737-301	23512 / 1291	N343US	0086	0889	2 CFMI CFM56-3B2	62823	F12Y114		
☐ N559AU	Boeing 737-301	23513 / 1327	N344US	0086	0889	2 CFMI CFM56-3B2	62823	F12Y114		
☐ N560AU	Boeing 737-301	23514 / 1331	N345US	0086	0889	2 CFMI CFM56-3B2	62823	F12Y114		
☐ N562AU	Boeing 737-301	23550 / 1367	N347US	0087	0889	2 CFMI CFM56-3B2	62823	F12Y114		
☐ N563AU	Boeing 737-301	23551 / 1380	N348US	0087	0889	2 CFMI CFM56-3B2	62823	F12Y114		
☐ N573US	Boeing 737-301	23560 / 1463	N357US	0087	0889	2 CFMI CFM56-3B2	62823	F12Y114		
☐ N574US	Boeing 737-301	23739 / 1469	N358US	0087	0889	2 CFMI CFM56-3B2	62823	F12Y114		
☐ N575US	Boeing 737-301	23740 / 1477	N359US	0087	0889	2 CFMI CFM56-3B2	62823	F12Y114		
☐ N576US	Boeing 737-301	23741 / 1498	N360US	0088	0889	2 CFMI CFM56-3B2	62823	F12Y114		
☐ N577US	Boeing 737-301	23742 / 1502	N361US	0088	0889	2 CFMI CFM56-3B2	62823	F12Y114		
☐ N584US	Boeing 737-301	23743 / 1510	N355P	0088	0889	2 CFMI CFM56-3B2	62823	F12Y114		
☐ N585US	Boeing 737-301	23930 / 1539	N357P	0088	0889	2 CFMI CFM56-3B2	62823	F12Y114		
☐ N586US	Boeing 737-301	23931 / 1552	N358P	0088	0889	2 CFMI CFM56-3B2	62823	F12Y114		
☐ N587US	Boeing 737-301	23932 / 1554	N359P	0088	0889	2 CFMI CFM56-3B2	62823	F12Y114		
☐ N588US	Boeing 737-301	23933 / 1559		0088	0889	2 CFMI CFM56-3B2	62823	F12Y114		
☐ N589US	Boeing 737-301	23934 / 1563		0088	0889	2 CFMI CFM56-3B2	62823	F12Y114		
☐ N590US	Boeing 737-301	23935 / 1569		0088	0889	2 CFMI CFM56-3B2	62823	F12Y114		
☐ N591US	Boeing 737-301	23936 / 1575		0088	0889	2 CFMI CFM56-3B2	62823	F12Y114		
☐ N592US	Boeing 737-301	23937 / 1587		0088	0889	2 CFMI CFM56-3B2	62823	F12Y114		
☐ N404US	Boeing 737-401	23886 / 1487	N73700*	0088	0889	2 CFMI CFM56-3B2	64637	F12Y132		
☐ N405US	Boeing 737-401	23885 / 1512		0088	0889	2 CFMI CFM56-3B2	64637	F12Y132		
☐ N406US	Boeing 737-401	23876 / 1528		0088	0889	2 CFMI CFM56-3B2	64637	F12Y132		Thomas H. Davis Pacemaker
☐ N407US	Boeing 737-401	23877 / 1543		0088	0889	2 CFMI CFM56-3B2	64637	F12Y132		
☐ N408US	Boeing 737-401	23878 / 1561		0088	0889	2 CFMI CFM56-3B2	64637	F12Y132		
☐ N409US	Boeing 737-401	23879 / 1573		0088	0889	2 CFMI CFM56-3B2	64637	F12Y132		
☐ N411US	Boeing 737-401	23880 / 1596		0088	0889	2 CFMI CFM56-3B2	64637	F12Y132		
☐ N412US	Boeing 737-401	23881 / 1610		0088	0889	2 CFMI CFM56-3B2	64637	F12Y132		
☐ N413US	Boeing 737-401	23882 / 1621		0088	0889	2 CFMI CFM56-3B2	64637	F12Y132		
☐ N415US	Boeing 737-401	23883 / 1631		0088	0889	2 CFMI CFM56-3B2	64637	F12Y132		
☐ N417US	Boeing 737-401	23984 / 1674		0089	0889	2 CFMI CFM56-3B2	64637	F12Y132		
☐ N418US	Boeing 737-401	23985 / 1676		0089	0889	2 CFMI CFM56-3B2	64637	F12Y132		
☐ N419US	Boeing 737-401	23986 / 1684		0089	0889	2 CFMI CFM56-3B2	64637	F12Y132		
☐ N420US	Boeing 737-401	23987 / 1698		0089	0889	2 CFMI CFM56-3B2	64637	F12Y132		
☐ N421US	Boeing 737-401	23988 / 1714		0089	0889	2 CFMI CFM56-3B2	64637	F12Y132		Thomas H. Davis
☐ N422US	Boeing 737-401	23989 / 1716		0089	0889	2 CFMI CFM56-3B2	64637	F12Y132		
☐ N423US	Boeing 737-401	23990 / 1732		0089	0889	2 CFMI CFM56-3B2	64637	F12Y132		
☐ N424US	Boeing 737-401	23991 / 1746		0089	0889	2 CFMI CFM56-3B2	64637	F12Y132		
☐ N425US	Boeing 737-401	23992 / 1764		0089	0889	2 CFMI CFM56-3B2	64637	F12Y132		
☐ N426US	Boeing 737-4B7	24548 / 1789		0089	1089	2 CFMI CFM56-3B2	64637	F12Y132		
☐ N427US	Boeing 737-4B7	24549 / 1791		0089	1189	2 CFMI CFM56-3B2	64637	F12Y132		
☐ N428US	Boeing 737-4B7	24550 / 1793		0089	1289	2 CFMI CFM56-3B2	64637	F12Y132		
☐ N429US	Boeing 737-4B7	24551 / 1795		0089	1289	2 CFMI CFM56-3B2	64637	F12Y132		
☐ N430US	Boeing 737-4B7	24552 / 1797		0089	1289	2 CFMI CFM56-3B2	64637	F12Y132		
☐ N431US	Boeing 737-4B7	24553 / 1799		0089	1289	2 CFMI CFM56-3B2	64637	F12Y132		
☐ N432US	Boeing 737-4B7	24554 / 1817		0090	0290	2 CFMI CFM56-3B2	64637	F12Y132		
☐ N433US	Boeing 737-4B7	24555 / 1819		0090	0290	2 CFMI CFM56-3B2	64637	F12Y132		
☐ N434US	Boeing 737-4B7	24556 / 1821		0090	0290	2 CFMI CFM56-3B2	64637	F12Y132		
☐ N435US	Boeing 737-4B7	24557 / 1835		0090	0390	2 CFMI CFM56-3B2	64637	F12Y132		
☐ N436US	Boeing 737-4B7	24558 / 1845		0090	0490	2 CFMI CFM56-3B2	64637	F12Y132		
☐ N437US	Boeing 737-4B7	24559 / 1847		0090	0490	2 CFMI CFM56-3B2	64637	F12Y132		

	registration	type of aircraft	cn/fn	ex/ex*	mfd	del	powered by	mtow kg	configuration	selcal	name/fln/specialitites/remarks
☐	N438US	Boeing 737-4B7	24560 / 1849		0090	0490	2 CFMI CFM56-3B2	64637	F12Y132		
☐	N439US	Boeing 737-4B7	24781 / 1874		0090	0690	2 CFMI CFM56-3B2	64637	F12Y132		
☐	N440US	Boeing 737-4B7	24811 / 1890		0090	0790	2 CFMI CFM56-3B2	64637	F12Y132		
☐	N441US	Boeing 737-4B7	24812 / 1892		0090	0790	2 CFMI CFM56-3B2	64637	F12Y132		
☐	N442US	Boeing 737-4B7	24841 / 1906		0090	0890	2 CFMI CFM56-3B2	64637	F12Y132		
☐	N443US	Boeing 737-4B7	24842 / 1908		0090	0890	2 CFMI CFM56-3B2	64637	F12Y132		
☐	N444US	Boeing 737-4B7	24862 / 1910		0090	0890	2 CFMI CFM56-3B2	64637	F12Y132		
☐	N445US	Boeing 737-4B7	24863 / 1914		0090	0990	2 CFMI CFM56-3B2	64637	F12Y132		
☐	N446US	Boeing 737-4B7	24873 / 1931		0090	1090	2 CFMI CFM56-3B2	64637	F12Y132		
☐	N447US	Boeing 737-4B7	24874 / 1936		0090	1090	2 CFMI CFM56-3B2	64637	F12Y132		
☐	N448US	Boeing 737-4B7	24892 / 1944		0090	1190	2 CFMI CFM56-3B2	64637	F12Y132	PQ-FJ	
☐	N449US	Boeing 737-4B7	24893 / 1946		0090	1190	2 CFMI CFM56-3B2	64637	F12Y132	PQ-FK	
☐	N775AU	Boeing 737-4B7	24933 / 1954		0090	1190	2 CFMI CFM56-3B2	64637	F12Y132	HR-GQ	
☐	N776AU	Boeing 737-4B7	24934 / 1956		0090	1190	2 CFMI CFM56-3B2	64637	F12Y132	HR-GS	
☐	N777AU	Boeing 737-4B7	24979 / 1980		0091	0191	2 CFMI CFM56-3B2	64637	F12Y132	HR-JK	
☐	N778AU	Boeing 737-4B7	24980 / 1982		0091	0191	2 CFMI CFM56-3B2	64637	F12Y132	HR-JL	
☐	N779AU	Boeing 737-4B7	24996 / 1986		0091	0191	2 CFMI CFM56-3B2	64637	F12Y132	HR-JM	
☐	N780AU	Boeing 737-4B7	24997 / 1990		0091	0291	2 CFMI CFM56-3B2	64637	F12Y132	HR-JP	
☐	N781AU	Boeing 737-4B7	25020 / 1992		0091	0291	2 CFMI CFM56-3B2	64637	F12Y132	HR-JQ	
☐	N782AU	Boeing 737-4B7	25021 / 1995		0091	0291	2 CFMI CFM56-3B2	64637	F12Y132	HR-JS	
☐	N783AU	Boeing 737-4B7	25022 / 2010		0091	0391	2 CFMI CFM56-3B2	64637	F12Y132	PQ-FG	
☐	N784AU	Boeing 737-4B7	25023 / 2020		0091	0491	2 CFMI CFM56-3B2	64637	F12Y132		
☐	N785AU	Boeing 737-4B7	25024 / 2026		0091	0491	2 CFMI CFM56-3B2	64637	F12Y132	PQ-FM	
☐	N700UW	Airbus Industrie A319-112	885	D-AVYF*	0098	1098	2 CFMI CFM56-5B6/P	64000	F12Y108		
☐	N701UW	Airbus Industrie A319-112	890	D-AVYG*	0098	1098	2 CFMI CFM56-5B6/P	64000	F12Y108		
☐	N702UW	Airbus Industrie A319-112	896	D-AVYH*	0098	1198	2 CFMI CFM56-5B6/P	64000	F12Y108		
☐	N703UW	Airbus Industrie A319-112	904	D-AVYI*	0098	1198	2 CFMI CFM56-5B6/P	64000	F12Y108		
☐	N704US	Airbus Industrie A319-112	922	D-AVYQ*	0098	1298	2 CFMI CFM56-5B6/P	64000	F12Y108		
☐	N705UW	Airbus Industrie A319-112	929	D-AVYA*	0098	1298	2 CFMI CFM56-5B6/P	64000	F12Y108		
☐	N706US	Airbus Industrie A319-112	946	D-AVYD*	0099	0199	2 CFMI CFM56-5B6/P	64000	F12Y108		
☐	N707UW	Airbus Industrie A319-112	949	D-AVYG*	0099	0199	2 CFMI CFM56-5B6/P	64000	F12Y108		
☐	N708UW	Airbus Industrie A319-112	972		0099	0399	2 CFMI CFM56-5B6/P	64000	F12Y108		
☐	N709UW	Airbus Industrie A319-112	997				2 CFMI CFM56-5B6/P	64000	F12Y108		oo-delivery 0499
☐	N710UW	Airbus Industrie A319-112					2 CFMI CFM56-5B6/P	64000	F12Y108		oo-delivery 0599
☐	N711UW	Airbus Industrie A319-112					2 CFMI CFM56-5B6/P	64000	F12Y108		oo-delivery 0699
☐	N712US	Airbus Industrie A319-112					2 CFMI CFM56-5B6/P	64000	F12Y108		oo-delivery 0699
☐	N713UW	Airbus Industrie A319-112					2 CFMI CFM56-5B6/P	64000	F12Y108		oo-delivery 0699
☐	N714US	Airbus Industrie A319-112					2 CFMI CFM56-5B6/P	64000	F12Y108		oo-delivery 0799
☐	N715UW	Airbus Industrie A319-112					2 CFMI CFM56-5B6/P	64000	F12Y108		oo-delivery 0799
☐	N716UW	Airbus Industrie A319-112					2 CFMI CFM56-5B6/P	64000	F12Y108		oo-delivery 0799
☐	N717UW	Airbus Industrie A319-112					2 CFMI CFM56-5B6/P	64000	F12Y108		oo-delivery 0899
☐	N718UW	Airbus Industrie A319-112					2 CFMI CFM56-5B6/P	64000	F12Y108		oo-delivery 0899
☐	N719US	Airbus Industrie A319-112					2 CFMI CFM56-5B6/P	64000	F12Y108		oo-delivery 0999
☐	N720US	Airbus Industrie A319-112					2 CFMI CFM56-5B6/P	64000	F12Y108		oo-delivery 0999
☐	N721UW	Airbus Industrie A319-112					2 CFMI CFM56-5B6/P	64000	F12Y108		oo-delivery 1099
☐	N722US	Airbus Industrie A319-112					2 CFMI CFM56-5B6/P	64000	F12Y108		oo-delivery 1099
☐	N723UW	Airbus Industrie A319-112					2 CFMI CFM56-5B6/P	64000	F12Y108		oo-delivery 1099
☐	N724UW	Airbus Industrie A319-112					2 CFMI CFM56-5B6/P	64000	F12Y108		oo-delivery 1199
☐	N725UW	Airbus Industrie A319-112					2 CFMI CFM56-5B6/P	64000	F12Y108		oo-delivery 1199
☐	N726US	Airbus Industrie A319-112					2 CFMI CFM56-5B6/P	64000	F12Y108		oo-delivery 1199
☐	N727UW	Airbus Industrie A319-112					2 CFMI CFM56-5B6/P	64000	F12Y108		oo-delivery 1299
☐	N728UW	Airbus Industrie A319-112					2 CFMI CFM56-5B6/P	64000	F12Y108		oo-delivery 1299
☐	N729US	Airbus Industrie A319-112					2 CFMI CFM56-5B6/P	64000	F12Y108		oo-delivery 1299
☐	N730US	Airbus Industrie A319-112					2 CFMI CFM56-5B6/P	64000	F12Y108		oo-delivery 0100
☐	N732US	Airbus Industrie A319-112					2 CFMI CFM56-5B6/P	64000	F12Y108		oo-delivery 0100
☐	N733UW	Airbus Industrie A319-112					2 CFMI CFM56-5B6/P	64000	F12Y108		oo-delivery 0200
☐	N736US	Airbus Industrie A319-112					2 CFMI CFM56-5B6/P	64000	F12Y108		oo-delivery 0200
☐	N737US	Airbus Industrie A319-112					2 CFMI CFM56-5B6/P	64000	F12Y108		oo-delivery 0200
☐	N738US	Airbus Industrie A319-112					2 CFMI CFM56-5B6/P	64000	F12Y108		oo-delivery 0300
☐	N739US	Airbus Industrie A319-112					2 CFMI CFM56-5B6/P	64000	F12Y108		oo-delivery 0300
☐	N740UW	Airbus Industrie A319-112					2 CFMI CFM56-5B6/P	64000	F12Y108		oo-delivery 0300
☐	N741UW	Airbus Industrie A319-112					2 CFMI CFM56-5B6/P	64000	F12Y108		oo-delivery 0400
☐	N742US	Airbus Industrie A319-112					2 CFMI CFM56-5B6/P	64000	F12Y108		oo-delivery 0400
☐	N743UW	Airbus Industrie A319-112					2 CFMI CFM56-5B6/P	64000	F12Y108		oo-delivery 0400
☐	N744US	Airbus Industrie A319-112					2 CFMI CFM56-5B6/P	64000	F12Y108		oo-delivery 0500
☐	N745UW	Airbus Industrie A319-112					2 CFMI CFM56-5B6/P	64000	F12Y108		oo-delivery 0500
☐	N747UW	Airbus Industrie A319-112					2 CFMI CFM56-5B6/P	64000	F12Y108		oo-delivery 0600
☐	N748UW	Airbus Industrie A319-112					2 CFMI CFM56-5B6/P	64000	F12Y108		oo-delivery 0600
☐	N749US	Airbus Industrie A319-112					2 CFMI CFM56-5B6/P	64000	F12Y108		oo-delivery 0600
☐	N750UW	Airbus Industrie A319-112					2 CFMI CFM56-5B6/P	64000	F12Y108		oo-delivery 0700
☐	N751UW	Airbus Industrie A319-112					2 CFMI CFM56-5B6/P	64000	F12Y108		oo-delivery 0700
☐	N752US	Airbus Industrie A319-112					2 CFMI CFM56-5B6/P	64000	F12Y108		oo-delivery 0700
☐	N753US	Airbus Industrie A319-112					2 CFMI CFM56-5B6/P	64000	F12Y108		oo-delivery 0800
☐	N754UW	Airbus Industrie A319-112					2 CFMI CFM56-5B6/P	64000	F12Y108		oo-delivery 0800
☐	N755US	Airbus Industrie A319-112					2 CFMI CFM56-5B6/P	64000	F12Y108		oo-delivery 0800
☐	N756US	Airbus Industrie A319-112					2 CFMI CFM56-5B6/P	64000	F12Y108		oo-delivery 0900
☐	N757UW	Airbus Industrie A319-112					2 CFMI CFM56-5B6/P	64000	F12Y108		oo-delivery 0900
☐	N758US	Airbus Industrie A319-112					2 CFMI CFM56-5B6/P	64000	F12Y108		oo-delivery 1000
☐	N760US	Airbus Industrie A319-112					2 CFMI CFM56-5B6/P	64000	F12Y108		oo-delivery 1000
☐	N762US	Airbus Industrie A319-112					2 CFMI CFM56-5B6/P	64000	F12Y108		oo-delivery 1000
☐	N763US	Airbus Industrie A319-112					2 CFMI CFM56-5B6/P	64000	F12Y108		oo-delivery 1100
☐	N764US	Airbus Industrie A319-112					2 CFMI CFM56-5B6/P	64000	F12Y108		oo-delivery 1100
☐	N765US	Airbus Industrie A319-112					2 CFMI CFM56-5B6/P	64000	F12Y108		oo-delivery 1100
☐	N766US	Airbus Industrie A319-112					2 CFMI CFM56-5B6/P	64000	F12Y108		oo-delivery 1200
☐	N767UW	Airbus Industrie A319-112					2 CFMI CFM56-5B6/P	64000	F12Y108		oo-delivery 1200
☐	N768US	Airbus Industrie A319-112					2 CFMI CFM56-5B6/P	64000	F12Y108		oo-delivery 1200
☐	N769US	Airbus Industrie A319-112					2 CFMI CFM56-5B6/P	64000	F12Y108		oo-delivery 0101
☐	N770UW	Airbus Industrie A319-112					2 CFMI CFM56-5B6/P	64000	F12Y108		oo-delivery 0101
☐	N771UW	Airbus Industrie A319-112					2 CFMI CFM56-5B6/P	64000	F12Y108		oo-delivery 0201
☐	N772UW	Airbus Industrie A319-112					2 CFMI CFM56-5B6/P	64000	F12Y108		oo-delivery 0201
☐	N773US	Airbus Industrie A319-112					2 CFMI CFM56-5B6/P	64000	F12Y108		oo-delivery 0301
☐	N774US	Airbus Industrie A319-112					2 CFMI CFM56-5B6/P	64000	F12Y108		oo-delivery 0301
☐	N775UW	Airbus Industrie A319-112					2 CFMI CFM56-5B6/P	64000	F12Y108		oo-delivery 0401
☐	N776UW	Airbus Industrie A319-112					2 CFMI CFM56-5B6/P	64000	F12Y108		oo-delivery 0401
☐	N777UW	Airbus Industrie A319-112					2 CFMI CFM56-5B6/P	64000	F12Y108		oo-delivery 0501
☐	N778US	Airbus Industrie A319-112					2 CFMI CFM56-5B6/P	64000	F12Y108		oo-delivery 0501
☐	N779US	Airbus Industrie A319-112					2 CFMI CFM56-5B6/P	64000	F12Y108		oo-delivery 0601
☐	N780US	Airbus Industrie A319-112					2 CFMI CFM56-5B6/P	64000	F12Y108		oo-delivery 0601
☐	N781US	Airbus Industrie A319-112					2 CFMI CFM56-5B6/P	64000	F12Y108		oo-delivery 0701
☐	N782US	Airbus Industrie A319-112					2 CFMI CFM56-5B6/P	64000	F12Y108		oo-delivery 0701
☐	N783US	Airbus Industrie A319-112					2 CFMI CFM56-5B6/P	64000	F12Y108		oo-delivery 0701
☐	N784US	Airbus Industrie A319-112					2 CFMI CFM56-5B6/P	64000	F12Y108		oo-delivery 0801
☐	N785US	Airbus Industrie A319-112					2 CFMI CFM56-5B6/P	64000	F12Y108		oo-delivery 0801
☐	N786US	Airbus Industrie A319-112					2 CFMI CFM56-5B6/P	64000	F12Y108		oo-delivery 0901
☐	N787US	Airbus Industrie A319-112					2 CFMI CFM56-5B6/P	64000	F12Y108		oo-delivery 0901
☐	N788US	Airbus Industrie A319-112					2 CFMI CFM56-5B6/P	64000	F12Y108		oo-delivery 1001
☐	N789UW	Airbus Industrie A319-112					2 CFMI CFM56-5B6/P	64000	F12Y108		oo-delivery 1001
☐	N790UW	Airbus Industrie A319-112					2 CFMI CFM56-5B6/P	64000	F12Y108		oo-delivery 1101
☐	N791US	Airbus Industrie A319-112					2 CFMI CFM56-5B6/P	64000	F12Y108		oo-delivery 1101
☐	N792US	Airbus Industrie A319-112					2 CFMI CFM56-5B6/P	64000	F12Y108		oo-delivery 1201
☐	N793US	Airbus Industrie A319-112					2 CFMI CFM56-5B6/P	64000	F12Y108		oo-delivery 1201
☐	N794US	Airbus Industrie A319-112					2 CFMI CFM56-5B6/P	64000	F12Y108		oo-delivery 1201
☐	N795US	Airbus Industrie A319-112					2 CFMI CFM56-5B6/P	64000	F12Y108		oo-delivery 0002
☐	N796US	Airbus Industrie A319-112					2 CFMI CFM56-5B6/P	64000	F12Y108		oo-delivery 0002
☐	N797UW	Airbus Industrie A319-112					2 CFMI CFM56-5B6/P	64000	F12Y108		oo-delivery 0002
☐	N798US	Airbus Industrie A319-112					2 CFMI CFM56-5B6/P	64000	F12Y108		oo-delivery 0002
☐	N799US	Airbus Industrie A319-112					2 CFMI CFM56-5B6/P	64000	F12Y108		oo-delivery 0002
☐	N	Airbus Industrie A319-112					2 CFMI CFM56-5B6/P	64000	F12Y108		oo-delivery 0002
☐	N	Airbus Industrie A319-112					2 CFMI CFM56-5B6/P	64000	F12Y108		oo-delivery 0002
☐	N	Airbus Industrie A319-112					2 CFMI CFM56-5B6/P	64000	F12Y108		oo-delivery 0002

☐	N	Airbus Industrie A319-112					2 CFMI CFM56-5B6/P	64000	F12Y108		oo-delivery 0002
☐	N	Airbus Industrie A319-112					2 CFMI CFM56-5B6/P	64000	F12Y108		oo-delivery 0002
☐	N	Airbus Industrie A319-112					2 CFMI CFM56-5B6/P	64000	F12Y108		oo-delivery 0002
☐	N	Airbus Industrie A319-112					2 CFMI CFM56-5B6/P	64000	F12Y108		oo-delivery 0002
☐	N	Airbus Industrie A319-112					2 CFMI CFM56-5B6/P	64000	F12Y108		oo-delivery 0002
☐	N	Airbus Industrie A319-112					2 CFMI CFM56-5B6/P	64000	F12Y108		oo-delivery 0002
☐	N	Airbus Industrie A319-112					2 CFMI CFM56-5B6/P	64000	F12Y108		oo-delivery 0002
☐	N	Airbus Industrie A319-112					2 CFMI CFM56-5B6/P	64000	F12Y108		oo-delivery 0002
☐	N	Airbus Industrie A319-112					2 CFMI CFM56-5B6/P	64000	F12Y108		oo-delivery 0002
☐	N	Airbus Industrie A319-112					2 CFMI CFM56-5B6/P	64000	F12Y108		oo-delivery 0002
☐	N	Airbus Industrie A319-112					2 CFMI CFM56-5B6/P	64000	F12Y108		oo-delivery 0002
☐	N	Airbus Industrie A319-112					2 CFMI CFM56-5B6/P	64000	F12Y108		oo-delivery 0002
☐	N800US	Boeing (Douglas) MD-81 (DC-9-81)	48034 / 946	N924PS	0080	0488	2 PW JT8D-217	63503	F12Y130		
☐	N801US	Boeing (Douglas) MD-81 (DC-9-81)	48037 / 965	N927PS	0081	0488	2 PW JT8D-217	63503	F12Y130		
☐	N802US	Boeing (Douglas) MD-81 (DC-9-81)	48036 / 963	N926PS	0080	0488	2 PW JT8D-217	63503	F12Y130		
☐	N803US	Boeing (Douglas) MD-81 (DC-9-81)	48035 / 955	N925PS	0080	0488	2 PW JT8D-217	63503	F12Y130		
☐	N804US	Boeing (Douglas) MD-81 (DC-9-81)	48052 / 974	N928PS	0081	0488	2 PW JT8D-217	63503	F12Y130		
☐	N805US	Boeing (Douglas) MD-81 (DC-9-81)	48053 / 986	N929PS	0081	0488	2 PW JT8D-217	63503	F12Y130		
☐	N806US	Boeing (Douglas) MD-81 (DC-9-81)	48038 / 1002	N930PS	0081	0488	2 PW JT8D-217	63503	F12Y130		
☐	N807US	Boeing (Douglas) MD-81 (DC-9-81)	48039 / 1003	N931PS	0081	0488	2 PW JT8D-217	63503	F12Y130		
☐	N808US	Boeing (Douglas) MD-81 (DC-9-81)	48040 / 1006	N932PS	0081	0488	2 PW JT8D-217	63503	F12Y130		
☐	N809US	Boeing (Douglas) MD-81 (DC-9-81)	48041 / 1008	N933PS	0081	0488	2 PW JT8D-217	63503	F12Y130		
☐	N810US	Boeing (Douglas) MD-81 (DC-9-81)	48042 / 1009	N934PS	0081	0488	2 PW JT8D-217	63503	F12Y130		
☐	N811US	Boeing (Douglas) MD-81 (DC-9-81)	48043 / 1010	N935PS	0081	0488	2 PW JT8D-217	63503	F12Y130		
☐	N812US	Boeing (Douglas) MD-81 (DC-9-81)	48092 / 1034	N936PS	0082	0488	2 PW JT8D-217	63503	F12Y130		
☐	N813US	Boeing (Douglas) MD-81 (DC-9-81)	48093 / 1049	N937PS	0082	0488	2 PW JT8D-217	63503	F12Y130		
☐	N814US	Boeing (Douglas) MD-81 (DC-9-81)	48094 / 1053	N938PS	0082	0488	2 PW JT8D-217	63503	F12Y130		
☐	N815US	Boeing (Douglas) MD-82 (DC-9-82)	48095 / 1055	N940PS	0082	0488	2 PW JT8D-217	66678	F12Y130		
☐	N816US	Boeing (Douglas) MD-82 (DC-9-82)	48096 / 1057	N941PS	0082	0488	2 PW JT8D-217	66678	F12Y130		
☐	N817US	Boeing (Douglas) MD-82 (DC-9-82)	48097 / 1059	N942PS	0082	0488	2 PW JT8D-217	66678	F12Y130		
☐	N818US	Boeing (Douglas) MD-82 (DC-9-82)	48098 / 1060	N943PS	0082	0488	2 PW JT8D-217	66678	F12Y130		
☐	N819US	Boeing (Douglas) MD-81 (DC-9-81)	48099 / 1067	N939PS	0082	0488	2 PW JT8D-217	63503	F12Y130		
☐	N820US	Boeing (Douglas) MD-82 (DC-9-82)	49119 / 1070	N944PS	0082	0488	2 PW JT8D-217	66678	F12Y130		
☐	N821US	Boeing (Douglas) MD-82 (DC-9-82)	49138 / 1090	N945PS	0082	0488	2 PW JT8D-217	66678	F12Y130		
☐	N822US	Boeing (Douglas) MD-82 (DC-9-82)	49139 / 1091	N946PS	0082	0488	2 PW JT8D-217	66678	F12Y130		
☐	N823US	Boeing (Douglas) MD-82 (DC-9-82)	49142 / 1094	N947PS	0082	0488	2 PW JT8D-217	66678	F12Y130		
☐	N824US	Boeing (Douglas) MD-82 (DC-9-82)	49143 / 1095	N948PS	0082	0488	2 PW JT8D-217	66678	F12Y130		
☐	N825US	Boeing (Douglas) MD-82 (DC-9-82)	49237 / 1144	N949PS	0084	0488	2 PW JT8D-217	66678	F12Y130		
☐	N826US	Boeing (Douglas) MD-81 (DC-9-81)	48026 / 960	N10028	0081	0488	2 PW JT8D-217	63503	F12Y130		
☐	N827US	Boeing (Douglas) MD-81 (DC-9-81)	48049 / 983	N10029	0081	0488	2 PW JT8D-217	63503	F12Y130		
☐	N828US	Boeing (Douglas) MD-81 (DC-9-81)	48028 / 979	N950PS	0080	0488	2 PW JT8D-217	63503	F12Y130		
☐	N829US	Boeing (Douglas) MD-82 (DC-9-82)	49429 / 1242	N951PS	0086	0488	2 PW JT8D-217	66678	F12Y130		
☐	N830US	Boeing (Douglas) MD-82 (DC-9-82)	49443 / 1291	N952PS	0086	0488	2 PW JT8D-217	66678	F12Y130		
☐	N101UW	Airbus Industrie A320-214	936	F-WWIT*	0099	0199	2 CFMI CFM56-5B4/P	73500	F16Y126		
☐	N102UW	Airbus Industrie A320-214					2 CFMI CFM56-5B4/P	73500	F16Y126		oo-delivery 0499
☐	N103US	Airbus Industrie A320-214					2 CFMI CFM56-5B4/P	73500	F16Y126		oo-delivery 0499
☐	N104UW	Airbus Industrie A320-214					2 CFMI CFM56-5B4/P	73500	F16Y126		oo-delivery 0599
☐	N105UW	Airbus Industrie A320-214					2 CFMI CFM56-5B4/P	73500	F16Y126		oo-delivery 0899
☐	N106US	Airbus Industrie A320-214					2 CFMI CFM56-5B4/P	73500	F16Y126		oo-delivery 0999
☐	N107US	Airbus Industrie A320-214					2 CFMI CFM56-5B4/P	73500	F16Y126		oo-delivery 0000
☐	N108UW	Airbus Industrie A320-214					2 CFMI CFM56-5B4/P	73500	F16Y126		oo-delivery 0000
☐	N109UW	Airbus Industrie A320-214					2 CFMI CFM56-5B4/P	73500	F16Y126		oo-delivery 0000
☐	N110UW	Airbus Industrie A320-214					2 CFMI CFM56-5B4/P	73500	F16Y126		oo-delivery 0000
☐	N111UW	Airbus Industrie A320-214					2 CFMI CFM56-5B4/P	73500	F16Y126		oo-delivery 0000
☐	N112UW	Airbus Industrie A320-214					2 CFMI CFM56-5B4/P	73500	F16Y126		oo-delivery 0000
☐	N113UW	Airbus Industrie A320-214					2 CFMI CFM56-5B4/P	73500	F16Y126		oo-delivery 0000
☐	N114UW	Airbus Industrie A320-214					2 CFMI CFM56-5B4/P	73500	F16Y126		oo-delivery 0000
☐	N115US	Airbus Industrie A320-214					2 CFMI CFM56-5B4/P	73500	F16Y126		oo-delivery 0000
☐	N116US	Airbus Industrie A320-214					2 CFMI CFM56-5B4/P	73500	F16Y126		oo-delivery 0000
☐	N117UW	Airbus Industrie A320-214					2 CFMI CFM56-5B4/P	73500	F16Y126		oo-delivery 0002
☐	N118US	Airbus Industrie A320-214					2 CFMI CFM56-5B4/P	73500	F16Y126		oo-delivery 0002
☐	N119US	Airbus Industrie A320-214					2 CFMI CFM56-5B4/P	73500	F16Y126		oo-delivery 0002
☐	N600AU	Boeing 757-225	22192 / 3	N502EA	0082	0692	2 RR RB211-535E4	104326	F24Y158	KL-BH	lsf GECC
☐	N601AU	Boeing 757-225	22193 / 4	N503EA	0082	0392	2 RR RB211-535E4	104326	F24Y158	KL-BE	lsf GECC
☐	N602AU	Boeing 757-225	22196 / 7	N506EA	0082	0592	2 RR RB211-535E4	104326	F24Y158	CF-AM	lsf GECC
☐	N603AU	Boeing 757-225	22198 / 12	N508EA	0083	0792	2 RR RB211-535E4	104326	F24Y158		lsf GECC
☐	N604AU	Boeing 757-225	22199 / 17	N509EA	0083	1291	2 RR RB211-535E4	104326	F24Y158	CF-BD	lsf GECC
☐	N605AU	Boeing 757-225	22201 / 21	N511EA	0083	0192	2 RR RB211-535E4	104326	F24Y158	JM-GL	lsf GECC
☐	N606AU	Boeing 757-225	22202 / 22	N512EA	0083	0692	2 RR RB211-535E4	104326	F24Y158	GJ-HM	lsf GECC
☐	N607AU	Boeing 757-225	22203 / 26	N513EA	0083	0492	2 RR RB211-535E4	104326	F24Y158	GJ-KL	lsf GECC
☐	N608AU	Boeing 757-225	22204 / 27	N514EA	0083	0292	2 RR RB211-535E4	104326	F24Y158	GJ-LM	lsf GECC
☐	N609AU	Boeing 757-225	22205 / 28	N515EA	0083	0292	2 RR RB211-535E4	104326	F24Y158	HM-EL	lsf GECC
☐	N610AU	Boeing 757-2B7	27122 / 525		0093	0293	2 RR RB211-535E4	104326	F24Y158		Ideas that Fly
☐	N611AU	Boeing 757-2B7	27123 / 534		0093	0393	2 RR RB211-535E4	104326	F24Y158	BR-MS	
☐	N612AU	Boeing 757-2B7	27124 / 540		0093	0493	2 RR RB211-535E4	104326	F24Y158		
☐	N613AU	Boeing 757-2B7	27144 / 544		0093	0493	2 RR RB211-535E4	104326	F24Y158		
☐	N614AU	Boeing 757-2B7	27145 / 546		0093	0593	2 RR RB211-535E4	104326	F24Y158		
☐	N615AU	Boeing 757-2B7	27146 / 551		0093	0593	2 RR RB211-535E4	104326	F24Y158		
☐	N616AU	Boeing 757-2B7	27147 / 552		0093	0593	2 RR RB211-535E4	104326	F24Y158		
☐	N617AU	Boeing 757-2B7	27148 / 564		0093	0793	2 RR RB211-535E4	104326	F24Y158	BR-JS	
☐	N618AU	Boeing 757-225	22210 / 42	N520EA	0084	1192	2 RR RB211-535E4	104326	F24Y158	CE-BD	
☐	N619AU	Boeing 757-2B7	27198 / 584		0093	1193	2 RR RB211-535E4	104326	F24Y158		
☐	N620AU	Boeing 757-2B7	27199 / 586		0093	1193	2 RR RB211-535E4	104326	F24Y158		
☐	N621AU	Boeing 757-2B7	27200 / 589		0093	1293	2 RR RB211-535E4	104326	F24Y158		
☐	N622AU	Boeing 757-2B7	27201 / 605		0094	0394	2 RR RB211-535E4	104326	F24Y158		
☐	N623AU	Boeing 757-2B7	27244 / 607		0094	0394	2 RR RB211-535E4	104326	F24Y158		
☐	N624AU	Boeing 757-2B7	27245 / 630		0094	0794	2 RR RB211-535E4	104326	F24Y158		
☐	N625VJ	Boeing 757-2B7	27246 / 643		0094	1094	2 RR RB211-535E4	104326	F24Y158		
☐	N626AU	Boeing 757-2B7	27303 / 647		0094	1194	2 RR RB211-535E4	104326	F24Y158		
☐	N627AU	Boeing 757-2B7	27805 / 655		0094	0195	2 RR RB211-535E4	104326	F24Y158		
☐	N628AU	Boeing 757-2B7	27806 / 657		0094	0195	2 RR RB211-535E4	104326	F24Y158		
☐	N629AU	Boeing 757-2B7	27807 / 662		0095	0295	2 RR RB211-535E4	104326	F24Y158		
☐	N630AU	Boeing 757-2B7	27808 / 666		0095	0395	2 RR RB211-535E4	104326	F24Y158		
☐	N631AU	Boeing 757-2B7	27809 / 673		0095	0595	2 RR RB211-535E4	104326	F24Y158		
☐	N632AU	Boeing 757-2B7	27810 / 678		0095	0695	2 RR RB211-535E4	104326	F24Y158		
☐	N633AU	Boeing 757-2B7	27811 / 681		0095	0795	2 RR RB211-535E4	104326	F24Y158		
☐	N645US	Boeing 767-201 (ER)	23897 / 173	N603P	0087	0889	2 GE CF6-80C2B2	159211	C24Y179	BF-AP	
☐	N646US	Boeing 767-201 (ER)	23898 / 175	N604P	0087	0889	2 GE CF6-80C2B2	159211	C24Y179	BF-CP	
☐	N647US	Boeing 767-201 (ER)	23899 / 182	N607P	0087	0889	2 GE CF6-80C2B2	159211	C24Y179	BF-DP	
☐	N648US	Boeing 767-201 (ER)	23900 / 190	N608P	0088	0889	2 GE CF6-80C2B2	159211	C24Y179	BF-EP	
☐	N649US	Boeing 767-201 (ER)	23901 / 197	N614P	0087	0488	2 GE CF6-80C2B2	159211	C24Y179	BF-GP	
☐	N650US	Boeing 767-201 (ER)	23902 / 217	N617P	0088	0889	2 GE CF6-80C2B2	159211	C24Y179	BF-HP	
☐	N651US	Boeing 767-2B7 (ER)	24764 / 306		0090	0590	2 GE CF6-80C2B2	159211	C24Y179	BF-JP	
☐	N652US	Boeing 767-2B7 (ER)	24765 / 308		0090	0590	2 GE CF6-80C2B2	159211	C24Y179	BF-KP	
☐	N653US	Boeing 767-2B7 (ER)	24894 / 338		0090	1190	2 GE CF6-80C2B2	159211	C24Y179	BF-LP	
☐	N654US	Boeing 767-2B7 (ER)	25225 / 375		0091	0691	2 GE CF6-80C2B2	159211	C24Y179	BF-MP	
☐	N655US	Boeing 767-2B7 (ER)	25257 / 383		0091	0791	2 GE CF6-80C2B2	159211	C24Y179	BG-AP	Edwin L. Colodny
☐	N656US	Boeing 767-2B7 (ER)	26847 / 486		0093	0493	2 GE CF6-80C2B2	159211	C24Y179	BG-CP	
☐	N	Airbus Industrie A330-323					2 PW PW4168A	217000	FCY278		oo-delivery 1299
☐	N	Airbus Industrie A330-323					2 PW PW4168A	217000	FCY278		oo-delivery 0100
☐	N	Airbus Industrie A330-323					2 PW PW4168A	217000	FCY278		oo-delivery 0300
☐	N	Airbus Industrie A330-323					2 PW PW4168A	217000	FCY278		oo-delivery 0500
☐	N	Airbus Industrie A330-323					2 PW PW4168A	217000	FCY278		oo-delivery 0700
☐	N	Airbus Industrie A330-323					2 PW PW4168A	217000	FCY278		oo-delivery 0900
☐	N	Airbus Industrie A330-323					2 PW PW4168A	217000	FCY278		oo-delivery 1100

US AIRWAYS LEASING & SALES, Inc. = (USAL) (Subsidiary of US Airways Group, Inc.) Arlington, VA

2345 Crystal Drive, Arlington, VA 22227, USA ☎ (703) 872-7500 Tx: 892645 us agtn Fax: (703) 872-7515 SITA: n/a
F: 1985 👥 6 Head: Stuart Peebles Net: n/a New and used aircraft leasing & sales company.
Lessor of following (main) aircraft (ex US Airways) types: BAe 146-200, F28-1000/-4000 & McDonnell Douglas DC-9-31. Aircraft listed from US Airways Leasing & Sales are listed and mentioned as lsf USAL under the leasing carriers.

462 registration type of aircraft cn/fn ex/ex* mfd del powered by mtow kg configuration selcal name/fln/specialitites/remarks

US AIRWAYS SHUTTLE = TB / USS (Shuttle Inc. dba / Subsidiary of US Airways Group / formerly Trump Shuttle Inc.) — New York-La Guardia, NY

PO Box 710616, Flushing, NY 11371, USA ☎ (718) 397-6364 Tx: n/a Fax: (718) 397-6035 SITA: n/a
F: 1989 620 Head: Rita M. Cuddihy IATA: 857 ICAO: US SHUTTLE Net: http://www.us-airways.com

☐ N912TS	Boeing 727-254	20438 / 799	N536EA	0070	0689	3 PW JT8D-7B	78245	Y165		
☐ N913TS	Boeing 727-254	20250 / 781	N547EA	0069	0689	3 PW JT8D-7B	78245	Y165		
☐ N914TS	Boeing 727-254	20251 / 782	N548EA	0069	0689	3 PW JT8D-7B	78245	Y165		
☐ N916TS	Boeing 727-254	20437 / 798	N584EA	0070	0689	3 PW JT8D-7B	78245	Y165		
☐ N918TS	Boeing 727-225	20445 / 840	N8847E	0070	0689	3 PW JT8D-7B (HK3/FDX)	78245	Y165		
☐ N919TS	Boeing 727-225	20447 / 843	N8849E	0070	0689	3 PW JT8D-7B (HK3/FDX)	78245	Y165		
☐ N922TS	Boeing 727-225	20415 / 833	N8841E	0070	1093	3 PW JT8D-7B	78245	Y165		
☐ N923TS	Boeing 727-225	20441 / 835	N8843E	0070	1093	3 PW JT8D-7B	78245	Y165		
☐ N924TS	Boeing 727-227 (A)	21041 / 1104	N559PE	0075	0695	3 PW JT8D-9A (HK3/FDX)	79651	Y165		
☐ N925TS	Boeing 727-227 (A)	21244 / 1201	N568PE	0076	0895	3 PW JT8D-9A (HK3/FDX)	79651	Y165		
☐ N926TS	Boeing 727-227 (A)	20774 / 997	N553PE	0073	0696	3 PW JT8D-9A (HK3/FDX)	79651	Y165		
☐ N927TS	Boeing 727-227 (A)	20837 / 1016	N555PE	0074	0696	3 PW JT8D-9A	79651	Y165		

USA JET AIRLINES, Inc. = U7 / JUS (Active Aero Charter) (Member of Active Aero Group) — Detroit-Willow Run, MI

2064 D Street, Belleville, MI 48111-1278, USA ☎ (734) 480-0200 Tx: none Fax: (734) 480-0202 SITA: n/a
F: 1994 320 Head: Martin R. Goldman IATA: 184 ICAO: JET USA Net: http://www.activeaero.com King Air & Falcon 20 aircraft are operated under the name ACTIVE AERO (an internal division, same headquarters).

☐ N984AA	Beech King Air B90	LJ-429	N811AA	0068	0496	2 PWC PT6A-28	4377	Freighter		
☐ N811AA	Dassault Falcon 20D (C)	187	N750R	0068	0496	2 GE CF700-2D2	13000	Freighter		cvtd D
☐ N812AA	Dassault Falcon 20C (C)	57	N711KG	0966	0496	2 GE CF700-2D2	13000	Freighter		cvtd C
☐ N815AA	Dassault Falcon 20D (C)	205	N4LH	0669	0496	2 GE CF700-2D2	13000	Freighter		cvtd D
☐ N816AA	Dassault Falcon 20E (C)	290	I-TIAL	0973	0496	2 GE CF700-2D2	13000	Freighter		cvtd E
☐ N817AA	Dassault Falcon 20D (C)	233	I-TIAG	0370	0496	2 GE CF700-2D2	13000	Freighter		cvtd D
☐ N818AA	Dassault Falcon 20C (C)	36	OE-GUS	0466	0496	2 GE CF700-2D2	13000	Freighter		cvtd C
☐ N819AA	Dassault Falcon 20C (C)	26	N11827	0266	0496	2 GE CF700-2D2	13000	Freighter		cvtd C
☐ N820AA	Dassault Falcon 20C (C)	118	F-GGKE	1167	0496	2 GE CF700-2D2	13000	Freighter		cvtd C
☐ N821AA	Dassault Falcon 20D (C)	203	N36P	0069	0496	2 GE CF700-2D2	13000	Freighter		cvtd D
☐ N822AA	Dassault Falcon 20D (C)	195	N195MP	0069	0496	2 GE CF700-2D2	13000	Freighter		cvtd D
☐ N823AA	Dassault Falcon 20D (C)	228	OE-GRU	0070	0496	2 GE CF700-2D2	13000	Freighter		cvtd D
☐ N826AA	Dassault Falcon 20C (C)	67	F-BTML	0067	0496	2 GE CF700-2D2	13000	Freighter		cvtd C
☐ N827AA	Dassault Falcon 20E (C)	298	OE-GNN	0174	0496	2 GE CF700-2D2	13000	Freighter		cvtd E
☐ N192US	Boeing (Douglas) DC-9-15F (RC)	47156 / 228	N9357	1267	1197	2 PW JT8D-7B	41141	Freighter		
☐ N193US	Boeing (Douglas) DC-9-15F (RC)	45828 / 242	N566PC	0068	0796	2 PW JT8D-7B	41141	Freighter		
☐ N194US	Boeing (Douglas) DC-9-15F (RC)	47016 / 173	N9349	1067	0694	2 PW JT8D-7B (HK3/ABS)	41141	Freighter	EF-CM	
☐ N195US	Boeing (Douglas) DC-9-15F (RC)	47017 / 186	N9352	1067	1194	2 PW JT8D-7B (HK3/ABS)	41141	Freighter	EH-AC	
☐ N196US	Boeing (Douglas) DC-9-15F (RC)	47155 / 216	N9355	1267	1294	2 PW JT8D-7B (HK3/ABS)	41141	Freighter	EH-BD	
☐ N197US	Boeing (Douglas) DC-9-15F (RC)	47154 / 201	N901CK	0067	1294	2 PW JT8D-7B (HK3/ABS)	41141	Freighter		cvtd -15F (RC)
☐ N198US	Boeing (Douglas) DC-9-15F (MC)	47045 / 184	N902CK	1167	1294	2 PW JT8D-7B (HK3/ABS)	41141	Freighter		
☐ N199US	Boeing (Douglas) DC-9-15F (RC)	47153 / 185	N567PC	1067	0796	2 PW JT8D-7B (HK3/ABS)	41141	Freighter		

US HELICOPTERS, Inc. — Wingate-US Heliport, NC

PO Box 625, Marshville, NC 28103, USA ☎ (704) 233-4254 Tx: none Fax: (704) 233-4255 SITA: n/a
F: 1979 n/a Head: Cresful W. Horne, Jr. Net: n/a

☐ N109US	Bell 206B JetRanger II	2164	N164A	0077	0889	1 AN 250-C20	1451			
☐ N203FC	Bell 206B JetRanger III	3645		0082	1196	1 AN 250-C20J	1451			
☐ N313TV	Bell 206B JetRanger III	2379	N98CH	0078	0190	1 AN 250-C20B	1451			
☐ N3898G	Bell 206B JetRanger III	3207		0080	1095	1 AN 250-C20B	1451			
☐ N515TV	Bell 206B JetRanger II	2130	N97CH	0076	0290	1 AN 250-C20	1451			
☐ N905CA	Bell 206B JetRanger III	4027		0088	1095	1 AN 250-C20J	1451			
☐ N97CW	Bell 206B JetRanger II	2048	N3NJ	0076	1092	1 AN 250-C20	1451			
☐ N98CH	Bell 206B JetRanger III	3489	N202TV	0081	1191	1 AN 250-C20B	1451			
☐ N44TV	Bell 206L-1 LongRanger II	45208	N222LK	0078	1095	1 AN 250-C28B	1882			
☐ N811TV	Bell 206L-1 LongRanger II	45290	N2769Z	0079	0896	1 AN 250-C28B	1882			

UYAK AIR SERVICE, Inc. (Affiliated with Pacific Rim Wilderness Adventures / Seasonal April-October ops only) — Kodiak-Trident SPB, AK

PO Box 4188, Kodiak, AK 99615, USA ☎ (907) 486-3407 Tx: none Fax: (907) 486-2267 SITA: n/a
F: 1979 4 Head: Oliver K. Tovsen, Jr. Net: n/a

☐ N10RM	De Havilland DHC-2 Beaver I	1022	N64393	0057	0298	1 PW R-985	2313			Floats
☐ N123UA	De Havilland DHC-2 Beaver I	1493	C-GBWS	0062	0790	1 PW R-985	2313			Floats
☐ N12UA	De Havilland DHC-2 Beaver I	700	C-GSIN	0054	1094	1 PW R-985	2313			Floats
☐ N613WB	De Havilland DHC-2 Beaver I	672	N90409	0053	0597	1 PW R-985	2309			Floats

VALET AIR SERVICES = VAR (Valley Air Services, Inc. dba / affiliated with Valley Aviation, Inc.) — Burlington-Int'l, VT

PO Box 2366, South Burlington, VT 05401, USA ☎ (802) 863-3626 Tx: none Fax: (802) 658-9573 SITA: n/a
F: 1984 25 Head: Frank E. Donahue ICAO: VALLEY AIR Net: n/a

☐ N15338	Piper PA-34-200 Seneca	34-7350051		0073	0793	2 LY IO-360-C1E6	1905			
☐ N6681L	Beech Baron 58	TH-1088		0080	0597	2 CO IO-520-C	2449			lsf Spirit Leasing Inc.
☐ N27820	Piper PA-31-350 Navajo Chieftain	31-7952002		0079	0487	2 LY TIO-540-J2BD	3175			lsf HCA Aircraft Leasing Inc.
☐ N711EB	Piper PA-31-350 Navajo Chieftain	31-7305049		0073	1286	2 LY TIO-540-J2BD	3175			
☐ N771A	Piper PA-31-350 Navajo Chieftain	31-7852027		0078	0594	2 LY TIO-540-J2BD	3175			lsf Big Bird Leasing Co.
☐ N100GV	Beech King Air A100	B-116	N531DF	0072	0296	2 PWC PT6A-28	5216			lsf King Air Corp.
☐ N153ML	Beech King Air 200	BB-23	N814KA	0074	0197	2 PWC PT6A-41	5670			lsf DNH Leasing Inc.

VALLEY EXECUTIVE CHARTER (Avtrans Corporation dba) — Long Beach-Daugherty Field, CA

333 East Spring Street, Suite 132, Long Beach, CA 90806, USA ☎ (562) 989-4321 Tx: none Fax: (562) 989-4316 SITA: n/a
F: 1992 n/a Head: Shale K. Parker Net: n/a

☐ N1944G	Cessna 421B Golden Eagle	421B0844		0075	0797	2 CO GTSIO-520-H	3379			lsf pvt
☐ N43TT	Beech King Air A90 (65-A90)	LJ-210	N11UC	0067	0298	2 PWC PT6A-20	4218			lsf pvt

VALLEY HELICOPTER SERVICE (James R. Pope dba) — Clarkston-Heliport, WA

PO Box 54, Clarkston, WA 99403, USA ☎ (509) 758-1900 Tx: none Fax: (509) 243-1396 SITA: n/a
F: 1968 n/a Head: James R. Pope Net: n/a Aircraft below MTOW 1361kg: Hiller UH-12E

☐ N14837	Bell 206B JetRanger	850		0072	1095	1 AN 250-C20	1451			

VALLEY RESOURCES, Inc. — Plainville-Robertson Field, CT

PO Box 425, Farmington, CT 06034-0425, USA ☎ (860) 747-5082 Tx: none Fax: (860) 793-0630 SITA: n/a
F: 1986 n/a Head: Victor F. Tomasso Net: n/a Operates presentation flights at air-shows but no transport flights.

☐ N3006	Boeing (Douglas) DC-3D	42961	N3000	0046	0386	2 PW R-1830	12202	Exec 9 seats		

VANGUARD AIRLINES, Inc. = NJ / VGD — Kansas City-Int'l, MO

533 Mexico City Avenue, Kansas City, MO 64153, USA ☎ (816) 243-2177 Tx: none Fax: (816) 243-2154 SITA: n/a
F: 1994 450 Head: Robert J. Spane IATA: 311 ICAO: VANGUARD AIR Net: http://www.flyvanguard.com

☐ N120NJ	Boeing 737-2T5 (A)	22979 / 950	HA-LEC	0083	0299	2 PW JT8D-15	53070	Y128		lsf GECA
☐ N204AU	Boeing 737-247	19603 / 51	N758N	0068	1294	2 PW JT8D-9A	49442	Y128		lsf FSBU Trustee
☐ N208AU	Boeing 737-222	19547 / 107	N749N	0068	1194	2 PW JT8D-9A	49442	Y128		lsf FSBU Trustee
☐ N209US	Boeing 737-222	19548 / 114	N751N	0068	0195	2 PW JT8D-9A (HK3/NOR)	49442	Y128		lsf FSBU Trustee
☐ N219US	Boeing 737-281	20414 / 244	N776N	0070	1194	2 PW JT8D-9A	49442	Y128		lsf FSBU Trustee
☐ N412CE	Boeing 737-205	20412 / 225	PK-IJC	0071	0195	2 PW JT8D-15 (HK3/AVA)	54204	Y128		lsf IALI
☐ N5WM	Boeing 737-297 (A)	22629 / 842	N728AL	0082	1097	2 PW JT8D-15 (HK3/AVA)	53070	Y128		lsf Interlease Aviation Investors
☐ N603DJ	Boeing 737-222	19955 / 210	PH-TVH	0069	0296	2 PW JT8D-9A (HK3/NOR)	49442	Y128		lsf Mimi Leasing Corp.
☐ N620PC	Boeing 737-244	19708 / 87	N236TA	1068	0697	2 PW JT8D-9A (HK3/AVA)	49442	Y128		lsf Interlease Aviation Investors
☐ N912MP	Boeing 737-247	19607 / 70	N4510W	0968	1297	2 PW JT8D-9A (HK3/AVA)	49442	Y128		lsf INTL
☐ N	Boeing 737-2Q8 (A)	21735 / 582	HA-LEA	0079		2 PW JT8D-15	54204	Y128		to be lsf GECA 0499

VEE NEAL AVIATION, Inc. — Latrobe-Westmoreland County, PA

200 Pleasant Unity Road, Suite 211, Latrobe, PA 15650, USA ☎ (724) 539-1621 Tx: none Fax: (724) 539-4538 SITA: n/a
F: 1994 n/a Head: Charles V. Frey Net: http://www.veeneal.com

☐ N646SA	BAe 3101 Jetstream 31	646	N646JX	0084	1096	2 GA TPE331-10UR-513H	6900	C12		
☐ N651VN	BAe 3101 Jetstream 31	651	ZK-JSX	0085	1298	2 GA TPE331-10UR-513H	6900	C10		
☐ N8000J	BAe 3112 Jetstream 31	733	C-GJPC	0086	0997	2 GA TPE331-10UR-514H	6950	C10		

VERNAIR, Inc. (Subsidiary of Ulmer, Inc.) — Anchorage-Merrill Field, AK

1704 East 5th Ave., Anchorage, AK 99501, USA ☎ (907) 258-7822 Tx: none Fax: (907) 258-0909 SITA: n/a
F: 1978 n/a Head: Lavern O. Ulmer Net: http://www.alaska.net/vernair

☐ N3389W	Piper PA-32-260 Cherokee SIX	32-247		0065	0996	1 LY O-540-E4B5	1542			lsf Alaska Flight Tours Inc.

VICTORY AVIATION (Southern Aircraft Services, Inc. dba) — Fort Lauderdale-Hollywood Int'l, FL

288 SW 34th Street, Fort Lauderdale, FL 33315, USA ☎ (954) 359-0444 Tx: none Fax: (954) 359-0411 SITA: n/a
F: 1990 30 Head: David Lennemeier Net: n/a Operates non-commercial VIP-flights exclusively for the owner and for associated sport-teams/American football & hockey.

☐ N430WH	Bell 430	49012	N6284Q	0096	1196	2 AN 250-C40	4082	VIP		

463 registration type of aircraft cn/fn ex/ex* mfd del powered by mtow kg configuration selcal name/fln/specialitites/remarks

N431WH	Bell 430	49022	N1175B	0097	0597	2 AN 250-C40	4082	VIP		
N61WH	GAC (Grumman) G-1159B Gulfstream IIB	048	N711MC	0069	0695	2 RR Spey 511-8	31615	VIP		cvtd G-1159
N37WH	GAC G-IV Gulfstream IV (SP)	1243	N39WH	0095	1097	2 RR Tay 611-8	33838	VIP		
N737WH	Boeing 737-2V6 (A)	22431 / 803	HB-IEH	0081	1297	2 PW JT8D-17 (HK3/AVA)	58105	VIP		
N700WH	Boeing 737-75T (BBJ)	29142 / 167	N1782B*	0098	1298	2 CFMI CFM56-7B26	69400	VIP		

VIEQUES AIR LINK, Inc. = VI / VES

Vieques, PR

PO Box 487, Vieques, PR 00765, USA ☎ (787) 253-3644 Tx: none Fax: (787) 253-4000 SITA: n/a
F: 1965 ‹staff› 32 Head: Osvaldo Gonzalez IATA: 381 ICAO: VIEQUES Net: n/a

N663VL	Britten-Norman BN-2B-26 Islander	2110	N663J	0081	1189	2 LY O-540-E4B5	2812	Y9		
N861VL	Britten-Norman BN-2B-26 Islander	2155	N861JA*	0084	1191	2 LY O-540-E4B5	2812	Y9		
N902VL	Britten-Norman BN-2B-26 Islander	2128	8P-TAC	0082	0496	2 LY O-540-E4C5	2994	Y9		
N903VL	Britten-Norman BN-2A-26 Islander	2019	N2159X	0079	1289	2 LY O-540-E4B5	2812	Y9		
N904VL	Britten-Norman BN-2A-26 Islander	3014	HK-3813	0086	0297	2 LY O-540-E4C5	2994	Y9		
N907VL	Britten-Norman BN-2B-26 Islander	2192	HK-3812	0086	0297	2 LY O-540-E4C5	2994	Y9		
N901VL	Britten-Norman BN-2A Mk.III-1 Trislander	1003	N901TA	0074	0591	3 LY O-540-E4C5	4241	Y9		
N905VL	Britten-Norman BN-2A Mk.III-2 Trislander	1048	N905GD*	0083	1089	3 LY O-540-E4C5	4241	Y9		
N906VL	Britten-Norman BN-2A Mk.III-2 Trislander	1060	N906GD	0083	1089	3 LY O-540-E4C5	4241	Y9		

VIKING EXPRESS, Inc. = WCY

Chicago-Aurora Municipal, IL

Aurora Municipal Airport, 43W518 Route 30, Sugar Grove, IL 60554, USA ☎ (630) 466-7500 Tx: none Fax: (630) 466-7041 SITA: n/a
F: 1979 ‹staff› n/a Head: Robert B. Burwell ICAO: TITAN AIR Net: http://www.vikjet.com

N102VE	Cessna 208B Grand Caravan	208B0619		0097	0397	1 PWC PT6A-114A	3969	Freighter		
N103VE	Cessna 208B Grand Caravan	208B0620		0097	0397	1 PWC PT6A-114A	3969	Freighter		
N104VE	Cessna 208B Grand Caravan	208B0623		0097	0397	1 PWC PT6A-114A	3969	Freighter		
N102SA	Beech E18S	BA-441	N1230S	0059	1190	2 PW R-985-AN14B	4581	Freighter		lsf pvt
N124TS	Learjet 24D (XR)	24D-233	N500RW	0071	1196	2 GE CJ610-6	6124	Freighter		lsf Kittyhawk Enterprises Llc
N777NJ	Learjet 25B (XR)	25B-173	N780AQ	0074	1293	2 GE CJ610-6	6804	Freighter		lsf Dragon Leasing Corp.

VINTAGE AVIATION (Vintage Wings & Things, Llc dba)

Lafayette-Regional, LA

301 Sheppard, Lafayette, LA 70508, USA ☎ (318) 266-5833 Tx: none Fax: (318) 266-5837 SITA: n/a
F: 1997 ‹staff› n/a Head: David Jeansonne Net: n/a Operates FAR125 special flights to airshows and executive flights for the company. Also has other airworthy, vintage planes, in private collection & for private use only.

N900JC	Learjet 35A	35A-178	N35GG	0078	0398	2 GA TFE731-2-2B	8301	Executive		
N33VW	Boeing (Douglas) DC-3C (C-47A-90-DL)	20401	N12RB	0044	1197	2 PW R-1830	12202	20 Pax		

VINTAGE PROPS & JETS, Inc.

New Smyrna Beach-Municipal, FL

601 Skyline Drive, New Smyrna Beach, FL 32168, USA ☎ (904) 423-1773 Tx: none Fax: (904) 423-1774 SITA: n/a
F: 1992 ‹staff› n/a Head: William T. Crevasse, Jr. Net: n/a

N51HN	Piper PA-31-350 Navajo Chieftain	31-7552068		0075	0295	2 LY TIO-540-J2BD	3175	9 Pax		
N59905	Piper PA-31-350 Navajo Chieftain	31-7652135		0076	0694	2 LY TIO-540-J2BD	3175	9 Pax		
N7559L	Piper PA-31-310 Navajo B	31-7300946		0073	0496	2 LY TIO-540-A2C	2948	6 Pax		
N112CH	De Havilland DHC-4A Caribou	63	C-GVYZ	0063	0497	2 PW R-2000	12927	Freighter		lsf C C & H Aviation Inc.

VIRGINIA AVIATION (Aviation Resources, Inc. dba)

Lynchburg-Regional/Preston Glenn Field, VA

PO Box 4209, Lynchburg, VA 24502, USA ☎ (757) 237-8420 Tx: none Fax: (757) 237-8433 SITA: n/a
F: 1986 ‹staff› 40 Head: Stewart B. Hobbs Net: n/a Aircraft below MTOW 1361kg: Cessna 172

N8295C	Piper PA-44-180T Turbo Seminole	44-8107028		0080	1294	2 LY TO-360-E1A6D	1780			

VOLCANO HELI-TOURS (Manuiwa Airways, Inc. dba)

Kilauea-Volcano Heliport, HI

1655 Makaloa Street, Suite 2701, Honolulu, HI 96814, USA ☎ (808) 949-1722 Tx: none Fax: (808) 955-5915 SITA: n/a
F: 1982 ‹staff› n/a Head: Richard Y. Okita Net: n/a

N121VT	MD Helicopters MD 500D (Hughes 369D)	480301D	N58218	0078	0986	1 AN 250-C20B	1361			lsf Heli Logistics Inc.

VULCAN NORTHWEST - Flight Operations (Flight Operations of Vulcan Northwest, Inc.)

Seattle-Tacoma Int'l, WA

110-110th Ave. NE, Suite 550, Bellevue, WA 98004, USA ☎ (425) 453-1940 Tx: none Fax: none SITA: n/a
F: 1991 ‹staff› n/a Head: William D. Savoy Net: n/a Operates non-commercial executive flights for its parent company only.

N900AF	MD Helicopters MD 900 Explorer	900-00023	N9015Y	0096	0396	2 PWC PW206A	2722	Executive		
N108CJ	Cessna 525 CitationJet	525-0108	N5211Q	0095	0895	2 WRR FJ44-1A	4717	Executive		
N601AF	Canadair CL-601-3A (CL-600-2B16) Challen.	5045	N500GS	0089	0491	2 GE CF34-3A	20500	Executive		
N757AF	Boeing 757-2J4	25155 / 371	N115FS	0091	0395	2 RR RB211-535E4	113398	Executive		lsf Citicorp North America Inc.

WACHOVIA - Air Transportation Dept. (Air Transportation Dept. of Wachovia Corporation)

Atlanta-Fulton County/Brown Field, GA

Wachovia Bldg, 191 Peachtree Street, 21st Floor, Atlanta, GA 30303, USA ☎ (404) 332-6310 Tx: none Fax: (404) 332-1259 SITA: n/a
F: 1990 ‹staff› n/a Head: Jim Hall Net: n/a Operates non-commerical corporate flights for its parent, multibank company, only.

N17NC	Beech King Air 350 (B300)	FL-42	N315P	0091	0492	2 PWC PT6A-60A	6804	Corporate		
N1865A	Beech King Air 350 (B300)	FL-103	N8192M	0093	0195	2 PWC PT6A-60A	6804	Corporate		
N995WS	Beech 1900D Airliner	UE-175		0095	1095	2 PWC PT6A-67D	7688	Corporate		

WALTERS HELICOPTER SERVICE (Ronnie T. Walters dba)

San Diego-El Cajon/Gillespie Field, CA

1739 North Marshall Avenue, El Cajon, CA 92020, USA ☎ (760) 562-9949 Tx: none Fax: none SITA: n/a
F: 1995 ‹staff› n/a Head: Ronnie T. Walters Net: n/a

N4734F	Bell UH-1H (205)	4613	65-9569	0065	0695	1 LY T53-L-13	4309			to be re-reg. N205WH

WARBELOW'S AIR VENTURES, Inc. = 4W / VNA

Fairbanks-Int'l, AK

PO Box 60649, Fairbanks, AK 99706, USA ☎ (907) 474-0518 Tx: none Fax: (907) 479-5054 SITA: n/a
F: 1990 ‹staff› 37 Head: Arthur W. Warbelow ICAO: VENTAIRE Net: n/a Aircraft below MTOW 1361kg: Piper PA-18.

N756DJ	Cessna U206G Stationair	U20604005		0077	0790	1 CO IO-520-F	1633			
N6207H	Cessna 207A Stationair 7 II	20700551		0079	0994	1 CO IO-520-F	1724			
N7380U	Cessna 207A Stationair 7 II	20700428		0078	0790	1 CO IO-520-F	1724			
N27755	Piper PA-31-350 Navajo Chieftain	31-7852148		0078	0594	2 LY TIO-540-J2BD	3175			lsf pvt
N3527U	Piper PA-31-350 Navajo Chieftain	31-7952141		0079	0495	2 LY TIO-540-J2BD	3175			
N3582P	Piper PA-31-350 Navajo Chieftain	31-8052103		0080	1294	2 LY TIO-540-J2BD	3295			lsf pvt
N4082T	Piper PA-31-350 Navajo Chieftain	31-8152089		0081	0693	2 LY TIO-540-J2BD	3175			
N4434D	Piper PA-31-350 Navajo Chieftain	31-7552020		0075	0598	2 LY TIO-540-J2BD	3175			
N59764	Piper PA-31-350 Navajo Chieftain	31-7652037		0076	0792	2 LY TIO-540-J2BD	3175			
N59829	Piper PA-31-350 Navajo Chieftain	31-7652081		0076	1090	2 LY TIO-540-J2BD	3175			
N792FC	Piper PA-31-350 Navajo Chieftain	31-7552108	N492SC	0075	0895	2 LY TIO-540-J2BD	3175			lsf pvt

WARD AIR, Inc.

Juneau-Int'l, AK

8991 Yandukin Drive, Juneau, AK 99801, USA ☎ (907) 789-9150 Tx: none Fax: (907) 789-7002 SITA: n/a
F: 1975 ‹staff› 8 Head: Edward K. Kiesel Net: http://www.wardair.com

N93025	Cessna A185F Skywagon	18503163		0077	1188	1 CO IO-520-D	1520			Amphibian
N93311	Cessna A185F Skywagon	18503217		0077	0597	1 CO IO-520-D	1520			lsf pvt / Amphibian
N62353	De Havilland DHC-2 Beaver I	1363	58-2031	0058	1078	1 PW R-985	2313			lsf pvt / Amphibian
N62357	De Havilland DHC-2 Beaver I	1145	N64391	0057	0784	1 PW R-985	2313			Amphibian
N67897	De Havilland DHC-2 Beaver I	1045	CF-JXQ	0056	0594	1 PW R-985	2313			Amphibian
N63354	De Havilland DHC-3 Otter	30	C-FWAF	0053	0496	1 PW R-1340	3629			lsf pvt / Amphibian

WAUKEGAN AVIATION (Waukegan Aviation, Ltd dba / Subsidiary of Waukegan Avionics, Inc.)

Chicago-Waukegan Regional, IL

3550 North McAree Road, Waukegan, IL 60087, USA ☎ (847) 336-1120 Tx: none Fax: (847) 336-1422 SITA: n/a
F: 1985 ‹staff› n/a Head: Truman Aaron Net: n/a

N6242Q	Cessna 310R II	310R0067		0074	0590	2 CO IO-520-M	2495			lsf pvt
N532AS	Cessna 340	3400189		0072	0292	2 CO TSIO-520-N	2710			lsf pvt

WAYFARER AVIATION, Inc. (formerly Wayfarer Ketch Corporation)

White Plains-Westchester County, NY

Hangar G, Westchester County Airport, Westchester, NY 10604, USA ☎ (914) 949-4424 Tx: none Fax: (914) 949-5206 SITA: n/a
F: 1956 ‹staff› 150 Head: James C. Christiansen Net: http://wayfareraviation.com Beside aircraft listed, additional corporate jets & turboprops are operated under management for private owners.

N500WK	Agusta A109A II	7341	N109EA	0085	0389	2 AN 250-C20B	2600			lsf pvt
N200WK	Dassault Falcon 20F-5	261	N4368F	0072	0173	2 GA TFE731-5BR-2C	13200			lsf pvt / cvtd 20F

WEDGE AVIATION, Inc. (Subsidiary of Wedge Group / Associated with Transair, Paris-Le Bourget, France)

North America & Europe

PO Box 204, NL-1180-AE Amstelveen, Netherlands ☎ (20) 647 22 12 Tx: none Fax: (20) 643 54 78 SITA: n/a
F: 1981 ‹staff› n/a Head: Gary W. Harp Net: n/a Operates non-commerical executive flights exclusively for its parent company, a multi-national corporation.

N721MF	Boeing 727-2X8 (A)	22687 / 1784	N4523N	0081	1181	3 PW JT8D-17	88400	Executive	DJ-KL	

WELCH AVIATION, Inc. = TDB

Alpena-County Regional, MI

Alpena County Regional Airport, Alpena, MI 49707, USA ☎ (517) 356-9051 Tx: none Fax: (517) 356-1262 SITA: n/a
F: 1948 ‹staff› n/a Head: Jeffrey J. Welch ICAO: THUNDER BAY Net: n/a

N3112W	Beech King Air C90	LJ-612		0074	1196	2 PWC PT6A-20	4377			

464 registration type of aircraft cn/fn ex/ex* mfd del powered by mtow kg configuration selcal name/fln/specialitites/remarks

WELLSVILLE FLYING SERVICE, INC.
Wellsville-Municipal/Tarantine Field, NY

2600 Tarantine Road, Wellsville, NY 14895-9690, USA ☎ (716) 593-3350 Tx: none Fax: (716) 593-1543 SITA: n/a
F: 1960 ⁂ 8 Head: Gary Barnes Net: n/a

registration	type of aircraft	cn/fn	ex/ex*	mfd	del	powered by	mtow kg	configuration	selcal	name/fln/specialitites/remarks
N8AP	Piper PA-23-250 Aztec E	27-7305072		0073	0773	2 LY IO-540-C4B5	2359			
N9AP	Piper PA-23-250 Aztec E	27-7305129		0073	0773	2 LY IO-540-C4B5	2359			
N14AP	Piper PA-31-350 Navajo Chieftain	31-7752060		0077	0377	2 LY TIO-540-J2BD	3175			
N722CF	Piper PA-31-310 Navajo B	31-7300968		0073	0489	2 LY TIO-540-A2C	2948			lsf Luftladder Inc.

WEST AIR, Inc. = PCM (Subsidiary of FGO, Inc.)
Fresno-Air Terminal & Chico-Municipal, CA

5005 East Anderson, Fresno, CA 93727, USA ☎ (209) 294-6915 Tx: none Fax: (209) 291-5784 SITA: n/a
F: 1989 ⁂ 60 Head: Lawrence O. Olson ICAO: PAC VALLEY Net: n/a

registration	type of aircraft	cn/fn	ex/ex*	mfd	del	powered by	mtow kg	configuration	selcal	name/fln/specialitites/remarks
N707FX	Cessna 208B Caravan I Super Cargomaster	208B0427		0095	0395	1 PWC PT6A-114A	3969	Freighter		lsf/opf FDX in FedEx Feeder-colors
N713FX	Cessna 208B Caravan I Super Cargomaster	208B0438		0095	0595	1 PWC PT6A-114A	3969	Freighter		lsf/opf FDX in FedEx Feeder-colors
N722FX	Cessna 208B Caravan I Super Cargomaster	208B0454		0095	0895	1 PWC PT6A-114A	3969	Freighter		lsf/opf FDX in FedEx Feeder-colors
N726FX	Cessna 208B Caravan I Super Cargomaster	208B0465		0095	0995	1 PWC PT6A-114A	3969	Freighter		lsf/opf FDX in FedEx Feeder-colors
N744FX	Cessna 208B Caravan I Super Cargomaster	208B0492		0095	1295	1 PWC PT6A-114A	3969	Freighter		lsf/opf FDX in FedEx Feeder-colors
N748FX	Cessna 208B Caravan I Super Cargomaster	208B0503		0096	0196	1 PWC PT6A-114A	3969	Freighter		lsf/opf FDX in FedEx Feeder-colors
N750FX	Cessna 208B Caravan I Super Cargomaster	208B0511		0096	0296	1 PWC PT6A-114A	3969	Freighter		lsf/opf FDX in FedEx Feeder-colors
N754FX	Cessna 208B Caravan I Super Cargomaster	208B0526		0096	0396	1 PWC PT6A-114A	3969	Freighter		lsf/opf FDX in FedEx Feeder-colors
N758FX	Cessna 208B Caravan I Super Cargomaster	208B0539		0096	0596	1 PWC PT6A-114A	3969	Freighter		lsf/opf FDX in FedEx Feeder-colors
N759FX	Cessna 208B Caravan I Super Cargomaster	208B0542		0096	0696	1 PWC PT6A-114A	3969	Freighter		lsf/opf FDX in FedEx Feeder-colors
N762FE	Cessna 208B Caravan I Super Cargomaster	208B0255		0091	0291	1 PWC PT6A-114A	3969	Freighter		lsf/opf FDX in FedEx Feeder-colors
N763FE	Cessna 208B Caravan I Super Cargomaster	208B0256		0091	0391	1 PWC PT6A-114A	3969	Freighter		lsf/opf FDX in FedEx Feeder-colors
N768FE	Cessna 208B Caravan I Super Cargomaster	208B0263		0091	0491	1 PWC PT6A-114A	3969	Freighter		lsf/opf FDX in FedEx Feeder-colors
N771FE	Cessna 208B Caravan I Super Cargomaster	208B0267		0091	0691	1 PWC PT6A-114A	3969	Freighter		lsf/opf FDX in FedEx Feeder-colors
N772FE	Cessna 208B Caravan I Super Cargomaster	208B0268		0091	0691	1 PWC PT6A-114A	3969	Freighter		lsf/opf FDX in FedEx Feeder-colors
N781FE	Cessna 208B Caravan I Super Cargomaster	208B0278		0091	0891	1 PWC PT6A-114A	3969	Freighter		lsf/opf FDX in FedEx Feeder-colors
N782FE	Cessna 208B Caravan I Super Cargomaster	208B0280		0091	0991	1 PWC PT6A-114A	3969	Freighter		lsf/opf FDX in FedEx Feeder-colors
N785FE	Cessna 208B Caravan I Super Cargomaster	208B0283		0091	1091	1 PWC PT6A-114A	3969	Freighter		lsf/opf FDX in FedEx Feeder-colors
N790FE	Cessna 208B Caravan I Super Cargomaster	208B0288		0091	1191	1 PWC PT6A-114A	3969	Freighter		lsf/opf FDX in FedEx Feeder-colors
N844FE	Cessna 208B Caravan I Super Cargomaster	208B0149		0089	0289	1 PWC PT6A-114	3969	Freighter		lsf/opf FDX in FedEx Feeder-colors
N857FE	Cessna 208B Caravan I Super Cargomaster	208B0177		0089	0689	1 PWC PT6A-114	3969	Freighter		lsf/opf FDX in FedEx Feeder-colors
N872FE	Cessna 208B Caravan I Super Cargomaster	208B0200		0089	1289	1 PWC PT6A-114	3969	Freighter		lsf/opf FDX in FedEx Feeder-colors
N879FE	Cessna 208B Caravan I Super Cargomaster	208B0213		0090	0490	1 PWC PT6A-114	3969	Freighter		lsf/opf FDX in FedEx Feeder-colors
N886FE	Cessna 208B Caravan I Super Cargomaster	208B0190		0089	0989	1 PWC PT6A-114	3969	Freighter		lsf/opf FDX in FedEx Feeder-colors
N891FE	Cessna 208B Caravan I Super Cargomaster	208B0221		0090	0690	1 PWC PT6A-114	3969	Freighter		lsf/opf FDX in FedEx Feeder-colors
N892FE	Cessna 208B Caravan I Super Cargomaster	208B0222		0090	0690	1 PWC PT6A-114	3969	Freighter		lsf/opf FDX in FedEx Feeder-colors
N908FE	Cessna 208B Caravan I Super Cargomaster	208B0008		0086	1286	1 PWC PT6A-114	3969	Freighter		lsf/opf FDX in FedEx Feeder-colors
N920FE	Cessna 208B Caravan I Super Cargomaster	208B0020		0087	0487	1 PWC PT6A-114	3969	Freighter		lsf/opf FDX in FedEx Feeder-colors
N930FE	Cessna 208B Caravan I Super Cargomaster	208B0030		0087	0687	1 PWC PT6A-114	3969	Freighter		lsf/opf FDX in FedEx Feeder-colors
N968FE	Cessna 208B Caravan I Super Cargomaster	208B0090		0088	0588	1 PWC PT6A-114	3969	Freighter		lsf/opf FDX in FedEx Feeder-colors
N969FE	Cessna 208B Caravan I Super Cargomaster	208B0092		0088	0588	1 PWC PT6A-114	3969	Freighter		lsf/opf FDX in FedEx Feeder-colors
N984FE	Cessna 208B Caravan I Super Cargomaster	208B0115		0088	0988	1 PWC PT6A-114	3969	Freighter		lsf/opf FDX in FedEx Feeder-colors
N985FE	Cessna 208B Caravan I Super Cargomaster	208B0117		0088	0988	1 PWC PT6A-114	3969	Freighter		lsf/opf FDX in FedEx Feeder-colors
N987FE	Cessna 208B Caravan I Super Cargomaster	208B0201		0089	1289	1 PWC PT6A-114	3969	Freighter		lsf/opf FDX in FedEx Feeder-colors

WESTCHESTER AIR, Inc.
White Plains-Westchester County, NY

Hangar C-1, Westchester City Airport, White Plains, NY 10604-1304, USA ☎ (914) 761-3000 Tx: none Fax: (914) 761-3291 SITA: n/a
F: 1982 ⁂ 16 Head: Millie Hernandez-Becker Net: n/a

registration	type of aircraft	cn/fn	ex/ex*	mfd	del	powered by	mtow kg	configuration	selcal	name/fln/specialitites/remarks
N150AL	Piper PA-31-350 Navajo Chieftain	31-7405251		0074	0885	2 LY TIO-540-J2BD	3175			
N850DB	Beech King Air 100	B-53	N879K	0070	0295	2 PWC PT6A-28	4808			

WEST COAST AIR CHARTER, Inc.
El Paso-Int'l, TX

2211 East Missouri, Suite N291B, El Paso, TX 79903, USA ☎ (734) 482-4030 Tx: none Fax: (734) 482-4032 SITA: n/a
F: 1974 ⁂ n/a Head: Jorge Quinones Net: n/a

registration	type of aircraft	cn/fn	ex/ex*	mfd	del	powered by	mtow kg	configuration	selcal	name/fln/specialitites/remarks
N268WC	Learjet 25D	25D-268	XA-SPL	0079	0894	2 GE CJ610-8A	6804			lsf Mega Air Inc.
N148WC	Dassault Falcon 20C	148	N888WS	0068	0295	2 GE CF700-2C	12000			lsf Mega Air Inc.

WESTCOR AVIATION, Inc.
Scottsdale, AZ

15035 North 73rd Street, Scottsdale, AZ 85260, USA ☎ (520) 991-6558 Tx: none Fax: (520) 991-7827 SITA: n/a
F: 1982 ⁂ n/a Head: Robert J. Oliver Net: n/a

registration	type of aircraft	cn/fn	ex/ex*	mfd	del	powered by	mtow kg	configuration	selcal	name/fln/specialitites/remarks
N700TV	Eurocopter (Aerosp.) AS350B AStar	1838		0085	1191	1 TU Arriel 1B	1950			
N311RL	Eurocopter (Aerosp.) AS355F2 TwinStar	5436		0090	1190	2 AN 250-C20F	2540			
N64VM	Beech Beechjet 400	RJ-1		0085	0785	2 PWC JT15D-5	7158			lsf Nektor Industries Inc.

WESTERN AIR EXPRESS = WAE (Transportation Systems, Inc. dba)
Boise, ID

815 Park Blvd., Suite 330, Boise, ID 83712, USA ☎ (208) 343-2756 Tx: none Fax: (208) 343-2878 SITA: n/a
F: 1994 ⁂ n/a Head: Eugene D. Heil ICAO: WESTERN EXPRESS Net: n/a

registration	type of aircraft	cn/fn	ex/ex*	mfd	del	powered by	mtow kg	configuration	selcal	name/fln/specialitites/remarks
N6367X	Cessna 402B II	402B1330		0078	0894	2 CO TSIO-520-E	2858			
N7947Q	Cessna 402B	402B0397		0073	0894	2 CO TSIO-520-E	2858			lsf Western Airlines Lc
N98680	Cessna 402B II	402B1044		0076	0894	2 CO TSIO-520-E	2858			
N341PL	Fairchild (Swearingen) SA226TC Metro II	TC-334	C-GBWF	0080	0894	2 GA TPE331-10UA-511G	5670			
N56EA	Fairchild (Swearingen) SA226TC Metro IIA	TC-399	N602AS	0081	0298	2 GA TPE331-10UA-511G	5987			lsf Western Airlines Lc / cvtd II
N5974V	Fairchild (Swearingen) SA226TC Metro II	TC-411	SX-BSG	0081	0498	2 GA TPE331-10UA-511G	5670			lsf Western Airlines Lc

WESTERN AIR EXPRESS, Inc.
Lubbock-Int'l, TX

Lubbock Int'l Airport, 2608 West Cuthbert, Midland, TX 79701, USA ☎ (915) 687-5004 Tx: none Fax: (915) 687-1025 SITA: n/a
F: 1996 ⁂ n/a Head: Jim Nyerges Net: n/a

registration	type of aircraft	cn/fn	ex/ex*	mfd	del	powered by	mtow kg	configuration	selcal	name/fln/specialitites/remarks
N20NP	Beech Queen Air B80 (65-B80)	LD-433		0070	1296	2 LY IGSO-540-A1D	3992	Freighter		lsf pvt
N5376M	Beech Queen Air B80 (65-B80)	LD-301		0066	1296	2 LY IGSO-540-A1D	3992	Freighter		lsf pvt
N6AQ	Beech Queen Air A80 (65-A80)	LD-214		0064	1296	2 LY IGSO-540-A1A	3856	Freighter		lsf pvt
N7817L	Beech Queen Air B80 (65-B80)	LD-340		0067	1296	2 LY IGSO-540-A1D	3992	Freighter		lsf pvt
N8071R	Beech Queen Air B80 (65-B80)	LD-420		0069	1296	2 LY IGSO-540-A1D	3992	Freighter		lsf pvt
N70NP	Beech 99 Airliner	U-14	N914Y	0068	1296	2 PWC PT6A-20	4717	Freighter		lsf pvt

WESTERN AIR FREIGHT = WZ (IBC Pacific, Inc. dba)
Los Angeles-Int'l, CA

5793 West Imperial Highway, Los Angeles, CA 90045, USA ☎ (650) 692-8106 Tx: none Fax: (650) 692-9635 SITA: n/a
F: 1997 ⁂ n/a Head: Charles H. Shea IATA: 017 Net: n/a

registration	type of aircraft	cn/fn	ex/ex*	mfd	del	powered by	mtow kg	configuration	selcal	name/fln/specialitites/remarks
N69628	Cessna 310Q	310Q0824		0073	0997	2 CO IO-470-VO	2404	Freighter		lsf pvt

WESTERN AVIATORS, Inc. = WTV (Air Colorado)
Grand Junction-Walker Field, CO

2867 Aviator's Way, Grand Junction, CO 81506, USA ☎ (970) 242-6805 Tx: none Fax: (970) 243-1871 SITA: n/a
F: 1978 ⁂ n/a Head: Richard L. Fowler ICAO: WESTAVIA Net: n/a AIR COLORADO is a marketing name used for ski-charter flights (same fleet, headquarters).

registration	type of aircraft	cn/fn	ex/ex*	mfd	del	powered by	mtow kg	configuration	selcal	name/fln/specialitites/remarks
N159SW	Piper PA-31-350 Navajo Chieftain	31-7405229		0074	1290	2 LY TIO-540-J2BD	3175			lsf pvt
N4051X	Fairchild (Swearingen) SA26AT Merlin IIB	T26-124		0069	1089	2 GA TPE331-1-151G	4536			lsf pvt

WESTERN OPERATIONS, Inc. – Helicopter division
Rialto-Municipal, CA

PO Box 2450, Rialto, CA 92376, USA ☎ (909) 829-1056 Tx: none Fax: (909) 869-2550 SITA: n/a
F: 1996 ⁂ n/a Head: Rufus L. Greene Net: http://www.westernops.com Aircraft below MTOW 1361kg: Schweizer 269C (300C)

registration	type of aircraft	cn/fn	ex/ex*	mfd	del	powered by	mtow kg	configuration	selcal	name/fln/specialitites/remarks
N105JL	MD Helicopters MD 500D (Hughes 369D)	900807D	C-GDFF	0080	0496	1 AN 250-C20B	1361			lsf Joda Partnership

WEST ISLE AIR, Inc. = WIL (Sister company of Aeronautical Services, Inc.)
Anacortes, WA

4000 Airport Road, Anacortes, WA 98221, USA ☎ (360) 293-4691 Tx: none Fax: (360) 293-0517 SITA: n/a
F: 1980 ⁂ 45 Head: Steve D. Franklin IATA: 590 ICAO: WEST ISLE AIR Net: n/a Aircraft below MTOW 1361 kg: Cessna 172

registration	type of aircraft	cn/fn	ex/ex*	mfd	del	powered by	mtow kg	configuration	selcal	name/fln/specialitites/remarks
N29068	Cessna U206C Super Skywagon	U206-1049		0068	0990	1 CO IO-520-F	1633			
N8313Q	Cessna U206F Stationair II	U20603174		0076	0392	1 CO IO-520-F	1633			
N8768Q	Cessna U206F Stationair II	U20603521		0076	0591	1 CO IO-520-F	1633			
N9428G	Cessna U206E Stationair	U20601628		0071	0198	1 CO IO-520-F	1633			lsf Raven Air Inc.
N1584U	Cessna 207 Skywagon	20700184		0070	0198	1 CO IO-520-F	1724			lsf Aeronautical Services
N7405	Cessna T207 Turbo Skywagon	20700147		0070	0194	1 CO TSIO-520-G	1724			

WESTJET (Westjet Air Center, Inc. dba)
Rapid City-Regional, SD

4160 Firestation Road, Rapid City, SD 57701-8703, USA ☎ (605) 393-2500 Tx: none Fax: (605) 393-1631 SITA: n/a
F: 1949 ⁂ n/a Head: Donald H. Rydstrom Net: n/a

registration	type of aircraft	cn/fn	ex/ex*	mfd	del	powered by	mtow kg	configuration	selcal	name/fln/specialitites/remarks
N5034Q	Cessna 310N	310N0134		0068	0181	2 CO IO-470-V	2359			
N7863Q	Cessna 310Q	310Q0649		0073	0377	2 CO IO-470-VO	2404			
N766CF	Piper PA-31-350 Navajo Chieftain	31-7305102		0073	1091	2 LY TIO-540-J2BD	3175			
N777DA	Piper PA-31-350 Navajo Chieftain	31-7552004		0075	0189	2 LY TIO-540-J2BD	3175			

WEST MICHIGAN AIR CARE, Inc. **Kalamazoo-Heliport, MI**

1535 Gull Road, Suite 100, Kalamazoo, MI 49001, USA ☎ (616) 337-2505 Tx: none Fax: (616) 337-2506 SITA: n/a
F: 1993 ☗☗☗ n/a Head: Edward R. Eroe Net: n/a

☐ N365SJ	Eurocopter (Aerosp.) SA365N Dauphin 2	6018	N365UC	0082	0393	2 TU Arriel 1C	4000	EMS		
☐ N365WM	Eurocopter (Aerosp.) AS365N2 Dauphin 2	6429		0091	0993	2 TU Arriel 1C2	4250	EMS		

WESTWIND AVIATION, Inc. **Phoenix-Deer Valley Municipal, AZ**

732 West Deer Valley Road, Suite J, Phoenix, AZ 85027, USA ☎ (916) 869-0866 Tx: none Fax: (916) 780-8484 SITA: n/a
F: 1985 ☗☗☗ n/a Head: Ron Haarer Net: http://www.westwindaviation.com Aircraft below MTOW 1361kg: Cessna 172 & 177

☐ N456MA	Cessna U206G Stationair 6 II	U20604325		0078	0295	1 CO IO-520-F	1633			lsf Dalessio Enterprises Inc.
☐ N4756Z	Cessna TU206G Turbo Stationair 6 II	U20606012		0081	0596	1 CO TSIO-520-M	1633			lsf Dalessio Enterprises Inc.
☐ N756LK	Cessna U206G Stationair 6 II	U20604174		0078	0393	1 CO IO-520-F	1633			
☐ N8329Q	Cessna TU206F Turbo Stationair II	U20603190		0076	0493	1 CO TSIO-520-C	1633			lsf pvt
☐ N6241B	Cessna T210M Turbo Centurion II	21062719		0078	0694	1 CO TSIO-520-R	1724			
☐ N402AT	Cessna 402B	402B0612		0074	1193	2 CO TSIO-520-E	2858			lsf S&P Leasing Inc.
☐ N2656B	Cessna 421C Golden Eagle III	421C0711		0079	0595	2 CO GTSIO-520-L	3379			lsf Keys Family Llc

WESTWIND HELICOPTERS, Inc. **Rancho Cordova-Sunrise One Heliport, CA**

11353 Sunrise Gold Circle, Rancho Cordova, CA 95742, USA ☎ (530) 852-0476 Tx: none Fax: (530) 852-0390 SITA: n/a
F: 1975 ☗☗☗ n/a Head: Scott Baker Net: n/a

☐ N123WF	Bell 206B JetRanger III	3058	N72BL	0080	0294	1 AN 250-C20B	1451			
☐ N2296N	Bell 206B JetRanger III	3575		0082	0795	1 AN 250-C20J	1451			
☐ N2297E	Bell 206B JetRanger III	3656		0082	0690	1 AN 250-C20J	1451			
☐ N4480	Bell UH-1B (204)	1030	N49CD	0064	0495	1 LY T53-L-11	3856			
☐ N64770	Bell UH-1B (204)	946	63-8721	0063	0889	1 LY T53-L-11	3856			lsf Infinity Aviation Inc.

WEYERHAEUSER AVIATION (Weyerhaeuser Company dba) **Seattle-Tacoma Int'l, WA**

Mailstop Airport, PO Box 2999, Tacoma, WA 98477-2999, USA ☎ (206) 241-2858 Tx: none Fax: (206) 244-0256 SITA: n/a
F: 1975 ☗☗☗ n/a Head: Thomas J. Gustafson Net: n/a Beside (commercial) listed helicopters, also operates non-commercial corporate fixed-wing (Beechcraft King Air 350, Cessna 560/650 & Falcon 2000) aircraft.

☐ N53W	Bell 206B JetRanger III	3587	N22955	0082	0187	1 AN 250-C20J	1451			
☐ N86W	Bell 206B JetRanger III	4142		0091	0191	1 AN 250-C20J	1451			
☐ N108W	Bell 206L-4 LongRanger IV	52034		0093	0693	1 AN 250-C30P	2018			
☐ N404W	Bell 206L-4 LongRanger IV	52055		0093	0594	1 AN 250-C30P	2018			
☐ N62W	Bell 206L-3 LongRanger III	51343		0090	0390	1 AN 250-C30P	1882			
☐ N181W	Bell 212	35058	C-FOKZ	0092	0893	2 PWC PT6T-3B TwinPac	5080			
☐ N82W	Bell 212	31177	N3911B	0081	0484	2 PWC PT6T-3B TwinPac	5080			
☐ N98W	Bell 212	35100		0096	0696	2 PWC PT6T-3B TwinPac	5080			

WHITES AIR SERVICE (Carl H. White dba) **Kenai, AK**

PO Box 412, Kenai, AK 99611, USA ☎ (907) 283-4646 Tx: none Fax: none SITA: n/a
F: 1992 ☗☗☗ n/a Head: Carl H. White Net: n/a

☐ N80124	Cessna A185F Skywagon	18503094		0076	0592	1 CO IO-520-D	1520			Floats / Wheel-Skis

WIGGINS AIRWAYS = WIG (Wiggins Air Cargo, Inc. & Wiggins Airways, Inc. dba / Associated with Piper East, Inc.) **Norwood-Memorial, MA**

Wiggins Airways

PO Box 250, Norwood, MA 02062, USA ☎ (781) 762-5690 Tx: none Fax: (781) 762-1958 SITA: n/a
F: 1929 ☗☗☗ 120 Head: David L. Ladd IATA: 035 Net: http://www.wiggins-air.com

☐ N112SC	Bell 206B JetRanger III	3096		0080	0184	1 AN 250-C20B	1451			lsf Piper East Inc./opf WCVB Television
☐ N27WA	Bell 206B JetRanger III	3568	N2266K	0082	0288	1 AN 250-C20B	1451			lsf Piper East Inc.
☐ N37WA	Bell 206B JetRanger III	3433	N70TV	0081	0184	1 AN 250-C20B	1451			lsf Piper East Inc.
☐ N5749U	Bell 206B JetRanger III	3106		0080	0590	1 AN 250-C20B	1451			lsf Piper East Inc./opf WBZ Television
☐ N701FX	Cessna 208B Caravan I Super Cargomaster	208B0420		0095	0195	1 PWC PT6A-114A	3969	Freighter		lsf/opf FDX in FedEx Feeder-colors
☐ N725FX	Cessna 208B Caravan I Super Cargomaster	208B0460		0095	0895	1 PWC PT6A-114A	3969	Freighter		lsf/opf FDX in FedEx Feeder-colors
☐ N731FX	Cessna 208B Caravan I Super Cargomaster	208B0480		0095	1195	1 PWC PT6A-114A	3969	Freighter		lsf/opf FDX in FedEx Feeder-colors
☐ N748FE	Cessna 208B Caravan I Super Cargomaster	208B0241		0090	1190	1 PWC PT6A-114A	3969	Freighter		lsf/opf FDX in FedEx Feeder-colors
☐ N755FX	Cessna 208B Caravan I Super Cargomaster	208B0529		0096	0496	1 PWC PT6A-114A	3969	Freighter		lsf/opf FDX in FedEx Feeder-colors
☐ N757FX	Cessna 208B Caravan I Super Cargomaster	208B0535		0096	0496	1 PWC PT6A-114A	3969	Freighter		lsf/opf FDX in FedEx Feeder-colors
☐ N780FE	Cessna 208B Caravan I Super Cargomaster	208B0277		0091	0891	1 PWC PT6A-114A	3969	Freighter		lsf/opf FDX in FedEx Feeder-colors
☐ N783FE	Cessna 208B Caravan I Super Cargomaster	208B0281		0091	0991	1 PWC PT6A-114A	3969	Freighter		lsf/opf FDX in FedEx Feeder-colors
☐ N789FE	Cessna 208B Caravan I Super Cargomaster	208B0287		0091	1191	1 PWC PT6A-114A	3969	Freighter		lsf/opf FDX in FedEx Feeder-colors
☐ N804FE	Cessna 208B Caravan I Super Cargomaster	208B0039	F-GETN	0087	0987	1 PWC PT6A-114	3969	Freighter		lsf/opf FDX in FedEx Feeder-colors
☐ N807FE	Cessna 208B Caravan I Super Cargomaster	208B0041	F-GETO	0087	0987	1 PWC PT6A-114	3969	Freighter		lsf/opf FDX in FedEx Feeder-colors
☐ N865FE	Cessna 208B Caravan I Super Cargomaster	208B0188		0089	0989	1 PWC PT6A-114	3969	Freighter		lsf/opf FDX in FedEx Feeder-colors
☐ N870FE	Cessna 208B Caravan I Super Cargomaster	208B0196		0089	1189	1 PWC PT6A-114	3969	Freighter		lsf/opf FDX in FedEx Feeder-colors
☐ N888FE	Cessna 208B Caravan I Super Cargomaster	208B0217		0090	0590	1 PWC PT6A-114	3969	Freighter		lsf/opf FDX in FedEx Feeder-colors
☐ N898FE	Cessna 208B Caravan I Super Cargomaster	208B0228		0090	0990	1 PWC PT6A-114	3969	Freighter		lsf/opf FDX in FedEx Feeder-colors
☐ N901FE	Cessna 208B Caravan I Super Cargomaster	208B0001	N9767F*	0086	1186	1 PWC PT6A-114	3969	Freighter		lsf/opf FDX in FedEx Feeder-colors
☐ N909FE	Cessna 208B Caravan I Super Cargomaster	208B0009		0086	1286	1 PWC PT6A-114	3969	Freighter		lsf/opf FDX in FedEx Feeder-colors
☐ N911FE	Cessna 208B Caravan I Super Cargomaster	208B0011		0087	0187	1 PWC PT6A-114	3969	Freighter		lsf/opf FDX in FedEx Feeder-colors
☐ N919FE	Cessna 208B Caravan I Super Cargomaster	208B0019		0087	0387	1 PWC PT6A-114	3969	Freighter		lsf/opf FDX in FedEx Feeder-colors
☐ N931FE	Cessna 208B Caravan I Super Cargomaster	208B0031		0087	0687	1 PWC PT6A-114	3969	Freighter		lsf/opf FDX in FedEx Feeder-colors
☐ N935FE	Cessna 208B Caravan I Super Cargomaster	208B0035		0087	0787	1 PWC PT6A-114	3969	Freighter		lsf/opf FDX in FedEx Feeder-colors
☐ N937FE	Cessna 208B Caravan I Super Cargomaster	208B0037		0087	0887	1 PWC PT6A-114	3969	Freighter		lsf/opf FDX in FedEx Feeder-colors
☐ N947FE	Cessna 208B Caravan I Super Cargomaster	208B0050		0087	1087	1 PWC PT6A-114	3969	Freighter		lsf/opf FDX in FedEx Feeder-colors
☐ N958FE	Cessna 208B Caravan I Super Cargomaster	208B0071		0088	0288	1 PWC PT6A-114	3969	Freighter		lsf/opf FDX in FedEx Feeder-colors
☐ N959FE	Cessna 208B Caravan I Super Cargomaster	208B0073		0088	0288	1 PWC PT6A-114	3969	Freighter		lsf/opf FDX in FedEx Feeder-colors
☐ N963FE	Cessna 208B Caravan I Super Cargomaster	208B0080		0088	0388	1 PWC PT6A-114	3969	Freighter		lsf/opf FDX in FedEx Feeder-colors
☐ N966FE	Cessna 208B Caravan I Super Cargomaster	208B0086		0088	0488	1 PWC PT6A-114	3969	Freighter		lsf/opf FDX in FedEx Feeder-colors
☐ N974FE	Cessna 208B Caravan I Super Cargomaster	208B0099		0088	0688	1 PWC PT6A-114	3969	Freighter		lsf/opf FDX in FedEx Feeder-colors
☐ N981FE	Cessna 208B Caravan I Super Cargomaster	208B0110		0088	0888	1 PWC PT6A-114	3969	Freighter		lsf/opf FDX in FedEx Feeder-colors
☐ N989FE	Cessna 208B Caravan I Super Cargomaster	208B0124		0088	1088	1 PWC PT6A-114	3969	Freighter		lsf/opf FDX in FedEx Feeder-colors
☐ N996FE	Cessna 208B Caravan I Super Cargomaster	208B0135		0088	1288	1 PWC PT6A-114	3969	Freighter		lsf/opf FDX in FedEx Feeder-colors
☐ N998FE	Cessna 208B Caravan I Super Cargomaster	208B0139		0088	1288	1 PWC PT6A-114	3969	Freighter		lsf/opf FDX in FedEx Feeder-colors
☐ N191WA	Beech 99A Airliner	U-136	C-GPCF	0070	1198	2 PWC PT6A-28	4717			lsf Piper East Inc.
☐ N192WA	Beech B99 Airliner	U-152	C-GEOI	0074	0199	2 PWC PT6A-28	4944			lsf Piper East Inc.
☐ N193WA	Beech 99 Airliner	U-17	N10MV	0068	0695	2 PWC PT6A-27	4717			lsf Piper East Inc.
☐ N194WA	Beech B99 Airliner	U-64	C-FAWX	0068	1197	2 PWC PT6A-27	4944			lsf Piper East Inc.
☐ N195WA	Beech 99 Airliner	U-91	N533SK	0069	0794	2 PWC PT6A-27	4717			lsf Piper East Inc.
☐ N196WA	Beech 99 Airliner	U-68	N900AR	0069	0594	2 PWC PT6A-20	4717			lsf Piper East Inc.
☐ N199WA	Beech B99 Airliner	U-154	N99CH	0074	0292	2 PWC PT6A-27	4944			lsf Piper East Inc.
☐ N656WA	De Havilland DHC-6 Twin Otter 100	47	N56AN	0067	0586	2 PWC PT6A-20	5252	Freighter		lsf Piper East Inc.

WILDERNESS AIR, Inc. **Juneau-Int'l, AK**

1873 Shell Simmons Drive, Juneau, AK 99801-9398, USA ☎ (907) 789-7818 Tx: none Fax: (907) 789-4228 SITA: n/a
F: 1997 ☗☗☗ n/a Head: Peter D. Devaris Net: n/a

☐ N480DB	Beech C-45F (18)		N8033H	0044	0397	2 PW R-985-AN14B	3969			Floats

WILLOW AIR (Bal, Inc. dba / Seasonal May-October ops only) **Willow-Lake SPB, AK**

PO Box 42, Willow, AK 99688, USA ☎ (907) 495-6370 Tx: none Fax: (907) 495-6370 SITA: n/a
F: 1997 ☗☗☗ n/a Head: Steven White Net: n/a

☐ N98JH	De Havilland DHC-2 Beaver I	953	S-3 RNAF	0056	0897	1 PW R-985	2309			lsf Northern Alps Inn / Floats

WILL SQUYRES HELICOPTER TOURS **Lihue, HI**

3222 Kuhio Highway, Lihue, HI 96766, USA ☎ (808) 245-8881 Tx: none Fax: (808) 245-8075 SITA: n/a
F: 1984 ☗☗☗ n/a Head: William W. Squyres Net: n/a

☐ N4010K	Eurocopter (Aerosp.) AS350BA AStar	2841		0095	0396	1 TU Arriel 1B	2100			lsf Geneva Transport Equipment Co.
☐ N699W	Eurocopter (Aerosp.) AS350BA AStar	2424		0090	0996	1 TU Arriel 1B	2100			lsf Geneva Transport Equipment/cvtd350B

WINAIR, Inc. = WNA **Salt Lake City-Int'l, UT**

303 North 2370 West, Salt Lake City, UT 84116, USA ☎ (801) 519-2100 Tx: none Fax: (801) 519-2200 SITA: n/a
F: 1997 ☗☗☗ n/a Head: Steven Kästler ICAO: WINAIR Net: n/a

☐ N118RW	Boeing 737-2Y5 (A)	23040 / 955	5B-DBF	0083	0298	2 PW JT8D-15A (HK3/NOR)	56472	Y122		
☐ N4361R	Boeing 737-236 (A)	21800 / 661	G-BGDK	0080	1098	2 PW JT8D-15A (HK3/NOR)	52752	Y122		lsf BOUL / to be re-reg. N923WA
☐ N920WA	Boeing 737-236 (A)	21791 / 626	G-BGDB	0079	0398	2 PW JT8D-15A (HK3/NOR)	52752	Y122		lsf BOUL
☐ N921WA	Boeing 737-2Y5 (A)	23039 / 954	ZK-NAH	0083	0798	2 PW JT8D-15A (HK3/NOR)	56472	Y122		lsf INGO
☐ N930WA	Boeing 737-3U3	28732 / 2966	N1792B*	1297	1198	2 CFMI CFM56-3C1	63276	Y136		lsf ANZ
☐ N931WA	Boeing 737-3U3	28733 / 2969	N6066Z*	1297	0299	2 CFMI CFM56-3C1	63276	Y136		lsf ANZ
☐ TC-AFA	Boeing 737-4Q8	26306 / 2653		0094	1198	2 CFMI CFM56-3C1	68040	Y170	DG-HQ	lsf PGT in winter
☐ TC-AFM	Boeing 737-4Q8	26279 / 2221		0092	1198	2 CFMI CFM56-3C1	68040	Y170	BP-ER	lsf PGT in winter
☐ TC-APP	Boeing 737-4Q8	28202 / 3009		0098	1198	2 CFMI CFM56-3C1	68040	Y170	GS-DJ	lsf PGT in winter

WINCO, Inc. **Molalla-Heliport, OR**

32299 South Goodtime Road, Molalla, OR 97038, USA ☎ (541) 829-4354 Tx: none Fax: (541) 829-8579 SITA: n/a
F: 1992 ☗☗☗ n/a Head: Gordon Winfree Net: n/a

☐ N11054	MD Helicopters MD 500D (Hughes 369D)	310910D		0081	0492	1 AN 250-C20B	1361			

466 registration type of aircraft cn/fn ex/ex* mfd del powered by mtow kg configuration selcal name/fln/specialitites/remarks

☐ N520WH	MD Helicopters MD 500E (Hughes 369E)	0288E	N381F	0088	1195	1 AN 250-C20R	1361			

WINDHAM AVIATION, Inc. — Willimantic-Windham, CT

PO Box 136, Willimantic, CT 06226, USA ☎ (860) 456-4156 Tx: none Fax: (860) 456-2540 SITA: n/a
F: 1975 ⁂ n/a Head: Norvald Oygard Net: n/a Aircraft below MTOW 1361kg: Piper PA-28

☐ N2930Y	Piper PA-34-200 Seneca	34-7450099		0074	1091	2 LY IO-360-C1E6	1905			
☐ N23605	Beech King Air A100	B-236		0077	0794	2 PWC PT6A-28	5216			
☐ N424SW	Beech King Air 100	B-80	N99KA	0071	0895	2 PWC PT6A-28	4808			
☐ N44882	Beech King Air F90	LA-102	YV-399CP	0081	1288	2 PWC PT6A-135	4967			lsf Spirol International Corp.
☐ N842DS	Beech King Air A100	B-244	N942DS	0077	0896	2 PWC PT6A-28	5216			
☐ N999BT	Beech King Air 200	BB-400	N164AB	0078	1196	2 PWC PT6A-41	5670			lsf Sanford Farms Inc.

WINDWARD AVIATION, Inc. — Kahului, HI

333 Dairy Road, Suite 103, Kahului, HI 96732, USA ☎ (808) 877-3368 Tx: none Fax: (808) 877-0532 SITA: n/a
F: 1991 ⁂ n/a Head: Donald R. Shearer Net: n/a

☐ N114HD	MD Helicopters MD 500D (Hughes 369D)	280261D	C-GKNP	0078	0994	1 AN 250-C20B	1361			

WINGS (Robert C. Gretzke dba) — Anchorage-Merrill Field, AK

PO Box 112221, Anchorage, AK 99515, USA ☎ (907) 345-7121 Tx: none Fax: none SITA: n/a
F: 1993 ⁂ n/a Head: Robert C. Gretzke Net: n/a

☐ N1531F	Cessna 185D Skywagon	185-0874		0065	0793	1 CO IO-470-F	1451			Amphibian

WINGS, Inc. — Springdale-Municipal, AR

214 Center Drive, Lowell, AR 72745, USA ☎ (501) 770-6052 Tx: none Fax: (501) 770-0733 SITA: n/a
F: 1996 ⁂ n/a Head: Rhonda M. Schossow Net: n/a

☐ N585B	Piper PA-23-250 Aztec E	27-4819		0072	0996	2 LY IO-540-C4B5	2359			

WINGS OF ALASKA = K5 / WAK (Alaska Juneau Aeronautics, Inc. dba) — Juneau-Int'l, AK

8421 Livingston Way, Juneau, AK 99801, USA ☎ (907) 789-9863 Tx: none Fax: (907) 789-3130 SITA: n/a
F: 1982 ⁂ 80 Head: Robert N. Jacobsen ICAO: WINGS ALASKA Net: http://www.alaskaone.com/wingsofak/

☐ N43AK	Cessna U206G Stationair 6 II	U20605545	N4811X	0080	1188	1 CO IO-520-F	1633	4 Pax		Amphibian
☐ N51AK	Cessna U206G Stationair	U20603785	N8273G	0077	1087	1 CO IO-520-F	1633	5 Pax		lsf pvt / Floats
☐ N53AK	Cessna U206G Stationair 6 II	U20604823	N734CX	0078	1288	1 CO IO-520-F	1633	5 Pax		Floats
☐ N56AK	Cessna U206G Stationair 6 II	U20605353	N6156U	0079	0787	1 CO IO-520-F	1633	5 Pax		Floats
☐ N39AK	Cessna 207A Stationair 8 II	20700597	N73482	0080	0683	1 CO IO-520-F	1724	6 Pax		
☐ N62AK	Cessna 207A Stationair 8 II	20700780	N9997M	0084	0889	1 CO IO-520-F	1724	6 Pax		
☐ N450DB	De Havilland DHC-2 Beaver I	1309	C-GWPF	0059	0394	1 PW R-985	2313	6 Pax		lsf Wings Air Group Inc. / Floats
☐ N47AK	De Havilland DHC-2 Beaver I	726	N43447	0053	0784	1 PW R-985	2313	6 Pax		lsf pvt / Amphibian
☐ N90AK	De Havilland DHC-2 Beaver I	438	N5158G	0052	0189	1 PW R-985	2313	6 Pax		Floats
☐ N91AK	De Havilland DHC-2 Beaver I	737	C-GAEU	0053	0689	1 PW R-985	2313	6 Pax		Floats
☐ N92AK	De Havilland DHC-2 Beaver I	1031	C-GFNR	0056	0689	1 PW R-985	2313	6 Pax		lsf pvt / Floats
☐ N93AK	De Havilland DHC-2 Beaver I	809	N64395	0054	0189	1 PW R-985	2313	6 Pax		Floats
☐ N28TH	De Havilland DHC-3 Otter	454	C-FDIY	0066	0393	1 PW R-1340	3629	10 Pax		Floats
☐ N335AK	De Havilland DHC-3 Otter	263	C-FOMS	0058	0498	1 PW R-1340	3629	10 Pax		lsf Wings Airline Services Inc./Floats
☐ N336AK	De Havilland DHC-3 Otter	333	N567KA	0059	0393	1 PW R-1340	3629	10 Pax		Floats
☐ N337AK	De Havilland DHC-3 Otter	418	N2783J	0061	0393	1 PW R-1340	3629	10 Pax		lsf Wings Airline Services Inc./Floats
☐ N338AK	De Havilland DHC-3 Otter	262	N62355	0058	0393	1 PW R-1340	3629	10 Pax		lsf Wings Airline Services Inc./Floats
☐ N330AK	Cessna 208B Grand Caravan	208B0569		0096	1296	1 PWC PT6A-114A	3969	9 Pax		lsf First Security Bank NA Owner

WINGS = WAW (Pennsylvania Aviation, Inc. dba) — Blue Bell-Wings Field, PA

Wings Field, Blue Bell, PA 19422, USA ☎ (215) 646-1800 Tx: none Fax: (215) 628-3594 SITA: n/a
F: 1976 ⁂ n/a Head: James J. Vincenzo ICAO: WING SHUTTLE Net: n/a

☐ N521WA	Piper PA-31-350 Navajo Chieftain	31-7752103	N27200	0077	0990	2 LY TIO-540-J2BD	3175			
☐ N771HM	Beech King Air B200	BB-1078		0082	0982	2 PWC PT6A-42	5670			lsf HHMC Inc.

WITHROTOR AVIATION — Lakeview-Lake County, OR

PO Box 653, Lakeview, OR 97630, USA ☎ (541) 947-5265 Tx: none Fax: (541) 947-3321 SITA: n/a
F: 1997 ⁂ n/a Head: Kyle Witham Net: n/a

☐ N453CC	Bell UH-1E (204)	6208	155352	0068	0597	1 LY T53-L-11	3856			lsf Billings Flying Service

WOODLAND AVIATION, Inc. — Woodland-Watts & Davis Woodland Winters-Yolo County, CA

PO Box 1157, Woodland, CA 95776, USA ☎ (530) 669-3129 Tx: none Fax: (530) 662-3055 SITA: n/a
F: 1952 ⁂ n/a Head: Milton B. Watts Net: http://www.woodlandaviation.com

☐ N67933	Beech Bonanza A36	E-2137		0084	0384	1 CO IO-520-BB	1633			
☐ N7208V	Beech Baron 58	TH-1432		0084	0389	2 CO IO-520-C	2449			lsf Luhdorff & Scalmanini Consulting
☐ N931R	Beech Baron 58	TH-1616		0090	0896	2 CO IO-520-CB	2449			
☐ N703JT	Beech King Air F90	LA-39	YV-342CP	0080	0497	2 PWC PT6A-135	4967			lsf Cessna Finance Corp.
☐ N399BM	Beech King Air 200	BB-399	F-GIRM	0078	0697	2 PWC PT6A-41	5670			lsf Robert B. Currey & Associates
☐ N1556S	Beech Starship 2000	NC-6		0090	0995	2 PWC PT6A-67A	6627			lsf Raytheon Aircraft Credit Corp.

WOODS AIR FUEL, Inc. (Affiliated with Woods Air Service, Inc.) — Palmer-Municipal, AK

PO Box 840, Palmer, AK 99645, USA ☎ (907) 745-4831 Tx: none Fax: (907) 745-6063 SITA: n/a
F: 1962 ⁂ n/a Head: Warren G. Woods, Jr. Net: n/a

☐ N400UA	Boeing (Douglas) DC-6A	44258 / 467	YV-296C	0054	0698	4 PW R-2800	47083	Fuel Tanker/Frtr		Miss Karon

WOODS AIR SERVICE, Inc. (Affiliated with Woods Air Fuel, Inc.) — Palmer-Municipal, AK

PO Box 840, Palmer, AK 99645, USA ☎ (907) 745-4831 Tx: none Fax: (907) 745-6063 SITA: n/a
F: 1962 ⁂ n/a Head: Warren G. Woods, Jr. Net: n/a

☐ N4130R	Piper PA-32-300 Cherokee SIX	32-40448		0068	1195	1 LY IO-540-K1A5	1542			
☐ N29245	Cessna U206C Super Skywagon	U206-1190		0068	1289	1 CO IO-520-F	1633			
☐ N9119M	Cessna U206E Super Skywagon	U20601519		0070	0291	1 CO IO-520-F	1633			
☐ N41755	De Havilland DHC-3 Otter	339	58-1720	0059	0478	1 PW R-1340	3629			Wheel-Skis
☐ N50CM	Boeing (Douglas) DC-3C (C-47A-25-DK)	13445	N462T	0044	1289	2 PW R-1830	12202	Freighter		
☐ N777YA	Boeing (Douglas) DC-3C (C-47B-1-DK)	25634	N777PG	0044	0191	2 PW R-1830	12202	Freighter		

WOODSTONE Corporation — Loma-Private Heliport, CO

1271-0, 1/2 Road, Loma, CO 81524, USA ☎ (970) 858-9009 Tx: none Fax: (970) 858-8978 SITA: n/a
F: 1996 ⁂ n/a Head: Benny Hastings Net: n/a

☐ N3276M	Bell UH-1H (205)	9732	67-17534	0067	0996	1 LY T53-L-13	4309			

WOODY HELICOPTERS (Woody Contracting, Inc. dba) — La Grande-Union County, OR

63210 McKenzie Lane, Summerville, OR 97876, USA ☎ (541) 534-4741 Tx: none Fax: (541) 534-4650 SITA: n/a
F: 1992 ⁂ n/a Head: Tom Woody Net: n/a

☐ N134KA	Kaman K-1200 K-Max	A94-0006		0094	0896	1 LY T5317A-1	2722			

WORLD AIRWAYS, Inc. = WO / WOA (Subsidiary of WorldCorp. / Associated with Malaysian Helicopter Services Berhad) — Charleston-Int'l, SC

13873 Park Center Road, Suite 490, Herndon, VA 20171, USA ☎ (703) 834-9200 Tx: n/a Fax: (703) 834-9412 SITA: n/a
F: 1948 ⁂ 800 Head: Russell L. Ray IATA: 468 ICAO: WORLD Net: http://www.worldair.com

☐ N107WA	Boeing (Douglas) DC-10-30F (CF)	46836 / 280		0079	0579	3 GE CF6-50C2	259455	Freighter	JM-GK	lsf DPF Airlease Inc.
☐ N117WA	Boeing (Douglas) DC-10-30	48318 / 446	N3024W	0088	0495	3 GE CF6-50C2	259455	Y380	CM-BD	lsf Star & Sun Leasing Inc.
☐ 9M-MAW	Boeing (Douglas) DC-10-30	46959 / 234	OY-KDC	0077	0695	3 GE CF6-50C2	259455	Y380	AC-DG	lsf MAS
☐ 9M-MAZ	Boeing (Douglas) DC-10-30	46933 / 159	N109WA	0074	1295	3 GE CF6-50C2	256280	Y380	EG-AC	lsf MAS
☐ N271WA	Boeing (Douglas) MD-11	48518 / 525		0093	0393	3 PW PW4460	280320	Y409	GH-AR	lsf ILFC
☐ N272WA	Boeing (Douglas) MD-11	48437 / 506		0093	0493	3 PW PW4460	280320	Y409	GH-AS	lsf ILFC/to be sub-lst/opf EIN 05-1099
☐ N273WA	Boeing (Douglas) MD-11	48519 / 539		0093	0493	3 PW PW4460	280320	Y409	GH-BR	lsf ILFC
☐ N274WA	Boeing (Douglas) MD-11F	48633 / 563		0094	0394	3 PW PW4460	280320	Freighter	GH-DR	lsf ILFC / opf EWW
☐ N275WA	Boeing (Douglas) MD-11F (CF)	48631 / 579		0095	0395	3 PW PW4462	280320	Freighter	GH-CR	lsf ILFC/sub-lst/opf MAS in MASkargo-cs
☐ N276WA	Boeing (Douglas) MD-11F (CF)	48632 / 582		0095	0395	3 PW PW4462	280320	Freighter	GH-CS	lsf ILFC / sub-lst / opf STU in STAF-cs
☐ N277WA	Boeing (Douglas) MD-11	48743 / 590	N6203D*	0095	0396	3 PW PW4462	285990	Y409	JM-FL	lsf MDFC-Knoxville Co.
☐ N278WA	Boeing (Douglas) MD-11	48746 / 597	N9020Q*	0096	0396	3 PW PW4462	285990	Y409	JM-GH	lsf MDFC-Memphis Co.

WORLDWIND HELICOPTERS, Inc. — Seattle-Boeing Field/King County Int'l, WA

8535 Perimeter Road South, Box 11, Seattle, WA 98108, USA ☎ (206) 763-1120 Tx: none Fax: (206) 763-1192 SITA: n/a
F: 1995 ⁂ n/a Head: George R. Dillon Net: n/a

☐ N4MS	Bell 206B JetRanger III	1345	N101DQ	0074	0595	1 AN 250-C20B	1451			cvtd JetRanger

WRANGELL MOUNTAIN AIR, Inc. — McCarthy, AK

PO Box MXY 25, Glennallen, AK 99588, USA ☎ (907) 554-4411 Tx: none Fax: (907) 554-4400 SITA: n/a
F: 1988 ⁂ 10 Head: Kelly M. Bay Net: http://www.wrangellmountainair.com Aircraft below MTOW 1361kg: Cessna 172 & Piper PA-18

☐ N8209U	Cessna 185 Skywagon	185-0213		0061	0191	1 CO IO-520-D	1451			
☐ N61273	Cessna U206F Stationair	U20602067		0073	0995	1 CO IO-520-F	1633			
☐ N6369Z	Cessna U206G Stationair 6 II	U20606254		0081	0197	1 CO IO-520-F	1633			

467 registration type of aircraft cn/fn ex/ex* mfd del powered by mtow kg configuration selcal name/fln/specialitites/remarks

WRIGHT AIR SERVICE, Inc. = 8V
Fairbanks-Int'l, AK **WRIGHT AIR SERVICE**

PO Box 60142, Fairbanks, AK 99706, USA ☎ (907) 474-0502 Tx: none Fax: (907) 474-0375 SITA: n/a
F: 1967 ⁂ 17 Head: Robert P. Bursiel Net: n/a

registration	type of aircraft	cn/fn	ex/ex*	mfd	del	powered by	mtow kg	configuration	name/fln/specialitites/remarks
☐ N27532	Cessna A185F Skywagon II	18503688		0078	1282	1 CO IO-520-D	1520		lsf pvt / Floats / Wheel-Skis
☐ N42DC	Helio H-295 Super Courier	1454		0073	1190	1 LY GO-480-G1A6	1542		Wheel-Skis
☐ N6465V	Helio H-295 Super Courier	1417		0069	0984	1 LY GO-480-G1A6	1542		Wheel-Skis
☐ N4637U	Cessna U206G Stationair 6 II	U20605017		0079	0181	1 CO IO-520-F	1633		lsf pvt
☐ N2043X	Beech Bonanza A36	E-1387		0078	0383	1 CO IO-520-B	1633		lsf pvt
☐ N73463	Cessna 207A Stationair 8 II	20700593		0080	0281	1 CO IO-520-F	1724		
☐ N91027	Cessna 207 Skywagon	20700018		0069	0679	1 CO IO-520-F	1724		
☐ N54WA	Piper PA-31-350 Navajo Chieftain	31-7652067	N942LU	0076	0577	2 LY TIO-540-J2BD	3175		
☐ N63MB	Piper PA-31-350 Navajo Chieftain	31-7852117		0078	0693	2 LY TIO-540-J2BD	3175		lsf pvt
☐ N7426L	Piper PA-31-310 Navajo B	31-812		0072	0689	2 LY TIO-540-A2C	2948		
☐ N9FW	Piper PA-31-350 Navajo Chieftain	31-7405468		0074	0388	2 LY TIO-540-J2BD	3175		
☐ N32WA	Cessna 208B Grand Caravan	208B0234	C-FKEL	0090	0591	1 PWC PT6A-114A	3969		
☐ N4365U	Cessna 208B Grand Caravan	208B0253		0091	0592	1 PWC PT6A-114A	3969		
☐ N900WA	Cessna 208B Grand Caravan	208B0659		0098	0698	1 PWC PT6A-114A	3969		

WSG EXECUTIVE AIR SERVICE (Airstat) (WSG, Inc. dba / Sister company of Airstat, Inc.)
Chicago-Midway, IL

211 East Ontario, Suite 1110, Chicago, IL 60611, USA ☎ (773) 582-0860 Tx: none Fax: (773) 582-0806 SITA: n/a
F: 1994 ⁂ n/a Head: James A. Mecha Net: n/a Organ-transport flights are carried out under the name of AIRSTAT.

registration	type of aircraft	cn/fn	ex/ex*	mfd	del	powered by	mtow kg	configuration	name/fln/specialitites/remarks
☐ N37BW	Twin (Aero) Turbo Commander 690A	11129	N57129	0073	0994	2 GA TPE331-5-251K	4679		to be re-registered N500AL
☐ N395DA	Beech King Air B90	LJ-495	N803SM	0070	1095	2 PWC PT6A-20	4377		lsf Aerolease Inc./to be re-reg. N600AL
☐ N700AL	Dassault Falcon 10	55	N702NG	0075	1195	2 GA TFE731-2-1C	8755		lsf Aerolease Inc.

XEROX – Flight Department = XER (Flight Department of Xerox Corporation)
White Plains-Westchester County, NY

Hangar G, Westchester County Airport, White Plains, NY 10604, USA ☎ (914) 397-1300 Tx: none Fax: (914) 397-1316 SITA: n/a
F: 1965 ⁂ n/a Head: Kraig H. Kenney ICAO: XEROX Net: n/a

registration	type of aircraft	cn/fn	ex/ex*	mfd	del	powered by	mtow kg	configuration	name/fln/specialitites/remarks
☐ N914X	Canadair CL-601-3R (CL-600-2B16) Challen.	5185	N611CC	0095	0196	2 GE CF34-3A1	20457	Corporate	
☐ N9700X	Canadair CL-601-3R (CL-600-2B16) Challen.	5186	N612CC	0095	0196	2 GE CF34-3A1	20457	Corporate	
☐ N5100X	Canadair Regional Jet 100ER (CL-600-2B19)	7008	C-FMKV*	0092	0193	2 GE CF34-3A1	23133	Corporate	

XL HELICOPTERS, Inc.
Denver-Centennial, CO

PO Box 3229, Boulder, CO 80307, USA ☎ (303) 662-1741 Tx: none Fax: (303) 662-0141 SITA: n/a
F: 1998 ⁂ n/a Head: Eric R. Darsonval Net: http://www.xlhelicopters.com Aircraft below MTOW 1361kg: Robinson R22

registration	type of aircraft	cn/fn	ex/ex*	mfd	del	powered by	mtow kg	configuration	name/fln/specialitites/remarks
☐ N504	Sikorsky S-58E	58-895	N33504	0058	0698	1 WR R-1820	5897		cvtd H-34A
☐ N214NS	Bell 214B-1 BigLifter	28055	N314CR	0080	0098	1 LY T5508D	5670		lsf pvt

XPRESS AIR, Inc.
Chattanooga-Lovell Field, TN

2931 South Market Street, Chattanooga, TN 37410, USA ☎ (423) 510-3208 Tx: none Fax: (423) 265-5715 SITA: n/a
F: 1993 ⁂ n/a Head: Max L. Fuller Net: n/a

registration	type of aircraft	cn/fn	ex/ex*	mfd	del	powered by	mtow kg	configuration	name/fln/specialitites/remarks
☐ N32SJ	Fairchild (Swear.) SA227TT Merlin IIIC	TT-453	N453SA	0082	1093	2 GA TPE331-10U-503G	5670		

YINGLING AIRCRAFT, Inc.
Wichita-Mid Continent, KS **Yingling Aircraft**

PO Box 9248, Wichita, KS 67277-0248, USA ☎ (316) 943-3246 Tx: none Fax: (316) 943-2484 SITA: n/a
F: 1946 ⁂ 65 Head: Jack Feiden Net: http://www.yinglingaircraft.com

registration	type of aircraft	cn/fn	ex/ex*	mfd	del	powered by	mtow kg	configuration	name/fln/specialitites/remarks
☐ N4203A	Beech Baron 58	TH-22		0070	1289	2 CO IO-520-C	2404		
☐ N12436	Cessna 414A Chancellor III	414A1004		0084	1184	2 CO TSIO-520-NB	3062		lsf pvt
☐ N628JW	Cessna 414A Chancellor III	414A0241		0079	0986	2 CO TSIO-520-NB	3062		lsf Bulldog Inc.

YOUNKIN AIR SERVICE, Inc.
Springdale-Municipal, AR

PO Box 1785, Springdale, AR 72765-1785, USA ☎ (501) 751-0030 Tx: none Fax: (501) 751-0030 SITA: n/a
F: 1987 ⁂ n/a Head: Robert A. Younkin Net: n/a

registration	type of aircraft	cn/fn	ex/ex*	mfd	del	powered by	mtow kg	configuration	name/fln/specialitites/remarks
☐ N8191Y	Piper PA-30-160 Twin Comanche B	30-1308		0066	0995	2 LY IO-320-B1A	1633		
☐ N18RY	Beech E18S	BA-325	N26BB	0057	0393	2 PW R-985-AN14B	4218	Freighter	
☐ N911E	Beech E18S	BA-10		0054	0997	2 PW R-985-AN14B	4218	Freighter	

YUKON AIR SERVICE, Inc. (Seasonal April-October ops only)
Fort Yukon, AK

PO Box 90, Fort Yukon, AK 99740, USA ☎ (907) 662-2445 Tx: none Fax: (907) 662-2445 SITA: n/a
F: 1986 ⁂ 2 Head: Donald E. Ross Net: n/a Winter address: 2532 Roland Road, Fairbanks, AK 99701. Phone (907) 479-3792, Fax (907) 479-3792.

registration	type of aircraft	cn/fn	ex/ex*	mfd	del	powered by	mtow kg	configuration	name/fln/specialitites/remarks
☐ N4443R	Cessna A185F Skywagon	18502957		0076	0195	1 CO IO-520-D	1520		

YUKON AVIATION (Yukon Helicopters, Inc. dba)
Bethel, AK

PO Box 976, Bethel, AK 99559, USA ☎ (907) 543-3280 Tx: n/a Fax: (907) 543-3244 SITA: n/a
F: 1986 ⁂ 4 Head: Thomas D. Ratledge Net: n/a Aircraft below MTOW 1361kg: Cessna 172

registration	type of aircraft	cn/fn	ex/ex*	mfd	del	powered by	mtow kg	configuration	name/fln/specialitites/remarks
☐ N150HH	Bell 206B JetRanger III	701		0071	0187	1 AN 250-C20B	1451		lsf pvt / cvtd 206A
☐ N1322F	Cessna A185F Skywagon	18502825		0075	1292	1 CO IO-520-D	1520		lsf pvt
☐ N29970	Cessna A185F Skywagon II	18504292		0081	1185	1 CO IO-520-D	1481		lsf pvt
☐ N7318U	Cessna 207A Skywagon	20700396		0077	0192	1 CO IO-520-F	1724		
☐ N24165	Beech Baron 58TC	TK-78		0078	1096	2 CO TSIO-520-LB	2767		
☐ N4237V	Bell 204 (UH-1B)	261	60-3615	0060	0187	1 LY T5311D	3856		lsf pvt

YUTE AIR ALASKA, Inc. = 4Y / UYA
Dillingham, AK **YUTE AIR ALASKA**

4451 Aircraft Drive, Anchorage, AK 99502, USA ☎ (907) 243-1011 Tx: none Fax: (907) 243-2811 SITA: n/a
F: 1963 ⁂ 18 Head: Jeffrey R. Pereira ICAO: YUTE AIR Net: http://www.yuteair.com Aircraft below MTOW 1361kg: Cessna 172 Entered Chapter 11 bankruptcy protection 0199. Operations continue.

registration	type of aircraft	cn/fn	ex/ex*	mfd	del	powered by	mtow kg	configuration	name/fln/specialitites/remarks
☐ N4466T	Piper PA-32-300E Cherokee SIX	32-7240067		0072	0381	1 LY IO-540-K1A5	1542		lsf pvt
☐ N35952	Cessna U206F Stationair II	U20602825		0075	0393	1 CO IO-520-F	1633		
☐ N60491	Cessna U206F Stationair	U20602025		0073	0194	1 CO IO-520-F	1633		
☐ N756ZV	Cessna U206G Stationair 6 II	U20604495		0078	1079	1 CO IO-520-F	1633		lsf pvt
☐ N1549U	Cessna 207 Skywagon	20700149		0070	0785	1 CO IO-520-F	1724		
☐ N1704U	Cessna 207 Skywagon	20700304		0075	1182	1 CO IO-520-F	1724		
☐ N1763U	Cessna 207A Skywagon	20700363		0076	0192	1 CO IO-520-F	1724		
☐ N36CF	Cessna 207 Skywagon	20700269		0074	0791	1 CO IO-520-F	1724		
☐ N54GV	Cessna 207A Stationair 7 II	20700447		0078	1193	1 CO IO-520-F	1724		
☐ N6282H	Cessna 207A Stationair 7 II	20700465		0078	0292	1 CO IO-520-F	1724		
☐ N6470H	Cessna 207A Stationair 7 II	20700534		0079	0785	1 CO IO-520-F	1724		
☐ N73036	Cessna 207A Stationair 7 II	20700555		0079	0991	1 CO IO-520-F	1724		lsf pvt
☐ N7336U	Cessna 207A Skywagon	20700405		0077	0791	1 CO IO-520-F	1724		
☐ N755AB	Cessna 207A Stationair 8 II	20700622		0080	0192	1 CO IO-520-F	1724		
☐ N54272	Piper PA-31-350 Navajo Chieftain	31-7405422		0074	0287	2 LY TIO-540-J2BD	3175		
☐ N59985	Piper PA-31-350 Navajo Chieftain	31-7552077		0075	0988	2 LY TIO-540-J2BD	3175		
☐ N1232Y	Cessna 208B Grand Caravan	208BB0566		0096	1296	1 PWC PT6A-114A	3969		lsf Textron Financial Corp.
☐ N90LN	Cessna 208B Grand Caravan	208B0462		0095	0697	1 PWC PT6A-114A	3969		lsf FSBU Trustee

ZANTOP INTERNATIONAL AIRLINES, Inc. = ZAN
Detroit-Willow Run, MI & Macon, GA **ZANTOP**

840 Willow Run Airport, Ypsilanti, MI 48198-0840, USA ☎ (734) 485-8900 Tx: none Fax: (734) 485-4813 SITA: n/a
F: 1972 ⁂ 200 Head: Duane A. Zantop ICAO: ZANTOP Net: n/a Since 010497, company and its aircraft are offered for sale. Limited operations continue.

registration	type of aircraft	cn/fn	ex/ex*	mfd	del	powered by	mtow kg	configuration	selcal	name/fln/specialitites/remarks
☐ N5509K	Convair 640 (F) (SCD)	66		0053	1273	2 RR Dart 542-4	24948	Freighter		cvtd CV340-36 / std YIP / for sale
☐ N5510K	Convair 640 (F) (SCD)	76		0053	1273	2 RR Dart 542-4	24948	Freighter		cvtd CV340-36 / std YIP / for sale
☐ N5511K	Convair 640 (F) (SCD)	171	VH-BZE	0054	1273	2 RR Dart 542-4	24948	Freighter		cvtd CV340-51A / std YIP / for sale
☐ N5512K	Convair 640 (F) (SCD)	134	PH-CGN	0053	1273	2 RR Dart 542-4	24948	Freighter		cvtd CV340-48 / std YIP / for sale
☐ N5515K	Convair 640 (F) (SCD)	133	PH-CGM	0053	1273	2 RR Dart 542-4	24948	Freighter		cvtd CV340-48 / for sale
☐ N7529U	Convair 640 (F) (SCD)	58	CC-CBI	0053	1273	2 RR Dart 542-4	24948	Freighter		cvtd CV340-36 / std YIP / for sale
☐ N282F	Lockheed L-188A (F) Electra	1084	N5006K	0059	1074	4 AN 501-D13A	51256	Freighter		cvtd L-188A / std YIP / for sale
☐ N284F	Lockheed L-188A (F) Electra	1104	N5011K	0059	0974	4 AN 501-D13A	51256	Freighter		cvtd L-188A / std YIP / for sale
☐ N286F	Lockheed L-188A (F) Electra	1146	N5013K	0060	1074	4 AN 501-D13A	51256	Freighter		cvtd L-188A / std YIP / for sale
☐ N290F	Lockheed L-188C (F) Electra	1133	N863U	0060	0474	4 AN 501-D13A	52617	Freighter		cvtd L-188C / std YIP / for sale
☐ N340HA	Lockheed L-188C (F) Electra	1109	N172PS	0060	0980	4 AN 501-D13A	52617	Freighter		lst TMM / cvtd L-188C
☐ N341HA	Lockheed L-188PF Electra	1035	N415MA	0059	0980	4 AN 501-D13A	52617	Freighter		cvtd L-188A / std YIP / for sale
☐ N343HA	Lockheed L-188A (F) Electra	1053	N429MA	0059	0980	4 AN 501-D13A	51256	Freighter		cvtd L-188A / std YIP / for sale
☐ N344HA	Lockheed L-188A (F) Electra	1038	N5525	0059	0980	4 AN 501-D13A	51256	Freighter		lst TMM / cvtd L-188A
☐ N346HA	Lockheed L-188A (F) Electra	1043	N61AJ	0059	0980	4 AN 501-D13A	51256	Freighter		lst TMM / cvtd L-188A
☐ N5507	Lockheed L-188A (F) Electra	1012		0059	0178	4 AN 501-D13A	51256	Freighter		cvtd L-188A / std YIP / for sale
☐ N5510L	Lockheed L-188A (F) Electra	1014	HK-557	0058	1277	4 AN 501-D13A	51256	Freighter		cvtd L-188A / std YIP / for sale
☐ N5512	Lockheed L-188A (F) Electra	1017		0058	1077	4 AN 501-D13A	51256	Freighter		cvtd L-188A
☐ N5522	Lockheed L-188A (F) Electra	1033		0058	1277	4 AN 501-D13A	51256	Freighter		cvtd L-188A / std YIP / for sale
☐ N8041U	Boeing (Douglas) DC-8-54F (JT)	45675 / 200		0064	0391	4 PW JT3D-3B (HK2/QNC)	142882	Freighter	AC-BM	std MCN / for sale
☐ N8042U	Boeing (Douglas) DC-8-54F (JT)	45676 / 197	N42UA	0064	0391	4 PW JT3D-3B (HK2/QNC)	142882	Freighter	AC-DF	for sale

ZEBRA AIR, Inc.
Dallas-Love Field, TX

PO Box 7005, Dallas, TX 75209, USA ☎ (214) 358-7200 Tx: none Fax: (214) 358-7203 SITA: n/a
F: 1988 ⁂ 5 Head: James C. Rhoades Net: http://www.zebraair.com

registration	type of aircraft	cn/fn	ex/ex*	mfd	del	powered by	mtow kg	configuration	name/fln/specialitites/remarks
☐ N1037	Bell 206B JetRanger III	2717	XA-SNQ	0079	1296	1 AN 250-C20B	1451		
☐ N1080N	Bell 206B JetRanger III	3549	VH-JWD	0081	1295	1 AN 250-C20B	1451		

OB = PERU (Republic of Peru) (Republica de Peru)

Capital: Lima Official Language: Spanish Population: 24,0 million Square Km: 1285216 Dialling code: +51 Year established: 1821 Acting political head: Alberto Fujimori (President)

AERO ANDINO, SA (Affiliated with Aero Servicio Andino, Srl) — Chiclayo

PO Box 382, Chiclayo, Peru ☎ (74) 23 31 61 Tx: none Fax: (74) 24 15 75 SITA: n/a
F: 1990 ⁂ 15 Head: Rudolf & Micaela Wiedler-Eberli Net: http://www.llampayec.rcp.net.pe/aeroandino

registration	type of aircraft	cn/fn	ex/ex*	mfd	del	powered by	mtow kg	configuration	selcal	name/fln/specialitites/remarks
☐ OB-788	Helio H-295 Super Courier	1205		0065		1 LY GO-480-G1D6	1542	6 Pax		
☐ OB-1600	Pilatus PC-6/B2-H2 Turbo Porter	789	HC-BHL	0077	0594	1 PWC PT6A-27	2770	11 Pax		
☐ OB-	Britten-Norman BN-2A-6 Islander	187	C-GKMJ	0070	0198	2 LY O-540-E4C5	2858	9 Pax		being rebuilt 1999
☐ OB-	Britten-Norman BN-2A-20 Islander	404	C-GIRH	0076	0198	2 LY IO-540-K1B5	2994	9 Pax		being rebuilt 1999

AERO CONDOR, S.A. - Servicio de Transporte Aéreo Turistico = P2 / CDP — Lima / Nazca & / Ica

Juan de Arona 781, San Isidro, Lima, Peru ☎ (1) 442 52 15 Tx: 25650 pe pb hsher Fax: (1) 442 94 87 SITA: n/a
F: 1975 ⁂ 100 Head: Carlos Palacin Fernandez IATA: 537 ICAO: CONDOR-PERU Net: n/a Aircraft below MTOW 1361 kg: Cessna 172

registration	type of aircraft	cn/fn	ex/ex*	mfd	del	powered by	mtow kg	configuration	selcal	name/fln/specialitites/remarks
☐ OB-1192	Cessna U206G Stationair 6 II	CU20605538		0080	0885	1 CO IO-520-F	1633	Y5		
☐ OB-1616	Cessna U206B Super Skywagon	U206-0878	N3878G	0067	0495	1 CO IO-520-F	1633	Y5		based Ica
☐ OB-1001	Cessna 207 Skywagon	20700055		0069		1 CO IO-520-F	1724	Y6		
☐ N839MA	Cessna 208 Caravan I	20800198	F-OGPU	0090	0096	1 PWC PT6A-114	3629	Y9		lsf Joda Partnership
☐ N1132D	Cessna 208B Grand Caravan	208B0670		0098	0598	1 PWC PT6A-114A	3969	Y12 / Freighter		lsf Cessna Finance Corp.
☐ N9448B	Cessna 208B Grand Caravan	208B0121		0088	0798	1 PWC PT6A-114A	3969	Y12 / Freighter		lsf Joda Partnership
☐ OB-952	Beech Excalibur Queenaire 8800	LD-348		0067		2 LY IO-720-A1B	3992	Y10		cvtd Queen Air 65-B80
☐ OB-1297	Beech King Air B90 Taurus	LJ-326	N7702	0068	1186	2 PWC PT6A-28	4377	Y11		Fray Gregorio / cvtd King Air
☐ OB-1593	Beech King Air B90 Taurus	LJ-477	N7777	0069	0390	2 PWC PT6A-28	4377	Y11		cvtd King Air B90
☐ OB-1594	Beech King Air B90 Taurus	LJ-322	N45SC	0068	0293	2 PWC PT6A-28	4377	Y11		cvtd King Air B90
☐ OB-1700	Beech Catpass 250	BB-214	N26LE	0077	0098	2 PWC PT6A-41	5670	Y13		cvtd King Air 200
☐ N869MA	Beech Catpass 250	BB-170	C-FIWH	0076	0497	2 PWC PT6A-41	5670	Y13		lsf Joda Partnership/cvtd King Air 200
☐ OB-1709	Let 410UVP	790204	LY-ABO	0079	0098	2 WA M-601D	5800	Y15		
☐ N3107P	Fairchild (Swearingen) SA227AC Metro III	AC-496		0082	0893	2 GA TPE331-11U-611G	6577	Y19		lsf Joda Partnership
☐ N386PH	Fairchild (Swearingen) SA227AC Metro III	AC-597	N3116T	0084	0997	2 GA TPE331-11U-611G	6577	Y19 / Freighter		lsf Joda Partnership/opf LC Busre Cargo
☐ OB-1627	Fokker F27 Friendship 100 (F27 Mk100)	10116	N145PM	0059	0296	2 RR Dart 514-7	18370	Y44		
☐ OB-1693	Fokker F27 Friendship 200 (F27 Mk200)	10181	N863MA	0061	0298	2 RR Dart 532-7R	19731	Y44		lsf Joda Partnership

AERO CONTINENTE, SA = N6 / ACQ — Lima

Av. Pardo 651, Miraflores, Lima 18, Peru ☎ (1) 242 42 60 Tx: none Fax: (1) 444 50 14 SITA: n/a
F: 1992 ⁂ 850 Head: Fernando Zevallos IATA: 929 ICAO: AERO CONTINENTE Net: http://www.aerocontinente.com.pe/

registration	type of aircraft	cn/fn	ex/ex*	mfd	del	powered by	mtow kg	configuration	selcal	name/fln/specialitites/remarks
☐ OB-1589	Fairchild Ind. F-27J	68	N276BT	1259	1294	2 RR Dart 532-7	19051	Y44		cvtd F-27A
☐ OB-1591	Fairchild Ind. F-27J	69	N43675	1259	1094	2 RR Dart 532-7	19051	Y44		cvtd F-27 / std LIM
☐ OB-1636	Fokker F28 Fellowship 1000 (F28 Mk1000)	11009	N37RT	0069	0296	2 RR Spey 555-15	28580	Y65		lsf Int'l Airline Investors Ltd
☐ P4-ASA	Boeing 737-130	19014 / 3	XA-LBM	0068	0796	2 PW JT8D-7B	44180	Y106		lsf Air Sweden AVV
☐ P4-ASB	Boeing 737-130	19017 / 7	XA-GBM	0269	0996	2 PW JT8D-7B	43999	Y109		lsf Air Sweden AVV
☐ OB-1493	Boeing 737-204	19712 / 162	N199AW	0469	0492	2 PW JT8D-9A	53070	Y122		lsf Int'l Pacific Trading
☐ OB-1620	Boeing 737-247	19615 / 125	N4518W	0169	0995	2 PW JT8D-9A	49442	Y116		lsf Int'l Airline Inv./dmgd/std Piura
☐ P4-ARA	Boeing 737-281	20277 / 235	OB-1511	0070	0992	2 PW JT8D-9A	49442	Y125		lsf Int'l Pacific Trading
☐ P4-ARB	Boeing 737-247	19616 / 126	OB-1619	0169	0795	2 PW JT8D-9A / -15	49442	Y121		lsf Int'l Airline Investors Ltd
☐ P4-CAD	Boeing 737-201	19422 / 61	N206AU	0868	0998	2 PW JT8D-9A	49442	Y125		lsf Skyways Aviation, Aruba
☐ P4-SYX	Boeing 737-222	19059 / 50	XA-SYX	0768	0494	2 PW JT8D-7B	49442	Y122		lsf Int'l Pacific Trading
☐ OB-1570	Boeing 727-22	19153 / 508	N286AT	0067	1194	3 PW JT8D-7B / -9A	72802	Y129	JM-BG	lsf Int'l Airline Investors Ltd
☐ OB-1588	Boeing 727-51	18942 / 198	N289AT	0065	1194	3 PW JT8D-7B / -9A	72802	Y129	BH-CL	lsf Int'l Airline Investors Ltd
☐ OB-1601	Boeing 727-51	18943 / 203	N288AT	0065	1194	3 PW JT8D-7B	72802	Y129	BH-CM	lsf Int'l Airline Investors Ltd
☐ P4-BAA	Boeing 727-23	18433 / 44	ZS-IJG	0564	0598	3 PW JT8D-7B	72847	F10Y108		lsf CSAV
☐ P4-BAC	Boeing 727-23	18432 / 43	N1976	0564	0598	3 PW JT8D-7B	72847	F10Y108		lsf CSAV
☐ P4-JAA	Lockheed L-1011-385-1 TriStar 1	193B-1013	SE-DSE	0072		3 RR RB211-22B	195050	Y341		to be lsf Jet Aircraft Leasing AVV 0599
☐ P4-JAB	Lockheed L-1011-385-1-15 TriStar 100	193B-1215	N204RC	0081		3 RR RB211-22B	211380	Y341		to be lsf Jet Aircraft Leasing AVV 0599

AERO ICA, S.C.R.L. — Nazca, Ica & Lima

Tudela y Varela 150, Lima 27, Peru ☎ (1) 421 03 35 Tx: none Fax: (1) 440 10 30 SITA: n/a
F: 1978 ⁂ 26 Head: Franklin Horler Net: n/a Aircraft below MTOW 1361kg: Cessna 170 & 182

registration	type of aircraft	cn/fn	ex/ex*	mfd	del	powered by	mtow kg	configuration	selcal	name/fln/specialitites/remarks
☐ OB-1329	Beech Baron B55 (95-B55)	TC-1084	N8263N	0068	1188	2 CO IO-470-L	2313			
☐ OB-1343	Cessna 421A	421A0090	N238BH	0069	1289	2 CO GTSIO-520-D	3103			

AERO MONTECARLO (Affiliated with Hosteria Montecarlo) — Nazca

Las Camelias 511, Of. 401, Lima 27, Peru ☎ (34) 52 25 77 Tx: n/a Fax: (34) 52 25 52 SITA: n/a
F: n/a ⁂ n/a Head: Luis Guillermo Elias A. Net: n/a

registration	type of aircraft	cn/fn	ex/ex*	mfd	del	powered by	mtow kg	configuration	selcal	name/fln/specialitites/remarks
☐ OB-1187	Cessna U206G Stationair 6 II	U20605560	OB-Z-1187	0080		1 CO IO-520-F	1633	5 Pax		

AERO NASCA, Srl. — Nazca

Ignacio Morsesky 120, Nazca, Peru ☎ (34) 52 22 97 Tx: n/a Fax: (34) 52 20 85 SITA: n/a
F: n/a ⁂ n/a Head: Aurelio Perla Net: n/a

registration	type of aircraft	cn/fn	ex/ex*	mfd	del	powered by	mtow kg	configuration	selcal	name/fln/specialitites/remarks
☐ OB-1302	Cessna U206E Stationair	U20601621		0071	0695	1 CO IO-520-F	1633	5 Pax		

AEROPERU = PL / PLI (Member of Aeroméxico Group / Empresa de Transporte Aéreo del Peru dba) — Lima

Av. José Pardo 601, Miraflores, Lima 18, Peru ☎ (1) 241 17 97 Tx: 21382 pe aeroperu Fax: (1) 444 39 74 SITA: n/a
F: 1973 ⁂ n/a Head: Roberto Abusada IATA: 210 ICAO: AEROPERU Net: n/a
Suspended all flights 110399 for an initial period of 2 months while debt renegotiations take place. Most aircraft (Boeing 727/737/757) returned to lessors.

registration	type of aircraft	cn/fn	ex/ex*	mfd	del	powered by	mtow kg	configuration	selcal	name/fln/specialitites/remarks
☐ OB-1546	Boeing 727-22	19150 / 485	N283AT	1267	0893	3 PW JT8D-7B	72802	C12Y107	HM-BD	Intihuatana / std LIM

AEROTAXI LORETO, S.A. — Iquitos

Jr. Progreso 1038, Iquitos, (Dep. Loreto), Peru ☎ (94) 23 23 24 Tx: none Fax: (94) 24 22 38 SITA: n/a
F: 1984 ⁂ 6 Head: Magno Reategui Alencar Net: n/a

registration	type of aircraft	cn/fn	ex/ex*	mfd	del	powered by	mtow kg	configuration	selcal	name/fln/specialitites/remarks
☐ OB-1293	Cessna U206F Stationair II Rob. STOL	U20603072	N7092Q	0076		1 CO IO-520-F	1633	5 Pax		Santa Rosa / Floats

AERO TAXIS Carlos Palacin (Subsidiary of Aero Condor, SA) — Lima

Juan de Arona 781, San Isidro, Lima, Peru ☎ (1) 442 52 15 Tx: 25650 pe pb hsher Fax: (1) 442 94 87 SITA: n/a
F: 1973 ⁂ 10 Head: Carlos Palacin Fernandez Net: n/a Aircraft below MTOW 1361kg: Piper PA-25

registration	type of aircraft	cn/fn	ex/ex*	mfd	del	powered by	mtow kg	configuration	selcal	name/fln/specialitites/remarks
☐ OB-517	Beech Travel Air B95	TD-259		0059		2 LY O-360-A1A	1860			Espiritu de San Martin
☐ OB-1327	Beech Baron B55 (95-B55)	TC-1611	N25711	0074	0889	2 CO IO-470-L	2313			

AERO TAXI SEMINARIO (Rafael Seminario R. dba) — Piura

Libertad 624, Piura, Peru ☎ (74) 32 47 02 Tx: n/a Fax: none SITA: n/a
F: 1986 ⁂ n/a Head: Rafael Seminario R. Net: n/a

registration	type of aircraft	cn/fn	ex/ex*	mfd	del	powered by	mtow kg	configuration	selcal	name/fln/specialitites/remarks
☐ OB-845	Piper PA-30-160 Twin Comanche B	30-1199		0066		2 LY IO-320-B1A	1633			

AERO TRANSPORTE, S.A. - ATSA = AMP (formerly Asesoramientos Tecnicos, SA) — Lima

PO Box 3592, Lima 100, Peru ☎ (1) 575 17 02 Tx: none Fax: (1) 575 36 41 SITA: n/a
F: 1980 ⁂ 21 Head: Dionisio Romero Seminario ICAO: ATSA Net: n/a

registration	type of aircraft	cn/fn	ex/ex*	mfd	del	powered by	mtow kg	configuration	selcal	name/fln/specialitites/remarks
☐ OB-1629	Piper PA-42 Cheyenne III	42-8001067	N183CC	0082	0893	2 PWC PT6A-41	5080	9 Pax		
☐ OB-1630	Piper PA-42 Cheyenne III	42-8001022	N145CA	0081	1092	2 PWC PT6A-41	5080	9 Pax		
☐ OB-1633	Piper PA-42 Cheyenne III	42-7801003	N134KM	0078	1095	2 PWC PT6A-41	5080	9 Pax		
☐ OB-1687	Piper PA-42 Cheyenne III	42-8001016	N69PC	0081	0897	2 PWC PT6A-41	5080	9 Pax		
☐ OB-1667	Beech 1900C Airliner	UB-54	N815BE	0086	1296	2 PWC PT6A-65B	7530	19 Pax		
☐ OB-1694	Beech 1900C Airliner	UB-41	N806BE	0085	0198	2 PWC PT6A-65B	7530	19 Pax		
☐ OB-1703	IAI 1125 Astra	004	N425TS	0086	0998	2 GA TFE731-3A-200G	10659	8 Pax		

AIR ATLANTIC, Srl — Pucallpa

Durero 499, Lima 41, Peru ☎ (1) 455 21 59 Tx: none Fax: (1) 451 91 30 SITA: n/a
F: n/a ⁂ n/a Head: Sergio Beltran R. Net: n/a

registration	type of aircraft	cn/fn	ex/ex*	mfd	del	powered by	mtow kg	configuration	selcal	name/fln/specialitites/remarks
☐ OB-1567	Beech King Air A90 (65-A90)	LJ-228	N946K	0067	1292	2 PWC PT6A-20	4218			

ALAS DEL ORIENTE, SA - OSA — Pucallpa

Andalucia 899-404, Lima 21, Peru ☎ (1) 463 39 49 Tx: none Fax: (1) 463 39 49 SITA: n/a
F: 1984 ⁂ 7 Head: Hilter Gonzales Reategui Net: n/a

registration	type of aircraft	cn/fn	ex/ex*	mfd	del	powered by	mtow kg	configuration	selcal	name/fln/specialitites/remarks
☐ OB-1345	Boeing (Douglas) DC-3A (C-53D-DO)	11771	FAP 315	0043	0089	2 PW R-1830	12202	21 Pax		

AMAZON HELICOPTEROS, S.A. — Iquitos

Av. Santa Cruz 1012, Of. 302, Lima 18, Peru ☎ (1) 442 67 60 Tx: none Fax: (1) 440 58 12 SITA: n/a
F: 1984 ⁂ n/a Head: Miguel A. Revoredo Net: n/a

registration	type of aircraft	cn/fn	ex/ex*	mfd	del	powered by	mtow kg	configuration	selcal	name/fln/specialitites/remarks
☐ OB-1645	Mil Mi-8T	8115		0080		2 IS TV2-117A	12000	Utility		

AQP – Servicios Aéreos AQP, SA

Lima

Los Castanos 462, Lima 27, Peru ☎ (1) 264 24 60 Tx: none Fax: (4) 264 18 77 SITA: n/a
F: 1990 ⁂ 19 Head: Andres Von Wedemeyer Net: n/a

☐ OB-1649	Piper PA-42 Cheyenne III	42-8001009	N151PC	0081	0096	2 PWC PT6A-41	5080			
☐ OB-1714	Piper PA-42 Cheyenne III	42-8001013	N275AB	0081	1298	2 PWC PT6A-41	5080			

AVIACION LIDER, SA

Lima

Villareal 235, Lima 18, Peru ☎ (1) 441 32 85 Tx: none Fax: (1) 440 90 15 SITA: n/a
F: 1989 ⁂ 9 Head: Luis Redin Net: n/a

☐ OB-1435	Cessna 402C II	402C0316	N36915	0080	0490	2 CO TSIO-520-VB	3107	9 Pax		
☐ N90WT	Beech King Air E90	LW-31	N17GD	0072	0696	2 PWC PT6A-28	4581			lsf Joda Partnership

AVIASUR – Aviacion del Sur, S.A.

Iquitos

Carlos Concha 267, Lima 27, Peru ☎ (1) 264 31 52 Tx: none Fax: (1) 264 18 14 SITA: n/a
F: 1996 ⁂ 45 Head: Luis Guerrero Arias Net: n/a

☐ OB-1646	Mil Mi-8AMT	59489603704		0094	0097	2 IS TV3-117VM	13000			
☐ OB-1668	Mil Mi-8AMT	59489605817	OB-1582	0092	0096	2 IS TV3-117VM	13000			
☐ OB-1662	Mil Mi-17	94394		0086	0096	2 IS TV3-117MT-3	13000			
☐ OB-1663	Mil Mi-17	94704		0087	0096	2 IS TV3-117VM	13000			
☐ RA-70882	Mil Mi-17	212M150	CCCP-70882	0091	0097	2 IS TV3-117MT-3	13000			lsf Mil
☐ RA-70883	Mil Mi-17	212M151	CCCP-70883	0091	0097	2 IS TV3-117MT-3	13000			lsf Mil

CIELOS DEL PERU, S.A. = EXD (Subsidiary of STAF, Argentina / formerly dba Export Air Cargo)

Lima

Avenida Faucett 4800, Lima-Callao, Peru ☎ (1) 484 02 33 Tx: none Fax: (1) 484 04 05 SITA: n/a
F: n/a ⁂ n/a Head: Alfonso Rey B. IATA: 529 ICAO: EXPORT Net: n/a

☐ OB-1696	Boeing 707-331C	18711 / 370	N777FB	0064	0898	4 PW JT3D-3B (HK2/COM)	151500	Freighter		Petete / lsf Daedalus Aviation Fin.Inc.
☐ OB-1699	Boeing 707-369C	20084 / 758	N851JB	0068	0798	4 PW JT3D-3B (HK2/COM)	151500	Freighter		Petete / lsf Daedalus Aviation Fin.Inc.
☐ OB-1716	Boeing 707-321C	20017 / 753	N517MA	0068	1098	4 PW JT3D-3B (HK2/COM)	151500	Freighter		Petete / lsf Jetlease Inc.

COLIBRI – Servicios Aéreos Colibri, S.A.

Lima

Av. 2 de Mayo 1545-217, Lima 27, Peru ☎ (1) 221 74 89 Tx: none Fax: (1) 221 74 89 SITA: n/a
F: 1994 ⁂ n/a Head: n/a Net: n/a

☐ OB-1461	Antonov 32B	2801		0090	0097	2 IV AI-20D	27000	Y50 / Combi		std LIM
☐ OB-1462	Antonov 32B	2802		0090	1194	2 IV AI-20D	27000	Y50 / Combi		Espiritu Santo I
☐ OB-1485	Antonov 72				1298	2 LO D-36	34800	Combi		
☐ OB-1486	Antonov 72				1298	2 LO D-36	34800	Combi		

FAUCETT PERU = CF / CFP (Faucett, S.A. dba / Subsidiary of Corporacion Asesora, S.A.)

Lima

Apartado 1429, Lima 100, Peru ☎ (1) 575 09 61 Tx: 25225 limdacf pe Fax: (1) 575 09 70 SITA: LIMDACF
F: 1928 ⁂ n/a Head: Roberto Leigh R. IATA: 163 ICAO: FAUCETT Net: n/a Suspended operations in 1197, intends to restart.

☐ OB-1288	Boeing 737-112	19769 / 194	N40AF	0769	0685	2 PW JT8D-9A	49895	Y117		std LIM
☐ OB-1476	Boeing 737-212 (A)	20492 / 281	HR-SHJ	0671	0492	2 PW JT8D-9A	53070	Y117		lsf INGL / std LIM
☐ OB-1538	Boeing 737-269 (A)	21206 / 448	EI-CHB	0276	0593	2 PW JT8D-17	54204	Y117		lsf GECA / std LIM
☐ OB-1544	Boeing 737-2A9 (A)	20956 / 386	VT-EWA	1174	0893	2 PW JT8D-9A	53070	Y117		lsf INGL / std LIM
☐ OB-1635	Boeing 737-222	19554 / 123	N67AF	0269	1195	2 PW JT8D-9A	49442	Y117		lsf IALI / std LIM
☐ OB-1541	Boeing 727-264 (A)	21072 / 1145	XA-FIE	0675	0394	3 PW JT8D-17	83461	Y164		lsf INGL / std LIM

FUERZA AEREA DEL PERU – Grupo Aéreo No 3

Lima

Avda Faucett sn, Lima-Callao, Peru ☎ (1) 451 70 29 Tx: none Fax: (1) 451 70 29 SITA: n/a
F: n/a ⁂ n/a Head: n/a Net: n/a Operates non-profit passenger/cargo/inspection flights for oil companies.

☐ OB-1405	Eurocopter (MBB) BO105LS-A3	2026		0089		2 AN 250-C28C	2600			
☐ OB-1406	Eurocopter (MBB) BO105LS-A3	2027		0089		2 AN 250-C28C	2600			
☐ OB-1409	Eurocopter (MBB) BO105LS-A3	2028		0089		2 AN 250-C28C	2600			
☐ OB-1410	Eurocopter (MBB) BO105LS-A3	2029		0089		2 AN 250-C28C	2600			
☐ OB-1418	Eurocopter (MBB) BO105LS-A3	2030		0089		2 AN 250-C28C	2600			
☐ OB-1419	Eurocopter (MBB) BO105LS-A3	2031		0089		2 AN 250-C28C	2600			

FUERZA AEREA DEL PERU – Grupo Aéreo No 8 = FPR

Lima

Aeropuerto Internacional Jorge Chavez, Rampa Norte, Lima-Callao, Peru ☎ (1) 574 24 41 Tx: none Fax: (1) 574 22 59 SITA: n/a
F: 1960 ⁂ n/a Head: Col. Oscar Salinas Ortega Net: n/a Grupo Aereo N 8, the transport group of the FAP, operates non-profit pax/cargo flights where civil airlines do not have any services.
Additional aircraft are used from the Fuerza Aérea del Peru when required.

☐ OB-1379	Antonov 32	0909		0086		2 IV AI-20D	27000	Combi		362
☐ OB-1380	Antonov 32	0910		0086		2 IV AI-20D	27000	Combi		363
☐ OB-1381	Antonov 32	1001		0086		2 IV AI-20D	27000	Combi		366
☐ OB-1382	Antonov 32	1002		0086		2 IV AI-20D	27000	Combi		367
☐ OB-1383	Antonov 32	1003		0086		2 IV AI-20D	27000	Combi		376
☐ OB-1385	Antonov 32	1107		0087		2 IV AI-20D	27000	Combi		378
☐ OB-1386	Antonov 32	1108		0087		2 IV AI-20D	27000	Combi		379
☐ OB-1387	Antonov 32	1109		0087		2 IV AI-20D	27000	Combi		386
☐ OB-1391	Antonov 32	1302		0087		2 IV AI-20D	27000	Combi		391
☐ OB-1392	Antonov 32	1303		0087		2 IV AI-20D	27000	Combi		392
☐ OB-1393	Antonov 32	1305		0087		2 IV AI-20D	27000	Combi		387
☐ OB-1640	Antonov 32B	3002	TS-LCA	0091	1295	2 IV AI-20D	27000	Combi		322
☐ OB-1641	Antonov 32B	2809	48052	0090	0096	2 IV AI-20D	27000	Combi		323
☐ OB-1642	Antonov 32B	2907	RA-48129	0091	0096	2 IV AI-20D	27000	Combi		324
☐ OB-1685	Antonov 32B				0098	2 IV AI-20D	27000	Combi		326
☐ OB-1686	Antonov 32B				0098	2 IV AI-20D	27000	Combi		327
☐ OB-1395	Lockheed L-182 (C-130A) Hercules	1A-3177	57-0470	0058	1187	4 AN T56-A-9D	56336	Combi		396
☐ PRP-001	Boeing 737-528	27426 / 2739		0095	0995	2 CFMI CFM56-3C1	53977	VIP		
☐ OB-1374	Lockheed L-382E (L-100-20) Hercules	26C-4358	OB-R-1188	0070	1070	4 AN 501-D22A	70307	Combi		394
☐ OB-1375	Lockheed L-382E (L-100-20) Hercules	47C-4850	N4115M*	0080	0281	4 AN 501-D22A	70307	Combi		397
☐ OB-1376	Lockheed L-382E (L-100-20) Hercules	47C-4853	N4119M*	0080	0281	4 AN 501-D22A	70307	Combi		398
☐ OB-1377	Lockheed L-382E (L-100-20) Hercules	37C-4706	OB-R-1183	0076	1176	4 AN 501-D22A	70307	Combi		382
☐ OB-1378	Lockheed L-382E (L-100-20) Hercules	37C-4715		0077	0177	4 AN 501-D22A	70307	Combi		384
☐ OB-1371	Boeing 707-323C	19575 / 714	HP-1028	0068	0288	4 PW JT3D-3B	151046	Combi/Tanker		319
☐ OB-1372	Boeing (Douglas) DC-8-62F (CF)	46078 / 475	HB-IDK	0069	1281	4 PW JT3D-3B (HK3/BAC)	151953	Combi		370
☐ OB-1373	Boeing (Douglas) DC-8-62F (CF)	45984 / 370	HB-IDH	0067	1281	4 PW JT3D-3B (HK2)	151953	Combi		371 / std LIM

HELICA DEL PERU, S.A.

Lima

Calle Redi 150, Lima 41, Peru ☎ (1) 225 30 58 Tx: none Fax: (1) 476 14 87 SITA: n/a
F: 1995 ⁂ n/a Head: n/a Net: n/a

☐ N6748D	Bell 206L-3 LongRanger III	51106	HC-BVB	0084	0096	1 AN 250-C30P	1882			lsf PHM

HELICUSCO – Helicopteros del Cusco, SA

Cuzco

Arias Araguez 369, Lima 18, Peru ☎ (1) 445 61 26 Tx: none Fax: (1) 444 87 08 SITA: n/a
F: 1994 ⁂ 30 Head: Enrique Illich K. Net: http://www.rcp.net.pe/helicusco/

☐ OB-1639	Mil Mi-8AMT	59489607212		0094	0096	2 IS TV3-117VM	13000	Y24		Apuchin

HELISUR – Helicopteros del Sur, S.A.

Iquitos

Carlos Concha 267, Lima 27, Peru ☎ (1) 264 18 80 Tx: none Fax: (1) 264 18 14 SITA: n/a
F: 1993 ⁂ 71 Head: Luis Guerrero Arias Net: n/a

☐ C-FPMR	Bell 212	31115	N48ZP	0080	0096	2 PWC PT6T-3 TwinPac	5080			lsf Canadian Helicopters
☐ C-GBPH	Bell 212	30630	N947AA	0074	0098	2 PWC PT6T-3 TwinPac	5080			lsf Canadian Helicopters
☐ OB-1584	Mil Mi-17	95432		0090	0094	2 IS TV3-117MT-3	13000			
☐ OB-1585	Mil Mi-17	223M103		0090	0094	2 IS TV3-117MT-3	13000			
☐ OB-1586	Mil Mi-17	223M104		0090	0094	2 IS TV3-117MT-3	13000			
☐ OB-1691	Mil Mi-17	96153	RA-27193	0093	0094	2 IS TV3-117MT-3	13000			

HELI-UNION PERU, S.A. (Heli-Union Selva, S.A.) (Subsidiary of Heli-Union, France)

Lima & Iquitos

Av. Santa Luisa 174, San Isidro-Lima, Peru ☎ (1) 440 12 64 Tx: none Fax: (1) 422 58 60 SITA: n/a
F: 1995 ⁂ 20 Head: José Miguel Raffo Net: n/a Services within the Selva-aerea of Peru are operated under the name HELI-UNION SELVA, S.A. (same headquarters & fleet).
Beside helicopters listed, also uses additional (AS350BA Ecureuil & SA315B Lama) from the Heli-Union France (F-) fleet, when required.

☐ C-FFHB	Bell 205A-1	30294	VH-HHW	0079		1 LY T5313B	4309			lsf Frontier Helicopters
☐ C-GFHM	Bell 205A-1	30289	VH-HHM	0079		1 LY T5313B	4309			lsf Frontier Helicopters
☐ C-GFRS	Bell 212	30716	I-ZCMA	0075		2 PWC PT6T-3 TwinPac	5080			lsf Frontier Helicopters
☐ N241CH	Boeing Vertol 234UT Chinook	MJ-016	N224TA	0083		2 LY 5512	19278			lsf Columbia Helicopters / cvtd 234LR

470 registration type of aircraft cn/fn ex/ex* mfd del powered by mtow kg configuration selcal name/fln/specialitites/remarks

IBERICO Aérotaxi
Tarapoto

Apartado 63, Tarapoto, Peru ☎ (94) 52 20 73 Tx: 93870 cptapto Fax: (94) 52 21 11 SITA: n/a
F: 1970 ♦♦♦ 16 Head: Humberto Iberico Net: n/a

registration	type of aircraft	cn/fn	ex/ex*	mfd	del	powered by	mtow kg	configuration	selcal	name/fln/specialitites/remarks
☐ OB-1551	Cessna 337G Super Skymaster	33701544	N72238	0073	0092	2 CO IO-360-G	2100	6 Pax		
☐ OB-1022	Evangel 4500	003		0073		2 LY IO-540-K1B5	2495	8 Pax		std TPP

SAN – Servicio Aerofotografico Nacional (Division of Fuerza Aérea del Peru)
Lima-Las Palmas

Base Aérea de Las Palmas, Barranco, Lima, Peru ☎ (1) 467 67 26 Tx: none Fax: (1) 477 36 82 SITA: n/a
F: 1942 ♦♦♦ 240 Head: Mayor General Miguel Moron Buleje Net: n/a

☐ OB-1429	Learjet 25B	25B-159	N66JD	0074	0074	2 GE CJ610-8A	6804	VIP / Photo		FAP522
☐ OB-1430	Learjet 25B	25B-164		0074	0074	2 GE CJ610-8A	6804	VIP / Photo		FAP523
☐ OB-1431	Learjet 36A	36A-051	N4290J*	0083	0083	2 GA TFE731-2-2B	8301	VIP / Photo		FAP524
☐ OB-1432	Learjet 36A	36A-052	N4291K*	0083	0083	2 GA TFE731-2-2B	8301	VIP / Photo		FAP525
☐ OB-1433	Dassault Falcon 20F	434	F-WRQP*	0081	0783	2 GE CF700-2D2	13000	VIP		FAP300

SAOSA – Servicios Aéreos del Oriente, SA (formerly Aero Selva, SA)
Pucallpa

Crnel Portillo 644, Pucallpa, Peru ☎ (64) 57 11 38 Tx: n/a Fax: (64) 57 11 38 SITA: n/a
F: 1990 ♦♦♦ n/a Head: Federico Frantzen Martinez Net: n/a

☐ OB-1220	Cessna U206G Stationair 6 II	U20606187		0081	0095	1 CO IO-520-F	1633			
☐ OB-1415	Cessna U206G Stationair 6 II	U20604877	N734VG	0079	1090	1 CO IO-520-F	1633			
☐ OB-1558	Beech King Air B90	LJ-405	N68RT	0068	1293	2 PWC PT6A-20	4377			

SAT – Servicios Aereos Transandinos, SA
Puerto Bermudez

Baltazar La Torre 720, Lima 27, Peru ☎ (1) 422 13 45 Tx: none Fax: (1) 422 13 45 SITA: n/a
F: 1987 ♦♦♦ 5 Head: Luis A. Bordo Garcia Rosell Net: n/a

☐ OB-1320	Cessna TU206G Turbo Stationair 6 II	U20605485	N6461U	0080	0988	1 CO TSIO-520-M	1633			Juana Corina

SIPESA – Servicios Aeronauticos Sipesa, S.A.
Lima

Mariscal Miller 2621, Lima 14, Peru ☎ (1) 221 30 66 Tx: none Fax: (1) 440 62 75 SITA: n/a
F: n/a ♦♦♦ n/a Head: Raul La Madrid Jimenez Net: n/a

☐ OB-1666	Twin (Aero) Shrike Commander 500S	3083	N500DJ	0070	0096	2 LY IO-540-E1B5	3062			1
☐ OB-1689	Twin (Aero) Shrike Commander 500S	500S-1756-2	N635SP	0068	0097	2 LY IO-540-E1B5	3062			5
☐ OB-1690	Twin (Aero) Shrike Commander 500S	3262	N57288	0075	0096	2 LY IO-540-E1B5	3062			6

STAR UP, S.A.
Lima

Las Camelias 410, 2do. Piso, Lima 27, Peru ☎ (1) 441 26 26 Tx: none Fax: (1) 442 07 68 SITA: n/a
F: 1998 ♦♦♦ n/a Head: n/a Net: n/a

☐ ER-AFU	Antonov 24RV	27308010	RA-46482	0972	0299	2 IV AI-24VT	21800	Y48		lsf MCC
☐ OB-1488	Antonov 32	1608		0086	0098	2 IV AI-20D	27000	Y50 / Combi		std LIM
☐ OB-1610	Antonov 32B	3202	UR-48130	0092	0098	2 IV AI-20D	27000	Freighter		
☐ OB-1652	Antonov 32B	3204	UR-48131	0091	0098	2 IV AI-20D	27000	Freighter		

TANS – Transportes Aéreos Nacionales de la Selva = ELV (Division of Fuerza Aérea del Peru)
Iquitos-Moronacocha & Lima

Sgto Lores 127, Iquitos, (Dep. Loreto), Peru ☎ (94) 23 46 32 Tx: n/a Fax: (94) 23 46 32 SITA: n/a
F: 1964 ♦♦♦ n/a Head: Mayor Gral FAP Jesus Vassallo Bedoya ICAO: AEREOS SELVA Net: n/a

☐ OB-1164	Pilatus PC-6/B2-H2 Turbo Porter	760			0073	1 PWC PT6A-27	2200	7 Pax		316 / Floats
☐ OB-1165	Pilatus PC-6/B2-H2 Turbo Porter	720			0071	1 PWC PT6A-27	2200	7 Pax		320
☐ OB-1166	Pilatus PC-6/B2-H2 Turbo Porter	722			0071	1 PWC PT6A-27	2200	7 Pax		331 / Floats
☐ OB-1500	Harbin Yunshuji Y12 II	0051			0092 0592	2 PWC PT6A-27	5300	17 Pax		335
☐ OB-1501	Harbin Yunshuji Y12 II	0052			0092 0592	2 PWC PT6A-27	5300	17 Pax		336
☐ OB-1502	Harbin Yunshuji Y12 II	0053			0092 0592	2 PWC PT6A-27	5300	17 Pax		337
☐ OB-1503	Harbin Yunshuji Y12 II	0054			0092 0592	2 PWC PT6A-27	5300	17 Pax		338
☐ OB-1621	Harbin Yunshuji Y12 II	0072			0093	2 PWC PT6A-27	5300	17 Pax		
☐ OB-1622	Harbin Yunshuji Y12 II	0073			0093	2 PWC PT6A-27	5300	17 Pax		
☐ OB-1623	Harbin Yunshuji Y12 II	0074			0093	2 PWC PT6A-27	5300	17 Pax		
☐ OB-1154	De Havilland DHC-6 Twin Otter 300	274	N86TC	0070		2 PWC PT6A-27	5670	20 Pax		305
☐ OB-1157	De Havilland DHC-6 Twin Otter 300	378		0073	0973	2 PWC PT6A-27	5670	20 Pax		302
☐ OB-1159	De Havilland DHC-6 Twin Otter 300	385		0073	1073	2 PWC PT6A-27	5670	20 Pax		311
☐ OB-1160	De Havilland DHC-6 Twin Otter 300	322		0071	0771	2 PWC PT6A-27	5670	20 Pax		312 / Floats
☐ OB-1161	De Havilland DHC-6 Twin Otter 300	324		0071	0971	2 PWC PT6A-27	5670	20 Pax		317 / Floats
☐ OB-1336	De Havilland DHC-6 Twin Otter 300	483		0076	0576	2 PWC PT6A-27	5670	20 Pax		303
☐ 308	De Havilland DHC-6 Twin Otter 300	266	N85TC	0069	0980	2 PWC PT6A-27	5670	20 Pax		
☐ OB-1396	Fokker F28 Fellowship 1000 (F28 Mk1000)	11100	PH-EXY*	0075	0098	2 RR Spey 555-15	29484	Y65		390
☐ OB-	Boeing 737-244	19707	XA-SFR	1068	0598	2 PW JT8D-9A	49442	Y120		
☐ OB-	Boeing 737-248	19424 / 147	CC-CVA	0069	1298	2 PW JT8D-9A	49442	Y120		lsf IALI
☐ OB-	Boeing 737-248	20221 / 227	CC-CVB	0070	1298	2 PW JT8D-9A	49442	Y120		lsf IALI
☐ OB-	Boeing 737-282 (A)	23042 / 967	VT-PDC	0083	0299	2 PW JT8D-17A	56472	Y120		

TAR AERO REGIONAL – Transporte Aéreo Regional, S.A.
Lima

Calle Grau 151, Lima 18, Peru ☎ (1) 241 75 43 Tx: none Fax: n/a SITA: n/a
F: 1998 ♦♦♦ n/a Head: n/a Net: n/a Presently being set-up. Intends to start operations during 1999 with Cessna 208 Caravan aircraft.

TASA – Transportes Aéreos, S.A. (formerly Transportes Turisticos Aéreos, SA)
Pucallpa

Jr. Progreso 547, Pucallpa, Peru ☎ (64) 57 52 21 Tx: 575221 Fax: (64) 57 31 28 SITA: n/a
F: 1979 ♦♦♦ 10 Head: Martha L. de Chavez Net: n/a

☐ OB-1247	Cessna U206G Stationair 6 II	U20606478	OB-T-1247	0082		1 CO IO-520-F	1633			
☐ OB-1298	Cessna U206F Stationair II	U20603059		0076		1 CO IO-520-F	1633			
☐ OB-1557	Cessna T210N Turbo Centurion II	21063363	N5314A	0079	1193	1 CO TSIO-520-R	1814			

TAUSA – Transportes Aéreos Unidos de la Selva Amazonica, S.A. (formerly TAUSA – Transportes Aeros Uchiza, SA)
Tarapoto

Soledad 111, Of. 302, Lima 14, Peru ☎ (1) 442 87 70 Tx: 20053 pb limtc pe Fax: (1) 441 13 82 SITA: n/a
F: 1980 ♦♦♦ 30 Head: Fernando Zevallos Net: n/a Aircraft below MTOW 1361kg: Piper PA-24-250.

☐ OB-1237	Cessna U206G Stationair 6 II Rob STOL	CU20606439	OB-T-1237	0081		1 CO IO-520-F	1633	5 Pax		

T doble A – Transportes Aéreos Andahuaylas, SA = TEA
Cuzco

Av. Pardo 640, Mezzanine T2, Miraflores, Lima 18, Peru ☎ (1) 242 56 39 Tx: none Fax: (1) 446 21 20 SITA: n/a
F: 1994 ♦♦♦ 60 Head: Herlinda Mendoza de Campos ICAO: TEE-DOBLE Net: n/a

☐ OB-1653	Yakovlev 40	9041860	OB-1606	0080	0096	3 IV AI-25	16800	Y34		Cristo Ascencion / lst Aerosur
☐ OB-1650	Antonov 24RV	37308802	OB-1562	0073	0096	2 IV AI-24VT	21800	Y50		Virgen de Guadalupe
☐ OB-1651	Antonov 24RV	27308303	OB-1571	0072	0096	2 IV AI-24VT	21800	Y50		Nino Jesus de Praga

TRANS AM AIRLINES = ES (TransAm, S.A. dba)
Lima

Avenida Comandante Espinar 331, Miraflores, Lima 18, Peru ☎ (1) 445 18 79 Tx: none Fax: (1) 445 17 87 SITA: n/a
F: 1998 ♦♦♦ n/a Head: Daniel Ratti IATA: 530 Net: n/a Presently being set-up. Intends to start operations during 1999 with Boeing 727-200 & 737-200 aircraft.

OD = LEBANON (Republic of Lebanon) (al-Jumhouriya al-Lubnaniya)
Capital: Beirut Official Language: Arabic Population: 4,0 million Square Km: 10400 Dialling code: +961 Year established: 1941 Acting political head: Salim al-Hoss (Prime Minister)

Government / Corporate / Executive / VIP Aircraft

☐ OD-PAL	Dassault Falcon 20F	395	F-WRQX*	0079	1179	2 GE CF700-2D2	13000	VIP		Government

MEA – Middle East Airlines = ME / MEA
Beirut

PO Box 206, Beirut, Lebanon ☎ (1) 62 92 50 Tx: 20820 cedars le Fax: (1) 62 92 60 SITA: n/a
F: 1945 ♦♦♦ 4300 Head: Mohamad A. El-Hout IATA: 076 ICAO: CEDAR JET Net: http://www.mea.com.lb

☐ F-OHMO	Airbus Industrie A320-232	640	F-WWDF*	0096	0197	2 IAE V2527-A5	75500	C24Y114		lsf ILFC
☐ F-OHMR	Airbus Industrie A320-232	676	F-WWBG*	0097	0597	2 IAE V2527-A5	75500	C24Y114		lsf ILFC
☐ F-OHMP	Airbus Industrie A321-231	663	D-AVZK*	0097	0597	2 IAE V2533-A5	89000	C24Y145		lsf ILFC
☐ F-OHMQ	Airbus Industrie A321-231	668	D-AVZN*	0097	0597	2 IAE V2533-A5	89000	C24Y145		lsf ILFC
☐ 3B-STI	Airbus Industrie A310-222	347	9V-STI	0084	0797	2 PW JT9D-7R4E1	142000	C40Y140		lsf SALE
☐ 3B-STJ	Airbus Industrie A310-222	350	9V-STJ	0084	1097	2 PW JT9D-7R4E1	142000	C40Y140		lsf SALE
☐ 3B-STK	Airbus Industrie A310-222	357	9V-STK	0085	0598	2 PW JT9D-7R4E1	142000	C40Y140		lsf SALE
☐ OD-AFD	Boeing 707-3B4C	20259 / 822		0069	1069	4 PW JT3D-3B (HK2/COM)	146200	C22Y128	BE-DL	std BEY / for sale or lease
☐ OD-AGV	Boeing 707-347C	19967 / 745	N1505W	0068	0680	4 PW JT3D-3B (HK2/COM)	146200	C22Y128	BE-HM	std BEY / for sale or lease
☐ OD-AHC	Boeing 707-323C	19589 / 701	N8410	0068	0582	4 PW JT3D-3B (HK2/COM)	146200	C22Y128	DG-EL	std BEY / for sale or lease
☐ OD-AHD	Boeing 707-323C	19515 / 608	N7595A	0067	1182	4 PW JT3D-3B (HK2/COM)	146200	C22Y128	KM-BC	std BEY / for sale or lease
☐ OD-AHE	Boeing 707-323C	19516 / 612	N7596A	0067	1282	4 PW JT3D-3B (HK2/COM)	146200	C22Y128	BE-CL	std BEY / for sale or lease
☐ OD-AHF	Boeing 707-323B	20170 / 795	N708PC	0469	0190	4 PW JT3D-3B (HK2/COM)	146200	C22Y130	BG-FL	std BEY / for sale or lease
☐ F-OHLH	Airbus Industrie A310-304	447	D-APOL	0387	0993	2 GE CF6-80C2A2	157000	C30Y156	BG-FH	lsf GECA
☐ F-OHLI	Airbus Industrie A310-304	481	D-APOP	0088	0694	2 GE CF6-80C2A2	157000	C30Y156	CL-FJ	lsf GECA

471 registration	type of aircraft		cn/fn	ex/ex*	mfd	del	powered by		mtow kg	configuration	selcal	name/fln/specialitites/remarks

TMA OF LEBANON = TL / TMA (Trans Mediterranean Airways, S.A.L. dba) — Beirut

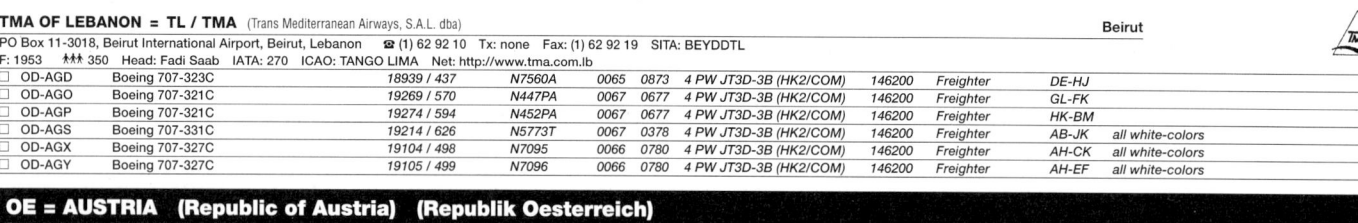

PO Box 11-3018, Beirut International Airport, Beirut, Lebanon ☎ (1) 62 92 10 Tx: none Fax: (1) 62 92 19 SITA: BEYDDTL
F: 1953 ✱✱✱ 350 Head: Fadi Saab IATA: 270 ICAO: TANGO LIMA Net: http://www.tma.com.lb

☐ OD-AGD	Boeing 707-323C	18939 / 437	N7560A	0065	0873	4 PW JT3D-3B (HK2/COM)	146200	Freighter	DE-HJ	
☐ OD-AGO	Boeing 707-321C	19269 / 570	N447PA	0067	0677	4 PW JT3D-3B (HK2/COM)	146200	Freighter	GL-FK	
☐ OD-AGP	Boeing 707-321C	19274 / 594	N452PA	0067	0677	4 PW JT3D-3B (HK2/COM)	146200	Freighter	HK-BM	
☐ OD-AGS	Boeing 707-331C	19214 / 626	N5773T	0067	0378	4 PW JT3D-3B (HK2/COM)	146200	Freighter	AB-JK	all white-colors
☐ OD-AGX	Boeing 707-327C	19104 / 498	N7095	0066	0780	4 PW JT3D-3B (HK2/COM)	146200	Freighter	AH-CK	all white-colors
☐ OD-AGY	Boeing 707-327C	19105 / 499	N7096	0066	0780	4 PW JT3D-3B (HK2/COM)	146200	Freighter	AH-EF	all white-colors

OE = AUSTRIA (Republic of Austria) (Republik Oesterreich)

Capital: Vienna Official Language: German Population: 8,5 million Square Km: 83856 Dialling code: +43 Year established: 1918 Acting political head: Viktor Klima (Federal Chancellor)

AERIAL-HELIKOPTER — Gross Harras

Diepolz 45, A-2034 Gross Harras, Austria ☎ (2526) 73 81 Tx: none Fax: (2526) 73 21 37 SITA: n/a
F: 1996 ✱✱✱ n/a Head: Leopold Reidinger Net: n/a Aircraft below MTOW 1361kg: Schweizer 300C (269C)

☐ OE-XLM	Agusta-Bell 206B JetRanger	8046	G-COUR	0068	0598	1 AN 250-C20	1451			cvtd 206A
☐ OE-XRF	Agusta-Bell 206A JetRanger	8246	G-BNRE	0070	1296	1 AN 250-C20	1361			

AERZTEFLUGAMBULANZ, GmbH = OAF (Austrian Air Ambulance / AirMed) — Vienna-Schwechat

Albertgasse 1A, A-1080 Wien, Austria ☎ (1) 401 44 Tx: 136613 jetd a Fax: (1) 401 55 SITA: n/a
F: 1978 ✱✱✱ 15 Head: Gerhard Flekatsch ICAO: AUSTRIAN AMBULANCE Net: n/a

☐ OE-GMD	Learjet 36A	36A-047	N36SK	0081	0594	2 GA TFE731-2-2B	8301	EMS		

AIRLINK Luftverkehrs, GmbH = JAR — Salzburg

Innsbrucker Bundesstr. 95, A-5035 Salzburg, Austria ☎ (662) 85 08 63 Tx: none Fax: (662) 850 86 33 SITA: n/a
F: 1979 ✱✱✱ 8 Head: Johanna Wurzinger ICAO: AIRLINK Net: n/a Aircraft below MTOW 1361kg: Cessna 152 & Piper PA-28.

☐ OE-FBR	Piper PA-34-220T Seneca III	3448009	D-GCWO	0090	0693	2 CO TSIO-360-KB	1999			
☐ OE-FSM	Piper PA-34-200T Seneca II	34-7970359	D-GIAS	0079		2 CO TSIO-360-E	1999			
☐ OE-FDR	Cessna 421C Golden Eagle III	421C1413	N1205P	0084	0990	2 CO GTSIO-520-N	3379			
☐ OE-FKG	Piper PA-31T Cheyenne II	31T-8020036	N30DJ	0080		2 PWC PT6A-28	4082			
☐ OE-FKH	Piper PA-31T1 Cheyenne I	31T-8104029	N803CA	0081	0298	2 PWC PT6A-11	3946			
☐ OE-FHL	Beech King Air C90A	LJ-1115	D-IBPE	0085	0392	2 PWC PT6A-21	4377			
☐ OE-FGN	Cessna 500 Citation	500-0291	N291DS	0075	1297	2 PWC JT15D-1A	5375			
☐ OE-FME	Beech King Air 300LW	FA-228	HB-GJC	0093	0796	2 PWC PT6A-60A	5670			
☐ OE-FBS	Cessna 551 Citation II/SP	551-0574	N60GF	0088	0592	2 PWC JT15D-4	5670			
☐ OE-FPA	Cessna 551 Citation II/SP	551-0552		0087	0291	2 PWC JT15D-4	5670			

AIR-STYRIA Luftfahrtunternehmen, GmbH – AST — Graz

Flughafen, A-8073 Feldkirchen, Austria ☎ (316) 29 10 08 Tx: n/a Fax: (316) 42 69 97 SITA: n/a
F: 1993 ✱✱✱ 6 Head: Robert Hoess Net: n/a

☐ OE-GIL	Cessna 550 Citation II	550-0060	N315CK	0079	0893	2 PWC JT15D-4	6033			

AIR-TAXI KLAGENFURT KFbg (Kärtner Flughafenbetriebs, GmbH dba) — Klagenfurt

Flughafen Klagenfurt, A-9020 Klagenfurt, Austria ☎ (463) 41 500 Tx: 422375 apklu a Fax: (463) 41 50 02 36 SITA: n/a
F: 1958 ✱✱✱ 3 Head: Dkfm. Hans-Herbert Laubreiter Net: n/a

☐ OE-DER	Cessna P206B Super Skylane	P206-0342	N4742F	0066		1 CO IO-520-A	1633			

ALBUS Air Flugbetrieb, GmbH (formerly Albus-Flugdienst, GmbH) — Salzburg

Franz-Josef-Str. 15, A-5020 Salzburg, Austria ☎ (662) 88 66 90 Tx: none Fax: (662) 88 66 90 22 SITA: n/a
F: 1928 ✱✱✱ 2 Head: Andreas Moder Net: n/a

☐ OE-GLZ	Cessna 550 Citation II	550-0690		0091	0098	2 PWC JT15D-4	6396			occ lsf/jtly opw Taxiflug

ALPENFLUG, GmbH & Co. KG (formerly Alpenflug Gesellschaft Zell am See, Leitinger & Co.) — Zell am See

Flugplatz, A-5700 Zell am See, Austria ☎ (6542) 57 937 Tx: none Fax: (6542) 572 40 41 SITA: n/a
F: 1960 ✱✱✱ 2 Head: Paul Empl Net: n/a

☐ OE-KAZ	Piper PA-32-301 Saratoga	3206044	N9150G	0088		1 LY IO-540-K1G5	1633	Executive		

AMERER AIR, GmbH = AMK — Linz

Flughafenstr. 1, A-4063 Hörsching, Austria ☎ (7221) 64 752 Tx: none Fax: (7221) 64 753 SITA: LNZAMCR
F: 1995 ✱✱✱ 40 Head: Heinz Peter Amerer ICAO: AMER AIR Net: n/a

☐ OE-DAA	Piper PA-32RT-300T Turbo Lance II	32R-7887053	D-ETAS	0078	0896	1 LY TIO-540-S1AD	1633	6 Pax/Frtr500kg		
☐ OE-ILW	Fokker F27 Friendship 500 (F27 Mk500)	10681	N505AW	0085	0295	2 RR Dart 552-7R	20820	Freighter		Sissy
☐ OE-ILA	Lockheed L-188C (F) Electra	1145	LN-FOH	0061	0997	4 AN 501-D13	52617	Freighter		cvtd L-188A
☐ OE-ILB	Lockheed L-188A (F) Electra	1039	N356Q	0059	1296	4 AN 501-D13	51256	Freighter		cvtd L-188A

AUSTRIAN AIRLINES, Oesterreichische Luftverkehrs AG = OS / AUA (Member of The Qualiflyer Group) — Vienna-Schwechat

Postfach 50, A-1107 Wien, Austria ☎ (1) 17 66 Tx: 131811 osxm a Fax: (1) 68 55 05 SITA: VIETOOB
F: 1957 ✱✱✱ 4150 Head: Dr. Rudolf Streicher IATA: 257 ICAO: AUSTRIAN Net: http://www.aua.com
Some regional services on behalf of Austrian Airlines are operated by associated TYROLEAN AIRWAYS (Austrian Regional) with Canadair RJ100LR, De Havilland DHC-8 & Fokker 70 aircraft – for details – see under that company.

☐ OE-LFO	Fokker 70 (F28 Mk0070)	11559	PH-EZV*	0095	0995	2 RR Tay 620-15	37995	CY80	JS-FQ	Wiener Neustadt
☐ OE-LFP	Fokker 70 (F28 Mk0070)	11560	PH-EZW*	0095	1095	2 RR Tay 620-15	37995	CY80	JS-FR	Wels
☐ OE-LFQ	Fokker 70 (F28 Mk0070)	11568	PH-EZC*	0096	0496	2 RR Tay 620-15	37995	CY80	LP-DR	Dornbirn
☐ OE-LFR	Fokker 70 (F28 Mk0070)	11572	PH-EZD*	0096	0496	2 RR Tay 620-15	37995	CY80	LP-DS	Steyr
☐ OE-LFS	Fokker 70 (F28 Mk0070)	11528	PH-JCH	0095	0997	2 RR Tay 620-15	39915	CY80	AP-JS	Schwechat
☐ OE-LFT	Fokker 70 (F28 Mk0070)	11537	PH-JCT	0095	1097	2 RR Tay 620-15	39915	CY80	BC-KP	Tulln
☐ OE-LMK	Boeing (Douglas) MD-87 (DC-9-87)	49411 / 1412		0087	1187	2 PW JT8D-219	57833	CY107	JM-KL	St. Pölten
☐ OE-LML	Boeing (Douglas) MD-87 (DC-9-87)	49412 / 1424		0087	1287	2 PW JT8D-219	57833	CY107	JM-AB	Salzburgstadt
☐ OE-LMM	Boeing (Douglas) MD-87 (DC-9-87)	49413 / 1681		0290	0390	2 PW JT8D-217C	57833	CY107	BJ-CD	Innsbruck
☐ OE-LMN	Boeing (Douglas) MD-87 (DC-9-87)	49414 / 1682		0290	0390	2 PW JT8D-217C	57833	CY107	JL-EF	Klagenfurt
☐ OE-LMO	Boeing (Douglas) MD-87 (DC-9-87)	49888 / 1692		0090	0390	2 PW JT8D-217C	57833	CY107	JL-EH	Bregenz
☐ OE-LDP	Boeing (Douglas) MD-81 (DC-9-81)	48015 / 924	N1002W*	0081	0581	2 PW JT8D-217C	64410	CY137	AD-HJ	Niederösterreich / lsf Airfl.Cred.-0599
☐ OE-LDS	Boeing (Douglas) MD-81 (DC-9-81)	48017 / 958		1280	0181	2 PW JT8D-217C	64410	CY141	AD-KM	Burgenland / lsf Airfleet Credit -0699
☐ OE-LDX	Boeing (Douglas) MD-82 (DC-9-82)	48021 / 1078		0083	0283	2 PW JT8D-217C	67810	CY137	AG-BF	Tirol / lsf Airfleet Credit / cvtd -81
☐ OE-LDY	Boeing (Douglas) MD-82 (DC-9-82)	49115 / 1135		0084	0584	2 PW JT8D-217C	67810	CY137	AG-CL	Vorarlberg / lsf Airfleet Credit/cvtd-81
☐ OE-LDZ	Boeing (Douglas) MD-82 (DC-9-82)	49164 / 1182		0085	0285	2 PW JT8D-217C	67810	CY137	AH-CJ	Graz / lsf Airfleet Credit / cvtd -81
☐ OE-LMA	Boeing (Douglas) MD-82 (DC-9-82)	49278 / 1183		0185	0285	2 PW JT8D-217C	67810	CY137	JM-AE	Linz / cvtd -81
☐ OE-LMB	Boeing (Douglas) MD-82 (DC-9-82)	49279 / 1230		0985	1085	2 PW JT8D-217C	67810	CY137	JM-AD	Eisenstadt / cvtd -81
☐ OE-LMC	Boeing (Douglas) MD-82 (DC-9-82)	49372 / 1252		0086	0286	2 PW JT8D-217C	67810	Y161	JM-AC	Baden / cvtd -81
☐ OE-LMD	Boeing (Douglas) MD-83 (DC-9-83)	49933 / 1837		0091	0391	2 PW JT8D-219	72575	Y161	AC-PS	Villach
☐ OE-LME	Boeing (Douglas) MD-83 (DC-9-83)	53377 / 2057		0093	0493	2 PW JT8D-219	72575	Y161	CE-DS	Krems
☐ OE-LBN	Airbus Industrie A320-214	768	F-WWDH*	0098	0198	2 CFMI CFM56-5B4/2P	75500	CY144	DG-BP	Osttirol
☐ OE-LBO	Airbus Industrie A320-214	776	F-WWDM*	0098	0298	2 CFMI CFM56-5B4/2P	75500	CY144	DP-QR	Pyhrn-Eisenwurzen
☐ OE-LBP	Airbus Industrie A320-214	797	F-WWDV*	0098	0398	2 CFMI CFM56-5B4/2P	75500	CY144	DP-RS	Neusiedler See
☐ OE-LBQ	Airbus Industrie A320-214					2 CFMI CFM56-5B4/2P	75500	CY144		oo-delivery 1200
☐ OE-LBR	Airbus Industrie A320-214					2 CFMI CFM56-5B4/2P	75500	CY144		oo-delivery 0301
☐ OE-LBS	Airbus Industrie A320-214					2 CFMI CFM56-5B4/2P	75500	CY144		oo-delivery 0601
☐ OE-LBT	Airbus Industrie A320-214					2 CFMI CFM56-5B4/2P	75500	CY144		oo-delivery 0002
☐ OE-LBU	Airbus Industrie A320-214					2 CFMI CFM56-5B4/2P	75500	CY144		oo-delivery 0002
☐ OE-LBV	Airbus Industrie A320-214					2 CFMI CFM56-5B4/2P	75500	CY144		oo-delivery 0003
☐ OE-LBW	Airbus Industrie A320-214					2 CFMI CFM56-5B4/2P	75500	CY144		oo-delivery 0003
☐ OE-LBX	Airbus Industrie A320-214					2 CFMI CFM56-5B4/2P	75500	CY144		oo-delivery 0004
☐ OE-LBY	Airbus Industrie A320-214					2 CFMI CFM56-5B4/2P	75500	CY144		oo-delivery 0004
☐ OE-LBZ	Airbus Industrie A320-214					2 CFMI CFM56-5B4/2P	75500	CY144		oo-delivery 0005
☐ OE-LBA	Airbus Industrie A321-111	552	D-AVZH*	0095	1295	2 CFMI CFM56-5B1	83000	CY186	LP-BS	Salzkammergut
☐ OE-LBB	Airbus Industrie A321-111	570	D-AVZQ*	0096	0296	2 CFMI CFM56-5B1	83000	CY186	LP-CR	Pinzgau / special Millienum colors
☐ OE-LBC	Airbus Industrie A321-111	581	D-AVZS*	0096	0296	2 CFMI CFM56-5B1	83000	CY186	LP-CS	Südtirol
☐ OE-LBD	Airbus Industrie A321-211	920	D-AVZN*	0098	1298	2 CFMI CFM56-5B3/P	89000	CY186	BP-JK	Steirisches Weinland
☐ OE-LBE	Airbus Industrie A321-211	935	D-AVZR*	0098	1298	2 CFMI CFM56-5B3/P	89000	CY186	AD-HK	Wachau
☐ OE-LBF	Airbus Industrie A321-211					2 CFMI CFM56-5B3/P	89000	CY186		oo-delivery 0599
☐ OE-LBG	Airbus Industrie A321-211					2 CFMI CFM56-5B3/P	89000	CY186		oo-delivery 0601
☐ OE-LAA	Airbus Industrie A310-324 (ET)	489	F-WWCK*	0088	1288	2 PW PW4152	157000	C30Y166	BM-HK	New York
☐ OE-LAB	Airbus Industrie A310-324 (ET)	492	F-WWCP*	0089	0189	2 PW PW4152	157000	C30Y166	BM-JK	Tokyo
☐ OE-LAC	Airbus Industrie A310-324 (ET)	568	F-WWCE*	0091	0391	2 PW PW4152	157000	C18Y195	AC-BR	Paris / lsf Airbus Industrie
☐ OE-LAD	Airbus Industrie A310-325 (ET)	624	F-WWCE*	0092	0392	2 PW PW4156A	164000	C30Y166	BR-HL	Chicago
☐ OE-LAM	Airbus Industrie A330-223	223	F-WWKQ*	0098	0898	2 PW PW4168A	230000	C30Y235	FL-JQ	Dachstein
☐ OE-LAN	Airbus Industrie A330-223	181	F-WWKA*	0897		2 PW PW4168A	230000	C30Y235	GH-BQ	Grossglockner / oo-del.0599 / cvtd -242
☐ OE-LAO	Airbus Industrie A330-223	195	F-WWKJ*	1297		2 PW PW4168A	230000	C30Y235		oo-delivery 0100 / cvtd -222
☐ OE-LAP	Airbus Industrie A330-223	317				2 PW PW4168A	230000	C30Y235		to be lsf ILFC 0100

472 registration type of aircraft cn/fn ex/ex* mfd del powered by mtow kg configuration selcal name/fln/specialitites/remarks

registration	type of aircraft	cn/fn	ex/ex*	mfd	del	powered by	mtow kg	configuration	selcal	name/fln/specialitites/remarks
☐ OE-LAG	Airbus Industrie A340-211	075	F-WWJR*	0095	0395	4 CFMI CFM56-5C2	253500	C36Y227	GP-AR	Europe
☐ OE-LAH	Airbus Industrie A340-211	081	F-WWJO*	0095	0395	4 CFMI CFM56-5C2	253500	C36Y227	GR-EF	Asia
☐ OE-LAK	Airbus Industrie A340-313	169	F-WWJC*	0097	0497	4 CFMI CFM56-5C4	271000	C36Y261	CP-JR	Africa
☐ OE-LAL	Airbus Industrie A340-313	263	F-WWJU*	0099	0399	4 CFMI CFM56-5C4	271000	C36Y261	GH-AQ	America

AUSTRIAN AIRTRANSPORT, Oesterreichische Flugbetriebs GmbH = AAT (Subsidiary of Austrian Airlines)
Vienna-Schwechat

Postfach 50, A-1107 Wien, Austria ☎ (1) 688 16 91 Tx: none Fax: (1) 688 11 91 SITA: VIEBAOS
F: 1964 ♦♦♦ 11 Head: Dr. Herbert Koschier IATA: 663 ICAO: AUSTRIAN CHARTER Net: n/a Operates charter flights with aircraft used from the fleet of AUSTRIAN AIRLINES when required.

AUSTRO CONTROL, GmbH (The Austrian Civil Aviation Administration / Oesterreichische Gesellschaft für Zivilluftfahrt)
Vienna-Schwechat

Schnirchgasse 11, A-1030 Wien, Austria ☎ (1) 17 03 70 00 Tx: none Fax: (1) 17 03 76 SITA: n/a
F: 1994 ♦♦♦ 1050 Head: Richard Wolf Net: n/a Aircraft below MTOW 1361kg: Ce. 182P Non-commercial federal organisation conducting VIP transports, search & rescue, ambulance and business flights.

| ☐ OE-GDA | Cessna 560 Citation V | 560-0200 | | 0092 | 0498 | 2 PWC JT15D-5A | 7212 | Executive | | jtly opw MGR |

AUTOMOBILVERTRIEBS, AG = MBA (Subsidiary of Mercedes-Benz)
Salzburg

Flughafen, A-5035 Salzburg, Austria ☎ (662) 85 20 84 Tx: none Fax: (662) 85 20 84 SITA: n/a
F: 1975 ♦♦♦ n/a Head: Alexander Pappas ICAO: AVAG AIR Net: n/a Operates non-commerical corporate flights for Mercedes-Benz Austria and its affiliates companies.

| ☐ OE-FAM | Cessna 425 Conquest I | 425-0131 | OE-FIB | 0083 | | 2 PWC PT6A-112 | 3901 | Corporate | | |
| ☐ OE-GAP | Cessna 560XL Citation Excel | 560-5004 | N5148N* | 0098 | 0998 | 2 PWC PW545A | 8709 | Corporate | | |

AVANTI-AIR Bedarfsflug, GmbH = ATV (formerly Avanti Touristik, GmbH)
Vienna-Schwechat

Parkring 12a, A-1010 Wien, Austria ☎ (1) 51 460 Tx: 111581 a Fax: (1) 514 60 12 50 SITA: n/a
F: 1981 ♦♦♦ 6 Head: Ing. Hannes Nouza ICAO: AVANTI Net: n/a

| ☐ OE-FAN | Cessna 500 Citation | 500-0289 | N939KS | 0076 | | 2 PWC JT15D-1A | 5375 | 7 Pax | | |

B.A.C.H. Flugbetriebs, GmbH
Wien-Schwechat

Bachgasse 21, A-1160 Wien, Austria ☎ (1) 480 19 53 Tx: none Fax: (1) 48 01 9 53 20 SITA: n/a
F: 1993 ♦♦♦ 2 Head: Norbert Amberger Net: n/a

☐ OE-KIK	Cessna P210N Pressurized Centurion II	P21000445	N731DP	0079	0299	1 CO TSIO-520-P	1814			
☐ OE-KIM	Cessna P210N Pressurized Centurion II	P21000211	N4583K	0079	1093	1 CO TSIO-520-P	1814			
☐ OE-FFE	Cessna 421C Golden Eagle II	421C0120	N811VQ	0076	0797	2 CO GTSIO-520-L	3429			

BANNERT AIR Bedarfsflugunternehmen, GmbH = BBA (Affiliated with Alfred Bannert, GmbH)
Vienna-Schwechat

Wagramerstrasse 56, A-1220 Wien, Austria ☎ (1) 203 55 89 12 Tx: none Fax: (1) 203 55 89 26 SITA: n/a
F: 1994 ♦♦♦ n/a Head: Alfred Bannert ICAO: BANAIR Net: http://www.bannert.com

| ☐ OE-GBA | Cessna 550 Citation II | 550-0085 | N57AJ | 0079 | 0896 | 2 PWC JT15D-4 | 6577 | 8 Pax | | |

BRAUNEGG LUFTTAXI, GmbH
Vienna-Schwechat

Obere Donaustr. 37, A-1020 Wien, Austria ☎ (1) 330 40 40 Tx: none Fax: (1) 330 40 44 SITA: n/a
F: 1996 ♦♦♦ n/a Head: Dr. Rolf Braunegg Net: n/a

☐ OE-FGT	Cessna T303 Crusader	T30300086		0082	0796	2 CO L/TSIO-520-AE	2336			
☐ OE-FGL	Cessna 414A Chancellor III	414A0450	D-IFEP	0080	0796	2 CO TSIO-520-NB	3062			
☐ OE-FEG	Cessna 421C Golden Eagle III	421C1078	D-IBMF	0081	0796	2 CO GTSIO-520-N	3379			

BUNDESAMT FUER EICH- & VERMESSUNGSWESEN – BEV (Federal Office for Metrology & Surveying)
Vienna-Schwechat

Abteilung Fernerkundung, Krotenthallergasse 3, A-1080 Wien, Austria ☎ (1) 40 14 62 10 Tx: none Fax: (1) 406 99 92 SITA: n/a
F: 1957 ♦♦♦ 50 Head: Dipl. Ing. Michael Franzen Net: n/a Non-commercial federal organisation conducting aerial photography flights for Geoinformation purposes.

| ☐ OE-BBL | Pilatus PC-6/B2-H2 Turbo Porter | 664 | | 0068 | 0968 | 1 PWC PT6A-27 | 2200 | Photo / Survey | | |
| ☐ OE-BBB | Beech King Air 200 | BB-526 | | 0079 | 0679 | 2 PWC PT6A-41 | 5675 | Photo / Survey | | |

BUNDESMINISTERIUM FUER INNERES – Flugpolizei (Federal Ministry for the Interior-Airpolice)
Vienna-Meidling

Abt. II/21, Am Hof 4, A-1010 Wien, Austria ☎ (1) 531 26 47 00 Tx: none Fax: (1) 531 26 47 18 SITA: n/a
F: 1956 ♦♦♦ 88 Head: Mag. Robert Czoba Net: n/a Non-commercial federal organisation conducting police surveillance flights with JetRangers and ambulance (Notarzt) flights with Ecureuil helicopters from 1 main & 7 sub-bases.

☐ OE-BXA	Agusta-Bell 206B JetRanger III	8613		0081	0281	1 AN 250-C20B	1450	Police survey		
☐ OE-BXB	Agusta-Bell 206B JetRanger III	8644		0081	1081	1 AN 250-C20B	1450	Police survey		
☐ OE-BXC	Agusta-Bell 206B JetRanger III	8618		0082	0882	1 AN 250-C20B	1450	Police survey		
☐ OE-BXE	Agusta-Bell 206B JetRanger III	8666		0083	0783	1 AN 250-C20B	1450	Police survey		
☐ OE-BXO	Bell 206B JetRanger III	4440		0097	0597	1 AN 250-C20J	1450	Police survey		
☐ OE-BXP	Bell 206B JetRanger III	4410	C-FYDD*	0096	0796	1 AN 250-C20J	1450	Police survey		
☐ OE-BXR	Bell 206B JetRanger III	4413	C-FYDH*	0096	0796	1 AN 250-C20J	1450	Police survey		
☐ OE-BXS	Agusta-Bell 206B JetRanger III	8403		0074	0974	1 AN 250-C20J	1450	Police survey		
☐ OE-BXT	Bell 206B JetRanger III	4441		0097	0597	1 AN 250-C20J	1450	Police survey		
☐ OE-BXY	Agusta-Bell 206B JetRanger III	8604		0080	0780	1 AN 250-C20B	1450	Police survey		
☐ OE-BXZ	Agusta-Bell 206B JetRanger III	8605		0080	0880	1 AN 250-C20B	1450	Police survey		
☐ OE-BXF	Bell 206L-3 LongRanger III	51112		0084	1184	1 AN 250-C30P	1882	Policesurvey/EMS		
☐ OE-BXH	Eurocopter (Aerosp.) AS350B1 Ecureuil	1898		0086	0586	1 TU Arriel 1D	2200	EMS		
☐ OE-BXI	Eurocopter (Aerosp.) AS350B1 Ecureuil	1899		0086	0586	1 TU Arriel 1D	2200	EMS		
☐ OE-BXK	Eurocopter (Aerosp.) AS350B1 Ecureuil	1900		0086	0586	1 TU Arriel 1D	2200	EMS		
☐ OE-BXL	Eurocopter (Aerosp.) AS350B1 Ecureuil	2049		0087	0987	1 TU Arriel 1D	2200	EMS		
☐ OE-BXM	Eurocopter (Aerosp.) AS350B1 Ecureuil	2113		0088	0688	1 TU Arriel 1D	2200	EMS		
☐ OE-BXN	Eurocopter (Aerosp.) AS350B1 Ecureuil	2214		0089	0689	1 TU Arriel 1D	2200	EMS		
☐ OE-BXD	Eurocopter (Aerosp.) AS355N Ecureuil 2	5581	F-WYMK*	0094	1194	2 TU Arrius 1A	2540	EMS		
☐ OE-BXU	Eurocopter (Aerosp.) AS355F2 Ecureuil 2	5485	F-WYMA*	0091	0791	2 AN 250-C20F	2540	EMS		
☐ OE-BXW	Eurocopter (Aerosp.) AS355F2 Ecureuil 2	5528		0092	0992	2 AN 250-C20F	2540	EMS		
☐ OE-BXX	Eurocopter (Aerosp.) AS355N Ecureuil 2	5558		0093	1293	2 TU Arrius 1A	2540	EMS		

CHARTER AIR, GmbH & Co. KG = CHW
Vienna-Schwechat

Flughafen, Halle 03, Raum 052, A-1300 Wien Flughafen, Austria ☎ (1) 70 07 3 53 63 Tx: n/a Fax: (1) 70 07 3 53 64 SITA: n/a
F: n/a ♦♦♦ 6 Head: Capt. Karl Zimmermann ICAO: CHARTER WIEN Net: n/a

| ☐ OE-FRW | Cessna 414 II | 414-0825 | N98726 | 0076 | | 2 CO TSIO-520-N | 2880 | 5 Pax / EMS | | |
| ☐ OE-FOW | Fairchild (Swearingen) SA226T Merlin IIIB | T-318 | D-IBBD | 0070 | 0890 | 2 GA TPE331-10U-501G | 5670 | 9 Pax / EMS | | |

CHARTERFLUG FRUEHWALD (Dipl. Ing. Frühwald & Söhne, KG dba)
Vienna-Schwechat

Börseplatz 7, A-1010 Wien, Austria ☎ (1) 98 04 44 10 Tx: none Fax: (1) 98 04 44 16 SITA: n/a
F: 1998 ♦♦♦ n/a Head: Dipl Ing. Frühwald Net: n/a

| ☐ OE-FCI | Cessna 340A II | 340A0690 | N6347X | 0079 | | 2 CO TSIO-520-NB | 2717 | | | |

CHRISTOPHORUS FLUGRETTUNGSVEREIN – CFV (An organisation of OeAMTC / associated HELIAIR-Helikopter Air Transport)
Innsbruck

Postfach 71, Flughafen, A-6026 Innsbruck, Austria ☎ (512) 28 88 80 Tx: none Fax: (512) 28 62 00 SITA: n/a
F: 1997 ♦♦♦ 24 Head: Kurt Nordberg Net: n/a Operates Medical/EMS/Rescue flights in conjunction with OeAMTC & HELIAIR-Helikopter Air Transport.

☐ OE-FXA	Eurocopter (Aerosp.) AS355F1 Ecureuil 2	5056		0081	0398	2 AN 250-C20F	2400	EMS		Christophorus 2 / cvtd AS355F
☐ OE-FXH	Eurocopter (Aerosp.) AS355F2 Ecureuil 2	5429	F-WZKH*	0089	0398	2 AN 250-C20F	2540	EMS		Christophorus 3
☐ OE-XHN	Eurocopter (Aerosp.) AS355N Ecureuil 2	5546		0093	0398	2 TU Arrius 1A	2600	EMS		for sale
☐ OE-XEA	Eurocopter EC135T1	0025		0097	0398	2 TU Arrius 2B	2720	EMS		Christophorus 1
☐ OE-XEB	Eurocopter EC135T1	0050		0098	0498	2 TU Arrius 2B	2720	EMS		Christophorus 5
☐ OE-XEC	Eurocopter EC135T1	0053		0098	0498	2 TU Arrius 2B	2720	EMS		Christophorus 4
☐ OE-XED	Eurocopter EC135T1	0072		0098	1098	2 TU Arrius 2B	2720	EMS		Christophorus 6
☐ OE-XEE	Eurocopter EC135T1	0097		0099	0399	2 TU Arrius 2B	2720	EMS		Christophorus 2
☐ OE-	Eurocopter EC135T1					2 TU Arrius 2B	2720	EMS		oo-delivery 0099
☐ OE-	Eurocopter EC135T1					2 TU Arrius 2B	2720	EMS		oo-delivery 0099
☐ OE-	Eurocopter EC135T1					2 TU Arrius 2B	2720	EMS		oo-delivery 0099

CITY-JET Luftfahrt, GmbH = CIT
Vienna-Schwechat

General Aviation Center, A-1300 Schwechat, Austria ☎ (1) 70 07 97 01 Tx: 75314249 city a Fax: (1) 70 07 3 63 33 SITA: n/a
F: 1992 ♦♦♦ 17 Head: Dr. Ernst C. Strobl ICAO: CITY VIENNA Net: n/a

| ☐ OE-FYC | Cessna 501 Citation I/SP | 501-0207 | N968DM | 0081 | 1198 | 2 PWC JT15D-1A | 5380 | | | |
| ☐ OE-GCJ | Dassault Falcon 20C | 184 | F-GAPC | 0072 | 0795 | 2 GE CF700-2C | 13000 | | | |

COMTEL FLUG = COE (Comtel Messeflug- Veranstaltungs-GmbH & Co. Bedarfsflüge KG dba / Member of Comtel Group)
Vienna-Schwechat

Computerstr. 6, A-1101 Wien, Austria ☎ (664) 308 78 66 Tx: none Fax: (1) 70 07 59 76 SITA: n/a
F: 1988 ♦♦♦ 4 Head: Edi Meisel ICAO: COMTEL-AIR Net: n/a

| ☐ OE-FHW | Cessna 501 Citation I/SP | 501-0121 | D-IANO | 0079 | 0793 | 2 PWC JT15D-1A | 5375 | | | |
| ☐ OE-GCN | Cessna 650 Citation III | 650-0014 | C-GHOO | 0083 | 0496 | 2 GA TFE731-3-100S | 9752 | | | |

EAGLE AIRLINES Luftverkehrs, GmbH = ZN / EAV (formerly Eagle Aviation Luftfahrt, GmbH)
Klagenfurt

Ebentalerstr. 50, A-9020 Klagenfurt, Austria ☎ (316) 243 95 00 Tx: none Fax: (316) 243 95 05 SITA: n/a
F: 1991 ♦♦♦ 10 Head: Gert Litscher IATA: 528 ICAO: MAYFLOWER Net: n/a Aircraft below MTOW 1361kg: Cessna 152 & Piper PA-28.

| ☐ OE-FFL | Cessna 340A II | 340A0021 | N3KP | 0076 | | 2 CO TSIO-520-N | 2717 | Y4 | | |
| ☐ OE-LEA | Beech 1300 Airliner | BB-468 | TF-ELT | 0079 | 0496 | 2 PWC PT6A-42 | 5670 | Y11 | | cvtd Super King Air 200 |

registration   type of aircraft   cn/fn   ex/ex*   mfd   del   powered by   mtow kg   configuration   selcal   name/fln/specialitites/remarks

FLUGTAXI GmbH Suben

Linz

Schillerstr. 19, A-4910 Ried im Innkreis, Austria ☎ (7752) 82 412 Tx: none Fax: (7752) 82 412 SITA: n/a
F: 1987 n/a Head: Dipl.Ing. Alois Hatzmann Net: n/a Beside aircraft listed, also uses Cessna 550 Citation II aircraft, lsf/opb TRANSAIR (OE-), when required.

☐ OE-DEI	Cessna 210F Centurion	21058615	N4915U	0065		1 CO IO-520-A	1406			
☐ OE-FGA	Piper PA-34-200T Seneca II	34-7870207	N9661C	0078		2 CO TSIO-360-EB	1999			
☐ OE-FLX	Cessna 421C Golden Eagle II	421C0248	N5536G	0077	0797	2 CO GTSIO-520-L	3379			

GOLDECK-FLUG, GmbH

Klagenfurt

Flughafen Klagenfurt, A-9020 Klagenfurt, Austria ☎ (463) 45 975 Tx: none Fax: (463) 41 556 SITA: n/a
F: 1991 n/a Head: Dr. Hanspeter Haselsteiner Net: n/a

☐ OE-XHA	MD Helicopters MD 500E (Hughes 369E)	0336E	D-HABC	0089	0398	1 AN 250-C20B	1361			
☐ OE-XCC	Bell 206BR+ JetRanger III	4256		0092	1192	1 AN 250-C20R/4	1451			cvtd 206B
☐ OE-FBO	Piper PA-31T Cheyenne II	31T-7820051	D-IGAK	0078	0992	2 PWC PT6A-28	4082			
☐ OE-FDM	Cessna 501 Citation I/SP	501-0140	N96CF	0079	1091	2 PWC JT15D-1A	5375			
☐ OE-GCC	Cessna 560 Citation V	560-0125	N6809V	0091	0791	2 PWC JT15D-5A	7212			
☐ OE-GRR	Learjet 55	55-059	D-CAEP	0082	1296	2 GA TFE731-3A-2B	9752			

GROSSMANN AIR SERVICE Bedarfsflugunternehmen, GmbH & Co. KG

Vienna-Schwechat

Brünnerstr. 170, A-1210 Wien, Austria ☎ (1) 292 34 56 Tx: none Fax: (1) 292 45 56 18 SITA: n/a
F: 1991 10 Head: Hans Grossmann Net: n/a

☐ OE-GRO	Learjet 55	55-122	C-FHJB	0085	0698	2 GA TFE731-3AR-2B	9752	7 Pax		
☐ OE-HET	Canadair CL-600S (CL-600-1A11) Challenger	1085	N600ST	0083	0197	2 LY ALF502L-2C	18711	14 Pax		

HAAS HELIKOPTER FLUGDIENST, Ges. mbH

Bad Vöslau

Rotenhofgasse 58-2-10, A-1100 Wien, Austria ☎ (1) 602 44 12 Tx: 14343 advoe a Fax: (1) 603 02 00 SITA: n/a
F: 1976 5 Head: Sylvia Haas Net: n/a In addition to helicopters, also operates a Cameron A-105 Hot-Air Balloon (OE-PZK).

☐ OE-DXM	Bell 206A JetRanger	042	D-HEAS	0067		1 AN 250-C18B	1361			
☐ OE-KXM	Bell 206B JetRanger III	2997	D-HMHS	0080		1 AN 250-C20B	1451			
☐ OE-KXH	Eurocopter (Aerosp.) AS350B Ecureuil	1761	D-HAFP	0083		1 TU Arriel 1B	1950			
☐ OE-FXB	Eurocopter (Aerosp.) AS355F1 Ecureuil 2	5252	D-HLTK	0082	1198	2 AN 250-C20F	2400			cvtd AS355F1
☐ OE-XFH	Agusta A109A II	7318	VH-AUG	0085		2 AN 250-C20B	2600			
☐ OE-XHD	Agusta A109E Power	11033		0098	1298	2 PWC PW206C	2850			

HAIL AIR Hagelabwehr, GmbH

Graz

Pichlbergstr. 15, A-8561 Söding, Austria ☎ (3137) 61 29 Tx: none Fax: (3137) 61 29 SITA: n/a
F: 1998 n/a Head: Josef Harrer Net: n/a Operates hail prevention flights for private customers & state organisations.

☐ OE-DON	Cessna 182R Skylane II	18267887	D-EDGN	0081	0798	1 CO O-470-U	1406			

HELIAIR – Helikopter Air Transport GmbH (Sister company of Christophorus Flugrettungsverein)

Innsbruck

Postfach 71, Flughafen, A-6026 Innsbruck, Austria ☎ (512) 28 88 80 Tx: none Fax: (512) 28 62 00 SITA: n/a
F: 1977 30 Head: Kurt Nordberg Net: n/a

☐ OE-XHG	Eurocopter (Aerosp.) AS350B2 Ecureuil	2576	F-WZKH*	0091	1191	1 TU Arriel 1D1	2250	5 Pax / Utility		

HELI ALPIN KNAUS, GmbH (formerly Heli Alpin Service)

Trieben, Zell am See & Salzburg

Maschl 47, A-5600 St. Johann im Pongau, Austria ☎ (6412) 73 10 Tx: none Fax: (6412) 78 92 SITA: n/a
F: 1982 8 Head: Roy Knaus Net: n/a

☐ OE-KXW	MD Helicopters MD 500D (Hughes 369D)	700748D	G-BNMY	0080	0896	1 AN 250-C20B	1361			
☐ OE-EXF	Eurocopter (Aerosp.) SA315B Lama	2278	F-BVUF	0072	0298	1 TU Artouste IIIB	1950			
☐ OE-XKI	MD Helicopters MD 520N (Hughes 500N)	LN033	OO-MRI	0092	0595	1 AN 250-C20R	1520			

HELI AUSTRIA, GmbH

Salzburg

Hof 249, A-5310 Mondsee, Austria ☎ (6232) 40 74 Tx: 632311 heli a Fax: (6232) 40 74 15 SITA: n/a
F: 1995 5 Head: Martin Schiessl & Michael Häberle Net: n/a

☐ OE-XXY	Eurocopter (Aerosp.) AS350B2 Ecureuil	2652	D-HWPH	0092	1298	1 TU Arriel 1D1	2250			
☐ OE-XXZ	Eurocopter (Aerosp.) AS355F1 Ecureuil 2	5214	N378E	0082	0197	2 AN 250-C20F	2400			cvtd AS355F

HELICOPTER WUCHER, GmbH & Co. KG

Ludesch

Walgaustr. 214, A-6713 Ludesch, Austria ☎ (5550) 38 80 Tx: n/a Fax: (5550) 388 06 SITA: n/a
F: 1975 24 Head: Ing. Gerhard Huber Net: n/a

☐ OE-EXE	Eurocopter (Aerosp.) SA315B Lama	2406	F-WXFS	0074		1 TU Artouste IIIB	1950			
☐ OE-EXU	Eurocopter (Aerosp.) SA315B Lama	2478		0077		1 TU Artouste IIIB	1950			
☐ OE-OXR	Eurocopter (Aerosp.) SA315B Lama	1025 / 34		0090	0690	1 TU Artouste IIIB	1950			cvtd Alouette II
☐ OE-OXA	Eurocopter (Aerosp.) AS350B2 Ecureuil	2158		0088		1 TU Arriel 1D1	2250			cvtd AS350B1
☐ OE-XHB	Eurocopter (Aerosp.) AS350B2 Ecureuil	2536		0091	0891	1 TU Arriel 1D1	2250			
☐ OE-EXS	Bell 205A-1	30265	N5002N	0078		1 LY T5317A	4309			

HELI-LINE Hubschraubertransporte, GmbH

Seitenstetten

Oed am seichten Graben 9, A-3250 Wieselburg-Land, Austria ☎ (7416) 55 100 Tx: n/a Fax: (7416) 55 10 04 SITA: n/a
F: 1994 n/a Head: Gerold Simon Net: n/a Aircraft below MTOW 1361kg: Robinson R44

☐ OE-XKH	Bell 206B JetRanger III	3814	N3189T	0084	0895	1 AN 250-C20B	1451			

HELIOS Hubschraubertransport, GmbH

Salzburg

Bahnhofstr. 36, A-5102 Anthering, Austria ☎ (6223) 29 94 Tx: n/a Fax: (6223) 33 70 SITA: n/a
F: 1995 3 Head: Walter Enthammer Net: http://www.helios.at

☐ OE-XHE	MD Helicopters MD 500D (Hughes 369D)	770166D	D-HHOP	0077	0395	1 AN 250-C20B	1360			

HELI TEAM Bedarfsflug, GmbH

Krems

Ringstr. 10/3D, A-3500 Krems, Austria ☎ (664) 102 14 19 Tx: none Fax: (2732) 81 216 SITA: n/a
F: 1992 n/a Head: Peter Steiner Net: n/a

☐ D-HHBI	Bell 206BR+ JetRanger III	4210		0092	0098	1 AN 250-C20R/4	1450			occ lsf Betzler Heli-Line / cvtd 206B

HUBI-FLY Helicopter Bedarfsflug & Flugschule (Hubi-Fly Helikopterschule, GmbH dba)

Bad Vöslau

Flugplatzstrasse, Flugplatz Bad Vöslau, A-2540 Bad Vöslau, Austria ☎ (2252) 73 555 Tx: n/a Fax: (2252) 73 555 SITA: n/a
F: 1991 5 Head: André Dobias & Henrik Wojnar Net: n/a Aircraft below MTOW 1361kg: Hughes 269C (300C) & Robinson R22B

☐ OE-XCD	Bell 206B JetRanger III	3750	N45EA	0083	0592	1 AN 250-C20J	1451			

HUBSCHRAUBER FLUG (Affiliated with Aviation Consulting & Leasing Luftfahrzeugberatungs- & Vermietungs, GmbH)

Graz

Moserhofgasse 31, A-8010 Graz, Austria ☎ (663) 83 53 95 Tx: none Fax: (316) 291 58 39 SITA: n/a
F: 1985 n/a Head: Helmut Leitner Net: http://homepage.sime.com/airtransport Aircraft below MTOW 1361kg: Cessna 150 & 172

☐ D-EKGD	Commander (Rockwell) 114	14397	OE-KGD	0078		1 LY IO-540-T4A5D	1424			lsf pvt
☐ OE-FHD	Piper PA-44-180 Seminole	44-7995111	N61624	0079	1193	2 LY 0-360-E1AD	1724			
☐ OE-KXE	Bell 206LR+ LongRanger	45028	D-HAVS	0076	0490	1 AN 250-C20R	1814			Aquila / cvtd 206L

HUBSCHRAUBER TRANSPORT, GmbH

Innsbruck

Kranebitter Allee 24, A-6020 Innsbruck, Austria ☎ (512) 278 55 80 Tx: none Fax: (512) 27 85 57 SITA: n/a
F: 1998 n/a Head: Franz Giakomini Net: n/a

☐ OE-XMH	Eurocopter (Aerosp.) SA315B Lama	2587	HB-XTR	0080	1098	1 TU Artouste IIIB	1950			
☐ OE-OXT	Eurocopter (Aerosp.) AS350B2 Ecureuil	2393	F-WZFN*	0090	1198	1 TU Arriel 1D1	2250			

KLM alps (AAA Austria / Air Alps Aviation, Alpenländische Luftfahrt, GmbH dba / Assoc. with Air Engiadina)

Innsbruck & Salzburg

Fürstenweg 180, A-6020 Innsbruck, Austria ☎ (512) 29 27 29 Tx: none Fax: (512) 29 27 29 27 SITA: n/a
F: 1998 n/a Head: Helmut Wurm Net: n/a Operates scheduled services in conjunction with KLM-Royal Dutch Airlines, using KL flight numbers.

☐ OE-LKA	Dornier 328-110	3110		0099	0399	2 PWC PW119B	13990	Y31		
☐ OE-LKB	Dornier 328-110	3036	HB-AEH	0095	0399	2 PWC PW119B	13990	Y31		

LAUDA AIR Luftfahrt, AG = NG / LDA (Assoc. with Lufthansa & Austrian Airlines/Member of European Leisure Group)

Vienna-Schwechat

Postfach 56, A-1300 Wien-Flughafen, Austria ☎ (1) 70 00 Tx: 133850 lauda a Fax: (1) 70 00 78 005 SITA: VIESONG
F: 1979 1200 Head: Niki Lauda IATA: 231 ICAO: LAUDA AIR Net: http://www.laudaair.com

☐ OE-GLL	Learjet 60	60-				2 PWC PW305A	10659	Exec 7 Pax		oo-delivery 0099
☐ OE-GNL	Learjet 60	60-032	N5013D	0094	1094	2 PWC PW305A	10319	Exec 7 Pax		
☐ OE-HLE	Canadair CL-601-1A (CL-600-2A12) Challen.	3047	N602TJ	0085	0698	2 GE CF34-1A	19550	Exec 14 Pax		
☐ OE-LRA	Canadair Regional Jet 100LR (CL-600-2B19)	7032	C-FRKQ*	0093	0394	2 GE CF34-3A1	23995	CY50	FS-BG	Herbert von Karajan / cvtd 100ER
☐ OE-LRB	Canadair Regional Jet 100LR (CL-600-2B19)	7033	C-FMNX*	0094	0394	2 GE CF34-3A1	23995	CY50	FS-BH	Leonard Bernstein / cvtd 100ER
☐ OE-LRC	Canadair Regional Jet 100LR (CL-600-2B19)	7036	C-FROL*	0094	0394	2 GE CF34-3A1	23995	CY50	HL-CR	lst CLH as D-ACLX / cvtd 100ER
☐ OE-LRD	Canadair Regional Jet 100LR (CL-600-2B19)	7052	C-FMMN*	0094	0195	2 GE CF34-3A1	23995	CY50	HL-CS	Egon Schiele
☐ OE-LRE	Canadair Regional Jet 100LR (CL-600-2B19)	7059		0095	0295	2 GE CF34-3A1	23995	CY50	HL-DR	Gustav Klimt
☐ OE-LRF	Canadair Regional Jet 100LR (CL-600-2B19)	7061	C-FMNQ*	0095	0395	2 GE CF34-3A1	23995	CY50	HL-DS	Oskar Kokoschka
☐ OE-LRG	Canadair Regional Jet 100LR (CL-600-2B19)	7063	C-FMNY*	0095	0395	2 GE CF34-3A1	23995	CY50	HL-ER	Jean Tinguely
☐ OE-LRH	Canadair Regional Jet 100LR (CL-600-2B19)	7125	C-FMMB*	0396	0796	2 GE CF34-3A1	23995	CY50	HL-ES	Jochen Rindt
☐ OE-ILF	Boeing 737-3Z9	23601 / 1254		0086	0786	2 CFMI CFM56-3B1	61990	CY139	FH-JL	Bob Marley
☐ OE-ILG	Boeing 737-3Z9	24081 / 1515		0088	0388	2 CFMI CFM56-3B1	61990	CY139	BL-HP	John Lennon
☐ OE-	Boeing 737-6Z9					2 CFMI CFM56-7B20	65091			oo-delivery 0300
☐ OE-	Boeing 737-6Z9					2 CFMI CFM56-7B20	65091			oo-delivery 0700

474 registration type of aircraft cn/fn ex/ex* mfd del powered by mtow kg configuration selcal name/fln/specialitites/remarks

☐ OE-	Boeing 737-7Z9					2 CFMI CFM56-7B24	69400			oo-delivery 0101
☐ OE-	Boeing 737-7Z9					2 CFMI CFM56-7B24	69400			oo-delivery 0002
☐ OE-	Boeing 737-7Z9					2 CFMI CFM56-7B24	69400			oo-delivery 0002
☐ OE-	Boeing 737-7Z9					2 CFMI CFM56-7B24	69400			oo-delivery 0002
☐ OE-LNH	Boeing 737-4Z9	25147 / 2043		0091	0591	2 CFMI CFM56-3C1	67999	Y164	GJ-DQ	Elvis Presley
☐ OE-LNI	Boeing 737-4Z9	27094 / 2432		0093	0293	2 CFMI CFM56-3C1	67999	Y164	BL-JK	Janis Joplin
☐ OE-LNJ	Boeing 737-8Z9	28177 / 69		0098	0798	2 CFMI CFM56-7B26	77997	Y184		Falco
☐ OE-LNK	Boeing 737-8Z9	28178 / 222	N1786B*	0099	0399	2 CFMI CFM56-7B26	77997	Y184		
☐ OE-LAS	Boeing 767-33A (ER)	27909 / 591		0095	0895	2 PW PW4056	186880	C24Y220	JS-MQ	Ayrton Senna / lsf AWAS / sub-lst LDI
☐ OE-LAT	Boeing 767-31A (ER)	25273 / 393	PH-MCK	1291	1291	2 PW PW4060	184612	C24Y234	DH-BC	Enzo Ferrari / lst LDI
☐ OE-LAU	Boeing 767-3Z9 (ER)	23765 / 165	N6009F*	0087	0588	2 PW PW4056	173725	C24Y220	BL-JP	Marilyn Monroe / cvtd -3T9
☐ OE-LAW	Boeing 767-3Z9 (ER)	26417 / 448		0092	0892	2 PW PW4060	184612	C24Y220	CE-AS	Franz Schubert
☐ OE-LAX	Boeing 767-3Z9 (ER)	27095 / 467		0092	1292	2 PW PW4060	184612	C24Y220	CE-BR	James Dean
☐ OE-LAY	Boeing 767-3Z9 (ER)	29867 / 731		1298	1298	2 PW PW4060	186880	C36Y209		
☐ OE-LAZ	Boeing 767-3Z9 (ER)					2 PW PW4060	186880	C36Y209		oo-delivery 0899
☐ OE-LPA	Boeing 777-2Z9 (ER)	28698 / 87	N5022E*	0097	0997	2 GE GE90-92B	286897	C42Y302	DR-MS	Inspiration
☐ OE-LPB	Boeing 777-2Z9 (ER)	28699 / 163		0998	0998	2 GE GE90-92B	286897	C42Y302	AE-BQ	Ernest Hemmingway
☐ OE-LPC	Boeing 777-2Z9 (ER)					2 GE GE90-92B	286897	C42Y302		oo-delivery 0002
☐ OE-LPD	Boeing 777-2Z9 (ER)					2 GE GE90-92B	286897	C42Y302		oo-delivery 0003

LVD Luftfahrzeug-Vermietungs-Dienst, GmbH — Graz

Wielandgasse 14-16, A-8010 Graz, Austria ☎ (316) 818 90 00 Tx: none Fax: (316) 81 89 00 99 SITA: n/a
F: 1996 ⚲ n/a Head: Guenther Matheis Net: n/a

☐ OE-FBI	Piper PA-34-220T Seneca III	34-8433062	N4361N	0084	0397	2 CO TSIO-360-KB	1999			
☐ OE-FLD	Piper PA-34-200T Seneca II	34-7870076	N2271M	0077	0898	2 CO TSIO-360-E	1999			
☐ OE-FBY	Cessna 421B Golden Eagle	421B0931	OE-BAY	0075	1198	2 CO GTSIO-520-H	3379			

MAGNA AIR Luftfahrt, GmbH = MGR (Subsidiary of Magna International Inc., Toronto, Canada) — Vienna-Schwechat

Magna-Str. 1, A-2522 Oberwaltersdorf, Austria ☎ (2253) 60 020 Tx: none Fax: (2253) 60 05 58 SITA: n/a
F: 1996 ⚲ n/a Head: Lukas Lichtner-Hoyer ICAO: MAGNA AIR Net: n/a

☐ OE-FGI	Cessna 525 CitationJet	525-0254		0098	0598	2 WRR FJ44-1A	4717	Executive		lsf Orest-Immorent Leasing GmbH
☐ HB-VLM	Beech Beechjet 400A	RK-66	N400Y	0093	1098	2 PWC JT15D-5	7303	Executive		lsf/opf Corpavia Jets
☐ HB-VLN	Beech Beechjet 400A	RK-94	N3051S	0094	1098	2 PWC JT15D-5	7303	Executive		lsf/opf Corpavia Jets
☐ OE-GDA	Cessna 560 Citation V	560-0200		0092	0397	2 PWC JT15D-5A	7212	Executive		jtly opw Austro Control
☐ OE-GMI	Cessna 560 Citation V Ultra	560-0362		0096	0596	2 PWC JT15D-5D	7394	Executive		
☐ OE-IMI	Dassault Falcon 900B	147	N900FJ	0094	0596	3 GA TFE731-5BR-1C	21099	Executive		

MALI AIR Luftverkehr, GmbH — Graz

Reitbach 22, A-8763 Möderbrugg, Austria ☎ (3571) 26 326 Tx: none Fax: (3571) 26 326 SITA: n/a
F: 1996 ⚲ 9 Head: Karl-Heinz Mali Net: http://members.magnet.at/mali

☐ OE-FMH	Cessna 340A II	340A0289	D-IAAB	0077		2 CO TSIO-520-N	2717			

PHOENIX, GmbH — Vienna-Schwechat

Fröbelgasse 48, A-1160 Wien, Austria ☎ (1) 495 10 10 Tx: none Fax: (1) 495 10 10 SITA: n/a
F: 1987 ⚲ n/a Head: Peter Kukla Net: n/a

☐ OE-FCV	Cessna 340A II	340A1263		0081		2 CO TSIO-520-NB	2717			

PINK AVIATION SERVICES Luftverkehrsunternehmen, GmbH & Co KG (formerly Burli Air Arbeitsflüge, GmbH) — Vienna-Schwechat

Endresstr. 79/4, A-1238 Wien, Austria ☎ (1) 888 58 88 Tx: none Fax: (1) 889 26 26 SITA: n/a
F: 1985 ⚲ 8 Head: Thomas Lewetz Net: n/a

☐ OE-FDE	Shorts Skyvan 3 Variant 100 (SC-7)	SH1886	C9-ASN	0070	0199	2 GA TPE331-2-201A	5670	Para		

PUNITZ FLUG Betrieb, GmbH — Punitz

Untere Hauptstr. 165, A-7535 St. Michael, Austria ☎ (3327) 86 84 Tx: none Fax: (3327) 86 84 SITA: n/a
F: 1985 ⚲ 3 Head: Reinhard Kremsner Net: n/a Aircraft below MTOW 1361kg: Cessna 150 & Piper PA-28

☐ OE-FPU	Cessna 414A Chancellor III	414A0505	D-IHAB	0080	0591	2 CO TSIO-520-NB	3062			

QUICK AIR-Bedarfsflug, GmbH — Vienna-Neustadt Ost

Stadiongasse 5, A-7350 Oberpullendorf, Austria ☎ (2612) 45 923 Tx: none Fax: (2612) 424 54 85 SITA: n/a
F: 1998 ⚲ n/a Head: Andreas Geldner Net: http://www.geldner.at/quickair

☐ OE-FCA	Cessna 421C Golden Eagle II	421C0099	D-IACS	0076	0398	2 CO GTSIO-520-L	3379			

RHEINTALFLUG = WE / RTL (Team Lufthansa) (Rheintalflug Seewald, GmbH dba) — Vienna-Schwechat

Bahnhofstr. 10A, A-6900 Bregenz, Austria ☎ (5574) 48 800 Tx: none Fax: (5574) 48 80 08 SITA: ACHRRWE
F: 1973 ⚲ 80 Head: Rolf Seewald IATA: 915 ICAO: RHEINTAL Net: n/a Some scheduled flights are operated in conjunction with LH as a Team franchise partner (in full Team Lufthansa colors & titles) using LH flight numbers.

☐ OE-LRS	De Havilland DHC-8-103 Dash 8	175	OE-HRS	0089	0989	2 PWC PW121	15649	Y37		Silvretta / lsf VIP-Air
☐ OE-LRW	De Havilland DHC-8-311 Dash 8	307	C-FTUX	0091	0495	2 PWC PW123	18643	Y50		Valbella / lsf GECA / op in Team LH-cs
☐ OE-LSA	De Havilland DHC-8-314 Dash 8Q	487	C-GEWI*	0097	0298	2 PWC PW123B	19505	Y50		Löwental / op in Team Lufthansa-colors
☐ OE-LSB	De Havilland DHC-8-314 Dash 8Q	525	C-FDHY*	0099	0299	2 PWC PW123B	19505	Y50		Fürstentum Liechtenstein
☐ OE-	De Havilland DHC-8-314 Dash 8Q					2 PWC PW123B	19505	Y50		oo-delivery 0300
☐ OE-	De Havilland DHC-8-401 Dash 8Q					2 PWC PW150A	28690	Y72		oo-delivery 0600

RUESCHER HELICOPTER, GmbH – Air-Service — Feldkirch & Hohenems

Münkafeld 7, A-6800 Feldkirch, Austria ☎ (5522) 82 23 80 Tx: none Fax: (5522) 31 965 SITA: n/a
F: 1995 ⚲ 2 Head: Walter Rüscher Net: http://www.ruescher.com

☐ OE-XRA	Bell 206B JetRanger III	3968	N206RP	0087	0798	1 AN 250-C20J	1451			
☐ OE-XRB	Bell 206B JetRanger III	2311	D-HAUO	0077	0598	1 AN 250-C20B	1451			lsf Meravo

SHS HELICOPTER TRANSPORTE, GmbH – Schider Helicopter Service — Waidring Heliport & Zell am See

Unterwasser 59, A-6384 Waidring, Austria ☎ (5353) 63 02 Tx: none Fax: (5353) 63 02 22 SITA: n/a
F: 1993 ⚲ 6 Head: Rudolf Schider Net: n/a

☐ OE-XRS	Eurocopter (Aerosp.) AS350B1 Ecureuil	2021	F-GEOD	0087	0694	1 TU Arriel 1D	2200			

STEIRISCHE MOTORFLUG-UNION & Airtaxi — Graz

Flughafen Graz-Thalerhof, A-8073 Graz, Austria ☎ (316) 29 10 09 Tx: none Fax: (316) 29 25 10 SITA: n/a
F: 1961 ⚲ 2 Head: Josef Zöhrer Net: http://www.motorflugunion.com Aircraft below MTOW 1361 kg: Cessna 150 / 152 & Piper PA-28.

☐ OE-KMH	Piper PA-32R-301T Turbo Saratoga SP	32R-8529007	N6912B	0085	0192	1 LY TIO-540-S1AD	1633			
☐ OE-FEE	Piper PA-34-220T Seneca III	34-8133066	D-GILS	0081		2 CO TSIO-360-KB	1999			

TAXIFLUG, GmbH Dornbirn (Subsidiary of Zumtobel, AG) — Hohenems-Dornbirn

Hoechster Str. 8, A-6850 Dornbirn, Austria ☎ (5572) 390 12 29 Tx: 59126 zumt a Fax: (5572) 39 06 02 SITA: n/a
F: 1975 ⚲ 10 Head: Jürg Zumtobel Net: n/a

☐ OE-GLZ	Cessna 550 Citation II	550-0690		0091	0691	2 PWC JT15D-4	6396			occ lst/jtly opw Albus Air

THE FLYING BULLS, GmbH (Sister company of Red Bull, GmbH) — Innsbruck

Alpenstr. 54, A-5020 Salzburg, Austria ☎ (664) 358 82 33 Tx: none Fax: (512) 29 10 36 SITA: n/a
F: 1998 ⚲ 3 Head: Martin Lener Net: n/a Operates historical flights to airshows & fly-inns.

☐ OE-FWS	Grumman G-44A Widgeon (Scan-30)	30	N151SA	0056	0898	2 LY GO-480	2495			Amphibian
☐ OE-ESA	North American T-28B Texan	200-250	N3905H	0054	0898	1 PW R-1340	3496			
☐ N6123C	North American B-25J Mitchell		44-86893A	0044	0098	2 WR R-2800	15876			lsf Red Bull Aviation Inc.

TIROLER FLUGHAFENBETRIEBS, GmbH – Bedarfsflugunternehmen — Innsbruck

Postfach 89, A-6026 Innsbruck, Austria ☎ (512) 22 52 51 03 Tx: none Fax: (512) 29 25 40 SITA: INNAPXH
F: 1966 ⚲ 3 Head: Dipl. Ing. Reto Manitz Net: http://www.tirol.com/flughafen

☐ OE-FTI	Piper PA-34-220T Seneca III	34-8533002	N4376N	0085	0291	2 CO L/TSIO-360-KB	1999			

TRANSAIR Bedarfsflugunternehmen, GmbH — Vienna-Schwechat

Kärntner Ring 4, A-1015 Wien, Austria ☎ (1) 505 51 50 Tx: 134543 vimpx a Fax: (1) 505 41 92 SITA: n/a
F: 1985 ⚲ n/a Head: Nabil Kuzbari Net: n/a

☐ OE-GCI	Cessna 550 Citation II	550-0041	N177HH	0078	1296	2 PWC JT15D-4	6032			

TYROLEAN AIRWAYS, Tiroler Luftfahrt AG = VO / TYR (Member of Austrian Airlines Group) — Innsbruck

Postfach 81, A-6026 Innsbruck, Austria ☎ (512) 22 22 0 Tx: none Fax: (512) 22 22 90 05 SITA: INNTJXH
F: 1958 ⚲ 1050 Head: Fritz A. Feitl IATA: 734 ICAO: TYROLEAN Net: http://www.tjs.at

☐ OE-LLE	De Havilland DHC-8-106 Dash 8	355	C-GFEN*	0094	0194	2 PWC PW121	16466	Y37	NONE	Zillertal
☐ OE-LLF	De Havilland DHC-8-106 Dash 8	351	C-FWBB*	0093	0293	2 PWC PW121	16466	Y37	NONE	Seefeld
☐ OE-LLG	De Havilland DHC-8-106 Dash 8	345	C-GFQL*	0092	0193	2 PWC PW121	16466	Y37	NONE	Kufstein
☐ OE-LLH	De Havilland DHC-8-106 Dash 8	268	C-GFBW*	0091	0391	2 PWC PW121	16466	Y37	NONE	Kitzbühel / cvtd -103
☐ OE-LLJ	De Havilland DHC-8-106 Dash 8	317	OE-LRU	0092	0694	2 PWC PW121	16466	Y37	NONE	Arlberg / cvtd -103
☐ OE-LLL	De Havilland DHC-8-106 Dash 8	253	C-GETI*	0090	1290	2 PWC PW121	16466	Y37	NONE	lst AUB as D-BDUS / cvtd -103
☐ OE-LLX	De Havilland DHC-8-314 Dash 8	323	C-GFEN*	0092	0492	2 PWC PW123B	19505	Y50	NONE	Land Salzburg
☐ OE-LLY	De Havilland DHC-8-314 Dash 8	370	C-GFUM*	0094	0294	2 PWC PW123B	19505	Y50	NONE	Land Vorarlberg
☐ OE-LLZ	De Havilland DHC-8-314 Dash 8	340	C-GLOT*	0093	0294	2 PWC PW123B	19505	Y50	NONE	Land Burgenland
☐ OE-LTD	De Havilland DHC-8-314 Dash 8	400		0095	0495	2 PWC PW123B	19505	Y50	NONE	Land Oberösterreich / SOS Kinderdorf-cs

475 registration | type of aircraft | cn/fn | ex/ex* | mfd | del | powered by | mtow kg | configuration | selcal | name/fln/specialitites/remarks

☐ OE-LTF	De Havilland DHC-8-314 Dash 8	423	C-GDIU*	0096	0296	2 PWC PW123B	19505	Y50	NONE	Land Niederösterreich
☐ OE-LTG	De Havilland DHC-8-314 Dash 8Q	438	C-GDFT*	0096	0597	2 PWC PW123B	19505	Y50	NONE	Land Tirol
☐ OE-LTH	De Havilland DHC-8-314 Dash 8Q	442	C-GFUM*	0096	0697	2 PWC PW123B	19505	Y50	NONE	
☐ OE-LTI	De Havilland DHC-8-314 Dash 8Q	466	C-GFQL*	0096	0697	2 PWC PW123B	19505	Y50	NONE	special The Sounds of Silence-colors
☐ OE-LTJ	De Havilland DHC-8-314 Dash 8Q	481	C-GDOE*	0097	1297	2 PWC PW123B	19505	Y50	NONE	cvtd -311
☐ OE-LTK	De Havilland DHC-8-314 Dash 8Q	483	C-GDFT*	0097	1197	2 PWC PW123B	19505	Y50	NONE	cvtd -311
☐ OE-LTL	De Havilland DHC-8-314 Dash 8Q	485	C-GFYI*	0097	1297	2 PWC PW123B	19505	Y50	NONE	cvtd -311
☐ OE-LTM	De Havilland DHC-8-314 Dash 8Q	527		0098	1298	2 PWC PW123B	19505	Y50	NONE	
☐ OE-LTN	De Havilland DHC-8-314 Dash 8Q	531		0098	1298	2 PWC PW123B	19505	Y50	NONE	
☐ OE-LLU	De Havilland DHC-7-102 Dash 7	113	C-GFCF*	0088	1288	4 PWC PT6A-50	19958	Y48	LQ-AH	for sale
☐ OE-LCF	Canadair Regional Jet 200LR (CL-600-2B19)	7094		0095	0196	2 GE CF34-3B1	23995	Y50	JR-GM	Stadt Düsseldorf
☐ OE-LCG	Canadair Regional Jet 200LR (CL-600-2B19)	7103		0096	0296	2 GE CF34-3B1	23995	Y50	JR-GP	Stadt Köln
☐ OE-LCH	Canadair Regional Jet 200LR (CL-600-2B19)	7110	C-FMMB*	0096	0496	2 GE CF34-3B1	23995	Y50	JR-GQ	Stadt Amsterdam
☐ OE-LCI	Canadair Regional Jet 200LR (CL-600-2B19)	7133	C-FMNB*	0096	0996	2 GE CF34-3B1	23995	Y50	MQ-DS	Stadt Zürich
☐ OE-LCJ	Canadair Regional Jet 200LR (CL-600-2B19)	7142	C-FMMN*	0096	1096	2 GE CF34-3B1	23995	Y50	MQ-EJ	Stadt Hannover
☐ OE-LCK	Canadair Regional Jet 200LR (CL-600-2B19)	7148	C-FMNB*	0096	0297	2 GE CF34-3B1	23995	Y50	BF-MR	Stadt Brüssel
☐ OE-LCL	Canadair Regional Jet 200LR (CL-600-2B19)	7167	C-FMLT*	0097	0397	2 GE CF34-3B1	23995	Y50	BF-MS	Stadt Oslo
☐ OE-LCM	Canadair Regional Jet 200LR (CL-600-2B19)	7205		0097	1297	2 GE CF34-3B1	23995	Y50	JR-EP	Stadt Bologna
☐ OE-	Canadair Regional Jet 200LR (CL-600-2B19)					2 GE CF34-3B1	23995	Y50		oo-delivery 0100
☐ OE-	Canadair Regional Jet 200LR (CL-600-2B19)					2 GE CF34-3B1	23995	Y50		oo-delivery 0200
☐ OE-	Canadair Regional Jet 200LR (CL-600-2B19)					2 GE CF34-3B1	23995	Y50		oo-delivery 0201
☐ OE-	Canadair Regional Jet 200LR (CL-600-2B19)					2 GE CF34-3B1	23995	Y50		oo-delivery 1001
☐ OE-	De Havilland DHC-8-401 Dash 8Q					2 PWC PW150A	28690	Y72		oo-delivery 1299
☐ OE-	De Havilland DHC-8-401 Dash 8Q					2 PWC PW150A	28690	Y72		oo-delivery 1299
☐ OE-	De Havilland DHC-8-401 Dash 8Q					2 PWC PW150A	28690	Y72		oo-delivery 0100
☐ OE-	De Havilland DHC-8-401 Dash 8Q					2 PWC PW150A	28690	Y72		oo-delivery 0900
☐ OE-	De Havilland DHC-8-401 Dash 8Q					2 PWC PW150A	28690	Y72		oo-delivery 0101
☐ OE-LFG	Fokker 70 (F28 Mk0070)	11549	PH-EZW*	0095	0595	2 RR Tay 620-15	37995	Y80	JR-EK	Stadt Innsbruck
☐ OE-LFH	Fokker 70 (F28 Mk0070)	11554	PH-EZN*	0095	0895	2 RR Tay 620-15	37995	Y80	JR-EL	Stadt Salzburg
☐ OE-LFI	Fokker 70 (F28 Mk0070)	11529	PH-WXF	0094	1098	2 RR Tay 620-15	37995	Y80	LS-DP	Stadt Klagenfurt
☐ OE-LFJ	Fokker 70 (F28 Mk0070)	11532	PH-WXG	0095	0298	2 RR Tay 620-15	37995	Y80	LS-EP	Stadt Graz
☐ OE-LFK	Fokker 70 (F28 Mk0070)	11555	PH-EZP*	0095	0895	2 RR Tay 620-15	37995	Y80	JR-EM	Stadt Wien
☐ OE-LFL	Fokker 70 (F28 Mk0070)	11573	PH-WXE	0095	0897	2 RR Tay 620-15	37995	Y80	NONE	Stadt Linz

TYROLEAN JET SERVICE, GmbH = TYJ (Tyrolean Air Ambulance) (Associated with Tyrolean Airways)

Innsbruck

Postfach 71, A-6026 Innsbruck Flughafen, Austria ☎ (512) 224 22 Tx: 534314 tyjet a Fax: (512) 28 88 88 SITA: INNDAVO
F: 1984 ⁂ 50 Head: Mag. Jakob Ringler Net: http://www.tjs.co.at Uses the marketing name "Tyrolean Air Ambulance" for ambulance and medical services (net, http://www.taa.co.at).

☐ OE-FMS	Cessna 501 Citation I/SP	501-0239	N164CB	0082		2 PWC JT15D-1A	5375	Executive		
☐ OE-GAA	Cessna 560 Citation V	560-0111		0091	0591	2 PWC JT15D-5A	7212	EMS		
☐ OE-GSW	Cessna 560 Citation V	560-0088		0090	1190	2 PWC JT15D-5A	7212	Executive		
☐ OE-GSC	Dassault Falcon 10	122	N312AT	0078	0695	2 GA TFE731-2-1C	8500	EMS		
☐ OE-GBB	Dornier 328-110	3078	D-CDXG*	0096	1196	2 PWC PW119B	13990	Y31orC19orEMS		Rotterdam
☐ OE-HCC	Dornier 328JET (328-300)					2 PWC PW306B	14990	Y32orExecorEMS		oo-delivery 0899
☐ OE-	Dornier 328JET (328-300)					2 PWC PW306B	14990	Y32orExecorEMS		oo-delivery 1000
☐ OE-ILS	Dassault Falcon 900	58		0088		3 GA TFE731-5AR-1C2	20638	Executive		

VIP-AIR Flug, GmbH = VPI (Sister company of Rheintalflug / formerly part of Rheintalflug)

Hohenems-Dornbirn

Flugplatz, A-6845 Hohenems, Austria ☎ (5576) 73 142 Tx: 59458 rtfl a Fax: (5576) 73 559 SITA: n/a
F: 1973 ⁂ 3 Head: Rolf Seewald Net: n/a Aircraft below MTOW 1361kg: Piper PA-28.

☐ OE-KRS	Piper PA-32-301 Saratoga	32-8106096	N8435H	0081		1 LY IO-540-K1G5D	1633			
☐ OE-FLH	Piper PA-34-200T Seneca II	34-7670323	N3899F	0076	0298	2 CO TSIO-360-E	1999			lsf pvt
☐ OE-LRS	De Havilland DHC-8-103 Dash 8	175	OE-HRS	0089	0698	2 PWC PW121	15649	Y37		Silvretta / lst RTL

VOESLAUER FLUGBETRIEB Ing. Watschinger, GmbH

Bad Vöslau

Flugplatz, A-2540 Bad Vöslau, Austria ☎ (2252) 772 16 Tx: n/a Fax: (2252) 897 97 SITA: n/a
F: 1987 ⁂ 3 Head: Ing. Günter Watschinger Net: n/a Aircraft below MTOW 1361 kg: DA 20, DV 20 Katana & Piper PA-28

☐ OE-DHY	Piper PA-32-300 Cherokee SIX	32-7940119	N28581	0079		1 LY IO-540-K1G5D	1542			
☐ OE-FAR	Piper PA-34-200T Seneca II	34-8070053	D-GMOX	0080	1298	2 CO TSIO-360-EB	1999			

WACHAUFLUG, GmbH (Subsidiary of B.A.C.H. Flugbetriebs, GmbH)

Wien-Schwechat

Bachgasse 21, A-1160 Wien, Austria ☎ (1) 480 19 53 Tx: none Fax: (1) 48 01 97 04 SITA: n/a
F: 1989 ⁂ 21 Head: Norbert Amberger Net: n/a

☐ OE-FRH	Cessna 414A Chancellor II	414A0027		0078	0790	2 CO TSIO-520-N	3062			
☐ OE-FRF	Beech King Air B200	BB-933	D-IAWS	0081	0299	2 PWC PT6A-42	5670			

OH = FINLAND (Republic of Finland) (Suomen Tasavalta)

Capital: Helsinki Official Language: Finnish Population: 5,1 million Square Km: 338145 Dialling code: +358 Acting political head: Paavo Lipponen (Prime Minister)

Government / Corporate / Executive / VIP Aircraft

☐ LJ-1	Learjet 35A	35A-430	N10870*	0081	0982	2 GA TFE731-2-2B	8301	VIP/miltrans/Svy		Ilmavoimat/Finnish Air Force
☐ LJ-2	Learjet 35A	35A-451	N1462B*	0082	0982	2 GA TFE731-2-2B	8301	VIP/miltrans/Svy		Ilmavoimat/Finnish Air Force
☐ LJ-3	Learjet 35A	35A-470	N3810G*	0082	0982	2 GA TFE731-2-2B	8301	VIP/miltrans/Svy		Ilmavoimat/Finnish Air Force

AIR BOTNIA = KF / KFB (Oy Air Botnia, Ab dba / Subsidiary of Scandinavian Airlines SAS)

Helsinki-Vantaa

PL 168, FIN-01531 Vantaa, Finland ☎ (9) 61 51 29 00 Tx: none Fax: (9) 61 51 29 19 SITA: n/a
F: 1987 ⁂ 50 Head: Heikki Jolula IATA: 142 ICAO: BOTNIA Net: n/a

☐ OH-JAB	BAe 3201 Jetstream 32	835	G-BUIO	0088	0293	2 GA TPE331-12UAR-705H	7350	Y19		lsf BAMT
☐ OH-JAD	BAe 3201 Jetstream 32	836	N836JX	0089	0894	2 GA TPE331-12UAR-705H	7350	Y19		lsf BAMT
☐ OH-JAE	BAe 3201 Jetstream 32	840	N840JX	0089	1094	2 GA TPE331-12UAR-705H	7350	Y19		lsf BAMT
☐ OH-JAF	BAe 3201 Jetstream 32	847	N847JX	0089	1296	2 GA TPE331-12UAR-704H	7350	Y19		lsf BAMT
☐ OH-JAG	BAe 3201 Jetstream 32	845	N845JX	0089	0497	2 GA TPE331-12UAR-704H	7350	Y19		lsf BAMT
☐ OH-SAC	Saab SF340A	340A-081	N374DC	0087	0798	2 GE CT7-5A2	12700	Y34		lsf De Havilland Corp.
☐ OH-SAD	Saab SF340A	340A-083	N376DC	0087	0998	2 GE CT7-5A2	12700	Y34		lsf De Havilland Corp.
☐ OH-SAE	Saab SF340A	340A-117	N378DC	0088	0998	2 GE CT7-5A2	12700	Y34		lsf De Havilland Corp.
☐ OH-SAF	Saab SF340A	340A-143	N375DC	0089	0798	2 GE CT7-5A2	12700	Y34		lsf De Havilland Corp.
☐ SE-DGO	Fokker F28 Fellowship 4000 (F28 Mk4000)	11190	PH-EXU*	0082	0399	2 RR Spey 555-15P	33115	Y75		lsf Nordbanken Finans AB
☐ SE-DGR	Fokker F28 Fellowship 4000 (F28 Mk4000)	11204	PH-EXR*	0083	0399	2 RR Spey 555-15P	33115	Y75		lsf Nordbanken Finans AB
☐ SE-DGS	Fokker F28 Fellowship 4000 (F28 Mk4000)	11236	PH-EZA*	0086	0399	2 RR Spey 555-15P	33115	Y75		lsf Nordbanken Finans AB
☐ SE-DGU	Fokker F28 Fellowship 4000 (F28 Mk4000)	11241	PH-EZT*	0087		2 RR Spey 555-15P	33115	Y75		to be lsf Kjölen SCL Co.Ltd 0999/ex SAS
☐ SE-DGX	Fokker F28 Fellowship 4000 (F28 Mk4000)	11225	PH-EZX*	0085		2 RR Spey 555-15P	33115	Y75		to be lsf SCL Aero Service 0999/ex SAS

AIRDEAL, Oy = ADU

Helsinki-Vantaa

Liikelentoterminaali, Helsinki-Vantaan lentoasema, FIN-01530 Vantaa, Finland ☎ (9) 870 20 41 Tx: none Fax: (9) 870 21 07 SITA: n/a
F: 1989 ⁂ 3 Head: Juhani Tuominen ICAO: AIRDEAL Net: n/a

☐ OH-ADA	Fairchild (Swearingen) SA226T Merlin III	T-248	N120TT	0074	0594	2 GA TPE331-3U-303G	5670			lsf Oy Condex KM Ltd
☐ OH-GLB	Learjet 24D	24D-262	N110PS	0073		2 GE CJ610-6	6123			

AIRECON (Juris Economica Oy Airecon dba)

Helsinki-Vantaa

Kyläkirkontie 38, FIN-00370 Helsinki, Finland ☎ (9) 55 77 99 Tx: n/a Fax: (9) 55 53 44 SITA: n/a
F: 1979 ⁂ n/a Head: Kyösti Ratilainen Net: n/a

☐ OH-PYE	Piper PA-31T Cheyenne II	31T-7920094	SE-ICS	0079		2 PWC PT6A-28	4082			

AIR VERTICAL, Oy

Joensuu

Suvisrannantie 28, FIN-83500 Outokumpu, Finland ☎ (13) 55 22 40 Tx: n/a Fax: (13) 55 22 40 SITA: n/a
F: 1993 ⁂ n/a Head: n/a Net: n/a Aircraft below MTOW 1361kg: Cessna 150, 172 & Hughes 269C (300C)

☐ OH-CEG	Cessna 185D Skywagon	185-0863		0065		1 CO IO-470-F	1450			lsf Itä-Suomen Lento Oy

BF-LENTO, Oy = BKF (BF-Air)

Helsinki-Malmi

Helsinki-Malmin lentoasema, FIN-00700 Helsinki, Finland ☎ (9) 37 61 70 Tx: none Fax: (9) 37 99 37 SITA: n/a
F: 1969 ⁂ 10 Head: Mark Baker ICAO: BAKERFLIGHT Net: n/a Aircraft below MTOW 1361kg: Cessna 150/152/172/175 & Piper PA-28.

☐ OH-PEO	Piper PA-23-250 Aztec B	27-2104	SE-ECO	0062		2 LY O-540-A1D5	2180			lsf Ring-Sky Oy / E Nose mod.
☐ OH-PST	Piper PA-23-250 Aztec E	27-7305013	OY-BJR	0073	1093	2 LY IO-540-C4B5	2360			lsf Aerotrain Oy
☐ OH-CGA	Cessna 402B	402B0208	SE-FXO	0072	0095	2 CO TSIO-520-E	2860			lsf pvt
☐ OH-MRS	Piper PA-31-310 Navajo B	31-7400984		0074	0096	2 LY TIO-540-A2C	2950			

COPTER ACTION, Oy

Helsinki-Malmi

Helsinki-Malmin lentoasema, FIN-00700 Helsinki, Finland ☎ (9) 350 52 10 Tx: n/a Fax: (9) 374 33 77 SITA: n/a
F: 1989 ⁂ 9 Head: Kari Ljungberg Net: http://www.copteraction.fi Aircraft below MTOW 1361kg: Hughes 269C (300C), 369C/HM (500C)

☐ OH-HCG	Eurocopter (Aerosp.) AS350B2 Ecureuil	2710	SE-JBX	0093	0598	1 TU Arriel 1D1	2250			

476 registration type of aircraft cn/fn ex/ex* mfd del powered by mtow kg configuration selcal name/fln/specialitites/remarks

☐ OH-HCB	Eurocopter (MBB) BO105CBS	S-396	N10360	0079	0896	2 AN 250-C20B	2400			
☐ OH-HCC	Eurocopter (MBB) BO105CBS	S-546	AB-6	0081	0697	2 AN 250-C20B	2400			
☐ OH-HCD	Eurocopter (MBB) BO105CBS	S-547	AB-7	0081	1197	2 AN 250-C20B	2400			
☐ OH-HCH	Eurocopter EC135P1	0008	D-HPOZ	0096	0299	2 PWC PW206B	2720			

DC-YHDISTYS, Ry (DC-Association)

Helsinki-Malmi

HKI-Malmin lentoasema, Huone 55, FIN-00700 Helsinki, Finland ☎ (50) 511 01 11 Tx: none Fax: (9) 88 73 82 04 SITA: n/a
F: n/a ✱✱✱ n/a Head: Lars Nyqvist Net: n/a Non-profit/commercial organisation conducting historical flights with DC-3 aircraft.

☐ OH-LCH	Boeing (Douglas) DC-3A (C-53C-DO)	6346	DO-11	0042		2 PW R-1830-S1C3G	12200	32 Pax		lsf Airveteran Oy/Finnish Airl.-AERO cs

DELTACRAFT, Oy = DEC

Turku

Piiskakuja 1, FIN-20380 Turku, Finland ☎ (2) 255 00 55 Tx: n/a Fax: (2) 255 02 84 SITA: n/a
F: 1995 ✱✱✱ n/a Head: Timo Koski ICAO: DELTACRAFT Net: n/a Aircraft below MTOW 1361kg: Cessna 172 & Piper PA-28

☐ OH-CCY	Cessna A185E Skywagon	185-1352	N2200T	0068	0095	1 CO IO-520-D	1520			
☐ OH-CBC	Cessna 421A	421A0013	N2213Q	0069	0096	2 CO GTSIO-520-D	3103			
☐ OH-CDC	Cessna 404 Titan II	404-0046	SE-GZH	0077	1196	2 CO GTSIO-520-M	3810			
☐ OH-CZG	Cessna 404 Titan II	404-0033	SE-GZG	0077	0098	2 CO GTSIO-520-M	3810			
☐ OH-BKA	Beech King Air 100	B-39	HB-GEN	0070	0098	2 PWC PT6A-28	4800			lsf Airwings Oy

FINNAIR, Oyj = AY / FIN (Member of Oneworld Alliance / formerly Aero, Oy)

Helsinki-Vantaa

FINNAIR

PL 15, FIN-01053 Finnair Vantaa, Finland ☎ (9) 818 81 Tx: 124946 fnair sf Fax: (9) 818 40 90 SITA: n/a
F: 1923 ✱✱✱ 10780 Head: Antti Potila IATA: 105 ICAO: FINNAIR Net: http://www.finnair.fi

☐ OH-KOG	De Havilland DHC-6 Twin Otter 300	642		0079	1079	2 PWC PT6A-27	5670	Surveyer		lst Malmilento Oy
☐ OH-FAD	Saab SF340A (QC)	340A-135	SE-F35*	0088	1288	2 GE CT7-5A2	12700	Y34 / Frtr		Riekko-Snoeripan
☐ OH-FAE	Saab SF340A (QC)	340A-139	SE-F39*	0088	1288	2 GE CT7-5A2	12700	Y34 / Frtr		
☐ OH-FAF	Saab 340B	340B-167	SE-F67*	0089	1189	2 GE CT7-9B	12930	Y34 / Executive		
☐ OH-KRA	ATR 72-201	126	F-WWEJ*	0089	0190	2 PWC PW124B	21500	Y66		
☐ OH-KRB	ATR 72-201	140	F-WWER*	0089	1089	2 PWC PW124B	21500	Y66		lsf Merita Rahoitus Oy
☐ OH-KRC	ATR 72-201	145	F-WWES*	0089	1189	2 PWC PW124B	21500	Y66		
☐ OH-KRD	ATR 72-201	162	F-WWEM*	0090	0490	2 PWC PW124B	21500	Y66		
☐ OH-KRE	ATR 72-201	174	F-WWEE*	0090	0590	2 PWC PW124B	21500	Y66		
☐ OH-KRF	ATR 72-201	324	F-WWEU*	0092	0992	2 PWC PW124B	21500	Y66		
☐ OH-KRH	ATR 72-201	212	F-WQIU	0091	0199	2 PWC PW124B	21500	Y66		
☐ OH-KRK	ATR 72-201	251	B-22706	0091	0199	2 PWC PW124B	21500	Y66		
☐ OH-KRL	ATR 72-201	332	B-22710	0092	0199	2 PWC PW124B	21500	Y66		
☐ OH-LYN	Boeing (Douglas) DC-9-51	47694 / 805		1275	0176	2 PW JT8D-17A	54900	CY122	NONE	
☐ OH-LYO	Boeing (Douglas) DC-9-51	47695 / 806		0176	0176	2 PW JT8D-17A	54900	CY122	NONE	
☐ OH-LYP	Boeing (Douglas) DC-9-51	47696 / 808	N9MD	0176	0276	2 PW JT8D-17A	54900	CY122	NONE	
☐ OH-LYR	Boeing (Douglas) DC-9-51	47736 / 827		0676	0976	2 PW JT8D-17A	55450	CY122	NONE	
☐ OH-LYS	Boeing (Douglas) DC-9-51	47737 / 829	9Y-TFF	0676	0177	2 PW JT8D-17A	54900	CY122	NONE	
☐ OH-LYT	Boeing (Douglas) DC-9-51	47738 / 830		0776	1076	2 PW JT8D-17A	54900	CY122	NONE	
☐ OH-LYU	Boeing (Douglas) DC-9-51	47771 / 883		0878	0978	2 PW JT8D-17A	55450	CY122	NONE	
☐ OH-LYV	Boeing (Douglas) DC-9-51	47772 / 890	N8713Q	1078	0480	2 PW JT8D-17A	55450	CY122	NONE	
☐ OH-LYW	Boeing (Douglas) DC-9-51	47773 / 891	N8714Q	1178	1180	2 PW JT8D-17A	55450	CY122	NONE	
☐ OH-LYX	Boeing (Douglas) DC-9-51	48134 / 980		1280	0181	2 PW JT8D-17A	55450	CY122	NONE	
☐ OH-LYY	Boeing (Douglas) DC-9-51	48135 / 987		0281	0381	2 PW JT8D-17A	55450	CY122	NONE	
☐ OH-LYZ	Boeing (Douglas) DC-9-51	48136 / 993		0381	0481	2 PW JT8D-17A (HK3/ABS)	55450	CY122	NONE	
☐ OH-LMA	Boeing (Douglas) MD-87 (DC-9-87)	49403 / 1404	N19B*	0087	1187	2 PW JT8D-219	63500	CY112	DJ-AC	
☐ OH-LMB	Boeing (Douglas) MD-87 (DC-9-87)	49404 / 1430		0087	0188	2 PW JT8D-219	63500	CY112	DK-HL	
☐ OH-LMC	Boeing (Douglas) MD-87 (DC-9-87)	49405 / 1525		0088	1088	2 PW JT8D-219	63500	CY112	DK-JL	
☐ OH-LVA	Airbus Industrie A319-112	1073				2 CFMI CFM56-5B6/2	64000	CY126		oo-delivery 0899
☐ OH-LVB	Airbus Industrie A319-112	1107				2 CFMI CFM56-5B6/2	64000	CY126		oo-delivery 1099
☐ OH-LVC	Airbus Industrie A319-112					2 CFMI CFM56-5B6/2	64000	CY126		oo-delivery 0800
☐ OH-LVD	Airbus Industrie A319-112					2 CFMI CFM56-5B6/2	64000	CY126		oo-delivery 1000
☐ OH-LVE	Airbus Industrie A319-112					2 CFMI CFM56-5B6/2	64000	CY126		oo-delivery 1001
☐ OH-LMG	Boeing (Douglas) MD-83 (DC-9-83)	49625 / 1503		0088	0888	2 PW JT8D-219	72550	Y156	DK-JM	
☐ OH-LMH	Boeing (Douglas) MD-82 (DC-9-82)	53245 / 1978		0092	0492	2 PW JT8D-219	67800	CY140	DK-FL	lsf K/S UL MD-82
☐ OH-LMN	Boeing (Douglas) MD-82 (DC-9-82)	49150 / 1087		0982	0383	2 PW JT8D-219	67800	CY141	BG-CF	lsf Investors Asset Holding Corp.
☐ OH-LMO	Boeing (Douglas) MD-82 (DC-9-82)	49151 / 1088		1082	0383	2 PW JT8D-219	67800	CY140	BG-CL	lsf Investors Asset Holding Corp.
☐ OH-LMP	Boeing (Douglas) MD-82 (DC-9-82)	49152 / 1089		1082	0483	2 PW JT8D-219	67800	CY140	BG-CM	
☐ OH-LMR	Boeing (Douglas) MD-83 (DC-9-83)	49284 / 1209		0685	0685	2 PW JT8D-219	67800	CY141	DJ-AF	lsf Aviation 49284 Corp./cvtd MD-82
☐ OH-LMS	Boeing (Douglas) MD-83 (DC-9-83)	49252 / 1169	N19B*	1184	1085	2 PW JT8D-219	72550	CY141	DJ-AG	lsf Aviation 49252 Corp.
☐ OH-LMT	Boeing (Douglas) MD-82 (DC-9-82)	49877 / 1594		0089	0589	2 PW JT8D-219	67800	CY141	EF-AM	
☐ OH-LMU	Boeing (Douglas) MD-83 (DC-9-83)	49741 / 1630		0089	0989	2 PW JT8D-219	72550	Y156	EF-BG	
☐ OH-LMV	Boeing (Douglas) MD-83 (DC-9-83)	49904 / 1680		0090	0290	2 PW JT8D-219	72550	Y156	EF-BH	
☐ OH-LMW	Boeing (Douglas) MD-82 (DC-9-82)	49905 / 1767		0990	1090	2 PW JT8D-219	67800	CY140	EM-GJ	lsf K/S UL MD-82
☐ OH-LMX	Boeing (Douglas) MD-82 (DC-9-82)	49906 / 1786		0090	1190	2 PW JT8D-219	67800	CY140	EM-JK	
☐ OH-LMY	Boeing (Douglas) MD-82 (DC-9-82)	53244 / 1901	N19B*	0091	0891	2 PW JT8D-219	67800	CY140	DH-EM	lsf Kemi Lease Co. Ltd
☐ OH-LMZ	Boeing (Douglas) MD-82 (DC-9-82)	53246 / 1918		0991	0991	2 PW JT8D-219	67800	CY140	DK-EJ	lsf Turku Lease Co. Ltd
☐ OH-LPA	Boeing (Douglas) MD-82 (DC-9-82)	49900 / 1765	EC-FJQ	0990	1195	2 PW JT8D-219	67800	CY140	LR-AG	lsf Unileasing A/S
☐ OH-LPB	Boeing (Douglas) MD-83 (DC-9-83)	49966 / 2047	SE-DLX	0093	0495	2 PW JT8D-219	72550	Y156	LR-AH	lsf Sanwa Business Credit Corp.
☐ OH-LPC	Boeing (Douglas) MD-83 (DC-9-83)	49965 / 2044	SE-DLV	0093	0495	2 PW JT8D-219	72550	Y156	LR-AJ	
☐ OH-LPD	Boeing (Douglas) MD-83 (DC-9-83)	49710 / 1547	EC-GFJ	0088	1096	2 PW JT8D-219	67800	CY140	QS-AP	lsf Nordbanken Finans AB
☐ OH-LPE	Boeing (Douglas) MD-83 (DC-9-83)	49401 / 1357	EC-FZQ	0487	1096	2 PW JT8D-219	67800	CY140	QS-AR	
☐ OH-LPF	Boeing (Douglas) MD-83 (DC-9-83)	49574 / 1413	EC-FVR	1087	0497	2 PW JT8D-219	67800	CY140	QS-BC	
☐ OH-LPG	Boeing (Douglas) MD-83 (DC-9-83)	49708 / 1561	EC-GKS	0089	0397	2 PW JT8D-219	67800	CY140	QS-BD	lsf Nordbanken Finans AB
☐ OH-LPH	Boeing (Douglas) MD-83 (DC-9-83)	49623 / 1499	SE-DHN	0688	1295	2 PW JT8D-219	72550	Y162	QS-BE	
☐ OH-LXA	Airbus Industrie A320-214					2 CFMI CFM56-5B4/P	73500	CY150		oo-delivery 0201
☐ OH-LXB	Airbus Industrie A320-214					2 CFMI CFM56-5B4/P	73500	CY150		oo-delivery 0501
☐ OH-LXC	Airbus Industrie A320-214					2 CFMI CFM56-5B4/P	73500	CY150		oo-delivery 0801
☐ OH-LZA	Airbus Industrie A321-211	941	D-AVZT*	0099	0199	2 CFMI CFM56-5B3/P	89000	CY188		
☐ OH-LZB	Airbus Industrie A321-211	961		0099	0299	2 CFMI CFM56-5B3/P	89000	CY188		
☐ OH-LZC	Airbus Industrie A321-211					2 CFMI CFM56-5B3/P	89000	CY188		oo-delivery 0200
☐ OH-LZD	Airbus Industrie A321-211					2 CFMI CFM56-5B3/P	89000	CY188		oo-delivery 0500
☐ OH-LBO	Boeing 757-2Q8	28172 / 772	N1789B*	0097	1097	2 PW PW2040	115666	Y219	LQ-FH	lsf ILFC
☐ OH-LBR	Boeing 757-2Q8	28167 / 775		1097	1097	2 PW PW2040	115666	Y219	LQ-FJ	lsf ILFC
☐ OH-LBS	Boeing 757-2Q8	27623 / 792	N5573K*	0098	0398	2 PW PW2040	115666	Y219	LQ-FK	lsf ILFC
☐ OH-LBT	Boeing 757-2Q8	28170 / 801		0098	0598	2 PW PW2040	115666	Y219	LQ-FM	lsf ILFC
☐ OH-LBU	Boeing 757-2Q8	29377		0099	0499	2 PW PW2040	115666	Y219		lsf ILFC
☐ OH-LGA	Boeing (Douglas) MD-11	48449 / 455		0090	1290	3 GE CF6-80C2D1F	283722	C31Y332	DE-AG	
☐ OH-LGB	Boeing (Douglas) MD-11	48450 / 479		0091	1291	3 GE CF6-80C2D1F	283722	C35Y280	DE-CG	
☐ OH-LGC	Boeing (Douglas) MD-11	48512 / 529		0092	0293	3 GE CF6-80C2D1F	283722	C35Y280	DE-CH	
☐ OH-LGD	Boeing (Douglas) MD-11	48513 / 564		0094	0394	3 GE CF6-80C2D1F	283722	C31Y332	DE-FM	

FINNAIR TRAINING CENTER (Finnairin Ilmailuopisto) (Subsidiary of Finnair, Oyj)

Helsinki-Vantaa & Pori

Pyhtdäskorvantie 6, FIN-01530 Vantaa, Finland ☎ (9) 818 47 01 Tx: none Fax: (9) 818 47 03 SITA: n/a
F: 1963 ✱✱✱ 18 Head: Mrs Soili Johansson Net: n/a Trainer aircraft below MTOW 5000kg: Beechcraft Bonanza A36 & Cessna 152

☐ OH-BSA	Beech King Air 300	FA-205	N5672A	0089	0690	2 PWC PT6A-60A	6350	Trainer		
☐ OH-BSB	Beech King Air 300	FA-206		0090	0890	2 PWC PT6A-60A	6350	Trainer		

FIRST INVEST, Oy

Kerava Heliport & Helsinki-Malmi

Pihlajakatu 2, FIN-04260 Kerava, Finland ☎ (9) 294 50 96 Tx: none Fax: (9) 294 50 96 SITA: n/a
F: n/a ✱✱✱ n/a Head: n/a Net: n/a Aircraft below MTOW 1361kg: Hughes 300C (269C)

☐ OH-HLP	Bell 206B JetRanger	1766	N49587	0075	0097	1 AN 250-C20	1451			

FRONTIER GUARD – Air Patrol Squadron = FNG (Vartiolentolaivue) (Division of Ministry of Interior)

Helsinki, Rovaniemi & Turku

Finnish Frontier Guard

PO Box 3, FIN-00131 Helsinki, Finland ☎ (20) 410 66 14 Tx: none Fax: (20) 410 66 21 SITA: n/a
F: 1981 ✱✱✱ 100 Head: Pertti Ruotsalainen ICAO: FINNGUARD Net: http://www.intermin.fi Non-commercial government organisation conducting border/maritime patrol & SAR flights.

☐ OH-HRF	Agusta-Bell 206B JetRanger III	8286		0071	1072	1 AN 250-C20B	1450	Border Patrol		cvtd 206A
☐ OH-HRG	Agusta-Bell 206B JetRanger III	8295		0071	1071	1 AN 250-C20B	1450	Border Patrol		cvtd 206A
☐ OH-HRH	Agusta-Bell 206B JetRanger	8380		0074	0774	1 AN 250-C20	1450	Border Patrol		
☐ OH-HRI	Agusta-Bell 206B JetRanger III	8599		0080	0280	1 AN 250-C20B	1450	Border Patrol		
☐ OH-HVD	Agusta-Bell 412	25540		0085	1085	2 PWC PT6T-3B TwinPac	5400	SAR		
☐ OH-HVE	Agusta-Bell 412	25541		0086	0187	2 PWC PT6T-3B TwinPac	5400	SAR		
☐ OH-HVH	Agusta-Bell 412	25609		0090	0790	2 PWC PT6T-3B TwinPac	5400	SAR		
☐ OH-HVJ	Agusta-Bell 412EP	25903		0096	1296	2 PWC PT6T-3D TwinPac	5400	SAR		
☐ OH-MVN	Dornier 228-212	8233	D-CATE*	0095	0695	2 GA TPE331-5AB-252D	6400	Maritime Patrol		Pollution/Radarcontrol
☐ OH-MVO	Dornier 228-212	8232	D-CATD*	0095	0595	2 GA TPE331-5AB-252D	6400	Maritime Patrol		Pollution/Radarcontrol
☐ OH-HVF	Eurocopter (Aerosp.) AS332L1 Super Puma	2218	F-WMHE*	0087	1287	2 TU Makila 1A1	8600	SAR		
☐ OH-HVG	Eurocopter (Aerosp.) AS332L1 Super Puma	2221		0087	0488	2 TU Makila 1A1	8600	SAR		
☐ OH-HVI	Eurocopter (Aerosp.) AS332L1 Super Puma	2341		0092	0192	2 TU Makila 1A1	8600	SAR		

477 registration type of aircraft cn/fn ex/ex* mfd del powered by mtow kg configuration selcal name/fln/specialitites/remarks

GOSPEL FLIGHT, Ry — Helsinki-Malmi

Helsinki Malmin Lentoasema, FIN-00700 Helsinki, Finland ☎ (9) 374 15 57 Tx: n/a Fax: (9) 37 34 43 SITA: n/a
F: 1982 ⁂ 0 Head: Raine Haikarainen Net: n/a Aircraft below MTOW 1361 kg: Cessna 180

☐ OH-MAF	Cessna U206A Super Skywagon	U206-0639	N4939F*	0066		1 CO IO-520-A	1635			lsf MAF England

HELIKOPTERIKESKUS Oy Helsinki (Helicopter Centre Helsinki) (formerly Bee-Air, Oy) — Helsinki-Hernesaari Heliport

Hernesaarenranta 13, FIN-00150 Helsinki, Finland ☎ (9) 17 71 12 Tx: n/a Fax: (9) 62 44 15 SITA: n/a
F: 1973 ⁂ 6 Head: Timo Heloaho Net: n/a

☐ OH-HMP	MD Helicopters MD 500D (Hughes 369D)	510981D	N7012G	0081	0698	1 AN 250-C20B	1360			lsf Pro-Collection Oy Ltd
☐ OH-HAU	Agusta-Bell 206B JetRanger	8257	LN-OTK	0070		1 AN 250-C20	1451			cvtd 206A
☐ OH-HLK	Agusta-Bell 206B JetRanger II	8532	G-BEPP	0077		1 AN 250-C20	1451			
☐ OH-HOT	Bell 206B JetRanger III	3552	JA9321	0081	0292	1 AN 250-C20B	1451			lsf Northeastern Helicopters Inc.

HELIKOPTERIPALVELU, Oy (Helicopter Service) (formerly Helilift, Oy) — Helsinki-Vantaa, Jyväskylä & Rovaniemi

Siipitie 11, FIN-01530 Vantaa, Finland ☎ (9) 61 51 41 80 Tx: none Fax: (9) 61 51 41 88 SITA: n/a
F: 1960 ⁂ 24 Head: Jan Krogerus Net: http://www.helikopteripalvelu.com Aircraft below MTOW 1361 kg: Robinson R22.

☐ OH-HIF	Agusta-Bell 206B JetRanger	8372		0073		1 AN 250-C20	1451			
☐ OH-HOH	Bell 206L LongRanger	45030	C-GIIP	0076		1 AN 250-C20B	1814			lsf HK-Copterflite Oy
☐ OH-HKI	Eurocopter (MBB) BO105CBS-4	S-731	D-HECB	0086	0796	2 AN 250-C20B	2500	SAR		
☐ OH-HMS	Eurocopter (MBB) BO105CBS-4	S-723		0086	0394	2 AN 250-C20B	2500	EMS		
☐ OH-HNS	Eurocopter (MBB) BO105CBS	S-762	D-HNWI	0087	1097	2 AN 250-C20B	2500			lsf Neste Oy
☐ OH-HAQ	Eurocopter (Aerosp.) AS355F Ecureuil 2	5090		0081	0096	2 AN 250-C20F	2300			
☐ OH-HAW	Agusta A109A II	7327	N1BN	0085	0689	2 AN 250-C20B	2600			lsf Neste Oy

HELITOUR, Oy (formerly Lapin keskuslentokoulu, Oy) — Helsinki-Malmi

Helsinki-Malmin lentoasema, FIN-00700 Helsinki, Finland ☎ (9) 374 51 00 Tx: none Fax: (9) 37 38 87 SITA: n/a
F: 1990 ⁂ n/a Head: Pentti Torronen Net: n/a Aircraft below MTOW 1361 kg: Hughes 369HS (500C), Robinson R22 & R44

☐ OH-HIE	Agusta-Bell 206A JetRanger	8177		0070	0097	1 AN 250-C18	1361			lsf Profitoff Oy

IVALON LENTOPALVELU, Ky (Ivalon Air Service) (formerly Reino Huhtamella) — Ivalo

PPA 2, Huhtamella, FIN-99800 Ivalo, Finland ☎ (16) 66 77 41 Tx: none Fax: (16) 66 76 02 SITA: n/a
F: 1988 ⁂ 3 Head: Reino Huhtamella Net: n/a

☐ OH-DAK	Cessna A185F Skywagon	18502880		0076		1 CO IO-520-D	1520	5 Pax / SAR		Floats / Wheel-Skis

JETFLITE, Oy = JEF (Euro-Flite Air Ambulance/Air Cargo) — Helsinki-Vantaa

PL 86, FIN-01531 Vantaa, Finland ☎ (9) 82 27 66 Tx: 122520 jetfl sf Fax: (9) 870 32 02 SITA: n/a
F: 1980 ⁂ 15 Head: Matti Korpivaara ICAO: JETFLITE Net: n/a
Ambulance/EMS flights are operated under the marketing name EURO-FLITE AIR AMBULANCE, cargo flights under EURO-FLITE AIR CARGO (both same headquarters & fleets).

☐ OH-PNT	Piper PA-31T Cheyenne II	31T-7520007		0074	0580	2 PWC PT6A-28	4082			
☐ OH-ACN	Twin (Aero) Turbo Commander 690A	11301	N81405	0075		2 GA TPE331-5-251K	4649	Surveyer		lsf Maanmittaushallitus
☐ OH-KNE	Mitsubishi MU-300 Diamond I	A014SA	N339DM	0083	0098	2 PWC JT15D-4	6636			lsf ESA Ja Kari Rannila
☐ OH-AMB	Dassault Falcon 10	193	N3BY	0082	1298	2 GA TFE731-2-1C	8755	EMS		lsf Wihuri Oy
☐ OH-BAP	Hawker 700B (HS 125-700B)	257212	G-5-659*	0084		2 GA TFE731-3R-1H	11567			lsf Microhierax Oy
☐ OH-JET	Hawker 700B (HS 125-700B)	257136	G-BIRU	0081		2 GA TFE731-3R-1H	11567			lsf Wihuri Oy
☐ OH-WIH	Canadair CL-600S (CL-600-1A11) Challenger	1029	N205A	0082	1196	2 LY ALF502L-2C	18711			lsf Wihuri Oy

KONEKORHONEN, Oy — Tikkakoski

PL 11, FIN-41161 Tikkakoski, Finland ☎ (14) 445 59 90 Tx: none Fax: (14) 445 59 95 SITA: n/a
F: 1996 ⁂ n/a Head: Kari Katainen Net: http://www.konekorhonen.com Aircraft below MTOW 1361kg: Hughes 300C (269C)

☐ OH-CHO	Cessna TU206G Turbo Stationair	U20603634	N7364N	0076	0098	1 CO TSIO-520-M	1633			Floats
☐ OH-CGT	Cessna A188B AgTruck	18801959T	N78763	0075	0698	1 CO IO-520-D	1905	Fuel hauling		
☐ OH-PPG	Piper PA-36-300 Brave	36-7560005	SE-GIV	0075	0097	1 LY IO-540-K1G5	1995	Fuel hauling		lsf Autorep Oy
☐ OH-CHM	Cessna 401A	401A0125	LN-TVN	0069	0096	2 CO TSIO-520-E	2860	7 Pax		
☐ OH-HTR	Eurocopter (Aerosp.) SA360C Dauphin	1024		0078	0096	1 TU Astazou XVIIIA	3000	9 Pax		
☐ OH-PRB	Piper PA-31-310 Navajo C	31-7812124	N27793	0078	0096	2 LY TIO-540-A2C	2950	7 Pax		

LILLBAKA JETAIR, Oy = FPC (formerly Lillbacka, Oy/Sky Blue Jet Service) — Kauhava

PL 38, FIN-62201 Kauhava, Finland ☎ (6) 428 21 11 Tx: 72188 sf Fax: (6) 428 26 35 SITA: n/a
F: 1969 ⁂ 5 Head: Jorma Lillbacka ICAO: FINNPOWER Net: n/a

☐ OH-HJL	Bell 206L LongRanger	45084	SE-HSO	0077		1 AN 250-C20B	1815			
☐ OH-FPC	Dassault Falcon 20F	345	N133AP	0076	0896	2 GE CF700-2D2	13000			

LOMAKYLA INARIN LENTOPALVELU, Oy (Lomakylä Inarin Flight Service) — Inari-SPB

n/a, FIN-99870 Inari, Finland ☎ (16) 67 11 08 Tx: none Fax: (16) 67 14 80 SITA: n/a
F: 1996 ⁂ n/a Head: n/a Net: n/a

☐ OH-CHU	Cessna TU206G Turbo Stationair 6 II	U20604332		0078	0097	1 CO TSIO-520-M	1633			Floats / Wheels

MALMILENTO, Oy (Geological Air Service) — Helsinki-Vantaa

Tietotie 11, FIN-01530 Vantaa, Finland ☎ (9) 818 68 02 Tx: none Fax: (9) 818 68 03 SITA: n/a
F: 1996 ⁂ 5 Head: Pekka Välimaki Net: n/a

☐ OH-KOG	De Havilland DHC-6 Twin Otter 300	642		0079	0096	2 PWC PT6A-27	5670	Surveyer		lsf FIN

NORDIC AIR AMBULANCE (Metro Jet, Oy dba) — Helsinki-Vantaa

PL 60, FIN-01301 Vantaa, Finland ☎ (9) 870 06 70 Tx: none Fax: (9) 87 00 67 20 SITA: n/a
F: 1992 ⁂ n/a Head: Jarmo Kammonen Net: n/a

☐ OH-BCX	Beech King Air C90	LJ-770	N88CG	0078	0092	2 PWC PT6A-21	4377	EMS		

OULUN TILAUSLENTO, Oy (Oulu Business Flight) — Oulu

Kajaanintie 247, FIN-90240 Oulu, Finland ☎ (49) 68 39 30 Tx: n/a Fax: (8) 557 17 02 SITA: n/a
F: 1992 ⁂ 3 Head: Antti Kontio Net: n/a

☐ OH-KYC	Piper PA-31-350 Navajo Chieftain	31-8052186	SE-KYC	0080	0294	2 LY TIO-540-J2BD	3175			

PLAANI-LIIKELENNOT, Oy (Plaani Business Flights) — Helsinki-Malmi

Korkeavuorenkatu 1, FIN-00140 Helsinki, Finland ☎ (9) 62 26 56 22 Tx: none Fax: (9) 62 42 24 SITA: n/a
F: n/a ⁂ n/a Head: n/a Net: n/a

☐ OH-CGB	Cessna U206F Stationair	U20602237	N1526U	0074	1296	1 CO IO-520-F	1633			

POLAR-LENTO, Oy — Kilpisjärvi

Lentosatama, FIN-99490 Kilpisjärvi, Finland ☎ (16) 53 78 10 Tx: none Fax: (16) 53 78 10 SITA: n/a
F: 1991 ⁂ n/a Head: n/a Net: n/a

☐ OH-CVT	Cessna A185F Skywagon	18502977	N500BW	0076	0191	1 CO IO-520-D	1520			Floats / Wheels-Skis

REIJO RAUMALA AIR SERVICE — Inari

Kittilän ratsutie 6, FIN-99870 Inari, Finland ☎ (16) 67 14 01 Tx: n/a Fax: n/a SITA: n/a
F: n/a ⁂ n/a Head: Reijo Raumala Net: n/a

☐ OH-CDO	Cessna A185E Skywagon	18501773	N5804J	0070		1 CO IO-520-D	1520			Floats / Wheel-Skis

SAVAIR, Ky — Helsinki-Vantaa

Laippatie 17, FIN-00880 Helsinki, Finland ☎ (9) 755 78 99 Tx: none Fax: (9) 755 51 03 SITA: n/a
F: 1952 ⁂ 3 Head: Vanhatalo Pekka Net: n/a

☐ OH-PVA	Partenavia P.68	10		0073		2 LY IO-360-A1B	1960			lsf Fm-Kartta Oy
☐ OH-PNB	Piper PA-31-310 Navajo	31-609	N6714L	0070	0097	2 LY TIO-540-A1A	2950			lsf FM-Kartta Oy
☐ OH-PNO	Piper PA-31-310 Navajo	31-273	SE-FDR	0068		2 LY TIO-540-A1A	2948			
☐ OH-UTI	Twin (Aero) Turbo Commander 690A	11204	SE-GSR	0074	0097	2 GA TPE331-5-251K	4649			

SCANWINGS, Oy = ABF (formerly Aerial, Oy) — Helsinki-Vantaa

PL 22, FIN-04401 Järvenpää, Finland ☎ (9) 870 39 39 Tx: n/a Fax: (9) 870 29 39 SITA: n/a
F: 1969 ⁂ 20 Head: Kari Pekka Tiihonen ICAO: SKYWINGS Net: http://www.scanwings.fi

☐ OH-CIO	Cessna TU206G Turbo Stationair 6 II	U20606090		0081	0098	1 CO TSIO-520-M	1633			lsf pvt
☐ OH-BAX	Beech King Air C90	LJ-948	N4495U	0081		2 PWC PT6A-21	4585			
☐ OH-BEX	Beech King Air C90	LJ-978	N725KR	0081	0897	2 PWC PT6A-21	4377			

SKAERGARDSFLYG, Ab = 5Q / LND — Mariehamn

Mariehamns Flygplats, FIN-22100 Mariehamn, Finland ☎ (18) 12 515 Tx: none Fax: (18) 19 405 SITA: n/a
F: 1956 ⁂ 5 Head: Sven Lemberg ICAO: AALAND Net: n/a

☐ OH-CTF	Cessna U206G Stationair 6 II	U20606837	N9339R	0084	0991	1 CO IO-520-F	1633	Y5		Floats / Wheel-Skis
☐ OH-BND	Britten-Norman BN-2B-21 Islander	2171	G-BKOH*	0087		2 LY IO-540-K1B5	2996	Y9		lsf Aelands Landskapsstyrelsen
☐ OH-EBC	Embraer 110P1 Bandeirante (EMB-110P1)	110258	PT-SAX*	0080		2 PWC PT6A-34	5670	Y19		
☐ OH-EBD	Embraer 110P1A Bandeirante (EMB-110P1A)	110439	N110EB	0084	0097	2 PWC PT6A-34	5670	Y19		

478 registration type of aircraft cn/fn ex/ex* mfd del powered by mtow kg configuration selcal name/fln/specialitites/remarks

SKAERGARDSHAVETS HELIKOPTERTJAENST, Ab (Skaergardshavets Helicopter Service) Mariehamn

Norra Esplanadgatan 1A, FIN-22100 Mariehamn, Finland ☎ (18) 17 271 Tx: n/a Fax: (18) 17 517 SITA: n/a
F: 1991 4 Head: Matti Aalto Net: n/a

☐ OH-HMA	Eurocopter (MBB) BO105C	S-88	D-HDCM	0073		2 AN 250-C20	2400			lsf Wiklöf Holding Ab

SUOMEN LASKUVARJOKERHO, Ry (Finnish Parachuting Club) Helsinki-Malmi

Helsinki-Malmin lentoasema, FIN-00700 Helsinki, Finland ☎ (9) 37 88 27 Tx: n/a Fax: (9) 374 14 59 SITA: n/a
F: n/a n/a Head: n/a Net: n/a Mainly operates para-flights for club-members only.

☐ OH-SLK	De Havilland DHC-6 Twin Otter 300	260	SE-GEG	0069	0288	2 PWC PT6A-27	5670	Para		

TAMPEREEN HELIKOPTERIKESKUS, Oy Tampere

Tampere-Pirkkalan lentoasema, FIN-33960 Pirkkala, Finland ☎ (3) 342 30 05 Tx: none Fax: (3) 342 30 05 SITA: n/a
F: 1991 n/a Head: Avoin Yhtiö Net: n/a Aircraft below MTOW 1361kg: Hughes 269C (300C)

☐ OH-HWA	MD Helicopters MD 500E (Hughes 369E)	0487E	D-HWAG	0091	0696	1 AN 250-C20B	1361			
☐ OH-HWE	MD Helicopters MD 500E (Hughes 369E)	0427E	D-HFAZ	0090	0997	1 AN 250-C20R2	1361			

TURKU AIR, Oy Turku

PL 167, FIN-20101 Turku, Finland ☎ (2) 276 49 66 Tx: 62233 cftu sf Fax: (2) 276 49 69 SITA: n/a
F: 1974 4 Head: Matti Tähtinen Net: n/a Aircraft below MTOW 1361 kg: Cessna 150, 152, 172 & Piper PA-28

☐ OH-CAC	Cessna U206F Stationair	U20602364	SE-GGI	0074	0098	1 CO IO-520-F	1633			lsf pvt
☐ OH-PNU	Piper PA-31-350 Navajo Chieftain	31-7752027	N62993	0077		2 LY TIO-540-J2BD	3175			
☐ OH-PNX	Piper PA-31-350 Navajo Chieftain	31-8052040	ES-PAG	0079	0997	2 LY TIO-540-J2BD	3175			
☐ OH-PNY	Piper PA-31-350 Navajo Chieftain	31-7652079	LN-SAB	0076	0696	2 LY TIO-540-J2BD	3175			

TV-LENTO, Ky Rovaniemi

Kiviniementie 6A, FIN-96400 Rovaniemi, Finland ☎ (49) 29 52 00 Tx: none Fax: (16) 31 82 70 SITA: n/a
F: n/a n/a Head: Teijo Hietala Net: n/a Aircraft below MTOW 1361kg: Cessna 172 & Hughes 269C (300C)

☐ OH-CEV	Cessna A185E Skywagon	185-1180	N4726Q	0067	0096	1 CO IO-520-D	1520			Floats / Wheel-Skis
☐ OH-CMT	Cessna U206F Stationair II	U20602702	LN-HAP	0075		1 CO IO-520-F	1633			Floats / Wheels

UTIN LENTO, Oy Utti

Utin Lentoasema, FIN-45410 Utti, Finland ☎ (5) 36 84 42 22 Tx: none Fax: (5) 368 44 23 SITA: n/a
F: 1989 n/a Head: Jussi Sistonen Net: n/a Aircraft below MTOW 1361 kg: Cessna 150/152/172/180

☐ OH-CSU	Cessna U206A Super Skywagon	U206-0620	N4920F	0066	0098	1 CO IO-520-A	1633			lsf Imatran Ilmailukerho Ry
☐ OH-UDZ	Cessna T207A Turbine Skywagon	20700388	D-EXWG	0077	0498	1 AN 250-C20S	1814			lsf Utin Laskuvarj./Soloy cvtd Skywagon
☐ OH-ACA	Twin (Aero) Commander 500	500-803-80	N8464C	0059	0098	2 LY O-540-A2B	2722			lsf First Invest Oy
☐ OH-USI	Cessna 208 Caravan I	20800275		0098	0498	1 PWC PT6A-114	3629			

VESIAIR, Oy Savonlinna

Rengastie 8, FIN-57100 Savonlinna, Finland ☎ (400) 67 06 90 Tx: none Fax: (15) 51 48 10 SITA: n/a
F: 1992 2 Head: Antti Ojanen Net: n/a

☐ OH-CHZ	Cessna TU206G Turbo Stationair 6 II	U20604970		0079		1 CO TSIO-520-M	1633			Amphibian

VUOTSON LENTOPALVELU, Oy (Vuotson Air Service) Vuotso

Säpitkästie 25, FIN-99690 Vuotso, Finland ☎ (16) 62 61 70 Tx: n/a Fax: (16) 62 61 70 SITA: n/a
F: 1994 n/a Head: n/a Net: n/a

☐ OH-CJJ	Cessna A185E Skywagon	18501418	LN-VIX	0068		1 CO IO-520-D	1520			

WESTBIRD AVIATION = WBA (Etela-Pohjanmaan lentokeskus, Oy dba) Seinajoki

PI 61, FIN-60511 Hyllykallio, Finland ☎ (6) 420 20 02 Tx: none Fax: (6) 420 20 03 SITA: n/a
F: 1993 6 Head: Johan Pakari ICAO: WESTBIRD Net: http://www.lentokeskus.pss.fi

☐ OH-CHS	Cessna 402B II	402B1082	CB-52	0076	0097	2 CO TSIO-520-E	2860			
☐ OH-WBA	Mitsubishi MU-2N (MU-2B-36A)	718SA	N150BA	0078	0298	2 GA TPE331-5-252M	5250			

OK = CZECH REPUBLIC / CZECHIA (Czech Republic) (Ceska Republika)

Capital: Prague Official Language: Czech Population: 10,5 million Square Km: 78852 Dialling code: +420 Year established: 1993 Acting political head: Vaclav Havel (President)

Government / Corporate / Executive / VIP Aircraft

CZECH AIR FORCE uses ICAO 3-letter code: CEF, call sign: CZECH AIR FORCE

☐ OK-024	Let 610	X-03	OK-132*	0089	0089	2 WA M-602	14000	Testbed		VZLU Aeronautical Research & Test Inst.
☐ OK-130	Let 610	X-01	OK-TZB*	1288	1288	2 WA M-602	14000	Testbed		Let, Kunovice/Prototype / std Kunovice
☐ OK-CDB	Let 410UVP-E20	972730		0093	0093	2 WA M-601E	6400	Corporate		Let, Kunovice
☐ OK-CZD	Let 610G	970301	*	0097	0097	2 GE CT7-9B	14500	Testbed		Let, Kunovice
☐ OK-IYA	Let 410UVP-T	770101	OK-026	0078		2 WA M-601D	6100	Testbed		VZLU Aeronautical Research & Test Inst.
☐ OK-XZA	Let 610G	920102	OK-136*	0092	0092	2 GE CT7-9B	14500	Testbed		Let, Kunovice
☐ 0005	Let 610	X-05	OK-VZC*	0390	0893	2 WA M-602	14000	Testbed/miltrans		Czech Air Force
☐ 0260	Yakovlev 40	9940260	OK-BYK	0079	0199	3 IV AI-25	16000	VIP 18 Pax		Czech Air Force
☐ 0601	Tupolev 154B-2	601	OK-BYD	0585	0291	3 KU NK-8-2U	98000	VIP 98 Pax		Czech Air Force
☐ 1016	Tupolev 154M	1016	OK-BYZ	1296	0199	3 SO D-30KU-154-II	100000	VIP		Czech Air Force
☐ 1107	Antonov 30	1107	LZ-AEG	0076	0091	2 IV AI-24T	23000	Surveyer		Czech Air Force
☐ 1257	Yakovlev 40K	9821257	OK-BYJ	0078	0199	3 IV AI-25	16000	VIP / miltrans		Czech Air Force
☐ 2710	Let 410UVP-E20C	922710	OK-BYF	0292	0199	2 WA M-601E	6400	VIP / miltrans		Czech Air Force
☐ 5105	Canadair CL-601-3A (CL-600-2B16) Challen.	5105	OK-BYA	0092	0199	2 GE CF34-3A	20500	VIP 12-17 Pax	AE-KP	Czech Air Force

ABA-AIR, a.s. = ABP Prague-Kbely

Mladoboleslavska 902, CZ-197 00 Praha 9, Czech Republic / Czechia ☎ (2) 20 11 29 77 Tx: none Fax: (2) 859 04 59 SITA: n/a
F: 1996 32 Head: Daniel Tucek ICAO: BAIR Net: n/a Beside aircraft listed, also leases Let 410UVP-E from DELTA SYSTEM-AIR when required.

☐ OK-JKS	Piper PA-34-200T Seneca II	34-7970494		0079	0596	2 CO TSIO-360-EB1	1999	EMS		
☐ OK-BKS	Beech King Air C90B	LJ-1430	N3251U	0096	0596	2 PWC PT6A-21	4608	EMS		
☐ OK-NDG	Let 410UVP	831138	OK-NZG	0083	0096	2 WA M-601D	5800	Y17		occ lsf Le Cygne Sportif
☐ OK-YES	Beech King Air 350 (B300)	FL-221	N3030S*	1298	0399	2 PWC PT6A-60A	6780	EMS		
☐ OK-ABA	Fokker F27 Friendship 500CRF(F27Mk500CRF)	10530	N737A	0076	0998	2 RR Dart 532-7	20410	Freighter		
☐ OK-ABB	Fokker F27 Friendship 500CRF(F27Mk500CRF)	10531	N739A	0076	1298	2 RR Dart 532-7	20410	Freighter		

ABAS, spol. s r.o. = MRP Plasy

Airport, CZ-331 01 Plasy, Czech Republic / Czechia ☎ (182) 20 06 Tx: none Fax: (182) 20 06 SITA: n/a
F: 1995 n/a Head: Vladimir Janousek ICAO: ABAS Net: n/a Ag-aircraft below MTOW 5000kg: 6 Z-37A/C & 2 Z-137T

☐ OK-AAG	Cessna TU206G Turbo Stationair 6 II	U20604336		0078	0098	1 CO TSIO-520-M	1633	Photo / Survey		
☐ OK-OFI	Let 200A Morava	170614		0060	0097	2 WA M-337	1950	4 Pax		

AEROCENTRUM, Ltd Mlada Boleslav

Regnerova ul., letiste Mlada Boleslav, CZ-293 01 Mlada Boleslav, Czech Republic / Czechia ☎ (326) 28 300 Tx: none Fax: (326) 24 672 SITA: n/a
F: 1994 14 Head: Jaroslav Rakos Net: n/a

☐ OK-UIC	PZL Swidnik (Mil) Mi-2	548149053	YL-LHL	0583	0097	2 IS GTD-350-4	3550	Utility		lst Tech-Mont
☐ OK-FXE	Mil Mi-8T	10546		0075	0096	2 IS TV2-117AG	12000	transport/crane		lsf Aircraft Repair Works
☐ OK-XYB	Mil Mi-8TP	99254381	CCCP-27014	0392	0394	2 IS TV2-117AG	12000	transport/crane		
☐ OK-XYC	Mil Mi-8T	99250952		0392	0394	2 IS TV2-117AG	12000	transport/crane		
☐ OK-XYD	Mil Mi-8T	99254392		0392	0394	2 IS TV2-117AG	12000	transport/crane		

AERO VODOCHODY, a.s. = AOD (Flying division of Aero Vodochody, Aviation production plant) Odolena Voda-Vodochody

Flying division, CZ-250 70 Odolena Voda, Czech Republic / Czechia ☎ (2) 688 09 71 Tx: 121169 c Fax: (2) 82 31 72 SITA: n/a
F: 1989 n/a Head: Adam Stranak ICAO: AERO CZECH Net: n/a Flying division of the Aviation production plant conducting non-commercial corporate flights for its own purposes only.

☐ OK-WDC	Let 410UVP-E8D	912531		0991	1091	2 WA M-601E	6400	Corporate Y17		

AIRCRAFT REPAIR WORKS (LOK-Letecke opravny Kbely) (Commercial division of Aircraft Repair Works) Prague-Kbely

Commercial Division, Touzimska 583, CZ-197 03 Praha 9-Kbely, Czech Republic / Czechia ☎ (2) 850 76 85 Tx: 121407 lok c Fax: (2) 850 78 06 SITA: n/a
F: 1996 n/a Head: Milan Siroky Net: n/a

☐ OK-FXA	Mil Mi-8T	10539		0075	0097	2 IS TV2-117AG	12000	transport/crane		
☐ OK-FXE	Mil Mi-8T	10546		0075	0097	2 IS TV2-117AG	12000	transport/crane		lst Aerocentrum

AIR OSTRAVA, Ltd = 8K / VTR (Member of the Chemapol Group & ERA/European Regional Airlines Association / formerly Air Vitkovice, spol. s r.o) Ostrava-Mosnov

Ostrava Int'l Airport, CZ-742 51 Mosnov, Czech Republic / Czechia ☎ (69) 665 94 55 Tx: none Fax: (69) 665 94 90 SITA: n/a
F: 1977 160 Head: Milan Rousar IATA: 183 ICAO: VITEK Net: n/a

☐ OK-PEP	Saab SF340A	340A-018	HB-AHD	0085	0496	2 GE CT7-5A2	12250	Y33		lsf Saab Aircraft / Skoda Octavia-cs
☐ OK-REK	Saab SF340A	340A-071	SE-E71*	0086	1295	2 GE CT7-5A2	12250	Y33		lsf Saab Aircraft Credit AB
☐ OK-TOP	Saab SF340A	340A-132	SE-KFA	0088	0497	2 GE CT7-5A2	12700	Y33		lsf Saab Aircraft Credit AB
☐ OK-UFO	Saab SF340A	340A-141	ZK-NSL	0089	0198	2 GE CT7-5A2	12700	Y33		lsf Saab Aircraft Credit AB

479 registration type of aircraft cn/fn ex/ex* mfd del powered by mtow kg configuration selcal name/fln/specialitites/remarks

AIR SERVICE CS

Strunkovice nad Blanici

Airfield, CZ-384 26 Strunkovice nad Blanici, Czech Republic / Czechia ☎ (338) 32 73 02 Tx: none Fax: (338) 32 72 02 SITA: n/a
F: 1993 👥 2 Head: Jaroslav Kristof Net: n/a Aircraft below MTOW 1361kg: 1 Cessna 172FR

☐ OK-VHC	PZL Mielec (Antonov) An-2	*1G238-24*		*0090*	*0191*	*1 SH ASh-62IR*	*5500*			

AIR SPECIAL, a.s. = ASX (formerly part of Slov-Air)

Prague/Ces.Budej.,/Liberec/Rakovnik/Marianské Lazne/Tabor

Airport Ruzyne, CZ-160 08 Praha 6, Czech Republic / Czechia ☎ (2) 20 11 24 00 Tx: 127060 c Fax: (2) 32 17 59 SITA: n/a
F: 1991 👥 66 Head: Vodnanska Jarmila ICAO: AIRSPEC Net: n/a Aircraft/Ag-aircraft below MTOW 1361/5000kg (mainly used as sprayers, trainers & couriers): 74 Z-37A, 11 Z-37T, 1 Z-42 & 6 Z-43.
Trainers are operated by subsidiary AIR SPECIAL SCHOOL in Marianské Lazne and Liberec.

☐ OK-OHD	Let 200D Morava	*170212*	*OK-BYA*	*0060*	*0060*	*2 WA M-337*	*1950*	*4 Pax*		
☐ OK-PLV	Let 200A Morava	*170815*	*SP-NXX*	*0061*	*0098*	*2 WA M-337*	*1950*	*4 Pax*		
☐ OK-JIJ	PZL Mielec (Antonov) An-2R	*1G186-24*		*0079*	*0080*	*1 SH ASh-62IR*	*5500*	*Sprayer/11 Pax*		
☐ OK-JIL	PZL Mielec (Antonov) An-2R	*1G186-26*		*0079*	*0098*	*1 SH ASh-62IR*	*5500*	*Sprayer/11 Pax*		
☐ OK-JIM	PZL Mielec (Antonov) An-2R	*1G186-27*		*0079*	*0099*	*1 SH ASh-62IR*	*5500*	*Sprayer/11 Pax*		
☐ OK-JIQ	PZL Mielec (Antonov) An-2R	*1G186-28*		*0079*	*0080*	*1 SH ASh-62IR*	*5500*	*Sprayer/11 Pax*		
☐ OK-KIC	PZL Mielec (Antonov) An-2R	*1G186-34*		*0080*	*0099*	*1 SH ASh-62IR*	*5500*	*Sprayer/11 Pax*		
☐ OK-KIE	PZL Mielec (Antonov) An-2R	*1G186-36*		*0080*	*0099*	*1 SH ASh-62IR*	*5500*	*Sprayer/11 Pax*		
☐ OK-KIF	PZL Mielec (Antonov) An-2R	*1G186-37*		*0080*	*0099*	*1 SH ASh-62IR*	*5500*	*Sprayer/11 Pax*		
☐ OK-KII	PZL Mielec (Antonov) An-2R	*1G190-04*		*0080*	*0080*	*1 SH ASh-62IR*	*5500*	*Sprayer/11 Pax*		
☐ OK-KIK	PZL Mielec (Antonov) An-2R	*1G190-06*		*0080*	*0099*	*1 SH ASh-62IR*	*5500*	*Sprayer/11 Pax*		
☐ OK-KIL	PZL Mielec (Antonov) An-2R	*1G190-07*		*0080*	*0099*	*1 SH ASh-62IR*	*5500*	*Sprayer/11 Pax*		
☐ OK-KIP	PZL Mielec (Antonov) An-2R	*1G190-10*		*0080*	*0080*	*1 SH ASh-62IR*	*5500*	*11 Pax*		
☐ OK-KIQ	PZL Mielec (Antonov) An-2R	*1G190-11*		*0080*	*0099*	*1 SH ASh-62IR*	*5500*	*Sprayer/11 Pax*		
☐ OK-KIV	PZL Mielec (Antonov) An-2R	*1G190-16*		*0080*	*0099*	*1 SH ASh-62IR*	*5500*	*Sprayer/11 Pax*		

AIR-TRANSA, a.s.

Hradec Kralove

Horova 180, CZ-500 02 Hradec Kralove, Czech Republic / Czechia ☎ (49) 39 83 59 Tx: none Fax: (49) 39 83 71 SITA: n/a
F: 1993 👥 n/a Head: Josef Vanek Net: n/a

☐ OK-KIZ	PZL Swidnik (Mil) Mi-2	*526847100*	*UR-20808*	*0080*	*0094*	*2 IS GTD-350-4*	*3550*	*Transport*		
☐ OK-EXC	Mil Mi-8T	*9743714*		*0074*	*0095*	*2 IS TV2-117AG*	*12000*	*Transport/Crane*		

AIR WIN, a.s.

Prague-Ruzyne

Srobarova 49, CZ-130 00 Praha 3, Czech Republic / Czechia ☎ (2) 74 96 98 Tx: none Fax: (2) 74 96 98 SITA: n/a
F: 1997 👥 n/a Head: Erwin Junker Net: n/a

☐ OK-GTJ	Beech King Air 300LW	*FA-223*	*D-IHHB*	*0092*	*0098*	*2 PWC PT6A-60A*	*5670*	*Executive*		Melnik

ALFA HELIKOPTER, Spol s r.o.

Brno-Cernovice / Jihlava / Olomouc

Starobrnenska 13, PO Box 720, CZ-663 20 Brno, Czech Republic / Czechia ☎ (5) 42 21 74 60 Tx: none Fax: (5) 42 21 74 60 SITA: n/a
F: 1991 👥 18 Head: Miroslav Pospisil Net: n/a

☐ OK-WIR	Bell 206L-3 LongRanger III	*51511*		*0091*	*0592*	*1 AN 250-C30P*	*1883*	*EMS*		
☐ OK-XIS	Bell 206L-3 LongRanger III	*51602*		*0092*	*0393*	*1 AN 250-C30P*	*1883*	*Executive*		
☐ OK-YIP	Bell 206L-4 LongRanger IV	*52068*	*N2137P*	*0094*	*0894*	*1 AN 250-C30P*	*2018*	*EMS*		
☐ OK-ZIU	Bell 206LT TwinRanger	*52032*	*N93LT*	*0094*	*0296*	*2 AN 250-C20R*	*2061*	*EMS*		

ARGUS GEO SYSTEM, spol. s r.o.

Hradec Kralova

Hradecka 1151, CZ-500 02 Hradec Kralove, Czech Republic / Czechia ☎ (49) 521 08 49 Tx: none Fax: (49) 521 08 49 SITA: n/a
F: 1994 👥 9 Head: Ladislav Nagy Net: n/a

☐ OK-EKT	Cessna TU206F Turbo Stationair	*U20602276*	*D-EEVR*	*0074*	*0094*	*1 CO TSIO-520-C*	*1633*	*Photo / Survey*		
☐ OK-EKU	Piper PA-23-250 Aztec E	*27-7405402*	*G-JASP*	*0074*	*0097*	*2 LY TIO-540-C1A*	*1950*	*Photo / Survey*		

BEMOINVEST, spol. s r.o. (Affiliated with Letecka skola Bemoair Benesov)

Benesov

Na Bezdekove 2056, CZ-256 01 Benesov u Prahy, Czech Republic / Czechia ☎ (301) 93 144 Tx: none Fax: (301) 93 529 SITA: n/a
F: 1997 👥 n/a Head: Josef Drab Net: n/a Aircraft below MTOW 1361kg: 2 Cessna 172, 2 Zlin Z-142, 2 Z-43, 1 Z-126 & 4 gliders

☐ OK-PLH	Let 200A Morava	*170722*		*0061*	*0097*	*2 WA M-337*	*1950*	*Y4*		*lsf pvt*
☐ OK-PLR	Let 200A Morava	*170801*		*0061*	*0097*	*2 WA M-337*	*1950*	*Y4*		

BOHEMIA AIR SERVICE - BAS, s r.o.

Prague

Nebovidska 2, CZ-110 00 Praha 1, Czech Republic / Czechia ☎ (2) 57 31 00 42 Tx: none Fax: (2) 57 31 21 88 SITA: n/a
F: 1994 👥 5 Head: Vladimir Koukal Net: n/a

☐ OK-VHJ	PZL Mielec (Antonov) An-2	*1G234-02*		*0090*	*0094*	*1 SH ASh-62IR*	*5250*	*11Pax/Cargo/Para*		*opf Para-Club Praha-Letnany & Probest*

BUDVAIR, a.s.

Ceske Budejovice

PO Box 164, Letiste Plana, CZ-370 04 Ceske Budejovice, Czech Republic / Czechia ☎ (38) 32 445 Tx: none Fax: (38) 32 445 SITA: n/a
F: 1995 👥 7 Head: Josef Spilka Net: n/a

☐ OK-PDB	Let 410FG	*851522*	*1522*	*0085*	*0296*	*2 WA M-601D*	*5800*	*Photo / Survey*		
☐ OK-PDC	Let 410FG	*851524*	*1524*	*0085*	*0596*	*2 WA M-601D*	*5800*	*Photo / Survey*		

CIS-AIR International, Ltd = CSR (formerly Cis-Air)

Slusovice-Bila Hlina

PO Box 86, CZ-763 15 Slusovice, Czech Republic / Czechia ☎ (67) 798 13 72 Tx: none Fax: (67) 38 103 SITA: n/a
F: 1990 👥 4 Head: Zdenek Cisar ICAO: CISAIR Net: n/a

☐ OK-VHB	PZL Mielec (Antonov) An-2	*1G238-54*		*0590*	*1290*	*1 SH ASh-62IR*	*5250*			

CROWN AIR, s r.o. = OWR

Prague-Ruzyne

Letiste Ruzyne-Jih, Suite 239, CZ-160 00 Praha 6, Czech Republic / Czechia ☎ (2) 20 11 22 35 Tx: none Fax: (2) 20 11 24 88 SITA: n/a
F: 1997 👥 n/a Head: Zdenek Pejskar ICAO: AIR CROWN Net: n/a

☐ OK-HKS	Piper PA-23-250 Aztec F	*27-7754134*	*N95EB*	*0077*	*0097*	*2 LY IO-540-C4B5*	*2359*	*Executive*		
☐ OK-	Cessna 750 Citation X	*750-*				*2 AN AE3007C*	*16193*	*Executive*		*oo-delivery 0699*

CSA Czech Airlines = OK / CSA (formerly CSA Czechoslovak Airlines/Ceskoslovenské Aerolinie)

Prague-Ruzyne

Ruzyne Airport, CZ-160 08 Praha 6, Czech Republic / Czechia ☎ (2) 36 26 14 Tx: 120338 took c Fax: (2) 316 27 74 SITA: n/a
F: 1923 👥 3900 Head: Antonin Jakubse IATA: 064 ICAO: CSA Net: http://www.csa.cz

☐ OK-AFE	ATR 42-400	*487*	*F-WWEF**	*0095*	*0396*	*2 PWC PW121A*	*17900*	*CY42*		Kolin
☐ OK-AFF	ATR 42-400	*491*	*F-WWLC**	*0095*	*0396*	*2 PWC PW121A*	*17900*	*CY42*		Kutna Hora
☐ OK-BFG	ATR 42-320	*409*	*F-OKMR*	*0095*		*2 PWC PW121*	*16700*	*CY42*		*to be lsf ATR 0599*
☐ OK-BFH	ATR 42-320	*412*	*F-OKMS*	*0095*		*2 PWC PW121*	*16700*	*CY42*		*to be lsf ATR 0999*
☐ OK-XFA	ATR 72-202	*285*	*F-WWLO**	*0092*	*0492*	*2 PWC PW124B*	*21500*	*CY64*		Cesky Krumlov
☐ OK-XFB	ATR 72-202	*297*	*F-WWLW**	*0092*	*0492*	*2 PWC PW124B*	*21500*	*CY64*		Znojmo
☐ OK-XFC	ATR 72-202	*299*	*F-WWLX**	*0092*	*0492*	*2 PWC PW124B*	*21500*	*CY64*		Nitra
☐ OK-XFD	ATR 72-202	*303*	*F-WWLB**	*0092*	*0592*	*2 PWC PW124B*	*21500*	*CY64*		Mlada Boleslav
☐ OK-CGH	Boeing 737-55S	*28469 / 2849*		*0097*	*0397*	*2 CFMI CFM56-3C1*	*55999*	*CY108*		Usti n./Labem
☐ OK-CGJ	Boeing 737-55S	*28470 / 2861*		*0097*	*0397*	*2 CFMI CFM56-3C1*	*55999*	*CY108*		Hradec Kralove
☐ OK-CGK	Boeing 737-55S	*28471 / 2885*		*0597*	*0597*	*2 CFMI CFM56-3C1*	*55999*	*CY108*		Pardubice
☐ OK-DGL	Boeing 737-55S	*28472 / 3004*		*0398*	*0398*	*2 CFMI CFM56-3C1*	*55999*	*CY108*	*RS-EK*	Tabor
☐ OK-EGO	Boeing 737-55S	*28475 / 3096*	*N1786B**	*0099*	*0299*	*2 CFMI CFM56-3C1*	*55999*	*CY108*		Jindrichuv Hradec
☐ OK-XGA	Boeing 737-55S	*26539 / 2300*	*N1790B**	*0092*	*0692*	*2 CFMI CFM56-3C1*	*55565*	*CY108*	*CR-KS*	Plzen
☐ OK-XGB	Boeing 737-55S	*26540 / 2317*		*0092*	*0792*	*2 CFMI CFM56-3C1*	*55565*	*CY108*	*CR-LM*	Olomouc
☐ OK-XGC	Boeing 737-55S	*26541 / 2319*		*0092*	*0792*	*2 CFMI CFM56-3C1*	*55565*	*CY108*	*CR-LP*	Ceske Budejovice
☐ OK-XGD	Boeing 737-55S	*26542 / 2337*		*0092*	*0792*	*2 CFMI CFM56-3C1*	*55565*	*CY108*	*CR-LQ*	Poprad
☐ OK-XGE	Boeing 737-55S	*26543 / 2339*		*0092*	*0892*	*2 CFMI CFM56-3C1*	*55565*	*CY108*	*CR-LS*	Kosice
☐ OK-DGM	Boeing 737-45S	*28473 / 3014*		*0098*	*0498*	*2 CFMI CFM56-3C1*	*64999*	*CY144*	*RS-EL*	Trebon
☐ OK-DGN	Boeing 737-45S	*28474 / 3028*		*0098*	*0598*	*2 CFMI CFM56-3C1*	*64999*	*CY144*	*RS-EM*	Trebic
☐ OK-EGP	Boeing 737-45S	*28476 / 3103*		*0099*	*0399*	*2 CFMI CFM56-3C1*	*64999*	*CY144*		Kladno
☐ OK-WGF	Boeing 737-4Y0	*24903 / 1978*	*9M-MJN*	*0091*	*0495*	*2 CFMI CFM56-3C1*	*64636*	*CY144*	*JQ-BS*	Jihlava / *lsf GECA*
☐ OK-WGG	Boeing 737-4Y0	*24693 / 1972*	*9M-MJM*	*0091*	*0395*	*2 CFMI CFM56-3C1*	*64636*	*CY144*	*JQ-CD*	Liberec / *lsf GECA*
☐ OK-TCD	Tupolev 154M	*792*		*1288*	*0189*	*3 SO D-30KU-154-II*	*92000*	*CY136*		Trencianské Teplice
☐ OK-UCE	Tupolev 154M	*804*		*0089*	*0689*	*3 SO D-30KU-154-II*	*92000*	*CY136*		Marianske Lazne
☐ OK-UCF	Tupolev 154M	*807*		*0089*	*0789*	*3 SO D-30KU-154-II*	*92000*	*CY136*		Smokovec
☐ OK-VCG	Tupolev 154M	*838*		*0090*	*0790*	*3 SO D-30KU-154-II*	*92000*	*CY136*		Luhacovice
☐ OK-WAA	Airbus Industrie A310-304 (ET)	*564*	*F-WWCB**	*0291*	*0291*	*2 GE CF6-80C2A2*	*157000*	*C21Y188*	*CK-AQ*	Praha
☐ OK-WAB	Airbus Industrie A310-304 (ET)	*567*	*F-WWCD**	*0391*	*0391*	*2 GE CF6-80C2A2*	*157000*	*C21Y188*	*CK-BQ*	Bratislava

DELTA SYSTEM-AIR

Hradec Královéj

Vita Nejedlého 951, CZ-500 82 Hradec Králové, Czech Republic / Czechia ☎ (49) 44 549 Tx: none Fax: (49) 44 549 SITA: n/a
F: 1991 👥 26 Head: Tomas Suchanek Net: n/a Aircraft below MTOW 1361kg: Cessna 172, Schweizer 269C (300C) & Zlin Z-142 & Z-226

☐ OK-DKP	Piper PA-34-200 Seneca	*34-7350288*	*C-GCZA*	*0073*	*0595*	*2 LY IO-360-C1E6*	*1910*	*Y5*		
☐ OK-AIA	Eurocopter (Aerosp.) AS355F2 Ecureuil 2	*5512*	*RP-C355*	*0091*	*1295*	*2 AN 250-C20F*	*2540*	*EMS*		*lsf Eurocopter France*
☐ OK-BIC	Eurocopter (Aerosp.) AS355F2 Ecureuil 2	*5388*		*0089*	*0096*	*2 AN 250-C20F*	*2540*	*EMS*		
☐ OK-MIA	Eurocopter (Aerosp.) AS355F1 Ecureuil 2	*5187*	*N5799W*	*0082*	*0098*	*2 AN 250-C20F*	*2400*	*EMS*		
☐ OK-WIQ	Eurocopter (Aerosp.) AS355F2 Ecureuil 2	*5483*	*OM-WIQ*	*0691*	*0293*	*2 AN 250-C20F*	*2540*	*EMS*		
☐ OK-JIX	PZL Swidnik (Mil) Mi-2	*536012029*	*OM-JIX*	*0079*	*0092*	*2 IS GTD-350-4*	*3550*	*EMS*		
☐ OK-LJR	PZL Swidnik (Mil) Mi-2	*537327091*	*OM-LJR*	*0081*	*0092*	*2 IS GTD-350-4*	*3550*	*EMS*		
☐ OK-NDG	Let 410UVP	*831138*	*OK-NZG*	*0083*	*0392*	*2 WA M-601D*	*5800*	*Y17*		*occ lsf Le Cygne Sportif*

480 registration type of aircraft *cn/fn* *ex/ex** *mfd* *del* *powered by* *mtow kg* *configuration* *selcal* *name/fln/specialitites/remarks*

F AIR, Ltd
Benesov

Masarykovo nam. 225, CZ-256 01 Benesov, Czech Republic / Czechia ☎ (301) 79 38 20 Tx: none Fax: (301) 79 38 20 SITA: n/a
F: 1991 ⁂ 9 Head: Michal Markovic Net: n/a Aircraft/Ag-aircraft below MTOW 1361/5000kg: 1 Cessna 150, 1 Cessna 152, 1 Cessna 172, 1 Piper PA-28, 1 Zlin Z-37A Cmelak, 1 Z-43, 3 glider & 7 ultralights

☐ OK-MKR	Piper PA-44-180T Turbo Seminole	44-8207014	D-GJOY	0082	0097	2 LY TO-360-E1A6D	1776			

FISCHER AIR, s r.o. = 8F / FFR
Prague-Ruzyne

PO 68, PO Box 15, Ruzyne Airport, CZ-160 08 Praha 6, Czech Republic / Czechia ☎ (2) 20 11 61 70 Tx: none Fax: (2) 20 11 54 39 SITA: PRGZOPF
F: 1996 ⁂ 90 Head: Michal Tomis ICAO: FISCHER Net: n/a

☐ OK-FAN	Boeing 737-33A	27469 / 2864		0097	0397	2 CFMI CFM56-3C1	61235	Y148		
☐ OK-FIT	Boeing 737-36N	28590 / 3097		0099	0399	2 CFMI CFM56-3C1	62822	Y148		lsf GECA
☐ OK-FUN	Boeing 737-33A	27910 / 2873		0097	0497	2 CFMI CFM56-3C1	61235	Y148		

FRYDLANTSKE STROJIRNY - RASL A SYN, a.s.
Hodkovice nad Mohelkou

Chrastavska 263/8, CZ-360 01 Liberec 2, Czech Republic / Czechia ☎ (329) 77 01 81 Tx: none Fax: (48) 510 50 40 SITA: n/a
F: 1996 ⁂ n/a Head: Mnichovo Hradiste Net: n/a

☐ OK-IKL	Cessna R182 Skylane RG II	R18200161	D-ETAT	0078	0096	1 LY O-540-J3C5D	1406			
☐ OK-PHJ	Let 200A Morava	170802		0061	0096	2 WA M-337	1950			
☐ OK-VHA	PZL Mielec (Antonov) An-2	1G238-53		0590	0096	1 SH ASh-62IR	5700			

GEODIS BRNO, spol. s r.o.
Brno-Cernovice

Lazaretni 11a, CZ-615 00 Brno, Czech Republic / Czechia ☎ (5) 45 21 20 40 Tx: none Fax: (5) 45 21 20 61 SITA: n/a
F: 1995 ⁂ n/a Head: Karel Sukup Net: n/a

☐ OK-HKE	Cessna TU206G Turbo Stationair	U20603877		0077	0095	1 CO TSIO-520-M	1633	Photo / Survey		

HELICOPTER, spol. s r.o. = HCP
Pribor, Ceske Budejovice-Hosin

Nam. S. Freuda 4, PO Box 29, CZ-742 58 Pribor, Czech Republic / Czechia ☎ (656) 91 11 93 Tx: none Fax: (656) 91 11 93 SITA: n/a
F: 1994 ⁂ 12 Head: Stanislav Ambroz ICAO: HELI CZECH Net: n/a

☐ OK-AIH	PZL Swidnik (Mil) Mi-2	542209121	SP-FDH	0071	0498	2 IS GTD-350-4	3550	EMS/Inspection		
☐ OK-MIK	PZL Swidnik Kania Model 1	900103	SP-SSA	0082	0098	2 AN 250-C20B	3550	EMS/Inspection		
☐ OK-VIL	PZL Swidnik Kania Model 1	900305		0696	0796	2 AN 250-C20B	3550	EMS/Inspection		

JAS AIR, spol. s r.o.
Ceské Budjovice-Hosin

Airfield Hosin, CZ-373 41 Hosin, Czech Republic / Czechia ☎ (38) 722 07 83 Tx: none Fax: (38) 722 07 88 SITA: n/a
F: 1993 ⁂ n/a Head: n/a Net: n/a Aircraft / Ag-aircraft below MTOW 1361 / 5000kg (mainly used as trainers & sprayers): 1 Cessna FR172, 3 Z-37A Cmelak

☐ OK-JID	PZL Mielec (Antonov) An-2R	1G186-18		0080	0098	1 SH ASh-62IR	5500	Sprayer / 11 Pax		

LE CYGNE SPORTIF, a.s.
Prague-Kbely

Zavisova 13/66, CZ-140 00 Praha 4, Czech Republic / Czechia ☎ (2) 21 59 81 12 Tx: none Fax: (2) 21 59 81 48 SITA: n/a
F: 1995 ⁂ n/a Head: Pavel Dvorak Net: n/a

☐ OK-NDG	Let 410UVP	831138	OK-NZG	0083	0096	2 WA M-601D	5800	Y17		occ lst ABA-Air & Delta System-Air

LETECKE PRACE A SLUZBY-LPS, spol. s r.o. (Aerial Works & Services)
Melnik

Palackého 967/11, CZ-412 01 Litomerice 1, Czech Republic / Czechia ☎ (206) 62 22 77 Tx: none Fax: (206) 62 22 77 SITA: n/a
F: 1998 ⁂ n/a Head: Lubomir Ogurcak Net: n/a Aircraft below MTOW 1361kg: 1 Robinson R22 & 1 L-13SE glider

☐ OK-OIT	PZL Swidnik (Mil) Mi-2	528919104	OM-OIT	0084	0098	2 IS GTD-350-4	3550	Utility		

LR AIRLINES, Ltd = LRB
Ostrava

Ostrava International Airport, CZ-762 51 Mosnov, Czech Republic / Czechia ☎ (69) 665 91 49 Tx: none Fax: (69) 665 92 11 SITA: n/a
F: 1997 ⁂ n/a Head: Klement Bilek ICAO: LADY RACINE Net: n/a

☐ OK-LRA	Let 410UVP-E	892216	CCCP-67605	0089	0697	2 WA M-601E	6400	Exec 15 Pax		Lady Racine

LSC Letecké sportovni centrum (Flying Sport Center)
Moravska Trebova

Airfield Stare Mesto, CZ-569 32 Moravska Trebova, Czech Republic / Czechia ☎ (462) 31 25 36 Tx: none Fax: (462) 31 25 36 SITA: n/a
F: 1990 ⁂ 13 Head: Petr Poborsky Net: http://www./sc.cz Aircraft below MTOW 1361kg: Cessna 152/172, Extra 300/S, L-40, Z-50LE/LS, Z-142 & Z-526F/AS.

☐ OK-PLE	Let 200A Morava	170718		0061		2 WA M-337	1950			
☐ OK-PLG	Let 200A Morava	170720		0061		2 WA M-337	1950			
☐ OK-UIA	PZL Mielec (Antonov) An-2	1G237-36		0089		1 SH ASh-62IR	5500			
☐ OK-XIG	PZL Mielec (Antonov) An-2	1G98-70		0068		1 SH ASh-62IR	5500			

OLIMEX, spol. s r.o. = OLX
Prerov

Travnik 31, CZ-750 02 Prerov, Czech Republic / Czechia ☎ (641) 83 95 Tx: none Fax: (641) 83 95 SITA: n/a
F: 1993 ⁂ 15 Head: Petr Navratil ICAO: OLIMEX Net: n/a

☐ OK-RDA	Let 410UVP-E9	861813	OM-RAY	0086	1198	2 WA M-601E	6400	Y17		
☐ OK-UDS	Let 410UVP-E13	892321		0089	0098	2 WA M-601E	6400	Y17		lsf Tory Leasing
☐ OK-WDR	Let 410UVP-E	912607		0091	1095	2 WA M-601E	6400	Y17		

PETR NAVRATIL Aerotaxi & Airschool
Prerov

Travnik 31, CZ-750 00 Prerov, Czech Republic / Czechia ☎ (602) 50 33 24 Tx: none Fax: (641) 83 95 SITA: n/a
F: 1995 ⁂ 7 Head: Petr Navratil Net: n/a Aircraft below MTOW 1361kg: Zlin Z-43

☐ OK-PHG	Let 200A Morava	170805		0061		2 WA M-337	1950	Y4 / Trainer		
☐ OK-RHH	Let 200D Morava	171418	YU-BBI	0062		2 WA M-337	1950	Y4 / Trainer		
☐ OK-PDO	Let 410UVP	851411	UR-67507	0085	0098	2 WA M-601D	5800	Y17/Para/Frtr		

POLICIE – Letecka sluzba Policie Ceské Republiky (Police Aviation) (Aviation Service of the Czech Republic Police)
Prague-Ruzyne

PO 614, Box 35, CZ-161 00 Praha, Czech Republic / Czechia ☎ (2) 33 32 33 07 Tx: none Fax: (2) 61 43 35 33 SITA: n/a
F: 1993 ⁂ 120 Head: Capt. Vladimir Panenka Net: n/a Non-commercial government organisation conducting police patrol and ambulance flights.

☐ B-5265	Eurocopter (MBB) BO105CBS-4	S-865	D-HBKB*	0292	0392	2 AN 250-C20B	2500	Patrol		
☐ B-5278	Eurocopter (MBB) BO105CBS-4	S-878	D-HMBK*	0892	0992	2 AN 250-C20B	2500	Patrol		
☐ B-5292	Eurocopter (MBB) BO105CBS-4	S-592	D-HDQO*	1282	0791	2 AN 250-C20B	2500	EMS		
☐ B-4362	Bell 412HP	36062	N6181Y*	0493	0893	2 PWC PT6T-3BE TwinPac	5398	Patrol		
☐ B-4363	Bell 412HP	36063	N6199J*	0493	0893	2 PWC PT6T-3BE TwinPac	5398	EMS		
☐ B-4369	Bell 412HP	36069	N70890*	0093	1093	2 PWC PT6T-3BE TwinPac	5398	EMS / Patrol		
☐ B-4370	Bell 412HP	36070	N70904*	0093	1093	2 PWC PT6T-3BE TwinPac	5398	EMS / Patrol		
☐ B-8733	Mil Mi-8P	10833		0887	1087	2 IS TV2-117A	12000	EMS / Patrol		
☐ B-8938	Mil Mi-8P	10838		0389	0489	2 IS TV2-117A	12000	EMS / Patrol		

SILVER AIR, spol. s r.o. = SLD
Prague-Ruzyne

Pernerova 16, CZ-186 00 Praha 8, Czech Republic / Czechia ☎ (2) 24 81 57 54 Tx: none Fax: (2) 232 14 05 SITA: n/a
F: 1996 ⁂ 7 Head: Zdenek Skoda ICAO: SOLID Net: n/a

☐ OK-WDO	Let 410UVP-E19A	912538	J2-KBE	0091	0097	2 WA M-601E	6400	Y17		lsf Omnipol / sub-lst TDR as 9A-BTA
☐ OK-WDT	Let 410UVP-E	912615		0091	0098	2 WA M-601E	6400	Y17		lsf VZLU Aeronautical Research & Test

SLOVACKY AEROKLUB
Uherske Hradiste-Kunovice

PO Box 34, CZ-686 04 Kunovice, Czech Republic / Czechia ☎ (632) 54 96 80 Tx: none Fax: (632) 54 96 80 SITA: n/a
F: 1945 ⁂ 5 Head: Stanislav Sklenar Net: n/a Aircraft below MTOW 1361kg: Cessna 172, Zlin Z-126/226/326 & gliders and powered gliders

☐ OK-UJD	Let Z-37A Cmelak	005		0065	0069	1 AV M-462RF	1950	Sprayer/Towing		
☐ OK-PLJ	Let 200D Morava	170724		0061	0093	2 WA M-337	1950	Y4		
☐ OK-DZA	Let 410MA	730207	OK-158	0073	0190	2 WA M-601B	5700	Y17		

TRAVEL SERVICE AIRLINES = TVS (Associated with Canaria Travel)
Prague-Ruzyne

PO Box 87, Postovni urad 61, CZ-161 00 Praha 6, Czech Republic / Czechia ☎ (2) 20 11 18 86 Tx: none Fax: (2) 20 11 18 87 SITA: n/a
F: 1997 ⁂ n/a Head: Jiri Kaplan ICAO: SKYTRAVEL Net: n/a

☐ OK-TVR	Boeing 737-4Y0	23870 / 1647	G-OBMG	0089	0399	2 CFMI CFM56-3C1	64637	Y168	DF-GP	lsf GECA
☐ OK-TVS	Boeing 737-4Y0	24911 / 2033	SE-DTB	0091	0598	2 CFMI CFM56-3C1	68040	Y168	BE-LP	Bubu / lsf GECA
☐ OK-VCP	Tupolev 154M	858	OK-BYP	1290	0997	3 SO D-30KU-154-II	100000	Y148		

UCL-Urad pro civilni letectvi CR = CBA (CAA-Civil Aviation Authority, Flight Inspeciton div.)
Prague-Ruzyne

Letiste Praha Ruzyne, CZ-160 08 Praha 6, Czech Republic / Czechia ☎ (2) 36 79 23 Tx: 120321 c Fax: (2) 316 27 78 SITA: n/a
F: 1997 ⁂ 133 Head: Boleslav Stavovcik ICAO: CALIBRA Net: n/a Aircraft below MTOW 1361kg: Zlin Z-43. Non-commercial state organisation conducting aerial inspection and calibration missions.
UCL shares with the Ministry of Transport, Civil Aviation Dept. the duties of C.A.A. in Czechia.

☐ OK-HYA	Let Z-37-2C Cmelak	23-08		0077	0497	1 AV M-462RF	1850	3 Pax / Courier		
☐ OK-OGB	Let 200D Morava	170318	OK-BYC	0060	0497	2 WA M-337	1950	4 Pax		
☐ OK-SLI	Beech Baron 58	TH-1757	N3257N	0095	0497	2 CO IO-550-C	2495	Corporate		
☐ OK-WYI	Let 410UVP-E	912616	CCCP-67685	0091	0497	2 WA M-601E	6400	Calibrator		
☐ OK-UZI	Beech Beechjet 400	RJ-56	G-BSZP	0089	0497	2 PWC JT15D-5	7158	Calibrator		

ZLIN AIR (Zlin Air School dba / Subsidiary of Moravan Otrokovice)
Zlin-Otrokovice

Otrokovice, CZ-765 81 Otrokovice, Czech Republic / Czechia ☎ (67) 92 20 41 Tx: 67240 morav c Fax: (67) 92 23 40 SITA: n/a
F: 1964 ⁂ 7 Head: Vladimir Nemec Net: n/a Aircraft below MTOW 1361 kg: Zlin 42MU, 50M, 142, 142C, 143L & 242L

☐ OK-OHH	Let 200A Morava	170619	0619	0060	0190	2 WA M-337	1950	4 Pax/Trainer		

481 registration type of aircraft cn/fn ex/ex* mfd del powered by mtow kg configuration selcal name/fln/specialitites/remarks

OM = SLOVAKIA (Slovak Republic) (Slovenska Republika)

Capital: Bratislava Official Language: Slovak Population: 5,4 million Square Km: 49014 Dialling code: +421 Year established: 1993 Acting political head: Mikolas Dzorinda (Prime Minister)

AERO SLOVAKIA, a.s. = ASO

Nitra

Airport Janikovce, SK-949 07 Nitra, Slovakia ☎ (87) 53 48 77 Tx: none Fax: (87) 53 46 50 SITA: n/a

F: 1992 👥 36 Head: Lubomir Kovacik ICAO: AERO NITRA Net: n/a Aircraft/Ag-aircraft below MTOW 1361/5000kg: 3 PZL M-18 Dromader, 44 Zlin 37A/A2 Cmelak, 6 Zlin 37T & 1 Zlin 42M.

registration	type of aircraft	cn/fn	ex/ex*	mfd	del	powered by	mtow kg	configuration	selcal	name/fln/specialitites/remarks
☐ OM-AES	Cessna U206F Stationair II	U20602718	OM-FCB	0075	0097	1 CO IO-520-F	1633	Utility		
☐ OM-JIG	PZL Mielec (Antonov) An-2R	1G186-21	OK-JIG	0079	0097	1 SH ASh-62IR	5500	Photo		
☐ OM-JIH	PZL Mielec (Antonov) An-2R	1G186-22	OK-JIH	0079	0092	1 SH ASh-62IR	5500	Sprayer		
☐ OM-KIJ	PZL Mielec (Antonov) An-2R	1G190-05	OK-KIJ	0080	0092	1 SH ASh-62IR	5500	Sprayer		
☐ OM-KIN	PZL Mielec (Antonov) An-2R	1G190-09	OK-KIN	0080	0097	1 SH ASh-62IR	5500	Para		
☐ OM-KIR	PZL Mielec (Antonov) An-2R	1G190-12	OK-KIR	0080	0092	1 SH ASh-62IR	5500	Sprayer		
☐ OM-KIT	PZL Mielec (Antonov) An-2R	1G190-14	OK-KIT	0080	0092	1 SH ASh-62IR	5500	Sprayer		
☐ OM-LIA	PZL Mielec (Antonov) An-2R	1G194-30	HA-MEV	0081	0094	1 SH ASh-62IR	5500	Y12 / Freighter		

AGROLET, Ltd = AGZ

Trnava

Halova 10, SK-851 01 Bratislava, Slovakia ☎ (7) 53 41 74 25 Tx: none Fax: (7) 53 41 74 25 SITA: n/a

F: 1991 👥 40 Head: Daniel Svrcek ICAO: AGROLET Net: n/a Ag- & Trainer aircraft below MTOW 5000kg: 1 Let Z-37-2 Cmelak, 3 UL Zenair Zodiac CH-601 & 20 Zlin Z-37A

registration	type of aircraft	cn/fn	ex/ex*	mfd	del	powered by	mtow kg	configuration	selcal	name/fln/specialitites/remarks
☐ OM-EIB	PZL Mielec (Antonov) An-2P	1G151-53	HA-YHA	0074		1 SH ASh-62IR	5500	Y12		
☐ OM-KID	PZL Mielec (Antonov) An-2P	1G86-35	OK-KID	0067		1 SH ASh-62IR	5500	Sprayer		

AIR CARPATIA, a.s.

Bratislava-M.R. Stefanik

Gercenova 29, SK-851 01 Bratislava, Slovakia ☎ (7) 43 71 21 39 Tx: none Fax: (7) 437 12 67 SITA: n/a

F: 1998 👥 n/a Head: Capt. Pavel Rychtarik Net: http://www.aircarpatia.sk Aircraft below MTOW 1361kg: Cessna 172N & P-220ULR

registration	type of aircraft	cn/fn	ex/ex*	mfd	del	powered by	mtow kg	configuration	selcal	name/fln/specialitites/remarks
☐ OM-FKO	Piper PA-34-200T Seneca II	34-7570019	OK-FKO	0075	0598	2 CO TSIO-360-E	2073	5 Pax		

AIR SERVICE, a.s. = CSV (formerly Cassovia Air Service, a.s. & part of Slov-Air)

Kosice-Barca

Airport, SK-041 75 Kosice, Slovakia ☎ (95) 622 00 65 Tx: none Fax: (95) 622 17 89 SITA: n/a

F: 1992 👥 12 Head: Stefan Sanislo ICAO: CASSOVIA SERVICE Net: n/a Aircraft/Ag-aircraft below MTOW 1361/5000kg: 2 PZL M-18 Dromader & 20 Z-37A Cmelak.

registration	type of aircraft	cn/fn	ex/ex*	mfd	del	powered by	mtow kg	configuration	selcal	name/fln/specialitites/remarks
☐ OM-CAS	Zlin Z-37-C2	0220	HA-MFB	0071	0792	1 WA M-462RF	1750	Trainer/Courier		
☐ OM-YXO	Zlin Z-37-C3	0822	OK-YJO	0071	0792	1 WA M-462RF	1750	Trainer/Courier		

AIR SLOVAKIA BWJ, Ltd = GM / SVK (formerly Air Slovakia, Ltd & Air Terrex Slovakia, Ltd)

Bratislava-M.R. Stefanik

PO Box 2, SK-820 01 Bratislava, Slovakia ☎ (7) 43 42 27 42 Tx: none Fax: (7) 43 42 27 44 SITA: BTSKX7X

F: 1993 👥 40 Head: Augustin Bernat ICAO: SLOVAKIA Net: n/a

registration	type of aircraft	cn/fn	ex/ex*	mfd	del	powered by	mtow kg	configuration	selcal	name/fln/specialitites/remarks
☐ OM-BWJ	Boeing 737-2E3 (A)	22703 / 811	9M-VMB	0081	0399	2 PW JT8D-15A (HK3/NOR)	54204	Y128		
☐ OM-CHD	Boeing 727-230	20526 / 871	N879UM	0072	0894	3 PW JT8D-15	79800	Y165		Devin

AIR TRANSPORT EUROPE, Ltd = EAT

Poprad-Tatry/Kosice & Bratislava-M.R. Stefanik

Airport Tatry, SK-058 98 Poprad, Slovakia ☎ (92) 61 911 Tx: none Fax: (92) 61 945 SITA: n/a

F: 1991 👥 37 Head: Milan Hoholik ICAO: TRANS EUROPE Net: http://www.trynet.sk/ate/popis.htm

registration	type of aircraft	cn/fn	ex/ex*	mfd	del	powered by	mtow kg	configuration	selcal	name/fln/specialitites/remarks
☐ OM-MIQ	Eurocopter (Aerosp.) AS355F1 Ecureuil 2	5160	OK-MIQ	0082	0392	2 AN 250-C20F	2400	EMS		Eva
☐ OM-OTO	Eurocopter (Aerosp.) AS355N Ecureuil 2	5113	N5786D	1281	1297	2 TU Arrius 1A	2600	EMS		Lucia / cvtd AS355F1
☐ OM-EIR	PZL Swidnik (Mil) Mi-2	513831114	OK-EIR	0074	0192	2 IS GTD-350-4	3550	EMS		
☐ OM-FIN	PZL Swidnik (Mil) Mi-2	514307095	OK-FIN	0075	0392	2 IS GTD-350-4	3550	EMS		
☐ OM-KJN	PZL Swidnik (Mil) Mi-2	516625040	OK-KJN	0080	0392	2 IS GTD-350-4	3550	EMS		
☐ OM-KJO	PZL Swidnik (Mil) Mi-2	516626040	OK-KJO	0080	0392	2 IS GTD-350-4	3550	EMS		
☐ OM-LJO	PZL Swidnik (Mil) Mi-2	527225071	OK-LJO	0081	0192	2 IS GTD-350-4	3550	EMS		
☐ OM-OIU	PZL Swidnik (Mil) Mi-2	529012124	OK-OIU	0084	0894	2 IS GTD-350-4	3550	EMS		
☐ OM-TFA	PZL Swidnik Kania Model 1	900202	SP-SSE	0588	0697	2 AN 250-C20B	3550	EMS / 9 Pax		
☐ OM-RDE	Let 410UVP-E1 Turbolet	861801	LZ-LSA	1186	0397	2 WA M-601E	6400	Y17/EMS/Para/Ph		Michal / for sale
☐ OM-DXO	Mil Mi-8T	10825	OK-DXO	0073	0192	2 IS TV2-117A	12000	transport/crane		Chrudim
☐ OM-EVA	Mil Mi-8T	98417157	RA-22896	0084	1097	2 IS TV2-117AG	12000	transport/crane		Kristina
☐ OM-	Mil Mi-8T					2 IS TV2-117AG	12000	Transport/Crane		oo-delivery 0099
☐ OM-GAT	Tupolev 134A	48565	ES-AAF	0876	0595	2 SO D-30-II	47000	Y76		David / lst VPB

CASSOVIA AIR, a.s. = CVI (Associated with Vychodoslovenské zeleziarne, a.s.)

Kosice-Barca

Airport, SK-041 75 Kosice, Slovakia ☎ (95) 680 22 76 Tx: none Fax: (95) 622 17 89 SITA: n/a

F: 1991 👥 7 Head: Daniel Böhm ICAO: CASSOVIA Net: n/a

registration	type of aircraft	cn/fn	ex/ex*	mfd	del	powered by	mtow kg	configuration	selcal	name/fln/specialitites/remarks
☐ OM-VKE	Beech King Air C90A	LJ-1222	OK-VKE	0089	1091	2 PWC PT6A-21	4581	Pax / EMS		for sale
☐ OM-SKY	Hawker 800XP	258314	N314XP*	0096	0297	2 GA TFE731-5BR-1H	12701	Executive		lsf Raytheon Aircraft / opf VSZ Kosice

FLIGT SERVICE, Ltd

Nitra

Airport M.R. Stefanik, SK-821 23 Bratislava, Slovakia ☎ (7) 48 57 61 50 Tx: none Fax: (7) 43 29 14 68 SITA: n/a

F: 1997 👥 n/a Head: Jaroslav Pajdlhauser Net: n/a Aircraft below MTOW 1361kg: Hughes 300C (269C)

registration	type of aircraft	cn/fn	ex/ex*	mfd	del	powered by	mtow kg	configuration	selcal	name/fln/specialitites/remarks
☐ OM-SPP	Agusta-Bell 206B JetRanger III	8255	D-HAFW	0070	0798	1 AN 250-C20B	1451	Patrol/Survey		opf Tranzitny plynovod s.p./cvtd 206A
☐ OM-SIF	Eurocopter (Aerosp.) AS350B2 Ecureuil	3066	F-WPDS*	1297	1297	1 TU Arriel 1D1	2250	Patrol/Survey		opf Slovenske elektarne a.s.

LETECKY URAD SLOVENSKEJ REPUBLIKY = CIA (CAA-Civil Aviation Authority of the Slovak Republic) (formerly SLI)

Bratislava-M.R. Stefanik

Airport M.R. Stefanik, SK-823 05 Bratislava, Slovakia ☎ (7) 43 42 32 10 Tx: 92264 slib sk Fax: (7) 43 42 03 31 SITA: n/a

F: 1993 👥 62 Head: Jan Kassak ICAO: CALIMERA Net: n/a Non-commercial state organisation conducting inspection & calibration missions.

Shares with Ministry of Transport, Post & Communications, Civil Aviation Dept., the duties of the CAA.

registration	type of aircraft	cn/fn	ex/ex*	mfd	del	powered by	mtow kg	configuration	selcal	name/fln/specialitites/remarks
☐ OM-HYU	Let Z-37-2C Cmelak	23-09	OK-HYU	0077	0193	1 AV M-462RF	1850	3 Pax / Courier		
☐ OM-OFS	Let 200D Morava	170213	OK-OFS	0060	0193	2 WA M-337	1950	4 Pax / Courier		
☐ OM-SYI	Let 410UVP-E6	872019	OK-SYI	0087	0194	2 WA M-601E	6400	Calibrator		
☐ OM-DYA	Yakovlev 40	9341230	OK-DYA	0073	0194	3 IV AI-25	16000	Calibrator		

SEAGLE AIR, letecko-obchodna spolocnost = CGL

Trencin

Letisko, SK-911 04 Trencin, Slovakia ☎ (831) 58 73 34 Tx: none Fax: (831) 58 73 33 SITA: n/a

F: 1995 👥 9 Head: Lubomir Hlavac ICAO: SEAGLE Net: n/a Aircraft/Ag-aircraft below MTOW 1361/5000kg: ST-4 Aztek, Zlin Z-37-2, Z-42, Z-43, Z-50LX & Z-142

registration	type of aircraft	cn/fn	ex/ex*	mfd	del	powered by	mtow kg	configuration	selcal	name/fln/specialitites/remarks
☐ OM-HLB	Let 410UVP-E3	871914	1914	0087	0897	2 WA M-601E	6400	Freighter/Para		
☐ OM-SDA	Let 410UVP-E	872006	CCCP-67600	0087	0395	2 WA M-601E	6400	Y19		lst CSB

SLOV AIR, a.s. = OIR (formerly Tatra Air Group, a.s. dba Slov-Air Special, Slov-Air Transport / Slov-Air, State company)

Bratislava-M.R. Stefanik

M.R. Stefanik Airport, SK-823 12 Bratislava, Slovakia ☎ (7) 43 33 67 20 Tx: 93270 oird sk Fax: (7) 43 42 36 21 SITA: BTSSACR

F: 1969 👥 94 Head: Milan Gajdos ICAO: SLOVAIR Net: n/a

registration	type of aircraft	cn/fn	ex/ex*	mfd	del	powered by	mtow kg	configuration	selcal	name/fln/specialitites/remarks
☐ OM-NDP	Let 410UVP	831028	OK-NDP	0083	1192	2 WA M-601D	5800	Y15		
☐ OM-WDA	Let 410UVP-E8C	912540	OK-WDA	0091	0491	2 WA M-601E	6400	Y17		
☐ OM-WDB	Let 410UVP-E8B	912539	OK-WDB	0091	0591	2 WA M-601E	6400	Y17		lst TDR

SLOVAK AIRLINES, Inc. = 6Q / SLL (Slovenske Aerolinie)

Bratislava-M.R. Stefanik

Trnavska cesta 56, SK-821 02 Bratislava, Slovakia ☎ (7) 44 45 00 96 Tx: none Fax: (7) 44 45 00 97 SITA: BTSKK6Q

F: 1997 👥 n/a Head: Pavol Mlady IATA: 921 ICAO: SLOV LINE Net: n/a Suspended operations 310199. Intends to restart.

registration	type of aircraft	cn/fn	ex/ex*	mfd	del	powered by	mtow kg	configuration	selcal	name/fln/specialitites/remarks
☐ OM-AAA	Tupolev 154M	1014		0097	0198	3 SO D-30KU-154-II	100000	CY157		Puchov / lsf Gvmt / std BRS
☐ OM-AAB	Tupolev 154M	1015		0098	0598	3 SO D-30KU-154-II	100000	CY157		Gerlach / lsf Gvmt / std BRS
☐ OM-AAC	Tupolev 154M	1018		0098	0998	3 SO D-30KU-154-II	100000	CY157		Detva / lsf Gvmt / std BTS

SLOVAK GOVERNMENT FLYING SERVICE = SSG (Letecky Utvar) (Division of the Ministry of the Interior/Ministerstva vnutra Slovenskej republiky)

Bratislava-M.R. Stefanik

Airport M.R. Stefanik, SK-823 03 Bratislava, Slovakia ☎ (7) 43 33 74 01 Tx: none Fax: (7) 43 29 41 85 SITA: n/a

F: 1993 👥 85 Head: Capt. Viliam Polniser ICAO: SLOVAK GOVERNMENT Net: n/a Non-commercial government organisation conducting mainly VIP flights, police patrol & commercial flights through leasing forms.

registration	type of aircraft	cn/fn	ex/ex*	mfd	del	powered by	mtow kg	configuration	selcal	name/fln/specialitites/remarks
☐ B-	MD Helicopters MD 902 Explorer (900 Adv.)					2 PWC PW206E	2840	Police Patrol		oo-delivery 0099
☐ B-	MD Helicopters MD 902 Explorer (900 Adv.)					2 PWC PW206E	2840	Police Patrol		oo-delivery 0099
☐ B-	MD Helicopters MD 902 Explorer (900 Adv.)					2 PWC PW206E	2840	Police Patrol		oo-delivery 0099
☐ B-2048	PZL Swidnik (Mil) Mi-2	5311148060		0690	0193	2 IS GTD-350-4	3550	Police Patrol		
☐ B-2405	PZL Swidnik (Mil) Mi-2	539005124		1284	0193	2 IS GTD-350-4	3550	Police Patrol		
☐ B-2406	PZL Swidnik (Mil) Mi-2	539006124		1284	0193	2 IS GTD-350-4	3550	Police Patrol		
☐ B-2744	PZL Swidnik (Mil) Mi-2	5310344097		0987	0193	2 IS GTD-350-4	3550	Police Patrol		
☐ B-2950	PZL Swidnik (Mil) Mi-2	535950019		0279	0193	2 IS GTD-350-4	3550	Patrol/Trainer		
☐ B-8231	Mil Mi-8P	10831		0682	0193	2 IS TV2-117A	12000	Patrol/Transport		
☐ B-8427	Mil Mi-8P	10827		0279	1193	2 IS TV2-117A	12000	Patrol		
☐ B-8532	Mil Mi-8PS	10832		0885	0193	2 IS TV2-117A	12000	VIP / Patrol		
☐ OM-BYE	Yakovlev 40	9440338	OK-BYE	1174	0193	3 IV AI-25	16000	VIP / C24		
☐ OM-BYL	Yakovlev 40	9940560	OK-BYL	1279	0193	3 IV AI-25	16000	VIP / C24orY31		
☐ OM-BYO	Tupolev 154M	803	OK-BYO	0489	0193	3 SO D-30KU-154-II	100000	VIP / CY130		
☐ OM-BYR	Tupolev 154M	1012		0098	0398	3 SO D-30KU-154-II	100000	VIP		

TATRA AIR, a.s. = QS / TTR — Bratislava-M.R. Stefanik

M.R. Stefanik Airport, SK-823 14 Bratislava, Slovakia ☎ (7) 43 29 23 18 Tx: none Fax: (7) 43 29 42 59 SITA: BTSKKQS
F: 1990 ⁂ 68 Head: Capt. Frantisek Nemcek IATA: 904 ICAO: TATRA Net: n/a Suspended operations 0299. Intends to restart.

registration	type of aircraft	cn/fn	ex/ex*	mfd	del	powered by	mtow kg	configuration	selcal	name/fln/specialitites/remarks
☐ OM-UGT	Saab 340B	340B-171	OK-UGT	1289	0392	2 GE CT7-9B	12927	Y35		
☐ OM-UGU	Saab 340B	340B-163	OK-UGU	1289	0892	2 GE CT7-9B	12927	Y35		

TECH-MONT, Ltd (formerly part of L.O.S. Ltd) — Spiska Nova Ves

Na letisko 100, SK-058 98 Poprad, Slovakia ☎ (92) 772 41 68 Tx: none Fax: (92) 772 21 26 SITA: n/a
F: 1996 ⁂ 40 Head: Pavel Orolin Net: http://www.techmont.sk Ag-aircraft below MTOW 5000kg: Zlin Z-37A Cmelak

registration	type of aircraft	cn/fn	ex/ex*	mfd	del	powered by	mtow kg	configuration	selcal	name/fln/specialitites/remarks
☐ OM-MIO	PZL Swidnik (Mil) Mi-2	527735072	OK-MIO	0082	1297	2 IS GTD-350-4	3550	Utility		
☐ OM-OIN	PZL Swidnik (Mil) Mi-2	528522014	OK-OIN	0084	1297	2 IS GTD-350-4	3550	Utility		
☐ OK-UIC	PZL Swidnik (Mil) Mi-2	548149053	YL-LHL	0583	0399	2 IS GTD-350-4	3550	Utility		lsf Aerocentrum
☐ OM-AXZ	Mil Mi-8T	2142	UR-25526	0071	0297	2 IS TV2-117A	12000	Transport/Crane		
☐ OM-ORO	Mil Mi-8PS	10448		0089	0298	2 IS TV2-117A	12000	Transport/Crane		
☐ OM-WXC	Mil Mi-8T	99150520	UR-25604	0071	0697	2 IS TV2-117AG	12000	Transport/Crane		

OO = BELGIUM (Kingdom of Belgium) (Koninkrijk Belgiê / Royaume Belge)

Capital: Brussels Official Language: Flemish, French Population: 10,1 million Square Km: 30519 Dialling code: +32 Year established: 1830 Acting political head: Jean-Luc Dahaene (Prime Minister)

ABELAG Aviation, S.A. = AAB — Brussels-National

Rue de Livourne 66 B 1, B-1000 Brussels, Belgium ☎ (2) 720 58 80 Tx: 24833 abelag b Fax: (2) 721 22 88 SITA: n/a
F: 1964 ⁂ 47 Head: Denis Solvay ICAO: ABG Net: n/a

registration	type of aircraft	cn/fn	ex/ex*	mfd	del	powered by	mtow kg	configuration	selcal	name/fln/specialitites/remarks
☐ OO-TJK	Partenavia P.68 Observer	372-28		0086	0894	2 LY IO-360-A1B6	1990			
☐ OO-LFL	Cessna 441 Conquest II	441-0184		0080	1080	2 GA TPE331-8-401S	4468			
☐ OO-DCM	Cessna 500 Citation Eagle	500-0182	N13HJ	0074	0096	2 PWC JT15D-1	5215			lsf Lambda Jet S.A.
☐ OO-LCM	Cessna 500 Citation R/STOL Longwing	500-0036	N18HJ	0072	0096	2 PWC JT15D-1A	5215			lsf Lambda Jet S.A. / cvtd Citation
☐ OO-GBL	Learjet 35A	35A-284	D-CCAX	0080	1283	2 GA TFE731-2-2B	8165			
☐ OO-LFV	Learjet 35A	35A-481	N27NR	0082	0790	2 GA TFE731-2-2B	8165			
☐ OO-LFS	Learjet 45	45-018	N418LJ*	0098	1198	2 GA TFE731-20	9163			
☐ OO-LFT	Dassault Falcon 50	42	OE-HCS	0081	0189	3 GA TFE731-3-1C	17600			lsf Air Business & Co.

AERODATA International Surveys — Antwerp-Deurne

Airport Business Center, Luchthavenlei 7, B10, B-2100 Deurne, Belgium ☎ (3) 287 00 30 Tx: none Fax: (3) 287 00 38 SITA: n/a
F: 1992 ⁂ 6 Head: W. Philipse Net: http://www.aerodata-surveys.com

registration	type of aircraft	cn/fn	ex/ex*	mfd	del	powered by	mtow kg	configuration	selcal	name/fln/specialitites/remarks
☐ OO-MSN	Cessna 310R II	310R0562	LX-III	0076	1193	2 CO IO-520-M	2495	Photo/Survey		

AIR BELGIUM = AJ / ABB (Air Belgium International, N.V. dba/Subs.of Airtours Int'l/formerly Abelag Airways) — Brussels-National

Brucargo, Building 726, B-1931 Zaventem, Belgium ☎ (2) 753 05 10 Tx: 64803 airbel b Fax: (2) 753 05 11 SITA: BRUKKAJ
F: 1979 ⁂ 80 Head: Marc van Moerkerke ICAO: AIR BELGIUM Net: n/a

registration	type of aircraft	cn/fn	ex/ex*	mfd	del	powered by	mtow kg	configuration	selcal	name/fln/specialitites/remarks
☐ OO-ILJ	Boeing 737-46B	25262 / 2088		0091	0791	2 CFMI CFM56-3C1	65990	Y170	AQ-DR	lsf BOUL
☐ OO-AEY	Airbus Industrie A320-212	301	OY-CNM	0092	0599	2 CFMI CFM56-5A3	77000	Y177	AL-FR	lsf VKG
☐ OO-AEZ	Airbus Industrie A320-212	349	OY-CNR	0092	0499	2 CFMI CFM56-5A3	77000	Y177	AL-GS	lsf VKG

AIR DAKOTA, S.A. — Brussels-Melsbroek

Namur-Suarlée-Airport, B-5020 Suarlée, Belgium ☎ (81) 56 61 46 Tx: none Fax: (81) 56 96 00 SITA: n/a
F: 1996 ⁂ 4 Head: Georges Bertrand Net: n/a

registration	type of aircraft	cn/fn	ex/ex*	mfd	del	powered by	mtow kg	configuration	selcal	name/fln/specialitites/remarks
☐ N49AG	Boeing (Douglas) DC-3A (C-53D-DO)	11737	TJ-AJW	0043	0396	2 PW R-1830	12202	Y30		lsf Aircr.Guaranty / BAF K-16/OT-CWG cs

AIR LIMO = LIM (Lucorp, B.V.B.A. dba) — Liege

Langveldstraat 17, B-3570 Alken, Belgium ☎ (11) 31 44 19 Tx: none Fax: (11) 59 13 88 SITA: n/a
F: 1989 ⁂ 1 Head: Ludo Bosmans ICAO: LIMO Net: n/a

registration	type of aircraft	cn/fn	ex/ex*	mfd	del	powered by	mtow kg	configuration	selcal	name/fln/specialitites/remarks
☐ OO-LSA	Partenavia P.68C	279	D-GIMI	0083	0097	2 LY IO-360-A1B6	1990			
☐ OO-STG	Cessna 421C Golden Eagle III	421C0879	D-IXXX	0080	0498	2 CO GTSIO-520-L	3379			

AIR RENT SERVICES, S.A. – ARS (formerly Air Rent Service, S.P.R.L.) — Charleroi-Brussels South

Route de Mons 96, B-7390 Wasmuel, Belgium ☎ (65) 62 10 10 Tx: none Fax: (65) 62 34 34 SITA: n/a
F: 1985 ⁂ n/a Head: Michel Henry Net: n/a Aircraft below MTOW 1361 kg: AA1B, AA5A/B, Cessna 150 & 172.

registration	type of aircraft	cn/fn	ex/ex*	mfd	del	powered by	mtow kg	configuration	selcal	name/fln/specialitites/remarks
☐ OO-GSM	Reims/Cessna FR182 Skylane RG II	FR182-0013	OO-HNN	0078		1 LY O-540-J3C5D	1406			
☐ OO-GZM	Reims/Cessna FR182 Skylane RG II	FR182-0045	D-EIYO	0079	0491	1 LY O-540-J3C5D	1406			
☐ OO-MCA	Piper PA-32-301 Saratoga	32-8006013	N81648	0080		1 LY IO-540-K1G5	1633			
☐ OO-GHM	Piper PA-34-220T Seneca III	34-8133021	N8341U	0081		2 CO TSIO-360-KB	2155			

AIRVENTURE, B.V.B.A. = RVE — Antwerp-Deurne

Bus 23, Antwerp Airport, B-2100 Deurne, Belgium ☎ (3) 285 66 66 Tx: n/a Fax: (3) 285 66 66 SITA: n/a
F: 1989 ⁂ 8 Head: Martin Franck ICAO: VENTURELINER Net: http://www.airventure.be Aircraft below MTOW 1361 kg: Zlin Z.526F.

registration	type of aircraft	cn/fn	ex/ex*	mfd	del	powered by	mtow kg	configuration	selcal	name/fln/specialitites/remarks
☐ OO-DVJ	Cessna R182 Skylane RG II	R18200142	N129	0078		1 LY O-540-J3C5D	1406			
☐ OO-SXB	Embraer 121A Xingu (EMB-121A)	121040	PT-MBH*	0081	0393	2 PWC PT6A-28	5670	5 Pax / EMS		

ANTWERP AVIATION, N.V. — Antwerp-Deurne

PB 66, B-2100 Deurne, Belgium ☎ (3) 287 00 51 Tx: none Fax: (3) 287 41 87 SITA: n/a
F: 1998 ⁂ 3 Head: Desmet Frank Net: n/a Aircraft below MTOW 1361kg: Robinson R22

registration	type of aircraft	cn/fn	ex/ex*	mfd	del	powered by	mtow kg	configuration	selcal	name/fln/specialitites/remarks
☐ OO-SKE	Agusta-Bell 206A JetRanger	8331		0072	0098	1 AN 250-C18	1361			

ASL – Air Service Liège, N.V. — Maastricht

Stadsheide 7, B-3500 Hasselt, Belgium ☎ (11) 29 50 16 Tx: none Fax: (11) 29 50 18 SITA: n/a
F: 1994 ⁂ 1 Head: Phillipe Bodson Net: n/a

registration	type of aircraft	cn/fn	ex/ex*	mfd	del	powered by	mtow kg	configuration	selcal	name/fln/specialitites/remarks
☐ OO-MLF	Piper PA-34-200T Seneca II	34-7970216	N2245Z	0079		2 CO TSIO-360-E	1999			
☐ OO-LET	Beech King Air B200	BB-1473	PT-OXG	0093	0399	2 PWC PT6A-42	5670			

AVIASUD, S.C. — Liege

Aéroport de Bierset-Liège, B-4460 Grace-Hollogne, Belgium ☎ (41) 34 85 31 Tx: none Fax: (41) 50 54 20 SITA: n/a
F: n/a ⁂ n/a Head: n/a Net: n/a Aircraft below MTOW 1361kg: Cessna 150, 152 & 172

registration	type of aircraft	cn/fn	ex/ex*	mfd	del	powered by	mtow kg	configuration	selcal	name/fln/specialitites/remarks
☐ OO-BPW	Piper PA-32-300B Cherokee SIX	32-40765	N8970N	0069		1 LY IO-540-K1A5	1542			

AVIATION SANS FRONTIERES Belgium – A.S.F. — Brussels-National & Overseas

Brussels National Airport, Building 706, Box 60, B-1931 Brucargo, Belgium ☎ (2) 753 24 70 Tx: none Fax: (2) 753 24 71 SITA: n/a
F: 1983 ⁂ n/a Head: Alain Peeters Net: n/a Non-commerical organisation conducting flights for relief & development agencies & missions in remote areas of third world countries with aircraft leased when required.
Beside aircraft listed also occasionally uses Lockheed C-130H Hercules leased from/operated by Belgian Air Force & other aircraft when required.

registration	type of aircraft	cn/fn	ex/ex*	mfd	del	powered by	mtow kg	configuration	selcal	name/fln/specialitites/remarks
☐ OO-PKS	Cessna TU206G Turbo Stationair 6 II	U20605455		0080	0299	1 CO TSIO-520-M	1633			
☐ LX-ASF	Cessna 207A Stationair 8 II	20700582	OO-PZG	0080	0598	1 CO IO-520-F	1724			op. from Kisangani, Congo

BELGIAN AIR FORCE – Rescue Flight Group (Force Aérienne Belge-Grp.Sauvetage/Belg.Luchtmacht-Reddings Vluchten Groep) — Koksijde

Koksijde Operations, 100R Vandammestraat, B-8670 Koksijde, Belgium ☎ (58) 53 22 11 Tx: none Fax: (58) 53 24 01 SITA: n/a
F: 1961 ⁂ 60 Head: Maj. VL J.L. Feuillen Net: n/a Helicopter-SAR division of the Air Force (40 Sqn) conducting non-commercial rescue (SAR) flights, both for the armed forces and for civilians.

registration	type of aircraft	cn/fn	ex/ex*	mfd	del	powered by	mtow kg	configuration	selcal	name/fln/specialitites/remarks
☐ RS-01	Westland Sea King Mk.48	WA831	G-17-1*	0076	0576	2 RR Gnome H.1400-1	9525	SAR		BAF91
☐ RS-02	Westland Sea King Mk.48	WA832	G-17-2*	0076	0576	2 RR Gnome H.1400-1	9525	SAR		BAF92
☐ RS-03	Westland Sea King Mk.48	WA833	G-17-3*	0076	0676	2 RR Gnome H.1400-1	9525	SAR		BAF93
☐ RS-04	Westland Sea King Mk.48	WA834	G-17-4*	0076	0676	2 RR Gnome H.1400-1	9525	SAR		BAF94
☐ RS-05	Westland Sea King Mk.48	WA835	G-17-5*	0076	0776	2 RR Gnome H.1400-1	9525	SAR		BAF95

BELGIAN AIR FORCE – Transport Fleet = BAF (Force Aérienne Belge-Flotte de Transp./Belgische Luchtmacht-Transp.Vloot) — Brussels-Melsbroek

Melsbroek Operations, B-1820 Melsbroek, Belgium ☎ (2) 752 45 04 Tx: none Fax: (2) 752 44 01 SITA: n/a
F: 1946 ⁂ 1000 Head: n/a ICAO: BAF 6XX Net: n/a Transport division (20th & 21st Sqn) of the Air Force, a military organisation, which beside military transport-duties, also conducting int'l relief & VIP flights for the government.

registration	type of aircraft	cn/fn	ex/ex*	mfd	del	powered by	mtow kg	configuration	selcal	name/fln/specialitites/remarks
☐ CF-01	Fairchild (Swearingen) SA226T Merlin IIIA	T-259	N5374M*	0076	0376	2 GA TPE331-3U-303G	5670	VIP / mil trans		
☐ CF-02	Fairchild (Swearingen) SA226T Merlin IIIA	T-260	N5373M*	0076	0476	2 GA TPE331-3U-303G	5670	VIP / mil trans		
☐ CF-04	Fairchild (Swearingen) SA226T Merlin IIIA	T-264	N5378M*	0076	0776	2 GA TPE331-3U-303G	5670	VIP / mil trans		
☐ CF-05	Fairchild (Swearingen) SA226T Merlin IIIA	T-265	N5381M*	0076	0876	2 GA TPE331-3U-303G	5670	VIP / mil trans		
☐ CF-06	Fairchild (Swearingen) SA226T Merlin IIIA	T-267	N5382M*	0076	0976	2 GA TPE331-3U-303G	5670	VIP / mil trans		
☐ CM-01	Dassault Falcon 20E	276	F-WNGL*	0073	0273	2 GE CF700-2D2	13000	VIP / mil trans		
☐ CM-02	Dassault Falcon 20E	278	F-WNGM*	0073	0473	2 GE CF700-2D2	13000	VIP / mil trans		
☐ CS-01	BAe (HS) 748-288 Srs 2A (SCD)	1741 / 222		0076	0576	2 RR Dart 535-2	21092	VIP / mil trans		
☐ CS-02	BAe (HS) 748-288 Srs 2A (SCD)	1742 / 223		0076	0776	2 RR Dart 535-2	21092	VIP / mil trans		
☐ CS-03	BAe (HS) 748-288 Srs 2A (SCD)	1743 / 224	G-BEEM*	0076	0976	2 RR Dart 535-2	21092	VIP / mil trans		
☐ CD-01	Dassault Falcon 900B	109	G-BTIB	0091	0195	3 GA TFE731-5BR-1C	20640	VIP / mil trans	JQ-KR	

☐ CH-01	Lockheed L-382C (C-130H) Hercules	25D-4455	71-1797	0072	0772	4 AN T56-A-15	70307	Frtr/mil trans	BG-AS	
☐ CH-02	Lockheed L-382C (C-130H) Hercules	25D-4460	71-1798	0072	0772	4 AN T56-A-15	70307	Frtr/mil trans	BG-CR	
☐ CH-03	Lockheed L-382C (C-130H) Hercules	25D-4461	71-1799	0072	0872	4 AN T56-A-15	70307	Frtr/mil trans	BG-CS	
☐ CH-04	Lockheed L-382C (C-130H) Hercules	25D-4467	71-1800	0072	0972	4 AN T56-A-15	70307	Frtr/mil trans	BG-DR	
☐ CH-05	Lockheed L-382C (C-130H) Hercules	25D-4470	71-1801	0072	1172	4 AN T56-A-15	70307	Frtr/mil trans	BG-DS	
☐ CH-07	Lockheed L-382C (C-130H) Hercules	25D-4476	71-1803	0072	0173	4 AN T56-A-15	70307	Frtr/mil trans	BG-ES	
☐ CH-08	Lockheed L-382C (C-130H) Hercules	25D-4478	71-1804	0072	0173	4 AN T56-A-15	70307	Frtr/mil trans	BG-FR	
☐ CH-09	Lockheed L-382C (C-130H) Hercules	25D-4479	71-1805	0073	0273	4 AN T56-A-15	70307	Frtr/mil trans	BG-FS	
☐ CH-10	Lockheed L-382C (C-130H) Hercules	25D-4481	71-1806	0073	0273	4 AN T56-A-15	70307	Frtr/mil trans	BG-HR	
☐ CH-11	Lockheed L-382C (C-130H) Hercules	25D-4482	71-1807	0073	0373	4 AN T56-A-15	70307	Frtr/mil trans	BG-HS	
☐ CH-12	Lockheed L-382C (C-130H) Hercules	25D-4483	71-1808	0073	0373	4 AN T56-A-15	70307	Frtr/mil trans	BG-JR	
☐ CA-01	Airbus Industrie A310-222	372	9V-STN	0085	0997	2 PW JT9D-7R4E1	142000	VIP / mil trans	EM-CP	
☐ CA-02	Airbus Industrie A310-222	367	9V-STM	0085	0498	2 PW JT9D-7R4E1	142000	VIP / mil trans		

BELGIAN ARMY - Light Aviation = AYB (Force Terrestre Belge-Aviation Légère/Belg. Landmacht-Lichte Vliegweze) **Brasschaat & Bierset**

Army Aviation School, Airfield, B-2930 Brasschaat, Belgium ☎ (3) 630 27 33 Tx: none Fax: (3) 630 27 39 SITA: n/a
F: 1956 ♟♟♟ 180 Head: n/a ICAO: BELGIAN ARMY Net: n/a
Military organisation which, beside military duties (with other aircraft), also conducting non-commercial pollution control flights for the Ministry of Environment & photoflights for the National Geografic Institute.

☐ B-02	Britten-Norman BN-2B-21 Islander	468	G-BDHG*	0076	0576	2 LY IO-540-K1B5	2994	PollutionControl		OT-ALB / opf Ministry of Environment
☐ B-12	Britten-Norman BN-2A-21 Islander	553	G-BEFI*	0076	0277	2 LY IO-540-K1B5	2994	Vertical Photo		OT-ALL / opf National Geografic Inst.

BELGIAN C.A.A. - Technical Dept. (Admin.de l'Aéronautique/Bestuur van de Luchtvaart) **Brussels-National**

Admin. de l'Aéronautique-Bestuur van de Luchtvaar, DTAé, Rue de la Fusée 90, B-1130 Brussels, Belgium ☎ (2) 724 02 11 Tx: none Fax: (2) 724 02 01 SITA: n/a
F: n/a ♟♟♟ n/a Head: E. van Nuffel Net: n/a Technical Dept. of the Belgian Civil Aviation Authority, a government organisation conducting non-commercial calibration flights.

☐ OO-SNA	Beech King Air A100	B-217		0075	0775	2 PWC PT6A-28	5216	Calibrator		

BELGIAN GENDARMERIE - Air Support Unit = GDB (Gendarmerie/Rijkswacht) **Brussels-Melsbroek**

Dét. d'Appui Aérien/Luchtsteundetachement, Quartier Groenveld, Chaussée de Haecht 138, B-1820 Melsbroek, Belgium ☎ (2) 753 03 11 Tx: none Fax: (2) 753 03 09 SITA: n/a
F: 1993 ♟♟♟ 32 Head: Lt. Col. Herman Perdu ICAO: BELGIAN GENDARMERIE Net: n/a Non-commercial state organisation conducting patrol, police & EMS missions.

☐ G-01	Cessna 182Q Skylane II	18267696	N5411N	0080	0594	1 CO O-470-U	1338	Patrol		OT-GLB
☐ G-03	Cessna 182R Skylane II	18267742	N5472N	0081	0597	1 CO O-470-U	1406	Patrol		OT-GLC
☐ G-04	Cessna 182R Skylane II	18267850	N4885H	0081	0694	1 CO O-470-U	1406	Patrol		OT-GLD
☐ G-90	Eurocopter (Aerosp.) SA318C Alouette II	1991	A-90	0068	0268	1 TU Astazou IIA	1650	Patrol		OT-GCA / Hi Skids
☐ G-93	Eurocopter (Aerosp.) SA318C Alouette II	2004	A-93	0068	0568	1 TU Astazou IIA	1650	Patrol		OT-GCC / Hi Skids
☐ G-94	Eurocopter (Aerosp.) SA318C Alouette II	2102	A-94	1069	1069	1 TU Astazou IIA	1650	Patrol		OT-GCD / Hi Skids
☐ G-10	MD Helicopters MD 900 Explorer	900-00034	N91960	0096	0197	2 PWC PW206B	2722	Patrol / EMS		OT-GIA / Hoist/Emergency Floats
☐ G-11	MD Helicopters MD 900 Explorer	900-00045	N92047	0097	0897	2 PWC PW206B	2722	Patrol / EMS		OT-GIB / Hoist/Emergency Floats
☐ G-05	Britten-Norman BN-2T Turbine Islander	2146	G-DEMO	0084	0093	2 AN 250-B17C	3175	Survey / Patrol		OT-GLA / cvtd BN-2B-26
☐ G-02	Eurocopter (Aerosp.) SA330L Puma	1237	OL-G02	0073	1073	2 TU Turmo IVC	7400	Survey / EMS		OT-GIB / cvtd 330C/H

BELGIAN NAVY - Heliflight = NYB (Marine Belge/Belgische Marine) **Koksijde**

Koksijde Operations, 100R Vandammestraat, B-8670 Koksijde, Belgium ☎ (58) 53 22 11 Tx: none Fax: (58) 53 24 01 SITA: n/a
F: 1946 ♟♟♟ 20 Head: Lt.Col. Pierre Lejeune ICAO: BELGIAN NAVY Net: n/a Military organisation (40th Sdn), which beside military duties, also conducting non-commercial governmental VIP transport, EMS & SAR flights.

☐ M-1	Eurocopter (Aerosp.) SA316B Alouette III	1812	F-ZWBE*	0071	0071	1 TU Artouste IIIB	2200	VIP/SAR/miltrans		OT-ZPA
☐ M-2	Eurocopter (Aerosp.) SA316B Alouette III	1816	F-ZWBF*	0071	0071	1 TU Artouste IIIB	2200	VIP/SAR/miltrans		OT-ZPB
☐ M-3	Eurocopter (Aerosp.) SA316B Alouette III	1817		0071	0071	1 TU Artouste IIIB	2200	VIP/SAR/miltrans		OT-ZPC

BELGIAN WORLD AIRLINES, S.A. - BWA (formerly Challengair, S.A.) **Brussels-National**

Avenue Louise 416, Bte 17, B-1050 Brussels, Belgium ☎ (2) 647 25 15 Tx: 25369 bwa ops b Fax: (2) 646 59 97 SITA: BRUBW7X
F: 1994 ♟♟♟ n/a Head: Luc F.R. Mellaerts ICAO: BELGIAN WORLD Net: n/a

☐ OO-VAS	Boeing 767-33A (ER)	25535 / 491	V5-NMB	0093	0298	2 PW PW4060	185065	Y301		lsf AWAS

CASTEL AIR, N.V. **Kortrijk-Wevelgem**

Dwarsstraat 20, B-8531 Bavikhove, Belgium ☎ (56) 36 31 33 Tx: none Fax: (56) 36 31 18 SITA: n/a
F: 1997 ♟♟♟ n/a Head: Jean Werbrouck Net: n/a

☐ OO-SOO	MD Helicopters MD 500E (Hughes 369E)	0447E	D-HGWM	0091	1097	1 AN 250-C20R	1361			

CICADE Aerial Photo (Div. of CICADE, S.A.-Compagnie d'Informatique et de Cartographie Digitale) **Namur-Suarlée & Nancy**

Av. de la Pairelle 11, B-5000 Namur, Belgium ☎ (81) 22 32 61 Tx: none Fax: (81) 23 03 50 SITA: n/a
F: 1985 ♟♟♟ 15 Head: Pierre Louis Net: n/a

☐ OO-DAD	Cessna T303 Crusader	T30300281	N4837V	0084	0196	2 CO TSIO-520-AE	2336	Photo / Survey		

CITY BIRD, S.A. = H2 / CTB (Member of City Hotels Group / associated with Sabena, S.A.) **Brussels-National**

Building 117D, Melsbroek Airport, B-1820 Melsbroek, Belgium ☎ (2) 752 52 11 Tx: none Fax: (2) 752 52 10 SITA: BRUOWH2
F: 1996 ♟♟♟ 300 Head: Victor Hasson ICAO: DREAM FLIGHT Net: http://www.citybird.com

☐ OO-CTT	Airbus Industrie A300C-605R (A300C4-605R)	755	F-WWAX*	0095		2 GE CF6-80C2A5	170500	Freighter		to be lsf Airbus Industrie 0699
☐ OO-CTU	Airbus Industrie A300C-605R (A300C4-605R)	758	F-WWAR*	0095		2 GE CF6-80C2A5	170500	Freighter		to be lsf Airbus Industrie 0799
☐ OO-CTQ	Boeing 767-33A (ER)	28159 / 689		0098	0298	2 GE CF6-80C2B6F	186880	C36Y223	BP-LQ	Falcon / lsf AWAS
☐ OO-CTR	Boeing 767-33A (ER)	28495 / 643	VH-NOA	0097	0598	2 GE CF6-80C2B6F	186880	C26Y220	DJ-AP	Harrier / lsf AWAS
☐ OO-CTB	Boeing (Douglas) MD-11	48766 / 600	N6203U*	0096	1296	3 GE CF6-80C2D1F	285990	C36Y335	CG-LP	Albatros
☐ OO-CTC	Boeing (Douglas) MD-11	48780 / 624		0098	0498	3 GE CF6-80C2D1F	285990	C48Y249	AK-DP	lst / opf SAB in Sabena-colors
☐ OO-CTS	Boeing (Douglas) MD-11	48756 / 623		0098	0398	3 PW PW4460	285990	C48Y249	BE-CP	lst / opf SAB in Sabena-colors
☐ OO-	Boeing 747-400F (SCD)					4	396893	Freighter		oo-delivery 0600
☐ OO-	Boeing 747-400F (SCD)					4	396893	Freighter		oo-delivery 0700

CONSTELLATION INTERNATIONAL AIRLINES, S.A. = CQ / CIN **Brussels-Zaventem**

Vilvoordelaan 170, B-1930 Zaventem, Belgium ☎ (2) 720 77 66 Tx: none Fax: (2) 720 27 25 SITA: BRUSSCQ
F: 1995 ♟♟♟ 110 Head: Eray Serimözü ICAO: CONSTELLATION Net: n/a

☐ OO-COF	Airbus Industrie A320-232	542	F-WWIH*	0095	0597	2 IAE V2527-A5	75500	Y179	HS-BQ	lsf ILFC / cvtd -212
☐ OO-COH	Airbus Industrie A320-232	543	F-WWIY*	0095	0597	2 IAE V2527-A5	75500	Y179	HS-CE	lsf ILFC / cvtd -212
☐ OO-COL	Airbus Industrie A320-231	344	F-WIHX	0692	0499	2 IAE V2500-A1	75500	Y179		lsf Airbus Industrie Financial Services

DAT - Delta Air Transport, N.V. = DAT (Subsidiary of Sabena, S.A.) **Brussels-National**

Airport Building 117, B-1820 Melsbroek, Belgium ☎ (2) 754 19 00 Tx: 32602 delta b Fax: (2) 754 19 99 SITA: BRUDFSN
F: 1966 ♟♟♟ 600 Head: Willy Buysse ICAO: DELTAIR Net: n/a All aircraft are operated in Sabena-colors (& both titles) and using SN flights numbers when operating scheduled Sabena-flights.

☐ OO-DJE	BAe 146-200	E2164	G-6-164*	0090	0790	4 LY ALF502R-5	42180	CY84		op in Sabena-colors
☐ OO-DJF	BAe 146-200	E2167	G-6-167*	0090	0890	4 LY ALF502R-5	42180	CY84		op in Sabena-colors
☐ OO-DJG	BAe 146-200	E2180	G-BSZZ*	0090	1290	4 LY ALF502R-5	42180	CY84		op in Sabena-colors
☐ OO-DJH	BAe 146-200	E2172	G-BSSG*	0090	1290	4 LY ALF502R-5	42180	CY84		op in Sabena-colors
☐ OO-DJJ	BAe 146-200	E2196	G-6-196*	0091	0791	4 LY ALF502R-5	42180	CY84		op in Sabena-colors
☐ OO-DJK	Avro RJ85 (Avro 146-RJ85)	E2271	G-6-271*	0095	1295	4 LY LF507-1F	44000	CY82		op in Sabena-colors
☐ OO-DJL	Avro RJ85 (Avro 146-RJ85)	E2273	G-6-273*	0095	1295	4 LY LF507-1F	44000	CY82		op in Sabena-colors
☐ OO-DJN	Avro RJ85 (Avro 146-RJ85)	E2275	G-6-275*	0095	1295	4 LY LF507-1F	44000	CY82		op in Sabena-colors
☐ OO-DJO	Avro RJ85 (Avro 146-RJ85)	E2279	G-6-279*	0095	1295	4 LY LF507-1F	44000	CY82		op in Sabena-colors
☐ OO-DJP	Avro RJ85 (Avro 146-RJ85)	E2287	G-6-287*	0096	0596	4 LY LF507-1F	44000	CY82		op in Sabena-colors
☐ OO-DJQ	Avro RJ85 (Avro 146-RJ85)	E2289	G-6-289*	0096	0696	4 LY LF507-1F	44000	CY82		op in Sabena-colors
☐ OO-DJR	Avro RJ85 (Avro 146-RJ85)	E2290	G-6-290*	0096	0796	4 LY LF507-1F	44000	CY82		op in Sabena-colors
☐ OO-DJS	Avro RJ85 (Avro 146-RJ85)	E2292	G-6-292*	0096	0896	4 LY LF507-1F	44000	CY82		op in Sabena-colors
☐ OO-DJT	Avro RJ85 (Avro 146-RJ85)	E2294	G-6-294*	0096	0996	4 LY LF507-1F	44000	CY82		op in Sabena-colors
☐ OO-DJV	Avro RJ85 (Avro 146-RJ85)	E2295	G-6-295*	0096	1096	4 LY LF507-1F	44000	CY82		op in Sabena-colors
☐ OO-DJW	Avro RJ85 (Avro 146-RJ85)	E2296	G-6-296*	0096	1096	4 LY LF507-1F	44000	CY82		op in Sabena-colors
☐ OO-DJX	Avro RJ85 (Avro 146-RJ85)	E2297	G-6-297*	0096	1196	4 LY LF507-1F	44000	CY82		op in Sabena-colors
☐ OO-DJY	Avro RJ85 (Avro 146-RJ85)	E2302	G-6-302*	0097	0397	4 LY LF507-1F	44000	CY82		op in Sabena-colors
☐ OO-DJZ	Avro RJ85 (Avro 146-RJ85)	E2305	G-6-305*	0097	0497	4 LY LF507-1F	44000	CY82		op in Sabena-colors
☐ OO-MJE	BAe 146-200	E2192	G-6-192*	0091	0491	4 LY ALF502R-5	42180	CY84		op in Sabena-colors
☐ OO-DWA	Avro RJ100 (Avro 146-RJ100)	E3308	G-6-308*	0097	0697	4 LY LF507-1F	46040	CY97		op in Sabena-colors
☐ OO-DWB	Avro RJ100 (Avro 146-RJ100)	E3315	G-6-315*	0097	1097	4 LY LF507-1F	46040	CY97		op in Sabena-colors
☐ OO-DWC	Avro RJ100 (Avro 146-RJ100)	E3322	G-6-322*	0098	0298	4 LY LF507-1F	46040	CY97		op in Sabena-colors
☐ OO-DWD	Avro RJ100 (Avro 146-RJ100)	E3324	G-6-324*	0098	0498	4 LY LF507-1F	46040	CY97		op in Sabena/special 75th year anniv.cs
☐ OO-DWE	Avro RJ100 (Avro 146-RJ100)	E3327	G-6-327*	0098	0598	4 LY LF507-1F	46040	CY97		op in Sabena-colors
☐ OO-DWF	Avro RJ100 (Avro 146-RJ100)	E3332	G-6-332*	0098	0898	4 LY LF507-1F	46040	CY97		op in Sabena-colors
☐ OO-DWG	Avro RJ100 (Avro 146-RJ100)	E3336	G-6-336*	0098	1198	4 LY LF507-1F	46040	CY97		op in Sabena-colors
☐ OO-DWH	Avro RJ100 (Avro 146-RJ100)	E3340	G-6-340*	0098	1298	4 LY LF507-1F	46040	CY97		op in Sabena-colors
☐ OO-DWI	Avro RJ100 (Avro 146-RJ100)	E3342	G-6-342*	0099	0199	4 LY LF507-1F	46040	CY97		op in Sabena-colors
☐ OO-DWJ	Avro RJ100 (Avro 146-RJ100)					4 LY LF507-1F	46040	CY97		to be lsf GATX 0799/op in Sabena-colors
☐ OO-DWK	Avro RJ100 (Avro 146-RJ100)					4 LY LF507-1F	46040	CY97		to be lsf GATX 0999/op in Sabena-colors
☐ OO-DWL	Avro RJ100 (Avro 146-RJ100)					4 LY LF507-1F	46040	CY97		to be lsf GATX 1099/op in Sabena-colors

484 registration type of aircraft cn/fn ex/ex* mfd del powered by mtow kg configuration selcal name/fln/specialitites/remarks

EAT – European Air Transport, N.V. = QY / BCS (a DHL Company) — Brussels-National

Building 4-5, Brussels National Airport, B-1930 Zaventem, Belgium ☎ (2) 718 14 14 Tx: 23818 eat b Fax: (2) 718 15 55 SITA: BRUOOQY
F: 1971 ⁂ 310 Head: Gordon D. Olafson IATA: 615 ICAO: EUROTRANS Net: n/a All aircraft operated on behalf of DHL Int'l (in full DHL colors) in in the evening & during the night, while charter-flights for outside customers are conducted during the day. Additional aircraft (Airbus Industrie A300B4 freighters) are operated on behalf of DHL (managed by EAT) in DHL-colors by: AIR CONTRACTORS (EI-) & TULIP AIR CHARTER (PH-). For details – see under both carriers.

☐	OO-JPA	Fairchild (Swearingen) SA226AT Merlin IVA	AT-041	N6FJ	0075	0785	2 GA TPE331-3UW-303G	5670	Y18 / Freighter		Ist SWT as EC-GBI
☐	OO-JPI	Fairchild (Swearingen) SA226TC Metro II	TC-221		0075	0276	2 GA TPE331-3UW-303G	5670	Y18 / Freighter		Ist SWT as EC-FZB
☐	OO-JPN	Fairchild (Swearingen) SA226AT Merlin IVA	AT-038	N5FJ	0075	0785	2 GA TPE331-3UW-303G	5670	Y18 / Freighter		Ist SWT as EC-FUX
☐	OO-DHB	Convair 580 (F) (SCD)	458	N537SA	0057	0987	2 AN 501-D13	24766	Freighter		Ist SWT as EC-GBF / cvtd 440-97
☐	OO-DHC	Convair 580 (F) (SCD)	68	N535SA	0053	1087	2 AN 501-D13	24766	Freighter		cvtd 340-31 / op in DHL-colors
☐	OO-DHD	Convair 580 (F) (SCD)	135	N536SA	0053	1087	2 AN 501-D13	24766	Freighter		Ist SWT as EC-GKH / cvtd 340-48
☐	OO-DHE	Convair 580 (F) (SCD)	52	C-GDTE	0053	0688	2 AN 501-D13	26379	Freighter		cvtd 340-31 / op in DHL-colors
☐	OO-DHF	Convair 580 (F) (SCD)	147	C-GQHA	0054	1088	2 AN 501-D13	26379	Freighter		cvtd 340-63 / op in DHL-colors
☐	OO-DHG	Convair 580 (F) (SCD)	25	N73117	0052	0988	2 AN 501-D13	26379	Freighter		Ist SWT as EC-GDY / cvtd 340-31
☐	OO-DHH	Convair 580 (F) (SCD)	186	N73156	0053	0988	2 AN 501-D13	26379	Freighter		Ist SWT as EC-GHN / cvtd 440-31
☐	OO-DHL	Convair 580 (F) (SCD)	459	C-GGWF	0057	0188	2 AN 501-D13	24766	Freighter		cvtd 440-97 / op in DHL-colors
☐	OO-HUB	Convair 580 (F) (SCD)	130	C-GGWG	0053	0388	2 AN 501-D13	24766	Freighter		Ist SWT as EC-GSJ / cvtd 340-47
☐	OO-DHM	Boeing 727-31C	20114 / 712	N7892	0069	0890	3 PW JT8D-7B (HK3/FDX)	76885	Freighter	AD-CJ	cvtd -31 / op in DHL-colors
☐	OO-DHN	Boeing 727-31C	20113 / 711	N260NE	0069	1190	3 PW JT8D-7B (HK3/FDX)	76885	Freighter	AD-CH	cvtd -31 / op in DHL-colors
☐	OO-DHO	Boeing 727-31C	20112 / 700	N250NE	0069	1190	3 PW JT8D-7B (HK3/FDX)	76885	Freighter		cvtd -31 / op in DHL-colors
☐	OO-DHP	Boeing 727-35 (F)	19166 / 303	N150FN	0866	0892	3 PW JT8D-7B (HK3/FDX)	76885	Freighter		Ist DHL Guatemala as TG-DHP / cvtd -35
☐	OO-DHQ	Boeing 727-35 (F)	19167 / 325	N152FN	1066	0992	3 PW JT8D-7B (HK3/FDX)	76885	Freighter		Ist VEC as YV-846C / cvtd -35
☐	OO-DHR	Boeing 727-35 (F)	19834 / 489	N932FT	0067	0294	3 PW JT8D-7B (HK3/FDX)	76885	Freighter		cvtd -35 / op in DHL-colors
☐	OO-DHK	Boeing 727-277 (F) (A)	22643 / 1762	N70415	0081	0997	3 PW JT8D-15 (HK3/FDX)	89358	Freighter		cvtd -277 / op in DHL-colors
☐	OO-DHS	Boeing 727-223 (F)	20189 / 733	N6836	0669	1094	3 PW JT8D-9A (HK3/FDX)	80559	Freighter		cvtd -223 / op in DHL-colors
☐	OO-DHT	Boeing 727-223 (F)	19489 / 593	N6814	0668	1294	3 PW JT8D-9A (HK3/FDX)	80559	Freighter		cvtd -223 / op in DHL-colors
☐	OO-DHU	Boeing 727-223 (F) (A)	20992 / 1187	N851AA	0576	0795	3 PW JT8D-9A (HK3/FDX)	78457	Freighter		cvtd -223 / op in DHL-colors
☐	OO-DHV	Boeing 727-223 (F) (A)	21084 / 1199	N857AA	0476	0795	3 PW JT8D-9A (HK3/FDX)	78457	Freighter		Ist SWT as EC-HAH / cvtd -223
☐	OO-DHW	Boeing 727-223 (F) (A)	20993 / 1189	N852AA	0576	0795	3 PW JT8D-9A (HK3/FDX)	80559	Freighter		cvtd -223 / op in DHL-colors
☐	OO-DHX	Boeing 727-223 (F) (A)	20994 / 1190	N853AA	0576	0795	3 PW JT8D-9A (HK3/FDX)	78457	Freighter		cvtd -223 / op in DHL-colors
☐	OO-DHY	Boeing 727-230 (F) (A)	20905 / 1091	N626DH	0075	0697	3 PW JT8D-15 (HK3/FDX)	82782	Freighter		cvtd -230 / op in DHL-colors
☐	OO-DHZ	Boeing 727-2Q4 (F) (A)	22424 / 1683	N7563Q	0080	0797	3 PW JT8D-17R (HK3/FDX)	79605	Freighter		cvtd -2Q4 / op in DHL-colors
☐	OO-DLB	Boeing 727-277 (F) (A)	22642 / 1759	N86330	0081	1097	3 PW JT8D-15 (HK3/FDX)	89358	Freighter		cvtd -277 / op in DHL-colors
☐	VH-DHE	Boeing 727-2J4 (F) (A)	22080 / 1598	N729DH	0080	0595	3 PW JT8D-17 (HK3/FDX)	90517	Freighter	BM-CJ	Ist Asian Express Airlines / cvtd -2J4
☐	OO-DLC	Airbus Industrie A300B4-203 (F)	152	N221EA	0081	0299	2 GE CF6-50C2	165000	Freighter		cvtd -203 / op in DHL-colors
☐	OO-DLD	Airbus Industrie A300B4-203 (F)	259	N865PA	0883	0499	2 GE CF6-50C2	165000	Freighter		cvtd -203 / op in DHL-colors
☐	OO-DLE	Airbus Industrie A300B4-203 (F)	238	PK-JID	0083	0199	2 GE CF6-50C2	165000	Freighter		oo-del. 0999/cvtd -203/tb op in DHL-cs
☐	OO-DLF	Airbus Industrie A300B4-203 (F)	208	F-OHPN	0082		2 GE CF6-50C2	165000	Freighter		oo-del. 1299/cvtd -203/tb op in DHL-cs

EG HELISERVICE, N.V. (Member of EG Group) — Mechelen-Walem Heliport

Battenbroek 10, B-2800 Mechelen, Belgium ☎ (15) 28 91 91 Tx: none Fax: (15) 28 91 90 SITA: n/a
F: 1989 ⁂ 6 Head: Eric Geboers Net: n/a Aircraft below MTOW 1361kg: Robinson R22 & R44

☐	OO-DOU	Agusta-Bell 206B JetRanger III	8718	G-RNGR	0089	0793	1 AN 250-C20J	1451			lsf Vervoer Van Roey N.V.
☐	OO-EGM	Bell 206B JetRanger	1097	G-BBBM	0073	0596	1 AN 250-C20	1451			lsf Carfin N.V.
☐	OO-FVR	Agusta-Bell 206B JetRanger III	8590	D-HORA	0080	1295	1 AN 250-C20B	1451			lsf Rotor Wings N.V.
☐	OO-AHE	Agusta A109A II	7325	OO-XHE	0085	0492	2 AN 250-C20B	2600			lsf Vervoer Van Roey N.V.

EUROSENSE BELFOTOP, N.V. (Sister company of Eurosense, GmbH) — Brussels-National

Nervierslaan 54, B-1780 Wemmel, Belgium ☎ (2) 460 70 00 Tx: none Fax: (2) 460 49 58 SITA: n/a
F: 1962 ⁂ 49 Head: Emil Maes Net: n/a

☐	OO-GPS	Cessna 404 Titan II	404-0609	N26835	0080	0493	2 CO GTSIO-520-M	3810	Photo/Survey		

FLYING SUPPORT, N.V. = IBS (formerly Ibis, N.V.) — Antwerp-Deurne

Antwerp Airport, Luchthaven Bus 18, B-2100 Deurne, Belgium ☎ (3) 286 86 06 Tx: none Fax: (3) 230 98 59 SITA: n/a
F: 1984 ⁂ 7 Head: Bernard Van Milders ICAO: SPIDER Net: n/a

☐	OO-OSA	Cessna S550 Citation S/II	S550-0147	N1296N	1187	0498	2 PWC JT15D-4B	6849	9 Pax		lsf B. van Milders N.V.

HELIFLY, B.V.B.A. — Halen

Kuringersteenweg 170A, B-3500 Hasselt, Belgium ☎ (13) 44 24 46 Tx: none Fax: (13) 44 47 73 SITA: n/a
F: 1990 ⁂ 8 Head: Tom Piron Net: n/a Aircraft below MTOW 1361kg: Hughes 269A

☐	OO-HFS	MD Helicopters MD 500D (Hughes 369D)	1200880D	LX-HLE	1280	0898	1 AN 250-C20B	1361			lsf Jan Construct N.V.
☐	OO-SZO	MD Helicopters MD 520N (Hughes 500N)	LN027	OY-HEN	0092	1096	1 AN 250-C20R	1520			
☐	OO-EMS	MD Helicopters MD 900 Explorer	900-00020	SE-JCG	0095	0596	2 PWC PW206A	2722	EMS		Ist Luxembourg Air Rescue

HELI-JET, N.V. (formerly E.G. Helicopters, N.V.) — Antwerp-Tielen

Gierlebaan 100, B-2460 Tielen, Belgium ☎ (14) 55 92 39 Tx: none Fax: (14) 55 92 00 SITA: n/a
F: 1991 ⁂ n/a Head: A. Janssens Net: n/a Aircraft below MTOW 1361kg: Robinson R22

☐	OO-KBM	Bell 206B JetRanger	1786	G-BVWS	0075	1295	1 AN 250-C20	1451			lsf Kempische Bouwmaterialen N.V.

HELIMO, N.V. — Antwerp-Private Heliport

d'Herbouvillekaai 80, B-2020 Antwerpen, Belgium ☎ (3) 457 34 01 Tx: none Fax: (3) 457 70 20 SITA: n/a
F: 1992 ⁂ n/a Head: William Wilford Net: n/a

☐	OO-WGW	Agusta A109C	7647	I-SEIG	0091	0097	2 AN 250-C20R/1	2720			

HELI SERVICE BELGIUM, N.V. (formerly Q.S. Helicopters & V.C. Helicopters, N.V.) — Halle-Heliport

Gaasbeek Steenweg 140, B-1500 Halle, Belgium ☎ (2) 361 21 21 Tx: none Fax: (2) 360 27 70 SITA: n/a
F: 1991 ⁂ 8 Head: Bernard Slegten Net: n/a Aircraft below MTOW 1361 kg: Robinson R22 & R44

☐	OO-EAN	Bell 206B JetRanger	1595	G-BORX	0075		1 AN 250-C20	1451			lsf Echo Alpha November N.V.
☐	OO-LER	Bell 206B JetRanger II	2043	G-BVWT	0076	0098	1 AN 250-C20	1451			
☐	OO-VCC	Bell 206B JetRanger III	4057	PH-VCK	0089	0789	1 AN 250-C20J	1451			lsf Q-Invest N.V.
☐	OO-HSB	Eurocopter (Aerosp.) AS355F1 Ecureuil 2	5223	G-PLAX	0082	0397	2 AN 250-C20F	2400	EMS		opf Mugheli Inst.,Brugge-Sint Jan Hosp.
☐	OO-HSG	Eurocopter (Aerosp.) AS355F1 Ecureuil 2	5116	N5791M	0182	0997	2 AN 250-C20F	2400			

HELI VAN WULPEN, N.V. — Kortrijk-Wevelgem

Krekelstraat 50, B-8770 Ingelmunster, Belgium ☎ (51) 48 90 91 Tx: n/a Fax: (51) 48 81 61 SITA: n/a
F: 1990 ⁂ 2 Head: Eddy Van Wulpen Net: n/a

☐	OO-VWE	Agusta-Bell 206B JetRanger III	8563	G-NATO	0079	0590	1 AN 250-C20B	1451			
☐	OO-VWK	Piper PA-34-220T Seneca III	34-8133182	HB-LQL	0081	0894	2 CO TSIO-360-KB	1999			

LVC HELICOPTERS, N.V. — Wevelgem-Kortijk

Luchtvaarstraat 1, Bus 12, B-8560 Wevelgem, Belgium ☎ (64) 33 33 18 Tx: none Fax: (64) 36 77 80 SITA: n/a
F: 1995 ⁂ n/a Head: Eddy Leyn Net: n/a Aircraft below MTOW 1361kg: Hughes 269C (300C)

☐	OO-LVK	MD Helicopters MD 500D (Hughes 369D)	1200881D	OE-XBB	1280	0296	1 AN 250-C20B	1361			cvtd with a MD 500E front-section

NAMUR AIR PROMOTION — Namur

Rue du Maka 31, B-6280 Gougnies, Belgium ☎ (71) 50 17 10 Tx: n/a Fax: (71) 50 17 10 SITA: n/a
F: 1994 ⁂ n/a Head: André Duculot Net: n/a

☐	OO-NAP	Pilatus PC-6/B2-H4 Turbo Porter	914		0095	0495	1 PWC PT6A-27	2800	Para		

NOORDZEE HELIKOPTERS VLAANDEREN, N.V. — Ostend

Watersportlaan 3c, B-8620 Nieuwpoort, Belgium ☎ (59) 30 61 68 Tx: none Fax: (59) 30 61 67 SITA: n/a
F: 1997 ⁂ n/a Head: Eric Van Hal Net: n/a

☐	OO-NHV	Eurocopter (Aerosp.) AS365N3 Dauphin 2	6510	F-WWOZ*	1297	1297	2 TU Arriel 2C	4250			Flipper 1 / IFR/Hoist/Emergency Floats

PUBLI AIR, S.A. — Namur

Namur Airport, B-5020 Suarlée, Belgium ☎ (81) 56 61 46 Tx: none Fax: (81) 56 96 00 SITA: n/a
F: 1959 ⁂ 15 Head: Georges Bertrand Net: n/a Aircraft below MTOW 1361kg: Cessna 150/172, Piper PA-18 & Robinson R22.

☐	OO-COP	Agusta-Bell 206B JetRanger	8284	D-HAVA	0071	0673	1 AN 250-C20	1451	4 Pax		cvtd 206A
☐	OO-HOP	Agusta-Bell 206B JetRanger	8418	PH-HAP	0074	0790	1 AN 250-C20	1451	4 Pax		
☐	OO-VCI	Agusta-Bell 206B JetRanger III	8732	PH-VCP	0091	0593	1 AN 250-C20J	1451	4 Pax		

RST AVIATION, N.V. = DMD — Antwerp-Deurne

Luchthaven Antwerpen, Bus 59, B-2100 Deurne, Belgium ☎ (3) 281 27 59 Tx: none Fax: (3) 281 27 61 SITA: n/a
F: 1991 ⁂ 10 Head: Dirk Van Lint Net: n/a

☐	OO-SXD	Embraer 121A Xingu (EMB-121A)	121043	PT-MBK*	0081		2 PWC PT6A-28	5670			lsf Fast Air N.V.
☐	OO-RSE	Sabreliner 65 (Rockwell NA265-65)	465-72	N857W	0081	0493	2 GA TFE731-3R-1D	10886			

485 registration type of aircraft cn/fn ex/ex* mfd del powered by mtow kg configuration selcal name/fln/specialitites/remarks

SABENA, S.A. = SN / SAB (Subsidiary of SAirLines/Member of SAirGroup & The Qualiflyer Group) **Brussels-National** **sabena**

Avenue E. Mounier 2, B-1200 Brussels, Belgium ☎ (2) 723 31 11 Tx: 63697 sabcom b Fax: (2) 723 58 99 SITA: BRUSSSN
F: 1923 ✈ 9200 Head: Paul Reutlinger IATA: 082 ICAO: SABENA Net: http://www.sabena.com Beside aircraft listed, additional (Avro RJ85/100 & BAe 146-200) are operated on behalf of Sabena by subsidiary company DAT-Delta Air Transport in full Sabena-colors & both titles & using SN-flight numbers. For details – see under that company.

registration	type of aircraft	cn/fn	ex/ex*	mfd	del	powered by	mtow kg	configuration	selcal	name/fln/specialitites/remarks
☐ PH-SDM	De Havilland DHC-8-311 Dash 8	298	N511SK	0092	0393	2 PWC PW123	19500	CY46		lsf / opb SCH in Sabena-colors
☐ PH-SDP	De Havilland DHC-8-311 Dash 8	300	N501DC	0091	0993	2 PWC PW123	19500	CY46		lsf / opb SCH in Sabena-colors
☐ PH-SDR	De Havilland DHC-8-311 Dash 8	283	EI-CED	0091	0394	2 PWC PW123	19500	CY46		lsf / opb SCH in Sabena-colors
☐ PH-SDT	De Havilland DHC-8-311 Dash 8	276	C-FZBL	0091	0996	2 PWC PW123	19500	CY46		lsf / opb SCH in Sabena-colors
☐ PH-SDU	De Havilland DHC-8-311 Dash 8	232	C-FXXU	0090	1096	2 PWC PW123	19500	CY46		lsf / opb SCH in Sabena-colors
☐ OO-SDA	Boeing 737-229 (A)	20907 / 351	LX-LGN	0074	0474	2 PW JT8D-15 (HK3/NOR)	52750	CY109	EL-CF	lsf European Aviation Ltd -0099
☐ OO-SDD	Boeing 737-229 (A)	20910 / 358	EC-EEG	0074	0674	2 PW JT8D-15 (HK3/NOR)	52750	CY109	EL-GK	lsf European Aviation Ltd -0000
☐ OO-SDE	Boeing 737-229 (A)	20911 / 360	C-GNDX	0074	0674	2 PW JT8D-15/15A	54200	CY109	EL-GM	lsf European Aviation Ltd -0099
☐ OO-SDF	Boeing 737-229 (A)	20912 / 365		0074	0774	2 PW JT8D-15/15A	52750	CY109	EL-HJ	lsf European Aviation Ltd -0000
☐ OO-SDG	Boeing 737-229 (A)	21135 / 418		0075	0675	2 PW JT8D-15/15A	52750	CY109	EL-CJ	lsf European Aviation Ltd -0000
☐ OO-SDJ	Boeing 737-229C (A)	20915 / 401		0075	0375	2 PW JT8D-15/15A	52750	CY109	EM-CJ	lsf European Aviation Ltd -0000
☐ OO-SDK	Boeing 737-229C (A)	20916 / 403		0075	0375	2 PW JT8D-15/15A	52750	CY109	FG-BM	lsf European Aviation Ltd -0000
☐ OO-SDL	Boeing 737-229 (A)	21136 / 420		0075	0675	2 PW JT8D-15/15A	52750	CY109	EL-DG	lsf European Aviation Ltd -0000
☐ OO-SDM	Boeing 737-229 (A)	21137 / 421		0075	0675	2 PW JT8D-15/15A	54200	CY109	EL-DK	lsf European Aviation Ltd -0099
☐ OO-SDN	Boeing 737-229 (A)	21176 / 431	9M-MBP	0075	1275	2 PW JT8D-15/15A	54200	CY109	EL-FH	lsf European Aviation Ltd -0000
☐ OO-SDO	Boeing 737-229 (A)	21177 / 433		0075	1275	2 PW JT8D-15/15A	54200	CY109	EL-FJ	lsf European Aviation Ltd -0000
☐ OO-SDP	Boeing 737-229C (A)	21139 / 437		0075	1175	2 PW JT8D-15/15A	52750	CY109	FG-AK	lsf European Aviation Ltd -0000
☐ OO-SDR	Boeing 737-229C (A)	21738 / 576		0079	0579	2 PW JT8D-15/15A	52750	CY109	EL-DJ	lsf European Aviation Ltd -0099
☐ OO-SYE	Boeing 737-529	25218 / 2111		0091	0991	2 CFMI CFM56-3C1	52390	CY111	GJ-KQ	lsf S.N.C.I.
☐ OO-SYG	Boeing 737-529	25249 / 2145		0091	1091	2 CFMI CFM56-3C1	52390	CY111	GJ-MQ	
☐ OO-SYH	Boeing 737-529	25418 / 2163		0091	1191	2 CFMI CFM56-3C1	52390	CY111	EM-DG	lsf CITG
☐ OO-SYI	Boeing 737-529	25419 / 2165		0091	1191	2 CFMI CFM56-3C1	52390	CY111	AL-RS	lsf CITG
☐ OO-SYJ	Boeing 737-529	26537 / 2296		0092	0692	2 CFMI CFM56-3C1	52390	CY111	BL-FR	
☐ OO-SYK	Boeing 737-529	26538 / 2298		0092	0692	2 CFMI CFM56-3C1	52390	CY111	BL-FS	
☐ OO-SDV	Boeing 737-329	23771 / 1430		0087	0887	2 CFMI CFM56-3B2	59870	CY126	EM-DG	lsf CITG
☐ OO-SDW	Boeing 737-329	23772 / 1432		0087	0887	2 CFMI CFM56-3B2	59870	CY126	EM-GL	lsf CITG
☐ OO-SDX	Boeing 737-329	23773 / 1441		0087	0987	2 CFMI CFM56-3B2	59870	CY126	EM-FJ	
☐ OO-SDY	Boeing 737-329	23774 / 1443		0087	0987	2 CFMI CFM56-3B2	59870	CY126	EM-FL	
☐ OO-SYA	Boeing 737-329	24355 / 1709		0089	0489	2 CFMI CFM56-3B2	59870	CY126	EM-GH	lsf SL SAB Co. Ltd
☐ OO-SYB	Boeing 737-329	24356 / 1711		0089	0589	2 CFMI CFM56-3B2	59870	CY126	EL-FG	lsf SL SAB Co. Ltd
☐ OO-SYC	Boeing 737-429	25226 / 2104		0091	0891	2 CFMI CFM56-3C1	65770	CY144	GJ-FQ	
☐ OO-SYD	Boeing 737-429	25247 / 2106		0091	0891	2 CFMI CFM56-3C1	65770	CY144	GJ-HQ	lsf CITG
☐ OO-SYF	Boeing 737-429	25248 / 2120		0091	0991	2 CFMI CFM56-3C1	65770	CY144	GJ-LQ	lsf CITG
☐ OO-SSA	Airbus Industrie A319-112	1048				2 CFMI CFM56-5B6/2P	64000			oo-delivery 0799
☐ OO-SSB	Airbus Industrie A319-112	1068				2 CFMI CFM56-5B6/2P	64000			oo-delivery 0899
☐ OO-SSC	Airbus Industrie A319-112	1086				2 CFMI CFM56-5B6/2P	64000			oo-delivery 0999
☐ OO-SSD	Airbus Industrie A319-112	1102				2 CFMI CFM56-5B6/2P	64000			oo-delivery 1099
☐ OO-SSE	Airbus Industrie A319-112	1124				2 CFMI CFM56-5B6/2P	64000			oo-delivery 1199
☐ OO-SSF	Airbus Industrie A319-112					2 CFMI CFM56-5B6/2P	64000			oo-delivery 1299
☐ OO-SSG	Airbus Industrie A319-112					2 CFMI CFM56-5B6/2P	64000			oo-delivery 0100
☐ OO-SSH	Airbus Industrie A319-112					2 CFMI CFM56-5B6/2P	64000			oo-delivery 0200
☐ OO-SSI	Airbus Industrie A319-112					2 CFMI CFM56-5B6/2P	64000			oo-delivery 0300
☐ OO-SSJ	Airbus Industrie A319-112					2 CFMI CFM56-5B6/2P	64000			oo-delivery 0400
☐ OO-SSK	Airbus Industrie A319-112					2 CFMI CFM56-5B6/2P	64000			oo-delivery 0500
☐ OO-SSL	Airbus Industrie A319-112					2 CFMI CFM56-5B6/2P	64000			oo-delivery 0600
☐ OO-SSM	Airbus Industrie A319-112					2 CFMI CFM56-5B6/2P	64000			oo-delivery 0800
☐ OO-SSN	Airbus Industrie A319-112					2 CFMI CFM56-5B6/2P	64000			oo-delivery 0900
☐ OO-SSO	Airbus Industrie A319-112					2 CFMI CFM56-5B6/2P	64000			oo-delivery 1000
☐ OO-SSP	Airbus Industrie A319-112					2 CFMI CFM56-5B6/2P	64000			oo-delivery 1200
☐ OO-SSQ	Airbus Industrie A319-112					2 CFMI CFM56-5B6/2P	64000			oo-delivery 0101
☐ OO-SSR	Airbus Industrie A319-112					2 CFMI CFM56-5B6/2P	64000			oo-delivery 0201
☐ OO-SSS	Airbus Industrie A319-112					2 CFMI CFM56-5B6/2P	64000			oo-delivery 0301
☐ OO-SST	Airbus Industrie A319-112					2 CFMI CFM56-5B6/2P	64000			oo-delivery 0401
☐ OO-SSU	Airbus Industrie A319-112					2 CFMI CFM56-5B6/2P	64000			oo-delivery 0501
☐ OO-SSV	Airbus Industrie A319-112					2 CFMI CFM56-5B6/2P	64000			oo-delivery 0601
☐ OO-SSW	Airbus Industrie A319-112					2 CFMI CFM56-5B6/2P	64000			oo-delivery 0701
☐ OO-SSX	Airbus Industrie A319-112					2 CFMI CFM56-5B6/2P	64000			oo-delivery 0801
☐ OO-SSY	Airbus Industrie A319-112					2 CFMI CFM56-5B6/2P	64000			oo-delivery 0901
☐ OO-SSZ	Airbus Industrie A319-112					2 CFMI CFM56-5B6/2P	64000			oo-delivery 1001
☐ OO-	Airbus Industrie A320-214					2 CFMI CFM56-5B4/2	73500			oo-delivery 0699
☐ OO-	Airbus Industrie A320-214					2 CFMI CFM56-5B4/2	73500			oo-delivery 1099
☐ OO-	Airbus Industrie A320-214					2 CFMI CFM56-5B4/2	73500			oo-delivery 0200
☐ OO-	Airbus Industrie A320-214					2 CFMI CFM56-5B4/2	73500			oo-delivery 0800
☐ OO-	Airbus Industrie A320-214					2 CFMI CFM56-5B4/2	73500			oo-delivery 0401
☐ OO-SUA	Airbus Industrie A321-211	970	D-AVZY*	0099	0299	2 CFMI CFM56-5B3/P	89000			
☐ OO-SUB	Airbus Industrie A321-211	995	D-AVZG*	0099	0399	2 CFMI CFM56-5B3/P	89000			
☐ OO-SUC	Airbus Industrie A321-211	1012		0099	0499	2 CFMI CFM56-5B3/P	89000			
☐ OO-SFM	Airbus Industrie A330-301	030	F-GMDA	0093	0797	2 GE CF6-80E1A2	215000	C50Y222	RS-DP	lsf Airbus Industrie Financial Services
☐ OO-SFN	Airbus Industrie A330-301	037	F-GMDB	0093	0797	2 GE CF6-80E1A2	215000	C50Y222	RS-DQ	lsf Airbus Industrie Financial Services
☐ OO-SFO	Airbus Industrie A330-301	045	F-GMDC	0093	1197	2 GE CF6-80E1A2	215000	C50Y222	DR-AQ	lsf Airbus Industrie Financial Services
☐ OO-SFX	Airbus Industrie A330-322	096	9M-MKZ	0095	0499	2 PW PW4168	212000	C50Y222		lsf ILFC
☐ OO-SFP	Airbus Industrie A330-223	230	F-WWKT*	0098	0998	2 PW PW4168A	230000	C54Y187		lsf Bi Mandala Lease Co. Ltd
☐ OO-SFQ	Airbus Industrie A330-223	290				2 PW PW4168A	230000	C54Y187		to be lsf ILFC 0799
☐ OO-SFR	Airbus Industrie A330-223	296				2 PW PW4168A	230000	C54Y187		to be lsf ILFC 0999
☐ OO-SFS	Airbus Industrie A330-223	305				2 PW PW4168A	230000	C54Y187		to be lsf ILFC 1099
☐ OO-SFT	Airbus Industrie A330-223	322				2 PW PW4168A	230000	C54Y187		oo-delivery 0200
☐ OO-SFU	Airbus Industrie A330-223	328				2 PW PW4168A	230000	C54Y187		oo-delivery 0300
☐ OO-SCW	Airbus Industrie A340-211	014	F-GNIB	0093	0693	4 CFMI CFM56-5C2	257000	C54Y198	DR-AP	lsf Atrix Aviation S.A.
☐ OO-SCX	Airbus Industrie A340-211	022	F-GNIC	0093	0693	4 CFMI CFM56-5C2	257000	C54Y198	DR-AS	lsf Atrix Aviation S.A.
☐ OO-SCY	Airbus Industrie A340-311	047	F-GNID	0094	0394	4 CFMI CFM56-5C2	257000	C52Y242	DR-BC	lsf Senne Aviation S.A.
☐ OO-SCZ	Airbus Industrie A340-311	051	F-GNIE	0094	0494	4 CFMI CFM56-5C2	257000	C52Y242	DR-BE	lsf Senne Aviation S.A.
☐ OO-CTC	Boeing (Douglas) MD-11	48780 / 624		0098	0598	3 GE CF6-80C2D1F	285990	C48Y249	AK-DP	lsf / opb CTB in Sabena-colors
☐ OO-CTS	Boeing (Douglas) MD-11	48756 / 623		0098	0498	3 PW PW4460	285990	C48Y249	BE-CP	lsf / opb CTB in Sabena-colors
☐ OO-SGC	Boeing 747-329 (M)	23439 / 646	N6005C*	0086	0686	4 GE CF6-50E2	377800	C74Y311	EM-FH	to be wfu/sold 0899
☐ OO-SGD	Boeing 747-329 (M)	24837 / 810		0090	0990	4 GE CF6-50E2	377800	C74Y311	JQ-CP	to be wfu/sold 1099

SKY-SERVICE, B.V.B.A. = SKS **Kortrijk-Wevelgem**

Kortrijkstraat 317, B-8560 Wevelgem, Belgium ☎ (56) 40 39 11 Tx: none Fax: (56) 40 42 08 SITA: n/a
F: 1980 ✈ 20 Head: Bart Foucart ICAO: SKY SERVICE Net: n/a

registration	type of aircraft	cn/fn	ex/ex*	mfd	del	powered by	mtow kg	configuration	selcal	name/fln/specialitites/remarks
☐ LX-LTX	Beech King Air E90	LW-297	SE-IKD	0078	0495	2 PWC PT6A-28	4384	Corporate 8 Pax		lsf Creditlease SA
☐ OO-SXC	Embraer 121A Xingu (EMB-121A)	121042	PT-MBJ*	0081	0992	2 PWC PT6A-28	5670	5 Pax		
☐ OO-SXE	Embraer 121A Xingu (EMB-121A)	121045	PT-MBM*	0081		2 PWC PT6A-28	5670	5 Pax		
☐ N57LM	Beech King Air 200C	BL-16	F-GFAA	0080	0399	2 PWC PT6A-41	5670	Corporate 9 Pax		lsf Latexco N.V. / to be LX re-reg.
☐ LX-SKS	Embraer 110P1 Bandeirante (EMB-110P1)	110381	F-GFYZ	0082	0491	2 PWC PT6A-34	5670	14 Pax / Frtr		lsf Creditlease SA
☐ OO-MMP	Cessna 551 Citation II/SP	551-0559	D-ICHE	0087	0498	2 PWC JT15D-4	5670	9 Pax/EMS/Frtr		
☐ OO-SKS	Cessna 551 Citation II/SP	551-0117	N11AB	0079	0696	2 PWC JT15D-4	5670	9 Pax/EMS/Frtr		lsf Deli Consult/cvtd Ce 550 550-0063

SKYTECH HELICOPTER SERVICE, SàRL (Joint venture with Mil, Russia) **Ostend & Overseas**

Rue de la Lasne 11A, B-1380 Lasne, Belgium ☎ (2) 633 58 90 Tx: none Fax: (2) 633 58 84 SITA: n/a
F: 1989 ✈ n/a Head: Thierry Lakhanisky Net: n/a Beside aircraft listed, also leases Antonov 32 & Yakovlev 40 aircraft from Komiavia, Sterkh, Trans-Charter (RA-) when required.

registration	type of aircraft	cn/fn	ex/ex*	mfd	del	powered by	mtow kg	configuration	selcal	name/fln/specialitites/remarks
☐ RA-31007	Kamov Ka-32	5703	CCCP-31007	0387		2 IS TV3-117V	12600	Freighter 5t		lsf Pankh
☐ RA-31064	Kamov Ka-32	8606	CCCP-31064	0890		2 IS TV3-117V	12600	Freighter 5t		lsf Pankh
☐ RA-31571	Kamov Ka-32	6220	CCCP-31571	0391		2 IS TV3-117V	12600	Freighter 5t		lsf Pankh
☐ RA-31576	Kamov Ka-32	6225	CCCP-31576	0591		2 IS TV3-117V	12600	Freighter 5t		lsf Pankh / based Malaysia
☐ RA-31577	Kamov Ka-32	6226	CCCP-31577	0591		2 IS TV3-117V	12600			lsf Pankh / based Malaysia
☐ RA-31579	Kamov Ka-32	8601	CCCP-31579	0691		2 IS TV3-117V	12600	Freighter 5t		lsf Pankh
☐ RA-31595	Kamov Ka-32T	8802	CCCP-31595	0692		2 IS TV3-117VK	11000	Freighter 5t		lsf Nefteyugansk Air Enterprise
☐ RA-25441	Mil Mi-8MTV-1	95582	CCCP-25441	0090		2 IS TV3-117MT	13000	Y22 / Frtr 4t		lsf KMA
☐ RA-25750	Mil Mi-8AMT	59489607833		0093		2 IS TV3-117MT	13000	Y22 / Frtr 4t		lsf KMA / std OST
☐ RA-27041	Mil Mi-8MTV-1	95875	CCCP-27041	0092		2 IS TV3-117MT	13000	Y22 / Frtr 4t		lsf KMA
☐ RA-06038	Mil Mi-26	34001212428	CCCP-06038	1090		2 LO D-136	56000	Freighter 20t		lsf Pankh

SOBELAIR, N.V. = Q7 / SLR (Subsidiary of Sabena, S.A./Member of European Leisure Group) **Brussels-National** **sobelair**

Airport Building 117A, B-1820 Melsbroek, Belgium ☎ (2) 754 12 11 Tx: 22095 soblr b Fax: (2) 754 12 88 SITA: BRUXOSN
F: 1946 ✈ 300 Head: Mrs. Sylviane Lust ICAO: SOBELAIR Net: n/a

registration	type of aircraft	cn/fn	ex/ex*	mfd	del	powered by	mtow kg	configuration	selcal	name/fln/specialitites/remarks
☐ OO-SBX	Boeing 737-3M8	25040 / 2017	TC-BIR	0091	0596	2 CFMI CFM56-3B2	61235	Y149	LQ-DP	lsf BBAM
☐ OO-SBZ	Boeing 737-329	23775 / 1412		0087	0787	2 CFMI CFM56-3B2	61910	Y149	EM-FK	

☐ OO-SLK	Boeing 737-33S	29072 / 3012		0398	0398	2 CFMI CFM56-3C1	61235	Y149	EL-FM	lsf PEMB
☐ OO-SBJ	Boeing 737-46B	24573 / 1844	G-BROC	0090	0490	2 CFMI CFM56-3C1	66990	Y170	JQ-DE	
☐ OO-SBM	Boeing 737-429	25729 / 2217		0092	0292	2 CFMI CFM56-3C1	66990	Y170	AL-QS	
☐ OO-SBY	Boeing 767-33A (ER)	27310 / 545		0094	0694	2 GE CF6-80C2B6F	184200	Y272	CF-ES	lsf AWAS
☐ OO-STF	Boeing 767-328 (ER)	27212 / 531	F-GHGK	0094	0696	2 GE CF6-80C2B6F	184610	Y271	EH-LR	lsf SUNR

T.I.A. – Travaux Internationaux Aériens, S.A. Charleroi-Brussels South

Rue Sylvain Guyaux 40, B-7100 La Louvière, Belgium ☎ (3) 218 43 83 Tx: none Fax: (3) 218 94 78 SITA: n/a
F: 1994 n/a Head: Amedée Vermeire Net: n/a Aircraft below MTOW 1361kg: Piper PA-28 & PA-38

☐ OO-RAG	Piper PA-32R-301 Saratoga II HP	3213004	G-WILI	1287	0495	1 LY IO-540-K1G5D	1633	Pax/Photo/Exec		

VIRGIN EXPRESS, S.A. = TV / VEX (Member of Virgin Group / formerly EBA Eurobelgian Airlines, S.A.) Brussels-National

Building 116, B-1820 Melsbroek Airport, Belgium ☎ (2) 752 05 11 Tx: 21886 b Fax: (2) 752 05 06 SITA: BRUDTTV
F: 1991 600 Head: James Swigart IATA: 665 ICAO: VIRGIN EXPRESS Net: http://www.virgin-exp.com

☐ OO-LTL	Boeing 737-3M8	25041 / 2024		0491	0392	2 CFMI CFM56-3B2	61235	Y149	LQ-EF	lsf TOMB
☐ OO-LTM	Boeing 737-3M8	25070 / 2037	F-GMTM	0591	0292	2 CFMI CFM56-3B2	61235	Y149	LQ-FG	lsf Locabel
☐ OO-LTP	Boeing 737-33A	25032 / 2014	PP-SOG	0491	0293	2 CFMI CFM56-3C1	61235	Y142	LQ-DP	lsf AWAS
☐ OO-LTU	Boeing 737-33A	27455 / 2709		0095	0495	2 CFMI CFM56-3C1	61235	Y142	LQ-BS	lsf AWAS
☐ OO-LTV	Boeing 737-3Y0	23924 / 1542	XA-SEM	0088	0296	2 CFMI CFM56-3B2	61235	Y142	LQ-BR	lsf BBAM
☐ OO-LTW	Boeing 737-33A	25010 / 2008	VH-OAM	0091	0495	2 CFMI CFM56-3C1	61235	Y142	LQ-CJ	lsf AWAS
☐ OO-LTY	Boeing 737-3Y0	23925 / 1544	XA-SEO	0088	0296	2 CFMI CFM56-3B2	61235	Y142	LQ-CM	lsf BBAM
☐ OO-VEB	Boeing 737-36M	28333 / 2810		0096	0896	2 CFMI CFM56-3C1	61235	Y149	LR-DE	lsf GECA
☐ OO-VEE	Boeing 737-3Y0	23922 / 1538	TF-ABK	0088	0297	2 CFMI CFM56-3B2	62822	Y142	FQ-LP	lsf Cauff, Lippman Aviation
☐ OO-VEG	Boeing 737-36N	28568 / 2987		0098	0298	2 CFMI CFM56-3C1	61235	Y142	LQ-CK	lsf GECA
☐ OO-VEH	Boeing 737-36N	28571 / 3022		0098	0498	2 CFMI CFM56-3C1	61235	Y148	LQ-DM	lsf GECA
☐ OO-VEX	Boeing 737-36N	28670 / 2948		0097	1197	2 CFMI CFM56-3C1	61235	Y142	GS-AB	lsf GECA
☐ OO-VBR	Boeing 737-4Y0	24314 / 1680	F-GMBR	0089	0397	2 CFMI CFM56-3C1	64636	Y170	GR-FP	lsf Antwerp Co. Ltd
☐ OO-VEC	Boeing 737-46M	28549 / 2844	C-GBIW	0097	0197	2 CFMI CFM56-3C1	64636	Y170	LQ-CP	lsf BBAM / sub-lst TSC,C-GBIW in winter
☐ OO-VED	Boeing 737-46M	28550 / 2847	C-GBIX	0097	0197	2 CFMI CFM56-3C1	64636	Y170	LQ-DK	lsf TOMB / sublst TSC, C-GBIX in winter
☐ OO-VEF	Boeing 737-430	27000 / 2311	D-ABKA	0092	0597	2 CFMI CFM56-3C1	62822	Y164		lsf INGO
☐ OO-VEJ	Boeing 737-405	24271 / 1738	LN-BRB	0089	0499	2 CFMI CFM56-3C1	67998	Y170		lsf BRA
☐ OO-VEK	Boeing 737-405	24270 / 1726	LN-BRA	0089	0599	2 CFMI CFM56-3C1	67998	Y170		lsf BRA
☐ OO-VJO	Boeing 737-4Y0	23980 / 1667	F-GMJO	0089	0397	2 CFMI CFM56-3C1	64636	Y170	GR-FM	lsf CITG
☐ OO-	Boeing 737-86M					2 CFMI CFM56-7B26	78245	Y184		oo-delivery 0600
☐ OO-	Boeing 737-86M					2 CFMI CFM56-7B26	78245	Y184		oo-delivery 0600
☐ EI-TLL	Airbus Industrie A300B4-203	158	N225GE	0081		2 GE CF6-50C2	165000	Y314	KL-EF	to be lsf / opb TLA 06-1099

VLM Vlaamse Luchttransportmaatschappij, N.V. = VG / VLM (Wings of Flanders) (Member of Frevag Group) Antwerp-Deurne

Antwerp Airport, Luchthavengebouw Bus 50, B-2100 Deurne, Belgium ☎ (3) 230 90 00 Tx: none Fax: (3) 281 32 00 SITA: ANRKOVG
F: 1992 100 Head: Jaap Rosen Jacobson IATA: 978 ICAO: RUBENS Net: http://www.vlm-r.com

☐ OO-VLE	Fokker 50 (F27 Mk050)	20132	D-AFKD	0088	0394	2 PWC PW125B	20820	Y50		City of Düsseldorf / lsf Frevag
☐ OO-VLG	Fokker 50 (F27 Mk050)	20104	PH-ARD	0087	0897	2 PWC PW125B	20820	Y50		Princess Diana / lsf PEMB
☐ OO-VLJ	Fokker 50 (F27 Mk050)	20105	PH-ARE	0087	0897	2 PWC PW125B	20820	Y50		Diana Princess of Wales / lsf PEMB
☐ OO-VLK	Fokker 50 (F27 Mk050)	20122	PH-FZF	0088	0396	2 PWC PW125B	20820	Y50		Cityof Mönchengladbach / lsfAeroCentury
☐ OO-VLR	Fokker 50 (F27 Mk050)	20121	PH-ARF	0088	0299	2 PWC PW125B	20820	Y50		City of Luxembourg / lsf Debis AirFin.
☐ PH-VLM	Fokker 50 (F27 Mk050)	20135	OO-VLM	0088	0493	2 PWC PW125B	20820	Y50		Rotterdam / lsf Mass Holding N.V.
☐ PH-VLN	Fokker 50 (F27 Mk050)	20145	OO-VLN	0089	0493	2 PWC PW125B	20820	Y50		City of Antwerp / lsf Mass Holding N.V.

WALAIR, B.V.B.A. Kortrijk-Wevelgem

Muizendale 2, B-9850 Nevele-Landegem, Belgium ☎ (9) 371 52 92 Tx: none Fax: (9) 371 52 92 SITA: n/a
F: n/a n/a Head: Walter de Roose Net: n/a Aircraft below MTOW 1361 kg: Cessna 152 & 172.

☐ OO-WAL	Cessna 182R Skylane II	18268083	N9870H	0081		1 CO O-470-U	1406			

WALPHOT, S.A. (Associated with Eurosense-Belfotop, N.V.) Brussels-National

Rue van Opré 97, B-5100 Namur, Belgium ☎ (81) 30 24 01 Tx: none Fax: (81) 30 41 67 SITA: n/a
F: 1972 22 Head: Emil Maes Net: n/a

☐ OO-TOP	Britten-Norman BN-2A-27 Islander	424	G-BCSI	0075		2 LY IO-540-E4C5	2994	Photo		

WAUTERS AIR SERVICE, S.A. – W.A.S. Charleroi-Brussels South

Rue Grogerie 114, B-6120 Ham-sur-Heure, Belgium ☎ (71) 21 63 67 Tx: none Fax: (71) 21 63 67 SITA: n/a
F: 1983 1 Head: Baudouin Wauters Net: n/a

☐ OO-PCZ	Cessna T207A Turbine Stationair 7 II	20700520	HB-CJL	0079		1 AN 250-C20S	1814	Para		Soloy cvtd

OY = DENMARK (Kingdom of Denmark) (Kongeriget Danmark)

Including: Faroe Islands & Greenland
Capital: Copenhagen Official Language: Danish Population: 5,2 million Square Km: 43092 Dialling code: +45 Year established: 800 Acting political head: Poul Nyrup Rasmussen (Prime Minister)

FAROE ISLANDS (Foroyar)
Capital: Thorshavn Official Language: Danish, Faroe Population: 0,1 million Square Km: 1399 Dialling code: +298 Acting political head: Edmund Joensen (Prime Minister)
GREENLAND (Kalaallit Nunaat)
Capital: Nuuk Official Language: Danish, Eskimo Population: 0,1 million Square Km: 2175600 Dialling code: +299 Acting political head: Jonathan Motzfeldt (Prime Minister)

Government / Corporate / Executive / VIP Aircraft Royal Danish Air Force / Kongelige Danske Flyvevaben uses the ICAO three letter code: DAF and ICAO call sign: DANISH AIR FORCE.

☐ C-066	Canadair CL-604 (CL-600-2B16) Challen.	5366	N604DD	0098	0698	2 GE CF34-3B	21909	VIP / mil trans		RDAF / lsf Canadair till 0699
☐ C-080	Canadair CL-604 (CL-600-2B16) Challen.	5380	C-GEGM*	0098		2 GE CF34-3B	21909	VIP / mil trans		RDAF / oo-delivery 0799
☐ F-249	GAC G-1159A Gulfstream SMA-3	249	N901GA*	0079	0482	2 RR Spey 511-8	30935	Surveyer/VIP/mil	DK-BH	Kongelige Danske Flyvevaben/RDAF
☐ F-313	GAC G-1159A Gulfstream SMA-3	313		0080	0482	2 RR Spey 511-8	30935	Surveyer/VIP/mil	DK-BJ	Kongelige Danske Flyvevaben/RDAF

AIR ALPHA, A/S = AHA (formerly Alpha Air, A/S) Odense

Odense Lufthavn 50, Box 630, DK-5270 Odense N, Denmark ☎ 65 95 54 54 Tx: none Fax: 65 95 54 76 SITA: n/a
F: 1986 35 Head: Poul Lübbert ICAO: AIR ALPHA Net: n/a Aircraft below MTOW 1361kg: Piper PA-28. Beside operating air-taxi/charter flights, Air Alpha now also acts as a Piper aircraft-dealer.

☐ OY-TUS	Pilatus PC-12/45	230	HB-FSY	0098	0199	1 PWC PT6A-67B	4500			
☐ OY-GRB	Beech King Air 200	BB-845	N486DC	0081		2 PWC PT6A-41	5670			lst BSF / Raisbeck mod.
☐ OY-JAO	Beech King Air 200	BB-401		0078	0394	2 PWC PT6A-41	5670			lst APW as SX-APJ
☐ OY-JAR	Beech King Air 200C	BL-13	PH-ILG	0080	0893	2 PWC PT6A-41	5670			lsf AL Aviation Leasing GmbH/sublst BSF
☐ OY-LKH	Beech King Air B200	BB-1325	G-KMCD	0089	0498	2 PWC PT6A-42	5670			lsf Rederiet Danstruplund A/S
☐ ZS-OFW	Learjet 31A	31A-031	N31HA	0091	1098	2 GA TFE731-2-3B	7484			lsf Foster Webb Air Charter
☐ OY-LJA	Learjet 35A	35A-594	N7007V	0084	1198	2 GA TFE731-2-2B	8301			lsf Lamburne Corp.
☐ OY-	Learjet 45	45-092				2 GA TFE731-20	9163			oo-delivery 0899
☐ OY-JKH	Learjet 60	60-141				2 PWC PW305A	10659			oo-delivery 0599

AIR ALPHA GREENLAND, A/S (Subsidiary of Air Alpha, A/S) Ilulissat

PO Box 1, DK-3952 Ilulissat, Greenland ☎ 94 30 04 Tx: none Fax: 94 34 00 SITA: n/a
F: 1994 16 Head: Poul Lübbert Net: http://www.airalphagreenland

☐ OY-HBF	Bell 206B JetRanger	1468		0074	0597	1 AN 250-C20	1451			
☐ OY-HDC	Agusta-Bell 206B JetRanger III	8499	SE-HGU	0075		1 AN 250-C20B	1451			lsf pvt / cvtd JetRanger
☐ OY-HII	Bell 206L-1 LongRanger III	45339	SE-HVH	0079	0598	1 AN 250-C30P	1882			lsf ABN Amro Leasing / cvtd LR II
☐ OY-HIA	Bell 222UT	47529	TC-HCS	0084	0198	2 LY LTS101-750C.1	3810			
☐ OY-HIB	Bell 222U	47519	D-HCED	0083	0598	2 LY LTS101-750C.1	3742			lsf ABN Ambro Leasing

AIR ALSIE, A/S = MMD Soenderborg

PO Box 240, Soenderborg Lufthavn, DK-6400 Soenderborg, Denmark ☎ 74 42 98 88 Tx: 52362 airals dk Fax: 74 43 42 82 SITA: n/a
F: 1988 38 Head: Jens Oesterlund ICAO: MERMAID Net: http://www.alsie.com

☐ OY-JMC	Cessna 525 CitationJet	525-0277	N277CJ	0098	1298	2 WRR FJ44-1A	4717	5 Pax		
☐ OY-CKT	Cessna 560 Citation V	560-0078	SE-DLI	0090	0593	2 PWC JT15D-5A	7212	10 Pax / EMS		
☐ OY-CCG	Cessna 650 Citation III	650-0003	N92LA	0083	0598	2 GA TFE731-3B-100S	9980	Executive		lsf / opf pvt
☐ OY-RAC	Hawker 800XP	258335	N335XP*	0097	1097	2 GA TFE731-5BR-1H	12701	9 Pax		lsf pvt
☐ OY-BDS	Dassault Falcon 20C-5	180	F-WMKF*	0070		2 GE TFE731-5BR-2C	13200	9 Pax / EMS		cvtd 20C / Danfoss-colors
☐ OY-CKN	Dassault Falcon 2000	76	F-WWML*	0098	0299	2 CFE CFE738-1-1B	16556	10 Pax		
☐ OY-LIN	Dassault Falcon 50	230	3B-NSY	0093	1297	3 GA TFE731-3-1C	18500	9 Pax / EMS		lsf pvt

AIR CENTER WEST = BDI (Sister company of Jetcopter & Training Center West/Subsidiary of Hangar 5 Airservice, ApS) Stauning

Hangar 5, Stauning Airport, DK-6900 Skjern, Denmark ☎ 97 36 92 06 Tx: none Fax: 97 36 96 10 SITA: n/a
F: 1990 6 Head: Bent Larsen ICAO: BIRDIE Net: http://www.daa.dk/air.center Aircraft below MTOW 1361kg: AA1, Cessna 172/182 & Piper PA-28.

☐ OY-DZW	Beech Travel Air D95A	TD-529	OE-FSA	0063		2 LY IO-360-B1B	1910			lsf pvt
☐ OY-PBA	Pilatus PC-6/B2-H4 Turbo Porter	678	LN-VIT	0068	0395	1 PWC PT6A-27	2800			lsf Alebco Corp. ApS
☐ OY-BYK	Cessna 421B Golden Eagle	421B0593	SE-IND	0074	0395	2 CO GTSIO-520-H	3379			lsf pvt
☐ OY-PBF	Cessna 208B Grand Caravan	208B0584	G-MART	0096	0497	1 PWC PT6A-114A	3969			lsf Alebco Corp. ApS
☐ OY-PBG	Reims/Cessna F406 Caravan II	F406-0015	G-TINI	0087	0998	2 PWC PT6A-112	4468			lsf Alebco Corp. ApS

487 registration type of aircraft cn/fn ex/ex* mfd del powered by mtow kg configuration selcal name/fln/specialitites/remarks

☐ OY-JEO	Fairchild (Swearingen) SA226TC Metro II	TC-318	N5476M	0079	0097	2 GA TPE331-10UA-511G	5670			lsf Bent Dall ApS
☐ OY-BZT	Cessna 550 Citation II	550-0259	N810JT	0081		2 PWC JT15D-4	6032			lsf Alebco Corp. ApS

AIR GATE, ApS
Roskilde

Lufthavnsvej 44, DK-4000 Roskilde, Denmark ☎ 46 19 14 22 Tx: none Fax: 46 19 14 74 SITA: n/a
F: 1993 👥 4 Head: Povl Michelsen Net: n/a Aircraft below MTOW 1361kg: Piper PA-28R

☐ OY-BSI	Piper PA-34-200 Seneca	34-7350334	OO-TNT	0073	0093	2 LY IO-360-C1E6	1905			
☐ OY-CFC	Cessna 414	414-0067	SE-GOT	0070	0299	2 CO TSIO-520-N	2880			

AIR TAXI DENMARK, A/S (formerly Air Denmark, A/S)
Roskilde

Norreskov Bakke 51, DK-8600 Silkeborg, Denmark ☎ 70 10 11 71 Tx: none Fax: 70 10 11 61 SITA: n/a
F: 1996 👥 2 Head: Ole Vadum Dahl Net: http://www.airtaxi.dk

☐ OY-OLE	Piper PA-31-350 Navajo Chieftain	31-7752061	PH-DAE	0077	1296	2 LY TIO-540-J2BD	3288			jtly opw Ikaros Fly

ATB, ApS
Sonderborg

Kaervej 98, DK-6400 Sonderborg, Denmark ☎ 74 42 08 78 Tx: none Fax: 74 42 15 78 SITA: n/a
F: 1995 👥 2 Head: Mogens Clausen Net: n/a

☐ OY-PCF	Piper PA-32-300C Cherokee SIX	32-40755	OH-PCF	0069	1095	1 LY IO-540-K1A5	1542	6 Pax / Cargo		

ATLANTIC AIRWAYS (Faroe Islands), P/F = RC / FLI
Faroe Islands-Vagar

Vagar Airport, FR-380 Soervagur, Faroe Islands ☎ 33 37 00 Tx: 82440 atlant fa Fax: 33 33 80 SITA: FAEADRC
F: 1987 👥 46 Head: Eydfinnur Jacobsen IATA: 767 ICAO: FAROELINE Net: n/a

☐ OY-HMB	Bell 212	30686	LN-OSR	0075	0494	2 PWC PT6T-3 TwinPac	5080	13 Pax		
☐ OY-CRG	BAe 146-200A	E2075	N369PS	0087	0388	4 LY ALF502R-5	42184	CY81		

AVIATION ASSISTANCE, A/S
Copenhagen-Roskilde

Kobenhavns Lufthavn Roskilde, DK-4000 Roskilde, Denmark ☎ 46 14 16 00 Tx: 22905 beech dk Fax: 46 14 16 01 SITA: n/a
F: 1991 👥 30 Head: Michael Burgess Net: n/a Aircraft below MTOW 1361kg: Bellanca 8KCAB & Piper PA-28

☐ OY-BVR	Beech Bonanza F33A	CE-1200		0087	1091	1 CO IO-520-BB	1542			
☐ OY-BVV	Beech Bonanza F33A	CE-1123		0087	1091	1 CO IO-520-BB	1542			occ lsf pvt
☐ OY-TFB	Beech Bonanza A36	E-3003	N821SA	0096	0497	1 CO IO-550-B	1656			
☐ OY-TFC	Beech Bonanza A36	E-3009	N1109Q	0096	0297	1 CO IO-550-B	1656			
☐ OY-TFD	Beech Bonanza A36	E-3013	N1113J	0096	0597	1 CO IO-550-B	1656			
☐ OY-TFE	Beech Bonanza A36	E-3034	N1096Y	0096	0297	1 CO IO-550-B	1656			
☐ OY-BTR	Beech King Air 200	BB-211	LN-ASI	0076	0493	2 PWC PT6A-41	5670			lsf pvt/sub-lst Air Bateleur as 5Y-BMC
☐ OY-BVB	Beech King Air 200	BB-419	N256EN	0079	1091	2 PWC PT6A-41	5670			lsf pvt
☐ OY-BVE	Beech King Air 200C	BL-2	N690G	0079	1091	2 PWC PT6A-41	5670			lsf pvt/sub-lst Air Bateleur as 5Y-EKO
☐ OY-CBP	Beech King Air 200	BB-235	N9BK	0078	1091	2 PWC PT6A-41	5670			lsf pvt
☐ OY-GEB	Beech King Air B200C	BL-40	VH-NSR	0081	0792	2 PWC PT6A-42	5670			lsf pvt
☐ OY-GEH	Beech King Air 200C	BB-155	SE-GHS	0076	0195	2 PWC PT6A-41	5670			lst Air Bateleur as 5Y-BMA/cvtd K.A.200
☐ OY-GRB	Beech King Air 200	BB-845	N486DC	0081	0096	2 PWC PT6A-41	5670			lsf AHA / Raisbeck mod.
☐ OY-JAR	Beech King Air 200C	BL-13	PH-ILG	0080	0096	2 PWC PT6A-41	5670			lsf AHA
☐ OY-GER	Beech 1300 Airliner	BB-1343	VT-SAF	0089	0998	2 PWC PT6A-42	5670			lsf Rayth./lst AirBatel.5Y-ECO/cvtdB200
☐ OY-GES	Beech 1300 Airliner	BB-1305	VT-SAB	0089	0199	2 PWC PT6A-42	5670			lsf Rayth./lst AirBatel.5Y-EOB/cvtdB200
☐ OY-GEU	Beech 1300 Airliner	BB-1341	VT-SAD	0089	0498	2 PWC PT6A-42	5670			lsf Raytheon / cvtd King Air B200
☐ OY-GEW	Beech 1300 Airliner	BB-1342	VT-SAE	0089	0498	2 PWC PT6A-42	5670			lsf Raytheon / cvtd King Air B200
☐ OY-GIG	Beech King Air 350 (B300)	FL-167		0097	0897	2 PWC PT6A-60A	6804			lsf pvt
☐ OY-MEN	Beech King Air 350 (B300)	FL-229	N9WV	0098	0399	2 PWC PT6A-60A	6804			lsf pvt
☐ OY-BVI	Beech 1900C-1 Airliner	UC-55	OK-UEA	0089	0196	2 PWC PT6A-65B	7530			lsf pvt/sub-lst Air Bateleur as 5Y-BVI
☐ OY-GEG	Beech 1900C-1 Airliner	UC-132	N55201	0090	0294	2 PWC PT6A-65B	7530			lsf Raytheon Credit
☐ OY-GEN	Beech 1900C Airliner	UB-4	SE-KSX	0084	0096	2 PWC PT6A-65B	7530			lsf pvt

BILLUND AIR CENTER, A/S = BIL
Billund

Postboks 6, Lufthavnsvej 43, DK-7190 Billund, Denmark ☎ 75 33 89 07 Tx: none Fax: 75 35 39 66 SITA: n/a
F: 1990 👥 7 Head: Pia Bragen ICAO: BILAIR Net: n/a Aircraft below MTOW 1361kg: Cessna 172 & Piper PA-28

☐ OY-PEM	Piper PA-44-180 Seminole	44-8195020	N333X	0081	0093	2 LY O-360-E1A6D	1724			
☐ OY-SUR	Partenavia P.68 Observer	246-04-OB	D-GEMG	0081	0097	2 LY IO-360-A1B6	1990	Survey/Photo		lsf / opf Bio Consult A/S
☐ OY-BZN	Cessna 421C Golden Eagle II	421C0045	SE-INC	0075	0394	2 CO GTSIO-520-L	3379			lsf Air Service Int'l A/S
☐ OY-PHN	Dassault Falcon 100	209	HB-VKR	0086	0498	2 GA TFE731-2-1C	8755			lsf Pharma-Nord

BILLUND FLY (Billund Rundflyvning, ApS dba)
Billund

Moelleparken 180, DK-7190 Billund, Denmark ☎ 75 33 82 17 Tx: n/a Fax: none SITA: n/a
F: n/a 👥 n/a Head: Mogens Anker Net: n/a Aircraft below MTOW 1361kg: Cessna 172.

☐ OY-SUC	Cessna 207A Stationair 8 II	20700781	N9999M	0084		1 CO IO-520-F	1724			

CENTER FLIGHT, ApS (Center Air)
Roskilde

Hangarvej A4, Kobenhavens Lufthavn, DK-4000 Roskilde, Denmark ☎ 46 19 19 19 Tx: none Fax: 46 19 08 37 SITA: n/a
F: 1988 👥 3 Head: Jens Kristian Frost Net: n/a Aircraft below MTOW 1361kg: Piper PA-28 Training flights/school is operated under the name CENTER AIR, ApS (a sister company, same fleet/headquarters).

☐ OY-FRA	Piper PA-34-200 Seneca	34-7250017	G-AZJB	0071		2 LY IO-360-C1E6	1905			lsf pvt
☐ OY-RAV	Cessna 340A II Rob. STOL/RAM	340A0716	N98976	0079		2 CO TSIO-520-NB	2898			lsf Stig Ravns A/S
☐ OY-SAV	Cessna 402B	402B0201		0071		2 CO TSIO-520-E	2858			jtly opw Kampsax Geoplan
☐ OY-SUN	Cessna 402C II	402C0461	ZS-KUU	0081		2 CO TSIO-520-VB	3107			jtly opw Kampsax Geoplan

CIMBER AIR, A/S = QI / CIM (formerly Cimber Air Service)
Soenderborg

Soenderborg Lufthavn, DK-6400 Soenderborg, Denmark ☎ 74 42 22 77 Tx: 52315 eksbqi dk Fax: 74 42 65 11 SITA: SGDADQI
F: 1946 👥 280 Head: Jorgen Nielsen IATA: 647 ICAO: CIMBER Net: n/a

☐ OY-FFB	Cessna 501 Citation I/SP	500-0406	SE-DET	0081	0992	2 PWC JT15D-1A	5375	Corporate		cvtd Cessna 500
☐ OY-CIB	ATR 42-300	007	F-WWEC*	0086	0286	2 PWC PW120	16150	Y46		op in Team Lufthansa colors
☐ OY-CID	ATR 42-300	079	D-BATA	0088	0388	2 PWC PW120	16700	Y46		
☐ OY-CIE	ATR 42-300	082	D-BATB	0088	0388	2 PWC PW120	16700	Y46		
☐ OY-CIG	ATR 42-300	019	YU-ALK	0086	1290	2 PWC PW120	16700	Y46		
☐ OY-CIH	ATR 42-300	238	F-WWEC*	0091	0491	2 PWC PW120	16700	Y50		
☐ OY-CIJ	ATR 42-500	497	F-WWLR*	0096	0396	2 PWC PW127E	18600	Y46		
☐ OY-CIK	ATR 42-500	501	F-WWEE*	0096	0496	2 PWC PW127E	18600	Y46		
☐ OY-CIL	ATR 42-500	514	F-WWLO*	0096	1196	2 PWC PW127E	18600	Y46		
☐ OY-CIR	ATR 42-300	107	F-GHPX	0088	1096	2 PWC PW120	16700	Y46		lsf GECA
☐ OY-CIS	ATR 42-300	161	EI-BYO	0089	1196	2 PWC PW120	16700	Y46		lsf GECA
☐ OY-CIT	ATR 42-300	196	C-FZVZ	0090	0397	2 PWC PW120	16700	Y48		lsf GECA
☐ OY-CIU	ATR 42-300	112	C-FIQB	0088	1097	2 PWC PW120	16700	Y48		lsf GECA
☐ OY-CIM	ATR 72-500 (72-212A)	468	F-WWLV*	0099	0299	2 PWC PW127F	22500	Y70		
☐ OY-CIN	ATR 72-500 (72-212A)	568	F-WWEH*	0099	0399	2 PWC PW127F	22500	Y70		

COPENHAGEN AIRTAXI, A/S = CAT (Associated with Copenhagen Aviation Trading, A/S)
Copenhagen-Roskilde

Kobenhavns Lufthavn, Lufthavnsvej 20, DK-4000 Roskilde, Denmark ☎ 46 19 11 14 Tx: 43234 aircat dk Fax: 46 19 11 15 SITA: n/a
F: 1961 👥 10 Head: Kenneth A. Larsen ICAO: AIRCAT Net: n/a Light single engine aircraft mainly used for training & trading: SOCATA TB9, TB10, TB20, Cessna 172 / 182 & Piper PA-28

☐ OY-ASW	Piper PA-34-200T Seneca II	34-7670105	D-ILBI	0076		2 CO TSIO-360-E	1999			
☐ OY-CAA	Partenavia P.68B	48		0075		2 LY IO-360-A1B6	1990			
☐ OY-CAB	Partenavia P.68B	72		0076		2 LY IO-360-A1B6	1990			lsf FLS Overseas A/S
☐ OY-CAC	Partenavia P.68B	179		0079		2 LY IO-360-A1B6	1990			
☐ OY-CDC	Partenavia P.68C	211	D-GEMD	0080	0098	2 LY IO-360-A1B6	1990			lsf FLS Real Estate A/S
☐ OY-AUH	Piper PA-31-310 Navajo C	31-7512072	LN-PAB	0075		2 LY TIO-540-A2C	2948			
☐ OY-CFV	Britten-Norman BN-2B-27 Islander	2174	G-BKOK	0084	1297	2 LY O-540-E4C5	2994			
☐ OY-CKA	Piper PA-31P Pressurized Navajo	31P-7300136	N150TT	0073		2 LY TIGO-541-E1A	3538			lsf pvt

DANISH AIR SURVEY, ApS
Copenhagen-Roskilde

Abjergvej 10D, DK-2720 Vanloese, Denmark ☎ 38 79 19 92 Tx: none Fax: 38 79 28 28 SITA: n/a
F: 1983 👥 2 Head: Leif Petersen Net: n/a

☐ OY-CAG	Partenavia P.68 Observer	243-03-OB		0081		2 LY IO-360-A1B6	1990	Surveyer		

DANISH DAKOTA FRIENDS (Foreningen For Flyvende Museumsfly/Club for flying museum aircraft dba)
Vaerloese Air Base

c/o John V. Blaagreen, Rusgaards Bakke 44, DK-4100 Ringsted, Denmark ☎ 57 52 56 95 Tx: none Fax: 48 30 33 63 SITA: n/a
F: 1992 👥 31 Head: John V. Blaagreen Net: http://home6.inet.tele.dk/dakota-d Non-commercial flying club conducting historical DC-3 flights.

☐ OY-BPB	Boeing (Douglas) DC-3C (C-47A-85-DL)	20019	K-682	0044	0892	2 PW R-1830	11454	19 Pax		DC-3 Vennerne / RDAF-colors

DAT - Danish Air Transport, K/S = DX / DTR
Vamdrup-Kolding

PO Box 80, DK-6580 Vamdrup, Denmark ☎ 75 58 37 77 Tx: none Fax: 75 58 37 22 SITA: n/a
F: 1989 👥 40 Head: Jesper Rungholm ICAO: DANISH Net: http://www.dat.dk Aircraft below MTOW 1361kg: Cessna 195 & Lake LA4-200

☐ OY-PAB	Reims/Cessna F406 Caravan II	F406-0034	PH-PHO	0088	1098	2 PWC PT6A-112	4468	Y12		lsf Muninn Aviation K/S
☐ OY-PEU	Reims/Cessna F406 Caravan II	F406-0045	5Y-LAN	0089	0997	2 PWC PT6A-112	4468	Freighter		lsf NAC Nordic Aviation Contractor A/S
☐ OY-BVS	Beech King Air B90	LJ-418	SE-LEN	0068	1197	2 PWC PT6A-20	4377	Y8		

488 registration type of aircraft cn/fn ex/ex* mfd del powered by mtow kg configuration selcal name/fln/specialitites/remarks

☐ OY-JRO	Beech King Air B90 (CargoLiner)	LJ-327	N827K	0068	0891	2 PWC PT6A-20	4377	Freighter		cvtd B90 / large cargodoors
☐ OY-CPW	Cessna 501 Citation I/SP	501-0120	N487LS	0079	1293	2 PWC JT15D-1A	5375	Y6		
☐ OY-JRN	Beech King Air 200	BB-364	F-GHYV	0078	0198	2 PWC PT6A-41	5670	Y10		
☐ OY-JRK	Shorts Skyvan 3 Variant 100 (SC-7)	SH1901	N8117V	0072	0489	2 GA TPE331-2-201A	5670	Freighter		
☐ OY-JRL	Shorts Skyvan 3 Var.100 (SC-7) Super-2	SH1854	EI-BNN	0069	0890	2 GA TPE331-2-201A	5670	Freighter		lsf pvt / cvtd Variant 100
☐ OY-JRF	Beech 1900C Airliner	UB-66	F-GTOT	0086	0997	2 PWC PT6A-65B	7530	Y19		lsf pvt
☐ OY-JRV	Beech 1900D Airliner	UE-338	N23381*	0098	1298	2 PWC PT6A-67D	7688	Y19		lsf pvt
☐ OY-JRT	Embraer 120ER Brasilia (EMB-120ER)	120014	F-WQGG	0086	1197	2 PWC PW118	11990	Y30		cvtd 120RT
☐ G-RUNG	Saab SF340A	340A-086	F-GGBV	0087	0697	2 GE CT7-5A2	12700	Y33		lst GNT
☐ OY-JRJ	ATR 42-320	036	F-WQIS	0086	0599	2 PWC PW121	16700	Y46		cvtd -300

EXECUJET SCANDINAVIA, A/S

Copenhagen-Roskilde

Hangarvej H11, Copenhagen Airport Roskilde, DK-4000 Roskilde, Denmark ☎ 46 14 15 16 Tx: none Fax: 46 14 15 17 SITA: n/a

F: 1997 ✱✱✱ 11 Head: Christian Gravengaard Net: http://www.execujet.co.za/ Sales agent for Bombardier Aerospace & Pilatus, EXECUJET intends to start own AOC charter operations with 5 Executive-aircraft during 1999.

GROENLANDSFLY, A/S = GL / GRL (Greenlandair, Inc. / GLACE-Greenlandair Charter) (Subs.of Danish & Greenland Gvmts & Scandinavian Airlines SAS)

Nuuk

Box 1012, DK-3900 Nuuk, Greenland ☎ 28 888 Tx: none Fax: 27 288 SITA: n/a

F: 1960 ✱✱✱ 410 Head: Jonathon Motzfeldt IATA: 631 ICAO: GREENLANDAIR Net: http://www.greenland-guide.dk/gla/ Aircraft below MTOW 1361 kg: Cessna 172P & Piper PA-18.

Charter services are operated under the name GLACE – Greenlandair Charter (same fleet & headquarters).

☐ OY-HGB	MD Helicopters MD 500D (Hughes 369D)	1146D	CS-HCI	0082	0695	1 AN 250-C20B	1361			
☐ OY-HGD	MD Helicopters MD 500D (Hughes 369D)	480294D	SE-JBU	0078	0696	1 AN 250-C20B	1361			
☐ OY-HGE	MD Helicopters MD 500D (Hughes 369D)	470112D	D-HOLG	0077	0696	1 AN 250-C20B	1361			
☐ OY-HGF	MD Helicopters MD 500D (Hughes 369D)	980347D	D-HILS	0078	0696	1 AN 250-C20B	1361			
☐ OY-HEL	Eurocopter (Aerosp.) AS350B2 Ecureuil	2616		0092		1 TU Arriel 1D1	2250			
☐ OY-HEY	Eurocopter (Aerosp.) AS350B2 Ecureuil	2904	N4027Q	0096	1097	1 TU Arriel 1D1	2250			lsf Roberts Aircraft Co.
☐ OY-HGA	Eurocopter (Aerosp.) AS350B2 Ecureuil	2600		0092		1 TU Arriel 1D1	2250			
☐ OY-HGJ	Eurocopter (Aerosp.) AS350B2 Ecureuil	2401	C-GHMD	0090	0596	1 TU Arriel 1D1	2250			lsf ABN Amro Leasing
☐ OY-HGK	Eurocopter (Aerosp.) AS350B2 Ecureuil	2570	C-FNJW	0091	0596	1 TU Arriel 1D1	2250			lsf ABN Amro Leasing
☐ OY-HGL	Eurocopter (Aerosp.) AS350B2 Ecureuil	2950	N4074E	0096	0298	1 TU Arriel 1D1	2250			lsf Roberts Aircraft Co.
☐ OY-HGH	Bell 407	53008	SE-JCL*	0096	0496	1 AN 250-C47B	2268			
☐ OY-HCU	Bell 212	31155		0081	0081	2 PWC PT6T-3B TwinPac	5080			Piivi / lst HHH as EC-GLS
☐ OY-HCY	Bell 212	31166		0081	0081	2 PWC PT6T-3B TwinPac	5080			Piseeq / Pop-out Floats
☐ OY-HDM	Bell 212	31142	N57545	0080	0091	2 PWC PT6T-3B TwinPac	5080			Pop-out Floats
☐ OY-HDN	Bell 212	31136	N5752K	0080	0087	2 PWC PT6T-3B TwinPac	5080			Miteq / Pop-out Floats
☐ OY-HMD	Bell 212	31125		0080	0693	2 PWC PT6T-3B TwinPac	5080			lsf DNK Leasing GroupLtd/Pop-out Floats
☐ OY-NUK	Beech King Air 200	BB-634	N101CP	0080	0596	2 PWC PT6A-41	5670			
☐ OY-ATY	De Havilland DHC-6 Twin Otter 300	561	C-GRZH-X*	0077	0178	2 PWC PT6A-27	6350	Surveyer		Naaja / Ice-Patrol
☐ OY-POF	De Havilland DHC-6 Twin Otter 300	235	N6868	0069	1176	2 PWC PT6A-27	5670			Bulk fuel hauling-provision
☐ OY-HAF	Sikorsky S-61N	61267	N10045	0065	0065	2 GE CT58-140-1	9299	Y25		Nattoralik
☐ OY-HAG	Sikorsky S-61N	61268	N10046	0065	0065	2 GE CT58-140-1	9299	Y25		Kussak
☐ OY-HAH	Sikorsky S-61N	61365		0068	0068	2 GE CT58-140-1	9299	Y25		Tulugaq
☐ OY-HDO	Sikorsky S-61N	61740	LN-OSU	0075	1193	2 GE CT58-140-2	9299	Y25		lsf HKS
☐ OY-CBT	De Havilland DHC-7-103 Dash 7	010	C-GRQB*	0079	0279	4 PWC PT6A-50	19958	Y50/Combi/Frtr		Papikkaaq
☐ OY-CBU	De Havilland DHC-7-103 Dash 7	020		0080	0280	4 PWC PT6A-50	19958	Y50/Combi/Frtr		Nipiki
☐ OY-CTC	De Havilland DHC-7-102 Dash 7	101	G-BNDC	0084	0588	4 PWC PT6A-50	19958	Y50		Minniki
☐ OY-GRD	De Havilland DHC-7-103 Dash 7	009	A6-ALM	0078	1094	4 PWC PT6A-50	19958	Y50/Combi/Frtr		
☐ OY-GRE	De Havilland DHC-7-103 Dash 7	106	N54026	0085	0398	4 PWC PT6A-50	19958	Y50/Combi/Frtr		
☐ TF-GRL	Boeing 757-236	25620 / 449	G-CSVS	0092	0598	2 RR RB211-535E4	113398	CY209	AQ-EM	Kunuunnguaq / lsf FIH Lsng/lst/opb ICE

HELI-FLIGHT EAST, ApS

Copenhagen-Roskilde

Hangarvej 12, DK-4000 Roskilde, Denmark ☎ 46 19 00 11 Tx: none Fax: 46 19 08 05 SITA: n/a

F: 1990 ✱✱✱ 2 Head: John Rosasco Net: n/a Aircraft below MTOW 1361kg: Robinson R22/R22M & R44.

☐ OY-HHT	Bell 206B JetRanger III	3128	G-BWBX	0080	0096	1 AN 250-C20B	1451			lsf pvt

HELIKOPTER-SERVICE, A/S

Copenhagen-Roskilde

Lufthavnsvej 32, Roskilde Lufthavn, DK-4000 Roskilde, Denmark ☎ 46 19 15 11 Tx: n/a Fax: 46 19 15 33 SITA: n/a

F: 1993 ✱✱✱ 2 Head: Peter K. Hansen Net: n/a Aircraft below MTOW 1361kg: Hughes 269C (300C)

☐ OY-HSH	Bell 206L LongRanger	45014	SE-HOL	0075		1 AN 250-C20B	1815			

IKAROS FLY, ApS = IKR

Copenhagen-Roskilde

Hangarvej A12, Kobenhavns Lufthavn, DK-4000 Roskilde, Denmark ☎ 46 19 10 10 Tx: n/a Fax: 46 19 05 15 SITA: n/a

F: 1981 ✱✱✱ 10 Head: Claus L.A. Thomsen ICAO: IKAROS Net: http://www.ikaros.dk Aircraft below MTOW 1361 kg: AA1, Cessna 172, 177RG, Piper PA-28 & PA-28R

☐ OY-BVU	Beech Bonanza F33A	CE-1139		0087		1 CO IO-520-BB	1542			lsf Piko Fly I/S
☐ OY-ASJ	Beech Travel Air D95A	TD-541	SE-EEX	0063		2 LY IO-360-B1B	1905	3 Pax		lsf Flyudlejning ApS
☐ OY-ELK	Piper PA-31-350 Navajo Panther II	31-8252028	N803DM	0082	0995	2 LY TIO-540-J2BD	3265	8 Pax		lsf pvt / cvtd Navajo Chieftain
☐ OY-OLE	Piper PA-31-350 Navajo Chieftain	31-7752061	PH-DAE	0077	1296	2 LY TIO-540-J2BD	3288			jtly opw Air Taxi Denmark

JETAIR FLIGHT ACADEMY (Peva Management dba)

Copenhagen-Roskilde

Lufthavnsvej 50, DK-4000 Roskilde, Denmark ☎ 46 19 15 55 Tx: none Fax: 46 19 16 50 SITA: n/a

F: 1996 ✱✱✱ 2 Head: Peter Slaatorn Net: n/a

☐ OY-MST	Piper PA-31-310 Navajo B	31-7300967	G-BNDD	0073		2 LY TIO-540-A2C	2948	PollutionPatrol		lsfpvt/opf Danish Environment Pr.Agency

JETCOPTER = JCP (Sister company of Air Center West/Subsidiary of Hangar 5 Airservice, ApS)

Stauning

Stauning Airport, DK-6900 Skjern, Denmark ☎ 97 36 92 66 Tx: none Fax: 97 36 92 10 SITA: n/a

F: 1990 ✱✱✱ 16 Head: Peter Bennedsen ICAO: JETCOPTER Net: http://www.benair.com Aircraft below MTOW 1361kg: Cessna 172 & Hughes 269C (300C)

☐ OY-HDD	Bell 206B JetRanger III	3649	N130S	0082		1 AN 250-C20B	1451			
☐ N109PB	Agusta A109A II	7344	OH-HEI	0085	0793	2 AN 250-C20B	2600			lsf Alebco Corp. Trustee

KALUNDBORG LUFTFART (Egon Kargaard Soerensen dba)

Kalundborg

Kalundborg Flyveplads, DK-4593 Eskebjerg, Denmark ☎ 59 29 11 23 Tx: none Fax: 59 29 28 27 SITA: n/a

F: 1973 ✱✱✱ 1 Head: Egon Kargaard Soerensen Net: n/a Aircraft below MTOW 1361kg: Piper PA-28.

☐ OY-BCR	Piper PA-32-260 Cherokee SIX	32-838	N3892W	0067		1 LY O-540-E4B5	1542			

KAMPSAX GEOPLAN - Aerial Photo/Survey (Subsidiary of Kampsax A/S & Sun-Air of Scandinavia A/S)

Copenhagen-Roskilde

Stamholmen 112, DK-2650 Hvidovre, Denmark ☎ 36 39 09 00 Tx: none Fax: 36 77 24 21 SITA: n/a

F: 1960 ✱✱✱ 120 Head: Ule Valbjörn Net: n/a

☐ OY-SAV	Cessna 402B	402B0201		0071		2 CO TSIO-520-E	2858	Photo/Survey		jtly opw Center Flight
☐ OY-SUN	Cessna 402C II	402C0461	ZS-KUU	0081	0295	2 CO TSIO-520-VB	3107	Photo/Survey		jtly opw Center Flight

KARLOG AIR, A/S = KLG

Sonderborg

Veesbaek 1, Sonderborg Lufthavn, DK-6400 Sonderborg, Denmark ☎ 74 42 22 85 Tx: none Fax: 74 42 90 85 SITA: n/a

F: 1994 ✱✱✱ 5 Head: Henning Karlog Mortensen ICAO: KARLOG Net: n/a Aircraft below MTOW 1361kg: Cessna 150, 152, 172 & 182.

☐ OY-AJI	Piper PA-34-200 Seneca	34-7250312		0072	0097	2 LY IO-360-C1E6	1905			lsf pvt

KLIPPEFLY, I/S

Roenne

Roenne Lufthavn, S. Landevej 2, DK-3700 Roenne, Denmark ☎ 56 95 35 73 Tx: n/a Fax: 56 95 22 54 SITA: n/a

F: 1972 ✱✱✱ 6 Head: Kaj Munk Net: http://www.europage.dk/bornholm/klippefly Aircraft below MTOW 1361 kg: Cessna 172, KZ III & KZ VII.

☐ OY-ECI	Piper PA-32-260 Cherokee SIX	32-7300024	LN-BNR	0073		1 LY O-540-E4B5	1542			

KORTFLY, K/S

Copenhagen-Roskilde

Brodersens Alle 3, DK-2900 Hellerup, Denmark ☎ 31 62 73 33 Tx: n/a Fax: 31 62 64 80 SITA: n/a

F: 1970 ✱✱✱ 45 Head: Erik H. Petersen Net: n/a

☐ OY-DJV	Partenavia P.68B	22		0074		2 LY IO-360-A1B6	1960	Photo		
☐ OY-BHF	Piper PA-31-310 Navajo	31-245	G-BXAZ	0068		2 LY TIO-540-A1A	2948	Photo		

MAERSK AIR, A/S = DM / DAN (Member of A.P. Moeller Group / formerly Maersk Air I/S)

Copenhagen-Kastrup & Esbjerg

Copenhagen Airport South, DK-2791 Dragoer, Denmark ☎ 32 31 44 44 Tx: 31125 dmair dk Fax: 32 31 44 90 SITA: CPHDSDM

F: 1969 ✱✱✱ 1250 Head: Ole Dietz IATA: 349 ICAO: MAERSKAIR Net: http://www.maersk-air.com

☐ OY-APM	Canadair CL-601-3R (CL-600-2B16) Challen.	5153	N604BA	0094	1297	2 GE CF34-3A1	20457	Executive		
☐ OY-MMI	Fokker 50 (F27 Mk050)	20126	PH-EXK*	0088	0788	2 PWC PW125B	20820	Y56		lsf Greyhound Fin./sub-lst EEL, ES-AFK
☐ OY-MMJ	Fokker 50 (F27 Mk050)	20127	PH-EXL*	0088	0788	2 PWC PW125B	20820	Y56		lsf Greyhound Fin./sub-lst ELL, ES-AFL
☐ OY-MMS	Fokker 50 (F27 Mk050)	20148	PH-EXU*	0089	0289	2 PWC PW125B	20820	Y56		lsf Finova Capital Ltd -0400
☐ OY-APA	Boeing 737-5L9	28083 / 2784		0096	0496	2 CFMI CFM56-3C1	54884	CY104		lst ELL as ES-ABE
☐ OY-APB	Boeing 737-5L9	28084 / 2788		0096	0496	2 CFMI CFM56-3C1	54884	CY114		lst MSK as G-MSKE
☐ OY-APC	Boeing 737-5L9	28129 / 2823		0096	1096	2 CFMI CFM56-3C1	50938	CY104	JQ-AM	
☐ OY-APD	Boeing 737-5L9	28130 / 2825		0096	1096	2 CFMI CFM56-3C1	50938	CY104		
☐ OY-APG	Boeing 737-5L9	28131 / 2828		0096	1196	2 CFMI CFM56-3C1	50938	CY104		
☐ OY-APH	Boeing 737-5L9	28721 / 2856		0097	0297	2 CFMI CFM56-3C1	54884	CY104	DM-BS	
☐ OY-API	Boeing 737-5L9	28722 / 2868		0097	0397	2 CFMI CFM56-3C1	54884	CY104	FS-BE	
☐ OY-APK	Boeing 737-5L9	28995 / 2947		1097	1097	2 CFMI CFM56-3C1	50938	CY104	MQ-HP	

489 registration type of aircraft cn/fn ex/ex* mfd del powered by mtow kg configuration selcal name/fln/specialitites/remarks

registration	type of aircraft	cn/fn	ex/ex*	mfd	del	powered by	mtow kg	configuration	selcal	name/fln/specialitites/remarks
☐ OY-APL	Boeing 737-5L9	28996 / 2998		0098	0298	2 CFMI CFM56-3C1	50938	CY104		
☐ OY-APN	Boeing 737-5L9	28997 / 3008		0098	0398	2 CFMI CFM56-3C1	50938	CY104		
☐ OY-APP	Boeing 737-5L9	29234 / 3068	N1786B*	0898	0898	2 CFMI CFM56-3C1	50938	CY104		
☐ OY-APR	Boeing 737-5L9	29235 / 3076	N1786B*	0098	1098	2 CFMI CFM56-3C1	50938	CY104		
☐ OY-MAA	Boeing 737-5L9	24778 / 1816		0090	0490	2 CFMI CFM56-3B1	55566	CY114	MS-BQ	lst MSK as G-MSKD
☐ OY-MAE	Boeing 737-5L9	25066 / 2038		0091	0591	2 CFMI CFM56-3B1	55566	CY114	CR-GP	lst MSK as G-MSKC
☐ OY-MAF	Boeing 737-5L9	28128 / 2817		0096	0996	2 CFMI CFM56-3C1	50938	CY104	JQ-AK	lsf F. Salling A/S
☐ OY-MAL	Boeing 737-3L9	26441 / 2250		0092	0392	2 CFMI CFM56-3B2	62822	Y136		lsf PEMB -1099 / sub-lst BAG,D-ADBA
☐ OY-MAM	Boeing 737-3L9	26442 / 2277		0092	0592	2 CFMI CFM56-3B2	63276	Y136	BR-AM	lsf INGO -1099 / sub-lst BAG, D-ADBC
☐ OY-MAO	Boeing 737-3L9	27336 / 2587		0094	0394	2 CFMI CFM56-3C1	58849	Y136		lsf Heller Fin.-0101/sub-lst BAG,D-ADBH
☐ OY-MAP	Boeing 737-3L9	27337 / 2594		0094	0394	2 CFMI CFM56-3C1	58849	Y136		lsf Heller Fin.-0401/sub-lst BAG,D-ADBI
☐ OY-MRA	Boeing 737-7L9	28004 / 10	N35153*	0097	0398	2 CFMI CFM56-7B22	69399	Y145	DM-AR	
☐ OY-MRB	Boeing 737-7L9	28005 / 11	N35161*	0098	0398	2 CFMI CFM56-7B22	69399	Y145	DM-BR	
☐ OY-MRC	Boeing 737-7L9	28006 / 26	N5573K*	0098	0598	2 CFMI CFM56-7B22	69399	Y145		
☐ OY-MRD	Boeing 737-7L9	28007 / 136	N1786B*	0098	1198	2 CFMI CFM56-7B22	69399	Y145		
☐ OY-MRE	Boeing 737-7L9	28008 / 203	N1786B*	0099	0299	2 CFMI CFM56-7B22	69399	Y145		
☐ OY-MRF	Boeing 737-7L9	28009 / 221	N1787B*	0099	0399	2 CFMI CFM56-7B22	69399	Y145		
☐ OY-MRG	Boeing 737-7L9					2 CFMI CFM56-7B22	69399	Y148		oo-delivery 1099
☐ OY-	Boeing 737-7L9					2 CFMI CFM56-7B22	69399	Y148		oo-delivery 0000
☐ OY-	Boeing 737-7L9					2 CFMI CFM56-7B22	69399	Y148		oo-delivery 0001
☐ OY-	Boeing 737-7L9					2 CFMI CFM56-7B22	69399	Y148		oo-delivery 0001
☐ OY-	Boeing 737-7L9					2 CFMI CFM56-7B22	69399	Y148		oo-delivery 0002
☐ OY-	Boeing 737-7L9					2 CFMI CFM56-7B22	69399	Y148		oo-delivery 0002

MAERSK HELICOPTERS (Sister company of Maersk Air & Member of A.P. Moeller Group) **Esbjerg**

Esbjerg Airport, John Tranumsvej, DK-6705 Esbjerg East, Denmark ☎ 75 16 03 88 Tx: none Fax: 75 16 03 24 SITA: n/a

F: 1975 ⁂ 85 Head: Jan Hagemann Net: n/a

☐ OY-HMW	Eurocopter (Aerosp.) AS365N2 Dauphin 2	6448	F-WYMR*	0093	0893	2 TU Arriel 1C2	4250	11 Pax		lsf Danbor Service A/S
☐ OY-HMY	Eurocopter (Aerosp.) AS365N2 Dauphin 2	6446	F-WYMN*	0093	0993	2 TU Arriel 1C2	4250	11 Pax		lsf Danbor Service A/S
☐ OY-HMH	Eurocopter (Aerosp.) AS332L Super Puma	2053	LN-OME	0083	0591	2 TU Makila 1A	8600	18 Pax		lsf HKS
☐ OY-HMI	Eurocopter (Aerosp.) AS332L Super Puma	2103	LN-OLD	0084	1295	2 TU Makila 1A	8600	18 Pax		lsf HKS
☐ OY-HMJ	Eurocopter (Aerosp.) AS332L Super Puma	2082	LN-OLB	0083	0596	2 TU Makila 1A	8600	18 Pax		lsf HKS

MUK AIR, A/S = ZR / MUK (formerly Muk Air & Muk Air Taxi) **Copenhagen-Kastrup**

Copenhagen Airport, DK-2791 Dragoer, Denmark ☎ 32 82 00 00 Tx: none Fax: 32 82 00 79 SITA: CPHHQZR

F: 1979 ⁂ 120 Head: Capt. Knut Lindau IATA: 796 ICAO: MUKAIR Net: http://www.mukair.dk

☐ OY-ASY	Embraer 110P1 Bandeirante (EMB-110P1)	110308	EI-BPI	0080	0493	2 PWC PT6A-34	5670	Y18 / Frtr		
☐ OY-BHT	Embraer 110P2 Bandeirante (EMB-110P2)	110161	N4942S	0077	0486	2 PWC PT6A-34	5670	Y18 / Frtr		
☐ OY-BNM	Embraer 110P2 Bandeirante (EMB-110P2)	110200	N892AC	0078	0287	2 PWC PT6A-34	5670	Y18 / Frtr		
☐ OY-MUA	Embraer 110P1 Bandeirante (EMB-110P1)	110263	N431A	0080	1188	2 PWC PT6A-34	5670	Y18 / Frtr		
☐ OY-MUE	BAe 3100 Jetstream 31	758	G-BTAI	0087	0995	2 GA TPE331-10UGR-514H	6950	Y18		
☐ OY-MUB	Shorts 330-200 (SD3-30)	SH3069	G-BITX	0081	0490	2 PWC PT6A-45R	10387	Y30 / Frtr		
☐ OY-MMA	Shorts 360-200 (SD3-60)	SH3632	EI-BYU	0083	0693	2 PWC PT6A-65AR	11999	Y35 / Frtr		
☐ OY-MUD	Shorts 360-200 (SD3-60)	SH3692	N693PC	0086	0695	2 PWC PT6A-65AR	11999	Y35 / Frtr		lsf Security Pacific Equipment Leasing
☐ OY-MUG	Shorts 360-300 (SD3-60)	SH3716	G-BNDM	0087	1097	2 PWC PT6A-67R	12292	Y35 / Frtr		
☐ OY-MUK	ATR 42-300	176	EI-CBF	0090	0499	2 PWC PW120	16700	Y48		lsf GECA

NEWAIR Airservice = NAW **Billund**

Billund Lufthavn, DK-7190 Billund, Denmark ☎ 75 35 47 45 Tx: none Fax: 75 33 23 03 SITA: n/a

F: 1977 ⁂ 35 Head: Per Arpe ICAO: NEWDAN Net: n/a

☐ OY-EBC	Fokker F27 Friendship 200 (F27 Mk200)	10675	LN-AKD	0084	1096	2 RR Dart 552-7R	20412	Y44		lsf Viking Air A/S / cvtd 200MAR
☐ OY-MUF	Fairchild Ind. F-27	40	LN-BSE	0059	0392	2 RR Dart 514-7	17871	Freighter		
☐ EI-CLF	Fairchild Ind. FH-227E	505	SE-KBP	0066	0098	2 RR Dart 532-7L	19730	Freighter		lsf Ireland Airways Holdings Ltd
☐ OY-	Fokker 50 (F27 Mk050)					2 PWC PW125B	20820	Y52		oo-delivery 0599
☐ OY-	Fokker 50 (F27 Mk050)					2 PWC PW125B	20820	Y52		oo-delivery 0799

NORTH FLYING, A/S = NFA **Aalborg, Aarhus & Copenhagen**

Aalborg Lufthavn, DK-9400 Noerresundby, Denmark ☎ 98 17 38 11 Tx: 69924 north dk Fax: 98 17 90 52 SITA: n/a

F: 1969 ⁂ 45 Head: Soren Ibent ICAO: NORTH FLYING Net: http://www.northflying.com Aircraft below MTOW 1361 kg: Cessna 172 / 182 & Piper PA-28

☐ OY-CDN	Socata TB 21 Trinidad TC	969	F-GKVQ	0089	0793	1 LY TIO-540-AB1AD	1400			
☐ OY-BED	Beech Duchess 76	ME-352	EI-BHS	0080		2 LY O-360-A1G6D	1769			
☐ OY-CFT	Partenavia P.68C	213	I-VCID	0080		2 LY IO-360-A1B6	1990			
☐ OY-DLY	Piper PA-31-310 Navajo	31-229	G-AWOW	0068		2 LY TIO-540-A1A	3100			
☐ OY-FRE	Piper PA-31-310 Navajo	31-632	G-AXYA	0070	1192	2 LY TIO-540-A2B	3102			
☐ OY-CEV	Cessna 500 Citation	500-0329	N4999H	0076	0798	2 PWC JT15D-1A	5375			
☐ OY-NPA	Fairchild (Swearingen) SA226TC Metro II	TC-258	C-GBDF	0078	1291	2 GA TPE331-3UW-303G	5670			
☐ OY-CYV	Cessna 550 Citation II	550-0440	N120TC	0082	0798	2 PWC JT15D-4	6033			
☐ OY-SBR	Aerospatiale SN601 Corvette	23	F-BVPF	0075	1096	2 PWC JT15D-4	7000			
☐ OY-SBT	Aerospatiale SN601 Corvette	33	F-BTTT	0076	1096	2 PWC JT15D-4	7000			
☐ OY-BPH	Fairchild (Swearingen) SA227AC Metro III	AC-580B	TC-FBU	0084	0197	2 GA TPE331-11U-601G	7257			cvtd cn AC-580
☐ OY-NPB	Fairchild (Swearingen) SA227AC Metro III	AC-420	N67TC	0081	1095	2 GA TPE331-11U-611G	6580			
☐ OY-NPC	Fairchild (Swearingen) SA227AC Metro III	AC-748B	OE-LIZ	0089	0995	2 GA TPE331-11U-612G	7257			
☐ OY-NPD	Fairchild (Swearingen) SA227DC Metro 23	DC-865B	9M-BCH	0094	0198	2 GA TPE331-12U-701G	7485			
☐ OY-CCJ	Learjet 35A	35A-468	N468LM	0082	0798	2 GA TFE731-2-2B	8891			

PREMIAIR, A/S = DK / VKG (Subsidiary of Airtours Plc, UK) **Copenhagen-Kastrup**

Hangar 276, Copenhagen Airport, DK-2791 Dragoer, Denmark ☎ 32 45 45 00 Tx: 31423 dk Fax: 32 45 12 20 SITA: CPHAPDK

F: 1994 ⁂ 1300 Head: Tom Clausen IATA: 630 ICAO: VIKING Net: http://www.premiair.dk Beside aircraft listed, also leases Lockheed TriStar from Novair (SE-) when required.

☐ OY-CNB	Airbus Industrie A320-212	221	G-DRVE	0091	0397	2 CFMI CFM56-5A3	77000	Y177	AL-ER	lsf AIH
☐ OY-CNC	Airbus Industrie A320-212	222	G-RRJE	0091	0397	2 CFMI CFM56-5A3	77000	Y177	AL-ES	lsf AIH
☐ OY-CNM	Airbus Industrie A320-212	301	G-JANM	0092	1196	2 CFMI CFM56-5A3	77000	Y177	AL-FR	lsf AIH / sub-lst ABB as OO-AEY
☐ OY-CNP	Airbus Industrie A320-212	294	G-HBAP	0092	0297	2 CFMI CFM56-5A3	77000	Y177	AL-GR	lsf AIH
☐ OY-CNR	Airbus Industrie A320-212	349	G-DACR	0092	0197	2 CFMI CFM56-5A3	77000	Y177	AL-GS	lsf AIH / sub-lst ABB as OO-AEZ
☐ OY-CNW	Airbus Industrie A320-212	299	G-JDFW	0092	1296	2 CFMI CFM56-5A3	77000	Y177	AL-FS	lsf AIH
☐ OY-CNA	Airbus Industrie A300B4-120	079	LN-RCA	0079	0194	2 PW JT9D-59A	160000	Y298	AK-DG	cvtd B2-320
☐ OY-CNK	Airbus Industrie A300B4-120	094	SE-DFK	0079	0194	2 PW JT9D-59A	160000	Y298		cvtd B2-320
☐ OY-CNL	Airbus Industrie A300B4-120	128	SE-DFL	0081	0194	2 PW JT9D-59A	160000	Y298	AK-DH	cvtd B2-320
☐ OY-CNS	Boeing (Douglas) DC-10-10	46646 / 285	SE-DHS	0079	0194	3 GE CF6-6D1A	206385	Y379	EJ-CG	lsf Scandinavian Leisure Group AB
☐ OY-CNT	Boeing (Douglas) DC-10-10	47833 / 322	SE-DHT	0080	0194	3 GE CF6-6D1A	206385	Y379	BC-AF	lsf Scandinavian Leisure Group AB
☐ OY-CNU	Boeing (Douglas) DC-10-10	47832 / 318	SE-DHU	0080	0194	3 GE CF6-6D1A	206385	Y379	EL-BD	lsf Scandinavian Leisure Group AB
☐ OY-CNY	Boeing (Douglas) DC-10-10	46983 / 252	SE-DHY	0078	0494	3 GE CF6-6D1A	206385	Y379	BF-CL	lsf Scandinavian Leisure Group AB
☐ OY-	Airbus Industrie A330-243	301	G-			2 RR Trent 772B-60	230000	C49Y311		to be lsf AIH 1299
☐ OY-	Airbus Industrie A330-243	309	G-			2 RR Trent 772B-60	230000	C49Y311		to be lsf AIH 1299
☐ OY-CNO	Boeing (Douglas) DC-10-30	46990 / 260	XA-SYE	0078	0597	3 GE CF6-50C2	259455	Y359	DM-EF	lsf Finova Capital / sub-lst AIH

Q-FALDSKAERMSCENTER (Q-Para Center) (Steen Ulrich dba) **Aalborg**

Lufthavnsvej 41, DK-9400 Noerresundby, Denmark ☎ 98 19 00 60 Tx: none Fax: 98 17 83 00 SITA: n/a

F: 1988 ⁂ 4 Head: Bent Kock Net: n/a

☐ OY-CJG	Cessna U206E Super Skywagon	U20601567	LN-BEI	0070		1 CO IO-520-F	1633	Para/Cargo		lsf pvt
☐ OY-TRZ	Cessna P206E Super Skylane	P20600621	D-EDEV	0069		1 CO IO-520-A	1633	Para		lsf pvt
☐ OY-JRR	De Havilland DHC-2 Turbo Beaver III	1632TB18	N911CC	0066	0493	1 PWC PT6A-20	2436	Para/Cargo		lst pvt / based Spa, Belgium

SCANDINAVIAN AIRLINES COMMUTER / SAS – see under SE-markings

SLV – Statens Luftfartsvaesen, Danmark (CAA – Civil Aviation Administration, Denmark) (Aerodrome division of CAA – Civil Aviation Administration, Denmark) **Copenhagen**

Aerodrome Division, Ellebjergvej 50, DK-2450 Copenhagen SV, Denmark ☎ 36 44 48 48 Tx: 27096 dk Fax: 36 44 03 03 SITA: n/a

F: 1954 ⁂ 8 Head: Ole Asmussen Net: n/a Non-commercial state organisation conducting calibration missions.

☐ OY-IVA	Aerospatiale (Nord) 262A-42	57		0069	1070	2 TU Bastan VIC1	10600	Calibration		

STAR AIR, A/S = SRR (formerly Star Air I/S / Sister company of Maersk Air, A/S) **Copenhagen-Kastrup**

Copenhagen Airport South, DK-2791 Dragoer, Denmark ☎ 32 31 43 43 Tx: none Fax: 32 31 43 90 SITA: CPHDQDM

F: 1984 ⁂ 85 Head: Bjarne Hansen ICAO: WHITESTAR Net: http://www.maersk-air.com

☐ OY-UPA	Boeing 727-31C (QF)	19233 / 458	N926UP	0967	0796	3 RR Tay 651-54	76884	Freighter	BL-KQ	lsf/opf UPS / cvtd -31C
☐ OY-UPB	Boeing 727-180C (QF)	19874 / 534	N921UP	0268	0897	3 RR Tay 651-54	76884	Freighter	BL-EQ	lsf/opf UPS / cvtd -180C
☐ OY-UPD	Boeing 727-22C (QF)	19103 / 341	N944UP	1166	0495	3 RR Tay 651-54	76884	Freighter	BP-FQ	lsf/opf UPS / cvtd -22C
☐ OY-UPJ	Boeing 727-22C (QF)	19102 / 336	N943UP	1166	0894	3 RR Tay 651-54	76884	Freighter	BP-EQ	lsf/opf UPS / cvtd -22C
☐ OY-UPM	Boeing 727-31C (QF)	19229 / 390	N923UP	0367	0196	3 RR Tay 651-54	76884	Freighter	BL-GQ	lsf/opf UPS / cvtd -31C
☐ OY-UPS	Boeing 727-31C (QF)	19232 / 425	N927UP	0667	1093	3 RR Tay 651-54	76884	Freighter	BL-MQ	lsf/opf UPS / cvtd -31C
☐ OY-UPT	Boeing 727-22C (QF)	19094 / 295	N945UP	0766	1093	3 RR Tay 651-54	76884	Freighter	BP-GQ	lsf/opf UPS / cvtd -22C

STARLING AIR — Marstal-Aero

Hangar 1, Aero Flygplats, DK-5690 Marstal, Denmark ☎ 62 53 33 94 Tx: none Fax: 62 53 33 94 SITA: n/a
F: 1988 👥 2 Head: Peter Nordquist Net: n/a Aircraft below MTOW 1361 kg: Cessna 172.

☐ OY-BUY	Cessna U206G Stationair	U20603631	N7359N	0076	0994	1 CO IO-520-F	1635			Smaragdstaeren
☐ OY-BSE	Partenavia P.68B	174	SE-GEU	0079	0489	2 LY IO-360-A1B6	1990			Pragtstaeren

STERLING EUROPEAN AIRLINES - SEA = SNB (Sterling European Kommanditaktieselskab dba / Subsidiary of Ganger Rolf, A/S) — Copenhagen-Kastrup

Copenhagen Airport, DK-2791 Dragoer, Denmark ☎ 32 45 45 45 Tx: 31331 stair dk Fax: 32 45 13 91 SITA: CPHOPNB
F: 1994 👥 280 Head: Lars O. Svenheim ICAO: STERLING Net: n/a

☐ OY-SEG	Boeing 737-59D	26419 / 2186	G-OBMY	1291	0998	2 CFMI CFM56-3C1	57153	Y128		lsf Charlston Partners Ltd
☐ OY-SEE	Boeing 737-3Y0	24463 / 1701	N955WP	0089	0198	2 CFMI CFM56-3B2	63276	Y148		
☐ OY-SEF	Boeing 737-382	25162 / 2241	CS-TIL	0092	0498	2 CFMI CFM56-3B2	63276	Y148		lsf ILFC
☐ OY-SEA	Boeing 737-8Q8	28213 / 50	N3521N*	0098	0698	2 CFMI CFM56-7B26	78245	Y189	HK-BL	lsf ILFC/sublst/opf BAL in Britannia-cs
☐ OY-SEB	Boeing 737-8Q8	28214 / 78		0098	0798	2 CFMI CFM56-7B26	78245	Y189	EG-FK	lsf ILFC
☐ OY-SEC	Boeing 737-8Q8	28221 / 226		0099	0399	2 CFMI CFM56-7B26	78245	Y189		lsf ILFC
☐ OY-SEH	Boeing 737-85H	29444 / 178	N1787B*	0199	0199	2 CFMI CFM56-7B26	78245	Y189	HM-CP	lsf ITOH
☐ OY-SEI	Boeing 737-85H	29445 / 186	N1786B*	0199	0199	2 CFMI CFM56-7B26	78245	Y189	HM-CQ	lsf ITOH / Candy Apple Red-colors
☐ OY-SER	Boeing 727-232 (F) (A)	20639 / 927	N16784	0073	0698	3 PW JT8D-15 (HK3/FDX)	86409	Freighter		lsf/opf TNT Int'l in TNT-cs/cvtd -232
☐ OY-SES	Boeing 727-251 (F)	19977 / 690	N258US	0269	0398	3 PW JT8D-7B (HK3/FDX)	78245	Freighter		lsf/opf TNT Int'l in TNT-cs/cvtd -251
☐ OY-SET	Boeing 727-227 (F) (A)	21245 / 1202	EI-PAK	0076	1197	3 PW JT8D-7B (HK3/FDX)	80558	Freighter		lsf/opf TNT Int'l in TNT-cs/cvtd -227
☐ OY-SEU	Boeing 727-243 (F) (A)	21269 / 1230	EI-EWW	0076	1197	3 PW JT8D-7B (HK3/FDX)	80558	Freighter		lsf/opf TNT Int'l in TNT-cs/cvtd -243
☐ OY-SEV	Boeing 727-281 (F)	20571 / 884	EI-SKY	0072	1197	3 PW JT8D-7B (HK3/FDX)	80558	Freighter		lsf/opf TNT Int'l in SkyPak-cs/cvtd-281
☐ OY-SEW	Boeing 727-287 (F) (A)	21688 / 1415	N920PG	0078	0997	3 PW JT8D-7B (HK3/FDX)	80558	Freighter		lsf/opf TNT Int'l in TNT-cs/cvtd -287
☐ OY-SEY	Boeing 727-224 (F) (A)	20659 / 979	N29730	1073	0297	3 PW JT8D-7B (HK3/FDX)	78245	Freighter	FG-HM	lsf/opf TNT Int'l in TNT-cs/cvtd -224
☐ OY-SEZ	Boeing 727-2M7 (A)	21202 / 1221	N723RW	1276	0596	3 PW JT8D-17 (HK3/FDX)	88359	Y182		lsf PEGA
☐ OY-TNT	Boeing 727-281 (F)	20725 / 958	EI-TNT	0073	1197	3 PW JT8D-7B (HK3/FDX)	80558	Freighter		lsf/opf TNT Int'l in TNT-cs/cvtd -281

SUN-AIR of Scandinavia, A/S = EZ / SUS — Billund

PO Box 40, Billund Lufthavn, DK-7190 Billund, Denmark ☎ 76 50 01 00 Tx: 60892 sunair dk Fax: 75 33 86 18 SITA: BLLOPEZ
F: 1977 👥 150 Head: Niels Sundberg IATA: 947 ICAO: SUNSCAN Net: n/a Aircraft below MTOW 1361 kg: Mooney M20 & Piper PA-28.
All scheduled services (with ATP, Jetstream 31/41) are operated under a franchise agreement with BRITISH AIRWAYS (in full such colors & both titles) & using BA-flight numbers.

☐ OY-INI	Cessna 501 Citation I/SP	501-0166	I-CIPA	0080	1294	2 PWC JT15D-1A	5375	Executive		lsf Jet Plan Corp. ApS
☐ OY-ONE	Cessna 501 Citation I/SP	501-0143	D-IGGK	0080	0395	2 PWC JT15D-1A	5375	Executive		lsf Magpie Aviation ApS
☐ OY-SVF	BAe 3102 Jetstream 31	686	G-BSFG	0085	0891	2 GA TPE331-10UR-513H	7059	Y19		op in BA Waves of the City-colors
☐ OY-SVJ	BAe 3102 Jetstream 31	711	G-BTYG	0086	0392	2 GA TPE331-10UR-513H	7059	Y19		Skien / op in BA Blomsterang-colors
☐ OY-SVR	BAe 3100 Jetstream 31	701	D-CONA	0086	1193	2 GA TPE331-10UR-513H	7059	Y19		op in BA Rendezvous-colors
☐ OY-SVZ	BAe 3100 Jetstream 31	641	G-MACX	0084	0593	2 GA TPE331-10UR-513H	7059	Y19		op in BA Colum-colors
☐ OY-SVS	BAe 4100 Jetstream 41	41014	G-4-014*	0093	0693	2 GA TPE331-14HR-801H	10433	Y30		Spirit of Aarhus / op in BA Ndebele-cs
☐ OY-SVW	BAe 4102 Jetstream 41	41047	G-BVZC*	0095	0595	2 GA TPE331-14HR-801H	10433	Y30		Port of Arhus / op in BA Wings-colors
☐ OY-SVI	BAe ATP	2061	G-BUYW	0295	0198	2 PWC PW126A	22930	Y64		BA Benyhone Tartan/Mtn of the Birds-cs
☐ OY-SVT	BAe ATP	2062	G-11-062*	0093	1298	2 PWC PW126A	22930	Y64		op in BA Colum-colors
☐ OY-SVU	BAe ATP	2063	G-BWYT	0295	1197	2 PWC PW126A	22930	Y64		op in BA Wings-colors

UNI-FLY (Uni-Fly Bjarne Stuhr Petersen, ApS dba) — Svendborg

Tordensgardsvej 4, DK-5700 Svendborg, Denmark ☎ 62 21 31 44 Tx: none Fax: 62 22 95 74 SITA: n/a
F: 1969 👥 3 Head: Bjarne Stuhr Petersen Net: n/a Aircraft below MTOW 1361 kg: Bell 47G-5, Hughes 269C (300C).

☐ OY-HJM	Eurocopter EC120B Colibri	007		0098	0398	1 TU Arrius 2F	1680			
☐ OY-HJN	Eurocopter EC120B Colibri					1 TU Arrius 2F	1680			oo-delivery 1299

P = KOREA (Democratic People's Republic of Korea) (Choson Minjujui Inmin Konghuaguk)

Capital: Pyongyang Official Language: Korean Population: 24,0 million Square Km: 120538 Dialling code: +850 Year established: 1948 Acting political head: Kim Jong Il (President)

AIR KORYO = JS / KOR (formerly Chosonminhang Korean Airways / CAAK) — Pyongyang

Sunan District, Pyongyang, Democratic People's Republic of Korea ☎ (2) 32 143 Tx: 5471 js kp Fax: (2) 81 46 25 SITA: n/a
F: 1954 👥 2500 Head: Choe Yong Gu IATA: 120 ICAO: AIR KORYO Net: n/a

☐ P-527	Antonov 24					2 IV AI-24	21000	Y50		
☐ P-528	Antonov 24					2 IV AI-24	21000	Y50		
☐ P-529	Antonov 24					2 IV AI-24	21000	Y50		
☐ P-531	Antonov 24					2 IV AI-24	21000	Y50		
☐ P-532	Antonov 24					2 IV AI-24	21000	Y50		
☐ P-533	Antonov 24					2 IV AI-24	21000	Y50		
☐ P-534	Antonov 24					2 IV AI-24	21000	Y50		
☐ P-537	Antonov 24					2 IV AI-24	21000	Y50		
☐ P-813	Tupolev 134B-3	66215		0083		2 SO D-30-III	49000	Y76		
☐ P-814	Tupolev 134B-3	66368		0083		2 SO D-30-III	49000	Y76		
☐ P-835	Ilyushin 18D	188011205		0068	0369	4 IV AI-20M	64000	Y100		
☐ P-836	Ilyushin 18V	185008204		0065		4 IV AI-20M	64000	Y100		
☐ P-551	Tupolev 154B	129		1275	0075	3 KU NK-8-2U	98000	F18Y102		P5-CVA / cvtd 154A
☐ P-552	Tupolev 154B	143		0376	0076	3 KU NK-8-2U	98000	F18Y102		P5-CVB / cvtd 154A
☐ P-553	Tupolev 154B	191		0177	0077	3 KU NK-8-2U	98000	F18Y102		
☐ P-561	Tupolev 154B-2	573		0483	0083	3 KU NK-8-2U	98000	F18Y102		
☐ P-618	Ilyushin 62M	2546624		0085	0085	4 SO D-30KU	167000	F33Y136		
☐ P-881	Ilyushin 62M	3647853		0086	0086	4 SO D-30KU	167000	VIP		
☐ P-882	Ilyushin 62M	2850236		0088	0088	4 SO D-30KU	167000	F33Y136		
☐ P-885	Ilyushin 62M	3933913		0079	0679	4 SO D-30KU	167000	F33Y136		P5-XIC
☐ P-912	Ilyushin 76MD	1003403104		0090	0090	4 SO D-30KP	190000	Freighter		
☐ P-913	Ilyushin 76MD	1003404126		0090	0090	4 SO D-30KP	190000	Freighter		
☐ P-914	Ilyushin 76MD	1003404146		0090	0090	4 SO D-30KP	190000	Freighter		

PH = NETHERLANDS (Kingdom of the Netherlands) (Koninkrijk der Nederlanden)

Capital: Amsterdam Official Language: Dutch Population: 15,5 million Square Km: 41473 Dialling code: +31 Year established: 1581 Acting political head: Wim Kok (Prime Minister)

Government / Corporate / Executive / VIP Aircraft Royal Netherlands Air Force / Koninklijke Luchtmacht uses the ICAO three-letter-code NAF.

☐ PH-KBX	Fokker 70 (F28 Mk0070)	11547		0995	0396	2 RR Tay 620-15	39915	VIP 26 Pax	JR-DE	Gvmt/Dutch Royal Flight / opb MPH
☐ T-235	Boeing (Douglas) KDC-10-30F (CF)	46956 / 235	PH-MBP	0076	0295	3 GE CF6-50C	256280	Tanker/Frtr/milt	CG-HJ	Royal Netherlands A.F./cvtd DC-10-30F
☐ T-264	Boeing (Douglas) KDC-10-30F (CF)	46985 / 264	PH-MBT	0078	0295	3 GE CF6-50C	256280	Tanker/Frtr/milt	CG-HL	Prins Bernhard / RNAF / cvtd DC-10-30F
☐ U-05	Fokker 50 (F27 Mk0502)	20253	PH-KXO*	0092	1296	2 PWC PW127B	20820	VIP		Fons Aler / Royal Netherlands Air Force
☐ U-06	Fokker 50 (F27 Mk0502)	20287	PH-MXI*	0096	1196	2 PWC PW127B	20820	VIP		Robbie Wijting / Royal Netherlands A.F.
☐ V-11	GAC G-IV Gulfstream IV	1009	VR-BOY	0086	1295	2 RR Tay 610-8	31615	VIP / miltrans	MR-FG	Royal Netherlands Air Force

ACE AIR CHARTERS = RCC (Air Charters Eelde, B.V. dba) — Groningen-Eelde

Machlaan 20, NL-9761 TK Eelde, Netherlands ☎ (50) 309 11 44 Tx: none Fax: (50) 309 48 88 SITA: n/a
F: 1996 👥 11 Head: C.J. Rooijens ICAO: RACER Net: n/a

☐ PH-JMV	Piper PA-31-350 Navajo Chieftain	31-8052088	N180CR	0080		2 LY TIO-540-J2BD	3175	Y8 / Freighter		
☐ PH-ACZ	Beech King Air B200	BB-1215	D-IEEE	0085	0297	2 PWC PT6A-42	5670	Y9/VIP/Frtr		lsf Air-Cover Holding B.V.
☐ D-CBSG	Beech 1900D Airliner	UE-44	OK-YES	0093	0798	2 PWC PT6A-67D	7688	Y18		lsf Air-Cover Holding / sub-lst/opf BRO

AIR HOLLAND = GG / AHR (Air Holland Charter, B.V. dba / formerly Air Holland, N.V.) — Amsterdam-Schiphol

PO Box 75116, NL-1117 ZR Schiphol, Netherlands ☎ (20) 316 44 44 Tx: 15272 nl Fax: (20) 316 44 45 SITA: SPLHQGG
F: 1985 👥 425 Head: Jan C Heppener IATA: 895 ICAO: ORANGE Net: n/a

☐ PH-OZA	Boeing 737-3L9	23718 / 1402	G-BOZA	0087	0492	2 CFMI CFM56-3B2	62822	Y148	HJ-BM	lsf Air Holland Leasing I B.V.
☐ PH-OZB	Boeing 737-3Y0	23921 / 1513	5B-CIO	0288	0494	2 CFMI CFM56-3B2	62822	Y148	GR-FH	lsf BBAM
☐ PH-OZC	Boeing 737-36N	28559 / 2882		0097	0597	2 CFMI CFM56-3C1	62822	Y148	LQ-JM	lsf GECA
☐ PH-AHE	Boeing 757-27B	24135 / 165	OY-SHE	0088	0388	2 RR RB211-535E4	113398	Y219	CE-DM	lsf Finova Capital Ltd
☐ PH-AHI	Boeing 757-27B	24137 / 178	G-OAHI	0088	0588	2 RR RB211-535E4	113398	Y219	CE-GM	lsf Air Holland Leasing II B.V.
☐ PH-AHK	Boeing 757-23A	24291 / 215	N916AW	0089	0498	2 RR RB211-535E4	113398	Y219	GK-CQ	lsf AWAS
☐ PH-AHP	Boeing 757-23A	24528 / 250	G-BXOL	0089	0499	2 RR RB211-535E4	108860	Y219		lsf TOMB

ANWB Medical Air Assistance, B.V. (Division of ANWB) — Amsterdam-Hospital Heliport & Rotterdam

Donklaan 76, NL-2254 AD Voorschoten, Netherlands ☎ (70) 314 73 58 Tx: none Fax: (70) 314 73 37 SITA: n/a
F: 1996 👥 12 Head: Wil Botman ICAO: LIFELINE Net: n/a

☐ PH-KHD	Eurocopter (MBB) BO105CBS-4	S-324	HB-XGM	0077	0896	2 AN 250-C20B	2500	EMS		lsf Schreiner Northsea Helicopters
☐ PH-KHE	Eurocopter (MBB) BO105CBS-4	S-329	HB-XGT	0077	0896	2 AN 250-C20B	2500	EMS		lsf Schreiner Northsea Helicopters
☐ D-HHBG	Eurocopter (MBB) BO105CBS-4	S-625	VH-NSL	0083	0797	2 AN 250-C20B	2500	EMS		lsf ADAC Luftrettung

491 registration type of aircraft cn/fn ex/ex* mfd del powered by mtow kg configuration selcal name/fln/specialitites/remarks

BASE Airlines = 5E / BRO (Business Aviation Services Eindhoven, B.V. dba) — **Eindhoven**

PO Box 7165, NL-5605 JD Eindhoven, Netherlands ☎ (40) 257 15 50 Tx: none Fax: (40) 252 38 01 SITA: n/a
F: 1985 ⁂ 38 Head: Hans Noorlander IATA: 228 ICAO: COASTRIDER Net: n/a
Some scheduled services are operated under a franchise agreement with BRITISH AIRWAYS (in full such colors & both titles) & using BA-flight numbers.

☐ PH-KJB	BAe 3108 Jetstream 31	648	G-31-648*	0084	0191	2 GA TPE331-10UG-513H	6899	Y16		op in British Airways-colors
☐ PH-KJG	BAe 3108 Jetstream 31	690	G-LOGT	0086	0993	2 GA TPE331-10UG-513H	6950	Y16		op in British Airways-colors
☐ D-CBSG	Beech 1900D Airliner	UE-44	OK-YES	0093	0798	2 PWC PT6A-67D	7688	Y18		lsf / opb RCC in white-colors
☐ PH-BRI	Embraer 120ER Brasilia (EMB-120ER)	120235	OO-DTN	0091	0697	2 PWC PW118	11990	Y28		
☐ PH-BRK	Embraer 120ER Brasilia (EMB-120ER)	120253	OO-DTO	0091	0697	2 PWC PW118	11990	Y28		
☐ PH-BRL	Embraer 120RT Brasilia (EMB-120RT)	120083	N278UE	0688	0499	2 PWC PW118	11500	Y28		op in British Airways-colors
☐ PH-BRM	Embraer 120RT Brasilia (EMB-120RT)	120090	N280UE	0088	0499	2 PWC PW118	11500	Y28		op in British Airways-colors
☐ PH-BRP	Embraer 120RT Brasilia (EMB-120RT)	120175	N286UE	0390	0499	2 PWC PW118	11500	Y28		op in British Airways-colors

DELTA PHOT Luchtfotografie — **Midden Zeeland**

Nw. Kleverkerkseweg 25, NL-4338 PP Middelburg, Netherlands ☎ (118) 63 71 00 Tx: n/a Fax: (118) 62 59 54 SITA: n/a
F: 1978 ⁂ 6 Head: A.T. & T.C. Slagboom Net: n/a

☐ PH-DPX	Cessna T207A Turbo Stationair 8 II	20700727	D-EBMO	0081	0394	1 CO TSIO-520-M	1724	Photo / Survey		

DENIM AIR, B.V. = 3D / DNM — **Eindhoven**

Luchthavenweg 81-41, NL-5657 EA Eindhoven, Netherlands ☎ (40) 251 70 13 Tx: none Fax: (40) 251 16 38 SITA: EINDAXH
F: 1996 ⁂ 65 Head: Hamid Kerboua IATA: 973 ICAO: DENIM Net: n/a

☐ PH-DMB	Fokker 50 (F27 Mk050)	20264	OE-LFF	0092	0496	2 PWC PW125B	20820	Y50		Frits Philips / lsf Austrian Lease Fin.
☐ PH-DMC	Fokker 50 (F27 Mk050)	20227	OE-LFE	0091	1196	2 PWC PW125B	20820	Y50		lsf Austrian Lease Finance Co. Ltd
☐ PH-DMD	Fokker 50 (F27 Mk050)	20144	SE-LEM	0089	0199	2 PWC PW125B	20820	Y50		lsf Austrian Lease Finance Co. Ltd
☐ PH-DMG	Fokker 50 (F27 Mk050)	20203	5Y-BHK	0090	0698	2 PWC PW125B	20820	Y50		lst ANM as EC-GTE
☐ PH-DMK	Fokker 50 (F27 Mk050)	20137	5Y-BFN	0088	0698	2 PWC PW125B	20820	Y50		
☐ PH-DMO	Fokker 50 (F27 Mk050)	20103	OY-MBM	0087	0598	2 PWC PW125B	20820	Y50		lsf PEMB/sub-lst EAE European Air Expr.

DUTCH DAKOTA Association, B.V. – DDA (Member of Dutch Historical Aircraft Federation) — **Amsterdam-Schiphol**

PO Box 75090, NL-1117 ZP Schiphol, Netherlands ☎ (20) 374 77 00 Tx: none Fax: (20) 601 08 58 SITA: n/a
F: 1982 ⁂ 4 Head: Anne-Cor Groeneveld Net: n/a Aircraft below MTOW 1361 kg: Stinson L-5B-VW Sentinel. Non-profit organisation conducting historical aircraft flights.

☐ PH-AJU	Boeing (Douglas) DC-2-112	1288	VH-CRH	0034		2 WR R-1820-F2B	8618			std AMS / to be made operational 2010
☐ PH-DDZ	Boeing (Douglas) DC-3C (C-47A-80-DL)	19754	SU-BFY	0043	0287	2 PW R-1830-92	11885	27 Pax		old Martin's Air Charter-colors
☐ PH-PBA	Boeing (Douglas) DC-3C (C-47A-75-DL)	19434	42-100971	0042		2 PW R-1830-92	11885	17-27 Pax		old Gvmt/Prins Bernhard-colors
☐ PH-DDS	Boeing (Douglas) DC-4-1009	42934 / D4 13	ZS-NUR	0046	0596	4 PW R-2000-11	30240	50 Pax		old KLM De Vliegende Hollander-colors
☐ PH-DDY	Boeing (Douglas) DC-4 (C-54A-5-DO)	7488 / DO 96	ZS-IPR	0044	0697	4 PW R-2000-11	30240			std AMS

DYNAMIC AIRLINES = QG / DYE (Dynamic Air, B.V. dba) — **Eindhoven**

Luchthavenweg 43, NL-5657 EA Eindhoven, Netherlands ☎ (40) 252 89 55 Tx: none Fax: (40) 251 39 39 SITA: n/a
F: 1982 ⁂ 40 Head: Huub J. van den Hout ICAO: DYNAMITE Net: n/a

☐ PH-CTY	Cessna 500 Citation	500-0044	OO-ATS	0072	0399	2 PWC JT15D-1A	5375	6 Pax		
☐ PH-CTX	Cessna 550 Citation II	550-0398	N398S	0081	0297	2 PWC JT15D-4	6577	9 Pax		
☐ PH-CTZ	Cessna 550 Citation II	550-0052	N67TM	0079	1297	2 PWC JT15D-4	6577	9 Pax		

EUROSENSE, B.V. (Subsidiary of Eurosense-Belfotop, N.V.) — **Brussels-National**

Postbus 4923, NL-4803 EX Breda, Netherlands ☎ (76) 565 88 50 Tx: none Fax: (76) 565 59 99 SITA: n/a
F: 1981 ⁂ 5 Head: I.C.A. Kuijlaars Net: n/a

☐ PH-ITC	Piper PA-31-350 Navajo Chieftain	31-7405491	N61479	0074	0590	2 LY TIO-540-J2BD	3185	Photo / Survey		Nadar

F27 FRIENDSHIP FLIGHT ASSOCIATION (Operational division of F27 Friendship Assocation / Member of Dutch Historical Aircraft Federation) — **Amsterdam-Schiphol**

PO Box 497, NL-2130 AL Hoofddorp, Netherlands ☎ (320) 25 20 27 Tx: none Fax: (320) 25 20 27 SITA: n/a
F: 1987 ⁂ 0 Head: Peter de Raaf ICAO: FRIENDSHIP Net: http://home.wxs.nl/f27fligh/ Non-commercial historical organisation conducting F27 Friendship flights at airshows or other special arrangements.

☐ PH-NVF	Fokker F27 Friendship 100 (F27 Mk100)	10102	D-BAKI	0056	1195	2 RR Dart 514-7E	18370			being made operational at Eindhoven

HELICON, B.V. (Affiliated with sister co. A.T.A.S. Air advertising & Star Airservice, aircraft maintenance) — **Teuge**

Patrijsstraat 22, NL-6971 VR Brummen, Netherlands ☎ (55) 323 21 74 Tx: none Fax: (55) 323 49 04 SITA: n/a
F: 1998 ⁂ 10 Head: Ericq van 't Spijker Net: n/a Aircraft below MTOW 1361kg: Robinson R22

☐ PH-NSW	Eurocopter (Aerosp.) SE313B Alouette II	1185	G-BUIV	0058	0593	1 TU Artouste IIC6	1600			

HELI-HOLLAND, B.V. = HHE — **Emmer Helipad**

Postbus 16, NL-7880 AA Emmer-Compascuum, Netherlands ☎ (591) 35 12 51 Tx: none Fax: (591) 35 27 69 SITA: n/a
F: 1976 ⁂ 5 Head: René van der Haring ICAO: HELI HOLLAND Net: n/a Aircraft below MTOW 1361kg: Hughes 269C (300C) & 369HS (500C).

☐ PH-HWH	Agusta-Bell 206B JetRanger	8076	G-AWLL	0068	0993	1 AN 250-C20	1451			lsf Heli-Holland Holding B.V./cvtd 206A
☐ PH-HXH	Bell 206L LongRanger	45103	SE-HSA	0077	0494	1 AN 250-C20B	1814			lsf Heli-Holland Holding B.V.
☐ PH-BGS	Eurocopter (Aerosp.) AS350B2 Ecureuil	3107		0098	0798	1 TU Arriel 1D1	2250			lsf Heliflight Holland Holding BV
☐ PH-HHC	Eurocopter (Aerosp.) AS355F1 Ecureuil 2	5049	I-VIEY	0081	1197	2 AN 250-C20F	2400			
☐ PH-HVH	Eurocopter (Aerosp.) AS355F1 Ecureuil 2	5215	ZS-HMF	0082	0992	2 AN 250-C20F	2400			lsf Heli-Holland Holding B.V.

ING LEASE INTERNATIONAL EQUIPMENT MANAGEMENT, B.V. = (INGL) (Subsidiary of ING Group) — **Amsterdam**

PO Box 1971, NL-1000 BZ Amsterdam, Netherlands ☎ (20) 652 57 01 Tx: none Fax: (20) 652 57 04 SITA: n/a
F: 1981 ⁂ 17 Head: Cees Leys Net: http://www.inglease.com/iem New & used aircraft management, leasing, sales & financing company.
Owner / lessor of following aircraft types: Airbus Industrie A300B4, Boeing 727/737/747/757 & MD-80. Aircraft leased from ING Lease are listed & mentioned as lsf INGL under the leasing carriers.

JET LINK HOLLAND, B.V. = JLH — **Amsterdam-Schiphol**

Jupiterstraat 51-69, NL-2132 HC Hoofddorp, Netherlands ☎ (23) 562 45 60 Tx: none Fax: (23) 561 77 60 SITA: SPLJHCR
F: 1995 ⁂ n/a Head: Sobhy Abdel Messeh IATA: 712 Net: http://www.jetlink.nl

☐ PH-JLH	Airbus Industrie A300B4-203 (F)	123	N59123	0080	0698	2 GE CF6-50C2	165000	Freighter		lsf CSAV / cvtd -203

JET SOLUTION AMSTERDAM, B.V. (Associated with Aerodynamics, B.V. / formerly Hezemans Air, AG) — **Amsterdam**

PO Box 75138, NL-1117 ZR Schiphol East, Netherlands ☎ (20) 405 00 92 Tx: none Fax: (20) 648 41 74 SITA: n/a
F: 1997 ⁂ 4 Head: Pieter Bas Mijinster Net: n/a

☐ PH-JSL	Mitsubishi MU-300 Diamond IA	A087SA	HB-VIA	0085	0997	2 PWC JT15D-4D	6636	Y6		

KLM – Royal Dutch Airlines = KL / KLM ("The Flying Dutchman") (Koninklijke Luchtvaart Maatschappij, N.V., dba) — **Amsterdam-Schiphol**

PO Box 7700, NL-1117 ZL Schiphol-Oost, Netherlands ☎ (20) 649 91 23 Tx: 11252 klm nl Fax: (20) 41 28 72 SITA: n/a
F: 1919 ⁂ 25500 Head: Leo M. Wijk IATA: 074 ICAO: KLM Net: http://www.klm.nl Boeing 747-206B which have been modified with a series 300 stretched upper deck retain the designation -206B but are marked with (SUD).
Some regional flights are op. by partner companies: KLM alps (OE-), KLM cityhopper (PH-), KLM exel (PH-) & KLM uk (G-) using KL flight flight numbers. For details see under each co. Scheduled freighter flights on behalf of KLM using KL-flight numbers are operated by: Atlas Air (B747-200F), HeavyLift Cargo Airlines (with Airbus Industrie A300B4-203F) & Martinair (with Boeing 747-200F) – for details see under each company.
Flights to Taiwan are operated under the name KLM asia (with such titles / same headquarters).

☐ PH-BDA	Boeing 737-306	23537 / 1275		0086	1086	2 CFMI CFM56-3B1	56959	CY109	HL-AF	Willem Barentsz / lsf Ben Air SpA
☐ PH-BDB	Boeing 737-306	23538 / 1288		0086	1086	2 CFMI CFM56-3B1	56959	CY109	HL-AG	Olivier van Noort / lsf Ben Air SpA
☐ PH-BDC	Boeing 737-306	23539 / 1295		0086	1186	2 CFMI CFM56-3B1	56959	CY109	HL-AJ	Cornelis de Houtman / lsf Ben Air SpA
☐ PH-BDD	Boeing 737-306	23540 / 1303		0086	1186	2 CFMI CFM56-3B1	56959	CY109	HL-AK	Anthony van Diemen / lsf Ben Air SpA
☐ PH-BDE	Boeing 737-306	23541 / 1309		0086	1286	2 CFMI CFM56-3B1	56959	CY109	HL-AM	Abel J. Tasman / lsf Molen Aircraft Ltd
☐ PH-BDG	Boeing 737-306	23542 / 1317		0086	1286	2 CFMI CFM56-3B1	56959	CY109	HL-BC	Michiel A. de Ruyter / lsf Orient Ac
☐ PH-BDH	Boeing 737-306	23543 / 1325		0086	0187	2 CFMI CFM56-3B1	56959	CY109	HL-BD	Petrus Plancius / lsf Orient Aircraft
☐ PH-BDI	Boeing 737-306	23544 / 1335		0087	0287	2 CFMI CFM56-3B1	56959	CY109	HK-GL	Maarten H. Tromp / lsf Orient Aircraft
☐ PH-BDK	Boeing 737-306	23545 / 1343		0087	0287	2 CFMI CFM56-3B1	56959	CY109	DL-AJ	Jan H. van Linschoten / lsf Orient Ac
☐ PH-BDL	Boeing 737-306	23546 / 1349		0087	0387	2 CFMI CFM56-3B1	56959	CY109	DM-BG	Piet Heyn / lsf Orient Aircraft
☐ PH-BDN	Boeing 737-306	24261 / 1640		0088	1188	2 CFMI CFM56-3B1	56959	CY109	EH-DJ	Willem van Ruysbroeck / lsf Labora B.V.
☐ PH-BDO	Boeing 737-306	24262 / 1642		0088	1288	2 CFMI CFM56-3B1	56959	CY109	EH-DK	Jacob van Heemskerck / lsf Bora N.V.
☐ PH-BDP	Boeing 737-306	24404 / 1681		0089	0389	2 CFMI CFM56-3B1	56959	CY109	EH-CG	Jacob Roggeveen / lsf ORIX
☐ PH-BTD	Boeing 737-306	27420 / 2406		0092	1292	2 CFMI CFM56-3B1	56959	CY109	HL-PQ	James Cook / lsf DIA Ltd
☐ PH-BTE	Boeing 737-306	27421 / 2438		0093	0393	2 CFMI CFM56-3B1	56959	CY109	HP-MQ	Roald Amundsen / lsf Dia Ltd
☐ PH-BTH	Boeing 737-306	28719 / 2930		0097	1097	2 CFMI CFM56-3B1	56959	CY109	HL-KQ	Heike Kamerling-Onnes
☐ PH-BTI	Boeing 737-306	28720 / 2957	N1786B*	0097	1297	2 CFMI CFM56-3B1	56959	CY109	HK-PQ	Niels Bohr
☐ PH-BDR	Boeing 737-406	24514 / 1768		0089	0989	2 CFMI CFM56-3B2	62822	CY129	EH-BJ	Willem C. Schouten / lsf Knight Ac
☐ PH-BDS	Boeing 737-406	24529 / 1770		0089	0989	2 CFMI CFM56-3B2	62822	CY129	EH-AD	Joris van Spilbergen / lsf Castle Ac
☐ PH-BDT	Boeing 737-406	24530 / 1772		0089	0989	2 CFMI CFM56-3B2	62822	CY129	EH-AC	Gerrit de Veer / lsf Bishop Aircraft
☐ PH-BDU	Boeing 737-406	24857 / 1902		0090	0890	2 CFMI CFM56-3B2	62822	CY129	DL-AF	Marco Polo / lsf Libra Leasing
☐ PH-BDW	Boeing 737-406	24858 / 1903		0090	0890	2 CFMI CFM56-3B2	62822	CY129	EH-BD	Leifur Eiriksson / lsf Libra Leasing
☐ PH-BDY	Boeing 737-406	24959 / 1949		0090	1190	2 CFMI CFM56-3B2	62822	CY129	HK-CQ	Vasco da Gama / lsf Molen Aerospace
☐ PH-BDZ	Boeing 737-406	25355 / 2132		0091	1091	2 CFMI CFM56-3B2	62822	CY129	HK-GQ	Christophorus Columbus
☐ PH-BPA	Boeing 737-4Y0	23865 / 1582	G-UKLA	0088	0597	2 CFMI CFM56-3C1	62822	CY129		Albert Einstein / lsf GECA
☐ PH-BPB	Boeing 737-4Y0	24344 / 1723	G-UKLB	0089	0997	2 CFMI CFM56-3C1	62822	CY129		Jan Tinbergen / lsf GECA
☐ PH-BPC	Boeing 737-4Y0	24468 / 1747	G-UKLE	0089	1097	2 CFMI CFM56-3C1	62822	CY129		Ernest Hemingway / lsf GECA
☐ PH-BPD	Boeing 737-42C	24231 / 1871	G-UKLC	0090	0696	2 CFMI CFM56-3C1	62822	CY129	BP-AE	Guglielmo Marconi / lsf Kuria Ltd
☐ PH-BPE	Boeing 737-42C	24232 / 2060	G-UKLD	0091	0696	2 CFMI CFM56-3C1	62822	CY129	BP-HJ	Henri Dunant / lsf Kuria Ltd
☐ PH-BPF	Boeing 737-42C	24813 / 2062	G-UKLF	0091	0696	2 CFMI CFM56-3C1	62822	CY129	BP-JQ	Wilhelm Röntgen / lsfTFID FSC Piper Inc
☐ PH-BPG	Boeing 737-42C	24814 / 2270	G-UKLG	0092	0796	2 CFMI CFM56-3C1	62822	CY129		Max Planck / lsf FM FSC UK Ltd

492 registration type of aircraft cn/fn ex/ex* mfd del powered by mtow kg configuration selcal name/fln/specialitites/remarks

☐ PH-BTA	Boeing 737-406	25412 / 2161		0091	1191	2 CFMI CFM56-3B2	62822	CY129	HK-JQ	Fernao de Magelhaes / lsf BlueWingLease
☐ PH-BTB	Boeing 737-406	25423 / 2184		0091	0192	2 CFMI CFM56-3B2	62822	CY129	HK-LQ	Henry Hudson / lsf CF Topaz Leasing
☐ PH-BTC	Boeing 737-406	25424 / 2200		0092	0292	2 CFMI CFM56-3B2	62822	CY129	HK-MQ	David Livingstone / lsf SF Canal 3 Ltd
☐ PH-BTF	Boeing 737-406	27232 / 2591		0094	0394	2 CFMI CFM56-3B2	62822	CY129	DH-BS	Alexander von Humboldt / lsf Wood Lsng
☐ PH-BTG	Boeing 737-406	27233 / 2601		0094	0494	2 CFMI CFM56-3B2	62822	CY129	DH-ER	Sir Henry Morton Stanley / lsfFreshLsng
☐ PH-BXA	Boeing 737-8K2	29131 / 198	N1786B*	0099	0299	2 CFMI CFM56-7B26	73700	CY158		Swan
☐ PH-BXB	Boeing 737-8K2	29132 / 261		0099	0499	2 CFMI CFM56-7B26	73700	CY158		
☐ PH-BXC	Boeing 737-8K2	29133				2 CFMI CFM56-7B26	73700	CY158		oo-delivery 0699
☐ PH-BXD	Boeing 737-8K2	29134				2 CFMI CFM56-7B26	73700	CY158		oo-delivery 0899
☐ PH-BXE	Boeing 737-8K2					2 CFMI CFM56-7B26	73700	CY158		oo-delivery 0500
☐ PH-BXF	Boeing 737-8K2					2 CFMI CFM56-7B26	73700	CY158		oo-delivery 0600
☐ PH-BXG	Boeing 737-8K2					2 CFMI CFM56-7B26	73700	CY158		oo-delivery 0800
☐ PH-BXH	Boeing 737-8K2					2 CFMI CFM56-7B26	73700	CY158		oo-delivery 0900
☐ PH-BXI	Boeing 737-8K2					2 CFMI CFM56-7B26	73700	CY158		oo-delivery 0900
☐ PH-BXK	Boeing 737-8K2					2 CFMI CFM56-7B26	73700	CY158		oo-delivery 1000
☐ PH-BXL	Boeing 737-8K2					2 CFMI CFM56-7B26	73700	CY158		oo-delivery 1000
☐ PH-BXM	Boeing 737-8K2					2 CFMI CFM56-7B26	73700	CY158		oo-delivery 1100
☐ PH-BXN	Boeing 737-8K2					2 CFMI CFM56-7B26	73700	CY158		oo-delivery 1200
☐ PH-	Boeing 737-9K2					2 CFMI CFM56-7B26	79016	CY190		oo-delivery 0501
☐ PH-	Boeing 737-9K2					2 CFMI CFM56-7B26	79016	CY190		oo-delivery 0701
☐ PH-	Boeing 737-9K2					2 CFMI CFM56-7B26	79016	CY190		oo-delivery 0901
☐ PH-	Boeing 737-9K2					2 CFMI CFM56-7B26	79016	CY190		oo-delivery 1101
☐ PH-BZA	Boeing 767-306 (ER)	27957 / 587		0095	0795	2 GE CF6-80C2B6F	181400	C36Y188	EQ-GP	Blauwbrug / Blue Bridge / lsf ILFC
☐ PH-BZB	Boeing 767-306 (ER)	27958 / 589		0095	0895	2 GE CF6-80C2B6F	181400	C36Y188	EQ-GH	Pont Neuf / lsf ILFC
☐ PH-BZC	Boeing 767-306 (ER)	26263 / 592		0095	1095	2 GE CF6-80C2B6F	181400	C36Y188	EQ-GJ	Brooklyn Bridge / lsf ILFC
☐ PH-BZD	Boeing 767-306 (ER)	27610 / 605		0096	0396	2 GE CF6-80C2B6F	181400	C36Y188	ER-DL	King Hussain Bridge / lsf ILFC
☐ PH-BZE	Boeing 767-306 (ER)	28098 / 607		0096	0596	2 GE CF6-80C2B6F	181400	C36Y188	ER-LM	Ponte Rialto / lsf ILFC
☐ PH-BZF	Boeing 767-306 (ER)	27959 / 609		0096	0696	2 GE CF6-80C2B6F	181400	C36Y188	ER-LS	Golden Gate Bridge / lsf ILFC
☐ PH-BZG	Boeing 767-306 (ER)	27960 / 625	N6009F*	0096	0896	2 GE CF6-80C2B6F	181400	C36Y188	ES-HL	Erasmus Brug/Bridge / lsf ILFC
☐ PH-BZH	Boeing 767-306 (ER)	27611 / 633		0096	1096	2 GE CF6-80C2B6F	181400	C36Y188	KM-DS	Tower Bridge / lsf ILFC
☐ PH-BZI	Boeing 767-306 (ER)	27612 / 647		0097	0297	2 GE CF6-80C2B6F	181400	C36Y188	KM-ER	Bosporus Bridge / lsf ILFC
☐ PH-BZK	Boeing 767-306 (ER)	27614 / 661		0597	0597	2 GE CF6-80C2B6F	181400	C36Y188	KM-ES	Zeelandbrug/Zeeland Bridge / lsf ILFC
☐ PH-BZM	Boeing 767-306 (ER)	28884 / 738		0299	0299	2 GE CF6-80C2B6F	181400	C36Y188		Garibaldi Bridge / lsf ILFC
☐ PH-	Boeing 767-306 (ER)					2 GE CF6-80C2B6F	181400	C36Y188		to be lsf ILFC 0200
☐ PH-KCA	Boeing (Douglas) MD-11	48555 / 557	N6202D*	0093	1293	3 GE CF6-80C2D1F	280320	C37Y260	AF-ER	Amy Johnson / lsf SK Alpha Co. Ltd
☐ PH-KCB	Boeing (Douglas) MD-11	48556 / 561		0094	0394	3 GE CF6-80C2D1F	280320	C37Y260	AF-ES	Maria Montessori / lsf WTC Trustee
☐ PH-KCC	Boeing (Douglas) MD-11	48557 / 569		0094	0694	3 GE CF6-80C2D1F	280320	C37Y260	AF-GR	Marie Curie / lsf WTC Trustee
☐ PH-KCD	Boeing (Douglas) MD-11	48558 / 573		0094	0994	3 GE CF6-80C2D1F	280320	C37Y260	AF-HR	Florence Nightingale / lsf WTC Trustee
☐ PH-KCE	Boeing (Douglas) MD-11	48559 / 575		0094	1194	3 GE CF6-80C2D1F	280320	C37Y260	AF-LS	Audrey Hepburn / lsf WTC Trustee
☐ PH-KCF	Boeing (Douglas) MD-11	48560 / 579		0094	1294	3 GE CF6-80C2D1F	280320	C37Y260	AF-MR	Annie Romein / lsf FT Melon Leasing Ltd
☐ PH-KCG	Boeing (Douglas) MD-11	48561 / 585		0095	0595	3 GE CF6-80C2D1F	280320	C37Y260	AG-DP	Maria Callas / lsf WTC Trustee
☐ PH-KCH	Boeing (Douglas) MD-11	48562 / 591		0095	0895	3 GE CF6-80C2D1F	280320	C37Y260	AG-RS	Anna Pavlova / lsf Occabot Beheer B.V.
☐ PH-KCI	Boeing (Douglas) MD-11	48563 / 593	PP-SPM	0095	1195	3 GE CF6-80C2D1F	280320	C37Y260	AH-BR	Moeder / Mother Theresa
☐ PH-KCK	Boeing (Douglas) MD-11	48564 / 612		0097	0497	3 GE CF6-80C2D1F	280320	C37Y260	AH-GP	Ingrid Bergman / lsf Governor & Co.
☐ PH-BUH	Boeing 747-206B (SF) (SUD)	21110 / 271		0075	1075	4 GE CF6-50E2	377842	Freighter	DM-BH	Dr. Albert Plesman / cvtd -206B (M)
☐ PH-BUI	Boeing 747-206B (SF) (SUD)	21111 / 276	N8297V*	0075	1275	4 GE CF6-50E2	377842	Freighter	DK-BM	Willbur Wright / cvtd -206B (M)
☐ PH-BUK	Boeing 747-206B (M) (SUD)	21549 / 336		0078	0978	4 GE CF6-50E2	377842	C56Y241 / Plts	BK-GJ	Louis Blériot / lsfNCLBLse/cvtd-206B(M)
☐ PH-BUL	Boeing 747-206B (M) (SUD)	21550 / 344		0078	1178	4 GE CF6-50E2	377842	C56Y241 / Plts	DK-AJ	Charles A. Lindbergh / cvtd -206B (M)
☐ PH-BUM	Boeing 747-206B (M) (SUD)	21659 / 369	N1792B*	0079	0579	4 GE CF6-50E2	377842	C56Y241 / Plts	GL-FJ	Sir Charles E.Kingsford Smith / cvtd(M)
☐ PH-BUN	Boeing 747-206B (M) (SUD)	21660 / 389		0079	0879	4 GE CF6-50E2	377842	C56Y241 / Plts	GL-JK	Anthony HG.Fokker / lsfWTC/cvtd-206B(M)
☐ PH-BUO	Boeing 747-206B (SUD)	21848 / 397		0079	0979	4 GE CF6-50E2	371945	C34Y432	HJ-CG	The Missouri / lsf WTC Trust/cvtd-206B
☐ PH-BUP	Boeing 747-206B (SUD)	22376 / 474	N1295E	0080	0980	4 GE CF6-50E2	371945	C34Y432	DK-BL	The Ganges / lsf ILFC/cvtd-206B
☐ PH-BUR	Boeing 747-206B (SUD)	22379 / 491	N1298E	0080	1280	4 GE CF6-50E2	371945	C34Y432	BM-CG	The Indus / lsf SPA Inc./cvtd -206B
☐ PH-BUT	Boeing 747-206B (M) (SUD)	22380 / 539	N1309E	0081	0981	4 GE CF6-50E2	377842	C56Y241 / Plts	DL-AM	Adm. Richard E.Byrd / lsf ILFC/cvtd (M)
☐ PH-BUU	Boeing 747-306 (M)	23056 / 587	N4548M	0083	1083	4 GE CF6-50E2	374850	C56Y241 / Plts	DM-AF	Sir Frank Whittle / lsf ILFC
☐ PH-BUV	Boeing 747-306 (M)	23137 / 600	N4551N	0084	0984	4 GE CF6-50E2	374850	C56Y241 / Plts	BM-AE	Sir Geoffrey de Havilland / lsf WTC Tr.
☐ PH-BUW	Boeing 747-306 (M)	23508 / 657	N6055X*	0086	1086	4 GE CF6-50E2	374850	C56Y241 / Plts	DK-BG	Leonardo da Vinci / lsf Orient Aircraft
☐ PH-BFA	Boeing 747-406	23999 / 725	N6018N*	0089	0589	4 GE CF6-80C2B1F	377842	C52Y372	DJ-BG	City of Atlanta / lsf Crown Aircraft
☐ PH-BFB	Boeing 747-406	24000 / 732		0089	0689	4 GE CF6-80C2B1F	377842	C52Y372	EH-BC	City of Bangkok / lsf Westriba One Ltd
☐ PH-BFC	Boeing 747-406 (M)	23982 / 735	N6038E*	0089	0989	4 GE CF6-80C2B1F	396893	C52Y232 / Plts	DK-AC	City of Calgary / lsf Westriba/asia-TL
☐ PH-BFD	Boeing 747-406 (M)	24001 / 737		0089	0989	4 GE CF6-80C2B1F	396893	C52Y232 / Plts	DK-AF	City of Dubai/Doebai / lsfBNECo/asia-TL
☐ PH-BFE	Boeing 747-406 (M)	24201 / 763	N6046P*	0090	0190	4 GE CF6-80C2B1F	396893	C52Y232 / Plts	DM-AJ	City of Melbourne / lsf ORIX
☐ PH-BFF	Boeing 747-406 (M)	24202 / 770	N6046P*	0090	0290	4 GE CF6-80C2B1F	396893	C52Y232 / Plts	DM-AL	City of Freetown / lsf ORIX
☐ PH-BFG	Boeing 747-406	24517 / 782		0090	0490	4 GE CF6-80C2B1F	377842	C52Y372	DM-BE	City of Guayaquil / lsf Barnesbury Ltd
☐ PH-BFH	Boeing 747-406 (M)	24518 / 783	N60668*	0090	0490	4 GE CF6-80C2B1F	396893	C52Y232 / Plts	EH-AF	City of HongKong / lsf Windmill/asia-TL
☐ PH-BFI	Boeing 747-406 (M)	25086 / 850		0091	0591	4 GE CF6-80C2B1F	396893	C52Y232 / Plts	EH-BK	City of Jakarta / lsf JL Windmill Lease
☐ PH-BFK	Boeing 747-406 (M)	25087 / 854		0091	0591	4 GE CF6-80C2B1F	396893	C52Y232 / Plts	EH-BL	City of Karachi / lsf LG Best Leasing
☐ PH-BFL	Boeing 747-406	25356 / 888		0091	1291	4 GE CF6-80C2B1F	377842	C52Y372	DM-AK	City of Lima
☐ PH-BFM	Boeing 747-406 (M)	26373 / 896		0092	0292	4 GE CF6-80C2B1F	396893	C52Y232 / Plts	CG-LR	City of Mexico / lsf CIT FSC / asia-TL
☐ PH-BFN	Boeing 747-406	26372 / 969		0093	0493	4 GE CF6-80C2B1F	377842	C52Y372	KL-JP	City of Nairobi / lsf Amstelveen FSC
☐ PH-BFO	Boeing 747-406 (M)	25413 / 938		0092	1092	4 GE CF6-80C2B1F	396893	C52Y232 / Plts	BQ-EJ	City of Orlando / lsf Rochester FSC Ltd
☐ PH-BFP	Boeing 747-406 (M)	26374 / 992		0093	0993	4 GE CF6-80C2B1F	396893	C52Y232 / Plts	KL-MP	City of Paramaribo / lsf NightWatch FSC
☐ PH-BFR	Boeing 747-406 (M)	27202 / 1014		0094	0194	4 GE CF6-80C2B1F	396893	C52Y232 / Plts	CG-KS	City of Rio de Janeiro / lsf WTC Tr.
☐ PH-BFS	Boeing 747-406 (M)	28195 / 1090		0096	1096	4 GE CF6-80C2B1F	396893	C52Y232 / Plts	KL-HP	City of Seoul / lsf WTC Trustee
☐ PH-BFT	Boeing 747-406 (M)	28459 / 1112		0597	0597	4 GE CF6-80C2B1F	396893	C52Y232 / Plts	KM-DR	Tokio / City of Tokyo / lsf WTC Trustee
☐ PH-BFU	Boeing 747-406 (M)	28196 / 1127		0097	0997	4 GE CF6-80C2B1F	396893	C52Y232 / Plts	DM-BC	City of Beijing
☐ PH-BFV	Boeing 747-406 (M)	28460		0099		4 GE CF6-80C2B1F	396893	C52Y232 / Plts		City of Vancouver / oo-delivery 0899
☐ PH-BFW	Boeing 747-406 (M)					4 GE CF6-80C2B1F	396893	C52Y232 / Plts		oo-delivery 0000
☐ PH-BFX	Boeing 747-406 (M)					4 GE CF6-80C2B1F	396893	C52Y232 / Plts		oo-delivery 0001
☐ PH-BFY	Boeing 747-406 (M)					4 GE CF6-80C2B1F	396893	C52Y232 / Plts		oo-delivery 0004
☐ PH-BFZ	Boeing 747-406 (M)					4 GE CF6-80C2B1F	396893	C52Y232 / Plts		oo-delivery 0005

KLM aerocarto (KLM Aerocarto, B.V. dba) **Rotterdam & Teuge**

PO Box 7002, NL-6801 HA Arnhem, Netherlands ☎ (26) 377 83 90 Tx: none Fax: (26) 362 12 20 SITA: n/a
F: 1921 ♙♙♙ 55 Head: Gerrit Maten Net: http://web.klmaerocarto.com Aircraft below MTOW 1361kg: Cessna 172

☐ PH-OTJ	Cessna T207A Turbo Stationair 8 II	20700590	N37443	0080	0680	1 CO TSIO-520-M	1725	Photo / Survey		
☐ PH-OTH	Piper PA-31-350 Navajo Chieftain	31-7552075	G-BXUV	0075	0775	2 LY TIO-540-J2BD	3185	Photo / Survey		

KLM cityhopper = WA / KLC (KLM Cityhopper B.V. dba/Subs.of KLM Royal Dutch Airl./formerly NetherLines B.V. & NLM CityHopper B.V.) **Amsterdam-Schiphol** KLM cityhopper

Postbus 7700, NL-1117 ZL Schiphol-Oost, Netherlands ☎ (20) 649 22 27 Tx: 11252 klm nl Fax: (20) 649 23 79 SITA: SPLZAKL
F: 1966 ♙♙♙ 670 Head: Elfrieke Van Galen ICAO: CITY Net: n/a Operates scheduled flights in conjunction with KLM-Royal Dutch Airlines using KL flight numbers.

☐ PH-KSA	Saab 340B	340B-175	SE-F75*	0089	0190	2 GE CT7-9B	13155	Y33	NONE	Straatsburg / std AMS / for sale
☐ PH-KSB	Saab 340B	340B-178	SE-F78*	0090	0290	2 GE CT7-9B	13155	Y33	NONE	Bristol / std AMS / for sale
☐ PH-KSC	Saab 340B	340B-179	SE-F79*	0090	0390	2 GE CT7-9B	13155	Y33	NONE	Cardiff / std AMS / for sale
☐ PH-KSD	Saab 340B	340B-183	SE-F83*	0090	0590	2 GE CT7-9B	13155	Y33	NONE	Neurenberg / std AMS / for sale
☐ PH-KSE	Saab 340B	340B-186	SE-F86*	0090	0490	2 GE CT7-9B	13155	Y33	NONE	Southampton / std AMS / for sale
☐ PH-JXJ	Fokker 50 (F27 Mk050)	20232	PT-SLJ	0091	0398	2 PWC PW125B	20820	Y50	JR-AP	lsf Debis AirFinance B.V.
☐ PH-JXK	Fokker 50 (F27 Mk050)	20233	PT-SLK	0091	0198	2 PWC PW125B	20820	Y50	JR-BP	lsf Debis AirFinance B.V.
☐ PH-KVA	Fokker 50 (F27 Mk050)	20189	PH-EXC*	0090	0790	2 PWC PW125B	20820	Y50	HK-DE	City of Bremen / lsf Libra Leasing
☐ PH-KVB	Fokker 50 (F27 Mk050)	20190	PH-EXD*	0090	0890	2 PWC PW125B	20820	Y50	HK-DF	City of Brussels/Brussel / lsf Libra L.
☐ PH-KVC	Fokker 50 (F27 Mk050)	20191	PH-EXF*	0090	0890	2 PWC PW125B	20820	Y50	HK-DM	City of Stavanger / lsf Libra Leasing
☐ PH-KVD	Fokker 50 (F27 Mk050)	20197		0090	1090	2 PWC PW125B	20820	Y50	HK-CG	City of Düsseldorf / lsf Libra Leasing
☐ PH-KVE	Fokker 50 (F27 Mk050)	20206		0090	0191	2 PWC PW125B	20820	Y50	HK-CJ	City of Amsterdam / lsf DB Export Lsng
☐ PH-KVF	Fokker 50 (F27 Mk050)	20207		0090	0191	2 PWC PW125B	20820	Y50	HK-CL	City of Paris/Parijs / lsf DB Exp.Lsng
☐ PH-KVG	Fokker 50 (F27 Mk050)	20211		0090	0391	2 PWC PW125B	20820	Y50	HK-CM	City of Stuttgart / lsf DB Export Lsng
☐ PH-KVH	Fokker 50 (F27 Mk050)	20217		0091	0591	2 PWC PW125B	20820	Y50	HK-DQ	City of Hanover/Hannover / lsf DB Exp.
☐ PH-KVI	Fokker 50 (F27 Mk050)	20218		0091	0691	2 PWC PW125B	20820	Y50	HK-EQ	City of Bordeaux / lsf DB Export Lsng
☐ PH-KVK	Fokker 50 (F27 Mk050)	20219		0091	0691	2 PWC PW125B	20820	Y50	HK-FQ	City of London/Londen / lsf DB Exp.Lsng
☐ PH-KXM	Fokker 50 (F27 Mk050)	20252	PT-SLO	0092	0298	2 PWC PW125B	20820	Y50	JR-CP	lsf Debis AirFinance B.V.
☐ PH-KZA	Fokker 70 (F28 Mk0070)	11567		0096	0296	2 RR Tay 620-15	37995	Y80	KR-JS	
☐ PH-KZB	Fokker 70 (F28 Mk0070)	11562		0096	0296	2 RR Tay 620-15	37995	Y80	KR-LM	
☐ PH-KZC	Fokker 70 (F28 Mk0070)	11566		0096	0596	2 RR Tay 620-15	37995	Y80	KR-LP	
☐ PH-KZD	Fokker 70 (F28 Mk0070)	11582		0097	0197	2 RR Tay 620-15	37995	Y80	KR-LQ	
☐ PH-KZE	Fokker 70 (F28 Mk0070)	11576		0096	1096	2 RR Tay 620-15	37995	Y80	PQ-HR	
☐ PH-KZF	Fokker 70 (F28 Mk0070)	11577		0096	1096	2 RR Tay 620-15	37995	Y80	PQ-HS	
☐ PH-KZG	Fokker 70 (F28 Mk0070)	11578		0096	1196	2 RR Tay 620-15	37995	Y80	PQ-JR	
☐ PH-KZH	Fokker 70 (F28 Mk0070)	11583		0097	0297	2 RR Tay 620-15	37995	Y80	PQ-JS	
☐ PH-KZI	Fokker 70 (F28 Mk0070)	11579		0097	0397	2 RR Tay 620-15	37995	Y80	PQ-KM	
☐ PH-KZK	Fokker 70 (F28 Mk0070)	11581		0097	0497	2 RR Tay 620-15	37995	Y80	PQ-KR	
☐ PH-WXA	Fokker 70 (F28 Mk0070)	11570	I-REJO	0096	1297	2 RR Tay 620-15	37995	Y80	JR-HP	
☐ PH-WXC	Fokker 70 (F28 Mk0070)	11574	I-REJI	0095	1297	2 RR Tay 620-15	37995	Y80	JR-KP	

493 registration type of aircraft cn/fn ex/ex* mfd del powered by mtow kg configuration selcal name/fln/specialitites/remarks

KLM exel = 4X / AXL (Air Exel Netherlands, B.V. dba / Assw. with Schreiner Airways / Quirine Excellent Holding & LIOF) — Maastricht

PO Box 300, NL-6190 AH Maastricht-Aachen Airport, Netherlands ☎ (43) 358 85 85 Tx: none Fax: (43) 358 85 86 SITA: MSTXTKL
F: 1991 ⁂ 75 Head: Roberto Stinga IATA: 824 ICAO: EXEL COMMUTER Net: n/a Operates scheduled flights in conjunction with KLM-Royal Dutch Airlines using KL & 4X-flight numbers.

registration	type of aircraft	cn/fn	ex/ex*	mfd	del	powered by	mtow kg	configuration	selcal	name/fln/specialitites/remarks
☐ PH-XLA	Embraer 120RT Brasilia (EMB-120RT)	120081	G-BRAZ	0088	0192	2 PWC PW118	11500	Y30		Mosae Trajectum (Maastricht)
☐ PH-XLB	Embraer 120RT Brasilia (EMB-120RT)	120091	F-GFTB	0088	0792	2 PWC PW118	11500	Y30		Aquis Grani (Aachen)
☐ PH-XLF	Embraer 120ER Brasilia (EMB-120ER)	120082	OO-DTF	0088	0198	2 PWC PW118	11990	Y30		cvtd 120RT
☐ PH-XLG	Embraer 120ER Brasilia (EMB-120ER)	120121	OO-DTI	0089	0198	2 PWC PW118	11990	Y28		cvtd 120RT
☐ PH-XLC	ATR 42-320	060	F-WQBX	0087	0497	2 PWC PW121	16700	Y48		lsf Bartholdi Bail / cvtd -300
☐ PH-XLD	ATR 42-320	075	F-WQBS	0088	0397	2 PWC PW121	16700	Y48		lsf Cleveland Bail
☐ PH-XLE	ATR 42-320	090	F-WQBR	0088	0397	2 PWC PW121	16700	Y48		lsf Lax Bail
☐ PH-XLH	ATR 72-201	195	F-WQGO	0090	1298	2 PWC PW124B	21500	Y66		lsf ATR

MARTINAIR = MP / MPH (Martinair Holland N.V. dba / Subsidiary of KLM-Royal Dutch Airlines) — Amsterdam-Schiphol

PO Box 7507, NL-1118 ZG Schiphol, Netherlands ☎ (20) 601 12 22 Tx: 11678 macair nl Fax: (20) 601 13 03 SITA: SPLPRMP
F: 1958 ⁂ 2055 Head: Aart Van Bochove IATA: 129 ICAO: MARTINAIR Net: http://www.travelx.com/martinairholland.hmtl

registration	type of aircraft	cn/fn	ex/ex*	mfd	del	powered by	mtow kg	configuration	selcal	name/fln/specialitites/remarks
☐ PH-MNZ	Dornier 228-212	8206	D-CDIV*	0092	0692	2 GA TPE331-5A-252D	6400	Surveyer		opf Rijkswaterstaat/Kustwacht
☐ PH-MEX	Cessna 650 Citation VI	650-0217		0092	0792	2 GA TFE731-3B-100S	9979	7 Pax	DF-JR	
☐ PH-MFX	Cessna 650 Citation VI	650-0240	N51143	0094	1294	2 GA TFE731-3B-100S	9979	7 Pax	HK-AS	
☐ PH-MGX	Embraer 120ER Brasilia (EMB-120ER)	120149	OO-DTK	0089	0296	2 PWC PW118	11990	Y28 Crew feeder		cvtd 120RT / based Santo Domingo
☐ PH-BPS	Dassault Falcon 20F-5	321	N104SB	0074	0998	2 GA TFE731-5BR-2C	13200	9 Pax		cvtd 20F
☐ PH-KBX	Fokker 70 (F28 Mk0070)	11547		0995	0396	2 RR Tay 620-15	39915	VIP 26 Pax	JR-DE	opf Gvmt/Dutch Royal Flight
☐ PH-MCG	Boeing 767-31A (ER)	24428 / 279		0089	0989	2 PW PW4060	184611	C24Y248	CQ-BH	Prins Johan Friso / lsf Mega-Flight KB
☐ PH-MCH	Boeing 767-31A (ER)	24429 / 294		0090	0290	2 PW PW4060	184611	C24Y248	CQ-BJ	Prins Constantijn / lsf Mega-Flight KB
☐ PH-MCI	Boeing 767-31A (ER)	25312 / 400		0091	1191	2 PW PW4060	184611	C24Y248	AR-LM	Prins Pieter-Christiaan / lsf Ruby Ac.
☐ PH-MCL	Boeing 767-31A (ER)	26469 / 415		0092	0292	2 PW PW4060	184611	C24Y248	BJ-PR	Koningin Beatrix / lsf JL Zodiac Lease
☐ PH-MCM	Boeing 767-31A (ER)	26470 / 416		0092	0292	2 PW PW4060	184611	C24Y248	CE-BS	Prins Floris / lsf Apple Ac.&6 other co
☐ PH-MCV	Boeing 767-31A (ER)	27619 / 595		0095	1195	2 PW PW4060	184611	C24Y248	JM-DS	lsf ILFC
☐ PH-MCP	Boeing (Douglas) MD-11F (CF)	48616 / 577	N90187*	0094	1294	3 PW PW4462	285990	C24Y344 / Frtr	BP-ES	lsf MGT Kumiai
☐ PH-MCR	Boeing (Douglas) MD-11F (CF)	48617 / 581		0095	0395	3 PW PW4462	283722	C24Y344 / Frtr	BQ-CS	lsf Yamasa Planet Lease Co. Ltd
☐ PH-MCS	Boeing (Douglas) MD-11F (CF)	48618 / 584		0095	0495	3 PW PW4462	285990	C24Y344 / Frtr	BQ-EG	lsf JL Royal Lease Co. Ltd
☐ PH-MCT	Boeing (Douglas) MD-11F (CF)	48629 / 586		0095	0595	3 PW PW4462	285990	C24Y344 / Frtr	BQ-EH	
☐ PH-MCU	Boeing (Douglas) MD-11F	48757 / 606		0096	1096	3 PW PW4462	285990	Freighter	PR-EQ	
☐ PH-MCW	Boeing (Douglas) MD-11F	48788 / 632		0098	1198	3 PW PW4462	285990	Freighter	CS-BP	
☐ PH-MCE	Boeing 747-21AC (M)	23652 / 669	N6038E*	0086	0287	4 GE CF6-50E2	377842	C18Y498 / Frtr	KL-AB	Prins van Oranje / lsf Mitsui Finance
☐ PH-MCF	Boeing 747-21AC (M)	24134 / 712	N6009F*	0088	0988	4 GE CF6-50E2	377842	C18Y498 / Frtr	FG-BC	Prins Claus / lsf Mega Carrier Komm.
☐ PH-MCN	Boeing 747-228F (SCD)	25266 / 878	F-GCBN	0091	1091	4 GE CF6-50E2	377842	Freighter	AF-HM	Prins Bernhard jr. / lsf Stellar Lsng

NATIONALE LUCHTVAART SCHOOL - NLS = NLS (B.V. Nationale Luchtvaartschool dba / Member of Schreiner Aviation Group, B.V.) — Maastricht

PO Box 204, NL-6190 AE Beek, Netherlands ☎ (43) 364 84 84 Tx: 56394 nlsaw nl Fax: (43) 364 66 19 SITA: n/a
F: 1927 ⁂ 50 Head: Walter H. Visser ICAO: PANDER Net: n/a Trainer-aircraft below MTOW 5000kg: Piper PA-28-161, PA-34-220T & Socata TB20

registration	type of aircraft	cn/fn	ex/ex*	mfd	del	powered by	mtow kg	configuration	selcal	name/fln/specialitites/remarks
☐ PH-SBK	Beech King Air 200	BB-180	G-BHVX	0076	0880	2 PWC PT6A-41	5670	Trainer		

NLR - Nationaal Lucht- & Ruimtevaartlaboratorium (National Aerospace Laboratory) — Amsterdam-Schiphol

Postbus 90502, NL-1006 BM Amsterdam, Netherlands ☎ (20) 511 31 13 Tx: none Fax: (20) 511 32 10 SITA: n/a
F: 1937 ⁂ 850 Head: Dr. Ir. B.M. Spee Net: n/a National organisation conducting aeronautical & space research work.

registration	type of aircraft	cn/fn	ex/ex*	mfd	del	powered by	mtow kg	configuration	selcal	name/fln/specialitites/remarks
☐ PH-NLZ	Fairchild (Swearingen) SA226TC Metro II	TC-277	N5651M*	0079	0479	2 GA TPE331-3UW-304G	6350	Research		
☐ PH-LAB	Cessna 550 Citation II	550-0712	N12030*	0093	0393	2 PWC JT15D-4	6396	Research		

POLITIE LUCHTVAART DIENST (Police Air Support Services) (Div. of National Police Agency / Dept. of the Technical & Operational Support division) — Amsterdam-Schiphol

PO Box 75014, NL-1117 ZN Schiphol-Oost, Netherlands ☎ (20) 502 56 00 Tx: none Fax: (20) 502 56 02 SITA: n/a
F: n/a ⁂ 76 Head: H.J.A. Remers Net: n/a Non-commercial state organisation conducting police aerial work, traffic surveillance & EMS flights when required.

registration	type of aircraft	cn/fn	ex/ex*	mfd	del	powered by	mtow kg	configuration	selcal	name/fln/specialitites/remarks
☐ PH-RPH	Cessna 182R Skylane II	18267808	N6243N	0081	0384	1 CO O-470-U	1406	Police survey		
☐ PH-RPI	Cessna 182R Skylane II	18267809	N6245N	0081	0384	1 CO O-470-U	1406	Police survey		
☐ PH-RPJ	Cessna 182R Skylane II	18267833	N6390N	0081	0584	1 CO O-470-U	1406	Police survey		
☐ PH-PLA	Eurocopter (Aerosp.) AS350B2 Ecureuil	2878		0095	0795	1 TU Arriel 1D1	2250	Policesurvey/EMS		opf Korps Landelijke Politie Diensten
☐ PH-PLB	Eurocopter (Aerosp.) AS350B2 Ecureuil	2884		0095	0795	1 TU Arriel 1D1	2250	Policesurvey/EMS		opf Korps Landelijke Politie Diensten
☐ PH-RPR	Eurocopter (MBB) BO105C	S-356	D-HDGS*	0078	0479	2 AN 250-C20	2400	Policesurvey/EMS		Dries
☐ PH-RPS	Eurocopter (MBB) BO105C	S-355	D-HDGR*	0078	0879	2 AN 250-C20	2400	Policesurvey/EMS		Jacques
☐ PH-RPV	Eurocopter (MBB) BO105C	S-249	D-HDHI*	0076	0676	2 AN 250-C20	2400	Policesurvey/EMS		Wim
☐ PH-RPW	Eurocopter (MBB) BO105C	S-250	D-HDHJ*	0076	0676	2 AN 250-C20	2400	Policesurvey/EMS		Henk
☐ PH-RPM	Britten-Norman BN-2T Turbine Islander	2190	G-BLNK*	0088	1288	2 AN 250-B17C	3175	Police survey		
☐ PH-RPN	Britten-Norman BN-2T Turbine Islander	2191	G-BLNL*	0088	1288	2 AN 250-B17C	3175	Police survey		

QUICK AIRWAYS HOLLAND = QAH (Quick Airways, B.V. dba) — Groningen-Eelde

Machlaan 10d, NL-9761 TK Eelde, Netherlands ☎ (50) 309 43 41 Tx: none Fax: (50) 309 17 94 SITA: n/a
F: 1984 ⁂ 10 Head: Ing. Gerard Huizinga ICAO: QUICK Net: http://www.quickairways.nl

registration	type of aircraft	cn/fn	ex/ex*	mfd	del	powered by	mtow kg	configuration	selcal	name/fln/specialitites/remarks
☐ PH-PTC	Piper PA-31-350 Navajo Chieftain	31-7852052	G-CLAN	0078	0584	2 LY TIO-540-J2BD	3342	6-8 Pax		
☐ PH-PTD	Piper PA-31-350 Navajo Chieftain	31-7852066	G-BRGV	0078	0984	2 LY TIO-540-J2BD	3342	6-8 Pax		
☐ PH-BOA	Mitsubishi MU-2B-60 Marquise	1507SA	N888FS	0081	0693	2 GA TPE331-10-511M	5250	6-8 Pax / EMS		

RAS - Rijnmond Air Services, B.V. = RAZ (Subsidiary of Quick Airways, B.V.) — Rotterdam

PO Box 12051, NL-3004 GB Rotterdam, Netherlands ☎ (10) 437 81 22 Tx: none Fax: (10) 437 17 77 SITA: n/a
F: 1980 ⁂ 30 Head: Wiebe Bosma ICAO: RIJNMOND Net: n/a Aircraft below MTOW 1361 kg: Cessna F172.

registration	type of aircraft	cn/fn	ex/ex*	mfd	del	powered by	mtow kg	configuration	selcal	name/fln/specialitites/remarks
☐ PH-AST	Piper PA-31-350 Navajo Chieftain	31-7752046	N63722	0077	1283	2 LY TIO-540-J2BD	3342	8 Pax/Frtr		
☐ PH-XPI	Piper PA-31-350 Navajo Chieftain	31-7752187	G-BFFR	0077	0183	2 LY TIO-540-J2BD	3342	8 Pax/Frtr		
☐ PH-FWM	Mitsubishi MU-2B-60 Marquise	1548SA	N474MA	0082	1286	2 GA TPE331-10-511M	5250	8 Pax/Frtr/EMS		
☐ PH-RAX	Fairchild (Swearingen) SA227AT Merlin IVC	AT-493	F-GGLG	0081	0199	2 GA TPE331-11U-611G	6350	19 Pax/Frtr/EMS		
☐ PH-RAZ	Fairchild (Swearingen) SA226TC Metro II	TC-252	OY-AZW	0078	0894	2 GA TPE331-3UW-303G	5670	17 Pax/Frtr/EMS		

SCHREINER AIRWAYS, B.V. = AW / SCH (Member of Schreiner Aviation Group) — Rotterdam, Maastricht & Overseas

PO Box 381, NL-2130 AJ Hoofddorp, Netherlands ☎ (23) 555 55 55 Tx: none Fax: (23) 555 55 00 SITA: n/a
F: 1945 ⁂ 350 Head: Evert van Schaik ICAO: SCHREINER Net: n/a

registration	type of aircraft	cn/fn	ex/ex*	mfd	del	powered by	mtow kg	configuration	selcal	name/fln/specialitites/remarks
☐ PH-SKP	Beech King Air 200C	BL-11	F-GIMD	0080	0497	2 PWC PT6A-41	5670			lsf Charis Finance Ltd
☐ PH-SDH	De Havilland DHC-8-102 Dash 8	222	C-GFUM*	0090	0790	2 PWC PW120A	15650	Y36		
☐ PH-TTA	De Havilland DHC-8-102 Dash 8	237	G-BRYG	0090	1096	2 PWC PW120A	15650	Y36		lsf GECA / sub-lst TRQ
☐ PH-TTB	De Havilland DHC-8-102 Dash 8	241	G-BRYH	0090	0298	2 PWC PW120A	15650	Y36		lsf GECA / sub-lst TRQ
☐ PH-SDK	De Havilland DHC-8-311 Dash 8	254	C-GFYI*	0091	0191	2 PWC PW123	19500	Y46		
☐ PH-SDM	De Havilland DHC-8-311 Dash 8	298	N511SK	0092	0393	2 PWC PW123	19500	CY46		lsf GECA/sub-lst/opf SAB in Sabena-cs
☐ PH-SDP	De Havilland DHC-8-311 Dash 8	300	N501DC	0092	0993	2 PWC PW123	19500	CY46		lsf GECA/sub-lst/opf SAB in Sabena-cs
☐ PH-SDR	De Havilland DHC-8-311 Dash 8	283	EI-CED	0091	0394	2 PWC PW123	19500	CY46		lsf GECA/sub-lst/opf SAB in Sabena-cs
☐ PH-SDT	De Havilland DHC-8-311 Dash 8	276	C-FZBL	0091	0996	2 PWC PW123	19500	CY46		lsf GECA/sub-lst/opf SAB in Sabena-cs
☐ PH-SDU	De Havilland DHC-8-311 Dash 8	232	C-FXXU	0090	1096	2 PWC PW123	19500	CY46		lsf GECA/sub-lst/opf SAB in Sabena-cs

SCHREINER NORTHSEA HELICOPTERS, B.V. - SNH (Member of Schreiner Aviation Group / formerly KLM ERA Helicopters B.V. & KLM Helikopters, B.V.) — Den Helder

Luchthavenweg 6B, NL-1786 PP Den Helder, Netherlands ☎ (223) 67 75 55 Tx: none Fax: (223) 67 75 01 SITA: n/a
F: 1965 ⁂ 215 Head: Tjapko J. van Wijk Net: n/a

registration	type of aircraft	cn/fn	ex/ex*	mfd	del	powered by	mtow kg	configuration	selcal	name/fln/specialitites/remarks
☐ PH-KHD	Eurocopter (MBB) BO105CBS-4	S-324	HB-XGM	0077	0896	2 AN 250-C20B	2500	EMS		lst ANWB Medical Air Assistance
☐ PH-KHE	Eurocopter (MBB) BO105CBS-4	S-329	HB-XGT	0077	0896	2 AN 250-C20B	2500	EMS		lst ANWB Medical Air Assistance
☐ PH-SSK	Eurocopter (Aerosp.) SA365C2 Dauphin 2	5010	5N-BAO	0079	1085	2 TU Arriel 1A2	3500	9 Pax		
☐ PH-SST	Eurocopter (Aerosp.) SA365N Dauphin 2	6077	EC-EEP	0084	0185	2 TU Arriel 1C	4000	9 Pax		
☐ PH-SSW	Eurocopter (Aerosp.) SA365N Dauphin 2	6103	V8-UDW	0084	1193	2 TU Arriel 1C	4000	9 Pax		lsf DNK Leasing Group Ltd
☐ PH-SSX	Eurocopter (Aerosp.) SA365N Dauphin 2	6030	5N-BAR	0082	0595	2 TU Arriel 1C	4000	9 Pax		
☐ PH-SSY	Eurocopter (Aerosp.) SA365C2 Dauphin 2	5055	EC-GVU	0080	0496	2 TU Arriel 1A2	3500	9 Pax		
☐ PH-KHA	Sikorsky S-76B	760310	N638ME	0085	0795	2 PWC PT6B-36A	5307	12 Pax		
☐ PH-KHC	Sikorsky S-76B	760350	D-HMDE	0089	1095	2 PWC PT6B-36A	5307	12 Pax		
☐ PH-NZS	Sikorsky S-76B	760325	G-UKLS	0086	1286	2 PWC PT6B-36A	5307	12 Pax		
☐ PH-NZT	Sikorsky S-76B	760326	G-UKLT	0086	1286	2 PWC PT6B-36A	5307	12 Pax		
☐ PH-NZU	Sikorsky S-76B	760329	G-UKLU	0086	0287	2 PWC PT6B-36A	5307	12 Pax		
☐ PH-NZV	Sikorsky S-76B	760336	G-UKLM	0086	0487	2 PWC PT6B-36A	5307	12 Pax		
☐ PH-NZW	Sikorsky S-76B	760381	G-OKLE	0091	0791	2 PWC PT6B-36A	5307	12 Pax		
☐ PH-NZZ	Sikorsky S-76B	760316	N373G	0086	0498	2 PWC PT6B-36A	5307	12 Pax		
☐ PH-NZD	Sikorsky S-61N	61489		0071	1171	2 GE CT58-140-1	9298	24 Pax		opf UN
☐ PH-NZG	Sikorsky S-61N	61753		0075	1275	2 GE CT58-140-1	9298	24 Pax		
☐ PH-NZK	Sikorsky S-61N	61773	LN-OMO	0077	0278	2 GE CT58-140-1	9298	24 Pax		

SPECIAL AIR SERVICES, B.V. - SAS — Teuge

De Zanden 11C, NL-7395 PA Twello, Netherlands ☎ (55) 323 17 89 Tx: none Fax: (55) 323 19 24 SITA: n/a
F: 1983 ⁂ 50 Head: Gerard Klaver Net: http://www.aviation.nl/sas Aircraft below MTOW 1361kg: Cessna 150, 172 & Piper PA-18.

registration	type of aircraft	cn/fn	ex/ex*	mfd	del	powered by	mtow kg	configuration	selcal	name/fln/specialitites/remarks
☐ PH-RVS	Partenavia P.68B	98		0077	0186	2 LY IO-360-A1B6	1960			
☐ PH-HNK	Cessna 340A II	340A0546	OO-DKE	0078	0892	2 CO TSIO-520-N	2853			

TESSEL AIR, B.V.

Texel

Postweg 128, NL-1795 JS De Cocksdorp, Netherlands ☎ (222) 31 14 64 Tx: none Fax: (222) 31 14 14 SITA: n/a
F: 1973 ⁂ n/a Head: Bob D. Rinks Net: n/a Aircraft below MTOW 1361 kg: Cessna F172.

registration	type of aircraft	cn/fn	ex/ex*	mfd	del	powered by	mtow kg	configuration	selcal	name/fln/specialitites/remarks
☐ PH-LMR	Piper PA-32-260 Cherokee SIX	32-7700021	N38982	0077	1078	1 LY O-540-E4B5	1542			lsf Industr.Disconto Maatschappij N.V.
☐ PH-JAS	Cessna 208 Caravan I	20800226		0093	0393	1 PWC PT6A-114	3629	Para		

TRANSAVIA AIRLINES, C.V. = HV / TRA (Subsidiary of KLM-Royal Dutch Airlines / formerly Transavia Holland N.V.)

Amsterdam-Schiphol

PO Box 7777, NL-1118 ZM Schiphol Airport Centre, Netherlands ☎ (20) 604 65 55 Tx: 13067 tras nl Fax: (20) 601 50 93 SITA: SPLDDHV
F: 1966 ⁂ 1130 Head: Peter J. Legro IATA: 979 ICAO: TRANSAVIA Net: n/a

registration	type of aircraft	cn/fn	ex/ex*	mfd	del	powered by	mtow kg	configuration	selcal	name/fln/specialitites/remarks
☐ PH-HVF	Boeing 737-3K2	23411 / 1195	XA-STM	0086	0286	2 CFMI CFM56-3B2	61915	Y149	LM-CF	
☐ PH-HVG	Boeing 737-3K2	23412 / 1198	XA-STN	0086	0386	2 CFMI CFM56-3B2	61869	Y149	LM-BH	
☐ PH-HVJ	Boeing 737-3K2	23738 / 1360		0087	0387	2 CFMI CFM56-3B2	61915	Y149	LM-CH	lsf SL Air Leasing Co. Ltd
☐ PH-HVK	Boeing 737-3K2	23786 / 1386	XA-SVQ	0087	0587	2 CFMI CFM56-3B2	61869	Y149	LM-DE	lsf SL Air Leasing
☐ PH-HVM	Boeing 737-3K2	24326 / 1683		0089	0389	2 CFMI CFM56-3B2	60962	Y149	HM-AB	lsf CMK Aircraft Lease (One) B.V.
☐ PH-HVN	Boeing 737-3K2	24327 / 1712		0089	0589	2 CFMI CFM56-3B2	61915	Y149	HM-AL	lsf CMK Aircraft Lease (Two) B.V.
☐ PH-HVT	Boeing 737-3K2	24328 / 1856		0090	0590	2 CFMI CFM56-3C1	61915	Y149	HM-CD	lsf CMK Aircraft Lease (Three) B.V.
☐ PH-HVV	Boeing 737-3K2	24329 / 1858		0090	0590	2 CFMI CFM56-3C1	61915	Y149	GQ-AP	lsf CMK Aircraft Lease (Four) B.V.
☐ PH-TSU	Boeing 737-3Y0	24905 / 2001	CS-TKE	0091	0295	2 CFMI CFM56-3C1	62142	C24Y102	GQ-BC	lsf GECA
☐ PH-TSW	Boeing 737-3L9	24219 / 1600	OY-MMO	0088	0395	2 CFMI CFM56-3B2	61915	Y149	GQ-BE	lsf CITG
☐ PH-TSX	Boeing 737-3K2	26318 / 2731		0095	0695	2 CFMI CFM56-3C1	62822	Y149	GQ-BD	lsf ILFC
☐ PH-TSY	Boeing 737-3K2	28085 / 2722		0095	0595	2 CFMI CFM56-3C1	62822	Y149	GQ-BF	lsf ILFC
☐ PH-TSZ	Boeing 737-3K2	27635 / 2721		0095	0595	2 CFMI CFM56-3C1	62822	Y149	GQ-BH	lsf ILFC
☐ PH-HZA	Boeing 737-8K2	28373 / 51		0098	0698	2 CFMI CFM56-7B26	78245	Y184	LS-GR	
☐ PH-HZB	Boeing 737-8K2	28374 / 57		0098	0698	2 CFMI CFM56-7B26	78245	Y184	LS-HJ	
☐ PH-HZC	Boeing 737-8K2	28375 / 85		0898	0898	2 CFMI CFM56-7B26	78245	Y184		City of Rotterdam
☐ PH-HZD	Boeing 737-8K2	28376 / 252		0099	0399	2 CFMI CFM56-7B26	78245	Y184		
☐ PH-HZE	Boeing 737-8K2	28377				2 CFMI CFM56-7B26	78245	Y184		oo-delivery 0599
☐ PH-HZF	Boeing 737-8K2	28378				2 CFMI CFM56-7B26	78245	Y184		oo-delivery 0899
☐ PH-HZG	Boeing 737-8K2	28379				2 CFMI CFM56-7B26	78245	Y184		oo-delivery 0300
☐ PH-HZI	Boeing 737-8K2	28380				2 CFMI CFM56-7B26	78245	Y184		oo-delivery 0600
☐ PH-TKA	Boeing 757-2K2	26633 / 519		0093	0293	2 RR RB211-535E4	105519	Y218	MQ-GL	lsf JL Canal Lease Co. Ltd
☐ PH-TKB	Boeing 757-2K2	26634 / 545		0093	0593	2 RR RB211-535E4	105519	Y218	MQ-GP	Isle of Kos / lsf JL Delft Lease Co.Ltd
☐ PH-TKC	Boeing 757-2K2	26635 / 608		0094	0494	2 RR RB211-535E4	105519	Y218	MQ-HJ	lsf JL Polder Lease Co. Ltd
☐ PH-TKD	Boeing 757-2K2	26330 / 717	C-GTSR	0096	0696	2 RR RB211-535E4	105519	Y218	MQ-HK	lsf ILFC/sublst TEJ as XA-TMU in winter

TTA - Trans Travel Airlines, B.V. = 6N / TRQ (formerly Turdus Airways, B.V.)

Lelystad

Arendweg 21, NL-8218 PE Lelystad, Netherlands ☎ (320) 28 84 00 Tx: none Fax: (320) 28 84 01 SITA: LEYRC6N
F: 1985 ⁂ 25 Head: Ode Groot IATA: 556 ICAO: HUNTER Net: n/a Aircraft below MTOW 1361 kg: Cessna 150 & Piper PA-28.

registration	type of aircraft	cn/fn	ex/ex*	mfd	del	powered by	mtow kg	configuration	selcal	name/fln/specialitites/remarks
☐ PH-DUS	Beech 1300 Airliner	BB-1296	N296YV	0088	1292	2 PWC PT6A-42	5670	Y13 / EMS		lsf Turdus Harderwijk B.V./cvtd KA B200
☐ PH-TTA	De Havilland DHC-8-102 Dash 8	237	G-BRYG	0090	1096	2 PWC PW120A	15650	Y36		lsf SCH
☐ PH-TTB	De Havilland DHC-8-102 Dash 8	241	G-BRYH	0090	0298	2 PWC PW120A	15650	Y36		lsf SCH

TULIP AIR, B.V. = TLP (Sister company of Tulip Air Charter, B.V.)

Rotterdam

PO Box 12059, NL-3004 GB Rotterdam, Netherlands ☎ (10) 437 81 00 Tx: none Fax: (10) 437 21 64 SITA: n/a
F: 1988 ⁂ n/a Head: Frans W.M. Stevens ICAO: TULIPAIR Net: n/a Aircraft below MTOW 1361kg: Cessna 172

registration	type of aircraft	cn/fn	ex/ex*	mfd	del	powered by	mtow kg	configuration	selcal	name/fln/specialitites/remarks
☐ PH-ABD	Piper PA-31-350 Navajo Chieftain	31-7305048	F-BTMU	0073	0589	2 LY TIO-540-J2BD	3342			
☐ PH-EEF	Piper PA-31-350 Navajo Chieftain	31-7552017	SE-GIM	0075	0593	2 LY TIO-540-J2BD	3342			
☐ PH-GYN	Piper PA-31-350 Navajo Chieftain	31-7305119	G-BDMD	0073	0488	2 LY TIO-540-J2BD	3342			
☐ PH-IDA	Piper PA-31-350 Navajo Chieftain	31-7852160	N27806	0078	0091	2 LY TIO-540-J2BD	3342			lsf Dejoha B.V.
☐ N5BU	Piper PA-31-350 Navajo Chieftain	31-7305029	G-IFTA	0073	0492	2 LY TIO-540-J2BD	3289			lsf Aircraft Guaranty Corp.
☐ PH-ATM	Beech Catpass 200	BB-123	N120DA	0076	0894	2 PWC PT6A-41	5670			lsf Tulip Air II B.V./cvtd King Air 200
☐ PH-DDB	Beech King Air 200	BB-221	SE-KYL	0077	0797	2 PWC PT6A-41	5670			lsf Tulip Air II B.V.

TULIP AIR CHARTER, B.V. = FRN (Sister co.of Tulip Air B.V./Member of Farnair Europe, European Aviation Alliance)

Rotterdam

PO Box 12110, NL-3004 GC Rotterdam, Netherlands ☎ (10) 238 09 09 Tx: none Fax: (10) 238 09 00 SITA: n/a
F: 1995 ⁂ n/a Head: Co van der Meer ICAO: FARNAIR EUROPE Net: n/a

registration	type of aircraft	cn/fn	ex/ex*	mfd	del	powered by	mtow kg	configuration	selcal	name/fln/specialitites/remarks
☐ PH-FNV	Fokker F27 Friendship 500 (F27 Mk500)	10397	F-BPUK	0069	0695	2 RR Dart 532-7R	20820	Freighter		lsf Tulip Air II B.V. / sub-lst MNL
☐ PH-FNW	Fokker F27 Friendship 500 (F27 Mk500)	10398	F-BPUL	0069	1195	2 RR Dart 532-7R	20820	Freighter		lsf Tulip Air II B.V./Farnair Europe-cs
☐ PH-FOZ	Fokker F27 Friendship 500 (F27 Mk500)	10425	G-BVZW	0069	1298	2 RR Dart 532-7R	20820	Freighter		lsf Farnair SPC/op in Farnair Europe-cs
☐ PH-JLN	Fokker F27 Friendship 500 (F27 Mk500)	10449	F-BSUO	0071	0298	2 RR Dart 532-7R	20820	Freighter		lsf FAT / op in Farnair Europe-colors
☐ PH-CLA	Airbus Industrie A300B4-103 (F)	044	N204EA	0077	0998	2 GE CF6-50C2	157500	Freighter		lsf Farnair SPC/cvtd-2C/103/opin DHL-cs
☐ PH-EAN	Airbus Industrie A300B4-103 (F)	041	N201EA	0077	0498	2 GE CF6-50C2	157500	Freighter		lsf Farnair SPC/cvtd-2C/103/opin DHL-cs
☐ PH-GIR	Airbus Industrie A300B4-103 (F)	042	N202EA	0077	0698	2 GE CF6-50C2	157500	Freighter		lsf Farnair SPC/cvtd-2C/103/opin DHL-cs

WINGS OVER HOLLAND, B.V. (Associated with Wings over Europe & Wings over Aruba)

Lelystad

Emoeweg 28, NL-8218 PC Lelystad, Netherlands ☎ (320) 28 82 60 Tx: none Fax: (320) 28 83 74 SITA: n/a
F: 1983 ⁂ 10 Head: Bert Huizenga Net: n/a

registration	type of aircraft	cn/fn	ex/ex*	mfd	del	powered by	mtow kg	configuration	selcal	name/fln/specialitites/remarks
☐ PH-PNA	Partenavia P.68B	38	N777EW	0075	0387	2 LY IO-360-A1B6	1960			lsf Eltee Onroerend Goed B.V.

PJ = NETHERLANDS ANTILLES

Capital: Willemstad/Curacao Official Language: Dutch, Papiamento Population: 0,2 million Square Km: 800 Dialling code: +599 Acting political head: Susanne Camelia-Römer (Prime Minister)

AIR ALM = LM / ALM (ALM 1997 Airline Inc. dba/formerly ALM Antillean Airlines & ALM-Antillaanse Luchtvaart Maatschappij N.V.)

Curaçao-Hato

Aeropuerto Hato, Curaçao, Netherlands Antilles ☎ (9) 833 88 88 Tx: 1114 alm na Fax: (9) 833 83 00 SITA: n/a
F: 1964 ⁂ 1000 Head: Duncan Fisher IATA: 119 ICAO: ANTILLEAN Net: http://www.ALM-Airlines.com

registration	type of aircraft	cn/fn	ex/ex*	mfd	del	powered by	mtow kg	configuration	selcal	name/fln/specialitites/remarks
☐ PJ-DHA	De Havilland DHC-8-311 Dash 8	301	C-GFBW*	0092	0692	2 PWC PW123	18643	Y50		Wayaka
☐ PJ-DHB	De Havilland DHC-8-311 Dash 8	303	C-GESR*	0092	0692	2 PWC PW123	18643	Y50		Tuturutu
☐ PJ-DHE	De Havilland DHC-8-311 Dash 8 (SCD)	242	C-FZPS	0090	1296	2 PWC PW123	18643	Y50 / Combi		lsf Avmax Group Inc.
☐ PJ-DHI	De Havilland DHC-8-311 Dash 8 (SCD)	230	C-FZVU	0090	0397	2 PWC PW123	18643	Y50 / Combi		lsf Avmax Group Inc.
☐ PJ-SEF	Boeing (Douglas) MD-82 (DC-9-82)	49123 / 1075		0082	1082	2 PW JT8D-217	66678	Y146	AC-HM	Flamboyant
☐ PJ-SEG	Boeing (Douglas) MD-82 (DC-9-82)	49124 / 1077		0082	1082	2 PW JT8D-217	66678	Y146	AC-JK	Kibrahacha
☐ PJ-SEH	Boeing (Douglas) MD-82 (DC-9-82)	49661 / 1452	EC-EVY	0288	0591	2 PW JT8D-217C	67812	Y146		lsf Kolding Ltd

AIR CARIBBEAN = XC / CLT

Curaçao-Hato

Hato Cargo Center 120, Hato Airport, Curaçao, Netherlands Antilles ☎ (9) 868 09 18 Tx: none Fax: (9) 868 03 97 SITA: n/a
F: 1962 ⁂ 180 Head: Ronald Nezea IATA: 918 ICAO: CARIBBEAN Net: n/a Operates cargo flights with freighter aircraft leased from other companies when required.

FLEXAIR (Member of BAC Aero Leasing, N.V.)

Curaçao-Hato

c/o BAC Aero Leasing, Motetwerf, Willemstad, Curaçao, Netherlands Antilles ☎ (9) 462 89 95 Tx: none Fax: (9) 462 89 96 SITA: n/a
F: 1992 ⁂ 6 Head: Jhr Mark B.H. van den Brandeler Net: n/a

registration	type of aircraft	cn/fn	ex/ex*	mfd	del	powered by	mtow kg	configuration	selcal	name/fln/specialitites/remarks
☐ PJ-PLA	Piper PA-31-350 Navajo Chieftain	31-7305038	PH-KID	0073	1093	2 LY TIO-540-J2BD	3175	Y9 / Freighter		
☐ PJ-PLB	Beech Queen Air 80 (65-80)	LD-148	HB-GEY	0064	0495	2 LY IGSO-540-A1A6	3629	Aerial Survey		KLM aerocarto-colors

PELICAN AIR, N.V.

Curaçao-Downtown Helipad

Motetwerf, Willemstad, Curaçao, Netherlands Antilles ☎ (9) 462 81 55 Tx: none Fax: (9) 462 81 82 SITA: n/a
F: 1993 ⁂ 5 Head: George Tielen Net: n/a

registration	type of aircraft	cn/fn	ex/ex*	mfd	del	powered by	mtow kg	configuration	selcal	name/fln/specialitites/remarks
☐ PJ-PLD	Bell 206B JetRanger	29	EC-EFE	0067	0095	1 AN 250-C20	1451			cvtd 206A / opf Police

WINAIR = WM / WIA (Windward Islands Airways International, N.V. dba)

St. Maarten

PO Box 2088, Princess Juliana Int'l Airport, St. Maarten, Netherlands Antilles ☎ (5) 52 568 Tx: none Fax: (5) 54 229 SITA: SXMGMWM
F: 1962 ⁂ 91 Head: Michael Ferrier IATA: 295 ICAO: WINAIR Net: n/a

registration	type of aircraft	cn/fn	ex/ex*	mfd	del	powered by	mtow kg	configuration	selcal	name/fln/specialitites/remarks
☐ PJ-WIE	De Havilland DHC-6 Twin Otter 300	542		0077	0777	2 PWC PT6A-27	5670	Y20		
☐ PJ-WIF	De Havilland DHC-6 Twin Otter 300	543		0077	0777	2 PWC PT6A-27	5670	Y20		
☐ PJ-WIH	De Havilland DHC-6 Twin Otter 300	766	N304CH	0081	0985	2 PWC PT6A-27	5670	Y20		

PK = INDONESIA (Republic of Indonesia) (Republik Indonesia)

Capital: Jakarta Official Language: Indonesian Population: 210,0 million Square Km: 1904569 Dialling code: +62 Year established: 1945 Acting political head: Bakharuddin Jusuf Habibie (President)

Government / Corporate / Executive / VIP Aircraft

Industri Pesawat Terbang Nusantara P.T. – IPTN uses ICAO three-letter code IPN & call sign NUSANTARA.

registration	type of aircraft	cn/fn	ex/ex*	mfd	del	powered by	mtow kg	configuration	selcal	name/fln/specialitites/remarks
☐ A-2801	Fokker F28 Fellowship 1000 (F28 Mk1000)	11042	PK-PJT	0071	1283	2 RR Spey 555-15	29484	VIP / mil trans		TNI-AU / Indonesian Air Force
☐ A-2802	Fokker F28 Fellowship 3000 (F28 Mk3000)	11113	PK-GFR	0076	1194	2 RR Spey 555-15	29484	VIP / mil trans		TNI-AU / Indonesian Air Force
☐ A-2803	Fokker F28 Fellowship 3000 (F28 Mk3000)	11117	PK-GFQ	0076	1194	2 RR Spey 555-15	29484	VIP / mil trans		TNI-AU / Indonesian Air Force
☐ A-7002	Boeing 707-3M1C	21092 / 899	PK-GAU	0075		4 PW JT3D-3B	151046	VIP / mil trans		TNI-AU / Indonesian Air Force
☐ AI-7301	Boeing 737-2X9 (A)	22777 / 868	N1779B*	0082	0582	2 PW JT8D-17	58060	Survey/F14Y88		TNI-AU / Indonesian Air Force
☐ AI-7302	Boeing 737-2X9 (A)	22778 / 947	N8288V*	0083	0683	2 PW JT8D-17	58060	Survey/F14Y88		TNI-AU / Indonesian Air Force

☐ AI-7303	Boeing 737-2X9 (A)	22779 / 985	N1786B*	0083	1083	2 PW JT8D-17	58060	Survey/F14Y88		TNI-AU / Indonesian Air Force
☐ PK-CAE	Beech King Air A100	B-222		0075	0176	2 PWC PT6A-28	5216	Calibrator		Ditjen Perhubungan Udara / CAA
☐ PK-CAG	Dassault Falcon 20F	408	F-WRQS*	0079	0580	2 GE CF700-2D2	13000	Calibrator		Dewa Rud / Ditjen Perhub. Udara / CAA
☐ PK-CAH	Learjet 31A	31A-066	N26006*	0094	1194	2 GA TFE731-2-3B	7484	Calibrator		Ditjen Perhubungan Udara / CAA
☐ PK-CAJ	Learjet 31A	31A-077	N26002*	0094	0894	2 GA TFE731-2-3B	7484	Calibrator		Ditjen Perhubungan Udara / CAA
☐ PK-CAK	Beech King Air B200C	BL-140	N82410	0093	0097	2 PWC PT6A-42	5670	Calibrator		Ditjen Perhubungan Udara / CAA
☐ PK-PJF	BAe (BAC) One-Eleven 401AK	065	N117MR	0066		2 RR Spey 511-14	40143	VIP		Citra Group
☐ PK-XNG	IPTN N-250-50	PA1/A9996		0095	0895	2 AN AE2100C	24800	Testbed		IPTN / Prototype

ADVENTIST AVIATION Indonesia (SDA Masehi Advent Hari Ketujuh Indonesia) — Doyo-Baru & Jayapura

PO Box 1303, Manado 95105, Indonesia ☎ (431) 85 81 91 Tx: none Fax: none SITA: n/a
F: 1970 ✱✱✱ 6 Head: A. Rantung Net: n/a

☐ PK-SDC	Cessna A185F Skywagon	18502381	N1685R	0074	0974	1 CO IO-520-D	1520			
☐ PK-SDF	Cessna A185F Skywagon II	18503645		0078	1080	1 CO IO-520-D	1520			

AIRFAST Indonesia = AFE (P.T. Airfast Indonesia dba) — Singapore-Seletar, Balikpapan & Jayapura

Plaza Kuningan-Menara Utara 035, Jalan H.R. Rasuna Said Kav C11-14, Jakarta 12940, Indonesia ☎ (21) 520 06 96 Tx: 62151 airfas ia Fax: (21) 520 25 57 SITA: n/a
F: 1971 ✱✱✱ 339 Head: Frank D. Reuneker ICAO: AIRFAST Net: http://www.airfast.co.id

☐ PK-OBG	Bell 206B JetRanger	67	VH-UHC	0067	0679	1 AN 250-C20	1451	Y4		cvtd 206A
☐ PK-OBI	Bell 206B JetRanger	48	P2-AJJ	0067	0879	1 AN 250-C20	1451	Y4		cvtd 206A
☐ PK-OCD	Bell 206B+ JetRanger	893	PK-VBP	0072	0291	1 AN 250-C20R	1451	Y4		cvtd 206B
☐ PK-OCO	Bell 206B JetRanger	580	PK-EBL	0070	0996	1 AN 250-C20	1451	Y4		cvtd 206A
☐ PK-OAQ	Piper PA-23-250 Aztec D	27-4416	PK-KSB	0069	0972	1 LY IO-540-C4B5	2359	Y5 / Freighter		Large freight door
☐ PK-OAW	Beech Queen Air B80 (65-B80)	LD-308	PK-JBF	0069	0979	2 LY IGSO-540-A1D	3992	Y10		
☐ PK-OAT	Agusta-Bell 204B	3169	PK-LBC	0066	0979	1 LY T5311A	3856	Y10		rebuilt
☐ PK-OBA	Bell 204B	2050	VH-UTW	0069	0675	1 LY T5311A	3856	Y10		
☐ PK-HCF	Bell 212	30629	VR-BFB	0074	0096	2 PWC PT6T-3 TwinPac	5080	Y14		
☐ PK-HCK	Bell 212	30533		0071	0096	2 PWC PT6T-3 TwinPac	5080	Y14		std Seletar
☐ PK-OCE	Bell 212	30981	PK-VBZ	0079	0291	2 PWC PT6T-3 TwinPac	5080	Y14		
☐ PK-OCA	Bell (IPTN) 412	NB09/34009	PK-XFJ*	0089	1089	2 PWC PT6T-3B TwinPac	5398	Y14		opf Freeport Indonesia
☐ PK-OCB	Bell (IPTN) 412	NB07/34007	PK-XFH*	0089	0590	2 PWC PT6T-3B TwinPac	5398	Y14		
☐ PK-OAD	Sikorsky S-58T	58-601	N1159U	0057	1174	1 PWC PT6T-6 TwinPac	5897	Y16		cvtd S-58E
☐ PK-OBN	Sikorsky S-58T	58-1492	PH-NZE	0061	0380	1 PWC PT6T-3 TwinPac	5897	Y16		cvtd S-58D
☐ PK-OBO	Sikorsky S-58T	58-721	PH-POC	0057	0480	1 PWC PT6T-6 TwinPac	5897	Y16		cvtd S-58E / std Seletar
☐ PK-OCJ	De Havilland DHC-6 Twin Otter 300	522	A6-MBM	0077	0092	2 PWC PT6A-27	5670	Y18		
☐ PK-OCK	De Havilland DHC-6 Twin Otter 300	616	G-BGEN	0079	1292	2 PWC PT6A-27	5670	Y18		
☐ PK-OCL	De Havilland DHC-6 Twin Otter 300	689	N689WJ	0080	0794	2 PWC PT6A-27	5670	Y18		
☐ PK-OCM	Grumman G-73 Turbo Mallard	J-50	N686FM	0050	1194	2 PWC PT6A-34	6350	Y13		Amphibian
☐ PK-OCC	IPTN (CASA) 212-CC4 Aviocar Srs 200	50N/210	PK-NZJ	0082	0391	2 GA TPE331-10R-511C	7450	Y24		
☐ PK-OAZ	Boeing (Douglas) DC-3C (C-47A-80-DL)	19623	PK-GDF	0043	0979	2 PW R-1830-92	12202	Y21 / Freighter		
☐ PK-OBQ	BAe (HS) 748-209 Srs 2A	1638 / 93	RP-C1016	0067	0580	2 RR Dart 534-2	20192	Y44		
☐ PK-OCF	Boeing 737-247	19601 / 45	N466AC	0768	1091	2 PW JT8D-9	49442	C87	HL-AG	opf Freeport Indonesia
☐ PK-OCG	Boeing 737-293	20335 / 237	N469AC	1070	0991	2 PW JT8D-7A	46947	C87	BL-DM	opf Freeport Indonesia
☐ PK-OCI	Boeing 737-230C	20255 / 234	N800WA	0170	0293	2 PW JT8D-9A	54204	C87 / Freighter	HM-DF	opf Freeport Indonesia

AMA - Associated Mission Aviation (Penerbangan Misi Katolik) — Jayapura

Kotak Pos 243, Sentani 99352, Irian Jaya, Indonesia ☎ (967) 59 10 09 Tx: none Fax: (967) 59 15 85 SITA: n/a
F: 1959 ✱✱✱ 30 Head: Piet Bots Net: n/a

☐ PK-RCH	Cessna A185F Skywagon II	18503526	N2717Q	0078	0778	1 CO IO-520-D	1520			
☐ PK-RCL	Cessna A185F Skywagon	18503063	N56KW	0076	0783	1 CO IO-520-D	1520			
☐ PK-RCM	Cessna A185F Skywagon II	18504222	N61514	0081	0587	1 CO IO-520-D	1520			
☐ PK-RCT	Cessna A185F Skywagon	18502824	N1319F	0075	1190	1 CO IO-520-D	1520			
☐ PK-RCU	Cessna A185F Skywagon	18503385	N602BM	0077	0893	1 CO IO-520-D	1520			
☐ PK-RCV	Cessna A185F Skywagon II	18503926	N185KS	0079	0694	1 CO IO-520-D	1520			
☐ PK-RCW	Cessna A185F Skywagon II	18504391	N714EX	0082	0396	1 CO IO-520-D	1520			
☐ PK-RCX	Pilatus PC-6/B2-H4 Turbo Porter	922	HB-FLO*	0298	0398	1 PWC PT6A-27	2800			
☐ PK-RCY	Pilatus PC-6/B2-H4 Turbo Porter	923	HB-FLP*	0298	0398	1 PWC PT6A-27	2800			

BALI AIR = BLN (P.T. Bali International Air Servics dba / Subsidiary of Bouraq Indonesia Airlines) — Banjarmasin

Jalan Angkasa 1-3, PO Box 2965, Jakarta 10720, Indonesia ☎ (21) 628 88 15 Tx: 41247 bo ia Fax: (21) 624 91 83 SITA: n/a
F: 1973 ✱✱✱ 67 Head: Danny R. Sumendap ICAO: BIAR Net: n/a

☐ PK-KNA	Britten-Norman BN-2A-3S Islander	308	G-BAAE	0072	1173	2 LY IO-540-K1B5	2994	Y9		
☐ PK-KND	Britten-Norman BN-2A-3 Islander	692	G-AZXY	0072	0374	2 LY IO-540-K1B5	2858	Y9		
☐ PK-KTA	Britten-Norman BN-2A Mk.III-2 Trislander	1006	G-BCXU	0075	1275	3 LY O-540-E4C5	4536	Y16		
☐ PK-KTH	Britten-Norman BN-2A Mk.III-2 Trislander	1022	G-BDOK	0076	1076	3 LY O-540-E4C5	4536	Y16		
☐ PK-KTJ	Britten-Norman BN-2A Mk.III-2 Trislander	1033	G-BDWT	0076	0777	3 LY O-540-E4C5	4536	Y16		

BOURAQ INDONESIA AIRLINES = BO / BOU (P.T. Bouraq Indonesia Airlines dba) — Jakarta-Soekarno-Hatta Int'l

Jalan Angkasa 1-3, PO Box 2965, Jakarta 10720, Indonesia ☎ (21) 629 53 64 Tx: none Fax: (21) 629 86 51 SITA: n/a
F: 1970 ✱✱✱ 1730 Head: Danny A. Sumendap IATA: 666 ICAO: BOURAQ Net: http://www.promindo.com/tourism/bouraq/ On order (subject to reconfirmation): 5 IPTN N-250-100 for delivery starting 1999.

☐ PK-IHG	BAe (HS) 748-235 Srs 2A	1627 / 109	PP-VDP	0068	1276	2 RR Dart 534-2	20183	Y48		
☐ PK-IHH	BAe (HS) 748-235 Srs 2A	1629 / 111	PP-VDR	0068	0277	2 RR Dart 534-2	20183	Y48		
☐ PK-IHJ	BAe (HS) 748-235 Srs 2A	1630 / 112	PP-VDS	0068	0177	2 RR Dart 534-2	20183	Y48		
☐ PK-IHO	BAe (HS) 748-402 Srs 2B	1774 / 253	G-BKLD*	0082	0683	2 RR Dart 536-2	21092	Y48		
☐ PK-IHV	BAe (HS) 748-402 Srs 2B	1795 / 276	G-BKLI*	0082	0583	2 RR Dart 536-2	21092	Y48		
☐ PK-IJH	Boeing 737-2K2 (A)	21397 / 507	PH-TVP	0077	1293	2 PW JT8D-15A	56699	Y116		
☐ PK-IJI	Boeing 737-230 (A)	22125 / 734	D-ABFS	0081	0294	2 PW JT8D-15	52390	Y106		lsf PT Pann Multi Finance
☐ PK-IJJ	Boeing 737-230 (A)	22130 / 762	D-ABFZ	0081	0294	2 PW JT8D-15	52390	Y106		lsf PT Pann Multi Finance
☐ PK-IJK	Boeing 737-230 (A)	22143 / 838	D-ABHU	0082	0794	2 PW JT8D-15	52390	Y106		lsf PT Pann Multi Finance

DAS - P.T. Dirgantara Air Services = AW / DIR — Jakarta-Halim & Banjarmasin & Pontianak

PO Box 6154, Jakarta 13610, Indonesia ☎ (21) 809 72 43 Tx: 49130 dasair jkt Fax: (21) 809 43 48 SITA: n/a
F: 1971 ✱✱✱ 100 Head: Makki Perdanakusuma ACM ICAO: DIRGANTARA Net: n/a

☐ PK-VIA	Britten-Norman BN-2B-20 Islander	2250	PK-HNF	0092	0097	2 LY IO-540-K1B5	2976			
☐ PK-VIM	Britten-Norman BN-2A-3 Islander	634	9V-BEB	0071	0672	2 LY IO-540-K1B5	2858			
☐ PK-VIN	Britten-Norman BN-2A-3 Islander	351	G-BBJA	0073	0574	2 LY IO-540-K1B5	2858			
☐ PK-VIS	Britten-Norman BN-2A-21 Islander	485	G-BEGB	0076	0978	2 LY IO-540-K1B5	2994			
☐ PK-VIU	Britten-Norman BN-2A-21 Islander	781	PK-KNH	0076	0579	2 LY IO-540-K1B5	2994			
☐ PK-VIW	Britten-Norman BN-2A-21 Islander	2026	G-BIPD*	0081	1081	2 LY IO-540-K1B5	2994			
☐ PK-VIX	Britten-Norman BN-2A-21 Islander	2027	G-BIUF*	0081	1281	2 LY IO-540-K1B5	2994			
☐ PK-VIY	Britten-Norman BN-2A-21 Islander	2133	G-BJOR*	0081	0882	2 LY IO-540-K1B5	2994			
☐ PK-VIZ	Britten-Norman BN-2A-21 Islander	697	PK-ESS	0073	0584	2 LY IO-540-K1B5	2994			
☐ PK-HJA	IPTN (CASA) 212-CC4 Aviocar Srs 200	87N/282	PK-XEJ*	0088	0097	2 GA TPE331-10R-512C	7450			
☐ PK-HJC	IPTN (CASA) 212-CC4 Aviocar Srs 200	90N/410	PK-XEN*	0092	0097	2 GA TPE331-10R-512C	7450			
☐ PK-HJD	IPTN (CASA) 212-CC4 Aviocar Srs 200	91N/411	PK-XEO*	0093	0097	2 GA TPE331-10R-512C	7450			
☐ PK-HJE	IPTN (CASA) 212-CC4 Aviocar Srs 200	90N/412		0093	0097	2 GA TPE331-10R-512C	7450			
☐ PK-VSN	IPTN (CASA) 212-A4 Aviocar Srs 100	22N/136	PK-XCU*	0080	1080	2 GA TPE331-5-251C	6500			
☐ PK-VSP	IPTN (CASA) 212-A4 Aviocar Srs 100	7N/78	PK-NCE	0077	1088	2 GA TPE331-5-251C	6500			

DERAYA AIR TAXI = DRY (P.T. Deraya Air Taxi dba) — Jakarta-Halim / Palembang / Pontianak

Terminal Bldg, 1/F, Room 150/HT, Halim Perdanakusuma Airport, Jakarta 13610, Indonesia ☎ (21) 809 36 27 Tx: 48179 dazona ia (att Fax: (21) 809 57 70 SITA: n/a
F: n/a ✱✱✱ 153 Head: Miss Siti Rahayu Sumadi ICAO: DERAYA Net: n/a Aircraft below MTOW 1361 kg: Cessna 150, 152, 172 & Gelatik PZL104.

☐ PK-UFO	Cessna U206F Stationair II	U20602789	N35902	0075	0095	1 CO IO-520-F	1633	5 Pax		
☐ PK-DGF	Piper PA-23-250 Aztec F	27-4745		0071	0178	2 LY IO-540-C4B5	2359	5 Pax		
☐ PK-DCC	Cessna 402C II	402C0250	N444DS	0079	0491	2 CO TSIO-520-VB	3107	8 Pax		
☐ PK-DCJ	Cessna 402B	402B0615	N3759C	0074	0775	2 CO TSIO-520-E	2858	8 Pax		
☐ PK-DCK	Cessna 402B	402B0627	N3780C	0074	0775	2 CO TSIO-520-E	2858	8 Pax		
☐ PK-DCY	Cessna 402C III	402C0801	N1233G	0084	0391	2 CO TSIO-520-VB	3107	8 Pax		
☐ PK-DCZ	Cessna 402B	402B0890	N5203J	0075	0391	2 CO TSIO-520-E	2858	8 Pax		
☐ PK-DYR	Piper PA-31T Cheyenne II	31T-7820054	VH-MWT	0078	1182	2 PWC PT6A-28	4082	5 Pax		
☐ PK-DSU	Shorts Skyvan 3 Variant 100 (SC-7)	SH1924	PK-PSJ	0074	1183	2 GA TPE331-2-201A	5670	17 Pax		
☐ PK-DSV	Shorts Skyvan 3 Variant 100 (SC-7)	SH1910	PK-PSH	0073	1084	2 GA TPE331-2-201A	5670	17 Pax		
☐ PK-DCO	IPTN (CASA) 212-A4 Aviocar Srs 100	13N/93	PK-XCL	0078	0979	2 GA TPE331-5-251C	6500	19 Pax		
☐ PK-DCP	IPTN (CASA) 212-A4 Aviocar Srs 100	14N/101	PK-XCM	0079	0979	2 GA TPE331-5-251C	6500	19 Pax		
☐ PK-DCQ	IPTN (CASA) 212-A4 Aviocar Srs 100	16N/112	PK-XCO	0079	1079	2 GA TPE331-5-251C	6500	19 Pax		

DERAZONA HELICOPTERS (P.T. Derazona Air Service dba / Member of The Boedihardjo Group) — Jakarta-Halim

Halim Perdanakusuma Airport, Jakarta 13610, Indonesia ☎ (21) 809 34 27 Tx: 48179 dazona ia Fax: (21) 809 14 57 SITA: n/a
F: 1971 ✱✱✱ 75 Head: Asril Lamisi Net: n/a

☐ PK-DAL	Bell 206B JetRanger	1624	PK-DGD	0075	0291	1 AN 250-C20	1451			

496 registration type of aircraft cn/fn ex/ex* mfd del powered by mtow kg configuration selcal name/fln/specialitites/remarks

registration	type of aircraft	cn/fn	ex/ex*	mfd	del	powered by	mtow kg	configuration	selcal	name/fln/specialitites/remarks
☐ PK-DAT	Bell 206B JetRanger	1625	PK-DGE	0075	0291	1 AN 250-C20	1451			
☐ PK-DBA	Bell 206B JetRanger	110	PK-VBS	0067	0277	1 AN 250-C20	1451			cvtd 206A
☐ PK-DBB	Bell 206B JetRanger	1127	N58031	0073	1079	1 AN 250-C20	1451			
☐ PK-DBC	Bell 206B JetRanger	1140	VR-HHH	0073	0779	1 AN 250-C20	1451			
☐ PK-DBE	Bell 206B JetRanger	376	N1432W	0069	0771	1 AN 250-C20	1451			cvtd 206A
☐ PK-DBH	Bell 206B JetRanger	157	N6296N	0068	1272	1 AN 250-C20	1451			cvtd 206A
☐ PK-DBQ	Bell 206B JetRanger	822	N14803	0072	0774	1 AN 250-C20	1451			
☐ PK-DAS	Bell (IPTN) 412	NB16/34016	PK-YPH	0091	0395	2 PWC PT6T-3B TwinPac	5398			
☐ PK-LNA	Bell (IPTN) 412	NB05/34005	PK-XFE*	0090	0098	2 PWC PT6T-3B TwinPac	5398			

EASTINDO (P.T. East Indonesia Air Taxi & Charter Service dba) — Jakarta-Halim — EASTINDO

Terminal Bldg 2/F, Halim Perdanakusuma Airport, PO Box 4714, Jakarta 13610, Indonesia ☎ (21) 809 35 00 Tx: 48340 asi jkt Fax: (21) 809 27 10 SITA: n/a

F: 1982 ⁂ 29 Head: Capt. Sigit Tri Wahyono Net: n/a

registration	type of aircraft	cn/fn	ex/ex*	mfd	del	powered by	mtow kg	configuration	selcal	name/fln/specialitites/remarks
☐ PK-RGP	Britten-Norman BN-2B-20 Islander	2249	PK-HNG	0091	0896	2 LY IO-540-K1B5	2976			
☐ PK-RGM	Hawker 800B (BAe 125-800B)	258106	PK-WSJ	0087	0189	2 GA TFE731-5R-1H	12428			

GARUDA INDONESIA = GA / GIA (P.T. Garuda Indonesian Airways dba) — Jakarta-Soekarno-Hatta Int'l — Garuda Indonesia

Medan Merdeka Selatan 13, Jakarta 10110, Indonesia ☎ (21) 380 19 01 Tx: 49113 gia jkt Fax: (21) 380 66 52 SITA: n/a

F: 1949 ⁂ 14000 Head: Abdul Gani IATA: 126 ICAO: INDONESIA Net: http://www.garudaindonesia.com

registration	type of aircraft	cn/fn	ex/ex*	mfd	del	powered by	mtow kg	configuration	selcal	name/fln/specialitites/remarks
☐ PK-GFS	Fokker F28 Fellowship 3000 (F28 Mk3000)	11119	PH-EXX*	0077	0977	2 RR Spey 555-15	29484	Y65		for sale
☐ PK-GFT	Fokker F28 Fellowship 3000 (F28 Mk3000)	11129	PH-EXS*	0078	0478	2 RR Spey 555-15	29484	Y65		for sale
☐ PK-GFW	Fokker F28 Fellowship 3000C (F28 MK3000C)	11134	PH-EXZ*	0078	0778	2 RR Spey 555-15	29484	Y65		for sale
☐ PK-GKZ	Fokker F28 Fellowship 4000 (F28 Mk4000)	11216	PH-EZD*	0084	0984	2 RR Spey 555-15H	32205	Y85		for sale
☐ PK-GQB	Fokker F28 Fellowship 4000 (F28 Mk4000)	11218	PH-EZP*	0084	1184	2 RR Spey 555-15H	32205	Y85		for sale
☐ PK-GGA	Boeing 737-5U3	28726 / 2920		0097	1297	2 CFMI CFM56-3C1	52390	C12Y72		
☐ PK-GGC	Boeing 737-5U3	28727 / 2937	N1786B*	0097	1297	2 CFMI CFM56-3C1	52390	C12Y72		
☐ PK-GGD	Boeing 737-5U3	28728 / 2938	N1786B*	0097	1297	2 CFMI CFM56-3C1	52390	C12Y72		
☐ PK-GGE	Boeing 737-5U3	28729 / 2950	N60436*	1297	1298	2 CFMI CFM56-3C1	52390	C12Y72		
☐ PK-GGF	Boeing 737-5U3	28730 / 2952		0097	1297	2 CFMI CFM56-3C1	52390	C12Y72		
☐ PK-GGG	Boeing 737-3U3	28731 / 2949		0097	1297	2 CFMI CFM56-3C1	63276	C26Y76		
☐ PK-GGN	Boeing 737-3U3	28735 / 3029	N5573K*	0598	1298	2 CFMI CFM56-3C1	63276	C26Y76		
☐ PK-GGO	Boeing 737-3U3	28736 / 3032	N3134C*	0598	1298	2 CFMI CFM56-3C1	63276	C26Y76		
☐ PK-GGP	Boeing 737-3U3	28737 / 3037	N1020L*	0598	1298	2 CFMI CFM56-3C1	63276	C26Y76		
☐ PK-GGQ	Boeing 737-3U3	28739 / 3064	N1024A*	0898	1298	2 CFMI CFM56-3C1	63276	C26Y76		
☐ PK-GGR	Boeing 737-3U3	28741 / 3079	N1026G*	1098	1298	2 CFMI CFM56-3C1	63276	C26Y76		
☐ PK-GWA	Boeing 737-3Q8	24403 / 1706		0089	0489	2 CFMI CFM56-3B1	56472	C26Y76	DQ-CG	lsf ILFC
☐ PK-GWI	Boeing 737-3Q8	24701 / 1957		0090	1190	2 CFMI CFM56-3B1	56472	C26Y76		lsf ILFC
☐ PK-GWJ	Boeing 737-3Q8	24702 / 1994		0090	0291	2 CFMI CFM56-3B1	56472	C26Y76		lsf ILFC
☐ PK-GWK	Boeing 737-4U3	25713 / 2531		0093	1093	2 CFMI CFM56-3C1	62822	C22Y102		
☐ PK-GWL	Boeing 737-4U3	25714 / 2535	N6067B*	0093	1293	2 CFMI CFM56-3C1	62822	C22Y102		
☐ PK-GWM	Boeing 737-4U3	25715 / 2537		0093	1093	2 CFMI CFM56-3C1	62822	C22Y102		
☐ PK-GWN	Boeing 737-4U3	25716 / 2540		0093	1193	2 CFMI CFM56-3C1	62822	C22Y102		
☐ PK-GWO	Boeing 737-4U3	25717 / 2546		0093	1193	2 CFMI CFM56-3C1	62822	C22Y102		
☐ PK-GWP	Boeing 737-4U3	25718 / 2548		0093	1293	2 CFMI CFM56-3C1	62822	C22Y102		
☐ PK-GWQ	Boeing 737-4U3	25719 / 2549		0093	1293	2 CFMI CFM56-3C1	62822	C22Y102		
☐ PK-GAA	Airbus Industrie A300B4-220FF	159	F-WZMH*	0081	0382	2 PW JT9D-59A	165000	C26Y218	HK-GK	
☐ PK-GAC	Airbus Industrie A300B4-220FF	164	F-WZMK*	0081	0282	2 PW JT9D-59A	165000	C26Y218	HL-JK	
☐ PK-GAD	Airbus Industrie A300B4-220FF	165	F-WZML*	0081	0182	2 PW JT9D-59A	165000	C26Y218	HM-BF	
☐ PK-GAE	Airbus Industrie A300B4-220FF	166	F-WZMM*	0081	0182	2 PW JT9D-59A	165000	C26Y218	HM-BG	
☐ PK-GAF	Airbus Industrie A300B4-220FF	167	F-WZMN*	0081	0282	2 PW JT9D-59A	165000	C26Y218	HM-BJ	std CGK
☐ PK-GAG	Airbus Industrie A300B4-220FF	168	F-WZMO*	0081	0282	2 PW JT9D-59A	165000	C26Y218	HM-GJ	
☐ PK-GAH	Airbus Industrie A300B4-220FF	213	F-WZMT*	0082	1182	2 PW JT9D-59A	165000	C26Y218	DK-BH	
☐ PK-GAJ	Airbus Industrie A300B4-220FF	215	F-WZMY*	0082	1182	2 PW JT9D-59A	165000	C26Y218	DK-CL	
☐ PK-GPA	Airbus Industrie A330-341	138	F-WWKH*	0096	1296	2 RR Trent 768-60	212000	C42Y251		
☐ PK-GPC	Airbus Industrie A330-341	140	F-WWKU*	0096	1296	2 RR Trent 768-60	212000	C42Y251		
☐ PK-GPD	Airbus Industrie A330-341	144	F-WWKG*	0097	0197	2 RR Trent 768-60	212000	C42Y251		
☐ PK-GPE	Airbus Industrie A330-341	148	F-WWKD*	0097	0297	2 RR Trent 768-60	212000	C42Y251		
☐ PK-GPF	Airbus Industrie A330-341	153	F-WWKY*	0097	0397	2 RR Trent 768-60	212000	C42Y251		
☐ PK-GPG	Airbus Industrie A330-341	165	F-WWKL*	0097	0497	2 RR Trent 768-60	212000	C42Y251		
☐ PK-GPH	Airbus Industrie A330-341					2 RR Trent 768-60	212000	C42Y251		oo-delivery 00XX
☐ PK-GPI	Airbus Industrie A330-341					2 RR Trent 768-60	212000	C42Y251		oo-delivery 00XX
☐ PK-GPJ	Airbus Industrie A330-341					2 RR Trent 768-60	212000	C42Y251		oo-delivery 00XX
☐ PK-	Boeing 777-2U3 (ER)					2 GE GE90-92B	297562			oo-delivery 0002
☐ PK-	Boeing 777-2U3 (ER)					2 GE GE90-92B	297562			oo-delivery 0002
☐ PK-	Boeing 777-2U3 (ER)					2 GE GE90-92B	297562			oo-delivery 0003
☐ PK-	Boeing 777-2U3 (ER)					2 GE GE90-92B	297562			oo-delivery 0003
☐ PK-	Boeing 777-2U3 (ER)					2 GE GE90-92B	297562			oo-delivery 0004
☐ PK-	Boeing 777-2U3 (ER)					2 GE GE90-92B	297562			oo-delivery 0004
☐ PK-GIA	Boeing (Douglas) DC-10-30	46918 / 223		0076	0376	3 GE CF6-50C	251744	F12C24Y214	FG-CH	
☐ PK-GIB	Boeing (Douglas) DC-10-30	46919 / 226		0076	0676	3 GE CF6-50C	251744	F12C24Y214	HL-DG	
☐ PK-GIC	Boeing (Douglas) DC-10-30	46964 / 239		0077	1077	3 GE CF6-50C	251744	F12C24Y214	AE-DG	
☐ PK-GID	Boeing (Douglas) DC-10-30	46951 / 246		0077	0178	3 GE CF6-50C	251744	F12C24Y214	AE-DH	
☐ PK-GIF	Boeing (Douglas) DC-10-30	46686 / 286		0079	0879	3 GE CF6-50C	251744	F12C24Y214	AE-DL	
☐ PK-GSA	Boeing 747-2U3B	22246 / 452		0080	0680	4 PW JT9D-7Q	371946	C24Y374	HM-EL	
☐ PK-GSB	Boeing 747-2U3B	22247 / 459		0080	0780	4 PW JT9D-7Q	371946	C24Y374	HM-FG	
☐ PK-GSC	Boeing 747-2U3B	22248 / 461		0080	0880	4 PW JT9D-7Q	371946	C24Y374	HM-FJ	
☐ PK-GSD	Boeing 747-2U3B	22249 / 468		0080	0880	4 PW JT9D-7Q	371946	C24Y374	HM-FK	
☐ PK-GSG	Boeing 747-4U3	25704 / 1011		0093	0194	4 GE CF6-80C2B1F	394625	F18C64Y323	DR-EM	
☐ PK-GSH	Boeing 747-4U3	25705 / 1029	N6038E*	0094	0594	4 GE CF6-80C2B1F	394625	F18C64Y323	EH-FR	
☐ PK-GSI	Boeing 747-441	24956 / 917	N791LF	0092	0395	4 GE CF6-80C2B1F	385553	F18C64Y323	HS-DK	lsf ILFC

GATARI AIR = GHS (P.T. Gatari Air Service dba/formerly P.T. Gatari Hutama Airservice) — Jakarta-Halim/Balikpapan/Denpasar & Duri Aumatera — GATARI AIR SERVICE

Halim Perdana Kusuma Airport, 2nd Floor, Jakarta 13610, Indonesia ☎ (21) 809 00 91 Tx: 48476 gat ia Fax: (21) 809 29 00 SITA: n/a

F: 1983 ⁂ 440 Head: Mrs. Titik W. Pudjoko ICAO: GATARI Net: n/a

registration	type of aircraft	cn/fn	ex/ex*	mfd	del	powered by	mtow kg	configuration	selcal	name/fln/specialitites/remarks
☐ PK-AVA	Bell 206B JetRanger	1709		0075		1 AN 250-C20	1451			opf Pusdiklat Perhub. Udara
☐ PK-AVD	Bell 206B JetRanger	1711		0075		1 AN 250-C20	1451			opf Pusdiklat Perhub. Udara
☐ PK-HMN	Bell 206B JetRanger III	2575	PK-PGL	0078	0691	1 AN 250-C20B	1451			
☐ PK-HMO	Bell 206B JetRanger III	2569	PK-PGM	0078	0691	1 AN 250-C20B	1451			
☐ PK-HNC	Bell 206B JetRanger	1710	PK-AVC	0075	0392	1 AN 250-C20	1451			
☐ PK-DKH	Eurocopter (IPTN/MBB) NBO105CB	N24/S-260	HH-1501	0082	1290	2 AN 250-C20B	2400			opf Departemen Kehutanan
☐ PK-DKP	Eurocopter (IPTN/MBB) NBO105CB	N61/S-459	HH-1510	0082	1290	2 AN 250-C20B	2400			opf Departemen Kehutanan
☐ PK-HNY	Kawasaki (Eurocopter/MBB) BK117B-1	1052	JA6614	0090	0694	2 LY LTS101-750B.1	3200			
☐ PK-HMA	Bell 212	30674	PK-DBW	0074	0186	2 PWC PT6T-3 TwinPac	5080			
☐ PK-HMB	Bell 212	30502	PK-DBY	0072	0186	2 PWC PT6T-3 TwinPac	5080			
☐ PK-HMC	Bell 212	30648	PK-DBZ	0074	0186	2 PWC PT6T-3 TwinPac	5080			
☐ PK-HML	Bell 212	30540	PK-PDZ	0072	0691	2 PWC PT6T-3 TwinPac	5080			
☐ PK-HMM	Bell 212	30958	PK-PGF	0079	0791	2 PWC PT6T-3 TwinPac	5080			
☐ PK-HMY	Bell 212	30713	PK-DBT	0075	0186	2 PWC PT6T-3 TwinPac	5080			
☐ PK-HNB	Bell 212	30959	PK-PGG	0079	0691	2 PWC PT6T-3 TwinPac	5080			lsf Amro Duta Leasing
☐ PK-HMI	Bell (IPTN) 412	NB01/34001		0089	0989	2 PWC PT6T-3B TwinPac	5262			
☐ PK-HMJ	Bell (IPTN) 412	NB02/34002	PK-XFG*	0089	0890	2 PWC PT6T-3B TwinPac	5262			
☐ PK-HMP	Bell 412	33102		0083	0783	2 PWC PT6T-3B TwinPac	5262			
☐ PK-HMS	Bell 412	33105		0083	0883	2 PWC PT6T-3B TwinPac	5262			
☐ PK-HMT	Bell 412	33106		0083	1083	2 PWC PT6T-3B TwinPac	5262			
☐ PK-HMU	Bell 412	33107		0083	1083	2 PWC PT6T-3B TwinPac	5262			
☐ PK-HMV	Bell 412	33098	N3186H	0083	0385	2 PWC PT6T-3B TwinPac	5262			
☐ PK-HNI	Bell (IPTN) 412	NB19/34019	PK-CND	0092	0193	2 PWC PT6T-3B TwinPac	5262			
☐ PK-HTI	Beech King Air B200	BB-1255	N125CU	0086	0793	2 PWC PT6A-42	5670			
☐ PK-HJB	IPTN (CASA) 212-CC4 Aviocar Srs 200	88N/283	PK-XEL*	0088	0194	2 GA TPE331-10R-511C	7450			
☐ PK-HJI	IPTN (CASA) 212-CC4 Aviocar Srs 200	93N/413	PK-XEQ*	0093	1094	2 GA TPE331-10R-511C	7450			

INDONESIA AIR TRANSPORT – IAT = IDA (P.T. Indonesia Air Transport dba) — Jakarta-Halim / -Pondok Cabe & Balikpapan — iat

PO Box 2485, Jakarta 10001, Indonesia ☎ (21) 749 02 13 Tx: 47063 iat ia Fax: (21) 749 12 87 SITA: n/a

F: 1968 ⁂ 390 Head: Azhar Mualim ICAO: INTRA Net: n/a

registration	type of aircraft	cn/fn	ex/ex*	mfd	del	powered by	mtow kg	configuration	selcal	name/fln/specialitites/remarks
☐ PK-TSA	Eurocopter (Aerosp.) SA315B Lama	2473	ZK-HNQ	0076	0896	1 TU Artouste IIIB	1950	6 Pax		
☐ PK-TSD	Eurocopter (Aerosp.) AS350BA Ecureuil	1818	F-GETP	0085	0497	1 TU Arriel 1B	2100	5 Pax		cvtd AS350B
☐ PK-TSE	Euroc.(Helibras/Aerosp.)HB350BA Ecureuil	1581 / HB1039	F-GKMD	0082	0497	1 TU Arriel 1B	2100	5 Pax		cvtd HB350B
☐ PK-TPV	Eurocopter (Aerosp.) SE316B Alouette III	1762	PH-NNV	0071	0571	1 TU Artouste IIIB	2200	6 Pax		
☐ PK-TPW	Eurocopter (Aerosp.) SE316B Alouette III	1760	PH-NNU	0071	0571	1 TU Artouste IIIB	2200	6 Pax		

☐ PK-TRY	Eurocopter (Aerosp.) SA316B Alouette III	1770	EC-EZG	0070	0096	1 TU Artouste IIIB1	2200	6 Pax		
☐ PK-TRZ	Eurocopter (Aerosp.) SA316B Alouette III	1669	PK-OAC	0070	0096	1 TU Artouste IIIB1	2200	6 Pax		
☐ PK-TRC	Britten-Norman BN-2A-21 Islander	545	G-BEEB	0077	0178	2 LY IO-540-K1B5	2994	9 Pax		
☐ PK-TRD	Eurocopter (Aerosp.) SA365C2 Dauphin 2	5058		0080	0681	2 TU Arriel 1A2	3500	12 Pax		
☐ PK-TRE	Eurocopter (Aerosp.) SA365C2 Dauphin 2	5004		0079	0581	2 TU Arriel 1A2	3500	12 Pax		
☐ PK-TSH	Eurocopter (Aerosp.) SA365N Dauphin 2	6008	N801BA	0082	0797	2 TU Arriel 1C	3850	12 Pax		
☐ PK-TSI	Eurocopter (Aerosp.) SA365N Dauphin 2	6026	N87SV	0083	0997	2 TU Arriel 1C	3850	12 Pax		
☐ PK-TSF	Bell 212	30974	N27664	0079	0897	2 PWC PT6T-3 TwinPac	5080	14 Pax		
☐ PK-TSG	Bell 212	30753	N81FC	0075	0497	2 PWC PT6T-3 TwinPac	5080	14 Pax		
☐ PK-TRA	Beech King Air 200	BB-113		0075	0176	2 PWC PT6A-41	5670	11 Pax		
☐ PK-TRQ	Shorts Skyvan 3 Variant 200 (SC-7)	SH1851	PK-WSA	0068	1190	2 GA TPE331-2-201A	6123	18 Pax/Freighter		
☐ PK-TRR	Shorts Skyvan 3A Variant 100 (SC-7)	SH1926	PK-FCD	0074	0293	2 GA TPE331-2-201A	6215	18 Pax/Freighter		
☐ PK-TRS	Shorts Skyvan 3 Variant 200 (SC-7)	SH1874	PK-HME	0069	0594	2 GA TPE331-2-201A	6123	18 Pax/Freighter		
☐ PK-TRT	Shorts Skyliner 3A Variant 100 (SC-7)	SH1925	PK-HMF	0074	0594	2 GA TPE331-2-201A	6215	18 Pax/Freighter		
☐ PK-TDR	Beech King Air 350 (B300)	FL-30	PK-NSI	0090	0097	2 PWC PT6A-60A	6804	11 Pax		
☐ PK-TRW	Beech 1900D Airliner	UE-177	N3237H	0095	0296	2 PWC PT6A-67D	7688	18 Pax		
☐ PK-TRX	Beech 1900D Airliner	UE-186	N3233J	0095	0296	2 PWC PT6A-67D	7688	18 Pax		
☐ PK-TIR	Dassault Falcon 20E	297	N121EU	0074	0986	2 GE CF700-2D2	13000	VIP 9 Pax		
☐ PK-TRI	Dassault Falcon 20F	173	N729S	0070	1284	2 GE CF700-2D2	13000	VIP 9 Pax		
☐ PK-TRL	GAC (Grumman) G-159 Gulfstream I	060	C-FIOM	0060	0488	2 RR Dart 529-8X	16329	18 Pax		
☐ PK-TRN	GAC (Grumman) G-159 Gulfstream I	193	N754G	0068	0190	2 RR Dart 529-8X	16329	18 Pax		
☐ PK-TRO	GAC (Grumman) G-159 Gulfstream I	130	N3416	0064	0490	2 RR Dart 529-8X	16329	18 Pax		
☐ PK-TSK	Fokker F27 Friendship 600 (F27 Mk600)	10441	VH-TQS	0070	0697	2 RR Dart 532-7R	19731	Y35 / Freighter		
☐ PK-TSL	Fokker F27 Friendship 600 (F27 Mk600)	10458	VH-TQT	0071	1097	2 RR Dart 532-7R	19731	Y35 / Freighter		
☐ PK-TSJ	Fokker F27 Friendship 500CRF(F27Mk500CRF)	10525	N702A	0076	0697	2 RR Dart 532-7R	20412	Y35 / Freighter		
☐ PK-TRU	BAe (BAC) One-Eleven 492GM	262	G-BLDH	0084	1294	2 RR Spey 511-14DW	44679	VIP 20 Pax		
☐ PK-TSR	BAe (BAC) One-Eleven 422EQ	126	N51387	0067	0697	2 RR Spey 511-14W	40143	VIP 20 Pax		
☐ PK-TST	BAe (BAC) One-Eleven 423ET	118	G-BEJM	0068	0498	2 RR Spey 511-14W	40143	VIP 20 Pax		

INTAN ANGKASA AIR (P.T. Intan Angkasa Air dba)

Jakarta-Halim

Sentra Mulia, Bldg, Suite 1112, Jalan HR. Rasuna Said, Kav.X/6 No.8, Jakarta 12940, Indonesia ☎ (21) 522 20 40 Tx: none Fax: (21) 522 67 42 SITA: n/a
F: n/a ⁂ n/a Head: n/a Net: n/a

☐ PK-IWE	Eurocopter (IPTN/MBB) NBO105CB	N26/S-262	PK-FGG	0082	0092	2 AN 250-C20B	2400			
☐ PK-IWC	Piper PA-31-350 Navajo Chieftain	31-7552045		0075	0892	2 LY TIO-540-J2BD	3175			
☐ PK-IWH	Piper PA-31-350 Navajo Chieftain	31-7852065	VH-TMN	0078	1295	2 LY TIO-540-J2BD	3175			

MAF Indonesia – Mission Aviation Fellowship = MAF (Branch of MAF USA)

Irian Jaya & Kalimantan & Sulawesi

PO Box 29, Grogol, Jakarta Barat 11450, Indonesia ☎ (21) 560 38 36 Tx: 46811 fslink ia Fax: (21) 560 38 37 SITA: n/a
F: 1955 ⁂ 140 Head: Robert J. Breuker ICAO: MAF Net: n/a Aircraft below MTOW 1361kg: Hughes 369HS (500C).
Non-commercial multinational ecclesistical consortium conducting flights for relief & development agencies & missions in remote areas of third world countries.

☐ PK-MCB	Cessna A185E Skywagon	185-1526	N2776J	0069	0270	1 CO IO-520-D	1520			
☐ PK-MCD	Cessna A185E Skywagon	185-0459	VH-BVK	0062	0676	1 CO IO-520-D	1520			cvtd 185A
☐ PK-MCF	Cessna A185E Skywagon	18502087	N70270	0072	0173	1 CO IO-520-D	1520			
☐ PK-MCG	Cessna A185F Skywagon	18502214	N3964Q	0073	1173	1 CO IO-520-D	1520			
☐ PK-MCJ	Cessna A185F Skywagon	18502199	PK-LIG	0073	1074	1 CO IO-520-D	1520			
☐ PK-MCK	Cessna A185F Skywagon	18502340	N53051	0074	0874	1 CO IO-520-D	1520			
☐ PK-MCM	Cessna A185F Skywagon	18502564	N1849R	0074	0675	1 CO IO-520-D	1520			
☐ PK-MCO	Cessna A185F Skywagon	18502702	N1045F	0075	0676	1 CO IO-520-D	1520			
☐ PK-MCU	Cessna A185F Skywagon	18503449	N9575H	0077	0679	1 CO IO-520-D	1520			
☐ PK-MCX	Cessna A185F Skywagon II	18504060		0080	0181	1 CO IO-520-D	1520			
☐ PK-MPD	Cessna A185E Skywagon	185-0665	PI-C672	0064	0372	1 CO IO-520-D	1520			cvtd 185C
☐ PK-MPL	Cessna A185E Skywagon	185-1612	N2412F	0066	0166	1 CO IO-520-D	1520			cvtd 180H
☐ PK-MAA	Cessna TU206G Turbo Stationair 6 II	U20606093	N206MF	0081	0387	1 CO TSIO-520-M	1633			
☐ PK-MAB	Cessna TU206G Turbo Stationair 6 II	U20606806	N1779R	0084	0687	1 CO TSIO-520-M	1633			
☐ PK-MAJ	Cessna U206G Stationair 6 II	U20606868	N9461R	0085	1088	1 CO IO-520-F	1633			
☐ PK-MAQ	Cessna TU206G Turbo Stationair 6 II	U20605164		0079	0792	1 CO TSIO-520-M	1633			
☐ PK-MAR	Cessna TU206G Turbo Stationair 6 II	U20606231	N6317Z	0081	0593	1 CO TSIO-520-M	1633			
☐ PK-MAT	Cessna TU206G Turbo Stationair 6 II	U20604164	N206ST	0078	0494	1 CO TSIO-520-M	1633			
☐ PK-MAU	Cessna TU206G Turbo Stationair 6 II	U20606365	N7551Z	0081	0295	1 CO TSIO-520-M	1633			
☐ PK-MCA	Cessna TU206D Turbo Skywagon	U206-1269	N72054	0069	0969	1 CO TSIO-520-C	1633			
☐ PK-MCP	Cessna TU206F Turbo Stationair II	U20603000	N2816Q	0075	0376	1 CO TSIO-520-C	1633			
☐ PK-MCZ	Cessna TU206F Stationair	U20602142	PK-OBR	0073	0683	1 CO TSIO-520-C	1633			cvtd U206F
☐ PK-MPO	Cessna TU206G Turbo Stationair 6 II	U20605255	N5374U	0079	0384	1 CO TSIO-520-M	1633			
☐ PK-MPP	Cessna U206G Stationair	U20603719	9M-AVW	0077	0884	1 CO IO-520-F	1633			
☐ PK-MAN	Cessna 208 Caravan I	20800048	N88TJ	0075	0689	1 PWC PT6A-114	3629			
☐ PK-MAO	Cessna 208 Caravan I	20800162	N9738F	0089	0990	1 PWC PT6A-114	3629			

MANDALA AIRLINES = MDL (P.T. Mandala Airlines dba)

Jakarta-Soekarno-Hatta Int'l

Jalan Garuda 76, PO Box 3706, Jakarta 10620, Indonesia ☎ (21) 420 66 46 Tx: 45425 mal ia Fax: (21) 424 94 91 SITA: n/a
F: 1969 ⁂ 770 Head: Gunadi Sugoto ICAO: MANDALA Net: n/a Beside aircraft listed, also leases Antonov 12 & Antonov 26 freighters from AIR MARK AVIATION, Singapore when required.

☐ PK-YPJ	Fokker F28 Fellowship 4000 (F28 Mk4000)	11148	PK-PJW	0079	0895	2 RR Spey 555-15H	32205	Y85		lsf Trigana Air Service
☐ PK-RII	Boeing 737-2E7 (A)	22876 / 922	G-BLDE	0082	0393	2 PW JT8D-17A	58105	C16Y84		
☐ PK-RIJ	Boeing 737-210 (A)	21820 / 578	G-BKNH	0079	0393	2 PW JT8D-17	56472	C16Y84		
☐ PK-RIK	Boeing 737-2V5 (A)	22531 / 724	N167PL	0080	0294	2 PW JT8D-15A	53070	C16Y84		lsf POLA
☐ PK-RIL	Boeing 737-230 (A)	22137 / 788	D-ABHL	0081	1294	2 PW JT8D-15	50893	C16Y84		lsf PT Pann Multi Finance
☐ PK-RIM	Boeing 737-230 (A)	22136 / 783	D-ABHK	0081	1194	2 PW JT8D-15	52390	C16Y84		lsf PT Pann Multi Finance
☐ PK-RIQ	Boeing 737-291 (A)	23023 / 957	TF-ABI	0083	0394	2 PW JT8D-17A	53070	C16Y84		lsf Elasis Lease
☐ PK-RIR	Boeing 737-2L9 (A)	22735 / 825	N164PL	0081	0494	2 PWC JT8D-17A	56472	C16Y84		lsf POLA

MANUNGGAL AIR (P.T. Manunggal Air dba)

Jakarta-Halim & -Soekarno-Hatta Int'l

Jalan Bangka 11a-4, Salatan, Jakarta 12710, Indonesia ☎ (21) 719 51 31 Tx: none Fax: (21) 719 51 31 SITA: n/a
F: 1997 ⁂ n/a Head: n/a Net: n/a

☐ PK-VFA	Fokker F28 Fellowship 4000 (F28 Mk4000)	11142	F-GDUY	0079	1297	2 RR Spey 555-15H	33110	Y85		
☐ PK-VTP	Aerospatiale/MBB Transall C-160NG	233	PK-PTO	0085	0097	2 RR Tyne 522	49000	Combi		
☐ PK-VTQ	Aerospatiale/MBB Transall C-160NG	234	PK-PTP	0085	0097	2 RR Tyne 522	49000	Combi		
☐ PK-VTR	Aerospatiale/MBB Transall C-160NG	235	PK-PTQ	0085	0097	2 RR Tyne 522	49000	Combi		
☐ PK-VTS	Aerospatiale/MBB Transall C-160P	205	PK-PTX	0082	0097	2 RR Tyne 522	49000	Combi		
☐ PK-VTT	Aerospatiale/MBB Transall C-160P	207	PK-PTY	0082	0097	2 RR Tyne 522	49000	Combi		
☐ PK-VTZ	Aerospatiale/MBB Transall C-160P	208	PK-PTZ	0082	0097	2 RR Tyne 522	49000	Combi		

MAPINDO PARAMA (P.T. Mapindo Parama dba)

Jakarta-Halim

Jalan Mabes Hankam 60, Jakarta 13820, Indonesia ☎ (21) 845 07 74 Tx: none Fax: (21) 845 07 79 SITA: n/a
F: n/a ⁂ n/a Head: Ir. Herman Hidayat Net: n/a

☐ PK-VRA	Dornier DO 28D-1 Skyservant	4026	PK-LDI	0069	0188	2 LY IGSO-540-A1E	3700	Photo / Survey		
☐ PK-VRB	Dornier DO 28D-1 Skyservant	4031	PK-LDJ	0069	0188	2 LY IGSO-540-A1E	3700	Photo / Survey		

MERPATI = MZ / MNA (P.T. Merpati Nusantara Airlines dba)

Jakarta-Soekarno-Hatta Int'l

Kotak Pos 1323, Jakarta 10720, Indonesia ☎ (21) 424 36 08 Tx: 49154 merpati ia Fax: (21) 654 06 20 SITA: n/a
F: 1962 ⁂ 4800 Head: Budiarto Subroto IATA: 621 ICAO: MERPATI Net: n/a On order (subject to reconfirmation): 16 IPTN CN-235-200 & 15 IPTN N-250-100 for delivery starting 1999.

☐ PK-NUH	De Havilland DHC-6 Twin Otter 300	383		0073	1273	2 PWC PT6A-27	5670	Y20		Natuna
☐ PK-NUI	De Havilland DHC-6 Twin Otter 300	386		0073	0174	2 PWC PT6A-27	5670	Y20		Karimun
☐ PK-NUO	De Havilland DHC-6 Twin Otter 300	487		0076	0376	2 PWC PT6A-27	5670	Y20		Singkep
☐ PK-NUR	De Havilland DHC-6 Twin Otter 300	484		0076	0276	2 PWC PT6A-27	5670	Y20		Muna
☐ PK-NUS	De Havilland DHC-6 Twin Otter 300	481		0075	1175	2 PWC PT6A-27	5670	Y20		Peleng
☐ PK-NUU	De Havilland DHC-6 Twin Otter 300	478		0075	1075	2 PWC PT6A-27	5670	Y20		Manterawu
☐ PK-NUV	De Havilland DHC-6 Twin Otter 300	472		0075	0975	2 PWC PT6A-27	5670	Y20		Tanimbar
☐ PK-NUZ	De Havilland DHC-6 Twin Otter 300	443	PK-NUM	0074	0175	2 PWC PT6A-27	5670	Y20		Alor
☐ PK-NCH	IPTN (CASA) 212-AB4 Aviocar Srs 200	30N/173	PK-XAD*	0080	0481	2 GA TPE331-10-511C	7450	Y24		Weh
☐ PK-NCL	IPTN (CASA) 212-AB4 Aviocar Srs 200	34N/185	PK-XAH*	0081	0781	2 GA TPE331-10-511C	7450	Y24		Berbak
☐ PK-NCM	IPTN (CASA) 212-AB4 Aviocar Srs 200	35N/188	PK-XAI*	0081	0881	2 GA TPE331-10-511C	7450	Y24		Tabuan
☐ PK-NCN	IPTN (CASA) 212-AB4 Aviocar Srs 200	36N/191	PK-XAJ*	0081	0981	2 GA TPE331-10-511C	7450	Y24		Seribu
☐ PK-NCO	IPTN (CASA) 212-AB4 Aviocar Srs 200	37N/194	PK-XAK*	0081	0981	2 GA TPE331-10-511C	7450	Y24		Panaitan
☐ PK-NCP	IPTN (CASA) 212-AB4 Aviocar Srs 200	38N/197	PK-XAL*	0081	1081	2 GA TPE331-10-511C	7450	Y24		Mondoliko
☐ PK-NCU	IPTN (CASA) 212-CC4 Aviocar Srs 200	74N/254	PK-XDW*	0085	0186	2 GA TPE331-10R-511C	7450	Y24		Pantar
☐ PK-NCV	IPTN (CASA) 212-CC4 Aviocar Srs 200	75N/255	PK-XDX*	0085	0186	2 GA TPE331-10R-511C	7450	Y24		Misool
☐ PK-NCX	IPTN (CASA) 212-CC4 Aviocar Srs 200	77N/257	PK-XDZ*	0085	0186	2 GA TPE331-10R-511C	7450	Y24		Batudata
☐ PK-NCZ	IPTN (CASA) 212-CC4 Aviocar Srs 200	79N/274	PK-XEC*	0086	0486	2 GA TPE331-10R-511C	7450	Y24		Tanah Massa
☐ PK-MNA	IPTN (CASA) CN-235-10	N001	PK-XNA*	0087	0188	2 GE CT7-7A	14400	Y40		Obira

498 registration type of aircraft cn/fn ex/ex* mfd del powered by mtow kg configuration selcal name/fln/specialitites/remarks

☐ PK-MNC	IPTN (CASA) CN-235-10	N002	PK-XND*	0087	0288	2 GE CT7-7A	14400	Y40		Wokam
☐ PK-MND	IPTN (CASA) CN-235-10	N003	PK-XNE*	0088	0588	2 GE CT7-7A	14400	Y40		Sermata
☐ PK-MNE	IPTN (CASA) CN-235-10	N004	PK-XNF*	0088	1188	2 GE CT7-7A	14400	Y40		Leti
☐ PK-MNF	IPTN (CASA) CN-235-10	N005	PK-XNG*	0088	1288	2 GE CT7-7A	14400	Y40		Wowoni
☐ PK-MNG	IPTN (CASA) CN-235-10	N006	PK-XNH*	0089	1089	2 GE CT7-7A	14400	Y40		Timor
☐ PK-MNH	IPTN (CASA) CN-235-10	N008	PK-XNJ*	0089	1289	2 GE CT7-7A	14400	Y40		Kaibesar
☐ PK-MNI	IPTN (CASA) CN-235-10	N007	PK-XNI*	0089	0290	2 GE CT7-7A	14400	Y40		Babar
☐ PK-MNJ	IPTN (CASA) CN-235-10	N009	PK-XNK*	0089	0390	2 GE CT7-7A	14400	Y40		Damar
☐ PK-MNK	IPTN (CASA) CN-235-10	N010	PK-XNL*	0089	1289	2 GE CT7-7A	14400	Y40		Kobroor
☐ PK-MNL	IPTN (CASA) CN-235-10	N011	PK-XNM*	0090	0990	2 GE CT7-7A	14400	Y40		Lakor
☐ PK-MNM	IPTN (CASA) CN-235-10	N012	PK-XNN*	0090	1190	2 GE CT7-7A	14400	Y40		Moa
☐ PK-MNO	IPTN (CASA) CN-235-10	N014	PK-XNP*	0091	0091	2 GE CT7-7A	14400	Y40		Romang
☐ PK-MNP	IPTN (CASA) CN-235-10	N015	PK-XNQ*	0091	0091	2 GE CT7-7A	14400	Y40		Kaledupa
☐ PK-MFF	Fokker F27 Friendship 500 (F27 Mk500)	10551	ZK-NFA	0077	0292	2 RR Dart 532-7R	20412	Y56		Tanah Bela
☐ PK-MFG	Fokker F27 Friendship 500F (F27 Mk500F)	10552	ZK-NFB	0077	0292	2 RR Dart 532-7R	20412	Y56		Lingga
☐ PK-MFJ	Fokker F27 Friendship 500F (F27 Mk500F)	10598	ZK-NFE	0080	0592	2 RR Dart 532-7R	20412	Y56		Adanora
☐ PK-MFK	Fokker F27 Friendship 500F (F27 Mk500F)	10607	ZK-NFF	0080	0692	2 RR Dart 532-7R	20412	Y56		Wangi-Wangi
☐ PK-MFL	Fokker F27 Friendship 500F (F27 Mk500F)	10609	ZK-NFH	0080	0492	2 RR Dart 532-7R	20412	Y56		Tapu Landang
☐ PK-MFM	Fokker F27 Friendship 500F (F27 Mk500F)	10614	ZK-NFI	0081	0492	2 RR Dart 532-7R	20412	Y56		Obi
☐ PK-MFN	Fokker F27 Friendship 500F (F27 Mk500F)	10618	ZK-NFJ	0081	0692	2 RR Dart 532-7R	20412	Y56		Batanta
☐ PK-MFQ	Fokker F27 Friendship 500RF (F27 Mk500RF)	10623	PK-GRF	0081	0182	2 RR Dart 536-7	20412	Y56		Bintan
☐ PK-MFU	Fokker F27 Friendship 500RF (F27 Mk500RF)	10624	PK-GRG	0081	0282	2 RR Dart 536-7	20412	Freighter		Kabaena
☐ PK-MFV	Fokker F27 Friendship 500RF (F27 Mk500RF)	10625	PK-GRH	0082	0282	2 RR Dart 536-7	20412	Y56		Kabia
☐ PK-MFW	Fokker F27 Friendship 500RF (F27 Mk500RF)	10626	PK-GRI	0082	0382	2 RR Dart 536-7	20412	Y56		Maja
☐ PK-MFX	Fokker F27 Friendship 500RF (F27 Mk500RF)	10628	PK-GRJ	0082	0482	2 RR Dart 536-7	20412	Freighter		Nusa Barung
☐ PK-MFY	Fokker F27 Friendship 500RF (F27 Mk500RF)	10629	PK-GRK	0082	0482	2 RR Dart 536-7	20412	Y56		Halmahera
☐ PK-MTV	BAe ATP	2046	G-BTZG*	0092	0292	2 PWC PW126	22930	Y68		Sipora / lsf BAMT / std CGK
☐ PK-MTW	BAe ATP	2047	G-BTZH*	0092	0392	2 PWC PW126	22930	Y68		Pulau Laut / lsf BAMT / std CGK
☐ PK-MTY	BAe ATP	2049	G-BTZJ*	0092	0692	2 PWC PW126	22930	Y68		Selayar / lsf BAMT / std CGK
☐ PK-MTZ	BAe ATP	2050	G-BTZK*	0092	0792	2 PWC PW126	22930	Y68		Numfoor / lsf BAMT / std CGK
☐ PK-GKC	Fokker F28 Fellowship 4000 (F28 Mk4000)	11157	PH-ZBW*	0080	0091	2 RR Spey 555-15H	32205	Y85		to be re-reg. PK-MGD
☐ PK-GKF	Fokker F28 Fellowship 4000 (F28 Mk4000)	11170	PH-EXU*	0081	0490	2 RR Spey 555-15H	32205	Y85		to be re-reg. PK-MGG
☐ PK-GKN	Fokker F28 Fellowship 4000 (F28 Mk4000)	11196	PH-EXU*	0083	0091	2 RR Spey 555-15H	32205	Y85		lsf Arthasaka Nusapala / tbr PK-MGU
☐ PK-GKO	Fokker F28 Fellowship 4000 (F28 Mk4000)	11198	PH-EXP*	0083	0091	2 RR Spey 555-15H	32205	Y85		lsf Arthasaka Nusapala / tbr PK-MGV
☐ PK-GKQ	Fokker F28 Fellowship 4000 (F28 Mk4000)	11201	PH-EXO*	0083	0091	2 RR Spey 555-15H	32205	Y85		lsf Arthasaka Nusapala / tbr PK-MGW
☐ PK-GKR	Fokker F28 Fellowship 4000 (F28 Mk4000)	11202	PH-EXT*	0083	0091	2 RR Spey 555-15H	32205	Y85		to be re-reg. PK-MGN
☐ PK-GKS	Fokker F28 Fellowship 4000 (F28 Mk4000)	11206	PH-EXU*	0083	0091	2 RR Spey 555-15H	32205	Y85		lsf Arthas.Nusapala/std CGK/tbr PK-MGX
☐ PK-GKT	Fokker F28 Fellowship 4000 (F28 Mk4000)	11209	PH-EXF*	0083	0091	2 RR Spey 555-15H	32205	Y85		to be re-reg. PK-MGO
☐ PK-GKV	Fokker F28 Fellowship 4000 (F28 Mk4000)	11211	PH-EXU*	0083	0093	2 RR Spey 555-15H	32205	Y85		lsf Arthasaka Nusapala / tbr PK-MGY
☐ PK-GQA	Fokker F28 Fellowship 4000 (F28 Mk4000)	11217	PK-EZZ*	0084	0093	2 RR Spey 555-15H	32205	Y85		lsf Arthasaka Nusapala / sub-lst VUN
☐ PK-MGA	Fokker F28 Fellowship 4000 (F28 Mk4000)	11154	PK-GKA	0080	0490	2 RR Spey 555-15H	32205	Y85		
☐ PK-MGC	Fokker F28 Fellowship 4000 (F28 Mk4000)	11155	PK-GKB	0080	0490	2 RR Spey 555-15H	32205	Y85		
☐ PK-MGE	Fokker F28 Fellowship 4000 (F28 Mk4000)	11158	PK-GKD	0080	0091	2 RR Spey 555-15H	32205	Y85		
☐ PK-MGF	Fokker F28 Fellowship 4000 (F28 Mk4000)	11160	PK-GKE	0080	0091	2 RR Spey 555-15H	32205	Y85		
☐ PK-MGH	Fokker F28 Fellowship 4000 (F28 Mk4000)	11171	PK-GKG*	0081	0689	2 RR Spey 555-15H	32205	Y85		std CGK
☐ PK-MGI	Fokker F28 Fellowship 4000 (F28 Mk4000)	11174	PK-GKH	0081		2 RR Spey 555-15H	32205	Y85		
☐ PK-MGJ	Fokker F28 Fellowship 4000 (F28 Mk4000)	11175	PK-GKL	0081	0091	2 RR Spey 555-15H	32205	Y85		
☐ PK-MGK	Fokker F28 Fellowship 4000 (F28 Mk4000)	11188	PK-GKI	0082		2 RR Spey 555-15H	32205	Y85		
☐ PK-MGL	Fokker F28 Fellowship 4000 (F28 Mk4000)	11189	PK-GKJ	0082	0091	2 RR Spey 555-15H	32205	Y85		
☐ PK-MGM	Fokker F28 Fellowship 4000 (F28 Mk4000)	11199	PK-GKP	0083	0091	2 RR Spey 555-15H	32205	Y85		
☐ PK-MGP	Fokker F28 Fellowship 4000 (F28 Mk4000)	11213	PK-GKW	0084	0093	2 RR Spey 555-15H	32205	Y85		
☐ PK-MGQ	Fokker F28 Fellowship 4000 (F28 Mk4000)	11214	PK-GKX	0084	0093	2 RR Spey 555-15H	32205	Y85		
☐ PK-MGR	Fokker F28 Fellowship 4000 (F28 Mk4000)	11215	PK-GKY	0084	0093	2 RR Spey 555-15H	32205	Y85		
☐ PK-MGS	Fokker F28 Fellowship 4000 (F28 Mk4000)	11177	PK-GKM	0082	0091	2 RR Spey 555-15H	32205	Y85		lsf Arthasaka Nusapala
☐ PK-MJA	Fokker 100 (F28 Mk0100)	11453	PH-MXO*	0093	1093	2 RR Tay 650-15	44452	C32Y70		Bawal
☐ PK-MJC	Fokker 100 (F28 Mk0100)	11463	PH-EZV*	0093	1093	2 RR Tay 650-15	44452	C32Y70		Sabu
☐ PK-MJD	Fokker 100 (F28 Mk0100)	11474	PH-EZW*	0094	0394	2 RR Tay 650-15	44452	C32Y70		Rupat
☐ PK-MBC	Boeing 737-230 (A)	22129 / 754	D-ABFY	0081	1294	2 PW JT8D-15	50893	CY103		lsf PT Pann Multi Finance
☐ PK-MBD	Boeing 737-230 (A)	22141 / 795	D-ABHR	0081	1294	2 PW JT8D-15	50893	CY103		lsf PT Pann Multi Finance
☐ PK-MBE	Boeing 737-230 (A)	22142 / 797	D-ABHS	0081	0395	2 PW JT8D-15	50893	CY103		lsf PT Pann Multi Finance

NATIONAL UTILITY HELICOPTERS – NUH (P.T. National Utility Helicopters dba)

Balikpapan & Singapore

Jl. Tanah Abang 1/11-E, Jakarta 10160, Indonesia ☎ (21) 380 46 83 Tx: 46377 nuheli ia Fax: (21) 380 99 34 SITA: n/a

F: 1970 ✈✈✈ 60 Head: Capt. Wibisono Rusmiputro Net: n/a

☐ PK-UHM	Bell 206B JetRanger	64	N7876S	0067	0673	1 AN 250-C20	1451			cvtd 206A
☐ PK-UHC	Bell 205A-1	30036	N1441W	0069	0671	1 LY T5313B	4309			
☐ PK-UHE	Bell 205A-1	30087		0070	0770	1 LY T5313B	4309			
☐ PK-UHI	Bell 205A-1	30006	N4045G	0068	0770	1 LY T5313B	4309			
☐ PK-UHJ	Bell 205A-1	30031	N1405W	0068	0571	1 LY T5313B	4309			
☐ PK-UHR	Bell 205A-1	30061	N2223W	0069	0571	1 LY T5313B	4309			
☐ PK-UHT	Bell 205A-1	30098	N7033J	0071	0872	1 LY T5313B	4309			
☐ PK-UHU	Bell 205A-1	30107	N2979W	0072	0872	1 LY T5313B	4309			

PELITA AIR = PAS (P.T. Pelita Air Service dba / Subsidiary of Pertamina)

Jakarta-Halim & -Pondok Cabe

Jalan Abdul Muis 52-56A, Jakarta 10160, Indonesia ☎ (21) 231 20 30 Tx: 46462 pelita ia Fax: (21) 231 20 63 SITA: n/a

F: 1970 ✈✈✈ 1080 Head: Capt. Oedyono Adiwisastro ICAO: PELITA Net: n/a

☐ PK-PGI	Eurocopter (IPTN/MBB) NBO105CB	N47/S-375	PK-XZP*	0082	1182	2 AN 250-C20B	2400			
☐ PK-PGJ	Eurocopter (IPTN/MBB) NBO105CB	N56/S-454		0082	0183	2 AN 250-C20B	2400			
☐ PK-PGQ	Eurocopter (IPTN/MBB) NBO105CB	N60/S-458		0082	0483	2 AN 250-C20B	2400			
☐ PK-PGR	Eurocopter (IPTN/MBB) NBO105CB	N62/S-460		0082	0983	2 AN 250-C20B	2400			
☐ PK-PGS	Eurocopter (IPTN/MBB) NBO105CB	N63/S-551		0083	1183	2 AN 250-C20B	2400			
☐ PK-PGT	Eurocopter (IPTN/MBB) NBO105CB	N64/S-552		0083	1283	2 AN 250-C20B	2400			
☐ PK-PGU	Eurocopter (IPTN/MBB) NBO105CB	N12/S-218	PK-XZJ*	0081	0681	2 AN 250-C20B	2400			
☐ PK-PGZ	Eurocopter (IPTN/MBB) NBO105CB	N65/S-553		0083	1283	2 AN 250-C20B	2400			
☐ PK-PIF	Eurocopter (IPTN/MBB) NBO105CB	N66/S-554		0083	1283	2 AN 250-C20B	2400			
☐ PK-PIG	Eurocopter (IPTN/MBB) NBO105CB	N67/S-555		0083	0184	2 AN 250-C20B	2400			
☐ PK-PIH	Eurocopter (IPTN/MBB) NBO105CB	N68/S-556		0083	0184	2 AN 250-C20B	2400			
☐ PK-PII	Eurocopter (IPTN/MBB) NBO105CB	N69/S-557		0083	0184	2 AN 250-C20B	2400			
☐ PK-PIJ	Eurocopter (IPTN/MBB) NBO105CB	N70/S-558	PK-XYN*	0083	0284	2 AN 250-C20B	2400			
☐ PK-PIK	Eurocopter (IPTN/MBB) NBO105CB	N71/S-559	PK-XYO*	0084	0484	2 AN 250-C20B	2400			
☐ PK-PIM	Eurocopter (IPTN/MBB) NBO105CB	N72/S-560	PK-XYP*	0084	0484	2 AN 250-C20B	2400			
☐ PK-PIO	Eurocopter (IPTN/MBB) NBO105CB	N74/S-562	PK-XYR*	0084	0584	2 AN 250-C20B	2400			
☐ PK-PIP	Eurocopter (IPTN/MBB) NBO105CB	N75/S-563	PK-XYS*	0084	0684	2 AN 250-C20B	2400			
☐ PK-PIR	Eurocopter (IPTN/MBB) NBO105CB	N77/S-565	PK-XYU*	0084	0784	2 AN 250-C20B	2400			
☐ PK-PIS	Eurocopter (IPTN/MBB) NBO105CB	N78/S-566	PK-XYV*	0084	1084	2 AN 250-C20B	2400			
☐ PK-PIT	Eurocopter (IPTN/MBB) NBO105CB	N79/S-567	PK-XYW*	0084	1184	2 AN 250-C20B	2400			
☐ PK-PIV	Eurocopter (IPTN/MBB) NBO105CB	N81/S-569	PK-XYY*	0084	1284	2 AN 250-C20B	2400			
☐ PK-PIX	Eurocopter (IPTN/MBB) NBO105CB	N83/S-651	PK-XWA*	0084	0285	2 AN 250-C20B	2400			
☐ PK-PIY	Eurocopter (IPTN/MBB) NBO105CB	N50/S-378	PK-XZS*	0082	0387	2 AN 250-C20B	2400			
☐ PK-PUA	Sikorsky S-76A	760179	N5446U*	0082	0183	2 AN 250-C30S	4672			
☐ PK-PUC	Sikorsky S-76A	760194	N3120Y*	0082	0183	2 AN 250-C30S	4672			
☐ PK-PUD	Sikorsky S-76A	760195	N3121A*	0082	0183	2 AN 250-C30S	4672			
☐ PK-PUE	Sikorsky S-76A	760200		0082	0183	2 AN 250-C30S	4672			
☐ PK-PCN	IPTN (CASA) 212-CC4 Aviocar Srs 200	56N/216	PK-XDE*	0083	0283	2 GA TPE331-10R-511C	7450			
☐ PK-PCO	IPTN (CASA) 212-CC4 Aviocar Srs 200	55N/215	PK-XDD*	0082	0283	2 GA TPE331-10R-511C	7450			
☐ PK-PCP	IPTN (CASA) 212-CC4 Aviocar Srs 200	48N/208	PK-XAV*	0082	1082	2 GA TPE331-10R-511C	7450			
☐ PK-PCQ	IPTN (CASA) 212-AB4 Aviocar Srs 200	47N/207	PK-XAU*	0082	0782	2 GA TPE331-10R-511C	7450			
☐ PK-PCR	IPTN (CASA) 212-AB4 Aviocar Srs 200	46N/206	PK-XAT*	0082	0782	2 GA TPE331-10R-511C	7450			
☐ PK-PCS	IPTN (CASA) 212-AB4 Aviocar Srs 200	45N/205	PK-XAS*	0082	0582	2 GA TPE331-10R-511C	7450			
☐ PK-PCT	IPTN (CASA) 212-CC4 Aviocar Srs 200	44N/204	PK-XAR*	0082	0482	2 GA TPE331-10R-511C	7450			
☐ PK-PCU	IPTN (CASA) 212-AB4 Aviocar Srs 200	43N/203	PK-XAQ*	0082	0382	2 GA TPE331-10-501C	7450			
☐ PK-PCV	IPTN (CASA) 212-A4 Aviocar Srs 100	21N/132	PK-XCT*	0080	0681	2 GA TPE331-5-251C	6500			
☐ PK-PCW	IPTN (CASA) 212-A4 Aviocar Srs 100	24N/144	PK-XCW*	0080	0681	2 GA TPE331-5-251C	6500			
☐ PK-PCY	IPTN (CASA) 212-A4 Aviocar Srs 100	2N/39	PK-PCL	0075	1275	2 GA TPE331-5-251C	6500			
☐ PK-PCZ	IPTN (CASA) 212-A4 Aviocar Srs 100	1N/34	PK-PCK	0075	0875	2 GA TPE331-5-251C	6500			
☐ PK-PDT	Eurocopter (Aerosp.) SA330G Puma	1264	F-WTNB*	0074	0574	2 TU Turmo IVA	7400			
☐ PK-PDY	Eurocopter (Aerosp.) SA330G Puma	1160		0072	1272	2 TU Turmo IVA	7400			
☐ PK-PEH	Eurocopter (Aerosp.) SA330J Puma	1304		0075	0575	2 TU Turmo IVC	7400			
☐ PK-PEI	Eurocopter (Aerosp.) SA330J Puma	1299		0074	1274	2 TU Turmo IVC	7400			
☐ PK-PEK	Eurocopter (Aerosp.) SA330G Puma	1283		0074	1074	2 TU Turmo IVC	7400			

499 registration type of aircraft cn/fn ex/ex* mfd del powered by mtow kg configuration selcal name/fln/specialitites/remarks

☐ PK-PEM	Eurocopter (Aerosp.) SA330J Puma	1268		0074	0774	2 TU Turmo IVC	7400			
☐ PK-PEN	Eurocopter (Aerosp.) SA330G Puma	1275		0074	0174	2 TU Turmo IVC	7400			
☐ PK-PEO	Eurocopter (Aerosp.) SA330J Puma	1261		0074	0774	2 TU Turmo IVC	7400			
☐ PK-PEP	Eurocopter (Aerosp.) SA330G Puma	1253		0074	0374	2 TU Turmo IVC	7400	VIP		
☐ PK-PHW	Eurocopter (Aerosp.) SA330G Puma	1082	F-OCRQ	0071	0771	2 TU Turmo IVC	7400			
☐ PK-PIA	Eurocopter (IPTN/Aerosp.) SA330J Puma	NP1/1661	PK-XPA*	0081	0681	2 TU Turmo IVC	7400			
☐ PK-PIC	Eurocopter (IPTN/Aerosp.) SA330J Puma	NP2/1664	PK-XPB*	0081	0781	2 TU Turmo IVC	7400			
☐ PK-PID	Eurocopter (IPTN/Aerosp.) SA330J Puma	NP3/1668	PK-XPC*	0082	0282	2 TU Turmo IVC	7400			
☐ PK-PIE	Eurocopter (IPTN/Aerosp.) SA330J Puma	NP7/1670	PK-XPD*	0082	0582	2 TU Turmo IVC	7400			
☐ PK-PUG	Eurocopter (IPTN/Aerosp.) AS332C S.Puma	NSP2/2020	PK-XSB*	0083	0784	2 TU Makila 1A	8600			
☐ PK-PUH	Eurocopter (IPTN/Aerosp.) AS332C S.Puma	NSP3/2021	PX-XSC*	0083	0884	2 TU Makila 1A	8600			
☐ PK-PKT	De Havilland DHC-7-110 Dash 7	054	C-FYXV	0081	0398	4 PWC PT6A-50	19958			
☐ PK-PSV	De Havilland DHC-7-103 Dash 7	105	C-GFOD*	0084	0784	4 PWC PT6A-50	19958			
☐ PK-PSW	De Havilland DHC-7-103 Dash 7	100	C-GFCF*	0084	0684	4 PWC PT6A-50	19958			
☐ PK-PSX	De Havilland DHC-7-103 Dash 7	094	C-GFYI*	0082	1182	4 PWC PT6A-50	19958			
☐ PK-PSY	De Havilland DHC-7-103 Dash 7	086	C-GFUM*	0082	0782	4 PWC PT6A-50	19958			
☐ PK-PSZ	De Havilland DHC-7-103 Dash 7	075	C-GFCF*	0082	0282	4 PWC PT6A-50	19958			
☐ PK-PJA	GAC G-1159A Gulfstream III	395	N1761Q	0083	0184	2 RR Spey 511-8	31615	VIP		lst Eagle Aviation
☐ PK-PJK	Fokker F28 Fellowship 4000 (F28 Mk4000)	11192	PH-EXW*	0083	0583	2 RR Spey 555-15H	32205			opf Caltex
☐ PK-PJL	Fokker F28 Fellowship 4000 (F28 Mk4000)	11111	PH-EZA*	0076	0591	2 RR Spey 555-15H	32205			
☐ PK-PJM	Fokker F28 Fellowship 4000 (F28 Mk4000)	11178	PH-EXW*	0081	1081	2 RR Spey 555-15H	32205			Matak
☐ PK-PJS	Fokker F28 Fellowship 1000 (F28 Mk1000)	11030	D-ABAM	0070	0874	2 RR Spey 555-15	29484			Jatibarang
☐ PK-PJY	Fokker F28 Fellowship 4000 (F28 Mk4000)	11146	PH-EXN*	0079	0380	2 RR Spey 555-15H	32205			Arun / std HLP
☐ PK-PFE	Fokker 70 (F28 Mk0070)	11553	PH-MXN*	0095	0995	2 RR Tay 620-15	36740	Y79		lsf Avignon Location
☐ PK-PJJ	Avro RJ85 (Avro 146-RJ85)	E2239	G-BVAE*	0093	1293	4 LY LF507-1F	43999	VIP		

PENAS = PNS (P.T. Survai Udara Penas (Persero) dba) **Jakarta-Halim**

Jalan Kran 11, Kemayoran, Jakarta 10610, Indonesia ☎ (21) 421 67 43 Tx: 49193 penas ia Fax: (21) 421 67 43 SITA: n/a
F: 1961 ⁂ 125 Head: Mr. Soedarma ICAO: PENAS Net: n/a

☐ PK-VCD	Cessna 402B	402B0024	N5424M	0070	0271	2 CO TSIO-520-E	2858	Surveyer		
☐ PK-VKY	Beech Jetcrafters Taurus A90	LJ-197	N2510L	0066	0781	2 PWC PT6A-135	4353	Surveyer		opf Bakosurtanal/cvtd King Air
☐ PK-VKZ	Beech Jetcrafters Taurus A90	LJ-189	N123KA	0066	0681	2 PWC PT6A-135	4353	Surveyer		opf Bakosurtanal/cvtd King Air
☐ PK-VKA	Beech King Air 200	BB-732	N3716D	0080	0681	2 PWC PT6A-41	5670	Surveyer		
☐ PK-VKB	Beech King Air 200	BB-794	N3720U	0081	0681	2 PWC PT6A-41	5670	Surveyer		
☐ PK-CAP	GAC G-1159A Gulfstream III	316	N26018	0080	0194	2 RR Spey 511-8	30935	Executive		lsf Mitraguna Tribakti
☐ PK-VBA	Boeing 727-25	18970 / 229	N680AM	0066	0595	3 PW JT8D-7B (HK3/FDX)	72802	VIP F35		opf Bakrie Brothers

RAJAWALI AIR (P.T. Rajawali Air Transport dba) **Jakarta-Halim**

Jalan Jend. Sudirman, Kav. 34, Floor 3A, Wisma Rajawali, Jakarta 10220, Indonesia ☎ (21) 573 68 52 Tx: 62264 rajwl ia Fax: (21) 573 68 53 SITA: n/a
F: n/a ⁂ n/a Head: Rustam Suhando Net: n/a

☐ PK-RJA	GAC (Grumman) G-159 Gulfstream I	191	VH-JPJ	0068	0392	2 RR Dart 529-8X	16329	C12		
☐ PK-RJW	Fokker F28 Fellowship 1000 (F28 Mk1000)	11045	PH-PBX	0071	0596	2 RR Spey 555-15	29480	Y80		Anugerah

SATUAN UDARA F.A.S.I. (Federasi Aero Sport Indonesia/Flying Association of the Indonesian Services dba/Div. of the Air Force) **Jakarta-Halim**

Terminal Bldg, Halim Perdanakusuma Airport, Jakarta 13610, Indonesia ☎ (21) 801 91 25 Tx: none Fax: (21) 800 39 15 SITA: n/a
F: n/a ⁂ n/a Head: Marshall TNI Rilo Tambudi Net: n/a Non-commercial state association conducting mainly flights carrying member parachutists.

☐ AF-4775	Boeing (Douglas) DC-3C (C-47A)				0093	2 PW R-1830	12202			RI-001/Seulawah / old Indonesian Aw.cs
☐ AF-4776	Boeing (Douglas) DC-3C (C-47A-25-DK)	13334	PK-VTO	0044	0093	2 PW R-1830	12202			
☐ AF-4777	Boeing (Douglas) DC-3C (C-47B-45-DK)	34228	PK-VTM	0045	0093	2 PW R-1830	12202			
☐ AF-4790	Boeing (Douglas) DC-3C (C-47A)				0093	2 PW R-1830	12202			RI-007/Djakarta / old Indonesian Aw.cs

SEMPATI AIR = SG / SSR (P.T. Sempati Air dba/formerly P.T. Sempati Air Transport/Associated with Asean Aviation) **Jakarta-Soekarno-Hatta Int'l**

Ground Floor, Terminal Bldg, Halim Perdana Kusuma Airport, Jakarta 13610, Indonesia ☎ (21) 809 16 12 Tx: 46641 asb sinar ia Fax: (21) 809 44 20 SITA: n/a
F: 1968 ⁂ n/a Head: n/a IATA: 821 ICAO: SPIROW Net: http://www.sempati.co.id/teknik/ Suspended operations 0698. Intends to restart.

☐ PK-JFG	Fokker F27 Friendship 600 (F27 Mk600)	10413	F-GBGI	0069	0880	2 RR Dart 532-7	19731	Y44		Selamat / std CGK
☐ PK-JFH	Fokker F27 Friendship 600 (F27 Mk600)	10396	PH-SFH	0069	0177	2 RR Dart 532-7	19731	Y44		Natalus / std CGK
☐ PK-JFI	Fokker F27 Friendship 600 (F27 Mk600)	10362	PK-CFD	0068	0985	2 RR Dart 532-7	19731	Y44		Immanuel / cvtd -400 / std CGK
☐ PK-JFK	Fokker F27 Friendship 200 (F27 Mk200)	10226	9M-AMJ	0063	0572	2 RR Dart 532-7	19051	Y44		Anugerah / std Seletar
☐ PK-JFN	Fokker F27 Friendship 200 (F27 Mk200)	10242	9M-MCZ	0064	0781	2 RR Dart 532-7	19051	C8Y32		Kasih / std CGK
☐ PK-JHA	Boeing 737-281	20450 / 262	JA8409	0070	1192	2 PW JT8D-9A	49442	C16Y81		White Rose / lsf Asia Market / std CGK
☐ PK-JHC	Boeing 737-281 (A)	20506 / 280	JA8412	0071	0093	2 PW JT8D-9A	49442	C16Y81		lsf Asia Market Investments / std CGK
☐ PK-JHD	Boeing 737-281	20451 / 266	JA8410	0070	1192	2 PW JT8D-9A	49442	C20Y81		Red Rose / lsf Asia Market / std CGK
☐ PK-JHE	Boeing 737-281	20452 / 270	JA8411	0070	0093	2 PW JT8D-9A	49442	Y126		lsf Asia Market Investments / std CGK
☐ PK-JHG	Boeing 737-281 (A)	20507 / 282	JA8413	0071	1193	2 PW JT8D-9A	49442	C16Y81		Orange Rose / lsf Asia Market / std CGK

S.M.A.C – P.T. Sabang Merauke Raya Air Charter = SMC (Associated with Merpati) **Medan & Singapore-Seletar**

Jalan Imam Bonjol No. 59, Medan 20157, Indonesia ☎ (61) 53 77 60 Tx: 51895 smac ia Fax: (61) 53 86 43 SITA: n/a
F: 1969 ⁂ 130 Head: Toto Iman Dewanto ICAO: SAMER Net: n/a
Scheduled feeder-services are operated for Merpati & Garuda in Sumatra.

☐ PK-ZAE	Britten-Norman BN-2A-21 Islander	565	G-BEGH	0076	1077	2 LY IO-540-K1B5	2994	Y9		
☐ PK-ZAM	Britten-Norman BN-2A-21 Islander	782	G-BDRO	0076	0189	2 LY IO-540-K1B5	2994	Y9		
☐ PK-ZAK	Piper PA-31-310 Navajo	31-407	PK-FJH	0068	0678	2 LY TIO-540-A1A	2948	Y7		
☐ PK-ZAT	Piper PA-31-350 Navajo Chieftain	31-7652070	PK-PPF	0076	0380	2 LY TIO-540-J2BD	3175	Y9		
☐ PK-ZAB	IPTN (CASA) 212-A4 Aviocar Srs 100	23N/140	PK-XCV*	0080	1080	2 GA TPE331-5-251C	6500	Y19		
☐ PK-ZAI	IPTN (CASA) 212-A4 Aviocar Srs 100	18N/120	PK-XCQ*	0080	0880	2 GA TPE331-5-251C	6500	Y19		
☐ PK-ZAN	IPTN (CASA) 212-A4 Aviocar Srs 100	5N/60	A-2102	0076	0093	2 GA TPE331-5-251C	6500	Y19		
☐ PK-ZAO	IPTN (CASA) 212-A4 Aviocar Srs 100	4N/64	A-2101	0076	0093	2 GA TPE331-5-251C	6500	Y19		
☐ PK-ZAF	Fokker F27 Friendship 200 (F27 Mk200)	10222	PK-MFA	0063	0994	2 RR Dart 532-7	19731	Y44		lsf Aviona Leasing

TRANSINDO (P.T. Dayajasa Transindo Pratama dba) **Jakarta-Halim**

Terminal Bldg, Halim Perdanakusuma Airport, Jakarta 13610, Indonesia ☎ (21) 809 72 25 Tx: n/a Fax: (21) 809 72 27 SITA: n/a
F: 1990 ⁂ 75 Head: G. Goguen Net: http://www.guides.com/acg/transindo

☐ PK-CHA	Eurocopter (IPTN/MBB) NBO105CB	N97/S-665	PK-XWP*	0086	1090	2 AN 250-C20B	2400			
☐ PK-CHC	Bell (IPTN) 412	NB18/34018	PK-XFS	0091	0192	2 PWC PT6T-3B TwinPac	5398			
☐ PK-CTA	Hawker 700A (HS 125-700A)	257153 / NA0313	N18G	0081	0890	2 GA TFE731-3R-1H	11567			
☐ PK-CTC	Hawker 700A (HS 125-700A)	257099 / NA0270	N621JA	0080	0691	2 GA TFE731-3R-1H	11567			
☐ PK-CTE	GAC (Grumman) G-159 Gulfstream I	177	G-BRWN	0068	0292	2 RR Dart 529-8X	16329			

TRIGANA AIR SERVICE (P.T. Trigana Air Service dba) **Jakarta-Halim**

Komplex Puri Centra Niaga, Jalan Wiraloka 686, Blok D, Jakarta-Malan 13970, Indonesia ☎ (21) 860 48 67 Tx: none Fax: (21) 860 48 66 SITA: n/a
F: 1991 ⁂ n/a Head: Capt. Rubyanto Adisarwono Net: n/a

☐ PK-YPI	Bell (IPTN) 412	NB17/34017	PK-XFR*	0091	0293	2 PWC PT6T-3B TwinPac	5398	Y14		
☐ PK-YPF	De Havilland DHC-6 Twin Otter 300	210	C-FYFT	0069	0293	2 PWC PT6A-27	5670	Y19		cvtd 200
☐ PK-YPS	Beech King Air B200	BB-920	N83TJ	0081	0193	2 PWC PT6A-42	5670	Y10		
☐ PK-YPL	Fokker F27 Friendship 600 (F27 Mk600)	10435	PK-MFO	0070	0793	2 RR Dart 532-7	19731	Y44		Biak / std HLP
☐ PK-YPN	Fokker F27 Friendship 400 (F27 Mk400)	10299	PK-MFT	0066	0094	2 RR Dart 532-7	19731	Y44		Morotai
☐ PK-YPO	Fokker F27 Friendship 600 (F27 Mk600)	10400	PK-MFE	0069	1195	2 RR Dart 532-7	19731	Y44		std HLP
☐ PK-YPJ	Fokker F28 Fellowship 4000 (F28 Mk4000)	11148	PK-PJW	0079	0795	2 RR Spey 555-15H	32205	Y85		lst MDL

YAJASI AVIATION (Yayasan Jasa Aviasi) (formerly Summer Institute of Linguistics) **Jayapura**

PO Box 1800, Jayapura 99018, Irian Jaya, Indonesia ☎ (967) 91 094 Tx: n/a Fax: (967) 81 302 SITA: n/a
F: 1976 ⁂ 31 Head: Jongky Sarioa Net: n/a Aircraft below MTOW 1361 kg: Hiller UH-12E.

☐ PK-UCA	Helio H-295 Super Courier	1408	N6460V	0069	0876	1 LY GO-480-G1D6	1542	Pax / Frtr		Belly pod / opf Universitas Cendrawasih
☐ PK-UCB	Helio H-295 Super Courier	1235		0066	0378	1 LY GO-480-G1D6	1542	Pax / Frtr		Freight door/Belly pod/opf Univ.Cendra.
☐ PK-UCD	Helio H-295 Super Courier	1246	66-14344	0066	0483	1 LY GO-480-G1D6	1542	Pax / Frtr		Freight door/Belly pod/opf Univ.Cendra.
☐ PK-UCC	Piper PA-23-250 Aztec C	27-3042	N6TM	0065	0981	2 LY IO-540-C4B5	2359	Pax / Frtr		Large freight door/opf Univers.Cendraw.
☐ PK-UPD	Piper PA-23-250 Aztec C	27-3827	N6534Y	0067	0187	2 LY IO-540-C4B5	2359	Pax / Frtr		Large frtdoor/opf Universitas Pattimura

YAYASAN AVIASI Indonesia **Jakarta-Halim**

Bandara Halim Perdanakusuma Airport, Jakarta 13610, Indonesia ☎ (21) 809 69 23 Tx: none Fax: (21) 800 97 09 SITA: n/a
F: n/a ⁂ n/a Head: n/a Net: n/a Aircraft below MTOW 1361kg: Cessna 172 & FFA AS202/18 Bravo

☐ PK-AGG	Beech Baron 58	TH-972	N2068C	0078	0195	2 CO IO-520-C	2449			
☐ PK-AGE	Cessna 402A	402A0046	L-4021	0068	0995	2 CO TSIO-520-E	2858			
☐ PK-AGF	Cessna 402A	402A0047	L-4022	0068	0595	2 CO TSIO-520-E	2858			

500 registration type of aircraft cn/fn ex/ex* mfd del powered by mtow kg configuration selcal name/fln/specialitites/remarks

PP = BRAZIL (Federative Republic of Brazil) (Republica Federativa do Brasil)

Capital: Brasilia Official Language: Portuguese Population: 165,0 million Square Km: 8511965 Dialling code: +55 Year established: 1822 Acting political head: Fernando Henrique Cardoso (President)

Government / Corporate / Executive / VIP Aircraft

☐ PP-EAM	Embraer 110P1 Bandeirante (EMB-110P1)	110498	PT-SBS*	0093	0396	2 PWC PT6A-34	5670	VIP		Governo do Estado do Amazonas, Manaus
☐ PP-EIC	Embraer 121A Xingu (EMB-121A)	121039	PT-MBG*	0081		2 PWC PT6A-28	5670	VIP		SEVOP Belem
☐ PP-EIF	Cessna 500 Citation I	500-0680	PT-LFR	0084		2 PWC JT15D-1B	5216	VIP		Gov.do Parana CWB/cvtd Ce501 cn 5010680
☐ PP-EIJ	Embraer 121A1 Xingu II (EMB-121A1)	121094	PT-MCH*	0085		2 PWC PT6A-135	5670	VIP		Governo do Piaui Teresina
☐ PP-EIX	Embraer 110P1 Bandeirante (EMB-110P1)	110468	PT-SHW*	0087	1289	2 PWC PT6A-34	5670	VIP		Governo de Amapa, Macapa
☐ PP-EMG	Embraer 110E Bandeirante (EMB-110E)	110032	PT-GJV*	0074	1076	2 PWC PT6A-27	5600	VIP		Governo de Minas Gerais BHZ
☐ PP-EMN	Embraer 121A Xingu (EMB-121A)	121035	PT-MBC*	0080		2 PWC PT6A-28	5670	VIP		Governo de Minas Gerais BHZ
☐ PP-EON	Embraer 110C Bandeirante (EMB-110C)	110038	PT-KOK	0074	0492	2 PWC PT6A-27	5600	VIP		Governo de Roraima
☐ PP-EOO	Embraer 110C Bandeirante (EMB-110C)	110025	PT-FVH	0074	0592	2 PWC PT6A-27	5600	VIP		Governo de Roraima
☐ PP-ERN	Embraer 110P1 Bandeirante (EMB-110P1)	110344	PT-FAV	0081	0694	2 PWC PT6A-34	5670	VIP		Governo de Rio Grande do Norte
☐ PP-FFV	Embraer 110B1 Bandeirante (EMB-110B1)	110284	PT-SBO*	0080		2 PWC PT6A-27	5600	Corporate		INPE S.J. dos Campos
☐ PP-FHE	Embraer 121A1 Xingu II (EMB-121A1)	121051	PT-FAY	0082	0588	2 PWC PT6A-135	5670	VIP		Mirad Brasilia
☐ PP-FOY	Beech King Air A100	B-142		0073		2 PWC PT6A-28	5216	VIP		Ministerio de Interior Brasilia
☐ PT-FAX	Embraer 121A Xingu (EMB-121A)	121049	PT-MBR*	0082		2 PWC PT6A-28	5670	VIP		SUDENE Recife
☐ PT-FDL	Embraer 110E Bandeirante (EMB-110E)	110069	PT-GJO	0075	0283	2 PWC PT6A-27	5600	VIP		Gov. do Amapa/Minter Macapa
☐ PT-FRF	Embraer 110E Bandeirante (EMB-110E)	110115	PT-GKK*	0076	0876	2 PWC PT6A-27	5600	VIP		DNER Rio de Janeiro
☐ PT-FRG	Embraer 121A Xingu (EMB-121A)	121044	PT-MBL*	0081		2 PWC PT6A-28	5670	VIP		DNER Brasilia
☐ PT-LHB	Hawker 800B (BAe 125-800B)	258031	PT-ZAA	0085		2 GA TFE731-5R-1H	12428	Corporate		CESP Sao Paulo
☐ PT-SCE	Embraer 110P1 Bandeirante (EMB-110P1)	110296		0080	1080	2 PWC PT6A-34	5670	Corporate		CHESF Recife
☐ PT-SCY	Embraer 110P1 Bandeirante (EMB-110P1)	110319		0081	0181	2 PWC PT6A-34	5670	Corporate		CODAGRO Fortaleza
☐ PT-SHO	Embraer 110P1 Bandeirante (EMB-110P1)	110461		0085	0585	2 PWC PT6A-34	5670	Corporate		FURNAS Rio de Janeiro
☐ PT-SHP	Embraer 110P1 Bandeirante (EMB-110P1)	110462		0085	1186	2 PWC PT6A-34	5670	Corporate		CHESF Recife
☐ PT-SHR	Embraer 110P1 Bandeirante (EMB-110P1)	110464		0085	0985	2 PWC PT6A-34	5670	Corporate		FURNAS Rio de Janeiro
☐ PT-SHU	Embraer 110P1 Bandeirante (EMB-110P1)	110466		0085	1285	2 PWC PT6A-34	5670	Corporate		CEMIG Belo Horizonte
☐ PT-SRM	Embraer 110P1 Bandeirante (EMB-110P1)	110463	PT-SHQ*	0085	0387	2 PWC PT6A-34	5670	Corporate		Sao Raimundo Mineraçao Itaituba
☐ PT-ZJA	Embraer RJ135 (EMB-135)	145801		0095	0895	2 AN AE3007A3	19000	Test/Demo		Embraer / 1st Prototype / cvtd RJ145ER
☐ PT-ZJB	Embraer RJ145ER (EMB-145ER)	145001		0095	1195	2 AN AE3007A	20600	Test/Demo		Embraer / 2nd Prototype
☐ PT-ZJC	Embraer RJ135 (EMB-135)	145002		0096	0296	2 AN AE3007A3	19000	Test/Demo		Embraer / 2nd Prototype / cvtd RJ145ER
☐ PT-ZJD	Embraer RJ145ER (EMB-145ER)	145003		0096	0496	2 AN AE3007A	20600	Test/Demo		Embraer / 3rd Prototype
☐ PT-ZVB	Embraer-FAMA CBA-123 Vector	802		0091		2 GA TPF351-20	8500	Test/Demo		Embraer / 2nd Prototype
☐ PT-ZVE	Embraer-FAMA CBA-123 Vector	801		0090		2 GA TPF351-20	8500	Test/Demo		Embraer / 1st Prototype
☐ 2000	Embraer 120RT (VC-97) (EMB-120RT)	120003	PT-ZBB*	0083	0787	2 PWC PW118	11500	VIP / mil transp		Força Aérea Brasileira, GTE
☐ 2002	Embraer 120RT (VC-97) (EMB-120RT)	120040	PT-SJO*	0087	0287	2 PWC PW118	11500	VIP / mil transp		Força Aérea Brasileira, GTE
☐ 2003	Embraer 120RT (VC-97) (EMB-120RT)	120055	PT-SJY*	0087	0987	2 PWC PW118	11500	VIP / mil transp		Força Aérea Brasileira, GTE
☐ 2004	Embraer 120RT (VC-97) (EMB-120RT)	120066	PT-SKJ*	0088	0288	2 PWC PW118	11500	VIP / mil transp		Força Aérea Brasileira, GTE
☐ 2005	Embraer 120ER (VC-97) (EMB-120ER)	120337		0098	0698	2 PWC PW118A	11990	VIP / mil transp		Força Aérea Brasileira, GTE
☐ 2114	Hawker 400A (VU-93) (HS 125-400A)	25212 / NA740	N702P	0069		2 RR Viper 522	10569	VIP / mil transp		Força Aérea Brasileira, GTE
☐ 2115	Boeing 737-2N3 (A) (VC-96)	21165 / 441		0075	0376	2 PW JT8D-17	53070	VIP / mil transp		Força Aérea Brasileira, GTE
☐ 2116	Boeing 737-2N3 (A) (VC-96)	21166 / 445		0075	0476	2 PW JT8D-17	53070	VIP / mil transp		Força Aérea Brasileira, GTE
☐ 2117	Hawker 400A (VU-93) (HS 125-400A)	25210 / NA738	N702D	0069		2 RR Viper 522	10569	VIP / mil transp		Força Aérea Brasileira, GTE
☐ 2118	Hawker 400A (VU-93) (HS 125-400A)	25200 / NA729	N702SS	0069		2 RR Viper 522	10569	VIP / mil transp		Força Aérea Brasileira, GTE
☐ 2120	Hawker 3B/RC (VC-93) (HS 125-3B/RC)	25162		0068		2 RR Viper 522	10342	VIP / mil transp		Força Aérea Brasileira, GTE
☐ 2123	Hawker 3B/RC (VC-93) (HS 125-3B/RC)	25167		0068		2 RR Viper 522	10342	VIP / mil transp		Força Aérea Brasileira, GTE
☐ 2124	Hawker 3B/RC (VC-93) (HS 125-3B/RC)	25168		0068		2 RR Viper 522	10342	VIP / mil transp		Força Aérea Brasileira, GTE
☐ 2126	Hawker 403B (VU-93) (HS 125-403B)	25277	G-5-11*	0072		2 RR Viper 522	10569	VIP / mil transp		Força Aérea Brasileira, GTE
☐ 2127	Hawker 403B (VU-93) (HS 125-403B)	25288		0073		2 RR Viper 522	10569	VIP / mil transp		Força Aérea Brasileira, GTE
☐ 2128	Hawker 403B (VU-93) (HS 125-403B)	25289	G-5-16*	0073		2 RR Viper 522	10569	VIP / mil transp		Força Aérea Brasileira, GTE
☐ 2401	Boeing 707-345C (KC-137E)	19840 / 679	PP-VJY	0068	0786	4 PW JT3D-3B	151046	VIP / Tanker	EF-CJ	Força Aérea Brasileira / cvtd 707-345C

ABC TAXI AEREO, SA (Member of Grupo Algar, SA) — Uberlandia, (MG)

Aeroporto Eduardo Gomes, Hangar Walter Garcia, CEP-38407-026 Uberlandia, (Minas Gerais), Brazil ☎ (34) 212 55 55 Tx: none Fax: (34) 212 01 01 SITA: n/a

F: 1981 ⁂ n/a Head: Rogério Montalvao Elian Net: n/a

☐ PT-MAM	Embraer 121A Xingu (EMB-121A)	121020		0080		2 PWC PT6A-28	5670			
☐ PT-MAV	Embraer 121A Xingu (EMB-121A)	121029		0080	0097	2 PWC PT6A-28	5670			
☐ PT-OPJ	Learjet 35A	35A-396	N74JL	0081	0097	2 GA TFE731-2-2B	7711			lsf Delta Nat. Bank & Trust Co.

ABELHA Taxi Aéreo, Ltda — Cuiaba, (MT)

Aeroporto Marechal Rondon, Box Abelha, CEP-78110-971 Varzea Grande, (Mato Grosso), Brazil ☎ (65) 381 12 23 Tx: n/a Fax: n/a SITA: n/a

F: 1988 ⁂ n/a Head: n/a Net: n/a

☐ PT-WEL	Cessna 210M Centurion II	21062086		0077	1095	1 CO IO-520-L	1724			
☐ PT-LRP	Beech Baron 58	TH-928		0078		2 CO IO-520-C	2449			
☐ PT-EFY	Embraer 820C Navajo (EMB-820C)	820035		0076		2 LY TIO-540-J2BD	3175			

ABSA CARGO = M3 / TUS (ABSA-Aerolinhas Brasileiras, S.A. dba/formerly Brasil Transair-Transportes Charter Turismo, Ltda) — Sao Paulo-Viracopos, (SP)

Rua Laplace 96-7andar, CEP-04622-000 Brooklin-Sao Paulo, (Sao Paulo), Brazil ☎ (11) 532 00 55 Tx: none Fax: (11) 530 69 30 SITA: n/a

F: 1994 ⁂ 120 Head: Vlamir Domic IATA: 549 ICAO: TURISMO Net: http://www.absacargo.com

☐ PP-ABS	Boeing (Douglas) DC-8-71F	45810 / 252	CC-CYQ	0066	0896	4 CFMI CFM56-2C	147418	Freighter		lsf FST / cvtd DC-8-61/-71

ADEY Taxi Aéreo, Ltda — Salvador, (BA)

Aeroport Int'l Dois de Julho s/n, Box Adey, CEP-41510-250 Salvador, (Bahia), Brazil ☎ (71) 358 84 98 Tx: n/a Fax: (71) 377 19 93 SITA: n/a

F: 1992 ⁂ n/a Head: n/a Net: n/a

☐ PT-VIJ	Embraer 720D Minuano (EMB-720D)	720244		0090	0097	1 LY IO-540-K1G5	1633			
☐ PT-VMQ	Embraer 720D Minuano (EMB-720D)	720268		0090		1 LY IO-540-K1G5	1633			
☐ PT-WKZ	Embraer 810C Seneca II (EMB-810C)	810440	PP-EHR	0082	0797	2 CO TSIO-360-EB	2073			
☐ PT-JIZ	Cessna 402B	402B0393		0073		2 CO TSIO-520-E	2858			
☐ PT-EHG	Embraer 820C Navajo (EMB-820C)	820043		0077	0097	2 LY TIO-540-J2BD	3175			

ADMIRAL Taxi Aéreo, Ltda — Sao Paulo-Congonhas, (SP)

Rua Visconde de Aguiar Toledo 40, Bairro Aeroporto, CEP-04612-100 Sao Paulo (Sao Paulo), Brazil ☎ (11) 533 18 07 Tx: none Fax: (11) 533 18 07 SITA: n/a

F: 1994 ⁂ 10 Head: Walfredo Herkenhoff Net: n/a

☐ PT-WBG	Embraer 110 Bandeirante (EMB-110)	110019	FAB2139	0074	0097	2 PWC PT6A-27	5600			
☐ PT-WTL	Embraer 110 Bandeirante (EMB-110)	110104	FAB2180	0076		2 PWC PT6A-27	5600			

AEB Taxi Aéreo, Ltda (Associated with AEB – Estruturas Metalicas, Ltda) — Porto Alegre-Salgado Filho, (RS)

CP 8021, Aeroporto Int'l Salgado Filho, CEP-90201-970 Porto Alegre, (Rio Grande do Sul), Brazil ☎ (51) 341 80 66 Tx: 513034 aeb br Fax: (51) 472 53 98 SITA: n/a

F: 1970 ⁂ 9 Head: José Luiz Teixeira Barichello Net: n/a

☐ PT-EVP	Embraer 810C Seneca II (EMB-810C)	810250		0079		2 CO TSIO-360-EB	2073	5 Pax		
☐ PT-IUD	Piper PA-31-350 Navajo Chieftain	31-7305037	N74915	0073	0789	2 LY TIO-540-J2BD	3175	6 Pax		
☐ PT-JEH	Piper PA-31-350 Navajo Chieftain	31-7305057	N74928	0073		2 LY TIO-540-J2BD	3175	6 Pax		lsf BCN Leasing

AEROEXECUTIVOS Taxi Aéreo, Ltda — Sao Paulo-Congonhas, (SP) & Rio de Janeiro-Int'l, (RJ)

Rua Joao Carlos Mallet, 62 Pla. Paulistao, CEP-04072-040 Sao Paulo, (Sao Paulo), Brazil ☎ (11) 583 12 12 Tx: n/a Fax: (11) 583 12 12 SITA: n/a

F: 1992 ⁂ n/a Head: n/a Net: n/a

☐ PT-LIX	Cessna 500 Citation	500-0171	N728US	0074		2 PWC JT15D-1	5216			
☐ PT-LEN	Learjet 25B	25B-093	N33NM	0072		2 GE CJ610-6	6804			

AEROLEO Taxi Aéreo, Ltda — Rio de Janeiro-Santos Dumont, (RJ)

Aeroporto Santos Dumont, Praca Senador Salgado Filho sn, Hangar 01, Bairro Centro, CEP-20021-340 Rio de Janeiro (RJ), Brazil ☎ (21) 210 24 34 Tx: 2123175 cpdb br Fax: (21) 220 41 67 SITA: n/a

F: 1968 ⁂ 250 Head: Newton Nascimento Lins Net: n/a

☐ PT-HQV	Bell 206B JetRanger III	3657	N2147V	0082		1 AN 250-C20J	1451			
☐ PT-HOR	Sikorsky S-76A	760003	N476AL	0079		2 AN 250-C30S	4672			lsf Airlog International Inc.
☐ PT-HUI	Sikorsky S-76A	760027	N764AL	0079		2 AN 250-C30S	4672			lsf Airlog International Inc.
☐ PT-YAU	Sikorsky S-76A	760175	N5446E	0081	1095	2 AN 250-C30S	4672			lsf Airlog International Inc.
☐ PT-YAY	Sikorsky S-76A	760277	N708AL	0084	1095	2 AN 250-C30S	4672			lsf Airlog International Inc.
☐ PT-HQG	Bell 212	31123	N1087B	0080		2 PWC PT6T-3B TwinPac	5080			
☐ PT-HRO	Bell 212	31269	N31860	0084		2 PWC PT6T-3B TwinPac	5080			
☐ PT-HRP	Bell 212	31270	N31861	0084		2 PWC PT6T-3B TwinPac	5080			
☐ PT-HUO	Bell 412SP	33159	N18099	0088		2 PWC PT6T-3B TwinPac	5398			
☐ PT-HUV	Bell 412SP	33184	N32130	0089	1289	2 PWC PT6T-3B TwinPac	5398			
☐ PT-YCF	Sikorsky S-61N	61757	LN-OQH	0076	1096	2 GE CT58-140-2	9299			lsf HKS / opf Petrobras
☐ PT-YEK	Sikorsky S-61N	61825	G-BHOG	0080	0997	2 GE CT58-140-2	9299			lsf Bristow Helicopters

AEROMIL Taxi Aéreo, Ltda — Sao Paulo-CGH, (SP) / RIO-Jacarepagua, (RJ) & Brasilia, (DF)

Rua General Pantaleao Telles 40, Aeroporto de Congonhas, CEP-04355-040 Sao Paulo, (SP), Brazil ☎ (11) 533 58 60 Tx: none Fax: (11) 533 58 60 SITA: n/a

F: 1993 ⁂ 50 Head: Capt. Paulo S. Carinha Net: n/a

☐ PT-HYP	Eurocopter (Aerosp.) AS350B2 Esquilo	2678		0092		1 TU Arriel 1D1	2250			

501 registration type of aircraft cn/fn ex/ex* mfd del powered by mtow kg configuration selcal name/fln/specialitites/remarks

□ PT-HYQ	Eurocopter (Aerosp.) AS350B2 Esquilo	2692		0092		1 TU Arriel 1D1	2250			
□ PT-YRJ	Eurocopter (MBB) BK117C-1	7519		0098	0598	2 TU Arriel 1E2	3350			lsf Eurocopter Deutschland GmbH
□ PT-YSP	Eurocopter (MBB) BK117C-1	7518		0097	0198	2 TU Arriel 1E2	3350			lsf Eurocopter Deutschland GmbH
□ PT-LKS	Cessna S550 Citation S/II	S550-0114	N1292A	0086		2 PWC JT15D-4B	6668			

AERONAUS Comercio de Aeronaves e Aerotaxi, Ltda — Curitiba-Bacacheri, (PR)

Rua Cicero Jaime Bley 76, Aeroporto Bacacheri, CEP-82515-230 Curitiba, (Parana), Brazil ☎ (41) 256 22 92 Tx: n/a Fax: n/a SITA: n/a

F: 1993 n/a Head: n/a Net: n/a

□ PT-DYK	Piper PA-31-310 Navajo	31-718		0071		2 LY TIO-540-A2C	2948			

AERO STAR Taxi Aéreo, Ltda — Salvador, (BA)

Aeroporto 2 de Julho, Box Aero Star, CEP-41520-970 Salvador, (Bahia), Brazil ☎ (71) 379 28 55 Tx: none Fax: (71) 377 17 63 SITA: n/a

F: 1995 n/a Head: n/a Net: n/a

□ PT-VFP	Embraer 720D Minuano (EMB-720D)	720222		0086		1 LY IO-540-K1G5	1633			
□ PT-JGX	Cessna 310Q II	310Q0932		0074	0098	2 CO IO-470-VO	2404			
□ PT-EDF	Embraer 820C Navajo (EMB-820C)	820014		0076		2 LY TIO-540-J2BD	3175			
□ PT-EZN	Embraer 820C Navajo (EMB-820C)	820106		0080	0097	2 LY TIO-540-J2BD	3175			

AEROSUL, SA - Levantamentos Aeroespaciais e Consultoria — Curitiba, (PR)

Av. Brasilia 5547, Novo Mundo, CEP-81020-010 Curitiba, (Parana), Brazil ☎ (41) 346 35 53 Tx: 415558 aesu br Fax: (41) 246 20 15 SITA: n/a

F: 1969 200 Head: Antonio Carlos Bogo Net: n/a

□ PT-EIY	Embraer 810C Seneca II (EMB-810C)	810084		0077		2 CO TSIO-360-E	2073	Photo		

AEROTAXI JACAREPAGUA, Ltda — Rio de Janeiro-Jacarepagua, (RJ)

Av. Ayrton Senna 2541, Aeroporto de Jacarapagua, CEP-22775-000 Rio de Janeiro, (Rio de Janeiro), Brazil ☎ (21) 325 64 86 Tx: none Fax: none SITA: n/a

F: 1995 n/a Head: n/a Net: n/a

□ PT-WHJ	Embraer 810C Seneca II (EMB-810C)	810154	FAB2610	0078	0996	2 CO TSIO-360-EB	2073			
□ PT-EZM	Embraer 820C Navajo (EMB-820C)	820105		0079		2 LY TIO-540-J2BD	3175			
□ PT-WAP	Embraer 110 Bandeirante (EMB-110)	110044	FAB2152	0075		2 PWC PT6A-27	5600			

AEROTAXI POTY, Ltda — Teresina, (PI)

Aeroporto Santos Dumont, CEP-64006-970 Teresina, (Piaui), Brazil ☎ (86) 225 11 23 Tx: n/a Fax: (86) 225 11 23 SITA: n/a

F: 1974 n/a Head: n/a Net: n/a

□ PT-EAK	Embraer 810C Seneca II (EMB-810C)	810008		0075		2 CO TSIO-360-E	2073			
□ PT-RCG	Embraer 810C Seneca II (EMB-810C)	810329		0080		2 CO TSIO-360-EB	2073			
□ PT-RUC	Embraer 810D Seneca III (EMB-810D)	810518		0083	0098	2 CO TSIO-360-KB	2155			
□ PT-VJE	Embraer 810D Seneca III (EMB-810D)	810690		0088		2 CO TSIO-360-KB	2155			
□ PT-JYE	Piper PA-31-350 Navajo Chieftain	31-7405154	N74994	0074	0690	2 LY TIO-540-J2BD	3175			
□ PT-RCL	Embraer 820C Navajo (EMB-820C)	820119		0080	0097	2 LY TIO-540-J2BD	3175			

AEROTAXI RIO PRETO, Ltda - AERP — Sao Jose do Rio Preto, (SP)

Av. dos Estudantes s/n, Jd. Aeroporto, CEP-15035-010 Sao José do Rio Preto, (Sao Paulo), Brazil ☎ (17) 233 74 78 Tx: n/a Fax: (17) 233 77 33 SITA: n/a

F: 1993 n/a Head: n/a Net: n/a

□ PT-LJV	Cessna T210N Turbo Centurion II	21064762	N1992U	0082		1 CO TSIO-520-R	1814			

AEROTEC Taxi Aéreo, Ltda — Goiania, (GO)

Av. Santos Dumont sn, Hangar Aerotec, Aeroporto, CEP-74672-420 Goiania, (Goias), Brazil ☎ (62) 207 13 13 Tx: n/a Fax: n/a SITA: n/a

F: 1987 n/a Head: n/a Net: n/a

□ PT-LJB	Embraer 810C Seneca II (EMB-810C)	810275	PP-EGY	0079	0098	2 CO TSIO-360-EB	2073			
□ PT-LKX	Embraer 810C Seneca II (EMB-810C)	810272		0079		2 CO TSIO-360-EB	2073			
□ PT-RGA	Embraer 810C Seneca II (EMB-810C)	810389		0080		2 CO TSIO-360-EB	2073			
□ PT-RGM	Embraer 810C Seneca II (EMB-810C)	810405		0081		2 CO TSIO-360-EB	2073			

AGUIA Taxi Aéreo, Ltda — Toledo, (PR)

Av. Tiradentes 59-Centro, CEP-85900-230 Toledo, (Parana), Brazil ☎ (45) 252 11 55 Tx: none Fax: n/a SITA: n/a

F: 1996 n/a Head: n/a Net: n/a

□ PT-RGD	Embraer 810C Seneca II (EMB-810C)	810393		0080	1296	2 CO TSIO-360-EB	2073			

ALA - Abaete Linhas Aéreas, SA = ABJ (Sister company of ATA-Aerotaxi Abaete, Ltda — Salvador, (BA)

Aeroporto Dois de Julho, Box Abaete, CEP-41520-970 Salvador, (Bahia), Brazil ☎ (71) 377 39 55 Tx: 712825 atab br Fax: (71) 377 28 02 SITA: n/a

F: 1994 n/a Head: n/a Net: n/a

□ PT-GKO	Embraer 110P Bandeirante (EMB-110P)	110119		0076		2 PWC PT6A-27	5600	Y15		cvtd 110E
□ PT-MFN	Embraer 110 Bandeirante (EMB-110)	110040	FAB2148	0074	0996	2 PWC PT6A-27	5600	Y15		
□ PT-MFO	Embraer 110 Bandeirante (EMB-110)	110058	FAB2158	0075	0295	2 PWC PT6A-27	5600	Y15		
□ PT-MFP	Embraer 110 Bandeirante (EMB-110)	110105	FAB2181	0076	1294	2 PWC PT6A-27	5600	Y15		
□ PT-MFQ	Embraer 110 Bandeirante (EMB-110)	110121	FAB2188	0076	0795	2 PWC PT6A-27	5600	Y15		
□ PT-MFS	Embraer 110 Bandeirante (EMB-110)	110054	FAB2160	0075	0396	2 PWC PT6A-27	5600	Y15		

AMAPIL Taxi Aéreo, Ltda — Campo Grande, (MS)

Rua Jornalista Belizario Lima 677, VS Filomena, CEP-79004-270 Campo Grande, (Mato Grosso do Sul), Brazil ☎ (67) 721 07 33 Tx: none Fax: (67) 721 07 22 SITA: n/a

F: 1993 n/a Head: n/a Net: n/a

□ PT-KJU	Cessna U206F Stationair	U20602508		0074		1 CO IO-520-F	1633			
□ PT-KHH	Cessna 210L Centurion II	21060473	N93981	0074		1 CO IO-520-L	1724			
□ PT-RUH	Embraer 810D Seneca III (EMB-810D)	810523		0083	0098	2 CO TSIO-360-KB	2155			

AMAZON Taxi Aéreo, Ltda — Manaus, (AM)

Estrado do Aeroclub s/n, Hangar 03, SL.2, CEP-69048-790 Manaus, (Amazonas), Brazil ☎ (92) 654 10 43 Tx: n/a Fax: n/a SITA: n/a

F: 1994 n/a Head: n/a Net: n/a

□ PT-EOO	Embraer 721C Sertanejo (EMB-721C)	721095		0078		1 LY IO-540-K1G5D	1633			

ANDIRA Taxi Aéreo, Ltda — Casa Branca, (SP)

Av. Garces N. 1282, Caixa Postal 05, CEP-13710-000 Tambau, (Sao Paulo), Brazil ☎ (19) 673 17 25 Tx: none Fax: (19) 673 10 75 SITA: n/a

F: 1989 5 Head: Ivan Ot.del Favaro & Paulo S.M. Filho Net: n/a Aircraft below MTOW 1361kg: Cessna 172

□ PT-RBP	Embraer 810C Seneca II (EMB-810C)	810315		0080		2 CO TSIO-360-EB	2073			
□ PT-RYP	Embraer 810D Seneca III (EMB-810D)	810568		0085		2 CO TSIO-360-KB	2155			
□ PT-VBC	Embraer 810D Seneca III (EMB-810D)	810608		0086	0097	2 CO TSIO-360-KB	2155			

AQUILA Taxi Aéreo, Ltda — Santarém, (PA)

Aeroporto Internacional de Santarém, Hangar Flavio Cesar, CEP-68100 Santarém, (Para), Brazil ☎ (91) 522 18 48 Tx: 915544 aqla br Fax: (91) 522 19 20 SITA: n/a

F: 1980 n/a Head: Galdino Flavio de Almeida Net: n/a

□ PT-JTP	Cessna U206F Stationair	U20602256	N1554U	0074		1 CO IO-520-F	1633			
□ PT-DQU	Piper PA-31-310 Navajo	31-640	PP-EEN	0070	1089	2 LY TIO-540-A1A	2948			

ATA - AEROTAXI ABAETE, Ltda (Sister company of ALA-Abaete Linhas Aéreas, SA) — Salvador, (BA)

Lot Jardim Santa Julia, Qdra D-Lote 32-Itinga, Bairro Lauro de Freitas, CEP-42700-000 Salvador (Bahia), Brazil ☎ (71) 378 19 88 Tx: 712825 atab br Fax: (71) 378 15 07 SITA: n/a

F: 1979 n/a Head: Jorge Ney Barreto Mello Net: n/a

□ PT-JST	Cessna 310Q II	310Q0998		0074	0098	2 CO IO-470-VO	2404			
□ PP-ATS	Cessna 402B	402B0372		0073		2 CO TSIO-520-E	2858			
□ PT-IUW	Cessna 402B	402B0380		0073		2 CO TSIO-520-E	2858			
□ PT-JRT	Cessna 402B	402B0552	N1634T	0074		2 CO TSIO-520-E	2858			
□ PT-JTZ	Cessna 402B	402B0532		0074	0991	2 CO TSIO-520-E	2858			
□ PT-KAK	Cessna 402B	402B0548		0074		2 CO TSIO-520-E	2858			
□ PT-EBU	Embraer 820C Navajo (EMB-820C)	820005		0076		2 LY TIO-540-J2BD	3175			
□ PT-EFA	Embraer 820C Navajo (EMB-820C)	820025		0076		2 LY TIO-540-J2BD	3175			
□ PT-ENH	Embraer 820C Navajo (EMB-820C)	820067		0078		2 LY TIO-540-J2BD	3175			
□ PT-ETT	Embraer 820C Navajo (EMB-820C)	820093		0079		2 LY TIO-540-J2BD	3175			
□ PT-RAT	Embraer 820C Navajo (EMB-820C)	820108		0080	0789	2 LY TIO-540-J2BD	3175			
□ PT-OGK	Cessna 208A Caravan I Cargomaster	20800078	N831FE	0086		1 PWC PT6A-114	3629	Freighter		lsf Cessna Finance Corp.
□ PT-OGP	Cessna 208A Caravan I Cargomaster	20800050	N817FE	0085	0092	1 PWC PT6A-114	3629	Freighter		
□ PT-OGR	Cessna 208A Caravan I Cargomaster	20800100	N838FE	0086	0092	1 PWC PT6A-114	3629	Freighter		
□ PT-OGS	Cessna 208A Caravan I Cargomaster	20800034	N811FE	0085	0092	1 PWC PT6A-114	3629	Freighter		
□ PT-OGT	Cessna 208A Caravan I Cargomaster	20800038	N815FE	0085	0092	1 PWC PT6A-114	3629	Freighter		
□ PT-OGU	Cessna 208A Caravan I Cargomaster	20800066	N826FE	0085	0092	1 PWC PT6A-114	3629	Freighter		
□ PT-VCH	Neiva NE-821 Caraja	821012		0084	0097	2 PWC PT6A-34	3629			cvtd 820C c/n 820143
□ PT-VCI	Neiva NE-821 Caraja	820144		0087	0097	2 PWC PT6A-34	3629			cvtd 820C
□ PT-VKD	Neiva NE-821 Caraja	820159		0086	0097	2 PWC PT6A-34	3629			cvtd 820C
□ PT-WFL	Neiva NE-821 Caraja	820150		0087	0396	2 PWC PT6A-34	3629			cvtd 820C
□ PT-OZA	Cessna 208B Grand Caravan	208B0157	N4615B	0089		1 PWC PT6A-114	3969			
□ PT-OMS	Cessna 500 Citation	500-0251	N790EA	0075		2 PWC JT15D-1	5216			
□ PT-OMT	Cessna 500 Citation	500-0179	N179EA	0074		2 PWC JT15D-1	5216			

502 registration type of aircraft cn/fn ex/ex* mfd del powered by mtow kg configuration selcal name/fln/specialitites/remarks

☐ PP-ACM	Embraer 121A Xingu (EMB-121A)	121021	PT-MAN	0080	0097	2 PWC PT6A-28	5670			
☐ PT-MCA	Embraer 121A1 Xingu II (EMB-121A1)	121058		0082	0097	2 PWC PT6A-135	5670			
☐ PT-LPK	Cessna 550 Citation II	550-0010	N806C	0078	0098	2 PWC JT15D-4	6033			

ATLANTA Taxi Aéreo, Ltda — Salvador, (BA)

Aeroporto Dois de Julho, CEP-40520-970 Salvador, (Bahia), Brazil ☎ (71) 377 25 55 Tx: 711215 br Fax: (71) 204 11 44 SITA: n/a
F: 1957 ✱✱✱ n/a Head: n/a Net: n/a

☐ PP-ATT	Cessna 402B	402B0631		0074		2 CO TSIO-520-E	2858			
☐ PT-LKZ	Cessna 402B	402B1074	N1554G	0076		2 CO TSIO-520-E	2858			

ATLANTICO SUL Aerotaxi, Ltda — Balneario Camborio, (SC)

Av. Beira Rio 1366, CEP-86330-000, (Santa Catarina), Brazil ☎ (47) 361 08 80 Tx: none Fax: (47) 361 08 80 SITA: n/a
F: 1997 ✱✱✱ 13 Head: Maria Helena de Almeida Net: n/a

☐ PT-HQX	Bell 206B JetRanger III	3673		0082		1 AN 250-C20J	1451	4 Pax		
☐ PT-HTL	Bell 206B JetRanger	1408	N-7035	0074		1 AN 250-C20	1451	4 Pax		

ATP - Empresa de Aerotaxi e Manutençao Pampulha, Ltda — Belo Horizonte-Pampulha, (MG)

Rua Boaventura 2312, CEP-31270-310 Belo Horizonte, (Minas Gerais), Brazil ☎ (31) 448 75 00 Tx: none Fax: (31) 441 11 49 SITA: n/a
F: 1987 ✱✱✱ 150 Head: Otavio de Paula Net: n/a

☐ PT-HNA	Eurocopter (Aerosp.) AS355F2 Ecureuil 2	5376		0088		2 AN 250-C20F	2540			lsf Construtora Andrade Gutierrez SA
☐ PT-OFB	Beech King Air F90	LA-200	N6685H	0082	1290	2 PWC PT6A-135	4967			lsf Constructora Andrade Gutierrez SA
☐ PT-LZP	Learjet 35A	35A-339	N1500	0080	0390	2 GA TFE731-2-2B	7711			

AVIEXPREX Taxi Aéreo, Ltda (formerly AVIA Taxi Aéreo, Ltda) — Sao Paulo-Congonhas, (SP)

Rua Alagoas 41, CEP-09520-000 Sao Caetano do Sul, (Sao Paulo), Brazil ☎ (11) 743 37 46 Tx: none Fax: n/a SITA: n/a
F: 1989 ✱✱✱ n/a Head: n/a Net: n/a

☐ PT-HMN	Euroc.(Helibras/Aerosp.)HB350B Esquilo	1978 / HB1097		0087	0690	1 TU Arriel 1B	1950			

BANJET Taxi Aéreo, Ltda (Associated with Banco Bandeirantes & Bamaq SA Bandeirantes Maq.) — Belo Horizonte-Pampulha, (MG)

BANJET

Rua dos Hangares 14, Aeroporto Pampulha, CEP-31710-970 Belo Horizonte, (Minas Gerais), Brazil ☎ (31) 494 62 11 Tx: 311096 br Fax: (31) 494 60 85 SITA: n/a
F: 1987 ✱✱✱ 30 Head: José Americo Leao Net: n/a

☐ PT-MAB	Embraer 121A1 Xingu II (EMB-121A1)	121007		0082		2 PWC PT6A-135	5670	6 Pax		
☐ PT-ODZ	Cessna 550 Citation II	550-0645	N1310C*	0090		2 PWC JT15D-4	6033	8 Pax		lsf pvt
☐ PT-GAF	Hawker 800	258261	N958H	0094	0196	2 GA TFE731-5R-1H	12428	8 Pax		lsf FSBU Trustees

BASE Aerofotogrametria e Projetos, SA — Sao Paulo-Congonhas, (SP)

Rua Romao Puiggari 757, V1 das Merces, CEP-04164 Sao Paulo, (Sao Paulo), Brazil ☎ (11) 946 91 91 Tx: 1154821 br Fax: (11) 946 91 91 SITA: n/a
F: 1974 ✱✱✱ 78 Head: Antonio Cobo Neto Net: n/a

☐ PT-RAZ	Embraer 820C Navajo (EMB-820C)	820114		0080		2 LY TIO-540-J2BD	3175	Photo/Survey		
☐ PT-JPU	Piper PA-31-350 Navajo Chieftain	31-7405153	N74992	0074		2 LY TIO-540-J2BD	3175	Photo/Survey		

BATA - BAHIA Taxi Aéreo, Ltda — Salvador, (BA)

Rua Rui Barbosa 15-905, CEP-40020-070 Salvador, (Bahia), Brazil ☎ (71) 377 28 97 Tx: 712575 bata br Fax: (71) 377 25 49 SITA: n/a
F: 1967 ✱✱✱ 45 Head: Gildo Caldas Raimundo Net: n/a

☐ PT-JCY	Cessna 310Q	310Q0744		0073		2 CO IO-470-VO	2404			
☐ PT-EHM	Embraer 820C Navajo (EMB-820C)	820049		0077		2 LY TIO-540-J2BD	3175			
☐ PT-ENP	Embraer 820C Navajo (EMB-820C)	820075		0078		2 LY TIO-540-J2BD	3175			
☐ PP-SEC	Twin (Aero) Shrike Commander 500S	3094		0071		2 LY IO-540-E1B5	3062			

BERTOL Aerotaxi, Ltda — Porto Alegre, (RS)

Rodovia RST 153, KM2, N.S. Aparecida, CEP-99001-970 Passo Fundo, (Rio Grande do Sul), Brazil ☎ (54) 314 17 22 Tx: none Fax: (54) 314 17 22 SITA: n/a
F: 1995 ✱✱✱ 5 Head: Joao Oliveira (ATP) Net: n/a

☐ PT-VAP	Neiva NE-821 Caraja	821008		0084		2 PWC PT6A-34	3629	6 Pax		cvtd 820C c/n 820139
☐ PT-WIB	Cessna S550 Citation S/II	S550-0137	N100TB	0088		2 PWC JT15D-4B	6849	9 Pax		lsf BB Leasing Co. Ltda

BETA CARGO, Ltda = BSI (formerly BRASAIR Transportes Aéreos, Ltda) — Sao Paulo-Guarulhos, (SP)

Aeroporto Int'l de Guarulhos, CP 3101, CEP-07141-970 Sao Paulo, (Sao Paulo), Brazil ☎ (11) 64 45 68 30 Tx: none Fax: (11) 64 45 56 66 SITA: SAOBACR
F: 1990 ✱✱✱ 50 Head: Roberto Kfouri Net: n/a

☐ PP-BRI	Boeing 707-351C	19776 / 732	N8091J	0768	0194	4 PW JT3D-3B (HK2/COM)	148327	Freighter	CF-BM	
☐ PP-BRR	Boeing 707-323C	20088 / 727	PT-TCN	0768	0297	4 PW JT3D-3B (HK2/COM)	151182	Freighter	EG-BL	lsf OMEG
☐ PP-BSE	Boeing 707-330C	19317 / 557	PT-TCM	0367	1296	4 PW JT3D-3B	148327	Freighter		lsf OMEG

BRABO Taxi Aéreo, Ltda — Belem, (PA)

Travessa Bom Jardim 1918, Bro Jurunas, CEP-66120-000 Belem, (Para), Brazil ☎ (91) 233 48 84 Tx: n/a Fax: n/a SITA: n/a
F: 1987 ✱✱✱ n/a Head: n/a Net: n/a

☐ PT-JPW	Cessna U206F Stationair	U20602357	N2287U	0074		1 CO IO-520-F	1633			
☐ PT-JAV	Cessna 210L Centurion II	21059994	N35481	0073	0097	1 CO IO-520-L	1724			
☐ PT-JBL	Cessna 210L Centurion II	21060070	N59074	0073		1 CO IO-520-L	1724			

BRATA - BRASILIA Taxi Aéreo, Ltda — Brasilia, (DF)

SGCV/SUL, Conj. 07/08, Sede Aviplan, CEP-71215-100 Brasilia, (Distrito Federal), Brazil ☎ (61) 365 11 21 Tx: 212286 br Fax: (61) 233 40 67 SITA: n/a
F: 1988 ✱✱✱ n/a Head: n/a Net: n/a

☐ PT-OCZ	Learjet 35A	35A-361	PT-FAT	0081	0696	2 GA TFE731-2-2B	8165			
☐ PT-LDR	Learjet 55B	55B-134	N7261D	0087		2 GA TFE731-3A-2B	9525			lsf BB Leasing Co. Inc.

CARAJAS Taxi Aéreo, Ltda — Conceiçao do Araguaia, (PA)

Táxi Aéreo Carajás

Aeroporto Municipal de Redençao, Box 09, CEP-68550-000 Redençao, (Para), Brazil ☎ (91) 424 13 90 Tx: none Fax: none SITA: n/a
F: 1980 ✱✱✱ 4 Head: Angelo Mario de Nadal Net: n/a

☐ PT-ROK	Embraer 721D Sertanejo (EMB-721D)	721190		0083		1 LY IO-540-K1G5D	1633			
☐ PT-IFE	Cessna 210L Centurion II	21059647	N5147Q	0072	0097	1 CO IO-520-L	1724			

CAVOK Taxi Aéreo, Ltda — Rio de Janeiro-Santos Dumont, (RJ)

CAVOK TAXI AÉREO

Av. Rio Branco 257, 16 andar, CEP-20040-009 Rio de Janeiro, (Rio de Janeiro), Brazil ☎ (21) 220 57 71 Tx: 2132835 br Fax: (21) 240 48 83 SITA: n/a
F: 1986 ✱✱✱ 5 Head: Murilo Madureira Saade Net: n/a

☐ PT-LZO	Cessna 550 Citation II	550-0249	N201U	0080	0390	2 PWC JT15D-4	6033			

CBM Taxi Aéreo, Ltda — Belo Horizonte-Pampulha, (MG)

Av. Portugal 4851, Sala 02, Pampulha, CEP-30000 Belo Horizonte, (Minas Gerais), Brazil ☎ (31) 445-2977 Tx: n/a Fax: n/a SITA: n/a
F: 1987 ✱✱✱ n/a Head: n/a Net: n/a

☐ PT-LPN	Cessna 550 Citation II	550-0294	N323CJ	0081	0388	2 PWC JT15D-4	6033			

CENTAURUS Taxi Aéreo, Ltda — Rio de Janeiro-Santos Dumont, (RJ)

Praia de Botafogo 300, 11andar, CEP-22250-040 Rio de Janeiro, (Rio de Janeiro), Brazil ☎ (21) 536 34 05 Tx: 2123279 br Fax: (21) 536 32 42 SITA: n/a
F: 1990 ✱✱✱ n/a Head: n/a Net: n/a

☐ PT-OTC	Hawker 800B (BAe 125-800B)	258194	G-5-692*	0091	0491	2 GA TFE731-5R-1H	12428			lsf CIBC Finance Plc
☐ PT-OSA	Canadair CL-601-3A (CL-600-2B16) Challen.	5075	N810D	0090	1091	2 GE CF34-3A	19550			lsf CIBC Finance Plc

CETTA - Celso Tinoco Taxi Aéreo, Ltda — Fortaleza

BR 116 sn, Aeroclube do Ceara, SL02, CEP-60850 Fortaleza, (Ceara), Brazil ☎ (85) 272 21 12 Tx: none Fax: n/a SITA: n/a
F: 1996 ✱✱✱ n/a Head: n/a Net: n/a

☐ PT-ECC	Embraer 810C Seneca II (EMB-810C)	810025		0076		2 CO TSIO-360-E	2073			
☐ PT-ELC	Embraer 810C Seneca II (EMB-810C)	810099		0077	0098	2 CO TSIO-360-E	2073			
☐ PT-ELZ	Embraer 820C Navajo (EMB-820C)	820064		0078	0098	2 LY TIO-540-J2BD	3175			

CMS Taxi Aéreo, Ltda — Belo Horizonte-Pampulha, (MG)

Av. Alvares Cabral 1600, 3andar, CEP-30170-001 Belo Horizonte, (Minas Gerais), Brazil ☎ (31) 292 21 66 Tx: 313128 br Fax: (31) 291 69 44 SITA: n/a
F: 1987 ✱✱✱ n/a Head: n/a Net: n/a

☐ PT-OAB	Beech King Air C90-1	LJ-1022	N6280P	0082	0390	2 PWC PT6A-21	4377			

COBRAS Taxi Aéreo, Ltda — Sao Luiz, (MA)

Rua do Egito 218, CEP-65010-190 Sao Luiz, (Maranhao), Brazil ☎ (98) 222 32 43 Tx: none Fax: (98) 222 51 67 SITA: n/a
F: 1967 ✱✱✱ 18 Head: Olivar Weba de Amorim Alves Net: n/a Aircraft below MTOW 1361 kg: Cessna 182E & K.

☐ PT-KHT	Piper PA-23-250 Aztec E	27-7405431	N54135	0074		2 LY IO-540-C4B5	2359			
☐ PT-KHU	Piper PA-23-250 Aztec E	27-7405420	N54108	0074		2 LY IO-540-C4B5	2359			
☐ PT-DJP	Piper PA-31-310 Navajo	31-622		0070	0489	2 LY TIO-540-A2B	2948			
☐ PT-KZS	Piper PA-31-350 Navajo Chieftain	31-7405126	PT-EFQ	0073		2 LY TIO-540-J2BD	3175			

503 registration type of aircraft cn/fn ex/ex* mfd del powered by mtow kg configuration selcal name/fln/specialitites/remarks

COMETA Taxi Aéreo, Ltda — Goiania, (GO)

Aerodromo Brigadeiro Eppinghaus, Lote 8-A-GO-070, KM5, CEP-74501-970 Goiania (Goias), Brazil ☎ (62) 297 14 89 Tx: n/a Fax: n/a SITA: n/a
F: 1975 n/a Head: n/a Net: n/a Aircraft below MTOW 1361 kg: Beechcraft Bonanza C35

☐ PT-BZH	Cessna 205 (210-5)	205-0325	N8325Z	0063		1 CO IO-470-S	1497			

COMPLEMENTO Taxi Aéreo, Ltda — Sao Paulo-Congonhas, (SP)

Av. Maria Coelho Aguiar 573, Edif. VII, CEP-05805 Jd Sao Luiz-Sao Paulo, (Sao Paulo), Brazil ☎ (11) 524 89 77 Tx: none Fax: none SITA: n/a
F: 1990 n/a Head: n/a Net: n/a

☐ PT-LPZ	Cessna 500 Citation	500-0015	N14JL	0072		2 PWC JT15D-1	5216			lsf BFB Leasing SA

CONTINENTAL Taxi Aéreo, Ltda — Altamira, (PA)

Tv Pedro Gomes 1171, CP 124, CEP-68371-150 Altamira, (Para), Brazil ☎ (91) 515 10 27 Tx: none Fax: (91) 515 20 26 SITA: n/a
F: 1981 4 Head: Mauro Gumercindo Machado Net: n/a

☐ PT-RLE	Embraer 720D Minuano (EMB-720D)	720154		0080		1 LY IO-540-K1G5	1633			
☐ PT-EAF	Embraer 810C Seneca II (EMB-810C)	810005		0075	1282	2 CO TSIO-360-E	2073			

COPASOJA Taxi Aéreo, Ltda — Campinos-Viracopos, (SP)

Rua Emilio Ribas 172, Cambui, CEP-13025-140 Campinas, (Sao Paulo), Brazil ☎ (19) 241 83 77 Tx: none Fax: none SITA: n/a
F: 1987 n/a Head: n/a Net: n/a

☐ PT-LYA	Cessna 550 Citation II	550-0620	N1254G	0089	0290	2 PWC JT15D-4	6033			

DELMAR Taxi Aéreo, Ltda — Tatui, (SP)

Rodovia Tatui-Tiete, KM113, Jardim Tokio, CP08, CEP-18270-000 Tatui, (Sao Paulo), Brazil ☎ (152) 51 58 21 Tx: n/a Fax: (152) 51 52 71 SITA: n/a
F: 1992 3 Head: Claudio Del Fiol Net: n/a

☐ PT-HHV	Bell 206B JetRanger	1081	N83171	0073		1 AN 250-C20	1451			

DIASA, S.A. Taxi Aéreo — Sao Paulo-Marte, (SP)

Av. Queiroz dos Santos 1333, CEP-09015-311 Santo Andre, (Sao Paulo), Brazil ☎ (11) 440 16 66 Tx: 1144221 br Fax: (11) 440 18 01 SITA: n/a
F: 1990 n/a Head: Mario Cordeiro de Menezes Junior Net: n/a

☐ PT-HNU	Euroc.(Helibras/Aerosp.)HB350B Esquilo	2419 / HB1146		0091	0891	1 TU Arriel 1B	1950			

DS AIR Taxi Aéreo, Ltda — Rio de Janeiro-Santos Dumont, (RJ)

Aeroporto Santos Dumont, Sala DS Air, CEP-20021-340 Rio de Janeiro, (Rio de Janeiro), Brazil ☎ (21) 220 33 72 Tx: none Fax: (21) 262 34 61 SITA: n/a
F: 1990 n/a Head: Cmte Daniel Ribeiro Monteiro Net: n/a

☐ PT-RSM	Embraer 810D Seneca III (EMB-810D)	810479		0083		2 CO TSIO-360-KB	2155			

EMBRATAXI - Empresa Brasileira de Taxi Aéreo, SA — Belo Horizonte-Pampulha, (MG)

Aeroporto da Pampulha, CEP-31270-410 Belo Horizonte, (Minas Gerais), Brazil ☎ (31) 441 65 35 Tx: none Fax: (31) 491 13 04 SITA: n/a
F: 1970 11 Head: Ronaldo Fuscaldi Net: n/a

☐ PT-LZS	Learjet 55C	55C-139	N1039L	0090	0396	2 GA TFE731-3A-2B	9525			

EMPRESA BAIANA DE TAXI AEREO, Ltda - EBTA — Salvador, (BA)

Aeroporto Dois de Julho, Area de Aviaçao Geral, CEP-41511-970 Salvador, (Bahia), Brazil ☎ (71) 377 03 55 Tx: none Fax: (71) 377 03 57 SITA: n/a
F: 1988 4 Head: Eudelio Carlos Dourado Net: n/a

☐ PT-ENQ	Embraer 810C Seneca II (EMB-810C)	810126		0077	0790	2 CO TSIO-360-E	2073			
☐ PT-OSM	Cessna S550 Citation S/II	S550-0160	N550GT	0088	0791	2 PWC JT15D-4B	6849			lsf Citicorp Leasing Int'l Inc.

EQUIP Taxi Aéreo, Ltda — Curitiba-Afonso Pena, (PR)

Rua Joao Bettega 5700, Cidade Industrial, CEP-81000 Curitiba, (Parana), Brazil ☎ (41) 382 12 37 Tx: none Fax: (41) 382 12 37 SITA: n/a
F: 1988 6 Head: n/a Net: n/a

☐ PT-OAC	Cessna 550 Citation II	550-0613	N1250P	0089		2 PWC JT15D-4	6033			

ESPECIAL Taxi Aéreo, Ltda — Porto Velho, (RO)

Rua Campos Salles-Areal 1262, CEP-78916-260 Porto Velho, (Rondonia), Brazil ☎ (69) 225 30 00 Tx: none Fax: (69) 225 24 00 SITA: n/a
F: 1984 4 Head: Ayrton Brasil Ribeiro Souza Net: n/a

☐ PT-HGB	Bell 206B JetRanger III	4298	C-FRIN	0094		1 AN 250-C20J	1451			lsf Bamerindus Leasing
☐ PT-ENY	Embraer 810C Seneca II (EMB-810C)	810134		0078		2 CO TSIO-360-E	2073			
☐ PT-ESM	Embraer 810C Seneca II (EMB-810C)	810186		0078	0789	2 CO TSIO-360-E	2073			
☐ PT-DHQ	Piper PA-23-250 Aztec C	27-3939		0068		2 LY IO-540-C4B5	2359			

ESTEIO Engenharia e Aerolevantamentos, SA — Curitiba, (PR)

Rua Reinaldo Machado 1151, Bairro Prado Velho, CEP-80210 Curitiba, (Parana), Brazil ☎ (41) 332 42 99 Tx: 415412 eeea br Fax: (41) 332 32 73 SITA: n/a
F: 1969 270 Head: Marlus Coelho Net: n/a

☐ PT-EJE	Embraer 810C Seneca II (EMB-810C)	810088		0077		2 CO TSIO-360-E	2073	Photo		
☐ PT-RQA	Embraer 810C Seneca II (EMB-810C)	810448		0082		2 CO TSIO-360-EB	2073	Photo		
☐ PT-VDO	Embraer 810D Seneca III (EMB-810D)	810630		0086		2 CO TSIO-360-KB	2155	Photo		

ETA - Empresa de Taxi Aéreo, Ltda — Uberaba, (MG)

Av. Nene Sabino 169, CEP-38100 Uberaba, (Minas Gerais), Brazil ☎ (34) 314 74 33 Tx: n/a Fax: n/a SITA: n/a
F: 1989 n/a Head: n/a Net: n/a

☐ PT-VKY	Embraer 810D Seneca III (EMB-810D)	810714		0089		2 CO TSIO-360-KB	2155			

EUCATUR Taxi Aéreo, Ltda — Cascavel, (PR)

Av. Tancredo Neves 2222, CEP-85804-260 Cascavel, (Parana), Brazil ☎ (452) 24 50 50 Tx: none Fax: (452) 24 54 33 SITA: n/a
F: 1980 10 Head: Armando Ribeiro Prata Net: n/a

☐ PT-HSM	Bell 206B JetRanger III	4274	N61478	0093		1 AN 250-C20J	1451			
☐ PT-HKP	Bell 206L-4 LongRanger IV	52003	N6170X	0092	0098	1 AN 250-C30P	2018			
☐ PT-ODM	Piper PA-31T Cheyenne II	31T-8120042	N131CC	0081	0990	2 PWC PT6A-28	4082			
☐ PT-OVC	Learjet 35A	35A-399	N399AZ	0081		2 GA TFE731-2-2B	7711			lsf BB Leasing Co. Ltd

FLYING TAXI AEREO, Ltda — Rio de Janeiro-Santos Dumont, (RJ)

Rua Luiz Zanchetta 127, Riachnelo, CEP-20970-120 Rio de Janeiro, (Rio de Janeiro), Brazil ☎ (21) 586 66 58 Tx: none Fax: (21) 581 66 58 SITA: n/a
F: 1995 5 Head: Haroldo Rego Net: n/a

☐ PT-YHA	Bell 206L-3 LongRanger III	51593	N93AH	0792	0095	1 AN 250-C30P	1882	6 Pax		
☐ PT-OXH	Beech King Air C90A	LJ-1127	N7254B	0085		2 PWC PT6A-21	4581	6 Pax		

FLY, S.A. Linhas Aéreas = FLB — Sao Paulo-Guarulhos, (SP)

Rua Evaristo da Veiga 47, Gr. 501, Centro, CEP-20031-040 Rio de Janeiro, (Rio de Janeiro), Brazil ☎ (21) 533 76 05 Tx: none Fax: (21) 532 17 05 SITA: GRULAXH
F: 1994 48 Head: Ten. Brig. R/R Sérgio Luiz Bürger ICAO: AEREAFLY Net: n/a

☐ PP-LBF	Boeing 727-2B6 (A)	20705 / 945	N609AG	0073	0795	3 PW JT8D-15	86409	Y163		
☐ PP-LBO	Boeing 727-2B6 (A)	22377 / 1633	N614AG	0080	0397	3 PW JT8D-15	86409	Y163		

FLYSUL Aerotaxi, Ltda — Porto Alegre-Salgado Filho, (RS)

Caixa Postal 8003 - Anchieta, CEP-90201-970 Porto Alegre, (Rio Grande do Sul), Brazil ☎ (51) 341 48 66 Tx: 512957 fagi br Fax: (51) 341 48 66 SITA: n/a
F: 1986 15 Head: Joao Vicente Cortazzi Net: n/a

☐ PT-MFW	Piper PA-31T2 Cheyenne II XL	31T-8166067	N9179C	0081	0196	2 PWC PT6A-135	4297	6 Pax		lsf Marcep Finance
☐ PT-LMO	Dassault Falcon 10	49	N700TT	0075		2 GA TFE731-2-1C	8755	8 Pax		
☐ PT-WSF	Dassault Falcon 10	169	F-GHFB	0080	1296	2 GA TFE731-2-1C	8755	8 Pax		lsf Carleton Enterprises Inc.

GAL AIR Taxi Aéreo, Ltda — Recife, (PE)

Rodov. BR 101, KM07, No.7123-Parte, CEP-50910-520 Dois Irmaos-Recife, (Pernambuco), Brazil ☎ (81) 441 38 22 Tx: 811460 br Fax: (81) 441 28 42 SITA: n/a
F: 1986 n/a Head: Rubia Clea M. de Oliveira Net: n/a

☐ PT-RGS	Embraer 810C Seneca II (EMB-810C)	810412		0081	0489	2 CO TSIO-360-EB	2073			
☐ PT-LXY	Beech King Air F90	LA-195	N70132	0082	1189	2 PWC PT6A-135	4967			

GEOMAG, SA - Prospeçoes Aerogeofisica (Member of Grupo Rocha Miranda) — Rio de Janeiro-Santos Dumont, (RJ)

Rua Santa Alexandrina 1011, Rio Comprido, CEP-20261-230 Rio de Janeiro, (Rio de Janeiro), Brazil ☎ (21) 503 62 12 Tx: none Fax: (21) 503 62 31 SITA: n/a
F: 1991 35 Head: Antonio Carlos Godoy Net: n/a

☐ PT-KRO	Britten-Norman BN-2A-21 Islander	742	G-BCVL	0075		2 LY IO-540-K1B5	2994	Surveyer		tailmagnetometer
☐ PP-XBJ	CASA 212-CC40 Aviocar Srs 200	196	C-FDKM	0081	1198	2 GA TPE331-10-501C	7700	Surveyer		

GIRASSOL Aerotaxi, Ltda — Manaus, (AM)

Aeroporto Internacional Eduardo Gomes 11, CEP-69072-690 Manaus, (Amazonas), Brazil ☎ (92) 621 11 12 Tx: n/a Fax: (92) 621 11 12 SITA: n/a
F: 1981 n/a Head: n/a Net: n/a

☐ PT-EME	Embraer 720C Minuano (EMB-720C)	720066		0077	0098	1 LY IO-540-K1G5	1542			
☐ PT-EAA	Embraer 810C Seneca II (EMB-810C)	810001		0075		2 CO TSIO-360-E	2073			
☐ PT-EAX	Embraer 810C Seneca II (EMB-810C)	810014		0076		2 CO TSIO-360-E	2073			
☐ PT-EJC	Embraer 810C Seneca II (EMB-810C)	810086		0077		2 CO TSIO-360-E	2073			
☐ PT-DKO	Beech Baron B55 (95-B55)	TC-1335		0070	0097	2 CO IO-470-L	2313			
☐ PT-JBT	Piper PA-31-350 Navajo Chieftain	31-7305101	N94953	0073		2 LY TIO-540-J2BD	3175			

504 registration type of aircraft cn/fn ex/ex* mfd del powered by mtow kg configuration selcal name/fln/specialitites/remarks

☐ PT-LYH	Piper PA-31-350 Navajo Chieftain	*31-7305124*	*PP-EFS*	*0073*	*0191*	*2 LY TIO-540-J2BD*	*3175*			
☐ PT-EBN	Embraer 820C Navajo (EMB-820C)	*820001*		*0076*	*1189*	*2 LY TIO-540-J2BD*	*3175*			
☐ PT-KTR	Britten-Norman BN-2A-27 Islander	*495*	*G-BDNN*	*0076*		*2 LY O-540-E4C5*	*2994*			

GLOBAL Taxi Aéreo, Ltda — **Sao Paulo-Congonhas, (SP)**

Aeroporto de Congonhas, Box 3, Terminal Ala Sul, CEP-04072-900 Sao Paulo, (Sao Paulo), Brazil ☎ (11) 583 18 78 Tx: n/a Fax: n/a SITA: n/a
F: 1994 n/a Head: n/a Net: n/a

☐ PT-WCM	Embraer 110 Bandeirante (EMB-110)	*110041*	*FAB2149*	*0074*		*2 PWC PT6A-27*	*5600*			

GOIATAX Taxi Aéreo, Ltda — **Itaituba, (PA)**

Travessa Justo Chermont 278, Esquina Com. A Rua Nova de Santana, CEP-68180-030 Itaituba (Para), Brazil ☎ (91) 518 14 11 Tx: 915351 gtax br Fax: n/a SITA: n/a
F: 1981 3 Head: Manoel Costa Souza Net: n/a

☐ PT-KKD	Cessna U206F Stationair	*U20602500*	*N1175V*	*0074*		*1 CO IO-520-F*	*1633*			
☐ PT-JOH	Beech Bonanza A36	*E-491*		*0074*		*1 CO IO-520-BA*	*1633*			

GONAIR Taxi Aéreo, Ltda — **Belo Horizonte-Pampulha, (MG)**

Rua dos Hangares 10, Aeroporto Pampulha, CEP-31710-410 Belo Horizonte, (Minas Gerais), Brazil ☎ (31) 494 61 12 Tx: n/a Fax: (31) 494 61 12 SITA: n/a
F: 1987 n/a Head: n/a Net: n/a

☐ PT-ODY	Embraer 110 Bandeirante (EMB-110)	*110039*	*FAB2147*	*0074*		*2 PWC PT6A-27*	*5600*			

GUARA Taxi Aéreo, Ltda — **Cuiaba, (MT)**

Aeroporto Marechal Rondon s/n, CEP-78150 Varzea Grande, (Mato Grosso), Brazil ☎ (65) 381 28 63 Tx: 651146 br Fax: (65) 381 22 88 SITA: n/a
F: 1974 n/a Head: n/a Net: n/a

☐ PT-RFB	Embraer 810C Seneca II (EMB-810C)	*810365*		*0080*		*2 CO TSIO-360-E*	*2073*			

GUAXUPE Taxi Aéreo, Ltda — **Guaxupe, (MG)**

R. José A. Ribeiro Valle 1159, CEP-37800-000 Guaxupe, (Minas Gerais), Brazil ☎ (35) 551 38 00 Tx: 357265 br Fax: (35) 551 29 19 SITA: n/a
F: 1986 3 Head: Orostrado Olavo Silva Barbosa Net: n/a

☐ PT-NMD	Embraer 710C Carioca (EMB-710C)	*710177*		*0078*		*1 LY O-540-B4B5*	*1361*			
☐ PT-OTS	Cessna 560 Citation V	*560-0213*	*N12845*	*0093*		*2 PWC JT15D-5A*	*7212*			*lsf Citicorp Leasing Int'l Inc.*

H&A Taxi Aéreo, Ltda — **Sao Paulo-Congonhas, (SP)**

Rua Eng. Leopoldo Sydow 91, Alto Boa Vista, CEP-04748-010 Sao Paulo (SP), Brazil ☎ (11) 842 25 42 Tx: n/a Fax: (11) 247 72 92 SITA: n/a
F: 1992 n/a Head: n/a Net: n/a

☐ PT-YYE	Bell 206L-4 LongRanger IV	*52201*	*N52262**	*0098*	*0998*	*1 AN 250-C30P*	*2018*			
☐ PT-HSE	Eurocopter (Aerosp.) AS350B Esquilo	*2166*	*N6027F*	*0088*		*1 TU Arriel 1B*	*1950*			
☐ PT-YAE	Eurocopter (Aerosp.) AS350BA Esquilo	*2533*	*N93TH*	*0091*		*1 TU Arriel 1B*	*2100*			

HELISUL Linhas Aéreas, S.A. = H9 / SUL (Sister company of HELISUL Taxi Aéreo, Ltda / Member of TAM Group) — **Foz do Iguaçu, (PR)**

Aeroporto Int'l de Foz do Iguaçu, CP1131, CEP-85863-000 Foz do Iguaçu, (Parana), Brazil ☎ (455) 23 11 90 Tx: 455233 br Fax: (455) 74 41 14 SITA: n/a
F: 1997 n/a Head: Eloy & Celso Biesuz IATA: 153 ICAO: HELISUL Net: n/a

☐ PT-SDB	Embraer 110P1 Bandeirante (EMB-110P1)	*110323*		*0082*		*2 PWC PT6A-34*	*5670*	*Y16*		
☐ PT-SFS	Embraer 110P1 Bandeirante (EMB-110P1)	*110401*		*0082*		*2 PWC PT6A-34*	*5670*	*Y18*		
☐ PT-SHY	Embraer 110P1 Bandeirante (EMB-110P1)	*110470*		*0087*		*2 PWC PT6A-34*	*5670*	*Y18*		
☐ PT-WDM	Embraer 110 Bandeirante (EMB-110)	*110094*	*FAB2174*	*0076*		*2 PWC PT6A-27*	*5600*	*Y15*		

HELISUL Taxi Aéreo, Ltda (Sister company of HELISUL Linhas Aéreas, S.A.) — **Foz do Iguaçu, (PR)**

Aeroporto Int'l Foz do Iguaçu, CP1131, CEP-85863-000 Foz do Iguaçu, (Parana), Brazil ☎ (455) 23 11 90 Tx: none Fax: (455) 74 41 14 SITA: n/a
F: 1972 n/a Head: Eloy & Celso Biesuz Net: n/a

☐ PT-HSN	Bell 206B JetRanger III	*2953*		*0080*	*1092*	*1 AN 250-C20B*	*1451*	*4 Pax*		*lsf Banestado Leasing SA*
☐ PT-HSU	Bell 206B JetRanger	*1411*		*0074*	*0988*	*1 AN 250-C20*	*1451*	*4 Pax*		*lsf Banestado Leasing SA*
☐ PT-HSY	Bell 206B JetRanger	*1409*	*N-5026*	*0074*	*0687*	*1 AN 250-C20*	*1451*	*4 Pax*		
☐ PT-HTC	Bell 206B JetRanger III	*3449*	*N2113Z*	*0081*		*1 AN 250-C20J*	*1451*	*4 Pax*		*lsf Banestado Leasing SA*
☐ PT-YEG	Bell 206B JetRanger III	*4414*	*N75492*	*0096*	*1096*	*1 AN 250-C20J*	*1450*	*4 Pax*		*lsf Textron Financial Corp.*
☐ PT-YEE	Bell 206L-4 LongRanger IV	*52173*	*N6257J*	*0096*	*1096*	*1 AN 250-C30P*	*2018*	*6 Pax*		*lsf Textron Financial Corp.*
☐ PT-YEF	Bell 206L-4 LongRanger IV	*52171*	*N6257B*	*0096*	*1096*	*1 AN 250-C30P*	*2018*	*6 Pax*		*lsf Textron Financial Corp.*
☐ PT-HLL	Euroc.(Helibras/Aerosp.)HB350B Esquilo	*1426 / HB1021*		*0081*		*1 TU Arriel 1B*	*1950*	*5 Pax*		*lsf Real Leasing*
☐ PT-HLO	Euroc.(Helibras/Aerosp.)HB350B Esquilo	*1498 / HB1024*		*0081*	*0291*	*1 TU Arriel 1B*	*1950*	*5 Pax*		
☐ PT-HMI	Euroc.(Helibras/Aerosp.)HB350B Esquilo	*1639 / HB1046*		*0083*		*1 TU Arriel 1B*	*1950*	*5 Pax*		*lsf Safra Leasing SA*
☐ PT-HML	Euroc.(Helibras/Aerosp.)HB350B Esquilo	*1642 / HB1049*		*0083*		*1 TU Arriel 1B*	*1950*	*5 Pax*		*lsf Banestado Leasing SA*
☐ PT-YCJ	Euroc.(Helibras/Aerosp.)HB350B Esquilo	*2120 / HB1120*		*0088*	*0098*	*1 TU Arriel 1B*	*1950*			

HELITRANS Taxi Aéreo, Ltda — **Rio de Janeiro-Jacarepagua, (RJ)**

Av. Almirante Barroso 139, Grupo 201, CEP-20031 Rio de Janeiro, (Rio de Janeiro), Brazil ☎ (21) 210 21 15 Tx: n/a Fax: n/a SITA: n/a
F: 1992 n/a Head: n/a Net: n/a

☐ PT-HZH	Euroc.(Helibras/Aerosp.) AS350B2 Esquilo	*AS2794*		*0094*		*1 TU Arriel 1D1*	*2250*			

HELIVIA Aero Taxi, Ltda — **Manaus-Eduardo Gomes, (AM)**

Rua Barao do Flamengo 32-2andar, CEP-22220-080 Flamengo, (Rio de Janeiro), Brazil ☎ (21) 285 73 35 Tx: 2136080 hvia br Fax: (21) 205 04 48 SITA: n/a
F: 1987 100 Head: James H. Bianchi Net: n/a

☐ PT-HVA	Eurocopter (MBB) BO105CBS-4	*S-795*	*N5416X*	*0088*	*0590*	*2 AN 250-C20B*	*2400*	*5 Pax*		*lsf Eurocopter Deutschland GmbH*
☐ PT-HVB	Eurocopter (MBB) BO105CBS-4	*S-792*	*N7062W*	*0088*	*0690*	*2 AN 250-C20B*	*2400*	*5 Pax*		*lsf Eurocopter Deutschland GmbH*
☐ PT-HXI	Eurocopter (MBB) BO105CBS	*S-724*	*N105RM*	*0086*	*1091*	*2 AN 250-C20B*	*2500*	*5 Pax*		*lsf Eurocopter Deutschland GmbH*
☐ PT-HXK	Eurocopter (MBB) BO105CBS-4	*S-785*	*N54125*	*0088*		*2 AN 250-C20B*	*2500*	*5 Pax*		*lsf Eurocopter Deutschland GmbH*
☐ PT-HAO	Eurocopter (Aerosp.) SA330J Puma	*1571*	*LX-HUC*	*0078*		*2 TU Turmo IVC*	*7400*	*17 Pax*		*lsf HLU*
☐ PT-YAW	Eurocopter (Aerosp.) SA330J Puma	*1590*	*F-GEQI*	*0078*		*2 TU Turmo IVC*	*7400*	*17 Pax*		*lsf HLU*

HENRIMAR Taxi Aéreo, Ltda — **Rio de Janeiro-Jacarapagua, (RJ)**

Rua Ayrton Senna 2541, Aeroporto de Jacarapagua, CEP-22775-001 Rio de Janeiro, (Rio de Janeiro), Brazil ☎ (21) 262 14 38 Tx: none Fax: n/a SITA: n/a
F: 1996 n/a Head: n/a Net: n/a

☐ PT-HMG	Euroc.(Helibras/Aerosp.)HB350B Esquilo	*1620 / HB1044*		*0083*	*1096*	*1 TU Arriel 1B*	*1950*	*Y5*		

HERINGER Taxi Aéreo, Ltda — **Imperatriz, (MA)**

Aeroporto Municipal, Hangar II, CEP-65900 Imperatriz, (Maranhao), Brazil ☎ (86) 721 18 21 Tx: n/a Fax: n/a SITA: n/a
F: 1981 n/a Head: n/a Net: n/a

☐ PT-EXE	Embraer 810C Seneca II (EMB-810C)	*810253*		*0079*	*0097*	*2 CO TSIO-360-EB*	*2073*			
☐ PT-RCB	Embraer 810C Seneca II (EMB-810C)	*810324*		*0080*		*2 CO TSIO-360-EB*	*2073*			
☐ PT-RDJ	Embraer 810C Seneca II (EMB-810C)	*810344*		*0080*		*2 CO TSIO-360-EB*	*2073*			
☐ PT-RFU	Embraer 810C Seneca II (EMB-810C)	*810383*		*0080*		*2 CO TSIO-360-EB*	*2073*			
☐ PT-VDI	Embraer 810D Seneca III (EMB-810D)	*810624*		*0086*	*0496*	*2 CO TSIO-360-KB*	*2155*			
☐ PT-VDL	Embraer 810D Seneca III (EMB-810D)	*810627*		*0086*	*0097*	*2 CO TSIO-360-KB*	*2155*			
☐ PT-VGT	Embraer 810D Seneca III (EMB-810D)	*810670*		*0086*	*0097*	*2 CO TSIO-360-KB*	*2155*			
☐ PT-WYQ	Embraer 810D Seneca III (EMB-810D)	*810487*		*0083*	*0098*	*2 CO TSIO-360-KB*	*2155*			
☐ PT-KPB	Cessna 500 Citation	*500-0188*	*N5223J*	*0074*		*2 PWC JT15D-1*	*5216*			

HORUS AEROTAXI, Ltda — **Joinville, (SC)**

Rua Nilo Pecanha 149, FlorestaSL10, CEP-89211-400 Joinville, (Santa Catarina), Brazil ☎ (47) 426 36 00 Tx: none Fax: (47) 426 06 12 SITA: n/a
F: 1996 n/a Head: n/a Net: n/a

☐ PT-HQB	Bell 206B JetRanger III	*3428*	*N20795*	*0081*	*0097*	*1 AN 250-C20B*	*1451*			
☐ PT-HUS	Bell 206B JetRanger	*1059*	*N58150*	*0073*	*1296*	*1 AN 250-C20*	*1451*			
☐ PT-YBJ	Bell 206A JetRanger	*249*	*FAB8581*	*0068*	*0097*	*1 AN 250-C18*	*1361*			

INDAIA Taxi Aéreo, Ltda – INTA — **Recife, (PE)**

Rua Imperial-B. Sao José 822, CEP-50020-000 Recife, (Pernambuco), Brazil ☎ (81) 224 04 00 Tx: 8115623 itla br Fax: (81) 471 17 49 SITA: n/a
F: 1983 50 Head: Henrique Silveira Net: n/a Aircraft below MTOW 1361 kg: Cessna 172.

☐ PT-WVI	Beech King Air C90B	*LJ-1331*	*N8089J*	*0094*		*2 PWC PT6A-21*	*4581*			*lsf Citicorp Leasing Int'l Inc.*
☐ PT-MVI	Learjet 31A	*31A-082*	*N4022X*	*0094*		*2 GA TFE731-2-3B*	*7031*			*lsf Learjet Latin America Sales Inc.*

INTER AIR Taxi Aéreo, Ltda — **Rio de Janeiro-Santos Dumont, (RJ)**

Rua do Parque 31, S. Cristovao, CEP-20940-200 Rio de Janeiro, (Rio de Janeiro), Brazil ☎ (21) 99 77 81 61 Tx: 2121815 br Fax: (21) 589 89 22 SITA: n/a
F: 1988 n/a Head: Mrs Tania Fontenelle Net: n/a

☐ PT-LYM	Beech King Air F90	*LA-185*	*N61DH*	*0082*	*0190*	*2 PWC PT6A-135*	*4967*			*lsf pvt*

INTERAVIA Taxi Aéreo, Ltda — **Sao Paulo-Congonhas, (SP)**

Av. Jurandyr 356, Aeroporto, CEP-04072 Sao Paulo, (Sao Paulo), Brazil ☎ (11) 581 45 31 Tx: n/a Fax: n/a SITA: n/a
F: 1986 n/a Head: n/a Net: n/a

☐ PT-YGV	Agusta A109C	*7662*	*N771AT*	*0092*	*0098*	*2 AN 250-C20R/1*	*2720*			
☐ PT-LQJ	Cessna 550 Citation II	*550-0578*	*N1300N**	*0088*		*2 PWC JT15D-4*	*6033*			
☐ PT-LHC	Cessna 650 Citation III	*650-0086*		*0085*		*2 GA TFE731-3B-100S*	*9525*			

505 registration type of aircraft *cn/fn* *ex/ex** *mfd* *del* *powered by* *mtow kg* *configuration* *selcal* *name/fln/specialitites/remarks*

INTERBRASIL STAR = Q9 / ITB (Interbrasil STAR, S.A.-Sistema de Transporte Aéreo Regional dba/Subsidiary of Transbrasil) — **Sao Paulo-Congonhas, (SP)**

Rua Tamoio 696-Jardim Aeroporto, CEP-04630-001 Sao Paulo, (Sao Paulo), Brazil ☎ (11) 532 49 47 Tx: n/a Fax: (11) 532 49 23 SITA: n/a
F: 1994 ⁂ n/a Head: Dr. Omar Fontana IATA: 151 ICAO: INTERBRASIL Net: n/a

□ PP-ISA	Embraer 120ER (QC) Brasilia	120219	PT-SSO*	0090	0695	2 PWC PW118	11990	Y30 / Frtr 3,5t		
□ PP-ISB	Embraer 120ER (QC) Brasilia	120232	PT-STE*	0091	0695	2 PWC PW118	11990	Y30 / Frtr 3,5t		
□ PP-ISC	Embraer 120ER (QC) Brasilia	120300	PT-SVU*	0095	0995	2 PWC PW118	11990	Y30 / Frtr 3,5t		
□ PP-ISD	Embraer 120RT Brasilia (EMB-120RT)	120041	PT-SLH	0087	0997	2 PWC PW118	11500	Y30		lsf DLT of USA Inc.
□ PP-ISE	Embraer 120RT Brasilia (EMB-120RT)	120246	N6222Z	0091	1198	2 PWC PW118	11500	Y30		lsf CITG
□ PP-ISF	Embraer 120RT Brasilia (EMB-120RT)	120183	N287UR	0490	0199	2 PWC PW118	11500	Y30		lsf CITG

ITA - IMPERATRIZ Taxi Aéreo, Ltda — **Imperatriz, (MA)**

Av. Dorgival Pinheiro de Sousa 211, CEP-65900 Imperatriz, (Maranhao), Brazil ☎ (86) 721 38 99 Tx: n/a Fax: n/a SITA: n/a
F: 1980 ⁂ n/a Head: n/a Net: n/a

□ PT-CPE	Cessna 310K	310K0196	N7096L	0066		2 CO IO-470-V	2359			

ITAPARICA Taxi Aéreo, Ltda — **Salvador, (BA)**

Aeroporto Int'l 2 de Julho s/n, CEP-41511-250 Salvador, (Bahia), Brazil ☎ (71) 204 13 32 Tx: n/a Fax: (71) 204 13 32 SITA: n/a
F: 1988 ⁂ n/a Head: n/a Net: n/a Aircraft below MTOW 1361kg: Embraer 711C

□ PT-IUQ	Cessna 402B	402B0351	N5087Q	0073		2 CO TSIO-520-EB	2858			

ITAPEMIRIM Taxi Aéreo, Ltda (Affiliated with Viaçao Itapemirim, SA / Member of Itapemirim Transport Group) — **Cachoeiro do Itapemirim, (ES)**

Caixa Postal 178 - Parque Rodoviario, CEP-29304-900 Cachoeiro do Itapemirim, (Espirito Santo), Brazil ☎ (27) 521 09 44 Tx: 273571 br Fax: (27) 521 09 44 SITA: n/a
F: 1987 ⁂ 10 Head: Camilo Cola Net: n/a

□ PT-LVK	Beech King Air C90A	LJ-1201		0089	1089	2 PWC PT6A-21	4581			

ITAPEMIRIM Transportes Aéreos, S.A. - ITA = 5W / ITM (Member of Itapemirim Transport Group) — **Rio de Janeiro-Internacional, (RJ)**

Pça Pio X, No 15, 4 andar, CEP-20040-020 Rio de Janeiro, (Rio de Janeiro), Brazil ☎ (21) 263 42 55 Tx: 278064 vita br Fax: (21) 233 42 61 SITA: n/a
F: 1990 ⁂ 2000 Head: Camilo Cola IATA: 660 Net: n/a

□ PP-ITY	Cessna 208B Grand Caravan	208B0560		0096	0596	1 PWC PT6A-114A	3969			lsf Banco de Credito Nacional SA
□ PP-ITZ	Cessna 208B Grand Caravan	208B0499		0096	0596	1 PWC PT6A-114A	3969			lsf Banco de Credito Nacional SA
□ PP-ITA	Boeing 727-25 (F)	18968 / 223	PP-CJL	0065	0890	3 PW JT8D-7B	76657	Freighter		cvtd -25
□ PP-ITL	Boeing 727-46 (F)	20078 / 686	N746EV	0067	1093	3 PW JT8D-9A	76657	Freighter		cvtd -46
□ PP-ITM	Boeing 727-173C	19507 / 449	PP-VLW	0067	0991	3 PW JT8D-7B	76657	Freighter		lsf Citibank Leasing SA
□ PP-ITP	Boeing 727-30C	19313 / 411	N727MJ	0067	0993	3 PW JT8D-7B	79152	Freighter		
□ PP-ITR	Boeing 727-225 (F) (A)	22549 / 1737	N812EA	0081	0495	3 PW JT8D-15	88677	Freighter		
□ PP-ITV	Boeing 727-259 (F) (A)	22476 / 1747	N205AV	0081	0395	3 PW JT8D-17R	88677	Freighter		

IVAL ALVES Taxi Aéreo, Ltda — **Maraba, (PA)**

Rua Castelo Branco 1500, CEP-68501-970 Maraba, (Para), Brazil ☎ (91) 324 16 61 Tx: n/a Fax: n/a SITA: n/a
F: 1983 ⁂ n/a Head: Ival Alves Net: n/a

□ PT-EEA	Embraer 721C Sertanejo (EMB-721C)	721013		0076		1 LY IO-540-K1G5D	1633			
□ PT-EGM	Embraer 721C Sertanejo (EMB-721C)	721033		0076		1 LY IO-540-K1G5D	1633			
□ PT-BUT	Piper PA-23-250 Aztec B	27-2208		0062		2 LY O-540-A1D5	2177			

JAGUAR Taxi Aéreo, Ltda — **Conceicao do Araguaia, (PA)**

Aeroporto de Redençao, CEP-68550-970 Redençao, (Para), Brazil ☎ (91) 424 08 92 Tx: n/a Fax: n/a SITA: n/a
F: 1984 ⁂ n/a Head: n/a Net: n/a

□ PT-KII	Cessna T210L Turbo Centurion II	21060417		0074		1 CO TSIO-520-H	1724			
□ PT-RGC	Embraer 810C Seneca II (EMB-810C)	810392		0080		2 CO TSIO-360-EB	2073			

JANDAIA Aerotaxi, Ltda — **Itaituba, (PA)**

Travessa Campos 281, C.P. 95, CEP-68180 Itaituba, (Para), Brazil ☎ (91) 518 12 00 Tx: 912991 jand br Fax: n/a SITA: n/a
F: 1982 ⁂ n/a Head: Paulo Alvez da Silva Net: n/a

□ PT-KBY	Cessna U206F Stationair	U20602495		0074	0190	1 CO IO-520-F	1633			
□ PT-KYD	Cessna U206G Stationair	U20603586	N7255N	0077	0689	1 CO IO-520-F	1633			
□ PT-KFT	Cessna 210L Centurion II	21060310		0074		1 CO IO-520-L	1724			

JAO Taxi Aéreo, Ltda — **Cuiaba, (MT)**

Aeroporto Marechal Rondon, Box 5, CEP-78110-971 Varzea Grande, (Mato Grosso), Brazil ☎ (65) 381 10 67 Tx: n/a Fax: (65) 682 25 55 SITA: n/a
F: 1986 ⁂ n/a Head: n/a Net: n/a

□ PT-JLQ	Beech Baron E55	TE-951		0074		2 CO IO-520-C	2404			

JAPI Taxi Aéreo, Ltda — **Jundiai, (SP)**

Aeroporto de Jndiai, CP 559, CEP-13200-970 Jundiai, (Sao Paulo), Brazil ☎ (11) 732 60 79 Tx: n/a Fax: (11) 732 60 79 SITA: n/a
F: 1984 ⁂ n/a Head: n/a Net: n/a

□ PT-LGP	Twin (Aero) Shrike Commander 500S	3319	N49AC	0079		2 LY IO-540-E1B5	3062			
□ PT-OFH	Piper PA-31T Cheyenne II	31T-7920034	N29KR	0079	1290	2 PWC PT6A-28	4082			

JATO AEROTAXI, Ltda — **Alta Floresta, (MT)**

Rua A 461 Setor A, CP267, CEP-78580-000 Alta Floresta, (Mato Grosso), Brazil ☎ (65) 521 32 55 Tx: none Fax: n/a SITA: n/a
F: 1995 ⁂ n/a Head: n/a Net: n/a

□ PT-KSG	Cessna T210L Turbo Centurion II	21060962		0075	0896	1 CO TSIO-520-H	1724			
□ PT-LRS	Beech Baron 58	TH-439	N8LE	0074	0896	2 CO IO-520-C	2449			
□ PT-RCI	Embraer 820C Navajo (EMB-820C)	820116		0080		2 LY TIO-540-J2BD	3175			

JATO Taxi Aéreo (Division of JATO Taxi Aéreo & Manumiento de Aeronaves, Ltda) — **Brasilia, (DF)**

Aeropuerto Internacional, Hangar 18-Lgo.Sul, CEP-71609-000 Brasilia, (Distrito Federal), Brazil ☎ (61) 365 37 01 Tx: none Fax: n/a SITA: n/a
F: 1996 ⁂ n/a Head: n/a Net: n/a

□ PT-OKH	Embraer 810C Seneca II (EMB-810C)	810439		0081	0096	2 CO TSIO-360-EB	2073			

JET SERVICE Taxi Aéreo, Ltda — **Brasilia, (DF)**

SHIS Q1, 15, Conj. 5, Casa 2/4, CEP-71635-250 Brasilia, (Distrito Federal), Brazil ☎ (61) 248 67 77 Tx: none Fax: (61) 248 11 75 SITA: n/a
F: 1985 ⁂ 20 Head: Ozéas Almeida Net: n/a

□ PT-LEA	Learjet 25B	25B-155	N24TA	0074		2 GE CJ610-6	6804			

JET SUL Taxi Aéreo, Ltda — **Curitiba-Afonso Pena, (PR)**

Aeroporto Afonso Pena, Hangar Jet Sul, CEP-83010-620 Sao Jose dos Pinhais, (Parana), Brazil ☎ (41) 381 15 00 Tx: none Fax: (41) 381 15 05 SITA: n/a
F: 1993 ⁂ 33 Head: Cmte. José W. Rodrigues Cordeiro Net: http://www.jetsul.com

□ PT-LZA	Beech King Air A100	B-200	PT-FOB	0074		2 PWC PT6A-28	5216	Executive		lsf BCN Leasing
□ PT-OOK	Cessna 500 Citation	500-0039	N555CC	0072	0097	2 PWC JT15D-1A	5216	Executive		lsf Pedro Muffato Ltda
□ PT-MMC	Beech King Air 300	FA-113	N299GS	0087		2 PWC PT6A-60A	6350	Executive		
□ PT-WAK	Embraer 110 Bandeirante (EMB-110)	110071	FAB2167	0075		2 PWC PT6A-27	5600	Executive		lsf Bamerindus Lease
□ PT-WSJ	Beech King Air 350 (B300)	FL-152	N1092S	0096	0797	2 PWC PT6A-60A	6804	Executive		lsf Raytheon Aircraft Receivables Corp.
□ PT-LOE	Learjet 35A	35A-393	N700WJ	0081		2 GA TFE731-2-2B	7711	Executive		lsf BCN Leasing

KARINA Taxi Aéreo, Ltda — **Bebedouro, (SP)**

Rua Coronel Joao Monoel 1313, CP140, CEP-14700 Bebedouro, (Sao Paulo), Brazil ☎ (175) 42 27 22 Tx: n/a Fax: (175) 42 21 24 SITA: n/a
F: 1988 ⁂ n/a Head: n/a Net: n/a

□ PT-LXF	Beech Baron 58	TH-1383	N513MB	0082		2 CO IO-520-CB	2449			

LASA Engenharia e Prospecçoes, SA — **Rio de Janeiro-Santos Dumont, (RJ)**

Avenida Almirante Frontin 381, Ramos, CEP-21030-040 Rio de Janeiro, (Rio de Janeiro), Brazil ☎ (21) 270 84 89 Tx: none Fax: (21) 270 14 89 SITA: n/a
F: 1947 ⁂ 20 Head: Dr.Dacci Matos & Dr.Jorge D.Hildenbrand Net: n/a

□ PT-KNE	Britten-Norman BN-2A-21 Islander	696	G-BAYH	0073		2 LY IO-540-K1B5	2994	Surveyer		tailmagnetometer

LIDER Taxi Aéreo, SA — **Belo Horizonte-Pampulha, (MG) / SDU / CGH**

Avenida Santa Rosa 123, Pampulha, CEP-31270-750 Belo Horizonte, (Minas Gerais), Brazil ☎ (31) 448 47 00 Tx: 311275 lder br Fax: (31) 443 41 79 SITA: n/a
F: 1958 ⁂ 680 Head: Capt. José Afonso Assumpçao Net: http://www.lidertaxiaereo.com.br/
Company is also a Beechcraft, Bell (under the name Rotorbras) & Hawker sales agent / distributor and owns / operates additional aircraft for short periods.

□ PT-HPQ	Bell 206B JetRanger III	3546	N2219G	0081	0097	1 AN 250-C20B	1451			
□ PT-HRC	Bell 206B JetRanger III	3486	N81WE	1081		1 AN 250-C20B	1451			
□ PT-HSJ	Bell 206L-3 LongRanger III	51096	N3188F	0084		1 AN 250-C30P	1882			
□ PT-YBE	Bell 206L-3 LongRanger III	51398	N33GH	0190	1095	1 AN 250-C30P	1882			lsf Airsupport Services Corp.
□ PT-HQR	Sikorsky S-76A	760184	N3120A	0581		2 AN 250-C30S	4763			lsf Atlantic Corp.
□ PT-HRD	Sikorsky S-76A	760203	N3123B	0881		2 AN 250-C30S	4763			lsf Atlantic Corp.
□ PT-HRE	Sikorsky S-76A	760206	N3123F	0881		2 AN 250-C30S	4763			lsf Atlantic Corp.
□ PT-YAX	Sikorsky S-76A	760174	N5444X	0681		2 AN 250-C30S	4763			lsf Airsupport Services Corp.
□ PT-LSO	Beech King Air C90	LJ-794	N57JHB	0078		2 PWC PT6A-21	4377			
□ PT-HKV	Bell 212	31119	N57485	0080	0992	2 PWC PT6T-3 TwinPac	5080			lsf Atlantic Corp.
□ PT-HOW	Bell 212	32130	N2103D	0081	0792	2 PWC PT6T-3B TwinPac	5080			

506 registration type of aircraft cn/fn ex/ex* mfd del powered by mtow kg configuration selcal name/fln/specialitites/remarks

☐ PT-HOX	Bell 212	31175	N212CE	0081	0992	2 PWC PT6T-3B TwinPac	5080			lsf Atlantic Corp.
☐ PT-HPO	Bell 212	32138	N2143C	0081	0194	2 PWC PT6T-3B TwinPac	5080			
☐ PT-HTP	Bell 212	31132	N5748Z	0080	0787	2 PWC PT6T-3B TwinPac	5080			
☐ PT-HUJ	Bell 412SP	33154	N3206A	0087	0688	2 PWC PT6T-3B TwinPac	5262			
☐ PT-HUK	Bell 412SP	33156	N32051	0087	0688	2 PWC PT6T-3B TwinPac	5262			
☐ PT-HUW	Bell 412SP	33183	N3213U	0088	0190	2 PWC PT6T-3B TwinPac	5262			
☐ PT-HUX	Bell 412SP	33182	N3213P	0088	0190	2 PWC PT6T-3B TwinPac	5262			
☐ PT-LQR	Cessna 500 Citation	500-0246	N277VG	0074	0097	2 PWC JT15D-1A	5216			
☐ PT-MAD	Embraer 121A Xingu (EMB-121A)	121010		0079		2 PWC PT6A-28	5670			
☐ PT-WHB	Beech Beechjet 400A	RK-73	N8070Q	0193	1195	2 PWC JT15D-5	7303			lsf Raytheon Aircraft Credit Corp.
☐ PT-WHC	Beech Beechjet 400A	RK-58	N56356	1192	1095	2 PWC JT15D-5	7303			lsf Raytheon Aircraft Credit Corp.
☐ PT-WHD	Beech Beechjet 400A	RK-77	N8277Y	0693	1195	2 PWC JT15D-5	7303			lsf Raytheon Aircraft Credit Corp.
☐ PT-WHE	Beech Beechjet 400A	RK-81	N8167G	0194	1095	2 PWC JT15D-5	7303			lsf Raytheon Aircraft Credit Corp.
☐ PT-WHF	Beech Beechjet 400A	RK-82	N8282E	0194	1295	2 PWC JT15D-5	7303			lsf Raytheon Aircraft Credit Corp.
☐ PT-WHG	Beech Beechjet 400A	RK-54	N80938	0192	1295	2 PWC JT15D-5	7303			lsf Raytheon Aircraft Credit Corp.
☐ PP-JAA	Learjet 36A	36A-055	N365AS	0086	0295	2 GA TFE731-2-2B	7711			lsf Learjet Latin America Sales Inc.
☐ PT-KZR	Learjet 35A	35A-252	N28CR	0079	0097	2 GA TFE731-2-2B	7711			
☐ PT-LGS	Learjet 35A	35A-299	N244FC	0080	0992	2 GA TFE731-2-2B	8301			lsf FSBU Trustee
☐ PT-LGW	Learjet 35A	35A-598	N8567T	0084		2 GA TFE731-2-2B	7711			
☐ PT-LJK	Learjet 35A	35A-372	N372AS	0081		2 GA TFE731-2-2B	8301			

LRC Taxi Aéreo, Ltda — Sao Paulo-Marte, (SP)

Av. Bem-Te-Vi 333, Conj. 834, CEP-04088 (Moema) Sao Paulo, (Sao Paulo), Brazil ☎ (11) 535 54 53 Tx: none Fax: none SITA: n/a
F: 1989 ✱✱✱ 8 Head: Luis Roberto Coutinho Nogueira Net: n/a Aircraft below MTOW 1361kg: Robinson R44

☐ PT-YCD	Euroc.(Helibras/Aerosp.)HB350BA Esquilo	2892		0095	0796	1 TU Arriel 1B	2100			

LUG Taxi Aéreo, Ltda — Campo dos Palmares-Maceio (AL)

Aeroporto Campo dos Palmares-Maceio, Hangar 02, CEP-57110-100 Rio Largo, (Alagoas), Brazil ☎ (82) 322 15 28 Tx: 823127 br Fax: (82) 322 15 93 SITA: n/a
F: 1987 ✱✱✱ n/a Head: Luiz Brandao Net: n/a

☐ PT-HPL	Bell 206B JetRanger III	4187	N47AJ	0091		1 AN 250-C20J	1451			
☐ PT-VRM	Embraer 810D Cuesta (EMB-810D)	810831		0093		2 CO TSIO-360-KB	2155			
☐ PT-LET	Learjet 55	55-080	N85632	0083	0097	2 GA TFE731-3AR-2B	9752			

MADRI Taxi Aéreo, Ltda — Ribeirao Preto, (SP)

Aeroporto Leite Lopez, Hangar 12, CEP-14075-510 Ribeirao Preto, (Sao Paulo), Brazil ☎ (16) 628 37 35 Tx: n/a Fax: n/a SITA: n/a
F: 1995 ✱✱✱ n/a Head: n/a Net: n/a

☐ PT-IXC	Cessna 310Q	310Q0709	N8232Q	0073		2 CO IO-470-VO	2404			

MALAGA Taxi Aéreo, Ltda — Osasco, (SP)

Av. Alberto Jackson Byngton 2786, CEP-06276-903 Osasco, (Sao Paulo), Brazil ☎ (11) 72 01 46 30 Tx: none Fax: (11) 72 01 31 70 SITA: n/a
F: 1989 ✱✱✱ 11 Head: n/a Net: n/a

☐ PT-YFM	Bell 206B JetRanger III	4179	N206TA	0091	0595	1 AN 250-C20J	1451			lsf BCN Leasing

MANACA Taxi Aéreo, Ltda — Sao Paulo-Congonhas, (SP)

Rua Frei Egidio Laurent 308, Sala 2, Vila Remedios, CEP-06290 Osasco, Brazil ☎ (11) 702 81 11 Tx: n/a Fax: n/a SITA: n/a
F: 1987 ✱✱✱ n/a Head: n/a Net: n/a

☐ PT-LEM	Learjet 24D	24D-270	N3779P	0073		2 GE CJ610-6	6123			

MAPLAN AEROLEVANTAMENTOS, SA — Vitoria, (ES)

Av. Paulino Müller 845, Jucutuquara, CEP-29042-571 Vitoria, (Espirito Santo), Brazil ☎ (27) 223 21 88 Tx: none Fax: (27) 223 20 92 SITA: n/a
F: 1972 ✱✱✱ 60 Head: Eng. Lécio Passos Narciso Net: n/a

☐ PT-EGQ	Embraer 810C Seneca II (EMB-810C)	810058		0076		2 CO TSIO-360-E	2073	4 Pax/Photo		

MARGIRIUS Taxi Aéreo, SA — Sao Paulo-Congonhas, (SP)

Av. Paulista 1499, 15 andar, CEP-01311-200 Sao Paulo, (Sao Paulo), Brazil ☎ (11) 253 24 72 Tx: none Fax: (11) 261 54 50 SITA: n/a
F: 1987 ✱✱✱ 10 Head: n/a Net: n/a

☐ PT-HAC	Bell 222	47025	N997RS	0080		2 LY LTS101-650C.3A	3561			

MARICA Taxi Aéreo, Ltda — Rio de Janeiro-Santos Dumont, (RJ)

Avenida Passoa 101, Gr.1.301, CEP-20051-040 Rio de Janeiro, (Rio de Janeiro), Brazil ☎ (21) 325 30 83 Tx: 2121875 iiel br Fax: (21) 325 56 83 SITA: n/a
F: 1987 ✱✱✱ n/a Head: Ricardo Assad Net: n/a

☐ PT-HYV	Eurocopter (Aerosp.) AS350BA Esquilo	2720		0094	0098	1 TU Arriel 1B	2100			lsf SEC Consultoria
☐ PT-YJC	Eurocopter (Aerosp.) AS350B2 Esquilo	1216	G-BXNI	0079	0098	1 TU Arriel 1D1	2250			lsf Canair Gestora
☐ PT-EBD	Embraer 810C Seneca II (EMB-810C)	810017		0076		2 CO TSIO-360-E	2073			

MATO GROSSO DO SUL Taxi Aéreo, Ltda — Campo Grande, (MS)

Av. Duque de Caxias sn, CEP-79104 Campo Grande, (Mato Grosso do Sul), Brazil ☎ (67) 763 12 64 Tx: n/a Fax: n/a SITA: n/a
F: 1977 ✱✱✱ 6 Head: n/a Net: n/a

☐ PT-KGC	Cessna U206F Stationair	U20602494		0074	0097	1 CO IO-520-F	1633			
☐ PT-RVJ	Embraer 810D Seneca III (EMB-810D)	810550		0085	1196	2 CO TSIO-360-KB	2155			
☐ PT-VAR	Embraer 810D Seneca III (EMB-810D)	810597		0086		2 CO TSIO-360-KB	2155			

META – MESQUITA Transportes Aéreos, Ltda = MSQ (formerly META – MESQUITA Taxi Aéreo, Ltda) — Boa Vista, (RR)

Aerop. Int'l Boa Vista, Area dos Hangares, CEP-69304-000 Boa Vista, (Roraima), Brazil ☎ (95) 224 77 80 Tx: none Fax: (95) 224 73 00 SITA: n/a
F: 1990 ✱✱✱ 8 Head: Cmt. Fco. A. Mesquita ICAO: META Net: n/a

☐ PT-EMD	Embraer 720C Minuano (EMB-720C)	720065		0077		1 LY IO-540-K1G5	1542			
☐ PT-RVS	Embraer 720D Minuano (EMB-720D)	720174		0084		1 LY IO-540-K1G5	1633			
☐ PT-LMZ	Cessna U206F Stationair	U20602184		0073		1 CO IO-520-F	1633			
☐ PT-OND	Cessna U206G Stationair 6 II	U20606542	N9529Z	0082		1 CO IO-520-F	1633			
☐ PT-ONV	Cessna 210N Centurion II	21064298	N6215Y	0081		1 CO IO-520-L	1724			
☐ PT-LNW	Embraer 110P1 Bandeirante (EMB-110P1)	110346	N697RA	0081	1294	2 PWC PT6A-34	5670			

METRO Taxi Aéreo, SA — Sao Paulo-Congonhas, (SP)

Av. Paulista 1374, 3 andar, CEP-01310-916 Bela Vista, (Sao Paulo), Brazil ☎ (11) 285-1109 Tx: 1131811 br Fax: (11) 251-5499 SITA: n/a
F: 1988 ✱✱✱ 5 Head: n/a Net: n/a

☐ PT-HNH	Eurocopter (Aerosp.) AS355F2 Ecureuil 2	5419		0089	1089	2 AN 250-C20F	2540			lsf Itauleasing
☐ PT-AAF	Dassault Falcon 50	234	N233FJ*	0093	0093	3 GA TFE731-3-1C	17600		DM-FP	lsf Citicorp Leasing Int'l Inc.

MORRO VERMELHO Taxi Aéreo, Ltda — Sao Paulo-Congonhas (SP)

Rua Funchal 160, Vila Olimpia, CEP-04551 Sao Paulo, (Sao Paulo), Brazil ☎ (11) 577 57 33 Tx: none Fax: (11) 578 95 43 SITA: n/a
F: 1985 ✱✱✱ 33 Head: Dr. Fernando de Arruda Botelho Net: n/a

☐ PT-MMV	Cessna 550 Citation Bravo	550-0811	N5221Y	0097	0097	2 PWC PW530A	6713	7 Pax		
☐ PT-LJI	Dassault Falcon 50	173	N172FJ	0087	0097	3 GA TFE731-3-1C	17600	9 Pax		

MOURAN Taxi Aéreo, Ltda — Sao Paulo-Congonhas, (SP)

Rua Jorgé Faleiros 260, CEP-04342 Congonhas, (Sao Paulo), Brazil ☎ (11) 853 27 99 Tx: none Fax: (11) 853 19 42 SITA: n/a
F: 1986 ✱✱✱ 6 Head: Sergio Belem Net: n/a

☐ PT-WCB	Beech King Air B200	BB-1419	N8248W	0092	0895	2 PWC PT6A-42	5670			lsf Sattin Leasing

NAVEGANTES Taxi Aéreo, Ltda — Navegantes, (SC)

Estrada Geral, Aeroporto de Navegantes, CP25, CEP-88375-000 Navegantes, (Santa Catarina), Brazil ☎ (47) 342 15 57 Tx: 473235 ceva br Fax: (47) 331 23 34 SITA: n/a
F: 1990 ✱✱✱ 3 Head: Capt. Joao Uriarte Net: n/a

☐ PT-LZQ	Cessna 560 Citation V	560-0045	N2665Y*	0089	0891	2 PWC JT15D-5A	7212			

NORDESTE Linhas Aéreas Regionais, SA = JH / NES (Subsidiary of Rio-Sul) — Salvador, (BA)

Avenida Tancredo Neves 1672, 1andar, CEP-41820-020 Pituba, (Bahia), Brazil ☎ (71) 341 75 33 Tx: none Fax: (71) 341 09 63 SITA: SSAUZJH
F: 1976 ✱✱✱ 410 Head: Percy Rodrigues IATA: 264 ICAO: NORDESTE Net: http://www.nordeste.com

☐ PT-MNF	Embraer 120ER Brasilia (EMB-120ER)	120332		0097	1097	2 PWC PW118	11990	Y30		lsf RS Ltd
☐ PT-MNG	Embraer 120ER Brasilia (EMB-120ER)	120333		0097	1097	2 PWC PW118	11990	Y30		lsf RS Ltd
☐ PT-OQJ	Embraer 120RT Brasilia (EMB-120RT)	120242	C-GUOE	0091	1094	2 PWC PW118	11500	Y30		lsf CITG
☐ PT-SRF	Embraer 120RT Brasilia (EMB-120RT)	120192		0090	0992	2 PWC PW118	11500	Y30		
☐ PT-MNA	Fokker 50 (F27 Mk050)	20298	PH-MXR*	0094	0595	2 PWC PW125B	20820	Y50		lsf Brazilian Aircraft Finance XIV B.V.
☐ PT-MNB	Fokker 50 (F27 Mk050)	20302	PH-JCE*	0094	0695	2 PWC PW125B	20820	Y50		lsf Brazilian Aircraft Finance XV B.V.
☐ PT-MND	Boeing 737-53A	24786 / 1898	HL7261	0090	1097	2 CFMI CFM56-3C1	60554	Y111		lsf AWAS
☐ PT-MNE	Boeing 737-53A	24787 / 1900	HL7262	0090	1097	2 CFMI CFM56-3C1	60554	Y111		lsf AWAS

507 registration type of aircraft cn/fn ex/ex* mfd del powered by mtow kg configuration selcal name/fln/specialitites/remarks

NTA - NACIONAL Taxi Aéreo, Ltda

Goiania, (GO) & Brasilia, (DF)

Aeroporto Sta. Genoveva, Hangar do NTA, CEP-74671 Goiania, (Goiania), Brazil ☎ (62) 249 00 11 Tx: 622117 br Fax: (62) 249 01 76 SITA: n/a
F: 1986 n/a Head: n/a Net: n/a

☐ PT-ODP	Lake LA-250 Renegade	*029*	*N14026*	*0085*	*1190*	*1 LY IO-540-C4B5*	*1383*			*Amphibian*
☐ PT-RME	Embraer 810C Seneca II (EMB-810C)	*810424*		*0081*		*2 CO TSIO-360-EB*	*2073*			
☐ PT-LMM	Learjet 25D	*25D-323*	*N6YY*	*0080*	*0589*	*2 GE CJ610-8A*	*6804*			

OESTE REDES AEREAS, SA - ORA Taxi Aéreo

Cuiaba, (MT)

Aeroporto Marechal Rondon, Hangar ORA, CEP-78110-971 Varzea Grande, (Mato Grosso), Brazil ☎ (65) 381 18 77 Tx: n/a Fax: n/a SITA: n/a
F: 1967 n/a Head: n/a Net: n/a

☐ PT-BOY	Mitsubishi MU-2F (MU-2B-20)	*145*	*N769Q*	*0068*		*2 GA TPE331-1-151A*	*4500*			
☐ PT-LOS	Cessna 500 Citation	*500-0239*	*N6034F*	*0075*	*0097*	*2 PWC JT15D-1*	*5216*			

ONIX Taxi Aéreo, Ltda

Marilia, (SP)

Av. Brigadeiro Eduardo Gomes 2260, CEP-17514-000 Marilia, (Sao Paulo), Brazil ☎ (191) 22 69 99 Tx: n/a Fax: n/a SITA: n/a
F: 1988 n/a Head: n/a Net: n/a

☐ PT-WOX	Beech Bonanza A36	*E-2703*	*N8034E*	*0092*	*1095*	*1 CO IO-550-B*	*1656*			
☐ PT-WEK	Beech Baron 58	*TH-1654*	*N258BF*	*0092*	*0595*	*2 CO IO-520-CB*	*2449*			

PANTANAL Linhas Aéreas Sul-Matogrossenses, SA = P8 / PTN (formerly Pantanal Taxi Aéreo, Ltda)

Sao Paulo-Congonhas, (SP) & Campo Grande, (MS)

Av. Nacoes Unidas 10989, Cj 81, CEP-04578-000 Villa Olimpia-Sao Paulo, (Sao Paulo), Brazil ☎ (11) 30 40 39 00 Tx: none Fax: (11) 828 03 06 SITA: n/a
F: 1990 200 Head: Marcos Sampaio Ferreira ICAO: PANTANAL Net: http://www.pantanal-airlines.com.br

☐ PT-SOG	Embraer 110P1 Bandeirante (EMB-110P1)	*110490*		*0091*	*0591*	*2 PWC PT6A-34*	*5670*	*Y18*		
☐ PT-MFA	Embraer 120RT Brasilia (EMB-120RT)	*120204*	PT-SRW*	*0090*	*1092*	*2 PWC PW118*	*11500*	*Y30*		
☐ PT-MFH	ATR 42-300	*029*	*F-GFJP*	*0086*	*0297*	*2 PWC PW120*	*16700*	*Y50*		*lsf Aviation Enterprises Inc.*
☐ PT-MFI	ATR 42-320	*302*	*F-OKNG*	*0092*	*0797*	*2 PWC PW121*	*16700*	*Y50*		*lsf Prop. Lease & Trading Co. Ltd*
☐ PT-MFJ	ATR 42-320	*343*	*F-WQHV*	*0093*	*0298*	*2 PWC PW121*	*16700*	*Y48*		*lsf Joh Bail*
☐ PT-MFK	ATR 42-300	*225*	*F-GKNA*	*0091*	*0198*	*2 PWC PW120*	*16700*	*Y50*		*lsf Prop Bail No1*
☐ PT-MFM	ATR 42-300	*376*	*F-GKNH*	*0094*	*0598*	*2 PWC PW120*	*16700*	*Y50*		*lsf Prop Leasing & Trading Co. Ltd*
☐ PT-MFT	ATR 42-320	*306*	*G-BXEH*	*0092*	*0798*	*2 PWC PW121*	*16700*	*Y50*		*lsf Fuselage Finance Ltd*

PARAMAZONIA Taxi Aéreo, Ltda

Boa Vista, (RR)

Rua Souza Junior 209, Sao Francisco, CEP-69308-050 Boa Vista, (Roraima), Brazil ☎ (95) 224 87 07 Tx: n/a Fax: (95) 224 84 22 SITA: n/a
F: 1995 n/a Head: n/a Net: n/a Aircraft below MTOW 1361kg: Hughes 369HS (500C)

☐ PT-RZX	Embraer 720D Minuano (EMB-720D)	*720194*		*0084*	*0796*	*1 LY IO-540-K1G5*	*1633*			

PARANA JET Taxi Aéreo, Ltda

Curitiba-Afonso Pena, (PR)

Rua Rocha Pombo s/n, Aeroporto Afonso Pena, Hangar Aerodata, CEP-83100 Sao José dos Pinhais (Parana), Brazil ☎ (41) 282 23 22 Tx: n/a Fax: n/a SITA: n/a
F: 1989 n/a Head: n/a Net: n/a

☐ PT-OKP	Cessna 550 Citation II	*550-0460*	*N6523A*	*0083*		*2 PWC JT15D-4*	*6033*			

PASSAREDO Transportes Aéreos, S.A. - PAZ = Y8 / PTB (Member of Passaredo Group)

Ribeirao Preto, (SP)

Av. Nove de Julho 549, CEP-14015-070 Ribeirao Preto, (Sao Paulo), Brazil ☎ (16) 625 37 37 Tx: none Fax: (16) 625 10 70 SITA: n/a
F: 1995 70 Head: José L. Felicio IATA: 837 ICAO: PASSAREDO Net: n/a

☐ PP-PSA	Embraer 120ER (QC) Brasilia	*120302*		*0095*	*0995*	*2 PWC PW118A*	*11990*	*Y30 / Frtr 3,5t*		
☐ PP-PSB	Embraer 120ER (QC) Brasilia	*120303*		*0095*	*0396*	*2 PWC PW118A*	*11990*	*Y30 / Frtr 3,5t*		
☐ PP-PSC	Embraer 120ER (QC) Brasilia	*120313*		*0096*	*0197*	*2 PWC PW118A*	*11990*	*Y30 / Frtr 3,5t*		*lsf Embraer Finance Ltd*
☐ PP-PSF	ATR 42-320	*340*	*F-WQIK*	*0093*	*1298*	*2 PWC PW121*	*16700*	*Y47*		*lsf ATR*
☐ PP-PSG	ATR 42-320	*300*	*F-WQGR*	*0092*		*2 PWC PW121*	*16700*	*Y47*		*to be lsf ATR 0599*
☐ PP-PSD	Airbus Industrie A310-322	*437*	*OO-SCC*	*0087*	*1297*	*2 PW JT9D-7R4E1*	*153000*	*Y247*		*lsf ILFC*
☐ PP-PSE	Airbus Industrie A310-324	*535*	*N535KR*	*0090*	*0698*	*2 PW PW4152*	*157000*	*Y247*		*lsf ILFC*

PAULICOPTER - CIA. PAULISTA DE HELICOPTERO, Ltda-Taxi Aéreo (formerly Selecta Aero Taxi, Ltda)

Sao Paulo-Marte, (SP)

Avenida Olavo Fontoura 950, CEP-02012-021 Sao Paulo, (Sao Paulo), Brazil ☎ (11) 267 52 22 Tx: 1138884 sela br Fax: (11) 267 78 31 SITA: n/a
F: 1982 42 Head: José Octaviano Cury Net: n/a

☐ PT-HNN	Euroc.(Helibras/Aerosp.)HB350B Esquilo	*1641 / HB1048*		*0083*	*0489*	*1 TU Arriel 1B*	*1950*			

PENTA - Pena Transportes Aéreos, S.A. = 5P / PEP (formerly PENA Taxi Aéreo, Ltda)

Santarem (PA)

Praça Eduardo Gomes, Aeroporto de Santarém, CEP-68025-710 Santarém, (Para), Brazil ☎ (91) 522 10 14 Tx: none Fax: (91) 522 60 25 SITA: n/a
F: 1989 n/a Head: Cesar Pena Fernandes IATA: 308 ICAO: AERO PENA Net: n/a

☐ PT-MPA	Cessna 208B Grand Caravan	*208B0627*		*0097*	*0097*	*1 PWC PT6A-114A*	*3969*	*Y9*		*lsf Cessna Finance Corp.*
☐ PT-MPB	Cessna 208B Grand Caravan	*208B0630*		*0097*	*0097*	*1 PWC PT6A-114A*	*3969*	*Y9*		*lsf Cessna Finance Corp.*
☐ PT-MPD	Cessna 208B Grand Caravan	*208B0644*		*0097*	*0498*	*1 PWC PT6A-114A*	*3969*	*Y9*		*lsf Cessna Finance Corp.*
☐ PT-MPG	Cessna 208B Grand Caravan	*208B0645*		*0097*	*0498*	*1 PWC PT6A-114A*	*3969*	*Y9*		
☐ PT-OSG	Cessna 208B Grand Caravan	*208B0300*	*N5516B*	*0092*		*1 PWC PT6A-114A*	*3969*	*Y9*		*lsf Cessna Finance Corp.*
☐ PT-LLC	Embraer 110P1 Bandeirante (EMB-110P1)	*110427*	*N302EB*	*0083*	*0197*	*2 PWC PT6A-34*	*5670*	*Y19*		
☐ PT-SOF	Embraer 110P1 Bandeirante (EMB-110P1)	*110486*		*0089*	*0591*	*2 PWC PT6A-34*	*5670*	*Y19*		
☐ PT-MFB	Embraer 120RT Brasilia (EMB-120RT)	*120167*	*P4-EMA*	*0089*	*1196*	*2 PWC PW118*	*11500*	*Y30*		*lsf Embraer Finance Ltd*
☐ PT-MPJ	Embraer 120RT Brasilia (EMB-120RT)	*120068*	*PT-SLG*	*0087*	*1197*	*2 PWC PW118*	*11500*	*Y30*		*lsf Embraer Finance Ltd*
☐ PT-SXP	Embraer 120ER Brasilia (EMB-120ER)	*120323*		*0096*	*1296*	*2 PWC PW118A*	*11990*	*Y30*		*lsf Embraer Finance Ltd*
☐ PT-MPH	De Havilland DHC-8-315 Dash 8	*395*	*C-GBQZ*	*0095*	*1297*	*2 PWC PW123B*	*19505*	*Y50*		Monte Dourado / *lsf Bombardier/cvtd-314*
☐ PT-MPI	De Havilland DHC-8-315 Dash 8	*397*	*C-GBRA*	*0095*	*1297*	*2 PWC PW123B*	*19505*	*Y50*		Porto Trombetas / *lsf Bombard./cvtd-314*
☐ PT-	Embraer RJ145ER (EMB-145ER)					*2 AN AE3007A*	*20600*	*Y50*		*oo-delivery 0599*

PERFIL Taxi Aéreo, Ltda

Curitiba-Bacacheri, (PR)

Aeroporto de Bacacheri, Hangar 41, CEP-82501 Curitiba, (Parana), Brazil ☎ (41) 256 99 46 Tx: n/a Fax: n/a SITA: n/a
F: 1988 n/a Head: n/a Net: n/a

☐ PT-LAX	Cessna 500 Citation	*500-0194*	*N310U*	*0074*	*0098*	*2 PWC JT15D-1*	*5216*			
☐ PT-CXJ	Learjet 24	*24-176*		*0068*		*2 GE CJ610-4*	*5897*			

PLANAR Taxi Aéreo, Ltda

Goiania, (GO)

Pca. Cap. Frazao sn, HG. Jaime Camara, CEP-74672 Goiania, (Goias), Brazil ☎ (62) 233 44 23 Tx: n/a Fax: n/a SITA: n/a
F: 1992 n/a Head: n/a Net: n/a

☐ PT-ERY	Embraer 810C Seneca II (EMB-810C)	*810176*		*0078*		*2 CO TSIO-360-E*	*2073*			

PONTAX - PONTA GROSSA Taxi Aéreo, Ltda

Sao Paulo (SP)

Rua Enxovia 455, Santo Amaro, CEP-19055 Sao Paulo, (Parana), Brazil ☎ (11) 548 55 00 Tx: n/a Fax: n/a SITA: n/a
F: 1975 n/a Head: n/a Net: n/a

☐ PT-LTB	Cessna 650 Citation III	*650-0166*	*N1313J*	*0089*		*2 GA TFE731-3B-100S*	*9072*			

PRATICA Taxi Aéreo, Ltda (Affiliated with PRATICA Escola de Pilotos de Helicoptero)

Rio de Janeiro-Jacarepagua, (RJ)

Rua Parana 798, Galpao, Posse, CEP-26282-130 Nova Iguacu, (Rio de Janeiro), Brazil ☎ (21) 767 04 54 Tx: n/a Fax: n/a SITA: n/a
F: 1994 n/a Head: n/a Net: n/a

☐ PT-HBJ	Bell 206A JetRanger	*152*		*0068*		*1 AN 250-C18*	*1361*			
☐ PT-HIZ	Bell 206B JetRanger II	*2203*		*0077*	*0097*	*1 AN 250-C20*	*1451*			
☐ PT-HVF	Bell 206B JetRanger	*1366*	*N-7028*	*0074*		*1 AN 250-C20*	*1451*			

PROGRESSO Taxi Aéreo, Ltda

Belo Horizonte, (MG)

Av. Afonso Pena 550, 11 andar, CEP-30130-001 Belo Horizonte, (Minas Gerais), Brazil ☎ (31) 201 45 80 Tx: 311972 br Fax: (21) 224 42 30 SITA: n/a
F: 1987 n/a Head: n/a Net: n/a

☐ PT-EHH	Embraer 820C Navajo (EMB-820C)	*820044*		*0077*	*0097*	*2 LY TIO-540-J2BD*	*3175*			
☐ PT-LTO	Beech King Air F90	*LA-156*	*N1827F*	*0081*	*0098*	*2 PWC PT6A-135*	*4967*			
☐ PT-KQT	Learjet 36	*36-011*		*0075*	*0098*	*2 GA TFE731-2-2B*	*7711*			
☐ PT-LSJ	Learjet 35A	*35A-181*	*N5114G*	*0078*	*0098*	*2 GA TFE731-2-2B*	*7711*			

REDENCAO Taxi Aéreo Ltda - RTA

Carlos Roberto Bueno

Rua da Prata N. 06, Alto Parano, CEP-68540 Redençao, (Para), Brazil ☎ (91) 424 14 61 Tx: none Fax: n/a SITA: n/a
F: 1981 n/a Head: n/a Net: n/a Aircraft below MTOW 1361kg: Cessna 182

☐ PT-VMH	Embraer 720D Minuano (EMB-720D)	*720259*		*0089*	*1091*	*1 LY IO-540-K1G5*	*1633*			
☐ PT-JHF	Piper PA-32-260 Cherokee SIX	*32-7300065*		*0073*	*1091*	*1 LY O-540-E4B5*	*1542*			
☐ PT-LFX	Mitsubishi MU-2J (MU-2B-35)	*650*	*N990M*	*0074*	*0098*	*2 GA TPE331-6-251M*	*4899*			

RIANA Taxi Aéreo, Ltda

Rio de Janeiro-Jacarepagua, (RJ)

Av. Ayrton Senna 2541, Hangar 23, 19 e 07, CEP-22775-001 Rio de Janeiro, (Rio de Janeiro), Brazil ☎ (21) 325 05 10 Tx: n/a Fax: (21) 325 25 75 SITA: n/a
F: 1992 n/a Head: n/a Net: n/a

☐ PT-HTQ	Bell 206L-3 LongRanger III	*51197*	*N3303W*	*0086*		*1 AN 250-C30P*	*1882*			
☐ PT-HMP	Euroc.(Helibras/Aerosp.)HB350B Esquilo	*1658 / HB1053*		*0082*		*1 TU Arriel 1B*	*1950*			*lsf Sudameris Leasing*
☐ PT-HND	Euroc.(Helibras/Aerosp.)HB350B Esquilo	*2068 / HB1117*		*0089*	*0197*	*1 TU Arriel 1B*	*1950*			
☐ PT-OOY	Beech King Air C90	*LJ-882*	*N181GA*	*0080*		*2 PWC PT6A-21*	*4377*			*lsf Safra Leasing*

508 registration type of aircraft *cn/fn* *ex/ex** *mfd* *del* *powered by* *mtow kg* *configuration* *selcal* *name/fln/specialitites/remarks*

RICO Linhas Aéreas, S.A. = RLE (formerly RICO Taxi Aéreo, Ltda)

Manaus, (AM)

Aeroporto Internacional Eduardo Gomes, TPS II, CP 3501, Flores, CEP-69092 Manaus (Amazonas), Brazil ☎ (92) 652 15 53 Tx: none Fax: (92) 652 12 44 SITA: n/a
F: 1979 ✈✈✈ 35 Head: Atila Yurtsever ICAO: RICO Net: n/a

registration	type of aircraft	cn/fn	ex/ex*	mfd	del	powered by	mtow kg	configuration	selcal	name/fln/specialitites/remarks
☐ PT-YAV	Bell 206L-4 LongRanger IV	52072	N56757	0094	0795	1 AN 250-C30P	2018	Y6		lsf Air Support Services Corp.
☐ PT-ETZ	Embraer 810C Seneca II (EMB-810C)	810211		0078		2 CO TSIO-360-EB	2073	Y5		
☐ PT-ELW	Neiva NE-821 Caraja	820061		0078		2 PWC PT6A-27	3629	Y6		cvtd 820C
☐ PT-MAA	Embraer 121A1 Xingu II (EMB-121A1)	121001	PT-ZCT*	0078		2 PWC PT6A-135	5670	Y5		cvtd 121
☐ PT-GJC	Embraer 110E Bandeirante (EMB-110E)	110055		0075	0090	2 PWC PT6A-27	5600	Y15		
☐ PT-OCV	Embraer 110P1 Bandeirante (EMB-110P1)	110359	N97PB	0081	0493	2 PWC PT6A-34	5670	Y19		
☐ PT-WDB	Embraer 110 Bandeirante (EMB-110)	110051	FAB2159	0075	0896	2 PWC PT6A-27	5600	Y15		
☐ PT-WGE	Embraer 120RT Brasilia (EMB-120RT)	120004	XA-SQN	0086	0497	2 PWC PW118	11500	Y30		
☐ PT-WRO	Embraer 120ER Brasilia (EMB-120RT)	120070	PT-SLB	0088	0698	2 PWC PW118	11990	Y30		lsf Embraer Finance Ltd / cvtd 120RT
☐ PT-WRQ	Embraer 120ER Brasilia (EMB-120RT)	120043	PT-SLF	0087	1297	2 PWC PW118	11990	Y30		lsf Embraer Finance Ltd / cvtd 120RT

RIO NORTE Taxi Aéreo Ltda

Macapóa, (AP)

Box do Aeroporto Internacional de Macapóa, CEP-68900 Macapóa, (Amapa), Brazil ☎ (96) 222 00 33 Tx: n/a Fax: n/a SITA: n/a
F: 1986 ✈✈✈ 12 Head: Ivan Machado Net: n/a

registration	type of aircraft	cn/fn	ex/ex*	mfd	del	powered by	mtow kg	configuration	selcal	name/fln/specialitites/remarks
☐ PT-ETW	Embraer 720C Minuano (EMB-720C)	720088		0079		1 LY IO-540-K1G5D	1542			
☐ PT-EZA	Embraer 810C Seneca II (EMB-810C)	810277		0079	0989	2 CO TSIO-360-EB	2073			
☐ PT-JYD	Piper PA-23-250 Aztec E	27-7405343	N40596	0074		2 LY IO-540-C4B5	2359			

RIO-SUL Serviços Aéreos Regionais SA = SL / RSL (Subsidiary of VARIG, SA)

Rio de Janeiro, (RJ)

Av. Rio Branco 85-10 Andar, CEP-20040-004 Rio de Janeiro, (Rio de Janeiro), Brazil ☎ (21) 263 25 65 Tx: n/a Fax: (21) 253 20 44 SITA: n/a
F: 1976 ✈✈✈ 1760 Head: Paulo Enrique Coco IATA: 293 ICAO: RIOSUL Net: http://www.rio-sul.com

registration	type of aircraft	cn/fn	ex/ex*	mfd	del	powered by	mtow kg	configuration	selcal	name/fln/specialitites/remarks
☐ PT-SLC	Embraer 120RT Brasilia (EMB-120RT)	120094	PT-SML*	0088	0988	2 PWC PW118A	11500	Y30		
☐ PT-SLD	Embraer 120RT Brasilia (EMB-120RT)	120147		0089	0989	2 PWC PW118A	11500	Y30		
☐ PT-SLE	Embraer 120RT Brasilia (EMB-120RT)	120161		0089	1289	2 PWC PW118A	11500	Y30		
☐ PT-SRB	Embraer 120ER Brasilia (EMB-120ER)	120309	PT-SXB*	0096	0897	2 PWC PW118A	11990	Y30		lsf RS Ltd
☐ PT-SRC	Embraer 120ER Brasilia (EMB-120ER)	120311	PT-SXD*	0096	0897	2 PWC PW118A	11990	Y30		lsf RS Ltd
☐ PT-SRD	Embraer 120ER Brasilia (EMB-120ER)	120315	PT-SXH*	0096	0897	2 PWC PW118A	11990	Y30		lsf RS Ltd
☐ PT-SRE	Embraer 120ER Brasilia (EMB-120ER)	120324	PT-SXQ*	0096	0897	2 PWC PW118A	11990	Y30		lsf RS Ltd
☐ PT-SRG	Embraer 120ER Brasilia (EMB-120ER)	120331	PT-SXX*	0097	0897	2 PWC PW118A	11990	Y30		lsf RS Ltd
☐ PT-SPA	Embraer RJ145ER (EMB-145ER)	145020	PT-SYQ*	0097	0897	2 AN AE3007A	20600	Y50		lsf River One Ltd
☐ PT-SPB	Embraer RJ145ER (EMB-145ER)	145023	PT-SYT*	0097	0997	2 AN AE3007A	20600	Y50		lsf River One Ltd
☐ PT-SPC	Embraer RJ145ER (EMB-145ER)	145027	PT-SYX*	0097	1097	2 AN AE3007A	20600	Y50		lsf River One Ltd
☐ PT-SPD	Embraer RJ145ER (EMB-145ER)	145028	PT-SYY*	0097	1097	2 AN AE3007A	20600	Y50		lsf River One Ltd
☐ PT-SPE	Embraer RJ145ER (EMB-145ER)	145032		0097	1197	2 AN AE3007A	20600	Y50		lsf River One Ltd
☐ PT-SPF	Embraer RJ145ER (EMB-145ER)	145034		0097	1297	2 AN AE3007A	20600	Y50		lsf River One Ltd
☐ PT-SPG	Embraer RJ145ER (EMB-145ER)	145038		0097	1297	2 AN AE3007A	20600	Y50		lsf River One Ltd
☐ PT-SPH	Embraer RJ145ER (EMB-145ER)	145060		0098	0698	2 AN AE3007A	20600	Y50		
☐ PT-SPI	Embraer RJ145ER (EMB-145ER)	145065		0098	0798	2 AN AE3007A	20600	Y50		
☐ PT-SPJ	Embraer RJ145ER (EMB-145ER)	145083		0098	1098	2 AN AE3007A	20600	Y50		
☐ PT-SPK	Embraer RJ145ER (EMB-145ER)	145089		0098	1198	2 AN AE3007A	20600	Y50		
☐ PT-SPL	Embraer RJ145ER (EMB-145ER)	145090		0098	1298	2 AN AE3007A	20600	Y50		
☐ PT-SPM	Embraer RJ145ER (EMB-145ER)					2 AN AE3007A	20600	Y50		oo-delivery 0499
☐ PT-SPN	Embraer RJ145ER (EMB-145ER)					2 AN AE3007A	20600	Y50		oo-delivery 0599
☐ PT-SPO	Embraer RJ145ER (EMB-145ER)					2 AN AE3007A	20600	Y50		oo-delivery 0799
☐ PT-SLX	Fokker 50 (F27 Mk050)	20283	PH-MXF*	0095	0395	2 PWC PW125B	20820	Y50		lsf Brazilian Aircraft Fin. XIII B.V.
☐ PT-SLY	Fokker 50 (F27 Mk050)	20260	PH-KXV*	0092	1295	2 PWC PW125B	20820	Y50		lsf Dasa Aircraft Finance XIII B.V.
☐ PT-SLZ	Fokker 50 (F27 Mk050)	20237	PH-JXM*	0091	1295	2 PWC PW125B	20820	Y50		lsf Dasa Aircraft Finance XI B.V.
☐ PT-SRA	Fokker 50 (F27 Mk050)	20261	PH-KXW*	0092	0496	2 PWC PW125B	20820	Y50		lsf Brazilian Aircraft Fin. XXVII B.V.
☐ PT-SLN	Boeing 737-5Y0	26075 / 2374		0092	1092	2 CFMI CFM56-3B1	60554	Y111		lsf GECA
☐ PT-SLP	Boeing 737-5Y0	26097 / 2534		0093	1093	2 CFMI CFM56-3B1	60554	Y111		lsf GECA
☐ PT-SLS	Boeing 737-5Y0	26104 / 2552		0093	1293	2 CFMI CFM56-3B1	60554	Y111		lsf GECA
☐ PT-SLT	Boeing 737-5Y0	26105 / 2553		0093	0194	2 CFMI CFM56-3B1	60554	Y111		lsf GECA
☐ PT-SLU	Boeing 737-5Y0	25186 / 2236	XA-RKP	0092	0695	2 CFMI CFM56-3B1	60554	Y111		lsf GECA
☐ PT-SLV	Boeing 737-5Y0	25189 / 2240	XA-RKQ	0092	0395	2 CFMI CFM56-3B1	60554	Y111		lsf GECA
☐ PT-SLW	Boeing 737-53A	24922 / 1964	CN-RMU	0090	1295	2 CFMI CFM56-3B1	56472	Y111		lsf AWAS
☐ PT-SSA	Boeing 737-5Y0	25192 / 2262	XA-SAC	0092	0596	2 CFMI CFM56-3B1	60554	Y111		lsf GECA
☐ PT-SSB	Boeing 737-5Q8	27629 / 2834		0096	1296	2 CFMI CFM56-3C1	60554	Y111		lsf ILFC
☐ PT-SSC	Boeing 737-5Q8	27634 / 2889		0597	0597	2 CFMI CFM56-3C1	60554	Y111		lsf ILFC
☐ PT-SSD	Boeing 737-56N	28565 / 2944		0097	1197	2 CFMI CFM56-3C1	60554	Y111		lsf GECA
☐ PT-SSE	Boeing 737-5Q8	28052 / 2965		0097	1297	2 CFMI CFM56-3C1	60554	Y111		lsf ILFC
☐ PT-SSF	Boeing 737-5Q8	28201 / 2999		0098	0298	2 CFMI CFM56-3C1	60554	Y111		lsf ILFC
☐ PT-SSG	Boeing 737-5Q8	28055 / 3024		0098	0498	2 CFMI CFM56-3C1	60554	Y111		lsf ILFC
☐ PT-SSH	Boeing 737-58E	29122 / 2991	N291SR	0098	0698	2 CFMI CFM56-3C1	60554	Y111		lsf SUNR
☐ PT-	Boeing 737-548	24878 / 1939	EI-CDA	0090		2 CFMI CFM56-3B1	55000	Y117		to be lsf EIN 0699

SELVA Taxi Aéreo, Ltda

Manaus, (AM)

Aeroporto Int'l Eduardo Gomes, TPS2, CEP-69092 Manaus, (Amazonas), Brazil ☎ (92) 633 41 35 Tx: n/a Fax: n/a SITA: n/a
F: 1993 ✈✈✈ n/a Head: n/a Net: n/a

registration	type of aircraft	cn/fn	ex/ex*	mfd	del	powered by	mtow kg	configuration	selcal	name/fln/specialitites/remarks
☐ PT-EIT	Embraer 810C Seneca II (EMB-810C)	810079		0077		2 CO TSIO-360-E	2073			
☐ PT-LGB	Embraer 110C Bandeirante (EMB-110C)	110047	PT-FAD	0075		2 PWC PT6A-27	5600			

SETE Taxi Aéreo, Ltda

Goiania, (GO)

Aeroporto Santa Genoveva, CEP-74671-970 Goiania, (Goias), Brazil ☎ (62) 207 12 00 Tx: 621223 stxa br Fax: (62) 207 12 00 SITA: n/a
F: 1976 ✈✈✈ 93 Head: Luiz Roberto Vilella Net: n/a

registration	type of aircraft	cn/fn	ex/ex*	mfd	del	powered by	mtow kg	configuration	selcal	name/fln/specialitites/remarks
☐ PT-EVA	Embraer 810C Seneca II (EMB-810C)	810235		0080	0097	2 CO TSIO-360-EB	2073			lsf Unibanco Leasing SA
☐ PT-RFH	Embraer 810C Seneca II (EMB-810C)	810373		0080	0097	2 CO TSIO-360-E	2073			lsf Safra Leasing SA
☐ PT-RGO	Embraer 810C Seneca II (EMB-810C)	810407		0080	0098	2 CO TSIO-360-EB	2073			lsf Safra Leasing SA
☐ PT-RQH	Embraer 810D Seneca III (EMB-810D)	810455		0083	0098	2 CO TSIO-360-KB	2155			
☐ PT-RQI	Embraer 810D Seneca III (EMB-810D)	810456		0083	0496	2 CO TSIO-360-KB	2155			
☐ PT-RQT	Embraer 810D Seneca III (EMB-810D)	810467		0083		2 CO TSIO-360-KB	2155			
☐ PT-RQX	Embraer 810D Seneca III (EMB-810D)	810471		0083	0097	2 CO TSIO-360-KB	2155			lsf Unibanco Leasing SA
☐ PT-RSO	Embraer 810D Seneca III (EMB-810D)	810481		0083	0097	2 CO TSIO-360-KB	2155			lsf pvt
☐ PT-RSP	Embraer 810D Seneca III (EMB-810D)	810482		0083	0099	2 CO TSIO-360-KB	2155			lsf Rural Leasing SA
☐ PT-RTV	Embraer 810D Seneca III (EMB-810D)	810511		0083	0097	2 CO TSIO-360-KB	2155			
☐ PT-VAF	Embraer 810D Seneca III (EMB-810D)	810587		0086		2 CO TSIO-360-KB	2155			lsf pvt
☐ PT-EHE	Embraer 820C Navajo (EMB-820C)	820041		0077	0098	2 LY TIO-540-J2BD	3175			lsf Rural Leasing SA
☐ PT-LDC	Embraer 820C Navajo (EMB-820C)	820008		0076	0098	2 LY TIO-540-J2BD	3175			
☐ PT-LFP	Embraer 820C Navajo (EMB-820C)	820038	PP-EGB	0076	0098	2 LY TIO-540-J2BD	3175			lsf BB Leasing Co. Ltd
☐ PT-RBA	Embraer 820C Navajo (EMB-820C)	820115		0080	0097	2 LY TIO-540-J2BD	3175			lsf Safra Leasing SA
☐ PT-DTL	Mitsubishi MU-2F (MU-2B-20)	196	N116MA	0071		2 GA TPE331-1-151A	4500			
☐ PT-WST	Mitsubishi MU-2N (MU-2B-36A)	711SA	N171CA	0078	0497	2 GA TPE331-5-252M	5250			
☐ PT-WYT	Mitsubishi MU-2N (MU-2B-36A)	722SA	N722MU	0078	0098	2 GA TPE331-5-252M	5250			lsf BB Leasing Co. Ltd

SKYMASTER AIRLINES, Ltda = SKC

Manaus, (AM)

Av. Efigenio Sales 3050, Bairro Aleixo, CEP-69063-020 Manaus, (Amazonas), Brazil ☎ (11) 64 45 40 09 Tx: none Fax: (11) 64 45 50 13 SITA: n/a
F: 1997 ✈✈✈ n/a Head: n/a ICAO: SKYMASTER AIR Net: n/a

registration	type of aircraft	cn/fn	ex/ex*	mfd	del	powered by	mtow kg	configuration	selcal	name/fln/specialitites/remarks
☐ PT-WSM	Boeing 707-351C	19773 / 705	N149DM	0068	0697	4 PW JT3D-3B (HK2/COM)	148400	Freighter		lsf OMEG
☐ PT-WSZ	Boeing 707-338C	18808 / 404	HK-3030X	0265	1298	4 PW JT3D-3B (HK2/COM)	145331	Freighter		lsf Citizen Holdings Ltd

SKYTOUR Taxi Aéreo, Ltda

Marica, (RJ)

Aeroporto Municipal de Marica, Hangar 16 & 20, CEP-24900-00 Marica, (Rio de Janeiro), Brazil ☎ (21) 240 73 74 Tx: none Fax: n/a SITA: n/a
F: 1992 ✈✈✈ n/a Head: n/a Net: n/a

registration	type of aircraft	cn/fn	ex/ex*	mfd	del	powered by	mtow kg	configuration	selcal	name/fln/specialitites/remarks
☐ PT-BUK	Cessna 337D Super Skymaster	337-1004		0069		2 CO IO-360-C/D	1996			
☐ PT-KQS	Britten-Norman BN-2A-8 Islander	434	N94JA	0075		2 LY O-540-E4C5	2812			

SOCIEDADE DE TAXI AEREO WESTON, Ltda

Recife, (PE)

Aeroporto Int'l dos Guararapes s/n, CP4400, CEP-51032-970 Recife, (Pernambuco), Brazil ☎ (81) 471 14 70 Tx: 814277 staw br Fax: (81) 339 43 54 SITA: n/a
F: 1968 ✈✈✈ 62 Head: Dr. F.J. & J.B. Pereira dos Santos Net: n/a

registration	type of aircraft	cn/fn	ex/ex*	mfd	del	powered by	mtow kg	configuration	selcal	name/fln/specialitites/remarks
☐ PT-LVB	Cessna 501 Citation I/SP	501-0205	N6784T	0081		2 PWC JT15D-1A	5375			
☐ PT-LAA	Learjet 35A	35A-295		0080		2 GA TFE731-2-2B	8165			
☐ PT-LEB	Learjet 35A	35A-474	N37975	0082		2 GA TFE731-2-2B	8165			
☐ PT-LUK	Learjet 55	55-086	N8227P	0082	1289	2 GA TFE731-3A-2B	8845			
☐ PT-ORA	Learjet 55C	55C-146	N9125M	0090	0591	2 GA TFE731-3A-2B	9525			

SOTAN - SOCIEDADE DE TAXI AEREO NORDESTE, Ltda (Associated with Usina Caete, SA)

Maceio, (AL)

Via Expressa 99, Tabuleiro do Martins, CEP-57046-000 Maceio, (Alagoas), Brazil ☎ (82) 324 22 22 Tx: 818886 br Fax: (82) 324 21 81 SITA: n/a
F: 1986 ✈✈✈ n/a Head: Senador Carlos Lyra Neto Net: n/a

registration	type of aircraft	cn/fn	ex/ex*	mfd	del	powered by	mtow kg	configuration	selcal	name/fln/specialitites/remarks
☐ PT-RSE	Embraer 710D Carioca (EMB-710D)	710286		0082		1 LY O-540-J3A5D	1361			

☐ PT-VNY	Embraer 810D Seneca III (EMB-810D)	810759		0090	0391	2 CO TSIO-360-KB	2155			
☐ PT-OIF	Beech King Air F90	LA-49	N200BM	0080		2 PWC PT6A-135	4967			
☐ PT-LHR	Learjet 55	55-044	N3797C	0082		2 GA TFE731-3A-2B	8845			

SOURE Taxi Aéreo, Ltda

Belem, (PA)

Av. Senador Lomes 4635, Sacramento, CEP-66120-970 Belém, (Para), Brazil ☎ (91) 233 49 86 Tx: n/a Fax: n/a SITA: n/a
F: 1988 n/a Head: n/a Net: n/a

☐ PT-EOT	Embraer 720C Minuano (EMB-720C)	720073		0078	1089	1 LY IO-540-K1G5	1542			
☐ PT-DGK	Cessna U206C Super Skywagon	U206-1070		0068		1 CO IO-520-F	1633			
☐ PT-ETG	Embraer 810C Seneca II (EMB-810C)	810206		0079	0097	2 CO TSIO-360-EB	2073			

SULESTE Taxi Aéreo, Ltda

Pocos de Caldas, (MG)

Av. Teofilo de Olivera sn, Municipal de Pocos de Caldas, CEP-37700 Pocos de Caldas, (Minas Gerais), Brazil ☎ (35) 721-3524 Tx: n/a Fax: n/a SITA: n/a
F: 1989 n/a Head: n/a Net: n/a

☐ PT-OME	Cessna T210N Turbo Centurion II	21064612	N9828Y	0082		1 CO TSIO-520-R	1814			

SUPERJET Aerotaxi, Ltda

Florianopolis, (SC)

Rua Leoberto Leal 1280, Barreiros, CEP-88110-000 Sao José, (Santa Catarina), Brazil ☎ (48) 246 91 00 Tx: none Fax: (48) 246 91 00 SITA: n/a
F: 1992 n/a Head: n/a Net: n/a Aircraft below MTOW 1361kg: Cessna 177

☐ PT-VBA	Embraer 810D Seneca III (EMB-810D)	810606		0086	1296	2 CO TSIO-360-KB	2155			
☐ PT-VEO	Embraer 810D Seneca III (EMB-810D)	810647		0087	0098	2 CO TSIO-360-KB	2155			
☐ PT-YPF	Eurocopter (Aerosp.) AS350BA Esquilo	2947		0096	0697	1 TU Arriel 1B	2100			
☐ PT-OQD	Cessna 500 Citation	500-0244	N516AB	0075		2 PWC JT15D-1	5216			
☐ PT-LYE	Learjet 24F	24F-354	N678SP	0078	0098	2 GE CJ610-8A	6123			
☐ PT-LJJ	Cessna 550 Citation II	550-0247	N928DS	0081		2 PWC JT15D-4	6033			lsf pvt
☐ PT-OHD	Learjet 25D	25D-296	N55MJ	0080	0098	2 GE CJ610-8A	6804			

TABA – Transportes Aéreos Regionais da Bacia Amazonica, SA = TAB

Belém, (PA)

Av. Governador José Malcher 883, Bro Nazaré, CEP-66055-260 Belém, (Para), Brazil ☎ (91) 242 63 00 Tx: 911314 tar br Fax: (91) 225 13 10 SITA: n/a
F: 1976 750 Head: Col. Marcelio J. Gibson IATA: 863 ICAO: TABA Net: n/a

☐ PT-GJS	Embraer 110C Bandeirante (EMB-110C)	110085		0076	0976	2 PWC PT6A-27	5600	Y15		
☐ PT-GJT	Embraer 110C Bandeirante (EMB-110C)	110086		0076	0976	2 PWC PT6A-27	5600	Y15		
☐ PT-GJU	Embraer 110C Bandeirante (EMB-110C)	110089		0076	0976	2 PWC PT6A-27	5600	Y15		
☐ PT-GKV	Embraer 110P Bandeirante (EMB-110P)	110132		0076	0177	2 PWC PT6A-27	5600	Y18		
☐ PT-GKX	Embraer 110P Bandeirante (EMB-110P)	110129		0077	0177	2 PWC PT6A-27	5600	Y18		
☐ PT-GKZ	Embraer 110P Bandeirante (EMB-110P)	110137		0076	0177	2 PWC PT6A-27	5600	Y18		
☐ PT-GLK	Embraer 110P2 Bandeirante (EMB-110P2)	110189		0078	1079	2 PWC PT6A-34	5670	Y21		
☐ PT-OHE	Embraer 110P1 Bandeirante (EMB-110P1)	110244	N59PB	0080	0291	2 PWC PT6A-34	5670	Y19		
☐ PP-BUG	Fairchild Ind. FH-227B	565	N2738R*	0067	0676	2 RR Dart 532-7	19731	Y44		
☐ PT-LBF	Fairchild Ind. FH-227B	528	N851TA	0066	0980	2 RR Dart 532-7	19731	Y44		lsf Nacional Leasing
☐ PT-LBG	Fairchild Ind. FH-227B	539	G-SKYB	0067	1080	2 RR Dart 532-7	19731	Y44		lsf Nacional Leasing

TAF Linhas Aéreas, SA = TSD (formerly TAF – Taxi Aéreo Fortaleza, Ltda)

Fortaleza, (CE)

Hangar, Aeroporto Pinto Martins, CEP-60420-290 Fortaleza, (Ceara), Brazil ☎ (85) 272 73 33 Tx: none Fax: (85) 272 51 44 SITA: n/a
F: 1971 n/a Head: Joao Ariston Pessoa de Araujo Net: n/a

☐ PT-KZD	Twin (Aero) Shrike Commander 500S	3140		0073	0098	2 LY IO-540-E1B5	3062			
☐ PT-OGG	Cessna 208A Caravan I Cargomaster	20800041	N813FE	0085		1 PWC PT6A-114	3629	Freighter		lsf Cessna Finance Corp.
☐ PT-OGL	Cessna 208A Caravan I Cargomaster	20800102	N839FE	0086		1 PWC PT6A-114	3629	Freighter		lsf Cessna Finance Corp.
☐ PT-OGV	Cessna 208A Caravan I Cargomaster	20800019	N805FE	0085		1 PWC PT6A-114	3629	Freighter		lsf Cessna Finance Corp.
☐ PT-OHA	Cessna 208A Caravan I Cargomaster	20800097	N837FE	0086		1 PWC PT6A-114	3629	Freighter		lsf Cessna Finance Corp.
☐ PT-OQT	Cessna 208B Grand Caravan	208B0314	N1018X	0092		1 PWC PT6A-114A	3969	Y9 / Freighter		lsf Cessna Finance Corp.
☐ PT-LDI	Cessna 500 Citation I	500-0335	N2937L	0076		2 PWC JT15D-1A	5375	Executive		
☐ PP-SBF	Embraer 110C Bandeirante (EMB-110C)	110023		0074	0596	2 PWC PT6A-27	5600	Y15		
☐ PT-GJD	Embraer 110E Bandeirante (EMB-110E)	110056		0075	0086	2 PWC PT6A-27	5600	Y15		
☐ PT-LBU	Embraer 110C Bandeirante (EMB-110C)	110033	PT-FAE	0075	1291	2 PWC PT6A-27	5600	Y15		
☐ PT-TAF	Embraer 110 Bandeirante (EMB-110)	110103	FAB2179	0076	0695	2 PWC PT6A-27	5600	Y15		
☐ PT-WKI	Embraer 120RT Brasilia (EMB-120RT)	120074	N336JS	0088	0397	2 PWC PW118	11500	Y30		lsf DLT of USA Inc. / opf Aluminal

TAMANDARE Taxi Aéreo, Ltda

Teresina (PI)

Rua Desembargador Freitas 685, CEP-64025 Teresina, (Piaui), Brazil ☎ (86) 222 62 67 Tx: n/a Fax: n/a SITA: n/a
F: 1989 n/a Head: n/a Net: n/a

☐ PT-KLQ	Cessna T210L Turbo Centurion II	21060449		0074	0490	1 CO TSIO-520-H	1724			
☐ PT-VJV	Embraer 810D Seneca III (EMB-810D)	810707		0089		2 CO TSIO-360-KB	2155			
☐ PT-OSO	Beech King Air C90	LJ-927	N4492D	0080		2 PWC PT6A-21	4377			

TAM Brasil = KK / TAM (Transportes Aéreos Regionais, S.A. dba / Member of TAM Group)

Sao Paulo-Congonhas, (SP)

Rua Gal. Pantaleo Telles 210, (Jardim Aeroporto), CEP-04355-040 Sao Paulo (SP), Brazil ☎ (11) 55 82 87 31 Tx: 1156641 tamr br Fax: (11) 533 24 69 SITA: n/a
F: 1976 2140 Head: Cmte. Rolim Adolfo Amaro IATA: 877 ICAO: TAM Net: http://www.tam.com.br On order (Letter of intent): 38 Airbus Industrie A319/A320 & further 5 A330 for delivery 2000-2005.

☐ PT-LAG	Fokker F27 Friendship 600 (F27 Mk600)	10197	PH-FDM*	0062	0480	2 RR Dart 532-7	19731	Y44		cvtd F27-200
☐ PT-LAH	Fokker F27 Friendship 600 (F27 Mk600)	10178	PH-FCS*	0061	0780	2 RR Dart 532-7	19731	Y44		cvtd F27-200
☐ PT-LAJ	Fokker F27 Friendship 500 (F27 Mk500)	10632	PH-FSJ*	0082	0183	2 RR Dart 532-7	20412	Y52		Ribeirao Preto
☐ PT-LAK	Fokker F27 Friendship 500 (F27 Mk500)	10634	PH-FSL*	0082	0183	2 RR Dart 532-7	20412	Y52		Maringa
☐ PT-LAL	Fokker F27 Friendship 500 (F27 Mk500)	10341	N272FA	0067	0386	2 RR Dart 532-7	20412	Y52		
☐ PT-MLA	Fokker 50 (F27 Mk050)	20182	PH-FZE*	0090	1095	2 PWC PW125B	20820	Y46	JS-AD	lsf Dasa Aircraft Finance VI B.V.
☐ PT-MLB	Fokker 50 (F27 Mk050)	20192	PH-LMT*	0090	1195	2 PWC PW125B	20820	Y46	JS-AE	lsf Dasa Aircraft Finance VII B.V.
☐ PT-MLC	Fokker 50 (F27 Mk050)	20202	PH-FZG*	0090	1195	2 PWC PW125B	20820	Y46	JS-AF	lsf Dasa Aircraft Finance VIII B.V.
☐ PT-MLD	Fokker 50 (F27 Mk050)	20210	PH-FZH*	0091	1295	2 PWC PW125B	20820	Y46	JS-AG	lsf Dasa Aircraft Finance IX B.V.
☐ PT-MLE	Fokker 50 (F27 Mk050)	20220	PH-RRF*	0091	1295	2 PWC PW125B	20820	Y46	JS-AH	lsf Dasa Aircraft Finance X B.V.
☐ PT-MLF	Fokker 50 (F27 Mk050)	20316	PH-EXK*	0096	0496	2 PWC PW125B	20820	Y46		lsf Brazilian Aircraft Fin. XXII B.V.
☐ PT-MLG	Fokker 50 (F27 Mk050)	20317	PH-EXA*	0096	1196	2 PWC PW125B	20820	Y46		lsf Brazilian Aircraft Fin. XXIII B.V.
☐ PT-MLH	Fokker 50 (F27 Mk050)	20254	D-AFFE	0092	0397	2 PWC PW125B	20820	Y46		lsf BD Industrie Beteiligungs GmbH
☐ PT-MLI	Fokker 50 (F27 Mk050)	20255	D-AFFF	0092	0497	2 PWC PW125B	20820	Y46		lsf BD Industrie Beteiligungs GmbH
☐ PT-MQA	Fokker 100 (F28 Mk0100)	11296	PH-TAC	0090	1296	2 RR Tay 650-15	44455	Y100		lsf Dasa Aircraft Finance XVIII B.V.
☐ PT-MQB	Fokker 100 (F28 Mk0100)	11350	PH-LNN	0891	0697	2 RR Tay 650-15	44455	Y100		lsf GPA Fokker 100 Finance Ltd
☐ PT-MQC	Fokker 100 (F28 Mk0100)	11371	PH-JXP	1291	0597	2 RR Tay 650-15	44455	Y100		lsf GPA Fokker 100 Finance Ltd
☐ PT-MQD	Fokker 100 (F28 Mk0100)	11383	B-2231	0092	0398	2 RR Tay 650-15	44455	Y100		lsf GPA Fokker 100 Finance Ltd
☐ PT-MQE	Fokker 100 (F28 Mk0100)	11389	B-2232	0092	0598	2 RR Tay 650-15	44455	Y100		lsf GPA Fokker 100 Finance Ltd
☐ PT-MQF	Fokker 100 (F28 Mk0100)	11401	B-2234	0093	0798	2 RR Tay 650-15	44455	Y100		lsf GPA Fokker 100 Finance Ltd
☐ PT-MQG	Fokker 100 (F28 Mk0100)	11527	F-WQGZ	0094	0898	2 RR Tay 650-15	44455	Y100		lsf Debis AirFinance
☐ PT-MQH	Fokker 100 (F28 Mk0100)	11512	F-WQGY	0094	0798	2 RR Tay 650-15	44455	Y100		lsf Debis AirFinance
☐ PT-MQI	Fokker 100 (F28 Mk0100)	11517	F-WQGX	0094	0898	2 RR Tay 650-15	44455	Y100		lsf Debis AirFinance
☐ PT-MQJ	Fokker 100 (F28 Mk0100)	11347	PH-LNL	0091	0998	2 RR Tay 650-15	44452	Y100		lsf GPA Fokker 100 Finance Ltd
☐ PT-MQK	Fokker 100 (F28 Mk0100)	11336	PH-LNF	0091	1198	2 RR Tay 650-15	44452	Y100		lsf GPA Fokker 100 Finance Ltd
☐ PT-MQL	Fokker 100 (F28 Mk0100)	11394	B-2233	0092	1198	2 RR Tay 650-15	44455	Y100		lsf GPA Fokker 100 Finance Ltd
☐ PT-MQM	Fokker 100 (F28 Mk0100)	11301	PH-LMV	0090	0199	2 RR Tay 650-15	44452	Y100		lsf GPA Fokker 100 Finance Ltd
☐ PT-MRA	Fokker 100 (F28 Mk0100)	11284	PH-LMI*	0090	0990	2 RR Tay 650-15	44455	Y100		lsf GPA Fokker 100 Finance Ltd
☐ PT-MRB	Fokker 100 (F28 Mk0100)	11285	PH-LMK*	0090	0990	2 RR Tay 650-15	44455	Y100		lsf GPA Fokker 100 Finance Ltd
☐ PT-MRC	Fokker 100 (F28 Mk0100)	11320	PH-LND*	0091	0591	2 RR Tay 650-15	44455	Y100		lsf GPA Fokker 100 Finance Ltd
☐ PT-MRD	Fokker 100 (F28 Mk0100)	11322	PH-LNE*	0091	0691	2 RR Tay 650-15	44455	Y100		lsf GPA Fokker 100 Finance Ltd
☐ PT-MRE	Fokker 100 (F28 Mk0100)	11348	PH-LNM*	0092	0792	2 RR Tay 650-15	44455	Y100		lsf GPA Fokker 100 Finance Ltd
☐ PT-MRF	Fokker 100 (F28 Mk0100)	11351	PH-LNO*	0092	0792	2 RR Tay 650-15	44455	Y100		lsf Aircraft Leasing P.S. Ltd
☐ PT-MRG	Fokker 100 (F28 Mk0100)	11304	PH-LMX*	0091	1192	2 RR Tay 650-15	44455	Y100		lsf GPA Fokker 100 Finance Ltd
☐ PT-MRH	Fokker 100 (F28 Mk0100)	11305	PH-LMY*	0091	1192	2 RR Tay 650-15	44455	Y100		lsf GPA Fokker 100 Finance Ltd
☐ PT-MRI	Fokker 100 (F28 Mk0100)	11442	PH-MXK*	0093	0593	2 RR Tay 650-15	44455	Y100		lsf BBV Leasing Fonds GmbH & Co.
☐ PT-MRJ	Fokker 100 (F28 Mk0100)	11451	PH-EZT*	0093	0693	2 RR Tay 650-15	44455	Y100		lsf BBV Leasing Fonds GmbH & Co.
☐ PT-MRL	Fokker 100 (F28 Mk0100)	11441	PH-LXS*	0093	1093	2 RR Tay 650-15	44455	Y100		lsf BBV Leasing
☐ PT-MRM	Fokker 100 (F28 Mk0100)	11422	PH-LXI*	0093	0394	2 RR Tay 650-15	44455	Y100		lsf Lufthansa Leasing
☐ PT-MRN	Fokker 100 (F28 Mk0100)	11443	PH-MXB*	0093	0594	2 RR Tay 650-15	44455	Y100		lsf Lufthansa Leasing
☐ PT-MRO	Fokker 100 (F28 Mk0100)	11470	PH-EZR*	0094	1194	2 RR Tay 650-15	44455	Y100		lsf Brazilian Aircraft Finance X B.V.
☐ PT-MRP	Fokker 100 (F28 Mk0100)	11472	PH-EZU*	0095	0295	2 RR Tay 650-15	44455	Y100		lsf Brazilian Aircraft Finance XI B.V.
☐ PT-MRQ	Fokker 100 (F28 Mk0100)	11473	PH-EZU*	0095	0495	2 RR Tay 650-15	44455	Y100		lsf Brazilian Aircraft Finance XII B.V.
☐ PT-MRR	Fokker 100 (F28 Mk0100)	11461	PH-EZT*	0095	0895	2 RR Tay 650-15	44455	Y100		lsf Brazilian Aircraft Finance XVI B.V.
☐ PT-MRS	Fokker 100 (F28 Mk0100)	11462	PH-EZX*	0095	0895	2 RR Tay 650-15	44455	Y100		lsf Brazilian Aircraft Fin. XVII B.V.
☐ PT-MRT	Fokker 100 (F28 Mk0100)	11505	PH-JCJ*	0095	1295	2 RR Tay 650-15	44455	Y100	KQ-DR	lsf Brazilian Aircraft Fin. XVIII B.V.
☐ PT-MRU	Fokker 100 (F28 Mk0100)	11511	PH-JCK*	0096	0296	2 RR Tay 650-15	44455	Y100		lsf Lazard Frères
☐ PT-MRV	Fokker 100 (F28 Mk0100)	11516	PH-JCL*	0096	0296	2 RR Tay 650-15	44455	Y100		lsf Lazard Frères
☐ PT-MRW	Fokker 100 (F28 Mk0100)	11518	PH-JCM*	0096	0396	2 RR Tay 650-15	44455	Y100		lsf Lazard Frères
☐ PT-MRX	Fokker 100 (F28 Mk0100)	11341	PH-LNH	0091	0796	2 RR Tay 650-15	44455	Y100		lsf GPA Fokker 100 Finance Ltd
☐ PT-MRY	Fokker 100 (F28 Mk0100)	11343	PH-LNK	0092	0896	2 RR Tay 650-15	44455	Y100		lsf GPA Fokker 100 Finance Ltd
☐ PT-MRZ	Fokker 100 (F28 Mk0100)	11290	PH-TAB	0090	1296	2 RR Tay 650-15	44455	Y100		lsf Dasa Aircraft Finance XVII B.V.

510 registration type of aircraft cn/fn ex/ex* mfd del powered by mtow kg configuration selcal name/fln/specialitites/remarks

registration	type of aircraft	cn/fn	ex/ex*	mfd	del	powered by	mtow kg	configuration	selcal	name/fln/specialitites/remarks
☐ PT-WHK	Fokker 100 (F28 Mk0100)	11452	PH-RRN	0093	0196	2 RR Tay 650-15	44455	Y100		lsf PEMB
☐ PT-WHL	Fokker 100 (F28 Mk0100)	11471	PH-MXW	0093	0496	2 RR Tay 650-15	44455	Y100		lsf PEMB
☐ PT-	Fokker 100 (F28 Mk0100)	11409	B-2235	0093		2 RR Tay 650-15	44455	Y100		tblsf GPA Fokker100 Fin.Ltd 0099/ex CES
☐ PT-	Fokker 100 (F28 Mk0100)	11430	B-2236	0093		2 RR Tay 650-15	44455	Y100		tblsf GPA Fokker100 Fin.Ltd 0099/ex CES
☐ PT-	Fokker 100 (F28 Mk0100)	11421	B-2237	0093		2 RR Tay 650-15	44455	Y100		tblsf GPA Fokker100 Fin.Ltd 0099/ex CES
☐ PT-	Fokker 100 (F28 Mk0100)	11423	B-2238	0093		2 RR Tay 650-15	44455	Y100		tblsf GPA Fokker100 Fin.Ltd 0099/ex CES
☐ PT-	Fokker 100 (F28 Mk0100)	11429	B-2239	0093		2 RR Tay 650-15	44455	Y100		tblsf GPA Fokker100 Fin.Ltd 0099/ex CES
☐ PT-	Fokker 100 (F28 Mk0100)	11431	B-2240	0093		2 RR Tay 650-15	44455	Y100		tblsf GPA Fokker100 Fin.Ltd 0099/ex CES
☐ PT-MZA	Airbus Industrie A319-132	976	D-AVYT	0099	0399	2 IAE V2524-A5	64000			
☐ PT-MZB	Airbus Industrie A319-132	1010		0099	0499	2 IAE V2524-A5	64000			
☐ PT-	Airbus Industrie A319-132					2 IAE V2524-A5	64000			oo-delivery 1099
☐ PT-	Airbus Industrie A319-132					2 IAE V2524-A5	64000			oo-delivery 1099
☐ PT-	Airbus Industrie A319-132					2 IAE V2524-A5	64000			oo-delivery 1199
☐ PT-	Airbus Industrie A319-132					2 IAE V2524-A5	64000			oo-delivery 0100
☐ PT-	Airbus Industrie A319-132					2 IAE V2524-A5	64000			oo-delivery 0200
☐ PT-	Airbus Industrie A319-132					2 IAE V2524-A5	64000			oo-delivery 0400
☐ PT-	Airbus Industrie A319-132					2 IAE V2524-A5	64000			oo-delivery 0700
☐ PT-	Airbus Industrie A319-132					2 IAE V2524-A5	64000			oo-delivery 0900
☐ PT-	Airbus Industrie A319-132					2 IAE V2524-A5	64000			oo-delivery 1200
☐ PT-	Airbus Industrie A319-132					2 IAE V2524-A5	64000			oo-delivery 0201
☐ PT-	Airbus Industrie A319-132					2 IAE V2524-A5	64000			oo-delivery 0501
☐ PT-	Airbus Industrie A319-132					2 IAE V2524-A5	64000			oo-delivery 0701
☐ PT-	Airbus Industrie A319-132					2 IAE V2524-A5	64000			oo-delivery 0901
☐ PT-	Airbus Industrie A319-132					2 IAE V2524-A5	64000			oo-delivery 1201
☐ PT-	Airbus Industrie A319-132					2 IAE V2524-A5	64000			oo-delivery 0002
☐ PT-	Airbus Industrie A319-132					2 IAE V2524-A5	64000			oo-delivery 0002
☐ PT-	Airbus Industrie A319-132					2 IAE V2524-A5	64000			oo-delivery 0002
☐ PT-	Airbus Industrie A319-132					2 IAE V2524-A5	64000			oo-delivery 0002
☐ PT-	Airbus Industrie A319-132					2 IAE V2524-A5	64000			oo-delivery 0002
☐ PT-	Airbus Industrie A319-132					2 IAE V2524-A5	64000			oo-delivery 0003
☐ PT-	Airbus Industrie A319-132					2 IAE V2524-A5	64000			oo-delivery 0003
☐ PT-	Airbus Industrie A319-132					2 IAE V2524-A5	64000			oo-delivery 0003
☐ PT-	Airbus Industrie A319-132					2 IAE V2524-A5	64000			oo-delivery 0003
☐ PT-MVA	Airbus Industrie A330-223	232	F-WWKV*	0098	1198	2 PW PW4168A	230000	CY235		lsf Airbus Finance Co. Ltd
☐ PT-MVB	Airbus Industrie A330-223	238	F-WWKY*	0098	1198	2 PW PW4168A	230000	CY235		lsf Airbus Finance Co. Ltd
☐ PT-MVC	Airbus Industrie A330-223	247	F-WWKH*	0098	1298	2 PW PW4168A	230000	CY235		lsf Frusco Ltd
☐ PT-MVD	Airbus Industrie A330-223	259	F-WWKP*	0099	0299	2 PW PW4168A	230000	CY235		
☐ PT-MVE	Airbus Industrie A330-223	300				2 PW PW4168A	230000	CY235		oo-delivery 0999
☐ PT-	Airbus Industrie A320-232					2 IAE V2527-A5	73500			oo-delivery 1099
☐ PT-	Airbus Industrie A320-232					2 IAE V2527-A5	73500			oo-delivery 1199
☐ PT-	Airbus Industrie A320-232					2 IAE V2527-A5	73500			oo-delivery 1199
☐ PT-	Airbus Industrie A320-232					2 IAE V2527-A5	73500			oo-delivery 1299
☐ PT-	Airbus Industrie A320-232					2 IAE V2527-A5	73500			oo-delivery 1299
☐ PT-	Airbus Industrie A320-232					2 IAE V2527-A5	73500			oo-delivery 0400
☐ PT-	Airbus Industrie A320-232					2 IAE V2527-A5	73500			oo-delivery 0600
☐ PT-	Airbus Industrie A320-232					2 IAE V2527-A5	73500			oo-delivery 0800
☐ PT-	Airbus Industrie A320-232					2 IAE V2527-A5	73500			oo-delivery 1000
☐ PT-	Airbus Industrie A320-232					2 IAE V2527-A5	73500			oo-delivery 0101
☐ PT-	Airbus Industrie A320-232					2 IAE V2527-A5	73500			oo-delivery 0401
☐ PT-	Airbus Industrie A320-232					2 IAE V2527-A5	73500			oo-delivery 0701
☐ PT-	Airbus Industrie A320-232					2 IAE V2527-A5	73500			oo-delivery 0901

TAM Express = JJ / BLC (TAM-Transportes Aéreos Meridionais S.A. dba/formerly Brasil Central-Linha Regional S.A./Member of TAM Group) — Sao Paulo-Congonhas, (SP)

Rua Gal. Pantaleo Telles 210, (Jardim Aeroporto), CEP-04355-040 Sao Paulo (SP), Brazil ☎ (11) 55 82 88 11 Tx: 1154565 bcla br Fax: (11) 55 30 41 31 SITA: SAODBKK
F: 1986 ⁂ 300 Head: Cmte. Rolim Adolfo Amaro IATA: 957 ICAO: TAM-MERIDIONAL Net: n/a

registration	type of aircraft	cn/fn	ex/ex*	mfd	del	powered by	mtow kg	configuration	selcal	name/fln/specialitites/remarks
☐ PT-OGA	Cessna 208A Caravan I	20800042	N814FE	0085	0191	1 PWC PT6A-114	3629	Y9 / Freighter		lsf Cessna Finance / cvtd Cargomaster
☐ PT-OGB	Cessna 208A Caravan I	20800047	N821FE	0085	0191	1 PWC PT6A-114	3629	Y9 / Freighter		lsf Cessna Finance / cvtd Cargomaster
☐ PT-OGD	Cessna 208A Caravan I	20800074	N829FE	0085	0191	1 PWC PT6A-114	3629	Y9 / Freighter		lsf Cessna Finance / cvtd Cargomaster
☐ PT-OGH	Cessna 208A Caravan I	20800012	N802FE	0085	0691	1 PWC PT6A-114	3629	Y9 / Freighter		lsf Cessna Finance / cvtd Cargomaster
☐ PT-OGQ	Cessna 208A Caravan I	20800032	N809FE	0085	1291	1 PWC PT6A-114	3629	Y9 / Freighter		lsf Cessna Finance / cvtd Cargomaster
☐ PT-OGX	Cessna 208A Caravan I	20800076	N825FE	0085	1191	1 PWC PT6A-114	3629	Y9 / Freighter		lsf Cessna Finance / cvtd Cargomaster
☐ PT-MEA	Cessna 208B Grand Caravan	208B0333	N1037L*	0093	0693	1 PWC PT6A-114A	3969	Y12 / Freighter		lsf Cessna Finance Corp.
☐ PT-MEB	Cessna 208B Grand Caravan	208B0335	N1038G*	0093	0693	1 PWC PT6A-114A	3969	Y12 / Freighter		lsf Cessna Finance Corp.
☐ PT-MEC	Cessna 208B Grand Caravan	208B0342	N1045C*	0093	0693	1 PWC PT6A-114A	3969	Y12 / Freighter		lsf Cessna Finance Corp.
☐ PT-MED	Cessna 208B Grand Caravan	208B0343	N1052C*	0093	0693	1 PWC PT6A-114A	3969	Y12 / Freighter		lsf Cessna Finance Corp.
☐ PT-MEE	Cessna 208B Grand Caravan	208B0344	N1054M*	0093	0693	1 PWC PT6A-114A	3969	Y12 / Freighter		lsf Cessna Finance Corp.
☐ PT-MEG	Cessna 208B Grand Caravan	208B0352		0093	0893	1 PWC PT6A-114A	3969	Y12 / Freighter		lsf Cessna Finance Corp.
☐ PT-MEH	Cessna 208B Grand Caravan	208B0354		0093	0893	1 PWC PT6A-114A	3969	Y12 / Freighter		lsf Cessna Finance Corp.
☐ PT-MEI	Cessna 208B Grand Caravan	208B0358		0093	0893	1 PWC PT6A-114A	3969	Y12 / Freighter		lsf Cessna Finance Corp.
☐ PT-MEJ	Cessna 208B Grand Caravan	208B0359		0093	0993	1 PWC PT6A-114A	3969	Y12 / Freighter		lsf Cessna Finance Corp.
☐ PT-MEK	Cessna 208B Grand Caravan	208B0360		0093	0993	1 PWC PT6A-114A	3969	Y12 / Freighter		lsf Cessna Finance Corp.
☐ PT-MEL	Cessna 208B Grand Caravan	208B0361		0093	0993	1 PWC PT6A-114A	3969	Y12 / Freighter		lsf Cessna Finance Corp.
☐ PT-MEM	Cessna 208B Grand Caravan	208B0405		0094	0994	1 PWC PT6A-114A	3969	Y12 / Freighter		lsf Cessna Finance Corp.
☐ PT-MEN	Cessna 208B Grand Caravan	208B0408		0094	0994	1 PWC PT6A-114A	3969	Y12 / Freighter		lsf Cessna Finance Corp.
☐ PT-MEO	Cessna 208B Grand Caravan	208B0412		0094	1194	1 PWC PT6A-114A	3969	Y12 / Freighter		lsf Cessna Finance Corp.
☐ PT-MEP	Cessna 208B Grand Caravan	208B0413		0094	1194	1 PWC PT6A-114A	3969	Y12 / Freighter		lsf Cessna Finance Corp.
☐ PT-MER	Cessna 208B Grand Caravan	208B0506		0096	0596	1 PWC PT6A-114A	3969	Y12 / Freighter		lsf Cessna Finance Corp.
☐ PT-MES	Cessna 208B Grand Caravan	208B0507		0096	0596	1 PWC PT6A-114A	3969	Y12 / Freighter		lsf Cessna Finance Corp.
☐ PT-MET	Cessna 208B Grand Caravan	208B0509		0096	0596	1 PWC PT6A-114A	3969	Y12 / Freighter		lsf Cessna Finance Corp.
☐ PT-MEU	Cessna 208B Grand Caravan	208B0510		0096	0596	1 PWC PT6A-114A	3969	Y12 / Freighter		lsf Cessna Finance Corp.
☐ PT-MEV	Cessna 208B Grand Caravan	208B0512		0096	0596	1 PWC PT6A-114A	3969	Y12 / Freighter		lsf Cessna Finance Corp.
☐ PT-MEW	Cessna 208B Grand Caravan	208B0513		0096	0596	1 PWC PT6A-114A	3969	Y12 / Freighter		lsf Cessna Finance Corp.
☐ PT-MEX	Cessna 208B Grand Caravan	208B0515		0096	0596	1 PWC PT6A-114A	3969	Y12 / Freighter		lsf Cessna Finance Corp.
☐ PT-MEY	Cessna 208B Grand Caravan	208B0518		0096	0596	1 PWC PT6A-114A	3969	Y12 / Freighter		lsf Cessna Finance Corp.
☐ PT-MEZ	Cessna 208B Grand Caravan	208B0519		0096	0596	1 PWC PT6A-114A	3969	Y12 / Freighter		lsf Cessna Finance Corp.
☐ PT-MHA	Cessna 208B Grand Caravan	208B0533		0096	0696	1 PWC PT6A-114A	3969	Y12 / Freighter		lsf Cessna Finance Corp.
☐ PT-MHB	Cessna 208B Grand Caravan	208B0534		0096	0696	1 PWC PT6A-114A	3969	Y12 / Freighter		lsf Cessna Finance Corp.
☐ PT-MHC	Cessna 208B Grand Caravan	208B0543		0096	0896	1 PWC PT6A-114A	3969	Y12 / Freighter		lsf Cessna Finance Corp.
☐ PT-MHD	Cessna 208B Grand Caravan	208B0544		0096	0896	1 PWC PT6A-114A	3969	Y12 / Freighter		lsf Cessna Finance Corp.
☐ PT-MHE	Cessna 208B Grand Caravan	208B0545		0096	0896	1 PWC PT6A-114A	3969	Y12 / Freighter		lsf Cessna Finance Corp.
☐ PT-MHF	Cessna 208B Grand Caravan	208B0549		0096	0896	1 PWC PT6A-114A	3969	Y12 / Freighter		lsf Cessna Finance Corp.

TAMIG - TAXI AEREO MINAS GERAIS, Ltda (Affiliated with Mendes Junior Engenharia, SA) — Belo Horizonte-Pampulha, (MG)

Rua Lider 22, Hangar CMJ, Aeroporto da Pampulha, CEP-31270-480 Belo Horizonte, (Minas Gerais), Brazil ☎ (31) 441 31 22 Tx: 314141 comj br Fax: (31) 441 65 30 SITA: n/a
F: 1962 ⁂ 100 Head: Alberto Laborne Valle Mendes Net: n/a

registration	type of aircraft	cn/fn	ex/ex*	mfd	del	powered by	mtow kg	configuration	selcal	name/fln/specialitites/remarks
☐ PT-JRU	Cessna 402B	402B0453		0073		2 CO TSIO-520-E	2858	6 Pax		
☐ PT-JYK	Cessna 402B	402B0530		0074		2 CO TSIO-520-E	2858	6 Pax		
☐ PT-LIT	Cessna 402C II	402C0302	5T-DPR	0080		2 CO TSIO-520-VB	3107	6 Pax		opf Mendes Junior Engenharia SA
☐ PT-LDY	IAI 1124 Westwind I	251	CX-CMJ	0079		2 GA TFE731-3-1G	10659	9 Pax		opf Mendes Junior Engenharia SA

TAM Jatos Executivos Marilia, S.A. (Member of TAM Group / formerly TAM-Taxi Aéreo Marilia, S.A.) — Sao Paulo-Congonhas, (SP)

TAM

Rua Monsenhor Antonio Pepe 94, Parque Jabaquara, CEP-04357-080 Sao Paulo (SP), Brazil ☎ (11) 55 82 88 11 Tx: none Fax: (11) 55 82 87 56 SITA: n/a
F: 1961 ⁂ 281 Head: Cmte. Rolim Adolfo Amoro Net: n/a Aircraft below MTOW 1361kg: Cessna 180

registration	type of aircraft	cn/fn	ex/ex*	mfd	del	powered by	mtow kg	configuration	selcal	name/fln/specialitites/remarks
☐ PT-OEL	Beech Baron B55 (95-B55)	TC-2407		0082		2 CO IO-470-L	2313			
☐ PT-YCE	Agusta A109A II	7394	N48FA	0087	1096	2 AN 250-C20B	2600			
☐ PT-WGD	Cessna 525 CitationJet	525-0120	N5264M	0095	1295	2 WRR FJ44-1A	4717			lsf Banco Itamarati S.A.
☐ PT-LUE	Cessna 650 Citation III	650-0091	N58HC	0085	0689	2 GA TFE731-3B-100S	9072			
☐ PT-LVF	Cessna 650 Citation III	650-0171	N1345G	0089		2 GA TFE731-3B-100S	9979			lsf Itamarati Leasing
☐ PT-OMU	Cessna 650 Citation III	650-0205	N2630N	0091		2 GA TFE731-3B-100S	9525			lsf ASI Aircraft Holdings Inc.

TAPAJOS Taxi Aéreo, Ltda — Santarem, (PA)

Av. Francisco Guilhon 100, Maracana, CEP-68035-000 Santarém, (Para), Brazil ☎ (91) 522 49 09 Tx: n/a Fax: n/a SITA: n/a
F: 1981 ⁂ n/a Head: n/a Net: n/a Aircraft below MTOW 1361kg: Cessna 182

registration	type of aircraft	cn/fn	ex/ex*	mfd	del	powered by	mtow kg	configuration	selcal	name/fln/specialitites/remarks
☐ PT-IAZ	Cessna U206F Stationair	U20601726		0072	0097	1 CO IO-520-F	1633			
☐ PT-BXD	Beech Baron A55 (95-A55)	TC-423		0063	0490	2 CO IO-470-L	2214			

TAP - Transportes Aéreos Presidente, S.A. = TPE (formerly Taxi Aéreo Presidente, Ltda) — Presidente Prudente, (SP)

Rua dos Pardais 467/B-Jardim Yolanda, CEP-19013-410 Presidente Prudente, (Sao Paulo), Brazil ☎ (18) 221 25 70 Tx: none Fax: (18) 222 23 83 SITA: n/a
F: 1987 ⁂ n/a Head: Antonio José Aldrighi dos Santos ICAO: PRESIDENTE Net: n/a

registration	type of aircraft	cn/fn	ex/ex*	mfd	del	powered by	mtow kg	configuration	selcal	name/fln/specialitites/remarks
☐ PT-EHL	Embraer 820C Navajo (EMB-820C)	820048		0077		2 LY TIO-540-J2BD	3175	Y9		
☐ PT-GJH	Embraer 110C Bandeirante (EMB-110C)	110050		0075	0096	2 PWC PT6A-27	5600	Y15		

☐ PT-ODG	Embraer 110 Bandeirante (EMB-110)	110035	FAB2145	0074	0096	2 PWC PT6A-27	5600	Y15		
☐ PT-SCD	Embraer 110P2 Bandeirante (EMB-110P2)	110295		0080	0396	2 PWC PT6A-34	5670	Y18		

TASUL – TAXI AEREO SUL, Ltda   Porto Alegre-Salgado Filho, (RS)

Aeroporto Salgado Filho, CP 8010, CEP-90201-270 Porto Alegre, (Rio Grande do Sul), Brazil   ☎ (51) 325 20 55 Tx: none Fax: (51) 325 12 98 SITA: n/a
F: 1968   ♦♦♦ 20 Head: Mauricio W. Engelke Net: n/a

☐ PT-KDA	Cessna 310Q II	310Q1087		0074	0996	2 CO IO-470-VO	2404			
☐ PT-JGH	Cessna 402B	402B0441		0073		2 CO TSIO-520-E	2858			
☐ PT-JJB	Cessna 402B	402B0399	N8063Q	0073		2 CO TSIO-520-E	2858			
☐ PT-WFT	Cessna 500 Citation Eagle	500-0154	N54MC	0074	1095	2 PWC JT15D-1A	5670			cvtd Citation
☐ PT-MAL	Embraer 121A Xingu (EMB-121A)	121019		0080	0097	2 PWC PT6A-28	5670			
☐ PT-GKB	Embraer 110P Bandeirante (EMB-110P)	110091		0076		2 PWC PT6A-27	5600			

TAVAJ – Transportes Aéreos Regulares, SA = 4U / TVJ (formerly Tavaj-Taxi Aéreo Vale do Jurua, Ltda)   Rio Branco, (AC)

Caixa Postal 484, CEP-69901-320 Rio Branco, (Acre), Brazil   ☎ (68) 221 28 66 Tx: none Fax: (68) 221 36 54 SITA: n/a
F: 1972   ♦♦♦ 150 Head: José Idalberto da Cunha ICAO: TAVAJ Net: n/a

☐ PT-GJP	Embraer 110E Bandeirante (EMB-110E)	110065		0075	0098	2 PWC PT6A-27	5600	Y15		
☐ PT-LRB	Embraer 110P1 Bandeirante (EMB-110P1)	110409	N720RA	0083	0095	2 PWC PT6A-34	5900	Y19		
☐ PT-LRJ	Embraer 110P1 Bandeirante (EMB-110P1)	110384	N699RA	0082	0095	2 PWC PT6A-34	5900	Y19		
☐ PT-LTN	Embraer 110P1 Bandeirante (EMB-110P1)	110418	N860AC	0083	0095	2 PWC PT6A-34	5900	Y19		
☐ PT-OCW	Embraer 110P1 Bandeirante (EMB-110P1)	110273	N90PB	0080	0193	2 PWC PT6A-34	5900	Y19		
☐ PT-OCX	Embraer 110P1 Bandeirante (EMB-110P1)	110316	N94PB	0080	0193	2 PWC PT6A-34	5900	Y19		
☐ PT-TVB	De Havilland DHC-8-202 Dash 8Q	439	C-GHRI*	0096	0397	2 PWC PW123D	16465	Combi Y29		
☐ PT-TVC	De Havilland DHC-8-202 Dash 8Q	453	C-FDHD*	0096	0397	2 PWC PW123D	16465	Combi Y29		
☐ PT-TVA	Fokker F27 Friendship 600 (F27 Mk600)	10334	G-BNAL	0067	0995	2 RR Dart 532-7	20412	Y44		lsf Fokker Aircraft B.V.

TAXI AEREO DOURADO, Ltda – TAD   Belem, (PA)

Av. Dr. Freitas 2198, CEP-66120-590 Belém, (Para), Brazil   ☎ (91) 226 23 51 Tx: n/a Fax: n/a SITA: n/a
F: 1969   ♦♦♦ n/a Head: Manuel Dourado Costa Net: n/a

☐ PT-COF	Cessna P206B Super Skylane	P206-0219	N4619F	0066		1 CO IO-520-A	1633			
☐ PT-DDG	Cessna U206C Super Skywagon	U206-0968		0068		1 CO IO-520-F	1633			
☐ PT-KPN	Cessna U206E Super Skywagon	U20601566	PT-FOV	0070		1 CO IO-520-F	1633			
☐ PT-DED	Cessna 401	401-0192		0068		2 CO TSIO-520-E	2858			
☐ PT-IUX	Cessna 402B	402B0378		0073		2 CO TSIO-520-E	2858			

TAXI AEREO ITAITUBA, Ltda   Santarem, (PA)

Travessa Turiano Meira 42, Centro, CEP-68100-000 Santarém, (Para), Brazil   ☎ (91) 522 35 39 Tx: n/a Fax: n/a SITA: n/a
F: 1975   ♦♦♦ n/a Head: n/a Net: n/a

☐ PT-JZL	Cessna T210L Turbo Centurion II	21060394		0074	0098	1 CO TSIO-520-H	1724			
☐ PT-EFX	Neiva NE-821 Caraja	820034		0076	0097	2 PWC PT6A-27	3629			cvtd 820C
☐ PT-GJR	Embraer 110E Bandeirante (EMB-110E)	110070		0075	0789	2 PWC PT6A-27	5600			
☐ PT-GKE	Embraer 110B1 Bandeirante (EMB-110B1)	110096	PP-ZKE	0076	0097	2 PWC PT6A-27	5600			

TAXI AEREO JET NEWS, Ltda   Belem, (PA)

Rodovia BR316, KM5, CEP-67020-010 Belém, (Para), Brazil   ☎ (91) 235 41 00 Tx: 911083 br Fax: (91) 235 42 42 SITA: n/a
F: 1989   ♦♦♦ n/a Head: n/a Net: n/a

☐ PT-VBE	Embraer 810D Seneca III (EMB-810D)	810610		0086		2 CO TSIO-360-KB	2155			
☐ PT-LTH	Beech Baron 58P	TJ-450	N6867W	0084		2 CO TSIO-520-WB	2812			

TAXI AEREO KOVACS, SA   Belem, (PA)

Psg Dr. Freitas 160, CEP-66120-590 Belém, (Para), Brazil   ☎ (91) 233 16 00 Tx: 911663 taki br Fax: (91) 233 29 53 SITA: n/a
F: 1958   ♦♦♦ 80 Head: Adalberto Kovacs Nogueira Net: n/a

☐ PT-HVE	Bell 206B JetRanger III	2502	N99BP	0078		1 AN 250-C20B	1451			
☐ PT-BXX	Cessna 205	205-0295	N8295Z	0063		1 CO IO-470-S	1497			
☐ PT-BBW	Cessna U206C Super Skywagon	U206-1039		0068		1 CO IO-520-F	1633			
☐ PT-JNG	Cessna 402B	402B0446		0073		2 CO TSIO-520-E	2858			

TAXI AEREO NORTAO, Ltda   Cuiaba, (MT)

Travessa Palmas 11, Bairro Nova, CEP-78130-840 Varzea Grande, (Mato Grosso), Brazil   ☎ (65) 381 20 90 Tx: none Fax: n/a SITA: n/a
F: 1995   ♦♦♦ n/a Head: n/a Net: n/a

☐ PT-EPN	Embraer 810C Seneca II (EMB-810C)	810146		0078		2 CO TSIO-360-E	2073			
☐ PT-ERD	Embraer 810C Seneca II (EMB-810C)	810165		0078		2 CO TSIO-360-E	2073			
☐ PT-RYT	Embraer 810D Seneca III (EMB-810D)	810572		0086		2 CO TSIO-360-KB	2155			
☐ PT-VAA	Embraer 810D Seneca III (EMB-810D)	810582		0086		2 CO TSIO-360-KB	2155			
☐ PT-VRP	Embraer 810D Cuesta (EMB-810D)	810834		0093		2 CO TSIO-360-KB	2155			
☐ PT-VSB	Embraer 810D Cuesta (EMB-810D)	810845		0093		2 CO TSIO-360-KB	2155			

TAXI AEREO PALMAS, Ltda   Palmas

Aeropuerto Municipal de Palmas, Arso 42 sn, CEP-77054-970 Palmas, (Tocantins), Brazil   ☎ (63) 216 17 16 Tx: none Fax: n/a SITA: n/a
F: 1993   ♦♦♦ n/a Head: n/a Net: n/a Aircraft below MTOW 1361kg: Embraer 711ST

☐ PP-ODI	Cessna T210L Turbo Centurion II	21059688	PP-ATQ	0072		1 CO TSIO-520-H	1724			
☐ PT-ETH	Embraer 810C Seneca II (EMB-810C)	810207		0079		2 CO TSIO-360-EB	2073			

TAXI AEREO PINHAL, Ltda   Mogi Mirim, (SP)

Rodovia SP 342-KM204, CEP-13990 Espirito Santo do Pinhal, (Sao Paulo), Brazil   ☎ (196) 51 18 67 Tx: n/a Fax: (196) 51 39 19 SITA: n/a
F: 1987   ♦♦♦ n/a Head: n/a Net: n/a

☐ PT-LNN	Mitsubishi MU-300 Diamond IA	A048SA	N335DM	0083		2 PWC JT15D-4D	6636			

TAXI AEREO QUARTIN, Ltda – TAQ   Campo Grande, (MS)

Rua Prof. Severino Ramos de Queiroz 110, CEP-79004-250 Campo Grande, (Mato Grosso do Sul), Brazil   ☎ (67) 384 40 28 Tx: n/a Fax: n/a SITA: n/a
F: 1975   ♦♦♦ n/a Head: n/a Net: n/a

☐ PT-LEY	Embraer 810C Seneca II (EMB-810C)	810322	PT-RBZ	0080		2 CO TSIO-360-EB	2073			

TAXI AEREO RONDONIA, Ltda   Boa Vista, (RR)

Aeroporto Internacional Boa Vista, Sala 3, CEP-69304-000 Boa Vista, (Roraima), Brazil   ☎ (95) 224-5068 Tx: n/a Fax: (95) 224 50 68 SITA: n/a
F: 1968   ♦♦♦ n/a Head: n/a Net: n/a

☐ PT-NLL	Embraer 710C Carioca (EMB-710C)	710161		0078	0097	1 LY O-540-B4B5	1361			
☐ PT-DQZ	Piper PA-23-250 Aztec E	27-4595		0071		2 LY IO-540-C4B5	2359			

TAXI AEREO SINUELO, Ltda   Rio de Janeiro-Santos Dumont (RJ)

Av. Marechal Camara 160, 5 andar, CEP-20020-080 Rio de Janeiro, (Rio de Janeiro), Brazil   ☎ (21) 297 66 22 Tx: 2121305 br Fax: (21) 262 00 25 SITA: n/a
F: 1967   ♦♦♦ n/a Head: n/a Net: n/a

☐ PT-LJQ	Cessna S550 Citation S/II	S550-0113	N553CC	0086		2 PWC JT15D-4B	6668			

TAXI AEREO WILSON, Ltda   Osasco, (SP)

Av. Presidente Kennedy, 2463 V. Tiete, CEP-06298-190 Osasco, (Sao Paulo), Brazil   ☎ (11) 707 51 44 Tx: 1134202 ccbv br Fax: (11) 707 56 50 SITA: n/a
F: 1977   ♦♦♦ 20 Head: Wilson Urbano Netto Net: n/a

☐ PT-HPN	Bell 206B JetRanger III	3538		0081		1 AN 250-C20B	1451	4 Pax		
☐ PT-HUH	Bell 206B JetRanger III	4001	C-FBGY	0088		1 AN 250-C20J	1451	4 Pax		
☐ PT-RDR	Embraer 820C Navajo (EMB-820C)	820125		0082		2 LY TIO-540-J2BD	3175	6 Pax		lsf Finasa Leasing

TBS Taxi Aéreo, Ltda   Santos, (SP)

Rua Dr. Arthur Assis 31, Boqueirao, CEP-11045-540 Santos, (Sao Paulo), Brazil   ☎ (13) 234 99 02 Tx: n/a Fax: n/a SITA: n/a
F: 1995   ♦♦♦ n/a Head: n/a Net: n/a

☐ PT-EST	Embraer 810C Seneca II (EMB-810C)	810193		0078		2 CO TSIO-360-E	2073			

TECNOFLY Taxi Aéreo, Ltda   Santo Andre-Heliport, (SP)

Av. Joao Cachoeira 488-10andar, Conj.1002, CEP-04535-001 Chacara Itaim, (Sao Paulo), Brazil   ☎ (11) 822 72 28 Tx: none Fax: (11) 866 89 89 SITA: n/a
F: 1990   ♦♦♦ 7 Head: Roberto de Castro Visnevski Net: n/a

☐ PT-HBV	Bell 206B JetRanger III	2341	N16913	0078		1 AN 250-C20B	1451			
☐ PT-HXL	Bell 206L-3 LongRanger III	51233	CC-PSB	0088		1 AN 250-C30P	1882			
☐ PT-HNC	Euroc.(Helibras/Aerosp.)HB350B Esquilo	2067 / HB1116		0088		1 TU Arriel 1B	1950			

TIQUARA Taxi Aéreo, Ltda   Recife, (PE)

Rua da Aurora 1675, 1andar, Sala 4, Bairro Santo Amaro, CEP-50040-090 Recife (Pernambuco), Brazil   ☎ (81) 231 43 10 Tx: n/a Fax: n/a SITA: n/a
F: 1990   ♦♦♦ n/a Head: n/a Net: n/a

☐ PT-OUJ	Beech King Air F90	LA-155	N155GA	0081		2 PWC PT6A-135	4967			lsf The First National Bank of Boston

registration   type of aircraft   cn/fn   ex/ex*   mfd   del   powered by   mtow kg   configuration   selcal   name/fln/specialitites/remarks

TIRRENO Taxi Aéreo, Ltda
Sao Paulo-Congonhas, (SP)

Rua Bandeirantes 530, CEP-09912-230 Diadema, (Sao Paulo), Brazil ☎ (11) 445 42 22 Tx: 1144377 br Fax: (11) 456 57 11 SITA: n/a
F: 1989 n/a Head: n/a Net: n/a

☐ PT-HXC	Bell 222U	47522	N77UT	0085	0591	2 LY LTS101-750C.1	3742			

TOTAL Linhas Aéreas, SA = TTL (Member of Grupo Empresarial Rota / formerly Total Aerotaxi, SA)
Belo Horizonte, (MG) & Rio de Janeiro-SDU, (RJ)

Rua Boa Ventura 2312-Jaragua, CEP-32170-310 Belo Horizonte, (Minas Gerais), Brazil ☎ (31) 441 64 44 Tx: none Fax: (31) 441 69 22 SITA: n/a
F: 1988 n/a Head: Alfredo Meister ICAO: TOTAL Net: n/a

☐ PT-JHG	Embraer 110C Bandeirante (EMB-110C)	110012		0073	1189	2 PWC PT6A-27	5600	Y15		
☐ PP-PTA	Embraer 120RT Brasilia (EMB-120RT)	120061	F-GFEN	0087	0797	2 PWC PW118	11500	Y30		lsf A.T.R.
☐ PP-PTB	Embraer 120RT Brasilia (EMB-120RT)	120080	F-GFEP	0088	0997	2 PWC PW118	11500	Y30		lsf A.T.R. / opf Caprioli
☐ PT-STN	Embraer 120ER Brasilia (QC)	120241		0091	0593	2 PWC PW118	11990	Y30		cvtd 120RT
☐ PP-ATV	ATR 42-300	298	F-GIVG	0093	0895	2 PWC PW120	16700	Y48		lsf Letizia Leasing Ltd
☐ PT-MFE	ATR 42-300	295	F-WWLU*	0092	0597	2 PWC PW120	16700	Y48		lsf Regional Aircraft Leasing Ltd
☐ PT-TTL	ATR 42-320	380	N988MA	0094	0896	2 PWC PW121	16700	Y48		lsf Surf's Up Ltd

TRANSAIR INTERNATIONAL Linhas Aéreas, Ltda = TNI (Sister company of Pegasus, Inc.)
Rio de Janeiro-Internacional, (RJ)

Av. Rio Branco 99, CEP-20040-003 Rio de Janeiro, (Rio de Janeiro), Brazil ☎ (21) 516 66 41 Tx: none Fax: (21) 516 04 53 SITA: RIOTRXH
F: 1997 70 Head: Paulo Constant Marques ICAO: TRANSINTER Net: n/a

☐ PP-OOO	Boeing (Douglas) DC-10-15	48258 / 346	V2-LEX	0080	0198	3 GE CF6-50C2F	206385	F14Y339		lsf Finova Capital Corp.

TRANSAR Taxi Aéreo, SA
Sao Paulo-Congonhas, (SP)

Rua Jorge Faleiros 250, CEP-04342-110 Sao Paulo, (Sao Paulo), Brazil ☎ (11) 275 11 09 Tx: 24979 ugaz br Fax: (11) 275 13 55 SITA: n/a
F: 1969 20 Head: Pery Igel Net: n/a

☐ PT-LDL	Twin (Aero) Turbo Commander 690	11037	PP-FRD	0072		2 GA TPE331-5-252K	4649			
☐ PT-LHV	Twin (Aero) Turbo Commander 690B	11376	N81567	0077		2 GA TPE331-5-251K	4683			

TRANSBRASIL = TR / TBA (Transbrasil, SA Linhas Aéreas dba / formerly Sadia, SA)
Sao Paulo-Congonhas, (SP) & Brasilia, (DF)

Rua General Pantaleao Telles 40, (Parque Jabaquara), CEP-04355-040 Sao Paulo (SP), Brazil ☎ (11) 532 46 00 Tx: 1153708 tsbr br Fax: (11) 533 49 83 SITA: n/a
F: 1955 5290 Head: Dr. Antonio Celso Cipriani IATA: 653 ICAO: TRANSBRASIL Net: http://www.transbrasil.com.br

☐ PT-TEF	Boeing 737-3Q4	24208 / 1490		1287	0188	2 CFMI CFM56-3B2	61235	Y132	FG-HM	lsf ILFC
☐ PT-TEG	Boeing 737-3Q4	24209 / 1492		1287	0188	2 CFMI CFM56-3B2	61235	Y132	FG-JL	Brigadeiro Eduardo Gomes / lsf ILFC
☐ PT-TEH	Boeing 737-3Q4	24210 / 1577		0788	0788	2 CFMI CFM56-3B2	61235	Y132	FG-LM	lsf ACG Institutional Investors
☐ PT-TEI	Boeing 737-3Y0	23812 / 1511		0288	0388	2 CFMI CFM56-3B1	61235	Y135	FG-DM	lsf CITG
☐ PT-TEP	Boeing 737-36N	28564 / 2936		0097	1197	2 CFMI CFM56-3C1	61235	Y148		lsf GECA
☐ PT-TEQ	Boeing 737-33A	25057 / 2046	PP-SOK	0591	1292	2 CFMI CFM56-3C1	61235	Y132	FJ-AD	lsf AWAS
☐ PT-TER	Boeing 737-33A	25119 / 2069	PP-SOL	0691	1292	2 CFMI CFM56-3C1	61235	Y132	FJ-AK	lsf AWAS
☐ PT-TDE	Boeing 737-4Y0	24545 / 1805	G-OABE	0090	1198	2 CFMI CFM56-3C1	65770	Y158		lsf FUA in winter
☐ PT-TDF	Boeing 737-4Y0	24682 / 1824	N682GE	0090	1198	2 CFMI CFM56-3C1	65770	Y158		lsf GECA
☐ PT-TDG	Boeing 737-4Y0	25180 / 2201	EC-GOB	0092	1298	2 CFMI CFM56-3C1	65770	Y158		lsf FUA
☐ PT-TEL	Boeing 737-4Y0	24467 / 1733		0689	0689	2 CFMI CFM56-3C1	64636	Y158	KL-BF	lsf GECA
☐ PT-TEM	Boeing 737-4Y0	24511 / 1759		0789	0889	2 CFMI CFM56-3C1	64636	Y158	KL-BG	lsf GECA
☐ PT-TEN	Boeing 737-4Y0	24513 / 1779		0989	1089	2 CFMI CFM56-3C1	64636	Y158	KL-BH	lsf GECA
☐ PT-TEO	Boeing 737-4Y0	24692 / 1963	EI-CBT	1290	0191	2 CFMI CFM56-3C1	68038	Y158	KL-BE	lsf GECA
☐ PT-TAA	Boeing 767-2Q4	22921 / 55	N4574M*	0683	0683	2 GE CF6-80A	136078	C24Y186	JK-BQ	
☐ PT-TAB	Boeing 767-2Q4	22922 / 57	N45742*	0783	0783	2 GE CF6-80A	136078	C24Y186	JK-BR	
☐ PT-TAC	Boeing 767-2Q4	22923 / 59	N4575L*	0783	0783	2 GE CF6-80A	136078	C24Y186	JK-BS	
☐ PT-TAG	Boeing 767-219 (ER)	24150 / 239	ZK-NBE	0088	0593	2 GE CF6-80A2	159211	F15C36Y132	JK-CR	lsf ILFC
☐ PT-TAH	Boeing 767-216 (ER)	23624 / 144	CC-CJV	0086	0295	2 GE CF6-80A2	159211	F16C24Y153	KR-BQ	lsf ILFC
☐ PT-TAI	Boeing 767-283 (ER)	24727 / 301	SE-DKP	0690	0993	2 PW PW4056	175540	F15C32Y127	JK-CS	lsf SAS -0699
☐ PT-TAJ	Boeing 767-283 (ER)	24728 / 305	LN-RCC	0090	0993	2 PW PW4056	175540	F15C32Y127	JK-DQ	lsf PLMI
☐ PT-TAK	Boeing 767-2B1 (ER)	25421 / 407	EI-CEM	0092	1095	2 PW PW4056	175540	F15C22Y154	JK-DR	lsf GECA
☐ PT-TAE	Boeing 767-3Y0 (ER)	24948 / 380	N6005C*	0391	0891	2 PW PW4060	184612	F15C26Y167	JK-CQ	lsf GECA
☐ PT-TAL	Boeing 767-3P6 (ER)	23764 / 158	A4O-GF	0086	1294	2 GE CF6-80C2B4	175540	F15C18Y189	JK-DS	lsf PEGA / cvtd -3T8 (ER)
☐ PT-TAM	Boeing 767-3P6 (ER)	24349 / 244	A4O-GG	1188	0295	2 GE CF6-80C2B4	175540	F15C18Y179	JK-EQ	lsf PEGA

TRANSPORTES CHARTER DO BRASIL, Ltda - TCB = TCJ
Sao Paulo-Viracopos (SP)

Aeroporto Internacional Viracopos, CEP-13051-970 Sao Paulo, (Sao Paulo), Brazil ☎ (192) 45 59 35 Tx: none Fax: (192) 45 59 35 SITA: n/a
F: 1994 n/a Head: n/a ICAO: CHARTER BRASIL Net: n/a

☐ PP-TNZ	Boeing (Douglas) DC-8-54F (FM)	45768 / 240	HK-2632X	0065	0298	4 PW JT3D-3B (HK2/QNC)	142882	Freighter		lsf Air Transport Corp. / cvtd -53
☐ PP-TPC	Boeing (Douglas) DC-8-52F	45752 / 233	N42920	0065	0197	4 PW JT3D-3B (HK2/QNC)	136078	Freighter		Daniel / lsf FB Air Inc. / cvtd DC-8-52

TRANSUL Taxi Aéreo, Ltda
Porto Alegre, (RS)

Aeroporto Salgado Filho sn, Caixa Postal 8004, CEP-90201 Porto Alegre, (Rio Grande do Sul), Brazil ☎ (51) 341 07 76 Tx: none Fax: (51) 342 42 11 SITA: n/a
F: 1974 10 Head: Darci Canazaro Net: n/a

☐ PT-DHD	Piper PA-24-260 Comanche B	24-4753		0068		1 LY IO-540-D4A5	1406			
☐ PT-IBW	Piper PA-34-200 Seneca	34-7250069		0072		2 LY IO-360-C1E6	1814			

TTA - Teresina Taxi Aéreo, Ltda
Teresina, (PI)

Rua Coelho Rodrigues 1274, CEP-64000-080 Teresina, (Piaui), Brazil ☎ (86) 223 42 81 Tx: none Fax: n/a SITA: n/a
F: 1993 n/a Head: n/a Net: n/a

☐ PT-RSI	Embraer 810D Seneca III (EMB-810D)	810475		0083		2 CO TSIO-360-KB	2155			
☐ PT-OOL	Cessna 500 Citation	500-0060	N712G	0073		2 PWC JT15D-1	5216			

UNEX AIRLINES = UNX (Universal Express Linhas Aéreas, Ltda dba)
Sao Paulo-Congonhas

Avda Indianapolis 2504, Planalto Paulista, CEP-04062-002 Sao Paulo, (Sao Paulo), Brazil ☎ (11) 55 83 28 28 Tx: none Fax: (11) 276 00 12 SITA: n/a
F: 1997 n/a Head: José Manoel de Lima ICAO: UNEX Net: n/a

☐ PT-MFF	ATR 42-300	384	F-WWEG*	0094	0997	2 PWC PW120	16700	Y48		lsf Regional Aircraft Leasing Ltd II
☐ PT-MFG	ATR 42-300	388	F-WWLA*	0095	0997	2 PWC PW120	16700	Y48		lsf Regional Aircraft Leasing Ltd II

UNIAIR Taxi Aéreo, Ltda
Vitória, (ES)

Av. F. Ferrari sn, Aeroporto de Vitoria, CEP-29075-052 Vitoria, (Espirito Santo), Brazil ☎ (27) 327 02 44 Tx: none Fax: (27) 327 02 38 SITA: n/a
F: 1986 7 Head: Jair Coser Net: n/a

☐ PT-VRD	Embraer 810D Cuesta (EMB-810D)	810822		0093	0098	2 CO TSIO-360-KB	2155			
☐ PT-LJS	Mitsubishi MU-2B-60 Marquise	1568SA	N501MA	0085		2 GA TPE331-10-501M	5250			lsf Itauleasing

UNIMED AIR (Flamingo Unimed Air Taxi Aéreo, Ltda dba / formerly Taxi Aéreo Flamingo, S.A.)
Sao Paulo-Congonhas, (SP)

Av. Jurandir, sn, Hangar Flamingo, CEP-04072-000 Sao Paulo (SP), (Sao Paulo), Brazil ☎ (11) 55 81 44 84 Tx: none Fax: (11) 55 81 53 36 SITA: n/a
F: 1968 48 Head: Plinio de Macedo Vieira Net: http://www.unimedair.com.br

☐ PT-OPK	Beech Bonanza F33A	CE-1653		0092		1 CO IO-520-BB	1542			
☐ PT-WKF	Pilatus PC-12	141	N141BL	0096	0796	1 PWC PT6A-67B	4500	EMS		lsf BB Leasing Co. Ltd
☐ PT-YBG	Sikorsky S-76A	760288	N770AM	0085	0396	2 AN 250-C30S	4763	EMS		lsf ITC Aerospace Inc.

UNIVERSAL Taxi Aéreo, Ltda
Cuiaba, (MT)

Aeroporto Marechal Rondon, Box Universal, CEP-78110-971 Varzea Grande, (Mato Grosso), Brazil ☎ (65) 381 23 52 Tx: n/a Fax: n/a SITA: n/a
F: 1988 n/a Head: n/a Net: n/a

☐ PT-VAE	Embraer 810D Seneca III (EMB-810D)	810586		0086	0097	2 CO TSIO-360-KB	2155			

UPPERFLY Aerotaxi, Ltda
Sao Paulo-Marte, (SP)

Rua Bage 20/113, Vila Mariana, CEP-04012-140 Sao Paulo, (Sao Paulo), Brazil ☎ (11) 221 11 44 Tx: n/a Fax: (11) 221 11 44 SITA: n/a
F: 1994 n/a Head: n/a Net: n/a Aircraft below MTOW 1361kg: Robinson R22

☐ PT-HQD	Bell 206B JetRanger II	2111	N23SC	0076		1 AN 250-C20	1451			

VARIG Brasil = RG / VRG (Varig, Viaçao Aérea Rio-Grandense, SA dba / Member of Star Alliance)
Rio de Janeiro, (RJ)

Av. Almirante Silvio de Noronha 365, CEP-20021-010 Rio de Janeiro, (Rio de Janeiro), Brazil ☎ (21) 814 50 00 Tx: 2122363 vrigc br Fax: (21) 814 57 00 SITA: n/a
F: 1927 18200 Head: Fernando Abs da Cruz de Souza Pinto IATA: 042 ICAO: VARIG Net: http://www.varig.com.br

☐ PP-CJN	Boeing 737-2C3 (A)	21012 / 392		0074	0193	2 PW JT8D-17A	52390	Y109	AB-KL	lsf PLMI
☐ PP-CJP	Boeing 737-2C3 (A)	21014 / 397		0075	0193	2 PW JT8D-17A	52390	Y109	AB-KM	
☐ PP-CJR	Boeing 737-2C3 (A)	21015 / 404		0075	0193	2 PW JT8D-17A	52390	Y109	AC-BD	
☐ PP-CJS	Boeing 737-2C3 (A)	21016 / 406		0075	0193	2 PW JT8D-17A	52390	Y109	AC-BE	
☐ PP-CJT	Boeing 737-2C3 (A)	21017 / 410		0075	0193	2 PW JT8D-17A	52390	Y109	AC-BH	lsf PLMI
☐ PP-VME	Boeing 737-241 (A)	21000 / 378		0074	1074	2 PW JT8D-17A	52390	Y109	HL-DE	lsf PLMI
☐ PP-VMF	Boeing 737-241 (A)	21001 / 384		0074	1174	2 PW JT8D-17A	52390	Y109	HL-DF	
☐ PP-VMG	Boeing 737-241 (A)	21002 / 385		0074	1174	2 PW JT8D-17A	52390	Y109	HL-DJ	lsf PLMI
☐ PP-VMH	Boeing 737-241 (A)	21003 / 389		0074	1274	2 PW JT8D-17A	52390	Y109	HL-DK	lsf PLMI
☐ PP-VMI	Boeing 737-241 (A)	21004 / 390		0074	0175	2 PW JT8D-17A	52390	Y109	HL-DM	lst PUA
☐ PP-VMJ	Boeing 737-241 (A)	21005 / 394		0075	0175	2 PW JT8D-17A	52390	Y109	HL-EF	lsf PLMI
☐ PP-VML	Boeing 737-241 (A)	21007 / 400		0075	0375	2 PW JT8D-17A	52390	Y109	HL-EJ	lsf PLMI
☐ PP-VMM	Boeing 737-241 (A)	21008 / 402		0075	0375	2 PW JT8D-17A	52390	Y109	HL-EK	lsf PLMI

513 registration type of aircraft cn/fn ex/ex* mfd del powered by mtow kg configuration selcal name/fln/specialitites/remarks

registration	type of aircraft	cn/fn	ex/ex*	mfd	del	powered by	mtow kg	configuration	selcal	name/fln/specialitites/remarks
□ PP-VMN	Boeing 737-241 (A)	21009 / 417		0075	0675	2 PW JT8D-17A	52390	Y109	HL-CM	lsf PLMI
□ PP-VNF	Boeing 737-2K9 (A)	22504 / 804	N4529W*	0081	0582	2 PW JT8D-17A	52390	Y109	DG-JM	lsf PLMI
□ PP-VNG	Boeing 737-2K9 (A)	22505 / 815	N4530W*	0081	0582	2 PW JT8D-17A	55311	Y109	FJ-BD	
□ PP-VPD	Boeing 737-2Q8 (A)	21518 / 522	ZP-CAC	0078	1196	2 PW JT8D-17	52390	Y109	ER-DP	lsf INGO / sub-lst PUA CX-FAT
□ PP-VPE	Boeing 737-219 (A)	21130 / 426	HC-BTI	0075	0297	2 PW JT8D-17	52390	Y109	CL-BD	lsf INGO
□ PP-VNT	Boeing 737-33A	23828 / 1446		0087	1187	2 CFMI CFM56-3B2	61235	Y132	AF-HK	lsf AWAS
□ PP-VNU	Boeing 737-3K9	23797 / 1416		0087	0987	2 CFMI CFM56-3B2	61235	Y132	FJ-CM	lsf BAVA
□ PP-VNV	Boeing 737-3K9	23798 / 1429		0087	0987	2 CFMI CFM56-3B2	61235	Y132	FJ-DE	lsf BAVA
□ PP-VNX	Boeing 737-33A	23829 / 1460		0087	1187	2 CFMI CFM56-3B2	61235	Y132	AF-HL	lsf AWAS
□ PP-VNY	Boeing 737-3K9	24864 / 1918		0090	0990	2 CFMI CFM56-3B2	61235	Y132	CD-HL	lsf BAVA
□ PP-VNZ	Boeing 737-3K9	24869 / 1926		0090	1090	2 CFMI CFM56-3B2	61235	Y132	CD-HM	lsf BAVA
□ PP-VOD	Boeing 737-341	24275 / 1637		0088	1188	2 CFMI CFM56-3B2	61235	Y132	CD-FG	lsf GATX
□ PP-VOE	Boeing 737-341	24276 / 1645		0088	1288	2 CFMI CFM56-3B2	61235	Y132	CD-FJ	lsf GATX
□ PP-VOF	Boeing 737-341	24277 / 1658		0088	0189	2 CFMI CFM56-3B2	61235	Y132	CD-GH	lsf GATX
□ PP-VOG	Boeing 737-341	24278 / 1660		0088	0189	2 CFMI CFM56-3B2	61235	Y132	CD-GJ	lsf GATX
□ PP-VOH	Boeing 737-341	24279 / 1673		0089	0289	2 CFMI CFM56-3B2	61235	Y132	CD-GL	lsf GATX
□ PP-VON	Boeing 737-341	24935 / 1935		0090	1190	2 CFMI CFM56-3B2	61235	Y132	FJ-BK	lsf Mitsui
□ PP-VOO	Boeing 737-341	24936 / 1951		0090	1190	2 CFMI CFM56-3B2	61235	Y132	FJ-BM	lsf Mitsui
□ PP-VOR	Boeing 737-33A	24093 / 1727	G-PATE	0089	0590	2 CFMI CFM56-3B2	61235	Y132	AB-DF	lsf AWAS
□ PP-VOS	Boeing 737-341	25048 / 2085		0091	0791	2 CFMI CFM56-3B2	61235	Y132	AD-FH	lsf ORIX
□ PP-VOT	Boeing 737-341	25049 / 2091		0091	0791	2 CFMI CFM56-3B2	61235	Y132	AD-GL	lsf SL VRG Ltd
□ PP-VOU	Boeing 737-341	25050 / 2125		0091	1291	2 CFMI CFM56-3B2	61235	Y132	AD-GM	lsf Wilmington Trust Co.
□ PP-VOV	Boeing 737-341	25051 / 2127		0091	1291	2 CFMI CFM56-3B2	61235	Y132	CL-AF	lsf Wilmington Trust Co.
□ PP-VOW	Boeing 737-3Q8	24961 / 2133		0091	1091	2 CFMI CFM56-3B2	61235	Y132	AS-LQ	lsf ILFC
□ PP-VOY	Boeing 737-3K9	25210 / 2090		0091	0791	2 CFMI CFM56-3B2	61235	Y132	BF-RS	lsf BAVA
□ PP-VOZ	Boeing 737-3K9	25239 / 2100		0091	0891	2 CFMI CFM56-3B2	61235	Y132	BG-AR	lsf BAVA / World Championship-colors
□ PP-VPA	Boeing 737-341	26852 / 2273		0092	0592	2 CFMI CFM56-3B2	61235	Y132	CL-AH	lsf CITG
□ PP-VPB	Boeing 737-341	26856 / 2321		0092	0792	2 CFMI CFM56-3B2	61235	Y132	CL-AJ	lsf BAVA
□ PP-VPC	Boeing 737-341	26857 / 2326		0092	0792	2 CFMI CFM56-3B2	61235	F12Y108	CL-AK	lsf BAVA
□ PP-VPF	Boeing 737-3S1	24834 / 1896	N371TA	0790	0897	2 CFMI CFM56-3B2	62142	Y136	RS-FP	lsf TAI
□ PP-VPQ	Boeing 737-36Q	28664 / 2940	N1786B*	0097	1097	2 CFMI CFM56-3C1	61235	Y132	RS-AL	lsf BOUL
□ PP-VPR	Boeing 737-36Q	28761 / 3011		0098	0398	2 CFMI CFM56-3C1	61235	Y132	AB-KM	lsf BOUL
□ PP-VPS	Boeing 737-36N	28671 / 2955		0097	1197	2 CFMI CFM56-3C1	61235	Y132	AM-PR	lsf GECA
□ PP-VPT	Boeing 737-36N	28566 / 2964		0097	1297	2 CFMI CFM56-3C1	61235	Y132	AM-PS	lsf GECA
□ PP-VPU	Boeing 737-36N	28567 / 2971		0097	1297	2 CFMI CFM56-3C1	61235	Y132	AE-CP	lsf GECA
□ PP-VPX	Boeing 737-33R	28870 / 2899	N965WP	0697	0598	2 CFMI CFM56-3C1	62823	Y132		lsf GATX
□ PP-VPY	Boeing 737-33R	28871 / 2900	N966WP	0097	0598	2 CFMI CFM56-3C1	62823	Y132		lsf SUNR
□ PP-VPZ	Boeing 737-3S3	29245 / 3061		0098	0998	2 CFMI CFM56-3C1	62823	Y132		lsf SUNR
□ PP-VQA	Boeing 737-76N	28580 / 135	N1003N*	0098	1198	2 CFMI CFM56-7B24	69400	Y132		lsf GECA
□ PP-VQB	Boeing 737-76N	28582 / 154		0098	1298	2 CFMI CFM56-7B24	69400	Y132		lsf GECA
□ PP-VQC	Boeing 737-76N	28583	N1786B*	0098	1298	2 CFMI CFM56-7B24	69400	Y132		lsf GECA
□ PP-VQD	Boeing 737-76N	28584 / 170	N5573L*	1298	1298	2 CFMI CFM56-7B24	69400	Y132		lsf GECA
□ PP-VQE	Boeing 737-76N	28585 / 173	N1780B*	0199	0199	2 CFMI CFM56-7B24	69400	Y132		lsf GECA
□ PP-	Boeing 737-741					2 CFMI CFM56-7B24	69400	Y132		oo-delivery 0300
□ PP-	Boeing 737-741					2 CFMI CFM56-7B24	69400	Y132		oo-delivery 0600
□ PP-	Boeing 737-741					2 CFMI CFM56-7B24	69400	Y132		oo-delivery 1000
□ PP-	Boeing 737-741					2 CFMI CFM56-7B24	69400	Y132		oo-delivery 0201
□ PP-VLD	Boeing 727-41 (F)	20425 / 824		0070	1070	3 PW JT8D-9A	76884	Freighter	HM-BK	cvtd -41
□ PP-VLE	Boeing 727-172C	19666 / 480	N726AL	0067	0473	3 PW JT8D-9A	76884	Freighter	JL-FK	
□ PP-VLG	Boeing 727-41 (F)	20423 / 810		0070	1070	3 PW JT8D-9A	76884	Freighter	FH-CD	cvtd -41
□ PP-VLS	Boeing 727-173C	19508 / 457	N694WA	0067	0174	3 PW JT8D-9A	76884	Freighter	HL-FM	
□ PP-VLV	Boeing 727-30C	19009 / 374	N705EV	0067	1279	3 PW JT8D-7B	76884	Freighter	JL-CD	
□ PP-	Boeing 737-841					2 CFMI CFM56-7B26	78245			oo-delivery 0300
□ PP-	Boeing 737-841					2 CFMI CFM56-7B26	78245			oo-delivery 0600
□ PP-	Boeing 737-841					2 CFMI CFM56-7B26	78245			oo-delivery 0201
□ PP-	Boeing 737-841					2 CFMI CFM56-7B26	78245			oo-delivery 1001
□ PP-	Boeing 737-841					2 CFMI CFM56-7B26	78245			oo-delivery 0002
□ PP-	Boeing 737-841					2 CFMI CFM56-7B26	78245			oo-delivery 0003
□ PP-	Boeing 737-841					2 CFMI CFM56-7B26	78245			oo-delivery 0003
□ PP-	Boeing 737-841					2 CFMI CFM56-7B26	78245			oo-delivery 0004
□ PP-	Boeing 737-841					2 CFMI CFM56-7B26	78245			oo-delivery 0005
□ PP-	Boeing 737-841					2 CFMI CFM56-7B26	78245			oo-delivery 0005
□ PP-VNN	Boeing 767-241 (ER)	23803 / 161	N60668*	0087	0787	2 GE CF6-80C2B2	159210	C18Y176	AP-JK	lsf WTC Trustee
□ PP-VNO	Boeing 767-241 (ER)	23801 / 170	N6009F*	0087	0787	2 GE CF6-80C2B2	159210	C18Y176	AP-JL	lsf WTC Trustee
□ PP-VNP	Boeing 767-241 (ER)	23802 / 172	N6018N*	0087	0787	2 GE CF6-80C2B2	159210	C18Y176	AP-JM	lsf WTC Trustee
□ PP-VNQ	Boeing 767-241 (ER)	23804 / 178	N6009F*	0087	0787	2 GE CF6-80C2B2	159210	C18Y176	AP-KL	lsf GECA
□ PP-VNR	Boeing 767-241 (ER)	23805 / 180	N6005C*	0087	0787	2 GE CF6-80C2B2	159210	C18Y176	AP-KM	lsf GECA
□ PP-VNS	Boeing 767-241 (ER)	23806 / 181	N6018N*	0087	0887	2 GE CF6-80C2B2	159210	C18Y176	AP-LM	lsf GECA
□ PP-VOI	Boeing 767-341 (ER)	24752 / 289		0089	1289	2 GE CF6-80C2B6	181436	F10C18Y185	FQ-EM	lsf Nissho Iwai Corp.
□ PP-VOJ	Boeing 767-341 (ER)	24753 / 291		0090	0290	2 GE CF6-80C2B6	181436	F10C18Y185	FQ-EP	lsf Nissho Iwai Corp.
□ PP-VOK	Boeing 767-341 (ER)	24843 / 314		0090	0690	2 GE CF6-80C2B6	181436	F10C18Y185	FQ-GH	lsf ITOH
□ PP-VOL	Boeing 767-341 (ER)	24844 / 324		0090	0890	2 GE CF6-80C2B6	181436	F10C18Y185	FQ-GJ	lsf ITOH
□ PP-VPV	Boeing 767-375 (ER)	24086 / 248	C-FCAJ	0089	1297	2 GE CF6-80C2B6F	184612	F10C18Y185	BL-PR	lsf SUNR
□ PP-VPW	Boeing 767-375 (ER)	24087 / 249	C-FCAU	0089	1197	2 GE CF6-80C2B6F	184612	F10C18Y185	BL-PS	lsf CITG
□ PP-	Boeing 767-341 (ER)					2 GE CF6-80C2B7F	186882	F10C18Y185		oo-delivery 0699
□ PP-	Boeing 767-341 (ER)					2 GE CF6-80C2B7F	186882	F10C18Y185		oo-delivery 0999
□ PP-	Boeing 767-341 (ER)					2 GE CF6-80C2B7F	186882	F10C18Y185		oo-delivery 0500
□ PP-	Boeing 767-341 (ER)					2 GE CF6-80C2B7F	186882	F10C18Y185		oo-delivery 0101
□ PP-	Boeing 767-341 (ER)					2 GE CF6-80C2B7F	186882	F10C18Y185		oo-delivery 0801
□ PP-	Boeing 767-341 (ER)					2 GE CF6-80C2B7F	186882	F10C18Y185		oo-delivery 0002
□ PP-	Boeing 777-241 (ER)					2 GE GE90-92B	297562			to be lsf ILFC 0300
□ PP-	Boeing 777-241 (ER)					2 GE GE90-92B	297562			to be lsf ILFC 0400
□ PP-	Boeing 777-241 (ER)					2 GE GE90-92B	297562			oo-delivery 0301
□ PP-	Boeing 777-241 (ER)					2 GE GE90-92B	297562			oo-delivery 0601
□ PP-	Boeing 777-241 (ER)					2 GE GE90-92B	297562			oo-delivery 1001
□ PP-	Boeing 777-241 (ER)					2 GE GE90-92B	297562			oo-delivery 0002
□ PP-VMA	Boeing (Douglas) DC-10-30	46944 / 133		0074	0574	3 GE CF6-50C2	256280	F12C49Y181	CD-HK	lsf Global Aircraft Leasing/sub-lst AVE
□ PP-VMB	Boeing (Douglas) DC-10-30	46945 / 156		0074	0674	3 GE CF6-50C2	256280	F12C49Y181	EF-CK	lsf PEGA / sub-lst AVE as YV-50C
□ PP-VMQ	Boeing (Douglas) DC-10-30	46941 / 176		0074	1174	3 GE CF6-50C2	256280	F12C49Y181	BL-FJ	lsf Aircraft 46941 Inc.
□ PP-VMT	Boeing (Douglas) DC-10-30F	47841 / 329		0080	0780	3 GE CF6-50C2	263084	Freighter	GM-AB	lsf GECA / cvtd -30
□ PP-VMU	Boeing (Douglas) DC-10-30F	47842 / 332		0080	0980	3 GE CF6-50C2	263084	Freighter	GM-AC	lsf GECA / cvtd -30
□ PP-VMV	Boeing (Douglas) DC-10-30	47843 / 335		0080	1080	3 GE CF6-50C2	263084	F12C49Y181	GM-AD	lsf Mitsui -0699 / for SKJ
□ PP-VMX	Boeing (Douglas) DC-10-30	47845 / 356		0081	0681	3 GE CF6-50C2	263084	F12C49Y181	GM-AF	
□ PP-VMY	Boeing (Douglas) DC-10-30	48282 / 355		0081	0481	3 GE CF6-50C2	263084	F12C49Y181	CM-BD	
□ PP-VOP	Boeing (Douglas) MD-11	48434 / 476		0091	1191	3 GE CF6-80C2D1F	280320	F12C49Y221	AM-FP	lsf GECA
□ PP-VOQ	Boeing (Douglas) MD-11	48435 / 478		0091	1291	3 GE CF6-80C2D1F	280320	F12C49Y221	AM-GP	lsf GECA
□ PP-VPJ	Boeing (Douglas) MD-11	48404 / 523		0092	1292	3 GE CF6-80C2D1F	280320	F12C49Y221	CR-FH	lsf Compass Rose Leasing Ltd
□ PP-VPK	Boeing (Douglas) MD-11	48405 / 524		0092	1292	3 GE CF6-80C2D1F	280320	F12C49Y221	CR-FJ	lsf Compass Rose Leasing Ltd
□ PP-VPL	Boeing (Douglas) MD-11	48406 / 547	N9166X*	0093	1293	3 GE CF6-80C2D1F	280320	F12C49Y221	CR-FK	lsf Compass Rose Leasing Ltd
□ PP-VPM	Boeing (Douglas) MD-11	48439 / 554		0093	1293	3 GE CF6-80C2D1F	280320	F12C49Y221	CR-FL	lsf Compass Rose Leasing Ltd
□ PP-VPN	Boeing (Douglas) MD-11	48499 / 486	EI-CDI	0091	1296	3 GE CF6-80C2D1F	280320	F12C49Y221	GS-MR	lsf GECA
□ PP-VPO	Boeing (Douglas) MD-11	48500 / 493	EI-CDJ	0092	0497	3 GE CF6-80C2D1F	280320	F12C49Y221	AS-ER	lsf GECA
□ PP-VPP	Boeing (Douglas) MD-11	48501 / 513	EI-CDK	0092	0997	3 GE CF6-80C2D1F	280320	F12C49Y221	CE-MP	lsf GECA
□ PP-VQF	Boeing (Douglas) MD-11	48502 / 520	N540MD	0093	0199	3 GE CF6-80C2D1F	280320	F12C49Y221		lsf Boeing Capital Corp.
□ PP-VQG	Boeing (Douglas) MD-11	48503 / 528	N538MD	0093	1198	3 GE CF6-80C2D1F	280320	F12C49Y221		lsf Boeing Capital Corp.
□ PP-VQH	Boeing (Douglas) MD-11	48504 / 548	N539MD	0093	1298	3 GE CF6-80C2D1F	280320	F12C49Y221		lsf Boeing Capital Corp.
□ PP-VQI	Boeing (Douglas) MD-11	48753 / 608	PK-GIK	0096	0998	3 GE CF6-80C2D1F	285990	F12C49Y221		lsf Boeing Capital Corp.
□ PP-VNH	Boeing 747-341 (M)	23394 / 627	N6005C*	0085	1285	4 GE CF6-50E2	377842	F16Y65Y184 / Plt	JL-EM	lsf Nissho Iwai Corp.
□ PP-VNI	Boeing 747-341 (M)	23395 / 629	N6009F*	0085	1285	4 GE CF6-50E2	377842	F16C65Y184 / Plt	JM-AD	lsf Nissho Iwai Corp.
□ PP-VOA	Boeing 747-341	24106 / 701	N6046P*	0088	0488	4 GE CF6-80C2B1	377842	F16C65Y318	AH-BJ	lsf ILFC
□ PP-VOB	Boeing 747-341	24107 / 702	N6018N*	0088	0588	4 GE CF6-80C2B1	377842	F16C65Y318	AH-BK	lsf ILFC
□ PP-VOC	Boeing 747-341	24108 / 703	N6005C*	0088	0588	4 GE CF6-80C2B1	377842	F16C65Y318	AH-BL	lsf ILFC

VASP = VP / VSP (Vaspex) (Viação Aérea Sao Paulo, S.A. dba)   Sao Paulo-Congonhas, (SP)
Pça. Cte. Lineu Gomes sn, Ed. Sede VASP, Aeroporto de Congonhas, CEP-04626-910 Sao Paulo (Sao Paulo), Brazil   ☎ (11) 532 30 00   Tx: 1156575 br   Fax: (11) 542 08 80   SITA: n/a
F: 1933   ✦✦✦ 7160   Head: Wagner Canhedo Azevedo   IATA: 343   ICAO: VASP   Net: http://www.vasp.com.br
VASPEX is the marketing name used by the CARGO-division (same headquarters) and is painted as such on the Freighter-aircraft.

□ PP-SFI	Boeing 737-2Q3 (A)	21478 / 591	JA8445	0079	0798	2 PW JT8D-17	52390	Y112		lsf BAVA
□ PP-SMA	Boeing 737-2A1	20092 / 161		0469	0769	2 PW JT8D-17	52390	Y112	AE-CM	
□ PP-SMB	Boeing 737-2A1 (F)	20093 / 169		0569	0769	2 PW JT8D-17	52390	Freighter	AE-DK	cvtd -2A1 / Vaspex-colors

registration	type of aircraft	cn/fn	ex/ex*	mfd	del	powered by	mtow kg	configuration	selcal	name/fln/specialitites/remarks
☐ PP-SMC	Boeing 737-2A1	20094 / 182		0769	0769	2 PW JT8D-17	52390	Y112	AE-DL	
☐ PP-SMF	Boeing 737-2A1 (A)	20589 / 301		0672	0772	2 PW JT8D-17	52390	Y112	AE-DF	
☐ PP-SMG	Boeing 737-2A1 (A)	20777 / 324		0773	0773	2 PW JT8D-17	52390	Y112	AE-DG	
☐ PP-SMH	Boeing 737-2A1 (A)	20778 / 325		0873	0873	2 PW JT8D-17	52390	Y112	AE-DH	
☐ PP-SMP	Boeing 737-2A1 (A)	20779 / 327		0973	0973	2 PW JT8D-17	52390	Y112	AE-DJ	
☐ PP-SMQ	Boeing 737-214	20155 / 180	N382PS	0669	0574	2 PW JT8D-17	52390	Y112	BD-CJ	Isf Rural Leasing SA
☐ PP-SMR	Boeing 737-214	20157 / 189	N984PS	0769	0574	2 PW JT8D-17	52390	Y112	BD-CL	
☐ PP-SMS	Boeing 737-214	20159 / 193	N986PS	0769	0574	2 PW JT8D-17	52390	Y112	BD-EF	
☐ PP-SMT	Boeing 737-214	20160 / 195	N987PS	0869	0574	2 PW JT8D-17	52390	Y112	BD-EG	
☐ PP-SMU	Boeing 737-2A1 (A)	20967 / 364	N1799B*	0974	0974	2 PW JT8D-17	52390	Y112	AE-CF	
☐ PP-SMV	Boeing 737-2A1 (A)	20968 / 367		0874	0874	2 PW JT8D-17	52390	Y112	AE-CG	std GRU
☐ PP-SMW	Boeing 737-2H4C	20346 / 258	N23SW	1170	0874	2 PW JT8D-17	52390	Freighter	BM-EL	Vaspex-colors
☐ PP-SMZ	Boeing 737-2A1 (A)	20971 / 382		1174	1174	2 PW JT8D-17	52390	Y112	AE-CK	
☐ PP-SNA	Boeing 737-2A1 (A)	21094 / 412		0875	0875	2 PW JT8D-17	54204	Y112	BM-EG	
☐ PP-SNB	Boeing 737-2A1 (A)	21095 / 432		0875	0875	2 PW JT8D-17	52390	Y112	BM-EH	
☐ PP-SPF	Boeing 737-2L7C (A)	21073 / 419	C2-RN3	0075	0595	2 PW JT8D-17	52390	Y112	AF-BC	
☐ PP-SPG	Boeing 737-2L7 (A)	21616 / 533	C2-RN6	0078	0894	2 PW JT8D-17	52390	Y112	AF-BL	
☐ PP-SPH	Boeing 737-2L9 (A)	22070 / 614	C2-RN8	0079	0894	2 PW JT8D-17	52390	Y112	GJ-FL	
☐ PP-SPI	Boeing 737-2Q3 (A)	21476 / 519	JA8443	0078	0595	2 PW JT8D-17	52390	Y112	AH-FJ	
☐ PP-SPJ	Boeing 737-2M9 (A)	21236 / 461	9J-AEG	0076	0795	2 PW JT8D-17	52390	Y112	BF-GM	
☐ PP-SFJ	Boeing 737-3K9	24212 / 1633	N945WP	0088	0598	2 CFMI CFM56-3B2	62823	Y132		Isf BAVA
☐ PP-SFK	Boeing 737-33R	28868 / 2881	N963WP	0097	0398	2 CFMI CFM56-3C1	62823	Y132		Isf ILFC
☐ PP-SFL	Boeing 737-3S3	23787 / 1374	N375TA	0487	0498	2 CFMI CFM56-3B2	62142	Y132		Isf KG Leasing
☐ PP-SFM	Boeing 737-3Q8	24299 / 1598	N956WP	0088	0498	2 CFMI CFM56-3B2	62823	Y132		Isf ILFC
☐ PP-SFN	Boeing 737-3L9	27925 / 2763	OY-MAU	0095	0798	2 CFMI CFM56-3C1	63276	Y132		Isf Vitoria Regia Leasing Ltd
☐ PP-SOT	Boeing 737-3L9	25150 / 2074	OY-MMY	0691	0891	2 CFMI CFM56-3B2	63276	Y132	CD-GK	
☐ PP-SOU	Boeing 737-3L9	25360 / 2140	OY-MMZ	0891	1091	2 CFMI CFM56-3B2	61235	Y132	AH-EJ	
☐ PP-SFC	Boeing 727-264 (F) (A)	21071 / 1143	N171G	0075	1096	3 PW JT8D-17R	78015	Freighter	LM-EG	cvtd -264 / Vaspex-colors
☐ PP-SFE	Boeing 727-243 (F) (A)	22166 / 1725	N58414	0081	1296	3 PW JT8D-9A	78015	Freighter	CG-DL	Isf PACA / cvtd -243 / Vaspex-colors
☐ PP-SFF	Boeing 727-2J7 (F) (A)	20880 / 1037	N129NA	0474	0697	3 PW JT8D-15	78015	Freighter		Isf PACA / cvtd -2J7 / Vaspex-colors
☐ PP-SFG	Boeing 727-2Q4 (F) (A)	22425 / 1698	N63063	0080	0997	3 PW JT8D-17R	78015	Freighter		cvtd -2Q4 / Vaspex-colors
☐ PP-SFQ	Boeing 727-2J4 (F) (A)	22079 / 1588	CP-2294	0080	1298	3 PW JT8D-17	92124	Freighter		cvtd -2J4 / Vaspex-colors
☐ PP-SFH	Airbus Industrie A310-304	552	F-GKTD	0090	1097	2 GE CF6-80C2A2	157000		LQ-CJ	Isf Air Invest VII / sub-Isf EEA
☐ PP-SNL	Airbus Industrie A300B2-203	202	F-WZMJ*	0682	1182	2 GE CF6-50C2	142000	F26Y214	DH-AK	
☐ PP-SNM	Airbus Industrie A300B2-203	205	F-WZMP*	0782	1182	2 GE CF6-50C2	142000	F26Y214	DH-AL	Isf Rural Leasing SA
☐ PP-SNN	Airbus Industrie A300B2-203	225	F-WZMB*	1282	0183	2 GE CF6-50C2	142000	F26Y214	DH-BG	
☐ PP-SFB	Boeing (Douglas) DC-10-30	46575 / 57	HC-BKO	0072	0596	3 GE CF6-50C	256284	F18Y251	AE-CG	Ist EEA
☐ PP-SFA	Boeing (Douglas) MD-11	48768 / 601	N9134D*	0096	0696	3 GE CF6-80C2D1F	280320	F10C21Y294	BC-EH	Isf Golden Gate Leasing Ltd
☐ PP-SFD	Boeing (Douglas) MD-11	48769 / 603	N9166N*	0096	1196	3 GE CF6-80C2D1F	283722	F10C21Y294	JM-AE	Nossa Senhora Aparecida / IsfGoldenGate
☐ PP-SOW	Boeing (Douglas) MD-11	48413 / 488		0192	0292	3 GE CF6-80C2D1F	280320	F10C21Y294	CE-BD	Armando Sales de Oliveira / Isf Mitsui
☐ PP-SOZ	Boeing (Douglas) MD-11	48414 / 491		0292	0392	3 GE CF6-80C2D1F	280320	F10C21Y294	CF-JK	Isf Mitsui
☐ PP-SPD	Boeing (Douglas) MD-11	48411 / 453	N891DL	1290	0194	3 GE CF6-80C2D1F	280320	F10C21Y294	DL-CF	Isf TOMB
☐ PP-SPE	Boeing (Douglas) MD-11	48412 / 454	N892DL	0090	0194	3 GE CF6-80C2D1F	280320	F10C21Y294	DL-CM	Isf TOMB
☐ PP-SPK	Boeing (Douglas) MD-11	48744 / 592		0095	1195	3 GE CF6-80C2D1F	280320	F10C21Y294	DL-EH	Isf Golden Gate Leasing Ltd
☐ PP-SPL	Boeing (Douglas) MD-11	48745 / 596	N90187*	0095	1295	3 GE CF6-80C2D1F	280320	F10C21Y294	DL-EJ	Isf Golden Gate Leasing Ltd

VATICANO Taxi Aéreo, Ltda
Sao Paulo-Marte, (SP)

Av. Roberto Gordon 222, Vila Mary, CEP-09990-090 Diadema, (Sao Paulo), Brazil ☎ (11) 445 67 76 Tx: n/a Fax: (11) 456 71 81 SITA: n/a

F: 1988 ♦♦♦ n/a Head: n/a Net: n/a

| ☐ PT-HLP | Euroc.(Helibras/Aerosp.)HB350B Esquilo | 1499 / HB1025 | | 0081 | 0489 | 1 TU Arriel 1B | 1950 | | | |

VECTOR Taxi Aéreo, Ltda
Sao Paulo-Congonhas, (SP) & Belo Horizonte-Pampulha, (MG)

Rua Gal. Pantaleao Telles 1000, J. Aeroporto, CEP-04355-040 Sao Paulo, (Sao Paulo), Brazil ☎ (11) 241 82 11 Tx: none Fax: (11) 240 55 84 SITA: n/a

F: 1987 ♦♦♦ n/a Head: Altamirando Ribeiro Silva Net: n/a

| ☐ PT-OZR | Beech King Air C90 | LJ-1059 | N6581B | 0083 | | 2 PWC PT6A-21 | 4377 | | | Isf Atlantic Corp. |
| ☐ PT-WGF | Learjet 35A | 35A-322 | N305SC | 0080 | | 2 GA TFE731-2-2B | 7711 | | | Isf Learjet Latin America Sales Inc. |

VETA VELANO Taxi Aéreo, Ltda
Alfenas, (MG)

Aeroporto Municipal de Alfenas, CP23, CEP-37130-000 Alfenas, (Minas Gerais), Brazil ☎ (35) 292 34 22 Tx: none Fax: (35) 292 10 68 SITA: n/a

F: 1993 ♦♦♦ 7 Head: Andrei L. Costa de Faria Net: n/a

| ☐ PT-MAJ | Embraer 121A1 Xingu II (EMB-121A1) | 121017 | | 0079 | | 2 PWC PT6A-135 | 5670 | | | Isf Safra Leasing |

VIABRASIL – Air Club Transportes Aéreos, Ltda = VBR
Sao Paulo-Congonhas, (SP)

Avda. San Luis 86, 15th Floor, CEP-01046-000 Centro Sao Paulo, (Sao Paulo), Brazil ☎ (11) 255 35 05 Tx: none Fax: (11) 255 35 05 SITA: n/a

F: 1998 ♦♦♦ n/a Head: Raul Medeiros ICAO: VIABRASIL Net: n/a

| ☐ PT-MLM | Boeing 727-2B6 (A) | 21299 / 1247 | CN-RMQ | 0077 | 0998 | 3 PW JT8D-15 | 86409 | Y173 | | |

VICA AIRLINES = VCA (Viaçao Charter Aérea, Ltda dba)
Sao Paulo-Guarulhos (SP)

Aeroporto Int'l de Guarulhos, Wing A, 5.P, CEP-07141-970 Sao Paulo, (Sao Paulo), Brazil ☎ (11) 64 45 39 21 Tx: none Fax: (11) 64 45 32 18 SITA: n/a

F: 1997 ♦♦♦ n/a Head: Ernesto Marli ICAO: VICA Net: n/a

| ☐ PT-LAF | Fokker F27 Friendship 600 (F27 Mk600) | 10177 | PH-FCR* | 0061 | 1097 | 2 RR Dart 532-7 | 19731 | Y48 | | Isf Tavares de A.Participaçoes/cvtd 200 |

WANAIR Taxi Aéreo, Ltda
Belo Horizonte-Pampulha, (MG)

Rua Boaventura 2312, Aeroporto da Pampula, CEP-31270-480 Belo Horizonte, (Minas Gerais), Brazil ☎ (31) 448 89 00 Tx: none Fax: (31) 448 89 01 SITA: n/a

F: 1984 ♦♦♦ n/a Head: Enge Eduardo F. Lanza Net: n/a Aircraft below MTOW 1361kg: Cessna 182

☐ PT-LMG	Cessna 182R Skylane B	18268569	N9632X	0086		1 CO O-470-U	1406			
☐ PT-IRO	Cessna U206F Stationair	U20602078		0073		1 CO IO-520-F	1633			
☐ PT-LIF	Beech King Air F90-1	LA-223	N83KA	0084		2 PWC PT6A-135A	4967			

WEE AIR Taxi Aéreo, Ltda
Blumenau, (SC)

Rua Dr. Pedro Zimmermann 5073, CP637, CEP-89068-000 Blumenau, (Santa Catarina), Brazil ☎ (47) 337 11 19 Tx: none Fax: n/a SITA: n/a

F: 1996 ♦♦♦ n/a Net: n/a

| ☐ PT-WAM | Embraer 110 Bandeirante (EMB-110) | 110066 | FAB2163 | 0075 | 0096 | 2 PWC PT6A-27 | 5600 | | | |

WIRLAND FREIRE Taxi Aéreo, Ltda
Santarem, (PA)

Av. Tapajos 1671, Bairro de Aldeia, CEP-68107 Santarém, (Para), Brazil ☎ (91) 523 21 41 Tx: n/a Fax: n/a SITA: n/a

F: 1992 ♦♦♦ n/a Head: n/a Net: n/a

| ☐ PT-KJA | Cessna U206F Stationair | U20602477 | | 0074 | 0098 | 1 CO IO-520-F | 1633 | | | |
| ☐ PT-LLD | Embraer 110P1 Bandeirante (EMB-110P1) | 110392 | N69DA | 0082 | | 2 PWC PT6A-34 | 5900 | | | |

WORLD AEROTAXI, Ltda
Belo Horizonte, (MG)

Rua Lider 84, CEP-31280-480 Belo Horizonte, (Minas Gerais), Brazil ☎ (31) 491 32 66 Tx: none Fax: (31) 492 28 18 SITA: n/a

F: 1996 ♦♦♦ n/a Head: Ligo Costa Net: n/a

| ☐ PT-MAG | Embraer 121A1 Xingu II (EMB-121A1) | 121013 | | 0079 | 0597 | 2 PWC PT6A-135 | 5670 | | | |
| ☐ PT-SGM | Embraer 110P1 Bandeirante (EMB-110P1) | 110420 | 8R-GFO | 0083 | 0598 | 2 PWC PT6A-34 | 5670 | | | |

YAPO Aerotaxi, Ltda
Curitiba-Afonso Pena, (PR)

Rua Alferes Poli 405, Conj.102 Centro, CEP-80230-090 Curitiba, (Parana), Brazil ☎ (41) 335 03 66 Tx: n/a Fax: (41) 338 67 34 SITA: n/a

F: 1982 ♦♦♦ n/a Head: n/a Net: n/a

| ☐ PT-YAP | Bell 206B JetRanger III | 3481 | N215BG | 0081 | | 1 AN 250-C20B | 1451 | | | Isf BCN Leasing |

PZ = SURINAME (Republic of Suriname) (Republiek van Surinam)
Capital: Paramaribo Official Language: Dutch Population: 0,6 million Square Km: 163265 Dialling code: +597 Year established: 1975 Acting political head: Jules Wijdenbosch (President)

Government / Corporate / Executive / VIP Aircraft

| ☐ SAF-212 | CASA 212 Aviocar Srs 400 | 466 | | 0098 | 1298 | 2 GA TPE331-12JR-701C | 8100 | VIP/milt/Frt/EMS | | Suriname Air Force |

GUM AIR, NV (Associated with Suriname Sky Farmers, NV)
Paramaribo-Zorg en Hoop

PO Box 390, Paramaribo, Suriname ☎ 49 87 60 Tx: 216 gumair sn Fax: 49 17 40 SITA: n/a

F: 1971 ♦♦♦ 21 Head: Pieter H. Gummels Net: n/a

☐ PZ-TBD	Cessna U206G Stationair	U20603786	N8286G	0077		1 CO IO-520-F	1633	Y6		
☐ PZ-TBE	Cessna U206G Stationair 6 II	U20606776	N9959Z	0083	1193	1 CO IO-550-F	1633	Y6		
☐ PZ-TVU	Cessna TU206G Turbo Stationair II	U20604783	PZ-PVU	0078		1 CO TSIO-520-M	1633	Y6		
☐ PZ-TBL	Britten-Norman BN-2B-26 Islander	2153	N633BB	0082	0696	2 LY O-540-E4C5	2812	Y9		
☐ PZ-TBA	GAF N22B Nomad	N22B-66		0078	0778	2 AN 250-B17B	3856	Y14		
☐ PZ-TBM	GAF Nomad N24A	N24A-42	ZK-ECN	0077	0497	2 AN 250-B17B	4264	Y16		

INTER TROPICAL AVIATION
Paramaribo-Zorg en Hoop

PO Box 9067, Paramaribo, Suriname ☎ 43 17 55 Tx: none Fax: 43 17 55 SITA: n/a

F: 1987 ♦♦♦ 22 Head: Amichand Thauw Net: n/a Aircraft below MTOW 1361kg: Cessna 172

| ☐ PZ-TGP | Cessna U206G Stationair | U20604041 | PZ-PGP | 0077 | 0094 | 1 CO IO-520-F | 1633 | | | |

registration	type of aircraft	cn/fn	ex/ex*	mfd	del	powered by	mtow kg	configuration	selcal	name/fln/specialitites/remarks
☐ PZ-TGQ	Cessna U206G Stationair 6 II	U20605917	PZ-TAO	0080		1 CO IO-520-F	1633			
☐ PZ-TLV	Cessna U206G Stationair 6 II	U20606951		0086		1 CO IO-520-F	1633			
☐ PZ-TGT	Britten-Norman BN-2B-21 Islander	2116	SAF003	0081	1197	2 LY IO-540-K1B5	2994			
☐ PZ-TGR	Let 410UVP	831027	LY-ANR	0083	0197	2 WA M-601D	5800			

MAF Suriname – Mission Aviation Fellowship (SZV-Surinaamse Zendings Vliegdienst) (Branch of MAF USA) Paramaribo-Zorg en Hoop

PO Box 2031, Paramaribo-Zuid, Suriname ☎ 49 77 16 Tx: 216 gumairsn/att SZV Fax: 49 77 16 SITA: n/a
F: 1969 ♦♦♦ 4 Head: Harry Debisarun Net: n/a Non-commercial multinational ecclesiastical consortium conducting flights for relief & development agencies & missions in remote areas of third world countries.

☐ PZ-NAU	Cessna U206F Stationair II	U20602902	N1462Q	0075		1 CO IO-520-F	1724			Flint Tip tanks
☐ PZ-NAV	Cessna U206F Stationair II	U20602776	N35876	0075		1 CO IO-520-F	1633			

OVEREEM AIR SERVICE Nickerie

Karang Anjar, Pc. 70, District Nickerie, Suriname ☎ 23 19 91 Tx: n/a Fax: 23 21 74 SITA: n/a
F: 1991 ♦♦♦ n/a Head: Robert G. Overeem Net: n/a Ag-aircraft below MTOW 5000kg: Grumman G-164A/B

☐ PZ-TRJ	Cessna T210R Turbo Centurion	21065002		0086		1 CO TSIO-520-CE	1860			
☐ PZ-TRR	Cessna 207 Skywagon	20700313	PZ-MAF	0075	0095	1 CO IO-520-F	1724			

SKY LINERS, NV = LNR Paramaribo-Zorg en Hoop

Anton Dragtenweg 103a, Paramaribo, Suriname ☎ 45 46 63 Tx: none Fax: 45 28 00 SITA: n/a
F: 1991 ♦♦♦ 20 Head: Dennis Levens ICAO: LINERSERVICE Net: n/a

☐ PZ-TDL	Cessna U206G Stationair 6 II	U20605065	N4697U	0079	0192	1 CO IO-520-F	1633			

SURINAM AIRWAYS = PY / SLM (SLM – Surinaamse Luchtvaart Maatschappij) Paramaribo-Zorg en Hoop & Zanderij International 🦅 SURINAM AIRWAYS

PO Box 2029, Paramaribo, Suriname ☎ 46 57 00 Tx: 292 surair sn Fax: 49 12 13 SITA: n/a
F: 1954 ♦♦♦ 400 Head: Motilal Mungra IATA: 192 ICAO: SURINAM Net: n/a Scheduled services to Amsterdam are operated with Boeing 747 aircraft in a code-sharing agreement with KLM using PY/KL flight numbers.

☐ PZ-TCD	De Havilland DHC-6 Twin Otter 300	646		0079	1179	2 PWC PT6A-27	5670	Y20		
☐ PZ-TCE	De Havilland DHC-6 Twin Otter 300	656		0079	1279	2 PWC PT6A-27	5670	Y20		
☐ PZ-TCG	Boeing (Douglas) MD-87 (DC-9-87)	49671 / 1463	N107PY	0388	0196	2 PW JT8D-219	67812	Y137		District of Para / lsf ILFC

P2 = PAPUA NEW GUINEA (Independent State of Papua New Guinea) Papua New Guinea

Capital: Port Moresby Official Language: English Population: 4,5 million Square Km: 462840 Dialling code: +675 Year established: 1975 Acting political head: Bill Skate (Prime Minister)

Government / Corporate / Executive / VIP Aircraft

☐ P2-CAA	Beech King Air 200	BB-415	P2-PNH	0078		2 PWC PT6A-41	5670	Liaison		Department of Civil Aviation

AIRLINK, Ltd = ND Madang AIRLINK

PO Box 1208, Madang, Papua New Guinea ☎ 852 29 33 Tx: none Fax: 852 27 25 SITA: n/a
F: 1989 ♦♦♦ 120 Head: Colin B. Bubner IATA: 159 Net: n/a

☐ P2-ALB	Cessna 402B	402B0006	P2-GKL	0070	0090	2 CO TSIO-520-E	2858			
☐ P2-ALC	Britten-Norman BN-2A Islander	36	P2-ATS	0068	0695	2 LY O-540-E4B5	2858			
☐ P2-ALD	Britten-Norman BN-2A Islander	76	P2-DNB	0069	0695	2 LY O-540-E4B5	2858			
☐ P2-ALE	Britten-Norman BN-2A-26 Islander	100	P2-SAB	0069	0695	2 LY O-540-E4C5	2994			
☐ P2-ALI	Britten-Norman BN-2A-26 Islander	73	P2-ISI	0069	0091	2 LY O-540-E4C5	2994			
☐ P2-ALM	Britten-Norman BN-2A-26 Islander	124	P2-NAA	0069	0097	2 LY O-540-E4C5	2994			
☐ P2-ALG	Cessna 404 Titan II	404-0653	VH-SON	0080	0091	2 CO GTSIO-520-M	3810			
☐ P2-ALK	Cessna 404 Titan II	404-0222	VH-TMX	0078	0091	2 CO GTSIO-520-M	3810			
☐ P2-ALX	Embraer 110P2 Bandeirante (EMB-110P2)	110210	VH-WDF	0079	0794	2 PWC PT6A-34	5670			
☐ P2-ALZ	Embraer 110P1 Bandeirante (EMB-110P1)	110233	VH-HVS	0079	0893	2 PWC PT6A-34	5670			

AIR MANUBADA (Caloundra, Pty Ltd dba) Port Moresby

PO Box 7373, Boroko, Papua New Guinea ☎ 325 40 37 Tx: none Fax: 323 48 52 SITA: n/a
F: 1991 ♦♦♦ n/a Head: n/a Net: n/a Aircraft below MTOW 1361kg: Piper PA-28

☐ P2-MFX	Cessna A185F Skywagon	18502146	VH-MFX	0073		1 CO IO-520-D	1520			Koiari Kekeni
☐ P2-CBL	Cessna U206G Stationair 6 II	U20604799	VH-HIK	0079		1 CO IO-520-F	1633			Goilala Kekeni
☐ P2-SAV	Cessna 402A	402A0069	P2-GKI	0069		2 CO TSIO-520-E	2858			Rigo Kekeni

AIR NIUGINI, Pty Ltd = PX / ANG (Subsidiary of National Airline Commission) Port Moresby 🦅 Air Niugini

PO Box 7186, Boroko, (N.C.D.), Papua New Guinea ☎ 327 32 00 Tx: 22225 airng ne Fax: 327 33 04 SITA: POMPRPX
F: 1973 ♦♦♦ 1780 Head: Joseph Tauvasa IATA: 656 ICAO: NIUGINI Net: http://www.datec.com.au/airniugini

☐ P2-ANK	De Havilland DHC-8-202 Dash 8Q	461	C-GFBW*	0097	0597	2 PWC PW123D	16465	Y36orCombiorFrtr		
☐ P2-ANL	De Havilland DHC-8-202 Dash 8Q	470	C-GDKL*	0097	0797	2 PWC PW123D	16465	Y36orCombiorFrtr		
☐ P2-ANC	Fokker F28 Fellowship 1000 (F28 Mk1000)	11089	RMAF M28-02	0075	1188	2 RR Spey 555-15	30164	Y60		
☐ P2-AND	Fokker F28 Fellowship 4000 (F28 Mk4000)	11118	PH-RRJ	0077	1092	2 RR Spey 555-15H	33112	Y74		
☐ P2-ANE	Fokker F28 Fellowship 1000 (F28 Mk1000)	11033	C-FTAV	0071	0679	2 RR Spey 555-15	30164	Y60		
☐ P2-ANF	Fokker F28 Fellowship 1000 (F28 Mk1000)	11038	C-FTAY	0071	0279	2 RR Spey 555-15	30164	Y60		
☐ P2-ANI	Fokker F28 Fellowship 4000 (F28 Mk4000)	11223	PH-RRB	0085	1294	2 RR Spey 555-15P	33112	Y74		
☐ P2-ANJ	Fokker F28 Fellowship 4000 (F28 Mk4000)	11219	PH-RRA	0084	0296	2 RR Spey 555-15P	33112	Y74		
☐ P2-ANU	Fokker F28 Fellowship 1000 (F28 Mk1000)	11041	C2-RN1	0071	1077	2 RR Spey 555-15	30164	Y60		
☐ P2-ANW	Fokker F28 Fellowship 1000 (F28 Mk1000)	11056	C2-RN2	0072	1077	2 RR Spey 555-15	30164	Y60		
☐ P2-ANA	Airbus Industrie A310-324	378	LZ-JXA	0085	0093	2 PW PW4152	153000	C30Y179	AE-HM	cvtd -322
☐ P2-ANG	Airbus Industrie A310-324	549	F-WWCX*	0090	1290	2 PW PW4152	153000	C42Y156	KM-EQ	

FUBILAN AIR TRANSPORT, Pty Ltd (Subsidiary of National Jet Systems, Pty Ltd / formerly Asia Pacific Airlines, Pty Ltd) Tabubil

PO Box 293, Tabubil, (W.P.), Papua New Guinea ☎ 548 94 77 Tx: none Fax: 548 94 66 SITA: n/a
F: 1991 ♦♦♦ n/a Head: Warren Seymour Net: n/a

☐ P2-NAZ	De Havilland DHC-8-106 Dash 8	316	C-GFUM*	0092	0993	2 PWC PW121	16465	Y36		Spirit of Tabubil / lsf ELVE

GOROKA AIR SERVICES, Pty Ltd Goroka

PO Box 882, Goroka, (E.H.P.), Papua New Guinea ☎ 732 16 81 Tx: none Fax: 732 1722 SITA: n/a
F: 1995 ♦♦♦ n/a Head: n/a Net: n/a

☐ P2-MDK	De Havilland DHC-6 Twin Otter 200	164	P2-MBU	0068	0096	2 PWC PT6A-20	5252	Y19		
☐ P2-MRN	De Havilland DHC-6 Twin Otter 310	610	P2-MBT	0079	0097	2 PWC PT6A-27	5670			

GOVERNMENT FLYING UNIT Port Moresby

PO Box 6605, Boroko, Papua New Guinea ☎ 325 22 80 Tx: none Fax: 325 63 67 SITA: n/a
F: n/a ♦♦♦ n/a Head: n/a Net: n/a

☐ P2-PNG	Beech King Air 350 (B300)	FL-79	N8246Q*	0092	0093	2 PWC PT6A-60A	6804	VIP / Charter		

HELI NIUGINI, Pty Ltd Madang

PO Box 914, Madang, Papua New Guinea ☎ 852 24 22 Tx: none Fax: 852 25 20 SITA: n/a
F: 1987 ♦♦♦ 37 Head: Horst Allman Net: n/a

☐ P2-HBB	Bell 206L-1 LongRanger III	45323	YV-320CP	0079		1 AN 250-C30P	1882			cvtd LongRanger II
☐ P2-HBC	Bell 206L-3 LongRanger III	51396	VH-SBC	0090	1293	1 AN 250-C30P	1882			
☐ P2-HBG	Bell 206L-3 LongRanger III	51432	JA6059	0091	0196	1 AN 250-C30P	1882			
☐ P2-HBH	Bell 206L-3 LongRanger III	51012	SE-HOR	0082	0997	1 AN 250-C30P	1882			
☐ VH-WTT	Bell 206L-1 LongRanger II	45262	N2183X	0079	0098	1 AN 250-C28B	1882			lsf pvt

HEVI LIFT (PNG), Pty Ltd Mount Hagen

PO Box 49, Mount Hagen, (W.H.P.), Papua New Guinea ☎ 545 12 40 Tx: 52066 rotowok ne Fax: 545 12 61 SITA: n/a
F: 1982 ♦♦♦ 270 Head: Trevor Pook Net: n/a

☐ P2-HCC	Bell 206L-1 LongRanger III	45427	N5019T	0080		1 AN 250-C30P	1882			cvtd LongRanger II
☐ P2-HCD	Bell 206L-1 LongRanger III	45528	C-GGHZ	0080		1 AN 250-C30P	1882			cvtd LongRanger II
☐ P2-HCE	Bell 206L-3 LongRanger III	51291		0089		1 AN 250-C30P	1882			
☐ P2-HCI	Bell 206L-3 LongRanger III	51297	P2-BHK	0089		1 AN 250-C30P	1882			
☐ P2-HCM	Bell 206L-1 LongRanger III	45608	P2-NHE	0081	1090	1 AN 250-C30P	1882			cvtd LongRanger II
☐ P2-HCO	Bell 206L-3 LongRanger III	51178	N3204K	0086	0391	1 AN 250-C30P	1882			
☐ P2-HCP	Bell 206L-3 LongRanger III	51014	N2291K	0082	0191	1 AN 250-C30P	1882			
☐ P2-HCT	Bell 206L-3 LongRanger III	51387	N250EV	0090	0594	1 AN 250-C30P	1882			
☐ P2-HCU	Bell 206L-3 LongRanger III	51416	N254EV	0090	0594	1 AN 250-C30P	1882			
☐ P2-HCB	Bell 212	30895	VH-EMK	0078	0086	2 PWC PT6T-3 TwinPac	5080			
☐ P2-HCQ	Bell 212	30860	JA9528	0077	0091	2 PWC PT6T-3 TwinPac	5080			
☐ P2-HCV	Bell 212	30508	PK-EBN	0071	0095	2 PWC PT6T-3 TwinPac	5080			
☐ P2-HCW	Bell 212	30520	PK-EBO	0071	0095	2 PWC PT6T-3 TwinPac	5080			
☐ VH-EMJ	Bell 212	30799		0076		2 PWC PT6T-3 TwinPac	5080			
☐ VH-HHW	Bell 212	30983	P2-HCK	0080	1090	2 PWC PT6T-3 TwinPac	5080			
☐ P2-HCN	Beech King Air 200C	BL-22	P2-PJV	0081		2 PWC PT6A-41	5670			
☐ P2-VIC	Beech King Air B200	BB-990	N61369	0082		2 PWC PT6A-42	5670			
☐ P2-HCF	De Havilland DHC-6 Twin Otter 300	528	N528SA	0077	1193	2 PWC PT6A-27	5670			
☐ P2-HCX	De Havilland DHC-6 Twin Otter 300	485	CP-2035	0076	0395	2 PWC PT6A-27	5670			
☐ VH-FNV	De Havilland DHC-6 Twin Otter 320	313	P2-RDJ	0071	0498	2 PWC PT6A-27	5670			lsf Cape York Air
☐ P2-RAA	Kamov Ka-32S	8705	P2-HCR	0091	0092	2 IS TV3-117VK	11000			

☐ RA-31031	Kamov Ka-32S	6106	CCCP-31031	0089		2 IS TV3-117VK	11000			lsf Aerolift Int'l P/L
☐ RA-31032	Kamov Ka-32S	6107	CCCP-31032	0089		2 IS TV3-117VK	11000			lsf Aerolift Int'l P/L
☐ RA-31036	Kamov Ka-32T	6111	CCCP-31036	0091		2 IS TV3-117VK	11000			lsf Aerolift Int'l P/L
☐ RA-31586	Kamov Ka-32A	8708		0092	0595	2 IS TV3-117VMA	11000			lsf Aerolift Int'l P/L
☐ P2-HLA	Embraer 120ER Brasilia (EMB-120ER)	120030	N271UE	1286	0898	2 PWC PW118	11990			cvtd 120RT
☐ RA-27101	Mil Mi-8AMT (Mi-171)	59489605182		0092		2 IS TV3-117MT	13000			lsf Aerolift Int'l P/L
☐ RA-27106	Mil Mi-8AMT (Mi-171)	59489607904		0092		2 IS TV3-117MT	13000			lsf Aerolift Int'l P/L
☐ RA-27158	Mil Mi-8AMT (Mi-171)	59489611156		0093		2 IS TV3-117MT	13000			lsf Aerolift Int'l P/L

ISLAND AIRWAYS, Pty Ltd — Madang

PO Box 747, Madang, Papua New Guinea ☎ 852 26 01 Tx: none Fax: 852 23 53 SITA: n/a
F: 1988 ⁂ 20 Head: J. Cheung Net: n/a

☐ P2-CBA	Britten-Norman BN-2A-20 Islander	753	P2-MFF	0075	0096	2 LY IO-540-K1B5	2994			
☐ P2-CBB	Britten-Norman BN-2A-26 Islander	140	VH-UBD	0070	0197	2 LY O-540-E4C5	2994			
☐ P2-CBC	Cessna 402B	402B0909	VH-LCF	0075		2 CO TSIO-520-E	2858			

ISLANDS NATIONAIR = CN (Islands Helicopter Services, Pty Ltd & Stolip Aviation, Pty Ltd dba) — Port Moresby

PO Box 488, Boroko, Papua New Guinea ☎ 325 40 55 Tx: none Fax: 325 50 59 SITA: n/a
F: 1984 ⁂ n/a Head: David Pidduck IATA: 920 Net: n/a

☐ P2-CMM	Cessna U206F Stationair	U20601978	VH-CMM	0073		1 CO IO-520-F	1633			
☐ P2-IHA	Bell 206L-1 LongRanger II	45333	VH-BLV	0079		1 AN 250-C28B	1882			
☐ P2-IHC	Bell 206L-1 LongRanger III	45614	VH-HIV	0081		1 AN 250-C30P	1882			cvtd LongRanger II
☐ P2-IHD	Bell 206L-1 LongRanger II	45387	VH-BJY	0080		1 AN 250-C28B	1882			
☐ P2-IHE	Bell 206L-1 LongRanger III	45238	N140VG	0079		1 AN 250-C30P	1882			cvtd LongRanger II
☐ P2-IHF	Bell 206L-3 LongRanger III	51322		0089	0090	1 AN 250-C30P	1882			
☐ P2-IHH	Bell 206L-1 LongRanger III	45255	P2-NHD	0079		1 AN 250-C30P	1882			cvtd LongRanger II
☐ P2-IHK	Bell 206L-1 LongRanger II	45450	VH-WCS	0080	0994	1 AN 250-C28B	1882			
☐ P2-IHJ	Bell 407	53105	N4116	0097	0597	1 AN 250-C47B	2268			
☐ P2-IAB	Beech Baron 58	TH-760	VH-NET	0076		2 CO IO-520-C	2449			
☐ P2-IAC	Britten-Norman BN-2A-21 Islander	425	P2-KAF	0075	0091	2 LY IO-540-K1B5	2994			
☐ P2-IAA	De Havilland DHC-6 Twin Otter 310	244	VH-TNM	0069	0791	2 PWC PT6A-27	5670			
☐ P2-IAE	De Havilland DHC-6 Twin Otter 320	255	VH-TNS	0069	1291	2 PWC PT6A-27	5670			
☐ P2-IAF	De Havilland DHC-6 Twin Otter 300	261	VH-IAM	0069	0793	2 PWC PT6A-27	5670			
☐ P2-IAJ	Embraer 110P1 Bandeirante (EMB-110P1)	110254	VH-FCE	0080	0694	2 PWC PT6A-34	5670			
☐ P2-IAK	Embraer 110P2 Bandeirante (EMB-110P2)	110394	ZS-LGM	0082	0894	2 PWC PT6A-34	5670			
☐ P2-IAL	Embraer 110P2 Bandeirante (EMB-110P2)	110412	ZS-LGN	0082	0894	2 PWC PT6A-34	5670			
☐ P2-IAH	Beech King Air 200	BB-297	VH-IBD	0077	1193	2 PWC PT6A-41	5670			

KIUNGA AVIATION, Pty Ltd — Lae

PO Box 1404, Lae, (Morobe Province), Papua New Guinea ☎ 472 64 88 Tx: none Fax: 472 40 86 SITA: n/a
F: 1982 ⁂ 18 Head: John Richard Leahy Net: n/a

☐ P2-MJL	Cessna A185E Skywagon	18501947	VH-MJL	0072		1 CO IO-520-D	1520			
☐ P2-KAA	Cessna 402C II	402C0247	N2748X	0080		2 CO TSIO-520-VB	3107			

MAF Papua New Guinea, Ltd (Associated with MAF Missionary Aviation Fellowship of Australia & New Zealand) — Mount Hagen

Box 273, Mount Hagen, (W.H.P.), Papua New Guinea ☎ 545 14 77 Tx: none Fax: 545 13 87 SITA: n/a
F: 1951 ⁂ 130 Head: G.W. Butler Net: n/a Aircraft below MTOW 1361kg: Cessna 172 (for flight training).
Multinational ecclesiastical consortium conducting flights for relief & development agencies & missions in remote areas of third world countries.

☐ P2-MAA	Cessna U206E Stationair	U20602051	P2-CMA	0073		1 CO IO-520-F	1633			
☐ P2-MAE	Cessna U206G Stationair 6 II	U20606661	VH-HBP	0082		1 CO IO-520-F	1633			
☐ P2-MAG	Cessna TU206G Turbo Stationair	U20603806	VH-JLN	0077		1 CO TSIO-520-M	1633			
☐ P2-MAI	Cessna TU206G Turbo Stationair II	U20605734	P2-DMH	0081		1 CO TSIO-520-M	1633			
☐ P2-MAJ	Cessna TU206G T. Stationair 6 II R/STOL	U20606295	P2-SIK	0081	0098	1 CO TSIO-520-M	1633			
☐ P2-MAX	Cessna U206G Stationair	U20603716	VH-SFW	0077	0393	1 CO IO-520-F	1633			
☐ P2-MDC	Cessna U206G Stationair II	U20602738	N1753C	0075		1 CO IO-520-F	1633			cvtd F
☐ P2-MFG	Cessna TU206G Turbo Stationair II	U20602875	N1759C	0075		1 CO TSIO-520-M	1633			cvtd F
☐ P2-MFJ	Cessna TU206G Turbo Stationair R/STOL	U20602447	P2-BLA	0074		1 CO TSIO-520-M	1633			
☐ P2-MFM	Cessna TU206G Turbo Stationair 6 II	U20605380		0079		1 CO TSIO-520-M	1633			
☐ P2-MFN	Cessna TU206G Turbo Stationair 6 II	U20605541	N6346U	0080		1 CO TSIO-520-M	1633			
☐ P2-MFP	Cessna TU206G T. Stationair 6 II R/STOL	U20605793	N4809M	0080		1 CO TSIO-520-M	1633			
☐ P2-MFV	Cessna TU206G T. Stationair 6 II R/STOL	U20606252	N6359Z	0081		1 CO TSIO-520-M	1633			
☐ P2-MFA	Beech Baron D55	TE-469	P2-SQC	0067		2 CO IO-520-C	2404			
☐ P2-MFI	Britten-Norman BN-2A-20 Islander	188	N8000J	0070	0789	2 LY IO-540-K1B5	2994			
☐ P2-MFT	Britten-Norman BN-2A-21 Islander	421	P2-FHR	0075	0091	2 LY IO-540-K1B5	2994			
☐ P2-MFW	Britten-Norman BN-2A-20 Islander	521	JA5255	0076	0389	2 LY IO-540-K1B5	2994			
☐ P2-MFB	De Havilland DHC-6 Twin Otter 300	289	N910HD	0070	1095	2 PWC PT6A-27	5670			
☐ P2-MFQ	De Havilland DHC-6 Twin Otter 300	174	N9762J	0068	0091	2 PWC PT6A-34	5670			cvtd Twin Otter 200
☐ P2-MFR	De Havilland DHC-6 Twin Otter 200	118	N63118	0068	0883	2 PWC PT6A-20	5252			
☐ P2-MFU	De Havilland DHC-6 Twin Otter 200	182	TJ-AHV	0068	1196	2 PWC PT6A-20	5252			
☐ P2-MFY	De Havilland DHC-6 Twin Otter 200	219	VH-BMG	0069	0788	2 PWC PT6A-20	5252			

MAPMAKERS, Pty Ltd (Aerial Mapping Consultants) — Port Moresby

PO Box 6575, Boroko, Papua New Guinea ☎ 325 74 88 Tx: none Fax: 325 77 35 SITA: n/a
F: 1964 ⁂ 20 Head: Ronald Douglas Firns Net: n/a

☐ P2-COC	Piper PA-23-250 Turbo Aztec C	27-3328	VH-COC	0066		2 LY TIO-540-C1A	2359			

MBA, Ltd = CG (formerly Milne Bay Air, Pty Ltd) — Port Moresby

PO Box 170, Port Moresby, Papua New Guinea ☎ 325 20 11 Tx: none Fax: 325 22 19 SITA: POMDZCG
F: 1987 ⁂ n/a Head: John R. Wild IATA: 626 Net: n/a

☐ P2-MBD	Britten-Norman BN-2A Islander	158	VH-FLD	0070	0090	2 LY O-540-E4B5	2722			
☐ P2-MBF	Britten-Norman BN-2A-8 Islander	646	P2-WGT	0071		2 LY O-540-E4C5	2722			
☐ P2-MBA	De Havilland DHC-6 Twin Otter 300	353	C-FWAX	0073	0196	2 PWC PT6A-27	5670			
☐ P2-MBC	De Havilland DHC-6 Twin Otter 200	218	N604MA	0069	0090	2 PWC PT6A-20	5252			Kutubu Kwin
☐ P2-MBS	De Havilland DHC-6 Twin Otter 200	124	P2-RDH	0068	0294	2 PWC PT6A-20	5252			
☐ P2-MCB	De Havilland DHC-6 Twin Otter 300	441	C-GNHB	0075	0197	2 PWC PT6A-27	5670			
☐ P2-MCD	De Havilland DHC-6 Twin Otter 300	592	C-GOVG	0078	0197	2 PWC PT6A-27	5670			
☐ P2-MCE	De Havilland DHC-6 Twin Otter 300	673	C-GHRB	0080	0197	2 PWC PT6A-27	5670			
☐ P2-MCF	De Havilland DHC-6 Twin Otter 300	741	C-GRBY	0081	0197	2 PWC PT6A-27	5670			
☐ P2-MBX	Beech 1900D Airliner	UE-102	N82928*	0094	0894	2 PWC PT6A-67D	7688			Wildthing
☐ P2-MBY	Beech 1900D Airliner	UE-115	N15317*	0094	1194	2 PWC PT6A-67D	7688			
☐ P2-CHD	Boeing Vertol 107-II	2003	N191CH	0062	0796	2 GE CT58-140-2	9752			lsf Columbia Helicopters
☐ P2-MCG	De Havilland DHC-8-102 Dash 8	006	C-GJCB	0084	0397	2 PWC PW120A	15649	Y36 or Combi		
☐ P2-MCH	De Havilland DHC-8-102 Dash 8	012	C-GPYD	0085	0197	2 PWC PW120A	15649	Y36 or Combi		
☐ P2-CHI	Boeing Vertol 234UT Chinook	MJ-003	N237CH	0081	0195	2 LY 5512	19278			lsf Columbia Helicopters / cvtd 234LR

NORTH COAST AVIATION = N9 — Lae, Popondetta & Wau

PO Box 350, Lae, (Morobe Province), Papua New Guinea ☎ 472 25 25 Tx: none Fax: 472 05 75 SITA: n/a
F: 1990 ⁂ n/a Head: Bs Potts Net: n/a

☐ P2-DQU	Cessna U206B Super Skywagon	U206-0892	VH-DQU	0067		1 CO IO-520-F	1633			
☐ P2-OHS	Cessna P206B Super Skylane	P206-0392	P2-HCM	0067		1 CO IO-520-C	1633			
☐ P2-GKB	Cessna 402	402-0141	VH-GKB	0067		2 CO TSIO-520-E	2858			
☐ P2-NCD	Cessna 402B II	402B1027	VH-USV	0075	0894	2 CO TSIO-520-E	2858			
☐ P2-DWA	Britten-Norman BN-2A-26 Islander	113	VH-EQE	0069		2 LY O-540-E4C5	2994			
☐ P2-ISA	Britten-Norman BN-2A-20 Islander	758	P2-SWB	0075	0297	2 LY IO-540-K1B5	2994			
☐ P2-ISB	Britten-Norman BN-2A-20 Islander	709	P2-MKW	0074		2 LY IO-540-K1B5	2994			
☐ P2-ISL	Britten-Norman BN-2A-20 Islander	806	G-BDYT*	0076	0392	2 LY IO-540-K1B5	2994			
☐ P2-ISM	Britten-Norman BN-2A-20 Islander	227	VH-EDI	0077		2 LY IO-540-K1B5	2994			
☐ P2-NCE	Britten-Norman BN-2A-20 Islander	768	P2-IAD	0075	0097	2 LY IO-540-K1B5	2994			
☐ P2-SAC	Britten-Norman BN-2A-20 Islander	94	P2-DNY	0069		2 LY IO-540-K1B5	2994			

NTM AVIATION (Division of New Tribes Mission) — Goroka

PO Box 149, Goroka, (E.H.P.), Papua New Guinea ☎ 732 20 78 Tx: none Fax: 732 20 90 SITA: n/a
F: 1975 ⁂ 17 Head: Ole Ottosen Net: n/a

☐ P2-NTC	Bell 206B JetRanger III	3822	P2-NHB	0084	0093	1 AN 250-C20J	1451			
☐ P2-NTA	Cessna U206G Stationair 6 II	U20604089	N756GW	0078	0390	1 CO IO-550-F	1633			
☐ P2-NTD	Cessna U206G Stationair 6 II	U20606346	VH-LQO	0081	0091	1 CO IO-550-F	1633			
☐ P2-NTE	Cessna U206F Stationair	U20602226	P2-SDP	0074	0093	1 CO IO-520-F	1633			
☐ P2-NTF	Cessna TU206G Turbo Stationair 6 II	U20605043	N4669U	0079	0495	1 CO TSIO-520-M	1633			
☐ P2-NTM	Cessna TU206G Turbo Stationair	U20603580	N7243N	0077		1 CO TSIO-520-M	1633			
☐ P2-NTT	Piper PA-31-350 Navajo Chieftain	31-8152041	N40751	0081	0493	2 LY TIO-540-J2BD	3175			

517 registration type of aircraft cn/fn ex/ex* mfd del powered by mtow kg configuration selcal name/fln/specialitites/remarks

PACAIR, Pty Ltd (Sister company of Pacific Helicopters, Pty Ltd) — **Goroka**

PO Box 342, Goroka, (E.H.P.), Papua New Guinea ☎ 732 26 66 Tx: none Fax: 732 15 03 SITA: n/a
F: 1975 n/a Head: Malcolm Smith Net: n/a

☐ P2-GKW	Beech Baron D55	TE-618	VH-FWJ	0068	0098	2 CO IO-520-C	2404	
☐ P2-SWD	Britten-Norman BN-2A-21 Islander	660	VH-OCH	0071	0098	2 LY IO-540-K1B5	2994	

PACIFIC HELICOPTERS, Pty Ltd (Sister company of Pacair, Pty Ltd) — **Goroka**

PO Box 342, Goroka, (E.H.P.), Papua New Guinea ☎ 732 18 33 Tx: none Fax: 732 15 03 SITA: n/a
F: 1975 160 Head: Malcolm Smith Net: n/a

☐ P2-PAK	MD Helicopters MD 500E (Hughes 369E)	0384E		0090	0090	1 AN 250-C20R2	1361	
☐ P2-PAO	MD Helicopters MD 500E (Hughes 369E)	0156E	N5239V	0086		1 AN 250-C20B	1361	
☐ P2-PAP	MD Helicopters MD 500E (Hughes 369E)	0304E		0088		1 AN 250-C20R2	1361	
☐ P2-PAS	MD Helicopters MD 500E (Hughes 369E)	0315E		0088		1 AN 250-C20R2	1361	
☐ P2-PHU	MD Helicopters MD 500E (Hughes 369E)	0448E	VH-PMA	0091		1 AN 250-C20R2	1361	
☐ P2-PHP	Eurocopter (Aerosp.) SA315B Lama	2472	N1217N	0076	0097	1 TU Artouste IIIB	1950	
☐ P2-MJB	Cessna U206 Super Skywagon	U206-0434	VH-MJB	0065		1 CO IO-520-A	1496	
☐ P2-PBA	Bell 206L-1 LongRanger III	45642	VH-SCV	0081	0193	1 AN 250-C30P	1882	cvtd LongRanger II
☐ P2-PBB	Bell 206L-3 LongRanger III	51400	N86CE	0090	0095	1 AN 250-C30P	1882	
☐ P2-PBC	Bell 206L-1 LongRanger III	45349	N1077N	0079	0397	1 AN 250-C30P	1882	cvtd LongRanger II
☐ P2-PBD	Bell 206L-3 LongRanger III	51275	VH-CKI	0089	0696	1 AN 250-C30P	1882	
☐ P2-PAC	Eurocopter (Aerosp.) AS350BA Ecureuil	1196	RP-C370	0079		1 TU Arriel 1B	2100	lst Dynasty Heli. as 9N-ACR/cvtd AS350B
☐ P2-PHA	Eurocopter (Aerosp.) AS350BA Ecureuil	1181	P2-PHU	0079		1 AN 250-C30M	2100	cvtd AS350B
☐ P2-PHC	Eurocopter (Aerosp.) AS350BA Ecureuil	1526		0082		1 TU Arriel 1B	2100	cvtd AS350B
☐ P2-PHD	Eurocopter (Aerosp.) AS350BA Ecureuil	1067	9N-ACQ	0079		1 TU Arriel 1B	2100	cvtd AS350B
☐ P2-PHG	Eurocopter (Aerosp.) AS350BA Ecureuil	1687		0083		1 TU Arriel 1B	2100	cvtd AS350B
☐ P2-PHH	Eurocopter (Aerosp.) AS350BA Ecureuil	1608	VH-CHO	0082	1294	1 TU Arriel 1B	2100	cvtd AS350A
☐ P2-PHX	Eurocopter (Aerosp.) AS350BA Ecureuil	1817		0086		1 TU Arriel 1B	2100	cvtd AS350B
☐ P2-PAU	Bell 212	30793	A6-BBG	0076	0095	2 PWC PT6T-3 TwinPac	5080	
☐ P2-PAV	Bell 212	30913	G-GLEN	0079		2 PWC PT6T-3 TwinPac	5080	
☐ P2-PAW	Bell 212	30547	I-SNAE	0072	0090	2 PWC PT6T-3 TwinPac	5080	
☐ P2-PAX	Bell 212	30786	A6-BBF	0076	0095	2 PWC PT6T-3 TwinPac	5080	
☐ P2-PAY	Eurocopter (Aerosp.) SA330J Puma	1502	N3263U	0078		2 TU Turmo IVC	7400	
☐ P2-PAZ	Eurocopter (Aerosp.) SA330J Puma	1459	N3263P	0077		2 TU Turmo IVC	7400	
☐ P2-PHZ	Eurocopter (Aerosp.) SA330J Puma	1472	VH-WOB	0077		2 TU Turmo IVC	7400	

PAPUAN HELICOPTERS (National Aviation Services, Pty Ltd dba) — **Port Moresby**

PO Box 5786, Boroko, Papua New Guinea ☎ 325 05 26 Tx: none Fax: 323 46 09 SITA: n/a
F: n/a n/a Head: n/a Net: n/a

☐ P2-JNA	Bell 206L-3 LongRanger III	51422	9M-TAN	0090	0094	1 AN 250-C30P	1882	
☐ P2-JND	Bell 206L-1 LongRanger II	45645	VH-MQA	0081	0193	1 AN 250-C28B	1882	

PNG ADVENTIST AVIATION SERVICES (Division of PNG Adventist Association) — **Lae**

PO Box 86, Lae, (Morobe Province), Papua New Guinea ☎ 732 12 64 Tx: none Fax: 732 10 30 SITA: n/a
F: 1964 8 Head: Trevor D. Robinson Net: n/a

☐ P2-SDA	Cessna TU206G Turbo Stationair 6 II	U20605399	N6277U	0080	0794	1 CO TSIO-520-M	1633	
☐ P2-SDB	Cessna TU206G Turbo Stationair 6 II	U20605456	C-GATQ	0080	0894	1 CO TSIO-520-M	1633	
☐ P2-SDC	Cessna U206F Stationair II	U20603255	N8394Q	0076		1 CO IO-520-F	1633	

REGIONAL AIR, Ltd = QT (Member of the Booij Group of Companies / formerly KSS Aviation, Pty Ltd) — **Madang**

PO Box 373, Madang, Papua New Guinea ☎ 852 39 77 Tx: none Fax: 852 39 76 SITA: n/a
F: 1993 22 Head: Jan Booij IATA: 361 Net: n/a

☐ P2-KSA	Beech King Air B200	BB-1527	N170W	0096	0299	2 PWC PT6A-42	5670	
☐ P2-KSG	De Havilland DHC-6 Twin Otter 320	509	VH-WPT	0076	1197	2 PWC PT6A-27	5670	
☐ P2-KSR	De Havilland DHC-6 Twin Otter 300	507	N720CA	0076	0696	2 PWC PT6A-27	5670	
☐ P2-KSS	De Havilland DHC-6 Twin Otter 300	578	N578SA	0078	0494	2 PWC PT6A-27	5670	

SIL AVIATION (Aviation Department of Summer Institute of Linguistics) — **Aiyura**

PO Box 402, Ukarumpa EHP 444, Papua New Guinea ☎ 640 44 03 Tx: none Fax: 640 44 00 SITA: n/a
F: 1956 40 Head: Donald C. Archibald Net: n/a

☐ P2-SIL	Bell 206B JetRanger III	3498	ZK-HTF	0081		1 AN 250-C20B	1451	
☐ P2-SIG	Cessna TU206G T. Stationair 6 II R/STOL	U20606029	VH-XAA	0080	0095	1 CO TSIO-520-M	1633	
☐ P2-SIJ	Cessna TU206G T. Stationair 6 II R/STOL	U20605805	N5491X	0080		1 CO TSIO-520-M	1633	
☐ P2-SIT	Cessna TU206G T. Stationair 6 II R/STOL	U20606158	N181PK	0081	0698	1 CO TSIO-520-M	1633	
☐ P2-SIB	Cessna 402C II R/STOL	402C0263	N379P	0080	0295	2 CO TSIO-520-VB	3107	
☐ P2-SIR	Cessna 402C II R/STOL	402C0422	N6787Z	0081		2 CO TSIO-520-VB	3107	
☐ P2-SIV	Britten-Norman BN-2T Turbine Islander	2138	9M-TIR	0083	0092	2 AN 250-B17C	3175	cvtd-26

SOUTHWEST AIR, Pty Ltd (Subsidiary of Floras, Pty Ltd) — **Mendi**

PO Box 71, Mendi, (S.H.P.), Papua New Guinea ☎ 549 10 31 Tx: none Fax: 549 13 58 SITA: n/a
F: n/a n/a Head: J. Sauverian Net: n/a

☐ P2-SHA	Bell 206L-3 LongRanger III	51533	VH-IRE	0091	0697	1 AN 250-C30P	1882	
☐ P2-SHB	Bell 206L-3 LongRanger III	51153		0085	0097	1 AN 250-C30P	1882	
☐ P2-SWF	Embraer 110P1 Bandeirante (EMB-110P1)	110237	N691RA	0079	0294	2 PWC PT6A-34	5670	
☐ P2-SWE	De Havilland DHC-6 Twin Otter 300	480	P2-RDL	0076	0793	2 PWC PT6A-27	5670	

TRANS AIR, Pty Ltd (Sister company of MBA, Pty Ltd) — **Port Moresby**

PO Box 170, Port Moresby, Papua New Guinea ☎ 325 20 11 Tx: none Fax: 325 22 19 SITA: n/a
F: 1997 n/a Head: John R. Wild Net: n/a

☐ P2-MBN	Cessna 550 Citation II	550-0145	VH-TFQ	0080	0097	2 PWC JT15D-4	6033	

TRANSNIUGINI AIRWAYS, Pty Ltd — **Port Moresby**

PO Box 529, Kundiawa, Papua New Guinea ☎ 735 13 78 Tx: none Fax: 735 11 73 SITA: n/a
F: 1991 20 Head: Gerard Phillip Net: n/a

☐ P2-TNC	Cessna A185E Skywagon	185-1233	P2-TAC	0067		1 CO IO-520-D	1520	
☐ P2-TND	Britten-Norman BN-2A-21 Islander	813	P2-COD	0076	0492	2 LY IO-540-K1B5	2994	
☐ P2-TNQ	Beech Queen Air B80 (65-B80)	LD-508	VH-FDL	0075	0593	2 LY IGSO-540-A1D	3992	

VAN AIR (Division of Garamut Exploration, Pty Ltd / formerly Garamut Aviation) — **Port Moresby & Vanimo**

PO Box 167, Vanimo, Papua New Guinea ☎ 857 10 56 Tx: none Fax: 857 15 76 SITA: n/a
F: 1992 n/a Head: Philipp John Net: n/a

☐ P2-CMV	Cessna U206G Stationair 6 II	U20604481	VH-SAJ	0078	0397	1 CO IO-520-F	1633	
☐ P2-VAC	Cessna U206F Stationair	U20602408	P2-AAC	0074	0396	1 CO IO-520-F	1633	
☐ P2-VAB	Britten-Norman BN-2A-20 Islander	759	P2-MFZ	0075	0396	2 LY IO-540-K1B5	2994	
☐ P2-TSJ	Cessna 208B Grand Caravan	208B0339	N1045Y*	0093	0593	1 PWC PT6A-114A	3969	
☐ P2-VAD	Embraer 110P1 Bandeirante (EMB-110P1)	110281	VH-WPI	0081	0696	2 PWC PT6A-34	5670	Township of Vanimo / std TWB/for sale

P4 = ARUBA

Capital: Oranjestad Official Language: Dutch Population: 0,1 million Square Km: 193 Dialling code: +2978 Acting political head: Jan Hendrik A. Eman (Prime Minister)

Government / Corporate / Executive / VIP Aircraft

☐ P4-AMO	BAe (BAC) One-Eleven 401AK	086	HR-AMO	0066	0792	2 RR Spey 511-14	40597	Executive		ABCO Aruba AVV
☐ P4-DPD	Airbus Industrie A310-304	431	V8-DPD	0087	1098	2 GE CF6-80C2A2	153000	VIP		Praeda AVV
☐ P4-FDH	Boeing 707-351B	18586 / 345	HZ-SAK1	0063	0596	4 PW JT3D-3B (HK2/COM)	146500	VIP		Omega Air / Azza AVV
☐ P4-JLD	Boeing 727-193	19620 / 377	VP-CWC	0067	0797	3 PW JT8D-7B	72802	VIP		Joylud Dist International
☐ P4-MDJ	Boeing 707-3L6C	21096 / 900	A6-HRM	0075	1295	4 PW JT3D-7 (HK2/COM)	150000	VIP F22Y70		Comtran Int'l
☐ P4-SKI	Boeing 727-212 (A/RE) (Super 27)	21460 / 1340	VP-CBQ	0078	0196	3 PW JT8D-217C/17 (BFG)	89358	Executive	JK-CD	Precision Air Ltd/based BOH / cvtd -212
☐ P4-TBN	Boeing 707-3L6B	21049 / 896	A6-HPZ	0075	1195	4 PW JT3D-7 (HK2/COM)	151046	Corporate		TBN Aircraft Aruba

AIR ARUBA, N.V. = FQ / ARU (Subsidiary of Aserca Airlines) — **Aruba**

PO Box 1017, Oranjestad, Aruba ☎ (8) 30 005 Tx: 5189 aua aw Fax: (8) 38 138 SITA: n/a
F: 1988 300 Head: Karl van der Linden & Nelson Croes IATA: 276 ICAO: ARUBA Net: http://www.interknowledge.com/air-aruba

☐ P4-DCA	Boeing (Douglas) DC-9-32	47638 / 730	N19504	0074	0998	2 PW JT8D-9A	49895	C8Y95		lsf Cari Avn Leasing Ltd / cvtd DC-9-31
☐ N11FQ	Boeing (Douglas) MD-88 (DC-9-88)	49759 / 1606	P4-MDA	0089	0392	2 PW JT8D-219	72575	C8Y135	BJ-FQ	Barica Geel / lsf POLA
☐ N12FQ	Boeing (Douglas) MD-88 (DC-9-88)	49766 / 1657	P4-MDC	1189	0792	2 PW JT8D-219	72575	C8Y135	BJ-GQ	Arikok / lsf POLA
☐ P4-MDF	Boeing (Douglas) MD-90-30	53578 / 2238		0098	1198	2 IAE V2525-D5	70760	C12Y143		lsf Hwa-Hsai Leasing Ltd
☐ P4-MDG	Boeing (Douglas) MD-90-30	53579 / 2242		0098	1198	2 IAE V2525-D5	70760	C12Y143		lsf Hwa-Hsai Leasing Ltd
☐ P4-MDH	Boeing (Douglas) MD-90-30	53580 / 2246		0098	1198	2 IAE V2525-D5	70760	C12Y143		lsf Hwa-Hsai Leasing Ltd / sub-lst OCA

AVIA AIR, N.V. = 8R / ARB — **Aruba**

PO Box 69, Queen Beatrix Int'l Airport, Aruba ☎ (8) 34 600 Tx: none Fax: (8) 26 355 SITA: n/a
F: 1987 30 Head: n/a ICAO: AVIAIR Net: n/a

☐ P4-AVA	Cessna 402B	402B0911	N9000C	0075	0694	2 CO TSIO-520-E	2858	Y7		

518 registration type of aircraft cn/fn ex/ex* mfd del powered by mtow kg configuration selcal name/fln/specialitites/remarks

☐ P4-AVD	Embraer 110P1 Bandeirante (EMB-110P1)	110336	N76CZ	0081	1094	2 PWC PT6A-34	5670	Y18		
☐ P4-AVE	Embraer 110P1 Bandeirante (EMB-110P1)	110283	N404AS	0080	1195	2 PWC PT6A-34	5670	Y18		

FIA – First International Airlines — Ostend

European HQ:, Airport Terminal, B-8400 Ostend, Belgium ☎ (59) 80 49 04 Tx: none Fax: (59) 80 86 80 SITA: n/a
F: 1996 ⁂ n/a Head: Capt. Hossein Taghdis Net: n/a

☐ 9G-LCA	Canadair CL-44-0 Guppy	16	4K-GUP	0061	0798	4 RR Tyne 515-10	95254	Freighter		lsf ALGI/sub-lst/jtly opw JON/cvtd -D4
☐ 9G-FIA	Boeing 707-331C	20069 / 815	P4-YYY	0769	0997	4 PW JT3D-3B (HK2/COM)	146500	Freighter		lsf ALGI / sub-lst / jtly opw JON
☐ 9G-OLD	Boeing 707-324C	19350 / 537	YA-PAM	0066	1197	4 PW JT3D-3B (HK2/COM)	146500	Freighter	DJ-EF	lsf ALGI / sub-lst / jtly opw JON
☐ 9G-OOD	Boeing 707-399C	19415 / 601	9G-ALD	0067	0998	4 PW JT3D-3B (HK2/COM)	146500	Freighter		lsf ALGI / sub-lst / jtly opw JON

PRO AIR AMBULANCE (Pro Air Charter Aruba, N.V. dba) — Aruba

Airport, Queen Beatrix Int'l Airport, Aruba ☎ (8) 29 197 Tx: none Fax: (8) 32 791 SITA: n/a
F: 1990 ⁂ n/a Head: Rupert Richard Net: n/a

☐ P4-AMB	Hawker 400B (HS 125-400B)	25252	N48US	0071	0793	2 RR Viper 522	10569	EMS		

SUPER SHRIMP – Flight Dept. (Flight Dept. of Super Shrimp AVV, a division of Sea Hatch Laboratory, N.V.) — Aruba

PO Box 382, Salvaneta, Aruba ☎ (8) 42 776 Tx: none Fax: (8) 42 348 SITA: n/a
F: 1997 ⁂ n/a Head: Jochen Van der Falk Net: n/a Operates cargo charter flights primarily for iself.

☐ P4-SSG	Convair 340-71 (C-131F)	282	N14099	0055	0598	2 PW R-2800	21772	Freighter		

RA = RUSSIA / RUSSIAN FEDERATION (Rossia / Rossiskaya Federatsia)

(Includes autonomous "republics")
Capital: Moscow Official Language: Russian Population: 148,4 million Square Km: 17075400 Dialling code: +7 Year established: 1991 Acting political head: Boris N. Yeltsin (President)

ADYGHEYA
Capital: Maikop Official Language: Adygheyan, Russian Population: 0,5 million Square Km: 7600 Dialling code: +7 Acting political head: Aslan Djarimov (President)
ALTAI
Capital: Gorno-Altaisk Official Language: Russian Population: 0,2 million Square Km: 92600 Dialling code: +7 Acting political head: V.V. Volkov (Prime Minister)
BASHKORTOSTAN (Bashkiria)
Capital: Ufa Official Language: Bashkirian, Russian Population: 4,0 million Square Km: 143600 Dialling code: +7 Acting political head: Murtaza Rakhimov (President)
BURYATIA
Capital: Ulan-Ude Official Language: Buryatian, Russian Population: 1,1 million Square Km: 351300 Dialling code: +7 Acting political head: Leonid V. Potapov (Prime Minister)
CHECHENIA
Capital: Grozny Official Language: Chechen, Russian Population: 0,6 million Square Km: 9500 Dialling code: +7 Acting political head: Aslan Maskhadov (President)
CHUVASHIA
Capital: Cheboksary Official Language: Chuvashian, Russian Population: 1,4 million Square Km: 18300 Dialling code: +7 Acting political head: Nikolai Fyodorov (President)
DAGESTAN
Capital: Makhachkala Official Language: Russian Population: 2,1 million Square Km: 50300 Dialling code: +7 Acting political head: Magomedali A. Magamedov (Prime Minister)
INGUSHETIA
Capital: Nazryan Official Language: Ingush, Russian Population: 0,3 million Square Km: 19300 Dialling code: +7 Acting political head: Ruslan Ashuyev (President)
KABARDINO-BALKARIA
Capital: Nalchik Official Language: Kabardino-Balkarian, Russian Population: 0,8 million Square Km: 12500 Dialling code: +7 Acting political head: Valery Kokov (President)
KALMYKIA
Capital: Elista Official Language: Kalmykian, Russian Population: 0,4 million Square Km: 76100 Dialling code: +7 Acting political head: Kirsan Ilyumzhinov (President)
KARELIA
Capital: Petrozavodsk Official Language: Karelian, Russian, Finnish Population: 0,8 million Square Km: 172400 Dialling code: +7 Acting political head: Viktor M. Stepanov (Prime Minister)
KARYACHEVO-CHERKESIA
Capital: Cherkassk Official Language: Cherkessk (Circassian), Russian Population: 0,5 million Square Km: 14100 Dialling code: +7 Acting political head: Vladimir Chubiyev (President)
KHAKASIA
Capital: Abakan Official Language: Khakasian, Russian Population: 0,6 million Square Km: 61900 Dialling code: +7 Acting political head: Vladimir Lebed (Chief of Administration)
KOMI
Capital: Syktyvkar Official Language: Komi, Russian Population: 1,3 million Square Km: 415900 Dialling code: +7 Acting political head: Yuri Spiridonov (President)
MARI-EL
Capital: Yoshkar-Ola Official Language: Mari, Russian Population: 0,8 million Square Km: 23200 Dialling code: +7 Acting political head: Vjatcheslav A. Kislitsin (President)
MORDOVIA
Capital: Saransk Official Language: Russian Population: 1,0 million Square Km: 26200 Dialling code: +7 Acting political head: I.N. Merkushkin (President)
SAKHA (Yakutia)
Capital: Yakutsk Official Language: Yakutian, Russian Population: 1,1 million Square Km: 3103200 Dialling code: +7 Acting political head: Mikhail Nikolayev (President)
SEVERNAYA OSETIA-ALANIA
Capital: Vladikavkaz Official Language: Osetian, Russian Population: 0,7 million Square Km: 8000 Dialling code: +7 Acting political head: Alexander Dsasokhov (President)
TATARSTAN
Capital: Kazan Official Language: Tatar, Russian Population: 3,7 million Square Km: 68000 Dialling code: +7 Acting political head: Mintimer Shaimiyev (President)
TUVA
Capital: Kyzyl Official Language: Tuva, Russian Population: 0,4 million Square Km: 170500 Dialling code: +7 Acting political head: Sherig-ool Orshak (President)
UDMURTIA
Capital: Izhevsk Official Language: Russian Population: 1,7 million Square Km: 42100 Dialling code: +7 Acting political head: Alexander A. Volkov (Prime Minister)

Government / Corporate / Executive / VIP Aircraft

Ministry of Defence aircraft are still in former Aeroflot colors with or without Aeroflot titles.

☐ FLARF02299	Ilyushin 14P	8344001	CCCP-48106	0058		2 SH ASh-82T	17500	Executive C20		FLARF / South Express-colors
☐ RA-01301	Ilyushin 14M	146001042	01 RED	0056	0094	2 SH ASh-82T	17250	12Pax/flyingdisp		private / based Moscow-Zhukovsky
☐ RA-08829	Antonov 22A	053483302	CCCP-08829	0075		4 KU NK-12MA	250000	Freighter		Ministry of Defence
☐ RA-08830	Antonov 22A	053483308	CCCP-08830	0075		4 KU NK-12MA	250000	Freighter		Ministry of Defence
☐ RA-08831	Antonov 22A	053483311	CCCP-08831	0075		4 KU NK-12MA	250000	Freighter		Ministry of Defence
☐ RA-08832	Antonov 22A	053484317	CCCP-08832	0075		4 KU NK-12MA	250000	Freighter		Ministry of Defence
☐ RA-08833	Antonov 22A	053484321	CCCP-08833	0075		4 KU NK-12MA	250000	Freighter		Ministry of Defence
☐ RA-08834	Antonov 22A	053484327	CCCP-08834	0075		4 KU NK-12MA	250000	Freighter		Ministry of Defence
☐ RA-08835	Antonov 22A	053484331	CCCP-08835	0075		4 KU NK-12MA	250000	Freighter		Ministry of Defence
☐ RA-08836	Antonov 22A	053485336	CCCP-08836	0075		4 KU NK-12MA	250000	Freighter		Ministry of Defence
☐ RA-09302	Antonov 22	8340202	CCCP-09302	0068		4 KU NK-12MA	250000	Freighter		Ministry of Defence
☐ RA-09304	Antonov 22	9340204	CCCP-09304	0069		4 KU NK-12MA	250000	Freighter		Ministry of Defence
☐ RA-09305	Antonov 22A	043481240	CCCP-09305	0074		4 KU NK-12MA	250000	Freighter		Ministry of Defence
☐ RA-09306	Antonov 22	9340206	CCCP-09306	0070		4 KU NK-12MA	250000	Freighter		Ministry of Defence
☐ RA-09308	Antonov 22	00340301	CCCP-09308	0070		4 KU NK-12MA	250000	Freighter		Ministry of Defence
☐ RA-09312	Antonov 22A	043481256	CCCP-09312	0074		4 KU NK-12MA	250000	Freighter		Ministry of Defence
☐ RA-09313	Antonov 22	01340307	CCCP-09313	0071		4 KU NK-12MA	250000	Freighter		Ministry of Defence
☐ RA-09315	Antonov 22	00340302	CCCP-09315	0071		4 KU NK-12MA	250000	Freighter		Ministry of Defence
☐ RA-09316	Antonov 22	01340308	CCCP-09316	0071		4 KU NK-12MA	250000	Freighter		Ministry of Defence
☐ RA-09319	Antonov 22	02340406	CCCP-09319	0072		4 KU NK-12MA	250000	Freighter		Ministry of Defence
☐ RA-09320	Antonov 22A	033480209	CCCP-09320	0073		4 KU NK-12MA	250000	Freighter		Ministry of Defence
☐ RA-09321	Antonov 22	01340303	CCCP-09321	0071		4 KU NK-12MA	250000	Freighter		Ministry of Defence
☐ RA-09322	Antonov 22	01340309	CCCP-09322	0071		4 KU NK-12MA	250000	Freighter		Ministry of Defence
☐ RA-09323	Antonov 22	01340304	CCCP-09323	0071		4 KU NK-12MA	250000	Freighter		Ministry of Defence
☐ RA-09324	Antonov 22	02340407	CCCP-09324	0072		4 KU NK-12MA	250000	Freighter		Ministry of Defence
☐ RA-09325	Antonov 22	00340208	CCCP-09325	0070		4 KU NK-12MA	250000	Freighter		Ministry of Defence
☐ RA-09327	Antonov 22A	033480212	CCCP-09327	0073		4 KU NK-12MA	250000	Freighter		Ministry of Defence
☐ RA-09329	Antonov 22A	043482276	CCCP-09329	0074		4 KU NK-12MA	250000	Freighter		Ministry of Defence
☐ RA-09332	Antonov 22	02340401	CCCP-09332	0072		4 KU NK-12MA	250000	Freighter		Ministry of Defence
☐ RA-09333	Antonov 22	02340402	CCCP-09333	0072		4 KU NK-12MA	250000	Freighter		Ministry of Defence
☐ RA-09335	Antonov 22	02340403	CCCP-09335	0072		4 KU NK-12MA	250000	Freighter		Ministry of Defence
☐ RA-09336	Antonov 22	01340306	CCCP-09336	0071		4 KU NK-12MA	250000	Freighter		Ministry of Defence
☐ RA-09337	Antonov 22A	033480225	CCCP-09337	0073		4 KU NK-12MA	250000	Freighter		Ministry of Defence
☐ RA-09338	Antonov 22A	033480228	CCCP-09338	0073		4 KU NK-12MA	250000	Freighter		Ministry of Defence
☐ RA-09340	Antonov 22A	033481234	CCCP-09340	0073		4 KU NK-12MA	250000	Freighter		Ministry of Defence
☐ RA-09341	Antonov 22A	043482266	CCCP-09341	0075		4 KU NK-12MA	250000	Freighter		Ministry of Defence
☐ RA-09342	Antonov 22A	043482282	CCCP-09342	0074		4 KU NK-12MA	250000	Freighter		Ministry of Defence
☐ RA-09345	Antonov 22	02340404	CCCP-09345	0072		4 KU NK-12MA	250000	Freighter		Ministry of Defence
☐ RA-09346	Antonov 22	00340210	CCCP-09346	0070		4 KU NK-12MA	250000	Freighter		Ministry of Defence
☐ RA-09348	Antonov 22A	053483292	CCCP-09348	0075		4 KU NK-12MA	250000	Freighter		Ministry of Defence
☐ RA-11037	Antonov 12B		CCCP-11037			4 IV AI-20M	61000	Freighter		Ministry of Defence
☐ RA-11240	Antonov 12BP	402706	CCCP-11240	0063		4 IV AI-20M	61000	Freighter		Ministry of Defence
☐ RA-11265	Antonov 12BP	402107	CCCP-11265	0062		4 IV AI-20M	61000	Freighter		Ministry of Defence
☐ RA-11266	Antonov 12		CCCP-11266			4 IV AI-20M	61000	Freighter		Ministry of Defence
☐ RA-11286	Antonov 12BP		CCCP-11286	0063		4 IV AI-20M	61000	Freighter		Ministry of Defence
☐ RA-11341	Antonov 12	00347606	CCCP-11341	0070		4 IV AI-20M	61000	Freighter		Ministry of Defence
☐ RA-11343	Antonov 12	00347503	CCCP-11343	0070		4 IV AI-20M	61000	Freighter		Ministry of Defence
☐ RA-11344	Antonov 12	00347409	CCCP-11344	0070		4 IV AI-20M	61000	Freighter		Ministry of Defence
☐ RA-11393	Antonov 12BP		CCCP-11393			4 IV AI-20M	61000	Freighter		Ministry of Defence
☐ RA-11400	Antonov 12BP		CCCP-11400			4 IV AI-20M	61000	Freighter		Ministry of Defence
☐ RA-11406	Antonov 12BP		CCCP-11406			4 IV AI-20M	61000	Freighter		Ministry of Defence
☐ RA-11412	Antonov 12BP		CCCP-11412			4 IV AI-20M	61000	Freighter		Ministry of Defence
☐ RA-11420	Antonov 12BP		CCCP-11420			4 IV AI-20M	61000	Freighter		Ministry of Defence
☐ RA-11426	Antonov 12BP	4342204	CCCP-11426	0064		4 IV AI-20M	61000	Freighter		Ministry of Defence
☐ RA-11431	Antonov 12BP	5343001	CCCP-11431	0065		4 IV AI-20M	61000	Freighter		Ministry of Defence
☐ RA-11660	Antonov 12BP		CCCP-11660			4 IV AI-20M	61000	Freighter		Ministry of Defence
☐ RA-11740	Antonov 12BP		CCCP-11740			4 IV AI-20M	61000	Freighter		Ministry of Defence

519 registration type of aircraft cn/fn ex/ex* mfd del powered by mtow kg configuration selcal name/fln/specialitites/remarks

registration	type of aircraft	cn/fn	ex/ex*	mfd	del	powered by	mtow kg	configuration	selcal	name/fln/specialitites/remarks
☐ RA-11742	Antonov 12BP		CCCP-11742			4 IV AI-20M	61000	Freighter		Ministry of Defence
☐ RA-11746	Antonov 12	7345007	CCCP-11746	0067		4 IV AI-20M	61000	Freighter		Ministry of Defence
☐ RA-11780	Antonov 12BP	7345102	CCCP-11780	0067		4 IV AI-20M	61000	Freighter		Ministry of Defence
☐ RA-11786	Antonov 12BP		CCCP-11786			4 IV AI-20M	61000	Freighter		Ministry of Defence
☐ RA-11792	Antonov 12BP	402701	CCCP-11792	0063		4 IV AI-20M	61000	Freighter		Ministry of Defence
☐ RA-11814	Antonov 12	7345008	CCCP-11814	0067		4 IV AI-20M	61000	Freighter		Ministry of Defence
☐ RA-11835	Antonov 12BP		CCCP-11835			4 IV AI-20M	61000	Freighter		Ministry of Defence
☐ RA-11844	Antonov 12BP		CCCP-11844			4 IV AI-20M	61000	Freighter		Ministry of Defence
☐ RA-11877	Antonov 12BP		CCCP-11877			4 IV AI-20M	61000	Freighter		Ministry of Defence
☐ RA-11894	Antonov 12BP	402602	CCCP-11894	0063		4 IV AI-20M	61000	Freighter		Ministry of Defence
☐ RA-11908	Antonov 12	6344501	CCCP-11908	0066		4 IV AI-20M	61000	Freighter		Ministry of Defence
☐ RA-11922	Antonov 12	7345005	CCCP-11922	0067		4 IV AI-20M	61000	Freighter		Ministry of Defence
☐ RA-11923	Antonov 12BP	1340101	CCCP-11923	0061		4 IV AI-20M	61000	Freighter		Ministry of Defence
☐ RA-11924	Antonov 12BP	6344508	CCCP-11924	0066		4 IV AI-20M	61000	Freighter		Ministry of Defence
☐ RA-11945	Antonov 12BP		CCCP-11945			4 IV AI-20M	61000	Freighter		Ministry of Defence
☐ RA-11965	Antonov 12BP		CCCP-11965			4 IV AI-20M	61000	Freighter		Ministry of Defence
☐ RA-12101	Antonov 12BP	402509	CCCP-12101	0063		4 IV AI-20M	61000	Freighter		Ministry of Defence
☐ RA-12103	Antonov 12BP		CCCP-12103			4 IV AI-20M	61000	Freighter		Ministry of Defence
☐ RA-12115	Antonov 12BP		CCCP-12115			4 IV AI-20M	61000	Freighter		Ministry of Defence
☐ RA-12126	Antonov 12BP	402507	CCCP-12126	0063		4 IV AI-20M	61000	Freighter		Ministry of Defence
☐ RA-12131	Antonov 12BP		CCCP-12131			4 IV AI-20M	61000	Freighter		Ministry of Defence
☐ RA-12132	Antonov 12		CCCP-12132			4 IV AI-20M	61000	Freighter		Ministry of Defence
☐ RA-12133	Antonov 12BP		CCCP-12133			4 IV AI-20M	61000	Freighter		Ministry of Defence
☐ RA-12137	Antonov 12BP		CCCP-12137			4 IV AI-20M	61000	Freighter		Ministry of Defence
☐ RA-12143	Antonov 12		CCCP-12143			4 IV AI-20M	61000	Freighter		Ministry of Defence
☐ RA-21500	Yakovlev 40K	9741356	CCCP-21500	0078		3 IV AI-25	16800	Corporate		Baltic Finance Industrial Group
☐ RA-26165	Antonov 26		CCCP-26165	0083		2 IV AI-24VT	24000	Freighter		Ministry of Defence
☐ RA-30078	Antonov 30	0507	CCCP-30078	0077		2 IV AI-24T	23000	Survey / Combi		Ministry of Defence
☐ RA-42423	Yakovlev 42D	4520424216606		0093		3 LO D-36	56500	Corporate		Yakovlev Design Bureau
☐ RA-42434	Yakovlev 42D	4520424305017		1093	0797	3 LO D-36	56500	C84		KhrunachevSpaceCtr/Proton-Tl/jtlyopwBKU
☐ RA-42644	Yakovlev 42F	4520424914090	CCCP-42644	0089		3 LO D-36	56500	Testbed / Demo		Yakovlev Design Bureau
☐ RA-46454	Antonov 26		CCCP-46454			2 IV AI-24VT	24000	Freighter		Ministry of Defence
☐ RA-46704	Antonov 24T		CCCP-46704			2 IV AI-24VT	22500	Freighter		Ministry of Defence
☐ RA-47403	Antonov 26					2 IV AI-24VT	24000	Freighter		Ministry of Defence
☐ RA-47407	Antonov 26		CCCP-47407			2 IV AI-24VT	24000	Freighter		Ministry of Defence
☐ RA-47411	Antonov 26					2 IV AI-24VT	24000	Freighter		Ministry of Defence
☐ RA-54000	Ilyushin 114	1001	CCCP-54000	0090		2 KL TV7-117	22700	Testbed		Ilyushin / Prototype
☐ RA-64001	Tupolev 234		CCCP-64001	0089		2 SO PS-90P	103000	Testbed		Tupolev Design Bur./Prototype/cvtd -204
☐ RA-64002	Tupolev 204		CCCP-64002	0090		2 SO PS-90A	94600	Testbed		Tupolev Design Bureau / Aeroflot colors
☐ RA-64003	Tupolev 204		CCCP-64003	0090		2 SO PS-90A	94600	Testbed		Tupolev Design Bureau / Aeroflot colors
☐ RA-64004	Tupolev 204		CCCP-64004	0091		2 SO PS-90A	94600	Testbed		Tupolev Design Bureau / Aeroflot colors
☐ RA-64006	Tupolev 204-120	1450743164006	CCCP-64006	0091		2 RR RB211-535E4	103000	Testbed		Sirocco Aerospace / Tupolev-Bravia cs
☐ RA-64026	Tupolev 234			0096		2 SO PS-90P	103000	Testbed		Tupolev / 2nd Prototype / cvtd 204
☐ RA-64501	Tupolev 214			0096		2 SO PS-90A	110750	Testbed		Tupolev Design Bureau / Prototype
☐ RA-65682	Tupolev 134A	62120	CCCP-65682	0072		2 SO D-30-II	49000	Y76		Ministry of Defence / Rossia titles
☐ RA-65684	Tupolev 134A	62205	CCCP-65684	0079		2 SO D-30-II	49000	Y76		Ministry of Defence
☐ RA-65685	Tupolev 134A	62375	CCCP-65685	0072		2 SO D-30-II	49000	Y76		Ministry of Defence
☐ RA-65688	Tupolev 134A	62575	CCCP-65688	0079		2 SO D-30-II	49000	VIP		Ministry of Defence / Rossia titles
☐ RA-65739	Tupolev 134A	2351509	CCCP-65739	0072		2 SO D-30-II	49000	Corporate		MAP-Ministerstvo aviats.promyshlennosti
☐ RA-65940	Tupolev 134A-3	3351906	LZ-TUM	0073	0097	2 SO D-30-III	49000	Exec 28 Pax		Shans Company / cvtd Tu-134A
☐ RA-65980	Tupolev 134A	63207	CCCP-65980	0081		2 SO D-30-II	49000	Y76		Ministry of Defence
☐ RA-65981	Tupolev 134A	63250	CCCP-65981	0080		2 SO D-30-II	49000	Y76		Ministry of Defence
☐ RA-72908	Antonov 72		CCCP-72908	0088		2 LO D-36	34500	Freighter		Ministry of Defence
☐ RA-72909	Antonov 72		CCCP-72909	0088		2 LO D-36	34500	Freighter		Ministry of Defence
☐ RA-72911	Antonov 72		CCCP-72911	0088		2 LO D-36	34500	Freighter		Ministry of Defence
☐ RA-72926	Antonov 72		CCCP-72926	0089		2 LO D-36	34500	Freighter		Ministry of Defence
☐ RA-72930	Antonov 72		CCCP-72930	0089		2 LO D-36	34500	Freighter		Ministry of Defence
☐ RA-72942	Antonov 72		CCCP-72942	0090		2 LO D-36	34500	Freighter		Ministry of Defence
☐ RA-72952	Antonov 72		CCCP-72952	0090		2 LO D-36	34500	Freighter		Ministry of Defence
☐ RA-72958	Antonov 72	36572092841	CCCP-72958	0090		2 LO D-36	34500	Freighter		Ministry of Defence
☐ RA-72961	Antonov 72		CCCP-72961	0090		2 LO D-36	34500	Freighter		Ministry of Defence
☐ RA-72962	Antonov 72		CCCP-72962	0090		2 LO D-36	34500	Freighter		Ministry of Defence
☐ RA-72972	Antonov 72	36572094883	CCCP-72972	0090		2 LO D-36	34500	Freighter		Ministry of Defence
☐ RA-72974	Antonov 72		CCCP-72974	0090		2 LO D-36	34500	Freighter		Ministry of Defence
☐ RA-75482	Ilyushin 18D		CCCP-75482			4 IV AI-20M	64000	Y100		Ministry of Defence
☐ RA-75895	Ilyushin 22 (modif. 18D)	0393607850	CCCP-75895	0074		4 IV AI-20M	64000	VIP/Command Post		Ministry of Defence
☐ RA-75902	Ilyushin 22 (modif. 18D)	0393610226	CCCP-75902	0074		4 IV AI-20M	64000	VIP/Command Post		Ministry of Defence
☐ RA-75903	Ilyushin 22 (modif. 18D)	0393610235	CCCP-75903	0074		4 IV AI-20M	64000	VIP/Command Post		Ministry of Defence
☐ RA-75911	Ilyushin 22 (modif. 18D)	0394011096	CCCP-75911	0074		4 IV AI-20M	64000	VIP/Command Post		Ministry of Defence
☐ RA-75912	Ilyushin 22 (modif. 18D)	0394011097	CCCP-75912	0074		4 IV AI-20M	64000	VIP/Command Post		Ministry of Defence
☐ RA-75913	Ilyushin 22 (modif. 18D)	0394011098	CCCP-75913	0074		4 IV AI-20M	64000	VIP/Command Post		Ministry of Defence
☐ RA-75920	Ilyushin 22 (modif. 18D)	2964017551	CCCP-75920	0074		4 IV AI-20M	64000	VIP/Command Post		Ministry of Defence
☐ RA-75923	Ilyushin 22 (modif. 18D)		CCCP-75923	0074		4 IV AI-20M	64000	VIP/Command Post		Ministry of Defence
☐ RA-75924	Ilyushin 22 (modif. 18D)	2964017554	CCCP-75924	0074		4 IV AI-20M	64000	VIP/Command Post		Ministry of Defence
☐ RA-75925	Ilyushin 22 (modif. 18D)		CCCP-75925	0074		4 IV AI-20M	64000	VIP/Command Post		Ministry of Defence
☐ RA-75927	Ilyushin 22 (modif. 18D)		CCCP-75927	0074		4 IV AI-20M	64000	VIP/Command Post		Ministry of Defence
☐ RA-76450	Ilyushin 76MD		CCCP-76450	0081		4 SO D-30KP	190000	Command Post		Ministry of Defence
☐ RA-76453	Ilyushin 76MD (A50 Mainstay)	0063466995	CCCP-76453	0086		4 SO D-30KP	190000	Surveyer		Ministry of Defence
☐ RA-76454	Ilyushin 76MD (A50 Mainstay)		CCCP-76454	0086		4 SO D-30KP	190000	Surveyer		Ministry of Defence
☐ RA-76455	Ilyushin 76MD (A50 Mainstay)		CCCP-76455	0086		4 SO D-30KP	190000	Surveyer		Ministry of Defence
☐ RA-76530	Ilyushin 76MD		CCCP-76530	0082		4 SO D-30KP	190000	Freighter		Ministry of Defence
☐ RA-76533	Ilyushin 76MD		CCCP-76533	0082		4 SO D-30KP	190000	Freighter		Ministry of Defence
☐ RA-76538	Ilyushin 76MD		CCCP-76538	0083		4 SO D-30KP	190000	Freighter		Ministry of Defence
☐ RA-76547	Ilyushin 76MD		CCCP-76547	0083		4 SO D-30KP	190000	Freighter		Ministry of Defence
☐ RA-76552	Ilyushin 76MD		CCCP-76552	0083		4 SO D-30KP	190000	Freighter		Ministry of Defence
☐ RA-76553	Ilyushin 76MD		CCCP-76553	0083		4 SO D-30KP	190000	Freighter		Ministry of Defence
☐ RA-76554	Ilyushin 76MD		CCCP-76554	0083		4 SO D-30KP	190000	Freighter		Ministry of Defence
☐ RA-76556	Ilyushin 78	0033445294	CCCP-76556	0083		4 SO D-30KP	190000	Freighter/Tanker		Ministry of Defence
☐ RA-76572	Ilyushin 76MD		CCCP-76572	0084		4 SO D-30KP	190000	Freighter		Ministry of Defence
☐ RA-76604	Ilyushin 76MD		CCCP-76604	0084		4 SO D-30KP	190000	Freighter		Ministry of Defence
☐ RA-76613	Ilyushin 76MD		CCCP-76613	0084		4 SO D-30KP	190000	Freighter		Ministry of Defence
☐ RA-76632	Ilyushin 78		CCCP-76632	0085		4 SO D-30KP	190000	Freighter/Tanker		Ministry of Defence
☐ RA-76634	Ilyushin 76MD	0053459770	CCCP-76634	0085		4 SO D-30KP	190000	Freighter		Ministry of Defence
☐ RA-76639	Ilyushin 76MD	0053460805	CCCP-76639	0085		4 SO D-30KP	190000	Freighter		Ministry of Defence
☐ RA-76643	Ilyushin 76MD		CCCP-76643	0085		4 SO D-30KP	190000	Freighter		Ministry of Defence
☐ RA-76648	Ilyushin 76MD		CCCP-76648	0085		4 SO D-30KP	190000	Freighter		Ministry of Defence
☐ RA-76668	Ilyushin 76MD		CCCP-76668	0085		4 SO D-30KP	190000	Freighter		Ministry of Defence
☐ RA-76701	Ilyushin 78		CCCP-76701	0086		4 SO D-30KP	190000	Freighter/Tanker		Ministry of Defence
☐ RA-76714	Ilyushin 76MD		CCCP-76714	0086		4 SO D-30KP	190000	Freighter		Ministry of Defence
☐ RA-76723	Ilyushin 76MD		CCCP-76723	0086		4 SO D-30KP	190000	Freighter		Ministry of Defence
☐ RA-76726	Ilyushin 76MD		CCCP-76726	0086		4 SO D-30KP	190000	Freighter		Ministry of Defence
☐ RA-76731	Ilyushin 76MD		CCCP-76731	0086		4 SO D-30KP	190000	Freighter		Ministry of Defence
☐ RA-76733	Ilyushin 76MD	0073476304	CCCP-76733	0087		4 SO D-30KP	190000	Freighter		Ministry of Defence
☐ RA-76762	Ilyushin 76MD		CCCP-76762	0087		4 SO D-30KP	190000	Freighter		Ministry of Defence
☐ RA-76776	Ilyushin 76MD	0083482486	CCCP-76776	0088		4 SO D-30KP	190000	Freighter		Ministry of Defence
☐ RA-76779	Ilyushin 76MD		CCCP-76779	0088		4 SO D-30KP	190000	Freighter		Ministry of Defence
☐ RA-76780	Ilyushin 76T	0013430901	CCCP-76780	0081		4 SO D-30KP	170000	Freighter		Ministry of Defence
☐ RA-76800	Ilyushin 76TD	0093493810	CCCP-76800	0089		4 SO D-30KP	190000	Freighter		Ministry of Defence
☐ RA-76801	Ilyushin 76MD	0093495866	CCCP-76801	0089		4 SO D-30KP	190000	Freighter		Ministry of Defence
☐ RA-76803	Ilyushin 76TD		CCCP-76803	0090		4 SO D-30KP	190000	Freighter		Ministry of Defence
☐ RA-76825	Ilyushin 76MD		CCCP-76825	0089		4 SO D-30KP	190000	Freighter		Ministry of Defence
☐ RA-76900	Ilyushin 76MF	1053417563	IS-76900	0095		4 SO PS-90AN	190000	Freighter		Ilyushin Design Bureau / Prototype
☐ RA-77114	Tupolev 144LL	08-2	CCCP-77114	0081		4 ST NK-321	199580	SST Research		Tupolev/joint-vent.program w/NASA,cvtdD
☐ RA-78762	Ilyushin 76MD		CCCP-78762	0088		4 SO D-30KP	190000	Freighter		Ministry of Defence
☐ RA-78766	Ilyushin 76MD	0083486595	CCCP-78766	0388		4 SO D-30KP	190000	Freighter		Ministry of Defence
☐ RA-78770	Ilyushin 76MDK	0083487617	CCCP-78770	0088		4 SO D-30KP	190000	Freighter		Ministry of Defence
☐ RA-78795	Ilyushin 76MD		CCCP-78795	0089		4 SO D-30KP	190000	Freighter		Ministry of Defence
☐ RA-78798	Ilyushin 76MD		CCCP-78798	0089		4 SO D-30KP	190000	Freighter		Ministry of Defence
☐ RA-78803	Ilyushin 76MD		CCCP-78803	0089		4 SO D-30KP	190000	Freighter		Ministry of Defence
☐ RA-78807	Ilyushin 76MD	00903493791	CCCP-78807	0089		4 SO D-30KP	190000	Freighter		Ministry of Defence

registration	type of aircraft	cn/fn	ex/ex*	mfd	del	powered by	mtow kg	configuration	selcal	name/fln/specialitites/remarks
☐ RA-78810	Ilyushin 76MD		CCCP-78810	0089		4 SO D-30KP	190000	Freighter		Ministry of Defence
☐ RA-78811	Ilyushin 76MD		CCCP-78811	0089		4 SO D-30KP	190000	Freighter		Ministry of Defence
☐ RA-78813	Ilyushin 76MD		CCCP-78813	0089		4 SO D-30KP	190000	Freighter		Ministry of Defence
☐ RA-78814	Ilyushin 78		CCCP-78814	0089		4 SO D-30KP	190000	Freighter/Tanker		Ministry of Defence
☐ RA-78829	Ilyushin 76MD		CCCP-78829	0090		4 SO D-30KP	190000	Freighter		Ministry of Defence
☐ RA-78830	Ilyushin 76MD	1003401010	CCCP-78830	0090		4 SO D-30KP	190000	Freighter		Ministry of Defence
☐ RA-78844	Ilyushin 76MD		CCCP-78844	0090		4 SO D-30KP	190000	Freighter		Ministry of Defence
☐ RA-78845	Ilyushin 76MD		CCCP-78845	0090		4 SO D-30KP	190000	Freighter		Ministry of Defence
☐ RA-78850	Ilyushin 76MD	1013405196	CCCP-78850	0091		4 SO D-30KP	190000	Freighter		Ministry of Defence
☐ RA-78878	Ilyushin 76MD		CCCP-78878	0091		4 SO D-30KP	190000	Freighter		Ministry of Defence
☐ RA-82006	Antonov 124 Ruslan	19530501004	CCCP-82006	0086		4 LO D-18T	392000	Freighter		fn 01-04 / Ministry of Defence
☐ RA-82011	Antonov 124 Ruslan	9773054646023	CCCP-82011	0087		4 LO D-18T	392000	Freighter		fn 01-10 / Ministry of Defence
☐ RA-82013	Antonov 124 Ruslan		CCCP-82013	0087		4 LO D-18T	392000	Freighter		fn 05-02 / Ministry of Defence
☐ RA-82020	Antonov 124 Ruslan	19530502001	CCCP-82020	0088		4 LO D-18T	392000	Freighter		fn 02-01 / Ministry of Defence
☐ RA-82022	Antonov 124 Ruslan	19530502003	CCCP-82022	0088		4 LO D-18T	392000	Freighter		fn 02-03 / Ministry of Defence
☐ RA-82025	Antonov 124 Ruslan	19530502106	CCCP-82025	0088		4 LO D-18T	392000	Freighter		fn 02-06 / Ministry of Defence
☐ RA-82031	Antonov 124 Ruslan	9773051832049	CCCP-82031	0088		4 LO D-18T	392000	Freighter		fn 05-05 / Ministry of Defence
☐ RA-82035	Antonov 124 Ruslan		CCCP-82035	0089		4 LO D-18T	392000	Freighter		fn 05-09 / Ministry of Defence
☐ RA-82037	Antonov 124 Ruslan	9773052955071	CCCP-82037	0089		4 LO D-18T	392000	Freighter		fn 06-01 / Ministry of Defence
☐ RA-85052	Tupolev 154B	052	CCCP-85052	0074		3 KU NK-8-2U	98000	Y164		Ministry of Defence / cvtd 154
☐ RA-85353	Tupolev 154B-2	353	CCCP-85353	0079		3 KU NK-8-2U	98000	Y164		Ministry of Defence
☐ RA-85380	Tupolev 154B-2	380	CCCP-85380	0079		3 KU NK-8-2U	98000	Y164		Ministry of Defence
☐ RA-85463	Tupolev 154B-2	463	CCCP-85463	0080		3 KU NK-8-2U	98000	Y164		Ministry of Defence
☐ RA-85655	Tupolev 154M	798	CCCP-85655	0089		3 SO D-30KU-154-II	100000	Cosmo Trainer		Ministry of Defence
☐ RA-86022	Ilyushin 76M		CCCP-86022	0079		4 SO D-30KP	170000	Freighter		Ministry of Defence
☐ RA-86023	Ilyushin 76M		CCCP-86023	0079		4 SO D-30KP	170000	Freighter		Ministry of Defence
☐ RA-86025	Ilyushin 76M		CCCP-86025	0079		4 SO D-30KP	170000	Freighter		Ministry of Defence
☐ RA-86026	Ilyushin 76M		CCCP-86026	0079		4 SO D-30KP	170000	Freighter		Ministry of Defence
☐ RA-86027	Ilyushin 76M		CCCP-86027	0079		4 SO D-30KP	170000	Freighter		Ministry of Defence
☐ RA-86032	Ilyushin 76M		CCCP-86032	0079		4 SO D-30KP	170000	Freighter		fn 13-01 / Ministry of Defence
☐ RA-86033	Ilyushin 76M		CCCP-86033	0079		4 SO D-30KP	170000	Freighter		Ministry of Defence
☐ RA-86037	Ilyushin 76M		CCCP-86037	0079		4 SO D-30KP	170000	Freighter		Ministry of Defence
☐ RA-86038	Ilyushin 76M		CCCP-86038	0079		4 SO D-30KP	170000	Freighter		Ministry of Defence
☐ RA-86040	Ilyushin 76M		CCCP-86040	0079		4 SO D-30KP	170000	Freighter		Ministry of Defence
☐ RA-86042	Ilyushin 76M		CCCP-86042	0079		4 SO D-30KP	170000	Freighter		Ministry of Defence
☐ RA-86043	Ilyushin 76M	093418539	CCCP-86043	0079		4 SO D-30KP	170000	Freighter		Ministry of Defence
☐ RA-86048	Ilyushin 76M		CCCP-86048	0079		4 SO D-30KP	170000	Freighter		Ministry of Defence
☐ RA-86049	Ilyushin 76M		CCCP-86049	0079		4 SO D-30KP	170000	Freighter		Ministry of Defence
☐ RA-86146	Ilyushin 86		CCCP-86146	0091		4 KU NK-86	215000	Command Post		Ministry of Defence
☐ RA-86147	Ilyushin 86		CCCP-86147	0091		4 KU NK-86	215000	Command Post		Ministry of Defence
☐ RA-86148	Ilyushin 86		CCCP-86148	0091		4 KU NK-86	215000	Command Post		Ministry of Defence
☐ RA-86149	Ilyushin 86		CCCP-86149	0091		4 KU NK-86	215000	Command Post		Ministry of Defence
☐ RA-86505	Ilyushin 62M	4934847	CCCP-86505	0079		4 SO D-30KU	167000	Y168		fn 3404 / Ministry of Defence
☐ RA-86556	Ilyushin 62	31401	CCCP-86556	0073		4 KU NK-8-4	161600	Y168		fn 1401 / Ministry of Defence
☐ RA-86557	Ilyushin 62	2725456	CCCP-86557	0077		4 KU NK-8-4	161600	Y168		fn 2505 / Ministry of Defence
☐ RA-86625	Ilyushin 76M		CCCP-86625	0076		4 SO D-30KP	170000	Freighter		Ministry of Defence
☐ RA-86642	Ilyushin 76M		CCCP-86642	0077		4 SO D-30KP	170000	Freighter		Ministry of Defence
☐ RA-86731	Ilyushin 76M		CCCP-86731	0078		4 SO D-30KP	170000	Freighter		Ministry of Defence
☐ RA-86734	Ilyushin 76M		CCCP-86734	0078		4 SO D-30KP	170000	Freighter		Ministry of Defence
☐ RA-86736	Ilyushin 76M		CCCP-86736	0078		4 SO D-30KP	170000	Freighter		Ministry of Defence
☐ RA-86738	Ilyushin 76M		CCCP-86738	0078		4 SO D-30KP	170000	Freighter		Ministry of Defence
☐ RA-86740	Ilyushin 76M		CCCP-86740	0078		4 SO D-30KP	170000	Freighter		Ministry of Defence
☐ RA-86741	Ilyushin 76M		CCCP-86741	0078		4 SO D-30KP	170000	Freighter		Ministry of Defence
☐ RA-86743	Ilyushin 76M		CCCP-86743	0078		4 SO D-30KP	170000	Freighter		Ministry of Defence
☐ RA-86744	Ilyushin 76M		CCCP-86744	0078		4 SO D-30KP	170000	Freighter		Ministry of Defence
☐ RA-86748	Ilyushin 76M		CCCP-86748	0078		4 SO D-30KP	170000	Freighter		Ministry of Defence
☐ RA-86749	Ilyushin 76M		CCCP-86749	0078		4 SO D-30KP	170000	Freighter		Ministry of Defence
☐ RA-86810	Ilyushin 76M		CCCP-86810	0075		4 SO D-30KP	170000	Freighter		Ministry of Defence/opf Azerbaijan MoD
☐ RA-86825	Ilyushin 76M		CCCP-86825	0075		4 SO D-30KP	170000	Freighter		VTA/Ministry of Defence
☐ RA-86826	Ilyushin 76M		CCCP-86826	0075		4 SO D-30KP	170000	Freighter		Ministry of Defence
☐ RA-86827	Ilyushin 76M		CCCP-86827	0075		4 SO D-30KP	170000	Freighter		Ministry of Defence
☐ RA-86830	Ilyushin 76M		CCCP-86830	0075		4 SO D-30KP	170000	Freighter		Ministry of Defence
☐ RA-86832	Ilyushin 76M		CCCP-86832	0075		4 SO D-30KP	170000	Freighter		Ministry of Defence
☐ RA-86833	Ilyushin 76M		CCCP-86833	0075		4 SO D-30KP	170000	Freighter		Ministry of Defence
☐ RA-86835	Ilyushin 76M		CCCP-86835	0075		4 SO D-30KP	170000	Freighter		Ministry of Defence
☐ RA-86836	Ilyushin 76M	0003422661	CCCP-86836	0080		4 SO D-30KP	170000	Freighter		Ministry of Defence
☐ RA-86837	Ilyushin 76M		CCCP-86837	0080		4 SO D-30KP	170000	Freighter		Ministry of Defence
☐ RA-86838	Ilyushin 76M		CCCP-86838	0080		4 SO D-30KP	170000	Freighter		Ministry of Defence
☐ RA-86839	Ilyushin 76M		CCCP-86839	0080		4 SO D-30KP	170000	Freighter		Ministry of Defence
☐ RA-86841	Ilyushin 76M		CCCP-86841	0080		4 SO D-30KP	170000	Freighter		Ministry of Defence
☐ RA-86842	Ilyushin 76M		CCCP-86842	0080		4 SO D-30KP	170000	Freighter		Ministry of Defence
☐ RA-86843	Ilyushin 76M		CCCP-86843	0080		4 SO D-30KP	170000	Freighter		Ministry of Defence
☐ RA-86847	Ilyushin 76M		CCCP-86847	0080		4 SO D-30KP	170000	Freighter		Ministry of Defence
☐ RA-86855	Ilyushin 76M		CCCP-86855	0080		4 SO D-30KP	170000	Freighter		Ministry of Defence
☐ RA-86857	Ilyushin 76M	0003425744	CCCP-86857	0080		4 SO D-30KP	170000	Freighter		Ministry of Defence
☐ RA-86858	Ilyushin 76M		CCCP-86858	0080		4 SO D-30KP	170000	Freighter		fn 19-08 / Ministry of Defence
☐ RA-86863	Ilyushin 76M	0003428809	CCCP-86863	0080		4 SO D-30KP	170000	Freighter		fn 21-03 / Ministry of Defence
☐ RA-86866	Ilyushin 76M	0003428821	CCCP-86866	0080		4 SO D-30KP	170000	Freighter		Ministry of Defence
☐ RA-86868	Ilyushin 76M		CCCP-86868	0080		4 SO D-30KP	170000	Freighter		Ministry of Defence
☐ RA-86870	Ilyushin 76M		CCCP-86870	0080		4 SO D-30KP	170000	Freighter		Ministry of Defence
☐ RA-86871	Ilyushin 76MD		CCCP-86871	0081		4 SO D-30KP	190000	Freighter		Ministry of Defence
☐ RA-86872	Ilyushin 76MD		CCCP-86872	0081		4 SO D-30KP	190000	Freighter		Ministry of Defence
☐ RA-86873	Ilyushin 76M		CCCP-86873	0080		4 SO D-30KP	170000	Freighter		Ministry of Defence
☐ RA-86876	Ilyushin 76MD		CCCP-86876	0081		4 SO D-30KP	190000	Freighter		Ministry of Defence
☐ RA-86891	Ilyushin 76M	093421628	YI-AKV	0079		4 SO D-30KP	170000	Freighter		Ministry of Defence
☐ RA-86893	Ilyushin 76M		CCCP-86893	0081		4 SO D-30KP	170000	Freighter		Ministry of Defence
☐ RA-86894	Ilyushin 76M		CCCP-86894	0081		4 SO D-30KP	170000	Freighter		Ministry of Defence
☐ RA-86895	Ilyushin 76M		CCCP-86895	0081		4 SO D-30KP	170000	Freighter		Ministry of Defence
☐ RA-86898	Ilyushin 76MD		CCCP-86898	0081		4 SO D-30KP	190000	Freighter		Ministry of Defence
☐ RA-86902	Ilyushin 76MD		CCCP-86902	0082		4 SO D-30KP	190000	Freighter		Ministry of Defence
☐ RA-86908	Ilyushin 76MD		CCCP-86908	0082		4 SO D-30KP	190000	Freighter		Ministry of Defence
☐ RA-86925	Ilyushin 76MD		CCCP-86925	0082		4 SO D-30KP	190000	Freighter		Ministry of Defence
☐ RA-87659	Yakovlev 40	9240325	CCCP-87659	0072		3 IV AI-25	16800	Corporate		Yakovlev Design Bureau
☐ RA-87807	Yakovlev 40	9231723	CCCP-87807	0772		3 IV AI-25	16100	VIP 13 Pax		International Industrial Bank
☐ RA-91005	Ilyushin 114T	0301		0996		2 KL TV7-117	23500	Freighter		Ilyushin / Freighter Prototype
☐ RA-94001	Tupolev 334	01-001		0095		2 LO D-436T1	46100	Testbed		Tupolev Design Bureau / Prototype
☐ RA-96000	Ilyushin 96M	0101	CCCP-96000	0088		4 PW PW2337	270000	Testbed		Ilyushin / Prototype / cvtd IL96-300
☐ RA-96001	Ilyushin 96-300	0103	CCCP-96001	0089		4 SO PS-90A	216000	Testbed		Ilyushin Design Bureau / Aeroflot cs
☐ RA-96002	Ilyushin 96-300		CCCP-96002	0089		4 SO PS-90A	216000	Testbed / Pax		Ilyushin Design Bur./occ opf AFL/AFL cs

ABAKAN-AVIA = ABG

Abakan

Kantegir Hotel, Airport, 662608 Abakan, (Republic of Khakasia), Russia ☎ (39022) 56 408 Tx: 150113 tppsu Fax: (39022) 56 418 SITA: n/a

F: 1992 n/a Head: Vladimir A. Belousov ICAO: ABAKAN-AVIA Net: n/a

☐ RA-76504	Ilyushin 76T	073411330	CCCP-76504	0077		4 SO D-30KP	170000	Freighter		
☐ RA-76505	Ilyushin 76T	073411331	CCCP-76505	0077		4 SO D-30KP	170000	Freighter		

ADYGHEYA AVIA, Joint-Stock Company = MKP (formerly Aeroflot Maikop division)

Maikop

Maikop Airport, 352710 Maikop, (Republic of Adygheya), Russia ☎ (87722) 31 004 Tx: none Fax: (87722) 31 656 SITA: n/a

F: n/a n/a Head: Yuri G. Soldatov ICAO: ADYGHEYA Net: n/a Beside aircraft listed, also own 70 Antonov 2 (Sprayers). Many are stored and for sale.

☐ RA-46479	Antonov 24RV	27308007	CCCP-46479	0072		2 IV AI-24VT	21800	Y48		
☐ RA-47190	Antonov 24B		CCCP-47190	0069		2 IV AI-24	21000	Y48		
☐ RA-47690	Antonov 24RV	27307507	CCCP-47690	0072		2 IV AI-24VT	21800	Y48		

AEROFLOT Russian International Airlines = SU / AFL (formerly Aeroflot International directorate)

Moscow-Sheremetyevo

Sheremetyevo Airport, 103340 Moskva, Russia ☎ (095) 155 66 41 Tx: none Fax: (095) 155 66 47 SITA: MOWDDSU

F: 1923 15000 Head: Valeri Okulov IATA: 555 ICAO: AEROFLOT Net: http://www.aeroflot.org Flights from Khabarovsk are contracted to/operated by KHABAROVSK AVIATION ENTERPRISE, international flights (beside CIS) by PULKOVO AVIATION ENTERPRISE using SU flight numbers. For details – see under both companies.

☐ RA-65559	Tupolev 134A	49909	101	0077	0093	2 SO D-30-II	49000	VIP F7Y48		
☐ RA-65566	Tupolev 134A	63952	9A-ADL	0082	0093	2 SO D-30-II	49000	F8Y60		
☐ RA-65567	Tupolev 134A-3	63967	9A-ADP	0082	0093	2 SO D-30-III	49000	F8Y60		

☐	RA-65568	Tupolev 134A	66135	9A-ADR	0083	0093	2 SO D-30-II	49000	F8Y60		
☐	RA-65623	Tupolev 134A	49985	SP-LHI	0077		2 SO D-30-II	49000	F8Y60		
☐	RA-65697	Tupolev 134A-3	63307	CCCP-65697	0080		2 SO D-30-III	49000	F8Y60		
☐	RA-65717	Tupolev 134A-3	63657	CCCP-65717	0081		2 SO D-30-III	49000	F8Y60		
☐	RA-65769	Tupolev 134A-3	62415	CCCP-65769	0079	0979	2 SO D-30-III	49000	F8Y60		
☐	RA-65770	Tupolev 134A-3	62430	CCCP-65770	0079	0979	2 SO D-30-III	49000	F8Y60		
☐	RA-65781	Tupolev 134A-3	62645	CCCP-65781	0079	0180	2 SO D-30-III	49000	F8Y60		
☐	RA-65783	Tupolev 134A-3	62708	CCCP-65783	0079	0180	2 SO D-30-III	49000	F8Y60		
☐	RA-65784	Tupolev 134A-3	62715	CCCP-65784	0079		2 SO D-30-III	49000	F8Y60		
☐	VP-BAH	Boeing 737-4M0	29201 / 3018		0098	0598	2 CFMI CFM56-3C1	68040	C20Y111	QS-BK	lsf Sailplane Leasing
☐	VP-BAI	Boeing 737-4M0	29202 / 3025		0098	0598	2 CFMI CFM56-3C1	68040	C20Y111	QS-DE	lsf Sailplane Leasing
☐	VP-BAJ	Boeing 737-4M0	29203 / 3049		0098	0798	2 CFMI CFM56-3C1	68040	C20Y111	QS-DF	lsf Sailplane Leasing
☐	VP-BAL	Boeing 737-4M0	29204 / 3051		0098	0798	2 CFMI CFM56-3C1	68040	C20Y111	QS-AL	lsf Sailplane Leasing
☐	VP-BAM	Boeing 737-4M0	29205 / 3056		0098	0798	2 CFMI CFM56-3C1	68040	C20Y111	QS-AM	lsf Sailplane Leasing
☐	VP-BAN	Boeing 737-4M0	29206 / 3058		0098	0898	2 CFMI CFM56-3C1	68040	C20Y111	QS-BL	lsf Sailplane Leasing
☐	VP-BAO	Boeing 737-4M0	29207 / 3078	N1786B*	0098	1198	2 CFMI CFM56-3C1	68040	C20Y111	QS-BM	lsf Sailplane Leasing
☐	VP-BAP	Boeing 737-4M0	29208 / 3081	N1003W*	0098	1298	2 CFMI CFM56-3C1	68040	C20Y111	QS-CM	lsf Sailplane Leasing
☐	VP-BAQ	Boeing 737-4M0	29209 / 3087		1298	1298	2 CFMI CFM56-3C1	68040	C20Y111	QS-CP	lsf Sailplane Leasing
☐	VP-BAR	Boeing 737-4M0	29210 / 3091	N1786B*	0099	0399	2 CFMI CFM56-3C1	68040	C20Y111	QS-DG	lsf Sailplane Leasing
☐	RA-85363	Tupolev 154B-2	363	CCCP-85363	0079	0979	3 KU NK-8-2U	98000	F12C18Y102		
☐	RA-85564	Tupolev 154B-2	564	CCCP-85564	0082	0183	3 KU NK-8-2U	98000	F12C18Y102		
☐	RA-85570	Tupolev 154B-2	570	CCCP-85570	0083	0383	3 KU NK-8-2U	98000	F12C18Y102		
☐	RA-85592	Tupolev 154B-2	592	CCCP-85592	0083	0184	3 KU NK-8-2U	98000	F12C18Y102		
☐	RA-85625	Tupolev 154M	752	CCCP-85625	0087	0787	3 SO D-30KU-154-II	100000	F12C18Y102		
☐	RA-85626	Tupolev 154M	753	CCCP-85626	0087	0787	3 SO D-30KU-154-II	100000	F12C18Y102		
☐	RA-85634	Tupolev 154M	763	CCCP-85634	0087	1287	3 SO D-30KU-154-II	100000	F12C18Y102		
☐	RA-85637	Tupolev 154M	767	CCCP-85637	0087	0188	3 SO D-30KU-154-II	100000	F12C18Y102		
☐	RA-85638	Tupolev 154M	768	CCCP-85638	0087	0288	3 SO D-30KU-154-II	100000	F12C18Y102		
☐	RA-85639	Tupolev 154M	771	CCCP-85639	0088	0488	3 SO D-30KU-154-II	100000	F12C18Y102		
☐	RA-85640	Tupolev 154M	772	CCCP-85640	0088	0488	3 SO D-30KU-154-II	100000	F12C18Y102		
☐	RA-85641	Tupolev 154M	773	CCCP-85641	0088	0488	3 SO D-30KU-154-II	100000	F12C18Y102		
☐	RA-85642	Tupolev 154M	778	CCCP-85642	0088	0788	3 SO D-30KU-154-II	100000	F12C18Y102		
☐	RA-85643	Tupolev 154M	779	CCCP-85643	0088	0788	3 SO D-30KU-154-II	100000	F12C18Y102		
☐	RA-85644	Tupolev 154M	780	MPR-85644	0088	0788	3 SO D-30KU-154-II	100000	F12C18Y102		
☐	RA-85646	Tupolev 154M	784	CCCP-85646	0088	0988	3 SO D-30KU-154-II	100000	F12C18Y102		
☐	RA-85647	Tupolev 154M	785	CCCP-85647	0288	1088	3 SO D-30KU-154-II	100000	F12C18Y102		
☐	RA-85648	Tupolev 154M	786	CCCP-85648	0088	1088	3 SO D-30KU-154-II	100000	F12C18Y102		
☐	RA-85649	Tupolev 154M	787	CCCP-85649	0088	1088	3 SO D-30KU-154-II	100000	F12C18Y102		
☐	RA-85650	Tupolev 154M	788	CCCP-85650	0088	1188	3 SO D-30KU-154-II	100000	F12C18Y102		
☐	RA-85661	Tupolev 154M	811	CCCP-85661	0089	0889	3 SO D-30KU-154-II	100000	F12C18Y102		
☐	RA-85662	Tupolev 154M	816	CCCP-85662	0089	1089	3 SO D-30KU-154-II	100000	F12C18Y102		
☐	RA-85663	Tupolev 154M	817	CCCP-85663	0089	1089	3 SO D-30KU-154-II	100000	F12C18Y102		
☐	RA-85665	Tupolev 154M	819	CCCP-85665	0089	1089	3 SO D-30KU-154-II	100000	F12C18Y102		
☐	RA-85668	Tupolev 154M	826	CCCP-85668	0089	0190	3 SO D-30KU-154-II	100000	F12C18Y102		
☐	RA-85669	Tupolev 154M	827	CCCP-85669	0089	0190	3 SO D-30KU-154-II	100000	F12C18Y102		
☐	RA-85670	Tupolev 154M	828	CCCP-85670	0089	0190	3 SO D-30KU-154-II	100000	F12C18Y102		
☐	RA-85797	Tupolev 154M	981		1293	0797	3 SO D-30KU-154-II	100000	F12C18Y104		lsf/jtly opw ERG
☐	RA-85809	Tupolev 154M	985		1294	0997	3 SO D-30KU-154-II	100000	F12C18Y104		lsf/jtly opw ERG
☐	RA-85810	Tupolev 154M	824	SP-LCM	1289	0994	3 SO D-30KU-154-II	100000	F12C18Y102		
☐	RA-85811	Tupolev 154M	831	SP-LCN	0290	0994	3 SO D-30KU-154-II	100000	F12C18Y102		
☐	F-OGQQ	Airbus Industrie A310-308 (ET)	592	F-WWCN*	0092	0892	2 GE CF6-80C2A8	164000	F12C35Y138	CS-DH	Tchaikovski / lsf Alex Bail
☐	F-OGQR	Airbus Industrie A310-308 (ET)	593	F-WWCP*	0092	0892	2 GE CF6-80C2A8	164000	F12C35Y138	CS-DJ	Rachmaninov / lsf Quark Leasing
☐	F-OGQT	Airbus Industrie A310-308 (ET)	622	F-WWCD*	0092	0792	2 GE CF6-80C2A8	164000	F12C35Y138	CS-DL	Moussorgski / lsf Kat.Bail
☐	F-OGQU	Airbus Industrie A310-308 (ET)	646	F-WWCT*	0092	0692	2 GE CF6-80C2A8	164000	F12C35Y138	CS-DM	Skriabin / lsf Cladel Bail
☐	F-OGYP	Airbus Industrie A310-324 (ET)	442	N812PA	0087	0896	2 PW PW4152	160000	F12C35Y138	PR-JQ	Rimsky Korsakov / lsf WTC Trustee
☐	F-OGYT	Airbus Industrie A310-325 (ET)	660	N836AB	0093	0796	2 PW PW4156A	164000	F12C35Y138	PR-JS	Borodin / lsf WTC Trustee/cvtd -324
☐	F-OGYU	Airbus Industrie A310-325 (ET)	687	N842AB	0093	0896	2 PW PW4156A	164000	F12C35Y138	PR-KL	Alyabiev / lsf WTC Trustee/cvtd -324
☐	F-OGYV	Airbus Industrie A310-325 (ET)	689	N843AB	0093	0796	2 PW PW4156A	164000	F12C35Y138	PR-KM	Dargomyzhsky / lsf WTC Trustee/cvtd-324
☐	VP-BAF	Airbus Industrie A310-304 (ET)	472	N472GE	0088	0398	2 GE CF6-80C2A2	157000	F12C38Y138		lsf POLA
☐	VP-BAG	Airbus Industrie A310-304 (ET)	475	N475GE	0088	0398	2 GE CF6-80C2A2	157000	F12C35Y138		lsf POLA
☐	RA-86130	Ilyushin 62M	3255333		1092	0998	4 SO D-30KU	167000	F12CY126		lsf/jtly opw ERG / fn 5503
☐	RA-86489	Ilyushin 62M	4830456	CCCP-86489	0078	0078	4 SO D-30KU	167000	F12C18Y102		fn 3005
☐	RA-86497	Ilyushin 62M	1931253	CCCP-86497	0079	0379	4 SO D-30KU	167000	F12C18Y102		fn 3105
☐	RA-86502	Ilyushin 62M	3933345	CCCP-86502	0079	1079	4 SO D-30KU	167000	F12C18Y102		fn 3304
☐	RA-86506	Ilyushin 62M	1035324	CCCP-86506	0080	0480	4 SO D-30KU	167000	F12C18Y102		fn 3502
☐	RA-86510	Ilyushin 62M	1035213	CCCP-86510	0080	0280	4 SO D-30KU	167000	F12C18Y102		fn 3501
☐	RA-86512	Ilyushin 62M	3037314	CCCP-86512	0080	0080	4 SO D-30KU	167000	F12C18Y102		fn 3701
☐	RA-86514	Ilyushin 62M	4037647	CCCP-86514	0080	1280	4 SO D-30KU	167000	F12C18Y102		fn 3704
☐	RA-86517	Ilyushin 62M	3139732	CCCP-86517	0081	0881	4 SO D-30KU	167000	F12C18Y102		fn 3903
☐	RA-86518	Ilyushin 62M	3139956	CCCP-86518	0081	1081	4 SO D-30KU	167000	F12C18Y102		fn 3905
☐	RA-86520	Ilyushin 62M	1241314	CCCP-86520	0082	0482	4 SO D-30KU	167000	F12C18Y102		fn 4101
☐	RA-86522	Ilyushin 62M	2241536	CCCP-86522	0082	0682	4 SO D-30KU	167000	F12C18Y102		fn 4103
☐	RA-86523	Ilyushin 62M	2241647	CCCP-86523	0082	0782	4 SO D-30KU	167000	F12C18Y102		fn 4104
☐	RA-86524	Ilyushin 62M	3242321	CCCP-86524	0082	0882	4 SO D-30KU	167000	F12C18Y102		fn 4202
☐	RA-86531	Ilyushin 62M	4242654	CCCP-86531	0082	1282	4 SO D-30KU	167000	F12C18Y102		fn 4205
☐	RA-86532	Ilyushin 62M	4243111	CCCP-86532	0082	0183	4 SO D-30KU	167000	F12C18Y102		fn 4301
☐	RA-86533	Ilyushin 62M	1343123	CCCP-86533	0083	0283	4 SO D-30KU	167000	F12C18Y102		fn 4302
☐	RA-86534	Ilyushin 62M	1343332	CCCP-86534	0083	0483	4 SO D-30KU	167000	F12C18Y102		fn 4303
☐	RA-86558	Ilyushin 62M	1052128	CCCP-86558	1289	0090	4 SO D-30KU	167000	F12C18Y102		fn 5202
☐	RA-86562	Ilyushin 62M	4831517	CCCP-86562	1078	1090	4 SO D-30KU	167000	F12C18Y102		fn 3101
☐	RA-86565	Ilyushin 62M	2546812	CCCP-86565	0485	1290	4 SO D-30KU	167000	F12C18Y102		fn 4601
☐	RA-86566	Ilyushin 62M	4255152		1292	1093	4 SO D-30KU	167000	F12C18Y102		lsf/opb FEW / fn 5505
☐	RA-86583	Ilyushin 62M	1356851		0796	0098	4 SO D-30KU	167000	F12CY126		lsf/jtly opw ERG / fn 5605
☐	EI-CKD	Boeing 767-3Y0 (ER)	26205 / 474	N6046P*	0093	0994	2 PW PW4060	184600	C44Y188	GR-HL	lsf GECA
☐	EI-CKE	Boeing 767-3Y0 (ER)	26208 / 505	N6009F*	0093	0994	2 PW PW4060	184600	C44Y188	GR-HM	lsf GECA
☐	VP-BAV	Boeing 767-36N (ER)	30107				2 PW PW4060	186882	C44Y188		to be lsf GECA 099
☐	VP-BAX	Boeing 767-36N (ER)	30109				2 PW PW4060	186882	C44Y188		to be lsf GECA 0499
☐	VP-BAY	Boeing 767-36N (ER)	30110				2 PW PW4060	186882	C44Y188		to be lsf GECA 0599
☐	VP-BAZ	Boeing 767-36N (ER)	30111				2 PW PW4060	186882	C44Y188		to be lsf GECA 0899
☐	RA-76467	Ilyushin 76TD	0023440157	CCCP-76467	0082	1082	4 SO D-30KP	190000	Freighter		
☐	RA-76468	Ilyushin 76TD	0023441195	CCCP-76468	0082	1282	4 SO D-30KP	190000	Freighter		
☐	RA-76469	Ilyushin 76TD	0033444286	CCCP-76469	0082		4 SO D-30KP	190000	Freighter		
☐	RA-76470	Ilyushin 76TD	0033444291	CCCP-76470	0083	0583	4 SO D-30KP	190000	Freighter		
☐	RA-76476	Ilyushin 76TD	0043451528	CCCP-76476	0084	0684	4 SO D-30KP	190000	Freighter		
☐	RA-76478	Ilyushin 76TD	0053459788	CCCP-76478	0085	0785	4 SO D-30KP	190000	Freighter		
☐	RA-76479	Ilyushin 76TD	0053460790	CCCP-76479	0085	0785	4 SO D-30KP	190000	Freighter		
☐	RA-76482	Ilyushin 76TD	0053460832	CCCP-76482	0085	0985	4 SO D-30KP	190000	Freighter		
☐	RA-76488	Ilyushin 76TD	0073479371	CCCP-76488	0587	1087	4 SO D-30KP	190000	Freighter		
☐	RA-76750	Ilyushin 76TD	0083485561	CCCP-76750	0987	0688	4 SO D-30KP	190000	Freighter		
☐	RA-76785	Ilyushin 76TD	0093495863	CCCP-76785	0089	1289	4 SO D-30KP	190000	Freighter		
☐	RA-76795	Ilyushin 76TD	0093498962	CCCP-76795	0089	0290	4 SO D-30KP	190000	Freighter		
☐	RA-86002	Ilyushin 86	0103	CCCP-86002	0077		4 KU NK-86	210000	Y350orY200&Cargo		
☐	RA-86015	Ilyushin 86	51483202013	CCCP-86015	0082	0582	4 KU NK-86	210000	F20CY296		
☐	RA-86054	Ilyushin 86	51483203021	CCCP-86054	0083	0783	4 KU NK-86	210000	F20CY296		
☐	RA-86058	Ilyushin 86	51483203025	CCCP-86058	0083	0883	4 KU NK-86	210000	F20CY296		
☐	RA-86059	Ilyushin 86	51483203026	CCCP-86059	0083	1083	4 KU NK-86	215000	F20CY296		
☐	RA-86066	Ilyushin 86	51483204033	CCCP-86066	0084	0784	4 KU NK-86	210000	F20CY296		
☐	RA-86067	Ilyushin 86	51483204034	CCCP-86067	0084	1284	4 KU NK-86	210000	F20CY296		
☐	RA-86074	Ilyushin 86	51483205041	CCCP-86074	0085	0885	4 KU NK-86	210000	F20CY296		
☐	RA-86075	Ilyushin 86	51483205044	CCCP-86075	0085	1085	4 KU NK-86	210000	F20CY296		
☐	RA-86079	Ilyushin 86	51483205050	CCCP-86079	1085	0686	4 KU NK-86	210000	F20CY296		
☐	RA-86080	Ilyushin 86	51483206051	CCCP-86080	0086	0786	4 KU NK-86	210000	F20CY296		
☐	RA-86087	Ilyushin 86	51483206058	CCCP-86087	0086	0587	4 KU NK-86	210000	F20CY296		
☐	RA-86088	Ilyushin 86	51483206059	CCCP-86088	0086	0787	4 KU NK-86	210000	F20CY296		
☐	RA-86095	Ilyushin 86	51483207066	CCCP-86095	0087	0788	4 KU NK-86	210000	F20CY296		
☐	RA-86096	Ilyushin 86	51483207067	CCCP-86096	0088	1088	4 KU NK-86	210000	F20CY296		
☐	RA-86103	Ilyushin 86	51483208071	CCCP-86103	0089	0589	4 KU NK-86	210000	F20CY296		
☐	RA-86110	Ilyushin 86	51483208078	CCCP-86110	0089	0590	4 KU NK-86	210000	F20CY296		
☐	RA-86113	Ilyushin 86	51483209081	CCCP-86113	0090		4 KU NK-86	210000	F20CY296		
☐	RA-86124	Ilyushin 86	51483210092	CCCP-86124	0092	1092	4 KU NK-86	210000	F20CY296		

522 registration type of aircraft cn/fn ex/ex* mfd del powered by mtow kg configuration selcal name/fln/specialitites/remarks

registration	type of aircraft	cn/fn	ex/ex*	mfd	del	powered by	mtow kg	configuration	selcal	name/fln/specialitites/remarks
RA-96005	Ilyushin 96-300	74393201002	CCCP-96005	0091		4 SO PS-90AN	240000	F22C40Y173		lsf VASO-Leasing
RA-96007	Ilyushin 96-300	74393201004		0092		4 SO PS-90AN	240000	F22C40Y173		
RA-96008	Ilyushin 96-300	74393201005		0092		4 SO PS-90AN	240000	F22C40Y173		
RA-96010	Ilyushin 96-300	74393201007		0094		4 SO PS-90AN	240000	F22C40Y173		
RA-96011	Ilyushin 96-300	74393201008		0094		4 SO PS-90AN	240000	F22C40Y173		
RA-96015	Ilyushin 96-300	74393202012		0095	0296	4 SO PS-90AN	240000	F22C40Y173		
VP-BAS	Boeing 777-2Q8 (ER)	27607 / 135	N5022E*	0098	0698	2 GE GE90-92B	286900		QR-GS	lsf ILFC
VP-BAU	Boeing 777-2Q8 (ER)	27608 / 164		0098	1098	2 GE GE90-92B	286900		QR-HJ	lsf ILFC
N524MD	Boeing (Douglas) DC-10-30F	46999 / 289	S2-ADA	0079	0995	3 GE CF6-50C2	263300	Freighter	KM-CE	lsf MDFC / cvtd DC-10-30
RA-96101	Ilyushin 96T			0597		4 PW PW2340	270000	Freighter 92t		oo-delivery 0099
RA-	Ilyushin 96T					4 PW PW2340	270000	Freighter 92t		oo-delivery 0000
RA-	Ilyushin 96T					4 PW PW2340	270000	Freighter 92t		oo-delivery 0000
RA-	Ilyushin 96M					4 PW PW2337	270000			oo-delivery 0001
RA-	Ilyushin 96M					4 PW PW2337	270000			oo-delivery 0001
RA-	Ilyushin 96M					4 PW PW2337	270000			oo-delivery 0001
RA-	Ilyushin 96M					4 PW PW2337	270000			oo-delivery 0001
RA-	Ilyushin 96M					4 PW PW2337	270000			oo-delivery 0001
RA-	Ilyushin 96M					4 PW PW2337	270000			oo-delivery 0001
RA-	Ilyushin 96M					4 PW PW2337	270000			oo-delivery 0001
RA-	Ilyushin 96M					4 PW PW2337	270000			oo-delivery 0001
RA-	Ilyushin 96M					4 PW PW2337	270000			oo-delivery 0001
RA-	Ilyushin 96M					4 PW PW2337	270000			oo-delivery 0001
RA-	Ilyushin 96M					4 PW PW2337	270000			oo-delivery 0002
RA-	Ilyushin 96M					4 PW PW2337	270000			oo-delivery 0002
RA-	Ilyushin 96M					4 PW PW2337	270000			oo-delivery 0002

AEROFREIGHT AIRLINES, Joint-Stock Company = FRT (Aviakompania Aerofrakht) Moscow-Domodedovo

Ul. Verkhnyaya Maslovka 20, 125083 Moskva, Russia ☎ (095) 212 04 41 Tx: none Fax: (095) 212 01 91 SITA: n/a
F: 1997 ♔♔♔ n/a Head: Viktor I. Merkulov ICAO: AEROFREIGHT Net: n/a

registration	type of aircraft	cn/fn	ex/ex*	mfd	del	powered by	mtow kg	configuration	remarks
RA-65719	Tupolev 134A	63637	CCCP-65719	0281	0098	2 SO D-30-II	49000	Exec 40 Pax	lsf/jtly opw KSM
RA-65726	Tupolev 134A	63720	CCCP-65726	0381	0098	2 SO D-30-II	49000	Exec 44 Pax	lsf/jtly opw KSM
RA-65956	Tupolev 134A	2351709	CCCP-65956	0273	0098	2 SO D-30-II	49000	Exec 55 Pax	lsf/jtly opw KSM
RA-11025	Antonov 12TB	6344103	CCCP-11025	1066	0098	4 IV AI-20M	61000	Freighter	lsf/jtly opw KSM
RA-11408	Antonov 12BP	3341209	CCCP-11408	0063	0098	4 IV AI-20M	61000	Freighter	lsf/jtly opw OBM
RA-11529	Antonov 12B	6344109	CCCP-11529	0666	0098	4 IV AI-20M	61000	Freighter	lsf/jtly opw FUE
RA-69314	Antonov 12BP	5343004	CCCP-69314	0465	0098	4 IV AI-20M	61000	Freighter	lsf/jtly opw FUE
RA-76499	Ilyushin 76TD	0023441186	CCCP-76499	1082	0098	4 SO D-30KP	190000	Freighter	lsf/jtly opw KSM

AERO-KAMOV = MSV (Subsidiary of Kamov Design Bureau) Moscow-Lyubertsy Heliport

Ul. 8-ogo Marta 8, 140007 Lyubertsy, (Moscow Region), Russia ☎ (095) 700 31 60 Tx: 206112 kamov Fax: (095) 373 42 20 SITA: n/a
F: 1995 ♔♔♔ n/a Head: n/a ICAO: AERAFKAM Net: n/a

registration	type of aircraft	cn/fn	ex/ex*	mfd	del	powered by	mtow kg	configuration	remarks
RA-31065	Kamov Ka-32T		CCCP-31065	0090		2 IS TV3-117V	12600		
RA-31072	Kamov Ka-32A1		CCCP-31072	0092		2 IS TV3-117V	12600		opf Moscow Firebrigade
RA-31073	Kamov Ka-32A1	8907	CCCP-31073	0092		2 IS TV3-117V	12600		opf Moscow Firebrigade
RA-31585	Kamov Ka-32A	8707	CCCP-31585	0091		2 IS TV3-117V	12600		lst VIH Logging
RA-31594	Kamov Ka-32A		CCCP-31594	0092		2 IS TV3-117V	12600		lst VIH Logging
RA-31603	Kamov Ka-32S	9102		0092		2 IS TV3-117V	12600		

AEROKUZNETSK, Joint-Stock Company = AKZ (formerly Aeroflot Novokuznetsk division) Novokuznetsk

Novokuznetsk Airport, 654043 Novokuznetsk, (Kemerovo Region), Russia ☎ (3843) 43 32 31 Tx: none Fax: (3843) 45 94 54 SITA: n/a
F: 1952 ♔♔♔ 1025 Head: Viktor D. Belozerov ICAO: AEROKUZNETSK Net: n/a

registration	type of aircraft	cn/fn	ex/ex*	mfd	del	powered by	mtow kg	configuration	remarks
RA-14069	PZL Swidnik (Mil) Mi-2	5210548048	CCCP-14069	0088	0088	2 IS GTD-350-4	3550	Utility	
RA-20270	PZL Swidnik (Mil) Mi-2	527231071	CCCP-20270	0081	0081	2 IS GTD-350-4	3550	Utility	
RA-20884	PZL Swidnik (Mil) Mi-2	528305083	CCCP-20884	0083	0083	2 IS GTD-350-4	3550	Utility	
RA-22413	Mil Mi-8T	5105	CCCP-22413	0075	0076	2 IS TV2-117A	12000	Transport	
RA-22725	Mil Mi-8T	98308700	CCCP-22725	0083	0083	2 IS TV2-117A	12000	Transport	
RA-22843	Mil Mi-8T	7644	CCCP-22843	0078	0082	2 IS TV2-117A	12000	Transport	
RA-24140	Mil Mi-8T	98841391	CCCP-24140	0088	0088	2 IS TV2-117A	12000	Transport	
RA-24142	Mil Mi-8T	98841432	CCCP-24142	0088	0088	2 IS TV2-117A	12000	Transport	
RA-24167	Mil Mi-8T	98941977	CCCP-24167	0089	0089	2 IS TV2-117A	12000	Transport	
RA-24647	Mil Mi-8T	9815707	CCCP-24647	0081	0081	2 IS TV2-117A	12000	Transport	
RA-26019	Antonov 26B	10203	CCCP-26019	0080	0080	2 IV AI-24VT	24000	Freighter	for sale
RA-85237	Tupolev 154B-1	237	CCCP-85237	0077	0092	3 KU NK-8-2U	98000	Y164	
RA-85392	Tupolev 154B-2	392	CCCP-85392	0080	0091	3 KU NK-8-2U	98000	Y164	
RA-85471	Tupolev 154B-2	471	CCCP-85471	0081	0092	3 KU NK-8-2U	102000	Y164	
RA-85747	Tupolev 154M	930		0092	0092	3 SO D-30KU-154-II	102000	Y166	
RA-85749	Tupolev 154M	931		0092	0092	3 SO D-30KU-154-II	102000	Y166	
RA-85758	Tupolev 154M	940		0092	0092	3 SO D-30KU-154-II	102000	Y166	lst IRQ as EP-TQE

AERO RENT, Joint-Stock Company = NRO (Aviakompania Aero Rent) (Member of Master Group) Moscow-Vnukovo

Kaloshin pereulok 2/24, 121002 Moskva, Russia ☎ (095) 241 84 42 Tx: none Fax: (095) 241 83 74 SITA: n/a
F: 1995 ♔♔♔ n/a Head: Mikhail G. Balyanin ICAO: AEROMASTER Net: n/a

registration	type of aircraft	cn/fn	ex/ex*	mfd	del	powered by	mtow kg	configuration	remarks
RA-02807	Hawker 800B (BAe 125-800B)	258076	G-BVAS	0087	1195	2 GA TFE731-5R-1H	12428	8 Pax	

AEROVOLGA = VOG (Air Volga) Samara-Int'l

Ul. Leningradskaya 75, 443020 Samara, Russia ☎ (8462) 33 45 92 Tx: 214166 rtv Fax: (8462) 32 58 34 SITA: n/a
F: 1993 ♔♔♔ 150 Head: n/a ICAO: AIR VOLGA Net: n/a
Company will be integrated into SAMARA AIRLINES during 1999.

registration	type of aircraft	cn/fn	ex/ex*	mfd	del	powered by	mtow kg	configuration	remarks
RA-85716	Tupolev 154M	892	CCCP-85716	0091	0093	3 SO D-30KU-154-II	100000	Y166	lst BRZ
RA-85739	Tupolev 154M	925	CCCP-85739	0092	0093	3 SO D-30KU-154-II	100000	Y164	lst BRZ

AIRSTAN, Joint-Stock Company = JSC (ASN Aerostan) Kazan

Ul. Z. Sultana 12, 420022 Kazan, (Republic of Tatarstan), Russia ☎ (8432) 93 04 48 Tx: none Fax: (8432) 93 04 81 SITA: n/a
F: 1994 ♔♔♔ n/a Head: Anatoly Yu. Galunov ICAO: AIRSTAN Net: http://www.kazan.ru/air

registration	type of aircraft	cn/fn	ex/ex*	mfd	del	powered by	mtow kg	configuration	remarks
RA-98113	Yakovlev 40	9710253	CCCP-98113	0377	0095	3 IV AI-25	17200	Executive	
RA-06199	Antonov 26B	11802	CCCP-06199	1281	0095	2 IV AI-24VT	24000	Freighter	
RA-76369	Ilyushin 76TD	1033414480		0393	0094	4 SO D-30KP	190000	Freighter	
RA-76842	Ilyushin 76TD	1033418616		1194	0094	4 SO D-30KP	190000	Freighter	

AIRTRANSSERVICE – ATS = AAS (Aviatransservice) Moscow-Vnukovo

Ul. I-aya Reisovaya 12, 103027 Moskva, Russia ☎ (095) 436 75 13 Tx: 412692 su Fax: (095) 436 88 95 SITA: n/a
F: 1995 ♔♔♔ n/a Head: Alexei A. Timofeyev ICAO: AVIASERVICE Net: n/a Operates passenger flights with Tupolev 134A leased from KOMIAVIA when required.

AIR TROIKA = TKA Moscow

Kuznetsky most 6/3, 103775 Moskva, Russia ☎ (095) 927 83 03 Tx: none Fax: (095) 924 35 82 SITA: n/a
F: 1992 ♔♔♔ n/a Head: Sergei E. Andreyev ICAO: TROIKA Net: n/a

registration	type of aircraft	cn/fn	ex/ex*	mfd	del	powered by	mtow kg	configuration	remarks
RA-24345	Kamov Ka-26		CCCP-24345	0076		2 VE M-14V-26	3250	Utility	
RA-24800	Mil Mi-8T			0084		2 IS TV2-117A	12000	Utility	
RA-24880	Mil Mi-8T			0084		2 IS TV2-117A	12000	Utility	
RA-26101	Antonov 26B	11908	CCCP-26101	0282		2 IV AI-24VT	24000	Freighter	lsf KTA / opf UN
RA-26677	Antonov 26	8603	CCCP-26677	0879		2 IV AI-24VT	24000	Freighter	lsf KTA / opf UN

AJT AIR INTERNATIONAL, Joint-Stock Company = E9 / TRJ (Asian Joint Transport dba) Moscow-Sheremetyevo

Leningradsky Prospekt 37/7, Suite 235, 125167 Moskva, Russia ☎ (095) 155 64 64 Tx: none Fax: (095) 155 64 32 SITA: MOWDDE9
F: 1992 ♔♔♔ 117 Head: Sergei A. Gusak IATA: 766 ICAO: TURJET Net: n/a Beside aircraft listed, additional (Tupolev 154) are leased from other Russian carriers when required.

registration	type of aircraft	cn/fn	ex/ex*	mfd	del	powered by	mtow kg	configuration	remarks
RA-86065	Ilyushin 86	51483204032	CCCP-86065	0084	0098	4 KU NK-86	215000	Y350	
RA-86073	Ilyushin 86	51483204040	CCCP-86073	0084	0098	4 KU NK-86	215000	Y350	lsf PLK
RA-86115	Ilyushin 86	51483209083	CCCP-86115	0090	0397	4 KU NK-86	215000	Y350	lsf VASO-Leasing
RA-86140	Ilyushin 86	51483211102		0095	0095	4 KU NK-86	215000	Y350	lsf VASO-Leasing
RA-86141	Ilyushin 86	51483211103		0097	0097	4 KU NK-86	215000	Y350	lsf VASO-Leasing

ALANIA, Leasing Airline = OST (Lizingovaya aviakompania ALANIA) Vladikavkaz

Ul. Gorkogo 41, 360040 Vladikavkaz, (Republic of Severnaya Osetia-Alania), Russia ☎ (8672) 75 75 57 Tx: none Fax: (8672) 75 75 57 SITA: n/a
F: 1996 ♔♔♔ n/a Head: Boris K. Daurov ICAO: ALANIA Net: n/a

registration	type of aircraft	cn/fn	ex/ex*	mfd	del	powered by	mtow kg	configuration	remarks
RA-65616	Tupolev 134A-3	4352206	D-AOBF	0374	0097	2 SO D-30-III	47000	Y80	lsf KMV
RA-65622	Tupolev 134A-3	60495	D-AOBM	0678	0098	2 SO D-30-III	47600	C16Y52	

ALMAZY ROSSII SAKHA Aviakompania = DRU (Diamonds of Russia-Sakha) (Subsidiary of Almazy Rossii Sakha Trade Company / formerly Aeroflot Mirny division) Mirny

Mirny Airport, 678170 Mirny, (Republic of Sakha-Yakutia), Russia ☎ (41136) 25 487 Tx: none Fax: (41136) 23 192 SITA: n/a

F: n/a ⁂ n/a Head: Nikolai N. Tereshchenko ICAO: MIRNY Net: n/a Most aircraft are still in Aeroflot colors but will be repainted in due course.

☐ RA-01440	PZL Mielec (Antonov) An-2		CCCP-01440	0088		1 SH ASh-62IR	5500	Utility		
☐ RA-02503	PZL Mielec (Antonov) An-2	1G119-46	CCCP-02503	0070		1 SH ASh-62IR	5500	Utility		
☐ RA-02522	PZL Mielec (Antonov) An-2	1G119-65	CCCP-02522	0070		1 SH ASh-62IR	5500	Utility		
☐ RA-07224	PZL Mielec (Antonov) An-2		CCCP-07224	0073		1 SH ASh-62IR	5500	Utility		
☐ RA-07408	PZL Mielec (Antonov) An-2	1G150-43	CCCP-07408	0073		1 SH ASh-62IR	5500	Utility		
☐ RA-07418	PZL Mielec (Antonov) An-2		CCCP-07418	0073		1 SH ASh-62IR	5500	Utility		
☐ RA-07649	PZL Mielec (Antonov) An-2	1G157-34	CCCP-07649	0074		1 SH ASh-62IR	5500	Utility		
☐ RA-40480	PZL Mielec (Antonov) An-2	1G224-57	CCCP-40480	0087		1 SH ASh-62IR	5500	Utility		
☐ RA-40642	PZL Mielec (Antonov) An-2	1G213-49	CCCP-40642	0085		1 SH ASh-62IR	5500	Utility		
☐ RA-70159	PZL Mielec (Antonov) An-2		CCCP-70159	0071		1 SH ASh-62IR	5500	Utility		
☐ RA-70576	PZL Mielec (Antonov) An-2	1G127-44	CCCP-70576	0071		1 SH ASh-62IR	5500	Utility		
☐ RA-70583	PZL Mielec (Antonov) An-2	1G127-51	CCCP-70583	0071		1 SH ASh-62IR	5500	Utility		
☐ RA-70679	PZL Mielec (Antonov) An-2		CCCP-70679	0071		1 SH ASh-62IR	5500	Utility		
☐ RA-70736	PZL Mielec (Antonov) An-2	1G130-37	CCCP-70736	0071		1 SH ASh-62IR	5500	Utility		
☐ RA-22394	Mil Mi-8		CCCP-22394	0077		2 IS TV2-117A	12000	Utility		
☐ RA-22570	Mil Mi-8		CCCP-22570	0079		2 IS TV2-117A	12000	Utility		
☐ RA-22571	Mil Mi-8		CCCP-22571	0079		2 IS TV2-117A	12000	Utility		
☐ RA-22731	Mil Mi-8		CCCP-22731	0083		2 IS TV2-117A	12000	Utility		
☐ RA-22744	Mil Mi-8		CCCP-22744	0083		2 IS TV2-117A	12000	Utility		
☐ RA-22777	Mil Mi-8		CCCP-22777	0083		2 IS TV2-117A	12000	Utility		
☐ RA-22879	Mil Mi-8		CCCP-22879	0084		2 IS TV2-117A	12000	Utility		
☐ RA-22899	Mil Mi-8		CCCP-22899	0084		2 IS TV2-117A	12000	Utility		
☐ RA-22902	Mil Mi-8		CCCP-22902	0084		2 IS TV2-117A	12000	Utility		
☐ RA-24240	Mil Mi-8		CCCP-24240	0087		2 IS TV2-117A	12000	Utility		
☐ RA-24256	Mil Mi-8		CCCP-24256	0087		2 IS TV2-117A	12000	Utility		
☐ RA-24257	Mil Mi-8		CCCP-24257	0087		2 IS TV2-117A	12000	Utility		
☐ RA-24400	Mil Mi-8		CCCP-24400	0086		2 IS TV2-117A	12000	Utility		
☐ RA-24417	Mil Mi-8		CCCP-24417	0086		2 IS TV2-117A	12000	Utility		
☐ RA-24435	Mil Mi-8		CCCP-24435	0086		2 IS TV2-117A	12000	Utility		
☐ RA-24451	Mil Mi-8		CCCP-24451	0086		2 IS TV2-117A	12000	Utility		
☐ RA-24506	Mil Mi-8		CCCP-24506	0085		2 IS TV2-117A	12000	Utility		
☐ RA-24536	Mil Mi-8		CCCP-24536	0085		2 IS TV2-117A	12000	Utility		
☐ RA-24564	Mil Mi-8		CCCP-24564	0085		2 IS TV2-117A	12000	Utility		
☐ RA-24692	Mil Mi-8		CCCP-24692	0081		2 IS TV2-117A	12000	Utility		
☐ RA-24741	Mil Mi-8		CCCP-24741	0084		2 IS TV2-117A	12000	Utility		
☐ RA-25228	Mil Mi-8		CCCP-25228	0079		2 IS TV2-117A	12000	Utility		
☐ RA-25313	Mil Mi-8		CCCP-25313	0082		2 IS TV2-117A	12000	Utility		
☐ RA-25333	Mil Mi-8		CCCP-25333	0082		2 IS TV2-117A	12000	Utility		
☐ RA-25376	Mil Mi-8		CCCP-25376	0082		2 IS TV2-117A	12000	Utility		
☐ RA-25943	Mil Mi-8		CCCP-25943	0075		2 IS TV2-117A	12000	Utility		
☐ RA-46352	Antonov 24B	97305801	CCCP-46352	0069		2 IV AI-24	21000	Y48		
☐ RA-46488	Antonov 24RV	27308106	CCCP-46488	0072		2 IV AI-24VT	21800	Y48		
☐ RA-46501	Antonov 24RV	37308306	CCCP-46501	0073		2 IV AI-24VT	21800	Y48		
☐ RA-46580	Antonov 24B	87304909	CCCP-46580	0068		2 IV AI-24	21000	Y48		
☐ RA-46621	Antonov 24RV	37308708	CCCP-46621	0073		2 IV AI-24VT	21800	Y48		
☐ RA-47272	Antonov 24B	07306402	CCCP-47272	0070		2 IV AI-24	21000	Y48		
☐ RA-47298	Antonov 24RV		CCCP-47298	0070		2 IV AI-24VT	21800	Y48		
☐ RA-47694	Antonov 24B	27307601	CCCP-47694	0072		2 IV AI-24	21000	Y48		
☐ RA-47807	Antonov 24B	17306909	CCCP-47807	0071		2 IV AI-24	21000	Y48		
☐ RA-26552	Antonov 26		CCCP-26552	0075		2 IV AI-24VT	24000	Freighter		
☐ RA-26607	Antonov 26		CCCP-26607	0076		2 IV AI-24VT	24000	Freighter		
☐ RA-26628	Antonov 26	5309	CCCP-26628	0077		2 IV AI-24VT	24000	Freighter		
☐ RA-26668	Antonov 26		CCCP-26668	0079		2 IV AI-24VT	24000	Freighter		
☐ RA-06027	Mil Mi-26		CCCP-06027	0090		2 LO D-136	56000	Freighter		
☐ RA-06036	Mil Mi-26		CCCP-06036	0091		2 LO D-136	56000	Freighter		
☐ RA-06081	Mil Mi-26			0092		2 LO D-136	56000	Freighter		
☐ RA-76357	Ilyushin 76TD	1023414467		0092		4 SO D-30KP	190000	Freighter		
☐ RA-76360	Ilyushin 76TD	1033414492	CCCP-76360	0093		4 SO D-30KP	190000	Freighter		
☐ RA-76373	Ilyushin 76TD	1033415507		0093		4 SO D-30KP	190000	Freighter		
☐ RA-76420	Ilyushin 76TD	1023413446		0092		4 SO D-30KP	190000	Freighter		

ALROSA-AVIA = LRO (Sister company of Almazy Rossii Sakha) Moscow-Zhukovsky

Zhukovsky Airport, 140160 Zhukovsky, (Moscow Region), Russia ☎ (095) 556 79 10 Tx: n/a Fax: (095) 556 53 91 SITA: n/a

F: n/a ⁂ n/a Head: Valentin G. Mikhailov ICAO: ALROSA Net: n/a

☐ RA-65907	Tupolev 134A	63996	CCCP-65907	0083		2 SO D-30-II	49000	Executive		

ALTAI AIRLINES (Altaiskie avialinii) (formerly part of Barnaul Air Enterprise & Aeroflot Barnaul division) Barnaul

Barnaul Airport, 656030 Barnaul, Russia ☎ (3852) 29 95 17 Tx: none Fax: (352) 29 95 17 SITA: n/a

F: n/a ⁂ n/a Head: n/a Net: n/a Most aircraft are still in Aeroflot colors but will be repainted in due course.

☐ RA-14067	PZL Swidnik (Mil) Mi-2	5210546038	CCCP-14067	0088		2 IS GTD-350-4	3550	Utility		
☐ RA-14151	PZL Swidnik (Mil) Mi-2	5210409107	CCCP-14151	0087		2 IS GTD-350-4	3550	Utility		
☐ RA-20867	PZL Swidnik (Mil) Mi-2	528228063	CCCP-20867	0083		2 IS GTD-350-4	3550	Utility		
☐ RA-20987	PZL Swidnik (Mil) Mi-2	549722046	CCCP-20987	0083		2 IS GTD-350-4	3550	Utility		
☐ RA-23224	PZL Swidnik (Mil) Mi-2	5210210047	CCCP-23224	0087		2 IS GTD-350-4	3550	Utility		
☐ RA-01422	PZL Mielec (Antonov) An-2		CCCP-01422	0088		1 SH ASh-62IR	5500	Utility		
☐ RA-01437	PZL Mielec (Antonov) An-2		CCCP-01437	0088		1 SH ASh-62IR	5500	Utility		
☐ RA-17753	PZL Mielec (Antonov) An-2		CCCP-17753	0083		1 SH ASh-62IR	5500	Utility		
☐ RA-33336	PZL Mielec (Antonov) An-2		CCCP-33336	0087		1 SH ASh-62IR	5500	Utility		
☐ RA-33390	PZL Mielec (Antonov) An-2		CCCP-33390	0087		1 SH ASh-62IR	5500	Utility		
☐ RA-33420	PZL Mielec (Antonov) An-2		CCCP-33420	0087		1 SH ASh-62IR	5500	Utility		
☐ RA-33496	PZL Mielec (Antonov) An-2		CCCP-33496	0088		1 SH ASh-62IR	5500	Utility		
☐ RA-35513	PZL Mielec (Antonov) An-2		CCCP-35513	0069		1 SH ASh-62IR	5500	Utility		
☐ RA-40295	PZL Mielec (Antonov) An-2	1G221-25	CCCP-40295	0086		1 SH ASh-62IR	5500	Utility		
☐ RA-40296	PZL Mielec (Antonov) An-2	1G221-26	CCCP-40296	0086		1 SH ASh-62IR	5500	Utility		
☐ RA-40484	PZL Mielec (Antonov) An-2		CCCP-40484	0087		1 SH ASh-62IR	5500	Utility		
☐ RA-40488	PZL Mielec (Antonov) An-2	1G225-05	CCCP-40488	0087		1 SH ASh-62IR	5500	Utility		
☐ RA-40617	PZL Mielec (Antonov) An-2		CCCP-40617	0085		1 SH ASh-62IR	5500	Utility		
☐ RA-40618	PZL Mielec (Antonov) An-2		CCCP-40618	0085		1 SH ASh-62IR	5500	Utility		
☐ RA-40646	PZL Mielec (Antonov) An-2		CCCP-40646	0085		1 SH ASh-62IR	5500	Utility		
☐ RA-40647	PZL Mielec (Antonov) An-2		CCCP-40647	0085		1 SH ASh-62IR	5500	Utility		
☐ RA-40738	PZL Mielec (Antonov) An-2		CCCP-40738	0076		1 SH ASh-62IR	5500	Utility		
☐ RA-62586	PZL Mielec (Antonov) An-2		CCCP-62586	0077		1 SH ASh-62IR	5500	Utility		
☐ RA-84533	PZL Mielec (Antonov) An-2		CCCP-84533	0080		1 SH ASh-62IR	5500	Utility		
☐ RA-22285	Mil Mi-8		CCCP-22285	0076		2 IS TV2-117A	12000	Utility		
☐ RA-24629	Mil Mi-8		CCCP-24629	0081		2 IS TV2-117A	12000	Utility		
☐ RA-25248	Mil Mi-8		CCCP-25248	0072		2 IS TV2-117A	12000	Utility		
☐ RA-25332	Mil Mi-8		CCCP-25332	0082		2 IS TV2-117A	12000	Utility		
☐ RA-87252	Yakovlev 40	9310926	CCCP-87252	0073		3 IV AI-25	16800	Y32		
☐ RA-87297	Yakovlev 40	9321428	CCCP-87297	0073		3 IV AI-25	16800	Y32		
☐ RA-87326	Yakovlev 40	9330530	CCCP-87326	0073		3 IV AI-25	16800	Y32		
☐ RA-87460	Yakovlev 40	9431936	CCCP-87460	0074		3 IV AI-25	16800	Y32		
☐ RA-87474	Yakovlev 40	9441937	CCCP-87474	0074		3 IV AI-25	16800	Y32		
☐ RA-87502	Yakovlev 40	9510140	CCCP-87502	0075		3 IV AI-25	16800	Y32		
☐ RA-87530	Yakovlev 40	9521241	CCCP-87530	0075		3 IV AI-25	16800	Y32		
☐ RA-87557	Yakovlev 40	9210821	CCCP-87557	0072		3 IV AI-25	16800	Y32		
☐ RA-87558	Yakovlev 40	9210921	CCCP-87558	0072		3 IV AI-25	16800	Y32		
☐ RA-88179	Yakovlev 40	9621947	CCCP-88179	0076		3 IV AI-25	16800	Y32		
☐ RA-88190	Yakovlev 40	9621048	CCCP-88190	0076		3 IV AI-25	16800	Y32		
☐ RA-26110	Antonov 26B		CCCP-26110	0082		2 IV AI-24VT	24000	Freighter		
☐ RA-26116	Antonov 26B		CCCP-26116	0082		2 IV AI-24VT	24000	Freighter		
☐ RA-26122	Antonov 26B	12401	CCCP-26122	0082		2 IV AI-24VT	24000	Freighter		
☐ RA-26130	Antonov 26B	12704	CCCP-26130	0082		2 IV AI-24VT	24000	Freighter		
☐ RA-26692	Antonov 26		CCCP-26692	0079		2 IV AI-24VT	24000	Freighter		lst Vostsibaero
☐ RA-76446	Ilyushin 76MD	1023412418	CCCP-76446	0092		4 SO D-30KP	190000	Freighter		lst Polyus
☐ RA-76833	Ilyushin 76TD	1023411363	CCCP-76833	0092		4 SO D-30KP	190000	Freighter		lst Polyus

524 registration type of aircraft *cn/fn* *ex/ex** *mfd* *del* *powered by* *mtow kg* *configuration* *selcal* name/fln/*specialitites/remarks*

AMUR Aviakompania (Flying division of Arteli staratelei Amur / Arteli Amur Geologists) **Mar-Kyuel**

Flying division / Letny otryad, Vostochnoe shosse 10, 680014 Khabarovsk, Russia ☎ (4212) 37 65 84 Tx: none Fax: (4212) 37 23 46 SITA: n/a
F: 1993 n/a Head: Alexander A. Lebedev Net: n/a

☐ RA-14330	PZL Swidnik (Mil) Mi-2	545335097		0077	0093	2 IS GTD-350-4	3550	Utility/Trainer		
☐ RA-15678	PZL Swidnik (Mil) Mi-2	5411010089		0089	0097	2 IS GTD-350-4	3550	Utility/Trainer		
☐ RA-33362	PZL Mielec (Antonov) An-2	1G226-21	CCCP-33362	0887	0097	1 SH ASh-62IR	5500	Utility		
☐ RA-40652	PZL Mielec (Antonov) An-2	1G213-59	CCCP-40652	0085	0094	1 SH ASh-62IR	5500	Utility		
☐ RA-40653	PZL Mielec (Antonov) An-2	1G213-60	CCCP-40653	0085	0094	1 SH ASh-62IR	5500	Utility		
☐ RA-24654	Mil Mi-8T	9815714	CCCP-24654	0081	0095	2 IS TV2-117A	12000	Utility		
☐ RA-26048	Antonov 26B	10901	CCCP-26048	0081	0096	2 IV AI-24VT	24000	Freighter		

ANTEY = TEY (Flying division of Polet Omsk Aviation Factory / APO Polet / Member of MAP Group) **Omsk**

Ul. Inzhinernaya 1, 644013 Omsk, Russia ☎ (3812) 35 77 14 Tx: none Fax: (3812) 16 45 77 SITA: n/a
F: 1992 n/a Head: n/a ICAO: ANTEY Net: n/a Operates cargo flights for itself & commercial charter flights. Most aircraft are still in Aeroflot colors with or without titles.

☐ RA-11301	Antonov 12BP	00347107	71 RED	0470	0696	4 IV AI-20M	61000	Freighter		
☐ RA-11302	Antonov 12BP	8346004		1068	0296	4 IV AI-20M	61000	Freighter		
☐ RA-11367	Antonov 12BP	8345607		0468	0496	4 IV AI-20M	61000	Freighter		
☐ RA-11368	Antonov 12BP	8346006	75 RED	1068	0496	4 IV AI-20M	61000	Freighter		lst Georgian Express
☐ RA-11369	Antonov 12BP	00346909		0170	0496	4 IV AI-20M	61000	Freighter		
☐ RA-11665	Antonov 12BP	6343903		0466	0092	4 IV AI-20M	61000	Freighter		

ARGO, Ltd **Surgut-Pobedit Heliport**

Ul. Lenina 27, 626400 Surgut, (Tyumen Region), Russia ☎ (3462) 24 81 28 Tx: none Fax: (3462) 24 81 72 SITA: n/a
F: n/a n/a Head: Yevgeni F. Kovalenko Net: n/a

☐ RA-20351	PZL Swidnik (Mil) Mi-2	549746056	CCCP-20351	0086		2 IS GTD-350-4	3550	Utility		
☐ RA-22550	Mil Mi-8		CCCP-22550	0079		2 IS TV2-117A	12000	Utility		
☐ RA-22608	Mil Mi-8		CCCP-22608	0079		2 IS TV2-117A	12000	Utility		
☐ RA-22626	Mil Mi-8		CCCP-22626	0080		2 IS TV2-117A	12000	Utility		lsf Uraiavia
☐ RA-24409	Mil Mi-8		CCCP-24409	0086		2 IS TV2-117A	12000	Utility		
☐ RA-24520	Mil Mi-8		CCCP-24520	0085		2 IS TV2-117A	12000	Utility		
☐ RA-24716	Mil Mi-8		CCCP-24716	0084		2 IS TV2-117A	12000	Utility		lsf Uraiavia

ARKHANGELSK 2nd Aviation Enterprise = OAO (Vtoroe Arkhangelskoe aviapredpriatie) (formerly Aeroflot Arkhangelsk 2nd division) **Arkhangelsk-Vaskovo**

Vaskovo Airport, 163036 Arkhangelsk, Russia ☎ (8182) 45 01 65 Tx: 242210 trap Fax: (8182) 45 17 94 SITA: n/a
F: 1963 n/a Head: Yuri E. Davydov ICAO: DVINA Net: n/a Most aircraft are still in Aeroflot colors but will be repainted in due course.

☐ RA-02322	PZL Mielec (Antonov) An-2	1G239-26	CCCP-02322	1290	0191	1 SH ASh-62IR	5500	Utility		
☐ RA-02324	PZL Mielec (Antonov) An-2	1G239-28	CCCP-02324	1290	0191	1 SH ASh-62IR	5500	Utility		
☐ RA-07515	PZL Mielec (Antonov) An-2	1G152-43	CCCP-07515	1173	1273	1 SH ASh-62IR	5500	Utility		
☐ RA-31400	PZL Mielec (Antonov) An-2	1G197-23	CCCP-31400	0582	0682	1 SH ASh-62IR	5500	Utility		
☐ RA-31401	PZL Mielec (Antonov) An-2	1G197-24	CCCP-31401	0582	0682	1 SH ASh-62IR	5500	Utility		
☐ RA-40243	PZL Mielec (Antonov) An-2	1G220-33	CCCP-40243	0786	0886	1 SH ASh-62IR	5500	Utility		
☐ RA-40633	PZL Mielec (Antonov) An-2	1G213-40	CCCP-40633	0585	0685	1 SH ASh-62IR	5500	Utility		
☐ RA-56530	PZL Mielec (Antonov) An-2	1G183-30	CCCP-56530	0579	0679	1 SH ASh-62IR	5500	Utility		
☐ RA-84674	PZL Mielec (Antonov) An-2	1G191-52	CCCP-84674	0381	0696	1 SH ASh-62IR	5500	Utility		
☐ RA-67551	Let 410UVP-E	851428	CCCP-67551	0985	1085	2 WA M-601E	6400	Y19		lst MLI
☐ RA-67553	Let 410UVP-E	851430	CCCP-67553	0985	1085	2 WA M-601E	6400	Y19		
☐ RA-67562	Let 410UVP-E	861602	CCCP-67562	0386	0486	2 WA M-601E	6400	Y19		
☐ RA-67563	Let 410UVP-E	861603	CCCP-67563	0386	0486	2 WA M-601E	6400	Y19		
☐ RA-67564	Let 410UVP-E	861604	CCCP-67564	0386	0486	2 WA M-601E	6400	Y19		
☐ RA-67565	Let 410UVP-E	861605	CCCP-67565	0386	0486	2 WA M-601E	6400	Y19		
☐ RA-67567	Let 410UVP-E	861607	CCCP-67567	0386	0486	2 WA M-601E	6400	Y19		
☐ RA-67569	Let 410UVP-E	861609	CCCP-67569	0386	0486	2 WA M-601E	6400	Y19		
☐ RA-22341	Mil Mi-8T	7166	CCCP-22341	0477	0577	2 IS TV2-117A	12000	Utility		
☐ RA-22762	Mil Mi-8T	98311485	CCCP-22762	0683	0787	2 IS TV2-117A	12000	Utility		
☐ RA-24010	rel Mi-8MTV-1	95711	CCCP-24010	0791	0891	2 IS TV3-117MT	13000	Utility		
☐ RA-24012	Mil Mi-8MTV-1	95713	CCCP-24012	0891	0991	2 IS TV3-117MT	13000	Utility		
☐ RA-24485	Mil Mi-8T	98628927	CCCP-24485	1186	1286	2 IS TV2-117A	12000	Utility		
☐ RA-25455	Mil Mi-8MTV-1	95595	CCCP-25455	0291	0391	2 IS TV3-117MT	13000	Utility		
☐ RA-21077	Mil Mi-6T	705302B	CCCP-21077	0171	1279	2 SO D-25V	42000	Utility		
☐ RA-21161	Mil Mi-6T	0533	CCCP-21161	0575	1187	2 SO D-25V	42000	Utility		
☐ RA-06039	Mil Mi-26T	34001212429	CCCP-06039	1090	1190	2 LO D-136	56000	Freighter		
☐ RA-06042	Mil Mi-26T	34001212432	CCCP-06042	1190	1290	2 LO D-136	56000	Freighter		
☐ RA-06044	Mil Mi-26T	34001212434	CCCP-06044	1290	0191	2 LO D-136	56000	Freighter		

ASHAB AIR, Joint-Stock Company = HAB (Aviakompania Askhab) **Moscow-Vnukovo & Grozny**

Yauzsky bulvar 9/6, Bldg 3, 129010 Moskva, Russia ☎ (095) 916 21 81 Tx: none Fax: (095) 916 27 82 SITA: n/a
F: 1997 n/a Head: n/a ICAO: ASHAB Net: n/a

☐ RA-65124	Tupolev 134A	60560	ES-AAN	0778	0097	2 SO D-30-II	49000	Y76		

ASTRAKHAN Airlines = ASZ (AST-Astrakhanskie avialinii) (formerly Aeroflot Astrakhan division) **Astrakhan**

Narimanovo Airport, 414023 Astrakhan, Russia ☎ (8512) 24 93 96 Tx: 254170 Fax: (8512) 24 44 87 SITA: n/a
F: 1994 n/a Head: Vladimir M. Stepanovich Net: n/a Some aircraft are still in Aeroflot colors without titles but will be repainted in due course.

☐ RA-19412	Kamov Ka-26	7404406	CCCP-19412	0674		2 VE M-14V-26	3250	Utility		
☐ RA-19413	Kamov Ka-26	7404407	CCCP-19413	0674		2 VE M-14V-26	3250	Utility		
☐ RA-19417	Kamov Ka-26	7404411	CCCP-19417	0674		2 VE M-14V-26	3250	Patrol		
☐ RA-19428	Kamov Ka-26	7706209	CCCP-19428	1077		2 VE M-14V-26	3250	Utility		
☐ RA-19429	Kamov Ka-26	7706210	CCCP-19429	1177		2 VE M-14V-26	3250	Utility		
☐ RA-19433	Kamov Ka-26	7706214	CCCP-19433	1177		2 VE M-14V-26	3250	Patrol		
☐ RA-19526	Kamov Ka-26	7404518	CCCP-19526	0974		2 VE M-14V-26	3250	Utility		
☐ RA-19566	Kamov Ka-26	7504807	CCCP-19566	0775		2 VE M-14V-26	3250	Utility		
☐ RA-19609	Kamov Ka-26	7505012	CCCP-19609	0675		2 VE M-14V-26	3250	Utility		
☐ RA-19619	Kamov Ka-26	7505103	CCCP-19619	0575		2 VE M-14V-26	3250	Patrol		
☐ RA-19620	Kamov Ka-26	7505104	CCCP-19620	0575		2 VE M-14V-26	3250	Patrol		
☐ RA-24303	Kamov Ka-26	7705920	CCCP-24303	0177		2 VE M-14V-26	3250	Utility		
☐ RA-24344	Kamov Ka-26	7605602	CCCP-24344	0676		2 VE M-14V-26	3250	Utility		
☐ RA-24353	Kamov Ka-26	7605617	CCCP-24353	0876		2 VE M-14V-26	3250	Utility		
☐ RA-24396	Kamov Ka-26	7705913	CCCP-24396	0377		2 VE M-14V-26	3250	Utility		
☐ RA-24399	Kamov Ka-26	7705916	CCCP-24399	0377		2 VE M-14V-26	3250	Utility		
☐ RA-01442	PZL Mielec (Antonov) An-2	1G231-23	CCCP-01442	0888		1 SH ASh-62IR	5250	Utility		
☐ RA-31483	PZL Mielec (Antonov) An-2	1G198-48	CCCP-31483	0882		1 SH ASh-62IR	5250	Utility		
☐ RA-31495	PZL Mielec (Antonov) An-2	1G198-60	CCCP-31495	0982		1 SH ASh-62IR	5250	Utility		
☐ RA-32624	PZL Mielec (Antonov) An-2	1G219-23	CCCP-32624	0586		1 SH ASh-62IR	5250	Utility		
☐ RA-32625	PZL Mielec (Antonov) An-2	1G219-24	CCCP-32625	0586		1 SH ASh-62IR	5250	Utility		
☐ RA-33337	PZL Mielec (Antonov) An-2	1G225-56	CCCP-33337	0687		1 SH ASh-62IR	5250	Utility		
☐ RA-40264	PZL Mielec (Antonov) An-2	1G220-54	CCCP-40264	0786		1 SH ASh-62IR	5250	Utility		
☐ RA-40300	PZL Mielec (Antonov) An-2	1G221-30	CCCP-40300	0786		1 SH ASh-62IR	5250	Utility		
☐ RA-56487	PZL Mielec (Antonov) An-2	1G182-44	CCCP-56487	0279		1 SH ASh-62IR	5250	Utility		
☐ RA-71295	PZL Mielec (Antonov) An-2	1G201-23	CCCP-71295	0283		1 SH ASh-62IR	5250	Utility		
☐ RA-46208	Antonov 24B	67303003	CCCP-46208	1266		2 IV AI-24-II	21500	Y48		
☐ RA-46294	Antonov 24B	77303806	CCCP-46294	1067		2 IV AI-24-II	21500	Y48		
☐ RA-46308	Antonov 24B	97305208	CCCP-46308	0469		2 IV AI-24-II	21500	Y48		
☐ RA-46402	Antonov 24B	77303905	CCCP-46402	1167		2 IV AI-24-II	21500	Y48		
☐ RA-46687	Antonov 24RV	47309804	CCCP-46687	0974		2 IV AI-24VT	22500	Y48 or Combi		
☐ RA-46834	Antonov 24RV	17306801	CCCP-46834	0371		2 IV AI-24VT	22500	Y48 or Combi		
☐ RA-47260	Antonov 24RV	27307802	CCCP-47260	0572		2 IV AI-24VT	22500	Y48 or Combi		
☐ RA-65055	Tupolev 134A-3	49856	CCCP-65055	0477		2 SO D-30-III	47000	Y76		
☐ RA-65080	Tupolev 134A-3	60065	CCCP-65080	0977		2 SO D-30-III	49000	Y76 or Combi		
☐ RA-65102	Tupolev 134A-3	60267	CCCP-65102	0278		2 SO D-30-III	47000	Y76 or Combi		
☐ RA-65825	Tupolev 134A-3	09078	CCCP-65825	0674		2 SO D-30-III	47000	Y76 or Combi		
☐ RA-65828	Tupolev 134A-3	12086	CCCP-65828	0674		2 SO D-30-III	47000	Y76		
☐ RA-42415	Yakovlev 42D	4520422219089	CCCP-42415	0792		3 LO D-36	56500	Y120 or Combi		
☐ RA-42417	Yakovlev 42D	4520423219110	CCCP-42417	0792		3 LO D-36	56500	Y120 or Combi		lst ESL

ATLANT-SOYUZ AIRLINES, Joint-Stock Company = 3G / AYZ **Moscow-Chkalovskaya & -Sheremetyevo**

Ul. Nikolskaya 10/2, 103012 Moskva, Russia ☎ (095) 923 97 17 Tx: none Fax: (095) 921 43 60 SITA: n/a
F: 1993 n/a Head: Stanislav D. Leichenko IATA: 411 ICAO: ATLANT-SOYUZ Net: n/a Some aircraft are still in former Aeroflot colors with or without titles.

☐ RA-65679	Tupolev 134A	23249	CCCP-65679	0075	0095	2 SO D-30-II	47000	C44		lsf CHD
☐ RA-65680	Tupolev 134A-3	49020	680 BLACK	0076	0095	2 SO D-30-III	47000	C44		lsf CHD
☐ RA-65681	Tupolev 134A-3	49760	CCCP-65681	0077	0095	2 SO D-30-III	47000	C44		lsf CHD
☐ RA-11125	Antonov 12BP	3341006	CCCP-11125	0263	0096	4 IV AI-20M	61000	Freighter		lsf KNM
☐ RA-11516	Antonov 12B	4341909		0064	0097	4 IV AI-20M	61000	Freighter		lsf EFE

525 registration type of aircraft cn/fn ex/ex* mfd del powered by mtow kg configuration selcal name/fln/specialitites/remarks

☐ RA-11916	Antonov 12AP	*2400901*	*CCCP-11916*	*0062*	*0097*	*4 IV AI-20M*	*61000*	*Freighter*		*lsf EFE*
☐ RA-74295	Ilyushin 18D	*187010602*	*CCCP-74295*	*0068*	*0095*	*4 IV AI-20M*	*61000*	*Y80*		*lsf CHD*
☐ RA-75496	Ilyushin 18D	*185011303*	*CCCP-75496*	*0065*	*0095*	*4 IV AI-20M*	*61000*	*Y80*		*lsf CHD*
☐ RA-75499	Ilyushin 18D	*188011004*	*CCCP-75499*	*0068*	*0095*	*4 IV AI-20M*	*61000*	*Y80*		*lsf CHD*
☐ RA-85360	Tupolev 154B-2	*360*	*CCCP-85360*	*0079*	*0095*	*3 KU NK-8-2U*	*98000*	*C120*		*lsf CHD*
☐ RA-85554	Tupolev 154B-2	*554*	*CCCP-85554*	*0082*	*0095*	*3 KU NK-8-2U*	*98000*	*Y155*		*lsf CHD*
☐ RA-85559	Tupolev 154B-2	*559*	*CCCP-85559*	*0082*	*0095*	*3 KU NK-8-2U*	*98000*	*Y155*		*lsf CHD*
☐ RA-85563	Tupolev 154B-2	*563*	*CCCP-85563*	*0082*	*0095*	*3 KU NK-8-2U*	*98000*	*Y155*		*lsf CHD*
☐ RA-86495	Ilyushin 62M	*2726628*	*CCCP-86495*	*0077*	*0095*	*4 SO D-30KU*	*165000*	*C108*		*lsf CHD / fn 2602*
☐ RA-86496	Ilyushin 62M	*3829859*	*CCCP-86496*	*0078*	*0095*	*4 SO D-30KU*	*165000*	*C108*		*lsf CHD / fn 2905*
☐ RA-76362	Ilyushin 76TD	*1033416533*		*0793*	*0096*	*4 SO D-30KP*	*190000*	*Freighter*		*jtly opw SUM*
☐ RA-76363	Ilyushin 76TD	*1033417540*		*0793*	*0096*	*4 SO D-30KP*	*190000*	*Freighter*		*jtly opw SUM*
☐ RA-76367	Ilyushin 76TD	*1033414474*		*1192*	*0095*	*4 SO D-30KP*	*190000*	*Freighter*		
☐ RA-76409	Ilyushin 76TD	*1023410355*		*1192*	*0095*	*4 SO D-30KP*	*190000*	*Freighter*		*lsf KNM*
☐ RA-76425	Ilyushin 76TD	*1003405167*		*0391*	*0095*	*4 SO D-30KP*	*190000*	*Freighter*		*lsf KNM*
☐ RA-76471	Ilyushin 76TD	*0033446345*	*EP-MKA*	*0083*	*0098*	*4 SO D-30KP*	*190000*	*Freighter*		
☐ RA-76483	Ilyushin 76TD	*0063468042*	*CCCP-76483*	*0086*	*0097*	*4 SO D-30KP*	*190000*	*Freighter*		*lsf MGD / fn 52-01*
☐ RA-76489	Ilyushin 76TD	*0083485554*	*CCCP-76489*	*1287*	*0097*	*4 SO D-30KP*	*190000*	*Freighter*		*lsf MGD*
☐ RA-76787	Ilyushin 76TD	*0093495854*	*CCCP-76787*	*0889*	*0097*	*4 SO D-30KP*	*190000*	*Freighter*		*lsf MGD*
☐ RA-76840	Ilyushin 76TD	*1033417553*		*1094*	*0096*	*4 SO D-30KP*	*190000*	*Freighter*		*lsf/jtly opw SUM*
☐ RA-76841	Ilyushin 76TD	*1033418601*		*0094*	*0097*	*4 SO D-30KP*	*190000*	*Freighter*		*lsf/jtly opw SUM*
☐ RA-76845	Ilyushin 76TD	*1043420696*		*0395*	*0096*	*4 SO D-30KP*	*190000*	*Freighter*		*lsf/jtly opw SUM*
☐ EW-78801	Ilyushin 76MD	*0093492763*	*CCCP-78801*	*0089*	*0097*	*4 SO D-30KP*	*190000*	*Freighter*		*lsf TXC / fn 7001*
☐ EW-78827	Ilyushin 76MD	*1003499997*	*CCCP-78827*	*0090*	*0097*	*4 SO D-30KP*	*190000*	*Freighter*		*lsf TXC / fn 7510*
☐ RA-86062	Ilyushin 86	*51483203029*	*EW-86062*	*0083*	*0098*	*4 KU NK-86*	*215000*	*Y350*		*lsf UHS*
☐ RA-86139	Ilyushin 86	*51483210098*		*0093*	*0096*	*4 KU NK-86*	*210000*	*Y350*		

ATRAN – Aviatrans Cargo Airlines = V8 / VAS (formerly Aviatrans Cargo Airlines)

Moscow-Domodedovo & -Myachkovo

Zemlyanoy val 66, 109004 Moscow, Russia ☎ (095) 244 40 72 Tx: 412204 atran ru Fax: (095) 244 49 33 SITA: MOWFFV8
F: 1942 👥 450 Head: Roman R. Krishtal IATA: 868 ICAO: ATRAN Net: n/a

☐ RA-26217	Antonov 26	*5405*	*FAP 362*	*0777*		*2 IV AI-24VT*	*24000*	*Freighter*		
☐ RA-26218	Antonov 26	*5408*	*FAP 363*	*0877*		*2 IV AI-24VT*	*24000*	*Freighter*		
☐ RA-26595	Antonov 26B	*13401*	*CCCP-26595*	*0184*		*2 IV AI-24VT*	*24000*	*Freighter*		
☐ RA-27210	Antonov 26	*5410*	*CCCP-27210*	*0077*		*2 IV AI-24VT*	*24000*	*Freighter*		
☐ RA-93916	Antonov 26	*9105*	*CCCP-93916*	*1279*		*2 IV AI-24VT*	*24000*	*Freighter*		
☐ RA-93917	Antonov 26	*10610*	*CCCP-93917*	*0181*		*2 IV AI-24VT*	*24000*	*Freighter*		
☐ RA-11868	Antonov 12BP	*9346310*	*OB-1448*	*0569*		*4 IV AI-20M*	*61000*	*Freighter*		
☐ RA-12990	Antonov 12B	*00347304*	*OB-1449*	*0770*		*4 IV AI-20M*	*61000*	*Freighter*		
☐ RA-93912	Antonov 12BP	*4341709*	*CCCP-93912*	*0164*		*4 IV AI-20M*	*61000*	*Freighter*		
☐ RA-93913	Antonov 12BP	*4342609*	*CCCP-93913*	*1264*		*4 IV AI-20M*	*61000*	*Freighter*		
☐ RA-93915	Antonov 12BP	*4342103*	*CCCP-93915*	*0564*		*4 IV AI-20M*	*61000*	*Freighter*		
☐ RA-98117	Antonov 12BP	*402301*	*CCCP-98117*	*0564*		*4 IV AI-20M*	*61000*	*Freighter*		
☐ RA-98118	Antonov 12BP	*6344304*	*CCCP-98118*	*0866*		*4 IV AI-20M*	*61000*	*Freighter*		
☐ RA-76754	Ilyushin 76T	*093421637*	*YI-AKU*	*0380*		*4 SO D-30KP*	*170000*	*Freighter*		*lst KRI*
☐ RA-76755	Ilyushin 76T	*0013433984*	*CCCP-76755*	*0282*		*4 SO D-30KP*	*170000*	*Freighter*		*lst INV as YL-LAL*
☐ RA-76757	Ilyushin 76T	*0013433990*	*YI-AKX*	*1281*		*4 SO D-30KP*	*170000*	*Freighter*		
☐ RA-76788	Ilyushin 76T	*0013433996*	*CCCP-76788*	*0382*		*4 SO D-30KP*	*170000*	*Freighter*		
☐ RA-76789	Ilyushin 76T	*0013433999*	*YI-ALP*	*0482*		*4 SO D-30KP*	*170000*	*Freighter*		
☐ RA-76809	Ilyushin 76TD	*1013408252*	*CCCP-76809*	*0891*		*4 SO D-30KP*	*190000*	*Freighter*		
☐ RA-76820	Ilyushin 76TD	*1013409295*	*CCCP-76820*	*0292*		*4 SO D-30KP*	*190000*	*Freighter*		

ATRUVERA Air Transport Company = AUV (Aviatransportnaya kompania ATRUVERA)

St. Petersburg-Pulkovo & Moscow-Zhukovsky

Ul. Basseinaya 33, 196070 St. Petersburg, Russia ☎ (812) 294 53 74 Tx: none Fax: (812) 294 53 74 SITA: n/a
F: 1992 👥 n/a Head: Alexander Ivanov ICAO: ATRUVERA Net: n/a

☐ RA-76659	Ilyushin 76MD	*0053463908*	*CCCP-76659*	*1085*	*0093*	*4 SO D-30KP*	*190000*	*Freighter*		*fn 4807*
☐ RA-76672	Ilyushin 76MD	*0063466981*	*CCCP-76672*	*0087*	*0093*	*4 SO D-30KP*	*190000*	*Freighter*		

AVCOM – Aviation Commercial = J6 / AOC (AVKOM-Kommercheskaya aviatsia)

Moscow-Domodedovo & -Sheremetyevo

Sheremetyevo Airport, K340, GosNII GA, 103340 Moskva, Russia ☎ (095) 578 52 12 Tx: 411700 avcom Fax: (095) 578 00 19 SITA: SVOAPJ6
F: 1992 👥 n/a Head: Yevgeni Bakhtin IATA: 415 ICAO: AVCOM Net: n/a

☐ RA-02803	Hawker 700B (HS 125-700B)	*257139*	*G-MHIH*	*0081*		*2 GA TFE731-3R-1H*	*11567*	*Executive 7 Pax*		*opf Ward Business Inc.*
☐ RA-09003	Dassault Falcon 20D	*183*	*EC-EFR*	*0069*	*0097*	*2 GE CF700-2D2*	*12900*	*Executive 9 Pax*		

AVIACON ZITOTRANS, Joint-Stock Company = AZS (Aviacon Tsitotrans)

Ekaterinburg-Koltsovo

Ul. Dobrolyubova 8a, 620014 Ekaterinburg, Russia ☎ (3432) 51 63 17 Tx: none Fax: (3432) 51 63 17 SITA: SVXAZ8X
F: 1995 👥 117 Head: Andrei A. Kuznetsov IATA: 620 ICAO: ZITOTRANS Net: n/a

☐ RA-85636	Tupolev 154M	*766*	*CCCP-85636*	*0087*	*0097*	*3 SO D-30KU-154-II*	*100000*	*Y164*		*lsf UHS*
☐ RA-85671	Tupolev 154M	*829*	*CCCP-85671*	*0089*	*0096*	*3 SO D-30KU-154-II*	*100000*	*Y164*		*lsf MVL*
☐ RA-85696	Tupolev 154M	*869*	*CCCP-85696*	*0091*	*0098*	*3 SO D-30KU-154-II*	*100000*	*Y164*		*lsf MVL*
☐ RA-76666	Ilyushin 76MD	*0053464934*	*CCCP-76666*	*0085*	*0096*	*4 SO D-30KP*	*190000*	*Freighter*		
☐ RA-76783	Ilyushin 76TD	*0093498974*	*CCCP-76783*	*0089*	*0097*	*4 SO D-30KP*	*190000*	*Freighter*		*lsf UHS*
☐ RA-76807	Ilyushin 76TD	*1013405176*	*CCCP-76807*	*0091*	*0098*	*4 SO D-30KP*	*190000*	*Freighter*		*lsf TYM*

AVIAEKSPRESSKRUIZ, Joint-Stock Company = BKS (Aviaexpresscruise)

Moscow-Vnukovo

Leningradsky prospekt 37, K1, Room 218A, 125836 Moskva, Russia ☎ (095) 155 58 39 Tx: none Fax: (095) 155 62 81 SITA: n/a
F: 1993 👥 n/a Head: Alexander A. Beznikin ICAO: AVIACRUISE Net: n/a

☐ RA-87511	Yakovlev 40	*9521340*	*CCCP-87511*	*0075*	*0096*	*3 IV AI-25*	*17200*	*Y32*		
☐ RA-87535	Yakovlev 40	*9521941*	*CCCP-87535*	*0075*	*0097*	*3 IV AI-25*	*17200*	*F15*		*Kalmykia-titles*
☐ RA-87905	Yakovlev 40K	*9720954*	*CCCP-87905*	*0077*	*0098*	*3 IV AI-25*	*17200*	*Y32*		
☐ RA-87917	Yakovlev 40	*9730755*	*CCCP-87917*	*0077*	*0096*	*3 IV AI-25*	*17200*	*Y32*		
☐ RA-65144	Tupolev 134A-3	*60977*	*ES-AAK*	*0179*	*0098*	*2 SO D-30-III*	*49000*	*C8Y64*		
☐ RA-85604	Tupolev 154B-2	*604*	*CCCP-85604*	*0084*	*0098*	*3 KU NK-8-2U*	*98000*	*Y164*		*lsf ORB*
☐ RA-85713	Tupolev 154M	*889*	*CCCP-85713*	*0091*	*0098*	*3 SO D-30KU-154-II*	*100000*	*C8Y146*		

AVIAENERGO, Joint-Stock Company = ERG (Subs.of RAO EES Rossii/United Energy System of Russia)

Moscow-Sheremetyevo/-Vnukovo & Dolgoprudny Heliport

Alleya 1-oi Mayovki 15, 111395 Moskva, Russia ☎ (095) 374 63 20 Tx: none Fax: (095) 374 70 41 SITA: MOWTO7U
F: 1994 👥 n/a Head: Capt. Alexander R. Blagonravov ICAO: AVIAENERGO Net: n/a

☐ RA-22152	Mil Mi-8T	*99357595*		*0493*		*2 IS TV2-117AG*	*12000*	*Utility*		
☐ RA-22153	Mil Mi-8T	*99357712*		*0893*		*2 IS TV2-117AG*	*12000*	*Utility*		
☐ RA-87216	Yakovlev 40	*9510440*	*CCCP-87216*	*0075*		*3 IV AI-25*	*16800*	*C17*		
☐ RA-74040	Antonov 74	*36547097930*		*0293*		*2 LO D-36*	*34500*	*Freighter*		
☐ RA-65693	Tupolev 134B-3	*63221*	*YL-LBC*	*0080*	*0496*	*2 SO D-30-III*	*49000*	*VIP 36 Pax*		*ALLA-Alla Pugacheva-titles*
☐ RA-85797	Tupolev 154M	*981*		*1293*		*3 SO D-30KU-154-II*	*100000*	*F12C18Y104/Y160*		*lst/jtly opw AFL*
☐ RA-85809	Tupolev 154M	*985*		*1294*		*3 SO D-30KU-154-II*	*100000*	*F12C18Y104/Y160*		*lst/jtly opw AFL*
☐ RA-86130	Ilyushin 62M	*3255333*		*1092*	*0895*	*4 SO D-30KU*	*167000*	*Y168orF12CY126*		*lst / jtly opw AFL / fn 5503*
☐ RA-86583	Ilyushin 62M	*1356851*		*0796*	*0796*	*4 SO D-30KU*	*167000*	*Y168orF12CY126*		*lst/jtly opw AFL / fn 5605*
☐ RA-76366	Ilyushin 76TD	*1043418628*		*0396*	*0496*	*4 SO D-30KP*	*190000*	*Freighter*		*lst/jtly opw ESL*
☐ RA-76843	Ilyushin 76TD	*1033418584*		*0195*		*4 SO D-30KP*	*190000*	*Freighter*		*lst/jtly opw ESL*

AVIAGARANT

Noyabrsk

Ul. Izyskatelei 36/1, 626600 Noyabrsk, (Tyumen Region), Russia ☎ (34564) 51 547 Tx: 235737 astra Fax: (34564) 51 548 SITA: n/a
F: n/a 👥 n/a Head: Vladimir Yu. Obnivin Net: n/a

☐ RA-22294	Mil Mi-8		*CCCP-22294*	*0077*		*2 IS TV2-117A*	*12000*	*Utility*		
☐ RA-24674	Mil Mi-8T			*0081*		*2 IS TV2-117A*	*12000*	*Utility*		
☐ RA-25238	Mil Mi-8		*CCCP-25238*	*0072*		*2 IS TV2-117A*	*12000*	*Utility*		
☐ RA-25631	Mil Mi-8		*CCCP-25631*	*0072*		*2 IS TV2-117A*	*12000*	*Utility*		
☐ RA-25644	Mil Mi-8		*CCCP-25644*	*0072*		*2 IS TV2-117A*	*12000*	*Utility*		

AVIAL Aviation Company, Ltd = RLC

Moscow-Domodedovo, -Sheremetyevo & -Zhukovsky

Ul. Bolshaya Kommunisticheskaya 40/14-1, 109000 Moscow, Russia ☎ (095) 912 38 99 Tx: 411182 aflsu Fax: (095) 912 42 37 SITA: MOWAUXH
F: 1991 👥 50 Head: Georgi Shishkin IATA: 450 Net: n/a

☐ RA-11112	Antonov 12BP	*01347907*	*CCCP-11112*	*0071*		*4 IV AI-20M*	*61000*	*Freighter*		*lst/jtly opw ESL*
☐ RA-11324	Antonov 12BP	*2340805*	*82 RED*	*0062*		*4 IV AI-20M*	*61000*	*Freighter*		
☐ RA-11766	Antonov 12BP	*401605*	*CCCP-11766*	*0063*		*4 IV AI-20M*	*61000*	*Freighter*		*lst/jtly opw ESL*
☐ RA-11899	Antonov 12BP	*402601*	*CCCP-11899*	*0064*		*4 IV AI-20M*	*61000*	*Freighter*		
☐ RA-12992	Antonov 12BP	*00347306*	*CCCP-12992*	*0070*		*4 IV AI-20M*	*61000*	*Freighter*		*lst/jtly opw ESL*

AVIALIFT VLADIVOSTOK

Vladivostok

Ul. Portovaya 41, 692800 Artem, (Primorsky region), Russia ☎ (4232) 30 76 52 Tx: none Fax: (4232) 30 76 51 SITA: n/a
F: 1996 👥 n/a Head: Alexei I. Gurko Net: n/a Beside aircraft listed, also operates Kamov Ka-32 & Mil Mi-8T. Full details not yet known.

☐ RA-15677	PZL Swidnik (Mil) Mi-2	*547950122*		*0082*	*0096*	*2 IS GTD-350-4*	*3550*	*Utility*		

526 registration type of aircraft *cn/fn* *ex/ex** *mfd* *del* *powered by* *mtow kg* *configuration* *selcal* *name/fln/specialitites/remarks*

AVIAMOST = MSG (Member of Most Group) — Moscow-Vnukovo

Ul. Novy Arbat 36, 121205 Moskva, Russia ☎ (095) 290 79 96 Tx: n/a Fax: (095) 290 78 93 SITA: n/a
F: 1993 ⁂ n/a Head: Alexander Reikhtman ICAO: AVIAMOST Net: n/a

registration	type of aircraft	cn/fn	ex/ex*	mfd	del	powered by	mtow kg	configuration	selcal	name/fln/specialitites/remarks
☐ RA-88231	Yakovlev 40K	9642050	CCCP-88231	1176	0097	3 IV AI-25	17200	VIP F5Y12		

AVIAOBSHCHEMASH Aviakompania = OBM (AOM Air Company) — Troitsk

Ul. 3-ya Mytishchinskaya 3, room 505, 129626 Moskva, Russia ☎ (095) 287 78 59 Tx: n/a Fax: (095) 278 78 59 SITA: n/a
F: 1992 ⁂ n/a Head: Gennady P. Onoprienko ICAO: OBSCHEMASH Net: n/a Most aircraft are still in Aeroflot colors but will be repainted in due course.

registration	type of aircraft	cn/fn	ex/ex*	mfd	del	powered by	mtow kg	configuration	selcal	name/fln/specialitites/remarks
☐ RA-88201	Yakovlev 40	9630349	CCCP-88201	0076		3 IV AI-25	16800	Y20		
☐ RA-26191	Antonov 24B	19902309	CCCP-26191	0071		2 IV AI-24	21000	Y32		
☐ RA-47771	Antonov 24B	67303005	CCCP-47771	0066		2 IV AI-24	21000	Y32		
☐ RA-79162	Antonov 24B	99902009	CCCP-79162	0069		2 IV AI-24	21000	Y32		
☐ RA-26090	Antonov 26	11506	CCCP-26090	0081		2 IV AI-24VT	24000	Freighter		
☐ RA-26136	Antonov 26B	12808	CCCP-26136	0083		2 IV AI-24VT	24000	Freighter		
☐ RA-26180	Antonov 26	7810	CCCP-26180	0079		2 IV AI-24VT	24000	Freighter		
☐ RA-26182	Antonov 26	8006	CCCP-26182	0079		2 IV AI-24VT	24000	Freighter		Rossia-titles
☐ RA-26193	Antonov 26	5301	CCCP-26193	0077		2 IV AI-24VT	24000	Freighter		
☐ RA-48092	Antonov 26	5005	CCCP-48092	0077		2 IV AI-24VT	24000	Freighter		
☐ RA-48099	Antonov 26	1404		0072		2 IV AI-24VT	24000	Freighter		
☐ RA-69336	Antonov 32	1810	CCCP-69336	0089		2 IV AI-20D	27000	Freighter		
☐ RA-69344	Antonov 32B	2009	CCCP-69344	0089		2 IV AI-20D	27000	Freighter		
☐ RA-72982	Antonov 72	36572096914	CCCP-72982	0092		2 LO D-36	31200	Freighter		
☐ RA-11327	Antonov 12	1400104		0061		4 IV AI-20M	61000	Freighter		
☐ RA-11408	Antonov 12BP	3341209	CCCP-11408	0063		4 IV AI-20M	61000	Freighter		lst/jtly opw FRT
☐ RA-11532	Antonov 12TB	402007	CCCP-11532	0064		4 IV AI-20M	61000	Freighter		
☐ RA-11756	Antonov 12	4342208	CCCP-11756	0064		4 IV AI-20M	61000	Freighter		
☐ RA-11795	Antonov 12	8900704	CCCP-11795	0059		4 IV AI-20M	61000	Freighter		
☐ RA-11830	Antonov 12BP	4342210	CCCP-11830	0064		4 IV AI-20M	61000	Freighter		
☐ RA-11851	Antonov 12TB	402003	CCCP-11851	0064		4 IV AI-20M	61000	Freighter		
☐ RA-76494	Ilyushin 76TD	0053465956	CCCP-76494	0085		4 SO D-30KP	190000	Freighter		lst RXM

AVIAPRAD = VID (Subsidiary of Ural Engines Repair Plant) — Ekaterinburg-Koltsovo

Ul. Belinskogo 262M, 620089 Ekaterinburg, Russia ☎ (3432) 26 69 61 Tx: none Fax: (3432) 26 69 61 SITA: n/a
F: 1996 ⁂ n/a Head: Sergei V. Kozin ICAO: AVIAPRAD Net: n/a

registration	type of aircraft	cn/fn	ex/ex*	mfd	del	powered by	mtow kg	configuration	selcal	name/fln/specialitites/remarks
☐ RA-76352	Ilyushin 76TD	1023411378	UK-76352	0092	0096	4 SO D-30KP	190000	Freighter		
☐ RA-76386	Ilyushin 76TD	1033418600	UK-76386	0993	0096	4 SO D-30KP	190000	Freighter		

AVIASTAR = FUE (Flying division of Aviastar Aircraft Factory / Member of MAP Group) — Ulyanovsk-Vostochny

Flying division / Letny otryad, Prospekt Leninskogo Komsomola 38, 432000 Ulyanovsk, Russia ☎ (8422) 20 18 93 Tx: none Fax: (8422) 20 18 93 SITA: n/a
F: 1997 ⁂ n/a Head: M.P. Pilnik ICAO: AVIASTAR-VOLGA Net: n/a Operates corporate & cargo flights for itself & commercial charter flights.

registration	type of aircraft	cn/fn	ex/ex*	mfd	del	powered by	mtow kg	configuration	selcal	name/fln/specialitites/remarks
☐ RA-06128	Mil Mi-8T	98315175		1083		2 IS TV2-117A	12000	Utility		
☐ RA-93924	Mil Mi-8T	6977		1276	0097	2 IS TV2-117A	12000	Utility		
☐ RA-87244	Yakovlev 40	9531243	CCCP-87244	1075		3 IV AI-25	17200	Executive		
☐ RA-87755	Yakovlev 40	9021011	CCCP-87755	0670		3 IV AI-25	17200	Executive		
☐ RA-26088	Antonov 26	11209	CCCP-26088	0781		2 IV AI-24VT	24000	Combi		
☐ RA-26093	Antonov 26B	12602	CCCP-26093	1082		2 IV AI-24VT	24000	Combi		
☐ RA-26625	Antonov 26	5203	CCCP-26625	0577		2 IV AI-24VT	24000	Survey/Research		
☐ RA-11529	Antonov 12B	6344109	CCCP-11529	0666		4 IV AI-20M	61000	Freighter		lst/jtly opw FRT
☐ RA-69314	Antonov 12BP	5343004	CCCP-69314	0465		4 IV AI-20M	61000	Freighter		lst/jtly opw FRT
☐ RA-76491	Ilyushin 76T	093421630	CCCP-76491	0180		4 SO D-30KP	170000	Freighter		

AVIATA, Joint-Stock Company = TVL (Aviatsia Tambova) (formerly Aeroflot Tambov division) — Tambov

Tambov Airport, 392019 Tambov, Russia ☎ (0752) 35 68 18 Tx: none Fax: (0752) 35 68 18 SITA: n/a
F: n/a ⁂ n/a Head: Sergei V. Talanov ICAO: AVIATA Net: n/a Most aircraft are still in Aeroflot colors but will be repainted in due course.

registration	type of aircraft	cn/fn	ex/ex*	mfd	del	powered by	mtow kg	configuration	selcal	name/fln/specialitites/remarks
☐ RA-07202	PZL Mielec (Antonov) An-2	1G146-31	CCCP-07202	0073		1 SH ASh-62IR	5500	Utility		
☐ RA-07587	PZL Mielec (Antonov) An-2	1G155-42	CCCP-07587	0074		1 SH ASh-62IR	5500	Utility		
☐ RA-17828	PZL Mielec (Antonov) An-2	1G204-29	CCCP-17828	0083		1 SH ASh-62IR	5500	Utility		
☐ RA-31492	PZL Mielec (Antonov) An-2	1G198-57	CCCP-31492	0082		1 SH ASh-62IR	5500	Utility		
☐ RA-31516	PZL Mielec (Antonov) An-2	1G199-25	CCCP-31516	0082		1 SH ASh-62IR	5500	Utility		
☐ RA-33010	PZL Mielec (Antonov) An-2	1G217-57	CCCP-33010	0085		1 SH ASh-62IR	5500	Utility		
☐ RA-33046	PZL Mielec (Antonov) An-2	1G218-33	CCCP-33046	0086		1 SH ASh-62IR	5500	Utility		
☐ RA-35183	PZL Mielec (Antonov) An-2	1G114-07	CCCP-35183	0069		1 SH ASh-62IR	5500	Utility		
☐ RA-35193	PZL Mielec (Antonov) An-2	1G114-17	CCCP-35193	0069		1 SH ASh-62IR	5500	Utility		
☐ RA-40228	PZL Mielec (Antonov) An-2	1G220-18	CCCP-40228	0086		1 SH ASh-62IR	5500	Utility		
☐ RA-40283	PZL Mielec (Antonov) An-2	1G221-13	CCCP-40283	0086		1 SH ASh-62IR	5500	Utility		
☐ RA-40355	PZL Mielec (Antonov) An-2	1G222-32	CCCP-40355	0086		1 SH ASh-62IR	5500	Utility		
☐ RA-40380	PZL Mielec (Antonov) An-2	1G223-04	CCCP-40380	0087		1 SH ASh-62IR	5500	Utility		
☐ RA-40489	PZL Mielec (Antonov) An-2	1G225-06	CCCP-40489	0087		1 SH ASh-62IR	5500	Utility		
☐ RA-40669	PZL Mielec (Antonov) An-2	1G214-27	CCCP-40669	0086		1 SH ASh-62IR	5500	Utility		
☐ RA-40713	PZL Mielec (Antonov) An-2	1G171-50	CCCP-40713	0076		1 SH ASh-62IR	5500	Utility		
☐ RA-40714	PZL Mielec (Antonov) An-2	1G171-51	CCCP-40714	0076		1 SH ASh-62IR	5500	Utility		
☐ RA-54908	PZL Mielec (Antonov) An-2		CCCP-54908	0079		1 SH ASh-62IR	5500	Utility		
☐ RA-54909	PZL Mielec (Antonov) An-2	1G186-57	CCCP-54909	0079		1 SH ASh-62IR	5500	Utility		
☐ RA-54910	PZL Mielec (Antonov) An-2	1G186-58	CCCP-54910	0079		1 SH ASh-62IR	5500	Utility		
☐ RA-56391	PZL Mielec (Antonov) An-2	1G180-21	CCCP-56391	0078		1 SH ASh-62IR	5500	Utility		
☐ RA-56411	PZL Mielec (Antonov) An-2		CCCP-56411	0078		1 SH ASh-62IR	5500	Utility		
☐ RA-56445	PZL Mielec (Antonov) An-2	1G181-29	CCCP-56445	0078		1 SH ASh-62IR	5500	Utility		
☐ RA-68162	PZL Mielec (Antonov) An-2	1G196-57	CCCP-68162	0081		1 SH ASh-62IR	5500	Utility		
☐ RA-70262	PZL Mielec (Antonov) An-2	1G139-21	CCCP-70262	0072		1 SH ASh-62IR	5500	Utility		
☐ RA-70714	PZL Mielec (Antonov) An-2	1G130-15	CCCP-70714	0071		1 SH ASh-62IR	5500	Utility		
☐ RA-82824	PZL Mielec (Antonov) An-2	1G166-56	CCCP-82824	0075		1 SH ASh-62IR	5500	Utility		
☐ RA-82838	PZL Mielec (Antonov) An-2	1G167-52	CCCP-82838	0076		1 SH ASh-62IR	5500	Utility		
☐ RA-84583	PZL Mielec (Antonov) An-2	1G189-50	CCCP-84583	0080		1 SH ASh-62IR	5500	Utility		
☐ RA-84584	PZL Mielec (Antonov) An-2	1G189-51	CCCP-84584	0080		1 SH ASh-62IR	5500	Utility		
☐ RA-46291	Antonov 24B	77303803	CCCP-46291	0067		2 IV AI-24	21800	Y48		
☐ RA-46519	Antonov 24RV	37308505	CCCP-46519	0073		2 IV AI-24VT	21800	Y48		
☐ RA-46581	Antonov 24B	97304910	CCCP-46581	0069		2 IV AI-24	21000	Y48		
☐ RA-46657	Antonov 24RV	47309303	CCCP-46657	0074		2 IV AI-24VT	21800	Y48		
☐ RA-46691	Antonov 24RV	47309902	CCCP-46691	0074		2 IV AI-24VT	21800	Y48		
☐ RA-46848	Antonov 24RV	27307506	CCCP-46848	0072		2 IV AI-24VT	21800	Y48		
☐ RA-47199	Antonov 24RV	27307703	CCCP-47199	0072		2 IV AI-24VT	21800	Y48		
☐ RA-47800	Antonov 24RV	17306809	CCCP-47800	0071		2 IV AI-24VT	21800	Y48		
☐ RA-47828	Antonov 24B	17307209	CCCP-47828	0071		2 IV AI-24	21000	Y48		
☐ RA-47835	Antonov 24B	17307307	CCCP-47835	0071		2 IV AI-24	21000	Y48		

AVIATION COMPANY PILOT (Aviakompania PILOT) — Krasnodar

PO Box 1712, 350051 Krasnodar, Russia ☎ (8612) 54 42 27 Tx: none Fax: (8612) 54 42 27 SITA: n/a
F: 1992 ⁂ 70 Head: Vadim L. Lakhtin Net: n/a

registration	type of aircraft	cn/fn	ex/ex*	mfd	del	powered by	mtow kg	configuration	selcal	name/fln/specialitites/remarks
☐ RA-07787	PZL Mielec (Antonov) An-2	1G162-37	CCCP-07787	0075		1 SH ASh-62IR	5500	Y12		lst ANP as 7P-AND
☐ RA-11038	Antonov 12BP	2340709	CCCP-11038	0062		4 IV AI-20M	61000	Freighter		lst ANP as 7P-ANA
☐ RA-11658	Antonov 12BP	9346608	CCCP-11658	0069		4 IV AI-20M	61000	Freighter		lst ANP as 7P-ANC
☐ RA-11760	Antonov 12BP	4342404	CCCP-11760	0064		4 IV AI-20M	64000	Freighter		lst ANP as 7P-ANB

AVITEK-Vyatskoe mashinostroitel'noe predpriatie (Flying division of Vyatka Machines Production Enterprise/Member of MAP Group) — Kirov-Pobedilovo

Flying division / Letny otryad, Oktyabrsky Prospekt 1A, 610047 Kirov, Russia ☎ (8332) 69 66 41 Tx: n/a Fax: (8332) 23 61 22 SITA: n/a
F: n/a ⁂ n/a Head: Alexei E. Bakhtirev Net: n/a Operates corporate flights for itself & commercial charter flights. Aircraft are still in Aeroflot colors with or without titles.

registration	type of aircraft	cn/fn	ex/ex*	mfd	del	powered by	mtow kg	configuration	selcal	name/fln/specialitites/remarks
☐ RA-26086	Antonov 26			0081		2 IV AI-24VT	24000	Freighter		
☐ RA-46741	Antonov 12					4 IV AI-20M	61000	Freighter		

AVL – Arkhangelskie vozdushnye linii = 5N / AUL (Arkhangelsk Airlines) (formerly part of Aeroflot Arkhangelsk directorate) — Arkhangelsk

Talagi Airport, 163053 Arkhangelsk, Russia ☎ (8182) 46 62 16 Tx: 242317 bort Fax: (8182) 46 68 16 SITA: n/a
F: 1961 ⁂ n/a Head: Vladimir M. Korotyaev IATA: 316 ICAO: ARCHANGELSK AIR Net: n/a Most aircraft are still in Aeroflot colors but will be repainted in due course.

registration	type of aircraft	cn/fn	ex/ex*	mfd	del	powered by	mtow kg	configuration	selcal	name/fln/specialitites/remarks
☐ RA-46214	Antonov 24B	77302908	CCCP-46214	0066		2 IV AI-24	21000	Y48		
☐ RA-46260	Antonov 24B	77303501	CCCP-46260	0067		2 IV AI-24	21000	Y40		
☐ RA-46275	Antonov 24B	77303608	CCCP-46275	0067		2 IV AI-24	21000	Y48		
☐ RA-46424	Antonov 24B	87304109	CCCP-46424	0068		2 IV AI-24	21000	Y48		
☐ RA-46528	Antonov 24RV	47310007	CCCP-46528	0074		2 IV AI-24VT	21800	Y40		
☐ RA-46560	Antonov 24B	87304609	CCCP-46560	0068		2 IV AI-24	21000	Y48		
☐ RA-46564	Antonov 24B		CCCP-46564	0068		2 IV AI-24	21000	Y48		
☐ RA-46588	Antonov 24B	97305008	CCCP-46588	0069		2 IV AI-24	21000	Y48		
☐ RA-46651	Antonov 24RV	47309202	CCCP-46651	0074		2 IV AI-24VT	21800	Y40		

registration	type of aircraft	cn/fn	ex/ex*	mfd del	powered by	mtow kg	configuration	selcal	name/fin/specialitites/remarks
☐ RA-46667	Antonov 24RV	47309508	CCCP-46667	0774	2 IV AI-24VT	21800	Y40		
☐ RA-46820	Antonov 24B	67302608	CCCP-46820	0071	2 IV AI-24	21000	Y48		
☐ RA-47305	Antonov 24RV	57310305	CCCP-47305	0075	2 IV AI-24VT	21800	Y40		
☐ RA-26024	Antonov 26B	10306	CCCP-26024	0080	2 IV AI-24VT	24000	Freighter		
☐ RA-26052	Antonov 26B	10908	CCCP-26052	0081	2 IV AI-24VT	24000	Freighter		
☐ RA-26076	Antonov 26B	11601	CCCP-26076	0081	2 IV AI-24VT	24000	Freighter		
☐ RA-26104	Antonov 26B	12002	CCCP-26104	0082	2 IV AI-24VT	24000	Freighter		
☐ RA-26119	Antonov 26B	12208	CCCP-26119	0082	2 IV AI-24VT	24000	Freighter		
☐ RA-26135	Antonov 26B	12806	CCCP-26135	0083	2 IV AI-24VT	24000	Freighter		
☐ RA-26542	Antonov 26	2708	CCCP-26542	0075	2 IV AI-24VT	24000	Freighter		
☐ RA-26551	Antonov 26		CCCP-26551	0075	2 IV AI-24VT	24000	Freighter		
☐ RA-26556	Antonov 26	3204	CCCP-26556	0075	2 IV AI-24VT	24000	Freighter		
☐ RA-26601	Antonov 26		CCCP-2660	0076	2 IV AI-24VT	24000	Freighter		
☐ RA-26615	Antonov 26	5001	CCCP-26615	0077	2 IV AI-24VT	24000	Freighter		
☐ RA-26682	Antonov 26	8706	CCCP-26682	0079	2 IV AI-24VT	24000	Freighter		
☐ RA-65052	Tupolev 134A	49825	CCCP-65052	0077	2 SO D-30-II	49000	Y76		
☐ RA-65066	Tupolev 134A-3	49898	CCCP-65066	0077	2 SO D-30-III	49000	Y76		
☐ RA-65083	Tupolev 134A-3	60090	CCCP-65083	0077	2 SO D-30-III	49000	Y76		
☐ RA-65084	Tupolev 134A-3	60115	CCCP-65084	0077	2 SO D-30-III	49000	Y76		
☐ RA-65096	Tupolev 134A-3	60257	CCCP-65096	0078	2 SO D-30-III	49000	Y76		
☐ RA-65103	Tupolev 134A-3	60297	CCCP-65103	0078	2 SO D-30-III	49000	Y76		
☐ RA-65116	Tupolev 134A-3	60420	CCCP-65116	0078	2 SO D-30-III	49000	Y76		
☐ RA-65132	Tupolev 134A-3	60639	CCCP-65132	0078	2 SO D-30-III	49000	Executive		lst/opf Clintondale Aviation
☐ RA-65811	Tupolev 134A-3	4352202	CCCP-65811	0074	2 SO D-30-II	49000	Y76		
☐ RA-65819	Tupolev 134A	4352304	CCCP-65819	0074	2 SO D-30-II	49000	Y76		
☐ RA-65846	Tupolev 134A	23132	CCCP-65846	0074	2 SO D-30-II	49000	Y76		
☐ RA-65898	Tupolev 134A-3	42220	CCCP-65898	0075	2 SO D-30-III	49000	Y76		
☐ RA-65955	Tupolev 134A-3	2351708	CCCP-65955	0072	2 SO D-30-III	49000	Y76		
☐ RA-65976	Tupolev 134A-3	3352007	CCCP-65976	0073	2 SO D-30-III	49000	Y76		
☐ RA-85302	Tupolev 154B-2	302	CCCP-85302	0078	3 KU NK-8-2U	98000	Y180		
☐ RA-85365	Tupolev 154B-2	365	CCCP-85365	0079	3 KU NK-8-2U	98000	Y164		lst LAZ as LZ-LTB
☐ RA-85386	Tupolev 154B-2	386	CCCP-85386	0079	3 KU NK-8-2U	98000	Y164		lst ESL
☐ RA-85468	Tupolev 154B-2	468	CCCP-85468	0081	3 KU NK-8-2U	98000	Y164		lst ESL
☐ RA-85551	Tupolev 154B-2	551	CCCP-85551	0082	3 KU NK-8-2U	98000	Y164		lst ESL

BAIKAL AIRLINES = X3 / BKL (Aviakompania Baikal) (formerly Aeroflot Irkutsk division)   Irkutsk-International

Ul. Shiryamova 8, 664009 Irkutsk, Russia   ☎ (3952) 54 37 70   Tx: 231822 azia   Fax: (3952) 54 37 69   SITA: n/a
F: n/a   ♠♠♠ n/a   Head: Vladimir N. Kovalenko   IATA: 483   ICAO: BAIKAL   Net: n/a   Some aircraft are still in former Aeroflot colors but will be repainted in due course.

registration	type of aircraft	cn/fn	ex/ex*	mfd del	powered by	mtow kg	configuration	selcal	name/fin/specialitites/remarks
☐ RA-35117	PZL Mielec (Antonov) An-2	1G111-43	CCCP-35117	1269	1 SH ASh-62IR	5250	Y12		
☐ RA-40627	PZL Mielec (Antonov) An-2	1G213-34	CCCP-40627	0585	1 SH ASh-62IR	5250	Y12		
☐ RA-71281	PZL Mielec (Antonov) An-2	1G207-52	CCCP-71281	0584	1 SH ASh-62IR	5250	Y12		
☐ RA-84672	PZL Mielec (Antonov) An-2	1G191-50	CCCP-84672	0381	1 SH ASh-62IR	5250	Y12		
☐ RA-22267	Mil Mi-8T	6916	CCCP-22267	1177	2 IS TV2-117A	12000	Utility		
☐ RA-22361	Mil Mi-8T	7225	CCCP-22361	0677	2 IS TV2-117A	12000	Utility		
☐ RA-22877	Mil Mi-8T	98475795	CCCP-22877	0584	2 IS TV2-117A	12000	Utility		
☐ RA-22975	Mil Mi-8T	5882	CCCP-22975	0975	2 IS TV2-117A	12000	Utility		
☐ RA-24632	Mil Mi-8P	8407	CCCP-24632	0883	2 IS TV2-117A	12000	C8		
☐ RA-25502	Mil Mi-8MTV-1	95650	CCCP-25502	0691	2 IS TV3-117VM	13000	Utility		
☐ RA-25504	Mil Mi-8MTV-1	95652	CCCP-25504	0691	2 IS TV3-117VM	13000	Utility		
☐ RA-25857	Mil Mi-8T	5122	CCCP-25857	0375	2 IS TV2-117A	12000	Utility		
☐ RA-46629	Antonov 24RV	37308808	CCCP-46629	0073	2 IV AI-24VT	21000	Y48		
☐ RA-46673	Antonov 24RV	47309605	CCCP-46673	0074	2 IV AI-24VT	21000	Y48		
☐ RA-46689	Antonov 24RV	47309806	CCCP-46689	0074	2 IV AI-24VT	21000	Y48		
☐ RA-46697	Antonov 24RV	47309908	CCCP-46697	0074	2 IV AI-24VT	21000	Y48		
☐ RA-47263	Antonov 24RV	27307805	CCCP-47263	0072	2 IV AI-24VT	21000	Y48		
☐ RA-47302	Antonov 24RV	57310302	CCCP-47302	0075	2 IV AI-24VT	21000	Y48		
☐ RA-47803	Antonov 24RV	17306902	CCCP-47803	0071	2 IV AI-24VT	21000	Y48		
☐ RA-47815	Antonov 24RV	17307101	CCCP-47815	0071	2 IV AI-24VT	21000	Y48		
☐ RA-26006	Antonov 26	9810	CCCP-26006	0080	2 IV AI-24VT	24000	Freighter		
☐ RA-26062	Antonov 26B	11110	CCCP-26062	0081	2 IV AI-24VT	24000	Freighter		
☐ RA-26530	Antonov 26	7402	CCCP-26530	0078	2 IV AI-24VT	24000	Freighter		
☐ RA-26539	Antonov 26	2103	CCCP-26539	0074	2 IV AI-24VT	24000	Freighter		
☐ RA-26614	Antonov 26	4910	CCCP-26614	0077	2 IV AI-24VT	24000	Freighter		
☐ RA-11032	Antonov 12B	7345004	CCCP-11032	0067	4 IV AI-20M	61000	Freighter		
☐ RA-11034	Antonov 12B	7345010	CCCP-11034	0067	4 IV AI-20M	61000	Freighter		
☐ RA-11116	Antonov 12B	01348006	CCCP-11116	0071	4 IV AI-20M	61000	Freighter		
☐ RA-11124	Antonov 12B	02348106	CCCP-11124	0072	4 IV AI-20M	61000	Freighter		
☐ RA-11996	Antonov 12B	402504	CCCP-11996	0064	4 IV AI-20M	61000	Freighter		
☐ RA-12988	Antonov 12B	00347206	CCCP-12988	0670	4 IV AI-20M	61000	Freighter		
☐ RA-85453	Tupolev 154B-2	453	CCCP-85453	0080	3 KU NK-8-2U	98000	Y164		
☐ RA-85462	Tupolev 154B-2	462	CCCP-85462	0080	3 KU NK-8-2U	98000	Y164		
☐ RA-85503	Tupolev 154B-2	503	CCCP-85503	0081	3 KU NK-8-2U	100000	Y164		
☐ RA-85512	Tupolev 154B-2	512	CCCP-85512	0081	3 KU NK-8-2U	100000	Y164		
☐ RA-85613	Tupolev 154M	722	CCCP-85613	0085	3 SO D-30KU-154-II	100000	Y164		
☐ RA-85652	Tupolev 154M	794	CCCP-85652	0088	3 SO D-30KU-154-II	100000	Y164		
☐ RA-85654	Tupolev 154M	796	CCCP-85654	0088	3 SO D-30KU-154-II	100000	Y164		
☐ RA-85657	Tupolev 154M	802	CCCP-85657	0089	3 SO D-30KU-154-II	100000	Y164		
☐ RA-85690	Tupolev 154M	861	CCCP-85690	1290	3 SO D-30KU-154-II	100000	Y164		
☐ RA-85695	Tupolev 154M	868	CCCP-85695	0091	3 SO D-30KU-154-II	100000	Y164		
☐ RA-76458	Ilyushin 76T	0013430888	CCCP-76458	0081	4 SO D-30KP	170000	Freighter		lst ESL
☐ RA-76462	Ilyushin 76T	0013432955	CCCP-76462	0081	4 SO D-30KP	170000	Freighter		lst ESL
☐ RA-76484	Ilyushin 76TD	0063469081	CCCP-76484	0086	4 SO D-30KP	190000	Freighter		
☐ RA-76525	Ilyushin 76T	0003427787	CCCP-76525	0080	4 SO D-30KP	170000	Freighter		
☐ RA-76526	Ilyushin 76T	0003427792	CCCP-76526	0080	4 SO D-30KP	170000	Freighter		
☐ RA-76808	Ilyushin 76TD	1013405177	CCCP-76808	0091	4 SO D-30KP	190000	Freighter		

BAIKIT AIR ENTERPRISE (Baikitskoe aviaprepriatie) (formerly Aeroflot Baikit division)   Baikit

Baikit Airport, Box 18, 663360 Baikit, (Krasnoyarsk Region), Russia   ☎ 21 245 (via Moscow)   Tx: none   Fax: none   SITA: n/a
F: 1980   ♠♠♠ n/a   Head: Leonid B. Kaminsky   Net: n/a   Most aircraft are still in Aeroflot colors but will be repainted in due course.

registration	type of aircraft	cn/fn	ex/ex*	mfd del	powered by	mtow kg	configuration	selcal	name/fin/specialitites/remarks
☐ RA-01714	PZL Mielec (Antonov) An-2	1G113-01	CCCP-01714	0070	1 SH ASh-62IR	5500			
☐ RA-62585	PZL Mielec (Antonov) An-2	1G176-54	CCCP-62585	0077	1 SH ASh-62IR	5500			
☐ RA-22680	Mil Mi-8T	8135	CCCP-22680	0080	2 IS TV2-117A	12000			
☐ RA-22737	Mil Mi-8T	98308999	CCCP-22737	0083	2 IS TV2-117A	12000			
☐ RA-22901	Mil Mi-8T	98420092	CCCP-22901	0084	2 IS TV2-117A	12000			
☐ RA-24414	Mil Mi-8T	98625247	CCCP-24414	0086	2 IS TV2-117A	12000			
☐ RA-24473	Mil Mi-8T	98628785	CCCP-24473	0086	2 IS TV2-117A	12000			
☐ RA-24695	Mil Mi-8T	98109116	CCCP-24695	0081	2 IS TV2-117A	12000			

BALAKOVO AIR ENTERPRISE (Balakovskoe aviapredpriatie) (formerly Aeroflot Balakovo division)   Balakovo

Balakovo Airport, 413800 Balakovo, (Saratov Region), Russia   ☎ (84570) 20 119   Tx: n/a   Fax: none   SITA: n/a
F: n/a   ♠♠♠ n/a   Head: Anatoly N. Niktin   Net: n/a   Most aircraft are still in Aeroflot colors but will be repainted in due course.

registration	type of aircraft	cn/fn	ex/ex*	mfd del	powered by	mtow kg	configuration	selcal	name/fin/specialitites/remarks
☐ RA-01482	PZL Mielec (Antonov) An-2		CCCP-01482	0088	1 SH ASh-62IR	5500	Utility		
☐ RA-01486	PZL Mielec (Antonov) An-2		CCCP-01486	0088	1 SH ASh-62IR	5500	Utility		
☐ RA-02206	PZL Mielec (Antonov) An-2		CCCP-02206	0090	1 SH ASh-62IR	5500	Utility		
☐ RA-02693	PZL Mielec (Antonov) An-2		CCCP-02693	0071	1 SH ASh-62IR	5500	Utility		
☐ RA-06256	PZL Mielec (Antonov) An-2		CCCP-06256	0071	1 SH ASh-62IR	5500	Utility		
☐ RA-07414	PZL Mielec (Antonov) An-2		CCCP-07414	0073	1 SH ASh-62IR	5500	Utility		
☐ RA-07467	PZL Mielec (Antonov) An-2		CCCP-07467	0073	1 SH ASh-62IR	5500	Utility		
☐ RA-07470	PZL Mielec (Antonov) An-2		CCCP-07470	0073	1 SH ASh-62IR	5500	Utility		
☐ RA-07476	PZL Mielec (Antonov) An-2		CCCP-07476	0073	1 SH ASh-62IR	5500	Utility		
☐ RA-16064	PZL Mielec (Antonov) An-2		CCCP-16064	0075	1 SH ASh-62IR	5500	Utility		
☐ RA-16065	PZL Mielec (Antonov) An-2		CCCP-16065	0075	1 SH ASh-62IR	5500	Utility		
☐ RA-19720	PZL Mielec (Antonov) An-2		CCCP-19720	0075	1 SH ASh-62IR	5500	Utility		
☐ RA-32634	PZL Mielec (Antonov) An-2		CCCP-32634	0086	1 SH ASh-62IR	5500	Utility		
☐ RA-33060	PZL Mielec (Antonov) An-2		CCCP-33060	0086	1 SH ASh-62IR	5500	Utility		
☐ RA-33061	PZL Mielec (Antonov) An-2		CCCP-33061	0086	1 SH ASh-62IR	5500	Utility		
☐ RA-33322	PZL Mielec (Antonov) An-2	1G225-41	CCCP-33322	0087	1 SH ASh-62IR	5500	Utility		
☐ RA-33375	PZL Mielec (Antonov) An-2	1G226-34	CCCP-33375	0087	1 SH ASh-62IR	5500	Utility		
☐ RA-33376	PZL Mielec (Antonov) An-2		CCCP-33376	0087	1 SH ASh-62IR	5500	Utility		
☐ RA-33534	PZL Mielec (Antonov) An-2		CCCP-33534	0088	1 SH ASh-62IR	5500	Utility		
☐ RA-33579	PZL Mielec (Antonov) An-2		CCCP-33579	0088	1 SH ASh-62IR	5500	Utility		

☐ RA-33617	PZL Mielec (Antonov) An-2		CCCP-33617	0088		1 SH ASh-62IR	5500	Utility
☐ RA-33674	PZL Mielec (Antonov) An-2		CCCP-33674	0089		1 SH ASh-62IR	5500	Utility
☐ RA-35089	PZL Mielec (Antonov) An-2		CCCP-35089	0069		1 SH ASh-62IR	5500	Utility
☐ RA-35197	PZL Mielec (Antonov) An-2		CCCP-35197	0069		1 SH ASh-62IR	5500	Utility
☐ RA-40220	PZL Mielec (Antonov) An-2		CCCP-40220	0086		1 SH ASh-62IR	5500	Utility
☐ RA-40351	PZL Mielec (Antonov) An-2		CCCP-40351	0086		1 SH ASh-62IR	5500	Utility
☐ RA-40352	PZL Mielec (Antonov) An-2		CCCP-40352	0086		1 SH ASh-62IR	5500	Utility
☐ RA-40353	PZL Mielec (Antonov) An-2		CCCP-40353	0086		1 SH ASh-62IR	5500	Utility
☐ RA-40358	PZL Mielec (Antonov) An-2		CCCP-40358	0086		1 SH ASh-62IR	5500	Utility
☐ RA-40365	PZL Mielec (Antonov) An-2	1G222-44	CCCP-40365	0086		1 SH ASh-62IR	5500	Utility
☐ RA-40383	PZL Mielec (Antonov) An-2		CCCP-40383	0087		1 SH ASh-62IR	5500	Utility
☐ RA-40384	PZL Mielec (Antonov) An-2		CCCP-40384	0087		1 SH ASh-62IR	5500	Utility
☐ RA-40385	PZL Mielec (Antonov) An-2		CCCP-40385	0087		1 SH ASh-62IR	5500	Utility
☐ RA-40728	PZL Mielec (Antonov) An-2		CCCP-40728	0076		1 SH ASh-62IR	5500	Utility
☐ RA-40730	PZL Mielec (Antonov) An-2		CCCP-40730	0076		1 SH ASh-62IR	5500	Utility
☐ RA-40733	PZL Mielec (Antonov) An-2		CCCP-40733	0076		1 SH ASh-62IR	5500	Utility
☐ RA-40792	PZL Mielec (Antonov) An-2		CCCP-40792	0077		1 SH ASh-62IR	5500	Utility
☐ RA-40794	PZL Mielec (Antonov) An-2		CCCP-40794	0077		1 SH ASh-62IR	5500	Utility
☐ RA-40875	PZL Mielec (Antonov) An-2		CCCP-40875	0085		1 SH ASh-62IR	5500	Utility
☐ RA-54842	PZL Mielec (Antonov) An-2		CCCP-54842	0079		1 SH ASh-62IR	5500	Utility
☐ RA-56435	PZL Mielec (Antonov) An-2		CCCP-56435	0078		1 SH ASh-62IR	5500	Utility
☐ RA-56470	PZL Mielec (Antonov) An-2		CCCP-56470	0079		1 SH ASh-62IR	5500	Utility
☐ RA-56505	PZL Mielec (Antonov) An-2		CCCP-56505	0079		1 SH ASh-62IR	5500	Utility
☐ RA-62610	PZL Mielec (Antonov) An-2		CCCP-62610	0078		1 SH ASh-62IR	5500	Utility
☐ RA-62611	PZL Mielec (Antonov) An-2		CCCP-62611	0078		1 SH ASh-62IR	5500	Utility
☐ RA-70082	PZL Mielec (Antonov) An-2		CCCP-70082	0071		1 SH ASh-62IR	5500	Utility
☐ RA-70085	PZL Mielec (Antonov) An-2		CCCP-70085	0071		1 SH ASh-62IR	5500	Utility
☐ RA-70131	PZL Mielec (Antonov) An-2		CCCP-70131	0071		1 SH ASh-62IR	5500	Utility
☐ RA-70191	PZL Mielec (Antonov) An-2		CCCP-70191	0072		1 SH ASh-62IR	5500	Utility
☐ RA-70519	PZL Mielec (Antonov) An-2		CCCP-70519	0073		1 SH ASh-62IR	5500	Utility
☐ RA-70840	PZL Mielec (Antonov) An-2		CCCP-70840	0071		1 SH ASh-62IR	5500	Utility
☐ RA-70843	PZL Mielec (Antonov) An-2		CCCP-70843	0071		1 SH ASh-62IR	5500	Utility
☐ RA-82823	PZL Mielec (Antonov) An-2		CCCP-82823	0075		1 SH ASh-62IR	5500	Utility
☐ RA-84566	PZL Mielec (Antonov) An-2		CCCP-84566	0080		1 SH ASh-62IR	5500	Utility
☐ RA-84662	PZL Mielec (Antonov) An-2		CCCP-84662	0080		1 SH ASh-62IR	5500	Utility
☐ RA-46318	Antonov 24B		CCCP-46318	0069		2 IV AI-24	21000	Y48
☐ RA-46520	Antonov 24RV		CCCP-46520	0073		2 IV AI-24VT	21800	Y48
☐ RA-47264	Antonov 24RV		CCCP-47264	0070		2 IV AI-24VT	21800	Y48

BAL – Bashkirskie avialinii = V9 / BTC (Bashkirian Airlines) (formerly Aeroflot Bashkirian directorate)

Ufa

Airport, 450056 Ufa, (Republic of Bashkortostan), Russia ☎ (3472) 14 34 45 Tx: 161125 ptb su Fax: (3472) 23 29 56 SITA: n/a

F: 1991 n/a Head: Vilgelm V. Kapp IATA: 940 ICAO: BASHKIRIAN Net: n/a

☐ RA-04003	Mil Mi-34	9783001501005		0696	0697	1 VO M-14V-26	1450	Utility
☐ RA-04004	Mil Mi-34	9783002501002		1096	0091	1 VO M-14V-26	1450	Utility
☐ RA-04005	Mil Mi-34	9783003500203		0397	0797	1 VO M-14V-26	1450	Utility
☐ RA-04006	Mil Mi-34	9783003502001		0895	1297	1 VO M-14V-26	1450	Utility
☐ RA-19313	Kamov Ka-26	7706015	CCCP-19313	0677	0091	2 VE M-14V-26	3250	Utility
☐ RA-19321	Kamov Ka-26	7706113	CCCP-19321	0977	0091	2 VE M-14V-26	3250	Utility
☐ RA-19418	Kamov Ka-26	7404412	CCCP-19418	0674	0091	2 VE M-14V-26	3250	Utility
☐ RA-19431	Kamov Ka-26	7706212	CCCP-19431	1177	0091	2 VE M-14V-26	3250	Utility
☐ RA-19435	Kamov Ka-26	7706216	CCCP-19435	1177	0091	2 VE M-14V-26	3250	Utility
☐ RA-19479	Kamov Ka-26	7304002	CCCP-19479	0374	0091	2 VE M-14V-26	3250	Utility
☐ RA-19665	Kamov Ka-26	7605505	CCCP-19665	0476	0091	2 VE M-14V-26	3250	Utility
☐ RA-01487	PZL Mielec (Antonov) An-2	1G232-21	CCCP-01487	1088	0091	1 SH ASh-62IR	5250	Utility
☐ RA-07652	PZL Mielec (Antonov) An-2	1G157-37	CCCP-07652	0674	0091	1 SH ASh-62IR	5250	Utility
☐ RA-07655	PZL Mielec (Antonov) An-2	1G157-40	CCCP-07655	0674	0091	1 SH ASh-62IR	5250	Utility
☐ RA-07753	PZL Mielec (Antonov) An-2	1G159-31	CCCP-07753	1174	0091	1 SH ASh-62IR	5500	Y12
☐ RA-17743	PZL Mielec (Antonov) An-2	1G203-04	CCCP-17743	0583	0091	1 SH ASh-62IR	5250	Sprayer
☐ RA-17823	PZL Mielec (Antonov) An-2	1G204-24	CCCP-17823	0883	0091	1 SH ASh-62IR	5250	Sprayer
☐ RA-19718	PZL Mielec (Antonov) An-2	1G165-32	CCCP-19718	0975	0091	1 SH ASh-62IR	5250	Sprayer
☐ RA-31462	PZL Mielec (Antonov) An-2	1G198-27	CCCP-31462	0882	0091	1 SH ASh-62IR	5250	Sprayer
☐ RA-32602	PZL Mielec (Antonov) An-2	1G219-01	CCCP-32602	0486	0091	1 SH ASh-62IR	5250	Sprayer
☐ RA-32672	PZL Mielec (Antonov) An-2	1G211-31	CCCP-32672	0285	0091	1 SH ASh-62IR	5250	Sprayer
☐ RA-33355	PZL Mielec (Antonov) An-2	1G226-14	CCCP-33355	0787	0091	1 SH ASh-62IR	5250	Sprayer
☐ RA-33614	PZL Mielec (Antonov) An-2	1G232-48	CCCP-33614	1188	0091	1 SH ASh-62IR	5250	Sprayer
☐ RA-33615	PZL Mielec (Antonov) An-2	1G232-49	CCCP-33615	1188	0091	1 SH ASh-62IR	5250	Sprayer
☐ RA-33676	PZL Mielec (Antonov) An-2	1G234-28	CCCP-33676	0289	0091	1 SH ASh-62IR	5250	Sprayer
☐ RA-40204	PZL Mielec (Antonov) An-2	1G219-54	CCCP-40204	0686	0091	1 SH ASh-62IR	5250	Sprayer
☐ RA-40394	PZL Mielec (Antonov) An-2	1G223-18	CCCP-40394	0187	0091	1 SH ASh-62IR	5250	Sprayer
☐ RA-40399	PZL Mielec (Antonov) An-2	1G223-23	CCCP-40399	0287	0091	1 SH ASh-62IR	5250	Sprayer
☐ RA-40538	PZL Mielec (Antonov) An-2	1G83-41	CCCP-40538	0667	0091	1 SH ASh-62IR	5250	Utility
☐ RA-40932	PZL Mielec (Antonov) An-2	1G216-12	CCCP-40932	1085	0192	1 SH ASh-62IR	5250	Sprayer
☐ RA-40933	PZL Mielec (Antonov) An-2	1G216-13	CCCP-40933	1085	0091	1 SH ASh-62IR	5250	Sprayer
☐ RA-40934	PZL Mielec (Antonov) An-2	1G216-14	CCCP-40934	1085	0091	1 SH ASh-62IR	5250	Sprayer
☐ RA-40935	PZL Mielec (Antonov) An-2	1G216-15	CCCP-40935	1085	0091	1 SH ASh-62IR	5250	Sprayer
☐ RA-54833	PZL Mielec (Antonov) An-2	1G184-40	CCCP-54833	0879	0091	1 SH ASh-62IR	5250	Sprayer
☐ RA-68172	PZL Mielec (Antonov) An-2	1G197-07	CCCP-68172	0482	0091	1 SH ASh-62IR	5250	Sprayer
☐ RA-70729	PZL Mielec (Antonov) An-2	1G130-30	CCCP-70729	0971	0091	1 SH ASh-62IR	5500	Y12
☐ RA-71160	PZL Mielec (Antonov) An-2	1G200-03	CCCP-71160	1182	0091	1 SH ASh-62IR	5250	Sprayer
☐ RA-82820	PZL Mielec (Antonov) An-2	1G166-52	CCCP-82820	1275	0091	1 SH ASh-62IR	5250	Sprayer
☐ RA-84578	PZL Mielec (Antonov) An-2	1G189-45	CCCP-84578	1080	0091	1 SH ASh-62IR	5250	Sprayer
☐ RA-92976	PZL Mielec (Antonov) An-2	1G171-33	CCCP-92976	0976	0091	1 SH ASh-62IR	5250	Sprayer
☐ RA-22722	Mil Mi-8T	98308600	CCCP-22722	0383	0091	2 IS TV2-117A	12000	Utility
☐ RA-22733	Mil Mi-8T	98308882	CCCP-22733	0583	0091	2 IS TV2-117A	12000	Utility
☐ RA-22734	Mil Mi-8T	98308901	CCCP-22734	0583	0091	2 IS TV2-117A	12000	Utility
☐ RA-22794	Mil Mi-8T	98315111	CCCP-22794	1083	0091	2 IS TV2-117A	12000	Utility
☐ RA-22858	Mil Mi-8T	98415421	CCCP-22858	0484	0091	2 IS TV2-117A	12000	Utility
☐ RA-22872	Mil Mi-8T	98415700	CCCP-22872	0684	0091	2 IS TV2-117A	12000	Utility
☐ RA-24018	Mil Mi-8T	99150898	CCCP-24018	0891	0492	2 IS TV2-117A	12000	Utility
☐ RA-24020	Mil Mi-8T	99150914	CCCP-24020	1091	0492	2 IS TV2-117A	12000	Utility
☐ RA-24486	Mil Mi-8T	98628934	CCCP-24486	1286	0091	2 IS TV2-117A	12000	Utility
☐ RA-25390	Mil Mi-8T	98208187	CCCP-25390	1082	0091	2 IS TV2-117A	12000	Utility
☐ RA-25394	Mil Mi-8T	98208227	CCCP-25394	0382	0091	2 IS TV2-117A	12000	Utility
☐ RA-46485	Antonov 24RV	27308103	CCCP-46485	0972	0091	2 IV AI-24VT	21800	Y48
☐ RA-46649	Antonov 24RV	47309102	CCCP-46649	0374	0091	2 IV AI-24VT	22500	Y48
☐ RA-74014	Antonov 74	36547098968		0095	0097	2 LO D-36-3	36500	Combi
☐ RA-74015	Antonov 74	36547098969		1197	1197	2 LO D-36-3	36500	Combi
☐ RA-74046	Antonov 74	36547097935		0293	0893	2 LO D-36-2A	34800	Combi
☐ RA-74047	Antonov 74	36547097941		0793	0893	2 LO D-36-2A	34800	Combi
☐ RA-74048	Antonov 74	36547098943		0294	0294	2 LO D-36-2A	34800	Combi
☐ RA-65026	Tupolev 134A-3	48470	CCCP-65026	0676	0091	2 SO D-30-III	49000	Y76
☐ RA-65028	Tupolev 134A-3	48490	CCCP-65028	0776	0791	2 SO D-30-III	49000	Y74
☐ RA-65040	Tupolev 134A-3	49100	LY-ABC	1076	0994	2 SO D-30-III	47600	C39 or Y56
☐ RA-65961	Tupolev 134A-3	3351807	CCCP-65961	0573	0091	2 SO D-30-III	47000	C39 or Y56
☐ RA-85347	Tupolev 154B-2	347	CCCP-85347	0679	0091	3 KU NK-8-2U	98000	Y164
☐ RA-85525	Tupolev 154B-2	525	CCCP-85525	0182	0091	3 KU NK-8-2U	100000	Y164
☐ RA-85773	Tupolev 154M	955	EP-TOB	0493	0493	3 SO D-30KU-154-II	100000	Y166
☐ RA-85777	Tupolev 154M	959	EP-TOA	0593	0593	3 SO D-30KU-154-II	100000	Y166
☐ RA-85816	Tupolev 154M	1006		0795	0795	3 SO D-30KU-154-II	100000	Y166
☐ RA-85824	Tupolev 154M	769	SP-LCE	0288	1295	3 SO D-30KU-154-II	102000	CY150
☐ RA-85825	Tupolev 154M	776	SP-LCH	0588	0196	3 SO D-30KU-154-II	102000	CY150
☐ RA-85826	Tupolev 154M	812	SP-LCL	0789	0496	3 SO D-30KU-154-II	100000	CY150
☐ RA-85831	Tupolev 154M	774	SP-LCF	0488	0497	3 SO D-30KU-154-II	100000	CY150

BALTIC AIRLINES = BLL (Baltiskie avialinii)

St. Peterburg-Pulkovo

Nevsky prospekt 7/9, Of. 12, 191186 St. Petersburg, Russia ☎ (812) 311 00 84 Tx: none Fax: (812) 311 00 84 SITA: n/a

F: 1993 33 Head: Valerian G. Fofanov ICAO: BALTIC AIRLINES Net: n/a

☐ RA-24111	Mil Mi-8	98839574		0088	0093	2 IS TV2-117A	12000	Utility
☐ RA-24620	Mil Mi-8T	8248		0081	0096	2 IS TV2-117A	12000	Utility
☐ RA-25237	Mil Mi-8	3106	CCCP-25237	0072	0094	2 IS TV2-117A	12000	Utility

529 registration type of aircraft cn/fn ex/ex* mfd del powered by mtow kg configuration selcal name/fln/specialitites/remarks

☐ RA-25329	Mil Mi-8	98203999		0082	0095	2 IS TV2-117A	12000	Utility		
☐ RA-25774	Mil Mi-8	4265		0074	0096	2 IS TV2-117A	12000	VIP Salon		
☐ RA-25775	Mil Mi-8	4270		0074	0096	2 IS TV2-117A	12000	VIP Salon		

BARGUZIN Aviakompania = BAZ (Bargouzin Airline) (Flying div. of Ulan Ude Aviation Plant/Member of MAP Group) — Ulan Ude-Vostochny

Ul. Khorinskaya 1, 670009 Ulan Ude, (Republic of Buryatia), Russia ☎ (3012) 25 15 51 Tx: 288110 avia Fax: (3012) 25 21 47 SITA: n/a
F: n/a 👪 n/a Head: Vasily V. Kovtunenko ICAO: BARGOUZIN Net: n/a

☐ RA-87222	Yakovlev 40	9832058	CCCP-87222	0078		3 IV AI-25	16800	Combi		
☐ RA-48102	Antonov 24RV					2 IV AI-24VT	21800	Combi		
☐ RA-93934	Antonov 24B	09902310	CCCP-93934	0070		2 IV AI-24	21000	Combi		
☐ RA-29120	Antonov 32		CCCP-29120			2 IV AI-20D	27000	Freighter		
☐ RA-65560	Tupolev 134A-3	60321	YU-AJW	0078		2 SO D-30-III	49000	Combi		Rossia-titles

BELGOROD AIR ENTERPRISE = BED (Belgorodskoe aviapredpriatie) (formerly part of Central Districts Airlines & Aeroflot Belgorod division) — Belgorod

Ul. B. Khmelnitskogo 166, 308029 Belgorod, Russia ☎ (0722) 34 02 05 Tx: none Fax: (0722) 34 02 05 SITA: n/a
F: n/a 👪 n/a Head: Sergei P. Sidorov ICAO: BELGORYE Net: n/a Also operates Antonov 2 & Kamov Ka-26. Full fleet details not yet known. Most aircraft are still in Aeroflot colors but will be repainted in due course.

☐ RA-87304	Yakovlev 40	9322028	CCCP-87304	0073		3 IV AI-25	16800	Y32		
☐ RA-87371	Yakovlev 40	9340232	CCCP-87371	0073		3 IV AI-25	16800	Y32		
☐ RA-87378	Yakovlev 40	9241425	UK-87378	0072		3 IV AI-25	16100	VIP		lsf UZB
☐ RA-87465	Yakovlev 40	9430437	CCCP-87465	0074		3 IV AI-25	16800	Y32		
☐ RA-87648	Yakovlev 40	9140920	CCCP-87648	0071		3 IV AI-25	16800	Y32		Rossia-titles
☐ RA-87809	Yakovlev 40	9231923	CCCP-87809	0072		3 IV AI-25	16800	Y32		
☐ RA-87919	Yakovlev 40K	9730955	CCCP-87919	0077		3 IV AI-25	16800	Y32		
☐ RA-87959	Yakovlev 40K	9822057	CCCP-87959	0078		3 IV AI-25	16800	Y32		
☐ RA-87993	Yakovlev 40	9541744	CCCP-87993	0075		3 IV AI-25	16800	Y32		

BEREZNIKI MUNICIPAL AIR ENTERPRISE (Bereznikovskoe munitsipalnoe aviapredpriatie) — Berezniki

Berezniki Airport, 618400 Berezniki, (Perm Region), Russia ☎ (34242) 66 349 Tx: none Fax: (34242) 66 349 SITA: n/a
F: 1996 👪 n/a Head: Vladimir G. Ryazantsev Net: n/a

☐ RA-22301	Mil Mi-8T	5863	CCCP-22301	0075	0096	2 IS TV2-117A	12000	Utility		
☐ RA-13344	Antonov 24RV	37308310		0073	0096	2 IV AI-24VT	21800	Y48		

BERKUT Aviakompania — Ermolino

Ul. Krymsky val 9, kv. 21, 117049 Moskva, Russia ☎ (095) 237 07 10 Tx: n/a Fax: (095) 237 12 69 SITA: n/a
F: n/a 👪 n/a Head: n/a Net: n/a

☐ RA-22178	Mil Mi-8MTV-1					2 IS TV3-117MT	13000	Utility		

BIOSTIM Aviakompania — Zelenogorsk

Ul. Lenina 18, Box 287, 663690 Zelenogorsk, (Krasnoyarsk Region), Russia ☎ (39169) 22 275 Tx: none Fax: (39169) 22 275 SITA: n/a
F: 1996 👪 n/a Head: Yuri F. Poberezhny Net: n/a

☐ RA-23773	PZL Swidnik (Mil) Mi-2	514209055		0775	0096	2 IS GTD-350-4	3550	Utility		

BLAGOVESHCHENSKAVIA, Ltd = BLD (Blagoveshchensk Air) — Blagoveshchensk

Ul. Kalinina 127, 675016 Blagoveshchensk, Russia ☎ (4162) 44 45 07 Tx: none Fax: (4162) 44 97 06 SITA: n/a
F: 1996 👪 n/a Head: Viktor A. Medvedev ICAO: BLAGAVIA Net: n/a Operates passenger & cargo flights with Mil Mi-8 & Yakovlev 40 aircraft, leased from other companies when required.

BODAIBO AIR ENTERPRISE (Bodaibinskoe aviapredpriatie) (formerly Aeroflot Bodaibo division) — Bodaibo

Ul. Pervomaiskaya 5, 666910 Bodaibo, (Irkutsk Region), Russia ☎ 75 666 Tx: n/a Fax: n/a SITA: n/a
F: n/a 👪 n/a Head: G.N. Mesyatsev Net: n/a Beside aircraft listed, also operates Antonov 2, & Mil Mi-8. Full details not yet known. Most aircraft are still in Aeroflot colors but will be repainted in due course.

☐ RA-46700	Antonov 24T	7910402		0067		2 IV AI-24VT	22500	Combi		
☐ RA-46713	Antonov 24T					2 IV AI-24VT	22500	Combi		
☐ RA-26655	Antonov 26	7802	CCCP-26655	0079		2 IV AI-24VT	24000	Combi		

BRATSK AVIA, Joint-Stock Company = BTK (formerly Bratsk Air Enterprise & Aeroflot Bratsk division) — Bratsk

Bratsk Airport, 665711 Bratsk 11, Russia ☎ (3953) 33 13 25 Tx: 268772 krilo Fax: (3953) 33 13 25 SITA: n/a
F: 1967 👪 n/a Head: Sergei F. Tatarnikov ICAO: BRATSK AIR Net: n/a Most aircraft are still in Aeroflot colors but will be repainted in due course.

☐ RA-07488	PZL Mielec (Antonov) An-2	1G152-16	CCCP-07488	1173	1173	1 SH ASh-62IR	5500	Y12		
☐ RA-33371	PZL Mielec (Antonov) An-2	1G226-30	CCCP-33371	0887	0887	1 SH ASh-62IR	5500	Y12		
☐ RA-35042	PZL Mielec (Antonov) An-2	1G110-08	CCCP-35042	0969	0781	1 SH ASh-62IR	5500	Y12		
☐ RA-40210	PZL Mielec (Antonov) An-2	1G219-60	CCCP-40210	0686	0786	1 SH ASh-62IR	5500	Y12		
☐ RA-40476	PZL Mielec (Antonov) An-2	1G224-53	CCCP-40476	0487	0687	1 SH ASh-62IR	5500	Y12		
☐ RA-40656	PZL Mielec (Antonov) An-2	1G214-14	CCCP-40656	0685	0785	1 SH ASh-62IR	5500	Y12		
☐ RA-40657	PZL Mielec (Antonov) An-2	1G214-15	CCCP-40657	0685	0785	1 SH ASh-62IR	5500	Y12		
☐ RA-22748	Mil Mi-8T	98311211	CCCP-22748	0583	0683	2 IS TV2-117A	12000	Y17		
☐ RA-24152	Mil Mi-8T	98941711	CCCP-24152	0389	0389	2 IS TV2-117A	12000	Y17		
☐ RA-24183	Mil Mi-8T	98943323	CCCP-24183	0789	0789	2 IS TV2-117A	12000	Y17		
☐ RA-24251	Mil Mi-8T	98734017	CCCP-24251	0787	1187	2 IS TV2-117A	12000	Y17		
☐ RA-24261	Mil Mi-8T	98734147	CCCP-24261	0887	1187	2 IS TV2-117A	12000	Y17		
☐ RA-87414	Yakovlev 40	9420634	CCCP-87414	0574	0674	3 IV AI-25	16800	Y30		
☐ RA-87448	Yakovlev 40	9430536	CCCP-87448	0874	0280	3 IV AI-25	16800	Y30		
☐ RA-87524	Yakovlev 40	9520641	CCCP-87524	0675	0675	3 IV AI-25	16800	Y36		
☐ RA-87545	Yakovlev 40	9531042	CCCP-87545	0875	0875	3 IV AI-25	16800	Y36		
☐ RA-87974	Yakovlev 40K	9041960	CCCP-87974	0181	0181	3 IV AI-25	16800	Y32		
☐ RA-88205	Yakovlev 40	9630749	CCCP-88205	0976	0976	3 IV AI-25	16800	Y32		
☐ RA-88215	Yakovlev 40K	9630150	CCCP-88215	1076	1076	3 IV AI-25	17200	Y32		
☐ RA-88228	Yakovlev 40	9641750	CCCP-88228	1176	1176	3 IV AI-25	16800	Y32		
☐ RA-85429	Tupolev 154B-2	429	CCCP-85429	0780	0292	3 KU NK-8-2U	98000	Y164		
☐ RA-85660	Tupolev 154M	810	EP-ITL	0789	0693	3 SO D-30KU-154-II	100000	Y164		lst IRB as EP-ITV
☐ RA-85689	Tupolev 154M	860	EP-ITF	1290	0492	3 SO D-30KU-154-II	100000	Y164		lst IRB as EP-MBA

BRYANSK AIR ENTERPRISE (Bryanskoe aviapredpriatie) (formerly Aeroflot Bryansk division) — Bryansk

Airport, 242042 pos. Oktyabrsky, (Bryansk Region), Russia ☎ (0832) 44 85 24 Tx: 182129 vzlet Fax: (0832) 74 39 93 SITA: n/a
F: 1946 👪 n/a Head: Vasily S. Yushchenko Net: n/a Most aircraft are still in Aeroflot colors but will be repainted in due course.

☐ RA-14147	PZL Swidnik (Mil) Mi-2	5210405097	CCCP-14147	1087	1187	2 IS GTD-350-4	3550	Utility		
☐ RA-15642	PZL Swidnik (Mil) Mi-2	5410113017	CCCP-15642	0187	0287	2 IS GTD-350-4	3550	Utility		
☐ RA-20381	PZL Swidnik (Mil) Mi-2	529828066	CCCP-20381	0686	0886	2 IS GTD-350-4	3550	Utility		
☐ RA-20412	PZL Swidnik (Mil) Mi-2	529910086	CCCP-20412	0886	1086	2 IS GTD-350-4	3550	Utility		
☐ RA-20828	PZL Swidnik (Mil) Mi-2	548101033	CCCP-20828	0383	0786	2 IS GTD-350-4	3550	Utility		
☐ RA-20978	PZL Swidnik (Mil) Mi-2	529703036	CCCP-20978	0386	0486	2 IS GTD-350-4	3550	Utility		
☐ RA-20979	PZL Swidnik (Mil) Mi-2	529704036	CCCP-20979	0386	0486	2 IS GTD-350-4	3550	Utility		
☐ RA-20999	PZL Swidnik (Mil) Mi-2	549744056	CCCP-20999	0586	0686	2 IS GTD-350-4	3550	Utility		
☐ RA-23249	PZL Swidnik (Mil) Mi-2	5210305067	CCCP-23249	0687	0887	2 IS GTD-350-4	3550	Utility		
☐ RA-17786	PZL Mielec (Antonov) An-2	1G203-47	CCCP-17786	0783	0783	1 SH ASh-62IR	5250	Utility		
☐ RA-17891	PZL Mielec (Antonov) An-2	1G205-32	CCCP-17891	1183	1283	1 SH ASh-62IR	5250	Utility		
☐ RA-31505	PZL Mielec (Antonov) An-2	1G199-14	CCCP-31505	1082	1182	1 SH ASh-62IR	5250	Utility		
☐ RA-32662	PZL Mielec (Antonov) An-2	1G211-21	CCCP-32662	0185	0285	1 SH ASh-62IR	5250	Utility		
☐ RA-32732	PZL Mielec (Antonov) An-2	1G212-37	CCCP-32732	0385	0485	1 SH ASh-62IR	5250	Utility		
☐ RA-32734	PZL Mielec (Antonov) An-2	1G212-39	CCCP-32734	0385	0485	1 SH ASh-62IR	5250	Utility		
☐ RA-33535	PZL Mielec (Antonov) An-2	1G229-27	CCCP-33535	0488	0488	1 SH ASh-62IR	5250	Utility		
☐ RA-40668	PZL Mielec (Antonov) An-2	1G214-26	CCCP-40668	0685	0785	1 SH ASh-62IR	5250	Utility		
☐ RA-40881	PZL Mielec (Antonov) An-2	1G215-16	CCCP-40881	0885	0985	1 SH ASh-62IR	5250	Utility		
☐ RA-40924	PZL Mielec (Antonov) An-2	1G216-04	CCCP-40924	0985	1085	1 SH ASh-62IR	5250	Utility		
☐ RA-40957	PZL Mielec (Antonov) An-2	1G216-57	CCCP-40957	1185	0186	1 SH ASh-62IR	5250	Utility		
☐ RA-68054	PZL Mielec (Antonov) An-2	1G193-26	CCCP-68054	0681	0881	1 SH ASh-62IR	5250	Utility		
☐ RA-68119	PZL Mielec (Antonov) An-2	1G195-24	CCCP-68119	0182	0182	1 SH ASh-62IR	5250	Utility		
☐ RA-68157	PZL Mielec (Antonov) An-2	1G196-50	CCCP-68157	0382	0482	1 SH ASh-62IR	5250	Utility		
☐ RA-71208	PZL Mielec (Antonov) An-2	1G200-51	CCCP-71208	1282	0183	1 SH ASh-62IR	5250	Utility		
☐ RA-71234	PZL Mielec (Antonov) An-2	1G207-05	CCCP-71234	0384	0484	1 SH ASh-62IR	5250	Utility		
☐ RA-87373	Yakovlev 40	9410732	CCCP-87373	1273	0674	3 IV AI-25	17200	Y36		
☐ RA-87440	Yakovlev 40	9431635	CCCP-87440	0774	0375	3 IV AI-25	17200	C10		
☐ RA-87510	Yakovlev 40	9521240	CCCP-87510	0475	0875	3 IV AI-25	17200	Y36		
☐ RA-87513	Yakovlev 40	9521540	CCCP-87513	0775	0485	3 IV AI-25	16100	C13		
☐ RA-87904	Yakovlev 40K	9720854	CCCP-87904	0677	0977	3 IV AI-25	17200	C13		
☐ RA-87906	Yakovlev 40K	9731054	CCCP-87906	0777	0777	3 IV AI-25	17200	C13		
☐ RA-88240	Yakovlev 40	9641151	CCCP-88240	0177	0485	3 IV AI-25	17200	C13		
☐ RA-88276	Yakovlev 40	9721453	CCCP-88276	0577	0185	3 IV AI-25	16800	C10		
☐ RA-46394	Antonov 24B	07306208	CCCP-46394	0770	0492	2 IV AI-24	21000	Y52		
☐ RA-46674	Antonov 24RV	47309606	CCCP-46674	0874	0191	2 IV AI-24VT	21800	Y48		

530 registration type of aircraft cn/fn ex/ex* mfd del powered by mtow kg configuration selcal name/fln/specialitites/remarks

BUGURUSLAN FLYING SCHOOL (Buguruslanskoe letnoe uchilishche GA) (former Aeroflot Buguruslan Flying School)   Buguruslan-Central & -Yushny

Ul. Aerodromnaya 1, 461600 Buguruslan, (Orenburg Region), Russia   ☎ (35352) 27 200   Tx: none   Fax: (35352) 27 314   SITA: n/a
F: 1940   ⋆⋆⋆ n/a   Head: Vasily Ya. Ruzov   Net: n/a   Operates aircraft for training purposes but also for commercial charter flights & for leasing. Most aircraft are in former Aeroflot colors without titles.

registration	type of aircraft	cn/fn	ex/ex*	mfd	del	powered by	mtow kg	configuration	selcal	name/fln/specialitites/remarks
☐ RA-01732	PZL Mielec (Antonov) An-2	1G106-29	CCCP-01732	0069		1 SH ASh-62IR	5250	Y12		
☐ RA-01737	PZL Mielec (Antonov) An-2	1G106-34	CCCP-01737	0069		1 SH ASh-62IR	5250	Y12		
☐ RA-01739	PZL Mielec (Antonov) An-2	1G106-36	CCCP-01739	0069		1 SH ASh-62IR	5250	Y12		
☐ RA-01748	PZL Mielec (Antonov) An-2	1G106-45	CCCP-01748	0069		1 SH ASh-62IR	5250	Y12		
☐ RA-01749	PZL Mielec (Antonov) An-2	1G106-46	CCCP-01749	0069		1 SH ASh-62IR	5250	Y12		
☐ RA-02416	PZL Mielec (Antonov) An-2	1G117-27	CCCP-02416	0070		1 SH ASh-62IR	5250	Y12		
☐ RA-02462	PZL Mielec (Antonov) An-2	1G119-05	CCCP-02462	0070		1 SH ASh-62IR	5250	Y12		
☐ RA-02464	PZL Mielec (Antonov) An-2	1G119-07	CCCP-02464	0070		1 SH ASh-62IR	5250	Y12		
☐ RA-02473	PZL Mielec (Antonov) An-2	1G119-16	CCCP-02473	0070		1 SH ASh-62IR	5250	Y12		
☐ RA-02475	PZL Mielec (Antonov) An-2	1G119-18	CCCP-02475	0070		1 SH ASh-62IR	5250	Y12		
☐ RA-02478	PZL Mielec (Antonov) An-2	1G119-21	CCCP-02478	0070		1 SH ASh-62IR	5250	Y12		
☐ RA-02486	PZL Mielec (Antonov) An-2	1G119-29	CCCP-02486	0070		1 SH ASh-62IR	5250	Y12		
☐ RA-02488	PZL Mielec (Antonov) An-2	1G119-31	CCCP-02488	0070		1 SH ASh-62IR	5250	Y12		
☐ RA-02519	PZL Mielec (Antonov) An-2	1G119-62	CCCP-02519	0070		1 SH ASh-62IR	5250	Y12		
☐ RA-02521	PZL Mielec (Antonov) An-2	1G119-64	CCCP-02521	0070		1 SH ASh-62IR	5250	Y12		
☐ RA-02732	PZL Mielec (Antonov) An-2	1G125-10	CCCP-02732	0071		1 SH ASh-62IR	5250	Y12		
☐ RA-02733	PZL Mielec (Antonov) An-2	1G125-11	CCCP-02733	0071		1 SH ASh-62IR	5250	Y12		
☐ RA-02737	PZL Mielec (Antonov) An-2	1G125-15	CCCP-02737	0071		1 SH ASh-62IR	5250	Y12		
☐ RA-02738	PZL Mielec (Antonov) An-2	1G125-16	CCCP-02738	0071		1 SH ASh-62IR	5250	Y12		
☐ RA-02749	PZL Mielec (Antonov) An-2	1G125-27	CCCP-02749	0071		1 SH ASh-62IR	5250	Y12		
☐ RA-02759	PZL Mielec (Antonov) An-2	1G125-37	CCCP-02759	0071		1 SH ASh-62IR	5250	Y12		
☐ RA-02764	PZL Mielec (Antonov) An-2	1G125-42	CCCP-02764	0071		1 SH ASh-62IR	5250	Y12		
☐ RA-02769	PZL Mielec (Antonov) An-2	1G125-47	CCCP-02769	0071		1 SH ASh-62IR	5250	Y12		
☐ RA-02841	PZL Mielec (Antonov) An-2	1G54-46	CCCP-02841	0065		1 SH ASh-62IR	5250	Y12		
☐ RA-02844	PZL Mielec (Antonov) An-2	1G54-49	CCCP-02844	0065		1 SH ASh-62IR	5250	Y12		
☐ RA-02859	PZL Mielec (Antonov) An-2	1G55-44	CCCP-02859	0065		1 SH ASh-62IR	5250	Y12		
☐ RA-02867	PZL Mielec (Antonov) An-2	1G56-02	CCCP-02867	0065		1 SH ASh-62IR	5250	Y12		
☐ RA-09622	PZL Mielec (Antonov) An-2	1G75-06	CCCP-09622	0066		1 SH ASh-62IR	5250	Y12		
☐ RA-09640	PZL Mielec (Antonov) An-2	1G75-24	CCCP-09640	0066		1 SH ASh-62IR	5250	Y12		
☐ RA-28885	PZL Mielec (Antonov) An-2	1G06-19	CCCP-28885	0061		1 SH ASh-62IR	5250	Y12		
☐ RA-33392	PZL Mielec (Antonov) An-2	1G226-51	CCCP-33392	0087		1 SH ASh-62IR	5250	Y12		
☐ RA-33407	PZL Mielec (Antonov) An-2	1G227-06	CCCP-33407	0087		1 SH ASh-62IR	5250	Y12		
☐ RA-33408	PZL Mielec (Antonov) An-2	1G227-07	CCCP-33408	0087		1 SH ASh-62IR	5250	Y12		
☐ RA-33409	PZL Mielec (Antonov) An-2	1G227-08	CCCP-33409	0087		1 SH ASh-62IR	5250	Y12		
☐ RA-33410	PZL Mielec (Antonov) An-2	1G227-09	CCCP-33410	0087		1 SH ASh-62IR	5250	Y12		
☐ RA-33412	PZL Mielec (Antonov) An-2	1G227-18	CCCP-33412	0087		1 SH ASh-62IR	5250	Y12		
☐ RA-33415	PZL Mielec (Antonov) An-2	1G227-21	CCCP-33415	0087		1 SH ASh-62IR	5250	Y12		
☐ RA-33416	PZL Mielec (Antonov) An-2	1G227-22	CCCP-33416	0087		1 SH ASh-62IR	5250	Y12		
☐ RA-33417	PZL Mielec (Antonov) An-2	1G227-23	CCCP-33417	0087		1 SH ASh-62IR	5250	Y12		
☐ RA-33419	PZL Mielec (Antonov) An-2	1G227-25	CCCP-33419	0087		1 SH ASh-62IR	5250	Y12		
☐ RA-33437	PZL Mielec (Antonov) An-2	1G227-43	CCCP-33437	0087		1 SH ASh-62IR	5250	Y12		
☐ RA-33438	PZL Mielec (Antonov) An-2	1G227-44	CCCP-33438	0087		1 SH ASh-62IR	5250	Y12		
☐ RA-33439	PZL Mielec (Antonov) An-2	1G227-49	CCCP-33439	0087		1 SH ASh-62IR	5250	Y12		
☐ RA-33440	PZL Mielec (Antonov) An-2	1G227-50	CCCP-33440	0087		1 SH ASh-62IR	5250	Y12		
☐ RA-33441	PZL Mielec (Antonov) An-2	1G227-51	CCCP-33441	0087		1 SH ASh-62IR	5250	Y12		
☐ RA-33442	PZL Mielec (Antonov) An-2	1G227-52	CCCP-33442	0087		1 SH ASh-62IR	5250	Y12		
☐ RA-33452	PZL Mielec (Antonov) An-2	1G228-02	CCCP-33452	0087		1 SH ASh-62IR	5250	Y12		
☐ RA-33460	PZL Mielec (Antonov) An-2	1G228-10	CCCP-33460	0087		1 SH ASh-62IR	5250	Y12		
☐ RA-33461	PZL Mielec (Antonov) An-2	1G228-11	CCCP-33461	0087		1 SH ASh-62IR	5250	Y12		
☐ RA-33471	PZL Mielec (Antonov) An-2	1G228-21	CCCP-33471	0088		1 SH ASh-62IR	5250	Y12		
☐ RA-33472	PZL Mielec (Antonov) An-2	1G228-22	CCCP-33472	0088		1 SH ASh-62IR	5250	Y12		
☐ RA-35000	PZL Mielec (Antonov) An-2	1G109-06	CCCP-35000	0069		1 SH ASh-62IR	5250	Y12		
☐ RA-35020	PZL Mielec (Antonov) An-2	1G109-26	CCCP-35020	0069		1 SH ASh-62IR	5250	Y12		
☐ RA-35022	PZL Mielec (Antonov) An-2	1G109-28	CCCP-35022	0069		1 SH ASh-62IR	5250	Y12		
☐ RA-35026	PZL Mielec (Antonov) An-2	1G109-32	CCCP-35026	0069		1 SH ASh-62IR	5250	Y12		
☐ RA-35052	PZL Mielec (Antonov) An-2	1G110-18	CCCP-35052	0069		1 SH ASh-62IR	5250	Y12		
☐ RA-35053	PZL Mielec (Antonov) An-2	1G110-19	CCCP-35053	0069		1 SH ASh-62IR	5250	Y12		
☐ RA-35514	PZL Mielec (Antonov) An-2	1G114-26	CCCP-35514	0070		1 SH ASh-62IR	5250	Y12		
☐ RA-35515	PZL Mielec (Antonov) An-2	1G114-27	CCCP-35515	0070		1 SH ASh-62IR	5250	Y12		
☐ RA-35518	PZL Mielec (Antonov) An-2	1G114-30	CCCP-35518	0070		1 SH ASh-62IR	5250	Y12		
☐ RA-35519	PZL Mielec (Antonov) An-2	1G114-31	CCCP-35519	0070		1 SH ASh-62IR	5250	Y12		
☐ RA-41362	PZL Mielec (Antonov) An-2	1G65-37	CCCP-41362	0065		1 SH ASh-62IR	5250	Y12		
☐ RA-41391	PZL Mielec (Antonov) An-2	1G67-09	CCCP-41391	0066		1 SH ASh-62IR	5250	Y12		
☐ RA-62435	PZL Mielec (Antonov) An-2	1G41-05	CCCP-62435	0063		1 SH ASh-62IR	5250	Y12		
☐ RA-70598	PZL Mielec (Antonov) An-2	1G128-07	CCCP-70598	0071		1 SH ASh-62IR	5250	Y12		
☐ RA-70651	PZL Mielec (Antonov) An-2	1G129-01	CCCP-70651	0071		1 SH ASh-62IR	5250	Y12		
☐ RA-70658	PZL Mielec (Antonov) An-2	1G129-08	CCCP-70658	0071		1 SH ASh-62IR	5250	Y12		
☐ RA-70659	PZL Mielec (Antonov) An-2	1G129-09	CCCP-70659	0071		1 SH ASh-62IR	5250	Y12		
☐ RA-70660	PZL Mielec (Antonov) An-2	1G129-10	CCCP-70660	0071		1 SH ASh-62IR	5250	Y12		
☐ RA-70676	PZL Mielec (Antonov) An-2	1G129-26	CCCP-70676	0071		1 SH ASh-62IR	5250	Y12		
☐ RA-70681	PZL Mielec (Antonov) An-2	1G129-31	CCCP-70681	0071		1 SH ASh-62IR	5250	Y12		
☐ RA-70691	PZL Mielec (Antonov) An-2	1G129-41	CCCP-70691	0071		1 SH ASh-62IR	5250	Y12		
☐ RA-70693	PZL Mielec (Antonov) An-2	1G129-43	CCCP-70693	0071		1 SH ASh-62IR	5250	Y12		
☐ RA-70694	PZL Mielec (Antonov) An-2	1G129-44	CCCP-70694	0071		1 SH ASh-62IR	5250	Y12		
☐ RA-70698	PZL Mielec (Antonov) An-2	1G129-48	CCCP-70698	0071		1 SH ASh-62IR	5250	Y12		
☐ RA-92891	PZL Mielec (Antonov) An-2	1G53-43	CCCP-92891	0064		1 SH ASh-62IR	5250	Y12		
☐ RA-87287	Yakovlev 40	9320228	CCCP-87287	0073		3 IV AI-25	16800	Y27		
☐ RA-87299	Yakovlev 40	9341528	CCCP-87299	0073		3 IV AI-25	16800	Y32		
☐ RA-87324	Yakovlev 40	9330330	CCCP-87324	0073		3 IV AI-25	16800	Y32		
☐ RA-87497	Yakovlev 40	9542045	CCCP-87497	0075		3 IV AI-25	16800	Y32		
☐ RA-87506	Yakovlev 40	9520840	CCCP-87506	0075		3 IV AI-25	16800	Y32		
☐ RA-87580	Yakovlev 40	9221222	CCCP-87580	0072		3 IV AI-25	16800	Y27		
☐ RA-87653	Yakovlev 40	9211620	CCCP-87653	0072		3 IV AI-25	16800	VIP C12		
☐ RA-87815	Yakovlev 40	9230624	CCCP-87815	0072		3 IV AI-25	16800	Y27		
☐ RA-87823	Yakovlev 40	9241524	CCCP-87823	0072		3 IV AI-25	16800	Y27		
☐ RA-88160	Yakovlev 40	9611446	CCCP-88160	0076		3 IV AI-25	16800	Y32		
☐ RA-88204	Yakovlev 40	9630649	CCCP-88204	0076		3 IV AI-25	16800	Y32		
☐ RA-88206	Yakovlev 40	9630949	CCCP-88206	0076		3 IV AI-25	16800	Y32		

BURYATIA AIRLINES (Buryatskie avialinii) (formerly Ulan Ude Air Enterprise)   Ulan Ude-Mukhino

Ulan Ude-Mukhino Airport, 670018 Ulan Ude, (Republic of Buryatia), Russia   ☎ (3012) 22 79 65   Tx: none   Fax: (3012) 22 71 41   SITA: n/a
F: 1993   ⋆⋆⋆ n/a   Head: Anatoly P. Abasheev   Net: n/a   Most aircraft are still in Aeroflot colors but will be repainted in due course.

registration	type of aircraft	cn/fn	ex/ex*	mfd	del	powered by	mtow kg	configuration	selcal	name/fln/specialitites/remarks
☐ RA-14316	PZL Swidnik (Mil) Mi-2		CCCP-14316	0075	0093	2 IS GTD-350-4	3550	Utility		
☐ RA-14317	PZL Swidnik (Mil) Mi-2	514227065	CCCP-14317	0075	0093	2 IS GTD-350-4	3550	Utility		
☐ RA-14318	PZL Swidnik (Mil) Mi-2	514229065	CCCP-14318	0075	0093	2 IS GTD-350-4	3550	Utility		
☐ RA-15761	PZL Swidnik (Mil) Mi-2	532538082	CCCP-15761	0072	0093	2 IS GTD-350-4	3550	Utility		
☐ RA-20145	PZL Swidnik (Mil) Mi-2	533411024	CCCP-20145	0074	0093	2 IS GTD-350-4	3550	Utility		
☐ RA-20777	PZL Swidnik (Mil) Mi-2	527819092	CCCP-20777	0082	0093	2 IS GTD-350-4	3550	Utility		
☐ RA-23962	PZL Swidnik (Mil) Mi-2	543816104	CCCP-23962	0074	0093	2 IS GTD-350-4	3550	Utility		
☐ RA-02517	PZL Mielec (Antonov) An-2		CCCP-02517	0070	0093	1 SH ASh-62IR	5250	Utility		
☐ RA-02626	PZL Mielec (Antonov) An-2		CCCP-02626	0071	0093	1 SH ASh-62IR	5250	Utility		
☐ RA-02680	PZL Mielec (Antonov) An-2		CCCP-02680	0071	0093	1 SH ASh-62IR	5250	Utility		
☐ RA-07305	PZL Mielec (Antonov) An-2		CCCP-07305	0073	0093	1 SH ASh-62IR	5250	Utility		
☐ RA-07394	PZL Mielec (Antonov) An-2		CCCP-07394	0073	0093	1 SH ASh-62IR	5250	Utility		
☐ RA-07622	PZL Mielec (Antonov) An-2		CCCP-07622	0074	0093	1 SH ASh-62IR	5250	Utility		
F: ☐ RA-07731	PZL Mielec (Antonov) An-2	1G159-06	CCCP-07731	0074	0093	1 SH ASh-62IR	5250	Utility		
☐ RA-19706	PZL Mielec (Antonov) An-2		CCCP-19706	0075	0093	1 SH ASh-62IR	5250	Utility		
☐ RA-32035	PZL Mielec (Antonov) An-2		CCCP-32035	0068	0093	1 SH ASh-62IR	5250	Utility		
☐ RA-32111	PZL Mielec (Antonov) An-2	1G93-17	CCCP-32111	0068	0093	1 SH ASh-62IR	5250	Utility		
☐ RA-32315	PZL Mielec (Antonov) An-2		CCCP-32315	0068	0093	1 SH ASh-62IR	5250	Utility		
☐ RA-35109	PZL Mielec (Antonov) An-2		CCCP-35109	0069	0093	1 SH ASh-62IR	5250	Utility		
☐ RA-35135	PZL Mielec (Antonov) An-2		CCCP-35135	0069	0093	1 SH ASh-62IR	5250	Utility		
☐ RA-40671	PZL Mielec (Antonov) An-2	1G214-29	CCCP-40671	0085	0093	1 SH ASh-62IR	5250	Utility		
☐ RA-56379	PZL Mielec (Antonov) An-2	1G180-09	CCCP-56379	0078	0093	1 SH ASh-62IR	5250	Utility		
☐ RA-56525	PZL Mielec (Antonov) An-2	1G183-25	CCCP-56525	0079	0093	1 SH ASh-62IR	5250	Utility		
☐ RA-62584	PZL Mielec (Antonov) An-2	1G176-53	CCCP-62584	0077	0093	1 SH ASh-62IR	5250	Utility		
☐ RA-71277	PZL Mielec (Antonov) An-2	1G207-48	CCCP-71277	0084	0093	1 SH ASh-62IR	5250	Utility		
☐ RA-84701	PZL Mielec (Antonov) An-2		CCCP-84701	0080	0093	1 SH ASh-62IR	5250	Utility		

☐ RA-84726	PZL Mielec (Antonov) An-2	1G201-44	CCCP-84726	0083	0093	1 SH ASh-62IR	5250	Utility		
☐ RA-22206	Mil Mi-8		CCCP-22206	0077	0093	2 IS TV2-117A	12000	Utility		
☐ RA-22326	Mil Mi-8T		CCCP-22326	0077	0093	2 IS TV2-117A	12000	Utility		lst Delta-K Enterprise
☐ RA-22653	Mil Mi-8		CCCP-22653	0080	0093	2 IS TV2-117A	12000	Utility		
☐ RA-24200	Mil Mi-8		CCCP-24200	0087	0093	2 IS TV2-117A	12000	Utility		
☐ RA-25129	Mil Mi-8MTV-1		CCCP-25129	0089	0093	2 IS TV3-117MT	13000	Utility		lst Delta-K Enterprise
☐ RA-25323	Mil Mi-8		CCCP-25323	0082	0093	2 IS TV2-117A	12000	Utility		
☐ RA-25642	Mil Mi-8	3057	CCCP-25642	0072	0093	2 IS TV2-117A	12000	Utility		
☐ RA-25747	Mil Mi-8		CCCP-25747	0075	0093	2 IS TV2-117A	12000	Utility		
☐ RA-25861	Mil Mi-8		CCCP-25861	0075	0093	2 IS TV2-117A	12000	Utility		
☐ RA-25894	Mil Mi-8		CCCP-25894	0075	0093	2 IS TV2-117A	12000	Utility		
☐ RA-25952	Mil Mi-8T		CCCP-25952	0075	0093	2 IS TV2-117A	12000	Utility		
☐ RA-46213	Antonov 24B	77302907	CCCP-46213	0067	0093	2 IV AI-24	21000	Y48		
☐ RA-46222	Antonov 24B	77303102	CCCP-46222	0067	0093	2 IV AI-24	21000	Y48		
☐ RA-46300	Antonov 24B	97305110	CCCP-46300	0069	0093	2 IV AI-24	21000	Y48		
☐ RA-46408	Antonov 24B	77304003	CCCP-46408	0067	0093	2 IV AI-24	21000	Y48		
☐ RA-46506	Antonov 24RV	37308402	CCCP-46506	0073	0093	2 IV AI-24VT	21800	Y48		
☐ RA-46570	Antonov 24B	87304804	CCCP-46570	0068	0093	2 IV AI-24	21000	Y48		
☐ RA-46614	Antonov 24RV	37308701	CCCP-46614	0073	0093	2 IV AI-24VT	21800	Y48		
☐ RA-46803	Antonov 24B	57302104	CCCP-46803	0065	0093	2 IV AI-24	21000	Y48		
☐ RA-47799	Antonov 24B	17306808	CCCP-47799	0071	0093	2 IV AI-24	21000	Y48		
☐ RA-26118	Antonov 26B	12207	CCCP-26118	0082	0093	2 IV AI-24VT	24000	Freighter		
☐ RA-26560	Antonov 26	3310	CCCP-26560	0075	0093	2 IV AI-24VT	24000	Freighter		
☐ RA-26679	Antonov 26	8608	CCCP-26679	0079	0093	2 IV AI-24VT	24000	Freighter		
☐ RA-85827	Tupolev 154M	745	SP-LCC	0087	0397	3 SO D-30KU-154-II	100000	CY150		lst ESL
☐ RA-85829	Tupolev 154M	755	SP-LCD	0087	1097	3 SO D-30KU-154-II	100000	CY150		lst ESL

BURYAT AVIA — **Ulan Ude-Mukhino**

Ul. Klyuchevskaya 39, Box 2342, 670013 Ulan Ude, (Republic of Buryatia), Russia ☎ (30122) 75 684 Tx: none Fax: (30122) 70 591 SITA: n/a
F: 1991 n/a Head: Viktor Z. Khamarkhanov Net: n/a

☐ RA-22946	Mil Mi-8T	99257083		0092	0092	2 IS TV2-117A	12000	Utility		

BYKOVO AVIA, Joint-Stock Company = BKU (Aviakompania Bykovo Avia) (formerly Aeroflot Bykovo division) — **Moscow-Bykovo**

Ul. Sovetskaya 19, 140150 Bykovo, (Moscow Region), Russia ☎ (095) 558 40 24 Tx: 111812 Fax: (095) 554 83 68 SITA: n/a
F: n/a n/a Head: Gennady I. Sytnik ICAO: BYKOVO AVIA Net: n/a Some aircraft are still in Aeroflot colors but will be repainted in due course.

☐ RA-46395	Antonov 24RV	07306209	CCCP-46395	0070	0074	2 IV AI-24VT	21800	Research/Survey		
☐ RA-26521	Antonov 26	7102	CCCP-26521	0078	0078	2 IV AI-24VT	24000	Research/Survey		
☐ RA-26528	Antonov 26	7210	CCCP-26528	0078	0078	2 IV AI-24VT	24000	Freighter		
☐ RA-26631	Antonov 26	5503	CCCP-26631	0077	0077	2 IV AI-24VT	24000	Research/Survey		
☐ RA-42313	Yakovlev 42	11030503	CCCP-42313	0080	0080	3 LO D-36	54000	Y120		std BKA
☐ RA-42321	Yakovlev 42	4520423402088	CCCP-42321	0084	0084	3 LO D-36	54000	Y120		
☐ RA-42322	Yakovlev 42	4520423402108	CCCP-42322	0084	0084	3 LO D-36	54000	Y120		
☐ RA-42324	Yakovlev 42	4520421402125	CCCP-42324	0084	0084	3 LO D-36	54000	Y120		
☐ RA-42341	Yakovlev 42	4520421706292	CCCP-42341	0087	0087	3 LO D-36	54000	Y120		
☐ RA-42356	Yakovlev 42	4520422811400	CCCP-42356	0088	0088	3 LO D-36	54000	Y120		
☐ RA-42368	Yakovlev 42D	4520422914166	CCCP-42368	0089	0089	3 LO D-36	56500	Y120		
☐ RA-42385	Yakovlev 42D	4520423016309	CCCP-42385	0090	0090	3 LO D-36	56500	Y120		
☐ RA-42434	Yakovlev 42D	4520424305017		1093	0797	3 LO D-36	56500	C84		jtly opw Khrunichev Space Ctr/PROTON-TL
☐ RA-42524	Yakovlev 42	11030603	CCCP-42524	0080	0084	3 LO D-36	54000	Y120		
☐ RA-42531	Yakovlev 42	11130304	CCCP-42531	0081	0081	3 LO D-36	54000	Y120		std BKA
☐ RA-42542	Yakovlev 42	11140804	CCCP-42542	0081	0086	3 LO D-36	54000	Y120		
☐ RA-42549	Yakovlev 42	11040105	CCCP-42549	0082	0084	3 LO D-36	54000	Y120		std BKA

CENTER-SOUTH AIRLINES = CTS (Tsentr-Yug Aviakompania) — **Belgorod**

Ul. B. Khmelnitskogo 166, 308029 Belgorod, Russia ☎ (07265) 34 21 07 Tx: none Fax: (07265) 13 640 SITA: n/a
F: 1990 n/a Head: n/a ICAO: CENTER-SOUTH Net: n/a

☐ RA-87467	Yakovlev 40	9440637	CCCP-87467	0074		3 IV AI-25	17200	C17		
☐ RA-87550	Yakovlev 40	9210121	CCCP-87550	0072		3 IV AI-25	17200	C15		

CENTRAL DISTRICTS AIRLINES = CDS (ACR-Avialinii tsentralnykh rayonov) (formerly Aeroflot Central Districts directorate) — **Moscow-Bykovo**

Oktyabrski prospekt 15, 140002 Lyubertsy 2, (Moscow Region), Russia ☎ (095) 503 51 27 Tx: none Fax: (095) 503 51 36 SITA: n/a
F: n/a n/a Head: Anatoly A. Mukhin ICAO: CENTRAL AVIA Net: n/a Operates charter flights with aircraft leased from airlines belonging to Regional Civil Aviation Department of Central Districts, when required.

☐ RA-42411	Yakovlev 42D	4520421219043	CCCP-42411	0091		3 LO D-36	56500	Y118		lst STZ

CHEBOKSARY AIR ENTERPRISE = CBK (Cheboksarskoe aviapredpriatie) (formerly Aeroflot Cheboksary division) — **Cheboksary**

Cheboksary Airport, 428021 Cheboksary, (Republic of Chuvakhia), Russia ☎ (8352) 25 91 10 Tx: none Fax: (8352) 26 49 35 SITA: n/a
F: n/a n/a Head: Yevgeni V. Bystryakov ICAO: AIR CHEBOKSARY Net: n/a Company will be transformed to the new national airlines of the Chuvashian Republic.
Most aircraft are still in Aeroflot colors but will be repainted in due course.

☐ RA-05735	PZL Mielec (Antonov) An-2		CCCP-05735	0074		1 SH ASh-62IR	5500	Utility		
☐ RA-07332	PZL Mielec (Antonov) An-2		CCCP-07332	0073		1 SH ASh-62IR	5500	Utility		
☐ RA-07641	PZL Mielec (Antonov) An-2		CCCP-07641	0074		1 SH ASh-62IR	5500	Utility		
☐ RA-07817	PZL Mielec (Antonov) An-2		CCCP-07817	0076		1 SH ASh-62IR	5500	Utility		
☐ RA-07818	PZL Mielec (Antonov) An-2		CCCP-07818	0076		1 SH ASh-62IR	5500	Utility		
☐ RA-09664	PZL Mielec (Antonov) An-2		CCCP-09664	0066		1 SH ASh-62IR	5500	Utility		
☐ RA-17724	PZL Mielec (Antonov) An-2		CCCP-17724	0083		1 SH ASh-62IR	5500	Utility		
☐ RA-17791	PZL Mielec (Antonov) An-2		CCCP-17791	0083		1 SH ASh-62IR	5500	Utility		
☐ RA-17820	PZL Mielec (Antonov) An-2		CCCP-17820	0083		1 SH ASh-62IR	5500	Utility		
☐ RA-31540	PZL Mielec (Antonov) An-2		CCCP-31540	0082		1 SH ASh-62IR	5500	Utility		
☐ RA-32309	PZL Mielec (Antonov) An-2		CCCP-32309	0068		1 SH ASh-62IR	5500	Utility		
☐ RA-40662	PZL Mielec (Antonov) An-2		CCCP-40662	0086		1 SH ASh-62IR	5500	Utility		
☐ RA-40845	PZL Mielec (Antonov) An-2		CCCP-40845	0073		1 SH ASh-62IR	5500	Utility		
☐ RA-44695	PZL Mielec (Antonov) An-2		CCCP-44695	0067		1 SH ASh-62IR	5500	Utility		
☐ RA-54844	PZL Mielec (Antonov) An-2		CCCP-54844	0079		1 SH ASh-62IR	5500	Utility		
☐ RA-56385	PZL Mielec (Antonov) An-2	1G180-15	CCCP-56385	0078		1 SH ASh-62IR	5500	Utility		
☐ RA-56387	PZL Mielec (Antonov) An-2		CCCP-56387	0078		1 SH ASh-62IR	5500	Utility		
☐ RA-62532	PZL Mielec (Antonov) An-2		CCCP-62532	0077		1 SH ASh-62IR	5500	Utility		
☐ RA-62688	PZL Mielec (Antonov) An-2		CCCP-62688	0078		1 SH ASh-62IR	5500	Utility		
☐ RA-62697	PZL Mielec (Antonov) An-2		CCCP-62697	0078		1 SH ASh-62IR	5500	Utility		
☐ RA-70317	PZL Mielec (Antonov) An-2		CCCP-70317	0072		1 SH ASh-62IR	5500	Utility		
☐ RA-70379	PZL Mielec (Antonov) An-2		CCCP-70379	0073		1 SH ASh-62IR	5500	Utility		
☐ RA-70523	PZL Mielec (Antonov) An-2		CCCP-70523	0073		1 SH ASh-62IR	5500	Utility		
☐ RA-70719	PZL Mielec (Antonov) An-2		CCCP-70719	0071		1 SH ASh-62IR	5500	Utility		
☐ RA-70755	PZL Mielec (Antonov) An-2		CCCP-70755	0071		1 SH ASh-62IR	5500	Utility		
☐ RA-92982	PZL Mielec (Antonov) An-2		CCCP-92982	0076		1 SH ASh-62IR	5500	Utility		
☐ RA-46263	Antonov 24B	77303504	UN-46263	0067		2 IV AI-24	21000	Y48		
☐ RA-46428	Antonov 24B	87304207	CCCP-46428	0068		2 IV AI-24	21000	Y48		
☐ RA-46499	Antonov 24RV	27308302	CCCP-46499	0072		2 IV AI-24VT	21800	Y48		
☐ RA-46583	Antonov 24B		CCCP-46583	0069		2 IV AI-24	21000	Y48		
☐ RA-47294	Antonov 24RV		CCCP-47294	0070		2 IV AI-24RV	21800	Y48		
☐ RA-47714	Antonov 24B		CCCP-47714	0066		2 IV AI-24	21000	Y48		
☐ RA-65007	Tupolev 134A-3	46100	CCCP-65007	0076		2 SO D-30-III	49000	Y76		
☐ RA-65015	Tupolev 134A	48325	CCCP-65015	0076		2 SO D-30-II	49000	Y76		
☐ RA-65021	Tupolev 134A	48390	CCCP-65021	0076		2 SO D-30-II	49000	Y76		
☐ RA-65024	Tupolev 134A	48420	CCCP-65024	0776		2 SO D-30-II	49000	Y76		
☐ RA-65033	Tupolev 134A-3	48540	CCCP-65033	0776		2 SO D-30-III	49000	Y76		

CHELYABINSK AIR ENTERPRISE, Joint-Stock Company = H6 / CHB (Chelyabinskoe aviapredpriatie) (formerly CHELAL & Aeroflot Chelyabinsk division) — **Chelyabinsk**

Chelyabinsk Airport, 454133 Chelyabinsk, Russia ☎ (3512) 79 33 25 Tx: 124611 port su Fax: (3512) 79 14 63 SITA: CEKAPH6
F: 1994 n/a Head: Sergei V. Yashin ICAO: CHELYABINSK Net: n/a

☐ RA-87444	Yakovlev 40	9430136	CCCP-87444	0874		3 IV AI-25	16800	Y30		
☐ RA-88234	Yakovlev 40	9640351	CCCP-88234	1176		3 IV AI-25	16800	Y32		
☐ RA-88243	Yakovlev 40K	9641651	CCCP-88243	1176		3 IV AI-25	16800	Y32		
☐ RA-65118	Tupolev 134A-3	60462	CCCP-65118	0678		2 SO D-30-III	49000	C8Y60		
☐ RA-65131	Tupolev 134A-3	60637	CCCP-65131	0978		2 SO D-30-III	49000	C8Y60		
☐ RA-65786	Tupolev 134A-3	62775	CCCP-65786	1279		2 SO D-30-III	49000	C8Y60		
☐ RA-42387	Yakovlev 42D	4520424016436	CCCP-42387	1190		3 LO D-36	57500	C16Y84		
☐ RA-42388	Yakovlev 42D	4520424016510	CCCP-42388	1290		3 LO D-36	57500	Y120		
☐ RA-42401	Yakovlev 42D	4520421116567	CCCP-42401	0291		3 LO D-36	57500	C16Y84		
☐ RA-42408	Yakovlev 42D	4520424116698	CCCP-42408	0192		3 LO D-36	57500	Y120		lst IRB as EP-YAC
☐ RA-42412	Yakovlev 42D	4520422219055	CCCP-42412	0592		3 LO D-36	57500	Y120		lst IRB as EP-YAA

532 registration type of aircraft cn/fn ex/ex* mfd del powered by mtow kg configuration selcal name/fln/specialitites/remarks

☐ RA-42413	Yakovlev 42D	4520422219066	CCCP-42413	0792		3 LO D-36	57500	Y120		lst IRB as EP-YAB
☐ RA-42430	Yakovlev 42D	4520423408016		0894		3 LO D-36	57500	Y120		
☐ RA-85180	Tupolev 154B	180	CCCP-85180	1076		3 KU NK-8-2U	100000	Y164		
☐ RA-85183	Tupolev 154B-1	183	CCCP-85183	1176		3 KU NK-8-2U	100000	Y164		cvtd 154B
☐ RA-85467	Tupolev 154B-2	467	CCCP-85467	0181		3 KU NK-8-2U	100000	C26Y102		
☐ RA-85725	Tupolev 154M	907	EW-85725	0092	0096	3 SO D-30KU-154-II	100000	Y164		
☐ RA-85754	Tupolev 154M	936		0092	0098	3 SO D-30KU-154-II	100000	C26Y102		

CHERNOMOR-AVIA = CMK (formerly Chernomorskie Airlines) — Sochi

Sochi Airport, A-355, 354355 Sochi, Russia ☎ (8622) 44 81 86 Tx: none Fax: (8622) 44 73 21 SITA: n/a
F: 1994 n/a Head: Eduard A. Akopyan ICAO: CHERAVIA Net: n/a

☐ RA-65565	Tupolev 134A	63998	EW-65565	0283	0098	2 SO D-30-II	49000	Y64		lsf BLI
☐ RA-65575	Tupolev 134A	62350	ES-AAL	0679	0096	2 SO D-30-II	49000	Y72		
☐ RA-85291	Tupolev 154B-1	291	CCCP-85291	0278	0098	3 KU NK-8-2U	98000	Y164		

CHITAAVIA, Joint-Stock Company = X7 / CHF (formerly Aeroflot Chita division) — Chita-Kadala

Chita-Kadala Airport, 672018 Chita, Russia ☎ (30222) 41 121 Tx: 225113 mart su Fax: (30222) 66 396 SITA: n/a
F: 1991 n/a Head: Nikolai Semyonov IATA: 637 ICAO: CHITA Net: n/a Most aircraft are still in Aeroflot colors but will be repainted in due course.

☐ RA-32597	PZL Mielec (Antonov) An-2		CCCP-32597	0069		1 SH ASh-62IR	5500	Utility		
☐ RA-33426	PZL Mielec (Antonov) An-2	1G227-32	CCCP-33426	0087		1 SH ASh-62IR	5500	Utility		
☐ RA-33429	PZL Mielec (Antonov) An-2	1G227-35	CCCP-33429	0087		1 SH ASh-62IR	5500	Utility		
☐ RA-33499	PZL Mielec (Antonov) An-2		CCCP-33499	0088		1 SH ASh-62IR	5500	Utility		
☐ RA-33501	PZL Mielec (Antonov) An-2		CCCP-33501	0088		1 SH ASh-62IR	5500	Utility		
☐ RA-40904	PZL Mielec (Antonov) An-2	1G215-41	CCCP-40904	0085		1 SH ASh-62IR	5500	Utility		
☐ RA-71280	PZL Mielec (Antonov) An-2	1G207-51	CCCP-71280	0084		1 SH ASh-62IR	5500	Utility		
☐ RA-71289	PZL Mielec (Antonov) An-2	1G201-17	CCCP-71289	0083		1 SH ASh-62IR	5500	Utility		
☐ RA-22951	Mil Mi-8MTV-1	96169		0594		2 IS TV3-117MT	13000	EMS		opf Chita Ambulance
☐ RA-24745	Mil Mi-8T	98420005	CCCP-24745	1184		2 IS TV2-117A	12000	Y22		
☐ RA-25225	Mil Mi-8T	7760	CCCP-25225	0679		2 IS TV2-117A	12000	Y22		
☐ RA-25813	Mil Mi-8MTV-1	96157		1093		2 IS TV3-117MT	13000	Y24		
☐ RA-25814	Mil Mi-8MTV-1	96158		0793		2 IS TV3-117MT	13000	Y24		
☐ RA-46246	Antonov 24B	77303204	CCCP-46246	0367		2 IV AI-24	21000	Y48		
☐ RA-46557	Antonov 24B	87304604	CCCP-46557	0868		2 IV AI-24	21000	Y48		
☐ RA-47169	Antonov 24B	89901801	CCCP-47169	0968		2 IV AI-24	21000	Y48		
☐ RA-47268	Antonov 24B	07306306	CCCP-47268	0870		2 IV AI-24	21000	Y48		
☐ RA-47764	Antonov 24B	79901308	CCCP-47764	1067		2 IV AI-24	21000	Y48		
☐ RA-47838	Antonov 24B	17307310	CCCP-47838	1171		2 IV AI-24	21000	Y48		
☐ RA-26018	Antonov 26B	10201	CCCP-26018	0980		2 IV AI-24VT	24000	Frtr / Y31		
☐ RA-26053	Antonov 26B	10909	CCCP-26053	0381		2 IV AI-24VT	24000	Frtr / Y33		
☐ RA-26543	Antonov 26	2709	CCCP-26543	0275		2 IV AI-24VT	24000	Frtr / Y32		
☐ RA-85280	Tupolev 154B-2	280	CCCP-85280	0678		3 KU NK-8-2U	98000	Y164		cvtd 154B-1
☐ RA-85506	Tupolev 154B-2	506	CCCP-85506	0881		3 KU NK-8-2U	98000	Y164		
☐ RA-85684	Tupolev 154M	851	CCCP-85684	1090		3 SO D-30KU-154-II	102000	Y151		
☐ RA-85735	Tupolev 154M	917	B-2627	0092		3 SO D-30KU-154-II	100000	Y164		
☐ RA-85765	Tupolev 154M	922	B-2628	0092		3 SO D-30KU-154-II	100000	Y164		
☐ RA-85766	Tupolev 154M	923		1092		3 SO D-30KU-154-II	102000	Y151		lst IRB as EP-MAP
☐ RA-85802	Tupolev 154M	961		1293		3 SO D-30KU-154-II	102000	Y153		lst IRB as EP-MAN

CHKALOV NATIONAL AEROCLUB OF RUSSIA (Natsionalny aeroclub Rossii im. Chkalova) — Moscow-Tushino

Volokolamskoe shosse 88/1, 123424 Moskva, Russia ☎ (095) 490 48 59 Tx: 411852 tanta Fax: (095) 491 74 47 SITA: n/a
F: 1993 n/a Head: Albert Sh. Nazarov Net: n/a

☐ RA-23776	PZL Swidnik (Mil) Mi-2	5411036099	FLA-04	0089		2 IS GTD-350-4	3550	Utility		
☐ RA-23777	PZL Swidnik (Mil) Mi-2	5411034109	FLA-09	0089		2 IS GTD-350-4	3550	Utility		
☐ RA-25770	Mil Mi-8PS-11	8709		0093	0097	2 IS TV2-117A	12000	VIP Salon		2nd active registered RA-25770
☐ RA-27142	Mil Mi-8T	9744121	RA-27132	0074		2 IS TV2-117A	12000	Utility		
☐ RA-27183	Mil Mi-8T	9754905	RA-27133	0075		2 IS TV2-117A	12000	Utility		
☐ RA-13339	Antonov 26	1208	CCCP-01208	0072		2 IV AI-24VT	24000	Combi		

CHUKOTAVIA — Anadyr / Keperveyem / Mys Shmidta & Pevek

Ul. Portovaya 6, 686720 pos. Uqolnye Kopi, (Anadyr Region, Chukotka AO), Russia ☎ (42722) 56 569 Tx: none Fax: (42722) 56 531 SITA: n/a
F: 1996 n/a Head: Gennady A. Baiborodov Net: n/a Company consists of ANADYR, CHAUNSK, KEPERVEYEM & MYS SHMIDTA Air Enterprises of Chukotavia.
Most aircraft are still in Aeroflot colors but will be repainted in due course.

☐ RA-01107	PZL Mielec (Antonov) An-2		CCCP-01107	0091		1 SH ASh-62IR	5500	Utility		
☐ RA-01108	PZL Mielec (Antonov) An-2		CCCP-01108	0091		1 SH ASh-62IR	5500	Utility		
☐ RA-01110	PZL Mielec (Antonov) An-2		CCCP-01110	0091		1 SH ASh-62IR	5500	Utility		
☐ RA-01114	PZL Mielec (Antonov) An-2		CCCP-01114	0091		1 SH ASh-62IR	5500	Utility		
☐ RA-32651	PZL Mielec (Antonov) An-2		CCCP-32651	0085		1 SH ASh-62IR	5500	Utility		
☐ RA-33627	PZL Mielec (Antonov) An-2		CCCP-33627	0089		1 SH ASh-62IR	5500	Utility		
☐ RA-33661	PZL Mielec (Antonov) An-2		CCCP-33661	0089		1 SH ASh-62IR	5500	Utility		
☐ RA-33662	PZL Mielec (Antonov) An-2		CCCP-33662	0089		1 SH ASh-62IR	5500	Utility		
☐ RA-41314	PZL Mielec (Antonov) An-2		CCCP-41314	0065		1 SH ASh-62IR	5500	Utility		
☐ RA-41965	Antonov An-2		CCCP-41965	0060		1 SH ASh-62IR	5500	Utility		
☐ RA-43882	Antonov An-2		CCCP-43882	0060		1 SH ASh-62IR	5500	Utility		
☐ RA-55551	Antonov An-2		CCCP-55551	0060		1 SH ASh-62IR	5500	Utility		
☐ RA-79912	Antonov An-2		CCCP-79912	0060		1 SH ASh-62IR	5500	Utility		
☐ RA-91740	PZL Mielec (Antonov) An-2		CCCP-91740	0063		1 SH ASh-62IR	5500	Utility		
☐ RA-92876	PZL Mielec (Antonov) An-2		CCCP-92876	0064		1 SH ASh-62IR	5500	Utility		
☐ RA-28701	PZL Mielec (Antonov) An-28	1AJ006-12	CCCP-28701	0089		2 GS TVD-10B	6500	Y17		
☐ RA-28752	PZL Mielec (Antonov) An-28	1AJ004-01	CCCP-28752	0087		2 GS TVD-10B	6500	Y17		
☐ RA-28758	PZL Mielec (Antonov) An-28	1AJ004-07	CCCP-28758	0087		2 GS TVD-10B	6500	Y17		
☐ RA-28760	PZL Mielec (Antonov) An-28	1AJ004-09	CCCP-28760	0087		2 GS TVD-10B	6500	Y17		
☐ RA-28792	PZL Mielec (Antonov) An-28	1AJ005-25	CCCP-28792	0089		2 GS TVD-10B	6500	Y17		
☐ RA-28797	PZL Mielec (Antonov) An-28	1AJ006-05	CCCP-28797	0089		2 GS TVD-10B	6500	Y17		
☐ RA-22240	Mil Mi-8		CCCP-22240	0077		2 IS TV2-117A	12000	Utility		
☐ RA-22262	Mil Mi-8		CCCP-22262	0077		2 IS TV2-117A	12000	Utility		
☐ RA-22293	Mil Mi-8		CCCP-22293	0077		2 IS TV2-117A	12000	Utility		
☐ RA-22383	Mil Mi-8		CCCP-22383	0077		2 IS TV2-117A	12000	Utility		
☐ RA-22385	Mil Mi-8		CCCP-22385	0077		2 IS TV2-117A	12000	Utility		
☐ RA-22390	Mil Mi-8		CCCP-22390	0077		2 IS TV2-117A	12000	Utility		
☐ RA-22499	Mil Mi-8T		CCCP-22499	0075		2 IS TV2-117A	12000	Utility		
☐ RA-22728	Mil Mi-8		CCCP-22728	0083		2 IS TV2-117A	12000	Utility		
☐ RA-22820	Mil Mi-8		CCCP-22820	0078		2 IS TV2-117A	12000	Utility		
☐ RA-22918	Mil Mi-8		CCCP-22918	0085		2 IS TV2-117A	12000	Utility		
☐ RA-24188	Mil Mi-8		CCCP-24188	0089		2 IS TV2-117A	12000	Utility		
☐ RA-24189	Mil Mi-8		CCCP-24189	0089		2 IS TV2-117A	12000	Utility		
☐ RA-24199	Mil Mi-8		CCCP-24199	0089		2 IS TV2-117A	12000	Utility		
☐ RA-24295	Mil Mi-8		CCCP-24295	0087		2 IS TV2-117A	12000	Utility		
☐ RA-24415	Mil Mi-8		CCCP-24415	0086		2 IS TV2-117A	12000	Utility		
☐ RA-24422	Mil Mi-8		CCCP-24422	0086		2 IS TV2-117A	12000	Utility		
☐ RA-24484	Mil Mi-8		CCCP-24484	0086		2 IS TV2-117A	12000	Utility		
☐ RA-24497	Mil Mi-8		CCCP-24497	0086		2 IS TV2-117A	12000	Utility		
☐ RA-24498	Mil Mi-8		CCCP-24498	0086		2 IS TV2-117A	12000	Utility		
☐ RA-24503	Mil Mi-8		CCCP-24503	0085		2 IS TV2-117A	12000	Utility		
☐ RA-24513	Mil Mi-8		CCCP-24513	0085		2 IS TV2-117A	12000	Utility		
☐ RA-24531	Mil Mi-8		CCCP-24531	0085		2 IS TV2-117A	12000	Utility		
☐ RA-24542	Mil Mi-8		CCCP-24542	0085		2 IS TV2-117A	12000	Utility		
☐ RA-24554	Mil Mi-8		CCCP-24554	0085		2 IS TV2-117A	12000	Utility		
☐ RA-24703	Mil Mi-8		CCCP-24703	0084		2 IS TV2-117A	12000	Utility		
☐ RA-24719	Mil Mi-8		CCCP-24719	0084		2 IS TV2-117A	12000	Utility		
☐ RA-24738	Mil Mi-8		CCCP-24738	0084		2 IS TV2-117A	12000	Utility		
☐ RA-25470	Mil Mi-8MTV-1		CCCP-25470	0091		2 IS TV3-117MT	13000	Utility		
☐ RA-25565	Mil Mi-8		CCCP-25565	0091		2 IS TV2-117A	12000	Utility		
☐ RA-25643	Mil Mi-8		CCCP-25643	0072		2 IS TV2-117A	12000	Utility		
☐ RA-25690	Mil Mi-8		CCCP-25690	0073		2 IS TV2-117A	12000	Utility		
☐ RA-25792	Mil Mi-8		CCCP-25792	0074		2 IS TV2-117A	12000	Utility		
☐ RA-25823	Mil Mi-8		CCCP-25823	0074		2 IS TV2-117A	12000	Utility		
☐ RA-25988	Mil Mi-8		CCCP-25988	0077		2 IS TV2-117A	12000	Utility		
☐ RA-46616	Antonov 24RV	37308703	CCCP-46616	0073		2 IV AI-24VT	21800	Y48		
☐ RA-47159	Antonov 24B	89901701	CCCP-47159	0068		2 IV AI-24	21000	Y48		
☐ RA-26099	Antonov 26B		CCCP-26099	0082		2 IV AI-24VT	24000	Freighter		
☐ RA-26117	Antonov 26B		CCCP-26117	0082		2 IV AI-24VT	24000	Freighter		

533 registration type of aircraft cn/fn ex/ex* mfd del powered by mtow kg configuration selcal name/fln/specialitites/remarks

registration	type of aircraft	cn/fn	ex/ex*	mfd	del	powered by	mtow kg	configuration	selcal	name/fln/specialitites/remarks
☐ RA-26128	Antonov 26B	12702	CCCP-26128	0082		2 IV AI-24VT	24000	Freighter		
☐ RA-26590	Antonov 26B		CCCP-26590	0083		2 IV AI-24VT	24000	Freighter		
☐ RA-26591	Antonov 26B	14001	CCCP-26591	0083		2 IV AI-24VT	24000	Freighter		

CLINTONDALE AVIATION, Inc. (Member of Clintondale Group Inc., Clintondale, N.Y., USA) — Moscow-Vnukovo

Leningradsky Prospekt 37, Business Center Westbridge, 125167 Moskva, Russia ☎ (095) 258 06 54 Tx: n/a Fax: (095) 258 06 55 SITA: n/a
F: n/a ♦♦♦ n/a Head: Yuri P. Konovalov Net: n/a   Offers aviation management & charter services mainly on behalf of Oil companies.
Flight services are operated on behalf of Clintondale Aviation by AVL – Arkhangelskie vozdushnye linii / Arkhangelsk Airlines (with Tupolev 134A aircraft) in full Clintondale colors.

registration	type of aircraft	cn/fn	ex/ex*	mfd	del	powered by	mtow kg	configuration	selcal	name/fln/specialitites/remarks
☐ RA-65088	Tupolev 134A-3	60172	LY-ABF	0078	0098	2 SO D-30-III	47600	Executive		
☐ RA-65132	Tupolev 134A-3	60639	CCCP-65132	0078	0394	2 SO D-30-III	49000	Executive		lsf/opb AVL-Arkhangelskie vozd. linii

CNG TRANSAVIA = CGT (KNG Transavia) — Voronezh

Ul. Voroshilova 22, 394066 Voronezh, Russia ☎ (0732) 34 85 16 Tx: none Fax: (0732) 36 23 36 SITA: n/a
F: 1995 ♦♦♦ n/a Head: Viktor V. Panevin ICAO: TRANSGAZ Net: n/a

registration	type of aircraft	cn/fn	ex/ex*	mfd	del	powered by	mtow kg	configuration	selcal	name/fln/specialitites/remarks
☐ RA-21506	Yakovlev 40KD	9840259	CCCP-21506	0078	0095	3 IV AI-25	17200	Executive		lst NRD
☐ RA-98103	Antonov 12BP	00347003	CCCP-98103	0070	0095	4 IV AI-20M	61000	Freighter		
☐ RA-98119	Antonov 12BP	7344801		0067	0095	4 IV AI-20M	61000	Freighter		

CONTINENTAL AIRWAYS, Joint-Stock Company = PC / PVV (Kontinentalnye avialinii) — Moscow-Sheremetyevo

Hotel Complex Sheremetyevo 2, 103339 Moskva, Russia ☎ (095) 578 03 70 Tx: none Fax: (095) 578 03 74 SITA: n/a
F: 1995 ♦♦♦ n/a Head: Yuri O. Lengarov IATA: 922 ICAO: CONTAIR Net: n/a

registration	type of aircraft	cn/fn	ex/ex*	mfd	del	powered by	mtow kg	configuration	selcal	name/fln/specialitites/remarks
☐ RA-86136	Ilyushin 86	51483210094	CCCP-86136	0091	0095	4 KU NK-86	215000	Y350		lsf F-16 Leasing
☐ RA-86138	Ilyushin 86	51483210096	CCCP-86138	0091	0095	4 KU NK-86	215000	Y350		lsf F-16 Leasing

DAGHESTAN AIRLINES = DAG (Avialinii Dagestana) (formerly Makhachkala Air Enterprise & Aeroflot Makhachkala division) — Makhachkala

Makhachkala Airport, 367016 Makhachkala, (Republic of Dagestan), Russia ☎ (8722) 65 49 20 Tx: none Fax: (8722) 65 49 25 SITA: n/a
F: 1927 ♦♦♦ n/a Head: Alexei D. Dzhabrailov ICAO: DAGAL Net: n/a   Most aircraft are still in Aeroflot colors but will be repainted in due course.

registration	type of aircraft	cn/fn	ex/ex*	mfd	del	powered by	mtow kg	configuration	selcal	name/fln/specialitites/remarks
☐ RA-33381	PZL Mielec (Antonov) An-2	1G226-40	CCCP-33381	0887	0987	1 SH ASh-62IR	5500	Y12		
☐ RA-71193	PZL Mielec (Antonov) An-2	1G200-36	CCCP-71193	1282	0093	1 SH ASh-62IR	5500	Y12		
☐ RA-71194	PZL Mielec (Antonov) An-2	1G200-37	CCCP-71194	1282	0093	1 SH ASh-62IR	5500	Y12		
☐ RA-71195	PZL Mielec (Antonov) An-2	1G200-38	CCCP-71195	1282	0093	1 SH ASh-62IR	5500	Y12		
☐ RA-71200	PZL Mielec (Antonov) An-2	1G200-43	CCCP-71200	1282	0183	1 SH ASh-62IR	5500	Y12		
☐ RA-71201	PZL Mielec (Antonov) An-2	1G200-44	CCCP-71201	1282	0183	1 SH ASh-62IR	5500	Y12		
☐ RA-71260	PZL Mielec (Antonov) An-2	1G207-31	CCCP-71260	0484	0484	1 SH ASh-62IR	5500	Y12		
☐ RA-81647	PZL Mielec (Antonov) An-2	1G209-41	CCCP-81647	0984	0984	1 SH ASh-62IR	5500	Y12		
☐ RA-81648	PZL Mielec (Antonov) An-2	1G209-42	CCCP-81648	0984	0984	1 SH ASh-62IR	5500	Y12		
☐ RA-22859	Mil Mi-8T	98415435	CCCP-22859	0484	0584	2 IS TV2-117A	12000	Y22		
☐ RA-25760	Mil Mi-8MTV-1	96123		0993	0993	2 IS TV3-117MT	13000	EMS		
☐ RA-46369	Antonov 24B	07305910	CCCP-46369	0073	0072	2 IV AI-24	21000	Y48		
☐ RA-46654	Antonov 24RV	47309209	CCCP-46654	0274	0076	2 IV AI-24VT	21800	Y36 & Cargo		
☐ RA-85728	Tupolev 154M	910	CCCP-85728	0592	0994	3 SO D-30KU-154-II	100000	Y164		
☐ RA-85756	Tupolev 154M	938		1192	0694	3 SO D-30KU-154-II	100000	Y166		op in ex Conveyor/Touch & Go colors
☐ RA-85828	Tupolev 154M	1009		1297	0398	3 SO D-30KU-154-II	100000	F12C18Y104		
☐ RA-85840	Tupolev 154M	1011		1298	1298	3 SO D-30KU-154-II	100000	Y166		

DALAVIA = H8 / KHB (Dalnevostochnye avialinii) (formerly Khabarovsk Avn Enterprise, part of Far East Avia Corp. & AFL Khabarovsk div.) — Khabarovsk-Central

Khabarovsk Airport, 680012 Khabarovsk, Russia ☎ (4212) 37 25 77 Tx: 141801 port Fax: (4212) 22 60 09 SITA: n/a
F: 1953 ♦♦♦ 5000 Head: Pavel I. Sevastianov IATA: 560 ICAO: KHABAROVSK AIR Net: n/a   All aircraft are still in Aeroflot colors but will be repainted in due course.
International flights are operated under contract to Aeroflot Russian International Airlines using SU/AFL flight codes.

registration	type of aircraft	cn/fn	ex/ex*	mfd	del	powered by	mtow kg	configuration	selcal	name/fln/specialitites/remarks
☐ RA-46474	Antonov 24RV	27308002	CCCP-46474	0872	0972	2 IV AI-24	21800	Y48		
☐ RA-46522	Antonov 24RV	47310001	CCCP-46522	1274	1274	2 IV AI-24VT	21800	Y48		
☐ RA-46529	Antonov 24RV	57310008	CCCP-46529	0375	1187	2 IV AI-24VT	21800	Y48		
☐ RA-46565	Antonov 24B	87304704	CCCP-46565	1068	0472	2 IV AI-24	21000	Y48		
☐ RA-46643	Antonov 24RV	37309001	CCCP-46643	1073	0274	2 IV AI-24VT	21800	Y48		
☐ RA-47156	Antonov 24B	89901608	CCCP-47156	0668	0768	2 IV AI-24	21000	Combi Y36		
☐ RA-47170	Antonov 24B	89901802	CCCP-47170	0968	1068	2 IV AI-24	21000	Y48		
☐ RA-47184	Antonov 24B	99901909	CCCP-47184	0369	0469	2 IV AI-24	21000	Y48		
☐ RA-47188	Antonov 24B	99902003	CCCP-47188	0569	0569	2 IV AI-24	21000	Combi Y36		
☐ RA-47290	Antonov 24B	07306510	CCCP-47290	1170	1186	2 IV AI-24	21000	Y48		
☐ RA-47354	Antonov 24RV	67310603	CCCP-47354	0776	0976	2 IV AI-24	21800	Y48		
☐ RA-47367	Antonov 24RV	77310806	CCCP-47367	0977	0678	2 IV AI-24VT	21800	Y48		
☐ RA-47748	Antonov 24B	79901201	CCCP-47748	0367	0467	2 IV AI-24	21000	Combi Y36		
☐ RA-47758	Antonov 24B	79901301	CCCP-47758	0667	0767	2 IV AI-24	21000	Y48		
☐ RA-47766	Antonov 24B	79901401	CCCP-47766	0967	1067	2 IV AI-24	21000	Combi Y36		
☐ RA-47819	Antonov 24RV	17307108	CCCP-47819	0771	0871	2 IV AI-24VT	21800	Y48		
☐ RA-47831	Antonov 24B	17307302	CCCP-47831	0971	1071	2 IV AI-24	21000	Y48		
☐ RA-26000	Antonov 26	9604	CCCP-26000	0480	1282	2 IV AI-24VT	24000	Freighter		
☐ RA-26001	Antonov 26	9705	CCCP-26001	0580	0680	2 IV AI-24VT	24000	Freighter		
☐ RA-26043	Antonov 26B		CCCP-26043	0281	0282	2 IV AI-24VT	24000	Freighter		
☐ RA-26058	Antonov 26B	11101	CCCP-26058	0681	0781	2 IV AI-24VT	24000	Freighter		
☐ RA-26500	Antonov 26	6307	CCCP-26500	0378	0478	2 IV AI-24VT	24000	Freighter		
☐ RA-26562	Antonov 26	3505	CCCP-26562	1275	0176	2 IV AI-24VT	24000	Freighter		
☐ RA-26564	Antonov 26	3507	CCCP-26564	1275	0176	2 IV AI-24VT	24000	Freighter		
☐ RA-26571	Antonov 26	3909	CCCP-26571	0476	1291	2 IV AI-24VT	24000	Frtr / Research		
☐ RA-26673	Antonov 26	8408	CCCP-26673	0779	0879	2 IV AI-24VT	24000	Frtr / Research		
☐ RA-85178	Tupolev 154B-1	178	CCCP-85178	1176	0690	3 KU NK-8-2U	98000	Y164		cvtd 154B
☐ RA-85190	Tupolev 154B-1	190	CCCP-85190	0677	0690	3 KU NK-8-2U	98000	Y164		cvtd 154B
☐ RA-85205	Tupolev 154B-1	205	CCCP-85205	0577	0677	3 KU NK-8-2U	98000	Y164		cvtd 154B
☐ RA-85206	Tupolev 154B-1	206	CCCP-85206	0477	0278	3 KU NK-8-2U	98000	Y164		cvtd 154B
☐ RA-85207	Tupolev 154B-1	207	CCCP-85207	0477	0977	3 KU NK-8-2U	98000	Y164		cvtd 154B
☐ RA-85216	Tupolev 154B-1	216	CCCP-85216	0677	0879	3 KU NK-8-2U	98000	Y164		cvtd 154B
☐ RA-85220	Tupolev 154B-2	220	CCCP-85220	0677	0881	3 KU NK-8-2U	98000	Y164		cvtd 154B
☐ RA-85266	Tupolev 154B-2	266	CCCP-85266	0378	0891	3 KU NK-8-2U	98000	Y164		cvtd 154B-1
☐ RA-85336	Tupolev 154B-2	336	CCCP-85336	0479	0479	3 KU NK-8-2U	98000	Y164		
☐ RA-85341	Tupolev 154B-2	341	CCCP-85341	0579	0579	3 KU NK-8-2U	98000	Y164		
☐ RA-85443	Tupolev 154B-2	443	CCCP-85443	0980	1080	3 KU NK-8-2U	98000	Y164		
☐ RA-85477	Tupolev 154B-2	477	CCCP-85477	0281	0381	3 KU NK-8-2U	98000	Y164		
☐ RA-86128	Ilyushin 62M	2255719	CCCP-86128	0792	0892	4 SO D-30KU	167000	Y168		fn 5501
☐ RA-86131	Ilyushin 62M	4255244	CCCP-86131	1292	0193	4 SO D-30KU	167000	Y174orF12CY126		fn 5504
☐ RA-86452	Ilyushin 62M	1622212	CCCP-86452	0376	0281	4 SO D-30KU	165000	Y168		fn 2201
☐ RA-86464	Ilyushin 62M	4624151	CCCP-86464	1276	1183	4 SO D-30KU	165000	Y168		fn 2405
☐ RA-86471	Ilyushin 62M	2725345	CCCP-86471	0377	0880	4 SO D-30KU	165000	Y168		fn 2504
☐ RA-86476	Ilyushin 62M	4728229	CCCP-86476	0478	0880	4 SO D-30KU	165000	Y168		fn 2802
☐ RA-86479	Ilyushin 62M	4728118	CCCP-86479	1277	1277	4 SO D-30KU	165000	Y168		fn 2801
☐ RA-86481	Ilyushin 62M	2829415	CCCP-86481	0378	0478	4 SO D-30KU	165000	Y168		fn 2901
☐ RA-86486	Ilyushin 62M	3830123	CCCP-86486	0878	0880	4 SO D-30KU	165000	Y168		fn 3002
☐ RA-86493	Ilyushin 62M	4140748	CCCP-86493	0282	1286	4 SO D-30KU	167000	Y168		fn 4004
☐ RA-86503	Ilyushin 62M	4934512	CCCP-86503	0680	0892	4 SO D-30KU	167000	Y168		fn 3401
☐ RA-86504	Ilyushin 62M	4934621	CCCP-86504	1179	1190	4 SO D-30KU	167000	F12CY126orCombi		fn 3402
☐ RA-86525	Ilyushin 62M	4851612	CCCP-86525	0489	0589	4 SO D-30KU	167000	Y168		fn 5101
☐ RA-86560	Ilyushin 62M	2153347	CCCP-86560	0591	0691	4 SO D-30KU	167000	Combi Y102		fn 5304
☐ RA-86618	Ilyushin 62M	3520422	CCCP-86618	0775	0380	4 SO D-30KU	165000	Y168		fn 2002
☐ RA-86620	Ilyushin 62M	3520345	CCCP-86620	0875	1279	4 SO D-30KU	165000	Y168		fn 2004
☐ RA-86623	Ilyushin 62M	4521728	CCCP-86623	1175	1180	4 SO D-30KU	165000	Y168		fn 2102
☐ RA-86700	Ilyushin 62M	31503	CCCP-86700	1273	1277	4 SO D-30KU	165000	Y168		fn 1503
☐ RA-86702	Ilyushin 62M	31505	CCCP-86702	1273	0578	4 SO D-30KU	165000	Y168		fn 1505

DELTA-K Enterprise (Delta-K aviapredpriatie) — Neryungri

Neryungri Airport, 678930 Chulman, (Republic of Sakha-Yakutia), Russia ☎ (41147) 37 249 Tx: none Fax: (41147) 40 934 SITA: n/a
F: 1992 ♦♦♦ n/a Head: Ivan G. Shapoval Net: n/a

registration	type of aircraft	cn/fn	ex/ex*	mfd	del	powered by	mtow kg	configuration	selcal	name/fln/specialitites/remarks
☐ RA-23663	PZL Swidnik (Mil) Mi-2	546434129	CCCP-23663	0079	0092	2 IS GTD-350-4	3550	Utility		
☐ RA-23664	PZL Swidnik (Mil) Mi-2		CCCP-23664	0079	0092	2 IS GTD-350-4	3550	Utility		
☐ RA-23665	PZL Swidnik (Mil) Mi-2		CCCP-23665	0079	0092	2 IS GTD-350-4	3550	Utility		
☐ RA-05822	PZL Mielec (Antonov) An-2			0074	0092	1 SH ASh-62IR	5500	Utility		
☐ RA-05823	PZL Mielec (Antonov) An-2			0074	0092	1 SH ASh-62IR	5500	Utility		
☐ RA-05824	PZL Mielec (Antonov) An-2			0074	0092	1 SH ASh-62IR	5500	Utility		
☐ RA-22326	Mil Mi-8T		CCCP-22326	0077	0093	2 IS TV2-117A	12000	Utility		lsf Ulan-Ude Air Enterprise
☐ RA-25129	Mil Mi-8MTV-1		CCCP-25129	0089	0093	2 IS TV3-117MT	13000	Utility		lsf Ulan-Ude Air Enterprise

DOBROLET AIRLINES = DOB (formerly NSA Soyuz)

Moscow-Sheremetyevo

Sheremetyevo Airport, Gosnii GA Bldg 1, Room 328, 103340 Moskva, Russia ☎ (095) 578 43 73 Tx: none Fax: (095) 578 47 55 SITA: n/a

F: 1992 ⁂ n/a Head: Viskhan M. Shakhabov ICAO: DOBROLET Net: n/a

☐ RA-76389	Ilyushin 76MD	1013407212	RA-78852	0091	0098	4 SO D-30KP	190000	Freighter		lsf TUP
☐ RA-76416	Ilyushin 76T	043402041	21 RED	0074	0092	4 SO D-30KP	172000	Freighter		
☐ RA-76417	Ilyushin 76T	043402046		1074	0092	4 SO D-30KP	172000	Freighter		
☐ RA-76418	Ilyushin 76T	073409237	CCCP-86640	1076	0092	4 SO D-30KP	172000	Freighter		

DOMODEDOVO AIRLINES, Joint-Stock Company = E3 / DMO (Domodedovskie avialinii)

Moscow-Domodedovo

Domodedovo Airport, 142045 Domodedovo, (Moscow Region), Russia ☎ (095) 323 89 91 Tx: none Fax: (095) 952 86 51 SITA: DMECDE3

F: 1997 ⁂ n/a Head: Alexander I. Akimov IATA: 497 ICAO: DOMODEDOVO Net: n/a Some aircraft are still painted with former operators-name DOMODEDOVO C.A.P.A.-Civil Aviation Production Association.

☐ RA-86127	Ilyushin 62M	1254851	CCCP-86127	0592	0097	4 SO D-30KU	167000	Y174 or C18Y138		fn 5405
☐ RA-86129	Ilyushin 62M	2255525		0992	0097	4 SO D-30KU	167000	Y174 or C18Y138		fn 5502
☐ RA-86475	Ilyushin 62M	3727213	CCCP-86475	0977	0097	4 SO D-30KU	165000	Y174 or C18Y138		fn 2701
☐ RA-86490	Ilyushin 62M	4831739	CCCP-86490	1278	0097	4 SO D-30KU	167000	Y174 or C18Y138		fn 3103
☐ RA-86494	Ilyushin 62M	4140859	CCCP-86494	0283	0097	4 SO D-30KU	167000	Y174 or C18Y138		fn 4005
☐ RA-86499	Ilyushin 62M	2932637	CCCP-86499	0479	0097	4 SO D-30KU	167000	Y174 or C18Y138		fn 3203
☐ RA-86509	Ilyushin 62M	2036829	CCCP-86509	0880	0097	4 SO D-30KU	167000	Y174 or C18Y138		fn 3602
☐ RA-86516	Ilyushin 62M	2139524	CCCP-86516	0682	0097	4 SO D-30KU	167000	Y174 or C18Y138		fn 3902
☐ RA-86519	Ilyushin 62M	4140212	CCCP-86519	0282	0097	4 SO D-30KU	167000	Y174 or C18Y138		fn 4001
☐ RA-86521	Ilyushin 62M	1241425	CCCP-86521	0482	0097	4 SO D-30KU	167000	Y174 or C18Y138		fn 4102
☐ RA-86526	Ilyushin 62M	2951447	CCCP-86526	1089	0097	4 SO D-30KU	167000	Y174 or C18Y138		fn 5104
☐ RA-86530	Ilyushin 62M	4242543	CCCP-86530	1082	0097	4 SO D-30KU	167000	Y174 or C18Y138		fn 4204
☐ RA-86535	Ilyushin 62M	2444555	CCCP-86535	0584	0097	4 SO D-30KU	167000	Y174 or C18Y138		fn 4405
☐ RA-86541	Ilyushin 62M	3951359	CCCP-86541	1289	0097	4 SO D-30KU	167000	Y174 or C18Y138		fn 5105
☐ RA-86542	Ilyushin 62M	3952714	CCCP-86542	1289	0097	4 SO D-30KU	167000	Y174 or Y18C138		fn 5201
☐ RA-86552	Ilyushin 62M	2052345	CCCP-86552	0290	0097	4 SO D-30KU	167000	Y174 or C18Y138		fn 5204
☐ RA-86673	Ilyushin 62M	3154416	CCCP-86673	1191	0097	4 SO D-30KU	167000	Y174 or C18Y138		fn 5401
☐ RA-76786	Ilyushin 76TD	0093496923	CCCP-76786	1189	0097	4 SO D-30KP	190000	Freighter		
☐ RA-76799	Ilyushin 76TD	1003403075	CCCP-76799	0790	0097	4 SO D-30KP	190000	Freighter		
☐ RA-76806	Ilyushin 76TD	1003403121	CCCP-76806	1190	0097	4 SO D-30KP	190000	Freighter		
☐ RA-76812	Ilyushin 76TD	1013407230	CCCP-76812	0791	0097	4 SO D-30KP	190000	Freighter		
☐ RA-96006	Ilyushin 96-300	74393201003	CCCP-96006	0793	0097	4 SO PS-90A	224000	Y294 or C22Y230		
☐ RA-96009	Ilyushin 96-300	74393201006		0494	0097	4 SO PS-90AN	240000	Y294 or C22Y230		
☐ RA-96013	Ilyushin 96-300	74393202013		0299	0399	4 SO PS-90AN	240000	Y294 or C22Y230		

DONAVIA, Joint-Stock Company = D9 / DNV (Don Airlines)

Rostov-na-Donu

АКЦИОНЕРНАЯ АВИАКОМПАНИЯ ДОНАВИА

Prospekt Sholokhova 272, 344009 Rostov-na-Donu, Russia ☎ (8632) 58 98 11 Tx: n/a Fax: (8632) 52 05 67 SITA: n/a

F: 1993 ⁂ n/a Head: Pavel D. Duzhnikov IATA: 733 ICAO: DONAVIA Net: n/a Some aircraft are still in Aeroflot colours without titles but will be repainted in due course.

☐ RA-65016	Tupolev 134A-3	48340	CCCP-65016	0076	0893	2 SO D-30-III	47000	C8Y60		
☐ RA-65100	Tupolev 134A-3	60258	CCCP-65100	0078	0893	2 SO D-30-III	49000	C8Y60		
☐ RA-65104	Tupolev 134A-3	60301	CCCP-65104	0078	0893	2 SO D-30-III	49000	C8Y60		
☐ RA-65666	Tupolev 134A-3	1351202	CCCP-65666	0071	0893	2 SO D-30-III	47000	C8Y60		
☐ RA-65771	Tupolev 134A-3	62445	CCCP-65771	0079	0893	2 SO D-30-III	49000	C8Y60		
☐ RA-65796	Tupolev 134A-3	63150	CCCP-65796	0080	0893	2 SO D-30-III	49000	C8Y60		
☐ RA-65834	Tupolev 134A-3	17109	CCCP-65834	0074	0893	2 SO D-30-III	47000	C8Y60		
☐ RA-65863	Tupolev 134A-3	28283	CCCP-65863	0075	0893	2 SO D-30-III	47000	C8Y60		
☐ RA-11115	Antonov 12BP	01348003	CCCP-11115	0071	0893	4 IV AI-20M	61000	Freighter		
☐ RA-12960	Antonov 12BP	9346602	CCCP-12960	0069	0893	4 IV AI-20M	61000	Freighter		
☐ RA-12965	Antonov 12BP	9346409	CCCP-12965	0069	0893	4 IV AI-20M	61000	Freighter		
☐ RA-12974	Antonov 12BP	9346506	CCCP-12974	0069	0893	4 IV AI-20M	61000	Freighter		
☐ RA-12994	Antonov 12BP	00347401	CCCP-12994	0070	0893	4 IV AI-20M	61000	Freighter		
☐ RA-85295	Tupolev 154B-2	295	CCCP-85295	0078	0893	3 KU NK-8-2U	98000	C14Y119orCombi		cvtd 154B-1
☐ RA-85305	Tupolev 154B-2	305	CCCP-85305	0078	0893	3 KU NK-8-2U	98000	C14Y119		
☐ RA-85306	Tupolev 154B-2	306	CCCP-85306	0078	0893	3 KU NK-8-2U	98000	Y180		
☐ RA-85308	Tupolev 154B-2	308	CCCP-85308	0078	0893	3 KU NK-8-2U	98000	Y180		
☐ RA-85309	Tupolev 154B-2	309	CCCP-85309	0078	0893	3 KU NK-8-2U	98000	C14Y119		
☐ RA-85400	Tupolev 154B-2	400	CCCP-85400	0080	0893	3 KU NK-8-2U	98000	C14Y119		
☐ RA-85409	Tupolev 154B-2	409	CCCP-85409	0080	0893	3 KU NK-8-2U	98000	Y164		
☐ RA-85414	Tupolev 154B-2	414	CCCP-85414	0080	0893	3 KU NK-8-2U	98000	C14Y119		
☐ RA-85425	Tupolev 154B-2	425	CCCP-85425	0080	0893	3 KU NK-8-2U	98000	Y164		
☐ RA-85435	Tupolev 154B-2	435	CCCP-85435	0080	0893	3 KU NK-8-2U	98000	C14Y119		
☐ RA-85436	Tupolev 154B-2	436	CCCP-85436	0080	0893	3 KU NK-8-2U	98000	C14Y119		
☐ RA-85437	Tupolev 154B-2	437	CCCP-85437	0080	0893	3 KU NK-8-2U	98000	C14Y119orCombi		
☐ RA-85452	Tupolev 154B-2	452	CCCP-85452	0080	0893	3 KU NK-8-2U	98000	Y164		
☐ RA-85454	Tupolev 154B-2	454	CCCP-85454	0080	0893	3 KU NK-8-2U	98000	Y164 or Combi		
☐ RA-85495	Tupolev 154B-2	495	CCCP-85495	0081	0893	3 KU NK-8-2U	98000	Y164 or Combi		
☐ RA-85527	Tupolev 154B-2	527	CCCP-85527	0082	0893	3 KU NK-8-2U	98000	C14Y119		

DONSKAYA TRANSPORTNAYA Aviakompania (Don Transport Aircompany)

Rostov-na-Donu

Prospekt Sholokhova 272, 344009 Rostov-na-Donu, Russia ☎ (8632) 52 34 87 Tx: none Fax: none SITA: n/a

F: 1995 ⁂ 50 Head: Vladimir N. Pivovarov Net: n/a Most aircraft are still in Aeroflot colors but will be repainted in due course.

☐ RA-15205	PZL Swidnik (Mil) Mi-2	525807098	CCCP-15205	0078		2 IS GTD-350-4	3550	Utility		
☐ RA-20316	PZL Swidnik (Mil) Mi-2	527522022	CCCP-20316	0082		2 IS GTD-350-4	3550	Utility		
☐ RA-20731	PZL Swidnik (Mil) Mi-2	527548032	CCCP-20731	0082		2 IS GTD-350-4	3550	Utility		
☐ RA-20824	PZL Swidnik (Mil) Mi-2	548047033	CCCP-20824	0083		2 IS GTD-350-4	3550	Utility		
☐ RA-20900	PZL Swidnik (Mil) Mi-2	538339093	CCCP-20900	0083		2 IS GTD-350-4	3550	Utility		
☐ RA-20903	PZL Swidnik (Mil) Mi-2	528432113	CCCP-20903	0083		2 IS GTD-350-4	3550	Utility		
☐ RA-20914	PZL Swidnik (Mil) Mi-2	528546024	CCCP-20914	0084		2 IS GTD-350-4	3550	Utility		
☐ RA-20926	PZL Swidnik (Mil) Mi-2	528608034	CCCP-20926	0084		2 IS GTD-350-4	3550	Utility		
☐ RA-23454	PZL Swidnik (Mil) Mi-2		CCCP-23454	0079		2 IS GTD-350-4	3550	Utility		
☐ RA-23455	PZL Swidnik (Mil) Mi-2		CCCP-23455	0079		2 IS GTD-350-4	3550	Utility		
☐ RA-01433	PZL Mielec (Antonov) An-2	1G231-13	CCCP-01433	0088		1 SH ASh-62IR	5500	Utility		
☐ RA-02262	PZL Mielec (Antonov) An-2		CCCP-02262	0090		1 SH ASh-62IR	5500	Utility		
☐ RA-02451	PZL Mielec (Antonov) An-2		CCCP-02451	0070		1 SH ASh-62IR	5500	Utility		
☐ RA-32387	PZL Mielec (Antonov) An-2		CCCP-32387	0068		1 SH ASh-62IR	5500	Utility		
☐ RA-70420	PZL Mielec (Antonov) An-2	1G141-74	CCCP-70420	0073		1 SH ASh-62IR	5500	Utility		

EAST LINE AIRLINES, Joint-Stock Company = P7 / ESL

Moscow-Domodedovo

Domodedovo Airport, 142045 Domodedovo, (Moscow Region), Russia ☎ (095) 795 34 57 Tx: none Fax: (095) 795 34 89 SITA: MOWTOP7

F: 1996 ⁂ n/a Head: Amiran G. Kurtanidze IATA: 215 ICAO: EASTLINE EXPRESS Net: n/a

☐ RA-42417	Yakovlev 42D	4520423219110	CCCP-42417	0792	0097	3 LO D-36	56500	Y120 or Combi		lsf ASZ
☐ RA-11112	Antonov 12BP	01347907	CCCP-11112	0071	0098	4 IV AI-20M	61000	Freighter		lsf jtly opw RLC
☐ RA-11766	Antonov 12BP	401605	CCCP-11766	0063	0098	4 IV AI-20M	61000	Freighter		lsf/jtly opw RLC
☐ RA-12992	Antonov 12BP	00347306	CCCP-12992	0070	0098	4 IV AI-20M	61000	Freighter		lsf/jtly opw RLC
☐ RA-85386	Tupolev 154B-2	386	CCCP-85386	0079	0098	3 KU NK-8-2U	98000	Y164		lsf AUL
☐ RA-85468	Tupolev 154B-2	468	CCCP-85468	0081	0097	3 KU NK-8-2U	98000	Y164		lsf AUL
☐ RA-85551	Tupolev 154B-2	551	CCCP-85551	0082	0098	3 KU NK-8-2U	98000	Y164		lsf AUL
☐ RA-85827	Tupolev 154M	745	SP-LCC	0087	0098	3 SO D-30KU-154-II	100000	CY150		lsf Buryatia Airlines
☐ RA-85829	Tupolev 154M	755	SP-LCD	0087	0098	3 SO D-30KU-154-II	100000	CY150		lsf Buryatia Airlines
☐ RA-86567	Ilyushin 62M	4256314		0095	0098	4 SO D-30KU	167000	F12C18Y102		fn 5601
☐ RA-76366	Ilyushin 76TD	1043418628		0396	0097	4 SO D-30KP	190000	Freighter		lsf/jtly opw ERG
☐ RA-76400	Ilyushin 76TD	1023413438		0092	0098	4 SO D-30KP	190000	Freighter		lsf VLK
☐ RA-76403	Ilyushin 76TD	1023412414		0092	0098	4 SO D-30KP	190000	Freighter		Igor Bykov / lsf VLK
☐ RA-76458	Ilyushin 76T	0013430888	CCCP-76458	0081	0098	4 SO D-30KP	170000	Freighter		lsf BKL
☐ RA-76462	Ilyushin 76T	0013432955	CCCP-76462	0081	0098	4 SO D-30KP	170000	Freighter		lsf BKL
☐ RA-76492	Ilyushin 76T	093418548	YI-AKT	0479	0098	4 SO D-30KP	170000	Freighter		lsf VLK / cvtd Ilyushin 76M
☐ RA-76814	Ilyushin 76TD	1013408269	CCCP-76814	0091	0098	4 SO D-30KP	190000	Freighter		
☐ RA-76843	Ilyushin 76TD	1033418584		0195	0098	4 SO D-30KP	190000	Freighter		lsf/jtly opw ERG
☐ EW-78799	Ilyushin 76MD	0093491754	CCCP-78799	1188	0095	4 SO D-30KP	190000	Freighter		lsf TXC
☐ EW-78808	Ilyushin 76MD	0093493794	CCCP-78808	0089	0098	4 SO D-30KP	190000	Freighter		lsf TXC
☐ EW-78819	Ilyushin 76MD	0093495883	CCCP-78819	0089	0098	4 SO D-30KP	190000	Freighter		lsf TXC
☐ EW-78826	Ilyushin 76MD	1003499991	CCCP-78826	0090	0098	4 SO D-30KP	190000	Freighter		lsf TXC
☐ EW-78828	Ilyushin 76MD	1003401004	CCCP-78828	0090	0098	4 SO D-30KP	190000	Freighter		lsf TXC / fn 7601
☐ EW-78839	Ilyushin 76MD	1003402047	CCCP-78839	0090	0098	4 SO D-30KP	190000	Freighter		lsf TXC
☐ EW-78843	Ilyushin 76MD	1003403082	CCCP-78843	0090	0098	4 SO D-30KP	190000	Freighter		lsf TXC
☐ UK-76351	Ilyushin 76TD	1023408240		1292	0097	4 SO D-30KP	190000	Freighter		lsf UZB / fn 8110
☐ UK-76353	Ilyushin 76TD	1023414454		0193	0098	4 SO D-30KP	190000	Freighter		lsf UZB
☐ UK-76448	Ilyushin 76TD	1023413443		0992	0798	4 SO D-30KP	190000	Freighter		lsf UZB
☐ UK-76449	Ilyushin 76TD	1023403058		1192	0098	4 SO D-30KP	190000	Freighter		Shenyang / lsf UZB / fn 7705
☐ UK-76782	Ilyushin 76TD	0093498971	CCCP-76782	0190	0097	4 SO D-30KP	190000	Freighter		lsf UZB

535 registration type of aircraft cn/fn ex/ex* mfd del powered by mtow kg configuration selcal name/fln/specialitites/remarks

☐ UK-76824	Ilyushin 76TD	1023410327		0492	0097	4 SO D-30KP	190000	Freighter		lsf UZB
☐ UK-86053	Ilyushin 86	51483202020	RA-86053	0183	0098	4 KU NK-86	215000	Y350		lsf UZB

ELBRUS-AVIA = NLK (formerly Nalchik Air Enterprise & AFL Nalchik div.) **Nalchik**

Ul. Kabardinskaya 195, 360000 Nalchik, (Republic of Kabardino-Balkaria), Russia ☎ (86622) 13 301 Tx: none Fax: (86622) 11 898 SITA: n/a

F: n/a ✈✈✈ n/a Head: Khaupi K. Metov ICAO: ELAVIA Most helicopters are still in AFL colors but will be repainted in due course. Beside helicopters listed, also leases Yak 40 aircraft from other Russian companies when required.

☐ RA-14105	PZL Swidnik (Mil) Mi-2	5210724098	CCCP-14105	0088		2 IS GTD-350-4	3550	Utility		
☐ RA-14188	PZL Swidnik (Mil) Mi-2	5410529028	CCCP-14188	0088		2 IS GTD-350-4	3550	Utility		
☐ RA-14189	PZL Swidnik (Mil) Mi-2	5410530028	CCCP-14189	0088		2 IS GTD-350-4	3550	Utility		
☐ RA-14386	PZL Swidnik (Mil) Mi-2	525305077	CCCP-14386	0077		2 IS GTD-350-4	3550	Utility		
☐ RA-14387	PZL Swidnik (Mil) Mi-2	525306077	CCCP-14387	0077		2 IS GTD-350-4	3550	Utility		
☐ RA-14388	PZL Swidnik (Mil) Mi-2	525307077	CCCP-14388	0077		2 IS GTD-350-4	3550	Utility		
☐ RA-14389	PZL Swidnik (Mil) Mi-2	525308077	CCCP-14389	0077		2 IS GTD-350-4	3550	Utility		
☐ RA-15202	PZL Swidnik (Mil) Mi-2	525804088	CCCP-15202	0078		2 IS GTD-350-4	3550	Utility		
☐ RA-15206	PZL Swidnik (Mil) Mi-2	525808088	CCCP-15206	0078		2 IS GTD-350-4	3550	Utility		
☐ RA-15298	PZL Swidnik (Mil) Mi-2	525911118	CCCP-15298	0078		2 IS GTD-350-4	3550	Utility		
☐ RA-15299	PZL Swidnik (Mil) Mi-2	525912118	CCCP-15299	0078		2 IS GTD-350-4	3550	Utility		
☐ RA-15629	PZL Swidnik (Mil) Mi-2	5210050017	CCCP-15629	0087		2 IS GTD-350-4	3550	Utility		
☐ RA-15630	PZL Swidnik (Mil) Mi-2	5210101017	CCCP-15630	0087		2 IS GTD-350-4	3550	Utility		
☐ RA-20241	PZL Swidnik (Mil) Mi-2	527129051	CCCP-20241	0081		2 IS GTD-350-4	3550	Utility		
☐ RA-20248	PZL Swidnik (Mil) Mi-2	527136051	CCCP-20248	0081		2 IS GTD-350-4	3550	Utility		
☐ RA-20251	PZL Swidnik (Mil) Mi-2	527139051	CCCP-20251	0081		2 IS GTD-350-4	3550	Utility		
☐ RA-20274	PZL Swidnik (Mil) Mi-2	547314091	CCCP-20274	0081		2 IS GTD-350-4	3550	Utility		
☐ RA-20286	PZL Swidnik (Mil) Mi-2	527405111	CCCP-20286	0081		2 IS GTD-350-4	3550	Utility		
☐ RA-20355	PZL Swidnik (Mil) Mi-2	549750056	CCCP-20355	0086		2 IS GTD-350-4	3550	Utility		
☐ RA-20356	PZL Swidnik (Mil) Mi-2	529801056	CCCP-20356	0086		2 IS GTD-350-4	3550	Utility		
☐ RA-20388	PZL Swidnik (Mil) Mi-2	529835076	CCCP-20388	0086		2 IS GTD-350-4	3550	Utility		
☐ RA-20389	PZL Swidnik (Mil) Mi-2	529836076	CCCP-20389	0086		2 IS GTD-350-4	3550	Utility		
☐ RA-20425	PZL Swidnik (Mil) Mi-2	529928096	CCCP-20425	0086		2 IS GTD-350-4	3550	Utility		
☐ RA-20426	PZL Swidnik (Mil) Mi-2	529929096	CCCP-20426	0086		2 IS GTD-350-4	3550	Utility		
☐ RA-20427	PZL Swidnik (Mil) Mi-2	529930096	CCCP-20427	0086		2 IS GTD-350-4	3550	Utility		
☐ RA-20428	PZL Swidnik (Mil) Mi-2	529931096	CCCP-20428	0086		2 IS GTD-350-4	3550	Utility		
☐ RA-20429	PZL Swidnik (Mil) Mi-2	529932096	CCCP-20429	0086		2 IS GTD-350-4	3550	Utility		
☐ RA-20630	PZL Swidnik (Mil) Mi-2	535608048	CCCP-20630	0078		2 IS GTD-350-4	3550	Utility		
☐ RA-20636	PZL Swidnik (Mil) Mi-2	535615048	CCCP-20636	0078		2 IS GTD-350-4	3550	Utility		
☐ RA-20639	PZL Swidnik (Mil) Mi-2	525706068	CCCP-20639	0078		2 IS GTD-350-4	3550	Utility		
☐ RA-20689	PZL Swidnik (Mil) Mi-2	526724070	CCCP-20689	0080		2 IS GTD-350-4	3550	Utility		
☐ RA-20691	PZL Swidnik (Mil) Mi-2	526726070	CCCP-20691	0080		2 IS GTD-350-4	3550	Utility		
☐ RA-20692	PZL Swidnik (Mil) Mi-2	526727070	CCCP-20692	0080		2 IS GTD-350-4	3550	Utility		
☐ RA-20693	PZL Swidnik (Mil) Mi-2	526728070	CCCP-20693	0080		2 IS GTD-350-4	3550	Utility		
☐ RA-20694	PZL Swidnik (Mil) Mi-2	526729070	CCCP-20694	0080		2 IS GTD-350-4	3550	Utility		
☐ RA-20742	PZL Swidnik (Mil) Mi-2	527639052	CCCP-20742	0082		2 IS GTD-350-4	3550	Utility		
☐ RA-20757	PZL Swidnik (Mil) Mi-2	547712062	CCCP-20757	0082		2 IS GTD-350-4	3550	Utility		
☐ RA-20758	PZL Swidnik (Mil) Mi-2	547713062	CCCP-20758	0082		2 IS GTD-350-4	3550	Utility		
☐ RA-20902	PZL Swidnik (Mil) Mi-2	538341093	CCCP-20902	0083		2 IS GTD-350-4	3550	Utility		
☐ RA-20916	PZL Swidnik (Mil) Mi-2	528548024	CCCP-20916	0084		2 IS GTD-350-4	3550	Utility		
☐ RA-20917	PZL Swidnik (Mil) Mi-2	528549024	CCCP-20917	0084		2 IS GTD-350-4	3550	Utility		
☐ RA-20918	PZL Swidnik (Mil) Mi-2	528550024	CCCP-20918	0084		2 IS GTD-350-4	3550	Utility		
☐ RA-20928	PZL Swidnik (Mil) Mi-2	528610034	CCCP-20928	0084		2 IS GTD-350-4	3550	Utility		
☐ RA-20929	PZL Swidnik (Mil) Mi-2	528611034	CCCP-20929	0084		2 IS GTD-350-4	3550	Utility		
☐ RA-23209	PZL Swidnik (Mil) Mi-2	5210130037	CCCP-23209	0087		2 IS GTD-350-4	3550	Utility		
☐ RA-23210	PZL Swidnik (Mil) Mi-2	5210131037	CCCP-23210	0087		2 IS GTD-350-4	3550	Utility		
☐ RA-23256	PZL Swidnik (Mil) Mi-2	5210330087	CCCP-23256	0087		2 IS GTD-350-4	3550	Utility		
☐ RA-23321	PZL Swidnik (Mil) Mi-2	529210045	CCCP-23321	0085		2 IS GTD-350-4	3550	Utility		
☐ RA-23322	PZL Swidnik (Mil) Mi-2	529211045	CCCP-23322	0085		2 IS GTD-350-4	3550	Utility		
☐ RA-23324	PZL Swidnik (Mil) Mi-2	529213045	CCCP-23324	0085		2 IS GTD-350-4	3550	Utility		
☐ RA-23347	PZL Swidnik (Mil) Mi-2	529327075	CCCP-23347	0085		2 IS GTD-350-4	3550	Utility		
☐ RA-23373	PZL Swidnik (Mil) Mi-2	528801074	CCCP-23373	0084		2 IS GTD-350-4	3550	Utility		
☐ RA-23374	PZL Swidnik (Mil) Mi-2	528802074	CCCP-23374	0084		2 IS GTD-350-4	3550	Utility		
☐ RA-23386	PZL Swidnik (Mil) Mi-2	528832084	CCCP-23386	0084		2 IS GTD-350-4	3550	Utility		
☐ RA-23387	PZL Swidnik (Mil) Mi-2	528833084	CCCP-23387	0084		2 IS GTD-350-4	3550	Utility		
☐ RA-23427	PZL Swidnik (Mil) Mi-2		CCCP-23427	0085		2 IS GTD-350-4	3550	Utility		
☐ RA-23433	PZL Swidnik (Mil) Mi-2	529348085	CCCP-23433	0085		2 IS GTD-350-4	3550	Utility		
☐ RA-23436	PZL Swidnik (Mil) Mi-2	529401085	CCCP-23436	0085		2 IS GTD-350-4	3550	Utility		
☐ RA-23440	PZL Swidnik (Mil) Mi-2	529405095	CCCP-23440	0085		2 IS GTD-350-4	3550	Utility		
☐ RA-23442	PZL Swidnik (Mil) Mi-2	529407095	CCCP-23442	0085		2 IS GTD-350-4	3550	Utility		
☐ RA-23448	PZL Swidnik (Mil) Mi-2	539421095	CCCP-23448	0085		2 IS GTD-350-4	3550	Utility		
☐ RA-23449	PZL Swidnik (Mil) Mi-2	539422095	CCCP-23449	0085		2 IS GTD-350-4	3550	Utility		
☐ RA-24255	Mil Mi-8		CCCP-24255	0087		2 IS TV2-117A	12000	Utility		
☐ RA-24416	Mil Mi-8		CCCP-24416	0086		2 IS TV2-117A	12000	Utility		
☐ RA-24461	Mil Mi-8		CCCP-24461	0086		2 IS TV2-117A	12000	Utility		
☐ RA-25114	Mil Mi-8MTV-1	95730	CCCP-25114	0091		2 IS TV3-117MT	13000	Utility		
☐ RA-25497	Mil Mi-8MTV-1		CCCP-25497	0091		2 IS TV3-117MT	13000	Utility		
☐ RA-25498	Mil Mi-8MTV-1		CCCP-25498	0091		2 IS TV3-117MT	13000	Utility		

ELF AIR, Ltd = EFR (Division of LIIP-Letnye ispitania i proizvodstva/Flight testing & productions) **Moscow-Zhukovsky**

Zhukovsky Airport, LIIP, 140160 Zhukovsky, (Moscow Region), Russia ☎ (095) 556 54 91 Tx: none Fax: (095) 556 23 58 SITA: n/a

F: 1991 ✈✈✈ n/a Head: Alexander K. Minchenok IATA: 934 ICAO: ELFAIR Net: n/a

☐ RA-87219	Yakovlev 40K	9932059	CCCP-87219	0079		3 IV AI-25	16100	Executive/Combi		
☐ RA-88238	Yakovlev 40	9640951	CCCP-88238	0076		3 IV AI-25	16100	Y32		
☐ RA-88239	Yakovlev 40	9641051	CCCP-88239	0076		3 IV AI-25	16100	Executive		
☐ RA-13398	Antonov 26	2607	CCCP-13398	0074		2 IV AI-24VT	24000	Combi		
☐ RA-65097	Tupolev 134A	60540	CCCP-65097	0078		2 SO D-30-II	47200	Combi		
☐ RA-65908	Tupolev 134A	63870	CCCP-65908	0083		2 SO D-30-II	47600	Executive		opf VAP Group
☐ RA-13321	Antonov 12BP	2340301	CCCP-13321	0062		4 IV AI-20M	61200	Freighter		
☐ RA-75431	Ilyushin 18D	186009405	CCCP-75431	0066		4 IV AI-20M	61200	Combi		
☐ RA-75811	Ilyushin 18V	182004504	CCCP-75811	0062	0097	4 IV AI-20M	61200	Combi		
☐ RA-75834	Ilyushin 18V	182005104	CCCP-75834	0062	0097	4 IV AI-20M	61200	Combi		
☐ RA-75851	Ilyushin 18V	182005501	CCCP-75851	0062		4 IV AI-20M	61200	Combi		
☐ RA-76756	Ilyushin 76T	0013428839	CCCP-76756	0081		4 SO D-30KP	170000	Freighter		
☐ RA-76819	Ilyushin 76TD	1013409274	ES-NIT	1191	0098	4 SO D-30KP	190000	Freighter		
☐ RA-76823	Ilyushin 76TD	0023441189	YI-ALQ	0082		4 SO D-30KP	190000	Freighter		

ELIIP - Ermolinskoe letnoe ispitatel'no-issledovatelskoe predpriatie = EFE (Ermolino Flying Test Research Enterprise) **Ermolino**

Balabanovo 1, 249000 Balabanovo, (Kaluga region), Russia ☎ (095) 546 34 85 Tx: none Fax: (095) 546 34 92 SITA: n/a

F: 1992 ✈✈✈ n/a Head: Sergei A. Sevastianov ICAO: ERMOLINO AIR Net: n/a Operates test/research flights & commercial charter flights. Aircraft are still in Aeroflot colors without titles.

☐ RA-08827	Antonov 26B	11801		0081		2 IV AI-24VT	24000	Freighter		
☐ RA-26644	Antonov 26	7407	CCCP-26644	0078		2 IV AI-24VT	24000	Freighter		
☐ RA-11049	Antonov 12TB	8346109	CCCP-11049	0068		4 IV AI-20M	61000	Freighter		
☐ RA-11356	Antonov 12BK	7345206	CCCP-11356	0067		4 IV AI-20M	61000	Freighter		
☐ RA-11516	Antonov 12B	4341909		0064		4 IV AI-20M	61000	Freighter		lst AYZ
☐ RA-11768	Antonov 12BP	5343103	36 BLUE	0065		4 IV AI-20M	61000	Freighter		
☐ RA-11916	Antonov 12AP	2400901	CCCP-11916	0062		4 IV AI-20M	61000	Freighter		lst AYZ

ENERGETIK-AVIA **Yakutsk-Magan**

Ul. Popova 14, 677000 Yakutsk, (Republic of Sakha-Yakutia), Russia ☎ (4112) 45 32 44 Tx: 111135 splav Fax: (4112) 49 76 16 SITA: n/a

F: 1995 ✈✈✈ n/a Head: n/a Net: n/a

☐ RA-27004	Mil Mi-8AMT		CCCP-27004	0091		2 IS TV3-117MT	13000	Utility		

ENKOR, Joint-Stock Company = 5Z / ENK (Associated with Chelyabinsk Air Enterprise) **Moscow-Domodedovo**

Ul. Priorova 2A, 125299 Moskva, Russia ☎ (095) 450 62 24 Tx: none Fax: (095) 450 08 00 SITA: n/a

F: 1997 ✈✈✈ n/a Head: Oleg Bolshedvorsky IATA: 816 ICAO: ENKOR Net: n/a

☐ RA-85514	Tupolev 154B-2	514	CCCP-85514	1081	0098	3 KU NK-8-2U	100000	C26Y102		
☐ RA-85724	Tupolev 154M	906	EW-85724	0092	0098	3 SO D-30KU-154-II	100000	C26Y102		

ETELEAIR Air Company, Ltd = ETO **Moscow-Bykovo & -Zhukovsky**

Ul. Bolshaya Pochtovaya 18/20, Bldg 5, 107082 Moskva, Russia ☎ (095) 234 17 54 Tx: none Fax: (095) 267 69 91 SITA: n/a

F: 1996 ✈✈✈ n/a Head: Vladimir T. Lyashchenko ICAO: ETELEAIR Net: n/a

☐ RA-87280	Yakovlev 40	9322025	CCCP-87280	0073	0096	3 IV AI-25	16800	VIP		
☐ RA-11117	Antonov 12BP	402707	CCCP-11117	0065	0098	4 IV AI-20M	61000	Freighter		

536 registration type of aircraft cn/fn ex/ex* mfd del powered by mtow kg configuration selcal name/fln/specialitites/remarks

EURASIA Air Company = EUS

Moscow-Bykovo

Shmitovsky proezd 2, Room 413, 123100 Moskva, Russia ☎ (095) 319 82 54 Tx: none Fax: (095) 319 82 54 SITA: n/a
F: 1997 n/a Head: Rustam N. Khakimov ICAO: EURASIA Net: n/a Operates passenger flights with Yakovlev 40, currently leased from other companies when required.

EXPRESS, Joint-Stock Company = PSR

Moscow-Domodedovo

Bul. Sireneviy 21, 105425 Moskva, Russia ☎ (095) 164 56 51 Tx: none Fax: (095) 164 56 06 SITA: n/a
F: 1995 n/a Head: Nikolai A. Bomko ICAO: EXAVIA Net: n/a

RA-11530	Antonov 12BP	6344503	CCCP-11530	0066	0097	4 IV AI-20M	61000	Freighter		
RA-76372	Ilyushin 76T	073410279	CCCP-86723	0277	0096	4 SO D-30KP	175000	Freighter		
RA-76708	Ilyushin 76MD	0063473171	CCCP-76708	0086	0095	4 SO D-30KP	190000	Freighter		

FAR EASTERN CARGO AIRLINES = FEW (Dal'nevostochnye gruzovie avialinii)

Khabarovsk

Ul. Marsovaya 8, 680011 Khabarovsk, Russia ☎ (4212) 22 73 81 Tx: n/a Fax: (4212) 71 31 01 SITA: n/a
F: 1993 n/a Head: Sergey A. Samoilov ICAO: EASTERN CARGO Net: n/a Beside aircraft listed, also operates Ilyushin 76, leased from other companies when required.

RA-86566	Ilyushin 62M	4255152		1292	1093	4 SO D-30KU	167000	F12CY120		lst/opf AFL in AFL cs / fn 5505
RA-86931	Ilyushin 62M	3344724	C9-BAE	0983		4 SO D-30KU	167000	Y168		fn 4402

FLIGHT Air Company = FLV (Aviakompania Flait)

Moscow & Astrakhan

Ul. Zhelyabova 53a, 414000 Astrakhan, Russia ☎ (8512) 22 55 44 Tx: none Fax: (8512) 22 55 44 SITA: n/a
F: 1995 n/a Head: Vladimir L. Rezhets ICAO: BELOUGA Net: n/a

RA-25601	Mil Mi-8T	99150428	CCCP-25601	0091	0097	2 IS TV2-117A	12000	Utility		

GAZPROMAVIA, Ltd = GZP (Member of Gazprom Group)

Moscow-VKO/Kaluga/Perm/Samara-Smyshlaevka/Ukhta & Yugorsk

Ul. Nametkina 16, 117884 Moskva, Russia ☎ (095) 719 18 30 Tx: none Fax: (095) 719 11 85 SITA: MOWFUOC
F: 1995 n/a Head: Vladimir S. Krasnov ICAO: GAZPROM Net: n/a

RA-19427	Kamov Ka-26	7706208	CCCP-19427	1077	0098	2 VE M-14V-26	3250	Y6 / Utility		
RA-19430	Kamov Ka-26	7706211	CCCP-19430	1177	0497	2 VE M-14V-26	3250	Y6 / Utility		
RA-19434	Kamov Ka-26	7706215	CCCP-19434	1177	0497	2 VE M-14V-26	3250	Y6 / Utility		
RA-19489	Kamov Ka-26	7404104	CCCP-19489	0374	0497	2 VE M-14V-26	3250	Y6 / Utility		
RA-19537	Kamov Ka-26	7404611	CCCP-19537	1074	0497	2 VE M-14V-26	3250	Y6 / Utility		
RA-19538	Kamov Ka-26	7404612	CCCP-19538	1074	0497	2 VE M-14V-26	3250	Y6 / Utility		
RA-19540	Kamov Ka-26	7404614	CCCP-19540	1074	0497	2 VE M-14V-26	3250	Y6 / Utility		
RA-19552	Kamov Ka-26	7404711	CCCP-19552	1274	0497	2 VE M-14V-26	3250	Y6 / Utility		
RA-19584	Kamov Ka-26	7504911	CCCP-19584	0576	0497	2 VE M-14V-26	3250	Y6 / Utility		
RA-19604	Kamov Ka-26	7505005	CCCP-19604	0375	0497	2 VE M-14V-26	3250	Y6 / Utility		
RA-19639	Kamov Ka-26	7506304	CCCP-19639	1275	0497	2 VE M-14V-26	3250	Y6 / Utility		
RA-19648	Kamov Ka-26	7605320	CCCP-19648	0176	0497	2 VE M-14V-26	3250	Y6 / Utility		
RA-24306	Kamov Ka-26	7706008	CCCP-24306	0577	0497	2 VE M-14V-26	3250	Y6 / Utility		
RA-24316	Kamov Ka-26	7706018	CCCP-24316	0777	0497	2 VE M-14V-26	3250	Y6 / Utility		
RA-24335	Kamov Ka-26	7605315	CCCP-24335	0176	0497	2 VE M-14V-26	3250	Y6 / Utility		
RA-24363	Kamov Ka-26	7605708	CCCP-24363	1076	0497	2 VE M-14V-26	3250	Y6 / Utility		
RA-24370	Kamov Ka-26	7605717	CCCP-24370	1176	0497	2 VE M-14V-26	3250	Y6 / Utility		
RA-24371	Kamov Ka-26	7605718	CCCP-24371	1176	0497	2 VE M-14V-26	3250	Y6 / Utility		
RA-24373	Kamov Ka-26	7605720	CCCP-24373	1176	0497	2 VE M-14V-26	3250	Y6 / Utility		
RA-24378	Kamov Ka-26	7605810	CCCP-24378	1276	0497	2 VE M-14V-26	3250	Y6 / Utility		
RA-24382	Kamov Ka-26	7605814	CCCP-24382	0277	0497	2 VE M-14V-26	3250	Y6 / Utility		
RA-20947	PZL Swidnik (Mil) Mi-2	528647044	CCCP-20947	0584	0097	2 IS GTD-350-4	3550	Y8 / Utility		
RA-23740	PZL Swidnik (Mil) Mi-2	5410638068		0688	0098	2 IS GTD-350-4	3550	Y8 / Utility		
RA-23741	PZL Swidnik (Mil) Mi-2	5410639068		0688	0098	2 IS GTD-350-4	3550	Y8 / Utility		
RA-23742	PZL Swidnik (Mil) Mi-2	5410640068		0688	0097	2 IS GTD-350-4	3550	Y8 / Utility		
RA-23743	PZL Swidnik (Mil) Mi-2	5410641078		0788	0097	2 IS GTD-350-4	3550	Y8 / Utility		
RA-23748	PZL Swidnik (Mil) Mi-2	549225055	CCCP-23748	0585	0097	2 IS GTD-350-4	3550	Y8 / Utility		
RA-67693	Let 410UVP-E	952624		0495	0497	2 WA M-601E	6400	Y17		
RA-67694	Let 410UVP-E	952625		0595	0497	2 WA M-601E	6400	Y17		
RA-06106	Mil Mi-8T	4589	CCCP-06106	0874	0098	2 IS TV2-117A	12000	Freighter		
RA-06162	Mil Mi-8T	98943931		1289	0097	2 IS TV2-117A	12000	Freighter		
RA-22844	Mil Mi-8PS	7645	CCCP-22844	0679	0497	2 IS TV2-117A	11550	VIP C9		
RA-22952	Mil Mi-8MTV-1	96188		1094	0797	2 IS TV3-117VM	13000	Y22 / Utility		
RA-22962	Mil Mi-8T	99357695		0395	0097	2 IS TV2-117A	12000	Freighter		
RA-22963	Mil Mi-8T	99457734		0395	0097	2 IS TV2-117A	12000	Freighter		
RA-22964	Mil Mi-8T	99357706		0295	0097	2 IS TV2-117A	12000	Freighter		
RA-22965	Mil Mi-8T	99357303		0695	0097	2 IS TV2-117A	12000	Freighter		
RA-22967	Mil Mi-8AMT	59489614234		0696	0097	2 IS TV3-117MT	13000	Y22 / Utility		
RA-24019	Mil Mi-8MTV-1	312M82		1192	0797	2 IS TV3-117MT	13000	Y22 / Utility		
RA-25382	Mil Mi-8T	98208118	CCCP-24382	0882	0099	2 IS TV2-117A	12000	Freighter		
RA-25410	Mil Mi-8MTV-1	96126		0493	0098	2 IS TV3-117MT	13000	Y22 / Utility		
RA-25411	Mil Mi-8MTV-1	96127		0493	0098	2 IS TV3-117MT	13000	Y22 / Utility		
RA-25412	Mil Mi-8MTV-1	96148		0793	0098	2 IS TV3-117MT	13000	Y22 / Utility		
RA-25616	Mil Mi-8T	99150834	CCCP-25616	0691	0097	2 IS TV2-117A	12000	Freighter		
RA-25776	Mil Mi-8MTV-1	96103		0393	0098	2 IS TV3-117MT	13000	Y22 / Utility		
RA-25794	Mil Mi-8MTV-1	96203		0295	0797	2 IS TV3-117VM	13000	Y22 / Utility		
RA-25798	Mil Mi-8MTV-1	96009		0992	0797	2 IS TV3-117VM	13000	Y22 / Utility		
RA-25799	Mil Mi-8MTV-1	96010		0992	0797	2 IS TV3-117VM	13000	Y22 / Utility		
RA-25800	Mil Mi-8MTV-1	96012		0992	0797	2 IS TV3-117VM	13000	Y22 / Utility		
RA-27077	Mil Mi-8MTV-1	95915		0992	0797	2 IS TV3-117VM	13000	Y22 / Utility		
RA-27078	Mil Mi-8MTV-1	95916		0492	0797	2 IS TV3-117VM	13000	Y22 / Utility		
RA-27140	Mil Mi-8MTV-1	96202		0396	0797	2 IS TV3-117VM	13000	Y22 / Utility		
RA-27159	Mil Mi-8T	99257231		1092	0797	2 IS TV2-117A	12000	Y22 / Utility		
RA-27196	Mil Mi-8PS	8434	CCCP-27196	0183	0098	2 IS TV2-117A	11550	VIP C9		
RA-27197	Mil Mi-8MTV-1	96011		0092	0098	2 IS TV3-117MT	13000	Y22 / Utility		
RA-27199	Mil Mi-8MTV-1	95014		0092	0097	2 IS TV3-117MT	13000	Y22 / Utility		
RA-21505	Yakovlev 40K	9830159	CCCP-21505	0078	0098	3 IV AI-25	17200	VIP C14		
RA-88186	Yakovlev 40K	9620648	CCCP-88186	0876	0797	3 IV AI-25	17200	VIP C14		
RA-88300	Yakovlev 40K	9641451	OK-GEO	1276	0497	3 IV AI-25	17200	VIP C14		
RA-88306	Yakovlev 40K	9640651	OK-GEL	1176	0497	3 IV AI-25	17200	Y32		
RA-09000	Dassault Falcon 900B	118	F-GNFI	0493	0095	3 GA TFE731-5BR-1C	20640	Executive		
RA-09001	Dassault Falcon 900B	123	F-WWFL*	0394	0095	3 GA TFE731-5BR-1C	20640	Executive		
RA-74005	Antonov 74	36547094892	CCCP-74005	0492	0098	2 LO D-36	34800	Freighter		
RA-74008	Antonov 74T-100	36547095900	UR-74008	0492	0097	2 LO D-36	36500	Freighter		
RA-74012	Antonov 74D	36547098959		0296	0398	2 LO D-36	36500	VIP C12		
RA-74031	Antonov 74-200	36547098961	UN-74031	0894	0097	2 LO D-36	36500	Freighter		
RA-74032	Antonov 74-200	36547098962		1094	0096	2 LO D-36	36500	Freighter		
RA-74035	Antonov 74-200	36547098963		1294	0797	2 LO D-36	36850	Freighter		
RA-74036	Antonov 74-200	36547098965		1194	0797	2 LO D-36	36850	Freighter		
RA-74044	Antonov 74-200	36547097936	UN-74044	0694	0097	2 LO D-36	36500	Freighter		
RA-74045	Antonov 74-200	36547097938		0694	0097	2 LO D-36	36500	Freighter		
RA-74056	Antonov 74-200	36547098951		1095	0095	2 LO D-36	36500	Freighter		
RA-74058	Antonov 74-200	36547098956		1195	0095	2 LO D-36	36500	Freighter		
RA-74060	Antonov 74-200	36547098966		1194	0797	2 LO D-36	37500	Freighter		
RA-65045	Tupolev 134A	49500	CCCP-65045	0177	0398	2 SO D-30-II	49000	VIP C46		
RA-65983	Tupolev 134A-3	63350	CCCP-65983	0780	0498	2 SO D-30-III	49000	Y70		
RA-42436	Yakovlev 42D	4520421605018		0496	0096	3 LO D-36	57500	Y120		
RA-42437	Yakovlev 42D	4520423606018		0796	0096	3 LO D-36	57800	Y120		
RA-42438	Yakovlev 42D	4520423609018		0996	1196	3 LO D-36	57800	Y120 or Exec		
RA-42439	Yakovlev 42D					3 LO D-36	57800	Y120		oo-delivery 0099
RA-42451	Yakovlev 42D	4520422708018		0697	0097	3 LO D-36	57500	Y120 or Exec		
RA-85751	Tupolev 154M	933		1192	0096	3 SO D-30KU-154-II	100000	Y164		
RA-85774	Tupolev 154M	956		0493	0698	3 SO D-30KU-154-II	100000	Y164		
RA-85778	Tupolev 154M	962		0593	0097	3 SO D-30KU-154-II	100000	Y164		
RA-76370	Ilyushin 76TD	1033414458		0293	0096	4 SO D-30KP	191000	Freighter		
RA-76402	Ilyushin 76TD	1023413430		0992	0096	4 SO D-30KP	191000	Freighter		

GORNY ALTAI Aviakompania (formerly Aeroflot Gorno-Altaisk division)

Gorno-Altaisk

Gorno-Altaisk Airport, 659700 Gorno Altaisk, (Republic of Altai), Russia ☎ (385412) 21 96 Tx: n/a Fax: n/a SITA: n/a
F: n/a n/a Head: Valery P. Glukhovskikh Net: n/a

RA-87438	Yakovlev 40		CCCP-87438	0074		3 IV AI-25	16800	Y32		
RA-87802	Yakovlev 40	9230523	CCCP-87802	0072		3 IV AI-25	16800	Y32		

537 registration type of aircraft cn/fn ex/ex* mfd del powered by mtow kg configuration selcal name/fln/specialitites/remarks

GROMOV AIR = LII (Subs.of Flight Research Institute M.M.Gromov/LII-Lento-issledovalel'ski institut im.M.M. Gromova) — Moscow-Zhukovsky

LII im.M.M. Gromova, 140160 Zhukovsky, (Moscow Region), Russia ☎ (095) 556 54 33 Tx: 412710 sokol Fax: (095) 556 53 34 SITA: n/a
F: 1995 ⁂ n/a Head: Alexander V. Petrov ICAO: GROMOV AIR Net: n/a Operates non-commercial research & test flights & commercial charter flights. Most aircraft are still in Aeroflot colors with or without titles.

registration	type of aircraft	cn/fn	ex/ex*	mfd	del	powered by	mtow kg	configuration	selcal	name/fln/specialitites/remarks
☐ RA-87791	Yakovlev 40	9910203	CCCP-87791	0069		3 IV AI-25	16800	Y32		
☐ RA-88265	Yakovlev 40	9722052	CCCP-88265	0077		3 IV AI-25	16800	C18		
☐ RA-26038	Antonov 26	8002	CCCP-26038	0080		2 IV AI-24VT	24000	Combi		
☐ RA-64454	Tupolev 134A	66140	CCCP-64454	0083		2 SO D-30-II	49000	Research		
☐ RA-65562	Tupolev 134Sh	2350204	CCCP-65562	0072	0090	2 SO D-30-II	49000	Research		cvtd military aircraft
☐ RA-65740	Tupolev 134A	2351510	CCCP-65740	0072		2 SO D-30-II	49000	Research		
☐ RA-65926	Tupolev 134A	66101	CCCP-65926	0083	0097	2 SO D-30-II	49000	F6Y47		
☐ RA-65927	Tupolev 134A	66198	CCCP-65927	0083		2 SO D-30-II	49000	VIP		
☐ RA-65939	Tupolev 134A-3	1351409	LZ-TUU	0071		2 SO D-30-III	49000	Y72		cvtd Tu-134A
☐ RA-83962	Antonov 12BP	402210		0065		4 IV AI-20M	61600	Freighter		
☐ RA-78732	Ilyushin 18V	181004103	CCCP-78732	0061		4 IV AI-20M	61200	Y56		
☐ RA-85317	Tupolev 154M	317	CCCP-85317	0078		3 SO D-30KU-154-II	100000	Research/Testbed		cvtd 154B-2
☐ RA-85606	Tupolev 154M	701	CCCP-85606	0085		3 SO D-30KU-154-II	100000	Combi		
☐ RA-86674	Ilyushin 62	80304	CCCP-86674	0068		4 KU NK-8-4	161600	Y140		fn 0304
☐ RA-76528	Ilyushin 76T	073410293	CCCP-76528	0077		4 SO D-30KP	170000	Freighter		fn 0804
☐ RA-76623	Ilyushin 76MD		CCCP-76623	0084		4 SO D-30KP	190000	Research		
☐ RA-78738	Ilyushin 76TD	0033442247	YI-ALS	0083		4 SO D-30KP	190000	Freighter		fn 3202 / cvtd 76MD

HELICOPTERS MI (Vertolety Mi NPP) (Member of MAP Group) — Kazan

Ul. Tetsevskaya 20, 420112 Kazan, (Republic of Tatarstan), Russia ☎ (8432) 54 54 64 Tx: none Fax: (8432) 36 43 55 SITA: n/a
F: n/a ⁂ n/a Head: Alexander A. Talov Net: n/a Operates Mil Mi-8 & Mi-8MTV-1 helicopters. Full details not yet known.

IAPO - Irkutskoe aviatsionnoe PO Irkut-Avia (Flying division of Irkutsk Aircraft Production Factory / Member of MAP Group) — Irkutsk 2

Ul. Novatorov 3, 664020 Irkutsk 20, Russia ☎ (3952) 42 11 68 Tx: n/a Fax: (3952) 33 60 06 SITA: n/a
F: 1934 ⁂ n/a Head: Alexei I. Doroshchenko Net: n/a Operates corporate flights for itself & commercial charter flights. Aircraft are still in Aeroflot colors with or without titles.

registration	type of aircraft	cn/fn	ex/ex*	mfd	del	powered by	mtow kg	configuration	selcal	name/fln/specialitites/remarks
☐ RA-26187	Antonov 24T	0911308	CCCP-26187	0070	0070	2 IV AI-24VT	22500	Combi		
☐ RA-69354	Antonov 32	1606	CCCP-69354	0088	0089	2 IV AI-20D	27000	Combi		
☐ RA-69355	Antonov 32	1607	CCCP-69355	0088	0089	2 IV AI-20D	27000	Combi		
☐ RA-65934	Tupolev 134A-3	66143	CCCP-65934	0083	0083	2 SO D-30-III	49000	Combi		
☐ RA-93929	Tupolev 134A-3	1351206	YU-AJA	0071	0091	2 SO D-30-III	49000	Combi		
☐ RA-11309	Antonov 12	00347510	CCCP-11309	0070	0092	4 IV AI-20M	61000	Combi		
☐ RA-12162	Antonov 12BP	3341509	CCCP-12162	0063	0089	4 IV AI-20M	61000	Combi		
☐ RA-13391	Antonov 12	5342805	CCCP-13391	0065	0091	4 IV AI-20M	61000	Combi		

IDF - Iron Dragonfly = IDF — Kazan-International

PO Box 652, 420044 Kazan, (Republic of Tatarstan), Russia ☎ (8432) 76 94 75 Tx: none Fax: (8432) 76 94 95 SITA: n/a
F: 1993 ⁂ n/a Head: Oleg M. Gorlik Net: n/a

registration	type of aircraft	cn/fn	ex/ex*	mfd	del	powered by	mtow kg	configuration	selcal	name/fln/specialitites/remarks
☐ RA-85358	Tupolev 154B-2	358	CCCP-85358	0779	0096	3 KU NK-8-2U	100000	Y164		Tatarstan IDF-titles
☐ RA-85842	Tupolev 154B-2	420	0420	0780	0598	3 KU NK-8-2U	100000	Y140		
☐ RA-76495	Ilyushin 76T	073410292	ST-SFT	0077	0097	4 SO D-30KP	170000	Freighter		fn 0803

IGAP -Ivanovskoe gosudarstvennoe aviapredpriatie = IGP (Ivanovo Air Enterprise) (formerly part of Central Districts Airline & AFL Ivanovo division) — Ivanovo-Zhukovka

Ivanovo Airport, 153041 Ivanovo, Russia ☎ (0932) 29 48 69 Tx: none Fax: (0932) 23 42 89 SITA: n/a
F: n/a ⁂ n/a Head: Vadim D. Gladyshev ICAO: AIR IGAP Net: n/a Most aircraft are still in Aeroflot colors but will be repainted in due course.

registration	type of aircraft	cn/fn	ex/ex*	mfd	del	powered by	mtow kg	configuration	selcal	name/fln/specialitites/remarks
☐ RA-46341	Antonov 24B	97305609	CCCP-46341	0069		2 IV AI-24	21000	Y48		
☐ RA-46351	Antonov 24B	97305710	CCCP-46351	0069		2 IV AI-24	21000	Y48		
☐ RA-46355	Antonov 24B	07305805	CCCP-46355	0070		2 IV AI-24	21000	Y48		
☐ RA-46393	Antonov 24B		CCCP-46393	0070		2 IV AI-24	21000	Y48		
☐ RA-46663	Antonov 24RV		CCCP-46663	0074		2 IV AI-24VT	21800	Y48		
☐ RA-47813	Antonov 24RV	17307006	CCCP-47813	0071		2 IV AI-24VT	21800	Y48		
☐ RA-65550	Tupolev 134A-3	66200	CCCP-65550	0083		2 SO D-30-III	49000	Y76		lst SFD
☐ RA-65722	Tupolev 134A-3	66420	CCCP-65722	0084		2 SO D-30-III	49000	Agri research		
☐ RA-65725	Tupolev 134A-3	66472	CCCP-65725	0084		2 SO D-30-III	49000	Agri research		
☐ RA-65756	Tupolev 134A-3	62179	CCCP-65756	0079		2 SO D-30-III	49000	Y76		
☐ RA-65928	Tupolev 134A-3	66491	CCCP-65928	0084		2 SO D-30-III	49000	Agri Research		

IKAR (Ikar, TOO) — Magadan

Ul. Gagarina 9a, Room 2, 685024 Magadan, Russia ☎ (41322) 35 285 Tx: n/a Fax: (41322) 24 515 SITA: n/a
F: n/a ⁂ n/a Head: Sergey V. Izyumov Net: n/a

registration	type of aircraft	cn/fn	ex/ex*	mfd	del	powered by	mtow kg	configuration	selcal	name/fln/specialitites/remarks
☐ RA-24735	Mil Mi-8		CCCP-22735	0084		2 IS TV2-117A	12000	Utility		

ILAVIA Airlines, Joint-Stock Company = ILV (Sister company of Ilyushin Design Bureau) — Moscow-Zhukovsky

PO Box 100, 125438 Moskva, Russia ☎ (095) 456 65 91 Tx: none Fax: (095) 456 65 91 SITA: n/a
F: 1994 ⁂ n/a Head: Emil G. Akopyan ICAO: ILAVIA Net: n/a

registration	type of aircraft	cn/fn	ex/ex*	mfd	del	powered by	mtow kg	configuration	selcal	name/fln/specialitites/remarks
☐ RA-76473	Ilyushin 76TD	0033448404	CCCP-76473	1083	0095	4 SO D-30KP	190000	Freighter 50t		lst IRH as EP-ALG
☐ RA-76474	Ilyushin 76TD	0033448407	CCCP-76474	0983	0095	4 SO D-30KP	190000	Freighter 50t		lst IRH as EP-ALF
☐ RA-76477	Ilyushin 76TD	0043453575	CCCP-76477	0784	0095	4 SO D-30KP	190000	Freighter 50t		lst IRH as EP-ALE
☐ RA-76516	Ilyushin 76T	093418556	CCCP-76516	0079	0097	4 SO D-30KP	170000	Freighter 40t		fn 1409
☐ RA-76519	Ilyushin 76T	093420599	CCCP-76519	0079	0096	4 SO D-30KP	170000	Freighter 40t		
☐ RA-76712	Ilyushin 76MD	0063473190	CCCP-76712	0086	0098	4 SO D-30KP	190000	Freighter 50t		
☐ RA-76735	Ilyushin 76TD	0073476314	CCCP-76735	0087	0098	4 SO D-30KP	190000	Freighter 50t		cvtd 76MD
☐ RA-76737	Ilyushin 76MD	0073477323	CCCP-76737	0087	0097	4 SO D-30KP	190000	Freighter 50t		
☐ RA-76818	Ilyushin 76TD	1013408264	CCCP-76818	0091	0098	4 SO D-30KP	190000	Freighter 50t		
☐ RA-78792	Ilyushin 76TD	0093490718	CCCP-78792	0089	0096	4 SO D-30KP	190000	Freighter 50t		

IRS AERO, Joint-Stock Company = LDF — Moscow-Zhukovsky

Leningradsky prospekt 37/1, 125836 Moskva, Russia ☎ (095) 155 62 11 Tx: none Fax: (095) 155 59 63 SITA: n/a
F: 1997 ⁂ n/a Head: Vladimir A. Kotelnikov ICAO: ELBRUS Net: n/a

registration	type of aircraft	cn/fn	ex/ex*	mfd	del	powered by	mtow kg	configuration	selcal	name/fln/specialitites/remarks
☐ RA-75598	Ilyushin 18V	186008802	CCCP-75598	0066	0097	4 IV AI-20M	64000	Freighter		

IRTYSHAVIATRANS (Sister company of Tyumenaviatrans) — Tobolsk

Tobolsk Airport, 626100 Tobolsk, (Tyumen Region), Russia ☎ (34511) 62 652 Tx: none Fax: (34511) 62 652 SITA: n/a
F: n/a ⁂ n/a Head: Alexander G. Selyukov Net: n/a

registration	type of aircraft	cn/fn	ex/ex*	mfd	del	powered by	mtow kg	configuration	selcal	name/fln/specialitites/remarks
☐ RA-20875	PZL Swidnik (Mil) Mi-2	528236063	CCCP-20875	0083		2 IS GTD-350-4	3550	Utility		
☐ RA-23311	PZL Swidnik (Mil) Mi-2	529142045	CCCP-23311	0085		2 IS GTD-350-4	3550	Utility		
☐ RA-23428	PZL Swidnik (Mil) Mi-2	529343085	CCCP-23428	0085		2 IS GTD-350-4	3550	Utility		
☐ RA-23562	PZL Swidnik (Mil) Mi-2	526201069	CCCP-23562	0079		2 IS GTD-350-4	3550	Utility		
☐ RA-23810	PZL Swidnik (Mil) Mi-2					2 IS GTD-350-4	3550	Utility		
☐ RA-23811	PZL Swidnik (Mil) Mi-2					2 IS GTD-350-4	3550	Utility		
☐ RA-01491	PZL Mielec (Antonov) An-2		CCCP-01491	0088		1 SH ASh-62IR	5500	Utility		
☐ RA-70540	PZL Mielec (Antonov) An-2		CCCP-70540	0073		1 SH ASh-62IR	5500	Utility		
☐ RA-22208	Mil Mi-8		CCCP-22208	0077		2 IS TV2-117A	12000	Utility		
☐ RA-22618	Mil Mi-8		CCCP-22618	0079		2 IS TV2-117A	12000	Utility		
☐ RA-25164	Mil Mi-8T		CCCP-25164	0090		2 IS TV2-117A	12000	Utility		

IZHAVIA = IZA (Izhevskie avialinii / Izhevsk Airlines) (formerly Izhevsk Air Enterprise / Izhevsk division of Aeroflot) — Izhevsk

Izhevsk Airport, 426015 Izhevsk, (Republic of Udurmutia), Russia ☎ (3412) 31 16 75 Tx: none Fax: (3412) 78 05 43 SITA: n/a
F: n/a ⁂ n/a Head: Valter F. Krauter ICAO: IZHAVIA Net: n/a Most aircraft are still in Aeroflot colors but will be repainted in due course.

registration	type of aircraft	cn/fn	ex/ex*	mfd	del	powered by	mtow kg	configuration	selcal	name/fln/specialitites/remarks
☐ RA-06260	PZL Mielec (Antonov) An-2		CCCP-06260	0071		1 SH ASh-62IR	5500	Utility		
☐ RA-07350	PZL Mielec (Antonov) An-2		CCCP-07350	0073		1 SH ASh-62IR	5500	Utility		
☐ RA-09645	PZL Mielec (Antonov) An-2		CCCP-09645	0066		1 SH ASh-62IR	5500	Utility		
☐ RA-46620	Antonov 24RV	37308707	CCCP-46620	0073		2 IV AI-24VT	21800	Y48		
☐ RA-46637	Antonov 24RV	37308903	CCCP-46637	0073		2 IV AI-24VT	21800	Y48		
☐ RA-46805	Antonov 24B		CCCP-46805	0065		2 IV AI-24	21000	Y48		
☐ RA-47173	Antonov 24B		CCCP-47173	0068		2 IV AI-24	21000	Y48		
☐ RA-26529	Antonov 26		CCCP-26529	0078		2 IV AI-24VT	24000	Freighter		
☐ RA-26669	Antonov 26	8202	CCCP-26669	0079		2 IV AI-24VT	24000	Freighter		
☐ RA-26683	Antonov 26		CCCP-26683	0079		2 IV AI-24VT	24000	Freighter		
☐ RA-65002	Tupolev 134A-3	44020	CCCP-65002	0075		2 SO D-30-III	49000	Y76		
☐ RA-65056	Tupolev 134A-3	49860	CCCP-65056	0077		2 SO D-30-III	49000	Y76		
☐ RA-65141	Tupolev 134A-3	60945	CCCP-65141	0078		2 SO D-30-III	49000	Y76		
☐ RA-65842	Tupolev 134A	18121	CCCP-65842	0074		2 SO D-30-II	49000	Y76		
☐ RA-42450	Yakovlev 42D			0094	0097	3 LO D-36	56500	Y120		Udmurtia-titles

KALININGRADAVIA = K8 / KLN (Kaliningrad Air) (former Kaliningrad Air Enterprise & Aeroflot Kaliningrad division) — Kaliningrad-Khrabrovo

Khrabrovo Airport, 238315 Kaliningrad, Russia ☎ (0112) 45 94 11 Tx: none Fax: (0112) 45 95 80 SITA: n/a
F: 1976 n/a Head: Vladislav S. Filipenko IATA: 097 ICAO: KALININGRAD AIR Net: n/a Some aircraft are still in Aeroflot colors but will be repainted in due course.

☐ RA-65010	Tupolev 134A	46130	CCCP-65010	0376	0280	2 SO D-30-II	49000	Y76		
☐ RA-65011	Tupolev 134A-3	46140	CCCP-65011	0276	0178	2 SO D-30-III	49000	Y76		
☐ RA-65019	Tupolev 134A	48375	CCCP-65019	0476	1276	2 SO D-30-II	49000	Y76		
☐ RA-65027	Tupolev 134A	48485	CCCP-65027	0676	0584	2 SO D-30-II	49000	Y76		
☐ RA-65054	Tupolev 134A-3	49840	CCCP-65054	0277	0377	2 SO D-30-III	49000	Y76		
☐ RA-65087	Tupolev 134A	60155	CCCP-65087	1277	0986	2 SO D-30-II	49000	Y76		
☐ RA-65090	Tupolev 134A	60185	CCCP-65090	1277	1188	2 SO D-30-II	49000	Y76		
☐ RA-65824	Tupolev 134A-3	09074	HA-LBS	0674	1078	2 SO D-30-III	49000	Y76		
☐ RA-65845	Tupolev 134A	23131	CCCP-65845	1174	0279	2 SO D-30-II	49000	Y76		
☐ RA-65870	Tupolev 134A-3	28310	CCCP-65870	0475	0678	2 SO D-30-III	49000	Y76		
☐ RA-85788	Tupolev 154M	972	EP-ITS	0993	0993	3 SO D-30KU-154-II	100000	Y166		
☐ RA-85789	Tupolev 154M	973		0993	0993	3 SO D-30KU-154-II	100000	Y166		

KAMCHATSKIE AVIALINII (Kamchatka Airlines) — Yelizovo Heliport

Ul. Podstantsionnaya 5a, 684010 Yelizovo, (Kamchatka Region), Russia ☎ (4152) 11 17 44 Tx: none Fax: (4152) 11 17 44 SITA: n/a
F: 1992 n/a Head: Nikolai G. Batishchev Net: n/a

☐ RA-22536	Mil Mi-8T	9765123		0076	0096	2 IS TV2-117A	12000	Utility		
☐ RA-22643	Mil Mi-8T	8028	CCCP-22643	0080	0097	2 IS TV2-117A	12000	Utility		
☐ RA-22740	Mil Mi-8T	98311054	CCCP-22740	0083	0097	2 IS TV2-117A	12000	Utility		
☐ RA-24402	Mil Mi-8T	98625131		0086	0097	2 IS TV2-117A	12000	Utility		
☐ RA-24744	Mil Mi-8T	98417949	CCCP-24744	0084	0094	2 IS TV2-117A	12000	Utility / Y24		
☐ RA-25612	Mil Mi-8T	9744414		0074	0092	2 IS TV2-117A	12000	Utility		
☐ RA-25817	Mil Mi-8T	9722114		0072	0095	2 IS TV2-117A	12000	Utility		

KAMCHATSKIE VITYAZI — Petropavlovsk Kamchatsky-Khalaktyrka

Ul. Toporkova 10, 683031 Petropavlovsk-Kamchatsky, Russia ☎ (41522) 58 340 Tx: n/a Fax: (41522) 58 340 SITA: n/a
F: n/a n/a Head: Mikhail I. Drobot Net: n/a

☐ RA-22368	Mil Mi-8		CCCP-22368	0077		2 IS TV2-117A	12000	22 Pax		

KAPO - Kazanskoe aviatsionnoe PO im. Gorbunova = KAO (Flying div. of Gorbunov Kazan Aviation Prod. Ass. / Member of MAP Group) — Kazan-Borisoglebskoe

Flying division / Letny otryad, Ul. Dementyeva, 420036 Kazan 36 (Republic of Tatarstan), Russia ☎ (8432) 54 00 02 Tx: none Fax: (8432) 54 36 93 SITA: n/a
F: n/a n/a Head: Vozikh M. Gaptrakhanov ICAO: KAZAVIA Net: n/a Operates corporate flights for itself & commercial charter flights. Aircraft are still in Aeroflot colors without titles or with Tatarstan flag.

☐ RA-87341	Yakovlev 40	9511039	CCCP-87341	0475		3 IV AI-25	16800	Executive		
☐ RA-87834	Yakovlev 40	9241125	CCCP-87834	1272		3 IV AI-25	16800	Executive		
☐ RA-26597	Antonov 26B	13310	CCCP-26597	1283		2 IV AI-24VT	24000	Combi		
☐ RA-13392	Antonov 12BK	00347210	CCCP-13392	0670		4 IV AI-20M	61000	Freighter		
☐ RA-93922	Antonov 12BK	8345403	CCCP-93922	1167		4 IV AI-20M	61000	Freighter		

KARAT, Joint-Stock Company = 2U / AKT (Aviakompania Karat) (formerly Rikor Aviakompania) — Moscow-Vnukovo

Prospekt Vernadskogo 37/2, 117415 Moskva, Russia ☎ (095) 938 19 92 Tx: none Fax: (095) 938 26 44 SITA: MOWTP7X
F: 1994 n/a Head: Viktor V. Mikheyev ICAO: AVIAKARAT Net: n/a

☐ RA-47361	Antonov 24RV	67310705	CCCP-47361	0076	0097	2 IV AI-24VT	21800	Y44		lsf Vladimir Air Enterprise
☐ RA-42333	Yakovlev 42	4520422606156	CCCP-42333	0486	0095	3 LO D-36	54000	Y120		lsf KAZ
☐ RA-42402	Yakovlev 42D	4520422116583	CCCP-42402	0091	0097	3 LO D-36	56500	Y120		lsf LIP
☐ RA-42427	Yakovlev 42D	4520422305016		0093		3 LO D-36	56500	Y120		lsf LIP
☐ RA-42528	Yakovlev 42D	11041003	CCCP-42528	0080	0096	3 LO D-36	56500	F8Y96		lsf UHS / cvtd 42
☐ RA-42539	Yakovlev 42	11140504	CCCP-42539	0082	0096	3 LO D-36	56500	F8Y96		lsf UHS
☐ RA-42543	Yakovlev 42	11250904	CCCP-42543	0085	0095	3 LO D-36	56500	F8Y96		lsf UHS

KATEKAVIA, Ltd = KTK — Sharypovo

Sharypovo Airport, 662320 Sharypovo, (Krasnayarsk Region), Russia ☎ (39153) 24 106 Tx: none Fax: (39153) 24 106 SITA: n/a
F: 1996 n/a Head: Sergei V. Rodkin ICAO: KATEKAVIA Net: n/a

☐ RA-46358	Antonov 24B	07305808	CCCP-46358	0070	0097	2 IV AI-24	21000	Y48		
☐ RA-46493	Antonov 24RV	27308206	CCCP-46493	0072	0097	2 IV AI-24VT	21800	Y48		

KAVKAZSKIE AVIATRASSY, Joint-Stock Company = KAV — Moscow-Vnukovo

Prospekt Vernadskogo 53, Druzhba Centre, Room 614, 117415 Moskva, Russia ☎ (095) 433 24 14 Tx: none Fax: (095) 433 24 14 SITA: n/a
F: 1998 n/a Head: Nikolai N. Kovalenko ICAO: KATRASS Net: n/a Operates regular passenger charter flights with Tupolev 134A aircraft, leased from other Russian companies (RA-) & Tajikistan Airlines (EY-), when required.

KAZAN AVIATION SPORT CLUB (Kazansky aviatsionno-sportivny klub) — Kazan 2

Ul. P. Lumumby 4, 420045 Kazan, (Republic of Tatarstan), Russia ☎ (8432) 76 51 42 Tx: none Fax: none SITA: n/a
F: n/a n/a Head: Radik I. Khaliullin Net: n/a

☐ RA-17790	PZL Mielec (Antonov) An-2	1G203-51	CCCP-17790	0683		1 SH ASh-62IR	5500	Utility/Trainer		
☐ RA-33602	PZL Mielec (Antonov) An-2	1G232-36	CCCP-33602	1188		1 SH ASh-62IR	5500	Utility/Trainer		
☐ RA-70781	PZL Mielec (Antonov) An-2	1G132-36	CCCP-70781	0971		1 SH ASh-62IR	5500	Utility/Trainer		

KAZAN 2nd Aviation Enterprise (Vtoroe Kazanskoe aviapredpriatie) (formerly Aeroflot 2nd Kazan division) — Kazan 2

Airport, Kazan 2, 420045 Kazan, (Republic of Tatarstan), Russia ☎ (8432) 76 50 22 Tx: none Fax: (8432) 76 80 55 SITA: n/a
F: n/a n/a Head: n/a Net: n/a Company will be renamed (KAZANAVIA is expected) in 1999.

☐ RA-23710	PZL Swidnik (Mil) Mi-2	5410516018	CCCP-23710	0288		2 IS GTD-350-4	3550	Utility		
☐ RA-23723	PZL Swidnik (Mil) Mi-2	548011013	CCCP-23723	0283		2 IS GTD-350-4	3550	Utility		
☐ RA-05807	PZL Mielec (Antonov) An-2	1G154-47	CCCP-05807	0274		1 SH ASh-62IR	5500	Utility		
☐ RA-07161	PZL Mielec (Antonov) An-2	1G145-37	CCCP-07161	0373		1 SH ASh-62IR	5500	Utility		
☐ RA-07656	PZL Mielec (Antonov) An-2	1G157-41	CCCP-07656	0674		1 SH ASh-62IR	5500	Utility		
☐ RA-16077	PZL Mielec (Antonov) An-2	1G165-01	CCCP-16077	0875		1 SH ASh-62IR	5500	Utility		
☐ RA-16082	PZL Mielec (Antonov) An-2	1G165-06	CCCP-16082	0875		1 SH ASh-62IR	5500	Freighter		
☐ RA-35693	PZL Mielec (Antonov) An-2	1G134-57	CCCP-35693	0871		1 SH ASh-62IR	5500	Utility		
☐ RA-40731	PZL Mielec (Antonov) An-2	1G172-03	CCCP-40731	1076		1 SH ASh-62IR	5500	Freighter		
☐ RA-40788	PZL Mielec (Antonov) An-2	1G173-15	CCCP-40788	0077		1 SH ASh-62IR	5500	Utility		
☐ RA-40878	PZL Mielec (Antonov) An-2	1G215-13	CCCP-40878	0885		1 SH ASh-62IR	5500	Utility		
☐ RA-54848	PZL Mielec (Antonov) An-2	1G184-55	CCCP-54848	0879		1 SH ASh-62IR	5500	Utility		
☐ RA-70211	PZL Mielec (Antonov) An-2	1G138-29	CCCP-70211	0172		1 SH ASh-62IR	5500	Utility		
☐ RA-70215	PZL Mielec (Antonov) An-2	1G138-33	CCCP-70215	0772		1 SH ASh-62IR	5500	Utility		
☐ RA-70574	PZL Mielec (Antonov) An-2	1G127-42	CCCP-70574	0671		1 SH ASh-62IR	5500	Utility		
☐ RA-70824	PZL Mielec (Antonov) An-2	1G133-27	CCCP-70824	1271		1 SH ASh-62IR	5500	Utility		
☐ RA-92984	PZL Mielec (Antonov) An-2	1G171-41	CCCP-92984	0976		1 SH ASh-62IR	5500	Utility		
☐ RA-67006	Let 410UVP	810607	CCCP-67006	0281		2 WA M-601D	5800	Y15		
☐ RA-67015	Let 410UVP	810616	CCCP-67015	0381		2 WA M-601D	5800	Y15		
☐ RA-67142	Let 410UVP	800408	CCCP-67142	0980		2 WA M-601D	5800	Y15		
☐ RA-67171	Let 410UVP	790207	CCCP-67171	0979		2 WA M-601D	5800	Y15		
☐ RA-67406	Let 410UVP	831034	CCCP-67406	0683		2 WA M-601D	5800	Y15		
☐ RA-67667	Let 410UVP-E	902408		0290	0097	2 WA M-601E	6400	Y19		
☐ RA-67668	Let 410UVP-E	902413		0390	0097	2 WA M-601E	6400	Y19		
☐ RA-67669	Let 410UVP-E	902409		0290	0097	2 WA M-601E	6400	Y19		
☐ RA-67670	Let 410UVP-E	902416		0390	0097	2 WA M-601E	6400	Y19		
☐ RA-67671	Let 410UVP-E	902410		0290	0097	2 WA M-601E	6400	Y19		
☐ RA-06171	Mil Mi-8T	98420128	CCCP-06171	1284		2 IS TV2-117A	12000	Utility		
☐ RA-22959	Mil Mi-8T	4734	CCCP-22959	0974		2 IS TV2-117A	12000	Utility		
☐ RA-25130	Mil Mi-8MTV	95746	CCCP-25130	0991		2 IS TV3-117MT-3	13000	VIP		
☐ RA-25408	Mil Mi-8T	98233135	CCCP-25408	0183		2 IS TV2-117A	12000	Utility		
☐ RA-27023	Mil Mi-8T	9754622	CCCP-27023	0475		2 IS TV2-117A	12000	Utility		
☐ RA-27198	Mil Mi-8MTV-1	96013		0992		2 IS TV3-117MT	13000	Utility		

KHAKASIA AIRLINES, Joint-Stock Company = BKN (Aviakompania Khakasia) (formerly Abakan Air Enterprise) — Abakan

Abakan Airport, 662608 Abakan, (Republic of Khakasia), Russia ☎ (39022) 63 061 Tx: none Fax: (39022) 50 588 SITA: n/a
F: 1993 n/a Head: Nikolai V. Metelkov ICAO: AIR ABAKAN Net: n/a Most aircraft are still in Aeroflot colors but will be repainted in due course,

☐ RA-15643	PZL Swidnik (Mil) Mi-2	5410114017	CCCP-15643	0087	0093	2 IS GTD-350-4	3550	Utility		
☐ RA-23398	PZL Swidnik (Mil) Mi-2	528908094	CCCP-23398	0984	0093	2 IS GTD-350-4	3550	Y6		
☐ RA-24489	Mil Mi-8T	98628960	CCCP-24489	1286	0093	2 IS TV2-117A	11300	Y22		
☐ RA-24611	Mil Mi-8T	8238	CCCP-24611	0581	0093	2 IS TV2-117A	11300	Y22		
☐ RA-25326	Mil Mi-8T	98203991	CCCP-25326	0382	0093	2 IS TV2-117A	11300	Y22		
☐ RA-46470	Antonov 24RV	27307908	CCCP-46470	0872	0093	2 IV AI-24VT	21800	Y48		
☐ RA-46497	Antonov 24RV	27308210	CCCP-46497	1272	0093	2 IV AI-24VT	21800	Y48		
☐ RA-46662	Antonov 24RV	47309410	CCCP-46662	0474	0093	2 IV AI-24VT	21800	Y48		
☐ RA-46683	Antonov 24RV	47309706	CCCP-46683	0874	0093	2 IV AI-24VT	21800	Y48		
☐ RA-85160	Tupolev 154B	160	CCCP-85160	0676	0093	3 KU NK-8-2U	100000	Y164		
☐ RA-85195	Tupolev 154B	195	CCCP-85195	0277	0093	3 KU NK-8-2U	100000	Y144		
☐ RA-85223	Tupolev 154B-1	223	CCCP-85223	0777	0093	3 KU NK-8-2U	100000	Y144		cvtd 154B
☐ RA-85676	Tupolev 154M	836	EP-MAM	0490	0093	3 SO D-30KU-154-II	100000	Y164		
☐ RA-85681	Tupolev 154M	848	EP-LAU	0990	0093	3 SO D-30KU-154-II	100000	Y164		lst SIB

539 registration type of aircraft cn/fn ex/EX* mfd del powered by mtow kg configuration selcal name/fln/specialitites/remarks

KHALAKTYRKA Aviakompania (Khalaktyrka Aircompany) (formerly Aeroflot Khalaktyrka division) Petropavlovsk Kamchatsky-Khalaktyrka

Ul. Nevelskogo 1, Airport, 683011 Petropavlovsk-Kamchatsky, Russia ☎ (41522) 76 925 Tx: none Fax: none SITA: n/a
F: 1942 ⁂ n/a Head: Alexander V. Posukhov Net: n/a Most aircraft are still in Aeroflot colors but will be repainted in due course.

☐ RA-17993	PZL Mielec (Antonov) An-2	1G210-17	CCCP-17993	1084	1184	1 SH ASh-62IR	5500	Utility		
☐ RA-40874	PZL Mielec (Antonov) An-2	1G215-09	CCCP-40874	0885	0885	1 SH ASh-62IR	5500	Utility		
☐ RA-44688	PZL Mielec (Antonov) An-2	1G88-15	CCCP-44688	1167	1267	1 SH ASh-62IR	5500	Utility		
☐ RA-28954	PZL Mielec (Antonov) An-28	1AJ009-20	CCCP-28954	0791	0891	2 GS TVD-10B	6500	Utility		
☐ RA-22213	Mil Mi-8T	6343	CCCP-22213	0277	1189	2 IS TV2-117A	12000	Utility		
☐ RA-22227	Mil Mi-8T	6357	CCCP-22227	0376	0676	2 IS TV2-117A	12000	Utility		
☐ RA-22592	Mil Mi-8T	7886	CCCP-22592	1279	1279	2 IS TV2-117A	12000	Utility		
☐ RA-24114	Mil Mi-8T	98839711	CCCP-24114	0788	0788	2 IS TV2-117A	12000	Utility		
☐ RA-24115	Mil Mi-8T	98839750	CCCP-24115	0688	0788	2 IS TV2-117A	12000	Utility		
☐ RA-24198	Mil Mi-8T	98943817	CCCP-24198	1089	1089	2 IS TV2-117A	12000	Utility		
☐ RA-24253	Mil Mi-8T	98734031	CCCP-24253	0787	0987	2 IS TV2-117A	12000	Utility		
☐ RA-24408	Mil Mi-8T	98625174	CCCP-24408	0286	0386	2 IS TV2-117A	12000	Utility		
☐ RA-24551	Mil Mi-8T	98522925	CCCP-24551	1085	1185	2 IS TV2-117A	12000	Utility		
☐ RA-24668	Mil Mi-8T	9815728	CCCP-24668	0681	0781	2 IS TV2-117A	12000	Utility		
☐ RA-25172	Mil Mi-8MTV-1	95481	CCCP-25172	0890	1090	2 IS TV3-117MT	13000	Utility		
☐ RA-25194	Mil Mi-8T	99047315	CCCP-25194	0690	0790	2 IS TV2-117A	12000	Utility		
☐ RA-25357	Mil Mi-8T	98206778	CCCP-25357	0782	0782	2 IS TV2-117A	12000	Utility		
☐ RA-25433	Mil Mi-8MTV-1	95574	CCCP-25433	1290	0391	2 IS TV3-117MT	13000	Utility		
☐ RA-25434	Mil Mi-8MTV-1	95575	CCCP-25434	1290	0491	2 IS TV3-117MT	13000	Utility		

KIRENSK AIR ENTERPRISE (Kirenskoe aviapredpriatie) (formerly Aeroflot Kirensk division) Kirensk

Ul. Ozernaya 9, 666710 Kirensk, (Irkutsk Region), Russia ☎ (39568) 21 345 Tx: none Fax: (39568) 21 345 SITA: n/a
F: 1943 ⁂ n/a Head: Viktor V. Chamovskikh Net: n/a Most aircraft are still in Aeroflot colors but will be repainted in due course.

☐ RA-02753	PZL Mielec (Antonov) An-2	1G125-31	CCCP-02753	0071		1 SH ASh-62IR	5500	Utility		
☐ RA-02771	PZL Mielec (Antonov) An-2	1G125-49	CCCP-02771	0071		1 SH ASh-62IR	5500	Utility		
☐ RA-07737	PZL Mielec (Antonov) An-2	1G159-12	CCCP-07737	0074		1 SH ASh-62IR	5500	Utility		
☐ RA-07774	PZL Mielec (Antonov) An-2	1G161-49	CCCP-07774	0075		1 SH ASh-62IR	5500	Utility		
☐ RA-07781	PZL Mielec (Antonov) An-2	1G161-56	CCCP-07781	0075		1 SH ASh-62IR	5500	Utility		
☐ RA-07851	PZL Mielec (Antonov) An-2	1G170-10	CCCP-07851	0076		1 SH ASh-62IR	5500	Utility		
☐ RA-07855	PZL Mielec (Antonov) An-2	1G170-14	CCCP-07855	0076		1 SH ASh-62IR	5500	Utility		
☐ RA-35038	PZL Mielec (Antonov) An-2	1G110-04	CCCP-35038	0069		1 SH ASh-62IR	5500	Utility		
☐ RA-35581	PZL Mielec (Antonov) An-2	1G115-32	CCCP-35581	0070		1 SH ASh-62IR	5500	Utility		
☐ RA-40915	PZL Mielec (Antonov) An-2	1G215-52	CCCP-40915	0085		1 SH ASh-62IR	5500	Utility		
☐ RA-56408	PZL Mielec (Antonov) An-2	1G180-38	CCCP-56408	0078		1 SH ASh-62IR	5500	Utility		
☐ RA-62571	PZL Mielec (Antonov) An-2	1G176-40	CCCP-62571	0077		1 SH ASh-62IR	5500	Utility		
☐ RA-62597	PZL Mielec (Antonov) An-2	1G177-44	CCCP-62597	0078		1 SH ASh-62IR	5500	Utility		
☐ RA-70571	PZL Mielec (Antonov) An-2	1G127-39	CCCP-70571	0071		1 SH ASh-62IR	5500	Utility		
☐ RA-96246	PZL Mielec (Antonov) An-2	1G72-30	CCCP-96246	0066		1 SH ASh-62IR	5500	Utility		
☐ RA-22247	Mil Mi-8T	6577	CCCP-22247	0076		2 IS TV2-117A	12000	Utility		
☐ RA-22648	Mil Mi-8T	8095	CCCP-22648	0080		2 IS TV2-117A	12000	Utility		
☐ RA-22875	Mil Mi-8T	98415757	CCCP-22875	0084		2 IS TV2-117A	12000	Utility		
☐ RA-24162	Mil Mi-8T	98941888	CCCP-24162	0089		2 IS TV2-117A	12000	Utility		
☐ RA-24192	Mil Mi-8T	98943711	CCCP-24192	0089		2 IS TV2-117A	12000	Utility		
☐ RA-24250	Mil Mi-8T	98730968	CCCP-24250	0087		2 IS TV2-117A	12000	Utility		
☐ RA-24731	Mil Mi-8T	98417546	CCCP-24731	0084		2 IS TV2-117A	12000	Utility		
☐ RA-25190	Mil Mi-8T	98943839	CCCP-25190	0089		2 IS TV2-117A	12000	Utility		
☐ RA-25191	Mil Mi-8T	98943845	CCCP-25191	0089		2 IS TV2-117A	12000	Utility		
☐ RA-25387	Mil Mi-8T	98208153	CCCP-25387	0082		2 IS TV2-117A	12000	Utility		

KIROV AIR ENTERPRISE = KTA (Kirovskoe aviapredpriatie) (formerly Aeroflot Kirov division) Kirov

Kirov Airport, 610009 Kirov, Russia ☎ (8332) 62 73 62 Tx: none Fax: (8332) 62 46 83 SITA: n/a
F: n/a ⁂ n/a Head: Alexander Ya. Solostey ICAO: VYATKA-AVIA Net: n/a Beside aircraft listed, also owns 40 Antonov 2, many of them stored & for sale. Most aircraft are still in Aeroflot colors but will be repainted in due course.

☐ RA-15211	PZL Swidnik (Mil) Mi-2	535815098	CCCP-15211	0078		2 IS GTD-350-4	3550	Utility		
☐ RA-20267	PZL Swidnik (Mil) Mi-2	527228071	CCCP-20267	0081		2 IS GTD-350-4	3550	Utility		
☐ RA-20564	PZL Swidnik (Mil) Mi-2	534635026	CCCP-20564	0086		2 IS GTD-350-4	3550	Utility		
☐ RA-20623	PZL Swidnik (Mil) Mi-2	535029126	CCCP-20623	0076		2 IS GTD-350-4	3550	Utility		
☐ RA-20705	PZL Swidnik (Mil) Mi-2	536813080	CCCP-20705	0080		2 IS GTD-350-4	3550	Utility		
☐ RA-20706	PZL Swidnik (Mil) Mi-2	536814080	CCCP-20706	0080		2 IS GTD-350-4	3550	Utility		
☐ RA-20894	PZL Swidnik (Mil) Mi-2	538333093	CCCP-20894	0083		2 IS GTD-350-4	3550	Utility		
☐ RA-23592	PZL Swidnik (Mil) Mi-2	534613016	CCCP-23592	0076		2 IS GTD-350-4	3550	Utility		
☐ RA-23593	PZL Swidnik (Mil) Mi-2	534614016	CCCP-23593	0076		2 IS GTD-350-4	3550	Utility		
☐ RA-46374	Antonov 24B	07306005	CCCP-46374	0470		2 IV AI-24	21000	Y48		
☐ RA-46382	Antonov 24B	07306105	CCCP-46382	0770		2 IV AI-24	21000	Y48		
☐ RA-46660	Antonov 24RV	47309307	CCCP-46660	0374		2 IV AI-24VT	21800	Y48		opf UN
☐ RA-47154	Antonov 24B	89901606	CCCP-47154	0668		2 IV AI-24	21000	Y48		
☐ RA-47295	Antonov 24RV	07306608	CCCP-47295	0171		2 IV AI-24VT	21800	Y48		lst MLI
☐ RA-47848	Antonov 24B	17307410	CCCP-47848	1271		2 IV AI-24	21000	Y48		
☐ RA-26101	Antonov 26B	11908	CCCP-26101	0282		2 IV AI-24VT	24000	Freighter		lst TKA
☐ RA-26664	Antonov 26	7905	CCCP-26664	0479		2 IV AI-24VT	24000	Combi		
☐ RA-26677	Antonov 26	8603	CCCP-26677	0879		2 IV AI-24VT	24000	Freighter		lst TKA
☐ RA-65035	Tupolev 134A-3	48590	CCCP-65035	0876		2 SO D-30-III	47000	Y76		
☐ RA-65060	Tupolev 134A	49872	CCCP-65060	0577		2 SO D-30-II	47000	Y76		
☐ RA-65137	Tupolev 134A-3	60890	CCCP-65137	1178		2 SO D-30-III	47000	Y76		

KMPO – Kazanskoe motorostroitel'noe proizvodstvennoe ob'yedinenie (Flying div.of Kazan Motors Prod.Ass./Member of MAP Group) Kazan-Borisoglebskoe

Flying division / Letny otryad, Ul. Dementyeva 1, 420036 Kazan 36 (Republic of Tatarstan), Russia ☎ (8432) 54 14 21 Tx: n/a Fax: (8432) 54 10 34 SITA: n/a
F: n/a ⁂ n/a Head: Yevgeni L. Balabanov Net: n/a Operates corporate flights for itself & commercial charter flights. Aircraft are still in Aeroflot colors without titles or with Tatarstan flag.

☐ RA-48110	Yakovlev 40	9230623	CCCP-48110	0972		3 IV AI-25	16800	Executive		
☐ RA-26212	Antonov 26B	14401	CCCP-26212	1285		2 IV AI-24VT	24000	Combi		
☐ RA-69309	Antonov 32	1605	CCCP-69309	0588		2 IV AI-20D	27000	Freighter		lst TCH

KMV – Kavkazskie Mineralnye Vody = KV / MVD (Kavminvodyavia) (formerly Min. Vody C.A.P.O. & Aeroflot Min. Vody prod. & flying unit) Mineralnye Vody

Mineralnye Vody Airport, 357310 Mineralny Vody 5, (Stavropol Region), Russia ☎ (86531) 77 000 Tx: 223226 brmv ru Fax: (86531) 31 828 SITA: n/a
F: n/a ⁂ 3360 Head: Vasili V. Babaskin IATA: 348 ICAO: AIR MINVODY Net: n/a Some aircraft are still in Aeroflot colors but will be repainted in due course.

☐ RA-65074	Tupolev 134A-3	49987	CCCP-65074	0077		2 SO D-30-III	49000	Y76		
☐ RA-65126	Tupolev 134A-3	60588	CCCP-65126	0078		2 SO D-30-III	49000	Y76		
☐ RA-65139	Tupolev 134A	60915	CCCP-65139	0078		2 SO D-30-II	49000	Y76		
☐ RA-65844	Tupolev 134A	18125	CCCP-65844	0074		2 SO D-30-II	49000	Y80		
☐ RA-65887	Tupolev 134A	36170	CCCP-65887	0075		2 SO D-30-II	49000	Y76		
☐ RA-85226	Tupolev 154B	226	CCCP-85226	0077		3 KU NK-8-2U	98000	Combi Y60&Cargo		
☐ RA-85303	Tupolev 154B-2	303	CCCP-85303	0078		3 KU NK-8-2U	98000	Y180		
☐ RA-85307	Tupolev 154B-2	307	CCCP-85307	0078		3 KU NK-8-2U	98000	Y180		
☐ RA-85330	Tupolev 154B-2	330	CCCP-85330	0079		3 KU NK-8-2U	98000	Y164		
☐ RA-85340	Tupolev 154B-2	340	CCCP-85340	0079		3 KU NK-8-2U	98000	Y164		
☐ RA-85371	Tupolev 154B-2	371	CCCP-85371	0079		3 KU NK-8-2U	98000	Y164		
☐ RA-85373	Tupolev 154B-2	373	CCCP-85373	0079		3 KU NK-8-2U	98000	Y164		
☐ RA-85382	Tupolev 154B-2	382	CCCP-85382	0079		3 KU NK-8-2U	98000	Y164		
☐ RA-85393	Tupolev 154B-2	393	CCCP-85393	0079		3 KU NK-8-2U	98000	F12Y120		
☐ RA-85457	Tupolev 154B-2	457	CCCP-85457	0080		3 KU NK-8-2U	98000	F12Y120		
☐ RA-85494	Tupolev 154B-2	494	CCCP-85494	0081		3 KU NK-8-2U	98000	Y164		
☐ RA-85715	Tupolev 154M	891	EP-LAI	0091	0091	3 SO D-30KU-154-II	100000	F12Y120		lst BON as EP-BOM
☐ RA-85722	Tupolev 154M	904	EP-ARH	0092		3 SO D-30KU-154-II	100000	F12Y120		lst BON as EP-BOJ
☐ RA-85746	Tupolev 154M	929	EP-LAD	0092		3 SO D-30KU-154-II	100000	Y166		lst BON as EP-BON
☐ RA-64016	Tupolev 204-100	1450742364016		0093	0398	2 SO PS-90A	103000	C36Y136		

KNAAPO – Komsomolsk-na-Amure aviatsionnoe PO im. Gagarina = KNM (Flying div. of Gagarin Aviation Prod. Ass. / Member of MAP Group) Komsomolsk-na-Amure-Dzemgi

Flying division / Letny otryad, Ul. Sovetskaya 1, 681014 Komsomolsk-na-Amure, Russia (Khabarovsk Region) ☎ (42172) 28 504 Tx: 141149 Fax: (42172) 29 851 SITA: n/a
F: n/a ⁂ n/a Head: Viktor P. Yevseyev ICAO: KNAAPO Net: n/a Operates flights for itself & commercial charter flights. Most aircraft are still in Aeroflot colors without titles.

☐ RA-06150	Mil Mi-8	98841531	CCCP-06150	1288	0088	2 IS TV2-117A	12000	Utility		
☐ RA-22154	Mil Mi-8	99357401		0193	0096	2 IS TV2-117A	12000	Utility		
☐ RA-22502	Mil Mi-8	99357419		0393	0096	2 IS TV2-117A	12000	Utility		
☐ RA-26185	Antonov 26	8303	CCCP-26185	0679	0079	2 IV AI-24VT	24000	Freighter		
☐ RA-48101	Antonov 32	2106	CCCP-48101	0989	0089	2 IV AI-20D	27000	Freighter		
☐ RA-48979	Antonov 32	1409	CCCP-48979	1287	0088	2 IV AI-20D	27000	Freighter		lst TCH
☐ RA-65564	Tupolev 134A-3	63165	CCCP-65564	0380	0084	2 SO D-30-III	47600	Combi		
☐ RA-93927	Tupolev 134A-3	2351508	YU-AJD	0372	0090	2 SO D-30-III	47600	Combi		
☐ RA-11125	Antonov 12BP	3341006	CCCP-11125	0263	0082	4 IV AI-20M	61000	Freighter		lst AYZ
☐ RA-11230	Antonov 12BP	5342708	LZ-BFA	0165	0085	4 IV AI-20M	61000	Freighter		

540 registration type of aircraft cn/fn ex/ex* mfd del powered by mtow kg configuration selcal name/fln/specialitites/remarks

registration	type of aircraft	cn/fn	ex/ex*	mfd	del	powered by	mtow kg	configuration	selcal	name/fln/specialitites/remarks
☐ RA-11789	Antonov 12BP	6343905	LZ-BFB	0466	0083	4 IV AI-20M	61000	Freighter		
☐ RA-48978	Antonov 12	9346410	CCCP-48978	1269	0080	4 IV AI-20M	61000	Freighter		
☐ RA-76409	Ilyushin 76TD	1023410355		1192	0093	4 SO D-30KP	190000	Freighter		lst AYZ
☐ RA-76425	Ilyushin 76TD	1003405167		0391	0093	4 SO D-30KP	190000	Freighter		lst AYZ

KODAAVIA

Nyagan'

Oktyabrsky Airport, 626250 pos. Oktyabrski, (Tyumen Region), Russia ☎ (34678) 22 525 Tx: none Fax: none SITA: n/a
F: n/a ☆☆☆ n/a Head: Viktor A. Pan'kov Net: n/a

registration	type of aircraft	cn/fn	ex/ex*	mfd	del	powered by	mtow kg	configuration	selcal	name/fln/specialitites/remarks
☐ RA-23729	PZL Swidnik (Mil) Mi-2					2 IS GTD-350-4	3550	Utility		
☐ RA-23730	PZL Swidnik (Mil) Mi-2		CCCP-23730			2 IS GTD-350-4	3550	Utility		
☐ RA-23731	PZL Swidnik (Mil) Mi-2		CCCP-23731			2 IS GTD-350-4	3550	Utility		
☐ RA-22277	Mil Mi-8		CCCP-22277	0076		2 IS TV2-117A	12000	Utility		lsf Uraiavia

KOLAVIA, Joint-Stock Company = 7K / KGL (Kogalymavia)

Kogalym & Surgut

Kogalym Airport, 626481 Kogalym, (Tyumen Region), Russia ☎ (34667) 23 101 Tx: none Fax: (34667) 29 695 SITA: SGCKIXH
F: 1993 ☆☆☆ n/a Head: Nikolai N. Zolnikov ICAO: KOGALYM Net: n/a

registration	type of aircraft	cn/fn	ex/ex*	mfd	del	powered by	mtow kg	configuration	selcal	name/fln/specialitites/remarks
☐ RA-22501	Mil Mi-8T	99357415		0193	0096	2 IS TV2-117A	12000	Utility		
☐ RA-22599	Mil Mi-8T	7895	CCCP-22599	1279	0998	2 IS TV2-117A	12000	Utility		
☐ RA-22641	Mil Mi-8T	8026	CCCP-22641	0780	0097	2 IS TV2-117A	12000	Utility		
☐ RA-25328	Mil Mi-8T	98203998	CCCP-25328	0482	0095	2 IS TV2-117A	12000	Utility		
☐ RA-25342	Mil Mi-8T	98206652	CCCP-25342	0582	0095	2 IS TV2-117A	12000	Utility		dmgd/std/to be repaired
☐ RA-25761	Mil Mi-8MTV-1	96073		0293	0093	2 IS TV3-117MT	13000	Utility		
☐ RA-25762	Mil Mi-8MTV-1	96074		0293	0093	2 IS TV3-117MT	13000	Utility		
☐ RA-65861	Tupolev 134A-3	1351407	EW-65861	1271	0499	2 SO D-30-III	49000	VIP or CY62		cvtd 134A
☐ RA-65942	Tupolev 134A-3	17103	HA-LBO	0074	0599	2 SO D-30-III	49000	Y76		cvtd 134A
☐ RA-65943	Tupolev 134A-3	12096	HA-LBN	0074	0599	2 SO D-30-III	49000	Y76		cvtd 134A
☐ RA-65944	Tupolev 134A-3	63580	HA-LBR	0080	0499	2 SO D-30-III	49000	CY68		cvtd 134A
☐ RA-85335	Tupolev 154B-2	335	CCCP-85335	0079	0798	3 KU NK-8-2U	98000	Y164		lsf TYM
☐ RA-85395	Tupolev 154B-2	395	UR-85395	0080	0097	3 KU NK-8-2U	98000	Y164		lsf LHS
☐ RA-85761	Tupolev 154M	944		0393		3 SO D-30KU-154-II	100000	Y166		
☐ RA-85784	Tupolev 154M	968		0793		3 SO D-30KU-154-II	100000	F12C18Y104		
☐ RA-85786	Tupolev 154M	970		1093	0397	3 SO D-30KU-154-II	100000	Y166		
☐ RA-85787	Tupolev 154M	971		0993		3 SO D-30KU-154-II	100000	Y166		
☐ RA-85801	Tupolev 154M	960	LZ-BTR	0793	0598	3 SO D-30KU-154-II	100000	Y166		

KOLPASHEVO AIR ENTERPRISE (Kolpashevskoe aviapredpriatie) (formerly Aeroflot Kolpashevo division)

Kolpashevo

Lazo 6, 636420 Kolpashevo, (Tomsk Region), Russia ☎ (38254) 75 200 Tx: n/a Fax: (38254) 23 761 SITA: n/a
F: n/a ☆☆☆ n/a Head: Kamil I. Kuzmin Net: n/a Beside aircraft listed, also operates Antonov 2. Full details not yet known. Most aircraft are still in Aeroflot colors but will be repain- ted in due course.

registration	type of aircraft	cn/fn	ex/ex*	mfd	del	powered by	mtow kg	configuration	selcal	name/fln/specialitites/remarks
☐ RA-14359	PZL Swidnik (Mil) Mi-2	535107017	CCCP-14359			2 IS GTD-350-4	3550	Utility		
☐ RA-14367	PZL Swidnik (Mil) Mi-2	535115027	CCCP-14367			2 IS GTD-350-4	3550	Utility		
☐ RA-14380	PZL Swidnik (Mil) Mi-2	525238067	CCCP-14380			2 IS GTD-350-4	3550	Utility		
☐ RA-14394	PZL Swidnik (Mil) Mi-2	535528028	CCCP-14394			2 IS GTD-350-4	3550	Utility		
☐ RA-20410	PZL Swidnik (Mil) Mi-2	529908086	CCCP-20410			2 IS GTD-350-4	3550	Utility		
☐ RA-20625	PZL Swidnik (Mil) Mi-2	535031126	CCCP-20625			2 IS GTD-350-4	3550	Utility		
☐ RA-23447	PZL Swidnik (Mil) Mi-2	539420095	CCCP-23447			2 IS GTD-350-4	3550	Utility		
☐ RA-28719	PZL Mielec (Antonov) An-28	1AJ007-04	CCCP-28719	0089		2 GS TVD-10B	6500	Y17		
☐ RA-28721	PZL Mielec (Antonov) An-28	1AJ007-06	CCCP-28721	0089		2 GS TVD-10B	6500	Y17		
☐ RA-28723	PZL Mielec (Antonov) An-28	1AJ007-08	CCCP-28723	0089		2 GS TVD-10B	6500	Y17		
☐ RA-28726	PZL Mielec (Antonov) An-28	1AJ007-11	CCCP-28726	0090		2 GS TVD-10B	6500	Y17		
☐ RA-28755	PZL Mielec (Antonov) An-28	1AJ005-01	CCCP-28755	0088		2 GS TVD-10B	6500	Y17		
☐ RA-28767	PZL Mielec (Antonov) An-28	1AJ004-16	CCCP-28767	0088		2 GS TVD-10B	6500	Y17		
☐ RA-28769	PZL Mielec (Antonov) An-28	1AJ004-18	CCCP-28769	0088		2 GS TVD-10B	6500	Y17		
☐ RA-28770	PZL Mielec (Antonov) An-28	1AJ004-19	CCCP-28770	0088		2 GS TVD-10B	6500	Y17		
☐ RA-28771	PZL Mielec (Antonov) An-28	1AJ004-20	CCCP-28771	0088		2 GS TVD-10B	6500	Y17		
☐ RA-28794	PZL Mielec (Antonov) An-28	1AJ006-02	CCCP-28794	0089		2 GS TVD-10B	6500	Y17		
☐ RA-28927	PZL Mielec (Antonov) An-28	1AJ008-14	CCCP-28927	0090		2 GS TVD-10B	6500	Y17		
☐ RA-28928	PZL Mielec (Antonov) An-28	1AJ008-15	CCCP-28928	0090		2 GS TVD-10B	6500	Y17		
☐ RA-28937	PZL Mielec (Antonov) An-28	1AJ009-03	CCCP-28937	0090		2 GS TVD-10B	6500	Y17		
☐ RA-28939	PZL Mielec (Antonov) An-28	1AJ009-05	CCCP-28939	0090		2 GS TVD-10B	6500	Y17		
☐ RA-28940	PZL Mielec (Antonov) An-28	1AJ009-06	CCCP-28940	0090		2 GS TVD-10B	6500	Y17		
☐ RA-22265	Mil Mi-8		CCCP-22265	0077		2 IS TV2-117A	12000	Utility		
☐ RA-22590	Mil Mi-8		CCCP-22590	0079		2 IS TV2-117A	12000	Utility		
☐ RA-22646	Mil Mi-8		CCCP-22646	0080		2 IS TV2-117A	12000	Utility		
☐ RA-22671	Mil Mi-8		CCCP-22671	0080		2 IS TV2-117A	12000	Utility		
☐ RA-22739	Mil Mi-8		CCCP-22739	0083		2 IS TV2-117A	12000	Utility		
☐ RA-22751	Mil Mi-8		CCCP-22751	0083		2 IS TV2-117A	12000	Utility		
☐ RA-22752	Mil Mi-8		CCCP-22752	0083		2 IS TV2-117A	12000	Utility		
☐ RA-22757	Mil Mi-8		CCCP-22757	0083		2 IS TV2-117A	12000	Utility		
☐ RA-22916	Mil Mi-8		CCCP-22916	0085		2 IS TV2-117A	12000	Utility		
☐ RA-24143	Mil Mi-8		CCCP-24143	0088		2 IS TV2-117A	12000	Utility		
☐ RA-24163	Mil Mi-8		CCCP-24163	0089		2 IS TV2-117A	12000	Utility		
☐ RA-24166	Mil Mi-8		CCCP-24166	0089		2 IS TV2-117A	12000	Utility		
☐ RA-24210	Mil Mi-8		CCCP-24210	0087		2 IS TV2-117A	12000	Utility		
☐ RA-24242	Mil Mi-8		CCCP-24242	0087		2 IS TV2-117A	12000	Utility		
☐ RA-24268	Mil Mi-8		CCCP-24268	0087		2 IS TV2-117A	12000	Utility		
☐ RA-24439	Mil Mi-8		CCCP-24439	0086		2 IS TV2-117A	12000	Utility		
☐ RA-24481	Mil Mi-8		CCCP-24481	0086		2 IS TV2-117A	12000	Utility		
☐ RA-24501	Mil Mi-8		CCCP-24501	0085		2 IS TV2-117A	12000	Utility		
☐ RA-24510	Mil Mi-8		CCCP-24510	0085		2 IS TV2-117A	12000	Utility		
☐ RA-24570	Mil Mi-8		CCCP-24570	0088		2 IS TV2-117A	12000	Utility		
☐ RA-24581	Mil Mi-8		CCCP-24581	0088		2 IS TV2-117A	12000	Utility		
☐ RA-24582	Mil Mi-8		CCCP-24582	0088		2 IS TV2-117A	12000	Utility		
☐ RA-24601	Mil Mi-8		CCCP-24601	0081		2 IS TV2-117A	12000	Utility		
☐ RA-24643	Mil Mi-8		CCCP-24643	0081		2 IS TV2-117A	12000	Utility		
☐ RA-24656	Mil Mi-8		CCCP-24656	0081		2 IS TV2-117A	12000	Utility		
☐ RA-24661	Mil Mi-8		CCCP-24661	0081		2 IS TV2-117A	12000	Utility		
☐ RA-24675	Mil Mi-8		CCCP-24675	0081		2 IS TV2-117A	12000	Utility		
☐ RA-24723	Mil Mi-8		CCCP-24723	0084		2 IS TV2-117A	12000	Utility		
☐ RA-24737	Mil Mi-8		CCCP-24737	0084		2 IS TV2-117A	12000	Utility		
☐ RA-25105	Mil Mi-8MTV-1		CCCP-25105	0091		2 IS TV3-117MT	13000	Utility		
☐ RA-25106	Mil Mi-8MTV-1		CCCP-25106	0091		2 IS TV3-117MT	13000	Utility		
☐ RA-25147	Mil Mi-8		CCCP-25147	0090		2 IS TV2-117A	12000	Utility		
☐ RA-25155	Mil Mi-8T		CCCP-25155	0090		2 IS TV2-117A	12000	Utitlity		
☐ RA-25192	Mil Mi-8		CCCP-25192	0090		2 IS TV2-117A	12000	Utility		
☐ RA-25457	Mil Mi-8MTV-1		CCCP-25457	0091		2 IS TV3-117MT	13000	Utility		
☐ RA-25493	Mil Mi-8MTV-1		CCCP-25493	0091		2 IS TV3-117MT	13000	Utility		
☐ RA-25850	Mil Mi-8		CCCP-25850	0075		2 IS TV2-117A	12000	Utility		
☐ RA-87232	Yakovlev 40	9531742	CCCP-87232	0075		3 IV AI-25	16800	Y32		
☐ RA-87493	Yakovlev 40		CCCP-87493	0075		3 IV AI-25	16800	Y32		
☐ RA-87494	Yakovlev 40		CCCP-87494	0075		3 IV AI-25	16800	Y32		
☐ RA-87984	Yakovlev 40	9540744	CCCP-87984	0075		3 IV AI-25	16800	Y32		
☐ RA-88164	Yakovlev 40	9611846	CCCP-88164	0076		3 IV AI-25	16800	Y32		

KOMIAVIATRANS = KMA (formerly part of Komiavia & Aeroflot Komi directorate)

Syktyvkar / Pechora / Ukhta & Vorkuta

Ul. Sovetskaya 67, 167610 Syktyvkar, (Republic of Komi), Russia ☎ (8212) 42 26 01 Tx: 181288 centr ru Fax: (8212) 42 11 96 SITA: n/a
F: 1967 ☆☆☆ n/a Head: Anatoly K. Zatsepin ICAO: KOMIAVIA Net: n/a Some aircraft are still in Aeroflot colors but will be repainted in due course.

registration	type of aircraft	cn/fn	ex/ex*	mfd	del	powered by	mtow kg	configuration	selcal	name/fln/specialitites/remarks
☐ RA-14061	PZL Swidnik (Mil) Mi-2	5310537038	CCCP-14061	0088		2 IS GTD-350-4	3550	Frtr700kg or Y8		
☐ RA-14063	PZL Swidnik (Mil) Mi-2	5410542038	CCCP-14063	0088	0488	2 IS GTD-350-4	3550	Frtr700kg or Y8		
☐ RA-14099	PZL Swidnik (Mil) Mi-2	5310708088	CCCP-14099	0088		2 IS GTD-350-4	3550	Frtr700kg or Y8		
☐ RA-14122	PZL Swidnik (Mil) Mi-2	5310834029	CCCP-14122	0089		2 IS GTD-350-4	3550	Frtr700kg or Y8		
☐ RA-14127	PZL Swidnik (Mil) Mi-2	5410839029	CCCP-14127	0089	0489	2 IS GTD-350-4	3550	Frtr700kg or Y8		
☐ RA-14128	PZL Swidnik (Mil) Mi-2	5410840029	CCCP-14128	0089		2 IS GTD-350-4	3550	Frtr700kg or Y8		
☐ RA-14138	PZL Swidnik (Mil) Mi-2	5210342087	CCCP-14138	0087	1087	2 IS GTD-350-4	3550	Frtr700kg or Y8		
☐ RA-14140	PZL Swidnik (Mil) Mi-2	5210347047	CCCP-14140	0087	1087	2 IS GTD-350-4	3550	Frtr700kg or Y8		
☐ RA-14141	PZL Swidnik (Mil) Mi-2	5410348097	CCCP-14141	0087	0188	2 IS GTD-350-4	3550	Frtr700kg or Y8		
☐ RA-14142	PZL Swidnik (Mil) Mi-2	5210349097	CCCP-14142	0087		2 IS GTD-350-4	3550	Frtr700kg or Y8		
☐ RA-14143	PZL Swidnik (Mil) Mi-2	5210350097	CCCP-14143	0087		2 IS GTD-350-4	3550	Frtr700kg or Y8		
☐ RA-14193	PZL Swidnik (Mil) Mi-2	5310534038	CCCP-14193	0088		2 IS GTD-350-4	3550	Frtr700kg or Y8		
☐ RA-14194	PZL Swidnik (Mil) Mi-2	5310535038	CCCP-14194	0088		2 IS GTD-350-4	3550	Frtr700kg or Y8		
☐ RA-14195	PZL Swidnik (Mil) Mi-2	5310536038	CCCP-14195	0088		2 IS GTD-350-4	3550	Frtr700kg or Y8		
☐ RA-14275	PZL Swidnik (Mil) Mi-2	5311228051	CCCP-14275	0091		2 IS GTD-350-4	3550	Frtr700kg or Y8		

	registration	type of aircraft	cn/fn	ex/ex*	mfd	del	powered by	mtow kg	configuration	selcal	name/fln/specialitites/remarks
□	RA-14276	PZL Swidnik (Mil) Mi-2	5311229051	CCCP-14276	0091		2 IS GTD-350-4	3550	Frtr700kg or Y8		
□	RA-20380	PZL Swidnik (Mil) Mi-2	539827066	CCCP-20380	0086		2 IS GTD-350-4	3550	Frtr700kg or Y8		
□	RA-20400	PZL Swidnik (Mil) Mi-2	549848076	CCCP-20400	0086		2 IS GTD-350-4	3550	Frtr700kg or Y8		
□	RA-20714	PZL Swidnik (Mil) Mi-2	536832100	CCCP-20714	0080		2 IS GTD-350-4	3550	Frtr700kg or Y8		
□	RA-20857	PZL Swidnik (Mil) Mi-2	548138043	CCCP-20857	0083		2 IS GTD-350-4	3550	Frtr700kg or Y8		
□	RA-20964	PZL Swidnik (Mil) Mi-2	549520115	CCCP-20964	0085	0286	2 IS GTD-350-4	3550	Frtr700kg or Y8		
□	RA-20965	PZL Swidnik (Mil) Mi-2	549525125	CCCP-20965	0085		2 IS GTD-350-4	3550	Frtr700kg or Y8		
□	RA-20972	PZL Swidnik (Mil) Mi-2	539645036	CCCP-20972	0086		2 IS GTD-350-4	3550	Frtr700kg or Y8		
□	RA-23217	PZL Swidnik (Mil) Mi-2	5210203037	CCCP-23217	0087		2 IS GTD-350-4	3550	Frtr700kg or Y8		
□	RA-23251	PZL Swidnik (Mil) Mi-2	5210325087	CCCP-23251	0087	0987	2 IS GTD-350-4	3550	Frtr700kg or Y8		
□	RA-23252	PZL Swidnik (Mil) Mi-2	5210326087	CCCP-23252	0087	0987	2 IS GTD-350-4	3550	Frtr700kg or Y8		
□	RA-23266	PZL Swidnik (Mil) Mi-2	5210344087	CCCP-23266	0087	1287	2 IS GTD-350-4	3550	Frtr700kg or Y8		
□	RA-23289	PZL Swidnik (Mil) Mi-2	539110025	CCCP-23289	0085		2 IS GTD-350-4	3550	Frtr700kg or Y8		
□	RA-23401	PZL Swidnik (Mil) Mi-2	538923104	CCCP-23401	0084	1284	2 IS GTD-350-4	3550	Frtr700kg or Y8		
□	RA-23402	PZL Swidnik (Mil) Mi-2	548924104	CCCP-23402	0084		2 IS GTD-350-4	3550	Frtr700kg or Y8		
□	RA-23404	PZL Swidnik (Mil) Mi-2	548926104	CCCP-23404	0084		2 IS GTD-350-4	3550	Frtr700kg or Y8		
□	RA-23445	PZL Swidnik (Mil) Mi-2	539418095	CCCP-23445	0085		2 IS GTD-350-4	3550	Frtr700kg or Y8		
□	RA-01111	PZL Mielec (Antonov) An-2	1G240-49	CCCP-01111	0091	0691	1 SH ASh-62IR	5250	Freighter		
□	RA-01460	PZL Mielec (Antonov) An-2	1G231-51	CCCP-01460	0088		1 SH ASh-62IR	5250	Y12		
□	RA-01878	Antonov An-2	115347310	CCCP-01878	0061		1 SH ASh-62IR	5250	Y12		
□	RA-02232	PZL Mielec (Antonov) An-2	1G235-03	CCCP-02232	0089	0991	1 SH ASh-62IR	5250	Ambulance		
□	RA-05755	PZL Mielec (Antonov) An-2	1G151-65	CCCP-05755	0074		1 SH ASh-62IR	5250	Y12		
□	RA-32305	PZL Mielec (Antonov) An-2	1G97-17	CCCP-32305	0068		1 SH ASh-62IR	5250	Y12		
□	RA-33623	PZL Mielec (Antonov) An-2	1G232-59	CCCP-33623	0088		1 SH ASh-62IR	5250	Y12		
□	RA-40236	PZL Mielec (Antonov) An-2	1G221-41	CCCP-40236	0086	1086	1 SH ASh-62IR	5250	Ambulance		
□	RA-40277	PZL Mielec (Antonov) An-2	1G221-07	CCCP-40277	0086		1 SH ASh-62IR	5250	Y12		
□	RA-44991	PZL Mielec (Antonov) An-2	1G27-14	CCCP-44991	0062	1085	1 SH ASh-62IR	5250	Freighter		
□	RA-22244	Mil Mi-8P	6370	CCCP-22244	0076		2 IS TV2-117A	12000	Frtr4t or Y24		
□	RA-22258	Mil Mi-8T	6599	CCCP-22258	0076		2 IS TV2-117A	12000	Frtr4t or Y22		
□	RA-22308	Mil Mi-8T	7126	CCCP-22308	0077		2 IS TV2-117A	12000	Frtr4t or Y22		
□	RA-22345	Mil Mi-8T	7250	CCCP-22345	0077		2 IS TV2-117A	12000	Frtr4t or Y22		
□	RA-22668	Mil Mi-8T	8120	CCCP-22668	0080		2 IS TV2-117A	12000	Frtr4t or Y22		
□	RA-22726	Mil Mi-8T	98308741	CCCP-22726	0083		2 IS TV2-117A	12000	Frtr4t or Y22		
□	RA-22800	Mil Mi-8T	7528	CCCP-22800	0078		2 IS TV2-117A	12000	Frtr4t or Y22		
□	RA-22818	Mil Mi-8T	7586	CCCP-22818	0078		2 IS TV2-117A	12000	Frtr4t or Y22		
□	RA-24117	Mil Mi-8T	98839833	CCCP-24117	0088		2 IS TV2-117A	12000	Frtr4t or Y22		
□	RA-24136	Mil Mi-8T	98841316	CCCP-24136	0088		2 IS TV2-117A	12000	Frtr4t or Y22		
□	RA-24154	Mil Mi-8T	98941754	CCCP-24154	0089		2 IS TV2-117A	12000	Frtr4t or Y22		
□	RA-24220	Mil Mi-8T	98730485	CCCP-24220	0087		2 IS TV2-117A	12000	Frtr4t or Y22		
□	RA-24221	Mil Mi-8T	98730492	CCCP-24221	0087		2 IS TV2-117A	12000	Frtr4t or Y22		
□	RA-24230	Mil Mi-8T	98730602	CCCP-24230	0087		2 IS TV2-117A	12000	Frtr4t or Y22		
□	RA-24244	Mil Mi-8T	98730871	CCCP-24244	0087		2 IS TV2-117A	12000	Frtr4t or Y22		
□	RA-24270	Mil Mi-8T	98734231	CCCP-24270	0087		2 IS TV2-117A	12000	Frtr4t or Y22		
□	RA-24271	Mil Mi-8T	98734242	CCCP-24271	0087		2 IS TV2-117A	12000	Frtr4t or Y22		
□	RA-24277	Mil Mi-8T	98734317	CCCP-24277	0087		2 IS TV2-117A	12000	Frtr4t or Y22		
□	RA-24278	Mil Mi-8T	98734322	CCCP-24278	0087		2 IS TV2-117A	12000	Frtr4t or Y22		
□	RA-24448	Mil Mi-8T	98628198	CCCP-24448	0086		2 IS TV2-117A	12000	Frtr4t or Y22		
□	RA-24449	Mil Mi-8T	98628211	CCCP-24449	0086		2 IS TV2-117A	12000	Frtr4t or Y22		
□	RA-24454	Mil Mi-8T	98628334	CCCP-24454	0086		2 IS TV2-117A	12000	Frtr4t or Y22		
□	RA-24462	Mil Mi-8T	98628551	CCCP-24462	0086		2 IS TV2-117A	12000	Frtr4t or Y22		
□	RA-24571	Mil Mi-8T	98839087	CCCP-24571	0088		2 IS TV2-117A	12000	Frtr4t or Y22		
□	RA-24583	Mil Mi-8T	98839354	CCCP-24583	0088		2 IS TV2-117A	12000	Frtr4t or Y22		
□	RA-24626	Mil Mi-8T	8255	CCCP-24626	0081		2 IS TV2-117A	12000	Frtr4t or Y22		
□	RA-25162	Mil Mi-8T	99047923	CCCP-25162	0090		2 IS TV2-117A	12000	Frtr4t or Y22		
□	RA-25334	Mil Mi-8T	98206217	CCCP-25334	0082		2 IS TV2-117A	12000	Frtr4t or Y22		
□	RA-25359	Mil Mi-8T	98206785	CCCP-25359	0082		2 IS TV2-117A	12000	Frtr4t or Y22		
□	RA-25425	Mil Mi-8MTV-1	95535	CCCP-25425	0090		2 IS TV3-117MT	13000	Frtr4t or Y22		
□	RA-25441	Mil Mi-8MTV-1	95582	CCCP-25441	0090		2 IS TV3-117MT	13000	Frtr4t or Y22		lst Skytech Helicopter Service
□	RA-25515	Mil Mi-8MTV-1	95663	CCCP-25515	0091		2 IS TV3-117MT	13000	Frtr4t or Y22		
□	RA-25750	Mil Mi-8AMT	59489607833		0093		2 IS TV3-117MT	13000	Frtr4t or Y22		lst Skytech Helicopter Service
□	RA-27041	Mil Mi-8MTV-1	95875	CCCP-27041	0092		2 IS TV3-117MT	13000	Frtr4t or Y22		lst Skytech Helicopter Service
□	RA-27053	Mil Mi-8MTV-1	95887	CCCP-27053	0092		2 IS TV3-117MT	13000	Frtr4t or Y22		
□	RA-27141	Mil Mi-8MTV-1	95991		0092		2 IS TV3-117MT	13000	Frtr4t or Y22		
□	RA-21004	Mil Mi-6A	0234	CCCP-21004	0074		2 SO D-25V	42500	Freighter 12t		
□	RA-21015	Mil Mi-6A	0455	CCCP-21015	0074		2 SO D-25V	42500	Freighter 12t		
□	RA-21016	Mil Mi-6A	0457	CCCP-21016	0074		2 SO D-25V	42500	Freighter 12t		
□	RA-21031	Mil Mi-6A	0633	CCCP-21031	0077		2 SO D-25V	42500	Freighter 12t		
□	RA-21032	Mil Mi-6A	0634	CCCP-21032	0077		2 SO D-25V	42500	Freighter 12t		
□	RA-21057	Mil Mi-6A	0678	CCCP-21057	0079		2 SO D-25V	42500	Freighter 12t		
□	RA-21080	Mil Mi-6	7683509	CCCP-21080	0067		2 SO D-25V	42500	Freighter 12t		
□	RA-21136	Mil Mi-6A	715402V	CCCP-21136	0071		2 SO D-25V	42500	Freighter 12t		

KOMIINTERAVIA, Joint-Stock Company = KMV

Syktyvkar

Ul. Sovetskaya 69, 167610 Syktyvkar, (Republic of Komi), Russia ☎ (8212) 21 67 32 Tx: none Fax: (8212) 21 67 16 SITA: n/a
F: 1996 ✈✈✈ n/a Head: Mikhail V. Kutuzov ICAO: KOMIINTER Net: n/a

	registration	type of aircraft	cn/fn	ex/ex*	mfd	del	powered by	mtow kg	configuration	selcal	name/fln/specialitites/remarks
□	RA-87439	Yakovlev 40	9431535	CCCP-87439	0074	0998	3 IV AI-25	16800	Y30		opf UN
□	RA-87533	Yakovlev 40	9521741	CCCP-87533	0075	0998	3 IV AI-25	16800	VIP F5Y8		opf UN
□	RA-88216	Yakovlev 40	9630250	CCCP-88216	0076	0998	3 IV AI-25	16800	Y32		
□	RA-46307	Antonov 24B	97305207	CCCP-46307	0469	0998	2 IV AI-24-II	21000	Y48		
□	RA-46411	Antonov 24B	87304006	CCCP-46411	0168	0998	2 IV AI-24-II	21000	Y48		
□	RA-46468	Antonov 24RV	27307906	CCCP-46468	0772	0998	2 IV AI-24-II	21800	Y48		
□	RA-46494	Antonov 24RV	27308207	CCCP-46494	1272	0998	2 IV AI-24-II	21800	Y48		
□	RA-46578	Antonov 24B	97304907	CCCP-46578	0169	0998	2 IV AI-24-II	21000	Y48		
□	RA-46590	Antonov 24B	97305010	CCCP-46590	0269	0998	2 IV AI-24-II	21000	Y48		
□	RA-46610	Antonov 24RV	37308607	CCCP-46610	0573	0998	2 IV AI-24-II	21800	Y48		
□	RA-47276	Antonov 24B	07306406	CCCP-47276	0970	0998	2 IV AI-24-II	21000	Y48		
□	RA-47696	Antonov 24RV	27307603	CCCP-47696	0272	0998	2 IV AI-24-II	21800	Y48		
□	RA-47820	Antonov 24RV	17307201	CCCP-47820	0871	0998	2 IV AI-24-II	21800	Y48		
□	RA-26017	Antonov 26B	10109	CCCP-26017	1080	0998	2 IV AI-24VT	24000	Y19 / Frtr 5,5t		
□	RA-26050	Antonov 26B	10905	CCCP-26050	0381	0998	2 IV AI-24VT	24000	Y19 / Frtr 5,5t		
□	RA-26072	Antonov 26B	11409	CCCP-26072	0981	0998	2 IV AI-24VT	24000	Y19 / Frtr 5,5t		
□	RA-26081	Antonov 26B	11703	CCCP-26081	1181	0998	2 IV AI-24VT	24000	Y19 / Frtr 5,5t		
□	RA-26234	Antonov 26	14308	RA-49274	1185	0998	2 IV AI-24VT	24000	Y19 / Frtr 5,5t		
□	RA-26239	Antonov 26	14307	RA-49269	1185	0998	2 IV AI-24VT	24000	Y19 / Frtr 5,5t		
□	RA-65148	Tupolev 134A	61025	CCCP-65148	0279	0998	2 SO D-30-II	47000	Y80		
□	RA-65606	Tupolev 134A	46300	D-AOBR	0376	0998	2 SO D-30-II	47000	C16Y52		
□	RA-65607	Tupolev 134A	48560	D-AOBS	0876	0998	2 SO D-30-II	47000	VIP F9Y52		
□	RA-65608	Tupolev 134A	38040	D-AOBO	0975	0998	2 SO D-30-II	47000	Y80		
□	RA-65609	Tupolev 134A	46155	D-AOBQ	0276	0998	2 SO D-30-II	47000	Y80		lst NLB
□	RA-65610	Tupolev 134A	40150	D-AOBP	1075	0998	2 SO D-30-II	47000	Y80		
□	RA-65611	Tupolev 134A	3351903	D-AOBA	0573	0998	2 SO D-30-II	47000	Y80		
□	RA-65612	Tupolev 134A	3352102	D-AOBC	1173	0998	2 SO D-30-II	47000	Y80		
□	RA-65613	Tupolev 134A	3352106	D-AOBD	1273	0998	2 SO D-30-II	47000	Y80		lst Yamal Air Transport
□	RA-65614	Tupolev 134A-3	4352207	D-AOBG	0374	0998	2 SO D-30-III	47000	C8Y60		
□	RA-65615	Tupolev 134A-3	4352205	D-AOBE	0274	0998	2 SO D-30-III	47000	Y80		
□	RA-65616	Tupolev 134A-3	4352206	D-AOBF	0374	0998	2 SO D-30-III	47000	C8Y60		lst OST
□	RA-65618	Tupolev 134A-3	12095	D-AOBJ	0774	0998	2 SO D-30-III	47000	Y80		
□	RA-65619	Tupolev 134A-3	31218	D-AOBK	0575	0998	2 SO D-30-III	47000	Y80		
□	RA-65620	Tupolev 134A-3	35180	D-AOBN	0675	0998	2 SO D-30-III	47000	Y80		
□	RA-65621	Tupolev 134A-3	48320	D-AOBL	0376	0998	2 SO D-30-III	47000	Y80		
□	RA-65716	Tupolev 134B-3	63595	CCCP-65716	0281	1297	2 SO D-30-III	47600	C16Y52		
□	RA-65755	Tupolev 134A-3	62165	CCCP-65755	0379	0998	2 SO D-30-III	47600	Y80		
□	RA-65777	Tupolev 134A-3	62552	CCCP-65777	1079	0998	2 SO D-30-III	47600	Y80		
□	RA-65780	Tupolev 134A-3	62622	CCCP-65780	1179	0998	2 SO D-30-III	47600	Y80		
□	RA-65793	Tupolev 134A-3	63128	CCCP-65793	0280	0998	2 SO D-30-III	47600	Y80		
□	RA-65901	Tupolev 134A-3	63731	CCCP-65901	0481	0998	2 SO D-30-III	47600	C16Y52		
□	RA-65902	Tupolev 134A-3	63742	CCCP-65902	0481	0998	2 SO D-30-III	47600	Y80		
□	RA-65977	Tupolev 134A-3	63245	CCCP-65977	0580	1196	2 SO D-30-III	49000	C16Y52		
□	RA-11114	Antonov 12BP	01347909	CCCP-11114	1071	0998	4 IV AI-20M	61000	Freighter 20t		
□	RA-11526	Antonov 12BP	02348207	CCCP-11526	0772	0998	4 IV AI-20M	61000	Freighter 20t		
□	RA-12972	Antonov 12BP	9346504	CCCP-12972	0669	0998	4 IV AI-20M	61000	Freighter 20t		opf UN

KONVERS AVIA

Tver

Ulanski pereulok 22, Room 423, 101000 Moskva, Russia ☎ (095) 925 90 00 Tx: none Fax: (095) 207 03 72 SITA: n/a

F: 1995 n/a Head: Marina L. Popovich Net: n/a

☐ RA-23705	PZL Swidnik (Mil) Mi-2			0088	0095	2 IS GTD-350-4	3550	Utility		
☐ RA-23706	PZL Swidnik (Mil) Mi-2			0088	0095	2 IS GTD-350-4	3550	Utility		
☐ RA-23707	PZL Swidnik (Mil) Mi-2			0088	0095	2 IS GTD-350-4	3550	Utility		
☐ RA-23721	PZL Swidnik (Mil) Mi-2			0085	0095	2 IS GTD-350-4	3550	Utility		

KORSAR Airlines = KRS (Korsar Aviakompania)

Moscow-Vnukovo

Pl. Suvorova 1, 103473 Moskva, Russia ☎ (095) 284 44 65 Tx: 413761 yox mo Fax: (095) 281 74 52 SITA: n/a

F: 1991 n/a Head: Sergei V. Cheremnykh ICAO: KORSAR AVIA Net: n/a Also leases Antonov 12, Ilyushin 18/76 & Tupolev 134/154 from Aeroflot Russian Int'l Airlines, Kosmos & 223rd Flight Unit when required.

Most aircraft are still in former Aeroflot colors with or without titles.

☐ RA-88298	Yakovlev 40K	9930160	CCCP-88298	0079		3 IV AI-25	16800	Y32 or VIP		

KORYAK AIR ENTERPRISE (Koryakskoe aviapredpriatie) (formerly Aeroflot Koryak division)

Tilichiki

Ul. Pilota 15, 684810 pos. Korf, (Kamchatka Region), Russia ☎ (41532) 59 299 Tx: 244122 akor su Fax: (41532) 52 703 SITA: n/a

F: 1956 n/a Head: Vladimir M. Shevelenko Net: n/a Most aircraft are still in Aeroflot colors but will be repainted in due course.

☐ RA-28713	PZL Mielec (Antonov) An-28	1AJ006-23	CCCP-28713	0089	0089	2 GS TVD-10B	6500	Y17 / Combi		
☐ RA-28714	PZL Mielec (Antonov) An-28	1AJ006-24	CCCP-28714	0089	0089	2 GS TVD-10B	6500	Y17 / Combi		
☐ RA-28715	PZL Mielec (Antonov) An-28	1AJ006-25	CCCP-28715	0089	0090	2 GS TVD-10B	6500	Y17 / Combi		
☐ RA-28716	PZL Mielec (Antonov) An-28	1AJ007-01	CCCP-28716	0089	0090	2 GS TVD-10B	6500	Y17 / Combi		
☐ RA-28722	PZL Mielec (Antonov) An-28	1AJ007-07	CCCP-28722	0089	0090	2 GS TVD-10B	6500	Y17 / Combi		
☐ RA-28950	PZL Mielec (Antonov) An-28	1AJ009-16	CCCP-28950	0091	0091	2 GS TVD-10B	6500	Y17 / Combi		
☐ RA-22670	Mil Mi-8	8122	CCCP-22670	0080	0080	2 IS TV2-117A	12000	Combi		
☐ RA-24209	Mil Mi-8	98730181	CCCP-24209	0087	0087	2 IS TV2-117A	12000	Combi		
☐ RA-24411	Mil Mi-8	98625206	CCCP-24411	0086	0086	2 IS TV2-117A	12000	Combi		
☐ RA-24740	Mil Mi-8	98417864	CCCP-24740	0084	0084	2 IS TV2-117A	12000	Combi		
☐ RA-25195	Mil Mi-8	99047350	CCCP-25195	0090	0090	2 IS TV2-117A	12000	Combi		
☐ RA-25388	Mil Mi-8	98208166	CCCP-25388	0082	0082	2 IS TV2-117A	12000	Combi		
☐ RA-25617	Mil Mi-8	99150838	CCCP-25617	0091	0091	2 IS TV2-117A	12000	Combi		
☐ RA-25618	Mil Mi-8	99150841	CCCP-25618	0091	0091	2 IS TV2-117A	12000	Combi		
☐ RA-74039	Antonov 74	36547097931		0093	0094	2 LO D-36	34800	Freighter		
☐ RA-74050	Antonov 74	36547181011		0094	0094	2 LO D-36	34800	Freighter		

KOSMOS Aviakompania = KSM

Moscow-Vnukovo 3

Borovskoe shosse 1, 103027 Moskva, Russia ☎ (095) 436 89 00 Tx: none Fax: (095) 436 89 00 SITA: n/a

F: 1995 n/a Head: Alexander N. Ilyukhin ICAO: KOSMOS Net: n/a

☐ RA-13371	Antonov 26	1910	CCCP-13371	1173		2 IV AI-24VT	24000	Freighter		
☐ RA-65719	Tupolev 134A	63637	CCCP-65719	0281		2 SO D-30-II	49000	Exec 40 Pax		lst/jtly opw FRT
☐ RA-65726	Tupolev 134A	63720	CCCP-65726	0381		2 SO D-30-II	49000	Exec 44 Pax		lst/jtly opw FRT
☐ RA-65941	Tupolev 134A	60642	LZ-TUS	0978	0696	2 SO D-30-II	47600	VIP 28 Pax		
☐ RA-65956	Tupolev 134A	2351709	CCCP-65956	0273		2 SO D-30-II	49000	Exec 55 Pax		lst/jtly opw FRT
☐ RA-11025	Antonov 12TB	6344103	CCCP-11025	1066		4 IV AI-20M	61000	Freighter		lst/jtly opw FRT
☐ RA-76499	Ilyushin 76TD	0023441186	CCCP-76499	1082		4 SO D-30KP	190000	Freighter		lst/jtly opw FRT

KOSTROMA AIR ENTERPRISE (Kostromskoe aviapredpriatie) (formerly part of Central Districts Airlines & Aeroflot Kostroma division)

Kostroma

Kostroma Airport, 156012 Kostroma, Russia ☎ (0942) 55 36 51 Tx: n/a Fax: (0942) 55 36 51 SITA: n/a

F: n/a n/a Head: Boris B. Anokhin Net: n/a Beside aircraft listed, also operates Antonov 2 & Mil Mi-2. Full details not yet known. Most aircraft are still in Aeroflot colors but will be repainted in due course.

☐ RA-67105	Let 410UVP	841331	CCCP-67105	0084		2 WA M-601D	5800	Y15		
☐ RA-67143	Let 410UVP	800409	CCCP-67143	0080		2 WA M-601D	5800	Y15		
☐ RA-67338	Let 410UVP	820838	CCCP-67338	0082		2 WA M-601D	5800	Y15		
☐ RA-67401	Let 410UVP	831029	CCCP-67401	0083		2 WA M-601D	5800	Y15		
☐ RA-67402	Let 410UVP	831030	CCCP-67402	0083		2 WA M-601D	5800	Y15		
☐ RA-67443	Let 410UVP	841208	SP-FTP	0084		2 WA M-601D	5800	Y15		
☐ RA-67483	Let 410UVP	841308	SP-FTR	0084		2 WA M-601D	5800	Y15		
☐ RA-67501	Let 410UVP	851405	CCCP-67501	0085		2 WA M-601D	5800	Y15		

KOTLASAVIA = KTS (Kotlas Air Enterprise) (formerly Aeroflot Kotlas division)

Kotlas

Kotlas Airport, 165400 Kotlas, Russia ☎ (81837) 44 555 Tx: n/a Fax: (81837) 44 269 SITA: n/a

F: n/a n/a Head: Vyacheslav N. Logachev ICAO: KOTLASAVIA Net: n/a Also operates Antonov 2 & Mil Mi-8. Full details not yet known. Most aircraft are still in Aeroflot colors but will be repainted in due course.

☐ RA-87235	Yakovlev 40	9530143	CCCP-87235	0975		3 IV AI-25	16800	Y27		
☐ RA-87336	Yakovlev 40	9510539	CCCP-87336	0375		3 IV AI-25	16800	Y32		
☐ RA-87392	Yakovlev 40	9410433	CCCP-87392	0274		3 IV AI-25	16800	Y32		
☐ RA-87456	Yakovlev 40	9431336	CCCP-87456	0274		3 IV AI-25	16800	Y32		
☐ RA-87843	Yakovlev 40	9331130	CCCP-87843	0973		3 IV AI-25	16800	Y32		
☐ RA-87956	Yakovlev 40K	9821757	CCCP-87956	0578		3 IV AI-25	16800	Y27		
☐ RA-87957	Yakovlev 40K	9821857	CCCP-87957	0578		3 IV AI-25	16800	Y32		
☐ RA-88308	Yakovlev 40	9230224	SP-GEA	0072	0096	3 IV AI-25	16000	Y32		

KRAS AIR – Krasnoyarsk Airlines, Joint-Stock Company = 7B / KJC (Krasnoyarskie avialinii)

Krasnoyarsk-Yemelianovo & Achinsk

Yemelianovo Airport, 663020 Krasnoyarsk, Russia ☎ (3912) 23 63 66 Tx: 288182 Fax: (3912) 23 62 00 SITA: n/a

F: 1993 n/a Head: Capt. Boris M. Abramovich IATA: 499 ICAO: KRASNOYARSKY AIR Net: n/a

☐ RA-87473	Yakovlev 40	9441837	CCCP-87473	0074		3 IV AI-25	16800	Y32		
☐ RA-87916	Yakovlev 40	9730655	CCCP-87916	0077		3 IV AI-25	16800	Y32		
☐ RA-88224	Yakovlev 40	9641150	CCCP-88224	0076		3 IV AI-25	16800	Y32		
☐ RA-46693	Antonov 24RV	47309904	CCCP-46693	1174	0098	2 IV AI-24VT	21800	Y48		
☐ RA-49278	Antonov 24RV	47309808	YR-AMJ	0074	0097	2 IV AI-24VT	21800	Y48		
☐ RA-49279	Antonov 24RV	17306905	YR-AMB	0071	0097	2 IV AI-24VT	21800	Y48		
☐ RA-49287	Antonov 24RV	27307607	YR-AME	0072	0097	2 IV AI-24VT	21800	Y48		
☐ RA-26133	Antonov 26B	12709	CCCP-26133	0083		2 IV AI-24VT	24000	Freighter		
☐ RA-26139	Antonov 26B	12901	CCCP-26139	0083		2 IV AI-24VT	24000	Freighter		
☐ RA-26588	Antonov 26B	13908	CCCP-26588	0085		2 IV AI-24VT	24000	Freighter		
☐ RA-26593	Antonov 26B	14003	CCCP-26593	0085		2 IV AI-24VT	24000	Freighter		
☐ RA-85184	Tupolev 154B	184	CCCP-85184	0076		3 KU NK-8-2U	100000	Y164		
☐ RA-85201	Tupolev 154B	201	CCCP-85201	0077		3 KU NK-8-2U	100000	Y164		
☐ RA-85202	Tupolev 154B	202	CCCP-85202	0077		3 KU NK-8-2U	100000	Y164		
☐ RA-85417	Tupolev 154B-2	417	CCCP-85417	0080		3 KU NK-8-2U	100000	Y164		
☐ RA-85418	Tupolev 154B-2	418	CCCP-85418	0080		3 KU NK-8-2U	100000	Y164		
☐ RA-85489	Tupolev 154B-2	489	CCCP-85489	0081		3 KU NK-8-2U	100000	F12Y120		
☐ RA-85505	Tupolev 154B-2	505	CCCP-85505	0081		3 KU NK-8-2U	100000	F12Y120		
☐ RA-85529	Tupolev 154B-2	529	CCCP-85529	0082		3 KU NK-8-2U	100000	Y164		
☐ RA-85672	Tupolev 154M	830	CCCP-85672	0089		3 SO D-30KU-154-II	100000	Y164		
☐ RA-85678	Tupolev 154M	841	EP-LAS	0090		3 SO D-30KU-154-II	100000	Y164		
☐ RA-85679	Tupolev 154M	842	EP-LAT	0090		3 SO D-30KU-154-II	100000	Y164		
☐ RA-85682	Tupolev 154M	849	CCCP-85682	0090		3 SO D-30KU-154-II	100000	Y164		
☐ RA-85683	Tupolev 154M	850	EP-LAQ	0090		3 SO D-30KU-154-II	100000	Y164		
☐ RA-85694	Tupolev 154M	867	EP-MAE	0191		3 SO D-30KU-154-II	100000	Y164		
☐ RA-85702	Tupolev 154M	877	EP-ITK	0791		3 SO D-30KU-154-II	100000	Y164		
☐ RA-85704	Tupolev 154M	879	EP-LAV	0091		3 SO D-30KU-154-II	100000	Y164		
☐ RA-85708	Tupolev 154M	883	EP-ITJ	0091		3 SO D-30KU-154-II	100000	Y164		
☐ RA-85720	Tupolev 154M	902	EP-ITA	0091		3 SO D-30KU-154-II	100000	Y164		
☐ RA-86453	Ilyushin 62	1622323	CCCP-86453	0076		4 KU NK-8-4	161600	Y180		fn 2202
☐ RA-86459	Ilyushin 62	3623945	CCCP-86459	0076		4 KU NK-8-4	161600	Y180		fn 2304
☐ RA-86619	Ilyushin 62	3520233	CCCP-86619	0075		4 KU NK-8-4	161600	Y180		fn 2003
☐ RA-86706	Ilyushin 62	21105	CCCP-86706	0072		4 KU NK-8-4	161600	Y180		fn 1105
☐ RA-86707	Ilyushin 62	41604	CCCP-86707	0074		4 KU NK-8-4	161600	Y180		fn 1604
☐ RA-86708	Ilyushin 62	41802	CCCP-86708	0074		4 KU NK-8-4	161600	Y180		lst NLB / fn 1802
☐ RA-86709	Ilyushin 62	62204	CCCP-86709	0076		4 KU NK-8-4	161600	Y180		fn 2204
☐ RA-76459	Ilyushin 76T	0013430890	CCCP-76459	0081		4 SO D-30KP	170000	Freighter		fn 2303
☐ RA-76463	Ilyushin 76T	0013432960	CCCP-76463	0081		4 SO D-30KP	170000	Freighter		fn 2410
☐ RA-76464	Ilyushin 76TD	0023437090	CCCP-76464	0082		4 SO D-30KP	190000	Freighter		fn 2803
☐ RA-76465	Ilyushin 76TD	0023438101	CCCP-76465	0682		4 SO D-30KP	190000	Freighter		fn 2806
☐ RA-76508	Ilyushin 76T	083413412	CCCP-76508	0078		4 SO D-30KP	170000	Freighter		fn 1103
☐ RA-76509	Ilyushin 76T	083413415	CCCP-76509	0078		4 SO D-30KP	170000	Freighter		fn 1104
☐ RA-76515	Ilyushin 76T	093417526	CCCP-76515	0079		4 SO D-30KP	170000	Freighter		fn 1402
☐ RA-76517	Ilyushin 76T	093418560	CCCP-76517	0079		4 SO D-30KP	170000	Freighter		fn 1410
☐ RA-76524	Ilyushin 76T	0003425746	CCCP-76524	0080		4 SO D-30KP	170000	Freighter		fn 1907
☐ RA-76792	Ilyushin 76TD	0093497942	CCCP-76792	0089		4 SO D-30KP	190000	Freighter		lst RXM / fn 7406
☐ RA-86121	Ilyushin 86	51483209089	CCCP-86121	0091		4 KU NK-86	215000	Y350		
☐ RA-86122	Ilyushin 86	51483209090	CCCP-86122	0092		4 KU NK-86	215000	Y350		
☐ RA-86137	Ilyushin 86	51483210095	CCCP-86137	0092		4 KU NK-86	215000	Y350		
☐ RA-86145	Ilyushin 86	51483211101		0093		4 KU NK-86	215000	Y350		

543 registration type of aircraft cn/fn ex/ex* mfd del powered by mtow kg configuration selcal name/fln/specialitites/remarks

KRECHET — Petropavlovsk Kamchatsky-Yelizovo

Ul. Solochnaya 13, 684010 Yelizovo, (Kamchatka Region), Russia ☎ (41551) 61 493 Tx: n/a Fax: n/a SITA: n/a
F: n/a 👥 n/a Head: n/a Net: n/a

registration	type of aircraft	cn/fn	ex/ex*	mfd	del	powered by	mtow kg	configuration	selcal	name/fln/specialitites/remarks
☐ RA-22513	Mil Mi-8T		*CCCP-22513*			*2 IS TV2-117A*	*12000*	*Utility*		
☐ RA-22515	Mil Mi-8P		*CCCP-22515*			*2 IS TV2-117A*	*12000*	*Utility*		
☐ RA-93921	Mil Mi-8T		*CCCP-93921*			*2 IS TV2-117A*	*12000*	*Utility*		
☐ RA-93925	Mil Mi-8T		*CCCP-93925*			*2 IS TV2-117A*	*12000*	*Utility*		

KRYLO Aviakompania = KRI — Moscow-Bykovo & -Zhukovsky

PO Box 39, 109386 Moskva, Russia ☎ (095) 919 91 42 Tx: none Fax: (095) 919 91 36 SITA: MOWRACR
F: 1990 👥 65 Head: Yevgeni A. Gorbunov ICAO: KRYLO Net: n/a Some aircraft are still in Aeroflot colors without titles but will be repainted in due course.

registration	type of aircraft	cn/fn	ex/ex*	mfd	del	powered by	mtow kg	configuration	selcal	name/fln/specialitites/remarks
☐ RA-87487	Yakovlev 40	*9441538*	*CCCP-87487*	*0074*	*0090*	*3 IV AI-25*	*16800*	*VIP F12*		
☐ RA-26044	Antonov 26B	*10803*	*CCCP-26044*	*0081*	*0090*	*2 IV AI-24VT*	*24000*	*Frtr 3,5t/orY19*		*opf ACS-Air Cargo Service broker*
☐ RA-76379	Ilyushin 76TD	*1033417569*		*0093*	*0093*	*4 SO D-30KP*	*190000*	*Freighter 40t*		
☐ RA-76754	Ilyushin 76T	*093421637*	*YI-AKU*	*0380*	*0097*	*4 SO D-30KP*	*170000*	*Freighter 40t*		*lsf VAS*

KRYLYA SAMOTLORA (Samotlor Wings) — Nizhnevartovsk

Ul. Permskaya 5, 626440 Nizhnevartovsk, (Tyumen Region), Russia ☎ (3466) 24 80 53 Tx: none Fax: (3466) 24 80 53 SITA: n/a
F: n/a 👥 n/a Head: Sergei V. Blinov Net: n/a

registration	type of aircraft	cn/fn	ex/ex*	mfd	del	powered by	mtow kg	configuration	selcal	name/fln/specialitites/remarks
☐ RA-01439	PZL Mielec (Antonov) An-2		*CCCP-01439*	*0088*		*1 SH ASh-62IR*	*5500*	*Utility*		
☐ RA-07862	PZL Mielec (Antonov) An-2	*1G170-21*	*CCCP-07862*	*0076*		*1 SH ASh-62IR*	*5500*	*Utility*		
☐ RA-70320	PZL Mielec (Antonov) An-2		*CCCP-70320*	*0072*		*1 SH ASh-62IR*	*5500*	*Utility*		
☐ RA-70705	PZL Mielec (Antonov) An-2		*CCCP-70705*	*0071*		*1 SH ASh-62IR*	*5500*	*Utility*		
☐ RA-70733	PZL Mielec (Antonov) An-2		*CCCP-70733*	*0071*		*1 SH ASh-62IR*	*5500*	*Utility*		

KUBAN AIRLINES, Joint-Stock Company = GW / KIL (ALK-Avialinii Kubani) (formerly Krasnodar Avia & Aeroflot Krasnodar division) — Krasnodar

Krasnodar Airport, 350026 Krasnodar, Russia ☎ (8612) 37 05 00 Tx: 211116 port Fax: (8612) 37 38 11 SITA: n/a
F: n/a 👥 n/a Head: Ivan R. Babichev IATA: 113 ICAO: AIR KUBAN Net: n/a Some aircraft are still in Aeroflot colors but will be repainted in due course.

registration	type of aircraft	cn/fn	ex/ex*	mfd	del	powered by	mtow kg	configuration	selcal	name/fln/specialitites/remarks
☐ RA-46668	Antonov 24RV	*47309406*	*CCCP-46668*	*0474*		*2 IV AI-24VT*	*21800*	*Y48*		
☐ RA-47817	Antonov 24RV	*17307103*	*LZ-VPB*	*0771*		*2 IV AI-24VT*	*21800*	*Y48*		
☐ RA-47842	Antonov 24B	*17307404*	*CCCP-47842*	*1171*		*2 IV AI-24*	*21000*	*Y48*		
☐ RA-26096	Antonov 26B	*11901*	*CCCP-26096*	*0182*		*2 IV AI-24VT*	*24000*	*Freighter*		
☐ RA-26114	Antonov 26B	*12201*	*CCCP-26114*	*0582*		*2 IV AI-24VT*	*24000*	*Freighter*		
☐ RA-26126	Antonov 26B	*12610*	*CCCP-26126*	*1282*		*2 IV AI-24VT*	*24000*	*Freighter*		
☐ RA-42331	Yakovlev 42	*4520424505128*	*CCCP-42331*	*1085*		*3 LO D-36*	*56500*	*Y120*		
☐ RA-42336	Yakovlev 42	*4520422606220*	*CCCP-42336*	*0686*		*3 LO D-36*	*56500*	*Y120*		
☐ RA-42350	Yakovlev 42	*4520424711372*	*CCCP-42350*	*1187*		*3 LO D-36*	*56500*	*Y120*		
☐ RA-42363	Yakovlev 42D	*4520424811438*	*CCCP-42363*	*1188*		*3 LO D-36*	*56500*	*Y120*		
☐ RA-42367	Yakovlev 42D	*4520421914133*	*CCCP-42367*	*0389*		*3 LO D-36*	*56500*	*Y120*		
☐ RA-42375	Yakovlev 42D	*4520424914410*	*CCCP-42375*	*0190*		*3 LO D-36*	*56500*	*Y120*		
☐ RA-42386	Yakovlev 42D	*4520424016310*	*CCCP-42386*	*1190*		*3 LO D-36*	*56500*	*Y120*		
☐ RA-42421	Yakovlev 42D	*4520422303017*		*0793*		*3 LO D-36*	*56500*	*Y120*		
☐ RA-42526	Yakovlev 42	*11040803*	*CCCP-42526*	*0481*		*3 LO D-36*	*56500*	*Y120*		
☐ RA-42538	Yakovlev 42	*11130404*	*CCCP-42538*	*0981*		*3 LO D-36*	*54000*	*Y120*		
☐ RA-42541	Yakovlev 42	*11140704*	*CCCP-42541*	*1181*		*3 LO D-36*	*56500*	*Y120*		

KUBANAVIAUSLUGA (formerly Aeroflot Krasnodar 2nd division) — Enem

Enem Airport, 353321 poselok Enem, (Krasnodar Region), Russia ☎ (8612) 37 68 86 Tx: 211239 krylo Fax: (8612) 37 26 05 SITA: n/a
F: n/a 👥 n/a Head: Igor V. Voronov Net: n/a Beside listed aircraft, also own about 80 Antonov 2 (Sprayer) aircraft, many of them are currently stored and for sale. Most aircraft still in former Aeroflot colors.

registration	type of aircraft	cn/fn	ex/ex*	mfd	del	powered by	mtow kg	configuration	selcal	name/fln/specialitites/remarks
☐ RA-14082	PZL Swidnik (Mil) Mi-2	*5210626058*	*CCCP-14082*	*0088*		*2 IS GTD-350-4*	*3550*	*Utility*		
☐ RA-14083	PZL Swidnik (Mil) Mi-2	*5210627058*	*CCCP-14083*	*0088*		*2 IS GTD-350-4*	*3550*	*Utility*		
☐ RA-14084	PZL Swidnik (Mil) Mi-2	*5210628058*	*CCCP-14084*	*0088*		*2 IS GTD-350-4*	*3550*	*Utility*		
☐ RA-14107	PZL Swidnik (Mil) Mi-2	*5210726098*	*CCCP-14107*	*0088*		*2 IS GTD-350-4*	*3550*	*Utility*		
☐ RA-15601	PZL Swidnik (Mil) Mi-2	*529934096*	*CCCP-15601*	*0086*		*2 IS GTD-350-4*	*3550*	*Utility*		
☐ RA-15631	PZL Swidnik (Mil) Mi-2	*5210102017*	*CCCP-15631*	*0087*		*2 IS GTD-350-4*	*3550*	*Utility*		
☐ RA-15632	PZL Swidnik (Mil) Mi-2	*5210103017*	*CCCP-15632*	*0087*		*2 IS GTD-350-4*	*3550*	*Utility*		
☐ RA-20214	PZL Swidnik (Mil) Mi-2	*547001011*	*CCCP-20214*	*0081*		*2 IS GTD-350-4*	*3550*	*Utility*		
☐ RA-20272	PZL Swidnik (Mil) Mi-2	*547312091*	*CCCP-20272*	*0081*		*2 IS GTD-350-4*	*3550*	*Utility*		
☐ RA-20348	PZL Swidnik (Mil) Mi-2	*544034035*	*CCCP-20348*	*0075*		*2 IS GTD-350-4*	*3550*	*Utility*		
☐ RA-20358	PZL Swidnik (Mil) Mi-2	*529803056*	*CCCP-20358*	*0086*		*2 IS GTD-350-4*	*3550*	*Utility*		
☐ RA-20359	PZL Swidnik (Mil) Mi-2	*529804056*	*CCCP-20359*	*0086*		*2 IS GTD-350-4*	*3550*	*Utility*		
☐ RA-20390	PZL Swidnik (Mil) Mi-2	*529837076*	*CCCP-20390*	*0086*		*2 IS GTD-350-4*	*3550*	*Utility*		
☐ RA-20391	PZL Swidnik (Mil) Mi-2	*529838076*	*CCCP-20391*	*0086*		*2 IS GTD-350-4*	*3550*	*Utility*		
☐ RA-20405	PZL Swidnik (Mil) Mi-2	*529903086*	*CCCP-20405*	*0086*		*2 IS GTD-350-4*	*3550*	*Utility*		
☐ RA-20602	PZL Swidnik (Mil) Mi-2	*524742046*	*CCCP-20602*	*0076*		*2 IS GTD-350-4*	*3550*	*Utility*		
☐ RA-20681	PZL Swidnik (Mil) Mi-2	*526646050*	*CCCP-20681*	*0080*		*2 IS GTD-350-4*	*3550*	*Utility*		
☐ RA-20682	PZL Swidnik (Mil) Mi-2	*526647050*	*CCCP-20682*	*0080*		*2 IS GTD-350-4*	*3550*	*Utility*		
☐ RA-20683	PZL Swidnik (Mil) Mi-2		*CCCP-20683*	*0080*		*2 IS GTD-350-4*	*3550*	*Utility*		
☐ RA-20798	PZL Swidnik (Mil) Mi-2	*527920112*	*CCCP-20798*	*0082*		*2 IS GTD-350-4*	*3550*	*Utility*		
☐ RA-20811	PZL Swidnik (Mil) Mi-2	*528009013*	*CCCP-20811*	*0083*		*2 IS GTD-350-4*	*3550*	*Utility*		
☐ RA-20812	PZL Swidnik (Mil) Mi-2	*528010013*	*CCCP-20812*	*0083*		*2 IS GTD-350-4*	*3550*	*Utility*		
☐ RA-20823	PZL Swidnik (Mil) Mi-2	*548046033*	*CCCP-20823*	*0083*		*2 IS GTD-350-4*	*3550*	*Utility*		
☐ RA-20834	PZL Swidnik (Mil) Mi-2	*548107033*	*CCCP-20834*	*0083*		*2 IS GTD-350-4*	*3550*	*Utility*		
☐ RA-20860	PZL Swidnik (Mil) Mi-2	*548141043*	*CCCP-20860*	*0083*		*2 IS GTD-350-4*	*3550*	*Utility*		
☐ RA-20861	PZL Swidnik (Mil) Mi-2	*548142043*	*CCCP-20861*	*0083*		*2 IS GTD-350-4*	*3550*	*Utility*		
☐ RA-20996	PZL Swidnik (Mil) Mi-2	*549731046*	*CCCP-20996*	*0086*		*2 IS GTD-350-4*	*3550*	*Utility*		
☐ RA-20997	PZL Swidnik (Mil) Mi-2	*549732046*	*CCCP-20997*	*0086*		*2 IS GTD-350-4*	*3550*	*Utility*		
☐ RA-23213	PZL Swidnik (Mil) Mi-2	*5210135037*	*CCCP-23213*	*0087*		*2 IS GTD-350-4*	*3550*	*Utility*		
☐ RA-23214	PZL Swidnik (Mil) Mi-2	*5210136037*	*CCCP-23214*	*0087*		*2 IS GTD-350-4*	*3550*	*Utility*		
☐ RA-23242	PZL Swidnik (Mil) Mi-2	*5210248067*	*CCCP-23242*	*0087*		*2 IS GTD-350-4*	*3550*	*Utility*		
☐ RA-23248	PZL Swidnik (Mil) Mi-2	*5210304067*	*CCCP-23248*	*0087*		*2 IS GTD-350-4*	*3550*	*Utility*		
☐ RA-23500	PZL Swidnik (Mil) Mi-2	*526331109*	*CCCP-23500*	*0079*		*2 IS GTD-350-4*	*3550*	*Utility*		
☐ RA-23504	PZL Swidnik (Mil) Mi-2	*526417119*	*CCCP-23504*	*0079*		*2 IS GTD-350-4*	*3550*	*Utility*		
☐ RA-23505	PZL Swidnik (Mil) Mi-2	*526418119*	*CCCP-23505*	*0079*		*2 IS GTD-350-4*	*3550*	*Utility*		
☐ RA-23506	PZL Swidnik (Mil) Mi-2	*526419129*	*CCCP-23506*	*0079*		*2 IS GTD-350-4*	*3550*	*Utility*		
☐ RA-23755	PZL Swidnik (Mil) Mi-2			*0074*		*2 IS GTD-350-4*	*3550*	*Utility*		
☐ RA-23756	PZL Swidnik (Mil) Mi-2			*0074*		*2 IS GTD-350-4*	*3550*	*Utility*		
☐ RA-23757	PZL Swidnik (Mil) Mi-2	*543740094*		*0074*		*2 IS GTD-350-4*	*3550*	*Utility*		
☐ RA-23758	PZL Swidnik (Mil) Mi-2			*0074*		*2 IS GTD-350-4*	*3550*	*Utility*		
☐ RA-23759	PZL Swidnik (Mil) Mi-2			*0074*		*2 IS GTD-350-4*	*3550*	*Utility*		
☐ RA-23760	PZL Swidnik (Mil) Mi-2			*0074*		*2 IS GTD-350-4*	*3550*	*Utility*		
☐ RA-23761	PZL Swidnik (Mil) Mi-2			*0074*		*2 IS GTD-350-4*	*3550*	*Utility*		
☐ RA-23762	PZL Swidnik (Mil) Mi-2			*0074*		*2 IS GTD-350-4*	*3550*	*Utility*		

KUDYMKAR AIR ENTERPRISE (Kudymkarskoe aviapredpriatie) (formerly Aeroflot Kudymkar division) — Kudymkar

Kudymkar Airport, 617240 Kudymkar, (Perm Region), Russia ☎ (34262) 20 046 Tx: 684919 pilot Fax: (34262) 20 046 SITA: n/a
F: n/a 👥 n/a Head: Alexander L. Rychkov Net: n/a

registration	type of aircraft	cn/fn	ex/ex*	mfd	del	powered by	mtow kg	configuration	selcal	name/fln/specialitites/remarks
☐ RA-20893	PZL Swidnik (Mil) Mi-2	*538332093*	*CCCP-20893*	*0083*		*2 IS GTD-350-4*	*3550*	*EMS*		
☐ RA-02467	PZL Mielec (Antonov) An-2	*1G119-10*	*CCCP-02467*	*0070*		*1 SH ASh-62IR*	*5500*	*12 Pax*		
☐ RA-07683	PZL Mielec (Antonov) An-2		*CCCP-07683*	*0074*		*1 SH ASh-62IR*	*5500*	*12 Pax*		

KUMERTAU EXPRESS (Flying division of Kumertau Production Aviation Enterprise / Kumertauskoe APP / Member of MAP Group) — Kumertau

Kumertau Airport, 453350 Kumertau, (Republic of Bashkortostan), Russia ☎ (34761) 22 300 Tx: n/a Fax: (34761) 23 913 SITA: n/a
F: 1992 👥 n/a Head: Boris S. Malyshev Net: n/a Operates corporate flights for itself & commercial charter flights.

registration	type of aircraft	cn/fn	ex/ex*	mfd	del	powered by	mtow kg	configuration	selcal	name/fln/specialitites/remarks
☐ RA-87223	Yakovlev 40K	*9840359*	*CCCP-87223*	*0078*		*3 IV AI-25*	*16800*	*Combi*		
☐ RA-46632	Antonov 30	*0201*	*CCCP-46632*	*0073*		*2 IV AI-24T*	*23000*	*Survey / Combi*		
☐ RA-27204	Antonov 8		*CCCP-27204*	*0059*		*2 IV AI-20D*	*38000*	*Freighter*		
☐ RA-48970	Antonov 12	*2400502*	*LZ-BFC*	*0061*		*4 IV AI-20M*	*61000*	*Freighter*		

KURGAN AIR ENTERPRISE (Kurganskoe aviaprepriatie) (formerly Aeroflot Kurgan division) — Kurgan

Kurgan Airport, 640015 Kurgan, Russia ☎ (35222) 33 224 Tx: none Fax: (35222) 34 853 SITA: n/a
F: n/a 👥 n/a Head: Viniamin A. Selyaev Net: n/a Most aircraft are still in Aeroflot colors but will be repainted in due course.

registration	type of aircraft	cn/fn	ex/ex*	mfd	del	powered by	mtow kg	configuration	selcal	name/fln/specialitites/remarks
☐ RA-35059	PZL Mielec (Antonov) An-2		*CCCP-35059*	*0069*		*1 SH ASh-62IR*	*5500*	*Utility*		
☐ RA-62453	PZL Mielec (Antonov) An-2		*CCCP-62453*	*0064*		*1 SH ASh-62IR*	*5500*	*Utility*		
☐ RA-46286	Antonov 24B	*77303708*	*CCCP-46286*	*0067*		*2 IV AI-24*	*21000*	*Y48*		
☐ RA-46366	Antonov 24B		*CCCP-46366*	*0070*		*2 IV AI-24*	*21000*	*Y48*		
☐ RA-47273	Antonov 24B	*07306403*	*CCCP-47273*	*0070*		*2 IV AI-24*	*21000*	*Y48*		
☐ RA-26029	Antonov 26B		*CCCP-26029*	*0080*		*2 IV AI-24VT*	*24000*	*Freighter*		
☐ RA-26032	Antonov 26B		*CCCP-26032*	*0080*		*2 IV AI-24VT*	*24000*	*Freighter*		

KURSKAVIA = KUS (Kursk Air Enterprise) (formerly part of Central Districts Airline & Aeroflot Kursk division) — Kursk-Vostochny

Kursk Airport, 305022 Kursk, Russia ☎ (07122) 61 205 Tx: none Fax: (07122) 20 300 SITA: n/a
F: n/a ✈ n/a Head: Valery V. Darakhvelidze ICAO: KURSK AVIA Net: n/a Most aircraft are still in Aeroflot colors but will be repainted in due course.

registration	type of aircraft	cn/fn	ex/ex*	mfd	del	powered by	mtow kg	configuration	selcal	remarks
RA-01446	PZL Mielec (Antonov) An-2		CCCP-01446	0088		1 SH ASh-62IR	5500	Utility		
RA-05702	PZL Mielec (Antonov) An-2		CCCP-05702	0074		1 SH ASh-62IR	5500	Utility		
RA-07529	PZL Mielec (Antonov) An-2		CCCP-07529	0073		1 SH ASh-62IR	5500	Utility		
RA-07654	PZL Mielec (Antonov) An-2		CCCP-07654			1 SH ASh-62IR	5500	Utility		
RA-07823	PZL Mielec (Antonov) An-2		CCCP-07823	0076		1 SH ASh-62IR	5500	Utility		
RA-16048	PZL Mielec (Antonov) An-2		CCCP-16048	0075		1 SH ASh-62IR	5500	Utility		
RA-17894	PZL Mielec (Antonov) An-2	1G205-35	CCCP-17894	0083		1 SH ASh-62IR	5500	Utility		
RA-17972	PZL Mielec (Antonov) An-2		CCCP-17972	0084		1 SH ASh-62IR	5500	Utility		
RA-32664	PZL Mielec (Antonov) An-2		CCCP-32664	0085		1 SH ASh-62IR	5500	Utility		
RA-33009	PZL Mielec (Antonov) An-2		CCCP-33009	0086		1 SH ASh-62IR	5500	Utility		
RA-33045	PZL Mielec (Antonov) An-2		CCCP-33045	0086		1 SH ASh-62IR	5500	Utility		
RA-33315	PZL Mielec (Antonov) An-2		CCCP-33315	0087		1 SH ASh-62IR	5500	Utility		
RA-33474	PZL Mielec (Antonov) An-2		CCCP-33474	0088		1 SH ASh-62IR	5500	Utility		
RA-33552	PZL Mielec (Antonov) An-2		CCCP-33552	0088		1 SH ASh-62IR	5500	Utility		
RA-40304	PZL Mielec (Antonov) An-2		CCCP-40304	0086		1 SH ASh-62IR	5500	Utility		
RA-40321	PZL Mielec (Antonov) An-2		CCCP-40321	0086		1 SH ASh-62IR	5500	Utility		
RA-40490	PZL Mielec (Antonov) An-2		CCCP-40490	0087		1 SH ASh-62IR	5500	Utility		
RA-40705	PZL Mielec (Antonov) An-2		CCCP-40705	0085		1 SH ASh-62IR	5500	Utility		
RA-40706	PZL Mielec (Antonov) An-2		CCCP-40706	0085		1 SH ASh-62IR	5500	Utility		
RA-40721	PZL Mielec (Antonov) An-2		CCCP-40721	0076		1 SH ASh-62IR	5500	Utility		
RA-40722	PZL Mielec (Antonov) An-2	1G171-59	CCCP-40722	0076		1 SH ASh-62IR	5500	Utility		
RA-40723	PZL Mielec (Antonov) An-2	1G171-60	CCCP-40723	0076		1 SH ASh-62IR	5500	Utility		
RA-40724	PZL Mielec (Antonov) An-2		CCCP-40724	0076		1 SH ASh-62IR	5500	Utility		
RA-41343	PZL Mielec (Antonov) An-2	1G65-18	CCCP-41343	0065		1 SH ASh-62IR	5500	Utility		
RA-50504	PZL Mielec (Antonov) An-2		CCCP-50504	0067		1 SH ASh-62IR	5500	Utility		
RA-54904	PZL Mielec (Antonov) An-2		CCCP-54904	0080		1 SH ASh-62IR	5500	Utility		
RA-56389	PZL Mielec (Antonov) An-2	1G180-19	CCCP-56389	0078		1 SH ASh-62IR	5500	Utility		
RA-56407	PZL Mielec (Antonov) An-2		CCCP-56407	0078		1 SH ASh-62IR	5500	Utility		
RA-56430	PZL Mielec (Antonov) An-2		CCCP-56430	0078		1 SH ASh-62IR	5500	Utility		
RA-56448	PZL Mielec (Antonov) An-2		CCCP-56448	0078		1 SH ASh-62IR	5500	Utility		
RA-56451	PZL Mielec (Antonov) An-2		CCCP-56451	0079		1 SH ASh-62IR	5500	Utility		
RA-62634	PZL Mielec (Antonov) An-2	1G178-26	CCCP-62634	0078		1 SH ASh-62IR	5500	Utility		
RA-62668	PZL Mielec (Antonov) An-2		CCCP-62668	0078		1 SH ASh-62IR	5500	Utility		
RA-62687	PZL Mielec (Antonov) An-2	1G179-17	CCCP-62687	0078		1 SH ASh-62IR	5500	Utility		
RA-68055	PZL Mielec (Antonov) An-2		CCCP-68055	0081		1 SH ASh-62IR	5500	Utility		
RA-70577	PZL Mielec (Antonov) An-2		CCCP-70577	0071		1 SH ASh-62IR	5500	Utility		
RA-71186	PZL Mielec (Antonov) An-2		CCCP-71186	0082		1 SH ASh-62IR	5500	Utility		
RA-71187	PZL Mielec (Antonov) An-2		CCCP-71187	0082		1 SH ASh-62IR	5500	Utility		
RA-71270	PZL Mielec (Antonov) An-2		CCCP-71270	0084		1 SH ASh-62IR	5500	Utility		
RA-82806	PZL Mielec (Antonov) An-2		CCCP-82806	0075		1 SH ASh-62IR	5500	Utility		
RA-82818	PZL Mielec (Antonov) An-2		CCCP-82818	0075		1 SH ASh-62IR	5500	Utility		
RA-82836	PZL Mielec (Antonov) An-2		CCCP-82836	0076		1 SH ASh-62IR	5500	Utility		
RA-84650	PZL Mielec (Antonov) An-2		CCCP-84650	0081		1 SH ASh-62IR	5500	Utility		
RA-46386	Antonov 24B		CCCP-46386	0070		2 IV AI-24	21000	Y48		
RA-46432	Antonov 24B	87304302	CCCP-46432	0068		2 IV AI-24	21000	Y48		
RA-46484	Antonov 24RV	27308102	CCCP-46484	0072		2 IV AI-24VT	21800	Y48		
RA-46574	Antonov 24B		CCCP-46574	0068		2 IV AI-24	21000	Y48		
RA-46641	Antonov 24RV		CCCP-46641	0073		2 IV AI-24VT	21800	Y48		
RA-47283	Antonov 24B	07306503	CCCP-47283	0070		2 IV AI-24	21000	Y48		
RA-47843	Antonov 24B		CCCP-47843	0071		2 IV AI-24	21000	Y48		
RA-26031	Antonov 26B	10503	CCCP-26031	0080		2 IV AI-24VT	24000	Freighter		
RA-26067	Antonov 26B		CCCP-26067	0081		2 IV AI-24VT	24000	Freighter		
RA-26070	Antonov 26B	11404	CCCP-26070	0081		2 IV AI-24VT	24000	Freighter		
RA-26082	Antonov 26B	11705	CCCP-26082	0081		2 IV AI-24VT	24000	Freighter		
RA-26098	Antonov 26B		CCCP-26098	0082		2 IV AI-24VT	24000	Freighter		

KVZ – Kazansky vertoletny zavod = KPH (Flying div. of Kazan Helicopters Prod. Ass. / Member of MAP Group) — Kazan-Int'l

Flying division / Letny otryad, Ul. Tetsevskaya, 420085 Kazan (Republic of Tatarstan), Russia ☎ (8432) 37 97 79 Tx: n/a Fax: (8432) 37 97 79 SITA: n/a
F: n/a ✈ n/a Head: Vilyr V. Batirov ICAO: KAMA Net: n/a Operates corporate flights for itself & commercial charter flights. Most aircraft are still in Aeroflot colors with or without titles or with Tatarstan flag.

registration	type of aircraft	cn/fn	ex/ex*	mfd	del	powered by	mtow kg	configuration	selcal	remarks
RA-06175	Mil Mi-8T	8621	CCCP-06175	0686		2 IS TV2-117A	12000	Utility		
RA-70897	Mil Mi-8MTV-1	95824	CCCP-70897	0192	0097	2 IS TV3-117MT	13000	Utility		
RA-70900	Mil Mi-8MTV-1	95831	CCCP-70900	0192	0097	2 IS TV3-117MT	13000	Utility		
RA-47715	Antonov 24B	69900505	CCCP-47715	0766		2 IV AI-24	21800	Y48		
RA-26060	Antonov 26B	11107	CCCP-26060	0581		2 IV AI-24VT	24000	Freighter		lst TUL

LENSIBAVIA = LSB (Nauchny letno-metodicheski kompleks / Scientific Flight & Methodical Complex dba) — St. Petersburg-Pulkovo

Ul. Pilotov 38, 196210 St. Petersburg, Russia ☎ (812) 104 15 31 Tx: n/a Fax: (812) 104 18 69 SITA: n/a
F: 1992 ✈ n/a Head: Vladimir V. Romanenko ICAO: LENSIBAVIA Net: n/a Aircraft below MTOW 1361: Ilyushin 103

registration	type of aircraft	cn/fn	ex/ex*	mfd	del	powered by	mtow kg	configuration	selcal	remarks
RA-17963	PZL Mielec (Antonov) An-2	1G209-47	CCCP-17963	0084		1 SH ASh-62IR	5500	Trainer		
RA-35016	PZL Mielec (Antonov) An-2	1G109-22	CCCP-35016	0069		1 SH ASh-62IR	5500	Trainer		
RA-70686	PZL Mielec (Antonov) An-2	1G129-36	CCCP-70686	0071		1 SH ASh-62IR	5500	Trainer		
RA-25537	Mil Mi-8		CCCP-25537	0091		2 IS TV2-117A	12000	Trainer		

LESHUKONSKOE AIR ENTERPRISE (Aviapredpriatie Leshukonskoe) (formerly Aeroflot Leshukonskoe division) — Leshukonskoe

Leshukonskoe Airport, 164670 Leshukonskoe, (Arkhangelsk Region), Russia ☎ 31 718 (via Moscow) Tx: 242665 sever Fax: none SITA: n/a
F: n/a ✈ n/a Head: Gennady V. Gromak Net: n/a Most aircraft are still in Aeroflot colors but will be repainted in due course.

registration	type of aircraft	cn/fn	ex/ex*	mfd	del	powered by	mtow kg	configuration	selcal	remarks
RA-02284	PZL Mielec (Antonov) An-2		CCCP-02284	0090		1 SH ASh-62IR	5500	Utility		
RA-07230	PZL Mielec (Antonov) An-2		CCCP-07230	0073		1 SH ASh-62IR	5500	Utility		
RA-07481	PZL Mielec (Antonov) An-2		CCCP-07481	0073		1 SH ASh-62IR	5500	Utility		
RA-07513	PZL Mielec (Antonov) An-2		CCCP-07513	0073		1 SH ASh-62IR	5500	Utility		
RA-07516	PZL Mielec (Antonov) An-2		CCCP-07516	0073		1 SH ASh-62IR	5500	Utility		
RA-07525	PZL Mielec (Antonov) An-2		CCCP-07525	0073		1 SH ASh-62IR	5500	Utility		
RA-07526	PZL Mielec (Antonov) An-2		CCCP-07526	0073		1 SH ASh-62IR	5500	Utility		
RA-07528	PZL Mielec (Antonov) An-2		CCCP-07528	0073		1 SH ASh-62IR	5500	Utility		
RA-07534	PZL Mielec (Antonov) An-2		CCCP-07534	0073		1 SH ASh-62IR	5500	Utility		
RA-07536	PZL Mielec (Antonov) An-2		CCCP-07536	0073		1 SH ASh-62IR	5500	Utility		
RA-07638	PZL Mielec (Antonov) An-2		CCCP-07638	0074		1 SH ASh-62IR	5500	Utility		
RA-07866	PZL Mielec (Antonov) An-2		CCCP-07866	0076		1 SH ASh-62IR	5500	Utility		
RA-07879	PZL Mielec (Antonov) An-2		CCCP-07879	0076		1 SH ASh-62IR	5500	Utility		
RA-17756	PZL Mielec (Antonov) An-2		CCCP-17756	0083		1 SH ASh-62IR	5500	Utility		
RA-17855	PZL Mielec (Antonov) An-2		CCCP-17855	0083		1 SH ASh-62IR	5500	Utility		
RA-31536	PZL Mielec (Antonov) An-2		CCCP-31536	0082		1 SH ASh-62IR	5500	Utility		
RA-33393	PZL Mielec (Antonov) An-2		CCCP-33393	0087		1 SH ASh-62IR	5500	Utility		
RA-33394	PZL Mielec (Antonov) An-2		CCCP-33394	0087		1 SH ASh-62IR	5500	Utility		
RA-40318	PZL Mielec (Antonov) An-2		CCCP-40318	0086		1 SH ASh-62IR	5500	Utility		
RA-40880	PZL Mielec (Antonov) An-2		CCCP-40880	0085		1 SH ASh-62IR	5500	Utility		
RA-40907	PZL Mielec (Antonov) An-2		CCCP-40907	0085		1 SH ASh-62IR	5500	Utility		
RA-40981	PZL Mielec (Antonov) An-2	1G217-21	CCCP-40981	0085		1 SH ASh-62IR	5500	Utility		
RA-54939	PZL Mielec (Antonov) An-2		CCCP-54939	0080		1 SH ASh-62IR	5500	Utility		
RA-56534	PZL Mielec (Antonov) An-2		CCCP-56534	0079		1 SH ASh-62IR	5500	Utility		
RA-56535	PZL Mielec (Antonov) An-2		CCCP-56535	0079		1 SH ASh-62IR	5500	Utility		
RA-62573	PZL Mielec (Antonov) An-2		CCCP-62573	0077		1 SH ASh-62IR	5500	Utility		
RA-62574	PZL Mielec (Antonov) An-2		CCCP-62574	0077		1 SH ASh-62IR	5500	Utility		
RA-62575	PZL Mielec (Antonov) An-2		CCCP-62575	0077		1 SH ASh-62IR	5500	Utility		
RA-70411	PZL Mielec (Antonov) An-2		CCCP-70411	0073		1 SH ASh-62IR	5500	Utility		
RA-71166	PZL Mielec (Antonov) An-2		CCCP-71166	0082		1 SH ASh-62IR	5500	Utility		
RA-81533	PZL Mielec (Antonov) An-2		CCCP-81533	0084		1 SH ASh-62IR	5500	Utility		

LIPETSK AIR ENTERPRISE = LIP (Lipetskoe aviapredpriatie) (formerly part of Central Districts Airlines & Aeroflot Lipetsk division) — Lipetsk

Lipetsk Airport, 398000 Lipetsk, Russia ☎ (0742) 25 01 06 Tx: 101113 yastreb Fax: (0742) 72 00 95 SITA: n/a
F: n/a ✈ n/a Head: Peter D. Zubrev ICAO: LIPETSK-AVIA Net: n/a Most aircraft are still in Aeroflot colors but will be repainted in due course. Also owns 40 Antonov An-2 aircraft but are wfu and for sale.

registration	type of aircraft	cn/fn	ex/ex*	mfd	del	powered by	mtow kg	configuration	selcal	remarks
RA-14178	PZL Swidnik (Mil) Mi-2	5210514018	CCCP-14178	0088		2 IS GTD-350-4	3550	Utility		
RA-14345	PZL Swidnik (Mil) Mi-2	535043126	CCCP-14345	0076		2 IS GTD-350-4	3550	Utility		
RA-14355	PZL Swidnik (Mil) Mi-2	535103017	CCCP-14355	0077		2 IS GTD-350-4	3550	Utility		
RA-15638	PZL Swidnik (Mil) Mi-2	5410109017	CCCP-15638	0087		2 IS GTD-350-4	3550	Utility		
RA-15639	PZL Swidnik (Mil) Mi-2	5410110017	CCCP-15639	0087		2 IS GTD-350-4	3550	Utility		
RA-20235	PZL Swidnik (Mil) Mi-2	527103031	CCCP-20235	0081		2 IS GTD-350-4	3550	Utility		
RA-20236	PZL Swidnik (Mil) Mi-2	527104031	CCCP-20236	0081		2 IS GTD-350-4	3550	Utility		

☐ RA-20310	PZL Swidnik (Mil) Mi-2	527516022	CCCP-20310	0082		2 IS GTD-350-4	3550	Utility		
☐ RA-20311	PZL Swidnik (Mil) Mi-2	527517022	CCCP-20311	0082		2 IS GTD-350-4	3550	Utility		
☐ RA-20312	PZL Swidnik (Mil) Mi-2	527518022	CCCP-20312	0082		2 IS GTD-350-4	3550	Utility		
☐ RA-20350	PZL Swidnik (Mil) Mi-2	549745056	CCCP-20350	0086		2 IS GTD-350-4	3550	Utility		
☐ RA-20382	PZL Swidnik (Mil) Mi-2	529829066	CCCP-20382	0086		2 IS GTD-350-4	3550	Utility		
☐ RA-20419	PZL Swidnik (Mil) Mi-2	529922086	CCCP-20419	0086		2 IS GTD-350-4	3550	Utility		
☐ RA-20420	PZL Swidnik (Mil) Mi-2	529923086	CCCP-20420	0086		2 IS GTD-350-4	3550	Utility		
☐ RA-20736	PZL Swidnik (Mil) Mi-2	527633052	CCCP-20736	0082		2 IS GTD-350-4	3550	Utility		
☐ RA-23212	PZL Swidnik (Mil) Mi-2	5210134037	CCCP-23212	0087		2 IS GTD-350-4	3550	Utility		
☐ RA-23222	PZL Swidnik (Mil) Mi-2		CCCP-23222	0087		2 IS GTD-350-4	3550	Utility		
☐ RA-23308	PZL Swidnik (Mil) Mi-2	529129035	CCCP-23308	0085		2 IS GTD-350-4	3550	Utility		
☐ RA-23420	PZL Swidnik (Mil) Mi-2	529015124	CCCP-23420	0084		2 IS GTD-350-4	3550	Utility		
☐ RA-23425	PZL Swidnik (Mil) Mi-2	529020124	CCCP-23425	0084		2 IS GTD-350-4	3550	Utility		
☐ RA-23484	PZL Swidnik (Mil) Mi-2	526243089	CCCP-23484	0079		2 IS GTD-350-4	3550	Utility		
☐ RA-23485	PZL Swidnik (Mil) Mi-2	526244089	CCCP-23485	0079		2 IS GTD-350-4	3550	Utility		
☐ RA-23549	PZL Swidnik (Mil) Mi-2	526138059	CCCP-23549	0079		2 IS GTD-350-4	3550	Utility		
☐ RA-87281	Yakovlev 40	9311627	CCCP-87281	0073		3 IV AI-25	16800	C15		
☐ RA-87372	Yakovlev 40	9340332	CCCP-87372	0073		3 IV AI-25	16800	C12		
☐ RA-87406	Yakovlev 40	9421833	CCCP-87406	0074		3 IV AI-25	16800	Y32		
☐ RA-87845	Yakovlev 40	9331430	CCCP-87845	0073		3 IV AI-25	17200	C15		
☐ RA-87921	Yakovlev 40K	9731155	CCCP-87921	0077		3 IV AI-25	17200	Y32		
☐ RA-87986	Yakovlev 40	9540944	CCCP-87986	0075		3 IV AI-25	16800	Y32		
☐ RA-88229	Yakovlev 40	9641850	CCCP-88229	0076		3 IV AI-25	17200	C15		
☐ RA-88236	Yakovlev 40	9640551	CCCP-88236	0076		3 IV AI-25	17200	C15		op in STINOL-colors
☐ RA-42402	Yakovlev 42D	4520422116583	CCCP-42402	0091		3 LO D-36	56500	Y120		Ist AKT
☐ RA-42427	Yakovlev 42D	4520422305016		0093		3 LO D-36	56500	Y120		Ist AKT

LUKIAVIATRANS — **Balandino**

Ul. Portovaya, 182100 Balandino, (Velikie Luki District, Pskov Region), Russia ☎ 92 967 (via Moscow) Tx: none Fax: none SITA: n/a
F: n/a ✈✈✈ n/a Head: Mikhail A. Tumanov Net: n/a

☐ RA-05811	PZL Mielec (Antonov) An-2					1 SH ASh-62IR	5500	Utility		
☐ RA-05812	PZL Mielec (Antonov) An-2					1 SH ASh-62IR	5500	Utility		

LUKOIL AVIA (Division of Lukoil Company) — **Moscow-Sheremetyevo**

GosNII GA, Sheremetyevo I Airport, 103340 Moskva, Russia ☎ (095) 578 43 04 Tx: none Fax: (095) 578 38 39 SITA: n/a
F: n/a ✈✈✈ n/a Head: Mrs. Larisa V. Shchepachenko Net: n/a

☐ RA-87221	Yakovlev 40K	9831958	CCCP-87221	0078		3 IV AI-25	17200	Exec 14 Pax		
☐ RA-87353	Yakovlev 40	9330231	CCCP-87353	0073		3 IV AI-25	16800	Exec 14 Pax		
☐ RA-88297	Yakovlev 40	9530142	01 RED	0775		3 IV AI-25	17200	Exec 14 Pax		
☐ RA-42424	Yakovlev 142	4520421502016		0095		3 LO D-36	57500	Executive		fn 0216 / cvtd 42D

MADINA = MND — **Makhachkala & Moscow-Vnukovo**

Pr. Lenina 97, 367025 Makhachkala, (Republic of Dagestan), Russia ☎ (8722) 67 85 85 Tx: none Fax: (8722) 67 71 82 SITA: n/a
F: n/a ✈✈✈ n/a Head: Murad G. Kuyaev ICAO: AIR MADINA Net: n/a Operates Ilyushin 18V leased from NPP MIR & Tupolev 134A leased from VORONEZHAVIA when required.

MAD – Malaya Aviatsia Dona = MKK (SDA-Small Don Aviation) (formerly Aeroflot Rostov-na-Donu 2nd division) — **Rostov-na-Donu**

Prospekt Sholokhova 262/3, 344009 Rostov-na-Donu, Russia ☎ (8632) 52 47 28 Tx: none Fax: (8632) 52 47 28 SITA: n/a
F: 1994 ✈✈✈ n/a Head: Konstantin K. Miroshnichenko ICAO: AEROKEY Net: n/a

☐ RA-23717	PZL Swidnik (Mil) Mi-2	519917086		0086	0094	2 IS GTD-350-4	3550	Utility		
☐ RA-23778	PZL Swidnik (Mil) Mi-2	546910110		0080	0094	2 IS GTD-350-4	3550	Utility		
☐ RA-23790	PZL Swidnik (Mil) Mi-2	546920110		0080	0094	2 IS GTD-350-4	3550	Utility		
☐ RA-23791	PZL Swidnik (Mil) Mi-2	548111032		0082	0094	2 IS GTD-350-4	3550	Utility		
☐ RA-22960	Mil Mi-8	9743711		0074	0094	2 IS TV2-117A	12000	Utility		
☐ RA-22961	Mil Mi-8	9765410		0074	0094	2 IS TV2-117A	12000	Utility		
☐ RA-25131	Mil Mi-8	3475		0074	0094	2 IS TV2-117A	12000	Utility		
☐ RA-27007	Mil Mi-8	9732809		0073	0094	2 IS TV2-117A	12000	Utility		

MAGADAN 2nd Aviation Enterprise (Vtoroe Magadanskoe aviapredpriatie) (formerly Aeroflot Magadan 2nd division) — **Magadan-13km**

13km Osnovnoi Trassy, 685009 Magadan 9, Russia ☎ (41322) 46 302 Tx: n/a Fax: n/a SITA: n/a
F: n/a ✈✈✈ n/a Head: Eduard E. Shatilov Net: n/a Most aircraft are still in Aeroflot colors but will be repainted in due course.

☐ RA-04351	Antonov An-2	113547309	CCCP-04351	0060		1 SH ASh-62IR	5500	Utility		
☐ RA-22593	Mil Mi-8		CCCP-22593	0079		2 IS TV2-117A	12000	Combi		
☐ RA-22863	Mil Mi-8		CCCP-22863	0084		2 IS TV2-117A	12000	Combi		
☐ RA-22881	Mil Mi-8		CCCP-22881	0084		2 IS TV2-117A	12000	Combi		
☐ RA-22919	Mil Mi-8		CCCP-22919	0085		2 IS TV2-117A	12000	Combi		
☐ RA-24423	Mil Mi-8		CCCP-24423	0084		2 IS TV2-117A	12000	Combi		
☐ RA-24442	Mil Mi-8		CCCP-24442	0086		2 IS TV2-117A	12000	Combi		
☐ RA-24524	Mil Mi-8		CCCP-24524	0085		2 IS TV2-117A	12000	Combi		
☐ RA-24541	Mil Mi-8		CCCP-24541	0085		2 IS TV2-117A	12000	Combi		
☐ RA-24671	Mil Mi-8		CCCP-24671	0081		2 IS TV2-117A	12000	Combi		
☐ RA-24704	Mil Mi-8		CCCP-24704	0084		2 IS TV2-117A	12000	Combi		
☐ RA-25321	Mil Mi-8		CCCP-25321	0082		2 IS TV2-117A	12000	Combi		
☐ RA-25450	Mil Mi-8MTV-1		CCCP-25450	0091		2 IS TV3-117MT	13000	Combi		
☐ RA-25827	Mil Mi-8		CCCP-25827	0074		2 IS TV2-117A	12000	Combi		
☐ RA-25986	Mil Mi-8		CCCP-25986	0077		2 IS TV2-117A	12000	Combi		

MAGNITOGORSK AIR ENTERPRISE = MNG (Magnitogorskoe aviapredpriatie) (formerly Aeroflot Magnitogrosk division) — **Magnitogorsk**

Magnitogorsk Airport, 455033 Magnitogorsk, (Chelyabinsk Region), Russia ☎ (3511) 32 94 25 Tx: n/a Fax: (3511) 34 63 74 SITA: n/a
F: n/a ✈✈✈ n/a Head: Vitali Martyniuk ICAO: MAGNITKA Net: n/a Beside aircraft listed, also operates Antonov 2 aircraft. Full details not yet known. Most aircraft are still in Aeroflot colors but will be repainted in due course.

☐ RA-46486	Antonov 24RV	27308104	CCCP-46486	0072		2 IV AI-24VT	21800	Y48		
☐ RA-46603	Antonov 24RV		CCCP-46603	0073		2 IV AI-24VT	21800	Y48		
☐ RA-46682	Antonov 24RV		CCCP-46682	0074		2 IV AI-24VT	21800	Y48		
☐ RA-46692	Antonov 24RV	47309903	CCCP-46692	0074		2 IV AI-24VT	21800	Y48		
☐ RA-47197	Antonov 24RV		CCCP-47197	0072		2 IV AI-24VT	21800	Y48		
☐ RA-47814	Antonov 24RV		CCCP-47814	0071		2 IV AI-24VT	21800	Y48		
☐ RA-26525	Antonov 26	7205	CCCP-26525	0078		2 IV AI-24VT	24000	Freighter		
☐ RA-26545	Antonov 26		CCCP-26545	0075		2 IV AI-24VT	24000	Freighter		
☐ RA-26558	Antonov 26	3305	CCCP-26558	0075		2 IV AI-24VT	24000	Freighter		
☐ RA-26611	Antonov 26	4304	CCCP-26611	0076		2 IV AI-24VT	24000	Freighter		

MARZ-AVIA (Subsidiary of Moscow Helicopter Repair Plant) — **Chernoe Heliport**

p/o Chernoye, 143991 Balashikha, (Moscow Region), Russia ☎ (095) 522 91 83 Tx: none Fax: (095) 522 92 05 SITA: n/a
F: 1997 ✈✈✈ n/a Head: Gennady V. Dolgov Net: n/a

☐ RA-15676	PZL Swidnik (Mil) Mi-2					2 IS GTD-350-4	3550	Utility		
☐ RA-15684	PZL Swidnik (Mil) Mi-2					2 IS GTD-350-4	3550	Utility		

MAUS – Myachkovskie aviatsionnye uslugi, Joint-Stock Company = MKV (Myachkovo Air Services) (formerly Myachkovo Avn&AFL Myachkovo) — **Moscow-Myachkovo**

PO Box 50, 140000 Lyubertsy, (Moscow Region), Russia ☎ (095) 552 35 35 Tx: none Fax: (095) 522 22 16 SITA: n/a
F: n/a ✈✈✈ n/a Head: Ivan I. Sharapov ICAO: LUBER Net: n/a Most aircraft are still in Aeroflot colors but will be repainted in due course.

☐ RA-25244	Mil Mi-8	3228	CCCP-25244	0072		2 IS TV2-117A	12000	Utility		
☐ RA-30001	Antonov 30	1402	CCCP-30001	0078		2 IV AI-24T	23000	Survey / Combi		
☐ RA-30006	Antonov 30	1407	CCCP-30006	0078		2 IV AI-24T	23000	Survey / Combi		
☐ RA-30021	Antonov 30	0403	CCCP-30021	0073		2 IV AI-24T	23000	Survey / Combi		
☐ RA-30023	Antonov 30	0501	CCCP-30023	0074		2 IV AI-24T	23000	Survey / Combi		
☐ RA-30027	Antonov 30	0506	CCCP-30027	0074		2 IV AI-24T	23000	Survey / Combi		
☐ RA-30032	Antonov 30	0607	CCCP-30032	0074		2 IV AI-24T	23000	Survey / Combi		
☐ RA-30033	Antonov 30	0610	CCCP-30033	0074		2 IV AI-24T	23000	Survey / Combi		
☐ RA-30035	Antonov 30	0702	CCCP-30035	0074		2 IV AI-24T	23000	Survey / Combi		
☐ RA-30039	Antonov 30	0710	CCCP-30039	0074		2 IV AI-24T	23000	Survey / Combi		
☐ RA-30042	Antonov 30	0901	CCCP-30042	0075		2 IV AI-24T	23000	Survey / Combi		
☐ RA-30043	Antonov 30	0905	CCCP-30043	0075		2 IV AI-24T	23000	Survey / Combi		
☐ RA-30045	Antonov 30	0907	CCCP-30045	0075		2 IV AI-24T	23000	Survey / Combi		
☐ RA-30047	Antonov 30	0909	CCCP-30047	0075		2 IV AI-24T	23000	Survey / Combi		
☐ RA-30050	Antonov 30	1005	CCCP-30050	0075		2 IV AI-24T	23000	Survey / Combi		
☐ RA-30054	Antonov 30	1010	CCCP-30054	0076		2 IV AI-24T	23000	Survey / Combi		
☐ RA-30055	Antonov 30	1101	CCCP-30055	0076		2 IV AI-24T	23000	Survey / Combi		
☐ RA-30061	Antonov 30	1110	CCCP-30061	0076		2 IV AI-24T	23000	Survey / Combi		
☐ RA-30064	Antonov 30	1203	CCCP-30064	0077		2 IV AI-24T	23000	Survey / Combi		
☐ RA-30065	Antonov 30	1204	CCCP-30065	0077		2 IV AI-24T	23000	Survey / Combi		
☐ RA-30066	Antonov 30	1206	CCCP-30066	0077		2 IV AI-24T	23000	Survey / Combi		
☐ RA-30069	Antonov 30	1210	CCCP-30069	0077		2 IV AI-24T	23000	Survey / Combi		

546 registration type of aircraft cn/fn ex/ex* mfd del powered by mtow kg configuration selcal name/fln/specialitites/remarks

☐ RA-30070	Antonov 30	1301	CCCP-30070	0077		2 IV AI-24T	23000	Survey / Combi		
☐ RA-30072	Antonov 30	1303	CCCP-30072	0077		2 IV AI-24T	23000	Survey / Combi		
☐ RA-30073	Antonov 30	1304	CCCP-30073	0077		2 IV AI-24T	23000	Survey / Combi		
☐ RA-30074	Antonov 30	1305	CCCP-30074	0077		2 IV AI-24T	23000	Survey / Combi		
☐ RA-30075	Antonov 30	1306	CCCP-30075	0077		2 IV AI-24T	23000	Survey / Combi		
☐ RA-46634	Antonov 30	0301	CCCP-46634	0075		2 IV AI-24T	23000	Survey / Combi		

MAVIAL – Magadanskie avialinii = H5 / MVL (Magadan Airlines) (formerly part of Aeroflot Magadan directorate) — Magadan-Sokol

Sokol Airport, 685018 Magadan, Russia ☎ (41322) 93 644 Tx: none Fax: (41322) 93 060 SITA: n/a
F: 1994 ☨☨☨ n/a Head: Alexander P. Shubaev IATA: 428 ICAO: MAVIAL Net: n/a

☐ RA-85540	Tupolev 154B-2	540	CCCP-85540	0582		3 KU NK-8-2U	100000	Y164		
☐ RA-85557	Tupolev 154B-2	557	CCCP-85557	0082		3 KU NK-8-2U	98000	Y164		
☐ RA-85562	Tupolev 154B-2	562	CCCP-85562	0082		3 KU NK-8-2U	98000	Y164		
☐ RA-85567	Tupolev 154B-2	567	CCCP-85567	0082		3 KU NK-8-2U	98000	Y164		
☐ RA-85584	Tupolev 154B-2	584	CCCP-85584	0083		3 KU NK-8-2U	98000	Y164		
☐ RA-85588	Tupolev 154B-2	588	CCCP-85588	0083		3 KU NK-8-2U	98000	Y164		lst VLK
☐ RA-85596	Tupolev 154B-2	596	CCCP-85596	0084		3 KU NK-8-2U	98000	Y164		lst VLK
☐ RA-85667	Tupolev 154M	825	CCCP-85667	0089		3 SO D-30KU-154-II	100000	Y164		
☐ RA-85671	Tupolev 154M	829	CCCP-85671	0090		3 SO D-30KU-154-II	100000	Y164		lst AZS
☐ RA-85677	Tupolev 154M	839	CCCP-85677	0090		3 SO D-30KU-154-II	100000	Y164		
☐ RA-85680	Tupolev 154M	843	CCCP-85680	0090		3 SO D-30KU-154-II	100000	Y164		
☐ RA-85685	Tupolev 154M	853	CCCP-85685	0090		3 SO D-30KU-154-II	100000	Y164		
☐ RA-85696	Tupolev 154M	869	CCCP-85696	0091		3 SO D-30KU-154-II	100000	Y164		lst AZS
☐ RA-86507	Ilyushin 62M	2035546	CCCP-86507	0080	0098	4 SO D-30KU	167000	Y156		lsf UHS / fn 3504

MCHS ROSSII Gosudarstvennoe unitarnoe aviatsionnoe predpriatie = SUM (State Unitary Air Enterprise of Ministry for Emergency Situations dba) — Moscow-Zhukovsky

Ul. Davydkovskaya 7, 121352 Moskva, Russia ☎ (095) 445 44 24 Tx: none Fax: (095) 445 44 14 SITA: n/a
F: 1995 ☨☨☨ n/a Head: Rafail Sh. Zakirov ICAO: SUMES Net: n/a

☐ RA-87482	Yakovlev 40	9441038	CCCP-87482	0074		3 IV AI-25	16100	Y24		
☐ RA-74029	Antonov 74	36547097940		1293		2 LO D-36	34800	Freighter		
☐ RA-74034	Antonov 74	47136012		0195		2 LO D-36	34800	Freighter		
☐ RA-42441	Yakovlev 42D	4520421402018		0094	0996	3 LO D-36	56500	VIP		
☐ RA-86570	Ilyushin 62M	1356344		0095	0696	4 SO D-30KU	167000	VIP 114 Pax		fn 5604
☐ RA-76362	Ilyushin 76TD	1033416533		0793		4 SO D-30KP	190000	Freighter		jtly opw AYZ
☐ RA-76363	Ilyushin 76TD	1033417540		0793		4 SO D-30KP	190000	Freighter		jtly opw AYZ
☐ RA-76429	Ilyushin 76TD	1043419639		0497	0097	4 SO D-30KP	190000	Freighter		
☐ RA-76840	Ilyushin 76TD	1033417553		1094		4 SO D-30KP	190000	Freighter		lst/jtly opw AYZ
☐ RA-76841	Ilyushin 76TD	1033418601		0094		4 SO D-30KP	190000	Freighter		lst/jtly opw AYZ
☐ RA-76845	Ilyushin 76TD	1043420696		0395		4 SO D-30KP	190000	Freighter		lst/jtly opw AYZ

MDA AIRLINES, Joint-Stock Company = KR / MDD — Rostov-na-Donu

Prospekt Sholokhova 272, 344009 Rostov-na-Donu, Russia ☎ (8632) 58 92 48 Tx: none Fax: (8632) 52 68 12 SITA: n/a
F: 1996 ☨☨☨ n/a Head: Yevgeni A. Kravchenko ICAO: DONLINES Net: n/a

☐ RA-87253	Yakovlev 40	9321026	CCCP-87253	0073	0097	3 IV AI-25	17200	C14		
☐ RA-87254	Yakovlev 40	9311126	CCCP-87254	0073	0097	3 IV AI-25	17200	Y27		
☐ RA-87268	Yakovlev 40	9310427	CCCP-87268	0073	0097	3 IV AI-25	17200	Y27		
☐ RA-87295	Yakovlev 40	9321228	CCCP-87295	0073	0097	3 IV AI-25	17200	Y27		
☐ RA-87307	Yakovlev 40	9320329	CCCP-87307	0073	0097	3 IV AI-25	17200	Y27		
☐ RA-87499	Yakovlev 40	9610246	EP-LBB	0076	0097	3 IV AI-25	17200	Y30		
☐ RA-87965	Yakovlev 40	9820858	CCCP-87965	0078	0097	3 IV AI-25	17200	C18		
☐ RA-88184	Yakovlev 40	9620448	CCCP-88184	0076	0097	3 IV AI-25	17200	Y32		
☐ RA-88218	Yakovlev 40	9630450	CCCP-88218	0076	0097	3 IV AI-25	17200	Y32		
☐ RA-88225	Yakovlev 40	9641250	EP-LBA	0076	0097	3 IV AI-25	17200	Y30		
☐ RA-88270	Yakovlev 40	9720853	CCCP-88270	0077	0097	3 IV AI-25	17200	Y32		

MERIDIAN AIR, Co. Ltd = MMM (Aviakompania Meridian) — Moscow-Vnukovo

PO Box 144, 103473 Moskva, Russia ☎ (095) 913 17 93 Tx: none Fax: (095) 284 59 49 SITA: n/a
F: 1982 ☨☨☨ n/a Head: Sergey E. Knyaguinichev ICAO: AVIAMERIDIAN Net: n/a

☐ RA-02801	Hawker 700B (HS 125-700B)	257097	G-BHTJ	0080	0197	2 GA TFE731-3R-1H	11567	8 Pax		opf Patina & Charter Air Centre

MI-AVIA = MIV (Division of Mil-Moskovsky vertoletny zavod im M.L. Mila/Mil-Moscow Helicopter Factory) — Moscow-Lyubertsy Heliport

Ul. Sokolnichesky Val 2, 107113 Moskva, Russia ☎ (095) 956 68 93 Tx: 112247 ubiliar Fax: (095) 956 68 92 SITA: n/a
F: 1992 ☨☨☨ n/a Head: Yury F. Chapaev ICAO: MIAVIA Net: n/a

☐ RA-04002	Mil Mi-34			0096		1 VO M-14V-26	1450	Utility		opf Police
☐ RA-06180	Mil Mi-26T	226205	CCCP-06180	0089		2 LO D-136	56000	Utility		
☐ RA-06181	Mil Mi-26		CCCP-06181	0089		2 LO D-136	56000	Utility		

MURMANSK AIRLINES, Joint-Stock Company = MNK (Murmanskie avialinii) (formerly Aeroflot Murmansk division) — Murmansk-Murmashi

Murmashi Airport, 184364 Murmansk, Russia ☎ (8152) 58 34 05 Tx: 126136 port ru Fax: Norway (789) 10 746 SITA: n/a
F: 1996 ☨☨☨ n/a Head: Vladimir V. Tolkachev ICAO: ARCTICA AIR Net: n/a Some aircraft are still in Aeroflot colors but will be repainted in due course.

☐ RA-14093	PZL Swidnik (Mil) Mi-2	5210702078	CCCP-14093	0088	0096	2 IS GTD-350-4	3550	Utility		
☐ RA-14094	PZL Swidnik (Mil) Mi-2	5210703078	CCCP-14094	0088	0096	2 IS GTD-350-4	3550	Utility		
☐ RA-14155	PZL Swidnik (Mil) Mi-2	5210413107	CCCP-14155	0087	0096	2 IS GTD-350-4	3550	Utility		
☐ RA-14156	PZL Swidnik (Mil) Mi-2	5210414107	CCCP-14156	0087	0096	2 IS GTD-350-4	3550	Utility		
☐ RA-20230	PZL Swidnik (Mil) Mi-2	527048021	CCCP-20230	0081	0096	2 IS GTD-350-4	3550	Utility		
☐ RA-20952	PZL Swidnik (Mil) Mi-2	528717064	CCCP-20952	0084	0096	2 IS GTD-350-4	3550	Utility		
☐ RA-23241	PZL Swidnik (Mil) Mi-2	5410247067	CCCP-23241	0087	0096	2 IS GTD-350-4	3550	Utility		
☐ RA-23443	PZL Swidnik (Mil) Mi-2	539416095	CCCP-23443	0085	0096	2 IS GTD-350-4	3550	Utility		
☐ RA-23444	PZL Swidnik (Mil) Mi-2	539417095	CCCP-23444	0085	0096	2 IS GTD-350-4	3550	Utility		
☐ RA-23458	PZL Swidnik (Mil) Mi-2	536147059		0079	0096	2 IS GTD-350-4	3550	Utility		
☐ RA-07733	PZL Mielec (Antonov) An-2	1G159-08	CCCP-07733	0074	0096	1 SH ASh-62IR	5500	Y12		
☐ RA-07748	PZL Mielec (Antonov) An-2	1G159-23	CCCP-07748	0074	0096	1 SH ASh-62IR	5500	Y12		
☐ RA-33374	PZL Mielec (Antonov) An-2	1G226-33	CCCP-33374	0087	0096	1 SH ASh-62IR	5500	Utility		
☐ RA-33665	PZL Mielec (Antonov) An-2	1G233-59	CCCP-33665	0089	0096	1 SH ASh-62IR	5500	Utility		
☐ RA-70709	PZL Mielec (Antonov) An-2	1G130-10	CCCP-70709	0071	0097	1 SH ASh-62IR	5500	Y12		
☐ RA-31002	Kamov Ka-32T	5503	CCCP-31002	0986	0096	2 IS TV3-117VK	12600	Utility		
☐ RA-31003	Kamov Ka-32T	5504	CCCP-31003	0986	0096	2 IS TV3-117VK	12600	Utility		
☐ RA-31015	Kamov Ka-32S	5902	CCCP-31015	0087	0096	2 IS TV3-117VK	12600	Utility		
☐ RA-31017	Kamov Ka-32S	6001	CCCP-31017	0089	0096	2 IS TV3-117VK	12600	Utility		
☐ RA-31018	Kamov Ka-32S	6002	CCCP-31018	0089	0096	2 IS TV3-117VK	12600	Utility		
☐ RA-31019	Kamov Ka-32S	6003	CCCP-31019	0089	0096	2 IS TV3-117VK	12600	Utility		
☐ RA-31027	Kamov Ka-32S	6102	CCCP-31027	0089	0096	2 IS TV3-117VK	12600	Utility		
☐ RA-31592	Kamov Ka-32T	8717		0492	0096	2 IS TV3-117V	12600	Utility		
☐ RA-31593	Kamov Ka-32T	8720		0092	0096	2 IS TV3-117V	12600	Utility		
☐ RA-22189	Mil Mi-8T	9765509		0076	0096	2 IS TV2-117A	12000	Utility		
☐ RA-24161	Mil Mi-8T	98941872	CCCP-24161	0089	0096	2 IS TV2-117A	12000	Utility		
☐ RA-25522	Mil Mi-8T	4111	CCCP-25522	0073	0096	2 IS TV2-117A	12000	Utility		
☐ RA-25523	Mil Mi-8T	9754718	CCCP-25523	0075	0096	2 IS TV2-117A	12000	Utility		
☐ RA-25735	Mil Mi-8MTV-1	95896		1292	0098	2 IS TV3-117MT	13000	EMS / Y24		
☐ RA-85733	Tupolev 154M	915	CCCP-85733	0092	0096	3 SO D-30KU-154-II	100000	Y164		
☐ RA-85755	Tupolev 154M	937		0092	0096	3 SO D-30KU-154-II	100000	Y166		
☐ RA-85759	Tupolev 154M	941		0092	0096	3 SO D-30KU-154-II	100000	Y166		
☐ RA-85799	Tupolev 154M	983		0094	0096	3 SO D-30KU-154-II	100000	Y166		

NADYM AIR ENTERPRISE (Nadymskoe aviapredpriatie) (Associated with Gazprom Company) — Nadym

Nadym Airport, 626711 Nadym, Russia ☎ (34595) 40 970 Tx: none Fax: (34595) 44 602 SITA: n/a
F: n/a ☨☨☨ n/a Head: Nikolai M. Rozhkov Net: n/a

☐ RA-02319	PZL Mielec (Antonov) An-2		CCCP-02319	0091		1 SH ASh-62IR	5500	Utility		
☐ RA-02320	PZL Mielec (Antonov) An-2		CCCP-02320	0091		1 SH ASh-62IR	5500	Utility		
☐ RA-02321	PZL Mielec (Antonov) An-2		CCCP-02321	0091		1 SH ASh-62IR	5500	Utility		
☐ RA-35532	PZL Mielec (Antonov) An-2		CCCP-35532	0069		1 SH ASh-62IR	5500	Utility		
☐ RA-35549	PZL Mielec (Antonov) An-2		CCCP-35549	0069		1 SH ASh-62IR	5500	Utility		
☐ RA-22401	Mil Mi-8		CCCP-22401	0077		2 IS TV2-117A	12000	Utility		
☐ RA-22576	Mil Mi-8		CCCP-22576	0079		2 IS TV2-117A	12000	Utility		
☐ RA-22577	Mil Mi-8		CCCP-22577	0079		2 IS TV2-117A	12000	Utility		
☐ RA-22582	Mil Mi-8		CCCP-22582	0079		2 IS TV2-117A	12000	Utility		
☐ RA-22583	Mil Mi-8		CCCP-22583	0079		2 IS TV2-117A	12000	Utility		
☐ RA-22612	Mil Mi-8		CCCP-22612	0079		2 IS TV2-117A	12000	Utility		
☐ RA-22636	Mil Mi-8		CCCP-22636	0080		2 IS TV2-117A	12000	Utility		
☐ RA-22773	Mil Mi-8		CCCP-22773	0083		2 IS TV2-117A	12000	Utility		

547 registration type of aircraft cn/fn ex/ex* mfd del powered by mtow kg configuration selcal name/fln/specialitites/remarks

registration	type of aircraft	cn/fn	ex/ex*	mfd	del	powered by	mtow kg	configuration	selcal	name/fln/specialitites/remarks
□ RA-22785	Mil Mi-8		CCCP-22785	0083		2 IS TV2-117A	12000	Utility		
□ RA-22807	Mil Mi-8		CCCP-22807	0078		2 IS TV2-117A	12000	Utility		
□ RA-22832	Mil Mi-8		CCCP-22832	0078		2 IS TV2-117A	12000	Utility		
□ RA-22836	Mil Mi-8		CCCP-22836	0078		2 IS TV2-117A	12000	Utility		
□ RA-22837	Mil Mi-8		CCCP-22837	0078		2 IS TV2-117A	12000	Utility		
□ RA-24158	Mil Mi-8		CCCP-24158	0089		2 IS TV2-117A	12000	Utility		
□ RA-24179	Mil Mi-8		CCCP-24179	0089		2 IS TV2-117A	12000	Utility		
□ RA-24659	Mil Mi-8		CCCP-24659	0081		2 IS TV2-117A	12000	Utility		
□ RA-25160	Mil Mi-8T		CCCP-25160	0090		2 IS TV2-117A	12000	Utility		
□ RA-25337	Mil Mi-8		CCCP-25337	0082		2 IS TV2-117A	12000	Utility		
□ RA-25392	Mil Mi-8		CCCP-25392	0082		2 IS TV2-117A	12000	Utility		
□ RA-25432	Mil Mi-8MTV-1		CCCP-25432	0091		2 IS TV3-117MT	13000	Utility		
□ RA-25469	Mil Mi-8MTV-1		CCCP-25469	0091		2 IS TV3-117MT	13000	Utility		
□ RA-25896	Mil Mi-8		CCCP-25896	0075		2 IS TV2-117A	12000	Utility		
□ RA-25962	Mil Mi-8		CCCP-25962	0074		2 IS TV2-117A	12000	Utility		
□ RA-25982	Mil Mi-8		CCCP-25982	0077		2 IS TV2-117A	12000	Utility		
□ RA-27054	Mil Mi-8MTV-1		CCCP-27054	0092		2 IS TV3-117MT	13000	Utility		
□ RA-27063	Mil Mi-8MTV-1		CCCP-27063	0092		2 IS TV3-117MT	13000	Utility		
□ RA-27082	Mil Mi-8MTV-1		CCCP-27082	0092		2 IS TV3-117MT	13000	Utility		
□ RA-27088	Mil Mi-8MTV-1		CCCP-27088	0092		2 IS TV3-117MT	13000	Utility		

NAPO-Aviatrans = NPO (Flying div.of Novosibirsk Aircr.Prod.Ass./Novosibirskoe aviatsionnoe proizvodstvennoe obyedinenie/Member of MAP Group) **Novosibirsk-Yeltsovka**

Ul. Polzunova 15, 630051 Novosibirsk, Russia ☎ (3832) 79 85 01 Tx: none Fax: (3832) 77 84 89 SITA: n/a

F: 1994 n/a Head: Viktor F. Sukhomlinov ICAO: NOVSIB Net: n/a Operates flights for itself & commercial charter flights.

registration	type of aircraft	cn/fn	ex/ex*	mfd	del	powered by	mtow kg	configuration	selcal	name/fln/specialitites/remarks
□ RA-06113	Mil Mi-8T	9775576		1277		2 IS TV2-117A	12000	Utility		
□ RA-06148	Mil Mi-8T	98315200		1083		2 IS TV2-117A	12000	Utility		
□ RA-06170	Mil Mi-8T	98841552	CCCP-06170	1288		2 IS TV2-117A	12000	Utility		
□ RA-87962	Yakovlev 40K	9820558	CCCP-87962	0778		3 IV AI-25	16800	Combi / Exec		
□ RA-65563	Tupolev 134A-3	60035	CCCP-65563	0877		2 SO D-30-III	49000	F12Y46		Ist SBI
□ RA-11328	Antonov 12BP	3341606	CCCP-11328	1263		4 IV AI-20M	61000	Freighter		
□ RA-12192	Antonov 12BP	5343305		0865	0095	4 IV AI-20M	61000	Freighter		
□ RA-12193	Antonov 12BK	9346805		1069	0096	4 IV AI-20M	61000	Freighter		
□ RA-12194	Antonov 12BK	00347203		0570		4 IV AI-20M	61000	Freighter		
□ RA-12195	Antonov 12BK	00347410		0970		4 IV AI-20M	61000	Freighter		
□ RA-12388	Antonov 12BP	5343405	CCCP-12388	0965		4 IV AI-20M	61000	Freighter		

NARYAN-MAR AIR ENTERPRISE (Naryan-Marskoe aviapredpriatie) (formerly Aeroflot Naryan-Mar division) **Naryan-Mar**

Naryan-Mar Airport, 164700 Naryan-Mar, (Arkhangelsk Region), Russia ☎ (81853) 23 157 Tx: none Fax: (81853) 23 168 SITA: n/a

F: n/a n/a Head: Valery P. Asanatyev Net: n/a Most aircraft are still in Aeroflot colors but will be repainted in due course.

registration	type of aircraft	cn/fn	ex/ex*	mfd	del	powered by	mtow kg	configuration	selcal	name/fln/specialitites/remarks
□ RA-07212	PZL Mielec (Antonov) An-2	1G146-41	CCCP-07212	0073		1 SH ASh-62IR	5500	Utility		
□ RA-07216	PZL Mielec (Antonov) An-2	1G146-45	CCCP-07216	0073		1 SH ASh-62IR	5500	Utility		
□ RA-07217	PZL Mielec (Antonov) An-2	1G146-46	CCCP-07217	0073		1 SH ASh-62IR	5500	Utility		
□ RA-07226	PZL Mielec (Antonov) An-2	1G146-55	CCCP-07226	0073		1 SH ASh-62IR	5500	Utility		
□ RA-07478	PZL Mielec (Antonov) An-2	1G152-06	CCCP-07478	0073		1 SH ASh-62IR	5500	Utility		
□ RA-07679	PZL Mielec (Antonov) An-2	1G157-64	CCCP-07679	0074		1 SH ASh-62IR	5500	Utility		
□ RA-17857	PZL Mielec (Antonov) An-2	1G204-58	CCCP-17857	0083		1 SH ASh-62IR	5500	Utility		
□ RA-17871	PZL Mielec (Antonov) An-2	1G205-12	CCCP-17871	0083		1 SH ASh-62IR	5500	Utility		
□ RA-32363	PZL Mielec (Antonov) An-2	1G100-14	CCCP-32363	0068		1 SH ASh-62IR	5500	Utility		
□ RA-32622	PZL Mielec (Antonov) An-2	1G219-21	CCCP-32622	0086		1 SH ASh-62IR	5500	Utility		
□ RA-33301	PZL Mielec (Antonov) An-2	1G225-18	CCCP-33301	0087		1 SH ASh-62IR	5500	Utility		
□ RA-33302	PZL Mielec (Antonov) An-2	1G225-19	CCCP-33302	0087		1 SH ASh-62IR	5500	Utility		
□ RA-35058	PZL Mielec (Antonov) An-2	1G110-24	CCCP-35058	0069		1 SH ASh-62IR	5500	Utility		
□ RA-40280	PZL Mielec (Antonov) An-2	1G221-10	CCCP-40280	0086		1 SH ASh-62IR	5500	Utility		
□ RA-40942	PZL Mielec (Antonov) An-2	1G216-42	CCCP-40942	0085		1 SH ASh-62IR	5500	Utility		
□ RA-40943	PZL Mielec (Antonov) An-2	1G216-43	CCCP-40943	0085		1 SH ASh-62IR	5500	Utility		
□ RA-62583	PZL Mielec (Antonov) An-2	1G176-52	CCCP-62583	0077		1 SH ASh-62IR	5500	Utility		
□ RA-70148	PZL Mielec (Antonov) An-2	1G137-22	CCCP-70148	0071		1 SH ASh-62IR	5500	Utility		
□ RA-70182	PZL Mielec (Antonov) An-2	1G137-56	CCCP-70182	0071		1 SH ASh-62IR	5500	Utility		
□ RA-71165	PZL Mielec (Antonov) An-2	1G200-08	CCCP-71165	0082		1 SH ASh-62IR	5500	Utility		
□ RA-81534	PZL Mielec (Antonov) An-2	1G208-38	CCCP-81534	0084		1 SH ASh-62IR	5500	Utility		
□ RA-22156	Mil Mi-8T			0093		2 IS TV2-117AG	12000	Utility		
□ RA-22276	Mil Mi-8		CCCP-22276	0077		2 IS TV2-117A	12000	Utility		
□ RA-22302	Mil Mi-8		CCCP-22302	0077		2 IS TV2-117A	12000	Utility		
□ RA-22786	Mil Mi-8		CCCP-22786	0083		2 IS TV2-117A	12000	Utility		
□ RA-22914	Mil Mi-8		CCCP-22914	0085		2 IS TV2-117A	12000	Utility		
□ RA-24011	Mil Mi-8MTV-1		CCCP-24011	0091		2 IS TV3-117MT	13000	Utility		
□ RA-24014	Mil Mi-8MTV-1		CCCP-24014	0091		2 IS TV3-117MT	13000	Utility		
□ RA-24205	Mil Mi-8		CCCP-24205	0087		2 IS TV2-117A	12000	Utility		
□ RA-24224	Mil Mi-8		CCCP-24224	0087		2 IS TV2-117A	12000	Utility		
□ RA-24425	Mil Mi-8		CCCP-24425	0086		2 IS TV2-117A	12000	Utility		
□ RA-24476	Mil Mi-8		CCCP-24476	0086		2 IS TV2-117A	12000	Utility		
□ RA-24533	Mil Mi-8		CCCP-24533	0085		2 IS TV2-117A	12000	Utility		
□ RA-24612	Mil Mi-8T		CCCP-24612	0081		2 IS TV2-117AG	12000	Utility		
□ RA-24618	Mil Mi-8P		CCCP-24618	0081		2 IS TV2-117A	12000	22 Pax		
□ RA-24707	Mil Mi-8		CCCP-24707	0084		2 IS TV2-117A	12000	Utility		
□ RA-24708	Mil Mi-8		CCCP-24708	0084		2 IS TV2-117A	12000	Utility		
□ RA-25141	Mil Mi-8T		CCCP-25141	0090		2 IS TV2-117AG	12000	Utility		
□ RA-25156	Mil Mi-8T		CCCP-25156	0090		2 IS TV2-117AG	12000	Utility		
□ RA-25166	Mil Mi-8T		CCCP-25166	0090		2 IS TV2-117AG	12000	Utility		
□ RA-25440	Mil Mi-8MTV-1		CCCP-25440	0090		2 IS TV3-117MT	13000	Utility		
□ RA-25456	Mil Mi-8MTV-1		CCCP-25456	0091		2 IS TV3-117MT	13000	Utility		
□ RA-25513	Mil Mi-8MTV-1		CCCP-25513	0091		2 IS TV3-117MT	13000	Utility		
□ RA-25608	Mil Mi-8T		CCCP-25608	0091		2 IS TV2-117AG	12000	Utility		
□ RA-25609	Mil Mi-8T		CCCP-25609	0091		2 IS TV2-117AG	12000	Utility		
□ RA-25812	Mil Mi-8T		CCCP-25812	0074		2 IS TV2-117AG	12000	Utility		
□ RA-25910	Mil Mi-8		CCCP-25910	0075		2 IS TV2-117A	12000	Utility		
□ RA-25937	Mil Mi-8		CCCP-25937	0075		2 IS TV2-117A	12000	Utility		
□ RA-25977	Mil Mi-8		CCCP-25977	0075		2 IS TV2-117A	12000	Utility		

NATIONAL AEROCLUB OF TATARSTAN (Natsionalny aeroklub Tatarstana) **Kazan 2**

Ul. P. Lumumby 4, 420045 Kazan, (Republic of Tatarstan), Russia ☎ (8432) 75 46 82 Tx: none Fax: none SITA: n/a

F: n/a n/a Head: Mansur G. Tukhbatullin Net: n/a

registration	type of aircraft	cn/fn	ex/ex*	mfd	del	powered by	mtow kg	configuration	selcal	name/fln/specialitites/remarks
□ RA-23650	PZL Swidnik (Mil) Mi-2	545138047		0971		2 IS GTD-350-4	3550	Utility/Trainer		
□ RA-23651	PZL Swidnik (Mil) Mi-2	545207057		0477		2 IS GTD-350-4	3550	Utility/Trainer		
□ RA-23652	PZL Swidnik (Mil) Mi-2	547723072		0577		2 IS GTD-350-4	3550	Utility/Trainer		
□ RA-23653	PZL Swidnik (Mil) Mi-2	547732072		0782		2 IS GTD-350-4	3550	Utility/Trainer		
□ RA-23654	PZL Swidnik (Mil) Mi-2	549201045		0182		2 IS GTD-350-4	3550	Utility/Trainer		
□ RA-23768	PZL Swidnik (Mil) Mi-2	549136062		0485		2 IS GTD-350-4	3550	Utility/Trainer		
□ RA-23769	PZL Swidnik (Mil) Mi-2	547650035		0782		2 IS GTD-350-4	3550	Utility/Trainer		
□ RA-02897	Antonov An-2			1259		1 SH ASh-62IR	5500	Utility/Trainer		
□ RA-02898	PZL Mielec (Antonov) An-2	1G98-39		0968		1 SH ASh-62IR	5500	Utility/Trainer		
□ RA-02899	PZL Mielec (Antonov) An-2	1G160-55		0275		1 SH ASh-62IR	5500	Utility/Trainer		
□ RA-17792	PZL Mielec (Antonov) An-2	1G203-55		0783		1 SH ASh-62IR	5500	Utility/Trainer		
□ RA-70650	PZL Mielec (Antonov) An-2	1G128-59		0971		1 SH ASh-62IR	5500	Utility/Trainer		

NAZ SOKOL – Nizhnegorodski aviastroitel'ny zavod Sokol (Flying div.of Nizhny Novgorod Aviation Prod.Ass. Sokol/Member of MAP Group) **Nizhny Novgorod**

Flying division / Letny otryad, Ul. Chaadaeva 2, 603035 Nizhny Novgorod, Russia ☎ (8312) 46 70 38 Tx: none Fax: (8312) 24 79 66 SITA: n/a

F: n/a n/a Head: Nikolai N. Guryev Net: n/a Operates flights for itself & commercial charter flights. Most aircraft are still in Aeroflot colors with or without titles.

registration	type of aircraft	cn/fn	ex/ex*	mfd	del	powered by	mtow kg	configuration	selcal	name/fln/specialitites/remarks
□ RA-06116	Mil Mi-8T					2 IS TV2-117A	12000	Utility		
□ RA-21502	Yakovlev 40K	9831858	CCCP-21502	0077		3 IV AI-25	16800	Combi		
□ RA-69321	Antonov 32					2 IV AI-20D	27000	Freighter		

NEFTEYUGANSK AIR ENTERPRISE, Joint-Stock Company = NFT (Nefteyuganskoe aviapredpriatie) (formerly part of Tyumenavia & AFL Nefteyugansk di **Nefteyugansk**

Nefteyugansk Airport, 626430 Nefteyugansk, (Tyumen Region), Russia ☎ (34612) 25 656 Tx: none Fax: (34612) 29 756 SITA: n/a

F: 1976 n/a Head: Murat G. Sabitov ICAO: NEFTEAVIA Net: n/a Most aircraft are still in Aeroflot colors but will be repainted in due course.

registration	type of aircraft	cn/fn	ex/ex*	mfd	del	powered by	mtow kg	configuration	selcal	name/fln/specialitites/remarks
□ RA-14233	PZL Swidnik (Mil) Mi-2	5311120020	CCCP-14233	0290	0390	2 IS GTD-350-4	3550	Utility / 7 Pax		
□ RA-14234	PZL Swidnik (Mil) Mi-2	5311121020	CCCP-14234	0290	0390	2 IS GTD-350-4	3550	Utility / 7 Pax		
□ RA-14242	PZL Swidnik (Mil) Mi-2	5311129040	CCCP-14242	0490	0690	2 IS GTD-350-4	3550	Utility / 7 Pax		
□ RA-14243	PZL Swidnik (Mil) Mi-2	5311130040	CCCP-14243	0490	0690	2 IS GTD-350-4	3550	Utility / 7 Pax		
□ RA-14244	PZL Swidnik (Mil) Mi-2	5311131040	CCCP-14244	0490	0690	2 IS GTD-350-4	3550	Utility / 7 Pax		
□ RA-14397	PZL Swidnik (Mil) Mi-2	535531028	CCCP-14397	0278	0678	2 IS GTD-350-4	3550	Utility / 7 Pax		

registration	type of aircraft	cn/fn	ex/ex*	mfd	del	powered by	mtow kg	configuration	selcal	name/fln/specialitites/remarks
☐ RA-23676	PZL Swidnik (Mil) Mi-2	542737013		0173	0592	2 IS GTD-350-4	3550	Utility / 7 Pax		
☐ RA-23678	PZL Swidnik (Mil) Mi-2	542932053		0173	0592	2 IS GTD-350-4	3550	Utility / 7 Pax		
☐ RA-23680	PZL Swidnik (Mil) Mi-2	543340024		0274	0392	2 IS GTD-350-4	3550	Utility / 7 Pax		
☐ RA-31010	Kamov Ka-32T	5706	CCCP-31010	0387	0494	2 IS TV3-117VK	12600	Utility / 15 Pax		
☐ RA-31074	Kamov Ka-32T	8907	CCCP-31074	1092	1193	2 IS TV3-117VK	12600	Utility / 15 Pax		
☐ RA-31595	Kamov Ka-32T	8802	CCCP-31595	0692	0793	2 IS TV3-117VK	12600	Utility / 15 Pax		Ist Skytech Helicopter Service
☐ RA-31596	Kamov Ka-32T	8803	CCCP-31596	0692	0793	2 IS TV3-117VK	12600	Utility / 15 Pax		
☐ RA-31597	Kamov Ka-32T	8804	CCCP-31597	0692	0793	2 IS TV3-117VK	12600	Utility / 15 Pax		
☐ RA-22218	Mil Mi-8T	6348	CCCP-22218	0376	0576	2 IS TV2-117A	12000	Utility / 17 Pax		
☐ RA-22248	Mil Mi-8T	6578	CCCP-22248	0876	0976	2 IS TV2-117A	12000	Utility / 17 Pax		
☐ RA-22561	Mil Mi-8T	7804	CCCP-22561	0979	0979	2 IS TV2-117A	12000	Utility / 17 Pax		
☐ RA-22607	Mil Mi-8T	7953	CCCP-22607	0380	0480	2 IS TV2-117A	12000	Utility / 17 Pax		
☐ RA-22611	Mil Mi-8T	7958	CCCP-22611	0380	0480	2 IS TV2-117A	12000	Utility / 17 Pax		
☐ RA-22657	Mil Mi-8T	8107	CCCP-22657	1080	1180	2 IS TV2-117A	12000	Utility / 17 Pax		
☐ RA-22693	Mil Mi-8T	8152	CCCP-22693	1280	0181	2 IS TV2-117A	12000	Utility / 17 Pax		
☐ RA-24197	Mil Mi-8T	98943809	CCCP-24197	0989	1291	2 IS TV2-117A	12000	Utility / 20 Pax		
☐ RA-25107	Mil Mi-8MTV-1	95723	CCCP-25107	0891	1291	2 IS TV3-117MT	13000	Utility / 20 Pax		
☐ RA-25127	Mil Mi-8MTV-1	95743	CCCP-25127	0991	1291	2 IS TV3-117MT	13000	Utility / 20 Pax		
☐ RA-25134	Mil Mi-8MTV-1	95750	CCCP-25134	0991	1291	2 IS TV3-117MT	13000	Utility / 20 Pax		
☐ RA-25206	Mil Mi-8T	7690	CCCP-25206	1278	1278	2 IS TV2-117A	12000	Utility / 17 Pax		
☐ RA-25207	Mil Mi-8T	7691	CCCP-25207	1278	0179	2 IS TV2-117A	12000	Utility / 17 Pax		
☐ RA-25208	Mil Mi-8T	7701	CCCP-25208	1178	1278	2 IS TV2-117A	12000	Utility / 17 Pax		
☐ RA-25222	Mil Mi-8T	7757	CCCP-25222	0679	0779	2 IS TV2-117A	12000	Utility / 17 Pax		
☐ RA-25485	Mil Mi-8MTV-1	95630	CCCP-25485	0391	1093	2 IS TV3-117MT	13000	Utility / 20 Pax		
☐ RA-25856	Mil Mi-8T	5121	CCCP-25856	0375	0076	2 IS TV2-117A	12000	Utility / 17 Pax		
☐ RA-25884	Mil Mi-8T	5155	CCCP-25884	0375	0076	2 IS TV2-117A	12000	Utility / 17 Pax		

NIIS ATP - Nauchno issledovatelski institut Izmeritelnykh Sistem = NII (Flying div. of Scientific Research Institut of IS) **Nizhny Novgorod-Strigino**

Flying division / Letny otryad, GSP 486, Ul. Tropinina 47, 603600 Nizhny Novgorod, Russia ☎ (8312) 66 60 50 Tx: 151124 Fax: (8312) 66 87 52 SITA: n/a
F: 1994 ⚇ n/a Head: Yuri E. Yukhrov ICAO: NIIS-AVIA Net: n/a Operates corporate/research flights for itself & commercial charter flights.

registration	type of aircraft	cn/fn	ex/ex*	mfd	del	powered by	mtow kg	configuration	selcal	name/fln/specialitites/remarks
☐ RA-26092	Antonov 26B	12705	CCCP-26092	0082	0094	2 IV AI-24VT	24000	Combi		

NIKOLAEVSK-NA-AMURE AIR ENTERPRISE (Nikolaevskoe-na-Amure aviapredpriatie) (formerly Aeroflot Nikolaevsk-na-Amure division) **Nikolaevsk-na-Amure**

Airport, 682430 Nikolaevsk-na-Amure, (Khabarovsk Region), Russia ☎ (42135) 23 402 Tx: none Fax: (42135) 23 402 SITA: n/a
F: n/a ⚇ n/a Head: Valery P. Dolmatov Net: n/a Most aircraft are still in Aeroflot colors but will be repainted in due course.

registration	type of aircraft	cn/fn	ex/ex*	mfd	del	powered by	mtow kg	configuration	selcal	name/fln/specialitites/remarks
☐ RA-14192	PZL Swidnik (Mil) Mi-2	5310533038	CCCP-14192	0088		2 IS GTD-350-4	3550	Utility		
☐ RA-15743	PZL Swidnik (Mil) Mi-2	532520072	CCCP-15743	0072		2 IS GTD-350-4	3550	Utility		
☐ RA-20147	PZL Swidnik (Mil) Mi-2	533413024	CCCP-20147	0074		2 IS GTD-350-4	3550	Utility		
☐ RA-20378	PZL Swidnik (Mil) Mi-2	529825066	CCCP-20378	0086		2 IS GTD-350-4	3550	Utility		
☐ RA-20398	PZL Swidnik (Mil) Mi-2	529846076	CCCP-20398	0086		2 IS GTD-350-4	3550	Utility		
☐ RA-20709	PZL Swidnik (Mil) Mi-2	536817080	CCCP-20709	0080		2 IS GTD-350-4	3550	Utility		
☐ RA-20744	PZL Swidnik (Mil) Mi-2	527641052	CCCP-20744	0082		2 IS GTD-350-4	3550	Utility		
☐ RA-20970	PZL Swidnik (Mil) Mi-2	549643026	CCCP-20970	0086		2 IS GTD-350-4	3550	Utility		
☐ RA-23314	PZL Swidnik (Mil) Mi-2	529145045	CCCP-23314	0085		2 IS GTD-350-4	3550	Utility		
☐ RA-23498	PZL Swidnik (Mil) Mi-2	526315099	CCCP-23498	0079		2 IS GTD-350-4	3550	Utility		
☐ RA-23974	PZL Swidnik (Mil) Mi-2	533920124	CCCP-23974	0074		2 IS GTD-350-4	3550	Utility		
☐ RA-01457	PZL Mielec (Antonov) An-2		CCCP-01457	0088		1 SH ASh-62IR	5500	Utility		
☐ RA-01784	PZL Mielec (Antonov) An-2		CCCP-01784	0069		1 SH ASh-62IR	5500	Utility		
☐ RA-02209	PZL Mielec (Antonov) An-2		CCCP-02209	0089		1 SH ASh-62IR	5500	Utility		
☐ RA-02210	PZL Mielec (Antonov) An-2		CCCP-02210	0089		1 SH ASh-62IR	5500	Utility		
☐ RA-02300	PZL Mielec (Antonov) An-2		CCCP-02300	0091		1 SH ASh-62IR	5500	Utility		
☐ RA-02306	PZL Mielec (Antonov) An-2		CCCP-02306	0091		1 SH ASh-62IR	5500	Utility		
☐ RA-02482	PZL Mielec (Antonov) An-2		CCCP-02482	0070		1 SH ASh-62IR	5500	Utility		
☐ RA-02513	PZL Mielec (Antonov) An-2		CCCP-02513	0070		1 SH ASh-62IR	5500	Utility		
☐ RA-02739	PZL Mielec (Antonov) An-2		CCCP-02739	0071		1 SH ASh-62IR	5500	Utility		
☐ RA-07300	PZL Mielec (Antonov) An-2		CCCP-07300	0073		1 SH ASh-62IR	5500	Utility		
☐ RA-07304	PZL Mielec (Antonov) An-2		CCCP-07304	0073		1 SH ASh-62IR	5500	Utility		
☐ RA-07360	PZL Mielec (Antonov) An-2		CCCP-07360	0073		1 SH ASh-62IR	5500	Utility		
☐ RA-07439	PZL Mielec (Antonov) An-2		CCCP-07439	0073		1 SH ASh-62IR	5500	Utility		
☐ RA-07743	PZL Mielec (Antonov) An-2		CCCP-07743	0074		1 SH ASh-62IR	5500	Utility		
☐ RA-16005	PZL Mielec (Antonov) An-2		CCCP-16005	0075		1 SH ASh-62IR	5500	Utility		
☐ RA-16013	PZL Mielec (Antonov) An-2		CCCP-16013	0075		1 SH ASh-62IR	5500	Utility		
☐ RA-17812	PZL Mielec (Antonov) An-2		CCCP-17812	0083		1 SH ASh-62IR	5500	Utility		
☐ RA-31437	PZL Mielec (Antonov) An-2		CCCP-31437	0082		1 SH ASh-62IR	5500	Utility		
☐ RA-31526	PZL Mielec (Antonov) An-2		CCCP-31526	0082		1 SH ASh-62IR	5500	Utility		
☐ RA-35040	PZL Mielec (Antonov) An-2		CCCP-35040	0069		1 SH ASh-62IR	5500	Utility		
☐ RA-35056	PZL Mielec (Antonov) An-2		CCCP-35056	0069		1 SH ASh-62IR	5500	Utility		
☐ RA-35069	PZL Mielec (Antonov) An-2		CCCP-35069	0069		1 SH ASh-62IR	5500	Utility		
☐ RA-35195	PZL Mielec (Antonov) An-2		CCCP-35195	0070		1 SH ASh-62IR	5500	Utility		
☐ RA-40320	PZL Mielec (Antonov) An-2		CCCP-40320	0086		1 SH ASh-62IR	5500	Utility		
☐ RA-62466	PZL Mielec (Antonov) An-2		CCCP-62466	0064		1 SH ASh-62IR	5500	Utility		
☐ RA-62581	PZL Mielec (Antonov) An-2		CCCP-62581	0077		1 SH ASh-62IR	5500	Utility		
☐ RA-70111	PZL Mielec (Antonov) An-2		CCCP-70111	0071		1 SH ASh-62IR	5500	Utility		
☐ RA-70331	PZL Mielec (Antonov) An-2		CCCP-70331	0072		1 SH ASh-62IR	5500	Utility		
☐ RA-70683	PZL Mielec (Antonov) An-2		CCCP-70683	0071		1 SH ASh-62IR	5500	Utility		
☐ RA-92968	PZL Mielec (Antonov) An-2		CCCP-92968	0076		1 SH ASh-62IR	5500	Utility		
☐ RA-67098	Let 410UVP	841322	CCCP-67098	0084		2 WA M-601D	5800	Y15		
☐ RA-67432	Let 410UVP	831123	CCCP-67432	0083		2 WA M-601D	5800	Y15		
☐ RA-67455	Let 410UVP	841220	CCCP-67455	0084		2 WA M-601D	5800	Y15		
☐ RA-67456	Let 410UVP	841221	CCCP-67456	0084		2 WA M-601D	5800	Y15		
☐ RA-67457	Let 410UVP	841222	CCCP-67457	0084		2 WA M-601D	5800	Y15		
☐ RA-67475	Let 410UVP	841240	CCCP-67475	0084		2 WA M-601D	5800	Y15		
☐ RA-67482	Let 410UVP	841307	CCCP-67482	0084		2 WA M-601D	5800	Y15		
☐ RA-67645	Let 410UVP-E	902438	CCCP-67645	0090		2 WA M-601E	6400	Y19		
☐ RA-67662	Let 410UVP-E	902520	CCCP-67662	0090		2 WA M-601E	6400	Y19		
☐ RA-22362	Mil Mi-8		CCCP-22362	0077		2 IS TV2-117A	12000	Utility		
☐ RA-22771	Mil Mi-8		CCCP-22771	0083		2 IS TV2-117A	12000	Utility		
☐ RA-22870	Mil Mi-8		CCCP-22870	0084		2 IS TV2-117A	12000	Utility		
☐ RA-22923	Mil Mi-8		CCCP-22923	0085		2 IS TV2-117A	12000	Utility		
☐ RA-24267	Mil Mi-8		CCCP-24267	0087		2 IS TV2-117A	12000	Utility		
☐ RA-24405	Mil Mi-8		CCCP-24405	0086		2 IS TV2-117A	12000	Utility		
☐ RA-24438	Mil Mi-8		CCCP-24438	0086		2 IS TV2-117A	12000	Utility		
☐ RA-24453	Mil Mi-8		CCCP-24453	0086		2 IS TV2-117A	12000	Utility		
☐ RA-24653	Mil Mi-8		CCCP-24653	0081		2 IS TV2-117A	12000	Utility		
☐ RA-24722	Mil Mi-8		CCCP-24722	0084		2 IS TV2-117A	12000	Utility		
☐ RA-25138	Mil Mi-8T		CCCP-25138	0090		2 IS TV2-117A	12000	Utility		
☐ RA-25196	Mil Mi-8		CCCP-25196	0090		2 IS TV2-117A	12000	Utility		
☐ RA-25421	Mil Mi-8MTV-1		CCCP-25421	0090		2 IS TV3-117MT	13000	Utility		
☐ RA-25422	Mil Mi-8MTV-1		CCCP-25422	0090		2 IS TV3-117MT	13000	Utility		
☐ RA-25489	Mil Mi-8MTV-1		CCCP-25489	0091		2 IS TV3-117MT	13000	Utility		
☐ RA-25503	Mil Mi-8MTV-1		CCCP-25503	0091		2 IS TV3-117MT	13000	Utility		
☐ RA-25709	Mil Mi-8		CCCP-25709	0073		2 IS TV2-117A	12000	Utility		
☐ RA-25759	Mil Mi-8T		CCCP-25759	0075		2 IS TV2-117A	12000	Utility		
☐ RA-25874	Mil Mi-8		CCCP-25874	0075		2 IS TV2-117A	12000	Utility		

NIZHEGORODSKIE AVIALINII = NGL (Nizhny Novgorod Airlines) (formerly Aeroflot Nizhny Novgorod (Gorkij) division) **Nizhny Novgorod-Strigino**

Nizhny Novgorod Airport, 603056 Nizhny Novgorod, Russia ☎ (8312) 59 65 23 Tx: none Fax: (8312) 54 71 22 SITA: n/a
F: n/a ⚇ n/a Head: Nikolai M. Moshkov ICAO: NIZHNOVAVIA Net: n/a Also owns 37 Antonov 2, many of them stored and for sale. Most aircraft are still in Aeroflot colors but will be repainted in due course.

registration	type of aircraft	cn/fn	ex/ex*	mfd	del	powered by	mtow kg	configuration	selcal	name/fln/specialitites/remarks
☐ RA-08824	Antonov 24RV	87310810B		0078		2 IV AI-24VT	21800	Y48		
☐ RA-46230	Antonov 24B	77303110	CCCP-46230	0067		2 IV AI-24	21000	Y48		
☐ RA-46405	Antonov 24B	77303910	CCCP-46405	0067		2 IV AI-24	21000	Y48		
☐ RA-46437	Antonov 24B	87304307	CCCP-46437	0068		2 IV AI-24	21000	Y48		
☐ RA-46463	Antonov 24RV	27307809	CCCP-46463	0072		2 IV AI-24VT	21800	Y48		
☐ RA-47315	Antonov 24RV	67310502	CCCP-47315	0076		2 IV AI-24VT	21800	Y48		
☐ RA-26691	Antonov 26B		CCCP-26691	0079		2 IV AI-24VT	24000	Freighter		
☐ RA-64451	Tupolev 134A-3	66550	XU-102	1286	0095	2 SO D-30-III	47000	Y76		ex Kampuchea colors
☐ RA-65043	Tupolev 134A-3	49400	CCCP-65043	0076		2 SO D-30-III	49000	Y76		
☐ RA-65065	Tupolev 134A-3	49890	XU-101	0577	0095	2 SO D-30-III	47000	Y76		
☐ RA-65823	Tupolev 134A	09073	CCCP-65823	0074		2 SO D-30-II	47000	Y76		
☐ RA-65829	Tupolev 134A-3	12087	CCCP-65829	0074		2 SO D-30-III	49000	Y76		
☐ RA-65867	Tupolev 134A-3	28296	CCCP-65867	0075		2 SO D-30-III	49000	Y76		

registration	type of aircraft	cn/fn	ex/ex*	mfd	del	powered by	mtow kg	configuration	selcal	name/fln/specialitites/remarks
☐ RA-65970	Tupolev 134A	3351910	CCCP-65970	0073		2 SO D-30-II	49000	Y76		
☐ RA-85080	Tupolev 154B	080	CCCP-85080	0074		3 KU NK-8-2U	98000	Y164		cvtd 154A
☐ RA-85228	Tupolev 154B-1	228	CCCP-85228	0077		3 KU NK-8-2U	98000	Y164		
☐ RA-85253	Tupolev 154B-1	253	CCCP-85253	0077		3 KU NK-8-2U	98000	Y164		
☐ RA-85263	Tupolev 154B-1	263	CCCP-85263	0078		3 KU NK-8-2U	98000	Y164		
☐ RA-85287	Tupolev 154B-1	287	CCCP-85287	0078		3 KU NK-8-2U	98000	Y164		
☐ RA-85318	Tupolev 154B-2	318	CCCP-85318	0078		3 KU NK-8-2U	98000	Y164		
☐ RA-85456	Tupolev 154B-2	456	CCCP-85456	0080		3 KU NK-8-2U	98000	Y164		
☐ RA-85458	Tupolev 154B-2	458	CCCP-85458	0080		3 KU NK-8-2U	98000	Y164		

NIZHNEUDINSK AIR ENTERPRISE (Nizhneudinskoe aviapredpriatie) (formerly Aeroflot Nizhneudinsk divsion)   Nizhneudinsk

Nizhneudinsk Airport, 665110 Nizhneudinsk, (Irkutsk Region), Russia   ☎ (39517) 41 668   Tx: none   Fax: none   SITA: n/a
F: n/a   ♔♔♔ n/a   Head: Viktor I. Poryadin   Net: n/a   Most aircraft are still in Aeroflot colors but will be repainted in due course.

registration	type of aircraft	cn/fn	ex/ex*	mfd	del	powered by	mtow kg	configuration	selcal	name/fln/specialitites/remarks
☐ RA-14348	PZL Swidnik (Mil) Mi-2	535046017	CCCP-14348	0077		2 IS GTD-350-4	3550	Utility		
☐ RA-20589	PZL Swidnik (Mil) Mi-2	534729046	CCCP-20589	0076		2 IS GTD-350-4	3550	Utility		
☐ RA-20620	PZL Swidnik (Mil) Mi-2	535026126	CCCP-20620	0076		2 IS GTD-350-4	3550	Utility		
☐ RA-20959	PZL Swidnik (Mil) Mi-2	549515115	CCCP-20959	0085		2 IS GTD-350-4	3550	Utility		
☐ RA-20967	PZL Swidnik (Mil) Mi-2	539640026	CCCP-20967	0086		2 IS GTD-350-4	3550	Utility		
☐ RA-20968	PZL Swidnik (Mil) Mi-2	539641026	CCCP-20968	0086		2 IS GTD-350-4	3550	Utility		
☐ RA-23464	PZL Swidnik (Mil) Mi-2					2 IS GTD-350-4	3550	Utility		
☐ RA-23594	PZL Swidnik (Mil) Mi-2	534615016	CCCP-23594	0076		2 IS GTD-350-4	3550	Utility		
☐ RA-02579	PZL Mielec (Antonov) An-2		CCCP-02579	0071		1 SH ASh-62IR	5500	Utility		
☐ RA-02609	PZL Mielec (Antonov) An-2		CCCP-02609	0071		1 SH ASh-62IR	5500	Utility		
☐ RA-70231	PZL Mielec (Antonov) An-2		CCCP-70231	0072		1 SH ASh-62IR	5500	Utility		
☐ RA-70415	PZL Mielec (Antonov) An-2		CCCP-70415	0073		1 SH ASh-62IR	5500	Utility		
☐ RA-67080	Let 410UVP	810717	CCCP-67080	0081		2 WA M-601D	5800	Y15		
☐ RA-67155	Let 410UVP	800421	CCCP-67155	0080		2 WA M-601D	5800	Y15		
☐ RA-67359	Let 410UVP	820919	CCCP-67359	0082		2 WA M-601D	5800	Y15		
☐ RA-67468	Let 410UVP	841233	CCCP-67468	0084		2 WA M-601D	5800	Y15		
☐ RA-67647	Let 410UVP-E	902440	CCCP-67647	0090		2 WA M-601E	6400	Y19		
☐ RA-67648	Let 410UVP-E	902501	CCCP-67648	0090		2 WA M-601E	6400	Y19		
☐ RA-67651	Let 410UVP-E	902504	CCCP-67651	0090		2 WA M-601E	6400	Y19		
☐ RA-67652	Let 410UVP-E	902505	CCCP-67652	0090		2 WA M-601E	6400	Y19		
☐ RA-24131	Mil Mi-8		CCCP-24131	0088		2 IS TV2-117A	12000	Utility		
☐ RA-24132	Mil Mi-8		CCCP-24132	0088		2 IS TV2-117A	12000	Utility		
☐ RA-24260	Mil Mi-8		CCCP-24260	0087		2 IS TV2-117A	12000	Utility		
☐ RA-24290	Mil Mi-8		CCCP-24290	0087		2 IS TV2-117A	12000	Utility		
☐ RA-24410	Mil Mi-8		CCCP-24410	0086		2 IS TV2-117A	12000	Utility		
☐ RA-24428	Mil Mi-8		CCCP-24428	0086		2 IS TV2-117A	12000	Utility		
☐ RA-24598	Mil Mi-8		CCCP-24598	0088		2 IS TV2-117A	12000	Utility		

NIZHNEVARTOVSK AIR ENTERPRISE (Nizhnevartovskoe aviapredpriatie) (formerly part of Tyumenavia & Aeroflot Nizhnevartovsk division)   Nizhnevartovsk

Nizhnevartovsk Airport, 626440 Nizhnevartovsk, (Tyumen Region), Russia   ☎ (3466) 23 44 80   Tx: none   Fax: (3466) 23 77 63   SITA: n/a
F: n/a   ♔♔♔ n/a   Head: Vladimir G. Pysenok   Net: n/a

registration	type of aircraft	cn/fn	ex/ex*	mfd	del	powered by	mtow kg	configuration	selcal	name/fln/specialitites/remarks
☐ RA-22222	Mil Mi-8T		CCCP-22222	0077		2 IS TV2-117A	12000	Utility		
☐ RA-22223	Mil Mi-8T		CCCP-22223	0077		2 IS TV2-117A	12000	Utility		
☐ RA-22238	Mil Mi-8T		CCCP-22238	0077		2 IS TV2-117A	12000	Utility		
☐ RA-22239	Mil Mi-8T		CCCP-22239	0077		2 IS TV2-117A	12000	Utility		
☐ RA-22251	Mil Mi-8T		CCCP-22251	0077		2 IS TV2-117A	12000	Utility		
☐ RA-22289	Mil Mi-8T		CCCP-22289	0076		2 IS TV2-117A	12000	Utility		
☐ RA-22310	Mil Mi-8T		CCCP-22310	0077		2 IS TV2-117A	12000	Utility		
☐ RA-22325	Mil Mi-8T		CCCP-22325	0077		2 IS TV2-117A	12000	Utility		
☐ RA-22358	Mil Mi-8T		CCCP-22358	0077		2 IS TV2-117A	12000	Utility		
☐ RA-22359	Mil Mi-8T		CCCP-22359	0077		2 IS TV2-117A	12000	Utility		
☐ RA-22510	Mil Mi-8T		CCCP-22510	0092		2 IS TV2-117A	12000	Utility		
☐ RA-22560	Mil Mi-8T		CCCP-22560	0079		2 IS TV2-117A	12000	Utility		
☐ RA-22564	Mil Mi-8T		CCCP-22564	0079		2 IS TV2-117A	12000	Utility		
☐ RA-22610	Mil Mi-8T		CCCP-22610	0079		2 IS TV2-117A	12000	Utility		
☐ RA-22637	Mil Mi-8T		CCCP-22637	0080		2 IS TV2-117A	12000	Utility		
☐ RA-22822	Mil Mi-8T		CCCP-22822	0078		2 IS TV2-117A	12000	Utility		
☐ RA-22846	Mil Mi-8T		CCCP-22846	0078		2 IS TV2-117A	12000	Utility		
☐ RA-24110	Mil Mi-8T		CCCP-24110	0088		2 IS TV2-117A	12000	Utility		
☐ RA-24133	Mil Mi-8T		CCCP-24133	0088		2 IS TV2-117A	12000	Utility		
☐ RA-24134	Mil Mi-8T		CCCP-24134	0088		2 IS TV2-117A	12000	Utility		
☐ RA-25146	Mil Mi-8T		CCCP-25146	0090		2 IS TV2-117A	12000	Utility		
☐ RA-25205	Mil Mi-8T		CCCP-25205	0078		2 IS TV2-117A	12000	Utility		
☐ RA-25217	Mil Mi-8T		CCCP-25217	0078		2 IS TV2-117A	12000	Utility		
☐ RA-25221	Mil Mi-8T		CCCP-25221	0078		2 IS TV2-117A	12000	Utility		
☐ RA-25748	Mil Mi-8AMT			0093		2 IS TV3-117MT	13000	Utility		
☐ RA-25749	Mil Mi-8AMT			0093		2 IS TV3-117MT	13000	Utility		
☐ RA-25851	Mil Mi-8T		CCCP-25851	0075		2 IS TV2-117A	12000	Utility		
☐ RA-25880	Mil Mi-8T		CCCP-25880	0075		2 IS TV2-117A	12000	Utility		
☐ RA-25891	Mil Mi-8T		CCCP-25891	0075		2 IS TV2-117A	12000	Utility		
☐ RA-25966	Mil Mi-8T		CCCP-25966	0075		2 IS TV2-117A	12000	Utility		
☐ RA-25973	Mil Mi-8T		CCCP-25973	0075		2 IS TV2-117A	12000	Utility		
☐ RA-25984	Mil Mi-8T		CCCP-25984	0075		2 IS TV2-117A	12000	Utility		
☐ RA-25990	Mil Mi-8T		CCCP-25990	0075		2 IS TV2-117A	12000	Utility		
☐ RA-27094	Mil Mi-8AMT			0092		2 IS TV3-117MT	13000	Utility		
☐ RA-27095	Mil Mi-8AMT			0092		2 IS TV3-117MT	13000	Utility		
☐ RA-27117	Mil Mi-8AMT		CCCP-27117	0091		2 IS TV3-117MT	13000	Utility		
☐ RA-27149	Mil Mi-8AMT			0092		2 IS TV3-117MT	13000	Utility		
☐ RA-21061	Mil Mi-6A		CCCP-21061	0077		2 SO D-25V	38000	Utility		
☐ RA-21070	Mil Mi-6A		CCCP-21070	0077		2 SO D-25V	38000	Utility		
☐ RA-21075	Mil Mi-6A		CCCP-21075	0077		2 SO D-25V	38000	Utility		
☐ RA-21150	Mil Mi-6		CCCP-21150	0073		2 SO D-25V	38000	Utility		
☐ RA-06028	Mil Mi-26T		CCCP-06028	0090		2 LO D-136	56000	Utility		
☐ RA-06031	Mil Mi-26T		CCCP-06031	0090		2 LO D-136	56000	Utility		
☐ RA-06035	Mil Mi-26T		CCCP-06035	0091		2 LO D-136	56000	Utility		

NORD AIR, Joint-Stock Company = NRD (Aviakompania Nord Air)   Lukhovitsy & Noyabrsk

Ul. Shipilovskaya 25/2, 115563 Moskva, Russia   ☎ (095) 393 53 71   Tx: none   Fax: (095) 394 44 14   SITA: n/a
F: 1995   ♔♔♔ n/a   Head: Roman A. Agranov   ICAO: NORD AIR   Net: n/a   Beside aircraft listed, also operates Antonov 74, Mil Mi-2 & Mi-8. Full details not yet known.

registration	type of aircraft	cn/fn	ex/ex*	mfd	del	powered by	mtow kg	configuration	selcal	name/fln/specialitites/remarks
☐ RA-21506	Yakovlev 40K	9840259	CCCP-21506	0078	0097	3 IV AI-25	17200	Executive		lsf CGT

NORILSK AIR ENTERPRISE (Norilskoe aviapredpriatie) (formerly part of Yeniseisky Meridian)   Norilsk

Ul. Sevastopolskaya 7, 663310 Norilsk, (Krasnoyarsk Region), Russia   ☎ (3919) 42 37 34   Tx: none   Fax: (3919) 42 37 29   SITA: n/a
F: 1993   ♔♔♔ n/a   Head: Stanislav Ye. Srebransky   Net: n/a   Most aircraft are still in former Aeroflot colors but will be repainted in due course.

registration	type of aircraft	cn/fn	ex/ex*	mfd	del	powered by	mtow kg	configuration	selcal	name/fln/specialitites/remarks
☐ RA-01813	PZL Mielec (Antonov) An-2		CCCP-01813	0070		1 SH ASh-62IR	5500	Utility		'
☐ RA-01814	PZL Mielec (Antonov) An-2		CCCP-01814	0070		1 SH ASh-62IR	5500	Utility		
☐ RA-07650	PZL Mielec (Antonov) An-2		CCCP-07650	0074		1 SH ASh-62IR	5500	Utility		
☐ RA-07860	PZL Mielec (Antonov) An-2		CCCP-07860	0076		1 SH ASh-62IR	5500	Utility		
☐ RA-07878	PZL Mielec (Antonov) An-2		CCCP-07878	0076		1 SH ASh-62IR	5500	Utility		
☐ RA-17773	PZL Mielec (Antonov) An-2		CCCP-17773	0083		1 SH ASh-62IR	5500	Utility		
☐ RA-17995	PZL Mielec (Antonov) An-2		CCCP-17995	0084		1 SH ASh-62IR	5500	Utility		
☐ RA-33629	PZL Mielec (Antonov) An-2		CCCP-33629	0088		1 SH ASh-62IR	5500	Utility		
☐ RA-33630	PZL Mielec (Antonov) An-2		CCCP-33630	0088		1 SH ASh-62IR	5500	Utility		
☐ RA-35004	PZL Mielec (Antonov) An-2		CCCP-35004	0069		1 SH ASh-62IR	5500	Utility		
☐ RA-35006	PZL Mielec (Antonov) An-2		CCCP-35006	0069		1 SH ASh-62IR	5500	Utility		
☐ RA-35008	PZL Mielec (Antonov) An-2		CCCP-35008	0069		1 SH ASh-62IR	5500	Utility		
☐ RA-35175	PZL Mielec (Antonov) An-2		CCCP-35175	0069		1 SH ASh-62IR	5500	Utility		
☐ RA-50565	PZL Mielec (Antonov) An-2		CCCP-50565	0071		1 SH ASh-62IR	5500	Utility		
☐ RA-50580	PZL Mielec (Antonov) An-2		CCCP-50580	0071		1 SH ASh-62IR	5500	Utility		
☐ RA-50584	PZL Mielec (Antonov) An-2		CCCP-50584	0071		1 SH ASh-62IR	5500	Utility		
☐ RA-62625	PZL Mielec (Antonov) An-2		CCCP-62625	0078		1 SH ASh-62IR	5500	Utility		
☐ RA-70724	PZL Mielec (Antonov) An-2		CCCP-70724	0071		1 SH ASh-62IR	5500	Utility		
☐ RA-81614	PZL Mielec (Antonov) An-2		CCCP-81614	0084		1 SH ASh-62IR	5500	Utility		
☐ RA-22228	Mil Mi-8		CCCP-22228	0077		2 IS TV2-117A	12000	Utility		
☐ RA-22229	Mil Mi-8		CCCP-22229	0077		2 IS TV2-117A	12000	Utility		
☐ RA-22295	Mil Mi-8		CCCP-22295	0077		2 IS TV2-117A	12000	Utility		
☐ RA-22382	Mil Mi-8		CCCP-22382	0077		2 IS TV2-117A	12000	Utility		
☐ RA-22396	Mil Mi-8		CCCP-22396	0077		2 IS TV2-117A	12000	Utility		

☐ RA-22677	Mil Mi-8		CCCP-22677	0080		2 IS TV2-117A	12000	Utility		
☐ RA-22781	Mil Mi-8		CCCP-22781	0083		2 IS TV2-117A	12000	Utility		
☐ RA-22792	Mil Mi-8		CCCP-22792	0083		2 IS TV2-117A	12000	Utility		
☐ RA-22803	Mil Mi-8		CCCP-22803	0078		2 IS TV2-117A	12000	Utility		
☐ RA-24120	Mil Mi-8		CCCP-24120	0088		2 IS TV2-117A	12000	Utility		
☐ RA-24121	Mil Mi-8		CCCP-24121	0088		2 IS TV2-117A	12000	Utility		
☐ RA-24122	Mil Mi-8		CCCP-24122	0088		2 IS TV2-117A	12000	Utility		
☐ RA-24138	Mil Mi-8		CCCP-24138	0088		2 IS TV2-117A	12000	Utility		
☐ RA-24164	Mil Mi-8		CCCP-24164	0089		2 IS TV2-117A	12000	Utility		
☐ RA-24182	Mil Mi-8		CCCP-24182	0089		2 IS TV2-117A	12000	Utility		
☐ RA-24294	Mil Mi-8		CCCP-24294	0087		2 IS TV2-117A	12000	Utility		
☐ RA-24585	Mil Mi-8		CCCP-24585	0088		2 IS TV2-117A	12000	Utility		
☐ RA-24586	Mil Mi-8		CCCP-24586	0088		2 IS TV2-117A	12000	Utility		
☐ RA-24658	Mil Mi-8		CCCP-24658	0081		2 IS TV2-117A	12000	Utility		
☐ RA-24687	Mil Mi-8		CCCP-24687	0081		2 IS TV2-117A	12000	Utility		
☐ RA-24742	Mil Mi-8		CCCP-24742	0084		2 IS TV2-117A	12000	Utility		
☐ RA-24747	Mil Mi-8		CCCP-24747	0084		2 IS TV2-117A	12000	Utility		
☐ RA-24748	Mil Mi-8		CCCP-24748	0084		2 IS TV2-117A	12000	Utility		
☐ RA-25360	Mil Mi-8		CCCP-25360	0082		2 IS TV2-117A	12000	Utility		
☐ RA-25367	Mil Mi-8		CCCP-25367	0082		2 IS TV2-117A	12000	Utility		
☐ RA-25381	Mil Mi-8		CCCP-25381	0082		2 IS TV2-117A	12000	Utility		
☐ RA-25383	Mil Mi-8		CCCP-25383	0082		2 IS TV2-117A	12000	Utility		
☐ RA-25393	Mil Mi-8		CCCP-25393	0082		2 IS TV2-117A	12000	Utility		
☐ RA-25907	Mil Mi-8		CCCP-25907	0075		2 IS TV2-117A	12000	Utility		
☐ RA-26013	Antonov 26B	10009	CCCP-26013	0080		2 IV AI-24VT	24000	Freighter		
☐ RA-26022	Antonov 26B	10302	CCCP-26022	0080		2 IV AI-24VT	24000	Freighter		
☐ RA-26045	Antonov 26	10804	CCCP-26045	0080		2 IV AI-24VT	24000	Freighter		
☐ RA-26056	Antonov 26B	11005	CCCP-26056	0081		2 IV AI-24VT	24000	Freighter		
☐ RA-26568	Antonov 26	3808	CCCP-26568	0076		2 IV AI-24VT	24000	Freighter		
☐ RA-26610	Antonov 26	4901	CCCP-26610	0076		2 IV AI-24VT	24000	Freighter		
☐ RA-26620	Antonov 26	5104	CCCP-26620	0077		2 IV AI-24VT	24000	Freighter		
☐ RA-74004	Antonov 74	36547094890	CCCP-74004	0090		2 LO D-36	34500	Freighter		
☐ RA-21011	Mil Mi-6		CCCP-21011	0074		2 SO D-25V	42500	Utility		
☐ RA-21048	Mil Mi-6A	0658	CCCP-21048	0078		2 SO D-25V	38000	Utility		
☐ RA-21073	Mil Mi-6A		CCCP-21073	0080		2 SO D-25V	38000	Utility		
☐ RA-21074	Mil Mi-6A		CCCP-21074	0080		2 SO D-25V	38000	Utility		
☐ RA-21890	Mil Mi-6		CCCP-21890	0066		2 SO D-25V	42500	Utility		
☐ RA-11100	Antonov 12B	01347702	CCCP-11100	0071		4 IV AI-20M	61000	Freighter		
☐ RA-11816	Antonov 12BP	3341003	CCCP-11816	0063		4 IV AI-20M	61000	Freighter		
☐ RA-11906	Antonov 12BP	2340802	CCCP-11906	0062		4 IV AI-20M	61000	Freighter		
☐ RA-11989	Antonov 12BP	401910	CCCP-11989	0063		4 IV AI-20M	61000	Freighter		
☐ RA-12957	Antonov 12B	8345508	CCCP-12957	0068		4 IV AI-20M	61000	Freighter		
☐ RA-12981	Antonov 12B	00347104	CCCP-12981	0070		4 IV AI-20M	61000	Freighter		

NORTHERN-EAST CARGO AIRLINES = MGD (SVGAL-severo-vostochnye gruzovie avialinii) — Magadan & Kent Int'l (U.K.)

Ul. Naberezhnaya Reki Magananki 7, 685000 Magadan, Russia ☎ (41322) 24 336 Tx: none Fax: (41322) 28 754 SITA: n/a

F: 1992 n/a Head: Vladimir K. Braynen ICAO: MAGADAN CARGO Net: n/a Some aircraft are still in Aeroflot colors but will be repainted in due course.

☐ RA-11242	Antonov 12BP	3341406	CCCP-11242	0063		4 IV AI-20M	61000	Freighter		
☐ RA-11421	Antonov 12BP	401711	CCCP-11421	0062		4 IV AI-20M	61000	Freighter		
☐ RA-12119	Antonov 12BP	402109	CCCP-12119	0063		4 IV AI-20M	61000	Freighter		
☐ RA-76361	Ilyushin 76TD	1033415497		0093		4 SO D-30KP	190000	Freighter		
☐ RA-76472	Ilyushin 76TD	0033446350	CCCP-76472	0083		4 SO D-30KP	190000	Freighter		
☐ RA-76483	Ilyushin 76TD	0063468042	CCCP-76483	0086		4 SO D-30KP	190000	Freighter		lst AYZ / fn 52-01
☐ RA-76489	Ilyushin 76TD	0083485554	CCCP-76489	1287		4 SO D-30KP	190000	Freighter		lst AYZ
☐ RA-76787	Ilyushin 76TD	0093495854	CCCP-76787	0889		4 SO D-30KP	190000	Freighter		lst AYZ

NOVGOROD AIR ENTERPRISE = NVG (Novgorodskoe aviapredpriatie) (formerly Aeroflot Novgorod division) — Novgorod

Yurievskoe Shosse, 173010 Novgorod, Russia ☎ (81622) 75 156 Tx: 237136 aport Fax: (81622) 75 223 SITA: n/a

F: 1944 n/a Head: Vladimir M. Zemskov ICAO: SADKO AVIA Net: n/a Most aircraft are still in Aeroflot colors but will be repainted in due course.

☐ RA-14272	PZL Swidnik (Mil) Mi-2	5311225051	CCCP-14272	0591	0593	2 IS GTD-350-4	3550	Utility		
☐ RA-14273	PZL Swidnik (Mil) Mi-2	5311226051	CCCP-14273	0591	0593	2 IS GTD-350-4	3550	Utility		
☐ RA-14274	PZL Swidnik (Mil) Mi-2	5311227051	CCCP-14274	0591	0593	2 IS GTD-350-4	3550	Utility		
☐ RA-31416	PZL Mielec (Antonov) An-2	1G197-39	CCCP-31416	0682	0682	1 SH ASh-62IR	5500	Utility		
☐ RA-32730	PZL Mielec (Antonov) An-2	1G212-35	CCCP-32730	0385	0385	1 SH ASh-62IR	5500	Utility		
☐ RA-32731	PZL Mielec (Antonov) An-2	1G212-36	CCCP-32731	0385	0385	1 SH ASh-62IR	5500	Utility		
☐ RA-87260	Yakovlev 40	9311126A	CCCP-87260	0373	0373	3 IV AI-25	16800	Y32		
☐ RA-87489	Yakovlev 40	9512038	CCCP-87489	0275	0275	3 IV AI-25	16800	Y32		
☐ RA-87575	Yakovlev 40	9220722	CCCP-87575	0472	0472	3 IV AI-25	16800	Y32		
☐ RA-87847	Yakovlev 40	9331630	CCCP-87847	0973	0973	3 IV AI-25	16800	Y30		lst RPI

NOVOROSSISK AIRLINES = NRL — Anapa

Ul. Engelsa 73/75, 353905 Novorossisk, (Krasnodar Region), Russia ☎ (86134) 50 967 Tx: none Fax: (86134) 50 967 SITA: n/a

F: 1995 n/a Head: Yuri A. Metelev ICAO: NOVAL Net: n/a Operates charter flights with Antonov 12, Ilyushin 76, Tupolev 134 & 154 aircraft, currently leased from other companies when required.

NOVOSIBIRSK AIR ENTERPRISE (Novosibirskoe aviapredpriatie) (formerly Aeroflot 2nd Novosibirsk division) — Novosibirsk-Severny

Severny Airport, 630021 Novosibirsk, Russia ☎ (3832) 28 39 00 Tx: none Fax: (3832) 25 55 65 SITA: n/a

F: 1995 n/a Head: Vitaly N. Preobrazhensky Net: n/a Most aircraft are still in Aeroflot colors but will be repainted in due course.

☐ RA-01435	PZL Mielec (Antonov) An-2	1G231-15	CCCP-01435	0088		1 SH ASh-62IR	5500	Utility		
☐ RA-07752	PZL Mielec (Antonov) An-2	1G159-30	CCCP-07752	0074		1 SH ASh-62IR	5500	Utility		
☐ RA-17851	PZL Mielec (Antonov) An-2	1G204-52	CCCP-17851	0083		1 SH ASh-62IR	5500	Utility		
☐ RA-17852	PZL Mielec (Antonov) An-2	1G204-53	CCCP-17852	0083		1 SH ASh-62IR	5500	Utility		
☐ RA-33494	PZL Mielec (Antonov) An-2		CCCP-33494	0088		1 SH ASh-62IR	5500	Utility		
☐ RA-40673	PZL Mielec (Antonov) An-2		CCCP-40673	0086		1 SH ASh-62IR	5500	Utility		
☐ RA-40674	PZL Mielec (Antonov) An-2		CCCP-40674	0086		1 SH ASh-62IR	5500	Utility		
☐ RA-40745	PZL Mielec (Antonov) An-2	1G172-17	CCCP-40745	0076		1 SH ASh-62IR	5500	Utility		
☐ RA-54935	PZL Mielec (Antonov) An-2		CCCP-54935	0080		1 SH ASh-62IR	5500	Utility		
☐ RA-62512	PZL Mielec (Antonov) An-2		CCCP-62512	0077		1 SH ASh-62IR	5500	Utility		
☐ RA-68091	PZL Mielec (Antonov) An-2		CCCP-68091	0081		1 SH ASh-62IR	5500	Utility		
☐ RA-68095	PZL Mielec (Antonov) An-2		CCCP-68095	0081		1 SH ASh-62IR	5500	Utility		
☐ RA-70602	PZL Mielec (Antonov) An-2		CCCP-70602	0071		1 SH ASh-62IR	5500	Utility		
☐ RA-71283	PZL Mielec (Antonov) An-2		CCCP-71283	0084		1 SH ASh-62IR	5500	Utility		
☐ RA-71284	PZL Mielec (Antonov) An-2		CCCP-71284	0084		1 SH ASh-62IR	5500	Utility		
☐ RA-82908	PZL Mielec (Antonov) An-2		CCCP-82908	0076		1 SH ASh-62IR	5500	Utility		
☐ RA-84671	PZL Mielec (Antonov) An-2	1G191-49	CCCP-84671	0081		1 SH ASh-62IR	5500	Utility		
☐ RA-67301	Let 410UVP	820801	CCCP-67301	0082		2 WA M-601D	5800	Y15		
☐ RA-67302	Let 410UVP	820802	CCCP-67302	0082		2 WA M-601D	5800	Y15		
☐ RA-67303	Let 410UVP	820803	CCCP-67303	0082		2 WA M-601D	5800	Y15		
☐ RA-67304	Let 410UVP	820804	CCCP-67304	0082		2 WA M-601D	5800	Y15		
☐ RA-67305	Let 410UVP	820805	CCCP-67305	0082		2 WA M-601D	5800	Y15		
☐ RA-67311	Let 410UVP	820811	CCCP-67311	0082		2 WA M-601D	5800	Y15		
☐ RA-67316	Let 410UVP	820816	CCCP-67316	0082		2 WA M-601D	5800	Y15		
☐ RA-67318	Let 410UVP	820818	CCCP-67318	0082		2 WA M-601D	5800	Y15		
☐ RA-67348	Let 410UVP	820908	CCCP-67348	0082		2 WA M-601D	5800	Y15		
☐ RA-67349	Let 410UVP	820909	CCCP-67349	0082		2 WA M-601D	5800	Y15		
☐ RA-67530	Let 410UVP	851437	CCCP-67530	0085		2 WA M-601D	5800	Y15		
☐ RA-22209	Mil Mi-8		CCCP-22209	0077		2 IS TV2-117A	12000	Utility		
☐ RA-22598	Mil Mi-8		CCCP-22598	0791		2 IS TV2-117A	12000	Utility		
☐ RA-22624	Mil Mi-8		CCCP-22624	0080		2 IS TV2-117A	12000	Utility		
☐ RA-24113	Mil Mi-8		CCCP-24113	0088		2 IS TV2-117A	12000	Utility		
☐ RA-24219	Mil Mi-8		CCCP-24219	0087		2 IS TV2-117A	12000	Utility		
☐ RA-24227	Mil Mi-8		CCCP-24227	0087		2 IS TV2-117A	12000	Utility		
☐ RA-24685	Mil Mi-8		CCCP-24685	0081		2 IS TV2-117A	12000	Utility		
☐ RA-25315	Mil Mi-8		CCCP-25315	0082		2 IS TV2-117A	12000	Utility		
☐ RA-46252	Antonov 24B	77303304	CCCP-46252	0067		2 IV AI-24	21000	Y48		
☐ RA-46321	Antonov 24B	97305407	CCCP-46321	0769	0098	2 IV AI-24	21000	Y48		
☐ RA-46354	Antonov 24B	07305804	CCCP-46354	0170	0098	2 IV AI-24	21000	Y48		
☐ RA-46571	Antonov 24B	87304805	CCCP-46571	0068		2 IV AI-24	21000	Y48		
☐ RA-46642	Antonov 24RV		CCCP-46642	0073		2 IV AI-24VT	21800	Y48		
☐ RA-46659	Antonov 24RV	47309306	CCCP-46659	0074		2 IV AI-24VT	21800	Y48		
☐ RA-47150	Antonov 24B	89901602	CCCP-47150	0068		2 IV AI-24	21000	Y48		
☐ RA-47165	Antonov 24B	89901707	CCCP-47165	0068		2 IV AI-24	21000	Y48		

551 registration type of aircraft cn/fn ex/ex* mfd del powered by mtow kg configuration selcal name/fln/specialitites/remarks

☐ RA-47185	Antonov 24B	99901910	CCCP-47185	0669	0098	2 IV AI-24	21000	Y48		
☐ RA-47189	Antonov 24B		CCCP-47189	0069		2 IV AI-24	21000	Y48		
☐ RA-47275	Antonov 24B	07306405	CCCP-47275	0970	0098	2 IV AI-24	21000	Y48		
☐ RA-47306	Antonov 24RV	57310306	CCCP-47306	0075		2 IV AI-24VT	21800	Y48		
☐ RA-47704	Antonov 24B	59900302	CCCP-47704	0065		2 IV AI-24	21000	Y48		
☐ RA-47731	Antonov 24B	69900904	CCCP-47731	1166	0098	2 IV AI-24	21000	Y48		
☐ RA-47759	Antonov 24B	79901303	CCCP-47759	0067		2 IV AI-24	21000	Y48		
☐ RA-47809	Antonov 24RV	17307001	XU-314	0571		2 IV AI-24VT	21800	Y48		
☐ RA-47821	Antonov 24RV		CCCP-47821	0071		2 IV AI-24VT	21800	Y48		
☐ RA-47839	Antonov 24B		CCCP-47839	0071		2 IV AI-24	21000	Y48		
☐ RA-30004	Antonov 30D	1405	CCCP-30004	0078		2 IV AI-24T	23000	Survey / Combi		
☐ RA-30007	Antonov 30D	1408	CCCP-30007	0078		2 IV AI-24T	23000	Survey / Combi		
☐ RA-30034	Antonov 30	0701	CCCP-30034	0074		2 IV AI-24T	23000	Survey / Combi		
☐ RA-30037	Antonov 30	0704	CCCP-30037	0074		2 IV AI-24T	23000	Survey / Combi		
☐ RA-30041	Antonov 30	0805	CCCP-30041	0075		2 IV AI-24T	23000	Survey / Combi		
☐ RA-30049	Antonov 30	1004	CCCP-30049	0075		2 IV AI-24T	23000	Survey / Combi		
☐ RA-30051	Antonov 30	1006	CCCP-30051	0076		2 IV AI-24T	23000	Survey / Combi		
☐ RA-30052	Antonov 30	1007	CCCP-30052	0076		2 IV AI-24T	23000	Survey / Combi		
☐ RA-30056	Antonov 30	1102	CCCP-30056	0076		2 IV AI-24T	23000	Survey / Combi		
☐ RA-30059	Antonov 30	1108	CCCP-30059	0076		2 IV AI-24T	23000	Survey / Combi		
☐ RA-30063	Antonov 30D	1202	CCCP-30063	0077		2 IV AI-24T	23000	Survey / Combi		
☐ RA-30068	Antonov 30D		CCCP-30068	0077		2 IV AI-24T	23000	Survey / Combi		

NOVOSIBIRSK AIRLINES, Joint-Stock Company = L8 / NLB (Novosibirskie avialinii) — Novosibirsk-Tolmachevo

Ul. Karla Marksa 30, Room 320, 630087 Novosibirsk, Russia ☎ (3832) 46 15 45 Tx: none Fax: (3832) 46 10 92 SITA: OVBKB7B
F: 1995 ✈✈✈ n/a Head: Vitali M. Chizhov ICAO: OBAIR Net: n/a

☐ RA-65057	Tupolev 134A-3	49865	CCCP-65057	0077	0097	2 SO D-30-III	49000	Y76		lsf VRN
☐ RA-65609	Tupolev 134A	46155	D-AOBQ	0276	0099	2 SO D-30-II	47000	Y80		lsf KMV
☐ RA-86708	Ilyushin 62	41802	CCCP-86708	0074	0098	4 KU NK-8-4	161600	Y180		lsf KJC / fn 1802
☐ RA-76445	Ilyushin 76MD	1023410330	CCCP-76445	0092	0098	4 SO D-30KP	190000	Freighter		

NOVOSIBIRSKY ASK (Novosibirsk Aviation Sport Club) — Barnaul

P/O Box 10, Box 11, 633190 Berdsk, (Novosibirsk Region), Russia ☎ (38341) 52 595 Tx: none Fax: (38341) 32 652 SITA: n/a
F: n/a ✈✈✈ n/a Head: Sergei S. Fedchenko Net: n/a

☐ RA-23689	PZL Swidnik (Mil) Mi-2			0081	0092	2 IS GTD-350-4	3700	Utility		
☐ RA-23691	PZL Swidnik (Mil) Mi-2			0081	0091	2 IS GTD-350-4	3700	Utility		
☐ RA-23693	PZL Swidnik (Mil) Mi-2			0089	0091	2 IS GTD-350-4	3700	Utility		
☐ RA-23694	PZL Swidnik (Mil) Mi-2			0089	0091	2 IS GTD-350-4	3700	Utility		
☐ RA-01147	PZL Mielec (Antonov) An-2			0082	0092	1 SH ASh-62IR	5500	Utility		
☐ RA-02889	PZL Mielec (Antonov) An-2			0082	0092	1 SH ASh-62IR	5500	Utility		

NOVY URENGOI AIR ENTERPRISE (Novourengoiskoe aviapredpriatie) (formerly part of Tyumenavia & Aeroflot Novy Urengoi division) — Novy Urengoi

Airport, 626718 Novy Urengoi, (Tyumen Region), Russia ☎ (34549) 41 919 Tx: none Fax: (34549) 41 010 SITA: n/a
F: n/a ✈✈✈ n/a Head: Vladimir T. Fedorov Net: n/a Most aircraft are still in Aeroflot colors but will be repainted in due course.

☐ RA-22507	Mil Mi-8T			0092		2 IS TV2-117A	12000	Utility		opf Urengoigasprom
☐ RA-22508	Mil Mi-8T	99357517		0493	0098	2 IS TV2-117A	12000	Freighter		
☐ RA-22613	Mil Mi-8		CCCP-22613	0079		2 IS TV2-117A	12000	Utility		
☐ RA-22655	Mil Mi-8		CCCP-22655	0080		2 IS TV2-117A	12000	Utility		
☐ RA-22742	Mil Mi-8		CCCP-22742	0083		2 IS TV2-117A	12000	Utility		
☐ RA-22754	Mil Mi-8		CCCP-22754	0083		2 IS TV2-117A	12000	Utility		
☐ RA-22883	Mil Mi-8		CCCP-22883	0084		2 IS TV2-117A	12000	Utility		
☐ RA-22908	Mil Mi-8		CCCP-22908	0084		2 IS TV2-117A	12000	Utility		
☐ RA-24127	Mil Mi-8		CCCP-24127	0088		2 IS TV2-117A	12000	Utility		
☐ RA-24214	Mil Mi-8		CCCP-24214	0087		2 IS TV2-117A	12000	Utility		
☐ RA-24239	Mil Mi-8		CCCP-24239	0087		2 IS TV2-117A	12000	Utility		
☐ RA-24641	Mil Mi-8		CCCP-24641	0081		2 IS TV2-117A	12000	Utility		
☐ RA-24642	Mil Mi-8		CCCP-24642	0081		2 IS TV2-117A	12000	Utility		
☐ RA-24660	Mil Mi-8		CCCP-24660	0081		2 IS TV2-117A	12000	Utility		
☐ RA-25220	Mil Mi-8		CCCP-25220	0079		2 IS TV2-117A	12000	Utility		
☐ RA-25223	Mil Mi-8		CCCP-25223	0079		2 IS TV2-117A	12000	Utility		
☐ RA-25224	Mil Mi-8		CCCP-25224	0079		2 IS TV2-117A	12000	Utility		
☐ RA-25306	Mil Mi-8		CCCP-25306	0082		2 IS TV2-117A	12000	Utility		
☐ RA-25316	Mil Mi-8		CCCP-25316	0082		2 IS TV2-117A	12000	Utility		
☐ RA-25339	Mil Mi-8		CCCP-25339	0082		2 IS TV2-117A	12000	Utility		

NPP MIR Aviakompania = NPP (Nauchno-proizvodstvennoe predpriatie MIR/MIR Scientific Indust. Enterprise, Joint-Stock/div. of Leninets Holding Co.) — St. Petersburg-Pushkin

Starogatchinskoe Shosse 2, 189620 St. Petersburg-Pushkin 3, Russia ☎ (812) 465 34 34 Tx: none Fax: (812) 465 47 00 SITA: n/a
F: 1959 ✈✈✈ n/a Head: Ruben V. Pirzadyan ICAO: MIR SCIENTIFIC Net: n/a Some aircraft are still in Aeroflot colors with or without titles but will be repainted in due course.

☐ RA-26196	Antonov 24B	17307303	CCCP-26196	0071	0071	2 IV AI-24	21000	Geo Survey		
☐ RA-47195	Antonov 24RV	07306202	CCCP-47195	0071	0090	2 IV AI-24VT	21000	Geo Survey		
☐ RA-65098	Tupolev 134Sh	73550815	CCCP-65098	0077	0079	2 SO D-30	42000	Geo Survey		cvtd military aircraft
☐ 100	Tupolev 134UBL	64010		0081	0083	2 SO D-30	42000	Geo Survey		
☐ RA-75411	Ilyushin 18V	186009205	CCCP-75411	0066	0074	4 IV AI-20M	61400	CombiY72&4,5tcgo		
☐ RA-75713	Ilyushin 18D	186009403	CCCP-75713	0068	0075	4 IV AI-20M	64000	Y110or13,5t cgo		
☐ RA-75786	Ilyushin 18V	181003905	CCCP-75786	0063	0068	4 IV AI-20M	61200	Geo Survey		
☐ RA-75804	Ilyushin 18V	182004305	CCCP-75804	0062	0067	4 IV AI-20M	61200	CombiY32&8,5Tcgo		

OMSKAVIA, Joint-Stock Company = OMS — Omsk

Ul. Inzhenernaya 1, 644103 Omsk, Russia ☎ (3812) 35 71 06 Tx: 216214 port Fax: (3812) 31 64 17 SITA: n/a
F: 1994 ✈✈✈ 800 Head: Yevgeni S. Romanyuk IATA: 753 ICAO: OMSK Net: n/a

☐ RA-47282	Antonov 24B	07306502	CCCP-47282	1070	0294	2 IV AI-24	21000	Y48		
☐ RA-85133	Tupolev 154B	133	YL-LAA	0778	0898	3 KU NK-8-2U	98000	Y164		lsf Alexandra-Avia Lease
☐ RA-85730	Tupolev 154M	912	CCCP-85730	0592	0494	3 SO D-30KU-154-II	100000	Y164		
☐ RA-85745	Tupolev 154M	928		0992	1197	3 SO D-30KU-154-II	100000	Y166		lst IRB as EP-MAT
☐ RA-85750	Tupolev 154M	932		1092	0296	3 SO D-30KU-154-II	100000	Y166		lst IRB as EP-MAR
☐ RA-85752	Tupolev 154M	934		1192	1296	3 SO D-30KU-154-II	102000	Y166		
☐ RA-85763	Tupolev 154M	946		0193	0399	3 SO D-30KU-154-II	100000	Y166		lsf TSK -1099
☐ RA-85818	Tupolev 154M	719	CU-T1276	1285	1295	3 SO D-30KU-154-II	100000	Y164		lst IRB as EP-MAJ
☐ RA-85830	Tupolev 154M	821	YN-CBT	1189	0797	3 SO D-30KU-154-II	100000	Y164		lst IRB as EP-MBB

OREL AIR ENTERPRISE = ORM (Orlovskoe aviapredpriatie) (formerly Aeroflot Orel division) — Orel

Ul. Planernaya, Airport, 302010 Orel, Russia ☎ (08622) 22 056 Tx: none Fax: (08622) 62 045 SITA: n/a
F: n/a ✈✈✈ n/a Head: Vladimir V. Kugel' ICAO: ORPRISE Net: n/a Most aircraft are still in Aeroflot colors but will be repainted in due course.

☐ RA-01426	PZL Mielec (Antonov) An-2		CCCP-01426	0088		1 SH ASh-62IR	5500	Utility		
☐ RA-01668	PZL Mielec (Antonov) An-2		CCCP-01668	0067		1 SH ASh-62IR	5500	Utility		
☐ RA-02238	PZL Mielec (Antonov) An-2		CCCP-02238	0090		1 SH ASh-62IR	5500	Utility		
☐ RA-02240	PZL Mielec (Antonov) An-2		CCCP-02240	0090		1 SH ASh-62IR	5500	Utility		
☐ RA-02241	PZL Mielec (Antonov) An-2		CCCP-02241	0090		1 SH ASh-62IR	5500	Utility		
☐ RA-02243	PZL Mielec (Antonov) An-2		CCCP-02243	0090		1 SH ASh-62IR	5500	Utility		
☐ RA-02244	PZL Mielec (Antonov) An-2		CCCP-02244	0090		1 SH ASh-62IR	5500	Utility		
☐ RA-02245	PZL Mielec (Antonov) An-2	1G235-16	CCCP-02245	0090		1 SH ASh-62IR	5500	Utility		
☐ RA-02265	PZL Mielec (Antonov) An-2		CCCP-02265	0090		1 SH ASh-62IR	5500	Utility		
☐ RA-02272	PZL Mielec (Antonov) An-2		CCCP-02272	0090		1 SH ASh-62IR	5500	Utility		
☐ RA-07319	PZL Mielec (Antonov) An-2		CCCP-07319	0073		1 SH ASh-62IR	5500	Utility		
☐ RA-07527	PZL Mielec (Antonov) An-2		CCCP-07527	0073		1 SH ASh-62IR	5500	Utility		
☐ RA-17817	PZL Mielec (Antonov) An-2		CCCP-17817	0083		1 SH ASh-62IR	5500	Utility		
☐ RA-17971	PZL Mielec (Antonov) An-2		CCCP-17971	0089		1 SH ASh-62IR	5500	Utility		
☐ RA-31510	PZL Mielec (Antonov) An-2		CCCP-31510	0082		1 SH ASh-62IR	5500	Utility		
☐ RA-32395	PZL Mielec (Antonov) An-2		CCCP-32395	0068		1 SH ASh-62IR	5500	Utility		
☐ RA-32607	PZL Mielec (Antonov) An-2		CCCP-32607	0086		1 SH ASh-62IR	5500	Utility		
☐ RA-32666	PZL Mielec (Antonov) An-2	1G211-25	CCCP-32666	0085		1 SH ASh-62IR	5500	Utility		
☐ RA-33310	PZL Mielec (Antonov) An-2		CCCP-33310	0087		1 SH ASh-62IR	5500	Utility		
☐ RA-33382	PZL Mielec (Antonov) An-2		CCCP-33382	0087		1 SH ASh-62IR	5500	Utility		
☐ RA-33530	PZL Mielec (Antonov) An-2		CCCP-33530	0088		1 SH ASh-62IR	5500	Utility		
☐ RA-33555	PZL Mielec (Antonov) An-2		CCCP-33555	0088		1 SH ASh-62IR	5500	Utility		
☐ RA-35641	PZL Mielec (Antonov) An-2		CCCP-35641	0070		1 SH ASh-62IR	5500	Utility		
☐ RA-40234	PZL Mielec (Antonov) An-2		CCCP-40234	0086		1 SH ASh-62IR	5500	Utility		
☐ RA-40250	PZL Mielec (Antonov) An-2		CCCP-40250	0086		1 SH ASh-62IR	5500	Utility		
☐ RA-40389	PZL Mielec (Antonov) An-2		CCCP-40389	0087		1 SH ASh-62IR	5500	Utility		
☐ RA-40441	PZL Mielec (Antonov) An-2	1G224-18	CCCP-40441	0087		1 SH ASh-62IR	5500	Utility		
☐ RA-40777	PZL Mielec (Antonov) An-2		CCCP-40777	0076		1 SH ASh-62IR	5500	Utility		

552 registration type of aircraft cn/fn ex/ex* mfd del powered by mtow kg configuration selcal name/fln/specialitites/remarks

☐ RA-40819	PZL Mielec (Antonov) An-2		CCCP-40819	0077		1 SH ASh-62IR	5500	Utility		
☐ RA-54882	PZL Mielec (Antonov) An-2		CCCP-54882	0079		1 SH ASh-62IR	5500	Utility		
☐ RA-54898	PZL Mielec (Antonov) An-2		CCCP-54898	0079		1 SH ASh-62IR	5500	Utility		
☐ RA-54907	PZL Mielec (Antonov) An-2		CCCP-54907	0079		1 SH ASh-62IR	5500	Utility		
☐ RA-56426	PZL Mielec (Antonov) An-2		CCCP-56426	0078		1 SH ASh-62IR	5500	Utility		
☐ RA-62500	PZL Mielec (Antonov) An-2		CCCP-62500	0077		1 SH ASh-62IR	5500	Utility		
☐ RA-62606	PZL Mielec (Antonov) An-2		CCCP-62606	0078		1 SH ASh-62IR	5500	Utility		
☐ RA-62614	PZL Mielec (Antonov) An-2		CCCP-62614	0078		1 SH ASh-62IR	5500	Utility		
☐ RA-62630	PZL Mielec (Antonov) An-2	1G178-22	CCCP-62630	0078		1 SH ASh-62IR	5500	Utility		
☐ RA-68113	PZL Mielec (Antonov) An-2	1G195-18	CCCP-68113	0082		1 SH ASh-62IR	5500	Utility		
☐ RA-70137	PZL Mielec (Antonov) An-2		CCCP-70137	0071		1 SH ASh-62IR	5500	Utility		
☐ RA-70319	PZL Mielec (Antonov) An-2		CCCP-70319	0072		1 SH ASh-62IR	5500	Utility		
☐ RA-71211	PZL Mielec (Antonov) An-2		CCCP-71211	0085		1 SH ASh-62IR	5500	Utility		
☐ RA-82797	PZL Mielec (Antonov) An-2		CCCP-82797	0075		1 SH ASh-62IR	5500	Utility		
☐ RA-84595	PZL Mielec (Antonov) An-2		CCCP-84595	0080		1 SH ASh-62IR	5500	Utility		
☐ RA-84597	PZL Mielec (Antonov) An-2		CCCP-84597	0080		1 SH ASh-62IR	5500	Utility		
☐ RA-84601	PZL Mielec (Antonov) An-2		CCCP-84601	0080		1 SH ASh-62IR	5500	Utility		
☐ RA-84641	PZL Mielec (Antonov) An-2		CCCP-84641	0080		1 SH ASh-62IR	5500	Utility		
☐ RA-87568	Yakovlev 40		CCCP-87568	0072		3 IV AI-25	17200	Y27		
☐ RA-87829	Yakovlev 40	9240125	CCCP-87829	0072		3 IV AI-25	17200	C15		
☐ RA-87838	Yakovlev 40	9240426	CCCP-87838	0072		3 IV AI-25	17200	C15		

ORENBURG AIRLINES = R2 / ORB (Orenburgskie avialinii) (formerly Orenburg Avia Enterprise & Aeroflot Orenburg division) — Orenburg-Tsentralny

Orenburg-Tsentralny Airport, 460049 Orenburg, Russia ☎ (3532) 33 02 68 Tx: 144261 port Fax: (3532) 41 98 78 SITA: n/a
F: n/a ✝✝✝ n/a Head: Boris A. Portnikov IATA: 291 ICAO: ORENBURG Net: n/a Some aircraft are still in Aeroflot colors but will be repainted in due course.

☐ RA-01427	PZL Mielec (Antonov) An-2		CCCP-01427	0088		1 SH ASh-62IR	5500	Utility		
☐ RA-01429	PZL Mielec (Antonov) An-2		CCCP-01429	0088		1 SH ASh-62IR	5500	Utility		
☐ RA-01430	PZL Mielec (Antonov) An-2		CCCP-01430	0088		1 SH ASh-62IR	5500	Utility		
☐ RA-19742	PZL Mielec (Antonov) An-2		CCCP-19742	0075		1 SH ASh-62IR	5500	Utility		
☐ RA-32394	PZL Mielec (Antonov) An-2		CCCP-32394	0068		1 SH ASh-62IR	5500	Utility		
☐ RA-32641	PZL Mielec (Antonov) An-2		CCCP-32641	0086		1 SH ASh-62IR	5500	Utility		
☐ RA-33038	PZL Mielec (Antonov) An-2		CCCP-33038	0086		1 SH ASh-62IR	5500	Utility		
☐ RA-33594	PZL Mielec (Antonov) An-2		CCCP-33594	0088		1 SH ASh-62IR	5500	Utility		
☐ RA-35520	PZL Mielec (Antonov) An-2		CCCP-35520	0070		1 SH ASh-62IR	5500	Utility		
☐ RA-35541	PZL Mielec (Antonov) An-2		CCCP-35541	0070		1 SH ASh-62IR	5500	Utility		
☐ RA-40312	PZL Mielec (Antonov) An-2		CCCP-40312	0086		1 SH ASh-62IR	5500	Utility		
☐ RA-40315	PZL Mielec (Antonov) An-2		CCCP-40315	0086		1 SH ASh-62IR	5500	Utility		
☐ RA-40337	PZL Mielec (Antonov) An-2		CCCP-40337	0086		1 SH ASh-62IR	5500	Utility		
☐ RA-40338	PZL Mielec (Antonov) An-2		CCCP-40338	0086		1 SH ASh-62IR	5500	Utility		
☐ RA-40413	PZL Mielec (Antonov) An-2		CCCP-40413	0087		1 SH ASh-62IR	5500	Utility		
☐ RA-40481	PZL Mielec (Antonov) An-2		CCCP-40481	0087		1 SH ASh-62IR	5500	Utility		
☐ RA-40493	PZL Mielec (Antonov) An-2	1G225-10	CCCP-40493	0087		1 SH ASh-62IR	5500	Utility		
☐ RA-40684	PZL Mielec (Antonov) An-2		CCCP-40684	0086		1 SH ASh-62IR	5500	Utility		
☐ RA-40969	PZL Mielec (Antonov) An-2		CCCP-40969	0085		1 SH ASh-62IR	5500	Utility		
☐ RA-43969	PZL Mielec (Antonov) An-2	1G210-46	CCCP-43969	0084		1 SH ASh-62IR	5500	Utility		
☐ RA-43990	PZL Mielec (Antonov) An-2	1G211-09	CCCP-43990	0085		1 SH ASh-62IR	5500	Utility		
☐ RA-62706	PZL Mielec (Antonov) An-2		CCCP-62706	0078		1 SH ASh-62IR	5500	Utility		
☐ RA-68130	PZL Mielec (Antonov) An-2		CCCP-68130	0082		1 SH ASh-62IR	5500	Utility		
☐ RA-70264	PZL Mielec (Antonov) An-2		CCCP-70264	0072		1 SH ASh-62IR	5500	Utility		
☐ RA-70765	PZL Mielec (Antonov) An-2		CCCP-70765	0071		1 SH ASh-62IR	5500	Utility		
☐ RA-70796	PZL Mielec (Antonov) An-2	1G132-51	CCCP-70796	0071		1 SH ASh-62IR	5500	Utility		
☐ RA-81631	PZL Mielec (Antonov) An-2	1G209-25	CCCP-81631	0084		1 SH ASh-62IR	5500	Utility		
☐ RA-82822	PZL Mielec (Antonov) An-2		CCCP-82822	0075		1 SH ASh-62IR	5500	Utility		
☐ RA-84569	PZL Mielec (Antonov) An-2		CCCP-84569	0080		1 SH ASh-62IR	5500	Utility		
☐ RA-92970	PZL Mielec (Antonov) An-2	1G171-27	CCCP-92970	0076		1 SH ASh-62IR	5500	Utility		
☐ RA-25765	Mil Mi-8MTV-1			0092		2 IS TV3-117MT	13000	Utility		
☐ RA-27172	Mil Mi-8MTV-1	96111		0093		2 IS TV3-117MT	13000	Utility		
☐ RA-27173	Mil Mi-8MTV-1	96112		0093		2 IS TV3-117MT	13000	Utility		
☐ RA-27174	Mil Mi-8MTV-1			0093		2 IS TV3-117MT	13000	Utility		
☐ RA-27175	Mil Mi-8MTV-1			0093		2 IS TV3-117MT	13000	Utility		
☐ RA-87272	Yakovlev 40	9330827	UN-87272	0873		3 IV AI-25	16100	Y32		
☐ RA-87352	Yakovlev 40	9330131	UN-87352	0973		3 IV AI-25	16100	Y32		
☐ RA-87471	Yakovlev 40	9441637	UN-87471	1174		3 IV AI-25	16100	Y32		
☐ RA-46315	Antonov 24B		CCCP-46315	0069		2 IV AI-24	21000	Y48		
☐ RA-46339	Antonov 24B	97305607	CCCP-46339	0069		2 IV AI-24	21000	Y48		
☐ RA-46388	Antonov 24B		CCCP-46388	0070		2 IV AI-24	21000	Y48		
☐ RA-46597	Antonov 24B	97305107	CCCP-46597	0069		2 IV AI-24	21000	Y48		
☐ RA-47847	Antonov 24B		CCCP-47847	0071		2 IV AI-24	21000	Y48		
☐ RA-65101	Tupolev 134A-3	60260	CCCP-65101	0278		2 SO D-30-III	47600	Y80		
☐ RA-65110	Tupolev 134A-3	60343	CCCP-65110	0378		2 SO D-30-III	47600	Y80		
☐ RA-65117	Tupolev 134A-3	60450	CCCP-65117	0578		2 SO D-30-III	47600	Y80		
☐ RA-65136	Tupolev 134A-3	60885	CCCP-65136	1078		2 SO D-30-III	47600	Y80		
☐ RA-65847	Tupolev 134A-3	23135	CCCP-65847	1274		2 SO D-30-III	47600	Y80		
☐ RA-65860	Tupolev 134A-3	28265	CCCP-65860	0275		2 SO D-30-III	47000	Y80		
☐ RA-85595	Tupolev 154B-2	595	CCCP-85595	1283		3 KU NK-8-2U	98000	Y164		
☐ RA-85602	Tupolev 154B-2	602	CCCP-85602	0084		3 KU NK-8-2U	98000	Y164		
☐ RA-85603	Tupolev 154B-2	603	CCCP-85603	0084		3 KU NK-8-2U	98000	Y164		
☐ RA-85604	Tupolev 154B-2	604	CCCP-85604	0084		3 KU NK-8-2U	98000	Y164		lst BKS
☐ RA-85768	Tupolev 154M	949		0393		3 SO D-30KU-154-II	100000	Y166		

PANKH Air Company — Krasnodar

Ul. Kirova 138, 350723 Krasnodar, Russia ☎ (8612) 55 65 95 Tx: 279136 lotos su Fax: (8612) 55 36 48 SITA: n/a
F: 1964 ✝✝✝ n/a Head: Vladimir B. Kozlovsky Net: n/a

☐ RA-19362	Kamov Ka-26	7202403	CCCP-19362	0372	0390	2 VE M-14V-26	3250	6 Pax		
☐ RA-20901	PZL Swidnik (Mil) Mi-2	548340093	CCCP-20901	1283	0490	2 IS GTD-350-4	3550	7 Pax		
☐ RA-02207	PZL Mielec (Antonov) An-2	1G234-38	CCCP-02207	0389	0197	1 SH ASh-62IR	5500	12 Pax		
☐ RA-07367	PZL Mielec (Antonov) An-2	1G150-02	CCCP-07367	1073	0891	1 SH ASh-62IR	5500	12 Pax		
☐ RA-16058	PZL Mielec (Antonov) An-2	1G164-11	CCCP-16058	0875	0292	1 SH ASh-62IR	5500	12 Pax		
☐ RA-32141	PZL Mielec (Antonov) An-2	1G94-02	CCCP-32141	0668	0192	1 SH ASh-62IR	5500	12 Pax		
☐ RA-32741	PZL Mielec (Antonov) An-2	1G212-46	CCCP-32741	0385	0197	1 SH ASh-62IR	5500	12 Pax		
☐ RA-33621	PZL Mielec (Antonov) An-2	1G232-55	CCCP-33621	0289	0592	1 SH ASh-62IR	5500	12 Pax		
☐ RA-35667	PZL Mielec (Antonov) An-2	1G116-58	CCCP-35667	0770	0992	1 SH ASh-62IR	5500	12 Pax		
☐ RA-56528	PZL Mielec (Antonov) An-2	1G183-28	CCCP-56528	0379	0197	1 SH ASh-62IR	5500	12 Pax		
☐ RA-68090	PZL Mielec (Antonov) An-2	1G193-60	CCCP-68090	0981	0197	1 SH ASh-62IR	5500	12 Pax		
☐ RA-71269	PZL Mielec (Antonov) An-2	1G207-40	CCCP-71269	0684	0693	1 SH ASh-62IR	5500	12 Pax		
☐ RA-22732	Mil Mi-8T	98308852	CCCP-22732	0483	0983	2 IS TV2-117A	12000	22 Pax		
☐ RA-22769	Mil Mi-8T	98311568	CCCP-22769	0783	0591	2 IS TV2-117A	12000	22 Pax		
☐ RA-25435	Mil Mi-8MTV-1	95576	CCCP-25435	0191	0491	2 IS TV3-117MT	13000	24 Pax		
☐ RA-31007	Kamov Ka-32	5703	CCCP-31007	0387	0488	2 IS TV3-117V	12600	9-12 Pax		lst Skytech Helicopter Service
☐ RA-31025	Kamov Ka-32	6009	CCCP-31025	0589	0689	2 IS TV3-117V	12600	9-12 Pax		
☐ RA-31064	Kamov Ka-32	8606	CCCP-31064	0890	0192	2 IS TV3-117V	12600	9-12 Pax		lst Skytech Helicopter Service
☐ RA-31571	Kamov Ka-32	6220	CCCP-31571	0391	0491	2 IS TV3-117V	12600	9-12 Pax		lst Skytech Helicopter Service
☐ RA-31576	Kamov Ka-32	6225	CCCP-31576	0591	0691	2 IS TV3-117V	12600	9-12 Pax		lst Skytech Helicopter Service
☐ RA-31577	Kamov Ka-32	6226	CCCP-31577	0591	0691	2 IS TV3-117V	12600	9-12 Pax		lst Skytech Helicopter Service
☐ RA-31579	Kamov Ka-32	8601	CCCP-31579	0691	1091	2 IS TV3-117V	12600	9-12 Pax		lst Skytech Helicopter Service
☐ RA-06038	Mil Mi-26	34001212428	CCCP-06038	1090	0191	2 LO D-136	56000	Freighter		lst Skytech Helicopter Service

PENZA AIR ENTERPRISE = PNZ (Penzenskoe aviapredpriatie) (formerly Aeroflot Penza division) — Penza

Ul. Tsentralnaya, Airport, 440021 Penza, Russia ☎ (8412) 34 04 34 Tx: none Fax: (8412) 55 32 78 SITA: n/a
F: n/a ✝✝✝ n/a Head: Anatoly S. Polzhunov ICAO: PENZA Net: n/a Most aircraft are still in Aeroflot colors but will be repainted in due course.

☐ RA-09670	PZL Mielec (Antonov) An-2		CCCP-09670	0066		1 SH ASh-62IR	5500	Freighter		
☐ RA-17788	PZL Mielec (Antonov) An-2		CCCP-17788	0083		1 SH ASh-62IR	5500	Freighter		
☐ RA-17800	PZL Mielec (Antonov) An-2		CCCP-17800	0083		1 SH ASh-62IR	5500	Freighter		
☐ RA-17807	PZL Mielec (Antonov) An-2		CCCP-17807	0083		1 SH ASh-62IR	5500	Freighter		
☐ RA-17816	PZL Mielec (Antonov) An-2		CCCP-17816	0083		1 SH ASh-62IR	5500	Freighter		
☐ RA-17821	PZL Mielec (Antonov) An-2	1G204-22	CCCP-17821	0083		1 SH ASh-62IR	5500	Freighter		
☐ RA-33031	PZL Mielec (Antonov) An-2		CCCP-33031	0086		1 SH ASh-62IR	5500	Freighter		
☐ RA-33470	PZL Mielec (Antonov) An-2		CCCP-33470	0088		1 SH ASh-62IR	5500	Freighter		
☐ RA-33505	PZL Mielec (Antonov) An-2		CCCP-33505	0088		1 SH ASh-62IR	5500	Freighter		
☐ RA-33506	PZL Mielec (Antonov) An-2		CCCP-33506	0088		1 SH ASh-62IR	5500	Freighter		
☐ RA-40275	PZL Mielec (Antonov) An-2		CCCP-40275	0086		1 SH ASh-62IR	5500	Freighter		

553 registration type of aircraft cn/fn ex/ex* mfd del powered by mtow kg configuration selcal name/fln/specialitites/remarks

□ RA-40415	PZL Mielec (Antonov) An-2		CCCP-40415	0087		1 SH ASh-62IR	5500	Freighter		
□ RA-40439	PZL Mielec (Antonov) An-2		CCCP-40439	0087		1 SH ASh-62IR	5500	Freighter		
□ RA-40610	PZL Mielec (Antonov) An-2		CCCP-40610	0085		1 SH ASh-62IR	5500	Freighter		
□ RA-40612	PZL Mielec (Antonov) An-2		CCCP-40612	0085		1 SH ASh-62IR	5500	Freighter		
□ RA-40643	PZL Mielec (Antonov) An-2		CCCP-40643	0085		1 SH ASh-62IR	5500	Freighter		
□ RA-40725	PZL Mielec (Antonov) An-2		CCCP-40725	0076		1 SH ASh-62IR	5500	Freighter		
□ RA-43991	PZL Mielec (Antonov) An-2		CCCP-43991	0085		1 SH ASh-62IR	5500	Freighter		
□ RA-54850	PZL Mielec (Antonov) An-2		CCCP-54850	0079		1 SH ASh-62IR	5500	Freighter		
□ RA-68173	PZL Mielec (Antonov) An-2		CCCP-68173	0082		1 SH ASh-62IR	5500	Freighter		
□ RA-81635	PZL Mielec (Antonov) An-2		CCCP-81635	0089		1 SH ASh-62IR	5500	Freighter		
□ RA-84568	PZL Mielec (Antonov) An-2		CCCP-84568	0080		1 SH ASh-62IR	5500	Freighter		
□ RA-46361	Antonov 24B		CCCP-46361	0070		2 IV AI-24	21000	Y48		
□ RA-46379	Antonov 24B	07306102	CCCP-46379	0070		2 IV AI-24	21000	Y48		
□ RA-46422	Antonov 24B		CCCP-46422	0068		2 IV AI-24	21000	Y48		
□ RA-46466	Antonov 24RV	27307904	CCCP-46466	0072		2 IV AI-24VT	21800	Y48		
□ RA-46531	Antonov 24RV	57310010	CCCP-46531	0075		2 IV AI-24VT	21800	Y48		
□ RA-46645	Antonov 24RV	37309104	CCCP-46645	0073		2 IV AI-24VT	21800	Y48		
□ RA-46678	Antonov 24RV	47309610	CCCP-46678	0074		2 IV AI-24VT	21800	Y48		
□ RA-46846	Antonov 24RV	27307504	CCCP-46846	0072		2 IV AI-24VT	21800	Y48		
□ RA-47805	Antonov 24RV		CCCP-47805	0071		2 IV AI-24VT	21800	Y48		
□ RA-26208	Antonov 26B	14205	CCCP-26208	0085		2 IV AI-24VT	24000	Freighter		
□ RA-11338	Antonov 12	3341506	ST-ANL	0063		4 IV AI-20M	61000	Freighter		
□ RA-11339	Antonov 12BP	6344310	CCCP-11339	0066		4 IV AI-20M	61000	Freighter		

PERM AIRLINES = PGP (PAL Permskie avialinii) (formerly Perm State Unitary Air Enterprise) **Perm-Bolshoe Savino**

Bolshoe Savino Airport, 614078 Perm, Russia ☎ (3422) 28 43 25 Tx: 134604 pilot ru Fax: (3422) 27 44 92 SITA: PEEDSSU

F: 1933 👥 1300 Head: Igor D. Grachev ICAO: PERM AIR Net: n/a

□ RA-87418	Yakovlev 40	9421034	CCCP-87418	0074	0997	3 IV AI-25	16800	Combi		
□ RA-47152	Antonov 24B	89901604	CCCP-47152	0568	0372	2 IV AI-24	21800	Y48		
□ RA-47756	Antonov 24B	79901209	CCCP-47756	0667	1167	2 IV AI-24	21000	Y48		
□ RA-47773	Antonov 24B	79901406	CCCP-47773	1167	1267	2 IV AI-24	21000	Y48		
□ RA-26520	Antonov 26	7101	CCCP-26520	0978	1078	2 IV AI-24VT	24000	Freighter		
□ RA-26603	Antonov 26	4505	CCCP-26603	1076	1078	2 IV AI-24VT	24000	Freighter		
□ RA-26636	Antonov 26	6306	EP-TPR	0378	0478	2 IV AI-24VT	24000	Freighter		
□ RA-65046	Tupolev 134A-3	49550	CCCP-65046	1276	1077	2 SO D-30-III	49000	Y76		
□ RA-65059	Tupolev 134A-3	49870	CCCP-65059	0377	0178	2 SO D-30-III	49000	Y76		
□ RA-65064	Tupolev 134A-3	49886	CCCP-65064	0577	0378	2 SO D-30-III	49000	Y76		
□ RA-65751	Tupolev 134A-3	61066	CCCP-65751	0279	0379	2 SO D-30-III	49000	CY66		
□ RA-65775	Tupolev 134A-3	62530	CCCP-65775	0979	0181	2 SO D-30-III	49000	Y76		
□ RA-85104	Tupolev 154B	104	CCCP-85104	0575	0693	3 KU NK-8-2U	98000	Y164		cvtd 154A
□ RA-85212	Tupolev 154B-1	212	CCCP-85212	0577	0693	3 KU NK-8-2U	98000	Y164		cvtd 154B
□ RA-85284	Tupolev 154B-1	284	CCCP-85284	0778	0693	3 KU NK-8-2U	98000	Y164		
□ RA-85312	Tupolev 154B-2	312	CCCP-85312	1278	0297	3 KU NK-8-2U	98000	Y164		
□ RA-64017	Tupolev 204-100	1450742564017		0095	0597	2 SO PS-90A	103000	C36Y136		

PERM 2nd Aviation Enterprise (Vtoroe Permskoe aviapredpriatie) (formerly Aeroflot Perm 2nd division) **Perm-Bakharevka**

Bakharevka Airport, 614600 Perm, Russia ☎ (3422) 27 59 71 Tx: none Fax: (3422) 27 59 71 SITA: n/a

F: 1972 👥 n/a Head: Vladimir A. Shubin Net: n/a Most aircraft are still in Aeroflot colors but will be repainted in due course.

□ RA-14095	PZL Swidnik (Mil) Mi-2	5310704078	CCCP-14095	0088	0189	2 IS GTD-350-4	3550	Utility		
□ RA-14096	PZL Swidnik (Mil) Mi-2	5310705088	CCCP-14096	0088	0389	2 IS GTD-350-4	3550	Utility		
□ RA-14097	PZL Swidnik (Mil) Mi-2	5310706088	CCCP-14097	0088	0189	2 IS GTD-350-4	3550	Utility		
□ RA-14110	PZL Swidnik (Mil) Mi-2	5210729098	CCCP-14110	0088	1288	2 IS GTD-350-4	3550	Utility		
□ RA-14111	PZL Swidnik (Mil) Mi-2	5210730098	CCCP-14111	0088	0289	2 IS GTD-350-4	3550	Utility		
□ RA-14125	PZL Swidnik (Mil) Mi-2	5310837029	CCCP-14125	0089	0389	2 IS GTD-350-4	3550	Utility		
□ RA-14129	PZL Swidnik (Mil) Mi-2	5410841039	CCCP-14129	0089	0489	2 IS GTD-350-4	3550	Utility		
□ RA-14201	PZL Swidnik (Mil) Mi-2	5310942069	CCCP-14201	0089	0889	2 IS GTD-350-4	3550	Utility		
□ RA-14202	PZL Swidnik (Mil) Mi-2	5310943069	CCCP-14202	0089	0889	2 IS GTD-350-4	3550	Utility		
□ RA-14208	PZL Swidnik (Mil) Mi-2	5311041119	CCCP-14208	0089	0290	2 IS GTD-350-4	3550	Utility		
□ RA-14209	PZL Swidnik (Mil) Mi-2	5311042119	CCCP-14209	0089	0190	2 IS GTD-350-4	3550	Utility		
□ RA-14260	PZL Swidnik (Mil) Mi-2	5411203051	CCCP-14260	0089	0791	2 IS GTD-350-4	3550	Utility		
□ RA-14261	PZL Swidnik (Mil) Mi-2	5411204051	CCCP-14261	0089	0791	2 IS GTD-350-4	3550	Utility		
□ RA-14268	PZL Swidnik (Mil) Mi-2	5411221041	CCCP-14268	0091	0691	2 IS GTD-350-4	3550	Utility		
□ RA-14269	PZL Swidnik (Mil) Mi-2	5411222041	CCCP-14269	0091	0691	2 IS GTD-350-4	3550	Utility		
□ RA-20231	PZL Swidnik (Mil) Mi-2	527049021	CCCP-20231	0081	0481	2 IS GTD-350-4	3550	Utility		
□ RA-20782	PZL Swidnik (Mil) Mi-2	527824092	CCCP-20782	0082	0383	2 IS GTD-350-4	3550	Utility		
□ RA-20941	PZL Swidnik (Mil) Mi-2	528641054	CCCP-20941	0084	0389	2 IS GTD-350-4	3550	Utility		
□ RA-20944	PZL Swidnik (Mil) Mi-2	528644044	CCCP-20944	0084	0389	2 IS GTD-350-4	3550	Utility		
□ RA-23950	PZL Swidnik (Mil) Mi-2	533718084	CCCP-23950	0074	0074	2 IS GTD-350-4	3550	Utility		
□ RA-07306	PZL Mielec (Antonov) An-2	1G149-10	CCCP-07306	0073	0073	1 SH ASh-62IR	5500	Utility		
□ RA-07315	PZL Mielec (Antonov) An-2	1G149-19	CCCP-07315	0073	0482	1 SH ASh-62IR	5500	Utility		
□ RA-16071	PZL Mielec (Antonov) An-2	1G164-25	CCCP-16071	0075	0085	1 SH ASh-62IR	5500	Utility		
□ RA-19707	PZL Mielec (Antonov) An-2	1G165-21	CCCP-19707	0075	0975	1 SH ASh-62IR	5500	Utility		
□ RA-19737	PZL Mielec (Antonov) An-2	1G165-51	CCCP-19737	0075	1075	1 SH ASh-62IR	5500	Utility		
□ RA-19740	PZL Mielec (Antonov) An-2	1G165-54	CCCP-19740	0075	1075	1 SH ASh-62IR	5500	Utility		
□ RA-19744	PZL Mielec (Antonov) An-2	1G165-58	CCCP-19744	0075	1275	1 SH ASh-62IR	5500	Utility		
□ RA-32631	PZL Mielec (Antonov) An-2	1G219-30	CCCP-32631	0086	0686	1 SH ASh-62IR	5500	Utility		
□ RA-32632	PZL Mielec (Antonov) An-2	1G219-31	CCCP-32632	0086	0686	1 SH ASh-62IR	5500	Utility		
□ RA-33353	PZL Mielec (Antonov) An-2	1G226-12	CCCP-33353	0086	0987	1 SH ASh-62IR	5500	Utility		
□ RA-33564	PZL Mielec (Antonov) An-2	1G230-01	CCCP-33564	0088	0688	1 SH ASh-62IR	5500	Utility		
□ RA-35654	PZL Mielec (Antonov) An-2	1G117-10	CCCP-35654	0070	0683	1 SH ASh-62IR	5500	Utility		
□ RA-62464	PZL Mielec (Antonov) An-2	1G41-33	CCCP-62464	0063	0483	1 SH ASh-62IR	5500	Utility		
□ RA-68018	PZL Mielec (Antonov) An-2	1G192-50	CCCP-68018	0081	0681	1 SH ASh-62IR	5500	Utility		
□ RA-70549	PZL Mielec (Antonov) An-2	1G145-25	CCCP-70549	0073	0073	1 SH ASh-62IR	5500	Utility		
□ RA-70688	PZL Mielec (Antonov) An-2	1G129-38	CCCP-70688	0071	0483	1 SH ASh-62IR	5500	Utility		
□ RA-70849	PZL Mielec (Antonov) An-2	1G119-35	CCCP-70849	0070	0072	1 SH ASh-62IR	5500	Utility		
□ RA-82793	PZL Mielec (Antonov) An-2	1G166-06	CCCP-82793	0075	1275	1 SH ASh-62IR	5500	Utility		
□ RA-22591	Mil Mi-8T	7884	CCCP-22591	0079	0180	2 IS TV2-117A	12000	Utility		
□ RA-22625	Mil Mi-8T	8010	CCCP-22625	0080	0680	2 IS TV2-117A	12000	Utility		
□ RA-22664	Mil Mi-8T	8116	CCCP-22664	0080	1280	2 IS TV2-117A	12000	Utility		
□ RA-22665	Mil Mi-8T	8117	CCCP-22665	0080	1280	2 IS TV2-117A	12000	Utility		
□ RA-22735	Mil Mi-8T	98308929	CCCP-22735	0083	0583	2 IS TV2-117A	12000	Utility		
□ RA-22795	Mil Mi-8T	98315133	CCCP-22795	0083	1083	2 IS TV2-117A	12000	Utility		
□ RA-24443	Mil Mi-8T	98628077	CCCP-24443	0086	0886	2 IS TV2-117A	12000	Utility		
□ RA-24628	Mil Mi-8T	8257	CCCP-24628	0081	0781	2 IS TV2-117A	12000	Utility		
□ RA-24702	Mil Mi-8T	98103238	CCCP-24702	0081	1181	2 IS TV2-117A	12000	Utility		
□ RA-24706	Mil Mi-8T	98103353	CCCP-24706	0081	1281	2 IS TV2-117A	12000	Utility		
□ RA-24714	Mil Mi-8T	98417229	CCCP-24714	0084	0984	2 IS TV2-117A	12000	Utility		
□ RA-25363	Mil Mi-8T	98206836	CCCP-25363	0082	0782	2 IS TV2-117A	12000	Utility		
□ RA-25372	Mil Mi-8T	98206945	CCCP-25372	0082	0882	2 IS TV2-117A	12000	Utility		
□ RA-25590	Mil Mi-8T	99047983	CCCP-25590	0091	0691	2 IS TV2-117A	12000	Utility		

PERMSKIE MOTORY Aviakompania = PMT (Flying div. of Perm Motors, Joint-Stock Company/Member of MAP Group) **Perm-Bolshoe Savino**

Komsomolsky prospekt 93, GSP 621, 614600 Perm, Russia ☎ (3422) 45 41 42 Tx: n/a Fax: (3422) 45 41 42 SITA: n/a

F: n/a 👥 n/a Head: Alexander L. Lensky ICAO: MOTORPERM Net: n/a Operates corporate flights for itself only as well as commercial charter flights.

□ RA-87416	Yakovlev 40	9420834	CCCP-87416	0074		3 IV AI-25	16800	Combi		
□ RA-26028	Antonov 26B	10408	CCCP-26028	0080		2 IV AI-24VT	24000	Freighter		
□ RA-26069	Antonov 26B	11401	CCCP-26069	0081	0097	2 IV AI-24VT	24000	Freighter		
□ RA-26085	Antonov 26B		CCCP-26085	0081	0097	2 IV AI-24VT	24000	Freighter		

PETRONORD-AVIA, Ltd = PRN **Moscow-Vnukovo & -Bykovo**

Sretenski bulvar 9/2, 103045 Moskva, Russia ☎ (095) 925 64 19 Tx: 412000 ben su Fax: (095) 925 12 87 SITA: n/a

F: 1993 👥 n/a Head: Sergei A. Mitichkin ICAO: PETRONORD Net: n/a

□ RA-87669	Yakovlev 40	9021760	EW-87669	0080	0093	3 IV AI-25	17200	VIP C14		
□ RA-88294	Yakovlev 40	9331029	031	0073	0093	3 IV AI-25	17200	VIP C17		

PETROPAVLOVSK-KAMCHATSKY AIR ENTERPRISE = PTK (Petropavlovsk-Kamchatskoe aviapredpriatie) **Petropavlovsk Kamchatsky-Yelizovo**

Yelizovo Airport, 684010 Yelizovo, (Kamchatka Region), Russia ☎ (41522) 62 470 Tx: none Fax: (41522) 62 470 SITA: n/a

F: n/a 👥 n/a Head: Alexei I. Tverdokhleb ICAO: PETROKAM Net: n/a Most aircraft are still in Aeroflot colors but will be repainted in due course. (formerly AFL Petropavlovsk-Kamchatsky div.)

□ RA-67032	Let 410UVP	800503	CCCP-67032	0080		2 WA M-601D	5800	Y15		
□ RA-67051	Let 410UVP	800522	CCCP-67051	0080		2 WA M-601D	5800	Y15		
□ RA-67052	Let 410UVP	800523	CCCP-67052	0080		2 WA M-601D	5800	Y15		

554 registration type of aircraft cn/fn ex/ex* mfd del powered by mtow kg configuration selcal name/fln/specialitites/remarks

☐ RA-67053	Let 410UVP	800528	CCCP-67053	0080		2 WA M-601D	5800	Y15		
☐ RA-67054	Let 410UVP	800529	CCCP-67054	0080		2 WA M-601D	5800	Y15		
☐ RA-67055	Let 410UVP	800530	CCCP-67055	0080		2 WA M-601D	5800	Y15		
☐ RA-67132	Let 410UVP	800328	CCCP-67132	0080		2 WA M-601D	5800	Y15		
☐ RA-67152	Let 410UVP	800418	CCCP-67152	0080		2 WA M-601D	5800	Y15		
☐ RA-67158	Let 410UVP	800424	CCCP-67158	0080		2 WA M-601D	5800	Y15		
☐ RA-87321	Yakovlev 40	9332029	CCCP-87321	0073		3 IV AI-25	16800	Y32		
☐ RA-87385	Yakovlev 40	9411632	CCCP-87385	0074		3 IV AI-25	16800	Y32		
☐ RA-87481	Yakovlev 40	9440938	CCCP-87481	0074		3 IV AI-25	16800	Y32		
☐ RA-87625	Yakovlev 40	9140619	CCCP-87625	0071		3 IV AI-25	16800	Y27		
☐ RA-87640	Yakovlev 40		CCCP-87640	0071		3 IV AI-25	16800	Y27		
☐ RA-87651	Yakovlev 40	9141220	CCCP-87651	0071		3 IV AI-25	16800	Y27		
☐ RA-87947	Yakovlev 40	9621145	CCCP-87947	0076		3 IV AI-25	16800	Y32		
☐ RA-87949	Yakovlev 40	9621345	CCCP-87949	0076		3 IV AI-25	16800	Y32		
☐ RA-87988	Yakovlev 40	9541244	CCCP-87988	0075		3 IV AI-25	16800	Y32		
☐ RA-88241	Yakovlev 40	9641351	CCCP-88241	0076		3 IV AI-25	16800	Y32		
☐ RA-88264	Yakovlev 40	9711952	CCCP-88264	0077		3 IV AI-25	16800	Y32		

PETROZAVODSK AIR Enterprise (Petrozavodskoe aviapredpriatie) (formerly Aeroflot Petrozavodsk division) — **Petrozavodsk**

Peski Airport, Solomenskoe chosse, 185006 Petrozavodsk, (Republic of Karelia), Russia ☎ (81422) 44 574 Tx: none Fax: (81422) 76 470 SITA: n/a

F: n/a ⁂ n/a Head: Vladimir A. Nikolaev Net: n/a Most aircraft are still in Aeroflot colors but will be repainted in due course. Company will be transformed to the new national airline of the Republic of Karelia.

☐ RA-19565	Kamov Ka-26		CCCP-19565	0074		2 VE M-14V-26	3250	Utility		
☐ RA-19667	Kamov Ka-26		CCCP-19667	0076		2 VE M-14V-26	3250	Utility		
☐ RA-24333	Kamov Ka-26		CCCP-24333	0076		2 VE M-14V-26	3250	Utility		
☐ RA-24348	Kamov Ka-26		CCCP-24348	0076		2 VE M-14V-26	3250	Utility		
☐ RA-24349	Kamov Ka-26		CCCP-24349	0076		2 VE M-14V-26	3250	Utility		
☐ RA-24354	Kamov Ka-26		CCCP-24354	0076		2 VE M-14V-26	3250	Utility		
☐ RA-02476	PZL Mielec (Antonov) An-2		CCCP-02476	0071		1 SH ASh-62IR	5500	Utility		
☐ RA-07203	PZL Mielec (Antonov) An-2		CCCP-07203	0073		1 SH ASh-62IR	5500	Utility		
☐ RA-07484	PZL Mielec (Antonov) An-2		CCCP-07484	0073		1 SH ASh-62IR	5500	Utility		
☐ RA-07853	PZL Mielec (Antonov) An-2		CCCP-07853	0076		1 SH ASh-62IR	5500	Utility		
☐ RA-29319	PZL Mielec (Antonov) An-2	1G77-02	CCCP-29319	0066		1 SH ASh-62IR	5500	Utility		
☐ RA-35534	PZL Mielec (Antonov) An-2		CCCP-35534	0069		1 SH ASh-62IR	5500	Utility		
☐ RA-50578	PZL Mielec (Antonov) An-2		CCCP-50578	0071		1 SH ASh-62IR	5500	Utility		
☐ RA-70623	PZL Mielec (Antonov) An-2		CCCP-70623	0071		1 SH ASh-62IR	5500	Utility		
☐ RA-22393	Mil Mi-8		CCCP-22393	0077		2 IS TV2-117A	12000	Utility		
☐ RA-24112	Mil Mi-8		CCCP-24112	0088		2 IS TV2-117A	12000	Utility		
☐ RA-24499	Mil Mi-8		CCCP-24499	0086		2 IS TV2-117A	12000	Utility		
☐ RA-24574	Mil Mi-8		CCCP-24574	0088		2 IS TV2-117A	12000	Utility		lst EGA
☐ RA-24575	Mil Mi-8		CCCP-24575	0088		2 IS TV2-117A	12000	Utility		
☐ RA-24631	Mil Mi-8		CCCP-24631	0083		2 IS TV2-117A	12000	Utility		
☐ RA-25499	Mil Mi-8MTV-1		CCCP-25499	0091		2 IS TV3-117MT	13000	Utility		
☐ RA-25524	Mil Mi-8T		CCCP-25524	0091		2 IS TV2-117A	12000	Utility		
☐ RA-25525	Mil Mi-8T		CCCP-25525	0091		2 IS TV2-117A	12000	Utility		

POLET Aviakompania, Joint-Stock Company = POT (FLIGHT Aircompany) — **Stary Oskol & Ulyanovsk-Vostochny**

Ul. Sofi Perovskoi 37A, 394035 Voronezh, Russia ☎ (0732) 53 06 46 Tx: none Fax: (0732) 55 67 10 SITA: n/a

F: 1989 ⁂ n/a Head: Anatoly S. Karpov ICAO: POLET Net: http://www.polet.ru

☐ RA-87541	Yakovlev 40	9530642	CCCP-87541	0075		3 IV AI-25	16800	C16		
☐ RA-88291	Yakovlev 40	9530541	CCCP-88291	0075	0098	3 IV AI-25	16800	VIP		
☐ RA-42428	Yakovlev 42D	4520422306016		0093	0095	3 LO D-36	56500	Y120		
☐ RA-82010	Antonov 124-100 Ruslan	9773053616017	CCCP-82010	0086	0099	4 LO D-18T	392000	Freighter 120t		fn 01-09 / cvtd 124
☐ RA-82014	Antonov 124-100 Ruslan	9773054732039	CCCP-82014	0087	0099	4 LO D-18T	392000	Freighter 120t		fn 05-03 / cvtd 124
☐ RA-82024	Antonov 124-100 Ruslan	19530502035	CCCP-82024	0089	0099	4 LO D-18T	392000	Freighter 120t		fn 02-05 / cvtd 124
☐ RA-82026	Antonov 124-100 Ruslan	19530502127	10	0090	0099	4 LO D-18T	392000	Freighter 120t		fn 02-07 / cvtd 124
☐ RA-82075	Antonov 124-100 Ruslan	9773053459147		0094	0094	4 LO D-18T	392000	Freighter 120t		fn 07-08
☐ RA-82077	Antonov 124-100 Ruslan	9773054459151		0095	0095	4 LO D-18T	392000	Freighter 120t		fn 07-09

POLYUS-Centre for Parachute & Expeditional Works = PLB — **Ermolino**

Ul. Lobachika 17/19, 107113 Moskva, Russia ☎ (095) 269 06 13 Tx: none Fax: (095) 269 06 13 SITA: n/a

F: 1996 ⁂ n/a Head: Peter I. Zadirov ICAO: ANTEX Net: n/a Beside aircraft listed, also operates Mil Mi-8 & Yakovlev 40, leased from other companies when required.

☐ RA-76446	Ilyushin 76MD	1023412418	CCCP-76446	0092	0097	4 SO D-30KP	190000	Freighter		lsf Altai Airlines
☐ RA-76833	Ilyushin 76TD	1023411363	CCCP-76833	0092	0097	4 SO D-30KP	190000	Freighter		lsf Altai Airlines

POVOLZHSKY RAO (Volga Regional Sport Aviation Association) — **Ulyanovsk**

Ul. Zapadny Bulvar 3, 432034 Ulyanovsk, Russia ☎ (8422) 36 34 82 Tx: none Fax: (8422) 36 34 82 SITA: n/a

F: n/a ⁂ n/a Head: Yuri B. Vasilenko Net: n/a

☐ RA-14294	PZL Swidnik (Mil) Mi-2					2 IS GTD-350-4	3550	Utility		
☐ RA-23724	PZL Swidnik (Mil) Mi-2					2 IS GTD-350-4	3550	Utility		
☐ RA-23725	PZL Swidnik (Mil) Mi-2					2 IS GTD-350-4	3550	Utility		
☐ RA-23726	PZL Swidnik (Mil) Mi-2					2 IS GTD-350-4	3550	Utility		
☐ RA-23727	PZL Swidnik (Mil) Mi-2					2 IS GTD-350-4	3550	Utility		
☐ RA-23728	PZL Swidnik (Mil) Mi-2					2 IS GTD-350-4	3550	Utility		
☐ RA-23770	PZL Swidnik (Mil) Mi-2					2 IS GTD-350-4	3550	Utility		
☐ RA-23795	PZL Swidnik (Mil) Mi-2					2 IS GTD-350-4	3550	Utility		
☐ RA-23800	PZL Swidnik (Mil) Mi-2					2 IS GTD-350-4	3550	Utility		
☐ RA-01121	PZL Mielec (Antonov) An-2			0091		1 SH ASh-62IR	5500	Sprayer		
☐ RA-01125	PZL Mielec (Antonov) An-2			0091		1 SH ASh-62IR	5500	Sprayer		
☐ RA-01126	PZL Mielec (Antonov) An-2			0091		1 SH ASh-62IR	5500	Sprayer		
☐ RA-01127	PZL Mielec (Antonov) An-2			0091		1 SH ASh-62IR	5500	Sprayer		
☐ RA-02818	PZL Mielec (Antonov) An-2			0074		1 SH ASh-62IR	5500	Sprayer		
☐ RA-02826	PZL Mielec (Antonov) An-2			0074		1 SH ASh-62IR	5500	Sprayer		

PROGRESS (Arsenevskaya avatsionnaya kompania Progress im. N.I. Sazykina) (Flying div. of Arsenev Aviation Factory/Member of MAP Group) — **Arsenev**

Flying division / Letny otryad, Ul. Lenina 5, 692330 Arsenev (Primorsky Region), Russia ☎ (42361) 25 246 Tx: none Fax: (42361) 26 130 SITA: n/a

F: n/a ⁂ n/a Head: n/a Net: n/a Operates corporate for itself only & commercial charter flights. Most aircraft are still in Aeroflot colors with or without titles.

☐ RA-06107	Mil Mi-8		CCCP-06107			2 IS TV2-117A	12000	Utility		
☐ RA-06139	Mil Mi-8		CCCP-06139			2 IS TV2-117A	12000	Utility		
☐ RA-70886	Mil Mi-17		CCCP-70886	0091		2 IS TV3-117MT-3	13000	Utility		
☐ RA-69302	Antonov 8		CCCP-69302	0059		2 IV AI-20D	38000	Freighter		
☐ RA-69327	Antonov 8		CCCP-69327	0059		2 IV AI-20D	38000	Freighter		
☐ RA-93926	Tupolev 134A-3	1351204	YU-AHY	0071		2 SO D-30-III	49000	Combi		
☐ RA-11650	Antonov 12BP	6344305	LZ-BAG	0066		4 IV AI-20M	61000	Freighter		lst SFB as LZ-BFG
☐ RA-98102	Antonov 12BP	5343005	CCCP-98102	0065		4 IV AI-20M	61000	Freighter		lsf BFB as LZ-BFD

PROLOG Aviakompania, Ltd — **Strezhevoi**

4-ty MKP 407B, Room 228, 636762 Strezhevoi, (Tomsk Region), Russia ☎ (38259) 32 230 Tx: none Fax: (38259) 32 230 SITA: n/a

F: 1996 ⁂ n/a Head: Alexander R. Inzarin Net: n/a Operates Mil Mi-8 helicopters. Full details not yet known.

PSKOVAVIA = PSW (formerly Aeroflot Pskov division) — **Pskov**

Ul. Germana 34, 180005 Pskov, Russia ☎ (8112) 16 46 53 Tx: 246161 sokol ru Fax: (8112) 16 52 24 SITA: n/a

F: 1944 ⁂ n/a Head: Anatoly I. Sulimov ICAO: PSKOVAVIA Net: n/a Beside aircraft listed, also operates Antonov 2. Full details not yet known. Some aircraft are still in Aeroflot colors but will be repainted in due course.

☐ RA-26107	Antonov 26B	12008	CCCP-26107	0082	0082	2 IV AI-24VT	24000	Freighter		
☐ RA-26120	Antonov 26B	12304	CCCP-26120	0082	0082	2 IV AI-24VT	24000	Freighter		
☐ RA-26123	Antonov 26B	12402	CCCP-26123	0083	0083	2 IV AI-24VT	24000	Freighter		
☐ RA-26134	Antonov 26B	12805	OB-1441	0083	0083	2 IV AI-24VT	24000	Freighter		
☐ RA-26142	Antonov 26B	12904	OB-1442	0083	0083	2 IV AI-24VT	24000	Freighter		

PULKOVO AVIATION ENTERPRISE = Z8 / PLK (Aviapredpriatie Pulkovo) (formerly Aeroflot St. Petersburg directorate) — **St. Petersburg-Pulkovo**

Ul. Pilotov 18/4, 196210 St. Petersburg, Russia ☎ (812) 104 33 02 Tx: 121519 afl su Fax: (812) 104 37 02 SITA: n/a

F: 1932 ⁂ n/a Head: Boris G. Demchenko IATA: 195 ICAO: PULKOVO Some aircraft are still in former AFL colors & international schedules flights beside CIS are operated under contract to AFL using SU-flight numbers.

☐ RA-65004	Tupolev 134A-3	44060	CCCP-65004	0076		2 SO D-30-III	49000	C16Y52		
☐ RA-65020	Tupolev 134A-3	48380	CCCP-65020	0076		2 SO D-30-III	49000	C16Y52		
☐ RA-65042	Tupolev 134A-3	49350	CCCP-65042	0076		2 SO D-30-III	49000	C16Y52		
☐ RA-65068	Tupolev 134A-3	49907	ES-AAG	0777	0895	2 SO D-30-III	49000	C4Y56		
☐ RA-65093	Tupolev 134A-3	60215	UR-65093	0078	0097	2 SO D-30-III	49000	C4Y56		
☐ RA-65109	Tupolev 134A	60339	UR-65109	0078	0098	2 SO D-30-II	49000	C4Y56		
☐ RA-65112	Tupolev 134A-3	60350	ES-AAI	0478	0596	2 SO D-30-III	49000	C4Y56		
☐ RA-65113	Tupolev 134A	60380	ES-AAM	0478	0895	2 SO D-30-II	49000	C4Y56		
☐ RA-65128	Tupolev 134A	60628	LY-ABI	0078	0397	2 SO D-30-II	49000	C4Y56		
☐ RA-65759	Tupolev 134A	62239	ES-AAO	0479	0895	2 SO D-30-II	49000	C4Y56		
☐ RA-65872	Tupolev 134A-3	29312	CCCP-65872	0075		2 SO D-30-III	47000	C16Y52		

555 registration type of aircraft cn/fn ex/ex* mfd del powered by mtow kg configuration selcal name/fln/specialitites/remarks

☐ RA-11127	Antonov 12B	02348202	LZ-PVL	0072	0082	4 IV AI-20M	61000	Freighter		
☐ RA-12995	Antonov 12B	00347402	CCCP-12995	0070	0070	4 IV AI-20M	61000	Freighter		lst HLA
☐ RA-85293	Tupolev 154B-1	293	CCCP-85293	0078		3 KU NK-8-2U	98000	Y152		
☐ RA-85334	Tupolev 154B-2	334	CCCP-85334	0079		3 KU NK-8-2U	98000	Y164		
☐ RA-85343	Tupolev 154B-2	343	CCCP-85343	0079		3 KU NK-8-2U	98000	Y164		
☐ RA-85346	Tupolev 154B-2	346	CCCP-85346	0079		3 KU NK-8-2U	98000	Y152		
☐ RA-85377	Tupolev 154B-2	377	CCCP-85377	0079		3 KU NK-8-2U	98000	Y152		
☐ RA-85381	Tupolev 154B-2	381	CCCP-85381	0079		3 KU NK-8-2U	98000	Y152		
☐ RA-85390	Tupolev 154B-2	390	CCCP-85390	0079		3 KU NK-8-2U	98000	Y152		
☐ RA-85441	Tupolev 154B-2	441	CCCP-85441	0080		3 KU NK-8-2U	98000	Y152		
☐ RA-85530	Tupolev 154B-2	530	CCCP-85530	0082		3 KU NK-8-2U	100000	F12C18Y102		
☐ RA-85542	Tupolev 154B-2	542	CCCP-85542	0082		3 KU NK-8-2U	100000	F12C18Y102		
☐ RA-85552	Tupolev 154B-2	552	CCCP-85552	0082		3 KU NK-8-2U	100000	F12C18Y102		
☐ RA-85553	Tupolev 154B-2	553	CCCP-85553	0082		3 KU NK-8-2U	100000	F12C18Y102		
☐ RA-85579	Tupolev 154B-2	579	CCCP-85579	0083		3 KU NK-8-2U	100000	F12C18Y102		
☐ RA-85753	Tupolev 154M	935		0092	0098	3 SO D-30KU-154-II	100000	Y166		
☐ RA-85767	Tupolev 154M	948		0093	0094	3 SO D-30KU-154-II	100000	Y166		
☐ RA-85769	Tupolev 154M	951		0093	0093	3 SO D-30KU-154-II	100000	Y166		
☐ RA-85770	Tupolev 154M	952		0093	0093	3 SO D-30KU-154-II	100000	Y166		
☐ RA-85771	Tupolev 154M	953		0093	0096	3 SO D-30KU-154-II	100000	Y166		
☐ RA-85779	Tupolev 154M	963		0093	0895	3 SO D-30KU-154-II	100000	F12C18Y104		
☐ RA-85785	Tupolev 154M	969		0093	0093	3 SO D-30KU-154-II	100000	Y166		
☐ RA-85800	Tupolev 154M	984		0094	0095	3 SO D-30KU-154-II	100000	F12C18Y104		
☐ RA-86050	Ilyushin 86	51483202017	CCCP-86050	0082		4 KU NK-86	215000	Y350		
☐ RA-86060	Ilyushin 86	51483203027	CCCP-86060	0083		4 KU NK-86	215000	Y350		
☐ RA-86061	Ilyushin 86	51483203028	CCCP-86061	0083		4 KU NK-86	215000	Y350		
☐ RA-86063	Ilyushin 86	51483203030	CCCP-86063	0083		4 KU NK-86	215000	Y350		
☐ RA-86070	Ilyushin 86	51483204037	CCCP-86070	0084		4 KU NK-86	215000	Y350		
☐ RA-86073	Ilyushin 86	51483204040	CCCP-86073	0084		4 KU NK-86	215000	Y350		lst TRJ
☐ RA-86092	Ilyushin 86	51483207063	CCCP-86092	0087		4 KU NK-86	215000	Y350		
☐ RA-86094	Ilyushin 86	51483207065	CCCP-86094	0087		4 KU NK-86	215000	Y350		
☐ RA-86106	Ilyushin 86	51483208074	CCCP-86106	0089		4 KU NK-86	215000	Y350		

PYATIGORSK AIR ENTERPRISE (formerly part of Min. Vody C.A.P.O.) **Pyatigorsk**

Ul. Yermolova 14, 357528 Pyatigorsk, (Stavropol Region), Russia ☎ (86533) 99 153 Tx: none Fax: none SITA: n/a

F: n/a ⁂ n/a Head: n/a Net: n/a Operates Antonov 2 aircraft. Full details not yet known.

RAM AIR, Joint-Stock Company = RMY (Associated with Phoenix FZE, Sharjah, UAE) **Chelyabinsk & Sharjah (UAE)**

Operations office:, c/o Phoenix FZE, PO Box 7801, SAIF Zone, Sharjah International Airport, United Arab Emirates ☎ (6) 57 00 53 Tx: none Fax: (6) 57 00 56 SITA: n/a

F: 1993 ⁂ n/a Head: Alexey V. Yanchuk ICAO: RAMAIR Net: n/a Flights from Sharjah (UAE) are operated for/in conjunction with associated company PHOENIX FZE. Some aircraft carry such titles.

☐ RA-87228	Yakovlev 40K	9841659	CCCP-87228	0279	0098	3 IV AI-25	16800	Combi		Phoenix-titles
☐ RA-74267	Ilyushin 18D	188011105	CCCP-74267	1168	0399	4 IV AI-20M	64000	Y102		
☐ RA-74268	Ilyushin 18D	188011201	CCCP-74268	1268	0399	4 IV AI-20M	64000	Y102		
☐ EX-75442	Ilyushin 18D	187009702	RA-75442	0067	0097	4 IV AI-20M	64000	Y100		
☐ EX-75466	Ilyushin 18D	187010403	RA-75466	0067	0097	4 IV AI-20M	64000	Y100		
☐ ST-APZ	Ilyushin 18D	187010004	RA-75449	0067	0097	4 IV AI-20M	64000	Y100		
☐ T9-ABB	Ilyushin 18V	184007405	EL-ADY	0664	0598	4 IV AI-20M	64000	Y95		
☐ ST-AQA	Ilyushin 76TD	0023442218	EP-ALC	0082	1198	4 SO D-30KP	190000	Freighter		
☐ ST-AQB	Ilyushin 76TD	0053460795	EP-ALA	0285	1198	4 SO D-30KP	190000	Freighter		
☐ T9-QAA	Ilyushin 76TD	0023437076	EP-ALB	0082	1198	4 SO D-30KP	190000	Freighter		
☐ T9-QAB	Ilyushin 76TD	1013408265	EP-ALD	0091	1198	4 SO D-30KP	190000	Freighter		Phoenix-titles

REMEX, Ltd = RXM **Moscow-Zhukovsky & -Chkalovskaya**

Ul. 2-ya Tverstaya-Yamskaya 52, 125047 Moskva, Russia ☎ (095) 250 35 92 Tx: none Fax: (095) 250 8951 SITA: MOWSTXH

F: 1997 ⁂ n/a Head: Konstantin G. Vartanov ICAO: REMEX Net: http://www.aha.ru/sky

☐ RA-76485	Ilyushin 76TD	0063470088	CCCP-76485	0086	0097	4 SO D-30KP	190000	Freighter		lsf IKT
☐ RA-76494	Ilyushin 76TD	0053465956	CCCP-76494	0085	0098	4 SO D-30KP	190000	Freighter		lsf OBM
☐ RA-76792	Ilyushin 76TD	0093497942	CCCP-76792	0089	0097	4 SO D-30KP	190000	Freighter		lsf KJC / fn 7406
☐ RA-78731	Ilyushin 76T		CCCP-78731	0080	0097	4 SO D-30KP	175000	Freighter		

ROSTVERTOL = RUZ (Flying div.of Rostvertol Heli.Corp./Rostovskoe vertoletnoe proizvodsvennoe predpriatie/Member of MAP Group) **Rostov-na-Donu**

Ul. Novatorov 5, 344038 Rostov-na-Donu, Russia ☎ (8632) 31 74 78 Tx: 614803 gromv su Fax: (8632) 31 65 88 SITA: n/a

F: 1992 ⁂ n/a Head: Igor Yu. Shmidt ICAO: ROSTVERTOL Net: n/a

☐ RA-70890	Mil Mi-8MT	212M146	CCCP-70890	0091		2 IS TV3-117MT	13000	24 Pax		
☐ RA-70892	Mil Mi-8MT	212M148	CCCP-70892	0091		2 IS TV3-117MT	13000	24 Pax		
☐ RA-70893	Mil Mi-8MT	212M149	CCCP-70893	0091		2 IS TV3-117MT	13000	24 Pax		
☐ RA-70955	Mil Mi-8MT	202M24	CCCP-70955	0091		2 IS TV3-117MT	13000	24 Pax		
☐ RA-70956	Mil Mi-8MT	202M25	CCCP-70956	0091		2 IS TV3-117MT	13000	24 Pax		
☐ RA-70957	Mil Mi-8MT	202M26	CCCP-70957	0091		2 IS TV3-117MT	13000	24 Pax		
☐ RA-70958	Mil Mi-8MT	202M27	CCCP-70958	0091		2 IS TV3-117MT	13000	24 Pax		
☐ RA-26089	Antonov 26	12203	CCCP-26089	0082		2 IV AI-24VT	24000	Freighter		
☐ RA-48983	Antonov 32	1603	CCCP-48983	0088		2 IV AI-20D	27000	Freighter		
☐ RA-06070	Mil Mi-26T	34001212493		0092		2 LO D-136	56000	Freighter		
☐ RA-06089	Mil Mi-26T	34001212499		0092		2 LO D-136	56000	Freighter		
☐ RA-06271	Mil Mi-26T	34001212495		0092		2 LO D-136	56000	Freighter		
☐ RA-06273	Mil Mi-26T	34001212501		0092		2 LO D-136	56000	Freighter		
☐ RA-06274	Mil Mi-26T	34001212502		0092		2 LO D-136	56000	Freighter		
☐ RA-06275	Mil Mi-26T	34001212503		0092		2 LO D-136	56000	Freighter		
☐ RA-06276	Mil Mi-26T	34001212504		0092		2 LO D-136	56000	Freighter		
☐ RA-29109	Mil Mi-26TC	226208	CCCP-29109	0090		2 LO D-136	49750	Freighter		

RUSAEROLEASING AIRLINE = KVM (Rosaerolising Aviakompania) **Moscow**

Tverskaya 20/1, Room 340, 103789 Moskva, Russia ☎ (095) 209 46 68 Tx: n/a Fax: (095) 209 46 68 SITA: n/a

F: 1995 ⁂ n/a Head: Viktor M. Kurilo ICAO: COMLEASE Net: n/a Operates Ilyushin 76 & Tupolev 154 aircraft leased from other companies when required.

RUSAIR, International Aviastransport, Corp. = 2Q / RMK (Rusavia) **Moscow-Sheremetyevo**

Leningradsky Prospekt 37, 125836 Moskva, Russia ☎ (095) 755 56 12 Tx: none Fax: none SITA: n/a

F: 1998 ⁂ n/a Head: n/a ICAO: RUSAVIA Net: n/a

☐ RA-87311	Yakovlev 40	9320629	CCCP-87311	0073	0098	3 IV AI-25	16800	Y32		
☐ RA-65005	Tupolev 134A-3	44065	CCCP-65005	0476	0098	2 SO D-30-III	47000	Y68		

RUSSIA State Transport Company = R4 / SDM (Gosudarstvennaya transportnaya kompania ROSSIA) (formerly Russia Special CAD) **Moscow-Vnukovo**

I-aya Reisovaya 2, 103027 Moskva, Russia ☎ (095) 436 26 65 Tx: n/a Fax: (095) 436 23 28 SITA: n/a

F: n/a ⁂ n/a Head: Vladimir A. Kachnov IATA: 948 ICAO: RUSSIA Net: n/a

State organisation conducting VIP & transport flights for the Russian Government & commercial scheduled & charter flights. Also frequently leases/operates on behalf of other airlines.

☐ RA-15294	PZL Swidnik (Mil) Mi-2	525907118	CCCP-15294	0078		2 IS GTD-350-4	3550	Utility		
☐ RA-24229	Mil Mi-8PS-9		CCCP-24229	0087		2 IS TV2-117A	12000	VIP 9 Pax		
☐ RA-24296	Mil Mi-8		CCCP-24296	0087		2 IS TV2-117A	12000	Utility		
☐ RA-24297	Mil Mi-8		CCCP-24297	0087		2 IS TV2-117A	12000	Utility		
☐ RA-24298	Mil Mi-8PS-7	8651	CCCP-24298	0087		2 IS TV2-117A	12000	VIP 7 Pax		
☐ RA-25137	Mil Mi-8		CCCP-25137	0087		2 IS TV2-117A	12000	Utility		
☐ RA-25187	Mil Mi-8		CCCP-25187	0090		2 IS TV2-117A	12000	Utility		
☐ RA-27080	Mil Mi-8PS-7		CCCP-27080	0092		2 IS TV2-117A	12000	VIP 7 Pax		
☐ RA-27186	Mil Mi-8MTV-1			0093		2 IS TV3-117MT	13000	Utility		
☐ RA-87203	Yakovlev 40	9741456	CCCP-87203	0077		3 IV AI-25	16800	VIP		
☐ RA-87334	Yakovlev 40D	9510738	CCCP-87334	0075		3 IV AI-25	17200	Y32		cvtd 40
☐ RA-87968	Yakovlev 40	9841258	CCCP-87968	0078		3 IV AI-25	16800	VIP		
☐ RA-87969	Yakovlev 40	9841358	CCCP-87969	0078		3 IV AI-25	16800	VIP		
☐ RA-87970	Yakovlev 40D	9831458	CCCP-87970	0078		3 IV AI-25	17200	VIP		cvtd 40
☐ RA-87971	Yakovlev 40	9831558	CCCP-87971	0078		3 IV AI-25	16800	VIP		
☐ RA-87972	Yakovlev 40	9921658	CCCP-87972	0079		3 IV AI-25	16800	VIP		
☐ RA-88200	Yakovlev 40	9630249	CCCP-88200	0076		3 IV AI-25	16800	Y32		
☐ RA-65552	Tupolev 134A-3	66270	CCCP-65552	0083		2 SO D-30-III	49000	VIP / F8Y60		
☐ RA-65553	Tupolev 134A-3	66300	CCCP-65553	0084		2 SO D-30-III	49000	VIP / F8Y60		
☐ RA-65554	Tupolev 134A-3	66320	CCCP-65554	0084		2 SO D-30-III	49000	VIP / F8Y60		
☐ RA-65555	Tupolev 134A-3	66350	CCCP-65555	0084		2 SO D-30-III	49000	VIP		
☐ RA-65557	Tupolev 134A-3	66380	CCCP-65557	0084		2 SO D-30-III	49000	VIP		
☐ RA-65904	Tupolev 134A-3	63953	CCCP-65904	0082		2 SO D-30-III	49000	VIP		
☐ RA-65905	Tupolev 134A-3	63965	CCCP-65905	0082		2 SO D-30-III	49000	VIP		
☐ RA-65911	Tupolev 134A-3	63972	CCCP-65911	0083		2 SO D-30-III	49000	VIP		
☐ RA-65912	Tupolev 134A-3	63985	CCCP-65912	0082		2 SO D-30-III	49000	VIP / F8Y60		
☐ RA-65914	Tupolev 134A-3	66109	TC-GRD	0083		2 SO D-30-III	49000	VIP / F8Y60		

556 registration type of aircraft cn/fn ex/ex* mfd del powered by mtow kg configuration selcal name/fln/specialitites/remarks

☐ RA-65915	Tupolev 134A-3	66120	TC-GRE	0083		2 SO D-30-III	49000	VIP / F8Y60		
☐ RA-65916	Tupolev 134A-3	66152	CCCP-65916	0083		2 SO D-30-III	49000	VIP / F8Y60		
☐ RA-65919	Tupolev 134A-3	66168	CCCP-65919	0083		2 SO D-30-III	49000	VIP / F8Y60		
☐ RA-65921	Tupolev 134A-3	63997	CCCP-65921	0083		2 SO D-30-III	49000	VIP / F8Y60		
☐ RA-65978	Tupolev 134A-3	63357	CCCP-65978	0080		2 SO D-30-III	49000	VIP		
☐ RA-65994	Tupolev 134A-3	66207	CCCP-65994	0083		2 SO D-30-III	49000	VIP		
☐ RA-65995	Tupolev 134A-3	66400	CCCP-65995	0084		2 SO D-30-III	49000	VIP		
☐ RA-75453	Ilyushin 18D	187010103	CCCP-75453	0067		4 IV AI-20M	61000	Y100		
☐ RA-75454	Ilyushin 18D	187010104	CCCP-75454	0067		4 IV AI-20M	61000	Y100		
☐ RA-75464	Ilyushin 18D	187010401	CCCP-75464	0067		4 IV AI-20M	61000	Y100		
☐ RA-85629	Tupolev 154M	758	CCCP-85629	0087		3 SO D-30KU-154-II	100000	F12Y120		
☐ RA-85630	Tupolev 154M	759	CCCP-85630	0087		3 SO D-30KU-154-II	100000	F12Y120		lst TEP
☐ RA-85631	Tupolev 154M	760	CCCP-85631	0087		3 SO D-30KU-154-II	100000	F12Y120		
☐ RA-85645	Tupolev 154M	782	CCCP-85645	0088		3 SO D-30KU-154-II	100000	F12Y120		
☐ RA-85651	Tupolev 154M	793	CCCP-85651	0088		3 SO D-30KU-154-II	100000	VIP		
☐ RA-85653	Tupolev 154M	795	CCCP-85653	0088		3 SO D-30KU-154-II	100000	VIP		
☐ RA-85658	Tupolev 154M	808	CCCP-85658	0089		3 SO D-30KU-154-II	100000	F12Y120		
☐ RA-85659	Tupolev 154M	809	CCCP-85659	0089		3 SO D-30KU-154-II	100000	VIP / Y164		
☐ RA-85666	Tupolev 154M	820	CCCP-85666	0089		3 SO D-30KU-154-II	100000	VIP		
☐ RA-85675	Tupolev 154M	835	CCCP-85675	0090		3 SO D-30KU-154-II	100000	VIP		
☐ RA-85686	Tupolev 154M	854	CCCP-85686	0090		3 SO D-30KU-154-II	100000	VIP		
☐ RA-64014	Tupolev 204			0093		2 SO PS-90A	94600	VIP		
☐ RA-64015	Tupolev 204			0093		2 SO PS-90A	94600	VIP		
☐ RA-86466	Ilyushin 62M	2749316	CCCP-86466	0087		4 SO D-30KU	167000	VIP / F12CY120		fn 4901
☐ RA-86467	Ilyushin 62M	3749733	CCCP-86467	0087		4 SO D-30KU	167000	F12CY120		fn 4903
☐ RA-86468	Ilyushin 62M	4749857	CCCP-86468	0087		4 SO D-30KU	167000	VIP		fn 4905
☐ RA-86536	Ilyushin 62M	4445948	CCCP-86536	0084		4 SO D-30KU	167000	F12CY120		fn 4504
☐ RA-86537	Ilyushin 62M	3546733	CCCP-86537	0085		4 SO D-30KU	167000	VIP / F12CY120		fn 4603
☐ RA-86540	Ilyushin 62M	3546548	CCCP-86540	0085		4 SO D-30KU	167000	VIP		fn 4604
☐ RA-86553	Ilyushin 62M	3052657	CCCP-86553	0090		4 SO D-30KU	167000	F12CY120		fn 5205
☐ RA-86554	Ilyushin 62M	4053514	CCCP-86554	0090		4 SO D-30KU	167000	VIP		fn 5301
☐ RA-86559	Ilyushin 62M	2153258	CCCP-86559	0091		4 SO D-30KU	167000	VIP		02 / fn 5305
☐ RA-86561	Ilyushin 62M	4154842	CCCP-86561	0091		4 SO D-30KU	167000	VIP		01 / fn 5404 / Presidential aircraft
☐ RA-86710	Ilyushin 62M	2647646	CCCP-86710	0086		4 SO D-30KU	167000	F12CY120		fn 4704
☐ RA-86711	Ilyushin 62M	4648414	CCCP-86711	0086		4 SO D-30KU	167000	VIP		fn 4801
☐ RA-86712	Ilyushin 62M	4648339	CCCP-86712	0086		4 SO D-30KU	167000	VIP		fn 4803
☐ RA-96012	Ilyushin 96-300	74393201009		0095		4 SO PS-90AN	240000	VIP		Presidential aircraft
☐ RA-96014	Ilyushin 96-300					4 SO PS-90AN	240000	VIP		oo-delivery 0099
☐ RA-82072	Antonov 124-100 Ruslan	9773053359136		0093	0094	4 LO D-18T	392000	Freighter		fn 07-05
☐ RA-82073	Antonov 124-100 Ruslan	9773054359139		0093	0094	4 LO D-18T	392000	Freighter		fn 07-06

RYAZANAVIATRANS = RYZ (formerly Ryazan Air Enterprise & part of Central Districts Airlines & Aeroflot Ryazan division) **Ryazan**

Turlatovo Airport, 391011 Ryazan, Russia ☎ (0912) 44 67 34 Tx: none Fax: (095) 973 00 95 SITA: n/a

F: n/a ⁂ n/a Head: Gennady D. Kravchenko ICAO: RYAZAN AIR Net: n/a Also owns 50 Antonov 2 but most are stored and for sale. Most aircraft are still in Aeroflot colors but will be repainted in due course.

☐ RA-14184	PZL Swidnik (Mil) Mi-2	5410525028	CCCP-14184	0088		2 IS GTD-350-4	3550	Utility		
☐ RA-20242	PZL Swidnik (Mil) Mi-2	527130051	CCCP-20242	0081		2 IS GTD-350-4	3550	Utility		
☐ RA-20309	PZL Swidnik (Mil) Mi-2	527515022	CCCP-20309	0082		2 IS GTD-350-4	3550	Utility		
☐ RA-20375	PZL Swidnik (Mil) Mi-2	529822066	CCCP-20375	0086		2 IS GTD-350-4	3550	Utility		
☐ RA-20416	PZL Swidnik (Mil) Mi-2	529914086	CCCP-20416	0086		2 IS GTD-350-4	3550	Utility		
☐ RA-23586	PZL Swidnik (Mil) Mi-2	534607016	CCCP-23586	0086		2 IS GTD-350-4	3550	Utility		
☐ RA-67106	Let 410UVP	851335	CCCP-67106	0085		2 WA M-601D	5800	Y15		
☐ RA-67107	Let 410UVP	851336	OK-PDM	0085		2 WA M-601D	5800	Y17		
☐ RA-67108	Let 410UVP	851337	CCCP-67108	0085		2 WA M-601D	5800	Y15		lst West Coast Airways as 9L-LBN
☐ RA-67109	Let 410UVP	841338	CCCP-67109	0084		2 WA M-601D	5800	Y15		lst West Coast Airways as 9L-LBM
☐ RA-67342	Let 410UVP	820902	CCCP-67342	0082		2 WA M-601D	5800	Y15		
☐ RA-67434	Let 410UVP	831125	CCCP-67434	0083		2 WA M-601D	5800	Y15		
☐ RA-67435	Let 410UVP	831139	CCCP-67435	0083		2 WA M-601D	5800	Y15		
☐ RA-67438	Let 410UVP	841202	HA-LAI	0084		2 WA M-601D	5800	Y15		lst West Coast Airways as 9L-LBJ
☐ RA-67495	Let 410UVP	851339	CCCP-67495	0085		2 WA M-601D	5800	Y15		

RYBINSK MOTORS, Joint-Stock Company = RMO (Rybinskie motory) (Flying division of Rybinsk Aircraft Motors Factory / Member of MAP Group) **Rybinsk-Staroselye**

Flying div./Letny otryad, Prospekt Lenina 163, 152903 Rybinsk, (Yaroslav' Region), Russia ☎ (0855) 24 32 27 Tx: 412559 topaz Fax: (0855) 21 74 13 SITA: n/a

F: 1914 ⁂ n/a Head: Alexander A. Belyaev ICAO: RYBMOTORS Net: n/a Operates corporate flights for itself only & commercial charter flights.

☐ RA-87211	Yakovlev 40	9440737	CCCP-87211	0074	0086	3 IV AI-25	17200	Executive		
☐ RA-87225	Yakovlev 40K	9841359	CCCP-87225	0078	0078	3 IV AI-25	17200	Combi		
☐ RA-87936	Yakovlev 40K	9740756	CCCP-87936	0077	0077	3 IV AI-25	16800	Combi		
☐ RA-88289	Antonov 26B	11804	CCCP-88289	0082	0082	2 IV AI-24VT	24000	Freighter		

RZHEVKA AIR ENTERPRISE = RZV (Aviapredpriatie Rzhevka) (formerly Aeroflot Rzhevka division) **St. Petersburg-Rzhevka**

Rzhevka Airport, 188679 pos. Kovalevo, (Vsevolozhsky District), Russia ☎ (812) 527 37 27 Tx: n/a Fax: (812) 527 39 82 SITA: n/a

F: n/a ⁂ n/a Head: Yevgeni P. Shestakov ICAO: RZHEVKA Net: n/a Also operates Antonov 2, Mil Mi-2 & Mi-8. Full details not yet known. Most aircraft are still in Aeroflot colors but will be repainted in due course.

☐ RA-30024	Antonov 30	0502	CCCP-30024	0074		2 IV AI-24T	23000	Survey / Combi		
☐ RA-30048	Antonov 30	0910	CCCP-30048	0075		2 IV AI-24T	23000	Survey / Combi		
☐ RA-30053	Antonov 30D	1008	CCCP-30053	0075		2 IV AI-24T	23000	Survey / Combi		
☐ RA-30062	Antonov 30	1207	CCCP-30062	0077		2 IV AI-24T	23000	Survey / Combi		
☐ RA-30067	Antonov 30	1208	CCCP-30067	0077		2 IV AI-24T	23000	Survey / Combi		
☐ RA-26227	Antonov 26	5509	CCCP-59502	0077		2 IV AI-24VT	24000	Freighter		
☐ RA-26228	Antonov 26	5602	FAP 378	0078		2 IV AI-24VT	24000	Freighter		

SAAK, Stavropol Joint-Stock Airline = SVL (Stavropolskaya aktsionernaya aviakompania) (formerly Aeroflot Stavropol division) **Stavropol**

Airport, 355010 Stavropol, Russia ☎ (8652) 32 61 47 Tx: 223221 saak ru Fax: (8652) 25 08 75 SITA: n/a

F: 1992 ⁂ n/a Head: Gennady S. Russkikh ICAO: STAVROPOL Net: n/a Some aircraft are still in Aeroflot colors without titles but will be repainted in due course.

☐ RA-22155	Mil Mi-8T	99257223		0092	0092	2 IS TV2-117A	12000	Y26 / Combi		
☐ RA-24013	Mil Mi-8MTV-1	95714	CCCP-24013	0891	0091	2 IS TV3-117MT	13000	Y24 / Combi		lst Golden Airways
☐ RA-27033	Mil Mi-8MTV-1	95867		0292	0092	2 IS TV3-117MT	13000	Y24 / Combi		
☐ RA-27056	Mil Mi-8MTV-1	95890		0392	0092	2 IS TV3-117MT	13000	Y24 / Combi		lst Trans Air Congo
☐ RA-27064	Mil Mi-8MTV-1	95900		0392	0092	2 IS TV3-117MT	13000	Y24 / Combi		
☐ RA-27143	Mil Mi-8P	8702	TC-HNA	1192	0093	2 IS TV2-117A	12000	Y28 / Combi		
☐ RA-27144	Mil Mi-8T	99257342		0092	0092	2 IS TV2-117A	12000	Y26 / Combi		
☐ RA-27145	Mil Mi-8T	99257347		1292	0093	2 IS TV2-117A	12000	Y26 / Combi		
☐ RA-27146	Mil Mi-8T	99257365		0092	0092	2 IS TV2-117A	12000	Y26 / Combi		
☐ RA-87939	Yakovlev 40	9640352		0177	0093	3 IV AI-25	16800	Y32		
☐ RA-87992	Yakovlev 40	9541644	CCCP-87992	1275	1275	3 IV AI-25	16800	Research Lab.		
☐ RA-88292	Yakovlev 40	9540446		0276	0093	3 IV AI-25	16800	Y32		
☐ RA-46323	Antonov 24B	97305409	CCCP-46323	0769	0069	2 IV AI-24	21000	Y48		
☐ RA-46324	Antonov 24B	97305410	CCCP-46324	0769	0069	2 IV AI-24	21000	Y48		
☐ RA-46380	Antonov 24B	07306103	CCCP-46380	0570	0070	2 IV AI-24	21000	Y48		
☐ RA-46462	Antonov 24RV	27307808	CCCP-46462	0672	0072	2 IV AI-24VT	21800	Y48		lst Golden Airways, Ghana
☐ RA-46495	Antonov 24RV	27308208	CCCP-46495	1272	0072	2 IV AI-24VT	21800	Y48		lst Trans Air Congo
☐ RA-46591	Antonov 24B	97305101	CCCP-46591	0269	0069	2 IV AI-24	21000	Y48		
☐ RA-46606	Antonov 24RV	37308603	CCCP-46606	0473	0073	2 IV AI-24VT	21800	Y48		lst Golden Airways, Ghana
☐ RA-47811	Antonov 24RV	17307003	TC-KHT	0571	0071	2 IV AI-24VT	21800	Y48		lst Trans Air Congo
☐ RA-26243	Antonov 26B	11102		0581	0094	2 IV AI-24VT	24000	Freighter		
☐ RA-65047	Tupolev 134A	49600	CCCP-65047	0877	0096	2 SO D-30-II	47600	CY72		
☐ RA-65935	Tupolev 134A	66180	CCCP-65935	1183	0097	2 SO D-30-II	49000	CY72		
☐ RA-42320	Yakovlev 42	4520421302075	CCCP-42320	0383	0096	3 LO D-36	56500	Y120 or Frtr		

SAKHAAVIA National Aircompany = K7 / IKT (Sakha Airlines) (formerly Yakutavia) **Yakutsk**

Ul. Gagarina 10, 677014 Yakutsk, (Republic of Sakha-Yakutia), Russia ☎ (4112) 44 30 83 Tx: 135116 alas su Fax: (4112) 44 32 12 SITA: n/a

F: 1993 ⁂ n/a Head: Alexander N. Manturov IATA: 840 ICAO: SAKHA-AVIA Net: n/a All aircraft are operated by the following Air Enterprise divisions (under the licence & colors & SAKHAAVIA):
CHOKURDAKH, KOLYMA-INDIGIRKA, MAGAN, NERYUNGRI, NYURBA, TIKSI, UST-NERA, YAKUTSK & ZYRYANKA.

☐ RA-20771	PZL Swidnik (Mil) Mi-2	547808082	CCCP-20771	0082	0093	2 IS GTD-350-4	3500	Utility		opb Magan Air Enterprise-division
☐ RA-23467	PZL Swidnik (Mil) Mi-2	536206069	CCCP-23467	0079	0093	2 IS GTD-350-4	3500	Utility		opb Magan Air Enterprise-division
☐ RA-23472	PZL Swidnik (Mil) Mi-2	536231079	CCCP-23472	0079	0093	2 IS GTD-350-4	3500	Utility		opb Magan Air Enterprise-division
☐ RA-01408	PZL Mielec (Antonov) An-2	1G230-48	CCCP-01408	0088	0093	1 SH ASh-62IR	5500	Utility or Y12		opb Magan Air Enterprise-division
☐ RA-01411	PZL Mielec (Antonov) An-2	1G230-51	CCCP-01411	0088	0093	1 SH ASh-62IR	5500	Utility or Y12		opb Magan Air Enterprise-division
☐ RA-01412	PZL Mielec (Antonov) An-2	1G230-52	CCCP-01412	0088	0093	1 SH ASh-62IR	5500	Utility or Y12		opb Kolyma-Indigirka Air Enterprise-div
☐ RA-01420	PZL Mielec (Antonov) An-2	1G230-60	CCCP-01420	0088	0093	1 SH ASh-62IR	5500	Utility or Y12		opb Nyurba Air Enterprise-division
☐ RA-01445	PZL Mielec (Antonov) An-2	1G231-49	CCCP-01445	0088	0093	1 SH ASh-62IR	5500	Utility or Y12		opb Chokurdakh Air Enterprise-division
☐ RA-01488	PZL Mielec (Antonov) An-2	1G232-22	CCCP-01488	0088	0093	1 SH ASh-62IR	5500	Utility or Y12		opb Chokurdakh Air Enterprise-division
☐ RA-01493	PZL Mielec (Antonov) An-2	1G232-27	CCCP-01493	0088	0093	1 SH ASh-62IR	5500	Utility or Y12		opb Chokurdakh Air Enterprise-division

557 registration type of aircraft cn/fn ex/ex* mfd del powered by mtow kg configuration selcal name/fln/specialitites/remarks

☐	RA-01740	PZL Mielec (Antonov) An-2	1G106-37	CCCP-01740	0069	0093	1 SH ASh-62IR	5500	Utility or Y12		opb Kolyma-Indigirka Air Enterprise-div
☐	RA-02250	PZL Mielec (Antonov) An-2	1G234-04	CCCP-02250	0089	0093	1 SH ASh-62IR	5500	Utility or Y12		opb Chokurdakh Air Enterprise-division
☐	RA-02251	PZL Mielec (Antonov) An-2	1G234-05	CCCP-02251	0089	0093	1 SH ASh-62IR	5500	Utility or Y12		opb Magan Air Enterprise-division
☐	RA-02252	PZL Mielec (Antonov) An-2	1G234-06	CCCP-02252	0089	0093	1 SH ASh-62IR	5500	Utility or Y12		opb Zyryanka Air Enterprise-division
☐	RA-02253	PZL Mielec (Antonov) An-2	1G243-07	CCCP-02253	0089	0093	1 SH ASh-62IR	5500	Utility or Y12		opb Kolyma-Indigirka Air Enterprise-div
☐	RA-02325	PZL Mielec (Antonov) An-2	1G239-29	CCCP-02325	0090	0093	1 SH ASh-62IR	5500	Utility or Y12		opb Magan Air Enterprise-division
☐	RA-02577	PZL Mielec (Antonov) An-2	1G120-37	CCCP-02577	0070	0093	1 SH ASh-62IR	5500	Utility or Y12		opb Ust-Nera Air Enterprise-division
☐	RA-02736	PZL Mielec (Antonov) An-2	1G125-14	CCCP-02736	0071	0093	1 SH ASh-62IR	5500	Utility or Y12		opb Chokurdakh Air Enterprise-division
☐	RA-05750	PZL Mielec (Antonov) An-2	1G151-58	CCCP-05750	0074	0093	1 SH ASh-62IR	5500	Utility or Y12		opb Kolyma-Indigirka Air Enterprise-div
☐	RA-05757	PZL Mielec (Antonov) An-2	1G151-66	CCCP-05757	0074	0093	1 SH ASh-62IR	5500	Utility or Y12		opb Tiksi Air Enterprise-division
☐	RA-07167	PZL Mielec (Antonov) An-2	1G145-56	CCCP-07167	0073	0093	1 SH ASh-62IR	5500	Utility or Y12		opb Tiksi Air Enterprise-division
☐	RA-07168	PZL Mielec (Antonov) An-2	1G145-57	CCCP-07168	0073	0093	1 SH ASh-62IR	5500	Utility or Y12		opb Magan Air Enterprise-division
☐	RA-07495	PZL Mielec (Antonov) An-2	1G152-23	CCCP-07495	0073	0093	1 SH ASh-62IR	5500	Utility or Y12		opb Kolyma-Indigirka Air Enterprise-div
☐	RA-07502	PZL Mielec (Antonov) An-2	1G152-30	CCCP-07502	0073	0093	1 SH ASh-62IR	5500	Utility or Y12		opb Zyryanka Air Enterprise-division
☐	RA-07512	PZL Mielec (Antonov) An-2	1G152-40	CCCP-07512	0073	0093	1 SH ASh-62IR	5500	Utility or Y12		opb Magan Air Enterprise-division
☐	RA-07658	PZL Mielec (Antonov) An-2	1G157-43	CCCP-07658	0074	0093	1 SH ASh-62IR	5500	Utility or Y12		opb Magan Air Enterprise-division
☐	RA-07666	PZL Mielec (Antonov) An-2	1G157-51	CCCP-07666	0074	0093	1 SH ASh-62IR	5500	Utility or Y12		opb Nyurba Air Enterprise-division
☐	RA-07740	PZL Mielec (Antonov) An-2	1G159-15	CCCP-07740	0074	0093	1 SH ASh-62IR	5500	Utility or Y12		opb Zyryanka Air Enterprise-division
☐	RA-07755	PZL Mielec (Antonov) An-2	1G159-33	CCCP-07755	0074	0093	1 SH ASh-62IR	5500	Utility or Y12		opb Nyurba Air Enterprise-division
☐	RA-07799	PZL Mielec (Antonov) An-2	1G162-49	CCCP-07799	0075	0093	1 SH ASh-62IR	5500	Utility or Y12		opb Nyurba Air Enterprise-division
☐	RA-07864	PZL Mielec (Antonov) An-2	1G170-23	CCCP-07864	0076	0093	1 SH ASh-62IR	5500	Utility or Y12		opb Ust-Nera Air Enterprise-division
☐	RA-07867	PZL Mielec (Antonov) An-2	1G170-26	CCCP-07867	0076	0093	1 SH ASh-62IR	5500	Utility or Y12		opb Chokurdakh Air Enterprise-division
☐	RA-07895	PZL Mielec (Antonov) An-2	1G170-57	CCCP-07895	0076	0093	1 SH ASh-62IR	5500	Utility or Y12		opb Nyurba Air Enterprise-division
☐	RA-16026	PZL Mielec (Antonov) An-2	1G163-31	CCCP-16026	0075	0093	1 SH ASh-62IR	5500	Utility or Y12		opb Ust-Nera Air Enterprise-division
☐	RA-17901	PZL Mielec (Antonov) An-2	1G205-42	CCCP-17901	0083	0093	1 SH ASh-62IR	5500	Utility or Y12		opb Nyurba Air Enterprise-division
☐	RA-17904	PZL Mielec (Antonov) An-2	1G205-45	CCCP-17904	0083	0093	1 SH ASh-62IR	5500	Utility or Y12		opb Nyurba Air Enterprise-division
☐	RA-17936	PZL Mielec (Antonov) An-2	1G206-41	CCCP-17936	0084	0093	1 SH ASh-62IR	5500	Utility or Y12		opb Magan Air Enterprise-division
☐	RA-17937	PZL Mielec (Antonov) An-2	1G206-42	CCCP-17937	0084	0093	1 SH ASh-62IR	5500	Utility or Y12		opb Magan Air Enterprise-division
☐	RA-32156	PZL Mielec (Antonov) An-2	1G94-17	CCCP-32156	0068	0093	1 SH ASh-62IR	5500	Utility or Y12		opb Ust-Nera Air Enterprise-division
☐	RA-32338	PZL Mielec (Antonov) An-2	1G97-50	CCCP-32338	0068	0093	1 SH ASh-62IR	5500	Utility or Y12		opb Kolyma-Indigirka Air Enterprise-div
☐	RA-32574	PZL Mielec (Antonov) An-2	1G106-02	CCCP-32574	0069	0093	1 SH ASh-62IR	5500	Utility or Y12		opb Zyryanka Air Enterprise-division
☐	RA-32577	PZL Mielec (Antonov) An-2	1G106-05	CCCP-32577	0069	0093	1 SH ASh-62IR	5500	Utility or Y12		opb Tiksi Air Enterprise-division
☐	RA-32661	PZL Mielec (Antonov) An-2	1G211-20	CCCP-32661	0085	0093	1 SH ASh-62IR	5500	Utility or Y12		opb Kolyma-Indigirka Air Enterprise-div
☐	RA-32676	PZL Mielec (Antonov) An-2	1G211-35	CCCP-32676	0085	0093	1 SH ASh-62IR	5500	Utility or Y12		opb Ust-Nera Air Enterprise-division
☐	RA-32688	PZL Mielec (Antonov) An-2	1G211-52	CCCP-32688	0085	0093	1 SH ASh-62IR	5500	Utility or Y12		opb Magan Air Enterprise-division
☐	RA-32699	PZL Mielec (Antonov) An-2	1G212-04	CCCP-32699	0085	0093	1 SH ASh-62IR	5500	Utility or Y12		opb Magan Air Enterprise-division
☐	RA-32708	PZL Mielec (Antonov) An-2	1G212-13	CCCP-32708	0085	0093	1 SH ASh-62IR	5500	Utility or Y12		opb Magan Air Enterprise-division
☐	RA-33011	PZL Mielec (Antonov) An-2	1G217-58	CCCP-33011	0086	0093	1 SH ASh-62IR	5500	Utility or Y12		opb Kolyma-Indigirka Air Enterprise-div
☐	RA-33037	PZL Mielec (Antonov) An-2	1G218-24	CCCP-33037	0086	0093	1 SH ASh-62IR	5500	Utility or Y12		opb Kolyma-Indigirka Air Enterprise-div
☐	RA-33391	PZL Mielec (Antonov) An-2	1G226-50	CCCP-33391	0087	0093	1 SH ASh-62IR	5500	Utility or Y12		opb Kolyma-Indigirka Air Enterprise-div
☐	RA-33395	PZL Mielec (Antonov) An-2	1G226-54	CCCP-33395	0087	0093	1 SH ASh-62IR	5500	Utility or Y12		opb Kolyma-Indigirka Air Enterprise-div
☐	RA-33559	PZL Mielec (Antonov) An-2	1G229-56	CCCP-33559	0088	0093	1 SH ASh-62IR	5500	Utility or Y12		opb Magan Air Enterprise-division
☐	RA-33562	PZL Mielec (Antonov) An-2	1G229-59	CCCP-33562	0088	0093	1 SH ASh-62IR	5500	Utility or Y12		opb Magan Air Enterprise-division
☐	RA-33631	PZL Mielec (Antonov) An-2	1G233-15	CCCP-33631	0088	0093	1 SH ASh-62IR	5500	Utility or Y12		opb Kolyma-Indigirka Air Enterprise-div
☐	RA-33633	PZL Mielec (Antonov) An-2	1G233-17	CCCP-33633	0088	0093	1 SH ASh-62IR	5500	Utility or Y12		opb Magan Air Enterprise-division
☐	RA-35009	PZL Mielec (Antonov) An-2	1G109-15	CCCP-35009	0069	0093	1 SH ASh-62IR	5500	Utility or Y12		opb Magan Air Enterprise-division
☐	RA-40284	PZL Mielec (Antonov) An-2	1G221-14	CCCP-40284	0086	0093	1 SH ASh-62IR	5500	Utility or Y12		opb Ust-Nera Air Enterprise-division
☐	RA-40287	PZL Mielec (Antonov) An-2	1G221-17	CCCP-40287	0086	0093	1 SH ASh-62IR	5500	Utility or Y12		opb Magan Air Enterprise-division
☐	RA-40292	PZL Mielec (Antonov) An-2	1G221-22	CCCP-40292	0086	0093	1 SH ASh-62IR	5500	Utility or Y12		opb Nyurba Air Enterprise-division
☐	RA-40297	PZL Mielec (Antonov) An-2	1G221-27	CCCP-40297	0086	0093	1 SH ASh-62IR	5500	Utility or Y12		opb Ust-Nera Air Enterprise-division
☐	RA-40336	PZL Mielec (Antonov) An-2	1G222-13	CCCP-40336	0086	0093	1 SH ASh-62IR	5500	Utility or Y12		opb Nyurba Air Enterprise-division
☐	RA-40393	PZL Mielec (Antonov) An-2	1G223-17	CCCP-40393	0087	0093	1 SH ASh-62IR	5500	Utility or Y12		opb Magan Air Enterprise-division
☐	RA-40396	PZL Mielec (Antonov) An-2	1G223-20	CCCP-40396	0087	0093	1 SH ASh-62IR	5500	Utility or Y12		opb Magan Air Enterprise-division
☐	RA-40405	PZL Mielec (Antonov) An-2	1G223-29	CCCP-40405	0087	0093	1 SH ASh-62IR	5500	Utility or Y12		opb Magan Air Enterprise-division
☐	RA-40430	PZL Mielec (Antonov) An-2	1G224-02	CCCP-40430	0087	0093	1 SH ASh-62IR	5500	Utility or Y12		opb Zyryanka Air Enterprise-division
☐	RA-40442	PZL Mielec (Antonov) An-2	1G224-19	CCCP-40442	0087	0093	1 SH ASh-62IR	5500	Utility or Y12		opb Magan Air Enterprise-division
☐	RA-40628	PZL Mielec (Antonov) An-2	1G213-35	CCCP-40628	0085	0093	1 SH ASh-62IR	5500	Utility or Y12		opb Ust-Nera Air Enterprise-division
☐	RA-43997	PZL Mielec (Antonov) An-2	1G211-16	CCCP-43997	0085	0093	1 SH ASh-62IR	5500	Utility or Y12		opb Nyurba Air Enterprise-division
☐	RA-62589	PZL Mielec (Antonov) An-2	1G176-58	CCCP-62589	0077	0093	1 SH ASh-62IR	5500	Utility or Y12		opb Nyurba Air Enterprise-division
☐	RA-62593	PZL Mielec (Antonov) An-2	1G177-40	CCCP-62593	0077	0093	1 SH ASh-62IR	5500	Utility or Y12		opb Nyurba Air Enterprise-division
☐	RA-62598	PZL Mielec (Antonov) An-2	1G177-45	CCCP-62598	0077	0093	1 SH ASh-62IR	5500	Utility or Y12		opb Chokurdakh Air Enterprise-division
☐	RA-70135	PZL Mielec (Antonov) An-2	1G137-09	CCCP-70135	0072	0093	1 SH ASh-62IR	5500	Utility or Y12		opb Magan Air Enterprise-division
☐	RA-70162	PZL Mielec (Antonov) An-2	1G137-36	CCCP-70162	0072	0093	1 SH ASh-62IR	5500	Utility or Y12		opb Magan Air Enterprise-division
☐	RA-70165	PZL Mielec (Antonov) An-2	1G137-39	CCCP-70165	0072	0093	1 SH ASh-62IR	5500	Utility or Y12		opb Ust-Nera Air Enterprise-division
☐	RA-70309	PZL Mielec (Antonov) An-2	1G140-13	CCCP-70309	0072	0093	1 SH ASh-62IR	5500	Utility or Y12		opb Tiksi Air Enterprise-division
☐	RA-70357	PZL Mielec (Antonov) An-2	1G141-11	CCCP-70357	0072	0093	1 SH ASh-62IR	5500	Utility or Y12		opb Kolyma-Indigirka Air Enterprise-div
☐	RA-70362	PZL Mielec (Antonov) An-2	1G141-16	CCCP-70362	0072	0093	1 SH ASh-62IR	5500	Utility or Y12		opb Nyurba Air Enterprise-division
☐	RA-70482	PZL Mielec (Antonov) An-2	1G141-76	CCCP-70482	0072	0093	1 SH ASh-62IR	5500	Executive C6		opb Magan Air Enterprise-division
☐	RA-71236	PZL Mielec (Antonov) An-2	1G207-07	CCCP-71236	0084	0093	1 SH ASh-62IR	5500	Utility or Y12		opb Magan Air Enterprise-division
☐	RA-71237	PZL Mielec (Antonov) An-2	1G207-08	CCCP-71237	0084	0093	1 SH ASh-62IR	5500	Utility or Y12		opb Magan Air Enterprise-division
☐	RA-71302	PZL Mielec (Antonov) An-2	1G201-36	CCCP-71302	0083	0093	1 SH ASh-62IR	5500	Utility or Y12		opb Magan Air Enterprise-division
☐	RA-92861	PZL Mielec (Antonov) An-2	1G53-13	CCCP-92861	0064	0093	1 SH ASh-62IR	5500	Utility or Y12		opb Kolyma-Indigirka Air Enterprise-div
☐	RA-67534	Let 410UVP	851501	CCCP-67534	0085	0093	2 WA M-601D	5800	Y17		opb Magan Air Enterprise-division
☐	RA-67535	Let 410UVP	851450	CCCP-67535	0085	0093	2 WA M-601D	5800	Y17		opb Magan Air Enterprise-division
☐	RA-67539	Let 410UVP	851506	CCCP-67539	0085	0093	2 WA M-601D	5800	Y17		opb Magan Air Enterprise-division
☐	RA-67540	Let 410UVP	851507	CCCP-67540	0085	0093	2 WA M-601D	5800	Y17		opb Magan Air Enterprise-division
☐	RA-67541	Let 410UVP	851508	CCCP-67541	0085	0093	2 WA M-601D	5800	Y17		opb Magan Air Enterprise-division
☐	RA-67542	Let 410UVP	851509	CCCP-67542	0085	0093	2 WA M-601D	5800	Y17		opb Magan Air Enterprise-division
☐	RA-67616	Let 410UVP-E	892401	CCCP-67616	0089	0093	2 WA M-601E	6400	Y19		opb Magan Air Enterprise-division
☐	RA-67617	Let 410UVP-E	892314	CCCP-67617	0089	0093	2 WA M-601E	6400	Y19		opb Magan Air Enterprise-division
☐	RA-67618	Let 410UVP-E	892315	CCCP-67618	0089	0093	2 WA M-601E	6400	Y19		opb Magan Air Enterprise-division
☐	RA-67621	Let 410UVP-E	902403	CCCP-67621	0090	0093	2 WA M-601E	6400	Y19		opb Nyurba Air Enterprise-division
☐	RA-67622	Let 410UVP-E	902404	CCCP-67622	0090	0093	2 WA M-601E	6400	Executive C10		opb Magan Air Enterprise-division
☐	RA-67623	Let 410UVP-E	902405	CCCP-67623	0090	0093	2 WA M-601E	6400	Y19		opb Magan Air Enterprise-division
☐	RA-67624	Let 410UVP-E	902406	CCCP-67624	0090	0093	2 WA M-601E	6400	Y19		opb Magan Air Enterprise-division
☐	RA-67629	Let 410UVP-E	902422	CCCP-67629	0090	0093	2 WA M-601E	6400	Y19		opb Nyurba Air Enterprise-division
☐	RA-67630	Let 410UVP-E	902423	CCCP-67630	0090	0093	2 WA M-601E	6400	Y19		opb Magan Air Enterprise-division
☐	RA-67642	Let 410UVP-E	902435	CCCP-67642	0090	0093	2 WA M-601E	6400	Y19		opb Nyurba Air Enterprise-division
☐	RA-67643	Let 410UVP-E	902436	CCCP-67643	0090	0093	2 WA M-601E	6400	Y19		opb Nyurba Air Enterprise-division
☐	RA-67646	Let 410UVP-E	902439	CCCP-67646	0090	0093	2 WA M-601E	6400	Y19		opb Nyurba Air Enterprise-division
☐	RA-67664	Let 410UVP-E	902526	CCCP-67664	0090	0093	2 WA M-601E	6400	Y19		opb Magan Air Enterprise-division
☐	RA-22257	Mil Mi-8	6597	CCCP-22257	0076	0093	2 IS TV2-117A	12000	Utility		opb Neryungri Air Enterprise-division
☐	RA-22307	Mil Mi-8	7125	CCCP-22307	0077	0093	2 IS TV2-117A	12000	Utility		opb Ust-Nera Air Enterprise-division
☐	RA-22340	Mil Mi-8	7165	CCCP-22340	0077	0093	2 IS TV2-117A	12000	Utility		opb Neryungri Air Enterprise-division
☐	RA-22372	Mil Mi-8	7251	CCCP-22372	0077	0093	2 IS TV2-117A	12000	Utility		opb Kolyma-Indigirka Air Enterprise-div
☐	RA-22409	Mil Mi-8	7454	CCCP-22409	0077	0093	2 IS TV2-117A	12000	Utility		opb Magan Air Enterprise-division
☐	RA-22647	Mil Mi-8	8082	CCCP-22647	0080	0093	2 IS TV2-117A	12000	VIP C9		opb Magan Air Enterprise-division
☐	RA-22661	Mil Mi-8	8112	CCCP-22661	0080	0093	2 IS TV2-117A	12000	Utility		opb Chokurdakh Air Enterprise-division
☐	RA-22696	Mil Mi-8	8155	CCCP-22696	0080	0093	2 IS TV2-117A	12000	Utility		opb Kolyma-Indigirka Air Enterprise-div
☐	RA-22720	Mil Mi-8	98308548	CCCP-22720	0083	0093	2 IS TV2-117A	12000	Utility		opb Zyryanka Air Enterprise-division
☐	RA-22743	Mil Mi-8	98311115	CCCP-22743	0083	0093	2 IS TV2-117A	12000	Utility		opb Neryungri Air Enterprise-division
☐	RA-22755	Mil Mi-8	98311374	CCCP-22755	0083	0093	2 IS TV2-117A	12000	Utility		opb Tiksi Air Enterprise-division
☐	RA-22766	Mil Mi-8	98311535	CCCP-22766	0083	0093	2 IS TV2-117A	12000	Utility		opb Neryungri Air Enterprise-division
☐	RA-22776	Mil Mi-8	98311765	CCCP-22776	0083	0093	2 IS TV2-117A	12000	Utility		opb Nyurba Air Enterprise-division
☐	RA-22787	Mil Mi-8	98311970	CCCP-22787	0083	0093	2 IS TV2-117A	12000	Utility		opb Magan Air Enterprise-division
☐	RA-22808	Mil Mi-8	7537	CCCP-22808	0078	0093	2 IS TV2-117A	12000	Utility		opb Neryungri Air Enterprise-division
☐	RA-22827	Mil Mi-8	7627	CCCP-22827	0078	0093	2 IS TV2-117A	12000	Utility		opb Ust-Nera Air Enterprise-division
☐	RA-22847	Mil Mi-8	7666	CCCP-22847	0078	0093	2 IS TV2-117A	12000	Y28		opb Magan Air Enterprise-division
☐	RA-22909	Mil Mi-8	98520163	CCCP-22909	0085	0093	2 IS TV2-117A	12000	Utility		opb Magan Air Enterprise-division
☐	RA-22929	Mil Mi-8	98520571	CCCP-22929	0085	0093	2 IS TV2-117A	12000	Utility		opb Chokurdakh Air Enterprise-division
☐	RA-24149	Mil Mi-8	98941646	CCCP-24149	0089	0093	2 IS TV2-117A	12000	Utility		opb Magan Air Enterprise-division
☐	RA-24174	Mil Mi-8	98943133	CCCP-24174	0089	0093	2 IS TV2-117A	12000	Utility		opb Magan Air Enterprise-division
☐	RA-24180	Mil Mi-8	98943224	CCCP-24180	0089	0093	2 IS TV2-117A	12000	Utility		opb Magan Air Enterprise-division
☐	RA-24191	Mil Mi-8	98943692	CCCP-24191	0089	0093	2 IS TV2-117A	12000	Utility		opb Magan Air Enterprise-division
☐	RA-24401	Mil Mi-8	98525126	CCCP-24401	0086	0093	2 IS TV2-117A	12000	Utility		opb Kolyma-Indigirka Air Enterprise-div
☐	RA-24418	Mil Mi-8	98625305	CCCP-24418	0086	0093	2 IS TV2-117A	12000	Utility		opb Magan Air Enterprise-division
☐	RA-24452	Mil Mi-8	98628297	CCCP-24452	0086	0093	2 IS TV2-117A	12000	Utility		opb Kolyma-Indigirka Air Enterprise-div
☐	RA-24458	Mil Mi-8	98628426	CCCP-24458	0086	0093	2 IS TV2-117A	12000	Utility		opb Tiksi Air Enterprise-division
☐	RA-24459	Mil Mi-8	98628462	CCCP-24459	0086	0093	2 IS TV2-117A	12000	Utility		opb Nyurba Air Enterprise-division
☐	RA-24465	Mil Mi-8	98628617	CCCP-24465	0086	0093	2 IS TV2-117A	12000	Utility		opb Tiksi Air Enterprise-division

558 registration type of aircraft *cn/fn* *ex/ex** *mfd* *del* *powered by* *mtow kg* *configuration* *selcal* name/fln/specialitites/remarks

registration	type of aircraft	cn/fn	ex/ex*	mfd	del	powered by	mtow kg	configuration	selcal	name/fln/specialitites/remarks
□ RA-24466	Mil Mi-8	98678638	CCCP-24466	0086	0093	2 IS TV2-117A	12000	Utility		opb Neryungri Air Enterprise-division
□ RA-24528	Mil Mi-8	98522317	CCCP-24528	0085	0093	2 IS TV2-117A	12000	Utility		opb Zyryanka Air Enterprise-division
□ RA-24529	Mil Mi-8	98522340	CCCP-24529	0085	0093	2 IS TV2-117A	12000	Utility		opb Magan Air Enterprise-division
□ RA-24548	Mil Mi-8	98522894	CCCP-24548	0085	0093	2 IS TV2-117A	12000	Utility		opb Zyryanka Air Enterprise-division
□ RA-24561	Mil Mi-8	98525005	CCCP-24561	0085	0093	2 IS TV2-117A	12000	Utility		opb Magan Air Enterprise-division
□ RA-24679	Mil Mi-8	98101126	CCCP-24679	0081	0093	2 IS TV2-117A	12000	Utility		opb Nyurba Air Enterprise-division
□ RA-24680	Mil Mi-8	98101227	CCCP-24680	0081	0093	2 IS TV2-117A	12000	Utility		opb Chokurdakh Air Enterprise-division
□ RA-24686	Mil Mi-8	98101547	CCCP-24686	0082	0093	2 IS TV2-117A	12000	Utility		opb Ust-Nera Air Enterprise-division
□ RA-24698	Mil Mi-8	98103225	CCCP-24698	0081	0093	2 IS TV2-117A	12000	Utility		opb Nyurba Air Enterprise-division
□ RA-24715	Mil Mi-8	98417245	CCCP-24715	0084	0093	2 IS TV2-117A	12000	Utility		opb Nyurba Air Enterprise-division
□ RA-25116	Mil Mi-8MTV-1	95732	CCCP-25116	0091	0093	2 IS TV3-117MT	13000	Utility		opb Magan Air Enterprise-division
□ RA-25132	Mil Mi-8MTV-1	95748	CCCP-25132	0091	0093	2 IS TV3-117MT	13000	Utility		opb Magan Air Enterprise-division
□ RA-25300	Mil Mi-8	98203671	CCCP-25300	0082	0093	2 IS TV2-117A	12000	Utility		opb Magan Air Enterprise-division
□ RA-25312	Mil Mi-8	99203716	CCCP-25312	0082	0093	2 IS TV2-117A	12000	Utility		opb Tiksi Air Enterprise-division
□ RA-25336	Mil Mi-8	98206230	CCCP-25336	0082	0093	2 IS TV2-117A	12000	Utility		opb Zyryanka Air Enterprise-division
□ RA-25350	Mil Mi-8	98206730	CCCP-25350	0082	0093	2 IS TV2-117A	12000	Utility		opb Ust-Nera Air Enterprise-division
□ RA-25373	Mil Mi-8	98206949	CCCP-25373	0082	0093	2 IS TV2-117A	12000	Utility		opb Tiksi Air Enterprise-division
□ RA-25374	Mil Mi-8	98206954	CCCP-25374	0082	0093	2 IS TV2-117A	12000	Utility		opb Chokurdakh Air Enterprise-division
□ RA-25375	Mil Mi-8	98206957	CCCP-25375	0082	0093	2 IS TV2-117A	12000	Utility		opb Magan Air Enterprise-division
□ RA-25377	Mil Mi-8	98206975	CCCP-25377	0082	0093	2 IS TV2-117A	12000	Utility		opb Ust-Nera Air Enterprise-division
□ RA-25385	Mil Mi-8	98208139	CCCP-25385	0082	0093	2 IS TV2-117A	12000	Utility		opb Magan Air Enterprise-division
□ RA-25477	Mil Mi-8MTV-1	95622	CCCP-25477	0091	0093	2 IS TV3-117MT	13000	Utility		opb Magan Air Enterprise-division
□ RA-25478	Mil Mi-8MTV-1	95623	CCCP-25478	0091	0093	2 IS TV3-117MT	13000	Utility		opb Magan Air Enterprise-division
□ RA-25479	Mil Mi-8MTV-1	95624	CCCP-25479	0091	0093	2 IS TV3-117MT	13000	Utility		opb Magan Air Enterprise-division
□ RA-25496	Mil Mi-8MTV-1	95641	CCCP-25496	0091	0093	2 IS TV3-117MT	13000	Utility		opb Magan Air Enterprise-division
□ RA-25889	Mil Mi-8	5160	CCCP-25889	0075	0093	2 IS TV2-117A	12000	Utility		opb Magan Air Enterprise-division
□ RA-25940	Mil Mi-8	5576	CCCP-25940	0075	0093	2 IS TV2-117A	12000	Utility		opb Nyurba Air Enterprise-division
□ RA-25955	Mil Mi-8	5594	CCCP-25955	0075	0093	2 IS TV2-117A	12000	Utility		opb Magan Air Enterprise-division
□ RA-25972	Mil Mi-8	6322	CCCP-25972	0076	0093	2 IS TV2-117A	12000	Utility		opb Kolyma-Indigirka Air Enterprise-div
□ RA-25991	Mil Mi-8	7523	CCCP-25991	0078	0093	2 IS TV2-117A	12000	Utility		opb Nyurba Air Enterprise-division
□ RA-27047	Mil Mi-8MTV-1	95881	CCCP-27047	0092	0093	2 IS TV3-117MT	13000	Utility		opb Nyurba Air Enterprise-division
□ RA-27051	Mil Mi-8MTV-1	95885	CCCP-27051	0092	0093	2 IS TV3-117MT	13000	Utility		opb Nyurba Air Enterprise-division
□ RA-27081	Mil Mi-8MTV-1	95917	CCCP-27081	0092	0093	2 IS TV3-117MT	13000	Utility		opb Kolyma-Indigirka Air Enterprise-div
□ RA-87205	Yakovlev 40	9810257	CCCP-87205	0078	0093	3 IV AI-25	17500	Y32		opb Neryungri Air Enterprise-division
□ RA-87238	Yakovlev 40	9530543	CCCP-87238	0075	0093	3 IV AI-25	17500	Y32		opb Neryungri Air Enterprise-division
□ RA-87393	Yakovlev 40	9410533	CCCP-87393	0074	0093	3 IV AI-25	17500	Y32		opb Neryungri Air Enterprise-division
□ RA-87431	Yakovlev 40	9420735	CCCP-87431	0074	0093	3 IV AI-25	17500	Y32		opb Neryungri Air Enterprise-division
□ RA-87472	Yakovlev 40	9441737	UN-87472	0074	0093	3 IV AI-25	17500	Y32		opb Neryungri Air Enterprise-division
□ RA-87483	Yakovlev 40	9441138	CCCP-87483	0074	0093	3 IV AI-25	17500	Y32		opb Neryungri Air Enterprise-division
□ RA-87943	Yakovlev 40	9540745	CCCP-87943	0076	0093	3 IV AI-25	17500	Y32		opb Neryungri Air Enterprise-division
□ RA-88150	Yakovlev 40	9610346	CCCP-88150	0076	0093	3 IV AI-25	17500	Y32		opb Neryungri Air Enterprise-division
□ RA-88166	Yakovlev 40	9612046	CCCP-88166	0076	0093	3 IV AI-25	17500	Y32		opb Neryungri Air Enterprise-division
□ RA-88175	Yakovlev 40	9621347	CCCP-88175	0076	0093	3 IV AI-25	17500	Y32		opb Neryungri Air Enterprise-division
□ RA-88192	Yakovlev 40	9621248	CCCP-88192	0076	0093	3 IV AI-25	17500	Y32		opb Neryungri Air Enterprise-division
□ RA-88261	Yakovlev 40	9711652	CCCP-88261	0077	0093	3 IV AI-25	17500	Y32		opb Neryungri Air Enterprise-division
□ RA-46344	Antonov 24B	97305704	CCCP-46344	0069	0093	2 IV AI-24	21800	Y48		opb Yakutsk Air Enterprise-division
□ RA-46670	Antonov 24RV	47309601	CCCP-46670	0074	0093	2 IV AI-24VT	21800	Y48		opb Yakutsk Air Enterprise-division
□ RA-47158	Antonov 24B	89901610	CCCP-47158	0068	0093	2 IV AI-24	21800	Y48		opb Nyurba Air Enterprise-division
□ RA-47181	Antonov 24B	99901906	CCCP-47181	0069	0093	2 IV AI-24	21800	Y48		opb Yakutsk Air Enterprise-division
□ RA-47193	Antonov 24B	99902008	CCCP-47193	0069	0093	2 IV AI-24	21800	Y48		opb Yakutsk Air Enterprise-division
□ RA-47352	Antonov 24RV	67310601	CCCP-47352	0076	0093	2 IV AI-24VT	21800	Y48		opb Yakutsk Air Enterprise-division
□ RA-47755	Antonov 24B	79901208	CCCP-47755	0067	0093	2 IV AI-24	21800	Y48		opb Yakutsk Air Enterprise-division
□ RA-47762	Antonov 24B	79901306	CCCP-47762	0067	0093	2 IV AI-24	21800	Y48		opb Yakutsk Air Enterprise-division
□ RA-47775	Antonov 24B	79901408	CCCP-47775	0067	0093	2 IV AI-24	21800	Y48		opb Yakutsk Air Enterprise-division
□ RA-47777	Antonov 24B	79901501	CCCP-47777	0067	0093	2 IV AI-24	21800	Y48		opb Yakutsk Air Enterprise-division
□ RA-47830	Antonov 24B	17307301	CCCP-47830	0071	0093	2 IV AI-24	21800	Y48		opb Yakutsk Air Enterprise-division
□ RA-47845	Antonov 24B	17307407	CCCP-47845	0071	0093	2 IV AI-24	21800	Y48		opb Yakutsk Air Enterprise-division
□ RA-26030	Antonov 26B	10501	CCCP-26030	0080	0093	2 IV AI-24VT	24000	Freighter		opb Kolyma-Indigirka Air Enterprise-div
□ RA-26037	Antonov 26	10608	CCCP-26037	0081	0093	2 IV AI-24VT	24000	Freighter		opb Yakutsk Air Enterprise-division
□ RA-26061	Antonov 26B	11108	CCCP-26061	0081	0093	2 IV AI-24VT	24000	Freighter		opb Kolyma-Indigirka Air Enterprise-div
□ RA-26509	Antonov 26	6705	CCCP-26509	0078	0093	2 IV AI-24VT	24000	Freighter		opb Kolyma-Indigirka Air Enterprise-div
□ RA-26516	Antonov 26	7001	CCCP-26516	0078	0093	2 IV AI-24VT	24000	Freighter		opb Yakusk Air Enterprise-division
□ RA-26635	Antonov 26	6305	CCCP-26635	0078	0093	2 IV AI-24VT	24000	Freighter		opb Kolyma-Indigirka Air Enterprise-div
□ RA-26652	Antonov 26	7709	CCCP-26652	0079	0093	2 IV AI-24VT	24000	Freighter		opb Yakutsk Air Enterprise-division
□ RA-26660	Antonov 26	8008	CCCP-26660	0079	0093	2 IV AI-24VT	24000	Freighter		opb Yakutsk Air Enterprise-division
□ RA-26665	Antonov 26	8108	CCCP-26665	0079	0093	2 IV AI-24VT	24000	Freighter		opb Nyurba Air Enterprise-division
□ RA-26674	Antonov 26	8506	CCCP-26674	0079	0093	2 IV AI-24VT	24000	Freighter		opb Kolyma-Indigirka Air Enterprise-div
□ RA-26686	Antonov 26	6302	CCCP-26686	0078	0093	2 IV AI-24VT	24000	Freighter		opb Nyurba Air Enterprise-division
□ RA-74000	Antonov 74	36547060649	CCCP-74000	0090	0093	2 LO D-36	36000	Combi		opb Kolyma-Indigirka Air Enterprise-div
□ RA-74001	Antonov 74TK-100	36547070655	CCCP-74001	0090	0093	2 LO D-36	36000	Combi or Y52		opb Kolyma-Indigirka Air Enterprise-div
□ RA-74003	Antonov 74	36547070690	CCCP-74003	0090	0093	2 LO D-36	36000	Combi		opb Kolyma-Indigirka Air Enterprise-div
□ RA-74006	Antonov 74	36547095896	CCCP-74006	0092	0093	2 LO D-36	36000	Combi		opb Kolyma-Indigirka Air Enterprise-div
□ RA-11236	Antonov 12BP	402111	CCCP-11236	0064	0093	4 IV AI-20M	61000	Freighter		opb Yakutsk Air Enterprise-division
□ RA-11345	Antonov 12BP	401801	CCCP-11345	0063	0093	4 IV AI-20M	61000	Freighter		opb Yakutsk Air Enterprise-division
□ RA-11354	Antonov 12BP	401812	CCCP-11354	0063	0093	4 IV AI-20M	61000	Freighter		opb Yakutsk Air Enterprise-division
□ RA-11767	Antonov 12BP	401909	CCCP-11767	0063	0093	4 IV AI-20M	61000	Freighter		opb Yakutsk Air Enterprise-division
□ RA-11884	Antonov 12BP	401710	CCCP-11884	0063	0093	4 IV AI-20M	61000	Freighter		opb Yakutsk Air Enterprise-division
□ RA-11991	Antonov 12BP	402006	CCCP-11991	0063	0093	4 IV AI-20M	61000	Freighter		opb Yakutsk Air Enterprise-division
□ RA-12953	Antonov 12B	8345504	CCCP-12953	0068	0093	4 IV AI-20M	61000	Freighter		opb Yakutsk Air Enterprise-division
□ RA-85217	Tupolev 154B-1	217	CCCP-85217	0077	0093	3 KU NK-8-2U	98000	Y164		opb Neryungri A.E.-division/cvtd 154B
□ RA-85323	Tupolev 154B-2	323	CCCP-85323	0079	0093	3 KU NK-8-2U	98000	Y164		opb Neryungri Air Enterprise-division
□ RA-85348	Tupolev 154B-2	348	CCCP-85348	0079	0093	3 KU NK-8-2U	98000	Y164		opb Yakutsk A.E./Respublika Sakha-title
□ RA-85354	Tupolev 154B-2	354	CCCP-85354	0079	0093	3 KU NK-8-2U	98000	Y164		opb Yakutsk Air Enterprise-division
□ RA-85367	Tupolev 154B-2	367	CCCP-85367	0079	0093	3 KU NK-8-2U	98000	Y164		opb Neryungri Air Enterprise-division
□ RA-85486	Tupolev 154B-2	486	CCCP-85486	0081	0093	3 KU NK-8-2U	98000	Y164		opb Neryungri Air Enterprise-division
□ RA-85520	Tupolev 154B-2	520	CCCP-85520	0081	0093	3 KU NK-8-2U	98000	Y164		opb Yakutsk Air Enterprise-division
□ RA-85577	Tupolev 154B-2	577	CCCP-85577	0083	0093	3 KU NK-8-2U	98000	Y164		opb Yakutsk Air Enterprise-division
□ RA-85597	Tupolev 154B-2	597	CCCP-85597	0084	0093	3 KU NK-8-2U	98000	Y164		opb Neryungri Air Enterprise-division
□ RA-85790	Tupolev 154M	974		0093		3 SO D-30KU-154-II	102000	Y164		lst LAZ,LZ-LTC / Yakutsk Air Enterprise
□ RA-85791	Tupolev 154M	975		0093		3 SO D-30KU-154-II	102000	VIP F12Y118		opb Yakutsk A.E./Respublika Sakha-title
□ RA-85793	Tupolev 154M	977		0094		3 SO D-30KU-154-II	102000	Y164		opb Yakutsk Air Enterprise-division
□ RA-85812	Tupolev 154M	1005		0095		3 SO D-30KU-154-II	102000	Y164		opb Yakutsk Air Enterprise-division
□ RA-76485	Ilyushin 76TD	0063470088	CCCP-76485	0086	0093	4 SO D-30KP	190000	Freighter		opb Yakutsk Air Enterpr.-div / lst RMX
□ RA-76486	Ilyushin 76TD	0073476281	CCCP-76486	0087	0093	4 SO D-30KP	190000	Freighter		opb Yakutsk Air Enterprise-division
□ RA-76487	Ilyushin 76TD	0073479367	CCCP-76487	0087	0093	4 SO D-30KP	190000	Freighter		lst BRZ
□ RA-76797	Ilyushin 76TD	1003403052	CCCP-76797	0090	0093	4 SO D-30KP	190000	Freighter		opb Yakutsk Air Enterprise-division

SAKHA AVIATION SCHOOL CENTER (Sakha tsentr podgotovki aviatsionnogo personala) — Yakutsk

Ul. Bykovskogo 6, 677014 Yakutsk, (Republic of Sakha-Yakutia), Russia ☎ (41122) 95 731 Tx: none Fax: none SITA: n/a

F: n/a ✈✈✈ n/a Head: Sergey I. Faybushevich Net: n/a Beside school & training flights, also operates passenger charter flights.

registration	type of aircraft	cn/fn	ex/ex*	mfd	del	powered by	mtow kg	configuration	selcal	name/fln/specialitites/remarks
□ RA-27052	Mil Mi-8MTV-1	95886	CCCP-27052	0092		2 IS TV3-117MT	13000	Utility		
□ RA-87656	Yakovlev 40	9211920	CCCP-87656	0072		3 IV AI-25	16800	C15		
□ RA-88177	Yakovlev 40	9621747	CCCP-88177	0076		3 IV AI-25	16800	Y32		
□ RA-88193	Yakovlev 40	9621348	CCCP-88193	0076		3 IV AI-25	16800	Y32		

SAKHAVIATRANS, Ltd = SVT (Sister company of ATRAN-Aviatrans Cargo Airlines) — Yuzhno-Sakhalinsk

SAKHAVIATRANS

PO Box 142, 639013 Yuzhno-Sakhalinsk, Russia ☎ (42422) 56 104 Tx: 213214 sfera su Fax: (42422) 23 521 SITA: n/a

F: 1992 ✈✈✈ n/a Head: Vladimir F. Rykunov ICAO: AIR SAKHALIN Net: n/a Operates cargo flights with Antonov 12/26 & Ilyushin 76 leased from ATRAN-Aviatrans Cargo Airlines when required.

SALSK AIR ENTERPRISE (Salskoe aviapredpriatie) (formerly Aeroflot Salsk division) — Salsk

Ul. Aerodromnaya 1, 347603 Salsk, (Rostov Region), Russia ☎ (86372) 26 259 Tx: none Fax: n/a SITA: n/a

F: n/a ✈✈✈ n/a Head: Vladimir I. Goncharov Net: n/a Most aircraft are still in Aeroflot colors but will be repainted in due course.

registration	type of aircraft	cn/fn	ex/ex*	mfd	del	powered by	mtow kg	configuration	selcal	name/fln/specialitites/remarks
□ RA-01421	PZL Mielec (Antonov) An-2		CCCP-01421	0088		1 SH ASh-62IR	5500	Utility		
□ RA-01432	PZL Mielec (Antonov) An-2		CCCP-01432	0088		1 SH ASh-62IR	5500	Utility		
□ RA-01441	PZL Mielec (Antonov) An-2		CCCP-01441	0088		1 SH ASh-62IR	5500	Utility		
□ RA-02218	PZL Mielec (Antonov) An-2		CCCP-02218	0089		1 SH ASh-62IR	5500	Utility		
□ RA-02254	PZL Mielec (Antonov) An-2		CCCP-02254	0089		1 SH ASh-62IR	5500	Utility		
□ RA-02261	PZL Mielec (Antonov) An-2		CCCP-02261	0090		1 SH ASh-62IR	5500	Utility		
□ RA-02295	PZL Mielec (Antonov) An-2		CCCP-02295	0091		1 SH ASh-62IR	5500	Utility		
□ RA-02309	PZL Mielec (Antonov) An-2		CCCP-02309	0091		1 SH ASh-62IR	5500	Utility		

☐ RA-17925	PZL Mielec (Antonov) An-2		CCCP-17925	0084		1 SH ASh-62IR	5500	Utility		
☐ RA-17926	PZL Mielec (Antonov) An-2		CCCP-17926	0084		1 SH ASh-62IR	5500	Utility		
☐ RA-31399	PZL Mielec (Antonov) An-2		CCCP-31399	0082		1 SH ASh-62IR	5500	Utility		
☐ RA-32705	PZL Mielec (Antonov) An-2		CCCP-32705	0085		1 SH ASh-62IR	5500	Utility		
☐ RA-33522	PZL Mielec (Antonov) An-2		CCCP-33522	0088		1 SH ASh-62IR	5500	Utility		
☐ RA-33524	PZL Mielec (Antonov) An-2		CCCP-33524	0088		1 SH ASh-62IR	5500	Utility		
☐ RA-33540	PZL Mielec (Antonov) An-2		CCCP-33540	0088		1 SH ASh-62IR	5500	Utility		
☐ RA-33542	PZL Mielec (Antonov) An-2		CCCP-33542	0088		1 SH ASh-62IR	5500	Utility		
☐ RA-33548	PZL Mielec (Antonov) An-2		CCCP-33548	0088		1 SH ASh-62IR	5500	Utility		
☐ RA-40387	PZL Mielec (Antonov) An-2		CCCP-40387	0087		1 SH ASh-62IR	5500	Utility		
☐ RA-40459	PZL Mielec (Antonov) An-2		CCCP-40459	0087		1 SH ASh-62IR	5500	Utility		
☐ RA-40760	PZL Mielec (Antonov) An-2		CCCP-40760	0076		1 SH ASh-62IR	5500	Utility		
☐ RA-40769	PZL Mielec (Antonov) An-2		CCCP-40769	0076		1 SH ASh-62IR	5500	Utility		
☐ RA-40812	PZL Mielec (Antonov) An-2		CCCP-40812	0077		1 SH ASh-62IR	5500	Utility		
☐ RA-40913	PZL Mielec (Antonov) An-2		CCCP-40913	0085		1 SH ASh-62IR	5500	Utility		
☐ RA-40997	PZL Mielec (Antonov) An-2		CCCP-40997	0085		1 SH ASh-62IR	5500	Utility		
☐ RA-40998	PZL Mielec (Antonov) An-2		CCCP-40998	0085		1 SH ASh-62IR	5500	Utility		
☐ RA-54797	PZL Mielec (Antonov) An-2		CCCP-54797	0079		1 SH ASh-62IR	5500	Utility		
☐ RA-54943	PZL Mielec (Antonov) An-2		CCCP-54943	0080		1 SH ASh-62IR	5500	Utility		
☐ RA-56353	PZL Mielec (Antonov) An-2		CCCP-56353	0078		1 SH ASh-62IR	5500	Utility		
☐ RA-56356	PZL Mielec (Antonov) An-2		CCCP-56356	0078		1 SH ASh-62IR	5500	Utility		
☐ RA-56437	PZL Mielec (Antonov) An-2		CCCP-56437	0078		1 SH ASh-62IR	5500	Utility		
☐ RA-56501	PZL Mielec (Antonov) An-2		CCCP-56501	0079		1 SH ASh-62IR	5500	Utility		
☐ RA-62648	PZL Mielec (Antonov) An-2		CCCP-62648	0078		1 SH ASh-62IR	5500	Utility		
☐ RA-68032	PZL Mielec (Antonov) An-2		CCCP-68032	0081		1 SH ASh-62IR	5500	Utility		
☐ RA-68076	PZL Mielec (Antonov) An-2		CCCP-68076	0081		1 SH ASh-62IR	5500	Utility		
☐ RA-68124	PZL Mielec (Antonov) An-2		CCCP-68124	0082		1 SH ASh-62IR	5500	Utility		
☐ RA-68168	PZL Mielec (Antonov) An-2		CCCP-68168	0082		1 SH ASh-62IR	5500	Utility		
☐ RA-71253	PZL Mielec (Antonov) An-2		CCCP-71253	0084		1 SH ASh-62IR	5500	Utility		
☐ RA-71254	PZL Mielec (Antonov) An-2		CCCP-71254	0084		1 SH ASh-62IR	5500	Utility		
☐ RA-81524	PZL Mielec (Antonov) An-2		CCCP-81524	0084		1 SH ASh-62IR	5500	Utility		
☐ RA-84537	PZL Mielec (Antonov) An-2		CCCP-84537	0080		1 SH ASh-62IR	5500	Utility		
☐ RA-84538	PZL Mielec (Antonov) An-2		CCCP-84538	0080		1 SH ASh-62IR	5500	Utility		
☐ RA-84619	PZL Mielec (Antonov) An-2		CCCP-84619	0080		1 SH ASh-62IR	5500	Utility		
☐ RA-84620	PZL Mielec (Antonov) An-2		CCCP-84620	0080		1 SH ASh-62IR	5500	Utility		
☐ RA-84740	PZL Mielec (Antonov) An-2		CCCP-84740	0083		1 SH ASh-62IR	5500	Utility		
☐ RA-84741	PZL Mielec (Antonov) An-2		CCCP-84741	0083		1 SH ASh-62IR	5500	Utility		

SALYUT Aviakompania

Samara-Int'l

Mekhzavod, 443028 Samara, Russia ☎ (8462) 57 12 72 Tx: n/a Fax: (8462) 57 23 86 SITA: n/a

F: n/a ⁂ n/a Head: Sergei P. Mlyavy Net: n/a Some aircraft are still in Aeroflot colors without titles but will be repainted in due course.

☐ RA-87587	Yakovlev 40		CCCP-87587	0072		3 IV AI-25	16800	Y32		lst GEA
☐ RA-26177	Antonov 26	7504	CCCP-26177	0083		2 IV AI-24VT	24000	Freighter		
☐ RA-74030	Antonov 74	36547098957		0093		2 LO D-36	34500	Freighter		

SAMARA AIRLINES, Joint-Stock Company = E5 / BRZ (Aviakompania Samara)

Samara-Int'l

Samara Airport, 443025 Samara, Russia ☎ (8462) 79 09 70 Tx: 173214 port Fax: (8462) 79 09 56 SITA: KUFAPE5

F: 1993 ⁂ n/a Head: Alexander F. Kozlov IATA: 906 ICAO: BERYOZA Net: n/a Beside aircraft listed, additional Yakovlev 40 are leased from TATARSTAN/Bugulma Air Enterprise, when required.

☐ RA-87248	Yakovlev 40K	9540144	CCCP-87248	0276	0697	3 IV AI-25	16800	Y32		lsf Priroda Corp.
☐ RA-88293	Yakovlev 40	9510138	SP-PGA	0075	1196	3 IV AI-25	17200	VIP 13 Pax		lsf Avtovaz Company
☐ RA-65105	Tupolev 134A-3	60308	LY-ABH	0078	0095	2 SO D-30-III	49000	Y76		
☐ RA-65122	Tupolev 134A-3	60518	CCCP-65122	0078	0093	2 SO D-30-III	49000	Y76		
☐ RA-65753	Tupolev 134A-3	61099	CCCP-65753	0079	0093	2 SO D-30-III	49000	Y76		
☐ RA-65758	Tupolev 134A-3	62230	CCCP-65758	0079	0093	2 SO D-30-III	49000	Y76		
☐ RA-65792	Tupolev 134A-3	63121	CCCP-65792	0080	0093	2 SO D-30-III	49000	Y76		
☐ RA-65797	Tupolev 134A-3	63173	CCCP-65797	0080	0093	2 SO D-30-III	49000	Y76		
☐ RA-65800	Tupolev 134A-3	3352009	CCCP-65800	0073	0093	2 SO D-30-III	47000	Y76		
☐ RA-65889	Tupolev 134A	38010	CCCP-65889	0075	0093	2 SO D-30-II	47000	Y76		
☐ RA-65932	Tupolev 134A-3	66405	CCCP-65932	0084	0997	2 SO D-30-III	49000	Y76		lsf SUH
☐ RA-42414	Yakovlev 42D	4520423219073	CCCP-42414	1092	0098	3 LO D-36	56500	Y120		
☐ RA-42418	Yakovlev 42D	4520423219118	CCCP-42418	1092	0098	3 LO D-36	56500	Y120		
☐ RA-12954	Antonov 12BP	8345505	CCCP-12954	0068	0093	4 IV AI-20M	61000	Freighter		std KUF / for sale
☐ RA-12986	Antonov 12BP	00347201	CCCP-12986	0070	0093	4 IV AI-20M	61000	Freighter		for sale
☐ RA-85267	Tupolev 154B-2	267	CCCP-85267	0078	0093	3 KU NK-8-2U	98000	Y164		cvtd 154B-1
☐ RA-85472	Tupolev 154B-2	472	CCCP-85472	0081	0093	3 KU NK-8-2U	100000	Y164		
☐ RA-85500	Tupolev 154B-2	500	CCCP-85500	0081	0093	3 KU NK-8-2U	100000	Y164		
☐ RA-85585	Tupolev 154B-2	585	CCCP-85585	0083	0093	3 KU NK-8-2U	100000	F12C18Y102		
☐ RA-85716	Tupolev 154M	892	CCCP-85716	0091	0399	3 SO D-30KU-154-II	100000	Y166		lsf VOG
☐ RA-85723	Tupolev 154M	905	CCCP-85723	0392	0093	3 SO D-30KU-154-II	100000	Y164		
☐ RA-85731	Tupolev 154M	913	EP-LAX	0592	0093	3 SO D-30KU-154-II	100000	Y164		lst IRK as EP-LBH
☐ RA-85739	Tupolev 154M	925	CCCP-85739	0092	0399	3 SO D-30KU-154-II	100000	Y164		lsf VOG
☐ RA-85792	Tupolev 154M	976		1293	0094	3 SO D-30KU-154-II	100000	Y166		lst IRK as EP-LAZ
☐ RA-85817	Tupolev 154M	1007		0995	0896	3 SO D-30KU-154-II	100000	F12C18Y104		
☐ RA-85821	Tupolev 154M	805	SP-LCI	0589	0995	3 SO D-30KU-154-II	100000	Y150		
☐ RA-85822	Tupolev 154M	806	SP-LCK	0589	1095	3 SO D-30KU-154-II	100000	Y150		
☐ RA-85823	Tupolev 154M	775	SP-LCG	0588	1195	3 SO D-30KU-154-II	100000	Y150		
☐ RA-76475	Ilyushin 76TD	0043451523	CCCP-76475	0384	0093	4 SO D-30KP	190000	Freighter		
☐ RA-76487	Ilyushin 76TD	0073479367	CCCP-76487	0087	0098	4 SO D-30KP	190000	Freighter		lsf IKT
☐ RA-76791	Ilyushin 76TD	0093497936	CCCP-76791	0089	0093	4 SO D-30KP	190000	Freighter		lst TIS
☐ RA-76798	Ilyushin 76TD	1003403063	CCCP-76798	0690	0093	4 SO D-30KP	190000	Freighter		std KUF

SAMARA-AVIA

Samara-Smyshlyaevka

Smyshlyaevka Airport, 443046 Samara, Russia ☎ (8462) 58 64 72 Tx: none Fax: (8462) 52 18 24 SITA: n/a

F: n/a ⁂ n/a Head: Alexander A. Borisoglebsky Net: n/a

☐ RA-32181	PZL Mielec (Antonov) An-2		CCCP-32181	0068		1 SH ASh-62IR	5500	Utility		
☐ RA-32738	PZL Mielec (Antonov) An-2		CCCP-32738	0085		1 SH ASh-62IR	5500	Utility		
☐ RA-33577	PZL Mielec (Antonov) An-2	1G230-14	CCCP-33577	0088		1 SH ASh-62IR	5500	Utility		
☐ RA-33578	PZL Mielec (Antonov) An-2		CCCP-33578	0088		1 SH ASh-62IR	5500	Utility		
☐ RA-50507	PZL Mielec (Antonov) An-2		CCCP-50507	0067		1 SH ASh-62IR	5500	Utility		
☐ RA-54851	PZL Mielec (Antonov) An-2		CCCP-54851	0079		1 SH ASh-62IR	5500	Utility		
☐ RA-62556	PZL Mielec (Antonov) An-2		CCCP-62556	0077		1 SH ASh-62IR	5500	Utility		
☐ RA-68156	PZL Mielec (Antonov) An-2		CCCP-68156	0082		1 SH ASh-62IR	5500	Utility		
☐ RA-70514	PZL Mielec (Antonov) An-2		CCCP-70514	0073		1 SH ASh-62IR	5500	Utility		
☐ RA-70532	PZL Mielec (Antonov) An-2		CCCP-70532	0073		1 SH ASh-62IR	5500	Utility		
☐ RA-70792	PZL Mielec (Antonov) An-2		CCCP-70792	0071		1 SH ASh-62IR	5500	Utility		

SARANSK AIR ENTERPRISE (Saranskoe aviapredpriatie) (formerly Aeroflot Saransk division)

Saransk

Saransk Airport, 430018 Saransk, (Republic of Mordovia), Russia ☎ (8342) 17 66 88 Tx: n/a Fax: (8342) 17 89 01 SITA: n/a

F: n/a ⁂ n/a Head: Anatoly I. Sakharov Net: n/a Most aircraft are still in Aeroflot colors but will be repainted in due course. Company will be transformed to the new national airline of the Republic of Mordovia.

☐ RA-01769	PZL Mielec (Antonov) An-2		CCCP-01769	0069		1 SH ASh-62IR	5500	Utility		
☐ RA-01771	PZL Mielec (Antonov) An-2		CCCP-01771	0069		1 SH ASh-62IR	5500	Utility		
☐ RA-02311	PZL Mielec (Antonov) An-2		CCCP-02311	0091		1 SH ASh-62IR	5500	Utility		
☐ RA-02312	PZL Mielec (Antonov) An-2		CCCP-02312	0091		1 SH ASh-62IR	5500	Utility		
☐ RA-02424	PZL Mielec (Antonov) An-2		CCCP-02424	0070		1 SH ASh-62IR	5500	Utility		
☐ RA-02587	PZL Mielec (Antonov) An-2		CCCP-02587	0071		1 SH ASh-62IR	5500	Utility		
☐ RA-05765	PZL Mielec (Antonov) An-2		CCCP-05765	0074		1 SH ASh-62IR	5500	Utility		
☐ RA-07819	PZL Mielec (Antonov) An-2		CCCP-07819	0076		1 SH ASh-62IR	5500	Utility		
☐ RA-29323	PZL Mielec (Antonov) An-2		CCCP-29323	0066		1 SH ASh-62IR	5500	Utility		
☐ RA-31486	PZL Mielec (Antonov) An-2		CCCP-31486	0082		1 SH ASh-62IR	5500	Utility		
☐ RA-32234	PZL Mielec (Antonov) An-2		CCCP-32234	0068		1 SH ASh-62IR	5500	Utility		
☐ RA-32285	PZL Mielec (Antonov) An-2		CCCP-32285	0068		1 SH ASh-62IR	5500	Utility		
☐ RA-33625	PZL Mielec (Antonov) An-2		CCCP-33625	0088		1 SH ASh-62IR	5500	Utility		
☐ RA-33677	PZL Mielec (Antonov) An-2		CCCP-33677	0089		1 SH ASh-62IR	5500	Utility		
☐ RA-33678	PZL Mielec (Antonov) An-2		CCCP-33678	0089		1 SH ASh-62IR	5500	Utility		
☐ RA-35118	PZL Mielec (Antonov) An-2		CCCP-35118	0069		1 SH ASh-62IR	5500	Utility		
☐ RA-35526	PZL Mielec (Antonov) An-2		CCCP-35526	0069		1 SH ASh-62IR	5500	Utility		
☐ RA-40581	PZL Mielec (Antonov) An-2		CCCP-40581	0067		1 SH ASh-62IR	5500	Utility		
☐ RA-40687	PZL Mielec (Antonov) An-2		CCCP-40687	0086		1 SH ASh-62IR	5500	Utility		
☐ RA-40801	PZL Mielec (Antonov) An-2		CCCP-40801	0077		1 SH ASh-62IR	5500	Utility		
☐ RA-40848	PZL Mielec (Antonov) An-2		CCCP-40848	0077		1 SH ASh-62IR	5500	Utility		
☐ RA-54834	PZL Mielec (Antonov) An-2		CCCP-54834	0079		1 SH ASh-62IR	5500	Utility		

560 registration type of aircraft *cn/fn* *ex/ex** *mfd* *del* *powered by* *mtow kg* *configuration* *selcal* *name/fln/specialitites/remarks*

☐ RA-56382	PZL Mielec (Antonov) An-2		CCCP-56382	0078		1 SH ASh-62IR	5500	Utility		
☐ RA-56384	PZL Mielec (Antonov) An-2		CCCP-56384	0078		1 SH ASh-62IR	5500	Utility		
☐ RA-62701	PZL Mielec (Antonov) An-2		CCCP-62701	0078		1 SH ASh-62IR	5500	Utility		
☐ RA-68135	PZL Mielec (Antonov) An-2		CCCP-68135	0082		1 SH ASh-62IR	5500	Utility		
☐ RA-70122	PZL Mielec (Antonov) An-2		CCCP-70122	0071		1 SH ASh-62IR	5500	Utility		
☐ RA-70508	PZL Mielec (Antonov) An-2		CCCP-70508	0073		1 SH ASh-62IR	5500	Utility		
☐ RA-70837	PZL Mielec (Antonov) An-2		CCCP-70837	0071		1 SH ASh-62IR	5500	Utility		
☐ RA-82852	PZL Mielec (Antonov) An-2		CCCP-82852	0076		1 SH ASh-62IR	5500	Utility		
☐ RA-82857	PZL Mielec (Antonov) An-2		CCCP-82857	0076		1 SH ASh-62IR	5500	Utility		
☐ RA-46255	Antonov 24B		CCCP-46255	0067		2 IV AI-24	21000	Y48		
☐ RA-46480	Antonov 24RV		CCCP-46480	0072		2 IV AI-24VT	21800	Y48		
☐ RA-46640	Antonov 24RV	37308908	CCCP-46640	0073		2 IV AI-24VT	21800	Y48		
☐ RA-46845	Antonov 24RV	27307503	CCCP-46845	0072		2 IV AI-24VT	21800	Y48		
☐ RA-47253	Antonov 24RV	27307705	CCCP-47253	0072		2 IV AI-24VT	21800	Y48		
☐ RA-47834	Antonov 24B		CCCP-47834	0071		2 IV AI-24	21000	Y48		
☐ RA-26246	Antonov 26					2 IV AI-24VT	24000	Freighter		

SARAVIA – Saratovskie avialinii = SOV (Saratov Airlines) (formerly Aeroflot Saratov division) — Saratov

Ul. Zhukovskogo 25, 410010 Saratov, Russia ☎ (8452) 69 65 02 Tx: 241121 polet Fax: (8452) 64 25 52 SITA: n/a

F: 1931 👥 n/a Head: Yuri K. Davydov ICAO: SARATOV AIR Net: n/a Most aircraft are still in Aeroflot colors but will be repainted in due course.

☐ RA-14130	PZL Swidnik (Mil) Mi-2	5410842039	CCCP-14130	0389		2 IS GTD-350-4	3550	Y8		
☐ RA-14171	PZL Swidnik (Mil) Mi-2	5210506127	CCCP-14171	0188		2 IS GTD-350-4	3550	Y8		
☐ RA-14172	PZL Swidnik (Mil) Mi-2	5210507127	CCCP-14172	0888		2 IS GTD-350-4	3550	Y8		
☐ RA-15289	PZL Swidnik (Mil) Mi-2	535820098	CCCP-15289	0978		2 IS GTD-350-4	3550	Y8		
☐ RA-15291	PZL Swidnik (Mil) Mi-2	535822098	CCCP-15291	0978		2 IS GTD-350-4	3550	Y8		
☐ RA-23309	PZL Swidnik (Mil) Mi-2	529130035	CCCP-23309	0385		2 IS GTD-350-4	3550	Y8		
☐ RA-46331	Antonov 24B	97305508	CCCP-46331	0869		2 IV AI-24	21000	Y48		
☐ RA-46601	Antonov 24RV	37308508	CCCP-46601	0473		2 IV AI-24VT	21800	Y52		
☐ RA-46648	Antonov 24RV	37309108	CCCP-46648	1273		2 IV AI-24VT	21800	Y48		
☐ RA-46812	Antonov 24B	67302401	CCCP-46812	0366		2 IV AI-24	21000	Y48		
☐ RA-47304	Antonov 24RV	57310304	CCCP-47304	0575		2 IV AI-24VT	21800	Y48		
☐ RA-42316	Yakovlev 42	4520422202030	CCCP-42316	0682		3 LO D-36	54000	Y120		
☐ RA-42326	Yakovlev 42	4520424402154	CCCP-42326	0385		3 LO D-36	54000	Y120		
☐ RA-42328	Yakovlev 42	4520421505058	CCCP-42328	0585		3 LO D-36	54000	Y120		
☐ RA-42329	Yakovlev 42D	4520422505093	CCCP-42329	0585		3 LO D-36	57500	Y120		lst STY
☐ RA-42361	Yakovlev 42D	4520423811427	CCCP-42361	0988		3 LO D-36	56500	Y120		
☐ RA-42365	Yakovlev 42D	4520424811447	CCCP-42365	1288		3 LO D-36	56500	Y120		
☐ RA-42378	Yakovlev 42D	4520421014494	TC-FAR	0290		3 LO D-36	56500	Y120		
☐ RA-42389	Yakovlev 42D	4520424016542	CCCP-42389	0491		3 LO D-36	56500	Y120		
☐ RA-42432	Yakovlev 42D	4520424410016	TC-ALY	1294		3 LO D-36	56500	Y120		lst AXX
☐ RA-42550	Yakovlev 42D	11040205	CCCP-42550	0382		3 LO D-36	56500	Y120		
☐ RA-42551	Yakovlev 42D	11140305	CCCP-42551	0482		3 LO D-36	56500	Y120		

SASOVO FLYING SCHOOL (Sasovskoe letnoe uchilishche) (formerly Aeroflot Sasovo Flying School) — Sasovo

Aviagorodok, 391600 Sasovo, (Ryazan Region), Russia ☎ (09133) 20 397 Tx: 136331 grom Fax: none SITA: n/a

F: n/a 👥 n/a Head: Valery I. Zaurov Net: n/a Beside aircraft listed, also operates 80 Antonov 2 on for training purposes only. Most aircraft are still in Aeroflot colors with or without titles.

☐ RA-67011	Let 410UVP	810612	CCCP-67011	0081		2 WA M-601D	5800	Y15 / Trainer		
☐ RA-67013	Let 410UVP	810614	CCCP-67013	0081		2 WA M-601D	5800	Y15 / Trainer		
☐ RA-67019	Let 410UVP	810620	CCCP-67019	0081		2 WA M-601D	5800	Y15 / Trainer		
☐ RA-67026	Let 410UVP	810628	CCCP-67026	0081		2 WA M-601D	5800	Y15 / Trainer		
☐ RA-67027	Let 410UVP	810629	CCCP-67027	0081		2 WA M-601D	5800	Y15 / Trainer		
☐ RA-67028	Let 410UVP	810630	CCCP-67028	0081		2 WA M-601D	5800	Y15 / Trainer		
☐ RA-67029	Let 410UVP	810631	CCCP-67029	0081		2 WA M-601D	5800	Y15 / Trainer		
☐ RA-67056	Let 410UVP	810632	CCCP-67056	0081		2 WA M-601D	5800	Y15 / Trainer		
☐ RA-67057	Let 410UVP	810633	CCCP-67057	0081		2 WA M-601D	5800	Y15 / Trainer		
☐ RA-67063	Let 410UVP	810639	CCCP-67063	0081		2 WA M-601D	5800	Y15 / Trainer		
☐ RA-67092	Let 410UVP	820733	CCCP-67092	0082		2 WA M-601D	5800	Y15 / Trainer		
☐ RA-67093	Let 410UVP	820734	CCCP-67093	0082		2 WA M-601D	5800	Y15 / Trainer		
☐ RA-67094	Let 410UVP	820735	CCCP-67094	0082		2 WA M-601D	5800	Y15 / Trainer		
☐ RA-67150	Let 410UVP	800416	CCCP-67150	0080		2 WA M-601D	5800	Y15 / Trainer		
☐ RA-67153	Let 410UVP	800419	CCCP-67153	0080		2 WA M-601D	5800	Y15 / Trainer		
☐ RA-67154	Let 410UVP	800420	CCCP-67154	0080		2 WA M-601D	5800	Y15 / Trainer		
☐ RA-67162	Let 410UVP	800428	CCCP-67162	0080		2 WA M-601D	5800	Y15 / Trainer		
☐ RA-67444	Let 410UVP	841209	CCCP-67444	0084		2 WA M-601D	5800	Y15 / Trainer		
☐ RA-67445	Let 410UVP	841210	CCCP-67445	0084		2 WA M-601D	5800	Y15 / Trainer		
☐ RA-67447	Let 410UVP	841212	CCCP-67447	0084		2 WA M-601D	5800	Y15 / Trainer		
☐ RA-67448	Let 410UVP	841213	CCCP-67448	0084		2 WA M-601D	5800	Y15 / Trainer		

SAT Airlines = HZ / SHU (Sakhalinskie Aviatrassy) — Yuzhno-Sakhalinsk

Sakhalinskie Aviatrassy
SAT Aircompany

Ul. Gorkogo 50A, 693023 Yuzhno-Sakhalinsk, Russia ☎ (4242) 25 19 17 Tx: 152112 mir ru Fax: (4242) 42 64 11 SITA: UUSATSU

F: 1992 👥 450 Head: Konstantin P. Sukhorebrik IATA: 598 ICAO: SATAIR Net: n/a Some aircraft are still in Aeroflot colors but will be repainted in due course.

☐ RA-22517	Mil Mi-8MTV-1	96106		0393	0098	2 IS TV3-117MT	13000	Freighter 4t		
☐ RA-24208	Mil Mi-8T	98730170	CCCP-24208	0287	0098	2 IS TV2-117A	12000	Freighter 4t		
☐ RA-24683	Mil Mi-8T	98101336	CCCP-24683	0881	0098	2 IS TV2-117A	12000	Freighter 4t		
☐ RA-25185	Mil Mi-8MTV-1	95524	CCCP-25185	0990	0098	2 IS TV3-117MT	13000	Freighter 4t		
☐ RA-25737	Mil Mi-8MTV-1	96058		1292	0195	2 IS TV3-117MT	13000	Y18 / Frtr 4t		
☐ RA-25738	Mil Mi-8MTV-1	96059		1292	0395	2 IS TV3-117VM	13000	Y18 / Frtr 4t		lsf Spektr, Khabarovsk
☐ RA-25739	Mil Mi-8MTV-1	96060		1292	0098	2 IS TV3-117VM	13000	Freighter 4t		
☐ RA-25893	Mil Mi-8T	5164	CCCP-25893	0375	0098	2 IS TV2-117A	12000	Freighter 4t		
☐ RA-31093	Kamov Ka-32S	9106		0592	0098	2 IS TV3-117V	12600	Freighter 5t		
☐ RA-46530	Antonov 24RV	57310009	CCCP-46530	0175	0092	2 IV AI-24VT	22500	Y36		
☐ RA-46639	Antonov 24RV	37308905	CCCP-46639	0973	0092	2 IV AI-24VT	21800	Y36		
☐ RA-47198	Antonov 24RV	27307702	CCCP-47198	0472	0092	2 IV AI-24VT	21800	Y44		
☐ RA-47317	Antonov 24RV	67310504	CCCP-47317	0376	0092	2 IV AI-24VT	21800	Y44		
☐ RA-47366	Antonov 24RV	77310804	CCCP-47366	0977	0092	2 IV AI-24VT	21800	Y36		
☐ RA-26132	Antonov 26B	12708	CCCP-26132	0183	0098	2 IV AI-24VT	24000	Freighter		
☐ RA-73003	Boeing 737-247	19611 / 92	N470TA	1168	0894	2 PW JT8D-9A	49442	F8Y101		lsf Whirlpool Financial

SAYANY AIRLINES, Joint-Stock Company = SYL — Irkutsk-Int'l

Ul. Gryaznova 1, 663003 Irkutsk, Russia ☎ (3952) 27 44 98 Tx: none Fax: (3952) 34 30 39 SITA: n/a

F: 1998 👥 n/a Head: Alexei I. Kulikov ICAO: SAYANY Net: n/a Operates regular passenger flights with 2 Tupolev 154B-2, leased from CHITAAVIA (RA-) when required.

SAZ – Saratovsky aviatsionny zavod = SVP (Saratov Aviation Plant) (Flying division of Saratov Aircraft Factory / Member of MAP Group) — Saratov

Flying division / Letny otryad, Pl. Ordzhonikidze 1, 410015 Saratov, Russia ☎ (8452) 44 82 98 Tx: 241110 sreza Fax: (8452) 44 36 07 SITA: n/a

F: 1943 👥 n/a Head: Alexei P. Spiridonov ICAO: SAZAVIA Net: n/a Operates corporate flights for itself & commercial charter flights. Aircraft are still in former Aeroflot colors with or without titles.

☐ RA-87317	Yakovlev 40	9331629	CCCP-87317	0073		3 IV AI-25	16800	Combi		
☐ RA-87621	Yakovlev 40	9130219	CCCP-87621	0071		3 IV AI-25	16800	Combi		
☐ RA-87849	Yakovlev 40K	9331830	CCCP-87849	0073		3 IV AI-25	16800	Combi		
☐ RA-87952	Yakovlev 40K	9821057	CCCP-87952	0078		3 IV AI-25	16800	Combi		
☐ RA-88301	Yakovlev 40K	9641251	EY-1251	0076		3 IV AI-25	16000	Combi		

SEVERAERO, Joint-Stock Company = NOT (Northaero) — Norilsk

Leninsky prospekt 1, Room 24, 663310 Norilsk, (Krasnoyarsk Region), Russia ☎ (3919) 46 83 92 Tx: none Fax: (3919) 46 83 92 SITA: n/a

F: 1998 👥 n/a Head: Yanik E. Zurnadzhyan ICAO: NORTHAERO Net: n/a

☐ RA-65605	Tupolev 134A	09070	EW-65605	0574	0098	2 SO D-30-II	47000	Y64		
☐ RA-85273	Tupolev 154B-1	273	CCCP-85273	0478	0098	3 KU NK-8-2U	98000	Y164		
☐ RA-85504	Tupolev 154B-2	504	CCCP-85504	0081	0098	3 KU NK-8-2U	100000	Y164		

SEVERSTAL (Subsidiary of Cherepovetsky metallurgichesky kombinat / Cherepovets Metalurgical Combine) — Cherepovets

Flying div./Letny otryad, Ul. Mira 30, 162600 Cherepovets, (Vologda Region), Russia ☎ (81736) 50 502 Tx: n/a Fax: (81736) 54 488 SITA: n/a

F: n/a 👥 n/a Head: Leonid A. Smirnov Net: n/a Beside aircraft listed, additional Yakovlev 40 are leased from VOLOGDA AIR ENTERPRISE when required.

☐ RA-22183	Mil Mi-8MTV-1		CCCP-22183	0092		2 IS TV3-117MT	13000	Combi		
☐ RA-87586	Yakovlev 40	9221822	CCCP-87586	0072		3 IV AI-25	16800	Executive		Rossia titles
☐ RA-88296	Yakovlev 40	9421634	VN-A445	0074		3 IV AI-25	16800	Executive		Rossia titles

SHAKHTINSKY ARZ (Flying division of Shakhty Aviation Repair Works / Shakhtinsky aviaremontny zavod) — Shakhty

Flying division / Letny otryad, Ul. Aeroflotskaya 1, 346523 Shakhty (Rostov Region), Russia ☎ (86362) 20 774 Tx: none Fax: (86362) 20 774 SITA: n/a

F: n/a 👥 n/a Head: Peter P. Gagaev Net: n/a

☐ RA-23633	PZL Swidnik (Mil) Mi-2					2 IS GTD-350-4	3550	Utility		
☐ RA-23634	PZL Swidnik (Mil) Mi-2					2 IS GTD-350-4	3550	Utility		
☐ RA-23635	PZL Swidnik (Mil) Mi-2					2 IS GTD-350-4	3550	Utility		
☐ RA-02819	PZL Mielec (Antonov) An-2			0065		1 SH ASh-62IR	5500	Utility		

561 registration type of aircraft cn/fn ex/ex* mfd del powered by mtow kg configuration selcal name/fln/specialitites/remarks

registration	type of aircraft	cn/fn	ex/ex*	mfd	del	powered by	mtow kg	configuration	selcal	name/fln/specialities/remarks
☐ RA-02874	PZL Mielec (Antonov) An-2			0065		1 SH ASh-62IR	5500	Utility		
☐ RA-02876	PZL Mielec (Antonov) An-2			0065		1 SH ASh-62IR	5500	Utility		
☐ RA-02884	PZL Mielec (Antonov) An-2			0065		1 SH ASh-62IR	5500	Utility		
☐ RA-02885	PZL Mielec (Antonov) An-2			0065		1 SH ASh-62IR	5500	Utility		
☐ RA-02886	PZL Mielec (Antonov) An-2			0065		1 SH ASh-62IR	5500	Utility		
☐ RA-02887	PZL Mielec (Antonov) An-2			0065		1 SH ASh-62IR	5500	Utility		

SHAKHTY AIR ENTERPRISE (Shakhtinskoe aviapredpriatie) (formerly Aeroflot Shakhty division) — Shakhty

Ul. Aeroflotovskaya 1, 346523 Shakhty, (Rostov Region), Russia   ☎ (86362) 27 431   Tx: n/a   Fax: none   SITA: n/a
F: n/a   ✈✈✈ n/a   Head: Alexander A. Svetenov   Net: n/a   Most aircraft are still in Aeroflot colors but will be repainted in due course.

registration	type of aircraft	cn/fn	ex/ex*	mfd	del	powered by	mtow kg	configuration	selcal	name
☐ RA-14081	PZL Swidnik (Mil) Mi-2	5210625058	CCCP-14081	0088		2 IS GTD-350-4	3550	Utility		
☐ RA-20205	PZL Swidnik (Mil) Mi-2	526844100	CCCP-20205	0080		2 IS GTD-350-4	3550	Utility		
☐ RA-20273	PZL Swidnik (Mil) Mi-2	547313091	CCCP-20273	0081		2 IS GTD-350-4	3550	Utility		
☐ RA-20325	PZL Swidnik (Mil) Mi-2	524011025	CCCP-20325	0075		2 IS GTD-350-4	3550	Utility		
☐ RA-20386	PZL Swidnik (Mil) Mi-2	529833076	CCCP-20386	0086		2 IS GTD-350-4	3550	Utility		
☐ RA-20422	PZL Swidnik (Mil) Mi-2	529925086	CCCP-20422	0086		2 IS GTD-350-4	3550	Utility		
☐ RA-20622	PZL Swidnik (Mil) Mi-2	535028126	CCCP-20622	0076		2 IS GTD-350-4	3550	Utility		
☐ RA-20660	PZL Swidnik (Mil) Mi-2	526537030	CCCP-20660	0080		2 IS GTD-350-4	3550	Utility		
☐ RA-20806	PZL Swidnik (Mil) Mi-2	528004013	CCCP-20806	0083		2 IS GTD-350-4	3550	Utility		
☐ RA-20807	PZL Swidnik (Mil) Mi-2	528005013	CCCP-20807	0083		2 IS GTD-350-4	3550	Utility		
☐ RA-20813	PZL Swidnik (Mil) Mi-2	528017013	CCCP-20813	0083		2 IS GTD-350-4	3550	Utility		
☐ RA-20814	PZL Swidnik (Mil) Mi-2	528018013	CCCP-20814	0083		2 IS GTD-350-4	3550	Utility		
☐ RA-20815	PZL Swidnik (Mil) Mi-2	528019013	CCCP-20815	0083		2 IS GTD-350-4	3550	Utility		
☐ RA-20858	PZL Swidnik (Mil) Mi-2	548139043	CCCP-20858	0083		2 IS GTD-350-4	3550	Utility		
☐ RA-20859	PZL Swidnik (Mil) Mi-2	548140043	CCCP-20859	0083		2 IS GTD-350-4	3550	Utility		
☐ RA-20899	PZL Swidnik (Mil) Mi-2	538338093	CCCP-20899	0083		2 IS GTD-350-4	3550	Utility		
☐ RA-20904	PZL Swidnik (Mil) Mi-2	528433113	CCCP-20904	0083		2 IS GTD-350-4	3550	Utility		
☐ RA-20906	PZL Swidnik (Mil) Mi-2	528435113	CCCP-20906	0083		2 IS GTD-350-4	3550	Utility		
☐ RA-20915	PZL Swidnik (Mil) Mi-2	528547024	CCCP-20915	0084		2 IS GTD-350-4	3550	Utility		
☐ RA-20925	PZL Swidnik (Mil) Mi-2	528607034	CCCP-20925	0084		2 IS GTD-350-4	3550	Utility		
☐ RA-20966	PZL Swidnik (Mil) Mi-2	539526115	CCCP-20966	0085		2 IS GTD-350-4	3550	Utility		
☐ RA-20982	PZL Swidnik (Mil) Mi-2	529707036	CCCP-20982	0086		2 IS GTD-350-4	3550	Utility		
☐ RA-20983	PZL Swidnik (Mil) Mi-2	529708036	CCCP-20983	0086		2 IS GTD-350-4	3550	Utility		
☐ RA-23327	PZL Swidnik (Mil) Mi-2	529216045	CCCP-23327	0085		2 IS GTD-350-4	3550	Utility		
☐ RA-23328	PZL Swidnik (Mil) Mi-2	529217045	CCCP-23328	0085		2 IS GTD-350-4	3550	Utility		
☐ RA-23348	PZL Swidnik (Mil) Mi-2	529328075	CCCP-23348	0085		2 IS GTD-350-4	3550	Utility		
☐ RA-23371	PZL Swidnik (Mil) Mi-2	528743074	CCCP-23371	0084		2 IS GTD-350-4	3550	Utility		
☐ RA-23385	PZL Swidnik (Mil) Mi-2	528831084	CCCP-23385	0084		2 IS GTD-350-4	3550	Utility		
☐ RA-23388	PZL Swidnik (Mil) Mi-2	528834084	CCCP-23388	0084		2 IS GTD-350-4	3550	Utility		
☐ RA-23456	PZL Swidnik (Mil) Mi-2					2 IS GTD-350-4	3550	Utility		
☐ RA-01434	PZL Mielec (Antonov) An-2		CCCP-01434	0088		1 SH ASh-62IR	5500	Utility		
☐ RA-02211	PZL Mielec (Antonov) An-2		CCCP-02211	0089		1 SH ASh-62IR	5500	Utility		
☐ RA-02212	PZL Mielec (Antonov) An-2		CCCP-02212	0089		1 SH ASh-62IR	5500	Utility		
☐ RA-02215	PZL Mielec (Antonov) An-2		CCCP-02215	0089		1 SH ASh-62IR	5500	Utility		
☐ RA-02217	PZL Mielec (Antonov) An-2		CCCP-02217	0089		1 SH ASh-62IR	5500	Utility		
☐ RA-02256	PZL Mielec (Antonov) An-2		CCCP-02256	0089		1 SH ASh-62IR	5500	Utility		
☐ RA-02263	PZL Mielec (Antonov) An-2		CCCP-02263	0090		1 SH ASh-62IR	5500	Utility		
☐ RA-02293	PZL Mielec (Antonov) An-2		CCCP-02293	0090		1 SH ASh-62IR	5500	Utility		
☐ RA-02294	PZL Mielec (Antonov) An-2		CCCP-02294	0090		1 SH ASh-62IR	5500	Utility		
☐ RA-02417	PZL Mielec (Antonov) An-2		CCCP-02417	0070		1 SH ASh-62IR	5500	Utility		
☐ RA-07462	PZL Mielec (Antonov) An-2	1G151-37	CCCP-07462	0073		1 SH ASh-62IR	5500	Utility		
☐ RA-07785	PZL Mielec (Antonov) An-2		CCCP-07785	0075		1 SH ASh-62IR	5500	Utility		
☐ RA-17738	PZL Mielec (Antonov) An-2		CCCP-17738	0083		1 SH ASh-62IR	5500	Utility		
☐ RA-17888	PZL Mielec (Antonov) An-2		CCCP-17888	0083		1 SH ASh-62IR	5500	Utility		
☐ RA-17889	PZL Mielec (Antonov) An-2		CCCP-17889	0083		1 SH ASh-62IR	5500	Utility		
☐ RA-17890	PZL Mielec (Antonov) An-2		CCCP-17890	0083		1 SH ASh-62IR	5500	Utility		
☐ RA-17908	PZL Mielec (Antonov) An-2		CCCP-17908	0083		1 SH ASh-62IR	5500	Utility		
☐ RA-17909	PZL Mielec (Antonov) An-2		CCCP-17909	0083		1 SH ASh-62IR	5500	Utility		
☐ RA-17910	PZL Mielec (Antonov) An-2		CCCP-17910	0083		1 SH ASh-62IR	5500	Utility		
☐ RA-32670	PZL Mielec (Antonov) An-2		CCCP-32670	0085		1 SH ASh-62IR	5500	Utility		
☐ RA-32671	PZL Mielec (Antonov) An-2		CCCP-32671	0085		1 SH ASh-62IR	5500	Utility		
☐ RA-33561	PZL Mielec (Antonov) An-2		CCCP-33561	0088		1 SH ASh-62IR	5500	Utility		
☐ RA-40266	PZL Mielec (Antonov) An-2		CCCP-40266	0086		1 SH ASh-62IR	5500	Utility		
☐ RA-40382	PZL Mielec (Antonov) An-2		CCCP-40382	0087		1 SH ASh-62IR	5500	Utility		
☐ RA-40438	PZL Mielec (Antonov) An-2		CCCP-40438	0087		1 SH ASh-62IR	5500	Utility		
☐ RA-40450	PZL Mielec (Antonov) An-2		CCCP-40450	0087		1 SH ASh-62IR	5500	Utility		
☐ RA-40472	PZL Mielec (Antonov) An-2		CCCP-40472	0087		1 SH ASh-62IR	5500	Utility		
☐ RA-40771	PZL Mielec (Antonov) An-2	1G172-43	CCCP-40771	0076		1 SH ASh-62IR	5500	Utility		
☐ RA-40939	PZL Mielec (Antonov) An-2		CCCP-40939	0085		1 SH ASh-62IR	5500	Utility		
☐ RA-40954	PZL Mielec (Antonov) An-2		CCCP-40954	0085		1 SH ASh-62IR	5500	Utility		
☐ RA-40976	PZL Mielec (Antonov) An-2		CCCP-40976	0085		1 SH ASh-62IR	5500	Utility		
☐ RA-40979	PZL Mielec (Antonov) An-2		CCCP-40979	0085		1 SH ASh-62IR	5500	Utility		
☐ RA-40993	PZL Mielec (Antonov) An-2		CCCP-40993	0085		1 SH ASh-62IR	5500	Utility		
☐ RA-40994	PZL Mielec (Antonov) An-2		CCCP-40994	0085		1 SH ASh-62IR	5500	Utility		
☐ RA-40995	PZL Mielec (Antonov) An-2		CCCP-40995	0085		1 SH ASh-62IR	5500	Utility		
☐ RA-54952	PZL Mielec (Antonov) An-2		CCCP-54952	0080		1 SH ASh-62IR	5500	Utility		
☐ RA-62659	PZL Mielec (Antonov) An-2		CCCP-62659	0078		1 SH ASh-62IR	5500	Utility		
☐ RA-68077	PZL Mielec (Antonov) An-2		CCCP-68077	0081		1 SH ASh-62IR	5500	Utility		
☐ RA-70403	PZL Mielec (Antonov) An-2		CCCP-70403	0072		1 SH ASh-62IR	5500	Utility		
☐ RA-71258	PZL Mielec (Antonov) An-2		CCCP-71258	0084		1 SH ASh-62IR	5500	Utility		
☐ RA-71259	PZL Mielec (Antonov) An-2		CCCP-71259	0084		1 SH ASh-62IR	5500	Utility		
☐ RA-81639	PZL Mielec (Antonov) An-2		CCCP-81639	0089		1 SH ASh-62IR	5500	Utility		
☐ RA-81644	PZL Mielec (Antonov) An-2		CCCP-81644	0089		1 SH ASh-62IR	5500	Utility		
☐ RA-84523	PZL Mielec (Antonov) An-2		CCCP-84523	0080		1 SH ASh-62IR	5500	Utility		
☐ RA-84552	PZL Mielec (Antonov) An-2		CCCP-84552	0080		1 SH ASh-62IR	5500	Utility		
☐ RA-84553	PZL Mielec (Antonov) An-2		CCCP-84553	0080		1 SH ASh-62IR	5500	Utility		
☐ RA-84629	PZL Mielec (Antonov) An-2		CCCP-84629	0080		1 SH ASh-62IR	5500	Utility		

SHAR INK, Ltd = UGP — Moscow-Ostafyevo & -Myachkovo

Ul. Butlerova 40, 117332 Moskva, Russia   ☎ (095) 334 93 44   Tx: none   Fax: (095) 334 93 97   SITA: n/a
F: n/a   ✈✈✈ n/a   Head: Vasily N. Klyuchnikov   ICAO: SHARINK   Net: n/a

registration	type of aircraft	cn/fn	ex/ex*	mfd	del	powered by	mtow kg	configuration	selcal	name
☐ RA-72905	Antonov 72		CCCP-72905	0087		2 LO D-36	36500	Combi		opf Urengoigasprom
☐ RA-74011	Antonov 74			0095		2 LO D-36	36500	Freighter		opf Urengoigasprom
☐ RA-74052	Antonov 74			0094		2 LO D-36	36500	Freighter		opf Urengoigasprom

SIBAVIATRANS, Joint-Stock Company = 5M / SIB (SIAT) (formerly Kramzavia & Flying div.of Krasnoyarsk Metallurgy Factory) — Krasnoyarsk-Yemelianovo

Ul. Vzletnaya 5a, 660077 Krasnoyarsk, Russia   ☎ (3912) 22 77 29   Tx: none   Fax: (3912) 66 11 58   SITA: n/a
F: n/a   ✈✈✈ n/a   Head: Alexander M. Abramovich   IATA: 842   ICAO: SIBAVIA   Net: n/a   Beside aircraft listed, additional (Ilyushin 62 & Tupolev 154) are leased from KRAS AIR when required.

registration	type of aircraft	cn/fn	ex/ex*	mfd	del	powered by	mtow kg	configuration	selcal	name
☐ RA-24515	Mil Mi-8T	98522029	CCCP-24521	0085		2 IS TV2-117A	12000	Freighter		
☐ RA-25400	Mil Mi-8PS-11	8587		1284		2 IS TV2-117A	12000	VIP 11 Pax		
☐ RA-25430	Mil Mi-8MTV-1	95462	CCCP-25430	0090	0096	2 IS TV3-117MT	13000	Freighter		
☐ RA-25490	Mil Mi-8MTV-1	95635	CCCP-25490	0091	0096	2 IS TV3-117VM	13000	Freighter		
☐ RA-27118	Mil Mi-8AMT	59489607093		0092	0096	2 IS TV3-117VM	13000	Freighter		
☐ RA-27119	Mil Mi-8AMT	59489607174		0092	0096	2 IS TV3-117VM	13000	Freighter		
☐ RA-27162	Mil Mi-8T	99257249		0092	0096	2 IS TV2-117AG	12000	Freighter		
☐ RA-27163	Mil Mi-8T	99257258		0092	0096	2 IS TV2-117AG	12000	Freighter		
☐ RA-02850	Hawker 700B (HS 125-700B)	257112	G-SVLB	0080	0398	2 GA TFE731-3R-1H	11567	Executive		
☐ RA-21503	Yakovlev 40K	9820358	CCCP-21503	0078		3 IV AI-25	17200	Combi		
☐ RA-87417	Yakovlev 40	9420934	CCCP-87417	0074	0096	3 IV AI-25	17200	Executive		
☐ RA-48113	Antonov 32	1709	CCCP-48113	0988	0096	2 IV AI-20D	27000	Freighter		
☐ RA-69356	Antonov 32A	1408		0087		2 IV AI-20D	27000	Freighter		
☐ RA-85681	Tupolev 154M	848	EP-LAU	0990	0098	3 SO D-30KU-154-II	100000	Y164		lsf BKN

SIBIA Aviakompania, Ltd = SBD — Kurgan

Kurgan Airport, Room 319, 640015 Kurgan, Russia   ☎ (35222) 99 785   Tx: none   Fax: (35222) 34 853   SITA: n/a
F: 1991   ✈✈✈ n/a   Head: Gennady Shironosov   ICAO: SIBIA   Net: n/a

registration	type of aircraft	cn/fn	ex/ex*	mfd	del	powered by	mtow kg	configuration	selcal	name
☐ RA-23379	PZL Swidnik (Mil) Mi-2	548822084	CCCP-23379	0884		2 IS GTD-350-4	3550	8 Pax		
☐ RA-07339	PZL Mielec (Antonov) An-2	1G149-43	CCCP-07339	0873		1 SH ASh-62IR	5500	12 Pax		
☐ RA-07433	PZL Mielec (Antonov) An-2	1G151-08	CCCP-07433	1073		1 SH ASh-62IR	5500	12 Pax		
☐ RA-32679	PZL Mielec (Antonov) An-2	1G211-38	CCCP-32679	0285		1 SH ASh-62IR	5500	12 Pax		
☐ RA-33036	PZL Mielec (Antonov) An-2	1G218-23	CCCP-33036	0286		1 SH ASh-62IR	5500	12 Pax		
☐ RA-33300	PZL Mielec (Antonov) An-2	1G225-17	CCCP-33300	0587		1 SH ASh-62IR	5500	12 Pax		

☐ RA-35032	PZL Mielec (Antonov) An-2	1G109-38	CCCP-35032	0969		1 SH ASh-62IR	5500	12 Pax		
☐ RA-40274	PZL Mielec (Antonov) An-2	1G221-04	CCCP-40274	0886		1 SH ASh-62IR	5500	12 Pax		
☐ RA-40487	PZL Mielec (Antonov) An-2	1G225-04	CCCP-40487	0487		1 SH ASh-62IR	5500	12 Pax		
☐ RA-54946	PZL Mielec (Antonov) An-2	1G187-55	CCCP-54946	0580		1 SH ASh-62IR	5500	12 Pax		
☐ RA-81506	PZL Mielec (Antonov) An-2	1G208-06	CCCP-81506	0584		1 SH ASh-62IR	5500	12 Pax		
☐ RA-82812	PZL Mielec (Antonov) An-2	1G166-44	CCCP-82812	1275		1 SH ASh-62IR	5500	12 Pax		

SIBIR AIRLINES, Joint-Stock Company = S7 / SBI (Aviakompania Sibir) — Novosibirsk-Tolmachevo, Barnaul, Kemerovo & Tomsk

Tolmachevo Airport, 633115 Ob'-4, (Novosibirsk Region), Russia ☎ (3832) 59 90 11 Tx: none Fax: (38373) 59 90 64 SITA: OVBDMS7
F: 1993 n/a Head: Vladislav F. Filev IATA: 421 ICAO: SIBERIA AIRLINES Net: n/a Some aircraft are still in Aeroflot colors but will be repainted in due course.

☐ RA-26137	Antonov 26B	12809	CCCP-26137	0283	0093	2 IV AI-24VT	24000	Freighter		
☐ RA-26563	Antonov 26	3506	CCCP-26563	1275	0093	2 IV AI-24VT	24000	Freighter		
☐ RA-26577	Antonov 26B	12909	CCCP-26577	0483	0093	2 IV AI-24VT	24000	Freighter		
☐ RA-26592	Antonov 26B	14002	CCCP-26592	0385	0093	2 IV AI-24VT	24000	Freighter		
☐ RA-48060	Antonov 32B	2910		0292	0696	2 IV AI-20D	27000	Combi		
☐ RA-65563	Tupolev 134A-3	60035	CCCP-65563	0877	0098	2 SO D-30-III	49000	F12Y46		lsf NPO
☐ RA-85106	Tupolev 154B	106	CCCP-85106	0575	0093	3 KU NK-8-2U	98000	Y164		cvtd 154A
☐ RA-85115	Tupolev 154B	115	CCCP-85115	0775	1298	3 KU NK-8-2U	98000	Y164		cvtd 154A
☐ RA-85261	Tupolev 154B-1	261	CCCP-85261	0278	0093	3 KU NK-8-2U	98000	Y164		
☐ RA-85292	Tupolev 154B-2	292	CCCP-85292	0878	0093	3 KU NK-8-2U	98000	Y164		cvtd 154B-1
☐ RA-85402	Tupolev 154B-2	402	CCCP-85402	0380	0398	3 KU NK-8-2U	98000	F8Y130		
☐ RA-85421	Tupolev 154B-2	421	CCCP-85421	0680	1298	3 KU NK-8-2U	98000	Y164		
☐ RA-85461	Tupolev 154B-2	461	CCCP-85461	1280	0093	3 KU NK-8-2U	98000	F8Y130		
☐ RA-85485	Tupolev 154B-2	485	CCCP-85485	0581	1298	3 KU NK-8-2U	100000	F8Y130		
☐ RA-85556	Tupolev 154B-2	556	YL-LAD	0982	0398	3 KU NK-8-2U	100000	F8Y130		
☐ RA-85583	Tupolev 154B-2	583	EW-85583	0883	0796	3 KU NK-8-2U	102000	F8Y130		
☐ RA-85687	Tupolev 154M	857	EP-MAC	1190	0093	3 SO D-30KU-154-II	102000	Y164		lst IRB as EP-MAZ
☐ RA-85688	Tupolev 154M	859	CCCP-85688	1290	0093	3 SO D-30KU-154-II	100000	F12Y120		
☐ RA-85693	Tupolev 154M	866	OM-VEA	0391	0093	3 SO D-30KU-154-II	102000	Y164		lst IRB as EP-MAS
☐ RA-85697	Tupolev 154M	870	EP-MAQ	0491	0093	3 SO D-30KU-154-II	102000	F8Y130		
☐ RA-85699	Tupolev 154M	874	CCCP-85699	0691	0093	3 SO D-30KU-154-II	102000	F8Y130		
☐ RA-85705	Tupolev 154M	880	EP-MAI	0891	0093	3 SO D-30KU-154-II	102000	F8Y130		
☐ RA-85709	Tupolev 154M	884	EP-ITM	0991	0093	3 SO D-30KU-154-II	102000	Y164		lst IRB as EP-MAK
☐ RA-86102	Ilyushin 86	51483207070	CCCP-86102	0389	0093	4 KU NK-86	210000	Y350		
☐ RA-86105	Ilyushin 86	51483208073	CCCP-86105	0889	0093	4 KU NK-86	210000	Y350		
☐ RA-86107	Ilyushin 86	51483208075	CCCP-86107	1189	0093	4 KU NK-86	210000	F20Y296		
☐ RA-86108	Ilyushin 86	51483208076	CCCP-86108	0190	0093	4 KU NK-86	210000	Y350		
☐ RA-86109	Ilyushin 86	51483208077	CCCP-86109	0390	0093	4 KU NK-86	210000	Y350		
☐ RA-86112	Ilyushin 86	51483208080	CCCP-86112	0890	0093	4 KU NK-86	210000	Y350		
☐ RA-86120	Ilyushin 86	51483209088	CCCP-86120	1191	0093	4 KU NK-86	210000	Y350		
☐ RA-86125	Ilyushin 86	51483210093	CCCP-86125	0992	0896	4 KU NK-86	210000	Y350		

SIBIRINTERAVIA, Joint-Stock Company = STQ (Siberia-Interavia) (Flying division of Tyumen Motors Factory / Member of MAP Group) — Tyumen

Tyumenskie motorostroiteli PO, 625014 Tyumen 14, Russia ☎ (3452) 21 49 94 Tx: none Fax: (3452) 21 49 94 SITA: n/a
F: 1996 n/a Head: Vladimir G. Gryazlov ICAO: SIBINTER Net: n/a

☐ RA-21504	Yakovlev 40K	9831758	CCCP-21504	0078		3 IV AI-25	16800	Combi		
☐ RA-27211	Antonov 26	5610	CCCP-27211	0078		2 IV AI-24VT	24000	Freighter		
☐ RA-48116	Antonov 32	2201	CCCP-48116	0087		2 IV AI-20D	27000	Freighter		

SIR AERO, Joint-Stock Company — Yakutsk

Ul. Dzerzhinskogo 20/1, 677018 Yakutsk, (Republic of Sakha-Yakutia), Russia ☎ (4112) 45 38 05 Tx: none Fax: (4112) 45 21 77 SITA: n/a
F: 1995 n/a Head: Nikolai N. Sofroneyev Net: n/a

☐ RA-47167	Antonov 24B	89901709	CCCP-47167	0068		2 IV AI-24	21000	Y48		

SKASP - Samarskaya kompania aviatsii spetsialnogo primechenia (Samara Co.of Aviation for Special Tasks) (form.SU 2nd Kuybyshev) — Samara-Smyshlyaevka

Smyshlyaevka Airport, 443046 Samara, Russia ☎ (8462) 58 64 77 Tx: none Fax: (8462) 58 83 88 SITA: n/a
F: n/a n/a Head: Alexander I. Kapustin Net: n/a Most aircraft are still in Aeroflot colors but will be repainted in due course.

☐ RA-14169	PZL Swidnik (Mil) Mi-2	5210504127	CCCP-14169	0087		2 IS GTD-350-4	3550	Utility		
☐ RA-14170	PZL Swidnik (Mil) Mi-2	5210505127	CCCP-14170	0087		2 IS GTD-350-4	3550	Utility		
☐ RA-14203	PZL Swidnik (Mil) Mi-2	5211001079	CCCP-14203	0089		2 IS GTD-350-4	3550	Utility		
☐ RA-14204	PZL Swidnik (Mil) Mi-2	5211002079	CCCP-14204	0089		2 IS GTD-350-4	3550	Utility		
☐ RA-20224	PZL Swidnik (Mil) Mi-2	527013021	CCCP-20224	0081		2 IS GTD-350-4	3550	Utility		
☐ RA-20225	PZL Swidnik (Mil) Mi-2	527014021	CCCP-20225	0081		2 IS GTD-350-4	3550	Utility		
☐ RA-20226	PZL Swidnik (Mil) Mi-2	527015021	CCCP-20226	0081		2 IS GTD-350-4	3550	Utility		
☐ RA-20227	PZL Swidnik (Mil) Mi-2	527045021	CCCP-20227	0081		2 IS GTD-350-4	3550	Utility		
☐ RA-20228	PZL Swidnik (Mil) Mi-2	527046021	CCCP-20228	0081		2 IS GTD-350-4	3550	Utility		
☐ RA-20249	PZL Swidnik (Mil) Mi-2	527137051	CCCP-20249	0081		2 IS GTD-350-4	3550	Utility		
☐ RA-20255	PZL Swidnik (Mil) Mi-2	547213071	CCCP-20255	0081		2 IS GTD-350-4	3550	Utility		
☐ RA-20256	PZL Swidnik (Mil) Mi-2	547214071	CCCP-20256	0081		2 IS GTD-350-4	3550	Utility		
☐ RA-20385	PZL Swidnik (Mil) Mi-2	549832076	CCCP-20385	0086		2 IS GTD-350-4	3550	Utility		
☐ RA-20729	PZL Swidnik (Mil) Mi-2	527546032	CCCP-20729	0082		2 IS GTD-350-4	3550	Utility		
☐ RA-20730	PZL Swidnik (Mil) Mi-2	527547032	CCCP-20730	0082		2 IS GTD-350-4	3550	Utility		
☐ RA-20886	PZL Swidnik (Mil) Mi-2	528307083	CCCP-20886	0083		2 IS GTD-350-4	3550	Utility		
☐ RA-20887	PZL Swidnik (Mil) Mi-2	528308083	CCCP-20887	0083		2 IS GTD-350-4	3550	Utility		
☐ RA-23229	PZL Swidnik (Mil) Mi-2	5210230057	CCCP-23229	0087		2 IS GTD-350-4	3550	Utility		
☐ RA-23246	PZL Swidnik (Mil) Mi-2	5210302067	CCCP-23246	0087		2 IS GTD-350-4	3550	Utility		
☐ RA-23247	PZL Swidnik (Mil) Mi-2	5210303067	CCCP-23247	0087		2 IS GTD-350-4	3550	Utility		
☐ RA-23502	PZL Swidnik (Mil) Mi-2	526415119	CCCP-23502	0079		2 IS GTD-350-4	3550	Utility		
☐ RA-02274	PZL Mielec (Antonov) An-2		CCCP-02274	0090		1 SH ASh-62IR	5500	Utility		
☐ RA-02275	PZL Mielec (Antonov) An-2		CCCP-02275	0090		1 SH ASh-62IR	5500	Utility		
☐ RA-02282	PZL Mielec (Antonov) An-2		CCCP-02282	0090		1 SH ASh-62IR	5500	Utility		
☐ RA-02283	PZL Mielec (Antonov) An-2		CCCP-02283	0090		1 SH ASh-62IR	5500	Utility		
☐ RA-33619	PZL Mielec (Antonov) An-2	1G232-53	CCCP-33619	0088		1 SH ASh-62IR	5500	Utility		
☐ RA-35528	PZL Mielec (Antonov) An-2		CCCP-35528	0070		1 SH ASh-62IR	5500	Utility		
☐ RA-35539	PZL Mielec (Antonov) An-2		CCCP-35539	0070		1 SH ASh-62IR	5500	Utility		
☐ RA-40216	PZL Mielec (Antonov) An-2	1G220-06	CCCP-40216	0086		1 SH ASh-62IR	5500	Utility		
☐ RA-40273	PZL Mielec (Antonov) An-2		CCCP-40273	0086		1 SH ASh-62IR	5500	Utility		
☐ RA-62537	PZL Mielec (Antonov) An-2	1G175-60	CCCP-62537	0077		1 SH ASh-62IR	5500	Utility		
☐ RA-70058	PZL Mielec (Antonov) An-2		CCCP-70058	0071		1 SH ASh-62IR	5500	Utility		
☐ RA-70115	PZL Mielec (Antonov) An-2	1G136-41	CCCP-70115	0071		1 SH ASh-62IR	5500	Utility		
☐ RA-70116	PZL Mielec (Antonov) An-2	1G136-42	CCCP-70116	0071		1 SH ASh-62IR	5500	Utility		
☐ RA-22374	Mil Mi-8		CCCP-22374	0077		2 IS TV2-117A	12000	Utility		
☐ RA-22391	Mil Mi-8		CCCP-22391	0077		2 IS TV2-117A	12000	Utility		
☐ RA-22402	Mil Mi-8		CCCP-22402	0077		2 IS TV2-117A	12000	Utility		
☐ RA-22679	Mil Mi-8		CCCP-22679	0080		2 IS TV2-117A	12000	Utility		
☐ RA-22681	Mil Mi-8		CCCP-22681	0080		2 IS TV2-117A	12000	Utility		
☐ RA-22871	Mil Mi-8		CCCP-22871	0084		2 IS TV2-117A	12000	Utility		
☐ RA-22873	Mil Mi-8		CCCP-22873	0084		2 IS TV2-117A	12000	Utility		
☐ RA-24128	Mil Mi-8		CCCP-24128	0088		2 IS TV2-117A	12000	Utility		
☐ RA-24129	Mil Mi-8		CCCP-24129	0088		2 IS TV2-117A	12000	Utility		
☐ RA-24156	Mil Mi-8		CCCP-24156	0089		2 IS TV2-117A	12000	Utility		
☐ RA-24159	Mil Mi-8		CCCP-24159	0089		2 IS TV2-117A	12000	Utility		
☐ RA-24160	Mil Mi-8		CCCP-24160	0089		2 IS TV2-117A	12000	Utility		
☐ RA-24169	Mil Mi-8		CCCP-24169	0089		2 IS TV2-117A	12000	Utility		
☐ RA-24170	Mil Mi-8		CCCP-24170	0089		2 IS TV2-117A	12000	Utility		
☐ RA-24175	Mil Mi-8		CCCP-24175	0089		2 IS TV2-117A	12000	Utility		
☐ RA-24185	Mil Mi-8		CCCP-24185	0089		2 IS TV2-117A	12000	Utility		
☐ RA-24196	Mil Mi-8		CCCP-24196	0089		2 IS TV2-117A	12000	Utility		
☐ RA-24236	Mil Mi-8		CCCP-24236	0087		2 IS TV2-117A	12000	Utility		
☐ RA-24283	Mil Mi-8		CCCP-24283	0087		2 IS TV2-117A	12000	Utility		
☐ RA-24477	Mil Mi-8		CCCP-24477	0086		2 IS TV2-117A	12000	Utility		
☐ RA-24594	Mil Mi-8		CCCP-24594	0088		2 IS TV2-117A	12000	Utility		
☐ RA-24621	Mil Mi-8		CCCP-24621	0081		2 IS TV2-117A	12000	Utility		
☐ RA-24627	Mil Mi-8		CCCP-24627	0081		2 IS TV2-117A	12000	Utility		
☐ RA-25150	Mil Mi-8		CCCP-24150	0090		2 IS TV2-117A	12000	Utility		
☐ RA-25163	Mil Mi-8T		CCCP-25163	0090		2 IS TV2-117A	12000	Utility		
☐ RA-25597	Mil Mi-8T		CCCP-25597	0091		2 IS TV2-117A	12000	Utility		
☐ RA-25599	Mil Mi-8T		CCCP-25599	0091		2 IS TV2-117A	12000	Utility		
☐ RA-25600	Mil Mi-8T		CCCP-25600	0091		2 IS TV2-117A	12000	Utility		
☐ RA-25614	Mil Mi-8T		CCCP-25614	0091		2 IS TV2-117A	12000	Utility		
☐ RA-25615	Mil Mi-8T		CCCP-25615	0091		2 IS TV2-117A	12000	Utility		

563 registration type of aircraft cn/fn ex/ex* mfd del powered by mtow kg configuration selcal name/fln/specialitites/remarks

SKYFIELD AIRLINES, Ltd = SFD

Moscow-Sheremetyevo

3-i proezd Marinoi roshchi 40, 127018 Moskva, Russia ☎ (095) 289 95 45 Tx: none Fax: (095) 289 95 27 SITA: n/a
F: 1997 ⁂ n/a Head: n/a ICAO: SKYFIELD Net: n/a

registration	type of aircraft	cn/fn	ex/ex*	mfd	del	powered by	mtow kg	configuration	selcal	name/fln/specialitites/remarks
☐ RA-65550	Tupolev 134A-3	*66200*	*CCCP-65550*	*0083*	*0098*	*2 SO D-30-III*	*49000*	*Executive*		Filipp Kirkorov / *Isf IGP*
☐ RA-65692	Tupolev 134B-3	*63215*	*YL-LBB*	*0080*	*0097*	*2 SO D-30-III*	*49000*	*Executive*		

SMOLENSKAVIA (formerly part of Central Districts Airlines & Aeroflot Smolensk division)

Smolensk

Smolensk Airport, 214019 Smolensk, Russia ☎ (0812) 52 13 96 Tx: none Fax: (0812) 52 13 96 SITA: n/a
F: 1993 ⁂ n/a Head: Yuri A. Berezin Net: n/a Most aircraft are still in Aeroflot colors but will be repainted in due course.

registration	type of aircraft	cn/fn	ex/ex*	mfd	del	powered by	mtow kg	configuration	selcal	name/fln/specialitites/remarks
☐ RA-20176	PZL Swidnik (Mil) Mi-2	*523444034*	*CCCP-20176*	*0074*		*2 IS GTD-350-4*	*3550*	*Utility*		
☐ RA-20237	PZL Swidnik (Mil) Mi-2	*527105031*	*CCCP-20237*	*0081*		*2 IS GTD-350-4*	*3550*	*Utility*		
☐ RA-20414	PZL Swidnik (Mil) Mi-2	*529912086*	*CCCP-20414*	*0086*		*2 IS GTD-350-4*	*3550*	*Utility*		
☐ RA-20670	PZL Swidnik (Mil) Mi-2	*526633040*	*CCCP-20670*	*0080*		*2 IS GTD-350-4*	*3550*	*Utility*		
☐ RA-20829	PZL Swidnik (Mil) Mi-2	*548102033*	*CCCP-20829*	*0083*		*2 IS GTD-350-4*	*3550*	*Utility*		
☐ RA-20998	PZL Swidnik (Mil) Mi-2	*549743056*	*CCCP-20998*	*0086*		*2 IS GTD-350-4*	*3550*	*Utility*		
☐ RA-23487	PZL Swidnik (Mil) Mi-2	*526246089*	*CCCP-23487*	*0079*		*2 IS GTD-350-4*	*3550*	*Utility*		
☐ RA-01497	PZL Mielec (Antonov) An-2		*CCCP-01497*	*0088*		*1 SH ASh-62IR*	*5500*	*Utility*		
☐ RA-01764	PZL Mielec (Antonov) An-2		*CCCP-01764*	*0069*		*1 SH ASh-62IR*	*5500*	*Utility*		
☐ RA-01801	PZL Mielec (Antonov) An-2		*CCCP-01801*	*0069*		*1 SH ASh-62IR*	*5500*	*Utility*		
☐ RA-02780	PZL Mielec (Antonov) An-2		*CCCP-02780*	*0071*		*1 SH ASh-62IR*	*5500*	*Utility*		
☐ RA-05718	PZL Mielec (Antonov) An-2		*CCCP-05718*	*0074*		*1 SH ASh-62IR*	*5500*	*Utility*		
☐ RA-05721	PZL Mielec (Antonov) An-2		*CCCP-05721*	*0074*		*1 SH ASh-62IR*	*5500*	*Utility*		
☐ RA-07407	PZL Mielec (Antonov) An-2		*CCCP-07407*	*0073*		*1 SH ASh-62IR*	*5500*	*Utility*		
☐ RA-07432	PZL Mielec (Antonov) An-2		*CCCP-07432*	*0073*		*1 SH ASh-62IR*	*5500*	*Utility*		
☐ RA-07643	PZL Mielec (Antonov) An-2		*CCCP-07643*	*0074*		*1 SH ASh-62IR*	*5500*	*Utility*		
☐ RA-07709	PZL Mielec (Antonov) An-2	*1G158-29*	*CCCP-07709*	*0074*		*1 SH ASh-62IR*	*5500*	*Utility*		
☐ RA-16049	PZL Mielec (Antonov) An-2		*CCCP-16049*	*0075*		*1 SH ASh-62IR*	*5500*	*Utility*		
☐ RA-16069	PZL Mielec (Antonov) An-2	*1G164-23*	*CCCP-16069*	*0075*		*1 SH ASh-62IR*	*5500*	*Utility*		
☐ RA-16084	PZL Mielec (Antonov) An-2		*CCCP-16084*	*0075*		*1 SH ASh-62IR*	*5500*	*Utility*		
☐ RA-32737	PZL Mielec (Antonov) An-2		*CCCP-32737*	*0085*		*1 SH ASh-62IR*	*5500*	*Utility*		
☐ RA-33539	PZL Mielec (Antonov) An-2		*CCCP-33539*	*0088*		*1 SH ASh-62IR*	*5500*	*Utility*		
☐ RA-33541	PZL Mielec (Antonov) An-2		*CCCP-33541*	*0088*		*1 SH ASh-62IR*	*5500*	*Utility*		
☐ RA-35005	PZL Mielec (Antonov) An-2		*CCCP-35005*	*0069*		*1 SH ASh-62IR*	*5500*	*Utility*		
☐ RA-40356	PZL Mielec (Antonov) An-2		*CCCP-40356*	*0086*		*1 SH ASh-62IR*	*5500*	*Utility*		
☐ RA-40747	PZL Mielec (Antonov) An-2		*CCCP-40747*	*0076*		*1 SH ASh-62IR*	*5500*	*Utility*		
☐ RA-40773	PZL Mielec (Antonov) An-2	*1G172-45*	*CCCP-40773*	*0076*		*1 SH ASh-62IR*	*5500*	*Utility*		
☐ RA-40833	PZL Mielec (Antonov) An-2		*CCCP-40833*	*0073*		*1 SH ASh-62IR*	*5500*	*Utility*		
☐ RA-40839	PZL Mielec (Antonov) An-2	*1G174-17*	*CCCP-40839*	*0073*		*1 SH ASh-62IR*	*5500*	*Utility*		
☐ RA-54878	PZL Mielec (Antonov) An-2		*CCCP-54878*	*0079*		*1 SH ASh-62IR*	*5500*	*Utility*		
☐ RA-54897	PZL Mielec (Antonov) An-2		*CCCP-54897*	*0079*		*1 SH ASh-62IR*	*5500*	*Utility*		
☐ RA-56360	PZL Mielec (Antonov) An-2		*CCCP-56360*	*0078*		*1 SH ASh-62IR*	*5500*	*Utility*		
☐ RA-56369	PZL Mielec (Antonov) An-2		*CCCP-56369*	*0078*		*1 SH ASh-62IR*	*5500*	*Utility*		
☐ RA-56381	PZL Mielec (Antonov) An-2		*CCCP-56381*	*0078*		*1 SH ASh-62IR*	*5500*	*Utility*		
☐ RA-56478	PZL Mielec (Antonov) An-2	*1G182-35*	*CCCP-56478*	*0079*		*1 SH ASh-62IR*	*5500*	*Utility*		
☐ RA-56479	PZL Mielec (Antonov) An-2	*1G182-36*	*CCCP-56479*	*0079*		*1 SH ASh-62IR*	*5500*	*Utility*		
☐ RA-62501	PZL Mielec (Antonov) An-2		*CCCP-62501*	*0077*		*1 SH ASh-62IR*	*5500*	*Utility*		
☐ RA-62620	PZL Mielec (Antonov) An-2		*CCCP-62620*	*0078*		*1 SH ASh-62IR*	*5500*	*Utility*		
☐ RA-62632	PZL Mielec (Antonov) An-2		*CCCP-62632*	*0078*		*1 SH ASh-62IR*	*5500*	*Utility*		
☐ RA-62685	PZL Mielec (Antonov) An-2		*CCCP-62685*	*0078*		*1 SH ASh-62IR*	*5500*	*Utility*		
☐ RA-67612	Let 410UVP-E	*892340*	*CCCP-67612*	*0089*		*2 WA M-601E*	*6400*	*Y19*		
☐ RA-67619	Let 410UVP-E	*892316*	*CCCP-67619*	*0089*		*2 WA M-601E*	*6400*	*Y19*		
☐ RA-67639	Let 410UVP-E	*902432*	*CCCP-67639*	*0090*		*2 WA M-601E*	*6400*	*Y19*		
☐ RA-67641	Let 410UVP-E	*902434*	*CCCP-67641*	*0090*		*2 WA M-601E*	*6400*	*Y19*		
☐ RA-67657	Let 410UVP-E	*902510*	*CCCP-67657*	*0090*		*2 WA M-601E*	*6400*	*Y19*		

SOCHISPETSAVIA = SOC (Sochi Special Aviation)

Sochi СочиСпецАвиа

Sochi Airport, 354355 Sochi, Russia ☎ (8622) 44 26 45 Tx: n/a Fax: (8622) 44 18 34 SITA: n/a
F: 1993 ⁂ n/a Head: Sergei A. Bozian ICAO: SOCHI Net: n/a Most aircraft are still in Aeroflot colors but will be repainted in due course.

registration	type of aircraft	cn/fn	ex/ex*	mfd	del	powered by	mtow kg	configuration	selcal	name/fln/specialitites/remarks
☐ RA-31005	Kamov Ka-32	*5701*	*CCCP-31005*	*0387*		*2 IS TV3-117V*	*12600*	*Utility*		
☐ RA-31006	Kamov Ka-32	*5702*	*CCCP-31006*	*0387*		*2 IS TV3-117V*	*12600*	*Utility*		
☐ RA-31035	Kamov Ka-32	*6117*	*CCCP-31035*	*0291*		*2 IS TV3-117V*	*12600*	*Utility*		
☐ RA-31067	Kamov Ka-32			*0092*		*2 IS TV3-117V*	*12600*	*Utility*		
☐ RA-31070	Kamov Ka-32	*8901*	*CCCP-31070*	*0992*		*2 IS TV3-117V*	*12600*	*Utility*		*Ist IRR as EP-TRZ*
☐ RA-31071	Kamov Ka-32	*8902*	*CCCP-31071*	*0992*		*2 IS TV3-117V*	*12600*	*Utility*		*Ist IRR as EP-TRA*
☐ RA-31097	Kamov Ka-32	*8910*		*1192*		*2 IS TV3-117V*	*12600*	*Utility*		
☐ RA-31582	Kamov Ka-32	*8604*	*CCCP-31582*	*0691*		*2 IS TV3-117V*	*12600*	*Utility*		*Ist IRR as EP-TRM*
☐ RA-31588	Kamov Ka-32S	*8710*		*0292*		*2 IS TV3-117V*	*12600*	*Utility*		
☐ RA-22174	Mil Mi-8P	*1844*	*CCCP-22174*	*1270*		*2 IS TV2-117A*	*12000*	*28 Pax*		
☐ RA-22526	Mil Mi-8P	*0823*	*CCCP-22526*	*1268*		*2 IS TV2-117A*	*12000*	*28 Pax*		
☐ RA-22710	Mil Mi-8T	*98308280*	*CCCP-22710*	*0283*		*2 IS TV2-117A*	*12000*	*22 Pax*		
☐ RA-24025	Mil Mi-8AMT	*59489611145*		*1094*		*2 IS TV3-117MT*	*13000*	*27 Pax*		
☐ RA-24279	Mil Mi-8T	*98734358*	*CCCP-24279*	*1187*		*2 IS TV2-117A*	*12000*	*Utility*		
☐ RA-24639	Mil Mi-8P	*8606*	*CCCP-24639*	*1285*		*2 IS TV2-117A*	*12000*	*23 Pax*		
☐ RA-25250	Mil Mi-8P	*0213*	*CCCP-25250*	*1067*		*2 IS TV2-117A*	*12000*	*28 Pax*		
☐ RA-25471	Mil Mi-8MTV-1	*95615*	*CCCP-25471*	*0291*		*2 IS TV3-117MT*	*13000*	*Utility*		
☐ RA-25472	Mil Mi-8MTV-1	*95616*	*CCCP-25472*	*0291*		*2 IS TV3-117MT*	*13000*	*Utility*		

SOKOL Aviakompania (formerly Sapsan)

Novotitarovskaya Heliport

Ul. Severnaya 279, 350020 Krasnodar, Russia ☎ (8612) 55 46 99 Tx: none Fax: (8612) 55 41 58 SITA: n/a
F: 1994 ⁂ n/a Head: Igor V. Plaksy Net: n/a

registration	type of aircraft	cn/fn	ex/ex*	mfd	del	powered by	mtow kg	configuration	selcal	name/fln/specialitites/remarks
☐ RA-15709	PZL Swidnik (Mil) Mi-2	*5410139037*	*CCCP-15709*	*0587*	*0897*	*2 IS GTD-350-4*	*3550*	*Utility*		
☐ RA-15710	PZL Swidnik (Mil) Mi-2	*5410218047*	*CCCP-15710*	*0487*	*0897*	*2 IS GTD-350-4*	*3550*	*Utility*		
☐ RA-23732	PZL Swidnik (Mil) Mi-2	*547512022*	*CCCP-23732*	*0382*	*0595*	*2 IS GTD-350-4*	*3550*	*Utility*		
☐ RA-23733	PZL Swidnik (Mil) Mi-2	*547531032*	*CCCP-23733*	*0382*	*0595*	*2 IS GTD-350-4*	*3550*	*Utility*		
☐ RA-23734	PZL Swidnik (Mil) Mi-2	*549028015*	*CCCP-23734*	*0185*	*0595*	*2 IS GTD-350-4*	*3550*	*Utility*		
☐ RA-23735	PZL Swidnik (Mil) Mi-2	*549029015*	*CCCP-23735*	*0185*	*0595*	*2 IS GTD-350-4*	*3550*	*Utility*		
☐ RA-23736	PZL Swidnik (Mil) Mi-2	*549530125*	*CCCP-23736*	*1285*	*0695*	*2 IS GTD-350-4*	*3550*	*Utility*		
☐ RA-27179	Mil Mi-8MTV-1	*96181*	*CCCP-27179*	*1293*	*0395*	*2 IS TV3-117MT*	*13000*	*Utility*		
☐ RA-27180	Mil Mi-8MTV-1	*96182*	*CCCP-27180*	*1293*	*0395*	*2 IS TV3-117MT*	*13000*	*Utility*		
☐ RA-31069	Kamov Ka-32T	*8701*	*CCCP-31069*	*0090*	*0096*	*2 IS TV3-117V*	*12600*	*Utility*		
☐ RA-06072	Mil Mi-26T	*34001212491*	*CCCP-06072*	*0492*	*0395*	*2 LO D-136*	*56000*	*Freighter 20t*		

SPAIR Air Transport Corporation = PAR (Aviatransportnaya korporatsia Spaer) (Associated with East Space, Ltd, Prague/Czechia)

Ekaterinburg-Koltsovo

Ul. Vishnevaya 69, 620078 Ekaterinburg, Russia ☎ (3432) 74 05 08 Tx: none Fax: (3432) 74 47 01 SITA: n/a
F: 1990 ⁂ 150 Head: Valeri Spurnov ICAO: SPAIR Net: n/a

registration	type of aircraft	cn/fn	ex/ex*	mfd	del	powered by	mtow kg	configuration	selcal	name/fln/specialitites/remarks
☐ RA-11415	Antonov 12	*401708*	*CCCP-11415*	*0062*		*4 IV AI-20M*	*61000*	*Freighter*		
☐ RA-76790	Ilyushin 76TD	*0093496903*	*CCCP-76790*	*0689*		*4 SO D-30KP*	*190000*	*Freighter*		

SPECIAL CARGO AIRLINES, Joint-Stock Company = C7 / SCI (Spetsialnye gruzovie avialinii)

Kaluga

Ul. Proizvodstvennaya 6, 119619 Moskva, Russia ☎ (095) 435 65 51 Tx: none Fax: (095) 435 59 83 SITA: n/a
F: 1991 ⁂ n/a Head: Igor M. Lebedev IATA: 424 ICAO: SPECIAL CARGO Net: n/a

registration	type of aircraft	cn/fn	ex/ex*	mfd	del	powered by	mtow kg	configuration	selcal	name/fln/specialitites/remarks
☐ RA-19522	Kamov Ka-26	*7404514*	*CCCP-19522*	*0074*		*2 VE M-14V-26*	*3250*	*7 Pax / Frtr*		
☐ RA-19640	Kamov Ka-26	*7505305*	*CCCP-19640*	*0075*		*2 VE M-14V-26*	*3250*	*7 Pax / Frtr*		
☐ RA-24301	Kamov Ka-26	*7705918*	*CCCP-24301*	*0077*		*2 VE M-14V-26*	*3250*	*7 Pax / Frtr*		
☐ RA-01572	PZL Mielec (Antonov) An-2	*1G81-16*	*CCCP-01572*	*0067*		*1 SH ASh-62IR*	*5500*	*12 Pax / Frtr*		
☐ RA-02414	PZL Mielec (Antonov) An-2	*1G117-25*	*CCCP-02414*	*0070*		*1 SH ASh-62IR*	*5500*	*12 Pax / Frtr*		
☐ RA-17895	PZL Mielec (Antonov) An-2	*1G205-36*	*CCCP-17895*	*0083*		*1 SH ASh-62IR*	*5500*	*12 Pax / Frtr*		
☐ RA-31511	PZL Mielec (Antonov) An-2	*1G199-20*	*CCCP-31511*	*0082*		*1 SH ASh-62IR*	*5500*	*12 Pax / Frtr*		
☐ RA-68125	PZL Mielec (Antonov) An-2	*1G195-30*	*CCCP-68125*	*0082*		*1 SH ASh-62IR*	*5500*	*12 Pax / Frtr*		
☐ RA-68170	PZL Mielec (Antonov) An-2	*1G197-05*	*CCCP-68170*	*0082*		*1 SH ASh-62IR*	*5500*	*12 Pax / Frtr*		
☐ RA-81646	PZL Mielec (Antonov) An-2	*1G209-40*	*CCCP-81646*	*0084*		*1 SH ASh-62IR*	*5500*	*12 Pax / Frtr*		
☐ RA-27092	Mil Mi-8AMT	*59489605201*		*0092*		*2 IS TV3-117MT*	*13000*	*27 Pax / Frtr*		
☐ RA-26172	Antonov 26B	*13906*	*CCCP-26172*	*0083*		*2 IV AI-24VT*	*24000*	*Freighter*		*Ist Santa Cruz Imperial as EL-ANZ*
☐ RA-26209	Antonov 26B		*CCCP-26209*	*0085*		*2 IV AI-24VT*	*24000*	*Freighter*		
☐ RA-26640	Antonov 26	*3504*	*CCCP-26640*	*0075*		*2 IV AI-24VT*	*24000*	*Freighter*		
☐ RA-11329	Antonov 12BP	*8346010*	*CCCP-11329*	*0068*		*4 IV AI-20M*	*61000*	*Freighter*		
☐ RA-11863	Antonov 12BP	*401905*	*CCCP-11863*	*0062*		*4 IV AI-20M*	*61000*	*Freighter*		
☐ RA-12191	Antonov 12BP	*8346202*	*EL-AKW*	*0068*		*4 IV AI-20M*	*61000*	*Freighter*		*Ist Santa Cruz Imperial as EL-ALJ*

STAERO, Ltd = STB Stavropol

Ul. Goleneva 73, room 213, 355012 Stavropol, Russia ☎ (8652) 26 26 53 Tx: none Fax: (8652) 26 13 47 SITA: n/a
F: 1996 n/a Head: Konstantin Yu. Mirzoyan ICAO: STAERO Net: n/a

☐ RA-46502	Antonov 24RV	*37308307*	*CCCP-46502*	*0173*	*0098*	*2 IV AI-24VT*	*21800*	*Y48*		
☐ RA-47252	Antonov 24RV	*27307704*	*CCCP-47252*	*0472*	*1297*	*2 IV AI-24VT*	*21800*	*Y48*		
☐ RA-26535	Antonov 26	*2001*	*CCCP-26535*	*1173*	*0896*	*2 IV AI-24VT*	*24000*	*Combi*		

START Air Transport Company = STW (Aviatransportnaya kompania START) Moscow-Zhukovsky

Kronshtadsky bulvar 7, 125212 Moskva, Russia ☎ (095) 452 41 96 Tx: none Fax: (095) 452 15 28 SITA: n/a
F: n/a n/a Head: Andrei A. Manukharov ICAO: START CHARTER Net: n/a

☐ RA-11113	Antonov 12B	*01347908*	*CCCP-11113*	*0071*	*0098*	*4 IV AI-20M*	*61000*	*Freighter*		
☐ RA-13331	Antonov 12BP	*6344510*	*10 ORANGE*	*0066*		*4 IV AI-20M*	*61000*	*Freighter*		

STELA Irkutsk

GSP Stela, 664000 Irkutsk, Russia ☎ (3952) 31 43 31 Tx: none Fax: (3952) 31 43 32 SITA: n/a
F: 1992 n/a Head: Alexander A. Stepanov Net: n/a

☐ RA-48121	Antonov 32B	*2410*		*0091*		*2 IV AI-20D*	*27000*	*Freighter*		*ex Sterkh-colors*
☐ RA-48122	Antonov 32B			*0091*		*2 IV AI-20D*	*27000*	*Freighter*		

STERLITAMAK AIR ENTERPRISE (Aviapredpriatie Sterlitamak) (formerly Aeroflot Sterlitamak division) Sterlitamak

Sterlitamak Airport, 453113 Sterlitamak, (Republic of Bashkortostan), Russia ☎ (34711) 43 062 Tx: none Fax: (34711) 52 105 SITA: n/a
F: n/a n/a Head: Renat M. Bainbetov Net: n/a Most aircraft are still in Aeroflot colors but will be repainted in due course.

☐ RA-29111	PZL Mielec (Antonov) An-2		*CCCP-29111*	*0066*		*1 SH ASh-62IR*	*5250*	*Utility*		
☐ RA-69317	PZL Mielec (Antonov) An-2		*CCCP-69317*	*0081*		*1 SH ASh-62IR*	*5250*	*Utility*		
☐ RA-49273	Antonov 24T	*7910405*		*0067*		*2 IV AI-24VT*	*22500*	*Combi*		
☐ RA-26245	Antonov 26					*2 IV AI-24VT*	*24000*	*Freighter*		

STREZHAVIA, Joint-Stock Company = STY (Strezhevskie avialinii / Strezhevoi Airlines) Strezhevoi

Strezhevoi Airport, 636762 Strezhevoi, (Tomsk Region), Russia ☎ (38259) 54 543 Tx: none Fax: (38259) 54 542 SITA: n/a
F: 1997 n/a Head: Stepan S. Tegza ICAO: STREZHAVIA Net: n/a

☐ RA-42329	Yakovlev 42D	*4520422505093*	*CCCP-42329*	*0585*	*0098*	*3 LO D-36*	*57500*	*Y120*		*lsf SOV*
☐ RA-42337	Yakovlev 42D	*4520423606235*	*LY-AAM*	*0986*	*0098*	*3 LO D-36*	*57500*	*Y120*		*cvtd 42*
☐ RA-42352	Yakovlev 42D	*4520421811395*	*LY-AAS*	*0488*	*0098*	*3 LO D-36*	*57500*	*Y120*		

STREZHEVOI AIR ENTERPRISE (Strezhevskoe aviapredpriatie) (formerly Aeroflot Strezhevoi division) Strezhevoi

Strezhevoi Airport, 636762 Strezhevoi, (Tomsk region), Russia ☎ (38259) 32 059 Tx: none Fax: (38259) 31 126 SITA: n/a
F: n/a n/a Head: Vladimir P. Mikhailov Net: n/a Most aircraft are still in Aeroflot colors but will be repainted in due course.

☐ RA-02501	PZL Mielec (Antonov) An-2		*CCCP-02501*	*0070*		*1 SH ASh-62IR*	*5500*	*Utility*		
☐ RA-02756	PZL Mielec (Antonov) An-2		*CCCP-02756*	*0071*		*1 SH ASh-62IR*	*5500*	*Utility*		
☐ RA-07368	PZL Mielec (Antonov) An-2		*CCCP-07368*	*0073*		*1 SH ASh-62IR*	*5500*	*Utility*		
☐ RA-35187	PZL Mielec (Antonov) An-2		*CCCP-35187*	*0069*		*1 SH ASh-62IR*	*5500*	*Utility*		
☐ RA-22243	Mil Mi-8		*CCCP-22243*	*0077*		*2 IS TV2-117A*	*12000*	*Utility*		
☐ RA-22377	Mil Mi-8		*CCCP-22377*	*0077*		*2 IS TV2-117A*	*12000*	*Utility*		
☐ RA-22565	Mil Mi-8		*CCCP-22565*	*0079*		*2 IS TV2-117A*	*12000*	*Utility*		
☐ RA-22644	Mil Mi-8		*CCCP-22644*	*0080*		*2 IS TV2-117A*	*12000*	*Utility*		
☐ RA-22672	Mil Mi-8		*CCCP-22672*	*0080*		*2 IS TV2-117A*	*12000*	*Utility*		
☐ RA-22790	Mil Mi-8		*CCCP-22790*	*0083*		*2 IS TV2-117A*	*12000*	*Utility*		
☐ RA-22911	Mil Mi-8		*CCCP-22911*	*0085*		*2 IS TV2-117A*	*12000*	*Utility*		
☐ RA-22924	Mil Mi-8		*CCCP-22924*	*0085*		*2 IS TV2-117A*	*12000*	*Utility*		
☐ RA-24211	Mil Mi-8		*CCCP-24211*	*0087*		*2 IS TV2-117A*	*12000*	*Utility*		
☐ RA-24269	Mil Mi-8		*CCCP-24269*	*0087*		*2 IS TV2-117A*	*12000*	*Utility*		
☐ RA-24412	Mil Mi-8		*CCCP-24412*	*0086*		*2 IS TV2-117A*	*12000*	*Utility*		
☐ RA-24445	Mil Mi-8		*CCCP-24445*	*0086*		*2 IS TV2-117A*	*12000*	*Utility*		
☐ RA-24470	Mil Mi-8		*CCCP-24470*	*0086*		*2 IS TV2-117A*	*12000*	*Utility*		
☐ RA-24530	Mil Mi-8		*CCCP-24530*	*0085*		*2 IS TV2-117A*	*12000*	*Utility*		
☐ RA-24545	Mil Mi-8		*CCCP-24545*	*0085*		*2 IS TV2-117A*	*12000*	*Utility*		
☐ RA-24644	Mil Mi-8		*CCCP-24644*	*0081*		*2 IS TV2-117A*	*12000*	*Utility*		
☐ RA-24648	Mil Mi-8		*CCCP-24648*	*0081*		*2 IS TV2-117A*	*12000*	*Utility*		
☐ RA-24662	Mil Mi-8		*CCCP-24662*	*0081*		*2 IS TV2-117A*	*12000*	*Utility*		
☐ RA-24663	Mil Mi-8		*CCCP-24663*	*0081*		*2 IS TV2-117A*	*12000*	*Utility*		
☐ RA-24684	Mil Mi-8		*CCCP-24684*	*0081*		*2 IS TV2-117A*	*12000*	*Utility*		
☐ RA-24696	Mil Mi-8		*CCCP-24696*	*0081*		*2 IS TV2-117A*	*12000*	*Utility*		
☐ RA-24733	Mil Mi-8		*CCCP-24733*	*0084*		*2 IS TV2-117A*	*12000*	*Utility*		
☐ RA-25133	Mil Mi-8MTV-1		*CCCP-25133*	*0091*		*2 IS TV3-117MT*	*13000*	*Utility*		
☐ RA-25226	Mil Mi-8		*CCCP-25226*	*0079*		*2 IS TV2-117A*	*12000*	*Utility*		
☐ RA-25476	Mil Mi-8MTV-1		*CCCP-25476*	*0091*		*2 IS TV3-117MT*	*13000*	*Utility*		
☐ RA-25699	Mil Mi-8		*CCCP-25699*	*0073*		*2 IS TV2-117A*	*12000*	*Utility*		
☐ RA-25992	Mil Mi-8		*CCCP-25992*	*0075*		*2 IS TV2-117A*	*12000*	*Utility*		
☐ RA-25994	Mil Mi-8		*CCCP-25994*	*0075*		*2 IS TV2-117A*	*12000*	*Utility*		

SUKHOI Aviakompania = SUH (Sister company of Sukhoi Design Bureau) Moscow-Zhukovsky

Ul. Polikarpova 23a, 125284 Moskva, Russia ☎ (095) 945 55 86 Tx: none Fax: (095) 945 55 93 SITA: n/a
F: 1997 n/a Head: Fidoil B. Shagiziganov Net: n/a Operates corporate flights for itself & commercial cargo charter flights. Beside aircraft listed, also operates Antonov 12 & Yakovlev 40, full details not yet known.

☐ RA-65932	Tupolev 134A-3	*66405*	*CCCP-65932*	*0084*		*2 SO D-30-III*	*49000*	*Y76*		*lst BRZ*
☐ RA-76759	Ilyushin 76T	*093418543*	*CCCP-76759*	*1078*		*4 SO D-30KP*	*170000*	*Freighter*		*fn 1406*

SVB AOLOP Aviakompania (Severo-vostochnaya baza aviatsionnoi okhrany lesov i olen'ikh pastvishch / North East Base for Forest protection dba) Seimchany

Marchekanskoe shosse 14, 685002 Magadan, Russia ☎ (41322) 52 536 Tx: 145168 voschod Fax: (41322) 52 661 SITA: n/a
F: n/a n/a Head: Boris V. Khobta Net: n/a Most aircraft are still in Aeroflot colors but will be repainted in due course.

☐ RA-01109	PZL Mielec (Antonov) An-2		*CCCP-01109*	*0091*		*1 SH ASh-62IR*	*5500*	*Utility*		
☐ RA-01115	PZL Mielec (Antonov) An-2		*CCCP-01115*	*0091*		*1 SH ASh-62IR*	*5500*	*Utility*		
☐ RA-01116	PZL Mielec (Antonov) An-2	*1G240-57*	*CCCP-01116*	*0091*		*1 SH ASh-62IR*	*5500*	*Utility*		
☐ RA-01117	PZL Mielec (Antonov) An-2	*1G240-58*	*CCCP-01117*	*0091*		*1 SH ASh-62IR*	*5500*	*Utility*		
☐ RA-01118	PZL Mielec (Antonov) An-2	*1G240-59*	*CCCP-01118*	*0091*		*1 SH ASh-62IR*	*5500*	*Utility*		
☐ RA-01119	PZL Mielec (Antonov) An-2	*1G240-60*	*CCCP-01119*	*0091*		*1 SH ASh-62IR*	*5500*	*Utility*		
☐ RA-01973	Antonov An-2		*CCCP-01973*	*0060*		*1 SH ASh-62IR*	*5500*	*Utility*		
☐ RA-05826	PZL Mielec (Antonov) An-2		*CCCP-05826*	*0065*		*1 SH ASh-62IR*	*5500*	*Utility*		
☐ RA-13751	Antonov An-2	*111147312*	*CCCP-13751*	*0060*		*1 SH ASh-62IR*	*5500*	*Utility*		
☐ RA-33115	Antonov An-2		*CCCP-33115*	*0060*		*1 SH ASh-62IR*	*5500*	*Utility*		
☐ RA-33663	PZL Mielec (Antonov) An-2		*CCCP-33663*	*0088*		*1 SH ASh-62IR*	*5500*	*Utility*		
☐ RA-33664	PZL Mielec (Antonov) An-2		*CCCP-33664*	*0088*		*1 SH ASh-62IR*	*5500*	*Utility*		
☐ RA-62438	PZL Mielec (Antonov) An-2	*1G41-08*	*CCCP-62438*	*0063*		*1 SH ASh-62IR*	*5500*	*Utility*		
☐ RA-80000	Antonov An-2		*CCCP-80000*	*0060*		*1 SH ASh-62IR*	*5500*	*Utility*		
☐ RA-91731	PZL Mielec (Antonov) An-2		*CCCP-91731*	*0063*		*1 SH ASh-62IR*	*5500*	*Utility*		
☐ RA-98249	Antonov An-2	*19947316*	*CCCP-98249*	*0060*		*1 SH ASh-62IR*	*5500*	*Utility*		
☐ RA-22594	Mil Mi-8T		*CCCP-22594*	*0079*		*2 IS TV2-117A*	*12000*	*Utility*		
☐ RA-22862	Mil Mi-8T		*CCCP-22862*	*0084*		*2 IS TV2-117A*	*12000*	*Utility*		
☐ RA-22913	Mil Mi-8T		*CCCP-22913*	*0085*		*2 IS TV2-117A*	*12000*	*Utility*		
☐ RA-24212	Mil Mi-8T		*CCCP-24212*	*0087*		*2 IS TV2-117A*	*12000*	*Utility*		
☐ RA-24213	Mil Mi-8T		*CCCP-24213*	*0087*		*2 IS TV2-117A*	*12000*	*Utility*		
☐ RA-24474	Mil Mi-8T		*CCCP-24474*	*0086*		*2 IS TV2-117A*	*12000*	*Utility*		
☐ RA-24502	Mil Mi-8T		*CCCP-24502*	*0085*		*2 IS TV2-117A*	*12000*	*Utility*		
☐ RA-25501	Mil Mi-8MTV-1		*CCCP-25501*	*0091*		*2 IS TV3-117MT*	*13000*	*Utility*		
☐ RA-26002	Antonov 26		*CCCP-26002*	*0079*		*2 IV AI-24VT*	*24000*	*Combi*		
☐ RA-26011	Antonov 26		*CCCP-26011*	*0080*		*2 IV AI-24VT*	*24000*	*Combi*		
☐ RA-26532	Antonov 26		*CCCP-26532*	*0078*		*2 IV AI-24VT*	*24000*	*FishSurvey/Combi*		

SVERDLOVSK 2nd Air Enterprise = UKU (Vtoroe Sverdlovskoe aviapredpriatie) (formerly Aeroflot Sverdlovsk 2nd division) Ekaterinburg-Uktus

Uktus Airport, 620097 Ekaterinburg, Russia ☎ (3432) 27 32 76 Tx: n/a Fax: (3432) 60 67 37 SITA: n/a
F: n/a n/a Head: Nikolai Makhnev ICAO: PYSHMA Net: n/a Most aircraft are still in Aeroflot colors but will be repainted in due course.

☐ RA-14262	PZL Swidnik (Mil) Mi-2					*2 IS GTD-350-4*	*3550*	*Utility*		
☐ RA-14263	PZL Swidnik (Mil) Mi-2					*2 IS GTD-350-4*	*3550*	*Utility*		
☐ RA-14264	PZL Swidnik (Mil) Mi-2					*2 IS GTD-350-4*	*3550*	*Utility*		
☐ RA-14265	PZL Swidnik (Mil) Mi-2					*2 IS GTD-350-4*	*3550*	*Utility*		
☐ RA-14266	PZL Swidnik (Mil) Mi-2					*2 IS GTD-350-4*	*3550*	*Utility*		
☐ RA-14267	PZL Swidnik (Mil) Mi-2					*2 IS GTD-350-4*	*3550*	*Utility*		
☐ RA-14281	PZL Swidnik (Mil) Mi-2	*547843102*	*CCCP-14281*	*0082*		*2 IS GTD-350-4*	*3550*	*Utility*		
☐ RA-20402	PZL Swidnik (Mil) Mi-2	*549850076*	*CCCP-20402*	*0086*		*2 IS GTD-350-4*	*3550*	*Utility*		
☐ RA-20561	PZL Swidnik (Mil) Mi-2	*534632026*	*CCCP-20561*	*0076*		*2 IS GTD-350-4*	*3550*	*Utility*		
☐ RA-20701	PZL Swidnik (Mil) Mi-2	*536809080*	*CCCP-20701*	*0080*		*2 IS GTD-350-4*	*3550*	*Utility*		
☐ RA-20703	PZL Swidnik (Mil) Mi-2	*536811080*	*CCCP-20703*	*0080*		*2 IS GTD-350-4*	*3550*	*Utility*		

565 registration type of aircraft *cn/fn* *ex/ex** *mfd* *del* *powered by* *mtow kg* *configuration* *selcal* *name/fln/specialitites/remarks*

☐ RA-01413	PZL Mielec (Antonov) An-2		CCCP-01413	0078		1 SH ASh-62IR	5500	Utility		lsf Uraiavia
☐ RA-02458	PZL Mielec (Antonov) An-2		CCCP-02458	0070		1 SH ASh-62IR	5500	Utility		
☐ RA-02468	PZL Mielec (Antonov) An-2		CCCP-02468	0070		1 SH ASh-62IR	5500	Utility		
☐ RA-02825	PZL Mielec (Antonov) An-2		CCCP-02825	0065		1 SH ASh-62IR	5500	Utility		
☐ RA-07200	PZL Mielec (Antonov) An-2		CCCP-07200	0073		1 SH ASh-62IR	5500	Utility		
☐ RA-07301	PZL Mielec (Antonov) An-2		CCCP-07301	0073		1 SH ASh-62IR	5500	Utility		lsf Uraiavia
☐ RA-07331	PZL Mielec (Antonov) An-2		CCCP-07331	0073		1 SH ASh-62IR	5500	Utility		
☐ RA-07361	PZL Mielec (Antonov) An-2		CCCP-07361	0073		1 SH ASh-62IR	5500	Utility		
☐ RA-07413	PZL Mielec (Antonov) An-2		CCCP-07413	0073		1 SH ASh-62IR	5500	Utility		
☐ RA-07631	PZL Mielec (Antonov) An-2		CCCP-07631	0074		1 SH ASh-62IR	5500	Utility		
☐ RA-07633	PZL Mielec (Antonov) An-2	1G157-18	CCCP-07633	0074		1 SH ASh-62IR	5500	Utility		
☐ RA-07637	PZL Mielec (Antonov) An-2		CCCP-07637	0074		1 SH ASh-62IR	5500	Utility		
☐ RA-07738	PZL Mielec (Antonov) An-2		CCCP-07738	0074		1 SH ASh-62IR	5500	Utility		
☐ RA-07745	PZL Mielec (Antonov) An-2		CCCP-07745	0074		1 SH ASh-62IR	5500	Utility		
☐ RA-19728	PZL Mielec (Antonov) An-2		CCCP-19728	0075		1 SH ASh-62IR	5500	Utility		
☐ RA-54945	PZL Mielec (Antonov) An-2	1G187-54	CCCP-54945	0080		1 SH ASh-62IR	5500	Utility		
☐ RA-62490	PZL Mielec (Antonov) An-2		CCCP-62490	0063		1 SH ASh-62IR	5500	Utility		
☐ RA-70140	PZL Mielec (Antonov) An-2		CCCP-70140	0071		1 SH ASh-62IR	5500	Utility		
☐ RA-70243	PZL Mielec (Antonov) An-2		CCCP-70243	0072		1 SH ASh-62IR	5500	Utility		lsf Uraiavia
☐ RA-70310	PZL Mielec (Antonov) An-2		CCCP-70310	0072		1 SH ASh-62IR	5500	Utility		
☐ RA-92979	PZL Mielec (Antonov) An-2		CCCP-92979	0076		1 SH ASh-62IR	5500	Utility		
☐ RA-92981	PZL Mielec (Antonov) An-2		CCCP-92981	0076		1 SH ASh-62IR	5500	Utility		
☐ RA-28737	PZL Mielec (Antonov) An-28	1AJ007-25	CCCP-28737	0090		2 GS TVD-10B	6500	Y17		
☐ RA-28739	PZL Mielec (Antonov) An-28	1AJ008-02	CCCP-28739	0090		2 GS TVD-10B	6500	Y17		
☐ RA-22281	Mil Mi-8		CCCP-22281	0076		2 IS TV2-117A	12000	Utility		
☐ RA-22387	Mil Mi-8	5398	CCCP-22387	0076		2 IS TV2-117A	12000	Utility		
☐ RA-22449	Mil Mi-8		CCCP-22449	0075		2 IS TV2-117A	12000	Utility		
☐ RA-22557	Mil Mi-8		CCCP-22557	0079		2 IS TV2-117A	12000	Utility		
☐ RA-22632	Mil Mi-8		CCCP-22632	0080		2 IS TV2-117A	12000	Utility		
☐ RA-22692	Mil Mi-8		CCCP-22692	0080		2 IS TV2-117A	12000	Utility		
☐ RA-24493	Mil Mi-8		CCCP-24493	0086		2 IS TV2-117A	12000	Utility		
☐ RA-24517	Mil Mi-8		CCCP-24517	0085		2 IS TV2-117A	12000	Utility		
☐ RA-24576	Mil Mi-8		CCCP-24576	0088		2 IS TV2-117A	12000	Utility		
☐ RA-24587	Mil Mi-8		CCCP-24587	0088		2 IS TV2-117A	12000	Utility		
☐ RA-24588	Mil Mi-8		CCCP-24588	0088		2 IS TV2-117A	12000	Utility		
☐ RA-25396	Mil Mi-8		CCCP-25396	0082		2 IS TV2-117A	12000	Utility		
☐ RA-87224	Yakovlev 40	9841259	CCCP-87224	0079	0095	3 IV AI-25	16100	Y28		
☐ RA-88189	Yakovlev 40	9620948	CCCP-88189	0076		3 IV AI-25	16800	Y32		

TAIMYRTUR — Valek

Ul. Naberezhnaya 9/28, 663303 Norilsk, Russia ☎ (3919) 35 10 41 Tx: none Fax: (3919) 35 10 42 SITA: n/a
F: n/a ☺ n/a Head: Alexander V. Golikov Net: n/a

☐ RA-23619	PZL Swidnik (Mil) Mi-2					2 IS GTD-350-4	3550	Utility		
☐ RA-23656	PZL Swidnik (Mil) Mi-2					2 IS GTD-350-4	3550	Utility		

TANTK - Taganrogski aviatsionny NTK im. Berieva = GMB (Flying div. of Beriev Taganrog Aviation Scientific & Techn. Complex/Member of MAP Group) — Taganrog-Yuzhny

Flying division / Letny otryad, Pl. Aviatorov 1, 347927 Taganrog, Russia ☎ (86344) 49 910 Tx: 298107 beta su Fax: (86344) 41 454 SITA: n/a
F: 1988 ☺ n/a Head: S. Yusopov ICAO: BERIEV-AIR Net: n/a Operates corporate flights for itself & commercial charter flights.

☐ RA-26176	Antonov An-2	111047308	CCCP-26176	0059		1 SH ASh-62IR	5500	Combi		
☐ RA-87200	Yakovlev 40	9811956	CCCP-87200	0078		3 IV AI-25	16800	Combi		
☐ RA-26170	Antonov 26	6004	CCCP-26170	0070		2 IV AI-24VT	24000	Combi		
☐ RA-48089	Antonov 32	2510	CCCP-48089	0089		2 IV AI-20D	27000	Combi		
☐ RA-48090	Antonov 32	2601	CCCP-48090	0091		2 IV AI-20D	27000	Combi		opf UN

TATARSTAN/BUGULMA AIR ENTERPRISE = BGM (Bugulminskoe aviapredpriatie) (formerly part of Tatarstan Airlines Concern & AFL Bugulma division) — Bugulma

Bugulma Airport, 423200 Bugulma, (Republic of Tatarstan), Russia ☎ (84314) 53 700 Tx: none Fax: (84314) 52 488 SITA: n/a
F: n/a ☺ n/a Head: Peter V. Trubaev ICAO: BUGAVIA Net: n/a

☐ RA-07461	PZL Mielec (Antonov) An-2	1G151-36	CCCP-07461	1073		1 SH ASh-62IR	5500	Utility		
☐ RA-87209	Yakovlev 40K	9810657	CCCP-87209	0478		3 IV AI-25	16100	Y32		
☐ RA-87239	Yakovlev 40	9530643	CCCP-87239	0975		3 IV AI-25	16100	Y32		
☐ RA-87247	Yakovlev 40	9531543	CCCP-87247	1175		3 IV AI-25	16100	Y30		
☐ RA-87342	Yakovlev 40	9511139	CCCP-87342	0375		3 IV AI-25	16100	VIP		
☐ RA-87404	Yakovlev 40	9411633	CCCP-87404	0474		3 IV AI-25	16100	Y30		
☐ RA-87447	Yakovlev 40	9430436	CCCP-87447	0874		3 IV AI-25	16100	Y30		
☐ RA-87462	Yakovlev 40	9430137	CCCP-87462	0974		3 IV AI-25	16100	Y30		
☐ RA-87505	Yakovlev 40	9510740	CCCP-87505	0475		3 IV AI-25	16100	Y36		
☐ RA-87517	Yakovlev 40	9521940	CCCP-87517	0575		3 IV AI-25	16100	VIP		
☐ RA-87588	Yakovlev 40	9222022	CCCP-87588	0672		3 IV AI-25	16100	Y27		
☐ RA-87991	Yakovlev 40	9541544	CCCP-87991	1275		3 IV AI-25	16100	Y30		
☐ RA-88156	Yakovlev 40	9611046	CCCP-88156	0276		3 IV AI-25	16100	Y32		
☐ RA-88165	Yakovlev 40	9611946	CCCP-88165	0476		3 IV AI-25	16100	Y32		
☐ RA-88176	Yakovlev 40	9621447	CCCP-88176	0576		3 IV AI-25	16100	Y32		
☐ RA-88182	Yakovlev 40	9620248	CCCP-88182	0676		3 IV AI-25	16100	Y32		

TATARSTAN/KAZAN AIR ENTERPRISE = KAZ (Kazanskoe aviapredpriatie) (formerly part of Tatarstan Airlines Concern) — Kazan-Int'l

Kazan Airport, 420017 Kazan, (Republic of Tatarstan), Russia ☎ (8432) 37 98 29 Tx: 224121 Fax: (8432) 75 47 07 SITA: n/a
F: 1992 ☺ n/a Head: Vladimir V. Nekrashevich ICAO: AIR TATARSTAN Net: n/a

☐ RA-87977	Yakovlev 40	9321128	OK-BYH	0773	0092	3 IV AI-25	16100	VIP		
☐ RA-46526	Antonov 24RV	47310005	CCCP-46526	1274	0092	2 IV AI-24VT	22500	Y48		
☐ RA-46562	Antonov 24B	87304701	CCCP-46562	0968	0092	2 IV AI-24	22000	Y48		
☐ RA-46625	Antonov 24RV	37308804	CCCP-46625	0773	0092	2 IV AI-24VT	22500	Y48		
☐ RA-47818	Antonov 24RV	17307107	CCCP-47818	0771	0092	2 IV AI-24VT	22500	Y48		
☐ RA-26647	Antonov 26	7409	CCCP-26647	1279	0093	2 IV AI-24VT	24000	Freighter		std KZN in Aeroflot-colors
☐ RA-42332	Yakovlev 42	4520421605135	CCCP-42332	0686	0092	3 LO D-36	54000	Y120		std KZN
☐ RA-42333	Yakovlev 42	4520422606156	CCCP-42333	0486	0092	3 LO D-36	54000	Y120		lst AKT
☐ RA-42347	Yakovlev 42	4520423711322	CCCP-42347	0887	0092	3 LO D-36	54000	Y120		
☐ RA-42374	Yakovlev 42D	4520423914340	CCCP-42374	1089	0092	3 LO D-36	56500	Y120 or F16Y78		
☐ RA-42380	Yakovlev 42D	4520422014549	CCCP-42380	0490	0092	3 LO D-36	56500	Y120		
☐ RA-42433	Yakovlev 42D	4520421301017		0493	0093	3 LO D-36	56500	Y120 or F16Y78		
☐ RA-85412	Tupolev 154B-2	412	CCCP-85412	0480	0092	3 KU NK-8-2U	98000	Y164		
☐ RA-85488	Tupolev 154B-2	488	OK-LCP	0481	0193	3 KU NK-8-2U	98000	Y158 or F12Y120		
☐ RA-85804	Tupolev 154B-2	517	OK-LCS	1181	1292	3 KU NK-8-2U	100000	F8Y125		

TATARSTAN/NIZHNEKAMSK AIR ENTERPRISE = NKM (Nizhnekamskoe aviapredpriatie) (formerly part of Tatarstan Airlines Concern & AFL Nizhnekamsk div.) — Nizhnekamsk

Begishevo Airport, 423550 Nizhnekamsk, (Republic of Tatarstan), Russia ☎ (8552) 42 1102 Tx: none Fax: (8552) 42 45 88 SITA: n/a
F: n/a ☺ n/a Head: Minifayaz N. Sharipov ICAO: CHELNY Net: n/a

☐ RA-46328	Antonov 24B	97305505	CCCP-46328	0869		2 IV AI-24	22000	Y48		
☐ RA-47804	Antonov 24RV	17306903	CCCP-47804	0471		2 IV AI-24VT	22500	Y48		
☐ RA-42335	Yakovlev 42	4520422606204	CCCP-42335	0686		3 LO D-36	54000	Y120		
☐ RA-42357	Yakovlev 42	4520422811408	CCCP-42357	0588		3 LO D-36	54000	Y120		

TATNEFTAERO = TNF — Kazan

Ul. Mushtary 9B, 420012 Kazan, (Republic of Tatarstan), Russia ☎ (8432) 38 09 88 Tx: none Fax: (8432) 38 09 69 SITA: n/a
F: 1998 ☺ n/a Head: Nail G. Akhmetshin ICAO: TATNEFT Net: n/a

☐ RA-85798	Tupolev 154M	982		0194	0098	3 SO D-30KU-154-II	100000	Y160		

TAVIA-Taganrog Aviation = TGR (Taganrogskaya aviatsia) — Taganrog

Pl. Aviatorov 1, 347928 Taganrog, (Rostov Region), Russia ☎ (86344) 49 438 Tx: 298142 bereg Fax: (86344) 41 752 SITA: n/a
F: 1995 ☺ n/a Head: Ivan S. Semchenko ICAO: TAVIA Net: n/a

☐ RA-46419	Antonov 24B	87303704	CCCP-46419	0068	0095	2 IV AI-24	21000	Y48		
☐ RA-46491	Antonov 24RV	27308204	CCCP-46491	0072	0095	2 IV AI-24VT	21800	Y48		
☐ RA-26195	Antonov 26	5210	CCCP-26195	0077	0095	2 IV AI-24VT	24000	Combi Y19		

TESIS, Ltd = UZ / TIS — Moscow-Domodedovo

Ul. Profsoyuznaya 93a, Room 406, 117858 Moskva, Russia ☎ (095) 330 09 60 Tx: none Fax: (095) 335 51 11 SITA: n/a
F: n/a ☺ n/a Head: Boris Panukov IATA: 246 ICAO: TESIS Net: n/a Beside aircraft listed, leases additional Ilyushin 76 from other companies when required.

☐ RA-76791	Ilyushin 76TD	0093497936	CCCP-76791	0089	0096	4 SO D-30KP-2	190000	Freighter		lsf Samara Airlines

TITAN CARGO = TIT (Titan Aircompany, Ltd dba) — Ulyanovsk-Vostochny

Ul. Barrikadnaya 8/5, 123242 Moskva, Russia ☎ (095) 254 83 22 Tx: none Fax: (095) 254 88 72 SITA: MOWTCXH
F: 1995 ☺ n/a Head: Igor N. Koshel ICAO: TITAVIA Net: n/a

☐ RA-82003	Antonov 124-100 Ruslan	19530502792	UR-UAP	0094	0095	4 LO D-18T	392000	Freighter		fn 03-02
☐ RA-82074	Antonov 124-100 Ruslan	9773051459142		0094	0095	4 LO D-18T	392000	Freighter		fn 07-07

566 registration type of aircraft cn/fn ex/ex* mfd del powered by mtow kg configuration selcal name/fln/specialitites/remarks

TOMSK AIR ENTERPRISE = TSK (Tomskoe aviapredpriatie) (formerly Aeroflot Tomsk division) — Tomsk

Tomsk Airport, 634011 Tomsk, Russia ☎ (3822) 44 35 75 Tx: none Fax: (3822) 44 61 27 SITA: n/a
F: n/a ⁂ n/a Head: Yuri A. Prokopiev ICAO: TOMSK-AVIA Net: n/a Beside aircraft listed, owns 17 Antonov 2 but all are stored and for sale. Most aircraft are still in Aeroflot colors but will be repainted in due course.

registration	type of aircraft	cn/fn	ex/ex*	mfd	del	powered by	mtow kg	configuration	selcal	name/fln/specialitites/remarks
☐ RA-46627	Antonov 24RV		CCCP-46627	0073		2 IV AI-24VT	21800	Y48		
☐ RA-46679	Antonov 24RV		CCCP-46679	0074		2 IV AI-24VT	21800	Y48		
☐ RA-47254	Antonov 24RV		CCCP-47254	0072		2 IV AI-24VT	21800	Y48		
☐ RA-47255	Antonov 24RV		CCCP-47255	0072		2 IV AI-24VT	21800	Y48		
☐ RA-47355	Antonov 24RV		CCCP-47355	0076		2 IV AI-24VT	21800	Y48		
☐ RA-47826	Antonov 24B	17307207	CCCP-47826	0071		2 IV AI-24	21000	Y48		
☐ RA-26039	Antonov 26B		CCCP-26039	0080		2 IV AI-24VT	24000	Freighter		
☐ RA-26518	Antonov 26		CCCP-26518	0078		2 IV AI-24VT	24000	Freighter		
☐ RA-26566	Antonov 26		CCCP-26566	0075		2 IV AI-24VT	24000	Freighter		
☐ RA-26589	Antonov 26B		CCCP-26589	0083		2 IV AI-24VT	24000	Freighter		
☐ RA-26688	Antonov 26		CCCP-26688	0079		2 IV AI-24VT	24000	Freighter		
☐ RA-85763	Tupolev 154M	946		0193		3 SO D-30KU-154-II	100000	Y166		lst OMS -1099

TOMSKNEFT, Joint-Stock Company = TMO — Tomsk

Ul. Burovikov 23, 636762 Strezhvoy, (Tomsk Region), Russia ☎ (38259) 32 171 Tx: none Fax: (38259) 34 389 SITA: n/a
F: 1994 ⁂ n/a Head: Leonid I. Filimonov ICAO: TOMSK-OIL Net: n/a

registration	type of aircraft	cn/fn	ex/ex*	mfd	del	powered by	mtow kg	configuration	selcal	name/fln/specialitites/remarks
☐ RA-02800	Hawker 700B (HS 125-700B)	257007	G-BUNL	0077		2 GA TFE731-3R-1H	11567	Executive		

TRANSAERO AIRLINES, Joint-Stock Company = UN / TSO — Moscow-Sheremetyevo

Sheremetyevo I Airport, GosNII GA, Building 3, 103340 Moscow, Russia ☎ (095) 578 50 38 Tx: none Fax: (095) 578 86 88 SITA: n/a
F: 1990 ⁂ 2200 Head: Nikolai V. Kozhevnikov IATA: 670 ICAO: TRANSERO Net: http://www.transaero.ru

registration	type of aircraft	cn/fn	ex/ex*	mfd	del	powered by	mtow kg	configuration	selcal	name/fln/specialitites/remarks
☐ EI-CLN	Boeing 737-2C9 (A)	21443 / 501	RA-73000	0077	0393	2 PW JT8D-15	52204	CY100		lsf IAS Group
☐ EI-CLO	Boeing 737-2C9 (A)	21444 / 516	RA-73001	0078	0393	2 PW JT8D-15	54204	CY100		lsf IAS Group
☐ YL-BAA	Boeing 737-236 (A)	22028 / 656	G-BGJG	0080	0494	2 PW JT8D-15A	54204	CY100		lsf Finavion SA
☐ YL-BAB	Boeing 737-236 (A)	22032 / 742	G-BGJK	0081	0694	2 PW JT8D-15A	54204	CY100		lsf Finavion SA
☐ YL-BAC	Boeing 737-236 (A)	22034 / 751	G-BGJM	0081	0395	2 PW JT8D-15A	54204	CY100		lsf Finavion SA
☐ N100UN	Boeing 737-7K9	28088 / 19		0098	0598	2 CFMI CFM56-7B24	69400	CY122	JP-KS	lsf BAVA
☐ N101UN	Boeing 737-7K9	28089 / 25		0098	0698	2 CFMI CFM56-7B24	69400	CY122		lsf BAVA
☐ N601LF	Boeing 767-3Q8 (ER)	28206 / 694		0398	0398	2 GE CF6-80C2B6F	186880	CY221		lsf ILFC
☐ RA-86123	Ilyushin 86	51483210091	CCCP-86123	0092	0092	4 KU NK-86	215000	CY255		Moskva

TRANSAERO-EXPRESS, Inc. = TXE (Sister company of Transaero Airlines) — Moscow-Sheremetyevo

Ul. Babakina 5a, 141400 Khimki, (Moscow Region), Russia ☎ (095) 575 00 03 Tx: none Fax: (095) 571 11 60 SITA: n/a
F: 1994 ⁂ n/a Head: Vasili M. Vysotsky ICAO: TAXI Net: n/a

registration	type of aircraft	cn/fn	ex/ex*	mfd	del	powered by	mtow kg	configuration	selcal	name/fln/specialitites/remarks
☐ RA-65830	Tupolev 134A-3	12093	CCCP-65830	0074	0096	2 SO D-30-III	47000	VIP 38 Pax		

TRANS AERO-SAMARA Aviakompania = TSL (Trans Aero-Samara Airlines, Ltd) — Samara-Bezymyanka

Smyshlyaevskoe shosse 1A, 443050 Samara, Russia ☎ (8462) 58 60 90 Tx: 214434 kvant Fax: (8462) 58 61 55 SITA: n/a
F: 1992 ⁂ n/a Head: Vladimir M. Ptashinkiy ICAO: AVIALUCH Net: n/a

registration	type of aircraft	cn/fn	ex/ex*	mfd	del	powered by	mtow kg	configuration	selcal	name/fln/specialitites/remarks
☐ RA-87380	Yakovlev 40		CCCP-87380	0074		3 IV AI-25	16800	Y32		
☐ RA-11363	Antonov 12B		CCCP-11363			4 IV AI-20M	61000	Freighter		
☐ RA-11962	Antonov 12BP		CCCP-11962			4 IV AI-20M	61000	Freighter		
☐ RA-76381	Ilyushin 76TD			0093		4 SO D-30KP	190000	Freighter		
☐ RA-76817	Ilyushin 76TD	1023412387	CCCP-76817	0092		4 SO D-30KP	190000	Freighter		

TRANS-CHARTER Airlines = TCH — Moscow-Bykovo / -Domodedovo & Ulyanovsk

Leningradsky prospekt 37, Room 1209, 125836 Moskva, Russia ☎ (095) 155 68 75 Tx: 411182 afl su Fax: (095) 232 29 56 SITA: n/a
F: 1994 ⁂ 160 Head: Vladimir F. Samokhvalov ICAO: TRANS-CHARTER Net: n/a Beside aircraft listed, also leases Tupolev 154M from Murmansk Airlines when required.

registration	type of aircraft	cn/fn	ex/ex*	mfd	del	powered by	mtow kg	configuration	selcal	name/fln/specialitites/remarks
☐ RA-48014	Antonov 32B	3401		0093	0096	2 IV AI-20D	27000	Freighter		
☐ RA-48076	Antonov 32B	3110		0092	0094	2 IV AI-20D	27000	Freighter		
☐ RA-48979	Antonov 32	1409	CCCP-48979	1287	0096	2 IV AI-20D	27000	Freighter		lsf KNM
☐ RA-69309	Antonov 32	1605	CCCP-69309	0588	0096	2 IV AI-20D	27000	Freighter		lsf KMPO
☐ RA-65099	Tupolev 134A	63700	CCCP-65099	0078	0097	2 SO D-30-II	47600	Executive		opf Stolichny Savings Bank

TRANSEUROPEAN AIRLINES = UE / TEP — Moscow-Sheremetyevo

Ul. Seleznevskaya 11A, 101485 Moskva, Russia ☎ (095) 973 08 00 Tx: none Fax: (095) 973 06 25 SITA: n/a
F: 1996 ⁂ n/a Head: Artur R. Tsomaya ICAO: TRANSEURLINE Net: n/a

registration	type of aircraft	cn/fn	ex/ex*	mfd	del	powered by	mtow kg	configuration	selcal	name/fln/specialitites/remarks
☐ RA-85630	Tupolev 154M	759	CCCP-85630	0087	0098	3 SO D-30KU-154-II	100000	F12Y120		lsf SDM

TRETYAKOVO Air Transport company = TKO (Aviatransportnaya kompania Tretyakovo) — Lukhovitsy

Leningradsky prospekt 37/1, room 520, 101977 Moskva, Russia ☎ (095) 928 26 38 Tx: none Fax: (095) 155 53 07 SITA: n/a
F: 1997 ⁂ n/a Head: Yevgeni F. Brezgin ICAO: TRETYAKOVO Net: n/a Operates cargo flight with Antonov 26 freighter aircraft. Full details not yet known.

TSENTROSPAS (Division of MCHS-Ministry for Emergency Situations) — Moscow-Zhukovsky

Ul. Narkomvod 8, 140160 Zhukovsky, (Moscow Region), Russia ☎ (095) 556 27 65 Tx: none Fax: (095) 913 72 90 SITA: n/a
F: n/a ⁂ n/a Head: Andrei D. Legoshin Net: n/a

registration	type of aircraft	cn/fn	ex/ex*	mfd	del	powered by	mtow kg	configuration	selcal	name/fln/specialitites/remarks
☐ 903	Eurocopter (MBB) BO105CBS-5SF	S-903		0095	0095	2 AN 250-C20B	2500	EMS / SAR		
☐ 910	Eurocopter (MBB) BO105CBS-5SF	S-903		0095	0095	2 AN 250-C20B	2500	EMS / SAR		
☐ 912	Eurocopter (MBB) BO105CBS-5SF	S-912		0095	0095	2 AN 250-C20B	2500	EMS / SAR		
☐ RA-27181	Mil Mi-8MTV-1			0093	0093	2 IS TV3-117MT	13000	EMS / SAR		

TSKB SPK - Tsentr.KB po sudam na podvodnykh krylyakh im.Alekseyeva ATP (Flying div.of Hydroplane Centr.Design Bureau/Member of MAP Group) — Nizhny Novgorod

Flying division / Letny otryad, Ul. Svobody 51, 603003 Nizhny Novgorod, Russia ☎ (8312) 25 10 37 Tx: 151348 krylo Fax: (8312) 25 02 48 SITA: n/a
F: n/a ⁂ n/a Head: I.M. Vasilevsky Net: n/a Operates corporate flights for itself only & commercial charter flights.

registration	type of aircraft	cn/fn	ex/ex*	mfd	del	powered by	mtow kg	configuration	selcal	name/fln/specialitites/remarks
☐ RA-26210	Antonov 26B	14301	CCCP-26210	0085		2 IV AI-24VT	24000	Combi		

TULA AIR ENTERPRISE (Tulskoe aviapredpriatie) (formerly part of Central Districts Airlines & Aeroflot Tula division) — Tula

Tula Airport, 300038 Tula, Russia ☎ (0872) 77 59 41 Tx: none Fax: (0872) 77 40 20 SITA: n/a
F: n/a ⁂ n/a Head: Vladimir S. Alyoshin Net: n/a Most aircraft are still in Aeroflot colors but will be repainted in due course.

registration	type of aircraft	cn/fn	ex/ex*	mfd	del	powered by	mtow kg	configuration	selcal	name/fln/specialitites/remarks
☐ RA-46303	Antonov 24B	97305203	CCCP-46303	0069		2 IV AI-24	21000	Y48		
☐ RA-46329	Antonov 24B	97305506	CCCP-46329	0069		2 IV AI-24	21000	Y48		
☐ RA-46347	Antonov 24B	97305706	CCCP-46347	0069		2 IV AI-24	21000	Y48		
☐ RA-46587	Antonov 24B	97305007	CCCP-46587	0069		2 IV AI-24	21000	Y48		
☐ RA-26121	Antonov 26B	12305	CCCP-26121	0082		2 IV AI-24VT	24000	Freighter		
☐ RA-26125	Antonov 26B	12603	OB-1348	0083		2 IV AI-24VT	24000	Freighter		

TULPAR Aviation Company = TUL (formerly TAN Aviakompania) — Kazan-Int'l

Prospekt Pobedy 15, Box 147, 420138 Kazan, (Republic of Tatarstan), Russia ☎ (8432) 35 64 34 Tx: none Fax: (8432) 35 64 44 SITA: n/a
F: 1991 ⁂ 40 Head: Magomed B. Zakarzhaev ICAO: URSAL Net: n/a

registration	type of aircraft	cn/fn	ex/ex*	mfd	del	powered by	mtow kg	configuration	selcal	name/fln/specialitites/remarks
☐ RA-87496	Yakovlev 40	9541945	CCCP-87496	0176	0098	3 IV AI-25	16800	Y32		lsf VLA
☐ RA-87503	Yakovlev 40	9520240	CCCP-87503	0675	0093	3 IV AI-25	17200	C14		
☐ RA-87938	Yakovlev 40K	9710153	CCCP-87938	0477	0097	3 IV AI-25	17200	Y30		
☐ RA-87966	Yakovlev 40	9820958	CCCP-87966	0678	0097	3 IV AI-25	17200	C18		
☐ RA-88287	Yakovlev 40K	9130360	CCCP-88287	1081	0098	3 IV AI-25	17200	C19		
☐ RA-98109	Yakovlev 40K	9740956	CCCP-98109	1177	0097	3 IV AI-25	17200	Y32		
☐ RA-26060	Antonov 26B	11107	CCCP-26060	0581	0098	2 IV AI-24VT	24000	Freighter		lsf KPH
☐ RA-42425	Yakovlev 42D	4520423303016	EP-LAH	0393	0095	3 LO D-36	57500	Y120		

TUPOLEV-AEROTRANS = TUP (Subsidiary of Tupolev Design Bureau) — Moscow-Zhukovsky

Ul. Tupoleva, 140160 Zhukovsky, (Moscow Region), Russia ☎ (095) 556 73 50 Tx: none Fax: (095) 556 51 75 SITA: n/a
F: n/a ⁂ n/a Head: Grigori I. Litinski ICAO: TUPOLEV AIR Net: n/a Most aircraft are still in Aeroflot colors without titles.

registration	type of aircraft	cn/fn	ex/ex*	mfd	del	powered by	mtow kg	configuration	selcal	name/fln/specialitites/remarks
☐ RA-65667	Tupolev 134A-3	1351207	CCCP-65667	0071		2 SO D-30-III	49000	Y72		
☐ RA-65720	Tupolev 134B-3	62820	CCCP-65720	0081		2 SO D-30-III	49000	Y72		
☐ RA-65966	Tupolev 134A-3	3351902	CCCP-65966	0073		2 SO D-30-III	49000	Y76		
☐ RA-85523	Tupolev 154B-2	523	CCCP-85523	0082		3 KU NK-8-2U	98000	Y164		
☐ RA-85627	Tupolev 154M	756	CCCP-85627	0087		3 SO D-30KU-154-II	100000	Y164		
☐ RA-76388	Ilyushin 76TD	1013406204		0391		4 SO D-30KP	190000	Freighter		
☐ RA-76389	Ilyushin 76MD	1013407212	RA-78852	0091		4 SO D-30KP	190000	Freighter		lst DOB

TURA AIR ENTERPRISE (Turinskoe aviapredpriatie) (formerly Aeroflot Tura division) — Tura

Ul. Gagarina 2, 663370 Tura, (Krasnoyarsk Region), Russia ☎ (39113) 22 230 Tx: none Fax: (39113) 22 230 SITA: n/a
F: n/a ⁂ n/a Head: Nikolay D. Fatyanov Net: n/a Most aircraft are still in Aeroflot colors but will be repainted in due course.

registration	type of aircraft	cn/fn	ex/ex*	mfd	del	powered by	mtow kg	configuration	selcal	name/fln/specialitites/remarks
☐ RA-07875	PZL Mielec (Antonov) An-2		CCCP-07875	0076		1 SH ASh-62IR	5500	Utility		
☐ RA-32691	PZL Mielec (Antonov) An-2		CCCP-32691	0085		1 SH ASh-62IR	5500	Utility		
☐ RA-40688	PZL Mielec (Antonov) An-2		CCCP-40688	0086		1 SH ASh-62IR	5500	Utility		
☐ RA-40857	PZL Mielec (Antonov) An-2		CCCP-40857	0077		1 SH ASh-62IR	5500	Utility		
☐ RA-70332	PZL Mielec (Antonov) An-2		CCCP-70332	0072		1 SH ASh-62IR	5500	Utility		
☐ RA-22363	Mil Mi-8		CCCP-22363	0077		2 IS TV2-117A	12000	Utility		
☐ RA-22381	Mil Mi-8		CCCP-22381	0077		2 IS TV2-117A	12000	Utility		

registration	type of aircraft	cn/fn	ex/ex*	mfd/del	powered by	mtow kg	configuration	selcal	name/fln/specialitites/remarks
☐ RA-22566	Mil Mi-8		CCCP-22566	0079	2 IS TV2-117A	12000	Utility		
☐ RA-22736	Mil Mi-8		CCCP-22736	0083	2 IS TV2-117A	12000	Utility		
☐ RA-22793	Mil Mi-8		CCCP-22793	0083	2 IS TV2-117A	12000	Utility		
☐ RA-22893	Mil Mi-8		CCCP-22893	0084	2 IS TV2-117A	12000	Utility		
☐ RA-24512	Mil Mi-8		CCCP-24512	0085	2 IS TV2-117A	12000	Utility		
☐ RA-24549	Mil Mi-8		CCCP-24549	0085	2 IS TV2-117A	12000	Utility		
☐ RA-25327	Mil Mi-8		CCCP-25327	0082	2 IS TV2-117A	12000	Utility		
☐ RA-25521	Mil Mi-8AMT		CCCP-25521	0092	2 IS TV3-117MT	13000	Utility		
☐ RA-25987	Mil Mi-8		CCCP-25987	0077	2 IS TV2-117A	12000	Utility		
☐ RA-27177	Mil Mi-8AMT			0093	2 IS TV3-117MT	13000	Utility		
☐ RA-27178	Mil Mi-8AMT			0093	2 IS TV3-117MT	13000	Utility		

TURUKHANSK AIR ENTERPRISE (Turukhanskoe aviapredpriatie) (formerly Aeroflot Turukhansk division)   Turukhansk

Ul. Portovaya 1, 663180 Turukhansk, (Krasnoyarsk Region), Russia ☎ (38382) 44 138 Tx: none Fax: (3912) 26 32 39 SITA: n/a
F: 1976 ♠♠♠ n/a Head: Nikolai A. Nikiforov Net: n/a Most aircraft are still in Aeroflot colors but will be repainted in due course.

registration	type of aircraft	cn/fn	ex/ex*	mfd/del	powered by	mtow kg	configuration	selcal	name/fln/specialitites/remarks
☐ RA-01462	PZL Mielec (Antonov) An-2	1G231-53	CCCP-01462	0088	1 SH ASh-62IR	5500	Utility		
☐ RA-07504	PZL Mielec (Antonov) An-2	1G152-32	CCCP-07504	0073	1 SH ASh-62IR	5500	Utility		
☐ RA-07881	PZL Mielec (Antonov) An-2	1G170-40	CCCP-07881	0076	1 SH ASh-62IR	5500	Utility		
☐ RA-07882	PZL Mielec (Antonov) An-2	1G170-41	CCCP-07882	0076	1 SH ASh-62IR	5500	Utility		
☐ RA-32436	PZL Mielec (Antonov) An-2	1G101-17	CCCP-32436	0068	1 SH ASh-62IR	5500	Utility		
☐ RA-33380	PZL Mielec (Antonov) An-2	1G226-39	CCCP-33380	0087	1 SH ASh-62IR	5500	Utility		
☐ RA-40232	PZL Mielec (Antonov) An-2	1G220-22	CCCP-40232	0086	1 SH ASh-62IR	5500	Utility		
☐ RA-50586	PZL Mielec (Antonov) An-2	1G131-28	CCCP-50586	0071	1 SH ASh-62IR	5500	Utility		
☐ RA-62576	PZL Mielec (Antonov) An-2	1G176-45	CCCP-62576	0077	1 SH ASh-62IR	5500	Utility		
☐ RA-70757	PZL Mielec (Antonov) An-2	1G132-12	CCCP-70757	0071	1 SH ASh-62IR	5500	Utility		
☐ RA-22682	Mil Mi-8	8140	CCCP-22682	0080	2 IS TV2-117A	12000	Utility		
☐ RA-22685	Mil Mi-8	8143	CCCP-22685	0080	2 IS TV2-117A	12000	Utility		
☐ RA-22697	Mil Mi-8	8156	CCCP-22697	0080	2 IS TV2-117A	12000	Utility		
☐ RA-22700	Mil Mi-8	9721617	CCCP-22700	0083	2 IS TV2-117A	12000	Utility		
☐ RA-22778	Mil Mi-8	98311800	CCCP-22778	0083	2 IS TV2-117A	12000	Utility		
☐ RA-22825	Mil Mi-8	7625	CCCP-22825	0078	2 IS TV2-117A	12000	Utility		
☐ RA-24285	Mil Mi-8	98734433	CCCP-24285	0087	2 IS TV2-117A	12000	Utility		
☐ RA-24441	Mil Mi-8	98625989	CCCP-24441	0086	2 IS TV2-117A	12000	Utility		
☐ RA-24519	Mil Mi-8	98522095	CCCP-24519	0085	2 IS TV2-117A	12000	Utility		
☐ RA-24689	Mil Mi-8	9815749	CCCP-24689	0081	2 IS TV2-117A	12000	Utility		
☐ RA-25361	Mil Mi-8	98206821	CCCP-25361	0082	2 IS TV2-117A	12000	Utility		

TUVA AIRLINES (Tuvinskie avialinii) (formerly Aeroflot Kyzyl division)   Kyzyl

Kyzyl Airport, 667008 Kyzyl, (Republic of Tuva), Russia ☎ (39422) 30 025 Tx: none Fax: (39422) 30 025 SITA: n/a
F: n/a ♠♠♠ n/a Head: Vladimir G. Muzalev Net: n/a Most aircraft are still in Aeroflot colors but will be repainted in due course.

registration	type of aircraft	cn/fn	ex/ex*	mfd/del	powered by	mtow kg	configuration	selcal	name/fln/specialitites/remarks
☐ RA-07179	PZL Mielec (Antonov) An-2		CCCP-07179	0073	1 SH ASh-62IR	5500	Utility		
☐ RA-07299	PZL Mielec (Antonov) An-2		CCCP-07299	0073	1 SH ASh-62IR	5500	Utility		
☐ RA-07308	PZL Mielec (Antonov) An-2		CCCP-07308	0073	1 SH ASh-62IR	5500	Utility		
☐ RA-07491	PZL Mielec (Antonov) An-2		CCCP-07491	0073	1 SH ASh-62IR	5500	Utility		
☐ RA-17771	PZL Mielec (Antonov) An-2		CCCP-17771	0083	1 SH ASh-62IR	5500	Utility		
☐ RA-33035	PZL Mielec (Antonov) An-2		CCCP-33035	0086	1 SH ASh-62IR	5500	Utility		
☐ RA-35060	PZL Mielec (Antonov) An-2		CCCP-35060	0069	1 SH ASh-62IR	5500	Utility		
☐ RA-40425	PZL Mielec (Antonov) An-2		CCCP-40425	0087	1 SH ASh-62IR	5500	Utility		
☐ RA-68098	PZL Mielec (Antonov) An-2		CCCP-68098	0081	1 SH ASh-62IR	5500	Utility		
☐ RA-70812	PZL Mielec (Antonov) An-2		CCCP-70812	0071	1 SH ASh-62IR	5500	Utility		
☐ RA-67609	Let 410UVP-E	892335	CCCP-67609	0089	2 WA M-601E	6400	Y19		
☐ RA-67610	Let 410UVP-E	892336	CCCP-67610	0089	2 WA M-601E	6400	Y19		
☐ RA-67631	Let 410UVP-E	902424	CCCP-67631	0090	2 WA M-601E	6400	Y19		
☐ RA-67632	Let 410UVP-E	902425	CCCP-67632	0090	2 WA M-601E	6400	Y19		
☐ RA-22727	Mil Mi-8		CCCP-22727	0083	2 IS TV2-117A	12000	Utility		
☐ RA-22849	Mil Mi-8T		CCCP-22849	0078	2 IS TV2-117A	12000	Utility		
☐ RA-24614	Mil Mi-8		CCCP-24614	0081	2 IS TV2-117A	12000	Utility		
☐ RA-24711	Mil Mi-8		CCCP-24711	0084	2 IS TV2-117A	12000	Utility		
☐ RA-25906	Mil Mi-8		CCCP-25906	0075	2 IS TV2-117A	12000	Utility		
☐ RA-87425	Yakovlev 40		CCCP-87425	0074	3 IV AI-25	16800	Y32		
☐ RA-87443	Yakovlev 40		CCCP-87443	0074	3 IV AI-25	16800	Y32		
☐ RA-87476	Yakovlev 40		CCCP-87476	0074	3 IV AI-25	16800	Y32		
☐ RA-87477	Yakovlev 40		CCCP-87477	0074	3 IV AI-25	16800	Y32		
☐ RA-87495	Yakovlev 40		CCCP-87495	0075	3 IV AI-25	16800	Y32		
☐ RA-87519	Yakovlev 40		CCCP-87519	0075	3 IV AI-25	16800	Y32		
☐ RA-87915	Yakovlev 40	9730455	CCCP-87915	0077	3 IV AI-25	16800	Y32		
☐ RA-87925	Yakovlev 40	9731655	CCCP-87925	0077	3 IV AI-25	16800	Y32		
☐ RA-88212	Yakovlev 40	9631849	CCCP-88212	0076	3 IV AI-25	16800	Y32		

TVER AIR ENTERPRISE (Tverskoe aviapredpriatie) (formerly Aeroflot Tver division)   Tver-Zmeyevo

Zmeyevo Airport, 170007 Tver, Russia ☎ (0822) 31 23 91 Tx: none Fax: (0822) 31 23 63 SITA: n/a
F: n/a ♠♠♠ n/a Head: Viktor A. Volkov Net: n/a Most aircraft are still in Aeroflot colors but will be repainted in due course.

registration	type of aircraft	cn/fn	ex/ex*	mfd/del	powered by	mtow kg	configuration	selcal	name/fln/specialitites/remarks
☐ RA-15293	PZL Swidnik (Mil) Mi-2	525750098	CCCP-15293	0078	2 IS GTD-350-4	3550	Utility		
☐ RA-20110	PZL Swidnik (Mil) Mi-2	543011053	CCCP-20110	0073	2 IS GTD-350-4	3550	Utility		
☐ RA-20674	PZL Swidnik (Mil) Mi-2	526637050	CCCP-20674	0080	2 IS GTD-350-4	3550	Utility		
☐ RA-23286	PZL Swidnik (Mil) Mi-2	529107025	CCCP-23286	0085	2 IS GTD-350-4	3550	Utility		
☐ RA-23601	PZL Swidnik (Mil) Mi-2				2 IS GTD-350-4	3550	Utility		
☐ RA-23766	PZL Swidnik (Mil) Mi-2				2 IS GTD-350-4	3550	Utility		
☐ RA-17780	PZL Mielec (Antonov) An-2		CCCP-17780	0083	1 SH ASh-62IR	5500	Utility		
☐ RA-17809	PZL Mielec (Antonov) An-2	1G204-10	CCCP-17809	0083	1 SH ASh-62IR	5500	Utility		
☐ RA-17885	PZL Mielec (Antonov) An-2	1G205-26	CCCP-17885	0083	1 SH ASh-62IR	5500	Utility		
☐ RA-17903	PZL Mielec (Antonov) An-2	1G205-44	CCCP-17903	0083	1 SH ASh-62IR	5500	Utility		
☐ RA-17964	PZL Mielec (Antonov) An-2	1G209-49	CCCP-17964	0084	1 SH ASh-62IR	5500	Utility		
☐ RA-32302	PZL Mielec (Antonov) An-2		CCCP-32302	0068	1 SH ASh-62IR	5500	Utility		
☐ RA-32380	PZL Mielec (Antonov) An-2	1G100-31	CCCP-32380	0068	1 SH ASh-62IR	5500	Utility		
☐ RA-33335	PZL Mielec (Antonov) An-2		CCCP-33335	0087	1 SH ASh-62IR	5500	Utility		
☐ RA-40341	PZL Mielec (Antonov) An-2		CCCP-40341	0086	1 SH ASh-62IR	5500	Utility		
☐ RA-43957	PZL Mielec (Antonov) An-2		CCCP-43957	0084	1 SH ASh-62IR	5500	Utility		

223rd FLIGHT UNIT, State Airlines = CHD (223 letny otrayd)   Moscow-Chkalovskaya

Chkalovskaya Airport, 141100 Stchelkovo 10, (Moscow Region), Russia ☎ (095) 584 29 43 Tx: n/a Fax: (095) 584 29 19 SITA: n/a
F: n/a ♠♠♠ n/a Head: Ardalyon V. Pavlov ICAO: CHKALOVSK-AVIA Net: n/a Operates non-commercial transport flights but aircraft listed are also available for commercial leasing/operating on behalf of other Russian companies.
All aircraft are in former Aeroflot colors including Aeroflot titles.

registration	type of aircraft	cn/fn	ex/ex*	mfd/del	powered by	mtow kg	configuration	selcal	name/fln/specialitites/remarks
☐ RA-46824	Antonov 24B		CCCP-46824	0071	2 IV AI-24	21000	Y48		
☐ RA-47707	Antonov 24B		CCCP-47707	0065	2 IV AI-24	21000	Y48		
☐ RA-47794	Antonov 24B	09902208	CCCP-47794	0070	2 IV AI-24	21000	Y48		
☐ RA-47797	Antonov 24B		CCCP-47797	0066	2 IV AI-24	21000	Y48		
☐ RA-47798	Antonov 24B		CCCP-47798	0066	2 IV AI-24	21000	Y48		
☐ RA-72928	Antonov 72		CCCP-72928	0089	2 LO D-36	34500	Freighter		
☐ RA-72929	Antonov 72		CCCP-72929	0089	2 LO D-36	34500	Freighter		
☐ RA-72940	Antonov 72		CCCP-72940	0090	2 LO D-36	34500	Freighter		
☐ RA-72963	Antonov 72		CCCP-72963	0090	2 LO D-36	34500	Freighter		
☐ RA-65679	Tupolev 134A	23249	CCCP-65679	0075	2 SO D-30-II	47000	C44		lst AYZ
☐ RA-65680	Tupolev 134A-3	49020	680 BLACK	0076	2 SO D-30-III	47000	C44		lst AYZ
☐ RA-65681	Tupolev 134A-3	49760	CCCP-65681	0077	2 SO D-30-III	47000	C44		lst AYZ
☐ RA-65689	Tupolev 134A	62655	CCCP-65689	0072	2 SO D-30-II	49000	VIP		
☐ RA-65690	Tupolev 134A	62805	CCCP-65690	0070	2 SO D-30-II	49000	VIP		
☐ RA-65962	Tupolev 134A-3	3351901	CCCP-65962	0073	2 SO D-30-III	49000	Y76		
☐ RA-65979	Tupolev 134A	63158	CCCP-65979	0080	2 SO D-30-II	49000	VIP		
☐ RA-65982	Tupolev 134A-3	63315	CCCP-65982	0081	2 SO D-30-III	49000	Y76		
☐ RA-65984	Tupolev 134A	63400	CCCP-65984	0081	2 SO D-30-II	49000	Y76		
☐ RA-65986	Tupolev 134A	63475	CCCP-65986	0081	2 SO D-30-II	49000	Y76		
☐ RA-65987	Tupolev 134A-3	63505	CCCP-65987	0081	2 SO D-30-III	49000	VIP		
☐ RA-65988	Tupolev 134A	63550	CCCP-65988	0081	2 SO D-30-II	49000	Y76		
☐ RA-65989	Tupolev 134A	63605	CCCP-65989	0081	2 SO D-30-II	49000	Y76		
☐ RA-65990	Tupolev 134A	63690	CCCP-65990	0081	2 SO D-30-II	49000	Y76		
☐ RA-65991	Tupolev 134A	63845	CCCP-65991	0081	2 SO D-30-II	49000	Y76		
☐ RA-65992	Tupolev 134A	63850	CCCP-65992	0081	2 SO D-30-II	49000	Y76		
☐ RA-65996	Tupolev 134A-3		CCCP-65996	0081	2 SO D-30-II	49000	Y76		
☐ RA-74295	Ilyushin 18D	187010602	CCCP-74295	0068	4 IV AI-20M	61000	Y80		lst AYZ
☐ RA-75478	Ilyushin 18D	189011302	CCCP-75478	0069	4 IV AI-20M	61000	Y80		

registration	type of aircraft	cn/fn	ex/ex*	mfd	del	powered by	mtow kg	configuration	selcal	name/fln/specialitites/remarks
RA-75496	Ilyushin 18D	185011303	CCCP-75496	0065		4 IV AI-20M	61000	Y80		lst AYZ
RA-75498	Ilyushin 18D	187009804	CCCP-75498	0067		4 IV AI-20M	61000	Y100		
RA-75499	Ilyushin 18D	188011004	CCCP-75499	0068		4 IV AI-20M	61000	Y80		lst AYZ
RA-75602	Ilyushin 18V	182004203	CCCP-75602	0062		4 IV AI-20M	61000	Y100		
RA-75606	Ilyushin 18V	182004405	CCCP-75606	0062		4 IV AI-20M	61000	Y100		
RA-85360	Tupolev 154B-2	360	CCCP-85360	0079		3 KU NK-8-2U	98000	C120		lst AYZ
RA-85426	Tupolev 154B-2	426	CCCP-85426	0080		3 KU NK-8-2U	98000	VIP		
RA-85446	Tupolev 154B-2	446	CCCP-85446	0080		3 KU NK-8-2U	98000	Y164		
RA-85510	Tupolev 154B-2	510	CCCP-85510	0081		3 KU NK-8-2U	98000	VIP		
RA-85534	Tupolev 154B-2	534	CCCP-85534	0082		3 KU NK-8-2U	98000	Y164		
RA-85554	Tupolev 154B-2	554	CCCP-85554	0082		3 KU NK-8-2U	98000	Y155		lst AYZ
RA-85555	Tupolev 154B-2	555	CCCP-85555	0082		3 KU NK-8-2U	98000	Y164		
RA-85559	Tupolev 154B-2	559	CCCP-85559	0082		3 KU NK-8-2U	98000	Y155		lst AYZ
RA-85563	Tupolev 154B-2	563	CCCP-85563	0082		3 KU NK-8-2U	98000	Y155		lst AYZ
RA-85571	Tupolev 154B-2	571	CCCP-85571	0083		3 KU NK-8-2U	98000	Y164		
RA-85572	Tupolev 154B-2	572	CCCP-85572	0083		3 KU NK-8-2U	98000	Y164		
RA-85574	Tupolev 154B-2	574	CCCP-85574	0083		3 KU NK-8-2U	98000	Y164		
RA-85586	Tupolev 154B-2	586	CCCP-85586	0083		3 KU NK-8-2U	98000	Y164		
RA-85587	Tupolev 154B-2	587	CCCP-85587	0083		3 KU NK-8-2U	98000	Y164		
RA-85594	Tupolev 154B-2	594	CCCP-85594	0083		3 KU NK-8-2U	98000	VIP		
RA-85605	Tupolev 154B-2	605	CCCP-85605	0084		3 KU NK-8-2U	98000	VIP		
RA-85614	Tupolev 154M	723	CCCP-85614	0085		3 SO D-30KU-154-II	100000	Y164		opb Far East division
RA-85616	Tupolev 154M	732	CCCP-85616	0086		3 SO D-30KU-154-II	100000	Y164		opb Far East division
RA-86495	Ilyushin 62M	2726628	CCCP-86495	0077		4 SO D-30KU	165000	C108		lst AYZ / fn 2602
RA-86496	Ilyushin 62M	3829859	CCCP-86496	0078		4 SO D-30KU	165000	C108		lst AYZ / fn 2905
RA-86538	Ilyushin 62M		CCCP-86538	0085		4 SO D-30KU	167000	VIP		fn 4105
RA-86539	Ilyushin 62M	2344615	CCCP-86539	0083		4 SO D-30KU	167000	VIP		fn 4401
RA-86555	Ilyushin 62M	4547315	CCCP-86555	0085		4 SO D-30KU	167000	VIP		fn 4701
RA-86572	Ilyushin 62M			0092		4 SO D-30KU	167000	Y168		
RA-76635	Ilyushin 76MD		CCCP-76635	0085		4 SO D-30KP	190000	Freighter		
RA-82033	Antonov 124 Ruslan	9773052832054	21	0088		4 LO D-18T	392000	Freighter		fn 05-07

224th FLIGHT UNIT, State Airlines = TTF (224 letny otryad)

Bryansk 2 & Tver 2

Ul. Matrosskaya tishina 10, 103160 Moskva K-160, Russia ☎ (095) 269 91 37 Tx: none Fax: (095) 269 31 62 SITA: n/a

F: n/a 👥 450 Head: V.V. Yefanov ICAO: CARGO UNIT Net: n/a Operates non-commercial transport flights but aircraft listed are also available for commercial leasing/operating on behalf of other Russian companies.

All aircraft are in former Aeroflot colors including Aeroflot titles.

registration	type of aircraft	cn/fn	ex/ex*	mfd	del	powered by	mtow kg	configuration	selcal	name/fln/specialitites/remarks
RA-76592	Ilyushin 76MD	0043452555	CCCP-76592	0084	0084	4 SO D-30KP	190000	Freighter		
RA-76638	Ilyushin 76MD	0053460802	CCCP-76638	0085	0085	4 SO D-30KP	190000	Freighter		
RA-76650	Ilyushin 76MD	0053462865	CCCP-76650	0085	0085	4 SO D-30KP	190000	Freighter		
RA-76669	Ilyushin 76MD	0063465949	CCCP-76669	0086	0086	4 SO D-30KP	190000	Freighter		
RA-76686	Ilyushin 76MD	0063468045	CCCP-76686	0086	0086	4 SO D-30KP	190000	Freighter		
RA-76713	Ilyushin 76MD	0063474193	CCCP-76713	0086	0086	4 SO D-30KP	190000	Freighter		
RA-76719	Ilyushin 76MD	0073474226	CCCP-76719	0087	0087	4 SO D-30KP	190000	Freighter		
RA-76738	Ilyushin 76MD	0073477326	CCCP-76738	0087	0087	4 SO D-30KP	190000	Freighter		
RA-78764	Ilyushin 76MD	0083486586	CCCP-78764	0088	0088	4 SO D-30KP	190000	Freighter		
RA-78776	Ilyushin 76MD	0083489652	CCCP-78776	0088	0088	4 SO D-30KP	190000	Freighter		
RA-78788	Ilyushin 76MD	0083490703	CCCP-78788	0088	0088	4 SO D-30KP	190000	Freighter		fn 68-06
RA-78789	Ilyushin 76MD	0083490706	CCCP-78789	0088	0088	4 SO D-30KP	190000	Freighter		
RA-78794	Ilyushin 76MD	0093490726	CCCP-78794	0089	0089	4 SO D-30KP	190000	Freighter		
RA-78796	Ilyushin 76MD	0093491735	CCCP-78796	0089	0089	4 SO D-30KP	190000	Freighter		
RA-78797	Ilyushin 76MD	0093491742	CCCP-78797	0089	0089	4 SO D-30KP	190000	Freighter		
RA-78809	Ilyushin 76MD	0093493807	CCCP-78809	0089	0089	4 SO D-30KP	190000	Freighter		
RA-78815	Ilyushin 76MD	0093494842	CCCP-78815	0089	0089	4 SO D-30KP	190000	Freighter		
RA-78816	Ilyushin 76MD	0093495846	CCCP-78816	0089	0089	4 SO D-30KP	190000	Freighter		
RA-78817	Ilyushin 76MD	0093495851	CCCP-78817	0089	0089	4 SO D-30KP	190000	Freighter		
RA-78818	Ilyushin 76MD	0093495858	CCCP-78818	0089	0089	4 SO D-30KP	190000	Freighter		
RA-78831	Ilyushin 76MD	1003401017	CCCP-78831	0090	0090	4 SO D-30KP	190000	Freighter		
RA-78833	Ilyushin 76MD	1003401025	CCCP-78833	0090	0090	4 SO D-30KP	190000	Freighter		
RA-78834	Ilyushin 76MD	1003401032	CCCP-78834	0090	0090	4 SO D-30KP	190000	Freighter		
RA-78835	Ilyushin 76MD	1003401006	CCCP-78835	0090	0090	4 SO D-30KP	190000	Freighter		
RA-78838	Ilyushin 76MD	1003402044	CCCP-78838	0090	0090	4 SO D-30KP	190000	Freighter		
RA-78840	Ilyushin 76MD	1003403056	CCCP-78840	0090	0090	4 SO D-30KP	190000	Freighter		
RA-78842	Ilyushin 76MD	1003403069	CCCP-78842	1289	0090	4 SO D-30KP	190000	Freighter		
RA-78846	Ilyushin 76MD	1003403113	CCCP-78846	0090	0090	4 SO D-30KP	190000	Freighter		
RA-78847	Ilyushin 76MD	1003404132	CCCP-78847	0090	0090	4 SO D-30KP	190000	Freighter		
RA-78854	Ilyushin 76MD	1013407220	CCCP-78854	0091	0091	4 SO D-30KP	190000	Freighter		
RA-82012	Antonov 124 Ruslan	9773052732028	CCCP-82012	0087	0087	4 LO D-18T	392000	Freighter		fn 05-01
RA-82021	Antonov 124 Ruslan	19530502002	CCCP-82021	0087	0087	4 LO D-18T	392000	Freighter		fn 02-02
RA-82023	Antonov 124 Ruslan	19530502012	CCCP-82023	0088	0088	4 LO D-18T	392000	Freighter		fn 02-04
RA-82028	Antonov 124 Ruslan	19530502599	CCCP-82028	0091	0091	4 LO D-18T	392000	Freighter		fn 02-09
RA-82030	Antonov 124 Ruslan	9773054732045	CCCP-82030	0087	0087	4 LO D-18T	392000	Freighter		fn 05-04
RA-82032	Antonov 124 Ruslan	9773052832051	CCCP-82032	0088	0088	4 LO D-18T	392000	Freighter		fn 05-06
RA-82034	Antonov 124 Ruslan	9773053832057	CCCP-82034	0388	0088	4 LO D-18T	392000	Freighter		fn 05-08
RA-82036	Antonov 124 Ruslan	9773054832068	CCCP-82036	0089	0089	4 LO D-18T	392000	Freighter		fn 05-10
RA-82039	Antonov 124 Ruslan	9773052055082	CCCP-82039	0090	0090	4 LO D-18T	392000	Freighter		fn 06-03
RA-82040	Antonov 124 Ruslan	9773053055086	CCCP-82040	0090	0090	4 LO D-18T	392000	Freighter		fn 06-04
RA-82041	Antonov 124 Ruslan	9773054055089	CCCP-82041	0091	0091	4 LO D-18T	392000	Freighter		fn 06-05

TYUMEN AIRLINES = 7M / TYM (Tyumenskie avialinii) (formerly Aeroflot Tyumen Roshchino division)

Tyumen-Roshchino

Roshchino Airport, 625033 Tyumen, Russia ☎ (3452) 39 44 12 Tx: 735518 asta ru Fax: (3452) 39 44 58 SITA: n/a

F: 1992 👥 2500 Head: Yuri Yu. Yermolaev IATA: 691 ICAO: AIR TYUMEN Net: n/a Some aircraft are still in Aeroflot colors but will be repainted in due course.

registration	type of aircraft	cn/fn	ex/ex*	mfd	del	powered by	mtow kg	configuration	selcal	name/fln/specialitites/remarks
RA-46267	Antonov 24B	77303510	EW-46267	0767	0095	2 IV AI-24	21000	Y48		
RA-46297	Antonov 24B	77303809	EW-46297	1167	0095	2 IV AI-24	21000	Y48		
RA-47160	Antonov 24B	89901702	CCCP-47160	0068		2 IV AI-24	21000	Y48		
RA-47166	Antonov 24B	89901708	CCCP-47166	0968		2 IV AI-24	21000	Y48		
RA-47719	Antonov 24B	69900702	CCCP-47719	0066		2 IV AI-24	21000	Y48		
RA-47727	Antonov 24B	69900805	CCCP-47727	0066		2 IV AI-24	21000	Y48		
RA-47741	Antonov 24B	79901104	CCCP-47741	0067		2 IV AI-24	21000	Y48		
RA-47744	Antonov 24B	79901107	CCCP-47744	0267		2 IV AI-24	21000	Y48		
RA-47745	Antonov 24B	79901108	CCCP-47745	0067		2 IV AI-24	21000	Y48		
RA-47768	Antonov 24B	79901403	CCCP-47768	0067		2 IV AI-24	21000	Y48		
RA-47774	Antonov 24B	79901407	CCCP-47774	0067		2 IV AI-24	21000	Y48		
RA-47778	Antonov 24B	79901502	CCCP-47778	1267		2 IV AI-24	21800	Y48		
RA-47780	Antonov 24B	89901505	CCCP-47780	0068		2 IV AI-24	21000	Y48		
RA-26534	Antonov 26	1810	CCCP-26534	0073		2 IV AI-24VT	24000	Freighter		
RA-26540	Antonov 26B	2105	CCCP-26540	0074		2 IV AI-24VT	24000	Freighter		
RA-26561	Antonov 26	3502	CCCP-26561	0075		2 IV AI-24VT	24000	Freighter		
RA-26619	Antonov 26	5103	CCCP-26619	0077		2 IV AI-24VT	24000	Freighter		
RA-26630	Antonov 26	5403	CCCP-26630	0777		2 IV AI-24VT	24000	Freighter		lst INV
RA-26662	Antonov 26	8101	CCCP-26662	0079		2 IV AI-24VT	24000	Freighter		
RA-46503	Antonov 26	1505	CCCP-46503	1272		2 IV AI-24VT	24000	Freighter		
RA-65009	Tupolev 134A	46120	CCCP-65009	0076		2 SO D-30-II	49000	Y76		
RA-65012	Tupolev 134A	46175	CCCP-65012	0076		2 SO D-30-II	49000	Y76		
RA-65017	Tupolev 134A-3	48360	CCCP-65017	0076		2 SO D-30-III	49000	Y76		
RA-65025	Tupolev 134A	48450	CCCP-65025	0076		2 SO D-30-II	49000	Y76		
RA-65038	Tupolev 134A	48950	CCCP-65038	0076		2 SO D-30-II	49000	Y76		
RA-65063	Tupolev 134A	49880	CCCP-65063	0077		2 SO D-30-II	49000	Y76		
RA-65127	Tupolev 134A-3	60627	EY-65127	0878	1193	2 SO D-30-III	49000	C40		
RA-65653	Tupolev 134A	0351009	CCCP-65653	0070	0094	2 SO D-30-II	49000	Y76		lsf Novosibirsky NII
RA-65661	Tupolev 134A	0351107	CCCP-65661	0070		2 SO D-30-II	49000	Y76		
RA-65738	Tupolev 134A	2351507	CCCP-65738	0072	0097	2 SO D-30-II	49000	Y76		lsf Novosibirsky NII
RA-65802	Tupolev 134A	3352101	CCCP-65802	0073		2 SO D-30-II	49000	C40		
RA-65838	Tupolev 134A	18116	CCCP-65838	0074		2 SO D-30-II	49000	Y76		
RA-65859	Tupolev 134A-3	23264	CCCP-65859	0075		2 SO D-30-III	49000	Y64		
RA-65899	Tupolev 134A-3	42225	CCCP-65899	0075		2 SO D-30-III	49000	Y76		
RA-65950	Tupolev 134A	2351702	CCCP-65950	0072		2 SO D-30-II	49000	Y76		
RA-65960	Tupolev 134A	3351806	CCCP-65960	0073	0094	2 SO D-30-II	49000	Y76		lsf Novosibirsky NII
RA-11128	Antonov 12B	02348203	CCCP-11128	0072		4 IV AI-20M	61000	Freighter		
RA-11973	Antonov 12BP	401606		0463		4 IV AI-20M	61000	Freighter		std Tyumen
RA-12973	Antonov 12B	9346505	CCCP-12973	0069		4 IV AI-20M	61000	Freighter		
RA-12976	Antonov 12	9346510	CCCP-12976	0069		4 IV AI-20M	61000	Freighter		opf UN

☐ RA-12980	Antonov 12B	00347103	CCCP-12980	0070	0893	4 IV AI-20M	61000	Freighter		
☐ RA-12998	Antonov 12B	01347610	CCCP-12998	0071		4 IV AI-20M	61000	Freighter		
☐ RA-85255	Tupolev 154B-1	255	CCCP-85255	0077		3 KU NK-8-2U	98000	Y164		
☐ RA-85314	Tupolev 154B-2	314	CCCP-85314	0078		3 KU NK-8-2U	98000	Y164		
☐ RA-85335	Tupolev 154B-2	335	CCCP-85335	0079		3 KU NK-8-2U	98000	Y164		lst KGL
☐ RA-85361	Tupolev 154B-2	361	CCCP-85361	0079		3 KU NK-8-2U	98000	Y164		
☐ RA-85366	Tupolev 154B-2	366	CCCP-85366	0079		3 KU NK-8-2U	98000	Y164		
☐ RA-85378	Tupolev 154B-2	378	CCCP-85378	0079		3 KU NK-8-2U	98000	Y164		
☐ RA-85427	Tupolev 154B-2	427	CCCP-85427	0080		3 KU NK-8-2U	98000	Y164		
☐ RA-85434	Tupolev 154B-2	434	CCCP-85434	0080		3 KU NK-8-2U	98000	Y164		
☐ RA-85450	Tupolev 154B-2	450	CCCP-85450	0080		3 KU NK-8-2U	98000	Y164		
☐ RA-85451	Tupolev 154B-2	451	CCCP-85451	0080		3 KU NK-8-2U	98000	Y164		
☐ RA-85481	Tupolev 154B-2	481	CCCP-85481	0081		3 KU NK-8-2U	100000	Y164		
☐ RA-85498	Tupolev 154B-2	498	CCCP-85498	0081		3 KU NK-8-2U	100000	Y164		
☐ RA-85502	Tupolev 154B-2	502	CCCP-85502	0081		3 KU NK-8-2U	100000	Y164		
☐ RA-85522	Tupolev 154B-2	522	CCCP-85522	0082		3 KU NK-8-2U	100000	Y164		
☐ RA-85550	Tupolev 154B-2	550	CCCP-85550	0082		3 KU NK-8-2U	100000	Y164		
☐ RA-85819	Tupolev 154M	1008		0397	0697	3 SO D-30KU-154-II	100000	Y166		lsf Yamalo-Nenetsky AO Administration
☐ RA-76507	Ilyushin 76T	073411338	CCCP-76507	0077		4 SO D-30KP	170000	Freighter		
☐ RA-76512	Ilyushin 76T	083414447	CCCP-76512	0378		4 SO D-30KP	170000	Freighter		
☐ RA-76514	Ilyushin 76T	083415453	CCCP-76514	0078		4 SO D-30KP	170000	Freighter		
☐ RA-76518	Ilyushin 76T	093420594	CCCP-76518	0579		4 SO D-30KP	170000	Freighter		
☐ RA-76523	Ilyushin 76T	0003425732	CCCP-76523	0080		4 SO D-30KP	170000	Freighter		opf ICRC
☐ RA-76527	Ilyushin 76T	0003427796	CCCP-76527	0080		4 SO D-30KP	170000	Freighter		
☐ RA-76807	Ilyushin 76TD	1013405176	CCCP-76807	0091	1291	4 SO D-30KP	190000	Freighter		lst AZS

TYUMENAVIATRANS, Joint-Stock Company = P2 / TMN

Tyumen-Plekhanovo / Khanty-Mansisk & Surgut

Plekhanovo Airport, 625025 Tyumen, Russia ☎ (3452) 43 21 24 Tx: none Fax: (3452) 42 24 34 SITA: n/a
F: 1991 n/a Head: Andrei Z. Martirosov IATA: 298 ICAO: TYUMAVI Net: n/a

☐ RA-01409	PZL Mielec (Antonov) An-2	1G230-49	CCCP-01409	0088	0091	1 SH ASh-62IR	5500	12 Pax / Frtr		
☐ RA-01414	PZL Mielec (Antonov) An-2	1G230-54	CCCP-01414	0088	0091	1 SH ASh-62IR	5500	12 Pax / Frtr		
☐ RA-01415	PZL Mielec (Antonov) An-2	1G230-55	CCCP-01415	0088	0091	1 SH ASh-62IR	5500	12 Pax / Frtr		
☐ RA-01417	PZL Mielec (Antonov) An-2	1G230-57	CCCP-01417	0088		1 SH ASh-62IR	5500	12 Pax / Frtr		
☐ RA-01456	PZL Mielec (Antonov) An-2	1G231-44	CCCP-01456	0088	0091	1 SH ASh-62IR	5500	12 Pax / Frtr		
☐ RA-01463	PZL Mielec (Antonov) An-2	1G231-54	CCCP-01463	0088	0091	1 SH ASh-62IR	5500	12 Pax / Frtr		
☐ RA-01489	PZL Mielec (Antonov) An-2	1G232-23	CCCP-01489	0088	0091	1 SH ASh-62IR	5500	12 Pax / Frtr		
☐ RA-01490	PZL Mielec (Antonov) An-2	1G232-24	CCCP-01490	0088	0091	1 SH ASh-62IR	5500	12 Pax / Frtr		
☐ RA-01492	PZL Mielec (Antonov) An-2	1G232-26	CCCP-01492	0088	0091	1 SH ASh-62IR	5500	12 Pax / Frtr		
☐ RA-01496	PZL Mielec (Antonov) An-2	1G232-30	CCCP-01496	0088	0091	1 SH ASh-62IR	5500	12 Pax / Frtr		
☐ RA-02299	PZL Mielec (Antonov) An-2	1G240-01	CCCP-02299	0090	0091	1 SH ASh-62IR	5500	Sprayer		
☐ RA-02303	PZL Mielec (Antonov) An-2	1G240-05	CCCP-02303	0090	0091	1 SH ASh-62IR	5500	Sprayer		
☐ RA-02310	PZL Mielec (Antonov) An-2	1G240-12	CCCP-02310	0090	0091	1 SH ASh-62IR	5500	Sprayer		
☐ RA-02412	PZL Mielec (Antonov) An-2	1G117-23	CCCP-02412	0070	0091	1 SH ASh-62IR	5500	12 Pax / Frtr		
☐ RA-05748	PZL Mielec (Antonov) An-2	1G151-56	CCCP-05748	0074	0091	1 SH ASh-62IR	5500	12 Pax / Frtr		
☐ RA-07310	PZL Mielec (Antonov) An-2	1G149-14	CCCP-07310	0073	0091	1 SH ASh-62IR	5500	12 Pax / Frtr		
☐ RA-07341	PZL Mielec (Antonov) An-2	1G149-45	CCCP-07341	0073	0091	1 SH ASh-62IR	5500	12 Pax / Frtr		
☐ RA-07431	PZL Mielec (Antonov) An-2	1G151-06	CCCP-07431	0073	0091	1 SH ASh-62IR	5500	12 Pax / Frtr		
☐ RA-07443	PZL Mielec (Antonov) An-2	1G151-18	CCCP-07443	0073	0091	1 SH ASh-62IR	5500	12 Pax / Frtr		
☐ RA-07458	PZL Mielec (Antonov) An-2	1G151-33	CCCP-07458	0073	0091	1 SH ASh-62IR	5500	12 Pax / Frtr		
☐ RA-07473	PZL Mielec (Antonov) An-2	1G151-48	CCCP-07473	0073	0091	1 SH ASh-62IR	5500	12 Pax / Frtr		
☐ RA-07838	PZL Mielec (Antonov) An-2	1G169-53	CCCP-07838	0076	0091	1 SH ASh-62IR	5500	Sprayer		
☐ RA-07858	PZL Mielec (Antonov) An-2	1G170-17	CCCP-07858	0076	0091	1 SH ASh-62IR	5500	12 Pax / Frtr		
☐ RA-32643	PZL Mielec (Antonov) An-2	1G219-42	CCCP-32643	0086	0091	1 SH ASh-62IR	5500	Sprayer		
☐ RA-32644	PZL Mielec (Antonov) An-2	1G219-43	CCCP-32644	0086	0091	1 SH ASh-62IR	5500	Sprayer		
☐ RA-33348	PZL Mielec (Antonov) An-2	1G226-07	CCCP-33348	0087	0091	1 SH ASh-62IR	5500	Sprayer		
☐ RA-33357	PZL Mielec (Antonov) An-2	1G226-16	CCCP-33357	0087	0091	1 SH ASh-62IR	5500	Sprayer		
☐ RA-33358	PZL Mielec (Antonov) An-2	1G226-17	CCCP-33358	0087	0091	1 SH ASh-62IR	5500	Sprayer		
☐ RA-33359	PZL Mielec (Antonov) An-2	1G226-18	CCCP-33359	0087	0091	1 SH ASh-62IR	5500	Sprayer		
☐ RA-33372	PZL Mielec (Antonov) An-2	1G226-31	CCCP-33372	0087	0091	1 SH ASh-62IR	5500	12 Pax / Frtr		
☐ RA-33373	PZL Mielec (Antonov) An-2	1G226-32	CCCP-33373	0087	0091	1 SH ASh-62IR	5500	12 Pax / Frtr		
☐ RA-33445	PZL Mielec (Antonov) An-2	1G227-55	CCCP-33445	0087	0091	1 SH ASh-62IR	5500	Sprayer		
☐ RA-33446	PZL Mielec (Antonov) An-2	1G227-56	CCCP-33446	0087	0091	1 SH ASh-62IR	5500	Utility		
☐ RA-33447	PZL Mielec (Antonov) An-2	1G227-57	CCCP-33447	0087	0091	1 SH ASh-62IR	5500	12 Pax / Frtr		
☐ RA-33448	PZL Mielec (Antonov) An-2	1G227-58	CCCP-33448	0087	0091	1 SH ASh-62IR	5500	12 Pax / Frtr		
☐ RA-33450	PZL Mielec (Antonov) An-2	1G227-60	CCCP-33450	0087	0091	1 SH ASh-62IR	5500	Sprayer		
☐ RA-33475	PZL Mielec (Antonov) An-2	1G228-26	CCCP-33475	0088	0091	1 SH ASh-62IR	5500	Sprayer		
☐ RA-33624	PZL Mielec (Antonov) An-2	1G232-60	CCCP-33624	0088	0091	1 SH ASh-62IR	5500	12 Pax / Frtr		
☐ RA-35021	PZL Mielec (Antonov) An-2	1G109-27	CCCP-35021	0069	0091	1 SH ASh-62IR	5500	12 Pax / Frtr		
☐ RA-40208	PZL Mielec (Antonov) An-2	1G219-58	CCCP-40208	0085	0091	1 SH ASh-62IR	5500	Sprayer		
☐ RA-40209	PZL Mielec (Antonov) An-2	1G219-59	CCCP-40209	0085	0091	1 SH ASh-62IR	5500	Sprayer		
☐ RA-40278	PZL Mielec (Antonov) An-2	1G221-08	CCCP-40278	0085	0091	1 SH ASh-62IR	5500	Sprayer		
☐ RA-40363	PZL Mielec (Antonov) An-2	1G222-42	CCCP-40363	0086	0091	1 SH ASh-62IR	5500	Sprayer		
☐ RA-40449	PZL Mielec (Antonov) An-2	1G224-26	CCCP-40449	0087	0091	1 SH ASh-62IR	5500	Sprayer		
☐ RA-40903	PZL Mielec (Antonov) An-2	1G215-40	CCCP-40903	0085	0091	1 SH ASh-62IR	5500	Sprayer		
☐ RA-54936	PZL Mielec (Antonov) An-2	1G187-45	CCCP-54936	0080	0091	1 SH ASh-62IR	5500	Sprayer		
☐ RA-70154	PZL Mielec (Antonov) An-2	1G137-28	CCCP-70154	0072	0091	1 SH ASh-62IR	5500	12 Pax / Frtr		
☐ RA-70267	PZL Mielec (Antonov) An-2	1G139-26	CCCP-70267	0072	0091	1 SH ASh-62IR	5500	12 Pax / Frtr		
☐ RA-70398	PZL Mielec (Antonov) An-2	1G141-52	CCCP-70398	0072	0091	1 SH ASh-62IR	5500	12 Pax / Frtr		
☐ RA-70416	PZL Mielec (Antonov) An-2	1G141-70	CCCP-70416	0072	0091	1 SH ASh-62IR	5500	12 Pax / Frtr		
☐ RA-70419	PZL Mielec (Antonov) An-2	1G141-73	CCCP-70419	0072	0091	1 SH ASh-62IR	5500	12 Pax / Frtr		
☐ RA-70433	PZL Mielec (Antonov) An-2	1G143-12	CCCP-70433	0072	0091	1 SH ASh-62IR	5500	12 Pax / Frtr		
☐ RA-70673	PZL Mielec (Antonov) An-2	1G129-23	CCCP-70673	0071	0091	1 SH ASh-62IR	5500	12 Pax / Frtr		
☐ RA-70716	PZL Mielec (Antonov) An-2	1G130-17	CCCP-70716	0071	0091	1 SH ASh-62IR	5500	12 Pax / Frtr		
☐ RA-70751	PZL Mielec (Antonov) An-2	1G132-06	CCCP-70751	0071	0091	1 SH ASh-62IR	5500	12 Pax / Frtr		
☐ RA-70756	PZL Mielec (Antonov) An-2	1G132-11	CCCP-70756	0071	0091	1 SH ASh-62IR	5500	12 Pax / Frtr		
☐ RA-84531	PZL Mielec (Antonov) An-2	1G188-56	CCCP-84531	0080	0091	1 SH ASh-62IR	5500	Sprayer		
☐ RA-84675	PZL Mielec (Antonov) An-2	1G191-53	CCCP-84675	0081	0091	1 SH ASh-62IR	5500	Sprayer		
☐ RA-06166	Mil Mi-8T	98943928	CCCP-06166	0089	0091	2 IS TV2-117A	12000	24 Pax / Frtr		
☐ RA-22221	Mil Mi-8T	6351	CCCP-22221	0076	0091	2 IS TV2-117A	12000	24 Pax / Frtr		
☐ RA-22231	Mil Mi-8T	6361	CCCP-22231	0076	0091	2 IS TV2-117A	12000	24 Pax / Frtr		
☐ RA-22245	Mil Mi-8T	6575	CCCP-22245	0076	0091	2 IS TV2-117A	12000	24 Pax / Frtr		
☐ RA-22253	Mil Mi-8T	6592	CCCP-22253	0076	0091	2 IS TV2-117A	12000	24 Pax / Frtr		
☐ RA-22254	Mil Mi-8T	6594	CCCP-22254	0076	0091	2 IS TV2-117A	12000	24 Pax / Frtr		
☐ RA-22255	Mil Mi-8T	6595	CCCP-22255	0076	0091	2 IS TV2-117A	12000	24 Pax / Frtr		
☐ RA-22256	Mil Mi-8T	6596	CCCP-22256	0076	0091	2 IS TV2-117A	12000	24 Pax / Frtr		
☐ RA-22260	Mil Mi-8T	6906	CCCP-22260	0076	0091	2 IS TV2-117A	12000	24 Pax / Frtr		
☐ RA-22269	Mil Mi-8T	6948	CCCP-22269	0076	0091	2 IS TV2-117A	12000	24 Pax / Frtr		
☐ RA-22270	Mil Mi-8T	6949	CCCP-22270	0076	0091	2 IS TV2-117A	12000	24 Pax / Frtr		
☐ RA-22300	Mil Mi-8T	7117	CCCP-22300	0077	0091	2 IS TV2-117A	12000	24 Pax / Frtr		
☐ RA-22303	Mil Mi-8T	7117	CCCP-22303	0077	0091	2 IS TV2-117A	12000	24 Pax / Frtr		
☐ RA-22309	Mil Mi-8T	7128	CCCP-22309	0077	0091	2 IS TV2-117A	12000	24 Pax / Frtr		
☐ RA-22311	Mil Mi-8T	7133	CCCP-22311	0077	0091	2 IS TV2-117A	12000	24 Pax / Frtr		
☐ RA-22319	Mil Mi-8T	7141	CCCP-22319	0077	0091	2 IS TV2-117A	12000	24 Pax / Frtr		
☐ RA-22335	Mil Mi-8T	7151	CCCP-22335	0077	0091	2 IS TV2-117A	12000	24 Pax / Frtr		
☐ RA-22337	Mil Mi-8T	7162	CCCP-22337	0077	0091	2 IS TV2-117A	12000	24 Pax / Frtr		
☐ RA-22343	Mil Mi-8T	7171	CCCP-22343	0077	0091	2 IS TV2-117A	12000	24 Pax / Frtr		
☐ RA-22350	Mil Mi-8T	7192	CCCP-22350	0077	0091	2 IS TV2-117A	12000	24 Pax / Frtr		
☐ RA-22352	Mil Mi-8T	7213	CCCP-22352	0077	0091	2 IS TV2-117A	12000	24 Pax / Frtr		
☐ RA-22353	Mil Mi-8T	7214	CCCP-22353	0077	0091	2 IS TV2-117A	12000	24 Pax / Frtr		
☐ RA-22355	Mil Mi-8T	7216	CCCP-22355	0077	0091	2 IS TV2-117A	12000	24 Pax / Frtr		
☐ RA-22356	Mil Mi-8T	7217	CCCP-22356	0077	0091	2 IS TV2-117A	12000	24 Pax / Frtr		
☐ RA-22357	Mil Mi-8T	7218	CCCP-22357	0077	0091	2 IS TV2-117A	12000	24 Pax / Frtr		
☐ RA-22364	Mil Mi-8T	7228	CCCP-22364	0077	0091	2 IS TV2-117A	12000	24 Pax / Frtr		
☐ RA-22553	Mil Mi-8T	7768	CCCP-22553	0079	0091	2 IS TV2-117A	12000	24 Pax / Frtr		
☐ RA-22555	Mil Mi-8T	7770	CCCP-22555	0079	0091	2 IS TV2-117A	12000	24 Pax / Frtr		
☐ RA-22558	Mil Mi-8T	7801	CCCP-22558	0079	0091	2 IS TV2-117A	12000	24 Pax / Frtr		
☐ RA-22559	Mil Mi-8T	7802	CCCP-22559	0079	0091	2 IS TV2-117A	12000	24 Pax / Frtr		
☐ RA-22563	Mil Mi-8T	7807	CCCP-22563	0079	0091	2 IS TV2-117A	12000	24 Pax / Frtr		
☐ RA-22575	Mil Mi-8T	7821	CCCP-22575	0079	0091	2 IS TV2-117A	12000	24 Pax / Frtr		
☐ RA-22578	Mil Mi-8T	7825	CCCP-22578	0079		2 IS TV2-117A	12000	24 Pax / Frtr		
☐ RA-22579	Mil Mi-8T	7826	CCCP-22579	0079		2 IS TV2-117A	12000	24 Pax / Frtr		

570 registration type of aircraft cn/fn ex/ex* mfd del powered by mtow kg configuration selcal name/fln/specialitites/remarks

registration	type of aircraft	cn/fn	ex/ex*	mfd	del	powered by	mtow kg	configuration	selcal	name/fln/specialitites/remarks
☐ RA-22580	Mil Mi-8T	7827	CCCP-22580	0079		2 IS TV2-117A	12000	24 Pax / Frtr		
☐ RA-22585	Mil Mi-8T	7876	CCCP-22585	0079		2 IS TV2-117A	12000	24 Pax / Frtr		
☐ RA-22588	Mil Mi-8T	7880	CCCP-22588	0079		2 IS TV2-117A	12000	24 Pax / Frtr		
☐ RA-22589	Mil Mi-8T	7881	CCCP-22589	0079		2 IS TV2-117A	12000	24 Pax / Frtr		
☐ RA-22602	Mil Mi-8T	7947	CCCP-22602	0080		2 IS TV2-117A	12000	24 Pax / Frtr		
☐ RA-22603	Mil Mi-8T	7948	CCCP-22603	0080	0091	2 IS TV2-117A	12000	24 Pax / Frtr		
☐ RA-22604	Mil Mi-8T	7949	CCCP-22604	0080	0091	2 IS TV2-117A	12000	24 Pax / Frtr		
☐ RA-22606	Mil Mi-8T	7951	CCCP-22606	0080	0091	2 IS TV2-117A	12000	24 Pax / Frtr		
☐ RA-22615	Mil Mi-8T	7962	CCCP-22615	0080	0091	2 IS TV2-117A	12000	24 Pax / Frtr		
☐ RA-22616	Mil Mi-8T	7963	CCCP-22616	0080	0091	2 IS TV2-117A	12000	24 Pax / Frtr		
☐ RA-22617	Mil Mi-8T	7964	CCCP-22617	0080	0091	2 IS TV2-117A	12000	24 Pax / Frtr		
☐ RA-22619	Mil Mi-8T	7966	CCCP-22619	0080	0091	2 IS TV2-117A	12000	24 Pax / Frtr		
☐ RA-22628	Mil Mi-8T	8013	CCCP-22628	0080	0091	2 IS TV2-117A	12000	24 Pax / Frtr		
☐ RA-22633	Mil Mi-8T	8018	CCCP-22633	0080		2 IS TV2-117A	12000	24 Pax / Frtr		
☐ RA-22635	Mil Mi-8T	8020	CCCP-22635	0080		2 IS TV2-117A	12000	24 Pax / Frtr		
☐ RA-22654	Mil Mi-8T	8102	CCCP-22654	0080		2 IS TV2-117A	12000	24 Pax / Frtr		
☐ RA-22656	Mil Mi-8T	8106	CCCP-22656	0080		2 IS TV2-117A	12000	24 Pax / Frtr		
☐ RA-22660	Mil Mi-8T	8111	CCCP-22660	0080		2 IS TV2-117A	12000	24 Pax / Frtr		
☐ RA-22694	Mil Mi-8T	8153	CCCP-22694	0080		2 IS TV2-117A	12000	24 Pax / Frtr		
☐ RA-22764	Mil Mi-8T	98311512	CCCP-22764	0083		2 IS TV2-117A	12000	24 Pax / Frtr		
☐ RA-22774	Mil Mi-8T	98311701	CCCP-22774	0083		2 IS TV2-117A	12000	24 Pax / Frtr		
☐ RA-22805	Mil Mi-8T	7533	CCCP-22805	0078		2 IS TV2-117A	12000	24 Pax / Frtr		
☐ RA-22812	Mil Mi-8T	7579	CCCP-22812	0078		2 IS TV2-117A	12000	24 Pax / Frtr		
☐ RA-22817	Mil Mi-8T	7585	CCCP-22817	0078		2 IS TV2-117A	12000	24 Pax / Frtr		
☐ RA-22819	Mil Mi-8T	7587	CCCP-22819	0078		2 IS TV2-117A	12000	24 Pax / Frtr		
☐ RA-22841	Mil Mi-8T	7641	CCCP-22841	0078		2 IS TV2-117A	12000	24 Pax / Frtr		
☐ RA-22884	Mil Mi-8T	98415943	CCCP-22884	0084		2 IS TV2-117A	12000	24 Pax / Frtr		
☐ RA-22885	Mil Mi-8T	98415975	CCCP-22885	0084		2 IS TV2-117A	12000	24 Pax / Frtr		
☐ RA-22890	Mil Mi-8T	98417035	CCCP-22890	0084		2 IS TV2-117A	12000	24 Pax / Frtr		
☐ RA-22891	Mil Mi-8T	98417043	CCCP-22891	0084		2 IS TV2-117A	12000	24 Pax / Frtr		lst Heyns Helicopters
☐ RA-22892	Mil Mi-8T	98417056	CCCP-22892	0084	0091	2 IS TV2-117A	12000	24 Pax / Frtr		
☐ RA-22903	Mil Mi-8T	98420107	CCCP-22903	0084		2 IS TV2-117A	12000	24 Pax / Frtr		
☐ RA-22922	Mil Mi-8T	98520370	CCCP-22922	0085		2 IS TV2-117A	12000	24 Pax / Frtr		
☐ RA-22925	Mil Mi-8T	98520442	CCCP-22925	0085		2 IS TV2-117A	12000	24 Pax / Frtr		lst Heyns Helicopters
☐ RA-22928	Mil Mi-8T	98520540	CCCP-22928	0085		2 IS TV2-117A	12000	24 Pax / Frtr		
☐ RA-24103	Mil Mi-8T	98839492	CCCP-24103	0088		2 IS TV2-117A	12000	24 Pax / Frtr		
☐ RA-24105	Mil Mi-8T	98839502	CCCP-24105	0088		2 IS TV2-117A	12000	24 Pax / Frtr		
☐ RA-24106	Mil Mi-8T	98839511	CCCP-24106	0088		2 IS TV2-117A	12000	24 Pax / Frtr		
☐ RA-24107	Mil Mi-8T	98839516	CCCP-24107	0088		2 IS TV2-117A	12000	24 Pax / Frtr		
☐ RA-24124	Mil Mi-8T	98841040	CCCP-24124	0088		2 IS TV2-117A	12000	24 Pax / Frtr		
☐ RA-24125	Mil Mi-8T	98841061	CCCP-24125	0088		2 IS TV2-117A	12000	24 Pax / Frtr		
☐ RA-24126	Mil Mi-8T	98841088	CCCP-24126	0088		2 IS TV2-117A	12000	24 Pax / Frtr		
☐ RA-24135	Mil Mi-8T	98841290	CCCP-24135	0088		2 IS TV2-117A	12000	24 Pax / Frtr		
☐ RA-24144	Mil Mi-8T	98841468	CCCP-24144	0088	0091	2 IS TV2-117A	12000	24 Pax / Frtr		
☐ RA-24145	Mil Mi-8T	98841500	CCCP-24145	0088		2 IS TV2-117A	12000	24 Pax / Frtr		
☐ RA-24146	Mil Mi-8T	98941594	CCCP-24146	0089		2 IS TV2-117A	12000	24 Pax / Frtr		
☐ RA-24147	Mil Mi-8T	98941613	CCCP-24147	0089		2 IS TV2-117A	12000	24 Pax / Frtr		
☐ RA-24157	Mil Mi-8T	98941813	CCCP-24157	0089		2 IS TV2-117A	12000	24 Pax / Frtr		
☐ RA-24171	Mil Mi-8T	98943075	CCCP-24171	0089		2 IS TV2-117A	12000	24 Pax / Frtr		lst Heyns Helicopters
☐ RA-24176	Mil Mi-8T	98943166	CCCP-24176	0089		2 IS TV2-117A	12000	24 Pax / Frtr		
☐ RA-24177	Mil Mi-8T	98943172	CCCP-24177	0089		2 IS TV2-117A	12000	24 Pax / Frtr		
☐ RA-24186	Mil Mi-8T	98943412	CCCP-24186	0089		2 IS TV2-117A	12000	24 Pax / Frtr		
☐ RA-24187	Mil Mi-8T	98943453	CCCP-24187	0089		2 IS TV2-117A	12000	24 Pax / Frtr		
☐ RA-24206	Mil Mi-8T	98730151	CCCP-24206	0087		2 IS TV2-117A	12000	24 Pax / Frtr		
☐ RA-24215	Mil Mi-8T	98730303	CCCP-24215	0087	0091	2 IS TV2-117A	12000	24 Pax / Frtr		
☐ RA-24222	Mil Mi-8T	98730507	CCCP-24222	0087		2 IS TV2-117A	12000	24 Pax / Frtr		
☐ RA-24223	Mil Mi-8T	98730510	CCCP-24223	0087		2 IS TV2-117A	12000	24 Pax / Frtr		
☐ RA-24238	Mil Mi-8T	98730777	CCCP-24238	0087		2 IS TV2-117A	12000	24 Pax / Frtr		
☐ RA-24248	Mil Mi-8T	98730937	CCCP-24248	0087		2 IS TV2-117A	12000	24 Pax / Frtr		lst Heyns Helicopters
☐ RA-24272	Mil Mi-8T	98734257	CCCP-24272	0087		2 IS TV2-117A	12000	24 Pax / Frtr		
☐ RA-24273	Mil Mi-8T	98734263	CCCP-24273	0087		2 IS TV2-117A	12000	24 Pax / Frtr		
☐ RA-24274	Mil Mi-8T	98734275	CCCP-24274	0087		2 IS TV2-117A	12000	24 Pax / Frtr		
☐ RA-24456	Mil Mi-8T	98628375	CCCP-24456	0086		2 IS TV2-117A	12000	24 Pax / Frtr		
☐ RA-24463	Mil Mi-8T	98628574	CCCP-24463	0086		2 IS TV2-117A	12000	24 Pax / Frtr		
☐ RA-24464	Mil Mi-8T	98628595	CCCP-24464	0086		2 IS TV2-117A	12000	24 Pax / Frtr		
☐ RA-24479	Mil Mi-8T	98628863	CCCP-24479	0086		2 IS TV2-117A	12000	24 Pax / Frtr		
☐ RA-24491	Mil Mi-8T	98628975	CCCP-24491	0086		2 IS TV2-117A	12000	24 Pax / Frtr		
☐ RA-24492	Mil Mi-8T	98628979	CCCP-24492	0086		2 IS TV2-117A	12000	24 Pax / Frtr		
☐ RA-24505	Mil Mi-8T	98520801	CCCP-24505	0085		2 IS TV2-117A	12000	24 Pax / Frtr		
☐ RA-24521	Mil Mi-8T	98522125	CCCP-24521	0085		2 IS TV2-117A	12000	24 Pax / Frtr		
☐ RA-24539	Mil Mi-8T	98522670	CCCP-24539	0085		2 IS TV2-117A	12000	24 Pax / Frtr		
☐ RA-24546	Mil Mi-8T	98522853	CCCP-24546	0085		2 IS TV2-117A	12000	24 Pax / Frtr		
☐ RA-24577	Mil Mi-8T	98839293	CCCP-24577	0088		2 IS TV2-117A	12000	24 Pax / Frtr		
☐ RA-24578	Mil Mi-8T	98839301	CCCP-24578	0088		2 IS TV2-117A	12000	24 Pax / Frtr		
☐ RA-24579	Mil Mi-8T	98839307	CCCP-24579	0088		2 IS TV2-117A	12000	24 Pax / Frtr		
☐ RA-24580	Mil Mi-8T	98839312	CCCP-24580	0088		2 IS TV2-117A	12000	24 Pax / Frtr		
☐ RA-24592	Mil Mi-8T	98839415	CCCP-24592	0088		2 IS TV2-117A	12000	24 Pax / Frtr		
☐ RA-24593	Mil Mi-8T	98839417	CCCP-24593	0088		2 IS TV2-117A	12000	24 Pax / Frtr		
☐ RA-24645	Mil Mi-8T	9815705	CCCP-24645	0081		2 IS TV2-117A	12000	24 Pax / Frtr		
☐ RA-24720	Mil Mi-8T	98417359	CCCP-24720	0084		2 IS TV2-117A	12000	24 Pax / Frtr		
☐ RA-24726	Mil Mi-8T	98417452	CCCP-24726	0084		2 IS TV2-117A	12000	24 Pax / Frtr		
☐ RA-24727	Mil Mi-8T	98417473	CCCP-24727	0084		2 IS TV2-117A	12000	24 Pax / Frtr		
☐ RA-25139	Mil Mi-8T	99047492	CCCP-25139	0090		2 IS TV2-117A	12000	24 Pax / Frtr		lst Heyns Helicopters
☐ RA-25142	Mil Mi-8T	99047543	CCCP-25142	0090		2 IS TV2-117A	12000	24 Pax / Frtr		
☐ RA-25145	Mil Mi-8T	99047632	CCCP-25145	0090		2 IS TV2-117A	12000	24 Pax / Frtr		
☐ RA-25154	Mil Mi-8T	99047792	CCCP-25154	0090		2 IS TV2-117A	12000	24 Pax / Frtr		
☐ RA-25159	Mil Mi-8T	99047892	CCCP-25159	0090		2 IS TV2-117A	12000	24 Pax / Frtr		
☐ RA-25161	Mil Mi-8T	99047911	CCCP-25161	0090		2 IS TV2-117A	12000	24 Pax / Frtr		
☐ RA-25165	Mil Mi-8T	99047964	CCCP-25165	0090		2 IS TV2-117A	12000	24 Pax / Frtr		lst Heyns Helicopters
☐ RA-25200	Mil Mi-8T	7684	CCCP-25200	0078		2 IS TV2-117A	12000	24 Pax / Frtr		
☐ RA-25201	Mil Mi-8T	7685	CCCP-25201	0078		2 IS TV2-117A	12000	24 Pax / Frtr		
☐ RA-25202	Mil Mi-8T	7686	CCCP-25202	0078		2 IS TV2-117A	12000	24 Pax / Frtr		
☐ RA-25204	Mil Mi-8T	7688	CCCP-25204	0078		2 IS TV2-117A	12000	24 Pax / Frtr		
☐ RA-25209	Mil Mi-8T	7702	CCCP-25209	0079	0091	2 IS TV2-117A	12000	24 Pax / Frtr		
☐ RA-25212	Mil Mi-8T	7725	CCCP-25212	0079	0091	2 IS TV2-117A	12000	24 Pax / Frtr		
☐ RA-25213	Mil Mi-8T	7726	CCCP-25213	0079	0091	2 IS TV2-117A	12000	24 Pax / Frtr		
☐ RA-25214	Mil Mi-8T	7727	CCCP-25214	0079	0091	2 IS TV2-117A	12000	24 Pax / Frtr		
☐ RA-25307	Mil Mi-8T	98203690	CCCP-25307	0082		2 IS TV2-117A	12000	24 Pax / Frtr		
☐ RA-25338	Mil Mi-8T	98206239	CCCP-25338	0082		2 IS TV2-117A	12000	24 Pax / Frtr		
☐ RA-25384	Mil Mi-8T	98208134	CCCP-25384	0082		2 IS TV2-117A	12000	24 Pax / Frtr		
☐ RA-25481	Mil Mi-8MTV-1	95626	CCCP-25481	0091	0091	2 IS TV3-117MT	13000	24 Pax / Frtr		lst Heli Harvest
☐ RA-25484	Mil Mi-8MTV-1	95629	CCCP-25484	0091		2 IS TV3-117MT	13000	24 Pax / Frtr		
☐ RA-25854	Mil Mi-8T	5112	CCCP-25854	0075	0091	2 IS TV2-117A	12000	24 Pax / Frtr		
☐ RA-25873	Mil Mi-8T	5141	CCCP-25873	0075		2 IS TV2-117A	12000	24 Pax / Frtr		
☐ RA-25875	Mil Mi-8T	5143	CCCP-25875	0075		2 IS TV2-117A	12000	24 Pax / Frtr		
☐ RA-25881	Mil Mi-8T	5149	CCCP-25881	0075		2 IS TV2-117A	12000	24 Pax / Frtr		
☐ RA-25882	Mil Mi-8T	5153	CCCP-25882	0075		2 IS TV2-117A	12000	24 Pax / Frtr		
☐ RA-25931	Mil Mi-8T	5567	CCCP-25931	0075		2 IS TV2-117A	12000	24 Pax / Frtr		
☐ RA-25934	Mil Mi-8T	5570	CCCP-25934	0075		2 IS TV2-117A	12000	24 Pax / Frtr		lst Heyns Helicopters
☐ RA-25935	Mil Mi-8T	5571	CCCP-25935	0075		2 IS TV2-117A	12000	24 Pax / Frtr		
☐ RA-25938	Mil Mi-8T	5574	CCCP-25938	0075		2 IS TV2-117A	12000	24 Pax / Frtr		
☐ RA-25944	Mil Mi-8T	5586	CCCP-25944	0075	0091	2 IS TV2-117A	12000	24 Pax / Frtr		
☐ RA-25947	Mil Mi-8T	4885	CCCP-25947	0075		2 IS TV2-117A	12000	24 Pax / Frtr		
☐ RA-25963	Mil Mi-8P	5831	CCCP-25963	0075	0091	2 IS TV2-117A	12000	28 Pax		
☐ RA-25964	Mil Mi-8P	5835	CCCP-25964	0075	0091	2 IS TV2-117A	12000	28 Pax		
☐ RA-25965	Mil Mi-8P	5849	CCCP-25965	0075	0091	2 IS TV2-117A	12000	28 Pax		
☐ RA-25970	Mil Mi-8T	6320	CCCP-25970	0075		2 IS TV2-117A	12000	24 Pax / Frtr		
☐ RA-25989	Mil Mi-8T	7521	CCCP-25989	0077		2 IS TV2-117A	12000	24 Pax / Frtr		
☐ RA-27065	Mil Mi-8MTV-1	95901	CCCP-27065	0092		2 IS TV3-117MT	13000	24 Pax / Frtr		
☐ RA-27066	Mil Mi-8MTV-1	95902	CCCP-27066	0092		2 IS TV3-117MT	13000	24 Pax / Frtr		

	registration	type of aircraft	cn/fn	ex	mfd	del	powered by	mtow kg	configuration	selcal	name/fln/specialitites/remarks
☐	RA-27067	Mil Mi-8MTV-1	95903	CCCP-27067	0092		2 IS TV3-117MT	13000	24 Pax / Frtr		
☐	RA-27068	Mil Mi-8MTV-1	95904	CCCP-27068	0092		2 IS TV3-117MT	13000	24 Pax / Frtr		
☐	RA-27069	Mil Mi-8MTV-1	95905	CCCP-27069	0092		2 IS TV3-117MT	13000	24 Pax / Frtr		
☐	RA-27071	Mil Mi-8MTV-1	95907	CCCP-27071	0092		2 IS TV3-117MT	13000	24 Pax / Frtr		
☐	RA-27113	Mil Mi-8MTV-1	95964	CCCP-27113	0092	0092	2 IS TV3-117MT	13000	24 Pax / Frtr		lst Heyns Helicopters as ZS-RIT
☐	RA-27114	Mil Mi-8MTV-1	95965	CCCP-27114	0092	0092	2 IS TV3-117MT	13000	24 Pax / Frtr		lst Heyns Helicopters as ZS-RIV
☐	RA-27128	Mil Mi-8MTV-1	95955	CCCP-27128	0092	0092	2 IS TV3-117MT	13000	24 Pax / Frtr		lst Heyns Helicopters as ZS-RIU
☐	RA-27129	Mil Mi-8MTV-1	95956	CCCP-27129	0092	0092	2 IS TV3-117MT	13000	24 Pax / Frtr		lst Heyns Helicopters
☐	RA-27130	Mil Mi-8MTV-1	95957	CCCP-27130	0092	0092	2 IS TV3-117MT	13000	24 Pax / Frtr		lst Heyns Helicopters as ZS-RIR
☐	RA-27131	Mil Mi-8MTV-1	95958	CCCP-27131	0092	0092	2 IS TV3-117MT	13000	24 Pax / Frtr		lst Heyns Helicopters as ZS-RIS
☐	RA-27132	Mil Mi-8MTV-1	95959	CCCP-27132	0092		2 IS TV3-117MT	13000	24 Pax / Frtr		
☐	RA-27133	Mil Mi-8MTV-1	95960	CCCP-27133	0092		2 IS TV3-117MT	13000	24 Pax / Frtr		
☐	RA-87240	Yakovlev 40	9530743	CCCP-87240	0075	0091	3 IV AI-25	17200	Y32		
☐	RA-87292	Yakovlev 40	9320728	CCCP-87292	0073	0091	3 IV AI-25	17200	Y32		
☐	RA-87343	Yakovlev 40	9511239	CCCP-87343	0075	0091	3 IV AI-25	17200	Y32		
☐	RA-87348	Yakovlev 40	9511739	CCCP-87348	0075	0091	3 IV AI-25	17200	Y32		
☐	RA-87365	Yakovlev 40	9341531	CCCP-87365	0073		3 IV AI-25	17200	Y32		
☐	RA-87383	Yakovlev 40	9411432	CCCP-87383	0074	0091	3 IV AI-25	16800	Y30		
☐	RA-87410	Yakovlev 40	9420234	CCCP-87410	0074	0091	3 IV AI-25	17200	Y32		
☐	RA-87422	Yakovlev 40	9421834	CCCP-87422	0074	0091	3 IV AI-25	16800	Y30		
☐	RA-87449	Yakovlev 40	9430636	CCCP-87449	0074	0091	3 IV AI-25	17200	Y32		
☐	RA-87516	Yakovlev 40	9521840	CCCP-87516	0075	0091	3 IV AI-25	17200	Y30		
☐	RA-87527	Yakovlev 40	9520941	CCCP-87527	0075	0091	3 IV AI-25	17200	Y32		
☐	RA-87901	Yakovlev 40	9720354	CCCP-87901	0077	0091	3 IV AI-25	17200	Y32		
☐	RA-87907	Yakovlev 40	9731254	CCCP-87907	0077	0091	3 IV AI-25	16800	Y36		
☐	RA-87941	Yakovlev 40	9540545	CCCP-87941	0076	0091	3 IV AI-25	16800	Y30		
☐	RA-87942	Yakovlev 40K	9610645	CCCP-87942	0076	0091	3 IV AI-25	17200	Y32		
☐	RA-87997	Yakovlev 40	9540145	CCCP-87997	0075	0091	3 IV AI-25	16800	Y32		
☐	RA-88209	Yakovlev 40	9710353	CCCP-88209	0077	0091	3 IV AI-25	16800	Y32		
☐	RA-88210	Yakovlev 40	9631649	CCCP-88210	0076	0091	3 IV AI-25	16800	Y32		
☐	RA-88213	Yakovlev 40	9631949	CCCP-88213	0076	0091	3 IV AI-25	16800	Y32		
☐	RA-88227	Yakovlev 40	9641550	CCCP-88227	0076	0091	3 IV AI-25	17200	Y36		
☐	RA-88244	Yakovlev 40	9641751	CCCP-88244	0076	0091	3 IV AI-25	16800	Y32		
☐	RA-88280	Yakovlev 40	9820658	CCCP-88280	0078	0091	3 IV AI-25	16800	C20		
☐	RA-46332	Antonov 24B	97305509	CCCP-46332	0069		2 IV AI-24	21800	Y48		
☐	RA-46337	Antonov 24B	97305604	CCCP-46337	0069		2 IV AI-24	21800	Y48		
☐	RA-46362	Antonov 24B	07305903	CCCP-46362	0070		2 IV AI-24	21800	Y48		
☐	RA-46481	Antonov 24RV	27308009	CCCP-46481	0072		2 IV AI-24VT	21800	Y48		
☐	RA-46609	Antonov 24RV	37308606	CCCP-46609	0073		2 IV AI-24VT	21800	Y48		
☐	RA-46828	Antonov 24B	17306705	CCCP-46828	0071		2 IV AI-24	21800	Y48		
☐	RA-47271	Antonov 24B	07306401	CCCP-47271	0070	0091	2 IV AI-24	21800	Y48		
☐	RA-47289	Antonov 24B	07306509	CCCP-47289	0070	0091	2 IV AI-24	21800	Y48		
☐	RA-47827	Antonov 24B	17307208	CCCP-47827	0071		2 IV AI-24	21800	Y48		
☐	RA-47841	Antonov 24B	17307403	CCCP-47841	0071		2 IV AI-24	21800	Y48		
☐	RA-26010	Antonov 26B	9906	CCCP-26010	0080		2 IV AI-24VT	24000	Frtr / Y39		
☐	RA-26012	Antonov 26B	10007	CCCP-26012	0080		2 IV AI-24VT	24000	Freighter		
☐	RA-26023	Antonov 26B	10304	CCCP-26023	0080	0091	2 IV AI-24VT	24000	Freighter		
☐	RA-26025	Antonov 26B	10308	CCCP-26025	0080	0091	2 IV AI-24VT	24000	Freighter		
☐	RA-26057	Antonov 26B	11008	CCCP-26057	0081	0091	2 IV AI-24VT	24000	Freighter		
☐	RA-26503	Antonov 26	6310	CCCP-26503	0076	0091	2 IV AI-24VT	24000	Freighter		
☐	RA-26513	Antonov 26	6810	CCCP-26513	0078	0091	2 IV AI-24VT	24000	Freighter		
☐	RA-26544	Antonov 26	2710	CCCP-26544	0075	0091	2 IV AI-24VT	24000	Freighter		
☐	RA-26608	Antonov 26	4805	CCCP-26608	0076	0091	2 IV AI-24VT	24000	Freighter		
☐	RA-26621	Antonov 26	5108	CCCP-26621	0077	0091	2 IV AI-24VT	24000	Freighter		
☐	RA-26678	Antonov 26	8607	CCCP-26678	0079	0091	2 IV AI-24VT	24000	Freighter		
☐	RA-26698	Antonov 26	9504	CCCP-26698	0079	0091	2 IV AI-24VT	24000	Freighter		
☐	RA-04121	Mil Mi-10K	2163	CCCP-04121	0076	0091	2 SO D-25V	38000	Freighter		
☐	RA-04122	Mil Mi-10K	2164	CCCP-04122	0076		2 SO D-25V	38000	Freighter		
☐	RA-04123	Mil Mi-10K	2265	CCCP-04123	0076		2 SO D-25V	38000	Freighter		
☐	RA-04126	Mil Mi-10K	2269	CCCP-04126	0076		2 SO D-25V	38000	Freighter		
☐	RA-04129	Mil Mi-10K	2293	CCCP-04129	0076		2 SO D-25V	38000	Freighter		
☐	RA-04132	Mil Mi-10K	2296	CCCP-04132	0076		2 SO D-25V	38000	Freighter		
☐	RA-04134	Mil Mi-10K	2298	CCCP-04134	0076		2 SO D-25V	38000	Freighter		
☐	RA-21030	Mil Mi-6A	0583	CCCP-21030	0076	0091	2 SO D-25V	42500	Freighter		
☐	RA-21042	Mil Mi-6A	0631	CCCP-21042	0077	0091	2 SO D-25V	42500	Freighter		
☐	RA-21043	Mil Mi-6A	0632	CCCP-21043	0077	0091	2 SO D-25V	42500	Freighter		
☐	RA-21046	Mil Mi-6A	0656	CCCP-21046	0078	0091	2 SO D-25V	42500	Freighter		
☐	RA-21047	Mil Mi-6A	0657	CCCP-21047	0078	0091	2 SO D-25V	42500	Freighter		
☐	RA-21049	Mil Mi-6A	0659	CCCP-21049	0078	0091	2 SO D-25V	42500	Freighter		
☐	RA-21050	Mil Mi-6A	0660	CCCP-21050	0078	0091	2 SO D-25V	42500	Freighter		
☐	RA-21052	Mil Mi-6A	0662	CCCP-21052	0078	0091	2 SO D-25V	42500	Freighter		
☐	RA-21053	Mil Mi-6A	0663	CCCP-21053	0078	0091	2 SO D-25V	42500	Freighter		
☐	RA-21054	Mil Mi-6A	0675	CCCP-21054	0079	0091	2 SO D-25V	42500	Freighter		
☐	RA-21055	Mil Mi-6A	0676	CCCP-21055	0079	0091	2 SO D-25V	42500	Freighter		
☐	RA-21056	Mil Mi-6A	0677	CCCP-21056	0079	0091	2 SO D-25V	42500	Freighter		
☐	RA-21066	Mil Mi-6A	0702	CCCP-21066	0080	0091	2 SO D-25V	42500	Freighter		
☐	RA-21067	Mil Mi-6A	0703	CCCP-21067	0080	0091	2 SO D-25V	42500	Freighter		
☐	RA-21068	Mil Mi-6A	0710	CCCP-21068	0080	0091	2 SO D-25V	42500	Freighter		
☐	RA-21071	Mil Mi-6A	0713	CCCP-21071	0080	0091	2 SO D-25V	42500	Freighter		
☐	RA-06004	Mil Mi-26T	34001212107	CCCP-06004	0091	0091	2 LO D-136	56000	Freighter		
☐	RA-06009	Mil Mi-26T	34001212135	CCCP-06009	0087	0091	2 LO D-136	56000	Freighter		
☐	RA-06010	Mil Mi-26T	34001212136	CCCP-06010	0087	0091	2 LO D-136	56000	Freighter		
☐	RA-06011	Mil Mi-26T	34001212168	CCCP-06011	0088	0091	2 LO D-136	56000	Freighter		
☐	RA-06012	Mil Mi-26T	34001212169	CCCP-06012	0088	0091	2 LO D-136	56000	Freighter		
☐	RA-06015	Mil Mi-26T	34001212303	CCCP-06015	0088	0091	2 LO D-136	56000	Freighter		
☐	RA-06016	Mil Mi-26T	34001212304	CCCP-06016	0088	0091	2 LO D-136	56000	Freighter		
☐	RA-06018	Mil Mi-26T	34001212319	CCCP-06018	0089	0091	2 LO D-136	56000	Freighter		
☐	RA-06034	Mil Mi-26T	34001212424	CCCP-06034	0090	0091	2 LO D-136	56000	Freighter		
☐	RA-06037	Mil Mi-26T	34001212427	CCCP-06037	0090	0091	2 LO D-136	56000	Freighter		
☐	RA-06045	Mil Mi-26T	34001212435	CCCP-06045	0090	0091	2 LO D-136	56000	Freighter		
☐	RA-06080	Mil Mi-26T	34001212470		0091	0091	2 LO D-136	56000	Freighter		
☐	RA-06082	Mil Mi-26T	34001212472		0091	0091	2 LO D-136	56000	Freighter		
☐	RA-85796	Tupolev 154M	980		0794	0094	3 SO D-30KU-154-II	100000	F12C18Y104orY166		
☐	RA-85805	Tupolev 154M	986		0794	0094	3 SO D-30KU-154-II	100000	F12C18Y104orY166		
☐	RA-85806	Tupolev 154M	987		0395	0095	3 SO D-30KU-154-II	100000	F12C18Y104orY166		
☐	RA-85808	Tupolev 154M	989		0795	0895	3 SO D-30KU-154-II	100000	F12C18Y104orY166		
☐	RA-85813	Tupolev 154M	990		0595	0595	3 SO D-30KU-154-II	100000	F12C18Y104orY166		
☐	RA-85820	Tupolev 154M	995		0898	0998	3 SO D-30KU-154-II	100000	F12C18Y104		

ULYANOVSK HIGHER CIVIL AVIATION SCHOOL = UHS (Ulyanovskoe vysshee aviatsionnoe uchilische GA) (formerly Civil Aviation Center) Ulyanovsk

Ul. Mozhaiskogo 8/8, 432033 Ulyanovsk, Russia ☎ (8422) 34 17 31 Tx: 263212 polet Fax: (8422) 31 87 51 SITA: n/a

F: n/a 👪 n/a Head: Vitaly M. Rzhevsky ICAO: PILOT AIR Net: n/a Operates aircraft for training purposes, as well as for commercial charter flights & leasing. Most aircraft are still in Aeroflot colors with or without titles.

	registration	type of aircraft	cn/fn	ex	mfd	del	powered by	mtow kg	configuration	selcal	name/fln/specialitites/remarks
☐	RA-65018	Tupolev 134A	48365	CCCP-65018	0076		2 SO D-30-II	49000	Y76		
☐	RA-65078	Tupolev 134A	60043	CCCP-65078	0077		2 SO D-30-II	49000	Y76		
☐	RA-65801	Tupolev 134A	3352010	CCCP-65801	0073		2 SO D-30-II	49000	Y76		
☐	RA-42528	Yakovlev 42D	11041003	CCCP-42528	0080		3 LO D-36	56500	F8Y96		lst AKT / cvtd 42
☐	RA-42539	Yakovlev 42	11140504	CCCP-42539	0082		3 LO D-36	56500	F8Y96		lst AKT
☐	RA-42543	Yakovlev 42	11250904	CCCP-42543	0085		3 LO D-36	56500	F8Y96		lst AKT
☐	RA-85013	Tupolev 154B	013	CCCP-85013	0071		3 KU NK-8-2U	98000	Y164		cvtd 154
☐	RA-85016	Tupolev 154B	016	CCCP-85016	0071		3 KU NK-8-2U	98000	Y164		cvtd 154A
☐	RA-85025	Tupolev 154B	025	CCCP-85025	0072		3 KU NK-8-2U	98000	Y164		cvtd 154
☐	RA-85061	Tupolev 154B	061	CCCP-85061	0074		3 KU NK-8-2U	98000	Y164		cvtd 154A
☐	RA-85078	Tupolev 154B	078	CCCP-85078	0074		3 KU NK-8-2U	98000	Y164		cvtd 154A
☐	RA-85091	Tupolev 154B	091	CCCP-85091	0074		3 KU NK-8-2U	98000	Y164		cvtd 154A
☐	RA-85315	Tupolev 154B-2	315	CCCP-85315	0078		3 KU NK-8-2U	98000	Y164		
☐	RA-85388	Tupolev 154B-2	388	CCCP-85388	0079		3 KU NK-8-2U	98000	Y164		
☐	RA-85470	Tupolev 154B-2	470	CCCP-85470	0081		3 KU NK-8-2U	98000	Y164		
☐	RA-85609	Tupolev 154M	704	CCCP-85609	0085		3 SO D-30KU-154-II	100000	Y164		
☐	RA-85617	Tupolev 154M	736	CCCP-85617	0086		3 SO D-30KU-154-II	100000	Y164		
☐	RA-85636	Tupolev 154M	766	CCCP-85636	0087		3 SO D-30KU-154-II	100000	Y164		lst AZS
☐	RA-86458	Ilyushin 62M	3623834	CCCP-86458	0076		4 SO D-30KU	165000	Y174		fn 2303

registration	type of aircraft	cn/fn	ex/εx*	mfd	del	powered by	mtow kg	configuration	selcal	name/fln/specialitites/remarks
☐ RA-86507	Ilyushin 62M	2035546	CCCP-86507	0080		4 SO D-30KU	167000	Y156		Ist MVL / fn 3504
☐ RA-76401	Ilyushin 76TD	1023412399	CCCP-76401	0792		4 SO D-30KP	190000	Freighter		Ist VDA
☐ RA-76783	Ilyushin 76TD	0093498974	CCCP-76783	0089		4 SO D-30KP	190000	Freighter		Ist AZS
☐ RA-86062	Ilyushin 86	51483203029	EW-86062	0083		4 KU NK-86	215000	Y350		Ist AYZ

UMPO – Ufimskoe motorstroitel'noe proizvodstvennoe ob'yedinenie (Flying div. of Ufa Motors Prod. Ass. / Member of MAP Group) — Ufa-Maximovka

Flying div./Letny otryad, Ul. Sosnovskaya, 450033 Ufa, Pos. Maximovka, (Republic of Bashkortostan), Russia ☎ (3472) 38 59 20 Tx: 214143 albus Fax: (3472) 38 36 54 SITA: n/a
F: n/a 👪 n/a Head: Alexander I. Akinin Net: n/a Operates non-commercial cargo flights for itself only.

registration	type of aircraft	cn/fn	ex/εx*	mfd	del	powered by	mtow kg	configuration	selcal	name/fln/specialitites/remarks
☐ RA-21509	Antonov An-2					1 SH ASh-62IR	5500	Freighter		
☐ RA-66757	Antonov An-2					1 SH ASh-62IR	5500	Freighter		
☐ RA-66758	Antonov An-2					1 SH ASh-62IR	5500	Freighter		
☐ RA-21501	Yakovlev 40K	9741756	CCCP-21501	0077		3 IV AI-25	16800	Freighter		
☐ RA-87227	Yakovlev 40K	9841559	CCCP-87227	0078		3 IV AI-25	16800	Freighter		
☐ RA-26186	Antonov 24RT	0911307	CCCP-26186	0070		2 IV AI-24VT	22500	Freighter		
☐ RA-21507	Antonov 26	1302	CCCP-21507	0072		2 IV AI-24VT	24000	Freighter		
☐ RA-26091	Antonov 26B	12608	CCCP-26091	0081		2 IV AI-24VT	24000	Freighter		
☐ RA-48098	Antonov 32B	2102		0088		2 IV AI-20D	27000	Freighter		
☐ RA-48972	Antonov 32	2103	CCCP-48972	0088		2 IV AI-20D	27000	Freighter		
☐ RA-69306	Antonov 32	2104	CCCP-69306	0089		2 IV AI-20D	27000	Freighter		

URAIAVIA = URV — Urai

Urai Airport, 626310 Urai, (Tyumen Region), Russia ☎ (34676) 31 735 Tx: none Fax: (34676) 31 735 SITA: n/a
F: n/a 👪 n/a Head: Alexander N. Bedny ICAO: URAI Net: n/a

registration	type of aircraft	cn/fn	ex/εx*	mfd	del	powered by	mtow kg	configuration	selcal	name/fln/specialitites/remarks
☐ RA-01413	PZL Mielec (Antonov) An-2		CCCP-01413	0078		1 SH ASh-62IR	5500	Utility		Ist Sverdlovsk 2nd Aviation Enterprise
☐ RA-07301	PZL Mielec (Antonov) An-2		CCCP-07301	0073		1 SH ASh-62IR	5500	Utility		Ist Sverdlovsk 2nd Aviation Enterprise
☐ RA-70243	PZL Mielec (Antonov) An-2		CCCP-70243	0072		1 SH ASh-62IR	5500	Utility		Ist Sverdlovsk 2nd Aviation Enterprise
☐ RA-22216	Mil Mi-8		CCCP-22216	0077		2 IS TV2-117A	12000	Utility		
☐ RA-22277	Mil Mi-8		CCCP-22277	0076		2 IS TV2-117A	12000	Utility		Ist Kodaavia
☐ RA-22305	Mil Mi-8		CCCP-22305	0077		2 IS TV2-117A	12000	Utility		
☐ RA-22314	Mil Mi-8		CCCP-22314	0077		2 IS TV2-117A	12000	Utility		Ist Yugorsk Air Company
☐ RA-22586	Mil Mi-8		CCCP-22586	0079		2 IS TV2-117A	12000	Utility		Ist Yugorsk Air Company
☐ RA-22600	Mil Mi-8		CCCP-22600	0079		2 IS TV2-117A	12000	Utility		
☐ RA-22601	Mil Mi-8		CCCP-22601	0079		2 IS TV2-117A	12000	Utility		
☐ RA-22626	Mil Mi-8		CCCP-22626	0080		2 IS TV2-117A	12000	Utility		Ist Argo
☐ RA-22630	Mil Mi-8		CCCP-22630	0080		2 IS TV2-117A	12000	Utility		
☐ RA-22806	Mil Mi-8		CCCP-22806	0078		2 IS TV2-117A	12000	Utility		
☐ RA-22821	Mil Mi-8		CCCP-22821	0078		2 IS TV2-117A	12000	Utility		Ist Yugorsk Air Company
☐ RA-22907	Mil Mi-8		CCCP-22907	0084		2 IS TV2-117A	12000	Utility		
☐ RA-24108	Mil Mi-8		CCCP-24108	0088		2 IS TV2-117A	12000	Utility		
☐ RA-24406	Mil Mi-8		CCCP-24406	0086		2 IS TV2-117A	12000	Utility		
☐ RA-24716	Mil Mi-8		CCCP-24716	0084		2 IS TV2-117A	12000	Utility		Ist Argo
☐ RA-24717	Mil Mi-8		CCCP-24717	0084		2 IS TV2-117A	12000	Utility		
☐ RA-25153	Mil Mi-8		CCCP-25153	0090		2 IS TV2-117A	12000	Utility		
☐ RA-25215	Mil Mi-8		CCCP-25215	0078		2 IS TV2-117A	12000	Utility		
☐ RA-25317	Mil Mi-8		CCCP-25317	0082		2 IS TV2-117A	12000	Utility		
☐ RA-25369	Mil Mi-8		CCCP-25369	0082		2 IS TV2-117A	12000	Utility		Ist Yugorsk Air Company
☐ RA-25370	Mil Mi-8		CCCP-25370	0082		2 IS TV2-117A	12000	Utility		
☐ RA-25717	Mil Mi-8		CCCP-25717	0073		2 IS TV2-117A	12000	Utility		
☐ RA-25734	Mil Mi-8P		CCCP-25734	0073		2 IS TV2-117A	12000	VIP 8 Pax		
☐ RA-25878	Mil Mi-8		CCCP-25878	0075		2 IS TV2-117A	12000	Utility		
☐ RA-25879	Mil Mi-8		CCCP-25879	0075		2 IS TV2-117A	12000	Utility		Ist Yugorsk Air Company
☐ RA-25914	Mil Mi-8		CCCP-25914	0075		2 IS TV2-117A	12000	Utility		
☐ RA-25916	Mil Mi-8		CCCP-25916	0075		2 IS TV2-117A	12000	Utility		
☐ RA-25926	Mil Mi-8		CCCP-25926	0075		2 IS TV2-117A	12000	Utility		Ist Yugorsk Air Company

URAL AIRLINES, Joint-Stock Company = U6 / SVR (Uralskie avialinii) — Ekaterinburg-Koltsovo

Ul. Sputnikov 6, 620025 Ekaterinburg, Russia ☎ (3432) 26 86 25 Tx: 721739 port Fax: (3432) 26 62 21 SITA: SVXTOU6
F: 1993 👪 n/a Head: Sergei N. Skuratov IATA: 262 ICAO: SVERDLOVSK AIR Net: n/a

registration	type of aircraft	cn/fn	ex/εx*	mfd	del	powered by	mtow kg	configuration	selcal	name/fln/specialitites/remarks
☐ RA-46532	Antonov 24RV	57310101	CCCP-46532	0075	1294	2 IV AI-24VT	21800	Y48		
☐ RA-47182	Antonov 24B	99901907	CCCP-47182	0069	0195	2 IV AI-24	21000	Y48		
☐ RA-47187	Antonov 24B	99902002	CCCP-47187	0069	0195	2 IV AI-24	21000	Y48		
☐ RA-26654	Antonov 26	7801	CCCP-26654	0079	0593	2 IV AI-24VT	24000	Freighter		
☐ RA-26681	Antonov 26	8610	CCCP-26681	0079	0593	2 IV AI-24VT	24000	Freighter		
☐ RA-12952	Antonov 12B	8345503	CCCP-12952	0068	0093	4 IV AI-20M	64000	Freighter		
☐ RA-12975	Antonov 12B	9346509	CCCP-12975	0069	0093	4 IV AI-20M	64000	Freighter		
☐ RA-12999	Antonov 12TB	01347701	4K-12999	0071	0093	4 IV AI-20M	64000	Freighter		
☐ RA-85141	Tupolev 154B-2	141	CCCP-85141	0076	0093	3 KU NK-8-2U	98000	Y164		cvtd 154B
☐ RA-85193	Tupolev 154B-2	193	CCCP-85193	0077	0093	3 KU NK-8-2U	98000	Y152		cvtd 154B
☐ RA-85219	Tupolev 154B-2	219	CCCP-85219	0077	0093	3 KU NK-8-2U	98000	Y152		cvtd 154B
☐ RA-85310	Tupolev 154B-2	310	CCCP-85310	0078	0093	3 KU NK-8-2U	98000	Y152		
☐ RA-85319	Tupolev 154B-2	319	CCCP-85319	0078	0093	3 KU NK-8-2U	98000	Y152		
☐ RA-85328	Tupolev 154B-2	328	CCCP-85328	0079	0093	3 KU NK-8-2U	98000	Y152		
☐ RA-85337	Tupolev 154B-2	337	CCCP-85337	0079	0093	3 KU NK-8-2U	100000	Y152		
☐ RA-85357	Tupolev 154B-2	357	CCCP-85357	0079	0093	3 KU NK-8-2U	100000	Y164		
☐ RA-85374	Tupolev 154B-2	374	CCCP-85374	0079	0093	3 KU NK-8-2U	100000	Y152		
☐ RA-85375	Tupolev 154B-2	375	CCCP-85375	0079	0093	3 KU NK-8-2U	100000	Y152		
☐ RA-85432	Tupolev 154B-2	432	CCCP-85432	0080	0093	3 KU NK-8-2U	100000	Y152		
☐ RA-85439	Tupolev 154B-2	439	CCCP-85439	0080	0093	3 KU NK-8-2U	100000	Y152		
☐ RA-85459	Tupolev 154B-2	459	CCCP-85459	0080	0093	3 KU NK-8-2U	100000	Y152		
☐ RA-85508	Tupolev 154B-2	508	CCCP-85508	0081	0093	3 KU NK-8-2U	100000	Y164		
☐ RA-85807	Tupolev 154M	988		0395	0395	3 SO D-30KU-154-II	100000	F12C18Y104		
☐ RA-85814	Tupolev 154M	994		0995	0995	3 SO D-30KU-154-II	100000	F12C18Y104		
☐ RA-86051	Ilyushin 86	51483202018	CCCP-86051	0082	0193	4 KU NK-86	215000	Y350		
☐ RA-86078	Ilyushin 86	51483205049	CCCP-86078	0085	0193	4 KU NK-86	215000	Combi Y97&Cargo		
☐ RA-86093	Ilyushin 86	51483207064	CCCP-86093	0087	0193	4 KU NK-86	215000	F20Y296		
☐ RA-86114	Ilyushin 86	51483209082	CCCP-86114	0090	1094	4 KU NK-86	215000	F20Y296		

UST-ILIMSK AIR ENTERPRISE (Aviapredpriatie Ust'-Ilimsk) (formerly Aeroflot Ust-Ilimsk division) — Ust-Ilimsk

Box 140, 665770 Ust'-Ilimsk, (Irkutsk Region), Russia ☎ (39535) 75 246 Tx: 231678 polet Fax: (39535) 75 246 SITA: n/a
F: n/a 👪 n/a Head: Alexander I. Akimov Net: n/a Beside aircraft listed, also leases/jointly operates Tupolev 154 with AVIAENERGO.
Most aircraft are still in Aeroflot colors without titles but will be repainted in due course.

registration	type of aircraft	cn/fn	ex/εx*	mfd	del	powered by	mtow kg	configuration	selcal	name/fln/specialitites/remarks
☐ RA-70350	PZL Mielec (Antonov) An-2		CCCP-70350	0073		1 SH ASh-62IR	5500	Utility		
☐ RA-70620	PZL Mielec (Antonov) An-2		CCCP-70620	0071		1 SH ASh-62IR	5500	Utility		
☐ RA-24436	Mil Mi-8		CCCP-24436	0086		2 IS TV2-117A	12000	Utility		
☐ RA-24516	Mil Mi-8		CCCP-24516	0085		2 IS TV2-117A	12000	Utility		
☐ RA-87294	Yakovlev 40	9320928	CCCP-87294	0073		3 IV AI-25	16800	Y32		
☐ RA-87339	Yakovlev 40	9510839	CCCP-87339	0075		3 IV AI-25	16800	Y32		
☐ RA-87399	Yakovlev 40	9411133	CCCP-87399	0074		3 IV AI-25	16800	Y32		
☐ RA-46384	Antonov 24B	07306107	CCCP-46384	0570	0098	2 IV AI-24	21000	Y48		
☐ RA-46830	Antonov 24RV	17306707	CCCP-46830	0071		2 IV AI-24VT	21800	Y48		
☐ RA-46836	Antonov 24RV	17306803	CCCP-46836	0071		2 IV AI-24VT	21800	Y48		

UST-KUTAVIA (formerly Aeroflot Ust'-Kut division) — Ust-Kut

Ust'-Kut Airport 12, 665780 Ust'-Kut, (Irkutsk Region), Russia ☎ (39565) 19 110 Tx: none Fax: none SITA: n/a
F: n/a 👪 n/a Head: Yuri A. Dyrda Net: n/a Most aircraft are still in Aeroflot colors but will be repainted in due course.

registration	type of aircraft	cn/fn	ex/εx*	mfd	del	powered by	mtow kg	configuration	selcal	name/fln/specialitites/remarks
☐ RA-22328	Mil Mi-8		CCCP-22328	0077		2 IS TV2-117A	12000	Utility		
☐ RA-22860	Mil Mi-8		CCCP-22860	0084		2 IS TV2-117A	12000	Utility		
☐ RA-22861	Mil Mi-8		CCCP-22861	0084		2 IS TV2-117A	12000	Utility		
☐ RA-22869	Mil Mi-8		CCCP-22869	0084		2 IS TV2-117A	12000	Utility		
☐ RA-24225	Mil Mi-8		CCCP-24225	0087		2 IS TV2-117A	12000	Utility		
☐ RA-24651	Mil Mi-8		CCCP-24651	0081		2 IS TV2-117A	12000	Utility		
☐ RA-24749	Mil Mi-8		CCCP-24749	0084		2 IS TV2-117A	12000	Utility		
☐ RA-25330	Mil Mi-8		CCCP-25330	0082		2 IS TV2-117A	12000	Utility		
☐ RA-25365	Mil Mi-8		CCCP-25365	0082		2 IS TV2-117A	12000	Utility		
☐ RA-25606	Mil Mi-8T		CCCP-25606	0091		2 IS TV2-117A	12000	Utility		
☐ RA-25607	Mil Mi-8T		CCCP-25607	0091		2 IS TV2-117A	12000	Utility		
☐ RA-25610	Mil Mi-8T		CCCP-25610	0091		2 IS TV2-117A	12000	Utility		
☐ RA-25680	Mil Mi-8		CCCP-25680	0072		2 IS TV2-117A	12000	Utility		
☐ RA-25886	Mil Mi-8		CCCP-25886	0075		2 IS TV2-117A	12000	Utility		
☐ RA-47250	Antonov 24RT	1304		0070		2 IV AI-24VT	22500	Combi		
☐ RA-26670	Antonov 26		CCCP-26670	0079		2 IV AI-24VT	24000	Combi		

VASO – Voronezhskoe aktsionernoe samoletostroitel'noe obchestvo = VSO (Flying div. of Voronezh Aviation Prod. Ass. / Member of MAP Group) — Voronezh

Flying division / Letny otryad, Ul. Tsiolkovskogo 27, 394029 Voronezh, Russia ☎ (0732) 55 27 33 Tx: 153113 mars Fax: (0732) 49 90 17 SITA: n/a
F: n/a 👥 n/a Head: n/a ICAO: VASO Net: n/a Operates corporate flights for itself & commercial charter flights. All aircraft are still in Aeroflot colors with or without titles.

☐ RA-93931	PZL Mielec (Antonov) An-2		CCCP-93931			1 SH ASh-62IR	5500	Combi		
☐ RA-48096	Antonov 24RV		CCCP-48096	0075		2 IV AI-24VT	21800	Y48		
☐ RA-26646	Antonov 26	7809	CCCP-26646	0078		2 IV AI-24VT	24000	Freighter		
☐ RA-76493	Ilyushin 76TD	0043456700	CCCP-76493	0084		4 SO D-30KP	190000	Freighter		

VERTICAL-T Air Transport Company (Vertikal-T aviatransportnaya firma) — Tver & Velkie Lukie

Ul. Krasnoarmeiskaya 39, Box 24, 172060 Torzhsk, (Tver Region), Russia ☎ (08251) 51 014 Tx: none Fax: (08251) 51 355 SITA: n/a
F: 1992 👥 n/a Head: Vladimir B. Skurikhin Net: n/a

☐ RA-24637	Mil Mi-8P	8607	CCCP-24637	0985	0098	2 IS TV2-117A	12000	22 Pax		
☐ RA-25974	Mil Mi-8T	5881	CCCP-25974	0975	0095	2 IS TV2-117A	12000	Utility		
☐ RA-29112	Mil Mi-26T	226210	CCCP-29112	0090	0099	2 LO D-136	56000	Utility		

VLADIKAVKAZ AIR ENTERPRISE (Vladikavkazskoe aviapredpriatie) (formerly Aeroflot Ordzhonikidze division) — Vladikavkaz

Beslan Airport, 363000 Vladikavkaz, (Republic of Severnaya Osetia-Alania), Russia ☎ (8672) 24 05 14 Tx: none Fax: (8672) 25 75 57 SITA: n/a
F: n/a 👥 n/a Head: Murat A. Karginov Net: n/a Most aircraft are still in Aeroflot colors but will be repainted in due course.

☐ RA-25459	Mil Mi-8MTV-1	95603	CCCP-25459	0091		2 IS TV3-117VM	13000	Y24		lst Gorkha Airlines as 9N-ADS
☐ RA-25460	Mil Mi-8MTV-1	95604	CCCP-25460	0091		2 IS TV3-117VM	13000	Y24		lst Gorkha Airlines as 9N-ADT
☐ RA-25492	Mil Mi-8MTV-1		CCCP-25492	0091		3 IS TV3-117MT	13000	EMS		
☐ RA-87286	Yakovlev 40	9310128	CCCP-87286	0073		3 IV AI-25	16800	C15		
☐ RA-87569	Yakovlev 40	9220222	UN-87569	0072		3 IV AI-25	16800	C15		

VLADIMIR AIR ENTERPRISE (Vladimirskoe aviapredpriatie) (formerly Aeroflot Vladimir division) — Vladimir

Vladimir Airport, 600001 Vladimir, Russia ☎ (09222) 31 663 Tx: none Fax: (09222) 31 663 SITA: n/a
F: n/a 👥 n/a Head: Viktor I. Lunev Net: n/a Most aircraft are still in Aeroflot colors but will be repainted in due course.

☐ RA-02421	PZL Mielec (Antonov) An-2		CCCP-02421	0070		1 SH ASh-62IR	5500	Utility		
☐ RA-07844	PZL Mielec (Antonov) An-2		CCCP-07844	0076		1 SH ASh-62IR	5500	Utility		
☐ RA-16089	PZL Mielec (Antonov) An-2		CCCP-16089	0075		1 SH ASh-62IR	5500	Utility		
☐ RA-17811	PZL Mielec (Antonov) An-2		CCCP-17811	0083		1 SH ASh-62IR	5500	Utility		
☐ RA-17996	PZL Mielec (Antonov) An-2		CCCP-17996	0084		1 SH ASh-62IR	5500	Utility		
☐ RA-29369	PZL Mielec (Antonov) An-2		CCCP-29369	0076		1 SH ASh-62IR	5500	Utility		
☐ RA-31513	PZL Mielec (Antonov) An-2		CCCP-31513	0082		1 SH ASh-62IR	5500	Utility		
☐ RA-32420	PZL Mielec (Antonov) An-2	1G101-38	CCCP-32420	0068		1 SH ASh-62IR	5500	Utility		
☐ RA-32609	PZL Mielec (Antonov) An-2		CCCP-32609	0086		1 SH ASh-62IR	5500	Utility		
☐ RA-33312	PZL Mielec (Antonov) An-2		CCCP-33312	0087		1 SH ASh-62IR	5500	Utility		
☐ RA-40333	PZL Mielec (Antonov) An-2		CCCP-40333	0086		1 SH ASh-62IR	5500	Utility		
☐ RA-40729	PZL Mielec (Antonov) An-2		CCCP-40729	0076		1 SH ASh-62IR	5500	Utility		
☐ RA-40815	PZL Mielec (Antonov) An-2		CCCP-40815	0077		1 SH ASh-62IR	5500	Utility		
☐ RA-40843	PZL Mielec (Antonov) An-2		CCCP-40843	0077		1 SH ASh-62IR	5500	Utility		
☐ RA-40928	PZL Mielec (Antonov) An-2		CCCP-40928	0085		1 SH ASh-62IR	5500	Utility		
☐ RA-40965	PZL Mielec (Antonov) An-2		CCCP-40965	0085		1 SH ASh-62IR	5500	Utility		
☐ RA-44691	PZL Mielec (Antonov) An-2		CCCP-44691	0067		1 SH ASh-62IR	5500	Utility		
☐ RA-54818	PZL Mielec (Antonov) An-2		CCCP-54818	0079		1 SH ASh-62IR	5500	Utility		
☐ RA-54893	PZL Mielec (Antonov) An-2		CCCP-54893	0079		1 SH ASh-62IR	5500	Utility		
☐ RA-56449	PZL Mielec (Antonov) An-2		CCCP-56449	0078		1 SH ASh-62IR	5500	Utility		
☐ RA-56485	PZL Mielec (Antonov) An-2	1G182-42	CCCP-56485	0079		1 SH ASh-62IR	5500	Utility		
☐ RA-62561	PZL Mielec (Antonov) An-2		CCCP-62561	0077		1 SH ASh-62IR	5500	Utility		
☐ RA-62631	PZL Mielec (Antonov) An-2		CCCP-62631	0078		1 SH ASh-62IR	5500	Utility		
☐ RA-62667	PZL Mielec (Antonov) An-2		CCCP-62667	0078		1 SH ASh-62IR	5500	Utility		
☐ RA-71210	PZL Mielec (Antonov) An-2		CCCP-71210	0082		1 SH ASh-62IR	5500	Utility		
☐ RA-82807	PZL Mielec (Antonov) An-2		CCCP-82807	0075		1 SH ASh-62IR	5500	Utility		
☐ RA-84582	PZL Mielec (Antonov) An-2		CCCP-84582	0080		1 SH ASh-62IR	5500	Utility		
☐ RA-84642	PZL Mielec (Antonov) An-2		CCCP-84642	0080		1 SH ASh-62IR	5500	Utility		
☐ RA-84694	PZL Mielec (Antonov) An-2		CCCP-84694	0080		1 SH ASh-62IR	5500	Utility		
☐ RA-96230	PZL Mielec (Antonov) An-2		CCCP-96230	0066		1 SH ASh-62IR	5500	Utility		
☐ RA-47361	Antonov 24RV	67310705	CCCP-47361	0076		2 IV AI-24VT	21800	Y44		lst AKT
☐ RA-47363	Antonov 24RV	67310707	CCCP-47363	0076		2 IV AI-24VT	21800	Y48		

VLADIVOSTOK AIR, Joint-Stock Company = XF / VLK (Vladivostokavia) (formerly Vladivostok Aviation & AFL Vladivostok div.) — Vladivostok

Ul. Portovaya 41, 692811 Artem, (Primorsky Region), Russia ☎ (4232) 22 80 40 Tx: none Fax: (4232) 30 71 23 SITA: n/a
F: n/a 👥 n/a Head: Vladimir A. Saibel IATA: 277 ICAO: VLADIVOSTOK AIR Net: n/a Beside aircraft listed, additional (Tupolev 154B/M) are leased from MAVIAL (MVL) when required.

☐ RA-23203	PZL Swidnik (Mil) Mi-2	5310124027	CCCP-23203	0087	0087	2 IS GTD-350-4	3550	Utility		
☐ RA-31008	Kamov Ka-32T	5704	CCCP-31008	0087	0088	2 IS TV3-117VK	11000	Y15		
☐ RA-31009	Kamov Ka-32T	5705	CCCP-31009	0087	0088	2 IS TV3-117VK	11000	Y15		
☐ RA-31020	Kamov Ka-32S	6004	CCCP-31020	0089	0089	2 IS TV3-117VK	11000	Y15		
☐ RA-31021	Kamov Ka-32S	6005	CCCP-31021	0089	0089	2 IS TV3-117VK	11000	Y15		
☐ RA-31022	Kamov Ka-32S	6006	CCCP-31022	0089	0089	2 IS TV3-117VK	11000	Y15		
☐ RA-31029	Kamov Ka-32S	6104	CCCP-31029	0089	0089	2 IS TV3-117VK	11000	Y15		
☐ RA-31030	Kamov Ka-32S	6105	CCCP-31030	0089	0094	2 IS TV3-117VK	11000	Y15		
☐ RA-31031	Kamov Ka-32S	6106	CCCP-31031	0089	0089	2 IS TV3-117VK	11000	Y15		lst Aerolift Int'l P/L
☐ RA-31032	Kamov Ka-32S	6107	CCCP-31032	0089	0089	2 IS TV3-117VK	11000	Y15		lst Aerolift Int'l P/L
☐ RA-31036	Kamov Ka-32T	6111	CCCP-31036	0091	0091	2 IS TV3-117VK	11000	Y15		lst Aerolift Int'l P/L
☐ RA-31076	Kamov Ka-32T			0093	0093	2 IS TV3-117VK	11000	Y15		
☐ RA-31586	Kamov Ka-32A	8708		0092	0092	2 IS TV3-117VMA	11000	Y15		lst Aerolift Int'l P/L
☐ RA-31589	Kamov Ka-32A	8711		0092	0092	2 IS TV3-117VMA	11000	Y15		
☐ RA-22669	Mil Mi-8T	8121	CCCP-22669	0080	0082	2 IS TV2-117A	12000	Y22		
☐ RA-22724	Mil Mi-8T	98308688	CCCP-22724	0083	0083	2 IS TV2-117A	12000	Y22		
☐ RA-22904	Mil Mi-8T	98420113	CCCP-22904	0085	0085	2 IS TV2-117A	12000	Y22		
☐ RA-24245	Mil Mi-8T	98730890	CCCP-24245	0087	0087	2 IS TV2-117A	12000	Y22		
☐ RA-24633	Mil Mi-8PS-9	8408		0083	0087	2 IS TV2-117A	12000	C9		
☐ RA-25463	Mil Mi-8MTV-1	95607	CCCP-25463	0091	0091	2 IS TV3-117MT	13000	Y24		
☐ RA-25898	Mil Mi-8T	5171	CCCP-25898	0075	0075	2 IS TV2-117A	12000	Y22		
☐ RA-27101	Mil Mi-8AMT	59489605182		0092	0092	2 IS TV3-117MT	13000	Y26		lst Aerolift Int'l P/L
☐ RA-87273	Yakovlev 40	9310927	CCCP-87273	0073	0081	3 IV AI-25	17200	Y32		
☐ RA-87325	Yakovlev 40	9330430	CCCP-87325	0073	0073	3 IV AI-25	16800	Y32		
☐ RA-87376	Yakovlev 40	9411032	CCCP-87376	0074	0074	3 IV AI-25	16800	Y36		
☐ RA-87518	Yakovlev 40	9522040	CCCP-87518	0075	0075	3 IV AI-25	16800	Y32		
☐ RA-87546	Yakovlev 40	9531142	CCCP-87546	0075	0075	3 IV AI-25	16800	Y32		
☐ RA-87958	Yakovlev 40K	9821957	CCCP-87958	0078	0078	3 IV AI-25	17200	Y32 / Combi		
☐ RA-88163	Yakovlev 40	9611746	CCCP-88163	0076	0076	3 IV AI-25	16800	Y32		
☐ RA-88172	Yakovlev 40K	9631047	CCCP-88172	0076	0076	3 IV AI-25	16800	Y32 / Combi		
☐ RA-88222	Yakovlev 40	9630850	CCCP-88222	0076	0076	3 IV AI-25	16800	Y32		
☐ RA-88223	Yakovlev 40	9640950	CCCP-88223	0076	0076	3 IV AI-25	16800	Y32		
☐ RA-88232	Yakovlev 40K	9640151	CCCP-88232	0076	0076	3 IV AI-25	16800	Y32 / Combi		
☐ RA-88255	Yakovlev 40K	9711052	CCCP-88255	0077	0077	3 IV AI-25	16800	Y32 / Combi		
☐ RA-85588	Tupolev 154B-2	588	CCCP-85588	0083	0097	3 KU NK-8-2U	98000	Y164		lsf MVL
☐ RA-85596	Tupolev 154B-2	596	CCCP-85596	0084	0097	3 KU NK-8-2U	98000	Y164		lsf MVL
☐ RA-85710	Tupolev 154M	885	CCCP-85710	0091	0795	3 SO D-30KU-154-II	100000	Y164		
☐ RA-76400	Ilyushin 76TD	1023413438		0092	0092	4 SO D-30KP	190000	Freighter		lst ESL
☐ RA-76403	Ilyushin 76TD	1023412414		0092	0092	4 SO D-30KP	190000	Freighter		lst ESL
☐ RA-76492	Ilyushin 76T	093418548	YI-AKT	0479	0094	4 SO D-30KP	170000	Freighter		lst ESL / cvtd Ilyushin 76M

VNUKOVO AIRLINES, Joint-Stock Company = V5 / VKO (Vnukovskie avialinii) (formerly AFL Vnukovo prod.& flying unit) — Moscow-Domodedovo & -Vnukovo

I-aya Reisovaya 12, 103027 Moskva, Russia ☎ (095) 436 27 52 Tx: none Fax: (095) 436 26 26 SITA: n/a
F: 1993 👥 n/a Head: Alexander P. Romanov IATA: 442 ICAO: VNUKOVO Net: n/a Some aircraft are still in Aeroflot colors but will be repainted in due course.

☐ RA-42422	Yakovlev 42D	4520424304017		1193	0097	3 LO D-36	57500	C84 or Y120		
☐ RA-42435	Yakovlev 42D	4520424306017		1093	0097	3 LO D-36	56500	C84 or Y120		
☐ RA-42446	Yakovlev 42D	4520423308017	UN-42446	0993	0098	3 LO D-36	56500	C84 or Y120		
☐ RA-85084	Tupolev 154S	084	CCCP-85084	0074		3 KU NK-8-2U	98000	Freighter		cvtd 154A
☐ RA-85099	Tupolev 154B	099	CCCP-85099	0075		3 KU NK-8-2U	98000	Y164		cvtd 154A
☐ RA-85156	Tupolev 154B-1	156	CCCP-85156	0076		3 KU NK-8-2U	98000	Y164		cvtd 154B / std VKO in Aeroflot colors
☐ RA-85182	Tupolev 154B-1	182	CCCP-85182	0076		3 KU NK-8-2U	98000	Y164		cvtd 154B
☐ RA-85215	Tupolev 154B-1	215	CCCP-85215	0077		3 KU NK-8-2U	98000	Y164		cvtd 154B
☐ RA-85299	Tupolev 154B-2	299	CCCP-85299	0078		3 KU NK-8-2U	98000	Y164		cvtd 154B-1
☐ RA-85301	Tupolev 154B-2	301	CCCP-85301	0078		3 KU NK-8-2U	98000	Y164		
☐ RA-85610	Tupolev 154M	705	CCCP-85610	0084		3 SO D-30KU-154-II	100000	Y164		
☐ RA-85611	Tupolev 154M	715	CCCP-85611	0084		3 SO D-30KU-154-II	100000	Y164		
☐ RA-85612	Tupolev 154M	721	CCCP-85612	0085		3 SO D-30KU-154-II	100000	Y164		
☐ RA-85615	Tupolev 154M	731	CCCP-85615	0086		3 SO D-30KU-154-II	100000	Y164		

574 registration type of aircraft cn/fn ex/ex* mfd del powered by mtow kg configuration selcal name/fln/specialitites/remarks

	registration	type of aircraft	cn/fn	ex/ex*	mfd	del	powered by	mtow kg	configuration	selcal	name/fln/specialitites/remarks
☐	RA-85618	Tupolev 154M	737	CCCP-85618	0086		3 SO D-30KU-154-II	100000	Y164		
☐	RA-85619	Tupolev 154M	738	CCCP-85619	0086		3 SO D-30KU-154-II	100000	Y164		
☐	RA-85620	Tupolev 154M	739	TC-ACT	0086		3 SO D-30KU-154-II	100000	Y164		
☐	RA-85622	Tupolev 154M	746	CCCP-85622	0086		3 SO D-30KU-154-II	100000	Y164		
☐	RA-85623	Tupolev 154M	749	CCCP-85623	0087		3 SO D-30KU-154-II	100000	Y164		
☐	RA-85624	Tupolev 154M	750	CCCP-85624	0087		3 SO D-30KU-154-II	100000	Y164		
☐	RA-85628	Tupolev 154M	757	CCCP-85628	0087		3 SO D-30KU-154-II	100000	Y164		
☐	RA-85632	Tupolev 154M	761	CCCP-85632	0087		3 SO D-30KU-154-II	100000	Y164		std VKO
☐	RA-85633	Tupolev 154M	762	CCCP-85633	0087		3 SO D-30KU-154-II	100000	Y164		
☐	RA-85635	Tupolev 154M	764	CCCP-85635	0087		3 SO D-30KU-154-II	100000	Y164		
☐	RA-85673	Tupolev 154M	833	TC-ACV	0090		3 SO D-30KU-154-II	100000	Y164		
☐	RA-85674	Tupolev 154M	834	TC-ACI	0090		3 SO D-30KU-154-II	100000	Y164		
☐	RA-85736	Tupolev 154M	918	CCCP-85736	0992	0395	3 SO D-30KU-154-II	100000	Y164		
☐	RA-85743	Tupolev 154M	926	CCCP-85743	0092	0094	3 SO D-30KU-154-II	100000	Y166		
☐	RA-64008	Tupolev 204-100C	1450743264008		0092	0098	2 SO PS-90A	103000	Freighter		cvtd 204
☐	RA-64011	Tupolev 204	1450741364011		0093		2 SO PS-90A	94600	Y210		
☐	RA-64012	Tupolev 204	1450742364012		0093	0094	2 SO PS-90A	94600	Y214		
☐	RA-64013	Tupolev 204	1450743364013		0093	0094	2 SO PS-90A	94600	Y214		
☐	RA-86004	Ilyushin 86	0002	CCCP-86004	0079		4 KU NK-86	215000	Y304		
☐	RA-86005	Ilyushin 86	0003	CCCP-86005	0080		4 KU NK-86	215000	Y350		std VKO
☐	RA-86006	Ilyushin 86	0004	CCCP-86006	0080		4 KU NK-86	215000	Y304		
☐	RA-86007	Ilyushin 86	0005	CCCP-86007	0080		4 KU NK-86	215000	Y350		
☐	RA-86008	Ilyushin 86	0006	CCCP-86008	0081		4 KU NK-86	215000	Y350		std VKO
☐	RA-86009	Ilyushin 86	0007	CCCP-86009	0081		4 KU NK-86	215000	Y350		
☐	RA-86010	Ilyushin 86	0008	CCCP-86010	0081		4 KU NK-86	215000	Y304		
☐	RA-86011	Ilyushin 86	0009	CCCP-86011	0081		4 KU NK-86	215000	Y350		
☐	RA-86013	Ilyushin 86	0011	CCCP-86013	0081		4 KU NK-86	215000	Y350		
☐	RA-86014	Ilyushin 86	0012	CCCP-86014	0081		4 KU NK-86	215000	Y350		std VKO
☐	RA-86017	Ilyushin 86	51483202015	CCCP-86017	0082		4 KU NK-86	215000	Y350		
☐	RA-86018	Ilyushin 86	51483202016	CCCP-86018	0082		4 KU NK-86	215000	Y350		std VKO
☐	RA-86055	Ilyushin 86	51483203022	CCCP-86055	0083		4 KU NK-86	215000	Y304		
☐	RA-86081	Ilyushin 86	51483206052	CCCP-86081	0086		4 KU NK-86	215000	Y350		
☐	RA-86082	Ilyushin 86	51483206053	CCCP-86082	0086		4 KU NK-86	215000	Y350		
☐	RA-86084	Ilyushin 86	51483206055	CCCP-86084	0086		4 KU NK-86	215000	Y350		
☐	RA-86085	Ilyushin 86	51483206056	CCCP-86085	0086		4 KU NK-86	215000	Y350		
☐	RA-86089	Ilyushin 86	51483206060	CCCP-86089	0087		4 KU NK-86	215000	Y350		
☐	RA-86091	Ilyushin 86	51483207062	CCCP-86091	0087		4 KU NK-86	215000	Y350		
☐	RA-86097	Ilyushin 86	51483207068	CCCP-86097	0088		4 KU NK-86	215000	Y350		
☐	RA-86104	Ilyushin 86	51483208072	CCCP-86104	0089		4 KU NK-86	215000	Y350		
☐	RA-86111	Ilyushin 86	51483208079	CCCP-86111	0090		4 KU NK-86	215000	Y350		

VOLGA AVIAEXPRESS, Joint-Stock Company = G6 / VLA (formerly Volga Airlines & Aeroflot Volgograd division) — Volgograd

Volgograd Airport, 400036 Volgograd, Russia ☎ (8442) 31 73 22 Tx: 117158 sky su Fax: (8442) 31 73 22 SITA: n/a

F: 1992 n/a Head: Yuri K. Balochkin IATA: 518 ICAO: AKHTUBA Net: n/a Most aircraft are still in Aeroflot colors but will be repainted in due course.

	registration	type of aircraft	cn/fn	ex/ex*	mfd	del	powered by	mtow kg	configuration	selcal	name/fln/specialitites/remarks
☐	RA-87436	Yakovlev 40	9431235	CCCP-87436	0074		3 IV AI-25	16800	Y30		
☐	RA-87496	Yakovlev 40	9541945	CCCP-87496	0176		3 IV AI-25	16800	Y32		lst TUL
☐	RA-87500	Yakovlev 40	9511939	CCCP-87500	0075		3 IV AI-25	16800	Y30		
☐	RA-87581	Yakovlev 40	9221322	CCCP-87581	0072		3 IV AI-25	16800	Y27		
☐	RA-87839	Yakovlev 40	9240526	CCCP-87839	0072		3 IV AI-25	16800	Y27		
☐	RA-88251	Yakovlev 40K	9710552	CCCP-88251	0077		3 IV AI-25	16800	Y32 / Frtr 4t		
☐	RA-88278	Yakovlev 40K	9732053	CCCP-88278	0077		3 IV AI-25	16800	Y32 / Frtr 4t		
☐	RA-65008	Tupolev 134A-3	46105	CCCP-65008	0076		2 SO D-30-III	47000	Y76		
☐	RA-65086	Tupolev 134A-3	60130	CCCP-65086	0077		2 SO D-30-III	47600	Y76		
☐	RA-65691	Tupolev 134A-3	63195	CCCP-65691	0080		2 SO D-30-III	47600	Y76		
☐	RA-65869	Tupolev 134A-3	28306	CCCP-65869	0075		2 SO D-30-III	47000	Y76		
☐	RA-65903	Tupolev 134A-3	63780	CCCP-65903	0081		2 SO D-30-III	47600	Y76		
☐	RA-42340	Yakovlev 42D	4520424606270	CCCP-42340	0086		3 LO D-36	57500	Y120		cvtd 42
☐	RA-42343	Yakovlev 42D	4520421708285	CCCP-42343	0087		3 LO D-36	57500	Y120		cvtd 42
☐	RA-42346	Yakovlev 42D	4520423708311	CCCP-42346	0087		3 LO D-36	57500	Y120		cvtd 42
☐	RA-42360	Yakovlev 42D	4520423811421	CCCP-42360	0088		3 LO D-36	57500	Y108		lst RSO / cvtd 42
☐	RA-42364	Yakovlev 42D	4520424811442	CCCP-42364	0088		3 LO D-36	57500	Y120		cvtd 42
☐	RA-42371	Yakovlev 42D	4520422914225	CCCP-42371	0089		3 LO D-36	57500	Y120		
☐	RA-42373	Yakovlev 42D	4520423914323	CCCP-42373	0089		3 LO D-36	57500	F8Y102		
☐	RA-42382	Yakovlev 42D	4520422016196	CCCP-42382	0090		3 LO D-36	57500	Y120		
☐	RA-42384	Yakovlev 42D	4520423016230	CCCP-42384	0090		3 LO D-36	57500	Y120		
☐	RA-42406	Yakovlev 42D	4520424116683	CCCP-42406	0091		3 LO D-36	57500	Y120		

VOLGA-DNEPR AIRLINES = VI / VDA — Ulyanovsk

Ul. Karbysheva 14, 432062 Ulyanovsk, Russia ☎ (8422) 20 26 71 Tx: 263838 vold ru Fax: (8422) 20 26 75 SITA: ULYOOVI

F: 1990 800 Head: Alexey Isaikin IATA: 412 ICAO: VOLGA DNEPR Net: http://www.voldn.ru/ Antonov 124 aircraft are jointly managed/operated with HEAVYLIFT (G-) subsidiary company HEAVYLIFT-VOLGA DNEPR Ltd.

	registration	type of aircraft	cn/fn	ex/ex*	mfd	del	powered by	mtow kg	configuration	selcal	name/fln/specialitites/remarks
☐	RA-87357	Yakovlev 40	9340631	CCCP-87357	1073	0693	3 IV AI-25	16100	Executive		
☐	RA-76401	Ilyushin 76TD	1023412399	CCCP-76401	0792	0595	4 SO D-30KP	190000	Freighter		lsf UHS / sub-lst HLA
☐	RA-76758	Ilyushin 76TD	0073474203	CCCP-76758	1286	0591	4 SO D-30KP	190000	Freighter		
☐	RA-	Ilyushin 96T					4 PW PW2340	270000	Freighter 92t		oo-delivery 0099
☐	RA-	Ilyushin 96T					4 PW PW2340	270000	Freighter 92t		oo-delivery 0099
☐	RA-	Ilyushin 96T					4 PW PW2340	270000	Freighter 92t		oo-delivery 0099
☐	RA-	Ilyushin 96T					4 PW PW2340	270000	Freighter 92t		oo-delivery 0099
☐	RA-82042	Antonov 124-100 Ruslan	9773054055093	CCCP-82042	0791	0891	4 LO D-18T	392000	Freighter		fn 06-06
☐	RA-82043	Antonov 124-100 Ruslan	9773054155101	CCCP-82043	1091	1191	4 LO D-18T	392000	Freighter		fn 06-07
☐	RA-82044	Antonov 124-100 Ruslan	9773054155109	CCCP-82044	0292	0292	4 LO D-18T	392000	Freighter		fn 06-08
☐	RA-82045	Antonov 124-100 Ruslan	9773052255113	CCCP-82045	0492	0692	4 LO D-18T	392000	Freighter		fn 06-09
☐	RA-82046	Antonov 124-100 Ruslan	9773052255117	RA-82067	0692	1292	4 LO D-18T	392000	Freighter		fn 06-10
☐	RA-82047	Antonov 124-100 Ruslan	9773053259121	CCCP-82068	0393	0393	4 LO D-18T	392000	Freighter		fn 07-01
☐	RA-82078	Antonov 124-100 Ruslan	9773054559153		0996	0996	4 LO D-18T	392000	Freighter		fn 07-10

VOLGODONSKY ASK (Volgodonsk Aviation Sport Club) — Volgodonsk

Ul. Volgodonskaya 22, 347340 Volgodonsk, (Rostov Region), Russia ☎ (86392) 21 833 Tx: none Fax: none SITA: n/a

F: n/a n/a Head: Vyacheslav S. Zolotarev Net: n/a

	registration	type of aircraft	cn/fn	ex/ex*	mfd	del	powered by	mtow kg	configuration	selcal	name/fln/specialitites/remarks
☐	RA-23609	PZL Swidnik (Mil) Mi-2					2 IS GTD-350-4	3550	Utility		
☐	RA-23610	PZL Swidnik (Mil) Mi-2					2 IS GTD-350-4	3550	Utility		
☐	RA-23611	PZL Swidnik (Mil) Mi-2					2 IS GTD-350-4	3550	Utility		
☐	RA-02870	PZL Mielec (Antonov) An-2		CCCP-02870	0065		1 SH ASh-62IR	5250	Utility		
☐	RA-02871	PZL Mielec (Antonov) An-2		CCCP-02871	0065		1 SH ASh-62IR	5250	Utility		
☐	RA-02872	PZL Mielec (Antonov) An-2		CCCP-02872	0065		1 SH ASh-62IR	5250	Utility		
☐	RA-02873	PZL Mielec (Antonov) An-2		CCCP-02873	0065		1 SH ASh-62IR	5250	Utility		

VOLOGDA AIR ENTERPRISE = VGV (Vologodskoe aviapredpriatie) (formerly Aeroflot Vologda division) — Vologda

Vologda Airport, 160015 Vologda, Russia ☎ (8172) 72 50 12 Tx: none Fax: (8172) 72 06 86 SITA: n/a

F: 1933 n/a Head: Yuri I. Palady ICAO: VOLOGDA AIR Net: n/a Most aircraft are still in Aeroflot colors but will be repainted in due course.

	registration	type of aircraft	cn/fn	ex/ex*	mfd	del	powered by	mtow kg	configuration	selcal	name/fln/specialitites/remarks
☐	RA-14271	PZL Swidnik (Mil) Mi-2					2 IS GTD-350-4	3550	Utility		
☐	RA-20229	PZL Swidnik (Mil) Mi-2	527047021	CCCP-20229	0081		2 IS GTD-350-4	3550	Utility		
☐	RA-20406	PZL Swidnik (Mil) Mi-2	529904086	CCCP-20406	0086		2 IS GTD-350-4	3550	Utility		
☐	RA-20699	PZL Swidnik (Mil) Mi-2	536807080	CCCP-20699	0080		2 IS GTD-350-4	3550	Utility		
☐	RA-20700	PZL Swidnik (Mil) Mi-2	536808080	CCCP-20700	0080		2 IS GTD-350-4	3550	Utility		
☐	RA-20743	PZL Swidnik (Mil) Mi-2	527640052	CCCP-20743	0082		2 IS GTD-350-4	3550	Utility		
☐	RA-20962	PZL Swidnik (Mil) Mi-2	549518115	CCCP-20962	0085		2 IS GTD-350-4	3550	Utility		
☐	RA-20963	PZL Swidnik (Mil) Mi-2	549519115	CCCP-20963	0085		2 IS GTD-350-4	3550	Utility		
☐	RA-20974	PZL Swidnik (Mil) Mi-2	549647026	CCCP-20974	0086		2 IS GTD-350-4	3550	Utility		
☐	RA-20975	PZL Swidnik (Mil) Mi-2	549648026	CCCP-20975	0086		2 IS GTD-350-4	3550	Utility		
☐	RA-20976	PZL Swidnik (Mil) Mi-2	549649026	CCCP-20976	0086		2 IS GTD-350-4	3550	Utility		
☐	RA-23292	PZL Swidnik (Mil) Mi-2	529113025	CCCP-23292	0085		2 IS GTD-350-4	3550	Utility		
☐	RA-23345	PZL Swidnik (Mil) Mi-2	539303065	CCCP-23345	0085		2 IS GTD-350-4	3550	Utility		
☐	RA-23409	PZL Swidnik (Mil) Mi-2	548931104	CCCP-23409	0084		2 IS GTD-350-4	3550	Utility		
☐	RA-23446	PZL Swidnik (Mil) Mi-2	539419095	CCCP-23446	0085		2 IS GTD-350-4	3550	Utility		
☐	RA-02408	PZL Mielec (Antonov) An-2		CCCP-02408	0070		1 SH ASh-62IR	5500	Utility		
☐	RA-07493	PZL Mielec (Antonov) An-2		CCCP-07493	0073		1 SH ASh-62IR	5500	Utility		
☐	RA-07746	PZL Mielec (Antonov) An-2		CCCP-07746	0074		1 SH ASh-62IR	5500	Utility		
☐	RA-07749	PZL Mielec (Antonov) An-2		CCCP-07749	0074		1 SH ASh-62IR	5500	Utility		
☐	RA-07782	PZL Mielec (Antonov) An-2		CCCP-07782	0075		1 SH ASh-62IR	5500	Utility		
☐	RA-17968	PZL Mielec (Antonov) An-2		CCCP-17968	0084		1 SH ASh-62IR	5500	Utility		
☐	RA-29337	PZL Mielec (Antonov) An-2		CCCP-29337	0066		1 SH ASh-62IR	5500	Utility		

registration	type of aircraft	cn/fn	ex/ex*	mfd	del	powered by	mtow kg	configuration	selcal	name/fln/specialitites/remarks
☐ RA-29346	PZL Mielec (Antonov) An-2		CCCP-29346	0066		1 SH ASh-62IR	5500	Utility		
☐ RA-32281	PZL Mielec (Antonov) An-2		CCCP-32281	0068		1 SH ASh-62IR	5500	Utility		
☐ RA-33067	PZL Mielec (Antonov) An-2		CCCP-33067	0086		1 SH ASh-62IR	5500	Utility		
☐ RA-33320	PZL Mielec (Antonov) An-2		CCCP-33320	0087		1 SH ASh-62IR	5500	Utility		
☐ RA-33568	PZL Mielec (Antonov) An-2		CCCP-33568	0088		1 SH ASh-62IR	5500	Utility		
☐ RA-35652	PZL Mielec (Antonov) An-2		CCCP-35652	0069		1 SH ASh-62IR	5500	Utility		
☐ RA-40224	PZL Mielec (Antonov) An-2		CCCP-40224	0086		1 SH ASh-62IR	5500	Utility		
☐ RA-40575	PZL Mielec (Antonov) An-2		CCCP-40575	0067		1 SH ASh-62IR	5500	Utility		
☐ RA-40869	PZL Mielec (Antonov) An-2		CCCP-40869	0085		1 SH ASh-62IR	5500	Utility		
☐ RA-40870	PZL Mielec (Antonov) An-2		CCCP-40870	0085		1 SH ASh-62IR	5500	Utility		
☐ RA-40896	PZL Mielec (Antonov) An-2		CCCP-40896	0085		1 SH ASh-62IR	5500	Utility		
☐ RA-70160	PZL Mielec (Antonov) An-2		CCCP-70160	0071		1 SH ASh-62IR	5500	Utility		
☐ RA-70179	PZL Mielec (Antonov) An-2		CCCP-70179	0071		1 SH ASh-62IR	5500	Utility		
☐ RA-70662	PZL Mielec (Antonov) An-2		CCCP-70662	0071		1 SH ASh-62IR	5500	Utility		
☐ RA-70697	PZL Mielec (Antonov) An-2		CCCP-70697	0071		1 SH ASh-62IR	5500	Utility		
☐ RA-81522	PZL Mielec (Antonov) An-2		CCCP-81522	0084		1 SH ASh-62IR	5500	Utility		
☐ RA-81537	PZL Mielec (Antonov) An-2		CCCP-81537	0084		1 SH ASh-62IR	5500	Utility		
☐ RA-28711	PZL Mielec (Antonov) An-28	1AJ006-21	CCCP-28711	0089		2 GS TVD-10B	6500	Y17		
☐ RA-28717	PZL Mielec (Antonov) An-28	1AJ007-02	CCCP-28717	0089		2 GS TVD-10B	6500	Y17		
☐ RA-28718	PZL Mielec (Antonov) An-28	1AJ007-03	CCCP-28718	0089		2 GS TVD-10B	6500	Y17		
☐ RA-25588	Mil Mi-8T		CCCP-25588	0091		2 IS TV2-117A	12000	Utility		
☐ RA-27194	Mil Mi-8T			0093		2 IS TV2-117A	12000	Utility		
☐ RA-27195	Mil Mi-8T			0093		2 IS TV2-117A	12000	Utility		
☐ RA-87277	Yakovlev 40	9321327	CCCP-87277	0073		3 IV AI-25	16800	Y32		
☐ RA-87284	Yakovlev 40	9311927	CCCP-87284	0073		3 IV AI-25	16800	Y32		
☐ RA-87429	Yakovlev 40	9420535	CCCP-87429	0074		3 IV AI-25	16800	Y32		
☐ RA-87433	Yakovlev 40	9420935	CCCP-87433	0074		3 IV AI-25	16800	Y32		
☐ RA-87582	Yakovlev 40	9221422	CCCP-87582	0072		3 IV AI-25	16800	Y32		
☐ RA-87606	Yakovlev 40	9120518	CCCP-87606	0071		3 IV AI-25	16800	Y32		
☐ RA-87611	Yakovlev 40		CCCP-87611	0071		3 IV AI-25	16800	Y32		
☐ RA-87665	Yakovlev 40	9240925	CCCP-87665	0072		3 IV AI-25	16800	Y32		
☐ RA-87837	Yakovlev 40	9240326	CCCP-87837	0072		3 IV AI-25	16800	Y32		
☐ RA-87842	Yakovlev 40		CCCP-87842	0073		3 IV AI-25	16800	Y32		
☐ RA-87844	Yakovlev 40	9331330	CCCP-87844	0073		3 IV AI-25	16800	Y32		
☐ RA-88170	Yakovlev 40	9620847	CCCP-88170	0076		3 IV AI-25	16800	Y32		
☐ RA-88171	Yakovlev 40	9620947	CCCP-88171	0376		3 IV AI-25	17200	Y36		lst IRK as EP-LBK
☐ RA-88247	Yakovlev 40	9642051	CCCP-88247	1276		3 IV AI-25	16800	Y36		lst IRK as EP-LBJ

VORONEZHAVIA = ZT / VRN (formerly Aeroflot Voronezh division) **Voronezh-Chertovitskoe**

Voronezh Airport, 394025 Voronezh, Russia ☎ (0732) 16 09 37 Tx: 153114 port Fax: (0732) 55 35 66 SITA: n/a

F: n/a ⁂ n/a Head: Evgeni D. Shabunin ICAO: VORONEZHAVIA Net: n/a Most aircraft are still in Aeroflot colors but will be repainted in due course.

registration	type of aircraft	cn/fn	ex/ex*	mfd	del	powered by	mtow kg	configuration	selcal	name/fln/specialitites/remarks
☐ RA-01428	PZL Mielec (Antonov) An-2	1G231-08	CCCP-01428	0088		1 SH ASh-62IR	5500	Utility		
☐ RA-02273	PZL Mielec (Antonov) An-2	1G238-50	CCCP-02273	0090		1 SH ASh-62IR	5500	Utility		
☐ RA-02286	PZL Mielec (Antonov) An-2	1G239-13	CCCP-02286	0090		1 SH ASh-62IR	5500	Utility		
☐ RA-02287	PZL Mielec (Antonov) An-2	1G239-14	CCCP-02287	0090		1 SH ASh-62IR	5500	Utility		
☐ RA-02288	PZL Mielec (Antonov) An-2	1G239-15	CCCP-02288	0090		1 SH ASh-62IR	5500	Utility		
☐ RA-02289	PZL Mielec (Antonov) An-2	1G239-16	CCCP-02289	0090		1 SH ASh-62IR	5500	Utility		
☐ RA-05714	PZL Mielec (Antonov) An-2	1G153-27	CCCP-05714	0074		1 SH ASh-62IR	5500	Utility		
☐ RA-07514	PZL Mielec (Antonov) An-2	1G152-42	CCCP-07514	0073		1 SH ASh-62IR	5500	Utility		
☐ RA-07524	PZL Mielec (Antonov) An-2	1G152-52	CCCP-07524	0073		1 SH ASh-62IR	5500	Utility		
☐ RA-07770	PZL Mielec (Antonov) An-2	1G161-45	CCCP-07770	0075		1 SH ASh-62IR	5500	Utility		
☐ RA-07813	PZL Mielec (Antonov) An-2	1G169-28	CCCP-07813	0076		1 SH ASh-62IR	5500	Utility		
☐ RA-31402	PZL Mielec (Antonov) An-2	1G197-25	CCCP-31402	0082		1 SH ASh-62IR	5500	Utility		
☐ RA-31455	PZL Mielec (Antonov) An-2	1G198-20	CCCP-31455	0082		1 SH ASh-62IR	5500	Utility		
☐ RA-32459	PZL Mielec (Antonov) An-2	1G99-26	CCCP-32459	0068		1 SH ASh-62IR	5500	Utility		
☐ RA-33361	PZL Mielec (Antonov) An-2	1G226-20	CCCP-33361	0087		1 SH ASh-62IR	5500	Utility		
☐ RA-33529	PZL Mielec (Antonov) An-2	1G229-21	CCCP-33529	0088		1 SH ASh-62IR	5500	Utility		
☐ RA-33596	PZL Mielec (Antonov) An-2	1G230-38	CCCP-33596	0088		1 SH ASh-62IR	5500	Utility		
☐ RA-33597	PZL Mielec (Antonov) An-2	1G230-39	CCCP-33597	0088		1 SH ASh-62IR	5500	Utility		
☐ RA-35316	PZL Mielec (Antonov) An-2	1G134-09	CCCP-35316	0071		1 SH ASh-62IR	5500	Utility		
☐ RA-40339	PZL Mielec (Antonov) An-2	1G222-16	CCCP-40339	0086		1 SH ASh-62IR	5500	Utility		
☐ RA-40709	PZL Mielec (Antonov) An-2	1G171-46	CCCP-40709	0076		1 SH ASh-62IR	5500	Utility		
☐ RA-40786	PZL Mielec (Antonov) An-2	1G173-13	CCCP-40786	0077		1 SH ASh-62IR	5500	Utility		
☐ RA-54913	PZL Mielec (Antonov) An-2	1G187-01	CCCP-54913	0080		1 SH ASh-62IR	5500	Utility		
☐ RA-56392	PZL Mielec (Antonov) An-2	1G180-22	CCCP-56392	0078		1 SH ASh-62IR	5500	Utility		
☐ RA-62633	PZL Mielec (Antonov) An-2	1G178-25	CCCP-62633	0078		1 SH ASh-62IR	5500	Utility		
☐ RA-68044	PZL Mielec (Antonov) An-2	1G193-16	CCCP-68044	0081		1 SH ASh-62IR	5500	Utility		
☐ RA-71180	PZL Mielec (Antonov) An-2	1G200-23	CCCP-71180	0082		1 SH ASh-62IR	5500	Utility		
☐ RA-82839	PZL Mielec (Antonov) An-2	1G167-53	CCCP-82839	0076		1 SH ASh-62IR	5500	Utility		
☐ RA-46243	Antonov 24B	77303306	CCCP-46243	0067		2 IV AI-24	21000	Y48		
☐ RA-46406	Antonov 24B	77304001	CCCP-46406	0067		2 IV AI-24	21000	Y48		
☐ RA-46420	Antonov 24B	87304105	CCCP-46420	0068		2 IV AI-24	21000	Y48		
☐ RA-46505	Antonov 24RV	37308309	CCCP-46505	0073		2 IV AI-24VT	21800	Y48		
☐ RA-46612	Antonov 24RV	37308609	CCCP-46612	0073		2 IV AI-24VT	21800	Y48		
☐ RA-46635	Antonov 24RV	37308901	CCCP-46635	0073		2 IV AI-24VT	21800	Y48		
☐ RA-46671	Antonov 24RV	47309603	TC-KAR	0074		2 IV AI-24VT	21800	Y48		
☐ RA-46676	Antonov 24RV	47309608	CCCP-46676	0074		2 IV AI-24VT	21800	Y48		
☐ RA-46690	Antonov 24RV	47309901	CCCP-46690	0074		2 IV AI-24VT	22500	Y48		
☐ RA-47321	Antonov 24RV	67310507	TC-TOR	0076		2 IV AI-24VT	21800	Y48		
☐ RA-65057	Tupolev 134A-3	49865	CCCP-65057	0077		2 SO D-30-III	49000	Y76		lst NLB
☐ RA-65062	Tupolev 134A	49875	CCCP-65062	0077		2 SO D-30-II	49000	Y76		
☐ RA-65067	Tupolev 134A-3	49905	CCCP-65067	0077		2 SO D-30-III	49000	Y76		
☐ RA-65721	Tupolev 134A	66130	CCCP-65721	0084		2 SO D-30-II	47600	Agri Research		
☐ RA-65723	Tupolev 134A	66440	CCCP-65723	0089		2 SO D-30-II	47600	Agri Research		
☐ RA-65724	Tupolev 134A-3	66445	CCCP-65724	0089		2 SO D-30-III	47600	Agri Research		
☐ RA-65762	Tupolev 134A-3	62279	CCCP-65762	0079		2 SO D-30-III	49000	Y76		
☐ RA-65794	Tupolev 134A-3	63135	CCCP-65794	0080		2 SO D-30-III	49000	Y76		
☐ RA-65880	Tupolev 134A-3	35200	CCCP-65880	0075		2 SO D-30-III	47000	Y76		
☐ RA-65881	Tupolev 134A-3	35220	CCCP-65881	0075		2 SO D-30-III	47000	Y76		
☐ RA-65918	Tupolev 134A	63995	CCCP-65918	0084		2 SO D-30-II	47600	Agri Research		
☐ RA-65929	Tupolev 134A	66495	CCCP-65929	0085		2 SO D-30-II	47600	Agri Research		
☐ RA-65930	Tupolev 134A-3	66500	CCCP-65930	0089		2 SO D-30-III	49000	Y76 / Agri Res.		
☐ RA-42323	Yakovlev 42D	4520423402116	CCCP-42323	0084		3 LO D-36	56500	Y120		cvtd 42
☐ RA-42379	Yakovlev 42D	4520421014543	CCCP-42379	0090		3 LO D-36	56500	Y120		

VOSTOK Airlines = VTK (East Air) (formerly Aeroflot 2nd Khabarovsk division) **Khabarovsk-MVL**

MVL Airport, 680012 Khabarovsk, Russia ☎ (4212) 37 25 62 Tx: 141225 nebo su Fax: (4212) 37 15 83 SITA: n/a

F: 1945 ⁂ n/a Head: Fanis M. Mirzayanov ICAO: VOSTOK Net: n/a Some aircraft are still in Aeroflot colors but will be repainted in due course.

registration	type of aircraft	cn/fn	ex/ex*	mfd	del	powered by	mtow kg	configuration	selcal	name/fln/specialitites/remarks
☐ RA-14324	PZL Swidnik (Mil) Mi-2	514244075	23 RED	0775	0794	2 IS GTD-350-4	3700	Trainer/Combi		
☐ RA-15715	PZL Swidnik (Mil) Mi-2	522319032	CCCP-15715	0472	0772	2 IS GTD-350-4	3700	Sprayer		
☐ RA-20772	PZL Swidnik (Mil) Mi-2	527814092	CCCP-20772	0982	1182	2 IS GTD-350-4	3700	Sprayer		
☐ RA-20775	PZL Swidnik (Mil) Mi-2	527817092	CCCP-20775	0982	1282	2 IS GTD-350-4	3700	Sprayer		
☐ RA-23368	PZL Swidnik (Mil) Mi-2	528740064	CCCP-23368	0784	0884	2 IS GTD-350-4	3700	Sprayer		
☐ RA-23377	PZL Swidnik (Mil) Mi-2	548820084	CCCP-23377	0884	0984	2 IS GTD-350-4	3700	Trainer/Combi		
☐ RA-23712	PZL Swidnik (Mil) Mi-2	514249075		0775	0794	2 IS GTD-350-4	3700	Trainer/Combi		
☐ RA-23793	PZL Swidnik (Mil) Mi-2	548542024	CCCP-23793	0384	0794	2 IS GTD-350-4	3700	Trainer/Combi		
☐ RA-01403	PZL Mielec (Antonov) An-2	1G230-43	CCCP-01403	0788	0788	1 SH ASh-62IR	5250	Sprayer		
☐ RA-01404	PZL Mielec (Antonov) An-2	1G230-44	CCCP-01404	0788	0788	1 SH ASh-62IR	5250	Sprayer		
☐ RA-01499	PZL Mielec (Antonov) An-2	1G232-33	CCCP-01499	1188	0189	1 SH ASh-62IR	5250	Sprayer		
☐ RA-02461	PZL Mielec (Antonov) An-2	1G119-04	CCCP-02461	0970	1170	1 SH ASh-62IR	5250	Combi		
☐ RA-05753	PZL Mielec (Antonov) An-2P	1G151-61	CCCP-05753	0274	0474	1 SH ASh-62IR	5250	Y12		
☐ RA-07363	PZL Mielec (Antonov) An-2P	1G149-67	CCCP-07363	0873	1173	1 SH ASh-62IR	5250	Y12		
☐ RA-07364	PZL Mielec (Antonov) An-2P	1G149-68	CCCP-07364	0873	1173	1 SH ASh-62IR	5250	Y12		
☐ RA-31425	PZL Mielec (Antonov) An-2	1G197-48	CCCP-31425	0682	0782	1 SH ASh-62IR	5250	Sprayer		
☐ RA-31426	PZL Mielec (Antonov) An-2	1G197-49	CCCP-31426	0682	0782	1 SH ASh-62IR	5250	Sprayer		
☐ RA-33324	PZL Mielec (Antonov) An-2	1G225-43	CCCP-33324	0687	0787	1 SH ASh-62IR	5250	Sprayer		
☐ RA-33325	PZL Mielec (Antonov) An-2	1G225-44	CCCP-33325	0687	0787	1 SH ASh-62IR	5250	Sprayer		
☐ RA-33492	PZL Mielec (Antonov) An-2	1G228-43	CCCP-33492	0288	0488	1 SH ASh-62IR	5250	Sprayer		
☐ RA-40262	PZL Mielec (Antonov) An-2	1G220-52	CCCP-40262	0786	0886	1 SH ASh-62IR	5250	Sprayer		
☐ RA-40485	PZL Mielec (Antonov) An-2	1G225-02	CCCP-40485	0587	0687	1 SH ASh-62IR	5250	Sprayer		

☐ RA-40898	PZL Mielec (Antonov) An-2	1G215-35	CCCP-40898	0885	1085	1 SH ASh-62IR	5250	Sprayer		
☐ RA-68037	PZL Mielec (Antonov) An-2	1G193-09	CCCP-68037	0681	0781	1 SH ASh-62IR	5250	Sprayer		
☐ RA-67308	Let 410UVP	820808	CCCP-67308	0382	1088	2 WA M-601D	5800	Y15		
☐ RA-67377	Let 410UVP	831005	CCCP-67377	0383	0689	2 WA M-601D	5800	Y15		
☐ RA-67544	Let 410UVP	851511	CCCP-67544	0885	0188	2 WA M-601D	5800	Y15		
☐ RA-67634	Let 410UVP-E	902427	CCCP-67634	0590	0890	2 WA M-601E	6400	Y19		
☐ RA-67635	Let 410UVP-E	902428	CCCP-67635	0590	0790	2 WA M-601E	6400	Y19		
☐ RA-67636	Let 410UVP-E	902429	CCCP-67636	0590	0790	2 WA M-601E	6400	Y19		
☐ RA-67644	Let 410UVP-E	902437	CCCP-67644	0790	0790	2 WA M-601E	6400	Y19		
☐ RA-28920	PZL Mielec (Antonov) An-28	1AJ008-06	CCCP-28920	1090	1090	2 GS TVD-10B	6500	Y17		
☐ RA-28929	PZL Mielec (Antonov) An-28	1AJ008-16	CCCP-28929	0990	0990	2 GS TVD-10B	6500	Y17		
☐ RA-28931	PZL Mielec (Antonov) An-28	1AJ008-18	CCCP-28931	0990	0990	2 GS TVD-10B	6500	Y17		
☐ RA-28941	PZL Mielec (Antonov) An-28	1AJ009-07	CCCP-28941	1190	1096	2 GS TVD-10B	6500	Y17		
☐ RA-41902	Antonov 38-100			0098	0098	2 GA TPE331-14GR-801E	8800	Y26		
☐ RA-	Antonov 38-100			0098	0098	2 GA TPE331-14GR-801E	8800	Y26		
☐ RA-	Antonov 38-100			0098	0098	2 GA TPE331-14GR-801E	8800	Y26		
☐ RA-22279	Mil Mi-8T	6958	CCCP-22279	1276	1276	2 IS TV2-117A	12000	Combi		
☐ RA-22749	Mil Mi-8T	98311253	CCCP-22749	0583	0683	2 IS TV2-117A	12000	Combi		
☐ RA-22829	Mil Mi-8T	7629	CCCP-22829	0978	1078	2 IS TV2-117A	12000	Combi		
☐ RA-22915	Mil Mi-8T	98520247	CCCP-22915	0285	0385	2 IS TV2-117A	12000	Combi		
☐ RA-24116	Mil Mi-8T	98839781	CCCP-24116	0688	0888	2 IS TV2-117A	12000	Combi		
☐ RA-24246	Mil Mi-8T	98730894	CCCP-24246	0687	1087	2 IS TV2-117A	12000	Combi		
☐ RA-24429	Mil Mi-8T	98625598	CCCP-24429	0586	0686	2 IS TV2-117A	12000	Combi		
☐ RA-24488	Mil Mi-8T	98628952	CCCP-24488	1286	0187	2 IS TV2-117A	12000	Combi		
☐ RA-24500	Mil Mi-8T	98520599	CCCP-24500	0385	0585	2 IS TV2-117A	12000	Combi		
☐ RA-24640	Mil Mi-8T	8635	CCCP-24640	1186	0287	2 IS TV2-117A	12000	VIP		
☐ RA-25341	Mil Mi-8T	98206650	CCCP-25341	0582	0682	2 IS TV2-117A	12000	Combi		
☐ RA-25355	Mil Mi-8T	98206769	CCCP-25355	0782	0882	2 IS TV2-117A	12000	Combi		
☐ RA-25429	Mil Mi-8MTV-1	95461	CCCP-25429	1190	1191	2 IS TV3-117MT	13000	EMS/Hospital		
☐ RA-25486	Mil Mi-8MTV-1	95631	CCCP-25486	0391	0491	2 IS TV3-117MT	13000	Combi		
☐ RA-25869	Mil Mi-8T	5135	CCCP-25869	0375	0475	2 IS TV2-117A	12000	Combi		
☐ RA-25915	Mil Mi-8T	5545	CCCP-25915	0475	0575	2 IS TV2-117A	12000	Combi		
☐ RA-21014	Mil Mi-6	0438	CCCP-21014	0874	0974	2 SO D-25V	42500	Combi		
☐ RA-21134	Mil Mi-6	8683803B	CCCP-21134	0668	1290	2 SO D-25V	42500	Combi		
☐ RA-21153	Mil Mi-6	737002B	CCCP-21153	0473	0573	2 SO D-25V	42500	Combi		
☐ RA-06074	Mil Mi-26	3400121251		0193	0294	2 LO D-136	56000	Combi		
☐ RA-06084	Mil Mi-26	3400121247	CCCP-06084	0891	0091	2 LO D-136	56000	Combi		

VOSTSIBAERO = VSA (East Siberia Air) — Irkutsk

Ul. Sovetskaya 139a, 664009 Irkutsk, Russia ☎ (3952) 28 68 02 Tx: none Fax: (3952) 27 72 40 SITA: n/a
F: 1995 ⁂ n/a Head: Michael Y. Shelkovnikov ICAO: VOSSIBAERO Net: n/a

☐ RA-26692	Antonov 26		CCCP-26692	0079		2 IV AI-24VT	24000	Freighter		lsf Barnaul Air Enterprise
☐ RA-74024	Antonov 74			0092		2 LO D-36	36500	Freighter		
☐ RA-74037	Antonov 74-200			0093		2 LO D-36	36500	Freighter		

VZLET, Joint-Stock Company = VZL (Vzlet-NIILITs) — Solntsevo-Heliport

Ul. Proizvodstvennaya 6, 119619 Moskva, Russia ☎ (095) 435 27 20 Tx: none Fax: (095) 435 32 75 SITA: n/a
F: 1992 ⁂ n/a Head: Alexander A. Peregon ICAO: VZLET Net: n/a

☐ RA-31060	Kamov Ka-32A	31033	RA-06144	0094	0095	2 IS TV3-117VMA	11000	Utility		
☐ RA-22503	Mil Mi-8MTV-1	96078		0093	0098	2 IS TV3-117VM	13000	Utility		lst Heli Harvest
☐ RA-22948	Mil Mi-8T	99257154		0092	0097	2 IS TV2-117A	12000	Utility		
☐ RA-22974	Mil Mi-8T	98208247		0082	0092	2 IS TV2-117A	12000	Utility		
☐ RA-25746	Mil Mi-8MTV-1	96121	CCCP-25746	0093	0098	2 IS TV3-117VM	13000	Utility		lst Heli Harvest
☐ RA-27125	Mil Mi-8MTV-1	95952		0092	0092	2 IS TV3-117VM	13000	Utility		
☐ RA-04127	Mil Mi-10K	2290	CCCP-04127	0076	0092	2 SO D-25V	38000	Utility		

YAK SERVICE = AKY (Subsidiary of Yakovlev Design Bureau / Associated with Panatech Aviation) — Moscow-Zhukovsky & -Vnukovo

Leningradsky Prospekt 68, Box 191, 125315 Moskva, Russia ☎ (095) 151 66 92 Tx: none Fax: (095) 956 16 13 SITA: n/a
F: 1993 ⁂ n/a Head: Oleg N. Silnitsky ICAO: YAK-SERVICE Net: n/a

☐ RA-87243	Yakovlev 40	9531143	CCCP-87243	0075		3 IV AI-25	16800	C13		opf Krasny Oktyabr Production Assoc.
☐ RA-88295	Yakovlev 40	9331329	035	0073		3 IV AI-25	17200	C15		
☐ RA-42429	Yakovlev 42D	4520423407016		0093		3 LO D-36	56500	Y102		

YAMAL AIR TRANSPORT COMPANY = YL (Aviatransportnaya kompania Yamal) — Salekhard

Ul. Aviatsionnaya 27, 626603 Salekhard, (Tyumen Region), Russia ☎ (34591) 43 910 Tx: none Fax: (34591) 40 671 SITA: n/a
F: 1997 ⁂ n/a Head: Vasili N. Kryuk IATA: 268 Net: n/a

☐ RA-65143	Tupolev 134A-3	60967	CCCP-65143	0079	0098	2 SO D-30-III	49000	Y76		
☐ RA-65613	Tupolev 134A	3352106	D-AOBD	1273	0098	2 SO D-30-II	47000	Y80		lsf KMV

YARAVIA — Yaroslavl

Prospekt Lenina 18/50, P.14, 150040 Yaroslavl', Russia ☎ (0852) 23 33 61 Tx: none Fax: (0852) 32 05 87 SITA: n/a
F: n/a ⁂ n/a Head: Viktor V. Kuznetsov Net: n/a

☐ RA-22539	Mil Mi-8		CCCP-22539			2 IS TV2-117A	12000	Utility		
☐ RA-25413	Mil Mi-8MTV-1		CCCP-25413	0090		2 IS TV3-117MT	13000	Utility		
☐ RA-25414	Mil Mi-8MTV-1		CCCP-25414	0090		2 IS TV3-117MT	13000	Utility		

YAROSLAVL' AVIATION (Aviatsia Yaroslavlia) (formerly Aeroflot Yaroslavl' division) — Yaroslavl

Yaroslavl' Airport, 150062 Yaroslavl', Russia ☎ (0852) 11 06 02 Tx: none Fax: (0852) 11 22 82 SITA: n/a
F: 1950 ⁂ n/a Head: Nikolai I. Kuprianov Net: n/a Most aircraft are still in Aeroflot colors but will be repainted in due course.

☐ RA-14177	PZL Swidnik (Mil) Mi-2	5210513018	CCCP-14177	0888		2 IS GTD-350-4	3550	8 Pax		
☐ RA-15622	PZL Swidnik (Mil) Mi-2	5210037126	CCCP-15622	1286		2 IS GTD-350-4	3550	8 Pax		
☐ RA-15623	PZL Swidnik (Mil) Mi-2	5210038126	CCCP-15623	1286		2 IS GTD-350-4	3550	8 Pax		
☐ RA-20243	PZL Swidnik (Mil) Mi-2	527131051	CCCP-20243	0681		2 IS GTD-350-4	3550	8 Pax		
☐ RA-20244	PZL Swidnik (Mil) Mi-2	527132051	CCCP-20244	0681		2 IS GTD-350-4	3550	8 Pax		
☐ RA-20245	PZL Swidnik (Mil) Mi-2	527133051	CCCP-20245	0681		2 IS GTD-350-4	3550	8 Pax		
☐ RA-20305	PZL Swidnik (Mil) Mi-2	527449012	CCCP-20305	0182		2 IS GTD-350-4	3550	8 Pax		
☐ RA-20306	PZL Swidnik (Mil) Mi-2	527450012	CCCP-20306	0282		2 IS GTD-350-4	3550	8 Pax		
☐ RA-20307	PZL Swidnik (Mil) Mi-2	527513022	CCCP-20307	0382		2 IS GTD-350-4	3550	8 Pax		
☐ RA-20383	PZL Swidnik (Mil) Mi-2	529830066	CCCP-20383	0786		2 IS GTD-350-4	3550	8 Pax		
☐ RA-20421	PZL Swidnik (Mil) Mi-2	529924096	CCCP-20421	0986		2 IS GTD-350-4	3550	8 Pax		
☐ RA-20668	PZL Swidnik (Mil) Mi-2	526631040	CCCP-20668	0580		2 IS GTD-350-4	3550	8 Pax		
☐ RA-20672	PZL Swidnik (Mil) Mi-2	526635050	CCCP-20672	0580		2 IS GTD-350-4	3550	8 Pax		
☐ RA-20732	PZL Swidnik (Mil) Mi-2	547549092	CCCP-20732	0382		2 IS GTD-350-4	3550	8 Pax		
☐ RA-20733	PZL Swidnik (Mil) Mi-2	547550032	CCCP-20733	0482		2 IS GTD-350-4	3550	8 Pax		
☐ RA-20980	PZL Swidnik (Mil) Mi-2	529705036	CCCP-20980	0386		2 IS GTD-350-4	3550	8 Pax		
☐ RA-23421	PZL Swidnik (Mil) Mi-2	529016124	CCCP-23421	1284		2 IS GTD-350-4	3550	8 Pax		
☐ RA-23422	PZL Swidnik (Mil) Mi-2	529017124	CCCP-23422	1284		2 IS GTD-350-4	3550	8 Pax		
☐ RA-23423	PZL Swidnik (Mil) Mi-2	529018124	CCCP-23423	1284		2 IS GTD-350-4	3550	8 Pax		
☐ RA-17759	PZL Mielec (Antonov) An-2	1G203-20	CCCP-17759	0583		1 SH ASh-62IR	5500	12 Pax		
☐ RA-71218	PZL Mielec (Antonov) An-2	1G201-01	CCCP-71218	0183		1 SH ASh-62IR	5500	12 Pax		
☐ RA-22745	Mil Mi-8	98311154	CCCP-22745	0583		2 IS TV2-117A	12000	Utility		
☐ RA-22746	Mil Mi-8	98311172	CCCP-22746	0583		2 IS TV2-117A	12000	Utility		
☐ RA-22747	Mil Mi-8	98311198	CCCP-22747	0583		2 IS TV2-117A	12000	Utility		
☐ RA-24216	Mil Mi-8	98730317	CCCP-24216	0387		2 IS TV2-117A	12000	Utility		lst Yugorsk Air Company
☐ RA-24259	Mil Mi-8	98734139	CCCP-24259	0887		2 IS TV2-117A	12000	Utility		
☐ RA-24420	Mil Mi-8	98625342	CCCP-24420	0486		2 IS TV2-117A	12000	Utility		lst Yugorsk Air Company
☐ RA-24478	Mil Mi-8	98628840	CCCP-24478	1086		2 IS TV2-117A	12000	Utility		

YASHEN Aviakompania — Kazan 2

Ul. Radina 7a, 420089 Kazan, (Republic of Tatarstan), Russia ☎ (8432) 76 47 61 Tx: n/a Fax: (8432) 56 89 32 SITA: n/a
F: n/a ⁂ n/a Head: Fail G. Ibragimov Net: n/a

☐ RA-17723	PZL Mielec (Antonov) An-2	1G202-43	CCCP-17723	0483		1 SH ASh-62IR	5250	Sprayer		
☐ RA-33595	PZL Mielec (Antonov) An-2	1G230-37	CCCP-33595	0688		1 SH ASh-62IR	5250	Sprayer		
☐ RA-40644	PZL Mielec (Antonov) An-2	1G213-51	CCCP-40644	0585		1 SH ASh-62IR	5250	Sprayer		
☐ RA-62703	PZL Mielec (Antonov) An-2	1G174-33	CCCP-62703	0478		1 SH ASh-62IR	5250	Sprayer		
☐ RA-68134	PZL Mielec (Antonov) An-2	1G195-39	CCCP-68134	0282		1 SH ASh-62IR	5250	Sprayer		
☐ RA-71161	PZL Mielec (Antonov) An-2	1G200-04	CCCP-71161	1182		1 SH ASh-62IR	5250	Sprayer		
☐ RA-71276	PZL Mielec (Antonov) An-2	1G207-47	CCCP-71276	0484		1 SH ASh-62IR	5250	Sprayer		
☐ RA-71278	PZL Mielec (Antonov) An-2	1G207-49	CCCP-71278	0484		1 SH ASh-62IR	5250	Sprayer		

577 registration type of aircraft cn/fn ex/ex* mfd del powered by mtow kg configuration selcal name/fln/specialitites/remarks

YESSENTUKSKY ASK (Yessentuki Aviation Sport Club) — Yessentuki

Ul. Gogolya 5, 357600 Yessentuki, (Stavropol Region), Russia ☎ (86534) 53 047 Tx: none Fax: none SITA: n/a
F: n/a ☃ n/a Head: Yaroslav N. Kostushenko Net: n/a

☐ RA-02868	Antonov An-2			0047	0093	1 SH ASh-62IR	5500	Para		
☐ RA-02869	Antonov An-2			0047	0093	1 SH ASh-62IR	5500	Para		

YOSHKAR-OLA AIR ENTERPRISE (Yoshkar-Olinskoe aviapredpriatie) (formerly Aeroflot Yoshkar-Ola division) — Yoshkar-Ola

Yoshkar-Ola Airport, 424010 Yoshkar-Ola, (Republic of Mari-El), Russia ☎ (8362) 59 88 22 Tx: 220229 port Fax: (8362) 55 60 60 SITA: n/a
F: n/a ☃ n/a Head: Alexander P. Balashov Net: n/a
Most aircraft are still in Aeroflot colors but will be repainted in due course. Company will be transformed to the new national airline of the Republic of Mari-El.

☐ RA-09625	PZL Mielec (Antonov) An-2		CCCP-09625	0066		1 SH ASh-62IR	5500	Utility		
☐ RA-44674	PZL Mielec (Antonov) An-2		CCCP-44674	0067		1 SH ASh-62IR	5500	Utility		
☐ RA-46200	Antonov 24B	67302609	CCCP-46200	0066		2 IV AI-24	21000	Y48		
☐ RA-46204	Antonov 24B		CCCP-46204	0066		2 IV AI-24	21000	Y48		
☐ RA-46496	Antonov 24RV		CCCP-46496	0072		2 IV AI-24VT	21800	Y48		
☐ RA-46509	Antonov 24RV		CCCP-46509	0073		2 IV AI-24VT	21800	Y48		
☐ RA-46589	Antonov 24B		CCCP-46589	0069		2 IV AI-24	21000	Y48		
☐ RA-47285	Antonov 24B	07306505	CCCP-47285	0070		2 IV AI-24	21000	Y48		
☐ RA-47357	Antonov 24RV	67310606	CCCP-47357	0076		2 IV AI-24VT	21800	Y48		

YUGORSKAVIA, Joint-Stock Company (Yugorskaya aviatsionnaya kompania) — Sovetsky

Airport, 627740 pos. Sovetsky, (Tyumen Region), Russia ☎ (34675) 32 571 Tx: none Fax: (34675) 32 571 SITA: n/a
F: n/a ☃ n/a Head: Vladimir V. Luchinin Net: n/a

☐ RA-23783	PZL Swidnik (Mil) Mi-2					2 IS GTD-350-4	3550	EMS		
☐ RA-23784	PZL Swidnik (Mil) Mi-2					2 IS GTD-350-4	3550	EMS		
☐ RA-22314	Mil Mi-8		CCCP-22314	0077		2 IS TV2-117A	12000	Utility		lsf Uraiavia
☐ RA-22586	Mil Mi-8		CCCP-22586	0079		2 IS TV2-117A	12000	Utility		lsf Uraiavia
☐ RA-22821	Mil Mi-8		CCCP-22821	0078		2 IS TV2-117A	12000	Utility		lsf Uraiavia
☐ RA-24216	Mil Mi-8	98730317	CCCP-24216	0387		2 IS TV2-117A	12000	Utility		lsf Yaroslavl' Aviation
☐ RA-24420	Mil Mi-8	98625342	CCCP-24420	0486		2 IS TV2-117A	12000	Utility		lsf Yaroslavl' Aviation
☐ RA-25369	Mil Mi-8		CCCP-25369	0082		2 IS TV2-117A	12000	Utility		lsf Uraiavia
☐ RA-25879	Mil Mi-8		CCCP-25879	0075		2 IS TV2-117A	12000	Utility		lsf Uraiavia
☐ RA-25926	Mil Mi-8		CCCP-25926	0075		2 IS TV2-117A	12000	Utility		lsf Uraiavia

YUKOSAVIA, Joint-Stock Company (Yukos Air) (Subsidiary of Yukos Oil Company) — Nefteyugansk

Nefteyugansk Airport, 626430 Nefteyugansk, (Tyumen Region), Russia ☎ (34612) 39 973 Tx: none Fax: (34612) 39 305 SITA: n/a
F: 1994 ☃ n/a Head: Alexander Posokhov Net: n/a Suspended operations (with Tupolev 134A aircraft) in 1998. Intends to restart.

ZENIT = EZT — Moscow-Zhukovsky

Leningradskoe Shosse 6, 125299 Moskva, Russia ☎ (095) 155 20 17 Tx: n/a Fax: (095) 150 39 16 SITA: n/a
F: n/a ☃ n/a Head: Vyacheslav V. Mikailovski ICAO: ZENIT Net: n/a Most aircraft are still in Aeroflot colors with or without titles but will be repainted in due course.

☐ RA-48112	Yakovlev 40	9211520	CCCP-48112	0072		3 IV AI-25	16800	Combi		
☐ RA-11312	Antonov 12	3340903	87 RED	0063		4 IV AI-20M	61000	Freighter		
☐ RA-11992	Antonov 12	402604	CCCP-11992	0064		4 IV AI-20M	61000	Freighter		
☐ RA-86896	Ilyushin 76TD	0013434018		1181		4 SO D-30KP	190000	Freighter		lst IRH as EP-ALJ / cvtd MD

ZONALNOE AIR ENTERPRISE (Aviapredpriatie Zonalnoe) (formerly Aeroflot Zonalnoe division) — Zonalnoe

Zonalnoe Airport, 694404 Zonalnoe, (Tymovski District, Sakhalin Region), Russia ☎ (42447) 96 138 Tx: none Fax: (42447) 22 755 SITA: n/a
F: n/a ☃ n/a Head: n/a Net: n/a

☐ RA-17819	PZL Mielec (Antonov) An-2		CCCP-17819	0083		1 SH ASh-62IR	5500	Utility		
☐ RA-32553	PZL Mielec (Antonov) An-2		CCCP-32553	0068		1 SH ASh-62IR	5500	Utility		
☐ RA-40759	PZL Mielec (Antonov) An-2		CCCP-40759	0076		1 SH ASh-62IR	5500	Utility		
☐ RA-82837	PZL Mielec (Antonov) An-2	1G167-51	CCCP-82837	0076		1 SH ASh-62IR	5500	Utility		
☐ RA-96255	PZL Mielec (Antonov) An-2		CCCP-96255	0066		1 SH ASh-62IR	5500	Utility		

RDPL = LAOS (Lao People's Democratic Republic) (Sathalanalat Paxathipatai Paxaxon Lao)

Capital: Vientiane Official Language: Lao Population: 5,0 million Square Km: 236800 Dialling code: +856 Year established: 1953 Acting political head: Khamtay Siphandone (President)

Government / Corporate / Executive / VIP Aircraft

☐ RDPL-34015	Xian Yunshuji Y7-100C	12703		0091	0393	2 WJ 5A-1	21800	VIP		Gvmt
☐ RDPL-34016	Xian Yunshuji Y7-100C	12704		0091	0393	2 WJ 5A-1	21800	VIP		Gvmt

LAO AVIATION = QV / LAO — Vientiane

BP 4169, Vientiane, Laos ☎ (21) 21 20 57 Tx: 4336 laoav ls Fax: (21) 21 20 50 SITA: n/a
F: 1979 ☃ 260 Head: Sisavath Boussamaly IATA: 627 ICAO: LAO Net: n/a

☐ RDPL-34115	Harbin Yunshuji Y12 II	0033		0090	0290	2 PWC PT6A-27	5300	Y17		
☐ RDPL-34116	Harbin Yunshuji Y12 II	0034		0090	0490	2 PWC PT6A-27	5300	Y17		
☐ RDPL-34118	Harbin Yunshuji Y12 II	0043		0090	0191	2 PWC PT6A-27	5300	Y17		std VTE
☐ RDPL-34129	Harbin Yunshuji Y12 II	0085		0894	1194	2 PWC PT6A-27	5300	Y17		std VTE
☐ RDPL-34130	Harbin Yunshuji Y12 II	0086		0894	1194	2 PWC PT6A-27	5300	Y17		
☐ RDPL-34131	Harbin Yunshuji Y12 II	0087		1094	1294	2 PWC PT6A-27	5300	Y17		
☐ RDPL-34040	Mil Mi-8	23510		0085		2 IS TV2-117A	11000	Y28		
☐ RDPL-34002	Yakovlev 40	9840559		0068		3 IV AI-25	16000	Y32		
☐ RDPL-34132	ATR 72-202	396	F-OLAO	0093	0995	2 PWC PW124B	21500	Y74		
☐ RDPL-34005	Antonov 24RV	67310609		0076		2 IV AI-24VT	21800	Y52		
☐ RDPL-34119	Xian Yunshuji Y7-100C	10707		0091	0891	2 WJ 5A-1	21800	Y52		std VTE
☐ RDPL-34127	Xian Yunshuji Y7-100C	12706		0094	0094	2 WJ 5A-1	21800	Y52		
☐ RDPL-34128	Xian Yunshuji Y7-100C	13701		0094	0094	2 WJ 5A-1	21800	Y52		
☐ RDPL-34018	Antonov 74TK-100			0090	1098	2 LO D-36	36000	Y52/Combi/VIP		

LAO WESTCOAST HELICOPTER Company – LWCH (Subsidiary of Helicopters Australia, Pty Ltd) — Vientiane

Airport, Vientiane, Laos ☎ (21) 51 20 23 Tx: none Fax: (21) 51 20 55 SITA: n/a
F: 1991 ☃ 13 Head: David Reed Net: n/a

☐ ZK-HBU	Eurocopter (Aerosp.) AS350B Squirrel	1558	SX-HBO	0082		1 TU Arriel 1B	1950			lsf Helicopters New Zealand
☐ ZK-HDK	Eurocopter (Aerosp.) AS350BA Squirrel	1466	F-ODVZ	0081	0098	1 TU Arriel 1B	2100			lsf Helicopters New Zealand/cvtd AS350B
☐ ZK-HDQ	Eurocopter (Aerosp.) AS350B Squirrel	1932	VH-BHX	0086		1 AN 250-C30	1950			lsf Helic. NZ / cvtd TU Arriel AS350B
☐ ZK-HNK	Eurocopter (Aerosp.) AS350B2 Squirrel	2349	VH-WCS	0090		1 TU Arriel 1D1	2250			lsf Helicopters New Zealand
☐ ZK-HNL	Eurocopter (Aerosp.) AS350B Squirrel	1550		0082	0097	1 TU Arriel 1B	1950			lsf Helicopters New Zealand
☐ ZK-HNZ	Eurocopter (Aerosp.) AS350B2 Squirrel	2463	HB-XVT	0091	1297	1 TU Arriel 1D1	2250			lsf Helicopters New Zealand
☐ ZK-HZK	Eurocopter (Aerosp.) AS350B Squirrel	1827		0085	0097	1 TU Arriel 1B	1950			lsf Helicopters New Zealand

RP = PHILIPPINES (Republic of the Philippines) (Republica Ng Pilipinas)

Capital: Manila Official Language: Pilipino, Tagalog, English Population: 72,0 million Square Km: 300000 Dialling code: +63 Year established: 1898 Acting political head: Joseph Estrada (President)

PALAU (Republic of Palau) (This country is registering its aircraft in the Philippines under a general agreement)
Capital: Koror Official Language: English Population: 0,1 million Square Km: 458 Dialling code: +680 Acting political head: Kuniwo Nakamura (President)

Government / Corporate / Executive / VIP Aircraft

☐ RP-1250	Fokker F28 Fellowship 3000 (F28 Mk3000)	11153	RP-C1177	0079	0880	2 RR Spey 555-15H	33112	VIP		Gvmt/Presidential Airlift Wing
☐ RP-1896	Bell 412EP	36141	N11598*	0096	1196	2 PWC PT6T-3D TwinPac	5398	VIP		Gvmt/Presidential Airlift Wing
☐ RP-1898	Bell 412EP	36138	N34962*	0096	1196	2 PWC PT6T-3D TwinPac	5398	VIP		Gvmt/Presidential Airlift Wing
☐ RP-1946	Bell 412EP	36136	N34948*	0096	1196	2 PWC PT6T-3D TwinPac	5398	VIP		Gvmt/Presidential Airlift Wing
☐ RP-1986	Bell 412EP	36127	N20573*	0096	1196	2 PWC PT6T-3D TwinPac	5398	VIP		Gvmt/Presidential Airlift Wing
☐ RP-1998	Bell 412HP	36079	N52972*	0094	0694	2 PWC PT6T-3D TwinPac	5398	VIP		Gvmt/Presidential Airlift Wing
☐ RP-2000	Bell 412HP	36080	N52973*	0094	0694	2 PWC PT6T-3D TwinPac	5398	VIP		Gvmt/Presidential Airlift Wing
☐ RP-2001	BAe (HS) 748-209 Srs 2A	1641 / 107	RP-211	0068	0379	2 RR Dart 533-2	20183	Liaison		Air Transportation Office
☐ RP-2100	Beech King Air B200	BB-1405	N8129A	0091	0194	2 PWC PT6A-42	5670	Liaison		Air Transportation Office
☐ RP-C752	Eurocopter (Aerosp.) SA330L Puma	1562		0078		2 TU Turmo IVC	7400	VIP		Gvmt/Presidential Airlift Wing
☐ RP-C753	Eurocopter (Aerosp.) SA330L Puma	1570		0078		2 TU Turmo IVC	7400	VIP		Jiggy / Gvmt/Presidential Airlift Wing
☐ RP-C8800	Bell 412EP	36139	N34972	0096	0996	2 PWC PT6T-3D TwinPac	5398	VIP		Gvmt/Presidential Airlift Wing
☐ 59-0259	Fokker F27 Friendship 200 (F27 Mk200)	10115	PH-FAM*	0059	0959	2 RR Dart 532-7	19731	VIP		The President / Philippine AF/cvtd -100

AAI Island Hopper (Air Ads, Inc. dba) — Manila

Andrews Ave, Domestic Airport, Pasay City, Metro Manila 1300, Philippines ☎ (2) 833 32 64 Tx: 63590 airads pn Fax: (2) 831 49 39 SITA: n/a
F: 1982 ☃ 90 Head: Jose Mari C. Roa Net: n/a Aircraft below MTOW 1361kg: Cessna 172 & Piper PA-18.

☐ RP-C1284	Bell 206B JetRanger III	3256		0081	0095	1 AN 250-C20B	1451	5 Pax		lsf Max's Ermita Inc.
☐ RP-C2068	Cessna U206F Stationair II	U20602652		0075	0095	1 CO IO-520-F	1633	6 Pax		lsf pvt
☐ RP-C1400	Bell 206L LongRanger	45013	OH-HHJ	0075		1 AN 250-C20B	1814	6 Pax		lsf Royal Duty Free Shops Inc.
☐ RP-C2077	Eurocopter (Aerosp.) AS350B Ecureuil	2489		0091		1 TU Arriel 1B	1950	5 Pax		lsf pvt
☐ RP-C1158	Beech Baron 58	TH-673	N4579S	0075		2 CO IO-520-C	2449	5 Pax		

578 registration type of aircraft cn/fn ex/EX* mfd del powered by mtow kg configuration selcal name/fln/specialitites/remarks

registration	type of aircraft	cn/fn	ex/ex*	mfd	del	powered by	mtow kg	configuration	selcal	name/fln/specialitites/remarks
☐ RP-C109	Agusta A109A II	7263	I-SEIE	0084	0095	2 AN 250-C20B	2600	5 Pax		lsf Home Component Corp.
☐ RP-C688	Britten-Norman BN-2A-26 Islander	2042		0090	0095	2 LY O-540-E4C5	2994	9 Pax		lsf LBC Group
☐ RP-C693	Britten-Norman BN-2A-26 Islander	2043		0090	0095	2 LY O-540-E4C5	2994	9 Pax		lsf LBC Group
☐ RP-C788	Britten-Norman BN-2T Turbine Islander	3010		0083		2 AN 250-B17C	3175	9 Pax		lsf LBC Group
☐ RP-C105	Cessna 421B Golden Eagle	421B0812	N1582G	0074		2 CO GTSIO-520-H	3379	6 Pax		
☐ RP-C143	Cessna 421B Golden Eagle	421B0463	N421AS	0073	0795	2 CO GTSIO-520-H	3379	6 Pax		lsf pvt
☐ RP-C1990	Beech King Air E90	LW-341	N3722G	0081		2 PWC PT6A-28	4581	7 Pax		lsf pvt
☐ RP-C1502	Beech King Air B200	BB-1500	N3199B*	0095	0495	2 PWC PT6A-42	5670	8 Pax		lsf Royal Duty Free Shop Inc.
☐ RP-C1023	BAe (HS) 748-209 Srs 2A	1659 / 126		0069	0095	2 RR Dart 533-2	20183	45 Pax		lsf LBC Group

AAOP HELICOPTERS (Asia Aircraft Overseas Philippines, Inc. dba / Associated with Petroleum Helicopters, Inc.)

Manila

AAOP Hangar, Domestic Road, Cor. MIA Road, Pasay City, Metro Manila 1301, Philippines ☎ (2) 831 93 22 Tx: none Fax: (2) 831 43 26 SITA: n/a
F: 1979 ⁂ 19 Head: Alexander L. Limjoco Net: n/a

registration	type of aircraft	cn/fn	ex/ex*	mfd	del	powered by	mtow kg	configuration	selcal	name/fln/specialitites/remarks
☐ RP-C1156	Bell 206B JetRanger III	3616	N2271Z	0482		1 AN 250-C20B	1451			lsf Petroleum Helicopters
☐ RP-C1526	Bell 206B JetRanger III	3132	N57526	0080	0896	1 AN 250-C20B	1451			
☐ RP-C1678	Bell 206B JetRanger III	933	N456A	0073	0796	1 AN 250-C20B	1451			cvtd JetRanger
☐ RP-C1775	Bell 206B JetRanger III	1289	RP-C2124	0074		1 AN 250-C20B	1451			cvtd JetRanger

ABOITIZ AIR = BOI (Midnight Express) (Aboitiz Air Transport Corp. dba / Member of The Soriano Group)

Manila

AATC Hangar, General Aviation Area, Domestic Airport, Pasay City, Metro Manila 1301, Philippines ☎ (2) 831 70 47 Tx: 62265 aboair pn Fax: (2) 831 39 78 SITA: n/a
F: 1988 ⁂ 400 Head: Jon Ramon Aboitiz ICAO: ABAIR Net: n/a

registration	type of aircraft	cn/fn	ex/ex*	mfd	del	powered by	mtow kg	configuration	selcal	name/fln/specialitites/remarks
☐ RP-C3201	NAMC YS-11A-609	2089	JA8756	0069	1191	2 RR Dart 543-10K	25400	Freighter		cvtd -309
☐ RP-C3202	NAMC YS-11A-614	2128	JA8821	0069	1191	2 RR Dart 543-10K	24500	Freighter		cvtd -314
☐ RP-C3204	NAMC YS-11-108	2016	JA8651	1265	0994	2 RR Dart 542-10J	23500	Freighter		
☐ RP-C3205	NAMC YS-11-102	2010	JA8644	0765	0595	2 RR Dart 543-10J/K	23500	Freighter		
☐ RP-C3207	NAMC YS-11-117	2029	JA8706	1166	0895	2 RR Dart 543-10K	23500	Freighter		
☐ RP-C3208	NAMC YS-11A-523	2138	JA8769	0070	0497	2 RR Dart 543-10J/K	24500	Freighter		
☐ RP-C3209	NAMC YS-11A-500	2098	JA8730	0069	0698	2 RR Dart 543-10J/K	24500	Freighter		cvtd -213
☐ RP-C3212	NAMC YS-11A-500	2111	JA8736	0069	1098	2 RR Dart 543-10J/K	24500	Freighter		cvtd -213

AIR LINK INTERNATIONAL AIRWAYS, Inc.

Manila

Air Link Bldg., Domestic Road, Domestic Airport, Pasay City, Metro Manila 1301, Philippines ☎ (2) 833 38 91 Tx: none Fax: (2) 833 38 91 SITA: n/a
F: 1983 ⁂ 100 Head: Capt. Geronimo A. Amurao Net: n/a Aircraft below MTOW 1361 kg: Beech 23 & Cessna 172

registration	type of aircraft	cn/fn	ex/ex*	mfd	del	powered by	mtow kg	configuration	selcal	name/fln/specialitites/remarks
☐ RP-C494	Cessna 210C	21058148	PI-C494	0063		1 CO IO-470-S	1361			
☐ RP-C484	Beech Travel Air 95	TD-138	PI-C484	0058		2 LY O-360-A1A	1814			
☐ RP-C818	Beech Baron 95-55	TC-88	PI-C818	0061		2 CO IO-470-L	2214			
☐ RP-C180	Cessna 414	414-0402	RP-180	0073		2 CO TSIO-520-J	2880			
☐ RP-C1102	Beech Queen Air 65-88	LP-44		0067		2 LY IGSO-540-A1D	3992			
☐ RP-C2252	NAMC YS-11A-500	2079	RP-C1931	0068	0098	2 RR Dart 542-10J/K	24500			cvtd -212

AIR PHILIPPINES, Corp. = 2P / GAP

Subic Bay

15th fl., Multinational Bancorporation Centre, 6805 Ayala Avenue, Makati City, Manila 1200, Philippines ☎ (2) 843 70 01 Tx: none Fax: (2) 845 19 75 SITA: n/a
F: 1995 ⁂ 750 Head: Augustus C. Paiso ICAO: ORIENT PACIFIC Net: n/a Beside aircraft listed (used on domestic flights), intends to start international flights during 1999 with leased 4 Boeing 747-200B.

registration	type of aircraft	cn/fn	ex/ex*	mfd	del	powered by	mtow kg	configuration	selcal	name/fln/specialitites/remarks
☐ RP-C1960	NAMC YS-11-109	2026	P4-KFJ	0866	0596	2 RR Dart 542-10J/K	23500	Y64		
☐ RP-C1983	NAMC YS-11-124	2037	P4-KFL	0467	0596	2 RR Dart 542-10J/K	23500	Y64		
☐ RP-C2014	NAMC YS-11-102	2013	JA8650	0065	1196	2 RR Dart 543-10J/K	23500	Y60		
☐ RP-C2015	NAMC YS-11A-208	2067	JA8698	0068	1096	2 RR Dart 543-10J/K	24500	Y60		
☐ RP-C1938	Boeing 737-222	19553 / 122	9M-PMR	0069	1195	2 PW JT8D-7B	49442	Y119		
☐ RP-C2020	Boeing 737-222	19943 / 179	N9062U	0069	0996	2 PW JT8D-7B	49442	F8Y97		
☐ RP-C2021	Boeing 737-222	19039 / 6	N9001U	0067	1096	2 PW JT8D-7B	49442	F8Y101		
☐ RP-C2022	Boeing 737-222	19942 / 175	N9061U	0669	0297	2 PW JT8D-7B	49442	F8Y101		
☐ RP-C2023	Boeing 737-222	19947 / 187	N9066U	0069	0497	2 PW JT8D-7B	49442	F8Y101		
☐ RP-C2024	Boeing 737-222	19056 / 42	N9018U	0067	0597	2 PW JT8D-7B	49442	F8Y101		
☐ RP-C2025	Boeing 737-222	19077 / 103	N9039U	0068	0898	2 PW JT8D-7B	49442	F8Y101		
☐ RP-C3010	Boeing 737-2H4 (A)	21447 / 508	N50SW	0078	0199	2 PW JT8D-9A	52390	Y122		lsf AARL
☐ RP-C3011	Boeing 737-2H4 (A)	21533 / 524	N52SW	0078	0199	2 PW JT8D-9A	52390	Y122		lsf AARL
☐ 9M-MQE	Boeing 737-4H6	26462 / 2542		0093	1298	2 CFMI CFM56-3C1	62822	F16Y128	CM-AR	lsf MAS
☐ B-88888	Boeing (Douglas) MD-82 (DC-9-82)	53479 / 2124	N9012S*	0095	0798	2 PW JT8D-217C	67812	Y165		lsf/opb U-Land Airlines
☐ B-88898	Boeing (Douglas) MD-82 (DC-9-82)	53481 / 2145		0096	1298	2 PW JT8D-217C	67812	Y165		lsf/opb U-Land Airlines
☐ B-88899	Boeing (Douglas) MD-82 (DC-9-82)	53542 / 2152		0096	0798	2 PW JT8D-217C	67812	Y165		lsf/opb U-Land Airlines

AIRSPAN Corporation (Sister company of Jaka Air)

Manila

PO Box 7442, Airmail Distribution Center, NAIA 1300, Philippines ☎ (2) 833 32 59 Tx: none Fax: (2) 833 32 58 SITA: n/a
F: 1984 ⁂ 60 Head: Katrina C. Pone Entile Net: n/a Aircraft below MTOW 1361kg: Hughes 369HS (500C), Robinson R22 & R44.

registration	type of aircraft	cn/fn	ex/ex*	mfd	del	powered by	mtow kg	configuration	selcal	name/fln/specialitites/remarks
☐ RP-C257	MD Helicopters MD 500D (Hughes 369D)	1160037D		1176	0090	1 AN 250-C20B	1361			
☐ RP-C2300	Bell 206B JetRanger III	4356		0094		1 AN 250-C20J	1451			
☐ RP-C2600	Bell 206B JetRanger III	4364		0095		1 AN 250-C20J	1451			
☐ RP-C979	Cessna U206B Super Skywagon	U206-0903	PI-C979	0067	0087	1 CO IO-520-F	1633			
☐ RP-C8080	Piper PA-34-200T Seneca II	34-7970491		0079	0096	2 CO TSIO-360-EB	2073			
☐ RP-C1800	Eurocopter (Aerosp.) AS350B Ecureuil	2329	JA9894	0090	0493	1 TU Arriel 1B	1950			
☐ RP-C2345	Bell 407	53094	N18756*	0096	0397	1 AN 250-C47B	2268			
☐ RP-C2468	Bell 407	53037	N1098Y*	0096	0996	1 AN 250-C47B	2268			
☐ RP-C637	Beech Baron E55	TE-1031		0075	0894	2 CO IO-520-C	2404			
☐ RP-C2400	Agusta A109A II	7289	I-MIIT	0085	0595	2 AN 250-C20B	2600			
☐ RP-C2900	Agusta A109A	7228	I-DEKO	0082	0095	2 AN 250-C20B	2600			

ASIAN SPIRIT = RIT (Airline Employees Cooperative dba)

Manila

PO Box 7593, Manila Domestic Airport, Pasay City 1300, Philippines ☎ (2) 551 17 22 Tx: none Fax: (2) 551 17 24 SITA: n/a
F: 1995 ⁂ 120 Head: Antonio G. Buendia, Jr. ICAO: ASIAN SPIRIT Net: n/a

registration	type of aircraft	cn/fn	ex/ex*	mfd	del	powered by	mtow kg	configuration	selcal	name/fln/specialitites/remarks
☐ RP-C3880	Let 410UVP-E	892228	RA-67601	0089		2 WA M-601E	6400	Y19		
☐ RP-C2788	De Havilland DHC-7-102 Dash 7	089	N62RA	0082	0396	4 PWC PT6A-50	19958	Y50		
☐ RP-C2988	De Havilland DHC-7-102 Dash 7	078	N60RA	0082	0396	4 PWC PT6A-50	19958	Y50		
☐ RP-C3587	NAMC YS-11A-209	2069	P4-KFA	0068	0197	2 RR Dart 542-10J/K	24500	Y64		
☐ RP-C3588	NAMC YS-11A-500	2168	JA8787	0072	1296	2 RR Dart 542-10J/K	24500	Y64		cvtd -214
☐ RP-C3590	NAMC YS-11A-600	2106	N219LC	0069	0197	2 RR Dart 542-10J/K	25000	Y64		cvtd -301

A. SORIANO AVIATION, Inc. = SOY (Member of A. Soriano Group of Companies)

Manila

A. Soriano Hangar, Andrews Ave., Pasay City, Metro Manila 1301, Philippines ☎ (2) 831 42 07 Tx: 66256 sorfob pn Fax: (2) 833 38 53 SITA: n/a
F: 1987 ⁂ 70 Head: Ben Hur D. Gomez ICAO: SORIANO Net: n/a

registration	type of aircraft	cn/fn	ex/ex*	mfd	del	powered by	mtow kg	configuration	selcal	name/fln/specialitites/remarks
☐ RP-C3282	Eurocopter (Aerosp.) SA365N Dauphin 2	6021	N917EG	0082	0097	2 TU Arriel 1C	4000	Corporate		opf Int'l Container Terminal Services
☐ RP-C1111	Beech Queen Air A65	LC-270	PI-C1111	0068	1196	2 LY IGSO-480-A1E6	3719	Private		opf RGV Development Corp.
☐ RP-C1807	Beech King Air C90A	LJ-1181	N90PE	0088	0196	2 PWC PT6A-21	4377	Corporate		opf Rikio Company
☐ RP-C282	Beech King Air 100	B-78	PI-C282	0071	1195	2 PWC PT6A-28	4808	Charter		
☐ RP-C1890	Beech King Air 300	FA-64	N7232L	0085	0287	2 PWC PT6A-60A	6350	Charter		lsf Timber Creek Properties
☐ RP-C1776	De Havilland DHC-6 Twin Otter 200	132	N501BA	0068	0689	2 PWC PT6A-20	5252	Charter		
☐ RP-C1008	Dornier 228-212	8193	D-CARD*	0091	0991	2 GA TPE331-5A-252D	6400	Charter		lsf Seven Seas Resorts & Leisure
☐ RP-C2282	Dornier 228-212	8181	D-CBDG	0090	0897	2 GA TPE331-5A-252D	6400	Charter		

AYALA AVIATION, Corporation (Subsidiary of Ayala, Corporation)

Manila

Ayala Hangar, Domestic Airport, Pasay City, Metro Manila 1301, Philippines ☎ (2) 832 35 95 Tx: none Fax: (2) 833 87 50 SITA: n/a
F: 1993 ⁂ 15 Head: Teodoro L. Ferrer Net: n/a

registration	type of aircraft	cn/fn	ex/ex*	mfd	del	powered by	mtow kg	configuration	selcal	name/fln/specialitites/remarks
☐ RP-C338	Eurocopter (Aerosp.) AS355F Ecureuil 2	5274		0082		2 AN 250-C20F	2300	5 Pax		
☐ RP-C716	Eurocopter (Aerosp.) AS355F2 Ecureuil 2	5504		0091		2 AN 250-C20F	2540	6 Pax		
☐ RP-C1728	Beech King Air 350 (B300)	FL-118	N1555E	0094	1295	2 PWC PT6A-60A	6804	10 Pax		

CARD'S AIR SERVICES, Inc.

Bacolod

Bacolod Airport, Bacolod, (Negros), Philippines ☎ (34) 433 34 84 Tx: n/a Fax: n/a SITA: n/a
F: n/a ⁂ n/a Head: Capt. Rodolfo S. Grecia Net: n/a

registration	type of aircraft	cn/fn	ex/ex*	mfd	del	powered by	mtow kg	configuration	selcal	name/fln/specialitites/remarks
☐ RP-C1708	Cessna U206C Super Skywagon	U206-1083	PI-C1708	0068		1 CO IO-520-F	1633			
☐ RP-C1119	Beech Bonanza 36	E-149	PI-C1119	0069		1 CO IO-520-B	1633			
☐ RP-C1402	Beech Baron A55 (95-A55)	TC-231		0061		2 CO IO-470-L	2214			
☐ RP-C808	Beech Baron C55 (95-C55)	TE-113		0066		2 CO IO-520-C	2404			

CEBU PACIFIC AIR, Inc. = 5J / CPI (Subsidiary of JG Summit Holdings / formerly Cebu Air, Inc.)

Manila

30 EDSA Corner, pioneer Street, Mandaluyong City, Metro Manila, Philippines ☎ (2) 637 18 10 Tx: none Fax: (2) 637 91 70 SITA: MNLRZ5V
F: 1995 ⁂ 690 Head: John Gokongwei IATA: 203 ICAO: CEBU AIR Net: http://www.cebupacific.com.ph

registration	type of aircraft	cn/fn	ex/ex*	mfd	del	powered by	mtow kg	configuration	selcal	name/fln/specialitites/remarks
☐ RP-C1503	Boeing (Douglas) DC-9-32	47789 / 906	PK-GNS	0079	1195	2 PW JT8D-9A	48988	Y115	AF-DJ	

☐ RP-C1504	Boeing (Douglas) DC-9-32	47792 / 910	PK-GNV	0079	1195	2 PW JT8D-9A	48988	Y115	AF-DM	
☐ RP-C1505	Boeing (Douglas) DC-9-32	47793 / 911	PK-GNW	0079	1195	2 PW JT8D-9A	48988	Y115	AF-EG	
☐ RP-C1506	Boeing (Douglas) DC-9-32	47795 / 916	PK-GNY	0079	1195	2 PW JT8D-9A	48988	Y115	AF-EJ	
☐ RP-C1508	Boeing (Douglas) DC-9-32	47070 / 176	C-FTLR	0067	0497	2 PW JT8D-9A / -7B	48988	Y110		
☐ RP-C1509	Boeing (Douglas) DC-9-32	47071 / 188	C-FTLS	0067	0497	2 PW JT8D-9A / -7B	48988	Y110		
☐ RP-C1535	Boeing (Douglas) DC-9-32	47266 / 352	C-FTMA	0068	1197	2 PW JT8D-9A / -7B	48988	Y110		
☐ RP-C1536	Boeing (Douglas) DC-9-32	47353 / 471	C-FTMO	0069	1098	2 PW JT8D-9A / -7B	48988	Y110		
☐ RP-C1537	Boeing (Douglas) DC-9-32	47570 / 684	S5-ABH	0073	1298	2 PW JT8D-9A	48988	Y115		
☐ RP-C1538	Boeing (Douglas) DC-9-32	47239 / 466	S5-ABF	0069	0299	2 PW JT8D-9A	48988	Y115		

CENTENNIAL AIR, Inc. — Manila

PAL Compound, International Cargo Terminal, Pasay City, Metro Manila, Philippines ☎ (2) 8311061 ext.124 Tx: none Fax: (2) 552 51 06 SITA: n/a
F: 1998 ✈✈✈ n/a Head: n/a Net: n/a

☐ 9M-PMM	Boeing 737-205C	20458 / 278	PK-GWR	0371	0698	2 PW JT8D-9A	53070	Freighter		lsf TSE

CERTEZA SURVEYING & AEROPHOTO SYSTEMS, Inc. — Manila

795 E. Delos Santos Avenue, Quezon City, Manila, Philippines ☎ (2) 928 15 36 Tx: none Fax: (2) 924 24 95 SITA: n/a
F: 1924 ✈✈✈ 93 Head: Federico M. Nadela Net: n/a Aircraft below MTOW 1361kg: Cessna 172

☐ RP-C621	Twin (Aero) Commander 500U	500U-1706-24	PI-C621	0067		2 LY IO-540-E1B5	3062	Photo / Survey		Pamulinawen I
☐ RP-C641	Twin (Aero) Commander 680F	680F-1003-41	PI-C641	0060		2 LY IGSO-540-B1C	3629	Photo / Survey		Pamulinawen II

CHEMTRAD AVIATION, Corp. — Manila

Ground Floor, Manila Aero Club Bldg., Domestic Airport, Pasay City, Metro Manila 1301, Philippines ☎ (2) 833 19 83 Tx: none Fax: (2) 833 03 38 SITA: n/a
F: 1978 ✈✈✈ n/a Head: Manny Barradas Net: n/a Ag-aircraft below MTOW 5000kg: Cessna A188B & Piper PA-25

☐ RP-C1289	Cessna U206F Stationair	U20602284	N1919U	0074		1 CO IO-520-F	1633			
☐ RP-C1574	Cessna 207 Skywagon	20700274		0074		1 CO IO-520-F	1724			
☐ RP-C2079	Cessna 207A Stationair 8 II	20700600	N73511	0080		1 CO IO-520-F	1724			
☐ RP-C3126	Cessna 207A Stationair 7 II	20700560	N73114	0079	0190	1 CO IO-520-F	1724			
☐ RP-C3216	Cessna 207 Skywagon	20700333	N1733U	0076		1 CO IO-520-F	1724			
☐ RP-C1262	Britten-Norman BN-2A-21 Islander	408	G-BCLE	0075	1295	2 LY IO-540-K1B5	2994			
☐ RP-C2141	Britten-Norman BN-2A-21 Islander	452	G-BDDL	0075		2 LY IO-540-K1B5	2994			
☐ RP-C2201	Britten-Norman BN-2A-21 Islander	718	RP-C2207	0076	0096	2 LY IO-540-K1B5	2994			
☐ RP-C28	Britten-Norman BN-2A-21 Islander	409	G-BCLF	0074	0298	2 LY IO-540-K1B5	2994			
☐ RP-C764	Britten-Norman BN-2A-26 Islander	318	G-BANL	0073	0097	2 LY O-540-E4C5	2994			
☐ RP-C868	Britten-Norman BN-2A-21 Islander	725	RP-C1966	0074		2 LY IO-540-K1B5	2994			

CLA AIR TRANSPORT, Inc. = C9 / CXX (Subsidiary of Philippine Aerospace Development Co. & IASS, Japan) — Manila

PO Box 7419, Domestic Airport Post Office, Pasay City 1301, Philippines ☎ (2) 551 71 92 Tx: none Fax: (2) 552 74 21 SITA: MNLFFC9
F: 1997 ✈✈✈ n/a Head: Leopoldo S. Acot, Jr. IATA: 226 ICAO: LOGISTIC Net: n/a

☐ N345JW	Boeing (Douglas) DC-8-63F	46042 / 421	N7043U	0068	1098	4 PW JT3D-7 (HK3/BAC)	161025	Freighter	KM-CH	lsf IALI / cvtd -63

C.M. AERO SERVICES (Subsidiary of Commuter Air Philippines) — Manila

Atesco Hangar, Domestic Airport, Pasay City, Metro Manila 1301, Philippines ☎ (2) 833 32 63 Tx: none Fax: (2) 833 18 98 SITA: n/a
F: 1985 ✈✈✈ n/a Head: Charles R. Miller, Jr. Net: n/a

☐ RP-C690	Beech E18S Tri-gear	BA-389	N691T	0058		2 PW R-985	4218			Panorama Windows
☐ RP-C984	Beech H18 Tri-gear	BA-669	N333DM	0064		2 PW R-985	4491			Panorama Windows
☐ RP-C986	Beech E18S	BA-557	N807P	0061		2 PW R-985	4218			Panorama Windows
☐ RP-C1101	Boeing (Douglas) DC-3C (C-47A-30-DL)	9525	RP-534	0043		2 PW R-1830	12202			std MNL / to be made operational
☐ RP-C1352	Boeing (Douglas) DC-3C (C-47A-30-DK)	25347	F-WZIG	0044	0097	2 PW R-1830-28	12202	Y28 / Freighter		std MNL
☐ RP-C1353	Boeing (Douglas) DC-3C (C-47A-30-DK)	25368	F-WZIR	0044	0097	2 PW R-1830-28	12202	Y28 / Freighter		std MNL
☐ RP-C1354	Boeing (Douglas) DC-3C (C-47B-1-DK)	25571	F-WZII	0044	0097	2 PW R-1830-28	12202	Freighter		std MNL

COMMUTER AIR PHILIPPINES — Manila

Atesco Hangar, Domestic Airport, Pasay City, Metro Manila 1301, Philippines ☎ (2) 833 32 63 Tx: none Fax: (2) 833 18 98 SITA: n/a
F: 1983 ✈✈✈ n/a Head: Charles R. Miller, Jr. Net: n/a

☐ RP-C692	Beech H18 Tri-gear	BA-763	JA5172	0069		2 PW R-985	4491			Panorama windows
☐ RP-C707	Beech E18S	BA-126	N8475D	0056		2 PW R-985	4218			std MNL / to be made operational
☐ RP-C709	Beech H18	BA-712	N8475E	0060		2 PW R-985	4491			std MNL / to be made operational
☐ RP-C798	Beech E18S	BA-200	N59K	0056		2 PW R-985	4218			

CORPORATE AIR, Inc. (Associated with Corporate Air, Montana/USA) — Subic Bay

3/F, U-Warehouse Bldg, Barangay Vitalez, Old MIA Rd, NAIA Complex, Paranaque, Metro Manila, Philippines ☎ (2) 831 01 09 Tx: none Fax: (2) 833 32 88 SITA: n/a
F: 1995 ✈✈✈ n/a Head: Alberto D. Lina Net: n/a

☐ RP-C1758	Twin (Aero) Commander 500B	500B-1502-178	N86RP	0065	0695	2 LY IO-540-B1A5	3062	Freighter		
☐ N760FE	Cessna 208B Caravan I Super Cargomaster	208B0252		0091	0795	1 PWC PT6A-114A	3969	Freighter		lsf/opf FDX in FedEx Feeder-colors
☐ N766FE	Cessna 208B Caravan I Super Cargomaster	208B0260		0091	0695	1 PWC PT6A-114A	3969	Freighter		lsf/opf FDX in FedEx Feeder-colors
☐ N702PV	De Havilland DHC-6 Twin Otter 300	702		0080	0596	2 PWC PT6A-27	5670	Freighter		lsf CPT

CYCLONE AIRWAYS, Inc. — Cauayan

PO Box 076634, Cauayan Airport 3305, (Negros), Philippines ☎ (76) 52 458 Tx: n/a Fax: (76) 634 53 87 SITA: n/a
F: n/a ✈✈✈ n/a Head: Honorio E. Camposagrado Net: n/a

☐ RP-C694	Cessna P206B Super Skylane	P206-0312	N4712F	0067		1 CO IO-520-A	1633			
☐ RP-C671	Cessna 207 Skywagon	20700169		0070	0097	1 CO IO-520-F	1724			

FLYING MEDICAL SAMARITANS – FMS (Associated with Pacific Missionary Aviation – PMA, Guam) — Manila

PO Box 7255, D.A.P.O. Lock Box, Domestic Road, Pasay City, Metro Manila 1300, Philippines ☎ (2) 831 11 23 Tx: n/a Fax: (2) 831 11 23 SITA: n/a
F: 1982 ✈✈✈ 24 Head: Rev. Edmund Kalau Net: n/a Non-profit, non-denominational ambulance & development organisation.

☐ RP-C809	Britten-Norman BN-2A-26 Islander	755	VH-FCP	0075	0593	2 LY O-540-E4C5	2994	Ambulance		

GRANDAIR = 8L / GDI (Grand International Airways, Inc. dba) — Manila

8/F Philippines Village Airport Hotel, Pasay City, Metro Manila, Philippines ☎ (2) 831 29 11 Tx: n/a Fax: (2) 891 76 82 SITA: n/a
F: 1994 ✈✈✈ n/a Head: Dante Santos Net: n/a

☐ RP-C8887	Boeing 737-247	20132 / 167	B-2607	0069	1296	2 PW JT8D-9A	49442	Y120		lsf EASCO Taiwan Leasing Co. / std TPE
☐ RP-C8890	Boeing 737-204	19711 / 155	N313VA	0069	0897	2 PW JT8D-9	53070	Y120		lsf Askar, Philippines
☐ RP-C8891	Boeing 737-204	20236 / 166	N312VA	0069	0897	2 PW JT8D-9	53070	Y120		lsf Askar, Philippines

HOUSE OF TRAVEL, Inc. — Davao

Anflocar Bldg, Quirino Ave., Quirino Ave., Cor. NAIA Road Pque., Metro Manila, Philippines ☎ (2) 831 88 01 Tx: none Fax: (2) 833 62 65 SITA: n/a
F: n/a ✈✈✈ n/a Head: Ms. Eileen Domingo Net: n/a

☐ RP-C117	Bell 206B JetRanger III	1894		0076		1 AN 250-C20B	1451			cvtd JetRanger II
☐ RP-C653	Cessna 550 Citation II	550-0181	N88826	0080		2 PWC JT15D-4	6033			lsf Tagum Agricultural Development Co.

JAKA TRANSPORT, Corp. (Sister company of Airspan Corporation) — Manila

Hangar 10, Manila Domestic Airport, Pasay City 1301, Philippines ☎ (2) 833 32 59 Tx: none Fax: (2) 833 25 09 SITA: n/a
F: 1988 ✈✈✈ n/a Head: Katrina C. Pone Enrile Net: n/a

☐ RP-C1350	Eurocopter (Aerosp.) AS350B2 Ecureuil	2454		0091		1 TU Arriel 1D1	2250			
☐ RP-C1430	Eurocopter (Aerosp.) AS350B Ecureuil	2283	VH-BPE	0089		1 TU Arriel 1B	1950			
☐ RP-C1591	Eurocopter (Aerosp.) AS350BA Ecureuil	2887		0095	1096	1 TU Arriel 1B	2100			
☐ RP-C1355	Eurocopter (Aerosp.) AS355F2 Ecureuil 2	5494		0091		2 AN 250-C20F	2540			
☐ RP-C1501	Eurocopter (Aerosp.) AS355F2 Ecureuil 2	5478	I-ALKE	0091	0097	2 AN 250-C20F	2540			

L & L CORPORATE JET AVIATION, Corp. — Manila

2263 Macondray Center, Pasong Tamo Extension, Magallanes, Makati, Metro Manila, Philippines ☎ (2) 812 06 59 Tx: none Fax: (2) 818 70 39 SITA: n/a
F: 1996 ✈✈✈ n/a Head: Martin P. Lorenzo Net: n/a

☐ RP-C125	Hawker 1A/522 (HS 125-1A/522)	25033	N125LL	0065	0096	2 RR Viper 522	9616			lsf Makar Properties Development Inc.
☐ RP-C1600	Hawker 600B (HS 125-600B)	256037	VH-NJA	0074	0096	2 RR Viper 522	11567			lsf FEB Leasing & Finance Corp.

LAOAG INTERNATIONAL AIRLINE, Inc. = L7 / LPN — Laoag

Cindy's Bldg, Rizal Street, Laoag City, Ilocos Norte 2900, Philippines ☎ (77) 772 15 55 Tx: none Fax: (77) 772 06 66 SITA: n/a
F: 1995 ✈✈✈ 65 Head: Ms. Shirley Ng ICAO: LAOAG AIR Net: n/a

☐ RP-C3888	Fokker F27 Friendship 100 (F27 Mk100)	10167	NZ2781	0061	0795	2 RR Dart 514-7	18370	Y40 / Freighter		
☐ RP-C6888	Fokker F27 Friendship 100 (F27 Mk100)	10169	NZ2783	0061	0795	2 RR Dart 514-7	18370	Y40 / Freighter		
☐ RP-C8889	Fokker F27 Friendship 100 (F27 Mk100)	10185	ZK-BXF	0061	0296	2 RR Dart 514-7	18370	Y40 / Freighter		
☐ XU-001	Fokker F28 Fellowship 1000 (F28 Mk1000)	11012	F-GIAH	0069	0098	2 RR Spey 555-15	30164	Y60		lsf PSD

MABUHAY AIRWAYS Philippines, Inc. (Subsidiary of Balesin Corporation) — Manila

Montepino Bldg, 4th floor, Amorsolo cor. Gamboa Sts, Legaspi Village, Makati, Metro Manila, Philippines ☎ (2) 892 88 06 Tx: n/a Fax: (2) 818 12 03 SITA: n/a
F: 1974 ✈✈✈ n/a Head: Manny Sumbilon Net: n/a

☐ RP-C596	Beech Twin Bonanza D50C	DH-248	PI-C596	0060		2 LY GO-480-G2D6	2858			
☐ RP-C74	Boeing (Douglas) DC-3C (C-47B-1-DK)	25572	RP-C10	0044		2 PW R-1830	12202	Freighter		Victoria / std MNL/tb made op.as backup
☐ RP-C473	Boeing (Douglas) Super DC-3S (C-117D)	43327	N873SN	0043	1295	2 WR R-1820	13301	Freighter		Super Dee / lsf pvt/cvtd R4D-5 cn 9756

MINDANAO EXPRESS, Inc. (Sister company of Corporate Air, Inc. & associated with Corporate Air, Montana/USA)

Subic Bay

3/5, U-Warehouse Bldg, Barangay Vitalez, Old MIA Rd, NAIA Comples, Paranaque, Metro Manila, Philippines ☎ (2) 831 01 09 Tx: none Fax: (2) 833 32 88 SITA: n/a
F: 1996 n/a Head: Alberto Lina Net: n/a

registration	type of aircraft	cn/fn	ex/ex*	mfd	del	powered by	mtow kg	configuration	selcal	name/fln/specialitites/remarks
☐ RP-C2317	Beech C99 Airliner	U-236	N236AL	0087	1196	2 PWC PT6A-36	5126	Freighter		
☐ RP-C2370	Beech C99 Airliner	U-237	N237SL	0087	1196	2 PWC PT6A-36	5126	Freighter		
☐ RP-C2380	Beech C99 Airliner	U-238	N238AL	0087	0197	2 PWC PT6A-36	5126	Freighter		
☐ RP-C2390	Beech C99 Airliner	U-239	N239AL	0087	0197	2 PWC PT6A-36	5126	Freighter		
☐ RP-C2318	Beech 1900C-1 Airliner	UC-106	N106YV	0090	0597	2 PWC PT6A-65B	7530	Freighter		
☐ RP-C2319	Beech 1900C-1 Airliner	UC-112	N112YV	0690	0696	2 PWC PT6A-65B	7530	Freighter		

NEGROS AIR TRANSPORT Cooperative

Cauayan

ATO Compound, Bacolod Airport, Bacolod, (Negros), Philippines ☎ (34) 23 570 Tx: none Fax: none SITA: n/a
F: 1994 n/a Head: Mario Bedayo Net: n/a

registration	type of aircraft	cn/fn	ex/ex*	mfd	del	powered by	mtow kg	configuration	selcal	name/fln/specialitites/remarks
☐ RP-C1379	Piper PA-32R-300 Lance	32R-7680015	N4424X	0076		1 LY IO-540-K1G5D	1633			lsf Orville Aviation Inc.

PACIFICAIR = GX (Pacific Airways Corp. dba)

Manila

3110 Domestic Airport Road, MIA, Pasay City, Metro Manila 1300, Philippines ☎ (2) 832 27 31 Tx: none Fax: (2) 833 74 30 SITA: n/a
F: 1947 120 Head: Nemesio Tejero Net: n/a Aircraft / Ag-aircraft below MTOW 1361 / 5000kg: AA5, Beech A23 & 35-33, Cessna 172, Grumman G-164, Mooney M20, Piper PA-25 & Pa-28.

registration	type of aircraft	cn/fn	ex/ex*	mfd	del	powered by	mtow kg	configuration	selcal	name/fln/specialitites/remarks
☐ RP-C2350	Piper PA-32-260 Cherokee SIX	32-7300061		0073		1 LY O-540-E4B5	1542			lsf Central Bancorp.
☐ RP-C1174	Cessna U206F Stationair	U20601905	N50145	0072		1 CO IO-520-F	1633			lsf Central Bancorp.
☐ RP-C1175	Cessna U206F Stationair	U20601943	N50625	0073		1 CO IO-520-F	1633			lsf Central Bancorp.
☐ RP-C165	Cessna U206F Stationair	U20602016	RP-165	0073		1 CO IO-520-F	1633			lsf Central Bancorp.
☐ RP-C24	Cessna U206F Stationair II	U20603026	N3578Q	0076	0096	1 CO IO-520-F	1633			lsf Philippine Island Corp.
☐ RP-C978	Cessna U206E Super Skywagon	U20601505	N9105M	0070	0096	1 CO IO-520-F	1633			lsf Central Bancorp.
☐ RP-C822	Beech Debonair B33 (35-B33)	CD-588		0062		1 CO IO-470-K	1361			
☐ RP-C1225	Cessna T207 Turbo Skywagon	20700235	N1635U	0073		1 CO TSIO-520-G	1724			lsf Central Bancorp.
☐ RP-C1226	Cessna 207 Skywagon	20700092	N519SA	0069		1 CO IO-520-F	1724			lsf Central Bancorp.
☐ RP-C108	Cessna 210L Centurion II	21060546	N94220	0074	0096	1 CO IO-520-L	1724			lsf Central Bancorp.
☐ RP-C409	Beech Twin Bonanza C50	CH-172	PI-C409	0054		2 LY GO-480-G2D6	2722			lsf Central Bancorp.
☐ RP-C1999	Cessna 401	401-0309	RP-C1303	0068		2 CO TSIO-520-E	2858			
☐ RP-C1320	Britten-Norman BN-2A-21 Islander	569	569	0078	0295	2 LY IO-540-K1B5	2994			lsf Central Bancorp.
☐ RP-C1321	Britten-Norman BN-2A-21 Islander	547	547	0078	0096	2 LY IO-540-K1B5	2994			lsf Central Bancorp.
☐ RP-C1323	Britten-Norman BN-2A-21 Islander	502	502	0077	0096	2 LY IO-540-K1B5	2994			lsf Central Bancorp.
☐ RP-C1324	Britten-Norman BN-2A-21 Islander	539	539	0077	0096	2 LY IO-540-K1B5	2994			lsf Central Bancorp.
☐ RP-C1325	Britten-Norman BN-2A-21 Islander	593	593	0077	0096	2 LY IO-540-K1B5	2994			lsf Central Bancorp.
☐ RP-C1801	Britten-Norman BN-2A-21 Islander	739	G-BCNI	0075		2 LY IO-540-K1B5	2994			
☐ RP-C2132	Britten-Norman BN-2A-21 Islander	422	G-BCSG	0074		2 LY IO-540-K1B5	2994			lsf Central Bancorp.
☐ RP-C2137	Britten-Norman BN-2A-21 Islander	443	G-BCZU	0075		2 LY IO-540-K1B5	2994			lsf Central Bancorp.
☐ RP-C2138	Britten-Norman BN-2A-21 Islander	445	G-BCZW	0075		2 LY IO-540-K1B5	2994			lsf Central Bancorp.
☐ RP-C2157	Britten-Norman BN-2A-21 Islander	505		0077		2 LY IO-540-K1B5	2994			lsf Central Bancorp.
☐ RP-C471	Britten-Norman BN-2A-21 Islander	473		0077		2 LY IO-540-K1B5	2994			lsf Central Bancorp.
☐ RP-C684	Britten-Norman BN-2A-21 Islander	723	G-BCHA	0074		2 LY IO-540-K1B5	2994			
☐ RP-C2346	Twin (Aero) Commander 560A	560-342		0056		2 LY GO-480-G1B6	2722			lsf Central Bancorp.
☐ RP-C1611	Cessna 421C Golden Eagle II	421C0155	N5282J	0076		2 CO GTSIO-520-L	3379			
☐ RP-C880	Beech Queen Air 65	LC-135	PI-C880	0062		2 LY IGSO-480-A1B6	3493			lsf Central Bancorp. / std DVO
☐ RP-C1103	Beech H18	BA-660	N638CZ	0063		2 PW R-985-AN14B	4491			
☐ RP-C1358	Beech H18 Tri-gear	BA-750	RP-C1986	0067		2 PW R-985-AN14B	4491			
☐ RP-C1152	De Havilland DHC-6 Twin Otter 100	113	N59AN	0068	0589	2 PWC PT6A-20	5252			std MNL
☐ RP-C1153	De Havilland DHC-6 Twin Otter 100	91	N34TC	0067	0589	2 PWC PT6A-20	5252			
☐ RP-C1155	De Havilland DHC-6 Twin Otter 200	134	N1373T	0068	0589	2 PWC PT6A-20	5252			
☐ RP-C663	De Havilland DHC-6 Twin Otter 200	208	DQ-FCY	0069	0896	2 PWC PT6A-20	5252			

PACIFIC EAST ASIA CARGO Airlines, Inc. = PEC (Associated with Philippines Aerospace Development Co. & TNT)

Manila

PO Box 7395, Post Office Lock Box, Manila Domestic Airport 1301, Philippines ☎ (2) 833 88 53 Tx: none Fax: (2) 832 34 01 SITA: n/a
F: 1990 65 Head: Capt. Benjamin S. Solis IATA: 515 ICAO: PAC-EAST CARGO Net: n/a

registration	type of aircraft	cn/fn	ex/ex*	mfd	del	powered by	mtow kg	configuration	selcal	name/fln/specialitites/remarks
☐ RP-C481	BAe 146-200 (QT)	E2109	G-TNTD	0088	1093	4 LY ALF502R-5	42184	Freighter	AQ-HP	lsf/opf TNT Int'l in TNT-cs/cvtd -200
☐ RP-C482	BAe 146-200 (QT)	E2112	F-GTNU	0088	1093	4 LY ALF502R-5	42184	Freighter	AQ-JK	lsf/opf TNT Int'l in TNT-cs/cvtd -200
☐ N6809	Boeing 727-223 (F)	19484 / 560		0468	0596	3 PW JT8D-9 (HK3/FDX)	80966	Freighter	BK-EL	lsf/opf TNT Intl'l in TNT-cs/cvtd -223

PARADISE AIR Services, Inc.

Koror-Airai

PO Box 488, Koror, Republic of Palau ☎ 488 23 48 Tx: none Fax: 488 23 48 SITA: n/a
F: 1982 n/a Head: Bob Keys Net: n/a

registration	type of aircraft	cn/fn	ex/ex*	mfd	del	powered by	mtow kg	configuration	selcal	name/fln/specialitites/remarks
☐ RP-C1047	Britten-Norman BN-2A-21 Islander	654	H4-WPB	0071		2 LY IO-540-K1B5	2994			

PHILIPPINES – Philippine Airlines = PR / PAL (Philippine Air Lines, Inc. dba / Associated with PR Holdings)

Manila

6754 Ayala Avenue, Makati City 0750, Philippines ☎ (2) 818 01 11 Tx: 63518 pal pn Fax: (2) 810 92 14 SITA: n/a
F: 1941 8770 Head: Lucio C. Tan IATA: 079 ICAO: PHILIPPINE Net: http://www.philippineair.com Trainer-aircraft below MTOW 5000kg: Beechcraft King Air E90, Cessna 152/172, Piper PA-38 & PA-44.

registration	type of aircraft	cn/fn	ex/ex*	mfd	del	powered by	mtow kg	configuration	selcal	name/fln/specialitites/remarks
☐ RP-C4006	Boeing 737-3S3	24059 / 1517	EC-FGG	0088	0592	2 CFMI CFM56-3B2	62142	Y141	BR-DH	lsf Nora Leasing
☐ RP-C4007	Boeing 737-332	25996 / 2488	RP-C2000	0093	1193	2 CFMI CFM56-3C1	61235	Y141	FR-DM	
☐ EI-BZE	Boeing 737-3Y0	24464 / 1753		0089	0889	2 CFMI CFM56-3B1	56472	Y141	GQ-FH	lsf BBAM
☐ EI-BZF	Boeing 737-3Y0	24465 / 1755		0089	0889	2 CFMI CFM56-3B1	56472	Y141	GQ-FJ	lsf GECA
☐ EI-BZJ	Boeing 737-3Y0	24677 / 1837		0090	0390	2 CFMI CFM56-3B1	56472	Y141	GQ-FP	lsf GECA
☐ EI-BZL	Boeing 737-3Y0	24680 / 1927		0090	1090	2 CFMI CFM56-3B1	56472	Y141	GQ-HK	lsf GECA
☐ EI-BZM	Boeing 737-3Y0	24681 / 1929		0090	1090	2 CFMI CFM56-3B1	56472	Y141	GQ-HL	lsf GECA
☐ EI-BZN	Boeing 737-3Y0	24770 / 1941		0090	1090	2 CFMI CFM56-3B1	56472	Y141	GQ-HM	lsf GECA
☐ RP-C3221	Airbus Industrie A320-214	706	F-WWIM*	0097	0897	2 CFMI CFM56-5B4	73500	C18Y138	MQ-CG	lsf Airbus Industrie Financial Services
☐ RP-C3223	Airbus Industrie A320-214	745	F-WWIR*	0097	1197	2 CFMI CFM56-5B4	73500	C18Y138	MQ-DL	lsf Airbus Industrie Financial Services
☐ RP-C3224	Airbus Industrie A320-214	753	F-WWIV*	0097	1297	2 CFMI CFM56-5B4	73500	C18Y138	MQ-DP	lsf Airbus Industrie Financial Services
☐ F-OHZM	Airbus Industrie A330-301	183	F-WWKP*	0097	0797	2 GE CF6-80E1A2	215000	C48Y230	LS-JK	lsf Airbus Industrie Financial Services
☐ F-OHZQ	Airbus Industrie A330-301	189	F-WWKS*	0097	1197	2 GE CF6-80E1A2	215000	C48Y230	MQ-AL	lsf Airbus Industrie Financial Services
☐ F-OHZR	Airbus Industrie A330-301	198	F-WWKT*	0097	0198	2 GE CF6-80E1A2	215000	C48Y230	MQ-AP	lsf Airbus Industrie Financial Services
☐ F-OHZS	Airbus Industrie A330-301	200	F-WWKH*	0097	0198	2 GE CF6-80E1A2	215000	C48Y230	MQ-BC	lsf Airbus Industrie Financial Services
☐ F-OHZT	Airbus Industrie A330-301	203	F-WWKI*	0098	0298	2 GE CF6-80E1A2	215000	C48Y230	MQ-CF	lsf Airbus Industrie Financial Services
☐ F-OHPJ	Airbus Industrie A340-313	173	F-WWJG*	0097	0597	4 CFMI CFM56-5C4	271000	F12C32Y220	LS-EM	lsf Airbus Industrie Financial Services
☐ F-OHPK	Airbus Industrie A340-313	176	F-WWJB*	0097	0697	4 CFMI CFM56-5C4	271000	F12C32Y220	LS-EP	lsf Airbus Industrie Financial Services
☐ N751PR	Boeing 747-4F6	27261 / 1005		0093	1193	4 GE CF6-80C2B1F	394625	F18C38Y383	DS-AE	lsf Wilmington Trust Co.
☐ N752PR	Boeing 747-4F6	27262 / 1012		0093	1293	4 GE CF6-80C2B1F	394625	F18C38Y383	DS-AF	lsf Wilmington Trust Co.
☐ N753PR	Boeing 747-4F6	27828 / 1039	N6038E*	0094	0495	4 GE CF6-80C2B1F	394625	F18C38Y383	BR-DJ	lsf Wilmington Trust Co.
☐ N754PR	Boeing 747-469 (M)	27663 / 1068	N6009F*	0095	0396	4 GE CF6-80C2B1F	394625	Combi	FG-AJ	lsf Wilmington Trust Co.

SEAIR, Inc.

Manila & Clark

Clark Hangar 7224, Clark Special Economic Zone, Clarkfield, Pampanga, Philippines ☎ (45) 599 23 84 Tx: none Fax: (45) 599 23 83 SITA: n/a
F: 1994 25 Head: Iren Dornier Net: n/a Aircraft below MTOW 1361kg: Piper PA-28

registration	type of aircraft	cn/fn	ex/ex*	mfd	del	powered by	mtow kg	configuration	selcal	name/fln/specialitites/remarks
☐ RP-C1179	Dornier DO 28D-2 Skyservant	4127	D-IDRH	0071	1296	2 LY IGSO-540-A1E	3842	Y9		
☐ RP-C673	Dornier DO 28D-2 Skyservant	4174	D-IBDE	0073	0496	2 LY IGSO-540-A1E	3842	Y9		lsf Vivere Isle Leisure Corp.
☐ RP-C748	Let 410UVP-E	892342	UR-67614	0089	1296	2 WA M-601E	6400	Y19		lsf Vivere Isle Leisure Corp.
☐ RP-C749	Let 410UVP-E	892343	UR-67615	0089	0297	2 WA M-601E	6400	Y19		

SOUTHSTAR AVIATION, Co. Inc.

Davao

Davao International Airport, SASA, Davao, (Mindanao), Philippines ☎ (82) 234 34 06 Tx: none Fax: (82) 234 34 06 SITA: n/a
F: 1990 n/a Head: Rose Elaine B. Alcantara Net: n/a

registration	type of aircraft	cn/fn	ex/ex*	mfd	del	powered by	mtow kg	configuration	selcal	name/fln/specialitites/remarks
☐ RP-C528	Cessna U206G Stationair 6 II	U20606595	N9647Z	0082		1 CO IO-520-F	1633			lsf C. Alcantara & Sons Inc.
☐ RP-C1235	Beech Bonanza A36	E-975		0077	0791	1 CO IO-520-BA	1633			
☐ RP-C308	Beech Duchess 76	ME-132	N2070K	0079	0791	2 LY O-360-A1G6D	1769			
☐ RP-C1995	Beech King Air B200	BB-1429	N8008A	0092	1295	2 PWC PT6A-42	5670			lsf Aeromin Inc.

SUBIC INTERNATIONAL AIR CHARTER, Inc.

Subic Bay & Manila

Bldg. 8133, Subic International Airport, Subic Bay Freeport Zone, Zambales, Philippines ☎ (47) 252 78 10 Tx: none Fax: (2) 832 20 57 SITA: n/a
F: 1995 25 Head: Jose Alvarez Net: n/a

registration	type of aircraft	cn/fn	ex/ex*	mfd	del	powered by	mtow kg	configuration	selcal	name/fln/specialitites/remarks
☐ RP-C1110	Eurocopter (Aerosp.) SA341G Gazelle	1110	N708EZ	0074		1 TU Astazou IIIA	1800			
☐ RP-C787	Eurocopter (Aerosp.) SA341G Gazelle	1363		0077		1 TU Astazou IIIA	1800			
☐ RP-C1764	Bell 206L-3 LongRanger III	51272		0089	0098	1 AN 250-C30P	1882			opf San Miguel Corp.
☐ RP-C1774	Bell 206L-3 LongRanger III	51324	N21300	0089	0098	1 AN 250-C30P	1882			opf San Miguel Corp.
☐ RP-C2242	Eurocopter (Aerosp.) AS350B Ecureuil	2350	JA9896	0090	1096	1 TU Arriel 1B	1950			
☐ RP-C1945	Piper PA-31-350 Navajo Chieftain	31-7752006	N62958	0077		2 LY TIO-540-J2BD	3175			
☐ RP-C1747	Learjet 24D (XR)	24D-264	PI-C1747	0073		2 GE CJ610-6	6123			cvtd 24D
☐ RP-C1426	Learjet 35A	35A-426	N1128J	0081	0796	2 GA TFE731-2-2B	8301			
☐ RP-C648	Learjet 60	60-093	N80683	0097	0597	2 PWC PW305A	10478			
☐ RP-C1926	Hawker 800B (BAe 125-800B)	258226	G-5-755*	0092	0098	2 GA TFE731-5R-1H	12428			opf San Miguel Corp.

SWIFTAIR, Inc.

Manila & Zamboanga **SWIFTAIR**

West Maintenance Area, Domestic Airport, Pasay City, Metro Manila 1301, Philippines ☎ (2) 832 25 58 Tx: none Fax: (2) 833 66 53 SITA: n/a
F: 1963 ✠✠✠ 35 Head: Alexander R. Lim Net: n/a Aircraft below MTOW 1361 kg: Beech Musketeer 23 & MS885.

registration	type of aircraft	cn/fn	ex/ex*	mfd	del	powered by	mtow kg	configuration	selcal	name/fln/specialitites/remarks
☐ RP-C147	Boeing (Douglas) DC-3C (C-47B-1-DL)	20767	PI-C147	0044		2 PW R-1830	12202	Freighter		
☐ RP-C368	Boeing (Douglas) DC-3 (DST-217B)	2217	PI-C368	0040		2 PW R-1830	12202	Freighter		

VICTORIA AIR, Inc.

Manila

West Maintenance Area, Domestic Airport, Pasay City, Metro Manila 1301, Philippines ☎ (2) 831 55 25 Tx: none Fax: (2) 831 55 25 SITA: n/a
F: 1984 ✠✠✠ 20 Head: Capt. Jerry O. Juane Net: n/a

registration	type of aircraft	cn/fn	ex/ex*	mfd	del	powered by	mtow kg	configuration	selcal	name/fln/specialitites/remarks
☐ RP-C535	Boeing (Douglas) DC-3C (C-47B-20-DK)	27016	RP-C95	0044		2 PW R-1830	12600	Freighter		
☐ RP-C550	Boeing (Douglas) DC-3C (C-47B-1-DK)	25737	43-48476	0044	0295	2 PW R-1830	12600	Freighter		
☐ RP-C631	Boeing (Douglas) DC-3C (C-47A-1-DK)	12037	292257 PAF	0043		2 PW R-1830	12600	Freighter		

SE = SWEDEN (Kingdom of Sweden) (Konungariket Sverige)

Capital: Stockholm Official Language: Swedish Population: 8,8 million Square Km: 449964 Dialling code: +46 Year established: 1523 Acting political head: Goeran Persson (Prime Minister)

Government / Corporate / Executive / VIP Aircraft   SWEDISH AIR FORCE uses the ICAO three-letter-code: SDC and call sign: SWEDIC.

registration	type of aircraft	cn/fn	ex/ex*	mfd	del	powered by	mtow kg	configuration	selcal	name/fln/specialitites/remarks
☐ 100001	Tp 100A (Saab 340B)	340B-170	SE-F70*	0089	0290	2 GE CT7-9B	12927	VIP		001 / Swedish A.F.-F16 Flyg/Royal Family Flt
☐ 102001	Tp 102A (GAC G-1159C Gulfstream IV)	1014	N779SW	0087	1092	2 RR Tay 610-8	33203	VIP	FS-BL	021 / Swedish A.F.-F16 Flygflottilj
☐ 103001	Cessna 550 Citation II	550-0272	SE-DVV	0081	1098	2 PWC JT15D-4	6035	VIP		031 / Swedish A.F.-F16 Flygflottilj

AIRBORNE OF SWEDEN, AB = ZF / MIW (formerly Sundsvall Aero)

Mora, Sundsvall & Sveg **AIRBORNE**

Airport, S-792 91 Mora, Sweden ☎ (250) 39 300 Tx: none Fax: (250) 39 301 SITA: n/a
F: 1984 ✠✠✠ 18 Head: Paul Hedman ICAO: MIDWING Net: n/a

registration	type of aircraft	cn/fn	ex/ex*	mfd	del	powered by	mtow kg	configuration	selcal	name/fln/specialitites/remarks
☐ SE-DUZ	Cessna 500 Citation	500-0143	N767BA	0074	1298	2 PWC JT15D-1	5375	Y7		Isf Karlebo Aviation AB
☐ SE-KHL	Dornier 228-100	7003	LN-HPA	0082	0996	2 GA TPE331-5-252D	5700	Y16		Isf Bromma Air Maintenance AB
☐ SE-KKX	Dornier 228-100	7004	LN-HPE	0083	1094	2 GA TPE331-5-252D	5700	Y16		
☐ SE-KTM	Dornier 228-100	7022	OY-CHG	0083	0795	2 GA TPE331-5-252D	5700	Y16		Isf Dansk Fondsselskab A/S
☐ SE-LDH	BAe 3102 Jetstream 31	772	OY-SVK	0087	0697	2 GA TPE331-10UGR-514H	7059	Y18		Isf ABN Amro Leasing
☐ SE-LDI	BAe 3112 Jetstream 31	785	C-FHOE	0088	1097	2 GA TPE331-10UGR-514H	6950	Y18		Isf Elicon Data AB/sublst/opf TravelAir

AIR EXPRESS i Norrköping, AB = XV / GOT

Norrköping-Kungsängen **air express**

Box 284, S-601 04 Norrköping 1, Sweden ☎ (11) 13 20 06 Tx: none Fax: (11) 14 21 21 SITA: n/a
F: 1986 ✠✠✠ 15 Head: Thomas Sjoe ICAO: GOTIC Net: n/a

registration	type of aircraft	cn/fn	ex/ex*	mfd	del	powered by	mtow kg	configuration	selcal	name/fln/specialitites/remarks
☐ SE-KDK	Beech King Air B200	BB-909	N171M	0081		2 PWC PT6A-42	5670			Isf Joh Sjö AB
☐ SE-KXX	Beech 1900C-1 Airliner	UC-44	N31261	0088	0896	2 PWC PT6A-65B	7530	Y19		Isf Raytheon Corporate Jets Inc.
☐ SE-KXV	Beech 1900D Airliner	UE-188		0095	0196	2 PWC PT6A-67D	7688	Y19		Isf ABN Amro Leasing
☐ SE-KXY	Beech 1900D Airliner	UE-236		0096	0996	2 PWC PT6A-67D	7688	Y19		Visby / Isf ABN Amro Leasing

AIR KLINTEN, AB

Visby

Box 1076, S-621 21 Visby, Sweden ☎ (498) 27 95 60 Tx: n/a Fax: (498) 27 85 20 SITA: n/a
F: 1993 ✠✠✠ n/a Head: n/a Net: n/a

registration	type of aircraft	cn/fn	ex/ex*	mfd	del	powered by	mtow kg	configuration	selcal	name/fln/specialitites/remarks
☐ SE-GGU	Cessna 402B	402B0109	D-IDAL	0071		2 CO TSIO-520-E	2858			

AIRLIFT HELIKOPTER Sweden, AB (formerly Airlift Helikopter i Sverige, AB/Airlift Helikopter, AB & Lycksele Helikopter, AB)

Lycksele

Boxfjäll 1168, S-920 64 Tärnaby, Sweden ☎ (954) 10 315 Tx: none Fax: (954) 10 314 SITA: n/a
F: 1991 ✠✠✠ n/a Head: Lars Anders Net: n/a Aircraft below MTOW 1361kg: Hughes 269C (300C).

registration	type of aircraft	cn/fn	ex/ex*	mfd	del	powered by	mtow kg	configuration	selcal	name/fln/specialitites/remarks
☐ SE-HNT	MD Helicopters MD 500E (Hughes 369E)	0146E		0085		1 AN 250-C20B	1360			Isf Lars-Anders AB
☐ SE-HMO	Bell 206L LongRanger	46605	G-JAMI	0078	1298	1 AN 250-C20B	1815			Isf Lars-Anders AB

ANDERSSON BUSINESS JET, AB

Stockholm-Bromma

Vetevägen 16, S-187 69 Täby, Sweden ☎ (8) 756 93 80 Tx: none Fax: (8) 756 40 67 SITA: n/a
F: 1994 ✠✠✠ 10 Head: Bertil Andersson Net: n/a

registration	type of aircraft	cn/fn	ex/ex*	mfd	del	powered by	mtow kg	configuration	selcal	name/fln/specialitites/remarks
☐ SE-DYB	Dassault Falcon 100	216	N999WJ	0088	0298	2 GA TFE731-2-1C	8755			
☐ SE-DLB	Dassault Falcon 100	183	N183SR	0083	0194	2 GA TFE731-2-1C	8500			
☐ SE-DVP	Dassault Falcon 100	224	N135FJ	0089	0998	2 GA TFE731-2-1C	8755			

ARCTIC AIR, AB (formerly Fjällfrakt i Arjeplog, AB)

Vuoggatjalme

Vuoggatjalme 952, S-930 95 Jäckvik, Sweden ☎ (961) 10 715 Tx: none Fax: (961) 61 357 SITA: n/a
F: 1986 ✠✠✠ 1 Head: Björn Helamb Net: n/a

registration	type of aircraft	cn/fn	ex/ex*	mfd	del	powered by	mtow kg	configuration	selcal	name/fln/specialitites/remarks
☐ SE-HKK	Agusta-Bell 206B JetRanger III	8603	06283/804	0080		1 AN 250-C20B	1450			

ARLANDA HELICOPTER, AB

Stockholm-Arlanda

Box 136, S-190 45 Stockholm-Arlanda, Sweden ☎ (8) 59 36 02 08 Tx: none Fax: (8) 59 36 10 20 SITA: n/a
F: 1989 ✠✠✠ 5 Head: Tomas Wallis Net: n/a

registration	type of aircraft	cn/fn	ex/ex*	mfd	del	powered by	mtow kg	configuration	selcal	name/fln/specialitites/remarks
☐ SE-HKP	Bell 206B JetRanger III	2987	LN-OSM	0080	0797	1 AN 250-C20B	1450			
☐ SE-HRM	Bell 206B JetRanger III	2323	N21CK	0078		1 AN 250-C20B	1450			
☐ SE-HTK	Bell 206L LongRanger	45091	N2652	0077		1 AN 250-C20B	1815			
☐ SE-JDB	Agusta A109A II	7287	TC-HMK	0083	0299	2 AN 250-C20B	2600			Isf ABN Amro Leasing

BEAR FLIGHT, AB

Gothenborg-Landvetter

Box 2178, S-438 14 Landvetter, Sweden ☎ (31) 94 29 10 Tx: none Fax: (31) 94 29 11 SITA: n/a
F: 1995 ✠✠✠ n/a Head: Nils Bokedal Net: n/a

registration	type of aircraft	cn/fn	ex/ex*	mfd	del	powered by	mtow kg	configuration	selcal	name/fln/specialitites/remarks
☐ SE-KUS	Cessna 414	414-0482	OY-CYB	0073	0698	2 CO TSIO-520-J	2880			Isf Karlbeo Aviation AB

BLUE CHIP JET, HB = VOL (Associated with Volvo, AB / formerly Volvo Flygservice)

Gothenburg-Saeve

Göteborg-Säve Flygplats 2025, S-423 73 Säve, Sweden ☎ (31) 92 77 00 Tx: none Fax: (31) 92 66 03 SITA: n/a
F: 1955 ✠✠✠ n/a Head: n/a Net: n/a Company conducting non-commercial corporate flights exclusively for the owners of the company.

registration	type of aircraft	cn/fn	ex/ex*	mfd	del	powered by	mtow kg	configuration	selcal	name/fln/specialitites/remarks
☐ SE-DYE	Hawker 800XP	258382	N23451*	0098	0199	2 GA TFE731-5BR-1H	12700	Corporate		
☐ SE-DYV	Hawker 800XP	258385	N23466*	0098	0299	2 GA TFE731-5BR-1H	12700	Corporate		
☐ SE-DVG	Dassault Falcon 50	104	N50VG	0082	0289	3 GA TFE731-3-1C	18500	Corporate		
☐ SE-DVE	Dassault Falcon 900EX	23	F-WWFS*	0098	0498	3 GA TFE731-60-1C	22226			

BRAATHENS Malmö Aviation, AB = BU / SCW (Subsidiary of Braathens ASA, Norway)

Malmö-Sturup & Stockholm-Arlanda

Box 1835, S-171 28 Solna, Sweden ☎ (8) 59 79 16 00 Tx: none Fax: (8) 59 79 16 10 SITA: n/a
F: 1999 ✠✠✠ 700 Head: Anders Widesjö IATA: 154 ICAO: SCANWINGS Net: n/a

registration	type of aircraft	cn/fn	ex/ex*	mfd	del	powered by	mtow kg	configuration	selcal	name/fln/specialitites/remarks
☐ SE-DRA	BAe 146-200	E2115	G-BRXT	0088	0299	4 LY ALF502R-5	42184	Y96		Isf BAMJ / Sydkraft-colors
☐ SE-DRB	BAe 146-200	E2057	N698AA	0086	0299	4 LY ALF502R-5	40595	Y96		Isf BAMJ / special Anastasia-colors
☐ SE-DRC	BAe 146-200	E2053	N695AA	0086	0299	4 LY ALF502R-5	40595	Y96		Isf BAMJ / special Dagens industri-cs
☐ SE-DRD	BAe 146-200	E2094	G-CSJH	0087	0299	4 LY ALF502R-5	42184	Y96		Isf AB Dendera/spec.Webware/Internet-cs
☐ SE-DRE	BAe 146-200	E2051	N694AA	0086	0299	4 LY ALF502R-5	40595	Y96		Isf BAMJ
☐ SE-DRF	BAe 146-200	E2055	N697A	0086	0299	4 LY ALF502R-5	40595	Y96		Isf BAMJ
☐ SE-DRG	BAe 146-200	E2054	N696AA	0086	0299	4 LY ALF502R-5	40595	Y96		Isf BAMJ
☐ SE-DRI	BAe 146-200	E2058	N699AA	0086	0299	4 LY ALF502R-5	40595	Y96		Isf BAMJ
☐ SE-DRK	BAe 146-200	E2108	N295UE	0088	0299	4 LY ALF502R-5	40595	Y96		Isf BAMJ
☐ SE-DRL	BAe 146-200	E2138	N138JV	0089	0299	4 LY ALF502R-5	42184	Y96		Isf BAMJ / spec.Europolitan Airwaves-cs
☐ SE-DUC	Fokker 100 (F28 Mk0100)	11324	PH-CFB*	0090	0299	2 RR Tay 650-15	44450	Y107		Cörnelis / Isf AMS Fokker B.V.
☐ SE-DUD	Fokker 100 (F28 Mk0100)	11325	PH-CFC*	0090	0299	2 RR Tay 650-15	44450	Y107		Tyst / Isf AMS Fokker B.V.
☐ SE-DUE	Fokker 100 (F28 Mk0100)	11326	PH-CFD*	0090	0299	2 RR Tay 650-15	44450	Y107		Emil / Isf AMS Fokker B.V.
☐ SE-DUR	Fokker 100 (F28 Mk0100)	11332	PH-FZK	0091	0299	2 RR Tay 650-15	44450	Y107		Isf Debis Aircraft Leasing I B.V.
☐ SE-DUT	Boeing 737-548	25165 / 2463	EI-CDT	0090	0299	2 CFMI CFM56-3B1	55000	Y125	CS-EH	Isf ILFC
☐ SE-DUS	Boeing 737-3Y0	24255 / 1625	HB-IID	1088	0299	2 CFMI CFM56-3B2	61235	Y148	HM-BE	Isf BBAM

BRITANNIA AIRWAYS, AB = 6B / BLX (Subs.of Britannia Airways, Ltd/Member of Thomson Travel Group/formerly Blue Scandinavia, AB)

Stockholm-Arlanda

PO Box 611, S-194 26 Upplands-Väsby, Sweden ☎ (8) 50 91 00 00 Tx: none Fax: (8) 59 91 50 01 SITA: n/a
F: 1996 ✠✠✠ n/a Head: Kjell Sredhaem ICAO: BLUESCAN Net: n/a

registration	type of aircraft	cn/fn	ex/ex*	mfd	del	powered by	mtow kg	configuration	selcal	name/fln/specialitites/remarks
☐ SE-DUK	Boeing 757-236	25054 / 362	N100FS	0091	0296	2 RR RB211-535E4	113400	Y223	FM-PQ	Isf BBAM
☐ SE-DUL	Boeing 757-2Y0	26151 / 472	SX-BBY	0092	0496	2 RR RB211-535E4	113400	Y223	BM-FR	Isf GECA
☐ SE-DUN	Boeing 757-225	22612 / 114	G-OOOM	0086	1196	2 RR RB211-535E4	109317	Y223	FH-MQ	Isf CITG / sub-lst BAL
☐ SE-DUO	Boeing 757-236	24792 / 279	G-BRJI	0090	0597	2 RR RB211-535E4	113400	Y223	JQ-BL	Isf BBAM
☐ SE-DUP	Boeing 757-236	24793 / 292	G-OOOT	0090	1297	2 RR RB211-535E4	113400	Y223	LQ-CP	Isf Aviation Capital Group
☐ G-BXOP	Boeing 767-3S1 (ER)	25221 / 384	N770TA	0891	1098	2 GE CF6-80C2B6F	172365	Y328	AQ-KR	Isf BAL / to be re-reg. SE-DZF

BROBY HELIKOPTER

Bettna-Landing Pad

Broby, S-640 33 Bettna, Sweden ☎ (150) 30 008 Tx: n/a Fax: (150) 30 048 SITA: n/a
F: 1989 ✠✠✠ 2 Head: Dieden Gustaf Net: n/a

registration	type of aircraft	cn/fn	ex/ex*	mfd	del	powered by	mtow kg	configuration	selcal	name/fln/specialitites/remarks
☐ SE-HUM	Eurocopter (Aerosp.) SA318C Alouette II	2189	N8264	0070	1092	1 TU Astazou IIA	1650			

BUSINESS JET SWEDEN, AB — Vasteras

Hässlö flygplats, S-721 31 Västeras, Sweden ☎ (21) 80 10 40 Tx: none Fax: (21) 80 10 41 SITA: n/a
F: 1996 n/a Head: n/a Net: n/a

☐ SE-GOY	Cessna A185F Skywagon	18503170	N93040	0077	0298	1 CO IO-520-D	1520			lsf Scanvac Control AB
☐ SE-DEZ	Cessna 501 Citation I/SP	501-0279	N43BG	0083	0297	2 PWC JT15D-1A	5375			lsf Scanvac Control AB

CAB AIR = CVN (Division of Bromma Flygskola, AB) — Stockholm-Bromma

Box 310, S-161 26 Bromma, Sweden ☎ (8) 28 24 60 Tx: none Fax: (8) 29 46 34 SITA: n/a
F: 1965 40 Head: Per A. Blomberg ICAO: CARAVAN Net: n/a

☐ SE-IPR	Cessna R182 Skylane RG II	R18200704	N9410R	0079	0595	1 LY O-540-J3C5D	1406			lsf Bio-Search Information AB
☐ SE-IBO	Cessna 340A II	340A0613	N8674K	0079	0296	2 CO TSIO-520-NB	2715			lsf Vima Air KB
☐ SE-KCA	Cessna 340A II	340A0541	D-ICBB	0078		2 CO TSIO-520-N	2715			

CASSEL AERO, AB (formerly Skogsflyg Cassel Aero, AB) — Oernsköldsvik

Oernsköldsviks flygplats, S-890 35 Husum, Sweden ☎ (660) 25 70 17 Tx: none Fax: (660) 25 70 16 SITA: n/a
F: 1960 10 Head: Ulf Cassel Net: http://www.sasims.com Aircraft below MTOW 1361 kg: Hughes 269B/C.

☐ SE-JCA	Eurocopter (Aerosp.) AS350B2 Ecureuil	2619	F-WYMG*	0092	0492	1 TU Arriel 1D1	2250			lsf Rotorcraft Rental Ltd
☐ SE-JCB	Eurocopter (Aerosp.) AS350B2 Ecureuil	2635		0092	0792	1 TU Arriel 1D1	2250			lsf Rotorcraft Rental Ltd

EURO EXEC EXPRESS = EXC (European Executive Express dba / Subsidiary of CNA International, AB) — Karlstad

Box 599, S-651 13 Karlstad, Sweden ☎ (54) 21 22 47 Tx: none Fax: (54) 21 22 31 SITA: n/a
F: 1997 12 Head: Goran S. Janson ICAO: ECHO EXPRESS Net: n/a

☐ SE-LGA	BAe 3101 Jetstream 31	636	N636JX	0084	0897	2 GA TPE331-10UR-513H	7059	C8orC10orY18		
☐ SE-LGB	BAe 3101 Jetstream 31	639	N639JX	0084	0697	2 GA TPE331-10UR-513H	7059	C12 or Y18		lsf GE Capital
☐ SE-LGC	BAe 3108 Jetstream 31	645	G-BXLM	0084	0299	2 GA TPE331-10UR-513H	7059	C12 or Y18		lsf GE Capital

EUROPEAN HELICOPTER CENTER, AB (Subsidiary of European Flight Center A/S, Norway) — Gothenburg-Saeve

Box 8958, S-402 74 Göteborg, Sweden ☎ (31) 55 62 10 Tx: none Fax: (31) 55 08 97 SITA: n/a
F: 1996 n/a Head: n/a Net: n/a Aircraft below MTOW 1361kg: Robinson R22 & R44

☐ SE-JDM	Eurocopter (Aerosp.) AS355F1 Ecureuil 2	5172	N302PS	0082	0796	2 AN 250-C20F	2400			lsf AS Blackbird

FALCON AIR, AB = IH / FCN (formerly Falcon Aviation, AB & Falcon Cargo, AB) — Malmö-Sturup

Box 36, S-230 32 Malmö-Sturup, Sweden ☎ (40) 50 05 00 Tx: 33014 falcon s Fax: (40) 50 01 49 SITA: MMXOPIH
F: 1986 130 Head: Rolf A. Johansson IATA: 759 ICAO: FALCON Net: http://www.falconair.se

☐ SE-DPA	Boeing 737-33A (QC)	25401 / 2067		0691	1091	2 CFMI CFM56-3C1	61230	Y142/Freighter	BE-QR	Aftonfalken / lsf AWAS / cvtd -33A
☐ SE-DPB	Boeing 737-33A (QC)	25402 / 2159	N33AW	0691	1191	2 CFMI CFM56-3C1	61235	Y142/Freighter	BF-AS	Pilgrimsfalken / lsf AWAS / cvtd -33A
☐ SE-DPC	Boeing 737-33A (QC)	25426 / 2172	N34AW	1291	0192	2 CFMI CFM56-3C1	61235	Y142/Freighter	BF-CR	Tornfalken / lsf AWAS / cvtd -33A

FISKFLYG, AB — Stora Sjöfallet & Porjus

PO Box 830, S-982 60 Porjus, Sweden ☎ (973) 10 245 Tx: none Fax: (973) 10 360 SITA: n/a
F: 1953 5 Head: Sören Lundkvist Net: n/a Aircraft below MTOW 1361 kg: Agusta-Bell 47G-4.

☐ SE-AXB	Republic RC-3 Seabee	268		0047		1 LY GO-480-G1A6	1430	4 Pax		Amphibian
☐ SE-AXY	Republic RC-3 Seabee	830		0047		1 LY GO-480-G1A6	1430	4 Pax		Amphibian
☐ SE-BXB	Republic RC-3 Seabee	953	LN-MAL	0047		1 LY GO-480-G1A6	1430	4 Pax		Amphibian
☐ SE-HII	Agusta-Bell 206B JetRanger	8290	D-HEPY	0071		1 AN 250-C20	1450	4 Pax		
☐ SE-HOM	Bell 206B JetRanger III	2394	N48EA	0078		1 AN 250-C20B	1450	4 Pax		
☐ SE-GOP	Cessna U206G Stationair	U20603528	N8776Q	0076		1 CO IO-520-F	1635	5 Pax		Floats
☐ SE-HVI	Bell 206L-3 LongRanger III	51407		0090	1290	1 AN 250-C30P	1880	5 Pax		

FJAELLFLYGARNA i ARJEPLOG, AB — Laisvall & Arjeplog

Adolfström, S-930 93 Laisvall, Sweden ☎ (961) 23 040 Tx: n/a Fax: (961) 230 23 SITA: n/a
F: n/a n/a Head: n/a Net: n/a Aircraft below MTOW 1361kg: Hughes 369HS (500C)

☐ SE-JDL	MD Helicopters MD 500E (Hughes 369E)	0018E	N501TS	0087	0299	1 AN 250-C20B	1361			

FLYGANDE VETERANER (Stiftelsen Flygande Veteraner dba) — Stockholm-Bromma

Flygplatsinfarten 39, S-161 69 Bromma Flygplats, Sweden ☎ (8) 764 52 08 Tx: none Fax: (8) 662 64 98 SITA: n/a
F: 1984 n/a Head: Jimmie Berglund Net: n/a Non-profit organization.

☐ SE-CFP	Boeing (Douglas) DC-3C (C-47A-DL)	13883	RSAF79006	0043		2 PW R-1830	12200	28 Pax		Fridtjof Viking / old SAS colours

FLYGTJAENST, AB — Vilhelmina & Klimpfjäll

Vilhelmina flygplats, Sagadal 7, S-912 90 Vilhelmina, Sweden ☎ (940) 31 080 Tx: none Fax: (940) 31 078 SITA: n/a
F: 1977 3 Head: Frans J.Viklund Net: n/a Aircraft below MTOW 1361 kg: Hughes 269C (300C).

☐ SE-JAA	MD Helicopters MD 500D (Hughes 369D)	1138D	TF-FIM	0082		1 AN 250-C20B	1360			
☐ SE-CGM	Noorduyn Norseman VI (UC-64A)	780	LN-TSN	0045		1 PW R-1340	3420			lsf pvt / Floats

FLYING ENTERPRISE, AB = F3 / FLY — Skövde

August Barks gata 25, S-421 32 Västra Frölunda, Sweden ☎ (31) 709 76 00 Tx: none Fax: (31) 709 76 76 SITA: n/a
F: 1986 140 Head: Alf Lindqvist IATA: 272 ICAO: FLYING Net: http://www.flying.se

☐ SE-KKS	Piper PA-31-350 Navajo Chieftain	31-7852135	N27739	0078	0889	2 LY TIO-540-J2BD	3175	Y8		lsf Tipp&Kran/opf Sw.Navy as 54203/543
☐ SE-KKT	Piper PA-31-350 Navajo Chieftain	31-8052019	N124BC	0080	0889	2 LY TIO-540-J2BD	3175	Y8		lsf Tipp&Kran/opf Sw.Navy as 54201/541
☐ SE-IKZ	Fairchild (Swearingen) SA226TC Metro II	TC-383	D-IBAN	0081	0593	2 GA TPE331-3UW-303G	5670	Y14		FE Flying Linn / lst MXL
☐ SE-FVP	BAe 3102 Jetstream 31	719	G-BTXG	0086	0697	2 GA TPE331-10UR-513H	7060	Y18		
☐ SE-LGM	BAe 3102 Jetstream 31	781	OY-SVY	0087	0197	2 GA TPE331-10UR-514H	7060	Y19		
☐ SE-LHP	BAe 3102 Jetstream 31	638	G-BUFL	0084	0497	2 GA TPE331-10UR-513H	7060	Y19		lsf BAMT
☐ SE-LHV	BAe 3102 Jetstream 31	720	G-BRGL	0087	0397	2 GA TPE331-10UR-513H	7060	Y19		lsf BAMT
☐ SE-INZ	Shorts 330-200 (SD3-30)	SH3097	G-BLGG*	0084	0194	2 PWC PT6A-45R	10385	Y28		
☐ SE-LCC	Shorts 360-300 (SD3-60)	SH3726	G-BNMW	0087	1195	2 PWC PT6A-67R	12292	Y36		
☐ SE-LDA	Shorts 360-200 (SD3-60)	SH3688	G-BMLC	0086	0496	2 PWC PT6A-65AR	11999	Y36		lsf Midland Montagu Leasing
☐ SE-LGE	Shorts 360-200 (SD3-60)	SH3686	G-BMHX	0085	0796	2 PWC PT6A-65AR	11999	Y36		lsf Midland Montagu Leasing
☐ SE-LHY	Shorts 360-300 (SD3-60)	SH3755	G-BVMY	0089	1197	2 PWC PT6A-67R	12292	Y36		lsf Capi.BankLsng/Lotto Svenska Spel-cs
☐ SE-KCR	Saab SF340A (QC)	340A-065	OH-FAA	0086	1198	2 GE CT7-5A2	12700	Y34 / Frtr		
☐ SE-KCS	Saab SF340A (QC)	340A-066	OH-FAB	0086	1298	2 GE CT7-5A2	12700	Y34 / Frtr		
☐ SE-KCT	Saab SF340A (QC)	340A-070	OH-FAC	0086	1298	2 GE CT7-5A2	12700	Y34 / Frtr		

GOLDEN AIR = DC / GAO (Golden Air Flyg, AB dba / formerly Golden Air, AB) — Trollhattan

Flygplats Vänersborg, S-461 93 Trollhättan, Sweden ☎ (520) 48 21 70 Tx: none Fax: (520) 48 44 43 SITA: n/a
F: 1989 21 Head: Anders Källsson ICAO: GOLDEN Net: n/a

☐ SE-DEG	Cessna 500 Citation	500-0276	N473LR	0075		2 PWC JT15D-1A	5375	Y6		
☐ SE-ISD	Saab SF340A	340A-145	ZK-FXQ	0489	0897	2 GE CT7-5A2	12700	Y36		
☐ SE-ISG	Saab 340B	340B-162	SE-F62*	0089	1089	2 GE CT7-9B	12930	Y36		lsf Erik Thun AB
☐ SE-LEP	Saab SF340A	340A-127	B-12200	0088	0298	2 GE CT7-5A2	12700	Y36		lsf SKX / sub-lst / opf TED
☐ SE-LES	Saab SF340A	340A-129	B-12299	0088	0398	2 GE CT7-5A2	12700	Y36		lsf SKS / sub-lst / opf TED

GOTEBORGS FALLSKARMSKLUBB — Gothenburg-Saeve

Ravekarrsgatan 457, S-431 33 Mölndal, Sweden ☎ (31) 704 88 60 Tx: none Fax: (31) 704 88 60 SITA: n/a
F: 1959 n/a Head: Leif Rudin Net: n/a Operates para flights exclusively for club members (850) only.

☐ SE-LDK	Shorts Skyvan 3 Variant 300 (SC-7)	SH1870	SX-BBO	0069	0394	2 GA TPE331-2-201A	5670	Para		lsf Flygbussen paa Zaeve Hills KB

HELIFLYG, AB = HFL (Member of Helikopter Service Group, Norway/formerly Heli Avia) — Borlange, Linkoping, Ostersund & Alta/Bodo/Voss (Norway)

Oeverstevägen 40, S-784 63 Borlänge, Sweden ☎ (243) 79 49 99 Tx: 50943 heliab s Fax: (243) 79 49 01 SITA: n/a
F: 1986 n/a Head: Jan Närlinge ICAO: HELIFLYG Net: http://www.heliflyg.com Aircraft below MTOW 1361 kg: Hughes 269C (300C) & 369HS (500C).

☐ SE-HLI	MD Helicopters MD 500D (Hughes 369D)	1200879D		0080		1 AN 250-C20B	1360			lsf Rotor Konsult i Borlänge AB
☐ SE-HLP	MD Helicopters MD 500D (Hughes 369D)	610986D		0081		1 AN 250-C20B	1360			lsf Rotor Konsult i Borlänge AB
☐ SE-HSI	MD Helicopters MD 500D (Hughes 369D)	811041D	D-HAFE	0081	0595	1 AN 250-C20B	1360			
☐ SE-JAD	MD Helicopters MD 500E (Hughes 369E)	0458E	N1610N	0091		1 AN 250-C20B	1361			lsf Sven Kahlbäck Entreprenad AB
☐ OH-HLA	MD Helicopters MD 500D (Hughes 369D)	500718D	SE-HLA	0080		1 AN 250-C20B	1361			
☐ SE-JDP	Eurocopter EC120B Colibri	1019		0099	0299	1 TU Arrius 2F	1680			lsf Sven Kahlbäck Entreprenad AB
☐ SE-HVN	Eurocopter (Aerosp.) AS350B1 Ecureuil	2157	HB-XSA	0088	0496	1 TU Arriel 1D	2200			
☐ SE-JCV	Eurocopter (Aerosp.) AS350B3 Ecureuil	3064		0098	0398	1 TU Arriel 2B	2250			lsf GE Capital
☐ SE-JDR	Eurocopter (Aerosp.) AS350B3 Ecureuil	3175		0099	0299	1 TU Arriel 2B	2250			lsf GE Capital
☐ LN-OPB	Eurocopter (Aerosp.) AS350B1 Ecureuil	1940		0086	0098	1 TU Arriel 1D	2200			lsf LTR
☐ LN-OPE	Eurocopter (Aerosp.) AS350B1 Ecureuil	2183		0089	0098	1 TU Arriel 1D	2200			lsf LTR
☐ LN-OTA	Eurocopter (Aerosp.) AS350B1 Ecureuil	1902	SE-JAC	0086	0098	1 TU Arriel 1D	2200			lsf LTR
☐ SE-HSG	Eurocopter (MBB) BO105CBS	S-439	D-HDMM	0080		2 AN 250-C20B	2400			
☐ SE-JCK	Eurocopter (Aerosp.) SA365N Dauphin 2	6090	G-BKXE	0083	1295	2 TU Arriel 1C	4000			
☐ SE-HLE	Bell 214B-1 BigLifter	28054	LN-ORM	0080	1298	1 LY T5508D	5670			lsf LTR

583 registration type of aircraft cn/fn ex/ex* mfd del powered by mtow kg configuration selcal name/fln/specialitites/remarks

HELI i ARJEPLOG, AB

Arjeplog

Hamnplan, S-930 90 Arjeplog, Sweden ☎ (961) 61 240 Tx: none Fax: (961) 10 596 SITA: n/a
F: 1970 ⁂ 3 Head: n/a Net: n/a

☐	SE-HMM	Eurocopter (Aerosp.) AS350B Ecureuil	*1693*		*0082*	*0195*	*1 TU Arriel 1B*	*1950*		

HELIKOPTERSERVICE Euro Air, AB = YQ / SCO (formerly Euro Air Helikopter Service, AB)

Helsingborg

Atlantgatan 6, S-252 25 Helsingborg, Sweden ☎ (42) 37 08 00 Tx: 72814 euro s Fax: (42) 18 74 15 SITA: JHEKPYQ
F: 1982 ⁂ 45 Head: Sten Gunnarsson ICAO: SWEDCOPTER Net: http://www.helikopterservice.com

☐	SE-HPN	Bell 206L-1 LongRanger II	*45320*		*0079*		*1 AN 250-C28B*	*1882*	*Y4*		
☐	SE-JFA	Sikorsky S-76C+	*760466*		*0097*	*0497*	*2 TU Arriel 2S1*	*5300*	*Y12*		*lsf ABN Amro Leasing*
☐	SE-JFB	Sikorsky S-76C+	*760468*		*0097*	*0497*	*2 TU Arriel 2S1*	*5300*	*Y12*		*lsf ABN Amro Leasing*
☐	SE-JFC	Sikorsky S-76C+	*760481*		*1297*	*0198*	*2 TU Arriel 2S1*	*5300*	*Y12*		*lsf ABN Amro Leasing*

HELIKOPTERTJAENST i Kittelfjäll, AB (formerly Fjällhäven Vip Air, AB)

Oernsköldsvik & Domsjö

Box 145, S-892 23 Domsjö, Sweden ☎ (10) 257 58 56 Tx: n/a Fax: (660) 74 200 SITA: n/a
F: n/a ⁂ n/a Head: Borge Marklund Net: n/a

☐	SE-HEL	Agusta-Bell 206B JetRanger	*8332*		*0072*	*0798*	*1 AN 250-C20*	*1450*			*lsf VIP Air i Lappland AB*
☐	SE-HOK	Bell 206B JetRanger	*1693*	*N73DH*	*0075*		*1 AN 250-C20*	*1451*			*lsf Fjällräven AB*
☐	SE-HRC	Eurocopter (Aerosp.) SE3130 Alouette II	*1128*	*02109*	*0057*	*0597*	*1 TU Artouste IIC6*	*1500*			

HELIKOPTERTRANSPORT = KTR (HT Helikoptertransport, AB dba)

Grillby Helipad

Box 42, S-740 81 Grillby, Sweden ☎ (171) 70 424 Tx: none Fax: (171) 70 708 SITA: n/a
F: 1989 ⁂ 5 Head: Göran Andersson ICAO: COPTER TRANS Net: n/a Aircraft below MTOW 1361 kg: Hughes 269C (300C).

☐	SE-HRK	MD Helicopters MD 500D (Hughes 369D)	*1187D*	*LN-OPM*	*0082*		*1 AN 250-C20B*	*1360*			
☐	SE-HUU	MD Helicopters MD 500D (Hughes 369D)	*1090594D*	*OY-HCJ*	*0079*		*1 AN 250-C20B*	*1360*			
☐	SE-HVY	MD Helicopters MD 500D (Hughes 369D)	*970188D*		*0077*		*1 AN 250-C20B*	*1360*			

HIGHLAND AIR, AB = HS / HIL (Subsidiary of Skyways, AB)

Hultsfred

Flygplatsen, S-577 91 Hultsfred, Sweden ☎ (495) 24 97 70 Tx: none Fax: (495) 13 303 SITA: n/a
F: 1995 ⁂ 50 Head: Sievert Andersson IATA: 990 ICAO: HIGHLAND Net: http://www.highlandair.se

☐	SE-IKY	Dornier 228-201	*8016*	*D-IBLH**	*0083*	*0995*	*2 GA TPE331-5-252D*	*5980*	*Y19*		*lsf Enar Lindström AB*
☐	SE-LHD	Dornier 228-201	*8108*	*G-CAYN*	*0087*	*0696*	*2 GA TPE331-5-252D*	*5980*	*Y16*		*cvtd -200*
☐	SE-LHA	BAe 3201 Jetstream 32	*842*	*N842JX*	*0089*	*0796*	*2 GA TPE331-12UHR-702H*	*7350*	*Y19*		*lsf BAMT*
☐	SE-LHB	BAe 3201 Jetstream 32	*844*	*N844JX*	*0089*	*0996*	*2 GA TPE331-12UHR-702H*	*7350*	*Y19*		*lsf BAMT*
☐	SE-LHC	BAe 3201 Jetstream 32	*846*	*N846JX*	*0089*	*0597*	*2 GA TPE331-12UHR-702H*	*7350*	*Y19*		*lsf BAMT*
☐	SE-LHE	BAe 3201 Jetstream 32	*854*	*N854JX*	*0089*	*0997*	*2 GA TPE331-12UHR-702H*	*7350*	*Y19*		*lsf BAMT*
☐	SE-LHF	BAe 3201 Jetstream 32	*855*	*N855JX*	*0089*	*0298*	*2 GA TPE331-12UHR-702H*	*7350*	*Y19*		*lsf BAMT*
☐	SE-LHG	BAe 3201 Jetstream 32EP	*857*	*N857JX*	*0089*	*1198*	*2 GA TPE331-12UHR-702H*	*7350*	*Y19*		*lsf BAMT / cvtd 32*
☐	SE-LHH	BAe 3201 Jetstream 32EP	*848*	*N848JX*	*0089*	*0199*	*2 GA TPE331-12UHR-702H*	*7350*	*Y19*		*lsf BAMT / cvtd 32*
☐	SE-LHI	BAe 3201 Jetstream 32EP	*841*	*N841JX*	*0089*	*0199*	*2 GA TPE331-12UHR-702H*	*7350*	*Y19*		*lsf BAMT / cvtd 32*

IBA International Business Air, AB = U5 / IBZ

Karlshamn & Stockholm-Bromma

Bodekullsvägen 1, S-374 35 Karlshamn, Sweden ☎ (454) 19 595 Tx: n/a Fax: (454) 19 596 SITA: n/a
F: 1983 ⁂ 50 Head: Jan-Eric Olsson ICAO: INTERBIZ Net: n/a

☐	SE-IKV	Piper PA-31-350 Navajo Chieftain	*31-7405148*	*G-BDFN*	*0074*		*2 LY TIO-540-J2BD*	*3290*	*Y9*		*lsf Volair AB*
☐	SE-IVA	Mitsubishi MU-2L (MU-2B-36)	*666*	*N826RC*	*0075*		*2 GA TPE331-6-251M*	*5255*	*Y6*		*lsf Volair AB*
☐	SE-LEF	Fairchild (Swearingen) SA227AC Metro III	*AC-451B*	*VH-NEM*	*0081*	*0396*	*2 GA TPE331-11U-611G*	*7260*	*Y19*		*lsf Finans Skandic AB*
☐	SE-LIL	Fairchild (Swearingen) SA227AC Metro III	*AC-432B*	*F-GLPE*	*0081*	*0197*	*2 GA TPE331-11U-611G*	*7260*	*Y19*		*lsf Finansskandic AB*
☐	SE-LKB	Embraer 120ER Brasilia (EMB-120ER)	*120016*	*N124AM*	*0086*	*0299*	*2 PWC PW118*	*11990*	*Y30*		*cvtd 120ER*
☐	SE-LKC	Embraer 120ER Brasilia (EMB-120ER)	*120046*	*N273UE*	*1187*	*0299*	*2 PWC PW118*	*11990*	*Y30*		*cvtd 120RT*

IFS International Flight Service, AB

Gothenburg-Saeve

Hangar C1, Säve Flygplats, S-423 73 Säve, Sweden ☎ (31) 92 78 58 Tx: none Fax: (31) 92 78 57 SITA: n/a
F: 1997 ⁂ 6 Head: n/a Net: n/a

☐	SE-GVZ	Piper PA-31-310 Navajo C	*31-7812079*		*0078*	*1097*	*2 LY TIO-540-A2C*	*2950*			
☐	SE-DVZ	Cessna 550 Citation Bravo	*550-0808*	*N1299B*	*0097*	*1197*	*2 PWC PW530A*	*6713*			*lsf BLN Förvaltnings AB*

INDIGO AVIATION, AB = (INGO)

Malmoe

Födra Förftad Gatan 4, S-211 43 Malmö, Sweden ☎ (40) 660 30 01 Tx: none Fax: (40) 30 23 50 SITA: n/a
F: 1988 ⁂ n/a Head: John Evans Net: n/a New and used aircraft leasing, sales and financing company.
Owner/lessor of following (main) aircraft types: Airbus Industrie A320/A321 & Boeing 737-200/-300/-500. Aircraft leased from Indigo Aviation are listed and mentioned as lsf INGO under the leasing carriers.
US business is handled by sister company INDIGO AIRLEASE CORP., Suite 800, 100NE 3rd Ave, Fort Lauderdale, FL 33301, USA. Phone (954) 760-7777, Fax (954) 760-7716.

INTER AIR, AB = INR

Malmö-Sturup

PO Box 27, S-230 32 Malmö-Sturup, Sweden ☎ (40) 50 03 00 Tx: 33591 intair s Fax: (40) 50 03 09 SITA: n/a
F: 1981 ⁂ 14 Head: Anders Lundstrom ICAO: INTERAIR Net: n/a

☐	SE-DEY	Cessna 500 Citation I	*500-0370*	*N36897*	*0077*		*2 PWC JT15D-1A*	*5375*	*7 Pax*		*lsf A.J. Produkter i Hyltebruk AB*
☐	SE-DDY	Cessna 550 Citation II	*550-0115*	*N127SC*	*0080*		*2 PWC JT15D-4*	*6035*	*8 Pax*		
☐	SE-DKC	Dassault Falcon 10	*123*	*N25FF*	*0078*		*2 GA TFE731-2-1C*	*8500*	*7 Pax*		*lsf Trelleborg AB*
☐	SE-DPK	Dassault Falcon 10	*152*	*F-GDRN*	*0079*	*0092*	*2 GA TFE731-2-1C*	*8760*	*6 Pax*		*lsf Mellby Gard Air AB*
☐	SE-DVY	Cessna 650 Citation VII	*650-7011*	*N700VP*	*0092*	*0298*	*2 GA TFE731-4R-2S*	*10185*	*9 Pax*		*lsf ABN Amro Leasing*

JAEMTLANDS FLYG, AB (formerly Jaemtlands Flyg & Fiske, AB)

Oestersund

Lugnviksväg 105, S-831 52 Oestersund, Sweden ☎ (63) 10 36 70 Tx: none Fax: (63) 13 36 70 SITA: n/a
F: n/a ⁂ n/a Head: Siv Grinde Net: n/a Aircraft below MTOW 1361kg: Hughes 269C (300C)

☐	SE-JFZ	Eurocopter EC120B Colibri	*1011*		*0098*	*0998*	*1 TU Arrius 2F*	*1680*			

JIVAIR (Jivair Marketing, AB dba)

Gothenburg-Saeve

Box 23, S-431 21 Mölndal, Sweden ☎ (31) 87 78 00 Tx: 28650 jivair s Fax: (31) 27 45 12 SITA: n/a
F: 1981 ⁂ 8 Head: Anders Jivegaard Net: http://www.jivairmarketing.se

☐	SE-GNA	Piper PA-31-310 Navajo C	*31-7612034*		*0076*		*2 LY TIO-540-A2C*	*2950*			
☐	SE-DLZ	Cessna 500 Citation I	*500-0411*	*G-NCMT*	*0082*	*0389*	*2 PWC JT15D-1A*	*5375*			

JONAIR AFFAERSFLYG, AB

Umea

Hartvigsgatan 4, S-902 48 Umea, Sweden ☎ (90) 12 12 00 Tx: n/a Fax: (90) 14 29 66 SITA: n/a
F: n/a ⁂ n/a Head: Per Jonsson Net: n/a

☐	SE-GLE	Piper PA-31-310 Navajo C	*31-7512056*		*0075*		*2 LY TIO-540-A2C*	*2950*			

KIRUNA FLYG, AB (formerly Tammert Aero, AB)

Kiruna

Box 214, S-981 24 Kiruna, Sweden ☎ (980) 20 250 Tx: none Fax: (980) 20 251 SITA: n/a
F: 1989 ⁂ n/a Head: Lars Levin Net: n/a

☐	SE-KKR	De Havilland DHC-2 Beaver I	*1551*	*N5595N*	*0064*	*0689*	*1 PW R-985*	*2315*			*Floats / Wheel-Skis*

KUSTBEVAKNING – Swedish Coast Guard = KBV

Nykoping-Skavsta

Flight Division, Stumholmen, Box 536, S-371 23 Karlskrona, Sweden ☎ (455) 35 34 00 Tx: 43268 coastg s Fax: (455) 105 21 SITA: n/a
F: 1988 ⁂ 28 Head: Lars Franzen ICAO: SWECOAST Net: n/a Non-commercial state organisation conducting surveillance flights.

☐	SE-IVE	CASA 212-CE4 Aviocar Srs 200	*343*		*0085*	*0886*	*2 GA TPE331-10R-512C*	*7700*	*Patrol / Survey*		
☐	SE-IVF	CASA 212-CE4 Aviocar Srs 200	*346*		*0085*	*0886*	*2 GA TPE331-10R-512C*	*7700*	*Patrol / Survey*		
☐	SE-KVG	CASA 212-CE4 Aviocar Srs 200	*229*	*FAU 534*	*0081*	*0291*	*2 GA TPE331-10R-512C*	*7700*	*Patrol / Survey*		

LAP AIR (AB, Lapplandsflyg dba)

Umea, Kiruna, Kvikkjokk & Tärnaby

Umea Flygplats, S-904 22 Umea, Sweden ☎ (90) 12 90 50 Tx: none Fax: (90) 12 90 55 SITA: n/a
F: 1953 ⁂ 8 Head: Bertil Johannson ICAO: LAPAIR Net: http://www.lapplandsflyg.se Aircraft below MTOW 1361 kg: Bell 47G-2

☐	SE-HEH	Bell 206B JetRanger	*734*	*N2915W*	*0071*		*1 AN 250-C20*	*1450*			*cvtd 206A*
☐	SE-HEI	Agusta-Bell 206B JetRanger	*8348*		*0073*		*1 AN 250-C20*	*1450*			
☐	SE-HLK	Agusta-Bell 206B JetRanger III	*8047*		*0067*		*1 AN 250-C20B*	*1450*			*cvtd 206A / rebuilt*
☐	SE-HTV	Bell 206B JetRanger III	*4049*		*0089*		*1 AN 250-C20J*	*1450*			
☐	SE-HKC	Bell 206L-1 LongRanger II	*45321*		*0079*		*1 AN 250-C28B*	*1882*			
☐	SE-HTR	Bell 206L-1 LongRanger II	*45395*	*C-GLMO*	*0080*		*1 AN 250-C28B*	*1882*			*lsf Flygtransporter*
☐	SE-JEB	Bell 407	*53006*	*C-FXDK**	*0096*	*0396*	*1 AN 250-C47B*	*2268*			

LE CARAVELLE CLUB

Stockholm-Arlanda

c/o Ola Carlsson, Karl Martins Väg 18, S-185 33 Vaxholm, Sweden ☎ (70) 717 67 48 Tx: none Fax: none SITA: n/a
F: 1998 ⁂ n/a Head: Ola Karlson Net: n/a Club conducting nostalgia passenger flights exclusively for the club members and presentation flights at airshows.

☐	SE-DAI	Aerospatiale (Sud) SE210 Caravelle III	*210*	*85210*	*0066*	*0199*	*2 RR Avon 527B*	*48000*	*40 Pax*		

MAF Sweden – Mission Aviation Fellowship (Branch of MAF Europe)

Dhaka (Bangladesh)

Gamla Tanneforsv. 17, S-582 54 Linköping, Sweden ☎ (13) 35 39 60 Tx: none Fax: (13) 35 39 65 SITA: n/a
F: 1982 ⁂ n/a Head: Göran Ahlin Net: n/a Non-commercial mulitnational ecclesiastical consortium conducting flights for relief & development agencies & missions in remote areas of third world countries.

☐	S2-ACE	De Havilland DHC-2 Beaver I	*1300*	*SE-LEV*	*0058*	*0596*	*1 PW R-985*	*2313*			

584 registration type of aircraft cn/fn ex/ex* mfd del powered by mtow kg configuration selcal name/fln/specialitites/remarks

MALMO AIR TAXI, AB
Malmö-Sturup

Hindbygarden, S-213 74 Malmö, Sweden ☎ (40) 21 05 74 Tx: none Fax: (40) 21 05 15 SITA: n/a
F: 1995 n/a Head: Willy Liljeheden Net: n/a

☐ SE-IDR	Piper PA-31-310 Navajo C	31-7712085	LN-DAB	0077	0695	2 LY TIO-540-A2C	2950			

MAXAIR, AB = 8M / MXL (formerly Kabair, HB)
Malmö-Sturup

PO Box 24, S-230 32 Malmö-Sturup, Sweden ☎ (40) 55 60 40 Tx: none Fax: (40) 55 60 49 SITA: n/a
F: 1994 3 Head: Steve Josefsson ICAO: MAXAIR Net: http://www.maxair.com

☐ SE-IKZ	Fairchild (Swearingen) SA226TC Metro II	TC-383	D-IBAN	0081	0798	2 GA TPE331-3UW-303G	5670	Y14		lsf FLY
☐ SE-KCP	Fairchild (Swearingen) SA226TC Metro II	TC-330	N7217N	0080	0299	2 GA TPE331-3UW-303G	5670	Y14		

MIDLAND AIR Oestersund, AB (formerly Midland Air, AB)
Oestersund

Box 2038, S-831 02 Oestersund, Sweden ☎ (63) 35 049 Tx: none Fax: (63) 35 074 SITA: n/a
F: 1985 2 Head: n/a Net: n/a Aircraft below MTOW 1361 kg: Hughes 269C (300C) & Piper PA-18.

☐ SE-IRI	Cessna A185F Skywagon	18503177	N93094	0077		1 CO IO-520-D	1520			lsf Sky Safari / Wheel-skis

NORDFLYG, AB = NEF
Eskilstuna

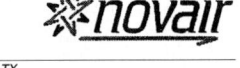

Flygplatsen, S-635 06 Eskilstuna, Sweden ☎ (16) 94 015 Tx: 46049 essutwr s Fax: (16) 94 090 SITA: n/a
F: 1952 8 Head: Ulf Darenius ICAO: NORDEX Net: n/a Aircraft below MTOW 1361 kg: Hughes 269C (300C).

☐ SE-HSN	MD Helicopters MD 500E (Hughes 369E)	0181E	OY-HEW	0086		1 AN 250-C20B	1360			lsf Investment AB Stammen
☐ SE-GBO	Piper PA-31-310 Navajo B	31-7400983		0074		2 LY TIO-540-A2C	2950			
☐ SE-ILL	Piper PA-31-350 Navajo Chieftain	31-7305117	4X-CCH	0073		2 LY TIO-540-J2BD	3175			lsf East Air KB
☐ SE-KYI	Cessna 208B Grand Caravan	208B0629		0097	1097	1 PWC PT6A-114A	4059			lsf ABN Amro Leasing

NORDKALOTTFLYG, AB
Lulea & Skelleftea

Box 80023, S-972 21 Lulea, Sweden ☎ (920) 22 74 74 Tx: none Fax: (920) 22 03 48 SITA: n/a
F: 1978 4 Head: Sune Lestander Net: n/a

☐ SE-GBG	Piper PA-31-310 Navajo B	31-7401234		0074		2 LY TIO-540-A2C	2950			

NORRLANDSFLYG, AB = HMF
Gällivare & Kiruna

Box 24, S-982 21 Gällivare, Sweden ☎ (970) 14 065 Tx: none Fax: (970) 16 055 SITA: n/a
F: 1960 33 Head: Knut Hedström ICAO: LIFEGUARD SWEDEN Net: http://www.grafiskform.se/norrflyg/

☐ SE-HUO	Eurocopter (Aerosp.) AS350B Ecureuil	1867	D-HHLL	0085	0789	1 TU Arriel 1B	1950			
☐ SE-JDZ	Eurocopter (Aerosp.) AS350B Ecureuil	2227	F-GGGU	0089	0698	1 TU Arriel 1B	1950			lsf Karlebo Aviation AB
☐ SE-JFK	Eurocopter (Aerosp.) AS350B1 Ecureuil	1983	F-GPAT	0086	1294	1 TU Arriel 1D	2200			
☐ SE-HLS	Eurocopter (Aerosp.) SA360C Dauphin	1016	F-BZAQ	0077	0881	1 TU Astazou XVIIIA	3000			
☐ SE-HGZ	Sikorsky S-55T	551252	N62540	0058	0675	1 GA TPE331-3U-303N	3270			cvtd S-55
☐ SE-JES	Sikorsky S-76A	760190	N110AG	0081	1094	2 AN 250-C30S	4765	EMS		lsf ABN Amro Leasing
☐ SE-JEZ	Sikorsky S-76A	760215	N72WW	0081	0793	2 AN 250-C30S	4765	EMS		lsf ABN Amro Leasing
☐ SE-JUZ	Sikorsky S-76A++	760282	N92RR	0085	1298	2 TU Arriel 1S1	4898	EMS Lifeguard		lsf ABN Amro Leasing / cvtd S-76A

NOVAIR = NVR (Nova Airlines, AB dba / Subsidiary of Apollo Resor, AB)
Stockholm-Arlanda

Box 94, S-190 45 Stockholm-Arlanda, Sweden ☎ (8) 797 53 44 Tx: none Fax: (8) 797 53 40 SITA: STOSO7I
F: 1997 250 Head: Thomas Rosenqvist ICAO: NAVIGATOR Net: n/a

☐ SE-DVO	Boeing 737-85F	28822 / 166	N1787B*	0098	0199	2 CFMI CFM56-7B26	79015	Y189		lsf GATX
☐ SE-DVR	Boeing 737-85F	28826 / 238		0099	0499	2 CFMI CFM56-7B26	79015	Y189		lsf GATX
☐ SE-DVF	Lockheed L-1011-385-3 TriStar 500	293B-1241	CS-TEC	0083	1097	3 RR RB211-524B4-02	231332	C19Y291	CF-DJ	lsf Finansskandic AB
☐ SE-DVI	Lockheed L-1011-385-3 TriStar 500	293A-1248	V2-LEK	0083	0398	3 RR RB211-524B4-02	231332	C19Y291	AB-CM	lsf Finansskandic AB
☐ SE-DVX	Lockheed L-1011-385-3 TriStar 500	193J-1183	N501GB	0080	1298	3 RR RB211-524B4-02	231332	C19Y291		lsf IALI

NYGE AERO, AB = TGT (Nyge Aero Specialflyg)
Nyköping

Box 321, S-611 27 Nyköping, Sweden ☎ (155) 77 100 Tx: none Fax: (155) 26 72 52 SITA: n/a
F: 1956 130 Head: Björn Sunden ICAO: TARGET Net: n/a Some flights are operated under the name NYGE AERO SPECIALFLYG, AB (a subsidiary, same fleet, headquarters).

☐ SE-GHA	Mitsubishi MU-2K (MU-2B-25)	283	N327MA	0073		2 GA TPE331-1-251M	4500	target towing		
☐ SE-GHB	Mitsubishi MU-2K (MU-2B-25)	287	N331MA	0073		2 GA TPE331-1-251M	4500	target towing		lsf Försvarets Materielverk
☐ SE-GHC	Mitsubishi MU-2K (MU-2B-25)	289	N334MA	0073		2 GA TPE331-1-251M	4500	target towing		lsf Försvarets Materielverk
☐ SE-GHD	Mitsubishi MU-2K (MU-2B-25)	293	N453MA	0073		2 GA TPE331-1-251M	4500	target towing		lsf Försvarets Materielverk
☐ SE-GHE	Mitsubishi MU-2K (MU-2B-25)	294	N454MA	0073		2 GA TPE331-1-251M	4500	target towing		lsf Försvarets Materielverk
☐ SE-GHF	Mitsubishi MU-2K (MU-2B-25)	299	N459MA	0073		2 GA TPE331-1-251M	4500	target towing		lsf Försvarets Materielverk
☐ SE-GHH	Mitsubishi MU-2F (MU-2B-20)	222	N9PN	0072		2 GA TPE331-1-151A	4500	target towing		
☐ SE-IOV	Mitsubishi MU-2M (MU-2B-26)	337	N522MA	0076		2 GA TPE331-6-252M	4750	target towing		
☐ SE-IOZ	Mitsubishi MU-2M (MU-2B-26)	320	N641KE	0075		2 GA TPE331-6-251M	4750	target towing		
☐ SE-IUA	Mitsubishi MU-2M (MU-2B-26)	345	N730MP	0076		2 GA TPE331-6-251M	4750	target towing		
☐ SE-DHO	Learjet 35A	35A-195	N555JE	0078	0989	2 GA TFE731-2-2B	8300	target towing		lsf Försvarets Materielverk
☐ SE-DHP	Learjet 35A	35A-075	N30FN	0076		2 GA TFE731-2-2B	8300	target towing		lsf Försvarets Materielverk

OREBRO AVIATION, AB
Orebro

Sommarvägen 7, S-702 30 Orebro, Sweden ☎ (19) 24 66 48 Tx: none Fax: (19) 24 66 69 SITA: n/a
F: 1995 n/a Head: Jon Perner Net: n/a

☐ SE-FNE	Piper PA-31-350 Navajo Chieftain	31-7405434	N54306	0074	0997	2 LY TIO-540-J2BD	3175			
☐ SE-GIT	Piper PA-31-310 Navajo C	31-7512041		0075		2 LY TIO-540-A2C	2950			

OSTERMAN HELICOPTER i Göteborg, AB (Member of Scandinavian Helicopter Group, AB)
Gothenburg-Saeve

PL 2005, S-423 73 Säve, Sweden ☎ (31) 92 60 00 Tx: n/a Fax: (31) 92 66 21 SITA: n/a
F: 1981 35 Head: Lennart Pihl Net: n/a Aircraft below MTOW 1361kg: Hughes 269C (300C)

☐ SE-HVE	Bell 206B JetRanger III	2949	G-OFAB	0080		1 AN 250-C20B	1450			
☐ SE-JEP	Eurocopter EC120B Colibri	1018		0099	0299	1 TU Arrius 2F	1680			lsf Karlebo Aviation AB
☐ SE-JMP	Eurocopter EC120B Colibri	1008		0098	0998	1 TU Arrius 2F	1680			
☐ SE-HKR	Bell 206L-1 LongRanger II	45444		0080		1 AN 250-C28B	1882			lsf Sjöfartsverket
☐ SE-JAX	Eurocopter (Aerosp.) AS350B2 Ecureuil	2618	F-WYMH*	0092	0792	1 TU Arriel 1D1	2250			lsf Vidinge Skärgardstransport AB
☐ SE-JCX	Eurocopter (Aerosp.) AS350B2 Ecureuil	2930		0096	0596	1 TU Arriel 1D1	2250			lsf Handelsbanken Finans AB
☐ SE-JDX	Eurocopter (Aerosp.) AS350B3 Ecureuil	3063		0098	0398	1 TU Arriel 2B	2250			lsf Finansskandic AB
☐ SE-JFX	Eurocopter (Aerosp.) AS350B3 Ecureuil	3077		0098	0798	1 TU Arriel 2B	2250			lsf Finansskandic AB
☐ SE-JUP	Eurocopter EC135T1	0005	D-HQQQ	0096	0299	2 TU Arrius 2B1	2720			
☐ SE-JLP	Bell 212	31146	N5756W	0080	0796	2 PWC PT6T-3 TwinPac	5080			lsf ABN Amro Leasing

POLAR-FLYG Lars Persson (formerly Polar-Flyg Paul Flodin)
Saxnäs / Strömsund / Järpen

Horneyvägen 53, S-830 04 Mörsil, Sweden ☎ (647) 60 206 Tx: none Fax: (647) 60 206 SITA: n/a
F: n/a n/a Head: Lars Persson Net: n/a Aircraft below MTOW 1361 kg: Cessna 172.

☐ SE-HRA	Eurocopter (Aerosp.) SE3130 Alouette II	1268	NAVY 02038	0059	0998	1 TU Artouste IIC6	1500			lsf Järpen Helikopter HB
☐ SE-JEH	Eurocopter (Aerosp.) SA316B Alouette III	1542	A-542	0069	0998	1 TU Artouste IIIB	2200			
☐ SE-BIO	De Havilland DHC-2 Beaver I	1056	C-FMAV	0057	0496	1 PW R-985	2315			Floats / Wheels

POLARHELIKOPTER i KIRUNA, AB
Kiruna

Box 170, S-981 23 Kiruna, Sweden ☎ (980) 83 055 Tx: n/a Fax: (980) 19 372 SITA: n/a
F: 1993 n/a Head: n/a Net: n/a

☐ SE-HLR	MD Helicopters MD 500D (Hughes 369D)	510987D	LN-OSR	0081		1 AN 250-C20B	1360			
☐ SE-JCH	MD Helicopters MD 500D (Hughes 369D)	1200892D	LN-OQV	0080	0597	1 AN 250-C20B	1360			lsf ABN Amro Leasing

REGULJAIR i SKELLEFTEA, AB = R8 / REF
Skelleftea

Skelleftea flygplats, S-931 92 Skelleftea, Sweden ☎ (910) 84 090 Tx: none Fax: (910) 84 091 SITA: SFTOPRB
F: 1996 9 Head: Ulf Gronlund ICAO: REGULJAIR Net: http://www.reguljair.se

☐ SE-IYZ	Embraer 110P1 Bandeirante (EMB-110P1)	110288	G-BIBE	0080	0896	2 PWC PT6A-34	5670	Y18		lsf Enar Lindström AB

ROSLAGENS HELIKOPTERFLYG, AB
Norrtälje

Sikvägen, S-761 43 Norrtälje, Sweden ☎ (176) 184 66 Tx: none Fax: (176) 100 95 SITA: n/a
F: 1972 n/a Head: Christer Ohlund Net: n/a Aircraft below MTOW 1361kg: Enstrom 280 & 480

☐ SE-HRE	Bell 206B JetRanger	642	N7905J	0071		1 AN 250-C20	1450			lsf Tamm Services AB / cvtd 206A

SAAB AIR, AB = SCT (Division of Saab, AB / formerly Saab-Scania)
Linköping

Airport, S-581 88 Linköping, Sweden ☎ (13) 18 70 50 Tx: 50113 saabair s Fax: (13) 18 70 55 SITA: n/a
F: 1957 21 Head: Ulf Jirstrand ICAO: SAAB-CRAFT Net: n/a

☐ SE-ITR	Beech Baron E55	TE-1021	N7253R	0075		2 CO IO-520-C	2405			
☐ SE-DSA	Dassault Falcon 20F-5	339	N19MX	0075	0195	2 GA TFE731-5BR-2C	13200			cvtd 20F
☐ SE-DVK	Dassault Falcon 50	249	N663MN	0094	0497	3 GA TFE731-3-1C	18500			lsf AB Rila
☐ SE-DVL	Dassault Falcon 50	238	N796A	0093	0397	3 GA TFE731-3-1C	18500			lsf Residuum AB

585 registration type of aircraft cn/fn ex/ex* mfd del powered by mtow kg configuration selcal name/fln/specialitites/remarks

SAE Swe Aviation Europe, AB = SWL

Gothenborg-Landvetter

Box 2157, S-438 14 Landvetter, Swerden ☎ (31) 94 66 55 Tx: none Fax: (31) 94 66 55 SITA: n/a
F: 1997 ⁂ n/a Head: n/a ICAO: SWING Net: n/a Currently all aircraft are on dry lease to other companies or stored but intends to start own charter operations in 1999.

registration	type of aircraft	cn/fn	ex/ex*	mfd	del	powered by	mtow kg	configuration	selcal	name/fln/specialitites/remarks
☐ SE-KZD	Fokker F27 Friendship 100 (F27 Mk100)	10245	LN-SUE	0064	0097	2 RR Dart 514-7	18370	Y44		lsf Swetrail Transport AB / std WOE
☐ SE-KZE	Fokker F27 Friendship 100 (F27 Mk100)	10248	LN-SUL	0064	0097	2 RR Dart 514-7	18370	Y44		lsf Swetrail Transport AB/sub-lst IFS
☐ SE-KZF	Fokker F27 Friendship 100 (F27 Mk100)	10266	LN-NPI	0064	0097	2 RR Dart 514-7	18370	Y44		lsf Swetrail Transport AB
☐ SE-KZG	Fokker F27 Friendship 100 (F27 Mk100)	10287	LN-NPM	0065	0097	2 RR Dart 514-7	18370	Y44		lsf Swetrail Transport AB/sub-lst IFS
☐ SE-KZH	Fokker F27 Friendship 100 (F27 Mk100)	10319	LN-NPD	0067	0097	2 RR Dart 514-7	18370	Y44		lsf Swetrail Transport AB/std Västeras

SALENIA AVIATION, AB = (SALA) (Member of Salenia Group)

Stockholm

PO Box 14237, S-104 40 Stockholm, Sweden ☎ (8) 670 98 70 Tx: none Fax: (8) 660 87 70 SITA: n/a
F: n/a ⁂ n/a Head: Peter Gullmarstrand Net: n/a New and used aircraft leasing, sales and financing company.
Owner/lessor of following (main) aircraft types: BAe 146-200, Saab SF340A/B, Saab 2000 (on order) and Swearingen SA227AC Metro III. Aircraft leased from SALA are listed and mentioned as such under the leasing carriers.

SCANDINAVIAN AIRLINES COMMUTER (Eurolink / Norlink / Swelink) (Sister company of SAS)

Copenhagen-Kastrup, Stockholm-Arlanda & Tromsoe-Langnes

Fluvervej, DK-2770 Kastrup, Denmark ☎ 32 32 00 00 Tx: none Fax: 32 32 28 78 SITA: n/a
F: 1988 ⁂ 375 Head: Ole Pedersen Net: n/a Scheduled commuter-services are operated on behalf of Scandinavian Airlines SAS, using SK-flight numbers.
Multinational state carrier of Denmark, Norway & Sweden. The owners of Scandinavian Commuter / SAS are in the proportion of 2:2:3: SAS Danmark A/S, SAS Norge ASA & SAS Sverige AB.

registration	type of aircraft	cn/fn	ex/ex*	mfd	del	powered by	mtow kg	configuration	selcal	name/fln/specialitites/remarks
☐ SE-LFA	Fokker 50 (F27 Mk050)	20165	PH-EXG*	0089	0989	2 PWC PW125B	20820	CY46	HQ-DM	Jorund Viking / Eurolink
☐ SE-LFB	Fokker 50 (F27 Mk050)	20169	PH-EXI*	0089	1189	2 PWC PW125B	20820	CY46	HQ-DP	Sture Viking / Eurolink
☐ SE-LFC	Fokker 50 (F27 Mk050)	20187	PH-EXN*	0090	0790	2 PWC PW125B	20820	CY46	HQ-FK	Ylva Viking / Eurolink/lsf Fin. Skandic
☐ SE-LFK	Fokker 50 (F27 Mk050)	20188	PH-EXB*	0090	0790	2 PWC PW125B	20820	CY46	HQ-FL	Alvar Viking / Eurolink/lsf Fin. Skandic
☐ SE-LFN	Fokker 50 (F27 Mk050)	20193	PH-EXP*	0090	0990	2 PWC PW125B	20820	CY46	HQ-FM	Edmund Viking / Eurolink/lsf Fin. Skandic
☐ SE-LFO	Fokker 50 (F27 Mk050)	20198	PH-EXG*	0090	1090	2 PWC PW125B	20820	CY46	HQ-GK	Folke Viking / Eurolink/lsf Fin. Skandic
☐ SE-LFP	Fokker 50 (F27 Mk050)	20199	PH-EXH*	0090	1190	2 PWC PW125B	20820	CY46	HQ-GL	Ingemar Viking / Eurolink/lsf Fin.Skandic
☐ SE-LFR	Fokker 50 (F27 Mk050)	20215	PH-RRD*	0091	0591	2 PWC PW125B	20820	CY46		Vagn Viking / Eurolink
☐ SE-LFS	Fokker 50 (F27 Mk050)	20216	PH-EXO*	0091	0591	2 PWC PW125B	20820	CY46		Vigge Viking / Eurolink
☐ LN-RNB	Fokker 50 (F27 Mk050)	20173	PH-EXX*	0089	1289	2 PWC PW125B	20820	CY46	HQ-EG	Brae Viking / Eurolink
☐ LN-RNC	Fokker 50 (F27 Mk050)	20176	PH-EXY*	0089	0290	2 PWC PW125B	20820	CY50	HQ-EJ	Eivind Viking / Norlink
☐ LN-RND	Fokker 50 (F27 Mk050)	20178	PH-EXZ*	0090	0390	2 PWC PW125B	20820	CY50	HQ-EK	Inge Viking / Norlink
☐ LN-RNE	Fokker 50 (F27 Mk050)	20179	PH-EXE*	0090	0390	2 PWC PW125B	20820	CY50	HQ-EL	Ebbe Viking / Norlink
☐ LN-RNF	Fokker 50 (F27 Mk050)	20183	PH-EXI*	0090	0490	2 PWC PW125B	20820	CY50	HQ-EM	Leif Viking / Norlink
☐ LN-RNG	Fokker 50 (F27 Mk050)	20184	PH-EXJ*	0090	0590	2 PWC PW125B	20820	CY50	HQ-EP	Gudrid Viking / Norlink
☐ LN-RNH	Fokker 50 (F27 Mk050)	20172	PH-EXW*	0089	1289	2 PWC PW125B	20820	CY46	HQ-EF	Harald Viking / Eurolink
☐ OY-KAE	Fokker 50 (F27 Mk050)	20162	PH-EXE*	0089	0989	2 PWC PW125B	20820	CY46	HQ-DK	Hans Viking / Eurolink
☐ OY-KAF	Fokker 50 (F27 Mk050)	20163	PH-EXF*	0089	0989	2 PWC PW125B	20820	CY46	HQ-DL	Sigvat Viking / Eurolink
☐ OY-KAG	Fokker 50 (F27 Mk050)	20185	PH-EXL*	0090	0690	2 PWC PW125B	20820	CY46	HQ-FG	Odensis Viking / Eurolink/lsf Fin.Skandic
☐ OY-KAH	Fokker 50 (F27 Mk050)	20186	PH-EXM*	0090	0690	2 PWC PW125B	20820	CY46	HQ-FJ	Grid Viking / Eurolink/lsf Fin. Skandic
☐ OY-KAI	Fokker 50 (F27 Mk050)	20194	PH-EXS*	0090	0990	2 PWC PW125B	20820	CY46	HQ-FP	Skjold Viking / Eurolink/lsf Fin. Skandic
☐ OY-KAK	Fokker 50 (F27 Mk050)	20195	PH-EXA*	0090	1090	2 PWC PW125B	20820	CY46	HQ-GJ	Turid Viking / Eurolink/lsf Fin. Skandic
☐ SE-LSA	Saab 2000	2000-042	SE-042*	0096	0197	2 AN AE2100A	22800	CY47		Tore Viking / lsf Saab / Swelink
☐ SE-LSB	Saab 2000	2000-043	SE-043*	0096	0197	2 AN AE2100A	22800	CY47		Rut Viking / lsf Saab / Swelink
☐ SE-LSC	Saab 2000	2000-044	SE-044*	0097	0397	2 AN AE2100A	22800	CY47		Karl Viking / lsf Saab / Swelink
☐ SE-LSE	Saab 2000	2000-046	SE-046*	0097	0497	2 AN AE2100A	22800	CY47		Gerd Viking / lsf Saab / Swelink
☐ SE-LSF	Saab 2000	2000-053	SE-053*	0097	0198	2 AN AE2100A	22800	CY47		Eir Viking / lsf Saab / Swelink
☐ SE-LSG	Saab 2000	2000-055	SE-055*	0098	0398	2 AN AE2100A	22999	CY47		Ake Viking / lsf Saab / Swelink
☐ SE-LRA	De Havilland DHC-8-401 Dash 8Q	4008				2 PWC PW150A	26989	CY72 or CY76		Toke Viking / oo-delivery 0799
☐ SE-LRB	De Havilland DHC-8-401 Dash 8Q					2 PWC PW150A	26989	CY72 or CY76		Ulv Viking / oo-delivery 1099
☐ SE-LRC	De Havilland DHC-8-401 Dash 8Q					2 PWC PW150A	26989	CY72 or CY76		Ingrid Viking / oo-delivery 1199
☐ SE-LRD	De Havilland DHC-8-401 Dash 8Q					2 PWC PW150A	26989	CY72 or CY76		oo-delivery 1299
☐ SE-LRE	De Havilland DHC-8-401 Dash 8Q					2 PWC PW150A	26989	CY72 or CY76		oo-delivery 0100
☐ SE-LRF	De Havilland DHC-8-401 Dash 8Q					2 PWC PW150A	26989	CY72 or CY76		oo-delivery 0100
☐ SE-LRG	De Havilland DHC-8-401 Dash 8Q					2 PWC PW150A	26989	CY72 or CY76		oo-delivery 0800
☐ SE-LRH	De Havilland DHC-8-401 Dash 8Q					2 PWC PW150A	26989	CY72 or CY76		oo-delivery 0900
☐ LN-RDA	De Havilland DHC-8-401 Dash 8Q					2 PWC PW150A	26989	CY72 or CY76		Fret Viking / oo-delivery 0999
☐ LN-RDB	De Havilland DHC-8-401 Dash 8Q					2 PWC PW150A	26989	CY72 or CY76		Kari Viking / oo-delivery 1299
☐ LN-RDC	De Havilland DHC-8-401 Dash 8Q					2 PWC PW150A	26989	CY72 or CY76		oo-delivery 0200
☐ LN-RDD	De Havilland DHC-8-401 Dash 8Q					2 PWC PW150A	26989	CY72 or CY76		oo-delivery 0300
☐ OY-KCA	De Havilland DHC-8-401 Dash 8Q					2 PWC PW150A	26989	CY72 or CY76		Huge Viking / oo-delivery 0899
☐ OY-KCB	De Havilland DHC-8-401 Dash 8Q					2 PWC PW150A	26989	CY72 or CY76		Herta Viking / oo-delivery 1199
☐ OY-KCC	De Havilland DHC-8-401 Dash 8Q					2 PWC PW150A	26989	CY72 or CY76		oo-delivery 0100
☐ OY-KCD	De Havilland DHC-8-401 Dash 8Q					2 PWC PW150A	26989	CY72 or CY76		oo-delivery 0200
☐ OY-KCE	De Havilland DHC-8-401 Dash 8Q					2 PWC PW150A	26989	CY72 or CY76		oo-delivery 0900

SCANDINAVIAN AIRLINES SAS = SK / SAS (Scandinavian Airlines System dba / Member of Star Alliance)

Copenhagen / Oslo / Stockholm-Arlanda

Fack, S-195 87 Stockholm-Bromma, Sweden ☎ (8) 797 00 00 Tx: Danmark 22263 sasxt Fax: (8) 85 79 80 SITA: n/a
F: 1946 ⁂ 20000 Head: Jan Stenberg IATA: 117 ICAO: SCANDINAVIAN Net: http://www.sas.se Multinational state carrier of Denmark, Norway & Sweden.
The owners of Scandinavian SAS are in the proportion of 2:2:3: SAS Danmark A/S, SAS Norge ASA & SAS Sverige AB. Scheduled commuter flights with Fokker 50 & Saab 2000 are operated by
SCANDINAVIAN AIRLINES COMMUTER (sister company) – see under that company. Beside aircraft listed, also uses a Boeing (Douglas) MD-11F, lsf/opb LUFTHANSA Cargo (D), when required for all cargo-services.
On order: further 11 Boeing 737-600/700/800 (model not yet decided) for delivery 1000-0203.

registration	type of aircraft	cn/fn	ex/ex*	mfd	del	powered by	mtow kg	configuration	selcal	name/fln/specialitites/remarks
☐ SE-DGF	Fokker F28 Fellowship 4000 (F28 Mk4000)	11115	PH-EXM*	0076	0193	2 RR Spey 555-15P	33115	Y75		Egil Viking / lsf Linjeflyg Lsng -0499
☐ SE-DGG	Fokker F28 Fellowship 4000 (F28 Mk4000)	11116	PH-EXV*	0077	0193	2 RR Spey 555-15P	33115	Y75		Gunnhild Viking / lsf Linjef.Lsng -0999
☐ SE-DGH	Fokker F28 Fellowship 4000 (F28 Mk4000)	11120	PH-EXY*	0077	0193	2 RR Spey 555-15P	33115	Y75		Hjalmar Viking / lsf Linjef.Lsng -0599
☐ SE-DGI	Fokker F28 Fellowship 4000 (F28 Mk4000)	11122	PH-EXP*	0077	0193	2 RR Spey 555-15P	33115	Y75		Ingeborg Viking / lsf Linjef.Lsng -0799
☐ SE-DGK	Fokker F28 Fellowship 4000 (F28 Mk4000)	11123	PH-EXZ*	0077	0193	2 RR Spey 555-15P	33115	Y75		Knut Viking / lsf Linjeflyg Lsng -0799
☐ SE-DGL	Fokker F28 Fellowship 4000 (F28 Mk4000)	11126	PH-EXV*	0077	0193	2 RR Spey 555-15P	33115	Y75		Loke Viking / lsf Linjeflyg Lsng -1099
☐ SE-DGM	Fokker F28 Fellowship 4000 (F28 Mk4000)	11128	PH-EXR*	0077	0193	2 RR Spey 555-15P	33115	Y75		Hild Viking / lsf Linjeflyg Lsng -1099
☐ SE-DGN	Fokker F28 Fellowship 4000 (F28 Mk4000)	11130	PH-JPV*	0078	0193	2 RR Spey 555-15P	33115	Y75		Gunnar Viking / lsf Linjef.Lsng -0799
☐ SE-DGP	Fokker F28 Fellowship 4000 (F28 Mk4000)	11191	PH-EXZ*	0082	0193	2 RR Spey 555-15P	33115	CY67		Steinar Viking / lsf Nordbank.Fin.-1099
☐ SE-DGT	Fokker F28 Fellowship 4000 (F28 Mk4000)	11239	PH-EZL*	0086	0193	2 RR Spey 555-15P	33115	Y75		Tola Viking / lsf Nordbanken Fin.-1099
☐ SE-DGU	Fokker F28 Fellowship 4000 (F28 Mk4000)	11241	PH-EZT*	0087	0193	2 RR Spey 555-15P	33115	Y75		Ulfljot Viking / lsf Kjölen/for KFB0999
☐ SE-DGX	Fokker F28 Fellowship 4000 (F28 Mk4000)	11225	PH-EZX*	0085	0193	2 RR Spey 555-15P	33115	CY67		Vemund Viking / lsf SCLAero/for KFB0999
☐ OY-KGF	Boeing (Douglas) DC-9-21	47308 / 474		0369	0369	2 PW JT8D-11 (HK3/ABS)	44450	CY75	FL-GM	Rolf Viking / lsf Crane Aviation
☐ OY-KIA	Boeing (Douglas) DC-9-21	47301 / 382	LN-RLL	0968	0369	2 PW JT8D-11 (HK3/ABS)	44450	CY75	FL-HJ	Guttorm Viking / lsf Crane Aviation
☐ OY-KID	Boeing (Douglas) DC-9-21	47360 / 475	SE-DBP	0369	0469	2 PW JT8D-11 (HK3/ABS)	44450	CY75	BF-AG	Rane Viking / lsf Crane Aviation
☐ OY-KIE	Boeing (Douglas) DC-9-21	47306 / 462	SE-DBR	0269	0269	2 PW JT8D-11 (HK3/ABS)	44450	CY75	BF-AH	Skate Viking / lsf Crane Aviation
☐ SE-DAS	Boeing (Douglas) DC-9-41	47610 / 725		0374	0474	2 PW JT8D-11 (HK3/ABS)	51710	CY105	BC-DM	Garder Viking / lsf Air 41 Llc
☐ SE-DAU	Boeing (Douglas) DC-9-41	47627 / 739		0074	0874	2 PW JT8D-11 (HK3/ABS)	51710	CY105	BF-CE	Hadding Viking / lsf Air 41 Llc
☐ SE-DAW	Boeing (Douglas) DC-9-41	47629 / 744		0074	0974	2 PW JT8D-11 (HK3/ABS)	51710	CY105	BC-HL	Gotrik Viking / lsf Air 41 Llc
☐ SE-DAX	Boeing (Douglas) DC-9-41	47631 / 743		0874	0874	2 PW JT8D-11	51710	CY105	BC-EG	Helsing Viking / lsf TOMB -0799
☐ SE-DBM	Boeing (Douglas) DC-9-41	47633 / 752		1074	1174	2 PW JT8D-11 (HK3/ABS)	51710	Y122	BC-AD	Ossur Viking / lsf Air 41 Llc
☐ SE-DDP	Boeing (Douglas) DC-9-41	47747 / 839	N19B*	0976	1176	2 PW JT8D-11 (HK3/ABS)	51710	Y122	AM-DL	Brun Viking / lsf Air 41 Llc
☐ SE-DDR	Boeing (Douglas) DC-9-41	47750 / 870		1177	1277	2 PW JT8D-11 (HK3/ABS)	51710	CY105	BC-KM	Atle Viking / lsf Air 41 Llc
☐ SE-DDS	Boeing (Douglas) DC-9-41	47777 / 896		0179	0279	2 PW JT8D-11 (HK3/ABS)	51710	CY105	BC-DG	Alrik Viking / lsf Air 41 Llc
☐ SE-DDT	Boeing (Douglas) DC-9-41	47779 / 898		0179	0379	2 PW JT8D-11 (HK3/ABS)	51710	CY105	EL-BJ	Amund Viking / lsf Air 41 Llc
☐ LN-RLA	Boeing (Douglas) DC-9-41	47599 / 716		0174	0174	2 PW JT8D-11 (HK3/ABS)	51710	CY105	BC-AE	Are Viking / lsf Air 41 Llc
☐ LN-RLH	Boeing (Douglas) DC-9-41	47748 / 855		1077	1177	2 PW JT8D-11 (HK3/ABS)	51710	CY105	BC-HM	Einar Viking / lsf Air 41 Llc
☐ LN-RLN	Boeing (Douglas) DC-9-41	47630 / 745		0074	0974	2 PW JT8D-11 (HK3/ABS)	51710	CY105	FL-EM	Halldor Viking / lsf Air 41 Llc
☐ LN-RLP	Boeing (Douglas) DC-9-41	47778 / 897		0179	0279	2 PW JT8D-11 (HK3/ABS)	51710	CY105	BF-DJ	Froste Viking / lsf Air 41 Llc
☐ LN-RLT	Boeing (Douglas) DC-9-41	47626 / 738		0774	0774	2 PW JT8D-11 (HK3/ABS)	51710	CY105	BC-EH	Audun Viking / lsf Air 41 Llc
☐ LN-RLZ	Boeing (Douglas) DC-9-41	47634 / 756		1174	1274	2 PW JT8D-11 (HK3/ABS)	51710	CY105	BC-DH	Bodvar Viking / lsf Air 41 Llc
☐ OY-KGL	Boeing (Douglas) DC-9-41	47597 / 713	N54631*	1273	0274	2 PW JT8D-11 (HK3/ABS)	51710	Y122	BC-FJ	Angantyr Viking / lsf Air 41 Llc
☐ OY-KGM	Boeing (Douglas) DC-9-41	47624 / 733		0074	0674	2 PW JT8D-11 (HK3/ABS)	51710	CY105	BF-AJ	Arnfinn Viking / lsf Air 41 Llc
☐ OY-KGO	Boeing (Douglas) DC-9-41	47632 / 748		0074	1074	2 PW JT8D-11 (HK3/ABS)	51710	CY105	BC-EK	Holte Viking / lsf Air 41 Llc
☐ OY-KGP	Boeing (Douglas) DC-9-41	47646 / 755		1174	1174	2 PW JT8D-11 (HK3/ABS)	51710	Y122	BF-EK	Torbern Viking / lsf Air 41 Llc
☐ OY-KGR	Boeing (Douglas) DC-9-41	47725 / 831		0776	0776	2 PW JT8D-11 (HK3/ABS)	51710	Y122	CG-JM	Holger Viking / lsf Air 41 Llc
☐ OY-KGS	Boeing (Douglas) DC-9-41	47766 / 886		0078	1078	2 PW JT8D-11 (HK3/ABS)	51710	CY105	BF-DG	Hall Viking / lsf Air 41 Llc
☐ SE-DNM	Boeing 737-683	28288 / 49	N1003M*	0098	0998	2 CFMI CFM56-7B20	57606	CY103	FL-EJ	Bernt Viking
☐ SE-DNN	Boeing 737-683	28291 / 112	N1787B*	0098	1098	2 CFMI CFM56-7B20	57606	CY103	BC-GK	Nanna Viking
☐ SE-DNO	Boeing 737-683	28292 / 116	N1780B*	0098	1098	2 CFMI CFM56-7B20	57606	CY103	BC-GL	Olof Viking
☐ SE-DNP	Boeing 737-683	28295 / 149	N1786B*	1198	1198	2 CFMI CFM56-7B20	57606	CY103	JM-CG	Gisela Viking
☐ SE-DNR	Boeing 737-683	28296 / 21	N7376*	0198	0199	2 CFMI CFM56-7B20	57606	CY103	EL-AM	Ragnfast Viking
☐ SE-DNS	Boeing 737-683	28297 / 30	N35135*	0398	0199	2 CFMI CFM56-7B20	57606	CY103	EL-BC	Signe Viking
☐ SE-DNT	Boeing 737-683	28302 / 243		0099	0499	2 CFMI CFM56-7B20	57606	Y116		Snefrid Viking
☐ SE-DNU	Boeing 737-683	28303 / 257		0099	0499	2 CFMI CFM56-7B20	57606	Y116		Unn Viking
☐ SE-DNX	Boeing 737-683	28304				2 CFMI CFM56-7B20	57606	Y116		Torvald Viking / oo-delivery 0599
☐ SE-DNY	Boeing 737-683	28308				2 CFMI CFM56-7B20	57606	CY103		Yngvar Viking / oo-delivery 0899
☐ SE-DNZ	Boeing 737-683	30190				2 CFMI CFM56-7B20	57606	CY103		Sigfrid Viking / oo-delivery 0899
☐ SE-DTF	Boeing 737-683	28309				2 CFMI CFM56-7B20	57606	CY103		Torbjörn Viking / oo-delivery 0999
☐ SE-DTH	Boeing 737-683	28313				2 CFMI CFM56-7B20	57606			Vile Viking / oo-delivery 1299
☐ SE-DTN	Boeing 737-683	30467				2 CFMI CFM56-7B20	57606			oo-delivery 0800

☐ SE-DTO	Boeing 737-683	*30194*				*2 CFMI CFM56-7B20*	*57606*			Gerda Viking / *oo-delivery 0900*
☐ SE-DTP	Boeing 737-683	*30468*				*2 CFMI CFM56-7B20*	*57606*			Ore Viking / *oo-delivery 0900*
☐ SE-DTU	Boeing 737-683	*28311*				*2 CFMI CFM56-7B20*	*57606*	*CY103*		Vilborg Viking / *oo-delivery 1099*
☐ LN-RPA	Boeing 737-683	*28290 / 100*	*N5002K**	*0098*	*1098*	*2 CFMI CFM56-7B20*	*57606*	*CY103*	*BC-AL*	Arnljot Viking
☐ LN-RPB	Boeing 737-683	*28294 / 137*	*N1787B**	*0098*	*1198*	*2 CFMI CFM56-7B20*	*57606*	*CY103*	*JL-CM*	Bure Viking
☐ LN-RPE	Boeing 737-683	*28306*				*2 CFMI CFM56-7B20*	*57606*	*Y116*		Edla Viking / *oo-delivery 0799*
☐ LN-RPF	Boeing 737-683	*28307*				*2 CFMI CFM56-7B20*	*57606*	*CY103*		Frede Viking / *oo-delivery 0799*
☐ LN-RPG	Boeing 737-683	*28310*				*2 CFMI CFM56-7B20*	*57606*	*CY103*		Geirmund Viking / *to be lsf PEMB 0599*
☐ LN-RPH	Boeing 737-683	*28605*				*2 CFMI CFM56-7B20*	*57606*	*CY103*		Hamder Viking / *to be lsf GECA 0999*
☐ LN-RPL	Boeing 737-683	*28322*				*2 CFMI CFM56-7B20*	*57606*			Ramveig Viking / *oo-delivery 0700*
☐ LN-RPM	Boeing 737-683	*28323*				*2 CFMI CFM56-7B20*	*57606*			Gyrd Viking / *oo-delivery 0800*
☐ OY-KKA	Boeing 737-683	*28289 / 92*	*N5002K**	*0098*	*0998*	*2 CFMI CFM56-7B20*	*57606*	*CY103*	*AM-DK*	Alvid Viking
☐ OY-KKB	Boeing 737-683	*28293 / 120*	*N1787B**	*0098*	*1198*	*2 CFMI CFM56-7B20*	*57606*	*CY103*	*KS-AB*	Bera Viking
☐ OY-KKC	Boeing 737-683	*28298 / 191*	*N1786B**	*0199*	*0199*	*2 CFMI CFM56-7B20*	*57606*	*Y116*	*AB-PR*	Gautrek Viking
☐ OY-KKD	Boeing 737-683	*28299 / 193*	*N1787B**	*0099*	*0299*	*2 CFMI CFM56-7B20*	*57606*	*Y116*	*AB-PS*	Ellida Viking
☐ OY-KKE	Boeing 737-683	*28305*				*2 CFMI CFM56-7B20*	*57606*	*Y116*		Elisabeth Viking / *oo-delivery 0699*
☐ OY-KKF	Boeing 737-683	*30189*				*2 CFMI CFM56-7B20*	*57606*	*CY103*		Fridlev Viking / *oo-delivery 0699*
☐ OY-KKG	Boeing 737-683	*28300 / 209*	*N1786B**	*0299*	*0299*	*2 CFMI CFM56-7B20*	*57606*	*Y116*		Sindre Viking
☐ OY-KKH	Boeing 737-683	*28301 / 227*	*N1795B**	*0099*	*0399*	*2 CFMI CFM56-7B20*	*57606*	*Y116*		Embla Viking
☐ OY-KKP	Boeing 737-683	*28312*				*2 CFMI CFM56-7B20*	*57606*	*CY103*		Ragna Viking / *oo-delivery 1199*
☐ SE-DIB	Boeing (Douglas) MD-87 (DC-9-87)	*49605 / 1501*	*N19B**	*0088*	*1188*	*2 PW JT8D-217C*	*61235*	*CY110*	*BK-FP*	Varin Viking
☐ SE-DIC	Boeing (Douglas) MD-87 (DC-9-87)	*49607 / 1512*		*0888*	*0988*	*2 PW JT8D-217C*	*61235*	*CY110*	*BK-GP*	Grane Viking
☐ SE-DIF	Boeing (Douglas) MD-87 (DC-9-87)	*49606 / 1569*		*0189*	*0389*	*2 PW JT8D-217C*	*61235*	*CY110*	*BL-DP*	Hjorulv Viking
☐ SE-DIH	Boeing (Douglas) MD-87 (DC-9-87)	*49608 / 1572*		*0289*	*0389*	*2 PW JT8D-217C*	*61235*	*CY110*	*BL-EP*	Slagfinn Viking
☐ SE-DIP	Boeing (Douglas) MD-87 (DC-9-87)	*53010 / 1921*	*N6202D**	*0991*	*1091*	*2 PW JT8D-217C*	*63503*	*CY110*	*KS-AM*	Margaret Viking / *lsf Orbit*
☐ SE-DIU	Boeing (Douglas) MD-87 (DC-9-87)	*53011 / 1931*		*0091*	*1191*	*2 PW JT8D-217C*	*63503*	*CY110*	*KS-AQ*	Torsten Viking / *lsf Torsten Leasing*
☐ SE-DMA	Boeing (Douglas) MD-87 (DC-9-87)	*53009 / 1916*		*0091*	*0991*	*2 PW JT8D-217C*	*63503*	*CY110*	*KS-AJ*	Lage Viking / *lsf Orbit Leasing*
☐ LN-RMG	Boeing (Douglas) MD-87 (DC-9-87)	*49611 / 1522*		*0988*	*1088*	*2 PW JT8D-217C*	*61235*	*CY110*	*BK-JP*	Snorre Viking / *lsf Aviation Business Co.*
☐ LN-RMH	Boeing (Douglas) MD-87 (DC-9-87)	*49612 / 1827*	*N6203U**	*0091*	*0291*	*2 PW JT8D-217C*	*63503*	*CY110*	*FL-EG*	Solmund Viking
☐ LN-RMK	Boeing (Douglas) MD-87 (DC-9-87)	*49610 / 1705*		*0490*	*0590*	*2 PW JT8D-217C*	*61235*	*CY110*	*DQ-EL*	Ragnhild Viking
☐ LN-RMP	Boeing (Douglas) MD-87 (DC-9-87)	*53337 / 1962*		*0092*	*0192*	*2 PW JT8D-217C*	*63503*	*CY110*	*BC-DF*	Reidun Viking
☐ LN-RMU	Boeing (Douglas) MD-87 (DC-9-87)	*53340 / 1967*	*SE-DMC*	*0192*	*0292*	*2 PW JT8D-217C*	*61235*	*CY110*	*AM-CG*	Grim Viking
☐ LN-RMX	Boeing (Douglas) MD-87 (DC-9-87)	*49585 / 1457*	*HB-IUA*	*0088*	*1195*	*2 PW JT8D-217C*	*66905*	*Y125*	*BC-JM*	Vidar Viking / *lsf Credit Lyonnais*
☐ LN-RMY	Boeing (Douglas) MD-87 (DC-9-87)	*49586 / 1472*	*HB-IUB*	*0088*	*1195*	*2 PW JT8D-217C*	*66905*	*Y125*	*BC-KL*	Ingolf Viking / *lsf Credit Lyonnais*
☐ OY-KHF	Boeing (Douglas) MD-87 (DC-9-87)	*49609 / 1517*		*0988*	*1088*	*2 PW JT8D-217C*	*61235*	*CY110*	*BK-HP*	Ragnar Viking
☐ OY-KHI	Boeing (Douglas) MD-87 (DC-9-87)	*49614 / 1556*		*1288*	*0389*	*2 PW JT8D-217C*	*61235*	*CY110*	*BL-CP*	Torkel Viking
☐ OY-KHU	Boeing (Douglas) MD-87 (DC-9-87)	*53336 / 1953*		*1191*	*0192*	*2 PW JT8D-217C*	*63503*	*CY110*	*BF-EH*	Ravn Viking
☐ OY-KHW	Boeing (Douglas) MD-87 (DC-9-87)	*53348 / 1985*		*0092*	*0392*	*2 PW JT8D-217C*	*61235*	*CY110*	*BC-EF*	Ingemund Viking
☐ SE-DTG	Boeing 737-783	*30191*				*2 CFMI CFM56-7B22*	*62823*	*Y131*		Solveig Viking / *oo-delivery 1199*
☐ SE-DTI	Boeing 737-783	*28314*				*2 CFMI CFM56-7B22*	*62823*	*Y131*		Erland Viking / *oo-delivery 0100*
☐ LN-RPJ	Boeing 737-783	*30192*				*2 CFMI CFM56-7B22*	*62823*	*Y131*		Grimhild Viking / *oo-delivery 0200*
☐ LN-RPK	Boeing 737-783	*28317*				*2 CFMI CFM56-7B22*	*62823*	*Y131*		Heimer Viking / *oo-delivery 0300*
☐ OY-KKI	Boeing 737-783	*28315*				*2 CFMI CFM56-7B22*	*62823*	*Y131*		Borgny Viking / *oo-delivery 0100*
☐ OY-KKR	Boeing 737-783	*28316*				*2 CFMI CFM56-7B22*	*62823*	*Y131*		Gjuke Viking / *oo-delivery 0200*
☐ SE-DFR	Boeing (Douglas) MD-82 (DC-9-82)	*49422 / 1264*	*SE-DFV*	*0386*	*0386*	*2 PW JT8D-217C*	*67812*	*CY130*	*BF-AL*	Ingjald Viking / *cvtd MD-81*
☐ SE-DFS	Boeing (Douglas) MD-82 (DC-9-82)	*49384 / 1237*		*0085*	*1285*	*2 PW JT8D-219*	*67812*	*Y156*	*BC-GJ*	Bjoern Viking
☐ SE-DFT	Boeing (Douglas) MD-82 (DC-9-82)	*49385 / 1244*		*1185*	*1285*	*2 PW JT8D-219*	*67812*	*Y156*	*BF-AD*	Assur Viking
☐ SE-DFU	Boeing (Douglas) MD-82 (DC-9-82)	*49421 / 1263*	*N841RA*	*0086*	*0386*	*2 PW JT8D-219*	*67812*	*Y156*	*BF-AK*	Isulv Viking
☐ SE-DFX	Boeing (Douglas) MD-82 (DC-9-82)	*49424 / 1284*	*N840RA*	*0086*	*0686*	*2 PW JT8D-219*	*67812*	*Y156*	*EH-FK*	Ring Viking
☐ SE-DFY	Boeing (Douglas) MD-82 (DC-9-82)	*49438 / 1353*		*0087*	*0487*	*2 PW JT8D-217C*	*67812*	*CY130*	*JL-CG*	Ottar Viking / *cvtd MD-81*
☐ SE-DIA	Boeing (Douglas) MD-82 (DC-9-82)	*49603 / 1442*	*N19B**	*0088*	*0488*	*2 PW JT8D-217C*	*67812*	*CY130*	*BC-JK*	Ulvrik Viking / *cvtd MD-81*
☐ SE-DID	Boeing (Douglas) MD-82 (DC-9-82)	*49615 / 1543*	*N843RA*	*1188*	*1288*	*2 PW JT8D-219*	*67812*	*Y156*	*BK-MP*	Spjute Viking
☐ SE-DII	Boeing (Douglas) MD-82 (DC-9-82)	*49909 / 1625*		*0089*	*0989*	*2 PW JT8D-217C*	*67812*	*CY130*	*BC-DL*	Sigtrygg Vik. / *lsfSigtryggLsng/cvtd-81*
☐ SE-DIK	Boeing (Douglas) MD-82 (DC-9-82)	*49728 / 1553*		*1288*	*0289*	*2 PW JT8D-217C*	*67812*	*Y156*	*BL-AP*	Stenkil Viking / *lsf NBB Sweden*
☐ SE-DIL	Boeing (Douglas) MD-82 (DC-9-82)	*49913 / 1665*		*1189*	*1289*	*2 PW JT8D-217C*	*67812*	*CY130*	*BL-GP*	Tord Viking / *lsf Tord Leasing/cvtd -81*
☐ SE-DIN	Boeing (Douglas) MD-82 (DC-9-82)	*49999 / 1803*		*1190*	*1290*	*2 PW JT8D-217C*	*67812*	*CY130*	*DQ-EP*	Eskil Viking / *lsf Red Airc.Ltd/cvtd-81*
☐ SE-DIR	Boeing (Douglas) MD-81 (DC-9-81)	*53004 / 1846*		*0391*	*0491*	*2 PW JT8D-217C*	*63503*	*CY130*	*KS-AC*	Nora Viking / *lsf Arlanda Aircraft Ltd*
☐ SE-DIS	Boeing (Douglas) MD-81 (DC-9-81)	*53006 / 1869*		*0591*	*0691*	*2 PW JT8D-217C*	*63503*	*CY130*	*KS-AE*	Sigmund Viking / *lsf Bromma Aircr.Ltd*
☐ SE-DIX	Boeing (Douglas) MD-82 (DC-9-82)	*49998 / 1800*		*0090*	*1290*	*2 PW JT8D-217C*	*67812*	*CY130*	*DQ-EM*	Anund Viking / *lsf White Aircr./cvtd-81*
☐ SE-DIY	Boeing (Douglas) MD-81 (DC-9-81)	*53008 / 1895*		*0091*	*0891*	*2 PW JT8D-217C*	*63503*	*CY130*	*KS-AG*	Albin Viking
☐ SE-DIZ	Boeing (Douglas) MD-82 (DC-9-82)	*53294 / 1917*		*0991*	*0991*	*2 PW JT8D-219*	*67812*	*Y156*	*KS-AL*	Sigyn Viking / *lsf Orbit Leasing*
☐ SE-DMB	Boeing (Douglas) MD-81 (DC-9-81)	*53314 / 1946*		*0091*	*1291*	*2 PW JT8D-217C*	*63503*	*CY130*	*BF-CH*	Bjarne Viking / *lsf Bjarne Leasing*
☐ SE-DMD	Boeing (Douglas) MD-81 (DC-9-81)	*53347 / 1979*	*N90125**	*0292*	*0392*	*2 PW JT8D-217C*	*63503*	*CY130*	*BC-AH*	Holmfrid Viking
☐ SE-DME	Boeing (Douglas) MD-81 (DC-9-81)	*53366 / 1999*		*0092*	*0592*	*2 PW JT8D-217C*	*63503*	*CY130*	*BF-AC*	Kristin Viking
☐ SE-DMT	Boeing (Douglas) MD-81 (DC-9-81)	*48003 / 944*	*HB-IND*	*0080*	*1297*	*2 PW JT8D-217C*	*64410*	*Y162*		Tora Viking / *lsf Credit Lyonnais*
☐ SE-DMU	Boeing (Douglas) MD-81 (DC-9-81)	*48005 / 957*	*HB-INF*	*0081*	*0896*	*2 PW JT8D-217C*	*64410*	*Y162*		Siv Viking / *lsf Finova Capital*
☐ SE-DMX	Boeing (Douglas) MD-81 (DC-9-81)	*48002 / 938*	*HB-INC*	*0080*	*0396*	*2 PW JT8D-217C*	*64410*	*Y162*		Sigvard Viking / *lsf Finova Capital*
☐ SE-DMY	Boeing (Douglas) MD-81 (DC-9-81)	*48010 / 992*	*HB-INL*	*0681*	*1195*	*2 PW JT8D-217C*	*64410*	*Y162*	*BC-HK*	Sten Viking / *lsf Credit Lyonnais*
☐ SE-DMZ	Boeing (Douglas) MD-81 (DC-9-81)	*48009 / 985*	*HB-INK*	*0081*	*0595*	*2 PW JT8D-217C*	*64410*	*Y162*	*AM-CJ*	Maria Viking / *lsf Finova Capital*
☐ SE-DPI	Boeing (Douglas) MD-83 (DC-9-83)	*49557 / 1436*	*LN-RMB*	*0088*	*0288*	*2 PW JT8D-219*	*72575*	*CY136*	*JM-CK*	Balder Viking
☐ LN-RLE	Boeing (Douglas) MD-82 (DC-9-82)	*49382 / 1232*		*0985*	*1085*	*2 PW JT8D-219*	*67812*	*Y156*	*BC-AG*	Kettil Viking / *cvtd MD-81*
☐ LN-RLF	Boeing (Douglas) MD-82 (DC-9-82)	*49383 / 1236*	*VH-LNJ*	*1085*	*1185*	*2 PW JT8D-219*	*67812*	*Y156*	*BC-EJ*	Finn Viking
☐ LN-RLG	Boeing (Douglas) MD-82 (DC-9-82)	*49423 / 1283*	*N844RA*	*0586*	*0686*	*2 PW JT8D-219*	*67812*	*Y156*	*BF-CJ*	Trond Viking
☐ LN-RLR	Boeing (Douglas) MD-82 (DC-9-82)	*49437 / 1345*	*VH-LNL*	*0087*	*0387*	*2 PW JT8D-219*	*67812*	*Y156*	*JL-CF*	Vegard Viking
☐ LN-RMA	Boeing (Douglas) MD-82 (DC-9-82)	*49554 / 1379*		*0687*	*0787*	*2 PW JT8D-217C*	*67812*	*CY130*	*JL-CM*	Hasting Viking / *lsf Orient Ac/cvtd MD-81*
☐ LN-RMD	Boeing (Douglas) MD-82 (DC-9-82)	*49555 / 1402*		*0887*	*0987*	*2 PW JT8D-219*	*67812*	*Y156*	*JM-CF*	Fenge Viking / *lsf Orient Aircraft Lsng*
☐ LN-RMF	Boeing (Douglas) MD-83 (DC-9-83)	*49556 / 1415*		*1187*	*0188*	*2 PW JT8D-219*	*72575*	*CY136*	*JM-CH*	Torgny Viking / *lsf Orient Aircr.Lsng*
☐ LN-RMJ	Boeing (Douglas) MD-82 (DC-9-82)	*49912 / 1659*		*1189*	*1289*	*2 PW JT8D-217C*	*67812*	*CY130*	*BL-FP*	Rand Viking / *lsf Rand Lsng/cvtd MD-81*
☐ LN-RML	Boeing (Douglas) MD-82 (DC-9-82)	*53002 / 1835*		*0091*	*0391*	*2 PW JT8D-217C*	*67812*	*CY130*	*BC-FG*	Aud Viking / *lsf CL Airfin./cvtd MD-81*
☐ LN-RMM	Boeing (Douglas) MD-81 (DC-9-81)	*53005 / 1855*		*0491*	*0591*	*2 PW JT8D-217C*	*63503*	*CY130*	*KS-AD*	Blenda Viking / *lsf Fornebu Aircr.Ltd*
☐ LN-RMN	Boeing (Douglas) MD-82 (DC-9-82)	*53295 / 1922*		*0091*	*1091*	*2 PW JT8D-219*	*67812*	*Y156*	*KS-AP*	Ivar Viking / *lsf Orbit Leasing Int'l*
☐ LN-RMO	Boeing (Douglas) MD-81 (DC-9-81)	*53315 / 1947*		*1191*	*1291*	*2 PW JT8D-217C*	*63503*	*CY130*	*BC-AJ*	Bergljot Viking / *lsf Bergljot Leasing*
☐ LN-RMR	Boeing (Douglas) MD-81 (DC-9-81)	*53365 / 1998*		*0092*	*0592*	*2 PW JT8D-217C*	*63503*	*CY130*	*BC-EM*	Olav Viking
☐ LN-RMS	Boeing (Douglas) MD-81 (DC-9-81)	*53368 / 2003*		*0592*	*0692*	*2 PW JT8D-217C*	*63503*	*CY130*	*BF-AM*	Nial Viking
☐ LN-RMT	Boeing (Douglas) MD-81 (DC-9-81)	*53001 / 1815*	*OY-KHS*	*1290*	*0291*	*2 PW JT8D-217C*	*63503*	*CY130*	*BF-EG*	Jarl Viking
☐ OY-KGT	Boeing (Douglas) MD-82 (DC-9-82)	*49380 / 1225*	*N845RA*	*0885*	*1085*	*2 PW JT8D-217C*	*67812*	*CY130*	*BC-AM*	Hake Viking / *cvtd MD-81*
☐ OY-KGY	Boeing (Douglas) MD-81 (DC-9-81)	*49420 / 1254*		*0186*	*0286*	*2 PW JT8D-217C*	*63503*	*CY130*	*BC-AK*	Rollo Viking
☐ OY-KGZ	Boeing (Douglas) MD-81 (DC-9-81)	*49381 / 1231*		*0985*	*1085*	*2 PW JT8D-217C*	*63503*	*CY130*	*BC-DJ*	Hagbard Viking
☐ OY-KHC	Boeing (Douglas) MD-82 (DC-9-82)	*49436 / 1303*		*0886*	*0986*	*2 PW JT8D-217C*	*67812*	*CY130*	*JL-CE*	Faste Viking / *cvtd MD-81*
☐ OY-KHE	Boeing (Douglas) MD-82 (DC-9-82)	*49604 / 1456*	*N842RA*	*0088*	*0488*	*2 PW JT8D-219*	*67812*	*Y156*	*BF-DH*	Saxo Viking
☐ OY-KHG	Boeing (Douglas) MD-82 (DC-9-82)	*49613 / 1519*		*0088*	*1088*	*2 PW JT8D-217C*	*67812*	*CY130*	*BK-LP*	Alle Viking / *cvtd MD-81*
☐ OY-KHK	Boeing (Douglas) MD-81 (DC-9-81)	*49910 / 1638*		*0989*	*0989*	*2 PW JT8D-217C*	*63503*	*CY130*	*BK-DP*	Roald Viking / *lsf Roald Leasing*
☐ OY-KHL	Boeing (Douglas) MD-81 (DC-9-81)	*49911 / 1653*		*0089*	*1189*	*2 PW JT8D-217C*	*63503*	*CY130*	*BK-EP*	Knud Viking / *lsf Knud Leasing*
☐ OY-KHM	Boeing (Douglas) MD-81 (DC-9-81)	*49914 / 1693*		*0390*	*0390*	*2 PW JT8D-217C*	*63503*	*CY130*	*DQ-EK*	Mette Viking / *lsf Mette Aircraft Ltd*
☐ OY-KHN	Boeing (Douglas) MD-81 (DC-9-81)	*53000 / 1812*		*1290*	*0191*	*2 PW JT8D-217C*	*63503*	*CY130*	*BC-FK*	Dan Viking
☐ OY-KHP	Boeing (Douglas) MD-81 (DC-9-81)	*53007 / 1882*		*0691*	*0791*	*2 PW JT8D-217C*	*63503*	*CY130*	*KS-AF*	Arild Viking / *lsf Aarhus Aircraft Ltd*
☐ OY-KHR	Boeing (Douglas) MD-81 (DC-9-81)	*53275 / 1896*		*0091*	*0891*	*2 PW JT8D-217C*	*63503*	*CY130*	*KS-AH*	Torkild Viking
☐ OY-KHT	Boeing (Douglas) MD-82 (DC-9-82)	*53296 / 1937*		*1091*	*1191*	*2 PW JT8D-219*	*67812*	*Y156*	*BC-DE*	Gorm Viking / *lsf Gorm Leasing Int'l*
☐ OY-KIG	Boeing (Douglas) MD-81 (DC-9-81)	*48006 / 966*	*HB-ING*	*0081*	*0395*	*2 PW JT8D-209*	*64410*	*Y162*	*AM-CH*	Igor Viking / *lsf Credit Lyonnais*
☐ OY-KIH	Boeing (Douglas) MD-81 (DC-9-81)	*48007 / 971*	*HB-INH*	*0381*	*0495*	*2 PW JT8D-217C*	*64410*	*Y162*	*BC-GH*	Oleg Viking / *lsf Credit Lyonnais*
☐ OY-KII	Boeing (Douglas) MD-81 (DC-9-81)	*48008 / 981*	*HB-INI*	*0581*	*0795*	*2 PW JT8D-217C*	*64410*	*Y162*	*BC-GM*	Ellisiv Viking / *lsf Finova Capital*
☐ OY-KIK	Boeing (Douglas) MD-81 (DC-9-81)	*48004 / 950*	*HB-INE*	*0080*	*0596*	*2 PW JT8D-217C*	*64410*	*Y162*		Ole Viking / *lsf Finova Capital*
☐ SE-DMF	Boeing (Douglas) MD-90-30	*53457 / 2138*		*0096*	*1096*	*2 IAE V2525-D5*	*70760*	*CY141*	*MP-DR*	Heidrek Viking / *lsf JL Venus Lease*
☐ SE-DMG	Boeing (Douglas) MD-90-30	*53461 / 2147*		*1096*	*1296*	*2 IAE V2525-D5*	*70760*	*CY141*	*MP-FR*	Hervor Viking / *lsf JL Bellona Lease*
☐ SE-DMH	Boeing (Douglas) MD-90-30	*53543 / 2194*		*0797*	*0797*	*2 IAE V2525-D5*	*70760*	*CY141*	*MP-GR*	Torolf Viking
☐ LN-ROA	Boeing (Douglas) MD-90-30	*53459 / 2141*		*0096*	*1196*	*2 IAE V2525-D5*	*70760*	*CY141*	*MP-ER*	Sigurd Viking / *lsf SCL Sierra Co.Ltd*
☐ LN-ROB	Boeing (Douglas) MD-90-30	*53462 / 2149*		*1196*	*1296*	*2 IAE V2525-D5*	*70760*	*CY141*	*MP-FS*	Isrid Viking / *lsf Baltic Aircraft Ltd*
☐ OY-KIL	Boeing (Douglas) MD-90-30	*53458 / 2140*		*0896*	*1096*	*2 IAE V2525-D5*	*70760*	*CY141*	*MP-DS*	Kaare Viking / *lsf JL Horizon Lease*
☐ OY-KIM	Boeing (Douglas) MD-90-30	*53460 / 2142*		*0096*	*1296*	*2 IAE V2525-D5*	*70760*	*CY141*	*MP-ES*	Jon Viking / *lsf SBL Aries Co.Ltd*
☐ OY-KIN	Boeing (Douglas) MD-90-30	*53544 / 2197*		*0097*	*0897*	*2 IAE V2525-D5*	*70760*	*CY141*	*MP-GS*	Tormod Viking
☐ SE-DTK	Boeing 737-883	*28318*				*2 CFMI CFM56-7B26*	*78245*	*Y179*		Hedrun Viking / *oo-delivery 0400*
☐ SE-DTL	Boeing 737-883	*28319*				*2 CFMI CFM56-7B26*	*78245*			Gunn Viking / *oo-delivery 0400*
☐ SE-DTM	Boeing 737-883	*28320*				*2 CFMI CFM56-7B26*	*78245*			Mimer Viking / *oo-delivery 0500*
☐ OY-KKL	Boeing 737-883	*28321*				*2 CFMI CFM56-7B26*	*78245*			Oddrun Viking / *oo-delivery 0600*
☐ OY-KKM	Boeing 737-883	*30193*				*2 CFMI CFM56-7B26*	*78245*			Thorgrim Viking / *oo-delivery 0600*
☐ SE-DKP	Boeing 767-283 (ER)	*24727 / 301*	*N6018N**	*0690*	*0690*	*2 PW PW4056*	*175540*	*F15C40Y129*	*BF-CK*	Sigrid Viking / *lst TBA as PT-TAI -0699*
☐ SE-DKZ	Boeing 767-3Y0 (ER)	*24952 / 357*	*N249WP*	*0091*	*1196*	*2 PW PW4060*	*184612*	*C154Y87*	*BF-CL*	Bjarke Viking / *lsf BBAM*
☐ LN-RCD	Boeing 767-383 (ER)	*24847 / 315*		*0790*	*0790*	*2 PW PW4060*	*186880*	*CY188*	*BF-DL*	Gyda Viking
☐ LN-RCE	Boeing 767-383 (ER)	*24846 / 309*	*SE-DKR*	*0090*	*0690*	*2 PW PW4060*	*186880*	*CY192*	*BF-DE*	Aase Viking
☐ LN-RCG	Boeing 767-383 (ER)	*24475 / 273*	*SE-DOA*	*0089*	*0889*	*2 PW PW4060*	*184612*	*CY190*	*BF-CD*	Yrsa Viking / *lsf AFGR*

587 registration type of aircraft *cn/fn* *ex/ex** *mfd* *del* *powered by* *mtow kg* *configuration* *selcal* name/fln/specialitites/remarks

☐ LN-RCH	Boeing 767-383 (ER)	24318 / 257	SE-DKO	0089	0389	2 PW PW4060	184612	CY190	BC-HJ	Ingegerd Viking / lsf SUNR
☐ LN-RCI	Boeing 767-383 (ER)	24476 / 274	SE-DOB	0089	0889	2 PW PW4060	184612	CY190	BF-CG	Helga Viking / lsf Kuta-Two Aircraft
☐ LN-RCK	Boeing 767-383 (ER)	24729 / 358	SE-DKU	0091	0391	2 PW PW4060	184612	CY190	FL-DM	Tor Viking / lsf Gilman Financial
☐ LN-RCL	Boeing 767-383 (ER)	25365 / 395	SE-DKX	0091	1091	2 PW PW4060	184612	CY190	EH-FJ	Sven Viking / lsf Aviation Investors
☐ LN-RCM	Boeing 767-383 (ER)	26544 / 412	SE-DOC	0092	0292	2 PW PW4060	186880	CY188	CG-JL	Gudrun Viking / lsf Nordbanken Finans
☐ OY-KDH	Boeing 767-383 (ER)	24358 / 263	I-AEJB	0089	0589	2 PW PW4060	184612	C109Y133	BF-AE	Tyra Viking / lsf BBAM/Star Alliance-cs
☐ OY-KDL	Boeing 767-383 (ER)	24477 / 337		0090	1190	2 PW PW4060	184612	CY190	EJ-DH	Tjodhild Viking / lsf DIA Companies
☐ OY-KDM	Boeing 767-383 (ER)	25088 / 359		0091	0391	2 PW PW4060	186882	CY188	JL-CH	Ingvar Viking / lsf Muzun Lsng One Ltd
☐ OY-KDN	Boeing 767-383 (ER)	24848 / 325	SE-DKS	0090	0990	2 PW PW4060	184612	CY188	BC-FL	Ulf Viking / lsf JL Baltic Lease Co.
☐ OY-KDO	Boeing 767-383 (ER)	24849 / 330	SE-DKT	0090	0990	2 PW PW4060	184612	CY188	BF-EJ	Svea Viking / lsf JL Bick Leasing Co.

SKYDIVE AIRLINES, AB — Gryttom

c/o Lars Orrje, Sköntorpsvägen 4, S-120 38 Arsta, Sweden ☎ (8) 91 63 42 Tx: n/a Fax: (8) 91 63 42 SITA: n/a
F: 1993 ⁂ n/a Head: Lars Orrje Net: n/a Operates para flights exclusively for the Stockholms Fallskärmsklubb.

☐ SE-GEE	De Havilland DHC-6 Twin Otter 300	364	F-GFAH	0073	0593	2 PWC PT6A-27	5675	Para		

SKYLINE HELIKOPTER (Nya Skyline Helikopter, AB dba) — Karlstad

Box 51, S-796 22 Aelvdalen, Sweden ☎ (250) 15 920 Tx: none Fax: (250) 12 399 SITA: n/a
F: 1984 ⁂ 7 Head: Christer Hagberg Net: n/a Aircraft below MTOW 1361 kg: Hughes 269C (300C) & 369HS (500C).

☐ SE-JFG	Eurocopter (Aerosp.) SA316B Alouette III	5377	F-GJGS	0077	0198	1 TU Artouste IIIB1	2200			

SKYWAYS, AB = JZ / SKX (formerly Avia, AB & Salair, AB / Associated with Salenia Aviation, AB & Scanadinavian SAS) — Linköping, Gothenburg & Stockholm-Arlanda

Box 1537, S-581 15 Linköping, Sweden ☎ (13) 37 55 00 Tx: none Fax: (13) 37 55 01 SITA: n/a
F: 1939 ⁂ 340 Head: Sven Salen IATA: 752 ICAO: SKY EXPRESS Net: http://www.skyways.se

☐ SE-ISL	Saab SF340A	340A-130	LN-SAA	0088	1088	2 GE CT7-5A2	12700	Y34		Oestergötland / lsf JBA Invest
☐ SE-ISP	Saab SF340A	340A-015	SE-E15*	0185	0395	2 GE CT7-5A2	12700	Y34		Småland / lsf ABN Amro Leasing
☐ SE-ISR	Saab SF340A	340A-017	SE-E17*	0185	0394	2 GE CT7-5A2	12700	Y34		Västergöland / lsf ABN Amro Leasing
☐ SE-ISV	Saab SF340A	340A-045	SE-E45*	0186	0494	2 GE CT7-5A2	12700	Y34		Jämtland / lsf ABN Amro Leasing
☐ SE-ISY	Saab SF340A	340A-080	SE-E80*	1286	0494	2 GE CT7-5A2	12700	Y34		lsf ABN Amro Leasing
☐ SE-KPD	Saab SF340A	340A-037	PH-KJL	0085	0893	2 GE CT7-5A2	12700	Y34		Närke / lsf ABN Amro Leasing
☐ SE-KPE	Saab SF340A	340A-055	PH-KJH	0086	0893	2 GE CT7-5A2	12700	Y34		Uppland / lsf ABN Amro Leasing
☐ SE-KRN	Saab SF340A	340A-159	D-CHBC	0089	0191	2 GE CT7-5A2	12700	Y34		
☐ SE-KUT	Saab SF340A	340A-087	LN-NVF	0087	0395	2 GE CT7-5A2	12700	Y34		Aengermanland / lsf Commuter Invest I
☐ SE-LEP	Saab SF340A	340A-127	B-12200	0088	0696	2 GE CT7-5A2	12700	Y36		lsf ABN Amro Leasing/sub-lst/opf TED
☐ SE-LES	Saab SF340A	340A-129	B-12299	0088	1196	2 GE CT7-5A2	12700	Y36		lsf ABN Amro Leasing/sub-lst/opf TED
☐ SE-DZA	Embraer RJ145EP (EMB-145EP)	145070	PT-SAO*	0098	1198	2 AN AE3007A1	20990	Y50		
☐ SE-DZB	Embraer RJ145EP (EMB-145EP)	145113		0299	0299	2 AN AE3007A1	20990	Y50		
☐ SE-LEA	Fokker 50 (F27 Mk050)	20116	PH-GHK	0088	0595	2 PWC PW125B	20820	Y50		Dalarna / lsf Ansett Industrie (HKG) Ltd
☐ SE-LEB	Fokker 50 (F27 Mk050)	20120	PH-JHD	0088	0895	2 PWC PW125B	20820	Y50		Gotland / lsf Heller Financial Inc.
☐ SE-LEC	Fokker 50 (F27 Mk050)	20112	VH-FNG	0088	0196	2 PWC PW125B	20820	Y50		Västerbotten / lsf Ansett Avn Equipment
☐ SE-LED	Fokker 50 (F27 Mk050)	20111	VH-FNF	0087	0396	2 PWC PW125B	20820	Y50		Södermanland / lsf Ansett Avn Equipment
☐ SE-LEH	Fokker 50 (F27 Mk050)	20108	VH-FNC	0087	0896	2 PWC PW125B	20820	Y50		lsf Ansett Aviation Equipment
☐ SE-LEL	Fokker 50 (F27 Mk050)	20110	VH-FNE	0087	0197	2 PWC PW125B	20820	Y50		lsf Ansett Aviation Equipment
☐ SE-LEU	Fokker 50 (F27 Mk050)	20115	9M-MGZ	0088	1097	2 PWC PW125B	20820	Y50		lsf Ansett Aviation Equipment
☐ SE-LEZ	Fokker 50 (F27 Mk050)	20128	PH-PRA	0088	0898	2 PWC PW125B	20820	Y50		lsf PEMB
☐ SE-LIN	Fokker 50 (F27 Mk050)	20138	PH-PRB	0088	0199	2 PWC PW125B	20820	Y50		lsf PEMB
☐ SE-LIO	Fokker 50 (F27 Mk050)	20146	PH-PRC	0089	0299	2 PWC PW125B	20820	Y50		lsf PEMB
☐ SE-LIP	Fokker 50 (F27 Mk050)	20147	PH-PRD	0089	0399	2 PWC PW125B	20820	Y50		lsf PEMB

SMAELANDSFLYG, AB = SMF — Ljungby

Björnbärsvägen 11, S-341 34 Ljungby, Sweden ☎ (372) 821 82 Tx: n/a Fax: (372) 838 82 SITA: n/a
F: 1994 ⁂ 4 Head: Frederik Svärd ICAO: GORDON Net: n/a

☐ SE-GIN	Piper PA-31-310 Navajo C	31-7512039		0075		2 LY TIO-540-A2C	2950			
☐ SE-KGH	Piper PA-31-350 Navajo Chieftain	31-7305007	OY-BYF	0073	0398	2 LY TIO-540-J2BD	3175			lsf Swanfly AB
☐ SE-LCM	Piper PA-31-350 Navajo Chieftain	31-7552114	OY-BLF	0075	0196	2 LY TIO-540-J2BD	3175			lsf ABN Amro Leasing

SOS FLYGAMBULANS, AB – SOS Air Ambulance, Ltd = SAG (formerly Svensk Flygambulans, AB) — Gothenburg-Saeve

Göteborg - Säve Flygplats, S-420 14 Säve, Sweden ☎ (31) 92 60 10 Tx: none Fax: (31) 92 61 10 SITA: n/a
F: 1975 ⁂ 25 Head: Lars Malmberg ICAO: MEDICAL AIR Net: http://www.sos.flygambulans.se

☐ SE-INI	Beech King Air 200	BB-687	EI-BIP	0080		2 PWC PT6A-41	5670	EMS		
☐ SE-IUX	Beech King Air 200	BB-675	N26SD	0080		2 PWC PT6A-41	5670	EMS		
☐ SE-IXC	Beech King Air B200	BB-1210	N7213J	0085		2 PWC PT6A-42	5670	EMS		
☐ SE-KFP	Beech King Air B200C	BL-132		0088		2 PWC PT6A-42	5670	EMS		
☐ SE-LCB	Beech King Air B200C	BL-139	N82431	0090	1294	2 PWC PT6A-42	5670	EMS		

SOS HELIKOPTERN GOTLAND, AB = MCG — Visby

Mickelgards, S-621 72 Visby, Sweden ☎ (498) 20 90 50 Tx: none Fax: (498) 21 01 17 SITA: n/a
F: 1992 ⁂ 2 Head: Lars Malmgren ICAO: MEDICOPTER Net: n/a

☐ SE-JUL	Eurocopter (MBB) BK117B-2	7186	D-HIMC	0090	0395	2 LY LTS101-750B.1	3350	EMS		

STANSON AIR, AB — Stockholm-Bromma

Box 7062, S-161 07 Bromma, Sweden ☎ (8) 87 13 01 Tx: n/a Fax: (8) 87 13 07 SITA: n/a
F: 1990 ⁂ n/a Head: n/a Net: n/a

☐ SE-LDL	Beech King Air A100	B-213	F-GFEV	0075	0197	2 PWC PT6A-28	5216			lsf ABN Amro Leasing

SVEA FLYG, AB = SI / SVB — Karlskoga

Flygplatsen, S-691 35 Karlskoga, Sweden ☎ (586) 35 350 Tx: none Fax: (586) 35 245 SITA: n/a
F: 1995 ⁂ 7 Head: Ragnar Nilsson ICAO: SVEAFLYG Net: n/a

☐ SE-IAC	Piper PA-31-310 Navajo C	31-7812095		0078		2 LY TIO-540-A2C	2950			
☐ SE-LGH	BAe 3102 Jetstream 31	773	OY-SVO	0087	0898	2 GA TPE331-10UR-514H	7060			

SWEDEWAYS AIR LINES, AB = HJ / SWE (formerly Holmstroem Air Sweden, AB & Holmstroem Air Hudiksvall, AB) — Hudiksvall

Skogstra 41, S-824 92 Hudiksvall, Sweden ☎ (650) 24 289 Tx: none Fax: (650) 24 224 SITA: n/a
F: 1993 ⁂ 45 Head: John-Olof Holmström ICAO: SWEDELINE Net: n/a

☐ SE-IXE	Shorts 360-200 (SD3-60 Variant 100)	SH3705	G-BNBA*	0086	0293	2 PWC PT6A-65AR	11999	Y34		lsf Skylease Sweden AB
☐ SE-KCI	Shorts 360-100 (SD3-60 Variant 100)	SH3648	G-OAAS	0084	0698	2 PWC PT6A-65R	11999	Y34		lsf Skylease Sweden AB
☐ SE-KGV	Shorts 360-100 (SD3-60 Variant 100)	SH3670	HR-IAT	0085	1097	2 PWC PT6A-65AR	11999	Y34		lsf Leasinair AB
☐ SE-KLO	Shorts 360-100 (SD3-60 Variant 100)	SH3609	N343MV	0083	0293	2 PWC PT6A-65AR	11999	Y34		lsf Skylease Sweden AB

TRAVEL AIR, AB — Borlange

Box 913, S-781 29 Borlange, Sweden ☎ (243) 22 42 50 Tx: none Fax: (243) 25 70 35 SITA: n/a
F: 1998 ⁂ 5 Head: Per Eliasson Net: http://www.travelair.se

☐ SE-LDI	BAe 3112 Jetstream 31	785	C-FHOE	0088	0598	2 GA TPE331-10UGR-514H	6950	Y18		lsf / opb Airborne of Sweden

TRYGG-FLYG Erik Trygg, AB = TYG (formerly Trygg-Flyg, AB) — Nyköping

Skavsta flygplats, S-611 92 Nyköping, Sweden ☎ (155) 26 77 25 Tx: n/a Fax: (155) 26 77 72 SITA: n/a
F: 1991 ⁂ n/a Head: Erik Trygg ICAO: TRYGG Net: http://www.trygg-flyg.se

☐ SE-LDB	CASA 212-CB Aviocar Srs 100	154	N125JM	0080	0396	2 GA TPE331-5-251C	6500			
☐ SE-LDC	CASA 212-CC Aviocar Srs 200	193	VH-ICJ	0081	0795	2 GA TPE331-10-501C	7700			
☐ SE-LDG	CASA 212-CC Aviocar Srs 200	192	N192MA	0081	0297	2 GA TPE331-10R-511C	7700			

V-AIR = T9 / SRL (AB Värmlandsflyg dba) — Torsby

PO Box 43, S-685 21 Torsby, Sweden ☎ (560) 71 515 Tx: none Fax: (560) 13 015 SITA: TYFKOT9
F: 1961 ⁂ 18 Head: John Andersson ICAO: STARLINE Net: n/a

☐ SE-FER	Cessna 207 Skywagon	20700042	LN-BIP	0069		1 CO IO-520-F	1724			
☐ SE-LCN	Twin (Aero) Shrike Commander 500S	3177	CS-APZ	0074	0794	2 LY IO-540-E1B5	3062			
☐ SE-GSS	Twin (Aero) Jetprop Commander 840 (690C)	11613	D-IBOB	0080		2 GA TPE331-5-254K	4685			
☐ SE-LCT	Beech King Air 300LW	FA-25	N147CA	0088	0396	2 PWC PT6A-60A	5670			
☐ SE-LCX	Beech 1900D Airliner	UE-275	N11189*	0097	0897	2 PWC PT6A-67D	7688			lsf Nordbanken Finans AB

WEST AIR SWEDEN, AB = SWN (formerly Air Sweden Executive & Abal Air, AB) — Gothenburg-Saeve & Lidkoeping

PO Box 5433, S-402 29 Göteborg, Sweden ☎ (31) 703 43 07 Tx: 66310 airswe s Fax: (31) 335 82 90 SITA: LIDOPPT
F: 1963 ⁂ 45 Head: Gustaf Thureborn ICAO: AIR SWEDEN Net: http://www.westair.se

☐ SE-LEG	BAe (HS) 748-244 Srs 2	1723 / 215	D-AFSF	0075	0995	2 RR Dart 550-2	20200	Freighter		lsf ABN Amro Leasing
☐ SE-LEK	BAe (HS) 748-244 Srs 2	1725 / 219	D-AFSH	0075	0995	2 RR Dart 550-2	20200	Freighter		lsf ABN Amro Leasing
☐ SE-LEO	BAe (HS) 748-244 Srs 2	1726 / 216	D-AFSI	0075	0995	2 RR Dart 550-2	20200	Freighter		lsf ABN Amro Leasing
☐ SE-LEX	BAe (HS) 748-244 Srs 2	1727 / 217	D-AFSJ	0076	0995	2 RR Dart 550-2	20200	Freighter		lsf ABN Amro Leasing
☐ SE-LEY	BAe (HS) 748-235 Srs 2A	1631 / 113	LN-FOM	0068	0996	2 RR Dart 532-2L	20185	Freighter		lsf ABN Amro Leasing
☐ SE-LIA	BAe (HS) 748-263 Srs 2A	1717 / 192	F-GFYM	0072	0397	2 RR Dart 534-2	20000	Freighter		lsf ABN Amro Leasing
☐ SE-LIB	BAe (HS) 748-371 Srs 2B (SCD)	1776 / 257	FAC1108	0080	0697	2 RR Dart 536-2	20200	Freighter		lsf ABN Amro Leasing
☐ SE-LIC	BAe (HS) 748-399 Srs 2B (SCD)	1778 / 259	C-FKTL	0081	0298	2 RR Dart 536-2	21090	Freighter		lsf ABN Amro Leasing
☐ SE-LID	BAe (HS) 748-333 Srs 2A	1760 / 241	J5-GAT	0078	0798	2 RR Dart 535-2	20200	Freighter		lsf ABN Amro Leasing
☐ SE-LIE	BAe (HS) 748-229 Srs 2	1595 / 86	A10-595	0067	0299	2 RR Dart 534-2	20200	Freighter		
☐ SE-LIF	BAe (HS) 748-229 Srs 2	1596 / 77	A10-596	0067	0299	2 RR Dart 534-2	20200	Freighter		

588 registration type of aircraft cn/fn ex/ex* mfd del powered by mtow kg configuration selcal name/fln/specialitites/remarks

SP = POLAND (Republic of Poland) (Rzeczpospolita Polska)

Capital: Warsaw Official Language: Polish Population: 38,5 million Square Km: 312683 Dialling code: +48 Year established: 1918 Acting political head: Aleksander Kwasnievski (President)

Government / Corporate / Executive / VIP Aircraft

☐ 032	Yakovlev 40	9331129		0073	0873	3 IV AI-25	16000	VIP / mil transp		Polskie Wojska Lotnicze/Polish A.F.
☐ 034	Yakovlev 40	9331229		0073	0873	3 IV AI-25	16000	VIP / mil transp		Polskie Wojska Lotnicze/Polish A.F.
☐ 037	Yakovlev 40	9510238		0075	0275	3 IV AI-25	16000	VIP / mil transp		Polskie Wojska Lotnicze/Polish A.F.
☐ 038	Yakovlev 40	9441237		0074	0275	3 IV AI-25	16000	VIP / mil transp		Polskie Wojska Lotnicze/Polish A.F.
☐ 039	Yakovlev 40	9441137		0074	1174	3 IV AI-25	16000	VIP / mil transp		Polskie Wojska Lotnicze/Polish A.F.
☐ 040	Yakovlev 40	9541643		0075	1275	3 IV AI-25	16000	VIP / mil transp		Polskie Wojska Lotnicze/Polish A.F.
☐ 041	Yakovlev 40	9541843	SP-LEB	0075	1275	3 IV AI-25	16000	VIP / mil transp		Polskie Wojska Lotnicze/Polish A.F.
☐ 042	Yakovlev 40	9541943	SP-LEC	0075	1275	3 IV AI-25	16000	VIP / mil transp		Polskie Wojska Lotnicze/Polish A.F.
☐ 043	Yakovlev 40	9542043	SP-LED	0075	1275	3 IV AI-25	16000	VIP / mil transp		Polskie Wojska Lotnicze/Polish A.F.
☐ 044	Yakovlev 40	9840659		0078	0479	3 IV AI-25	16000	VIP / mil transp		Polskie Wojska Lotnicze/Polish A.F.
☐ 045	Yakovlev 40	9840759		0078	0479	3 IV AI-25	16000	VIP / mil transp		Polskie Wojska Lotnicze/Polish A.F.
☐ 047	Yakovlev 40	9021560	SP-LEE	0080	0680	3 IV AI-25	16000	VIP / mil transp		Polskie Wojska Lotnicze/Polish A.F.
☐ 048	Yakovlev 40	9021660	SP-LEA	0080	0780	3 IV AI-25	16000	VIP / mil transp		Polskie Wojska Lotnicze/Polish A.F.
☐ 101	Tupolev 154M	837	837	0090	0090	3 SO D-30KU-154-II	100000	VIP / mil transp		01 / Polskie Wojska Lotnicze/Polish AF
☐ 102	Tupolev 154M	862	862	1290	0094	3 SO D-30KU-154-II	100000	VIP / mil transp		02 / Polskie Wojska Lotnicze/Polish AF

AEROGRYF, Spolka z o.o. = GRF (Associated with Aerotech, Spolka z o.o.) — Szczecin

ul. Przestrzenna 10, PL-70-800 Szczecin, Poland ☎ (91) 461 35 61 Tx: none Fax: (91) 461 33 42 SITA: n/a
F: 1991 ⁂ 42 Head: Jacek Kita ICAO: AEROGRYF Net: http://www.aerogryf.com.pl. Ag-/Firefighting aircraft below MTOW 5000kg: PZL M-18B Dromader

☐ SP-DMA	PZL Mielec M-20 Mewa	1AH001-01		0079		2 PZL-F6A-350C1L/R	2070			
☐ SP-FFN	PZL Mielec (Antonov) An-28	1AJ006-08	TC-FEB	0088		2 GS TVD-10B	6500			
☐ SP-FHP	PZL Mielec (Antonov) An-28	1AJ008-04	RA-28918	0090	0698	2 GS TVD-10B	6500			
☐ SP-FHR	PZL Mielec (Antonov) An-28	1AJ006-11	RA-28700	0089	0698	2 GS TVD-10B	6500			
☐ SP-FHS	PZL Mielec (Antonov) An-28	1AJ007-10	RA-28725	0090	1198	2 GS TVD-10B	6500			
☐ SP-FHU	PZL Mielec (Antonov) An-28	1AJ007-18	RA-28733	0090	1198	2 GS TVD-10B	6500			
☐ SP-FYV	PZL Mielec M-28 Skytruck	AJE001-01		0096	0496	2 PWC PT6A-65B	7000			

ALSI Przedsiebiorstwo Instalacji Przemystowych i Sanitarnych — Poznan-Lawica

Ul. Olszynowa 1, PL-62-064 Zakrzewo, Poland ☎ (61) 814 33 21 Tx: none Fax: (61) 8143321 ext.50 SITA: n/a
F: 1980 ⁂ n/a Head: Aleksander Siepnewski Net: n/a

☐ SP-FSP	PZL Swidnik (Mil) Mi-2	542503072	SP-FDI	0072	0398	2 IS GTD-350-4	3550			

EUROLOT, S.A. = ELO (Subsidiary of LOT Polish Airlines / Polskie Linie Lotnicze LOT, S.A.) — Warsaw-Okecie

ul. 17 Stycznia 39, PL-00-906 Warszawa, Poland ☎ (22) 606 64 67 Tx: none Fax: (22) 606 61 69 SITA: WAWOELO
F: 1997 ⁂ 152 Head: Marek Rymkiewicz ICAO: EUROLOT Net: http://www.eurolot.com.pl
Beside aircraft listed, also uses ATR72-202 from its parent company LOT & BAe 3102 Jetstream 31 from TASAWI AIR SERVICES (SP-), when required.

☐ SP-EEA	ATR 42-300	011	F-WQGF	0086	0798	2 PWC PW120	16700	Y48		lsf ATR
☐ SP-EEB	ATR 42-300	055	F-WQGI	0087	0798	2 PWC PW120	16700	Y48		lsf ATR
☐ SP-EEC	ATR 42-300	080	F-WQID	0088	0898	2 PWC PW120	16700	Y48		lsf ATR
☐ SP-	ATR 42-300					2 PWC PW120	16700	Y48		to be lsf ATR 0099
☐ SP-	ATR 42-300					2 PWC PW120	16700	Y48		to be lsf ATR 0099

EXIN Co. Ltd = EXN — Katowice

Rynek 18, PL-20-111 Lublin, Poland ☎ (81) 532 12 47 Tx: 642276 Fax: (81) 532 59 04 SITA: n/a
F: 1991 ⁂ 25 Head: Edward Kuvaszewicz ICAO: EXIN Net: http://www.exin.exe.pl

☐ SP-FTL	Antonov 26	5002	EW-26616	0377	0994	2 IV AI-24VT	24000	Freighter		op in DHL colors
☐ SP-FTZ	Antonov 26	5909	EW-26632	1277	0895	2 IV AI-24VT	24000	Freighter		

HELISECO - Helicopter Services Company (Lotnicze Przedsiebiorstwo Uslugowe HELISECO dba / Subsidiary of PZL, Swidnik) — Swidnik

Aleja Lotnikow 1, PL-21-045 Swidnik, Poland ☎ (81) 751 23 49 Tx: none Fax: (81) 468 09 23 SITA: n/a
F: 1975 ⁂ n/a Head: Wojciech Jablonski Net: n/a

☐ SP-SAS	PZL Swidnik (Mil) Mi-2	525612048		0078		2 IS GTD-350-4	3550			
☐ SP-SBL	PZL Swidnik (Mil) Mi-2	525147037		0077		2 IS GTD-350-4	3550			
☐ SP-SBN	PZL Swidnik (Mil) Mi-2	525149037	SU-BHY	0077		2 IS GTD-350-4	3550			
☐ SP-SCC	PZL Swidnik (Mil) Mi-2	529607016		0086		2 IS GTD-350-4	3550			
☐ SP-SCD	PZL Swidnik (Mil) Mi-2	529608016		0086		2 IS GTD-350-4	3550			
☐ SP-SCO	PZL Swidnik (Mil) Mi-2	529626026		0086		2 IS GTD-350-4	3550			
☐ SP-SCU	PZL Swidnik (Mil) Mi-2	529631026		0086		2 IS GTD-350-4	3550			
☐ SP-SCX	PZL Swidnik (Mil) Mi-2	529635026		0088		2 IS GTD-350-4	3550			
☐ SP-SCZ	PZL Swidnik (Mil) Mi-2	529633026		0086		2 IS GTD-350-4	3550			
☐ SP-SDC	PZL Swidnik (Mil) Mi-2	543908124		0075		2 IS GTD-350-4	3550			
☐ SP-SDI	PZL Swidnik (Mil) Mi-2	524005025		0075		2 IS GTD-350-4	3550			
☐ SP-SDM	PZL Swidnik (Mil) Mi-2	530322047	SP-PSC	0075		2 IS GTD-350-4	3550			
☐ SP-SEA	PZL Swidnik (Mil) Mi-2	542229012		0072		2 IS GTD-350-4	3550			
☐ SP-SEF	PZL Swidnik (Mil) Mi-2	525227067		0077		2 IS GTD-350-4	3550			
☐ SP-SEP	PZL Swidnik (Mil) Mi-2	525518028		0078		2 IS GTD-350-4	3550			
☐ SP-SES	PZL Swidnik (Mil) Mi-2	5210018116		0086		2 IS GTD-350-4	3550			
☐ SP-SFD	PZL Swidnik (Mil) Mi-2	526507010		0080		2 IS GTD-350-4	3550			
☐ SP-SFF	PZL Swidnik (Mil) Mi-2	5210008106		0086		2 IS GTD-350-4	3550			
☐ SP-SFG	PZL Swidnik (Mil) Mi-2	5210009106		0086		2 IS GTD-350-4	3550			
☐ SP-SFX	PZL Swidnik (Mil) Mi-2	5210308087		0087		2 IS GTD-350-4	3550			
☐ SP-SFY	PZL Swidnik (Mil) Mi-2	5210307067		0087		2 IS GTD-350-4	3550			
☐ SP-SGA	PZL Swidnik (Mil) Mi-2	5210415107		0087		2 IS GTD-350-4	3550			
☐ SP-SGB	PZL Swidnik (Mil) Mi-2	5210416107		0087		2 IS GTD-350-4	3550			
☐ SP-SGL	PZL Swidnik (Mil) Mi-2	5210434049		0089		2 IS GTD-350-4	3550			
☐ SP-SGP	PZL Swidnik (Mil) Mi-2	5210438069		0089		2 IS GTD-350-4	3550			
☐ SP-SGS	PZL Swidnik (Mil) Mi-2	5210440099		0089		2 IS GTD-350-4	3550			
☐ SP-SGT	PZL Swidnik (Mil) Mi-2	5210441099		0089		2 IS GTD-350-4	3550			
☐ SP-SLI	PZL Swidnik (Mil) Mi-2	525645068		0078		2 IS GTD-350-4	3550			
☐ SP-SLM	PZL Swidnik (Mil) Mi-2	525837108		0078		2 IS GTD-350-4	3550			
☐ SP-SPR	PZL Swidnik (Mil) Mi-2	535744098		0078		2 IS GTD-350-4	3550			opf Insitute of Geophysics
☐ SP-SUH	PZL Swidnik W-3 Sokol	310205		0088		2 PZL-10W	6400			
☐ SP-SUI	PZL Swidnik W-3 Sokol	310301		0089		2 PZL-10W	6400			
☐ SP-SUK	PZL Swidnik W-3 Sokol	310302		0089		2 PZL-10W	6400			
☐ SP-SUO	PZL Swidnik W-3 Sokol	310314		0090		2 PZL-10W	6400			
☐ SP-SUY	PZL Swidnik W-3 Sokol	310206		0088		2 PZL-10W	6400			
☐ SP-SUZ	PZL Swidnik W-3 Sokol	310207		0088		2 PZL-10W	6400			
☐ SP-SYA	PZL Swidnik W-3 Sokol	310204		0088		2 PZL-10W	6400			
☐ SP-SYB	PZL Swidnik W-3 Sokol	310310		0090		2 PZL-10W	6400			
☐ SP-SYC	PZL Swidnik W-3 Sokol	310311		0090		2 PZL-10W	6400			

INSTYTUT LOTNICTWA - Institute of Aviation — Warsaw-Okecie

Al. Krakowska 110/114, PL-02-256 Warszawa, Poland ☎ (22) 846 09 93 Tx: 813537 pl Fax: (22) 846 44 32 SITA: n/a
F: 1926 ⁂ 500 Head: Witold Wisniowski Net: n/a Aircraft below MTOW 1361kg: PZL-104 Wilga 35 Non-commercial national state organisation conducting scientific research & calibration flights.

☐ SP-GKA	Piper PA-34-200T Seneca II	34-7670279	N6299J	0076		2 CO TSIO-360-E1B	2073	Calibrator/Res.		
☐ SP-SER	PZL Swidnik (Mil) Mi-2	544535125		0075		2 IS GTD-350-4	3550	Calibrator/Res.		
☐ SP-GCA	PZL Mielec (Antonov) An-28	1AJ004-06		0087		2 GS TVD-10B	6500	Calibrator/Res.		

JET CLUB, Ltd = BOB — Warsaw-Okecie

Ul. Ostrobramska 75, PL-04-175 Warszawa, Poland ☎ (22) 611 39 07 Tx: none Fax: (22) 611 39 09 SITA: n/a
F: 1997 ⁂ 10 Head: Dion L.J. Heiymans ICAO: BOB JET Net: n/a

☐ SP-FCP	Dassault Falcon 20C	136	HB-VBM	0068	0797	2 GE CF700-2D2	12400	Executive		

LOT Polish Airlines / Polskie Linie Lotnicze LOT, S.A. = LO / LOT — Warszawa-Okecie

ul. 17 Stycznia 39, PL-00-906 Warszawa, Poland ☎ (22) 606 65 65 Tx: 813552 lot pl Fax: (22) 846 09 09 SITA: WAWNDLO
F: 1929 ⁂ 4100 Head: Jan Litwinski IATA: 080 ICAO: LOT Net: http://www.lot.com

☐ SP-LGA	Embraer RJ145EP (EMB-145EP)					2 AN AE3007A	20990	CY48		oo-delivery 0799
☐ SP-LGB	Embraer RJ145EP (EMB-145EP)					2 AN AE3007A	20990	CY48		oo-delivery 0899
☐ SP-LGC	Embraer RJ145EP (EMB-145EP)					2 AN AE3007A	20990	CY48		oo-delivery 0200
☐ SP-LGD	Embraer RJ145EP (EMB-145EP)					2 AN AE3007A	20990	CY48		oo-delivery 0400
☐ SP-LGE	Embraer RJ145EP (EMB-145EP)					2 AN AE3007A	20990	CY48		oo-delivery 0700
☐ SP-LGF	Embraer RJ145EP (EMB-145EP)					2 AN AE3007A	20990	CY48		oo-delivery 0900
☐ SP-LFA	ATR 72-202	246	F-WWEM*	0791	0891	2 PWC PW124B	21500	CY64		lsf Polka Bait, France
☐ SP-LFB	ATR 72-202	265	F-WWEJ*	1091	1291	2 PWC PW124B	21500	CY64		lsf Polka Bait, France
☐ SP-LFC	ATR 72-202	272	F-WWEN*	1291	1291	2 PWC PW124B	21500	CY64		lsf Polka Bait, France
☐ SP-LFD	ATR 72-202	279	F-WWLD*	0192	0292	2 PWC PW124B	21500	CY64		lsf Polka Bait, France

589 registration type of aircraft cn/fn ex/ex* mfd del powered by mtow kg configuration selcal name/fln/specialitites/remarks

□ SP-LFE	ATR 72-202	328	F-WWLJ*	1092	1092	2 PWC PW124B	21500	CY64		lsf Polka Bait, France
□ SP-LFF	ATR 72-202	402	F-WWLM*	0194	0394	2 PWC PW124B	21500	CY64		lsf Polka Bait, France
□ SP-LFG	ATR 72-202	411	F-WWEO*	0494	0794	2 PWC PW124B	21500	CY64		lsf Chopin Lease, France
□ SP-LFH	ATR 72-202	478	F-WWEK*	0496	0496	2 PWC PW124B	21500	CY64		lsf Polska Bait, France
□ SP-LKA	Boeing 737-55D	27416 / 2389		1192	1292	2 CFMI CFM56-3C1	58287	CY108	CJ-QS	lsf Marta Leasing Ltd, Cayman Islands
□ SP-LKB	Boeing 737-55D	27417 / 2392		1192	1292	2 CFMI CFM56-3C1	52390	CY108	CJ-RS	lsf Marta Leasing Ltd, Cayman Islands
□ SP-LKC	Boeing 737-55D	27418 / 2397		1192	1292	2 CFMI CFM56-3C1	52390	CY108	CJ-PR	lsf Marta Leasing Ltd, Cayman Islands
□ SP-LKD	Boeing 737-55D	27419 / 2401		1292	1292	2 CFMI CFM56-3C1	52390	CY108	CK-AR	lsf Marta Leasing Ltd, Cayman Islands
□ SP-LKE	Boeing 737-55D	27130 / 2448		0393	0393	2 CFMI CFM56-3C1	52390	CY108	CK-AS	lsf Marta Leasing Ltd, Cayman Islands
□ SP-LKF	Boeing 737-55D	27368 / 2603		0594	0594	2 CFMI CFM56-3C1	52390	CY108	FR-DK	lsf Marta Leasing Ltd, Cayman Islands
□ SP-LMC	Boeing 737-36N	28668 / 2890		0697	0797	2 CFMI CFM56-3C1	60985	Y145	JQ-HP	lsf GECA
□ SP-LMD	Boeing 737-36N	28669 / 2897		0697	0797	2 CFMI CFM56-3C1	60985	Y145	GK-BQ	lsf GECA
□ ZK-NGD	Boeing 737-3U3	28732 / 2966	N930WA	1297	0399	2 CFMI CFM56-3C1	63276	Y145		lsf ANZ -1099
□ SP-LLA	Boeing 737-45D	27131 / 2458		0493	0493	2 CFMI CFM56-3C1	62823	CY147	CK-BR	lsf Marta Leasing Ltd, Cayman Islands
□ SP-LLB	Boeing 737-45D	27156 / 2492		0693	0693	2 CFMI CFM56-3C1	62823	CY147	CK-BS	lsf Marta Leasing Ltd, Cayman Islands
□ SP-LLC	Boeing 737-45D	27157 / 2502		0793	0793	2 CFMI CFM56-3C1	62823	CY147	CK-DR	lsf Marta Leasing Ltd, Cayman Islands
□ SP-LLD	Boeing 737-45D	27256 / 2589		0394	0394	2 CFMI CFM56-3C1	62823	CY147	CK-DS	lsf Marta Leasing Ltd, Cayman Islands
□ SP-LLE	Boeing 737-45D	27914 / 2804	N1786B*	0696	0796	2 CFMI CFM56-3C1	62823	CY147	EP-FH	lsf Marta Leasing Ltd, Cayman Islands
□ SP-LLF	Boeing 737-45D	28752 / 2874		0497	0497	2 CFMI CFM56-3C1	62823	CY147	RS-AF	lsf FSBU Trustee, USA
□ SP-LLG	Boeing 737-45D	28753 / 2895		0697	0697	2 CFMI CFM56-3C1	62823	CY147	RS-AG	lsf FSBU Trustee, USA
□ SP-	Boeing 737-85D					2 CFMI CFM56-7B26	78245	CY165		oo-delivery 0503
□ SP-	Boeing 737-85D					2 CFMI CFM56-7B26	78245	CY165		oo-delivery 0503
□ SP-LOA	Boeing 767-25D (ER)	24733 / 261	N6046P*	0489	0489	2 GE CF6-80C2B4	156500	C12Y190	BQ-CL	Gniezno / lsf FSBU Trustee, USA
□ SP-LOB	Boeing 767-25D (ER)	24734 / 266		0589	0589	2 GE CF6-80C2B4	156500	C12Y190	BQ-CM	Krakow / lsf FSBU Trustee, USA
□ SP-LPA	Boeing 767-35D (ER)	24865 / 322		0890	0890	2 GE CF6-80C2B6	172400	C18Y225	LQ-GK	Warszawa / lsf FSBU Trustee, USA
□ SP-LPB	Boeing 767-35D (ER)	27902 / 577		0595	0595	2 GE CF6-80C2B6	172400	C18Y225	HS-CD	Gdansk / lsf FSBU Trustee, USA
□ SP-LPC	Boeing 767-35D (ER)	28656 / 659		0597	0597	2 GE CF6-80C2B6	172400	C18Y225	LM-JP	Poznan

PPL Przedsiebiorstwo Panstwowe "Porty Lotnicze" (Polish Airports State Enterprise-Flight Inspection Dept.) **Warsaw-Okecie**

Dzial Inspekcji Lotniczej, ul. Zwirki Wigury 1, PL-00-906 Warszawa, Poland ☎ (22) 650 14 29 Tx: 813553 zrl pl Fax: (22) 846 53 85 SITA: n/a
F: 1968 ⁂ 21 Head: Tadeusz Dalewski Net: n/a Non-commercial state organisation conducting navigation and flight-inspection flights.

□ SP-TPA	Let 410UVP-E15	892318		0089		2 WA M-601E	6400	Calibrator		
□ SP-TPB	Let 410UVP-E15	892329		0089		2 WA M-601E	6400	Calibrator		

SKYPOL = PZL (Division of PZL Panstwowe Zaklady Lotnicze Warszawa-Okecie, S.A.) **Warsaw-Okecie**

Aleja Krakowska 110/114, PL-00-971 Warszawa, Poland ☎ (22) 46 63 45 Tx: 813465 pl Fax: (22) 46 54 79 SITA: n/a
F: 1993 ⁂ n/a Head: Zdzislaw Jablonski ICAO: SKYPOL-AIR Net: n/a Suspended operations (with Fairchild SA227AC Metro III-aircraft) 0398. Intends to restart.

TASAWI AIR SERVICES, Ltd = 9X / TWI (Przedsiebiorstwo Lotnicze TASAWI, Spolka z o.o. dba) **Szczecin**

Ul. Przestrzenna 10, PL-70 800 Szczecin, Poland ☎ (91) 434 20 03 Tx: none Fax: (91) 434 25 03 SITA: n/a
F: 1989 ⁂ 20 Head: Andrzej Woitozuk ICAO: TASAWI Net: n/a Aircraft below MTOW 1361kg: PZL-104 & PZL-110

□ SP-FTG	BAe 3102 Jetstream 31	655	G-ENIS	0084	1095	2 GA TPE331-10UG-513H	6950	Y18		lsf BAMT
□ SP-FTH	BAe 3102 Jetstream 31	649	G-SWAD	0084	0196	2 GA TPE331-10UG-513H	6950	Y18		lsf BAMT

TURAVIA Air Transport & Travel, Ltd = TUV (Przedsiebiorstwo Uslug Lotniczych i Turystycznych TURAVIA, Spolka z o.o dba) **Katowice**

Katowice-Pyrzowice Airport, PL-41-960 Ozarowice, Poland ☎ (32) 284 50 25 Tx: none Fax: (32) 284 50 15 SITA: n/a
F: 1987 ⁂ 20 Head: Eugeniusz Piechoczek ICAO: TURAVIA Net: n/a Also leases Mil Mi-2 & Let 410UVP from WOKTRANS (SP-), BN-2A from WALPHOT (OO-) & Piper PA-31-350 from EUROSENSE (PH-), when required.

□ SP-FDM	PZL Swidnik (Mil) Mi-2	525141027	SP-SBE	0077	0097	2 IS GTD-350-4	3550			

URZAD MORSKI w Gdyni – Maritime Board in Gdynia **Gdynia**

Ul. Chrzanowskiego 10, PL-81-338 Gdynia, Poland ☎ (58) 620 69 11 Tx: none Fax: (58) 620 67 43 SITA: n/a
F: 1928 ⁂ 800 Head: Pawel Czerwinski Net: n/a Non-commercial state organisation conducting surveillance and inspection flights.

□ SP-SHO	PZL Swidnik (Mil) Mi-2	515039017		0077		2 IS GTD-350-4	3550	Surveyer		
□ SP-MBA	Let 410UVP-E2	861803		0086		2 WA M-601E	6400	Surveyer		

WHITE EAGLE AVIATION, Spolka z o.o = WEA (formerly White Eagle General Aviation, Ltd) **Warsaw-Okecie**

Zwirki-i-Wigury 1, PL-00-906 Warszawa, Poland ☎ (22) 650 10 30 Tx: none Fax: (22) 650 16 40 SITA: AWWEAXH
F: 1992 ⁂ 110 Head: Jan Szczepkowski ICAO: WHITE EAGLE Net: n/a Aircraft below MTOW 1361kg: Aero CSS-13 & PZL-104

□ SP-FNK	Beech Bonanza A36	E-3014	N3263W	0096		1 CO IO-550-B	1656			
□ SP-FDN	Bell 407	53051	N1119J	0096	0197	1 AN 250-C47B	2268			
□ SP-FMN	PZL Mielec (Antonov) An-2	1G177-21	SP-TWE	0077		1 SH ASh-62IR	5500			
□ SP-FYM	PZL Mielec (Antonov) An-2TP	1G137-58	SP-TBM	0071	0096	1 SH ASh-62IR	5500			
□ SP-FYO	PZL Mielec (Antonov) An-2P	1G185-56	SP-TBK	0080	0096	1 SH ASh-62IR	5500			
□ SP-FTN	Let 410UVP-E10	902515	SP-FGI	0090	0395	2 WA M-601E	6400	C14 or Y16		
□ SP-FTV	Let 410UVP-E	882038	SP-TAA	0088	0096	2 WA M-601E	6400	C14 or Y16		
□ SP-FTX	Let 410UVP-E10	892301	SP-TAB	0089	0096	2 WA M-601E	6400	C14 or Y16		
□ SP-FTY	Let 410UVP-E10	892317	SP-TAC	0089	0096	2 WA M-601E	6400	C14 or Y16		
□ SP-FNS	Beech King Air 350 (B300)	FL-134	N3252V	0096	0998	2 PWC PT6A-60A	6804			lsf Prokom Investments
□ SP-FES	Mil Mi-8	99150472		0091	0498	2 IS TV2-117A	12000			lsf Universal Leasing
□ SP-FYS	Yakovlev 40	9412032	LY-AAD	0074	1097	3 IV AI-25	16800	Y23		
□ SP-FYT	Yakovlev 40	9641851	LY-AAZ	0077	1097	3 IV AI-25	16800	Y23		
□ SP-FYU	Yakovlev 40	9211821	UR-87566	0072	0199	3 IV AI-25	16800	VIP C4 or Y12		
□ SP-FNF	Fokker F27 Friendship 600 (F27 Mk600)	10179	D-BAKD	0061	0797	2 RR Dart 532-7	19370	Freighter		Blue Eyes / lsf WDL/cvtd -200 / opf UPS

WOKTRANS – Wojewodzka Kolumna Transportu Sanitarnego = WKT (Ambulance Air Service of the Ministry of Health & Social Care) **Warsaw-Babice**

c/o Centralny Zespol Lotnictwa Sanitarnego, ul. Ksiezycowa 5, PL-01-934 Warszawa, Poland ☎ (22) 834 91 19 Tx: 816480 czls pl Fax: (22) 834 91 19 SITA: n/a
F: n/a ⁂ 100 Head: Zdzislaw Olszanski ICAO: WOKTRANS Net: n/a Operates EMS/Ambulance flights for the non-commercial state organisation LOTNICZE POGOTOWIE RATUNKOWE-Ambulance Air Service, a division of Centralny Zespol Lotnictwa Sanitarnego/Association of the Flight Ambulance Teams) through 14 units from 14 bases at: Bialystock, Bydgoszcz, Gdansk, Katowice, Kielce, Krakow, Lublin, Olsztyn, Poznan, Sanok, Szczecin, Warszawa, Wroclaw, Zielona Gora.

□ SP-NXK	Let 200D Morava	170908	SP-NRH	0061		2 WA M-337	1950	EMS		
□ SP-NXL	Let 200D Morava	171014	CCCP-34513	0061		2 WA M-337	1950	EMS		
□ SP-NXN	Let 200D Morava	171401	HB-LCU	0065	0796	2 WA M-337	1950	EMS		
□ SP-NXT	Let 200D Morava	171327	SP-NPB	0064		2 WA M-337	1950	EMS		
□ SP-NXX	Let 200D Morava	171206	HA-LDA	0062	1196	2 WA M-337	1950	EMS		
□ SP-NXY	Let 200D Morava	171402	SP-NAC	0065		2 WA M-337	1950	EMS		
□ SP-NXZ	Let 200D Morava	171203	SP-NAB	0062		2 WA M-337	1950	EMS		
□ SP-MXA	PZL Mielec M-20 Mewa	1AH002-08	SP-DMB	0090		2 CO T/LSIO-360-KB	2070	EMS		
□ SP-MXB	PZL Mielec M-20 Mewa	1AH002-12		0091	1291	2 CO T/LSIO-360-KB	2070	EMS		
□ SP-MXC	PZL Mielec M-20 Mewa	1AH002-14		0093		2 CO T/LSIO-360-KB	2070	EMS		
□ SP-MXD	PZL Mielec M-20 Mewa	1AH002-09	SP-FMI	0090		2 CO T/LSIO-360-KB	2070	EMS		
□ SP-SXB	PZL Swidnik (Mil) Mi-2	517301081		0081		2 IS GTD-350-4	3550	EMS		
□ SP-SXF	PZL Swidnik (Mil) Mi-2	519845076		0086		2 IS GTD-350-4	3550	EMS		
□ SP-SXG	PZL Swidnik (Mil) Mi-2	519943106		0086		2 IS GTD-350-4	3550	EMS		
□ SP-WXB	PZL Swidnik (Mil) Mi-2	542449072		0072		2 IS GTD-350-4	3550	EMS		
□ SP-WXD	PZL Swidnik (Mil) Mi-2	512723122		0072		2 IS GTD-350-4	3550	EMS		
□ SP-WXI	PZL Swidnik (Mil) Mi-2	513311123		0073		2 IS GTD-350-4	3550	EMS		
□ SP-WXL	PZL Swidnik (Mil) Mi-2	513901124		0075		2 IS GTD-350-4	3550	EMS		
□ SP-WXN	PZL Swidnik (Mil) Mi-2	513902015		0075		2 IS GTD-350-4	3550	EMS		
□ SP-WXS	PZL Swidnik (Mil) Mi-2	513906015		0075		2 IS GTD-350-4	3550	EMS		
□ SP-WXT	PZL Swidnik (Mil) Mi-2	513905015		0075		2 IS GTD-350-4	3550	EMS		
□ SP-WXU	PZL Swidnik (Mil) Mi-2	514045035		0075		2 IS GTD-350-4	3550	EMS		
□ SP-WXZ	PZL Swidnik (Mil) Mi-2	513911015		0075		2 IS GTD-350-4	3550	EMS		
□ SP-ZXC	PZL Swidnik (Mil) Mi-2	514408105		0075		2 IS GTD-350-4	3550	EMS		
□ SP-ZXE	PZL Swidnik (Mil) Mi-2	544304085		0075		2 IS GTD-350-4	3550	EMS		
□ SP-ZXO	PZL Swidnik (Mil) Mi-2	515032126		0076		2 IS GTD-350-4	3550	EMS		
□ SP-ZXP	PZL Swidnik (Mil) Mi-2	515032116		0076		2 IS GTD-350-4	3550	EMS		
□ SP-ZXU	PZL Swidnik (Mil) Mi-2	515823108		0078		2 IS GTD-350-4	3550	EMS		
□ SP-ZXY	PZL Swidnik (Mil) Mi-2	516531030		0080		2 IS GTD-350-4	3550	EMS		
□ SP-ZXZ	PZL Swidnik (Mil) Mi-2	515643068		0078		2 IS GTD-350-4	3550	EMS		opf Central Childrens Hospital
□ SP-UXE	PZL Mielec (Antonov) An-2S	1G211-01		0085		1 SH ASh-62IR	5500	EMS		
□ SP-UXI	PZL Mielec (Antonov) An-2S	1G214-07		0085		1 SH ASh-62IR	5500	EMS		
□ SP-TXA	Let 410UVP-E16	892319		0089		2 WA M-601E	6400	EMS		
□ SP-TXB	Let 410UVP-E16A	902414		0090	1090	2 WA M-601E	6400	EMS		
□ SP-SXU	PZL Swidnik W-3 Sokol	320210		0088		2 PZL-10W	6400	EMS		
□ SP-SXZ	PZL Swidnik W-3A Sokol	320507	SP-SYE	0094		2 PZL-10W	6400	EMS		

590 registration type of aircraft cn/fn ex/ex* mfd del powered by mtow kg configuration selcal name/fln/specialitites/remarks

Government / Corporate / Executive / VIP Aircraft

	registration	type of aircraft	cn/fn	ex/ex*	mfd	del	powered by	mtow kg	configuration	selcal	name/fln/remarks
☐	ST-AOQ	De Havilland DHC-6 Twin Otter 300	778	HB-LRE	0081	0195	2 PWC PT6A-27	5670	Corporate		A.M.C. Ariab Mining Company
☐	ST-PRS	Dassault Falcon 20F	372	F-WRQV*	0077	0178	2 GE CF700-2D2	13000	VIP		Gvmt
☐	ST-PSR	Dassault Falcon 50	114	F-WPXM*	0082	0783	3 GA TFE731-3-1C	17600	VIP		Gvmt

AIR WEST, Co. Ltd
Khartoum

PO Box 10217, Khartoum, Sudan   ☎ (11) 45 17 03   Tx: 23068 sd   Fax: (11) 45 17 03   SITA: n/a
F: 1992   ✠✠ 30   Head: Capt. Saif M.S. Omer   Net: n/a

	registration	type of aircraft	cn/fn	ex/ex*	mfd	del	powered by	mtow kg	configuration	selcal	remarks
☐	ST-AOZ	Antonov 26					2 IV AI-24VT	24000	Freighter		
☐	ST-APO	Antonov 26					2 IV AI-24VT	24000	Freighter		
☐	ST-AWM	Antonov 12B	5343704	RA-11003	0065	0098	4 IV AI-20M	61000	Freighter		

AZZA TRANSPORT Company Limited = AZZ
Khartoum

PO Box 16, Khartoum, Sudan   ☎ (11) 77 97 17   Tx: 22172 hisea sd   Fax: (11) 77 04 08   SITA: n/a
F: 1993   ✠✠ 90   Head: Dr. Gibril I. Mohd   ICAO: AZZA TRANSPORT   Net: n/a

	registration	type of aircraft	cn/fn	ex/ex*	mfd	del	powered by	mtow kg	configuration	selcal	remarks
☐	ST-JCC	Boeing 707-384C	18948 / 495	P4-JCC	0666	0597	4 PW JT3D-3B (HK2/COM)	152000	Freighter		lsf Comtran Int'l
☐	P4-AKW	Boeing 707-330C	20123 / 788	ST-AKW	0069	0894	4 PW JT3D-3B	150139	Freighter	HM-FG	lsf Ibis Aviation Aruba
☐	ST-APS	Ilyushin 76TD	1023409316	EW-76837	0092	0096	4 SO D-30KP	190000	Freighter		lsf BEL

BLUE BIRD AVIATION, Co. Ltd
Khartoum

PO Box 11025, Khartoum, Sudan   ☎ (11) 77 24 07   Tx: 22548 nico sd   Fax: (11) 77 63 28   SITA: n/a
F: n/a   ✠✠ n/a   Head: n/a   Net: n/a   Aircraft below MTOW 1361kg: Piper PA-28.

	registration	type of aircraft	cn/fn	ex/ex*	mfd	del	powered by	mtow kg	configuration	selcal	remarks
☐	ST-AIO	Cessna U206F Stationair	U20602107	5Y-HSP	0073		1 CO IO-520-F	1633			
☐	ST-AIP	Cessna 205 (210-5)	205-0229	5Y-ASC	0063		1 CO IO-470-S	1497			

CAMP AVIATION SERVICE, Ltd
Khartoum

PO Box 44887, Khartoum, Sudan   ☎ (11) 77 42 80   Tx: 24198 campa sd   Fax: n/a   SITA: n/a
F: n/a   ✠✠ n/a   Head: n/a   Net: n/a   Operates charter flights with aircraft leased from other companies when required.

DATA INTERNATIONAL AVIATION, Ltd
Khartoum

PO Box 8288 Al Amarat, Khartoum, Sudan   ☎ (11) 77 55 54   Tx: n/a   Fax: n/a   SITA: n/a
F: 1995   ✠✠ n/a   Head: n/a   ICAO: DATA AIR   Net: n/a

	registration	type of aircraft	cn/fn	ex/ex*	mfd	del	powered by	mtow kg	configuration	selcal	remarks
☐	ST-APU	Antonov 12B				0095	4 IV AI-20M	61000	Freighter		

ELDINDER AVIATION, Co. = DND
Khartoum

PO Box 2247, Khartoum, Sudan   ☎ (11) 44 52 53   Tx: 22955 icl sd   Fax: (11) 45 21 30   SITA: n/a
F: 1989   ✠✠ 30   Head: Salah Eldin Satti   ICAO: DINDER   Net: n/a

	registration	type of aircraft	cn/fn	ex/ex*	mfd	del	powered by	mtow kg	configuration	selcal	remarks
☐	ST-DND	Let 410UVP-E10A	912528	SP-FGH	0091	0995	2 WA M-601E	6400	Y19		

FARNAS AVIATION SERVICES = RAF
Khartoum

PO Box 3494, Khartoum, Sudan   ☎ (11) 77 96 98   Tx: n/a   Fax: n/a   SITA: n/a
F: 1993   ✠✠ n/a   Head: n/a   ICAO: FARNAS   Net: n/a

	registration	type of aircraft	cn/fn	ex/ex*	mfd	del	powered by	mtow kg	configuration	selcal	remarks
☐	ST-FAS	Antonov 32					2 IV AI-20D	27500	Freighter		

FEDERAL AIRLINES = FLL
Khartoum

PO Box 44887, Khartoum, Sudan   ☎ (11) 54 18 55   Tx: n/a   Fax: n/a   SITA: n/a
F: 1994   ✠✠ n/a   Head: n/a   ICAO: FEDERAL AIRLINES   Net: n/a

	registration	type of aircraft	cn/fn	ex/ex*	mfd	del	powered by	mtow kg	configuration	selcal	remarks
☐	ST-AOE	Antonov 24					2 IV AI-24	21250			
☐	ST-FAL	Antonov 24					2 IV AI-24	21250			

GOLDEN STAR AIR CARGO, Co Ltd = GLD
Khartoum

PO Box 4158, Khartoum, Sudan   ☎ (11) 78 43 21   Tx: 22575 gold sd   Fax: (11) 77 29 18   SITA: n/a
F: 1986   ✠✠ 30   Head: Omer Ali Abdel Magid   ICAO: GOLDEN STAR   Net: n/a   Operates all-cargo services with freighter-aircraft, leased from other companies when required.

IBK-PETRA AVIATION = AKI
Khartoum

PO Box 11874, Khartoum, Sudan   ☎ (11) 77 42 80   Tx: n/a   Fax: n/a   SITA: n/a
F: 1993   ✠✠ n/a   Head: n/a   Net: n/a

	registration	type of aircraft	cn/fn	ex/ex*	mfd	del	powered by	mtow kg	configuration	selcal	remarks
☐	ST-IPK	Antonov 26B	14402	RA-26213	0085	0094	2 IV AI-24VT	24000	Freighter		

NILE SAFARIS AVIATON, Ltd = NSA (formerly Nile Safaris, Co. Ltd)
Khartoum

PO Box 2711, Khartoum, Sudan   ☎ (11) 77 35 38   Tx: 22150 hunt sd   Fax: n/a   SITA: n/a
F: 1958   ✠✠ 80   Head: Joseph G. Kaikati   ICAO: NILE SAFARIS   Net: n/a

	registration	type of aircraft	cn/fn	ex/ex*	mfd	del	powered by	mtow kg	configuration	selcal	remarks
☐	ST-AGV	Cessna 210L Centurion II	21061205	G-BEOR	0076		1 CO IO-520-L	1724			
☐	ST-AIS	Cessna T210N Turbo Centurion II	21062987	N28DM	0079		1 CO TSIO-520-R	1814			
☐	ST-AJP	Cessna T210N Turbo Centurion II	21063022	PH-KJE	0079		1 CO TSIO-520-R	1814			
☐	ST-AGU	Cessna 402B II	402B1058	G-BEOP	0076		2 CO TSIO-520-E	2858			
☐	ST-AIY	Britten-Norman BN-2A-26 Islander	144	G-AXXH	0070		2 LY O-540-E4C5	2994			
☐	ST-AJE	Cessna 404 Titan II	404-0135	N37173	0077		2 CO GTSIO-520-M	3810			

OMRANCO TRANSPORT, Tourism & Trading, Co. Ltd (Subsidiary of Pezetel, Poland/Associated with Sudana Pezetel, Sudan)
Hasaheisa

PO Box 3841, Khartoum, Sudan   ☎ (11) 78 15 89   Tx: 22492 atab sd   Fax: (11) 77 40 97   SITA: n/a
F: 1990   ✠✠ 16   Head: Suliman El Bashir Hamid   Net: n/a   Ag-aircraft below MTOW 5000kg: PZL-106 Kruk.

	registration	type of aircraft	cn/fn	ex/ex*	mfd	del	powered by	mtow kg	configuration	selcal	remarks
☐	ST-ALZ	PZL Mielec (Antonov) An-2R	1G221-50	SP-ZFF	0086	0092	1 SH ASh-62IR	5500			

RIC AVIATION, Co. Ltd
Khartoum

PO Box 2669, Khartoum, Sudan   ☎ (11) 22 46 00   Tx: n/a   Fax: n/a   SITA: n/a
F: n/a   ✠✠ n/a   Head: n/a   Net: n/a

	registration	type of aircraft	cn/fn	ex/ex*	mfd	del	powered by	mtow kg	configuration	selcal	remarks
☐	ST-ANM	PZL Mielec (Antonov) An-2					1 SH ASh-62IR	5500			
☐	ST-AOF	Antonov 26					2 IV AI-24VT	24000	Freighter		
☐	ST-ANL	Antonov 12B					4 IV AI-20M	61000	Freighter		

SALPA AVIATION, Co. Ltd = SLP
Khartoum

PO Box 10421, Khartoum, Sudan   ☎ (11) 77 59 60   Tx: 22493 salpa sd   Fax: (11) 77 96 73   SITA: n/a
F: 1992   ✠✠ n/a   Head: n/a   ICAO: SALPA   Net: n/a   Operates charter flights, currently with aircraft leased from other companies when required.

SASCO AIR LINES = SAC (Sudanese Aeronautical Services, Co. Ltd dba/division of Nur Aviation Services)
Khartoum

PO Box 8260, Khartoum, Sudan   ☎ (11) 74 33 62   Tx: 22048 nurco sd   Fax: n/a   SITA: n/a
F: n/a   ✠✠ 40   Head: M.M. Nur   ICAO: SASCO   Net: n/a

	registration	type of aircraft	cn/fn	ex/ex*	mfd	del	powered by	mtow kg	configuration	selcal	remarks
☐	ST-NUR	Cessna T210N Turbo Centurion II	21063877	D-EJWS	0080		1 CO TSIO-520-R	1814			
☐	ST-ASH	Piper PA-23-250 Aztec E	27-7405257	G-BBYK	0074		2 LY IO-540-C4B5	2359			
☐	ST-AHL	Boeing (Douglas) DC-3C (C-47B-5-DK)	26095	5Y-BAX	0044		2 PW R-1830	12701			

SFT SUDANESE FLIGHT = STF (Sudanese Flight Trading & Services, Co. Ltd dba)
Khartoum

PO Box 2264, Khartoum, Sudan   ☎ (11) 77 71 62   Tx: n/a   Fax: n/a   SITA: n/a
F: 1992   ✠✠ n/a   Head: n/a   Net: n/a   Operates charter flights, currently with aircraft leased from other companies when required.

SUDAN AIRWAYS = SD / SUD
Khartoum

PO Box 253, Khartoum, Sudan   ☎ (11) 74 79 53   Tx: 22257 sudanair sd   Fax: (11) 74 79 78   SITA: n/a
F: 1947   ✠✠ 1900   Head: Dr. Elfatih Mohammed Ali   IATA: 200   ICAO: SUDANAIR   Net: n/a

	registration	type of aircraft	cn/fn	ex/ex*	mfd	del	powered by	mtow kg	configuration	selcal	name/remarks
☐	ST-ANH	Beech King Air C90	LJ-823	N580C	0079		2 PWC PT6A-21	4377	Exec / Trainer		
☐	ST-AHT	De Havilland DHC-6 Twin Otter 300	238	N5584H	0069	1081	2 PWC PT6A-27	5670	Y19		opf UNICEF
☐	ST-SFS	Beech King Air 200	BB-539	N555SK	0079		2 PWC PT6A-41	5670	Exec / Trainer		
☐	ST-AFK	Boeing 737-2J8C (A)	21169 / 429		0075	0975	2 PW JT8D-7	52617	F10Y94	DE-CK	White Nile
☐	ST-AFA	Boeing 707-3J8C	20897 / 885		0074	0674	4 PW JT3D-7	150411	F12Y141	DE-AJ	Blue Nile
☐	ST-AFB	Boeing 707-3J8C	20898 / 887		0074	0774	4 PW JT3D-7	150411	Freighter	DE-AK	Blue Nile
☐	ST-AIX	Boeing 707-369C	20086 / 764	9K-ACL	0068	0184	4 PW JT3D-3B	151364	F12Y141	DG-BF	Blue Nile
☐	F-ODTK	Airbus Industrie A300-622 (A300B4-622)	252	F-WZLR	0083	0594	2 PW PW4158	165000	F26Y249	AJ-DM	lsf Credit Lyonnais
☐	F-OIHA	Airbus Industrie A300-622R (A300B4-622R)	530	F-WHPI	0089	0898	2 PW PW4158	170500	F26Y249		lsf Airbus Industrie Financial Services

TRAMSON AIRLINES, Ltd = TRR
Khartoum

PO Box 2592, Khartoum, Sudan   ☎ (11) 77 85 88   Tx: 22209 sd   Fax: n/a   SITA: n/a
F: n/a   ✠✠ n/a   Head: n/a   ICAO: TRAMSON   Net: n/a   Operates charter flights with freighter aircraft, leased from other companies when required.

TRANS ARABIAN AIR TRANSPORT – T.A.A.T. = TRT
Khartoum   **TRANS ARABIAN** AIR TRANSPORT   ترانز ارابيان للنقل الجوى

PO Box 1461, Khartoum, Sudan   ☎ (11) 45 15 68   Tx: 24160 taat sd   Fax: (11) 45 15 44   SITA: n/a
F: 1983   ✠✠ 220   Head: Capt. M. Hassan Y. Kordofani   ICAO: TRANS ARABIAN   Net: n/a

	registration	type of aircraft	cn/fn	ex/ex*	mfd	del	powered by	mtow kg	configuration	selcal	name/remarks
☐	ST-AMF	Boeing 707-321C	19367 / 637	VR-HKL	0067	1092	4 PW JT3D-3B (HK2/COM)	150957	Freighter	GK-EL	lsf Transasian Air Leasing
☐	ST-APY	Boeing 707-351C	19412 / 563	N707DY	0067	0897	4 PW JT3D-3B (HK2/COM)	146193	Freighter	CD-JK	
☐	5X-ARJ	Boeing 707-351C	19632 / 649	ST-ANP	0067	0294	4 PW JT3D-3B (HK2/COM)	151500	Freighter	CF-AD	lsf TAAT Uganda Ltd

TROPICAL AVIATION, Ltd — Khartoum

PO Box 8151, Khartoum, Sudan ☎ (11) 77 71 91 Tx: n/a Fax: n/a SITA: n/a
F: n/a 👪 n/a Head: n/a Net: n/a Aircraft below MTOW 1361 kg: Piper PA-28.

☐ ST-AHI	Piper PA-31-310 Navajo	31-669	G-BGAC	0070		2 LY TIO-540-A1A	2948			
☐ ST-AHZ	Piper PA-31-310 Navajo	31-473	G-AXMR	0069		2 LY TIO-540-A1A	2948			

SU = EGYPT (Arab Republic of Egypt) (Jumhouriya Misr al-Arabiya)

Capital: Cairo Official Language: Arabic Population: 65,0 million Square Km: 1001449 Dialling code: +20 Year established: 1922 Acting political head: Mohamed Hosni Mubarak (President)

Government / Corporate / Executive / VIP Aircraft Hercules aircraft are operating cargo flights for Egypt Air from time to time.

☐ SU-ARR	Westland Commando Mk. 2E	WA867		0084		2 RR Gnome H.1400-1	9525	VIP		741 / Gvmt
☐ SU-AXJ	Boeing 707-366C	20919 / 888		0074	0974	4 PW JT3D-7 (HK2/COM)	151091	VIP 70 Pax	DK-CM	Egyptian 01 / Gvmt
☐ SU-AXN	Dassault Falcon 20E-5	294	F-BVPM	0073		2 GA TFE731-5AR-2C	13200	VIP		Gvmt / cvtd 20E
☐ SU-AYD	Dassault Falcon 20F	361	F-WMKF*	0077		2 GE CF700-2D2	13000	VIP		Gvmt
☐ SU-AZJ	Dassault Falcon 20F-5	358	F-WRQY*	0077		2 GA TFE731-5AR-2C	13200	VIP		Gvmt / cvtd 20F
☐ SU-BAM	Lockheed L-382C (VC-130H) Hercules	81D-4803	78-0760	0078	0179	4 AN T56-A-15	70307	VIP / Combi		1281 / Arab Republic of Egypt Air Force
☐ SU-BGM	GAC G-IV Gulfstream IV	1048	N448GA*	0088	0589	2 RR Tay 611-8	33203	VIP	AF-EQ	Gvmt
☐ SU-BGU	GAC G-1159A Gulfstream III	439	N17586*	0085		2 RR Spey 511-8	31615	VIP		Gvmt
☐ SU-BGV	GAC G-1159A Gulfstream III	442	N17587*	0085		2 RR Spey 511-8	31615	VIP		Gvmt
☐ SU-BNC	GAC G-IV Gulfstream IV (SP)	1329	N329GA*	0098	0098	2 RR Tay 611-8	33838	VIP		Gvmt
☐ SU-BND	GAC G-IV Gulfstream IV (SP)	1332	N332GA*	0098	0098	2 RR Tay 611-8	33838	VIP		Gvmt
☐ SU-GGG	Airbus Industrie A340-212	061	F-WWJI*	0094	0295	4 CFMI CFM56-5C3	257000	VIP 97Pax	GS-LR	Gvmt

AIR CAIRO (Associated with Kato Aromatic, Egypt) — Cairo

Export Centre, Cairo Int'l Airport, Helipolis, Cairo, Egypt ☎ (2) 267 14 56 Tx: none Fax: (2) 267 06 83 SITA: n/a
F: 1997 👪 n/a Head: Roger Braithwaite Net: n/a

☐ SU-EAF	Tupolev 204-120	1450743764027	RA-64027*	0097	1198	2 RR RB211-535E4-B	103000	Y208		lsf SIRO
☐ SU-EAG	Tupolev 204-120C	1450743764028		0097	1198	2 RR RB211-535E4-B	103000	Freighter 25t		lsf SIRO
☐ SU-	Tupolev 204-120					2 RR RB211-535E4-B	103000	Y208		to be lsf SIRO 0399
☐ SU-	Tupolev 204-120					2 RR RB211-535E4-B	103000	Y208		to be lsf SIRO 1199
☐ SU-	Tupolev 204-120C					2 RR RB211-535E4-B	103000	Freighter 25t		to be lsf SIRO 1199

AIR MEMPHIS, Inc. = MHS — Cairo

4 Ahmed Lotfy Street, Elnozha Elgedida, Heliopolis, Egypt ☎ (2) 296 66 20 Tx: none Fax: (2) 297 57 62 SITA: CAIAMCR
F: 1995 👪 100 Head: Hamdy Eisa ICAO: AIR MEMPHIS Net: n/a

☐ SU-AVZ	Boeing 707-366C	20762 / 868		0073	0598	4 PW JT3D-7 (HK2/COM)	151091	Freighter	AE-CJ	lsf TriStar Air Leasing
☐ SU-PBB	Boeing 707-328C	19916 / 762	SU-DAA	0068	1196	4 PW JT3D-3B (HK2/COM)	151046	Freighter		

AIR SINAI = 4D / ASD — Cairo

12 Kasr el Nil Street, Cairo, Egypt ☎ (2) 77 49 66 Tx: 95020 un Fax: (2) 574 47 11 SITA: CAIGC4D
F: 1982 👪 150 Head: Laurice Farid IATA: 903 ICAO: AIR SINAI Net: n/a

☐ SU-GAN	Boeing 737-2N7 (A)	21226 / 458	SU-AYN	0076	1089	2 PW JT8D-17	54204	Y121	FK-BD	occ lsf MSR / Air Sinai-titles
☐ SU-GBK	Boeing 737-566	26052 / 2276		0092	1097	2 CFMI CFM56-3C1	60555	F8Y96	DP-GQ	occ lsf MSR / Air Sinai-titles

AMC AVIATION = AMV (Aircraft Maintenance Company dba) — Cairo

5 El Nasr Street, El Nozha El Guedida, Cairo, Egypt ☎ (2) 299 02 22 Tx: 22243 amcho un Fax: (2) 299 23 02 SITA: n/a
F: 1994 👪 n/a Head: Eng. El Sayed Saber Mahmoud Net: n/a

☐ SU-AYK	Boeing 737-266 (A)	21194 / 455		0076	0993	2 PW JT8D-17	52390	Y127	GJ-BH	
☐ SU-BMQ	Boeing (Douglas) MD-90-30 (ER)	53576 / 2195		0097	0997	2 IAE V2528-D5	76204	Y170		
☐ SU-BMM	Airbus Industrie A300B4-203	175	SU-DAR	0082	0496	2 GE CF6-50C2	165000	Y287		Zeiad

EGYPT AIR = MS / MSR (formerly United Arab Airlines – UAA) — Cairo

Cairo International Airport, Heliopolis, Egypt ☎ (2) 390 24 44 Tx: 92116 egyop un Fax: (2) 390 15 57 SITA: CAIGCMS
F: 1932 👪 13000 Head: Eng. Mohamed Fahim Rayan IATA: 077 ICAO: EGYPTAIR Net: n/a

☐ SU-AYL	Boeing 737-266 (A)	21195 / 457		0076	0476	2 PW JT8D-17	54204	Y130	GJ-BK	Hapi / all white colors
☐ SU-AYO	Boeing 737-266 (A)	21227 / 466		0076	0776	2 PW JT8D-17	54204	Y130	FK-BE	Hathor
☐ SU-GAN	Boeing 737-2N7 (A)	21226 / 458	SU-AYN	0076	0686	2 PW JT8D-17	54204	Y121	FK-BD	occ lst ASD / Air Sinai-titles
☐ SU-GBH	Boeing 737-566	25084 / 2019		0091	0491	2 CFMI CFM56-3C1	60555	F8Y96	DP-CQ	Karnak
☐ SU-GBI	Boeing 737-566	25307 / 2135		0091	1091	2 CFMI CFM56-3C1	60555	F8Y96	DP-EQ	Abou Simbel
☐ SU-GBJ	Boeing 737-566	25352 / 2169		0091	1191	2 CFMI CFM56-3C1	60555	F8Y96	DP-FQ	Philae
☐ SU-GBK	Boeing 737-566	26052 / 2276		0092	0592	2 CFMI CFM56-3C1	60555	F8Y96	DP-GQ	Kalabsha / occ lst ASD/Air Sinai-titles
☐ SU-GBL	Boeing 737-566	26051 / 2282		0092	0592	2 CFMI CFM56-3C1	60555	F8Y96	DP-HQ	Ramesseum
☐ SU-GBA	Airbus Industrie A320-231	165	F-WWDV*	0091	0591	2 IAE V2500-A1	75500	F10Y135	HM-EQ	Aswan
☐ SU-GBB	Airbus Industrie A320-231	166	F-WWID*	0091	0591	2 IAE V2500-A1	75500	F10Y135	HM-FQ	Luxor
☐ SU-GBC	Airbus Industrie A320-231	178	F-WWIQ*	0091	0691	2 IAE V2500-A1	75500	F10Y135	HM-GQ	Hurghada
☐ SU-GBD	Airbus Industrie A320-231	194	F-WWIZ*	0091	1191	2 IAE V2500-A1	75500	F10Y135	HM-JQ	Taba
☐ SU-GBE	Airbus Industrie A320-231	198	F-WWDG*	0091	1191	2 IAE V2500-A1	75500	F10Y135	HM-KQ	El Alamein
☐ SU-GBF	Airbus Industrie A320-231	351	F-WWDM*	0092	0293	2 IAE V2500-A1	75500	F10Y134	HM-LQ	Sharm El Sheikh
☐ SU-GBG	Airbus Industrie A320-231	366	F-WWDD*	0092	0293	2 IAE V2500-A1	75500	F10Y134	HM-PQ	Saint Catherine
☐ SU-GBT	Airbus Industrie A321-231	680	D-AVZB*	0097	0597	2 IAE V2533-A5	89000	F10Y175	PR-AK	Red Sea
☐ SU-GBU	Airbus Industrie A321-231	687	D-AVZR*	0097	0697	2 IAE V2533-A5	89000	F10Y175	PR-AL	Sinai
☐ SU-GBV	Airbus Industrie A321-231	715	D-AVZX*	0097	0897	2 IAE V2533-A5	89000	F10Y175	PR-AM	Mediterranean
☐ SU-GBW	Airbus Industrie A321-231	725	D-AVZA*	0097	0997	2 IAE V2533-A5	89000	F10Y175	PR-AQ	The Nile
☐ SU-BDG	Airbus Industrie A300B4-203 (F)	200	F-WZMN*	0082	0882	2 GE CF6-50C2	165000	Freighter	BJ-FL	Toshki / cvtd -203
☐ SU-GAC	Airbus Industrie A300B4-203 (F)	255	F-WZMY*	0083	0783	2 GE CF6-50C2	165000	Freighter	BJ-DE	New Valley / cvtd -203
☐ SU-GAR	Airbus Industrie A300-622R (A300B4-622R)	557	F-WWAQ*	0090	0590	2 PW PW4158	170500	F10C13Y230	KQ-EH	Zoser
☐ SU-GAS	Airbus Industrie A300-622R (A300B4-622R)	561	F-WWAN*	0090	0890	2 PW PW4158	170500	F10C13Y230	KQ-EJ	Cheops
☐ SU-GAT	Airbus Industrie A300-622R (A300B4-622R)	572	F-WWAE*	0090	1190	2 PW PW4158	170500	F10C13Y230	KQ-EL	Chephren
☐ SU-GAU	Airbus Industrie A300-622R (A300B4-622R)	575	F-WWAF*	0090	1290	2 PW PW4158	170500	F10C13Y230	KQ-EM	Mycerinus
☐ SU-GAV	Airbus Industrie A300-622R (A300B4-622R)	579	F-WWAJ*	0091	0291	2 PW PW4158	170500	F10C13Y230	KQ-EP	Menes
☐ SU-GAW	Airbus Industrie A300-622R (A300B4-622R)	581	F-WWAL*	0091	0791	2 PW PW4158	170500	F10C13Y230	KQ-FG	Ahmose
☐ SU-GAX	Airbus Industrie A300-622R (A300B4-622R)	601	F-WWAP*	0091	0891	2 PW PW4158	170500	F10C13Y230	KQ-FH	Tut-Ankh-Amun
☐ SU-GAY	Airbus Industrie A300-622R (A300B4-622R)	607	F-WWAB*	0091	0991	2 PW PW4158	170500	F10C13Y230	KQ-FJ	Seti I
☐ SU-GAZ	Airbus Industrie A300-622R (A300B4-622R)	616	F-WWAJ*	0091	1291	2 PW PW4158	170500	F10C13Y230	KQ-FL	
☐ SU-GAO	Boeing 767-366 (ER)	24541 / 275		0089	0889	2 PW PW4060	181437	F10C22Y185	BQ-CJ	Ramses II
☐ SU-GAP	Boeing 767-366 (ER)	24542 / 282		0089	0989	2 PW PW4060	181437	F10C22Y185	BQ-CK	Thutmosis III
☐ SU-GBP	Boeing 777-266 (ER)	28423 / 71		0597	0597	2 PW PW4090	286897	F12C21Y286	PQ-CE	Nefertiti
☐ SU-GBR	Boeing 777-266 (ER)	28424 / 80		0097	0797	2 PW PW4090	286897	F12C21Y286	PQ-BR	Nefertari
☐ SU-GBS	Boeing 777-266 (ER)	28425 / 85		0097	0897	2 PW PW4090	286897	F12C21Y286	PQ-BS	Tyie
☐ SU-GBM	Airbus Industrie A340-212	156	F-WWJK*	0096	1196	4 CFMI CFM56-5C3	260000	F12C24Y224	LQ-HS	Osiris Express
☐ SU-GBN	Airbus Industrie A340-212	159	F-WWJV*	0096	1296	4 CFMI CFM56-5C3	260000	F12C24Y224	LQ-JR	Cleo Express
☐ SU-GBO	Airbus Industrie A340-212	178	F-WWJD*	0097	0697	4 CFMI CFM56-5C3	260000	F12C24Y224	LQ-JS	Hathor Express
☐ SU-	Airbus Industrie A340-642					4 RR Trent 556	365000			oo-delivery 0003
☐ SU-	Airbus Industrie A340-642					4 RR Trent 556	365000			oo-delivery 0004
☐ SU-GAL	Boeing 747-366 (M)	24161 / 704	N6038E*	0088	0688	4 PW JT9D-7R4G2	377842	F18C42Y390	DF-CK	Hatshepsut
☐ SU-GAM	Boeing 747-366 (M)	24162 / 707	N6018N*	0088	0688	4 PW JT9D-7R4G2	377842	F18C42Y390	CE-HL	Cleopatra

LOTUS AIR = TAS — Cairo

Villa 1, Kamal Hassan Ali Street, Behind Sheraton Helipolis Hotel, Heliopolis, Egypt ☎ (2) 266 67 01 Tx: none Fax: (2) 267 44 81 SITA: CAIOK8Q
F: 1997 👪 104 Head: Capt. Ali Dashti ICAO: LOTUS FLOWER Net: n/a

☐ SU-LBA	Airbus Industrie A320-211	371	TC-OND	1192	1297	2 CFMI CFM56-5A1	75500	Y174		The Spirit of Egypt / lsf ILFC
☐ SU-LBB	Airbus Industrie A320-212	814	F-WWII*	0098	0598	2 CFMI CFM56-5A3	75500	Y174		lsf ILFC
☐ SU-LBC	Airbus Industrie A320-212	937	F-WWIS*	0098	0399	2 CFMI CFM56-5A3	75500	Y174		
☐ TC-ONS	Airbus Industrie A321-131	364	D-AVZD*	0393	1098	2 IAE V2530-A5	83000	Y220		Funda / lsf OHY / cvtd -111

LUXOR AIR, Ltd = LXO — Cairo

43 Masr El-Tamir Bldg., Sheraton Heliopolis Housing, First Area, Heliopolis, Egypt ☎ (2) 267 79 36 Tx: none Fax: (2) 266 61 47 SITA: CAILXCR
F: 1997 👪 n/a Head: n/a Net: n/a

☐ SU-BMV	Boeing 707-3B4C	20260 / 823	OD-AFE	0069	0798	4 PW JT3D-3B (HK2/COM)	148325	Y174 or Combi	BE-DM	

NATIONAL AVIATION Company = GTY — Cairo

106 El Nil Street, Dokki-Giza, Egypt ☎ (2) 360 50 20 Tx: 22220 agaty un Fax: (2) 360 39 39 SITA: CAIJLCR
F: 1986 👪 130 Head: Capt. Yahia El Agaty Suspended own operations (with Boeing 707C aircraft) 0598 now acting as a aircraft handling company but intents to re-start own operations during 1999 with 1 Boeing 737.

NATIONAL OVERSEAS AIRLINE – N.O.A. = NOL — Cairo

PO Box 2520, El Horria, Heliopolis (11361), Egypt ☎ (2) 245 48 78 Tx: 23324 noa un Fax: (2) 244 31 20 SITA: n/a
F: 1979 👪 107 Head: Capt. Samir Auf ICAO: NAT AIRLINE Net: n/a

☐ SU-BGO	Reims/Cessna F337F Super Skymaster	F3370055	D-ICCI	0072		2 CO IO-360-C	2100	6 Pax		

592 registration type of aircraft cn/fn ex/ex* mfd del powered by mtow kg configuration selcal name/fln/specialitites/remarks

ORCAAIR = ORK
Sharm El Sheikh

40th Street, 254 Digla, Maadi, Cairo, Egypt ☎ (2) 352 35 29 Tx: 22328 sorat un Fax: (2) 518 28 58 SITA: n/a
F: 1996 ✝✝✝ 106 Head: Diaa El Gabbani ICAO: ORCA TAXI Net: http://www.orca-air.com

☐ SU-UAA	Beech King Air C90B (SE)	LJ-1418		0096	0196	2 PWC PT6A-42	4581	Y6		
☐ SU-UAB	Fairch. (Swearingen) SA227DC Metro 23 (E)	DC-878B		0096	0296	2 GA TPE331-12UHR-701G	7484	Y19		
☐ SU-UAC	Fairch. (Swearingen) SA227DC Metro 23 (E)	DC-879B	N3034P*	0096	0396	2 GA TPE331-12UHR-701G	7484	Y19		
☐ SU-UAD	De Havilland DHC-8-314 Dash 8	290	OE-LLV	0091	0897	2 PWC PW123B	19505	Y50		cvtd -311

PETROLEUM AIR SERVICES – PAS (Associated with Air Logistics International)
Cairo

PO Box 2711, Cairo, Egypt ☎ (2) 262 50 46 Tx: 21404 pas un Fax: (2) 260 21 84 SITA: n/a
F: 1982 ✝✝✝ 400 Head: Amir A. Riad Net: n/a

☐ SU-CAG	Bell 206B JetRanger III	3574		0082		1 AN 250-C20J	1451	4 Pax		
☐ SU-CAH	Bell 206B JetRanger III	3581		0082		1 AN 250-C20J	1451	4 Pax		
☐ SU-CAC	Bell 206L-3 LongRanger III	51004		0082		1 AN 250-C30P	1882	6 Pax		
☐ SU-CAD	Bell 206L-3 LongRanger III	51005		0082		1 AN 250-C30P	1882	6 Pax		
☐ SU-CAE	Bell 206L-3 LongRanger III	51030		0082		1 AN 250-C30P	1882	6 Pax		
☐ SU-CAF	Bell 206L-3 LongRanger III	51031		0082		1 AN 250-C30P	1882	6 Pax		
☐ SU-CAI	Bell 206L-3 LongRanger III	51018		0082		1 AN 250-C30P	1882	6 Pax		
☐ SU-CAK	Bell 206L-3 LongRanger III	51053		0083		1 AN 250-C30P	1882	6 Pax		
☐ SU-CAB	Bell 212	31223		0082		2 PWC PT6T-3B TwinPac	5080	14 Pax		
☐ SU-CAJ	Bell 212	31247		0083		2 PWC PT6T-3B TwinPac	5080	14 Pax		
☐ SU-CAL	Bell 212	31215	N3889A	0082		2 PWC PT6T-3B TwinPac	5080	14 Pax		
☐ SU-CAM	Bell 212	31249		0084		2 PWC PT6T-3B TwinPac	5080	14 Pax		
☐ SU-CAN	Bell 212	31250		0084		2 PWC PT6T-3B TwinPac	5080	14 Pax		
☐ SU-CAO	Bell 212	31260		0084		2 PWC PT6T-3B TwinPac	5080	14 Pax		
☐ SU-CAQ	Bell 212	31262		0084		2 PWC PT6T-3B TwinPac	5080	14 Pax		
☐ SU-CAR	Bell 212	31263		0084		2 PWC PT6T-3B TwinPac	5080	14 Pax		
☐ SU-CAS	Bell 212	31264		0084		2 PWC PT6T-3B TwinPac	5080	14 Pax		
☐ SU-CAU	Bell 212	35036		0091		2 PWC PT6T-3B TwinPac	5080	14 Pax		
☐ SU-CAV	Bell 412HP	36037		0091		2 PWC PT6T-3BE TwinPac	5398	14 Pax		
☐ SU-CAW	Bell 412HP	36038		0091		2 PWC PT6T-3BE TwinPac	5398	14 Pax		
☐ SU-CAX	Bell 412HP	36081	N2156S*	0094		2 PWC PT6T-3B TwinPac	5398	14 Pax		
☐ SU-CAY	Bell 412EP	36158	N6489P*	0097	0897	2 PWC PT6T-3D TwinPac	5398	14 Pax		
☐ SU-CAZ	Bell 412EP	36184	N52248*	0097	0198	2 PWC PT6T-3D TwinPac	5398	14 Pax		
☐ SU-CBA	De Havilland DHC-7-102 Dash 7	093	C-GFYI*	0084	0284	4 PWC PT6A-50	19958	50 Pax		
☐ SU-CBB	De Havilland DHC-7-102 Dash 7	096	C-GEWQ*	0084	0284	4 PWC PT6A-50	19958	50 Pax		
☐ SU-CBC	De Havilland DHC-7-102 Dash 7	097	C-GFQL*	0084	0284	4 PWC PT6A-50	19958	50 Pax		
☐ SU-CBD	De Havilland DHC-7-102 Dash 7	098	C-GEWQ*	0084	0684	4 PWC PT6A-50	19958	50 Pax		
☐ SU-CBE	De Havilland DHC-7-102 Dash 7	099	C-GFBW*	0084	0784	4 PWC PT6A-50	19958	50 Pax		

PHARAOH AIRLINES, S.A.E. = PHR (Al Farana Airline dba)
Cairo

30 Ammar Ibn Yasser Street, Heliopolis, Egypt ☎ (2) 245 45 79 Tx: none Fax: (2) 246 47 30 SITA: CAIPHCR
F: 1998 ✝✝✝ n/a Head: Tarik E-Tambouly ICAO: PHARAOH Net: n/a

☐ SU-PMA	Boeing 737-222	19064 / 63	F-GCLL	0068	0598	2 PW JT8D-7B	49442	Y123		Akhnaton

PYRAMID AIRLINES = PYR
Cairo

52 El Thawra Street, PO Box 340, Heliopolis West (11771), Egypt ☎ (2) 414 91 80 Tx: none Fax: (2) 414 91 82 SITA: n/a
F: 1977 ✝✝✝ n/a Head: Zaruq Shafi ICAO: PYAIR Net: n/a

☐ SU-OAE	Dassault Falcon 20D-5	175	HB-VJW	0069	1097	2 GA TFE731-5AR-2C	13200	Executive		cvtd 20D

RASLAN AIR SERVICE = MWR
Cairo

82 El-Merghani Street, Heliopolis (11341), Egypt ☎ (2) 418 28 83 Tx: n/a Fax: (2) 418 28 84 SITA: n/a
F: 1996 ✝✝✝ n/a Head: Motaz Raslan ICAO: RASLAN Net: n/a

☐ SU-PAB	Saab SF340A	340A-009	HB-AHC	0084	0596	2 GE CT7-5A2	12700	Y33		

SCORPIO AVIATION = SCP (Subsidiary of Scorpio Group)
Cairo

PO Box 221, Dokki-Giza (12411), Egypt ☎ (2) 346 37 09 Tx: 93837 souka un Fax: (2) 346 12 87 SITA: n/a
F: 1980 ✝✝✝ 75 Head: Mohamed A. Souka ICAO: SCORPIO Net: n/a

☐ SU-DML	ATR 42-320	091	F-WQIB	0088	0199	2 PWC PW121	16900	Y46		lsf ATR / cvtd -300

SHOROUK AIR = 7Q / SHK (Associated with Egypt Air & Kuwait Airways)
Cairo

PO Box 2684 Horreia, Heliopolis, Egypt ☎ (2) 417 23 09 Tx: 21766 shruk un Fax: (2) 417 23 11 SITA: CAIOK7Q
F: 1992 ✝✝✝ 162 Head: Dr. Mahmoud El Serafy IATA: 273 Net: n/a

☐ SU-RAA	Airbus Industrie A320-231	322	F-WWBL*	0092	0992	2 IAE V2500-A1	73500	Y174	CK-LP	
☐ SU-RAB	Airbus Industrie A320-231	326	F-WWDK*	0092	0992	2 IAE V2500-A1	73500	Y174	CM-KS	

TRISTAR AIR = TSY
Cairo

1S Sheraton Helipolis, Bldg Block 1227, Heliopolis, Egypt ☎ (2) 267 18 61 Tx: none Fax: (2) 267 18 73 SITA: n/a
F: 1998 ✝✝✝ n/a Head: n/a ICAO: TRIPLE STAR Net: n/a Operates cargo flights with Airbus Industrie A300B-203 (F), lsf/opb JET LINK HOLLAND (PH-) when required.

ULTRA AIR
Cairo

52 Mostafa El-Nahas Street, Nasr City, Cairo, Egypt ☎ (2) 271 88 90 Tx: none Fax: (2) 271 89 00 SITA: n/a
F: 1997 ✝✝✝ n/a Head: Ashraf Aboughazola Net: n/a

☐ SU-BMH	Cessna 421	421-0151	N42CS	0068	1097	2 CO GTSIO-520-D	3103			

SX = GREECE (Hellenic Republic) (Elleniki Dimokratia)

Capital: Athens Official Language: Greek Population: 10,5 million Square Km: 131957 Dialling code: +30 Year established: 1822 Acting political head: Costas Simitis (Prime Minister)

Government / Corporate / Executive / VIP Aircraft

☐ SX-ECG	Beech King Air 200	BB-372	N4937M	0078		2 PWC PT6A-41	5670	VIP		Civil Aviation Authority

AEGEAN AVIATION, S.A. = AEE (Aeroporia Aigaiou, A.E.) (Member of Th. Vassilakis Group)
Athens-Hellinikon

572 Vouliagmenis Avenue, GR-164 51 Athens, Greece ☎ (1) 996 81 81 Tx: none Fax: (1) 995 75 98 SITA: ATHTACR
F: 1988 ✝✝✝ 18 Head: Antonis N. Simigdalas ICAO: AEGEAN Net: http://www.hellas.de/agte/aegean

☐ SX-BNT	Learjet 35A	35A-228	N4GB	0079	0295	2 GA TFE731-2-2B	8301	Executive		
☐ SX-BNS	Learjet 55	55-072	N72ET	0083	1295	2 GA TFE731-3AR-2B	9752	Executive		
☐ SX-	Avro RJ100 (Avro 146-RJ100)	E3341	G-6-341*			4 LY LF507-1F	46040	Y112		oo-delivery 0599
☐ SX-	Avro RJ100 (Avro 146-RJ100)	E3343				4 LY LF507-1F	46040	Y112		oo-delivery 0599
☐ SX-	Fokker 100 (F28 Mk0100)	11476	HL7212	0093		2 RR Tay 650-15	44452	Y109		oo-delivery 0599 / ex KAL

AIR GREECE – Aerodromisis, S.A. = JG / AGJ (Subsidiary of Minoan Lines)
Heraklion

PO Box 1346, GR-712 02 Heraklion, Greece ☎ (81) 33 05 33 Tx: none Fax: (81) 33 05 34 SITA: n/a
F: 1994 ✝✝✝ 190 Head: Costas Bouvas IATA: 616 ICAO: AIR GREECE Net: n/a

☐ SX-BAO	ATR 72-202	326	F-GKOG	0092	0494	2 PWC PW124B	21500	Y70		Augusta / lsf Aircraft Int'l Renting
☐ SX-BAP	ATR 72-202	330	F-GKOH	0092	0594	2 PWC PW124B	21500	Y70		Gripas / lsf Aircraft Int'l Renting
☐ SX-BFK	ATR 72-202	313	F-GKOD	0092	0497	2 PWC PW124B	21500	Y70		Macedonia / lsf Aircraft Int'l Renting
☐ SX-	Fokker 100 (F28 Mk0100)	11387	HL7207	0092		2 RR Tay 650-15	44452	Y109		oo-delivery 0599 / ex KAL

AIR INTERSALONICA
Kalamaria-Private Heliport

19 N. Kountouriotou Street, GR-546 25 Thessaloniki, Greece ☎ (31) 55 46 41 Tx: none Fax: (31) 54 12 28 SITA: n/a
F: 1997 ✝✝✝ 3 Head: n/a Net: n/a

☐ SX-HDO	Eurocopter (Aerosp.) AS350BA Ecureuil	1191	F-GIPN	0079	1296	1 TU Arriel 1B	2100	Utility		cvtd AS350A

AIR MANOS, S.A. (Subsidiary of Manos Holidays)
Athens-Hellinikon

39 Panepiseinion Street, GR-105 64 Athens, Greece ☎ (1) 364 63 50 Tx: none Fax: (1) 325 38 85 SITA: n/a
F: 1999 ✝✝✝ n/a Head: Petros Kotiadis Net: n/a Operates charter flights with Avro RJ100, currently leased from Aegean Airlines (SX-), when required.

ARMADORA, S.A. = SIK
Athens-Hellinikon

1 Piraeus Street, GR-105 52 Athens, Greece ☎ (1) 324 28 05 Tx: none Fax: (1) 361 27 28 SITA: n/a
F: 1998 ✝✝✝ n/a Head: Skras Sikolas ICAO: ARMADORA Net: n/a Presently being set-up. Intends to start charter operations during 1999. Equipment not yet finalised.

AVIATOR, Ltd = AVW
Athens-Hellinikon

379 Syngrou Ave, GR-175 64 Athens, Greece ☎ (1) 942 68 09 Tx: 241618 gr Fax: (1) 942 85 79 SITA: n/a
F: 1991 ✝✝✝ 18 Head: Emmanuel G. Pantelides ICAO: AVIATOR Net: n/a Aircraft below MTOW 1361kg: Cessna 172

☐ SX-APP	Piper PA-31-350 Navajo Chieftain	31-8152171	N4093G	0081		2 LY TIO-540-J2BD	3175	8 Pax		
☐ SX-APJ	Beech King Air 200	BB-401	OY-JAO	0078	0594	2 PWC PT6A-41	5670	8 Pax		Captain John / lsf AHA

AVIONIC AIR SERVICES, Ltd = VIO
Athens-Hellinikon

12-14 Karageorgi Servias Street, GR-105 62 Athens, Greece ☎ (1) 323 76 97 Tx: 216272 gr Fax: (1) 322 84 16 SITA: n/a
F: 1994 ✝✝✝ n/a Head: n/a ICAO: AVIONIC Net: http://www.4gr.com/avionic/ Aircraft below MTOW 1361kg: Bell 47G, Hiller UH-12E & Robinson R22

☐ SX-HDI	Bell 206B JetRanger	976	N823C	0073		1 AN 250-C20	1451	Y4		

593 registration type of aircraft cn/fn ex/ex* mfd del powered by mtow kg configuration selcal name/fln/specialitites/remarks

registration	type of aircraft	cn/fn	ex/ex*	mfd	del	powered by	mtow kg	configuration	selcal	name/fln/specialitites/remarks
SX-HDJ	Bell 206B JetRanger III	3228	N824C	0081		1 AN 250-C20B	1451	Y4		
SX-HDN	Bell 407	53017		0096	0696	1 AN 250-C47B	2268	Y6		
SX-CRY	Cessna 310R II	310R0252	N44HB	0075		2 CO IO-520-M	2495	Y5		
SX-BFN	Shorts 360-300 (SD3-60)	SH3738	4X-CSL	0088	0597	2 PWC PT6A-67R	12292	Y37		
SX-BFW	Shorts 360-300 (SD3-60)	SH3739	EI-COR	0088	1298	2 PWC PT6A-67R	12292	Y37		

CRONUS AIRLINES = X5 / CUS (Member of Laskarides Group) — **Athens-Hellinikon**

500 Vouliagmenis Avenue, GR-174 56 Alimos, Greece ☎ (1) 995 64 00 Tx: none Fax: (1) 995 64 05 SITA: ATHGSXS
F: 1995 n/a Head: Iaonnis Manetas IATA: 198 ICAO: CRONUS Net: http://www.cronus.gr

registration	type of aircraft	cn/fn	ex/ex*	mfd	del	powered by	mtow kg	configuration	selcal	name/fln/specialitites/remarks
SX-BBT	Boeing 737-33A	25011 / 2012	F-GRSA	0491	0497	2 CFMI CFM56-3C1	61235	Y148		Kastalia / lsf AWAS
SX-BBU	Boeing 737-33A	25743 / 2206	EC-FMP	0092	0495	2 CFMI CFM56-3C1	62822	Y148		Joanna / lsf AWAS
SX-BGI	Boeing 737-3L9	27061 / 2347	D-ADBD	0092	0499	2 CFMI CFM56-3B2	63276	Y148		lsf TOMB
SX-	Boeing 737-700					2 CFMI CFM56-7B24	69400	Y148		oo-delivery 0701
SX-BGH	Boeing 737-4Y0	23866 / 1589	N4360W	0088	0498	2 CFMI CFM56-3C1	68040	Y170	MR-GL	Iniochos / lsf BOUL

EXPRESS HELICOPTER SERVICE (Division of Express Service, S.A.) — **Athens-Hellinikon**

234 Syngrou Avenue, GR-176 72 Athens, Greece ☎ (1) 952 49 52 Tx: none Fax: (1) 952 56 41 SITA: n/a
F: 1986 n/a Head: John Raptopoulos Net: n/a Operates EMS/ambulance & rescue flights for the members of its road assistance association only.

registration	type of aircraft	cn/fn	ex/ex*	mfd	del	powered by	mtow kg	configuration	selcal	name/fln/specialitites/remarks
SX-HBF	Bell 206B JetRanger III	3003		0080	0086	1 AN 250-C20B	1451	EMS		

HELLAS AIR SERVICES, S.A. — **Thermi-Private Heliport**

PO Box 180, GR-570 01 Thermi, Greece ☎ (31) 46 24 02 Tx: none Fax: (31) 46 47 93 SITA: n/a
F: 1997 5 Head: Dimitrioe Hatzopoulos Net: n/a

registration	type of aircraft	cn/fn	ex/ex*	mfd	del	powered by	mtow kg	configuration	selcal	name/fln/specialitites/remarks
SX-HDC	Eurocopter (Aerosp.) SA341G Gazelle	1205		0075		1 TU Astazou IIIA	1800			

HELLAS WINGS, Ltd = LJR (Subsidiary of Athens Aviation Service) — **Athens-Hellenikon**

E. Venizelou 32, GR-166 75 Glyfada, Greece ☎ (1) 964 64 69 Tx: none Fax: (1) 963 00 89 SITA: ATHAACR
F: 1998 n/a Head: Evangelos Stergiopoulos ICAO: HELLAS WINGS Net: http://www.united-hellas.com

registration	type of aircraft	cn/fn	ex/ex*	mfd	del	powered by	mtow kg	configuration	selcal	name/fln/specialitites/remarks
SX-BNV	Piper PA-31-350 Navajo Chieftain	31-7952088	N112GD	0079	0098	2 LY TIO-540-J2BD	3175	Y7		
SX-	Beech 1900D Airliner	UE-				2 PWC PT6A-67D	7688	Y19		to be lsf Raytheon Aircraft 0099
SX-	Beech 1900D Airliner	UE-				2 PWC PT6A-67D	7688	Y19		to be lsf Raytheon Aircraft 0099

INTERJET Hellenic Aviation & Tourist Enterprises, S.A. = INJ — **Athens-Hellinikon**

350 Syngrou Avenue, GR-176 74 Kallithea-Athens, Greece ☎ (1) 940 21 51 Tx: 214685 life gr Fax: (1) 940 21 52 SITA: ATHDWCR
F: 1992 25 Head: Kimon Daniilidis ICAO: INJET Net: n/a

registration	type of aircraft	cn/fn	ex/ex*	mfd	del	powered by	mtow kg	configuration	selcal	name/fln/specialitites/remarks
SX-HAY	Eurocopter (MBB) BO105CBS	S-389	D-HDLY*	0079	0993	2 AN 250-C20B	2500	4 Pax		
SX-HCK	Eurocopter (MBB) BO105CBS	S-593	D-HDQP*	0083	1292	2 AN 250-C20B	2500	4 Pax		
SX-HIN	Eurocopter (Aerosp.) AS355F2 Ecureuil 2	5406	F-WQEE	0089	0096	2 AN 250-C20F	2540	5 Pax		
SX-DCI	Cessna 560 Citation V Ultra	560-0366	N52352*	0096	0096	2 PWC JT15D-5D	7394	7 Pax		

KAL AVIATION, S.A. = CLV (Calavia) — **Athens-Hellinikon**

Pergamou 23, GR-116 75 Glyfada, Greece ☎ (1) 960 10 46 Tx: none Fax: (1) 965 17 95 SITA: n/a
F: 1990 34 Head: Soteris Antonakis ICAO: CALAVIA Net: n/a

registration	type of aircraft	cn/fn	ex/ex*	mfd	del	powered by	mtow kg	configuration	selcal	name/fln/specialitites/remarks
SX-BBX	Fairchild (Swearingen) SA227AC Metro III	AC-657	N26902	0086	0697	2 GA TPE331-11U-611G	6577	Freighter		lsf Finova Capital Corp.
SX-BGG	Fairchild (Swearingen) SA227AC Metro III	AC-656	N26895	0086	0897	2 GA TPE331-11U-611G	6577	Freighter		lsf Finova Capital Corp.

KAPA AIR, Ltd = KPR (formerly Agapitos Airlines) — **Athens-Hellinikon**

Hellinikon Airport, GR-167 77 Athens, Greece ☎ (1) 331 39 11 Tx: none Fax: (1) 321 46 77 SITA: n/a
F: 1997 n/a Head: Pantellis Tsollis ICAO: AIR KAPA Net: n/a

registration	type of aircraft	cn/fn	ex/ex*	mfd	del	powered by	mtow kg	configuration	selcal	name/fln/specialitites/remarks
SX-BFL	Piper PA-31-350 Navajo Chieftain	31-7952171	N64TT	0079	0197	2 LY TIO-540-J2BD	3175			
SX-BFM	Piper PA-31-350 Navajo Chieftain	31-8052204	N4504J	0080	0198	2 LY TIO-540-J2BD	3175			

MACEDONIAN AIRLINES = MCS (Subsidiary of Olympic Airways) — **Athens-Hellinikon**

120 Syngrou Avenue, GR-117 41 Athens, Greece ☎ (1) 926 73 59 Tx: none Fax: (1) 926 78 17 SITA: n/a
F: 1992 n/a Head: George Kalegyro IATA: 212 ICAO: MACAIR Net: n/a

registration	type of aircraft	cn/fn	ex/ex*	mfd	del	powered by	mtow kg	configuration	selcal	name/fln/specialitites/remarks
SX-	Boeing 737-400					2 CFMI CFM56-3C1	68040	Y170		to be lsd 0599
SX-	Boeing 737-400					2 CFMI CFM56-3C1	68040	Y170		to be lsd 0699
SX-	Boeing 737-400					2 CFMI CFM56-3C1	68040	Y170		to be lsd 0699
SX-CBG	Boeing 727-230 (A)	20918 / 1093	D-ABKJ	0475	0698	3 PW JT8D-15	82780	CY150	AM-EG	Mount Menalon / lsf OAL
SX-CBH	Boeing 727-230 (A)	20790 / 1021	N852SY	0374	0698	3 PW JT8D-15	86410	CY150	BD-HL	lsf OAL

OLYMPIC AIRWAYS, S.A. = OA / OAL — **Athens-Hellinikon**

96 Syngrou Avenue, GR-117 41 Athens, Greece ☎ (1) 926 72 95 Tx: 216488 oato gr Fax: (1) 926 71 23 SITA: n/a
F: 1957 8325 Head: George Zygoyiannis IATA: 050 ICAO: OLYMPIC Net: http://www.olympicair.com Charter services are operated by MACEDONIAN AIRLINES (a subsidiary) – see under that company.
Some scheduled commuter services are operated on behalf of Olympic Airways by OLYMPIC AVIATION (affiliate) using OA flight numbers – see under that company.

registration	type of aircraft	cn/fn	ex/ex*	mfd	del	powered by	mtow kg	configuration	selcal	name/fln/specialitites/remarks
SX-ECH	Dassault Falcon 900	26	HB-IAC	1187	1292	3 GA TFE731-5BR-1C	20640	VIP	GQ-CJ	King Minos / lsf Hellenic Air Force
SX-BCA	Boeing 737-284 (A)	21224 / 463		0676	0676	2 PW JT8D-9A	53070	CY117	DL-EH	Apollo
SX-BCB	Boeing 737-284 (A)	21225 / 464		0676	0676	2 PW JT8D-9A	53070	CY117	DL-EJ	Hermes
SX-BCC	Boeing 737-284 (A)	21301 / 474		1076	1076	2 PW JT8D-9A	53070	CY117	DL-FH	Hercules
SX-BCD	Boeing 737-284 (A)	21302 / 475	N40112*	1076	1076	2 PW JT8D-9A	53070	CY117	DL-HM	Hephaestus
SX-BCE	Boeing 737-284 (A)	22300 / 674		0680	0680	2 PW JT8D-9A	53070	CY117	DL-KM	Dionysus
SX-BCF	Boeing 737-284 (A)	22301 / 683		0780	0780	2 PW JT8D-9A	53070	CY117	DM-CH	Poseidon
SX-BCG	Boeing 737-284 (A)	22338 / 691	N8292V*	0880	0880	2 PW JT8D-9A	53070	CY117	DM-FG	Phoebus
SX-BCH	Boeing 737-284 (A)	22339 / 692		0880	0880	2 PW JT8D-9A	53070	CY117	DM-FH	Triton
SX-BCI	Boeing 737-284 (A)	22343 / 695		0980	0980	2 PW JT8D-9A	53070	CY117	JL-AC	Proteus
SX-BCK	Boeing 737-284 (A)	22400 / 766		0681	0681	2 PW JT8D-9A	53070	CY117	GH-CK	Nireus
SX-BCL	Boeing 737-284 (A)	22401 / 780		0781	0781	2 PW JT8D-9A	53070	CY117	GH-CL	Isle of Thassos
SX-BLA	Boeing 737-33R	28869 / 2887	N964WP	0097	0498	2 CFMI CFM56-3C1	62823	CY138		lsf BOUL
SX-BKA	Boeing 737-484	25313 / 2109		0991	0991	2 CFMI CFM56-3C1	68040	CY150	BL-EJ	Vergina
SX-BKB	Boeing 737-484	25314 / 2124		0991	0991	2 CFMI CFM56-3C1	68040	CY150	BL-EK	Olynthos
SX-BKC	Boeing 737-484	25361 / 2130		0991	0991	2 CFMI CFM56-3C1	68040	CY150	BL-EM	Philippi
SX-BKD	Boeing 737-484	25362 / 2142		1091	1091	2 CFMI CFM56-3C1	68040	CY150	BL-FH	Amphipoli
SX-BKE	Boeing 737-484	25417 / 2160		1191	1191	2 CFMI CFM56-3C1	68040	CY150	DM-AB	Stagira
SX-BKF	Boeing 737-484	25430 / 2174		1291	1291	2 CFMI CFM56-3C1	68040	CY150	DM-AE	Dion
SX-BKG	Boeing 737-484	27149 / 2471		0493	0693	2 CFMI CFM56-3C1	68040	CY150	BL-FM	Pella
SX-BKH	Boeing 737-4Q8	24703 / 1828	N407KW	0090	0698	2 CFMI CFM56-3C1	62823	CY150		lsf ILFC
SX-BKI	Boeing 737-4Y0	24915 / 2055	9M-MJT	0091	0598	2 CFMI CFM56-3C1	64636	CY150		lsf GECA
SX-BKK	Boeing 737-4Q8	25371 / 2195	N404KW	0092	0598	2 CFMI CFM56-3C1	65091	CY150		lsf ILFC
SX-BKL	Boeing 737-4Q8	24704 / 1855	N405KW	0090	0698	2 CFMI CFM56-3C1	62823	CY150	AF-QR	lsf ILFC
SX-BKM	Boeing 737-4Q8	24709 / 2115	N406KW	0091	0798	2 CFMI CFM56-3C1	62823	CY150		lsf ILFC
SX-BKN	Boeing 737-4Q8	26281 / 2380	N401KW	1092	0698	2 CFMI CFM56-3C1	65091	CY150	AF-QR	lsf ILFC
SX-	Boeing 737-884					2 CFMI CFM56-7B26	78245			oo-delivery 0300
SX-	Boeing 737-884					2 CFMI CFM56-7B26	78245			oo-delivery 0700
SX-	Boeing 737-884					2 CFMI CFM56-7B26	78245			oo-delivery 1100
SX-	Boeing 737-884					2 CFMI CFM56-7B26	78245			oo-delivery 0301
SX-	Boeing 737-884					2 CFMI CFM56-7B26	78245			oo-delivery 0701
SX-	Boeing 737-884					2 CFMI CFM56-7B26	78245			oo-delivery 1101
SX-	Boeing 737-884					2 CFMI CFM56-7B26	78245			oo-delivery 0002
SX-	Boeing 737-884					2 CFMI CFM56-7B26	78245			oo-delivery 0002
SX-CBG	Boeing 727-230 (A)	20918 / 1093	D-ABKJ	0475	0390	3 PW JT8D-15	82780	CY150	AM-EG	Mount Menalon / lst MCS
SX-CBH	Boeing 727-230 (A)	20790 / 1021	N852SY	0374	0490	3 PW JT8D-15	86410	CY150	BD-HL	Mount Vermion / lst MCS
SX-BED	Airbus Industrie A300B4-203	058	F-WZEH*	0280	0380	2 GE CF6-50C2	157500	C28Y232	JK-DL	Telemachus / lsf GECA / cvtd -103
SX-BEE	Airbus Industrie A300B4-203	103	F-WZEC*	0380	0480	2 GE CF6-50C2	157500	C28Y232	JK-EF	Nestor / lsf GECA / cvtd -103
SX-BEK	Airbus Industrie A300-605R (A300B4-605R)	632	F-WWAG*	0092	0692	2 GE CF6-80C2A5	170500	C28Y241	GQ-CF	Macedonia
SX-BEL	Airbus Industrie A300-605R (A300B4-605R)	696	F-WWAK*	0093	1093	2 GE CF6-80C2A5	170500	C28Y241	GQ-CH	Athena
SX-DFA	Airbus Industrie A340-313	235	F-WWJN*	0098	0199	4 CFMI CFM56-5C4	271000	C32Y267		Olympia
SX-DFB	Airbus Industrie A340-313	239	F-WWJC*	0098	0199	4 CFMI CFM56-5C4	271000	C32Y267		Delphi
SX-DFC	Airbus Industrie A340-313	280				4 CFMI CFM56-5C4	271000	C32Y267		oo-delivery 0799
SX-DFD	Airbus Industrie A340-313	292				4 CFMI CFM56-5C4	271000	C32Y267		oo-delivery 0899
SX-OAB	Boeing 747-284B	20825 / 223		1273	1273	4 PW JT9D-7J	351500	C49Y346	CH-DK	Olympic Eagle
SX-OAC	Boeing 747-212B	21683 / 387	9V-SQH	0779	0984	4 PW JT9D-7Q	371950	C44Y382	DG-HJ	Olympic Spirit
SX-OAD	Boeing 747-212B	21684 / 391	9V-SQI	0879	0485	4 PW JT9D-7Q	371950	C44Y382	CH-DJ	Olympic Flame
SX-OAE	Boeing 747-212B	21935 / 399	9V-SQJ	0979	1285	4 PW JT9D-7Q	371950	C44Y382	DL-BE	Olympic Peace

OLYMPIC AVIATION, S.A. = OLY (Affiliated with Olympic Airways, S.A.) — **Athens-Hellinikon**

West Airport Hellinikon, GR-166 04 Athens, Greece ☎ (1) 936 26 81 Tx: 215824 oaap gr Fax: (1) 936 34 73 SITA: ATHBQOA
F: 1971 680 Head: Dr. Petros Stefanou IATA: 898 ICAO: OLAVIA Net: http://www.olav.gr Aircraft below MTOW 1361kg: Cessna 152, Hughes 300CB & Piper PA-28.
Operates scheduled commuter-services in co-operation with Olympic Airways using OA-flight numbers.

registration	type of aircraft	cn/fn	ex/ex*	mfd	del	powered by	mtow kg	configuration	selcal	name/fln/specialitites/remarks
SX-HFA	Eurocopter (Aerosp.) AS355F2 Ecureuil 2	5563	F-WYMO*	0094	0894	2 AN 250-C20F	2540	Y5 / EMS		
SX-HFB	Eurocopter (Aerosp.) AS355F2 Ecureuil 2	5565		0094	0894	2 AN 250-C20F	2540	Y5 / EMS		

registration	type of aircraft	cn/fn	ex/ex*	mfd	del	powered by	mtow kg	configuration	selcal	name/fln/specialitites/remarks
☐ SX-HDA	Agusta A109A II Plus	7422		0089	0689	2 AN 250-C20R/1	2600	Y5 / EMS		
☐ SX-BHC	Dornier 228-201	8030	D-IDBB*	0084	0584	2 GA TPE331-5-252D	5980	Y18		Isle of Leros
☐ SX-BHD	Dornier 228-201	8034	D-IDBE*	0084	0784	2 GA TPE331-5-252D	5980	Y18		Isle of Skyros
☐ SX-BHE	Dornier 228-201	8050	D-IDBR*	0085	0585	2 GA TPE331-5-252D	5980	Y18		Isle of Kassos
☐ SX-BHF	Dornier 228-201	8057	D-CAPO*	0085	0585	2 GA TPE331-5-252D	5980	Y18		Isle of Astypalea
☐ SX-BHH	Dornier 228-201	8079	D-CLEC*	0086	0486	2 GA TPE331-5-252D	5980	Y18		Isle of Kythira
☐ SX-BHI	Dornier 228-201	8080	D-COLE*	0086	0586	2 GA TPE331-5-252D	5980	Y18		Isle of Karpathos
☐ SX-BIA	ATR 42-320	169	F-WWEW*	0090	0190	2 PWC PW121	16700	Y50		Platon
☐ SX-BIB	ATR 42-320	182	F-WWER*	0090	0490	2 PWC PW121	16700	Y50		Socrates
☐ SX-BIC	ATR 42-320	197	F-WWEE*	0090	0790	2 PWC PW121	16700	Y50		Aristotle
☐ SX-BID	ATR 42-320	219	F-WWEG*	0090	0591	2 PWC PW121	16700	Y50		Pythagora
☐ SX-BIE	ATR 72-202	239	F-WWED*	0091	0691	2 PWC PW124B	21500	Y68		Thales
☐ SX-BIF	ATR 72-202	241	F-WWEA*	0091	0891	2 PWC PW124B	21500	Y68		Demokritus
☐ SX-BIG	ATR 72-202	290	F-WWLQ*	0092	0492	2 PWC PW124B	21500	Y68		Homer
☐ SX-BIH	ATR 72-202	305	F-WWLC*	0092	0692	2 PWC PW124B	21500	Y68		Herodotus
☐ SX-BII	ATR 72-202	353	F-WWEK*	0093	0493	2 PWC PW124B	21500	Y68		Hippocrates
☐ SX-BIK	ATR 72-202	350	F-WWEG*	0093	0693	2 PWC PW124B	21500	Y68		Archimedes
☐ SX-BIL	ATR 72-202	437	F-WWLC*	0095	0695	2 PWC PW124B	21500	Y68		Melina-Eliada

PRINCESS AIRLINES, S.A. = PER — Athens-Hellinikon

24 Vouliagmenis Avenue, GR-166 75 Glyfada, Greece ☎ (1) 960 27 80 Tx: 224833 nord gr Fax: (1) 960 27 85 SITA: n/a
F: 1998 ⁂ n/a Head: Christozoulou Eviennou ICAO: PRINCESS Net: n/a

☐ SX-BFT	Boeing 737-3Q8	24470 / 1765	N470KB	0089	0698	2 CFMI CFM56-3B1	56472	Y148		lsf AARL

SUN AIR, S.A. — Athens-Hellinikon

57 Michalakopoulo Street, GR-115 28 Athens, Greece ☎ (1) 724 08 61 Tx: 219292 gr Fax: (1) 721 39 65 SITA: n/a
F: n/a ⁂ n/a Head: n/a Net: n/a

☐ SX-API	Beech Baron 58	TH-970		0078	0095	2 CO IO-520-C	2449			

TEA – Trans European Airlines, S.A. = TEG — Athens-Hellinikon

50 Patron Street, Nakfia, GR-145 64 Athens, Greece ☎ (1) 625 22 41 Tx: 210325 gr Fax: (1) 625 22 43 SITA: n/a
F: 1998 ⁂ n/a Head: Evangelos Papistas ICAO: EUROLINES Net: n/a

☐ SX-BNL	Embraer 110P1 Bandeirante (EMB-110P1)	110224	N614KC	0079	0498	2 PWC PT6A-34	5670	Y19		lsf Western Leasing Aviation Inc.

S2 = BANGLADESH (People's Republic of Bangladesh) (Gama Prajatantri Bangladesh)

Capital: Dhaka Official Language: Bengali Population: 122,0 million Square Km: 143998 Dialling code: +880 Year established: 1971 Acting political head: Mrs Sheikh Hasina (Prime Minister)

AERO BENGAL AIRLINES — Dhaka

House 17, Road 17, Block D, Dhaka-1212, Bangladesh ☎ (2) 88 11 45 Tx: 642912 iqbal bj Fax: (2) 88 31 26 SITA: n/a
F: 1995 ⁂ 50 Head: Air Commodore Moin-ul-Islam (Retd) Net: n/a

☐ S2-AAQ	Harbin Yunshuji Y12 II	0061		0092	0095	2 PWC PT6A-27	5300	Y17		
☐ S2-AAR	Harbin Yunshuji Y12 II	0062		0092	0095	2 PWC PT6A-27	5300	Y17		

AIR PARABAT, Ltd — Dhaka

Ibrahim Chamber, 1st Floor, 95 Motijheel Commercial Area, Dhaka, Bangladesh ☎ (2) 912 05 89 Tx: none Fax: n/a SITA: n/a
F: 1993 ⁂ n/a Head: Nadera Alam Net: n/a Aircraft below MTOW 1361kg: Cessna 150

☐ S2-ADD	Let 410UVP-E	912618	OK-WDV	0091	1297	2 WA M-601E	6400	Y17		
☐ S2-	Let 410UVP-E9D	962704	OK-BDG	0096	0499	2 WA M-601E	6600	Y17		

BIMAN BANGLADESH AIRLINES = BG / BBC — Dhaka

Biman BANGLADESH AIRLINES

Biman Bhaban, 100 Motijheel Commercial Area, Dhaka 1000, Bangladesh ☎ (2) 956 01 51 Tx: 642649 dabg bj Fax: (2) 86 30 05 SITA: n/a
F: 1972 ⁂ 5950 Head: Al-Ameen Chaudhury IATA: 997 ICAO: BANGLADESH Net: n/a

☐ S2-ACX	BAe ATP	2026	G-11-026*	0090	0890	2 PWC PW126	22930	Y70 or Y48 Combi		for sale
☐ S2-ACY	BAe ATP	2027	G-11-027*	0090	0990	2 PWC PW126	22930	Y70 or Y48 Combi		for sale
☐ S2-ACH	Fokker F28 Fellowship 4000 (F28 Mk4000)	11172	PH-EXX*	0081	0981	2 RR Spey 555-15H	32205	Y85		
☐ S2-	Fokker F28 Fellowship 4000 (F28 Mk4000)	11124	PK-YPV	0077	0499	2 RR Spey 555-15H	33112	Y85		
☐ S2-ADE	Airbus Industrie A310-325	698	F-WWCF*	0096	0696	2 PW PW4158A	164000	C25Y196	LP-AR	City of Hazrat Khan Jahan Ali (RA)
☐ S2-ADF	Airbus Industrie A310-325	700	F-WWCB*	0096	0896	2 PW PW4158A	164000	C25Y196		City of Chittagong
☐ S2-ACO	Boeing (Douglas) DC-10-30	46993 / 263	9V-SDB	0078	0883	3 GE CF6-50C2	259455	C28Y244	HL-CM	City of Hazrat Shah Makhdoom (R.A.)
☐ S2-ACP	Boeing (Douglas) DC-10-30	46995 / 275	9V-SDD	0079	0883	3 GE CF6-50C2	259455	C28Y244	HL-DE	City of Dhaka
☐ S2-ACQ	Boeing (Douglas) DC-10-30	47817 / 300	9V-SDF	0079	1183	3 GE CF6-50C2	259455	C28Y244	HL-DF	City of Hazrat Shah Jalal (R.A.)
☐ S2-ACR	Boeing (Douglas) DC-10-30	48317 / 445		0088	1288	3 GE CF6-50C2	259455	C28Y244	AC-BD	The New Era

GMG AIRLINES, Ltd = Z5 (Member of the GMG Industrial Group) — Dhaka

ABC House, 9th Floor, 8 Kemal Ataturk Avenue, Banani, Dhaka 1213, Bangladesh ☎ (2) 88 61 15 Tx: none Fax: (2) 88 61 15 SITA: n/a
F: 1997 ⁂ n/a Head: n/a Net: n/a

☐ S2-AAA	De Havilland DHC-8-102 Dash 8	245	N802MA	0090	0398	2 PWC PW120A	15649	Y37		In memory of Bangabondu / lsf DHC
☐ S2-ACZ	De Havilland DHC-8-102 Dash 8	251	N819MA	0090	0398	2 PWC PW120A	15649	Y37		In memory of Aziz Sattar / lsf DHC
☐ S2-	De Havilland DHC-8-311 Dash 8					2 PWC PW123	19500	Y50		to be lsf DHC 0099

S5 = SLOVENIA (Republic of Slovenia) (Republika Slovenija)

Capital: Ljubljana Official Language: Slovenian Population: 2,1 million Square Km: 20251 Dialling code: +386 Year established: 1991 Acting political head: Milan Kucan (President)

ADRIA AIRWAYS Slovenija = JP / ADR (formerly Inex Adria Aviopromet / Airways) — Ljubljana

ADRIA

Kuzmiceva 7, SLO-1001 Ljubljana, Slovenia ☎ (61) 133 43 36 Tx: 31268 adair si Fax: (61) 32 33 56 SITA: n/a
F: 1961 ⁂ 590 Head: Peter Grasek IATA: 165 ICAO: ADRIA Net: http://www.kabi.si/si21/aa/aa.html Aircraft below MTOW 1361kg: Piper PA-28R & PA-38

☐ S5-CAA	Piper PA-34-220T Seneca III	34-8233058	SL-CAA	0082		2 CO TSIO-360-KB	2155	Y4		
☐ S5-AAD	Canadair Regional Jet 200LR (CL-600-2B19)	7166	C-FZWS	0097	0198	2 GE CF34-3B1	23995	Y50		
☐ S5-AAE	Canadair Regional Jet 200LR (CL-600-2B19)	7170	C-GAIK	0097	0198	2 GE CF34-3B1	23995	Y50		
☐ S5-AAF	Canadair Regional Jet 200LR (CL-600-2B19)	7272	C-FMND*	0098	1198	2 GE CF34-3B1	23995	Y50		
☐ S5-AAA	Airbus Industrie A320-231	043	SX-BAS	0089	0589	2 IAE V2500-A1	73500	Y168	MR-AF	
☐ S5-AAB	Airbus Industrie A320-231	113	SX-BAT	0090	0990	2 IAE V2500-A1	73500	Y168	MR-AG	
☐ S5-AAC	Airbus Industrie A320-231	114	SX-BAU	0090	0990	2 IAE V2500-A1	73500	Y168	MR-AH	

ALFA HISTRIA, d.o.o. — Portoroz

Aerodrom Portoroz, Secovlje 19, SLO-6333 Secovlje, Slovenia ☎ (66) 79 091 Tx: none Fax: (66) 79 091 SITA: n/a
F: 1997 ⁂ 3 Head: Bivice Borivoi Net: n/a Aircraft below MTOW 1361kg: Cessna 172

☐ S5-CMO	Beech King Air C90B	LJ-1360	N1560U	0094		2 PWC PT6A-21	4581			

FALCON AIR (Sokolje Gnezdo, d.o.o. dba) — Bled

Sercerjeva 12, SLO-4240 Radovlyica, Slovenia ☎ (64) 70 48 50 Tx: none Fax: (64) 70 48 34 SITA: n/a
F: 1990 ⁂ 2 Head: Silvo Orozim Net: http://www.angelfinc.com/col.falconair/index Aircraft below MTOW 1361kg: Piper PA-28 & Yak-52

☐ S5-CAP	PZL Mielec (Antonov) An-2P	1G132-54	HA-ANH	0071	0697	1 SH ASh-62IR	5500			Tony Boy-Toncek
☐ S5-CAR	PZL Mielec (Antonov) An-2R	1G186-51	CCCP-54903	0080	1194	1 SH ASh-62IR	5500			Anuska

FRANC STROJ, s.p. — Begunje-Private Heliport

Dvorska vas 31c, SLO-4275 Begunje na Gorenjskem, Slovenia ☎ (64) 73 30 70 Tx: none Fax: (64) 73 30 70 SITA: n/a
F: n/a ⁂ n/a Head: n/a Net: n/a Aircraft below MTOW 1361kg: Enstrom F28C

☐ S5-HCB	Eurocopter (MBB) BO105CB-4	S-440	D-HDJB	0080		2 AN 250-C20B	2400			

GEODETSKI ZAVOD SLOVENIJE — Ljubljana

Aerial Survey Dept., Zemlsemerska 12, SLO-1000 Ljubljana, Slovenia ☎ (61) 132 71 21 Tx: none Fax: (61) 31 04 34 SITA: n/a
F: 1947 ⁂ n/a Head: Konstantin Divjak Net: n/a

☐ S5-CGC	Piper PA-31-350 Navajo Chieftain	31-7952153	S5-CAC	0079	0094	2 LY TIO-540-J2BD	3200	Photo/Survey/Pax		
☐ S5-CGB	Cessna 421A	421A0157	S5-CAB	0069	0094	2 CO GTSIO-520-D	3102	Photo/Survey/Pax		

REPUBLIC OF SLOVENIA – PRESIDENTIAL FLIGHT (Flight division of Republic of Slovenia Government/Vlada Republike Slovenije) — Ljubljana

Gregorciceva 20, SL-1000 Ljubljana, Slovenia ☎ (61) 178 14 22 Tx: none Fax: (61) 178 14 21 SITA: n/a
F: 1991 ⁂ n/a Head: Bojic Marian Net: n/a Government agency conducting non-commercial VIP flights to the government.

☐ S5-BAB	Learjet 24D	24D-320	SL-BAB	0075	0691	2 GE CJ610-6	6100	VIP		
☐ S5-BAA	Learjet 35A	35A-618	SL-BAA	0086	0691	2 GA TFE731-2-2B	7800	VIP		

SMELT AIR (Sister company of Smelt Intag, Switzerland) — Ljubljana

Dunajska 160, SLO-1000 Ljubljana, Slovenia ☎ (61) 168 12 31 Tx: none Fax: (61) 37 11 49 SITA: n/a
F: 1986 ⁂ n/a Head: Grigor Simonitis Net: n/a

☐ S5-CAE	Cessna 441 Conquest II	441-0150	SL-CAE	0080	0097	2 GA TPE331-8-402S	4468			
☐ HB-VHH	Cessna S550 Citation S/II	S550-0028		0084	0086	2 PWC JT15D-4B	6668			lsf Smelt Intag

SOLINAIR Portoroz, d.o.o. = SOP — Portoroz

Secovlje 19, SLO-6333 Secovlje, Slovenia ☎ (66) 79 001 Tx: 34159 adport si Fax: (66) 79 715 SITA: n/a
F: 1992 👥 n/a Head: Stane Potocnik ICAO: SOLINAIR Net: n/a Aircraft below MTOW 1361kg: Cessna 172, Piper PA-28 & Robinson R22.

registration	type of aircraft	cn/fn	ex/ex*	mfd	del	powered by	mtow kg	configuration	selcal	name/fln/specialitites/remarks
☐ S5-CAG	Piper PA-34-200 Seneca	34-7250356	N15052	0072	0593	2 LY IO-360-C1E6	1905			
☐ S5-CAI	Twin (Aero) Turbo Commander 690A	11121	D-IGAF	0073	1098	2 GA TPE331-5-251K	4679			
☐ S5-BAE	Let 410UVP-E	902503	RA-67650	0090	1297	2 WA M-601E	6400	Y19		
☐ S5-BAG	Let 410AB	750409	OK-FDE	0075	1194	2 PWC PT6A-27	5700	Y17		
☐ OK-DDU	Let 410A	730204	OK-DKC	0073	0093	2 PWC PT6A-27	5700	Y17 / Freighter		lsf Air Vitkovice / DHL colours

S7 = SEYCHELLES (Republic of Seychelles) (Repiblik Sesel)

Capital: Victoria Official Language: Creole, English Population: 0,1 million Square Km: 280 Dialling code: +248 Year established: 1976 Acting political head: France-Albert René (President)

AIR SEYCHELLES, Ltd = HM / SEY — Mahe

PO Box 386, Victoria Mahé, Seychelles ☎ 22 53 00 Tx: 2289 sz Fax: 22 51 59 SITA: n/a
F: 1979 👥 450 Head: Norman Weber IATA: 061 ICAO: SEYCHELLES Net: n/a

registration	type of aircraft	cn/fn	ex/ex*	mfd	del	powered by	mtow kg	configuration	selcal	name/fln/specialitites/remarks
☐ S7-AAA	Britten-Norman BN-2A-27 Islander	540	G-BDZP	0076		2 LY O-540-E4C5	2994	Y9		Isle of Remire
☐ S7-AAF	De Havilland DHC-6 Twin Otter 310	623	5N-ATN	0079	0192	2 PWC PT6A-27	5670	Y20		
☐ S7-AAJ	De Havilland DHC-6 Twin Otter 310	499	PH-STB	0076	0485	2 PWC PT6A-27	5700	Y20		Isle of Desroches
☐ S7-AAR	De Havilland DHC-6 Twin Otter 310	539	PH-STF	0077	0487	2 PWC PT6A-27	5700	Y20		Isle of Farquhar
☐ S7-AAT	De Havilland DHC-6 Twin Otter 320	721	VH-SHW	0080	0290	2 PWC PT6A-27	5700	Y20		Isle of Fregate
☐ S7-AAS	Boeing 767-2Q8 (ER)	24448 / 272		0089	0789	2 GE CF6-80C2B4	175540	C12Y196	BQ-CH	Isle of Aldabra / lsf ILFC
☐ S7-AHM	Boeing 767-37D (ER)	26328 / 637		0096	1296	2 GE CF6-80C2B6F	184612	C24Y222	PR-AB	Vallee de Mai / lsf ILFC

HELICOPTER SEYCHELLES, Ltd — Mahe

PO Box 595, Victoria Mahé, Seychelles ☎ 37 54 00 Tx: none Fax: 37 52 77 SITA: n/a
F: 1992 👥 13 Head: Capt. Vic Davies Net: n/a

registration	type of aircraft	cn/fn	ex/ex*	mfd	del	powered by	mtow kg	configuration	selcal	name/fln/specialitites/remarks
☐ S7-HBA	Bell 206B JetRanger III	3176	ZS-HJM	0080	0893	1 AN 250-C20B	1451			
☐ S7-HGN	Bell 206B JetRanger III	2212	ZS-HGN	0077		1 AN 250-C20B	1451			

IDC AIRCRAFT (IDC-Island Development Company dba) — Mahe

PO Box 638, Victoria Mahé, Seychelles ☎ 37 57 07 Tx: none Fax: 37 57 07 SITA: n/a
F: 1986 👥 n/a Head: Mike Stevenson Net: n/a

registration	type of aircraft	cn/fn	ex/ex*	mfd	del	powered by	mtow kg	configuration	selcal	name/fln/specialitites/remarks
☐ S7-AAU	Britten-Norman BN-2A-21 Islander	589	A2-01M	0075	1095	2 LY IO-540-K1B5	2994	Y9/SAR/Frtr		lsf Government of Seychelles
☐ S7-AAI	Reims/Cessna F406 Caravan II	F406-0051	N7148P	0090	1194	2 PWC PT6A-112	4468	Y12/SAR/Frtr		lsf Government of Seychelles
☐ S7-IDC	Beech 1900D Airliner	UE-212	N3217U*	0096	0398	2 PWC PT6A-67D	7688	Y19/SAR/Frtr		lsf Government of Seychelles

S9 = SAO TOME & PRINCIPE (Democratic Republic of Sao Tomé & Principe) (Republica Democratica de Sao Tomé e Principe)

Capital: Sao Tomé Official Language: Portuguese Population: 0,2 million Square Km: 964 Dialling code: +239 Year established: 1975 Acting political head: Miguel Trovoada (President)

AEROTEC International, Lda = (ATEC) — Sao Tome

PO Box 216, Sao Tome, Sao Tome & Principe ☎ (12) 22 455 Tx: none Fax: (12) 21 448 SITA: n/a
F: 1993 👥 n/a Head: Carlos Gomes & Jürgen Nappe Net: n/a Used aircraft operating leasing company.
Owner / lessor of following (main) aircraft types: Let 410, Mil Mi-8 & Mil Mi-14. Aircraft leased from Aerotec International (ATEC) are listed and mentioned as such under the leasing carriers.

AIR SAO TOME & PRINCIPE = KY / EQL (Linhas Aéreas de Sao Tomé & Principe dba) — Sao Tome

Caixa Postal 45, Sao Tomé, Sao Tomé & Principe ☎ (12) 21 976 Tx: 216 equat st Fax: (12) 21 375 SITA: n/a
F: 1993 👥 54 Head: Felisberto Neto IATA: 980 ICAO: EQUATORIAL Net: n/a

registration	type of aircraft	cn/fn	ex/ex*	mfd	del	powered by	mtow kg	configuration	selcal	name/fln/specialitites/remarks
☐ S9-CAD	Let 410UVP	841139	RA-67435	0084	0097	2 WA M-601D	5800	Y15		

SAL EXPRESS (Division of Golfo Air Service, S.A.) — Sao Tome

c/o Golfo International S.A., PO Box 5114, Sao Tomé, Sao Tomé & Principe ☎ (12) 22 023 Tx: none Fax: (12) 21 664 SITA: n/a
F: 1997 👥 n/a Head: Mario Matos Net: n/a

registration	type of aircraft	cn/fn	ex/ex*	mfd	del	powered by	mtow kg	configuration	selcal	name/fln/specialitites/remarks
☐ S9-CAC	Beech 1900C-1 Airliner	UC-93	N93YV	0190	0297	2 PWC PT6A-65B	7530	Y19 / Freighter		lsf Raytheon Aircraft Credit Corp.
☐ S9-CAE	Beech 1900C-1 Airliner	UC-142	N142YV	0291	0697	2 PWC PT6A-65B	7530	Y19 / Freighter		lsf Raytheon Aircraft Credit Corp.
☐ S9-CAF	Beech 1900C-1 Airliner	UC-91	N91YV	0089	0897	2 PWC PT6A-65B	7530	Y19 / Freighter		lsf Raytheon Aircraft Credit Corp.
☐ S9-	Beech 1900C-1 Airliner	UC-157	N157YV	0591	0298	2 PWC PT6A-65B	7530	Y19 / Freighter		lsf Raytheon Aircraft Credit Corp.

TAG – Transportes Aéreos Gerais — Maputo (Mozambique)

Operations office:, Apartado Postal 2054, Aeroporto Int'l, Maputo, Mozambique ☎ (1) 46 50 15 Tx: none Fax: (1) 49 27 04 SITA: n/a
F: n/a 👥 n/a Head: n/a Net: n/a

registration	type of aircraft	cn/fn	ex/ex*	mfd	del	powered by	mtow kg	configuration	selcal	name/fln/specialitites/remarks
☐ S9-TAS	PZL Mielec (Antonov) An-2P	1G162-54	UR-16004	0075	0295	1 SH ASh-62IR	5500	Y12/Frtr/Para		
☐ S9-TAT	PZL Mielec (Antonov) An-2P	1G139-09	UR-70250	0072	0295	1 SH ASh-62IR	5500	Y12/Frtr/Para		

TRANSAFRIK, Corporation Ltd — Sao Tome & Luanda (Angola)

Operations Office:, CP 2839, Luanda, Angola ☎ (2) 35 41 62 Tx: 4159 traklad an Fax: (2) 39 33 97 SITA: n/a
F: 1986 👥 145 Head: Erich F. Koch Net: n/a

registration	type of aircraft	cn/fn	ex/ex*	mfd	del	powered by	mtow kg	configuration	selcal	name/fln/specialitites/remarks
☐ S9-NAL	Lockheed L-382E (L-100-20) Hercules	25C-4385	ZS-GSK	0870	1189	4 AN 501-D22A	70307	Freighter		opf UN
☐ S9-CAI	Lockheed L-382G (L-100-30) Hercules	31C-4562	N904SJ	0074	0997	4 AN 501-D22A	70307	Freighter		lsf T.W.L. Ltd, Mauritius
☐ S9-CAJ	Lockheed L-382G (L-100-30) Hercules	31C-4565	N902SJ	0074	0997	4 AN 501-D22A	70307	Freighter		lsf T.W.L. Ltd, Mauritius
☐ S9-CAV	Lockheed L-382G (L-100-30) Hercules	11C-4301	N923SJ	0068	0798	4 AN 501-D22A	70307	Freighter		lsf T.W.L. Ltd, Mauritius/cvtd L-100-20
☐ S9-CAW	Lockheed L-382G (L-100-30) Hercules	13C-4300	N908SJ	0068	0798	4 AN 501-D22A	70307	Freighter		lsf T.W.L. Ltd, Mauritius/cvtd L-100-20
☐ S9-CAX	Lockheed L-382G (L-100-30) Hercules	14C-4248	N907SJ	0067	1298	4 AN 501-D22A	70307	Freighter	NONE	lst T.W.L. Ltd, Mauritius / cvtd L-100
☐ S9-CAY	Lockheed L-382G (L-100-30) Hercules	7C-4208	N918SJ	0067	0898	4 AN 501-D22A	70307	Freighter		lsf T.W.L. Ltd, Mauritius / cvtd L-100
☐ S9-CAA	Boeing 727-95 (F)	19836 / 494	HR-AMR	0067	1093	3 PW JT8D-7B	76884	Freighter		lsf Cargo Aircraft Leasing / cvtd -95
☐ S9-CAB	Boeing 727-23 (F)	19182 / 266	HR-AMI	0066	0393	3 PW JT8D-7B	76884	Freighter		lsf IALI / cvtd -23
☐ S9-CAH	Boeing 727-22 (F)	18849 / 178	ZS-NMW	0065	1293	3 PW JT8D-7B	72802	Freighter		lsf IALI / cvtd -22
☐ S9-NAZ	Boeing 727-82	19404 / 384	C-GWGP	1168	0293	3 PW JT8D-7B	76884	Fuel Tanker/Frtr		lsf Equatorial Aircraft Leasing Corp.
☐ S9-TAO	Boeing 727-23 (F)	19390 / 350	N931FT	0066	0694	3 PW JT8D-7B	76884	Freighter		lsf IALI / cvtd -23

TC = TURKEY (Republic of Turkey) (Türkiye Cumhuriyeti)

(including Northern Cyprus [Turkish Republic of Northern Cyprus / Kuzey Kibris Türk Cumhuriyeti] [figures not included])
Capital: Ankara Official Language: Turkish Population: 63,0 million Square Km: 779452 Dialling code: +90 Year established: 1923 Acting political head: Bülent Ecevit (Prime minister)

NORTHERN CYPRUS (Turkish Republic of Northern Cyprus) (Kuzey Kibris Türk Cumhuriyeti)
Capital: Nicosia Official Language: Turkish Population: 0,2 million Square Km: 3355 Dialling code: +90392 Acting political head: Rauf Denktash (President)

Government / Corporate / Executive / VIP Aircraft

registration	type of aircraft	cn/fn	ex/ex*	mfd	del	powered by	mtow kg	configuration	selcal	name/fln/specialitites/remarks
☐ TC-ATA	GAC G-IV Gulfstream IV	1043	TC-ANA	0088	0888	2 RR Tay 611-8	33203	VIP	EL-KP	Basbakanlik/Office of the PrimeMinister
☐ TC-GAP	GAC G-IV Gulfstream IV	1027	N1761B*	0088	0588	2 RR Tay 610-8	33203	VIP		Basbakanlik/Office of the PrimeMinister
☐ 064	Tusas Aerospace (CASA) CN-235M-100	064		0093	0993	2 GE CT7-9C	16500	VIP / mil trans		Turk Hava Kuvvetleri/Turkish Air Force
☐ 12-003	GAC G-IV Gulfstream IV	1163	N458GA*	0091	0392	2 RR Tay 611-8	33203	VIP / mil trans		Turk Hava Kuvvetleri/Turkish Air Force
☐ 93-7024	Cessna 650 Citation VII	650-7024	N1262Z*	0093	0693	2 GA TFE731-4R-2S	10183	VIP / mil trans		Turk Hava Kuvvetleri/Turkish Air Force
☐ 93-7026	Cessna 650 Citation VII	650-7026	N1263G*	0093	0693	2 GA TFE731-4R-2S	10183	VIP / mil trans		Turk Hava Kuvvetleri/Turkish Air Force

AIRSEALAND HELICOPTERS (Airsealand Havacilik Teknolojisi, A.S. dba) — Tuzla & Istanbul

Ayaza Aga Ticaret Merkezi, TR-80670 Maslak-Istanbul, Turkey ☎ (212) 285 15 00 Tx: none Fax: (212) 285 15 14 SITA: n/a
F: 1997 👥 n/a Head: Bülent Vardi Net: n/a

registration	type of aircraft	cn/fn	ex/ex*	mfd	del	powered by	mtow kg	configuration	selcal	name/fln/specialitites/remarks
☐ TC-HIB	MD Helicopters MD 520N (Hughes 500N)	LN058	N52244	0094		1 AN 250-C20R2	1520	VIP / Foto		

ALFA Hava Yollari, A.S. = H7 / LFA (Air Alfa) — Istanbul

Fatih Cad. 21, TR-34540 Günesli-Istanbul, Turkey ☎ (212) 630 33 48 Tx: 21006 alhy tr Fax: (212) 657 58 69 SITA: ISTSPH7
F: 1992 👥 450 Head: Necmettin Metiner IATA: 770 ICAO: ALFA Net: http://www.city-netz.com/airalfa

registration	type of aircraft	cn/fn	ex/ex*	mfd	del	powered by	mtow kg	configuration	selcal	name/fln/specialitites/remarks
☐ TC-ALL	Airbus Industrie A321-131	604	9Y-BWA	0096	0497	2 IAE V2530-A5	85000	Y210	MS-EH	lsf ILFC
☐ TC-ALO	Airbus Industrie A321-131	614	9Y-BWB	0096	0597	2 IAE V2530-A5	85000	Y210	MS-EJ	lsf ILFC
☐ TC-	Airbus Industrie A321-131					2 IAE V2530-A5	83000	Y210		to be lsf ILFC 0899
☐ TC-ALN	Airbus Industrie A300B4-103	065	OO-MKO	0078	0594	2 GE CF6-50C2	157500	Y323	FL-EJ	Umay-Ural / cvtd B4-2C
☐ TC-ALS	Airbus Industrie A300B4-103	066	OO-ING	0078	0196	2 GE CF6-50C2	157500	Y318	FL-EK	Mehmet Can / cvtd B4-2C
☐ TC-ALV	Airbus Industrie A300B4-203	261	N229KW	0083	0498	2 GE CF6-50C2	165000	Y318	KM-AB	lsf FSBU Trustee

ANADOLU UNIVERSITY – Air Taxi Operations (Aü. Shmo Döner Sermaye Isletmesi Müdürlügü dba) — Eskisehir

Muttalip Mevkü, TR-26470 Eskisehir, Turkey ☎ (222) 322 20 70 Tx: none Fax: (222) 322 16 19 SITA: n/a
F: 1996 👥 150 Head: Prof. Dr. Mustafa Oc Net: n/a Trainer-aircraft below MTOW 5000kg: AA5B, Piper PA-18, Socata TB9 & TB20

registration	type of aircraft	cn/fn	ex/ex*	mfd	del	powered by	mtow kg	configuration	selcal	name/fln/specialitites/remarks
☐ TC-HYS	Bell 206L-1 LongRanger II	45296	N77AR	0079		1 AN 250-C28B	1882			
☐ TC-AUT	Beech King Air C90	LJ-622	N104TT	0074		2 PWC PT6A-20	4377			
☐ TC-AUV	Beech King Air C90	LJ-587	N61KA	0073	0096	2 PWC PT6A-20	4377			
☐ TC-AUB	PZL Mielec (Antonov) An-2P	1G234-11	SP-DLD	0089		1 SH ASh-62IR	5500			
☐ TC-AUY	Beech King Air 200	BB-333	F-GHLH	0078	0096	2 PWC PT6A-41	5670			

ANATOLIA – Anadolu Havacilik, A.S. = TD / NTL (Air Anatolia) (Associated with Sultan Reizen / formerly GTI Airlines, Inc.) — Istanbul

Florya Caddesi, Ozgen Sok. 6, Senlikköy, TR-34810 Florya-Istanbul, Turkey ☎ (212) 624 07 57 Tx: none Fax: (212) 425 34 00 SITA: ISTSPTD
F: 1996 250 Head: Mehmet Hasançebi ICAO: AIR ANATOLIA Net: n/a

registration	type of aircraft	cn/fn	ex/ex*	mfd	del	powered by	mtow kg	configuration	selcal	name/fln/specialitites/remarks
☐ TC-GTA	Airbus Industrie A300B4-103	054	HS-THL	0078	0996	2 GE CF6-50C2	157500	Y310		Dila / lsf Tokai Denco CoLtd/cvtd B4-2C
☐ TC-GTB	Airbus Industrie A300B4-203	127	6Y-JMJ	0080	0397	2 GE CF6-50C2	165000	Y310		Ferit Toroluoglu / lsf GECA
☐ TC-GTC	Airbus Industrie A300B2-1C	048	F-BUAO	0077	0797	2 GE CF6-50C2R	142000	Y314		Umay & Ural / lsf Natiolocation
☐ TC-ONV	Airbus Industrie A300B4-2C	057	F-BUAQ	0078	0598	2 GE CF6-50C2R	150000	Y314		Ugras-Ugur / lsf OHY

AND AIR (AND Havacilik, A.S. dba) — Bursa

Kükürtlu Cad. Inci Sok., Yilmazer Apt. 2/2, Cekirge-Bursa, Turkey ☎ (224) 233 05 45 Tx: 32166 inki tr Fax: (222) 234 20 74 SITA: n/a
F: 1995 11 Head: Capt. Celal Decikoc Net: n/a Aircraft below MTOW 1361kg: Socata TB9 Tampico

registration	type of aircraft	cn/fn	ex/ex*	mfd	del	powered by	mtow kg	configuration	selcal	name/fln/specialitites/remarks
☐ TC-YSM	Beech King Air B200	BB-1086	TC-SDR	0082		2 PWC PT6A-42	5670			lsf Rant Finasal Kiralama A.S.
☐ TC-AND	Dassault Falcon 10	89	D-CENT	0077	0595	2 GA TFE731-2-1C	8800			lsf Albaraka Türk Ozel Finans Kurumu

BAYINDIR AVIATION (Bayindir Havacilik ve Ticaret, A.S. dba/Subsidiary of Bayindir Holding, A.S.) — Ankara-Esenboga

Tunus Cad. No. 24, TR-06680 Kavaklidere-Ankara, Turkey ☎ (312) 417 92 10 Tx: 944828 byindr tr Fax: (312) 398 02 08 SITA: n/a
F: 1984 7 Head: Kamuran Cörtük Net: n/a

registration	type of aircraft	cn/fn	ex/ex*	mfd	del	powered by	mtow kg	configuration	selcal	name/fln/specialitites/remarks
☐ TC-FAD	Piper PA-31P Pressurized Navajo	31P-7400225	N7341L	0074		2 LY TIGO-541-E1A	3538			
☐ TC-BAY	Cessna 550 Citation II	550-0283	N316CC	0081		2 PWC JT15D-4	6033			
☐ TC-BHO	Dassault Falcon 50EX	271	F-WWHV*	0098	0698	3 GA TFE731-40	18500			

BELKO AIR (BelKo, Ltd Sti dba) — Ankara

Kuloglu Sok. No. 13, A. Ayranci, TR-06540 Ankara, Turkey ☎ (312) 440 94 20 Tx: 44323 belk tr Fax: (312) 440 78 67 SITA: n/a
F: 1987 17 Head: Capt. Plt. Hilmi Emri Net: n/a

registration	type of aircraft	cn/fn	ex/ex*	mfd	del	powered by	mtow kg	configuration	selcal	name/fln/specialitites/remarks
☐ TC-HBH	Bell 222UT	47525	C-FVVA	0085	0896	2 LY LTS101-750C.1	3742	EMS		

BINTUR AIR (Bintur Havacilik Tasimacilik ve Ticaret, A.S. dba) — Izmir

Sehit Fethi Bey Cad. 120, TR-35210 Alsancak-Izmir, Turkey ☎ (232) 489 41 00 Tx: none Fax: (232) 489 65 64 SITA: n/a
F: 1995 7 Head: Korhan Solakoglu Net: n/a Aircraft below MTOW 1361kg: Piper PA-28

registration	type of aircraft	cn/fn	ex/ex*	mfd	del	powered by	mtow kg	configuration	selcal	name/fln/specialitites/remarks
☐ TC-YSR	Dassault Falcon 50	246	N246FJ	0093	1295	3 GA TFE731-3-1C	18500			lsf Tütün Finansal Kiralama A.S.

BOMAS AIR, Ltd Sti — Istanbul

Kemeralu Cad. Olcay Isham No.16, Kat 4, Daire 5, Karaköy-Istanbul, Turkey ☎ (212) 243 22 88 Tx: none Fax: (212) 243 07 28 SITA: n/a
F: 1995 n/a Head: n/a Net: n/a Aircraft below MTOW 1361kg: Cessna 172

registration	type of aircraft	cn/fn	ex/ex*	mfd	del	powered by	mtow kg	configuration	selcal	name/fln/specialitites/remarks
☐ TC-TLS	Beech Duke 60	P-117		0069		2 LY TIO-541-E1B4	3050			

BON AIR Havacilik ve Tic. Lim. Sti. — Istanbul

Sensilkköy Orman Sokak No. 10, TR-34810 Florya-Istanbul, Turkey ☎ (212) 663 18 29 Tx: none Fax: (212) 574 01 47 SITA: n/a
F: 1993 n/a Head: n/a Net: http://www.bonair.com.tr Aircraft below MTOW 1361kg: Cessna 172

registration	type of aircraft	cn/fn	ex/ex*	mfd	del	powered by	mtow kg	configuration	selcal	name/fln/specialitites/remarks
☐ TC-GIZ	Piper PA-32R-301 Saratoga SP	32R-8013064	N8160X	0080		1 LY IO-540-K1G5D	1633			lsf Kuvars Elektronik Sanayi ve Tic. AS
☐ TC-GPS	Cessna 421B Golden Eagle	421B0221	N5978M	0072		2 CO GTSIO-520-H	3379			
☐ TC-CAC	Piper PA-31P Pressurized Navajo	31P-57	F-BTQB	0072		2 LY TIGO-541-E1A	3538			
☐ TC-NMC	Cessna S550 Citation S/II	S550-0072	N686MC	0085	0398	2 PWC JT15D-4B	6849			
☐ TC-ROT	Cessna 560 Citation V Ultra	560-0454	N1216Z*	0098	0698	2 PWC JT15D-5D	7394			

BORONKAY HAVA Tasimaciligi, A.S. — Istanbul

Merkez Mah. Cinar, Sok No. 8, TR-34530 Yenibosna-Istanbul, Turkey ☎ (212) 654 17 07 Tx: none Fax: (212) 652 41 74 SITA: n/a
F: 1994 7 Head: Zoltan Boronkay Net: n/a Aircraft below MTOW 1361kg: Cessna 172

registration	type of aircraft	cn/fn	ex/ex*	mfd	del	powered by	mtow kg	configuration	selcal	name/fln/specialitites/remarks
☐ TC-YZB	Cessna 550 Citation II	550-0323	TC-FMB	0082		2 PWC JT15D-4	6033	8 Pax		

CUKUROVA AIR (Cukurova Havacilik, A.S. dba / Subsidiary of Cukurova Holding, A.S.) — Istanbul

Besyol Polis Egitim Merkezi Arkasi, özel Hangarlar Bölgesi, TR-34630 Sefaköy-Istanbul, Turkey ☎ (212) 541 60 20 Tx: none Fax: (212) 540 45 20 SITA: n/a
F: 1987 18 Head: Capt. Abdullah Kartal Net: n/a

registration	type of aircraft	cn/fn	ex/ex*	mfd	del	powered by	mtow kg	configuration	selcal	name/fln/specialitites/remarks
☐ TC-HCA	Agusta A109C	7632	N61453	0091	1293	2 AN 250-C20R/1	2720	4 Pax		
☐ TC-ELL	Learjet 60	60-030	N164PA	0094	0797	2 PWC PW305A	10659	7 Pax		
☐ TC-MEK	Learjet 60	60-016	N50163*	0093	1193	2 PWC PW305A	10659	6 Pax		

DARDANEL AIR = DRD (Dardanel Havacilik, A.S. dba) — Istanbul

Vali Konagi Caddesi YKB, Vakif Binasi 173, K8/1, TR-80220 Nisantasi-Istanbul, Turkey ☎ (212) 240 77 77 Tx: none Fax: (212) 234 27 38 SITA: n/a
F: 1996 n/a Head: Onder Diker ICAO: DARDANEL Net: n/a

registration	type of aircraft	cn/fn	ex/ex*	mfd	del	powered by	mtow kg	configuration	selcal	name/fln/specialitites/remarks
☐ TC-CNK	Beech 1900D Airliner	UE-288	N11320*	0097	1197	2 PWC PT6A-67D	7688	Y19		
☐ TC-TON	Beech 1900D Airliner	UE-294	N21334*	0097	0298	2 PWC PT6A-67D	7688	VIP		

DEMIR AIR (Demir Havacilik Sanayi ve Ticaret, A.S. dba) — Istanbul

Florya Caddesi, Cikmazi 3-1, TR-34810 Florya-Istanbul, Turkey ☎ (212) 598 03 71 Tx: none Fax: (212) 592 97 10 SITA: n/a
F: 1998 n/a Head: Göksal Sizan Net: n/a

registration	type of aircraft	cn/fn	ex/ex*	mfd	del	powered by	mtow kg	configuration	selcal	name/fln/specialitites/remarks
☐ TC-DEM	Dassault Falcon 200	489	N7654F	0084	0098	2 GA ATF3-6A-4C	14515			
☐ TC-CIN	Dassault Falcon 2000	26	F-WQFL*	0096	0098	2 CFE CFE738-1-1B	16556			

DHMI Hava Taksi (Division of DHMI-Devlet Hava Meydanlari Isletmesi Genel Müdürlügü/General Directorate State Airports) — Ankara

DHMI Gen. Md. Lügü, TR-06330 Etiler-Ankara, Turkey ☎ (312) 212 61 20 Tx: 44083 dhmi tr Fax: (312) 222 09 76 SITA: n/a
F: 1987 18 Head: Mustafa Ozatamer Net: n/a

registration	type of aircraft	cn/fn	ex/ex*	mfd	del	powered by	mtow kg	configuration	selcal	name/fln/specialitites/remarks
☐ TC-HAA	Eurocopter (Aerosp.) AS355F2 Ecureuil 2	5362		0087		2 AN 250-C20F	2540			
☐ TC-HAB	Eurocopter (Aerosp.) AS355F2 Ecureuil 2	5363		0087		2 AN 250-C20F	2540			
☐ TC-LAA	Cessna 560 Citation V	560-0212	N1284X*	0093	0993	2 PWC JT15D-5A	7212			
☐ TC-LAB	Cessna 560 Citation V	560-0216	N1285N*	0093	0993	2 PWC JT15D-5A	7212			

DOGUS AIR (Dogus Hava Tasimaciligi, A.S. dba) — Istanbul

Ozel Hangarlar Bölgesi No. 4, Atatürk Hava Limani, TR-34630 Sefaköy-Istanbul, Turkey ☎ (212) 541 14 31 Tx: n/a Fax: (212) 541 14 35 SITA: n/a
F: 1991 n/a Head: n/a Net: n/a

registration	type of aircraft	cn/fn	ex/ex*	mfd	del	powered by	mtow kg	configuration	selcal	name/fln/specialitites/remarks
☐ TC-DHD	Piper PA-32R-301 Saratoga II HP	3213090		0094		1 LY IO-540-K1G5D	1633			
☐ TC-HDO	Eurocopter (Aerosp.) AS365N2 Dauphin 2	6497	F-WQDC*	0096	0096	2 TU Arriel 1C2	4250			
☐ TC-DHB	Canadair CL-601-3A (CL-600-2B16) Challen.	5094	TC-OVA	0091		2 GE CF34-3A	20500			
☐ TC-DHE	Canadair CL-604 (CL-600-2B16) Challen.	5358	C-GBRQ*	0098	0798	2 GE CF34-3B	21591			

DORUK AIR (Doruk Turizm ve Tic, A.S./Doruk Tourism & Trade, Inc. dba) — Antalya

Burhanettin Onat Caddesi Osman Manavoglu, Apt. No. 92 Kat 1, Da 2, TR-07100 Zerdalilik-Antalya, Turkey ☎ (242) 321 00 32 Tx: none Fax: (242) 321 09 24 SITA: n/a
F: 1994 58 Head: Mehmet Sakir Acaroglu Net: n/a Aircraft below MTOW 1361kg: Piper PA-18

registration	type of aircraft	cn/fn	ex/ex*	mfd	del	powered by	mtow kg	configuration	selcal	name/fln/specialitites/remarks
☐ TC-HDA	Mil Mi-8PS	8562	UR-24636	0085	0694	2 IS TV2-117A	12000	Y20 / Utility		lsf Kremenchug Flight School
☐ TC-HDB	Mil Mi-8MTV-1	95479	UR-25170	0090	0795	2 IS TV3-117MT	13000	Y24 / Utility		lsf Kremenchug Flight School
☐ TC-HDD	Mil Mi-8MTV-1	95528	RA-25418	0090	0795	2 IS TV3-117MT	13000	Y24 / Utility		lsf Leningrad Leasing, Russia
☐ TC-HDF	Mil Mi-8MTV-1	95740	RA-25124	0091	0795	2 IS TV3-117MT	13000	Y24 / Utility		lsf Leningrad Leasing, Russia
☐ TC-HDG	Mil Mi-8MTV-1	95866	RA-27032	0092	0795	2 IS TV3-117MT	13000	Y24 / Utility		lsf Leningrad Leasing, Russia
☐ TC-HDH	Mil Mi-8MTV-1	95895	RA-27061	0092	0795	2 IS TV3-117MT	13000	Y24 / Utility		lsf Leningrad Leasing, Russia
☐ TC-HDK	Mil Mi-8PS	8561	UR-24635	0085	0795	2 IS TV2-117A	12000	Y20 / Utility		lsf Kremenchug Flight School

EMAIR (Emekli Ticaret Havacilik Ithalat-Ihracat, A.S. dba) — Ankara

Necatibey Cad. 88/6, TR-06430 Ankara, Turkey ☎ (312) 229 07 57 Tx: none Fax: (312) 230 68 08 SITA: n/a
F: 1961 18 Head: Haydar Gursan Net: n/a Aircraft & Ag-aircraft below MTOW 1361/5000kg: Cessna 172 & A188B

registration	type of aircraft	cn/fn	ex/ex*	mfd	del	powered by	mtow kg	configuration	selcal	name/fln/specialitites/remarks
☐ TC-FAE	Cessna U206G Stationair 6 II	U20606614	N9701Z	0082		1 CO IO-520-F	1633			
☐ TC-FAJ	Cessna U206G Stationair 6 II	U20605368	N6182U	0080		1 CO IO-520-F	1633			
☐ TC-EMR	Cessna 340A II	340A0269	EC-EVR	0077		2 CO TSIO-520-N	2717			

FIRAT AVIATION (Firat Havacilik Ticaret, A.S. dba) — Istanbul

Türkoba Köyü, PK12, TR-34907 Büyükcekmece-Istanbul, Turkey ☎ (212) 662 12 83 Tx: none Fax: (212) 662 12 83 SITA: n/a
F: 1996 n/a Head: Capt. Dinler Tamer Net: n/a Aircraft below MTOW 1361kg: Piper PA-18

registration	type of aircraft	cn/fn	ex/ex*	mfd	del	powered by	mtow kg	configuration	selcal	name/fln/specialitites/remarks
☐ TC-FIR	Beech King Air B200	BB-1082	N801BC	0082	1297	2 PWC PT6A-42	5670			

GENEL AIR (Genel Havacilik, A.S. dba) — Istanbul

Ozel Hangarlar Bölgesi, Atatürk Havalimani, TR-34630 Sefaköy-Istanbul, Turkey ☎ (212) 541 29 17 Tx: none Fax: (212) 541 29 23 SITA: n/a
F: 1993 n/a Head: n/a Net: n/a Aircraft below MTOW 1361kg: Cessna 172

registration	type of aircraft	cn/fn	ex/ex*	mfd	del	powered by	mtow kg	configuration	selcal	name/fln/specialitites/remarks
☐ TC-HNS	Bell 206B JetRanger II	1965	N922DR	0076		1 AN 250-C20	1451			
☐ TC-LEY	HFB 320 Hansa Jet	1043	TC-KHE	0069		2 GE CJ610-5	8800			
☐ TC-OMR	Lockheed L-1329 JetStar 731	5082 / 36	N82SR	0066	0098	4 GA TFE731-3-1E	20071			cvtd JetStar 6

GOKTURK AIR (Göktürk Havacilik Sanayi Ticaret Ltd. Sti. dba) — Bursa

Oulu Cd. Oylum Sitesi A/Blok D.1, TR-16070 Bursa, Turkey ☎ (224) 234 51 11 Tx: none Fax: (224) 234 51 12 SITA: n/a
F: 1993 n/a Head: n/a Net: n/a

registration	type of aircraft	cn/fn	ex/ex*	mfd	del	powered by	mtow kg	configuration	selcal	name/fln/specialitites/remarks
☐ TC-EEE	Piper PA-42-1000 Cheyenne 400LS	42-5527036	TC-SCM	0088	1194	2 GA TPE331-114	5466			
☐ TC-EYE	Dassault Falcon 50	161	N800BD	0086	0995	3 GA TFE731-3-1C	17600			lsf Demir Finansal Kiralama AS

GUNEYDOGU AIR = GDH (Güneydogu Havacilik, Ltd Sti dba) — **Ankara**

Kubilay Sok. 23/8, TR-06100 Maltepe-Ankara, Turkey ☎ (312) 232 49 58 Tx: none Fax: (312) 232 49 31 SITA: n/a
F: 1996 ✱✱✱ n/a Head: n/a ICAO: RISING SUN Net: n/a Aircraft below MTOW 1361kg: Cessna 172

☐ TC-FAV	Piper PA-34-200T Seneca II	34-7970113	N3979S	0079		2 CO TSIO-360-EB	2073			

GUVEN AIR (Güven Hava Yollari, A.S. dba) — **Istanbul**

Florya M. Catal S. Aiblok 5, TR-34810 Florya-Istanbul, Turkey ☎ (212) 662 03 62 Tx: none Fax: (212) 662 02 61 SITA: n/a
F: 1996 ✱✱✱ n/a Head: Ahmet Akpinar Net: http://www.guvenair.com.tr

☐ TC-HMD	Bell 430	49010	N62839*	0096	0096	2 AN 250-C40	4082			lsf ERA Leasing
☐ TC-MDE	Beech King Air B200	BB-1539	N1089S*	0096	1296	2 PWC PT6A-42	5670			lsf Raytheon Aircraft Credit Corp.
☐ TC-MDB	Beech Beechjet 400A	RK-164	N2164Z*	0097	0097	2 PWC JT15D-5	7303			
☐ TC-MDJ	Beech Beechjet 400A	RK-120	N3261Y*	0096	0097	2 PWC JT15D-5	7303			

HELIKOPTER 2000, A.S. (Associated with Air Ambulance Transportation Foundation) — **Istanbul**

Perpa Ticaret Merkezi, Kat. 8, No. 849, TR-80270 Okmeydoni-Istanbul, Turkey ☎ (212) 221 99 14 Tx: none Fax: (212) 220 37 28 SITA: n/a
F: 1994 ✱✱✱ 14 Head: H. Tahsin San Net: n/a Aircraft below MTOW 1361kg: Robinson R44

☐ TC-HAT	Agusta A109A	7191	D-HXXH	0080	1095	2 AN 250-C20B	2600	EMS / 8 Pax		lsf Aviation Leasing GmbH

IHLAS AVIATION (Ihlas Havacilik, A.S. dba) — **Istanbul**

29 Ekim Cad. 23, TR-34530 Yenibosna-Istanbul, Turkey ☎ (212) 454 22 62 Tx: none Fax: (212) 454 22 63 SITA: n/a
F: 1997 ✱✱✱ n/a Head: n/a Net: n/a

☐ TC-IHS	Lockheed L-1329 JetStar II	5225	N42KR	0078	0098	4 GA TFE731-3	20185			lsf IHLAS Finance Int'l

ISTANBUL AIRLINES = IL / IST (Istanbul Hava Yollari, A.S. dba) — **Istanbul**

Firuzköy Yolu 26, TR-34850 Avcilar-Istanbul, Turkey ☎ (212) 509 21 00 Tx: 21012 ihyo tr Fax: (212) 593 06 66 SITA: ISTOWIL
F: 1985 ✱✱✱ 1900 Head: Safi Ergin ICAO: ISTANBUL Net: n/a

☐ TC-IAC	Boeing 737-382	24450 / 1873	CS-TIE	0090	0798	2 CFMI CFM56-3B2	62000	Y148		lsf ORIX
☐ TC-IAD	Boeing 737-33A	25033 / 2025	OY-MBN	0091	0498	2 CFMI CFM56-3B1	61235	Y148		lsf CITG
☐ TC-IAE	Boeing 737-3L9	24571 / 1815	D-ADBF	0090	1198	2 CFMI CFM56-3B2	61235	Y148		lsf TOMB
☐ TC-ACA	Boeing 737-4Y0	24519 / 1781	VR-CAB	0089	0392	2 CFMI CFM56-3C1	68040	Y168	DR-JL	lsf BBAM
☐ TC-AGA	Boeing 737-4Y0	24512 / 1777	VR-CAL	0089	1291	2 CFMI CFM56-3C1	68040	Y168	DR-JK	lsf GECA
☐ TC-APA	Boeing 737-4S3	25595 / 2233	9M-MLG	0092	0393	2 CFMI CFM56-3C1	68040	Y168	EP-HR	lsf BOUL
☐ TC-AVA	Boeing 737-4S3	25594 / 2223	9M-MLJ	0092	0393	2 CFMI CFM56-3C1	68040	Y168	EP-HL	lsf BOUL
☐ TC-AYA	Boeing 737-4Y0	24683 / 1901	9M-MJR	0090	0493	2 CFMI CFM56-3C1	68040	Y168	DR-JS	lsf GECA
☐ TC-AZA	Boeing 737-4Y0	24691 / 1904	9M-MJS	0090	0593	2 CFMI CFM56-3C1	68040	Y168	DR-KL	lsf GECA
☐ TC-IAA	Boeing 737-46Q	29000 / 3033		0098	0698	2 CFMI CFM56-3C1	68040	Y168		lsf BOUL
☐ TC-IAB	Boeing 737-46Q	29001 / 3040		0098	0698	2 CFMI CFM56-3C1	68040	Y168		lsf BOUL
☐ TC-IAF	Boeing 737-43Q	28490 / 2830	B-18672	0096	1298	2 CFMI CFM56-3C1	62822	Y168		lsf GECA
☐ TC-IAG	Boeing 737-43Q	28491 / 2832	B-18673	0096	1298	2 CFMI CFM56-3C1	62822	Y168		lsf GECA
☐ TC-IAH	Boeing 737-86N	28591				2 CFMI CFM56-7B26	79015	Y189		to be lsf GECA 0599
☐ TC-	Boeing 737-86N					2 CFMI CFM56-7B26	79015	Y184		to be lsf GECA 0000
☐ TC-	Boeing 737-86N					2 CFMI CFM56-7B26	79015	Y184		to be lsf GECA 0000

KALE AIR (Kale Seramik Air Havacilik San ve Tic. A.S. dba) — **Istanbul**

Tevfikbey Mah.Istiklal Cad. 13, TR-34530 Sefköy-Istanbul, Turkey ☎ (212) 624 67 01 Tx: none Fax: (212) 624 18 95 SITA: n/a
F: 1994 ✱✱✱ 6 Head: Teoman Eke Net: n/a

☐ TC-HIK	Agusta A109A II MAX	7413	D-HAAY	0088	0097	2 AN 250-C20R/1	2600			
☐ TC-HKN	Sikorsky S-76B	760339	N22QP	0088	1294	2 PWC PT6B-36A	5350			

KALYON AIR (Kalyon Hava Tasimaciligi ve Turzim Ltd Sti dba) — **Ankara**

Silahtar Caddesi 16/3, TR-06560 Gazi-Ankara, Turkey ☎ (312) 212 30 33 Tx: none Fax: (312) 212 30 43 SITA: n/a
F: 1992 ✱✱✱ n/a Head: Turan Kalyoncu Net: n/a Aircraft below MTOW 1361kg: Cessna 172.

☐ TC-OTK	Cessna 340A II	340A0906	N2701X	0080		2 CO TSIO-520-N	2717			
☐ TC-ACN	Beech King Air 200	BB-791	N54LG	0081		2 PWC PT6A-41	5670			

KTHY – Kibris Türk Hava Yollari = KYV (Cyprus Turkish Airlines, Co. Ltd / Kibris Türk Hava Yollari, Ltd Sti dba / Associated with Turkish Airlines) — **Ercan**

Bedreddin Demirel Ave, Yenisehir, Nicosia, North Cyprus ☎ 228 39 01 Tx: 57133 thkf tr Fax: 228 14 62 SITA: ECNOWYK
F: 1974 ✱✱✱ 270 Head: Umit Utku ICAO: AIRKIBRIS Net: n/a

☐ TC-	Boeing 737-86N					2 CFMI CFM56-7B26	79015	Y189		to be lsf GECA 0400
☐ TC-	Boeing 737-86N					2 CFMI CFM56-7B26	79015	Y189		to be lsf GECA 0500
☐ TC-JBF	Boeing 727-2F2 (A)	20980 / 1085		0074	0096	3 PW JT8D-15	86409	Y164		Adana
☐ TC-JBG	Boeing 727-2F2 (A)	20981 / 1086		0074	0794	3 PW JT8D-15	86409	Y164	BJ-GM	Yavruvatan
☐ TC-JBJ	Boeing 727-2F2 (A)	20983 / 1088		0074	0794	3 PW JT8D-15	86409	Y164	BK-AJ	Besparmak
☐ TC-JEC	Boeing 727-228 (A)	22287 / 1710	F-GCDF	0081	0794	3 PW JT8D-15	86409	Y164	EK-GJ	Yesilada
☐ TC-JYK	Airbus Industrie A310-203	172	F-GEMF	0082	1294	2 GE CF6-80A3	142000	Y225	EH-GJ	Erenköy / lsf AFR / cvtd A310-221

MACH AIR (MAK Havacilik ve Turizm, Ltd Sti dba) — **Istanbul**

Ozel Hangarlar Bölgesi, Besyol, TR-34630 Sefaköy-Istanbul, Turkey ☎ (212) 541 14 23 Tx: 21068 Mak TR Fax: (212) 541 95 94 SITA: n/a
F: 1989 ✱✱✱ 48 Head: A. Birhan Temel Net: http://www.machair.com Aircraft below MTOW 1361kg: Cessna 172 & Robinson R22

☐ TC-HCC	Bell 206B JetRanger III	4024	C-FCYG	0088	0098	1 AN 250-C20J	1451			
☐ TC-HMH	Bell 222	47014	ZK-HFQ	0080	0895	2 LY LTS101-650C.2	3561			lsf Albaraka Türk Ozel Finans Kurumu
☐ TC-SKO	Beech King Air B200	BB-1334	N5545B	0089		2 PWC PT6A-42	5670			lsf Isko Tekstil San. Tic. A.S.
☐ TC-SBH	Cessna 650 Citation VI	650-0234	N334CM	0093		2 GA TFE731-3B-100S	9979			lsf Sabah Yayincilik A.S.
☐ TC-ANC	Hawker 800B (BAe 125-800B)	258208	G-BUID	0091		2 GA TFE731-5R-1H	12428			Henza / lsf Olakoglu Metalurji A.S.
☐ TC-AKK	Dassault Falcon 900B	171	F-WWFW*	0098	0498	3 GA TFE731-5BR-1C	21099			

MENEKSE AIR (Menekse Sivil Havacilik Ithalat, Ltd Sti dba) — **Ankara**

Bilir Sok. 6/15, TR-06700 Kavaklidere-Ankara, Turkey ☎ (312) 426 27 14 Tx: 46102 airm tr Fax: (312) 426 60 24 SITA: n/a
F: 1976 ✱✱✱ 12 Head: Erdogan Menekse Net: n/a Aircraft below MTOW 1361kg: Cessna 172 & Mooney M20J

☐ TC-CRO	Cessna 525 CitationJet	525-0102	N202CJ	0095	1195	2 WRR FJ44-1A	4717			lsf Bilfer Madencilik A.S.
☐ TC-LMK	Beech King Air C90A	LJ-1080	N6931W	0085		2 PWC PT6A-21	4377			lsf Interlease Fin. Kir. A.S.

METRO AIR (Metro Hava Tasm. san ve Tic. Ltd Sti dba) — **Istanbul**

Karaoglanoglu Caddesi 17, TR-34550 Bagcilar-Istanbul, Turkey ☎ (212) 630 85 00 Tx: none Fax: (212) 630 85 11 SITA: n/a
F: 1996 ✱✱✱ n/a Head: Baskurt Okaygün Net: n/a Aircraft below MTOW 1361kg: Cessna 172

☐ TC-OZY	Beech King Air B200	BB-1545	N1070E	0096	0498	2 PWC PT6A-42	5670			

MNG CARGO AIRLINES = MB / MNB (MNG Hava Yollari ve Tasimacilik, A.S. dba / Subsidiary of MNG Holdings) — **Istanbul**

Yesiköy Caddesi 9, TR-34810 Florya-Istanbul, Turkey ☎ (212) 663 83 52 Tx: none Fax: (212) 573 35 30 SITA: ISTGOXH
F: 1997 ✱✱✱ n/a Head: Kani Kurtulus IATA: 716 ICAO: BLACK SEA Net: http://www.mngaircargo.com

☐ TC-MNA	Airbus Industrie A300B4-203 (F)	019	N742SC	0075	0598	2 GE CF6-50C2	165000	Freighter		lsf CSAV / cvtd -203
☐ TC-MNG	Airbus Industrie A300C4-203	083	EI-BZB	0079	1097	2 GE CF6-50C2	165000	Freighter		Hayal / lsf GECA

NERGIS AIR (Nergis Havacilik, A.S. dba) — **Bursa**

Organize Sanayi Bölgesi, Bursa, Turkey ☎ (224) 243 19 55 Tx: 32050 nerg tr Fax: (224) 243 19 55 SITA: n/a
F: 1986 ✱✱✱ 7 Head: Capt. Sebahattin Oktay Net: n/a

☐ TC-HBK	Bell 206B JetRanger III	3950		0086	0098	1 AN 250-C20J	1451			
☐ TC-HCM	Bell 430	49032	N5254W*	0097	1097	2 AN 250-C40	4082			
☐ TC-HNH	Bell 430	49033	N8060J*	0097	1297	2 AN 250-C40	4082			
☐ TC-CMY	Cessna 650 Citation III	650-0141	N110TM	0087		2 GA TFE731-3B-100S	9979			lsf Iktisat Leasing A.S.
☐ TC-CAG	Dassault Falcon 900B	142	F-GSMF	0094	1096	3 GA TFE731-5BR-1C	21099			Caglar / lsf General Electric Capital

NUROL AVIATION (Nurol Havacilik, A.S. dba) — **Ankara**

Arjantin Cad. 7, TR-06700 Gop-Ankara, Turkey ☎ (312) 428 42 50 Tx: none Fax: (312) 427 85 01 SITA: n/a
F: 1997 ✱✱✱ 10 Head: Ahmet Erdem Net: n/a

☐ TC-NEO	Beech Beechjet 400A	RK-130	N1130B	0096	0397	2 PWC JT15D-5	7303			Eyup Sandel

ONUR AIR Tasimacilik, A.S. = 8Q / OHY (Subsidiary of Ten Tour International & Marmara tour operator) — **Istanbul**

Senlik Mahallesi, Catal Sokuk No. 3, TR-34810 Florya-Istanbul, Turkey ☎ (212) 663 23 00 Tx: 21207 onyt tr Fax: (212) 663 23 19 SITA: ISTTO8Q
F: 1992 ✱✱✱ 450 Head: Cankut Bagana ICAO: ONUR AIR Net: n/a

☐ TC-ONM	Boeing (Douglas) MD-88 (DC-9-88)	53546 / 2167		0097	0597	2 PW JT8D-219	72575	Y172		Yasemin
☐ TC-ONN	Boeing (Douglas) MD-88 (DC-9-88)	53547 / 2176		0097	0597	2 PW JT8D-219	72575	Y172		Ece
☐ TC-ONO	Boeing (Douglas) MD-88 (DC-9-88)	53548 / 2180		0097	0597	2 PW JT8D-219	72575	Y172		Yonca
☐ TC-ONP	Boeing (Douglas) MD-88 (DC-9-88)	53549 / 2185		0097	0597	2 PW JT8D-219	72575	Y172	AP-HS	Esra
☐ TC-ONR	Boeing (Douglas) MD-88 (DC-9-88)	53550 / 2187		0097	0697	2 PW JT8D-219	72575	Y172		Evren
☐ TC-ONG	Airbus Industrie A320-231	361	N431LF	0092	0695	2 IAE V2500-A1	73500	Y180		Gülnur / lsf ILFC / ex Leisure-colors
☐ TC-ONH	Airbus Industrie A321-131	591	D-AVZV*	0096	0496	2 IAE V2530-A5	83000	Y220		Nazar / lsf ILFC
☐ TC-ONI	Airbus Industrie A321-131	597	D-AVZY*	0096	0596	2 IAE V2530-A5	83000	Y220	CF-HM	Içli / lsf ILFC
☐ TC-ONJ	Airbus Industrie A321-131	385	D-AVZG*	0593	0796	2 IAE V2530-A5	83000	Y220		Kaptan Soray Sahin / cvtd -111
☐ TC-ONS	Airbus Industrie A321-131	364	D-AVZD*	0393	0698	2 IAE V2530-A5	83000	Y220		Funda / lst TAS / cvtd -111
☐ TC-ONK	Airbus Industrie A300B4-103	086	TC-TKA	0079	0196	2 GE CF6-50C2	157500	Y316		Pinar
☐ TC-ONL	Airbus Industrie A300B4-103	087	TC-TKB	0079	0196	2 GE CF6-50C2	157500	Y316		Selin
☐ TC-ONV	Airbus Industrie A300B4-2C	057	F-BUAQ	0078	0697	2 GE CF6-50C2R	150000	Y314		Ugras-Ugur / lsf Cebi Avn SA/sublst GTK

598 registration type of aircraft cn/fn ex/ex* mfd del powered by mtow kg configuration selcal name/fln/specialitites/remarks

ORMAN Helikopter (Forestry Helicopter) (Division of Orman Genel Müdürlügü / General Directorate of Forestry) — Ankara

c/o Orman Genel Müdürlügü, Havacilik Sb. Md., TR-06560 Gazi-Ankara, Turkey ☎ (312) 213 97 86 Tx: n/a Fax: (312) 222 50 76 SITA: n/a
F: 1988 n/a Head: Atilla Inal Net: n/a Non-commercial state organisation conducting flight for the surveillance of forests and national parks.

☐ TC-HCG	Eurocopter (Aerosp.) AS355F2 Ecureuil 2	5354	F-WYML*	0087		2 AN 250-C20F	2540			
☐ TC-HCH	Eurocopter (Aerosp.) AS355F2 Ecureuil 2	5369	F-WYMN*	0087		2 AN 250-C20F	2540			
☐ TC-HCJ	Eurocopter (Aerosp.) AS355F2 Ecureuil 2	5357	F-WYMM*	0087		2 AN 250-C20F	2540			
☐ TC-HCD	Eurocopter (Aerosp.) SA365N1 Dauphin 2	6303	F-WYMQ*	0087		2 TU Arriel 1C1	4100			
☐ TC-HCF	Eurocopter (Aerosp.) SA365N1 Dauphin 2	6302	F-WYMP*	0087		2 TU Arriel 1C1	4100			
☐ TC-HCK	Eurocopter (Aerosp.) SA365N2 Dauphin 2	6434	F-WYMN*	0091		2 TU Arriel 1C2	4250			

OZEK AIR (Ozek Havacilik, Ltd Sirketi dba) — Bursa

Yalova Yolu 4KM, TR-16107 Bursa, Turkey ☎ (224) 245 25 61 Tx: none Fax: (224) 245 25 61 SITA: n/a
F: 1996 n/a Head: Hüseyin Ozdilek Net: n/a Aircraft below MTOW 1361kg: Cessna 172

☐ TC-OZD	Beech King Air B200	BB-1496	N3047L	0094	0896	2 PWC PT6A-42	5670			

PARK EXPRESS (Member of Park Holding Group) — Istanbul

Sehit Muhtar Bey Caddesi 56, TR-80050 Taksim-Istanbul, Turkey ☎ (212) 254 71 00 Tx: none Fax: (212) 255 01 87 SITA: n/a
F: 1998 n/a Head: Atilla Celebi Net: n/a Presently being set-up. Intends to start operations during 2000.

☐ TC-RJA	Avro RJ100 (Avro 146-RJ100)					4 LY LF507-1F	46040	CY112		oo-delivery 0000
☐ TC-RJB	Avro RJ100 (Avro 146-RJ100)					4 LY LF507-1F	46040	CY112		oo-delivery 0000
☐ TC-RJC	Avro RJ100 (Avro 146-RJ100)					4 LY LF507-1F	46040	CY112		oo-delivery 0000
☐ TC-RJD	Avro RJ100 (Avro 146-RJ100)					4 LY LF507-1F	46040	CY112		oo-delivery 0000
☐ TC-RJE	Avro RJ100 (Avro 146-RJ100)					4 LY LF507-1F	46040	CY112		oo-delivery 0000

PEGASUS AIRLINES = PGT (Pegasus Hava Tasimaciligi, A.S. dba / Subsidiary of Enternasyonal Turizm Yatirim A.S.) — Istanbul

Istasyon Caddesi 24, Kat. 1, TR-34800 Yesilyurt-Istanbul, Turkey ☎ (212) 663 29 34 Tx: 21117 pegs tr Fax: (212) 663 66 86 SITA: ISTTOEI
F: 1990 330 Head: Osman Berkman ICAO: PEGASUS Net: n/a

☐ TC-AFA	Boeing 737-4Q8	26306 / 2653		0094	1094	2 CFMI CFM56-3C1	68040	Y170	DG-HQ	lsf ILFC / sub-lst WNA in winter
☐ TC-AFJ	Boeing 737-4Y0	23979 / 1661	OO-SBN	0089	0597	2 CFMI CFM56-3C1	64636	Y170	JQ-GK	lsf GECA
☐ TC-AFK	Boeing 737-4Y0	24684 / 1841		0090	0490	2 CFMI CFM56-3C1	68040	Y170	EM-DQ	lsf GECA
☐ TC-AFM	Boeing 737-4Q8	26279 / 2221		0092	0292	2 CFMI CFM56-3C1	68040	Y170	BP-ER	lsf ILFC / sub-lst WNA in winter
☐ TC-AFU	Boeing 737-4Y0	26081 / 2442	D-ABAF	0093	0396	2 CFMI CFM56-3C1	68000	Y170	DR-AH	lsf GECA
☐ TC-AFZ	Boeing 737-4Y0	23981 / 1678	EI-CEW	0089	0495	2 CFMI CFM56-3C1	64636	Y170	JK-AB	lsf GECA
☐ TC-APD	Boeing 737-42R	29107 / 2997		0098	0398	2 CFMI CFM56-3C1	68040	Y170	BS-HJ	lst SAI
☐ TC-APP	Boeing 737-4Q8	28202 / 3009		0098	0398	2 CFMI CFM56-3C1	68040	Y170	GS-DJ	lsf ILFC / sub-lst WNA in winter
☐ TC-APG	Boeing 737-82R	29329 / 224	N1786B*	0099	0399	2 CFMI CFM56-7B26	78245	Y189		

RED STAR AIR AMBULANCE (Red Star Acil özal Saglik Hizmetleri, A.S. dba) — Izmir

red st★r

Ziya Gökalp Bulvari 18, TR-35220 Alsancak-Izmir, Turkey ☎ (232) 464 52 12 Tx: 53730 mrj tr Fax: (232) 463 90 55 SITA: n/a
F: 1992 40 Head: Dr. Mustafa Atag Net: n/a

☐ TC-BBJ	PZL Swidnik (Mil) Mi-2	5210231057	RA-23230	0087	0693	2 IS GTD-350-4	3700	EMS		
☐ TC-EGE	PZL Swidnik (Mil) Mi-2	5210725098	RA-14106	0088	1093	2 IS GTD-350-4	3700	EMS		
☐ TC-MED	PZL Swidnik (Mil) Mi-2	5210126027	RA-23205	0087	1093	2 IS GTD-350-4	3700	EMS		
☐ TC-TIP	PZL Swidnik (Mil) Mi-2	5210624058	RA-14080	0088	0693	2 IS GTD-350-4	3700	EMS		

ROTA AIR (Rota Havacilik ve Ticaret AS, dba) — Istanbul

Konakli Sokak, Villa Ocak, no. 3/2, TR-34810 Florya-Istanbul, Turkey ☎ (212) 663 77 66 Tx: none Fax: (212) 663 77 89 SITA: n/a
F: 1997 n/a Head: Bülent Karasöy Net: http://www.escortnet.rotaair

☐ TC-ATC	Cessna 650 Citation VII	650-7043	N78DL	0095	0497	2 GA TFE731-4R-2S	10183			

RUBI AIR (Rubi Hava Tasimaciligi Ticaret, A.S. dba) — Istanbul

3 Beskardesler Sok. No. 18, Zeytinburnu-Istanbul, Turkey ☎ (212) 551 94 00 Tx: none Fax: (212) 552 24 99 SITA: n/a
F: 1995 5 Head: Capt. Pavel Podborsek Net: n/a Aircraft below MTOW 1361kg: Cessna 172

☐ TC-EMA	Cessna 525 CitationJet	525-0121	N5264S*	1195	1295	2 WRR FJ44-1A	4717	5 Pax		

SAFAK CIVIL AVIATION (Safak Sivil Havacilik, Ltd Sti dba) — Bursa

Bursa Havaalani, Ozel Sirketler Bölömuü, TR-16186 Bursa, Turkey ☎ (224) 245 90 82 Tx: none Fax: (224) 234 90 84 SITA: n/a
F: 1996 n/a Head: Metin Yelli Net: n/a Aircraft below MTOW 1361kg: Cessna 172

☐ TC-FAP	Cessna 421C Golden Eagle III	421C0513	N67Q	0078		2 CO GTSIO-520-L	3379			

SAGLAM AIR (Saglam Havacilik Hava Taksi, Isletmeciligi Ltd Sti dba) — Ankara

Tunali Hilmi Cad. 67/23, TR-06700 Kavaklidere-Ankara, Turkey ☎ (312) 467 19 00 Tx: none Fax: (312) 467 19 87 SITA: n/a
F: 1995 n/a Head: Halil Can Celik Net: n/a

☐ TC-HAG	Mil Mi-8MTV-1	95588	4L-25449	0191	0095	2 IS TV3-117VM	13000	Y24		lsf AISI
☐ TC-HIS	Mil Mi-8MTV-1	95486	4L-25176	0990	0095	2 IS TV3-117VM	13000	Y26		lsf AISI

SANCAK AIR, Inc. (Sancak Havacilik, A.S. dba) — Istanbul

SancakAir

Atatürk Hava Limani, Oezel Hangarlar Bölgesi, TR-34630 Sefaköy-Istanbul, Turkey ☎ (212) 541 41 41 Tx: 21037 koko tr Fax: (212) 541 02 85 SITA: n/a
F: 1986 105 Head: Mustafa Bayrak Net: http://www.sancakair.com.tr Aircraft below MTOW 1361kg: Enstrom F28

☐ TC-HBF	Agusta-Bell 206B JetRanger III	8702		0786	0786	1 AN 250-C20J	1451			
☐ TC-HBT	Bell 206B JetRanger III	2299	D-HKWF	0077	0097	1 AN 250-C20B	1451			

SANTAY AIR (Santay Havacilik Ticaret A.S. dba / formerly Santay Sanayi Tesileri ve Tic. A.S.) — Izmir

Santay

Atatürk Cad. 44/5, Konak, TR-35250 Izmir, Turkey ☎ (232) 274 27 00 Tx: none Fax: (232) 274 21 98 SITA: n/a
F: 1992 12 Head: Mehmet Dogan Atay Net: n/a

☐ TC-HEA	Bell 206B JetRanger III	4108		0090		1 AN 250-C20J	1451			
☐ TC-TAY	Piper PA-28-236 Dakota	2811032		0089		1 LY O-540-J3A5D	1361			
☐ TC-ARK	Dassault Falcon 100	218	F-GHSK	0089	0199	2 GA TFE731-2-1C	8755			

SET AIR (Set Air Hava Tasimaciligi ve Hizmetler, A.S. dba/Subs.of KOC Holding/Member of Setur/formerly Turyat Aviation) — Istanbul

Ozel Hangarlar Bolgesi Polis Egitim Merkezi Arkasi, TR-34630 Sefaköy-Istanbul, Turkey ☎ (212) 540 20 01 Tx: 27516 stur tr Fax: (212) 540 26 18 SITA: n/a
F: 1990 15 Head: Salih Keskin Net: n/a Aircraft below MTOW 1361kg: Cessna 150

☐ TC-HRM	Bell 430	49018		0096	1296	2 AN 250-C40	4082			lsf KOC Holding
☐ TC-MCK	Beech King Air C90	LJ-962	N1213P	0081	1293	2 PWC PT6A-21	4377			lsf KOC Holding
☐ TC-KOC	Cessna 650 Citation VII	650-7006	N966K	0092	1297	2 GA TFE731-4R-2S	10183			lsf KOC Holding

SKY LINE (Sky Line Ulasim Tic. A.S. dba / formerly Air Taksi Ulasim Tic. A.S.) — Ankara

Ozel Hangarlar Böl. Cubuk, TR-06600 Esenboga-Ankara, Turkey ☎ (312) 827 15 62 Tx: none Fax: (312) 827 15 63 SITA: n/a
F: 1994 15 Head: Eyup Tursucu Net: n/a

☐ TC-MSA	Beech Beechjet 400A	RK-124	N1124Z	0096	0096	2 PWC JT15D-5	7303			
☐ TC-MSB	Beech Beechjet 400A	RK-170	TC-MCX	0097	0098	2 PWC JT15D-5	7303			

SONMEZ AIRLINES = SMZ (Sönmez Hava Yollari, A.S. dba) — Bursa

DHMI Bursa Havaalani SHY Jet, Grubu, TR-16036 Hörriyet-Bursa, Turkey ☎ (224) 245 85 90 Tx: 32508 aos tr Fax: (224) 245 90 02 SITA: n/a
F: 1984 18 Head: Ali Osman Sönmez ICAO: SONMEZ Net: n/a

☐ TC-CAO	Cessna 650 Citation III	650-0060	N848US	0085	0396	2 GA TFE731-3B-100S	9752	Y10		
☐ TC-AOA	Shorts 360-100 (SD3-60)	SH3661	G-BLRT	0084	0693	2 PWC PT6A-65AR	11999	Y36		
☐ TC-SMA	GAC (Grumman) G-159 Gulfstream I	172	N712RD	0066	0598	2 RR Dart 529-8X	16329	Y15		

SUNEXPRESS = XQ / SXS (Sun Ekspres Hava Yollari, A.S. dba / Associated with Condor & THY Turkish Airlines) — Antalya

SunExpress

PO Box 28, TR-07100 Antalya, Turkey ☎ (242) 323 40 47 Tx: none Fax: (242) 323 40 57 SITA: AYTMDXQ
F: 1990 300 Head: Florian Hamm IATA: 564 Net: n/a

☐ TC-SUN	Boeing 737-3Y0	24676 / 1829		0090	0390	2 CFMI CFM56-3B2	62800	Y148	BP-JQ	lsf GECA
☐ TC-SUP	Boeing 737-3Y0	24908 / 2015		0091	0391	2 CFMI CFM56-3C1	62800	Y148	AE-MS	lsf GECA
☐ TC-SUR	Boeing 737-3Y0	24910 / 2030		0091	0491	2 CFMI CFM56-3C1	62800	Y148	AE-PR	lsf GECA
☐ TC-SUS	Boeing 737-430	27007 / 2367	D-ABKL	0092	0493	2 CFMI CFM56-3C1	65100	Y167		lsf DLH
☐ TC-SUT	Boeing 737-4Y0	25190 / 2256	OY-MBL	0092	1294	2 CFMI CFM56-3C1	68038	Y170	CR-JQ	lsf GECA

TARKIM AIR (Tarkim Ucak Bakim ve onarim Havacilik, Ltd Sti dba) — Adana

Sakirpasa Havaalani, TR-01070 Adana, Turkey ☎ (322) 435 78 57 Tx: none Fax: (322) 435 57 70 SITA: n/a
F: 1995 n/a Head: n/a Net: n/a Aircraft below MTOW 1361kg: Cessna 150/172, Lake LA4 & Piper PA-18

☐ TC-FAN	Piper PA-30-160 Twin Comanche B	30-1521	I-TJTJ	0067		2 LY IO-320-B1A	1633			
☐ TC-BAS	Cessna 421B Golden Eagle	421B0331	N77MH	0073	0297	2 CO GTSIO-520-H	3379			

TEKFEN AIR TRANSPORT (Tekfen Hava Tasimaciligi, A.S. dba) — Istanbul

Ulus Tekfen Sitesi, Blok A, TR-80600 Etiler-Istanbul, Turkey ☎ (212) 540 75 37 Tx: none Fax: (212) 540 75 37 SITA: n/a
F: 1995 2 Head: Ahmet Pekci Net: n/a

☐ TC-TEK	Hawker 800B (BAe 125-800B)	258229	N229RY	0091		2 GA TFE731-5R-1H	12428			

599 registration type of aircraft cn/fn ex/ex* mfd del powered by mtow kg configuration selcal name/fln/specialitites/remarks

THK - Türk Hava Kurumu/Hava Taksi Isletmesi = THK (Turkish Aeronautical Association/Air Taxi Enterprise) — Ankara

Atatürk Bulvari 33, Opera, TR-06100 Ankara, Turkey ☎ (312) 310 48 40 Tx: 44270 thkb tr Fax: (312) 310 04 13 SITA: n/a
F: 1925 ⁂ 100 Head: Prof. Dr. Attila Tacoy ICAO: HUR KUS Net: n/a Aircraft / Ag-& Trainer aircraft below MTOW 5000kg: Cessna T188C, Norman NAC-6 Fieldmaster, PZL 104 Wilga, PZL M-18A/B & Slingsby T67M Firefly

registration	type of aircraft	cn/fn	ex/ex*	mfd	del	powered by	mtow kg	configuration	selcal	name/fln/specialitites/remarks
☐ TC-CAE	Cessna U206B Super Skywagon	U206-0884	N11B	0067		1 CO IO-520-F	1633			
☐ TC-CAF	Cessna U206B Super Skywagon	U206-0885	N11B	0067		1 CO IO-520-F	1633			
☐ TC-CAN	Cessna TU206G Turbo Stationair 6 II	U20606181	N6185Z	0081		1 CO TSIO-520-M	1633			
☐ TC-CAP	Cessna U206G Stationair 6 II	U20606074	N5163Z	0081		1 CO IO-520-F	1633			
☐ TC-CAR	Cessna U206G Stationair 6 II	U20606128	N5517Z	0081		1 CO IO-520-F	1633			
☐ TC-CAT	Cessna TU206G Turbo Stationair 6 II	U20606230	N6314Z	0081		1 CO TSIO-520-M	1633			
☐ TC-CAM	Cessna 207 Skywagon	20700241	N69289	0074		1 CO IO-520-F	1724			
☐ TC-ZTP	Cessna 402B	402B0412	N69289	0073		2 CO TSIO-520-E	2858			
☐ TC-ZVJ	Cessna 402B II	402B1084	N1906G	0076		2 CO TSIO-520-E	2858			
☐ TC-TRL	Dornier DO 28D-1 Skyservant	4119	58+44	0073	0097	2 LY IGSO-540-A1E	4350			
☐ TC-TRM	Dornier DO 28D-1 Skyservant	4122	58+47	0073	0097	2 LY IGSO-540-A1E	4350			
☐ TC-TRO	Dornier DO 28D-1 Skyservant	4035		0072	0098	2 LY IGSO-540-A1E	4350			
☐ TC-CAU	Cessna 208 Caravan I	20800248	N1123X*	0096	1096	1 PWC PT6A-114	3629			
☐ TC-CAV	Cessna 208 Caravan I	20800256	N1249T*	0096	0896	1 PWC PT6A-114	3629			
☐ TC-FAH	Piper PA-42-720 Cheyenne IIIA	42-5501033		0085		2 PWC PT6A-61	5080			
☐ TC-THK	Piper PA-42-720 Cheyenne IIIA	42-5501031	TC-FAG	0085		2 PWC PT6A-61	5080			
☐ TC-ZAG	PZL Mielec (Antonov) An-2R	1G230-23	SP-ZZG	0088	0988	1 SH ASh-62IR	5500			
☐ TC-ZAH	PZL Mielec (Antonov) An-2R	1G230-24	SP-ZZH	0088	0988	1 SH ASh-62IR	5500			
☐ TC-ZAJ	PZL Mielec (Antonov) An-2R	1G230-25	SP-ZZI	0088	0988	1 SH ASh-62IR	5500			
☐ TC-ZAK	PZL Mielec (Antonov) An-2R	1G230-26	SP-ZZK	0088	0988	1 SH ASh-62IR	5500			
☐ TC-ZYF	PZL Mielec (Antonov) An-2R	1G185-58/1	SP-DMA	0080	0980	1 SH ASh-62IR	5500			
☐ TC-ZYG	PZL Mielec (Antonov) An-2R	1G185-59	SP-DBA	0079	0980	1 SH ASh-62IR	5500			
☐ TC-ZYH	PZL Mielec (Antonov) An-2R	1G191-01	SP-DBA	0081	0581	1 SH ASh-62IR	5500			
☐ TC-ZYİ	PZL Mielec (Antonov) An-2R	1G191-02	SP-DBB	0081	0581	1 SH ASh-62IR	5500			
☐ TC-ZYS	PZL Mielec (Antonov) An-2T	1G206-35	SP-ZYS	0084	0584	1 SH ASh-62IR	5500			
☐ TC-ZYT	PZL Mielec (Antonov) An-2T	1G208-03	SP-ZYT	0084	0584	1 SH ASh-62IR	5500			
☐ TC-ZYU	PZL Mielec (Antonov) An-2T	1G208-04	SP-ZYU	0084	0584	1 SH ASh-62IR	5500			
☐ TC-ZYV	PZL Mielec (Antonov) An-2R	1G208-01	SP-ZYV	0084	0584	1 SH ASh-62IR	5500			
☐ TC-ZYY	PZL Mielec (Antonov) An-2R	1G208-02	SP-ZYY	0084	0584	1 SH ASh-62IR	5500			
☐ TC-ZYZ	PZL Mielec (Antonov) An-2P	1G199-04	SP-ZYZ	0084	0784	1 SH ASh-62IR	5500			

TOP AIR Havacilik Sanayi ve Ticaret, A.S. = TOP — Istanbul

Atatürk Havalimani, E-Kapisi, TR-34640 Sefaköy-Istanbul, Turkey ☎ (212) 541 60 40 Tx: none Fax: (212) 598 50 60 SITA: n/a
F: 1990 ⁂ 60 Head: n/a ICAO: AIR TOP Net: n/a Aircraft below MTOW 1361kg: AA5B, Cessna 150 & 172

registration	type of aircraft	cn/fn	ex/ex*	mfd	del	powered by	mtow kg	configuration	selcal	name/fln/specialitites/remarks
☐ TC-DBI	Cessna 210L Centurion II	21060984	N2016S	0075		1 CO IO-520-L	1724	Y4		lsf Finans Finansal Kiralama
☐ TC-TBA	Cessna T210M Turbo Centurion II	21062303	N761JX	0077		1 CO TSIO-520-R	1724	Y4		
☐ TC-MST	Cessna 310Q	310Q0065	D-ILFS	0070		2 CO IO-470-VO	2404	Y4		
☐ TC-DBB	Cessna 340A II	340A0018	D-IFJB	0076		2 CO TSIO-520-N	2717	Y4		lsf Toprak Finansal Kiralama
☐ TC-VAN	Cessna 421C Golden Eagle II	421C0274	N248DA	0077	1190	2 CO GTSIO-520-L	3379	Y6		lsf Finans Finansal Kiralama
☐ TC-DBZ	Beech King Air C90	LJ-703	N793MA	0077		2 PWC PT6A-21	4377	Y6		lsf Finans Finansal Kiralama
☐ TC-DBY	Beech King Air 200	BB-821	N144TM	0080		2 PWC PT6A-41	5670	Y8		lsf Finans Finansal Kiralama

TOPRAK AVIATION (Toprak Hava Tasimacligi ve Tic. A.S. dba) — Istanbul

Kisikli Cad. 38, Altunizade-Istanbul, Turkey ☎ (216) 343 29 36 Tx: 26059 htha tr Fax: (216) 334 55 43 SITA: n/a
F: n/a ⁂ n/a Head: n/a Net: n/a

registration	type of aircraft	cn/fn	ex/ex*	mfd	del	powered by	mtow kg	configuration	selcal	name/fln/specialitites/remarks
☐ TC-HTS	Bell 230	23021	N5292L*	0094	0694	2 AN 250C-30G2	3810			
☐ TC-TOP	Cessna 650 Citation III	650-0083	N944CA	0085		2 GA TFE731-3B-100S	9525			lsf Albaraka Türk Ozel Finans Kurumu

TURKISH AIRLINES = TK / THY (Türk Hava Yollari, Anonim Ortakligi dba / Member of The Qualiflyer Group) — Istanbul

Genel Yönetim Binsai, Atatürk Hava Limani, TR-34830 Yesilköy-Istanbul, Turkey ☎ (212) 663 47 40 Tx: 28871 dxtk tr Fax: (212) 663 47 63 SITA: ISTDPTK
F: 1933 ⁂ 8958 Head: Yusuf Bolyirli IATA: 235 ICAO: TURKAIR Net: http://www.turkishairlines.com

registration	type of aircraft	cn/fn	ex/ex*	mfd	del	powered by	mtow kg	configuration	selcal	name/fln/specialitites/remarks
☐ TC-THI	Avro RJ70 (Avro 146-RJ70)	E1229	G-BUFI*	0092	0696	4 LY LF507-1F	40823	CY79		Erzincan / lsf BAMJ / cvtd BAe 146-100
☐ TC-THJ	Avro RJ70 (Avro 146-RJ70)	E1230	G-6-230*	0096	0396	4 LY LF507-1F	40823	CY79		Usak / lsf BAMJ
☐ TC-THL	Avro RJ70 (Avro 146-RJ70)	E1249	G-6-249*	0096	0696	4 LY LF507-1F	40823	CY79		Kahramanmaras / lsf BAMJ
☐ TC-THN	Avro RJ70 (Avro 146-RJ70)	E1252	G-6-252*	0096	0596	4 LY LF507-1F	40873	CY79		Mus / lsf BAMJ
☐ TC-THA	Avro RJ100 (Avro 146-RJ100)	E3232	G-6-232*	0093	0793	4 LY LF507-1F	46039	CY99		Denizli / lsf BAMJ
☐ TC-THB	Avro RJ100 (Avro 146-RJ100)	E3234	G-6-234*	0093	0893	4 LY LF507-1F	46039	CY99		Erzurum / lsf BAMJ
☐ TC-THC	Avro RJ100 (Avro 146-RJ100)	E3236	G-6-236*	0093	0993	4 LY LF507-1F	46039	CY99		Samsum / lsf BAMJ
☐ TC-THD	Avro RJ100 (Avro 146-RJ100)	E3237	G-6-237*	0093	1093	4 LY LF507-1F	46039	CY99		Van / lsf BAMJ
☐ TC-THE	Avro RJ100 (Avro 146-RJ100)	E3238	G-6-238*	0093	1193	4 LY LF507-1F	46039	CY99		Gaziantep / lsf BAMJ
☐ TC-THG	Avro RJ100 (Avro 146-RJ100)	E3241	G-6-241*	0094	0394	4 LY LF507-1F	46039	CY99		Konya / lsf BAMJ
☐ TC-THH	Avro RJ100 (Avro 146-RJ100)	E3243	G-6-243*	0094	0494	4 LY LF507-1F	46039	CY99		Kutahya / lsf BAMJ
☐ TC-THM	Avro RJ100 (Avro 146-RJ100)	E3264	G-6-264*	0095	0695	4 LY LF507-1F	46040	CY99		Slirt / lsf BAMJ
☐ TC-THO	Avro RJ100 (Avro 146-RJ100)	E3265	G-6-265*	0095	0695	4 LY LF507-1F	46040	CY99		Tokat / lsf BAMJ
☐ TC-JDU	Boeing 737-5Y0	25288 / 2286		0092	0692	2 CFMI CFM56-3C1	60553	CY117	CS-JM	Trabzon / lsf GECA
☐ TC-JDV	Boeing 737-5Y0	25289 / 2288	N6069D*	0092	0692	2 CFMI CFM56-3C1	60553	CY117	CS-JP	Bursa / lsf GECA
☐ TC-JDE	Boeing 737-4Y0	24904 / 1988		0091	0291	2 CFMI CFM56-3C1	68038	CY150	EH-CK	Kemer / lsf GECA
☐ TC-JDF	Boeing 737-4Y0	24917 / 2071		0091	0691	2 CFMI CFM56-3C1	68038	CY150	EH-CL	Ayvalik / lsf GECA
☐ TC-JDG	Boeing 737-4Y0	25181 / 2203		0092	0292	2 CFMI CFM56-3C1	68038	CY150	EH-CM	Marmaris / lsf GECA
☐ TC-JDH	Boeing 737-4Y0	25184 / 2227		0092	0392	2 CFMI CFM56-3C1	68038	CY150	GM-AH	Amasra / lsf GECA
☐ TC-JDI	Boeing 737-4Q8	25372 / 2280		0092	0592	2 CFMI CFM56-3C1	68038	CY150	GM-CK	Urgüp / lsf ILFC
☐ TC-JDT	Boeing 737-4Y0	25261 / 2258	N600SK	0092	0692	2 CFMI CFM56-3C1	68038	CY150	CS-DF	Alanya / lsf GECA
☐ TC-JDY	Boeing 737-4Y0	26065 / 2284		0092	0692	2 CFMI CFM56-3C1	68038	CY150	CS-JK	Antalya / lsf GECA
☐ TC-JDZ	Boeing 737-4Y0	26066 / 2301		0092	0692	2 CFMI CFM56-3C1	68038	CY150	CS-HM	Fethiye / lsf GECA
☐ TC-JEA	Boeing 737-42J	27143 / 2457		0093	0493	2 CFMI CFM56-3C1	68038	CY150	AH-DR	Kusadasi / lsf Arab Leasing
☐ TC-JEE	Boeing 737-4Q8	26290 / 2482		0093	0693	2 CFMI CFM56-3C1	68038	CY150	AM-CE	Cesme / lsf ILFC
☐ TC-JEF	Boeing 737-4Q8	26291 / 2513		0093	0893	2 CFMI CFM56-3C1	68038	CY150	EJ-BS	Göreme / lsf ILFC
☐ TC-JEG	Boeing 737-4Q8	25374 / 2562		0093	0194	2 CFMI CFM56-3C1	68038	CY150	ER-CK	Silifke / lsf ILFC
☐ TC-JEH	Boeing 737-4Q8	26320 / 2563		0093	0194	2 CFMI CFM56-3C1	68038	CY150	ER-CL	Tekirdag / lsf ILFC
☐ TC-JEI	Boeing 737-4Q8	26298 / 2564		0093	0394	2 CFMI CFM56-3C1	68038	CY150	ER-CM	Artvin / lsf ILFC
☐ TC-JEJ	Boeing 737-4Q8	25375 / 2598		0094	0494	2 CFMI CFM56-3C1	68038	CY150	ER-CP	Balikesir / lsf ILFC
☐ TC-JEK	Boeing 737-4Q8	26299 / 2602		0094	0494	2 CFMI CFM56-3C1	68038	CY150	ER-CQ	Bolu / lsf ILFC
☐ TC-JEL	Boeing 737-4Q8	26300 / 2604		0094	0594	2 CFMI CFM56-3C1	68038	CY150	ER-CS	Eskisehir / lsf ILFC
☐ TC-JEM	Boeing 737-4Q8	26302 / 2620		0094	0694	2 CFMI CFM56-3C1	68038	CY150	ER-DF	Malatya / lsf ILFC
☐ TC-JEN	Boeing 737-4Q8	25376 / 2689		0095	0295	2 CFMI CFM56-3C1	68038	CY150	ER-DG	Gelibolu / lsf ILFC
☐ TC-JEO	Boeing 737-4Q8	25377 / 2717		0095	0595	2 CFMI CFM56-3C1	68038	CY150	ER-BS	Anadolu / lsf ILFC
☐ TC-JEP	Boeing 737-4Q8	25378 / 2732		0095	0695	2 CFMI CFM56-3C1	68038	CY150	AP-DR	Trakya / lsf ILFC
☐ TC-JER	Boeing 737-4Y0	26073 / 2375		0093	0493	2 CFMI CFM56-3C1	68038	CY150	GL-DJ	Mugla / lsf GECA
☐ TC-JET	Boeing 737-4Y0	26077 / 2425		0093	0493	2 CFMI CFM56-3C1	68038	CY150	GL-DM	Canakkale / lsf GECA
☐ TC-JEU	Boeing 737-4Y0	26078 / 2431		0093	0493	2 CFMI CFM56-3C1	68038	CY150	GL-CD	Samsun / lsf GECA
☐ TC-JEV	Boeing 737-4Y0	26085 / 2468		0093	0593	2 CFMI CFM56-3C1	68038	CY150	GM-CJ	Efes / lsf GECA
☐ TC-JEY	Boeing 737-4Y0	26086 / 2475		0093	0593	2 CFMI CFM56-3C1	68038	CY150	AM-CD	Side / lsf GECA
☐ TC-JEZ	Boeing 737-4Y0	26088 / 2487		0093	0693	2 CFMI CFM56-3C1	68038	CY150	AM-DG	Bergama / lsf GECA
☐ TC-JFC	Boeing 737-8F2	29765 / 80		0098	1098	2 CFMI CFM56-7B26	79015	C20Y135		Diyarbakir
☐ TC-JFD	Boeing 737-8F2	29766 / 87		0098	1098	2 CFMI CFM56-7B26	79015	C20Y135		Rize
☐ TC-JFE	Boeing 737-8F2	29767 / 95	N1786B*	0098	1098	2 CFMI CFM56-7B26	79015	C20Y135		Hatay
☐ TC-JFF	Boeing 737-8F2	29768 / 99	N1786B*	0098	1098	2 CFMI CFM56-7B26	79015	C20Y135		Afyon
☐ TC-JFG	Boeing 737-8F2	29769 / 102	N1787B*	0098	1098	2 CFMI CFM56-7B26	79015	C20Y135		Sivas
☐ TC-JFH	Boeing 737-8F2	29770 / 114	N1787B*	0098	1098	2 CFMI CFM56-7B26	79015	C20Y135		Igdir
☐ TC-JFI	Boeing 737-8F2	29771 / 228		0099	0399	2 CFMI CFM56-7B26	79015	C20Y135		
☐ TC-JFJ	Boeing 737-8F2	29772 / 242		0099	0499	2 CFMI CFM56-7B26	79015	C20Y135		
☐ TC-JFK	Boeing 737-8F2	29773				2 CFMI CFM56-7B26	79015	C20Y135		oo-delivery 0599
☐ TC-JFL	Boeing 737-8F2	29774				2 CFMI CFM56-7B26	79015	C20Y135		oo-delivery 0699
☐ TC-JFM	Boeing 737-8F2	29775				2 CFMI CFM56-7B26	79015	C20Y135		oo-delivery 0799
☐ TC-JFN	Boeing 737-8F2	29776				2 CFMI CFM56-7B26	79015	C20Y135		oo-delivery 0899
☐ TC-JFO	Boeing 737-8F2	29777				2 CFMI CFM56-7B26	79015	C20Y135		oo-delivery 0999
☐ TC-JFP	Boeing 737-8F2	29778				2 CFMI CFM56-7B26	79015	C20Y135		oo-delivery 1199
☐ TC-JFR	Boeing 737-8F2					2 CFMI CFM56-7B26	79015	C20Y135		oo-delivery 1199
☐ TC-JFS	Boeing 737-8F2					2 CFMI CFM56-7B26	79015	C20Y135		oo-delivery 1299
☐ TC-JFT	Boeing 737-8F2					2 CFMI CFM56-7B26	79015	C20Y135		oo-delivery 0300
☐ TC-JFU	Boeing 737-8F2					2 CFMI CFM56-7B26	79015	C20Y135		oo-delivery 0500
☐ TC-JFV	Boeing 737-8F2					2 CFMI CFM56-7B26	79015	C20Y135		oo-delivery 0700
☐ TC-JFW	Boeing 737-8F2					2 CFMI CFM56-7B26	79015	C20Y135		oo-delivery 0900
☐ TC-JFX	Boeing 737-8F2					2 CFMI CFM56-7B26	79015	C20Y135		oo-delivery 1000
☐ TC-JFY	Boeing 737-8F2					2 CFMI CFM56-7B26	79015	C20Y135		oo-delivery 1100
☐ TC-JFZ	Boeing 737-8F2					2 CFMI CFM56-7B26	79015	C20Y135		oo-delivery 1200
☐ TC-JGA	Boeing 737-8F2					2 CFMI CFM56-7B26	79015	C20Y135		oo-delivery 0801
☐ TC-JGB	Boeing 737-8F2					2 CFMI CFM56-7B26	79015	C20Y135		oo-delivery 0002
☐ TC-JGC	Boeing 737-8F2					2 CFMI CFM56-7B26	79015	C20Y135		oo-delivery 0002

☐ TC-JCA	Boeing 727-2F2 (F) (A)	22992 / 1804		0082	0682	3 PW JT8D-15	86409	Freighter	BJ-HL	Edirne / cvtd -2F2 / for sale
☐ TC-JCB	Boeing 727-2F2 (F) (A)	22993 / 1808		0082	0782	3 PW JT8D-15	86409	Freighter	BJ-LM	Kars / cvtd -2F2 / for sale
☐ TC-JCD	Boeing 727-2F2 (F) (A)	22998 / 1810		0082	0882	3 PW JT8D-15	86409	Freighter	BK-AD	Sinop / cvtd -2F2 / for sale
☐ TC-JCL	Airbus Industrie A310-203	338	F-WZET*	0085	0585	2 GE CF6-80A3	142000	C18Y207	AM-JS	Seyhan
☐ TC-JCM	Airbus Industrie A310-203	375	F-WWBA*	0085	0585	2 GE CF6-80A3	142000	C18Y207	AM-KR	Ceyhan
☐ TC-JCN	Airbus Industrie A310-203	379	F-WWBB*	0085	0685	2 GE CF6-80A3	142000	C18Y207	AM-KS	Dicle
☐ TC-JCO	Airbus Industrie A310-203	386	F-WWBC*	0085	0685	2 GE CF6-80A3	142000	C18Y207	AM-LR	Firat
☐ TC-JCR	Airbus Industrie A310-203	370	F-WZLH*	0086	0286	2 GE CF6-80A3	142000	C18Y207	AM-LS	Kizilirmak
☐ TC-JCS	Airbus Industrie A310-203	389	F-WWBG*	0086	0486	2 GE CF6-80A3	142000	C18Y207	AM-PR	Yesilirmak
☐ TC-JCU	Airbus Industrie A310-203	390	F-WWBH*	0086	0386	2 GE CF6-80A3	142000	C18Y207	AM-PS	Sakarya
☐ TC-JCV	Airbus Industrie A310-304	476	F-WWCT*	0088	0488	2 GE CF6-80C2A2	153000	C18Y192	AM-QR	Aras
☐ TC-JCY	Airbus Industrie A310-304	478	F-WWCX*	0088	0688	2 GE CF6-80C2A2	153000	C18Y192	AM-QS	Coruh
☐ TC-JCZ	Airbus Industrie A310-304	480	F-WWCZ*	0088	0688	2 GE CF6-80C2A2	153000	C18Y192	AM-RS	Ergene
☐ TC-JDA	Airbus Industrie A310-304	496	F-WWCV*	0089	0489	2 GE CF6-80C2A2	153000	C18Y192	AP-BR	Aksu / lsf C.Itoh, Mitsui Finance
☐ TC-JDB	Airbus Industrie A310-304 (ET)	497	F-WWCH*	0089	0489	2 GE CF6-80C2A2	157000	F10C26Y140	AP-BS	Goksu / lsf C.Itoh, Mitsui Finance
☐ TC-JDC	Airbus Industrie A310-304 (ET)	537	F-WWCO*	0090	0390	2 GE CF6-80C2A2	157000	F10C26Y140	AP-CR	Meric / lsf Bosphorus Lease
☐ TC-JDD	Airbus Industrie A310-304 (ET)	586	F-WWCK*	0091	0791	2 GE CF6-80C2A2	157000	F10C26Y140	AP-CS	Dalaman
☐ TC-JDJ	Airbus Industrie A340-311	023	F-WWJN*	0093	0793	4 CFMI CFM56-5C2	257000	F10C24Y237	ER-CD	Istanbul / lsf Anatolia Aviation Lsng
☐ TC-JDK	Airbus Industrie A340-311	025	F-WWJP*	0093	0893	4 CFMI CFM56-5C2	257000	F10C24Y237	ER-CF	Isparta / lsf Anatolia Aviation Lsng
☐ TC-JDL	Airbus Industrie A340-311	057	F-WWJF*	0094	0794	4 CFMI CFM56-5C2	257000	F10C24Y237	ER-CG	Ankara / lsf Anatolia Aviation Lsng
☐ TC-JDM	Airbus Industrie A340-311	115	F-WWJN*	0096	0496	4 CFMI CFM56-5C2	257000	F10C24Y237	ER-CH	Izmir / lsf Anatolia Aviation Lsng
☐ TC-JDN	Airbus Industrie A340-313	180	F-WWJU*	0097	0897	4 CFMI CFM56-5C4	275000	F10C24Y237		Adana
☐ TC-JDO	Airbus Industrie A340-313	270	F-WWJF*	0099	0499	4 CFMI CFM56-5C4	275000	F10C24Y237		
☐ TC-JDP	Airbus Industrie A340-313					4 CFMI CFM56-5C4	275000	F10C24Y237		oo-delivery 0400

UPS Uensped Paket Servisi, A.S. – air operations = UNS (Subsidiary of United Parcel Service Co., USA) **Istanbul**

Ambarlir Caddesi 6A, UPS Building, TR-34786 Topkapi-Istanbul, Turkey ☎ (212) 547 12 20 Tx: none Fax: (212) 547 12 05 SITA: n/a
F: 1981 👥 10 Head: Hamdi Türker ICAO: UNSPED Net: n/a

☐ TC-APS	Cessna 340A II	340A0247	N3964G	0077		2 CO TSIO-520-N	2717	Freighter		
☐ TC-UPS	Fairchild (Swearingen) SA226AT Merlin IVA	AT-044	C-GGPT	0075	1093	2 GA TPE331-3UW-303G	5670	Freighter		Beril

URAYAIR (Uray Hava Tasimaciligi San, A.S. dba) **Istanbul**

Naima so Aydin Sitesi B1, Blok N4, TR-34800 Yesilköy-Istanbul, Turkey ☎ (212) 663 80 93 Tx: none Fax: (212) 663 80 94 SITA: n/a
F: 1992 👥 6 Head: Yalgin Sünnetcioglu Net: n/a

☐ TC-COS	Hawker 600B (HS 125-600B)	256048	N6567G	0075		2 RR Viper 601-22B	11340			

ZORLU AIR Havacilik, A.S. **Istanbul**

Petrol Ofis Dolum Tes. Yolu, TR-34840 Avcilar-Istanbul, Turkey ☎ (212) 690 18 80 Tx: none Fax: (212) 690 75 52 SITA: n/a
F: 1996 👥 5 Head: Mahmut Gayretlier Net: http://www.zorlu.com

☐ TC-HZT	Bell 206L-3 LongRanger III	51599		0792		1 AN 250-C30P	1882			
☐ TC-HZA	Bell 230	23031	N54387	0095		2 AN 250C-30G2	3810			
☐ TC-HZH	Bell 230	23038	N23890	0095	0898	2 AN 250C-30G2	3810			

TF = ICELAND (Republic of Iceland) (Lydveldid Island)

Capital: Reykjavik Official Language: Icelandic Population: 0,3 million Square Km: 103000 Dialling code: +354 Year established: 1918 Acting political head: David Oddsson (Prime Minister)

Government / Corporate / Executive / VIP Aircraft

☐ TF-FMS	Beech King Air B200	BB-1221	D-IUUU	0085	0297	2 PWC PT6A-42	5670	10 Pax		Flugmalastjorn (DCA)

AIR ATLANTA ICELAND = CC / ABD (Flugfelagid Atlanta e.h.f. dba) **Keflavik**

PO Box 80, IS-270 Mosfellssbaer, Iceland ☎ 566 77 00 Tx: none Fax: 566 77 66 SITA: REKOWCC
F: 1986 👥 740 Head: ThoraGudmundsdottir& ArngrimurJohannson ICAO: ATLANTA Net: http://www.atlanta.is

☐ TF-ABF	Boeing 737-230C	20258 / 276	D-ABHE	0071	0994	2 PW JT8D-15 (HK3/NOR)	50900	Freighter	FM-EH	
☐ TF-ABX	Boeing 737-230C	20257 / 274	D-ABGE	0070	0395	2 PW JT8D-15 (HK3/NOR)	50900	Freighter	FM-EG	lsf Cargo Corp.
☐ TF-ABD	Lockheed L-1011-385-1-15 TriStar 100	193B-1221	C-GRYU	0081	0596	3 RR RB211-22B	211374	Y360	EJ-DF	Ulfar Pordarson M.D.
☐ TF-ABE	Lockheed L-1011-385-1 TriStar 1	193A-1022	VR-HOA	0173	1295	3 RR RB211-22B	195045	Y362	GJ-BF	
☐ TF-ABH	Lockheed L-1011-385-1 TriStar 1	193A-1054	VR-HHX	1273	0196	3 RR RB211-22B	195045	Y362	HJ-BD	lsf Norske Finance
☐ TF-ABM	Lockheed L-1011-385-1 TriStar 50	193B-1072	SE-DPP	0074	0596	3 RR RB211-22B	204117	Y362	BJ-AC	cvtd TriStar 1
☐ TF-ABT	Lockheed L-1011-385-1-15 TriStar 100	193B-1231	N7035T	0082	1297	3 RR RB211-22B	211374	Y360	AB-HM	op in partial Caledonian-colors
☐ TF-ABU	Lockheed L-1011-385-1 TriStar 1	193A-1051	VR-HHY	1173	1196	3 RR RB211-22B	195045	Y362	CJ-AK	lsf Elmo Ventures Ltd
☐ TF-ABV	Lockheed L-1011-385-1 TriStar 1	193R-1033	SE-DTD	0573	0896	3 RR RB211-22B	195045	Y362	BG-CF	
☐ TF-ABA	Boeing 747-267B	22530 / 531	B-HID	0681	1198	4 RR RB211-524C2	377842	F12C32Y336		lsf CP Leasing/lst/opf IBE in Iberia-cs
☐ TF-ABG	Boeing 747-128	20377 / 176	F-BPVG	0072	0398	4 PW JT9D-7A	332937	Y486	EG-LM	lsf AGES
☐ TF-ABO	Boeing 747-1D1	20208 / 123	N502SR	0071	0394	4 PW JT9D-7AH	332937	Y480	DH-GJ	lsf Mido Ltd / op in SVA-colors
☐ TF-ABP	Boeing 747-267B	22429 / 493	B-HIC	1280	0199	4 RR RB211-524C4	377842	F12C32Y336		lsf CP Leasing/lst/opf IBE in Iberia-cs
☐ TF-ABR	Boeing 747-133	20014 / 121	N874UM	0071	0393	4 PW JT9D-7AH	332937	Y476	BF-HJ	lsf Mido Ltd
☐ TF-ABY	Boeing 747-246B	21030 / 251	JA8125	0074	1297	4 PW JT9D-7AW	346998	Y476	JL-BD	lsf FSBU Trustee / op in SVA-cs

AIR CHARTER ICELAND = LIO (L.I.O. e.h.f. dba / formerly Leiguflug Air Charter, Ltd & Sverrair) **Reykjavik**

Reykjavikurflugvelli, IS-101 Reykjavik, Iceland ☎ 562 80 11 Tx: none Fax: 552 84 20 SITA: n/a
F: 1974 👥 4 Head: Isleifur Ottesen Net: n/a Aircraft below MTOW 1361 kg: Beech 77, Cessna 152 & 172.

☐ TF-FTP	Partenavia P.68C	219	G-WTBC	0080	0098	2 LY IO-360-A1B6	1990	5 Pax		
☐ TF-GTO	Cessna 310Q	310Q0735		0073	0098	2 CO IO-470-VO	2404	5 Pax		
☐ TF-GTC	Cessna 402C II	402C0355	SE-IFH	0080	0694	2 CO TSIO-520-VB	3107	9 Pax		

FLUGFELAG ISLANDS, h.f. = NY / FXI (Air Iceland) (Subsidiary of Icelandair / formerly Flugfelag Nordurlands, h.f.) **Reykjavik**

Box 400, Akureyrarflugvelli, IS-602 Akureyri, Iceland ☎ 570 30 00 Tx: 2258 fn air is Fax: 570 30 01 SITA: REKAPFI
F: 1959 👥 220 Head: Jon Karl Oflafsson IATA: 882 ICAO: FAXI Net: http://www.airiceland.is Aircraft below MTOW 1361 kg: Piper PA-38.

☐ TF-JMG	Piper PA-31-350 Navajo Chieftain	31-7652093	G-BWAL	0076		2 LY TIO-540-J2BD	3175	Y9		
☐ TF-JMI	Piper PA-31-350 Navajo Chieftain	31-7652133	N62849	0076		2 LY TIO-540-J2BD	3290	Y9		
☐ TF-JMC	De Havilland DHC-6 Twin Otter 300	413	C-GIZR	0076	0687	2 PWC PT6A-27	5670	Y19		
☐ TF-JMD	De Havilland DHC-6 Twin Otter 300	475	C-GDAA	0076	0089	2 PWC PT6A-27	5670	Y19		
☐ TF-JME	Fairchild (Swearingen) SA227DC Metro 23	DC-880B	N3002K*	0097	0697	2 GA TPE331-12U-701G	7484	Y19		lsf Millennium Leasing Co.
☐ TF-JMK	Fairchild (Swearingen) SA227AC Metro III	AC-467	N3046L	0082	0291	2 GA TPE331-11U-601G	6577	Y19		
☐ TF-JML	Fairchild (Swearingen) SA227DC Metro 23	DC-881B	N3004D*	0097	0697	2 GA TPE331-12U-701G	7484	Y19		lsf Millennium Leasing Co./sub-lst EZE
☐ TF-FIR	Fokker 50 (F27 Mk050)	20243	PH-EXM*	0092	0397	2 PWC PW125B	20820	Y50		Asdis / lsf ICE
☐ TF-FIS	Fokker 50 (F27 Mk050)	20244	PH-EXN*	0092	0397	2 PWC PW125B	20820	Y50		Sigdis / lsf ICE
☐ TF-FIT	Fokker 50 (F27 Mk050)	20250	PH-EXT*	0092	0397	2 PWC PW125B	20820	Y50		Freydis / lsf ICE

FLUGFELAG VESTMANNAEYJA, h.f. (formerly Valur Andersen Flug) **Vestmannaeyjar**

Tungötu 9, IS-900 Vestmannaeyjar, Iceland ☎ 481 32 55 Tx: none Fax: 481 26 52 SITA: n/a
F: 1984 👥 n/a Head: Valur Andersen Net: n/a

☐ TF-VEY	Partenavia P.68B	109	G-JVMR	0077	1095	2 LY IO-360-A1B6	1990	6 Pax		
☐ TF-VEV	Piper PA-31-350 Navajo Chieftain	31-8152007	N4051Q	0081	0291	2 LY TIO-540-J2BD	3290	9 Pax		

GARDAFLUG, h.f. **Reykjavik**

Holtsbud 43, IS-210 Gardabae, Iceland ☎ 565 82 52 Tx: none Fax: 565 82 52 SITA: n/a
F: 1988 👥 2 Head: Ulfar Henningsson Net: n/a

☐ TF-BMW	Partenavia P.68 Observer 2	389-02-OB2	I-DOLF	1189	0295	2 LY IO-360-A1B6	2084	Pax/Photo/Survey		
☐ TF-BMX	Cessna 337G Skymaster II	33701701	N53559	0376	0288	2 CO IO-360-G	2110	Pax/Photo/Survey		

HALENDISFLUG, h.f. (Highland Air) (Subsidiary of Jorvik, h.f.) **Skaftafell National Park**

PO Box 5308, IS-125 Reykjavik, Iceland ☎ 562 51 01 Tx: none Fax: 562 52 01 SITA: n/a
F: 1993 👥 n/a Head: Jon Gretar Sigurdsson Net: n/a Operates airtaxi/charter flights with Cessna 337A/402B & Piper PA-23 aircraft, used from parent company JORVIK when required.

HELICOPTER SERVICE OF ICELAND (Pyrlubjonustan, h.f. dba) **Reykjavik**

Vidihlid 45, IS-105 Reykjavik, Iceland ☎ 561 61 00 Tx: n/a Fax: 561 61 00 SITA: n/a
F: n/a 👥 n/a Head: Albina Thordarson Net: n/a Aircraft below MTOW 1361kg: Hughes 269C (300C)

☐ TF-HHG	Bell 206L-1 LongRanger II	45677	F-GHHH	0081		1 AN 250-C28B	1882	6 Pax		lsf Féfang hf.

ICELANDAIR = FI / ICE (Flugleidir, h.f. dba) **Keflavik**

Reykjavik Airport, IS-101 Reykjavik, Iceland ☎ 505 03 00 Tx: 2021 iceair is Fax: 505 03 91 SITA: n/a
F: 1979 👥 1600 Head: Sigurdur Helgason IATA: 108 ICAO: ICEAIR Net: http://www.icelandair.is

☐ TF-FIR	Fokker 50 (F27 Mk050)	20243	PH-EXM*	0092	0292	2 PWC PW125B	20820	Y50		Asdis / lsf Iceland Ac.Fin./sublst FXI
☐ TF-FIS	Fokker 50 (F27 Mk050)	20244	PH-EXN*	0092	0392	2 PWC PW125B	20820	Y50		Sigdis / lsf Iceland Ac.Fin./sublst FXI
☐ TF-FIT	Fokker 50 (F27 Mk050)	20250	PH-EXT*	0092	0492	2 PWC PW125B	20820	Y50		Freydis / lsf IcelandAc.Fin./sublst FXI
☐ TF-FIE	Boeing 737-3S3 (QC)	23811 / 1445	N761LF	0087	0198	2 CFMI CFM56-3B2	62800	Freighter	QS-AH	lsf ILFC / cvtd -3S3
☐ TF-FIA	Boeing 737-408	24352 / 1705		0089	0489	2 CFMI CFM56-3C1	65990	CY153	FP-DH	Aldis / lsf SUNR
☐ TF-FIB	Boeing 737-408	24353 / 1721		0089	0589	2 CFMI CFM56-3C1	65990	CY153	FP-DJ	Eydis / lsf Wing Aerospace 2 Ltd
☐ TF-FID	Boeing 737-408	25063 / 2032		0091	0491	2 CFMI CFM56-3C1	65990	CY153	FM-JQ	Heiddis

601 registration type of aircraft cn/fn ex/ex* mfd del powered by mtow kg configuration selcal name/fln/specialitites/remarks

☐ TF-FIH	Boeing 757-208	24739 / 273		0090	0490	2 RR RB211-535E4	113398	C22Y167	FQ-AE	Hafdis / lsf BBAM
☐ TF-FII	Boeing 757-208	24760 / 281		0090	0590	2 RR RB211-535E4	113398	C22Y167	FQ-AG	Fanndis / lsf Heller Financial Inc.
☐ TF-FIJ	Boeing 757-208	25085 / 368	G-BTEJ	0091	0591	2 RR RB211-535E4	113398	C22Y167	FM-KQ	Svandis
☐ TF-FIK	Boeing 757-28A	26276 / 704		0096	0396	2 RR RB211-535E4	113398	C22Y167	KQ-FG	Soldis / lsf ILFC
☐ TF-FIN	Boeing 757-208	28989 / 780	N1790B*	0097	0198	2 RR RB211-535E4	113398	C22Y167		Bryndis
☐ TF-GRL	Boeing 757-236	25620 / 449	G-CSVS	0092	0598	2 RR RB211-535E4	113398	CY209	AQ-EM	lsf/opf GRL in Groenlandsfly-colors
☐ TF-	Boeing 757-208					2 RR RB211-535E4	113398	C22Y167		oo-delivery 0499
☐ TF-	Boeing 757-208					2 RR RB211-535E4	113398	C22Y167		oo-delivery 0200
☐ TF-	Boeing 757-208					2 RR RB211-535E4	113398	C22Y167		oo-delivery 0203
☐ TF-	Boeing 757-308					2 RR RB211-535E4B	122470			oo-delivery 0001
☐ TF-	Boeing 757-308					2 RR RB211-535E4B	122470			oo-delivery 0002

ISLANDSFLUG, h.f. = HH / ICB (Icebird Airlines, Ltd dba) — Reykjavik

Reykjavik Airport, IS-101 Reykjavik, Iceland ☎ 561 60 60 Tx: none Fax: 562 35 37 SITA: n/a
F: 1991 ⁂ 44 Head: Gunnar Thorvaldson IATA: 652 ICAO: ICEBIRD Net: n/a

☐ TF-EGU	Piper PA-31-350 Navajo Chieftain	31-7952033	N27895	0079	0096	2 LY TIO-540-J2BD	3290	Y9		lsf Flugfelag Austurlands
☐ TF-VLA	Piper PA-31-350 Navajo Chieftain	31-7952185	N25LS	0079	0191	2 LY TIO-540-J2BD	3290	Y9		lsf Glitnir hf.
☐ TF-ELA	Dornier 228-202K	8156	TC-FBN	0088	0193	2 GA TPE331-5-252D	6200	Y19		
☐ TF-ELF	Dornier 228-201	8046	LN-NVC	0084	0693	2 GA TPE331-5-252D	5980	Y19		lst VLF
☐ TF-ELH	Dornier 228-201	8070	SE-KVV	0085	0695	2 GA TPE331-5-252D	6200	Y19		lst Guard Air, Norway
☐ TF-BBG	Fairchild (Swearingen) SA227AC Metro III	AC-505B	F-GHVC	0082	0394	2 GA TPE331-11U-611G	7260	Y19		lst EZE / cvtd cn AC-505
☐ TF-ELJ	ATR 42-300 (QC)	118	C-FIQN	0088	0596	2 PWC PW120	16700	Y46 / Frtr 5t		lsf Shannon Aeronautique GIE
☐ TF-ELK	ATR 42-300 (QC)	059	F-OGNS	0087	0497	2 PWC PW120	16700	Y46 / Frtr 5t		lsf AL Aviation Leasing GmbH
☐ TF-ELL	Boeing 737-210C	20138 / 173	F-GGFI	0069	0897	2 PW JT8D-9A (HK3/NOR)	54430	Freighter 16t		lsf Business National Parcels / opf DHL
☐ TF-ELM	Boeing 737-2M8 (A)	21736 / 557	F-GLXG	0079	1298	2 PW JT8D-15	54204	Y131		lsf Localease Aviation B.V./sub-lst FWI

JORVIK, h.f. (Jorvik Aviation) — Reykjavik

PO Box 5308, IS-125 Reykjavik, Iceland ☎ 562 51 01 Tx: none Fax: 562 52 01 SITA: n/a
F: 1993 ⁂ n/a Head: Jon Gretar Sigurdsson Net: n/a Aircraft below MTOW 1361kg: Cessna 177RG & 180

☐ TF-SKY	Cessna 337A Super Skymaster	337-0397	G-ATPU	0066	0096	2 CO IO-360-C/D	1905	Y5/Photo/Survey		lsf pvt
☐ TF-JVD	Piper PA-23-250 Aztec D	27-4146	TF-JMA	0069	0897	2 LY IO-540-C4B5	2359	Y5/Photo/Survey		lsf Flugsport ehf
☐ TF-JVB	Cessna 402B	402B0875	TF-SUD	0075	0096	2 CO TSIO-520-E	2860	Y9/Photo/Survey		lsf SP Fjamögnun

LANDGRAEDSLA RIKISINS (State Soil Conservation Service) — Gunnarsholt

Gunnarsholti, Rangárvöllum, IS-851 Hella, Iceland ☎ 487 55 10 Tx: none Fax: 487 55 00 SITA: n/a
F: 1907 ⁂ 45 Head: Sveinn Runóolfsson Net: n/a

☐ TF-NPK	Boeing (Douglas) DC-3C (C-47A-DL)	13861	TF-ISH	0043		2 PW R-1830-92	13154	Spreader		Pall Sveinsson

LANDHELGISGAESLAN - Flight Department = ICG (Icelandic Coast Guard) (Flight Deptartment of the Icelandic Coast Guard) — Reykjavik

Reykjavik Airport, IS-101 Reykjavik, Iceland ☎ 511 22 22 Tx: 2048 vardsk is Fax: 511 22 44 SITA: n/a
F: 1955 ⁂ 25 Head: Pall Halldorsson ICAO: ICELAND COAST Net: n/a Non-commercial government Coast guard-organisation conducting SAR, EMS & VIP flights.

☐ TF-GRO	Eurocopter (Aerosp.) AS350B Ecureuil	1322	D-HKHL	0080	0086	1 TU Arriel 1B	1950	5 Pax/Patrol		
☐ TF-SIF	Eurocopter (Aerosp.) SA365N Dauphin 2	6136		0085	1185	2 TU Arriel 1C	4000	8 Pax/SAR/EMS		
☐ TF-LIF	Eurocopter (Aerosp.) AS332L1 Super Puma	2210		0086	0095	2 TU Makila 1A1	8600	18 Pax/SAR/EMS		
☐ TF-SYN	Fokker F27 Friendship 200 (F27 Mk200)	10545	PH-EXC*	0076	0177	2 RR Dart 536-7R	20412	20 Pax/SAR/VIP		

MK FLUGFELAGID, e.h.f. = MKI — Keflavik & London-Gatwick

Hofdabakki 9-BZ, IS-112 Reykjavik, Iceland ☎ 577 32 00 Tx: none Fax: 577 32 02 SITA: REKMKCR
F: 1997 ⁂ n/a Head: Ingimar Haukur Ingimarsson ICAO: KILO ICE Net: n/a

☐ TF-MKG	Boeing (Douglas) DC-8-62F	46027 / 437	N51CX	0269	0897	4 PW JT3D-7 (HK3/BAC)	158758	Freighter		cvtd -62
☐ TF-MKH	Boeing (Douglas) DC-8-62F	46153 / 551	N735PL	0071	0998	4 PW JT3D-7 (HK3/BAC)	151953	Freighter		lsf Kilo Golf Ltd / cvtd -62

MYFLUG, h.f. = MYA — Myvatn

Vogum, Myvatnssveit, IS-660 Reykjahlio, Iceland ☎ 464 44 00 Tx: none Fax: 464 43 41 SITA: n/a
F: 1985 ⁂ 1 Head: Leifur Hallgrimsson ICAO: MYFLUG Net: n/a

☐ TF-MYY	Cessna U206F Stationair II	U20602831	N35960	0075		1 CO IO-520-F	1633	5 Pax		
☐ TF-MYF	Piper PA-31-310 Navajo B	31-779	9H-ACF	0072	0096	2 LY TIO-540-A2C	2955	7 Pax		
☐ TF-MYV	Piper PA-31-350 Navajo Chieftain	31-7852139	TF-OOJ	0078	0690	2 LY TIO-540-J2BD	3363	9 Pax		

TG = GUATEMALA (Republic of Guatemala) (Republica de Guatemala)

Capital: Guatemala City Official Language: Spanish Population: 11,0 million Square Km: 108889 Dialling code: +502 Year established: 1839 Acting political head: Alvaro Arzu Irigoyen (President)

Government / Corporate / Executive / VIP Aircraft

☐ FAG-001	Bell 212	30760	N27EA	0076	0592	2 PWC PT6T-3 TwinPac	5080	VIP		Fuerza Aérea Guatemala/Presidential Ac.

AVCOM - Aviones Comerciales de Guatemala — Guatemala City-La Aurora

Avenida Hincapié, Zona 13, Hangar 21, Aeropuerto La Aurora, Guatemala City 01013, Guatemala ☎ 331 58 21 Tx: none Fax: 332 49 46 SITA: n/a
F: 1954 ⁂ 20 Head: n/a Net: n/a

☐ TG-JOI	Cessna 337E Super Skymaster	33701279		0070		2 CO IO-360-C/D	1996			
☐ TG-JAB	Twin (Aero) Shrike Commander 500S	3303		0078		2 LY IO-540-E1B5	3062			
☐ TG-JWC	Twin (Aero) Shrike Commander 500S	3209		0074		2 LY IO-540-E1B5	3062			
☐ TG-CAC	De Havilland DHC-6 Twin Otter 300	449		0075	0875	2 PWC PT6A-27	5670			
☐ TG-JAC	De Havilland DHC-6 Twin Otter 300	755	C-FCSG	0081	0893	2 PWC PT6A-27	5670			
☐ TG-JAJ	De Havilland DHC-6 Twin Otter 300	774	C-GFJQ	0081	0687	2 PWC PT6A-27	5670			
☐ TG-JEL	De Havilland DHC-6 Twin Otter 300	722	N3H	0080	1091	2 PWC PT6A-27	5670			
☐ TG-JAY	De Havilland DHC-7-102 Dash 7	046	C-FYMK	0081	1096	4 PWC PT6A-50	19958			

AVIATECA GUATEMALA = GU / GUG (Aviateca, S.A.-Aerolineas de Guatemala dba/Member of Grupo TACA) — Guatemala City-La Aurora

Avenida Hincapié 12-22, Zona 13, Aeropuerto La Aurora, Guatemala City 01013, Guatemala ☎ 331 82 61 Tx: 5960 avteca gu Fax: 331 74 12 SITA: n/a
F: 1945 ⁂ 500 Head: Ing. Julio O. Gomes IATA: 240 ICAO: AVIATECA Net: n/a Domestic flights are operated by subsidiary INTER (with Cessna 208B aircraft). For details – see under that company.

☐ N121GU	Boeing 737-2H6 (A)	20583 / 303	TG-ALA	0872	1191	2 PW JT8D-15 (HK3/NOR)	53070	Y125	AG-CF	lsf FSBU Trustee
☐ N122GU	Boeing 737-2H6 (A)	20586 / 307	TG-ALA	0972	0592	2 PW JT8D-15	53070	Y125		lsf FSBU Trustee
☐ N123GU	Boeing 737-2H6 (A)	20587 / 308	TG-AYA	0972	0892	2 PW JT8D-15 (HK3/NOR)	53070	Y125	AG-CL	lsf FSBU Trustee
☐ N126GU	Boeing 737-2H6 (A)	20582 / 302	TG-ADA	1072	0194	2 PW JT8D-15	53070	Y122	AG-CE	lsf FSBU Trustee
☐ N127GU	Boeing 737-242 (A)	22074 / 619	F-OHKA	1179	0995	2 PW JT8D-9A	53070	Y122		lsf INGO

DHL de Guatemala, SA = Z8 / JOS (Subsidiary of DHL Corporation) — Guatemala City-La Aurora

Air Operations Dept., Blvd. Juan Pablo II, 6-75, Zona 13, Guatemala City 01013, Guatemala ☎ 361 74 58 Tx: none Fax: 361 74 50 SITA: n/a
F: 1989 ⁂ 50 Head: Enrique Salazar IATA: 947 Net: n/a

☐ TG-DHL	Fairchild (Swearingen) SA227AC Metro III	AC-520	HC-BQR	0083	0094	2 GA TPE331-11U-611G	6577	Freighter		
☐ TG-DHP	Boeing 727-35 (F)	19166 / 303	OO-DHP	0866	0697	3 PW JT8D-7B (HK3/FDX)	76885	Freighter		lsf BCS / cvtd -35

HELI GUATEMALA - Helicopteros de Guatemala, SA — Guatemala City-La Aurora

Ave. Hincapie 23-30, Zona 13, Aeropuerto La Aurora, Guatemala City 01013, Guatemala ☎ 331 82 82 Tx: none Fax: 332 14 91 SITA: n/a
F: n/a ⁂ n/a Head: Hector Morataya Net: n/a

☐ TG-CEL	Bell 206B JetRanger III	2435		0078		1 AN 250-C20B	1451			
☐ TG-WAB	Bell 206B JetRanger II	2065		0076		1 AN 250-C20	1451			
☐ TG-WEV	Bell 206B JetRanger III	2227		0078		1 AN 250-C20B	1451			

INTER - Transportes Aéreos Inter, S.A. = TSP (Subsidiary of Aviateca Guatemala / Member of Grupo TACA) — Guatemala City-La Aurora

c/o Aviateca, Avenida Hincapié 12-22, Zona 13, Aeropuerto La Aurora, Guatemala City 01013, Guatemala ☎ 331 82 61 Tx: 5960 avteca gu Fax: 331 74 12 SITA: n/a
F: 1997 ⁂ n/a Head: Ing. Julio O. Gomes ICAO: TRANSPO-INTER Net: n/a Scheduled domestic flights are operated in conjunction with AVIATECA, using GU flight-numbers.

☐ TG-EAA	Cessna 208B Grand Caravan	208B0637	N1002Y	1097	1297	1 PWC PT6A-114A	3969	Y9		
☐ TG-RDC	Cessna 208B Grand Caravan	208B0636	N1038F	1097	1297	1 PWC PT6A-114A	3969	Y9		

JUNGLE FLYING TOURS — Guatemala City-La Aurora

Avenida Hincapie, Rua 8, Hangar 13-1, Aeropuerto Internacional La Aurora, Guatemala City 01013, Guatemala ☎ 360 49 20 Tx: none Fax: 331 49 95 SITA: n/a
F: n/a ⁂ n/a Head: n/a Net: n/a

☐ TG-JFT	Cessna 208B Grand Caravan	208B0622		0097	0897	1 PWC PT6A-114A	3969			

LINEAS AEREAS MAYAS, S.A. — Guatemala City-La Aurora

Avenida Hincapie y 18, Calle Interior, Hangar 60, Aeropuerto Internacional La Aurora, Guatemala City 01013, Guatemala ☎ 331 18 27 Tx: n/a Fax: 332 54 08 SITA: n/a
F: 1984 ⁂ n/a Head: Juan Adenolfo Galvez del Cio IATA: 558 Net: n/a Operates cargo flights with freighter aircraft leased from U.S. companies (N) when required.

MAYAN WORLD AIRLINES = EY / MYN — Guatemala City-La Aurora

7 Avenida 6-53, Zona 4, Edificio el Triangulo, Of. 49, 2do.nivel, Guatemala 00104, Guatemala ☎ 334 20 67 Tx: none Fax: 334 20 70 SITA: GUADGEY
F: 1996 ⁂ 73 Head: Santiago de la Rocha IATA: 987 ICAO: MAYAN WORLD Net: n/a Suspended operations 210998 (with ATR 42 aircraft). Intends to restart with Yakovlev 40 (lsf Aerocaribbean).

602 registration type of aircraft cn/fn ex/ex* mfd del powered by mtow kg configuration selcal name/fln/specialitites/remarks

RACSA – Rutas Aéreas Centro Americanas, S.A. — Guatemala City-La Aurora

Avenida Hincapié, Calle 18, Hangar 12, Aeropuerto La Aurora, Guatemala City 01013, Guatemala ☎ 334 79 35 Tx: none Fax: 334 79 35 SITA: n/a
F: 1998 n/a Head: Coronel Fernando Castillo Net: n/a

☐ TG-ANP	Aerospatiale (Nord) 262A-21	21	OY-BDD	0066	1098	2 TU Bastan VIC	10600	Y29		
☐ TG-NTR	Aerospatiale (Nord) 262A-26	21	N344PL	0067	1098	2 TU Bastan VIC	10600	Y29		

TAG – Transportes Aéreos Guatemaltecos, SA = GUM (TAG International Cargo, Corp. dba) — Guatemala City-La Aurora

Avenida Hincapié y 18 Calle, Zona 13, Hangar 15, Aeropuerto La Aurora, Guatemala City 01013, Guatemala ☎ 331 31 35 Tx: n/a Fax: 334 72 05 SITA: n/a
F: 1970 15 Head: José Antonio Gonzalez Aparicio Net: n/a

☐ TG-TAK	Piper PA-24-260 Comanche B	24-4667		0067		1 LY IO-540-D4A5	1406			
☐ TG-DOE	Cessna 185 Skywagon	1850039	N9839X	0061		1 CO IO-470-F	1451			
☐ TG-ANY	Beech D18S	A-429	N588B	0048		2 PW R-985	3969			

TAPSA – Transportes Aéreos Profesionales, SA — Guatemala City-La Aurora

Avenida Hincapié, Zona 13, Hangar 14, Aeropuerto La Aurora, Guatemala City 01013, Guatemala ☎ 331 48 60 Tx: none Fax: 334 55 72 SITA: n/a
F: n/a n/a Head: Guillermo Ponciano Net: n/a

☐ TG-SAM	Cessna TU206F Turbo Stationair					1 CO TSIO-520-C	1633			
☐ TG-TAM	Cessna TU206F Turbo Stationair					1 CO TSIO-520-M	1633			
☐ TG-TWO	Embraer 110P1 Bandeirante (EMB-110P1)	110219	N102VN	0079	0192	2 PWC PT6A-34	5670			

TIKAL AIRLINES (formerly Tikal Jets) — Guatemala City-La Aurora

Avenida Hincapié, Zona 13, Hangar 18, Aeropuerto La Aurora, Guatemala City 01013, Guatemala ☎ 332 50 70 Tx: none Fax: 361 33 42 SITA: n/a
F: 1990 n/a Head: Fernando Rodriquez Net: n/a

☐ TG-CFD	Let 410UVP-E	861704	YN-CFD	0086	1198	2 WA M-601E	6400	Y19		lsf AA-Atlantic Airlines Leasing
☐ TG-CFE	Let 410UVP-E	861705	YN-CFE	0086	1198	2 WA M-601E	6400	Y19		lsf AA-Atlantic Airlines Leasing
☐ TG-TJF	BAe (BAC) One-Eleven 401AK	089	N97JF	0066	0594	2 RR Spey 511-14	40597	Y84		Quirigua
☐ TG-TJK	BAe (BAC) One-Eleven 401AK	063	N217CA	0066	0896	2 RR Spey 511-14	40597	Y84		

TI = COSTA RICA (Republic of Costa Rica) (Republica de Costa Rica)

Capital: San José Official Language: Spanish Population: 3,5 million Square Km: 51100 Dialling code: +506 Year established: 1838 Acting political head: Miguel Angel Rodriguez Echeverria (President)

ACS – Air Cargo Service — San José-Juan Santamaria & Miami-Int'l, FL

USA operational office:, PO Box 527768, Miami, FL 33152, USA ☎ (305) 871-4599 Tx: none Fax: (305) 871-4992 SITA: n/a
F: 1997 n/a Head: n/a Net: n/a Operates cargo flights with DC-8F aircraft, lsf/opb AMERICAN INTERNATIONAL AIRWAYS (N), when required.

AERO COSTA SOL, SA — San José-Juan Santamaria

Aparatdao 782-4050, Alajuela, Costa Rica ☎ 441 14 44 Tx: n/a Fax: 441 26 71 SITA: n/a
F: n/a n/a Head: n/a Net: http://www.cool.co.cr/usr/costasol/

☐ TI-AVU	Let 410UVP-E9	952623	OK-ADS	0395	0495	2 WA M-601E	6400	Y19		

AERONAVES DE AMERICA, S.A. (formerly Aeronaves de Costa Rica, S.A.) — San José-Tobias Bolanos

Apartado 5771-1000, San José, Costa Rica ☎ 232 14 13 Tx: none Fax: 232 11 76 SITA: n/a
F: n/a n/a Head: José M. Ruiz Net: n/a Aircraft below MTOW 1361kg: Cessna 182.

☐ TI-AOX	Cessna 310R II	310R1674	N2640B	0079		2 CO IO-520-MB	2495			
☐ TI-ATR	Piper PA-31-310 Navajo	31-		0070	0293	2 LY TIO-540-A1A	2948			

AVIONES TAXI Aéreo, SA (Affiliated with TACSA – Taxi Aéreo Centroamericano, SA) — San José-Juan Santamaria

Apartado 605-4050, Alajuela, Costa Rica ☎ 441 20 62 Tx: n/a Fax: 441 27 13 SITA: n/a
F: 1970 n/a Head: Manuel E. Guerra V. Net: n/a Aircraft are intechanged with TACSA – Taxi Aéreo Centroamericano, SA as required.

☐ TI-ABA	Piper PA-23-250 Aztec D	27-4229	TI-1098C	0069		2 LY IO-540-C4B5	2359			
☐ TI-ACI	Piper PA-23-250 Aztec C	27-3515	TI-1058C	0066		2 LY IO-540-C4B5	2359			
☐ TI-AST	Piper PA-23-250 Aztec E	27-7554074		0075		2 LY IO-540-C4B5	2395			
☐ TI-ASR	Piper PA-31-325 Navajo C/R			0078		2 LY TIO-540-F2BD	2948			
☐ TI-ATZ	De Havilland DHC-6 Twin Otter 200	169	N931MA	0068	0693	2 PWC PT6A-20	5252			

JHM Cargo Expreso, S.A. = JHM (Member of Groupo TACA) — San José-Juan Santamaria & Miami-Int'l, FL (USA)

PO Box 527768, Miami, FL 33152, USA ☎ (305) 871-2355 Tx: none Fax: (305) 871-6016 SITA: n/a
F: 1998 n/a Head: Capt. Roberto Escalante Net: n/a

☐ N59106	Airbus Industrie A300B4-203 (F)	106	I-BUSC	0080	1298	2 GE CF6-50C2	165000	Freighter		lsf CSAV / cvtd -203
☐ N59107	Airbus Industrie A300B4-203 (F)	107	I-BUSD	0080	1198	2 GE CF6-50C2	165000	Freighter		lsf CSAV / cvtd -203
☐ N59140	Airbus Industrie A300B4-203 (F)	140	I-BUSH	0081	1198	2 GE CF6-50C2	165000	Freighter		lsf CSAV / cvtd -203
☐ N68142	Airbus Industrie A300B4-203 (F)	142	I-BUSJ	0081	1198	2 GE CF6-50C2	165000	Freighter		lsf CSAV / cvtd -203 / TACA-titles

LACSA Costa Rica = LR / LRC (Lineas Aéreas Costarricenses, S.A. dba / Member of Grupo TACA) — San José-Juan Santamaria

Apartado 1531-1000, San José, Costa Rica ☎ 231 60 64 Tx: 7006 lacric Fax: 232 91 85 SITA: SJOMRLR
F: 1945 1150 Head: José Guillermo Rojas IATA: 133 ICAO: LACSA Net: http://www.erupotaca.com
Domestic services are operated by subsidiary SANSA (with Cessna 208B aircraft) using LR-flight numbers. For details – see under that company.

☐ N238TA	Boeing 737-242 (A)	22075 / 630	C-GNDR	0180	1292	2 PW JT8D-17A	54204	Y125		lsf CITG
☐ N239TA	Boeing 737-25A (A)	23789 / 1392	N222AW	0687	0696	2 PW JT8D-17A (HK3/NOR)	54204	Y125		lsf FSBU Trustee
☐ N261LR	Boeing 737-230 (A)	22402 / 744	CS-TEV	0081	1295	2 PW JT8D-17 (HK3/NOR)	57000	Y125		lsf FSBU Trustee
☐ N271LR	Boeing 737-230 (A)	22636 / 808	CS-TER	1081	0196	2 PW JT8D-17A	58105	Y125		lsf FSBU Trustee
☐ N281LF	Boeing 737-2L9 (A)	22071 / 620	VR-HKP	1279	1093	2 PW JT8D-17 (HK3/NOR)	58105	Y125		lsf CITG
☐ N501NG	Boeing 737-2T5 (A)	22395 / 729	H4-SAL	0081	0596	2 PW JT8D-15 (HK3/NOR)	54204	Y125		lsf / opf NIS
☐ N340LA	Airbus Industrie A320-232	425	HC-BUH	1293	1197	2 IAE V2527-A5	77000	Y162		lsf CITG
☐ N941LF	Airbus Industrie A320-233	461	F-WWDP*	0394	0694	2 IAE V2527E-A5	77000	Y162		lsf ILFC / cvtd -232
☐ N951LF	Airbus Industrie A320-233	460	F-WWDN*	0394	0694	2 IAE V2527E-A5	77000	Y162		lsf ILFC / cvtd -232
☐ N981LR	Airbus Industrie A320-233	558	F-WWDF*	0895	1295	2 IAE V2527E-A5	77000	Y162		lsf FSBU Trustee
☐ N991LR	Airbus Industrie A320-233	561	F-WWDM*	0895	1295	2 IAE V2527E-A5	77000	Y162		lsf FSBU Trustee

SAETA – Servicio Aéreo Especiales Tomas Acevedo, SA — San José-Tobias Bolanos

Zona 9, Gion 163, Pavas, Costa Rica ☎ 232 14 74 Tx: n/a Fax: 232 95 14 SITA: n/a
F: 1979 n/a Head: José Tomas Acevedo Aguilar Net: n/a Aircraft below MTOW 1361kg: Cessna 180.

☐ TI-AGP	Cessna U206F Stationair	U20601915	TI-517L	0073		1 CO IO-520-F	1633			

SANSA – Servicios Aéreos Nacionales, SA = RZ / LRS (Subsidiary of LACSA) — San José-Juan Santamaria

Apartado 999-1007, Edificio Colon, San José, Costa Rica ☎ 221 94 14 Tx: none Fax: 255 21 76 SITA: n/a
F: 1980 n/a Head: Carlos M. Delgado IATA: 503 Net: n/a Scheduled services are operated on behalf of LACSA using their IATA code LR.

☐ TI-LRS	Cessna 208B Grand Caravan	208B0611	N1277Y	0597	0797	1 PWC PT6A-114A	3969	Y9		
☐ TI-LRT	Cessna 208B Grand Caravan	208B0613	N1133H	0597	0797	1 PWC PT6A-114A	3969	Y9		
☐ TI-LRU	Cessna 208B Grand Caravan	208B0570	N1024Y	1196	1296	1 PWC PT6A-114A	3969	Y9		
☐ TI-LRV	Cessna 208B Grand Caravan	208B0614	N12397	0597	0797	1 PWC PT6A-114A	3969	Y9		
☐ TI-LRW	Cessna 208B Grand Caravan	208B0571	N12030	1196	1296	1 PWC PT6A-114A	3969	Y9		
☐ TI-LRY	Cessna 208B Grand Caravan	208B0572	N1266Z	1196	1296	1 PWC PT6A-114A	3969	Y9		
☐ TI-LRZ	Cessna 208B Grand Caravan	208B0582	N1024V	1196	1296	1 PWC PT6A-114A	3969	Y9		

TACSA – Taxi Aéreo Centroamericano, SA (Affiliated with Aviones Taxi Aéreo, SA) — San José-Tobias Bolanos & Juan Santamaria

Apartado 3941-1000, San José, Costa Rica ☎ 232 15 79 Tx: none Fax: 232 14 69 SITA: n/a
F: 1971 35 Head: Manuel E. Guerra V. Net: n/a Aircraft below MTOW 1361kg: Cessna 180. Aircraft are interchanged with Aviones Taxi Aéreo, SA as required.

☐ TI-AML	Cessna TU206G Turbo Stationair 6 II	U20605181		0079		1 CO TSIO-520-M	1633			
☐ TI-ATL	Cessna U206G Stationair 6 II	U20605370	N6184U	0080	1293	1 CO IO-520-F	1633			
☐ TI-ATN	Cessna U206G Stationair 6 II	U20604231	N756NU	0078	1292	1 CO IO-520-F	1633			
☐ TI-AOW	Piper PA-34-200T Seneca II	34-7670124	N8312C	0076		2 CO TSIO-360-E	2073			
☐ TI-ADK	Piper PA-23-250 Aztec C	27-3209	TI-1087C	0066		2 LY IO-540-C4B5	2359			
☐ TI-ATM	Piper PA-23-250 Aztec E	27-7405413	N89SL	0074	1292	2 LY IO-540-C4B5	2359			
☐ TI-ADT	Piper PA-31-310 Navajo	31-403	F-OCOE	0069		2 LY TIO-540-A2B	2948			
☐ TI-ATT	Piper PA-31-325 Navajo C/R	31-7512030	N500PM	0075	0393	2 LY TIO-540-F2BD	2948			
☐ TI-ATU	Piper PA-31-325 Navajo C/R	31-7512011	N111MM	0075	0493	2 LY TIO-540-F2BD	2948			
☐ TI-AVF	Piper PA-31-310 Navajo	31-582		0070		2 LY TIO-540-A2B	2948			

TRANS COSTA RICA = TCR (Lineas Aereas Trans Costa Rica, SA dba) — San José-Tobias Bolanos & Juan Santamaria

Apartado 3499-1000, San José, Costa Rica ☎ 232 08 08 Tx: n/a Fax: 232 08 08 SITA: n/a
F: 1979 14 Head: Capt. Alejandro Nieto Y. ICAO: TICOS Net: n/a Aircraft below MTOW 1361 kg: Piper PA-28

☐ TI-AGM	Cessna U206F Stationair II	U20602734		0075	0093	1 CO IO-520-F	1633			
☐ TI-AQI	Cessna T207A Stationair 8 II	20700607	N73593	0080		1 CO TSIO-520-M	1724			Ray
☐ TI-TRB	Cessna 207 Skywagon	20700067	TI-AJR	0069	0987	1 CO IO-520-F	1724			Principe de Paz
☐ N469MA	Mitsubishi MU-2B-60 Marquise	1543SA	TF-FHM	0082		2 GA TPE331-10-501M	5250			lsf Executive Aviation of South Florida

603 registration type of aircraft cn/fn ex/ex* mfd del powered by mtow kg configuration selcal name/fln/specialitites/remarks

TRAVELAIR = U3 (Ace Air, Inc., Tok, AK/USA dba / Affiliated with 40-Mile Air, Tok, AK/USA)   San José-Tobias Bolanos

Apartado 8-4920, San José, Costa Rica   ☎ 220 30 54   Tx: none   Fax: 220 04 13   SITA: n/a
F: 1991   ⋔⋔ 40   Head: Howard Solomon

	registration	type of aircraft	cn/fn	ex/ex*	mfd	del	powered by	mtow kg	configuration	selcal	name/fln/specialitites/remarks
☐	N9424G	Cessna U206E Stationair	U20601624		0070	0097	1 CO IO-520-F	1633	Y6		lsf Charlie Inc.
☐	N66177	Britten-Norman BN-2A-8 Islander	626	F-OCQH	0071	0096	2 LY O-540-E4C5	2858			lst Arrow Express
☐	N414WA	Britten-Norman BN-2A Mk.III-2 Trislander	1034	G-BDWU	0076	1291	3 LY O-540-E4C5	4241	Y16		
☐	N420WA	Britten-Norman BN-2A Mk.III-2 Trislander	1040	G-BEDR	0076	0992	3 LY O-540-E4C5	4241	Y16		
☐	TI-AWY	Let 410UVP	841313	UR-67488	0984	0097	2 WA M-601D	5800	Y15		

VEASA – Viajes Especiales Aéreos, SA   San José-Tobias Bolanos

Apartado 430-1200, Pavas, Costa Rica   ☎ 232 80 43   Tx: 2775 mytire cr   Fax: 232 79 34   SITA: n/a
F: 1972   ⋔⋔ 14   Head: Rafael Oreamuno B.   Net: n/a

☐	TI-AQA	Cessna U206G Stationair 6 II	U20605214	TI-SAD	0079		1 CO IO-520-F	1633			
☐	TI-AQB	Cessna U206G Stationair	U20603908	TI-SAE	0077		1 CO IO-520-F	1633			

VIGILANCIA AEREA – Servicio de Vigilancia Aérea = MSP (Division of the M.S.P.-Ministerio de Seguridad Publica)   San José-Juan Santamaria

Apartado 1212-4050, Aeropuerto Juan Santamaria, Alajuela, Costa Rica   ☎ 442 00 20   Tx: none   Fax: 441 88 70   SITA: n/a
F: 1964   ⋔⋔ n/a   Head: Colonel Oldemas Madrigal   ICAO: SEGURIDAD   Net: n/a   Non-commercial state organisation conducting civil guard-patrol, liaison & SAR missions.

☐	MSP012	MD Helicopters MD 500E (Hughes 369E)	0081E			0084	1 AN 250-C20B	1361			
☐	MSP018	MD Helicopters MD 500E (Hughes 369E)	0142E			0085	1 AN 250-C20B	1361			
☐	MSP004	Cessna U206G Turbine Stationair 6 II	U20606879			0085	1 AN 250-C20S	1633			Soloy cvtd Stationair 6 II
☐	MSP005	Cessna U206G Turbine Stationair 6 II	U20606880			0085	1 AN 250-C20S	1633			Soloy cvtd Stationair 6 II
☐	MSP006	Cessna U206G Turbine Stationair 6 II	U20606895			0085	1 AN 250-C20S	1633			Soloy cvtd Stationair 6 II
☐	MSP007	Cessna U206G Turbine Stationair 6 II	U20606972			0086	1 AN 250-C20S	1633			Soloy cvtd Stationair 6 II
☐	MSP017	Piper PA-34-220T Seneca III	3433028			0087	2 CO TSIO-360-KB	2155			
☐	MSP001	Piper PA-31-310 Navajo	31-8012033			0080	2 LY TIO-540-A2C	2948			
☐	MSP003	Piper PA-31-350 Navajo Chieftain	31-8352002			0083	2 LY TIO-540-J2BD	3175			
☐	MSP016	Mil Mi-17	226M55			0085	2 IS TV3-117MT-3	13000			
☐	MSP002	De Havilland DHC-4A Caribou	149	63-9718		0064	2 PW R-2000	12927			

TJ = CAMEROON (Republic of Cameroon) (République de Cameroun)
Capital: Yaoundé   Official Language: French, English   Population: 13,5 million   Square Km: 475442   Dialling code: +237   Year established: 1960   Acting political head: Paul Biya (President)

Government / Corporate / Executive / VIP Aircraft

☐	TJ-AAM	Boeing 727-2R1 (A)	21636 / 1414		0078	1178	3 PW JT8D-15	89438	VIP	GL-HJ	Gvmt
☐	TJ-AAR	Eurocopter (Aerosp.) AS332L Super Puma	2119			0084	2 TU Makila 1A	8350	VIP		Gvmt
☐	TJ-AAW	GAC G-1159A Gulfstream III	486	N316GA*		0087	2 RR Spey 511-8	31615	VIP		Gvmt

AIR AFFAIRES AFRIQUE   Douala

BP 1325, Douala, Cameroon   ☎ 42 29 77   Tx: 5364 afrique kn   Fax: 42 99 03   SITA: n/a
F: 1978   ⋔⋔ 75   Head: Byron Byron-Exarcos   Net: n/a   Ag-Aircraft below MTOW 5000 kg: Cessna 188.

☐	TJ-AGY	Cessna 402B II	402B1035	D-IAAH	0076		2 CO TSIO-520-E	2858	Y6		
☐	TJ-AGD	Cessna 404 Titan II	404-0632		0080		2 CO GTSIO-520-M	3810	Y9		
☐	TJ-AHR	Aerospatiale SN601 Corvette	12	TR-LYM	0075		2 PWC JT15D-4	7000	Y12		
☐	TJ-AHU	Aerospatiale (Nord) 262A-37	20	F-BLHX	0066	0991	2 TU Bastan VIC1	10600	Y27		std DLA
☐	S9-TAD	Aerospatiale (Nord) 262A-44	18	F-BVFJ	0066	0095	2 TU Bastan VIC1	10600	Y27		

CAMEROON AIRLINES = UY / UYC (Cam-Air)   Douala   CAMEROON ✈ AIRLINES

BP 4092, Douala, Cameroon   ☎ 42 25 25   Tx: 5345 kn   Fax: 42 24 87   SITA: DLADGUY
F: 1971   ⋔⋔ 1500   Head: Aquille Etoundi Antagana   IATA: 604   ICAO: CAM-AIR   Net: n/a

☐	TJ-CCG	BAe (HS) 748-435 Super 2B	1805 / 286	G-11-11*	0085	1185	2 RR Dart 536-2	21092	Y44		Menchum / std DLA
☐	TJ-CBA	Boeing 737-2H7C (A)	20590 / 304		0072	0772	2 PW JT8D-15	51937	F12Y96	AF-CH	Benoue
☐	TJ-CBB	Boeing 737-2H7C (A)	20591 / 309		0072	0972	2 PW JT8D-15	51937	F12Y96	AF-CJ	Manyu
☐	TJ-CBF	Boeing 737-3Q8	23535 / 1301	SP-LMB	0086	0897	2 CFMI CFM56-3B2	60985			lsf GECA
☐	TJ-CBG	Boeing 737-33A	27458 / 2959		1197	1197	2 CFMI CFM56-3C1	61235	F12Y106		lsf AWAS
☐	TJ-CBH	Boeing 737-33A	27457 / 2756	9V-TRE	0095	1098	2 CFMI CFM56-3C1	61235	F12Y106		lsf AWAS
☐	TJ-CAB	Boeing 747-2H7B (M)	22378 / 508		0081	0281	4 PW JT9D-7Q	362800	F18C24Y212/Plts	AF-BC	Mont Cameroun

CAMEROON HELICOPTERS – Camhel (Associated with Héli-Union, France)   Douala

BP 5439, Douala, Cameroon   ☎ 42 02 22   Tx: 5395 camhel kn   Fax: n/a   SITA: n/a
F: 1984   ⋔⋔ 24   Head: Charles-Louis de Rochechouart   Net: n/a   Additional helicopters are leased from Heli-Union, France when required.

☐	TJ-AHP	Eurocopter (Aerosp.) SA318C Alouette II	2265	F-GBGX	0072		1 TU Astazou IIA2	1650	4 Pax		

TL = CENTRAL AFRICAN REPUBLIC (République Centrafricaine)
Capital: Bangui   Official Language: Sangho, French, Ubangi, Fulani   Population: 3,5 million   Square Km: 622984   Dialling code: +236   Year established: 1960   Acting political head: Ange-Félix Patassé (President)

AIR AFRIQUE = multinational state carrier – see under TU- markings

CAC – Compagnie Aérienne de Centrafrique (formerly Société Centrafricaine de Transport Aérien)   Bangui

BP 554, Bangui, Central African Republic   ☎ 61 35 35   Tx: none   Fax: 61 35 35   SITA: n/a
F: n/a   ⋔⋔ n/a   Head: Ismael Nimaga   Net: n/a

☐	TL-ABP	Cessna TU206C Super Skywagon	U206-0977	TN-AEM	0068		1 CO TSIO-520-C	1633			
☐	TL-ABK	Cessna 207A Stationair 7 II	20700511		0079		1 CO IO-520-F	1724			
☐	TL-ABV	Piper PA-23-250 Aztec D	27-4526		0070		2 LY TIO-540-C1A	2360			

CENTRAFRICAIN AIRLINES = GC / CET   Bangui & Sharjah (UAE)

Operations Office: c/o Transavia Travel Agency, PO Box 3962, Sharjah, United Arab Emirates   ☎ (6) 52 28 33   Tx: none   Fax: (6) 52 26 60n/a   SITA: n/a
F: 1998   ⋔⋔ n/a   Head: Victor Butt   ICAO: CENTRAFRICAIN   Net: n/a

☐	TL-ACI	Let 410UVP-E	892225	3D-LEA	0089	0998	2 WA M-601E	6400	Y17		
☐	TL-ACH	Yakovlev 40	9930407	CCCP-87709	0069	0898	3 IV AI-25	16800	Y32		
☐	TL-ACV	Antonov 72		3D-RTV		0998	2 LO D-36	34500	Freighter		
☐	TL-ACM	Antonov 8	9340706	EL-RDK	0798	0798	2 IV AI-20D	38000	Freighter		Katyusha
☐	TL-ACJ	Antonov 12BP	1340107	3D-AKV	0061	0998	4 IV AI-20M	64000	Freighter		
☐	TL-ACR	Antonov 12BP	2340809	3D-RDL	0062	1098	4 IV AI-20M	61000	Freighter		
☐	TL-ACF	Tupolev 154M	895	3D-RTP	0091	0998	3 SO D-30KU-154-II	102000	C12Y120		
☐	TL-ACL	Ilyushin 62M	3036142	3D-RTI	0080	0299	4 SO D-30KU	167000	C12Y140		fn 3604
☐	TL-ACN	Ilyushin 76T	053403072	3D-RTT	0075	1198	4 SO D-30KP-2	170000	Freighter		fn 0203
☐	TL-ACU	Ilyushin 76T	043402039	3D-RTX	0074	1198	4 SO D-30KP-2	170000	Freighter		fn 0110

MINAIR   Bangui   [MINAIR logo]

BP 333, Bangui, Central African Republic   ☎ 61 43 41   Tx: none   Fax: 61 91 00   SITA: n/a
F: 1994   ⋔⋔ 15   Head: Oumarou Mahamat   Net: n/a

☐	TL-ABY	Piper PA-23-250 Aztec C	27-2748	F-BTAR	0064	0494	2 LY IO-540-C4B5	2360			
☐	TL-ACE	Beech Baron 58	TH-746	TR-LBQ	0076	1295	2 CO IO-520-C	2449			
☐	TL-ABZ	Cessna 404 Titan II	404-0102	D-IACO	0077	0794	2 CO GTSIO-520-M	3810			
☐	TL-ACB	Cessna 404 Titan II	404-0650	EI-BUM	0080	1294	2 CO GTSIO-520-M	3810			

TN = CONGO BRAZZAVILLE (People's Republic of Congo) (République Populaire du Congo)
Capital: Brazzaville   Official Language: French   Population: 3,0 million   Square Km: 342000   Dialling code: +242   Year established: 1960   Acting political head: Denis Sassou-Nguesso (President)

AERO SERVICE = BF / RSR   Brazzaville & Pointe Noire

BP 1115, Brazzaville, Congo Brazzaville   ☎ 81 34 88   Tx: 5226 kg   Fax: 83 09 47   SITA: n/a
F: 1967   ⋔⋔ 65   Head: Ch. R. Griesbaum   ICAO: CONGOSERV   Net: n/a   Aircraft below MTOW 1361 kg: Cessna 172 & 182.

☐	TN-AEL	Cessna U206G Stationair 6 II	U20604793		0078		1 CO IO-520-F	1633	Y5		lsf Congo Timer COTIM
☐	TN-ADR	Beech Baron A55 (95-A55)	TC-363	TR-LYJ	0062		2 CO IO-470-L	2214	Y3		std BZV
☐	TN-ADN	Britten-Norman BN-2A-9 Islander	647	TL-AAQ	0076		2 LY O-540-E4C5	2858	Y9		
☐	TN-ADY	Britten-Norman BN-2A-9 Islander	764	TR-LWL	0076		2 LY O-540-E4C5	2858	Y8		
☐	TN-ACJ	Cessna 402B	402B0304	N3357Q	0072		2 CO TSIO-520-E	2858	Y9		
☐	TN-ACY	Cessna 402B	402B0810	TR-LTN	0074		2 CO TSIO-520-E	2858	Y9		std BZV
☐	TN-AEK	Cessna 404 Titan II	404-0312	TR-LXI	0077		2 CO GTSIO-520-M	3810	Y10		std BZV
☐	TN-ADP	Fairchild (Swearingen) SA226AT Merlin IV	AT-025	N52LB	0074		2 GA TPE331-3U-303G	5670	Y13		std BZV
☐	TN-ADI	Aerospatiale SN601 Corvette	9	F-OCRN	0075		2 PWC JT15D-4	6300	Y9		lsf Gvmt / std BZV
☐	TN-AFA	CASA 212-CB Aviocar Series 100	151	HB-LKX	0079	0492	2 GA TPE331-5-251C	6500	Y19		
☐	TN-AFC	CASA 212-DF Aviocar Srs 300	397	D4-CBA	0094	0094	2 GA TPE331-10R-513C	7450	Y26		Big Bill
☐	TN-AFD	CASA 212-DF Aviocar Srs 300	398	D4-CBB	0090	0094	2 GA TPE331-10R-513C	7450	Y26		
☐	F-GDFC	Fokker F28 Fellowship 4000 (F28 Mk4000)	11133	G-WWJC	0079	0398	2 RR Spey 555-15H	33110	Y80		lsf Regourd Aviation SA

registration   type of aircraft   cn/fn   ex/ex*   mfd   del   powered by   mtow kg   configuration   selcal   name/fln/specialitites/remarks

AIR AFRIQUE = multinational state carrier – see under TU- markings

---

CARGO EXPRESS CONGO (Subsidiary of ATO-Air Transport Office) — Brazzaville

Av. de l'Equateur 131, BP 180, Kinshasa 1, Democratic Republic of Congo ☎ (88) 45 340 Tx: none Fax: (212) 372 36 55 SITA: n/a
F: 1997 ✦✦✦ n/a Head: Patrick Latour & Herbert Skuvie Net: n/a

reg	type	cn/fn	ex/ex*	mfd	del	powered by	mtow	config	selcal	name/remarks
☐ EL-WLS	Boeing (Douglas) DC-4 (C-54D-1-DC)	10644 / DC 375	9Q-CLM	0045	0097	4 PW R-2000-7M2	30241			Freighter

---

EQUAFLIGHT, S.A. = 8H / EKA (Associated with Occitania Jet Fleet) — Pointe Noire

BP 4247, Pointe Noire, Congo Brazzaville ☎ 94 06 10 Tx: none Fax: 94 07 71 SITA: PNROP8X
F: 1998 ✦✦✦ n/a Head: Jacques Boulanger Net: n/a

| ☐ F-GNZB | Fokker F28 Fellowship 1000C (F28 Mk1000C) | 11073 | F-ODZB | 0073 | 1098 | 2 RR Spey 555-15 | 29480 | Y65 | | lsf Regourd Aviation SA / cvtd -1000 |

TRANS AIR CONGO – TAC = TSG — Brazzaville

CP 2422, Brazzaville, Congo Brazzaville ☎ 83 37 50 Tx: none Fax: 83 20 14 SITA: n/a
F: 1994 ✦✦✦ 129 Head: Bassam Elhage ICAO: TRANS-CONGO Net: n/a

☐ RA-27056	Mil Mi-8MTV-1 (Mi-17)	95890		0392	0395	2 IS TV3-117MT	13000	Y22		lsf SVL
☐ RA-46495	Antonov 24RV	27308208	CCCP-46495	0072	0895	2 IV AI-24VT	21800	Y44		lsf SVL
☐ RA-47811	Antonov 24RV	17307003	TC-KHT	0571	0996	2 IV AI-24VT	21800	Y48		lsf SVL

TR = GABON (Gabonese Republic) (République Gabonaise)

Capital: Libreville Official Language: French Population: 1,5 million Square Km: 267667 Dialling code: +241 Year established: 1960 Acting political head: El-Hadj Omar Albert-Bernard Bongo (President)

Government / Corporate / Executive / VIP Aircraft

☐ TR-KSP	GAC G-IV Gulfstream IV (SP)	1327	N327GA*	0098	1198	2 RR Tay 611-8	33838	VIP		Gvmt
☐ TR-LEX	Dassault Falcon 900EX	24	F-WWFU*	0098	0498	3 GA TFE731-60-1C	22226	VIP		Gvmt
☐ TR-LTZ	Boeing (Douglas) DC-8-73F (CF)	46053 / 446	N8638	0069	1174	4 CFMI CFM56-2C	161025	Combi	GL-AF	Franceville / Gvmt/cvtd -63CF

AIR AFFAIRES GABON — Libreville

BP 3962, Libreville, Gabon ☎ 73 25 13 Tx: 5360 afairgab go Fax: 73 49 98 SITA: n/a
F: 1975 ✦✦✦ 55 Head: R. Bellanger Net: n/a

☐ TR-LUG	Beech Baron 58	TH-622		0075	0575	2 CO IO-520-C	2449			
☐ TR-LVH	Beech King Air E90	LW-151	F-BXLF	0075	0875	2 PWC PT6A-28	4581			
☐ TR-LYK	Embraer 110P1 Bandeirante (EMB-110P1)	110195	PT-GLN*	0078	0179	2 PWC PT6A-34	5670			
☐ ZS-OCV	Beech 1900D Airliner	UE-313	N11354*	0098	0698	2 PWC PT6A-67D	7688			lsf Beech Sales (NAC) P/L
☐ ZS-OCX	Beech 1900D Airliner	UE-321	N22978*	0098	0898	2 PWC PT6A-67D	7688			lsf Beech Sales (NAC) P/L
☐ TR-LDB	Hawker 800B (BAe 125-800B)	258192	G-5-691*	0090	0391	2 GA TFE731-5R-1H	12428			lsf Better Services Ltd

---

AIR GABON = GN / AGN — Libreville

BP 2206, Libreville, Gabon ☎ 73 21 97 Tx: 5213 airgab go Fax: 73 11 56 SITA: LBVDAGN
F: 1977 ✦✦✦ 900 Head: Martin Bongo IATA: 185 ICAO: GOLF NOVEMBER Net: n/a

☐ TR-LSU	Fokker F28 Fellowship 2000 (F28 Mk2000)	11081	PH-EXD*	0074	0774	2 RR Spey 555-15	29480	Y79		Oyem
☐ TR-LXL	Boeing 737-2Q2C (A)	21467 / 515		0078	0778	2 PW JT8D-17	53070	F12Y96	GL-AE	Le Makokou
☐ 3B-LXM	Boeing 737-2H6 (A)	21732 / 559	ZK-JJD	0079	0898	2 PW JT8D-15	53070	F12Y94	AG-CD	lsf INGO
☐ TR-LEV	Boeing 727-228 (A)	22083 / 1605	F-OHOA	0480	0593	3 PW JT8D-15	86410	F12Y136	EK-CL	
☐ TR-LFH	Boeing 767-266 (ER)	23178 / 97	N767ER	0084	0599	2 PW JT9D-7R4E	156489	F10C24Y142		lsf Leopard Leasing Co.
☐ F-ODJG	Boeing 747-2Q2B (M)	21468 / 324	N1248E*	0078	1078	4 GE CF6-50E2	362800	F18C44Y188/Plts	AE-BK	President Leon Mba

---

AIR INTER GABON, SA = AIG — Port-Gentil

BP 240, Port-Gentil, Gabon ☎ 55 31 44 Tx: none Fax: 55 21 08 SITA: n/a
F: 1956 ✦✦✦ 64 Head: Maître Louis Gaston Mayila Net: n/a

☐ ZS-NED	Pilatus PC-12/45	245	HB-FRP*	0099	0299	1 PWC PT6A-67B	4500	Y10		lsf pvt
☐ TR-LEU	Beech 1900C-1 Airliner	UC-63	N15394	0089	1297	2 PWC PT6A-65B	7530	Y19		lsf Raytheon Aircraft Credit Corp.
☐ TR-LFA	Beech 1900D Airliner	UE-312	N11193*	0098	0598	2 PWC PT6A-67D	7688	Y19		Domicile / lsf Raytheon Aircraft
☐ TR-LFI	Beech 1900D Airliner	UE-329	N23183*	0098	1298	2 PWC PT6A-67D	7688	Y19		lsf Raytheon Aircraft Credit Corp.
☐ TR-LFD	ATR 42-320	337	F-OGXO	0093	0598	2 PWC PW121	16700	Y50		lsf Surf's Up Ltd

---

AIR SERVICE GABON, SA — Libreville

BP 2232, Libreville, Gabon ☎ 73 24 08 Tx: 5263 air svc go Fax: 73 60 69 SITA: n/a
F: 1965 ✦✦✦ 34 Head: Francis Lascombes Net: n/a

☐ TR-LBM	Cessna 404 Titan II	404-0453	D-ICRG	0079		2 CO GTSIO-520-M	3810	Y9		
☐ TR-LBW	Cessna 404 Titan II	404-0845	SE-IFO	0081		2 CO GTSIO-520-M	3810	Y9		
☐ F-GROI	Cessna 208B Grand Caravan	208B0220	JA8220	0090	0298	1 PWC PT6A-114A	3969	Y9		lsf ING Lease France SA
☐ TR-LEQ	Reims/Cessna F406 Caravan II	F406-0007	LX-LMS	0086	0298	2 PWC PT6A-112	4468	Y12		lsf CEB Gabon
☐ TR-LZW	CASA 212-CC29 Aviocar Series 200	180		0081	0481	2 GA TPE331-10-511C	7450	Y24		
☐ TR-LET	Beech 1900D Airliner	UE-106	F-GMSM	0094	0398	2 PWC PT6A-67D	7688	Y19		lsf Raytheon Aircraft Credit Corp.
☐ TR-LFC	Beech 1900D Airliner	UE-316	N21716*	0098	0798	2 PWC PT6A-67D	7688	Y19		lsf Raytheon Aircraft Credit Corp.
☐ TR-LFE	Beech 1900D Airliner	UE-310	N22873*	0098	0698	2 PWC PT6A-67D	7688	Y19		lsf Raytheon Aircraft Credit Corp.

GABON AIR TRANSPORT – GAT — Libreville

BP 173, Libreville, Gabon ☎ 73 02 02 Tx: 5740 go Fax: 73 08 80 SITA: n/a
F: 1978 ✦✦✦ 10 Head: Pierre Vialaret Net: n/a

☐ TR-LDI	Cessna TU206F Turbo Stationair II	U20603499	F-GELZ	0076	0492	1 CO TSIO-520-C	1633			
☐ TR-LYZ	Partenavia P.68B	201		0080	0690	2 LY IO-360-A1B6	1960			lsf S.E.E.F.
☐ TR-LCZ	Cessna 404 Titan II	404-0226	TL-ABJ	0078		2 CO GTSIO-520-M	3810			

HELI-GABON (Associated with Héli-Union, France) — Port-Gentil

BP 240, Port-Gentil, Gabon ☎ 55 29 23 Tx: 8204 air intr go Fax: 55 59 31 SITA: n/a
F: 1975 ✦✦✦ 10 Head: Christophe de Courlon Eurocopter (Aérospatiale) SA316B, AS365C3, AS365N/N2 & Sikorsky S-76A+ helicopters are leased from Héli-Union France when required – for fleet details see under that company.

SAFT Gabon – S.A. de Fret et de Transport — Libreville

BP 3987, Libreville, Gabon ☎ 73 45 56 Tx: none Fax: 73 18 21 SITA: n/a
F: 1996 ✦✦✦ n/a Head: Tital Boulingui Net: n/a

| ☐ N1092H | Beech King Air C90B | LJ-1454 | | 0096 | 0097 | 2 PWC PT6A-21 | 4581 | | | lsf Transair USA Inc. |
| ☐ D2-EPU | Antonov 24RV | | | 0071 | 0097 | 2 IV AI-24VT | 21800 | Y48 | | lsf Angola Gvmt |

TS = TUNISIA (Republic of Tunisia) (al-Jumhouriyah at-Tunisiyah)

Capital: Tunis Official Language: Arabic Population: 9,0 million Square Km: 163610 Dialling code: +216 Year established: 1956 Acting political head: Abidine Ben Ali (President)

NOUVELAIR TUNISIE = BJ / LBT (Member of TTS-Tunisian Travel Service Group / formerly Air Liberté Tunisie) — Monastir

Batiment Chaouachi, Route de Sousse, Monastir 5000, Tunisia ☎ (3) 52 06 00 Tx: 30933 tn Fax: (3) 52 06 00 SITA: n/a
F: 1990 ✦✦✦ 160 Head: Aziz Milad ICAO: NOUVELAIR Net: n/a

☐ EI-CBO	Boeing (Douglas) MD-83 (DC-9-83)	49442 / 1358	HB-IUL	0387	0396	2 PW JT8D-219	72575	Y167	DG-EH	lsf GECA
☐ EI-CGI	Boeing (Douglas) MD-83 (DC-9-83)	49624 / 1502	EC-EKM	0788	0494	2 PW JT8D-219	72575	Y167	DS-FK	lsf GECA
☐ EI-CNO	Boeing (Douglas) MD-83 (DC-9-83)	49672 / 1494	EC-FTU	0688	0397	2 PW JT8D-219	72575	Y167	EH-LP	lsf GECA
☐ F-GHEC	Boeing (Douglas) MD-83 (DC-9-83)	49662 / 1429	G-PATC	0088	0390	2 PW JT8D-219	72575	Y169	CP-AQ	lsf Airlease (101) Ltd
☐ TS-	Airbus Industrie A320-200					2	77000	Y174		oo-delivery 1299

TUNINTER = UG / TUI (Associated with Tunisair) — Tunis-Carthage

Immeuble Maghrebia Tour B, Bd. 7 Novembre 1987, Carthage, Tunis 2035, Tunisia ☎ (1) 70 17 17 Tx: none Fax: (1) 71 21 93 SITA: n/a
F: 1991 ✦✦✦ 300 Head: Ouerdani Abderrazak IATA: 150 Net: n/a

☐ TS-LBA	ATR 42-300	245	F-WWET*	0092	0292	2 PWC PW120	16700	Y48		Alyssa / lst GIL as G-BXBV
☐ TS-LBB	ATR 72-202	258	F-WWLE*	0092	0392	2 PWC PW124B	21500	Y70		Habib Bourguiba
☐ TS-LBC	ATR 72-202	281	F-WWLK*	0092	0592	2 PWC PW124B	21500	Y70		Tahar Haddad
☐ YU-AJI	Boeing (Douglas) DC-9-32	47563 / 687	N1346U*	0072	0198	2 PW JT8D-9A	48988	Y106	GJ-HK	lsf JAT / dmgd 130198 / std TUN
☐ TS-IEA	Boeing 737-2H6 (A)	23320 / 1120	PK-IJG	0085	0498	2 PW JT8D-15A	53070	Y130		lst INGO

TUNISAIR = TU / TAR — Tunis-Carthage

Boulevard 7 Novembre, Carthage, Tunis 2035, Tunisia ☎ (1) 70 01 00 Tx: 12283 tunair tn Fax: (1) 70 04 72 SITA: TUNXTTU
F: 1948 ✦✦✦ 6000 Head: Ahmed Smaoui IATA: 199 ICAO: TUNAIR Net: n/a

☐ TS-IOC	Boeing 737-2H3 (A)	21973 / 607		0079	1079	2 PW JT8D-9A	53070	Y126	CE-KL	Salammbo
☐ TS-IOD	Boeing 737-2H3C (A)	21974 / 615		0079	1179	2 PW JT8D-9A	53070	Y126	CE-KM	Bulla Regia
☐ TS-IOE	Boeing 737-2H3 (A)	22624 / 758		0081	0481	2 PW JT8D-17	58105	Y126	CE-JK	Zarzis
☐ TS-IOF	Boeing 737-2H3 (A)	22625 / 776		0081	0681	2 PW JT8D-17	58105	Y126	CE-JL	Sousse
☐ TS-IOG	Boeing 737-5H3	26639 / 2253		0092	0492	2 CFMI CFM56-3C1	56472	Y126	BF-QR	Sfax
☐ TS-IOH	Boeing 737-5H3	26640 / 2474		0093	0593	2 CFMI CFM56-3C1	56472	Y126	BM-GR	Hammamet
☐ TS-IOI	Boeing 737-5H3	27257 / 2583		0094	0394	2 CFMI CFM56-3C1	56472	Y126	EQ-KM	Mahdia
☐ TS-IOJ	Boeing 737-5H3	27912 / 2701		0095	0395	2 CFMI CFM56-3C1	56472	Y126	CG-MP	Monastir

---

605 registration type of aircraft cn/fn ex/ex* mfd del powered by mtow kg configuration selcal name/fln/specialitites/remarks

registration	type of aircraft	cn/fn	ex/ex*	mfd	del	powered by	mtow kg	configuration	selcal	name/fln/specialitites/remarks
☐ TS-	Boeing 737-6H3					2 CFMI CFM56-7B20	65091	Y126		oo-delivery 0599
☐ TS-	Boeing 737-6H3					2 CFMI CFM56-7B20	65091	Y126		oo-delivery 0599
☐ TS-	Boeing 737-6H3					2 CFMI CFM56-7B20	65091	Y126		oo-delivery 0799
☐ TS-	Boeing 737-6H3					2 CFMI CFM56-7B20	65091	Y126		oo-delivery 0200
☐ TS-	Boeing 737-6H3					2 CFMI CFM56-7B20	65091	Y126		oo-delivery 0300
☐ TS-	Boeing 737-6H3					2 CFMI CFM56-7B20	65091	Y126		oo-delivery 0500
☐ TS-IMJ	Airbus Industrie A319-114	869	D-AVYW*	0098	0898	2 CFMI CFM56-5A5	70000	Y144		El Kantaoui
☐ TS-IMK	Airbus Industrie A319-114	880	D-AVYD*	0098	0998	2 CFMI CFM56-5A5	70000	Y144		Kerkenah
☐ TS-	Airbus Industrie A319-114					2 CFMI CFM56-5A5	70000	Y144		oo-delivery 0401
☐ TS-IMB	Airbus Industrie A320-211	119	F-WWIJ*	0090	1090	2 CFMI CFM56-5A1	73500	C25Y120	CE-LM	Farhat Hached
☐ TS-IMC	Airbus Industrie A320-211	124	F-WWIS*	0090	1190	2 CFMI CFM56-5A1	73500	C25Y120	CF-AH	7 Novembre
☐ TS-IMD	Airbus Industrie A320-211	205	F-WWDO*	0091	0791	2 CFMI CFM56-5A1	73500	C25Y120	AH-FR	Khereddine
☐ TS-IME	Airbus Industrie A320-211	123	F-WWIP*	0090	0792	2 CFMI CFM56-5A1	73500	C25Y120	BS-AG	Tabarka
☐ TS-IMF	Airbus Industrie A320-211	370	F-WWIP*	0092	1292	2 CFMI CFM56-5A1	73500	Y174	BQ-DJ	Djerba
☐ TS-IMG	Airbus Industrie A320-211	390	F-WWDL*	0094	0394	2 CFMI CFM56-5A1	73500	Y174	FS-CP	Abou el Kacem Chebbi
☐ TS-IMH	Airbus Industrie A320-211	402	F-WWBN*	0094	0494	2 CFMI CFM56-5A1	73500	Y174	FS-CQ	Ali Belhaouane
☐ TS-IMI	Airbus Industrie A320-211	511	F-WWDC*	0094	0395	2 CFMI CFM56-5A1	73500	Y174	FJ-KS	Jugurtha / 50th anniversary-colors
☐ TS-IML	Airbus Industrie A320-211	958	F-WWBI*	0099	0399	2 CFMI CFM56-5A1	73500	Y174		
☐ TS-	Airbus Industrie A320-211	975	F-WWIR*			2 CFMI CFM56-5A1	73500	Y174		oo-delivery 0499
☐ TS-	Airbus Industrie A320-211					2 CFMI CFM56-5A1	73500	Y174		oo-delivery 0300
☐ TS-	Airbus Industrie A320-211					2 CFMI CFM56-5A1	73500	Y174		oo-delivery 0002
☐ TS-JHR	Boeing 727-2H3 (A)	21179 / 1171		0075	1175	3 PW JT8D-9A	79605	Y178	CE-AH	Bizerte
☐ TS-JHT	Boeing 727-2H3 (A)	21235 / 1210		0076	0676	3 PW JT8D-9A	79605	Y178	CE-AK	Sidi Bou Said
☐ TS-JHU	Boeing 727-2H3 (A)	21318 / 1252		0077	0377	3 PW JT8D-9A	79605	Y178	CD-HK	Hannibal
☐ TS-JHW	Boeing 727-2H3 (A)	21320 / 1271		0077	0677	3 PW JT8D-9A	79605	Y178	CD-LM	Ibn Khaldoun
☐ TS-IMA	Airbus Industrie A300B4-203	188	F-WZME*	0082	0582	2 GE CF6-50C2	165000	C24Y241	CF-AB	Amilcar

TUNISAVIA = TAJ (Société de Transports, Services et Travaux Aériens dba)   Tunis-Carthage

Immeuble Saadi Spric, Tour CD, El Menzah 1082, Tunisia   ☎ (1) 71 76 00   Tx: 13121 tunav tn   Fax: (1) 71 81 00   SITA: TUNTEBJ
F: 1974   ✈✈✈ 110   Head: Aziz Milad   ICAO: TUNISAVIA   Net: n/a

☐ TS-HAC	Eurocopter (Aerosp.) SA318C Alouette II	2372	F-ODRI	0074		1 TU Astazou IIA2	1650	4 Pax		
☐ TS-HSD	Eurocopter (Aerosp.) SA365N Dauphin 2	6117	F-WXFC*	0084		2 TU Arriel 1C	4000	11 Pax		
☐ TS-HSE	Eurocopter (Aerosp.) SA365N Dauphin 2	6150		0086		2 TU Arriel 1C	4000	11 Pax		
☐ TS-LIB	De Havilland DHC-6 Twin Otter 300	716	TS-DIB	0081	0481	2 PWC PT6A-27	5670	19 Pax		
☐ TS-LSF	De Havilland DHC-6 Twin Otter 300	575	TS-DSF	0078	0378	2 PWC PT6A-27	5670	19 Pax		

TT = CHAD (Republic of Chad) (République du Tchad)
Capital: N'Djamena Official Language: French, Arabic Population: 6,5 million Square Km: 1284000 Dialling code: +235 Year established: 1960 Acting political head: Idriss Déby (President)

Government / Corporate / Executive / VIP Aircraft
☐ TT-AAI	GAC (Grumman) G-1159 Gulfstream II	240	5A-DDR	0079	0691	2 RR Spey 511-8	29392	VIP		Gvmt

AIR AFRIQUE = multinational state carrier – see under TU- markings

AIR TCHAD = HTT   N'Djamena

BP 168, N'Djaména, Chad   ☎ 51 50 90   Tx: 5345 kd   Fax: n/a   SITA: n/a
F: 1966   ✈✈✈ 35   Head: Djibangar Madjirebaye   Net: n/a

☐ TT-AAK	Fokker F27 Friendship 600 (F27 Mk600)	10430	F-BYAR	0070	0683	2 RR Dart 532-7	19731	Y44		Le Chari

TU = IVORY COAST (Republic of the Ivory Coast) (République de Côte d'Ivoire)
Capital: Yamoussoukro+Abidjan Official Language: French Population: 15,0 million Square Km: 322463 Dialling code: +225 Year established: 1960 Acting political head: Henry Konan Bédié (President)

Government / Corporate / Executive / VIP Aircraft
☐ TU-VAA	Fokker 100 (F28 Mk0100)	11245	PH-CDI*	0088	0289	2 RR Tay 620-15	43091	VIP		FACI-GATL
☐ TU-VAD	GAC G-IV Gulfstream IV	1019	N17584*	0087		2 RR Tay 610-8	33203	VIP	BC-HP	FACI-GATL
☐ TU-VAF	GAC G-1159A Gulfstream III	462	N303GA*	0086		2 RR Spey 511-8	31615	VIP		FACI-GATL

AIR AFRIQUE = RK / RKA (Air Afrique Vacances)   Abidjan

01 BP 3927, Abidjan 01, Ivory Coast   ☎ 820 30 00   Tx: 22814 airaf ci   Fax: 820 30 03   SITA: ABJDGRK
F: 1961   ✈✈✈ 4330   Head: Tijane Sylla   IATA: 092   ICAO: AIRAFRIC   Net: http://www.airafrique-airline.com
Multinational state carrier of Benin, Burkina Faso, Central African Republic, Chad, Congo, Ivory Coast, Mali, Mauritania, Niger, Senegal and Togo.
Charter flights are operated under the name AIR AFRIQUE VACANCES (ICAO Code: AFV), an internal division, same headquarters & fleet.

☐ TU-TAJ	Boeing 737-3Q8	26333 / 2786	HB-IIF	0496	1098	2 CFMI CFM56-3C1	63276	CY148		lsf ILFC
☐ TU-TAK	Boeing 737-3Q8	28200 / 2854	HB-IIG	0297	1297	2 CFMI CFM56-3C1	63276	CY148		lsf ILFC
☐ YU-AND	Boeing 737-3H9	23329 / 1134		0085	0998	2 CFMI CFM56-3B1	61235	CY137	KL-HF	lsf / opb JAT
☐ YU-ANH	Boeing 737-3H9	23415 / 1171	TC-CYO	0085	0798	2 CFMI CFM56-3B1	61235	CY137	KL-GM	lsf / opb JAT
☐ LZ-SFN	Antonov 12BP	2340806	LZ-FEA	0062	0095	4 IV AI-20M	61000	Freighter		lsf SFB
☐ 9G-ADS	Boeing 707-323C	19587 / 686	F-GHFT	0368	0097	4 PW JT3D-3B (HK2/COM)	151092	Freighter	DF-AM	lsf Analinda Airlines / opb CCL
☐ F-OJAF	Airbus Industrie A310-324	638	F-GJEZ	0092	0998	2 PW PW4152	157000	C28Y146		lsf Green Four Ltd
☐ TU-TAO	Airbus Industrie A300B4-203	137	F-WZEP*	0081	0581	2 GE CF6-50C2	165000	F16J28Y167	DM-BC	Nouakchott / lsf Afrique Bail
☐ TU-TAS	Airbus Industrie A300B4-203	243	F-WZMJ*	0083	0783	2 GE CF6-50C2	165000	F16J28Y167	BL-HJ	Bangui
☐ TU-TAT	Airbus Industrie A300B4-203	282	F-WZXP*	0083	0984	2 GE CF6-50C2	165000	F16J28Y167	JK-EM	
☐ TU-TAH	Airbus Industrie A300-605R (A300B4-605R)	744	F-WWAK*	0095	0595	2 GE CF6-80C2A5	171700	F12C39Y173	HS-DF	lsf ILFC
☐ TU-TAI	Airbus Industrie A300-605R (A300B4-605R)	749	F-WWAN*	0095	0795	2 GE CF6-80C2A5	171700	F12C39Y173	HS-DG	lsf ILFC
☐ TU-TAM	Boeing (Douglas) DC-10-30	46892 / 204	HS-TGB	0075	0675	3 GE CF6-50C2	263084	C42Y275		lst AOM as F-GNEM

AIR INTER IVOIRE (Associated with Héli Union, France)   Abidjan

07 BP 62, Abidjan 07, Ivory Coast   ☎ 27 84 65   Tx: none   Fax: 27 71 65   SITA: n/a
F: 1968   ✈✈✈ 55   Head: n/a   Net: n/a   Aircraft below MTOW 1361 kg: Piper PA-28 & PA-38.

☐ TU-TJF	Piper PA-23-250 Aztec F	27-7654072	N62594	0076		2 LY IO-540-C4B5	2359			
☐ TU-TMP	Beech Baron 58	TH-1434		0084		2 CO IO-520-C	2449			lsf Ivoirienne Developpement Textiles
☐ TU-TGF	Piper PA-31-350 Navajo Chieftain	31-7305072	N74930	0073		2 LY TIO-540-J2BD	3175			lsf Sodelpalm
☐ TU-TLU	Piper PA-31-350 Navajo Chieftain	31-7752139	N27251	0077		2 LY TIO-540-J2BD	3175			
☐ TU-TJL	Piper PA-31T Cheyenne II	31T-7720033	N82152	0077		2 PWC PT6A-28	4082			lsf Sodelpalm

AIR IVOIRE = VU / VUN   Abidjan

01 BP 1027, Abidjan 01, Ivory Coast   ☎ 20 66 71   Tx: none   Fax: 33 26 26   SITA: n/a
F: 1963   ✈✈✈ n/a   Head: Col. Guidy Leopold   IATA: 084   ICAO: AIRIVOIRE   Net: n/a

☐ PK-GQA	Fokker F28 Fellowship 4000 (F28 Mk4000)	11217	PK-EZZ*	0084	0998	2 RR Spey 555-15H	32205	Y85		lsf MNA

IVOIRE HELICOPTERE   Abidjan

07 BP 244, Abidjan, Ivory Coast   ☎ 27 83 81   Tx: none   Fax: 27 71 36   SITA: n/a
F: 1980   ✈✈✈ 17   Head: Raymond Morean   Net: n/a   Aircraft & Ag-aircraft below MTOW 1361 / 5000kg: Agusta-Bell 47G-2 & Cessna A188B

☐ TU-THM	Eurocopter (Aerosp.) SE3130 Alouette II	1926	V-70	0064		1 TU Artouste IIC6	1500			
☐ F-OHFL	Eurocopter (Aerosp.) SA316B Alouette III	1512	23158	0068	0497	1 TU Artouste IIIB1	2200			

TY = BENIN (Republic of Benin) (République du Bénin)
Capital: Porto-Novo + Cotonou Official Language: French Population: 6,0 million Square Km: 112622 Dialling code: +229 Year established: 1960 Acting political head: Mathieu Kerekou (President)

AIR AFRIQUE = multinational state carrier – see under TU- markings

FORCE AERIENNE DU BENIN – Dept. Vols Commerciaux (Commercial Flt.Dept.of Force Aérienne du Benin/Benin Air Force, a div. of Forces Armées Beninoises/formerly Aviation Militaire) Cotonou

BP 331, Cotonou, Benin   ☎ 31 49 26   Tx: none   Fax: 31 43 52   SITA: n/a
F: 1961   ✈✈✈ n/a   Head: Lt.Col. Taffa Adam   Net: n/a   Air Force which beside non-commercial military flights, also operates commercial flights upon request.

☐ TY-AAJ	Eurocopter (Aerosp.) AS350B Ecureuil	1803		0084	0385	1 TU Arriel 1B	1950	5 Pax		
☐ TY-HBA	Eurocopter (Aerosp.) AS350B Ecureuil	1741		0083	0884	1 TU Arriel 1B	1950	5 Pax		
☐ TY-BBS	De Havilland DHC-6 Twin Otter 300	807	C-GESR*	0084	0984	2 PWC PT6A-27	5670	20 Pax		

TZ = MALI (Republic of Mali) (République du Mali)
Capital: Bamako Official Language: Bambara, French Population: 11,0 million Square Km: 1240192 Dialling code: +223 Year established: 1960 Acting political head: Alpha Oumar Konaré (President)

AFRIQUE AIR AFFAIRES = FAS   Bamako

BP 2838, Bamako, Mali   ☎ 22 59 52   Tx: none   Fax: 22 50 41   SITA: n/a
F: 1996   ✈✈✈ n/a   Head: n/a   ICAO: AIR AFFAIRES   Net: n/a   Operates charter flights with Cessna 402C aircraft from SAHEL AVIATION SERVICE (TZ-) when required.

AIR AFRIQUE = multinational state carrier – see under TU- markings

AIR MALI, SA = L9 / MLI   Bamako

BP 2690, Bamako, Mali ☎ 22 84 39 Tx: none Fax: 22 94 03 SITA: BKODGL9
F: 1993 ♦♦♦ 61 Head: Abderammane Berthe IATA: 109 ICAO: AIR MALI Net: n/a

	registration	type of aircraft	cn/fn	ex/ex*	mfd	del	powered by	mtow kg	configuration	selcal	name/fln/remarks
☐	RA-67551	Let 410UVP-E	851428	CCCP-67551	0985	0097	2 WA M-601E	6400	Y19		lsf OAO
☐	RA-47295	Antonov 24RV	07306608	CCCP-47295	0171	0097	2 IV AI-24VT	21800	Y48		lsf KTA
☐	TZ-ASH	Fokker F28 Fellowship 1000 (F28 Mk1000)	11003	C5-ADD	0067	0098	2 RR Spey 555-15H	29480	Y65		Bakary S.

SAHEL AVIATION SERVICE – S.A.S.   Bamako

BP 3272, Bamako, Mali ☎ 22 98 26 Tx: none Fax: 22 45 52 SITA: n/a
F: n/a ♦♦♦ n/a Head: Charles Kamkole Net: n/a

☐	TZ-AMB	Cessna 402C II	402C0018	N90108	0079		2 CO TSIO-520-VB	3107			
☐	TZ-AMS	Cessna 402C II	402C0517	N68802	0081		2 CO TSIO-520-VB	3107			

STA-MALI – Société de Transport Aérien du Mali = SBA   Bamako

BP 775, Bamako, Mali ☎ 77 03 85 Tx: none Fax: 23 09 81 SITA: n/a
F: n/a ♦♦♦ n/a Head: n/a ICAO: STA-MALI Net: n/a

☐	TZ-ASM	Britten-Norman BN-2A-9 Islander	700	6V-AES	0073		2 LY O-540-E4C5	2860			lsf Gestfin

T2 = TUVALU (The Tuvalu Islands)
Capital: Vaiaku Official Language: Tuvalu, English Population: 0,1 million Square Km: 26 Dialling code: +688 Year established: 1978 Acting political head: Bikenibeu Paeniu (Prime Minister)

At present there is no licenced commercial air operator in this country.

T3 = KIRIBATI (Republic of Kiribati) (Ribaberikin Kiribati)
(This country uses a country prefix [nationality mark] not notified to the ICAO)
Capital: Tarawa Official Language: Kiribati, English Population: 0,1 million Square Km: 728 Dialling code: +686 Year established: 1979 Acting political head: Teburoro Tito (President)

AIR KIRIBATI   Tarawa-Bonriki Int'l

PO Box 274, Tarawa, Republic of Kiribati ☎ 28 093 Tx: none Fax: 28 216 SITA: n/a
F: 1995 ♦♦♦ 63 Head: Sam Tira Net: n/a

☐	T3-ATE	Britten-Norman BN-2A Mk.III-2 Trislander	1004	DQ-FCE	0075	0796	3 LY O-540-E4C5	4536	Y16		
☐	T3-ATI	Harbin Yunshuji Y12 II	0077		0093	0097	2 PWC PT6A-27	5300	Y17		
☐	T3-ATC	CASA 212 Aviocar Srs 200	236		0082	0796	2 GA TPE331-10R-511C	7450	Y17		

T7 = SAN MARINO (Most Serene Republic of San Marino) (Serenissima Repubblica di San Marino)
Capital: San Marino Official Language: Italian Population: 0,1 million Square Km: 61 Dialling code: +378 Year established: 301 Acting political head: 2 co-regents in office for 6 months

At present there is no licenced commercial air operator in this country.

T9 = BOSNIA-HERZEGOVINA (Republic of Bosnia-Herzegovina) (Republika Bosna i Hercegovina)
(including the Muslim/Bosnian-Croatian Federation and the Serbian part-state 'Republika Srpska')
Capital: Sarajevo Official Language: Bosnian, Serbian, Croatian Population: 3,5 million Square Km: 51129 Dialling code: +387 Year established: 1992 Acting political head: Alija Izetbegovic (President)

AIR BOSNA = JA / BON   Sarajevo

Cemalasa 6, BA-71000 Sarajevo, Bosnia-Herzegovina ☎ (71) 66 79 53 Tx: none Fax: (71) 65 07 94 SITA: n/a
F: 1994 ♦♦♦ n/a Head: Mustafa Eminefendic IATA: 995 ICAO: AIR BOSNA Net: n/a

☐	T9-BIH	Cessna S550 Citation S/II	S550-0045	BH-BIH	0085	0094	2 PWC JT15D-4B	6849	VIP		
☐	T9-ABC	Yakovlev 42	11151004	UR-42544	0086	0098	3 LO D-36	56500	Y120		lsf UKR
☐	T9-ABD	Yakovlev 42D	4520422016201	UR-42383	0090	0097	3 LO D-36	56500	Y120		lsf UKR

AIR COMMERCE = CSB   Sarajevo

4C Radiceva Street, BA-71000 Sarajevo, Bosnia-Herzegovina ☎ (71) 66 33 95 Tx: none Fax: (71) 66 33 96 SITA: n/a
F: 1991 ♦♦♦ n/a Head: Mohamed Abadsic ICAO: AIR COMMERCE Net: n/a

☐	OM-SDA	Let 410UVP-E	872006	CCCP-67600	0087	0598	2 WA M-601E	6400	Y19		lsf CGL

AIR SRPSKA = R6 / SBK   Banja Luka

Yesilina Maslese 2, BA-78000 Banja Luka, (Serbian State), Bosnia-Herzegovina ☎ (78) 21 28 10 Tx: none Fax: (78) 21 28 14 SITA: n/a
F: 1998 ♦♦♦ n/a Head: n/a ICAO: AIR SERPSKA Net: n/a

☐	YU-ALO	ATR 72-202	186	F-WWEW*	0090	0199	2 PWC PW124B	21500	Y66		lsf JAT

BIO Air Company = BIO   Sarajevo

Ferhadija 14, BA-71000 Sarajevo, Bosnia-Herzegovina ☎ (71) 66 60 33 Tx: none Fax: (71) 20 51 30 SITA: n/a
F: 1997 ♦♦♦ n/a Head: Dzodzic Taric ICAO: BIO AIR Net: n/a

☐	T9-ABE	Antonov 74	36547097932	ES-NOE	0493	0098	2 LO D-36	34800	Combi		

SATAIR = SP / STZ   Banja Luka

Aerodrom, BA-78000 Banja Luka, (Serbian State), Bosnia-Herzegovina ☎ (78) 12 810 Tx: none Fax: (78) 12 814 SITA: n/a
F: 1998 ♦♦♦ n/a Head: n/a ICAO: AIR SAT Net: n/a

☐	RA-42411	Yakovlev 42D	4520421219043	CCCP-42411	0091	1198	3 LO D-36	56500	Y118		lsf CDS

SERB AIR = SRB   Banja Luka

Maladena Yanovica 69, BA-78000 Banja Luka, (Serbian State), Bosnia-Herzegovina ☎ (78) 23 01 36 Tx: none Fax: (78) 45 135 SITA: n/a
F: 1998 ♦♦♦ n/a Head: n/a ICAO: AIR SERB Net: n/a Operates charter flights with Yakovlev 42 aircraft, leased from other companies when required.

UK = UZBEKISTAN (Republic of Uzbekistan) (Uzbekiston Zumhuriyati)
Capital: Tashkent Official Language: Uzbek Population: 24,0 million Square Km: 447400 Dialling code: +7 Year established: 1991 Acting political head: Islam Karimov (President)

Government / Corporate / Executive / VIP Aircraft

☐	UK-22945	Mil Mi-17		CCCP-22945			2 IS TV3-117MT-3	13000	VIP		Gvmt
☐	UK-85050	Tupolev 154B	050	CCCP-85050	0073		3 KU NK-8-2U	98000	VIP		Ministry of Defence / cvtd 154 / UZB cs

AVIALEASING Aviation Company = AD / TWN (Uzbek-U.S. joint venture)   Tashkent-Int'l

Sergeli Airport, 700154 Tashkent, Uzbekistan ☎ (3712) 58 02 50 Tx: none Fax: (3712) 58 53 60 SITA: TASAVHY
F: 1992 ♦♦♦ 152 Head: Igor A. Smirnov ICAO: TWINARROW Net: n/a

☐	UK-76376	Ilyushin 76TD	1033417541		0093	0097	4 SO D-30KP	190000	Freighter		
☐	UK-76410	Ilyushin 76TD	1023412411	UN-76410	0092	0097	4 SO D-30KP	190000	Freighter		
☐	UK-76447	Ilyushin 76TD	1023412389		0592	0092	4 SO D-30KP	190000	Freighter		lst AHC

SAR – Spetsialnye aviatsionnye raboty (Sister company of Uzbekistan Airways)   Tashkent-Sergeli

Raikhon kuçasi, 700154 Tashkent, Uzbekistan ☎ (3712) 58 05 50 Tx: none Fax: (3712) 58 49 22 SITA: n/a
F: 1997 ♦♦♦ n/a Head: Rovshan Z. Ibragimov Net: n/a Beside aircraft listed, also owns another 163 Antonov 2 in Sprayer-configuration, most of them are stored and many still painted with former CCCP-registration.

☐	UK-20296	PZL Swidnik (Mil) Mi-2	537431121	CCCP-20296	0081		2 IS GTD-350-4	3250	Y7		
☐	UK-20301	PZL Swidnik (Mil) Mi-2	547436121	CCCP-20301	0082		2 IS GTD-350-4	3250	Y7		
☐	UK-20302	PZL Swidnik (Mil) Mi-2	547437121	CCCP-20302	0082		2 IS GTD-350-4	3250	Y7		
☐	UK-20848	PZL Swidnik (Mil) Mi-2	548219043	CCCP-20848	0083		2 IS GTD-350-4	3250	Y7		
☐	UK-20892	PZL Swidnik (Mil) Mi-2	538331093	CCCP-20892	0083		2 IS GTD-350-4	3250	Y7		
☐	UK-20958	PZL Swidnik (Mil) Mi-2	549424045	CCCP-20958	0085		2 IS GTD-350-4	3250	Y7		
☐	UK-23279	PZL Swidnik (Mil) Mi-2	539050025	CCCP-23279	0085		2 IS GTD-350-4	3250	Y7		
☐	UK-23376	PZL Swidnik (Mil) Mi-2	548819084	CCCP-23376	0084		2 IS GTD-350-4	3250	Y7		
☐	UK-01112	PZL Mielec (Antonov) An-2	1G240-50	CCCP-01112	0091		1 SH ASh-62IR	5250	Utility		
☐	UK-01113	PZL Mielec (Antonov) An-2	1G240-51	CCCP-01113	0091		1 SH ASh-62IR	5250	Utility		
☐	UK-07175	PZL Mielec (Antonov) An-2	1G146-04	CCCP-07175	0073		1 SH ASh-62IR	5250	Utility		
☐	UK-07244	PZL Mielec (Antonov) An-2	1G147-35	CCCP-07244	0073		1 SH ASh-62IR	5250	Utility		
☐	UK-07751	PZL Mielec (Antonov) An-2	1G159-29	CCCP-07751	0074		1 SH ASh-62IR	5250	Utility		
☐	UK-16028	PZL Mielec (Antonov) An-2	1G163-33	CCCP-16028	0075		1 SH ASh-62IR	5250	Combi 6 Pax		
☐	UK-32169	PZL Mielec (Antonov) An-2	1G94-30	CCCP-32169	0068		1 SH ASh-62IR	5250	Y12		
☐	UK-32423	PZL Mielec (Antonov) An-2	1G101-04	CCCP-32423	0069		1 SH ASh-62IR	5250	Utility		
☐	UK-32425	PZL Mielec (Antonov) An-2	1G101-06	CCCP-32425	0068		1 SH ASh-62IR	5250	Y12		
☐	UK-32429	PZL Mielec (Antonov) An-2	1G110-10	CCCP-32429	0069		1 SH ASh-62IR	5250	Y12		
☐	UK-32437	PZL Mielec (Antonov) An-2	1G101-18	CCCP-32437	0069		1 SH ASh-62IR	5250	Y12		
☐	UK-62670	PZL Mielec (Antonov) An-2	1G177-55	CCCP-62670	0078		1 SH ASh-62IR	5250	Combi 6 Pax		
☐	UK-70151	PZL Mielec (Antonov) An-2	1G137-25	CCCP-70151	0072		1 SH ASh-62IR	5250	Utility		
☐	UK-70152	PZL Mielec (Antonov) An-2	1G137-26	CCCP-70152	0072		1 SH ASh-62IR	5250	Utility		
☐	UK-70321	PZL Mielec (Antonov) An-2	1G140-25	CCCP-70321	0072		1 SH ASh-62IR	5250	Utility		
☐	UK-70487	PZL Mielec (Antonov) An-2	1G141-81	CCCP-70487	0073		1 SH ASh-62IR	5250	Combi 6 Pax		

registration	type of aircraft	cn/fn	ex/ex*	mfd	del	powered by	mtow kg	configuration	selcal	name/fln/specialitites/remarks
☐ UK-17200	Mil Mi-8MTV-1	860C01		0096		2 IS TV3-117VM	13000	VIP 8 Pax		
☐ UK-22658	Mil Mi-8T	8108	CCCP-22658	0080		2 IS TV2-117A	12000	Utility		
☐ UK-22767	Mil Mi-8T	98311548	CCCP-22767	0083		2 IS TV2-117A	12000	Utility		
☐ UK-22828	Mil Mi-8T	7628	CCCP-22828	0078		2 IS TV2-117A	12000	Utility		
☐ UK-22888	Mil Mi-8T	98417025	CCCP-22888	0084		2 IS TV2-117A	12000	Utility		
☐ UK-24016	Mil Mi-8T	99150884	CCCP-24016	0791		2 IS TV2-117A	12000	Utility		
☐ UK-24172	Mil Mi-8T	98943114	CCCP-24172	0089		2 IS TV2-117A	12000	Utility		
☐ UK-24184	Mil Mi-8T	98943332	CCCP-24184	0089		2 IS TV2-117A	12000	Utility		
☐ UK-24291	Mil Mi-8T	98734591	CCCP-24291	0087		2 IS TV2-117A	12000	Utility		
☐ UK-24591	Mil Mi-8T	98839409	CCCP-24591	0488		2 IS TV2-117A	12000	Utility		
☐ UK-24599	Mil Mi-8T	98839488	CCCP-24599	0088		2 IS TV2-117A	12000	Utility		
☐ UK-24613	Mil Mi-8T	8240	CCCP-24613	0081		2 IS TV2-117A	12000	Utility		
☐ UK-24617	Mil Mi-8T	8245	CCCP-24617	0081		2 IS TV2-117A	12000	Utility		
☐ UK-25109	Mil Mi-8MTV-1	95725	CCCP-25109	0991		2 IS TV3-117VM	13000	Utility		
☐ UK-25210	Mil Mi-8T	7723	CCCP-25210	0079		2 IS TV2-117A	12000	Utility		
☐ UK-25416	Mil Mi-8MTV-1	95526	CCCP-25416	0090		2 IS TV3-117VM	13000	Utility		
☐ UK-25417	Mil Mi-8MTV-1	95527	CCCP-25417	0990		2 IS TV3-117VM	13000			
☐ UK-25423	Mil Mi-8MTV-1	95533	CCCP-25423	0090		2 IS TV3-117VM	13000	Utility		
☐ UK-25424	Mil Mi-8MTV-1	95534	CCCP-25424	0090		2 IS TV3-117VM	13000	Utility		
☐ UK-25512	Mil Mi-8MTV-1	95660	CCCP-25512	0691		2 IS TV3-117VM	13000			
☐ UK-25619	Mil Mi-8T	99150848	CCCP-25619	0091		2 IS TV2-117A	12000	Utility		
☐ UK-27089	Mil Mi-8MTV-1	95925	CCCP-27089	1092		2 IS TV3-117VM	13000	Y24		lst PIA
☐ UK-27111	Mil Mi-8MTV-1	95936	CCCP-27111	0092		2 IS TV3-117VM	13000	Utility		

SIMURG UZBEKISTAN = JRP (Flying division of Tashkent Radioelectronic Plant Joint-Stock Company) — Tashkent-Vostochny

Flying division, Rechnaya kuçasi 2, 700007 Tashkent, Uzbekistan ☎ (3712) 68 12 43 Tx: none Fax: (3712) 68 04 20 SITA: n/a
F: 1987 ⁂ n/a Head: Taufik L. Khodzhaev ICAO: SIMURG Net: n/a Operates corporate flights for itself & commercial charter flights. Aircraft are in own colors but with Uzbekistan titles only.

registration	type of aircraft	cn/fn	ex/ex*	mfd	del	powered by	mtow kg	configuration	selcal	name/fln/specialitites/remarks
☐ UK-06105	Antonov 12BP	5343606	CCCP-06105	0065	0087	4 IV AI-20M	61000	Freighter		
☐ UK-11109	Antonov 12BP	01348005		0071	0089	4 IV AI-20M	61000	Freighter		
☐ UK-11418	Antonov 12BP	7344705	CCCP-11418	0067	0091	4 IV AI-20M	61000	Freighter		

TAPO-AVIA = PQ / CTP (Flying div.of Chkalov Tashkent Aircraft Factory/formerly Tashkent Aircraft Production Corp.) — Tashkent-Vostochny

Flying division, Elbek kuçasi 61, 700016 Tashkent, Uzbekistan ☎ (3712) 96 47 07 Tx: 1164775 tapo su Fax: (3712) 68 02 97 SITA: TASCDPQ
F: 1942 ⁂ n/a Head: Alexander S. Bushmanov ICAO: CORTAS Net: n/a
Operates corporate & cargo flights for itself and commercial charter flights. Some aircraft are still in Aeroflot colors without titles or with Uzbekistan titles and flag.

registration	type of aircraft	cn/fn	ex/ex*	mfd	del	powered by	mtow kg	configuration	selcal	name/fln/specialitites/remarks
☐ UK-08823	Antonov 24RV	87310810b	CCCP-08823	1278	0179	2 IV AI-24VT	21800	Combi		
☐ UK-91004	Ilyushin 114T	108380030		0096	0098	2 KL TV7-117	23500	Combi		
☐ UK-93914	Antonov 26	9104	CCCP-93914	0180	0280	2 IV AI-24VT	24000	Freighter		
☐ UK-11804	Antonov 12BP	2400406	CCCP-11804	0762	0878	4 IV AI-20M	61000	Freighter		
☐ UK-11807	Antonov 12BP	00346910	CCCP-11807	0170	0393	4 IV AI-20M	61000	Freighter		
☐ UK-58644	Antonov 12BP	2340303	CCCP-58644	0162	0362	4 IV AI-20M	61000	Freighter		
☐ UK-93920	Antonov 12BP	6344610	CCCP-93920	1266	0267	4 IV AI-20M	61000	Freighter		
☐ UK-76375	Ilyushin 76TD	1033414496		1191	0594	4 SO D-30KP	190000	Freighter		
☐ UK-76427	Ilyushin 76TD	1013406207		0491	0593	4 SO D-30KP	190000	Freighter		
☐ UK-76821	Ilyushin 76TD	0023441200	YI-ALR	1282	0491	4 SO D-30KP	190000	Freighter		cvtd 76MD
☐ UK-76831	Ilyushin 76TD	1013409287	CCCP-76831	0192	0292	4 SO D-30KP	190000	Freighter		
☐ UK-76844	Ilyushin 76TD	1033416525		0295	0495	4 SO D-30KP	190000	Freighter		

UZBEKISTAN AIRWAYS = HY / UZB (Uzbekistan Havo Jullary) — Tashkent-Int'l & Samarkand

Movarounnakhr kuçasi 41, 700060 Tashkent, Uzbekistan ☎ (3712) 33 70 36 Tx: 116169 polet su Fax: (3712) 33 18 85 SITA: n/a
F: 1992 ⁂ n/a Head: Arslan G. Ruzmetov IATA: 250 ICAO: UZBEK Net: n/a

registration	type of aircraft	cn/fn	ex/ex*	mfd	del	powered by	mtow kg	configuration	selcal	name/fln/specialitites/remarks
☐ UK-87263	Yakovlev 40	9311926	CCCP-87263	0373	0092	3 IV AI-25	14850	Y27		
☐ UK-87289	Yakovlev 40	9320428	CCCP-87289	0473	0092	3 IV AI-25	14850	Y27		
☐ UK-87367	Yakovlev 40	9341731	CCCP-87367	1173	0092	3 IV AI-25	16100	Y36		
☐ UK-87378	Yakovlev 40	9241425	CCCP-87378	0072	0092	3 IV AI-25	16100	VIP 13 Pax		lst BED as RA-87378
☐ UK-87396	Yakovlev 40	9410833	CCCP-87396	0374	0092	3 IV AI-25	16100	Y36		
☐ UK-87457	Yakovlev 40	9431636	CCCP-87457	0974	0092	3 IV AI-25	16100	Y30		
☐ UK-87542	Yakovlev 40	9530742	CCCP-87542	0875	0092	3 IV AI-25	16100	Y36		
☐ UK-87799	Yakovlev 40	9040316	CCCP-87799	0471	0092	3 IV AI-25	14850	Y27		
☐ UK-87846	Yakovlev 40	9331530	CCCP-87846	0973	0092	3 IV AI-25	16100	Y36		
☐ UK-87848	Yakovlev 40	9331730	CCCP-87848	0973	0092	3 IV AI-25	16100	Y36		
☐ UK-87923	Yakovlev 40	9731455	CCCP-87923	0178	0092	3 IV AI-25	16100	VIP 13 Pax		
☐ UK-87985	Yakovlev 40	9540844	CCCP-87985	1175	0092	3 IV AI-25	16100	Y36		
☐ UK-87989	Yakovlev 40	9541344	CCCP-87989	1275	0092	3 IV AI-25	16100	Y36		
☐ UK-87996	Yakovlev 40	9542044	CCCP-87996	1276	0092	3 IV AI-25	16100	Y32		
☐ UK-88194	Yakovlev 40	9621448	CCCP-88194	0776	0092	3 IV AI-25	16100	Y32		
☐ UK-88217	Yakovlev 40	9630350	CCCP-88217	1076	0092	3 IV AI-25	16100	VIP 20 Pax		
☐ UK-88242	Yakovlev 40	9641551	CCCP-88242	0177	0092	3 IV AI-25	16100	Y32		
☐ UK-46223	Antonov 24B	67303102	CCCP-46223	0066	0092	2 IV AI-24-II	21800	Y48		std SKD
☐ UK-46360	Antonov 24B	07305901	CCCP-46360	0070	0092	2 IV AI-24-II	21800	Y48		
☐ UK-46373	Antonov 24B	07306004	CCCP-46373	0370	0092	2 IV AI-24-II	21800	Y48		
☐ UK-46387	Antonov 24B	07306110	CCCP-46387	0770	0092	2 IV AI-24-II	21800	Y48		std SKD
☐ UK-46392	Antonov 24B	07306205	CCCP-46392	0670	0092	2 IV AI-24-II	21800	Y48		
☐ UK-46410	Antonov 24RV	77304005	CCCP-46410	0168	0092	2 IV AI-24VT	21800	Y48		
☐ UK-46573	Antonov 24B	87304807	CCCP-46573	1168	0092	2 IV AI-24-II	21800	Y48		
☐ UK-46594	Antonov 24B	97305104	CCCP-46594	0369	0092	2 IV AI-24-II	21800	Y48		
☐ UK-46623	Antonov 24RV	37308710	CCCP-46623	0673	0092	2 IV AI-24VT	21800	Y48		std SKD
☐ UK-46658	Antonov 24RV	47309304	CCCP-46658	0274	0092	2 IV AI-24VT	21800	Y48		
☐ UK-47274	Antonov 24B	07306404	CCCP-47274	0170	0092	2 IV AI-24-II	21800	Y48		
☐ UK-91000	Ilyushin 114	1033828025		1194	0094	2 KL TV7-117	23700	Y64		lsf IL for route proving flts / fn 0107
☐ UK-91001	Ilyushin 114	1023823024		0693	0094	2 KL TV7-117C	23700	Y64		lsf IL for route proving flts / fn 0106
☐ UK-80001	Avro RJ85 (Avro 146-RJ85)	E2312	G-6-312*	1097	1297	4 LY LF507-1F	42184	VIP 38 Pax		opf Gvmt
☐ UK-80002	Avro RJ85 (Avro 146-RJ85)	E2309	G-6-309*	0797	0797	4 LY LF507-1F	42184	Y85	HS-AD	
☐ UK-80003	Avro RJ85 (Avro 146-RJ85)	E2319	G-6-319*	1197	1297	4 LY LF507-1F	42184	Y85		
☐ UK-11369	Antonov 12B	6343810		0266	0097	4 IV AI-20M	61000	Freighter		
☐ UK-11372	Antonov 12B	5343204		0665	0096	4 IV AI-20M	64000	Freighter		
☐ UK-85272	Tupolev 154B-1	272	CCCP-85272	0078	0092	3 KU NK-8-2U	98000	Y155		
☐ UK-85286	Tupolev 154B-1	286	CCCP-85286	0678	0092	3 KU NK-8-2U	98000	Y155		
☐ UK-85344	Tupolev 154B-2	344	CCCP-85344	0579	0092	3 KU NK-8-2U	98000	Y155		
☐ UK-85356	Tupolev 154B-2	356	CCCP-85356	0779	0092	3 KU NK-8-2U	98000	Freighter		std TAS
☐ UK-85370	Tupolev 154B-2	370	CCCP-85370	0979	0092	3 KU NK-8-2U	98000	Y155		
☐ UK-85397	Tupolev 154B-2	397	CCCP-85397	0280	0092	3 KU NK-8-2U	98000	Y155		
☐ UK-85398	Tupolev 154B-2	398	CCCP-85398	0280	0092	3 KU NK-8-2U	98000	Y155		std TAS
☐ UK-85401	Tupolev 154B-2	401	CCCP-85401	0280	0092	3 KU NK-8-2U	98000	Y155		
☐ UK-85416	Tupolev 154B-2	416	CCCP-85416	0580	0092	3 KU NK-8-2U	98000	Y155		
☐ UK-85423	Tupolev 154B-2	423	CCCP-85423	0680	0092	3 KU NK-8-2U	98000	Y155		std TAS
☐ UK-85438	Tupolev 154B-2	438	CCCP-85438	0880	0092	3 KU NK-8-2U	98000	Y155		
☐ UK-85449	Tupolev 154B-2	449	CCCP-85449	1080	0092	3 KU NK-8-2U	98000	Y155		
☐ UK-85575	Tupolev 154B-2	575	CCCP-85575	0583	0092	3 KU NK-8-2U	100000	Y155		
☐ UK-85578	Tupolev 154B-2	578	CCCP-85578	0683	0092	3 KU NK-8-2U	100000	Y155		
☐ UK-85600	Tupolev 154B-2	600	CCCP-85600	0784	0092	3 KU NK-8-2U	100000	VIP		opf Gvmt
☐ UK-85711	Tupolev 154M	887	CCCP-85711	1091	0092	3 SO D-30KU-154-II	100000	Y155		
☐ UK-85764	Tupolev 154M	947	RA-85764	0393	0093	3 SO D-30KU-154-II	100000	Y155		
☐ UK-85776	Tupolev 154M	958		0593	0093	3 SO D-30KU-154-II	100000	Y155		
☐ UK-75700	Boeing 757-23P	28338 / 731		1096	1096	2 PW PW2037	115666	VIP		opf Gvmt
☐ UK-31001	Airbus Industrie A310-324	574	F-OGQY	0091	0693	2 PW PW4152	153000	F10C30Y150	ES-GM	
☐ UK-31002	Airbus Industrie A310-324	576	F-OGQZ	0091	0693	2 PW PW4152	153000	F10C30Y150	ES-GP	
☐ UK-31003	Airbus Industrie A310-324	706	F-WWCM*	0098	0698	2 PW PW4152	153000	F10C30Y150		Bukhara
☐ UK-86569	Ilyushin 62M	1356234		0593	0093	4 SO D-30KU	167000	VIP		fn 5603/opf Gvmt
☐ UK-86573	Ilyushin 62M	4140536	D-AOAG	1181	0092	4 SO D-30KU	167000	Y168		fn 4003
☐ UK-86574	Ilyushin 62M	3344833	D-AOAH	1183	0092	4 SO D-30KU	167000	Y168		fn 4403 / std TAS
☐ UK-86575	Ilyushin 62M	1647928	D-AOAJ	0386	0092	4 SO D-30KU	167000	Y168		fn 4702
☐ UK-86576	Ilyushin 62M	4546257	D-AOAK	1185	0092	4 SO D-30KU	167000	Y168		fn 4605 / std TAS
☐ UK-86577	Ilyushin 62M	2748552	D-AOAL	0687	0092	4 SO D-30KU	167000	Y168		lst TGZ / fn 4805
☐ UK-86578	Ilyushin 62M	1951525	D-AOAM	0689	0092	4 SO D-30KU	167000	Y168		fn 5102
☐ UK-86579	Ilyushin 62M	2951636	D-AOAN	0889	0092	4 SO D-30KU	167000	Y168		fn 5103
☐ UK-86659	Ilyushin 62	31404	CCCP-86659	0873	0092	4 KU NK-8-4	161000	Y180		fn 1404
☐ VP-BUA	Boeing 767-33P (ER)	28370 / 635	VR-BUA	1196	1196	2 PW PW4062	186882	F10C40Y157	MR-AL	Samarkand / lsf Uzb.Fin.Ltd/tbrUK-76701
☐ VP-BUZ	Boeing 767-33P (ER)	28392 / 650		0397	0397	2 PW PW4062	186882	F10C40Y157	MR-CL	Khiva / lsf Uzb.Fin.Ltd/tbr UK-76702
☐ UK-76351	Ilyushin 76TD	1023408240		1292	0092	4 SO D-30KP	190000	Freighter		lst ESL / fn 8110
☐ UK-76353	Ilyushin 76TD	1023414454		0193	0093	4 SO D-30KP	190000	Freighter		lst ESL

UK-76358	Ilyushin 76TD	1033410339		0593	0093	4 SO D-30KP	190000	Freighter		
UK-76359	Ilyushin 76TD	1033414483		0393	0093	4 SO D-30KP	190000	Freighter		fn 8801
UK-76426	Ilyushin 76TD	1043419644		0896	0096	4 SO D-30KP	190000	Freighter		
UK-76428	Ilyushin 76TD	1043419648		1096	0096	4 SO D-30KP	190000	Freighter		
UK-76448	Ilyushin 76TD	1023413443		0992	0092	4 SO D-30KP	190000	Freighter		lst ESL
UK-76449	Ilyushin 76TD	1023403058		1192	0092	4 SO D-30KP	190000	Freighter		lst ESL / fn 7705
UK-76782	Ilyushin 76TD	0093498971	CCCP-76782	0190	0092	4 SO D-30KP	190000	Freighter		lst ESL
UK-76793	Ilyushin 76TD	0093498951	CCCP-76793	1289	0092	4 SO D-30KP	190000	Freighter		
UK-76794	Ilyushin 76TD	0093498954	CCCP-76794	1289	0092	4 SO D-30KP	190000	Freighter		std TAS
UK-76805	Ilyushin 76TD	1003403109	CCCP-76805	0990	0092	4 SO D-30KP	190000	Freighter		
UK-76811	Ilyushin 76TD	1013407223	CCCP-76811	0791	0092	4 SO D-30KP	190000	Freighter		
UK-76813	Ilyushin 76TD	1013408246	CCCP-76813	0891	0092	4 SO D-30KP	190000	Freighter		
UK-76824	Ilyushin 76TD	1023410327		0492	0092	4 SO D-30KP	190000	Freighter		lst ESL
UK-86012	Ilyushin 86	0010	CCCP-86012	0981	0092	4 KU NK-86	215000	F20Y296		
UK-86016	Ilyushin 86	51483202014	CCCP-86016	0682	0092	4 KU NK-86	215000	Y350		std TAS
UK-86052	Ilyushin 86	51483202019	CCCP-86052	1182	0092	4 KU NK-86	215000	Y350		std TAS
UK-86053	Ilyushin 86	51483202020	RA-86053	0183	0092	4 KU NK-86	215000	Y350		lst ESL
UK-86056	Ilyushin 86	51483203023	CCCP-86056	0583	0092	4 KU NK-86	215000	Y350		std TAS
UK-86057	Ilyushin 86	51483203024	CCCP-86057	0683	0092	4 KU NK-86	215000	Y350		
UK-86064	Ilyushin 86	51483204031	CCCP-86064	0384	0092	4 KU NK-86	215000	Y350		std TAS
UK-86072	Ilyushin 86	51483204039	CCCP-86072	0485	0092	4 KU NK-86	215000	Y350		std TAS
UK-86083	Ilyushin 86	51483206054	CCCP-86083	1186	0092	4 KU NK-86	215000	Y350		std TAS
UK-86090	Ilyushin 86	51483207061	CCCP-86090	0987	0092	4 KU NK-86	215000	Y350		

UN = KAZAKHSTAN (Republic of Kazakhstan) (Kazak Respublikasy)

Capital: Almaty Official Language: Kazakh Population: 17,2 million Square Km: 2717300 Dialling code: +7 Year established: 1991 Acting political head: Nursultan Nazarbayev (President)

Government / Corporate / Executive / VIP Aircraft

UN-11367	Antonov 12BP	3341201	11 BLUE	0063		4 IV AI-20M	61000	Freighter		Ministry of Defence
UN-65683	Tupolev 134A	62199	CCCP-65683	0072		2 SO D-30-II	49000	VIP		Ministry of Defence
UN-85464	Tupolev 154B-2	464	CCCP-85464	0080		3 KU NK-8-2U	98000	VIP		Ministry of Defence

ABS-AVIA = GPS

Almaty

Pr. Dostik 240, 480051 Almaty, Kazakstan ☎ (3272) 64 13 40 Tx: none Fax: (3272) 64 18 97 SITA: n/a
F: 1997 n/a Head: Alexander M. Begun ICAO: ALATAU Net: n/a

UN-23521	PZL Swidnik (Mil) Mi-2	525924128	CCCP-23521	0078	0097	2 IS GTD-350-4	3550	6 Pax		
UN-27013	Mil Mi-8TP	99254376	CCCP-27013	0092	0097	2 IS TV2-117A	12000	12 Pax		
RA-25519	Mil Mi-8T		CCCP-25519	0076	0097	2 IS TV2-117A	12000	22 Pax/Utility		

AEROSERVICE-CARGO

Almaty

Ul. Algabaskaya 2a, 480074 Almaty, Kazakstan ☎ (3272) 36 66 71 Tx: none Fax: (3272) 36 64 17 SITA: n/a
F: 1996 n/a Head: Viktor N. Ivanov ICAO: TRAMP Net: n/a Beside aircraft listed, also leases Ilyushin 18 from other companies when required.

UN-26617	Antonov 26		RA-26617	0077		2 IV AI-24VT	24000	Freighter		

AEROSERVICE KAZAKSTAN AVIAKOMPANIASY = AVZ

Almaty

Algabasskaya 2a, 480028 Almaty, Kazakstan ☎ (3272) 36 69 26 Tx: none Fax: (3272) 52 93 45 SITA: n/a
F: 1991 n/a Head: Sabit Makhanov, Sr. ICAO: SABIT Net: n/a

UN-26026	Antonov 26B	10310	YL-LDA	0080	0093	2 IV AI-24VT	24000	Freighter		
UN-85516	Tupolev 154B-2	516	YL-LAC	0081	0093	3 KU NK-8-2U	100000	Y164		
UN-85539	Tupolev 154B-2	539	YL-LAF	0082	0093	3 KU NK-8-2U	100000	Y164		

AEROSERVICE-SABIT = CSM (Sister company of Aeroservice Kazakstan Aviakompaniasy)

Almaty

c/o Aeroservice Kazakstan Aviakompaniasy, Algabasskaya 2a, 480028 Almaty, Kazakstan ☎ (3272) 36 69 26 Tx: none Fax: (3272) 52 93 45 SITA: n/a
F: 1996 n/a Head: Sabit Makhanov, Jr. ICAO: LORRY Net: n/a Operates charter flights with Ilyushin 76 aircraft, currently leased from other companies when required.

AEROTEX = OTX

Almaty

M-N Almay 1, 480079 Almaty, Kazakstan ☎ (3272) 35 46 01 Tx: none Fax: (3272) 57 12 14 SITA: n/a
F: 1996 n/a Head: Anatoly F. Menshikov ICAO: ZOTEX Net: n/a Conducting aerial work/sprayer flights with Antonov 2 aircraft. Full details not yet known.

AIR KAZAKSTAN = 9Y / KZK

Almaty & Akmola

Ul. Ogareva 14, 480079 Almaty, Kazakstan ☎ (3272) 57 31 57 Tx: none Fax: (3272) 50 37 38 SITA: n/a
F: 1996 n/a Head: Rustem S. Bekturov IATA: 452 ICAO: AIR KAZAKSTAN Net: n/a

UN-46334	Antonov 24B	97305601	CCCP-46334	0069	0096	2 IV AI-24	21000	Y48		
UN-46342	Antonov 24B	97305610	CCCP-46342	0069	0096	2 IV AI-24	21000	Y48		
UN-46356	Antonov 24B	07305806	CCCP-46356	0070	0096	2 IV AI-24	21000	Y48		
UN-46396	Antonov 24B		CCCP-46396	0070	0096	2 IV AI-24	21000	Y48		
UN-46492	Antonov 24RV		CCCP-46492	0072	0096	2 IV AI-24VT	21800	Y48		
UN-46500	Antonov 24RV	37308305	CCCP-46500	0073	0096	2 IV AI-24VT	21800	Y48		
UN-46535	Antonov 24RV	57310109	CCCP-46535	0075	0096	2 IV AI-24VT	21800	Y48		
UN-46611	Antonov 24RV		CCCP-46611	0073	0096	2 IV AI-24VT	21800	Y48		
UN-46626	Antonov 24RV	37308805	CCCP-46626	0073	0096	2 IV AI-24VT	21800	Y48		
UN-46644	Antonov 24RV	37309002	CCCP-46644	0073	0096	2 IV AI-24VT	21800	Y48		
UN-46655	Antonov 24RV	47309301	CCCP-46655	0074	0096	2 IV AI-24VT	21800	Y48		
UN-46664	Antonov 24RV		RA-46664	0074	0096	2 IV AI-24VT	21800	Y48		
UN-46672	Antonov 24RV	47309604	CCCP-46672	0074	0096	2 IV AI-24VT	21800	Y48		
UN-46695	Antonov 24RV	47309906	CCCP-46695	0074	0096	2 IV AI-24VT	21800	Y48		
UN-46699	Antonov 24RV	47309910	UR-46699	0074	0096	2 IV AI-24VT	21800	Y48		lst Weasua Airtransport
UN-47186	Antonov 24B	99902001	CCCP-47186	0069	0096	2 IV AI-24	21000	Y48		
UN-47277	Antonov 24B	07306407	CCCP-47277	0070	0096	2 IV AI-24	21000	Y48		
UN-47284	Antonov 24B	07306504	CCCP-47284	0070	0096	2 IV AI-24	21800	Y48		
UN-47293	Antonov 24RV	07306603	CCCP-47293	0070	0096	2 IV AI-24VT	21800	Y48		
UN-47299	Antonov 24RV		CCCP-47299	0070	0096	2 IV AI-24VT	21800	Y48		
UN-47350	Antonov 24RV	67310509	CCCP-47350	0076	0096	2 IV AI-24VT	21800	Y40		
UN-47763	Antonov 24B	79901307	CCCP-47763	0067	0096	2 IV AI-24	21000	Y48		
UN-47802	Antonov 24RV	17306901	CCCP-47802	0071	0096	2 IV AI-24VT	21800	Y48		
UN-47822	Antonov 24RV	17307203	CCCP-47822	0071	0096	2 IV AI-24VT	21800	Y48		
UN-47832	Antonov 24B		CCCP-47832	0071	0096	2 IV AI-24	21000	Y48		
UN-47833	Antonov 24B		CCCP-47833	0071	0096	2 IV AI-24	21000	Y48		
UN-65115	Tupolev 134A-3	60405	CCCP-65115	0078	0096	2 SO D-30-III	49000	Y76		
UN-65130	Tupolev 134A-3	60635	CCCP-65130	0078	0096	2 SO D-30-III	49000	Y76		
UN-65138	Tupolev 134A	60907	CCCP-65138	0078	0096	2 SO D-30-II	49000	Y76		
UN-65147	Tupolev 134A-3	61012	CCCP-65147	0079	0096	2 SO D-30-III	49000	Y76		
UN-65551	Tupolev 134A-3	66212	CCCP-65551	0084	0096	2 SO D-30-III	49000	VIP		opf Gvmt
UN-65767	Tupolev 134A-3	62335	CCCP-65767	0079	0096	2 SO D-30-III	49000	Y76		
UN-65776	Tupolev 134A-3	62545	CCCP-65776	0079	0096	2 SO D-30-III	49000	Y76		
UN-65787	Tupolev 134A	62798	CCCP-65787	0079	0096	2 SO D-30-II	49000	Y76		
UN-B3706	Boeing 737-2M8 (A)	22090 / 664	HA-LEB	0080	1298	2 PW JT8D-15	54204	F14Y82		lsf GECA
P4-RMB	Boeing 737-291	20364 / 219	N730TJ	0069	0498	2 PW JT8D-9A	49442	F14Y82		Akmola / lsf Triple J Leasing Ltd
UN-85173	Tupolev 154B	173	CCCP-85173	0076	0096	3 KU NK-8-2U	98000	Y164		
UN-85194	Tupolev 154B-1	194	CCCP-85194	0077	0096	3 KU NK-8-2U	98000	Y164		cvtd 154B
UN-85221	Tupolev 154B-1	221	CCCP-85221	0077	0096	3 KU NK-8-2U	98000	Y164		cvtd 154B
UN-85230	Tupolev 154B-1	230	CCCP-85230	0077	0096	3 KU NK-8-2U	98000	Y164		
UN-85240	Tupolev 154B-1	240	CCCP-85240	0077	0096	3 KU NK-8-2U	98000	Y164		
UN-85271	Tupolev 154B-1	271	CCCP-85271	0078	0096	3 KU NK-8-2U	98000	Y164		
UN-85276	Tupolev 154B-1	276	CCCP-85276	0078	0096	3 KU NK-8-2U	98000	Y164		
UN-85396	Tupolev 154B-2	396	CCCP-85396	0080	0096	3 KU NK-8-2U	98000	Y164		
UN-85431	Tupolev 154B-2	431	CCCP-85431	0080	0096	3 KU NK-8-2U	98000	Y164		
UN-85478	Tupolev 154B-2	478	CCCP-85478	0081	0096	3 KU NK-8-2U	98000	Y164		
UN-85521	Tupolev 154B-2	521	CCCP-85521	0082	0096	3 KU NK-8-2U	98000	Y164		
UN-85537	Tupolev 154B-2	537	CCCP-85537	0082	0096	3 KU NK-8-2U	98000	Y164		
UN-85589	Tupolev 154B-2	589	CCCP-85589	0083	0096	3 KU NK-8-2U	98000	Y164		
UN-85719	Tupolev 154M	901	CCCP-85719	0091	0096	3 SO D-30KU-154-II	100000	Y164		
UN-85780	Tupolev 154M	964	RA-85780	0093	0096	3 SO D-30KU-154-II	100000	Y166		
UN-85781	Tupolev 154M	965	RA-85781	0093	0096	3 SO D-30KU-154-II	100000	Y166		
UN-76371	Ilyushin 76TD	1033414485		0293	0096	4 SO D-30KP	190000	Freighter		
UN-76374	Ilyushin 76TD	1033416520		0093	0096	4 SO D-30KP	190000	Freighter		
UN-76810	Ilyushin 76TD	1013409282	CCCP-76810	0091	0096	4 SO D-30KP	190000	Freighter		
UN-86068	Ilyushin 86	51483204035	CCCP-86068	0084	0096	4 KU NK-86	215000	Y350		
UN-86069	Ilyushin 86	51483204036	CCCP-86069	0084	0096	4 KU NK-86	215000	Y350		
UN-86071	Ilyushin 86	51483204038	CCCP-86071	0084	0096	4 KU NK-86	215000	Y350		

609 registration type of aircraft cn/fn ex/ex* mfd del powered by mtow kg configuration selcal name/fln/specialitites/remarks

☐ UN-86077	Ilyushin 86	51483205047	CCCP-86077	0085	0096	4 KU NK-86	215000	Y350	
☐ UN-86086	Ilyushin 86	51483206057	CCCP-86086	0086	0096	4 KU NK-86	215000	Y350	
☐ UN-86101	Ilyushin 86	51483207069	CCCP-86101	0089	0096	4 KU NK-86	215000	Combi Y200/Cargo	
☐ UN-86116	Ilyushin 86	51483209084	CCCP-86116	0090	0096	4 KU NK-86	215000	Y350	

AIR VIP = RIV — Almaty

Ul. Masanchi 86, 480072 Almaty, Kazakstan ☎ (3272) 50 92 98 Tx: none Fax: (3272) 67 81 10 SITA: n/a
F: 1997 n/a Head: Muratkhan Kh. Kudraliev ICAO: ASTANA Net: n/a

☐ UN-87337	Yakovlev 40	9510639	CCCP-87337	0075	0097	3 IV AI-25	16800	VIP	lsf Euro-Asia Air

AK-KANAT Aviakompania = KAN — Almaty & Shymkent

Mikrorayon Aksai-4, 70-100, 480063 Almaty, Kazakstan ☎ (3272) 39 32 58 Tx: none Fax: (3272) 33 36 18 SITA: n/a
F: 1996 n/a Head: Bauyrzhan S. Utepov ICAO: KANAT Net: n/a

☐ UN-11373	Antonov 12BP	02348304		0072	0098	4 IV AI-20M	61000	Freighter	
☐ UN-11374	Antonov 12BP	3341501		0063	0098	4 IV AI-20M	61000	Freighter	

ALTI Air Company = AID (Vysota Aviakompania) — Almaty

Pr. Abaya 141/5, 480065 Almaty, Kazakstan ☎ (3272) 69 61 57 Tx: none Fax: (3272) 69 53 73 SITA: n/a
F: 1995 n/a Head: Vyacheslav A. Kuklin ICAO: ALTI Net: n/a Operates passenger & cargo flights with Let 410 aircraft, leased from other companies when required.

ASIA SERVICE AIRLINES = ASQ — Almaty

Ul. Kabanbay Batyra 136, 480012 Almaty, Kazakstan ☎ (3272) 62 16 72 Tx: none Fax: (3272) 62 28 88 SITA: n/a
F: 1994 n/a Head: Vladimir Yu. Romenski ICAO: ASIA SERVICE Net: n/a
Operates passenger flights with Ilyushin 86 leased from PULKOVO AVIATION ENTERPRISE (RA-) & Tupolev 134A leased from TAJIKISTAN AIRLINES (EY-) when required.

ASTANAIR = A7 / STR — Almaty

Ul. Aiteke-be 78, 480091 Almaty, Kazakstan ☎ (3272) 62 68 14 Tx: none Fax: (3272) 62 85 90 SITA: ALATOJT
F: 1997 n/a Head: Malik Abyshev ICAO: ATNAR Net: n/a Operates charter flights with BAe (BAC) One-Eleven 500 aircraft, leased from JARO (YR-), when required.

ATYRAU AIRWAYS, Joint-Stock Company = JOL (Atyrau Aue Zholy) (formerly part of Kazakstan Airlines) — Atyrau

Atyrau Airport, 465050 Atyrau, Kazakstan ☎ (31222) 31 062 Tx: none Fax: (31222) 54 404 SITA: n/a
F: 1997 n/a Head: Zamirbek N. Bulekbaev ICAO: EDIL Net: n/a Beside aircraft listed, also operates Mil Mi-2 & Mi-8 helicopters. Full details not yet known.

☐ UN-46412	Antonov 24B	87304007	CCCP-46412	0068	0097	2 IV AI-24	21000	Y48	
☐ UN-46582	Antonov 24B	97305001	CCCP-46582	0069	0097	2 IV AI-24	21000	Y48	
☐ UN-47153	Antonov 24B	89901605	CCCP-47153	0068	0097	2 IV AI-24	21000	Y48	
☐ UN-65069	Tupolev 134A	49908	RA-65069	0077	0098	2 SO D-30-II	47600	C52	
☐ UN-65070	Tupolev 134A-3	49912	RA-65070	0077	0198	2 SO D-30-III	47600	Y72	

AVIATRACK = KAK — Karaganda

Ul. 40 let Kazakstana 5, 470061 Karaganda, Kazakstan ☎ (3212) 41 32 13 Tx: none Fax: (3212) 41 32 14 SITA: n/a
F: 1996 n/a Head: Vadim S. Aminov ICAO: AVIATRACK Net: n/a Operates charter flights with Ilyushin 18 aircraft, leased from CESSAVIA (3C-), when required.

AZAMAT = AZB — Almaty

Ul. Altysaryna 23a, 480036 Almaty, Kazakstan ☎ (3272) 28 47 00 Tx: n/a Fax: (3272) 63 77 95 SITA: n/a
F: 1991 n/a Head: Nurlan K. Akhmukhanov ICAO: TUMARA Net: n/a Operates charter flights with Tupolev 154M aircraft, leased from other companies when required.

BERKHUT Aviakompania = BPK — Uralsk

Uralsk Airport, 417027 Uralsk, Kazakstan ☎ (31122) 24 149 Tx: none Fax: (31122) 21 090 SITA: n/a
F: 1995 n/a Head: Ivan I. Lazhovsky ICAO: VENERA Net: n/a Beside aircraft listed, also operates Antonov 2 & Let 410 aircraft, full details not yet known.

☐ UN-07603	PZL Mielec (Antonov) An-2	1G155-58		0074	0095	1 SH ASh-62IR	5500	Utility	
☐ UN-29370	PZL Mielec (Antonov) An-2	1G79-01		0066	0095	1 SH ASh-62IR	5500	Utility	
☐ UN-82871	PZL Mielec (Antonov) An-2	1G168-47		0076	0095	1 SH ASh-62IR	5500	Utility	
☐ UN-67666	Let 410UVP-E	912612		0093	0095	2 WA M-601E	6400	Y17	
☐ UN-87306	Yakovlev 40	9320229	CCCP-87306	0073	0097	3 IV AI-25	17100	VIP	

BURUNDAIAVIA, Joint-Stock Company = IVR (formerly part of Kazakstan Airlines) — Almaty-Burundai

Burundai Airport, 483162 Almaty, Kazakstan ☎ (3272) 35 79 39 Tx: none Fax: (3272) 35 78 78 SITA: n/a
F: 1997 n/a Head: Toksholyk E. Akhmetov ICAO: BURUN Net: n/a

☐ UN-30003	Antonov 30	1404	CCCP-30003	0078	0097	2 IV AI-24T	23000	Survey / Combi	
☐ UN-30029	Antonov 30	0604	CCCP-30029	0074	0097	2 IV AI-24T	23000	Survey / Combi	
☐ UN-30031	Antonov 30	0606	CCCP-30031	0074	0097	2 IV AI-24T	23000	Survey / Combi	
☐ UN-30038	Antonov 30	0708	CCCP-30038	0074	0097	2 IV AI-24T	23000	Survey / Combi	
☐ UN-30040	Antonov 30	0801	CCCP-30040	0075	0097	2 IV AI-24T	23000	Survey / Combi	
☐ UN-30046	Antonov 30	0908	CCCP-30046	0075	0097	2 IV AI-24T	23000	Survey / Combi	
☐ UN-30057	Antonov 30	1106	CCCP-30057	0076	0097	2 IV AI-24T	23000	Survey / Combi	
☐ UN-30060	Antonov 30	1109	CCCP-30060	0076	0097	2 IV AI-24T	23000	Survey / Combi	
☐ UN-30071	Antonov 30	1302	CCCP-30071	0077	0097	2 IV AI-24T	23000	Survey / Combi	
☐ UN-26020	Antonov 26B	10205	CCCP-26020	0080	0097	2 IV AI-24VT	24000	Combi	
☐ UN-26033	Antonov 26B		CCCP-26033	0080	0097	2 IV AI-24VT	24000	Combi	
☐ UN-26054	Antonov 26B	10910	CCCP-26054	0081	0097	2 IV AI-24VT	24000	Combi	
☐ UN-26075	Antonov 26B	11508	CCCP-26075	0081	0097	2 IV AI-24VT	24000	Combi	
☐ UN-26579	Antonov 26B		CCCP-26579	0083	0097	2 IV AI-24VT	24000	Combi	
☐ UN-26649	Antonov 26	7506	CCCP-26649	0078	0097	2 IV AI-24VT	24000	Combi	

DIALOGUE-S-AERO = DAS — Kustaney

Airport, Hotel 101, 458007 Kustanay, Kazakstan ☎ (3142) 27 06 74 Tx: none Fax: (3142) 27 39 27 SITA: n/a
F: 1996 n/a Head: Dmitriy A. Senutrusov ICAO: DIALOGUE Net: n/a Operates charter flights with aircraft leased from other companies when required.

EURO-ASIA AIR, Joint-Stock Company = EAK (Evro-Azia aue zholy) — Aktau/Atyrau/Aktobe/Kzyl-Orda/Zhezkazgan

Ul. Mynbaeva 68/74, 480057 Almaty, Kazakstan ☎ (3272) 62 81 43 Tx: none Fax: (3272) 62 81 43 SITA: n/a
F: 1997 n/a Head: Batyrzhan K. Dzhantasov ICAO: EAKAZ Net: n/a

☐ UN-14218	PZL Swidnik (Mil) Mi-2	5411103129	CCCP-14218	1289	0097	2 IS GTD-350-4	3550	Utility	
☐ UN-23244	PZL Swidnik (Mil) Mi-2	5210250067	CCCP-23244	0687	0097	2 IS GTD-350-4	3550	Utility	
☐ UN-19723	PZL Mielec (Antonov) An-2	1G165-37	CCCP-19723	0975	0097	1 SH ASh-62IR	5500	Utility	
☐ UN-68052	PZL Mielec (Antonov) An-2	1G193-24	CCCP-68052	0781	0097	1 SH ASh-62IR	5500	Utility	
☐ UN-22683	Mil Mi-8T	8141	CCCP-22683	1280	0097	2 IS TV2-117A	12000	Utility	
☐ UN-22708	Mil Mi-8T	98308265	CCCP-22708	0283	0097	2 IS TV2-117A	12000	Utility	
☐ UN-22721	Mil Mi-8T	98308555	CCCP-22721	0383	0097	2 IS TV2-117A	12000	Utility	
☐ UN-22758	Mil Mi-8T	98311425	CCCP-22758	0683	0097	2 IS TV2-117A	12000	Utility	
☐ UN-22857	Mil Mi-8T	98415399	CCCP-22857	0384	0097	2 IS TV2-117A	12000	Utility	
☐ UN-22866	Mil Mi-8T	98415551	CCCP-22866	0484	0097	2 IS TV2-117A	12000	Utility	
☐ UN-22917	Mil Mi-8T	98520271	CCCP-22917	0385	0097	2 IS TV2-117A	12000	Utility	
☐ UN-24173	Mil Mi-8T	98417207	CCCP-24173	0884	0097	2 IS TV2-117A	12000	Utility	
☐ UN-24440	Mil Mi-8T	98625962	CCCP-24440	0686	0097	2 IS TV2-117A	12000	Utility	
☐ UN-24446	Mil Mi-8T	98628154	CCCP-24446	0786	0097	2 IS TV2-117A	12000	Utility	
☐ UN-24447	Mil Mi-8T	98628176	CCCP-24447	0883	0097	2 IS TV2-117A	12000	Utility	
☐ UN-24471	Mil Mi-8T	98628744	CCCP-24471	1086	0097	2 IS TV2-117A	12000	Utility	
☐ UN-24511	Mil Mi-8T	98522003	CCCP-24511	0585	0097	2 IS TV2-117A	12000	Utility	
☐ UN-24534	Mil Mi-8T	98522481	CCCP-24534	0785	0097	2 IS TV2-117A	12000	Utility	
☐ UN-24540	Mil Mi-8T	98522705	CCCP-24540	0885	0097	2 IS TV2-117A	12000	Utility	
☐ UN-24552	Mil Mi-8T	98522933	CCCP-24552	1185	0097	2 IS TV2-117A	12000	Utility	
☐ UN-24724	Mil Mi-8T	98417437	CCCP-24724	0984	0097	2 IS TV2-117A	12000	Utility	
☐ UN-25426	Mil Mi-8MTV-1	95458	CCCP-25426	0990	0097	2 IS TV3-117MT	13000	Utility	
☐ UN-25465	Mil Mi-8MTV-1	95609	CCCP-25465	0291	0097	2 IS TV3-117MT	13000	Utility	
☐ UN-25466	Mil Mi-8MTV-1	95610	CCCP-25466	0291	0097	2 IS TV3-117MT	13000	Utility	
☐ UN-25584	Mil Mi-8T	99257196	CCCP-25584	1092	0097	2 IS TV2-117A	12000	Utility	
☐ UN-27034	Mil Mi-8MTV-1	95840	CCCP-27034	0292	0097	2 IS TV3-117MT	13000	Utility	
☐ UN-27107	Mil Mi-8MTV-1	95931		0595	0097	2 IS TV3-117MT	13000	Utility	
☐ UN-27182	Mil Mi-8MTV-1	96185		0194	0097	2 IS TV3-117MT	13000	Utility	
☐ UN-87337	Yakovlev 40	9510639	CCCP-87337	0075	0097	3 IV AI-25	16800	VIP	lst Air Vip
☐ UN-87403	Yakovlev 40	9411533	CCCP-87403	0474	0097	3 IV AI-25	16800	Y32	
☐ UN-87935	Yakovlev 40K	9811856	CCCP-87935	0378	0097	3 IV AI-25	16800	Y32	
☐ UN-87990	Yakovlev 40	9541444	CCCP-87990	1275	0097	3 IV AI-25	16800	Y32	
☐ UN-88173	Yakovlev 40	9621147	CCCP-88173	0576	0097	3 IV AI-25	16800	Y32	
☐ UN-88266	Yakovlev 40K	9710453	CCCP-88266	0477	0097	3 IV AI-25	16800	Y32	

GVG AIR COMPANY = GDR — Almaty

Ul. Kozhmankulova 235, 480004 Almaty, Kazakstan ☎ (3272) 68 42 35 Tx: none Fax: (3272) 67 19 67 SITA: n/a
F: 1997 n/a Head: Valerian A. Matkala ICAO: VALIKO Net: n/a

☐ UN-75111	Ilyushin 18V	184007105	YR-IMF	0264	1197	4 IV AI-20M	64000	Combi	

610 registration type of aircraft cn/fn ex/ex* mfd del powered by mtow kg configuration selcal name/fln/specialitites/remarks

IRTYSH-AVIA = IRT
Pavlodar

Airport, 637023 Pavlodar, Kazakstan ☎ (3182) 32 06 17 Tx: none Fax: (3182) 32 49 58 SITA: n/a
F: 1996 ♦♦♦ n/a Head: Yuri P. Pogozhev ICAO: IRTYSH Net: n/a
It is expected that SEMEIAVIA (Yakovlev 40) & ULBA Aviakompania (Antonov 2, Yakovlev 40/42) will be bought/integrated into IRTYSH-AVIA during 1999.

	registration	type of aircraft	cn/fn	ex/ex*	mfd	del	powered by	mtow kg	configuration	selcal	name/fln/specialitites/remarks
☐	UN-87202	Yakovlev 40	9812056	CCCP-87202	0078	0096	3 IV AI-25	17200	Y36		
☐	UN-87491	Yakovlev 40	9621647	CCCP-87491	0076	0096	3 IV AI-25	17200	VIP F4Y16		
☐	UN-87501	Yakovlev 40	9512039	CCCP-87501	0075	0096	3 IV AI-25	17200	Y36		
☐	UN-87543	Yakovlev 40	9530842	CCCP-87543	0075	0096	3 IV AI-25	17200	VIP F4Y16		lsf PAV
☐	UN-88154	Yakovlev 40	9610846	CCCP-88154	0076	0096	3 IV AI-25	17200	Y36		
☐	UN-42338	Yakovlev 42D	4520423606256	LY-AAN	0086	1196	3 LO D-36	56500	Y120		
☐	UN-42342	Yakovlev 42	4520421706302	LY-AAP	0087	1297	3 LO D-36	56500	Y120		

JANA-ARKA = JAK
Almaty

Ul. Karasay Batyra 85, 480012 Almaty, Kazakstan ☎ (3272) 50 78 51 Tx: none Fax: (3272) 63 19 09 SITA: ALAJAKH
F: 1995 ♦♦♦ n/a Head: Yalken B. Vafin ICAO: YANZAR Net: n/a

☐	UN-85385	Tupolev 154B-2	385	EY-85385	1279	0096	3 KU NK-8-2U	100000	Y167		lsf TZK
☐	UN-85742	Tupolev 154B-2	320	RA-85742	0078	0098	3 KU NK-8-2U	98000	Y164		

KAZAIR WEST = KAW
Atyrau

Atyrau Airport, 465050 Atyrau, Kazakstan ☎ (31222) 54 244 Tx: none Fax: (31222) 54 244 SITA: n/a
F: 1996 ♦♦♦ n/a Head: Vyacheslav A. Chepurin ICAO: KAZWEST Net: n/a

☐	UN-67566	Let 410UVP-E	861606	RA-67566	0086	0097	2 WA M-601E	6400	Y19		
☐	UN-67611	Let 410UVP-E	892339	RA-67611	0089	0098	2 WA M-601E	6400	Y19		
☐	UN-27035	Mil Mi-8MTV-1	95869	RA-27035	0292	0098	2 IS TV3-117MT	13000	Y24		
☐	UN-65900	Tupolev 134A-3	63684	CCCP-65900	0081	0098	2 SO D-30-III	49000	C52		

KEVIS Air Company = KVS
Aktau

Microrajon 9, 10, Flat 58, 466200 Aktau, Kazakstan ☎ (3292) 43 77 33 Tx: none Fax: (3292) 43 77 43 SITA: n/a
F: 1997 ♦♦♦ n/a Head: Evgenij V. Lobarev ICAO: KEVIS Net: n/a Operates charter & aerial work flights with aircraft leased from other companies when required.

KOKSHETAU AIRLINES = KRT (Kokshetau Aue Zholy)
Kokshetau

Kokshetau Airport, 475017 Kokshetau, Kazakstan ☎ (31622) 65 729 Tx: none Fax: n/a SITA: n/a
F: 1997 ♦♦♦ n/a Head: Viktor D. Kudryavtsev ICAO: KOKTA Net: n/a Operates Antonov 24 (ex Kazakstan Airlines) aircraft. Full details not yet known.

LIP-AVIA = TTN
Aktobe

Aktyubinsk Airport, ARZ-406, 463025 Aktobe, Kazakstan ☎ (3132) 29 78 31 Tx: none Fax: (3132) 22 37 36 SITA: n/a
F: 1997 ♦♦♦ n/a Head: Gennadij V. Dolgov ICAO: ZAVOD Net: n/a Operates charter flights with aircraft leased from other companies when required.

MANGYSTAUAVIA
Aktau

Aktau Airport, 466200 Aktau, Kazakstan ☎ (3292) 42 13 20 Tx: none Fax: (3292) 33 47 97 SITA: n/a
F: 1997 ♦♦♦ n/a Head: n/a Net: n/a Operates Antonov 2 (ex Kazakstan Airlines) aircraft. Full details not yet known.

ORIENT EAGLE AIRWAYS = OEG
Almaty

276 Gornaya Street, 7th Floor, 480000 Almaty, Kazakstan ☎ (3272) 50 29 36 Tx: none Fax: (3272) 50 24 57 SITA: n/a
F: 1997 ♦♦♦ n/a Head: Sergei V. Sinitsin ICAO: ORIENT EAGLE Net: n/a

☐	P4-NEN	Boeing 737-2H4 (A)	20925 / 373	N24SW	0974	1097	2 PW JT8D-9A	52390	Y122		lsf Air Finance Europe Ltd
☐	P4-NSN	Boeing 757-2M6	23454 / 102	VR-CRK	0086	1297	2 RR RB211-535E4	108862	VIP	GJ-AC	lsf Air Fin.Europe / opf Kazakstan Gvmt

RUSLAN Aviakompania = RLN
Almaty

Ul. Masanchi 79/6, 480072 Almaty, Kazakstan ☎ (3272) 67 50 58 Tx: none Fax: (3272) 67 09 97 SITA: n/a
F: 1997 ♦♦♦ n/a Head: Bakhytkyri Santsyzbaev ICAO: RUSLAN Net: n/a Operates passenger flight with Tupolev 154 aircraft, leased from AIR KAZAKSTAN when required.

SAN Air Company = S3 / SND
Karaganda

201 Nurkena Abdirova Street, Office 3, 470032 Karaganda, Kazakstan ☎ (3212) 41 22 37 Tx: none Fax: (3212) 41 22 37 SITA: n/a
F: 1995 ♦♦♦ n/a Head: Valentin Kim IATA: 757 ICAO: NURLAN Net: n/a

☐	EY-65763	Tupolev 134A-3	62299	CCCP-65763	0579	0097	2 SO D-30-III	49000	Y80		lsf TZK
☐	EY-65788	Tupolev 134A-3	62835	CCCP-65788	0280	0097	2 SO D-30-III	49000	Y80		lsf TZK

SAYAKHAT, Ltd = W7 / SAH
Almaty

Bogenbay Batyra Street 124, 480091 Almaty, Kazakstan ☎ (3272) 62 26 28 Tx: none Fax: (3272) 62 28 70 SITA: n/a
F: 1989 ♦♦♦ n/a Head: Vladimir V. Kuropatenko IATA: 271 ICAO: SAYAKHAT Net: n/a

☐	UN-85835	Tupolev 154M	716	B-2601	0085	0198	3 SO D-30KU-154-II	100000	Y164		
☐	UN-85836	Tupolev 154M	717	B-2602	0085	0098	3 SO D-30KU-154-II	100000	Y164		
☐	UN-85837	Tupolev 154M	724	B-2604	0086	0198	3 SO D-30KU-154-II	100000	Y164		
☐	UN-76384	Ilyushin 76TD	1003401015			0090	4 SO D-30KP	190000	Freighter		
☐	UN-76385	Ilyushin 76TD	1033416515			0093	4 SO D-30KP	190000	Freighter		
☐	UN-76434	Ilyushin 76TD	1023412395	CCCP-76434		0092	4 SO D-30KP	190000	Freighter		
☐	UN-76442	Ilyushin 76TD	1023414450	CCCP-76442	0092	0092	4 SO D-30KP	190000	Freighter		

SBS AIRCRAFT = ALT
Almaty

Ul. Sakarpatskaya 48, 480079 Almaty, Kazakstan ☎ (3272) 57 75 35 Tx: none Fax: (3272) 57 16 25 SITA: n/a
F: n/a ♦♦♦ n/a Head: Anatoly I. Sorokopetov ICAO: GREEN-CRAFT Net: n/a

☐	EW-85748	Tupolev 154M	924	CCCP-85748	1092	0098	3 SO D-30KU-154-II	100000	Y164		lsf BRU

SEMEIAVIA = SMK (formerly part of Kazakstan Airlines)
Semipalatinsk

Semipalatinsk Airport, 490010 Semipalatinsk, Kazakstan ☎ (3222) 44 39 17 Tx: none Fax: (3222) 44 36 64 SITA: n/a
F: 1997 ♦♦♦ n/a Head: Nurtoleu M. Esenguzhanov ICAO: ERTIS Net: n/a
Company is expected to be integrated into IRTYSH-AVIA during 1999.

☐	UN-87420	Yakovlev 40		CCCP-87420	0074		3 IV AI-25	16800	Y32		

SEVER Aviakompania = KOT (Aviation Company North)
Petropavlovsk

Petropavlovsk Airport, 642000 Petropavlovsk, Kazakstan ☎ (3152) 46 52 00 Tx: none Fax: n/a SITA: n/a
F: 1997 ♦♦♦ n/a Head: Sergei R. Galyamov ICAO: SEVER Net: n/a Operates Antonov 2/24/26 (ex Kazakstan Airlines) aircraft. Full details not yet known.

SYR SUNKARY Aviakompania = SBM (formerly part of Kazakstan Airlines)
Kzyl-Orda

Kzyl-Orda Airport, 467021 Kzyl-Orda, Kazakstan ☎ (32422) 72671 Tx: none Fax: (32422) 76 759 SITA: n/a
F: 1997 ♦♦♦ n/a Head: Ualikhan A. Ashekov ICAO: SUNKAR Net: n/a Beside aircraft listed, also operates Mil Mi-8 helicopters. Full details not yet known.

☐	UN-87480	Yakovlev 40		CCCP-87480	0074	0097	3 IV AI-25	16800	Y32		
☐	UN-87525	Yakovlev 40	9520741	CCCP-87525	0075	0097	3 IV AI-25	16800	Y32		
☐	UN-88195	Yakovlev 40		CCCP-88195	0076	0097	3 IV AI-25	16800	Y32		
☐	UN-88197	Yakovlev 40	9631948	CCCP-88197	0076	0097	3 IV AI-25	16800	Y32		
☐	UN-88248	Yakovlev 40	9640152	CCCP-88248	0076	0097	3 IV AI-25	16800	Y32		

TAA – Trans Asian Airlines = T7 / SRT
Almaty

Tulebaeva Av. 4, 480016 Almaty, Kazakstan ☎ (3272) 30 65 71 Tx: none Fax: (3272) 30 15 58 SITA: n/a
F: 1996 ♦♦♦ n/a Head: Murlan Nurmagambetov IATA: 326 ICAO: TRASER Net: n/a

☐	UN-86501	Ilyushin 62M	4831628	YR-IRE	1178	0198	4 SO D-30KU	167000	Y179		
☐	UN-86502	Ilyushin 62	21305	YR-IRB	0473	0898	4 KU NK-8-4	161600	Y179		
☐	UN-86503	Ilyushin 62	51902	YR-IRC	0375	0299	4 KU NK-8-4	161600	Y179		

TARAZ WINGS = TWC (Krylya Taraza)
Zhambyl

Taraz Airport, 484020 Taraz, (Zhambyl Region), Kazakstan ☎ (32622) 50 795 Tx: none Fax: (32622) 50 896 SITA: n/a
F: 1996 ♦♦♦ n/a Head: Adilbek Kelimkulov ICAO: TARAZ Net: n/a Beside aircraft listed, also operates Antonov 2. Full details not yet known.

☐	UN-87282	Yakovlev 40	9321727	CCCP-87282	0073	0096	3 IV AI-25	16800	Y32		
☐	UN-87314	Yakovlev 40	9330929	CCCP-87314	0073	0096	3 IV AI-25	16800	Y32		
☐	UN-87377	Yakovlev 40	9411132	CCCP-87377	0074	0096	3 IV AI-25	16800	Y32		
☐	UN-87537	Yakovlev 40	9520242	CCCP-87537	0075	0096	3 IV AI-25	16800	Y32		
☐	UN-88162	Yakovlev 40	9611646	CCCP-88162	0076	0096	3 IV AI-25	16800	Y32		
☐	UN-88181	Yakovlev 40K	9620148	CCCP-88181	0076	0096	3 IV AI-25	16800	Y32		
☐	UN-88249	Yakovlev 40	9640252	CCCP-88249	0076	0096	3 IV AI-25	16800	Y32		
☐	UN-88268	Yakovlev 40	9720653	CCCP-88268	0077	0096	3 IV AI-25	16800	Y32		
☐	UN-85324	Tupolev 154B-2	324	ER-85324	0279	0098	3 KU NK-8-2U	98000	Y164		

TIEN-SHAN = TJN
Almaty

Ul. Rozybakieva 105B, Room 32, 480000 Almaty, Kazakstan ☎ (3272) 46 24 80 Tx: none Fax: (3272) 21 82 91 SITA: n/a
F: 1996 ♦♦♦ n/a Head: Vladimir A. Ansupov ICAO: NERON Net: n/a

☐	UN-79952	Antonov An-2			0060	0096	1 SH ASh-62IR	5500	Utility		
☐	UN-79954	Antonov An-2			0060	0096	1 SH ASh-62IR	5500	Utility		
☐	UN-79955	Antonov An-2			0060	0096	1 SH ASh-62IR	5500	Utility		
☐	UN-79956	Antonov An-2			0060	0096	1 SH ASh-62IR	5500	Utility		

registration   type of aircraft   cn/fn   ex/ex*   mfd   del   powered by   mtow kg   configuration   selcal   name/fln/specialitites/remarks

ULBA Aviakompania = ULB (formerly part of Kazakstan Airlines) — Ust-Kamenogorsk

Ul. Bazhova 566, Airport, 482080 Ust-Kamenogorsk, Kazakstan ☎ (3232) 42 77 64 Tx: none Fax: (3232) 49 69 51 SITA: n/a
F: 1997 ✦✦✦ n/a Head: Viktor N. Malygin ICAO: USKAM Net: n/a Beside aircraft listed, also operates Antonov 2 (ex Kazakstan Airlines). Full details not yet known.
Company is expected to be integrated into IRTYSH-AVIA during 1999.

	registration	type of aircraft	cn/fn	ex/ex*	mfd	del	powered by	mtow kg	configuration	name/fln/specialitites/remarks
☐	UN-87274	Yakovlev 40	9311027	CCCP-87274	0073		3 IV AI-25	16800	Y32	
☐	UN-87492	Yakovlev 40		CCCP-87492	0075		3 IV AI-25	16800	Y32	
☐	UN-87498	Yakovlev 40	9540146	CCCP-87498	0075		3 IV AI-25	16800	Y32	
☐	UN-87909	Yakovlev 40	9731454	CCCP-87909	0077		3 IV AI-25	16800	Y32	
☐	UN-87934	Yakovlev 40K	9740556	CCCP-87934	0079		3 IV AI-25	16800	Y32	
☐	UN-88271	Yakovlev 40K	9720953	CCCP-88271	0077		3 IV AI-25	16800	Y32	
☐	UN-42407	Yakovlev 42D	4520424116690	CCCP-42407	0091	0097	3 LO D-36	56500	Y120	
☐	UN-42447	Yakovlev 42D	4520424309017		0093	0097	3 LO D-36	56500	Y120	
☐	UN-42448	Yakovlev 42D	4520423310017		0093	0097	3 LO D-36	56500	Y120	
☐	UN-42558	Yakovlev 42D	4520423307017		0093	0097	3 LO D-36	56500	Y120	

VIPAIR AIRLINES, Ltd = 9V / VPA (VIP Aero) — Astana

Astana Airport, 473026 Astana, Kazakstan ☎ (3172) 32 43 29 Tx: none Fax: (3172) 32 01 03 SITA: n/a
F: 1996 ✦✦✦ n/a Head: Viktor S. Ostrovsky IATA: 434 ICAO: VIAIR Net: n/a

☐	UN-85775	Tupolev 154M	957	RA-85775	0093	0097	3 SO D-30KU-154-II	100000	Y166	
☐	UN-85782	Tupolev 154M	966	RA-85782	0093	0097	3 SO D-30KU-154-II	100000	Y166	

VIP AVIA = PAV — Almaty

Prospekt Abylay Khana 60, 480004 Almaty, Kazakstan ☎ (3272) 33 90 43 Tx: none Fax: (3272) 32 08 52 SITA: n/a
F: 1995 ✦✦✦ n/a Head: Anatoly A. Nekrasov ICAO: NICOL Net: n/a

☐	UN-87543	Yakovlev 40	9530842	CCCP-87543	0075	0096	3 IV AI-25	17200	VIP F4Y16	lsf IRT / opf Kazak Gas Company

ZHETYSU Aviakompania = JTU — Taldykorgan

Taldykorgan Airport, 488012 Taldykorgan, Kazakstan ☎ (32822) 10 006 Tx: none Fax: (32822) 10 006 SITA: n/a
F: 1997 ✦✦✦ n/a Head: Kalmukhamet Zh. Donsebaev ICAO: ZHETYSU Net: n/a Beside aircraft listed, also operates Antonov 2 (ex Kazakstan Airlines). Full details not yet known.

☐	UN-87271	Yakovlev 40	9310727	CCCP-87271	0073		3 IV AI-25	16800	Y32	
☐	UN-87329	Yakovlev 40		CCCP-87329	0073		3 IV AI-25	16800	Y32	
☐	UN-87926	Yakovlev 40K	9741755	CCCP-87926	0077		3 IV AI-25	16800	Y32	
☐	UN-87927	Yakovlev 40K	9741855	CCCP-87927	0077		3 IV AI-25	16800	Y32	
☐	UN-87929	Yakovlev 40		CCCP-87929	0077		3 IV AI-25	16800	Y32	
☐	UN-87931	Yakovlev 40		CCCP-87931	0077		3 IV AI-25	16800	Y32	

ZHEZAIR = KZH (Zhezkazgan Air/Zhezkazgan aue zholy) — Zhezkazgan

Airport, 477000 Zhezkazgan, Kazakstan ☎ (3102) 76 39 02 Tx: none Fax: (3102) 76 28 92 SITA: n/a
F: 1996 ✦✦✦ n/a Head: Rysmakhamed A. Iglikov ICAO: ULUTAU Net: n/a Beside aircraft listed, also operates Let 410 & Mil Mi-8 (ex Kazakstan Airlines). Full details not yet known.

☐	UN-87920	Yakovlev 40	9731055	CCCP-87920	0077	0096	3 IV AI-25	16800	Y32	
☐	UN-42557	Yakovlev 42D	4520423302017	RA-42557	0093	0096	3 LO D-36	56500	Y120	

UR = UKRAINE (Ukraïna)
Capital: Kiev Official Language: Ukrainian Population: 53,0 million Square Km: 603700 Dialling code: +380 Year established: 1991 Acting political head: Leonid Danilovich Kuchma (President)

Government / Corporate / Executive / VIP Aircraft

☐	UR-11352	Antonov 12BP		CCCP-11352	0063		4 IV AI-20M	61000	Freighter	Ministry of Defence
☐	UR-74033	Antonov 74			0094		2 LO D-36	34500	Freighter	ARTOS-Armadni Techniko Obchadni Servis
☐	UR-76560	Ilyushin 76MD	0033447363	CCCP-76560	0083		4 SO D-30KP	190000	Freighter	Ministry of Defence
☐	UR-76624	Ilyushin 76MD	0053457710	CCCP-76624	0085	0095	4 SO D-30KP	190000	Freighter	Ministry of Defence / fn 4308
☐	UR-76681	Ilyushin 76MD	0063467021	CCCP-76681	0086		4 SO D-30KP	190000	Freighter	Ministry of Defence
☐	UR-76699	Ilyushin 76MD		CCCP-76699	0086		4 SO D-30KP	190000	Freighter	Ministry of Defence
☐	UR-78778	Ilyushin 76MD		CCCP-78778	0088		4 SO D-30KP	190000	Freighter	Ministry of Defence
☐	UR-78820	Ilyushin 76MD	0093496907	RA-78820	0089		4 SO D-30KP	190000	Freighter	Ministry of Defence

AERO-CHARTER UKRAINE, Ltd = UCR — Kiev

23 Klimenko Street, 252110 Kiev, Ukraine ☎ (44) 277 21 44 Tx: none Fax: (44) 277 21 44 SITA: n/a
F: 1997 ✦✦✦ n/a Head: Georgiy Borishchuk ICAO: CHARTER UKRAINE Net: n/a

☐	UR-87479	Yakovlev 40	9441838	CCCP-87479	0075	0097	3 IV AI-25	16800	Y36	
☐	UR-88290	Yakovlev 40K	9840459	CCCP-88290	0078	0097	3 IV AI-25	16800	Executive	

AEROSTAR = UAR — Kiev-Zhulyany

PO Box NB-266, 252001 Kiev, Ukraine ☎ (44) 229 47 14 Tx: none Fax: (44) 462 03 10 SITA: n/a
F: 1997 ✦✦✦ n/a Head: Shahzeddin Askezov ICAO: AEROSTAR Net: n/a

☐	UR-87961	Yakovlev 40K	9820458	CCCP-87961	0078	0099	3 IV AI-25	17200	F12	
☐	UR-87998	Yakovlev 40	9540245	CCCP-87998	0176	0097	3 IV AI-25	16800	F12	lsf UZA

AEROSWEET AIRLINES = VV / AEW (Subsidiary of Air Ukraine) — Kiev-Borispol

Bulvar Shevchenko 58A, 252032 Kiev, Ukraine ☎ (44) 462 02 40 Tx: none Fax: (44) 296 75 33 SITA: IEVHQVV
F: 1994 ✦✦✦ n/a Head: Gregoriy Gurtovoy IATA: 870 ICAO: AEROSWEET Net: n/a

☐	UR-BFA	Boeing 737-2L9 (A)	21685 / 549	EI-CGZ	0179	0496	2 PW JT8D-17	54204	Y121	lsf GECA
☐	UR-BVY	Boeing 737-2Q8 (A)	22760 / 852	VP-BYC	0482	0597	2 PW JT8D-17	58105	Y120	
☐	UR-BVZ	Boeing 737-2Q8 (A)	22453 / 748	LY-GPA	0381	0299	2 PW JT8D-15	54204	Y120	lsf GECA

AIR KHARKOV = KHV — Kharkov

Ul. Sumskaya 104, 310031 Kharkov, Ukraine ☎ (572) 51 69 07 Tx: none Fax: (572) 51 68 51 SITA: n/a
F: 1998 ✦✦✦ n/a Head: n/a ICAO: AIR KHARKOV Net: n/a
Some aircraft are still in former AIR UKRAINE-colors & titles but will be repainted in due course.

☐	UR-26514	Antonov 26	6907	CCCP-26514	0078	0098	2 IV AI-24VT	24000	Freighter	
☐	UR-26555	Antonov 26	3203	CCCP-26555	0075	0098	2 IV AI-24VT	24000	Freighter	
☐	UR-26651	Antonov 26	7508	CCCP-26651	0079	0098	2 IV AI-24VT	24000	Freighter	
☐	UR-26676	Antonov 26B	8602	CCCP-26676	0079	0098	2 IV AI-24VT	24000	Freighter	
☐	UR-26689	Antonov 26B	9005	CCCP-26689	0079	0098	2 IV AI-24VT	24000	Freighter	
☐	UR-65037	Tupolev 134A-3	48850	CCCP-65037	0076	0098	2 SO D-30-III	49000	Y76	
☐	UR-65073	Tupolev 134A-3	49980	CCCP-65073	0074	0098	2 SO D-30-III	49000	Y76	
☐	UR-65114	Tupolev 134A-3	60395	CCCP-65114	0078	0098	2 SO D-30-III	49000	Y76	
☐	UR-65746	Tupolev 134A-3	2351608	CCCP-65746	0072	0098	2 SO D-30-III	49000	Y76	
☐	UR-65752	Tupolev 134A-3	61079	CCCP-65752	0079	0098	2 SO D-30-III	49000	Y76	
☐	UR-65761	Tupolev 134A-3	62244	CCCP-65761	0079	0098	2 SO D-30-III	49000	Y76	
☐	UR-65764	Tupolev 134A-3	62305	CCCP-65764	0079	0098	2 SO D-30-III	49000	Y76	
☐	UR-65773	Tupolev 134A-3	62495	CCCP-65773	0079	0098	2 SO D-30-III	49000	Y76	
☐	UR-65877	Tupolev 134A-3	31250	CCCP-65877	0075	0098	2 SO D-30-III	49000	Y76	

AIR KIROVOGRAD, Kompania Airlines = KAD — Kirovograd

Ul. Korolenko 1-A, 316005 Kirovograd, Ukraine ☎ (522) 22 68 57 Tx: none Fax: (522) 24 89 09 SITA: n/a
F: 1998 ✦✦✦ n/a Head: n/a ICAO: AIR KIROVOGRAD Net: n/a
Some aircraft are still in former AIR UKRAINE-colors & titles but will be repainted in due course.

☐	UR-01765	PZL Mielec (Antonov) An-2	1G107-12	CCCP-01765	0069	0098	1 SH ASh-62IR	5500	Y12	
☐	UR-17915	PZL Mielec (Antonov) An-2	1G205-56	CCCP-17915	0083	0098	1 SH ASh-62IR	5500	Y12	
☐	UR-17916	PZL Mielec (Antonov) An-2	1G205-57	CCCP-17916	0083	0098	1 SH ASh-62IR	5500	Y12	
☐	UR-17960	PZL Mielec (Antonov) An-2	1G209-44	CCCP-17960	0084	0098	1 SH ASh-62IR	5500	Y12	
☐	UR-31497	PZL Mielec (Antonov) An-2	1G199-06	CCCP-31497	0082	0098	1 SH ASh-62IR	5500	Y12	
☐	UR-33005	PZL Mielec (Antonov) An-2	1G217-45	CCCP-33005	0085	0098	1 SH ASh-62IR	5500	Y12	
☐	UR-40361	PZL Mielec (Antonov) An-2	1G222-40	CCCP-40361	0086	0098	1 SH ASh-62IR	5500	Y12	
☐	UR-40423	PZL Mielec (Antonov) An-2	1G223-49	CCCP-40423	0087	0098	1 SH ASh-62IR	5500	Y12	
☐	UR-40613	PZL Mielec (Antonov) An-2	1G213-20	CCCP-40613	0085	0098	1 SH ASh-62IR	5500	Y12	
☐	UR-43950	PZL Mielec (Antonov) An-2	1G210-27	CCCP-43950	0084	0098	1 SH ASh-62IR	5500	Y12	
☐	UR-43954	PZL Mielec (Antonov) An-2	1G230-31	CCCP-43954	0084	0098	1 SH ASh-62IR	5500	Y12	
☐	UR-62542	PZL Mielec (Antonov) An-2	1G176-05	CCCP-62542	0077	0098	1 SH ASh-62IR	5500	Y12	
☐	UR-81649	PZL Mielec (Antonov) An-2	1G209-43	CCCP-81649	0084	0098	1 SH ASh-62IR	5500	Y12	
☐	UR-84627	PZL Mielec (Antonov) An-2	1G190-59	CCCP-84627	0080	0098	1 SH ASh-62IR	5500	Y12	
☐	UR-87230	Yakovlev 40	9541542	CCCP-87230	0076	0098	3 IV AI-25	16800	Y32	lst MLV as ER-87230
☐	UR-87245	Yakovlev 40	9531343	RA-87245	0075	0098	3 IV AI-25	16800	Y36	
☐	UR-87276	Yakovlev 40	9311227	CCCP-87276	0073	0098	3 IV AI-25	16800	Y27	
☐	UR-87435	Yakovlev 40	9431135	CCCP-87435	0074	0098	3 IV AI-25	16800	Y36	
☐	UR-87562	Yakovlev 40	9211321	CCCP-87562	0072	0098	3 IV AI-25	16800	Y27	
☐	UR-87832	Yakovlev 40	9241825	CCCP-87832	0072	0098	3 IV AI-25	16800	Y27	

AIR UKRAINE = 6U / UKR (Avialinii Ukrainy) (formerly Aeroflot Kiev Directorate)

Kiev-Borispol & -Zhulyani

Prospekt Peremogy 14, 252135 Kiev, Ukraine ☎ (44) 226 25 67 Tx: none Fax: (44) 216 70 64 SITA: n/a

F: n/a ✈✈✈ 9500 Head: Vyachelsav V. Ilyin IATA: 891 ICAO: AIR UKRAINE Net: n/a Consists of the following Aviation Enterprises (divisions): CHERNOVTSY, LUGANSK, KHMELNITSKY, LVOV & VINNITSA.

All Aviation Enterprises operate their aircraft fleet under its own licence but under the name & color scheme of AIR UKRAINE. Air Ukraine itself has 2 bases: Kiev-Borispol & -Zhulyani.

All aircraft are listed here with operating remark. Some aircraft are still in former Aeroflot colors but with Air Ukraine titles.

registration	type of aircraft	cn/fn	ex/ex*	mfd	del	powered by	mtow kg	configuration	selcal	name/fln/specialitites/remarks
UR-17961	PZL Mielec (Antonov) An-2	1G209-45	CCCP-17961	0084	0084	1 SH ASh-62IR	5500	Y12		opb Lugansk Aviation Enterprise
UR-32637	PZL Mielec (Antonov) An-2	1G219-36	CCCP-32637	0086	0086	1 SH ASh-62IR	5500	Y12		opb Lugansk Aviation Enterprise
UR-32749	PZL Mielec (Antonov) An-2	1G212-54	CCCP-32749	0085	0085	1 SH ASh-62IR	5500	Y12		opb Lugansk Aviation Enterprise
UR-33388	PZL Mielec (Antonov) An-2	1G226-47	CCCP-33388	0087	0087	1 SH ASh-62IR	5500	Y12		opb Lugansk Aviation Enterprise
UR-33570	PZL Mielec (Antonov) An-2	1G230-07	CCCP-33570	0088	0088	1 SH ASh-62IR	5500	Y12		opb Lugansk Aviation Enterprise
UR-33571	PZL Mielec (Antonov) An-2	1G230-08	CCCP-33571	0088	0088	1 SH ASh-62IR	5500	Y12		opb Lugansk Aviation Enterprise
UR-33587	PZL Mielec (Antonov) An-2	1G230-29	CCCP-33587	0088	0088	1 SH ASh-62IR	5500	Y12		opb Lugansk Aviation Enterprise
UR-33590	PZL Mielec (Antonov) An-2	1G230-32	CCCP-33590	0088	0088	1 SH ASh-62IR	5500	Y12		opb Lugansk Aviation Enterprise
UR-40350	PZL Mielec (Antonov) An-2	1G222-27	CCCP-40350	0086	0086	1 SH ASh-62IR	5500	Y12		opb Lugansk Aviation Enterprise
UR-40885	PZL Mielec (Antonov) An-2	1G215-20	CCCP-40885	0085	0085	1 SH ASh-62IR	5500	Y12		opb Lugansk Aviation Enterprise
UR-40951	PZL Mielec (Antonov) An-2	1G216-51	CCCP-40951	0085	0085	1 SH ASh-62IR	5500	Y12		opb Lugansk Aviation Enterprise
UR-40952	PZL Mielec (Antonov) An-2	1G216-52	CCCP-40952	0085	0085	1 SH ASh-62IR	5500	Y12		opb Lugansk Aviation Enterprise
UR-71191	PZL Mielec (Antonov) An-2	1G200-34	CCCP-71191	0083	0083	1 SH ASh-62IR	5500	Y12		opb Lugansk Aviation Enterprise
UR-67065	Let 410UVP	810701	CCCP-67065	0081	0081	2 WA M-601D	5800	Y15		opb Chernovtsy Aviation Enterprise
UR-67141	Let 410UVP	800407	CCCP-67141	0080	0090	2 WA M-601D	5800	Y15		opb Vinnitsa Aviation Enterprise
UR-67335	Let 410UVP	820835	HA-LAB	0082	0082	2 WA M-601D	5800	Y15		opb Vinnitsa Aviation Enterprise
UR-67340	Let 410UVP	820840	CCCP-67340	0082	0082	2 WA M-601D	5800	Y15		opb Vinnitsa Aviation Enterprise
UR-67416	Let 410UVP	831104	CCCP-67416	0083	0092	2 WA M-601D	5800	Y15		opb Khmelnitsky Aviation Enterprise
UR-67422	Let 410UVP	831113	CCCP-67422	0083	0092	2 WA M-601D	5800	Y15		opb Khmelnitsky Aviation Enterprise
UR-67502	Let 410UVP	851406	CCCP-67502	0085	0092	2 WA M-601D	5800	Y15		lst AKO / opb Khmelnitsky A.E.
UR-67520	Let 410UVP	851424	CCCP-67520	0085	0085	2 WA M-601D	5800	Y15		opb Vinnitsa Aviation Enterprise
UR-67528	Let 410UVP	851435	CCCP-67528	0085	0085	2 WA M-601D	5800	Y15		opb Vinnitsa Aviation Enterprise
UR-67548	Let 410UVP	851515	CCCP-67548	0085	0085	2 WA M-601D	5800	Y15		opb Chernovtsy Aviation Enterprise
UR-46249	Antonov 24B	77303207	CCCP-46249	0067	0067	2 IV AI-24-II	21000	Y48		opb Lvov Airlines
UR-46278	Antonov 24B	07303701	CCCP-46278	0067	0067	2 IV AI-24-II	21000	Y48		opb Lvov Airlines
UR-46293	Antonov 24RV	77303805	CCCP-46293	0067	0067	2 IV AI-24VT	21800	Y48		based Kiev-Zhulyani
UR-46301	Antonov 24B	97305201	CCCP-46301	0069	0069	2 IV AI-24-II	21000	Y48		opb Lvov Airlines
UR-46305	Antonov 24B	97305205	CCCP-46305	0069	0069	2 IV AI-24-II	21000	Y48		opb Lvov Airlines
UR-46312	Antonov 24B	97305308	CCCP-46312	0069	0069	2 IV AI-24-II	21000	Y48		based Kiev-Zhulyani
UR-46326	Antonov 24B	97305503	CCCP-46326	0069	0069	2 IV AI-24-II	21000	Y48		opb Lvov Airlines
UR-46330	Antonov 24B	97305507	CCCP-46330	0069	0069	2 IV AI-24-II	21000	Y48		based Kiev-Zhulyani
UR-46372	Antonov 24B	07306003	CCCP-46372	0070	0070	2 IV AI-24-II	21000	Y48		based Kiev-Zhulyani
UR-46383	Antonov 24B	07306106	CCCP-46383	0070	0070	2 IV AI-24-II	21000	Y48		opb Lvov Airlines
UR-46397	Antonov 24B	07306301	RA-46397	0070	0097	2 IV AI-24-II	21000	Y36		opb Khmelnitsky Aviation Enterprise
UR-46434	Antonov 24B	87304304	CCCP-46434	0068	0068	2 IV AI-24-II	21000	Y48		based Kiev-Zhulyani
UR-46440	Antonov 24B	87304401	CCCP-46440	0068	0068	2 IV AI-24-II	21000	Y48		based Kiev-Zhulyani
UR-46469	Antonov 24RV	27307907	CCCP-46469	0072	0072	2 IV AI-24VT	21800	Y48		based Kiev-Zhulyani
UR-46475	Antonov 24RV	27308003	CCCP-46475	0072	0072	2 IV AI-24VT	21800	Y52		opb Lugansk Aviation Enterprise
UR-46514	Antonov 24RV	37308410	CCCP-46514	0073	0073	2 IV AI-24VT	21800	Y52		opb Lugansk Aviation Enterprise
UR-46517	Antonov 24RV	37308503	CCCP-46517	0073	0073	2 IV AI-24VT	21800	Y52		opb Lugansk Aviation Enterprise
UR-46527	Antonov 24RV	47310006	CCCP-46527	0074	0074	2 IV AI-24VT	21800	Y36		based Kiev-Zhulyani
UR-46596	Antonov 24B	97305106	CCCP-46596	0069	0069	2 IV AI-24-II	21000	Y48		based Kiev-Zhulyani
UR-46630	Antonov 24RV	37308809	CCCP-46630	0073	0073	2 IV AI-24VT	21800	Y52		opb Lugansk Aviation Enterprise
UR-46661	Antonov 24RV	47309305	CCCP-46661	0074	0074	2 IV AI-24VT	21800	Y52		opb Lugansk Aviation Enterprise
UR-46677	Antonov 24RV	47309609	RA-46677	0774	0073	2 IV AI-24VT	21800	Y52		opb Lugansk Aviation Enterprise
UR-46813	Antonov 24B	07302204	CCCP-46813	0066	0066	2 IV AI-24-II	21000	Y48		opb Lvov Airlines
UR-46838	Antonov 24RV	17306805	CCCP-46838	0071	0071	2 IV AI-24VT	21800	Y48		based Kiev-Zhulyani
UR-47257	Antonov 24RV	27307709	CCCP-47257	0072	0072	2 IV AI-24VT	21800	Y48		based Kiev-Zhulyani
UR-47266	Antonov 24B	07306304	CCCP-47266	0070	0070	2 IV AI-24-II	21000	Y48		based Kiev-Zhulyani
UR-47278	Antonov 24B	07306408	CCCP-47278	0070	0070	2 IV AI-24-II	21000	Y48		based Kiev-Zhulyani
UR-47281	Antonov 24B	07306501	CCCP-47281	0070	0070	2 IV AI-24-II	21000	Y48		based Kiev-Zhulyani
UR-47287	Antonov 24B	07306507	CCCP-47287	0070	0070	2 IV AI-24-II	21000	Y48		based Kiev-Zhulyani
UR-47297	Antonov 24RV	07306610	CCCP-47297	0071	0071	2 IV AI-24VT	21800	Y48		based Kiev-Zhulyani
UR-47308	Antonov 24RV	57310308	CCCP-47308	0075	0075	2 IV AI-24VT	21800	Y48		based Kiev-Zhulyani
UR-47311	Antonov 24RV	57310402	CCCP-47311	0075	0075	2 IV AI-24VT	21800	Y48		based Kiev-Zhulyani
UR-47312	Antonov 24RV	57310403	CCCP-47312	0075	0075	2 IV AI-24VT	21800	Y52		opb Lugansk Aviation Enterprise
UR-47801	Antonov 24RV	17306810	CCCP-47801	0071	0071	2 IV AI-24VT	21800	Y48		based Kiev-Zhulyani
UR-47824	Antonov 24B	17307205	CCCP-47824	0071	0071	2 IV AI-24-II	21000	Y48		based Kiev-Zhulyani
UR-47836	Antonov 24B	17307308	CCCP-47836	0071	0071	2 IV AI-24-II	21000	Y48		based Kiev-Zhulyani
UR-47837	Antonov 24B	17307309	CCCP-47837	0071	0071	2 IV AI-24-II	21000	Y48		based Kiev-Zhulyani
UR-30000	Antonov 30	1401	CCCP-30000	0078	0078	2 IV AI-24T	23000	Survey / Combi		based Kiev-Zhulyani
UR-30005	Antonov 30	1406	CCCP-30005	0378	0078	2 IV AI-24T	23000	Survey / Combi		based Kiev-Zhulyani
UR-30022	Antonov 30	0404	CCCP-30022	0074	0074	2 IV AI-24T	23000	Survey / Combi		based Kiev-Zhulyani
UR-30025	Antonov 30	0503	CCCP-30025	0074	0074	2 IV AI-24T	23000	Survey / Combi		based Kiev-Zhulyani
UR-30026	Antonov 30	0505	CCCP-30026	0074	0074	2 IV AI-24T	23000	Survey / Combi		based Kiev-Zhulyani
UR-30030	Antonov 30	0605	CCCP-30030	0075	0075	2 IV AI-24T	23000	Survey / Combi		based Kiev-Zhulyani
UR-30036	Antonov 30	0703	CCCP-30036	0075	0075	2 IV AI-24T	23000	Survey / Combi		based Kiev-Zhulyani
UR-30044	Antonov 30	0906	CCCP-30044	0076	0076	2 IV AI-24T	23000	Survey / Combi		based Kiev-Zhulyani
UR-46633	Antonov 30	0202	CCCP-46633	0073	0073	2 IV AI-24T	23000	Survey / Combi		based Kiev-Zhulyani
UR-65048	Tupolev 134A-3	49750	CCCP-65048	0077	0077	2 SO D-30-III	49000	Y76		based Kiev-Borispol
UR-65076	Tupolev 134A-3	60001	CCCP-65076	0077	0077	2 SO D-30-III	49000	Y76		opb Chernovtsy Aviation Enterprise
UR-65077	Tupolev 134A-3	60028	CCCP-65077	0077	0077	2 SO D-30-III	49000	C42		based Kiev-Borispol
UR-65089	Tupolev 134A	60180	CCCP-65089	0078	0078	2 SO D-30-II	49000	Y76		opb Chernovtsy Aviation Enterprise
UR-65107	Tupolev 134A	60328	CCCP-65107	0078	0078	2 SO D-30-II	49000	Y76		based Kiev-Borispol
UR-65134	Tupolev 134A-3	60647	CCCP-65134	0078	0078	2 SO D-30-III	49000	Y76		based Kiev-Borispol
UR-65135	Tupolev 134A-3	60648	CCCP-65135	0078	0078	2 SO D-30-III	49000	Y76		based Kiev-Borispol
UR-65757	Tupolev 134A-3	62215	CCCP-65757	0079	0079	2 SO D-30-III	49000	Y76		based Kiev-Borispol
UR-65765	Tupolev 134A	62315	CCCP-65765	0079	0079	2 SO D-30-II	49000	Y76		based Kiev-Borispol
UR-65790	Tupolev 134A-3	63100	CCCP-65790	0080	0080	2 SO D-30-III	49000	Y76		opb Chernovtsy Aviation Enterprise
UR-42317	Yakovlev 42	4520422202039	CCCP-42317	0085	0085	3 LO D-36	54000	Y120		opb Lvov Airlines
UR-42358	Yakovlev 42D	4520422811413	CCCP-42358	0088	0088	3 LO D-36	56500	Y120		opb Lvov Airlines
UR-42369	Yakovlev 42	4520422914190	CCCP-42369	0089	0089	3 LO D-36	54000	Y120		opb Lvov Airlines
UR-42403	Yakovlev 42D	4520422116588	CCCP-42403	0091	0091	3 LO D-36	56500	Y120		opb Lvov Airlines
UR-42527	Yakovlev 42	11040903	CCCP-42527	0085	0085	3 LO D-36	56500	Y120		opb Lvov Airlines
UR-42540	Yakovlev 42D	11140604	CCCP-42540	0085	0085	3 LO D-36	56500	Y120		opb Lvov Airlines / cvtd 42
UR-42544	Yakovlev 42	11151004	CCCP-42544	0086	0086	3 LO D-36	56500	Y120		lst BON as T9-ABC
UR-11314	Antonov 12BP	8345604		0068	0096	4 IV AI-20M	61000	Freighter		opb Lvov Airlines
UR-11346	Antonov 12BK	8345702	54 RED	0068	0096	4 IV AI-20M	61000	Freighter		opb Lvov Airlines
UR-85316	Tupolev 154B-2	316	CCCP-85316	0078	0078	3 KU NK-8-2U	98000	Y164		opb Lugansk Aviation Enterprise
UR-85350	Tupolev 154B-2	350	CCCP-85350	0079	0079	3 KU NK-8-2U	98000	Y164		based Kiev-Borispol
UR-85362	Tupolev 154B-2	362	CCCP-85362	0079	0079	3 KU NK-8-2U	98000	Y164		opb Lugansk Aviation Enterprise
UR-85368	Tupolev 154B-2	368	CCCP-85368	0079	0079	3 KU NK-8-2U	98000	Y164		based Kiev-Borispol
UR-85379	Tupolev 154B-2	379	CCCP-85379	0079	0079	3 KU NK-8-2U	98000	Y164		based Kiev-Borispol/opf UNO
UR-85395	Tupolev 154B-2	395	CCCP-85395	0080	0080	3 KU NK-8-2U	98000	Y164		lst KGL as RA-85395 / opb Lugansk A.E.
UR-85399	Tupolev 154B-2	399	CCCP-85399	0080	0080	3 KU NK-8-2U	98000	Y164		based Kiev-Borispol
UR-85407	Tupolev 154B-2	407	CCCP-85407	0080	0080	3 KU NK-8-2U	98000	Y164		based Kiev-Borispol
UR-85424	Tupolev 154B-2	424	CCCP-85424	0080	0080	3 KU NK-8-2U	98000	Y164		based Kiev-Borispol
UR-85460	Tupolev 154B-2	460	CCCP-85460	0080	0080	3 KU NK-8-2U	98000	Y164		based Kiev-Borispol
UR-85476	Tupolev 154B-2	476	CCCP-85476	0081	0081	3 KU NK-8-2U	98000	Y164		based Kiev-Borispol
UR-85482	Tupolev 154B-2	482	CCCP-85482	0081	0081	3 KU NK-8-2U	98000	Y164		based Kiev-Borispol
UR-85490	Tupolev 154B-2	490	CCCP-85490	0081	0081	3 KU NK-8-2U	98000	Y164		based Kiev-Borispol
UR-85499	Tupolev 154B-2	499	CCCP-85499	0081	0081	3 KU NK-8-2U	98000	Y164		based Kiev-Borispol
UR-85513	Tupolev 154B-2	513	CCCP-85513	0081	0081	3 KU NK-8-2U	98000	Y164		based Kiev-Borispol
UR-85526	Tupolev 154B-2	526	CCCP-85526	0082	0082	3 KU NK-8-2U	98000	Y164		based Kiev-Borispol
UR-85535	Tupolev 154B-2	535	CCCP-85535	0082	0082	3 KU NK-8-2U	98000	Y164		based Kiev-Borispol
UR-85700	Tupolev 154M	875	CCCP-85700	0091	0091	3 SO D-30KU-154-II	100000	Y164		based Kiev-Borispol
UR-85707	Tupolev 154M	882	CCCP-85707	0091	0091	3 SO D-30KU-154-II	100000	Y164		based Kiev-Borispol
UR-86132	Ilyushin 62M	1034152	CCCP-86132	0080	0091	4 SO D-30KU	167000	CY144		based Kiev-Borispol / fn 3405
UR-86133	Ilyushin 62M	1138234	CCCP-86133	0081	0091	4 SO D-30KU	167000	CY144		based Kiev-Borispol / fn 3803
UR-86134	Ilyushin 62M	1138546	CCCP-86134	0081	0091	4 SO D-30KU	167000	CY144	GK-HL	based Kiev-Borispol / fn 3804
UR-86135	Ilyushin 62M	1748445	CCCP-86135	0087	0091	4 SO D-30KU	167000	CY144	GL-AK	based Kiev-Borispol / fn 4804
UR-86580	Ilyushin 62M	2343554	CCCP-86580	0083	0091	4 SO D-30KU	167000	CY144		std Kiev-Borispol / fn 4305
UR-86581	Ilyushin 62M	2932526	CCCP-86581	0079	0091	4 SO D-30KU	167000	CY144	GK-HM	based Kiev-Borispol / fn 3202
UR-86582	Ilyushin 62M	3036253	CCCP-86582	0080	0091	4 SO D-30KU	167000	CY144	GK-HL	based Kiev-Borispol / fn 3605
UR-76705	Ilyushin 76MD	0063472158	CCCP-76705	0086	0086	4 SO D-30KP	190000	Freighter		opb Lvov Airlines

☐ UR-76778	Ilyushin 76MD	0083482502	CCCP-76778	0086	0086	4 SO D-30KP	190000	Freighter		opb Lvov Airlines

AIR URGA = 3N / URG — **Kirovograd**

Dobrovolskogo 1A, 316005 Kirovograd, Ukraine ☎ (522) 25 11 25 Tx: 282113 orlan ux Fax: (522) 25 11 25 SITA: KGOURG8
F: 1993 ⁂ 122 Head: Leonid Shmayevich IATA: 746 ICAO: URGA Net: n/a

☐ UR-46558	Antonov 24B	87304605	CCCP-46558	0068	0093	2 IV AI-24	21000	Y28		
☐ UR-46577	Antonov 24B	87304902	CCCP-46577	0068	0093	2 IV AI-24	21000	Y28		
☐ UR-47300	Antonov 24RV	57310203	CCCP-47300	0075	0093	2 IV AI-24VT	21800	Y48		lst SAV
☐ UR-47313	Antonov 24RV	57310410	CCCP-47313	0075	0093	2 IV AI-24VT	21800	Y48		
☐ UR-47316	Antonov 24RV	67310503	CCCP-47316	0076	0093	2 IV AI-24VT	21800	Y48		
☐ UR-47319	Antonov 24RV	67310506	CCCP-47319	0076	0093	2 IV AI-24VT	21800	Y48		
☐ UR-26111	Antonov 26B	12108	CCCP-26111	0082	0093	2 IV AI-24VT	24000	Frtr / Y19		
☐ UR-26143	Antonov 26B	12908	CCCP-26143	0083	0093	2 IV AI-24VT	24000	Frtr / Y19		
☐ UR-26201	Antonov 26B	14005	CCCP-26200	0085	0093	2 IV AI-24VT	24000	Frtr / Y19		
☐ UR-26202	Antonov 26B	14009	CCCP-26202	0085	0093	2 IV AI-24VT	24000	Frtr / Y19		
☐ UR-26203	Antonov 26B	14010	CCCP-26203	0085	0093	2 IV AI-24VT	24000	Frtr / Y19		UN964 / opf UN
☐ UR-26580	Antonov 26B	13408	TC-GZT	0084	0093	2 IV AI-24VT	24000	Frtr / Y19		UN182 / opf UN
☐ UR-26586	Antonov 26B	13805	CCCP-26586	0084	0093	2 IV AI-24VT	24000	Frtr / Y19		

ANTONOV AIRLINES = ADB (Avialinii Antonova) (Division of Antonov Design Bureau) — **Kiev-Gostomel**

Ul. Tupoleva 1, 252062 Kiev, Ukraine ☎ (44) 443 00 18 Tx: 131309 mirav su Fax: (44) 442 61 24 SITA: IEVANGS
F: 1989 ⁂ n/a Head: Anatoly G. Bulanenko ICAO: ANTONOV Net: n/a International cargo services are jointly marketed/operated with AIRFOYLE, Ltd (G-). For administration details see under that company.

☐ UR-46521	Antonov 24B	67302309	LZ-SFP	0066	0098	2 IV AI-24	22500	Y48		
☐ UR-48097	Antonov 24RV	57310409	CCCP-48097	0075	0089	2 IV AI-24VT	22500	Y48		
☐ UR-13395	Antonov 26	2605	CCCP-13395	0075	0089	2 IV AI-24VT	24000	Freighter		
☐ UR-48004	Antonov 32	1306		0086	0092	2 IV AI-20D	27000	Freighter		
☐ UR-48093	Antonov 32	0703	CCCP-48093	0086	0092	2 IV AI-20D	27000	Freighter		
☐ UR-74010	Antonov 74T	36547030450	CCCP-74010	0087	0098	2 LO D-36	34500	Freighter		
☐ UR-11315	Antonov 12BP	4342307	CCCP-11315	0064	0093	4 IV AI-20M	64000	Freighter		
☐ UR-11322	Antonov 12P	0901409	EW-11322	0060	0095	4 IV AI-20M	61000	Freighter		lsf VGS
☐ UR-11765	Antonov 12B	401705	LZ-SFM	0063	0098	4 IV AI-20M	64000	Freighter		
☐ UR-21510	Antonov 12AP	0901404		0060	0094	4 IV AI-20M	64000	Freighter		
☐ UR-09307	Antonov 22A	043481244	CCCP-09307	0074	0094	4 KU NK-12MA	225000	Freighter		
☐ UR-82007	Antonov 124-100 Ruslan	19530501005	CCCP-82007	0087	0089	4 LO D-18T	392000	Freighter		fn 01-05
☐ UR-82008	Antonov 124-100 Ruslan	19530501006	CCCP-82008	0086	0089	4 LO D-18T	392000	Freighter		fn 01-06
☐ UR-82009	Antonov 124-100 Ruslan	19530501007	CCCP-82009	0087	0089	4 LO D-18T	392000	Freighter		fn 01-08
☐ UR-82027	Antonov 124-100 Ruslan	19530502288	CCCP-82027	0090	0090	4 LO D-18T	392000	Freighter		fn 02-08
☐ UR-82029	Antonov 124-100 Ruslan	19530502630	CCCP-82029	0091	0091	4 LO D-18T	392000	Freighter		fn 02-10
☐ UR-82066	Antonov 124-100 Ruslan	19530502761	CCCP-82066	0092	0097	4 LO D-18T	392000	Freighter		fn 03-01
☐ UR-82060	Antonov 225 Mriya		CCCP-82060	0088	0089	6 LO D-18T	600000	Frtr/Shuttle-Tr		fn 01-01/Prototype / std Kiev-Gostomel

ARTEM-AVIA = ABA — **Kiev-Zhulyany**

Ul. Melnikova 2/10, 254050 Kiev, Ukraine ☎ (44) 213 20 97 Tx: none Fax: (44) 213 20 19 SITA: n/a
F: 1970 ⁂ n/a Head: Yuri D. Khokhlov ICAO: ARTEM-AVIA Net: n/a

☐ UR-26094	Antonov 26B	12706	CCCP-26094	0082	0082	2 IV AI-24VT	24000	Freighter		lst IVN
☐ UR-26214	Antonov 26B	14403	CCCP-26214	0086	0086	2 IV AI-24VT	24000	Freighter		lst UKL
☐ UR-26215	Antonov 26	4707	CCCP-26215	0077	0077	2 IV AI-24VT	24000	Freighter		
☐ UR-26216	Antonov 26	10704	CCCP-26216	0081	0081	2 IV AI-24VT	24000	Freighter		

AS Aviakompania, Joint-Stock Company = AOO — **Borodyanka**

Borodyanka Airport, 255770 Borodyanka, (Kiev Region), Ukraine ☎ (4477) 52 769 Tx: none Fax: (4477) 51 702 SITA: n/a
F: 1997 ⁂ n/a Head: Alexander K. Badurdinov ICAO: COMPANY AS Net: n/a Aircraft below MTOW 1361kg: Yakovlev 52

☐ UR-BEM	Yakovlev 18T	22202044533		0084	0097	1 VO M-14P	1650	Utility		
☐ UR-BEN	Yakovlev 18T	22202044541		0081	0097	1 VO M-14P	1650	Utility		
☐ UR-BEO	Yakovlev 18T	22202044261		0084	0097	1 VO M-14P	1650	Utility		
☐ UR-19333	Kamov Ka-26	7303409		0073	0097	2 VE M-14V-26	3250	Utility		
☐ UR-19391	Kamov Ka-26	7202805		0072	0097	2 VE M-14V-26	3250	Utility		
☐ UR-19474	Kamov Ka-26	7303903		0073	0097	2 VE M-14V-26	3250	Utility		
☐ UR-14302	PZL Swidnik (Mil) Mi-2	546042039	HA-BFI	0097	0097	2 IS GTD-350-4	3550	Utility		
☐ UR-35544	PZL Mielec (Antonov) An-2	1G114-56		0070	0097	1 SH ASh-62IR	5250	Utility		
☐ UR-56506	PZL Mielec (Antonov) An-2	1G183-04		0079	0097	1 SH ASh-62IR	5250	Utility		
☐ UR-68051	PZL Mielec (Antonov) An-2	1G193-23		0081	0097	1 SH ASh-62IR	5250	Utility		
☐ UR-70281	PZL Mielec (Antonov) An-2	1G139-40		0072	0097	1 SH ASh-62IR	5250	Utility		
☐ UR-BEJ	PZL Mielec (Antonov) An-2	1G172-46		0076	0097	1 SH ASh-62IR	5250	Utility		
☐ UR-BEL	PZL Mielec (Antonov) An-2	1G165-15		0075	0097	1 SH ASh-62IR	5500	Utility		
☐ UR-87405	Yakovlev 40	9421733	RA-87405	0074	0097	3 IV AI-25	16800	Y36		

ATI Aircompany = TII — **Kiev**

Ul. Yanvarskogo vosstania 17/2, 252015 Kiev, Ukraine ☎ (44) 290 40 78 Tx: none Fax: (44) 290 40 78 SITA: IEVAA8X
F: 1995 ⁂ n/a Head: Anatoly I. Levin ICAO: AIRATI Net: n/a

☐ UR-76629	Ilyushin 76MD	0053458745	CCCP-76629	0085	0097	4 SO D-30KP	190000	Freighter		
☐ UR-76700	Ilyushin 76MD	0063471134	CCCP-76700	0086	0097	4 SO D-30KP	190000	Freighter		
☐ UR-76716	Ilyushin 76MD	0073474211		0287	0097	4 SO D-30KP	190000	Freighter		
☐ UR-76759	Ilyushin 76MD	0083485558		0888	0097	4 SO D-30KP	190000	Freighter		cvtd 78
☐ UR-76767	Ilyushin 76MD	0083487598		0988	0097	4 SO D-30KP	190000	Freighter		cvtd 78
☐ UR-76777	Ilyushin 76TD	0083482490	CCCP-76777	0288	0097	4 SO D-30KP	190000	Freighter		
☐ UR-78752	Ilyushin 76MD	0083483519	CCCP-78752	0388	0097	4 SO D-30KP	190000	Freighter		
☐ UR-78758	Ilyushin 76MD	0083484551	CCCP-78758	0488	0097	4 SO D-30KP	190000	Freighter		
☐ UR-78772	Ilyushin 76MD	0083487627	CCCP-78772	1088	0097	4 SO D-30KP	190000	Freighter		

AVIAKOMPANIA TRANSAVIA – A.T. (Transavia Air Company) — **Kirovograd**

Ul. Poltavskaya 71, 316015 Kirovograd, Ukraine ☎ (522) 24 79 52 Tx: n/a Fax: (522) 24 79 11 SITA: n/a
F: n/a ⁂ n/a Head: Arkady G. Molodozhonov Net: n/a

☐ UR-49260	Antonov 26				0093	2 IV AI-24VT	24000	Freighter		
☐ UR-48012	Antonov 32B			0093	0093	2 IV AI-20D	27000	Freighter		

AVIANT – Kiev Aviation Plant = UAK (Kievski aviatsionny zavod AVIANT) — **Kiev-Gostomel & -Zhulyany**

Prospekt Peremogy 100, 252062 Kiev, Ukraine ☎ (44) 441 53 46 Tx: none Fax: (44) 442 62 13 SITA: n/a
F: 1993 ⁂ n/a Head: Alexander I. Kharlov ICAO: AVIATION PLANT Net: n/a

☐ UR-26175	Antonov 24RV	77310810A	CCCP-26175	0078		2 IV AI-24VT	21800	Y36		
☐ UR-46777	Antonov 24B	77301504	CCCP-46777	0067		2 IV AI-24	21000	C25 or Y36		
☐ UR-26194	Antonov 26	0202	CCCP-26194	0070		2 IV AI-24VT	24000	Freighter 5,4t		
☐ UR-79165	Antonov 26	5409		0077		2 IV AI-24VT	24000	Freighter 5,4t		
☐ UR-48016	Antonov 32B	3206		0093		2 IV AI-20D	27000	Freighter 6,7t		
☐ UR-48017	Antonov 32B	3302		0093		2 IV AI-20D	27000	Freighter 6,7t		
☐ UR-48047	Antonov 32B		RA-48047	0090	0097	2 IV AI-20D	27000	Tanker		
☐ UR-48081	Antonov 32B	3106	CCCP-48081	0091		2 IV AI-20D	27000	Freighter 6,7t		
☐ UR-48083	Antonov 32P	3001	CCCP-48083	0091		2 IV AI-20D	29700	Tanker/Frtr 8t		
☐ UR-48084	Antonov 32A	2602	CCCP-48084	0091		2 IV AI-20D	27000	Freighter 6,7t		
☐ UR-48085	Antonov 32A	2603	CCCP-48085	0091		2 IV AI-20D	27000	Freighter 6,7t		
☐ UR-48086	Antonov 32P	2901	CCCP-48086	0091		2 IV AI-20D	29700	Tanker/Frtr 8t		
☐ UR-48087	Antonov 32B	2904	CCCP-48087	0091		2 IV AI-20D	27000	Freighter 6,7t		
☐ UR-48125	Antonov 32A	2604	CCCP-48125	0091		2 IV AI-20D	27000	Freighter 6,7t		

AVIRCITI, Ltd = VTI (Ukrainian-Russian joint venture company) — **Odessa-Central**

Pr. Marshala Zhukova 32a, 270121 Odessa, Ukraine ☎ (482) 68 47 38 Tx: none Fax: (482) 68 33 23 SITA: n/a
F: 1996 ⁂ n/a Head: Nikolai P. Kritsov ICAO: AVIRCITI Net: n/a

☐ UR-11961	Antonov 12BP	2340403	CCCP-11961	0062	0096	4 IV AI-20M	61000	Freighter		

AVIS – Avia Service International = AIO — **Donetsk**

Ul. Universitetskaya 71, 340048 Donetsk, Ukraine ☎ (622) 93 81 77 Tx: 115199 senat su Fax: (622) 37 86 19 SITA: n/a
F: 1996 ⁂ n/a Head: Alexander V. Kutsev ICAO: AVIS Net: n/a

☐ UR-CCD	Dassault Falcon 20C	112	CS-ATF	0067	0097	2 GE CF700-2D2	12400	Executive		

AZOV-AVIA Aircompany = AZV — **Melitopol**

Airport 7-219, 332307 Melitopol, Ukraine ☎ (6142) 58 739 Tx: none Fax: (6142) 58 739 SITA: n/a
F: 1996 ⁂ n/a Head: Igor K. Konovalov ICAO: AZOV AVIA Net: n/a

☐ UR-76656	Ilyushin 76MD	0053463891	CCCP-76656	0085	0096	4 SO D-30KP	190000	Freighter		
☐ UR-76715	Ilyushin 76MD		CCCP-76715	0086	1296	4 SO D-30KP	190000	Freighter		

614 registration type of aircraft cn/fn ex/ex* mfd del powered by mtow kg configuration selcal name/fln/specialitites/remarks

CABI = CBI (Connection Aviation Business Information dba)
Donetsk

Ul. Universitetskaya 71, 340048 Donetsk, Ukraine ☎ (622) 92 12 94 Tx: none Fax: (622) 55 42 29 SITA: n/a
F: 1995 ⋏⋏⋏ Head: Yevgeni Glod ICAO: CABI Net: n/a

	registration	type of aircraft	cn/fn	ex/ex*	mfd	del	powered by	mtow kg	configuration	selcal	name/fln/remarks
☐	UR-CCA	Dassault Falcon 20F	256	F-GKME	0071	1294	2 GE CF700-2D2	13000	Executive		
☐	UR-CCB	Dassault Falcon 20C-5	141	F-BIHY	0068	0395	2 GA TFE731-5AR-2C	13200	Executive		cvtd 20C
☐	UR-CCC	Dassault Falcon 50	235	F-GKRU	0093	0195	3 GA TFE731-3-1C	17800	Executive		
☐	UR-74057	Antonov 74-200	36547098960		0093	0098	2 LO D-36	37500	Combi		

CHAIKA Aircompany = CHJ
Kiev

Ul. 50-letia Oktyabrya, 252162 Kiev, Ukraine ☎ (44) 476 09 92 Tx: none Fax: (44) 476 09 92 SITA: n/a
F: 1996 ⋏⋏⋏ n/a Head: Igor A. Polyakov ICAO: AIR CHAIKA Net: n/a Aircraft below MTOW 1361kg: PZL-104 Wilga 35A & Yakovlev 52

	registration	type of aircraft	cn/fn	ex/ex*	mfd	del	powered by	mtow kg	configuration	selcal	name/fln/remarks
☐	UR-BEY	PZL Mielec (Antonov) An-2			0075	0096	1 SH ASh-62IR	5500	Sprayer		
☐	UR-28808	PZL Mielec (Antonov) An-28	1AJ002-06	CCCP-28808	0085	0096	2 GS TVD-10B	6500	Executive		
☐	UR-22406	Mil Mi-8			0077	0098	2 IS TV2-117A	12000	Utility		opf UN
☐	UR-87266	Yakovlev 40	9310227	RA-87266	0073	0096	3 IV AI-25	16800	Y36		
☐	UR-87814	Yakovlev 40	9230524	RA-87814	0072	0096	3 IV AI-25	16800	Exec C14		

CHERNOVTSY AVIATION ENTERPRISE (Chernovtskoe aviapredpriatie) (Division of Air Ukraine / formerly Chernovtsy division of Aeroflot Ukraine directorate)
Chernovtsy

Ul. Chkalova 30, 274009 Chernovtsy, Ukraine ☎ (3722) 43 211 Tx: none Fax: (3722) 43 211 SITA: n/a
F: n/a ⋏⋏⋏ n/a Head: n/a Net: n/a Operates Let 410 & Tupolev 134A aircraft in AIR UKRAINE colors. For fleet details – see under AIR UKRAINE. Aircraft are marked opb Chernovtsy Aviation Enterprise.

COLUMBUS AVIA = CBS
Kiev-Zhulyany

Solomenskaya 16, 252110 Kiev, Ukraine ☎ (44) 277 80 43 Tx: none Fax: (44) 277 81 23 SITA: n/a
F: 1992 ⋏⋏⋏ n/a Head: Alexander Blokhin ICAO: COLUMBUS AVIA Net: n/a

	registration	type of aircraft	cn/fn	ex/ex*	mfd	del	powered by	mtow kg	configuration	selcal	name/fln/remarks
☐	UR-87308	Yakovlev 40	9320429	CCCP-87308	0073		3 IV AI-25	16800	Y32		
☐	UR-87432	Yakovlev 40	9420835	CCCP-87432	0074		3 IV AI-25	16800	Y32		

CONSTANTA Airlines = UZA (Konstanta Aviakompania)
Zaporozhye

Zaporozhye Airport, 310013 Zaporozhye, Ukraine ☎ (612) 64 40 18 Tx: none Fax: (612) 68 84 23 SITA: n/a
F: 1998 ⋏⋏⋏ n/a Head: Yevgeni K. Kozenko ICAO: CONSTANTA Net: n/a Some aircraft are still in former AIR UKRAINE-colors & titles but will be repainte in due course.

	registration	type of aircraft	cn/fn	ex/ex*	mfd	del	powered by	mtow kg	configuration	selcal	name/fln/remarks
☐	UR-87389	Yakovlev 40	9410133	CCCP-87389	0274	0098	3 IV AI-25	16800	Y36		
☐	UR-87463	Yakovlev 40	9430237	CCCP-87463	0874	0098	3 IV AI-25	16800	Y36		
☐	UR-87512	Yakovlev 40	9521440	CCCP-87512	0575	0098	3 IV AI-25	16800	Y36		
☐	UR-87547	Yakovlev 40	9531242	CCCP-87547	0875	0098	3 IV AI-25	16800	Y36		
☐	UR-87660	Yakovlev 40	9240425	CCCP-87660	1172	0098	3 IV AI-25	16800	Y27		
☐	UR-87806	Yakovlev 40	9231223	CCCP-87806	0772	0098	3 IV AI-25	16000	Y27		
☐	UR-87998	Yakovlev 40	9540245	CCCP-87998	0176	0098	3 IV AI-25	16800	F12		lst UAR
☐	UR-48053	Antonov 32	2803		0592	0098	2 IV AI-20D	27000	Freighter		
☐	UR-48054	Antonov 32	2804	CCCP-48054	0592	0098	2 IV AI-20D	27000	Freighter		
☐	UR-48055	Antonov 32	2805	CCCP-48055	0592	0098	2 IV AI-20D	27000	Freighter		

CRIMEA AIR = OR / CRF (Aviakompania Krim)
Simferopol

Tsentralny Airport, 333009 Simferopol, (Krim), Ukraine ☎ (652) 29 55 55 Tx: none Fax: (652) 27 22 88 SITA: n/a
F: 1993 ⋏⋏⋏ 2000 Head: Vladimir I. Kazanovsky IATA: 107 ICAO: CRIMEA AIR Net: n/a Beside aircraft listed, also leases Tupolev 154 & Yakovlev 42 from AIR UKRAINE when required.

	registration	type of aircraft	cn/fn	ex/ex*	mfd	del	powered by	mtow kg	configuration	selcal	name/fln/remarks
☐	UR-46477	Antonov 24RV	27308005		0072		2 IV AI-24VT	21800	Y48		
☐	UR-46622	Antonov 24RV	37308709	TC-JUZ	0073		2 IV AI-24VT	21800	C36		
☐	UR-46647	Antonov 24RV	37309107	CCCP-46647	0073		2 IV AI-24VT	21800	Y48		
☐	UR-46675	Antonov 24RV	47309607	CCCP-46675	0074		2 IV AI-24VT	21800	C36		
☐	UR-46688	Antonov 24RV	47309805	CCCP-46688	0074		2 IV AI-24VT	21800	Y48		
☐	UR-46833	Antonov 24RV	17306710	CCCP-46833	0071		2 IV AI-24VT	21800	Y48		
☐	UR-47256	Antonov 24RV	27307708	CCCP-47256	0072		2 IV AI-24VT	21800	Y48		
☐	UR-47265	Antonov 24RV	27307807	CCCP-47265	0072		2 IV AI-24VT	21800	Y48		
☐	UR-47296	Antonov 24RV	07306609	CCCP-47296	0070		2 IV AI-24VT	21800	C36		
☐	UR-42330	Yakovlev 42	4520422505122	RA-42330	0085	0199	3 LO D-36	54000	Y120		
☐	UR-42343	Yakovlev 42D	4520421708285	RA-42343	0087	0098	3 LO D-36	57500	Y120		cvtd 42

CRIMEA UNIVERSAL AVIA = KRM
Simferopol-Zavodskoe

Ul. Aeroflotskaya 5, 333021 Simferopol, (Crimea), Ukraine ☎ (652) 27 60 66 Tx: 222427 Fax: (652) 44 12 89 SITA: n/a
F: 1998 ⋏⋏⋏ n/a Head: Alexander Kovtun ICAO: TRANS-UNIVERSAL Net: n/a

	registration	type of aircraft	cn/fn	ex/ex*	mfd	del	powered by	mtow kg	configuration	selcal	name/fln/remarks
☐	UR-14090	PZL Swidnik (Mil) Mi-2	5210649078	CCCP-14090	0088	0098	2 IS GTD-350-4	3550	Sprayer		
☐	UR-14137	PZL Swidnik (Mil) Mi-2	5210909049	CCCP-14137	0089	0098	2 IS GTD-350-4	3550	Sprayer		
☐	UR-14222	PZL Swidnik (Mil) Mi-2	5211109010	CCCP-14222	0090	0098	2 IS GTD-350-4	3550	Sprayer		
☐	UR-20396	PZL Swidnik (Mil) Mi-2	5298443076	CCCP-20396	0086	0098	2 IS GTD-350-4	3550	Sprayer		
☐	UR-20769	PZL Swidnik (Mil) Mi-2	517806082	CCCP-20769	0082	0098	2 IS GTD-350-4	3550	Sprayer		
☐	UR-33512	PZL Mielec (Antonov) An-2	1G229-04	CCCP-33512	0088	0098	1 SH ASh-62IR	5250	Sprayer		
☐	UR-33516	PZL Mielec (Antonov) An-2	1G229-08	CCCP-33516	0088	0098	1 SH ASh-62IR	5250	Sprayer		
☐	UR-33639	PZL Mielec (Antonov) An-2	1G233-29	CCCP-33639	0088	0098	1 SH ASh-62IR	5250	Sprayer		
☐	UR-33640	PZL Mielec (Antonov) An-2	1G233-30	CCCP-33640	0088	0098	1 SH ASh-62IR	5250	Sprayer		
☐	UR-33641	PZL Mielec (Antonov) An-2	1G233-31	CCCP-33641	0088	0098	1 SH ASh-62IR	5250	Sprayer		
☐	UR-40435	PZL Mielec (Antonov) An-2	1G224-04	CCCP-40435	0087	0098	1 SH ASh-62IR	5250	Sprayer		
☐	UR-82895	PZL Mielec (Antonov) An-2	1G169-12	CCCP-82895	0076	0098	1 SH ASh-62IR	5250	Sprayer		
☐	UR-25444	Mil Mi-8MTV-1	95583	CCCP-25444	0090	0098	2 IS TV3-117MT	13000	Utility		
☐	UR-25514	Mil Mi-8MTV-1	95662	CCCP-25514	0091	0098	2 IS TV3-117MT	13000	Utility		

DESNA = DSN
Chernigov

Chernigov Airport, 250012 Chernigov, Ukraine ☎ (4622) 73 145 Tx: n/a Fax: (4622) 44 037 SITA: n/a
F: 1995 ⋏⋏⋏ n/a Head: Yuri D. Sidorov ICAO: DESNA Net: n/a Operates passenger & cargo flights with Antonov 2/24/28/74 aircraft, leased from other companies when required.

DNIPROAVIA, Joint-Stock Company = Z6 / UDN (Dnepr Air) (Subsidiary of Air Ukraine / formerly Dnieproavia)
Dnepropetrovsk

Dnepropetrovsk Airport, 320042 Dnepropetrovsk, Ukraine ☎ (562) 65 18 18 Tx: 143576 sprut Fax: (562) 65 04 96 SITA: DNKIRZ6
F: 1991 ⋏⋏⋏ 1300 Head: Mikhail V. Demidenko IATA: 181 ICAO: DNIPRO Net: n/a

	registration	type of aircraft	cn/fn	ex/ex*	mfd	del	powered by	mtow kg	configuration	selcal	name/fln/remarks
☐	UR-87528	Yakovlev 40	9521041	CCCP-87528	0075	0091	3 IV AI-25	17200	Y30		
☐	UR-87841	Yakovlev 40	9330930	CCCP-87841	0073	0091	3 IV AI-25	16800	Y30		
☐	UR-87918	Yakovlev 40	9730855	CCCP-87918	0077	0091	3 IV AI-25	17200	Y32		
☐	UR-88203	Yakovlev 40	9630549	CCCP-88203	0076	0091	3 IV AI-25	16800	Y32		
☐	UR-88237	Yakovlev 40	9640751	CCCP-88237	0076	0091	3 IV AI-25	17200	Y32		
☐	UR-42376	Yakovlev 42D	4520424914477	CCCP-42376	0090	0091	3 LO D-36	56500	Y120		
☐	UR-42405	Yakovlev 42D	4520423116624	CCCP-42405	0091	0091	3 LO D-36	56500	Y120		
☐	UR-42409	Yakovlev 42D	4520421216709	CCCP-42409	0392	0092	3 LO D-36	56500	C12Y84		lst MLV as ER-42409
☐	UR-42410	Yakovlev 42D	4520421219029	CCCP-42410	0092	0092	3 LO D-36	56500	Y120		lst CPN as EP-CPB
☐	UR-42416	Yakovlev 42D	4520423219102	EP-CPA	0092	0092	3 LO D-36	56500	Y120		lst CPN as EP-CPE
☐	UR-42419	Yakovlev 42D	4520423201016	CCCP-42419	0093	0093	3 LO D-36	56500	Y120		
☐	UR-42426	Yakovlev 42D	4520423304016	TC-IYI	0093	0093	3 LO D-36	56500	C12Y84		
☐	UR-42449	Yakovlev 42D	4520421401018	CCCP-42449	0094	0094	3 LO D-36	56500	Y120		lst CPN as EP-CPC

DONBASS AIR LINES = UDD
Donetsk

Donetsk Airport, 340021 Donetsk, Ukraine ☎ (622) 51 57 73 Tx: none Fax: (622) 51 56 27 SITA: n/a
F: n/a ⋏⋏⋏ n/a Head: Viktor Frolov ICAO: DONBASS Net: n/a

	registration	type of aircraft	cn/fn	ex/ex*	mfd	del	powered by	mtow kg	configuration	selcal	name/fln/remarks
☐	UR-85701	Tupolev 154M	876	CCCP-85701	0091		3 SO D-30KU-154-II	100000	Y164		

DONBASS-EASTERN UKRAINIAN AIRLINES = 7D / UDC
Donetsk

Donetsk Airport, 340021 Donetsk, Ukraine ☎ (622) 51 56 21 Tx: none Fax: (622) 55 53 47 SITA: n/a
F: 1998 ⋏⋏⋏ n/a Head: n/a IATA: 897 ICAO: AVIATION DONBASS Net: n/a Some aircraft are still in former Air Ukraine-colors & titles but will be repainted in due course.

	registration	type of aircraft	cn/fn	ex/ex*	mfd	del	powered by	mtow kg	configuration	selcal	name/fln/remarks
☐	UR-46251	Antonov 24B	77303303	CCCP-46251	0067	0098	2 IV AI-24-II	21000	Y48		
☐	UR-46279	Antonov 24B	77303702	CCCP-46279	0067	0098	2 IV AI-24-II	21000	Y48		
☐	UR-46302	Antonov 24B	97305202	CCCP-46302	0069	0098	2 IV AI-24-II	21000	Y48		
☐	UR-46416	Antonov 24B	87304101	CCCP-46416	0068	0098	2 IV AI-24-II	21000	Y48		
☐	UR-46585	Antonov 24B	97305004	CCCP-46585	0069	0098	2 IV AI-24-II	21000	Y48		
☐	UR-46586	Antonov 24B	97305006	CCCP-46586	0067	0098	2 IV AI-24-II	21000	Y48		
☐	UR-47846	Antonov 24B	17307408	CCCP-47846	0071	0098	2 IV AI-24-II	21000	Y48		
☐	UR-42308	Yakovlev 42	11040303	RA-42308	0081	0098	3 LO D-36	54000	Y120		
☐	UR-42310	Yakovlev 42	11040403	CCCP-42310	0081	0098	3 LO D-36	54000	Y120		
☐	UR-42318	Yakovlev 42	4520423402051	RA-42318	0084	0098	3 LO D-36	54000	Y120		
☐	UR-42319	Yakovlev 42	4520423402062	CCCP-42319	0084	0098	3 LO D-36	54000	Y120		
☐	UR-42327	Yakovlev 42	4520424402161	RA-42327	0085	0098	3 LO D-36	54000	Y120		
☐	UR-42348	Yakovlev 42	4520423711342	CCCP-42348	0087	0098	3 LO D-36	54000	Y120		
☐	UR-42366	Yakovlev 42	4520421814047	CCCP-42366	0089	0098	3 LO D-36	54000	Y120		
☐	UR-42372	Yakovlev 42D	4520423914266	CCCP-42372	0089	0098	3 LO D-36	56500	Y120		
☐	UR-42377	Yakovlev 42D	4520421014479	CCCP-42377	0090	0098	3 LO D-36	56500	Y120		
☐	UR-42381	Yakovlev 42D	4520422014576	CCCP-42381	0090	0098	3 LO D-36	56500	Y120		
☐	UR-42383	Yakovlev 42D	4520422016201	CCCP-42383	0090	0098	3 LO D-36	56500	Y120		lst BON as T9-ABD
☐	UR-42530	Yakovlev 42	11120204	CCCP-42530	0081	0098	3 LO D-36	54000	Y120		

615 registration   type of aircraft   cn/fn   ex/ex*   mfd   del   powered by   mtow kg   configuration   selcal   name/fln/specialitites/remarks

ICAR AIRLINES – Independent Carrier = C3 / IPR (Ikar) — Kharkov

Ul. Frunze 87/89, 254008 Kiev, Ukraine ☎ (44) 417 26 04 Tx: none Fax: (44) 462 59 92 SITA: n/a
F: 1993 ⚉ 145 Head: Viktor A. Vershigora IATA: 655 ICAO: AIR ICAR Net: n/a

☐ UR-67472	Let 410UVP	841237	CCCP-67472	0084	0096	2 WA M-601D	5800	Y15		lsf Kharkov Aviation Production Assoc.
☐ UR-98104	Antonov 24RV	67302310	CCCP-98104	0066	0096	2 IV AI-24VT	21800	Y48		lsf Kharkov Aviation Production Assoc.
☐ UR-PWA	Antonov 24B	67302608	RA-46820	0066	0098	2 IV AI-24	21000	Y48		
☐ UR-74007	Antonov 74-200	36547095903	HK-3809X	0592	0095	2 LO D-36	36500	Freighter 10t		lsf Kharkov Aviation Prod. / fn 1406
☐ UR-11819	Antonov 12B	6344009		0066	0095	4 IV AI-20M	61000	Freighter 18t		lsf Kharkov Aviation Production Assoc.
☐ UR-PWH	Antonov 12BP	6343707		0066	0098	4 IV AI-20M	61000	Freighter 18t		

INTERAVIATRANS, Ltd = IVT — Poltava

52 Shevchenko Street, 314000 Poltava, Ukraine ☎ (5322) 29 726 Tx: none Fax: (5322) 29 726 SITA: n/a
F: 1996 ⚉ 12 Head: Alexander G. Ionov ICAO: INTERAVIA Net: n/a

☐ UR-62569	PZL Mielec (Antonov) An-2	1G176-38	CCCP-62569	0077	0097	1 SH ASh-62IR	5500	Utility		

KHARKOV AVIATION PRODUCTION ASSOCIATION = WKH (Kharkovskoe aviatsionnoe proizvodstvennoe ob'yedinenie) (Flying div.of Kharkov Aviation [illegible]) — Kharkov

Flying division / letny otryad, Ul. Sumskaya 134, 310023 Kharkov, Ukraine ☎ (572) 47 42 74 Tx: n/a Fax: (572) 47 80 01 SITA: n/a
F: 1960 ⚉ n/a Head: Anatoly S. Nestertsov ICAO: WEST-KHARKOV Net: n/a Operates corporate flights for itself & commercial charter flights.

☐ UR-67472	Let 410UVP	841237	CCCP-67472	0084		2 WA M-601D	5800	Y14		lst IPR
☐ UR-46336	Antonov 24T	8910709	CCCP-46336	0068		2 IV AI-24VT	22500	Combi		
☐ UR-98104	Antonov 24RV	67302310	CCCP-98104	0066		2 IV AI-24VT	21800	Y48		lst IPR
☐ UR-26198	Antonov 26	5209	CCCP-26198	0084		2 IV AI-24VT	24000	Freighter		
☐ UR-26596	Antonov 26		CCCP-26596	0083		2 IV AI-24VT	24000	Freighter		
☐ UR-74007	Antonov 74-200	36547095903	HK-3809X	0592		2 LO D-36	36500	Freighter		lst IPR / fn 1406
☐ UR-74038	Antonov 74TK	36547097933		0093		2 LO D-36	36000	Freighter		
☐ UR-11819	Antonov 12B	6344009		0066		4 IV AI-20M	61000	Freighter		lst IPR
☐ UR-11833	Antonov 12BP	3341008	CCCP-11833	0063		4 IV AI-20M	61000	Freighter		

KHMELNITSKY AVIATION ENTERPRISE (Khmelnitskoe aviapredpriatie) (Division of Air Ukraine / formerly Khmelnitsky division of Aeroflot Ukraine directorate) — Khmelnitsky

Khmelnitsky Airport, 280000 Khmelnitsky, Ukraine ☎ (3822) 65 170 Tx: none Fax: (3822) 68 284 SITA: n/a
F: n/a ⚉ n/a Head: n/a Net: n/a Operates Antonov 26 & Let 410 aircraft in AIR UKRAINE colors. For fleet details – see under AIR UKRAINE. Aircraft are marked opb Khmelnitsky Aviation Enterprise.

KHORS Aircompany = X9 / KHO (Associated with Hungarian-Ukrainian Heavy Lift, Ltd) — Kiev

Bulvar Lesi Ukrainki 34, 253133 Kiev, Ukraine ☎ (44) 294 97 33 Tx: none Fax: (44) 294 98 11 SITA: n/a
F: 1990 ⚉ n/a Head: Anatoly F. Vysochansky IATA: 852 ICAO: AIRCOMPANY KHORS Net: n/a

☐ UR-46403	Antonov 24B	77303906	CCCP-46403	0067		2 IV AI-24-II	21800	Combi / Y30		
☐ UR-11332	Antonov 12BP	4342202	84 BLUE	0064		4 IV AI-20M	61000	Freighter		
☐ UR-UAA	Antonov 12BP	6344701		0066	0798	4 IV AI-20M	61000	Freighter		
☐ UR-76396	Ilyushin 76MD	0043451508	CCCP-76586	0084		4 SO D-30KP	190000	Freighter		
☐ UR-76397	Ilyushin 76MD	0043451517	CCCP-76587	0084		4 SO D-30KP	190000	Freighter		
☐ UR-76437	Ilyushin 76MD	0083484527	CCCP-76437	0088		4 SO D-30KP	190000	Freighter		
☐ UR-76438	Ilyushin 76TD	0083483513		0088		4 SO D-30KP	190000	Freighter		cvtd 76MD / ex EcoPatrol-colors
☐ UR-78775	Ilyushin 76MD	0083489647	CCCP-78775	0088		4 SO D-30KP	190000	Freighter		

KREMENCHUG FLIGHT SCHOOL (Kremenchugsky letny kolledzh) — Kremenchug-Bol. Kokhnovka

Ul. Pobedy 17/6, 315320 Kremenchug, (Poltava Region), Ukraine ☎ (5366) 31 028 Tx: 164520 almaz Fax: (532) 50 14 23 SITA: n/a
F: 1960 ⚉ n/a Head: Peter Kondratenko Net: n/a

☐ UR-20216	PZL Swidnik (Mil) Mi-2	547005011		0081	0081	2 IS GTD-350-4	3550	Y7		
☐ UR-20217	PZL Swidnik (Mil) Mi-2	547006011		0081	0081	2 IS GTD-350-4	3550	Trainer		
☐ UR-20219	PZL Swidnik (Mil) Mi-2	537008011		0081	0081	2 IS GTD-350-4	3550	Utility		
☐ UR-20221	PZL Swidnik (Mil) Mi-2	537010011		0081	0081	2 IS GTD-350-4	3550	Utility		
☐ UR-20222	PZL Swidnik (Mil) Mi-2	547011011		0081	0081	2 IS GTD-350-4	3550	Trainer		
☐ UR-20838	PZL Swidnik (Mil) Mi-2	548119033		0083	0083	2 IS GTD-350-4	3550	Utility		
☐ UR-20839	PZL Swidnik (Mil) Mi-2	548120043		0083	0083	2 IS GTD-350-4	3550	Utility		
☐ UR-20841	PZL Swidnik (Mil) Mi-2	548122043		0083	0083	2 IS GTD-350-4	3550	Y7		
☐ UR-23357	PZL Swidnik (Mil) Mi-2	548729064		0084	0085	2 IS GTD-350-4	3550	Y7		
☐ UR-23358	PZL Swidnik (Mil) Mi-2	528730064		0084	0084	2 IS GTD-350-4	3550	Utility		
☐ UR-23535	PZL Swidnik (Mil) Mi-2	546027029		0079	0079	2 IS GTD-350-4	3550	Trainer		
☐ UR-23540	PZL Swidnik (Mil) Mi-2	526032029		0079	0079	2 IS GTD-350-4	3550	Utility		
☐ UR-22234	Mil Mi-8T	6365		0076	0076	2 IS TV2-117A	12000	Trainer		
☐ UR-22283	Mil Mi-8T	6967		0079	0079	2 IS TV2-117A	12000	Utility		
☐ UR-22415	Mil Mi-8T	5107		0075	0075	2 IS TV2-117A	12000	Trainer		
☐ UR-22622	Mil Mi-8T	7969		0080	0080	2 IS TV2-117A	12000	Utility		
☐ UR-22623	Mil Mi-8T	7970		0080	0080	2 IS TV2-117A	12000	Utility		
☐ UR-22642	Mil Mi-8PS	8027	TC-HAK	0081	0083	2 IS TV2-117A	12000	Y24		
☐ UR-22715	Mil Mi-8T	98308422		0083	0083	2 IS TV2-117A	12000	Utility		
☐ UR-22886	Mil Mi-8T	98415987	SP-FSZ	0084	0084	2 IS TV2-117A	12000	Utility		
☐ UR-22887	Mil Mi-8T	98415999		0084	0084	2 IS TV2-117A	12000	Utility		
☐ UR-24444	Mil Mi-8T	98628099		0086	0086	2 IS TV2-117A	12000	Utility		
☐ UR-24558	Mil Mi-8T	98522979		0085	0085	2 IS TV2-117A	12000	Utility		
☐ UR-24604	Mil Mi-8T	8230		0081	0081	2 IS TV2-117A	12000	Utility		
☐ UR-24635	Mil Mi-8PS	8561		0085	0087	2 IS TV2-117A	12000	Y24		lst Doruk Air as TC-HDK
☐ UR-24636	Mil Mi-8PS	8562		0085	0087	2 IS TV2-117A	12000	Y24		lst Doruk Air as TC-HDA
☐ UR-25170	Mil Mi-8MTV-1	95479		0090	0090	2 IS TV3-117MT	13000	Utility		lst Doruk Air as TC-HDB
☐ UR-25852	Mil Mi-8T	5110		0075	0075	2 IS TV2-117A	12000	Trainer		
☐ UR-25855	Mil Mi-8T	5120		0075	0075	2 IS TV2-117A	12000	Trainer		
☐ UR-25899	Mil Mi-8T	5174		0075	0075	2 IS TV2-117A	12000	Trainer		

KRIMAVIAMONTAZH = KRG — Simferopol-Zavodskoe Heliport

Ul. Aeroflotskaya 5, 333021 Simferopol, (Crimea), Ukraine ☎ (652) 44 27 11 Tx: none Fax: (652) 44 27 11 SITA: n/a
F: 1997 ⚉ n/a Head: Alexander P. Stepko ICAO: AVIAMONTAZH Net: n/a

☐ UR-14091	PZL Swidnik (Mil) Mi-2	5210650078	CCCP-14091	0088	0097	2 IS GTD-350-4	3550	Utility		
☐ UR-23277	PZL Swidnik (Mil) Mi-2	529046025	CCCP-23277	0085	0097	2 IS GTD-350-4	3550	Utility		

KROONK Air Agency = KRO — Kiev-Zhulyany

Ul. Leipzigskaya 16, 252015 Kiev, Ukraine ☎ (44) 290 81 20 Tx: none Fax: (44) 290 42 78 SITA: n/a
F: 1993 ⚉ 25 Head: Grigori Bogodisty ICAO: KROONK Net: n/a

☐ UR-26244	Antonov 26	7705	20 BLUE	0078	0095	2 IV AI-24VT	24000	Freighter		
☐ UR-26602	Antonov 26	4407	CCCP-26602	0077	0095	2 IV AI-24VT	24000	Freighter		

KRYLA, Ltd = KRL (Subsidiary of Elektron Concern) — Lvov & Simferopol

Ul. Grabovskogo 11, 290205 Lvov, Ukraine ☎ (322) 97 11 49 Tx: none Fax: (322) 97 11 35 SITA: UKLLKRL
F: 1992 ⚉ n/a Head: Vladimir M. Servetnik ICAO: CITADEL AIR Net: n/a

☐ UR-75475	Ilyushin 18V	184007401	D-AOAQ	0664	0093	4 IV AI-20M	61200	Y110		ex Ber Line/Air Ukraine-colors
☐ UR-75850	Ilyushin 18E	185008503	75711	0965	0092	4 IV AI-20M	61400	Y110orY32&Cargo		

LUGANSK AVIATION ENTERPRISE = LHS (Luganskoe aviapredpriatie) (Division of Air Ukraine / formerly Lugansk division of Aeroflot Ukraine directorate) — Luhansk

Lugansk Airport, 348039 Lugansk, Ukraine ☎ (642) 54 01 01 Tx: none Fax: (642) 50 13 92 SITA: n/a
F: 1946 ⚉ 800 Head: Anatoly V. Nemlikher ICAO: ENTERPRISE LUGANSK Net: n/a Operates Antonov 2/24 & Tupolev 154B aircraft in AIR UKRAINE colors. For fleet details – see under AIR UKRAINE. Aircraft are marked opb Lugansk Aviation Enterprise.

LVOV AIRLINES = UKW (Lvovskie avialinii) (Division of Air Ukraine / formerly Lvov division of Aeroflot Ukraine directorate) — Lvov

Lvov Airport, 290003 Lvov, Ukraine ☎ (322) 69 22 16 Tx: none Fax: (322) 69 22 55 SITA: n/a
F: n/a ⚉ n/a Head: Leonti Zagreva ICAO: UKRAINE WEST Net: n/a Operates An 12/24, Il 76 & Yak 42 aircraft in AIR UKRAINE colors. For fleet details – see under AIR UKRAINE. Aircraft are marked opb Lvov Airlines.

MOTOR SICH Aviakompania = MSI — Zaporozhye

Ul. 8-ogo Marta 15, 330064 Zaporozhye, Ukraine ☎ (612) 61 44 43 Tx: 127435 apo Fax: (612) 64 45 87 SITA: n/a
F: 1984 ⚉ n/a Head: Valentin S. Shirochkin ICAO: MOTOR SICH Net: n/a

☐ UR-06130	Mil Mi-8T	22686		0075	0087	2 IS TV2-117A	12000	Combi		
☐ UR-06131	Mil Mi-8T	22688		0075	0087	2 IS TV2-117A	12000	Combi		
☐ UR-87215	Yakovlev 40	9510540	CCCP-87215	0075	0086	3 IV AI-25	16800	Executive		
☐ UR-88219	Yakovlev 40K	9630550	CCCP-88219	0076	0084	3 IV AI-25	16800	Y30		
☐ UR-46636	Antonov 24RV	37308902	RA-46636	0073	0098	2 IV AI-24VT	22500	Combi		
☐ UR-47258	Antonov 24RV	27307609	RA-47258	0072	0098	2 IV AI-24VT	22500	Combi		
☐ UR-26016	Antonov 26B	10105		0080	0086	2 IV AI-24VT	24000	Combi		
☐ UR-26113	Antonov 26B	12110	CCCP-26113	0082	0087	2 IV AI-24VT	24000	Combi		
☐ UR-26598	Antonov 26B	13905	CCCP-26598	0084	0085	2 IV AI-24VT	24000	Combi / Exec		
☐ UR-74026	Antonov 74-200	36547096919	HK-3810X	1192	0092	2 LO D-36	34800	Combi		fn 1506
☐ UR-11316	Antonov 12BK	9346810	RA-11316	0069	0092	4 IV AI-20M	61000	Freighter		
☐ UR-11528	Antonov 12AP	3341005	CCCP-11528	0063	0092	4 IV AI-20M	61000	Freighter		
☐ UR-13332	Antonov 12B	4341707	82 RED	0064	0092	4 IV AI-20M	61000	Freighter		
☐ UR-48975	Antonov 12A	1400101	CCCP-48975	0061	0090	4 IV AI-20M	61000	Freighter		

616 registration type of aircraft cn/fn ex/ex* mfd del powered by mtow kg configuration selcal name/fln/specialitites/remarks

ODESSA AIRLINES = 5K / ODS (Odeski avialinii)   Odessa-Central

Central Airport, 270054 Odessa, Ukraine ☎ (482) 25 00 52 Tx: none Fax: (482) 65 81 33 SITA: n/a
F: 1996 ⋆⋆⋆ n/a Head: Anatoly P. Rusalenko IATA: 654 ICAO: ODESSA AIR Net: n/a Some aircraft are still in former Air Ukraine colors with or without titles but will be repainted in due course.

	registration	type of aircraft	cn/fn	ex/ex*	mfd	del	powered by	mtow kg	configuration	selcal	name/fln/specialitites/remarks
☐	UR-87237	Yakovlev 40	9530343	CCCP-87237	0075		3 IV AI-25	17200	Y29		
☐	UR-87469	Yakovlev 40	9441437	CCCP-87469	0074		3 IV AI-25	17200	Y29		
☐	UR-87624	Yakovlev 40	9140519	CCCP-87624	0071		3 IV AI-25	17200	Y32		
☐	UR-88299	Yakovlev 40	9321028	OK-BYI	0073		3 IV AI-25	17200	Y27		Ironimpex-titles
☐	UR-85116	Tupolev 154B-1	116	CCCP-85116	0075		3 KU NK-8-2U	98000	Y164		cvtd 154A
☐	UR-85132	Tupolev 154B	132	CCCP-85132	0076		3 KU NK-8-2U	98000	Y164		
☐	UR-85148	Tupolev 154B	148	CCCP-85148	0076		3 KU NK-8-2U	98000	Y164		
☐	UR-85154	Tupolev 154B	154	CCCP-85154	0076		3 KU NK-8-2U	98000	Y164		
☐	UR-85179	Tupolev 154B-1	179	CCCP-85179	0076		3 KU NK-8-2U	98000	Y164		cvtd 154B
☐	UR-85218	Tupolev 154B	218	CCCP-85218	0077		3 KU NK-8-2U	98000	Y164		
☐	UR-85232	Tupolev 154B-1	232	CCCP-85232	0077		3 KU NK-8-2U	98000	Y164		

PRESTIGEAVIA = PGE (formerly Transago Borispol)   Kiev-Borispol

Ul. Bolshaya Zhitomirskaya 15B, 252025 Kiev, Ukraine ☎ (44) 212 35 72 Tx: none Fax: (44) 212 33 80 SITA: n/a
F: 1995 ⋆⋆⋆ n/a Head: Leonid V. Kisly ICAO: PRESTO Net: n/a

	registration	type of aircraft	cn/fn	ex/ex*	mfd	del	powered by	mtow kg	configuration	selcal	name/fln/specialitites/remarks
☐	UR-67502	Let 410UVP	851406	CCCP-67502	0085		2 WA M-601D	5800	Y15		lsf UKR / opb Khmelnitsky A.E.
☐	UR-65023	Tupolev 134A-3	48415	LY-ABB	0076	0797	2 SO D-30-III	47000	Y76		
☐	UR-65081	Tupolev 134A-3	60076	LY-ABE	0077	0796	2 SO D-30-III	47600	C12Y56		

ROVNO UNIVERSAL AVIA = UNR (Rivne Universal Avia)   Rovno

Ul. Aviatorov 1, 266010 Rovno, Ukraine ☎ (3622) 67 571 Tx: none Fax: (3622) 67 571 SITA: n/a
F: 1997 ⋆⋆⋆ n/a Head: Rostislav Batsovsky ICAO: RIVNE UNIVERSAL Net: n/a

	registration	type of aircraft	cn/fn	ex/ex*	mfd	del	powered by	mtow kg	configuration	selcal	name/fln/specialitites/remarks
☐	UR-20676	PZL Swidnik (Mil) Mi-2	526639050	CCCP-20676	0080	0097	2 IS GTD-350-4	3550	Utility		
☐	UR-BVH	PZL Swidnik (Mil) Mi-2	548028023		0083	0097	2 IS GTD-350-4	3550	Utility		
☐	UR-BVI	PZL Swidnik (Mil) Mi-2	548029023		0083	0097	2 IS GTD-350-4	3550	Utility		
☐	UR-07435	PZL Mielec (Antonov) An-2	1G151-10		0073	0097	1 SH ASh-62IR	5500	Utility		
☐	UR-17928	PZL Mielec (Antonov) An-2	1G206-09		0083	0097	1 SH ASh-62IR	5500	Utility		
☐	UR-17929	PZL Mielec (Antonov) An-2	1G206-10		0083	0097	1 SH ASh-62IR	5500	Utility		
☐	UR-19722	PZL Mielec (Antonov) An-2	1G165-36		0075	0097	1 SH ASh-62IR	5500	Sprayer		
☐	UR-32744	PZL Mielec (Antonov) An-2	1G212-51	SP-ZFS	0085	0097	1 SH ASh-62IR	5500	Sprayer		
☐	UR-40631	PZL Mielec (Antonov) An-2	1G213-38		0085	0097	1 SH ASh-62IR	5500	Utility		
☐	UR-40956	PZL Mielec (Antonov) An-2	1G216-56		0085	0097	1 SH ASh-62IR	5500	Sprayer		
☐	UR-43968	PZL Mielec (Antonov) An-2	1G210-45	SP-ZFT	0084	0097	1 SH ASh-62IR	5500	Sprayer		
☐	UR-84574	PZL Mielec (Antonov) An-2	1G189-41	CCCP-84574	0080	0097	1 SH ASh-62IR	5500	Sprayer		
☐	UR-67069	Let 410UVP	810705	CCCP-67069	0081	0097	2 WA M-601D	5800	Y17		
☐	UR-67082	Let 410UVP	810719	CCCP-67082	0081	0097	2 WA M-601D	5800	Y17		
☐	UR-67083	Let 410UVP	810720	CCCP-67083	0081	0097	2 WA M-601D	5800	Y17		
☐	UR-67084	Let 410UVP	810721	CCCP-67084	0081	0097	2 WA M-601D	5800	Y17		
☐	UR-67085	Let 410UVP	810722	CCCP-67085	0081	0097	2 WA M-601D	5800	Y17		
☐	UR-67102	Let 410UVP	841328	CCCP-67102	0084	0097	2 WA M-601D	5800	Y17		
☐	UR-67344	Let 410UVP	820904	CCCP-67344	0082	0097	2 WA M-601D	5800	Y17		
☐	UR-67372	Let 410UVP	830940	CCCP-67372	0083	0097	2 WA M-601D	5800	Y17		
☐	UR-67439	Let 410UVP	841204	CCCP-67439	0284	0097	2 WA M-601D	5800	Y17		
☐	UR-67477	Let 410UVP	841302	CCCP-67477	0084	0097	2 WA M-601D	5800	Y17		
☐	UR-67492	Let 410UVP	841317	HA-LAL	0084	0097	2 WA M-601D	5800	Y17		lst ELK as ES-LLD
☐	UR-67504	Let 410UVP	851408	CCCP-67504	0085	0097	2 WA M-601D	5800	Y17		lst BHU as HA-LAN
☐	UR-67524	Let 410UVP	851431	CCCP-67524	0085	0097	2 WA M-601D	5800	Y17		
☐	UR-67663	Let 410UVP-E	902525		0090	0097	2 WA M-601E	6400	C14		

SANAIR = SAV   Kiev-Zhulyani

Dmitrivskaya 18/24, 252054 Kiev, Ukraine ☎ (44) 246 82 23 Tx: none Fax: (44) 246 06 07 SITA: n/a
F: 1993 ⋆⋆⋆ 15 Head: Alexander N. Suvorov ICAO: SANAIR LINE Net: n/a

	registration	type of aircraft	cn/fn	ex/ex*	mfd	del	powered by	mtow kg	configuration	selcal	name/fln/specialitites/remarks
☐	UR-87345	Yakovlev 40	9511439	CCCP-87345	0075	0098	3 IV AI-25	16800	Y36		
☐	UR-47300	Antonov 24RV	57310203	CCCP-47300	0075	0099	2 IV AI-24VT	21800	Y48		lsf URG

SOKOL ATSK = SOK (Aviatsionno tekhnicheski sportivny klub SOKOL)   Volchansk

Ul. Frunze 1, 312510 Volchansk, (Kharkov Region), Ukraine ☎ (5741) 24 490 Tx: none Fax: (5741) 23 379 SITA: n/a
F: 1991 ⋆⋆⋆ n/a Head: Nikolai A. Shestakov ICAO: SOKOL Net: n/a

	registration	type of aircraft	cn/fn	ex/ex*	mfd	del	powered by	mtow kg	configuration	selcal	name/fln/specialitites/remarks
☐	UR-BDS	PZL Swidnik (Mil) Mi-2	547145061		0081	0091	2 IS GTD-350-4	3550	Utility		
☐	UR-BDT	PZL Swidnik (Mil) Mi-2	546113049		0079	0091	2 IS GTD-350-4	3550	Utility		
☐	UR-BDU	PZL Swidnik (Mil) Mi-2	546225079		0079	0091	2 IS GTD-350-4	3550	Utility		
☐	UR-BDV	PZL Swidnik (Mil) Mi-2	545619048		0078	0091	2 IS GTD-350-4	3550	Utility		
☐	UR-BDW	PZL Mielec (Antonov) An-2	1G159-55		0075	0091	1 SH ASh-62IR	5500	Utility		
☐	UR-BDX	PZL Mielec (Antonov) An-2	1G159-56		0075	0091	1 SH ASh-62IR	5500	Utility		

TAG AVIATION UKRAINE = AGK (Associated with TAG Aviation SA, Switzerland/formerly Aeroleasing Ukraine)   Kiev-Borispol

Prospekt Peremogy 14, 252135 Kiev, Ukraine ☎ (44) 216 26 71 Tx: 631307 ukaz Fax: (44) 216 44 78 SITA: n/a
F: 1991 ⋆⋆⋆ 35 Head: Alexander Gerkin ICAO: TAG AVIATION Net: n/a Beside aircraft listed, additional aircraft (Yakovlev 40) are leased from Air Ukraine when required.

	registration	type of aircraft	cn/fn	ex/ex*	mfd	del	powered by	mtow kg	configuration	selcal	name/fln/specialitites/remarks
☐	UR-EFA	Dassault Falcon 20C	55	CCCP-01100	0066	0192	2 GE CF700-2D2	12600	9 Pax		
☐	UR-EFB	Dassault Falcon 20C	75	N77QM	0067	0196	2 GE CF700-2D2	12400	9 Pax		

TAVRIA Aviakompania = T6 / TVR (Tavrey Air Company)   Odessa-Central

Prospekt Shevchenko 12, 270058 Odessa, Ukraine ☎ (482) 22 17 18 Tx: none Fax: (482) 21 00 06 SITA: ODSHQXH
F: 1995 ⋆⋆⋆ n/a Head: Alexei Yu. Zhilin IATA: 204 ICAO: TAVREY Net: n/a

	registration	type of aircraft	cn/fn	ex/ex*	mfd	del	powered by	mtow kg	configuration	selcal	name/fln/specialitites/remarks
☐	UR-85546	Tupolev 154B-2	546	YL-LAE	0082	0096	3 KU NK-8-2U	98000	Y164		

TAVRIA-MAK, Joint-Stock Company = TVM   Simferopol

Ul. Karla Marksa 18, Room 119, 333003 Simferopol, (Krim), Ukraine ☎ (652) 26 63 86 Tx: none Fax: (652) 25 91 70 SITA: n/a
F: 1992 ⋆⋆⋆ n/a Head: Ivan Djura ICAO: TAVRIA-MAK Net: n/a

	registration	type of aircraft	cn/fn	ex/ex*	mfd	del	powered by	mtow kg	configuration	selcal	name/fln/specialitites/remarks
☐	UR-46666	Antonov 24RV	47309507	YL-LCG	0074	0095	2 IV AI-24VT	22500	Y48		
☐	UR-47359	Antonov 24RV	67310608	RA-47359	0076	0097	2 IV AI-24VT	21800	Y48		
☐	UR-47362	Antonov 24RV	67310706	RA-47362	0177	0095	2 IV AI-24VT	21800	Y48		
☐	UR-BXA	Antonov 24RV				0098	2 IV AI-24VT	21800	Y48		
☐	UR-BXB	Antonov 24RV				0098	2 IV AI-24VT	21800	Y48		
☐	UR-	Antonov 26	6207		0078	0098	2 IV AI-24VT	24000	Freighter		

TRANS-KIEV = KCA   Kiev

Bulvar Lisi Ukrainki 34/315, 252159 Kiev, Ukraine ☎ (44) 295 33 72 Tx: n/a Fax: (44) 295 68 92 SITA: n/a
F: n/a ⋆⋆⋆ n/a Head: Anatoly E. Samsonov ICAO: TRANS-KIEV Net: n/a Operates charter flight, currently with aircraft leased from other companies when required.

UES-AVIA = UES (EES-Avia) (Subsidiary of United Energy System of Ukraine/EES Ukrainy)   Dnepropetrovsk

Dnepropetrovsk Airport, 320042 Dnepropetrovsk, Ukraine ☎ (562) 65 08 79 Tx: none Fax: (562) 65 03 42 SITA: n/a
F: 1996 ⋆⋆⋆ n/a Head: Alexander N. Davidov ICAO: AVIASYSTEM Net: n/a

	registration	type of aircraft	cn/fn	ex/ex*	mfd	del	powered by	mtow kg	configuration	selcal	name/fln/specialitites/remarks
☐	UR-87590	Yakovlev 40K	9741156	OK-HER	0077	0096	3 IV AI-25	16100	Executive		
☐	UR-87591	Yakovlev 40K	9741056	OK-HEQ	0077	0096	3 IV AI-25	17200	Executive		
☐	UR-87592	Yakovlev 40K	9730555	OK-HEP	0077	0096	3 IV AI-25	17200	Executive		

UKRAINA Aviapredpriatie = UKN (Ukraine-Air Enteprise)   Kiev-Borispol

Ul. Volozhskaya 62, 252070 Kiev, Ukraine ☎ (44) 417 07 90 Tx: none Fax: (44) 417 06 17 SITA: n/a
F: 1996 ⋆⋆⋆ n/a Head: Yuri N. Slavov ICAO: ENTERPRISE UKRAINE Net: n/a Company operate most flights on behalf on Ukrainian government but also leases Ilyushin 76 aircraft for commercial cargo flights when required.

	registration	type of aircraft	cn/fn	ex/ex*	mfd	del	powered by	mtow kg	configuration	selcal	name/fln/specialitites/remarks
☐	UR-87964	Yakovlev 40	9820758	CCCP-87964	0078	0097	3 IV AI-25	16800	VIP		
☐	UR-65556	Tupolev 134A-3	66372	CCCP-65556	0084		2 SO D-30-III	49000	VIP		
☐	UR-65718	Tupolev 134A-3	63668	CCCP-65718	0081		2 SO D-30-III	49000	VIP		
☐	UR-65782	Tupolev 134A-3	62672	CCCP-65782	0079		2 SO D-30-III	49000	VIP		
☐	UR-	Tupolev 154M	1017				3 SO D-30KU-154-II	100000	VIP		oo-delivery 0099
☐	UR-86527	Ilyushin 62M	4037758	CCCP-86527	0080		4 SO D-30KU	167000	VIP		fn 3705
☐	UR-86528	Ilyushin 62M	4038111	CCCP-86528	0081	0997	4 SO D-30KU	167000	VIP		

UKRAINE AIR ALLIANCE = UKL   Kiev-Borispol

PO Box 136, 253152 Kiev, Ukraine ☎ (44) 550 30 71 Tx: none Fax: (44) 553 49 69 SITA: n/a
F: 1992 ⋆⋆⋆ n/a Head: Valeri Marinichenko ICAO: UKRAINE AIRALLIANCE Net: n/a

	registration	type of aircraft	cn/fn	ex/ex*	mfd	del	powered by	mtow kg	configuration	selcal	name/fln/specialitites/remarks
☐	UR-49290	Antonov 24B	27307903	LZ-ANT	0072	0299	2 IV AI-24	21000	Y48		
☐	UR-26042	Antonov 26B	10710	CCCP-26042	0081	1298	2 IV AI-24VT	24000	Freighter		
☐	UR-26214	Antonov 26B	14403	CCCP-26214	0086	1298	2 IV AI-24VT	24000	Freighter		lsf ABA
☐	UR-BXF	Antonov 26B	12010	YL-LDC	0082	1198	2 IV AI-24VT	24000	Freighter		
☐	UR-11326	Antonov 12AP	2400802	CCCP-11326	0062	1298	4 IV AI-20M	61000	Freighter		

617 registration type of aircraft cn/fn ex/ex* mfd del powered by mtow kg configuration selcal name/fln/specialitites/remarks

UKRAINE FLIGHT STATE ACADEMY = UFA (Derzhavna lyotna akademia Ukrainy) — Kirovograd

Ul. Dobrovolskogo 1, 316005 Kirovograd, Ukraine ☎ (522) 29 45 70 Tx: none Fax: (522) 27 14 51 SITA: n/a
F: n/a ✈ n/a Head: Mikhail Rubets ICAO: FLIGHT ACADEMY Net: n/a Trainer-aircraft below MTOW 1361kg: 2 Yakovlev 18 Operates aircraft for training purposes but also for commercial charter flights & for leasing.
Most aircraft are still in Aeroflot colors without titles.

registration	type of aircraft	cn/fn	ex/ex*	mfd	del	powered by	mtow kg	configuration	selcal	name/fln/specialitites/remarks
☐ UR-02810	PZL Mielec (Antonov) An-2	1G54-15	CCCP-02810	0065	0089	1 SH ASh-62IR	5500	Y12		
☐ UR-33473	PZL Mielec (Antonov) An-2	1G228-23	CCCP-33473	0088		1 SH ASh-62IR	5500	Y12		
☐ UR-67000	Let 410UVP	810601	CCCP-67000	0081		2 WA M-601D	5800	Y15		std Kirovograd
☐ UR-67001	Let 410UVP	810602	CCCP-67001	0081		2 WA M-601D	5800	Y15		std Kirovograd
☐ UR-67004	Let 410UVP	810605	CCCP-67004	0081		2 WA M-601D	5800	Y15		
☐ UR-67010	Let 410UVP	810611	CCCP-67010	0081		2 WA M-601D	5800	Y15		std Dublin
☐ UR-67030	Let 410UVP	800501	CCCP-67030	0080		2 WA M-601D	5800	Y15		
☐ UR-67111	Let 410UVP	790307	CCCP-67111	0080	0089	2 WA M-601D	5800	Y15		
☐ UR-67122	Let 410UVP	790318	CCCP-67122	0080		2 WA M-601D	5800	Y15		
☐ UR-67128	Let 410UVP	790324	CCCP-67128	0080		2 WA M-601D	5800	Y15		
☐ UR-67129	Let 410UVP	790325	CCCP-67129	0080	0091	2 WA M-601D	5800	Y15		
☐ UR-67161	Let 410UVP	800427	CCCP-67161	0080		2 WA M-601D	5800	Y15		
☐ UR-67169	Let 410UVP	790205	CCCP-67169	0079	0090	2 WA M-601D	5800	Y15		
☐ UR-67197	Let 410UVP	790303	CCCP-67197	0079	0093	2 WA M-601D	5800	Y15		
☐ UR-67332	Let 410UVP	820832	CCCP-67332	0082		2 WA M-601D	5800	Y15		
☐ UR-67357	Let 410UVP	820917	CCCP-67357	0082	0089	2 WA M-601D	5800	Y15		
☐ UR-67389	Let 410UVP	831017	CCCP-67389	0083	0089	2 WA M-601D	5800	Y15		
☐ UR-67392	Let 410UVP	831020	CCCP-67392	0083	0089	2 WA M-601D	5800	Y15		
☐ UR-67393	Let 410UVP	831021	CCCP-67393	0083		2 WA M-601D	5800	Y15		
☐ UR-67395	Let 410UVP	831023	CCCP-67395	0083	0089	2 WA M-601D	5800	Y15		
☐ UR-67408	Let 410UVP	831036	CCCP-67408	0083		2 WA M-601D	5800	Y15		std Dublin
☐ UR-67409	Let 410UVP	831037	CCCP-67409	0083		2 WA M-601D	5800	Y15		
☐ UR-67411	Let 410UVP	831039	CCCP-67411	0083	0089	2 WA M-601D	5800	Y15		
☐ UR-67417	Let 410UVP	831108	CCCP-67417	0083	0090	2 WA M-601D	5800	Y19		
☐ UR-67419	Let 410UVP	831110	CCCP-67419	0083		2 WA M-601D	5800	Y19		
☐ UR-67449	Let 410UVP	841214	CCCP-67449	0084	0089	2 WA M-601D	5800	Y19		
☐ UR-67450	Let 410UVP	841215	CCCP-67450	0084	0088	2 WA M-601D	5800	Y19		
☐ UR-67526	Let 410UVP	851433	CCCP-67526	0085	0088	2 WA M-601D	5800	Y19		
☐ UR-67527	Let 410UVP	851434	CCCP-67527	0085	0089	2 WA M-601D	5800	Y19		
☐ UR-67543	Let 410UVP	851510	CCCP-67543	0085	0088	2 WA M-601D	5800	Y19		
☐ UR-67555	Let 410UVP	851519	CCCP-67555	0085	0088	2 WA M-601D	5800	Y19		
☐ UR-67658	Let 410UVP-E	902512	CCCP-67658	0090	0090	2 WA M-601E	6400	Y19		
☐ UR-67659	Let 410UVP-E	902513	CCCP-67659	0090	0090	2 WA M-601E	6400	Y19		
☐ UR-46205	Antonov 24B	67302803	CCCP-46205	0066	0066	2 IV AI-24-II	21000	Y48		
☐ UR-46217	Antonov 24B	67303006	CCCP-46217	0067	0067	2 IV AI-24-II	21000	Y28		
☐ UR-46311	Antonov 24B	97305307	LZ-MND	0069	0069	2 IV AI-24-II	21000	Y48		
☐ UR-46536	Antonov 24RV	57310110	OB-1587	0075	0075	2 IV AI-24VT	21800	Y48		
☐ UR-46608	Antonov 24RV	37308605	LZ-MNE	0073	0079	2 IV AI-24VT	21800	Y48		
☐ UR-46783	Antonov 24B	57301701	CCCP-46783	0065	0086	2 IV AI-24-II	21000	Y48		
☐ UR-47155	Antonov 24B	89901607	CCCP-47155	0068	0070	2 IV AI-24-II	21000	Y48		
☐ UR-47179	Antonov 24B	99901904	CCCP-47179	0069	0072	2 IV AI-24-II	21000	Y48		
☐ UR-47702	Antonov 24B	59900203	CCCP-47702	0065	0069	2 IV AI-24-II	21000	Y22		
☐ UR-47705	Antonov 24B	59900303	CCCP-47705	0065		2 IV AI-24-II	21000	Y20		
☐ UR-47711	Antonov 24B	69900501	CCCP-47711	0066	0067	2 IV AI-24-II	21000	Y20		
☐ UR-47743	Antonov 24B	79901106	CCCP-47743	0067		2 IV AI-24-II	21000	Y28		
☐ UR-47781	Antonov 24B	89901506	CCCP-47781	0067	0068	2 IV AI-24-II	21000	Y28		
☐ UR-47783	Antonov 24B	89901508	CCCP-47783	0068	0086	2 IV AI-24-II	21000	Y32		
☐ UR-26004	Antonov 26	9807	CCCP-26004	0080	0080	2 IV AI-24VT	24000	Frtr / Y39		lst Santa Cruz Imperial as EL-ALT
☐ UR-26015	Antonov 26B	10103	CCCP-26015	0080	0080	2 IV AI-24VT	24000	Frtr / Y39		
☐ UR-26103	Antonov 26B	12001	RA-26103	0082	0082	2 IV AI-24VT	24000	Frtr / Y19		
☐ UR-26115	Antonov 26B	12204	CCCP-26115	0082	0082	2 IV AI-24VT	24000	Frtr / Y19		
☐ UR-26124	Antonov 26B	12503	CCCP-26124	0082		2 IV AI-24VT	24000	Frtr / Y19		
☐ UR-26140	Antonov 26B	12902	CCCP-26140	0083	0083	2 IV AI-24VT	24000	Frtr / Y19		
☐ UR-26505	Antonov 26	3901	CCCP-26505	0076		2 IV AI-24VT	24000	Frtr / Y19		
☐ UR-26553	Antonov 26	3201	CCCP-26553	0075	0075	2 IV AI-24VT	24000	Frtr / Y39		
☐ UR-26583	Antonov 26B	13505	CCCP-26583	0384	0084	2 IV AI-24VT	24000	Frtr / Y19		

UKRAINE INTERNATIONAL AIRLINES = PS / AUI (Mizhnarodni avialinii Ukrainy) (formerly Air Ukraine International) — Kiev-Borispol

Міжнародні Авіалінії України Ukraine International

Prospekt Peremogy 14, Room 1103, 252135 Kiev, Ukraine ☎ (44) 216 67 30 Tx: 131371 ukair Fax: (44) 216 79 94 SITA: n/a
F: 1992 ✈ 215 Head: Vitaly M. Potemsky IATA: 566 ICAO: UKRAINEINTERNATIONAL Net: n/a

registration	type of aircraft	cn/fn	ex/ex*	mfd	del	powered by	mtow kg	configuration	selcal	name/fln/specialitites/remarks
☐ UR-GAC	Boeing 737-247 (A)	23188 / 1071	B-2509	0084	1194	2 PW JT8D-17A	56472	CY108		lsf GECA
☐ UR-GAD	Boeing 737-2T4 (A)	22802 / 901	B-610L	0082	0195	2 PW JT8D-17A	56472	CY108	EK-BL	lsf GECA
☐ UR-GAF	Boeing 737-35B	24237 / 1624	D-AGEG	0088	0398	2 CFMI CFM56-3B2	62822	CY135		lsf PEMB
☐ UR-GAG	Boeing 737-35B	24238 / 1626	D-AGEE	0088	0498	2 CFMI CFM56-3B2	62822	CY135		lsf PEMB
☐ UR-GAH	Boeing 737-32Q	29130				2 CFMI CFM56-3C1	62822	CY135		oo-delivery 0599

UKRAINIAN CARGO AIRWAYS - UCA = UKS — Zaporozhye

Ul. Frunze 19-21, 254080 Kiev, Ukraine ☎ (44) 417 73 35 Tx: none Fax: (44) 463 70 05 SITA: n/a
F: 1998 ✈ n/a Head: n/a ICAO: CARGOTRANS Net: n/a

registration	type of aircraft	cn/fn	ex/ex*	mfd	del	powered by	mtow kg	configuration	selcal	name/fln/specialitites/remarks
☐ UR-UCK	Antonov 12B				0098	4 IV AI-20M	61000	Freighter		
☐ UR-UCA	Ilyushin 76MD	0073479394		0087	0098	4 SO D-30KP	190000	Freighter		
☐ UR-UCC	Ilyushin 76MD	0083484531	UR-78755	0088	0098	4 SO D-30KP	190000	Freighter		
☐ UR-UCE	Ilyushin 76MD	0083484522	UR-76398	0088	0098	4 SO D-30KP	190000	Freighter		
☐ UR-UCF	Ilyushin 76MD				0098	4 SO D-30KP	190000	Freighter		
☐ UR-UCG	Ilyushin 76MD	0083482478	UR-76414	0088	0098	4 SO D-30KP	190000	Freighter		cvtd 78
☐ UR-UCH	Ilyushin 76MD	0083484536	UR-78756	0088	0098	4 SO D-30KP	190000	Freighter		
☐ UR-UCR	Ilyushin 76MD				0098	4 SO D-30KP	190000	Freighter		
☐ UR-UCY	Ilyushin 76MD	0083485566	UR-76399	0288	0098	4 SO D-30KP	190000	Freighter		

UKRAINIAN PILOT SCHOOL = UPL — Chaika

Aerodrome Chaika, 255500 Borschagivka, (Kiev Region), Ukraine ☎ (044) 444 82 93 Tx: none Fax: (044) 444 75 71 SITA: n/a
F: 1995 ✈ n/a Head: Victor Reznik ICAO: PILOT SCHOOL Net: n/a Aircraft below MTOW 1361kg: PZL-104 Wilga 35A & Yakovlev 52 Beside Flying School also operates commerical charter & aerial work flights.

registration	type of aircraft	cn/fn	ex/ex*	mfd	del	powered by	mtow kg	configuration	selcal	name/fln/specialitites/remarks
☐ UR-BWC	Yakovlev 18T	22202030003		0081	0098	1 VO M-14P	1650	Utility/Trainer		
☐ UR-BWY	PZL Mielec (Antonov) An-2	1G238-01	51	0090	0095	1 SH ASh-62IR	5500	Utility/Trainer		
☐ RA-28721	PZL Mielec (Antonov) An-28	1AJ007-06	CCCP-28721	0089	0099	2 GS TVD-10B	6500	Y17 / Trainer		

VETERAN AIRLINES = VPB — Dzhankoi

Moskovskaya 182a, Room 210, 334010 Dzhankoi, (Krim), Ukraine ☎ (6564) 33 112 Tx: none Fax: (6564) 30 122 SITA: SIPVT6U
F: 1992 ✈ n/a Head: Andrei Petrenko ICAO: VETERAN Net: n/a

registration	type of aircraft	cn/fn	ex/ex*	mfd	del	powered by	mtow kg	configuration	selcal	name/fln/specialitites/remarks
☐ UR-BVL	Yakovlev 18T	6200911		0076	0097	1 VO M-14P	1650	Utility		
☐ UR-17769	PZL Mielec (Antonov) An-2	1G203-30		0083	0096	1 SH ASh-62IR	5500	Utility		
☐ UR-33000	PZL Mielec (Antonov) An-2	1G217-40		0085	0096	1 SH ASh-62IR	5500	Utility		
☐ UR-82910	PZL Mielec (Antonov) An-2	1G167-16		0076	0097	1 SH ASh-62IR	5500	Utility		
☐ OM-GAT	Tupolev 134A	48565	ES-AAF	0876	0099	2 SO D-30-II	47000	Y76		David / lsf EAT
☐ UR-11303	Antonov 12BK	00347604		0070	0095	4 IV AI-20M	61000	Freighter		
☐ UR-11305	Antonov 12BK	01347803		0071	0096	4 IV AI-20M	61000	Freighter		
☐ UR-11306	Antonov 12BK	9346205		0069	0096	4 IV AI-20M	61000	Freighter		
☐ UR-PAS	Antonov 12B	2401105		0062	0098	4 IV AI-20M	61000	Freighter		Adrey
☐ UR-76676	Ilyushin 76MD	0063467003		0086	0093	4 SO D-30KP	190000	Freighter		
☐ UR-76691	Ilyushin 76MD	0063470089		0086	0093	4 SO D-30KP	190000	Freighter		
☐ UR-76697	Ilyushin 76MD	0063470118	CCCP-76697	0086	0093	4 SO D-30KP	190000	Freighter		
☐ UR-76698	Ilyushin 76MD	0063471123	CCCP-76698	0086	0093	4 SO D-30KP	190000	Freighter		
☐ UR-76729	Ilyushin 76MD	0073476275	CCCP-76729	1186	0093	4 SO D-30KP	190000	Freighter		

VINNITSA AVIATION ENTERPRISE (Vinnitskoe aviapredpriatie) (Division of Air Ukraine / formerly Vinnitsa division of Aeroflot Ukraine directorate) — Lvov

Vinnitsa Airport, 287125 Vinnitsa, Ukraine ☎ (4322) 26 077 Tx: none Fax: (4322) 25 660 SITA: n/a
F: n/a ✈ n/a Head: n/a Net: n/a Operates Let 410 aircraft in AIR UKRAINE colors. For fleet details – see under AIR UKRAINE. Aircraft are marked opb Vinnitsa Aviation Enterprise.

VOLARE AVIATION ENTERPRISE, Joint-Stock Company = F7 / VRE — Kiev & Krivoi Rog

Ul. Svyatoshinskaya 2, 252115 Kiev, Ukraine ☎ (44) 452 11 15 Tx: none Fax: (44) 452 28 29 SITA: IEVVRXH
F: 1994 ✈ n/a Head: Igor P. Likarenko IATA: 107 ICAO: UKRAINE VOLARE Net: http://www.volare-kiev.ua

registration	type of aircraft	cn/fn	ex/ex*	mfd	del	powered by	mtow kg	configuration	selcal	name/fln/specialitites/remarks
☐ UR-BWM	Antonov 12BP	00347004		0070	0097	4 IV AI-20M	61000	Freighter		
☐ UR-LIP	Antonov 12B	9346405	24 BLUE	0069	0098	4 IV AI-20M	61000	Freighter		
☐ UR-76628	Ilyushin 76MD	0053458741	CCCP-76628	0085	0097	4 SO D-30KP	190000	Freighter		
☐ UR-76636	Ilyushin 76MD	0053459781	CCCP-76636	0085	0094	4 SO D-30KP	190000	Freighter		
☐ UR-76687	Ilyushin 76MD	0063469051	CCCP-76687	0086	0097	4 SO D-30KP	190000	Freighter		

☐ UR-76704	Ilyushin 76MD	0063471150	CCCP-76704	0086		4 SO D-30KP	190000	Freighter		
☐ UR-76727	Ilyushin 76MD	0073475268	CCCP-76727	0087	0094	4 SO D-30KP	190000	Freighter		

YUZHMASHAVIA = UMK (Flying div. of Yuzhny mashinostroitel'ny zavod/Southern Engineering Plant) — **Dnepropetrovsk**

Ul. Rabochaya 99, 320008 Dnepropetrovsk, Ukraine ☎ (562) 92 68 97 Tx: none Fax: (562) 92 79 01 SITA: n/a
F: 1985 ✈ n/a Head: Nikolai B. Tiritenko ICAO: YUZHMAS Net: n/a

☐ UR-87298	Yakovlev 40	9241325	CCCP-87298	0072		3 IV AI-25	16100	VIP		
☐ UR-87508	Yakovlev 40	9521040	CCCP-87508	0075		3 IV AI-25	17200	Y32		
☐ UR-87951	Yakovlev 40K	9810957	CCCP-87951	0078		3 IV AI-25	16100	Combi		
☐ UR-88151	Yakovlev 40	9610546	CCCP-88151	0076		3 IV AI-25	16100	Y32		
☐ UR-78785	Ilyushin 76MD	0083489691	CCCP-78785	0088	0096	4 SO D-30KP	190000	Freighter		
☐ UR-78786	Ilyushin 76MD	0083490694	CCCP-78786	0088	0096	4 SO D-30KP	190000	Freighter		

YUZHNOE = UZH — **Kirvoi Rog**

Ul. Krivorozhskaya 3, 320008 Dnepropetrovsk, Ukraine ☎ (562) 42 00 18 Tx: none Fax: (562) 92 5041 SITA: n/a
F: 1998 ✈ n/a Head: Georgi G. Bednyak ICAO: YUZHNOE Net: n/a

☐ UR-78734	Ilyushin 76TD	1013409303	HA-TCA	0092	0098	4 SO D-30KP	190000	Freighter		

VH = AUSTRALIA (Commonwealth of Australia)

including Norfolk & Coral Sea Islands & Cocos Islands
Capital: Canberra Official Language: English Population: 17,9 million Square Km: 7686848 Dialling code: +61 Year established: 1901 Acting political head: John Howard (Prime Minister)

CHRISTMAS ISLAND / KIRITMATI
Official Language: English Population: 0,1 million Square Km: 134 Dialling code: +6724 Acting political head: Graham Nicholls (Administrator)
COCOS ISLANDS
Official Language: English Population: 0,1 million Square Km: 15 Dialling code: +6722 Acting political head: Ron Harvey (Administrator)
NORFOLK & CORAL SEA ISLANDS
Capital: Kingston Official Language: English Population: 0,1 million Square Km: 35 Dialling code: +6723 Acting political head: Tony Messner (Administrator)

Government / Corporate / Executive / VIP Aircraft

☐ A20-261	Boeing 707-368C	21261 / 919	N7486B	1276	0288	4 PW JT3D-3B	151046	VIP / mil transp	CF-EK	Royal Australian Air Force
☐ A20-623	Boeing 707-338C	19623 / 671	C-GRYN	0168	0683	4 PW JT3D-3B	151046	VIP/Tanker/miltr	GL-AK	City of Sydney / Royal Australian A.F.
☐ A20-624	Boeing 707-338C	19624 / 689	VH-EAD	0368	0379	4 PW JT3D-3B	151046	VIP/Tanker/miltr	FJ-EL	Richmond Town / Royal Australian A.F.
☐ A20-627	Boeing 707-338C	19627 / 707	VH-EAG	0468	0379	4 PW JT3D-3B	151046	VIP/Tanker/miltr	FJ-EM	Windsor Town / Royal Australian A.F.
☐ A20-629	Boeing 707-338C	19629 / 737	C-GGAB	0868	0683	4 PW JT3D-3B	151046	VIP/Tanker/miltr	GL-AJ	Royal Australian Air Force
☐ A26-070	Dassault Falcon 900	70	N450FJ*	0089	0989	3 GA TFE731-5A-1C2	20638	VIP / mil transp	LP-DJ	Royal Australian Air Force
☐ A26-073	Dassault Falcon 900	73	N452FJ*	0089	0089	3 GA TFE731-5A-1C2	20638	VIP / mil transp	LP-DK	Royal Australian Air Force
☐ A26-074	Dassault Falcon 900	74	N453FJ*	0089	0089	3 GA TFE731-5A-1C2	20638	VIP / mil transp	LP-DM	Royal Australian Air Force
☐ A26-076	Dassault Falcon 900	76	N454FJ*	0089	1189	3 GA TFE731-5A-1C2	20638	VIP / mil transp	LP-EF	Royal Australian Air Force
☐ A26-077	Dassault Falcon 900	77	N455FJ*	0089	0089	3 GA TFE731-5A-1C2	20638	VIP / mil transp	LP-EG	Royal Australian Air Force

ABRIL AVIATION (L R (No. 107) Pty Ltd dba) — **Springwood, QLD**

PO Box 158, Springwood, QLD 4127, Australia ☎ (7) 38 08 83 11 Tx: none Fax: (9) 38 08 68 44 SITA: n/a
F: 1997 ✈ n/a Head: John Anderson Net: n/a

☐ VH-ULX	Cessna 425 Conquest I	425-0124	N6882M	0082		2 PWC PT6A-112	3900			

AC AIRWAYS (Pieter & C. Mol dba / Affiliated with Air Centre Albury) — **Albury, NSW**

PO Box 521, Albury, NSW 2640, Australia ☎ (2) 60 21 29 29 Tx: n/a Fax: (2) 60 41 12 97 SITA: n/a
F: 1968 ✈ n/a Head: Pieter Mol Net: n/a Aircraft below MTOW 1361kg: Piper PA-28 & PA-38.

☐ VH-TWJ	Piper PA-30-160 Twin Comanche C	30-1977	N8819Y	0069		2 LY IO-320-C1A	1690			
☐ VH-TZF	Piper PA-34-200T Seneca II	34-7570223	N69NB	0075		2 CO TSIO-360-E	2073			
☐ VH-KMW	Piper PA-31-310 Navajo	31-726	N78EE	0071		2 LY TIO-540-A1A	2948			
☐ VH-MJA	Piper PA-31-350 Navajo Chieftain	31-8252026	N4105A	0082		2 LY TIO-540-J2BD	3175			

ACCESS AVIATION, Pty Ltd — **Brisbane-Archerfield, QLD**

PO Box 624, Archerfield, QLD 4108, Australia ☎ (7) 32 74 15 14 Tx: none Fax: (7) 32 74 12 64 SITA: n/a
F: 1990 ✈ 4 Head: Peter Boughen Net: n/a

☐ VH-JQK	Cessna 310R II	310R1355	N4046A	0078	0996	2 CO IO-520-M	2495			
☐ VH-JQS	Piper PA-31-350 Navajo Chieftain	31-7552095	VH-LHD	0075	1097	2 LY TIO-540-J2BD	3175			

AERIAL ENTERPRISES (Thousand Islands Airtours) (Roberton B. Richard & J. & A.B. dba) — **Derby, WA**

PO Box 61, Derby, WA 6728, Australia ☎ (8) 91 91 11 32 Tx: none Fax: (8) 91 93 12 01 SITA: n/a
F: n/a ✈ n/a Head: Richard B. Roberton Net: n/a
Some tourist flights are operated under the marketing name THOUSAND ISLANDS AIRTOURS (same headquarters).

☐ VH-AEH	Cessna U206F Stationair	U20601709	N1599C	0072		1 CO IO-520-F	1633			
☐ VH-AEI	Cessna U206F Stationair II	U20602868	N1205Q	0075		1 CO IO-520-F	1633			
☐ VH-AEX	Cessna U206G Stationair 6 II	U20606587	N9635Z	0083		1 CO IO-520-F	1633			
☐ VH-PJY	Cessna U206G Stationair 6 II	U20605120	N4829U	0079		1 CO IO-520-F	1633			
☐ VH-AEV	Cessna 337G Super Skymaster	33701578	N72413	0074		2 CO IO-360-G	2100			
☐ VH-AEY	Cessna 310R II	310R0685	N1217G	0076		2 CO IO-520-M	2495			
☐ VH-BIR	Cessna 310R II	310R0851	N3485G	0077	0297	2 CO IO-520-M	2495			
☐ VH-AEC	Britten-Norman BN-2B-26 Islander	2164	G-BKJO	0084	0586	2 LY O-540-E4C5	2994			
☐ VH-AEU	Britten-Norman BN-2B-26 Islander	2130	G-BJON	0082		2 LY O-540-E4C5	2994			

AERODATA, Holdings Ltd (World Geoscience Corp. Ltd dba / Affiliated with Questor Surveys Ltd, Canada) — **Perth, WA**

65 Brockway Road, Floreat, WA 6014, Australia ☎ (8) 92 73 64 00 Tx: none Fax: (8) 92 73 64 66 SITA: n/a
F: 1984 ✈ 120 Head: Ray Steedman Net: n/a

☐ VH-WGS	Cessna 404 Titan II	404-0686	N6763R	0080	1098	2 CO GTSIO-520-M	3810	Photo / Survey		
☐ VH-NKW	Britten-Norman BN-2A Mk.III-1 Trislander	381	C-GNKW	0074	0390	3 LY O-540-E4C5	4240	Photo / Survey		
☐ VH-WGG	Shorts Skyvan 3A Variant 100 (SC-7)	SH1913	700 SDF	0073	0894	2 GA TPE331-2-201A	6214	Photo / Survey		Ist pvt, Italy
☐ VH-WGT	Shorts Skyvan 3 Variant 100 (SC-7)	SH1960	ZS-MJS	0078	0996	2 GA TPE331-2-201A	5670	Photo / Survey		Ist pvt, Italy

AEROLINK AIR SERVICES, Pty Ltd (formerly Aero Connection, Pty Ltd) — **Sydney-Kingsford Smith, NSW**

PO Box 680, Mascot, NSW 2020, Australia ☎ (2) 96 69 64 20 Tx: none Fax: (2) 93 17 57 07 SITA: n/a
F: 1994 ✈ 10 Head: n/a Net: n/a

☐ VH-LJF	Cessna 310R II	310R0691	N41TV	0076	0295	2 CO IO-520-M	2495			
☐ VH-BWC	Embraer 110P1 Bandeirante (EMB-110P1)	110261	LN-FAP	0080	0797	2 PWC PT6A-34	5670	Y18		
☐ VH-MWF	Embraer 110P1 Bandeirante (EMB-110P1)	110447	N216EB	0084	1198	2 PWC PT6A-34	5670	Y18		
☐ VH-MWV	Embraer 110P2 Bandeirante (EMB-110P2)	110190	HS-SKG	0078	0998	2 PWC PT6A-34	5670	Y18		
☐ VH-WBI	Embraer 110P2 Bandeirante (EMB-110P2)	110292	PT-SCA*	0081	0397	2 PWC PT6A-34	5670	Y18		

AEROPELICAN Air Services, Pty Ltd = PEL (Subsidiary of Thomas Nationwide Transport & News Corp) — **Newcastle-Belmont Airport, NSW**

AEROPELICAN

PO Box 226, Belmont, NSW 2280, Australia ☎ (2) 49 45 09 88 Tx: 28092 aeropel aa Fax: (2) 49 45 88 24 SITA: n/a
F: 1971 ✈ 42 Head: Andrew Burkett Net: n/a

☐ VH-KZN	De Havilland DHC-6 Twin Otter 320	652	N479WW	0079	0687	2 PWC PT6A-27	5670	Y18		
☐ VH-KZO	De Havilland DHC-6 Twin Otter 320	753	C-GFBS*	0081	0581	2 PWC PT6A-27	5670	Y18		
☐ VH-KZP	De Havilland DHC-6 Twin Otter 320	758	C-GFBU*	0081	0581	2 PWC PT6A-27	5670	Y18		
☐ VH-KZQ	De Havilland DHC-6 Twin Otter 320	759	C-GFBY*	0081	0581	2 PWC PT6A-27	5670	Y18		

AEROPOWER, Pty Ltd (Subsidiary of Aeropower Holdings, Pty Ltd / formerly Masling Helicopters, Pty Ltd) — **Brisbane-Heliport, QLD**

AEROPOWER

PO Box 868, Hamilton Central, QLD 4007, Australia ☎ (7) 38 68 18 55 Tx: n/a Fax: (7) 38 68 11 85 SITA: n/a
F: 1991 ✈ 15 Head: n/a Net: n/a Aircraft below MTOW 1361kg: Hughes 269C (300C) & Hughes 369HS (500C).

☐ VH-HWD	MD Helicopters MD 500D (Hughes 369D)	110887D	ZK-HMD	0081	0598	1 AN 250-C20B	1361			
☐ VH-MHE	MD Helicopters MD 500D (Hughes 369D)	1160031D	P2-PHN	0076	0692	1 AN 250-C20B	1361			
☐ VH-PLD	MD Helicopters MD 500D (Hughes 369D)	510952D	P2-PHU	0081	0593	1 AN 250-C20B	1361			
☐ VH-PLF	MD Helicopters MD 500D (Hughes 369D)	890561D	P2-PHR	0079	0397	1 AN 250-C20B	1361			
☐ VH-PLI	MD Helicopters MD 500D (Hughes 369D)	990584D	P2-PHW	0079	1097	1 AN 250-C20B	1361			
☐ VH-PLJ	MD Helicopters MD 500D (Hughes 369D)	1280445D	P2-PHQ	0078	0793	1 AN 250-C20B	1361			
☐ VH-PLU	MD Helicopters MD 500D (Hughes 369D)	1190632D	ZS-RDU	0080	1096	1 AN 250-C20B	1361			
☐ VH-PLX	MD Helicopters MD 500D (Hughes 369D)	1170230D	P2-PHM	0078	1196	1 AN 250-C20B	1361			

AGRICAIR (Wee Waa), Pty Ltd — **Wee Waa, NSW**

PO Box 330, Wee Waa, NSW 2388, Australia ☎ (2) 67 95 43 76 Tx: none Fax: (2) 67 95 49 40 SITA: n/a
F: n/a ✈ n/a Head: David Baines Net: n/a

☐ VH-KMY	Beech Baron 58	TH-1020		0079	1198	2 CO IO-520-CB	2449			
☐ VH-LTU	Piper PA-31-350 Navajo Chieftain	31-7405462	VH-JJI	0074	0997	2 LY TIO-540-J2BD	3175			

AIR AUSTRALIA INTERNATIONAL, Pty Ltd — **Perth-Jandakot, WA**

37 Eagle Drive, Jandakot, WA 6164, Australia ☎ (8) 93 32 50 11 Tx: none Fax: (8) 94 17 22 46 SITA: n/a
F: 1992 ✈ n/a Head: n/a Net: n/a Aircraft below MTOW 1361kg: Beech C23, Cessna 152/172/177 & Robin R-2160

☐ VH-ESY	Piper PA-34-200 Seneca	34-7350075	N15553	0073	0196	2 LY IO-360-C1E6	1905			

619 registration type of aircraft cn/fn ex/ex* mfd del powered by mtow kg configuration selcal name/fln/specialitites/remarks

AIRBORNE RESEARCH AUSTRALIA (A Major National Research Facility at The Flinders University of South Australia) **Adelaide-Parafield, SA**

c/o FIAMS, PO Box 335, Salisbury South, SA 5106, Australia ☎ (8) 82 85 67 17 Tx: none Fax: (8) 82 85 67 10 SITA: n/a
F: 1995 ✈ 11 Head: Prof. Jörg M. Hacker Net: n/a Aircraft below MTOW 1361kg: Grob G-109B
National-organisation conducting non-commercial airborne tasks from between 15m-15000m covering research, contract survey & consultancy.

☐ VH-EOS	Cessna 404 Titan II	*404-0404*	*D-IFFG*	*0079*	*0996*	*2 CO GTSIO-520-M*	*3810*	*Research/Survey*		
☐ VH-ARA	Grob G-520T Egrett II	*10200*	*D-FARA*	*0093*	*0196*	*1 GA TPE331-14F-801L*	*4430*	*Research/Survey*		
☐ VH-LAB	Beech King Air 200T	*BT-23*	*N312D*	*0082*	*1197*	*2 PWC PT6A-41*	*6350*	*Research/Survey*		*cvtd 200 cn BB-1052*

AIRBORNE RESEARCH VEHICLES AUSTRALIA (Australian Flight Test Services, Pty Ltd dba) **Adelaide-Parafield, SA**

c/o Australian Flight Test Services P/L, Innovation House West, 1st Avenue, The Levels, SA 5095, Australia ☎ (8) 82 62 69 98 Tx: none Fax: (8) 83 43 88 88 SITA: n/a
F: 1986 ✈ 18 Head: Ian Martin Net: n/a Non-commercial semi-autonomous state organisation conducting scientific experiments in flight.

☐ VH-BDY	Cessna 310L	*310L0024*	*N2224F*	*0066*	*0297*	*2 CO IO-470-V*	*2359*	*Research*		
☐ VH-CAT	Fokker F27 Friendship 100 (F27 Mk100)	*10132*	*PH-FAZ**	*0059*	*1293*	*2 RR Dart 514-7*	*18370*	*Research*		Porcupine / *opf CSIRO Australia*

AIR CAIRNS (Kewarra Investments, Pty Ltd dba) **Cairns, QLD**

PO Box 835, Smithfield, QLD 4879, Australia ☎ (7) 40 57 63 06 Tx: none Fax: (7) 40 57 68 06 SITA: n/a
F: 1990 ✈ n/a Head: Victor Mail Net: n/a

☐ VH-WJQ	Piper PA-23-250 Aztec F	*27-7754043*	*N62830*	*0077*		*2 LY IO-540-C4B5*	*2359*			
☐ VH-BZK	Cessna 310R II	*310R1427*	*N5161C*	*0078*		*2 CO IO-520-M*	*2495*			

AIR CARGO AUSTRALIA (Aero Marine Consulting, Pty Ltd dba) **Melbourne-Tullamarine, VIC**

1-7 Silicon Place, Tullamarine, VIC 3043, Australia ☎ (3) 93 34 57 27 Tx: none Fax: (3) 93 34 57 30 SITA: n/a
F: 1989 ✈ 37 Head: William L. Cain ICAO: AUS CARGO Net: n/a

☐ VH-TBS	Boeing 727-77C	*20278 / 768*	*C2-RN7*	*0069*	*1195*	*3 PW JT8D-7A (HK3/FDX)*	*76884*	*Freighter*		*lsf Rothschild Lsng / sub-lst/opf XME*
☐ VH-AUP	Boeing 727-277 (F) (A)	*21695 / 1481*	*VH-RMN*	*0079*	*1197*	*3 PW JT8D-15 (HK3/FDX)*	*86409*	*Freighter*		*lsf Rothsch.Lsng/cvtd-277/sublst/opfXME*

AIR CHAMPAGNE, Pty Ltd **Tocumwal, NSW**

Tocumwal, Aerodrome Park, Tocumwal, NSW 2714, Australia ☎ (3) 58 74 20 63 Tx: none Fax: (3) 58 74 27 05 SITA: n/a
F: 1996 ✈ n/a Head: n/a Net: n/a Aircraft below MTOW 1361kg: Cessna 152 & Rockwell 112

☐ VH-MFS	Beech Duchess 76	*ME-421*	*N1838Y*	*0081*	*0898*	*2 LY O-360-A1G6D*	*1769*	*3 Pax / Trainer*		
☐ VH-OBI	BAe (DH) 104 Dove 8	*04525*	*G-LIDD*	*0061*	*0298*	*2 Gipsy Queen 70 Mk.3*	*4159*	*9 Pax*		
☐ VH-MAH	Grumman HU-16A Albatross	*368*	*N143DB*	*0054*	*0898*	*2 WR R-1820-76*	*15195*	*15 Pax / EMS*		*Amphibian*

AIR CHARTER AUSTRALIA, Pty Ltd (formerly Air Charter, Pty Ltd) **Adelaide-Int'l, SA**

PO Box 221, Stirling, SA 5152, Australia ☎ (8) 82 34 41 44 Tx: none Fax: (8) 82 34 37 63 SITA: n/a
F: 1988 ✈ 9 Head: Ms Coraine J. Sopru Net: n/a

☐ VH-KEZ	Cessna 402C II	*402C0262*	*N40BH*	*0080*		*2 CO TSIO-520-VB*	*3107*			
☐ VH-ROS	Cessna 402C II	*402C0038*	*N5764C*	*0079*		*2 CO TSIO-520-VB*	*3107*			
☐ VH-RCB	Reims/Cessna F406 Caravan II	*F406-0033*	*VT-SAC*	*0090*	*0298*	*2 PWC PT6A-112*	*4468*			
☐ VH-OCS	Cessna 441 Conquest II	*441-0030*	*N441MM*	*0078*		*2 GA TPE331-8-401S*	*4468*			

AIRCRAFT AND MARINE SERVICES (Elegna, Pty Ltd dba) **Caloundra, QLD**

PO Box 407, Caloundra, QLD 4551, Australia ☎ (7) 54 91 68 19 Tx: none Fax: (7) 54 91 68 19 SITA: n/a
F: 1985 ✈ n/a Head: Peter J. Norris Net: n/a Aircraft below MTOW 1361kg: Cessna 172

☐ VH-ROX	Cessna 402A	*402A0123*	*N7823Q*	*0069*	*0096*	*2 CO TSIO-520-E*	*2858*			

AIRCRUISING AUSTRALIA, Ltd = AIX **Sydney-Kingsford Smith, NSW**

PO Box 794, Mascot, NSW 2020, Australia ☎ (2) 96 93 22 33 Tx: none Fax: (2) 96 69 60 64 SITA: n/a
F: 1983 ✈ 24 Head: Gerald Garrett ICAO: CRUISER Net: http://www.broflo.com.au/aca.html

☐ VH-JSW	BAe 3107 Jetstream 31	*620*	*G-31-620**	*0083*	*0698*	*2 GA TPE331-10UF-511H*	*6950*	*Y19*		*lsf Skywest Airlines*
☐ VH-OSW	BAe 3107 Jetstream 31	*629*	*G-31-629**	*0084*	*0297*	*2 GA TPE331-10UF-511H*	*6950*	*Y19*		
☐ VH-NLS	Fokker F27 Friendship 100 (F27 Mk100)	*10105*	*ZK-NAH*	*0058*	*0186*	*2 RR Dart 514-7*	*18370*	*Y40*		

AIRESEARCH MAPPING, Pty Ltd **Darwin/NT, Brisbane/QLD & Melbourne-Tullamarine/VIC**

PO Box 186, Darwin, NT 0801, Australia ☎ (8) 89 81 90 51 Tx: none Fax: (8) 89 41 32 27 SITA: n/a
F: n/a ✈ n/a Head: John Murphy Net: n/a

☐ VH-AEA	Beech Baron 56TC	*TG-91*	*N9091Q*	*0070*		*2 LY TIO-541-E1B4*	*2717*	*Photo / Survey*		
☐ VH-SUV	Beech Baron 56TC	*TG-53*	*N6293V*	*0067*	*0397*	*2 LY TIO-541-E1B4*	*2717*	*Photo / Survey*		
☐ VH-BUR	Cessna 421C Golden Eagle III	*421C0524*	*N88594*	*0078*	*0298*	*2 CO GTSIO-520-L*	*3379*	*Photo / Survey*		
☐ VH-DRB	Cessna 421C Golden Eagle II	*421C0256*	*N5946G*	*0077*	*0895*	*2 CO GTSIO-520-L*	*3379*	*Photo / Survey*		

AIR FACILITIES = FZ (Arcas Airways, Pty Ltd dba) **Albury, NSW**

PO Box 675, Albury, NSW 2640, Australia ☎ (2) 60 41 12 10 Tx: none Fax: (2) 60 21 85 08 SITA: n/a
F: 1973 ✈ 12 Head: Les Sears Net: n/a

☐ VH-SKT	Cessna 310R II	*310R1815*	*N2645D*	*0080*		*2 CO IO-520-M*	*2495*			
☐ VH-MZI	Piper PA-31-350 Navajo Chieftain	*31-8152131*	*N4087S*	*0081*	*0393*	*2 LY TIO-540-J2BD*	*3175*			
☐ VH-MZV	Piper PA-31-350 Navajo Chieftain	*31-8152092*	*N4083C*	*0081*	*0893*	*2 LY TIO-540-J2BD*	*3175*			

AIRFLITE, Pty Ltd **Perth-Jandakot, WA**

37 Eagle Drive, Jandakot Airport, WA 6164, Australia ☎ (8) 93 32 52 44 Tx: none Fax: (8) 93 32 31 89 SITA: n/a
F: 1981 ✈ 190 Head: Homer Constantinides Net: n/a

☐ VH-KBH	Beech King Air B200	*BB-1189*	*N843CK*	*0084*	*0697*	*2 PWC PT6A-42*	*5670*			*lst / opf RAAF School of Air Navigation*
☐ VH-KCH	Beech King Air B200	*BB-1125*	*N12LD*	*0083*	*0697*	*2 PWC PT6A-42*	*5670*			*lst / opf RAAF School of Air Navigation*

AIR FRASER ISLAND (Gerry H. Geltch dba) **Pialba, QLD**

PO Box 121, Urangan, QLD 4655, Australia ☎ (71) 25 36 00 Tx: n/a Fax: (71) 25 36 05 SITA: n/a
F: 1992 ✈ 6 Head: Gerry H. Geltch Net: n/a

☐ VH-BPF	Cessna 205 (210-5)	*205-0092*	*N1867Z*	*0063*	*0795*	*1 CO IO-470-S*	*1497*			
☐ VH-COY	Cessna 205A (210-5A)	*205-0570*	*N4870U*	*0064*	*0298*	*1 CO IO-470-S*	*1497*			
☐ VH-HIS	Cessna U206G Stationair 6 II	*U20606348*	*N6621Z*	*0081*		*1 CO IO-520-F*	*1633*			
☐ VH-KRR	Cessna U206F Stationair II	*U20603210*		*0076*		*1 CO IO-520-F*	*1633*			
☐ VH-RLP	Cessna 205 (210-5)	*205-0213*		*0063*	*1195*	*1 CO IO-470-S*	*1497*			
☐ VH-FSA	Cessna 337G Super Skymaster	*33701566*	*N90239*	*0074*	*0996*	*2 CO IO-360-G*	*2100*			

AIR FRONTIER (Mooney Holdings, Pty Ltd dba) **Darwin, NT**

PO Box 2828, Darwin, NT 0801, Australia ☎ (8) 89 45 18 66 Tx: none Fax: (8) 89 45 36 99 SITA: n/a
F: 1985 ✈ n/a Head: John S. Hicks Net: n/a

☐ VH-MRK	Cessna U206G Stationair 6 II	*U20606086*	*N5251Z*	*0081*	*0197*	*1 CO IO-520-F*	*1633*			
☐ VH-DCQ	Piper PA-23-250 Aztec F	*27-7954012*	*N6576A*	*0079*		*2 LY IO-540-C4B5*	*2359*			
☐ VH-LIL	Piper PA-31-350 Navajo Chieftain	*31-7852061*	*N27399*	*0078*	*0895*	*2 LY TIO-540-J2BD*	*3175*			
☐ VH-KAK	Twin (Aero) Shrike Commander 500S	*3269*	*N57163*	*0076*		*2 LY IO-540-E1B5*	*3357*			*lsf Equipment Leasing P/L*
☐ VH-UJX	Twin (Aero) Shrike Commander 500S	*500S-1839-31*	*VH-EXI*	*0069*	*0796*	*2 LY IO-540-E1B5*	*3357*			*lsf GAM Air Services*

AIRLIFT HELICOPTERS, Pty Ltd **Perth, WA**

PO Box 653, Subiaco, WA 6008, Australia ☎ (8) 93 81 37 75 Tx: n/a Fax: n/a SITA: n/a
F: n/a ✈ n/a Head: n/a Net: n/a

☐ VH-TVJ	Bell 206B JetRanger	*761*	*VH-AZD*	*0072*	*1095*	*1 AN 250-C20*	*1451*			

AIRLINES OF SOUTH AUSTRALIA, Pty Ltd – ASA = RT / LRT (formerly Augusta Airways, Pty Ltd) **Port Augusta, SA**

PO Box 1756, Port Augusta, SA 5700, Australia ☎ (8) 86 42 31 00 Tx: 809627 augair aa Fax: (8) 86 41 08 60 SITA: n/a
F: 1978 ✈ 45 Head: Christine Kingham Net: n/a

☐ VH-KFO	Piper PA-44-180 Seminole	*44-7995208*	*N2203K*	*0079*		*2 LY O-360-E1A6D*	*1724*	*Y3 / Trainer*		
☐ VH-MEP	Piper PA-34-200 Seneca	*34-7350165*	*N55035*	*0073*		*2 LY IO-360-C1E6*	*1905*	*Y5*		
☐ VH-AZJ	Piper PA-31-350 Navajo Chieftain	*31-8152152*	*VH-OYY*	*0081*		*2 LY TIO-540-J2BD*	*3175*	*Y9*		
☐ VH-IJE	Piper PA-31-350 Navajo Chieftain	*31-7405463*	*N101BS*	*0074*	*1197*	*2 LY TIO-540-J2BD*	*3175*	*Y9*		
☐ VH-LMB	Piper PA-31-350 Navajo Chieftain	*31-8152142*	*N4090M*	*0081*	*0893*	*2 LY TIO-540-J2BD*	*3175*	*Y9*		
☐ VH-NPD	Piper PA-31-350 Navajo Chieftain	*31-7752126*	*N770SC*	*0077*		*2 LY TIO-540-J2BD*	*3175*	*Y9*		
☐ VH-ACZ	Twin (Aero) Shrike Commander 500S	*3176*	*N57029*	*0074*		*2 LY IO-540-E1B5*	*3062*	*Y6*		
☐ VH-LNB	Embraer 110P1 Bandeirante (EMB-110P1)	*110441*	*VH-WPE*	*0084*	*1197*	*2 PWC PT6A-34*	*5670*	*Y15*		City of Port Lincoln
☐ VH-LNC	Embraer 110P1 Bandeirante (EMB-110P1)	*110422*	*ZK-TRK*	*0083*	*1197*	*2 PWC PT6A-34*	*5670*	*Y15*		Spirit of Eyre Peninsula
☐ VH-PAG	Embraer 110P2 Bandeirante (EMB-110P2)	*110157*	*VH-FNP*	*0077*	*1298*	*2 PWC PT6A-34*	*5670*	*Y15*		Spirit of Augusta

AIRLINK, Pty Ltd (Member of Qantas Group / formerly Australian Airlink) **Perth, WA**

GPO Box D166, Perth, WA 6001, Australia ☎ (8) 92 25 83 83 Tx: none Fax: (8) 92 25 83 82 SITA: n/a
F: 1991 ✈ n/a Head: Grant Pitman Net: n/a Operates scheduled services on behalf of QANTAS using QF flight numbers.

☐ VH-NJC	BAe 146-100A	*E1013*	*G-6-013**	*0084*	*0091*	*4 LY ALF502R-5*	*37308*	*C6Y58*		City of Cairns / *lsf / opb NJS*
☐ VH-NJE	BAe 146-100	*E1104*	*G-BTXO*	*0089*	*0696*	*4 LY ALF502R-5*	*38101*	*C6Y58*		*lsf / opb NJS*
☐ VH-NJR	BAe 146-100	*E1152*	*G-BRLN*	*0090*	*0292*	*4 LY ALF502R-5*	*38101*	*C6Y58*		*lsf / opb NJS*
☐ VH-NJY	BAe 146-100	*E1005*	*G-SCHH*	*0083*	*0791*	*4 LY ALF502R-3A*	*37308*	*C6Y58*		*lsf / opb NJS*
☐ VH-NJZ	BAe 146-100	*E1009*	*G-6-009**	*0083*	*0795*	*4 LY ALF502R-3A*	*37308*	*C6Y58*		*lsf / opb NJS*
☐ VH-NJG	BAe 146-200	*E2170*	*G-BSOH*	*0090*	*0894*	*4 LY ALF502R-5*	*42184*	*C8Y68*		*lsf / opb NJS*
☐ VH-NJH	BAe 146-200	*E2178*	*G-BTCP*	*0091*	*0894*	*4 LY ALF502R-5*	*42184*	*C8Y68*		*lsf / opb NJS*

620 registration type of aircraft cn/fn ex/ex* mfd del powered by mtow kg configuration selcal name/fln/specialitites/remarks

registration	type of aircraft	cn/fn	ex/ex*	mfd	del	powered by	mtow kg	configuration	selcal	name/fln/specialitites/remarks
☐ VH-NJJ	BAe 146-200	E2184	G-BTKC	0091	0894	4 LY ALF502R-5	42184	C8Y68		lsf / opb NJS
☐ VH-NJQ	BAe 146-200A	E2072	G-BNJI	0087	0996	4 LY ALF502R-5	40597	C8Y68		lsf / opb NJS
☐ VH-NJU	BAe 146-200A	E2073	G-BVFV	0087	0996	4 LY ALF502R-5	40597	C8Y68		lsf / opb NJS
☐ VH-NJL	BAe 146-300	E3213	G-BVPE	0092	1194	4 LY ALF502R-5	44225	C8Y79		lsf / opb NJS
☐ VH-NJN	BAe 146-300	E3217	G-BUHW	0091	1194	4 LY ALF502R-5	44225	C8Y79		lsf / opb NJS

AIR LINK, Pty Ltd = DR

Dubbo, NSW

PO Box 223, Dubbo, NSW 2830, Australia ☎ (2) 68 84 24 35 Tx: none Fax: (2) 68 82 28 46 SITA: n/a
F: 1971 👥 11 Head: David Miller Net: n/a

registration	type of aircraft	cn/fn	ex/ex*	mfd	del	powered by	mtow kg	configuration	selcal	name/fln/specialitites/remarks
☐ VH-TDL	Piper PA-39-160 Twin Comanche C/R	39-152	VH-NHC	0072	0798	2 LY IO-320-B1A	1633			
☐ VH-BWQ	Cessna 310R II	310R1401	N4915A	0078	0892	2 CO IO-520-M	2495			cvtd T310R II
☐ VH-HSL	Cessna 310R II	310R0946	N8643G	0077		2 CO IO-520-M	2495			
☐ VH-JMP	Cessna 310R II	310R1270	N125SP	0078		2 CO IO-520-M	2495			
☐ VH-MXY	Cessna 310R II	310R1648	N2636N	0079	0397	2 CO IO-520-MB	2495			
☐ VH-DVR	Piper PA-31-350 Navajo Chieftain	31-7952052	N27936	0079	0492	2 LY TIO-540-J2BD	3175			
☐ VH-DVW	Piper PA-31-350 Navajo Chieftain	31-7952011	VH-LHH	0079	1093	2 LY TIO-540-J2BD	3175			
☐ VH-MWP	Piper PA-31-350 Navajo Chieftain	31-8352005	N4109C	0083	0295	2 LY TIO-540-J2BD	3175			
☐ VH-MZF	Piper PA-31-350 Navajo Chieftain	31-8252039	N41064	0082	0397	2 LY TIO-540-J2BD	3175			
☐ VH-MZM	Piper PA-31-350 Navajo Chieftain	31-8152187	N4096Y	0081	0199	2 LY TIO-540-J2BD	3175			

AIR MAREEBA (Angus Von Douglas dba)

Mareeba, QLD

PO Box 1400, Mareeba, QLD 4880, Australia ☎ (7) 40 92 21 81 Tx: none Fax: (7) 40 92 21 81 SITA: n/a
F: 1989 👥 1 Head: Angus Von Douglas Net: n/a

registration	type of aircraft	cn/fn	ex/ex*	mfd	del	powered by	mtow kg	configuration	selcal	name/fln/specialitites/remarks
☐ VH-AIA	Cessna A185F Skywagon	18502289	N3395S	0073		1 CO IO-520-D	1520			

AIR MOUNT ISA (Helicopter Operators, Pty Ltd dba / division of Simpson Aviation)

Mount Isa, QLD

PO Box 2168, Mount Isa, QLD 4825, Australia ☎ (7) 47 43 28 44 Tx: n/a Fax: (7) 47 43 61 80 SITA: n/a
F: 1971 👥 11 Head: Ross Lindsay Net: http://www.topend.com.au/ami

registration	type of aircraft	cn/fn	ex/ex*	mfd	del	powered by	mtow kg	configuration	selcal	name/fln/specialitites/remarks
☐ VH-MIJ	Cessna U206G Stationair 6 II	U20605297	N5453W	0079		1 CO IO-520-F	1633			
☐ VH-SQT	Cessna 210M Centurion II	21062874	N6005N	0078		1 CO IO-520-L	1724			
☐ VH-BPX	Cessna 402	402-0169	ZK-CSZ	0068		2 CO TSIO-520-E	2858			
☐ VH-RDZ	Cessna 402	402-0168	ZK-CSX	0068	1293	2 CO TSIO-520-E	2858			
☐ VH-HOA	Cessna 404 Titan II	404-0408	VH-SBV	0079		2 CO GTSIO-520-M	3810			

AIR NORTH EAST - Coastal Pacific Aviation (Alatron, Pty Ltd dba)

Lismore, NSW

PO Box 3014, Lismore, NSW 2480, Australia ☎ (66) 22 32 23 Tx: none Fax: (66) 22 32 23 SITA: n/a
F: 1992 👥 5 Head: Matthew Taylor Net: n/a Aircraft below MTOW 1361kg: Cessna 150 & Piper PA-28

registration	type of aircraft	cn/fn	ex/ex*	mfd	del	powered by	mtow kg	configuration	selcal	name/fln/specialitites/remarks
☐ VH-TBY	Cessna U206C Super Skywagon	U206-1006	VH-MRS	0068	0997	1 CO IO-520-F	1633			
☐ VH-TBE	Cessna 310R II	310R2119	VH-TXE	0081	0898	2 CO IO-520-M	2495			
☐ VH-TBG	Cessna 310R II	310R0299	VH-SGL	0076	0798	2 CO IO-520-M	2495			
☐ VH-TBI	Cessna 310R II	310R0801	VH-PPI	0077	0698	2 CO IO-520-M	2495			
☐ VH-PWV	AAC (Ted Smith) Aerostar 600A	60-0410-142	N9782Q	0078	0296	2 LY IO-540-K1F5	2495			
☐ VH-NEH	Piper PA-31-350 Navajo Chieftain	31-7405407	ZK-FIB	0074	0299	2 LY TIO-540-J2BD	3175			
☐ VH-SVV	Piper PA-31-350 Navajo Chieftain	31-7405175	VH-WGG	0074	0299	2 LY TIO-540-J2BD	3342			
☐ VH-TBJ	Piper PA-31-350 Navajo Chieftain	31-7552128	VH-SAJ	0075	0997	2 LY TIO-540-J2BD	3175			

AIRNORTH Regional = TL / ANO (Capiteq Ltd dba / formerly Air North Int'l, Ltd)

Alice Springs, Darwin & Katherine, NT

PO Box 39548, Winnellie, NT 0821, Australia ☎ (8) 89 45 29 99 Tx: none Fax: (8) 89 45 35 59 SITA: n/a
F: 1978 👥 n/a Head: Mike Bridge IATA: 935 Net: n/a

registration	type of aircraft	cn/fn	ex/ex*	mfd	del	powered by	mtow kg	configuration	selcal	name/fln/specialitites/remarks
☐ VH-AZO	Cessna 402C II	402C0508	N6874Y	0081	0297	2 CO TSIO-520-VB	3107	Y9		
☐ VH-NMQ	Cessna 402C II	402C0451	VH-RMQ	0081		2 CO TSIO-520-VB	3107	Y9		
☐ VH-RUY	Cessna 402C II	402C0273	N1774G	0080		2 CO TSIO-520-VB	3107	Y9		
☐ VH-CVN	Cessna 208B Grand Caravan	208B0676	N12372*	0098	0598	1 PWC PT6A-114A	3969	Y13		
☐ VH-NIA	Beech King Air 200	BB-470	N3018C	0079	1198	2 PWC PT6A-41	5670	Y9		
☐ VH-ANW	Fairchild (Swearingen) SA227DC Metro 23	DC-873B	N3031Q*	0095	0995	2 GA TPE331-12U-701G	7484	Y19		
☐ VH-MMA	Boeing (Douglas) DC-3C (C-47A-30-DL)	9583	VH-MWQ	0043		2 PW R-1830	11884	Y30		lsf Vintage Aircraft Co.

AIR SWIFT AVIATION = JOA (Division of Sea Swift, Pty Ltd)

Cairns, QLD

PO Box 6755, Cairns Mail Centre, Cairns, QLD 4870, Australia ☎ (7) 40 35 92 88 Tx: n/a Fax: (7) 40 35 92 54 SITA: n/a
F: 1986 👥 10 Head: S.W. Faithfull Net: n/a

registration	type of aircraft	cn/fn	ex/ex*	mfd	del	powered by	mtow kg	configuration	selcal	name/fln/specialitites/remarks
☐ VH-JOB	Cessna 310R II	310R1236	G-BOAT	0078		2 CO IO-520-MB	2495			
☐ VH-JOF	Cessna 310R II	310R0548	VH-HCB	0076		2 CO IO-520-MB	2495			
☐ VH-JOI	Cessna 310R II	310R0303	VH-BNR	0075	0792	2 CO IO-520-M	2495			
☐ VH-JOG	Twin (Aero) Shrike Commander 500S	500S-1856-38	VH-EXB	0069	1298	2 LY IO-540-E1B5	3357			
☐ VH-JOH	Cessna 402C II	402C0486	VH-JOC	0081	0895	2 CO TSIO-520-VB	3107			
☐ VH-JOV	Cessna 402C II	402C0087	VH-JOC	0079		2 CO TSIO-520-VB	3107			
☐ VH-MLM	Cessna 402B	402B0895	VH-JOG	0075	0591	2 CO TSIO-520-E	2858			
☐ VH-JOR	Cessna 404 Titan II	404-0642	D-IEEE	0080	0394	2 CO GTSIO-520-M	3810			

AIR TAXI AUSTRALIA, Pty Ltd

Brisbane-Eagle Farm, QLD

PO Box 1141, Eagle Farm, QLD 4009, Australia ☎ (7) 38 60 59 11 Tx: none Fax: (7) 38 60 59 22 SITA: n/a
F: 1996 👥 n/a Head: n/a Net: n/a

registration	type of aircraft	cn/fn	ex/ex*	mfd	del	powered by	mtow kg	configuration	selcal	name/fln/specialitites/remarks
☐ VH-KAD	Piper PA-31-310 Navajo B	31-7300924	N7495L	0073	0996	2 LY TIO-540-A2C	2948			

AIRTEX AVIATION (Avtex Air Services, Pty Ltd dba)

Sydney-Bankstown, NSW

501 Tower Road, Bankstown Airport, NSW 2200, Australia ☎ (2) 97 71 21 11 Tx: none Fax: (2) 97 92 16 61 SITA: n/a
F: 1984 👥 25 Head: Lester Peterson Net: http://www.airtexaviation.com

registration	type of aircraft	cn/fn	ex/ex*	mfd	del	powered by	mtow kg	configuration	selcal	name/fln/specialitites/remarks
☐ VH-XFA	Beech Baron E55	TE-791	P2-GKR	0070	0896	2 CO IO-520-C	2404			
☐ VH-UJF	Cessna 310R II	310R1342	N6215C	0078	0497	2 CO IO-520-M	2495			
☐ VH-IGN	AAC (Piper) Aerostar 601B	61-0682-7962142	N60700	0079		2 LY IO-540-S1A5	2722			
☐ VH-PWY	AAC (Ted Smith) Aerostar 601P	61P-0378-123	N9758Q	0077		2 LY IO-540-S1A5	2722			
☐ VH-HJE	Piper PA-31-350 Navajo Chieftain	31-7852074	N5038X	0078	0795	2 LY TIO-540-J2BD	3175			
☐ VH-HJH	Piper PA-31-350 Navajo Chieftain	31-7752127	VH-WZW	0077		2 LY TIO-540-J2BD	3175			
☐ VH-HJK	Piper PA-31-350 Navajo Chieftain	31-8052153	VH-JNX	0080	0696	2 LY TIO-540-J2BD	3175			
☐ VH-HJR	Piper PA-31-350 Navajo Chieftain	31-8252016	VH-MZX	0082	0497	2 LY TIO-540-J2BD	3175			
☐ VH-HJS	Piper PA-31-350 Navajo Chieftain	31-7652091	VH-TWB	0076	1098	2 LY TIO-540-J2BD	3175			
☐ VH-LGI	Piper PA-31-350 Navajo Chieftain	31-7952053	N667JT	0079	1298	2 LY TIO-540-J2BD	3175			
☐ VH-IGW	Piper PA-31P-350 Mojave	31P-8414019	N9233Y	0084		2 LY TIO-540-V2AD	3368			
☐ VH-DEG	Cessna 421B Golden Eagle	421B0637	VH-DEX	0074	0998	2 CO GTSIO-520-H	3379			
☐ VH-WGV	Fairchild (Swearingen) SA226TC Metro II	TC-287	ZK-SWD	0079	1098	2 GA TPE331-3UW-304G	5670			

AIRWAVES GOLD COAST, Pty Ltd

Main Beach, QLD

D Arm, Marina Mirage, Seaworld Drive, Main Beach, QLD 4215, Australia ☎ (7) 55 64 04 44 Tx: none Fax: (7) 55 28 00 90 SITA: n/a
F: 1996 👥 2 Head: N. Beissel Net: n/a

registration	type of aircraft	cn/fn	ex/ex*	mfd	del	powered by	mtow kg	configuration	selcal	name/fln/specialitites/remarks
☐ VH-ELQ	Cessna A185E Skywagon	185-1078	N4571F	0066	0996	1 CO IO-520-D	1520			Floats

AIR WHITSUNDAY SEAPLANES, Pty Ltd (Sister company of Coral Air Whitsunday, Pty Ltd)

Airlie Beach, QLD

PO Box 234, Airlie Beach, QLD 4802, Australia ☎ (7) 49 46 91 30 Tx: none Fax: (7) 49 46 91 85 SITA: n/a
F: 1974 👥 17 Head: Jon P. Davies Net: n/a Aircraft below MTOW 1361kg: Lake LA-250

registration	type of aircraft	cn/fn	ex/ex*	mfd	del	powered by	mtow kg	configuration	selcal	name/fln/specialitites/remarks
☐ VH-AWZ	De Havilland DHC-2 Beaver I	1618	VH-BSL	0065	1098	1 PW R-985	2309			Amphibian

AIRWORK HELICOPTERS (AMT Helicopters, Pty Ltd dba)

Caboolture, QLD

PO Box 857, Caboolture, QLD 4510, Australia ☎ (7) 54 95 80 00 Tx: none Fax: (7) 54 95 80 08 SITA: n/a
F: 1997 👥 n/a Head: Myles Tomkins Net: n/a Aircraft below MTOW 1361kg: Bell 47

registration	type of aircraft	cn/fn	ex/ex*	mfd	del	powered by	mtow kg	configuration	selcal	name/fln/specialitites/remarks
☐ VH-AJZ	Piper PA-31-310 Navajo	31-420	VH-KJD	0069	0998	2 LY TIO-540-A1A	2948			

ALICE SPRINGS AIR CHARTER, Pty Ltd (Rockayer)

Alice Springs, NT

PO Box 2987, Alice Springs, NT 0871, Australia ☎ (8) 89 55 52 00 Tx: n/a Fax: (8) 89 53 00 55 SITA: n/a
F: n/a 👥 n/a Head: n/a Net: n/a Aircraft below MTOW 1361kg: Cessna 172. Scenic flights are operated under the marketing name ROCKAYER.

registration	type of aircraft	cn/fn	ex/ex*	mfd	del	powered by	mtow kg	configuration	selcal	name/fln/specialitites/remarks
☐ VH-LTC	Piper PA-32R-301 Saratoga SP	32R-8113047	N740A	0081		1 LY IO-540-K1G5D	1633			
☐ VH-UAA	Cessna 207 Stationair 8 II	20700652	N75906	0080		1 CO IO-520-F	1724			
☐ VH-UBQ	Cessna 207 Skywagon	20700161	N1561U	0070	1193	1 CO IO-520-F	1724			
☐ VH-HMF	Beech Baron 58	TH-196	N9335Q	0072		2 CO IO-520-CB	2449			
☐ VH-JJN	Beech Baron 58	TH-1276	N3837M	0081	0193	2 CO IO-520-CB	2449			
☐ VH-AUG	Piper PA-31-350 Navajo Chieftain	31-7952132		0079	0898	2 LY TIO-540-J2BD	3175			
☐ VH-MNT	Piper PA-310 Navajo C	31-7812104	N27688	0078		2 LY TIO-540-A2C	2948			
☐ VH-SBN	Piper PA-31-350 Navajo Chieftain	31-7305070		0073		2 LY TIO-540-J2BD	3175			
☐ VH-TOT	Piper PA-31-350 Navajo Chieftain	31-7405438	N54315	0074		2 LY TIO-540-J2BD	3175			

ALLIGATOR AIRWAYS, Pty Ltd Kununurra, WA

PO Box 10, Kununurra, WA 6743, Australia ☎ (8) 91 68 13 33 Tx: none Fax: (8) 91 68 27 04 SITA: n/a
F: 1983 14 Head: Craig D. Muir Net: n/a

☐ VH-PQJ	Cessna U206F Stationair	U20602245	N1537U	0074		1 CO IO-550-F	1633			Floats / Wheels
☐ VH-RAS	Cessna 207 Skywagon	20700158	N1558U	0070		1 CO IO-520-F	1724			
☐ VH-WOT	Cessna 207 Skywagon	20700267	ZK-DEW	0075	0198	1 CO IO-520-F	1724			
☐ VH-WOU	Cessna 207 Skywagon	20700099	N91164	0069		1 CO IO-520-F	1724			
☐ VH-WOY	Cessna 207A Stationair 8 II	20800707	N9592M	0081		1 CO IO-520-F	1724			
☐ VH-EDE	Cessna 210L Centurion II	21060517		0074	0897	1 CO IO-520-L	1724			
☐ VH-FAP	Partenavia P.68B	45		0075		2 LY IO-360-A1B6	1960			
☐ VH-IXE	Partenavia P.68B	178		0078		2 LY IO-360-A1B6	1960			
☐ VH-WOG	De Havilland DHC-2 Beaver I	1561		0063		1 PW R-985	2313			Floats
☐ VH-MWJ	Beech Queen Air 70	LB-29	N4089A	0070	0895	2 LY IGSO-480-A1E6	3719			

ANINDILYAKWA AIR, Pty Ltd (Affiliated with Groote Island Aboriginal Trust/formerly Air Darwin) Darwin & Angurugu (Groote Eylandt), NT

PO Box 3395, Darwin, NT 0801, Australia ☎ (8) 89 45 22 30 Tx: none Fax: (8) 89 45 05 95 SITA: n/a
F: 1977 30 Head: Steve Chaplin Net: n/a

☐ VH-PZO	Cessna 210L Centurion II	21060298	N93185	0074	0796	1 CO IO-520-L	1724			
☐ VH-RDH	Cessna 210N Centurion II	21064374	N6427Y	0081	0596	1 CO IO-520-L	1724			
☐ VH-XGJ	Cessna 210N Centurion II	21063976	VH-NTZ	0080	0298	1 CO IO-520-L	1724			
☐ VH-COQ	Cessna 310R II	310R1643	N2635Y	0079	0796	2 CO IO-520-MB	2495			
☐ VH-DRP	Cessna 310R II	310R1557	N1738E	0079		2 CO IO-520-MB	2495			
☐ VH-JTS	Beech Baron B55 (95-B55)	TC-1992	N161Q	0076	1097	2 CO IO-470-L	2313			
☐ VH-BSE	Beech Baron 58	TH-526	N8182R	0075		2 CO IO-520-C	2449			
☐ VH-YJB	Beech Baron 58	TH-184	VH-NMT	0072	0898	2 CO IO-520-C	2449			
☐ VH-CYY	Piper PA-31-310 Navajo B	31-7401241	N913BT	0074		2 LY TIO-540-A2C	3102			
☐ VH-ENT	Cessna 404 Titan II	404-0818	ZK-ECP	0081	0398	2 CO GTSIO-520-M	3810			
☐ VH-KUZ	Cessna 441 Conquest II	441-0138	N311RR	0080	0297	2 GA TPE331-8-401S	4468			

ANSETT AIR FREIGHT, Ltd = AN / AAA (Subsidiary of Ansett Australia, Ltd) Sydney-Mascot, NSW

PO Box 558, Mascot, NSW 2020, Australia ☎ (2) 93 52 98 88 Tx: none Fax: (2) 93 52 97 79 SITA: n/a
F: n/a n/a Head: A. Markou IATA: 090 ICAO: ANSETT Net: n/a Beside aircraft listed, also uses Boeing (Douglas) DC-9-33F & Fokker F27-600, lsf/opb INDEPENDENT AIR FREIGHTERS (VH-), when required.

☐ VH-JJY	BAe 146-200 (QT)	E2113	G-BOXD*	0089	0589	4 LY ALF502R-5	42184	Freighter	FQ-DK	cvtd -200A
☐ VH-JJZ	BAe 146-200 (QT)	E2114	G-BOXE*	0089	0689	4 LY ALF502R-5	42184	Freighter	FQ-DL	cvtd -200A
☐ N6833	Boeing 727-223 (F)	20186 / 721		0569	0199	3 PW JT8D-9 (HK3/FDX)	80966	Freighter		lsf KHA / cvtd -223

ANSETT AUSTRALIA = AN / AAA (Ansett Austr.Ltd & Ansett Int'l Ltd dba/Subs.of Air New Zealand & The News Corp./Member of Star Alliance) Melbourne-Tullamarine, VIC

AnsettAustralia

501 Swanston Street, Melbourne, VIC 3000, Australia ☎ (3) 96 23 48 33 Tx: 30085 ansetts aa Fax: (3) 96 23 46 55 SITA: MELXTAN
F: 1936 9000 Head: Rod Eddington IATA: 090 ICAO: ANSETT Net: http://www.ansett.com.au
Commuter services in conjunction with Ansett using AN flight numbers are operated by: AEROPELICAN, IMPULSE, KENDELL, SKYWEST & SUNSHINE EXPRESS – for details see under each carrier.

☐ VH-ABR	Boeing (Douglas) DC-3-232A	2029	A30-3	0038	1038	2 WR R-1820	11884	Charters		Kanana / opb AN Hist.AvnSoc./old ANA cs
☐ VH-EWD	Fokker F28 Fellowship 4000 (F28 Mk4000)	11208	PH-EXT*	0084	1184	2 RR Spey 555-15P	33112	C72	CG-BK	
☐ VH-FKI	Fokker F28 Fellowship 4000 (F28 Mk4000)	11183	PH-EXZ*	0082	0782	2 RR Spey 555-15P	33112	C69		
☐ VH-FKJ	Fokker F28 Fellowship 4000 (F28 Mk4000)	11186	VH-EWH	0082	1282	2 RR Spey 555-15P	33112	C69	CK-HJ	
☐ VH-FKO	Fokker F28 Fellowship 4000 (F28 Mk4000)	11212	VH-LAR	0084	0790	2 RR Spey 555-15P	33112	C72		std MEL / for sale
☐ VH-JJP	BAe 146-200A	E2037		0085	0485	4 LY ALF502R-5	40597	C78	EH-DL	
☐ VH-JJQ	BAe 146-200A	E2038		0085	0685	4 LY ALF502R-5	40597	C78	EH-DM	
☐ VH-JJS	BAe 146-200	E2093	G-5-093*	0088	1088	4 LY ALF502R-5	42184	C78		
☐ VH-JJT	BAe 146-200	E2098	G-5-098*	0088	1188	4 LY ALF502R-5	42184	C78		
☐ VH-JJU	BAe 146-200	E2116	ZK-NZA	0089	0395	4 LY ALF502R-5	42184	C78		
☐ VH-JJW	BAe 146-200	E2110	G-5-110*	0088	0289	4 LY ALF502R-5	42184	C78	EP-JM	
☐ VH-JJX	BAe 146-200A	E2127	ZK-NZB	0089	0992	4 LY ALF502R-5	42184	C78		
☐ VH-EWI	BAe 146-300	E3171	G-6-171*	0090	0890	4 LY ALF502R-5	44225	C94		
☐ VH-EWM	BAe 146-300	E3179	G-6-179*	0090	1290	4 LY ALF502R-5	44225	C94		
☐ VH-EWR	BAe 146-300	E3195	G-6-195*	0091	0691	4 LY ALF502R-5	44225	C94		
☐ VH-EWS	BAe 146-300	E3197	G-6-197*	0091	0691	4 LY ALF502R-5	44225	C94		
☐ VH-CZA	Boeing 737-377	23653 / 1260		0086	0886	2 CFMI CFM56-3B1	61235	C24Y82	AD-GH	
☐ VH-CZB	Boeing 737-377	23654 / 1273	N5573B*	0086	0986	2 CFMI CFM56-3B1	61235	C24Y82		
☐ VH-CZC	Boeing 737-377	23655 / 1274		0086	0986	2 CFMI CFM56-3B1	61235	C24Y82	AD-GJ	
☐ VH-CZD	Boeing 737-377	23656 / 1279		0086	1086	2 CFMI CFM56-3B1	61235	C24Y82		
☐ VH-CZE	Boeing 737-377	23657 / 1280		0086	1086	2 CFMI CFM56-3B1	61235	C24Y82		
☐ VH-CZF	Boeing 737-377	23658 / 1281		0086	1086	2 CFMI CFM56-3B1	61235	C24Y82		
☐ VH-CZG	Boeing 737-377	23659 / 1292		0086	1186	2 CFMI CFM56-3B1	61235	C24Y82	BE-FM	
☐ VH-CZH	Boeing 737-377	23660 / 1294		0086	1186	2 CFMI CFM56-3B1	61235	C24Y82	AD-GH	
☐ VH-CZI	Boeing 737-377	23661 / 1314		0086	1286	2 CFMI CFM56-3B1	61235	C24Y82		
☐ VH-CZJ	Boeing 737-377	23662 / 1316		0086	1286	2 CFMI CFM56-3B1	61235	C24Y82		
☐ VH-CZK	Boeing 737-377	23663 / 1323		0086	0187	2 CFMI CFM56-3B1	61235	C24Y82		
☐ VH-CZL	Boeing 737-377	23664 / 1326		0086	0187	2 CFMI CFM56-3B1	61235	C24Y82		
☐ VH-CZM	Boeing 737-377	24302 / 1618	N113AW	0088	1088	2 CFMI CFM56-3B1	61235	C24Y82		
☐ VH-CZN	Boeing 737-377	24303 / 1620		0088	1088	2 CFMI CFM56-3B1	61235	C24Y82		
☐ VH-CZO	Boeing 737-377	24304 / 1622	N114AW	0088	1088	2 CFMI CFM56-3B1	61235	C24Y82		
☐ VH-CZP	Boeing 737-377	24305 / 1641	N115AW	0088	1188	2 CFMI CFM56-3B1	61235	C24Y82		
☐ VH-CZS	Boeing 737-33A	24030 / 1654	XA-SGJ	0089	0396	2 CFMI CFM56-3B1	61235	C24Y82		lsf AWAS
☐ VH-CZT	Boeing 737-33A	27454 / 2703		0095	0495	2 CFMI CFM56-3B1	61235	C24Y82	JP-BS	lsf AWAS
☐ VH-CZU	Boeing 737-33A	27267 / 2600		0094	0494	2 CFMI CFM56-3B1	61235	C24Y82		lsf AWAS
☐ VH-CZV	Boeing 737-33A	23831 / 1471	G-OBMA	0087	1293	2 CFMI CFM56-3B1	61235	C24Y82	DF-AP	lsf AWAS
☐ VH-CZW	Boeing 737-33A	23832 / 1473	G-OBMB	0087	0194	2 CFMI CFM56-3B1	61235	C24Y82	DF-BP	lsf AWAS
☐ VH-CZX	Boeing 737-33A	24029 / 1601	G-MONN	0088	0294	2 CFMI CFM56-3B1	61235	C24Y82	BQ-AK	
☐ VH-HYA	Airbus Industrie A320-211 (Skystar)	022	F-WWDR*	0088	1188	2 CFMI CFM56-5A1	73500	C28Y106	DL-MP	
☐ VH-HYB	Airbus Industrie A320-211 (Skystar)	023	F-WWDS*	0088	1188	2 CFMI CFM56-5A1	73500	C28Y106	EF-AP	Sydney 2000 Olympics-colors
☐ VH-HYC	Airbus Industrie A320-211 (Skystar)	024	F-WWDT*	0088	1288	2 CFMI CFM56-5A1	73500	C28Y106	EF-BP	
☐ VH-HYD	Airbus Industrie A320-211 (Skystar)	025	F-WWDU*	0088	0189	2 CFMI CFM56-5A1	73500	C28Y106	EF-CP	
☐ VH-HYE	Airbus Industrie A320-211 (Skystar)	026	F-WWDV*	0088	0289	2 CFMI CFM56-5A1	73500	C28Y106	EF-DP	
☐ VH-HYF	Airbus Industrie A320-211 (Skystar)	027	F-WWDD*	0088	0389	2 CFMI CFM56-5A1	73500	C28Y106	EF-GP	
☐ VH-HYG	Airbus Industrie A320-211 (Skystar)	029	F-WWDF*	0089	0489	2 CFMI CFM56-5A1	73500	C28Y106	EF-HP	
☐ VH-HYH	Airbus Industrie A320-211 (Skystar)	030	F-WWDI*	0089	0589	2 CFMI CFM56-5A1	73500	C28Y106	EF-JP	
☐ VH-HYI	Airbus Industrie A320-211 (Skystar)	140	F-WWDG*	0090	0191	2 CFMI CFM56-5A1	73500	C28Y106	AD-LR	
☐ VH-HYJ	Airbus Industrie A320-211 (Skystar)	142	F-WWDI*	0091	0191	2 CFMI CFM56-5A1	73500	C28Y106	AD-LS	
☐ VH-HYK	Airbus Industrie A320-211 (Skystar)	157	F-WWIB*	0091	0391	2 CFMI CFM56-5A1	73500	C28Y106	AD-MR	
☐ VH-HYL	Airbus Industrie A320-211 (Skystar)	229	F-WWIN*	0091	0492	2 CFMI CFM56-5A1	73500	C28Y106	AD-MS	
☐ VH-HYN	Airbus Industrie A320-211 (Skystar)	726	F-WWBP*	0097	1197	2 CFMI CFM56-5A1	73500	C28Y106		lsf ILFC
☐ VH-HYO	Airbus Industrie A320-211 (Skystar)	547	F-WWIU*	0095	0895	2 CFMI CFM56-5A1	73500	C28Y106		
☐ VH-HYQ	Airbus Industrie A320-211 (Skystar)	615	F-WWBR*	0096	0996	2 CFMI CFM56-5A1	73500	C28Y106		
☐ VH-HYR	Airbus Industrie A320-211 (Skystar)	622	F-WWBU*	0096	1096	2 CFMI CFM56-5A1	73500	C28Y106		
☐ VH-HYS	Airbus Industrie A320-211 (Skystar)	632	F-WWBI*	0096	1196	2 CFMI CFM56-5A1	73500	C28Y106		
☐ VH-HYT	Airbus Industrie A320-211 (Skystar)	662	F-WWDM*	0097	0397	2 CFMI CFM56-5A1	73500	C28Y106		
☐ VH-HYX	Airbus Industrie A320-211 (Skystar)	288	N491GX	0092	0596	2 CFMI CFM56-5A1	73500	C28Y106		lsf GATX
☐ VH-HYY	Airbus Industrie A320-211 (Skystar)	331	N490GX	0092	0596	2 CFMI CFM56-5A1	73500	C28Y106		lsf GATX
☐ VH-RMC	Boeing 767-219 (ER)	23326 / 124	HB-IIX	0085	0497	2 GE CF6-80A	159210	C25Y153	CP-GH	lsf ANZ
☐ VH-RMD	Boeing 767-277	22692 / 24	N8278V*	0083	0683	2 GE CF6-80A	140613	C30Y181	AD-FG	
☐ VH-RME	Boeing 767-277	22693 / 28	N8292V*	0083	0683	2 GE CF6-80A	140613	C30Y181	AD-FH	
☐ VH-RMF	Boeing 767-277	22694 / 32	N8287V*	0083	0683	2 GE CF6-80A	140613	C30Y181	AD-FJ	
☐ VH-RMG	Boeing 767-277	22695 / 35	N8289V*	0083	0883	2 GE CF6-80A	140613	C30Y181	AD-FK	
☐ VH-RMH	Boeing 767-277	22696 / 100	N1791B*	0084	0984	2 GE CF6-80A	140613	C30Y181	AD-FL	
☐ VH-RMK	Boeing 767-204	22981 / 79	G-BKVZ	0083	1194	2 GE CF6-80A	140613	C30Y181	HJ-GS	
☐ VH-RML	Boeing 767-204	22980 / 71	G-BKPW	0083	1195	2 GE CF6-80A	140613	C30Y181	KR-EM	
☐ VH-RMM	Boeing 767-216 (ER)	24973 / 347	N483GX	0091	0296	2 GE CF6-80A2	159210	C25Y153	LS-CJ	lsf GATX
☐ VH-RMO	Boeing 767-204	23807 / 184	G-BNCW	0087	0596	2 GE CF6-80A2	140613	C30Y181		lsf ILFC
☐ VH-BZF	Boeing 767-324 (ER)	27569 / 601	N6055X*	0096	0496	2 GE CF6-80C2B7F	186880	C25Y189	LS-CR	lsf GECA
☐ VH-INH	Boeing 747-312	23026 / 580	9V-SKA	0083	0894	4 PW JT9D-7R4G2	377842	F12C80Y326	FM-BD	lsf SIA -0899
☐ VH-INJ	Boeing 747-312	23029 / 590	9V-SKD	0083	0894	4 PW JT9D-7R4G2	377842	F12C80Y326	FM-BE	lsf SIA -0999 / Sydney 2000 Olympics-cs
☐ VH-ANA	Boeing 747-412	24062 / 722	9V-SMB	0089		4 PW PW4056	394625			to be lsf SIA 0899
☐ VH-ANB	Boeing 747-412	24064 / 755	9V-SMD	0089		4 PW PW4056	394625			to be lsf SIA 0999

ANSETT WORLDWIDE Aviation Services = (AWAS) (Subsidiary of TNT Ltd & News Corp. / Associated with Ansett Transport Ind.) Redfern, NSW / HKG / LON / MEL / SEA

Ansett Worldwide

Tower 1, TNT Plaza, Lawson Square, Redfern, NSW 2016, Australia ☎ (2) 96 99 22 22 Tx: 26536 aa Fax: (2) 96 99 13 49 SITA: n/a
F: 1985 n/a Head: Charles Graham IATA: 757 Net: n/a New and used aircraft leasing (dry & wet), sales and financing company.
Owner / Lessor of following (main) aircraft types: Airbus Industrie A300-600R, BAe 146, Boeing 737-300/500/700, 757-200/200F, 767-200/300 & McDonnell Douglas MD-83.
Aircraft leased from AWAS are listed and mentioned as such under the leasing carriers.

622 registration type of aircraft cn/fn ex/ex* mfd del powered by mtow kg configuration selcal name/fln/specialitites/remarks

AQUAFLIGHT AIRWAYS, Pty Ltd — Cairns, QLD

PO Box 664, Cairns, QLD 4870, Australia ☎ (7) 40 31 43 07 Tx: n/a Fax: (7) 40 41 25 40 SITA: n/a
F: 1985 👥 6 Head: David Presnell Net: n/a

☐ VH-IDQ	De Havilland DHC-2 Beaver I	1555		0064		1 PW R-985	2313			Floats
☐ VH-OTR	De Havilland DHC-3 Otter	373	C-FBEO	0060	0197	1 PW R-1340	3629			Floats

ARKAROOLA AIR SERVICES, Pty Ltd (Division of Arkaroola Travel Centre) — Arkaroola, SA

Arkaroola via Port Augusta, SA 5700, Australia ☎ (8) 86 48 48 48 Tx: none Fax: (8) 86 48 48 46 SITA: n/a
F: 1968 👥 26 Head: Doug Sprigg Net: n/a

☐ VH-SCI	Cessna 207 Skywagon	20700357	N1757U	0076		1 CO IO-520-F	1724	6 Pax		

ASIAN EXPRESS AIRLINES, Pty Ltd = HJ / AXF — Sydney-Mascot, NSW

PO Box 101, Mascot, NSW 2020, Australia ☎ (2) 96 67 19 91 Tx: none Fax: (2) 96 69 24 74 SITA: n/a
F: 1996 👥 n/a Head: Ross Howley ICAO: FREIGHTEXPRESS Net: n/a

☐ VH-DHE	Boeing 727-2J4 (F) (A)	22080 / 1598	N729DH	0080	1196	3 PW JT8D-17 (HK3/FDX)	90517	Freighter	BM-CJ	lsfBCS/lst/jtlyopwPremier/cvt-2J4/DHLcs

ASIA-PACIFIC AIRLINES (Auto Bake, Pty Ltd & Commander Land & Air Investments, Pty Ltd dba) — Sydney, NSW

PO Box 93, Hornsby, NSW 2077, Australia ☎ (2) 94 76 11 44 Tx: none Fax: (2) 94 82 10 74 SITA: n/a
F: n/a 👥 n/a Head: n/a Net: n/a

☐ VH-PCV	Twin (Aero) Turbo Commander 690A	11283	N57228	0076		2 GA TPE331-5-251K	4649			

ASSOCIATED AIRLINES, Pty Ltd — Melbourne-Essendon, VIC

Cnr Short Street & Nomad Road, Essendon Airport, VIC 3041, Australia ☎ (3) 93 74 17 77 Tx: none Fax: (3) 93 79 73 21 SITA: n/a
F: 1937 👥 34 Head: Peter A. Evans Net: n/a

☐ VH-EWP	Fokker F27 Friendship 500RF (F27 Mk500RF)	10534	PH-EXW*	0076	0292	2 RR Dart 536-7R	20410	Surveyer		lsf / opf LADS / R.A. Navy
☐ VH-CCA	GAC G-IV Gulfstream IV	1175	HB-ITJ	0091	0198	2 RR Tay 611-8	32590	Executive		opf Coca-Cola Amatil Ltd

AUS-AIR, Pty Ltd = NO / AUS (formerly Australian Air Charterers, Pty Ltd) — Melbourne-Moorabbin, VIC

116 Northern Avenue, Moorabbin Airport, VIC 3194, Australia ☎ (3) 95 80 61 66 Tx: none Fax: (3) 95 80 89 55 SITA: n/a
F: 1956 👥 28 Head: Bill Dart Net: n/a

☐ VH-OZM	Piper PA-31-350 Navajo Chieftain	31-7852003	VH-OAM	0078		2 LY TIO-540-J2BD	3175	Y9		
☐ VH-OZN	Piper PA-31-310 Navajo	31-285	VH-MBY	0068		2 LY TIO-540-A1A	2948	Y7		
☐ VH-OZO	Piper PA-31-310 Navajo	31-147	VH-RTO	0068		2 LY TIO-540-A1A	2948	Y7		
☐ VH-OZP	Piper PA-31-350 Navajo Chieftain	31-7752050	VH-MBP	0077		2 LY TIO-540-J2BD	3288	Y9		
☐ VH-OZT	Piper PA-31-350 Navajo Chieftain	31-7405157	VH-MBT	0074		2 LY TIO-540-J2BD	3175	Y9		
☐ VH-OZV	Piper PA-31-350 Navajo Chieftain	31-7405470	VH-TYV	0074		2 LY TIO-540-J2BD	3175	Y9		
☐ VH-OZF	Embraer 110P2 Bandeirante (EMB-110P2)	110201	G-EIIO	0079	0190	2 PWC PT6A-34	5670	Y15		
☐ VH-OZG	Embraer 110P1 Bandeirante (EMB-110P1)	110241	VH-XFJ	0080	0196	2 PWC PT6A-34	5670	Y15		City of Kingston

AUSSIE AIR, Pty Ltd — Adelaide-West Beach, SA

11 Rowell Road, Melrose Park, SA 5039, Australia ☎ (8) 82 77 47 41 Tx: n/a Fax: (8) 83 74 24 16 SITA: n/a
F: 1987 👥 2 Head: Brenton P. Hollitt Net: n/a

☐ VH-BIZ	Cessna 402B	402B0622	N3773C	0074		2 CO TSIO-520-E	2858			
☐ VH-RCA	Reims/Cessna F406 Caravan II	F406-0050	VT-SAA	0090	0698	2 PWC PT6A-112	4468			

AUSTCOPTERS, Pty Ltd — Brisbane-Archerfield, QLD

PO Box 584, Archerfield, QLD 4108, Australia ☎ (7) 32 74 14 77 Tx: none Fax: (7) 32 74 39 20 SITA: n/a
F: n/a 👥 n/a Head: n/a Net: n/a

☐ VH-HBK	Eurocopter (Aerosp.) AS350BA Squirrel	1360	ZK-HDV	0080	1297	1 TU Arriel 1B	2100			cvtd AS350B

AUSTRALASIAN JET, Pty Ltd — Melbourne-Essendon, VIC

Hangar 81, Essendon Airport, VIC 3041, Australia ☎ (3) 93 79 69 99 Tx: n/a Fax: (3) 93 79 59 49 SITA: n/a
F: 1990 👥 n/a Head: Alistair Lamb Net: http://www.ausjet.com.au

☐ VH-CGE	Cessna 337G Super Skymaster II	33701807	N1315L	0078	0199	2 CO IO-360-G	2100			
☐ VH-TTH	Beech Baron 58	TH-709	VH-BBT	0076		2 CO IO-520-C	2449			lsf pvt
☐ VH-TTM	Piper PA-31-310 Navajo	31-301	VH-PVL	0068	0995	2 LY TIO-540-A1A	2948			
☐ VH-TTK	Cessna 404 Titan II	404-0423	ST-AMA	0079	0295	2 CO GTSIO-520-M	3810			
☐ VH-TTZ	Cessna 404 Titan II	404-0095	VH-SBG	0077		2 CO GTSIO-520-M	3810			
☐ VH-TTD	Piper PA-31T Cheyenne II	31T-8020005	VH-DXI	0080	0995	2 PWC PT6A-28	4082			
☐ VH-NMA	Piper PA-42 Cheyenne III	42-8001066	N62WC	0082	0597	2 PWC PT6A-41	5080			
☐ VH-WCE	Piper PA-42 Cheyenne III	42-8001033	N582SW	0081	0498	2 PWC PT6A-41	5080			

AUSTRALASIAN MAPPING SERVICES (Papam, Pty Ltd dba) — Brisbane, QLD

159 Gailey Road, Taringa, QLD 4068, Australia ☎ (7) 38 70 33 27 Tx: n/a Fax: (7) 38 70 58 22 SITA: n/a
F: 1971 👥 6 Head: P. Strong Net: n/a

☐ VH-RLX	Cessna 320D SkyKnight	320D0097	N4197T	0066		2 CO TSIO-520-B	2359	Photo / Survey		
☐ VH-MWG	Cessna 402	402-0154	N4054Q	0067		2 CO TSIO-520-E	2858	Photo / Survey		

AUSTRALIAN AERIAL PATROL (City of Wollongong Aerial Patrol, Inc. dba) — Wollongong, NSW

PO Box 162, Dapto, NSW 2530, Australia ☎ (42) 57 32 00 Tx: none Fax: (42) 52 32 55 SITA: n/a
F: 1957 👥 n/a Head: n/a Net: n/a Non-commercial city-owned organisation conducting rescue & surveying flights.

☐ VH-APH	Partenavia P.68C-TC	351-36-TC	VH-SLS	0085	0896	2 LY TIO-360-C1A6D	1990	Aerial Patrol		

AUSTRALIAN AIR EXPRESS, Pty Ltd = XM / XME (Joint venture between Qantas & Australia Post) — Melbourne-Tullamarine, VIC

PO Box 1324L, Melbourne, VIC 3001, Australia ☎ (3) 92 41 65 33 Tx: none Fax: (3) 92 41 65 57 SITA: MELFXTN
F: 1992 👥 1150 Head: A. Buckley IATA: 524 Net: n/a Operates scheduled cargo services. All aircraft contracted out/operated by: AIR CARGO AUSTRALIA, NATIONAL JET & PEL-AIR on behalf of Australian Air Express.

☐ VH-EEN	Fairchild (Swearingen) SA227AT Expediter	AT-563	N563UP	0083	0297	2 GA TPE331-11U-611G	6577	Freighter		lsf/opb QWA / Australian Air Express-cs
☐ VH-EEO	Fairchild (Swearingen) SA227AT Expediter	AT-564	N564UP	0083	0297	2 GA TPE331-11U-611G	6577	Freighter		lsf/opb QWA / Australian Air Express-cs
☐ VH-EEP	Fairchild (Swearingen) SA227AT Expediter	AT-567	N565UP	0083	0297	2 GA TPE331-11U-611G	6577	Freighter		lsf/opb QWA / Australian Air Express-cs
☐ VH-NJV	BAe 146-100 (QC)	E1002	G-BSTA	0083	0995	4 LY ALF502R-3	37308	Freighter		lsf / opb National Jet / cvtd -100
☐ VH-NJF	BAe 146-300 (QT)	E3198	G-BTLD	0091	1092	4 LY ALF502R-5	44225	Freighter		lsf / opb National Jet / cvtd -300
☐ VH-NJM	BAe 146-300 (QT)	E3194	G-BTHT	0091	1195	4 LY ALF502R-5	44225	Freighter		lsf / opb National Jet / cvtd -300
☐ VH-TBS	Boeing 727-77C	20278 / 768	C2-RN7	0069	1195	3 PW JT8D-7A (HK3/FDX)	76884	Freighter		lsf / opb Air Cargo Australia
☐ VH-AUP	Boeing 727-277 (F) (A)	21695 / 1481	VH-RMN	0079	1197	3 PW JT8D-15 (HK3/FDX)	86409	Freighter		lsf / opb Air Cargo Australia/cvtd -277

AUSTRALIAN FLYERS, Pty Ltd — Albury, NSW

PO Box 796, Albury, NSW 2640, Australia ☎ (18) 57 28 11 Tx: none Fax: (18) 57 28 11 SITA: n/a
F: n/a 👥 n/a Head: Stirling Preston Net: n/a Aircraft below MTOW 1361kg: Cessna 152 & 172

☐ VH-JCC	Fokker F27 Friendship 700 (F27 Mk700)	10176	N146PM	0061	1197	2 RR Dart 514-7	18370	Y40 / Freighter		cvtd 100

AUSTRALIAN GEOPHYSICAL SURVEY (Durie, Pty Ltd dba) — Perth-Jandakot, WA

3 Baron Way, Jandakot, WA 6164, Australia ☎ (8) 94 14 12 66 Tx: none Fax: (8) 94 14 12 77 SITA: n/a
F: 1996 👥 n/a Head: n/a Net: n/a

☐ VH-AGS	Cessna 208B Grand Caravan	208B0615	N1215S	0097	0797	1 PWC PT6A-114A	3969	Surveyer		

AUSTRALIAN JET CHARTER, Pty Ltd – AJC (Subsidiary of British World Airlines, Ltd) — Sydney-Kingsford Smith, NSW

PO Box 205, Mascot, NSW 1460, Australia ☎ (2) 96 93 08 00 Tx: none Fax: (2) 96 93 08 80 SITA: n/a
F: 1984 👥 28 Head: Terry Sloane Net: n/a

☐ VH-XDD	Cessna 550 Citation II	550-0076	VH-TFY	0079		2 PWC JT15D-4	6033	Executive		lsf One Air P/L
☐ VH-BAE	BAe 3201 Jetstream 32EP	878	N878AE	0090	0998	2 GA TPE331-12UAR-704H	7350	Y19		lsf BAMT / cvtd 32

AUSTRALIA WORLD AIRWAYS, Pty Ltd — Melbourne-Tullamarine, VIC

Level 1, 9 Queen Street, Melbourne, VIC 3000, Australia ☎ (3) 96 21 12 99 Tx: none Fax: (3) 96 21 19 49 SITA: n/a
F: 1993 👥 12 Head: Simon Warrender Net: n/a Presently being set-up. Intends to start operations during 1999 with long-range wide body-aircraft.

AUSTREK AVIATION, Pty Ltd — Moree, NSW

Amaroo Tavern, Moree, NSW 2400, Australia ☎ (2) 67 52 72 66 Tx: n/a Fax: (2) 67 52 55 04 SITA: n/a
F: 1993 👥 n/a Head: Martin Taylor Net: n/a Aircraft below MTOW 1361kg: Cessna 172

☐ VH-DZU	Cessna 310R II	310R0123	VH-TXX	0075	1098	2 CO IO-520-M	2495			
☐ VH-DZX	Cessna 310R II	310R0294	VH-KGV	0075	1196	2 CO IO-520-M	2495			
☐ VH-DZY	Cessna 402A	402A0066	N4566Q	0069	0795	2 CO TSIO-520-E	2858			

AVIATION CENTRE, Pty Ltd (Affiliated with Aviation Centre (Maintenance) P/L & Aerospace Aviation,P/L) — Sydney-Kingsford Smith & -Bankstown, NSW

444 Marion Street, Bankstown Airport, NSW 2200, Australia ☎ (2) 97 91 02 44 Tx: 75016 avcen aa Fax: (2) 97 91 03 56 SITA: n/a
F: 1971 👥 14 Head: Brian Sorfleet Net: n/a

☐ VH-PNZ	Partenavia P.68B	77		0076		2 LY IO-360-A1B6	1960			
☐ VH-AVS	AAC (Piper) Aerostar 600A	60-0604-7961194	N8204J	0079		2 LY IO-540-K1F5	2495	Freighter		opf Security Express
☐ VH-IXA	AAC (Ted Smith) Aerostar 601B	61-0476-126	N9817Q	0078		2 LY IO-540-S1A5	2722	Freighter		opf Security Express
☐ VH-NOU	AAC (Piper) Aerostar 601P	61P-0668-7963312	N82RS	0079		2 LY IO-540-S1A5	2722			
☐ VH-DRQ	Cessna 340A II	340A0294	N4122G	0077		2 CO TSIO-520-N	2717			
☐ VH-DRN	Cessna 414A Chancellor II	414A0093	N4759A	0078		2 CO TSIO-520-N	3062			
☐ VH-AVF	Piper PA-31-350 Navajo Chieftain	31-7852118	ZK-PAI	0078		2 LY TIO-540-J2BD	3175			
☐ VH-SSL	Fairchild (Swearingen) SA226T Merlin III	T-210	N173SP	0070	1198	2 GA TPE331-3U-303G	5670			

623 registration type of aircraft cn/fn ex/ex* mfd del powered by mtow kg configuration selcal name/fln/specialitites/remarks

BAROSSA HELICOPTER SERVICE (Kies Aviation, Pty Ltd dba) — **Lyndoch, SA**

PO Box 58, Lyndoch, SA 5351, Australia ☎ (8) 85 24 42 09 Tx: none Fax: (8) 85 24 48 30 SITA: n/a
F: 1988 n/a Head: n/a Net: n/a Aircraft below MTOW 1361kg: Bell 47J-2A

registration	type of aircraft	cn/fn	ex/ex*	mfd	del	powered by	mtow kg	configuration	selcal	name/fln/specialitites/remarks
☐ VH-FRL	Bell 206B JetRanger	771	G-BRDL	0072	0697	1 AN 250-C20	1451			

BASS STRAIT AIR CHARTER, Pty Ltd — **Melbourne-Moorabbin, VIC**

PO Box 5030, Cheltenham East, VIC 3192, Australia ☎ (3) 95 80 65 56 Tx: none Fax: (3) 95 87 67 06 SITA: n/a
F: 1993 n/a Head: Anthony Norman Net: n/a

registration	type of aircraft	cn/fn	ex/ex*	mfd	del	powered by	mtow kg	configuration	selcal	name/fln/specialitites/remarks
☐ VH-EDV	Piper PA-31-350 Navajo Chieftain	31-7305025	N86588	0073		2 LY TIO-540-J2BD	3175			
☐ VH-PWA	Piper PA-31-350 Navajo Chieftain	31-7652072	N59819	0076	0697	2 LY TIO-540-J2BD	3175			

BATCHELOR AIR CHARTER (Batchelor Aviation, Pty Ltd dba) — **Batchelor, NT**

BATCHELOR AVIATION

Post Office, Batchelor, NT 0845, Australia ☎ (8) 89 76 00 23 Tx: none Fax: (8) 89 76 01 34 SITA: n/a
F: 1977 6 Head: R. Skinnor Net: n/a Aircraft below MTOW 1361kg: Cessna 182Q.

registration	type of aircraft	cn/fn	ex/ex*	mfd	del	powered by	mtow kg	configuration	selcal	name/fln/specialitites/remarks
☐ VH-FZO	Cessna 210M Centurion II	21061602	N732LS	0077		1 CO IO-520-L	1724			
☐ VH-JEV	Cessna 210N Centurion II	21063490	N5546A	0080		1 CO IO-520-L	1724			
☐ VH-SGX	Cessna 210N Centurion II	21064684	N1307U	0082		1 CO IO-520-L	1724			
☐ VH-TIJ	Cessna 210L Centurion II	21060591	N60105	0075		1 CO IO-520-L	1724			
☐ VH-WRD	Cessna 210M Centurion II	21062942	N6171N	0078		1 CO IO-520-L	1724			
☐ VH-BMN	Cessna 401A	401A0001	P2-BMN	0068		2 CO TSIO-520-E	2858			

BEAGLE AIRWAYS (William R. Leonard dba) — **Cairns, QLD**

PO Box 196, Trinity Beach, QLD 4879, Australia ☎ (7) 40 55 61 08 Tx: n/a Fax: (7) 40 55 62 11 SITA: n/a
F: 1974 2 Head: William R. Leonard Net: n/a

registration	type of aircraft	cn/fn	ex/ex*	mfd	del	powered by	mtow kg	configuration	selcal	name/fln/specialitites/remarks
☐ VH-WHE	Piper PA-31-310 Navajo	31-691	N6781L	0070		2 LY TIO-540-A2C	2948	7 Pax		

BEECHJET CHARTER (E. Brown, Pty Ltd dba) — **Sydney-Mascot, NSW**

Suite 17, 20-24 Gibbs Street, Miranda, NSW 2228, Australia ☎ (2) 94 89 67 22 Tx: none Fax: (2) 94 89 84 43 SITA: n/a
F: 1994 n/a Head: Warrick Brown Net: n/a

registration	type of aircraft	cn/fn	ex/ex*	mfd	del	powered by	mtow kg	configuration	selcal	name/fln/specialitites/remarks
☐ VH-BJC	Beech Beechjet 400A	RK-154	N2354B	0097	0498	2 PWC JT15D-5	7303			

BELLARINE AVIATION, Pty Ltd — **Queenscliff, VIC**

PO Box 158, Queenscliff, VIC 3225, Australia ☎ (3) 52 58 40 45 Tx: none Fax: (3) 52 58 40 46 SITA: n/a
F: n/a n/a Head: n/a Net: n/a

registration	type of aircraft	cn/fn	ex/ex*	mfd	del	powered by	mtow kg	configuration	selcal	name/fln/specialitites/remarks
☐ VH-FXK	Cessna 205 (210-5)	205-0133	VH-KXK	0063	0398	1 CO IO-470-S	1497			

BLUEWATER AVIATION, Pty Ltd (Affiliated with Armino, Pty Ltd) — **Townsville, QLD**

PO Box 7522, Garbutt, QLD 4814, Australia ☎ (77) 25 18 88 Tx: n/a Fax: (77) 25 14 51 SITA: n/a
F: 1985 n/a Head: n/a Net: n/a Aircraft below MTOW 1361kg: Cessna 152 & 172.

registration	type of aircraft	cn/fn	ex/ex*	mfd	del	powered by	mtow kg	configuration	selcal	name/fln/specialitites/remarks
☐ VH-IYC	Partenavia P.68B	119		0077		2 LY IO-360-A1B6	1960			
☐ VH-EZN	Beech Baron 58	TH-1222	N3722P	0081		2 CO IO-520-CB	2449			

BOB SMITH HELICOPTER SERVICES (Robert F. & M.P. Smith dba) — **Cairns, QLD**

20 Cayley Street, Trinity Beach, QLD 4871, Australia ☎ (7) 40 55 67 70 Tx: none Fax: (7) 40 55 67 70 SITA: n/a
F: n/a n/a Head: Robert F. Smith Net: n/a

registration	type of aircraft	cn/fn	ex/ex*	mfd	del	powered by	mtow kg	configuration	selcal	name/fln/specialitites/remarks
☐ VH-JMN	Bell 206B JetRanger	1353	N59530	0074		1 AN 250-C20	1451			

BRENCORP HELI, Pty Ltd — **Melbourne-Moorabbin, VIC**

367 Collins Street, 30th Floor, Melbourne, VIC 3000, Australia ☎ (3) 96 14 43 99 Tx: n/a Fax: (3) 93 79 94 54 SITA: n/a
F: 1990 n/a Head: Mark Robertson Net: n/a

registration	type of aircraft	cn/fn	ex/ex*	mfd	del	powered by	mtow kg	configuration	selcal	name/fln/specialitites/remarks
☐ VH-BHF	Bell 206L-1 LongRanger III	45164	N5000H	0078		1 AN 250-C30P	1882			cvtd LongRanger II
☐ VH-NNN	Bell 205A-1	30131	C-FMHA	0073	0997	1 LY T5313B	4763			

BRINDABELLA AIRLINES (Lara R. Corry dba) — **Canberra, ACT**

PO Box 1542, Fyshwick, ACT 2609, Australia ☎ (2) 62 48 87 11 Tx: none Fax: (6) 248 00 87 SITA: n/a
F: 1994 8 Head: Lara R. Corry Net: n/a

registration	type of aircraft	cn/fn	ex/ex*	mfd	del	powered by	mtow kg	configuration	selcal	name/fln/specialitites/remarks
☐ VH-BDT	Piper PA-34-200T Seneca II	34-7770398	N47470	0077		2 CO TSIO-360-EB1A	2073			lsf Purchasing Company P/L
☐ VH-KLS	Piper PA-31-310 Navajo	31-8112030	ZK-KPL	0081		2 LY TIO-540-A2C	2948			lsf Scientific Management Associates
☐ VH-TAR	Piper PA-31-350 Navajo Chieftain	31-7405207	ZK-PKC	0074	0997	2 LY TIO-540-J2BD	3175			
☐ VH-TAS	Piper PA-31-350 Navajo Chieftain	31-7652012	N38335	0076		2 LY TIO-540-J2BD	3175			lsf Purchasing Company P/L
☐ VH-WAL	Piper PA-31-310 Navajo B	31-7300943	N71TC	0073		2 LY TIO-540-A2C	2948			

BRISTOW HELICOPTERS (Australia), Pty Ltd (formerly Mayne-Bristow Helicopters, Pty Ltd) — **Perth/Karratha/Barrow Island, WA & Darwin, NT**

BRISTOW HELICOPTERS AUSTRALIA

135 Fauntleroy Ave, Redcliffe, WA 6104, Australia ☎ (8) 94 78 33 88 Tx: none Fax: (8) 94 78 38 44 SITA: n/a
F: 1967 75 Head: Phil Johns Net: n/a

registration	type of aircraft	cn/fn	ex/ex*	mfd	del	powered by	mtow kg	configuration	selcal	name/fln/specialitites/remarks
☐ VH-BHO	Bell 206L-3 LongRanger III	51354	JA9893	0090	0892	1 AN 250-C30P	1882	7 Pax		
☐ VH-BHI	Sikorsky S-76A+	760118	G-BVKS	0080	0595	2 TU Arriel 1S	4899	12 Pax		cvtd S-76A
☐ VH-BHL	Sikorsky S-76A+	760046	G-BHLY	0080	1298	2 TU Arriel 1S	4899	12 Pax		cvtd S-76A
☐ VH-BHM	Sikorsky S-76A+	760107	G-BVKO	0080	0994	2 TU Arriel 1S	4899	12 Pax		cvtd S-76A
☐ VH-BHQ	Sikorsky S-76A++	760090	G-BVKN	0080	0794	2 TU Arriel 1S1	4899	12 Pax		cvtd S-76A
☐ VH-WOD	Eurocopter (Aerosp.) SA330J Puma	1478	G-BFEU	0077		2 TU Turmo IVC	7400	16 Pax		
☐ VH-WOE	Eurocopter (Aerosp.) SA330J Puma	1475	G-BERH	0077		2 TU Turmo IVC	7400	16 Pax		
☐ VH-BHH	Eurocopter (Aerosp.) AS332L Tiger	2059	G-TIGW	0083	0399	2 TU Makila 1A	8600	18 Pax		
☐ VH-BHX	Eurocopter (Aerosp.) AS332L Tiger	2079	G-BRWE	0083		2 TU Makila 1A	8600	18 Pax		

BROOK ARMSTRONG AVIATION SERVICES, Pty Ltd — **Sydney-Bankstown, VIC**

Hangar 131, Cirrus Place, Bankstown Airport, NSW 2200, Australia ☎ (2) 97 91 05 48 Tx: none Fax: (2) 97 91 05 49 SITA: n/a
F: n/a n/a Head: n/a Net: n/a

registration	type of aircraft	cn/fn	ex/ex*	mfd	del	powered by	mtow kg	configuration	selcal	name/fln/specialitites/remarks
☐ VH-KOF	Mitsubishi MU-2G (MU-2B-30) Cargoliner	544	VH-WMW	0071	0898	2 GA TPE331-1-151A	4899			Cavenenaugh SCD conversion
☐ VH-MNU	Mitsubishi MU-2G (MU-2B-30)	527	VH-UZN	0070	0797	2 GA TPE331-1-151A	4900	Freighter		
☐ VH-UZB	Mitsubishi MU-2G (MU-2B-30)	528	ZK-ESM	0070	0697	2 GA TPE331-1-151A	4900	Freighter		

BROOME AVIATION, Pty Ltd — **Broome, WA**

PO Box 386, Broome, WA 6725, Australia ☎ (8) 91 92 13 69 Tx: none Fax: (8) 91 92 24 76 SITA: n/a
F: 1982 n/a Head: n/a Net: n/a

registration	type of aircraft	cn/fn	ex/ex*	mfd	del	powered by	mtow kg	configuration	selcal	name/fln/specialitites/remarks
☐ VH-OTV	De Havilland DHC-3 Turbo Otter	250	N373A	0058	1197	1 PWC PT6A-135A	3629			lsf Vazar P/L / Amphibian / cvtd Otter

CAPE YORK AIR = NS (Janlin, Pty Ltd dba / formerly Cape York Air Services & Cooktown Air Services) — **Cairns, QLD**

CAPE YORK AIR

PMB 13, Cairns Mail Centre, QLD 4871, Australia ☎ (7) 40 35 93 99 Tx: none Fax: (7) 40 35 91 08 SITA: CNSEWPX
F: 1974 30 Head: Robert Fulton Net: n/a

registration	type of aircraft	cn/fn	ex/ex*	mfd	del	powered by	mtow kg	configuration	selcal	name/fln/specialitites/remarks
☐ VH-IYI	Partenavia P.68B Victor	136		0078		2 LY IO-360-A1BD	1960			
☐ VH-CYV	Piper PA-31-310 Navajo	31-18	VH-DZZ	0067		2 LY TIO-540-A2B	3102			
☐ VH-DMF	Piper PA-31-310 Navajo	31-447	N6483L	0069		2 LY TIO-540-A2B	3102			
☐ VH-RTP	Britten-Norman BN-2A-6 Islander	79	G-AXIN	0070		2 LY O-540-E4C5	2858			
☐ VH-CYC	Cessna 208 Caravan I	20800108	N977A	0086	0196	1 PWC PT6A-114	3740			Sir Bob Norman
☐ VH-FNV	De Havilland DHC-6 Twin Otter 320	313	P2-RDJ	0071	0498	2 PWC PT6A-27	5670			lst Hevi Lift

CARDWELL AIR CHARTER (Margaret E. Prior dba) — **Cardwell, QLD**

PO Box 225, Cardwell, QLD 4849, Australia ☎ (7) 40 66 84 68 Tx: none Fax: (7) 40 66 84 68 SITA: n/a
F: 1996 1 Head: Margaret E. Prior Net: n/a

registration	type of aircraft	cn/fn	ex/ex*	mfd	del	powered by	mtow kg	configuration	selcal	name/fln/specialitites/remarks
☐ VH-UBX	Cessna 207 Skywagon	20700138	N1538U	0069	0297	1 CO IO-550-F2B	1724			

CAREFLIGHT (Associated with Careflight Queensland / Sponsored by NRMA) — **Westmead-Westmead Hospital, NSW**

CareFlight

PO Box 159, Westmead, NSW 2145, Australia ☎ (2) 98 91 61 44 Tx: none Fax: (2) 98 91 13 13 SITA: n/a
F: 1986 35 Head: Dr. Luis Gallur Net: n/a

registration	type of aircraft	cn/fn	ex/ex*	mfd	del	powered by	mtow kg	configuration	selcal	name/fln/specialitites/remarks
☐ VH-CFT	Bell 412HP	36050	N4383D	0092	1294	2 PWC PT6T-3BE TwinPac	5262	EMS		

CAREFLIGHT QUEENSLAND (Gold Coast Helicopter Rescue Service Ltd dba / Assoc.with Careflight, NSW / Sponsored by RACQ) — **Nerang, QLD**

CareFlight

PO Box 15, Tugun, QLD 4224, Australia ☎ (7) 55 98 02 22 Tx: n/a Fax: (7) 55 98 03 83 SITA: n/a
F: 1981 15 Head: P. Young Net: http://www.careflight.or.au/

registration	type of aircraft	cn/fn	ex/ex*	mfd	del	powered by	mtow kg	configuration	selcal	name/fln/specialitites/remarks
☐ VH-XCF	Bell 412	33019	N2070C	0081	0295	2 PWC PT6T-3B TwinPac	5262	EMS		

CENTRAL AIR, Pty Ltd — **Perth-Jandakot, WA**

PO Box 1116, Cloverdale, WA 6105, Australia ☎ (8) 94 79 74 40 Tx: none Fax: (8) 94 79 74 41 SITA: n/a
F: 1985 n/a Head: Ben Martinez Net: n/a

registration	type of aircraft	cn/fn	ex/ex*	mfd	del	powered by	mtow kg	configuration	selcal	name/fln/specialitites/remarks
☐ VH-SGT	Beech King Air 200	BB-73		0075	1096	2 PWC PT6A-41	5670			
☐ VH-SKC	Beech King Air 200	BB-47	RP-C200	0075	0299	2 PWC PT6A-41	5670			

CENTRAL HELICOPTERS, Pty Ltd
Adelaide-Parafield, SA

34 Croydon Road, Kesack, SA 5035, Australia ☎ (8) 82 97 91 55 Tx: none Fax: (8) 82 97 40 40 SITA: n/a
F: 1995 ⁂ n/a Head: n/a Net: n/a

	registration	type of aircraft	cn/fn	ex/ex*	mfd	del	powered by	mtow kg	configuration	selcal	name/fln/remarks
☐	VH-CHD	Bell 206B JetRanger II	2028	A6-BCG	0076	1096	1 AN 250-C20	1451			

CENTRAL HIGHLANDS AIR TRANSPORT, Pty Ltd (formerly Central Aerial Services – C.A.S.)
Emerald, QLD

PO Box 172, Emerald, QLD 4720, Australia ☎ (79) 87 55 66 Tx: n/a Fax: (79) 82 32 33 SITA: n/a
F: 1967 ⁂ 20 Head: James W. Johnson Net: n/a Aircraft / Ag-Aircraft below MTOW 1361 / 5000 kg: Airtrac 301, Ayres S2R & Piper PA-28.

☐ VH-BDG	Piper PA-32-300 Cherokee SIX	32-7740092	N38670	0077		1 LY IO-540-K1A5	1542		
☐ VH-LPW	Piper PA-32R-301 Saratoga SP	32R-8113095	N2889A	0081		1 LY IO-540-K1G5D	1633		
☐ VH-MSR	Piper PA-32-300 Cherokee SIX	32-7340106		0073		1 LY IO-540-K1A5	1542		
☐ VH-JMM	Piper PA-34-220T Seneca III	34-8233168	N8230Y	0082	0997	2 CO TSIO-360-KB	1999		
☐ VH-MRY	Piper PA-34-220T Seneca III	34-8233026	N8461M	0082	0896	2 CO TSIO-360-KB	2155		
☐ VH-TVZ	Piper PA-34-200T Seneca III	34-7770219	N3168Q	0077		2 CO TSIO-360-E	2073		
☐ VH-DXL	Piper PA-23-250 Aztec D	27-4033	N6706Y	0069		2 LY IO-540-C4B5	2359		
☐ VH-NCS	Piper PA-23-250 Aztec E	27-7654170	ZK-TNH	0076	0590	2 LY IO-540-C4B5	2359		
☐ VH-BCQ	Piper PA-31-350 Navajo Chieftain	31-7952134	N35265	0079		2 LY TIO-540-J2BD	3175		

CGA AUSTRALIA, Pty Ltd (formerly Courtenay & Gardner Aviation, Pty Ltd)
Melbourne-Moorabbin, VIC

Building 21, Bundora Parade, Moorabbin Airport, VIC 3194, Australia ☎ (3) 95 87 31 00 Tx: n/a Fax: (3) 95 87 38 30 SITA: n/a
F: 1985 ⁂ 3 Head: Robert A. Courtenay Net: n/a Aircraft below MTOW 1361kg: Cessna 180

☐ VH-AGF	Cessna 185A Skywagon	185-0495	VH-RKS	0062	1 CO IO-470-F	1451	
☐ VH-FLU	Cessna A185E Skywagon	185-1315	N3363L	0068	1 CO IO-520-D	1520	
☐ VH-DMG	Piper PA-23-250 Aztec B	27-2114	N5092Y	0062	2 LY O-540-A1D5	2177	
☐ VH-PDN	Piper PA-31-310 Navajo	31-177	N9131Y	0068	2 LY TIO-540-A1A	2948	

CHARTAIR = TL (Syncom, Pty Ltd dba / formerly Airnorth Central)
Alice Springs, Darwin, Katherine, Tennant Creek & Yulara, NT

PO Box 8170, Alice Springs, NT 0871, Australia ☎ (8) 89 52 66 66 Tx: 81359 lascah aa Fax: (8) 89 52 22 45 SITA: n/a
F: 1975 ⁂ 60 Head: Roger P.G. Leach Net: n/a

☐ VH-ARS	Cessna U206G Stationair 6 II	U20606898	N9605R	0085		1 CO IO-520-F	1633		
☐ VH-AOT	Cessna 210N Centurion II	21064124	N5217Y	0080		1 CO IO-520-L	1724		
☐ VH-HZL	Cessna 210N Centurion II	21063276	N9SA	0079		1 CO IO-520-L	1724		
☐ VH-LTB	Cessna 210N Centurion II	21064679	N670A	0082		1 CO IO-520-L	1724		
☐ VH-NQP	Cessna 210N Centurion II	21064572	N9678Y	0082		1 CO IO-520-L	1724		
☐ VH-SJW	Cessna 210M Centurion II	21062219	N761FJ	0077	0795	1 CO IO-520-L	1724		
☐ VH-TFF	Cessna 210N Centurion II	21064277	N6169Y	0081		1 CO IO-520-L	1724		
☐ VH-TFI	Cessna 210N Centurion II	21064255	N6114Y	0081		1 CO IO-520-L	1724		
☐ VH-WMP	Cessna 210M Centurion II	21062731	N6278B	0078	0497	1 CO IO-520-L	1724		
☐ VH-WTX	Cessna 210L Centurion II	21060222	N93025	0074	0895	1 CO IO-520-L	1724		
☐ VH-FTW	Beech Baron B55 (95-B55)	TC-2123	N24097	0078		2 CO IO-470-L	2313		
☐ VH-FWX	Beech Baron B55 (95-B55)	TC-1155	N7649N	0068		2 CO IO-470-L	2313		
☐ VH-CAJ	Cessna 402C II	402C0026	N5717C	0079		2 CO TSIO-520-VB	3107		
☐ VH-TFM	Cessna 402C II	402C0067	N2610Y	0079		2 CO TSIO-520-VB	3107		
☐ VH-TZH	Cessna 402C II	402C0617	N6880Y	0081		2 CO TSIO-520-VB	3107		
☐ VH-ANY	Fairchild (Swearingen) SA227DC Metro 23	DC-840B	N3022L*	0093	0295	2 GA TPE331-12U-701G	7484		
☐ VH-ASN	Embraer 120ER Brasilia (EMB-120ER)	120056	N334JS	0087	0497	2 PWC PW118	11990		cvtd 120RT

CHILD FLIGHT, Inc.
Sydney-Westmead Helipad, NSW

PO Box 563, Wentworthville, NSW 2145, Australia ☎ (2) 96 89 87 00 Tx: none Fax: (2) 96 89 87 80 SITA: n/a
F: 1989 ⁂ 7 Head: Jeremy Ovens Net: n/a Charity organisation doing inter-hospital flights for children only.

☐ VH-BKZ	Eurocopter (MBB) BK117B-2	7213	D-HFDD	0089	0196	2 LY LTS101-750B.1	3350	EMS	cvtd BK117B-1

CHOPPERLINE (Nimvale, Pty Ltd dba / Sister company of Choppermart)
Caloundra, QLD

Pathfinder Drive, Caloundra, QLD 4551, Australia ☎ (7) 54 91 46 00 Tx: none Fax: (7) 54 91 45 77 SITA: n/a
F: 1978 ⁂ 10 Head: Lewis Webb Net: n/a Aircraft below MTOW 1361kg: Robinson R22

☐ VH-ABO	Kawasaki (Eurocopter/MBB) BK117	1005	JA9605	0184	1196	2 LY LTS101-650B.1	2850		lsf Choppermart

COMMANDO SKYDIVERS, Inc.
Pakenham, VIC

PO Box 164, Pakenham, VIC 3810, Australia ☎ (3) 59 41 20 28 Tx: none Fax: none SITA: n/a
F: 1962 ⁂ n/a Head: n/a Net: n/a Operates Para-flights for its club-members only.

☐ VH-PQC	Cessna U206 Super Skywagon	U206-0407		0065		1 CO IO-520-A	1497	Para	
☐ VH-RUT	Britten-Norman BN-2A Islander	165	G-AXYT	0070		2 LY O-540-E4B5	2722	Para	
☐ VH-ATO	GAF Nomad N22C	N22B-108	F-ODMX	0079	1096	2 AN 250-B17C	3856	Para	

COMMERCIAL HELICOPTERS, Pty Ltd
Warren-Heliport, NSW

PO Box 201, Warren, NSW 2824, Australia ☎ (2) 68 47 37 22 Tx: none Fax: (2) 68 47 38 22 SITA: n/a
F: 1991 ⁂ n/a Head: Mark Rodgers Net: n/a

☐ VH-JAO	Bell 206B JetRanger III	2364	VH-THZ	0078	0199	1 AN 250-C20B	1451		
☐ VH-LEC	Agusta-Bell 206B JetRanger	8170	PK-HCC	0069	1298	1 AN 250-C20	1451		cvtd 206A

COOLAIR AVIATION (Brian M. Cool dba)
Adelaide, SA

7 Rutland Avenue, Lockleys, SA 5032, Australia ☎ (8) 82 34 94 84 Tx: none Fax: none SITA: n/a
F: 1995 ⁂ n/a Head: Brian M. Cool Net: n/a

☐ VH-JMD	Piper PA-31-310 Navajo B	31-7401260	VH-SOW	0074	0695	2 LY TIO-540-A2C	2948		

CORAL AIR WHITSUNDAY, Pty Ltd (Sister company of Air Whitsunday Seaplanes, Pty Ltd)
Airlie Beach, QLD

PO Box 234, Airlie Beach, QLD 4802, Australia ☎ (7) 49 46 91 30 Tx: none Fax: (7) 49 46 91 85 SITA: n/a
F: 1995 ⁂ n/a Head: n/a Net: n/a

☐ VH-HQE	De Havilland DHC-2 Beaver I	298	N88757	0051	1 PW R-985	2313	Amphibian
☐ VH-SSG	De Havilland DHC-2 Beaver I	1444	N9067F	0060	1 PW R-985	2313	Amphibian

CORAL SEA AIRLINES, Pty Ltd
Thursday Island, QLD

PO Box 288, Thursday Island, QLD 4875, Australia ☎ (3) 97 64 35 14 Tx: none Fax: (3) 97 64 49 44 SITA: n/a
F: 1997 ⁂ n/a Head: n/a Net: n/a

☐ VH-WZP	Partenavia P.68C	228	VH-AJX	0081	0498	2 LY IO-360-A1B6	1990		lsf Lip-Air
☐ VH-CSU	Britten-Norman BN-2A-26 Islander	81	YJ-RV6	0069	1097	2 LY O-540-E4C5	2994		lsf pvt
☐ VH-UJI	Twin (Aero) Shrike Commander 500S	3301	VH-TWS	0078	1097	2 LY IO-540-E1B5	3357		lsf GAM Air Services
☐ VH-YJP	Twin (Aero) Shrike Commander 500S	3060	VH-IBV	0070	0598	2 LY IO-540-E1B5	3357		lsf GAM Air Services

CORPORATE AIR (Vee H Aviation, Pty Ltd dba)
Canberra, ACT

PO Box 565, Canberra, ACT 2601, Australia ☎ (6) 62 48 67 66 Tx: n/a Fax: (6) 62 57 31 35 SITA: n/a
F: 1970 ⁂ 25 Head: Andrew H. Major Net: n/a Aircraft below MTOW 1361 kg: Cessna 152 & 172.

☐ VH-FRI	Piper PA-44-180 Seminole	44-8195015	N83376	0081	2 LY O-360-E1A6D	1724	3 Pax	
☐ VH-CYT	Beech Baron 58	TH-399	N3080W	0073	2 CO IO-520-C	2449	5 Pax	
☐ VH-ARQ	Cessna 404 Titan	404-0219	N88680	0078	2 CO GTSIO-520-M	3810	9 Pax / SAR	
☐ VH-CSV	Cessna 404 Titan	404-0217	VH-JOG	0078	2 CO GTSIO-520-M	3810	9 Pax / SAR	
☐ VH-IJQ	Cessna 441 Conquest II	441-0174	N441HW	0081	2 GA TPE331-8-401S	4468	9 Pax	

COUNTRY CONNECTION AIRLINES, Pty Ltd = XL / NSW
Cootamundra, NSW

PO Box 171, Cootamundra, NSW 2590, Australia ☎ (2) 69 42 35 00 Tx: none Fax: (2) 69 42 32 13 SITA: n/a
F: 1984 ⁂ 7 Head: Terry McKenzie Net: http://www.wagga.com.au/cc/ Aircraft below MTOW 1361kg: Cessna 172 & Hiller UH-12E

☐ VH-DOS	Beech Duchess 76	ME-157	N78AK	0079	1096	2 LY O-360-A1G6D	1769	
☐ VH-JCD	Beech Duchess 76	ME-375	N3711N	0080	1096	2 LY O-360-A1G6D	1769	
☐ VH-XLA	Piper PA-31-350 Navajo Chieftain	31-7952206	ZK-FQW	0079	0792	2 LY TIO-540-J2BD	3342	
☐ VH-XLB	Piper PA-31-350 Navajo Chieftain	31-7852104	VH-LHG	0078	0793	2 LY TIO-540-J2BD	3342	
☐ VH-XML	Piper PA-31-350 Navajo Chieftain	31-7852012	N27369	0078		2 LY TIO-540-J2BD	3342	

CRANE AIR, Pty Ltd
Sydney-Bankstown, NSW

PO Box 20, Condell Park, NSW 2200, Australia ☎ (2) 97 91 00 55 Tx: none Fax: (2) 97 91 01 94 SITA: n/a
F: 1981 ⁂ n/a Head: Rodney M. Crane Net: n/a

☐ VH-LBF	Beech Duchess 76	ME-344	N6753C	0080	0298	2 LY O-360-A1G6D	1769
☐ VH-WMY	AAC (Ted Smith) Aerostar 600A	60-0527-171	N8026J	0078		2 LY IO-540-K1F5	2495
☐ VH-LCE	Piper PA-31-350 Navajo Chieftain	31-7305088	N305SP	0073		2 LY TIO-540-J2BD	3342

CRITTENDEN AIR CHARTER (Crittenden Aviation Services, Pty Ltd dba)
Broken Hill, NSW

PO Box 346, Broken Hill, NSW 2880, Australia ☎ (80) 88 57 02 Tx: n/a Fax: n/a SITA: n/a
F: 1988 ⁂ 3 Head: Donald J. Crittenden Net: n/a

☐ VH-KNY	Piper PA-23-250 Aztec F	27-7854034	N2AN	0078	0597	2 LY IO-540-C4B5	2359	
☐ VH-EZF	Beech Baron E55	TE-1156	N2072C	0079		2 CO IO-520-CB	2404	

CROMARTY AIR, Pty Ltd (Paul Cromarty Investments, Pty Ltd dba) — **Albury, NSW**

3 Airport Drive, Albury, NSW 2640, Australia ☎ (2) 60 41 53 55 Tx: none Fax: (2) 60 41 54 55 SITA: n/a
F: 1993 ✈ n/a Head: Paul W. Cromarty Net: n/a

☐ VH-FEC	Cessna A185F Skywagon II	18503511	N2158Q	0078	0497	1 CO IO-520-D	1520			
☐ VH-MQM	Beech Baron 58	TH-576	N232LK	0075		2 CO IO-520-C	2449			
☐ VH-MDM	Piper PA-31-350 Navajo Chieftain	31-7952146	VH-LHL	0079		2 LY TIO-540-J2BD	3175			

DAKOTA DOWNUNDER (Ilereserve, Pty Ltd dba / formerly Splitters Creek Airlines) — **Albury, NSW**

RMB 668, Splitters Creek, Albury, NSW 2640, Australia ☎ (2) 60 21 11 36 Tx: none Fax: (2) 60 41 22 93 SITA: n/a
F: 1991 ✈ n/a Head: John G.O. Love Net: n/a

☐ VH-JGL	Boeing (Douglas) DC-3C (C-47B-15-DK)	26640	A65-64	0044		2 PW R-1830	11884	Frtr / 28 Pax		Louise

DAKOTA NATIONAL AIR (Dakota National Air (Aust.) Pty Ltd dba) — **Sydney-Bankstown, NSW**

444 Pacific Highway, North Gosford, NSW 2250, Australia ☎ (43) 24 49 77 Tx: none Fax: (43) 24 47 29 SITA: n/a
F: 1992 ✈ 10 Head: Peter P. Starr Net: n/a

☐ VH-BPN	Boeing (Douglas) DC-3C (C-47B-30-DK)	32945	VH-MML	0044	0895	2 PW R-1830	11884	Y28		07
☐ VH-DNA	Boeing (Douglas) DC-3C (C-47B-20-DK)	27130	P2-004	0045	0893	2 PW R-1830	11884	Freighter		04
☐ VH-DNF	Boeing (Douglas) DC-3C (C-47B-30-DK)	33109	P2-001	0045	0893	2 PW R-1830	11884	Y28		01 / std Warnervale, NSW
☐ VH-MIN	Boeing (Douglas) DC-3C (C-47A-25-DK)	13459	VH-SMI	0044	0598	2 PW R-1830	11884	Y30		08
☐ VH-PWN	Boeing (Douglas) DC-3C (C-47B-5-DK)	26001	P2-005	0044	0795	2 PW R-1830	11430	Freighter		05
☐ VH-SBL	Boeing (Douglas) DC-3C (C-47A-1-DK)	12056	P2-ANR	0043	0692	2 PW R-1830	11884	Y32		03
☐ VH-UPQ	Boeing (Douglas) DC-3C (C-47B-35-DK)	33300	A65-105	0045	0893	2 PW R-1830	11884	Y32		06

DEMAIR, Pty Ltd (Associated with Demed Association, Inc.) — **Oenpelli, NT**

PMB 89, Oenpelli, NT 0822, Australia ☎ (8) 89 79 04 40 Tx: none Fax: (8) 89 79 01 02 SITA: n/a
F: 1994 ✈ n/a Head: n/a Net: n/a

☐ VH-OEN	Cessna U206G Stationair 6 II	U20605763	VH-RPV	0080		1 CO IO-520-F	1633			lsf Demed Association Inc.
☐ VH-WDZ	Cessna U206G Stationair 6 II	U20605953		0080	0797	1 CO IO-520-F	1633			lsf Demed Association Inc.

DERBY AIR SERVICES (Napier Corporation, Pty Ltd dba / Subsidiary of Slingair, Pty Ltd) — **Derby, WA**

PO Box 706, Derby, WA 6728, Australia ☎ (8) 91 93 13 75 Tx: none Fax: (8) 91 91 17 22 SITA: n/a
F: 1992 ✈ 9 Head: Peter Leutenegger Net: n/a

☐ VH-NLG	Cessna U206G Stationair	U20603930	ZK-JGH	0077	0396	1 CO IO-520-F	1633			lsf Slingair
☐ VH-NLV	Cessna 210N Centurion II	21063093	VH-APU	0078	0297	1 CO IO-520-L	1724			lsf Slingair
☐ VH-NLZ	Cessna 210N Centurion II	21063769	VH-RZZ	0080	0595	1 CO IO-520-L	1724			lsf Slingair
☐ VH-TWD	Cessna 210N Centurion II	21064356	N6372Y	0081	0993	1 CO IO-520-L	1724			lsf Slingair
☐ VH-TWY	Cessna 310R II	310R0090	N69336	0075	0098	2 CO IO-520-M	2495			lsf Slingair

DICK LANGS DESERT-AIR SAFARIS (Richard "Dick" P. Lang dba) — **Adelaide, SA**

PO Box 80, Highbury, SA 5089, Australia ☎ (8) 82 64 72 00 Tx: n/a Fax: (8) 83 96 52 00 SITA: n/a
F: 1967 ✈ 6 Head: Richard "Dick" P. Lang Net: n/a

☐ VH-CJQ	Piper PA-31-350 Navajo Chieftain	31-8152151	N40906	0081	0895	2 LY TIO-540-J2BD	3175			

EASTERN AUSTRALIA AIRLINES, Pty Ltd = EAQ (Member of Qantas Group / formerly Eastern Airlines) — **Tamworth & Sydney-Mascot, NSW**

PO Box 566, Tamworth, NSW 2340, Australia ☎ (2) 67 60 72 24 Tx: none Fax: (2) 67 60 72 70 SITA: n/a
F: 1978 ✈ 290 Head: Bevan Coote Net: n/a Operates scheduled services in conjunction with QANTAS using QF flight numbers.

☐ VH-TQJ	BAe 3107 Jetstream 31	703	G-31-703*	0086	0388	2 GA TPE331-10UG-513H	6950	Y18		
☐ VH-TQK	BAe 3107 Jetstream 31	705	G-31-705*	0086	0388	2 GA TPE331-10UG-513H	6950	Y18		
☐ VH-TQL	BAe 3107 Jetstream 31	707	G-31-707*	0086	0388	2 GA TPE331-10UG-513H	6950	Y18		
☐ VH-TQM	BAe 3207 Jetstream 32	868	G-31-868*	0089	0290	2 GA TPE331-12UAR-701H	7350	Y18		
☐ VH-TQF	De Havilland DHC-8-102 Dash 8	067	N801AW	0087	1093	2 PWC PW120A	15650	Y36		
☐ VH-TQG	De Havilland DHC-8-201 Dash 8	430		0096	0296	2 PWC PW123D	16465	Y36		
☐ VH-TQN	De Havilland DHC-8-102 Dash 8	062	D-BEST	0086	0593	2 PWC PW120A	15650	Y36		
☐ VH-TQO	De Havilland DHC-8-102 Dash 8	004	C-GGPJ*	0083	0189	2 PWC PW120A	15650	Y36		
☐ VH-TQP	De Havilland DHC-8-102 Dash 8	135	C-GFQL*	0089	0289	2 PWC PW120A	15650	Y36		
☐ VH-TQQ	De Havilland DHC-8-102 Dash 8	204	C-GFUM*	0090	0390	2 PWC PW120A	15650	Y36		
☐ VH-TQR	De Havilland DHC-8-102 Dash 8	208	C-GESR*	0090	0490	2 PWC PW120A	15650	Y36		
☐ VH-TQS	De Havilland DHC-8-202 Dash 8	418	9M-EKB	0095	0398	2 PWC PW123D	16465	Y36		
☐ VH-TQT	De Havilland DHC-8-102 Dash 8	349	C-GBSW	0092	1098	2 PWC PW120A	15650	Y36		

EASTLAND AIR – Moore's Air Charter = DK (RR More & Co. Pty Ltd dba) — **Toowoomba, QLD**

PO Box 6021, Toowoomba West, QLD 4350, Australia ☎ (7) 46 34 13 66 Tx: none Fax: (7) 46 34 52 15 SITA: n/a
F: 1970 ✈ 22 Head: Cynthia Moore Net: n/a

☐ VH-MKC	Piper PA-31-350 Navajo Chieftain	31-7405201	VH-LNA	0074	0194	2 LY TIO-540-J2BD	3342	Y8		
☐ VH-MKK	Piper PA-31-350 Navajo Chieftain	31-7652068	VH-OZQ	0076	0895	2 LY TIO-540-J2BD	3175	Y8		
☐ VH-RNG	Piper PA-31-350 Navajo Chieftain	31-7852142	N27713	0078	1196	2 LY TIO-540-J2BD	3175	Y8		
☐ VH-LQH	Beech King Air C90	LJ-644	N66CN	0074	0498	2 PWC PT6A-20A	4377	EMS		opf QLD Gvmt/Flying Surgeon-contract
☐ VH-NQH	Beech King Air C90	LJ-655	N4095S	0075	0798	2 PWC PT6A-28	4377	EMS		opf QLD Gvmt/Flying Surgeon-contract
☐ VH-SQH	Beech King Air C90	LJ-730	N730WB	0077	0498	2 PWC PT6A-21	4377	EMS		opf QLD Gvmt/Flying Surgeon-contract
☐ VH-HEA	De Havilland DHC-6 Twin Otter 200	222	P2-ALU	0069	1198	2 PWC PT6A-20	5252	Y14		
☐ VH-JEA	De Havilland DHC-6 Twin Otter 200	117	P2-ALT	0068	1298	2 PWC PT6A-20	5252	Y14		
☐ VH-KEA	De Havilland DHC-6 Twin Otter 200	120	P2-ALS	0068	1198	2 PWC PT6A-20	5252	Y14		

EMU AIRWAYS (Emu Air Charter, Pty Ltd dba) — **Adelaide, SA**

General Aviation Terminal, Thomas Street, Adelaide Airport, SA 5950, Australia ☎ (8) 82 34 37 11 Tx: none Fax: (8) 82 34 37 47 SITA: n/a
F: n/a ✈ n/a Head: Lance McKean Net: n/a

☐ VH-FIA	Piper PA-31-350 Navajo Chieftain	31-7752032	ZK-FIA	0077	1196	2 LY TIO-540-J2BD	3175			
☐ VH-NMP	Piper PA-31-350 Navajo Chieftain	31-7852149	N27756	0078	0897	2 LY TIO-540-J2BD	3175			
☐ VH-ONC	Piper PA-31-350 Navajo Chieftain	31-7852151	N717PP	0078	1295	2 LY TIO-540-J2BD	3175			
☐ VH-AWS	Cessna 402A	402A0098	N4598Q	0069		2 CO TSIO-520-E	2858			
☐ VH-BYN	Cessna 402B II	402B1328	N104SX	0078	0894	2 CO TSIO-520-E	2858			
☐ VH-CEM	Cessna 402B II	402B1067	N98754	0076		2 CO TSIO-520-E	2858			

EXECUTIVE AIRLINES, Pty Ltd — **Melbourne-Essendon, VIC**

12 Airlie Road, Montmorency, VIC 3094, Australia ☎ (3) 94 32 17 77 Tx: n/a Fax: (3) 94 32 04 41 SITA: n/a
F: 1971 ✈ 5 Head: Geoffrey Hardinge Net: n/a

☐ VH-EXM	Cessna 550 Citation II	550-0228	N96CS	0081	0894	2 PWC JT15D-4	6577	7 Pax		

EXMOUTH AIR CHARTERS (J.E.J. & P.E.T. Arscott dba) — **Exmouth, WA**

PO Box 154, Exmouth, WA 6707, Australia ☎ (8) 99 49 11 80 Tx: n/a Fax: n/a SITA: n/a
F: n/a ✈ n/a Head: J.E.J. & P.E.T. Arscott Net: n/a

☐ VH-ESU	Cessna U206F Stationair	U20602258	N1556U	0074		1 CO IO-520-F	1633			
☐ VH-HUV	Cessna 310Q	310Q0726	N4155Q	0073		2 CO IO-470-VO	2404			

FARNSWAY AIR CHARTER SERVICES (division of Farnsway Australia, Pty Ltd / Member of Farnsway-Faminco Group) — **Brisbane, QLD**

PO Box 239, Samford, Queensland 4520, Australia ☎ (7) 32 89 20 66 Tx: none Fax: (7) 32 89 14 09 SITA: n/a
F: 1997 ✈ n/a Head: A. Derek Thompson Net: n/a

☐ VH-FAM	Pilatus PC-12/45	161	HB-FOK*	0096	0497	1 PWC PT6A-67B	4500			

FITZROY AVIATION QUEENSLAND, Pty Ltd — **Coolangatta, QLD**

PO Box 1062, Coolangatta, QLD 4225, Australia ☎ (7) 55 99 27 88 Tx: n/a Fax: (7) 55 99 27 90 SITA: n/a
F: 1991 ✈ 15 Head: Jason Ryder Net: n/a Aircraft below MTOW 1361 kg: Cessna 182Q.

☐ VH-IXH	Partenavia P.68B	186		0079	0695	2 LY IO-360-A1B6	1960			
☐ VH-HMV	AAC (Piper) Aerostar 600A	60-0685-7961215	N6071N	0079		2 LY IO-540-K1J5	2495			
☐ VH-EJE	Piper PA-31-310 Navajo	31-585	9M-ARF	0070	0199	2 LY TIO-540-A1A	2948			
☐ VH-MYF	Piper PA-31-350 Navajo Chieftain	31-7952165	VH-NEF	0079	1097	2 LY TIO-540-J2BD	3175			
☐ VH-MYG	Piper PA-31-310 Navajo B	31-7300976	VH-NEG	0073	1097	2 LY TIO-540-A2C	2948			
☐ VH-MYQ	Piper PA-31-350 Navajo Chieftain	31-7952128	N3526P	0079	0096	2 LY TIO-540-J2BD	3175			lsf Hoxcrest P/L
☐ VH-MYX	Piper PA-31-350 Navajo Chieftain	31-7552098	P2-SAS	0075	1197	2 LY TIO-540-J2BD	3175			
☐ VH-ELZ	Cessna 402	402-0206	N7857F	0068	1197	2 CO TSIO-520-E	2858			
☐ VH-NYA	Twin (Aero) Turbo Commander 690A	11152	N42MM	0074	0898	2 GA TPE331-5-251K	4649			
☐ VH-KGX	Fairchild (Swearingen) SA226TC Metro II	TC-326	VH-UUK	0080	0897	2 GA TPE331-3UW-304G	5670			
☐ VH-MYD	Fairchild (Swearingen) SA226TC Metro II	TC-303	C-FWWP	0079	1096	2 GA TPE331-10UA-511G	5670			
☐ VH-MYI	Fairchild (Swearingen) SA227DC Metro 23	DC-869B	9M-APB	0094	0298	2 GA TPE331-12U-701G	7366			
☐ VH-NEL	Fairchild (Swearingen) SA227AC Metro III	AC-611B	N611AV	0085	0997	2 GA TPE331-11U-612G	7257			cvtd cn AC-611

626 registration type of aircraft cn/fn ex/ex* mfd del powered by mtow kg configuration selcal name/fln/specialitites/remarks

FIVE STAR AVIATION, Pty Ltd — Coolangatta, QLD

PO Box 104, Coolangatta, QLD 4225, Australia ☎ (7) 32 74 01 11 Tx: n/a Fax: (7) 536 83 72 SITA: n/a
F: 1987 ⁂ n/a Head: Bryan Oxenford Net: n/a

☐ VH-OWN	Beech King Air B200	BB-936	N200NS	0081		2 PWC PT6A-42	5670			
☐ VH-OXF	Beech King Air 350 (B300)	FL-122	VH-BTL	0094	0795	2 PWC PT6A-60A	6804			

FLEET HELICOPTERS (Aerial Agriculture, Pty Ltd) — Armidale, NSW

PO Box 453, Armidale, NSW 2350, Australia ☎ (2) 67 72 23 48 Tx: none Fax: (2) 67 72 76 54 SITA: n/a
F: 1990 ⁂ n/a Head: RB Macarthur Onslow Net: n/a Aircraft below MTOW 1361kg: Cessna 182

☐ VH-ONZ	MD Helicopters MD 500E (Hughes 369E)	0190E	P2-PAM	0086	0597	1 AN 250-C20R	1361			
☐ VH-CHO	Bell 206B JetRanger III	714	P2-PAA	0071	0597	1 AN 250-C20B	1451			cvtd 206A
☐ VH-JVW	Bell 206B JetRanger	699	9M-AQU	0071		1 AN 250-C20	1451			cvtd 206A
☐ VH-ONS	Bell 206B JetRanger	109	P2-FHH	0067	1294	1 AN 250-C20	1451			cvtd 206A
☐ VH-ZHZ	De Havilland DHC-2 Beaver I	1060	VH-RAY	0057		1 PW R-985	2313			

FLIGHT CHARTER (Gemair, Pty Ltd & Flight Training Australia dba) — Brisbane-Archerfield, QLD

PO Box 523, Archerfield, QLD 4108, Australia ☎ (7) 32 77 85 44 Tx: none Fax: (7) 32 75 15 09 SITA: n/a
F: 1987 ⁂ 22 Head: n/a Net: n/a Aircraft below MTOW 1361kg: Bellanca 8KCAB, Cessna 152 & 172

☐ VH-DAA	Beech Duchess 76	ME-70	N4917M	0078		2 LY O-360-A1G6D	1769			
☐ VH-OFD	Beech Duchess 76	ME-403	N3831X	0081		2 LY O-360-A1G6D	1769			
☐ VH-SXS	Beech Baron 58	TH-181	ZK-EJJ	0071		2 CO IO-520-C	2449			
☐ VH-FUI	Piper PA-31-350 Navajo Chieftain	31-7652148	VH-STO	0076		2 LY TIO-540-J2BD	3342			

FLIGHT WEST AIRLINES, Pty Ltd = YC / FWQ (Queenslands Regional Airline) — Brisbane, QLD

PO Box 1126, Eagle Farm, QLD 4009, Australia ☎ (7) 32 12 12 12 Tx: none Fax: (7) 32 12 12 97 SITA: n/a
F: 1987 ⁂ 270 Head: Guy Buchanan IATA: 060 Net: http://www.fltwest.com.au/

☐ VH-SKN	Beech King Air 200	BB-690	ZK-WNL	0080	0687	2 PWC PT6A-41	5670	Y11		Sir Hudson Fysh KBE / for sale
☐ VH-XDB	Beech King Air 200	BB-533	LN-PAH	0079	0887	2 PWC PT6A-41	5670	Y11		Lores Bonney MBE / std BNE/for sale
☐ VH-XFB	BAe 3201 Jetstream 32EP	948	N948AE	0091	0698	2 GA TPE331-12UAR-704H	7350	Y19		Capt. Jack Treacy / cvtd 32
☐ VH-XFC	BAe 3201 Jetstream 32EP	949	N949AE	0091	0798	2 GA TPE331-12UAR-704H	7350	Y19		Lores Bonney / cvtd 32
☐ VH-XFD	BAe 3201 Jetstream 32EP	951	N951AE	0091	0798	2 GA TPE331-12UAR-704H	7350	Y19		Sir Robert Norman / cvtd 32
☐ VH-XFE	BAe 3201 Jetstream 32EP	953	N953LM	0091	1198	2 GA TPE331-12UAR-704H	7350	Y19		Arthur Affleck / cvtd 32
☐ VH-FNQ	Embraer 120ER Brasilia (EMB-120ER)	120054	N274UE	1187	0296	2 PWC PW118A	11990	Y30		cvtd 120RT / Cowboys North Qld-colors
☐ VH-XFH	Embraer 120ER Brasilia (EMB-120ER)	120079	N277UE	0588	0497	2 PWC PW118A	11990	Y30		cvtd 120RT / The Whitsundays-colors
☐ VH-XFQ	Embraer 120ER Brasilia (EMB-120ER)	120115	ZS-MIR	0088	1294	2 PWC PW118A	11990	Y30		cvtd 120RT
☐ VH-XFR	Embraer 120ER Brasilia (EMB-120ER)	120135	ZS-MMB	0089	0695	2 PWC PW118A	11990	Y30		cvtd 120RT
☐ VH-XFV	Embraer 120ER Brasilia (EMB-120ER)	120208	PT-SSA*	0090	1190	2 PWC PW118A	11990	Y30		cvtd 120RT
☐ VH-XFW	Embraer 120ER Brasilia (EMB-120ER)	120181	PT-SQT*	0090	0590	2 PWC PW118A	11990	Y30		John Campbell Miles / cvtd 120RT
☐ VH-XFX	Embraer 120ER Brasilia (EMB-120ER)	120116	G-EXEL	0088	0693	2 PWC PW118A	11990	Y30		cvtd 120RT
☐ VH-XFZ	Embraer 120ER Brasilia (EMB-120ER)	120140	D4-CAZ	0089	0194	2 PWC PW118A	11990	Y30		cvtd 120RT
☐ VH-EWA	Fokker F28 Fellowship 4000 (F28 Mk4000)	11195	PH-EXO*	0083	0397	2 RR Spey 555-15P	33112	C6Y60		Robert U. Paul / North QLD Cowboys-cs
☐ VH-EWB	Fokker F28 Fellowship 4000 (F28 Mk4000)	11205	PH-EXO*	0083	0397	2 RR Spey 555-15P	33112	C6Y60		Sir John Guise
☐ VH-EWC	Fokker F28 Fellowship 4000 (F28 Mk4000)	11207	PH-EXX*	0084	0397	2 RR Spey 555-15P	33112	C6Y60		Wing Commander RH "Bobby" Gibbes
☐ VH-FWH	Fokker 100 (F28 Mk0100)	11316	G-BXNF	0090	0998	2 RR Tay 650-15	44452	C16Y75		
☐ VH-FWI	Fokker 100 (F28 Mk0100)	11318	G-FIOR	0090	0998	2 RR Tay 650-15	44450	C16Y75		

FLINDERS RANGES TOURIST SERVICES, Pty Ltd — Wilpena Pound, SA

Wilpena Pound Motel, Wilpena Pound, SA 5434, Australia ☎ (8) 86 48 00 05 Tx: n/a Fax: (8) 86 48 00 28 SITA: n/a
F: 1957 ⁂ 28 Head: Keith Rasheed Net: n/a Aircraft below MTOW 1361kg: Cessna 182

☐ VH-WPN	Cessna U206G Stationair 6 II	U20606333	N6598Z	0081		1 CO IO-520-F	1633			

FLY DIRECT, Pty Ltd — Duncan Forbes

PO Box 4, Bankstown, NSW 2200, Australia ☎ (2) 97 91 05 59 Tx: none Fax: (2) 97 91 05 70 SITA: n/a
F: n/a ⁂ n/a Head: Sydney-Bankstown, NSW Net: n/a

☐ VH-TSW	Piper PA-31-350 Navajo Chieftain	31-8052195	N4503E	0080	0798	2 LY TIO-540-J2BD	3175			

FORESTRY COMMISSION OF NSW – Surveillance Flights/Air Charter — Sydney-Bankstown, NSW

Locked Bag 23, Pennant Hills, NSW 2120, Australia ☎ (2) 97 96 47 74 Tx: none Fax: (2) 97 91 00 60 SITA: n/a
F: 1978 ⁂ 2 Head: Terry Gors Net: n/a Commercial state organisation conducting surveillance & charter flights.

☐ VH-HLQ	Cessna 337G Super Skymaster	33701507	N71963	0073	0795	2 CO IO-360-G	2100			
☐ VH-NFW	Cessna 337A Super Skymaster	337-0253	N6253F	0066		2 CO IO-360-C/D	1905			
☐ VH-NFO	Eurocopter (Aerosp.) AS350B Squirrel	1823		0085		1 TU Arriel 1B	1950			

GAM AIR SERVICES (General Aviation Maintenance, Pty Ltd dba) — Melbourne-Essendon, VIC

Hangar 1, Essendon Airport, VIC 3041, Australia ☎ (3) 93 79 10 19 Tx: none Fax: (3) 93 74 26 20 SITA: n/a
F: 1986 ⁂ 50 Head: Steven R. Nott Net: n/a

☐ VH-ACJ	Twin (Aero) Shrike Commander 500S	3178	N57079	0074	0796	2 LY IO-540-E1B5	3357			opf Reefwatch Air Tours, Cairns
☐ VH-BAJ	Twin (Aero) Shrike Commander 500S	3130	N9182N	0073	0996	2 LY IO-540-E1B5	3357			lst Penguin Express
☐ VH-LET	Twin (Aero) Shrike Commander 500S	3264	N70343	0076	0597	2 LY IO-540-E1B5	3357			
☐ VH-LST	Twin (Aero) Shrike Commander 500S	3111	N9157N	0072	0295	2 LY IO-540-E1B5	3357	Freighter		
☐ VH-MDW	Twin (Aero) Shrike Commander 500S	3158	N801AC	0073	0398	2 LY IO-540-E1B5	3357			
☐ VH-PAR	Twin (Aero) Shrike Commander 500S	3311	N84SA	0077	0796	2 LY IO-540-E1B5	3357			opf Reefwatch Air Tours, Cairns
☐ VH-UJB	Twin (Aero) Shrike Commander 500S	3152	VH-EXJ	0073	0796	2 LY IO-540-E1B5	3357			opf Reefwatch Air Tours, Cairns
☐ VH-UJI	Twin (Aero) Shrike Commander 500S	3301	VH-TWS	0078		2 LY IO-540-E1B5	3357			lst Coral Sea Airlines
☐ VH-UJL	Twin (Aero) Shrike Commander 500S	3088	N9120N	0070		2 LY IO-540-E1B5	3357	Freighter		
☐ VH-UJM	Twin (Aero) Shrike Commander 500S	3117	N5007H	0072		2 LY IO-540-E1B5	3357	Freighter		opf Security Express Victoria
☐ VH-UJU	Twin (Aero) Shrike Commander 500S	3055	VH-PWO	0070		2 LY IO-540-E1B5	3357	Photo		
☐ VH-UJV	Twin (Aero) Shrike Commander 500S	3161	N712PC	0073		2 LY IO-540-E1B5	3357	Freighter		opf Security Express Victoria
☐ VH-UJX	Twin (Aero) Shrike Commander 500S	500S-1839-31	VH-EXI	0069	1195	2 LY IO-540-E1B5	3357			lst Air Frontier
☐ VH-UJZ	Twin (Aero) Shrike Commander 500S	3279	VH-EXY	0076	0296	2 LY IO-540-E1B5	3357			
☐ VH-YJE	Twin (Aero) Shrike Commander 500S	3053	VH-EXE	0070	1197	2 LY IO-540-E1B5	3357			
☐ VH-YJL	Twin (Aero) Shrike Commander 500S	500S-1875-48	VH-ACL	0069	0796	2 LY IO-540-E1B5	3357			
☐ VH-YJP	Twin (Aero) Shrike Commander 500S	3060	VH-IBV	0070	0894	2 LY IO-540-E1B5	3357			lst Coral Sea Airlines
☐ VH-YJR	Twin (Aero) Shrike Commander 500S	3231	VH-PCO	0075	0795	2 LY IO-540-E1B5	3357	Freighter		opf Security Express Victoria
☐ VH-YJS	Twin (Aero) Shrike Commander 500S	3315	VH-FGS	0078	0998	2 LY IO-540-E1B5	3357			
☐ VH-UJN	Twin (Aero) Turbo Commander 681B	681-6047	VH-NYE	0071	1096	2 GA TPE331-43BL	4264			
☐ VH-UJR	Twin (Aero) Commander 685	685-12034	VH-KCH	0073		2 CO GTSIO-520-K	4082			
☐ VH-UJA	Twin (Aero) RPM Commander 800L	680FL-1521-100	PK-MAG	0065		2 LY IO-720-B1BD	3856	Freighter		opf Sec.Express Vict./cvtd Grand 680FL
☐ VH-UJG	Twin (Aero) Turbo Commander 690	11062	VH-NEY	0073	0798	2 GA TPE331-5-251K	4649			
☐ VH-YJG	Twin (Aero) Turbo Commander 690	11026	VH-NYC	0072	0199	2 GA TPE331-5-251K	4649			

GAWNE AVIATION, Pty Ltd — Shepparton, VIC

PO Box 486, Shepparton, VIC 3630, Australia ☎ (3) 58 23 14 81 Tx: none Fax: (3) 58 23 20 49 SITA: n/a
F: 1977 ⁂ 6 Head: Allan G. Gawne Net: n/a Aircraft below MTOW 1361kg: Piper PA-28

☐ VH-EFS	Piper PA-30-160 Twin Comanche B	30-1377	N8251Y	0066	0795	2 LY IO-320-B1A	1633			lsf ASC P/L

GEELONG FLIGHT CENTER (Mahon Aviation, Pty Ltd dba) — Geelong, VIC

540 Surf Coast Highway, Mount Duneed, VIC 3216, Australia ☎ (3) 52 64 12 73 Tx: none Fax: (3) 52 64 10 06 SITA: n/a
F: 1993 ⁂ n/a Head: Jim Mahon Net: n/a Aircraft below MTOW 1361kg: Cessna 152

☐ VH-LJR	Partenavia P.68B	41	VH-FAO	0075		2 LY IO-360-A1B6	1960			lsf pvt
☐ VH-PNV	Partenavia P.68B	85		0076		2 LY IO-360-A1B6	1960			

GEIKIE AIR CHARTER (David G. Rundle dba) — Fitzroy Crossing, WA

PO Box 33, Fitzroy Crossing, WA 6765, Australia ☎ (8) 91 91 50 68 Tx: n/a Fax: n/a SITA: n/a
F: n/a ⁂ n/a Head: n/a Net: n/a

☐ VH-AJY	Piper PA-32R-300 Lance	32R-7680208	N9332K	0076	0199	1 LY IO-540-K1G5D	1633			
☐ VH-KDX	Cessna 210L Centurion II	21061427	N732DE	0076		1 CO IO-520-L	1724			

GEOCOMMANDER, Pty Ltd (formerly Western Commander, Pty Ltd) — Melbourne-Essendon, VIC

Hangar 6, Wirraway Road, Essendon Airport, VIC 3041, Australia ☎ (3) 93 74 20 44 Tx: none Fax: (3) 93 79 84 60 SITA: n/a
F: 1976 ⁂ n/a Head: Ron Smith Net: n/a

☐ VH-TEM	CASA 212 Aviocar Srs 200	138	P2-CNP	0078	0888	2 GA TPE331-10-501C	7450	Surveyer		opf Terra Surveys Ltd, Canada

GLOBAL AIR AUSTRALIA, Pty Ltd = GFR (Associated with Butler Aircraft Services Ltd, Gr. Brit.) — Brisbane, QLD

26 Norman Pde, Clanfield-Brisbane, QLD 4011, Australia ☎ (7) 38 62 12 55 Tx: none Fax: (7) 38 62 12 11 SITA: n/a
F: 1997 ⁂ 150 Head: Luke Butler ICAO: GLOBAL AIRFREIGHT Net: n/a Presently being set-up. Intends to start operations during 1999 with Boeing 737-400 & Boeing 747-200F freighter aircraft.

627 registration type of aircraft cn/fn ex/ex* mfd del powered by mtow kg configuration selcal name/fln/specialitites/remarks

GOLDEN EAGLE AIRLINES (Golden Eagle Aviation, Pty Ltd dba) **Port Hedland, WA**

PO Box 2208, South Hedland, WA 6722, Australia ☎ (8) 91 40 11 81 Tx: none Fax: (8) 91 40 23 41 SITA: n/a
F: 1990 ✱✱✱ 10 Head: Capt. Keith Russell Net: n/a

☐ VH-COT	Piper PA-34-200 Seneca	*34-7450082*	*N40815*	*0073*		*2 LY IO-360-C1E6*	*1905*			*lsf Stream Industry P/L*
☐ VH-FML	Piper PA-31-310 Navajo	*31-8112015*	*N45040*	*0081*	*0795*	*2 LY TIO-540-A2C*	*3053*			
☐ VH-NPA	Piper PA-31-350 Navajo Chieftain	*31-8452016*	*N41171*	*0084*	*0497*	*2 LY TIO-540-J2BD*	*3342*			

GOLDFIELDS AIR SERVICES – GAS = GOS (Trevlyn, Pty Ltd dba) **Kalgoorlie, WA**

PO Box 435, Kalgoorlie, WA 6430, Australia ☎ (8) 90 93 21 16 Tx: none Fax: (8) 90 93 19 79 SITA: n/a
F: 1982 ✱✱✱ 20 Head: David Horsley Net: n/a Aircraft below MTOW 1361kg: Piper PA-28.

☐ VH-LMX	Cessna 210N Centurion II	*21063509*	*VH-TFU*	*0079*	*0597*	*1 CO IO-520-L*	*1724*			
☐ VH-TDV	Cessna 210L Centurion II	*21061553*	*N732JR*	*0076*		*1 CO IO-520-L*	*1724*			
☐ VH-TYG	Cessna 210M Centurion II	*21061893*	*N1694C*	*0077*		*1 CO IO-520-L*	*1724*			
☐ VH-WXC	Cessna 210M Centurion II	*21062883*	*N6015N*	*0078*	*0397*	*1 CO IO-520-L*	*1724*			
☐ VH-ALY	Cessna 310R II	*310R1310*	*N6173X*	*0078*	*0995*	*2 CO IO-520-M*	*2495*			
☐ VH-CSO	Cessna 310R II	*310R1854*		*0080*	*0798*	*2 CO IO-520-M*	*2495*			
☐ VH-LCO	Cessna 310R II	*310R1216*	*N1386G*	*0079*		*2 CO IO-520-M*	*2495*			
☐ VH-OOT	Cessna 310R II	*310R1635*	*VH-PEE*	*0079*	*1196*	*2 CO IO-520-M*	*2495*			
☐ VH-HOR	Cessna 402C II	*402C0108*	*P2-KSR*	*0079*	*1295*	*2 CO TSIO-520-VB*	*3107*			
☐ VH-LAE	Cessna 402C II	*402C0097*	*N2614Z*	*0079*		*2 CO TSIO-520-VB*	*3107*			
☐ VH-MFF	Cessna 402B	*402B0874*	*N5187J*	*0075*		*2 CO TSIO-520-E*	*2858*			

GREAT WESTERN AVIATION, Pty Ltd (formerly Arthur Morris Aviation) **Brisbane, QLD**

PO Box 477, Hamilton Central, QLD 4007, Australia ☎ (7) 38 60 44 99 Tx: n/a Fax: (7) 38 60 44 98 SITA: n/a
F: 1961 ✱✱✱ n/a Head: Arthur B. Morris Net: n/a

☐ VH-DEH	Piper PA-31-310 Navajo C	*31-7812123*	*N27792*	*0078*		*2 LY TIO-540-A1A*	*2948*			
☐ VH-FMO	Piper PA-31-310 Navajo	*31-8012052*	*N35574*	*0080*	*1295*	*2 LY TIO-540-A2C*	*2948*			
☐ VH-FMU	Piper PA-31-310 Navajo	*31-8212015*	*N41033*	*0082*	*1296*	*2 LY TIO-540-A2C*	*2948*			
☐ VH-KTU	Piper PA-31-310 Navajo C	*31-7912079*	*N35301*	*0079*		*2 LY TIO-540-A1A*	*2948*			
☐ VH-SGV	Beech King Air 200	*BB-718*	*N6728N*	*0080*	*0497*	*2 PWC PT6A-41*	*5670*			

GREAT WESTERN AVIATION, Pty Ltd – G.W.A. **Perth, WA**

PO Box 1161, Cloverdale, WA 6105, Australia ☎ (8) 94 78 30 66 Tx: n/a Fax: (8) 92 77 77 62 SITA: n/a
F: 1986 ✱✱✱ n/a Head: Robert Ballantine Net: n/a

☐ VH-FWJ	Piper PA-31-310 Navajo C	*31-7712092*	*ZK-PNX*	*0077*	*1096*	*2 LY TIO-540-A2C*	*3270*			
☐ VH-NYZ	Beech Queen Air B80 (65-B80)	*LD-501*	*H4-ABC*	*0075*	*0890*	*2 LY IGSO-540-A1D*	*3992*			
☐ VH-FWA	Beech 1900C Airliner	*UB-61*	*N818BE*	*0086*	*0596*	*2 PWC PT6A-65B*	*7530*			
☐ VH-IYP	Beech 1900C Airliner	*UB-62*	*N819BE*	*0086*	*0297*	*2 PWC PT6A-65B*	*7530*			

GWYDIR AIR (Gwydir Air Charter, Pty Ltd dba) **Moree, NSW**

PO Box 243, Moree, NSW 2400, Australia ☎ (67) 52 24 99 Tx: 166833 gwyair aa Fax: n/a SITA: n/a
F: 1974 ✱✱✱ 14 Head: Fred Nolan Net: n/a Aircraft / Ag-aircraft below MTOW 1361/5000kg: Ayres S2RT & Cessna T188C.

☐ VH-NFE	Cessna 310Q II	*310Q1158*	*N157DN*	*0074*		*2 CO IO-470-VO*	*2404*			

HARDY AVIATION (NT), Pty Ltd **Darwin, NT**

PO Box 26, Parap, NT 0821, Australia ☎ (8) 89 41 13 79 Tx: none Fax: (8) 89 41 19 71 SITA: n/a
F: 1991 ✱✱✱ 5 Head: Mrs Marie V. Hardy Net: n/a

☐ VH-HPA	Cessna U206G Stationair 6 II	*U20605002*	*VH-WIW*	*0079*	*0698*	*1 CO IO-520-F*	*1633*			
☐ VH-RAP	Cessna U206F Stationair II	*U20602989*	*VH-DXU*	*0075*		*1 CO IO-520-F*	*1633*			
☐ VH-ANS	Cessna 210M Centurion II	*21062784*	*N784ED*	*0078*		*1 CO IO-520-L*	*1724*			
☐ VH-NOK	Cessna 210M Centurion II	*21062063*	*N9127M*	*0077*		*1 CO IO-520-L*	*1724*			
☐ VH-TFE	Cessna 210N Centurion II	*21064130*	*N52130*	*0080*		*1 CO IO-520-L*	*1724*			
☐ VH-SGO	Beech Baron 58	*TH-1185*	*N3702D*	*0080*	*1196*	*2 CO IO-520-CB*	*2449*			
☐ VH-ARJ	Cessna 402B	*402B0629*	*N3784C*	*0074*	*0798*	*2 CO TSIO-520-E*	*2858*			
☐ VH-UCI	Cessna 402C II	*402C0474*	*N6838H*	*0081*		*2 CO TSIO-520-VB*	*3107*			
☐ VH-ANM	Cessna 404 Titan II	*404-0010*	*VH-BPM*	*0077*		*2 CO GTSIO-520-M*	*3810*			
☐ VH-HMA	Cessna 404 Titan II	*404-0122*	*N37158*	*0077*	*0697*	*2 CO GTSIO-520-M*	*3810*			
☐ VH-MMY	Fairchild (Swearingen) SA226TC Metro II	*TC-256*	*VH-ANJ*	*0078*	*0998*	*2 GA TPE331-3UW-304G*	*5670*			

HAWDON OPERATIONS, Ltd **Melbourne, VIC**

PO Box 783, Caringbah, NSW 2229, Australia ☎ (2) 96 91 17 86 Tx: none Fax: (2) 95 23 05 58 SITA: n/a
F: 1987 ✱✱✱ n/a Head: Capt T.D. Wiltshire Net: n/a Operates non-commercial historical flights for Qantas – The Australian Airline staff & participates at air shows.

☐ VH-AES	Boeing (Douglas) DC-3C (C-47-DL)	*6021*	*VH-SBA*	*1042*	*0746*	*2 PW R-1830*	*11884*	*Y28*		Hawdon / *original TAA-colors*

HAZELTON AIRLINES = ZL / HZL (Hazelton Air Services, Pty Ltd – HAS dba) **Cudal, NSW**

PO Box 12, Cudal, NSW 2864, Australia ☎ (2) 63 61 58 15 Tx: none Fax: (2) 63 61 84 55 SITA: n/a
F: 1953 ✱✱✱ 220 Head: Stan Quinlivan IATA: 899 Net: n/a

☐ VH-DMI	Fairchild (Swearingen) SA227DC Metro 23	*DC-839B*	N3022F*	*0093*	*0993*	*2 GA TPE331-12U-701G*	*7366*	*Y19*		
☐ VH-DMO	Fairchild (Swearingen) SA227DC Metro 23	*DC-870B*		*0094*	*1294*	*2 GA TPE331-12U-701G*	*7366*	*Y19*		
☐ VH-HCB	Fairchild (Swearingen) SA227DC Metro 23	*DC-871B*		*0094*	*1294*	*2 GA TPE331-12U-701G*	*7366*	*Y19*		
☐ VH-HWR	Fairchild (Swearingen) SA227DC Metro 23	*DC-851B*	N3025T*	*0094*	*0195*	*2 GA TPE331-12U-701G*	*7366*	*Y19*		
☐ VH-CMH	Saab 340B	*340B-327*	SE-C27*	*0092*	*1292*	*2 GE CT7-9B*	*13155*	*Y36*		
☐ VH-LIH	Saab 340B	*340B-316*	SE-C16*	*0092*	*0293*	*2 GE CT7-9B*	*12930*	*Y36*		
☐ VH-OLM	Saab 340B	*340B-205*	SE-G05*	*0090*	*0990*	*2 GE CT7-9B*	*13155*	*Y36*		New Horizons
☐ VH-OLN	Saab 340B	*340B-207*	SE-G07*	*0090*	*1090*	*2 GE CT7-9B*	*13155*	*Y36*		
☐ VH-SBA	Saab 340B	*340B-311*	*SE-KXA*	*0092*	*1294*	*2 GE CT7-9B*	*13155*	*Y36*		
☐ VH-TCH	Saab 340B (Plus)	*340B-362*	SE-C62*	*0094*	*0794*	*2 GE CT7-9B*	*13155*	*Y36*		Our Selection
☐ VH-ZLY	Saab SF340A	*340A-026*	*HB-AHF*	*0085*	*1297*	*2 GE CT7-5A2*	*12700*	*Y36*		
☐ VH-ZLZ	Saab SF340A	*340A-038*	*HB-AHG*	*0085*	*1097*	*2 GE CT7-5A2*	*12700*	*Y36*		

HELI-ADVENTURES, Pty Ltd **Cairns, QLD**

PO Box 7192, Cairns, QLD 4870, Australia ☎ (7) 40 34 90 66 Tx: none Fax: (7) 40 34 90 77 SITA: n/a
F: 1997 ✱✱✱ n/a Head: n/a Net: n/a

☐ VH-HJG	Bell 206L-1 LongRanger II	*45731*	*F-GFHP*	*0081*	*1297*	*1 AN 250-C28B*	*1837*			
☐ VH-HJL	Bell 206L-1 LongRanger II	*45241*	*N96TH*	*0079*	*1297*	*1 AN 250-C28B*	*1837*			

HELICOPTER AERIAL SURVEYS (Barry E. Jones dba) **Sutherland, NSW**

PO Box 403, Sutherland, NSW 2232, Australia ☎ (2) 64 56 35 05 Tx: none Fax: (2) 97 91 19 78 SITA: n/a
F: 1995 ✱✱✱ n/a Head: Barry E. Jones Net: n/a Aircraft below MTOW 1361kg: Hughes 369HS (500C)

☐ VH-HWS	Bell 206B JetRanger	*920*	*N44AL*	*0073*	*0897*	*1 AN 250-C20*	*1451*			
☐ VH-KKY	Bell 206B JetRanger	*636*		*0071*	*0497*	*1 AN 250-C20*	*1451*			*cvtd 206A*
☐ VH-TFH	Bell 206B JetRanger	*1746*	*VH-CPA*	*0075*	*0696*	*1 AN 250-C20*	*1451*			
☐ VH-TMR	Bell 206B JetRanger	*952*		*0073*	*0097*	*1 AN 250-C20*	*1451*			

HELICOPTER CHARTER, Pty Ltd **Brisbane, QLD**

PO Box 138, Hamilton Central, QLD 4007, Australia ☎ (7) 32 68 40 77 Tx: none Fax: (7) 32 68 78 15 SITA: n/a
F: n/a ✱✱✱ n/a Head: n/a Net: n/a

☐ VH-HTA	Bell 206B JetRanger III	*3066*	*VH-PHY*	*0080*	*0198*	*1 AN 250-C20B*	*1451*			

HELICOPTER CHARTER FLIGHT (Helicopters No.1, Pty Ltd dba) **Sydney-Kingsford Smith, NSW**

PO Box 476, Mascot, NSW 2020, Australia ☎ (2) 96 93 11 88 Tx: none Fax: (2) 96 93 20 83 SITA: n/a
F: 1980 ✱✱✱ 4 Head: John Barnao Net: http://www.heli.com.au

☐ VH-BHU	Bell 206B JetRanger III	*2964*	*N1083T*	*0080*		*1 AN 250-C20B*	*1451*			

HELICOPTER OPERATORS AUSTRALIA, Pty Ltd **Warrnambol-Helipad, VIC**

136 Bromfield Street, Warrnambool, VIC 3280, Australia ☎ (3) 55 61 58 00 Tx: none Fax: (3) 55 61 58 60 SITA: n/a
F: 1990 ✱✱✱ n/a Head: n/a Net: n/a

☐ VH-KHR	Bell 206B JetRanger III	*3187*	*N38934*	*0081*	*0497*	*1 AN 250-C20B*	*1451*			

HELICOPTER RESOURCES, Pty Ltd (formerly Vowell Air Services (Helicopters)) **Tyabb, VIC / Redcliffe, WA / Cambridge,TAS**

110 Stuart Road, Tyabb, VIC 3913, Australia ☎ (3) 59 77 45 06 Tx: none Fax: (3) 59 77 44 91 SITA: n/a
F: 1970 ✱✱✱ 18 Head: William J. English Net: n/a

☐ VH-AFO	Eurocopter (Aerosp.) AS350B Squirrel	*1105*		*0079*		*1 TU Arriel 1B*	*1950*			
☐ VH-HBB	Eurocopter (Aerosp.) AS350B Squirrel	*1615*	*ZK-HGZ*	*0082*	*1192*	*1 TU Arriel 1B*	*1950*			
☐ VH-SES	Eurocopter (Aerosp.) AS350B Squirrel	*1053*		*0079*		*1 TU Arriel 1B*	*1950*	*EMS*		
☐ VH-SRB	Eurocopter (Aerosp.) AS350B Squirrel	*1106*		*0079*		*1 TU Arriel 1B*	*1950*			
☐ VH-XHB	Sikorsky S-76A	*760104*	*N9046H*	*0080*	*0697*	*2 AN 250-C30S*	*4763*			

HELICOPTERS AUSTRALIA, Pty Ltd **Perth, WA**

PO Box 263, Belmont, WA 6104, Australia ☎ (8) 92 77 83 99 Tx: none Fax: (8) 94 79 10 08 SITA: n/a
F: 1980 ✱✱✱ 35 Head: Dennis W. Troup Net: n/a

☐ VH-HRZ	Bell 206B JetRanger III	*3466*	*N21424*	*0081*	*1197*	*1 AN 250-C20B*	*1451*			

628 registration type of aircraft *cn/fn* *ex/ex** *mfd* *del* *powered by* *mtow kg* *configuration* *selcal* name/fln/*specialitites/remarks*

registration	type of aircraft	cn/fn	ex/ex*	mfd	del	powered by	mtow kg	configuration	selcal	name/fln/specialitites/remarks
☐ VH-WCF	Bell 206B JetRanger III	3134	N5754A	0080		1 AN 250-C20B	1451			
☐ VH-WCK	Bell 206B JetRanger	1141	ZK-HNE	0073	0595	1 AN 250-C20	1451			
☐ VH-HRD	Eurocopter (Aerosp.) AS350B Squirrel	1661	ZK-HND	0082	0698	1 TU Arriel 1B	1950			
☐ VH-WCD	Eurocopter (Aerosp.) AS350B Squirrel	1397	ZK-HDT	0080	0595	1 TU Arriel 1B	1950			
☐ VH-WCG	Eurocopter (Aerosp.) AS350B Squirrel	1572	ZK-HNM	0082	0492	1 TU Arriel 1B	1950			
☐ VH-WCI	Eurocopter (Aerosp.) AS350BA Squirrel	2073	ZK-HNZ	0088	0896	1 TU Arriel 1B	2100			
☐ VH-WCU	Eurocopter (Aerosp.) AS350B Squirrel	2132	HS-HTA	0088	0998	1 TU Arriel 1B	1950			
☐ VH-BJR	Sikorsky S-76A	760078	N89H	0880	0695	2 AN 250-C30S	4672			
☐ VH-BJS	Sikorsky S-76A	760224	N15464	1282	0695	2 AN 250-C30S	4672			

HELIJET SEAPLANES, Pty Ltd — Brisbane, QLD

GPO Box 1301, Brisbane, QLD 4001, Australia ☎ (7) 38 39 26 88 Tx: none Fax: (7) 38 39 26 44 SITA: n/a
F: 1973 ⁂ 2 Head: Gregory M. Schweikert Net: n/a

☐ VH-XHJ	De Havilland DHC-2 Beaver I	1040	RP-C738	0057	0192	1 PW R-985	2313			Floats

HELI-MUSTER, Pty Ltd (Heli-Australia) — Sydney-Bankstown, NSW & Victoria River Downs, NT

Hangar 480, Miles Street, Bankstown Airport, NSW 2200, Australia ☎ (2) 97 91 03 22 Tx: none Fax: (2) 97 91 03 60 SITA: n/a
F: 1976 ⁂ 80 Head: John V. Weymouth Net: n/a Aircraft / Ag-aircraft below MTOW 1361 / 5000kg: Aerotec Pitts S-2A, Bell 47G/J, CAC-25 Winjeel, Cessna 182 & Robinson R22.
Charter flights are operated under the name HELI-AUSTRALIA (Heli-Aust, Pty Ltd) a sister company (same HQ & fleet).

☐ VH-AZH	Bell 206B JetRanger III	3075	ZK-HWP	0080		1 AN 250-C20B	1451			
☐ VH-BLR	Bell 206B JetRanger	1309		0074		1 AN 250-C20	1451			
☐ VH-JWE	Bell 206A JetRanger	93	N6202N	0067		1 AN 250-C18	1361			
☐ VH-JWF	Bell 206B JetRanger III	3421	P2-AHB	0081	0194	1 AN 250-C20B	1451			
☐ VH-JWM	Bell 206B JetRanger	617	N7097J	0071		1 AN 250-C20	1451			cvtd 206A
☐ VH-MLI	Agusta-Bell 206B JetRanger	8072	VH-BHL	0068	0796	1 AN 250-C20	1451			cvtd 206A
☐ VH-RLV	Bell 206B JetRanger	781	ZK-HRO	0072		1 AN 250-C20	1451			
☐ VH-RMJ	Bell 206B JetRanger	428	ZK-HYG	0069		1 AN 250-C20	1451			cvtd 206A
☐ VH-SVW	Bell 206B JetRanger III	2814	VH-PHX	0079	1097	1 AN 250-C20B	1451			
☐ VH-PPG	Piper PA-32-300 Cherokee SIX	32-40010	N11C	0066		1 LY IO-540-K1A5	1542			
☐ VH-LMI	Cessna TU206G Turbo Stationair 6 II	U20606787	N9975Z	0084	0598	1 CO TSIO-520-M	1633			
☐ VH-SPC	Cessna P206B Super Skylane	P206-0413	VH-DPW	0067		1 CO IO-520-A	1633			
☐ VH-WHI	Cessna TU206G Turbo Stationair 6 II	U20605313	JA3903	0080	1198	1 CO TSIO-520-M	1633			
☐ VH-HIZ	Beech Bonanza F33C	CJ-129	JA3795	0077	0897	1 CO IO-520-BA	1542			
☐ VH-JVC	Eurocopter (Aerosp.) AS350B Squirrel	1516	P2-PHB	0082	0595	1 TU Arriel 1B	1950			
☐ VH-JWD	Eurocopter (Aerosp.) AS350D Squirrel	1135	N35974	0079	0895	1 LY LTS101-600A.2	1950			
☐ VH-IYF	Partenavia P.68B	128		0078	0798	2 LY IO-360-A1B6	1960			
☐ VH-AAM	De Havilland DHC-2 Beaver I	1492	VH-IMR	0060	0698	1 PW R-985	2313			
☐ VH-BVA	De Havilland DHC-2 Beaver I	245	N77WK	0052	0698	1 PW R-985	2313			
☐ VH-TOV	Beech Baron C55 (95-C55)	TE-157		0066		2 CO IO-520-C	2404			
☐ VH-BAK	Beech Baron 58	TH-327	N25626	0073		2 CO IO-520-C	2449			
☐ VH-EZB	Beech Baron 58	TH-97	9V-BCX	0070		2 CO IO-520-C	2449			
☐ VH-FMR	Beech Baron 58	TH-24	N4246A	0070	1096	2 CO IO-520-C	2404			
☐ VH-GJZ	Beech Baron 58	TH-334	VH-CSY	0073	1298	2 CO IO-520-C	2449			
☐ VH-WBR	Beech Baron 58	TH-71	N9028Q	0070	0695	2 CO IO-520-C	2449			
☐ VH-FAX	Cessna 401B	401B0221	N266EC	0072		2 CO TSIO-520-E	2858			
☐ VH-KRY	Cessna 401	401-0096	N3296Q	0067	1197	2 CO TSIO-520-E	2858			
☐ VH-BUD	Cessna 402	402-0079	N3279Q	0067		2 CO TSIO-520-E	2858			
☐ VH-RCT	Cessna 402A	402A0073	PK-LEE	0069		2 CO TSIO-520-E	2858			
☐ VH-SYU	Britten-Norman BN-2A-8 Islander	769	G-BDHW	0076	0997	2 LY O-540-E4C5	2858			
☐ VH-BKK	Kawasaki (Eurocopter/MBB) BK117B-1	1044	JA9993	0090	1197	2 LY LTS101-750B.1	3200			
☐ VH-ASE	Cessna 421B Golden Eagle	421B0501	N14DS	0074		2 CO GTSIO-520-H	3379			
☐ VH-BMX	Cessna 421	421-0108	N3127K	0068	0193	2 CO GTSIO-520-D	3084			
☐ VH-LTL	Cessna 421B Golden Eagle	421B0527	N74HG	0073	1294	2 CO GTSIO-520-H	3379			
☐ VH-YRK	Cessna 421B Golden Eagle	421B0522	N117JD	0074		2 CO GTSIO-520-H	3379			
☐ VH-UHJ	Bell 222U	47567	JA9689	0087	1097	2 LY LTS101-750C.1	3742			lsf Marpilots P/L
☐ VH-BQL	Beech Queen Air B80 (65-B80)	LD-288	DQ-FCQ	0066	0496	2 LY IGSO-540-A1D	3992			

HELIREEF, Pty Ltd — Airlie Beach, QLD

PO Box 715, Airlie Beach, QLD 4802, Australia ☎ (7) 49 46 91 02 Tx: none Fax: (7) 49 46 91 07 SITA: n/a
F: 1993 ⁂ n/a Head: Desmond K. Davey Net: n/a Aircraft below MTOW 1361kg: Bell 47G-5, Robinson R22 & R44

☐ VH-NIM	Bell 206B JetRanger III	2261	N321TC	0077		1 AN 250-C20B	1451			
☐ VH-MQB	Agusta A109A II	7282		0085	1196	2 AN 250-C20B	2600			

HELISERVICES NEWCASTLE & HUNTER (CHN Developments, P/L dba/formerly Helicruise Air Services, P/L) — Newcastle-Harbourside Heliport, NSW

PO Box 30, Wickham, NSW 2293, Australia ☎ (49) 62 10 45 Tx: none Fax: (49) 62 10 09 SITA: n/a
F: 1984 ⁂ 5 Head: Sonia Donolato Net: n/a

☐ VH-MXW	Bell 206B JetRanger	1198	ZK-HHH	0073		1 AN 250-C20	1451			

HELIWORK Western Australia, Pty Ltd (Affiliated with Slingair, Pty Ltd) — Kununurra, WA

PO Box 165, Kununurra, WA 6743, Australia ☎ (8) 91 68 18 11 Tx: n/a Fax: (8) 91 68 14 22 SITA: n/a
F: 1984 ⁂ 20 Head: Kerry Slingsby Net: n/a Aircraft below MTOW 1361kg: Bell 47G, Hughes 269C (300C), Robinson R22 R44

☐ VH-FHY	Bell 206B JetRanger III	3097	9M-PIE	0080		1 AN 250-C20B	1451			
☐ VH-UOD	Bell 206B JetRanger	475	ZK-HMT	0069		1 AN 250-C20	1451			cvtd 206A
☐ VH-UTS	Bell 206B JetRanger III	2328		0078		1 AN 250-C20B	1451			

HERON AIRLINES (IBJ International Aviation Consultants dba) — Sydney-Bankstown, NSW

601 Miles Street, Bankstown Airport, NSW 2200, Australia ☎ (2) 97 96 26 55 Tx: none Fax: (2) 97 96 25 34 SITA: n/a
F: 1991 ⁂ n/a Head: John Ives Net: n/a

☐ VH-CLW	BAe (DH) 114 Riley Heron	14108	DQ-FDY	0057	0795	4 LY IO-540-K1C5	6124	15 Pax		A. Avery / cvtd Srs 2D
☐ VH-CLX	BAe (DH) 114 Riley Heron	14098	G-ANPV	0056	0797	4 LY IO-540-K1C5	6124	15 Pax		Nammo / cvtd Srs 2D
☐ VH-NJI	BAe (DH) 114 Riley Heron	14061	DQ-FED	0055	1091	4 LY IO-540-K1C5	6124	15 Pax		Arthur Butler / cvtd Srs 2B
☐ VH-NJP	BAe (DH) 114 Heron 2	14072	G-ODLG	0054	0993	4 Gipsy Queen 30 Mk.2	5897	15 Pax		E.J. Connellan

HINTERLAND AVIATION (Subsidiary of Trailfinders, Pty Ltd) — Cairns, QLD

PO Box 5711, CMC, Cairns, QLD 4870, Australia ☎ (7) 40 35 93 23 Tx: 48271 aa Fax: (7) 40 35 94 58 SITA: n/a
F: 1984 ⁂ 5 Head: Richard Greenhill Net: n/a

☐ VH-TFC	Cessna U206G Stationair 6 II	U20604576	VH-CMT	0078	0895	1 CO IO-520-F	1633			
☐ VH-RMI	Cessna 402C II	402C0408	N6875T	0081	1198	2 CO TSIO-520-VB	3107			
☐ VH-TFK	Piper PA-31-310 Navajo B	31-759	VH-WZW	0071	0497	2 LY TIO-540-A2C	2948			
☐ VH-TFW	Twin (Aero) Shrike Commander 500S	500S-1798-13	VH-EPN	0068	1195	2 LY IO-540-E1B5	3357			
☐ VH-TFY	Twin (Aero) Shrike Commander 500S	3057	VH-IBY	0070	1094	2 LY IO-540-E1B5	3357			
☐ VH-INO	Britten-Norman BN-2B-20 Islander	2221	G-BRPA*	0090	0892	2 LY IO-540-K1B5	2976			
☐ VH-TFO	Cessna 404 Titan II	404-0076	VH-CAZ	0077	0498	2 CO GTSIO-520-M	3810			

HISTORICAL AIRCRAFT RESTORATION SOCIETY, Inc. — Sydney-Kingsford Smith, NSW

40 Kanadah Avenue, Baulkham Hills, NSW 2153, Australia ☎ (2) 96 74 19 85 Tx: none Fax: (2) 97 22 19 00 SITA: n/a
F: 1978 ⁂ volun Head: Robert de La Hunty Net: n/a Non-profit organisation conducting historical flying presentation with 300 volunteer members.

☐ VH-REK	Cessna 310B	35583	P2-REK	0057		2 CO O-470-M	2131	Support		
☐ VH-IOY	Lockheed P2V-7 (SP-2H) Neptune	726-7273	A89-273	0061		2 WR R-3350&2 WE J34jet	36287	fly-presentation		painted in RAAF-colors as A89-273
☐ VH-LRR	Lockheed P2V-7 (SP-2H) Neptune	726-7183	N8187Z	0060		2 WR R-3350&2 WE J34jet	36287	fly-presentation		painted in Aeronavale-colors as 147566
☐ VH-EAG	Lockh.L-1049F (C-121C) S.Const. (tip tks)	4176	N4115Q	0054	0994	4 WR R-3350	58967	fly.presentation		Southern Preservation

HORIZON AIRLINES, Pty Ltd = YK (Sister co. of Int'L Air Parts, Pty Ltd / formerly Int'l Aviation, Pty Ltd) — Sydney-Bankstown, NSW

PO Box CP311, Condell Park, NSW 2200, Australia ☎ (2) 97 91 93 89 Tx: none Fax: (2) 97 91 99 69 SITA: n/a
F: 1995 ⁂ n/a Head: Dennis Smith Net: n/a

☐ VH-IAU	Fairchild (Swearingen) SA226TC Metro II	TC-289	VH-KDR	0079	1295	2 GA TPE331-3UW-304G	5670	Y19 / Freighter		City of Mildura
☐ VH-WGX	Fairchild (Swearingen) SA226TC Metro II	TC-312	N1015B	0079	0195	2 GA TPE331-3UW-304G	5670	Y19 / Freighter		
☐ VH-WGQ	Shorts Skyvan 3 Variant 100 (SC-7)	SH1915	702 SDF	0073	0598	2 GA TPE331-2-201A	5670	Frtr / Para		
☐ VH-IAW	Fairchild (Swearingen) SA227AC Metro III	AC-600	N3117A	0084	0298	2 GA TPE331-11U-611G	6577	Y19 / Freighter		City of Adelaide
☐ VH-IMI	BAe (HS) 748-287 Srs 2B (SCD)	1736 / 210	G-BCOE	0075	0896	2 RR Dart 536-2	21092	Freighter		cvtd 2A
☐ VH-IMK	BAe (HS) 748-287 Srs 2B (SCD)	1737 / 213	G-BCOF	0075	0896	2 RR Dart 536-2	21092	Freighter		The Beast / cvtd 2A
☐ VH-	BAe (HS) 748-426 Srs 2B	1799 / 280	9N-ACX	0084	0399	2 RR Dart 536-2	21092	Y44 / Freighter		

IAF AIR FREIGHTERS (Independent Air Freighters, Pty Ltd dba / Associated with Australasian Jet) — Melbourne-Essendon, VIC

Hangar 81, Bristol Street, Essendon Airport, VIC 3041, Australia ☎ (3) 93 79 69 99 Tx: none Fax: (3) 93 79 59 49 SITA: n/a
F: 1993 ⁂ n/a Head: Alistair Lamb Net: n/a

☐ VH-WAN	Fokker F27 Friendship 600 (F27 Mk600)	10315	ZK-RTA	0066	0596	2 RR Dart 532-7	20412	Freighter		The Western Australian
☐ VH-RMX	Boeing 727-277 (F) (A) (QWS / winglets)	20551 / 1054		0074	0597	3 PW JT8D-15 (HK3/DUG)	86409	Freighter		lsf IPID / cvtd -277

IBIS AIRLINES = IU (Ibis Air, Pty Ltd dba) — West Sale, VIC

PO Box 181, Sale, VIC 3850, Australia ☎ (3) 51 43 24 68 Tx: none Fax: (3) 51 43 24 65 SITA: n/a
F: n/a ⁂ n/a Head: n/a Net: n/a

☐ VH-IBI	Piper PA-31-350 Navajo Chieftain	31-7552035	ZK-NSO	0075	0299	2 LY TIO-540-J2BD	3175	Y9	

IMPULSE AIRLINES, Pty Ltd = VQ (Member of Impulse Transportation Group, Pty Ltd) — Sydney-Kingsford Smith, NSW

Flight Facilities Terminal, 11th Street, Kingsford Smith Airport, NSW 2020, Australia ☎ (2) 93 17 54 00 Tx: none Fax: (2) 93 17 33 27 SITA: n/a
F: 1992 ⁂ 130 Head: Gerry McGowan IATA: 253 Net: http://www.wagga.com.au/impulse/

☐ VH-OST	Beech 1900C-1 Airliner	UC-56	VH-AFR	0089	0692	2 PWC PT6A-65B	7530	Y19	The Austr.Financial Review
☐ VH-AFR	Beech 1900D Airliner	UE-200	N3193Q*	0096	0396	2 PWC PT6A-67D	7688	Y19	
☐ VH-IMA	Beech 1900D Airliner	UE-7	VH-SMH	0092	0592	2 PWC PT6A-67D	7688	Y19	The Sydney Morning Herald
☐ VH-IMH	Beech 1900D Airliner	UE-230	N3252M*	0096	1196	2 PWC PT6A-67D	7688	Y19	
☐ VH-IMQ	Beech 1900D Airliner	UE-273	N11187*	0097	0697	2 PWC PT6A-67D	7688	Y19	
☐ VH-IMR	Beech 1900D Airliner	UE-324	N23143*	0098	0898	2 PWC PT6A-67D	7688	Y19	
☐ VH-IMS	Beech 1900D Airliner	UE-214	N3230V*	0096	0896	2 PWC PT6A-67D	7688	Y19	
☐ VH-MML	Beech 1900D Airliner	UE-10	N137MA	0092	0792	2 PWC PT6A-67D	7688	Y19	
☐ VH-NBN	Beech 1900D Airliner	UE-318	N22953*	0098	0798	2 PWC PT6A-67D	7688	Y19	Snowy Mountain-colors
☐ VH-NKN	Beech 1900D Airliner	UE-325	N23150*	0098	0998	2 PWC PT6A-67D	7688	Y19	
☐ VH-NTL	Beech 1900D Airliner	UE-117	VH-IPB*	0094	1194	2 PWC PT6A-67D	7688	Y19	
☐ VH-SMH	Beech 1900D Airliner	UE-191	N10326*	0095	0196	2 PWC PT6A-67D	7688	Y19	
☐ VH-TRW	Beech 1900D Airliner	UE-250	N10898*	0096	0197	2 PWC PT6A-67D	7688	Y19	500th 1900-stickers
☐ VH-	Beech 1900D Airliner	UE-				2 PWC PT6A-67D	7688	Y19	oo-delivery 0099
☐ VH-	Beech 1900D Airliner	UE-				2 PWC PT6A-67D	7688	Y19	oo-delivery 0099
☐ VH-	Beech 1900D Airliner	UE-				2 PWC PT6A-67D	7688	Y19	oo-delivery 0099
☐ VH-	Beech 1900D Airliner	UE-				2 PWC PT6A-67D	7688	Y19	oo-delivery 0099
☐ VH-	Beech 1900D Airliner	UE-				2 PWC PT6A-67D	7688	Y19	oo-delivery 0099
☐ VH-	Beech 1900D Airliner	UE-				2 PWC PT6A-67D	7688	Y19	oo-delivery 0099

INDEPENDENT CONTRACT SERVICES, Pty Ltd (Subsidiary of National Jet Systems, Pty Ltd) — Adelaide, SA

435 King William Street, Level 9, Adelaide, SA 5000, Australia ☎ (8) 83 04 56 00 Tx: none Fax: (8) 83 04 56 27 SITA: n/a
F: 1998 ⁂ n/a Head: Maurice Alexander Net: n/a

☐ VH-ICA	Embraer RJ145ER (EMB-145ER)	145095	PT-SBR*	0098	1198	2 AN AE3007A	20600	Y50	
☐ VH-ICD	Embraer RJ145ER (EMB-145ER)	145099		0098	1198	2 AN AE3007A	20600	Y50	

INLAND PACIFIC AIR (Island Link Air Charter, Pty Ltd dba) — Townsville, QLD

PO Box GE54, Garbutt, QLD 4814, Australia ☎ (74) 775 38 66 Tx: none Fax: (74) 775 38 68 SITA: n/a
F: 1993 ⁂ n/a Head: Anthony D. Suthers Net: n/a

☐ VH-PVU	Cessna 402C III	402C1011	N1237V	0085	1297	2 CO TSIO-520-VB	3107		
☐ VH-UCD	Cessna 402C II	402C0049		0078		2 CO TSIO-520-VB	3107		lsf Bencol P/L
☐ VH-TRC	Cessna 421C Golden Eagle II	421C0079		0076		2 CO GTSIO-520-L	3379		lsf Bencol P/L
☐ VH-TMP	Cessna 404 Titan II	404-0125	N37162	0077		2 CO GTSIO-520-M	3810		lsf Bencol P/L
☐ VH-MKS	Fairchild (Swearingen) SA226TC Metro II	TC-262	N49GW	0078	0798	2 GA TPE331-10UA-511G	5670		lsf Bencol P/L

INTERAIR, Pty Ltd — Melbourne-Essendon, VIC

Hangar 12, Essendon Airport, VIC 3041, Australia ☎ (3) 93 74 21 33 Tx: none Fax: (3) 93 79 82 80 SITA: n/a
F: 1981 ⁂ 4 Head: Ernie Shapanis Net: n/a

☐ N756Q	Mitsubishi MU-2F (MU-2B-20)	132		0068		2 GA TPE331-1-151A	4500		lsf Heetco Jet Center
☐ VH-ITA	Beech King Air 200	BB-344	P2-IAG	0078	0797	2 PWC PT6A-41	5670		
☐ VH-ITH	Beech King Air 200	BB-463	P2-NAT	0079	0797	2 PWC PT6A-41	5670		

INVERELL AVIATION (New England Air Training & Charter, Pty Ltd dba) — Inverell, NSW

PO Box 596, Inverell, NSW 2360, Australia ☎ (2) 67 23 13 44 Tx: none Fax: (2) 67 23 14 80 SITA: n/a
F: 1977 ⁂ n/a Head: John A. Newby Net: n/a

☐ VH-TCD	Beech Baron E55	TE-849		0072	0296	2 CO IO-520-C	2404		

ISLAND AIRLINES, Pty Ltd = DG — Hobart, TAS

372 Argyle Street, North Hobart, TAS 7000, Australia ☎ (362) 34 39 80 Tx: none Fax: (362) 34 42 77 SITA: n/a
F: 1996 ⁂ 7 Head: Rod Matthews Net: n/a

☐ VH-IAM	Piper PA-31-350 Navajo Chieftain	31-7952082	VH-TAR	0079	1096	2 LY TIO-540-J2BD	3175		
☐ VH-IAR	Piper PA-31-350 Navajo Chieftain	31-7305064	VH-PRJ	0073	0299	2 LY TIO-540-J2BD	3175		

ISLAND AIR SERVICES, Pty Ltd — Adelaide, SA

18 Charles Street, Allenby Gardens, SA 5009, Australia ☎ (8) 83 40 06 66 Tx: n/a Fax: (8) 83 40 32 58 SITA: n/a
F: 1984 ⁂ n/a Head: Jeremy Browne Net: n/a Aircraft below MTOW 1361kg: Cessna 182

☐ VH-OBL	Britten-Norman BN-2A-20 Islander	2035	A6-NHM	0086	0795	2 LY IO-540-K1B5	2994		

ISLAND AIR TAXIS, Pty Ltd — Airlie Beach, QLD

PO Box 463, Airlie Beach, QLD 4802, Australia ☎ (7) 49 46 99 33 Tx: none Fax: (7) 49 46 99 49 SITA: n/a
F: 1994 ⁂ 7 Head: Alan R. Hope Net: n/a Aircraft below MTOW 1361kg: Cessna 182

☐ VH-ECO	Partenavia P.68B	99	VH-PNS	0077	0396	2 LY IO-360-A1B6	1960		
☐ VH-PNP	Partenavia P.68B	51		0075	0595	2 LY IO-360-A1B6	1990		
☐ VH-ISL	Britten-Norman BN-2B-26 Islander	2131	P2-MCA	0082	0498	2 LY O-540-E4C5	2994		

JANDAKOT HELICOPTERS (Derek Doak dba) — Perth-Jandakot, WA

10 Eagle Drive, Jandakot Airport, Jandakot, WA 6164, Australia ☎ (8) 94 17 55 90 Tx: none Fax: (8) 94 17 59 20 SITA: n/a
F: n/a ⁂ n/a Head: Derek Doak Net: n/a

☐ VH-KHK	Bell 206B JetRanger III	4349	C-GLZK	0095	1297	1 AN 250-C20J	1451		

JAYROW HELICOPTERS, Pty Ltd (Affiliated with Lennox Management & Investments, Pty Ltd) — Melbourne-Moorabbin,VIC/Cairns,QLD/Perth,WA/Darwin,NT

JAYROW

PO Box 46, Mentone, VIC 3194, Australia ☎ (3) 95 87 18 33 Tx: none Fax: (3) 95 80 12 36 SITA: n/a
F: 1964 ⁂ 55 Head: Lindsay Rose Net: n/a

☐ VH-BJG	Bell 206B JetRanger III	2345		0078		1 AN 250-C20B	1451		
☐ VH-BLJ	Bell 206B JetRanger III	3244		0081		1 AN 250-C20B	1451		
☐ VH-BLN	Bell 206B JetRanger III	2846		0079		1 AN 250-C20B	1451		
☐ VH-BLO	Bell 206B JetRanger III	2557		0078		1 AN 250-C20B	1451		
☐ VH-BLP	Bell 206B JetRanger III	3092	P2-HCH	0080	0394	1 AN 250-C20B	1451		
☐ VH-FHV	Bell 206B JetRanger III	3112		0080	0497	1 AN 250-C20B	1451		
☐ VH-FHW	Bell 206B JetRanger III	2838		0079	0797	1 AN 250-C20B	1451		
☐ VH-FHX	Bell 206B JetRanger III	2822		0079		1 AN 250-C20B	1451		
☐ VH-FHZ	Bell 206B JetRanger III	2825		0079		1 AN 250-C20B	1451		
☐ VH-JRE	Bell 206B JetRanger III	2802	ZK-HPO	0079		1 AN 250-C20B	1451		
☐ VH-JRO	Bell 206B JetRanger III	2960	N1083P	0081		1 AN 250-C20B	1451		
☐ VH-KSD	Bell 206B JetRanger III	3658	P2-NHA	0082		1 AN 250-C20B	1451		
☐ VH-BLL	Bell 206L-1 LongRanger II	45174	VH-LKU	0077		1 AN 250-C28B	1882		
☐ VH-AWK	Eurocopter (Aerosp.) AS350D Squirrel	1920	JA9434	0086	0897	1 AN 250-C30	1950		
☐ VH-BLA	Eurocopter (Aerosp.) AS350B Squirrel	1651		0083		1 AN 250-C30	1950		
☐ VH-KVN	Eurocopter (Aerosp.) AS350B Squirrel	2235	JA9837	0089	0398	1 TU Arriel 1B	1950		cvtd AS350D
☐ VH-XMR	Eurocopter (Aerosp.) AS350B Squirrel	2292		0089	1292	1 AN 250-C30M	1950		cvtd TU Arriel Squirrel
☐ VH-OAI	Cessna 208 Caravan I	20800093	ZS-OAI	0086	1297	1 PWC PT6A-114	3629		

JET CHARTER SERVICES (Jet Charter Services, Pty Ltd dba) — Melbourne-Essendon, VIC

PO Box 499, Gisborne, VIC 3437, Australia ☎ (3) 54 28 37 54 Tx: none Fax: (3) 54 28 41 55 SITA: n/a
F: 1992 ⁂ 1 Head: John Morgan Net: n/a

☐ N166WC	GAC G-1159A Gulfstream III	413	249	0083	0394	2 RR Spey 511-8	31615		lsf Washington Corporations

JET CITY, Pty Ltd — Melbourne-Tullamarine, VIC

JET CITY

PO Box 1353, Tullamarine, VIC 3053, Australia ☎ (3) 93 30 15 55 Tx: n/a Fax: (3) 93 30 39 69 SITA: n/a
F: 1989 ⁂ 6 Head: L. Cole Net: n/a

☐ VH-SFH	Piper PA-31-350 Navajo Chieftain	31-7852109	N27709	0078	0395	2 LY TIO-540-J2BD	3175		
☐ VH-JCR	Learjet 35A	35A-231	N62DK	0079	0496	2 GA TFE731-2-2B	8301		

JETCRAFT AVIATION, Pty Ltd (Subsidiary of Pearljet Corporation/Sister co. of Pearl Aviation & Transtate Airlines) — Brisbane-Archerfield, QLD

PO Box 270, Archerfield, QLD 4108, Australia ☎ (7) 32 74 12 41 Tx: none Fax: (7) 32 77 34 81 SITA: n/a
F: 1989 ⁂ 85 Head: Randal W. McFarlane & Ian Foster Net: n/a

☐ VH-SWT	Beech Baron 58	TH-560	N9380S	0075		2 CO IO-520-C	2449		
☐ VH-WIM	Beech Baron 58	TH-822	N23938	0077		2 CO IO-520-C	2449		
☐ VH-TLL	AAC (Ted Smith) Aerostar 601P	61P-0239-037	N90431	0075		2 LY IO-540-S1A5	2722		
☐ VH-UUA	Fairchild (Swearingen) SA227AT Merlin IVC	AT-502	OY-CHH	0082	0696	2 GA TPE331-11U-611G	6577	Freighter	
☐ VH-UZQ	Fairchild (Swearingen) SA226TC Metro II	TC-259	N781S	0078	0591	2 GA TPE331-10UA-511G	5670	Freighter	
☐ VH-UZY	Fairchild (Swearingen) SA226TC Metro II	TC-343	N342PL	0080	0490	2 GA TPE331-10UA-511G	5700	Y19 / Freighter	

630 registration type of aircraft cn/fn ex/ex* mfd del powered by mtow kg configuration selcal name/fln/specialitites/remarks

☐ VH-UUB	Fairchild (Swearingen) SA227DC Metro 23	DC-894B	N3032F*	0097	1197	2 GA TPE331-12U-701G	7484	Y19		
☐ VH-UUG	Fairchild (Swearingen) SA227AC Metro III	AC-517	N3108X	0082	0696	2 GA TPE331-11U-611G	6577	Y19 / Freighter		
☐ VH-UUN	Fairchild (Swearingen) SA227AC Metro III	AC-686	N686AV	0087	0696	2 GA TPE331-11U-611G	6577	Y19		
☐ VH-UUO	Fairchild (Swearingen) SA227AC Metro III	AC-530	ZK-NST	0083	0596	2 GA TPE331-11U-611G	6577	Y19 / Freighter		
☐ VH-UUQ	Fairchild (Swearingen) SA227AC Metro III	AC-714	N433MA	0088	0897	2 GA TPE331-11U-612G	6577	Y19 / Freighter		
☐ VH-UZD	Fairchild (Swearingen) SA227AC Metro III	AC-490	N30693	0081	0395	2 GA TPE331-11U-611G	6577	Y19 / Freighter		
☐ VH-UZG	Fairchild (Swearingen) SA227AC Metro III	AC-553	N220CT	0083	0894	2 GA TPE331-11U-611G	6577	Y19 / Freighter		
☐ VH-UZI	Fairchild (Swearingen) SA227AT Expediter	AT-570	N570UP	0083	0397	2 GA TPE331-11U-601G	6577	Freighter		
☐ VH-UZP	Fairchild (Swearingen) SA227AC Metro III	AC-498	OY-BPL	0082	0193	2 GA TPE331-11U-611G	6577	Freighter		David Feil / opf Security Express
☐ VH-UZS	Fairchild (Swearingen) SA227AC Metro III	AC-616	N349AE	0085	0695	2 GA TPE331-11U-611G	6577	Y19		Copper Connection
☐ VH-UZW	Fairchild (Swearingen) SA227AC Metro III	AC-526	OY-GAW	0082	0693	2 GA TPE331-11U-611G	6577	Y19 / Freighter		Mount Hotham-Falls Creek Ski Resort-cs
☐ VH-CCJ	BAe 4100 Jetstream 41	41036	N436JX	0094	1097	2 GA TPE331-14HR-805H	10886	Y29		Copper Connection II
☐ VH-CCW	BAe 4100 Jetstream 41	41037	G-BWUI	1194	0298	2 GA TPE331-14HR-805H	10886	Y29		opf Queensland Phosphates
☐ VH-JPW	IAI 1124 Westwind I	317	P2-BCM	0081	0492	2 GA TFE731-3-1G	10659	Freighter		
☐ VH-UUM	De Havilland DHC-7-102 Dash 7	043	N705GW	0081	1295	4 PWC PT6A-50	19958	Y50		
☐ VH-UUX	De Havilland DHC-7-102 Dash 7	056	N175RA	0081	1297	4 PWC PT6A-50	19958	Y50		opf Western Mining

JET SYSTEMS, Pty Ltd

Adelaide, SA

28 James Schofield Drive, Adelaide Airport, SA 5950, Australia ☎ (8) 82 38 72 00 Tx: none Fax: (8) 82 38 72 60 SITA: n/a

F: 1989 ††† 4 Head: John Harvey Net: n/a

☐ VH-XCL	Bell 206B JetRanger III	2931	VH-CBI	0080	0398	1 AN 250-C20B	1451			
☐ VH-LMP	Hawker 1000B (BAe 125-1000B)	259022	G-5-734*	0092	0692	2 PWC PW305	14062			

JOHNSTON AVIATION SERVICES, Pty Ltd

Port Macquarie, NSW

Lot 11, Abbott Close, Port Macquarie Airport, Port Macquarie, NSW 2444, Australia ☎ (65) 84 04 84 Tx: none Fax: (65) 84 08 86 SITA: n/a

F: n/a ††† n/a Head: n/a Net: n/a

☐ VH-IJG	Beech Baron 58	TH-415	N24GT	0074	1098	2 CO IO-520-C	2449			

JONES AIR (St. George Air Famers, Pty Ltd dba)

St. George, QLD

Darryl Jones 152, The Terrace, St. George, QLD 4487, Australia ☎ (7) 54 25 31 54 Tx: none Fax: n/a SITA: n/a

F: n/a ††† n/a Head: n/a Net: n/a Aircraft / Ag-aircraft below MTOW 1361/5000kg: AirTractor AT-301, Ayres S2R & Cessna 180

☐ VH-JHF	Cessna 210N Centurion II	21063845	VH-LJE	0080	1296	1 CO IO-520-L	1724			

KAKADU AIR - Scenic Flights & Air Charter (Outback NT Air Safaris) (Kakadu Air Services, Pty Ltd dba)

Jabiru, NT

PO Box 95, Jabiru, NT 0886, Australia ☎ (8) 87 79 24 11 Tx: 85650 aa Fax: (8) 89 79 23 03 SITA: n/a

F: 1984 ††† 30 Head: Bob McDonald Net: n/a Outback safaris are operated under the marketing name OUTBACK NT AIR SAFARIS (sister company, same headquarter & fleet).

☐ VH-TFL	Cessna 210N Centurion II	21063678	N671AA	0080		1 CO IO-520-L	1724			
☐ VH-GKZ	Cessna 207 Skywagon	20700171	P2-SEB	0070		1 CO IO-520-F	1724			
☐ VH-KAX	Cessna T207A Turbo Stationair 8 II	20700630	N154SP	0080		1 CO TSIO-520-M	1724			
☐ VH-LFU	Cessna 207 Skywagon	20700296	ZK-DXT	0075		1 CO IO-520-F	1724			
☐ VH-NIV	Cessna 207A Stationair 8 II	20700627	N41JF	0080		1 CO IO-520-F	1724			
☐ VH-PFP	Partenavia P.68B	91		0077		2 LY IO-360-A1B6	1960			
☐ VH-AAP	Cessna 402B	402B0549	N1601T	0073	0497	2 CO TSIO-520-E	2858			
☐ VH-KQA	Cessna 402B	402B0567	VH-DTV	0074	1092	2 CO TSIO-520-E	2858			
☐ VH-PEK	Cessna 402B	402B0541	N19CW	0073	0397	2 CO TSIO-520-E	2858			
☐ VH-TWX	Cessna 402B	402B0639	N3809C	0074		2 CO TSIO-520-E	2858			
☐ VH-KNA	GAF Nomad N24A	N24A-117	ZK-ECM	0081	0594	2 AN 250-B17B	4264			

KALBARRI AIR CHARTER (Pexton Nominees, Pty Ltd dba)

Kalbarri, WA

PO Box 284, Kalbarri, WA 6536, Australia ☎ (8) 99 37 11 30 Tx: none Fax: (8) 99 37 13 23 SITA: n/a

F: 1981 ††† 3 Head: John Pexton Net: n/a Aircraft below MTOW 1361kg: Bel 47J-2A.

☐ VH-MIA	Cessna 207A Stationair 8 II	20700738	N9822M	0082		1 CO IO-520-F	1724			
☐ VH-MKY	Cessna 207A Turbo Skywagon	20700340	HB-CET	0076		1 CO IO-520-F	1724			cvtd T207A

KARRATHA FLYING SERVICES - KFS (Richard E. Pym dba)

Karratha, WA

12 Cossack Road, Karratha, WA 6714, Australia ☎ (8) 91 44 24 44 Tx: none Fax: (8) 91 44 11 72 SITA: n/a

F: 1986 ††† 7 Head: Richard E. Pym Net: n/a Aircraft below MTOW 1361kg: Cessna 172.

☐ VH-KFD	Cessna R182 Skylane RG II	R18200414	VH-UZI	0078	1196	1 LY O-540-J3C5D	1406			
☐ VH-TOE	Beech Baron C55 (95-C55)	TE-20	N2031W	0066		2 CO IO-520-C	2404			
☐ VH-KFK	Beech Baron 58	TH-969	VH-XMU	0078		2 CO IO-520-C	2449			
☐ VH-KFM	Beech Baron 58	TH-1339	VH-MOS	0082	0495	2 CO IO-520-CB	2449			
☐ VH-IHR	Piper PA-31-310 Navajo	31-8012077	N3257B	0080		2 LY TIO-540-A2C	2948			
☐ VH-KFF	Piper PA-31-350 Navajo Chieftain	31-7952125	VH-UOT	0079	0796	2 LY TIO-540-J2BD	3175			
☐ VH-KFQ	Piper PA-31-310 Navajo B	31-7401250	VH-SRZ	0074		2 LY TIO-540-A2C	2948			
☐ VH-KFW	Piper PA-31-310 Navajo	31-366	VH-WGU	0069		2 LY TIO-540-A1A	2948			

KARUMBA AIR SERVICES, Pty Ltd

Karumba, QLD

PO Box 125, Karumba, QLD 4891, Australia ☎ (77) 45 93 54 Tx: none Fax: (77) 45 93 54 SITA: n/a

F: n/a ††† n/a Head: n/a Net: n/a

☐ VH-CWK	Piper PA-32-300 Cherokee SIX	32-7840052	N2703M	0078	0698	1 LY IO-540-K1G5	1542			
☐ VH-MKH	Cessna P206 Super Skylane	P206-0143		0065	0796	1 CO IO-520-A	1497			
☐ VH-XGD	Cessna U206G Stationair	U20603669	VH-JDZ	0077		1 CO IO-520-F	1633			
☐ VH-XGR	Cessna U206A Super Skywagon	U206-0610	VH-RXE	0066	1198	1 CO IO-520-A	1633			
☐ VH-WPD	Cessna 210N Centurion II	21063998		0080	0998	1 CO IO-520-L	1724			
☐ VH-XGL	Piper PA-31-310 Navajo	31-30	N4513U	0069	0198	2 LY TIO-540-A2C	2948			

KENDELL AIRLINES (Australia), Pty Ltd = KD / KDA (Subsidiary of Ansett Australia)

Wagga Wagga, NSW

PO Box 78, Wagga Wagga, NSW 2650, Australia ☎ (2) 69 22 01 00 Tx: none Fax: (2) 69 22 01 16 SITA: n/a

F: 1966 ††† 220 Head: Geoff Breust IATA: 678 ICAO: KENDELL Net: http://www.kendell.com.au/

☐ VH-KAN	Fairchild (Swearingen) SA227DC Metro 23	DC-838B	N3021U*	0093	0893	2 GA TPE331-12U-701G	7366	Y19		The 1st settlement in SA-Kingscote,K.I.
☐ VH-KDJ	Fairchild (Swearingen) SA227DC Metro 23	DC-797B	N30042*	0092	0892	2 GA TPE331-12U-701G	7366	Y19		City of Portland
☐ VH-KDO	Fairchild (Swearingen) SA227DC Metro 23	DC-837B	N3012N*	0093	0893	2 GA TPE331-12U-701G	7366	Y19		Spirit of Coober Pedy
☐ VH-KDT	Fairchild (Swearingen) SA227DC Metro 23	DC-800B	N3005U*	0092	0992	2 GA TPE331-12U-701G	7366	Y19		Spirit of Ceduna
☐ VH-KED	Fairchild (Swearingen) SA227DC Metro 23	DC-845B	N3023Q*	0094	0294	2 GA TPE331-12U-701G	7366	Y19		Spirit of King Island
☐ VH-KEU	Fairchild (Swearingen) SA227DC Metro 23	DC-846B	N30326*	0094	0394	2 GA TPE331-12U-701G	7366	Y19		Sunraysia Chaffey Trail
☐ VH-KEX	Fairchild (Swearingen) SA227DC Metro 23	DC-872B	N3030X*	0295	0295	2 GA TPE331-12U-701G	7366	Y19		
☐ VH-EKD	Saab SF340A	340A-155	SE-F55*	0089	0889	2 GE CT7-5A2	12700	Y34		City of Wagga Wagga
☐ VH-EKG	Saab 340B	340B-367	SE-C67*	0095	0695	2 GE CT7-9B	13155	Y34		
☐ VH-EKH	Saab 340B	340B-369	SE-C69*	0095	0695	2 GE CT7-9B	13155	Y34		
☐ VH-EKK	Saab 340B	340B-223	SE-KSI	0090	0297	2 GE CT7-9B	12930	Y34		
☐ VH-EKN	Saab 340B	340B-372	SE-C72*	0095	1095	2 GE CT7-9B	13155	Y34		
☐ VH-EKT	Saab SF340A	340A-085	F-GGBJ	0087	0390	2 GE CT7-5A2	12700	Y34		City of Burnie
☐ VH-EKX	Saab 340B	340B-257	N257PX	0091	0696	2 GE CT7-9B	13155	Y34		
☐ VH-KDB	Saab SF340A	340A-008	PH-KJK	0084	1191	2 GE CT7-5A2	12700	Y34		
☐ VH-KDI	Saab SF340A	340A-131	SE-F31*	0088	1088	2 GE CT7-5A2	12700	Y34		City of Whyalla
☐ VH-KDK	Saab SF340A	340A-016	SE-E16*	0085	0285	2 GE CT7-5A2	12700	Y34		City of Mount Gambier
☐ VH-KDP	Saab SF340A	340A-052	SE-E52*	0086	0486	2 GE CT7-5A2	12700	Y34		City of Broken Hill
☐ VH-KDQ	Saab 340B	340B-325	SE-KVO	0092	0396	2 GE CT7-9B	12930	Y34		
☐ VH-KDR	Saab 340B	340B-229	SE-KSK	0091	0796	2 GE CT7-9B	12930	Y34		
☐ VH-KDV	Saab 340B	340B-322	SE-KVN	0092	0296	2 GE CT7-9B	12930	Y34		
☐ VH-KEQ	Saab SF340A	340A-011	9M-NSB	0084	0197	2 GE CT7-5A2	12371	Y34		Spirit of Devonport
☐ VH-LPI	Saab SF340A	340A-151	9M-NSC	0089	0797	2 GE CT7-5A2	12371	Y34		lsf Saab Aircraft Credit AB
☐ VH-	Canadair Regional Jet 200ER (CL-600-2B19)					2 GE CF34-3B1	23133	Y50		oo-delivery 1199
☐ VH-	Canadair Regional Jet 200ER (CL-600-2B19)					2 GE CF34-3B1	23133	Y50		oo-delivery 0000
☐ VH-	Canadair Regional Jet 200ER (CL-600-2B19)					2 GE CF34-3B1	23133	Y50		oo-delivery 0000
☐ VH-	Canadair Regional Jet 200ER (CL-600-2B19)					2 GE CF34-3B1	23133	Y50		oo-delivery 0000
☐ VH-	Canadair Regional Jet 200ER (CL-600-2B19)					2 GE CF34-3B1	23133	Y50		oo-delivery 0000
☐ VH-	Canadair Regional Jet 200ER (CL-600-2B19)					2 GE CF34-3B1	23133	Y50		oo-delivery 0000
☐ VH-	Canadair Regional Jet 200ER (CL-600-2B19)					2 GE CF34-3B1	23133	Y50		oo-delivery 0000
☐ VH-	Canadair Regional Jet 200ER (CL-600-2B19)					2 GE CF34-3B1	23133	Y50		oo-delivery 0000
☐ VH-	Canadair Regional Jet 200ER (CL-600-2B19)					2 GE CF34-3B1	23133	Y50		oo-delivery 0000
☐ VH-	Canadair Regional Jet 200ER (CL-600-2B19)					2 GE CF34-3B1	23133	Y50		oo-delivery 0001
☐ VH-	Canadair Regional Jet 200ER (CL-600-2B19)					2 GE CF34-3B1	23133	Y50		oo-delivery 0001
☐ VH-	Canadair Regional Jet 200ER (CL-600-2B19)					2 GE CF34-3B1	23133	Y50		oo-delivery 0001

KESTREL AVIATION (Jayswell, Pty Ltd dba)

Brisbane, QLD

PO Box 360, Mount Ommaney, QLD 4074, Australia ☎ (41) 972 95 58 Tx: none Fax: (41) 38 05 45 57 SITA: n/a

F: 1988 ††† 2 Head: Michael Braun Net: n/a

☐ VH-CUJ	Commander (Rockwell) 114	14107	N4772W	0076		1 LY IO-540-T4A5D	1424			

631 registration type of aircraft cn/fn ex/ex* mfd del powered by mtow kg configuration selcal name/fln/specialitites/remarks

KEVRON AERIAL SURVEY (Perth Air Charters) (Kevron, Pty Ltd dba / Member of Kevron Group) **Perth-Jandakot, WA**

121 Hill Street, Perth, WA 6004, Australia ☎ (8) 93 25 26 44 Tx: none Fax: (8) 94 21 16 58 SITA: n/a
F: n/a 👥 n/a Head: Kevin W. Radford Net: n/a Charter flights are operated under the marketing name PERTH AIR CHARTERS (same fleet & headquarters).

☐ VH-KPA	Cessna 185B Skywagon	185-0549	N2549Z	0063		1 CO IO-470-F	1451	Photo/Survey/Pax		
☐ VH-KPG	Cessna TU206G Turbo Stationair 6 II	U20605696	VH-AWR	0080	0698	1 CO TSIO-520-M	1633	Photo/Survey/Pax		
☐ VH-IFD	Beech Duke 60	P-40	N175U	0069		2 LY TIO-541-E1B4	3050	Photo/Survey/Pax		
☐ VH-KPB	Beech Duke B60	P-466	VH-SGG	0077	0296	2 LY TIO-541-E1C4	3073	Photo/Survey/Pax		
☐ VH-ANV	Cessna 404 Titan II	404-0820	N67674	0081		2 CO GTSIO-520-M	3810	Photo/Survey/Pax		
☐ VH-AZU	Cessna 404 Titan II	404-0803	N6765J	0082		2 CO GTSIO-520-M	3810	Photo/Survey/Pax		
☐ VH-LEM	Cessna 441 Conquest II	441-0081	N449OC	0079		2 GA TPE331-8-402S	4468	Photo/Survey/Pax		

KEVRON GEOPHYSICS (Kevron Geophysics, Pty Ltd dba / Member of Kevron Group) **Perth-Jandakot, WA**

Hangar 106, Compass Road, Jandakot Airport, WA 6164, Australia ☎ (8) 94 17 31 88 Tx: none Fax: (8) 94 17 35 58 SITA: n/a
F: n/a 👥 24 Head: Kevin W. Radford Net: n/a

☐ VH-EXS	Twin (Aero) Shrike Commander 500S	3069	N9083N	0070		2 LY IO-540-E1B5	3357	Photo/Survey		
☐ VH-KAC	Twin (Aero) Shrike Commander 500S	3185	N57242	0074		2 LY IO-540-E1B5	3357	Photo/Survey		
☐ VH-KAV	Twin (Aero) Shrike Commander 500S	3164	N474V	0073	1194	2 LY IO-540-E1B5	3357	Photo/Survey		
☐ VH-WAM	Twin (Aero) Shrike Commander 500S	3137	ZK-PAT	0073		2 LY IO-540-E1B5	3357	Photo/Survey		

KING ISLAND AIRLINES (Matakana Nominees, Pty Ltd dba) **Melbourne-Moorabbin, VIC**

PO Box 720, Cheltenham, VIC 3192, Australia ☎ (3) 95 80 37 77 Tx: none Fax: (3) 95 80 73 61 SITA: n/a
F: 1990 👥 14 Head: Leigh Faulkner Net: n/a

☐ VH-DMV	Piper PA-31-350 Navajo Chieftain	31-7405487	N61477	0074	0996	2 LY TIO-540-J2BD	3175			
☐ VH-HRL	Piper PA-31-350 Navajo Chieftain	31-7852146	N27811	0078	0998	2 LY TIO-540-J2BD	3175			
☐ VH-KGN	Piper PA-31-350 Navajo Chieftain	31-7952061	N27952	0079		2 LY TIO-540-J2BD	3175			
☐ VH-KGQ	Embraer 110P1 Bandeirante (EMB-110P1)	110221	VH-XFD	0079	0696	2 PWC PT6A-34	5670			

KING LEOPOLD AIR, Pty Ltd **Broome, WA**

PO Box 2632, Broome, WA 6725, Australia ☎ (8) 91 93 71 55 Tx: none Fax: (8) 91 92 24 84 SITA: n/a
F: 1992 👥 4 Head: Ian Lindsay Net: n/a Aircraft below MTOW 1361kg: Piper PA-28.

☐ VH-BIL	Cessna 210L Centurion II	21060429	N1660C	0074		1 CO IO-520-L	1724			lsf pvt
☐ VH-FYR	Cessna 210L Centurion II	21060314	N93229	0074		1 CO IO-520-L	1724			lsf pvt
☐ VH-UPN	Cessna 210N Centurion II	21064125	N5218Y	0080	0498	1 CO IO-520-L	1724			lsf Glowreef Holdings P/L

LADS – Flight Department (Div. of LADS Corp. Ltd – Laser Airborne Depth Sounder / Subsidiary of Vision Systems) **Cairns, QLD**

PO Box 316N, Cairns North, QLD 4870, Australia ☎ (7) 40 35 93 68 Tx: none Fax: (7) 40 35 94 69 SITA: n/a
F: 1991 👥 40 Head: Tom Spurling Net: http://www.vsl.com.au Company will operate its DHC-8 for own hydrographic survey of shallow coastal waters only.

☐ VH-LCL	De Havilland DHC-8-202 Dash 8Q	492	C-GEOA*	0097	0697	2 PWC PW123D	16465	Hydrogr.Survey		lst/opb Surveillance Australia
☐ VH-EWP	Fokker F27 Friendship 500RF (F27 Mk500RF)	10534	PH-EXW*	0076	0492	2 RR Dart 536-7R	20410	Surveyer		lst/opb Associated Airl. for R.A. Navy

LAYNHA-AIR (Laynhapuy Aviation, Pty Ltd dba) **Nhulunbuy, NT**

PO Box 721, Nhulunbuy, NT 0881, Australia ☎ (8) 89 87 19 22 Tx: n/a Fax: (8) 89 87 14 33 SITA: n/a
F: 1985 👥 12 Head: Adrian Wagg Net: n/a

☐ VH-PHA	Bell 206B JetRanger	1454		0074		1 AN 250-C20	1451			
☐ VH-LGN	Cessna U206G Stationair	U20603773	N8190G	0077		1 CO IO-520-F	1633			
☐ VH-PIY	Cessna U206G Stationair 6 II	U20604563	P2-PIY	0078		1 CO IO-520-F	1633			
☐ VH-RXT	Cessna U206B Super Skywagon	U206-0701	N3401L	0067	0295	1 CO IO-520-F	1633			
☐ VH-UBW	Cessna 207 Skywagon	20700137	N1537U	0069		1 CO IO-520-F	1724			
☐ VH-LHA	Britten-Norman BN-2A-26 Islander	856	JA5265	0080	1195	2 LY O-540-E4C5	2812			

LIDDLES AIR SERVICE, P/L **Ingham, QLD**

PO Box 1240, Ingham, QLD 4850, Australia ☎ (74) 776 57 55 Tx: none Fax: (74) 776 36 09 SITA: n/a
F: 1979 👥 n/a Head: Roger Liddle Net: n/a

☐ VH-TCL	Cessna U206F Stationair II	U20602627	N59171	0075	1297	1 CO IO-520-F	1633			

LIP-AIR, Pty Ltd **Cairns, QLD**

PO Box 147N, North Cairns, QLD 4870, Australia ☎ (7) 40 35 91 38 Tx: none Fax: (7) 40 35 99 85 SITA: n/a
F: 1995 👥 15 Head: Rick Lippmann Net: n/a

☐ VH-PNQ	Partenavia P.68B	63		0076	0198	2 LY IO-360-A1B6	1960			
☐ VH-WZP	Partenavia P.68C	228	VH-AJX	0081	1298	2 LY IO-360-A1B6	1990			lst Coral Sea Airlines
☐ VH-WZO	Beech Baron E55	TE-979	VH-EGJ	0074	1298	2 CO IO-520-C	2404			
☐ VH-WZW	Cessna 310R II	310R0719	VH-URS	0076	1298	2 CO IO-520-M	2495			
☐ VH-WZR	Beech Baron 58	TH-383	VH-ATL	0073	1298	2 CO IO-520-C	2449			
☐ VH-WZN	Piper PA-31-310 Navajo	31-657	VH-NOS	0070	1298	2 LY TIO-540-A2B	3102			
☐ VH-WZY	Piper PA-31-310 Navajo	31-302	VH-KJS	0068	1298	2 LY TIO-540-A2B	2948			
☐ VH-WZZ	Piper PA-31-310 Navajo B	31-775	VH-HHL	0071	1298	2 LY TIO-540-A2C	2948			
☐ VH-WZD	Britten-Norman BN-2A-21 Islander	450	VH-USD	0075	1298	2 LY IO-540-K1B5	2994			
☐ VH-WZF	Britten-Norman BN-2A-21 Islander	537	5Y-RAJ	0076	1298	2 LY IO-540-K1B5	2994			

LLOYD HELICOPTERS, Pty Ltd (Member of Helicopter Service Group, Norway) **Adelaide, SA**

45 Greenhill Road, Wayville, SA 5034, Australia ☎ (8) 83 73 07 00 Tx: 89619 heloyd aa Fax: (8) 83 73 33 66 SITA: n/a
F: 1969 👥 200 Head: Alan Latham Net: n/a

☐ VH-LAL	Bell 206B JetRanger III	2626	C-GJET	0079		1 AN 250-C20B	1451			
☐ VH-MIS	Bell 206B JetRanger III	2515		0078		1 AN 250-C20B	1451			opf National Nine News
☐ VH-UBH	Bell 206B JetRanger III	3350		0082		1 AN 250-C20B	1451	EMS		
☐ VH-BJX	Bell 206L-1 LongRanger III	45337	ZK-HQS	0079		1 AN 250-C30P	1882			cvtd LongRanger II
☐ VH-HHS	Bell 206L-1 LongRanger III	45404	N5735N	0080		1 AN 250-C30P	1882			cvtd LongRanger II
☐ VH-LHP	Bell 206L-3 LongRanger III	51002	G-CJCB	0082	0490	1 AN 250-C30P	1882	EMS CS RESQ		
☐ VH-PVM	Eurocopter (Aerosp.) AS350B Squirrel	2058	JA9705	0087	0796	1 TU Arriel 1B	1950	Police/SAR		lst Police Air Wing-Victoria
☐ VH-PVA	Eurocopter (Aerosp.) SA365C1 Dauphin 2	5025	F-WYMH*	0078	0796	2 TU Arriel 1A1	3400	Police/SAR/EMS		lst Police Air Wing-Victoria
☐ VH-PVF	Eurocopter (Aerosp.) SA365C1 Dauphin 2	5042		0078	0796	2 TU Arriel 1A1	3400	Police/SAR/EMS		lst Police Air Wing-Victoria
☐ VH-PVK	Eurocopter (Aerosp.) SA365C1 Dauphin 2	5033	F-WYMA*	0078	0796	2 TU Arriel 1A1	3400	Police/SAR/EMS		lst Police Air Wing-Victoria
☐ VH-HRP	Sikorsky S-76A+	760122	N176CH	0080		2 TU Arriel 1S	4899	SAR		opf RAAF Rescue / cvtd S-76A
☐ VH-HUB	Sikorsky S-76A++	760010	BPS-01	0079		2 TU Arriel 1S1	4899	SAR		opf RAAF Rescue / cvtd S-76A
☐ VH-HUC	Sikorsky S-76A+	760011	BPS-02	0079		2 TU Arriel 1S	4899			cvtd S-76A
☐ VH-HUD	Sikorsky S-76A	760138	G-BVGN	0081	1293	2 AN 250-C30S	4763			
☐ VH-JXL	Sikorsky S-76A+	760148	N31HA	0081		2 TU Arriel 1S	4899			cvtd S-76A
☐ VH-LAH	Sikorsky S-76A+	760089	RJAF 725	0080	0193	2 TU Arriel 1S	4899	SAR		cvtd S-76A
☐ VH-LAI	Sikorsky S-76A+	760103	RJAF 727	0080	0193	2 TU Arriel 1S	4899	SAR		cvtd S-76A
☐ VH-LAQ	Sikorsky S-76A++	760112	G-BNSH	0080	1293	2 TU Arriel 1S1	4899			cvtd S-76A
☐ VH-LAY	Sikorsky S-76A++	760198	G-BOFB	0081	1293	2 TU Arriel 1S1	4899			cvtd S-76A
☐ VH-LHY	Sikorsky S-76A+	760105	ABLE 9	0080	1192	2 TU Arriel 1S	4899	SAR		cvtd S-76A
☐ VH-LHZ	Sikorsky S-76A+	760113	RJAF 732	0080	1192	2 TU Arriel 1S	4899	SAR		cvtd S-76A
☐ VH-LAM	Bell 212	30814	SE-JBY	0077		2 PWC PT6T-3 TwinPac	5080			
☐ VH-NSA	Bell 212	30550	G-BAFN	0073		2 PWC PT6T-3 TwinPac	5080			opf Dept of Conservation & Nat.Res.
☐ VH-BZH	Bell 412	33044	N18098	0081		2 PWC PT6T-3B TwinPac	5262			
☐ VH-NSC	Bell 412	33029	VH-CRQ	0081		2 PWC PT6T-3B TwinPac	5262			
☐ VH-NSP	Bell 412	33091	N22976	0082		2 PWC PT6T-3B TwinPac	5262			
☐ VH-NSV	Bell 412	33084	N3172D	0082		2 PWC PT6T-3B TwinPac	5262	EMS		Air Ambulance
☐ VH-UAH	Bell 412	33034	N2141B	0082		2 PWC PT6T-3B TwinPac	5262			
☐ VH-LAF	Eurocopter (Aerosp.) AS332L1 Super Puma	2319	LN-OBT	0890	1194	2 TU Makila 1A1	8600			lsf HKS
☐ VH-LAG	Eurocopter (Aerosp.) AS332L1 Super Puma	2352	LN-OBU	0091	1294	2 TU Makila 1A1	8600			lsf HKS
☐ VH-LHG	Eurocopter (Aerosp.) AS332L1 Super Puma	2317	LN-OBR	0790	0495	2 TU Makila 1A1	8600			lsf HKS
☐ VH-LHH	Eurocopter (Aerosp.) AS332L1 Super Puma	2407	9M-STU	0094	0198	2 TU Makila 1A1	8600			

LONGREACH AIR CHARTER (John A. McNamara dba) **Longreach, QLD**

Tanamera, Longreach, QLD 4730, Australia ☎ (76) 58 17 51 Tx: n/a Fax: (76) 58 92 74 SITA: n/a
F: n/a 👥 n/a Head: John A. McNamara Net: n/a

☐ VH-TNR	Beech Baron 58	TH-842	N23950	0077		2 CO IO-520-C	2449			

MACAIR AIRLINES = CC (McKinlay Air Charter, Pty Ltd dba) **Townsville & McKinlay, QLD**

PO Box 7191, Garbutt, QLD 4814, Australia ☎ (7) 47 46 86 69 Tx: none Fax: (7) 47 46 86 38 SITA: n/a
F: 1996 👥 n/a Head: Peter Collins Net: n/a

☐ VH-EYH	Beech Baron 58	TH-246	N1564W	0072	0298	2 CO IO-520-C	2449			
☐ VH-AWU	Fairchild (Swearingen) SA226T Merlin IIIB	T-298	N5495M	0078	0397	2 GA TPE331-10U-512G	5670	Y19		
☐ VH-AKT	Beech King Air 200	BB-579	N6064B	0079	0798	2 PWC PT6A-41	5670	Y12		
☐ VH-CUZ	Fairchild (Swearingen) SA227AC Metro III	AC-610B	VH-ANW	0085	0596	2 GA TPE331-11U-612G	7257	Y19		Spirit of MacKinlay / cvtd cn AC-610
☐ VH-SSZ	Fairchild (Swearingen) SA227AC Metro III	AC-614	N614AV	0085	0698	2 GA TPE331-11U-611G	6577	Y19		lsf QWA
☐ VH-XDA	Saab 340B	340B-333	F-GMVX	0093	0698	2 GE CT7-9B	13155	Y34		
☐ VH-XDZ	Saab 340B	340B-328	F-GMVV	0092	0698	2 GE CT7-9B	13155	Y34		

632 registration type of aircraft cn/fn ex/ex* mfd del powered by mtow kg configuration selcal name/fln/specialitites/remarks

MAF Australia – Missionary Aviation Fellowship = FS — Gove, NT & Ballarat, VIC

PO Box 211, Box Hill, VIC 3128, Australia ☎ (3) 98 90 40 09 Tx: none Fax: (3) 98 99 60 63 SITA: n/a
F: 1947 👥 80 Head: J.L. Charlesworth Net: n/a Aircraft below MTOW 1361kg: Cessna 150, 152 & 172. Some services are operated under the name MAF Air Services, Ltd (same headquarters).
MAF also manages the operations for 4 Aboriginal groups - see under Marthakal Yolngu Airline, Ngaanyatarra Air, Ngurratjuta Air & P.Y. Non-commercial multinational ecclesistical consortium conducting flights for relief & development agencies & missions in remote areas of third world countries.

☐ VH-KBN	Cessna U206G Stationair 6 II	U20606630	N9731Z	0082		1 CO IO-520-F	1633
☐ VH-PGJ	Cessna U206F Stationair	U20601739	9V-BDZ	0072		1 CO IO-520-F	1633
☐ VH-UBR	Cessna U206G Stationair	U20603608	N7310N	0077		1 CO IO-520-F	1633
☐ VH-UBS	Cessna U206F Stationair	U20602148	P2-UBS	0074		1 CO IO-520-F	1633
☐ VH-UBV	Cessna U206G Stationair 6 II	U20605671	VH-WKH	0080	0997	1 CO IO-520-F	1633
☐ VH-UBY	Cessna U206G Stationair	U20603545	P2-IXP	0076		1 CO IO-520-F	1633
☐ VH-WOC	Cessna U206F Stationair II	U20603464	N8659Q	0076	0398	1 CO IO-520-F	1633
☐ VH-UBT	Cessna 207 Skywagon	20700116	N1516U	0069		1 CO IO-520-F	1724
☐ VH-IYE	Partenavia P.68B	124		0078		2 LY IO-360-A1B6	1960
☐ VH-AII	Cessna 402C II	402C0278	N3022M	0080		2 CO TSIO-520-VB	3107
☐ VH-UBB	Cessna 402C II	402C0412	N402MG	0081		2 CO TSIO-520-VB	3107
☐ VH-UBF	Cessna 402C II	402C0013	N4654N	0079		2 CO TSIO-520-VB	3107
☐ VH-UBZ	Cessna 402C II	402C0615	VH-UEZ	0082	0298	2 CO TSIO-520-VB	3107
☐ VH-UCM	Cessna 402C II	402C0472	N6838D	0081	0893	2 CO TSIO-520-VB	3107

MANN AVIATION SERVICES (Alan F. Mann dba) — Home Hill, QLD

PO Box 11, Home Hill, QLD 4806, Australia ☎ (7) 47 82 62 33 Tx: n/a Fax: (7) 47 82 62 44 SITA: n/a
F: 1986 👥 3 Head: Alan F. Mann Net: n/a

☐ VH-SOV	Cessna 210N Centurion II	21063082	N6526N	0079	0695	1 CO IO-520-L	1724

MARINE HELICOPTERS, Pty Ltd — Gladstone, QLD

Aerodrome Road, Gladstone Airport, QLD 4680, Australia ☎ (7) 49 78 11 77 Tx: none Fax: (7) 49 78 10 03 SITA: n/a
F: 1996 👥 10 Head: Banny Costa Net: n/a

☐ VH-HVO	MD Helicopters MD 500E (Hughes 369E)	0347E	N1606Z	0089	0697	1 AN 250-C20B	1361	
☐ VH-ONB	MD Helicopters MD 500E (Hughes 369E)	0320E	VH-ONE	0089	0698	1 AN 250-C20B	1361	
☐ VH-HPO	Eurocopter (Aerosp.) AS350BA Squirrel	2186	RP-C1900	0089	1298	1 TU Arriel 1B	2100	cvtd AS350B
☐ VH-HQO	Eurocopter (Aerosp.) AS350BA Squirrel	1607	VH-HCF	0082	0897	1 TU Arriel 1B	2100	cvtd AS350B
☐ VH-HRX	Eurocopter (Aerosp.) AS350B Squirrel	1592	C-GPHK	0082	0897	1 TU Arriel 1B	1950	

MAROOMBA AIRLINES = KN (Nantay, Pty Ltd dba / formerly Maroomba Air Service & Maroomba Aviation) — Perth, WA

Fauntleroy Avenue, Perth Airport, WA 6105, Australia ☎ (8) 94 78 38 50 Tx: none Fax: (8) 94 79 76 89 SITA: n/a
F: 1986 👥 14 Head: Steve F. Young Net: n/a

☐ VH-SMN	Cessna 310R II	310R0531	VH-AJB	0076		2 CO IO-520-M	2495
☐ VH-SMO	Cessna 441 Conquest II	441-0132	VH-ANJ	0080		2 GA TPE331-8-401S	4468
☐ VH-SMT	Beech King Air 200	BB-162	RP-C22	0076	0696	2 PWC PT6A-41	5670
☐ VH-SMZ	Beech King Air B200	BB-1155	VH-HPA	0083	0994	2 PWC PT6A-42	5670

MARTHAKAL YOLNGU AIRLINE, Pty Ltd — Darwin, NT

PMB 62, Winnellie, NT 0822, Australia ☎ (8) 89 87 90 40 Tx: none Fax: (8) 89 87 92 12 SITA: n/a
F: 1995 👥 6 Head: Ian McBride Net: n/a

☐ VH-FUY	Cessna U206G Stationair 6 II	U20604939	N735MF	0079	1195	1 CO IO-520-F	1633
☐ VH-SOP	Cessna U206G Stationair 6 II	U20606216	N6284Z	0081	1195	1 CO IO-520-F	1633
☐ VH-UBE	Cessna 207A Stationair 7 II	20700475	N6307H	0078	1195	1 CO IO-520-F	1724

MCALISTER AIRWAYS, Pty Ltd — Moree, NSW

PO Box 932, Moree, NSW 2400, Australia ☎ (67) 51 17 07 Tx: n/a Fax: (67) 52 20 78 SITA: n/a
F: 1989 👥 3 Head: Mrs Helen M. McAlister Net: n/a

☐ VH-JZW	Cessna 310R II	310R0073	N8213Q	0075		2 CO IO-520-M	2495

MCGEE AERIAL SERVICES (Charmbush, Pty Ltd dba) — Canberra, ACT

PMB Widgeon Road, Pialligo, ACT 2609, Australia ☎ (6) 247 77 99 Tx: none Fax: (6) 247 27 78 SITA: n/a
F: n/a 👥 n/a Head: n/a Net: n/a

☐ VH-HZD	Beech Duchess 76	ME-48	N5168M	0078	1096	2 LY O-360-A1G6D	1769

MCIVER AVIATION (Paulette D. McIver dba) — Hoxton Park, NSW

Hoxton Park Airport, McIver Ave, Hoxton Park, NSW 2171, Australia ☎ (2) 96 07 44 55 Tx: none Fax: (2) 96 08 47 04 SITA: n/a
F: 1972 👥 4 Head: Paulette D. McIver Net: n/a Aircraft below MTOW 1361kg: Cessna 152/172, Piper PA-28 & Robinson R22.

☐ VH-AGL	Bell 206B JetRanger	1308	VH-WHW	0074		1 AN 250-C20	1451

MIRAGE AIR, Pty Ltd — Melbourne-Moorabbin, VIC

Building 67, Northern Avenue, Moorabbin Airport, VIC 3194, Australia ☎ (3) 95 87 58 07 Tx: none Fax: (3) 95 80 21 19 SITA: n/a
F: 1995 👥 n/a Head: n/a Net: n/a

☐ VH-PGM	Twin (Aero) Shrike Commander 500S	3309	N81885	0077	0896	2 LY IO-540-E1B5	3357

MOORABBIN AIR CHARTER (Moorabbin Aviation Academy & General Flying Services, Pty Ltd dba) — Melbourne-Moorabbin, VIC

PO Box 40, Southland Centre, VIC 3192, Australia ☎ (3) 95 80 54 33 Tx: none Fax: (3) 95 87 29 55 SITA: n/a
F: 1968 👥 n/a Head: Ross Carrington Net: n/a Aircraft below MTOW 1361kg: Bellanca 8KCAB, Cessna 172, Piper PA-28, Robinson R22 & Zlin Z242

☐ VH-EUX	Cessna 182S Skylane	18280117		0098	0998	1 LY IO-540-AB1A5	1406
☐ VH-JDF	Piper PA-44-180 Seminole	44-7995304	N2904L	0079	0498	2 LY O-360-E1A6D	1724
☐ VH-KHG	Piper PA-44-180 Seminole	44-8095019	N81487	0080		2 LY O-360-E1A6D	1724
☐ VH-KJM	Piper PA-44-180 Seminole	44-7995122	VH-BNP	0079		2 LY O-360-E1A6D	1724
☐ VH-MHY	Piper PA-44-180 Seminole	44-7995059	N21793	0079		2 LY O-360-E1A6D	1724
☐ VH-NAV	Partenavia P.68C	275		0083	0298	2 LY IO-360-A1B6	1990
☐ VH-PCX	Partenavia P.68C	235		0081	0497	2 LY IO-360-A1B6	1990
☐ VH-CIR	Cessna 310R II	310R1813		0080	0397	2 CO IO-520-M	2495
☐ VH-SAR	Piper PA-31-350 Navajo Chieftain	31-7952027	VH-FDF	0079		2 LY TIO-540-J2BD	3175

MURCHISON RELINES (Bushstar, Pty Ltd dba) — Kalgoorlie, WA

PO Box 4777, Kalgoorlie, WA 6430, Australia ☎ (8) 90 91 51 77 Tx: none Fax: (8) 90 91 51 78 SITA: n/a
F: 1987 👥 n/a Head: Blair W. Howe & Dean W. Howe Net: n/a Aircraft below MTOW 1361kg: Cessna 150 Operates primarily corporate flights for itself but also commercial charter flights (using the AOC of a partner-company).

☐ VH-MRQ	Cessna 337G Super Skymaster	33701618	VH-MWD	0073		2 CO IO-360-G	2100
☐ VH-MRZ	Cessna 337A Super Skymaster	337-0446	N5346S	0066	1195	2 CO IO-360-C/D	1905
☐ VH-MRJ	Britten-Norman BN-2A Mk.III-1 Trislander	322	P2-DNX	0072	0595	3 LY O-540-E4C5	4240

NAT AVION, Pty Ltd — Canberra, ACT

PMB, Canberra Airport, Canberra, ACT 2609, Australia ☎ (6) 257 77 80 Tx: none Fax: (6) 257 77 81 SITA: n/a
F: 1996 👥 n/a Head: n/a Net: n/a

☐ VH-KTQ	Piper PA-34-200T Seneca II	34-7870298	N36158	0078	0298	2 CO TSIO-360-EB	2073
☐ VH-LAP	Beech Baron 58	TH-646	5N-ATC	0075	0797	2 CO IO-520-C	2449
☐ VH-RMT	Piper PA-31-310 Navajo B	31-7401216	N7600L	0073	0996	2 LY TIO-540-A2C	2948

NATIONAL JET SYSTEMS, Pty Ltd = NC / NJS — Adelaide, SA

28 James Schofield Drive, Adelaide Airport, SA 5950, Australia ☎ (8) 82 38 72 00 Tx: n/a Fax: (8) 82 38 72 60 SITA: ADLNJTN
F: 1990 👥 400 Head: Warren Seymour ICAO: NATIONAL JET Net: http://www.natjet.com.au Coastal survey operations are conducted by subsidiary SURVEILLANCE AUSTRALIA – for details see under that company.

☐ VH-OAO	Piper PA-31-350 Navajo Chieftain	31-8252021	N711BP	0082		2 LY TIO-540-J2BD	3175	Y9	
☐ VH-JSX	BAe 4107 Jetstream 41	41035	VH-IMQ	0094	1095	2 GA TPE331-14HR-805H	10886	Y29	lsf BAMT
☐ VH-JSH	De Havilland DHC-8-202 Dash 8	411	C-GHRI*	0095	0296	2 PWC PW123D	16465	Y37	
☐ VH-JSI	De Havilland DHC-8-103 Dash 8	229	VH-LAR	0090	0695	2 PWC PW121	15650	Y37	
☐ VH-JSJ	De Havilland DHC-8-103 Dash 8	170	VH-NJD	0089	1293	2 PWC PW121	15650	Y37	
☐ VH-JSY	De Havilland DHC-8-102 Dash 8	013	C-GAKZ	0085	1197	2 PWC PW120A	15649	Y37	lsf AVLI / cvtd -101
☐ VH-JSQ	De Havilland DHC-8-315 Dash 8	399	VH-NJT	0095	0495	2 PWC PW123B	19500	Y50	cvtd -311
☐ VH-NJA	BAe 146-100	E1004	PK-MTA	0082	1296	4 LY ALF502R-3	37308	Y77	lsf BAMJ / sub-lst DEB as G-DEBJ
☐ VH-NJC	BAe 146-100A	E1013	G-6-013*	0084	0690	4 LY ALF502R-5	37308	C6Y58	lsf BAMJ / sub-lst / opf Airlink
☐ VH-NJD	BAe 146-100	E1160	VH-JSF	0090	1195	4 LY ALF502R-5	38101	Y77	lsf BAMJ
☐ VH-NJE	BAe 146-100	E1104	G-BTXO	0089	0696	4 LY ALF502R-5	38101	C6Y58	lsf BAMJ / sub-lst / opf Airlink
☐ VH-NJR	BAe 146-100	E1152	G-BRLN	0090	0292	4 LY ALF502R-5	38101	C6Y58	lsf BAMJ / sub-lst / opf Airlink
☐ VH-NJT	Avro RJ70 (Avro 146-RJ70)	E1228	G-OLXX	0094	1295	4 LY LF507-1F	40823	Y83	lsf BAMJ
☐ VH-NJV	BAe 146-100 (QC)	E1002	G-BSTA	0083	0995	4 LY ALF502R-3	37308	Freighter	lsf BAMJ/lst/opf Aus.Air Exp./cvtd -100
☐ VH-NJW	Avro RJ70 (Avro 146-RJ70A)	E1223	YL-BAK	0093	0997	4 LY LF507-1F	40823	C6Y58	lsf BTI/sub-lst/opf Norfolk Jet Express
☐ VH-NJY	BAe 146-100	E1005	G-SCHH	0083	0791	4 LY ALF502R-3A	37308	C6Y58	lsf BAMJ / sub-lst / opf Airlink
☐ VH-NJZ	BAe 146-100	E1009	G-6-009*	0083	0791	4 LY ALF502R-3A	37308	C6Y58	lsf BAMJ / sub-lst / opf Airlink

633 registration type of aircraft cn/fn ex/ex* mfd del powered by mtow kg configuration selcal name/fln/specialitites/remarks

☐ VH-NJG	BAe 146-200	*E2170*	*G-BSOH*	*0090*	*0894*	*4 LY ALF502R-5*	*42184*	*C8Y68*		*lsf BAMJ / sub-lst / opf Airlink*
☐ VH-NJH	BAe 146-200	*E2178*	*G-BTCP*	*0091*	*0894*	*4 LY ALF502R-5*	*42184*	*C8Y68*		*lsf BAMJ / sub-lst / opf Airlink*
☐ VH-NJJ	BAe 146-200	*E2184*	*G-BTKC*	*0091*	*0894*	*4 LY ALF502R-5*	*42184*	*C8Y68*		*lsf BAMJ / sub-lst / opf Airlink*
☐ VH-NJQ	BAe 146-200A	*E2072*	*G-BNJI*	*0087*	*0996*	*4 LY ALF502R-5*	*40597*	*C8Y68*		*lsf ANZ Invest.Bank/sub-lst/opf Airlink*
☐ VH-NJU	BAe 146-200A	*E2073*	*G-BVFV*	*0087*	*0996*	*4 LY ALF502R-5*	*40597*	*C8Y68*		*lsf ANZ Invest.Bank/sub-lst/opf Airlink*
☐ VH-NJF	BAe 146-300 (QT)	*E3198*	*G-BTLD*	*0091*	*0992*	*4 LY ALF502R-5*	*44225*	*Freighter*		*lsf BAMJ/lst/opf Aus.Air Exp./cvtd -300*
☐ VH-NJL	BAe 146-300	*E3213*	*G-BVPE*	*0092*	*1194*	*4 LY ALF502R-5*	*44225*	*C8Y79*		*lsf BAMJ / sub-lst / opf Airlink*
☐ VH-NJM	BAe 146-300 (QT)	*E3194*	*G-BTHT*	*0091*	*1195*	*4 LY ALF502R-5*	*44225*	*Freighter*		*lsf BAMJ/lst/opf Aus.Air Exp./cvtd -300*
☐ VH-NJN	BAe 146-300	*E3217*	*G-BUHW*	*0091*	*1194*	*4 LY ALF502R-5*	*44225*	*C8Y79*		*lsf BAMJ / sub-lst / opf Airlink*

NATIONAL PARKS & WILDLIFE SERVICE NSW – Flight Section — **Sydney-Bankstown**

Hangar 609, Bankstown Airport, NSW 2200, Australia ☎ (2) 97 92 17 88 Tx: none Fax: (2) 97 92 16 02 SITA: n/a
F: 1970 ✈ 6 Head: George Foster Net: n/a Non-commercial national organisation conducting surveillance & transport flights.

☐ VH-NPW	Cessna U206G Stationair 6 II	*U20606775*	*N9958Z*	*0083*		*1 CO IO-520-F*	*1633*			
☐ VH-PTH	Eurocopter (Aerosp.) AS350BA Squirrel	*1653*		*0082*		*1 AN 250-C30M*	*2100*			*cvtd AS350B TU Arriel Squirrel*
☐ VH-WLO	Twin (Aero) Turbo Commander 690	*11030*	*VH-WLS*	*0072*		*2 GA TPE331-5-251K*	*4649*			

NAUTILUS AVIATION, Pty Ltd — **Townsville, QLD**

PO Box GE163, Garbutt, QLD 4814, Australia ☎ (7) 47 25 60 56 Tx: n/a Fax: (7) 47 25 42 83 SITA: n/a
F: 1993 ✈ 4 Head: Adrian Billing Net: n/a

☐ VH-OPH	Cessna 208 Caravan I	*20800157*	*N501P*	*0089*	*0895*	*1 PWC PT6A-114*	*3792*			Orpheus Island / *Amphibian*

NAVAIR (Frank Young Aviation, Pty Ltd dba) — **Sydney-Bankstown, NSW & Melbourne-Moorabbin, VIC**

Building 487, Avro Street, Bankstown Airport, NSW 2200, Australia ☎ (2) 97 08 12 22 Tx: none Fax: (2) 97 96 22 89 SITA: n/a
F: 1965 ✈ n/a Head: Frank Young Net: http://ww.navair.au Aircraft below MTOW 1361kg: Beech 23 / 24 / 77, Cessna 152 / 182, Piper PA-28 / 38.

☐ VH-HZK	Piper PA-44-180 Seminole	*44-7995044*	*N21234*	*0079*		*2 LY O-360-E1A6D*	*1724*			
☐ VH-WEC	Beech Duchess 76	*ME-257*	*N6062B*	*0079*		*2 LY O-360-A1G6D*	*1769*			
☐ VH-EPJ	Beech Baron 58	*TH-858*	*N23759*	*0077*	*0197*	*2 CO IO-520-C*	*2449*			

NETWORK AVIATION AUSTRALIA (Network Aviation, Pty Ltd dba) — **Perth, WA**

8 Rossmoyne Drive, Rossmoyne, WA 6148, Australia ☎ (8) 92 77 89 77 Tx: none Fax: (8) 92 77 89 66 SITA: n/a
F: 1998 ✈ 5 Head: Lindsay Evans Net: n/a

☐ VH-TFP	Cessna 310R II	*310R1844*	*N59EX*	*0080*	*0498*	*2 CO IO-520-MB*	*2567*	*5 Pax*		
☐ VH-NAX	Cessna 441 Conquest II	*441-0106*	*VH-YOL*	*0079*	*0498*	*2 GA TPE331-8-403S*	*4611*	*11 Pax*		

NGAANYATJARRA AIR (Div. of Aboriginal Air Services / Subs. of Ngaanyatjarra Council) — **Alice Springs, NT**

PO Box 1238, Alice Springs, NT 0871, Australia ☎ (8) 89 53 50 00 Tx: 81151 aa Fax: (8) 89 53 44 10 SITA: n/a
F: 1982 ✈ 7 Head: n/a Net: n/a

☐ VH-HXH	Cessna 210N Centurion II	*21063847*	*N6260C*	*0080*		*1 CO IO-520-L*	*1724*			
☐ VH-NGD	Cessna P210N Pressurized Centurion II	*P21000459*	*VH-DXA*	*0079*	*0298*	*1 CO TSIO-520-P*	*1814*			
☐ VH-NGE	Cessna P210N Pressurized Centurion II	*P21000830*	*VH-JPL*	*0083*	*0998*	*1 CO TSIO-520-P*	*1814*			
☐ VH-MJI	Cessna 402C II	*402C0500*	*N6842L*	*0081*		*2 CO TSIO-520-VB*	*3107*			
☐ VH-NGC	Cessna 402C II	*402C0419*	*N402GL*	*0081*	*0490*	*2 CO TSIO-520-VB*	*3107*			
☐ VH-NGS	Cessna 208B Grand Caravan	*208B0416*	*N1114W**	*0095*	*0595*	*1 PWC PT6A-114A*	*3969*			

NGURRATJUTA AIR, Pty Ltd (Div. of Aboriginal Air Services / Subs. of Ngaanyatjarra Council) — **Alice Springs, NT**

PO Box 1238, Alice Springs, NT 0871, Australia ☎ (8) 89 53 50 00 Tx: none Fax: (8) 89 53 44 10 SITA: n/a
F: 1987 ✈ 4 Head: n/a Net: n/a

☐ VH-MTJ	Cessna 210N Centurion II	*21064132*	*N5234Y*	*0080*		*1 CO IO-520-L*	*1724*			
☐ VH-NTQ	Cessna 208B Grand Caravan	*208B0635*	*N1216Q*	*0097*	*1197*	*1 PWC PT6A-114A*	*4059*			

NORDSTRESS (Australia), Pty Ltd = NDS = (NORD) (Subsidiary of TNT Ltd & News Corp. / Associated with Ansett Transport Ind.) — **Redfern, NSW**

Tower 1, TNT Plaza, Lawson Square, Redfern, NSW 2016, Australia ☎ (2) 96 99 22 22 Tx: 26536 aa Fax: (2) 96 99 13 49 SITA: n/a
F: 1993 ✈ n/a Head: Colin Smith Net: n/a New and used aircraft leasing, sales and financing company. Occasionally some aircraft are operated on contract basis for private companies.
Owner / Lessor of follwing (main) aircraft types: Airbus Industrie A300B4 & Boeing 737 Aircraft leased from Nordstress are listed and mentioned as lsf NORD under the leasing carriers.

NORFOLK JET EXPRESS, Pty Ltd — **Brisbane, QLD & Norfolk Island**

PO Box 876 GPO, Brisbane, QLD 4001, Australia ☎ (7) 32 21 66 77 Tx: none Fax: (7) 32 36 33 31 SITA: n/a
F: 1997 ✈ n/a Head: Peter Roberts Net: n/a

☐ VH-NJW	Avro RJ70 (Avro 146-RJ70A)	*E1223*	*YL-BAK*	*0093*	*0598*	*4 LY LF507-1F*	*40823*	*C6Y58*		*lsf/opb NJS*

NORIS DINAN AVIATION (SA Helicopters, Pty Ltd dba) — **Adelaide, SA**

PO Box 696, North Adelaide, SA 5006, Australia ☎ (8) 82 34 44 44 Tx: none Fax: (8) 82 34 44 11 SITA: n/a
F: n/a ✈ n/a Head: Douglas Dinan Net: n/a

☐ VH-NDE	Bell 206B JetRanger III	*3053*	*N345BB*	*0080*	*0795*	*1 AN 250-C20B*	*1451*			*opf Channel 10, Adelaide*
☐ VH-NDL	Bell 206B JetRanger III	*2710*	*VH-XHR*	*0079*	*1196*	*1 AN 250-C20B*	*1451*			
☐ VH-NDV	Bell 206B JetRanger III	*4071*	*VH-HHH*	*0089*	*0997*	*1 AN 250-C20B*	*1451*			*opf Channel 10, Melbourne*
☐ VH-NDY	Bell 206B JetRanger III	*3810*	*VH-BHY*	*0084*	*0397*	*1 AN 250-C20B*	*1451*			*opf Channel 7, Adelaide*
☐ VH-NDW	Bell 206L-3 LongRanger III	*51290*	*RP-C1650*	*0089*	*0198*	*1 AN 250-C30P*	*1882*			
☐ VH-ICB	Beech Baron 58	*TH-1096*	*N6067T*	*0079*	*0396*	*2 CO IO-520-CB*	*2449*			

NORTHERN AIR CHARTER (Stefan Wood dba) — **Darwin, NT & Halls Creek, WA**

PO Box 41859, Casuarina, NT 0811, Australia ☎ (8) 89 45 54 44 Tx: none Fax: (8) 89 45 59 77 SITA: n/a
F: 1995 ✈ n/a Head: Stefan Wood Net: n/a

☐ VH-BBI	Cessna 210L Centurion II	*21060471*	*N1672C*	*0074*		*1 CO IO-520-L*	*1724*			*lsf Castle Contracting P/L*
☐ VH-FTM	Cessna 210L Centurion II	*21061159*	*N2198S*	*0076*	*1298*	*1 CO IO-520-L*	*1724*			
☐ VH-KSS	Cessna 210L Centurion II	*21061536*	*N732HX*	*0076*	*1298*	*1 CO IO-520-L*	*1724*			
☐ VH-KST	Cessna 210M Centurion II	*21062521*	*ZK-KLG*	*0078*		*1 CO IO-520-L*	*1724*			*lsf pvt*
☐ VH-MJD	Cessna 210K Centurion II	*21059428*	*VH-EKO*	*0071*	*0398*	*1 CO IO-520-L*	*1724*			
☐ VH-LYD	Cessna 310R II	*310R0815*	*N3356G*	*0077*		*2 CO IO-520-M*	*2495*			*lsf pvt*
☐ VH-OKI	Beech Baron 58	*TH-788*	*N4571S*	*0077*	*1098*	*2 CO IO-520-C*	*2449*			
☐ VH-ATY	Cessna 402B	*402B0924*	*N87128*	*0075*		*2 CO TSIO-520-E*	*2858*			*lsf Centurio Rentals P/L*
☐ VH-LBB	Cessna 402C II	*402C0283*	*N470A*	*0080*		*2 CO TSIO-520-VB*	*3107*			*lsf Branir P/L*

NORTHERN AIR SERVICES, Pty Ltd — **Horn Island, QLD**

PMB 3, Thursday Island, QLD 4875, Australia ☎ (7) 40 69 27 77 Tx: none Fax: (7) 40 69 22 55 SITA: n/a
F: 1997 ✈ n/a Head: Wayne P. Robertson Net: n/a

☐ VH-PFD	Piper PA-23-250 Aztec D	*27-4432*		*0069*	*1097*	*2 LY IO-540-C4B5*	*2359*			*lsf The Robertson Aeroplane Co. P/L*
☐ VH-WRG	Piper PA-23-250 Aztec E	*27-4626*	*VH-MJG*	*0071*	*0097*	*2 LY IO-540-C4B5*	*2359*			*lsf The Robertson Aeroplane Co. P/L*
☐ VH-WRF	AAC (Ted Smith) Aerostar 601B	*61-0497-128*	*VH-UJG*	*0078*	*0097*	*2 LY IO-540-S1A5*	*2722*			*lsf The Robertson Aeroplane Co. P/L*
☐ VH-WRM	Britten-Norman BN-2A-26 Islander	*3015*	*VH-CFZ*	*0086*	*0697*	*2 LY O-540-E4C5*	*2994*			*lsf The Robertson Aeroplane Co. P/L*
☐ VH-WPY	Twin (Aero) Shrike Commander 500S	*3260*	*VH-AUU*	*0076*	*1197*	*2 LY IO-540-E1B5*	*3357*			*lsf The Robertson Aeroplane Co. P/L*
☐ VH-WRU	Twin (Aero) Commander 500B	*500B-1506-180*	*VH-WPP*	*0065*	*1197*	*2 LY IO-540-E1B5*	*3062*			*lsf The Robertson Aeroplane Co. P/L*

NORTHERN TERRITORY AIR SERVICES (Northern Territory Air Services P/L & Air Charter Aviation P/L dba/formerly Action Helicopters P/L) — **Darwin, NT**

PO Box 2006, Darwin, NT 0812, Australia ☎ (8) 89 45 00 83 Tx: none Fax: (8) 89 45 00 67 SITA: n/a
F: 1994 ✈ n/a Head: Cheryl Mactaggart Net: n/a

☐ VH-NTZ	Bell 206B JetRanger	*834*	*VH-JWN*	*0072*		*1 AN 250-C20*	*1451*			
☐ VH-JLK	Cessna U206F Stationair	*U20601914*	*N50288*	*0073*	*0597*	*1 CO IO-520-F*	*1633*			
☐ VH-NTK	Cessna U206G Stationair 6 II	*U20605862*	*P2-DOV*	*0080*	*1198*	*1 CO IO-520-F*	*1633*			
☐ VH-MOB	Cessna 210M Centurion II	*21062068*	*N1972C*	*0077*		*1 CO IO-520-L*	*1724*			
☐ VH-RJH	Cessna 210L Centurion II	*21059880*	*VH-EUT*	*0073*	*0598*	*1 CO IO-520-L*	*1724*			
☐ VH-LBT	Beech Baron 58	*TH-470*	*ZS-LBT*	*0074*		*2 CO IO-520-C*	*2449*			
☐ VH-NTG	Beech Baron 58	*TH-790*	*VH-MFM*	*0077*		*2 CO IO-520-C*	*2449*			
☐ VH-ASD	Piper PA-31-350 Navajo Chieftain	*31-8152030*	*N98CS*	*0081*	*1194*	*2 LY TIO-540-J2BD*	*3175*			
☐ VH-NTC	Cessna 208B Grand Caravan	*208B0418*	*VH-DEX*	*0095*	*0697*	*1 PWC PT6A-114A*	*3969*	*Y13*		
☐ VH-NTS	Cessna 208B Grand Caravan	*208B0348*	*N1288T*	*0093*	*0695*	*1 PWC PT6A-114A*	*3969*	*Y13*		
☐ VH-NTO	De Havilland DHC-6 Twin Otter 320	*371*	*LN-FAP*	*0073*	*0196*	*2 PWC PT6A-27*	*5670*	*Y19*		

NORTH QUEENSLAND AIR CHARTER (Division of North Queensland Aero Club) — **Cairns, QLD**

c/o North Queensland Aero Club, Bush Pilots Avenue, General Aviation, Cairns Airport, QLD 4870, Australia ☎ (7) 40 35 94 38 Tx: 48025 nqac aa Fax: (7) 40 35 98 91 SITA: n/a
F: 1941 ✈ n/a Head: Alex Popov Net: n/a Aircraft below MTOW 1361kg: Cessna 152/172 & Piper PA-28

☐ VH-TEA	Piper PA-44-180 Seminole	*44-7995119*	*VH-JAK*	*0079*		*2 LY O-360-E1A6D*	*1724*			*lsf Avionics & Calibration Service*

NORWEST CHARTERS (Zeiro, Pty Ltd dba / Associated with Bruce Hartwig Flying School) — **Adelaide-Parafield, SA**

Hangar 59, Parafield Airport, SA 5106, Australia ☎ (8) 82 58 42 44 Tx: none Fax: (8) 82 81 86 46 SITA: n/a
F: n/a ✈ n/a Head: Gregory R. Norris Net: n/a

☐ VH-FFJ	Cessna 402B II	*402B1016*	*N87188*	*0076*	*0995*	*2 CO TSIO-520-E*	*2858*			

634 registration type of aircraft *cn/fn* *ex/ex** *mfd* *del* *powered by* *mtow kg* *configuration* *selcal* name/fln/specialitites/remarks

NUMBURINDI AIR (Numbulwar Numburindi Community dba) — Katherine, NT

PO Box 821, Nhulunbuy, NT 0881, Australia ☎ (8) 89 75 47 65 Tx: none Fax: (8) 89 75 46 73 SITA: n/a
F: 1990 2 Head: Richard Rehrmann Net: n/a

registration	type of aircraft	cn/fn	ex/ex*	mfd	del	powered by	mtow kg	configuration	selcal	name/fln/specialitites/remarks
☐ VH-AEE	Cessna U206G Stationair 6 II	*U20605226*	*N5345U*	*0079*		*1 CO IO-520-F*	*1633*			

OASIS AIR, Pty Ltd — Halls Creek, WA

PO Box 116, Halls Creek, WA 6770, Australia ☎ (8) 91 68 64 62 Tx: n/a Fax: (8) 91 68 62 77 SITA: n/a
F: 1992 6 Head: Rolando E. Nanini Net: n/a

registration	type of aircraft	cn/fn	ex/ex*	mfd	del	powered by	mtow kg	configuration	selcal	name/fln/specialitites/remarks
☐ VH-FXG	Cessna U206F Stationair	*U20602449*		*0074*		*1 CO IO-520-F*	*1633*			
☐ VH-ALX	Cessna 210M Centurion II	*21062360*	*N761MH*	*0078*	*0299*	*1 CO IO-520-L*	*1724*			
☐ VH-OAP	Partenavia P.68B	*132*	*VH-IYG*	*0078*	*0497*	*2 LY IO-360-A1B6*	*1990*			*lsf pvt*
☐ VH-OAN	Piper PA-31-310 Navajo	*31-696*	*VH-SGQ*	*0071*	*0996*	*2 LY TIO-540-A2C*	*2948*			*lsf pvt*

O'CONNOR – Mount Gambier's Airline = UQ / OCM (O'Connors Air Services, Pty Ltd dba) — Mount Gambier, SA

Box 21, Mount Gambier, SA 5290, Australia ☎ (8) 87 23 06 66 Tx: none Fax: (8) 87 25 80 03 SITA: n/a
F: 1973 17 Head: Leigh O'Connor Net: n/a Aircraft below MTOW 1361 kg: Cessna 150 & 172.

registration	type of aircraft	cn/fn	ex/ex*	mfd	del	powered by	mtow kg	configuration	selcal	name/fln/specialitites/remarks
☐ VH-OAL	Cessna 210N Centurion II	*21063031*	*N6457N*	*0079*		*1 CO IO-520-L*	*1724*			
☐ VH-PNX	Partenavia P.68B	*66*		*0076*		*2 LY IO-360-A1B6*	*1960*			
☐ VH-OAA	Cessna 441 Conquest II	*441-0102*	*N4246Z*	*0079*		*2 GA TPE331-8-401S*	*4468*			
☐ VH-OAB	BAe 3201 Jetstream 32EP	*853*	*N853JX*	*0089*	*0397*	*2 GA TPE331-12UAR-704H*	*7350*	*Y19*		Spirit of Tantanoola / *lsf BAMT/cvtd 32*
☐ VH-OAE	BAe 3201 Jetstream 32EP	*851*	*N851JX*	*0089*	*0597*	*2 GA TPE331-12UAR-704H*	*7350*	*Y19*		Spirit of MountGambier / *lsfBAMT/cvtd32*

ODE Australia (OD & E, Pty Ltd dba) — Adelaide-Parafield, SA

15 Westport Road, Elizabeth West, SA 5113, Australia ☎ (8) 82 55 30 11 Tx: none Fax: (8) 82 52 02 72 SITA: n/a
F: n/a n/a Head: Garry White Net: n/a

registration	type of aircraft	cn/fn	ex/ex*	mfd	del	powered by	mtow kg	configuration	selcal	name/fln/specialitites/remarks
☐ VH-IOD	Piper PA-31-350 Navajo Chieftain	*31-8152076*	*N4079K*	*0081*		*2 LY TIO-540-J2BD*	*3178*			
☐ VH-ODE	Piper PA-31-350 Navajo Chieftain	*31-8352006*	*N41128*	*0083*		*2 LY TIO-540-J2BD*	*3178*			
☐ VH-OMM	Piper PA-31-350 Navajo Chieftain	*31-8152153*	*N4091B*	*0081*	*0497*	*2 LY TIO-540-J2BD*	*3175*			

ORD AIR CHARTER, Pty Ltd = RF — Kununurra, Wyndham & Derby, WA

PO Box 73, Wyndham, WA 6740, Australia ☎ (8) 91 61 13 35 Tx: none Fax: (8) 91 61 14 56 SITA: n/a
F: 1970 10 Head: Mrs. Maxine S. Reid Net: n/a Aircraft below MTOW 1361kg: Cessna 182

registration	type of aircraft	cn/fn	ex/ex*	mfd	del	powered by	mtow kg	configuration	selcal	name/fln/specialitites/remarks
☐ VH-BBU	Cessna U206G Stationair 6 II	*U20604109*	*N756HS*	*0078*		*1 CO IO-520-L*	*1633*	*5 Pax*		
☐ VH-IRY	Cessna U206F Stationair II	*U20602975*	*P2-MSC*	*0075*		*1 CO IO-520-F*	*1633*	*5 Pax*		
☐ VH-SHZ	Cessna U206G Stationair	*U20603726*	*N9909N*	*0077*		*1 CO IO-520-F*	*1633*	*5 Pax*		
☐ VH-AYV	Beech Baron 58	*TH-1231*	*N3723U*	*0081*		*2 CO IO-520-CB*	*2449*	*5 Pax*		
☐ VH-BBP	Beech Baron 58	*TH-750*	*N1535L*	*0076*		*2 CO IO-520-C*	*2449*	*5 Pax*		
☐ VH-MNH	Beech Baron 58	*TH-1137*	*N67249*	*0080*		*2 CO IO-520-C*	*2449*	*5 Pax*		
☐ VH-IOA	Britten-Norman BN-2A-20 Islander	*842*	*G-BESC*	*0077*		*2 LY IO-540-K1B5*	*2994*	*9 Pax*		
☐ VH-OAD	Cessna 402C II	*402C0014*	*ZK-LMP*	*0078*		*2 CO TSIO-520-VB*	*3107*	*9 Pax*		

OSPREY AIR (Gammadell, Pty Ltd dba) — Mackay, QLD

PO Box 8268, Mt Pleasant Mackay, QLD 4740, Australia ☎ (79) 57 84 88 Tx: none Fax: (79) 54 65 45 SITA: n/a
F: 1991 3 Head: M. Bell Net: n/a

registration	type of aircraft	cn/fn	ex/ex*	mfd	del	powered by	mtow kg	configuration	selcal	name/fln/specialitites/remarks
☐ VH-RJV	Piper PA-32-300 Cherokee SIX	*32-40068*		*0066*		*1 LY IO-540-K1A5*	*1542*			
☐ VH-DSC	Piper PA-30-160 Twin Comanche	*30-552*	*VH-TOO*	*0064*	*0596*	*2 LY IO-320-B1A*	*1633*			

PAGGIS AVIATION (Lino Paggi dba) — Carnarvon, WA

PO Box 247, Carnarvon, WA 6701, Australia ☎ (8) 99 41 15 87 Tx: none Fax: (8) 99 41 15 87 SITA: n/a
F: n/a n/a Head: Lino Paggi Net: n/a

registration	type of aircraft	cn/fn	ex/ex*	mfd	del	powered by	mtow kg	configuration	selcal	name/fln/specialitites/remarks
☐ VH-MHL	Cessna 207 Skywagon	*20700059*	*N91076*	*0069*		*1 CO IO-520-F*	*1724*			
☐ VH-PFR	Partenavia P.68B	*96*		*0077*		*2 LY IO-360-A1B6*	*1960*			
☐ VH-WZQ	Partenavia P.68B	*100*	*VH-PFU*	*0077*	*0496*	*2 LY IO-360-A1B6*	*1960*			

PARADISE HELICOPTERS (Paradise Holidays, Pty Ltd dba) — Coolangatta, QLD

PO Box 303, Coolangatta, QLD 4225, Australia ☎ (7) 55 38 88 86 Tx: none Fax: (7) 55 38 88 87 SITA: n/a
F: 1988 n/a Head: Ms Cheryl Lanham Net: n/a Aircraft below MTOW 1361kg: Cessna 150 & Kawasaki-Hughes 396HS (500C).

registration	type of aircraft	cn/fn	ex/ex*	mfd	del	powered by	mtow kg	configuration	selcal	name/fln/specialitites/remarks
☐ VH-UOR	Bell 206B JetRanger	*406*	*N1458W*	*0069*	*1097*	*1 AN 250-C20*	*1451*			*lsf pvt / cvtd 206A*

PAR-AVION = FP (Aerotechnology, Pty Ltd dba / Affiliated with Par Avion Wilderness Tours & Par Avion Wilderness Cruises) — Hobart-Cambridge, TAS

PO Box 324, Rosny Park, TAS 7018, Australia ☎ (3) 62 48 53 90 Tx: none Fax: (3) 62 48 51 17 SITA: n/a
F: 1977 12 Head: Don Wells Net: n/a Aircraft below MTOW 1361kg: Cessna 172.

registration	type of aircraft	cn/fn	ex/ex*	mfd	del	powered by	mtow kg	configuration	selcal	name/fln/specialitites/remarks
☐ VH-LCD	Cessna U206G Stationair 6 II	*U20604523*	*N673AA*	*0078*		*1 CO IO-520-F*	*1633*			
☐ VH-MYS	Cessna U206G Stationair 6 II	*U20605162*	*N4921U*	*0079*		*1 CO IO-520-F*	*1633*			
☐ VH-IFF	Cessna 310Q	*310Q0765*	*N2994Q*	*0073*		*2 CO IO-470-VO*	*2404*			
☐ VH-TWN	Cessna 310R II	*310R0650*	*N98925*	*0076*	*0197*	*2 CO IO-520-M*	*2495*			
☐ VH-BSF	Piper PA-31P Pressurized Navajo	*31P-58*	*N7305L*	*0072*		*2 LY TIGO-541-E1A*	*3538*			
☐ VH-SGA	Piper PA-31P Pressurized Navajo	*31P-7300166*		*0073*		*2 LY TIGO-541-E1A*	*3538*			
☐ VH-BTN	Twin (Aero) RPM Commander 800L	*680FLP-1695-35*	*D-IBME*	*0067*		*2 LY IO-720-B1B*	*3856*			*cvtd Grand 680FLP*
☐ VH-EXP	Twin (Aero) Grand Commander 680FL	*680FL-1490-94*	*N361K*	*0066*	*0898*	*2 LY IGSO-540-B1A*	*3856*			

PAUL LYONS AVIATION, Pty Ltd — Perth, WA

5 Culligan Road, Thornlie, WA 6108, Australia ☎ (8) 94 59 31 91 Tx: none Fax: (8) 94 59 22 60 SITA: n/a
F: 1986 4 Head: Paul Lyons Net: n/a

registration	type of aircraft	cn/fn	ex/ex*	mfd	del	powered by	mtow kg	configuration	selcal	name/fln/specialitites/remarks
☐ VH-INP	Beech Baron E55	*TE-898*	*N713JE*	*0072*		*2 CO IO-520-C*	*2404*			
☐ VH-XGF	Beech Baron 58	*TH-379*	*N3078V*	*0073*		*2 CO IO-520-C*	*2449*			

PAY'S AIR SERVICE, Pty Ltd – PAS — Scone, NSW

Box 158, Scone, NSW 2337, Australia ☎ (2) 65 45 15 55 Tx: 63287 payair aa Fax: (2) 65 45 29 55 SITA: n/a
F: 1961 42 Head: Colin Pay Net: n/a Aircraft / Historical-Aircraft below MTOW 1361 / 5000 kg: Bell 47G, CAC Mustang Mk 21, Cessna 182/188/305, Curtiss P-40, De Havilland DH-82 & North American T-6.

registration	type of aircraft	cn/fn	ex/ex*	mfd	del	powered by	mtow kg	configuration	selcal	name/fln/specialitites/remarks
☐ VH-JCO	Cessna A185F Skywagon	*18502629*	*N2303L*	*0075*		*1 CO IO-520-D*	*1520*			

PEARL AVIATION AUSTRALIA, Pty Ltd (Subsidiary of Pearljet Corporation/Sister company of Jetcraft Aviation) — Perth, WA

PO Box 894, Cloverdale, WA 6985, Australia ☎ (8) 94 79 25 55 Tx: none Fax: (8) 94 79 25 25 SITA: n/a
F: 1963 124 Head: Mike Hoar Net: n/a

registration	type of aircraft	cn/fn	ex/ex*	mfd	del	powered by	mtow kg	configuration	selcal	name/fln/specialitites/remarks
☐ VH-TSI	Cessna 402C II	*402C0492*	*N6841L*	*0081*		*2 CO TSIO-520-VB*	*3107*	*Charter*		
☐ VH-DUA	Cessna 414A Chancellor III	*414A0225*	*N5696C*	*0079*	*1198*	*2 CO TSIO-520-NB*	*3062*	*Charter*		
☐ VH-AMB	Beech King Air B200C	*BL-131*	N3228X*	*0089*		*2 PWC PT6A-42*	*5670*	*EMS*		*opf Ambulance Service of NSW*
☐ VH-AMM	Beech King Air B200C	*BL-125*	N72381*	*0085*		*2 PWC PT6A-42*	*5670*	*EMS*		*opf Ambulance Service of NSW*
☐ VH-AMR	Beech King Air B200C	*BL-126*	N72385*	*0085*		*2 PWC PT6A-42*	*5670*	*EMS*		*opf Ambulance Service of NSW*
☐ VH-AMS	Beech King Air B200C	*BL-133*	N15588*	*0090*		*2 PWC PT6A-42*	*5670*	*EMS*		*opf Ambulance Service of NSW*
☐ VH-KZL	Beech King Air 200C	*BL-9*	*VH-NSG*	*0080*		*2 PWC PT6A-41*	*5670*	*EMS*		*opf N.T. Aerial Medical Service*
☐ VH-MXK	Beech King Air 200	*BB-653*	*N67224*	*0080*		*2 PWC PT6A-41*	*5670*	*Charter / EMS*		
☐ VH-OYA	Beech King Air 200	*BB-365*	*P2-SML*	*0078*	*0896*	*2 PWC PT6A-41*	*5670*	*Charter / EMS*		
☐ VH-OYD	Beech King Air B200	*BB-1041*	*N200BK*	*0082*	*0197*	*2 PWC PT6A-42*	*5670*	*Charter / EMS*		
☐ VH-SMB	Beech King Air 200	*BB-355*	*P2-SMB*	*0078*		*2 PWC PT6A-41*	*5670*	*Charter / EMS*		
☐ VH-SWO	Beech King Air 200C	*BL-12*	*F-GILF*	*0080*	*1295*	*2 PWC PT6A-41*	*5670*	*EMS*		*opf N.T. Aerial Medical Service*
☐ VH-SWP	Beech King Air 200	*BB-529*	*F-GIQV*	*0079*	*1295*	*2 PWC PT6A-41*	*5670*	*EMS*		*opf N.T. Aerial Medical Service*
☐ VH-TLX	Beech King Air 200	*BB-550*	*P2-MBM*	*0079*		*2 PWC PT6A-41*	*5670*	*Charter / EMS*		
☐ VH-TNQ	Beech King Air 200C	*BL-30*	*N3723Y*	*0081*		*2 PWC PT6A-41*	*5670*	*EMS*		*opf N.T. Aerial Medical Service*
☐ VH-WNH	Beech King Air 200	*BB-148*	*C-GBGW*	*0076*		*2 PWC PT6A-41*	*5670*	*Charter / EMS*		
☐ VH-JPG	Cessna 550 Citation II	*550-0102*	*VH-JCG*	*0079*	*1096*	*2 PWC JT15D-4*	*6033*	*Charter / EMS*		
☐ VH-WGJ	Cessna 550 Citation II	*550-0054*	*N3301M*	*0079*		*2 PWC JT15D-4*	*6033*	*Charter / EMS*		
☐ VH-OYB	Fairchild (Swearingen) SA227DC Metro 23	*DC-848B*	*N452LA*	*0094*	*0996*	*2 GA TPE331-12U-701G*	*7484*	*Charter / EMS*		
☐ VH-OYC	Fairchild (Swearingen) SA227AC Metro III	*AC-619B*	*VH-UZA*	*0085*	*1298*	*2 GA TPE331-11U-611G*	*7257*	*Charter / EMS*		
☐ VH-SWM	Fairchild (Swearingen) SA227DC Metro 23	*DC-875B*	N3033B*	*0095*	*0995*	*2 GA TPE331-12U-701G*	*7484*	*Charter / EMS*		Callie
☐ VH-FIX	Beech King Air 350 (B300)	*FL-90*	*D-CKRA*	*0092*	*0497*	*2 PWC PT6A-60A*	*6804*	*Calibrator*		*opf Airservices Australia*
☐ VH-FIS	IAI 1125 Astra	*045*	*D-CFIS*	*0090*	*0497*	*2 GA TFE731-3A-200G*	*10659*	*Calibrator/VIP*		*opf Airservices Australia*

PEARL COAST AIRWAYS, Pty Ltd — Perth, WA

Unit 7/55 Hampden Road, Nedlands, WA 6009, Australia ☎ (8) 93 89 12 20 Tx: n/a Fax: (8) 93 89 82 32 SITA: n/a
F: n/a n/a Head: n/a Net: n/a

registration	type of aircraft	cn/fn	ex/ex*	mfd	del	powered by	mtow kg	configuration	selcal	name/fln/specialitites/remarks
☐ VH-MQX	Cessna U206G Stationair 6 II	*U20604924*	*N735HQ*	*0079*		*1 CO IO-520-F*	*1633*			*lsf Morgan & Co. P/L*
☐ VH-CWZ	Cessna 310R II	*310R1821*	*N2646D*	*0080*		*2 CO IO-520-M*	*2495*			
☐ VH-MOX	Cessna 208 Caravan I	*20800227*	*VH-NGD*	*0093*	*0595*	*1 PWC PT6A-114*	*3629*			*lsf Morgan & Co. P/L / Floats*

PEARSON AVIATION, Pty Ltd — Melbourne-Essendon, VIC

PO Box 85, Mount Macedon, VIC 3441, Australia ☎ (3) 93 79 16 44 Tx: none Fax: (3) 93 79 19 44 SITA: n/a
F: 1989 10 Head: Guy J. Pearson Net: n/a Operates airtaxi/charter (beside pilot training) flights, currently with aircraft leased from other companies when required.

PEL-AIR = QD / QWA (Qwestair) (Pel-Air Aviation, Pty Ltd, Pel-Air Express, Pty Ltd dba) **SYD-Mascot, NSW & BNE/DRW/MEB/NOA/PER**

PO Box 208, Mascot, NSW 1460, Australia ☎ (2) 96 69 35 55 Tx: 71025 peldal aa Fax: (2) 93 17 55 05 SITA: n/a
F: 1984 ✈✈✈ n/a Head: John Johnson Net: http://www.pelair.com.au Operations from PERTH-base/WA are operated under the marketing name QWESTAIR (same headquarters/aircraft).

☐ VH-EEQ	Fairchild (Swearingen) SA226TC Metro II	TC-251	VH-IAR	0078	0495	2 GA TPE331-3UW-303G	5670	Freighter		
☐ VH-EER	Fairchild (Swearingen) SA226TC Metro II	TC-284	VH-WGW	0079	0195	2 GA TPE331-3UW-304G	5670	Freighter		
☐ VH-EEN	Fairchild (Swearingen) SA227AT Expediter	AT-563	N563UP	0083	1296	2 GA TPE331-11U-611G	6577	Freighter		lst/opf XME / Australian Air Express-cs
☐ VH-EEO	Fairchild (Swearingen) SA227AT Expediter	AT-564	N564UP	0083	1296	2 GA TPE331-11U-611G	6577	Freighter		lst/opf XME / Australian Air Express-cs
☐ VH-EEP	Fairchild (Swearingen) SA227AT Expediter	AT-567	N565UP	0083	1296	2 GA TPE331-11U-611G	6577	Freighter		lst/opf XME / Australian Air Express-cs
☐ VH-SSM	Fairchild (Swearingen) SA227AC Metro III	AC-494	N605AS	0082	0195	2 GA TPE331-11U-611G	6577	Y19 / Freighter		
☐ VH-SST	Fairchild (Swearingen) SA227AC Metro III	AC-612	N347AE	0085	0195	2 GA TPE331-11U-611G	6577	Y19 / Freighter		opf DHL Worldwide Express
☐ VH-SSV	Fairchild (Swearingen) SA227AC Metro III	AC-617	N350AE	0085	0195	2 GA TPE331-11U-611G	6577	Y19 / Freighter		
☐ VH-SSW	Fairchild (Swearingen) SA227AC Metro III	AC-632	N346AE	0086	0195	2 GA TPE331-11U-611G	6577	Y19 / Freighter		
☐ VH-SSZ	Fairchild (Swearingen) SA227AC Metro III	AC-614	N614AV	0085	0195	2 GA TPE331-11U-611G	6577	Y19 / Freighter		lst Macair Airlines
☐ VH-SLD	Learjet 35A	35A-145	N145GJ	0077	0796	2 GA TFE731-2-2B	7711	Freighter		
☐ VH-SLE	Learjet 35A	35A-428	N17LH	0081	0696	2 GA TFE731-2-2B	8165	Executive		
☐ VH-SLF	Learjet 36A	36A-049	N136ST	0081	0696	2 GA TFE731-2-2B	8301	Executive		
☐ VH-SLJ	Learjet 36	36-014	N200Y	1075	0696	2 GA TFE731-2-2B	7711	Freighter		
☐ VH-AJJ	IAI 1124 Westwind I	248	N25RE	0079		2 GA TFE731-3-1G	10659	Executive		
☐ VH-AJK	IAI 1124 Westwind I	256	4X-CNG*	0079		2 GA TFE731-3-1G	10659	Freighter		
☐ VH-AJP	IAI 1124 Westwind I	238	4X-CMJ*	0078		2 GA TFE731-3-1G	10659	Freighter		
☐ VH-AJQ	IAI 1124 Westwind I	281	4X-CQA*	0080		2 GA TFE731-3-1G	10659	Freighter		
☐ VH-AJV	IAI 1124 Westwind I	282	N186G	0080		2 GA TFE731-3-1G	10659	Executive		
☐ VH-KNS	IAI 1124 Westwind I	323	N816H	0081		2 GA TFE731-3-1G	10659	Freighter		
☐ VH-NGA	IAI 1124A Westwind II	387	N97AL	0083		2 GA TFE731-3-1G	10659	Executive		

PENGUIN EXPRESS (Discover Flying / Essendon Air Charter) (Moloney Aviation, Pty Ltd dba / Affiliated with Sixth Canus, Pty Ltd) **Melbourne-Essendon, VIC**

Main Terminal Building, Essendon Airport, VIC 3041, Australia ☎ (3) 93 79 21 22 Tx: n/a Fax: (3) 93 74 20 86 SITA: n/a
F: 1983 ✈✈✈ 9 Head: Maurice G. Moloney ICAO: PENGUIN EXPRESS Net: n/a Marketing names DISCOVER FLYING & ESSENDON AIR CHARTER are used for some services occasionally.

☐ VH-BAJ	Twin (Aero) Shrike Commander 500S	3130	N9182N	0073	0097	2 LY IO-540-E1B5	3357			lsf GAM Air Services
☐ VH-ABM	BAe (DH) 104 Riley Dove	04097	G-ATGI	0047		2 LY IO-720	3992			Lady Di / cvtd Srs. 1
☐ VH-NBM	BAe (DH) 104 Riley Dove	04416	N711SK	0052		2 LY IO-720	3992			cvtd Srs. 2A

PITJANTJATJARA-YANKUNYTJATJARA AIR – P.Y. Air (Division of Yanap Aboriginal, Corp.) **Alice Springs, NT**

PO Box 2189, Alice Springs, NT 0871, Australia ☎ (8) 89 50 54 45 Tx: none Fax: (8) 89 53 44 10 SITA: n/a
F: 1985 ✈✈✈ 3 Head: n/a Net: n/a

☐ VH-TLU	Cessna U206G Stationair 6 II	U20604740	N732YS	0079		1 CO IO-520-F	1633			

POLAR AVIATION, Pty Ltd **Port Hedland, WA**

PO Box 772, Port Hedland, WA 6721, Australia ☎ (8) 91 73 31 33 Tx: n/a Fax: n/a SITA: n/a
F: n/a ✈✈✈ n/a Head: Clark A. Butson Net: n/a Aircraft below MTOW 1361kg: Piper PA-28.

☐ VH-BHW	Piper PA-32R-300 Lance	32R-7680496	N4989F	0076		1 LY IO-540-K1G5D	1633			
☐ VH-BIV	Cessna 210N Centurion II	21063398	N5373A	0079		1 CO IO-520-L	1724			
☐ VH-TRN	Cessna 310R II	310R1314	N6176C	0078		2 CO IO-520-M	2495			

POLICE AIRCRAFT SERVICES – South Australia (Division of South Australian Police) **Adelaide-West Beach, SA**

GPO Box 1539, Adelaide, SA 5001, Australia ☎ (8) 82 34 45 33 Tx: none Fax: (8) 82 34 36 48 SITA: n/a
F: 1972 ✈✈✈ 4 Head: Gregory E. Mellberg Net: n/a Non-commercial state organisation conducting aerial police & EMS work.

☐ VH-HMG	Cessna 402C III	402C1002	N1235B	0085		2 CO TSIO-520-VB	3107			
☐ VH-TAN	Cessna 402C III	402C1008	N1237D	0085		2 CO TSIO-520-VB	3107			

POLICE AIR WING – Northern Territory (Division of Northern Territory Police) **Darwin & Alice Springs, NT**

PO Box 39764, Winnellie, NT 0821, Australia ☎ (8) 89 22 31 08 Tx: 85020 aa Fax: (8) 89 22 31 06 SITA: n/a
F: 1979 ✈✈✈ 4 Head: Ronald Hart Net: n/a Non-commercial state organisation conducting aerial police & EMS work.

☐ VH-MWC	Piper PA-31-310 Navajo	31-8212011	N4103G	0082		2 LY TIO-540-A2C	3053			
☐ VH-NAD	Piper PA-31-310 Navajo	31-8212004	N4099T	0082		2 LY TIO-540-A2C	3053			

POLICE AIR WING – NSW (Division of NSW Police Department) **Sydney-Bankstown, NSW**

Sopwith Place, Hangar 276, Bankstown Airport, NSW 2200, Australia ☎ (2) 97 91 91 77 Tx: none Fax: (2) 97 91 90 20 SITA: n/a
F: 1979 ✈✈✈ 30 Head: Chief Inspector William McKinnon Net: n/a Non-commercial state organisation conducting aerial police & EMS work.

☐ VH-PHW	Bell 206B JetRanger III	2565		0078		1 AN 250-C20B	1451			Polair 1
☐ VH-PHB	Eurocopter (Aerosp.) AS350B2 Squirrel	2984		0097	0797	1 TU Arriel 1D1	2250			Polair 3
☐ VH-PHX	Eurocopter (Aerosp.) AS355N Tw.Squirrel	5623	F-OHKI	0096	0497	2 TU Arrius 1A	2540			Polair 2

POLICE AIR WING – Queensland (Division of Queensland Police Services) **Brisbane-Eagle Farm, QLD**

GPO Box 1440, Brisbane, QLD 4001, Australia ☎ (7) 38 60 46 24 Tx: none Fax: (7) 38 60 44 21 SITA: n/a
F: 1975 ✈✈✈ 8 Head: Mal Lynch Net: n/a Non-commercial state organisation conducting aerial police & EMS work.

☐ VH-PSQ	Cessna 208 Caravan I	20800213	N9798F*	0092	0592	1 PWC PT6A-114	3629			
☐ VH-PSY	Cessna 208B Grand Caravan	208B0577		0096	1296	1 PWC PT6A-114A	3969			
☐ VH-WNZ	Cessna 550 Citation II	550-0057	N2661N	0079	1286	2 PWC JT15D-4	6033			
☐ VH-PSK	Beech King Air 350 (B300)	FL-29	ZS-NAV	0091	0896	2 PWC PT6A-60A	6804			

POLICE AIR WING – Victoria (Division of Victoria Police Force) **Melbourne-Essendon, VIC**

Bldg 104, Lionel Street, Essendon Airport, VIC 3041, Australia ☎ (3) 93 79 73 47 Tx: none Fax: (3) 93 74 19 29 SITA: n/a
F: 1974 ✈✈✈ 57 Head: Chief Inspector Phil McSolvin Net: n/a Non-commercial state organisation conducting aerial police & EMS work.

☐ VH-PVM	Eurocopter (Aerosp.) AS350B Squirrel	2058	JA9705	0087	1091	1 TU Arriel 1B	1950	Police/SAR		lsf Lloyd Helicopters
☐ VH-PVA	Eurocopter (Aerosp.) SA365C1 Dauphin 2	5025	F-WYMH*	0078		2 TU Arriel 1A1	3400	Police/SAR/EMS		lsf Lloyd Helicopters
☐ VH-PVF	Eurocopter (Aerosp.) SA365C1 Dauphin 2	5042		0078		2 TU Arriel 1A1	3400	Police/SAR/EMS		lsf Lloyd Helicopters
☐ VH-PVK	Eurocopter (Aerosp.) SA365C1 Dauphin 2	5033	F-WYMA*	0078		2 TU Arriel 1A1	3400	Police/SAR/EMS		lsf Lloyd Helicopters

POLICE AIR WING – Western Australia (Division of Western Australia Police Department) **Perth-Jandakot, WA**

Hangar 149, Jandakot Airport, WA 6164, Australia ☎ (8) 94 17 36 93 Tx: n/a Fax: (8) 94 17 59 85 SITA: n/a
F: 1975 ✈✈✈ 22 Head: Inspector Lawrence Net: n/a Non-commercial state organisation conducting aerial police & EMS work.

☐ VH-HCP	Cessna 310R II	310R0849	N3475G	0077		2 CO IO-520-M	2495			
☐ VH-FLZ	Beech Baron 58	TH-274	VH-OTP	0073	1193	2 CO IO-520-C	2449			
☐ VH-DEP	Piper PA-31-310 Navajo C	31-7812125	N27794	0078		2 LY TIO-540-A2C	2948			
☐ VH-WAH	Kawasaki (Eurocopter/MBB) BK117B-1	1051	JA6607	0090	0992	2 LY LTS101-750B.1	3200			

PREMIER INTERNATIONAL (Premier Airlines, Pty Ltd dba) **Melbourne-Tullamarine, VIC**

PO Box 1317, Tullamarine, VIC 3043, Australia ☎ (3) 93 35 58 36 Tx: none Fax: (3) 93 35 58 46 SITA: n/a
F: 1994 ✈✈✈ 12 Head: Terrence Vickers Net: n/a

☐ VH-DHE	Boeing 727-2J4 (F) (A)	22080 / 1598	N729DH	0080	0595	3 PW JT8D-17 (HK3/FDX)	90517	Freighter	BM-CJ	lsf/jtlyopw AsianExp.in DHL-cs/cvtd-2J4

PROFESSIONAL HELICOPTER SERVICES, Pty Ltd (Affiliated with Newman Holdings, Pty Ltd & Newman Investments, Pty Ltd) **Melbourne-Moorabbin, VIC**

Bundora Parade, Moorabbin Airport, VIC 3194, Australia ☎ (3) 95 80 74 33 Tx: n/a Fax: (3) 95 87 38 21 SITA: n/a
F: n/a ✈✈✈ n/a Head: Ronald A. Newman Net: http://phs.com.au/ Aircraft below MTOW 1361kg: Hughes 269C (300C) & Robinson R22.

☐ VH-FHF	Bell 206B JetRanger III	1926		0076		1 AN 250-C20B	1451			cvtd JetRanger II
☐ VH-SWH	Bell 206B JetRanger III	1918		0076		1 AN 250-C20B	1451			cvtd JetRanger II

QANTAS Airways, Ltd = QF / QFA ("Spirit of Australia") (Assoc.with British Airways Plc / Member of Oneworld Alliance) **Sydney-Kingsford Smith, NSW**

Qantas Centre, Bldg A, 203 Coward Street, Sydney, NSW 2020, Australia ☎ (2) 96 91 36 36 Tx: 20113 qantas aa Fax: (2) 96 91 32 77 SITA: SYDXLQF
F: 1920 ✈✈✈ 30000 Head: Gary Pemberton IATA: 081 ICAO: QANTAS Net: http://www.qantas.com.au
Regional feeder services are operated on behalf of Qantas by subsidiary carriers: AIRLINK, AUSTRALIAN AIR EXPRESS, EASTERN AUSTRALIA AIRLINES, SOUTHERN AUSTRALIA AIRLINES & SUNSTATE AIRLINES, using QF flight numbers – for details see under each carrier. All Boeing 747-438 will be modified with RB211-524G/H-T engines starting 1999.

☐ VH-TAF	Boeing 737-376	23477 / 1225	N3281U*	0086	1093	2 CFMI CFM56-3C1	61235	F8CY108	DF-EQ	Courageous
☐ VH-TAG	Boeing 737-376	23478 / 1251		0086	1093	2 CFMI CFM56-3C1	61235	F8CY108	DF-ER	Advance
☐ VH-TAH	Boeing 737-376	23479 / 1259		0086	1093	2 CFMI CFM56-3C1	61235	F8CY108	DF-ES	Adventure
☐ VH-TAI	Boeing 737-376	23483 / 1264		0086	1093	2 CFMI CFM56-3C1	61235	F8CY108	EM-KR	Boldness
☐ VH-TAJ	Boeing 737-376	23484 / 1270		0086	1093	2 CFMI CFM56-3C1	61235	F8CY108	EM-KS	Challenge
☐ VH-TAK	Boeing 737-376	23485 / 1277		0086	1093	2 CFMI CFM56-3C1	61235	F8CY108	EM-LR	Daring
☐ VH-TAU	Boeing 737-376	23486 / 1286		0086	1093	2 CFMI CFM56-3C1	61235	F8CY108	EM-LS	Enterprise
☐ VH-TAV	Boeing 737-376	23487 / 1306		0086	1093	2 CFMI CFM56-3C1	61235	F8CY108	EM-PR	Intrepid
☐ VH-TAW	Boeing 737-376	23488 / 1352		0087	1093	2 CFMI CFM56-3C1	61235	F8CY108	EM-PS	Progress
☐ VH-TAX	Boeing 737-376	23489 / 1356		0087	1093	2 CFMI CFM56-3C1	61235	F8CY108	EM-QR	Success
☐ VH-TAY	Boeing 737-376	23490 / 1390		0087	1093	2 CFMI CFM56-3C1	61235	F8CY108	EM-QS	Valiant
☐ VH-TAZ	Boeing 737-376	23491 / 1391		0087	1093	2 CFMI CFM56-3C1	61235	F8CY108	EM-RS	Victory
☐ VH-TJA	Boeing 737-376	24295 / 1649		0088	1093	2 CFMI CFM56-3C1	61235	F8CY108	EP-AG	Resolute
☐ VH-TJB	Boeing 737-376	24296 / 1653		0088	1093	2 CFMI CFM56-3C1	61235	F8CY108	EG-DM	Guadalcanal / lst/jtly opw SOL
☐ VH-TJC	Boeing 737-376	24297 / 1740		0089	1093	2 CFMI CFM56-3C1	61235	F8CY108	EP-AR	Endeavour
☐ VH-TJD	Boeing 737-376	24298 / 1761		0089	1093	2 CFMI CFM56-3C1	61235	F8CY108	EP-AS	Gallant
☐ VH-TJE	Boeing 737-476	24430 / 1820		0090	1093	2 CFMI CFM56-3C1	68039	F8CY131	EP-BR	Kookaburra
☐ VH-TJF	Boeing 737-476	24431 / 1863		0090	1093	2 CFMI CFM56-3C1	68039	F8CY131	EP-BS	Brolga

636 registration type of aircraft cn/fn ex/ex* mfd del powered by mtow kg configuration selcal name/fln/specialitites/remarks

☐ VH-TJG	Boeing 737-476	24432 / 1879	9M-MLE	0090	1093	2 CFMI CFM56-3C1	68039	F8CY131	EP-CR	Eagle
☐ VH-TJH	Boeing 737-476	24433 / 1881		0090	1093	2 CFMI CFM56-3C1	68039	F8CY131	EP-CS	Falcon
☐ VH-TJI	Boeing 737-476	24434 / 1912	9M-MLD	0090	1093	2 CFMI CFM56-3C1	68039	F8CY131	EP-DR	Swan
☐ VH-TJJ	Boeing 737-476	24435 / 1959		0090	1093	2 CFMI CFM56-3C1	68039	F8CY131	EP-DS	Heron
☐ VH-TJK	Boeing 737-476	24436 / 1998		0091	1093	2 CFMI CFM56-3C1	68039	F8CY131	EP-FR	Ibis
☐ VH-TJL	Boeing 737-476	24437 / 2162		0091	1093	2 CFMI CFM56-3C1	68039	F8CY131	EP-FS	Swift
☐ VH-TJM	Boeing 737-476	24438 / 2171		0091	1093	2 CFMI CFM56-3C1	68039	F8CY131	EP-GJ	Kestrel
☐ VH-TJN	Boeing 737-476	24439 / 2265		0092	1093	2 CFMI CFM56-3C1	68039	F8CY131	EP-GR	Egret
☐ VH-TJO	Boeing 737-476	24440 / 2324		0092	1093	2 CFMI CFM56-3C1	68039	F8CY131	EP-GS	Lorikeet
☐ VH-TJP	Boeing 737-476	24441 / 2363		0092	1093	2 CFMI CFM56-3C1	68039	F8CY131	EP-HK	Petrel
☐ VH-TJQ	Boeing 737-476	24442 / 2371		0092	1093	2 CFMI CFM56-3C1	68039	F8CY131	EP-HM	Bellbird
☐ VH-TJR	Boeing 737-476	24443 / 2398		0092	1093	2 CFMI CFM56-3C1	68039	F8CY131	EP-HS	Cockatiel
☐ VH-TJS	Boeing 737-476	24444 / 2454		0093	1093	2 CFMI CFM56-3C1	68039	F8CY131	EP-JR	Jabiru
☐ VH-TJT	Boeing 737-476	24445 / 2539		0093	1093	2 CFMI CFM56-3C1	68039	F8CY131	EP-JS	Kingfisher
☐ VH-TJU	Boeing 737-476	24446 / 2569		0094	0294	2 CFMI CFM56-3C1	68039	F8CY131	EP-KL	Currawong
☐ VH-TJV	Boeing 737-4Q8	25163 / 2264	H4-SOL	0092	0694	2 CFMI CFM56-3C1	68039	F8CY130	DS-AJ	Swan / *lsf ILFC*
☐ VH-TJW	Boeing 737-4L7	26961 / 2517	C2-RN11	0093	0695	2 CFMI CFM56-3C1	68039	F8CY131	JR-DG	Sharing
☐ VH-TJX	Boeing 737-476	28150 / 2773		0096	0296	2 CFMI CFM56-3C1	64637	F8CY131	JS-CR	Trust
☐ VH-TJY	Boeing 737-476	28151 / 2785		0096	0496	2 CFMI CFM56-3C1	64637	F8CY131	JS-DE	Integrity
☐ VH-TJZ	Boeing 737-476	28152 / 2829		0096	1196	2 CFMI CFM56-3C1	64637	F8CY131	JS-DF	
☐ VH-EAJ	Boeing 767-238 (ER)	23304 / 119	N6055X*	0085	0785	2 PW JT9D-7R4E	145150	C30Y175	JM-DG	City of Wollongong
☐ VH-EAK	Boeing 767-238 (ER)	23305 / 120	N6009F*	0085	0785	2 PW JT9D-7R4E	145150	C30Y175	CE-AF	City of Townsville
☐ VH-EAL	Boeing 767-238 (ER)	23306 / 125	N6009F*	0085	0985	2 PW JT9D-7R4E	145150	C30Y175	CE-AG	City of Geelong
☐ VH-EAM	Boeing 767-238 (ER)	23309 / 129	N6018N*	0085	1285	2 PW JT9D-7R4E	145150	C30Y175	DK-GL	Lake Macquarie
☐ VH-EAN	Boeing 767-238 (ER)	23402 / 133	N6018N*	0086	0286	2 PW JT9D-7R4E	145150	C30Y175	DL-BJ	Alice Springs
☐ VH-EAO	Boeing 767-238 (ER)	23403 / 137	N6046P*	0086	0386	2 PW JT9D-7R4E	145150	C30Y175	DK-EL	City of Cairns
☐ VH-EAQ	Boeing 767-238 (ER)	23896 / 183	N6009F*	0087	0887	2 PW JT9D-7R4E	145150	C30Y175	AP-DJ	City of Launceston
☐ VH-OGA	Boeing 767-338 (ER)	24146 / 231	N6055X*	0088	0888	2 GE CF6-80C2B6	185065	C20Y208	EJ-HL	City of Whyalla
☐ VH-OGB	Boeing 767-338 (ER)	24316 / 242	N6005C*	0088	1088	2 GE CF6-80C2B6	185065	C20Y208	DK-JM	City of Kalgoorlie / Boulder
☐ VH-OGC	Boeing 767-338 (ER)	24317 / 246	N6005C*	0088	1188	2 GE CF6-80C2B6	185065	C20Y208	DG-AP	City of Bendigo
☐ VH-OGD	Boeing 767-338 (ER)	24407 / 247	N6009F*	0088	1288	2 GE CF6-80C2B6	172365	C20Y208	HJ-EP	City of Maitland
☐ VH-OGE	Boeing 767-338 (ER)	24531 / 278		0089	0989	2 GE CF6-80C2B6	172365	C20Y208	QR-AL	City of Orange
☐ VH-OGF	Boeing 767-338 (ER)	24853 / 319		0090	0790	2 GE CF6-80C2B6	172365	C20Y208	GQ-EP	City of Lismore
☐ VH-OGG	Boeing 767-338 (ER)	24929 / 343		0090	1290	2 GE CF6-80C2B6	172365	C20Y208	LQ-BF	City of Rockhampton
☐ VH-OGH	Boeing 767-338 (ER)	24930 / 344		0090	1290	2 GE CF6-80C2B6	172365	C20Y208	LQ-BG	City of Parramatta
☐ VH-OGI	Boeing 767-338 (ER)	25246 / 387		0091	0891	2 GE CF6-80C2B6	172365	C20Y208	LQ-BK	City of Port Augusta
☐ VH-OGJ	Boeing 767-338 (ER)	25274 / 396		0091	1091	2 GE CF6-80C2B6	172365	C20Y208	LQ-BM	City of Port Macquarie
☐ VH-OGK	Boeing 767-338 (ER)	25316 / 397	N6018N*	0091	1091	2 GE CF6-80C2B6	172365	C20Y208	LQ-BP	City of Mackay
☐ VH-OGL	Boeing 767-338 (ER)	25363 / 402	N6018N*	0091	1191	2 GE CF6-80C2B6	172365	C20Y208	LQ-CD	City of Wangaratta
☐ VH-OGM	Boeing 767-338 (ER)	25575 / 451		0092	0992	2 GE CF6-80C2B6	172365	C20Y208	QR-AG	City of Bundaberg
☐ VH-OGN	Boeing 767-338 (ER)	25576 / 549		0094	0894	2 GE CF6-80C2B6	172365	C20Y208	QR-AH	Partnership
☐ VH-OGO	Boeing 767-338 (ER)	25577 / 550		0094	0894	2 GE CF6-80C2B6	172365	C20Y208	QR-AJ	Unity
☐ VH-OGP	Boeing 767-338 (ER)	28153 / 615		0096	0596	2 GE CF6-80C2B6	172365	C20Y208	EG-DK	
☐ VH-OGQ	Boeing 767-338 (ER)	28154 / 623		0096	0896	2 GE CF6-80C2B6	172365	C20Y208	EG-DL	
☐ VH-OGR	Boeing 767-338 (ER)	28724 / 662		0097	0697	2 GE CF6-80C2B6	185065	C20Y208		
☐ VH-OGS	Boeing 767-338 (ER)	28725 / 665		0697	0697	2 GE CF6-80C2B6	185065	C20Y208		
☐ VH-OGT	Boeing 767-338 (ER)	29117 / 710		0098	0798	2 GE CF6-80C2B6	172365	C20Y208		
☐ VH-OGU	Boeing 767-338 (ER)	29118 / 713		0098	0898	2 GE CF6-80C2B6	172365	C20Y208		
☐ VH-OGV	Boeing 767-338 (ER)					2 GE CF6-80C2B6	172365	C20Y208		*oo-delivery 0099*
☐ VH-EAA	Boeing 747SP-38	22495 / 505		0081	0181	4 RR RB211-524D4	318422	C34Y262	EG-FM	City of Gold Coast/Tweed
☐ VH-EAB	Boeing 747SP-38	22672 / 537		0081	0881	4 RR RB211-524D4	318422	C34Y262	EG-FL	City of Traralgon
☐ VH-EBQ	Boeing 747-238B	22145 / 410		0079	1279	4 RR RB211-524D4	377842	C23Y421	DK-FM	City of Bunbury / *lst FJI as DQ-FJI*
☐ VH-EBR	Boeing 747-238B	22614 / 464	N8296V*	0080	0980	4 RR RB211-524D4	377842	C23Y421	DK-EM	City of Mt. Gambier / *lst FJI as DQ-FJE*
☐ VH-EBS	Boeing 747-238B	22616 / 543	N6005C*	0081	1181	4 RR RB211-524D4	377842	C48Y360	EG-FK	City of Broken Hill
☐ VH-ECB	Boeing 747-238B (M)	21977 / 409		0079	1179	4 RR RB211-524D4	377842	C48Y360	DK-EJ	City of Swan Hill
☐ VH-ECC	Boeing 747-238B (M)	22615 / 483		0080	1080	4 RR RB211-524D4	377842	C48Y360	JM-EG	City of Shepparton
☐ VH-EBT	Boeing 747-338	23222 / 602	N1784B*	0084	1184	4 RR RB211-524D4	377842	C50Y370	JM-EH	City of Wagga Wagga
☐ VH-EBU	Boeing 747-338	23223 / 606	N5573P*	0084	0185	4 RR RB211-524D4	377842	C50Y370	DL-BH	Nalanji Dreaming / *blue coral/fish cs*
☐ VH-EBV	Boeing 747-338	23224 / 610	N6005C*	0085	0485	4 RR RB211-524D4	377842	C50Y370	DL-BK	Geraldton
☐ VH-EBW	Boeing 747-338	23408 / 638	N6055X*	0086	0486	4 RR RB211-524D4	377842	C50Y370	CE-AB	City of Tamworth
☐ VH-EBX	Boeing 747-338	23688 / 662	N6005C*	0086	1186	4 RR RB211-524D4	377842	C50Y370	DL-BM	City of Wodonga
☐ VH-EBY	Boeing 747-338	23823 / 678	N6005C*	0087	0587	4 RR RB211-524D4	377842	C50Y370	EK-AF	City of Mildura
☐ VH-OEB	Boeing 747-48E (Longreach)	25778 / 983	HL7416	0093	0598	4 GE CF6-80C2B1F	394625	F16C65Y282		
☐ VH-OEC	Boeing 747-4H6 (Longreach)	24836 / 808	9M-MHN	0090	1198	4 GE CF6-80C2B1F	394625	F16C65Y282		
☐ VH-OED	Boeing 747-4H6 (Longreach)	25126 / 858	9M-MHO	0091	0998	4 GE CF6-80C2B1F	394625	F16C65Y282		
☐ VH-OJA	Boeing 747-438 (Longreach)	24354 / 731	N6046P*	0089	0889	4 RR RB211-524G	396893	F16C50Y330	HJ-FP	City of Canberra
☐ VH-OJB	Boeing 747-438 (Longreach)	24373 / 746		0089	0989	4 RR RB211-524G	396893	F16C50Y330	HJ-GP	City of Wunula Dreaming / *Aborigine-cs 7*
☐ VH-OJC	Boeing 747-438 (Longreach)	24406 / 751		0089	1089	4 RR RB211-524G	396893	F16C50Y330	HJ-KP	City of Melbourne
☐ VH-OJD	Boeing 747-438 (Longreach)	24481 / 764		0090	0190	4 RR RB211-524G	396893	F16C50Y330	HJ-LP	City of Brisbane
☐ VH-OJE	Boeing 747-438 (Longreach)	24482 / 765		0090	0190	4 RR RB211-524G	396893	F16C50Y330	DK-LM	City of Adelaide
☐ VH-OJF	Boeing 747-438 (Longreach)	24483 / 781		0090	0490	4 RR RB211-524G	396893	F16C50Y330	AQ-CE	City of Perth
☐ VH-OJG	Boeing 747-438 (Longreach)	24779 / 801	N6009F*	0090	0890	4 RR RB211-524G	396893	F16C50Y330	AQ-CF	City of Hobart
☐ VH-OJH	Boeing 747-438 (Longreach)	24806 / 807		0090	0890	4 RR RB211-524G	396893	F16C50Y330	AQ-CG	City of Darwin
☐ VH-OJI	Boeing 747-438 (Longreach)	24887 / 826	N6009F*	0090	1290	4 RR RB211-524G	396893	F16C50Y330	GQ-EL	Longreach
☐ VH-OJJ	Boeing 747-438 (Longreach)	24974 / 835		0091	0291	4 RR RB211-524G	396893	F16C50Y330	GQ-EM	Winton
☐ VH-OJK	Boeing 747-438 (Longreach)	25067 / 857		0091	0691	4 RR RB211-524G	396893	F16C50Y330	LQ-BH	City of Newcastle
☐ VH-OJL	Boeing 747-438 (Longreach)	25151 / 865		0091	0791	4 RR RB211-524G	396893	F16C50Y330	LQ-BJ	City of Ballaarat
☐ VH-OJM	Boeing 747-438 (Longreach)	25245 / 875		0091	0991	4 RR RB211-524G	396893	F16C65Y282	LQ-CE	City of Gosford
☐ VH-OJN	Boeing 747-438 (Longreach)	25315 / 883	N6009F*	0091	1191	4 RR RB211-524G	396893	F16C65Y282	QR-AB	City of Dubbo
☐ VH-OJO	Boeing 747-438 (Longreach)	25544 / 894	N6005C*	0092	0592	4 RR RB211-524G	396893	F16C65Y282	QR-AC	City of Toowoomba
☐ VH-OJP	Boeing 747-438 (Longreach)	25545 / 916		0092	0692	4 RR RB211-524G	396893	F16C65Y282	QR-AD	City of Albury
☐ VH-OJQ	Boeing 747-438 (Longreach)	25546 / 924	N6005C*	0092	0992	4 RR RB211-524G	396893	F16C65Y282	QR-AE	City of Mandurah
☐ VH-OJR	Boeing 747-438 (Longreach)	25547 / 936	N6018N*	0092	1092	4 RR RB211-524G	396893	F16C65Y282	QR-AF	City of Bathurst
☐ VH-OJS	Boeing 747-438 (Longreach)					4 RR RB211-524G/H-T	396893	F16C65Y282		*oo-delivery 1099*
☐ VH-OJT	Boeing 747-438 (Longreach)					4 RR RB211-524G/H-T	396893	F16C65Y282		*oo-delivery 0200*
☐ VH-OJU	Boeing 747-438 (Longreach)					4 RR RB211-524G/H-T	396893	F16C65Y282		*oo-delivery 0400*

QAS AERIAL AMBULANCE (Queensland Ambulance Service-Bundaberg Station & Rockhampton Station dba) — Bundaberg & Rockhampton, QLD

GPO Box 1425, Brisbane, QLD 4001, Australia ☎ (79) 21 15 86 Tx: none Fax: (79) 27 56 17 SITA: n/a
F: 1958 ♟♟♟ 5 Head: Chris Carr Net: n/a

☐ VH-JEH	Cessna 414A Chancellor III	414A0834	N3319M	0082		2 CO TSIO-520-NB	3062	EMS
☐ VH-JRK	Cessna 414A Chancellor III	414A0665	N6819X	0081		2 CO TSIO-520-NB	3062	EMS
☐ VH-BUY	Cessna 404 Titan II	404-0611	N2684R	0080		2 CO GTSIO-520-M	3810	EMS

QASCO (NSW), Pty Ltd (Queensland Air Survey Company dba) — Sydney-Bankstown, NSW & Brisbane, QLD

PO Box 233, Baulkham Hills, NSW 2153, Australia ☎ (2) 96 39 88 22 Tx: none Fax: (2) 96 86 26 20 SITA: n/a
F: n/a ♟♟♟ n/a Head: Keith Stapley Net: n/a

☐ VH-MAX	Cessna 402B II	402B1018	N87191	0076		2 CO TSIO-520-E	2858	Surveyer
☐ VH-SVQ	Cessna 402B	402B0601	ZK-FXS	0074	0199	2 CO TSIO-520-E	2858	Surveyer

QES RESCUE (Queensland Emergency Services dba / Division of The Queensland State Government) — Brisbane / Cairns & Townsville, QLD

GPO Box 1425, Brisbane, QLD 4001, Australia ☎ (7) 32 47 41 38 Tx: none Fax: (7) 32 47 42 07 SITA: n/a
F: 1989 ♟♟♟ 53 Head: n/a Net: n/a Non-commercial state organisation conducting EMS, Patrol & VIP flights.

☐ VH-SGK	Eurocopter (Aerosp.) AS350B Squirrel	1494		0081		1 TU Arriel 1B	1950	EMS/SAR/VIP
☐ VH-ESA	Bell 412HP	36022	N412VS	0091	1097	2 PWC PT6T-3B TwinPac	5262	EMS/SAR
☐ VH-ESB	Bell 412EP	36087	N2157A	0094	0795	2 PWC PT6T-3D TwinPac	5262	EMS/SAR
☐ VH-ESD	Bell 412HP	36026	N412TX	0091	0795	2 PWC PT6T-3B TwinPac	5262	EMS/SAR

Q.O.T.S. AIR CHARTER (Peter J. Evert / Queensland Outback Tourist Service dba) — Winton, QLD

PO Box 287, Winton, QLD 4735, Australia ☎ (7) 46 57 13 40 Tx: n/a Fax: (7) 46 57 15 41 SITA: n/a
F: 1975 ♟♟♟ 2 Head: Peter J. Evert Net: n/a

☐ VH-WMC	Piper PA-32R-301 Saratoga SP	32R-8013036	N3575G	0080		1 LY IO-540-K1G5D	1633

QUEENSLAND GOVERNMENT AIR WING (Division of The Queensland State Government) — Brisbane, QLD

GPO Box 1018, Eagle Farm, QLD 4009, Australia ☎ (7) 38 60 41 00 Tx: none Fax: (7) 38 60 44 21 SITA: n/a
F: 1996 ♟♟♟ n/a Head: n/a Net: n/a Non-commercial state organisation conducting EMS, Patrol & VIP flights.

☐ VH-SGQ	Beech King Air 350 (B300)	FL-150	N10691	0096	1296	2 PWC PT6A-60A	6804	EMS / VIP
☐ VH-SGY	Hawker 800XP	258328	N328XP*	0097	1297	2 GA TFE731-5BR-1H	12701	EMS / VIP

637 registration type of aircraft cn/fn ex/ex* mfd del powered by mtow kg configuration selcal name/fln/specialitites/remarks

REEF HELICOPTERS, Pty Ltd (Associated with Skytrans) — Cairns, QLD

PO Box 86, Stratford, QLD 4870, Australia ☎ (7) 40 35 94 44 Tx: none Fax: (7) 40 35 93 18 SITA: n/a
F: 1990 ⁂ 13 Head: David Barnard Net: n/a

☐ VH-FJE	Bell 206B JetRanger	1521	ZK-HZJ	0074		1 AN 250-C20	1451			
☐ VH-RHL	Bell 206B JetRanger III	2965	VH-ALV	0080	0494	1 AN 250-C20B	1451			
☐ VH-RHC	Bell 206L-4 LongRanger IV	52106		0095	0695	1 AN 250-C30P	2018	Coastal Survey		opf Customs Coastwatch
☐ VH-RHF	Bell 206L-3 LongRanger III	51115	VH-HTA	0084	0796	1 AN 250-C30P	1882			
☐ VH-TSP	Bell 222U	47532	N3189H	0085	0594	2 LY LTS101-750C.1	3742			

REEFWATCH AIR TOURS (Division of GAM Air Services) — Cairns, QLD

PO Box 2237, Cairns, QLD 4870, Australia ☎ (7) 40 35 98 08 Tx: none Fax: (7) 40 35 95 52 SITA: n/a
F: n/a ⁂ n/a Head: Steven R. Nott Net: n/a

☐ VH-ACJ	Twin (Aero) Shrike Commander 500S	3178	N57079	0074		2 LY IO-540-E1B5	3357			opb GAM Air Services
☐ VH-PAR	Twin (Aero) Shrike Commander 500S	3311	N84SA	0077		2 LY IO-540-E1B5	3357			opb GAM Air Services
☐ VH-UJB	Twin (Aero) Shrike Commander 500S	3152	VH-EXJ	0073	0796	2 LY IO-540-E1B5	3357			opb GAM Air Services

REGENT AIR SERVICES (Adnerva, Pty Ltd dba) — Perth, WA

1015 Coulston Roade, Boya, WA 6056, Australia ☎ (8) 92 99 88 88 Tx: none Fax: (9) 92 99 89 00 SITA: n/a
F: 1976 ⁂ n/a Head: Stuart Darbyshire Net: n/a

☐ VH-SJD	Piper PA-31-310 Navajo	31-8012008		0080		2 LY TIO-540-A2C	2948			

R.L. AVIATION (Russell J. Lee dba) — Ceres, VIC

195 Merrawarp Road, Ceres, VIC 3221, Australia ☎ (3) 52 49 13 87 Tx: none Fax: (3) 52 49 13 87 SITA: n/a
F: 1991 ⁂ 2 Head: Russell J. Lee Net: n/a

☐ VH-UPI	Cessna 185A Skywagon	185-0329	VH-CLH	0062		1 CO IO-470-F	1451			
☐ VH-PQT	Cessna U206 Super Skywagon	U206-0427	N8027Z	0065		1 CO IO-520-A	1497			
☐ VH-OMD	Beech Baron E55	TE-970	N4395W	0074		2 CO IO-520-C	2404			
☐ VH-LJI	Piper PA-31-310 Navajo C	31-7712021	N42BR	0077	0996	2 LY TIO-540-A2C	2948			

ROSSAIR CHARTER = RFS (Ross Aviation, Pty Ltd dba) — Adelaide, SA

Box 33, Private Box Centre, Adelaide Airport, SA 5950, Australia ☎ (8) 82 34 42 19 Tx: n/a Fax: (8) 82 34 30 46 SITA: n/a
F: 1991 ⁂ 5 Head: Bob Carr Net: n/a Aircraft below MTOW 1361kg: Cessna 152/172 & 182.

☐ VH-MAK	Cessna 414	414-0265	N1550T	0072		2 CO TSIO-520-J	2880			
☐ VH-BPO	Cessna 404 Titan II	404-0086	N8774G	0077	0496	2 CO GTSIO-520-M	3810			
☐ VH-TMU	Cessna 404 Titan II	404-0205	N6078G	0078		2 CO GTSIO-520-M	3810			
☐ VH-XMD	Cessna 441 Conquest II	441-0025	N441HD	0078	0697	2 GA TPE331-10-534S	4468			
☐ VH-XMG	Cessna 441 Conquest II	441-0130	VH-KDN	0080	1098	2 GA TPE331-8-401S	4468			
☐ VH-XMJ	Cessna 441 Conquest II	441-0113	N27TA	0080		2 GA TPE331-8-401S	4468			

ROTOR-LIFT, Pty Ltd — Sydney-Mascot, NSW

PO Box 694, Mascot, NSW 2020, Australia ☎ (2) 96 69 33 66 Tx: none Fax: (2) 96 67 19 19 SITA: n/a
F: 1998 ⁂ n/a Head: n/a Net: n/a

☐ VH-RLI	Kawasaki (Eurocopter/MBB) BK117A-4	1018	ZK-HNE	0089	0898	2 LY LTS101-650B.1	3200			

ROTORWAY AUSTRALIA, Pty Ltd — Newcastle, NSW

33 Buwa Street, Charlestown, NSW 2290, Australia ☎ Mobile(18) 68 07 53 Tx: none Fax: (49) 43 59 32 SITA: n/a
F: 1981 ⁂ 2 Head: Clive Lipscombe Net: n/a Aircraft below MTOW 1361kg: Robinson R22.

☐ VH-AAL	Bell 206B JetRanger	606		0070		1 AN 250-C20	1451			cvtd 206A

ROTORWEST & ABROLHOS HELICOPTERS (Fieldview Investments, Pty Ltd dba) — Perth

33B Saunders Street, Mosman Park, WA 6012, Australia ☎ (8) 94 81 08 99 Tx: none Fax: (8) 94 81 18 21 SITA: n/a
F: 1992 ⁂ n/a Head: Tim Roberts Net: n/a

☐ VH-ZZH	Eurocopter (Aerosp.) AS350BA Squirrel	1892	N929KR	0086	0396	1 TU Arriel 1B	2100			cvtd AS350B

ROYAL FLYING DOCTOR SERVICE – RFDS — Sydney, NSW

15-17 Young Street, Level 5, Sydney, NSW 2000, Australia ☎ (2) 92 41 24 11 Tx: none Fax: (2) 92 47 33 51 SITA: n/a
F: 1928 ⁂ 366 Head: Gerry Macdonald Net: n/a Non-profit and non-denominational organisation. Aircraft are assigned and operated by autonomous sections:
RFDS Central (based Northern Territory & South Australia), RFDS NSW (based New South Wales, Tasmania & Victoria), RFDS Queensland (based Queensland) & RFS Western Operations (based Western Australia).

☐ VH-LDW	Piper PA-31-325 Navajo C/R	31-7912032	N27918	0079	1089	2 LY TIO-540-F2BD	2948	EMS		Baden-Powell / opb RFDS Western Ops
☐ VH-TFX	Piper PA-31-350 Navajo Chieftain	31-8152143	N4090P	0081	0490	2 LY TIO-540-J2BD	3175	EMS		opb RFDS Central
☐ VH-HFD	Piper PA-31P-350 Mojave	31P-8414044	N2318X	0084	0589	2 LY TIO-540-V2AD	3368	EMS		Bruce Griffith / opb RFDS NSW
☐ VH-EGT	Cessna 425 Conquest I	425-0216	N1225J	0086	0794	2 PWC PT6A-112	3901	EMS		Kookynie / opb RFDS Western Ops
☐ VH-ANP	Cessna 404 Titan II	404-0064	N5447G	0077	1197	2 CO GTSIO-520-M	3810	EMS		opb RFDS NSW/opf Air Ambulance Victoria
☐ VH-LAD	Cessna 404 Titan II	404-0224	N88690	0078	1197	2 CO GTSIO-520-M	3810	EMS		opb RFDS NSW/opf Air Ambulance Victoria
☐ VH-WZK	Cessna 404 Titan II	404-0801	D-IFTG	0081	1197	2 CO GTSIO-520-M	3810	EMS		opb RFDS NSW/opf Air Ambulance Victoria
☐ VH-WZL	Cessna 404 Titan II	404-0834	N6807L	0081	1197	2 CO GTSIO-520-M	3810	EMS		opb RFDS NSW/opf Air Ambulance Victoria
☐ VH-WZM	Cessna 404 Titan II	404-0837	N68075	0081	1197	2 CO GTSIO-520-M	3810	EMS		opb RFDS NSW/opf Air Ambulance Victoria
☐ VH-FMC	Pilatus PC-12/45	109		0095	0395	1 PWC PT6A-67B	4500	EMS		opb RFDS Central
☐ VH-FMF	Pilatus PC-12/45	110		0095	0395	1 PWC PT6A-67B	4500	EMS		opb RFDS Central
☐ VH-FMP	Pilatus PC-12/45	122		0095	0995	1 PWC PT6A-67B	4500	EMS		opb RFDS Central
☐ VH-FMW	Pilatus PC-12/45	123		0095	0995	1 PWC PT6A-67B	4500	EMS		opb RFDS Central
☐ VH-FMZ	Pilatus PC-12/45	138		0096	0396	1 PWC PT6A-67B	4500	EMS		opb RFDS Central
☐ VH-CFD	Cessna 441 Conquest II	441-0141	N26267	0080	1292	2 GA TPE331-8-401S	4468	EMS		opb RFDS Western Operations
☐ VH-JFD	Cessna 441 Conquest II	441-0095	VH-JEB	0079	0386	2 GA TPE331-8-401S	4468	EMS		opb RFDS Western Operations
☐ VH-LFD	Cessna 441 Conquest II	441-0164	VH-LBC	0080	0187	2 GA TPE331-8-401S	4468	EMS		W.B.(Bill) Blown / opb RFDS Western Ops
☐ VH-NFD	Cessna 441 Conquest II	441-0159	N45FM	0080	0988	2 GA TPE331-8-401S	4468	EMS		opb RFDS Western Operations
☐ VH-YFD	Cessna 441 Conquest II	441-0157	N51LR	0080	1190	2 GA TPE331-8-401S	4468	EMS		James Hardie / opb RFDS Western Ops
☐ VH-FDM	Beech King Air C90-1	LJ-1024	N618DB	0082	0889	2 PWC PT6A-21	4377	EMS		Tim O'Leary / opb RFDS Queensland
☐ VH-FDP	Beech King Air C90	LJ-968	N102EP	0081	1185	2 PWC PT6A-21	4377	EMS		John Flynn / opb RFDS Queensland
☐ VH-FDT	Beech King Air C90	LJ-842	N6052F	0079	0486	2 PWC PT6A-21	4377	EMS		Sir Robert Law-Smith / opbRFDS West.Ops
☐ VH-FDW	Beech King Air C90-1	LJ-1011	N6139U	0083	0688	2 PWC PT6A-21	4377	EMS		Allan Vickers / opb RFDS Queensland
☐ VH-FDZ	Beech King Air C90	LJ-1021	N117D	0082	1286	2 PWC PT6A-21	4377	EMS		Alf Traeger / opb RFDS Queensland
☐ VH-CWO	Beech King Air B200C	BL-72	N43CE	0083	0196	2 PWC PT6A-42	5670	EMS		opb RFDS Western Operations
☐ VH-FDA	Beech King Air 200C	BL-55	VH-NSD	0082	1296	2 PWC PT6A-41	5670	EMS		RFDS Townsville / opb RFDS Queensland
☐ VH-FDB	Beech King Air 200C	BL-26	VH-WLH	0081	0984	2 PWC PT6A-41	5670	EMS		Alan Earnshaw / opb RFDS Queensland
☐ VH-FDG	Beech King Air B200C	BB-1172	G-OJGA	0084	0392	2 PWC PT6A-42	5670	EMS		Alec McLaughlan / opb West.Ops/cvtdB200
☐ VH-FDI	Beech King Air 200	BB-1037	VH-DAX	0082	0295	2 PWC PT6A-42	5670	EMS		RFDS Brisbane / opb RFDS Queensland
☐ VH-FDO	Beech King Air B200	BB-1056	VH-RFX	0082	0295	2 PWC PT6A-42	5670	EMS		RFDS Rockhampton / opb RFDS Queensland
☐ VH-FDR	Beech King Air B200C	BL-39	N75WR	0081	0488	2 PWC PT6A-42	5670	EMS		opb RFDS Central
☐ VH-FDS	Beech King Air B200C	BL-68	N83GA	0082	0491	2 PWC PT6A-42	5670	EMS		Marjorie Loveday / opb RFDS Queensland
☐ VH-FMN	Beech King Air B200C	BL-47	N6334F	0082	0589	2 PWC PT6A-42	5670	EMS		opb RFDS Central
☐ VH-HEO	Beech King Air B200C	BL-41	N100QR	0081	0487	2 PWC PT6A-42	5670	EMS		opb RFDS Central
☐ VH-KFN	Beech King Air 200C	BL-31	N200LG	0081	0889	2 PWC PT6A-41	5670	EMS		John Uhrig / opb RFDS Western Ops
☐ VH-MSH	Beech King Air B200	BB-1416	N8254H	0092	0696	2 PWC PT6A-42	5670	EMS		opb RFDS NSW
☐ VH-MSM	Beech King Air B200	BB-1430	N773AM	0092	0696	2 PWC PT6A-42	5670	EMS		Fred McKay / opb RFDS NSW
☐ VH-MSU	Beech King Air B200C	BL-48	N1860B	0081	0589	2 PWC PT6A-42	5670	EMS		Philip H. Bushell / opb RFDS NSW
☐ VH-MSZ	Beech King Air B200	BB-866	ZK-PBG	0081	1286	2 PWC PT6A-42	5670	EMS		Outback Trek / opb RFDS NSW
☐ VH-MVL	Beech King Air B200	BB-1333	N1101W	0089	1097	2 PWC PT6A-42	5670	EMS		opb RFDS NSW
☐ VH-MVY	Beech King Air B200	BB-1324	N7087N	0089	0998	2 PWC PT6A-42	5670	EMS		opb RFDS Queensland

RUDGE AIR (Rudge Enterprises, Pty Ltd dba) — Melbourne-Essendon, VIC

Hangar 4, Wirraway Road, Essendon Airport, VIC 3041, Australia ☎ (3) 93 79 85 54 Tx: none Fax: (3) 93 74 13 13 SITA: n/a
F: 1987 ⁂ 12 Head: Edward M. Rudge Net: n/a Aircraft below MTOW 1361kg: Boeing B75N1 Stearman.

☐ VH-DHA	BAe (DH) 104 Dove 6	04514	G-ARMT	0061	1191	2 Gipsy Queen 70 Mk.3	3992			
☐ VH-DHI	BAe (DH) 104 Dove 5	04410	XJ324	0053	1290	2 Gipsy Queen 70 Mk.3	3992			Belle's Dove / cvtd Srs 2A
☐ VH-DHQ	BAe (DH) 104 Dove 8	04533	VH-JGZ	0063	0489	2 Gipsy Queen 70 Mk.3	4159			

SAATAS, Pty Ltd (Affiliated with Cavill Power Products, Pty Ltd) — Adelaide, SA

315 Main North Road, Enfield, SA 5085, Australia ☎ (8) 82 58 19 02 Tx: 82196 cavpow aa Fax: (8) 82 69 60 86 SITA: n/a
F: 1965 ⁂ n/a Head: R.R. Cavill Net: n/a

☐ VH-BFP	Beech Duchess 76	ME-75	N4921M	0078		2 LY O-360-A1G6D	1769			
☐ VH-EYG	Beech Queen Air B80 (65-B80)	LD-334	N7834L	0067		2 LY IGSO-540-A1D	3992			

SAKHALIN ENERGY AVIATION (Division of Australian Jet Charter, Pty Ltd) — Yuzhno-Sakhalinsk

Operations office:, 556 Sakhalin Centre, 32 Communist Avenue, 693000 Yuzhno-Sakhalinsk, Russia ☎ (504) 416 24 26 Tx: none Fax: (504) 416 24 27 SITA: n/a
F: 1997 ⁂ n/a Head: n/a Net: n/a Operates exclusively under contract for the Sakhalin Energy Corp.

☐ VH-OZD	BAe 3101 Jetstream 31	668	N668SA	0085	1297	2 GA TPE331-10UR-513H	6900	Y19orExecorVIP		opf Sakhalin Energy Corp.

638 registration type of aircraft cn/fn ex/ex* mfd del powered by mtow kg configuration selcal name/fln/specialitites/remarks

SAVANNAH AVIATION (Dasap, Pty Ltd dba) — Burketown, QLD

PO Box 5, Burketown, QLD 4830, Australia ☎ (77) 45 51 77 Tx: none Fax: (77) 45 51 77 SITA: n/a
F: 1996 ⁂ n/a Head: n/a Net: n/a

☐ VH-KAG	Beech Bonanza A36	E-1006	N23906	0077	0796	1 CO IO-520-BA	1633			
☐ VH-LTF	Beech Baron 58	TH-640	N113MC	0075	0197	2 CO IO-520-C	2449			

SEAIR ADVENTURE CHARTERS (Stawilton No. 110 Pty Ltd dba) — Wynyard, TAS

PO Box 58, Wynyard, TAS 7325, Australia ☎ (3) 64 42 12 20 Tx: none Fax: (3) 64 42 32 08 SITA: n/a
F: n/a ⁂ n/a Head: n/a Net: n/a

☐ VH-HJT	MD Helicopters MD 500E (Hughes 369E)	0134E	N5217N	0085	0498	1 AN 250-C20B	1361			

SEAIR PACIFIC GOLD COAST (Istlecote, Pty Ltd dba) — Coolangatta & Runaway Bay-SPB, QLD

PO Box 348, Runaway Bay, QLD 4216, Australia ☎ (7) 55 91 86 68 Tx: none Fax: (7) 55 77 00 92 SITA: n/a
F: 1971 ⁂ 12 Head: Peter Gash Net: n/a

☐ VH-LMD	Cessna 208 Caravan I	20800217	9M-FBA	0092	1295	1 PWC PT6A-114	3629			Amphibian
☐ VH-MSF	GAF N22B Nomad	N22B-69		0078	0199	2 AN 250-B17B	3856			lsf Nomad Aviation P/L

SEAWING AIRWAYS (Krug Agencies, Pty Ltd dba) — Darwin, NT

PO Box 172, Darwin GPO, NT 0801, Australia ☎ (8) 89 45 43 37 Tx: none Fax: (8) 89 45 05 95 SITA: n/a
F: 1996 ⁂ n/a Head: Steve Krug Net: n/a

☐ VH-SWB	De Havilland DHC-2 Beaver I	1557	ZK-CKD	0064	0696	1 PW R-985	2313			Amphibian

SEA WORLD AVIATION (Village SWA Pty Ltd & Warner SWA Pty Ltd dba) — Surfers Paradise, QLD

PO Box 190, Surfers Paradise, QLD 4217, Australia ☎ (7) 55 88 22 24 Tx: 44593 seawld aa Fax: (7) 55 88 21 38 SITA: n/a
F: 1976 ⁂ 5 Head: Garry Liehm Net: n/a

☐ VH-JSM	Bell 206B JetRanger III	3411	N20711	0081		1 AN 250-C20B	1451			
☐ VH-SWL	Bell 206L-1 LongRanger II	45693	N66187	0081		1 AN 250-C28B	1882			
☐ VH-UTL	Bell 206L-1 LongRanger III	45202		0078		1 AN 250-C30P	1882			cvtd LongRanger II

SHARP AVIATION, Pty Ltd — Hamilton, VIC

PO Box 710, Hamilton, VIC 3300, Australia ☎ (3) 55 74 82 16 Tx: none Fax: (3) 55 74 82 58 SITA: n/a
F: n/a ⁂ n/a Head: Malcolm Sharp Net: n/a

☐ VH-JCH	Piper PA-31-350 Navajo Chieftain	31-8152106	N4084T	0081	0498	2 LY TIO-540-J2BD	3175			lsf ABGO P/L

SHAWFLIGHT AVIATION, Pty Ltd — Borroloola, NT

PO Box 432, Borroloola, NT 0854, Australia ☎ (8) 89 75 86 88 Tx: none Fax: (8) 89 75 86 85 SITA: n/a
F: n/a ⁂ n/a Head: n/a Net: n/a

☐ VH-AOV	Cessna T303 Crusader	T30300020	N9469T	0082	0198	2 CO TSIO-520-AE	2336			

SHEPPARTON AIRLINES, Pty Ltd = OB (Sister company of Gawne Aviation, Pty Ltd) — Shepparton, VIC

PO Box 486, Shepparton, VIC 3629, Australia ☎ (3) 58 23 14 81 Tx: none Fax: (3) 58 23 20 49 SITA: n/a
F: 1997 ⁂ n/a Head: Allan G. Gawne Net: n/a

☐ VH-JVD	Piper PA-31-350 Navajo Chieftain	31-7852041	N27523	0078	0697	2 LY TIO-540-J2BD	3175			

SHINE AVIATION SERVICES (Chrishine Nominees, Pty Ltd dba) — Geraldton, WA

Post Office, Moonyoonooka, WA 6532, Australia ☎ (8) 99 23 36 78 Tx: none Fax: (8) 99 23 37 93 SITA: n/a
F: 1981 ⁂ n/a Head: Chris Shine Net: n/a Aircraft below MTOW 1361kg: Cessna 172 & DH-82

☐ VH-HTO	Cessna U206E Stationair	U20601672	C-GPIF	0071	0795	1 CO IO-520-F	1633			Amphibian
☐ VH-JDJ	Beech Bonanza A36	E-1448	N1185T	0079		1 CO IO-520-BB	1633			
☐ VH-PHI	Beech Bonanza A36	E-394	N25621	0073		1 CO IO-520-BA	1633			
☐ VH-TYT	Beech Bonanza 36	E-35	N7483N	0068		1 CO IO-520-B	1633			
☐ VH-ADE	Piper PA-31-325 Navajo C/R	31-7712006	N62996	0077		2 LY TIO-540-F2BD	2948			
☐ VH-ITF	Piper PA-31-310 Navajo C	31-7812014	N27435	0078	0597	2 LY TIO-540-A2C	2948			

SHORLAND AIR SERVICES, Pty Ltd — Marlo, VIC

Lot 51, Healeys Road, Marlo, VIC 3888, Australia ☎ (3) 51 54 82 65 Tx: none Fax: (3) 51 54 83 30 SITA: n/a
F: 1996 ⁂ n/a Head: n/a Net: n/a

☐ VH-LXM	Bell 206B JetRanger II	2170	JA9173	0077	0198	1 AN 250-C20	1451			
☐ VH-ESE	Cessna A185F Skywagon II	18504133	N61254	0080	1096	1 CO IO-520-D	1520			Amphibian

SHORTSTOP JET CHARTER, Pty Ltd — Melbourne-Essendon, VIC

Hangar 5, Wirraway Road, Essendon Airport, VIC 3041, Australia ☎ (3) 93 79 92 99 Tx: n/a Fax: (3) 93 79 36 43 SITA: n/a
F: 1980 ⁂ 5 Head: Michael Falls, Sr. Net: n/a

☐ VH-OVO	North American SNJ-5 (AT-6D) Texan	43647	N3274G	0043		1 PW R-1340	2548			
☐ VH-JIG	Learjet 35A	35A-400	VH-TPR	0081	1296	2 GA TFE731-2-2B	8164			
☐ VH-OVM	Boeing (Douglas) DC-3C (C-47B-30-DK)	33092	VH-JXD	0045		2 PW R-1830	11793	28 Pax		Arthur Schutt MBE

SKIPPERS AVIATION, Pty Ltd = SY — Perth, WA

PO Box 1060, Osborne Park, WA 6917, Australia ☎ (8) 93 51 89 91 Tx: n/a Fax: (8) 94 78 31 84 SITA: n/a
F: 1990 ⁂ 10 Head: Stan J. Quinlivan Net: n/a

☐ VH-LKC	Cessna 402C II	402C0625	N6386X	0082		2 CO TSIO-520-VB	3107			
☐ VH-AZB	Cessna 441 Conquest II	441-0182	OO-NAN	0081	1092	2 GA TPE331-8-402S	4468			
☐ VH-AZW	Cessna 441 Conquest II	441-0026	VH-FWA	0078	0595	2 GA TPE331-8-401S	4468			
☐ VH-FMQ	Cessna 441 Conquest II	441-0109	N26226	0079		2 GA TPE331-8-402S	4468			
☐ VH-LBA	Cessna 441 Conquest II	441-0042	N46MR	0078		2 GA TPE331-8-402S	4468			
☐ VH-LBC	Cessna 441 Conquest II	441-0236	VH-TFG	0082		2 GA TPE331-8-403S	4468			
☐ VH-LBD	Cessna 441 Conquest II	441-0296	N6838K	0083	0493	2 GA TPE331-8-403S	4468			
☐ VH-LBX	Cessna 441 Conquest II	441-0091	VH-AZY	0079	1092	2 GA TPE331-8-402S	4468			
☐ VH-LBY	Cessna 441 Conquest II	441-0023	VH-TFW	0078		2 GA TPE331-8-402S	4468			
☐ VH-LBZ	Cessna 441 Conquest II	441-0038	VH-HWD	0078		2 GA TPE331-8-402S	4468			
☐ VH-LKB	Beech King Air 200	BB-259	VH-APA	0077	0794	2 PWC PT6A-41	5670			
☐ VH-LKF	Beech King Air 200	BB-660	N200TK	0080	0493	2 PWC PT6A-41	5670			
☐ VH-WAI	Fairchild (Swearingen) SA227DC Metro 23	DC-874B	N3032L*	0095	0795	2 GA TPE331-12U-701G	7484	Y19		
☐ VH-WAJ	Fairchild (Swearingen) SA227DC Metro 23	DC-876B	N3033U*	0095	1195	2 GA TPE331-12U-701G	7484	Y19		
☐ VH-WAX	Fairchild (Swearingen) SA227DC Metro 23	DC-877B	N30337*	0095	1195	2 GA TPE331-12U-701G	7484	Y19		
☐ VH-WBA	Fairchild (Swearingen) SA227DC Metro 23	DC-883B	N30042*	0096	0796	2 GA TPE331-12U-701G	7484	Y19		
☐ VH-WBQ	Fairchild (Swearingen) SA227DC Metro 23	DC-884B	N30046*	0096	0197	2 GA TPE331-12U-701G	7484	Y19		
☐ VH-XFT	De Havilland DHC-8-102 Dash 8	052	ZK-NEW	0086	0798	2 PWC PW120A	15650	Y37		
☐ VH-XFU	De Havilland DHC-8-102 Dash 8	151	ZK-NEV	0089	0798	2 PWC PW120A	15650	Y37		

SKYLINK AUSTRALIA, Pty Ltd — Melbourne-Essendon, VIC

RMB 7375A, Horsham, VIC 3401, Australia ☎ (3) 53 83 63 33 Tx: none Fax: (3) 53 83 63 00 SITA: n/a
F: 1981 ⁂ 8 Head: Paul Widmer Net: n/a

☐ VH-CCL	Piper PA-31-350 Navajo Chieftain	31-7752015	N62999	0077		2 LY TIO-540-J2BD	3175			
☐ VH-XMM	Piper PA-31-350 Navajo Chieftain	31-8052020	N3546L	0080		2 LY TIO-540-J2BD	3175			

SKYTRANS = NP (Barnard DJ & SJ, Pty Ltd dba / Associated with Reef Helicopters, Pty Ltd) — Cairns, QLD

PO Box 86, Stratford, QLD 4870, Australia ☎ (7) 40 35 94 44 Tx: none Fax: (7) 40 35 93 18 SITA: n/a
F: 1990 ⁂ 14 Head: David Barnard Net: n/a

☐ VH-SKJ	Piper PA-34-220T Seneca III	34-8133184	VH-JGW	0081		2 CO TSIO-360-KB	2155			
☐ VH-SKH	Cessna 310R II	310R1221	VH-LAF	0078	1193	2 CO IO-520-M	2495			
☐ VH-SKX	Cessna 310R II	310R0935	VH-UFS	0077	0497	2 CO IO-520-M	2495			
☐ VH-SKG	Britten-Norman BN-2A-27 Islander	609	ZK-CRA	0070	0199	2 LY O-540-E4C5	2994			
☐ VH-SKV	Cessna 404 Titan II	404-0412	VH-TLE	0079	0393	2 CO GTSIO-520-M	3810			
☐ VH-SKW	Cessna 404 Titan II	404-0042	VH-PNY	0077	1196	2 CO GTSIO-520-M	3810			
☐ VH-SKZ	Cessna 404 Titan II	404-0080	VH-JOH	0079	1194	2 CO GTSIO-520-M	3810			
☐ VH-SKU	Beech King Air 200	BB-165	VH-XRF	0076	0398	2 PWC PT6A-41	5670			

SKYWAYS AUSTRALIA (Robert J. Moss dba / formerly Nicholas Skyways, Pty Ltd) — Melbourne-Moorabbin, VIC

Second Street, Moorabbin-Airport, VIC 3194, Australia ☎ (3) 95 80 46 10 Tx: none Fax: (3) 95 80 16 26 SITA: n/a
F: 1961 ⁂ 3 Head: Robert J. Moss Net: n/a Aircraft below MTOW 1361 kg: Cessna 172.

☐ VH-JMW	Cessna T310R II	310R1802	N2641B	0081	0095	2 CO TSIO-520-BB	2495			lsf Remote Air P/L
☐ VH-RCG	Cessna 310K	310K0113	VH-RXY	0065	0095	2 CO IO-470-V	2359			lsf Remote Air P/L

SKYWEST AIRLINES, Pty Ltd = YT (Subsidiary of Ansett Holdings, Ltd) — Perth, WA

PO Box 176, Cloverdale, WA 6985, Australia ☎ (8) 94 78 99 99 Tx: none Fax: (8) 94 78 99 28 SITA: n/a
F: 1963 ⁂ 165 Head: Bob Mason IATA: 674 Net: http://www.skywest.com.au

☐ VH-ESW	BAe 3107 Jetstream 31	665	G-31-665*	0085		2 GA TPE331-10UF-511H	6950	Y19		std PER
☐ VH-HSW	BAe 3107 Jetstream 31	622	G-BLCB*	0083		2 GA TPE331-10UF-511H	6950	Y19		
☐ VH-JSW	BAe 3107 Jetstream 31	620	G-31-620*	0083		2 GA TPE331-10UF-511H	6950	Y19		lst Aircruising Australia

639 registration type of aircraft cn/fn ex/ex* mfd del powered by mtow kg configuration selcal name/fln/specialitites/remarks

☐ VH-FNA	Fokker 50 (F27 Mk050)	20106	PH-EXG*	0087	0895	2 PWC PW125B	20820	Y50		
☐ VH-FNB	Fokker 50 (F27 Mk050)	20107	PH-EXF*	0087	1295	2 PWC PW125B	20820	Y50		
☐ VH-FND	Fokker 50 (F27 Mk050)	20129	PH-EXB*	0088	1295	2 PWC PW125B	20820	Y50		
☐ VH-FNH	Fokker 50 (F27 Mk050)	20113	PH-EXY*	0088	0496	2 PWC PW125B	20820	Y50		
☐ VH-FNI	Fokker 50 (F27 Mk050)	20114	PH-EXZ*	0088	0996	2 PWC PW125B	20820	Y50		

SKYWORX AVIATION — Perth, WA

PO Box 6040, East Perth, WA 6892, Australia ☎ (8) 92 28 97 22 Tx: none Fax: (8) 92 28 97 00 SITA: n/a
F: 1995 n/a Head: Paul Beckster Net: n/a

☐ VH-KWW	Cessna 210L Centurion II	21059928	N30522	0073	0698	1 CO IO-520-L	1724			
☐ VH-SLY	Piper PA-30-160 Twin Comanche B	30-1486	VH-CLJ	0067	0598	2 LY IO-320-B1A	1633			

SLINGAIR, Pty Ltd (Subsidiary of Heliwork Western Australia, Pty Ltd) — Kununurra, WA

PO Box 612, Kununurra, WA 6743, Australia ☎ (8) 91 69 13 00 Tx: none Fax: (8) 91 68 11 29 SITA: n/a
F: 1976 55 Head: Kerry Slingsby Net: n/a Aircraft below MTOW 1361 kg: Cessna 172 & 182.

☐ VH-IEW	Cessna U206G Stationair 6	U20603695		0077	0997	1 CO IO-520-F	1633			
☐ VH-JDQ	Cessna U206 Super Skywagon	U206-0353	N2153F	0065		1 CO IO-520-A	1497			
☐ VH-NLG	Cessna U206G Stationair	U20603930	ZK-JGH	0077	0698	1 CO IO-520-F	1633			lst Derby Air Services
☐ VH-RGE	Cessna U206F Stationair	U20601981	N51221	0073		1 CO IO-520-F	1633			
☐ VH-IEU	Cessna 207 Skywagon	20700231	N1631U	0074		1 CO IO-520-F	1724			
☐ VH-AOI	Cessna 210N Centurion II	21064609	N9821Y	0082		1 CO IO-520-L	1724			
☐ VH-BKD	Cessna 210N Centurion II	21063127	N6635N	0079		1 CO IO-520-L	1724			
☐ VH-FOK	Cessna 210N Centurion II	21063109	N6559N	0079		1 CO IO-520-L	1724			
☐ VH-NLV	Cessna 210N Centurion II	21063093	VH-APU	0078	0498	1 CO IO-520-L	1724			lst Derby Air Services
☐ VH-NLZ	Cessna 210N Centurion II	21063769	VH-RZZ	0080	0498	1 CO IO-520-L	1724			lst Derby Air Services
☐ VH-OCM	Cessna 210N Centurion II	21064466	N9300Y	0081	1298	1 CO IO-520-L	1724			
☐ VH-TWD	Cessna 210N Centurion II	21064356	N6372Y	0081	0498	1 CO IO-520-L	1724			lst Derby Air Services
☐ VH-URX	Cessna 210N Centurion II	21064449	N6595Y	0081	1298	1 CO IO-520-L	1724			
☐ VH-FSI	Partenavia P.68B	80	ZS-LMJ	0076	0797	2 LY IO-360-A1B6	1960			
☐ VH-TWY	Cessna 310R II	310R0090	N69336	0075		2 CO IO-520-M	2495			lst Derby Air Services
☐ VH-DER	Piper PA-31-310 Navajo C	31-7912110	N3539D	0079	0199	2 LY TIO-540-A1A	2948			
☐ VH-RKD	Piper PA-31-350 Navajo Chieftain	31-8152048	N4076Z	0080	0796	2 LY TIO-540-J2BD	3175			
☐ VH-KSA	Cessna 208B Grand Caravan	208B0516	N6302B*	0096	0396	1 PWC PT6A-114A	3969			
☐ VH-LSA	Cessna 208B Grand Caravan	208B0421	N5192F*	0095	0395	1 PWC PT6A-114A	3969			

SOUTH-EAST AIR SERVICES, Pty Ltd — Naracoorte, SA

PO Box 381, Naracoorte, SA 5271, Australia ☎ (8) 87 62 18 62 Tx: none Fax: none SITA: n/a
F: 1969 1 Head: n/a Net: n/a

☐ VH-MGM	Beech Bonanza A36	E-584	N7394R	0074		1 CO IO-520-BA	1633			
☐ VH-DDG	Beech Baron B55 (95-B55)	TC-2137	N24145	0078		2 CO IO-470-L	2313			

SOUTHERN AUSTRALIA AIRLINES, Pty Ltd (Member of Qantas Group) — Mildura, VIC

PO Box 5010, Mildura, VIC 3502, Australia ☎ (3) 50 22 24 44 Tx: none Fax: (3) 50 22 16 39 SITA: n/a
F: 1986 160 Head: Tony Mathews IATA: 244 Net: n/a Operates scheduled services on behalf of QANTAS using QF flight numbers.

☐ VH-WZI	De Havilland DHC-8-102 Dash 8	014	N814CL	0085	0392	2 PWC PW120A	15650	Y36		Spirit of Sunraysia
☐ VH-WZJ	De Havilland DHC-8-102 Dash 8	027	N27CL	0086	0492	2 PWC PW120A	15650	Y36		City of Devonport
☐ VH-WZS	De Havilland DHC-8-102 Dash 8	005	N4229R	0084	0295	2 PWC PW120A	15650	Y36		City of Burnie
☐ VH-YAD	BAe 146-200A	E2097	N293UE	0088	1296	4 LY ALF502R-5	40597	C8Y68		City of Hobart / lsf BAMJ
☐ VH-YAE	BAe 146-200A	E2107	N294UE	0088	1296	4 LY ALF502R-5	42184	C8Y68		City of Launceston / lsf BAMJ

SOUTHERN COMMANDER, Pty Ltd — Melbourne-Essendon, VIC

Hangar 6, Wirraway Road, Essendon Airport, VIC 3041, Australia ☎ (3) 93 74 20 44 Tx: none Fax: (3) 93 79 84 60 SITA: n/a
F: 1992 n/a Head: Gordon Cox Net: n/a

☐ VH-XMO	Hawker 800B (BAe 125-800B)	258243	G-SHEB	0093	0396	2 GA TFE731-5R-1H	12428			

SOUTHERN CROSS AIR, Pty Ltd (formerly General Aviation Air Freighters, Pty Ltd) — Cairns, QLD

PO Box 14, Freshwater, QLD 4870, Australia ☎ (7) 40 35 94 04 Tx: none Fax: (7) 40 35 94 24 SITA: n/a
F: 1974 5 Head: Charles Noar Net: n/a Aircraft below MTOW 1361kg: Bellanca 8KCAB

☐ VH-TGA	Beech Excalibur Queenaire 8800	LD-152	N6868Q	0064		2 LY IO-720-A1B	3992	Freighter		cvtd Queen Air 65-A80

SOUTHERN SKY AIRLINES, Pty Ltd — Adelaide, SA

Level 8, 13 Grenfell Street, Adelaide, SA 5000, Australia ☎ (8) 82 34 33 00 Tx: none Fax: (8) 82 34 33 55 SITA: n/a
F: 1997 n/a Head: Evan Bartlett Net: n/a

☐ VH-UBA	Piper PA-31-310 Navajo	31-593	N6703L	0070	1298	2 LY TIO-540-A1A	2948			
☐ VH-OAS	Cessna 402C II	402C0326	N2635D	0080	0998	2 CO TSIO-520-VB	3107			

SOUTH WEST AIR SERVICE, Pty Ltd — Charleville, QLD

PO Box 421, Charleville, QLD 4470, Australia ☎ (7) 46 54 30 33 Tx: n/a Fax: (7) 46 54 30 30 SITA: n/a
F: 1990 2 Head: Peter Wade Net: n/a

☐ VH-KSE	Cessna 210M Centurion II	21062676	N6081B	0078		1 CO IO-520-L	1724			

STAR AIR CHARTER (Jeremy H. Trevor-Jones dba) — Kelso, NSW

73 Gilmour Street, Kelso, NSW 2795, Australia ☎ (2) 63 37 34 52 Tx: n/a Fax: (2) 63 37 33 18 SITA: n/a
F: 1977 3 Head: Jeremy H. Trevor-Jones Net: n/a Aircraft below MTOW 1361kg: Cessna 172

☐ VH-AZX	Beech Duchess 76	ME-28	N5268M	0078		2 LY O-360-A1G6D	1769			
☐ VH-MGR	Beech Baron E55	TE-1058	N6772S	0075		2 CO IO-520-C	2404			

STAR CHARTER (Transway Holdings, Pty Ltd dba) — Perth, WA

PO Box 688, West Perth Private Boxes, WA 6872, Australia ☎ (8) 93 22 72 66 Tx: none Fax: (8) 93 22 75 54 SITA: n/a
F: n/a n/a Head: n/a Net: n/a

☐ VH-LOI	Beech Baron 58	TH-743	N1824L	0076		2 CO IO-520-C	2449			

STATEWIDE AIR CHARTER – SWAC (Barry Hughes & E.Z. Hughes dba) — Brisbane-Eagle Farm, QLD

157 Bell Street, Kangaroo Point, QLD 4169, Australia ☎ (7) 33 91 30 13 Tx: none Fax: (7) 33 91 71 50 SITA: n/a
F: 1975 4 Head: Barry & E.Z. Hughes Net: n/a

☐ VH-SFC	Beech Baron 58	TH-824	N17806	0077		2 CO IO-520-C	2449			

SUDHOLZ AIR CHARTER, Pty Ltd — Goondiwindi, QLD

PO Box 883, Goondiwindi, QLD 4390, Australia ☎ (76) 71 10 44 Tx: n/a Fax: (76) 71 20 22 SITA: n/a
F: 1988 4 Head: R. Sudholz Net: n/a

☐ VH-JAA	Piper PA-32R-301 Saratoga SP	32R-8313003	N8317S	0083		1 LY IO-540-K1G5D	1633			
☐ VH-MRO	Cessna T303 Crusader	T30300041	N9739T	0082		2 CO TSIO-520-AE	2336			

SUNLOVER HELICOPTERS, Pty Ltd — Cairns, QLD

PO Box 84N, North Cairns, QLD 4870, Australia ☎ (7) 40 35 96 96 Tx: none Fax: (7) 40 35 94 14 SITA: n/a
F: 1996 13 Head: Chris Rose Net: http://www.sunloverheli.com.au

☐ VH-CLR	Bell 206B JetRanger III	3349	VH-HPO	0081	1198	1 AN 250-C20B	1451			
☐ VH-HZO	Bell 206B JetRanger III	2839	ZK-HPQ	0079	0798	1 AN 250-C20B	1451			

SUNSHINE COAST AIR CHARTER, Pty Ltd — Caloundra, QLD

PO Box 377, Caloundra, QLD 4551, Australia ☎ (7) 54 91 19 88 Tx: none Fax: (7) 54 91 83 46 SITA: n/a
F: 1979 5 Head: Lester E. Neideck Net: n/a Aircraft below MTOW 1361 kg: Cessna 172 & Piper PA-28.

☐ VH-JNW	Cessna U206F Stationair II	U20603081	N7211Q	0076	0698	1 CO IO-520-F	1633			opf Wide Bay Air Charter
☐ VH-SMM	Piper PA-34-200 Seneca	34-7450084	N40833	0073		2 LY IO-360-C1E6	1905			
☐ VH-BWZ	Cessna 310R II	310R1611	N2630C	0079		2 CO IO-520-MB	2495			
☐ VH-FCO	Britten-Norman BN-2A-8 Islander	845	G-BESF	0077		2 LY O-540-E4C5	2722			opf Wide Bay Air Charter
☐ VH-XFI	Britten-Norman BN-2A-26 Islander	605	P2-ISU	0070	1196	2 LY O-540-E4C5	2812			opf Wide Bay Air Charter

SUNSHINE COAST HELICOPTER RESCUE SERVICE, Ltd — Maroochydore-Sunshine Coast, QLD

Maroochydore Airport, MS 1102, David Low Way, Marcoola, QLD 4564, Australia ☎ (7) 54 48 77 77 Tx: none Fax: (7) 54 48 76 60 SITA: n/a
F: 1979 9 Head: Jim Campbell Net: n/a

☐ VH-COW	Bell 206B JetRanger III	2660		0079		1 AN 250-C20B	1451	Ambulance		Skids
☐ VH-JOW	Bell 206L-1 LongRanger III	45213	N91ZT	0079		1 AN 250-C30P	1882	Ambulance		cvtd LongRanger II
☐ VH-BKS	Kawasaki (Eurocopter/MBB) BK117B-1	1065	JA6631	0090	0797	2 LY LTS101-750B.1	3200	Ambulance		

SUNSHINE EXPRESS = CQ (Jet Lag, Pty Ltd dba) — Maroochydore-Sunshine Coast, QLD

Friendship Drive, Sunshine Coast Airport, Mudjimba, QLD 4564, Australia ☎ (7) 54 50 62 22 Tx: none Fax: (7) 54 50 63 33 SITA: n/a
F: 1998 n/a Head: Phil Laffer Net: n/a

☐ VH-SJP	Embraer 110P1 Bandeirante (EMB-110P1)	110347	YJ-AV7	0081	0998	2 PWC PT6A-34	5670	Y15		lsf Aeromil

640 registration type of aircraft cn/fn ex/ex* mfd del powered by mtow kg configuration selcal name/fln/specialitites/remarks

SUNSTATE AIRLINES (Qld), Pty Ltd = SSQ (Member of Qantas Group)

Brisbane, QLD

Level 2, Lobby 3, 153 Campbell Street, Bowen Hills, QLD 4006, Australia ☎ (7) 33 08 90 22 Tx: 140753 sunbne aa Fax: (7) 33 08 90 88 SITA: BNEKROF
F: 1974 ☗ 220 Head: Ashley Kilroy ICAO: SUNSTATE Net: n/a Operates scheduled services on behalf of QANTAS using QF flight numbers.

registration	type of aircraft	cn/fn	ex/ex*	mfd	del	powered by	mtow kg	configuration	selcal	name/fln/specialitites/remarks
☐ VH-BWO	Shorts 360-100 (SD3-60)	SH3651	9M-KGN	0084	1187	2 PWC PT6A-65R	11999	Y35		
☐ VH-MVW	Shorts 360-100 (SD3-60)	SH3626	G-14-3626*	0083	0787	2 PWC PT6A-65R	11999	Y35		std MBH/for sale
☐ VH-MVX	Shorts 360-100 (SD3-60)	SH3620	G-14-3620*	0083	1286	2 PWC PT6A-65R	11999	Y35		City of Mildura / std BNE/for sale
☐ VH-SUF	Shorts 360-300 (SD3-60)	SH3764	D-CBAS	0091	1196	2 PWC PT6A-67R	12292	Y35		
☐ VH-SUL	Shorts 360-300 (SD3-60)	SH3752	D-CAAS	0089	0796	2 PWC PT6A-67R	12292	Y35		
☐ VH-SUM	Shorts 360-300 (SD3-60)	SH3720	G-BNFD	0087	0495	2 PWC PT6A-67R	12292	Y35		lsf GECA
☐ VH-SUR	Shorts 360-300 (SD3-60)	SH3728	G-BNYF	0087	0395	2 PWC PT6A-67R	12292	Y35		lsf GECA
☐ VH-SDA	De Havilland DHC-8-202 Dash 8	482	C-GFQL*	0097	0498	2 PWC PW123D	16465	Y36		Torres Strait
☐ VH-TND	De Havilland DHC-8-102 Dash 8	036	N806MX	0086	0592	2 PWC PW120A	15650	Y36		
☐ VH-TNG	De Havilland DHC-8-102 Dash 8	041	N807MX	0086	0692	2 PWC PW120A	15650	Y36		
☐ VH-TNU	De Havilland DHC-8-102 Dash 8	203	OE-LLM	0090	0295	2 PWC PW120A	15650	Y36		
☐ VH-TNX	De Havilland DHC-8-102 Dash 8	033	N805MX	0086	0293	2 PWC PW120A	15650	Y36		cvtd -101

SURVEILLANCE AUSTRALIA, Pty Ltd (Subsidiary of National Jet Systems, Pty Ltd)

Adelaide, SA/Broome, WA/Cairns & Horn Island, QLD/Darwin, NT

Post Office, Adelaide Airport, SA 5000, Australia ☎ (8) 83 04 56 70 Tx: none Fax: (8) 83 04 56 74 SITA: n/a
F: 1994 ☗ 100 Head: Anthony Patterson ICAO: COASTWATCH Net: http://www.natjet.com.au

registration	type of aircraft	cn/fn	ex/ex*	mfd	del	powered by	mtow kg	configuration	selcal	name/fln/specialitites/remarks
☐ VH-ZZT	Britten-Norman BN-2B-20 Islander	2279	G-BVNC*	0095	0395	2 LY IO-540-K1B5	2994	Coastal Survey		opf Customs Coastwatch
☐ VH-ZZU	Britten-Norman BN-2B-20 Islander	2280	G-BVND*	0095	0395	2 LY IO-540-K1B5	2994	Coastal Survey		opf Customs Coastwatch
☐ VH-ZZV	Britten-Norman BN-2B-20 Islander	2281	G-BVNE*	0095	0695	2 LY IO-540-K1B5	2994	Coastal Survey		opf Customs Coastwatch
☐ VH-ZZW	Britten-Norman BN-2B-20 Islander	2282	G-BVNF*	0095	0795	2 LY IO-540-K1B5	2994	Coastal Survey		opf Customs Coastwatch
☐ VH-ZZX	Britten-Norman BN-2B-20 Islander	2283	G-BVSG*	0095	0895	2 LY IO-540-K1B5	2994	Coastal Survey		opf Customs Coastwatch
☐ VH-ZZY	Britten-Norman BN-2B-20 Islander	2284	G-BVSH*	0095	0895	2 LY IO-540-K1B5	2994	Coastal Survey		opf Customs Coastwatch
☐ VH-ZZS	Twin (Aero) Shrike Commander 500S	3071	N45WS	0070	0395	2 LY IO-540-E1B5	3357	Coastal Survey		opf Customs Coastwatch
☐ VH-ZZE	Reims/Cessna F406 Vigilant	F406-0076	F-WZDX*	0095	0995	2 PWC PT6A-112	4468	Coastal Survey		opf Customs Coastwatch
☐ VH-ZZF	Reims/Cessna F406 Vigilant	F406-0078	F-WZDY*	0095	1195	2 PWC PT6A-112	4468	Coastal Survey		opf Customs Coastwatch
☐ VH-ZZG	Reims/Cessna F406 Vigilant	F406-0079	F-WZDZ*	0095	0995	2 PWC PT6A-112	4468	Coastal Survey		opf Customs Coastwatch
☐ VH-LCL	De Havilland DHC-8-202 Dash 8	492	C-GEOA*	0097	0198	2 PWC PW123D	16465	Hydrogr.Survey		lsf / opf LADS
☐ VH-ZZA	De Havilland DHC-8-202 Dash 8	419	C-FWWU*	0096	0496	2 PWC PW123D	16465	Coastal Survey		opf Customs Coastwatch
☐ VH-ZZB	De Havilland DHC-8-202 Dash 8	424	C-FXBC*	0096	0496	2 PWC PW123D	16465	Coastal Survey		opf Customs Coastwatch
☐ VH-ZZC	De Havilland DHC-8-202 Dash 8	433	C-FXFK*	0096	0696	2 PWC PW123D	16465	Coastal Survey		opf Customs Coastwatch

SYDNEY AIR SCENICS (Mobile Carpet Cleaning Factory, P/L dba/Affiliated with Sydney Skydiving Centre/formerly Sydney Aerial Tours)

Sydney-Bankstown, NSW

677 Tower Road, Bankstown Airport, NSW 2200, Australia ☎ (2) 97 90 06 26 Tx: none Fax: (2) 97 90 00 76 SITA: n/a
F: 1996 ☗ n/a Head: Peter W. Onis Net: n/a

registration	type of aircraft	cn/fn	ex/ex*	mfd	del	powered by	mtow kg	configuration	selcal	name/fln/specialitites/remarks
☐ VH-DSP	Cessna U206C Super Skywagon	U206-0981	N3981G	0067		1 CO IO-520-F	1633			
☐ VH-AAX	De Havilland DHC-2 Turbo Beaver AI	1411		0058	0496	1 GA TPE331-61	2313			cvtd Beaver I
☐ VH-WGK	AAC (Ted Smith) Aerostar 601P	61P-0452-174	VH-PJC	0078	0598	2 LY IO-540-S1A5	2722			
☐ VH-SNX	GAF Nomad N22B	N22B-103		0080	0496	2 AN 250-B17B	3856			
☐ VH-WRT	GAF N22B Nomad	N22B-56		0077	0296	2 AN 250-B17B	3856			
☐ VH-OTA	De Havilland DHC-6 Twin Otter 100	90	N950SM	0067	0296	2 PWC PT6A-20	5252			
☐ VH-IBO	Shorts Skyvan 3M Variant 400 (SC-7)	SH1916	704 SDF	0073	1097	2 GA TPE331-2-201A	5670			

SYDNEY HARBOUR SEAPLANES, Pty Ltd

Sydney-Rose Bay SPB, NSW

PO Box 551, Avalon, NSW 2107, Australia ☎ (2) 93 88 19 78 Tx: none Fax: (2) 93 71 00 47 SITA: n/a
F: 1993 ☗ 12 Head: Rob Britten Net: http://www.sydneyseaplane.com.au

registration	type of aircraft	cn/fn	ex/ex*	mfd	del	powered by	mtow kg	configuration	selcal	name/fln/specialitites/remarks
☐ VH-AQA	De Havilland DHC-2 Beaver I	1467	N37761	0061		1 PW R-985	2313			Floats
☐ VH-AQU	De Havilland DHC-2 Beaver I	1544	VH-IDN	0064		1 PW R-985	2313			Floats
☐ VH-AQV	De Havilland DHC-2 Beaver I	1257	N67685	0057		1 PW R-985	2313			Floats / re-mfd 1996

SYDNEY HELICOPTER SERVICE, Pty Ltd

Sydney-Kingsford Smith, NSW

25 Wentworth Street, Granville, NSW 2142, Australia ☎ (2) 96 37 44 55 Tx: n/a Fax: (2) 96 37 27 72 SITA: n/a
F: 1983 ☗ 4 Head: David Gemmell Net: n/a

registration	type of aircraft	cn/fn	ex/ex*	mfd	del	powered by	mtow kg	configuration	selcal	name/fln/specialitites/remarks
☐ VH-SAI	Bell 206B JetRanger III	729	N6376	0071		1 AN 250-C20B	1451			cvtd 206A
☐ VH-SHH	Bell 206L LongRanger	45125	N16839	0077		1 AN 250-C20B	1814			

SYDNEY HELI-SCENIC, Pty Ltd

Sydney-Mascot, NSW

PO Box 46, Mascot, NSW 2020, Australia ☎ (2) 93 17 34 02 Tx: none Fax: (2) 96 67 31 42 SITA: n/a
F: 1997 ☗ n/a Head: Rachel Grier Net: n/a

registration	type of aircraft	cn/fn	ex/ex*	mfd	del	powered by	mtow kg	configuration	selcal	name/fln/specialitites/remarks
☐ VH-ATH	MD Helicopters MD 600N (Hughes 600N)	RN010	N9203N*	0097	1097	1 AN 250-C47M	1860			lsf pvt

TASAIR, Pty Ltd

Hobart, TAS

GPO Box 451E, Hobart, TAS 7001, Australia ☎ (3) 62 48 55 77 Tx: none Fax: (3) 62 48 55 07 SITA: n/a
F: 1965 ☗ 11 Head: George A. Ashwood Net: http://www.tasair.com.au

registration	type of aircraft	cn/fn	ex/ex*	mfd	del	powered by	mtow kg	configuration	selcal	name/fln/specialitites/remarks
☐ VH-TSR	Cessna U206E Stationair	U20601650	N9450G	0071		1 CO IO-520-F	1633			
☐ VH-EXC	Twin (Aero) Shrike Commander 500S	3251	N57162	0075		2 LY IO-540-E1B5	3357			
☐ VH-EXF	Twin (Aero) Shrike Commander 500S	500S-1797-12	N5024E	0068		2 LY IO-540-E1B5	3357			
☐ VH-LTW	Piper PA-31-350 Navajo Chieftain	31-8152025	N40725	0081	1096	2 LY TIO-540-J2BD	3175			

TASMAN AUSTRALIAN AIRLINES, Pty Ltd (Subsidiary of Fastbook Pacific Holidays/formerly Kentialink Australia, Pty Ltd)

Lord Howe Island, NSW

645 Harris Street, Level 1, Ultimo, NSW 2007, Australia ☎ (2) 92 11 07 75 Tx: none Fax: (2) 92 11 07 80 SITA: n/a
F: 1995 ☗ 3 Head: Ian Menzies Net: n/a

registration	type of aircraft	cn/fn	ex/ex*	mfd	del	powered by	mtow kg	configuration	selcal	name/fln/specialitites/remarks
☐ VH-TWR	Piper PA-31-350 Navajo Chieftain	31-7752097	VH-SVN	0077	0995	2 LY TIO-540-J2BD	3342			

THE HELICOPTER SERVICE AUSTRALIA, Pty Ltd

Melbourne-Essendon, VIC

PO Box 1070, Tullamarine, VIC 3043, Australia ☎ (3) 93 79 45 00 Tx: none Fax: (3) 93 79 99 88 SITA: n/a
F: 1984 ☗ 6 Head: John G. Eacott Net: n/a Aircraft below MTOW 1361kg: Cessna 150 & 172

registration	type of aircraft	cn/fn	ex/ex*	mfd	del	powered by	mtow kg	configuration	selcal	name/fln/specialitites/remarks
☐ VH-JGE	Bell 206B JetRanger III	528	VH-FHB	0070		1 AN 250-C20B	1451			cvtd 206A
☐ VH-JGT	Bell 206B JetRanger III	1822	P2-FHE	0075	0390	1 AN 250-C20B	1451			lsf Alpine Zone Helic. / cvtd JetRanger
☐ VH-TMA	Agusta A109A II	7288	N212DT	0083		2 AN 250-C20B	2600			lsf Bob Jane T-Marts P/L
☐ VH-BKL	Kawasaki (Eurocopter/MBB) BK117B-1	1087		0093	0797	2 LY LTS101-750B.1	3200			lsf MHSC HS P/L

TOORADIN FLYING (Glenn Balas dba)

Tooradin, VIC

PO Box 94, Tooradin, VIC 3980, Australia ☎ (3) 59 98 33 28 Tx: none Fax: (3) 59 98 33 67 SITA: n/a
F: 1972 ☗ n/a Head: Glenn Balas Net: n/a Aircraft below MTOW 1361kg: Cessna 172, Piper PA-28 & PA-38

registration	type of aircraft	cn/fn	ex/ex*	mfd	del	powered by	mtow kg	configuration	selcal	name/fln/specialitites/remarks
☐ VH-MWI	Beech Queen Air 70	LB-2	N8070R	0069	0697	2 LY IGSO-480-A1E6	3719			

TRANSAIR (Lessbrook, Pty Ltd dba)

Brisbane, QLD

Acacia Street, Brisbane Airport, QLD 4007, Australia ☎ (7) 38 60 46 00 Tx: none Fax: (7) 38 60 46 01 SITA: n/a
F: 1988 ☗ 10 Head: L.A. Wright Net: n/a

registration	type of aircraft	cn/fn	ex/ex*	mfd	del	powered by	mtow kg	configuration	selcal	name/fln/specialitites/remarks
☐ VH-TFB	Cessna 441 Conquest II	441-0260	N68597	0082		2 GA TPE331-8-403S	4468			
☐ VH-AAG	Twin (Aero) Turbo Commander 690A	11101	N57101	0073	1195	2 GA TPE331-5-251K	4649			
☐ VH-TFQ	Fairchild (Swearingen) SA226TC Metro II	TC-395	N20849	0081	0294	2 GA TPE331-3UW-303G	5670			
☐ VH-TFG	Fairchild (Swearingen) SA227AC Metro III	AC-504	N31072	0082	0796	2 GA TPE331-11U-611G	6577			cvtd SA227AT

TRANS EXECUTIVE AIR CHARTER (Miles C. Ford dba)

Cairns, QLD

PO Box 277H, Edge Hill, QLD 4870, Australia ☎ (7) 40 35 96 59 Tx: none Fax: (7) 40 35 99 66 SITA: n/a
F: 1993 ☗ n/a Head: Miles C. Ford Net: n/a Operates airtaxi/charter flights with Aero Commander aircraft, currently leased from other companies when required.

TRANS QUEENSLAND AIR SERVICES (Air Training Centre, Pty Ltd dba)

Brisbane-Archerfield, QLD

Terminal Bldg Area, Archerfield Aerodrome, QLD 4108, Australia ☎ (7) 32 77 65 66 Tx: none Fax: (7) 32 74 25 07 SITA: n/a
F: n/a ☗ n/a Head: George Bradberry Net: n/a Aircraft below MTOW 1361kg: Cessna 172/182 & Piper PA-28/38

registration	type of aircraft	cn/fn	ex/ex*	mfd	del	powered by	mtow kg	configuration	selcal	name/fln/specialitites/remarks
☐ VH-CBU	Piper PA-34-200 Seneca	34-7250212		0072	0397	2 LY IO-360-C1E6	1905			

TRANSTATE AIRLINES, Pty Ltd = BH (Subsidiary of Transset Corporation/Sister company of Jetcraft Aviation)

Cairns, QLD

PO Box 107, Cairns, QLD 4870, Australia ☎ (7) 40 35 97 22 Tx: none Fax: (7) 40 35 96 63 SITA: CNSRZBH
F: 1996 ☗ 40 Head: Russell King IATA: 374 Net: n/a

registration	type of aircraft	cn/fn	ex/ex*	mfd	del	powered by	mtow kg	configuration	selcal	name/fln/specialitites/remarks
☐ VH-UQN	Britten-Norman BN-2A-20 Islander	145	VH-ISD	0070	1198	2 LY IO-540-K1B5	2994	Y9		
☐ VH-FNU	De Havilland DHC-6 Twin Otter 320	286	P2-RDI	0070	1098	2 PWC PT6A-27	5670	Y18		
☐ VH-UQA	Embraer 110P2 Bandeirante (EMB-110P2)	110245	VH-XFL	0080	1196	2 PWC PT6A-34	5670	Y18		
☐ VH-UQB	Embraer 110P2 Bandeirante (EMB-110P2)	110253	VH-XFK	0080	1196	2 PWC PT6A-34	5670	Y18		
☐ VH-UQC	Embraer 110P2 Bandeirante (EMB-110P2)	110194	VH-XFM	0078	1196	2 PWC PT6A-34	5670	Y18		
☐ VH-UQD	Embraer 110P1 Bandeirante (EMB-110P1)	110208	VH-FWR	0079	1196	2 PWC PT6A-34	5670	Y18		
☐ VH-UQF	Embraer 110P1 Bandeirante (EMB-110P1)	110232	VH-XFO	0079	1196	2 PWC PT6A-34	5670	Y18		
☐ VH-UQG	Embraer 110P1 Bandeirante (EMB-110P1)	110236	VH-XFP	0079	1196	2 PWC PT6A-34	5670	Y18		

TRIPLE C AVIATION (Peter Johnson dba / Division of Triple C Furniture & Electrical, Pty Ltd) — Weipa, QLD

PO Box 111, Weipa, QLD 4874, Australia ☎ (7) 40 69 70 00 Tx: none Fax: (7) 40 69 78 30 SITA: n/a
F: 1996 n/a Head: Peter Johnson Net: n/a

☐ VH-IXB	Partenavia P.68B	154		0078	0698	2 LY IO-360-A1B6	1990			
☐ VH-IXC	Partenavia P.68B	164		0078		2 LY IO-360-A1B6	1990			

TROPICAIR (Tropic Air Services, Pty Ltd dba) — Carnarvon, WA

TropicAir

PO Box 26, Carnarvon, WA 6701, Australia ☎ (8) 99 41 10 07 Tx: n/a Fax: (8) 99 41 22 55 SITA: n/a
F: 1969 5 Head: Keith N. Hasleby Net: n/a

☐ VH-TEO	Cessna U206G Stationair 6 II	U20605045	N4671U	0079		1 CO IO-520-L	1633			
☐ VH-PNS	Partenavia P.68B Victor	71		0076		2 LY IO-360-A1B6	1960			Horrie Miller

TVW AVIATION, Pty Ltd — Perth, WA

TVW AVIATION

PO Box 77, Tuart Hill, WA 6060, Australia ☎ (8) 93 44 07 77 Tx: none Fax: (8) 93 44 08 25 SITA: n/a
F: 1986 2 Head: T. Boase Net: n/a

☐ VH-TVG	Eurocopter (Aerosp.) AS350BA Squirrel	1895		0086		1 TU Arriel 1B	2100			opf TVW TV Channel 7 / cvtd AS350B

TWIN PIONAIR (Sherwell Aviation, Pty Ltd dba) — Coolangatta, QLD

112 Worongary Road, Mudgeeraba, QLD 4213, Australia ☎ (7) 55 99 27 17 Tx: none Fax: (7) 55 99 27 17 SITA: n/a
F: 1997 n/a Head: Ray Sherwell Net: n/a

☐ VH-AIS	Scottish Aviation Twin Pioneer 3	540	G-APPH	0058	0497	2 ALV Leonides 531	6622	16 Pax		
☐ VH-EVB	Scottish Aviation Twin Pioneer 3	586	9M-ART	0059	0497	2 ALV Leonides 531	6622	16 Pax		

UZU AIR, Pty Ltd — Cairns, QLD

PO Box 1379, Cairns, QLD 4870, Australia ☎ (7) 40 31 57 76 Tx: none Fax: (7) 40 52 10 69 SITA: n/a
F: 1993 16 Head: Urs Felix Net: n/a Placed into administration 1296, operations continue.

☐ VH-URM	Cessna U206F Stationair II	U20602980	P2-KSG	0075	0297	1 CO IO-520-F	1633			
☐ VH-URJ	Britten-Norman BN-2A-21 Islander	402	VH-OIA	0074	0996	2 LY IO-540-K1B5	2994			
☐ VH-URT	Cessna 208B Grand Caravan	208B0428	N1288D*	0095	0595	1 PWC PT6A-114A	3969			

VERSATILE AVIATION (Versatile Helicopter Services, Pty Ltd dba) — Biloela-Heliport, QLD

PO 1010, Biloela, QLD 4715, Australia ☎ (7) 49 92 26 00 Tx: none Fax: (7) 49 92 26 66 SITA: n/a
F: 1997 n/a Head: David Davies Net: n/a

☐ VH-MFI	Bell 206B JetRanger	1060	RP-C1288	0073	1098	1 AN 250-C20	1451			
☐ VH-MFU	Bell 206B JetRanger	1029	RP-C1245	0073	1298	1 AN 250-C20	1451			
☐ VH-PMR	Bell 206B JetRanger	358		0069	0896	1 AN 250-C20	1451			

WAGGA AIR CENTRE (Mabena, Pty Ltd dba) — Wagga Wagga, NSW

Forest Hill Airport, Wagga Wagga, NSW 2650, Australia ☎ (2) 69 22 71 22 Tx: none Fax: (2) 69 22 71 16 SITA: n/a
F: 1997 n/a Head: n/a Net: n/a Aircraft below MTOW 1361kg: Cessna 172 & 182

☐ VH-ELB	Cessna 210J Centurion	21059134	N3334S	0069	0598	1 CO IO-520-J	1542			
☐ VH-WNI	Cessna 210M Centurion II	21062462	N761RR	0077	0197	1 CO IO-520-L	1724			
☐ VH-JUB	Cessna 310R II	310R1663	N1ML	0079	0197	2 CO IO-520-MB	2495			
☐ VH-LGK	Cessna 310R II	310R0890	N310ER	0076	0698	2 CO IO-520-MB	2495			
☐ VH-SFQ	Cessna 310R II	310R1274	N6106C	0078	0197	2 CO IO-520-M	2495			

WEBB HELICOPTERS (Central (Qld) Holdings, Pty Ltd dba) — Emerald, QLD

PO Box 722, Emerald, QLD 4720, Australia ☎ (79) 87 54 00 Tx: none Fax: (79) 82 33 73 SITA: n/a
F: 1984 n/a Head: Eric Webb Net: n/a Aircraft below MTOW 1361kg: Kawasaki-Bell 47G3B

☐ VH-EWH	Bell 206B JetRanger	1380	ZS-HTS	0075	0998	1 AN 250-C20	1451			
☐ VH-AMJ	Piper PA-32-300 Cherokee SIX	32-40343	N4045R	0068	0598	1 LY IO-540-K1A5	1542			
☐ VH-EWT	Piper PA-32-300 Cherokee SIX	32-40144	VH-PPR	0067		1 LY IO-540-K1A5	1542			
☐ VH-WEB	Bell 206L-1 LongRanger II	45275		0079	1097	1 AN 250-C28B	1837			

WEIPA AIR (Sky Charter, Pty Ltd dba) — Weipa, QLD

PO Box 105, Weipa, QLD 4814, Australia ☎ (70) 69 78 07 Tx: n/a Fax: (70) 69 78 15 SITA: n/a
F: 1990 8 Head: Robert Statton Net: n/a

☐ VH-HEC	Cessna 310R II	310R0522	N480A	0076	0597	2 CO IO-520-M	2495			
☐ VH-TFJ	Cessna 310R II	310R2123	N310CE	0080	0495	2 CO IO-520-MB	2495			

WESTCOAST AVIATION, Pty Ltd — Geelong, VIC

Locked Bag 8, Lara, VIC 3212, Australia ☎ (3) 52 64 10 43 Tx: n/a Fax: (3) 52 64 10 56 SITA: n/a
F: 1994 n/a Head: Geoffrey R. Staig Net: n/a Aircraft below MTOW 1361kg: Cessna 172

☐ VH-FTJ	Piper PA-23-250 Aztec F	27-7854088	N63957	0078	0295	2 LY IO-540-C4B5	2359			
☐ VH-WDR	Piper PA-31-310 Navajo	31-552		0070		2 LY TIO-540-A1A	2948			lsf pvt
☐ VH-MWK	Beech Queen Air B80 (65-B80)	LD-472	N25728	0073		2 LY IGSO-540-A1D	3992			

WESTERN AIRLINES = EM (Camstra, Pty Ltd dba / formerly Midstate Airlines) — Perth, WA

Domestic Terminal, Perth Airport, WA 6105, Australia ☎ (8) 92 77 40 22 Tx: none Fax: (8) 94 78 25 37 SITA: n/a
F: 1989 7 Head: Bob Biltoft Net: n/a

☐ VH-JVO	Cessna 310R II	310R0539	N145FB	0076		2 CO IO-520-M	2495			
☐ VH-TWU	Piper PA-31-350 Navajo Chieftain	31-7552110	N61387	0075		2 LY TIO-540-J2BD	3175			

WESTPAC LIFE-SAVER HELI RESCUE SERVICE – Brisbane Region (Brisbane Region Surf Life Saving Association Air Rescue Services, Ltd dba) — Brisbane, QLD

PO Box 2136, Fortitude Valley, QLD 4006, Australia ☎ (7) 38 52 14 96 Tx: n/a Fax: (7) 32 52 45 11 SITA: n/a
F: n/a n/a Head: Chris Lloyd Net: n/a

☐ VH-ELP	Eurocopter (Aerosp.) AS350B Squirrel	1724	DQ-FHA	0083	0595	1 TU Arriel 1B	1950	EMS		
☐ VH-ELR	Eurocopter (Aerosp.) AS350B Squirrel	2151	JA9790	0089	0998	1 TU Arriel 1B	1950	EMS		

WESTPAC LIFE-SAVER HELI RESCUE SERVICE – Hunter Region (Hunter Region Surf Life Saving Assocation Helicopter Rescue Services, Ltd dba) — Broadmeadow, NSW

PO Box 230, New Lambton, NSW 2305, Australia ☎ (49) 57 22 99 Tx: none Fax: (49) 52 82 63 SITA: n/a
F: 1975 17 Head: Richard Jones Net: n/a

☐ VH-HRM	Bell 206L-1 LongRanger III	45495	VH-AHV	0880	1194	1 AN 250-C30P	1882	EMS / SAR		Angel III / cvtd LongRanger II
☐ VH-HRS	Bell 412	33118	JA9638	0086	0693	2 PWC PT6T-3B TwinPac	5398	EMS / SAR		Angel II

WESTPAC LIFE-SAVER HELI RESCUE SERVICE – Northern Region (Northern Region Surf Life Saving Association Helicopter Rescue Service, Pty Ltd dba) — Lismore, NSW

PO Box 822, Lismore, NSW 2480, Australia ☎ (2) 96 94 52 70 Tx: none Fax: (2) 96 61 48 78 SITA: n/a
F: n/a n/a Head: n/a Net: n/a

☐ VH-LSL	Eurocopter (Aerosp.) SA365C1 Dauphin 2	5057	G-BSRM	0080		2 TU Arriel 1A1	3400	EMS		
☐ VH-NRL	Eurocopter (Aerosp.) SA365C1 Dauphin 2	5059	SE-JCJ	0080	1095	2 TU Arriel 1A1	3400	EMS		

WESTPAC LIFE-SAVER HELI RESCUE SERVICE – Southern Region (Southern Region Surf Life Saving Association Helicopter Rescue Service, Pty Ltd dba) — Sydney-Little Bay, NSW

LIFE SAVER

Cottage Five, Prince Henry Hospital, Little Bay, NSW 2036, Australia ☎ (2) 93 11 34 99 Tx: none Fax: (2) 96 61 48 78 SITA: n/a
F: 1973 25 Head: J.S. Klopper Net: n/a

☐ VH-SLA	Kawasaki (Eurocopter/MBB) BK117B-2	1048	JA6604	0090	0993	2 LY LTS101-750B.1	3350	EMS		Life Saver I / cvtd BK117B-1
☐ VH-SLS	Kawasaki (Eurocopter/MBB) BK117B-1	1050	JA6606	0090	0297	2 LY LTS101-750B.1	3200	EMS		

WESTRAC AVIATION, Pty Ltd — Perth, WA

128-134 Great Eastern Highway, South Guildford, WA 6055, Australia ☎ (8) 93 77 94 44 Tx: none Fax: (8) 93 77 17 91 SITA: n/a
F: n/a n/a Head: n/a Net: n/a

☐ VH-MNG	Beech King Air 350 (B300)	FL-162		0097	0598	2 PWC PT6A-60A	6804			

WETTENHALL AIR SERVICES (Wettenhall Air Service, Pty Ltd dba / formerly Macknight Airlines) — Deniliquin, NSW

PO Box 1233, Deniliquin, NSW 2710, Australia ☎ (3) 58 81 25 04 Tx: none Fax: (3) 58 81 31 15 SITA: n/a
F: 1970 6 Head: Nigel Wettenhall Net: n/a

☐ VH-MAB	Piper PA-39-160 Twin Comanche C/R	39-96	VH-MED	0071	0798	2 LY IO-320-B1A	1633			
☐ VH-MAC	Piper PA-30-160 Twin Comanche C	30-1869	VH-HHE	0069	1293	2 LY IO-320-B1A	1633			
☐ VH-MAV	Twin (Aero) Shrike Commander 500S	3280	N81512	0076		2 LY IO-540-E1B5	3357			

WHITAKER AIR CHARTERS (Lady Elliot Island) (BR Whitaker, Pty Ltd dba) — Hervey Bay, QLD

PO Box 186, Maryborough, QLD 4650, Australia ☎ (7) 41 25 53 44 Tx: none Fax: (7) 41 25 57 78 SITA: n/a
F: 1967 n/a Head: Bevan R. Whitaker Net: n/a
Some aircraft are painted with LADY ELLIOT ISLAND markings, a popular Whitaker Air Charters destination.

☐ VH-SMJ	GAF N22B Nomad	N22B-93	P2-IAM	0080	0199	2 AN 250-B17B	4060			
☐ VH-SNL	GAF Nomad N22C	N22C-95	9M-WKU	0079	0199	2 AN 250-B17B	4060			cvtd N22B
☐ VH-TZL	De Havilland DHC-6 Twin Otter 100	43	SE-FTO	0067	0889	2 PWC PT6A-20	4990			
☐ VH-TZR	De Havilland DHC-6 Twin Otter 200	145	DQ-FDD	0068		2 PWC PT6A-20	5252			

642 registration type of aircraft cn/fn ex/ex* mfd del powered by mtow kg configuration selcal name/fln/specialitites/remarks

WHITSUNDAY HELICOPTERS (Whitsunday Helicopter Group, Pty Ltd dba)
Mackay, QLD

PO Box 4025, Mackay South, QLD 4740, Australia ☎ (7) 49 53 30 61 Tx: none Fax: (7) 49 53 30 51 SITA: n/a
F: 1997 ♦♦♦ n/a Head: n/a Net: n/a

registration	type of aircraft	cn/fn	ex/ex*	mfd	del	powered by	mtow kg	configuration	remarks
☐ VH-WHC	MD Helicopters MD 500E (Hughes 369E)	0352E	P2-PAI	0089	0198	1 AN 250-C20R2	1361		

WHYALLA AIRLINES, Pty Ltd = WW / WWL (Affiliated with Des's Cabs, Pty Ltd)
Whyalla, SA

PO Box 209, Whyalla, SA 5600, Australia ☎ (8) 86 45 89 22 Tx: none Fax: (8) 86 45 19 51 SITA: n/a
F: 1990 ♦♦♦ 8 Head: Kym E. Brougham Net: n/a

registration	type of aircraft	cn/fn	ex/ex*	mfd	del	powered by	mtow kg	remarks
☐ VH-ROH	Cessna 210L Centurion II	21059630	VH-ROV	0072		1 CO IO-520-L	1724	
☐ VH-ION	Beech Baron 58	TH-14	RP-C958	0070		2 CO IO-520-C	2404	
☐ VH-UYU	AAC (Ted Smith) Aerostar 600A	60-0390-138	N9766Q	0077	0995	2 LY IO-540-K1F5	2495	
☐ VH-BYG	Piper PA-31-350 Navajo Chieftain	31-7852130	N350PA	0078		2 LY TIO-540-J2BD	3175	
☐ VH-MZK	Piper PA-31-350 Navajo Chieftain	31-8152180	N4095U	0081	0395	2 LY TIO-540-J2BD	3175	
☐ VH-NPB	Piper PA-31-350 Navajo Chieftain	31-7405215	N640A	0074		2 LY TIO-540-J2BD	3175	
☐ VH-XMC	Piper PA-31-350 Navajo Chieftain	31-7852055	N27539	0078		2 LY TIO-540-J2BD	3175	

WILDERNESS AIR (Outback Air, Pty Ltd dba)
Strahan-SPB, TAS

PO Box 92, Strahan, TAS 7468, Australia ☎ (3) 64 71 72 80 Tx: none Fax: (4) 64 71 73 03 SITA: n/a
F: 1985 ♦♦♦ 8 Head: Kevin J. Pearce Net: n/a

registration	type of aircraft	cn/fn	ex/ex*	mfd	del	powered by	mtow kg	remarks
☐ VH-JBM	Cessna A185F Skywagon	18502204		0073		1 CO IO-520-D	1520	Floats
☐ VH-SCH	Cessna A185F Skywagon	18503071	N21941	0076		1 CO IO-520-D	1520	Floats
☐ VH-TLO	Cessna A185F Skywagon II	18503068	N8332Q	0078	0795	1 CO IO-520-D	1520	Floats
☐ VH-KLP	Cessna 208 Caravan I	20800260	N12324	0097	0697	1 PWC PT6A-114	3629	lsf Angelhurst P/L

WIMMERA MALLEE CHARTER FLIGHTS (Wimdown, Pty Ltd dba)
Horsham, VIC

Box 635, Horsham, VIC 3402, Australia ☎ (53) 82 10 04 Tx: n/a Fax: (53) 82 66 00 SITA: n/a
F: n/a ♦♦♦ n/a Head: J.G. Moore Net: n/a

registration	type of aircraft	cn/fn	ex/ex*	mfd	del	powered by	mtow kg	remarks
☐ VH-WSK	Cessna 210M Centurion II	21062056	N9061M	0077		1 CO IO-520-L	1724	

WIMRAY AIR CHARTER (Raymond J. Allwright dba)
Darwin, NT

PO Box 1634, Darwin, NT 0801, Australia ☎ (8) 89 45 27 55 Tx: none Fax: (8) 89 41 27 31 SITA: n/a
F: 1977 ♦♦♦ n/a Head: Raymond J. Allwright Net: n/a

registration	type of aircraft	cn/fn	ex/ex*	mfd	del	powered by	mtow kg	remarks
☐ VH-FTP	Piper PA-32-300 Cherokee SIX	32-7940013	N2182F	0079	0195	1 LY IO-540-K1G5	1542	
☐ VH-PYC	Piper PA-32-300 Cherokee SIX	32-7540129	N1014X	0075		1 LY IO-540-K1G5	1542	
☐ VH-FER	Beech Baron 58	TH-602	N9398S	0075		2 CO IO-520-C	2449	
☐ VH-FDQ	Piper PA-31-350 Navajo Chieftain	31-7652150	N62894	0076		2 LY TIO-540-J2BD	3175	
☐ VH-TTX	Piper PA-31-350 Navajo Chieftain	31-8152034	N4074Z	0081		2 LY TIO-540-J2BD	3175	

WINDJAMMER PROMOTIONS (Robert A. Fisher dba)
Melbourne-Essendon, VIC

GPO Box 297B, Melbourne, VIC 3001, Australia ☎ (3) 96 29 15 05 Tx: none Fax: none SITA: n/a
F: 1996 ♦♦♦ n/a Head: Robert A. Fisher Net: n/a

registration	type of aircraft	cn/fn	ex/ex*	mfd	del	powered by	mtow kg	remarks
☐ VH-TMQ	Boeing (Douglas) DC-3C (C-47B-30-DK)	32884	A65-91	0045	0996	2 PW R-1830	11884	28 Pax / Para

WINGAWAY AIR, Pty Ltd
Port Macquarie, NSW

PO Box 5165, Port Macquarie, NSW 2444, Australia ☎ (65) 81 15 55 Tx: none Fax: (65) 81 15 67 SITA: n/a
F: 1993 ♦♦♦ n/a Head: William O. Redpath Net: n/a

registration	type of aircraft	cn/fn	ex/ex*	mfd	del	powered by	mtow kg	remarks
☐ VH-FSH	Partenavia P.68B	18		0074		2 LY IO-360-A1B6	1960	lst pvt

WINGS AIR, Pty Ltd
Melbourne-Essendon, VIC

Bldg 260, English Street, Essendon Airport, VIC 3041, Australia ☎ (3) 93 79 65 10 Tx: none Fax: (3) 93 51 00 05 SITA: n/a
F: 1995 ♦♦♦ 7 Head: Geoffrey F. Glenn Net: n/a Aircraft below MTOW 1361kg: Piper PA-28 & PA-38

registration	type of aircraft	cn/fn	ex/ex*	mfd	del	powered by	mtow kg	remarks
☐ VH-ZWH	Commander (Rockwell) 114	14290	VH-UKL	0077		1 LY IO-540-T4A5D	1424	lsf pvt
☐ VH-LRT	Piper PA-32RT-300 Lance II	32R-7885082	N30073	0078	1297	1 LY IO-540-K1G5D	1633	
☐ VH-ZWI	Piper PA-44-180 Seminole	44-7995219	VH-JCF	0079		2 LY O-360-E1A6D	1724	
☐ VH-ZWJ	Partenavia P.68B	112	VH-IYJ	0077	1197	2 LY IO-360-A1B6	1960	
☐ VH-ZWK	Piper PA-31-310 Navajo C	31-7912041	VH-EGF	0079		2 LY TIO-540-A2C	2948	lsf pvt

WRIGHTSAIR (Trevor W. Wright dba)
Boort, VIC & William Creek, SA

53 O'Neils Road, Melton, VIC 3337, Australia ☎ (3) 97 47 91 00 Tx: none Fax: (3) 97 43 19 23 SITA: n/a
F: 1991 ♦♦♦ 4 Head: Trevor W. Wright Net: n/a Aircraft below MTOW 1361kg: Cessna 172 & 182

registration	type of aircraft	cn/fn	ex/ex*	mfd	del	powered by	mtow kg	remarks
☐ VH-JEK	Cessna U206G Stationair 6 II	U20606774	N9954Z	0083	0398	1 CO IO-550-F	1633	
☐ VH-JGA	Cessna 210N Centurion II	21064222	N5482Y	0081	0597	1 CO IO-520-L	1724	
☐ VH-KTM	Cessna T210N Turbo Centurion II	21063269	N5101A	0079	0798	2 CO TSIO-520-R	1814	

YANDA AIRLINES = ST (Singleton Air Services, Pty Ltd dba)
Singleton, NSW

Private Mail Bag 5, Whittingham, NSW 2330, Australia ☎ (2) 65 72 31 00 Tx: none Fax: (5) 65 72 27 57 SITA: n/a
F: 1980 ♦♦♦ 10 Head: Paul D. Rees Net: n/a

registration	type of aircraft	cn/fn	ex/ex*	mfd	del	powered by	mtow kg	remarks
☐ VH-HVA	Embraer 820C Navajo (EMB-820C)	820045	PT-EHI	0077		2 LY TIO-540-J2BD	3175	
☐ VH-ATP	Piper PA-31-350 Navajo Chieftain	31-7405447	N61404	0074		2 LY TIO-540-J2BD	3175	
☐ VH-TXK	Piper PA-31-350 Navajo Chieftain	31-7405189	N66890	0074	0194	2 LY TIO-540-J2BD	3175	
☐ VH-WAD	Piper PA-31-350 Navajo Chieftain	31-7552018	N61506	0075		2 LY TIO-540-J2BD	3175	

YORKE AIR (BTT Nominees, Pty Ltd dba)
Adelaide, SA

2 Gilbert Close, Gilberton, SA 5081, Australia ☎ (8) 82 69 19 91 Tx: none Fax: (8) 82 69 10 01 SITA: n/a
F: n/a ♦♦♦ n/a Head: n/a Net: n/a Ag-aircraft below MTOW 1361kg: Air Tractor AT-502

registration	type of aircraft	cn/fn	ex/ex*	mfd	del	powered by	mtow kg	remarks
☐ VH-DTF	Piper PA-31-350 Navajo Chieftain	31-7852159	F-OHAS	0078	1298	2 LY TIO-540-J2BD	3175	

VN = VIETNAM (The Socialist Republic of Vietnam) (Cong Hoa Xa Hoi Chu Nghia Viet Nam)
Capital: Hanoi Official Language: Vietnamese Population: 75,0 million Square Km: 331689 Dialling code: +84 Year established: 1945 Acting political head: Tran Duc Luong (President)

PACIFIC AIRLINES, Co Ltd = BL / PIC (Associated with Vietnam Airlines, Ho Chi Minh City Peoples Committee & Saigon Tourist)
Ho Chi Minh City

112 Hong Ha Street, Tan Binh District, Ho Chi Minh City, Vietnam ☎ (8) 845 00 90 Tx: 812628 airhldg vt Fax: (8) 845 00 85 SITA: n/a
F: 1991 ♦♦♦ 273 Head: Duong Cao Tahi Nguyen IATA: 550 Net: n/a

registration	type of aircraft	cn/fn	ex/ex*	mfd	del	powered by	mtow kg	configuration	remarks
☐ B-88889	Boeing (Douglas) MD-82 (DC-9-82)	53480 / 2127		0095	0797	2 PW JT8D-217C	67812	Y165	lsf/opb U-Land Airlines

SFC VIETNAM – Service Flight Corp. of Vietnam (T.C. Ty Bay Dich Vu VN)
Da Nang/Conson/Hanoi/Ho Chi Minh City/Nam Can/Vung Tau

173 Truong Chinh Road, Hanoi, Vietnam ☎ (4) 852 17 73 Tx: none Fax: (4) 852 15 23 SITA: n/a
F: 1985 ♦♦♦ 370 Head: Nguyen Xuan Truong Net: n/a

registration	type of aircraft	cn/fn	ex/ex*	mfd	del	powered by	mtow kg	remarks
☐ VN-8605	Eurocopter (Aerosp.) SA330J Puma	1610		0079		2 TU Turmo IVC	7400	
☐ VN-8607	Eurocopter (Aerosp.) SA330J Puma	1407		0076		2 TU Turmo IVC	7400	
☐ VN-8608	Eurocopter (Aerosp.) AS332L2 S.Puma II	2348	F-GLHS	0093	0994	2 TU Makila 1A2	9300	
☐ VN-8609	Eurocopter (Aerosp.) AS332L2 S.Puma II	2366		0094	0595	2 TU Makila 1A2	9300	
☐ VN-7828	Mil Mi-8	20114		0079		2 IS TV2-117A	12000	
☐ VN-7846	Mil Mi-8MTV-1	95930		0092		2 IS TV3-117VM	13000	
☐ VN-8402	Mil Mi-8	201001		0084		2 IS TV2-117A	12000	
☐ VN-8404	Mil Mi-8	201002		0084		2 IS TV2-117A	12000	
☐ VN-8416	Mil Mi-8MTV-1	96052		0092		2 IS TV3-117VM	13000	
☐ VN-8406	Mil Mi-17	223M43		0087		2 IS TV3-117MT-3	13000	
☐ VN-8408	Mil Mi-17	223M44		0087		2 IS TV3-117MT-3	13000	
☐ VN-8410	Mil Mi-17	201M07		0092		2 IS TV3-117MT-3	13000	
☐ VN-8411	Mil Mi-17	201M08		0092		2 IS TV3-117MT-3	13000	
☐ VN-8414	Mil Mi-17	96167		0093		2 IS TV3-117MT-3	13000	
☐ VN-8415	Mil Mi-17	96168		0093		2 IS TV3-117MT-3	13000	

VASCO – Vietnam Air Service Company (Subsidiary of Vietnam Airlines Corp. - VAC)
Ho Chi Minh City & Hanoi

Aéroport, Ho Chi Minh City, Vietnam ☎ (8) 844 59 99 Tx: n/a Fax: (8) 844 52 24 SITA: n/a
F: 1993 ♦♦♦ 138 Head: Vu Ngoc Dinh Net: n/a

registration	type of aircraft	cn/fn	ex/ex*	mfd	del	powered by	mtow kg	remarks
☐ VN-C808	PZL Mielec (Antonov) An-2	1G235-24		0090		1 SH ASh-62IR	5500	Sprayer/Photo
☐ VN-C810	PZL Mielec (Antonov) An-2	1G235-25		0090		1 SH ASh-62IR	5500	Sprayer/Photo
☐ VN-B594	Beech King Air B200	BB-1329	VH-SWC	0089	0494	2 PWC PT6A-42	5670	Photo / Survey
☐ VN-B376	Antonov 30	1009		0076		2 IV AI-24T	23000	Survey/Freighter
☐ VN-B378	Antonov 30	1205		0077		2 IV AI-24T	23000	Survey/Freighter

VIETNAM AIRLINES = VN / HVN (Subsidiary of Vietnam Airlines Corp. - VAC / formerly Hang Khong Viet Nam)
Hanoi & Ho Chi Minh City

Gialam Airport, Hanoi 1000, Vietnam ☎ (4) 827 22 89 Tx: 412260 tchk vt Fax: (4) 827 22 91 SITA: HDQIIVN
F: 1976 ♦♦♦ 5700 Head: Me Dao Manh Nhuong IATA: 738 ICAO: VIETNAM AIRLINES Net: http://www.vietnamair.com

registration	type of aircraft	cn/fn	ex/ex*	mfd	del	powered by	mtow kg	configuration	remarks
☐ VN-B202	ATR 72-202	215	F-OKVN	0091	0592	2 PWC PW124B	21500	Y66	
☐ VN-B204	ATR 72-202	341	F-OKVM	0092	1292	2 PWC PW124B	21500	Y66	
☐ VN-B206	ATR 72-202	419	F-WWLW*	0094	1294	2 PWC PW124B	21500	Y66	

| 643 | registration | type of aircraft | | cn/fn | ex/ex* | mfd | del | powered by | | mtow kg | configuration | selcal | name/fln/specialtites/remarks |

☐ VN-B208	ATR 72-202	416	F-WWLE*	0094	1294	2 PWC PW124B	21500	Y66		
☐ F-GKOC	ATR 72-202	307	F-WWEG*	0092	0596	2 PWC PW124B	21500	Y66		lsf France Commuter Lease Co. Ltd
☐ F-OHOB	ATR 72-202	316	F-GKOE	0093	1295	2 PWC PW124B	21500	Y66		lsf Lodra Ltd
☐ VN-A502	Fokker 70 (F28 Mk0070)	11580	PH-EZL*	0096	0197	2 RR Tay 620-15	36740	Y79 / VIP		
☐ VN-A504	Fokker 70 (F28 Mk0070)	11585	PH-EZM*	0096	0197	2 RR Tay 620-15	36740	Y79 / VIP		
☐ VN-A116	Tupolev 134B-3	66230		0084		2 SO D-30-III	49000	F45		
☐ VN-A118	Tupolev 134B-3	66250		0084		2 SO D-30-III	49000	Y72		
☐ VN-A132	Tupolev 134A	63260	DDR-SDP	0080	0790	2 SO D-30-II	49000	Y72		
☐ VN-B198	Ilyushin 18D	189011304	5T-CJL	0069		4 IV AI-20M	64000	Y100		
☐ S7-ASA	Airbus Industrie A320-214	590	F-WWBE*	0096	0796	2 CFMI CFM56-5B4	73500	C12Y138	QS-AL	lsf STAR
☐ S7-ASB	Airbus Industrie A320-214	594	F-WWBG*	0096	0796	2 CFMI CFM56-5B4	73500	C12Y138	QS-AB	lsf STAR
☐ S7-ASC	Airbus Industrie A320-214	601	F-WWBJ*	0096	0796	2 CFMI CFM56-5B4	73500	C12Y138	QS-AC	lsf STAR
☐ S7-ASD	Airbus Industrie A320-214	605	F-WWBM*	0096	0796	2 CFMI CFM56-5B4	73500	C12Y138	QS-AD	lsf STAR
☐ S7-ASE	Airbus Industrie A320-214	607	F-WWBN*	0096	0896	2 CFMI CFM56-5B4	73500	C12Y138	QS-AE	lsf STAR
☐ S7-ASF	Airbus Industrie A320-214	611	F-WWBP*	0096	0896	2 CFMI CFM56-5B4	73500	C12Y138	QS-AF	lsf STAR
☐ S7-ASG	Airbus Industrie A320-214	617	F-WWBS*	0096	0996	2 CFMI CFM56-5B4	73500	C12Y138	QS-AG	lsf STAR
☐ S7-ASH	Airbus Industrie A320-214	619	F-WWBT*	0096	1096	2 CFMI CFM56-5B4	73500	C12Y138	QS-AH	lsf STAR
☐ S7-ASI	Airbus Industrie A320-214	648	F-WWDP*	0096	0197	2 CFMI CFM56-5B4	77000	C12Y138	QS-AJ	lsf STAR
☐ S7-ASJ	Airbus Industrie A320-214	650	F-WWDS*	0097	0197	2 CFMI CFM56-5B4	77000	C12Y138	QS-AK	lsf STAR
☐ S7-RGU	Boeing 767-324 (ER)	27568 / 593	EI-CMH	0095	0296	2 GE CF6-80C2B7F	186880	C25Y196	LS-CH	lsf GECA / opb RGA
☐ S7-RGV	Boeing 767-324 (ER)	27392 / 568	EI-CMD	0095	0196	2 GE CF6-80C2B7F	186880	C25Y196	LS-CF	lsf GECA / opb RGA
☐ S7-RGW	Boeing 767-324 (ER)	27393 / 571	EI-CME	0095	0296	2 GE CF6-80C2B7F	186880	C25Y196	LS-CG	lsf GECA / opb RGA
☐ V8-RBF	Boeing 767-33A (ER)	25530 / 414		0092	0496	2 PW PW4056	172365	C24Y224	BL-KR	lsf RBA

VP-A = ANGUILLA (Dependent UK-territory)

(Formerly VP-LA)
Capital: The Valley Official Language: English Population: 0,1 million Dialling code: +1-264 Acting political head: Hubert Hughes (Prime Minister)

AIR ANGUILLA, Inc.

Anguilla & St. Thomas-Cyril E. King, VI (USA)

Cyril E. King Airport, St. Thomas, VI 00802, USA ☎ (340) 776-5789 Tx: none Fax: (340) 777-8585 SITA: n/a
F: 1979 ⁂ n/a Head: Restormel M. Franklin Net: n/a

☐ N17BT	Cessna 402B	402B0515		0073	0894	2 CO TSIO-520-E	2858	Y9		lsf pvt

TRANS ANGUILLA, Inc.

Anguilla & St. Thomas-Cyril E. King, VI (USA)

PO Box 1329, The Valley, Anguilla ☎ (264) 497-8690 Tx: none Fax: (264) 497-8689 SITA: n/a
F: 1997 ⁂ n/a Head: Keithley F.T. Lake Net: n/a

☐ VP-AAE	Britten-Norman BN-2A-27 Islander	905	N993RA	0081	0198	2 LY O-540-E4C5	2884	Y9		
☐ N6371X	De Havilland DHC-6 Twin Otter 300	838	ZS-OEF	0088	0898	2 PWC PT6A-27	5670	Y19		

TYDEN AIR, Inc.

Anguilla & St. Thomas-Cyril E. King, VI (USA)

PO Box 107, The Valley, Anguilla ☎ (264) 497-3419 Tx: none Fax: (264) 497-3079 SITA: n/a
F: 1979 ⁂ n/a Head: Lesley Lloyd Net: n/a

☐ N62TA	Britten-Norman BN-2A-21 Islander	515	N65JA	0077	1086	2 LY IO-540-K1B5	2994	Y9		
☐ VP-AAB	Britten-Norman BN-2A-26 Islander	3008	V3-HEZ	0084	0098	2 LY O-540-E4C5	2994	Y9		lsf G.A. Roe & Sons Ltd, Belize

VP-B = BERMUDA (UK-Colony of Bermuda)

(Formerly VR-B. The nationality-mark had to be changed effective 1st July 1997 to VP-B, as the I.T.U. re-allocated the VR-A to VR-Q series to China)
Capital: Hamilton Official Language: English Population: 0,1 million Square Km: 54 Dialling code: +1-441 Acting political head: Mrs Pamela F. Gordon (Prime Minister)

Government / Corporate / Executive / VIP Aircraft

☐ VP-BAT	Boeing 747SP-21	21648 / 367	VR-BAT	0079	1095	4 PW JT9D-7A	318422	Executive		Worldwide Aircraft Holding Co.
☐ VP-BBJ	Boeing 737-72U (BBJ)	29273 / 146	N1011N*	0098	1298	2 CFMI CFM56-7B26	77564	Executive		Picton II Ltd
☐ VP-BDJ	Boeing 727-23	20046 / 605	VR-BDJ	0068	0494	3 PW JT8D-7B	72847	Executive	DJ-CG	D.J. Aerospace / opb Trump Group
☐ VP-BGW	Boeing 727-30	18366 / 98	VR-BGW	0064	1079	3 PW JT8D-7 (HK3/FDX)	72802	Executive	BE-FG	Sigair, Ltd
☐ VP-BHM	Boeing (Douglas) DC-8-62	46111 / 491	VR-BHM	0069	0482	4 PW JT3D-7 (HK3/BAC)	158757	Executive	AC-HL	Brisair, Ltd
☐ VP-BIF	Boeing 727-1H2 (RE) (Super 27/winglets)	20533 / 869	VP-BIL	0071	1198	3 PW JT8D-217C/9A (BFG)	76884	Executive		New Century Air Ltd / cvtd -1H2
☐ VP-BJR	Boeing (Douglas) DC-8-72	46067 / 455	VR-BJR	0069	1086	4 CFMI CFM56-2C	158757	Executive	DE-GH	Al Nassr Ltd
☐ VP-BLG	Boeing (Douglas) DC-8-62	46071 / 469	VR-BLG	0069	0591	4 PW JT3D-7 (HK3/BAC)	158757	Executive	BC-FJ	Sunningdale Investments Ltd
☐ VP-BNA	Boeing 727-21	19262 / 426	VR-BNA	0067	0692	3 PW JT8D-7B (HK3/FDX)	72802	VIP	DF-AH	Skyjet Ltd / lst Mid East Jet Inc.
☐ VP-BOC	Boeing 737-53A	24970 / 1977	VR-BOC	0090	0692	2 CFMI CFM56-3C1	60555	Executive	CJ-AD	Theberton Ltd
☐ VP-BRM	Boeing 737-75U (BBJ)	28976 / 158		0098	1298	2 CFMI CFM56-7B26	77564	Executive		Dobro Ltd

VP-C = CAYMAN ISLANDS (UK-Colony of Cayman Islands)

(Formerly VR-C. The nationality-mark had to be changed effective 1st July 1997 to VP-C, as the I.T.U. re-allocated the VR-A to VR-Q series to China)
Capital: Georgetown Official Language: English Population: 0,1 million Square Km: 259 Dialling code: +1-345 Acting political head: John Owen (Prime Minister)

Government / Corporate / Executive / VIP Aircraft

☐ VP-CCG	BAe (BAC) One-Eleven 401AK	081	VR-CCG	0066		2 RR Spey 511-14 (HK)	40597	Executive		private
☐ VP-CHK	Boeing 737-2S9 (A)	21957 / 618	N39BL	0079	0698	2 PW JT8D-17	53070	Executive		private / opb EXZ
☐ VP-CHM	BAe (BAC) One-Eleven 492GM	260	HZ-KA7	0080	0798	2 RR Spey 511-14DW	44679	Executive		Arabsco / opb Mercury Aviation
☐ VP-CJN	Boeing 727-76	20371 / 822	5X-AMM	0070	0598	3 PW JT8D-7B (HK3/FDX)	72802	Executive		Starling Aviation
☐ VP-CKA	Boeing 727-82	20489 / 856	VR-CKA	0071	0496	3 PW JT8D-7B (HK3/FDX)	72724	Executive		SAMCO Aviation
☐ VP-CLM	BAe (BAC) One-Eleven 401AK	072	N119DA	0066	1198	2 RR Spey 511-14 (HK2)	40597	Executive		TAG Aviation Inc., Grand Cayman
☐ VP-CMI	BAe (BAC) One-Eleven 212AR	183	VR-CMI	0069	0192	2 RR Spey 511-14	35834	Executive		Kinyaa Ltd
☐ VP-CMM	Boeing 727-30	18368 / 117	VR-CMM	0065	0287	3 PW JT8D-7B (HK3/RAI)	72802	Executive	BM-DG	Amel / MME Farms Maintenance Corp.
☐ VP-CMN	Boeing 727-46	19282 / 495	VR-CMN	0067	0396	3 PW JT8D-7B (HK3/FDX)	76884	Executive	AG-CH	IDG (Cayman) Ltd
☐ VP-CZY	Boeing 727-2P1 (A/RE) (Super 27/winglets)	21595 / 1406	N727MJ	0079	0997	3 PW JT8D-217C/17 (BFG)	89358	Corporate		Dunview Co. Ltd / opb PJS / cvtd -2P1

CAYMAN AIRWAYS, Ltd = KX / CAY

Georgetown

PO Box 1101, Georgetown, Grand Cayman, Cayman Islands ☎ (345) 949-8200 Tx: none Fax: (345) 949-7607 SITA: n/a
F: 1968 ⁂ 300 Head: Leonard Ebanks IATA: 378 ICAO: CAYMAN Net: n/a

☐ VP-CAL	Boeing 737-205 (A)	22022 / 616	VR-CAL	0079	0295	2 PW JT8D-17A (HK3/AVA)	53297	Y122	LQ-BD	lsf C.I. Gvmt
☐ VP-CKX	Boeing 737-236 (A)	23162 / 1056	VR-CKX	0084	0595	2 PW JT8D-15A (HK3/AVA)	52752	Y122		lsf BOUL

ISLAND AIR, Ltd

Georgetown

PO Box 2433, Georgetown, Grand Cayman, Cayman Islands ☎ (345) 949-0241 Tx: none Fax: (345) 949-7044 SITA: n/a
F: 1989 ⁂ 30 Head: Mirvin Cumber Net: http://cayman.com.ky/com/iair/iair.htm

☐ VP-CII	Britten-Norman BN-2A-26 Islander	883	VR-CII	0079	0191	2 LY O-540-E4C5	2994			
☐ VP-CIN	Piper PA-31-350 Navajo Chieftain	31-8152184	VR-CIN	0081	0191	2 LY TIO-540-J2BD	3175			
☐ VP-CTO	De Havilland DHC-6 Vista Liner 300	773	VR-CTO	0081	1094	2 PWC PT6A-27	5670			cvtd Twin Otter 300

VP-F = FALKLAND ISLANDS (UK-Dependency of Falkland Islands)

Capital: Port Stanley Official Language: English Population: 0,1 million Square Km: 12173 Dialling code: +500 Acting political head: Richard Ralph (Governor)

BRITISH ANTARCTIC SURVEY (Subsidiary of Natural Environment Research Council)

Rothera Base (Antarctica)

High Cross, Madingley Road, Cambridge CB3 0ET, Great Britain ☎ (1223) 22 14 00 Tx: 817725 bascam g Fax: (1223) 35 17 30 SITA: n/a
F: 1962 ⁂ 420 Head: Christopher G. Rapley Net: http://www.nerc-bas.ac.uk

☐ VP-FAZ	De Havilland DHC-6 Twin Otter 310	748	C-GEOA*	0081	0581	2 PWC PT6A-27	5670	Survey / Frtr		Wheel-Skis
☐ VP-FBB	De Havilland DHC-6 Twin Otter 310	783	C-GDKL*	0082	0382	2 PWC PT6A-27	5670	Survey / Frtr		Wheel-Skis
☐ VP-FBC	De Havilland DHC-6 Twin Otter 310	787	C-GDIU*	0082	0382	2 PWC PT6A-27	5670	Survey / Frtr		Wheel-Skis
☐ VP-FBL	De Havilland DHC-6 Twin Otter 310	839	C-GDCZ*	0088	0788	2 PWC PT6A-27	5670	Survey / Frtr		Wheel-Skis
☐ VP-FBQ	De Havilland DHC-7-110 Dash 7	111	G-BOAX	0088	0890	4 PWC PT6A-50	21319	Survey / Frtr		

FIGAS – FALKLAND ISLANDS GOVERNMENT AIR SERVICE

Stanley

Airport, Stanley, Falkland Islands ☎ 27 219 Tx: none Fax: 27 309 SITA: n/a
F: 1948 ⁂ 24 Head: Vernon Steen Net: n/a

☐ VP-FBD	Britten-Norman BN-2B-26 Islander	2160	G-BKJK	0085	1285	2 LY O-540-E4C5	2994	Y9		
☐ VP-FBI	Britten-Norman BN-2B-26 Islander	2188	G-BLNI*	0087	1087	2 LY O-540-E4C5	2994	Y9		
☐ VP-FBM	Britten-Norman BN-2B-26 Islander	2200	G-BLNZ*	0088	0589	2 LY O-540-E4C5	2994	Y9		
☐ VP-FBN	Britten-Norman BN-2B-26 Islander	2216	G-BRFY*	0089	0690	2 LY O-540-E4C5	2994	Fishery Patrol		
☐ VP-FBO	Britten-Norman BN-2B-26 Islander	2218	G-BRGA*	0089	0790	2 LY O-540-E4C5	2994	Fishery Patrol		
☐ VP-FBR	Britten-Norman BN-2B-26 Islander	2252	G-BTLX*	0091	0292	2 LY O-540-E4C5	2994	Y9		

644 registration type of aircraft cn/fn ex/ex* mfd del powered by mtow kg configuration selcal name/fln/specialitites/remarks

VP-G = GIBRALTAR

(Formerly VR-G. The nationality-mark had to be changed effective 1st July 1997 to VP-G, as the I.T.U. re-allocated the VR-A to VR-Q series to China)
Capital: Gibraltar Official Language: English, Spanish Population: 0,1 million Square Km: 8 Dialling code: +350 Acting political head: Peter Caruana (Chief Minister)

At present there is no licenced commercial air operator in this country.

VP-L = BRITISH VIRGIN ISLANDS (UK-Colony of B.V.I.)

(Formerly VP-LV)
Capital: Road Town Official Language: English Population: 0,1 million Square Km: 153 Dialling code: +1-284 Acting political head: Ralph O'Neill (Prime Minister)

FLY BVI, Ltd — Beef Island

PO Box 3347, Road Town, British Virgin Islands ☎ (284) 495-1747 Tx: none Fax: (284) 495-1973 SITA: n/a
F: 1993 ⁂ 10 Head: Nikki Abrams Net: http://www.duhe.com/wwsail/flybvi Aircraft below MTOW 1361kg: Cessna 172

☐ N6637Y	Piper PA-23-250 Aztec D	27-3949		0068	0594	2 LY IO-540-J4A5	2359			lsf High Ground Aviation Inc.
☐ N6884A	Piper PA-23-250 Aztec F	27-7954105		0079		2 LY IO-540-C4B5	2359			lsf PAR Investments Inc.
☐ N148ES	Britten-Norman BN-2A-26 Islander	685	N143FS	0073	1094	2 LY O-540-E4C5	2994			lsf High Ground Aviation BN2 Ltd
☐ N18AU	Cessna 404 Titan II	404-0823	ST-AWD	0081	1293	2 CO GTSIO-520-M	3810			lsf Expomax Enterprises Inc.

VP-M = MONTSERRAT (UK-Colony of Montserrat)

(Formerly VR-LM)
Capital: Port Diana Official Language: English Population: 0,1 million Square Km: 98 Dialling code: +1 809 Acting political head: David Brandt (Prime Minister)

At present there is no licenced commercial air operator in this country.

VQ-T = TURKS & CAICOS ISLANDS (UK-Colony of Turks & Caicos)

Capital: Cockburn Official Language: English Population: 0,1 million Square Km: 430 Dialling code: +1-649 Acting political head: Derek Taylor (Prime Minister)

FLAMINGO AIR SERVICES (B J Ventures, Inc. dba) — Grand Turk

Grand Turk International Airport, Grand Turk, Turks & Caicos Islands ☎ (649) 946-2109 Tx: n/a Fax: (649) 946-2108 SITA: n/a
F: 1980 ⁂ n/a Head: James Barrett Net: n/a

☐ N13898	Piper PA-23-250 Aztec D	27-4531		0071		2 LY IO-540-C4B5	2359			

INTERISLAND AIRWAYS = IWY (Division of Kermount InterIsland Airways Ltd) — Providenciales

PO Box 191, Providenciales, Turks & Caicos Islands ☎ (649) 941-5481 Tx: none Fax: (649) 946-4040 SITA: n/a
F: 1993 ⁂ 20 Head: Lyndon R. Gardiner ICAO: ISLANDWAYS Net: n/a

☐ VQ-TDC	Piper PA-23-250 Aztec D	27-4260	N6905Y	0069	0497	2 LY IO-540-C4B5	2359			lsf Azure Sky Holdings Ltd
☐ VQ-TGS	Piper PA-23-250 Aztec E	27-7554008		0075		2 LY IO-540-C4B5	2359			lsf Eagle One Ltd
☐ VQ-TRG	Cessna 401A	401A0061	N6261Q	0069		2 CO TSIO-520-E	2858			lsf Azure Sky Holdings Ltd
☐ VQ-TDG	Cessna 402B	402B0218	N7890Q	0072		2 CO TSIO-520-E	2858			lsf Azure Sky Holdings Ltd
☐ VQ-THL	Britten-Norman BN-2B-21 Islander	858	I-KUNO	0080	0798	2 LY IO-540-K1B5	2994			

ISLAND FLYERS — North Caicos

Bottle Creek, North Caicos, Turks & Caicos Islands ☎ (649) 946-7112 Tx: n/a Fax: (649) 946-7139 SITA: n/a
F: 1990 ⁂ n/a Head: n/a Net: n/a

☐ VQ-TAL	Piper PA-23-250 Aztec F	27-7954019	N6594A	0079		2 LY IO-540-C4B5	2359			

SKYKING AIRLINES = RU / SKI (TCI Skyking Limited dba) — Providenciales

Box 398, Providenciales, Turks & Caicos Islands ☎ (649) 941-5464 Tx: none Fax: (649) 941-5127 SITA: PLSTCXH
F: 1995 ⁂ 59 Head: Charles Harold ICAO: SKYKING Net: http://www.skyking.tc

☐ N255HC	Piper PA-23-250 Aztec F	27-7854009	N550MC	0078	0195	2 LY IO-540-C4B5	2359	Y5		
☐ VQ-TAK	Piper PA-23-250 Aztec F	27-8054009	C-GELI	0080		2 LY IO-540-C4B5	2359	Y5		
☐ VQ-TJS	Cessna 402C II	402C0476	N402MN	0081		2 CO TSIO-520-VB	3107	Y9		
☐ VQ-TAM	Cessna 404 Titan Ambassador II	404-0851	N681BA	0081		2 CO GTSIO-520-M	3810	Y10		
☐ VQ-THW	Beech 1900C-1 Airliner	UC-99	N80598	0089	1198	2 PWC PT6A-65B	7530	Y19		
☐ VQ-TSK	Shorts 360-300 (SD3-60)	SH3718	G-BNFB	0087	1296	2 PWC PT6A-67R	12292	Y36		

TURKS AIR, Ltd — Miami-Int'l, FL & Grand Turk

7295 NW 41st Street, Miami, FL 33166, USA ☎ (305) 871-1433 Tx: none Fax: (305) 871-1622 SITA: n/a
F: 1972 ⁂ 17 Head: Robert Kerivan Net: n/a Beside aircraft listed, also leases Boeing 727-200F & Douglas DC-8F from other carriers (N) when required.

☐ N101LM	Boeing (Douglas) DC-7BF	44921 / 666	N750Z	0056	1298	4 WR R-3350	53025	Freighter		cvtd -7B

TURKS & CAICOS AIRWAYS, Ltd = QW / TCI (formerly Turks & Caicos National Airline) — Grand Turk & Providenciales

PO Box 114, Providenciales, Turks & Caicos Islands ☎ (649) 946-4255 Tx: none Fax: (649) 946-5781 SITA: n/a
F: 1978 ⁂ 98 Head: A.V. Butterfield, Sr. IATA: 254 ICAO: TURK NATIONAL Net: n/a

☐ VQ-TAP	Piper PA-23-250 Aztec F	27-7854124	N43BD	0078		2 LY IO-540-C4B5	2359			
☐ VQ-TAA	Britten-Norman BN-2A-26 Islander	2016	N385KG	0079	0680	2 LY O-540-E4C5	2994			
☐ VQ-TAH	Britten-Norman BN-2A Islander	154	N154BN	0070		2 LY O-540-E4C5	2858			

VT = INDIA (Republic of India) (Bharatka Ganatantra)

Capital: New Delhi Official Language: Hindi, English Population: 970,0 million Square Km: 3287590 Dialling code: +91 Year established: 1947 Acting political head: Atel Bihari Vajpayee (Prime Minister)

Government / Corporate / Executive / VIP Aircraft

☐ K2412	Boeing 737-2A8 (A)	23036 / 977	VT-EHW	0083	0684	2 PW JT8D-17	52390	VIP / mil transp		Indian Air Force
☐ K2413	Boeing 737-2A8 (A)	23037 / 982	VT-EHX	0083	0384	2 PW JT8D-17	52390	VIP / mil transp		Indian Air Force
☐ K2899	Boeing 707-337C	19988 / 736	VT-DXT	0068	0487	4 PW JT3D-3B/7	148800	VIP/Frt/Research		Aviation Research Centre/opb Indian A.F
☐ K3186	Boeing 737-2A8	20484 / 275	VT-EAK	0071	0793	2 PW JT8D-9A	49442	VIP / mil transp	CD-BE	Indian Air Force
☐ K3187	Boeing 737-2A8	20483 / 273	VT-EAJ	0070	0793	2 PW JT8D-9A	49442	VIP / mil transp	CD-AM	Indian Air Force
☐ VT-DVB	Boeing 707-337C	19248 / 549	K2900	0070	0487	4 PW JT3D-3B/7	148800	VIP/Frt/Research		Aviation Research Centre/opb Indian A.F
☐ VT-EHB	Beech King Air B200	BB-972	N18409	0081		2 PWC PT6A-42	5670	VIP		Gvmt of Orissa State
☐ VT-ELX	De Havilland DHC-6 Twin Otter 300	825	C-GIIG*	0085	0886	2 PWC PT6A-27	6350	Surveyer		Dep of Mines Geological Survey/Scintrex
☐ VT-ENM	Beech King Air B200	BB-1236	N72473	0086		2 PWC PT6A-42	5675	VIP / Research		Aviation Research Centre/opb Indian AF
☐ VT-EPY	Beech King Air B200	BB-1277	N7241L	0087		2 PWC PT6A-42	5670	VIP		Gvmt of Maharashtra
☐ VT-EUX	Cessna 560 Citation V Ultra	560-0299	N5168F*	0095	1195	2 PWC JT15D-5D	7394	VIP		Gvmt of Tamil Nadu
☐ VT-JNK	Beech King Air 350 (B300)	FL-160	N1100A*	0097	0997	2 PWC PT6A-60A	6804	VIP		Gvmt of Jammu & Kashmir
☐ VT-MGJ	Beech King Air 350 (B300)	FL-192	N2192V*	0098	0298	2 PWC PT6A-60A	6804	VIP		Gvmt of Maharashtra
☐ VT-MPG	Beech King Air B200	BB-1445	N8121M	0093	0895	2 PWC PT6A-42	5670	VIP		Gvmt of Madhya Pradesh
☐ VT-TNA	Bell 412EP	36091	N21853*	0095	0795	2 PWC PT6T-3D TwinPac	5398	VIP		Gvmt of Tamil Nadu
☐ VT-UPA	Beech King Air 300LW	FA-230	N80679	0093	0494	2 PWC PT6A-60A	5670	VIP		Gvmt of Uttar Pradesh

AEROCOPTER SERVICES, Pvt Ltd — Mumbai-Juhu

Bellman Hangar No. 10, Juhu Airport, Santacruz (West), Mumbai 400054, India ☎ (22) 610 40 81 Tx: n/a Fax: (22) 610 40 82 SITA: n/a
F: 1991 ⁂ 75 Head: Ajit Karnik Net: n/a Currently a maintenance/overhaul (Helicopters & Dornier 228) company but intends to start commuter-type operations. Aircraft type not yet selected.

AIR-INDIA, Ltd = AI / AIC (formerly Air-India International) — Mumbai-Santa Cruz

Air-India Building, Nariman Point, Mumbai 400021, India ☎ (22) 202 41 42 Tx: 1178127 ai in Fax: (22) 202 48 97 SITA: n/a
F: 1948 ⁂ 18750 Head: Michael P. Mascarenhas IATA: 098 ICAO: AIRINDIA Net: http://www.airindia.com

☐ VT-EJG	Airbus Industrie A310-304	406	F-WWCG*	0086	0486	2 GE CF6-80C2A2	153000	C29Y181	HK-GJ	Yamuna
☐ VT-EJH	Airbus Industrie A310-304	407	F-WWCH*	0086	0586	2 GE CF6-80C2A2	153000	C29Y181	JK-CF	Tista
☐ VT-EJI	Airbus Industrie A310-304	413	F-WWCJ*	0086	0586	2 GE CF6-80C2A2	153000	C29Y181	JM-CF	Saraswati
☐ VT-EJJ	Airbus Industrie A310-304	428	F-WWCR*	0086	1086	2 GE CF6-80C2A2	153000	C29Y181	HK-FG	Beas
☐ VT-EJK	Airbus Industrie A310-304	429	F-WWCS*	0086	1286	2 GE CF6-80C2A2	153000	C29Y181	HK-GL	Gomati
☐ VT-EJL	Airbus Industrie A310-304	392	F-WWCB*	0085	0387	2 GE CF6-80C2A2	153000	C29Y181	HK-GM	Sabarmati
☐ VT-EQS	Airbus Industrie A310-304	538	F-WWCP*	0090	0890	2 GE CF6-80C2A2	153000	C29Y181	HL-AE	Krishna / lsf Orix Kite Corp.
☐ VT-EQT	Airbus Industrie A310-304	544	F-WWCL*	0090	0890	2 GE CF6-80C2A2	153000	C29Y181	JM-DF	Narmada / lsf Indus Two Barclays Bank
☐ VT-EHN	Airbus Industrie A300B4-203	177	F-WZMV*	0082	0782	2 GE CF6-50C2	165000	F22Y216	HK-FM	Ganga
☐ VT-EHO	Airbus Industrie A300B4-203	180	F-WZMX*	0082	0882	2 GE CF6-50C2	165000	F22Y216	HK-FJ	Godavari
☐ VT-EHQ	Airbus Industrie A300B4-203	190	F-WZMI*	0082	1182	2 GE CF6-50C2	165000	F22Y216	HK-FL	Cauveri
☐ VT-EBE	Boeing 747-237B	19960 / 130		0071	0471	4 PW JT9D-7J	362874	F16C40Y338	JM-CE	Shah Jehan
☐ VT-EBN	Boeing 747-237B	20459 / 185		0072	0372	4 PW JT9D-7J	362874	F16C40Y338	JL-CM	Rajendra Chola
☐ VT-EDU	Boeing 747-237B	21182 / 277		0075	1275	4 PW JT9D-7J	362874	F16C40Y338	JL-CH	Akbar
☐ VT-EFU	Boeing 747-237B	21829 / 390		0079		4 PW JT9D-7Q	362874	F16C40Y338	JM-CD	Krishna Deva Raya
☐ VT-EGA	Boeing 747-237B	21993 / 414		0079	1279	4 PW JT9D-7Q	362874	F16C40Y338	JM-CG	Samudra Gupta
☐ VT-EGB	Boeing 747-237B	21994 / 431		0080	0280	4 PW JT9D-7Q	362874	F16C40Y338	JM-CK	Mahendra Varman
☐ VT-EGC	Boeing 747-237B	21995 / 434		0080	0480	4 PW JT9D-7Q	362874	F16C40Y338	EL-AC	Harsha Vardhana

645 registration type of aircraft cn/fn ex/ex* mfd del powered by mtow kg configuration selcal name/fln/specialitites/remarks

registration	type of aircraft	cn/fn	ex/ex*	mfd	del	powered by	mtow kg	configuration	selcal	name/fln/specialitites/remarks
☐ VT-EPW	Boeing 747-337 (M)	24159 / 711	N6018N*	0088	1088	4 GE CF6-80C2B1	377842	F16C38Y227 / Plt	HK-JL	Shivaji
☐ VT-EPX	Boeing 747-337 (M)	24160 / 719	N6046P*	0088	1188	4 GE CF6-80C2B1	377842	F16C38Y227 / Plt	HK-JM	Narasimha Varman / lsf Linden City Ac
☐ VT-ESM	Boeing 747-437	27078 / 987		0093	0893	4 PW PW4056	394625	F16C42Y390	JL-CD	Konark
☐ VT-ESN	Boeing 747-437	27164 / 1003		0093	1193	4 PW PW4056	394625	F16C42Y390	JL-CF	Tanjore
☐ VT-ESO	Boeing 747-437	27165 / 1009		0093	1293	4 PW PW4056	394625	F16C42Y390	JL-CE	Khajuraho
☐ VT-ESP	Boeing 747-437	27214 / 1034		0094	0694	4 PW PW4056	394625	F16C42Y390	JL-CG	Ajanta
☐ VT-EVA	Boeing 747-437	28094 / 1089		0096	1096	4 PW PW4056	394625	F16C42Y390	JL-CK	Agra / lsf Veena Leasing Ltd
☐ VT-EVB	Boeing 747-437	28095 / 1093		0096	1196	4 PW PW4056	394625	F16C42Y390	JL-DF	Velha Goa / lsf Veena Leasing Ltd

ALLIANCE AIR = CD / LLR (Airline Allied Services, Ltd dba / Subsidiary of Indian Airlines, Ltd) — Delhi-Indira Gandhi Int'l

Domestic Arrival Hall, 1st Floor, IGI Airport, New Delhi 110037, India ☎ (11) 566 24 58 Tx: none Fax: (11) 566 20 06 SITA: n/a
F: 1996 n/a Head: J.R.D. Rao IATA: 296 ICAO: ALLIED Net: n/a

registration	type of aircraft	cn/fn	ex/ex*	mfd	del	powered by	mtow kg	configuration	selcal	name/fln/specialitites/remarks
☐ VT-EGD	Boeing 737-2A8 (A)	22280 / 671		0680	0197	2 PW JT8D-17A	52390	Y119	KL-EJ	
☐ VT-EGF	Boeing 737-2A8 (A)	22282 / 681	N8292V*	0780	1298	2 PW JT8D-17A	52390	Y119	KL-FG	
☐ VT-EGG	Boeing 737-2A8 (A)	22283 / 689		0880	0496	2 PW JT8D-17A	52390	Y119	KL-FH	
☐ VT-EGH	Boeing 737-2A8 (A)	22284 / 739		0281	0397	2 PW JT8D-17A	52390	Y119	KL-FJ	
☐ VT-EGI	Boeing 737-2A8 (A)	22285 / 798		0981	0496	2 PW JT8D-17A	52390	Y119	KL-FM	
☐ VT-EGJ	Boeing 737-2A8 (A)	22286 / 799		0981	1298	2 PW JT8D-17A	52390	Y119	KL-GH	
☐ VT-EHE	Boeing 737-2A8 (A)	22860 / 899		0882	0998	2 PW JT8D-17A	52390	Y119	BL-DH	
☐ VT-EHF	Boeing 737-2A8 (A)	22861 / 902		0882	1298	2 PW JT8D-17A	52390	Y119	CM-AF	
☐ VT-EHG	Boeing 737-2A8 (A)	22862 / 903		0882	0497	2 PW JT8D-17A	52390	Y119	CD-BG	
☐ VT-EHH	Boeing 737-2A8 (A)	22863 / 907		0982	0298	2 PW JT8D-17A	52390	Y119	BL-CH	

ARCHANA AIRWAYS, Ltd = F5 / ACY (Associated with Bhartiya Vehicles & Engineering, Co. Ltd) — Delhi-Indira Gandhi Int'l

41-A Friends Colony East, Mathura Road, New Delhi 110065, India ☎ (11) 684 20 01 Tx: 3175092 in Fax: (11) 684 77 62 SITA: n/a
F: 1991 240 Head: A.K. Bhartiya IATA: 679 ICAO: ARCHANA Net: n/a

registration	type of aircraft	cn/fn	ex/ex*	mfd	del	powered by	mtow kg	configuration	selcal	name/fln/specialitites/remarks
☐ VT-ETA	Let 410UVP-E9	922701		0092	0093	2 WA M-601E	6600	Y17		Divya
☐ VT-ETW	Let 410UVP-E9D	962632	OK-BDK*	0096	0397	2 WA M-601E	6600	Y17		

BENGAL AIR SERVICES, Pvt Ltd — Calcutta

EC-196 Salt Lake, Calcutta 700064, India ☎ (33) 358 27 01 Tx: none Fax: (33) 337 94 09 SITA: n/a
F: 1998 n/a Head: S. Mallick Net: n/a

registration	type of aircraft	cn/fn	ex/ex*	mfd	del	powered by	mtow kg	configuration	selcal	name/fln/specialitites/remarks
☐ VT-BAA	BAe (HS) 748-424 Super 2B	1800 / 281	C-GBCN	0084	1198	2 RR Dart 536-2	21092	Y44		
☐ VT-BAB	BAe (HS) 748-424 Super 2B	1801 / 282	C-GBCS	0084	0499	2 RR Dart 536-2	21092	Y44		

BHARATAIR (Bharat Commerce and Industries, Ltd dba) — Calcutta & Delhi-Safdarjung

No. 5 Bright Street, Calcutta 700019, India ☎ (33) 44 86 67 Tx: 213421 grup in Fax: (33) 29 50 37 SITA: n/a
F: 1946 40 Head: C.L. Kejriwal ICAO: BHARAT Net: n/a Aircraft below MTOW 1361 kg: Bell 47G & Piper PA-25.

registration	type of aircraft	cn/fn	ex/ex*	mfd	del	powered by	mtow kg	configuration	selcal	name/fln/specialitites/remarks
☐ VT-ASB	Reims/Cessna F406 Caravan II	F406-0031	D-IBOM	0089	0894	2 PWC PT6A-112	4468			lsf Century Textiles & Industries Ltd

BLUE DART AVIATION, Ltd (Subsidiary of Blue Dart Express, (P) Ltd) — Chennai

88/89 Old International Terminal, Meenambakkam Airport, Chennai 600027, India ☎ (44) 233 49 95 Tx: none Fax: (44) 234 90 67 SITA: n/a
F: 1994 350 Head: Niteen M.Gupte Net: n/a

registration	type of aircraft	cn/fn	ex/ex*	mfd	del	powered by	mtow kg	configuration	selcal	name/fln/specialitites/remarks
☐ VT-EDR	Boeing 737-2A8 (F) (A)	21163 / 434		0075	0596	2 PW JT8D-9A	52390	Freighter	BL-AG	Vision II / lsf Blue Dart Exp./cvtd-2A8
☐ VT-EDS	Boeing 737-2A8 (F) (A)	21164 / 435		0075	0596	2 PW JT8D-9A	52390	Freighter	BL-AM	lsf Blue Dart Express / cvtd -2A8

BORDER SECURITY FORCE – Flying Unit (Division of Ministry of Home Affairs) — Delhi-Indira Gandhi Int'l

Deputy Director Air, Nirman 1, New Delhi 110001, India ☎ (11) 436 00 16 Tx: n/a Fax: (11) 436 17 94 SITA: n/a
F: n/a n/a Head: n/a Net: n/a Non-commercial national organisation conducting surveillance, SAR & & liaison/transport missions.

registration	type of aircraft	cn/fn	ex/ex*	mfd	del	powered by	mtow kg	configuration	selcal	name/fln/specialitites/remarks
☐ VT-EBA	Eurocopter (HAL/Aerosp.) SA315B Cheetah	CH-243		0095	0197	1 TU Artouste IIIB	1950	Survey/Utility		
☐ VT-EQL	Eurocopter (HAL/Aerosp.) SA316B Chetak	AH-303		0090	1090	1 TU Artouste IIIB	2200	Survey/Utility		
☐ VT-BSA	Beech King Air B200	BB-1485	N1509X	0094	0795	2 PWC PT6A-42	5670	Survey/Liaison		
☐ VT-EHK	Beech King Air B200	BB-985	N1841Z	0082	0182	2 PWC PT6A-42	5670	Survey/Liaison		
☐ VT-DXH	HAL (BAe/HS) 748-224 Srs 2	K/748/513 / 65		0068	0094	2 RR Dart 533-2	20183	Survey/Liaison		std DEL
☐ VT-EAT	HAL (BAe/HS) 748-224 Srs 2	K/748/540		0072	0691	2 RR Dart 533-2	20183	Survey/Liaison		
☐ VT-EAV	HAL (BAe/HS) 748-224 Srs 2	K/748/542		0072	0691	2 RR Dart 533-2	20183	Survey/Liaison		
☐ VT-EHL	HAL (BAe/HS) 748-224 Srs 2	K/748/549	VT-EBC	0072	0382	2 RR Dart 533-2	20183	Survey/Liaison		
☐ VT-EIR	HAL (BAe/HS) 748-224 Srs 2M (SCD)	K/748/587		0083	0984	2 RR Dart 536-2T	20183	Svy/Frtr/Liaison		lsf Hindustan Aeronautics Ltd / std DEL

DECCAN AVIATION, (P) Ltd — Bangalore-Jakkur

Jakkur Aerodrome, Bellary Road, Bangalore 560064, India ☎ (80) 856 13 78 Tx: noen Fax: (80) 856 13 79 SITA: n/a
F: 1995 50 Head: Capt. G.R. Gopinath Net: http://www.deccan-air.com

registration	type of aircraft	cn/fn	ex/ex*	mfd	del	powered by	mtow kg	configuration	selcal	name/fln/specialitites/remarks
☐ VT-DAK	Bell 206L-3 LongRanger III	51612	9N-ADX	0092	0097	1 AN 250-C30P	1882	6 Pax		lsf ITC Leasing Inc.
☐ VT-DAL	Bell 206L-3 LongRanger III	51406	N87654	0090	0097	1 AN 250-C30P	1882	6 Pax		lsf ITC Leasing Inc.
☐ VT-DAM	Bell 212	31191	G-BXIK	0081	1198	2 PWC PT6T-3B TwinPac	5080	13 Pax		lsf BHL

DELHI GULF AIRWAYS SERVICES, (P) Ltd — Delhi-Safdarjung

Safdarjung Airport, New Delhi 110003, India ☎ (11) 463 11 70 Tx: 3161821 in Fax: none SITA: n/a
F: 1984 30 Head: Vinod Kumar Net: n/a

registration	type of aircraft	cn/fn	ex/ex*	mfd	del	powered by	mtow kg	configuration	selcal	name/fln/specialitites/remarks
☐ VT-EHP	Eurocopter (Aerosp.) AS350B Ecureuil	1539		0082		1 TU Arriel 1B	1950			

DWARKA AIR TAXI, Ltd — Delhi

B-14 Vasant Marg, Vasant Vihar, New Delhi 110057, India ☎ (11) 614 62 00 Tx: none Fax: (11) 614 41 23 SITA: n/a
F: 1998 n/a Head: n/a Net: n/a

registration	type of aircraft	cn/fn	ex/ex*	mfd	del	powered by	mtow kg	configuration	selcal	name/fln/specialitites/remarks
☐ VT-DAT	Cessna 404 Titan II	404-0855	N404N	0081	0398	2 CO GTSIO-520-M	3810			

EASTERN AIRWAYS, Ltd — Calcutta

Four Mangoe Lane, 7th Floor, 4 Surendra Mohan Ghosh Sarani, Calcutta, India ☎ (33) 220 23 91 Tx: none Fax: (33) 248 23 94 SITA: n/a
F: 1995 25 Head: R. Takru Net: n/a

registration	type of aircraft	cn/fn	ex/ex*	mfd	del	powered by	mtow kg	configuration	selcal	name/fln/specialitites/remarks
☐ VT-EAU	Hawker 800B (BAe 125-800B)	258120	HB-VLI	0089	1195	2 GA TFE731-5R-1H	12428	8 Pax	AQ-KP	lsf ITC Classic Finance Ltd

GESCO – Aviation Dept. (Joint venture of Gulf Helicopters & GESCO-The Great Eastern Shipping, Co. Ltd/formerly GAL Gulf Helicopters) — Mumbai

Offshore division, 35C Tardeo Road, Mumbai 400034, India ☎ (22) 496 57 33 Tx: 01171874 gesc in Fax: (22) 495 04 54 SITA: n/a
F: 1994 69 Head: S.K. Srivastava Net: n/a

registration	type of aircraft	cn/fn	ex/ex*	mfd	del	powered by	mtow kg	configuration	selcal	name/fln/specialitites/remarks
☐ VT-HGA	Bell 212	30902	A7-HAJ	0079		2 PWC PT6T-3 TwinPac	5080	13 Pax		lsf Gulf Helicopters
☐ VT-HGB	Bell 212	31124	A7-HAN	0080	0896	2 PWC PT6T-3 TwinPac	5080	13 Pax		lsf Gulf Helicopters
☐ VT-HGC	Bell 212	31149	A7-HAT	0080	0896	2 PWC PT6T-3B TwinPac	5080	13 Pax		lsf Gulf Helicopters
☐ VT-HGD	Bell 212	30918	A7-HAL	0078	1296	2 PWC PT6T-3 TwinPac	5080	13 Pax		lsf Gulf Helicopters

GUJARAT AIRWAYS, Ltd = G8 / GUJ — Vadodara

1st Floor, Sapna Shopping Centre, 20 Vishnas Colony, Alkapuri, Vadodara 390005, India ☎ (265) 32 29 26 Tx: none Fax: (265) 33 96 28 SITA: n/a
F: 1994 142 Head: Ms. Amerila Kaszarek ICAO: GUJARATAIR Net: http://www.gujarat.com

registration	type of aircraft	cn/fn	ex/ex*	mfd	del	powered by	mtow kg	configuration	selcal	name/fln/specialitites/remarks
☐ VT-AGA	Beech 1900D Airliner	UE-121	N3221A*	0094	0695	2 PWC PT6A-67D	7688	Y19		Pramukh I
☐ VT-AGB	Beech 1900D Airliner	UE-111	N3119U*	0094	0695	2 PWC PT6A-67D	7688	Y19		Pramukh II
☐ VT-AGC	Beech 1900D Airliner	UE-274	N11015*	0097	0997	2 PWC PT6A-67D	7688	Y19		
☐ VT-AGD	Beech 1900D Airliner	UE-280	N11284*	0097	1297	2 PWC PT6A-67D	7688	Y19		
☐ VT-AGE	Beech 1900D Airliner	UE-314	N22889*	0098	1098	2 PWC PT6A-67D	7688	Y19		Nina

INDIA INTERNATIONAL AIRWAYS, Ltd = IIL — Delhi

Thapar House, 3rd Floor, 124 Janpath, New Delhi 110001, India ☎ (11) 336 78 64 Tx: none Fax: (11) 336 89 51 SITA: n/a
F: 1990 50 Head: Surinder Singh Gill ICAO: INDIA INTER Net: n/a

registration	type of aircraft	cn/fn	ex/ex*	mfd	del	powered by	mtow kg	configuration	selcal	name/fln/specialitites/remarks
☐ VT-ERQ	Bell 206B JetRanger III	3455	N21197	0081	0191	1 AN 250-C20B	1451			Rani
☐ VT-ETM	Bell 206B JetRanger III	2494	G-KMAC	0078	1193	1 AN 250-C20B	1451			
☐ VT-MMT	Piper PA-31-350 Navajo Panther II	31-8052141	N35894	0080	0895	2 LY TIO-540-J2BD	3175			cvtd Navajo Chieftain
☐ VT-SAT	Bell 222U	47574	N50GH	0089	0895	2 LY LTS101-750C.1	3742			
☐ VT-EUN	Cessna 550 Citation II	550-0352	N352AM	0082	0894	2 PWC JT15D-4	6033			Shivani
☐ VT-EQZ	Hawker 3B (HS 125-3B)	25133	G-ILLS	0067	0190	2 RR Viper 522	9843			Raja

INDIAN AIRLINES, Ltd = IC / IAC — Delhi-Indira Gandhi Int'l

Airlines House, 113 Gurdware Rakabganj Road, Parliament St., New Delhi 110000, India ☎ (11) 371 89 51 Tx: 316110 ichq in Fax: (11) 371 45 46 SITA: n/a
F: 1953 21650 Head: Anil Baijal IATA: 058 ICAO: INDAIR Net: http://www.nic.in/indian-airlines

registration	type of aircraft	cn/fn	ex/ex*	mfd	del	powered by	mtow kg	configuration	selcal	name/fln/specialitites/remarks
☐ VT-EJN	HAL (Dornier) 228-201	K/228/1002		0086	0697	2 GA TPE331-5-252D	5980	Y19		lic.prod. of Dornier cn 8060
☐ VT-EIO	Dornier 228-201	8037	D-IDBG*	0084	0697	2 GA TPE331-5-252D	5980	Y19		
☐ VT-EJO	Dornier 228-201	8054	D-CALI*	0085	0697	2 GA TPE331-5-252D	5980	Y19		
☐ VT-EGE	Boeing 737-2A8 (A)	22281 / 679	N8291V*	0780	0780	2 PW JT8D-17A	52390	Y119	KL-EM	
☐ VT-EGM	Boeing 737-2A8C (A)	22473 / 747		0381	0381	2 PW JT8D-17A	52390	Y119	BL-CJ	
☐ VT-EPB	Airbus Industrie A320-231	045	F-WWDY*	0089	0689	2 IAE V2500-A1	73500	C20Y125	JP-EH	
☐ VT-EPC	Airbus Industrie A320-231	046	F-WWDG*	0089	0689	2 IAE V2500-A1	73500	C20Y125	JP-EK	
☐ VT-EPD	Airbus Industrie A320-231	047	F-WWDP*	0089	0789	2 IAE V2500-A1	73500	C20Y125	JP-EL	

☐ VT-EPE	Airbus Industrie A320-231	048	F-WWDU*	0089	0789	2 IAE V2500-A1	73500	C20Y125	JP-EM	
☐ VT-EPF	Airbus Industrie A320-231	049	F-WWIA*	0089	0789	2 IAE V2500-A1	73500	C20Y125	JP-FG	
☐ VT-EPG	Airbus Industrie A320-231	050	F-WWDR*	0089	0889	2 IAE V2500-A1	73500	C20Y125	JP-FH	
☐ VT-EPH	Airbus Industrie A320-231	051	F-WWIB*	0089	0989	2 IAE V2500-A1	73500	C20Y125	JP-FK	
☐ VT-EPI	Airbus Industrie A320-231	056	F-WWIC*	0089	0989	2 IAE V2500-A1	73500	C20Y125	JP-FL	
☐ VT-EPJ	Airbus Industrie A320-231	057	F-WWIF*	0089	0989	2 IAE V2500-A1	73500	C20Y125	JP-FM	
☐ VT-EPK	Airbus Industrie A320-231	058	F-WWID*	0089	1089	2 IAE V2500-A1	73500	C20Y125	JP-GH	
☐ VT-EPL	Airbus Industrie A320-231	074	F-WWIQ*	0089	1189	2 IAE V2500-A1	73500	C20Y125	JP-GK	
☐ VT-EPM	Airbus Industrie A320-231	075	F-WWIR*	0089	0190	2 IAE V2500-A1	73500	C20Y125	JP-GL	
☐ VT-EPO	Airbus Industrie A320-231	080	F-WWIX*	0089	0190	2 IAE V2500-A1	73500	C20Y125	JP-HK	
☐ VT-EPP	Airbus Industrie A320-231	089	F-WWDT*	0090	0290	2 IAE V2500-A1	73500	C20Y125	JP-HL	
☐ VT-EPQ	Airbus Industrie A320-231	090	F-WWDX*	0090	0990	2 IAE V2500-A1	73500	C20Y125	JP-HM	
☐ VT-EPR	Airbus Industrie A320-231	095	F-WWDS*	0090	0990	2 IAE V2500-A1	73500	C20Y125	JP-KL	
☐ VT-EPS	Airbus Industrie A320-231	096	F-WWDU*	0090	0990	2 IAE V2500-A1	73500	C20Y125	JP-KM	
☐ VT-EPT	Airbus Industrie A320-231	097	F-WWDV*	0090	0990	2 IAE V2500-A1	73500	C20Y125	JP-LM	
☐ VT-ESA	Airbus Industrie A320-231	396	F-WWBK*	0092	0293	2 IAE V2500-A1	73500	C20Y125		
☐ VT-ESB	Airbus Industrie A320-231	398	F-WWDQ*	0093	0393	2 IAE V2500-A1	73500	C20Y125		
☐ VT-ESC	Airbus Industrie A320-231	416	F-WWBP*	0093	0693	2 IAE V2500-A1	73500	C20Y125		
☐ VT-ESD	Airbus Industrie A320-231	423	F-WWIT*	0093	0693	2 IAE V2500-A1	73500	C20Y125		
☐ VT-ESE	Airbus Industrie A320-231	431	F-WWBQ*	0093	0793	2 IAE V2500-A1	73500	C20Y125		
☐ VT-ESF	Airbus Industrie A320-231	432	F-WWBS*	0093	0893	2 IAE V2500-A1	73500	C20Y125		
☐ VT-ESG	Airbus Industrie A320-231	451	F-WWIN*	0093	1293	2 IAE V2500-A1	73500	C20Y125		
☐ VT-ESH	Airbus Industrie A320-231	469	F-WWBD*	0094	0594	2 IAE V2500-A1	73500	C20Y125		
☐ VT-ESI	Airbus Industrie A320-231	486	F-WWBH*	0094	0994	2 IAE V2500-A1	73500	C20Y125		
☐ VT-ESJ	Airbus Industrie A320-231	490	F-WWDT*	0094	1094	2 IAE V2500-A1	73500	C20Y125		
☐ VT-ESK	Airbus Industrie A320-231	492	F-WWBU*	0094	1194	2 IAE V2500-A1	73500	C20Y125		
☐ VT-ESL	Airbus Industrie A320-231	499	F-WWDO*	0094	1294	2 IAE V2500-A1	73500	C20Y125		
☐ VT-EDW	Airbus Industrie A300B2-101	036	F-WUAT*	0076	1176	2 GE CF6-50C	142000	C33Y215		
☐ VT-EDY	Airbus Industrie A300B2-101	059	F-WZEI*	0078	0578	2 GE CF6-50C	142000	C30Y215	AM-CJ	cvtd -1C
☐ VT-EDZ	Airbus Industrie A300B2-101	060	F-WZEJ*	0078	0678	2 GE CF6-50C	142000	C33Y215	GH-CK	cvtd -1C
☐ VT-EFV	Airbus Industrie A300B2-101	088	F-WZED*	0079	1079	2 GE CF6-50C	142000	C33Y215		cvtd -1C
☐ VT-EFW	Airbus Industrie A300B2-101	111	F-WZEI*	0080	0780	2 GE CF6-50C	142000	C33Y215	AM-DE	
☐ VT-EFX	Airbus Industrie A300B2-101	113	F-WZEJ*	0080	0880	2 GE CF6-50C	142000	C33Y215	BL-AK	
☐ VT-EHC	Airbus Industrie A300B4-203	181	F-WZMY*	0082	0582	2 GE CF6-50C2	165000	C32Y215	BL-AJ	
☐ VT-EHD	Airbus Industrie A300B4-203	182	F-WZMZ*	0082	0582	2 GE CF6-50C2	165000	C32Y215		
☐ VT-ELW	Airbus Industrie A300B2-101	026	F-ODRE	0076	0886	2 GE CF6-50C	142000	C33Y215		cvtd -1C
☐ VT-EVC	Airbus Industrie A300B4-203	262	N262GE	0083	0698	2 GE CF6-50C2	165000	C32Y215		lsf GECA
☐ VT-EVD	Airbus Industrie A300B4-203	240	EI-CEB	0083	0598	2 GE CF6-50C2	165000	C32Y215		lsf GECA

JAGSON AIRLINES (Subsidiary of Jagson International, Ltd) — Delhi-Indira Gandhi Int'l

12E Vandana Building, 11 Tolstoy Marg, New Delhi 110001, India ☎ (11) 372 15 93 Tx: 03163083 jnbr in Fax: (11) 332 46 93 SITA: n/a
F: 1990 n/a Head: J.P. Gupta Net: n/a

☐ VT-ESS	Dornier 228-201	8017	A5-RGC	0083	0392	2 GA TPE331-5-252D	5980	Y18		cvtd -200
☐ VT-EUM	Dornier 228-201	8096	D-CAAL	0086	0594	2 GA TPE331-5-252D	5980	Y18		lsf Dornier / cvtd -200

JET AIRWAYS (India), Ltd = 9W / JAI (Member of Tailwinds Company, Dubai/UAE / formerly Jet Airways (India), Private Ltd) — Mumbai-Santa Cruz

S.M. Centre, Andheri-Kurla Road, Andheri (E), Mumbai 400059, India ☎ (22) 821 50 80 Tx: none Fax: (22) 822 10 40 SITA: n/a
F: 1992 2300 Head: Naresh Goyal IATA: 589 ICAO: JET AIRWAYS Net: http://www.jetairways.com

☐ VT-	ATR 72-500 (72-212A)	565	F-WWEE*			2 PWC PW127F	22500	Y70		oo-delivery 0099
☐ VT-	ATR 72-500 (72-212A)	570	F-WWEG*			2 PWC PW127F	22500	Y70		oo-delivery 0099
☐ VT-	ATR 72-500 (72-212A)	572	F-WWEI*			2 PWC PW127F	22500	Y70		oo-delivery 0099
☐ VT-	ATR 72-500 (72-212A)	575	F-WWEJ*			2 PWC PW127F	22500	Y70		oo-delivery 0099
☐ VT-	ATR 72-500 (72-212A)	582	F-WWEL*			2 PWC PW127F	22500	Y70		oo-delivery 0099
☐ VT-JAL	Boeing 737-5Y0	25191 / 2260	N191G	0092	1196	2 CFMI CFM56-3B1	60555	C16Y88		lsf GECA
☐ VT-JAW	Boeing 737-5H6	27355 / 2646	9M-MFH	0094	1298	2 CFMI CFM56-3C1	52389	C16Y88		lsf GECA
☐ VT-JAB	Boeing 737-33A	24791 / 1984	N222AW	0091	0493	2 CFMI CFM56-3C1	61235	C20Y100		lsf AWAS
☐ VT-JNE	Boeing 737-71Q	29043 / 138	N29879*	0098	1298	2 CFMI CFM56-7B24	69400	C20Y100		lsf TOMB
☐ VT-JNF	Boeing 737-71Q	29044 / 152	N29887*	0098	1298	2 CFMI CFM56-7B24	69400	C20Y100		lsf TOMB
☐ VT-JNG	Boeing 737-71Q	29045 / 169	N29945*	1298	1298	2 CFMI CFM56-7B24	69400	C20Y100		lsf TOMB
☐ VT-JNH	Boeing 737-71Q	29046 / 181	N29976*	0199	0199	2 CFMI CFM56-7B24	69400	C20Y100		lsf TOMB
☐ VT-JAE	Boeing 737-4H6	27086 / 2426	9M-MMO	0093	0494	2 CFMI CFM56-3C1	62822	C24Y112	MQ-CF	lsf ANZ Grindlays Export Finance Ltd
☐ VT-JAF	Boeing 737-4H6	27168 / 2435	9M-MMP	0093	0594	2 CFMI CFM56-3C1	62822	C24Y112	MQ-CG	lsf ANZ Grindlays Export Finance Ltd
☐ VT-JAG	Boeing 737-4Y0	24345 / 1731	EI-CEU	0089	0995	2 CFMI CFM56-3C1	62822	C24Y112		lsf GECA
☐ VT-JAI	Boeing 737-4S3	24165 / 1720	N690MA	0089	0596	2 CFMI CFM56-3C1	62822	C24Y112		lsf Hanway Corp.
☐ VT-JAJ	Boeing 737-4S3	24166 / 1722	N691MA	0089	0796	2 CFMI CFM56-3C1	62822	C24Y112		lsf Hanway Corp.
☐ VT-JAK	Boeing 737-4Y0	24687 / 1865	D-ABAC	0090	0796	2 CFMI CFM56-3C1	62822	C24Y112		lsf GECA
☐ VT-JAM	Boeing 737-48E	25773 / 2905	N773SR	0097	0997	2 CFMI CFM56-3C1	62822	C24Y112		lsf SUNR
☐ VT-JAN	Boeing 737-48E	25775 / 2925	N775SR	0097	1097	2 CFMI CFM56-3C1	62822	C24Y112		lsf SUNR
☐ VT-JAP	Boeing 737-497	25664 / 2393	F-GRSC	0092	1097	2 CFMI CFM56-3C1	65090	C24Y112		lsf GECA
☐ VT-JAQ	Boeing 737-497	25663 / 2382	F-GRSB	0092	1197	2 CFMI CFM56-3C1	65090	C24Y112		lsf GECA
☐ VT-JAR	Boeing 737-45R	29032 / 2943		0097	1197	2 CFMI CFM56-3C1	62822	C24Y112		
☐ VT-JAS	Boeing 737-45R	29033 / 2963		0097	1297	2 CFMI CFM56-3C1	62822	C24Y112		
☐ VT-JAT	Boeing 737-45R	29034 / 3015		0398	0398	2 CFMI CFM56-3C1	62822	C24Y112		
☐ VT-JAU	Boeing 737-45R	29035 / 3046		0098	0698	2 CFMI CFM56-3C1	62822	C24Y112		
☐ VT-JNA	Boeing 737-86N	28578 / 89	N578GE	0898	0998	2 CFMI CFM56-7B26	70530	C24Y136		lsf GECA
☐ VT-JNB	Boeing 737-86N	28575 / 91	N575GE	0098	0998	2 CFMI CFM56-7B26	70530	C24Y136		lsf GECA
☐ VT-JNC	Boeing 737-85R	29036 / 164	N1787B*	0098	1298	2 CFMI CFM56-7B26	70530	C24Y136		
☐ VT-JND	Boeing 737-85R	29037 / 177	N1787B*	1298	0199	2 CFMI CFM56-7B26	70530	C24Y136		
☐ VT-	Boeing 737-85R					2 CFMI CFM56-7B26	70530	C24Y136		oo-delivery 0699
☐ VT-	Boeing 737-85R					2 CFMI CFM56-7B26	70530	C24Y136		oo-delivery 0799
☐ VT-	Boeing 737-85R					2 CFMI CFM56-7B26	70530	C24Y136		oo-delivery 0100
☐ VT-	Boeing 737-85R					2 CFMI CFM56-7B26	70530	C24Y136		oo-delivery 0200

LUFTHANSA CARGO INDIA, Pvt. Ltd = LF / LCI (Hinduja Cargo Services) (Hinduja Lufthansa Cargo Venture) — Delhi-Indira Gandhi Int'l

Hotel Radisson, Commercial Plaza, Ground Floor, Wing A & B, National Highway 8, New Delhi 110037, India ☎ (11) 689 70 33 Tx: none Fax: (11) 689 57 80 SITA: DELUILH
F: 1996 281 Head: Joseph Matta IATA: 212 ICAO: LUFTHANSA INDIA Net: n/a

☐ VT-LCA	Boeing 727-243 (F) (A)	22052 / 1568	N12411	0080	1196	3 PW JT8D-15	88360	Freighter		lsf LAL Aircraft Leasing GmbH/cvtd -243
☐ VT-LCB	Boeing 727-243 (F) (A)	22053 / 1620	N59412	0080	0896	3 PW JT8D-15	88360	Freighter		lsf LAL Aircraft Leasing GmbH/cvtd -243
☐ VT-LCC	Boeing 727-243 (F) (A)	22167 / 1752	N34415	0081	0996	3 PW JT8D-15	88360	Freighter		lsf LAL Aircraft Leasing GmbH/cvtd -243
☐ VT-LCI	Boeing 727-243 (F) (A)	22168 / 1770	N14416	0081	0197	3 PW JT8D-15	88360	Freighter		lsf LAL Aircraft Leasing GmbH/cvtd -243

MEGAPODE AIRLINES, Ltd (Member of Taj Group of Hotels) — Mumbai-Santa Cruz

Malkani Chambers, Gr.Fl., nr Domestic Airport, Off. Nehru Road, Vile Parle East, Mumbai 400093, India ☎ (22) 617 56 24 Tx: none Fax: (22) 611 36 27 SITA: n/a
F: 1993 10 Head: Pradeep Thampi Net: n/a Company is expected to be renamed TAJ AIR during 1999 & plans to add commuter aircraft.

☐ VT-MPA	Hawker 700B (HS 125-700B)	257172	G-BKFS	0082	1093	2 GA TFE731-3R-1H	11567	Executive		

MESCO AIRLINES, Ltd (Subsidiary of Mid East Integrated Steel Company) — Mumbai-Juhu & Delhi

Hangar No. 10, Juhu Airport, S.V. Road, Mumbai 400054, India ☎ (22) 610 88 07 Tx: none Fax: (22) 610 33 06 SITA: n/a
F: 1992 140 Head: Jitendra Kumar Singh Net: n/a

☐ VT-JKS	Hiller UH-12E	5227		0092	0193	1 LY VO-540-C2A	1406			
☐ VT-RTA	Hiller UH-12E	5228		0092	0193	1 LY VO-540-C2A	1406			
☐ VT-MAB	Eurocopter (Aerosp.) AS350BA Ecureuil	2776		0094	0295	1 TU Arriel 1B	2100			
☐ VT-MAC	Eurocopter (Aerosp.) AS350BA Ecureuil	2838		0094	0295	1 TU Arriel 1B	2100			
☐ VT-MAD	Eurocopter (Aerosp.) AS350BA Ecureuil	1626	F-WYMH*	0082	0395	1 TU Arriel 1B	2100			cvtd AS350B
☐ VT-TAA	TAAL (Partenavia) P.68C Observer 2	NC-398-07-08		0094	0094	2 LY IO-360-A1B6	1990			lsf Mideast Integrated Steels Ltd
☐ VT-TAB	TAAL (Partenavia) AP68TP-600 Viator	9007		0094	0094	2 AN 250-B17C	2850			
☐ VT-MAA	Eurocopter (Aerosp.) SA365N Dauphin 2	6080	VH-AHO	0083	0195	2 TU Arriel 1C	3850			
☐ VT-MAE	Mil Mi-172	356C01		0095	0595	2 IS TV3-117VM-2	13000			
☐ VT-MAF	Mil Mi-172	356C04		0095	1195	2 IS TV3-117VM-2	13000			
☐ VT-MAG	Mil Mi-172	356C02		0096	0396	2 IS TV3-117VM-2	13000			

MILLION AIR (Member of Raymond Group) — Mumbai

c/o Raymonds Ltd, P. Budhkar Marg, Mahindra Towers, B Wing, Worli, Mumbai 400018, India ☎ (22) 493 90 30 Tx: none Fax: (22) 493 90 36 SITA: n/a
F: 1996 30 Head: Gautam Singhania Net: n/a

☐ VT-RLB	Bell 206L-3 LongRanger III	51565	N64EA	0092	0096	1 AN 250-C20P	1882	Executive		
☐ VT-RLC	Bell 206L-3 LongRanger III	51344	N71EA	0090	0096	1 AN 250-C20P	1882	Executive		
☐ VT-RLA	Eurocopter (Aerosp.) AS355N Ecureuil 2	5564	I-ELFE	0094	1295	2 TU Arrius 1A	2540	Executive		lsf Raymond Ltd
☐ VT-VPS	Cessna 550 Citation II	550-0390	N136BC	0082	0096	2 PWC JT15D-4	6033	Executive		

647 registration type of aircraft cn/fn ex/ex* mfd del powered by mtow kg configuration selcal name/fln/specialitites/remarks

NATIONAL AIRPORTS AUTHORITY – Flight Inspection Unit = YXA Delhi-Safdarjung & -Indira Gandhi Int'l

Flt Inspeciton Unit, Safdarjung Airport, New Delhi 110003, India ☎ (11) 61 97 01 Tx: 03174151 naa in Fax: (11) 463 39 90 SITA: n/a
F: 1986 ⋔⋔ 50 Head: n/a Net: n/a Non-commercial national organisation conducting airport/runway/ILS/ flight-inspection & control missions.

registration	type of aircraft	cn/fn	ex/ex*	mfd	del	powered by	mtow kg	configuration	selcal	name/fln/specialitites/remarks
☐ VT-EPU	HAL (Dornier) 228-201	K/228/2016		0088	0389	2 GA TPE331-5-252D	5980	Flight Inspect.		licence prod. of Dornier cn 8090
☐ VT-ENK	Dornier 228-201	8086	D-CANA*	0086	1087	2 GA TPE331-5-252D	5980	Flight Inspect.		
☐ VT-EFQ	HAL (BAe/HS) 748-224 Srs 2	K/748/546	VT-EAZ	0072	0278	2 RR Dart 533-2	20183	Flight Inspect.		
☐ VT-EFR	HAL (BAe/HS) 748-224 Srs 2	K/748/547	VT-EBA	0072	0978	2 RR Dart 533-2	20183	Flight Inspect.		

NATIONAL REMOTE SENSING AGENCY – Flying Unit Hyderabad

Plot No. 6 A&B, I.D.A. Jeedimetla, Hyderabad 500855, India ☎ (40) 309 59 84 Tx: none Fax: (40) 309 54 20 SITA: n/a
F: 1975 ⋔⋔ 50 Head: K. Kalyanaraman Net: n/a Non-commercial government organisation conducting remote sensing work.

registration	type of aircraft	cn/fn	ex/ex*	mfd	del	powered by	mtow kg	configuration	selcal	name/fln/specialitites/remarks
☐ VT-EBB	Beech King Air B200	BB-1486	N1542Z	0094	1296	2 PWC PT6A-42	5670	Surveyer		
☐ VT-EQK	Beech King Air B200	BB-1288	N30850	0088	1188	2 PWC PT6A-42	5670	Surveyer		

PAWAN HANS HELICOPTERS, Ltd = PHE (Swan of the Skies) (a Government of India Enterprise/formerly Pawan Hans, Ltd & Helicopter Corp. of India) Delhi-Safdarjung & Mumbai-Juhu

Safdarjung Airport, Corporate Office, New Delhi 110003, India ☎ (11) 463 25 38 Tx: 3162849 phl in Fax: (11) 460 25 96 SITA: n/a
F: 1985 ⋔⋔ 700 Head: Maj. Gen. (Ret'd) G.S. Hundal ICAO: PAWAN HANS Net: n/a Aircraft below MTOW 1361kg: Robinson R44.

registration	type of aircraft	cn/fn	ex/ex*	mfd	del	powered by	mtow kg	configuration	selcal	name/fln/specialitites/remarks
☐ VT-PHA	Bell 206L-4 LongRanger IV	52019	N6197Y*	0093	0493	1 AN 250-C30P	2018	5 Pax		
☐ VT-PHD	Bell 206L-4 LongRanger IV	52142	N64080*	0096	0596	1 AN 250-C30P	2018	5 Pax		opf Indian Customs
☐ VT-PHE	Bell 206L-4 LongRanger IV	52159	N9217Z*	0096	0596	1 AN 250-C30P	2018	5 Pax		opf Indian Customs
☐ VT-PHH	Bell 407	53210	N52263*	0097	1297	1 AN 250-C47B	2268	5 Pax		
☐ VT-PHI	Bell 407	53212	N52265*	0097	1297	1 AN 250-C47B	2268	5 Pax		
☐ VT-EKZ	Eurocopter (Aerosp.) SA365N Dauphin 2	6209		0086		2 TU Arriel 1C	4000	9 Pax		
☐ VT-ELA	Eurocopter (Aerosp.) SA365N Dauphin 2	6210		0086		2 TU Arriel 1C	4000	9 Pax		
☐ VT-ELB	Eurocopter (Aerosp.) SA365N Dauphin 2	6211	F-WYMI*	0086		2 TU Arriel 1C	4000	9 Pax		
☐ VT-ELD	Eurocopter (Aerosp.) SA365N Dauphin 2	6213		0086		2 TU Arriel 1C	4000	9 Pax		
☐ VT-ELE	Eurocopter (Aerosp.) SA365N Dauphin 2	6214		0086		2 TU Arriel 1C	4000	9 Pax		
☐ VT-ELF	Eurocopter (Aerosp.) SA365N Dauphin 2	6215		0086		2 TU Arriel 1C	4000	9 Pax		
☐ VT-ELG	Eurocopter (Aerosp.) SA365N Dauphin 2	6217		0086		2 TU Arriel 1C	4000	9 Pax		
☐ VT-ELI	Eurocopter (Aerosp.) SA365N Dauphin 2	6236		0087		2 TU Arriel 1C	4000	9 Pax		
☐ VT-ELJ	Eurocopter (Aerosp.) SA365N Dauphin 2	6239		0087		2 TU Arriel 1C	4000	9 Pax		
☐ VT-ELK	Eurocopter (Aerosp.) SA365N Dauphin 2	6245		0087		2 TU Arriel 1C	4000	9 Pax		
☐ VT-ELL	Eurocopter (Aerosp.) SA365N Dauphin 2	6246		0087		2 TU Arriel 1C	4000	9 Pax		
☐ VT-ELM	Eurocopter (Aerosp.) SA365N Dauphin 2	6248		0087		2 TU Arriel 1C	4000	9 Pax		
☐ VT-ELN	Eurocopter (Aerosp.) SA365N Dauphin 2	6254		0087		2 TU Arriel 1C	4000	9 Pax		
☐ VT-ELP	Eurocopter (Aerosp.) SA365N Dauphin 2	6260		0087		2 TU Arriel 1C	4000	9 Pax		
☐ VT-ELQ	Eurocopter (Aerosp.) SA365N Dauphin 2	6261		0087		2 TU Arriel 1C	4000	9 Pax		
☐ VT-ELR	Eurocopter (Aerosp.) SA365N Dauphin 2	6268		0087		2 TU Arriel 1C	4000	9 Pax		
☐ VT-ELS	Eurocopter (Aerosp.) SA365N Dauphin 2	6273		0087		2 TU Arriel 1C	4000	9 Pax		
☐ VT-ELT	Eurocopter (Aerosp.) SA365N Dauphin 2	6278		0087		2 TU Arriel 1C	4000	9 Pax		
☐ VT-ENZ	Eurocopter (Aerosp.) SA365N Dauphin 2	6163		0086		2 TU Arriel 1C	4000	9 Pax		
☐ VT-ASM	Mil Mi-172	356C03		0096	0098	2 IS TV3-117VM-2	13000	26 Pax		
☐ VT-PHF	Mil Mi-172	356C06		0096	1296	2 IS TV3-117VM-2	13000	26 Pax		
☐ VT-PHG	Mil Mi-172	356C07		0096	1296	2 IS TV3-117VM-2	13000	26 Pax		

SAHARA AIRLINES, Ltd = S2 (Member of Sahara India Group / formerly Sahara India Airlines, Ltd) Delhi-Indira Gandhi Int'l

7th Floor, Ambadeep Bldg, 14 Kasturba Gandhi Marg, Connaught Palce, New Delhi 110001, India ☎ (11) 332 00 13 Tx: none Fax: (11) 332 01 31 SITA: n/a
F: 1992 ⋔⋔ 1650 Head: Subrata Roy Sahara IATA: 705 Net: n/a

registration	type of aircraft	cn/fn	ex/ex*	mfd	del	powered by	mtow kg	configuration	selcal	name/fln/specialitites/remarks
☐ VT-SIL	Eurocopter (Aerosp.) AS355N Ecureuil 2	5612		0096	0597	2 TU Arrius 1A	2540	C5		
☐ VT-SIO	Eurocopter (Aerosp.) AS355N Ecureuil 2	5639		0097	0097	2 TU Arrius 1A	2540	C5		
☐ VT-SIP	Eurocopter (Aerosp.) AS355N Ecureuil 2	5640		0097	0097	2 TU Arrius 1A	2540	C5		
☐ VT-EWC	Boeing 737-2U4 (A)	22576 / 761	EI-BTZ	0081	0197	2 PW JT8D-15A	55111	C8Y101		lsf PLMI
☐ VT-SIB	Boeing 737-2U4 (A)	22161 / 652	G-WGEL	0080	1193	2 PW JT8D-15	55111	C8Y101	JL-BG	lsf PLMI
☐ VT-SIE	Boeing 737-2K9 (A)	22415 / 702	VT-PDA	0080	1197	2 PW JT8D-17	58105	C8Y101		
☐ VT-SIF	Boeing 737-2K9 (A)	22416 / 709	VT-PDB	0080	0198	2 PW JT8D-17	58105	C8Y101		
☐ VT-	Boeing 737-73A					2 CFMI CFM56-7B24	62823			to be lsf AWAS 0099
☐ VT-	Boeing 737-73A					2 CFMI CFM56-7B24	62823			to be lsf AWAS 0099
☐ VT-SIC	Boeing 737-4Q8	24708 / 2076	N631LF	0091	1094	2 CFMI CFM56-3C1	65090	C12Y138	RS-LQ	lsf ILFC
☐ VT-SID	Boeing 737-4Q8	24705 / 1971	N621LF	0090	1094	2 CFMI CFM56-3C1	65090	C12Y138	MQ-AJ	lsf ILFC

SGS AIRLINES (formerly UP Air) Lucknow

Roopali House, A-2, Defence Colony, New Delhi 110024, India ☎ (11) 461 91 45 Tx: n/a Fax: (11) 463 65 87 SITA: n/a
F: 1994 ⋔⋔ n/a Head: Subash Gulati Net: n/a

registration	type of aircraft	cn/fn	ex/ex*	mfd	del	powered by	mtow kg	configuration	selcal	name/fln/specialitites/remarks
☐ VT-UPC	Fokker F27 Friendship 500F (F27 Mk500F)	10667	G-JEAB	0084	0395	2 RR Dart 532-7	19731	Y52		
☐ VT-UPD	Fokker F27 Friendship 500F (F27 Mk500F)	10664	G-JEAA	0084	0795	2 RR Dart 532-7	19731	Y52		

SPAN AIR, Pvt. Ltd Delhi

Vijaya Building, 1st Floor, 17 Barakhamba Road, New Delhi 110000, India ☎ (11) 371 14 57 Tx: none Fax: (11) 335 21 72 SITA: n/a
F: 1995 ⋔⋔ n/a Head: Satrughan Gaur Net: n/a

registration	type of aircraft	cn/fn	ex/ex*	mfd	del	powered by	mtow kg	configuration	selcal	name/fln/specialitites/remarks
☐ VT-SPA	Bell 206L-4 LongRanger IV	52130	N9264J	0095	1095	1 AN 250-C30P	2018			
☐ VT-SPB	Bell 407	53000	N407BA	0096	0297	1 AN 250-C47B	2268			lsf Superama Int'l Inc.
☐ VT-EID	Beech King Air B200C	BL-56	N1844C	0082	0097	2 PWC PT6A-42	5670			

TRANS BHARAT AVIATION, (P) Ltd – TBA Delhi-Palam

Hindi Bhavan, 3rd Floor, 11 Vishnu Digambar Marg, New Delhi 110002, India ☎ (11) 323 70 09 Tx: none Fax: (11) 331 33 53 SITA: n/a
F: 1990 ⋔⋔ 23 Head: Prem N. Kumar Net: n/a

registration	type of aircraft	cn/fn	ex/ex*	mfd	del	powered by	mtow kg	configuration	selcal	name/fln/specialitites/remarks
☐ VT-ESU	Beech 99 Airliner	U-7	N205BH	0068	0592	2 PWC PT6A-20	4717	Y15		Krishan Raj

---

V2 = ANTIGUA & BARBUDA (State of Antigua and Barbuda)
Capital: St. John's Official Language: English Population: 0,1 million Square Km: 440 Dialling code: +1-268 Year established: 1981 Acting political head: Lester Bryant Bird (Prime Minister)

CARIB AVIATION, Ltd = K7 / DEL Antigua-V.C. Bird Int'l Carib Aviation

PO Box 318, St. John's, Antigua & Barbuda ☎ (268) 462-3452 Tx: none Fax: (268) 462-3125 SITA: n/a
F: 1973 ⋔⋔ 69 Head: Frank S. Delisle ICAO: RED TAIL Net: n/a

registration	type of aircraft	cn/fn	ex/ex*	mfd	del	powered by	mtow kg	configuration	selcal	name/fln/specialitites/remarks
☐ V2-LCM	Partenavia P.68C	280		0083	0083	2 LY IO-360-A1B6	1990	Y5		
☐ V2-LDC	Partenavia P.68C	365		0086	0086	2 LY IO-360-A1B6	1990	Y5		
☐ V2-LEG	Partenavia P.68C	302	YV-804CP	0084	0095	2 LY IO-360-A1B6	1990	Y5		
☐ V2-LCL	Britten-Norman BN-2A-26 Islander	2006	G-BESR*	0077		2 LY O-540-E4C5	2994	Y9		
☐ V2-LDI	Britten-Norman BN-2A-26 Islander	919	N662J	0081	1288	2 LY O-540-E4C5	2994	Y9		
☐ V2-LDL	Britten-Norman BN-2A-27 Islander	532	V4-AAA	0076		2 LY O-540-E4C5	2994	Y9		
☐ V2-LEW	Cessna 402B II	402B1220	N797A	0077	1096	2 CO TSIO-520-E	2858	Y7		
☐ V2-LDO	Beech Excalibur Queenaire 8800	LC-291	N8312N	0068	0094	2 LY IO-720-A1B	3992	Y6		cvtd Queen Air A65
☐ V2-LEY	De Havilland DHC-6 Vista Liner 300	389	N238SA	0073	1097	2 PWC PT6A-27	5670	Y19		lsf TWIN / cvtd Twin Otter
☐ V2-	De Havilland DHC-6 Vista Liner 300	615	N220SA	0079		2 PWC PT6A-27	5670	Y19		to be lsf TWIN 0599 / cvtd Twin Otter

CARIBBEAN HELICOPTERS, Ltd (Subsidiary of Skytech Aviation Ltd, Canada) St. John

PO Box 170, Jolly Harbour, Antigua & Barbuda ☎ (268) 460-5900 Tx: none Fax: (268) 460-5901 SITA: n/a
F: 1996 ⋔⋔ n/a Head: Michael Fleming Net: n/a

registration	type of aircraft	cn/fn	ex/ex*	mfd	del	powered by	mtow kg	configuration	selcal	name/fln/specialitites/remarks
☐ V2-LFA	Bell 206B JetRanger III	2313	C-GSZY	0077	0097	1 AN 250-C20B	1451			

CARIBJET, Inc. = CBJ Antigua

PO Box 1301, 60 Nevis Street, St. John's, Antigua & Barbuda ☎ Monaco 93 50 66 28 Tx: none Fax: Monaco 93 50 66 29 SITA: NCERMCR
F: 1992 ⋔⋔ n/a Head: Roger Nuyens ICAO: RIGEL Net: n/a Suspended operations (with Airbus Industrie A310 & Lockheed TriStar 500) 1196. Intends to restart.

GOLD AVIATION, Ltd Antigua

PO Box 789, St. John's, Antigua & Barbuda ☎ (268) 560-2063 Tx: none Fax: (268) 560-2063 SITA: n/a
F: 1997 ⋔⋔ 3 Head: Peter Notte Net: n/a

registration	type of aircraft	cn/fn	ex/ex*	mfd	del	powered by	mtow kg	configuration	selcal	name/fln/specialitites/remarks
☐ N440GA	Piper PA-34-200T Seneca II	34-8070213	D-GEMY	0080	0299	2 CO TSIO-360-EB1	2073			lsf Disko Leasing
☐ V2-LEZ	BAe 3103 Jetstream 31	603	OY-EDA	0082	0997	2 GA TPE331-10UR-513H	7059			lsf Aviation Leasing

LIAT – The Caribbean Airline = LI / LIA (LIAT (1974), Ltd dba / Associated with BWIA International) Antigua-V.C. Bird Int'l liat

PO Box 819, V.C. Bird Int'l Airport, Antigua & Barbuda ☎ (268) 462-0700 Tx: 2124 liat ak Fax: (268) 462-3455 SITA: n/a
F: 1956 ⋔⋔ 980 Head: Senator Aziz Hadeed IATA: 140 ICAO: LIAT Net: http://www.turq.com/antigua/liat.html Scheduled services to the Dominican Republic are operated in conjunction with Dominair (see also under HI- markings).

registration	type of aircraft	cn/fn	ex/ex*	mfd	del	powered by	mtow kg	configuration	selcal	name/fln/specialitites/remarks
☐ V2-LAG	Britten-Norman BN-2A Islander	163	VP-LAG	0070	0670	2 LY O-540-E4C5	2858	Y9		lst COU as J3-GAG
☐ V2-LCN	De Havilland DHC-6 Twin Otter 310	805	C-GEOA	0084	0384	2 PWC PT6A-27	5670	Y19		for sale
☐ V2-LCO	De Havilland DHC-6 Twin Otter 310	806	C-GETI	0084	0384	2 PWC PT6A-27	5670	Y19		for sale
☐ V2-LCV	De Havilland DHC-8-110 Dash 8	021	C-GIQK*	0085	1285	2 PWC PW120A	15649	Y37		
☐ V2-LCW	De Havilland DHC-8-110 Dash 8	029	C-GLOT*	0086	0386	2 PWC PW120A	15649	Y37		

648 registration   type of aircraft   cn/fn   ex/ex*   mfd   del   powered by   mtow kg   configuration   selcal   name/fln/specialitites/remarks

registration	type of aircraft	cn/fn	ex/ex*	mfd	del	powered by	mtow kg	configuration	selcal	name/fln/specialtites/remarks
☐ V2-LCX	De Havilland DHC-8-110 Dash 8	031	C-GESR*	0086	0486	2 PWC PW120A	15649	Y37		
☐ V2-LCY	De Havilland DHC-8-110 Dash 8	035	C-GESR*	0086	0486	2 PWC PW120A	15649	Y37		
☐ V2-LCZ	De Havilland DHC-8-110 Dash 8	048	C-GEOA*	0086	0986	2 PWC PW120A	15649	Y37		
☐ V2-LDP	De Havilland DHC-8-102 Dash 8	140	EI-BZC	0089	1090	2 PWC PW120A	15649	Y37		lsf GECA
☐ V2-LDQ	De Havilland DHC-8-102 Dash 8	113	EI-BWX	0088	1190	2 PWC PW120A	15649	Y37		lsf GECA
☐ V2-LDU	De Havilland DHC-8-103 Dash 8	270	EI-CBV	0091	1191	2 PWC PW121	15649	Y37		
☐ V2-LEF	De Havilland DHC-8-103 Dash 8	144	HS-SKH	0089	1194	2 PWC PW121	15649	Y37		lsf GECA
☐ V2-LES	De Havilland DHC-8-311 Dash 8	412	C-GETI*	0095	0696	2 PWC PW123	18643	Y50		lsf Bombardier
☐ V2-LET	De Havilland DHC-8-311 Dash 8	416	C-GFOD*	0090	0796	2 PWC PW123	18643	Y50		lsf Bombardier
☐ V2-LEU	De Havilland DHC-8-311 Dash 8	408	C-FWBB*	0095	1296	2 PWC PW123	18643	Y50		

NORMAN AVIATION, Ltd

Antigua

PO Box 1340, St. John's, Antigua & Barbuda ☎ (268) 462-2445 Tx: none Fax: (268) 462-2445 SITA: n/a
F: 1995   ⁂ n/a Head: n/a Net: n/a

☐ V2-LEB	Twin (Aero) Commander 560F	560F-1152-38	N870M	0062		2 LY IGSO-540-B1A	3402			
☐ V2-LDN	Piper PA-31-325 Navajo C/R	31-7612017	N59749	0076		2 LY TIO-540-F2BD	2948			

SKYJET, Inc. = SKJ (Sister company of Skyjet (Europe) S.A., Belgium)

Brussels-National (Belgium)   ⇶ SKYJET

Commercial & Management office:, Boulevard Louis Schmidt 75, B-1040 Brussels, Belgium ☎ (2) 735 67 37 Tx: 20550 ias b Fax: (2) 735 63 35 SITA: BRUSJXH
F: 1992   ⁂ 60 Head: Pierre Vandenbroucke Net: n/a   Flights are operated in conjunction with SKYJET (Europe), S.A., a sister. management company (same headquarters).

☐ V2-LER	Boeing (Douglas) DC-10-15	48294 / 372	N1004A	0082	0696	3 GE CF6-50C2F	206385	Y379		Gerhard Mercator / lsf Clipper Leasing
☐ V2-SKY	Boeing (Douglas) DC-10-15	48275 / 358	N10038	0081	0998	3 GE CF6-50C2F	206385	Y335		lsf Clipper Leasing
☐ V2-	Boeing (Douglas) DC-10-30	47843 / 335	PP-VMV	0080		3 GE CF6-50C2	263084	Freighter		tblsf Clipper 0699/exVRG/tb cvtd to-30F
☐ 9G-PHN	Boeing (Douglas) DC-10-30	46554 / 84	OO-PHN	0273	1192	3 GE CF6-50C	256280	C32Y238	JL-CH	lsf Clipper Leasing / sub-lst / opf GHA

V3 = BELIZE

Capital: Belmopan Official Language: English Population: 0,2 million Square Km: 22965 Dialling code: +501 Year established: 1973 Acting political head: Said Musa (Prime Minister)

AERO BELIZE, Ltd = ABZ

San Pedro

PO Box 25, San Pedro, Belize ☎ (26) 32 00 Tx: n/a Fax: (26) 27 00 SITA: n/a
F: n/a   ⁂ n/a Head: n/a ICAO: AERO BELIZE Net: n/a

☐ V3-HOT	Piper PA-23-150 Apache	23-1144	N3204P	0057	1294	2 LY O-320-A1A	1588			

CARIBEE AIR SERVICE, Ltd

Belize-Municipal   CARIBEE

PO Box 308, Belize City, Belize ☎ (2) 44 253 Tx: none Fax: (2) 31 031 SITA: n/a
F: 1980   ⁂ 8 Head: Arthur Hoy, Sr. Net: n/a Aircraft below MTOW 1361kg: Cessna 182.

☐ V3-HEQ	Piper PA-32-300 Cherokee SIX	32-40534	N4195R	0068		1 LY IO-540-K1A5	1542			

JAVIER'S FLYING SERVICE

Belize-Municipal

PO Box 1021, Belize City, Belize ☎ (2) 45 332 Tx: n/a Fax: (2) 31 731 SITA: n/a
F: 1984   ⁂ n/a Head: n/a Net: n/a Aircraft below MTOW 1361kg: Cessna 172.

☐ V3-HEA	Cessna U206G Stationair 6 II	U20605304		0079		1 CO IO-520-F	1633			

MAYA ISLAND AIR = MW / MYD (Belize Air Maya, Ltd dba)

Belize-Municipal & San Pedro

PO Box 458, Belize City, Belize ☎ (2) 35 795 Tx: 280 mayair bze Fax: (2) 30 576 SITA: n/a
F: 1997   ⁂ 80 Head: Brian Roe ICAO: MYLAND Net: http://www.belizenet.com/mayair.html Aircraft below MTOW 1361kg: Cessna 172

☐ V3-HER	Cessna 207A Stationair 8 II	20700606	N73591	0080	1297	1 CO IO-520-F17B	1724	Y6		
☐ V3-HMT	Cessna 207A Stationair 8 II	20700655		0080	1297	1 CO IO-520-F17B	1724	Y6		
☐ V3-HBI	Britten-Norman BN-2A-26 Islander	177	VP-HBI	0070	1297	2 LY O-540-E4C5	2994	Y9		
☐ V3-HFA	Britten-Norman BN-2A-26 Islander	839	G-BEMR*	0077	1297	2 LY O-540-E4C5	2994	Y9		
☐ V3-HFB	Britten-Norman BN-2A-26 Islander	907	N5252L	0080	1297	2 LY O-540-E4C5	2994	Y9		
☐ V3-HIA	Britten-Norman BN-2A-26 Islander	2015	N416WA	0077	1297	2 LY O-540-E4C5	2994	Y9		
☐ V3-HRT	Britten-Norman BN-2A-26 Islander	876	N610PA	0080	1297	2 LY O-540-E4C5	2994	Y9		
☐ V3-HFS	Cessna 208B Grand Caravan	208B0579		0096	1296	1 PWC PT6A-114A	3969	Y14		

TROPIC AIR = PM / TOS (Tropical Air Services dba)

San Pedro

PO Box 20, San Pedro, Belize ☎ (26) 20 12 Tx: none Fax: (26) 23 38 SITA: SPRSEXH
F: 1979   ⁂ 78 Head: Celi McCorkle ICAO: TROPISER Net: http://www.tropicair.com Aircraft below MTOW 1361 kg: Cessna 172.

☐ V3-HDT	Cessna 207A Stationair 8 II	20700716		0081		1 CO IO-520-F	1724	Y6		
☐ V3-HFP	Cessna 208B Grand Caravan	208B0478		0095	1295	1 PWC PT6A-114A	3969	Y14		
☐ V3-HFQ	Cessna 208B Grand Caravan	208B0575		0096	1296	1 PWC PT6A-114A	3969	Y14		
☐ V3-HFV	Cessna 208B Grand Caravan	208B0647		0097	1297	1 PWC PT6A-114A	3969	Y14		
☐ V3-HIK	Cessna 208B Grand Caravan	208B0707		0098	1198	1 PWC PT6A-114A	3969	Y14		
☐ V3-HSS	Cessna 208B Grand Caravan	208B0407	N1116V*	0094	1194	1 PWC PT6A-114A	3969	Y14		

V4 = ST. KITTS & NEVIS (Federation of St. Christopher and Nevis)

Capital: Basseterre Official Language: English Population: 0,1 million Square Km: 261 Dialling code: +1-809 Year established: 1983 Acting political head: Sir Denzil Douglas (Prime Minister)

AIR ST. KITTS & NEVIS (Kingfisher Air Services Air Safari dba)

Basseterre-Golden Rock

PO Box 529, Basseterre, (Kitts), St. Kitts & Nevis, West Indies ☎ (869) 465-8571 Tx: none Fax: (869) 465-9833 SITA: n/a
F: 1990   ⁂ n/a Head: Richard V. Hurley Net: n/a

☐ N403PA	Cessna 402B	402B0917		0075	0397	2 CO TSIO-520-E	2858			lsf Stella Sustralis Inc.
☐ N814CF	Cessna 402B	402B0335		0073	0398	2 CO TSIO-520-E	2858			lsf Stella Australis Inc.

ISLAND AVIATION, Ltd

Basseterre-Golden Rock

PO Box 1479, Basseterre, (Kitts), St. Kitts & Nevis, West Indies ☎ (869) 467-2930 Tx: none Fax: (869) 466-1363 SITA: n/a
F: 1998   ⁂ n/a Head: Bill Bailey Net: n/a

☐ V4-AAB	Bell 206L-1 LongRanger II	45232	G-OCRP	0079	0199	1 AN 250-C28B	1882			lsf OMG

NEVIS EXPRESS (Daystar Airways, Ltd dba)

Nevis-Newcastle   *Nevis Express*

1 Airport Road, Newcastle, (Nevis), St. Kitts & Nevis, West Indies ☎ (869) 469-9755 Tx: none Fax: (869) 469-9751 SITA: n/a
F: 1993   ⁂ 23 Head: Allen Haddadi Net: http://www.nevisexpress.com

☐ N100NE	Britten-Norman BN-2A-26 Islander	82	C-FYZU	0069	1294	2 LY O-540-E4C5	2812	Y9		Express One
☐ N102NE	Britten-Norman BN-2A-26 Islander	311	C-GAPZ	0073	0595	2 LY O-540-E4C5	2812	Y9		lsf BN Aircraft Llc
☐ N103NE	Britten-Norman BN-2A-26 Islander	911	HC-BTX	0081	0697	2 LY O-540-E4C5	2858	Y9		lsf BN Aircraft Inc.

V5 = NAMIBIA (Republic of Namibia)

Capital: Windhoek Official Language: English, German, Afrikaans, Herero Population: 1,8 million Square Km: 823168 Dialling code: +264 Year established: 1990 Acting political head: Samuel Nujoma (President)

Government / Corporate / Executive / VIP Aircraft

☐ V5-NAG	Learjet 31A	31A-091	N5019Y*	0094	0195	2 GA TFE731-2-3B	7484	VIP		Gvmt
☐ V5-NAM	Dassault Falcon 900B	103	F-WWFJ*	0091	0792	3 GA TFE731-5BR-1C	20638	VIP		Gvmt

AIR NAMIBIA – The National Airline of Namibia = SW / NMB (formerly South West Air Transport, (Pty) Ltd)

Windhoek-Eros & -Int'l   ◢ Air Namibia

PO Box 731, Windhoek, Namibia ☎ (61) 298 25 20 Tx: none Fax: (61) 298 20 60 SITA: WDHDZSW
F: 1946   ⁂ 410 Head: Wap Klein IATA: 186 ICAO: NAMIBIA Net: http://www.airnamibia.com.na/

☐ V5-LTB	Beech 1900C Airliner	UB-29	ZS-LTB	0086	0587	2 PWC PT6A-65B	7530	Y19		Caprivi
☐ V5-LTC	Beech 1900C Airliner	UB-73	ZS-LTC	0087	0687	2 PWC PT6A-65B	7530	Y19		Kalahari
☐ V5-MMN	Beech 1900C Airliner	UB-20	ZS-MMN	0086	1089	2 PWC PT6A-65B	7530	Y19		Khomas
☐ V5-ANA	Boeing 737-25A (A)	23790 / 1422	N724ML	0090	0591	2 PW JT8D-15A	54204	C20Y87		Ondekaremba
☐ 5H-MRK	Boeing 737-2R8C (A)	21711 / 573		0079	0399	2 PW JT8D-17	53070	C12Y94	BH-DK	lsf ATC
☐ ZS-SPC	Boeing 747SP-44	21134 / 288	3B-NAG	0076	0399	4 PW JT9D-7FW	317967	F8C28Y224	AF-BG	lsf SAA

ATLANTIC AVIATION, CC

Swakopmund

PO Box 465, Swakopmund, Namibia ☎ (64) 40 47 49 Tx: none Fax: (64) 40 58 32 SITA: n/a
F: 1994   ⁂ 10 Head: H.H. von Flotow Net: http://www.iml.com.na/tourist/aviation

☐ V5-FBJ	Cessna 210M Centurion II	21062190	N9239G	0077		1 CO IO-550-L	1724			
☐ V5-GWH	Cessna 210M Centurion II	21061648	N99113	0076		1 CO IO-520-L	1724			

BAY AIR AVIATION = NMD (Nomad Aviation, Ltd dba)

Walvis Bay

PO Box 357, Walvis Bay, Namibia ☎ (64) 20 43 19 Tx: none Fax: (64) 20 49 27 SITA: n/a
F: 1989   ⁂ 10 Head: Clifford Steydom ICAO: NOMAD AIR Net: n/a

☐ V5-FVP	Piper PA-30-160 Twin Comanche C	30-1824	ZS-FVP	0069		2 LY IO-320-B1A	1633			
☐ V5-EPL	Cessna 310N	310N0088	ZS-EPL	0068	0498	2 CO IO-470-V	2359			
☐ V5-FUR	Cessna 310Q	310Q0456	ZS-FUR	0072	0198	2 CO IO-470-VO	2404			

BUSH PILOT
Windhoek-Eros

PO Box 9224, Windhoek, Namibia ☎ (61) 24 83 16 Tx: none Fax: (61) 23 48 16 SITA: n/a
F: n/a ♦♦♦ n/a Head: n/a Net: n/a

registration	type of aircraft	cn/fn	ex/ex*	mfd	del	powered by	mtow kg	configuration	selcal	name/fln/specialites/remarks
☐ V5-BPN	Cessna 210L Centurion II	21060358	N93315	0074		1 CO IO-520-L	1724			

COMAV
Windhoek-Eros

PO Box 80300, Windhoek, Namibia ☎ (61) 22 75 12 Tx: none Fax: (61) 24 98 64 SITA: n/a
F: 1993 ♦♦♦ n/a Head: n/a Net: n/a

| ☐ V5-AAS | Cessna 402C II | 402C0437 | N6789D | 0081 | | 2 CO TSIO-520-VB | 3107 | | | |
| ☐ V5-JIH | Cessna 402B II | 402B1057 | | 0076 | | 2 CO TSIO-520-E | 2858 | | | |

DESERT AIR (Desert Air Partnership dba)
Windhoek-Eros

PO Box 11624, Windhoek, Namibia ☎ (61) 22 81 01 Tx: none Fax: (61) 25 43 45 SITA: n/a
F: 1995 ♦♦♦ n/a Head: Matthys Rall Net: n/a

☐ V5-AEM	Cessna 210L Centurion II	21061519		0076		1 CO IO-520-L	1724			
☐ V5-MKR	Cessna T210N Turbo Centurion II	21063060	ZS-LAS	0079		1 CO TSIO-520-R	1814			
☐ V5-MKS	Cessna T310R II	310R0583	N410AS	0076		2 CO TSIO-520-B	2495			

GUS UYS FLYING
Windhoek-Eros

PO Box 80378, Windhoek, Namibia ☎ (61) 23 56 62 Tx: none Fax: (61) 22 10 93 SITA: n/a
F: n/a ♦♦♦ n/a Head: n/a Net: n/a

| ☐ V5-NCE | Cessna 402B II | 402B1379 | ZS-MGY | 0078 | | 2 CO TSIO-520-E | 2858 | | | |

HELINAMIB (Subsidiary of Court Helicopters, South Africa)
Windhoek & Oranjemund

PO Box 82, Windhoek, Namibia ☎ (61) 23 79 70 Tx: none Fax: (61) 23 36 90 SITA: n/a
F: 1995 ♦♦♦ 30 Head: n/a Net: n/a

| ☐ ZS-HVJ | Sikorsky S-61N | 61493 | N9119Z | 0072 | 0096 | 2 GE CT58-140-1 | 9299 | | | lsf Court Helicopters |

KALAHARI EXPRESS AIRLINES, (Pty) Ltd = KEA (Subsidiary of TransNamib & Air Namibia)
Windhoek-Eros

c/o Air Namibia, PO Box 731, Windhoek, Namibia ☎ (61) 298 22 79 Tx: none Fax: (11) 298 20 60 SITA: n/a
F: 1997 ♦♦♦ n/a Head: n/a ICAO: KALAHARI Net: n/a Presently being set-up. Intends to start operations during 1999.

| ☐ V5-KEA | Fokker F28 Fellowship 3000 (F28 Mk3000) | 11151 | VH-EWG | 0079 | | 2 RR Spey 555-15P | 33112 | Y56 | | oo-delivery 0099 |
| ☐ V5-KEX | Fokker F28 Fellowship 3000 (F28 Mk3000) | 11143 | VH-EWF | 0079 | | 2 RR Spey 555-15P | 33112 | Y56 | | oo-delivery 0099 |

NCA – Namibia Commercial Aviation, (Pty) Ltd = MRE (NCA Classic Air Travel) (formerly Hire & Fly)
Windhoek-Eros

PO Box 30320, Windhoek, Namibia ☎ (61) 22 35 62 Tx: none Fax: (61) 23 45 83 SITA: n/a
F: 1977 ♦♦♦ 50 Head: Chris J. Schutte ICAO: MED RESCUE Net: n/a
DC-6B passenger flights are operated under the marketing name NCA Classic Air Travel. Medical rescue-flights (with Cessna 310Q) are operated under contract with the government.

☐ V5-KBV	Cessna 210J Centurion	21059126	ZS-KBV	0069		1 CO IO-520-J	1542			
☐ V5-NCD	Cessna 310R II	310R1563	N10SN	0078	0192	2 CO TSIO-520-M	2495			
☐ V5-RAT	Cessna 310Q II	310Q1089	ZS-RAT	0074		2 CO IO-470-VO	2404	Med Rescue		
☐ V5-NCF	Boeing (Douglas) DC-6B	45563 / 1034	GBM110	0058	1092	4 PW R-2800	47083	Y66		Fish Eagle
☐ V5-NCG	Boeing (Douglas) DC-6B	45564 / 1040	GBM112	0058	1092	4 PW R-2800	47083	Y66		Batuleur

PLEASURE FLIGHTS (Klein Aviation Enterprises dba)
Swakopmund

PO Box 537, Swakopmund, Namibia ☎ (64) 404 50 00 Tx: none Fax: (64) 404 50 00 SITA: n/a
F: 1993 ♦♦♦ n/a Head: Christian Klein Net: n/a

| ☐ V5-LSZ | Cessna 210L Centurion II | 21059872 | ZS-LSZ | 0073 | | 1 CO IO-520-L | 1724 | | | |

WEST AIR AVIATION, (Pty) Ltd = WAA
Windhoek-Eros

PO Box 407, Windhoek, Namibia ☎ (61) 23 72 30 Tx: n/a Fax: (61) 23 24 02 SITA: n/a
F: 1967 ♦♦♦ n/a Head: Wolfgang Grellmann ICAO: WESTAIR WINGS Net: n/a

☐ V5-WAD	Cessna 310R II	310R1340	ZS-KEE	0078	0692	2 CO IO-520-M	2495			
☐ V5-WAE	Cessna 402C II	402C0430	ZS-NPA	0081	0698	2 CO TSIO-520-VB	3107			
☐ V5-WAA	Cessna 404 Titan II/RAM	404-0210	N88668	0078	0991	2 CO GTSIO-520-M	3810			Ghost Rider

V6 = MICRONESIA (Federated States of Micronesia)
Capital: Palikir/Ponape Official Language: English Population: 0,1 million Square Km: 721 Dialling code: +691 Year established: 1990 Acting political head: Jacob Nena (President)

CAROLINE ISLAND AIR (formerly Caroline Pacific Air)
Pohnpei

Box 960, Pohnpei 96941, Federated States of Micronesia ☎ 320 84 06 Tx: none Fax: 320 85 30 SITA: n/a
F: 1995 ♦♦♦ n/a Head: Brian Caldwell Net: n/a

| ☐ V6-SFM | Britten-Norman BN-2A-27 Islander | 2014 | P2-KST | 0079 | 0098 | 2 LY O-540-E4C5 | 2994 | Y9 | | |

V7 = MARSHALL ISLANDS (Republic of The Marshall Islands)
Capital: Uliga Official Language: English Population: 0,1 million Square Km: 181 Dialling code: +692 Year established: 1990 Acting political head: Amata Kabua (President)

AIR MARSHALL ISLANDS, Inc. – AMI = CW / MRS (formerly Airline of The Marshall Islands)
Majuro Int'l

PO Box 1319, Majuro, MH 96960, Marshall Islands ☎ 625 37 31 Tx: none Fax: 625 37 30 SITA: n/a
F: 1980 ♦♦♦ 120 Head: Jack Chong-Gum IATA: 778 ICAO: MARSHALL ISLANDS Net: n/a

☐ V7-9206	Dornier 228-212	8194	MI-9206	0092	1291	2 GA TPE331-5A-252D	6400	Y19		
☐ V7-9207	Dornier 228-212	8201	MI-9207	0092	1291	2 GA TPE331-5A-252D	6400	Y19		
☐ V7-	Dornier 328-110	3100				2 PWC PW119B	13990	Y31		oo-delivery 0999
☐ V7-	Dornier 328-110	3109				2 PWC PW119B	13990	Y31		oo-delivery 0999
☐ V7-8203	BAe (HS) 748-400 Srs 2B	1796 / 277	MI-8203	0082	1282	2 RR Dart 536-2	21092	Y40		
☐ V7-9508	Saab 2000	2000-017	SE-017*	0095	0695	2 AN AE2100A	22800	Y50 / Freighter		lst AVN

V8 = BRUNEI (Negara Brunei Darussalam)
Capital: Bandar Seri Begawan Official Language: Malay, English Population: 0,4 million Square Km: 5765 Dialling code: +673 Year established: 1984 Acting political head: Hassan al-Bolkiah (Sultan)

BSP-SAV Flight Dept. (Flight Dept. of Brunei Shell Petroleum, Ltd)
Seria Heliport

Heliport, Seria 3534, Brunei ☎ (3) 37 39 99 Tx: none Fax: (3) 37 24 00 SITA: n/a
F: n/a ♦♦♦ n/a Head: Fredi Siewert Net: n/a Operates non-commercial coporate/personell flights for itself only.

☐ V8-SAV	Sikorsky S-61N	61775	PH-NZL	0077		2 GE CT58-140-2	9299	Coporate 24 Pax		
☐ V8-UDQ	Sikorsky S-61N	61488	VR-UDQ	0071		2 GE CT58-140-2	9299	Coporate 24 Pax		
☐ V8-UDU	Sikorsky S-61N	61364	VR-UDU	0067		2 GE CT58-140-2	9299	Coporate 24 Pax		
☐ V8-UDZ	Sikorsky S-61N	61717	VR-UDZ	0074		2 GE CT58-140-2	9299	Coporate 24 Pax		

ROYAL BRUNEI AIRLINES, Ltd = BI / RBA
Bandar Seri Begawan

PO Box 737, Bandar Seri Begawan 1907, Brunei Darussalam ☎ (2) 33 92 25 Tx: 2737 rba bu Fax: (2) 24 47 37 SITA: n/a
F: 1974 ♦♦♦ 1300 Head: Mohammad Alimin IATA: 672 ICAO: BRUNEI Net: n/a On order (MoU/Letter of Intent): 2 Airbus Industrie A319-132 for delivery 08 & 0999.

☐ V8-RB3	Fokker 100 (F28 Mk0100)	11253	HB-IVE	0088	1196	2 RR Tay 620-15	44452	Y109	AC-HP	for sale
☐ V8-RB4	Fokker 100 (F28 Mk0100)	11255	HB-IVG	0088	1196	2 RR Tay 620-15	44452	Y109	AD-HQ	for sale
☐ V8-RBA	Boeing 757-2M6	23452 / 94	N6666U*	0086	0586	2 RR RB211-535E4	108862	C24Y150	GH-JM	
☐ V8-RBB	Boeing 757-2M6	23453 / 100		0086	0686	2 RR RB211-535E4	108862	C24Y150	GJ-AB	
☐ V8-RBF	Boeing 767-33A (ER)	25530 / 414		0092	0292	2 PW PW4056	172365	C24Y224	BL-KR	lst HVN
☐ V8-RBG	Boeing 767-33A (ER)	25532 / 442	N6055X*	0092	0992	2 PW PW4056	172365	C24Y224	DP-QR	
☐ V8-RBH	Boeing 767-33A (ER)	25534 / 477	N6055X*	0093	0393	2 PW PW4056	172365	F13C28Y168	DR-JQ	
☐ V8-RBJ	Boeing 767-33A (ER)	25533 / 454	N67AW	0092	0293	2 PW PW4056	172365	F13C28Y168	EG-HR	
☐ V8-RBK	Boeing 767-33A (ER)	25536 / 504	N96AC	0093	0893	2 PW PW4056	172365	C24Y224	FJ-AS	
☐ V8-RBL	Boeing 767-33A (ER)	27189 / 521	N1794B*	0093	0194	2 PW PW4056	172365	F13C28Y168	GL-DS	
☐ V8-RBM	Boeing 767-328	27428 / 586	S7-RGT	0095	0396	2 GE CF6-80C2B6F	184612	C24Y196	LR-ES	
☐ V8-RBN	Boeing 767-328 (ER)	27427 / 579	3B-NAZ	0095	0496	2 GE CF6-80C2B6F	184612	C42Y196	MR-HK	

SULTAN'S FLIGHT (His Majesty The Sultan's Flight dba)
Bandar Seri Begawan

Brunei International Airport, Bandar Seri Begawan 3480, Brunei Darussalam ☎ (2) 43 00 43 Tx: none Fax: (2) 43 00 55 SITA: n/a
F: n/a ♦♦♦ n/a Head: BrG.Yang Amatmulia Pentipen Ratnawijaya Net: n/a Non-commercial state organisation conducting VIP passenger & cargo flights for the government.

☐ V8-001	GAC G-V Gulfstream V	509	V8-009	0098	0398	2 BR BR710A1-10	41232	VIP		
☐ V8-007	GAC G-V Gulfstream V	515	N599GA*	0098	0398	2 BR BR710A1-10	41232	VIP		
☐ V8-MJB	Boeing 767-27G (ER)	25537 / 517		0093	0695	2 GE CF6-80C2B4F	175500	VIP	EH-DR	op in Royal Brunei-colors
☐ V8-AC3	Airbus Industrie A340-213	204	F-WWJB*	0098	1198	4 CFMI CFM56-5C4	271000	VIP		std SXF in white-colors
☐ V8-AM1	Airbus Industrie A340-211	009	V8-JP1	0093	0393	4 CFMI CFM56-5C2	257000	VIP	BJ-FR	
☐ V8-BKH	Airbus Industrie A340-212	046	V8-PJB	0094	0394	4 CFMI CFM56-5C3	257000	VIP	FS-MR	op in Royal Brunei-colors
☐ V8-JBB	Airbus Industrie A340-213	151	F-WWJY*	0096	1096	4 CFMI CFM56-5C4	257000	VIP		
☐ V8-AL1	Boeing 747-430	26426 / 910	D-ABVM	0092	0492	4 GE CF6-80C2B1F	385553	VIP	CG-AD	

XA = MEXICO (United Mexican States) (Estados Unidos Mexicanos)

Capital: Mexico-City   Official Language: Spanish   Population: 96,0 million   Square Km: 1958201   Dialling code: +52   Year established: 1821   Acting political head: Ernesto Zedillo Ponce de Leon (President)

Government / Corporate / Executive / VIP Aircraft

reg	type	cn/fn	ex/ex*	mfd	del	powered by	mtow kg		configuration	selcal	name/fln/specialitites/remarks
B-12001	Boeing 737-247	20127 / 144	TP-03	0069	0680	2 PW JT8D-9	49442	VIP / mil trans			Fuerza Aérea Mexicana
JS-10201	Lockheed L-1329 JetStar 8	5144	N5508L*	0069	0771	4 PW JT12A-8	19005	VIP / mil trans			DN-01 / Fuerza Aérea Mexicana
MTX-01	Sabreliner 60 (Rockwell NA265-60)	306-34	MTX-02	0068		2 PW JT12A-8A	9072	VIP / mil trans			Armada de México
TP-01	Boeing 757-225	22690 / 151		0087	1187	2 RR RB211-535E4	104326	VIP		CG-BP	XC-CBD / Presidente Juarez / FAM
TP-02	Boeing 737-33A	24095 / 1737	N731XL	0089	0192	2 CFMI CFM56-3B1	61235	VIP / mil trans		FQ-JL	XC-UJB / Fuerza Aérea Mexicana
TP-03	Boeing 737-112	19772 / 217	XB-IBV	0069	0581	2 PW JT8D-7	49442	VIP / mil trans			XC-UJL / Fuerza Aérea Mexicána
TP-06	GAC G-1159A Gulfstream III	352	HB-ITM	0082	0390	2 RR Spey 511-8	30935	VIP / mil trans			XC-UJN / Fuerza Aérea Mexicana
TP-07	GAC G-1159A Gulfstream III	386	N902KB	0083	0790	2 RR Spey 511-8	30935	VIP / mil trans			XC-UJO / Fuerza Aérea Mexicana
TP-102	Sabreliner 75A (Rockwell NA265-80)	380-68	TP-104	0078	1278	2 GE CF700-2D2	10433	VIP / mil trans			XC-UJD / Fuerza Aérea Mexicana
TP-103	Sabreliner 60 (Rockwell NA265-60)	306-139	TP-105	0078	1278	2 PW JT12A-8	9150	VIP / mil trans			XC-UJE / Fuerza Aérea Mexicana
TP-104	Learjet 35	35-028	N135GL	0075	0092	2 GA TFE731-2-2B	8301	VIP / mil trans			XC-IPP / Fuerza Aérea Mexicana
TP-201	Lockheed L-188PF Electra	1051	XC-HDA	0059	0781	4 AN 501-D13A	51256	VIP/Combi/miltr			XC-UTA / Morelos / FAM/cvtd L-188A
TP-300	Lockheed L-182 (C-130A) Hercules	1A-3087	56-0479	0057	0089	4 AN T56-A	56336	VIP / miltrans			XC-UTP / Fuerza Aérea Mexicana
10501	Boeing 727-14	18912 / 169	XA-SEP	0065	0581	3 PW JT8D-7B	73028	VIP / mil trans			XC-FAD / Fuerza Aérea Mexicana
10503	Boeing 727-14	18908 / 133	XA-SER	0065	0981	2 PW JT8D-7B	73028	VIP / mil trans			XC-FAY / Fuerza Aérea Mexicana
10504	Boeing 727-14	18909 / 150	XA-SEU	0065	0981	3 PW JT8D-7B	73028	VIP / mil trans			XC-FAZ / Fuerza Aérea Mexicana
10506	Aerospatiale (Sud) SE210 Caravelle 10B3	211	HK-3836X	0067	0395	2 PW JT8D-7A	53000	Frtr / miltrans			Fuerza Aérea Mexicana / std MEX
10507	Aerosp. (Sud) SE210 Caravelle 10B1R	232	HK-3869X	0068	0894	2 PW JT8D-7B	52500	Frtr / miltrans			Fuerza Aérea Mexicana / std MEX

AEROASTRA, SA = OSA   Monterrey   Aeroastra

Padre Mier 578 Ote, 64000 Monterrey, (Nuevo Leon), México   ☎ (83) 43 34 85   Tx: none   Fax: (83) 44 13 39   SITA: n/a
F: 1977   ♦♦♦ 10   Head: Lic. Antonio Rodriguez   ICAO: ROSTRA   Net: n/a

reg	type	cn/fn	ex/ex*	mfd	del	powered by	mtow kg				
XA-GTR	Dassault Falcon 900	107	N470FJ	0092		3 GA TFE731-5BR-1C	20638				

AEROBANANA, S.A. de C.V. = OBA   Cozumel

Calle 2 Nte No. 99B, Av. Rafael e Melgar, Col. Centro, 77600 Cozumel (Quintana Roo), México   ☎ (987) 25 040   Tx: none   Fax: (987) 25 040   SITA: n/a
F: 1994   ♦♦♦ 10   Head: Juan J. Silverio Rachat   ICAO: AEROBANANA   Net: n/a

reg	type	cn/fn	ex/ex*	mfd	del	powered by	mtow kg	config			
XA-SOQ	Cessna U206F Stationair II	U20602631	XB-CZF	0075	0094	1 CO IO-520-F	1633	5 Pax			

AERO BARLOZ, SA de CV = BLZ   Monterrey

Av. San Jeronimo 801-Piso 2, 64640 Monterrey, (Nuevo Leon), México   ☎ (8) 340 75 30   Tx: n/a   Fax: (8) 340 75 30   SITA: n/a
F: 1988   ♦♦♦ n/a   Head: Alejandro Elizondo   ICAO: AEROLOZ   Net: n/a

reg	type	cn/fn	ex/ex*	mfd	del	powered by	mtow kg				
XA-MOB	Beech King Air B200	BB-1151	XA-MCB	0083		2 PWC PT6A-42	5670				
XA-MCB	Sabreliner 75A (Rockwell NA265-80)	380-36	N75HL	0076		2 GE CF700-2D2	10433				

AERO CALAFIA, S.A. de C.V.   Los Cabos

Plaza Las Glorias No. 4-A, 23410 Cabo San Lucas, (Baja California Sur), México   ☎ (114) 34 255   Tx: none   Fax: (114) 34 255   SITA: n/a
F: n/a   ♦♦♦ n/a   Head: n/a   Net: n/a

reg	type	cn/fn	ex/ex*	mfd	del	powered by	mtow kg				
XA-SJA	Cessna U206E Super Skywagon	U20601563	XB-CCP	0070		1 CO IO-520-F	1633				
XA-SFJ	Cessna 208B Grand Caravan	208B0301	N5538B	0092		1 PWC PT6A-114A	3969				

AEROCALIFORNIA, SA = JR / SER   La Paz

Calle Hidalgo, Esquina con Serdan 316, 23000 La Paz, (Baja California Sur), México   ☎ (112) 26 655   Tx: 01752237 easame   Fax: (112) 53 993   SITA: n/a
F: 1960   ♦♦♦ 1800   Head: Raul A. Archiga   IATA: 078   ICAO: AEROCALIFORNIA   Net: n/a

reg	type	cn/fn	ex/ex*	mfd	del	powered by	mtow kg	config			
XA-AGS	Boeing (Douglas) DC-9-15	45786 / 90	N968E	0067	0588	2 PW JT8D-7B	41141	CY85			lsf GECA
XA-BCS	Boeing (Douglas) DC-9-14	47043 / 88	N1302T	0067	1288	2 PW JT8D-7A	41141	CY85			lsf GECA
XA-CSL	Boeing (Douglas) DC-9-14	45743 / 29	N8902E	0066	0788	2 PW JT8D-7B	41141	CY85			lsf GECA
XA-GDL	Boeing (Douglas) DC-9-15	47085 / 139	EI-BZY	0067	1190	2 PW JT8D-7B	41141	CY85			lsf GECA
XA-LAC	Boeing (Douglas) DC-9-15	47126 / 405	EI-BZW	0068	1090	2 PW JT8D-7A	41141	CY85			lsf GECA
XA-LMM	Boeing (Douglas) DC-9-14	45736 / 45	N655TX	0066	0688	2 PW JT8D-7B	41141	CY85			lsf GECA
XA-RKT	Boeing (Douglas) DC-9-15	47122 / 224	EI-BZZ	0067	0390	2 PW JT8D-7A	41141	CY85			lsf GECA
XA-RNQ	Boeing (Douglas) DC-9-15	47059 / 125	EI-BZX	0067	1090	2 PW JT8D-7A	41141	CY85			lsf GECA
XA-RRY	Boeing (Douglas) DC-9-15	45785 / 64	EI-CBB	0066	1289	2 PW JT8D-7A	41141	CY85			lsf GECA
XA-RXG	Boeing (Douglas) DC-9-14	45714 / 7	N651TX	0066	0691	2 PW JT8D-7B	41141	CY85			lsf POLA
XA-SYQ	Boeing (Douglas) DC-9-14	45702 / 15	HB-IEF	0065	0595	2 PW JT8D-7A	41141	CY85			lsf Interglobal Inc.
XA-SWG	Boeing (Douglas) DC-9-32	47230 / 395	N277AW	0068	1294	2 PW JT8D-9A	48989	CY104			lsf Interglobal Inc.
XA-SWH	Boeing (Douglas) DC-9-32	47236 / 450	N274AW	0069	1294	2 PW JT8D-9A	48989	CY104			lsf Interglobal Inc.
XA-SYD	Boeing (Douglas) DC-9-32	47283 / 397	N2786S	0068	0495	2 PW JT8D-9A	48989	CY104			lsf Interglobal Inc.
XA-TAF	Boeing (Douglas) DC-9-32	47039 / 154	N4157A	0067	0795	2 PW JT8D-9A	48989	CY104			lsf PLMI
XA-TBQ	Boeing (Douglas) DC-9-32	47553 / 642	N136AA	0071	0995	2 PW JT8D-9A (HK3/ABS)	48989	CY104			lsf Jetfleet Aircraft
XA-THB	Boeing (Douglas) DC-9-32	47648 / 761	N942VV	0074	1097	2 PW JT8D-9A (HK3/ABS)	48988	CY104			lsf PLMI
XA-THC	Boeing (Douglas) DC-9-32	47666 / 772	N941VV	0075	1097	2 PW JT8D-9A (HK3/ABS)	48988	CY104			lsf PLMI
XA-	Boeing (Douglas) DC-9-32	48113 / 930	N12514	0079	0798	2 PW JT8D-15 (HK3/ABS)	49895	CY104			lsf Interglobal Inc.

AEROCARIBE, SA de CV = QA / CBE   (Inter)   (Subsidiary of CINTRA / Affiliated with Aerocozumel)   Merida & Cancun   aerocaribe

International Airport, 97000 Merida, (Yucatan), México   ☎ (99) 46 13 07   Tx: n/a   Fax: (99) 46 13 30   SITA: n/a
F: 1975   ♦♦♦ 350   Head: Jaime V. Tamariz   IATA: 723   ICAO: AEROCARIBE   Net: n/a
All aircraft are operated as AEROCARIBE/INTER, a commuter system to provide feeder connection at MX major hubs, using MX flight numbers.   Aircraft are interchanged with AEROCOZUMEL/INTER as required.

reg	type	cn/fn	ex/ex*	mfd	del	powered by	mtow kg	config			
XA-TFA	Cessna 208B Grand Caravan de Luxe	20880476	N1132V	0095	0096	1 PWC PT6A-114A	3969	Y9			
XA-TFB	Cessna 208B Grand Caravan de Luxe	20880525	N5202D	0096	0096	1 PWC PT6A-114A	3969	Y9			
N910AE	BAe 3201 Jetstream 32EP	910	G-31-910*	0090	1298	2 GA TPE331-12UAR-704H	7350	Y19			lsf BAMT / cvtd 32
N912FJ	BAe 3201 Jetstream 32EP	912	G-31-912*	0090	1298	2 GA TPE331-12UAR-704H	7350	Y19			lsf BAMT / cvtd 32
N915AE	BAe 3201 Jetstream 32EP	915	G-31-915*	0090	1298	2 GA TPE331-12UAR-704H	7350	Y19			lsf BAMT / cvtd 32
N916AE	BAe 3201 Jetstream 32EP	916	G-31-916*	0090	1298	2 GA TPE331-12UAR-704H	7350	Y19			lsf BAMT / cvtd 32
XA-MCJ	Fairchild Ind. F-27F	90	XC-UTD	0062	0087	2 RR Dart 529-7E	19051	Y40			Yucatan
XA-RJO	Fairchild Ind. F-27J	93	N383BA	0062	0791	2 RR Dart 532-7	19051	Y44			cvtd F-27F
XA-RPM	Fairchild Ind. F-27J	100	N384BA	0063	1189	2 RR Dart 532-7	19051	Y44			Veracruz / cvtd F-27F
XA-RUK	Fairchild Ind. F-27J	57	N380BA	0059	0391	2 RR Dart 532-7	19051	Y44			cvtd F-27F
XA-CZA	Fairchild Ind. FH-227D	577	XC-UTC	0071	0087	2 RR Dart 532-7L	20638	Y50			Capt'n Laffite
XA-NJI	Fairchild Ind. FH-227D	576	XC-UTB	0071	0087	2 RR Dart 532-7L	20638	Y50			Cancun
XA-RUL	Fairchild Ind. FH-227C	507	N376NE	0066	0793	2 RR Dart 532-7	19731	Y48			
XA-SKA	Boeing (Douglas) DC-9-14	47060 / 109	N38641	0067	0997	2 PW JT8D-7B	41141	Y85			Tatafieros / lsf IALI
XA-SSW	Boeing (Douglas) DC-9-14	45735 / 25	HK-3867X	0466	0794	2 PW JT8D-7B	41141	Y83			Chief / lsf ICT
XA-SVZ	Boeing (Douglas) DC-9-15	47125 / 388	HK-3486X	0968	0994	2 PW JT8D-7B	41141	Y83			lsf ICT
XA-TBX	Boeing (Douglas) DC-9-14	45716 / 13	HK-3833X	0166	0496	2 PW JT8D-7B	41141	Y83			Tlatoani / lsf ICT
XA-TGJ	Boeing (Douglas) DC-9-15	45783 / 128	HK-3720X	0667	0597	2 PW JT8D-7B	41141	Y83			Kukulcan / lsf ICT

AEROCEDROS   Ensenada

Aeropuerto Ensenada, 22700 Ensenada, (Baja California Norte), México   ☎ (617) 66 076   Tx: n/a   Fax: (617) 66 076   SITA: n/a
F: n/a   ♦♦♦ n/a   Head: I. Cedros   Net: n/a

reg	type	cn/fn	ex/ex*	mfd	del	powered by	mtow kg	config			
XA-STJ	Cessna 402B	402B0801	N3792C	0075	0494	2 CO TSIO-520-E	2858				opf Soc. Coop. Prod. Pesque Pescado
XA-RYV	Convair 440-0 Metropolitan	474	XB-CSE	1057	0594	2 PW R-2800	21772	Freighter			opf Soc. Coop. Prod. Pesque Pescado
XA-TFY	Convair 440-0 Metropolitan	472	N411GA	0059	0796	2 PW R-2800	21772	Freighter			opf Soc. Coop. Prod. Pesque Pescado
XA-TFZ	Convair 440-94 Metropolitan	439	N44829	0057	0197	2 PW R-2800	21772	Freighter			opf Soc. Coop. Prod. Pesque Pescado

---

AEROCOZUMEL, SA = AZM   (Inter)   (Subsidiary of CINTRA / Affiliated with Aerocaribe)   Cozumel

Aeropuerto Internacional, Apartado Postal 322, 77600 Cozumel, (Quintana Roo), México   ☎ (987) 23 456   Tx: none   Fax: (987) 20 503   SITA: n/a
F: 1990   ♦♦♦ n/a   Head: Jaime V. Tamariz   IATA: 686   ICAO: AEROCOZUMEL   Net: n/a   All aircraft are operated as AEROCOZUMEL/INTER, a commuter system to provide feeder connection at MX major hubs, using MX flight numbers.
Aircraft are technically maintained by AEROCARIBE/INTER & interchanged with AEROCARIBE/INTER as required.

reg	type	cn/fn	ex/ex*	mfd	del	powered by	mtow kg	config			
XA-KOP	Britten-Norman BN-2A Mk.III-2 Trislander	1046	G-BEHB	0077	0077	3 LY O-540-E4C5	4536	Y16			Isla Mujeres
XA-LIZ	Britten-Norman BN-2A Mk.III-2 Trislander	1043	G-BEGX	0077	0881	3 LY O-540-E4C5	4536	Y16			Playa del Carmen
XA-MIL	Fairchild Ind. F-27	59	N49CC	0059	0782	2 RR Dart 514-7	18370	Y40			

AERO CUAHONTE = CUO   Uruapan

Aeropuerto Federal de Uruapan, 60160 Uruapan, (Michoacan), México   ☎ (452) 40 032   Tx: none   Fax: (452) 49 360   SITA: n/a
F: 1957   ♦♦♦ 70   Head: Enrique & Martha Amezua Cuahonte   ICAO: CUAHONTE   Net: n/a

reg	type	cn/fn	ex/ex*	mfd	del	powered by	mtow kg				
XA-KAV	Cessna T210N Turbo Centurion II	21064055		0080		2 CO TSIO-520-R	1814				
XA-KOC	Cessna 402C II	402C0301	N3271M	0080		2 CO TSIO-520-VB	3107				
XA-TGG	Fairchild (Swearingen) SA226TC Metro II	TC-385	N48GW	0080	0497	2 GA TPE331-10UA-511G	5670				
XA-TML	Fairchild (Swearingen) SA227AC Metro III	AC-752	N27444	0089	1098	2 GA TPE331-11U-611G	6577				

AERO EMPRESA MEXICANA, SA – AEMSA = AFO   Toluca

Ave Revolucion 1387, Col. Campestre San Angel, 01040 México City, (Distrito Federal), México   ☎ (5) 662 50 73   Tx: n/a   Fax: (5) 662 24 71   SITA: n/a
F: 1976   ♦♦♦ 2   Head: Lic. Juan Diego Gutiérrez Cortina   ICAO: AERO EMPRESA   Net: n/a

reg	type	cn/fn	ex/ex*	mfd	del	powered by	mtow kg				
XA-DET	Learjet 24F	24F-337	XA-GEO	0076		2 GE CJ610-8A	6123				

651   registration   type of aircraft   cn/fn   ex/ex*   mfd   del   powered by   mtow kg   configuration   selcal   name/fln/specialitites/remarks

AEROEXO – Aeroejecutivo, S.A. de C.V. = SX / AJO — Monterrey

Humberto Lobo 660, Col. del Valle, 66220 Garza Garcia, (Nuevo Leon), México ☎ (83) 69 07 77 Tx: 0382016 aesame Fax: (83) 69 07 60 SITA: n/a
F: 1977 ꜱꜱꜱ 300 Head: Alejandro Morales Mega IATA: 456 ICAO: AEROEXO Net: n/a

☐ XA-RWG	Boeing 727-31	18572 / 46	N853TW	0064	0591	3 PW JT8D-7B	69264	Y118		std MTY
☐ XA-RYI	Boeing 727-31	19228 / 351	N889TW	0066	0192	3 PW JT8D-7B	72575	Y118		std MTY
☐ XA-RXI	Boeing 727-225	20150 / 771	N8831E	0069	0791	3 PW JT8D-7B	78245	Y164		std CAN
☐ XA-RXJ	Boeing 727-225	20154 / 780	N8835E	0069	0791	3 PW JT8D-7B	78245	Y164		std MTY
☐ XA-RZI	Boeing 727-225	20151 / 773	N8832E	0069	0192	3 PW JT8D-7B	78245	Y164		std MTY
☐ XA-SDR	Boeing 727-276 (A)	20555 / 1056	VH-TBJ	0074	0692	3 PW JT8D-15	86409	Y164		lst Aviacsa
☐ XA-SFG	Boeing 727-235	19474 / 607	N4754	0068	1192	3 PW JT8D-7B	78290	Y164		std MTY
☐ XA-SIE	Boeing 727-276 (A)	22069 / 1661	VH-TBR	0080	0493	3 PW JT8D-15	86409	Y164		
☐ XA-SIJ	Boeing 727-276 (A)	22017 / 1564	VH-TBQ	0080	0593	3 PW JT8D-15	86409	Y164		std MEX
☐ XA-SJE	Boeing 727-276 (A)	21479 / 1357	VH-TBN	0678	0993	3 PW JT8D-15	86409	Y164		lst Aviacsa
☐ XA-SJU	Boeing 727-276 (A)	20552 / 906	VH-TBG	0072	0993	3 PW JT8D-15	86409	Y164		std MTY
☐ XA-SLG	Boeing 727-276 (A)	21171 / 1232	VH-TBM	0076	0993	3 PW JT8D-15	86409	Y164		lst Aviacsa
☐ XA-SLM	Boeing 727-276 (A)	21696 / 1483	VH-TBP	0079	1293	3 PW JT8D-15	86409	Y164		
☐ XA-SMB	Boeing 727-276 (A)	21646 / 1434	VH-TBO	0079	1293	3 PW JT8D-15	86409	Y164		lst Aviacsa
☐ XA-SXC	Boeing 727-225 (A)	20619 / 902	N8857E	0072	0295	3 PW JT8D-15A	79923	Y164		
☐ XA-SXE	Boeing 727-225 (A)	20615 / 898	N8852E	0072	0795	3 PW JT8D-15A	79923	Y164		

AEROFERINCO, S.A. de C.V. — Playa del Carmen

Calle 3 Sur s/n, Esquina Con 15 Av., 77710 Playa del Carmen, (Quintana Roo), México ☎ (987) 31 919 Tx: none Fax: (987) 30 574 SITA: n/a
F: 1992 ꜱꜱꜱ 40 Head: Capt. Fernando Quintin Vargas Net: n/a Aircraft below MTOW 1361kg: Cessna 182 & Piper PA-18

☐ XA-TIT	Dornier DO 28D-2 Skyservant	4129	HP-1269	0071	0097	2 LY IGSO-540-A1E	3842			
☐ XA-TNA	Dornier DO 28D-2 Skyservant	4188	HK-3967	0073	0098	2 LY IGSO-540-A1E	3842			
☐ XA-SYJ	Let 410FG	851523	1523	0085	0098	2 WA M-601D	5800			
☐ XA-TAU	Let 410UVP	851529	CCCP-67557	0085		2 WA M-601D	5800			
☐ XA-TFG	Let 410UVP	851409	N41020	0085	1096	2 WA M-601D	5800			

AERO JUAREZ, S.A. de C.V. = JUA (Sister company of Aero Freight Inc., Texas/USA) — El Paso-Int'l, TX & Guadalajara

c/o Aero Freight, 6775 Convair Road, El Paso, TX 79925, USA ☎ (915) 772-3273 Tx: none Fax: (915) 772-9243 SITA: n/a
F: 1992 ꜱꜱꜱ 6 Head: Gail E. Beach ICAO: JUAREZ Net: n/a

☐ XA-SBM	Piper PA-31-350 Navajo Chieftain	31-7852138	N27749	0078		2 LY TIO-540-J2BD	3175			occ lst/jtly opw Aero Freight

AEROLINEAS DAMOJH, SA de CV (Affiliated with Aero Guadalajara SA de CV, aircraft maintenance company) — Guadalajara

Terminal de Aviacion General, Of. 4, 44900 Guadalajara, (Jalisco), México ☎ (3) 688 56 54 Tx: none Fax: (3) 688 56 54 SITA: n/a
F: n/a ꜱꜱꜱ n/a Head: n/a Net: n/a

☐ XA-RJB	GAC (Grumman) G-159 Gulfstream I	159	G-BNKN	0065		2 RR Dart 529-8X	16329			
☐ XA-RLK	GAC (Grumman) G-159 Gulfstream I	138	N126K	0064	0590	2 RR Dart 529-8X	16329			

AEROLINEAS EJECUTIVAS, S.A. de C.V. = LET (Aerotaxis de México, S.A. dba) — Toluca

Aeropuerto Int'l de Toluca, Lotes 14-18, 50130 Toluca (México), México ☎ (72) 73 11 35 Tx: none Fax: (72) 73 11 38 SITA: n/a
F: 1970 ꜱꜱꜱ 200 Head: Lic. Ruben Perez Maya ICAO: MEXEJECUTIV Net: n/a

☐ XA-APP	Beech Bonanza B36TC	EA-605		0097	1097	1 CO TSIO-520-UB	1746			
☐ XA-TVA	Bell 206L-3 LongRanger III	51336	N207FC	0092		1 AN 250-C30P	1882			
☐ XA-ALE	Agusta A109C	7611	N1ZU	0090		2 AN 250-C20R/1	2720			
☐ XA-SNP	Beech Beechjet 400A	RK-83	N8283C	0094		2 PWC JT15D-5	7303			
☐ XA-HOS	Learjet 35A	35A-341	D-CARE	0080		2 GA TFE731-2-2B	8165			
☐ XA-TCI	Learjet 35A	35A-349	N272T	0080		2 GA TFE731-2-2B	8165			
☐ XA-ZAP	Learjet 35A	35A-129	N229X	0077		2 GA TFE731-2-2B	8165			
☐ XA-DUC	Dassault Falcon 20F	269	XA-NAY	0073		2 GE CF700-2D2	13000			
☐ XA-RNB	Dassault Falcon 20C-5	142	N220RT	0068		2 GA TFE731-5AR-2C	12800			cvtd 20C
☐ XA-RUY	Hawker 800XP	258302	N302XP*	0096	1296	2 GA TFE731-5BR-1H	12701			
☐ XA-AVE	Dassault Falcon 50	22	XA-SFP	0080		3 GA TFE731-3-1C	17600			
☐ XA-FVK	Dassault Falcon 50	35	N350AF	0080	0194	3 GA TFE731-3-1C	17600			
☐ XA-RVV	Dassault Falcon 50	213	N295FJ	0090		3 GA TFE731-3-1C	17600			

AEROLINEAS EJECUTIVAS DE SAN LUIS, S.A. de C.V. = ELP — San Luis Potosi

5 de Mayo 435, Planta Baja Interior 2, 78000 San Luis Potosi, (San Luis Potosi), México ☎ (48) 14 00 54 Tx: none Fax: (48) 14 32 15 SITA: n/a
F: 1977 ꜱꜱꜱ 5 Head: n/a ICAO: AEROSANLUIS Net: n/a Aircraft below MTOW 1361kg: Piper PA-28.

☐ XA-PET	Twin (Aero) Commander 700	70028	XB-AVG	0079		2 LY TIO-540-R2AD	3151			

AEROLINEAS INTERNACIONALES, SA de CV = N2 / LNT — Cuernavaca

Blvd Vincente Guerrero 46, Lomas de la Selva, 62270 Cuernavaca, (Morelos), México ☎ (73) 11 22 63 Tx: n/a Fax: (73) 11 51 14 SITA: n/a
F: 1994 ꜱꜱꜱ n/a Head: n/a IATA: 440 ICAO: LINEAINT Net: http://www.iwm.com.mx/foroemp/aerint.html

☐ XA-RSQ	Boeing (Douglas) DC-9-14	45730 / 37	N930EA	0066	1096	2 PW JT8D-7A	41141			Oaxtepec / lsf IALI / cvtd -11
☐ XA-SKC	Boeing 727-23	19181 / 265	N1906	0566	0394	3 PW JT8D-7B	72847			
☐ XA-SNW	Boeing 727-23	18450 / 140	N1994	0565	0394	3 PW JT8D-7B	72847		BJ-FK	
☐ XA-SPU	Boeing 727-223	20181 / 699	N6828	0369	0694	3 PW JT8D-9	80966			Tepoztlan

AEROLINEAS MARCOS, SA de CV = MCO — Toluca

Calle Santo Domingo 14, Col. Cove, 01129 México City, (Distrito Federal), México ☎ (5) 589 81 44 Tx: none Fax: (5) 294 27 12 SITA: n/a
F: n/a ꜱꜱꜱ n/a Head: Joseph Rabi ICAO: MARCOS Net: n/a

☐ XA-POJ	IAI 1123 Jet Commander	1123-161	N33WD	0074		2 GE CJ610-9	9389			
☐ XA-PUF	IAI 1123 Jet Commander	1123-153	N223WW	0072		2 GE CJ610-9	9389			
☐ XA-LIJ	IAI 1124 Westwind	285	VR-CBK	0080		2 GA TFE731-3-1G	10365			

AEROLITORAL, S.A. de C.V. = SLI (Subsidiary of Aeromexico) — Monterrey & Veracruz

Carretera Miguel Aleman Km 22,8, 66600 Apodaca, (Nuevo Leon), México ☎ (83) 69 97 30 Tx: none Fax: (83) 38 61 61 SITA: n/a
F: 1989 ꜱꜱꜱ 297 Head: Alfonos Pasquel IATA: 642 ICAO: COSTERA Net: http://www.aerolitoral.com
All aircraft are operated on behalf of AEROMEXICO (in full Aerolitoral colours), to provide feeder connection at AM major hubs, using AM flight numbers.

☐ XA-RSB	Fairchild (Swearingen) SA227BC Metro III	BC-783B	N3001H*	0091	1091	2 GA TPE331-11U-611G	7257	Y19		
☐ XA-RVR	Fairchild (Swearingen) SA227BC Metro III	BC-771B	N71NE*	0091	0491	2 GA TPE331-11U-611G	7257	Y19		
☐ XA-RVS	Fairchild (Swearingen) SA227BC Metro III	BC-773B	N2757A*	0091	0491	2 GA TPE331-11U-611G	7257	Y19		
☐ XA-RWS	Fairchild (Swearingen) SA227BC Metro III	BC-770B	N27556*	0091	0591	2 GA TPE331-11U-611G	7257	Y19		
☐ XA-RXH	Fairchild (Swearingen) SA227BC Metro III	BC-774B	N27617*	0091	0691	2 GA TPE331-11U-611G	7257	Y19		
☐ XA-RXM	Fairchild (Swearingen) SA227BC Metro III	BC-777B	N27644*	0091	0891	2 GA TPE331-11U-611G	7257	Y19		
☐ XA-RXW	Fairchild (Swearingen) SA227BC Metro III	BC-779B	N27787*	0091	0991	2 GA TPE331-11U-611G	7257	Y19		
☐ XA-RYY	Fairchild (Swearingen) SA227BC Metro III	BC-781B	N3000R*	0091	0991	2 GA TPE331-11U-611G	7257	Y19		
☐ XA-SAQ	Fairchild (Swearingen) SA227BC Metro III	BC-787B	N3003A*	0092	0292	2 GA TPE331-11U-611G	7257	Y19		
☐ XA-SBD	Fairchild (Swearingen) SA227BC Metro III	BC-778B	N2775J*	0092	0392	2 GA TPE331-11U-611G	7257	Y19		
☐ XA-SBN	Fairchild (Swearingen) SA227BC Metro III	BC-768B	N27531*	0092	0392	2 GA TPE331-11U-611G	7257	Y19		
☐ XA-SCI	Fairchild (Swearingen) SA227BC Metro III	BC-780B	N27779*	0092	0592	2 GA TPE331-11U-611G	7257	Y19		
☐ XA-SCS	Fairchild (Swearingen) SA227BC Metro III	BC-786B	N3002K*	0092	0692	2 GA TPE331-11U-611G	7257	Y19		
☐ XA-SES	Fairchild (Swearingen) SA227BC Metro III	BC-789B	N3003T*	0092	0992	2 GA TPE331-11U-611G	7257	Y19		
☐ XA-SFC	Fairchild (Swearingen) SA227DC Metro 23	DC-805B	N3008L*	0092	0992	2 GA TPE331-12U-701G	7484	Y19		
☐ XA-SFX	Fairchild (Swearingen) SA227DC Metro 23	DC-808B	N3008M*	0092	1192	2 GA TPE331-12U-701G	7484	Y19		
☐ XA-SGG	Fairchild (Swearingen) SA227DC Metro 23	DC-818B	N3012Q*	0092	1292	2 GA TPE331-12U-701G	7484	Y19		
☐ XA-SGH	Fairchild (Swearingen) SA227DC Metro 23	DC-817B	N3010S*	0092	1292	2 GA TPE331-12U-701G	7484	Y19		
☐ XA-SGV	Fairchild (Swearingen) SA227DC Metro 23	DC-819B	N3012U*	0093	0293	2 GA TPE331-12U-701G	7484	Y19		
☐ XA-SHD	Fairchild (Swearingen) SA227DC Metro 23	DC-820B	N3013B*	0093	0293	2 GA TPE331-12U-701G	7484	Y19		
☐ XA-SHE	Fairchild (Swearingen) SA227DC Metro 23	DC-821B	N3013L*	0093	0393	2 GA TPE331-12U-701G	7484	Y19		
☐ XA-SNF	Fairchild (Swearingen) SA227DC Metro 23	DC-826B	N3025A*	0493	0693	2 GA TPE331-12U-701G	7484	Y19		
☐ XA-SVA	Fairchild (Swearingen) SA227DC Metro 23	DC-822B	N3013Q*	0093	0693	2 GA TPE331-12U-701G	7484	Y19		
☐ XA-SVB	Fairchild (Swearingen) SA227DC Metro 23	DC-823B	N30137*	0293	0693	2 GA TPE331-12U-701G	7484	Y19		
☐ XA-SVC	Fairchild (Swearingen) SA227DC Metro 23	DC-824B	N30134*	0093	0693	2 GA TPE331-12U-701G	7484	Y19		
☐ XA-TCJ	Fairchild (Swearingen) SA227DC Metro 23	DC-812B	N3008T*	0092	1192	2 GA TPE331-12U-701G	7484	Y19		
☐ XA-TIU	Saab 340B	340B-270	PH-KSL	0091	1197	2 GE CT7-9B	13155	Y33		lsf Boeing Capital Corp.
☐ XA-TJI	Saab 340B	340B-188	PH-KSF	0090	1297	2 GE CT7-9B	13155	Y33		Jalisco / lsf Boeing Capital Corp.
☐ XA-TJR	Saab 340B	340B-226	PH-KSK	0090	0298	2 GE CT7-9B	13155	Y33		lsf Boeing Capital Corp.
☐ XA-TKA	Saab 340B	340B-288	PH-KSM	0092	0498	2 GE CT7-9B	13155	Y33		lsf Boeing Capital Corp.
☐ XA-TKL	Saab 340B	340B-217	PH-KSI	0090	0498	2 GE CT7-9B	13155	Y33		lsf Boeing Capital Corp.
☐ XA-	Saab 340B	340B-189	PH-KSG	0090	0598	2 GE CT7-9B	13155	Y33		lsf Boeing Capital Corp.

AEROMAR AIRLINES = VW / TAO (Transportes Aeromar, S.A. de C.V. dba/ Member of Groupo Aeromar, S.A. de C.V.) — Mexico City

Hangar 7, Zone E, Terminal de Aviacion General, 15620 México City, (Distrito Federal), México ☎ (5) 627 02 05 Tx: none Fax: (5) 758 08 41 SITA: MEXRMVW
F: 1987 ꜱꜱꜱ 590 Head: Lic. Carlos F. Autrey IATA: 942 ICAO: TRANS-AEROMAR Net: http://www.aeromar-air.com

☐ XA-MAR	ATR 42-320	115	F-WWEL*	0088	1188	2 PWC PW121	16700	Y46		
☐ XA-RNP	ATR 42-320	213	F-WWEA*	0090	1090	2 PWC PW121	16700	Y48		
☐ XA-RXC	ATR 42-320	257	F-WWEO*	0091	1091	2 PWC PW121	16700	Y48		

652 registration type of aircraft cn/fn ex/ex* mfd del powered by mtow kg configuration selcal name/fln/specialitites/remarks

registration	type of aircraft	cn/fn	ex/ex*	mfd	del	powered by	mtow kg	configuration	selcal	name/fln/specialitites/remarks
☐ XA-SJJ	ATR 42-320	039	N71296	0087	0193	2 PWC PW121	16700	Y46		cvtd -300
☐ XA-SYH	ATR 42-320	062	XA-PEP*	0087	1087	2 PWC PW121	16700	Y46		Presidente Aleman
☐ XA-TAH	ATR 42-500	471	F-WWLS*	0095	1195	2 PWC PW127E	18600	Y48		
☐ XA-TAI	ATR 42-500	474	F-WWLF*	0095	1195	2 PWC PW127E	18600	Y48		
☐ XA-TIC	ATR 42-320	058	F-OGNF	0087	0797	2 PWC PW121	16700	Y48		cvtd -300
☐ XA-TKJ	ATR 42-500	561	F-WWLW*	0098	1098	2 PWC PW127E	18600	Y48		
☐ XA-TLN	ATR 42-500	564	F-WWEC*	0098	1098	2 PWC PW127E	18600	Y48		

AEROMEXICO = AM / AMX (Aerovias de México, S.A. de C.V. dba / Subsidiary of CINTRA / formerly Aeronaves de Mexico, S.A.) Mexico City

Paseo de la Reforma 445, 06500 México City, (Distrito Federal), México ☎ (5) 327 40 94 Tx: 01772765 amsame Fax: (5) 511 94 57 SITA: n/a
F: 1934 ⁂ 5510 Head: Ernesto M. Rebolledo IATA: 139 ICAO: AEROMEXICO Net: http://www.wotw.com/aeromexico/
A commuter system to provide feeder connection at AM major hubs, using AM flight numbers, is operated by subsidiary AEROLITORAL. For details see under that company.

☐ XA-AMA	Boeing (Douglas) DC-9-32	48125 / 947		0080	0480	2 PW JT8D-17	49442	C12Y90		lsf GECA
☐ XA-AMB	Boeing (Douglas) DC-9-32	48126 / 951		0080	0580	2 PW JT8D-17	49442	C12Y90		lsf GECA
☐ XA-AMC	Boeing (Douglas) DC-9-32	48127 / 961		0080	0780	2 PW JT8D-17	49442	C12Y90		lsf GECA
☐ XA-AMD	Boeing (Douglas) DC-9-32	48128 / 964		0080	0880	2 PW JT8D-17	49442	C12Y90		lsf GECA
☐ XA-AME	Boeing (Douglas) DC-9-32	48129 / 968		0080	1080	2 PW JT8D-17	49442	C12Y90		lsf GECA
☐ XA-AMF	Boeing (Douglas) DC-9-32	48130 / 976		0080	1280	2 PW JT8D-17	49442	C12Y90		lsf GECA
☐ XA-DEI	Boeing (Douglas) DC-9-32	47650 / 771		0075	0575	2 PW JT8D-17	49442	C12Y90	JM-BF	lsf GECA
☐ XA-DEK	Boeing (Douglas) DC-9-32	47602 / 718		0074	0374	2 PW JT8D-17	49442	C12Y90	CG-FJ	lsf GECA
☐ XA-DEL	Boeing (Douglas) DC-9-32	47607 / 721		0074	0374	2 PW JT8D-17	49442	C12Y90	CG-FK	lsf GECA
☐ XA-DEM	Boeing (Douglas) DC-9-32	47609 / 723		0074	0474	2 PW JT8D-17	49442	C12Y90	CG-FL	lsf GECA
☐ XA-JEB	Boeing (Douglas) DC-9-32	47394 / 458	YV-19C	0069	0580	2 PW JT8D-17	49442	C12Y90		
☐ XA-JEC	Boeing (Douglas) DC-9-32	47106 / 235	YV-73C	0068	0780	2 PW JT8D-17	49442	C12Y90		
☐ XA-SDF	Boeing (Douglas) DC-9-32	47006 / 99	VR-BMG	0067	0792	2 PW JT8D-17	49442	C12Y90		
☐ XA-TFO	Boeing (Douglas) DC-9-32	48151 / 1017	N1003U	0081	1181	2 PW JT8D-17	49442	C12Y90		
☐ N1003P	Boeing (Douglas) DC-9-32	48150 / 1014	XA-AMG ntu	0081	1081	2 PW JT8D-17	49442	C12Y90		lsf CCC Lease
☐ N935ML	Boeing (Douglas) DC-9-31	47549 / 639	VH-CZL	0071	0792	2 PW JT8D-17	49442	C12Y90		lsf FSBU Trustee
☐ N936ML	Boeing (Douglas) DC-9-31	47501 / 571	VH-CZG	0070	0792	2 PW JT8D-17	49442	C12Y90		lsf FSBU Trustee
☐ XA-SFO	Boeing (Douglas) MD-87 (DC-9-87)	49673 / 1508	EI-CBU	0088	1092	2 PW JT8D-219	67812	C12Y102		lsf GECA
☐ N1075T	Boeing (Douglas) MD-87 (DC-9-87)	49724 / 1549	SU-DAP	0089	1197	2 PW JT8D-219	67812	C12Y102		lsf CITG
☐ N803ML	Boeing (Douglas) MD-87 (DC-9-87)	49726 / 1610		0089	1292	2 PW JT8D-219	67812	C12Y102		lsf GECA
☐ XA-AMP	Boeing (Douglas) MD-82 (DC-9-82)	49189 / 1173		0084	1284	2 PW JT8D-217C	66678	C12Y135		lsf T&I Lease
☐ XA-AMQ	Boeing (Douglas) MD-82 (DC-9-82)	49190 / 1180		0085	0285	2 PW JT8D-217C	66678	C12Y135		lsf T&I Lease
☐ XA-AMS	Boeing (Douglas) MD-88 (DC-9-88)	49926 / 1715		0090	0590	2 PW JT8D-219	72575	C12Y125		lsf POLA
☐ XA-AMT	Boeing (Douglas) MD-88 (DC-9-88)	49927 / 1716		0090	0690	2 PW JT8D-219	72575	C12Y125		lsf POLA
☐ XA-AMU	Boeing (Douglas) MD-88 (DC-9-88)	49928 / 1732	N166PL	0090	0890	2 PW JT8D-219	72575	C12Y125		lsf POLA
☐ XA-AMV	Boeing (Douglas) MD-88 (DC-9-88)	49929 / 1741		0090	0890	2 PW JT8D-219	72575	C12Y125		lsf POLA
☐ XA-MRM	Boeing (Douglas) MD-82 (DC-9-82)	53066 / 1938	B-28005	0091	0998	2 PW JT8D-217C	67812	C12Y135		
☐ XA-SFL	Boeing (Douglas) MD-82 (DC-9-82)	48069 / 1032	N1003Z	0081	1281	2 PW JT8D-219	66678	C12Y135		lsf FSBU Trustee
☐ XA-TLH	Boeing (Douglas) MD-82 (DC-9-82)	53119 / 1956	B-28013	0092	0898	2 PW JT8D-219	67812	C12Y135		cvtd MD-83 (DC-9-83)
☐ EI-BTX	Boeing (Douglas) MD-82 (DC-9-82)	49660 / 1445		0088	1190	2 PW JT8D-219	66678	C12Y133		lsf GECA
☐ EI-BTY	Boeing (Douglas) MD-82 (DC-9-82)	49667 / 1466		0088	0790	2 PW JT8D-219	66678	C12Y133		lsf GECA
☐ N10033	Boeing (Douglas) MD-82 (DC-9-82)	48083 / 1043	XA-AML ntu	0081	0382	2 PW JT8D-217A	66678	C12Y135		lsf CITG
☐ N1003X	Boeing (Douglas) MD-82 (DC-9-82)	48067 / 1028	XA-AMI ntu	0081	1281	2 PW JT8D-217A	66678	C12Y135		lsf ACG Acquisition Corp.
☐ N1003Y	Boeing (Douglas) MD-82 (DC-9-82)	48068 / 1031	XA-SFK	0081	1281	2 PW JT8D-219	66678	C12Y135		lsf WTC Trustee
☐ N158PL	Boeing (Douglas) MD-88 (DC-9-88)	49761 / 1623		0089	1289	2 PW JT8D-219	72575	C12Y125		lsf POLA
☐ N160PL	Boeing (Douglas) MD-88 (DC-9-88)	49763 / 1626		0089	1289	2 PW JT8D-219	72575	C12Y125		lsf POLA
☐ N161PL	Boeing (Douglas) MD-88 (DC-9-88)	49764 / 1632		0089	1289	2 PW JT8D-219	72575	C12Y125		lsf POLA
☐ N162PL	Boeing (Douglas) MD-88 (DC-9-88)	49765 / 1645		0090	0190	2 PW JT8D-219	72575	C12Y125		lsf POLA
☐ N168PL	Boeing (Douglas) MD-88 (DC-9-88)	53174 / 1854		0091	0591	2 PW JT8D-219	72575	C12Y125		lsf POLA
☐ N169PL	Boeing (Douglas) MD-88 (DC-9-88)	53175 / 1868		0091	0691	2 PW JT8D-219	72575	C12Y125		lsf POLA
☐ N501AM	Boeing (Douglas) MD-82 (DC-9-82)	49188 / 1172	XA-AMO	0084	1284	2 PW JT8D-217A	66678	C12Y135		lsf Boeing Capital Corp.
☐ N505MD	Boeing (Douglas) MD-82 (DC-9-82)	49149 / 1086	XA-SFM	0082	1283	2 PW JT8D-217A	66678	C12Y135		lsf Finova Capital Corp.
☐ N583MD	Boeing (Douglas) MD-83 (DC-9-83)	49659 / 1438	YV-39C	0088	0897	2 PW JT8D-219	72575	C12Y125		lsf Boeing Capital Corp.
☐ N831LF	Boeing (Douglas) MD-83 (DC-9-83)	53050 / 1704	EC-EUZ	0090	0592	2 PW JT8D-219	67812	C12Y135		lsf ILFC
☐ N838AM	Boeing (Douglas) MD-83 (DC-9-83)	49397 / 1331	N830VV	0087	1296	2 PW JT8D-219	72575	C12Y125		lsf Boeing Capital Corp.
☐ N861LF	Boeing (Douglas) MD-83 (DC-9-83)	49826 / 1578	EC-EZR	0389	0692	2 PW JT8D-219	67812	C12Y135		lsf ILFC
☐ N881LF	Boeing (Douglas) MD-83 (DC-9-83)	53051 / 1718	EC-EVU	0090	0692	2 PW JT8D-219	67812	C12Y135		lsf ILFC
☐ N944AM	Boeing (Douglas) MD-82 (DC-9-82)	49440 / 1304	D-ALLT	0886	0297	2 PW JT8D-217	66678	C12Y135		lsf 49440 Corp.
☐ N945AS	Boeing (Douglas) MD-83 (DC-9-83)	49643 / 1423	G-BNSA	0087	0697	2 PW JT8D-219	72575	C12Y125		lsf ILFC
☐ N946AS	Boeing (Douglas) MD-83 (DC-9-83)	49658 / 1461	G-BNSB	0088	0597	2 PW JT8D-219	72575	C12Y125		lsf ILFC
☐ N380RM	Boeing 757-2Q8	29380 / 836	N1795B*	0098	1298	2 PW PW2037	104326	C12Y179		lsf ILFC
☐ N53AW	Boeing 757-23A	25490 / 510	XA-SMD	1292	1294	2 PW PW2037	108862	C18Y171	GJ-AS	lsf AWAS
☐ N592KA	Boeing 757-236	25592 / 453	SE-DSK	0092	0299	2 RR RB211-535E4	113398	C18Y170		lsf PEGA
☐ N801AM	Boeing 757-2Q8	25624 / 541	XA-SIK	0093	0493	2 PW PW2037	104326	C24Y151		lsf ILFC
☐ N802AM	Boeing 757-2Q8	26270 / 558	XA-SJD	0093	0693	2 PW PW2037	104326	C24Y151		lsf ILFC
☐ N803AM	Boeing 757-2Q8	26268 / 590	XA-SMJ	0094	0194	2 PW PW2037	104326	C12Y179		lsf ILFC
☐ N804AM	Boeing 757-2Q8	26271 / 592	XA-SMK	0094	0194	2 PW PW2037	104326	C12Y179		lsf ILFC
☐ N805AM	Boeing 757-2Q8	26272 / 594	XA-SML	0094	0394	2 PW PW2037	104326	C12Y179		lsf ILFC
☐ N806AM	Boeing 757-2Q8	26273 / 597	XA-SMM	0094	0494	2 PW PW2037	104326	C12Y179		lsf ILFC
☐ XA-JBC	Boeing 767-284 (ER)	24762 / 307	XA-RVY	0090	0696	2 PW PW4056	175540	C18Y172	BC-JR	lsf AWAS
☐ XA-RVZ	Boeing 767-284 (ER)	24716 / 297	CC-CDH	0090	0596	2 PW PW4056	175540	C18Y172	BC-JS	lsf AWAS
☐ XA-APB	Boeing 767-3Q8 (ER)	27618 / 727		1198	1198	2 PW PW4062	184612	C10Y223		lsf ILFC / 25th Anniversary-colors
☐ XA-RKI	Boeing 767-3Y0 (ER)	26200 / 450		0092	0992	2 PW PW4060	184612	C10Y223	BC-QR	lsf GECA
☐ XA-TJD	Boeing 767-3Y0 (ER)	25411 / 408	XA-EDE	0092	1197	2 PW PW4060	184612	C10Y223		lsf GECA

AEROMEXPRESS, SA de CV = QO / MPX (Subsidiary of CINTRA) Mexico City

Ave. Texcoco s/n, Esq. Av. Tahel, 15620 México City, (Distrito Federal), México ☎ (5) 133 02 03 Tx: none Fax: (5) 133 02 26 SITA: MEXXZQO
F: 1989 ⁂ 1200 Head: Alberto G. Obregon IATA: 976 ICAO: AEROMEXPRESS Net: n/a

☐ N909PG	Boeing 727-2K5 (F) (A)	21852 / 1553	A6-EMC	1179	0794	3 PW JT8D-17 (HK3/FDX)	89448	Freighter		Icarus / lsf PEGA / cvtd -2K5

AERO-MITLA Oaxaca

4A Martires de Tacubaya 401, 68000 Oaxaca, (Oaxaca), México ☎ (951) 30 318 Tx: none Fax: none SITA: n/a
F: 1979 ⁂ 12 Head: Capt. Roberto Yanez Cruz Net: n/a

☐ XA-KIK	Boeing (Douglas) DC-3C (C-47-DL)	4369	TG-ASA	0042		2 PW R-1830	12202	Freighter		

AERO PERSONAL, SA de C.V. = PNL Mexico City

Santos Dumont 220, Hangar 30, Colonia Federal, 15700 México City, (Distrito Federal), México ☎ (5) 558 12 11 Tx: none Fax: (5) 558 64 78 SITA: n/a
F: 1974 ⁂ 25 Head: Gustavo Anaya Canas ICAO: AEROPERSONAL Net: n/a

☐ XA-CCI	Eurocopter (Aerosp.) SA365N1 Dauphin 2	6365	N808JT	0090	0494	2 TU Arriel 1C1	4100			
☐ XA-SWT	Eurocopter (Aerosp.) AS365N2 Dauphin 2	6407	N488FA	0091	0797	2 TU Arriel 1C2	4250			
☐ XA-SPQ	Cessna 650 Citation VII	650-7028	N728CM	0093	0794	2 GA TFE731-4R-2S	10183			
☐ XA-GNI	Dassault Falcon 2000	60	N2147	0098	0898	2 CFE CFE738-1-1B	16556			

AEROPREMIER DE MEXICO, S.A. de C.V. = MIE Merida

Plataforma de Aviation General del, Aeropuerto International de Merida, 97000 Merida (Yucatan), México ☎ (99) 46 05 96 Tx: none Fax: (99) 46 16 31 SITA: n/a
F: 1991 ⁂ n/a Head: Leobardo Diaz R. ICAO: AEROPREMIER Net: n/a

☐ XA-SPW	Twin (Aero) Turbo Commander 690A	11175	N276H	0074	0894	2 GA TPE331-5-251K	4649			

AERORENT, SA de C.V. = REN Mexico City

Terminal Aviacion General, Hangar 1, Zona D, 15620 México City, (Distrito Federal), México ☎ (5) 558 02 13 Tx: n/a Fax: (5) 558 03 45 SITA: n/a
F: 1979 ⁂ n/a Head: n/a ICAO: AERORENT Net: n/a

☐ XA-POY	Beech King Air 300	FA-14	XA-VID	0084		2 PWC PT6A-60A	6350			
☐ XA-RXA	Learjet 24B	24B-197	N710TJ	0069		2 GE CJ610-6	6123			

AERO-REY, S.A. de C.V. = REY Monterrey

Apartado Postal 5326, 64000 Monterrey, (Nuevo Leon), México ☎ (8) 346 70 50 Tx: none Fax: (8) 348 83 47 SITA: n/a
F: 1989 ⁂ n/a Head: n/a ICAO: AEROREY Net: n/a

☐ XA-SBV	Sabreliner 60 (Rockwell NA265-60)	306-109	N602KB	0075	0492	2 PW JT12A-8	9150			

AERO SERVICIO ORTIZ, SA Culiacan

Colon 308 Oriente, 80000 Culiacan, (Sinaloa), México ☎ (67) 12 94 63 Tx: n/a Fax: (67) 60 14 22 SITA: n/a
F: n/a ⁂ n/a Head: n/a Net: n/a

☐ XA-FIO	Cessna TU206F Turbo Stationair II	U20602710		0075		1 CO TSIO-520-C	1633			
☐ XA-GIO	Cessna TU206F Turbo Stationair II	U20603368	N8511Q	0076		1 CO TSIO-520-C	1633			
☐ XA-IAE	Cessna TU206G Turbo Stationair 6 II	U20604194	XB-NAS	0078		1 CO TSIO-520-M	1633			
☐ XA-LUY	Cessna U206G Stationair 6 II	U20606267	N6396Z	0081		1 CO IO-520-F	1633			
☐ XA-NAC	Cessna TU206F Turbo Stationair	U20602529	XB-AUW	0074		1 CO TSIO-520-C	1633			
☐ XA-RAH	Cessna TU206G Turbo Stationair 6 II	U20606008	N4732Z	0080		1 CO TSIO-520-M	1633			

AEROSERVICIOS MONTERREY, S.A. de C.V. = SVM
Monterrey

Oscar Wilde 173, Colinas de San Jeronimo, 64630 Monterrey, (Nuevo Leon), México ☎ (8) 369 09 25 Tx: none Fax: (8) 369 09 25 SITA: n/a
F: n/a ⛹ n/a Head: n/a ICAO: SERVIMONTE Net: n/a

☐ XA-HAC	Piper PA-31-325 Navajo C/R	*31-7912088*	*N3532K*	*0072*		*2 LY TIO-540-F2BD*	*2948*

AEROTAXI VILLA RICA, SA de CV = VRI
Veracruz

Independencia 1633-5, 91700 Veracruz, (Veracruz), México ☎ (29) 32 78 12 Tx: n/a Fax: (29) 32 81 61 SITA: n/a
F: n/a ⛹ n/a Head: n/a ICAO: VILLARICA Net: n/a

☐ XA-JEX	Cessna 500 Citation I	*500-0395*	*N2651S*	*0078*		*2 PWC JT15D-1A*	*5375*

AEROTAX MONSE, SA de CV = TXO
Mexico City

Miramondis 3163, Col Hueso Benden Coada, 14320 México City, (Distrito Federal), México ☎ (5) 763 67 20 Tx: none Fax: (5) 627 67 06 SITA: n/a
F: 1989 ⛹ 8 Head: Capt. Monzano Walding ICAO: MONSE Net: n/a

☐ XA-SMF	Sabreliner 60 (Rockwell NA265-60)	*306-6*	*XA-ADC*	*0067*		*2 PW JT12A-8*	*9072*	*Exec 8 Pax*
☐ XA-RSP	Hawker 1A/522 (HS 125-1A/522)	*25091*	*N65FC*	*0066*		*2 RR Viper 522*	*9616*	*Exec 9 Pax*
☐ XA-RSR	Hawker 1A/522 (HS 125-1A/522)	*25017*	*N333M*	*0064*		*2 RR Viper 522*	*9616*	*Exec 7 Pax*
☐ XA-ADC	BAe (BAC) One-Eleven 211AH	*084*	*S9-TAE*	*0066*	*0694*	*2 RR Spey 511-14*	*35834*	*Exec 26 Pax*

AEROTONALA, SA de CV = TON
Guadalajara

Avda Ninos Hereos 961G, Sector Suarez, 44100 Guadalajara, (Jalisco), México ☎ (3) 658 19 62 Tx: n/a Fax: (3) 658 17 99 SITA: n/a
F: 1989 ⛹ n/a Head: Jaime Madrid Sanchez ICAO: AEROTONALA Net: n/a

☐ XA-SLL	Twin (Aero) Turbo Commander 690B II	*11521*	*XB-JYM*	*0079*		*2 GA TPE331-5-251K*	*4649*
☐ XA-RMF	Learjet 24D	*24D-290*	*N24TK*	*0074*		*2 GE CJ610-6*	*6123*
☐ XA-TII	Learjet 23	*23-070*	*XA-RZM*	*0065*	*1197*	*2 GE CJ610-4*	*5670*

AEROVENTAS, SA = AEV
Monterrey

Aeropuerto Int'l del Norte, Puerto No. 3, Apartado Postal 1309, 64000 Monterrey (Nuevo Leon), México ☎ (83) 45 43 02 Tx: 0382202 egzame Fax: (83) 45 53 54 SITA: n/a
F: 1974 ⛹ 22 Head: Francisco J. Garza Garza ICAO: AEROVENTAS Net: n/a

☐ XA-TDT	Agusta A109A II Plus	*7415*	*N75YA*	*0088*	*0996*	*2 AN 250-C20R/1*	*2600*

AEROVIAS CASTILLO, SA = CLL
Guadalajara

Avda Francia 1886, Colonia Moderno, 44000 Guadalajara, (Jalisco), México ☎ (3) 688 51 86 Tx: n/a Fax: (3) 812 86 61 SITA: n/a
F: n/a ⛹ n/a Head: n/a ICAO: AEROCASTILLO Net: n/a Aircraft below MTOW 1361kg: Cessna 182.

☐ XA-JUK	Cessna R182 Skylane RG II	*R18200994*		*0079*		*1 LY O-540-J3C5D*	*1406*
☐ XA-COJ	Cessna U206G Stationair 6 II	*U20605484*	*XB-ZIC*	*0080*		*1 CO IO-520-F*	*1633*
☐ XA-JIO	Cessna U206G Stationair 6 II	*U20605330*		*0079*		*1 CO IO-520-F*	*1633*
☐ XA-PEA	Cessna TU206G Turbo Stationair 6 II	*U20606379*		*0081*		*1 CO TSIO-520-M*	*1633*
☐ XA-RWO	Cessna T210L Turbo Centurion II	*21061474*		*0076*		*1 CO TSIO-520-H*	*1724*
☐ XA-KEB	Cessna T207A Turbo Stationair 8 II	*20700615*		*0080*		*1 CO TSIO-520-M*	*1724*
☐ XA-IUL	Cessna 402C II	*402C0091*		*0079*		*2 CO TSIO-520-VB*	*3107*
☐ XA-JON	Cessna 402C II	*402C0230*		*0080*		*2 CO TSIO-520-VB*	*3107*
☐ XA-POM	Cessna 421C Golden Eagle III	*421C0695*		*0079*		*2 CO GTSIO-520-L*	*3379*
☐ XA-SCE	Learjet 24D	*24D-271*	*N4305U*	*0073*		*2 GE CJ610-6*	*6123*

AEROVIAS MONTES AZULES, S.A. de C.V. = MZL
Tuxtla Gutierrez

Av. Central Poniente 927-A, 29000 Tuxtla Gutierrez, (Chiapas), México ☎ (961) 32 293 Tx: none Fax: (961) 22 993 SITA: n/a
F: 1994 ⛹ n/a Head: Fermin Rocha ICAO: MONTES AZULES Net: n/a

☐ XA-SOF	Cessna A185F Skywagon II	*18504177*	*XB-EFP*	*0081*		*1 CO IO-520-D*	*1520*
☐ XA-TMQ	Cessna TU206G Turbo Stationair 6 II	*U20604578*	*N9569E*	*0078*	*0098*	*1 CO TSIO-520-M*	*1633*
☐ XA-SOG	Piper PA-31-325 Navajo C/R	*31-7812056*	*XB-EGX*	*0078*		*2 LY TIO-540-F2BD*	*2948*

AEROVICS, SA de CV = ARI (formerly Cerveceria Moctezuma)
Toluca

Hangar 3, Calle 1, Aeropuerto Int'l de Toluca, 50200 Toluca, (México), México ☎ (72) 73 11 80 Tx: none Fax: (72) 73 12 19 SITA: n/a
F: 1984 ⛹ 36 Head: Fernando Fernandez Presas ICAO: AEROVICS Net: n/a

☐ XA-ALB	Eurocopter (Aerosp.) SA365N1 Dauphin 2	*6364*	*JA6639*	*0090*		*2 TU Arriel 1C1*	*4100*
☐ XA-ALT	Beech King Air 300	*FA-176*	*N1570H*	*0089*		*2 PWC PT6A-60A*	*6350*
☐ XA-TAB	Dassault Falcon 100	*204*	*F-WGTG**	*0086*		*2 GA TFE731-2-1C*	*8755*
☐ XA-BAL	GAC G-IV Gulfstream IV	*1114*	*N555WL*	*0089*		*2 RR Tay 611-8*	*33203*

AERO-ZANO, S.A. de C.V.
Monterrey

Blvd. Diaz Ordaz 200, Col. Santa Maria, Apartado Postal 843, 64650 Monterrey (Nuevo Leon), México ☎ (8) 346 30 90 Tx: none Fax: (8) 346 30 92 SITA: n/a
F: 1988 ⛹ 6 Head: Roberto Zambrano ICAO: ZANO Net: n/a

☐ XA-RRE	Mitsubishi MU-2B-60 Marquise	*757SA*	*XB-BLU*	*0080*		*2 GA TPE331-10-511M*	*5250*
☐ XA-THO	Cessna S550 Citation S/II	*S550-0035*	*N711JN*	*0085*		*2 PWC JT15D-4B*	*6849*

ALLEGRO AIR = LL / GRO (Lineas Aéreas Allegro, SA de CV dba)
Cancun

Jose Benitez 2709, Col. Obispado, 64060 Monterrey, (Nuevo Leon), México ☎ (83) 33 99 38 Tx: none Fax: (83) 33 99 40 SITA: n/a
F: 1992 ⛹ 95 Head: Fernando Padilla IATA: 902 ICAO: ALLEGRO Net: n/a

☐ XA-SPA	Boeing (Douglas) DC-9-14	*45698 / 5*	*N931EA*	*0065*	*0394*	*2 PW JT8D-7B*	*41141*	*Y90*	*CH-EK*	Cozumel
☐ XA-SWW	Boeing (Douglas) MD-83 (DC-9-83)	*49848 / 1592*	*SU-DAM*	*0489*	*0195*	*2 PW JT8D-219*	*72575*	*Y165*	*DG-EJ*	*lsf PEGA*
☐ XA-SXJ	Boeing (Douglas) MD-83 (DC-9-83)	*49845 / 1573*	*SU-DAL*	*0289*	*0395*	*2 PW JT8D-219*	*72575*	*Y165*	*CS-EG*	*lsf PEGA*
☐ XA-SXO	Boeing 727-247	*20268 / 764*	*N326AS*	*0069*	*0495*	*3 PW JT8D-15*	*78245*	*Y167*	*EK-BD*	*lsf IALI*
☐ XA-SYI	Boeing 727-247	*20264 / 756*	*N324AS*	*0069*	*0595*	*3 PW JT8D-15*	*78245*	*Y167*	*EK-BG*	Acapulco / *lsf IALI/sublst Air Atlantic*
☐ XA-TCX	Boeing 727-225 (A)	*22440 / 1692*	*N809EA*	*0080*	*1292*	*3 PW JT8D-15*	*86409*	*Y167*	*FK-JL*	El Regio / *lsf IALI*
☐ XA-TKO	Boeing 727-221 (A/RE) (Super 27)	*22536 / 1774*	*N727VA*	*0081*	*0598*	*3 PW JT8D-217C/17A(BFG)*	*89448*	*Y173*		*lsf Finova Capital Corp. / cvtd -221*
☐ XA-TKV	Boeing 727-221 (A/RE) (Super 27)	*22537 / 1779*	*N728VA*	*0081*	*0698*	*3 PW JT8D-217C/17A(BFG)*	*89448*	*Y173*		*lsf Finova Capital Corp. / cvtd -221*
☐ XA-TLZ	Boeing 727-2B7 (A)	*22163 / 1735*	*N923PG*	*0081*	*0199*	*3 PW JT8D-17A (HK3/FDX)*	*89999*	*Y182*		*lsf PACA*
☐ XA-TMA	Boeing 727-2B7 (A)	*22164 / 1743*	*N907PG*	*0481*	*1298*	*3 PW JT8D-17 (HK3/FDX)*	*89545*	*Y173*		*lsf PEGA*
☐ C-GNKF	Boeing 727-227 (A)	*20839 / 1031*	*N88770*	*0074*	*1197*	*3 PW JT8D-9A (HK3/FDX)*	*79605*	*Y170*	*AH-FL*	*lsf KFA*
☐ N891DB	Boeing 727-2K3 (A)	*22770 / 1807*	*OY-SBO*	*0082*	*1098*	*3 PW JT8D-17A*	*89999*	*Y182*		*lsf Riverhorse Investments Inc.*

ASESA – Aeroservicios Especializados, SA de CV (Member of Grupo Protexa)
Monterrey

Aeropuerto del Norte, Hangar Protexa, Apodaca, 64000 Monterrey, (Nuevo Leon), México ☎ (83) 40 14 08 Tx: 0382016 aesa me Fax: (83) 45 70 93 SITA: n/a
F: 1977 ⛹ 85 Head: Ing. Humberto Lobo Net: n/a

☐ XA-AKY	Piper PA-31-310 Navajo C	*31-7712061*		*0077*		*2 LY TIO-540-A2C*	*2948*
☐ XA-RTL	Eurocopter (Aerosp.) AS365N2 Dauphin 2	*6374*	*F-WYMD**	*0090*		*2 TU Arriel 1C2*	*4250*
☐ XA-RUZ	Eurocopter (Aerosp.) AS365N2 Dauphin 2	*6394*		*0091*		*2 TU Arriel 1C2*	*4250*
☐ XA-IOW	Bell 212	*30919*	*N5013K*	*0079*		*2 PWC PT6T-3 TwinPac*	*5080*
☐ XA-LAM	Bell 212	*31164*		*0080*		*2 PWC PT6T-3 TwinPac*	*5080*
☐ XA-LAO	Bell 212	*31165*		*0080*		*2 PWC PT6T-3 TwinPac*	*5080*

ATSA – Aero Taxis, SA de CV = TXI
Durango

Hidalgo 237 Nte, 34000 Durango, (Durango), México ☎ (18) 12 52 06 Tx: n/a Fax: (18) 13 56 11 SITA: n/a
F: 1961 ⛹ 25 Head: Capt. Hector Solómon Portillo ICAO: AEREOTAXIS Net: n/a

☐ XA-BUN	Cessna TU206F Turbo Stationair II	*U20602714*		*0075*		*1 CO TSIO-520-C*	*1633*
☐ XA-KOY	Cessna TU206G Turbo Stationair 6 II	*U20605742*	*N5426X*	*0080*		*1 CO TSIO-520-M*	*1633*

AVEMEX – Aviacion Ejecutiva Mexicana, SA = AVM
Mexico City

Hangar 2, Terminal Aviacion General, Aeropuerto Int'l, 15620 México City, (Distrito Federal), México ☎ (5) 763 68 44 Tx: 01762100 avzxme Fax: (5) 763 83 23 SITA: n/a
F: 1980 ⛹ 86 Head: José Lanzagorta Rosada ICAO: AVEMEX Net: n/a

☐ XA-TDS	Cessna 208B Grand Caravan	*208B0559*		*0096*		*1 PWC PT6A-114A*	*3969*
☐ XA-KMX	Cessna 550 Citation II	*550-0210*	*XA-SDN*	*0081*		*2 PWC JT15D-4*	*6577*
☐ XA-RUU	Learjet 31	*31-012*	*N917MC*	*0089*		*2 GA TFE731-2-3B*	*7484*
☐ XA-TCZ	Cessna 650 Citation VII	*650-7019*	*N12616*	*0092*	*1292*	*2 GA TFE731-4R-2S*	*10183*
☐ XA-XIS	Cessna 650 Citation VII	*650-7032*	*N12637*	*0094*	*0394*	*2 GA TFE731-4R-2S*	*10183*

AVIACSA – Consorcio Aviacsa, S.A. de C.V. = 6A / CHP (Subsidiary of Aeroexo-Aeroejecutivo, S.A. de C.V.)
Monterrey

Humberto Lobo 660, Col. del Valle, 66220 Garza Garcia, (Nuevo Leon), México ☎ (83) 69 07 77 Tx: 0382016 aesame Fax: (83) 69 07 60 SITA: n/a
F: 1990 ⛹ 370 Head: Alejandro Morales Mega IATA: 095 ICAO: AVIACSA Net: n/a

☐ XA-TIM	Boeing (Douglas) DC-9-15	*45778 / 82*	*N1064T*	*0067*	*0997*	*2 PW JT8D-7B*	*41141*	*Y90*	
☐ XA-TIZ	Boeing (Douglas) DC-9-15	*45782 / 114*	*N1068T*	*0067*	*1097*	*2 PW JT8D-7A/B*	*41141*	*Y90*	
☐ XA-TJS	Boeing (Douglas) DC-9-15	*45784 / 140*	*N1070T*	*0067*	*0298*	*2 PW JT8D-7B (HK3/ABS)*	*41141*	*Y90*	
☐ XA-SDR	Boeing 727-276 (A)	*20555 / 1056*	*VH-TBJ*	*0074*	*0097*	*3 PW JT8D-15*	*86409*	*Y164*	*lsf Aeroexo*
☐ XA-SJE	Boeing 727-276 (A)	*21479 / 1357*	*VH-TBN*	*0678*	*0097*	*3 PW JT8D-15*	*86409*	*Y164*	*lsf Aeroexo*
☐ XA-SLG	Boeing 727-276 (A)	*21171 / 1232*	*VH-TBM*	*0076*	*0097*	*3 PW JT8D-15*	*86409*	*Y164*	*lsf Aeroexo*
☐ XA-SMB	Boeing 727-276 (A)	*21646 / 1434*	*VH-TBO*	*0079*	*0097*	*3 PW JT8D-15*	*86409*	*Y164*	*lsf Aeroexo*

654 registration type of aircraft *cn/fn* *ex/ex** *mfd* *del* *powered by* *mtow kg* *configuration* *selcal* *name/fln/specialitites/remarks*

AVIONES ARE, SA de C.V. – Servicio de Transporte Aéreo = NRE (formerly Aviones BC, SA de CV) — Cuernavaca (Morelos)

Terminal Aviacion Gen'l, Hangar 6, Zona D, Aeropuerto Int'l, 15620 México City, (Distrito Federal), México ☎ (5) 558 65 00 Tx: 01777586 abcme Fax: (5) 558 01 95 SITA: n/a
F: 1971 ⁂ 14 Head: Isaias Chavez G. ICAO: AVIONES ARE Net: n/a

☐ XA-MEY	GAC G-1159A Gulfstream III	*252*	*N17582*	*0080*		*2 RR Spey 511-8*	*30935*	*12 Pax*		

AVIONES DE SONORA, SA = ADS — Hermosillo

Aeropuerto Internacional, Col. Manga, 83000 Hermosillo, (Sonora), México ☎ (62) 61 01 55 Tx: n/a Fax: (62) 14 23 69 SITA: n/a
F: n/a ⁂ n/a Head: n/a ICAO: SONORAV Net: n/a

☐ XA-KEA	Cessna 310R II	*310R1880*		*0080*		*2 CO IO-520-M*	*2495*			
☐ XA-KOA	Cessna 340A II	*340A0978*	*YV-1886P*	*0080*		*2 CO TSIO-520-NB*	*2717*			

AVIONES UNIDOS, S.A. de C.V. — Guamuchil

Aeropuerto Rural, Apartado Postal 293, 81400 Guamuchil, (Sinaloa), México ☎ (673) 24 710 Tx: none Fax: (673) 24 710 SITA: n/a
F: n/a ⁂ n/a Head: n/a Net: n/a Aircraft below MTOW 1361kg: Cessna 182

☐ XA-IAP	Cessna A185F Skywagon II	*18503605*	*N7433Q*	*0078*		*1 CO IO-520-D*	*1520*			
☐ XA-SHU	Cessna A185F Skywagon II	*18503515*	*XB-EPT*	*0078*		*1 CO IO-520-D*	*1520*			
☐ XA-GUP	Cessna U206G Stationair	*U20603848*		*0077*		*1 CO IO-520-F*	*1633*			
☐ XA-STC	Cessna TU206G Turbo Stationair 6 II	*U20605157*	*N4901U*	*0079*		*1 CO TSIO-520-M*	*1633*			

AVIOQUINTANA – Aviones de Renta de Quintana Roo, S.A. de C.V. = AQT — Chetumal

Av. Juarez 90, Centro, 77000 Chetumal, (Quintana Roo), México ☎ (983) 20 664 Tx: none Fax: (983) 28 597 SITA: n/a
F: 1990 ⁂ 18 Head: Capt. Mario A. Hermosillo Torres ICAO: AVIOQUINTANA Net: n/a

☐ XA-JAA	Piper PA-34-200T Seneca II	*34-7970400*	*N9600N*	*0079*		*2 CO TSIO-360-EB*	*2073*	*Y5*		
☐ XA-SXB	Fairchild (Swearingen) SA226TC Metro IIA	*TC-412*	*N253AM*	*0081*		*2 GA TPE331-10UA-511G*	*5987*	*Y19*		
☐ XA-TGD	Fairchild (Swearingen) SA227AC Metro III	*AC-720*	*N2724S*	*0088*	*0996*	*2 GA TPE331-11U-612G*	*6577*	*Y19*		*lsf Embraer S.A.*
☐ XA-TKE	Fairchild (Swearingen) SA227AC Metro III	*AC-732*	*N27278*	*0089*	*0497*	*2 GA TPE331-11U-612G*	*6577*	*Y19*		*lsf Pacific Coast Lease Corp.*
☐ XA-	Fairchild (Swearingen) SA227AC Metro III	*AC-718*	*N27220*	*0088*	*0598*	*2 GA TPE331-11U-612G*	*6577*	*Y19*		*lsf Pacific Coast Lease Corp.*
☐ XA-	Fairchild (Swearingen) SA227AC Metro III	*AC-735*	*N27297*	*0089*	*0198*	*2 GA TPE331-11U-612G*	*6577*	*Y19*		*lsf Pacific Coast Lease Corp.*
☐ XA-	Fairchild (Swearingen) SA227AC Metro III	*AC-723*	*N2725D*	*0088*	*0798*	*2 GA TPE331-11U-612G*	*6577*	*Y19*		*lsf Pacific Coast Lease Corp.*

CETTY Taxi Aéreo Nacional, SA de CV = CCT — Durango

707 Poniente, 34000 Durango, (Durango), México ☎ (18) 13 41 44 Tx: n/a Fax: (18) 13 41 44 SITA: n/a
F: n/a ⁂ n/a Head: n/a ICAO: CETTY Net: n/a Aircraft below MTOW 1361kg: Cessna 180.

☐ XA-HIS	Cessna TU206G Turbo Stationair 6 II	*U20604185*		*0078*		*1 CO TSIO-520-M*	*1633*			
☐ XA-KIW	Cessna TU206G Turbo Stationair 6 II	*U20605854*	*N6285X*	*0080*		*1 CO TSIO-520-M*	*1633*			
☐ XA-LEW	Cessna TU206G Turbo Stationair 6 II	*U20606145*		*0081*		*1 CO TSIO-520-M*	*1633*			
☐ XA-MUT	Cessna TU206G Turbo Stationair 6 II	*U20604817*	*N734BA*	*0079*		*1 CO TSIO-520-M*	*1633*			
☐ XA-RZJ	Cessna TU206G Turbo Stationair 6 II	*U20605062*	*XB-BDG*	*0079*		*1 CO TSIO-520-M*	*1633*			

COMERCIAL AEREA, SA de CV = CRS — Chihuahua

Apartado Postal 683, 31000 Chihuahua, (Chihuahua), México ☎ (14) 20 00 79 Tx: n/a Fax: (14) 20 41 95 SITA: n/a
F: n/a ⁂ n/a Head: n/a ICAO: COMERCIAL AEREA Net: n/a

☐ XA-HEW	Dassault Falcon 20F	*250*	*N111AM*	*0072*		*2 GE CF700-2D2*	*13000*			

COMMANDER MEXICANA, SA de CV = CRM — Mexico City

Hangar No. 18 Aviacion General, 15620 México City, (Distrito Federal), México ☎ (5) 558 06 11 Tx: n/a Fax: (5) 756 84 87 SITA: n/a
F: n/a ⁂ n/a Head: n/a ICAO: COMMANDERMEX Net: n/a

☐ XA-SPB	Eurocopter (Aerosp.) AS355N Ecureuil 2	*5560*		*0093*		*2 TU Arrius 1A*	*2540*			
☐ XA-SPC	Eurocopter (Aerosp.) AS355N Ecureuil 2	*5569*		*0093*		*2 TU Arrius 1A*	*2540*			
☐ XA-TGF	Bell 430	*49021*	*N3456W**	*0097*	*0397*	*2 AN 250-C40*	*4082*			
☐ XA-CYR	Piper PA-42-1000 Cheyenne 400LS	*42-5527032*	*N4120G*	*0088*		*2 GA TPE331-14-801A/B*	*5466*			
☐ XA-GAP	Sabreliner 65 (Rockwell NA265-65)	*465-8*	*N10581*	*0080*		*2 GA TFE731-3R-1D*	*10886*			
☐ XA-CPQ	GAC G-V Gulfstream V	*533*	*N533GA**	*0098*	*1198*	*2 BR BR710A1-10*	*41232*			

COMPANIA MEXICANA DE AEROPLANOS, SA = MDR — Toluca

Av. Fuerza Aérea Mexicana 465, Co. Federal, Deleg. V.C., 15700 México City, (Distrito Federal), México ☎ (5) 571 36 22 Tx: none Fax: (5) 785 33 65 SITA: n/a
F: 1946 ⁂ 3 Head: Aaron Saenz Couret ICAO: AEROPLANOS Net: n/a

☐ XA-KIT	Cessna 414A Chancellor III	*414A0465*	*N2735F*	*0080*		*2 CO TSIO-520-NB*	*3062*			
☐ XA-RYE	Cessna 500 Citation	*500-0068*	*XB-FDN*	*0073*		*2 PWC JT15D-1*	*5216*			

HELISERVICIO CAMPECHE, SA de CV = HEC — Mexico City & Campeche

Citlaltepetl 27, Col. Hipodromo, 06100 México City, (Distrito Federal), México ☎ (5) 553 60 06 Tx: n/a Fax: (5) 286 24 59 SITA: n/a
F: n/a ⁂ n/a Head: n/a ICAO: HELICAMPECHE Net: n/a

☐ XA-JOL	Bell 206B JetRanger	*786*	*N31AL*	*0072*		*1 AN 250-C20*	*1451*			
☐ XA-LOC	Bell 206B JetRanger III	*3284*		*0081*		*1 AN 250-C20B*	*1451*			
☐ XA-RVW	Bell 206L-3 LongRanger III	*51442*	*N353AL*	*0091*		*1 AN 250-C30P*	*1882*			
☐ XA-IUR	Bell 212	*30938*		*0079*		*2 PWC PT6T-3 TwinPac*	*5080*			
☐ XA-SBJ	Bell 412SP	*33212*	*N398AL*	*0089*	*0392*	*2 PWC PT6T-3B TwinPac*	*5398*			
☐ XA-SBZ	Bell 412SP	*33213*	*N399AL*	*0090*		*2 PWC PT6T-3B TwinPac*	*5262*			
☐ XA-STP	Bell 412	*33042*	*N2071C*	*0081*		*2 PWC PT6T-3B TwinPac*	*5262*			
☐ XA-TAM	Bell 412SP	*33169*	*N396AL*	*0087*		*2 PWC PT6T-3B TwinPac*	*5262*			

HOTELES DINAMICOS, S.A. de C.V. = HDI — Guadalajara

San Uriel 690, Piso 4, 44750 Guadalajara, (Jalisco), México ☎ (3) 688 51 46 Tx: none Fax: (3) 688 51 46 SITA: n/a
F: n/a ⁂ n/a Head: n/a ICAO: DINAMICOS Net: n/a

☐ XA-SDI	Cessna 501 Citation I/SP	*501-0031*	*N395SC*	*0078*		*2 PWC JT15D-1A*	*5375*			

JET RENT, SA = JRN — Mexico City

Terminal Aviacion General, Aeropuerto Internacional, 15620 México City, (Distrito Federal), México ☎ (5) 558 49 63 Tx: n/a Fax: none SITA: n/a
F: n/a ⁂ n/a Head: n/a ICAO: JET RENT Net: n/a

☐ XA-DIJ	Learjet 24D	*24D-269*		*0073*		*2 GE CJ610-6*	*6123*			
☐ XA-JOC	Learjet 25D	*25D-303*		*0080*		*2 GE CJ610-8A*	*6804*			

JETS EJECUTIVOS, SA = JEJ — Mexico City

JETS EJECUTIVOS

Terminal Aviacion General, Hangar 4, Aeropuerto Int'l, 15620 México City, (Distrito Federal), México ☎ (5) 558 83 00 Tx: none Fax: (5) 558 13 66 SITA: n/a
F: 1975 ⁂ 31 Head: Capt. David Nieto Escalona ICAO: MEXJETS Net: n/a

☐ XA-SNJ	Eurocopter (Aerosp.) AS365N2 Dauphin 2	*6463*	*F-WYMJ**	*0094*		*2 TU Arriel 1C2*	*4250*			
☐ XA-MIC	GAC G-1159A Gulfstream III	*323*		*0081*		*2 RR Spey 511-8*	*30935*	*Executive*	*FG-KM*	

LINEA AEREA MEXICANA DE CARGA, S.A. de C.V. = LMC (formerly Aero Internacional, S.A. de C.V.) — Monterrey & Laredo-Int'l, TX

US office: Hangar 182, Laredo Int'l Airport, Laredo, TX 78041, USA ☎ (210) 791 36 92 Tx: none Fax: (210) 791 36 44 SITA: n/a
F: 1995 ⁂ 15 Head: Eucario Leon R. ICAO: LINEA DE CARGA Net: n/a

☐ XA-TDF	Convair 240-53 (C-131A)	*53-11*	*N70636*	*0054*	*0596*	*2 PW R-2800*	*18956*	*Freighter*		
☐ XA-TDL	Convair 440-86 Metropolitan	*438*	*N442JM*	*0057*	*0896*	*2 PW R-2800*	*21772*	*Freighter*		

LINEAS AEREAS EJECUTIVAS de Durango, SA (formerly Valverde, SA) — Durango

Aeropuerto de Durango, 34000 Durango, (Durango), México ☎ (18) 17 82 11 Tx: n/a Fax: (18) 14 00 48 SITA: n/a
F: n/a ⁂ n/a Head: n/a Net: n/a

☐ XA-RIN	Learjet 25B	*25B-104*	*XA-JAX*	*0073*		*2 GE CJ610-6*	*6804*			

LINEAS AEREAS IXTLAN, SA de CV = IXT — Ixtlan

Hidalgo 129, Interior 10, 63940 Ixtlan, (Nayarit), México ☎ (324) 32 905 Tx: n/a Fax: none SITA: n/a
F: n/a ⁂ n/a Head: n/a ICAO: IXTLAN Net: n/a

☐ XA-RRF	Cessna TU206G Turbo Stationair 6 II	*U20606080*		*0081*		*1 CO TSIO-520-M*	*1633*			

MAGNICHARTERS = GMT (Grupo Turistico Magno, S.A. de C.V. dba / Subsidiary of Magnitur) — Monterrey

La Barca 1128, Col. Mitras Sur 4, 64020 Monterrey, (Nuevo Leon), México ☎ (8) 369 08 55 Tx: none Fax: (8) 369 09 77 SITA: n/a
F: 1994 ⁂ n/a Head: n/a ICAO: GRUPOMONTERREY Net: n/a

☐ XA-STB	Boeing 737-247	*20128 / 145*	*OB-1670*	*0069*	*0299*	*2 PW JT8D-9A*	*49442*	*Y130*		*lsf Int'l Pacific Trading*
☐ XA-SWL	Boeing 737-205 (A)	*20711 / 320*	*SE-DLD*	*0073*	*0195*	*2 PW JT8D-9A*	*54205*	*Y130*		*lsf Int'l Airline Investors*
☐ XA-SYT	Boeing 737-205	*19409 / 128*	*SE-DLP*	*0069*	*0795*	*2 PW JT8D-9A*	*54205*	*Y130*		*lsf Nyckeln Flygleasing*
☐ XA-SYX	Boeing 737-222	*19059 / 50*	*P4-SYX*	*0768*	*0399*	*2 PW JT8D-7B*	*49442*	*Y122*		*lsf ACQ*

MAS AIR CARGO = MY / MAA (Aerotransportes MAS de Carga, SA de CV dba) — Mexico City

Mas Air

Almacén 22, Aduana Interior del, Aeroport Internacional, 15520 México City (Distrito Federal), México ☎ (5) 786 95 55 Tx: none Fax: (5) 786 95 43 SITA: n/a
F: 1991 ⁂ 63 Head: Christian Ureta Larrain IATA: 865 ICAO: MAS CARGA Net: n/a

☐ XA-MAS	Boeing 707-323C	*19585 / 668*	*P4-CCC*	*0067*	*0796*	*4 PW JT3D-3B (HK2/COM)*	*151953*	*Freighter*		*lsf Pocahontes Investments*
☐ CC-CAX	Boeing (Douglas) DC-8-71F	*45970 / 343*	*N8080U*	*0068*	*0898*	*4 CFMI CFM56-2C*	*147418*	*Freighter*	*AJ-HL*	*lsf FST / cvtd DC-8-61/-71*

655 registration type of aircraft *cn/fn* *ex/ex** *mfd* *del* *powered by* *mtow kg* *configuration* *selcal* *name/fln/specialitites/remarks*

MAYAIR, S.A. de C.V. = MYI Cozumel

Calle 11 Sur No. 598, Col. Gonzalo Guerrera, 77663 Cozumel, (Quintana Roo), México ☎ (987) 20 433 Tx: none Fax: (987) 21 044 SITA: n/a
F: n/a ⁂ n/a Head: n/a ICAO: MAYAIR Net: n/a

☐ XA-SXX	Let 410UVP	800512	CCCP-67041	0080	0795	2 WA M-601D	5800	Y19		

MEXICANA = MX / MXA (Compania Mexicana de Aviacion, SA de CV dba / Subsidiary of CINTRA) Mexico City

Xola 535, 11th Floor, 03100 México City, (Distrito Federal), México ☎ (5) 448 30 96 Tx: 01771247 cmarme Fax: (5) 448 30 96 SITA: MEXDGMX
F: 1921 ⁂ 6580 Head: Fernando P. Flores IATA: 132 ICAO: MEXICANA Net: http://www.mexicana.com
A commuter system to provide feeder connection at MX major hubs, using MX flt no's, is operated under the marketing name INTER by AEROCARIBE & AEROCOZUMEL, for details – see under each co.

☐ XA-SGE	Fokker 100 (F28 Mk0100)	11382	PH-JXS*	0392	0193	2 RR Tay 650-15	44450	C8Y93	CS-DG	Cuernavaca / lsf Airplanes 100 Finance
☐ XA-SGF	Fokker 100 (F28 Mk0100)	11384	PH-JXU*	0392	0193	2 RR Tay 650-15	44450	C8Y93	CS-DJ	Puebla / lsf Airplanes 100 Finance
☐ XA-SHI	Fokker 100 (F28 Mk0100)	11309	PH-LMZ*	0491	0593	2 RR Tay 650-15	44450	C8Y93	EF-GS	Chihuahua / lsf Airplanes 100 Finance
☐ XA-SHJ	Fokker 100 (F28 Mk0100)	11319	PH-LNB*	0391	0593	2 RR Tay 650-15	44450	C8Y93	EL-RS	Torreon / lsf Airplanes 100 Finance
☐ XA-TCG	Fokker 100 (F28 Mk0100)	11374	PH-JXX*	0192	1292	2 RR Tay 650-15	44450	C8Y93	CQ-ER	Tuxpan / lsf Airplanes 100 Finance
☐ XA-TCH	Fokker 100 (F28 Mk0100)	11375	PH-JXR*	0192	1292	2 RR Tay 650-15	44450	C8Y93	CS-AP	Monclova / lsf Airplanes 100 Finance
☐ XA-TKP	Fokker 100 (F28 Mk0100)	11266	PK-JGD	0090	0698	2 RR Tay 650-15	44450	C8Y93	AD-BQ	San Antonio / lsf Airplanes 100 Finance
☐ XA-TKR	Fokker 100 (F28 Mk0100)	11339	PK-JGH	0091	0798	2 RR Tay 650-15	44450	C8Y93	AD-CQ	San Luis Potosi / lsf Airpl. 100 Fin.
☐ PH-JXW	Fokker 100 (F28 Mk0100)	11390	XA-SGS	0492	0393	2 RR Tay 650-15	44450	C8Y93	EF-CS	Mazatlan / lsf MAF I-Debis Airfinance
☐ PH-KXJ	Fokker 100 (F28 Mk0100)	11400	XA-SGT	0692	0393	2 RR Tay 650-15	44450	C8Y93	EF-DR	Ixtapa Zihuatanejo / lsf MAF II-Debis
☐ PH-KXR	Fokker 100 (F28 Mk0100)	11410	XA-SHG	0092	0493	2 RR Tay 650-15	44450	C8Y93	EF-DS	Coatzacoalcos / lsf MAF III-AFT
☐ PH-LXG	Fokker 100 (F28 Mk0100)	11420	XA-SHH	0392	0393	2 RR Tay 650-15	44450	C8Y93	EF-GR	Cancun / lsf MAF IV-AFT
☐	Airbus Industrie A320-232					2 IAE V2527-A5	73500	C12Y138		oo-delivery 00XX
☐	Airbus Industrie A320-232					2 IAE V2527-A5	73500	C12Y138		oo-delivery 00XX
☐	Airbus Industrie A320-232					2 IAE V2527-A5	73500	C12Y138		oo-delivery 00XX
☐	Airbus Industrie A320-232					2 IAE V2527-A5	73500	C12Y138		oo-delivery 00XX
☐	Airbus Industrie A320-232					2 IAE V2527-A5	73500	C12Y138		oo-delivery 00XX
☐	Airbus Industrie A320-232					2 IAE V2527-A5	73500	C12Y138		oo-delivery 00XX
☐	Airbus Industrie A320-232					2 IAE V2527-A5	73500	C12Y138		oo-delivery 00XX
☐	Airbus Industrie A320-232					2 IAE V2527-A5	73500	C12Y138		oo-delivery 00XX
☐ F-OHMA	Airbus Industrie A320-231	368	F-WWIF*	0193	0394	2 IAE V2500-A1	73500	C12Y138	EF-AR	Tampico / lsf AFC Jersey
☐ F-OHMD	Airbus Industrie A320-231	433	F-WWDC*	0993	0394	2 IAE V2500-A1	73500	Y174	EF-CR	Morelia / lsf AFC Jersey
☐ F-OHME	Airbus Industrie A320-231	252	XA-RZU	0991	1291	2 IAE V2500-A1	73500	C12Y138	BR-CF	Veracruz / mortgaged with Mexibus
☐ F-OHMF	Airbus Industrie A320-231	259	XA-RYQ	1091	1291	2 IAE V2500-A1	73500	C12Y138	BR-CG	Ciudad del Carmen / mortgaged w.Mexibus
☐ F-OHMG	Airbus Industrie A320-231	260	XA-RYS	1091	1291	2 IAE V2500-A1	73500	C12Y138	BR-CH	Monterrey / mortgaged with Mexibus
☐ F-OHMH	Airbus Industrie A320-231	261	XA-RYT	1091	1291	2 IAE V2500-A1	73500	C12Y138	BR-CJ	Chetumal / mortgaged with Mexibus
☐ F-OHMI	Airbus Industrie A320-231	275	XA-RJW	1091	0192	2 IAE V2500-A1	73500	C12Y138	CJ-PS	Playa del Carmen / mortgaged w. Mexibus
☐ F-OHMJ	Airbus Industrie A320-231	276	XA-RJX	1191	0292	2 IAE V2500-A1	73500	C12Y138	CJ-QR	Cozumel / mortgaged with Mexibus
☐ F-OHMK	Airbus Industrie A320-231	296	XA-RJY	0392	0392	2 IAE V2500-A1	73500	C12Y138	CR-EP	Tepic / mortgaged with Mexibus
☐ F-OHML	Airbus Industrie A320-231	320	XA-RJZ	0392	0692	2 IAE V2500-A1	73500	C12Y138	CS-GK	Puerto Vallarta / mortgaged w. Mexibus
☐ F-OHMM	Airbus Industrie A320-231	321	XA-RKA	0492	0692	2 IAE V2500-A1	73500	C12Y138	CS-GL	Querétaro / mortgaged with Mexibus
☐ F-OHMN	Airbus Industrie A320-231	353	XA-RKB	0792	1092	2 IAE V2500-A1	73500	C12Y138	CS-GM	San Luis Potosi / mortgaged w. Mexibus
☐ N280RX	Airbus Industrie A320-231	280	G-BVZU	0292	1097	2 IAE V2500-A1	75500	C12Y138	HP-AK	Lima / lsf ORIX
☐ N467RX	Airbus Industrie A320-231	467	G-BVJW	0794	1197	2 IAE V2500-A1	75500	C12Y138	BP-MS	Buenos Aires / lsf ORIX
☐ XA-HOH	Boeing 727-264 (A)	21577 / 1379		0878	0878	3 PW JT8D-17R	83824	C12Y138	EG-BC	Tijuana
☐ XA-HON	Boeing 727-264 (A)	21617 / 1416		0078	1178	3 PW JT8D-17R	86409	C12Y138	ED-BD	Caracas
☐ XA-HOV	Boeing 727-264 (A)	21637 / 1429		1278	1278	3 PW JT8D-17R	86409	C12Y138	HM-AF	Mexicali
☐ XA-HOX	Boeing 727-264 (A)	21638 / 1457		0379	0379	3 PW JT8D-17R	86409	C12Y138	KM-AG	Guadalajara
☐ XA-IEU	Boeing 727-264 (A)	21836 / 1497		0679	0679	3 PW JT8D-17R	83624	C12Y138	JK-CD	Huatulco
☐ XA-MEB	Boeing 727-264 (A)	21837 / 1545	XA-IEV	0079	1179	3 PW JT8D-17R	83824	C12Y138	JK-CG	Zacatecas
☐ XA-MEC	Boeing 727-264 (A)	21838 / 1547	XA-IEW	0079	1179	3 PW JT8D-17R (HK3/FDX)	83824	C12Y138	JK-CL	Guanajuato
☐ XA-MED	Boeing 727-264 (A)	22156 / 1607		0480	0480	3 PW JT8D-17R	83824	C12Y138	JM-CD	Durango
☐ XA-MEE	Boeing 727-264 (A)	22157 / 1619		0580	0580	3 PW JT8D-17R (HK3/FDX)	83824	C12Y138	JM-CE	Los Cabos
☐ XA-MEF	Boeing 727-264 (A)	22158 / 1642	N1786B*	0780	0780	3 PW JT8D-17R	83824	C12Y138	JM-CF	Campeche / Guadalajara Chivas-soccer cs
☐ XA-MEH	Boeing 727-264 (A)	22409 / 1676		1080	1080	3 PW JT8D-17R (HK3/FDX)	83824	C12Y138	GK-AB	Nuevo Laredo
☐ XA-MEI	Boeing 727-264 (A)	22410 / 1678		1080	1080	3 PW JT8D-17R	83824	C12Y138	GK-AC	Leon
☐ XA-MEJ	Boeing 727-264 (A)	22411 / 1696		1280	1280	3 PW JT8D-17R (HK3/FDX)	83824	C12Y138	GK-AD	Saltillo
☐ XA-MEK	Boeing 727-264 (A)	22412 / 1720		0281	0281	3 PW JT8D-17R (HK3/FDX)	83824	C12Y138	GK-AE	Hermosillo
☐ XA-MEL	Boeing 727-264 (A)	22413 / 1728		0381	0381	3 PW JT8D-17R	83824	C12Y138	GK-AF	Manzanillo
☐ XA-MEZ	Boeing 727-264 (A)	22676 / 1754		0581	0681	3 PW JT8D-17R	86409	C12Y138	HK-EF	Mérida
☐ XA-MXA	Boeing 727-264 (A)	22661 / 1757		0581	0681	3 PW JT8D-17R (HK3/FDX)	86409	C12Y138	HK-EG	Acapulco
☐ XA-MXB	Boeing 727-264 (A)	22662 / 1776		0881	0981	3 PW JT8D-17R	86409	C12Y138	HK-EJ	Villahermosa
☐ XA-MXC	Boeing 727-264 (A)	22663 / 1778		0981	1081	3 PW JT8D-17R (HK3/FDX)	86409	C12Y138	HK-EL	Tuxtla Gutiérrez
☐ XA-MXD	Boeing 727-264 (A)	22664 / 1780	N1779B*	0981	1081	3 PW JT8D-17R (HK3/FDX)	86409	C12Y138	HK-EM	Minatitlan
☐ XA-MXI	Boeing 727-2A1 (A)	21346 / 1675	XA-MXF	1080	1085	3 PW JT8D-17	86409	C12Y138	JK-AC	Oaxaca / lsf Airplanes III Lim.
☐ XA-MXJ	Boeing 727-2A1 (A)	21600 / 1679	XA-MXG	1080	0885	3 PW JT8D-17	86409	Y156	JK-AB	Puerto Escondido / lsf Airplanes III
☐ XA-TGP	Boeing 727-287 (A)	22604 / 1777	N919PG	1081	0397	3 PW JT8D-17	86409	C12Y138	EF-BG	Toluca / lsf PACA
☐ XA-TJC	Boeing 757-236	25133 / 374	SE-DSN	0691	1197	2 RR RB211-535E4	113500	C12Y171	GQ-DP	Siempre Si / lsf Pinewatch Lim.
☐ N755MX	Boeing 757-2Q8	24964 / 424	N754AT	0192	1296	2 PW PW2040	115892	C12Y171	EF-AS	No que no...? / lsf ILFC
☐ N758MX	Boeing 757-2Q8	24965 / 438	N755AT	0392	1296	2 PW PW2040	115892	C12Y171	EF-BR	Vamos por mas / lsf ILFC
☐ N762MX	Boeing 757-2Q8	29442 / 819		0098	0998	2 PW PW2040	115892	C12Y170	AD-EQ	S.S. Juan Pablo II / lsf ILFC
☐ N763MX	Boeing 757-2Q8	29443 / 821		0998	0998	2 PW PW2040	115892	C12Y170		Ciudad de México / lsf ILFC

MEXICARGO, S.A. de C.V. = GJ / MXC Mexico City

Norte 192 No. 640, Col. Pensador Mexicano, 15510 México City, (Distrito Federal), México ☎ (5) 760 09 99 Tx: none Fax: (5) 760 07 93 SITA: n/a
F: 1991 ⁂ 21 Head: Jose A. Mendiola IATA: 624 ICAO: MEXICARGO Net: n/a

☐ N8840E	Boeing 727-225 (F)	20383 / 831		0070	1295	3 PW JT8D-7B	80739	Freighter		lsf Joda Partnership / cvtd -225

MIDWEST HELICOPTERES MEXICO, SA de CV = HTE (Subsidiary of Midwest Helicopters, Canada) Mexico City

Insurgentes Sur 59-305, 03112 México City, (Distrito Federal), México ☎ (5) 543 56 13 Tx: n/a Fax: (5) 543 69 15 SITA: n/a
F: n/a ⁂ n/a Head: n/a ICAO: HELICOPTERSMEXICO Net: n/a

☐ XA-STL	Bell 206B JetRanger III	1493	C-GEHK	0074		1 AN 250-C20B	1450			cvtd JetRanger
☐ XA-THY	Bell 206B JetRanger III	2353	C-GNPI	0078	0697	1 AN 250-C20B	1451			
☐ XA-SXF	Bell 206L-1 LongRanger II	45447	C-GEAU	0080	1294	1 AN 250-C28B	1882			
☐ XA-TIJ	Bell 206L-3 LongRanger III	51256	C-FWXF	0088	0797	1 AN 250-C30P	1882			

PEGASO – Transportes Aéreos Pegaso, SA de CV = TPG Mexico City

Santander 15, Col. Insurgentes Mixcoac, 03920 México City, (Distrito Federal), México ☎ (5) 563 17 96 Tx: none Fax: (5) 611 53 76 SITA: n/a
F: 1980 ⁂ 70 Head: Enrique Zepeda Navarro ICAO: TRANSPEGASO Net: http://www.interacces.com.mx/pegaso

☐ XA-MBB	Eurocopter (MBB) BO105CBS-4	S-676	N4573H	0085		2 AN 250-C20B	2500			
☐ XA-NAT	Eurocopter (MBB) BO105LS-A3	2044	XA-TTT	0091		2 AN 250-C28C	2600			
☐ XA-TFP	Eurocopter (MBB) BO105LS-A3	2043	XA-SSS	0091		2 AN 250-C28C	2600			
☐ XA-THI	Eurocopter (MBB) BO105LS-A3	2046	C-GERG	0092	0097	2 AN 250-C28C	2600			
☐ XA-THJ	Eurocopter (MBB) BO105LS-A3	2049	D-HSLA	0093	0097	2 AN 250-C28C	2600			
☐ XA-THK	Eurocopter (MBB) BK117B-2	7131	D-HAEA	0087	0797	2 LY LTS101-750B.1	3350			cvtd BK117A-4
☐ XA-THM	Eurocopter (MBB) BK117B-2	7252	D-HAEC	0093	0897	2 LY LTS101-750B.1	3350			

SACSA – Servicios Aéreos del Centro, SA de CV Toluca

Aeropuerto Internacional, Calle 3, Hangar 12, 51130 Tolucax, (México), México ☎ (72) 79 26 00 Tx: none Fax: (72) 79 26 88 SITA: n/a
F: 1983 ⁂ 150 Head: Capt. Jesus Gaona D. Net: n/a

☐ XA-SJF	Bell 206B JetRanger III	3815	N3815H	0084		1 AN 250-C20J	1451			
☐ XA-SCW	Bell 206L-3 LongRanger III	51447	N6635R	0091		1 AN 250-C30P	1882			
☐ XA-SMX	Bell 206L-4 LongRanger IV	52005	N2064W	0092		1 AN 250-C30P	2018			
☐ XA-TBF	Bell 206L-4 LongRanger IV	52138	N20987	0095		1 AN 250-C30P	2018			
☐ XA-TFI	Bell 206L-4 LongRanger IV	52148		0095		1 AN 250-C30P	2018			
☐ XA-IKA	Bell 230	23028	N41144	0094		2 AN 250C-30G2	3810			
☐ XA-SYL	Bell 412EP	36101	N87746	0095		2 PWC PT6T-3D TwinPac	5400			
☐ XA-KAJ	Learjet 28	28-004	N225MS	0079		2 GE CJ610-8A	6804			
☐ XA-LRJ	Learjet 25D	25D-359	N116JR	0082		2 GE CJ610-8A	6804			
☐ XA-SJS	Learjet 25B	25B-076	N77KW	0071		2 GE CJ610-6	6804			
☐ XA-ICK	Sabreliner 60 (Rockwell NA265-60)	306-86	N60TG	0074		2 PW JT12A-8	9150			
☐ XA-RIR	Sabreliner 60 (Rockwell NA265-60)	306-36	N436CC	0068		2 PW JT12A-8A	9072			
☐ XA-MVT	Sabreliner 75A (Rockwell NA265-80)	380-42	N75AG	0076		2 GE CF700-2D2	10433			
☐ XA-JMN	Lockheed L-1329 JetStar 731	5134	N136MA	0069		4 GA TFE731-3	20071			cvtd JetStar 8

SAEMSA – Servicios Aéreos Especializados Mexicanos, S.A. de C.V. (Member of Grupo Protexa) Campeche/Tampico/Toluca

Zona A, Hangar 18, Aeropuerto Internacional, 15700 México City, (Distrito Federal), México ☎ (5) 700 20 49 Tx: none Fax: (5) 558 57 13 SITA: n/a
F: n/a ⁂ n/a Head: Gabino Salazar Saenz Net: n/a

☐ XA-SSO	Bell 206B JetRanger	1250	XC-GIJ	0074		1 AN 250-C20	1451			
☐ XA-SSP	Bell 206B JetRanger III	3962	XC-HIB	0087		1 AN 250-C20J	1451			
☐ XA-SRF	Cessna U206G Stationair 6 II	U20605823	XC-DOJ	0080		1 CO IO-520-F	1633			

656 registration type of aircraft cn/fn ex/ex* mfd del powered by mtow kg configuration selcal name/fln/specialitites/remarks

☐ XA-SRG	Cessna U206G Stationair 6 II	U20604684		0079		1 CO IO-520-F	1633			
☐ XA-SRI	Cessna U206G Stationair 6 II	U20604133	XC-MTT	0078		1 CO IO-520-F	1633			
☐ XA-SST	Cessna U206G Stationair 6 II	U20605820	XC-DOI	0080		1 CO IO-520-F	1633			
☐ XA-SRK	Cessna T210M Turbo Centurion II	21062532		0078		1 CO TSIO-520-R	1724			
☐ XA-SSQ	Eurocopter (Aerosp.) SA316B Alouette III	1744	XC-DOL	0071		1 TU Artouste IIIB	2200			
☐ XA-TFT	Eurocopter (Aerosp.) AS365N2 Dauphin 2	6495		0096		2 TU Arriel 1C2	4250			
☐ XA-TFU	Eurocopter (Aerosp.) AS365N2 Dauphin 2	6512		0097		2 TU Arriel 1C2	4250			
☐ XA-TFV	Eurocopter (Aerosp.) AS365N2 Dauphin 2	6513		0097		2 TU Arriel 1C2	4250			
☐ XA-TGS	Eurocopter (Aerosp.) AS365N2 Dauphin 2	6515		0097		2 TU Arriel 1C2	4250			
☐ XA-TGY	Eurocopter (Aerosp.) AS365N2 Dauphin 2	6516		0097		2 TU Arriel 1C2	4250			
☐ XA-TGZ	Eurocopter (Aerosp.) AS365N2 Dauphin 2	6517		0097		2 TU Arriel 1C2	4250			
☐ XA-SSR	Bell 205A-1	30167	XC-GOS	0074		1 LY T5313B	4309			
☐ XA-SRR	Sikorsky S-76A	760143	XC-HEC	0081		2 AN 250-C30S	4763			
☐ XA-SRV	Sikorsky S-76A	760162	XC-HEG	0081		2 AN 250-C30S	4763			
☐ XA-SRW	Sikorsky S-76A	760142	XC-FEK	0081		2 AN 250-C30S	4763			
☐ XA-SRX	Sikorsky S-76A	760094	XC-FES	0080		2 AN 250-C30S	4763			
☐ XA-SRY	Sikorsky S-76A	760091	XC-FEV	0080		2 AN 250-C30S	4763			
☐ XA-TIL	Piper PA-42 Cheyenne III	42-8001071	N65MC	0082		2 PWC PT6A-41	5080			
☐ XA-SRZ	Bell 212	30993	XC-DEY	0079		2 PWC PT6T-3 TwinPac	5080			
☐ XA-SSB	Bell 212	30845	XC-DAH	0077		2 PWC PT6T-3 TwinPac	5080			
☐ XA-SSC	Bell 212	30992	XC-DIA	0079		2 PWC PT6T-3 TwinPac	5080			
☐ XA-SSD	Bell 212	30988	XC-DIF	0079		2 PWC PT6T-3 TwinPac	5080			
☐ XA-SSE	Bell 212	30852	XC-SCO	0077		2 PWC PT6T-3 TwinPac	5080			
☐ XA-SSF	Bell 212	30987	XC-SER	0079		2 PWC PT6T-3 TwinPac	5080			
☐ XA-SSG	Bell 212	30939	XC-SET	0079		2 PWC PT6T-3 TwinPac	5080			
☐ XA-SSI	Bell 212	30562	XC-GAN	0073		2 PWC PT6T-3 TwinPac	5080			
☐ XA-SSJ	Bell 212	30588	XC-GEL	0073		2 PWC PT6T-3 TwinPac	5080			
☐ XA-SSK	Bell 212	30924	XC-HFI	0079		2 PWC PT6T-3 TwinPac	5080			
☐ XA-SSL	Bell 212	35031	XC-HHN	0091		2 PWC PT6T-3B TwinPac	5080			
☐ XA-SRC	Shorts Skyvan 3 Variant 100 (SC-7)	SH1909	XC-GAY	0072	0695	2 GA TPE331-2-201A	5670			
☐ XA-SQV	Cessna 550 Citation II	550-0198	XC-DOK	0080	0794	2 PWC JT15D-4	6033			
☐ XA-SRL	Eurocopter (Aerosp.) SA330J Puma	1625	XC-CME	0080		2 TU Turmo IVC	7400			
☐ XA-SRM	Eurocopter (Aerosp.) SA330J Puma	1614	XC-FEG	0080		2 TU Turmo IVC	7400			
☐ XA-SRN	Eurocopter (Aerosp.) SA330J Puma	1644	XC-FOI	0081		2 TU Turmo IVC	7400			
☐ XA-SRO	Eurocopter (Aerosp.) SA330J Puma	1615	XC-IMP	0080		2 TU Turmo IVC	7400			
☐ XA-SRP	Eurocopter (Aerosp.) SA330J Puma	1616	XC-OPS	0080		2 TU Turmo IVC	7400			
☐ XA-SRQ	Eurocopter (Aerosp.) SA330J Puma	1613	XC-SDE	0080		2 TU Turmo IVC	7400			
☐ XA-SQT	Fairchild Ind. FH-227B (SCD)	558	XC-LPG	0067	0695	2 RR Dart 532-7	20865			cvtd FH-227B

SARSA – Servicios Aéreos Regiomontanos, SA — Monterrey

Aeropuerto Internacional del Norte, Puerta 10, 66400 Apodaca, (Nuevo Leon), México ☎ (8) 345 40 07 Tx: none Fax: (8) 345 51 61 SITA: n/a
F: 1969 n/a Head: Carlos Merino E. ICAO: REGIOMONTANO Net: n/a

☐ XA-JAC	Piper PA-23-250 Aztec F	27-7954094		0079		2 LY IO-540-C4B5	2359			
☐ XA-KAC	Hawker 700A (HS 125-700A)	257110 / NA0271	G-5-15*	0080		2 GA TFE731-3R-1H	11567			

SERVICIOS DE ALQUILER AEREO, SA de CV = SQL — Mexico City

Hangar 2, Zona C, Aeropuerto Internacional, 15620 México City, (Distrito Federal), México ☎ (5) 558 19 20 Tx: n/a Fax: (5) 763 13 65 SITA: n/a
F: n/a n/a Head: n/a ICAO: ALQUILER Net: n/a

☐ XA-JIQ	Learjet 24D	24D-317	N45AJ	0075		2 GE CJ610-6	6123			

SETRA – Servicios de Transporte Aéreo, SA de CV = SVI (Subsidiary of Banco de México) — Mexico City

Avda Fuerza Aérea Mexicana 429, 15620 México City, (Distrito Federal), México ☎ (5) 785 58 07 Tx: n/a Fax: (5) 785 67 22 SITA: n/a
F: 1994 n/a Head: n/a ICAO: SETRA Net: n/a

☐ XA-BDM	Boeing (Douglas) DC-9-15F (RC)	47087 / 234	XC-BCO	0067	0894	2 PW JT8D-7	40823	Freighter		

SUDPACIFICO = SDP (Aero Sudpacifico, SA dba) — Uruapan

Manuel Perez Coronado 94, 60080 Uruapan, (Michoacan), México ☎ (452) 37 937 Tx: n/a Fax: (452) 44 773 SITA: n/a
F: 1990 55 Head: Cap. Manuel Arguelles Mejia ICAO: SUDPACIFICO Net: n/a

☐ XA-RTO	Piper PA-34-200 Seneca	34-7250214	XB-CUF	0072	0091	2 LY IO-360-C1E6	1905			
☐ XA-RML	Britten-Norman BN-2B-27 Islander	864	XC-DIB	0078		2 LY O-540-E4C5	2994			cvtd BN-2A-6
☐ XA-RRM	Britten-Norman BN-2A-8 Islander	390	XB-DVH	0074		2 LY O-540-E4C5	2858			
☐ XA-SJY	Fairchild (Swearingen) SA226TC Metro II	TC-340	N247AM	0080	1091	2 GA TPE331-10UA-511G	5670			
☐ N32AG	Fairchild (Swearingen) SA226TC Metro II	TC-386	EC-BRI	0081	1290	2 GA TPE331-10UA-511G	5670			lsf Metroliner Leasing Inc.

TACSA – Transportes Aéreos de Coahuila, SA de CV — Saltillo

Carretera Saltillo-Monterrey Km 30,5, 25900 Saltillo, (Coahuila), México ☎ (84) 88 18 90 Tx: n/a Fax: (84) 88 18 11 SITA: n/a
F: n/a n/a Head: n/a ICAO: TRANSCOAHUILA Net: n/a

☐ XA-SVM	Cessna 208B Grand Caravan	208B0214	N503TA	0090	1194	1 PWC PT6A-114A	3969			
☐ XA-SFS	Fairchild (Swearingen) SA226TC Metro II	TC-353	N53CS	0080	1192	2 GA TPE331-10UA-511G	5670			

TAESA – Transportes Aéreos Ejecutivos, SA de CV = GD / TEJ — Mexico City & Toluca

Hangar 2, Aeropuerto Internacional, Adolfo Lopez Mateos, 50130 Toluca (México), México ☎ (72) 73 12 06 Tx: none Fax: (72) 73 12 09 SITA: MEXOXGD
F: 1987 2800 Head: Capt. Alberto S. Abed IATA: 838 ICAO: TRANSEJECUTIVOS Net: http://www.taesa.com.mx

☐ XA-NNN	Eurocopter (MBB) BO105LS-A3	2034	N334MB	0089		2 AN 250-C28C	2600	Executive		
☐ XA-BBE	Eurocopter (Aerosp.) AS355N Ecureuil 2	5548	F-WYML*	0093		2 TU Arrius 1A	2540	Executive		
☐ XA-SMU	Learjet 24D	24D-255	XA-BBE	0072		2 GE CJ610-6	6123	Executive		
☐ XA-DAK	Learjet 25B	25B-190		0075		2 GE CJ610-6	6804	Executive		
☐ XA-NOG	Learjet 25D	25D-349	N20GT	0081		2 GE CJ610-8A	6804	Executive		
☐ XA-POG	Learjet 25B	25B-080	N30AP	0071		2 GE CJ610-6	6804	Executive		
☐ XA-RQI	Learjet 25	25-032	XA-ZYZ	0069		2 GE CJ610-6	6804	Executive		
☐ XA-HRM	Learjet 31A	31A-044	XA-MJG	0091	0098	2 GA TFE731-2-3B	7484	Executive		
☐ XA-PIC	Learjet 31A	31A-076	XA-SPR	0093	0098	2 GA TFE731-2-3B	7484	Executive		
☐ XA-RKY	Learjet 35A	35A-370	N8216Q	0081	0098	2 GA TFE731-2-2B	8301	Executive		
☐ XA-BEB	Lockheed L-1329 JetStar 731	5132 / 57	XA-PSD	0069		4 GA TFE731-3E	19845	Executive		cvtd JetStar 8
☐ XA-EMO	Lockheed L-1329 JetStar 8	5140	XA-JCG	0069		4 PW JT12A-8	19006	Executive		
☐ XA-FHR	Lockheed L-1329 JetStar II	5231	XA-TDG	0079		4 GA TFE731-3	20185	Executive		
☐ XA-OLI	Lockheed L-1329 JetStar 8	5148	XA-ROK	0071		4 PW JT12A-8	19006	Executive		
☐ XA-SWP	GAC (Grumman) G-1159 Gulfstream II (SP)	014	XA-RBS	0068	0195	2 RR Spey 511-8	29710	Executive		cvtd II
☐ XA-SXS	Boeing (Douglas) DC-9-14	45713 / 9	G-BMAI	0166	0595	2 PW JT8D-7A	41141	Y83		lsf ICT
☐ XA-SXT	Boeing (Douglas) DC-9-15	45719 / 18	G-BMAG	0166	0595	2 PW JT8D-7A	41141	Y83		lsf ICT
☐ XA-SXV	Boeing (Douglas) DC-9-14	45715 / 10	XA-SSZ	0166	0495	2 PW JT8D-7B	41141	Y83		lsf ICT
☐ XA-SYF	Boeing (Douglas) DC-9-15	45780 / 93	HK-3710X	0367	0695	2 PW JT8D-7B	41141	Y83		lsf ICT
☐ XA-SZC	Boeing (Douglas) DC-9-15	45739 / 56	G-BMAC	1066	0895	2 PW JT8D-7A	41141	Y83		lsf ICT
☐ XA-TKN	Boeing (Douglas) DC-9-31F	47418 / 570	N650UG	0070	0798	2 PW JT8D-7B	46720	Y117		lsf PACA / cvtd DC-9-31
☐ XA-PBA	Boeing 737-2H6 (A)	20631 / 310	XA-APB	0072	0998	2 PW JT8D-15	53070	Y133		lsf Airlease (106) Ltd
☐ XA-SIW	Boeing 737-2T4 (A)	22370 / 716	N139AW	0080	0693	2 PW JT8D-15	54204	Y133		
☐ XA-SIX	Boeing 737-2T4 (A)	22371 / 717	N140AW	0080	0693	2 PW JT8D-15	54204	Y133		
☐ XA-TLJ	Boeing 737-2H6 (A)	20926 / 372	PK-IJE	0074	0898	2 PW JT8D-15	53070	Y133		lsf Airlease (106) Ltd
☐ XA-SLY	Boeing 737-33A	24098 / 1763	PH-HVI	0089	1094	2 CFMI CFM56-3B2	61235	Y148	CS-GJ	lsf INGL
☐ XA-SNC	Boeing 737-3M8	24377 / 1719	OO-LTE	0089	0294	2 CFMI CFM56-3B2	61235	Y148	CE-DF	lsf INGL
☐ XA-SWO	Boeing 737-33A	27284 / 2606	CS-TKF	0094	1296	2 CFMI CFM56-3B2	62822	Y148		lsf AWAS / sub-lst BPA
☐ N492GD	Boeing 737-3Q8	24492 / 1808	XA-TMB	0090	0998	2 CFMI CFM56-3B1	56472	Y148		lsf TRIT
☐ N242GD	Boeing 737-4Q8	24234 / 1627	XA-TKM	0088	0598	2 CFMI CFM56-3C1	65091	Y170		lsf ILFC
☐ XA-ASS	Boeing 727-51	18800 / 116	XA-PAL	0065	1090	3 PW JT8D-7B	72802	Y131		
☐ XA-BBI	Boeing 727-24C	19528 / 465	N2475	0067	0591	3 PW JT8D-7B	76884	Y131		
☐ XA-RRB	Boeing 727-64	19427 / 375	TP-10502	0067	1289	3 PW JT8D-7B	72802	Y131		opf Aeroflash Travelagency
☐ XA-SQO	Boeing 727-31	18752 / 76	N727PJ	0064	0794	3 PW JT8D-7B	76884	Y131		
☐ XA-SXZ	Boeing 727-23	18436 / 58	N1980	0764	0399	3 PW JT8D-7B	72847	Y131		lsf CSAV
☐ XA-THU	Boeing 727-225 (A)	20625 / 941	N355PA	0473	0697	3 PW JT8D-15	79923	Y173		lsf CITG
☐ XA-RLM	Boeing 757-23A (ET)	24566 / 255	5Y-BGI	0089	1094	2 RR RB211-535E4	108862	Y223	MQ-CL	lsf AWAS
☐ XA-TDC	Boeing (Douglas) DC-10-30F (CF)	46891 / 127	N105WA	0973	0496	3 GE CF6-50C2	256280	Freighter		lsf CITG / sub-lst / opf NSW, Chile

TANSA – Transportes Aéreos de Nayarit, SA — Pantanal-Amado Nervo

Apartado Postal 221, 63190 Tepic, (Nayarit), México ☎ (321) 33 111 Tx: 61173 taname Fax: (321) 33 117 SITA: n/a
F: 1958 18 Head: Capt. P.A. Alberto Velasco Navarro Net: n/a

☐ XA-FAL	Cessna 402B	402B0205	XA-CAV	0072		2 CO TSIO-520-E	2858			
☐ XA-IUI	Boeing (Douglas) DC-3A (C-53D-DO)	11719	N4007C	0043		2 PW R-1830-92	12202			
☐ XA-RZF	Boeing (Douglas) DC-3C (C-47A-5-DK)	12192	C-FDTV	0042	0991	2 PW R-1830-92	12202			

657 registration type of aircraft cn/fn ex/ex* mfd del powered by mtow kg configuration selcal name/fln/specialitites/remarks

TAT – Transportes Aéreos Terrestres, SA

Durango

Avda Victoria 317, 34000 Durango, (Durango), México ☎ (17) 12 20 44 Tx: n/a Fax: (17) 12 20 44 SITA: n/a
F: n/a ⋔⋔ n/a Head: n/a Net: n/a

		cn/fn	ex/ex*	mfd	del	powered by	mtow kg	config	selcal	name/remarks
☐ XA-LOI	Eurocopter (MBB) BO105CBS	S-457	N8475A	0080		2 AN 250-C20B	2500			
☐ XA-TAT	De Havilland DHC-6 Twin Otter 300	237		0069	0669	2 PWC PT6A-27	5670			

TAXI AEREO DE MEXICO, SA = TXM

Mexico City

Zona D, Hangar 12, Terminal de Aviacion General, Ap. Int'l, 15620 México City, (Distrito Federal), México ☎ (5) 763 89 88 Tx: n/a Fax: (5) 763 84 50 SITA: n/a
F: 1975 ⋔⋔ 9 Head: Lic. Eduardo Ibarguengoitia Chico ICAO: TAXIMEX Net: http://www.iwm.com.mx/foroemp/aertax.html

| ☐ XA-KCM | Learjet 35A | 35A-418 | | 0081 | | 2 GA TFE731-2-2B | 7711 | | | |
| ☐ XA-KIM | Canadair CL-601-1A (CL-600-2A12) Challen. | 3015 | N374G | 0083 | | 2 GE CF34-1A | 19550 | | | |

TRANSPAIS AEREO, SA de CV

Monterrey

No. 473 y 108, Apartado Postal 108, 66400 San Nicolas de Las Garzas, (Nuevo Leon), México ☎ (83) 44 92 50 Tx: none Fax: (83) 34 94 06 SITA: n/a
F: 1992 ⋔⋔ n/a Head: Capt. Eduardo Rubio ICAO: TRANSPAIS Net: n/a

☐ XA-SAF	Cessna 210L Centurion II	21060186	N59271	0074		1 CO IO-520-L	1724			
☐ XA-CUS	Piper PA-23-250 Aztec E	27-7554002	N54204	0075		2 LY IO-540-C4B5	2359			
☐ XA-LIO	Dassault Falcon 10	40	N15SJ	0075		2 GA TFE731-2-1C	8500			
☐ XA-FLM	Dassault Falcon 20F	364	N285UR	0077		2 GE CF700-2D2	13000			
☐ XA-SAG	Dassault Falcon 20F	287	XB-ALO	0073		2 GE CF700-2D2	13000			
☐ XA-ILV	GAC (Grumman) G-1159 Gulfstream II	195	N71TP	0076		2 RR Spey 511-8	29393			

XT = BURKINA FASO (People's Democratic Republic of Burkina Faso) République Démocratique et Populaire de B.F.

Capital: Ouagadougou Official Language: French Population: 10,5 million Square Km: 274200 Dialling code: +226 Year established: 1960 Acting political head: Blaise Compaoré (President)

Government / Corporate / Executive / VIP Aircraft

| ☐ XT-BBE | Boeing 727-14 | 18990 / 238 | N21UC | 0066 | 0788 | 3 PW JT8D-7 | | VIP | AH-FL | Gvmt |

AIR AFRIQUE = multinational state carrier – see under TU- markings

AIR BURKINA = 2J / VBW (formerly Air Volta)

Ouagadougou

BP 1459, Ouagadougou, Burkina Faso ☎ 30 76 76 Tx: none Fax: 31 48 79 SITA: n/a
F: 1967 ⋔⋔ 91 Head: Mathieu Bouda IATA: 226 ICAO: BURKINA Net: n/a

| ☐ XT-ABJ | Embraer 110P2 Bandeirante (EMB-110P2) | 110193 | PT-GLL* | 0078 | 1178 | 2 PWC PT6A-34 | 5670 | Y18 | | |
| ☐ XT-FZP | Fokker F28 Fellowship 4000 (F28 Mk4000) | 11185 | PH-EXP* | 0082 | 0183 | 2 RR Spey 555-15P | 33110 | Y85 | | |

XU = CAMBODIA (Kingdom of Cambodia) (Preah Réachéanachakr Kampuchéa)

Capital: Phnom Penh Official Language: Cambodian Population: 11,0 million Square Km: 181035 Dialling code: +855 Year established: 1945 Acting political head: Norodom Sihanouk (King)

HELICOPTERS CAMBODIA, Ltd (Subsidiary of Helicopters New Zealand, Ltd)

Phnom Penh

Street 310, House 10, Phnom Penh, Cambodia ☎ (23) 21 37 06 Tx: none Fax: (23) 21 37 06 SITA: n/a
F: 1998 ⋔⋔ n/a Head: Kevin Treloar Net: n/a Operates Eurocopter (Aerosp.) AS350B Squirrel, leased from Helicopters New Zealand & Lao Westcoast Helicopter when required.

KAMPUCHEA AIRLINES = KT / KMP (Sister company of Orient Thai Airlines, Co. Ltd)

Phnom Penh-Pochentong

19 Preah Mohaksat Tiany Kosomak Road, Khan Daunpenh, Phnom Penh, Cambodia ☎ (23) 42 62 28 Tx: none Fax: (23) 42 63 13 SITA: n/a
F: 1991 ⋔⋔ n/a Head: Udom Tantiprasongchai IATA: 506 ICAO: KAMPUCHEA Net: n/a

| ☐ XU-800 | Lockheed L-1011-385-1 TriStar 1 | 193A-1040 | P4-IAH | 0073 | 0299 | 3 RR RB211-22B | 195045 | Y362 | | Isf IALI |
| ☐ XU-900 | Lockheed L-1011-385-1 TriStar 50 | 193P-1070 | N762BE | 0074 | 0299 | 3 RR RB211-22B | 204117 | Y362 | | Isf IALI / cvtd TriStar 1 |

PRESIDENT AIRLINES = TO / PSD (Subs. of Holiday Group Cambodia, Assoc. with Laoag Int'l Airline)

Phnom Penh

50 Norodom Boulevard, Phnom Penh, Cambodia ☎ (23) 21 28 87 Tx: none Fax: (23) 21 29 92 SITA: n/a
F: 1997 ⋔⋔ 20 Head: Capt. Paul Ng Net: n/a

☐ XU-999	Beech King Air A90 (65-A90)	LJ-281	RP-C3318	0067	0098	2 PWC PT6A-20	4377	Y10		
☐ XU-881	Fokker F27 Friendship 100 (F27 Mk100)	10168	RP-C5888	0061	0098	2 RR Dart 514-7	18370	Y40		
☐ XU-001	Fokker F28 Fellowship 1000 (F28 Mk1000)	11012	F-GIAH	0069	0098	2 RR Spey 555-15	30164	Y60		Ist LPN

ROYAL AIR CAMBODGE, Co. Ltd – RAC = VJ (Associated with Malaysian Helicopter Services Berhad)

Phnom Penh-Pochentong

206 Norodom Blvd, Phnom Penh, Cambodia ☎ (23) 42 88 21 Tx: none Fax: (18) 42 88 03 SITA: n/a
F: 1994 ⋔⋔ n/a Head: Pan Chan Tra IATA: 658 Net: n/a

☐ XU-701	Harbin Yunshuji Y12 II	0083		0094	0098	2 PWC PT6A-27	5300	Y17		
☐ XU-702	Harbin Yunshuji Y12 II	0084		0094	0098	2 PWC PT6A-27	5300	Y17		
☐ F-OMAR	ATR 72-201	108	F-GIGO	0089	0996	2 PWC PW124B	21500	Y70		Isf Protea Leasing Ltd
☐ F-ORAC	ATR 72-202	204	F-GKJK	0091	1194	2 PWC PW124B	21500	Y70		Isf Protea Leasing Ltd
☐ F-ORAN	ATR 72-202	207	F-WQAH*	0090	1094	2 PWC PW124B	21500	Y70		Isf Protea Leasing Ltd
☐ 9M-MMC	Boeing 737-4H6	26453 / 2332		0092	1096	2 CFMI CFM56-3C1	62822	F12Y134	BC-FS	Bayon / Isf MAS

XY = MYANMAR (Union of Myanmar) (Pyeidaungzu Myanma Naingngandaw)

Capital: Yangon Official Language: Burmese Population: 47,0 million Square Km: 676552 Dialling code: +95 Year established: 1948 Acting political head: General Than Shwe (President)

Government / Corporate / Executive / VIP Aircraft

| ☐ 5001 | Fokker F27 Friendship 600 (F27 Mk600) | 10392 | OY-SRR | 0069 | 0794 | 2 RR Dart 532-7 | 20412 | VIP / mil trans | | XY-AER / Myanma Air Force |

AIR MANDALAY, Limited = 6T (Joint venture between Kemayan Corp. Bhd, Malaysia & Myanma Airways Corp.)

Yangon

146 Damazedi Road, Bahan Township, Yangon, Myanmar ☎ (1) 52 76 18 Tx: none Fax: (1) 52 59 37 SITA: RGNTO6T
F: 1994 ⋔⋔ 143 Head: Eric Kang Tian Lye Net: n/a

| ☐ F-OHFS | ATR 72-212 | 393 | F-WWLI* | 0094 | 1094 | 2 PWC PW127 | 21500 | Y70 | | Isf Fransom Ltd |
| ☐ F-OHLB | ATR 72-212 | 422 | F-WWLZ* | 0094 | 1294 | 2 PWC PW127 | 21500 | Y70 | | Isf Fransom Ltd |

MYANMA AIRWAYS Corp. = UB / UBA (formerly Burma Airways, Corp.)

Yangon

123 Sule Pagoda Road, Yangon, Myanmar ☎ (1) 80 710 Tx: 21204 rgnbac bm Fax: (1) 89 583 SITA: n/a
F: 1948 ⋔⋔ 1100 Head: Capt. Thura U. Win Myint IATA: 209 ICAO: UNIONAIR Net: n/a

☐ XY-AFA	Eurocopter (Aerosp.) SA330J Puma	1422		0076		2 TU Turmo IVC	7400			
☐ XY-AFC	Eurocopter (Aerosp.) SA330J Puma	1450		0076		2 TU Turmo IVC	7400			
☐ XY-ADT	Fokker F27 Friendship 600 (F27 Mk600)	10523	PH-EXE*	0075	0176	2 RR Dart 532-7	20412			
☐ XY-ADZ	Fokker F27 Friendship 600 (F27 Mk600)	10574	PH-EXF*	0078	1078	2 RR Dart 532-7	20412			
☐ XY-AEO	Fokker F27 Friendship 600 (F27 Mk600)	10594	PH-ADJ	0079	1287	2 RR Dart 532-7	20412			
☐ XY-AEQ	Fokker F27 Friendship 400 (F27 Mk400)	10294	PH-SFA	0066	0694	2 RR Dart 532-7	20412			
☐ XY-AER	Fokker F27 Friendship 100 (F27 Mk100)	10124	5001	0060		2 RR Dart 514-7	18370			
☐ XY-ADU	Fokker F28 Fellowship 1000 (F28 Mk1000)	11019	PH-ZAO*	0070	0476	2 RR Spey 555-15	29484			
☐ XY-ADW	Fokker F28 Fellowship 4000 (F28 Mk4000)	11114	PH-EXU*	0077	0677	2 RR Spey 555-15H	33112			
☐ XY-AGA	Fokker F28 Fellowship 4000 (F28 Mk4000)	11232	PH-EZG*	0085	0386	2 RR Spey 555-15P	33112			

MYANMAR AIRWAYS INTERNATIONAL = UB / UBA (Joint venture of Myanma Airways Corp. & Highsonics Enterprise, Singapore)

Yangon

123 Sule Pagoda Road, Yangon, Myanmar ☎ (1) 80 710 Tx: n/a Fax: (1) 89 609 SITA: n/a
F: 1993 ⋔⋔ n/a Head: n/a IATA: 209 ICAO: UNIONAIR Net: n/a

| ☐ 9M-MMH | Boeing 737-4H6 | 27084 / 2391 | | 0092 | 0894 | 2 CFMI CFM56-3C1 | 62822 | F12Y134 | BC-LR | Isf MAS |
| ☐ 9M-MMY | Boeing 737-4H6 | 26455 / 2507 | | 0093 | 1294 | 2 CFMI CFM56-3C1 | 62822 | F12Y134 | CL-PR | Isf MAS |

YANGON AIRWAYS, Ltd = HK

Yangon

22/24 Pansondan Street, Yangon, Myanmar ☎ (1) 70 03 58 Tx: n/a Fax: (1) 25 19 32 SITA: n/a
F: 1996 ⋔⋔ 168 Head: Lt Kyaw Win Net: n/a

| ☐ F-OIYA | ATR 72-212 | 479 | F-WWEL* | 0096 | 1096 | 2 PWC PW127 | 21500 | Y70 | | Isf EVA Leasing Ltd |
| ☐ F-OIYB | ATR 72-212 | 481 | F-WWEQ* | 0096 | 1296 | 2 PWC PW127 | 21500 | Y70 | | Isf EVA Leasing Ltd |

YA = AFGHANISTAN (Islamic State of Afghanistan) (Di Afganistan Islami Dawlat)

Capital: Kabul Official Language: Pashtu, Tajik, Uzbek Population: 21,0 million Square Km: 652090 Dialling code: +93 Year established: 1919 Acting political head: Mullah Mohammed Omar (Chairman of the governing council)

ARIANA AFGHAN AIRLINES = FG / AFG (formerly Bakhtar Afghan Airlines)

Kabul

Operations office:, Suryakiran Bldg, 6F, 19 Kasturba Gandhi Marg, 110001 New Delhi, India ☎ (11) 331 24 78 Tx: none Fax: (11) 375 51 62 SITA: KBLDDFG
F: 1955 ⋔⋔ 1250 Head: Hafez Mohammed Younus IATA: 255 ICAO: ARIANA Net: n/a

☐ YA-DAG	Antonov 24B	87304504	EL-ASA	0068	0199	2 IV AI-24	21000	Y48		
☐ YA-DAA	Antonov 12B		RA-		0598	4 IV AI-20M	61000	Freighter		
☐ YA-DAB	Antonov 12BP	5342801	RA-11325	0065	0298	4 IV AI-20M	61000	Freighter		
☐ YA-FAU	Boeing 727-113C	20343 / 784		0069	0170	3 PW JT8D-9	77111	Combi	FL-BJ	
☐ YA-FAW	Boeing 727-155C	19619 / 470	TF-FLJ	0067	0671	3 PW JT8D-7	77111	Combi	KM-AL	
☐ YA-FAY	Boeing 727-228 (A)	22289 / 1719	F-GCDH	0081	1092	3 PW JT8D-15	86409		EK-DG	
☐ YA-TAR	Tupolev 154M	748		0087	0487	3 SO D-30KU-154-II	100000	Y164		Ist CPN

658 registration type of aircraft cn/fn ex/ex* mfd del powered by mtow kg configuration selcal name/fln/specialitites/remarks

YI = IRAQ (Republic of Iraq) (al-Jumhouriya al-Iraqiya)

Capital: Baghdad Official Language: Arabic Population: 22,0 million Square Km: 438317 Dialling code: +964 Year established: 1918 Acting political head: Saddam Hussein el-Takriti (President)

Government / Corporate / Executive / VIP Aircraft

registration	type of aircraft	cn/fn	ex/ex*	mfd	del	powered by	mtow kg	configuration	selcal	name/fln/specialitites/remarks
☐ YI-AHH	Dassault Falcon 20F	337	F-WRQR*	0076		2 GE CF700-2D2	13000	VIP		Gvmt/grounded
☐ YI-AHJ	Dassault Falcon 20F	343	F-WRQR*	0076		2 GE CF700-2D2	13000	VIP		Gvmt/grounded
☐ YI-ALC	Dassault Falcon 50	101	F-WPHX*	0082		3 GA TFE731-3-1C	17600	VIP		Gvmt/grounded
☐ YI-ALD	Dassault Falcon 50	120	F-WPXJ*	0083		3 GA TFE731-3-1C	17600	VIP		Gvmt/grounded
☐ YI-ALE	Dassault Falcon 50	122	F-WZHG*	0083		3 GA TFE731-3-1C	17600	VIP		Gvmt/grounded

IRAQI AIRWAYS = IA / IAW — Baghdad-Saddam Int'l & Baghdad-Muthenna

Saddam Int'l Airport, Baghdad, Iraq ☎ 886 39 99 Tx: 213453 iasda ik Fax: 887 58 08 SITA: n/a

F: 1945 ⁂ n/a Head: Rabie M.S. Abdulbaki IATA: 073 ICAO: IRAQI Net: n/a All aircraft are stored as indicated, in several locations in & outside Iraq, as a result of the political developments in 1991.
A solution to the pending problems has not yet been found. Currently all flights are suspended due to the U.N. sanctions.

registration	type of aircraft	cn/fn	ex/ex*	mfd	del	powered by	mtow kg	configuration	selcal	name/fln/specialitites/remarks
☐ YI-AGK	Boeing 727-270 (A)	21197 / 1186		0076	0376	3 PW JT8D-17	89448	F16Y126	AM-BG	Ninevah / std AMM
☐ YI-AGL	Boeing 727-270 (A)	21198 / 1191		0076	0376	3 PW JT8D-17	89448	F16Y126	AM-BH	Basrah / std AMM
☐ YI-AGM	Boeing 727-270 (A)	21199 / 1203		0076	0576	3 PW JT8D-17	89448	F16Y126	AM-BJ	Al Habbania / std
☐ YI-AGQ	Boeing 727-270 (A)	22261 / 1647	N8284V*	0080	0581	3 PW JT8D-17	89448	F16Y126	DG-CM	Ataameen / std AMM
☐ YI-AGR	Boeing 727-270 (A)	22262 / 1686	N8286V*	0080	0581	3 PW JT8D-17	89448	F16Y126	DG-EF	Babylon / std
☐ YI-AGS	Boeing 727-270 (A)	22263 / 1809	N1780B*	0082	0782	3 PW JT8D-17	89448	F16Y126	DH-FK	std AMM
☐ YI-AGE	Boeing 707-370C	20889 / 889		0074	0874	4 PW JT3D-7 (HK2/COM)	151091	Freighter	AM-FH	std AMM
☐ YI-AGG	Boeing 707-370C	20891 / 892		0074	1074	4 PW JT3D-7	151091	Freighter	AM-FL	Baghdad / std AMM
☐ YI-ALM	Boeing 747SP-70	22858 / 567		0082	0882	4 PW JT9D-7FW	317515	VIP	AM-EJ	std TOE
☐ YI-AGN	Boeing 747-270C (M)	21180 / 287		0076	0676	4 PW JT9D-7FW	362874	F25Y225 / Plt	AM-GL	Tigris / std
☐ YI-AGO	Boeing 747-270C (M)	21181 / 289		0076	0876	4 PW JT9D-7FW	362874	F25Y225 / Plt	AM-HL	Euphrates / std
☐ YI-AGP	Boeing 747-270C (M)	22366 / 565		0082	0782	4 PW JT9D-7FW	362874	F25Y225 / Plt	AM-EH	Shat-al-Arab / std

YJ = VANUATU (Republic of Vanuatu) (Ribablik blang Vanuatu)

Capital: Port Vila Official Language: English, Bislama Population: 0,2 million Square Km: 12189 Dialling code: +678 Year established: 1980 Acting political head: Donald Kalpokas (Prime Minister)

AIR VANUATU = NF / AVN (Air Vanuatu (Operations), Ltd dba) — Port Vila

PO Box 148, Port Vila, Vanuatu ☎ 23 838 Tx: none Fax: 23 250 SITA: VLIOZNF

F: 1987 ⁂ 206 Head: Jean-Paul Virelala IATA: 218 ICAO: AIR VAN Net: n/a

registration	type of aircraft	cn/fn	ex/ex*	mfd	del	powered by	mtow kg	configuration	selcal	name/fln/specialitites/remarks
☐ V7-9508	Saab 2000	2000-017	SE-017*	0095	0498	2 AN AE2100A	22800	Y50		lsf Air Marshall Islands
☐ YJ-AV18	Boeing 737-3Q8	28054 / 3016		0098	0498	2 CFMI CFM56-3C1	61235	C8Y118		Spirit of Vanuatu / lsf ILFC

HELICOPTER KOMPANI (Vanuatu) (formerly Helicopters Vanuatu, Ltd) — Port Vila

PO Box 366, Port Vila, Vanuatu ☎ 25 198 Tx: none Fax: 24 693 SITA: n/a

F: 1990 ⁂ 4 Head: Garrett Cloete Net: n/a

registration	type of aircraft	cn/fn	ex/ex*	mfd	del	powered by	mtow kg	configuration	selcal	name/fln/specialitites/remarks
☐ YJ-HV4	Bell 206B JetRanger III	1313	ZK-HIQ	0075	0994	1 AN 250-C20B	1451			cvtd JetRanger
☐ VH-HTB	Bell 206B JetRanger III	3398	P2-PHK	0081	0198	1 AN 250-C20B	1451			

VANAIR Ltd – Melanesian Connections (formerly Air Melanesiae, Ltd) — Port Vila

PMB 069, Port Vila, Vanuatu ☎ 22 643 Tx: n/a Fax: 23 910 SITA: n/a

F: 1989 ⁂ 90 Head: Willie N. Naripo Net: n/a

registration	type of aircraft	cn/fn	ex/ex*	mfd	del	powered by	mtow kg	configuration	selcal	name/fln/specialitites/remarks
☐ YJ-RV2	Britten-Norman BN-2A Islander	172	P2-ISW	0070	1189	2 LY O-540-E4B5	2858			
☐ YJ-RV1	De Havilland DHC-6 Twin Otter 300	491	HP-730AP	0076	0090	2 PWC PT6A-27	5670			Freedom
☐ YJ-RV5	De Havilland DHC-6 Twin Otter 300	520	5U-ABU	0077	0397	2 PWC PT6A-27	5670			
☐ YJ-RV8	De Havilland DHC-6 Twin Otter 300	703	F-ODGL	0080	0890	2 PWC PT6A-27	5670			Unity
☐ YJ-RV9	De Havilland DHC-6 Twin Otter 300	694	9M-PEH	0080	0590	2 PWC PT6A-27	5670			Victory
☐ YJ-RV10	De Havilland DHC-6 Twin Otter 300	679	OY-SLI	0080	0493	2 PWC PT6A-27	5670			Melanesian Princess

YK = SYRIA (Syrian Arab Republic) (al-Jamhouriya al-Arabiya as-Suriya)

Capital: Damascus Official Language: Arabic Population: 15,0 million Square Km: 185180 Dialling code: +963 Year established: 1941 Acting political head: Hafiz al-Assad (President)

SYRIANAIR – Syrian Arab Airlines = RB / SYR — Damascus

PO Box 417, Damascus, Syria ☎ (11) 222 07 00 Tx: 411593 sy Fax: (11) 221 49 23 SITA: DAMDGRB

F: 1961 ⁂ 4350 Head: Air Maj. Gen. Omar Rida IATA: 070 ICAO: SYRIANAIR Net: n/a

registration	type of aircraft	cn/fn	ex/ex*	mfd	del	powered by	mtow kg	configuration	selcal	name/fln/specialitites/remarks
☐ YK-ASA	Dassault Falcon 20F	328	F-WMKJ*	0075	1075	2 GE CF700-2D2	13000	VIP		opb Air Force in Syrianair-colors
☐ YK-ASB	Dassault Falcon 20F	331	F-WRQS*	0075	1175	2 GE CF700-2D2	13000	VIP		opb Air Force in Syrianair-colors
☐ YK-AQA	Yakovlev 40	9341932		0073	0074	3 IV AI-25	16000	Y32		opb Air Force in Syrianair-colors
☐ YK-AQB	Yakovlev 40	9530443		0075	0075	3 IV AI-25	16000	Y32		opb Air Force in Syrianair-colors
☐ YK-AQD	Yakovlev 40	9830158		0078	0078	3 IV AI-25	16000	Y32		opb Air Force in Syrianair-colors
☐ YK-AQE	Yakovlev 40	9830258		0078	0078	3 IV AI-25	16000	Y32		opb Air Force in Syrianair-colors
☐ YK-AQF	Yakovlev 40	9931859		0079	0079	3 IV AI-25	16000	Y32		opb Air Force in Syrianair-colors
☐ YK-AQG	Yakovlev 40K	9941959		0079	0079	3 IV AI-25	16000	Y32		opb Air Force in Syrianair-colors
☐ YK-ANA	Antonov 24B	87304203		0068	0068	2 IV AI-24	21000	Y50		opb Air Force in Syrianair-colors
☐ YK-ANC	Antonov 26	3007		0075	0075	2 IV AI-24VT	24000	Combi		opb Air Force in Syrianair-colors
☐ YK-AND	Antonov 26	3008		0075	0075	2 IV AI-24VT	24000	Combi		opb Air Force in Syrianair-colors
☐ YK-ANE	Antonov 26	3103		0075	0075	2 IV AI-24VT	24000	Combi		opb Air Force in Syrianair-colors
☐ YK-ANF	Antonov 26	3104		0075	0075	2 IV AI-24VT	24000	Combi		opb Air Force in Syrianair-colors
☐ YK-ANG	Antonov 26B	10907		0080	0080	2 IV AI-24VT	24000	Combi		opb Air Force in Syrianair-colors
☐ YK-AYA	Tupolev 134B-3	63992		0082	0082	2 SO D-30-III	49000	VIP		opb Air Force in Syrianair-colors
☐ YK-AYB	Tupolev 134B-3	63994		0082	0082	2 SO D-30-III	49000	VIP		opb Air Force in Syrianair-colors
☐ YK-AYC	Tupolev 134B-3	63989		0082	0082	2 SO D-30-III	49000	Y76		
☐ YK-AYD	Tupolev 134B-3	63990		0082	0082	2 SO D-30-III	49000	Y76		std DAM
☐ YK-AYE	Tupolev 134B-3	66187		0083	0083	2 SO D-30-III	49000	Y76		
☐ YK-AYF	Tupolev 134B-3	66190		0084	0084	2 SO D-30-III	49000	Y76		
☐ YK-AKA	Airbus Industrie A320-232	886	F-WWDH*	0098	1098	2 IAE V2527-A5	75500	C8Y144		Ugarit
☐ YK-AKB	Airbus Industrie A320-232	918	F-WWIJ*	0098	0399	2 IAE V2527-A5	75500	C8Y144		Ebla
☐ YK-AKC	Airbus Industrie A320-232	1032				2 IAE V2527-A5	75500	C8Y144		oo-delivery 0799
☐ YK-AKD	Airbus Industrie A320-232	1075				2 IAE V2527-A5	75500	C8Y144		oo-delivery 0999
☐ YK-AKE	Airbus Industrie A320-232	1117				2 IAE V2527-A5	75500	C8Y144		oo-delivery 1299
☐ YK-AKF	Airbus Industrie A320-232					2 IAE V2527-A5	75500	C8Y144		oo-delivery 0200
☐ YK-AGA	Boeing 727-294 (A)	21203 / 1188		0076	0376	3 PW JT8D-17	86409	F8Y141	BH-AJ	October 6
☐ YK-AGB	Boeing 727-294 (A)	21204 / 1194		0076	0376	3 PW JT8D-17	86409	F8Y141	BH-AK	Damascus
☐ YK-AGC	Boeing 727-294 (A)	21205 / 1198		0076	0476	3 PW JT8D-17	86409	F8Y141	BH-AL	Palmyra
☐ YK-AGD	Boeing 727-269 (A)	22360 / 1670	9K-AFB	0080	0494	3 PW JT8D-17R	89358	F8Y141	DG-HM	
☐ YK-AGE	Boeing 727-269 (A)	22361 / 1716	9K-AFC	0081	0194	3 PW JT8D-17R	89358	F8Y141	DL-AE	
☐ YK-AGF	Boeing 727-269 (A)	22763 / 1788	9K-AFD	0081	0194	3 PW JT8D-17R	89358	F8Y141	CG-DK	
☐ YK-AIA	Tupolev 154M	708		0084	0385	3 SO D-30KU-154-II	100000	F9Y134	DL-CE	
☐ YK-AIB	Tupolev 154M	709		0084	0485	3 SO D-30KU-154-II	100000	F9Y134	DL-CF	
☐ YK-AIC	Tupolev 154M	710		0084	0585	3 SO D-30KU-154-II	100000	F9Y134	DL-CG	
☐ YK-ATA	Ilyushin 76M	093421613		0079	0079	4 SO D-30KP	170000	Freighter		opb Air Force in Syrianair-colors
☐ YK-ATB	Ilyushin 76M	093421619		0079	0079	4 SO D-30KP	170000	Freighter		opb Air Force in Syrianair-colors
☐ YK-ATC	Ilyushin 76M	0013431911		0081	0081	4 SO D-30KP	170000	Freighter		opb Air Force in Syrianair-colors
☐ YK-ATD	Ilyushin 76M	0013431915		0081	0081	4 SO D-30KP	170000	Freighter		opb Air Force in Syrianair-colors
☐ YK-AHA	Boeing 747SP-94	21174 / 284		0076	0576	4 PW JT9D-7A	317515	F16Y308	BH-CJ	16 Novembre
☐ YK-AHB	Boeing 747SP-94	21175 / 290		0076	0776	4 PW JT9D-7A	317515	F16Y308	BH-CK	Arab Solidarity

YL = LATVIA (Republic of Latvia) (Latvijas Republika)

Capital: Riga Official Language: Latvian Population: 2,8 million Square Km: 64589 Dialling code: +371 Year established: 1990 Acting political head: Guntis Ulmanis (President)

AIR BALTIC, Corp. SIA = BT / BTI (Joint venture of Latvian Government & Scandinavian Airlines SAS) — Riga

Riga Airport, LV-1053 Riga, Latvia ☎ (7) 20 70 69 Tx: none Fax: (7) 20 73 69 SITA: RIXOZBT

F: 1995 ⁂ 210 Head: Rudi Schwab IATA: 657 ICAO: AIRBALTIC Net: http://www.airbaltic.lv

registration	type of aircraft	cn/fn	ex/ex*	mfd	del	powered by	mtow kg	configuration	selcal	name/fln/specialitites/remarks
☐ YL-BAG	Saab SF340A	340A-007	SE-LBP	0084	1095	2 GE CT7-5A2	12700	CY33		Zemgale / lsf Saab Aircraft Credit AB
☐ YL-BAP	Saab SF340A	340A-156	SE-ISE	0889	1097	2 GE CT7-5A2	12700	CY33		
☐ YL-BAR	Fokker 50 (F27 Mk050)	20149	PH-LVL	0089	1098	2 PWC PW125B	20820	CY50		Cesis / lsf Finova Capital Ltd
☐ YL-BAK	Avro RJ70 (Avro 146-RJ70A)	E1223	N832BE	0093	0396	4 LY LF507-1F	40823	CY70		Kurzeme / lsf BAMJ/sub-lst NJS, VH-NJW
☐ YL-BAL	Avro RJ70 (Avro 146-RJ70A)	E1224	N833BE	0093	0496	4 LY LF507-1F	40823	CY70		Latgale / lsf BAMJ
☐ YL-BAN	Avro RJ70 (Avro 146-RJ70A)	E1225	N834BE	0093	0596	4 LY LF507-1F	40823	CY70		Vidzeme / lsf BAMJ

BALTIC Express Line = LTB — Riga

Dzirnavu Street 100, LV-1050 Riga, Latvia ☎ (7) 28 10 37 Tx: none Fax: (2) 28 48 06 SITA: n/a

F: 1993 ⁂ 37 Head: Valery Litavar ICAO: SKY BEL Net: n/a Beside aircraft listed, also leases aircraft from other Latvian companies when required.

registration	type of aircraft	cn/fn	ex/ex*	mfd	del	powered by	mtow kg	configuration	selcal	name/fln/specialitites/remarks
☐ YL-LBI	Tupolev 134B-3	63365	CCCP-65701	0080	0096	2 SO D-30-III	49000	Y78		

CONCORS Latvian Air Service = COS
Riga

PO Box 63, LV-1029 Riga, Latvia ☎ (2) 20 74 04 Tx: none Fax: (7) 20 79 04 SITA: n/a
F: 1991 ♦♦♦ 20 Head: Sergej Ratnikov ICAO: CONCORS Net: n/a

registration	type of aircraft	cn/fn	ex/ex*	mfd	del	powered by	mtow kg	configuration	selcal	name/fln/remarks
☐ YL-CBL	Yakovlev 18T	1733		0093	0097	1 VO M-14P	1650	3 Pax		
☐ YL-KAC	Let 410UVP	851531	CCCP-67559	0085	0094	2 WA M-601D	5800	16 Pax		
☐ YL-KAE	Let 410UVP	790209	CCCP-67173	0079	0097	2 WA M-601D	5800	15 Pax		
☐ YL-KAI	Let 410UVP-E	861726	1726	0086	0098	2 WA M-601E	6600	Y19		
☐ YL-LAO	Ilyushin 18D	2964017102	CCCP-75916	0074	0698	4 IV AI-20M	64000	Combi		cvtd 22

INVERSIA, Ltd – Latvian Aviation Company = INV (Inversija)
Riga

Riga Airport, LV-1053 Riga, Latvia ☎ (7) 20 70 95 Tx: none Fax: (7) 20 74 78 SITA: RIXARXH
F: 1991 ♦♦♦ 110 Head: Efim Brook ICAO: INVER Net: n/a

registration	type of aircraft	cn/fn	ex/ex*	mfd	del	powered by	mtow kg	configuration	selcal	name/fln/remarks
☐ YL-LAJ	Ilyushin 76T	083414432	RA-76510	0078	0791	4 SO D-30KP	170000	Freighter		
☐ YL-LAK	Ilyushin 76T	0003424707	RA-76522	1279	0991	4 SO D-30KP	170000	Freighter		
☐ YL-LAL	Ilyushin 76T	0013433984	RA-76755	0282	0192	4 SO D-30KP	170000	Freighter		lsf VAS

LAT CHARTER Ltd = LTC
Riga

Riga Airport, LV-1053 Riga, Latvia ☎ (7) 20 73 92 Tx: 612486 ltc su Fax: (7) 20 73 98 SITA: RIXLAXH
F: 1993 ♦♦♦ 24 Head: Yury Rubenchik ICAO: LATCHARTER Net: n/a

registration	type of aircraft	cn/fn	ex/ex*	mfd	del	powered by	mtow kg	configuration	selcal	name/fln/remarks
☐ YL-LBE	Tupolev 134B-3	63285	CCCP-65695	0080	0094	2 SO D-30-III	49000	Y72		
☐ YL-LBG	Tupolev 134B-3	63333	CCCP-65699	0080	0097	2 SO D-30-III	49000	Y72		

LATGALES AVIO = LTG
Riga

Riga Airport, MTC-117, LV-1053 Riga, Latvia ☎ (7) 20 70 17 Tx: none Fax: (7) 20 70 17 SITA: n/a
F: 1996 ♦♦♦ n/a Head: Uldis Martinsons ICAO: LATGALE Net: n/a Aircraft below MTOW 1361kg: AA-5A Cheetah

registration	type of aircraft	cn/fn	ex/ex*	mfd	del	powered by	mtow kg	configuration	selcal	name/fln/remarks
☐ YL-LHS	PZL Swidnik (Mil) Mi-2			0096		2 IS GTD-350-4	3550	Utility		
☐ YL-LHT	PZL Swidnik (Mil) Mi-2			0096		2 IS GTD-350-4	3550	Utility		

LATPASS AIRLINES = QJ / LTP
Riga

Riga Airport, LV-1053 Riga, Latvia ☎ (7) 20 76 26 Tx: none Fax: (7) 20 71 26 SITA: RIXTOLY
F: 1995 ♦♦♦ 40 Head: Efim Ratner IATA: 937 ICAO: LATPASS Net: n/a

registration	type of aircraft	cn/fn	ex/ex*	mfd	del	powered by	mtow kg	configuration	selcal	name/fln/remarks
☐ YL-LAB	Tupolev 154B-2	515	CCCP-85515	0081	0096	3 KU NK-8-2U	98000	Y161		

RAF-AVIA = MTL
Riga

34 Duntes Street, LV-1005 Riga, Latvia ☎ (7) 39 20 92 Tx: none Fax: (7) 39 17 79 SITA: RIXRAXM
F: 1991 ♦♦♦ 79 Head: Youri Khemlevski ICAO: MITAVIA Net: n/a

registration	type of aircraft	cn/fn	ex/ex*	mfd	del	powered by	mtow kg	configuration	selcal	name/fln/remarks
☐ YL-RAA	Antonov 26B	11206	RA-26064	0681	1297	2 IV AI-24VT	24000	Combi		
☐ YL-RAB	Antonov 26B	10508	RA-26032	0080	0598	2 IV AI-24VT	24000	Combi		
☐ YL-RAC	Antonov 26	9903	CCCP-79169	0080	1092	2 IV AI-24VT	24000	Combi		
☐ YL-RAD	Antonov 26B	13909	RA-26589	0085	1198	2 IV AI-24VT	24000	Combi		

RIAIR – Riga Airlines = GV / RIG (Rigas Gaisas Linjas dba/Associated with Interlatvia Corp. & Software House, Riga)
Riga

1 Melluzu Street, LV-1067 Riga, Latvia ☎ (7) 42 42 83 Tx: none Fax: (7) 86 01 99 SITA: RIXTOGV
F: 1992 ♦♦♦ n/a Head: Maris Karklins IATA: 248 ICAO: RIGA LINER Net: http://www.riga-airlines.com Suspended operations (with Boeing 737-200 aircraft) 0199. Intends to restart.

RIGA AEROCLUB = RAK (Affiliated with Latvian Professional Air Sport Center)
Riga & Jelgava

1-17 Lienes Str., LV-1009 Riga, Latvia ☎ (2) 27 81 11 Tx: none Fax: (2) 29 59 61 SITA: n/a
F: 1992 ♦♦♦ n/a Head: Ildous Fahrutdinov ICAO: SPORT CLUB Net: n/a

registration	type of aircraft	cn/fn	ex/ex*	mfd	del	powered by	mtow kg	configuration	selcal	name/fln/remarks
☐ YL-KAB	PZL Mielec (Antonov) An-28	1AJ009-15	CCCP-28949	0090	0092	2 GS TVD-10B	6500	Y17/Para/Frtr		lst LIV
☐ YL-KAD	PZL Mielec (Antonov) An-28	1AJ004-02	RA-28753	0087	0095	2 GS TVD-10B	6500	Y17/Para/Frtr		lst ENI
☐ YL-KAF	PZL Mielec (Antonov) An-28	1AJ009-09	RA-28943	0090	0097	2 GS TVD-10B	6500	Y17/Para/Frtr		lst ENI
☐ YL-LCK	Antonov 24B	79901110	CCCP-47747	0067	0095	2 IV AI-24	21000	Y40		

TRANSEAST AIRLINES, Ltd = T4 / TRL
Riga

Riga Airport, LV-1053 Riga, Latvia ☎ (7) 20 77 71 Tx: none Fax: (7) 20 77 72 SITA: RIXRRT4
F: 1992 ♦♦♦ 20 Head: Igor N. Cherkasov IATA: 609 ICAO: LATTRANS Net: n/a

registration	type of aircraft	cn/fn	ex/ex*	mfd	del	powered by	mtow kg	configuration	selcal	name/fln/remarks
☐ YL-TRB	Yakovlev 40	9721353	RA-88275	0677	0897	3 IV AI-25	17200	Y30		

YN = NICARAGUA (Republic of Nicaragua) (Republica de Nicaragua)
Capital: Managua Official Language: Spanish Population: 4,5 million Square Km: 130682 Dialling code: +505 Year established: 1838 Acting political head: José Arnoldo Aleman Lacayo (President)

AEROSEGOVIA, S.A. = SGV
Managua

Aeropuerto Internacional A.C. Sandino, Managua, Nicaragua ☎ (2) 78 71 62 Tx: none Fax: (2) 78 71 62 SITA: n/a
F: 1996 ♦♦♦ n/a Head: n/a ICAO: SEGOVIA Net: n/a Beside aircraft listed, also leases Antonov 26 & Ilyushin 76 aircraft from other companies when required.

registration	type of aircraft	cn/fn	ex/ex*	mfd	del	powered by	mtow kg	configuration	selcal	name/fln/remarks
☐ YN-CBV	Antonov 32	1809		0088	0097	2 IV AI-20D	27000	Freighter		

LA COSTENA, S.A. (Member of Grupo TACA)
Managua

Aeropuerto Internacional A.C. Sandino, Terminal Vuelos Nacionales, Managua, Nicaragua ☎ (2) 63 12 28 Tx: none Fax: (2) 63 12 81 SITA: n/a
F: 1991 ♦♦♦ 85 Head: Julio Caballero ICAO: LACOSTENA Net: n/a

registration	type of aircraft	cn/fn	ex/ex*	mfd	del	powered by	mtow kg	configuration	selcal	name/fln/remarks
☐ YN-CDR	Cessna 208B Grand Caravan	208B0311	N1015G*	0092	1092	1 PWC PT6A-114A	3969	Y9		
☐ YN-CED	Cessna 208B Grand Caravan	208B0341	N1044V*	0093	0793	1 PWC PT6A-114A	3969	Y9		
☐ YN-CEQ	Cessna 208B Grand Caravan	208B0444		0095		1 PWC PT6A-114A	3969	Y9		
☐ YN-CFK	Cessna 208B Grand Caravan	208B0691		0095	1098	1 PWC PT6A-114A	3969	Y9		
☐ HP-1317APP	Shorts 360-200 (SD3-60)	SH3602	N360MQ	0082	0097	2 PWC PT6A-65AR	11999	Y36		lsf APP
☐ HP-1318APP	Shorts 360-200 (SD3-60)	SH3612	N362MQ	0083	0097	2 PWC PT6A-65AR	11999	Y36		lsf APP

NICA Nicaraguenses de Aviacion, SA = 6Y / NIS (Member of Grupo TACA)
Managua

Apartado Postal 6018, KM 10.5, Carretera del Norte, Managua, Nicaragua ☎ (2) 66 31 36 Tx: none Fax: (2) 63 18 22 SITA: n/a
F: 1992 ♦♦♦ 130 Head: Enrique Dreyfus IATA: 930 ICAO: NICA Net: http://www.flylatinamerica.com/acc_nica.html

registration	type of aircraft	cn/fn	ex/ex*	mfd	del	powered by	mtow kg	configuration	selcal	name/fln/remarks
☐ N501NG	Boeing 737-2T5 (A)	22395 / 729	H4-SAL	0081	0692	2 PW JT8D-15 (HK3/NOR)	54204	Y125		lsf CITG / sub-lst / opb LRC

YR = ROMANIA (Republic of Romania) (Republica Romania)
Capital: Bucharest Official Language: Romanian Population: 23,3 million Square Km: 237500 Dialling code: +40 Year established: 1859 Acting political head: Emil Constantinescu (President)

ACVILA AIR Romanian Carrier = WZ / RRM
Bucharest-Otopeni

Calea Victoriei 103, Ap. 10, Sector 1, Bucuresti, Romania ☎ (1) 312 60 85 Tx: none Fax: (1) 312 00 60 SITA: n/a
F: 1994 ♦♦♦ n/a Head: Johann Menchu ICAO: AIR ROMANIA Net: n/a Operates charter flights with Ilyushin 18D aircraft leased from ROMAVIA (YR-) & VICHI (ER-) when required.

AEROLION INTERNATIONAL, FZE = AOB
Sharjah (UAE)

Operations office:, PO Box 7810, Sharjah, United Arab Emirates ☎ (4) 22 94 29 Tx: none Fax: (4) 27 53 94 SITA: SHJALCR
F: 1998 ♦♦♦ n/a Head: Rafat Bakadah ICAO: INTERLION Net: n/a

registration	type of aircraft	cn/fn	ex/ex*	mfd	del	powered by	mtow kg	configuration	selcal	name/fln/remarks
☐ YR-BRB	RomBac One-Eleven 561RC	402	EI-BSS	0483	0398	2 RR Spey 512-14DW	47400	Y109		for sale or lease

ATS – Aviation Transport Services = ROS (Servicii de Transport Aerian)
Bucharest-Otopeni

Str. Piata Romana 9B, Suite 2, Bucuresti, Romania ☎ (1) 223 09 07 Tx: 12039 ats r Fax: (1) 312 95 35 SITA: n/a
F: 1991 ♦♦♦ 6 Head: Ioan Hasegan ICAO: ROMAS Net: n/a Operates non-scheduled passenger & cargo flights with Antonov 12/26, BAe One-Eleven 500, Boeing 707B/C & Ilyushin 18, leased from other companies when required.

AVIATIA UTILITARA, SA – AV.U = UTL (Utility Aviation)
Bucharest-Baneasa

Sos Bucurest-Ploiesti Km 8.5, Sct. 1, Cod 71557, Bucuresti, Romania ☎ (1) 679 23 40 Tx: 11359 r Fax: (1) 230 57 12 SITA: n/a
F: 1964 ♦♦♦ 476 Head: Ioan Chituu ICAO: AV UTIL Net: n/a

registration	type of aircraft	cn/fn	ex/ex*	mfd	del	powered by	mtow kg	configuration	selcal	name/fln/remarks
☐ YR-ELC	ICA IAR-316B Alouette III (Aero.SA316B)	1909		0071	0071	1 TU Artouste IIIB	2200	Utility		
☐ YR-ELR	ICA IAR-316B Alouette III (Aero.SA316B)	50		0074	0074	1 TU Artouste IIIB	2200	Utility		
☐ YR-ELS	ICA IAR-316B Alouette III (Aero.SA316B)	93		0077	0077	1 TU Artouste IIIB	2200	Utility		
☐ YR-ELU	ICA IAR-316B Alouette III (Aero.SA316B)	95		0077	0077	1 TU Artouste IIIB	2200	Utility		
☐ YR-CXA	Kamov Ka-26	7203003		0072	0597	2 VE M-14V-26	3250	Utility		
☐ YR-CXB	Kamov Ka-26	7203106		0072	0597	2 VE M-14V-26	3250	Utility		
☐ YR-CXC	Kamov Ka-26	7202606		0072	0597	2 VE M-14V-26	3250	Utility		
☐ YR-CXD	Kamov Ka-26	7202606		0072	0597	2 VE M-14V-26	3250	Utility		
☐ YR-CXG	Kamov Ka-26	7303206	ER-19323	0072	0698	2 VE M-14V-26	3250	Utility		
☐ YR-EAA	Kamov Ka-26	7706203		0077	0077	2 VE M-14V-26	3250	Utility		
☐ YR-EAD	Kamov Ka-26	7806412		0078	0078	2 VE M-14V-26	3250	Utility		
☐ YR-EAF	Kamov Ka-26	7806414		0078	0078	2 VE M-14V-26	3250	Utility		
☐ YR-EAJ	Kamov Ka-26	7806418		0078	0078	2 VE M-14V-26	3250	Utility		
☐ YR-EAM	Kamov Ka-26	7806501		0078	0078	2 VE M-14V-26	3250	Utility		
☐ YR-EAN	Kamov Ka-26	7303505	CCCP-19339	0073	0086	2 VE M-14V-26	3250	Utility		
☐ YR-EAO	Kamov Ka-26	7705912	CCCP-24395	0077	0086	2 VE M-14V-26	3250	Utility		
☐ YR-EKE	Kamov Ka-26	7000803		0070	0070	2 VE M-14V-26	3250	Utility		

☐ YR-EKL	Kamov Ka-26	7202806		0072	0072	2 VE M-14V-26	3250	Utility		
☐ YR-EKN	Kamov Ka-26	7202808		0072	0072	2 VE M-14V-26	3250	Utility		
☐ YR-EKO	Kamov Ka-26	7202809		0072	0072	2 VE M-14V-26	3250	Utility		
☐ YR-EKT	Kamov Ka-26	7706102		0077	0077	2 VE M-14V-26	3250	Utility		
☐ YR-EKV	Kamov Ka-26	7706202		0077	0077	2 VE M-14V-26	3250	Utility		
☐ YR-EKY	Kamov Ka-26	7706103		0077	1077	2 VE M-14V-26	3250	Utility		
☐ YR-AAP	PZL Mielec (Antonov) An-2	1G199-34	HA-MAP	0082		1 SH ASh-62IR	5500	Sprayer		
☐ YR-AER	PZL Mielec (Antonov) An-2	1G154-45	UR-05805	0082	0998	1 SH ASh-62IR	5500	Sprayer		
☐ YR-AOA	PZL Mielec (Antonov) An-2	1G197-38	UR-31415	0082	0498	1 SH ASh-62IR	5500	Sprayer		
☐ YR-AOB	PZL Mielec (Antonov) An-2	1G176-09	UR-62546	0077	0198	1 SH ASh-62IR	5500	Sprayer		
☐ YR-AOR	PZL Mielec (Antonov) An-2	1G145-03	HA-MBX	0073		1 SH ASh-62IR	5500	Sprayer		
☐ YR-APG	PZL Mielec (Antonov) An-2	1G124-27		0071	0071	1 SH ASh-62IR	5500	Sprayer		
☐ YR-APO	PZL Mielec (Antonov) An-2	1G124-36		0071	0071	1 SH ASh-62IR	5500	Sprayer		
☐ YR-APR	PZL Mielec (Antonov) An-2	1G124-37	37	0071	0071	1 SH ASh-62IR	5500	Sprayer		
☐ YR-APY	PZL Mielec (Antonov) An-2	1G124-45		0071	0071	1 SH ASh-62IR	5500	Sprayer		
☐ YR-BOR	PZL Mielec (Antonov) An-2	1G192-13	HA-MAN	0080	0596	1 SH ASh-62IR	5500	Sprayer		
☐ YR-CCF	PZL Mielec (Antonov) An-2	1G141-15	UR-70361	0072	0797	1 SH ASh-62IR	5500	Sprayer		
☐ YR-DAV	PZL Mielec (Antonov) An-2	1G183-17	UR-56519	0079	0397	1 SH ASh-62IR	5500	Sprayer		
☐ YR-FLA	PZL Mielec (Antonov) An-2	1G238-37	UR-02260	0090	0496	1 SH ASh-62IR	5500	Sprayer		
☐ YR-FLB	PZL Mielec (Antonov) An-2	1G190-57	UR-84625	0080	0496	1 SH ASh-62IR	5500	Sprayer		
☐ YR-FLC	PZL Mielec (Antonov) An-2	1G238-36	UR-02259	0090	0496	1 SH ASh-62IR	5500	Sprayer		
☐ YR-ION	PZL Mielec (Antonov) An-2	1G210-04	HA-MAO	0084		1 SH ASh-62IR	5500	Sprayer		
☐ YR-MAC	PZL Mielec (Antonov) An-2	1G209-53	HA-MAI	0084		1 SH ASh-62IR	5500	Sprayer		
☐ YR-PAD	PZL Mielec (Antonov) An-2	1G164-32		0075	0076	1 SH ASh-62IR	5500	Sprayer		
☐ YR-PAH	PZL Mielec (Antonov) An-2	1G164-35		0075	0076	1 SH ASh-62IR	5500	Sprayer		
☐ YR-PAK	PZL Mielec (Antonov) An-2	1G164-38		0075	0076	1 SH ASh-62IR	5500	Sprayer		
☐ YR-PAM	PZL Mielec (Antonov) An-2	1G164-40		0075	0076	1 SH ASh-62IR	5500	Sprayer		
☐ YR-PAO	PZL Mielec (Antonov) An-2	1G164-51		0075	0076	1 SH ASh-62IR	5500	Sprayer		
☐ YR-PAS	PZL Mielec (Antonov) An-2	1G164-53		0075	0076	1 SH ASh-62IR	5500	Sprayer		
☐ YR-PAT	PZL Mielec (Antonov) An-2	1G164-54		0075	0076	1 SH ASh-62IR	5500	Sprayer		
☐ YR-PAW	PZL Mielec (Antonov) An-2	1G164-57		0075	0076	1 SH ASh-62IR	5500	Sprayer		
☐ YR-PAX	PZL Mielec (Antonov) An-2	1G164-58		0075	0076	1 SH ASh-62IR	5500	Sprayer		
☐ YR-PBA	PZL Mielec (Antonov) An-2	1G166-36		0075	0084	1 SH ASh-62IR	5500	Sprayer		
☐ YR-PBC	PZL Mielec (Antonov) An-2	1G177-26		0077	0084	1 SH ASh-62IR	5500	Sprayer		
☐ YR-PBD	PZL Mielec (Antonov) An-2	1G177-27		0077	0084	1 SH ASh-62IR	5500	Sprayer		
☐ YR-PBG	PZL Mielec (Antonov) An-2	1G180-43		0078	0086	1 SH ASh-62IR	5500	Sprayer		
☐ YR-PBL	PZL Mielec (Antonov) An-2	1G196-36		0082	0082	1 SH ASh-62IR	5500	Sprayer		
☐ YR-PBM	PZL Mielec (Antonov) An-2	1G196-51		0082	0082	1 SH ASh-62IR	5500	Sprayer		
☐ YR-PBO	PZL Mielec (Antonov) An-2	1G202-21		0083	0083	1 SH ASh-62IR	5500	Sprayer		
☐ YR-PBP	PZL Mielec (Antonov) An-2	1G202-22		0083	0083	1 SH ASh-62IR	5500	Sprayer		
☐ YR-PBR	PZL Mielec (Antonov) An-2	1G202-23		0083	0083	1 SH ASh-62IR	5500	Sprayer		
☐ YR-PMB	PZL Mielec (Antonov) An-2	1G227-12		0087	0087	1 SH ASh-62IR	5500	Sprayer		
☐ YR-PMC	PZL Mielec (Antonov) An-2	1G227-13		0087	0087	1 SH ASh-62IR	5500	Sprayer		
☐ YR-PMD	PZL Mielec (Antonov) An-2	1G227-14		0087	0087	1 SH ASh-62IR	5500	Sprayer		
☐ YR-PME	PZL Mielec (Antonov) An-2	1G227-15		0087	0087	1 SH ASh-62IR	5500	Sprayer		
☐ YR-PMH	PZL Mielec (Antonov) An-2	1G231-34		0088	0088	1 SH ASh-62IR	5500	Sprayer		
☐ YR-PMI	PZL Mielec (Antonov) An-2	1G231-35		0088	0088	1 SH ASh-62IR	5500	Sprayer		
☐ YR-PMK	PZL Mielec (Antonov) An-2	1G231-37		0088	0088	1 SH ASh-62IR	5500	Sprayer		
☐ YR-PML	PZL Mielec (Antonov) An-2	1G231-38		0088	0088	1 SH ASh-62IR	5500	Sprayer		
☐ YR-PMM	PZL Mielec (Antonov) An-2	1G231-39		0088	0088	1 SH ASh-62IR	5500	Sprayer		
☐ YR-PMN	PZL Mielec (Antonov) An-2	1G231-40		0088	0088	1 SH ASh-62IR	5500	Sprayer		
☐ YR-PMO	PZL Mielec (Antonov) An-2	1G233-01		0088	0089	1 SH ASh-62IR	5500	Sprayer		
☐ YR-PMR	PZL Mielec (Antonov) An-2	1G233-03		0088	0089	1 SH ASh-62IR	5500	Sprayer		
☐ YR-PMS	PZL Mielec (Antonov) An-2	1G233-04		0088	0089	1 SH ASh-62IR	5500	Sprayer		
☐ YR-PMT	PZL Mielec (Antonov) An-2	1G233-05		0088	0089	1 SH ASh-62IR	5500	Sprayer		
☐ YR-PMU	PZL Mielec (Antonov) An-2	1G233-06		0088	0089	1 SH ASh-62IR	5500	Sprayer		
☐ YR-PMV	PZL Mielec (Antonov) An-2	1G233-07		0088	0089	1 SH ASh-62IR	5500	Sprayer		
☐ YR-PMX	PZL Mielec (Antonov) An-2	1G233-08		0088	0089	1 SH ASh-62IR	5500	Sprayer		
☐ YR-PSA	PZL Mielec (Antonov) An-2	1G177-22		0077	0078	1 SH ASh-62IR	5500	Sprayer		
☐ YR-PSD	PZL Mielec (Antonov) An-2	1G177-25		0077	0084	1 SH ASh-62IR	5500	Sprayer		
☐ YR-PVB	PZL Mielec (Antonov) An-2	1G175-02		0077	0077	1 SH ASh-62IR	5500	Sprayer		
☐ YR-PVC	PZL Mielec (Antonov) An-2	1G175-03		0077	0077	1 SH ASh-62IR	5500	Sprayer		
☐ YR-PVD	PZL Mielec (Antonov) An-2	1G175-04		0077	0077	1 SH ASh-62IR	5500	Sprayer		
☐ YR-PVF	PZL Mielec (Antonov) An-2	1G174-37		0077	0077	1 SH ASh-62IR	5500	Photo		
☐ YR-PVG	PZL Mielec (Antonov) An-2	1G175-06		0077	0077	1 SH ASh-62IR	5500	Sprayer		
☐ YR-PVH	PZL Mielec (Antonov) An-2	1G175-07		0077	0077	1 SH ASh-62IR	5500	Sprayer		
☐ YR-PVI	PZL Mielec (Antonov) An-2	1G175-08		0077	0077	1 SH ASh-62IR	5500	Sprayer		
☐ YR-PVM	PZL Mielec (Antonov) An-2	1G175-12		0077	0077	1 SH ASh-62IR	5500	Sprayer		
☐ YR-PVN	PZL Mielec (Antonov) An-2	1G175-13		0077	0077	1 SH ASh-62IR	5500	Sprayer		
☐ YR-PVO	PZL Mielec (Antonov) An-2	1G175-14		0077	0077	1 SH ASh-62IR	5500	Sprayer		
☐ YR-PVP	PZL Mielec (Antonov) An-2	1G175-15		0077	0077	1 SH ASh-62IR	5500	Sprayer		
☐ YR-PVR	PZL Mielec (Antonov) An-2	1G175-16		0077	0077	1 SH ASh-62IR	5500	Sprayer		

GRIVCO INTERNATIONAL, Ltd = GIV — Bucharest-Baneasa

Ploiesti 40, Baneasa-Airport, Bucuresti, Romania ☎ (1) 232 13 30 Tx: n/a Fax: (1) 212 13 30 SITA: n/a

F: 1993 ✱✱✱ 15 Head: Dar Tudorache ICAO: GRIVCO Net: n/a

☐ YR-DVA	Hawker 600B (HS 125-600B)	256024	G-OMGA	0073	0594	2 RR Viper 601-22A	11567			

ION TIRIAC AIR, S.A. = TIH — Bucurest-Otopeni

PO 21, Box 17, KM 16.5, Bucurest-Ploiesti Road, Otopeni-Bucurest Airport, Romania ☎ (1) 230 60 81 Tx: none Fax: (1) 230 60 81 SITA: BUHUXRO

F: 1997 ✱✱✱ 18 Head: Radu Stanescu ICAO: TIRIAC AIR Net: n/a

☐ YR-BEL	Bell 206L-1 LongRanger II	45375	N573W	0080	0097	1 AN 250-C28B	1882	4 Pax		lsf Salvahe Trading Ltd
☐ N1127K	Cessna 525 CitationJet	525-0293		1298	0199	2 WRR FJ44-1A	4717	5 Pax		lsf Interlease Aviation Corp.
☐ D-IOAN	Beech King Air B200	BB-872	F-GHMN	0081	0299	2 PWC PT6A-42	5670	8 Pax		lsf AL Aviation Leasing GmbH
☐ D-CION	Learjet 55	55-015	N550LJ	0081	0299	2 GA TFE731-3AR-2B	9750	7 Pax		lsf AL Aviation Leasing GmbH

JARO INTERNATIONAL, SA = MDJ — Bucharest-Baneasa

500 Bucuresti Ploesti 14-22, Bucuresti, Romania ☎ (1) 232 22 73 Tx: none Fax: (1) 230 77 81 SITA: BUHTOJT

F: 1991 ✱✱✱ 127 Head: Mirica Dimitrescu ICAO: JARO INTERNATIONAL Net: n/a

☐ YR-JBA	BAe (BAC) One-Eleven 528FL	234	G-BJRT	0071	1093	2 RR Spey 514-14DW	44000	C20Y55		Traian Vuia / lst ERT
☐ YR-JBB	BAe (BAC) One-Eleven 528FL	238	G-BJRU	0071	1093	2 RR Spey 514-14DW	44000	C12Y74		Aurel Vlaicu
☐ YR-JCB	Boeing 707-321B	20022 / 774	CC-CYB	0068	0295	4 PW JT3D-3B (HK2/COM)	152000	Y188	GK-LM	lsf Comtran Int'l / std BBU

MIRAVIA, Ltd = N3 / MRV — Bucarest-Otopeni

B-dul Magheru 41, Sector 1, Bucuresti, Romania ☎ (1) 659 45 16 Tx: n/a Fax: (1) 312 95 15 SITA: n/a

F: n/a ✱✱✱ n/a Head: n/a IATA: 581 ICAO: MIRAVIA Net: n/a Operates charter flights with Tupolev 134/154 aircraft, leased from othern companies when required.

ROMAVIA, R.A. = WQ / RMV — Bucharest-Baneasa & -Otopeni

B-dul Dimitrie Cantemir Nr. 1, Bl. B2, Sector 4, Bucuresti, Romania ☎ (1) 330 10 60 Tx: 11499 romav r Fax: (1) 330 10 49 SITA: BUHDDVQ

F: 1991 ✱✱✱ 320 Head: Iuliu A. Goleanu IATA: 534 ICAO: AEROMAVIA Net: n/a

☐ YR-MLB	Mil Mi-8PS	10735		0487	0491	2 IS TV2-117A	12000	Y14		
☐ YR-BRE	RomBac One-Eleven 561RC	405		0386	0491	2 RR Spey 512-14DW	47400	Y104	BH-GL	
☐ YR-BRH	RomBac One-Eleven 561RC	408		1288	0691	2 RR Spey 512-14DW	47400	Y109	BM-KL	
☐ YR-BRI	RomBac One-Eleven 561RC	409		0989	0491	2 RR Spey 512-14DW	47400	Y109	CD-AB	lst RSO
☐ YR-IMM	Ilyushin 18D	187009904		0567	0491	4 IV AI-20M	64000	Y105		
☐ YR-IMZ	Ilyushin 18GrM (SCD)	187009802		0767	0491	4 IV AI-20M	64000	Freighter		cvtd 18D
☐ YR-ABB	Boeing 707-3K1C	20804 / 883		0574	0491	4 PW JT3D-3B (HK2/COM)	150092	Y188	AB-EJ	

TAROM Romania = RO / ROT (Transporturile Aeriene Romane / Romanian Air Transport dba) — Bucharest-Otopeni & -Baneasa

Sos. Bucuresti-Ploiesti, Km 16.5, Sct. 1, R-11181 Bucuresti, Romania ☎ (1) 315 27 47 Tx: 11181 airbuh r Fax: (1) 314 05 24 SITA: BUHDTRO

F: 1946 ✱✱✱ 3300 Head: Gheorghe Racaru IATA: 281 ICAO: TAROM Net: n/a

☐ YR-ATA	ATR 42-500	566	F-WWLF*	0097	0698	2 PWC PW127E	18600	Y48		Dunarea
☐ YR-ATB	ATR 42-500	569	F-WWLH*	0097	0698	2 PWC PW127E	18600	Y48		Bistrita
☐ YR-ATC	ATR 42-500	589	F-WWLR*			2 PWC PW127E	18600	Y48		Mures / oo-delivery 0499
☐ YR-ATD	ATR 42-500	591	F-WWLS*			2 PWC PW127E	18600	Y48		Cris / oo-delivery 0599
☐ YR-ATE	ATR 42-500	596	F-WWLY*			2 PWC PW127E	18600	Y48		Olt / oo-delivery 0599
☐ YR-ATF	ATR 42-500	599	F-WWEB*			2 PWC PW127E	18600	Y48		Arges / oo-delivery 0699
☐ YR-ATG	ATR 42-500					2 PWC PW127E	18600	Y48		oo-delivery 0999
☐ YR-ATX	ATR 42-300	077	F-WQBU	0088	1296	2 PWC PW120	16900	Y48		Dimbovita
☐ YR-ATY	ATR 42-300	083	F-WQBV	0088	0197	2 PWC PW120	16900	Y48		Arges

661 registration type of aircraft cn/fn ex/ex* mfd del powered by mtow kg configuration selcal name/fln/specialitites/remarks

☐ YR-BMI	Antonov 24RV	57310408		0875	1175	2 IV AI-24VT	21800	Freighter		
☐ YR-BML	Antonov 24RV	77310805		0477	0777	2 IV AI-24VT	21800	Y52		
☐ YR-BMM	Antonov 24RV	77310807		0577	0777	2 IV AI-24VT	21800	Y52		
☐ YR-BMN	Antonov 24RV	77310808		0577	0777	2 IV AI-24VT	21800	C12Y30		std BBU
☐ YR-BMO	Antonov 24RV	77310710	TC-FPB	0377	0777	2 IV AI-24VT	21800	Y52		std BBU
☐ YR-BCR	BAe (BAC) One-Eleven 487GK (F)	267	G-TOMO	0681	0781	2 RR Spey 512-14DW	44679	Freighter		std OTP
☐ YR-BCI	BAe (BAC) One-Eleven 525FT	252		1276	0377	2 RR Spey 512-14DW	47400	C12Y77	AD-EJ	
☐ YR-BCJ	BAe (BAC) One-Eleven 525FT	253	TC-AKB	0377	0477	2 RR Spey 512-14DW	47400	Y104	AD-EK	
☐ YR-BCK	BAe (BAC) One-Eleven 525FT	254	TC-JCP	0477	0577	2 RR Spey 512-14DW	47400	Y104	AD-EM	
☐ YR-BCL	BAe (BAC) One-Eleven 525FT	255	EI-BVG	0677	0777	2 RR Spey 512-14DW	47400	C12Y77	AD-GK	
☐ YR-BCN	BAe (BAC) One-Eleven 525FT	266	EI-BSY	1180	0181	2 RR Spey 512-14DW	47400	C12Y77		
☐ YR-BRC	RomBac One-Eleven 561RC	403	YU-ANS	0484	0884	2 RR Spey 512-14DW	47400	C12Y77		
☐ YR-BGA	Boeing 737-38J	27179 / 2524	N5573K*	0093	1093	2 CFMI CFM56-3C1	56472	C12Y120	ER-AG	Alba Iulia
☐ YR-BGB	Boeing 737-38J	27180 / 2529		0093	1093	2 CFMI CFM56-3C1	56472	C32Y84	ER-AH	Bucuresti
☐ YR-BGC	Boeing 737-38J	27181 / 2662		0094	1194	2 CFMI CFM56-3C1	60100	C12Y120	ER-AJ	Constanta
☐ YR-BGD	Boeing 737-38J	27182 / 2663		0094	1194	2 CFMI CFM56-3C1	60100	C12Y120	ER-AK	Deva
☐ YR-BGE	Boeing 737-38J	27395 / 2671		0094	1194	2 CFMI CFM56-3C1	60100	C12Y120	ER-AL	Timisoara
☐ YR-BGX	Boeing 737-36Q	29326 / 3020		0098	0498	2 CFMI CFM56-3C1	61235	C12Y120		Galati / lsf BOUL
☐ YR-BGY	Boeing 737-36M	28332 / 2809	OO-VEA	0096	1298	2 CFMI CFM56-3C1	61235	C32Y89		lsf BOUL
☐ YR-TPB	Tupolev 154B-1	161		0676	0776	3 KU NK-8-2U	98000	C10Y135orY164		cvtd 154B / std OTP
☐ YR-TPG	Tupolev 154B-1	262		0278	0378	3 KU NK-8-2U	98000	C10Y135orY164		std OTP
☐ YR-ABA	Boeing 707-3K1C	20803 / 878		0274	0274	4 PW JT3D-3B (HK2/COM)	146000	Freighter	AB-EH	opf Key Aviation broker
☐ YR-ABC	Boeing 707-3K1C	20805 / 884		0074	0674	4 PW JT3D-3B (HK2/COM)	146000	Freighter	AB-EK	opf Key Aviation broker
☐ YR-LCA	Airbus Industrie A310-325 (ET)	636	F-WWCG*	0092	1292	2 PW PW4156A	164000	C20Y189	BJ-LS	Transilvania
☐ YR-LCB	Airbus Industrie A310-325 (ET)	644	F-WWCO*	0093	1292	2 PW PW4156A	164000	C20Y189	BJ-MR	Moldova

VEG AIR, Srl. = VEG

Bucharest-Baneasa

B-dul Iancu de Hunedoara 4, Ap. 25, Sector 1, Bucuresti, Romania ☎ (1) 659 69 09 Tx: none Fax: (1) 223 38 53 SITA: n/a
F: 1998 ⁂ n/a Head: n/a Net: n/a Presently being set-up. Intends to start operations during 1999 with 1 Yakovlev 40 aircraft.

YS = EL SALVADOR (Republic of El Salvador) (Republica de El Salvador)

Capital: San Salvador Official Language: Spanish Population: 6,2 million Square Km: 21041 Dialling code: +503 Year established: 1821 Acting political head: Francisco Flores (President)

LASA – Lineas Aéreas Salvadorianas, SA

San Salvador-Ilopango

71 Avenida Sur 328, Colonia Escalon, San Salvador, El Salvador ☎ 298 11 74 Tx: n/a Fax: 224 05 01 SITA: n/a
F: n/a ⁂ n/a Head: Juan Francisco Torres Net: n/a

☐ YS-65C	Fairchild Ind. F-27B	15	N4903	0058	0795	2 RR Dart 514-7	18370			

TACA International Airlines, SA = TA / TAI (Member of Grupo TACA)

San Salvador-Comalapa Int'l

Edificio Caribe, 2 Piso, San Salvador, El Salvador ☎ 298 50 55 Tx: 20456 tacair sal Fax: 223 37 57 SITA: n/a
F: 1931 ⁂ 2100 Head: Ing. Federico Bloch IATA: 202 ICAO: TACA Net: http://www.flylatinamerica.com/acc_taca.html

☐ N231TA	Boeing 737-2K5 (A)	22596 / 763	YU-AOF	0581	1096	2 PW JT8D-17 (HK3/NOR)	58105	Y125	EM-AH	lsf FSBU Trustee
☐ N232TA	Boeing 737-296 (A)	22277 / 675	LN-BRL	0680	1094	2 PW JT8D-17A (HK3/NOR)	54204	Y124	BC-GK	lsf FSBU Trustee
☐ N233TA	Boeing 737-2K5 (A)	22601 / 833	YU-AOG	0082	1096	2 PW JT8D-17 (HK3/NOR)	58105	Y125	EM-AB	lsf FSBU Trustee
☐ N235TA	Boeing 737-205 (A)	21765 / 595	N73FS	0879	1196	2 PW JT8D-17A (HK3/NOR)	58105	Y124		lsf FSBU Trustee
☐ N240TA	Boeing 737-205 (A)	21729 / 572	N73TH	0579	1196	2 PW JT8D-17A (HK3/NOR)	58105	Y124		lsf FSBU Trustee
☐ N4905W	Boeing 737-210C (A)	20917 / 344		0474	1284	2 PW JT8D-17 (HK3/NOR)	54204	Y125		lsf FSBU Trustee
☐ N371TA	Boeing 737-3S1	24834 / 1896		0790	0790	2 CFMI CFM56-3B2	62142	Y136	BH-AQ	lsf FSBU Trustee/sub-lst VRG as PP-VPF
☐ N372TA	Boeing 737-3S1	24856 / 1911		0990	0990	2 CFMI CFM56-3B2	62142	Y136		lsf FSBU Trustee
☐ N	Airbus Industrie A319-132	1066				2 IAE V2524-A5	64000			oo-delivery 0899
☐ N	Airbus Industrie A319-132					2 IAE V2524-A5	64000			oo-delivery 1099
☐ N	Airbus Industrie A319-132					2 IAE V2524-A5	64000			oo-delivery 1299
☐ N	Airbus Industrie A319-132					2 IAE V2524-A5	64000			oo-delivery 0600
☐ N	Airbus Industrie A319-132					2 IAE V2524-A5	64000			oo-delivery 0401
☐ N	Airbus Industrie A319-132					2 IAE V2524-A5	64000			oo-delivery 0801
☐ N	Airbus Industrie A319-132					2 IAE V2524-A5	64000			oo-delivery 1201
☐ N	Airbus Industrie A319-132					2 IAE V2524-A5	64000			oo-delivery 0002
☐ N	Airbus Industrie A319-132					2 IAE V2524-A5	64000			oo-delivery 0002
☐ N	Airbus Industrie A319-132					2 IAE V2524-A5	64000			oo-delivery 0002
☐ N	Airbus Industrie A319-132					2 IAE V2524-A5	64000			oo-delivery 0002
☐ N	Airbus Industrie A319-132					2 IAE V2524-A5	64000			oo-delivery 0003
☐ N	Airbus Industrie A319-132					2 IAE V2524-A5	64000			oo-delivery 0003
☐ N	Airbus Industrie A319-132					2 IAE V2524-A5	64000			oo-delivery 0003
☐ N	Airbus Industrie A319-132					2 IAE V2524-A5	64000			oo-delivery 0003
☐ N	Airbus Industrie A319-132					2 IAE V2524-A5	64000			oo-delivery 0003
☐ N	Airbus Industrie A319-132					2 IAE V2524-A5	64000			oo-delivery 0003
☐ N	Airbus Industrie A319-132					2 IAE V2524-A5	64000			oo-delivery 0003
☐ N	Airbus Industrie A319-132					2 IAE V2524-A5	64000			oo-delivery 0004
☐ N	Airbus Industrie A319-132					2 IAE V2524-A5	64000			oo-delivery 0004
☐ N	Airbus Industrie A319-132					2 IAE V2524-A5	64000			oo-delivery 0004
☐ N	Airbus Industrie A320-233					2 IAE V2527E-A5	77000	Y162		oo-delivery 0101
☐ N	Airbus Industrie A320-233					2 IAE V2527E-A5	77000	Y162		oo-delivery 0301
☐ N	Airbus Industrie A320-233					2 IAE V2527E-A5	77000	Y162		oo-delivery 0501
☐ N	Airbus Industrie A320-233					2 IAE V2527E-A5	77000	Y162		oo-delivery 0701
☐ N	Airbus Industrie A320-233					2 IAE V2527E-A5	77000	Y162		oo-delivery 0901
☐ N	Airbus Industrie A320-233					2 IAE V2527E-A5	77000	Y162		oo-delivery 1101
☐ N	Airbus Industrie A320-233					2 IAE V2527E-A5	77000	Y162		oo-delivery 0002
☐ N	Airbus Industrie A320-233					2 IAE V2527E-A5	77000	Y162		oo-delivery 0002
☐ N	Airbus Industrie A320-233					2 IAE V2527E-A5	77000	Y162		oo-delivery 0002
☐ N	Airbus Industrie A320-233					2 IAE V2527E-A5	77000	Y162		oo-delivery 0003
☐ N	Airbus Industrie A320-233					2 IAE V2527E-A5	77000	Y162		oo-delivery 0003
☐ N451TA	Airbus Industrie A320-233	733	F-WWBR*	0997	1197	2 IAE V2527E-A5	77000	Y162		lsf FSBU Trustee
☐ N452TA	Airbus Industrie A320-233	741	F-WWBK*	1097	1197	2 IAE V2527E-A5	77000	Y162		lsf FSBU Trustee
☐ N453TA	Airbus Industrie A320-233	747	F-WWIH*	1097	1297	2 IAE V2527E-A5	77000	Y162		lsf FSBU Trustee
☐ N454TA	Airbus Industrie A320-233	789	F-WWDT*	0298	0398	2 IAE V2527E-A5	77000	Y162		lsf FSBU Trustee
☐ N455TA	Airbus Industrie A320-233	874	F-WWBV*	0098	1098	2 IAE V2527E-A5	77000	Y162		lsf FSBU Trustee
☐ N457TA	Airbus Industrie A320-233	902	F-WWDN*	0098	1198	2 IAE V2527E-A5	77000	Y162		lsf FSBU Trustee
☐ N458TA	Airbus Industrie A320-233	912	F-WWDU*	0098	1298	2 IAE V2527E-A5	77000	Y162		lsf FSBU Trustee
☐ N459TA	Airbus Industrie A320-233	916	F-WWDX*	0098	1298	2 IAE V2527E-A5	77000	Y162		lsf FSBU Trustee
☐ N460TA	Airbus Industrie A320-233	1007				2 IAE V2527E-A5	77000	Y162		oo-delivery 0699
☐ N762TA	Boeing 767-216 (ER)	23623 / 142	CC-CJU	0586	0593	2 GE CF6-80A2	159211	Y234	CJ-BM	lsf FSBU Trustee / for sale
☐ N769TA	Boeing 767-3S1 (ER)	26608 / 559		1194	1194	2 GE CF6-80C2B4F	172365	Y283		lsf FSBU Trustee / for sale
☐ N770TA	Boeing 767-3S1 (ER)	25221 / 384	B-16688	0891	0891	2 GE CF6-80C2B6F	172365	Y283		lsf FSBU Trustee/sub-lst BAL as G-BXOP

YU = YUGOSLAVIA (Federal Republic of Yugoslavia) (Savezna Republika Jugoslavija)

Yugoslavia consists of the two federal units Serbia and Montenegro. Serbia also includes the autonomous provinces of Kosovo+Metohija and of Vojvodina (included in the Yugoslavia figures)
Capital: Belgrade Official Language: Serbian Population: 10,5 million Square Km: 102173 Dialling code: +381 Year established: 1918 Acting political head: Slobodan Milosevic (President)

MONTENEGRO
Capital: Podgorica Official Language: Serbian Population: 0,7 million Square Km: 13812 Dialling code: +381 Acting political head: Milo Djukanovic (President)
SERBIA
Capital: Belgrade Official Language: Serbian Population: 9,8 million Square Km: 88361 Dialling code: +381 Acting political head: Milan Milutinovic (President)

Government / Corporate / Executive / VIP Aircraft

☐ YU-BJG	Learjet 25B	25B-187		0075	0075	2 GE CJ610-6	6804	VIP		Gvmt
☐ YU-BKR	Learjet 25D	25D-221	N3819G*	0077	0077	2 GE CJ610-6	6804	VIP		Gvmt
☐ YU-BKZ	Cessna 500 Citation I	500-0373	N98449	0077	1277	2 PWC JT15D-1A	5375	VIP		Gvmt
☐ YU-BNA	Dassault Falcon 50	43	72102	0081	0581	3 GA TFE731-3-1C	17600	VIP	CD-AE	Gvmt
☐ YU-BPY	Learjet 35A	35A-173	N116EL	0078	0891	2 GA TFE731-2-2B	8165	VIP		Gvmt
☐ YU-BPZ	Dassault Falcon 50	25	72101	0081		3 GA TFE731-3-1C	17600	VIP	CD-AB	Gvmt
☐ YU-BRA	Learjet 25B	25B-202	70401	0076		2 GE CJ610-6	6804	VIP		Gvmt
☐ YU-SEB	Sikorsky S-76B	760444		0096	0096	2 PWC PT6B-36A	5307	VIP		Gvmt

AIR YUGOSLAVIA = YRG (Subsidiary of JAT Yugoslav Airlines)

Belgrade

Bul. Umetnosti 16, YU-11000 Belgrade, Yugoslavia ☎ (11) 311 22 23 Tx: 12125 yu juair Fax: (11) 311 14 54 SITA: BEGJRJU
F: 1969 ⁂ n/a Head: Mrs. Nada Lazic ICAO: YUGAIR Net: n/a Operates charter flights with aircraft leased from JAT Yugoslav Airlines when required.

662 registration type of aircraft cn/fn ex/ex* mfd del powered by mtow kg configuration selcal name/fln/specialitites/remarks

AVIOGENEX = AGX (Subsidiary of Genex Group / Associated with Yugotours) — Belgrade

Narodnih heroja 43, YU-11070 Novi Beograd, Yugoslavia ☎ (11) 60 92 90 Tx: 11711 genair yu Fax: (11) 60 41 53 SITA: n/a
F: 1968 ☘ 310 Head: Dragan Aksentijevic ICAO: GENEX Net: n/a

☐ YU-ANP	Boeing 737-2K3 (A)	23912 / 1401		0087	0687	2 PW JT8D-15 (HK3/NOR)	53070	Y125		
☐ YU-AKD	Boeing 727-2L8 (A)	21040 / 1142	OY-SBJ	0075	0283	3 PW JT8D-15	86409	Y178	KL-EF	lst NCH
☐ YU-AKH	Boeing 727-2L8 (A)	21080 / 1146	OY-SBP	0075	0283	3 PW JT8D-15	86409	Y178		lst NCH
☐ YU-AKM	Boeing 727-243 (A)	22702 / 1814	HK-3618X	0082	0585	3 PW JT8D-15	83007	Y178		lst NCH

FATCA FLIGHT INSPECTION (Division of Federal Air Traffic Control Authority/Savezna uprava za kontrolu letenja) — Belgrade

Dr. Ivana Ribara 91, YU-11070 Novi Beograd, Yugoslavia ☎ (11) 15 49 00 Tx: 11175 uciv yu Fax: (11) 15 41 51 SITA: n/a
F: n/a ☘ n/a Head: n/a Net: n/a Flight inspection division of non-commercial federal organisation conducting calibration check-flights for the ground navigation devices.

☐ YU-AKT	Yakovlev 40	9222020		0072		3 IV AI-25	16800	Calibrator		71503
☐ YU-AKV	Yakovlev 40	9630849		0076		3 IV AI-25	16800	Calibrator		71505

JAT Jugoslovenski Aerotransport/Yugoslav Airlines = JU / JAT — Belgrade

Bulevar Umetnosti 16, YU-11070 Novi Beograd, Yugoslavia ☎ (11) 311 42 22 Tx: 11401 jat yu Fax: (11) 13 77 56 SITA: n/a
F: 1947 ☘ 5000 Head: Zika Petrovic IATA: 115 ICAO: JAT Net: http://www.jat.com Trainer-aircraft below MTOW 5000kg: Cessna T310R & Piper PA31T Cheyenne II

☐ YU-ALN	ATR 72-202	180	F-WWEP*	0090	0790	2 PWC PW124B	21500	Y66		
☐ YU-ALO	ATR 72-202	186	F-WWEW*	0090	1090	2 PWC PW124B	21500	Y66		lst SBK
☐ YU-ALP	ATR 72-202	189	F-WWED*	0090	0191	2 PWC PW124B	21500	Y66		
☐ YU-AHN	Boeing (Douglas) DC-9-32	47470 / 591		0070	0570	2 PW JT8D-9A	48988	CY106	KL-BG	std BEG
☐ YU-AHU	Boeing (Douglas) DC-9-32	47532 / 626		0071	0571	2 PW JT8D-9A	48988	CY106	KL-CD	std BEG
☐ YU-AHV	Boeing (Douglas) DC-9-32	47460 / 627		0071	0571	2 PW JT8D-9A	48988	CY106	KL-CE	std BEG
☐ YU-AJH	Boeing (Douglas) DC-9-32	47562 / 685	N1345U*	0072	0273	2 PW JT8D-9A	48988	CY106	GJ-FM	lst BLV
☐ YU-AJI	Boeing (Douglas) DC-9-32	47563 / 687	N1346U*	0072	0273	2 PW JT8D-9A	48988	CY106	GJ-HK	lst TUI
☐ YU-AJJ	Boeing (Douglas) DC-9-32	47567 / 688	N1347U*	0373	0373	2 PW JT8D-9A (HK3/ABS)	48988	CY106	GJ-HL	lst MAK as Z3-ARE
☐ YU-AJK	Boeing (Douglas) DC-9-32	47568 / 689		0073	0473	2 PW JT8D-9A	48988	CY106	GJ-HM	lst MAK as Z3-ARD
☐ YU-AJL	Boeing (Douglas) DC-9-32	47571 / 695		0073	0573	2 PW JT8D-9A (HK3/ABS)	48988	CY106	GJ-KL	
☐ YU-AJM	Boeing (Douglas) DC-9-32	47582 / 701		0073		2 PW JT8D-9A	48988	CY106	GJ-KM	
☐ YU-AND	Boeing 737-3H9	23329 / 1134		0085	0785	2 CFMI CFM56-3B1	61235	CY137	KL-HF	City of Krusevac / lst/opf RKA
☐ YU-ANF	Boeing 737-3H9	23330 / 1136		0085	0885	2 CFMI CFM56-3B1	61235	CY137	KL-HM	
☐ YU-ANH	Boeing 737-3H9	23415 / 1171	TC-CYO	0085	1285	2 CFMI CFM56-3B1	61235	CY137	KL-GM	lst/opf RKA
☐ YU-ANI	Boeing 737-3H9	23416 / 1175		0085	1285	2 CFMI CFM56-3B1	61235	CY137	KL-JM	
☐ YU-ANJ	Boeing 737-3H9	23714 / 1305		0086	1186	2 CFMI CFM56-3B1	61235	CY137	KM-AJ	std IST as TC-MIO in BHY Bosphorus cs
☐ YU-ANK	Boeing 737-3H9	23715 / 1310		0086	1186	2 CFMI CFM56-3B1	61235	CY137	KM-AL	
☐ YU-ANL	Boeing 737-3H9	23716 / 1321	TS-IEC	0086	1286	2 CFMI CFM56-3B1	61235	CY137	KM-CF	lst MAK as Z3-ARF
☐ YU-ANV	Boeing 737-3H9	24140 / 1524		0088	0388	2 CFMI CFM56-3B1	61235	CY137	BH-FG	all white-colors
☐ YU-ANW	Boeing 737-3H9	24141 / 1526	TS-IED	0088	0388	2 CFMI CFM56-3B1	61235	CY137		
☐ YU-AKB	Boeing 727-2H9 (A)	20931 / 1045		0074	0674	3 PW JT8D-9A	83824	CY163	GK-BD	
☐ YU-AKE	Boeing 727-2H9 (A)	21037 / 1094		0074	1274	3 PW JT8D-9A	83824	CY163	KL-EH	
☐ YU-AKF	Boeing 727-2H9 (A)	21038 / 1118		0075	0375	3 PW JT8D-9A	83824	CY163	KL-EJ	
☐ YU-AKG	Boeing 727-2H9 (A)	21039 / 1119		0075	0375	3 PW JT8D-9A	83824	CY163	KL-EM	
☐ YU-AKI	Boeing 727-2H9 (A)	22393 / 1681		0080	1280	3 PW JT8D-9A	83824	CY163	EG-DK	all white-colors
☐ YU-AKJ	Boeing 727-2H9 (A)	22394 / 1691	N8281V*	0080	1280	3 PW JT8D-9A	83824	CY163	EG-DL	
☐ YU-AKK	Boeing 727-2H9 (A)	22665 / 1786	TS-JEA	0081	1281	3 PW JT8D-9A	83824	CY163	AL-BC	all white-colors
☐ YU-AKL	Boeing 727-2H9 (A)	22666 / 1790	TS-JEB	0081	1281	3 PW JT8D-9A	83824	CY163	AL-BD	all white-colors
☐ YU-AMB	Boeing (Douglas) DC-10-30	46988 / 278		0079	0579	3 GE CF6-50C1	259455	CY308	BL-DH	City of Belgrade

JAT Privredna Avijacija/Agricultural Aviation (Subsidiary of JAT Jugoslovenski Aerotransport/Yugoslav Airlines) — Belgrade

Aerodrom Beograd, Mali Hangar, YU-11003 Beograd, Yugoslavia ☎ (11) 60 32 60 Tx: none Fax: (11) 67 58 84 SITA: n/a
F: 1947 ☘ n/a Head: n/a Net: n/a Ag-aircraft below MTOW 5000kg: 15 PZL-Mielec M-18 Dromader

☐ YU-BJF	PZL Mielec (Antonov) An-2	1G160-03		0074		1 SH ASh-62IR	5500	Sprayer		
☐ YU-BKK	PZL Mielec (Antonov) An-2	1G167-08		0076		1 SH ASh-62IR	5500	Sprayer		
☐ YU-BKL	PZL Mielec (Antonov) An-2	1G167-11		0076		1 SH ASh-62IR	5500	Sprayer		
☐ YU-BKM	PZL Mielec (Antonov) An-2	1G172-49		0077		1 SH ASh-62IR	5500	Sprayer		
☐ YU-BKO	PZL Mielec (Antonov) An-2	1G172-51		0077		1 SH ASh-62IR	5500	Sprayer		
☐ YU-BOA	PZL Mielec (Antonov) An-2	1G216-02		0085		1 SH ASh-62IR	5500	Sprayer		
☐ YU-BOB	PZL Mielec (Antonov) An-2	1G216-01		0085		1 SH ASh-62IR	5500	Sprayer		
☐ YU-BON	PZL Mielec (Antonov) An-2	1G221-60		0086		1 SH ASh-62IR	5500	Sprayer		
☐ YU-BOT	PZL Mielec (Antonov) An-2	1G223-11		0086		1 SH ASh-62IR	5500	Sprayer		
☐ YU-BOU	PZL Mielec (Antonov) An-2	1G223-12		0086		1 SH ASh-62IR	5500	Sprayer		
☐ YU-BPA	PZL Mielec (Antonov) An-2	1G225-31		0087		1 SH ASh-62IR	5500	Sprayer		
☐ YU-BPE	PZL Mielec (Antonov) An-2	1G228-25		0088		1 SH ASh-62IR	5500	Sprayer		

MONTENEGRO AIRLINES = MGX — Podgorica & Tivat

Ul. Beogradska 10, YU-81000 Podgorica, (Montenegro), Yugoslavia ☎ (81) 62 26 41 Tx: none Fax: (81) 62 37 62 SITA: TGDOW1I
F: 1994 ☘ n/a Head: Dejan Radonjic ICAO: MONTENEGRO Net: http://www.montenegro-airlines

☐ YU-AOH	Fokker F28 Fellowship 4000 (F28 Mk4000)	11184	OO-DJB	0082	1296	2 RR Spey 555-15P	33112	Y75		
☐ YU-AOI	Fokker F28 Fellowship 4000 (F28 Mk4000)	11176	PH-CHN	0082	0798	2 RR Spey 555-15P	33112	Y75		

YV = VENEZUELA (Republic of Venezuela) (Republica de Venezuela)

Capital: Caracas Official Language: Spanish Population: 24,0 million Square Km: 912050 Dialling code: +58 Year established: 1810 Acting political head: Rafael Caldera (President)

Government / Corporate / Executive / VIP Aircraft

☐ FAV0001	Boeing 737-2N1 (A)	21167 / 442		0076	0176	2 PW JT8D-17	53070	VIP		Fuerza Aérea Venezolana
☐ FAV0002	Cessna 550 Citation II	550-0011	N98876	0078		2 PWC JT15D-4	6033	VIP		Fuerza Aérea Venezolana
☐ FAV0004	GAC (Grumman) G-1159 Gulfstream II	124	N203GA	0073		2 RR Spey 511-8	29710	VIP		Fuerza Aérea Venezolana
☐ FAV0005	GAC G-1159A Gulfstream III	400	N17585*	0083		2 RR Spey 511-8	30935	VIP		Fuerza Aérea Venezolana
☐ FAV0006	Learjet 24D	24D-250	N85CD	0072		2 GE CJ610-6	6123	VIP		Fuerza Aérea Venezolana
☐ FAV0222	Cessna 500 Citation	500-0092	N592CC	0073		2 PWC JT15D-1	5216	VIP		Fuerza Aérea Venezolana
☐ YV-O-GUR-1	Shorts 330UTT Sherpa (SD3-30)	SH3123	G-BMLG*	0086		2 PWC PT6A-45R	10387	Corporate		CVG Edelca
☐ YV-O-GURI-2	Shorts 360-300 (SD3-60)	SH3727	YV-O-GUR-2	0088		2 PWC PT6A-67R	12292	Corporate		CVG Edelca
☐ YV-O-INC-1	Canadair CL-215 (CL-215-1A10)	1062	YV-O-CFO-5	0078		2 PW R-2800-CA3	19731	Corporate		INC, Puerto Ordaz / Amphibian
☐ YV-O-MAR-3	IAI 102 Arava	050	4X-IBW*	0079		2 PWC PT6A-34	6804	Liaison		Min. del Ambiente
☐ YV-O-MRI-1	Learjet 35A	35A-270	N10871	0079		2 GA TFE731-2-2B	8165	Liaison		Min. de Relaciones Interior
☐ YV-O-MTC-1	Twin (Aero) Jetprop Commander 1000 (695A)	96016	YV-477CP	0082		2 GA TPE331-10-501K	5080	Liaison		Min. de Transp. y Communicaciones
☐ YV-O-MTC-20	Cessna 550 Citation II	550-0224	N6802Y	0081		2 PWC JT15D-4	6033	VIP		Min. de Transp. y Communicaciones
☐ YV-O-MTC-9	Shorts Skyvan 3 Variant 100 (SC-7)	SH1949	YV-O-MC-9	0076	0976	2 GA TPE331-2-201A	5670	Liaison		Min. de Transp. y Communicaciones
☐ YV-O-TFA-7	PZL Mielec (Antonov) An-2TP	1G238-21		0090	0291	1 SH ASh-62IR	5500	Liaison		Gobernacion Estado Amazonas
☐ YV-O-TFA-8	PZL Mielec (Antonov) An-2TP	1G238-21		0090	0291	1 SH ASh-62IR	5500	Liaison		Gobernacion Estado Amazonas

AEREO TRANSPORTE LA MONTANA, CA — Ciudad Bolivar

Avenida Jesus Soto, Aeropuerto de Ciudad Bolivar, Ciudad Bolivar, (Estado Bolivar), Venezuela ☎ (85) 29 367 Tx: n/a Fax: (85) 29 367 SITA: n/a
F: n/a ☘ n/a Head: Jaime Manduca Net: n/a

☐ YV-336C	Cessna U206G Stationair 6 II	U20604672	YV-360C	0079		1 CO IO-520-F	1633			
☐ YV-337C	Cessna U206G Stationair 6 II	U20605562	YV-364C	0080		1 CO IO-520-F	1633			
☐ YV-338C	Cessna U206G Stationair 6 II					1 CO IO-520-F	1633			
☐ YV-339C	Cessna U206G Stationair 6 II					1 CO IO-520-F	1633			
☐ YV-340C	Cessna U206G Stationair 6 II					1 CO IO-520-F	1633			
☐ YV-521C	Cessna U206G Stationair 6 II					1 CO IO-520-F	1633			
☐ YV-523C	Cessna 207A Stationair 8 II					1 CO IO-520-F	1724			
☐ YV-522C	Britten-Norman BN-2A-8 Islander	310	HP-1079KN	0072	0091	2 LY O-540-E4C5	2858			
☐ YV-889C	Antonov An-2P	19319	D-FKMF	0058	0095	1 SH ASh-62IR	5500			

AEROBOL - Aerovias Bolivar, C.A. — Ciudad Bolivar

Aeropuerto de Ciudad Bolivar, Ciudad Bolivar, (Estado Bolivar), Venezuela ☎ (85) 26 279 Tx: n/a Fax: (85) 26 279 SITA: n/a
F: n/a ☘ n/a Head: Herman Argumosa Net: n/a Aircraft below MTOW 1361 kg: Bell 47G-2.

☐ YV-315C	Cessna U206G Stationair 6 II	U20604323	YV-1465P	0078		1 CO IO-520-F	1633			
☐ YV-387C	Cessna U206G Stationair 6 II	U20605398		0080		1 CO IO-520-F	1633			
☐ YV-389C	Cessna U206G Stationair 6 II					1 CO IO-520-F	1633			
☐ YV-540C	Cessna U206G Stationair 6 II					1 CO IO-520-F	1633			
☐ YV-381C	Beech Bonanza A36	E-945		0077		1 CO IO-520-BA	1633			
☐ YV-382C	Beech Bonanza A36	E-282		0071		1 CO IO-520-BA	1633			
☐ YV-288C	Cessna 207A Stationair 8 II	20700708	YV-2143P	0081		1 CO IO-520-F	1724			
☐ YV-380C	Cessna 207A Stationair 8 II					1 CO IO-520-F	1724			
☐ YV-270C	Britten-Norman BN-2A-20 Islander	573	YV-142CP	0077		2 LY IO-540-K1B5	2994			
☐ YV-512C	PZL Mielec (Antonov) An-2	1G231-57		0088	0089	1 SH ASh-62IR	5500			

663 registration type of aircraft cn/fn ex/ex* mfd del powered by mtow kg configuration selcal name/fln/specialitites/remarks

AEROEJECUTIVOS, CA = VEJ

Caracas-Charallave & -Maiquetia/Simon Bolivar & -La Carlota

Base Aérea Francisco de Miranda, Sector Aeroclub, Local 4, La Carlota, Caracas, Venezuela ☎ (2) 92 99 52 Tx: none Fax: (2) 92 99 52 SITA: n/a

F: 1975 ጰጰጰ n/a Head: Hermann Zingg ICAO: VENEJECUTIV Net: n/a

registration	type of aircraft	cn/fn	ex/ex*	mfd	del	powered by	mtow kg	configuration	selcal	name/fln/specialitites/remarks
☐ YV-428C	Beech G18S	*BA-477*		*0059*		*2 PW R-985*	*4400*	*9 Pax / Cargo*		
☐ YV-426C	Boeing (Douglas) DC-3-201F	*4093*	*N888PR*	*0041*	*0186*	*2 PW R-1830*	*12202*	*25 Pax*		
☐ YV-440C	Boeing (Douglas) DC-3A	*2201*	*N31PB*	*0040*		*2 PW R-1830*	*12202*	*25 Pax*		
☐ YV-500C	Boeing (Douglas) DC-3C (C-47-DL)	*6135*	*C-FDBJ*	*0042*		*2 PW R-1830*	*12202*	*Freighter*		
☐ YV-223C	Convair 440 Metropolitan	*144*	*YV-58C*	*0053*	*0095*	*2 PW R-2800*	*21772*	*48 Pax*		*cvtd CV340-48*

AEROPOSTAL, Alas de Venezuela C.A. = VH / LAV

Caracas-Maiquetia/Simon Bolivar

Avenida Principal de la Castellana, Torre Banco LARA, 1er Piso, Chacao 1060 (Estada Miranda), Venezuela ☎ (2) 264 64 22 Tx: none Fax: (2) 264 11 50 SITA: n/a

F: 1930 ጰጰጰ 365 Head: Nelson Ramiz IATA: 152 ICAO: AEROPOSTAL Net: n/a

registration	type of aircraft	cn/fn	ex/ex*	mfd	del	powered by	mtow kg	configuration	selcal	name/fln/specialitites/remarks
☐ YV-24C	Boeing (Douglas) DC-9-32	*47727 / 848*		*0076*	*1276*	*2 PW JT8D-17*	*49895*	*Y112*		El Falconiano
☐ YV-25C	Boeing (Douglas) DC-9-32	*47721 / 847*		*0076*	*1276*	*2 PW JT8D-17*	*49895*	*Y112*		El Andino
☐ YV-37C	Boeing (Douglas) DC-9-34F (CF)	*47752 / 872*	*9Y-TFI*	*0077*	*1186*	*2 PW JT8D-17*	*54885*	*Y115*		El Llanero
☐ YV-20C	Boeing (Douglas) DC-9-51	*47705 / 842*		*0076*	*1076*	*2 PW JT8D-17*	*55429*	*Y135*		El Guayanes
☐ YV-21C	Boeing (Douglas) DC-9-51	*47719 / 845*		*0076*	*1176*	*2 PW JT8D-17*	*55429*	*Y135*		El Zuliano
☐ YV-22C	Boeing (Douglas) DC-9-51	*47703 / 841*		*0976*	*1076*	*2 PW JT8D-17*	*55429*	*Y135*		El Margariteno
☐ YV-32C	Boeing (Douglas) DC-9-51	*47770 / 892*		*0078*	*1178*	*2 PW JT8D-17*	*55429*	*Y135*		El Caraqueno
☐ YV-33C	Boeing (Douglas) DC-9-51	*47782 / 893*		*1178*	*1278*	*2 PW JT8D-17*	*55429*	*Y135*		El Venezolano
☐ YV-35C	Boeing (Douglas) DC-9-51	*47712 / 815*	*N649HA*	*0076*	*1279*	*2 PW JT8D-17*	*55429*	*Y137*		El Larense
☐ EI-TLP	Airbus Industrie A320-232	*760*	*F-WWDD**	*0097*	*1198*	*2 IAE V2527-A5*	*75500*	*Y180*	*BJ-DE*	*lsf / opb TLA*
☐ N280US	Boeing 727-251 (A)	*21159 / 1179*		*1275*	*0798*	*3 PW JT8D-15/-15A*	*80059*	*Y160*		*lsf / opb TRZ*
☐ F-OHPU	Airbus Industrie A310-324 (ET)	*439*	*F-WHPU*	*0087*	*1298*	*2 PW PW4152*	*157000*	*CY198*		*lsf Airbus Industrie Financial Services*
☐ F-OHPV	Airbus Industrie A310-324 (ET)	*449*	*F-WHPV*	*0087*	*0898*	*2 PW PW4152*	*157000*	*CY198*		*lsf Airbus Industrie Financial Services*

AEROSERVICIOS RANGER, C.A.

Caracas-La Carlota, Lagunillas (Zulia) & Tumeremo (Bolivar)

Avenida Las Acacias Sur, Edificio Inaltaca, Piso 1, Sector San Antonio, Sabana Grande, Caracas 1050, Venezuela ☎ (2) 782 98 62 Tx: none Fax: (2) 793 29 08 SITA: n/a

F: 1979 ጰጰጰ 45 Head: Dr. Enrique Luque Net: n/a Aircraft below MTOW 1361kg: Cessna 172 & Hughes 369C (500C).

registration	type of aircraft	cn/fn	ex/ex*	mfd	del	powered by	mtow kg	configuration	selcal	name/fln/specialitites/remarks
☐ YV-429C	Bell 206B JetRanger III	*1959*	*N9910K*	*0076*		*1 AN 250-C20B*	*1451*			*cvtd JetRanger II*
☐ YV-431C	Bell 206B JetRanger III	*2588*		*0079*		*1 AN 250-C20B*	*1451*			
☐ YV-433C	Bell 206B JetRanger II	*2106*	*YV-330CP*	*0076*		*1 AN 250-C20*	*1451*			
☐ YV-455C	Bell 206B JetRanger	*1481*	*N218AL*	*0074*		*1 AN 250-C20*	*1451*			
☐ YV-457C	Bell 206B JetRanger III	*2470*	*N50056*	*0078*		*1 AN 250-C20B*	*1451*			
☐ YV-571C	Bell 206B JetRanger	*273*	*N59Q*	*0068*		*1 AN 250-C20*	*1451*			*cvtd 206A*
☐ YV-572C	Bell 206B JetRanger	*644*	*N7906J*	*0071*		*1 AN 250-C20*	*1451*			*cvtd 206A*
☐ YV-573C	Bell 206B JetRanger	*527*	*C-FTUY*	*0070*		*1 AN 250-C20*	*1451*			*cvtd 206A*
☐ YV-897C	Bell 206L-1 LongRanger II	*45356*	*N1071B*	*1279*	*0093*	*1 AN 250-C28B*	*1882*			
☐ YV-920C	Britten-Norman BN-2A-26 Islander	*56*	*YR-BNY*	*0069*	*1095*	*2 LY O-540-E4C5*	*2994*			
☐ YV-921C	Britten-Norman BN-2A-26 Islander	*149*	*G-AXWR*	*0070*	*0195*	*2 LY O-540-E4C5*	*2994*			
☐ YV-922C	Bell 412	*33020*	*N2014K*	*0681*	*0297*	*2 PWC PT6T-3B TwinPac*	*5398*			

AEROTECNICA, SA - ATSA

Acarigua / Palo Negro / Caracas-La Carlota

Apartado de Correos 60107, Caracas 1060, Venezuela ☎ (2) 92 49 10 Tx: 55158 atsav vc Fax: (2) 92 73 90 SITA: n/a

F: n/a ጰጰጰ n/a Head: n/a Net: http://www.aerotecnica.com/ Aircraft / Ag-Aircraft below MTOW 1361 / 5000 kg: Bell 47G, Grumman G-164 & Piper PA-25.

registration	type of aircraft	cn/fn	ex/ex*	mfd	del	powered by	mtow kg	configuration	selcal	name/fln/specialitites/remarks
☐ YV-101C	Bell 206B JetRanger	*459*	*YV-C-GAA*	*0068*		*1 AN 250-C20*	*1451*			*cvtd 206A*
☐ YV-102C	Bell 206B JetRanger	*506*	*YV-C-GAB*	*0069*		*1 AN 250-C20*	*1451*			*cvtd 206A*
☐ YV-103C	Bell 206B JetRanger III	*3211*		*0080*		*1 AN 250-C20B*	*1451*			
☐ YV-104C	Bell 206B JetRanger	*467*	*YV-C-GAH*	*0069*		*1 AN 250-C20*	*1451*			*cvtd 206A*
☐ YV-105C	Bell 206B JetRanger	*889*	*YV-C-GAL*	*0072*		*1 AN 250-C20*	*1451*			
☐ YV-106C	Bell 206B JetRanger	*414*	*YV-C-GAM*	*0069*		*1 AN 250-C20*	*1451*			*cvtd 206A*
☐ YV-108C	Bell 206B JetRanger III	*2384*		*0078*		*1 AN 250-C20B*	*1451*			
☐ YV-109C	Bell 206B JetRanger III	*2402*		*0078*		*1 AN 250-C20B*	*1451*			
☐ YV-110C	Bell 206B JetRanger	*1119*	*N83005*	*0073*		*1 AN 250-C20*	*1451*			
☐ YV-112C	Bell 206B JetRanger III	*3213*		*0080*		*1 AN 250-C20B*	*1451*			
☐ YV-115C	Bell 206B JetRanger II	*2099*		*0076*		*1 AN 250-C20*	*1451*			
☐ YV-116C	Bell 206B JetRanger II	*2190*	*N103K*	*0077*		*1 AN 250-C20*	*1451*			
☐ YV-117C	Bell 206B JetRanger III	*2692*		*0079*		*1 AN 250-C20B*	*1451*			
☐ YV-118C	Bell 206B JetRanger III	*3409*		*0081*		*1 AN 250-C20B*	*1451*			
☐ YV-122C	Bell 206B JetRanger II	*1984*		*0076*		*1 AN 250-C20*	*1451*			
☐ YV-123C	Bell 206B JetRanger II	*2080*	*N9990K*	*0076*		*1 AN 250-C20*	*1451*			
☐ YV-124C	Bell 206B JetRanger III	*2215*		*0077*		*1 AN 250-C20B*	*1451*			
☐ YV-251C	Bell 206B JetRanger	*1106*	*YV-TAIN*	*0073*		*1 AN 250-C20*	*1451*			
☐ YV-254C	Bell 206B JetRanger II	*2059*	*N9934K*	*0076*		*1 AN 250-C20*	*1451*			
☐ YV-320C	Bell 206B JetRanger III	*2248*		*0077*		*1 AN 250-C20B*	*1451*			
☐ YV-321C	Bell 206B JetRanger III	*2496*		*0078*		*1 AN 250-C20B*	*1451*			
☐ YV-322C	Bell 206B JetRanger III	*3359*		*0081*		*1 AN 250-C20B*	*1451*			
☐ YV-323C	Bell 206B JetRanger	*874*		*0072*		*1 AN 250-C20*	*1451*			
☐ YV-324C	Bell 206B JetRanger III	*2266*	*YV-O-PTJ-2*	*0077*		*1 AN 250-C20B*	*1451*			
☐ YV-325C	Bell 206B JetRanger II	*2095*	*GN7635*	*0076*		*1 AN 250-C20*	*1451*			
☐ YV-326C	Bell 206B JetRanger	*1858*		*0075*		*1 AN 250-C20*	*1451*			
☐ YV-327C	Bell 206B JetRanger	*1355*	*YV-235CP*	*0074*		*1 AN 250-C20*	*1451*			
☐ YV-328C	Bell 206B JetRanger III	*3308*		*0081*		*1 AN 250-C20B*	*1451*			
☐ YV-329C	Bell 206B JetRanger III	*3336*		*0081*		*1 AN 250-C20B*	*1451*			
☐ YV-333C	Bell 206B JetRanger	*1699*	*YV-141CP*	*0075*		*1 AN 250-C20*	*1451*			
☐ YV-111C	Bell 206L-1 LongRanger II	*45343*		*0079*		*1 AN 250-C28B*	*1882*			
☐ YV-121C	Bell 206L-1 LongRanger II	*45501*		*0080*		*1 AN 250-C28B*	*1882*			
☐ YV-118CP	Beech King Air E90	*LW-234*		*0077*		*2 PWC PT6A-28*	*4581*	*Executive*		

AEROVENCA - Aeronautica Venezolana de Carga, CA = AVC

Caracas-Maiquetia/Simon Bolivar

Aeropuerto Int'l Simon Bolivar, Rampa Este, Maiquetia 1161, Venezuela ☎ (31) 28 595 Tx: none Fax: none SITA: n/a

F: 1987 ጰጰጰ n/a Head: Antonio Cabrera ICAO: AEROVENCA Net: n/a

registration	type of aircraft	cn/fn	ex/ex*	mfd	del	powered by	mtow kg	configuration	selcal	name/fln/specialitites/remarks
☐ YV-670C	Boeing (Douglas) DC-3C (C-47A-20-DK)	*13074*	*N902VC*	*0044*	*0391*	*2 PW R-1830*	*12202*	*Freighter*		

AIR VENEZUELA, Linea de Transporte Aéreo C.A. = VZA

Caracas-Maiquetia/Simon Bolivar

Aeropuerto Int'l Simon Bolivar, Rampa Este, Hangares Taven, Maiquetia 1161, Venezuela ☎ (31) 22 259 Tx: none Fax: (31) 26 711 SITA: n/a

F: 1995 ጰጰጰ 150 Head: Ing. William E. Medina C. ICAO: AIR VENEZUELA Net: n/a

registration	type of aircraft	cn/fn	ex/ex*	mfd	del	powered by	mtow kg	configuration	selcal	name/fln/specialitites/remarks
☐ YV-966C	Convair 580	*60*	*N4805C*	*0053*	*0197*	*2 AN 501-D13*	*24766*	*Y52*		508 / *cvtd CV340-38/440*
☐ YV-968C	Convair 580	*67*	*N2728R*	*0053*	*0197*	*2 AN 501-D13*	*24766*	*Y52*		516 / *cvtd CV340-35/440*
☐ YV-969C	Convair 580	*150*	*N2729R*	*0056*	*0596*	*2 AN 501-D13*	*24766*	*Y52*		517 / *cvtd CV340-68A/440*
☐ YV-970C	Convair 580	*55*	*N3430*	*0053*	*0596*	*2 AN 501-D13*	*24766*	*Y52*		518 / *cvtd CV340-42/440*
☐ YV-971C	Convair 580	*13*	*N7517U*	*0052*	*0197*	*2 AN 501-D13*	*24766*	*Y52*		519 / *cvtd CV340-34/440*
☐ YV-972C	Convair 580	*61*	*N3418*	*0053*	*0596*	*2 AN 501-D13*	*24766*	*Y52*		523 / *cvtd CV340-32*
☐ YV-973C	Convair 580	*77*	*N3423*	*0053*	*0596*	*2 AN 501-D13*	*24766*	*Y52*		524 / *cvtd CV340-32*
☐ YV-974C	Convair 580	*377*	*N4822C*	*0056*	*0197*	*2 AN 501-D13*	*24766*	*Y52*		546 / *cvtd CV440-38*
☐ YV-975C	Convair 580	*379*	*N4824C*	*0056*	*0596*	*2 AN 501-D13*	*24766*	*Y52*		550 / *cvtd CV440-38*

ASERCA AIRLINES - Aeroservicios Carabobo, C.A. = R7 / OCA

Valencia

Avda Bolivar Norte, Torre Exterior, Piso 8, Of. 8B, Valencia, Venezuela ☎ (41) 34 78 87 Tx: n/a Fax: (41) 34 74 75 SITA: n/a

F: n/a ጰጰጰ 890 Head: Simeon Garcia IATA: 717 ICAO: ASERCA Net: http://www.asercaairlines.com

registration	type of aircraft	cn/fn	ex/ex*	mfd	del	powered by	mtow kg	configuration	selcal	name/fln/specialitites/remarks
☐ YV-705C	Boeing (Douglas) DC-9-31	*45867 / 283*	*N8952E*	*0068*	*1294*	*2 PW JT8D-7B*	*47627*	*Y96*		Virgen del Valle / *lsf ARON*
☐ YV-706C	Boeing (Douglas) DC-9-31	*45875 / 365*	*YV-815C*	*0868*	*0896*	*2 PW JT8D-7B*	*47627*	*Y96*		Virgen de la Chinita
☐ YV-707C	Boeing (Douglas) DC-9-31	*47272 / 390*	*YV-816C*	*0068*	*0996*	*2 PW JT8D-7B*	*47627*	*Y96*		Virgen de la Coromato
☐ YV-708C	Boeing (Douglas) DC-9-31	*45864 / 130*	*N8927E*	*0067*	*0797*	*2 PW JT8D-7B*	*47627*	*Y96*		Virgen del Socorro
☐ YV-709C	Boeing (Douglas) DC-9-31	*47005 / 151*	*N937ML*	*0067*	*0797*	*2 PW JT8D-7B*	*46720*	*Y96*		
☐ YV-710C	Boeing (Douglas) DC-9-31	*47271 / 389*	*N975ML*	*0968*	*0398*	*2 PW JT8D-7B*	*47627*	*Y96*		Virgen de Loreto / *lsf Can Avn Lsng Ltd*
☐ YV-714C	Boeing (Douglas) DC-9-31	*47007 / 87*	*N938ML*	*0067*	*0792*	*2 PW JT8D-7B*	*46720*	*Y96*		El Pilar / *lsf ARON*
☐ YV-716C	Boeing (Douglas) DC-9-32	*47358 / 477*	*N1279L*	*0069*	*0493*	*2 PW JT8D-7B*	*48988*	*Y96*		*lsf MDFC*
☐ YV-718C	Boeing (Douglas) DC-9-31	*47187 / 282*	*XA-SHX*	*0068*	*0594*	*2 PW JT8D-7B*	*47627*	*Y96*		El Viajero / *lsf ARON*
☐ YV-719C	Boeing (Douglas) DC-9-31	*47157 / 322*	*N8959E*	*0068*	*0894*	*2 PW JT8D-7B*	*47627*	*Y96*	*CH-AG*	El Ejecutivos / *lsf ARON*
☐ YV-720C	Boeing (Douglas) DC-9-31	*45837 / 103*	*N8922E*	*0067*	*1294*	*2 PW JT8D-7B*	*47627*	*Y96*	*CF-BH*	El Industrial / *lsf ARON*
☐ P4-MDH	Boeing (Douglas) MD-90-30	*53580 / 2246*		*0098*	*1198*	*2 IAE V2525-D5*	*70760*	*C12Y143*		*lsf ARU*
☐ N500GX	Boeing 737-85F	*28824 / 180*	*N1782B**			*2 CFMI CFM56-7B26*	*78245*			*to be lsf GATX 0499*
☐ N501GX	Boeing 737-85F	*28825 / 188*	*N1784B**			*2 CFMI CFM56-7B26*	*78245*			*to be lsf GATX 0499*

AVENSA - Aerovias Venezolanas, S.A. = VE / AVE

Caracas-Maiquetia/Simon Bolivar

Base Aerea Francisco de Miranda, Hangar 20-21, Caracas 1080, Venezuela ☎ (2) 991 96 21 Tx: 22659 vc Fax: (2) 991 02 58 SITA: n/a

F: 1943 ጰጰጰ 2700 Head: Henry Lord Boulton IATA: 128 ICAO: AVE Net: http://www.avensa.com.ve

registration	type of aircraft	cn/fn	ex/ex*	mfd	del	powered by	mtow kg	configuration	selcal	name/fln/specialitites/remarks
☐ YV-82C	Boeing (Douglas) DC-9-31	*47121 / 277*	*N8989E*	*0068*	*0891*	*2 PW JT8D-7B*	*44452*		*BL-JM*	
☐ YV-85C	Boeing (Douglas) DC-9-51	*47683 / 792*	*N402EA*	*0075*	*0891*	*2 PW JT8D-17*	*54885*			

registration	type of aircraft	cn/fn	ex/ex*	mfd	del	powered by	mtow kg	configuration	selcal	name/fln/specialitites/remarks
☐ YV-87C	Boeing (Douglas) DC-9-51	47685 / 794	N403EA	0075	0891	2 PW JT8D-17	54885			AL-EK
☐ YV-838C	Boeing 727-35	19165 / 292	HK-3933X	0066	0986	3 PW JT8D-7B	74185			
☐ YV-839C	Boeing 727-22	18325 / 141	XA-LEX	0065	0483	3 PW JT8D-7B	74185			std CCS
☐ YV-840C	Boeing 727-114	19815 / 443	XA-NAD	0067	0786	3 PW JT8D-7B	72802			
☐ YV-89C	Boeing 727-22	18851 / 181	N7044U	0065	0985	3 PW JT8D-7B	74185			
☐ YV-94C	Boeing 727-281 (A)	20877 / 1029	N773BE	0074	0787	3 PW JT8D-17	86409			
☐ YV-95C	Boeing 727-281 (A)	20878 / 1034	N774BE	0074	1087	3 PW JT8D-9A	86409			std CCS
☐ YV-97C	Boeing 727-2D3 (A)	20885 / 1055	JY-ADR	0074	0688	3 PW JT8D-17	86409			
☐ YV-50C	Boeing (Douglas) DC-10-30	46945 / 156	PP-VMB	0074	1298	3 GE CF6-50C2	256280			lsf VRG
☐ PP-VMA	Boeing (Douglas) DC-10-30	46944 / 133		0074	1298	3 GE CF6-50C2	256280			lsf VRG

AVIOR EXPRESS – Aviones de Oriente, C.A. = 3B / ROI   Barcelona

Aeropuerto Int'l J.A. Anzoategui, Zona Hangares, Barcelona, (Edo. Barcelona), Venezuela ☎ (81) 76 02 66 Tx: none Fax: (81) 76 02 66 SITA: n/a
F: 1997   ✦✦✦ n/a Head: n/a IATA: 863 ICAO: AVIOR Net: n/a

registration	type of aircraft	cn/fn	ex/ex*	mfd	del	powered by	mtow kg	configuration	selcal	name/fln/remarks
☐ YV-658C	Cessna 208B Grand Caravan	208B0699		0098	0998	1 PWC PT6A-114A	3969	Y14		
☐ YV-923C	Beech 1900C-1 Airliner	UC-128	N15553	0090	0298	2 PWC PT6A-65B	7530	Y19		
☐ YV-401C	Beech 1900D Airliner	UE-		0097	0797	2 PWC PT6A-67D	7688	Y19		
☐ YV-402C	Beech 1900D Airliner	UE-		0097	1297	2 PWC PT6A-67D	7688	Y19		
☐ YV-403C	Beech 1900D Airliner	UE-		0097	0298	2 PWC PT6A-67D	7688	Y19		
☐ YV-404C	Beech 1900D Airliner	UE-		0097	0498	2 PWC PT6A-67D	7688	Y19		
☐ YV-405C	Beech 1900D Airliner	UE-		0098	1298	2 PWC PT6A-67D	7688	Y19		
☐ YV-406C	Beech 1900D Airliner	UE-		0098	1298	2 PWC PT6A-67D	7688	Y19		

CARIBBEAN FLIGHTS = CIF   Valencia

Apartado Correo 745, Valencia, Venezuela ☎ (41) 23 96 70 Tx: none Fax: (41) 23 88 34 SITA: n/a
F: n/a   ✦✦✦ n/a Head: Ivan Vasquez ICAO: CARFLIGHTS Net: n/a

registration	type of aircraft	cn/fn	ex/ex*	mfd	del	powered by	mtow kg	configuration	selcal	name/fln/remarks
☐ YV-912C	Boeing (Douglas) DC-3C (C-47B-5-DK)	25951	CP-2255	0044	0096	2 PW R-1830-94	11431	Y28		lsf Lineas Aéreas Canedo

CIACA – Centro Industrial Aeronautico, CA   Ciudad Bolivar   ⟁ CIACA

Avenida Jesus Soto, Edificio "Siljar", Aeropuerto, Ciudad Bolivar, (Estado Bolivar), Venezuela ☎ (85) 23 116 Tx: 85154 ciaca vc Fax: (85) 28 289 SITA: n/a
F: 1979   ✦✦✦ 40 Head: Manuel A. Silva J. Net: n/a Aircraft below MTOW 1361 kg: Hughes 369HS (500C)

registration	type of aircraft	cn/fn	ex/ex*	mfd	del	powered by	mtow kg	configuration	selcal	name/fln/remarks
☐ YV-451C	Cessna A185F Skywagon	18502591	YV-60CP	0075		1 CO IO-520-D	1520			
☐ YV-444C	Cessna U206G Stationair 6 II	U20604603	YV-2223P	0078		1 CO IO-520-F	1633			
☐ YV-450C	Cessna U206G Stationair 6 II	U20606380	YV-2193P	0081		1 CO IO-520-F	1633			
☐ YV-452C	Cessna U206G Stationair 6 II	U20605847	YV-1940P	0080		1 CO IO-520-F	1633			
☐ YV-978C	Let 410UVP	810702	CCCP-67066	0081	0896	2 WA M-601D	5800			
☐ YV-980C	Let 410UVP	830939	CCCP-67371	0083	0796	2 WA M-601D	5800			
☐ YV-981C	Let 410UVP	841306	CCCP-67481*	0084	0896	2 WA M-601D	5800			
☐ YV-982C	Let 410UVP	841329	CCCP-67103	0084	0796	2 WA M-601D	5800			
☐ YV-528C	PZL Mielec (Antonov) An-28	1AJ007-20	SP-FFL	0090	1196	2 GS TVD-10B	6500			
☐ YV-529C	PZL Mielec (Antonov) An-28	1AJ007-21	SP-FFM	0090	1196	2 GS TVD-10B	6500			

COMERAVIA – Comercial de Aviacion, Srl   Ciudad Bolivar

Apartado 319, Ciudad Bolivar, (Estado Bolivar), Venezuela ☎ (85) 25 208 Tx: n/a Fax: (85) 21 558 SITA: n/a
F: 1965   ✦✦✦ 10 Head: Noel Valery Net: n/a

registration	type of aircraft	cn/fn	ex/ex*	mfd	del	powered by	mtow kg	configuration	selcal	name/fln/remarks
☐ YV-185C	Cessna A185F Skywagon	18502484	YV-TAJR	0074		1 CO IO-520-D	1520			
☐ YV-179C	Cessna P206B Super Skylane	P206-0355	YV-C-CMD	0067		1 CO IO-520-A	1633			
☐ YV-180C	Cessna U206G Stationair 6 II	U20604092	YV-1279P	0078		1 CO IO-520-F	1633			
☐ YV-317C	Cessna U206G Stationair 6 II					1 CO IO-520-F	1633			
☐ YV-309C	Beech Baron C55 (95-C55)	TE-188	YV-35P	0066		2 CO IO-520-C	2404			
☐ YV-557C	PZL Mielec (Antonov) An-2TD	1G158-95	LSK 803	0074		1 SH ASh-62IR	5500			
☐ YV-860C	PZL Mielec (Antonov) An-2					1 SH ASh-62IR	5500			

HELICOPTEROS DEL CARIBE, CA   Caracas-Maiquetia/Simon Bolivar

Lado Oeste de la Torre de Control, Maiquetia, Helipuerto Simon Bolivar, La Guaira, Venezuela ☎ (31) 28 217 Tx: 31201 helic vc Fax: (31) 29 351 SITA: n/a
F: n/a   ✦✦✦ n/a Head: n/a Net: n/a Aircraft below MTOW 1361 kg: Beechcraft A24R, Bell 47G-4A & Enstrom 28

registration	type of aircraft	cn/fn	ex/ex*	mfd	del	powered by	mtow kg	configuration	selcal	name/fln/remarks
☐ YV-359C	Cessna U206G Stationair	U20603717	YV-1250P	0076		1 CO IO-520-F	1633			
☐ YV-893C	PZL Swidnik (Mil) Mi-2	535745098	YV-793CP	0078		2 IS GTD-350-4	3550			
☐ YV-894C	PZL Swidnik (Mil) Mi-2	529540125	YV-794CP	0085		2 IS GTD-350-4	3550			
☐ YV-895C	PZL Swidnik (Mil) Mi-2	529539125	YV-796CP	0085		2 IS GTD-350-4	3550			
☐ YV-355C	Sikorsky S-58ET			0064		1 PWC PT6T TwinPac	5897			cvtd S-58E
☐ YV-356C	Sikorsky S-58ET	58-1733	80+05	0064		1 PWC PT6T TwinPac	5897			cvtd S-58E
☐ YV-866C	Mil Mi-8MTV-1	95999		0092		2 IS TV3-117MT	13000			
☐ YV-867C	Mil Mi-8MTV-1	95998		0092		2 IS TV3-117MT	13000			
☐ YV-868C	Mil Mi-8T	23671		0085		2 IS TV2-117A	12000			

JET AIR INTERNATIONAL CHARTERS, C.A. = INC   Caracas-Maiqueta/Simon Bolivar

Avda. Francisco de Miranda, Edo. Menegrande, Ap. 80030, Caracas 1080, Venezuela ☎ (2) 285 23 75 Tx: n/a Fax: (2) 284 00 59 SITA: n/a
F: 1995   ✦✦✦ n/a Head: Jesus E. Noguera ICAO: INTERCHART Net: n/a Operates cargo flights, currently with McDonnell Douglas DC-8F aircraft leased from other companies when required.

LAI – Linea Aérea I.A.A.C.A. = KG   (Sister company of Industria Aérea Agricola, CA)   Barinas

Aeropuerto de Barinas, Barinas, (Estado Barinas), Venezuela ☎ (73) 22 668 Tx: n/a Fax: (73) 22 668 SITA: n/a
F: 1954   ✦✦✦ n/a Head: Arnaldo Bazichelli C. IATA: 102 Net: n/a

registration	type of aircraft	cn/fn	ex/ex*	mfd	del	powered by	mtow kg	configuration	selcal	name/fln/remarks
☐ YV-950C	ATR 42-320	397	F-WWLK*	0095	0895	2 PWC PW121	16700	Y48		
☐ YV-951C	ATR 42-320	400	F-WWLA*	0095	0895	2 PWC PW121	16700	Y48		
☐ YV-1004C	ATR 72-212	482	F-WWES*	0096	1296	2 PWC PW127	21500	Y70		
☐ YV-1005C	ATR 72-212	485	F-WWLE*	0097	0697	2 PWC PW127	21500	Y70		
☐ YV-1073C	ATR 72-212	486	F-WWLG*	0097	0198	2 PWC PW127	21500	Y70		

LASER – Linea Aérea de Servicio Ejecutivo Regional, C.A. = KZ / LER   Caracas-Maiquetia/Simon Bolivar

Avda. Principal La Castellana, Torre Lara, Planta Baha, Caracas 1029, Venezuela ☎ (2) 235 72 27 Tx: none Fax: (2) 263 04 28 SITA: n/a
F: 1993   ✦✦✦ 90 Head: José Augusto Azpurua IATA: 722 ICAO: LASER Net: n/a

registration	type of aircraft	cn/fn	ex/ex*	mfd	del	powered by	mtow kg	configuration	selcal	name/fln/remarks
☐ YV-977C	Boeing (Douglas) DC-9-14	45745 / 32	YV-852C	0566	0596	2 PW JT8D-7B	41141	C64		Aldebaran / lsf Int'l Airl. Support
☐ YV-880C	Boeing 727-224 (A)	20665 / 1149	N69736	0075	1098	3 PW JT8D-9A	78245	C98		lsf PEGA

LTA – Linea Turistica Aereotuy, C.A. = TUY   Caracas-Maiquetia/Simon Bolivar & Ciudad Bolivar

Apartado 2923, Caracas 1010A, Venezuela ☎ (2) 763 50 35 Tx: 29003 tuyca vc Fax: (2) 762 52 54 SITA: n/a
F: 1982   ✦✦✦ 400 Head: Peter Bottome ICAO: AEREOTUY Net: http://www.tuy.com

registration	type of aircraft	cn/fn	ex/ex*	mfd	del	powered by	mtow kg	configuration	selcal	name/fln/remarks
☐ YV-532C	Dornier 228-212	8182	D-CJRM*	0090	0690	2 GA TPE331-5A-252D	6400	Y19		
☐ YV-533C	Dornier 228-212	8183	D-CJPM*	0090	0690	2 GA TPE331-5A-252D	6400	Y19		
☐ YV-534C	Dornier 228-212	8184	D-CICA*	0090	1090	2 GA TPE331-5A-252D	6400	Y19		std CCS
☐ YV-647C	Dornier 228-212	8187	D-CAET	0091	0694	2 GA TPE331-5A-252D	6400	Y19		std CCS
☐ YV-575C	Beech 1900C-1 Airliner	UC-97	N97YV	0090	1297	2 PWC PT6A-65B	7530	Y19		lsf Raytheon Aircraft Credit Corp.
☐ YV-637C	De Havilland DHC-7-102 Dash 7	047	N701GG	0081	1095	4 PWC PT6A-50	19958	Y50		
☐ YV-638C	De Havilland DHC-7-102 Dash 7	030	N4309N	0080	0196	4 PWC PT6A-50	19958	Y50		lsf AGES
☐ YV-639C	De Havilland DHC-7-102 Dash 7	005	N702AC	0078	0296	4 PWC PT6A-50	19958	Y50		
☐ YV-640C	De Havilland DHC-7-102 Dash 7	017	N47RM	0079	0598	4 PWC PT6A-50	19958	Y50		lsf AGES

ORIENTAL DE AVIACION, S.A.   Cumana

Avenida Gran Mariscal, Edificio del Este, Piso 2, Cumana 6101, (Sucre), Venezuela ☎ (93) 32 53 14 Tx: none Fax: (93) 67 11 91 SITA: n/a
F: 1995   ✦✦✦ n/a Head: Manuel Molino Net: n/a

registration	type of aircraft	cn/fn	ex/ex*	mfd	del	powered by	mtow kg	configuration	selcal	name/fln/remarks
☐ YV-1072C	Yakovlev 40				0098	3 IV AI-25	16000	Y32		
☐ YV-594C	Yakovlev 40	9841159	CU-T1221	0078	1197	3 IV AI-25	16000	Y32		lsf CRN / std HAV
☐ YV-598C	Yakovlev 40	9641450	CU-T1203	0076	1195	3 IV AI-25	16000	Y32		lsf CRN
☐ YV-599C	Yakovlev 40	9731754	CU-T1212	0077	0096	3 IV AI-25	16000	Y32		lsf CRN / std HAV

RENTAVION, CA = RNT   Porlamar & Higuerote

Aeropuerto DelCaribe Gen. S. Marino, Porlamar, Venezuela ☎ (95) 62 55 75 Tx: none Fax: (95) 62 78 22 SITA: n/a
F: n/a   ✦✦✦ n/a Head: Mr. Sarmiento ICAO: RENTAVION Net: n/a

registration	type of aircraft	cn/fn	ex/ex*	mfd	del	powered by	mtow kg	configuration	selcal	name/fln/remarks
☐ YV-145C	Martin 404	14129	HI-501	0052	0589	2 PW R-2800	20366	Y48		
☐ YV-149C	Martin 404	14247	N982M	0053	1088	2 PW R-2800	20366	Y48		

RUTACA – Rutas Aéreas, CA = RUC   Ciudad Bolivar   ◤ RUTACA

Edificio Taller Mares, Aeropuerto de Ciudad Bolivar, Ciudad Bolivar, (Estado Bolivar), Venezuela ☎ (85) 24 010 Tx: 85395 boccardo vc Fax: (85) 25 955 SITA: n/a
F: 1974   ✦✦✦ 80 Head: Mrs. Rose Marie de Mares ICAO: RUTACA Net: n/a

registration	type of aircraft	cn/fn	ex/ex*	mfd	del	powered by	mtow kg	configuration	selcal	name/fln/remarks
☐ YV-208C	Cessna P206 Super Skylane	P206-0076	YV-C-HRH	0065		1 CO IO-520-F	1497			
☐ YV-209C	Cessna U206D Super Skywagon	U206-1338		0069		1 CO IO-520-F	1633			
☐ YV-210C	Cessna U206G Stationair 6 II	U20605354		0079		1 CO IO-520-F	1633			
☐ YV-214C	Cessna U206F Stationair	U20602386		0074		1 CO IO-520-F	1633			

☐ YV-219C	Cessna U206G Stationair	U20603977	YV-1296P	0077		1 CO IO-520-F	1633			
☐ YV-220C	Cessna U206G Stationair 6 II	U20606277		0081		1 CO IO-520-F	1633			
☐ YV-229C	Cessna U206G Stationair 6 II	U20603541		0077		1 CO IO-520-F	1633			
☐ YV-379C	Cessna U206G Stationair 6 II	U20604150		0078		1 CO IO-520-F	1633			
☐ YV-785C	Cessna U206G Stationair	U20603889	YV-1314P	0077		1 CO IO-520-F	1633			
☐ YV-786C	Cessna U206G Stationair 6 II	U20605125		0079		1 CO IO-520-F	1633			
☐ YV-789C	Cessna U206G Stationair 6 II	U20604803		0079	0096	1 CO IO-520-F	1633			
☐ YV-793C	Cessna U206F Stationair II	U20603193		0076	0097	1 CO IO-520-F	1633			
☐ YV-217C	Cessna 207A Stationair 7 II	20700440		0078		1 CO IO-520-F	1724			
☐ YV-788C	Cessna 210N Centurion II	21063295		0079		1 CO IO-520-L	1724			
☐ YV-790C	Cessna 208B Grand Caravan	208B0527		0096	0596	1 PWC PT6A-114A	3969			
☐ YV-791C	Cessna 208B Grand Caravan	208B0555		0096	0696	1 PWC PT6A-114A	3969			
☐ YV-792C	Cessna 208B Grand Caravan	208B0608		0097	0497	1 PWC PT6A-114A	3969			
☐ YV-205C	PZL Mielec (Antonov) An-2	1G185-58		0080	0780	1 SH ASh-62IR	5500			
☐ YV-206C	PZL Mielec (Antonov) An-2	1G233-42	SP-DLC	0088		1 SH ASh-62IR	5500			
☐ YV-245C	Embraer 110P1 Bandeirante (EMB-110P1)	110325	N103TN	0080	1291	2 PWC PT6A-34	5670			
☐ YV-246C	Embraer 110P1 Bandeirante (EMB-110P1)	110363	N104TN	0081	0292	2 PWC PT6A-34	5670			
☐ YV-247C	Embraer 110P1 Bandeirante (EMB-110P1)	110293	N901A	0080	1292	2 PWC PT6A-34	5670			
☐ YV-248C	Embraer 110P1 Bandeirante (EMB-110P1)	110376	N61DA	0081	1292	2 PWC PT6A-34	5670			
☐ YV-249C	Embraer 110P1 Bandeirante (EMB-110P1)	110382	N63DA	0081	1292	2 PWC PT6A-34	5670			
☐ YV-787C	Embraer 110P1 Bandeirante (EMB-110P1)	110403	N202EB	0082	0194	2 PWC PT6A-34	5900			
☐ YV-218C	Boeing (Douglas) DC-3D	43079	YV-108C	0044	0078	2 PW R-1830-92	12202			rebuilt C-47A-20-DK cn 12728
☐ YV-222C	Boeing (Douglas) DC-3C (C-47-DL)	7386	PP-CED	0043		2 PW R-1830-92	12202			
☐ YV-224C	Boeing (Douglas) DC-3C (C-47A-65-DL)	19055	PT-KXR	0043		2 PW R-1830-92	12202			
☐ YV-226C	Boeing (Douglas) DC-3C (C-47A-70-DL)	19121	YV-12C	0043		2 PW R-1830-92	12202			
☐ YV-227C	Boeing (Douglas) DC-3C (C-47A-65-DL)	19000	YV-115C	0043		2 PW R-1830-92	12202			

SANTA BARBARA AIRLINES, C.A. = BJ / BBR

Maracaibo

Av. 3H, No. 78-51, Maracaibo 4002, (Estado Zulia), Venezuela ☎ (61) 92 79 77 Tx: none Fax: (61) 93 02 50 SITA: n/a
F: 1995 ⁂ 80 Head: Heli S. Fernandez IATA: 249 ICAO: SANTA BARBARA Net: n/a

☐ YV-1014C	ATR 42-320	368	F-WSFB	0093	0297	2 PWC PW121	16700	Y45		Mi Chinita
☐ YV-1015C	ATR 42-320	360	F-GMGI	0093	0797	2 PWC PW121	16700	Y45		Virgen del Carmen

SERAMI – Servicios Aéreos Mineros, Srl

Ciudad Bolivar

Avenida Jesus Sota 1, Aeropuerto de Ciudad Bolivar, Ciudad Bolivar, (Estado Bolivar), Venezuela ☎ (85) 23 773 Tx: n/a Fax: none SITA: n/a
F: n/a ⁂ n/a Head: Capt. Reyes Rafael Muñoz Net: n/a

☐ YV-271C	Cessna A185F Skywagon	18502364	YV-177C	0074		1 CO IO-520-D	1520			
☐ YV-193C	Cessna U206F Stationair	U20602122	YV-322P	0073		1 CO IO-520-F	1633			
☐ YV-194C	Cessna U206F Stationair II	U20603107	YV-842P	0076		1 CO IO-520-F	1633			
☐ YV-221C	Cessna U206G Stationair	U20603975	YV-1372P	0077		1 CO IO-520-F	1633			
☐ YV-232C	Cessna U206G Stationair 6 II	U20604478	YV-1589P	0078		1 CO IO-520-F	1633			
☐ YV-233C	Cessna U206G Stationair 6 II	U20604456	YV-625P	0078		1 CO IO-520-F	1633			
☐ YV-234C	Cessna U206G Stationair 6 II	U20604554	YV-1604P	0078		1 CO IO-520-F	1633			
☐ YV-235C	Cessna U206G Stationair 6 II	U20604639	YV-1607P	0078		1 CO IO-520-F	1633			
☐ YV-341C	Cessna U206F Stationair II	U20602926	YV-837P	0075		1 CO IO-520-F	1633			
☐ YV-345C	Cessna U206G Stationair 6 II	U20605037	YV-1516P	0079		1 CO IO-520-F	1633			
☐ YV-346C	Cessna U206G Stationair 6 II	U20605055	YV-1481P	0079		1 CO IO-520-F	1633			

SERVIVENSA – Servicios Avensa, S.A. = VC / SVV (Subsidiary of AVENSA)

Caracas-Maiquetia/Simon Bolivar & Canaima

Av. Rio Caura, Urb. Parque Humboldt, Torre Humboldt, Piso 25, Caracas 101, Venezuela ☎ (2) 907 80 00 Tx: none Fax: (2) 563 96 96 SITA: n/a
F: 1990 ⁂ n/a Head: Henry Lord Boulton IATA: 985 ICAO: SERVIVENSA Net: n/a

☐ YV-467CP	Beech King Air E90	LW-94	N98ME	0074	0090	2 PWC PT6A-28	4581	Corporate		
☐ YV-147C	Boeing (Douglas) DC-3C (C-47A-30-DK)	25278	YV-2184P	0044	0098	2 PW R-1830	12202			
☐ YV-609C	Boeing (Douglas) DC-3C	43087	YV-98C	0043	0090	2 PW R-1830	12202	Freighter		
☐ YV-610C	Boeing (Douglas) DC-3C (C-47A-40-DL)	9894	YV-505C	0043	0090	2 PW R-1830	12202			
☐ YV-769C	Boeing (Douglas) DC-3C (C-47A-80-DL)	19513	HR-SHC	0043	0291	2 PW R-1830	12202			
☐ YV-612C	Boeing (Douglas) DC-9-32	45710 / 100	N939ML	0067	1290	2 PW JT8D-7B	48988			
☐ YV-613C	Boeing (Douglas) DC-9-32	47104 / 220	N901ML	0067	1290	2 PW JT8D-17	48988			
☐ YV-614C	Boeing (Douglas) DC-9-32	47105 / 221	N902ML	0067	1290	2 PW JT8D-7B	48988			std CCS
☐ YV-760C	Boeing (Douglas) DC-9-31	47098 / 108	N8988E	0067	0292	2 PW JT8D-7B	46720		GH-BE	std CCS
☐ YV-764C	Boeing (Douglas) DC-9-31	47331 / 408	N8982E	0068	0392	2 PW JT8D-7B	47627		BL-EJ	
☐ YV-817C	Boeing (Douglas) DC-9-31	47036 / 375	N972ML	0868	0992	2 PW JT8D-7B	47627			
☐ YV-766C	Boeing (Douglas) DC-9-51	47679 / 797	N421EA	1075	0692	2 PW JT8D-17	54885		JM-EL	std CCS
☐ YV-767C	Boeing (Douglas) DC-9-51	47745 / 863	N413EA	0077	0891	2 PW JT8D-17	54885		GJ-BC	
☐ YV-820C	Boeing (Douglas) DC-9-51	47743 / 859	9Y-TFH	0077	1192	2 PW JT8D-17	55429			
☐ YV-74C	Boeing 737-229 (A)	20909 / 353	OO-SDC	0074	1198	2 PW JT8D-15A (HK3/AVA)	54204		EL-GH	
☐ YV-79C	Boeing 737-229 (A)	20908 / 352	OO-SDB	0074	0497	2 PW JT8D-15A (HK3/AVA)	52753		EL-CG	
☐ YV-765C	Boeing 727-22	18855 / 195	YV-88C	0065	0092	3 PW JT8D-7B	74185			
☐ YV-845C	Boeing 727-27	19534 / 454	HK-3845X	0067	0198	3 PW JT8D-7B	76884			
☐ YV-608C	Boeing 727-227	20394 / 816	YV-76C	0070	0791	3 PW JT8D-9A	79606		AK-HM	
☐ YV-762C	Boeing 727-2D3 (A)	22268 / 1641	JY-AFT	0780	1291	3 PW JT8D-17	86409			std CCS
☐ YV-768C	Boeing 727-2M7 (A)	21457 / 1302	XA-MXE	0077	0992	3 PW JT8D-17R	86409			
☐ YV-823C	Boeing 727-2D3 (A/RE) (Super 27)	22269 / 1701	JY-AFU	1280	0496	3 PW JT8D-217C/17 (BFG)	86409			cvtd -2D3
☐ YV-843C	Boeing 727-281 (A)	20876 / 1026	XA-TGU	0374	0793	3 PW JT8D-17R	86409			
☐ YV-844C	Boeing 727-2D3 (A/RE) (Super 27)	22270 / 1709	JY-AFV	0181	0496	3 PW JT8D-217C/17	86409			cvtd -2D3
☐ YV-92C	Boeing 727-281 (A)	20724 / 954	N771BE	0073	1298	3 PW JT8D-17	86409			

TAAN – Transporte Aéreo Andino, SA = EAA

San Cristobal

Aeropuerto, San Cristobal, Venezuela ☎ (76) 56 53 01 Tx: n/a Fax: (76) 56 53 90 SITA: n/a
F: 1992 ⁂ n/a Head: Luiz Gomez ICAO: TANDINO Net: n/a

☐ YV-625C	BAe (H.P.) 137 Jetstream Century III	235	N10GA	0069	0992	2 GA TPE331-3U-303V	5670	Y18		Paco / cvtd Mk. 1
☐ YV-626C	BAe (H.P.) 137 Jetstream Century III	221	N12221	0069	0992	2 GA TPE331-3U-303V	5670	Y18		cvtd Mk. 1

TRANSMANDU – Transportes Aéreos Manduca, Srl

Ciudad Bolivar

Avenida Jesus Soto, Aeropuerto de Ciudad Bolivar, Ciudad Bolivar, (Estado Bolivar), Venezuela ☎ (85) 21 462 Tx: n/a Fax: (85) 21 462 SITA: n/a
F: n/a ⁂ n/a Head: n/a Net: n/a

☐ YV-278C	Cessna A185E Skywagon	185-1041	YV-56P	0066		1 CO IO-520-D	1497			
☐ YV-559C	Piper PA-32R-301 Saratoga SP	32-				1 LY IO-540-K1G5D	1633			
☐ YV-273C	Cessna U206F Stationair II	U20603431	YV-1107P	0076		1 CO IO-520-F	1633			
☐ YV-274C	Cessna U206G Stationair 6 II					1 CO IO-520-F	1633			
☐ YV-275C	Cessna U206G Stationair 6 II	U20604527	YV-1602P	0078		1 CO IO-520-F	1633			
☐ YV-276C	Cessna U206G Stationair 6 II					1 CO IO-520-F	1633			
☐ YV-280C	Cessna U206G Stationair 6 II	U20604874	YV-1763P	0079		1 CO IO-520-F	1633			
☐ YV-335C	Cessna U206G Stationair 6 II	U20605188	YV-1722P	0079		1 CO IO-520-F	1633			

VENESCAR INTERNACIONAL = VEC (Venezolana Servicios Expresos de Cargo, C.A. dba)

Caracas-Maiquetia/Simon Bolivar

Seccion Venscar, Aviacion General, Aeropuerto Int'l Simon Bolivar, Maiquetia 1161, Venezuela ☎ (2) 355 25 66 Tx: none Fax: (2) 355 15 15 SITA: MIQSNER
F: 1996 ⁂ n/a Head: Renaldo Marques ICAO: VECAR Net: n/a

☐ YV-876C	Dassault Falcon 20D	200	HC-BUP	0069	0098	2 GE CF700-2D2	13000	Freighter		opf DHL Venezuela in DHL-colors
☐ YV-846C	Boeing 727-35 (F)	19167 / 325	OO-DHQ	1066	0997	3 PW JT8D-7B (HK3/FDX)	76885	Freighter		lsf BCS/opf DHL Venez.in DHL-cs/cvtd-35

WAYUMI AERO-TAXI (Asociacion Cooperativa de Transporte Aero-Taxi Wayumi dba)

Puerto Ayacucho

Aeropuerto de Puerto Ayacucho, Puerto Ayacucho, (Amazonas), Venezuela ☎ (48) 21 635 Tx: n/a Fax: (48) 21 191 SITA: n/a
F: n/a ⁂ n/a Head: n/a Net: n/a

☐ YV-409C	Cessna U206G Stationair 6 II	U20606222	YV-2068P	0081		1 CO IO-520-F	1633			
☐ YV-410C	Cessna U206G Stationair 6 II	U20606399	YV-2072P	0081		1 CO IO-520-F	1633			
☐ YV-252C	Cessna 207A Stationair 8 II	20700719		0081		1 CO IO-520-F	1724			

Z = ZIMBABWE (Republic of Zimbabwe)

Capital: Harare Official Language: English Population: 13,0 million Square Km: 390759 Dialling code: +263 Year established: 1965 Acting political head: Robert Mugabe (President)

AFFRETAIR, (Private) Ltd = ZL / AFM

Harare-Int'l

PO Box AP13, Harare, Zimbabwe ☎ (4) 57 50 00 Tx: 40005 zw Fax: (4) 57 50 10 SITA: HRECMZL
F: 1965 ⁂ 120 Head: Godfrey Manhambara IATA: 292 ICAO: AFRO Net: n/a Operates cargo flights with Boeing (Douglas) DC-10-30F of DAS AIR CARGO (5X-), leased through DHL Worldwide Express (N) when required.

AIR ZIMBABWE, (Pvt) Ltd = UM / AZW (formerly Air Rhodesia, Corp.)

Harare-Int'l

PO Box AP.1, Harare Airport, Harare, Zimbabwe ☎ (4) 57 51 11 Tx: 24383 zw Fax: (4) 57 50 68 SITA: HRECRUM
F: 1961 ⁂ 1600 Head: Nick Nyandord IATA: 168 ICAO: AIR ZIMBABWE Net: n/a

☐ A2-ABD	BAe 146-100	E1101	G-5-101*	0089	0797	4 LY ALF502R-5	38102	Y77		lsf BOT

666 registration type of aircraft cn/fn ex/ex* mfd del powered by mtow kg configuration selcal name/fln/specialitites/remarks

☐ Z-WPD	BAe 146-200	E2065	G-5-065*	0087		4 LY ALF502R-5	40597	Y91	AE-KM	Jongwe / lsf Gvmt
☐ Z-WPA	Boeing 737-2N0 (A)	23677 / 1313		0086	1286	2 PW JT8D-17A	53070	CY113	AE-JL	Mbuya Nehanda
☐ Z-WPB	Boeing 737-2N0 (A)	23678 / 1405		0087	0687	2 PW JT8D-17A	53070	CY113	AE-JM	Great Zimbabwe
☐ Z-WPC	Boeing 737-2N0 (A)	23679 / 1415		0087	0787	2 PW JT8D-17A	53070	CY113	AE-KL	Matojeni
☐ Z-WPE	Boeing 767-2N0 (ER)	24713 / 287		0089	1189	2 PW PW4056	175540	C28Y175	EF-CH	Victoria Falls
☐ Z-WPF	Boeing 767-2N0 (ER)	24867 / 333		0090	1090	2 PW PW4056	175540	C28Y175	EF-CJ	Chimanimani

DEBONAIR (Pvt), Ltd — Harare-Int'l

Private Bag 6009, Harare, Zimbabwe ☎ (4) 30 60 13 Tx: none Fax: (4) 30 60 13 SITA: n/a
F: 1995 n/a Head: Kevin Smeda Net: n/a

☐ Z-EOS	Beech Bonanza A36	E-1994	Z-ROS	0082		1 CO IO-520-BB	1633			lsf Rosanna P/L
☐ Z-WLJ	Cessna 421B Golden Eagle	421B0474		0073		2 CO GTSIO-520-H	3379			lsf Tanganda Tee Co.

EXEC-AIR - Executive Air = AXE (Skyline Charters, (Pvt) Ltd dba) — Harare-Charles Prince

PO Box EH96, Emerald Hill, Harare, Zimbabwe ☎ (4) 30 22 48 Tx: 22393 zw Fax: (4) 30 39 87 SITA: n/a
F: 1972 54 Head: Mrs Kathleen R. Belford ICAO: AXAIR Net: n/a Aircraft below MTOW 1361kg: Cessna 172

☐ Z-WNK	Cessna U206F Stationair II	U20603007	ZS-IYN	0075		1 CO IO-520-F	1633			
☐ Z-WLW	Cessna 210M Centurion II	21061778	N732UE	0077		1 CO IO-520-L	1724			
☐ Z-WNM	Beech Baron B55 (95-B55)	TC-1338	ZS-IBO	0070		2 CO IO-470-L	2313			
☐ Z-WFP	Cessna 402A	402A0013		0069		2 CO TSIO-520-E	2858			
☐ Z-WRB	Cessna 402B	402B0032	N9475P	0070		2 CO TSIO-520-E	2858			
☐ Z-WRI	Cessna 402C II	402C0610	TR-LAN	0082		2 CO TSIO-520-VB	3107			
☐ Z-WOR	Piper PA-31-310 Navajo	31-35	ZS-JWF	0067		2 LY TIO-540-A1A	2948			
☐ Z-WOU	Piper PA-31-310 Navajo	31-118	ZS-SWA	0068		2 LY TIO-540-A1A	2948			

EXPEDITION AIRWAYS (Pvt), Ltd = FO / XPD — Harare-Int'l

PO Box AP12, Harare Airport, Harare, Zimbabwe ☎ (4) 72 29 83 Tx: none Fax: (4) 78 15 17 SITA: n/a
F: 1997 n/a Head: Capt. Denver Hornsby, Jr. ICAO: EXPEDITION Net: n/a

☐ Z-DHS	Beech 1900C Airliner	UB-18	N18ZR	0084	0797	2 PWC PT6A-65B	7530	Y19		

FLYWELL AIRLINES, Pvt Ltd = FEM — Harare-Int'l

PO Box 5687, Harare, Zimbabwe ☎ (4) 74 96 81 Tx: 24533 flywel zw Fax: (4) 74 96 86 SITA: HREFFCR
F: 1995 38 Head: Forbes E. Magadu IATA: 762 ICAO: FLYWELL Net: n/a Operates cargo flights with Boeing 707C & McDonnell Douglas DC-10-30F, leased from DAS AIR CARGO (5X-) when required.

INDEPENDENT CHARTER OPERATORS - I.C.O. — Harare-Int'l

PO Box AP51, Harare, Zimbabwe ☎ (4) 57 55 78 Tx: 26773 ico zw Fax: (4) 57 55 32 SITA: n/a
F: 1997 n/a Head: Robin Vetch Net: n/a

☐ Z-PTJ	Piper PA-34-200T Seneca II	34-7570095	G-BPTJ	0075		2 CO TSIO-360-E	2073			
☐ Z-SSS	Beech Baron 58	TH-594		0075		2 CO IO-520-C	2449			
☐ Z-AKV	Piper PA-31-310 Navajo B	31-782		0072		2 LY TIO-540-A2C	2948			
☐ Z-ICO	Piper PA-31-350 Navajo Chieftain	31-7405444	N103ZZ	0074	0597	2 LY TIO-540-J2BD	3175			
☐ Z-WRF	Beech Queen Air 80 (65-80)	LD-134	ZS-OOT	0063		2 LY IGSO-540-A1A6	3629			

MEDICAL AIR RESCUE SERVICE — Harare-Int'l

PO Box 7245, Belgravia, Harare, Zimbabwe ☎ (4) 73 45 13 Tx: 26344 mars zw Fax: (4) 73 45 17 SITA: n/a
F: 1991 70 Head: Willie Ford & Guy Edmunds Net: http://www.mars.co.zw

☐ Z-MRS	Beech King Air 200	BB-286	ZS-XGD	0077	0097	2 PWC PT6A-41	5670	EMS		

SOUTHEND CARGO AIRLINES = SYZ — Harare

PO Box HG-92, Highlands, Harare, Zimbabwe ☎ (4) 73 65 87 Tx: 26775 zw Fax: (4) 73 65 87 SITA: n/a
F: 1996 5 Head: S.J. Chituku ICAO: SOUTHEND Net: n/a Operates cargo flights, currently with aircraft leased from other companies when required.

SOUTHERN CROSS AVIATION, (Pvt) Ltd — Victoria Falls

PO Box 210, Victoria Falls, Zimbabwe ☎ (13) 46 18 Tx: 51689 zw Fax: (13) 46 09 SITA: n/a
F: 1990 10 Head: Trevor Lane Net: n/a Aircraft below MTOW 1361kg: Cessna 172

☐ Z-THL	Cessna U206F Stationair II	U20603233	N8372Q	0076		1 CO IO-520-F	1633			
☐ Z-WIA	Cessna U206F Stationair II	U20602581	VP-WIA	0075		1 CO IO-520-F	1633			
☐ Z-WFA	Cessna T207 Turbo Skywagon	20700098	VP-WFA	0069		1 CO TSIO-520-M	1724			
☐ Z-WTK	Piper PA-31-325 Navajo C/R	31-7812086		0078		2 LY TIO-540-F2BD	2948			

UNITED AIR SERVICES = UAC (Div. of Agricair (Pvt) Ltd dba / formerly Zambezi Air (Pvt) Ltd) — Harare-Charles Prince & -Int'l, Kariba & Victoria Falls

PO Box 3683, Harare, Zimbabwe ☎ (4) 30 20 76 Tx: 22234 zw Fax: (4) 30 48 71 SITA: n/a
F: 1946 100 Head: Steve A. Lampitt ICAO: UNITAIR Net: n/a Aircraft below MTOW 1361kg: Cessna 182

☐ Z-BWK	Cessna U206G Stationair	U20603546		0077		1 CO IO-520-F	1633	5 Pax		
☐ Z-WKL	Cessna U206F Stationair	U20601707	ZS-ILV	0072	0392	1 CO IO-520-F	1633	5 Pax		
☐ Z-WMG	Cessna U206 Super Skywagon	U206-0323	VP-WMG	0065		1 CO IO-520-A	1633	5 Pax		
☐ Z-WTA	Cessna U206F Stationair	U20602547	OO-SPX	0074	1094	1 CO IO-520-F	1633	5 Pax		
☐ Z-YHS	Cessna U206C Super Skywagon	U206-1029	VP-YHS	0068		1 CO IO-520-F	1633	5 Pax		
☐ Z-WAX	Beech Baron D55	TE-631	VP-WAX	0068		2 CO IO-520-C	2404	5 Pax		
☐ Z-WHG	Beech Baron D55	TE-761	VP-WHG	0069		2 CO IO-520-C	2404	5 Pax		
☐ Z-UAC	Beech Baron 58	TH-211		0072		2 CO IO-520-C	2404	5 Pax		
☐ Z-WHV	Beech Baron 58	TH-48	VP-WHV	0070		2 CO IO-520-C	2449	5 Pax		
☐ Z-WTG	Beech Baron 58	TH-262	ZS-BSP	0072	0395	2 CO IO-520-C	2449	5 Pax		
☐ Z-YKM	Beech Baron 58	TH-163	VP-YKM	0071		2 CO IO-520-C	2449	5 Pax		
☐ Z-WEX	Britten-Norman BN-2A Islander	619	VP-WEX	0070		2 LY O-540-E4B5	2858	9 Pax		
☐ Z-WHX	Britten-Norman BN-2A-7 Islander	192	VP-WHX	0070		2 LY O-540-E4C5	2858	9 Pax		
☐ Z-WTF	Cessna 414A Chancellor III	414A0062	G-METR	0078	0295	2 CO TSIO-520-NB	3062	7 Pax		
☐ Z-WHH	Beech Queen Air 80 (65-80)	LD-101	VP-WHH	0063		2 LY IGSO-540-A1A6	3629	5 Pax		
☐ Z-AIR	Britten-Norman BN-2A Mk.III-2 Trislander	1054	A2-AGX	0084		3 LY O-540-E4C5	4536	14 Pax		
☐ Z-UTD	Britten-Norman BN-2A Mk.III-2 Trislander	1055	A2-AGY	0084		3 LY O-540-E4C5	4536	14 Pax		

ZIMBABWE EXPRESS AIRLINES = Z7 / EZX (Tirez Aviation Services, Ltd dba) — Harare

PO Box 5130, Harare, Zimbabwe ☎ (4) 72 96 81 Tx: none Fax: (4) 73 71 17 SITA: n/a
F: 1994 n/a Head: Evans Ndebele IATA: 247 ICAO: ZIM EXPRESS Net: http://www.adventures.co.za/zim.htm

☐ ZS-NRD	Boeing (Douglas) DC-9-32	47037 / 121	N8270A	0667	0997	2 PW JT8D-7B	49898	C12Y86		Bulawayo - Business Express / lsf SSN
☐ ZS-NWA	Boeing 727-230 (A)	20757 / 1002	5N-CMB	0074	1197	3 PW JT8D-15	86409	CY146		lsf SFR

ZA = ALBANIA (Republic of Albania) (Republika Shqiperise)

(This country uses a prefix (nationality mark) not notified to the ICAO)
Capital: Tirana Official Language: Albanian Population: 3,5 million Square Km: 28748 Dialling code: +355 Year established: 1912 Acting political head: Rexhep Mejdani (President)

Government / Corporate / Executive / VIP Aircraft

☐ ZA-HOV	Bell 222UT	47555	AL-HOV	0086		2 LY LTS101-750C.1	3742	VIP		Gvmt

ADA AIR Albania = ZY / ADE (Member of ADA Group) — Tirana

Mine Peza P.218, Tirana, Albania ☎ (42) 35 522 Tx: none Fax: (42) 26 245 SITA: n/a
F: 1991 22 Head: Marsel Skendo IATA: 121 ICAO: ADA AIR Net: n/a

☐ ZA-ADA	Embraer 110P2 Bandeirante (EMB-110P2)	110303	F-GCMQ	0080	1091	2 PWC PT6A-34	5670	Y18		
☐ LZ-DOM	Yakovlev 40	9620447		0076	0097	3 IV AI-25	16000	Y32		lsf HMS

ALBANIAN AIRLINES, M.A.K. S.H.P.K. = LV / LBC (Subsidiary of MAK-Albania / Member of Kharafi Group, Kuwait) — Tirana

Rruga e Durresit 202, Tirana, Albania ☎ (42) 28 461 Tx: n/a Fax: (42) 42 857 SITA: n/a
F: 1995 n/a Head: n/a IATA: 639 ICAO: ALBANIAN Net: n/a

☐ LZ-TUH	Tupolev 134A	60142	OK-HFM	0077	0398	2 SO D-30-II	49000	Y72		lsf HMS
☐ LZ-TUJ	Tupolev 134A	49913	OK-HFL	0077	1098	2 SO D-30-II	49000	Y72		lsf HMS
☐ LZ-TUT	Tupolev 134B-3	63987		0082	1097	2 SO D-30-III	49000	Y76		lsf HMS

ZK = NEW ZEALAND (Dominion of New Zealand)

(including self-governing Cook Islands)
Capital: Wellington Official Language: English Population: 3,7 million Square Km: 270986 Dialling code: +64 Year established: 1907 Acting political head: James B. Bolger (Prime Minister)

COOK ISLANDS
Capital: Avarua/Rarotonga Official Language: English Population: 0,1 million Square Km: 241 Dialling code: +682 Acting political head: Sir Geoffrey A. Henry (Prime Minister)

Government / Corporate / Executive / VIP Aircraft

☐ NZ7271	Boeing 727-22C	19892 / 640	N7435U	0968	0781	3 PW JT8D-7	76884	VIP / mil transp	BG-CK	Royal New Zealand Air Force
☐ NZ7272	Boeing 727-22C	19895 / 658	N7438U	1168	0781	3 PW JT8D-7	76884	VIP / mil transp	BG-CM	Royal New Zealand Air Force

667 registration type of aircraft cn/fn ex/ex* mfd del powered by mtow kg configuration selcal name/fln/specialitites/remarks

AERIAL SURVEYS, Ltd = SUY — Nelson

29 Bolt Road, Tahunanui, Nelson 7001, New Zealand ☎ (3) 548 51 26 Tx: none Fax: (3) 548 51 26 SITA: n/a
F: 1948 ‡‡‡ 7 Head: Mr. Kearns ICAO: SURVEY Net: n/a

☐ ZK-EOP	Cessna TU206G Turbo Stationair 6 II	U20604697	N732MU	0079		1 CO TSIO-520-M	1633	Photo / Survey		

AIR ADVENTURES NEW ZEALAND, Ltd — Christchurch

PO Box 14028, Christchurch 8030, New Zealand ☎ (3) 358 83 34 Tx: none Fax: (3) 358 94 44 SITA: n/a
F: 1993 ‡‡‡ n/a Head: Michael B. Bannerman Net: http://www.airadventures.co.nz Aircraft below MTOW 1361kg: Piper PA-28

☐ ZK-MAN	Piper PA-32-300 Cherokee SIX	32-7840192	VH-MAN	0078	0394	1 LY IO-540-K1G5	1542			
☐ ZK-SFC	Piper PA-34-200T Seneca II	34-7770054	VH-PZG	0077	1198	2 CO TSIO-360-E	2073			
☐ ZK-DHB	Piper PA-23-250 Aztec C	27-3735	N6492Y	0067	1198	2 LY IO-540-C4B5	2359			

AIR CHARTER OTAGO (Commercial division of Otago Aero Club, (Inc.) — Dunedin

PO Box 25, Mosgiel 9032, New Zealand ☎ (3) 489 61 58 Tx: none Fax: (3) 489 61 58 SITA: n/a
F: 1927 ‡‡‡ n/a Head: John E. Penno Net: n/a Aircraft below MTOW 1361kg: Cessna 152/172 & Piper PA-28/38

☐ ZK-JDV	Cessna U206G Stationair 6 II	U20604775	VH-XMW	0078	0894	1 CO IO-520-D	1633			

AIR CHARTER TAUPO, (1995) Ltd (formerly Lakeland Flying School, Ltd) — Taupo

RD 2, Taupo 2730, New Zealand ☎ (7) 378 54 67 Tx: none Fax: (7) 378 54 68 SITA: n/a
F: 1982 ‡‡‡ 2 Head: Arthur Whitehead Net: http://www.airchartertaupo.co.nz Aircraft below MTOW 1361kg: AA-5.

☐ ZK-ERQ	Cessna U206F Stationair	U20601738	N9538G	0072		1 CO IO-520-F	1633			

AIR CHATHAMS, Ltd = CV / CVA — Chatham Islands

PO Box 52, Chatham Islands 8030, New Zealand ☎ (3) 305 02 09 Tx: n/a Fax: (3) 305 02 09 SITA: n/a
F: 1986 ‡‡‡ 9 Head: Craig Emeny ICAO: CHATHAM Net: n/a

☐ ZK-DOA	Cessna U206F Stationair	U20602203	N7450Q	0074		1 CO IO-520-F	1633			
☐ ZK-CIA	Beech Queen Air B80 (65-B80)	LD-430	N640K	0070		2 LY IGSO-540-A1D	3992			
☐ ZK-CIC	Fairchild (Swearingen) SA227AC Metro III	AC-623B	N623AV	0085	0993	2 GA TPE331-11U-611G	7257		HK-MP	cvtd cn AC-623
☐ ZK-CIB	Convair 580	327A	C-FCIB	0056	0596	2 AN 501-D13	26379	Combi/Y20-40/Cgo		cvtd 440-42
☐ ZK-KSA	Convair 580	507	C-GTTE	0058	0498	2 AN 501-D13	24766	Y52		cvtd 440-62

AIR COROMANDEL (Air Services Whitianga, Ltd dba / Sister company of Great Barrier Air / formerly Mercury Airlines) — Whitianga

PO Box 44, Whitianga 2856, New Zealand ☎ (7) 866 40 16 Tx: n/a Fax: (7) 866 40 17 SITA: n/a
F: 1986 ‡‡‡ 4 Head: Les Simpson Net: n/a Operates charter flights with aircraft used from GREAT BARRIER AIR when required.

AIR FIORDLAND (The Friendly Scenic Way) (Member of the Fiordland Experience Group, Ltd) — Te Anau, Milford Sound & Queenstown

Box 38, Te Anau 9681, New Zealand ☎ (3) 249 75 05 Tx: none Fax: (3) 249 70 80 SITA: n/a
F: 1984 ‡‡‡ 16 Head: Russell V. Baker Net: n/a Aircraft below MTOW 1361 kg: Cessna 172.

☐ ZK-CFI	Cessna 185B Skywagon	185-0598	N2598Z	0063		1 CO IO-520-D	1451			
☐ ZK-DOC	Cessna A185F Skywagon	18502318	N53017	0074	0792	1 CO IO-520-D	1520			
☐ ZK-KPM	Cessna U206G Stationair 6 II	U20606210	N6273Z	0081		1 CO IO-520-F	1633			
☐ ZK-KPW	Cessna U206G Stationair 6	U20603593	VH-AEZ	0077	1193	1 CO IO-520-F	1633			
☐ ZK-EJD	Cessna 207 Skywagon	20700362	N1791C	0076		1 CO IO-520-F	1724			
☐ ZK-FQY	Cessna 207 Skywagon	20700293	N1693U	0075	0589	1 CO IO-520-F	1724			
☐ ZK-SEV	Cessna 207 Skywagon	20700204	F-OCQK	0071	0596	1 CO IO-520-F	1724			
☐ ZK-UBU	Cessna 207 Skywagon	20700119	VH-UBU	0069	0894	1 CO IO-520-F	1724			

AIR FREIGHT NZ (Subsidiary of Ronberg Enterprises, Ltd) — Auckland-Int'l

PO Box 73-088, Auckland Airport 1030, New Zealand ☎ (9) 256 85 80 Tx: none Fax: (9) 256 85 83 SITA: n/a
F: 1989 ‡‡‡ 16 Head: M.D. Lasenby Net: n/a

☐ ZK-FTA	Convair 580 (F) (SCD)	168	C-GKFP	0054	0589	2 AN 501-D13	24766	Freighter		opf Parceline / cvtd CV340-31
☐ ZK-KFH	Convair 580	42	C-FKFL	0053	0297	2 AN 501-D13	24766	Freighter		cvtd CV340-31
☐ ZK-KFL	Convair 580 (F) (SCD)	372	C-FKFL	0056	0490	2 AN 501-D13	24766	Freighter		opf Parceline / cvtd CV440-90
☐ ZK-KFU	Convair 580 (F) (SCD)	17	C-GKFU	0052	0595	2 AN 501-D13	26379	Freighter		opf Parceline / cvtd CV340-31

AIR GISBORNE, Ltd — Gisborne

Gisborne Airport, Gisborne 3801, New Zealand ☎ (6) 867 46 84 Tx: n/a Fax: (6) 868 94 54 SITA: n/a
F: 1969 ‡‡‡ n/a Head: John E. Reid Net: n/a Aircraft below MTOW 1361 kg: Cessna 172 & Gulfstream American AA5.

☐ ZK-TLC	Piper PA-34-200T Seneca II	34-7970100	VH-STN	0079	1193	2 CO TSIO-360-EB	2073			

AIR MARLBOROUGH = SCS (Straits Air Charter (1996), Ltd dba / formerly Straits Air Charter, Ltd) — Blenheim

Hawkesbury Road, RD2, Blenheim 7321, New Zealand ☎ (3) 572 80 81 Tx: none Fax: (3) 572 81 96 SITA: n/a
F: 1991 ‡‡‡ n/a Head: Allan W. Graham ICAO: STRAITS AIR Net: n/a Aircraft below MTOW 1361kg: Piper PA-28.

☐ ZK-RUF	Piper PA-34-200T Seneca II	34-7870158	VH-AYN	0078	0493	2 CO TSIO-360-E	2073			
☐ ZK-JGA	Piper PA-31-310 Navajo C	31-7612102	VH-TRP	0076	0496	2 LY TIO-540-A2C	2948			

AIR NAPIER, Ltd = NPR — Napier

PO Box 12118, Ahuiri, Napier 4030, New Zealand ☎ (6) 835 61 92 Tx: none Fax: (6) 835 61 92 SITA: n/a
F: 1993 ‡‡‡ n/a Head: Gary Peacock Net: n/a Aircraft below MTOW 1361kg: Piper PA-28

☐ ZK-ELK	Piper PA-32-260 Cherokee	32-7400009	N8768C	0074	0598	1 LY O-540-E4B5	1542			
☐ ZK-MSL	Piper PA-34-200T Seneca II	34-7770224	N5600V	0077	0493	2 CO TSIO-360-E	2073			
☐ ZK-JEI	Piper PA-23-250 Aztec C	27-2638	DQ-FIB	0064	1298	2 LY IO-540-C4B5	2359			

AIR NATIONAL, Ltd (formerly Menzies Aviation) — Auckland-Int'l

PO Box 73-088, Auckland Airport 1030, New Zealand ☎ (9) 256 85 50 Tx: none Fax: (9) 256 85 52 SITA: n/a
F: 1988 ‡‡‡ 18 Head: Ian A. Gray Net: n/a Jetstream 32EP-aircraft is operated on behalf of ANSETT NEW ZEALAND (in own colors) & using AN-flight numbers.

☐ ZK-RDT	Embraer 820C Navajo (EMB-820C)	820127	PT-RDT	0082	0798	2 LY TIO-540-J2BD	3175	Y9		
☐ ZK-ECR	Mitsubishi MU-2P (MU-2B-26A)	371SA	VH-XMZ	0078	0695	2 GA TPE331-5-252M	4749	Y4		
☐ ZK-ECM	Embraer 110P1 Bandeirante (EMB-110P1)	110383	SE-KEL	0082	0794	2 PWC PT6A-34	5900	Y15		
☐ ZK-ECN	BAe 3201 Jetstream 32EP	967	N967JS	0092	1098	2 GA TPE331-12UAR-704H	7350	Y19		City of Rotorua / lsf BAMT / cvtd 32

AIR NELSON, Ltd = RLK (Air New Zealand Link) (Subsidiary of Air New Zealand) — Nelson

Private Bag 32, Nelson 7030, New Zealand ☎ (3) 547 87 00 Tx: none Fax: (3) 547 87 46 SITA: n/a
F: 1976 ‡‡‡ 400 Head: Steve Wilkes Net: n/a All aircraft are operated as AIR NEW ZEALAND LINK (in full such colours & both titles), a commuter system to provide feeder connection at NZ major hubs, using NZ flight numbers.

☐ ZK-NSI	Fairchild (Swearingen) SA227AC Metro III	AC-765	N2751N*	0090	1190	2 GA TPE331-11U-612G	6577	Y19		
☐ ZK-NSJ	Fairchild (Swearingen) SA227AC Metro III	AC-767	N27521*	0090	1290	2 GA TPE331-11U-612G	6577	Y19		
☐ ZK-NSU	Fairchild (Swearingen) SA227AC Metro III	AC-705	EI-BWU	0088	0490	2 GA TPE331-11U-612G	6577	Y19		lsf GECA
☐ ZK-NSV	Fairchild (Swearingen) SA227AC Metro III	AC-513	N3108H	0083	0389	2 GA TPE331-11U-611G	6577	Y19		
☐ ZK-NSY	Fairchild (Swearingen) SA227AC Metro III	AC-711	EI-BWV	0080	0390	2 GA TPE331-11U-612G	6577	Y19		lsf GECA
☐ ZK-NSZ	Fairchild (Swearingen) SA227AC Metro III	AC-712	EI-BWW	0088	0490	2 GA TPE331-11U-612G	6577	Y19		lsf GECA
☐ ZK-FXA	Saab SF340A	340A-120	HB-AHP	0088	1090	2 GE CT7-5A2	12700	Y33		
☐ ZK-FXB	Saab SF340A	340A-122	HB-AHQ	0088	1090	2 GE CT7-5A2	12700	Y33		
☐ ZK-FXD	Saab SF340A	340A-088	HB-AHN	0087	1290	2 GE CT7-5A2	12700	Y33		
☐ ZK-NLE	Saab SF340A	340A-067	SE-ISX	1086	0793	2 GE CT7-5A2	12700	Y33		lsf SAS Leasing
☐ ZK-NLH	Saab SF340A	340A-137	SE-ISN	1288	0694	2 GE CT7-5A2	12700	Y33		lsf SAS Leasing
☐ ZK-NLN	Saab SF340A	340A-136	N136AN	0088	0297	2 GE CT7-5A2	12700	Y33		lsf MCC Financial Corp.
☐ ZK-NLO	Saab SF340A	340A-153	N153AN	0089	0497	2 GE CT7-5A2	12700	Y33		lsf MCC Financial Corp.
☐ ZK-NLP	Saab SF340A	340A-042	SE-ISU	1285	0894	2 GE CT7-5A2	12700	Y33		lsf SAS Leasing
☐ ZK-NLQ	Saab SF340A	340A-124	D-CDID	0088	1196	2 GE CT7-5A2	12700	Y33		
☐ ZK-NLR	Saab SF340A	340A-097	SE-ISZ	0887	0794	2 GE CT7-5A2	12700	Y33		lsf SAS Leasing
☐ ZK-NLS	Saab SF340A	340A-134	HB-AHT	0088	0296	2 GE CT7-5A2	12700	Y33		lsf Saab Aircraft Leasing
☐ ZK-NLT	Saab SF340A	340A-116	D-CDIC	0088	1196	2 GE CT7-5A2	12700	Y33		
☐ ZK-NSK	Saab SF340A	340A-084	HB-AHM	0087	0392	2 GE CT7-5A2	12700	Y33		

AIR NEW PLYMOUTH (New Plymouth Aero Club, Inc. dba) — New Plymouth

RD3, New Plymouth 4621, New Zealand ☎ (6) 755 05 00 Tx: none Fax: (6) 755 14 78 SITA: n/a
F: 1929 ‡‡‡ 7 Head: Wayne Harrison Net: n/a

☐ ZK-NPC	Cessna 182R Skylane II	18268096	N9894H	0082		1 CO O-470-U	1406			
☐ ZK-NPA	Cessna 207A Stationair 7 II	20700479	N4997J	0078		1 CO IO-520-F	1724			
☐ ZK-JLR	Piper PA-34-220T Seneca III	34-8433030	N4340Q	0084	0598	2 CO TSIO-360-KB	2155			
☐ ZK-ECQ	Piper PA-31-325 Navajo C/R	31-7612090	VH-INX	0076	0896	2 LY TIO-540-F2BD	2948			

AIR NEW ZEALAND, Ltd = NZ / ANZ (Member of Star Alliance/Assoc.with Brierley Investements/formerly Tasman Empire Airways Ltd) — Auckland-Int'l

Private Bag 92007, Auckland 1020, New Zealand ☎ (9) 366 24 00 Tx: 2541 airnz ak nz Fax: (9) 366 26 67 SITA: AKLDANZ
F: 1940 ‡‡‡ 7000 Head: Selwyn Cushing IATA: 086 ICAO: NEW ZEALAND Net: http://www.airnz.co.nz A commuter system to provide feeder connection at NZ major hubs is operated under the marketing name AIR NEW ZEALAND LINK by: AIR NELSON, EAGLE AIRWAYS & MOUNT COOK AIRLINE. For details see under each company. Freighter services are operated with DC-8-73F & B747-200F aircraft lsf/opb U.S. carriers (N) when required.

☐ ZK-NAA	Boeing 737-204 (A)	22638 / 858	G-BJCT	0082	1193	2 PW JT8D-15A (HK3/NOR)	55111	C8Y105		Parekareka / lsf KB Flygplanet
☐ ZK-NAB	Boeing 737-204 (A)	22364 / 696	G-BHWE	0080	0294	2 PW JT8D-15A (HK3/NOR)	55111	C8Y105		Parera / lsf IAI Pacific Leasing Inc.
☐ ZK-NAF	Boeing 737-2Y5 (A)	23038 / 949	9H-ABA	0083	0994	2 PW JT8D-15A	56472	C8Y105	BJ-FH	Pohowhera / lsf INGO
☐ ZK-NAI	Boeing 737-204 (A)	22365 / 700	G-BHWF	0080	1293	2 PW JT8D-15A (HK3/NOR)	55111	C8Y105		Poaka / lsf KB Flygplanet
☐ ZK-NAT	Boeing 737-219 (A)	23470 / 1186		0086	0186	2 PW JT8D-15A (HK3/NOR)	53297	C8Y105	DE-GJ	Pihoihoi

668 registration type of aircraft cn/fn ex/ex* mfd del powered by mtow kg configuration selcal name/fln/specialitites/remarks

registration	type of aircraft	cn/fn	ex/ex*	mfd	del	powered by	mtow kg	configuration	selcal	name/fin/specialtitites/remarks
☐ ZK-NAU	Boeing 737-219 (A)	23471 / 1189		0086	0186	2 PW JT8D-15A (HK3/NOR)	53297	C8Y105		Pateke
☐ ZK-NAV	Boeing 737-219 (A)	23472 / 1194		0086	0286	2 PW JT8D-15A (HK3/NOR)	53297	C8Y105	HL-BC	Pukeko
☐ ZK-NAW	Boeing 737-219 (A)	23473 / 1197		0086	0286	2 PW JT8D-15A (HK3/NOR)	53297	C8Y105	DE-GK	Purourou
☐ ZK-NAX	Boeing 737-219 (A)	23474 / 1199		0086	0286	2 PW JT8D-15A (HK3/NOR)	53297	C8Y105	DE-GL	Piere
☐ ZK-NAY	Boeing 737-219 (A)	23475 / 1203		0086	0386	2 PW JT8D-15A (HK3/NOR)	53297	C8Y105		Piripiri
☐ ZK-NQC	Boeing 737-219C (A)	22994 / 928		0082	1282	2 PW JT8D-15A (HK3/NOR)	53297	C8Y105 / Frtr	HL-AM	Piopio
☐ ZK-NGA	Boeing 737-33R	28873 / 2975	N1787B*	0097	0198	2 CFMI CFM56-3C1	62823	C12Y102	CQ-DP	lsf GECA/spec. Millenium/America Cup-cs
☐ ZK-NGB	Boeing 737-36Q	29140 / 3013		0398	0398	2 CFMI CFM56-3C1	62823	C12Y102		lsf BOUL
☐ ZK-NGC	Boeing 737-36Q	29189 / 3057		0098	0898	2 CFMI CFM56-3C1	62823	C12Y102		lsf BOUL
☐ ZK-NGD	Boeing 737-3U3	28732 / 2966	N930WA	1297	1198	2 CFMI CFM56-3C1	63276	C8Y114		lsf LOT -1099
☐ ZK-NGE	Boeing 737-3U3	28733 / 2969	N931WA	1297	1298	2 CFMI CFM56-3C1	63276	C8Y114		lsf INGO / sub-lst ABD -1099
☐ ZK-NGF	Boeing 737-3U3	28734 / 2974	N309FL	1297	1298	2 CFMI CFM56-3C1	63276	C8Y114		lsf INGO / sub-lst FFT
☐ ZK-NGG	Boeing 737-319	25606				2 CFMI CFM56-3C1	63276	C8Y114		oo-delivery 1099
☐ ZK-NGH	Boeing 737-319	25607				2 CFMI CFM56-3C1	63276	C8Y114		oo-delivery 1199
☐ ZK-NGI	Boeing 737-319	25608				2 CFMI CFM56-3C1	63276	C8Y114		oo-delivery 1199
☐ ZK-NGJ	Boeing 737-319	25609				2 CFMI CFM56-3C1	63276	C8Y114		oo-delivery 1299
☐ ZK-NBA	Boeing 767-219 (ER)	23326 / 124	N6018N*	0085	0985	2 GE CF6-80A	163294	C25Y153	CP-GH	Aotearoa / lst AAA as VH-RMC
☐ ZK-NBB	Boeing 767-219 (ER)	23327 / 134	N6055X*	0086	0386	2 GE CF6-80A	163294	C24Y176	CP-GJ	Arahina
☐ ZK-NBC	Boeing 767-219 (ER)	23328 / 149	N6009F*	0086	0986	2 GE CF6-80A	163294	C24Y176	CP-GK	Atarau
☐ ZK-NBJ	Boeing 767-204 (ER)	23250 / 113	G-BLKW	0085	0990	2 GE CF6-80A	163294	C24Y176	FH-CQ	Awarua / lsf Aerospace Finance Ltd
☐ ZK-NCE	Boeing 767-319 (ER)	24875 / 371		0091	0691	2 GE CF6-80C2B6	185521	C24Y210	FH-DQ	lsf ILFC
☐ ZK-NCF	Boeing 767-319 (ER)	24876 / 413		0092	0292	2 GE CF6-80C2B6	185521	C24Y210	DJ-HR	lsf ILFC
☐ ZK-NCG	Boeing 767-319 (ER)	26912 / 509		0093	0893	2 GE CF6-80C2B6	186882	C24Y210	DJ-GS	
☐ ZK-NCH	Boeing 767-319 (ER)	26264 / 555		0094	1094	2 GE CF6-80C2B6	186882	C24Y210	FS-BQ	lsf ILFC
☐ ZK-NCI	Boeing 767-319 (ER)	26913 / 558	N6009F*	0094	1194	2 GE CF6-80C2B6	186882	C24Y210	HP-DK	
☐ ZK-NCJ	Boeing 767-319 (ER)	26915 / 574	N6018N*	0095	0495	2 GE CF6-80C2B6	186882	C24Y210	FS-BR	
☐ ZK-NCK	Boeing 767-319 (ER)	26971 / 663		0097	0697	2 GE CF6-80C2B6F	186882	C24Y210		
☐ ZK-NCL	Boeing 767-319 (ER)	28745 / 677		1097	1097	2 GE CF6-80C2B6F	186882	C24Y210		
☐ ZK-NCM	Boeing 767-35H (ER)	26389 / 459	N800CZ	0092	0496	2 GE CF6-80C2B6F	185521	C24Y212	CE-PR	lsf ITOH
☐ ZK-NCN	Boeing 767-319 (ER)	29388				2 GE CF6-80C2B6F	186882	C24Y210		to be lsf ILFC 0300
☐ ZK-NZX	Boeing 747-219B	22724 / 528	9M-MHG	0081	0681	4 RR RB211-524D4	377842	C32Y384	BG-AF	Takitimu / for VIR 0500 as G-VSSS
☐ ZK-NZY	Boeing 747-219B	22725 / 563	N6005C*	0082	0682	4 RR RB211-524D4	377842	C32Y384	BG-AD	Te Arawa / for VIR 0200 as G-VPUF
☐ ZK-NZZ	Boeing 747-219B	22791 / 568	9M-MHH	0082	0882	4 RR RB211-524D4	377842	C32Y384	EK-BC	Tokomaru / for VIR 0999 as G-VIBE
☐ ZK-NBS	Boeing 747-419	24386 / 756		0089	1289	4 RR RB211-524G	394625	F16C56Y324	JQ-EL	
☐ ZK-NBT	Boeing 747-419	24855 / 815	N6018N*	0090	1090	4 RR RB211-524G	394625	F16C56Y324	JQ-EM	
☐ ZK-NBU	Boeing 747-419	25605 / 933		0092	0992	4 RR RB211-524G	394625	F16C56Y324	DP-MS	
☐ ZK-NBV	Boeing 747-419	26910 / 1180		1098	1098	4 GE CF6-80C2B1F	394625	F16C56Y324		
☐ ZK-NBW	Boeing 747-419	29375				4 GE CF6-80C2B1F	394625	F16C56Y324		to be lsf ILFC 1099
☐ ZK-SUH	Boeing 747-475	24896 / 855	N891LF	0091	1194	4 GE CF6-80C2B1F	394625	F16C56Y324	GM-BR	lsf ILFC
☐ ZK-SUI	Boeing 747-441	24957 / 971	N821LF	0093	1294	4 GE CF6-80C2B1F	394625	F16C56Y324	CP-GL	lsf ILFC
☐ ZK-SUJ	Boeing 747-4F6	27602 / 1161	N756PR	0098	1098	4 GE CF6-80C2B1F	394625	F16C56Y324		lsf ILFC

AIR POST, Ltd = PST (Joint venture of Airwork (NZ), Ltd & New Zealand Post, Ltd)

Auckland, Wellington, Nelson & Christchurch

PO Box 516, Papakura 1733, New Zealand   ☎ (9) 298 72 02   Tx: none   Fax: (9) 298 14 55   SITA: n/a
F: 1990   ⁕⁕⁕ 40   Head: Hugh Jones   ICAO: POST   Net: n/a

☐ ZK-NSS	Fairchild (Swearingen) SA227AC Metro III	AC-692B	N2707D	0087	0391	2 GA TPE331-11U-612G	7257	Freighter		
☐ ZK-PAA	Fairchild (Swearingen) SA227AC Metro III	AC-582	N380PH	0084	0997	2 GA TPE331-11U-611G	6577	Freighter		
☐ ZK-POA	Fairchild (Swearingen) SA227AC Metro III	AC-551B	D-CABF	0083	1290	2 GA TPE331-11U-611G	7257	Freighter		cvtd c/n AC-551
☐ ZK-POE	Fairchild (Swearingen) SA227CC Metro 23	CC-843B	N30228*	0093	1094	2 GA TPE331-11U-611G	7484	Freighter		
☐ ZK-POF	Fairchild (Swearingen) SA227CC Metro 23	CC-844B	N30229*	0093	1094	2 GA TPE331-11U-611G	7484	Freighter		
☐ ZK-NAN	Fokker F27 Friendship 500 (F27 Mk500)	10365	9V-BCN	0068	1091	2 RR Dart 532-7R	20412	Freighter	HL-BC	
☐ ZK-NAO	Fokker F27 Friendship 500 (F27 Mk500)	10364	9V-BFK	0068	1091	2 RR Dart 532-7R	20412	Freighter	HL-BD	
☐ ZK-POH	Fokker F27 Friendship 500 (F27 Mk500)	10680	VT-NEH	0084	0798	2 RR Dart 552-7R	20820	Freighter		

AIR RAROTONGA, Ltd = GZ

Rarotonga   **Air Rarotonga**

PO Box 79, Rarotonga, Cook Islands   ☎ 21 669   Tx: none   Fax: 20 979   SITA: RARZQGZ
F: 1978   ⁕⁕⁕ 39   Head: Ewan F. Smith   IATA: 755   Net: http://www.ck/edairaro.htm   Aircraft below MTOW 1361 kg: Cessna 172.

☐ ZK-FTS	Embraer 110P1 Bandeirante (EMB-110P1)	110239	N107CA	0079	0689	2 PWC PT6A-34	5670	Y18		
☐ ZK-TAI	Embraer 110P1 Bandeirante (EMB-110P1)	110387	N134EM	0082	1291	2 PWC PT6A-34	5670	Y18		
☐ ZK-TAK	Embraer 110P1 Bandeirante (EMB-110P1)	110448	VH-KHA	0084	0898	2 PWC PT6A-34	5670	Y18		

AIR ROTORUA, Ltd

Rotorua

PO Box 7241, Rotorua 3215, New Zealand   ☎ (7) 345 75 00   Tx: none   Fax: (7) 349 22 07   SITA: n/a
F: 1997   ⁕⁕⁕ n/a   Head: M.F. & P.J. Malone   Net: n/a

☐ ZK-FNB	Piper PA-34-200T Seneca II	34-7970236	9M-AXV	0079	0197	2 CO TSIO-360-EB	2073			

AIR SAFARIS & SERVICES, (NZ) Ltd = SRI

Lake Tekapo   **AIR SAFARIS** AND SERVICES (NEW ZEALAND) LTD

PO Box 71, Lake Tekapo 8770, New Zealand   ☎ (3) 680 68 80   Tx: none   Fax: (3) 680 67 40   SITA: n/a
F: 1971   ⁕⁕⁕ 11   Head: Richard Rayward   ICAO: AIRSAFARI   Net: n/a   Aircraft below MTOW 1361kg: Cessna 177

☐ ZK-FJH	Cessna P206 Super Skylane	P20600634	G-BKSI	0070	0496	1 CO IO-520-A	1633			
☐ ZK-SEU	Cessna 207A Stationair 8 II	20700713	ZK-EWC	0081		1 CO IO-550-F	1724			
☐ ZK-SEW	Cessna T207A Turbo Stationair 8 II	20700584	N73394	0080		1 CO TSIO-520-M	1724			
☐ ZK-SEX	Cessna T207A Turbo Stationair 8 II	20700609	N73622	0080		1 CO TSIO-520-M	1724			
☐ ZK-SEY	Cessna T207A Turbo Stationair 8 II	20700661	N76012	0081		1 CO TSIO-520-M	1724			
☐ ZK-NMC	GAF Nomad N24A	N24A-34	VH-DHP	0077	0597	2 AN 250-B17B	4264			
☐ ZK-NMD	GAF Nomad N24A	N24A-60	VH-DHU	0078		2 AN 250-B17C	4264			
☐ ZK-NME	GAF Nomad N24A	N24A-122	5W-FAT	0082	0187	2 AN 250-B17C	4264			
☐ ZK-NMG	GAF Nomad N24A	N24A-73	VH-FHR	0078	0392	2 AN 250-B17C	4264			
☐ ZK-NMH	GAF Nomad N24A	N24A-74FA	N870US	0078	1294	2 AN 250-B17C	4264			

AIR TARANAKI, Ltd

Waitara

PO Box 290, Waitara 4656, New Zealand   ☎ (6) 754 43 75   Tx: none   Fax: (6) 754 40 78   SITA: n/a
F: 1994   ⁕⁕⁕ n/a   Head: Alan Warner   Net: n/a

☐ ZK-ERM	Piper PA-23-250 Aztec E	27-7405435	N54129	0074	1094	2 LY IO-540-C4B5	2359			

AIR WANGANUI COMMUTER, Ltd

Wanganui

PO Box 42, Wanganui 5015, New Zealand   ☎ (6) 348 92 00   Tx: none   Fax: (6) 342 97 26   SITA: n/a
F: 1987   ⁕⁕⁕ n/a   Head: George McKay   Net: n/a   Aircraft below MTOW 1361kg: Cessna 182

☐ ZK-WLV	Beech Baron 58	TH-698	VH-WLV	0075	0497	2 CO IO-520-C	2449			
☐ ZK-WTH	Piper PA-31P-350 Mojave	31P-8414003	N9187Y	0084		2 LY TIO-540-V2AD	3368	EMS / Charter		

AIRWEST HELICOPTERS, Ltd

Reefton

76 Shiel Street, Reefton 7853, New Zealand   ☎ (3) 732 88 82   Tx: none   Fax: (3) 732 89 46   SITA: n/a
F: n/a   ⁕⁕⁕ 3   Head: M.J. Rosanowski   Net: n/a   Aircraft below MTOW 1361 kg: Hughes 369HS (500C).

☐ ZK-HOL	MD Helicopters MD 500E (Hughes 369E)	0360E	G-OPRO	0089	0896	1 AN 250-C20R	1361			
☐ ZK-HSW	MD Helicopters MD 500D (Hughes 369D)	300675D	VH-KSY	0080		1 AN 250-C20B	1361			

AIRWORK (NZ), Ltd

Auckland & Wellington   **airwork**

PO Box 516, Papakura 1733, New Zealand   ☎ (9) 298 72 02   Tx: none   Fax: (9) 298 14 55   SITA: n/a
F: 1936   ⁕⁕⁕ 140   Head: Hugh Jones   Net: n/a

☐ ZK-HOJ	MD Helicopters MD 500D (Hughes 369D)	490491D		0079	1295	1 AN 250-C20B	1361			
☐ ZK-HPW	Bell OH-58A (206 JetRanger)	42104	72-21438	0072	0197	1 AN T63-A-700	1361			
☐ ZK-HGB	Eurocopter (Aerosp.) AS350B Squirrel	2550		0091	0995	1 TU Arriel 1B	1950			
☐ ZK-HZO	Eurocopter (Aerosp.) AS350B Squirrel	1034	VH-SRA	0078	1298	1 TU Arriel 1B	1950			
☐ ZK-HKG	Eurocopter (Aerosp.) AS355F1 Tw.Squirrel	5267	VH-NWA	0083	0994	2 AN 250-C20F	2400			
☐ ZK-EBT	Piper PA-31-350 Navajo Chieftain	31-7552044	N59929	0075		2 LY TIO-540-J2BD	3175			
☐ ZK-FOP	Piper PA-31-350 Navajo Chieftain	31-7405227	N888SG	0074		2 LY TIO-540-J2BD	3175	EMS		opf Auckland Regional Rescue Helicopter
☐ ZK-HFH	Kawasaki (Eurocopter/MBB) BK117B-1	1075	HL9212	0091	0896	2 LY LTS101-750B.1	3200			
☐ ZK-HJK	Kawasaki (Eurocopter/MBB) BK117A-4	1020	JA9911	0088	0698	2 LY LTS101-650B.1	3200			
☐ ZK-HMO	Kawasaki (Eurocopter/MBB) BK117B-1	1074	JA6650	0091	1094	2 LY LTS101-750B.1	3200			
☐ ZK-HSJ	Kawasaki (Eurocopter/MBB) BK117B-2	1076	JA6652	0091	1198	2 LY LTS101-750B.1	3350			cvtd BK117B-1
☐ ZK-HSS	Kawasaki (Eurocopter/MBB) BK117B-1	1040	JA9983	0090	0898	2 LY LTS101-750B.1	3200			
☐ ZK-POD	Piper PA-31T Cheyenne II	31T-7720009	ZK-MPI	0077	0592	2 PWC PT6A-28	4082	EMS		
☐ ZK-FPL	Piper PA-31T3-T1040	31T-8475001	N2464W	0084		2 PWC PT6A-11	4082			
☐ ZK-POB	Fairchild (Swearingen) SA227AC Metro III	AC-606B	D-CABG	0085	0391	2 GA TPE331-11U-611G	7257	EMS		opf Auckland Regional Rescue Helicopter

AMALGAMATED HELICOPTERS, Ltd

Carterton

PO Box 206, Carterton 8600, New Zealand   ☎ (6) 379 86 00   Tx: n/a   Fax: (6) 379 87 59   SITA: n/a
F: 1987   ⁕⁕⁕ 1   Head: Duncan Sutherland   Net: n/a

☐ ZK-HOM	MD Helicopters MD 500D (Hughes 369D)	590515D		0079		1 AN 250-C20B	1361			

AMURI HELICOPTERS, Ltd — Waikari

Pyramid Valley Road, Waikari 8276, New Zealand ☎ (3) 314 40 92 Tx: none Fax: (3) 314 49 20 SITA: n/a
F: 1987 n/a Head: Stephen Smith Net: n/a Aircraft below MTOW 1361kg: Robinson R44

☐ ZK-HDZ	MD Helicopters MD 500D (Hughes 369D)	510959D	P2-IHB	0081	1094	1 AN 250-C20B	1361			
☐ ZK-HYL	Bell 206B JetRanger	435	N12SX	0069	0991	1 AN 250-C20	1451			cvtd 206A

ANDERSON HELICOPTERS, Ltd — Hokitika

PO Box 187, Hokitika 7900, New Zealand ☎ (3) 755 66 06 Tx: n/a Fax: (3) 755 66 06 SITA: n/a
F: 1989 4 Head: Kevin J. Anderson Net: n/a

☐ ZK-HSG	Bell 206B JetRanger	1555	C-GLDR	0074		1 AN 250-C20	1451			

ANSETT NEW ZEALAND, Ltd = ZQ / AAA (Subsidiary of News Corp. / Member of Star Alliance / formerly Newmans Air) — Christchurch & Auckland

PO Box 14-139, Christchurch Airport 8030, New Zealand ☎ (9) 309 62 35 Tx: 4811 newair nz Fax: (9) 309 64 34 SITA: n/a
F: 1984 1150 Head: Kevin Doddwell IATA: 941 ICAO: ANSETT Net: n/a All flights are currently operated under the IATA 2-letter code AN of Ansett Australia.
Some flights are operated on behalf of Ansett NZ by: AIR NATIONAL (Jetstream 32) & ANSETT NZ REGIONAL (EMB-110P1 & Jetstream 32EP) using AN-flt no's. For details – see both companies.

☐ ZK-NES	De Havilland DHC-8-102 Dash 8	125	B-15203	0088	1295	2 PWC PW120A	15649	Y40		
☐ ZK-NET	De Havilland DHC-8-102 Dash 8	197	B-15205	0090	1095	2 PWC PW120A	15649	Y40		
☐ ZK-NEU	De Havilland DHC-8-102 Dash 8	218	B-15207	0090	0995	2 PWC PW120A	15649	Y40		
☐ ZK-NEZ	De Havilland DHC-8-102 Dash 8	060		0086	1286	2 PWC PW120A	15649	Y40		
☐ ZK-NZC	BAe 146-200 (QC)	E2119	G-BPBT*	0089	1089	4 LY ALF502R-5	42184	CY75 / Freighter		City of Manukau / cvtd -200
☐ ZK-NZF	BAe 146-300	E3134	G-5-134*	0089	1289	4 LY ALF502R-5	44225	CY90		City of Wellington
☐ ZK-NZG	BAe 146-300	E3135	G-5-135*	0089	1289	4 LY ALF502R-5	44225	CY90	DK-AC	City of Christchurch
☐ ZK-NZH	BAe 146-300	E3137	G-5-137*	0089	1289	4 LY ALF502R-5	44225	CY90	AH-DL	City of Auckland
☐ ZK-NZI	BAe 146-300	E3143	G-5-143*	0089	1289	4 LY ALF502R-5	44225	CY90		City of Dunedin
☐ ZK-NZJ	BAe 146-300	E3147	G-5-147*	0089	0290	4 LY ALF502R-5	44225	CY90	HK-AE	City of Nelson
☐ ZK-NZK	BAe 146-300	E3190	VH-EWN	0091	0192	4 LY ALF502R-5	44225	CY90		City of Invercargill
☐ ZK-NZL	BAe 146-300	E3175	VH-EWK	0090	0792	4 LY ALF502R-5	44225	CY90		City of Rotorua
☐ ZK-NZM	BAe 146-300	E3173	VH-EWJ	0090	0195	4 LY ALF502R-5	44225	CY90		Queenstown
☐ ZK-NZN	BAe 146-300	E3177	VH-EWL	0090	0297	4 LY ALF502R-5	44225	CY90		

ANSETT NEW ZEALAND REGIONAL = TNZ (Rex Aviation (NZ), Ltd dba) — Wellington

PO Box 14197, Kilbirnie, Wellington 6030, New Zealand ☎ (4) 387 29 07 Tx: none Fax: (4) 387 24 14 SITA: n/a
F: 1987 92 Head: John W. Lanham Net: n/a All aircraft are operated on behalf of ANSETT NEW ZEALAND (in full such colours & titles) using AN flight numbers.

☐ ZK-REU	Embraer 110P1 Bandeirante (EMB-110P1)	110298	VH-LSE	0080	1195	2 PWC PT6A-34	5670	Y15		
☐ ZK-REV	Embraer 110P1 Bandeirante (EMB-110P1)	110274	P2-NAL	0080	1093	2 PWC PT6A-34	5670	Y15		
☐ ZK-REZ	Embraer 110P1 Bandeirante (EMB-110P1)	110417	ZK-TRL	0083	0296	2 PWC PT6A-34	5670	Y15		
☐ ZK-REW	BAe 3201 Jetstream 32EP	968	N968AE	0092	0499	2 GA TPE331-12UAR-704H	7350	Y19		lsf BAMT / cvtd 32
☐ ZK-REX	BAe 3201 Jetstream 32EP	969	N969AE	0092	0499	2 GA TPE331-12UAR-704H	7350	Y19		lsf BAMT / cvtd 32
☐ ZK-REY	BAe 3201 Jetstream 32EP	946	N946AE	0091	0399	2 GA TPE331-12UAR-704H	7350	Y19		lsf BAMT / cvtd 32

AQUATIC & VINTAGE AIRWAYS, Ltd — Auckland-Int'l & Bay of Violence SPB

155 Trig Road, Whitford, Auckland 1750, New Zealand ☎ (9) 530 84 56 Tx: none Fax: (9) 402 83 88 SITA: n/a
F: 1991 n/a Head: Grant Harnish Net: n/a

☐ ZK-AVM	Grumman G-44A Widgeon	1466	P2-WET	0045	0796	2 CO IO-470-D	2359			Amphibian
☐ ZK-CFA	Grumman G-44A Widgeon	1439	N9096R	0045	0894	2 CO IO-470-D	2359			Amphibian
☐ ZK-CGX	De Havilland DHC-2 Beaver I	1548		0064	0695	1 PW R-985	2313			

ARDMORE AIR CHARTER (Division of Ardmore Flying School, Ltd) — Auckland-Ardmore

PO Box 744, Papakura 1730, New Zealand ☎ (9) 298 50 55 Tx: none Fax: (9) 298 30 07 SITA: n/a
F: 1978 n/a Head: Liz Needham Net: n/a Aircraft below MTOW 1361kg: Cessna 172, 177 & PA-38.

☐ ZK-JED	Beech Duchess 76	ME-386	N752BK	0080	1294	2 LY O-360-A1G6D	1769			

ASHWORTH HELICOPTERS, Ltd — Gisborne

PO Box 332, Gisborne 3815, New Zealand ☎ (6) 867 71 28 Tx: none Fax: (6) 867 11 78 SITA: n/a
F: 1981 n/a Head: Wayne Ashworth Net: n/a Aircraft below MTOW 1361kg: Hughes 369HS (500C).

☐ ZK-HHG	MD Helicopters MD 500D (Hughes 369D)	1160030D	BPS-9	0076	0393	1 AN 250-C20B	1361			
☐ ZK-HHC	Bell 206B JetRanger	1715	N101HC	0075	0696	1 AN 250-C20	1451			

ASPIRING AIR, Ltd = OI (formerly Aspiring Air (1981), Ltd) — Wanaka

PO Box 68, Wanaka 9192, New Zealand ☎ (3) 443 79 43 Tx: none Fax: (3) 443 89 49 SITA: n/a
F: 1981 5 Head: Barrie McHaffie Net: n/a

☐ ZK-EVO	Britten-Norman BN-2A-26 Islander	785	5W-FAQ	0076		2 LY O-540-E4C5	2994			
☐ ZK-EVT	Britten-Norman BN-2A-26 Islander	152	YJ-RV19	0070	0490	2 LY O-540-E4C5	2994			Lake Wanaka

ASSOCIATED AIRLINES, Ltd — Paraparaumu

PO Box 1594, Paraparaumu 6450, New Zealand ☎ (4) 298 62 94 Tx: none Fax: (4) 297 09 10 SITA: n/a
F: 1976 8 Head: Russell S. Jenkins Net: n/a Aircraft below MTOW 1361 kg: Cessna 152, 172 & Piper PA-28.

☐ ZK-NSN	Piper PA-31-310 Navajo	31-687	VH-CFP	0070	0197	2 LY TIO-540-A1A	2948			
☐ ZK-DCN	Cessna 421C Golden Eagle III	421C0688	N2654B	0079		2 CO GTSIO-520-L	3379			

AUCKLAND REGIONAL RESCUE HELICOPTER = WPR (Auckland Regional Rescue Helicopter Trust dba / formerly Helicopter Rescue Service, Ltd) — Auckland-Mechanics Bay

PO Box 2252, Auckland 1000, New Zealand ☎ (9) 309 68 93 Tx: none Fax: (9) 309 21 22 SITA: n/a
F: 1990 20 Head: I.S. Watson ICAO: WESTPAC RESCUE Net: n/a

☐ ZK-HPA	Eurocopter (Aerosp.) AS355F1 Tw.Squirrel	5010	N813CE	0080	0097	2 AN 250-C20F	2400	EMS		opb The Helicopter Line
☐ ZK-FOP	Piper PA-31-350 Navajo Chieftain	31-7405227	N888SG	0074		2 LY TIO-540-J2BD	3175	EMS		opb Airwork (NZ) Ltd
☐ ZK-HHV	Kawasaki (Eurocopter/MBB) BK117B-2	1022	JA9922	0088	1093	2 LY LTS101-750B.1	3350	EMS		opb The Helicopter Line / cvtd A-4
☐ ZK-POB	Fairchild (Swearingen) SA227AC Metro III	AC-606B	D-CABG	0085	0096	2 GA TPE331-11U-611G	7257	EMS		opb Airwork (NZ) Ltd

BACK COUNTRY HELICOPTERS, Ltd (formerly Maungawera Helicopters, Ltd) — Wanaka

Maungawera Road, RD 2, Wanaka 9192, New Zealand ☎ (3) 443 10 54 Tx: n/a Fax: (3) 443 10 51 SITA: n/a
F: n/a n/a Head: Harvey A. Hutton Net: n/a Aircraft below MTOW 1361kg: Robinson R22.

☐ ZK-HSR	MD Helicopters MD 500D (Hughes 369D)	1160024D	P2-AHN	0076	0193	1 AN 250-C20B	1361			

BAY OF ISLANDS AERO CLUB, (Inc.) — Kerikeri

PO Box 186, Kerikeri 0470, New Zealand ☎ (9) 407 84 00 Tx: none Fax: (9) 407 87 55 SITA: n/a
F: 1971 n/a Head: Ray Jefferis Net: n/a Aircraft below MTOW 1361kg: Cessna 172 & 177

☐ ZK-EXG	Cessna U206G Stationair 6 II	U20606459	N27330	0082	0197	1 CO IO-520-F	1633			

BECK HELICOPTERS, Ltd — Eltham

PO Box 81, Eltham 4751, New Zealand ☎ (6) 764 70 73 Tx: none Fax: (6) 764 70 70 SITA: n/a
F: 1973 n/a Head: Alan W. Beck Net: n/a

☐ ZK-HDU	Bell 206B JetRanger	1337	N59524	0074	1090	1 AN 250-C20	1451			
☐ ZK-HKO	Bell 206B JetRanger II	2140		0077	0077	1 AN 250-C20	1451			rebuilt 1996
☐ ZK-HHB	Bell UH-1B (204)	3114	N123MS	0065	1192	1 LY T53-L-13BA	3856			

BELLVIEW FLIGHT (Thomas D. Dick dba) — Christchurch

Hoskyns Road, RD5, Christchurch 8021, New Zealand ☎ (3) 358 75 73 Tx: none Fax: (3) 358 75 13 SITA: n/a
F: 1988 n/a Head: Thomas D. Dick Net: n/a

☐ ZK-TSD	Piper PA-34-200T Seneca II	34-8070356	ZK-DCQ	0080	0993	2 CO TSIO-360-EB	2073			

BUCKLEY AIR, Ltd = BUK — Auckland-Ardmore

PO Box 12804, Penrose, Auckland 1135, New Zealand ☎ (9) 299 66 79 Tx: none Fax: (9) 573 00 00 SITA: n/a
F: 1995 4 Head: Darren Mendoza ICAO: BUCKLEY Net: n/a

☐ ZK-SMB	Partenavia P.68C	308	G-JVJA	0084		2 LY IO-360-A1B6	1990			
☐ ZK-MVY	AAC (Piper) Aerostar 600A	60-0649-7961206	VH-MVY	0079	0295	2 LY IO-540-K1J5	2495			

CANTERBURY AERO CLUB, Inc. — Christchurch

PO Box 14-006, Christchurch Airport 8030, New Zealand ☎ (3) 359 21 21 Tx: n/a Fax: (3) 359 26 21 SITA: n/a
F: 1928 20 Head: Chris Bell Net: http://www.webwings.co.nz.cac Aircraft below MTOW 1361kg: PA-28 & PA-38

☐ ZK-DCO	Piper PA-34-200T Seneca II	34-8070354	N8263L	0080	0893	2 CO TSIO-360-EB	2073	EMS		
☐ ZK-MIR	Partenavia P.68C	227	VH-UUG	0080	0695	2 LY IO-360-A1B6	1990	EMS		
☐ ZK-NMK	Partenavia P.68B	114	VH-IYA	0077		2 LY IO-360-A1B6	1960	EMS		

CANTERBURY HELICOPTERS, Ltd — Rangiora

Claxby, R D 1, Rangiora 8254, New Zealand ☎ (3) 312 67 10 Tx: n/a Fax: (3) 312 67 10 SITA: n/a
F: 1980 n/a Head: Simon Spencer-Bower Net: n/a Aircraft below MTOW 1361kg: Robinson R22 & R44

☐ ZK-HYY	MD Helicopters MD 500D (Hughes 369D)	600739D	N913EG	0080	1195	1 AN 250-C20B	1361			
☐ ZK-HWQ	Bell 206B JetRanger	846	N40AL	0072	1095	1 AN 250-C20	1451			

670 registration type of aircraft cn/fn ex/ex* mfd del powered by mtow kg configuration selcal name/fln/specialitites/remarks

CHRISTIAN AVIATION (David William & Margaret Robyn Brown dba) — Auckland-Ardmore

PO Box 95, Takanini 1730, New Zealand ☎ (9) 298 98 46 Tx: none Fax: (9) 298 07 54 SITA: n/a
F: 1981 ☩ 10 Head: David W. Brown Net: http://www.chn.co.nz

☐ ZK-FMW	Piper PA-34-200T Seneca II	*34-8070181*	*N8186S*	*0080*		*2 CO TSIO-360-EB*	*2073*			
☐ ZK-CAL	Piper PA-31-350 Navajo Chieftain	*31-7405241*	*ZK-EVD*	*0074*		*2 LY TIO-540-J2BD*	*3175*			
☐ ZK-CAM	Piper PA-31-310 Navajo	*31-261*	*ZK-DCE*	*0068*		*2 LY TIO-540-A1A*	*2948*			
☐ ZK-RUR	Piper PA-42-1000 Cheyenne 400LS	*42-5527015*	*N42MD*	*0084*	*0496*	*2 GA TPE331-14-801A/B*	*5466*			*lsf Rural Aviation (1963) Ltd*

COASTWIDE HELICOPTERS, Ltd — Barrytown

1 Paroa Terrace, Paroa, Greymouth 7870, New Zealand ☎ (3) 762 61 17 Tx: none Fax: (3) 731 18 92 SITA: n/a
F: 1987 ☩ 2 Head: Christopher J. Cowan Net: n/a

☐ ZK-HUW	MD Helicopters MD 500D (Hughes 369D)	*1280415D*	*N58273*	*0078*		*1 AN 250-C20B*	*1361*			

CORPORATE AIR SERVICES, Ltd — Auckland-Ardmore

PO Box 62507, Auckland 1130, New Zealand ☎ (9) 529 99 60 Tx: none Fax: (9) 529 99 61 SITA: n/a
F: 1998 ☩ n/a Head: Edward Dougherty Net: n/a

☐ ZK-JGJ	Cessna 310B	*35738*	*VH-ATQ*	*0058*	*0399*	*2 CO O-470-M*	*2131*			

EAGLE AIRWAYS, Ltd (Air New Zealand Link) (Subsidiary of Air New Zealand) — Hamilton

Private Bag 3048, Hamilton 2020, New Zealand ☎ (7) 838 95 99 Tx: n/a Fax: (7) 838 95 05 SITA: n/a
F: 1969 ☩ 240 Head: John Hambleton Net: n/a All aircraft are operated as AIR NEW ZEALAND LINK (in full such colours & both titles), a commuter system to provide feeder connection NZ major hubs, using NZ flight numbers.

☐ ZK-DCH	Embraer 110P1 Bandeirante (EMB-110P1)	*110364*	*G-BLVG*	*0081*	*1095*	*2 PWC PT6A-34*	*5670*	*Y15*		
☐ ZK-ERU	Embraer 110P1 Bandeirante (EMB-110P1)	*110267*	*PT-SBF**	*0080*	*0580*	*2 PWC PT6A-34*	*5670*	*Y15*		
☐ ZK-FHX	Embraer 110P1 Bandeirante (EMB-110P1)	*110225*	*DQ-FCW*	*0079*	*0384*	*2 PWC PT6A-34*	*5670*	*Y15*		
☐ ZK-JCM	Embraer 110P1 Bandeirante (EMB-110P1)	*110305*	*N201AE*	*0081*	*1088*	*2 PWC PT6A-34*	*5670*	*Y15*		
☐ ZK-KIP	Embraer 110P1 Bandeirante (EMB-110P1)	*110286*	*VH-KIP*	*0080*	*0587*	*2 PWC PT6A-34*	*5670*	*Y15*		
☐ ZK-LBC	Embraer 110P1 Bandeirante (EMB-110P1)	*110345*	*N90427*	*0081*	*1088*	*2 PWC PT6A-34*	*5670*	*Y15*		
☐ ZK-MAS	Embraer 110P1 Bandeirante (EMB-110P1)	*110214*	*XC-COY*	*0079*	*1189*	*2 PWC PT6A-34*	*5670*	*Y15*		
☐ ZK-NDC	Embraer 110P1 Bandeirante (EMB-110P1)	*110379*	*G-OJAY*	*0082*	*1095*	*2 PWC PT6A-34*	*5670*	*Y15*		
☐ ZK-TRM	Embraer 110P1 Bandeirante (EMB-110P1)	*110436*	*N132EM*	*0083*	*0494*	*2 PWC PT6A-34*	*5670*	*Y15*		
☐ ZK-NSW	Fairchild (Swearingen) SA227AC Metro III	*AC-508*	*N31077*	*0083*	*0696*	*2 GA TPE331-11U-611G*	*6577*	*Y19*		
☐ ZK-NSX	Fairchild (Swearingen) SA227AC Metro III	*AC-542*	*N7063X*	*0083*	*0696*	*2 GA TPE331-11U-611G*	*6577*	*Y19*		
☐ ZK-OAA	Fairchild (Swearingen) SA227AC Metro III	*AC-546*	*N31108*	*0083*	*0591*	*2 GA TPE331-11U-611G*	*6577*	*Y19*		*cvtd SA227AT*
☐ ZK-PBA	Fairchild (Swearingen) SA227AC Metro III	*AC-547*	*N3111D*	*0083*	*0691*	*2 GA TPE331-11U-611G*	*6577*	*Y19*		*cvtd SA227AT*
☐ ZK-RCA	Fairchild (Swearingen) SA227AC Metro III	*AC-637*	*N352AE*	*0086*	*0894*	*2 GA TPE331-11U-611G*	*6577*	*Y19*		
☐ ZK-SDA	Fairchild (Swearingen) SA227AC Metro III	*AC-641*	*N351AE*	*0086*	*0894*	*2 GA TPE331-11U-611G*	*6577*	*Y19*		

EASTERN BAY/LAKELAND HELICOPTERS (Peter M. Bradley dba) — Murapara

Golf Road, RD 1, Murapara 3272, New Zealand ☎ (7) 349 47 08 Tx: none Fax: (7) 349 48 16 SITA: n/a
F: 1977 ☩ n/a Head: Peter M. Bradley Net: n/a

☐ ZK-HIX	Bell 206B JetRanger	*869*	*VH-YDA*	*0072*	*0194*	*1 AN 250-C20*	*1451*			
☐ ZK-HSX	Bell UH-1H (205)	*10320*	*N375AV*	*0068*	*0399*	*1 LY T53-L-13*	*4309*			

EMENY Helicopter Services (B.A. & J.C. Emeny Ltd dba) — New Plymouth

PO Box 70, Inglewood 4651, New Zealand ☎ (6) 756 72 49 Tx: n/a Fax: none SITA: n/a
F: 1989 ☩ 30 Head: Brett A. Emeny Net: n/a Aircraft below MTOW 1361kg: Bell 47G, Hughes 269C (300C) & Kawasaki-Bell 47G3B.

☐ ZK-HFC	Bell 206B JetRanger	*664*	*VH-XDM*	*0071*	*0293*	*1 AN 250-C20*	*1451*			*cvtd 206A*
☐ ZK-HXQ	Bell 206B JetRanger III	*3077*		*0080*		*1 AN 250-C20B*	*1451*			
☐ ZK-HYF	Bell 206B JetRanger	*422*	*N10SZ*	*0069*	*1191*	*1 AN 250-C20*	*1451*			*cvtd 206A*
☐ ZK-HSB	Sikorsky S-55BT	*551148*	*N6704*	*0057*	*0993*	*1 GA TPE331-3U-303N*	*3266*			*cvtd S-55B*
☐ ZK-HSC	Sikorsky S-55BT	*55238*	*N17754*	*0055*	*0495*	*1 GA TPE331-3U-303N*	*3266*			*cvtd S-55B*
☐ ZK-HSF	Garlick-Bell UH-1B (204)	*610*	*N80WF*	*0062*	*0595*	*1 LY T53-L-13*	*3856*			*cvtd Bell UH-1B*

FARAM HELICOPTERS, Ltd — Gisborne

PO Box 1019, Gisborne 3815, New Zealand ☎ (6) 868 85 00 Tx: none Fax: (6) 868 86 60 SITA: n/a
F: 1987 ☩ 6 Head: Jonathan G. Faram Net: n/a

☐ ZK-HHT	MD Helicopters MD 500D (Hughes 369D)	*790539D*	*C-GTZO*	*0079*		*1 AN 250-C20B*	*1361*			
☐ ZK-HJF	MD Helicopters MD 500D (Hughes 369D)	*510963D*		*0081*		*1 AN 250-C20B*	*1361*			
☐ ZK-HNR	MD Helicopters MD 500D (Hughes 369D)	*890580D*	*VH-LYM*	*0079*		*1 AN 250-C20B*	*1361*			
☐ ZK-HSD	MD Helicopters MD 500D (Hughes 369D)	*1090595D*		*0079*	*1295*	*1 AN 250-C20B*	*1361*			

FIORDLAND HELICOPTERS, Ltd — Te Anau

PO Box 180, Te Anau 9681, New Zealand ☎ (3) 249 75 75 Tx: none Fax: (3) 249 75 95 SITA: n/a
F: 1985 ☩ n/a Head: Kim E. Hollows Net: http://www.fiordlandhelicopters.co.nz

☐ ZK-HJN	MD Helicopters MD 530F (Hughes 369FF)	*0003F*	*P2-AHM*	*0084*	*0294*	*1 AN 250-C30*	*1406*			

FLIGHT 2000, Ltd — Auckland

Private Bag 14, Papakura 1733, New Zealand ☎ (9) 297 72 99 Tx: none Fax: (9) 298 23 25 SITA: n/a
F: 1998 ☩ n/a Head: n/a Net: n/a Flights are operated under the AOC of Lakeside Aviation.

☐ ZK-DAK	Boeing (Douglas) DC-3C (C-47B-10-DK)	*26480*	*VH-SBT*	*0044*	*0399*	*2 PW R-1830-92*	*12202*	*30 Pax*		

FLIGHT Corporation Ltd = FCP (Associated with Nelson Aviation College) — Nelson

PO Box 2196, Stoke, New Zealand ☎ (3) 547 81 75 Tx: none Fax: (3) 547 20 73 SITA: n/a
F: 1991 ☩ 6 Head: Cameron Rodgers ICAO: FLIGHTCORP Net: n/a

☐ ZK-JDH	Piper PA-34-200T Seneca II	*34-7970041*	*VH-IEE*	*0079*		*2 CO TSIO-360-EB*	*2073*			
☐ ZK-DOM	Piper PA-31-310 Navajo B	*31-777*	*VH-BZW*	*0072*		*2 LY TIO-540-A2C*	*2948*			
☐ ZK-KVW	Piper PA-31-350 Navajo Chieftain	*31-7752004*	*VH-JLC*	*0077*	*1196*	*2 LY TIO-540-J2BD*	*3175*			

FOX GLACIER HELICOPTER SERVICES — Fox Glacier

PO Box 40, Fox Glacier 7951, New Zealand ☎ (3) 751 08 66 Tx: none Fax: (3) 751 08 53 SITA: n/a
F: 1986 ☩ n/a Head: James P. Scott Net: n/a

☐ ZK-HBI	Eurocopter (Aerosp.) AS350B Squirrel	*2257*	*JA9851*	*0089*		*1 TU Arriel 1B*	*1950*			
☐ ZK-HYC	Eurocopter (Aerosp.) AS350D Squirrel	*1344*	*N5771N*	*0080*	*1298*	*1 LY LTS101-600A.3*	*1950*			

FREEDOM AIR INTERNATIONAL = FOM (South Pacific Air Charters, Ltd dba / Subsidiary of The Mount Cook Group, Ltd) — Auckland

PO Box 109698 New Market, Auckland 1001, New Zealand ☎ (9) 912 69 80 Tx: n/a Fax: (9) 912 69 98 SITA: n/a
F: 1995 ☩ n/a Head: Wayne Dodge ICAO: FREE AIR Net: http://www.clearfield.co.nz/freedom/

☐ ZK-FDM	Boeing 737-3M8	*25016 / 2004*	*HB-IIC*	*0291*	*0397*	*2 CFMI CFM56-3B2*	*63276*	*Y141*		*lsf Khassan Ltd (Ireland)*

GARDEN CITY HELICOPTERS, Ltd — Christchurch

PO Box 14-147, Christchurch 8030, New Zealand ☎ (3) 358 43 60 Tx: n/a Fax: (3) 358 41 50 SITA: n/a
F: 1985 ☩ 8 Head: John S. Currie Net: n/a Aircraft below MTOW 1361 kg: Enstrom 280FX, Hughes 369HS & Robinson R22.

☐ ZK-HGH	Eurocopter (Aerosp.) AS350B Squirrel	*1443*	*N144AE*	*0081*	*0489*	*1 TU Arriel 1B*	*1950*			
☐ ZK-HGT	Eurocopter (Aerosp.) AS350B Squirrel	*1609*	*JA9328*	*0082*	*0495*	*1 TU Arriel 1B*	*1950*			
☐ ZK-HQT	Eurocopter (Aerosp.) AS350B Squirrel	*1729*	*JA9359*	*0083*	*0595*	*1 TU Arriel 1B*	*1950*			
☐ ZK-HUG	Eurocopter (Aerosp.) AS350B Squirrel	*2038*	*JA9492*	*0087*	*0197*	*1 TU Arriel 1B*	*1950*			
☐ ZK-HJC	Kawasaki (Eurocopter/MBB) BK117B-1	*1061*	*JA6626*	*0090*	*0496*	*2 LY LTS101-750B.1*	*3200*			
☐ ZK-KBF	Cessna 421B Golden Eagle	*421B0943*	*VH-ADG*	*0075*	*1094*	*2 CO GTSIO-520-H*	*3379*			

GLACIER HELICOPTERS, Ltd — Fox Glacier & Franz Josef Glacier

PO Box 34, Fox Glacier 7951, New Zealand ☎ (3) 752 07 55 Tx: 4212 goldinn nz Fax: (3) 752 07 78 SITA: n/a
F: 1970 ☩ 19 Head: Graeme Catley Net: n/a Aircraft below MTOW 1361 kg: Hughes 269C (300C).

☐ ZK-HZE	Bell 206B JetRanger	*769*	*C-FTPG*	*0072*	*1096*	*1 AN 250-C20*	*1451*			*lsf Helicopters New Zealand*
☐ ZK-HJE	Eurocopter (Aerosp.) AS350D Squirrel	*1307*		*0080*	*0593*	*1 LY LTS101-600A.3*	*1950*			*lsf Helicopters New Zealand*
☐ ZK-HJQ	Eurocopter (Aerosp.) AS350D Squirrel	*1295*	*C-FBXE*	*0080*	*0594*	*1 LY LTS101-600A.3*	*1950*			*lsf Helicopters New Zealand*

GLENORCHY AIR SERVICES & Tourist Co, Ltd — Queenstown

91 McBride Street, Queenstown 9195, New Zealand ☎ (3) 442 22 07 Tx: none Fax: (3) 442 28 07 SITA: n/a
F: 1992 ☩ n/a Head: Robert J. Rutherford Net: n/a

☐ ZK-CHK	Cessna 185C Skywagon	*185-0755*	*N5855T*	*0064*	*0193*	*1 CO IO-470-F*	*1451*			
☐ ZK-DOJ	Piper PA-32S-300C Cherokee SIX	*32S-40638*	*N4252R*	*0069*	*0696*	*1 LY IO-540-K1A5*	*1542*			
☐ ZK-WGO	Piper PA-32-300 Cherokee SIX	*32-7340146*	*VH-WGO*	*0073*	*0797*	*1 LY IO-540-K1A5*	*1542*			

GREAT BARRIER AIRLINES (Flight Operations), Ltd – GBA (formerly Great Barrier Airlines, Ltd) — Auckland-Int'l

PO Box 53-091, Auckland Airport 1030, New Zealand ☎ (9) 275 91 20 Tx: none Fax: (9) 275 91 20 SITA: n/a
F: 1983 ☩ 35 Head: Mark Roberts Net: n/a Aircraft below MTOW 1361 kg: Piper PA-28.

☐ ZK-CNS	Piper PA-32-260 Cherokee SIX	*32-686R*		*0066*		*1 LY O-540-E4B5*	*1542*			
☐ ZK-DDF	Piper PA-32-260 Cherokee SIX	*32-480*	*N3586W*	*0066*		*1 LY O-540-E4B5*	*1542*			
☐ ZK-ENZ	Piper PA-32-260B Cherokee SIX	*32-1117*	*ZK-DBP*	*0069*	*0297*	*1 LY O-540-E4B5*	*1542*			
☐ ZK-REA	Beech Duchess 76	*ME-313*	*VH-BKK*	*0080*	*0596*	*2 LY O-360-A1G6D*	*1769*			
☐ ZK-DMA	Partenavia P.68B	*68*	*G-BECJ*	*0076*	*1198*	*2 LY IO-360-A1B6*	*1960*			

671 registration type of aircraft cn/fn ex/ex* mfd del powered by mtow kg configuration selcal name/fln/specialitites/remarks

☐ ZK-ERA	Partenavia P.68B	123	VH-IYD	0077	1097	2 LY IO-360-A1B6	1960			
☐ ZK-LAL	Partenavia P.68B	70	VH-PNY	0076	1198	2 LY IO-360-A1B6	1960			
☐ ZK-PLA	Partenavia P.68B	86	A6-ALO	0076	0696	2 LY IO-360-A1B6	1960			
☐ ZK-FVD	Britten-Norman BN-2A-26 Islander	316	G-BJWN	0073	1289	2 LY O-540-E4C5	2994			
☐ ZK-WNZ	Britten-Norman BN-2A-27 Islander	278	N8021M	0071	0297	2 LY O-540-E4C5	2994			cvtd BN-2A-3
☐ ZK-VNA	Piper PA-31-310 Navajo	31-8212003	VH-AYS	0082	1198	2 LY TIO-540-A2C	2948			
☐ ZK-EHS	Cessna 402B	402B0217	N7SA	0072	0199	2 CO TSIO-520-E	2858			

HASTINGS AIR CHARTER (Division of Hawkes Bay & East Coast Aero Club Inc.) — **Hastings**

PO Box 2199, Hastings 4200, New Zealand ☎ (6) 879 84 66 Tx: none Fax: (6) 879 98 05 SITA: n/a
F: 1980 ✈ 10 Head: P.L.H. Kidd Net: http://www.airacademy.hs.co.nz Aircraft below MTOW 1361kg: Cessna 172, Piper PA-28 & PA-38.

☐ ZK-DCI	Piper PA-34-200 Seneca	34-7350317	N56321	0073		2 LY IO-360-C1E6	1814			
☐ ZK-DCM	Piper PA-34-200 Seneca	34-7250058	N1068U	0072		2 LY IO-360-C1E6	1814			
☐ ZK-RSQ	Piper PA-34-220T Seneca III	34-8333001	N8239D	0083	0995	2 CO TSIO-360-KB	2155			
☐ ZK-LWN	Piper PA-31-310 Navajo	31-8112056	N40938	0081	0695	2 LY TIO-540-A2C	2948			occ lsf Skyline Aviation

HELE-TRANZ, Ltd — **Auckland**

PO Box 460, Albany, Auckland 1309, New Zealand ☎ (9) 479 19 91 Tx: none Fax: (9) 479 63 17 SITA: n/a
F: 1989 ✈ n/a Head: Anthony H. Monk Net: n/a

☐ ZK-HST	Eurocopter (Aerosp.) AS350BA Squirrel	1646	ZK-HZR	0082		1 TU Arriel 1B	2100			cvtd AS350B

HELICOPTER SERVICES B.O.P., Ltd (Affiliated with Funnell Aviation Services, Ltd & Just Law No. 16, Ltd) — **Taupo**

PO Box 158, Taupo 2730, New Zealand ☎ (7) 378 80 74 Tx: none Fax: (7) 378 04 68 SITA: n/a
F: 1983 ✈ 3 Head: W. John Funnell Net: n/a

☐ ZK-HGI	Eurocopter (Aerosp.) AS350B Squirrel	1614	VH-HRS	0082	0197	1 TU Arriel 1B	1950			
☐ ZK-HNP	Eurocopter (Aerosp.) AS350BA Squirrel	1611		0082		1 TU Arriel 1B	2100			cvtd AS350B
☐ ZK-HZL	Eurocopter (Aerosp.) AS350BA Squirrel	1218	N3610D	0079		1 TU Arriel 1B	2100			cvtd AS350B
☐ ZK-HZN	Eurocopter (Aerosp.) AS350BA Squirrel	1815		0085	0991	1 TU Arriel 1B	2100			cvtd AS350B

HELICOPTERS NEW ZEALAND, Ltd – HNZ — **Nelson**

Private Bag 9, Nelson 7020, New Zealand ☎ (3) 547 52 55 Tx: none Fax: (3) 547 55 98 SITA: n/a
F: 1955 ✈ 21 Head: Brian McDonald Net: http://icair.iac.org.nz/logistics/hnz/heli.htm

☐ ZK-HPB	Agusta-Bell 206B JetRanger	8002	SE-HPB	0067	0299	1 AN 250-C20	1451			cvtd 206A
☐ ZK-HZE	Bell 206B JetRanger	769	C-FTPG	0072	0698	1 AN 250-C20	1451			lst Glacier Helicopters
☐ ZK-HBU	Eurocopter (Aerosp.) AS350B Squirrel	1558	SX-HBO	0082		1 TU Arriel 1B	1950			lst Lao Westcoast Helicopter
☐ ZK-HBV	Eurocopter (Aerosp.) AS350D Squirrel	1265	N3608R	0080	0199	1 LY LTS101-600A.2	1950			
☐ ZK-HBX	Eurocopter (Aerosp.) AS350D Squirrel	1391	N5774X	0080	0698	1 LY LTS101-600A.2	1950			
☐ ZK-HDK	Eurocopter (Aerosp.) AS350BA Squirrel	1466	F-ODVZ	0081		1 TU Arriel 1B	2100			lst Lao Westcoast Helicopter/cvtdAS350B
☐ ZK-HDQ	Eurocopter (Aerosp.) AS350B Squirrel	1932	VH-BHX	0086		1 AN 250-C30	1950			lst Lao Westcoast/cvtd TU Arriel AS350B
☐ ZK-HFB	Eurocopter (Aerosp.) AS350BA Squirrel	2486		0091	0991	1 TU Arriel 1B	2100			cvtd AS350B
☐ ZK-HFE	Eurocopter (Aerosp.) AS350BA Squirrel	2518		0091	0991	1 TU Arriel 1B	2100			cvtd AS350B
☐ ZK-HJE	Eurocopter (Aerosp.) AS350D Squirrel	1307		0080	0698	1 LY LTS101-600A.3	1950			lst Glacier Helicopters
☐ ZK-HJQ	Eurocopter (Aerosp.) AS350D Squirrel	1295	C-FBXE	0080	0698	1 LY LTS101-600A.3	1950			lst Glacier Helicopters
☐ ZK-HJY	Eurocopter (Aerosp.) AS350BA Squirrel	2005	JA9463	0087	0098	1 TU Arriel 1B	2100			cvtd AS350B
☐ ZK-HKR	Eurocopter (Aerosp.) AS350D Squirrel	1234	N3606X	0080	0698	1 LY LTS101-600A.3	1950			
☐ ZK-HNK	Eurocopter (Aerosp.) AS350B2 Squirrel	2349	VH-WCS	0090	1096	1 TU Arriel 1D1	2250			lst Lao Westcoast Helicopter
☐ ZK-HNL	Eurocopter (Aerosp.) AS350B Squirrel	1550		0082		1 TU Arriel 1B	1950			lst Lao Westcoast Helicopter
☐ ZK-HNQ	Eurocopter (Aerosp.) AS350BA Squirrel	1972	JA9450	0086	0199	1 TU Arriel 1B	2100			cvtd AS350B
☐ ZK-HNU	Eurocopter (Aerosp.) AS350BA Squirrel	1120	N3595G	0081	0698	1 TU Arriel 1B	2100			cvtd AS350B
☐ ZK-HNZ	Eurocopter (Aerosp.) AS350B2 Squirrel	2463	HB-XVT	0091	1297	1 TU Arriel 1D1	2250			lst Lao Westcoast Helicopter
☐ ZK-HZK	Eurocopter (Aerosp.) AS350B Squirrel	1827		0085		1 TU Arriel 1B	1950			lst Lao Westcoast Helicopter
☐ ZK-HNO	Bell 212	31139	VH-BQH	0080		2 PWC PT6T-3B TwinPac	5080			
☐ ZK-HNI	Bell 412SP	33204	9M-AYW	0089	0199	2 PWC PT6T-3B TwinPac	5398			

HELICOPTERS OTAGO, Ltd (formerly Beck Aviation, Ltd) — **Dunedin**

PO Box 88, Mosgiel, Dunedin 9032, New Zealand ☎ (3) 489 73 22 Tx: none Fax: (3) 489 77 32 SITA: n/a
F: n/a ✈ n/a Head: Graeme Gale Net: n/a

☐ ZK-HWI	Bell 206B JetRanger	1685	C-GQYU	0075	0194	1 AN 250-C20	1451			
☐ ZK-HLU	Kawasaki (Eurocopter/MBB) BK117A-4	1021	JA9908	0088	0199	2 LY LTS101-650B.1	3200			

HELI HARVEST, Ltd (Joint venture of Helicopter Services B.O.P. Ltd & Rural Aviation (1963) Ltd) — **Taupo**

PO Box 158, Taupo 2730, New Zealand ☎ (7) 378 80 74 Tx: none Fax: (7) 378 04 68 SITA: n/a
F: 1993 ✈ n/a Head: W. John Funnell Net: n/a

☐ ZK-HUE	Bell UH-1L (204)	6046	N9770N	0067	0093	1 LY T53-L-13	3856			
☐ RA-22503	Mil Mi-8MTV-1	96078		0093	0098	2 IS TV3-117MT	13000			lsf VZL
☐ RA-25481	Mil Mi-8MTV-1	95626	CCCP-25481	0091	1293	2 IS TV3-117MT	13000			lsf TMN
☐ RA-25746	Mil Mi-8MTV-1	96121	CCCP-25746	0093	0098	2 IS TV3-117VM	13000	Utility		lsf VZL

HELIMAC HELICOPTERS, Ltd — **Oamaru**

RD 80, Oamaru 8921, New Zealand ☎ (3) 434 56 19 Tx: none Fax: (3) 439 56 56 SITA: n/a
F: 1988 ✈ n/a Head: John Oakes Net: n/a Aircraft below MTOW 1361kg: Hughes 269C (300C) & 369HS (500C)

☐ ZK-HWH	MD Helicopters MD 500D (Hughes 369D)	170072D	N8361F	0077	0496	1 AN 250-C20B	1361			

HELIPRO = HPR (Rick Lucas Helicopters Ltd dba) — **Palmerston North**

PO Box 7004, Palmerston North 5315, New Zealand ☎ (4) 472 15 50 Tx: none Fax: (4) 472 14 40 SITA: n/a
F: 1985 ✈ 10 Head: Rick Lucas ICAO: HELIPRO Net: n/a Aircraft below MTOW 1361kg: Hiller UH-12E, Hughes 369HS (500C) & Robinson R22

☐ ZK-HYD	Eurocopter (Aerosp.) AS350D Squirrel	1258	N36079	0080	1196	1 LY LTS101-600A.3	1950			
☐ ZK-HYO	Eurocopter (Aerosp.) AS350D Squirrel	1186	N155EH	0079	0197	1 LY LTS101-600A.3	1950			
☐ ZK-HYW	Eurocopter (Aerosp.) AS350D Squirrel	1420	N5782G	0080	0295	1 LY LTS101-600A.2	1950			
☐ ZK-HYB	Kawasaki (Eurocopter/MBB) BK117B-1	1034	JA9975	0089	0197	2 LY LTS101-750B.1	3200			
☐ ZK-HVY	Bell UH-1F (204)	7095	N2191J	0066	0596	1 GE T58-GE-3	3856			
☐ ZK-HVZ	Bell TH-1F (204)	7322	N224MS	0067	0596	1 GE T58-GE-3	3856			

HELIWING, Ltd (formerly Heliwork (East Cape), Ltd) — **Whakatane**

PO Box 498, Whakatane 3080, New Zealand ☎ (7) 312 55 55 Tx: none Fax: (7) 312 55 53 SITA: n/a
F: 1988 ✈ 3 Head: Denis L.R. Hartley Net: n/a

☐ ZK-HLC	Bell 206B JetRanger	1320	PK-EBE	0074	0495	1 AN 250-C20	1451			
☐ ZK-HLG	Bell 206B JetRanger III	2254		0077	0889	1 AN 250-C20B	1451			cvtd II

ISLAND AIR CHARTERS (Paul D. Ensor dba) — **Tauranga**

101 Aerodrome Road, Mount Maunganui 3002, New Zealand ☎ (7) 575 57 95 Tx: none Fax: none SITA: n/a
F: 1994 ✈ n/a Head: Paul D. Ensor Net: n/a

☐ ZK-DRD	Cessna P206 Super Skylane	P206-0135	F-OCFB	0065		1 CO IO-520-A	1497			
☐ ZK-SUN	Cessna TU206A Turbo Skywagon	U206-0511	ZK-MAP	0066	1196	1 CO TSIO-520-C	1633			

KAIKOURA HELICOPTERS (James P. Scott dba) — **Kaikoura**

PO Box 5, Kaikoura 8280, New Zealand ☎ (3) 319 66 09 Tx: none Fax: (3) 319 68 14 SITA: n/a
F: 1990 ✈ n/a Head: James P. Scott Net: n/a Aircraft below MTOW 1361kg: Hughes 369HS (500C)

☐ ZK-HNJ	MD Helicopters MD 500D (Hughes 369D)	1280406D	VH-PPD	0078	0596	1 AN 250-C20B	1361			
☐ ZK-HBO	Bell 206B JetRanger	570	N8190J	0070	0596	1 AN 250-C20	1451			cvtd 206A
☐ ZK-HHM	Eurocopter (Aerosp.) AS350B Squirrel	1076	JA9229	0079	0997	1 TU Arriel 1B	1950			

KAPITI DIRECT AIR CHARTER (Kapiti Districts Aero Club, (Inc.) dba) — **Paraparaumu**

PO Box 92, Paraparaumu 6450, New Zealand ☎ (4) 298 65 36 Tx: n/a Fax: (4) 298 65 34 SITA: n/a
F: 1982 ✈ n/a Head: Kevin Henderson Net: n/a Aircraft below MTOW 1361kg: Cessna 172, DH82A, Hughes 269C (300C) & Piper PA-28

☐ ZK-MIE	Piper PA-34-200T Seneca II	34-8170056		0081	0397	2 CO TSIO-360-EB	2073			

KITTO HELICOPTERS, Ltd — **Balclutha**

PO Box 199, Balclutha 9200, New Zealand ☎ (3) 418 01 58 Tx: none Fax: (3) 418 17 66 SITA: n/a
F: 1981 ✈ 3 Head: William G. Kitto Net: n/a

☐ ZK-HTO	Bell 206B JetRanger III	2265	N1689Z	0077		1 AN 250-C20B	1451			
☐ ZK-CGC	Cessna 185C Skywagon	185-0680	N2680Z	0064		1 CO IO-470-F	1451			

MAINLAND AIR SERVICES, Ltd — **Dunedin**

Fletchers Road, RD1, Milton 9250, New Zealand ☎ (3) 486 22 00 Tx: none Fax: (3) 486 22 00 SITA: n/a
F: 1991 ✈ 4 Head: Jeff McMillan Net: n/a Aircraft below MTOW 1361kg: Cessna 152 / 172 & 182.

☐ ZK-ROC	Piper PA-34-200 Seneca	34-7350084	N15668	0073	1196	2 LY IO-360-C1E6	1905			
☐ ZK-TBF	Piper PA-34-200T Seneca II	34-8070087	N3575Q	0080	0192	2 CO TSIO-360-EB	2073			

672 registration type of aircraft cn/fn ex/ex* mfd del powered by mtow kg configuration selcal name/fln/specialitites/remarks

MARINE HELICOPTERS, Ltd (Affiliated with Farm Helicopters, Ltd) — **Auckland-Ardmore**

PO Box 257, Papakura 1733, New Zealand ☎ (9) 299 91 80 Tx: none Fax: (9) 299 93 10 SITA: n/a
F: 1965 ⁂ 32 Head: Boyce C. Barrow Net: n/a Aircraft below MTOW 1361kg: Hughes 269C (300C) & 369HS (500C).

☐ ZK-HMG	MD Helicopters MD 500D (Hughes 369D)	990558D	P2-HBC	0079		1 AN 250-C20B	1361			
☐ ZK-HTX	Bell 206B JetRanger	1615	9M-AUE	0075		1 AN 250-C20	1451			
☐ ZK-HTZ	Bell 206B JetRanger	1179	9M-ATP	0073		1 AN 250-C20	1451			
☐ ZK-HSK	Eurocopter (Aerosp.) SA315B Lama	2586	VR-HIQ	0079		1 TU Artouste IIIB1	1950			
☐ ZK-HKU	Eurocopter (Aerosp.) AS350D Squirrel	1388	N5774U	0080	0195	1 LY LTS101-600A.2	1950			
☐ ZK-HKV	Eurocopter (Aerosp.) AS350D Squirrel	1132	N3598F	0079	0195	1 LY LTS101-600A.2	1950			

MARLBOROUGH HELICOPTERS (1981), Ltd — **Blenheim**

PO Box 731, Blenheim 7300, New Zealand ☎ (3) 578 96 84 Tx: none Fax: (3) 578 01 94 SITA: n/a
F: 1981 ⁂ 5 Head: John Sinclair Net: n/a Aircraft below MTOW 1361kg: Robinson R22B.

☐ ZK-HYH	Bell 206B JetRanger III	3290	ZK-HGS	0081	0493	1 AN 250-C20B	1451			

MEDIFLIGHT (Chardonnay Aircraft Leasing, Ltd dba) — **Christchurch**

PO Box 8885, Riccarton, Christchurch 8034, New Zealand ☎ (3) 341 31 63 Tx: none Fax: (3) 341 31 64 SITA: n/a
F: 1996 ⁂ 4 Head: Rod Bird Net: n/a

☐ ZK-JAN	Piper PA-34-200T Seneca II	34-8070027		0080	0297	2 CO TSIO-360-EB	2073	EMS		
☐ ZK-MED	Piper PA-31P Pressurized Navajo	31P-7530009	N777MB	0074	0298	2 LY TIGO-541-E1A	3538	EMS		
☐ ZK-ZNZ	Piper PA-31P Pressurized Navajo	31P-7300168	G-WITT	0073	0997	2 LY TIGO-541-E1A	3538	EMS		

MILFORD HELICOPTERS (David J. Shanks dba) — **Milford Sound**

State Highway 94, RD 2, Te Anau 9681, New Zealand ☎ (3) 249 78 45 Tx: none Fax: (3) 249 78 65 SITA: n/a
F: 1988 ⁂ n/a Head: David J. Shanks Net: n/a

☐ ZK-HMN	MD Helicopters MD 500D (Hughes 369D)	470108D	P2-AHP	0077	0992	1 AN 250-C20B	1361			
☐ ZK-HKZ	Eurocopter (Aerosp.) AS350BA Squirrel	2211	JA9829	0089	1196	1 TU Arriel 1B	2100			cvtd AS350B

MILLER HELICOPTER SERVICES, Ltd — **Thames**

PO Box 569, Thames 2815, New Zealand ☎ (7) 868 12 79 Tx: none Fax: (7) 868 12 08 SITA: n/a
F: 1986 ⁂ 3 Head: Paul Miller Net: n/a Aircraft below MTOW 1361kg: Hughes 269C (300C).

☐ ZK-HJO	MD Helicopters MD 500D (Hughes 369D)	1070204D	VH-AJZ	0078	0797	1 AN 250-C20B	1361			

MOUNTAIN AIR (Commercial Helicopters, Ltd dba) — **Taumarunui**

PO Box 152, Taumarunui 2600, New Zealand ☎ (7) 895 88 20 Tx: none Fax: (7) 895 34 05 SITA: n/a
F: 1980 ⁂ 10 Head: Keith L. McKenzie Net: n/a Aircraft below MTOW 1361kg: Cessna 172

☐ ZK-HNT	MD Helicopters MD 500D (Hughes 369D)	590514D		0079		1 AN 250-C20B	1361			
☐ ZK-DOV	Cessna 206 Super Skywagon	206-0248	N5248U	0064		1 CO IO-520-A	1497			
☐ ZK-PIW	Piper PA-23-250 Aztec E	27-7305089	VH-RCI	0073	0993	2 LY IO-540-C4B5	2359			
☐ ZK-PIX	Piper PA-23-250 Aztec E	27-4738	N14174	0071	0792	2 LY IO-540-C4B5	2359			
☐ ZK-PIY	Britten-Norman BN-2A-20 Islander	344	JA5218	0072	1196	2 LY IO-540-K1B5	2858			
☐ ZK-PIZ	Britten-Norman BN-2A-26 Islander	2012	N2132M	0077	1295	2 LY O-540-E4C5	2994			

MOUNT COOK AIRLINE = NM / NZM (Air New Zealand Link) (Div. of The Mount Cook Group/Subs. of Air New Zealand) **Christchurch / Mount Cook / Queenstown / Auckland**

MOUNT COOK AIRLINE

PO Box 14-020, Christchurch 8020, New Zealand ☎ (3) 435 18 49 Tx: 40073 airline nz Fax: (3) 435 18 86 SITA: CHCZVNM
F: 1921 ⁂ 220 Head: John Whittaker IATA: 445 ICAO: MOUNTCOOK Net: http://www.clearfield.co.nz/mount_cook/
All ATR72 aircraft are operated as AIR NEW ZEALAND LINK (in full such colors & both titles), a commuter system to provide feeder connection at NZ major hubs, using NZ flight numbers.

☐ ZK-MCC	ATR 72-212	464	F-WWLR*	0095	0995	2 PWC PW127	21500	Y66		
☐ ZK-MCL	ATR 72-212	465	F-WWLT*	0095	1095	2 PWC PW127	21500	Y66		
☐ ZK-MCQ	ATR 72-212	453	F-WWLB*	0095	1195	2 PWC PW127	21500	Y66		
☐ ZK-MCS	ATR 72-212	454	F-WWLI*	0095	1195	2 PWC PW127	21500	Y66		
☐ ZK-MCW	ATR 72-212	458	F-WWLO*	0095	1295	2 PWC PW127	21500	Y66		
☐ ZK-MCX	ATR 72-212	460	F-WWLH*	0096	0196	2 PWC PW127	21500	Y66		
☐ ZK-MCY	ATR 72-212	463	F-WWLQ*	0096	0296	2 PWC PW127	21500	Y66		
☐ ZK-	ATR 72-500 (72-212A)	597	F-WWEO*			2 PWC PW127F	22500	Y66		oo-delivery 1099
☐ ZK-	ATR 72-500 (72-212A)					2 PWC PW127F	22500	Y66		oo-delivery 1199
☐ ZK-	ATR 72-500 (72-212A)					2 PWC PW127F	22500	Y66		oo-delivery 1199
☐ ZK-	ATR 72-500 (72-212A)					2 PWC PW127F	22500	Y66		oo-delivery 1299
☐ ZK-	ATR 72-500 (72-212A)					2 PWC PW127F	22500	Y66		oo-delivery 1299
☐ ZK-	ATR 72-500 (72-212A)					2 PWC PW127F	22500	Y66		oo-delivery 0100
☐ ZK-	ATR 72-500 (72-212A)					2 PWC PW127F	22500	Y66		oo-delivery 0100

MOUNTAIN VIEW HELICOPTERS, Ltd — **Motueka**

Williams Road, RD1, Upper Moutere, Motueka 7152, New Zealand ☎ (3) 526 68 30 Tx: none Fax: (3) 526 68 30 SITA: n/a
F: 1990 ⁂ n/a Head: D. & S. Deaker Net: n/a

☐ ZK-HQW	MD Helicopters MD 500D (Hughes 369D)	180253D	N4282X	0077		1 AN 250-C20B	1361			lsf pvt

NELSON AIR CHARTER, Ltd — **Nelson**

13 Calamaras Street, Nelson 7001, New Zealand ☎ (3) 547 28 43 Tx: n/a Fax: none SITA: n/a
F: n/a ⁂ n/a Head: n/a Net: n/a

☐ ZK-CVF	Cessna 185A Skywagon	185-0504	ZK-CTN	0062	1193	1 CO IO-470-F	1451			
☐ ZK-JGI	Cessna A185E Skywagon	18501989		0072	0596	1 CO IO-520-D	1520			

NELSON HELICOPTERS, Ltd — **Nelson**

PO Box 3, Wakefield, Nelson 7000, New Zealand ☎ (3) 541 81 78 Tx: none Fax: (3) 541 95 00 SITA: n/a
F: 1983 ⁂ 7 Head: William J. Reid Net: n/a

☐ ZK-HNA	MD Helicopters MD 500E (Hughes 369E)	0477E	VH-BOL	0091	1295	1 AN 250-C20R2	1361			
☐ ZK-HSH	MD Helicopters MD 500D (Hughes 369D)	890562D	VH-TIY	0079		1 AN 250-C20B	1361			

NEW ZEALAND HELICOPTERS, Ltd (formerly Tarawera Helicopters, Ltd) — **Rotorua**

PO Box 6104, Rotorua 3215, New Zealand ☎ (7) 348 12 23 Tx: none Fax: (7) 349 37 09 SITA: n/a
F: 1978 ⁂ n/a Head: Steve Collins Net: http://www.new-zealand-heli-nzl-com Aircraft below MTOW 1361kg: Hughes 300C (269C)

☐ ZK-HRV	MD Helicopters MD 500D (Hughes 369D)	1192D	N5283C	0082	0498	1 AN 250-C20B	1361			

NEW ZEALAND HELIWORK (1988), Ltd — **Hamilton**

RD3, Cambridge 2351, New Zealand ☎ (7) 843 88 80 Tx: none Fax: (7) 843 88 84 SITA: n/a
F: 1986 ⁂ 4 Head: Dave J. Hogan Net: n/a Aircraft below MTOW 1361kg: Hiller UH-12E.

☐ ZK-HWN	Bell 206B JetRanger II	1995	C-GIZK	0076		1 AN 250-C20	1451			

NORTHERN AIR (North Island Air Services, Ltd dba) — **Auckland-Int'l**

PO Box 15-149, Auckland Airport 1030, New Zealand ☎ (9) 256 86 99 Tx: none Fax: (9) 256 86 97 SITA: n/a
F: 1995 ⁂ n/a Head: Ken Madden Net: n/a

☐ ZK-NPD	Cessna 210L Centurion II	21060331	N93270	0074	0595	1 CO IO-520-L	1724			

NORTHLAND EMERGENCY SERVICES Trust, Inc. — **Whangarei & Auckland-Int'l**

PO Box 8011, Kensington, Whangarei 0130, New Zealand ☎ (9) 437 21 40 Tx: none Fax: (9) 437 41 26 SITA: n/a
F: 1988 ⁂ 9 Head: Ian M. Webster Net: http://www.igrin.co.nz/deva/nest1.htm

☐ ZK-ISJ	Sikorsky S-76A	760012	VH-CFH	0079	0897	2 AN 250-C30	4763	EMS		opf St. John Ambulance

NORTH SHORE HELICOPTERS, Ltd — **Dairy Flat**

Postmans Road, RD4, Albany 1310, New Zealand ☎ (9) 426 82 87 Tx: none Fax: (9) 426 87 47 SITA: n/a
F: 1983 ⁂ 6 Head: Larry K. Bennett Net: n/a Aircraft below MTOW 1361kg: Robinson R22.

☐ ZK-HTC	Bell 206B JetRanger	1659	N90184	0075		1 AN 250-C20	1451			lsf Nimbus Properties Ltd
☐ ZK-HAF	Eurocopter (Aerosp.) AS350D Squirrel	1341	N5780A	0080		1 LY LTS101-600A.3	1950			
☐ ZK-HGF	Kawasaki (Eurocopter/MBB) BK117B-1	1053	JA6617	0090	0793	2 LY LTS101-750B.1	3200			lsf HGF Holdings Ltd
☐ ZK-HNB	Kawasaki (Eurocopter/MBB) BK117A-4	1024	JA9923	0088	0596	2 LY LTS101-650B.1	3200			

NZ AERIAL MAPPING, Ltd — **Hastings & Auckland**

PO Box 300-322, Albany 1331, New Zealand ☎ (9) 415 77 10 Tx: none Fax: (9) 415 77 10 SITA: n/a
F: 1936 ⁂ n/a Head: Craig Acheson Net: n/a

☐ ZK-FMU	Piper PA-23-250 Aztec C	27-2970	VH-ETJ	0065	0193	2 LY IO-540-C4B5	2359	Photo / Survey		
☐ ZK-CDK	Twin (Aero) Commander 680F	680F-1289-132	N78395	0063		2 LY IGSO-540-B1A	3629	Photo / Survey		
☐ ZK-AWP	Boeing (Douglas) DC-3C (C-47B-30-DK)	33135	5W-FAI	0044	0898	2 PW R-1830-92	12202	Y28 & Survey		

OCEANIA HELICOPTERS NZ, Ltd — **Auckland-Parnell Heliport**

PO Box 104-146, Auckland 1230, New Zealand ☎ (9) 358 17 27 Tx: none Fax: (9) 366 00 89 SITA: n/a
F: 1993 ⁂ n/a Head: Josh Camp & Jonathan Bowen Net: n/a

☐ ZK-HBA	MD Helicopters MD 500D (Hughes 369D)	510970D	N5110Y	0082	0897	1 AN 250-C20B	1361			

673 registration type of aircraft cn/fn ex/ex* mfd del powered by mtow kg configuration selcal name/fln/specialitites/remarks

ORIGIN PACIFIC AIRWAYS, Ltd = QO / OGN — Nelson

PO Box 7022, Nelson 7015, New Zealand ☎ (3) 547 20 20 Tx: none Fax: (3) 547 07 60 SITA: n/a
F: 1997 ⁂ n/a Head: Robert Inglis ICAO: ORIGIN Net: http://www.originpacific.co.nz

☐ ZK-JSA	BAe 3102 Jetstream 31	*839*	*G-GLAM*	*0088*	*0697*	*2 GA TPE331-10UGR-514H*	*7059*	*Y18*		
☐ ZK-JSH	BAe 3102 Jetstream 31	*838*	*G-IBLW*	*0088*	*0697*	*2 GA TPE331-10UGR-514H*	*7059*	*Y18*		
☐ ZK-JSI	BAe 3102 Jetstream 31	*761*	*G-LOGV*	*0087*	*0897*	*2 GA TPE331-10UGR-513H*	*7059*	*Y18*		

OWENSAIR = OWN (Owens Services B.O.P., Ltd dba) — Tauranga

Private Bag, Mount Maunganui 3020, New Zealand ☎ (7) 575 70 99 Tx: 21468 nz Fax: (7) 575 20 00 SITA: n/a
F: 1951 ⁂ 230 Head: J.A. Burn ICAO: OWENSAIR Net: n/a

☐ ZK-OSL	Cessna 414A Chancellor II	*414A0021*	*VH-GKA*	*0078*		*2 CO TSIO-520-N*	*3062*			

PETER GARDEN HELICOPTERS (Peter J. Garden dba) — Riversdale

The Terrace, Waipounamu, RD 6, Gore 9700, New Zealand ☎ (3) 202 56 50 Tx: n/a Fax: (3) 442 84 15 SITA: n/a
F: 1985 ⁂ n/a Head: Peter J. Garden Net: n/a

☐ ZK-HSL	Bell 206B JetRanger III	*2888*	*N40AA*	*0079*	*0597*	*1 AN 250-C20B*	*1451*			
☐ ZK-HWF	Bell 206B JetRanger	*1240*	*C-FKOJ*	*0074*	*0496*	*1 AN 250-C20*	*1451*			

PIONAIR (Pionair Adventures, Ltd dba) — Christchurch

PO Box 333, Christchurch 8000, New Zealand ☎ (3) 343 33 33 Tx: none Fax: (3) 343 30 35 SITA: n/a
F: 1991 ⁂ 7 Head: Tim Scott Net: n/a

☐ ZK-AMS	Boeing (Douglas) DC-3C (C-47A-20-DL)	*9286*	*VH-PWN*	*0042*	*0593*	*2 PW R-1830-92*	*12202*	*28 Pax*		

SEABOARD AIRLINES (NZ), Ltd (Subsidiary of Atlas Travel Club) — Auckland

PO Box 43060, Auckland, New Zealand ☎ (9) 275 67 88 Tx: none Fax: (9) 275 67 88 SITA: n/a
F: 1997 ⁂ n/a Head: Mike Bartlett Net: n/a Presently being set-up. Intends to start operations during 1999 with Boeing 747 aircraft.

SKYLINE AVIATION, Ltd (formerly Skyline Helicopters, Ltd) — Hastings

PO Box 2347, Hastings 4215, New Zealand ☎ (6) 878 31 78 Tx: none Fax: (6) 878 86 26 SITA: n/a
F: 1992 ⁂ n/a Head: Mike Toogood Net: n/a

☐ ZK-HFZ	Eurocopter (Aerosp.) AS350BA Squirrel	*1784*	*JA9373*	*0085*	*0292*	*1 TU Arriel 1B*	*2100*			*cvtd AS350B*
☐ ZK-HYP	Eurocopter (Aerosp.) AS350B Squirrel	*1393*	*N5774Y*	*0080*	*0596*	*1 TU Arriel 1B*	*1950*			*cvtd AS350D*
☐ ZK-LWN	Piper PA-31-310 Navajo	*31-8112056*	*N40938*	*0081*	*0695*	*2 LY TIO-540-A2C*	*2948*			*occ lst Hastings Air Charter*

SOUNDSAIR, Ltd — Wellington

PO Box 21006, Wellington 6041, New Zealand ☎ (4) 388 25 94 Tx: none Fax: (4) 380 88 81 SITA: n/a
F: 1985 ⁂ 7 Head: Willie Sage Net: n/a Aircraft below MTOW 1361kg: Lake LA-4-200.

☐ ZK-ENT	Cessna U206G Stationair	*U20603667*	*N7551N*	*0082*	*0697*	*1 CO IO-520-F*	*1633*			
☐ ZK-DCF	Twin (Aero) Commander 500A	*500A-1274-97*	*ZK-CTM*	*0063*	*1296*	*2 CO IO-470-M*	*2835*			
☐ ZK-PDM	Cessna 208 Caravan I	*20800240*	*N1289N*	*0095*	*0496*	*1 PWC PT6A-114*	*3629*			

SOUTH EAST AIR, Ltd — Invercargill

PO Box 87, Invercargill 9515, New Zealand ☎ (3) 214 55 22 Tx: none Fax: (3) 214 55 20 SITA: n/a
F: 1993 ⁂ n/a Head: Bill Moffatt Net: n/a

☐ ZK-JEM	Cessna A185E Skywagon	*18501780*	*VH-JBM*	*0070*	*0693*	*1 CO IO-520-D*	*1520*			*Floats / Wheels*
☐ ZK-RTS	Piper PA-32-300 Cherokee SIX	*32-7340070*	*VH-BTS*	*0073*	*0297*	*1 LY IO-540-K1A5*	*1542*			

SOUTHERN AIR (1997), Ltd = RKU (formerly Southern Air, Ltd & Stewart Island Air Services, Ltd) — Invercargill

PO Box 860, Invercargill 9500, New Zealand ☎ (3) 218 91 29 Tx: none Fax: (3) 214 46 81 SITA: n/a
F: 1976 ⁂ 20 Head: Allan Aikenson ICAO: RAKIURA Net: n/a Aircraft below MTOW 1361kg: Cessna 172

☐ ZK-FLU	Britten-Norman BN-2A-27 Islander	*104*	*F-OCFQ*	*0068*		*2 LY O-540-E4C5*	*2994*	*Y9*		*cvtd BN-2A-9*
☐ ZK-FWZ	Britten-Norman BN-2A-26 Islander	*52*	*T3-ATH*	*0069*	*1090*	*2 LY O-540-E4C5*	*2994*	*Y9*		*cvtd BN-2A-8*
☐ ZK-FXE	Britten-Norman BN-2A-26 Islander	*110*	*F-OCFR*	*0069*	*0691*	*2 LY O-540-E4C5*	*2994*	*Y9*		*cvtd BN-2A*

SOUTHERN ALPS AIR, Ltd (formerly Southern Alps Air Charter, Ltd) — Makarora

Makarora, V1A, Wanaka 9192, New Zealand ☎ (3) 443 83 72 Tx: none Fax: (3) 443 82 92 SITA: n/a
F: 1973 ⁂ 2 Head: Paul Cooper Net: n/a

☐ ZK-FMA	Cessna A185F Skywagon II	*18503513*	*N2177Q*	*0078*		*1 CO IO-520-D*	*1520*			

SOUTHERN LAKES HELICOPTERS, Ltd — Te Anau & Milford Sound

PO Box 156, Te Anau 9681, New Zealand ☎ (3) 249 71 67 Tx: none Fax: (3) 249 72 67 SITA: n/a
F: 1984 ⁂ 5 Head: Richard Hayes Net: n/a Aircraft below MTOW 1361kg: Hughes 369HS (500C).

☐ ZK-HUX	MD Helicopters MD 500D (Hughes 369D)	*1190607D*	*N9149F*	*0079*	*1094*	*1 AN 250-C20B*	*1361*			
☐ ZK-HRM	Eurocopter (Aerosp.) AS350B2 Squirrel	*2721*	*C-FCFM*	*0093*	*0598*	*1 TU Arriel 1D1*	*2250*			

SOUTHLAND AIR CHARTER (Southland Aero Club (Inc.) dba) — Invercargill

PO Box 1171, Invercargill 9500, New Zealand ☎ (3) 218 61 71 Tx: none Fax: (3) 218 61 71 SITA: n/a
F: 1929 ⁂ n/a Head: Allan Aitcheson Net: n/a Aircraft below MTOW 1361kg: Cessna 172, Piper PA-28 & PA-38.

☐ ZK-DIV	Piper PA-32-260 Cherokee	*32-7400015*	*N57306*	*0074*	*0192*	*1 LY O-540-E4B5*	*1542*			
☐ ZK-FUZ	Partenavia P.68C	*327*	*G-VJCT*	*0085*	*1198*	*2 LY IO-360-A1B6*	*1990*			

SOUTHLAND FLOAT PLANE SERVICES (Invercargill Holdings, Ltd dba) — Riverton

78 Russell Street, Invercargill 9501, New Zealand ☎ (3) 234 85 97 Tx: none Fax: (3) 234 82 66 SITA: n/a
F: n/a ⁂ n/a Head: n/a Net: n/a

☐ ZK-KMH	Cessna TU206G Turbo Stationair 6 II	*U20604075*	*N756GG*	*0077*	*1297*	*1 CO TSIO-520-M*	*1633*			*Floats*

SOUTH-WEST HELICOPTERS, Ltd — Te Anau & Tuatapere

PO Box 102, Te Anau 9681, New Zealand ☎ (3) 249 74 02 Tx: none Fax: (3) 249 74 09 SITA: n/a
F: 1996 ⁂ 4 Head: Ian Buick Net: http://www.southernlakes.co.nz/tenau/swestheli

☐ ZK-HBH	Eurocopter (Aerosp.) AS350B Squirrel	*1283*	*N3611B*	*0080*	*0796*	*1 TU Arriel 1B*	*1950*			
☐ ZK-HMY	Eurocopter (Aerosp.) AS350B Squirrel	*1052*		*0078*	*0796*	*1 TU Arriel 1B*	*1950*			

STEVENSON SKYWORK HELICOPTERS, Ltd — Warkworth

Baddeleys Beach Road, RD6, Warkworth 1241, New Zealand ☎ (9) 422 70 18 Tx: none Fax: (9) 422 70 64 SITA: n/a
F: 1996 ⁂ n/a Head: Roger Stevenson Net: n/a

☐ ZK-HQR	Bell 206B JetRanger	*1644*	*RP-C1941*	*0075*	*0597*	*1 AN 250-C20*	*1451*			
☐ ZK-HWG	Bell 206B JetRanger	*1262*	*C-FPZG*	*0074*	*0399*	*1 AN 250-C20*	*1451*			
☐ ZK-HWW	Eurocopter (Aerosp.) AS350B Squirrel	*1299*		*0080*	*0497*	*1 TU Arriel 1B*	*1950*			
☐ ZK-HZZ	Eurocopter (Aerosp.) AS350D Squirrel	*1382*	*N43677*	*0080*	*0499*	*1 LY LTS101-600A.3*	*1950*			

SUNAIR AVIATION, Ltd — Tauranga

PO Box 5153, Mount Maunganui 3030, New Zealand ☎ (7) 575 77 89 Tx: none Fax: (7) 575 77 99 SITA: n/a
F: 1984 ⁂ 10 Head: W. Daniel Power ICAO: SUNAIR Net: n/a Aircraft below MTOW 1361kg: Cessna 172.

☐ ZK-LGO	Partenavia P.68B	*25*	*HB-LGO*	*0074*	*0199*	*2 LY IO-360-A1B6*	*1960*			
☐ ZK-DIR	Piper PA-23-250 Aztec D	*27-4242*	*VH-PRB*	*0069*	*0695*	*2 LY IO-540-C4B5*	*2359*			
☐ ZK-FIL	Piper PA-31-310 Navajo C	*31-7712014*	*ZK-JFF*	*0077*	*0396*	*2 LY TIO-540-A2C*	*2948*			

TARARUA HELIWORK, Ltd — Pahiatua

508 Scarborough Road, RD3, Pahiatua 5470, New Zealand ☎ (6) 376 80 00 Tx: none Fax: (6) 376 68 68 SITA: n/a
F: 1989 ⁂ 6 Head: Robert Mangin Net: n/a Aircraft below MTOW 1361kg: Hughes 269C (300C)

☐ ZK-HRP	MD Helicopters MD 500D (Hughes 369D)	*1160013D*	*ZK-IRH*	*0076*	*1297*	*1 AN 250-C20B*	*1361*			

TAUPO AIR SERVICES, Ltd — Taupo

R.D.2, Taupo 2730, New Zealand ☎ (7) 378 53 25 Tx: none Fax: (7) 377 08 18 SITA: n/a
F: 1978 ⁂ 3 Head: Graeme Walker Net: n/a Aircraft below MTOW 1361 kg: Cessna 172, 177B & Piper PA-18.

☐ ZK-CAN	Cessna 185 Skywagon	*185-0134*	*N9934X*	*0061*	*0596*	*1 CO IO-470-F*	*1451*			
☐ ZK-TAM	Cessna U206F Stationair	*U20602042*	*VH-SAP*	*0073*	*0898*	*1 CO IO-520-F*	*1633*			

TAUPO'S FLOATPLANE, Ltd (formerly A.R.K. Aviation, Ltd) — Taupo-Lakefront

PO Box 238, Taupo 2730, New Zealand ☎ (7) 378 75 00 Tx: n/a Fax: (7) 377 08 43 SITA: n/a
F: 1978 ⁂ 4 Head: Mike Breen Net: n/a

☐ ZK-DXC	Cessna U206F Stationair II	*U20602986*	*N2665Q*	*0075*		*1 CO IO-520-F*	*1633*			*Floats*

THE CATALINA COMPANY NZ, Ltd — Auckland-Ardmore

PO Box 527, Papakura-Auckland 1730, New Zealand ☎ (9) 534 45 83 Tx: none Fax: (9) 534 45 83 SITA: n/a
F: 1994 ⁂ n/a Head: Ross Ewing Net: http://www.catalina.org.nz Operates non-commercial, non-profit historical/pleasure flights for The Catalina Club of NZ-members only.

☐ ZK-PBY	Consolidated PBY-5A Canso	*CV-357*	*Z-CAT*	*0044*	*0395*	*2 PW R-1830-92S*	*13835*	*16 Pax*		*Amphibian*

674 registration type of aircraft *cn/fn* *ex/ex** *mfd* *del* *powered by* *mtow kg* *configuration* *selcal* *name/fln/specialitites/remarks*

THE HELICOPTER LINE (Tourism Holdings, Ltd dba / formerly Alpine, Whirlwide & Wishart Helicopters, Ltd) — Dunedin — THE HELICOPTER LINE

PO Box 16, Dunedin 9000, New Zealand ☎ (3) 477 68 29 Tx: none Fax: (3) 477 99 87 SITA: n/a
F: 1986 ⁂ 60 Head: Murray Valentine Net: http://www.discover.co.nz/thlintro.html Aircraft below MTOW 1361 kg: Cessna 182.

☐ ZK-HIH	Eurocopter (Aerosp.) AS350B Squirrel	*1723*	*JA6018*	*0083*	*1193*	*1 TU Arriel 1B*	*1950*			
☐ ZK-HDG	Eurocopter (Aerosp.) AS355F1 Tw.Squirrel	*5212*	*N5802T*	*0083*	*0292*	*2 AN 250-C20F*	*2400*			*opf Police*
☐ ZK-HKF	Eurocopter (Aerosp.) AS355F1 Tw.Squirrel	*5200*	*VH-HJK*	*0083*		*2 AN 250-C20F*	*2400*			
☐ ZK-HKY	Eurocopter (Aerosp.) AS355F1 Tw.Squirrel	*5123*	*N909CH*	*0082*	*0595*	*2 AN 250-C20F*	*2400*			
☐ ZK-HMB	Eurocopter (Aerosp.) AS355F1 Tw.Squirrel	*5016*	*N57812*	*0081*	*0296*	*2 AN 250-C20F*	*2400*			
☐ ZK-HMI	Eurocopter (Aerosp.) AS355F1 Tw.Squirrel	*5029*	*N5775Y*	*0081*	*1295*	*2 AN 250-C20F*	*2400*			
☐ ZK-HML	Eurocopter (Aerosp.) AS355F1 Tw.Squirrel	*5032*	*N5776A*	*0081*	*0296*	*2 AN 250-C20F*	*2400*			
☐ ZK-HPA	Eurocopter (Aerosp.) AS355F1 Tw.Squirrel	*5010*	*N813CE*	*0080*	*0097*	*2 AN 250-C20F*	*2400*	*EMS*		*opf Auckland Regional Rescue Helicopter*
☐ ZK-HPE	Eurocopter (Aerosp.) AS355F1 Tw.Squirrel	*5229*	*N58021*	*0082*	*0297*	*2 AN 250-C20F*	*2400*			
☐ ZK-HPI	Eurocopter (Aerosp.) AS355F1 Tw.Squirrel	*5211*	*N5802N*	*0082*	*0797*	*2 AN 250-C20F*	*2400*			
☐ ZK-HPZ	Eurocopter (Aerosp.) AS355F1 Tw.Squirrel	*5107*	*N57906*	*0081*	*0297*	*2 AN 250-C20F*	*2400*			
☐ ZK-HHI	Kawasaki (Eurocopter/MBB) BK117B-1	*1077*	*JA6653*	*0091*	*0593*	*2 LY LTS101-750B.1*	*3200*	*EMS*		
☐ ZK-HHV	Kawasaki (Eurocopter/MBB) BK117B-2	*1022*	*JA9922*	*0088*	*1093*	*2 LY LTS101-750B.1*	*3350*	*EMS*		*opf Auckland Reg.Rescue Helic./cvtd A-4*

TOURISM FLIGHTSEEING (Tourism Holdings, Ltd dba / Joint venture with Fiordland Travel) — Queenstown

PO Box 920, Queenstown 9197, New Zealand ☎ (3) 442 26 80 Tx: none Fax: (3) 442 26 88 SITA: n/a
F: 1993 ⁂ 30 Head: Jules Tapper Net: n/a

☐ ZK-HOT	MD Helicopters MD 500D (Hughes 369D)	*670138D*	*N8628F*	*0077*	*0399*	*1 AN 250-C20B*	*1361*	*Y4*		
☐ ZK-CBS	Cessna 185A Skywagon	*185-0398*	*N4198Y*	*0062*	*0698*	*1 CO IO-470-F*	*1451*	*Y5*		*Wheel-Skis*
☐ ZK-CBY	Cessna 185A Skywagon	*185-0420*	*N1620Z*	*0062*	*0698*	*1 CO IO-470-F*	*1451*	*Y5*		*Wheel-Skis*
☐ ZK-DYH	Cessna A185E Skywagon	*18501848*	*N1645M*	*0071*	*1198*	*1 CO IO-520-D*	*1520*	*Y5*		*Wheel-Skis*
☐ ZK-ELQ	Cessna A185F Skywagon II	*18503619*	*N2275V*	*0078*	*0798*	*1 CO IO-520-D*	*1520*	*Y5*		*Wheel-Skis*
☐ ZK-ENW	Cessna A185F Skywagon	*18503133*	*N80651*	*0076*	*0199*	*1 CO IO-520-D*	*1520*	*Y5*		*Wheel-Skis*
☐ ZK-MCR	Cessna A185F Skywagon II	*18504429*	*N714XT*	*0084*	*0698*	*1 CO IO-520-D*	*1520*	*Y5*		*Wheel-Skis*
☐ ZK-MCU	Cessna A185F Skywagon II	*18504372*	*N9919N*	*0082*	*0698*	*1 CO IO-520-D*	*1520*	*Y5*		*Wheel-Skis*
☐ ZK-MCV	Cessna A185F Skywagon II	*18504395*	*N714FV*	*0083*	*0698*	*1 CO IO-520-D*	*1520*	*Y5*		*Wheel-Skis*
☐ ZK-MDA	Cessna A185F Skywagon II	*18503551*	*N4728Q*	*0078*	*0698*	*1 CO IO-520-D*	*1520*	*Y5*		*Wheel-Skis*
☐ ZK-MDB	Cessna A185F Skywagon II	*18504258*	*N61802*	*0081*	*0698*	*1 CO IO-520-D*	*1520*	*Y5*		*Wheel-Skis*
☐ ZK-JHT	Cessna U206G Stationair 6 II	*U20604237*	*N756PA*	*0078*	*1198*	*1 CO IO-520-F*	*1633*			
☐ ZK-LAW	Cessna 207A Stationair 8 II	*20700723*	*N9750M*	*0081*	*0793*	*1 CO IO-550-F*	*1724*	*Y6*		*Bonnaire modif.*
☐ ZK-MCK	Pilatus PC-6/B2-H4 Turbo Porter	*809*	*HB-FHO*	*0081*	*0798*	*1 PWC PT6A-27*	*2800*	*Y10*		*cvtd -H2 / Wheel-Skis*
☐ ZK-MCN	Pilatus PC-6/B2-H4 Turbo Porter	*824*	*HB-FCV*	*0083*	*0798*	*1 PWC PT6A-27*	*2800*	*Y10*		*cvtd -H2 / Wheel-Skis*
☐ ZK-MCT	Pilatus PC-6/B2-H4 Turbo Porter	*841*	*HB-FIO*	*0085*	*0798*	*1 PWC PT6A-27*	*2800*	*Y10*		*cvtd -H2 / Wheel-Skis*
☐ ZK-DBV	Britten-Norman BN-2A Islander	*164*	*VH-EQX*	*0070*	*0793*	*2 LY O-540-E4B5*	*2858*	*Y9*		
☐ ZK-MCD	Britten-Norman BN-2A-26 Islander	*719*	*G-BCAG*	*0074*	*0793*	*2 LY O-540-E4C5*	*2994*	*Y9*		
☐ ZK-MCE	Britten-Norman BN-2A-26 Islander	*724*	*G-BCHB*	*0074*	*0793*	*2 LY O-540-E4C5*	*2994*	*Y9*		
☐ ZK-FVU	GAF Nomad N22C	*N22C-55*	*VH-IIG*	*0077*	*0793*	*2 AN 250-B17C*	*3856*	*Y13*		*cvtd N22B*
☐ ZK-FVX	GAF Nomad N24A	*N24A-46*	*VH-FCX*	*0077*	*0793*	*2 AN 250-B17B*	*4264*	*Y15*		

TRANZGLOBAL = GLB (Tranzglobal Holdings, Ltd dba) — Auckland

PO Box 9139, Newmarket, Auckland 1031, New Zealand ☎ (9) 525 46 84 Tx: none Fax: (9) 525 46 82 SITA: n/a
F: 1994 ⁂ 35 Head: Steve J. Mosen ICAO: GLOBAL Net: http://www.tranzglobal.co.nz

☐ ZK-KML	Embraer 110P1 Bandeirante (EMB-110P1)	*110248*	*VH-SBH*	*0080*	*0794*	*2 PWC PT6A-34*	*5670*	*Y15 / Freighter*		
☐ ZK-TZL	Embraer 110P1 Bandeirante (EMB-110P1)	*110378*	*VH-FWI*	*0081*	*0697*	*2 PWC PT6A-34*	*5670*	*Y15 / Freighter*		
☐ ZK-TZM	Embraer 110P1 Bandeirante (EMB-110P1)	*110328*	*ZK-REW*	*0081*	*0998*	*2 PWC PT6A-34*	*5670*	*Y15 / Freighter*		

VINCENT AVIATION, Ltd — Wellington — VINCENT AVIATION

PO Box 21022, Wellington 6030, New Zealand ☎ (4) 388 89 83 Tx: none Fax: (4) 388 99 93 SITA: n/a
F: 1990 ⁂ 5 Head: Peter G. Vincent Net: n/a

☐ ZK-DCP	Piper PA-34-200T Seneca II	*34-8070355*	*N8263M*	*0080*	*1197*	*2 CO TSIO-360-EB*	*2073*	*Y5*		
☐ ZK-VAB	Cessna 402C III	*402C0803*	*VH-TAM*	*0084*	*0296*	*2 CO TSIO-520-VB*	*3107*	*Y9*		
☐ ZK-VAD	Cessna 402C II	*402C0076*	*VH-COH*	*0079*	*0397*	*2 CO TSIO-520-VB*	*3107*	*Y9*		

VIP AIR CHARTER, Ltd — Hamilton

Airport Road, RD2, Hamilton 2021, New Zealand ☎ (7) 843 65 30 Tx: none Fax: (7) 843 05 42 SITA: n/a
F: 1993 ⁂ 6 Head: Phillip Jones Net: http://infosys.co.nz/vip/vip.htm

☐ ZK-DFT	Cessna 337 Super Skymaster	*337-0176*	*VH-CJV*	*0065*	*1098*	*2 CO IO-360-C/D*	*1905*			
☐ ZK-DGT	Piper PA-23-250 Aztec C	*27-3437*	*9J-RCW*	*0066*	*0593*	*2 LY IO-540-C4B5*	*2359*			
☐ ZK-VIP	Piper PA-31-350 Navajo Chieftain	*31-7405482*	*N33WH*	*0074*	*0393*	*2 LY TIO-540-J2BD*	*3175*			

VOLCANIC AIR SAFARIS, Ltd — Rotorua — VOLCANIC AIR SAFARIS

PO Box 640, Rotorua 3200, New Zealand ☎ (7) 348 99 84 Tx: none Fax: (7) 348 40 69 SITA: n/a
F: 1991 ⁂ 6 Head: Laurie A. Barclay Net: n/a

☐ ZK-LAB	Cessna R182 Skylane RG II	*R18201089*	*N756KB*	*0079*		*1 LY O-540-J3C5D*	*1406*			
☐ ZK-HVA	Bell 206B JetRanger	*1299*	*N30DB*	*0074*	*0392*	*1 AN 250-C20*	*1451*			
☐ ZK-EFI	Cessna U206F Stationair II	*U20603525*	*N8772Q*	*0076*	*1293*	*1 CO IO-520-F*	*1633*			
☐ ZK-FEO	Cessna U206G Stationair	*U20603797*	*N90639*	*0078*		*1 CO IO-520-F*	*1633*			*Floats*
☐ ZK-ZAQ	Cessna 421C Golden Eagle II	*421C0060*	*VH-OYY*	*0076*	*1097*	*2 CO GTSIO-520-L*	*3379*			

WAIHEKE AIRSERVICES, Ltd — Waiheke Island

PO Box 215, Ostend, Waiheke Island 1240, New Zealand ☎ (9) 372 50 00 Tx: none Fax: (9) 372 50 01 SITA: n/a
F: 1995 ⁂ 2 Head: Terry Easthope Net: n/a Aircraft below MTOW 1361kg: Cessna 172

☐ ZK-EJG	Cessna U206G Stationair	*U20603549*	*N8797Q*	*0076*	*0796*	*1 CO IO-520-F*	*1633*			

WAIMANA HELICOPTERS, Ltd — Waimana

PO Box 10, Waimana, New Zealand ☎ (7) 312 32 43 Tx: n/a Fax: (7) 312 31 11 SITA: n/a
F: 1980 ⁂ n/a Head: Robert L. Fleming Net: n/a

☐ ZK-HIU	Kawasaki (Eurocopter/MBB) BK117A-4	*1029*	*JA9958*	*0089*	*1293*	*2 LY LTS101-650B.1*	*3200*			

WANGANUI AERO WORK, Ltd – WAW (Associated with Western Air Spray, Ltd / Aircraft Holdings, Ltd) — Wanganui

PO Box 509, Wanganui 5015, New Zealand ☎ (6) 345 39 94 Tx: n/a Fax: (6) 345 39 92 SITA: n/a
F: 1950 ⁂ 35 Head: Richmond J. Harding Net: n/a Aircraft & Ag-aircraft below MTOW 1361/5000 kg: Cessna 180, Fletcher FU-24 & Hughes 369HS (500C).

☐ ZK-HHX	MD Helicopters MD 500D (Hughes 369D)	*1070219D*	*P2-MID*	*0077*	*0293*	*1 AN 250-C20B*	*1361*			
☐ ZK-HSN	Bell 206B JetRanger III	*3062*	*DQ-FDL*	*0080*	*0895*	*1 AN 250-C20B*	*1451*			
☐ ZK-HTM	Bell 206B JetRanger III	*3305*		*0081*		*1 AN 250-C20B*	*1451*			
☐ ZK-HJH	Bell UH-1H (205)	*4530*	*N8230H*	*0066*	*0396*	*1 LY T53-L-13*	*4309*			

WATERWINGS AIRWAYS (Te Anau), Ltd (Milford Sound Scenic Flights) — Te Anau & Queenstown

PO Box 767, Te Anau 9681, New Zealand ☎ (3) 249 74 05 Tx: none Fax: (3) 249 79 39 SITA: n/a
F: 1983 ⁂ 11 Head: Chris Willett IATA: 914 Net: n/a Aircraft below MTOW 1361 kg: Cessna 172. Land-based aircraft are operated under the name MILFORD SOUND SCENIC FLIGHTS (with such titles).

☐ ZK-EKJ	Cessna U206G Stationair 6 II	*U20604282*	*N9392A*	*0078*		*1 CO IO-520-F*	*1633*			*Floats*
☐ ZK-DRY	Cessna 207 Skywagon	*20700196*	*5W-FAL*	*0071*		*1 CO IO-520-F*	*1724*			
☐ ZK-EAL	Cessna 207A Stationair 8 II	*20700728*	*ZK-FTL*	*0081*	*0993*	*1 CO IO-520-F*	*1724*			
☐ ZK-WET	Cessna 207A Skywagon	*20700375*	*VH-SLD*	*0077*		*1 CO IO-520-F*	*1724*			

WELAIR, Ltd (Air Wellington) — Paraparaumu — WELAIR

PO Box 392, Paraparaumu 6450, New Zealand ☎ (4) 298 73 28 Tx: none Fax: (4) 298 73 28 SITA: n/a
F: 1996 ⁂ n/a Head: Brian Davison Net: n/a Aircraft below MTOW 1361kg: Cessna 152/172/177/182 & Maule M5-235C
Scheduled flights are operated under the name AIR WELLINGTON Ltd (sister company, same headquarters & fleet).

☐ ZK-DAS	Cessna TU206A Turbo Skywagon	*U206-0554*	*N4854F*	*0066*	*1197*	*1 CO TSIO-520-C*	*1633*			
☐ ZK-DIO	Piper PA-23-250 Aztec E	*27-7305073*	*N40261*	*0073*	*1098*	*2 LY IO-540-C4B5*	*2359*			
☐ ZK-MCM	Piper PA-31-350 Navajo Chieftain	*31-7652032*	*N102LA*	*0076*	*0997*	*2 LY TIO-540-J2BD*	*3175*			
☐ ZK-WHW	Piper PA-31-310 Navajo	*31-437*	*N6476L*	*0069*	*0896*	*2 LY TIO-540-A1A*	*2948*			

WELLINGTON AIR CHARTER (Division of Wellington Aero Club, Inc.) — Wellington

PO Box 14-091, Wellington 6041, New Zealand ☎ (4) 388 84 44 Tx: none Fax: (4) 388 85 33 SITA: n/a
F: 1932 ⁂ n/a Head: Dennis Tindill Net: n/a Aircraft below MTOW 1361kg: AA5B, Cessna 182 & Piper PA-28

☐ ZK-DGS	Piper PA-23-250 Aztec E	*27-7304959*	*N14370*	*0072*	*1298*	*2 LY IO-540-C4B5*	*2359*			
☐ ZK-FHO	Piper PA-23-250 Aztec E	*27-4585*	*G-AYTP*	*0071*	*1298*	*2 LY IO-540-C4B5*	*2359*			

WESTAIR FLYING, Ltd — Hokitika

PO Box 69, Hokitika 7900, New Zealand ☎ (3) 755 77 56 Tx: none Fax: (3) 755 77 56 SITA: n/a
F: 1987 ⁂ n/a Head: Duncan Hamilton Net: n/a Aircraft below MTOW 1361kg: Cessna 172, Piper PA-28 & PA-38

☐ ZK-KVZ	Cessna U206G Stationair 6 II	*U20606144*	*N6110Z*	*0081*	*0698*	*1 CO IO-520-F*	*1633*			
☐ ZK-PCS	Cessna U206F Stationair	*U20602433*	*C-GBCS*	*0074*	*1097*	*1 CO IO-520-F*	*1633*			
☐ ZK-DSE	Cessna 207 Skywagon	*20700226*	*5W-FAP*	*0072*	*0497*	*1 CO IO-520-F*	*1724*			

675 registration type of aircraft cn/fn ex/EX* mfd del powered by mtow kg configuration selcal name/fln/specialitites/remarks

WHALEWATCH AIR, Ltd — Kaikoura

PO Box 55, Kaikoura 8280, New Zealand ☎ (3) 319 65 80 Tx: none Fax: (3) 319 66 68 SITA: n/a
F: 1990 ⁂ 4 Head: John Macphail Net: n/a Aircraft below MTOW 1361kg: Cessna 172.

☐ ZK-SFK	Britten-Norman BN-2A Islander	*236*	*VH-CPG*	*0070*		*2 LY O-540-E4B5*	*2722*			

WILDERNESS AIR & ACTIONFLITE (Peter R. Clarke dba) — Queenstown

PO Box 567, Queenstown 9197, New Zealand ☎ (3) 442 62 28 Tx: none Fax: (3) 442 68 16 SITA: n/a
F: n/a ⁂ n/a Head: Peter R. Clarke Net: n/a

☐ ZK-CHQ	Cessna U206 Super Skywagon	*U206-0314*	*ZK-TEM*	*0065*	*1297*	*1 CO IO-520-A*	*1497*			
☐ ZK-DXZ	Cessna U206F Stationair II	*U20602976*	*N2497Q*	*0075*	*0399*	*1 CO IO-520-F*	*1633*			

WINGSPAN NEW ZEALAND, Ltd — Auckland-Ardmore

Ardmore Airfield, Private Bag 14, Papakura 1730, New Zealand ☎ (9) 297 77 17 Tx: none Fax: (9) 297 77 57 SITA: n/a
F: 1994 ⁂ n/a Head: Bruce Roy Net: n/a Aircraft below MTOW 1361kg: Cessna 152 & 172

☐ ZK-JRV	Gulfstream American GA-7 Cougar	*GA7-0022*	*VH-IFX*	*0078*		*2 LY O-320-D1D*	*1724*			*lsf pvt*

ZP = PARAGUAY (Republic of Paraguay) (Republica de Paraguay)

Capital: Asuncion Official Language: Spanish Population: 5,0 million Square Km: 406752 Dialling code: +595 Year established: 1811 Acting political head: Gonzalez Macchi (President)

Government / Corporate / Executive / VIP Aircraft

☐ FAP-01	Boeing 707-321B	*18957 / 472*	*ZP-CCF*	*0066*	*0694*	*4 PW JT3D-3B (HK2/QNC)*	*152407*	*VIP*	*EL-CK*	*Fuerza Aérea Paraguaya*
☐ FAP-02	De Havilland DHC-6 Twin Otter 200	*137*	*FAP-01*	*0068*	*0768*	*2 PWC PT6A-20*	*5252*	*VIP*		*Fuerza Aérea Paraguaya*

ARPA – Aerolineas Paraguayas = A8 / PAY (Member of TAM Group) — Asuncion

Aeropuerto Internacional, Hangar de ARPA, Asuncion, Paraguay ☎ (21) 44 89 74 Tx: none Fax: (21) 21 51 11 SITA: n/a
F: 1994 ⁂ 26 Head: Miguel Candia IATA: 911 ICAO: ARPA Net: n/a Operates scheduled flights with Cessna 208A/B aircraft, leased from TAM Express (PP-) when required.

TAM Paraguay = PZ / LAP (TAM-Transportes Aéreos del Mercosur, S.A. dba/Member of TAM Group, Brazil/formerly LAPSA Air Paraguay) — Asuncion

Aeropuerto Internacional, Hangar de ARPA, Asuncion, Paraguay ☎ (21) 44 89 74 Tx: none Fax: (21) 21 51 11 SITA: n/a
F: 1963 ⁂ n/a Head: Miguel Candia IATA: 692 ICAO: PARAGUAYA Net: n/a Operates scheduled flights with Fokker 100 aircraft, leased from TAM Brasil (PT-) when required (various registrations).

TRANSPORTE AEREO MILITAR – TAM — Asuncion

Oliva 471, Asuncion, Paraguay ☎ (21) 44 69 95 Tx: n/a Fax: (21) 44 86 44 SITA: n/a
F: n/a ⁂ n/a Head: n/a Net: n/a Transport branch of FAP-Fuerza Aérea del Paraguay which beside non-commercial military flights also operates non-profit passenger & cargo flights to remote parts in Paraguay.

☐ 2027	CASA 212 Aviocar Srs 200	*307*		*0083*	*0684*	*2 GA TPE331-10-501C*	*7450*	*Pax*		
☐ 2029	CASA 212 Aviocar Srs 200	*310*		*0083*	*0684*	*2 GA TPE331-10-501C*	*7450*	*Pax*		
☐ 2031	CASA 212 Aviocar Srs 200	*315*		*0083*	*0784*	*2 GA TPE331-10-501C*	*7450*	*Pax*		
☐ 2033	CASA 212 Aviocar Srs 200	*316*		*0083*	*0784*	*2 GA TPE331-10-501C*	*7450*	*Executive Pax*		
☐ 2010	Boeing (Douglas) C-47B-25-DK (DC-3)	*32620*	*44-76288*	*0045*		*2 PW R-1830*	*12202*	*Pax*		
☐ 2030	Boeing (Douglas) C-47B-35-DK (DC-3)	*33415*	*44-77083*	*0045*		*2 PW R-1830*	*12202*	*Freighter*		
☐ 2032	Boeing (Douglas) C-47B-20-DK (DC-3)	*27098*	*FAB 2090*	*0045*		*2 PW R-1830*	*12202*	*Freighter*		

ZS = SOUTH AFRICA (Republic of South Africa) (Republiek van Zuid-Afrika)

Capital: Pretoria Official Language: Afrikaans, English Population: 44,0 million Square Km: 1119566 Dialling code: +27 Year established: 1910 Acting political head: Nelson Mandela (President)

Government / Corporate / Executive / VIP Aircraft

☐ ZS-CAI	Boeing (Douglas) DC-3C (C-47A-25-DK)	*13541*	*SAAF6838*	*0044*		*2 PW R-1830*	*12202*	*VIP / liaison*		*Directorate Civil Aviation*
☐ ZS-CAL	Hawker F3B/RA (HS 125-F3B/RA	*25172*	*G-AXEG*	*0069*		*2 GA TFE731-3R-1H*	*10342*	*VIP / liaison*		*Directorate Civil Aviation/cvtd 3B/RA*
☐ ZS-CAQ	Dassault Falcon 50	*133*	*HB-IEA*	*0083*		*3 GA TFE731-3-1C*	*17600*	*VIP*		*South African Air Force*
☐ ZS-CAR	Cessna S550 Citation S/II	*S550-0078*	*N1273X*	*0085*		*2 PWC JT15D-4B*	*6864*	*VIP / liaison*		*Directorate Civil Aviation*
☐ ZS-CAS	Dassault Falcon 50	*91*	*F-WZHY**	*0082*		*3 GA TFE731-3-1C*	*17600*	*VIP*		*South African Air Force*
☐ ZS-JBA	Hawker 400B (HS 125-400B)	*25259*	*SAAF 05*	*0071*	*0172*	*2 RR Viper 522*	*10569*	*VIP*		*South African Air Force*
☐ ZS-JIH	Hawker 400B (HS 125-400B)	*25260*	*SAAF 06*	*0071*	*1271*	*2 RR Viper 522*	*10569*	*VIP*		*South African Air Force*
☐ ZS-LME	Hawker 400B (HS 125-400B)	*25242*	*3D-ABZ*	*0070*		*2 RR Viper 522*	*10569*	*VIP*		*South African Air Force*
☐ ZS-LPE	Hawker 400B (HS 125-400B)	*25184*	*SAAF 04*	*0069*	*0570*	*2 RR Viper 522*	*10569*	*VIP*		*South African Air Force*
☐ ZS-LPF	Hawker 400B (HS 125-400B)	*25269*	*SAAF 07*	*0071*	*1271*	*2 RR Viper 522*	*10569*	*VIP*		*South African Air Force*
☐ ZS-NAN	Dassault Falcon 900	*99*	*F-WWFE**	*0091*	*1091*	*3 GA TFE731-5AR-1C*	*20639*	*VIP*		*South African Air Force*
☐ ZS-NYV	Learjet 31A	*31A-115*	*N31NR*	*0096*	*1196*	*2 GA TFE731-2-3B*	*7484*	*VIP*		*Kwazulu-Natal Provincial Administration*
☐ 1415	Boeing 707-328C	*19522 / 596*	*ZS-LSI*	*0067*	*0283*	*4 PW JT3D-7*	*151046*	*Tanker/Frtr/mil*		*AF-615 / South African Air Force*
☐ 1417	Boeing 707-328C	*19723 / 665*	*ZS-LSJ*	*0068*	*0383*	*4 PW JT3D-7*	*151046*	*Tanker/Frtr/mil*		*AF-617 / South African Air Force*
☐ 1419	Boeing 707-328C	*19917 / 763*	*ZS-LSK*	*0068*	*0383*	*4 PW JT3D-7*	*151046*	*Tanker/Frtr/mil*		*AF-619 / South African Air Force*
☐ 1421	Boeing 707-344C	*20283 / 691*	*EL-TBA*	*0069*	*0595*	*4 PW JT3D-7*	*151046*	*Elint/Frtr/mil*		*AF-621 / South African Air Force*
☐ 1423	Boeing 707-344C	*19706 / 691*	*ZS-LSL*	*0068*	*0595*	*4 PW JT3D-7*	*151046*	*Elint/Frtr/mil*		*AF-623 / South African Air Force*

ACACIA AIR, CC — Johannesburg-Lanseria

PO Box 497, Lanseria 1748, South Africa ☎ (11) 805 29 80 Tx: none Fax: (11) 805 29 80 SITA: n/a
F: 1998 ⁂ 3 Head: T.A. Smith Net: n/a

☐ ZS-MZS	Beech King Air B100	*BE-72*	*N20FL*	*0079*		*2 GA TPE331-6-252B*	*5352*			*lsf ZS-MZS Partnership*

AFRICA CARGO AIR, Pty Ltd — Johannesburg-Lanseria

PO Box 574, Lanseria 1748, South Africa ☎ (11) 701 33 09 Tx: none Fax: (11) 701 33 15 SITA: n/a
F: 1996 ⁂ n/a Head: Pik Mel Net: n/a

☐ ER-AEC	Antonov 32B	*3003*	*ER-ADC*	*0392*	*0096*	*2 IV AI-20D*	*27000*	*Combi*		*lsf VLN / to be re-reg. ZS-OIT*

AIR CHAMPAGNE, CC — Johannesburg-Lanseria

24 Sixth Avenue, Parktown North 2193, South Africa ☎ (11) 788 89 57 Tx: none Fax: (11) 788 89 57 SITA: n/a
F: 1992 ⁂ n/a Head: Reginald T. Weaver Net: n/a Beside aircraft listed, also leases DC-3 aircraft from AIRWORLD (ZS-), & DC-3 & DC-4 from SOUTH AFRICAN-Historic Flight (ZS-) when required.

☐ ZS-LEB	Cessna T303 Crusader	*T30300095*		*0082*		*2 CO TSIO-520-A*	*2336*			*lsf Kadet Investments P/L*
☐ ZS-LKH	Cessna 402C II	*402C0478*	*N6838Z*	*0081*		*2 CO TSIO-520-VB*	*3107*			*lsf VSA Aviation*
☐ ZS-JEY	Cessna 421B Golden Eagle	*421B0372*	*I-DUIN*	*0073*		*2 CO GTSIO-520-H*	*3379*			*lsf High Tech Backing*
☐ ZS-NVK	Twin (Aero) Grand Commander 680FL	*680FL-1671-133*	*ZS-ANP*	*0067*		*2 LY IGSO-540-B1A*	*3856*			*lsf pvt*

AIRWORLD, (Pty) Ltd = SPZ — Pretoria-Wonderboom & Cape Town-Int'l

PO Box 2634, Durbanville 7551, South Africa ☎ (21) 57 53 10 Tx: none Fax: (21) 57 53 16 SITA: n/a
F: 1996 ⁂ n/a Head: Basie Mouton ICAO: SPEED SERVICE Net: n/a

☐ ZS-MFY	Boeing (Douglas) DC-3C (C-47A-1-DK)	*12073*	*ZS-XXX*	*0043*	*0196*	*2 PW R-1830*	*12202*	*Freighter*		*lsf pvt / opf Speed Services Courier*
☐ ZS-MRU	Boeing (Douglas) DC-3C (R4D-1)	*4363*	*N234Z*	*0042*	*0796*	*2 PW R-1830*	*12202*	*Freighter*		*opf Speed Services Courier*
☐ ZS-NKK	AMI Turbo DC-3C	*13143*	*YV-32CP*	*0044*	*0196*	*2 PWC PT6A-65AR*	*12202*	*Freighter*		*cvtd Douglas C-47A-DK/opf Speed Serv.C.*

ALEX AIR (Alexandros Karatamoglou dba) — East London

51 Jan Smuts Ave, Greenfields, East London 5201, South Africa ☎ (431) 736 64 35 Tx: none Fax: (431) 736 64 36 SITA: n/a
F: 1994 ⁂ 3 Head: Alexandros Karatamoglou Net: n/a

☐ ZS-LOC	Beech Bonanza A36	*E-2149*	*N6923R*	*0084*		*1 CO IO-520-BB*	*1633*			*lsf Castellano-Beltrame P/L*
☐ ZS-KLE	Beech Baron B55 (95-B55)	*TC-2319*	*N67248*	*0081*		*2 CO IO-470-L*	*2313*			*lsf PE Industrial Installation CC*
☐ ZS-MCX	Beech Duke B60	*P-580*	*N1848S*	*0081*		*2 LY TIO-541-E1C4*	*3073*			*lsf Alex Air Partnership*

AOC SURVEYS (Aircraft Operating Company dba/Subs. of AOC Holdings (Pty) Ltd/affiliated with Aerial Surveys Botswana) — Lanseria

AOC Aircraft Operating Company

PO Box 2830, Johannesburg 2000, South Africa ☎ (11) 659 26 10 Tx: 450370 Fax: (11) 493 46 53 SITA: n/a
F: 1931 ⁂ 25 Head: M. Sanderson Net: n/a

☐ ZS-FFX	Cessna TU206C Super Skywagon	*U206-1078*	*A2-AEK*	*0068*		*1 CO TSIO-520-C*	*1633*	*Surveyer*		
☐ ZS-NKP	Cessna 320A SkyKnight	*320A0039*	*A2-AGE*	*0063*		*2 CO TSIO-470-B*	*2359*	*Surveyer*		
☐ ZS-KRG	Cessna 404 Titan II	*404-0676*	*N6761Y*	*0080*		*2 CO GTSIO-520-M*	*3810*	*Surveyer*		
☐ ZS-KUZ	Cessna 404 Titan II	*404-0678*	*A2-AGS*	*0080*		*2 CO GTSIO-520-M*	*3810*	*Surveyer*		

BEVERICK AIR — Welkom

PO Box 226, Welkom 9460, South Africa ☎ (57) 352 23 08 Tx: n/a Fax: (57) 357 10 49 SITA: n/a
F: 1988 ⁂ 8 Head: Alan Roebuck Net: n/a

☐ ZS-NEB	Beech Baron B55 (95-B55)	*TC-505*	*ZS-NLB*	*0064*		*2 CO IO-470-L*	*2313*			*lsf Dutec Aircraft Hire Services P/L*
☐ ZS-JOA	Piper PA-31-350 Navajo Chieftain	*31-7552132*	*N59715*	*0075*		*2 LY TIO-540-J2BD*	*3175*			
☐ ZS-KPU	Twin (Aero) Commander 500B	*500B-964-19*	*A2-ZHC*	*0060*		*2 LY IO-540-B1A5*	*3062*			*lsf Dutec Aircraft Hire Services P/L*

BOMA HELICOPTERS, (Pty) Ltd — Johannesburg-Lanseria

PO Box 30737, Kyalami 1684, South Africa ☎ (11) 702 14 16 Tx: none Fax: (11) 702 14 16 SITA: n/a
F: 1988 ⁂ n/a Head: Paul L. Davies Net: n/a Aircraft below MTOW 1361kg: Robinson R22.

☐ ZS-HSV	Bell 206B JetRanger III	*2442*	*N5003C*	*0078*	*0193*	*1 AN 250-C20B*	*1451*			

BUSH DRIFTERS, (Pty) Ltd — Johannesburg

PO Box 463, Fourways 2055, South Africa ☎ (11) 465 47 80 Tx: none Fax: 465 90 98 SITA: n/a
F: 1984 ⁂ n/a Head: John Matterson Net: n/a

☐ ZS-KDH	Cessna 210M Centurion II	*21062402*	*A2-AHY*	*0077*	*0392*	*1 CO IO-520-L*	*1724*			

676 registration type of aircraft cn/fn ex/ex* mfd del powered by mtow kg configuration selcal name/fln/specialitites/remarks

CAPE FLYING SERVICES (Associated with Todd Air Finance) — George

PO Box 2535, George 6530, South Africa ☎ (44) 876 92 17 Tx: none Fax: (44) 876 90 36 SITA: n/a
F: 1985 ✈ 8 Head: Gerald A. Todd Net: n/a Aircraft below MTOW 1361kg: Cessna 150 & Piper PA-28

☐ ZS-DSC	Piper PA-23-160 Apache	23-1877	VQ-ZEI	0059		2 LY O-320-B	1724			

CAPITAL AIR, (Pty) Ltd — Johannesburg-Rand

PO Box 18009, Rand Airport 1419, South Africa ☎ (11) 827 03 35 Tx: none Fax: (11) 827 38 98 SITA: n/a
F: 1982 ✈ 20 Head: Joao-Francisco Vinagre Net: n/a Aircraft below MTOW 1361kg: Robinson R22

☐ ZS-HJU	Bell 206B JetRanger III	3238		0081		1 AN 250-C20B	1451			
☐ ZS-REY	Bell 206B JetRanger III	3397	N688MS	0081	0195	1 AN 250-C20B	1451			
☐ ZS-RFD	Bell 206B JetRanger III	2940	C-GRVM	0080	0195	1 AN 250-C20B	1451			
☐ ZS-HIB	Bell 206L-1 LongRanger II	45303	N1068X	0079		1 AN 250-C28B	1882			

CARGO CARRIERS, (Pty) Ltd — Johannesburg

PO Box 201, Isando 1600, South Africa ☎ (11) 828 05 70 Tx: n/a Fax: (11) 828 03 46 SITA: n/a
F: n/a ✈ n/a Head: n/a Net: n/a

☐ ZS-KSU	Cessna 425 Conquest I	425-0115	N68807	0082		2 PWC PT6A-112	3901			

CIVAIR HELICOPTERS, CC — Cape Town

PO Box 120, Newlands 7725, South Africa ☎ (21) 419 51 82 Tx: none Fax: (21) 419 57 83 SITA: n/a
F: 1979 ✈ 15 Head: Andy Cluver Net: n/a Aircraft below MTOW 1361kg: Hughes 269C (300C).

☐ ZS-HVH	MD Helicopters MD 500E (Hughes 369E)	0234E	N1603S	0087	0293	1 AN 250-C20B	1361			
☐ ZS-HVN	Bell 206B JetRanger III	1966	5H-MPN	0076		1 AN 250-C20B	1451			cvtd JetRanger II
☐ ZS-RFS	Bell 206L-4 LongRanger IV	52116	N4252S	0095	0395	1 AN 250-C30P	2018			lsf Helitours Partnership
☐ ZS-RGG	Eurocopter (MBB) BO105C	S-52	N291CA	0072	0795	2 AN 250-C20	2300			

COMAIR, (Pty) Ltd = MN / CAW — Johannesburg-Int'l & -Rand

PO Box 7015, Bonaero Park 1622, South Africa ☎ (11) 921 01 11 Tx: 7-46738 sa Fax: (11) 973 39 13 SITA: n/a
F: 1967 ✈ 200 Head: Dave Novick IATA: 161 ICAO: COMMERCIAL Net: n/a Scheduled services are operated on a franchise agreement with BRITISH AIRWAYS (in full such colors and both titles) & using BA-flight numbers.

☐ ZS-NLN	Boeing 737-2L9 (A)	21686 / 550	TF-ABU	0079	1194	2 PW JT8D-17	53070	CY104	EG-DF	op in BA Waves & Cranes-colors
☐ ZS-NNG	Boeing 737-236 (A)	21793 / 635	PH-TSE	0080	0995	2 PW JT8D-15A	54204	CY104		lsf BOUL / op in BA Bauhaus-colors
☐ ZS-NNH	Boeing 737-236 (A)	21797 / 653	PH-TSD	0080	1095	2 PW JT8D-15A	54204	CY104		op in BA Blue Poole-colors
☐ ZS-SBN	Boeing 737-244	20229 / 214		0069	0894	2 PW JT8D-9	47000	CY102	FH-EM	op in BA Ndebele-colors
☐ ZS-SBO	Boeing 737-244	20329 / 250		0070	0892	2 PW JT8D-9	47000	CY102	BM-HK	op in BA Cockerel of Lowicz-colors
☐ ZS-SBR	Boeing 737-244	20331 / 260		0070	0793	2 PW JT8D-9	47000	CY102	BM-KL	op in BA Animals & Trees-colors
☐ ZS-NOU	Boeing 727-230 (A)	21113 / 1176	TC-TCA	1175	1096	3 PW JT8D-15	86409	CY148	AF-HK	lsf SFR / op in BA Blomsterang-colors
☐ ZS-NOV	Boeing 727-230 (A)	21114 / 1178	TC-TCB	1275	0996	3 PW JT8D-15	86409	CY148	AF-HL	lsf SFR/op in BA Delftblue Daybreak-cs
☐ ZS-NZV	Boeing 727-230 (A)	20792 / 1023	TC-RAC	0074	1297	3 PW JT8D-15	86409	CY150		lsf SFR / op in BA Column-colors
☐ ZS-OBO	Boeing 727-230 (A)	21623 / 1433	OK-JGY	0079	0598	3 PW JT8D-15	86409	CY148		lsfSFR/BA BenyhoneTartan/Mtn ofBirds-cs

COURT AIR = CUT (Divsion of Court Helicopters, (Pty) Ltd) — Cape Town-Int'l

PO Box 2546, Cape Town 8000, South Africa ☎ (21) 934 05 60 Tx: 5-20696 sa Fax: (21) 934 05 68 SITA: n/a
F: n/a ✈ n/a Head: Jeremy Labuschagne ICAO: COURT AIR Net: n/a

☐ ZS-KEI	Convair 580	141	N5822	0053	0993	2 AN 501-D13	26379			cvtd CV340-31
☐ ZS-LYL	Convair 580	39	N511GA	0052	0993	2 AN 501-D13	24766			cvtd CV340-38

COURT HELICOPTERS, (Pty) Ltd (Member of Helikopter Service Group, Norway) — CPT-Docks & DF Malan / JNB-Rand / Durban / George

PO Box 2546, Cape Town 8000, South Africa ☎ (21) 934 05 60 Tx: 5-20696 sa Fax: (21) 934 05 68 SITA: n/a
F: 1964 ✈ 150 Head: Jeremy Labuschagne Net: n/a

☐ ZS-HDV	Bell 206B JetRanger	1063	A2-HAA	0073		1 AN 250-C20	1451			
☐ ZS-HDZ	Bell 206B JetRanger III	1319	A2-ACM	0074		1 AN 250-C20B	1451			cvtd JetRanger
☐ ZS-HEK	Bell 206B JetRanger III	1477		0074		1 AN 250-C20B	1451			cvtd JetRanger
☐ ZS-HEM	Bell 206B JetRanger III	1608		0076		1 AN 250-C20B	1451			cvtd JetRanger
☐ ZS-HHW	Bell 206B JetRanger III	2551	N50137	0078		1 AN 250-C20B	1451			
☐ ZS-HJY	Bell 206B JetRanger III	3299		0081		1 AN 250-C20B	1451			
☐ ZS-HLZ	Bell 206B JetRanger III	3930		0086		1 AN 250-C20B	1451			lsf Gold Fields Security Ltd
☐ ZS-HVY	Bell 206B JetRanger	1471	N59605	0074		1 AN 250-C20	1451			lsf Zululand Baconry P/L
☐ ZS-HJN	Bell 206L-1 LongRanger II	45571		0080		1 AN 250-C28C	1882			
☐ ZS-HVV	Bell 206L-3 LongRanger III	51151	N151JB	0085		1 AN 250-C30P	1882			lsf Mostert Co.
☐ ZS-RDI	Bell 206L-3 LongRanger III	51392		0090		1 AN 250-C30P	1882			
☐ ZS-RCP	Eurocopter (MBB) BO105LS-A3	2001	VH-XLS	0085		2 AN 250-C28C	2600			lsf Eurocopter Southern Africa P/L
☐ ZS-RKL	Eurocopter (MBB) BO105DB	S-35	G-BAFD	0072	1298	2 AN 250-C20B	2400			
☐ ZS-HHK	Sikorsky S-62A	62062	3D-HAE	0060		1 GE CT58-110-1	3584			
☐ ZS-HNU	Sikorsky S-76A	760073	N721EW	0080		2 AN 250-C30S	4763			
☐ ZS-RBE	Sikorsky S-76A	760268	V5-HAB	0084	0898	2 AN 250-C30S	4763			
☐ ZS-RGX	Sikorsky S-76A	760132	VH-ECS	0081		2 AN 250-C30S	4763			lsf Esso
☐ ZS-RGZ	Sikorsky S-76A	760051	VH-EMM	0080	1295	2 AN 250-C30S	4763			lsf Esso
☐ ZS-RHB	Sikorsky S-76A++	760109	VH-EMX	0080	0396	2 TU Arriel 1S1	4899			lst Sonair-Helipetrol / cvtd S-76A
☐ ZS-RJS	Sikorsky S-76A+	760160	5N-DOS	0081	0198	2 TU Arriel 1S	4899			cvtd S-76A
☐ ZS-RKE	Sikorsky S-76A++	760042	LX-HUD	0079	0698	2 TU Arriel 1S1	4763			lsf Heli Union Int'l / cvtd S-76A
☐ ZS-RKO	Sikorsky S-76A++	760135	VH-LAX	0080	0199	2 TU Arriel 1S1	4899			cvtd S-76A
☐ ZS-RGV	Bell 212	30952	C-FRUU	0079	1095	2 PWC PT6T-3 TwinPac	5080			
☐ ZS-RKN	Bell 212	30849	VT-NSY	0077	0399	2 PWC PT6T-3 TwinPac	5080			
☐ ZS-HSZ	Sikorsky S-61N	61473	8Q-BUZ	0070		2 GE CT58-140-1	9299			
☐ ZS-HVJ	Sikorsky S-61N	61493	N9119Z	0072		2 GE CT58-140-1	9299			lst Helinamib
☐ ZS-RDV	Sikorsky S-61N	61716	G-BIHH	0074	0993	2 GE CT58-140-1	9299			

DEBON-AIR (Debon Air Tours, CC dba) — Johannesburg-Lanseria

PO Box 416, Lanseria 1748, South Africa ☎ (11) 760 40 10 Tx: none Fax: (11) 760 40 07 SITA: n/a
F: 1992 ✈ 12 Head: Denise Böttger Net: n/a

☐ ZS-OJD	Boeing (Douglas) DC-3C (C-53-DO)	4890	5Y-BGU	0042	1098	2 PW R-1830	12701	Y25		lsf Nerocro CC
☐ ZS-OJE	Boeing (Douglas) DC-3C (C-47B-25-DK)	32844	5Y-AAE	0345	1198	2 PW R-1830	12701	Y25		Delamere
☐ ZS-PTG	Boeing (Douglas) DC-3C (C-47A-25-DK)	13331	A2-ACG	0044	1295	2 PW R-1830	12202	Y30		Delaney

EAST COAST AIRWAYS, (Pty) Ltd = ECT — Durban-Virginia

PO Box 20245, Durban North 4016, South Africa ☎ (31) 564 93 44 Tx: 6-28656 sa Fax: (31) 83 14 14 SITA: n/a
F: 1977 ✈ 10 Head: E.I. Jamieson ICAO: EASTWAY Net: n/a

☐ ZS-LAX	Beech Baron 58	TH-1268	G-BMGI	0081		2 CO IO-520-CB	2449			lsf Kanberri Air Services P/L
☐ ZS-LFM	Beech King Air 200	BB-954	N1839S	0082		2 PWC PT6A-41	5670			lsf G.U.D. Filters
☐ ZS-NGC	Beech King Air 200	BB-215	7Q-YTC	0076		2 PWC PT6A-41	5670			lsf Kanberri Air Service

EASTERN CHARTERS, (Pty) Ltd — Ermelo

PO Box 1747, Ermelo 2350, South Africa ☎ (1341) 97 432 Tx: n/a Fax: (1341) 91 510 SITA: n/a
F: 1994 ✈ 3 Head: Jaco Skeen Net: n/a

☐ ZS-KKD	Piper PA-34-200T Seneca II	34-8070139	N8159Z	0081		2 CO TSIO-360-E	2073			lsf FHF Partnership

ELB FLYING SERVICES, Ltd (Subsidiary of El Bateman Ltd) — Johannesburg-Grand Central

PO Box 565, Boksburg 1460, South Africa ☎ (11) 899 22 61 Tx: none Fax: (11) 899 28 50 SITA: n/a
F: 1976 ✈ 2 Head: William G.L. Bateman Net: n/a

☐ ZS-MVX	Cessna 525 CitationJet	5250010	N210CJ	0093	0194	2 WRR FJ44-1A	4717		FR-HL	

EXECUJET AIR CHARTER, (Pty) Ltd (Affiliated with Execujet Aircraft Sales, (Pty) Ltd) — Johannesburg-Lanseria

PO Box 2, Lanseria 1748, South Africa ☎ (11) 659 27 57 Tx: none Fax: (11) 659 25 20 SITA: n/a
F: 1982 ✈ 18 Head: Niall Olver Net: n/a

☐ ZS-OEY	Piper PA-31-310 Navajo C	31-7912051	N350CB	0079	0198	2 LY TIO-540-A2C	2948			
☐ ZS-LXT	Cessna 501 Citation I/SP	501-0215	N50MM	0081		2 PWC JT15D-1A	5375			lsf Anerley Citation Partnership
☐ ZS-LIL	Beech King Air B200	BB-1047	V5-LIL	0082		2 PWC PT6A-42	5670			
☐ ZS-NGL	Cessna 560 Citation V	560-0202	N1283V	0092		2 PWC JT15D-5A	7212			lsf Sappi Manufacturing P/L
☐ ZS-EAG	Learjet 31A	31A-142	N142LJ	0097	1297	2 GA TFE731-2-3B	7711			
☐ ZS-MGK	Learjet 35A	35A-357	N1001L	0080		2 GA TFE731-2-2B	8300			
☐ ZS-AVL	Canadair CL-604 (CL-600-2B16) Challen.	5328	N712DG	0096	0798	2 GE CF34-3B	21863			

EXECUTIVE AEROSPACE = EAS (Executive Aerospace Operations, (Pty) Ltd dba) — Durban-Int'l

P.O., International Airport 4029, South Africa ☎ (31) 42 63 22 Tx: 625438 exec sa Fax: (31) 42 78 10 SITA: n/a
F: 1984 ✈ 35 Head: Keith Rosenweire ICAO: AEROSPACE Net: n/a

☐ ZS-KCA	Beech Baron 58	TH-871		0077		2 CO IO-520-CB	2449			lsf pvt
☐ ZS-LVK	Beech King Air B200	BB-1111	N600CM	0083		2 PWC PT6A-42	5670			lsf Aviation Africa II Partnership

677 registration type of aircraft cn/fn ex/ex* mfd del powered by mtow kg configuration selcal name/fln/specialitites/remarks

	registration	type of aircraft	cn/fn	ex/ex*	mfd	del	powered by	mtow kg	configuration	selcal	name/fln/specialities/remarks
☐	ZS-MIM	Beech King Air 200	BB-846	N846MW	0081		2 PWC PT6A-41	5670			lsf Cormorant Avn/sub-lst AD Avn,5Y-BKA
☐	ZS-LSO	BAe (HS) 748-FAA Srs 2B	1783 / 264	G-BMJU	0080	0796	2 RR Dart 535-2	21002	Y44		lsf Aerospace Express P/L
☐	ZS-NNW	BAe (HS) 748-378 Srs 2B	1785 / 266	G-BOHZ	0081	1194	2 RR Dart 536-2	19995	Y44		lsf Aerospace Express P/L
☐	ZS-NWW	BAe (HS) 748-378 Srs 2B	1786 / 269	G-HDBC	0081	1095	2 RR Dart 536-2	19995	Y44		lsf Aerospace Express P/L/sub-lst RWD
☐	ZS-OCF	BAe (HS) 748-242 Srs 2A	1647 / 131	ZK-CWJ	0068	0897	2 RR Dart 534-2	20183	Y44		lsf Aerospace Express P/L
☐	ZS-ODJ	BAe (HS) 748-263 Srs 2A	1680 / 165	F-GHKA	0070	0997	2 RR Dart 534-2	20183	Y44		lsf Aerospace Express P/L

EXPRESS AIR SERVICES, (Pty) Ltd = FLN
Cape Town, Johannesburg & Port Elizabeth

PO Box 39, International Airport, Cape Town 7525, South Africa ☎ (21) 934 08 18 Tx: none Fax: (21) 934 95 77 SITA: n/a
F: 1997 ♦♦♦ 50 Head: Eric W. Kingwill ICAO: FREIGHTLINE Net: n/a

	registration	type of aircraft	cn/fn	ex/ex*	mfd	del	powered by	mtow kg	configuration	selcal	name/fln/specialities/remarks
☐	ZS-NJP	Piaggio P.166S Albatross	457	SAAF895	0073	0297	2 LY GSO-480-B1C6	3680	Freighter		
☐	ZS-NJS	Piaggio P.166S Albatross	454	ZU-ADD	0073	0297	2 LY GSO-480-B1C6	3680	Freighter		
☐	ZS-NJT	Piaggio P.166S Albatross	453	SAAF891	0073	0297	2 LY GSO-480-B1C6	3680	Freighter		
☐	ZS-NJU	Piaggio P.166S Albatross	452	SAAF890	0073	0297	2 LY GSO-480-B1C6	3680	Freighter		
☐	ZS-NJV	Piaggio P.166S Albatross	450	SAAF888	0073	0297	2 LY GSO-480-B1C6	3680	Freighter		
☐	ZS-NJW	Piaggio P.166S Albatross	448	SAAF886	0073	0297	2 LY GSO-480-B1C6	3680	Freighter		
☐	ZS-NJX	Piaggio P.166S Albatross	446	SAAF884	0073	0297	2 LY GSO-480-B1C6	3680	Freighter		
☐	ZS-NJY	Piaggio P.166S Albatross	445	ZU-ADO	0073	0297	2 LY GSO-480-B1C6	3680	Freighter		
☐	ZS-NMY	Boeing 727-23 (F)	18447 / 127	N1991	0465	1097	3 PW JT8D-7B	72847	Freighter		cvtd -23
☐	ZS-NPX	Boeing 727-23 (F)	19131 / 218	N512FE	0066	0297	3 PW JT8D-7B	72575	Freighter		Xolani / lsf SFR / cvtd -23

EYETHU AIR CARGO (Division of Aero Air, Pty Ltd)
Johannesburg-Rand

PO Box 18025, Rand Airport 1419, South Africa ☎ (11) 827 88 91 Tx: none Fax: (11) 827 87 90 SITA: n/a
F: 1997 ♦♦♦ n/a Head: n/a Net: n/a

	registration	type of aircraft	cn/fn	ex/ex*	mfd	del	powered by	mtow kg	configuration	selcal	name/fln/specialities/remarks
☐	ZS-NTD	Boeing (Douglas) DC-3C (C-47B-10-DK)	26438	6848	0044		2 PW R-1830	12202	Freighter		
☐	ZS-NTE	Boeing (Douglas) DC-3C (C-47A-1-DK)	11926	6873	0043		2 PW R-1830	12202	Freighter		
☐	ZS-NZA	Boeing (Douglas) DC-3C (C-47A-50-DL)	10110	6862	0043		2 PW R-1830	12202	Freighter		

FALCONAIR, Ltd (Subsidiary of Rembrandt Group)
Cape Town-Int'l

PO Box 456, Stellenbosch 7600, South Africa ☎ (21) 934 01 23 Tx: none Fax: (21) 934 23 84 SITA: n/a
F: 1975 ♦♦♦ 31 Head: Dawid S. Laynes Net: n/a

	registration	type of aircraft	cn/fn	ex/ex*	mfd	del	powered by	mtow kg	configuration	selcal	name/fln/specialities/remarks
☐	ZS-NUZ	Cessna 560 Citation V Ultra	560-0398		0096	0197	2 PWC JT15D-5D	7394	VIP		lsf The Falcon Trust
☐	VP-BPI	Dassault Falcon 900B	149	VR-BPI	0095	0795	3 GA TFE731-5BR-1C	21099	VIP		lsf Intercont. Aviation (Bermuda) Ltd
☐	VP-BRO	Dassault Falcon 900EX	13	F-WWFK*	0097	0797	3 GA TFE731-60-1C	22226	VIP		lsf Flight Services (Bermuda) Ltd

FEDAIR = FDR (Federal Air, Pty Ltd dba)
Durban

PO Box 20400, Durban North 4016, South Africa ☎ (31) 562 82 21 Tx: none Fax: (31) 562 84 01 SITA: n/a
F: 1989 ♦♦♦ 40 Head: Greg J. McCurrach ICAO: FEDAIR Net: n/a

	registration	type of aircraft	cn/fn	ex/ex*	mfd	del	powered by	mtow kg	configuration	selcal	name/fln/specialities/remarks
☐	ZS-NDV	Cessna 208B Grand Caravan	208B0374	N1117Y*	0094	1097	1 PWC PT6A-114A	3969	Y14 / Freighter		
☐	ZS-NFY	Cessna 208B Grand Caravan	208B0294	N5275B*	0092		1 PWC PT6A-114A	3969	Y14 / Freighter		lsf Grand Caravan Charter P/L
☐	ZS-NGO	Cessna 208B Grand Caravan	208B0322	N1027S*	0092		1 PWC PT6A-114A	3969	Y14 / Freighter		
☐	ZS-NPD	Cessna 208B Grand Caravan	208B0369	N1117A*	0093	0997	1 PWC PT6A-114A	3969	Y14 / Freighter		
☐	ZS-NVH	Cessna 208B Grand Caravan	208B0473	N1287N*	0095		1 PWC PT6A-114A	3969	Y14 / Freighter		lsf Caravan Transport CC
☐	ZS-NXZ	Cessna 208B Grand Caravan	208B0357		0093	0997	1 PWC PT6A-114A	3969	Y14 / Freighter		
☐	ZS-ODS	Cessna 208B Grand Caravan	208B0538	C-FKAC	0096	1097	1 PWC PT6A-114A	3969	Y14 / Freighter		
☐	ZS-PAT	Cessna 208B Grand Caravan	208B0437		0095	0495	1 PWC PT6A-114A	3969	Y14 / Freighter		lsf The Flying Fish Airline CC
☐	TZ-NLM	Cessna 208B Grand Caravan	208B0375	ZS-NLM*	0094		1 PWC PT6A-114A	3969	Y14 / Freighter		

FLAMINGO FLIGHTS, CC
Cape Town-Int'l

PO Box 26481, Hout Bay 7872, South Africa ☎ (21) 790 10 10 Tx: n/a Fax: (21) 790 10 10 SITA: n/a
F: 1992 ♦♦♦ 5 Head: Peter E. Claxton Net: n/a

	registration	type of aircraft	cn/fn	ex/ex*	mfd	del	powered by	mtow kg	configuration	selcal	name/fln/specialities/remarks
☐	ZS-ECA	Beech Bonanza V35B	D-9279	ZS-INA	0071		1 CO IO-520-BA	1542			
☐	ZS-ITX	Piper PA-23-250 Aztec C	27-3914	3D-FLY	0068		2 LY IO-540-C4B5	2359			lsf pvt
☐	ZS-NKF	Piper PA-23-250 Aztec F	27-7654017		0076		2 LY IO-540-C4B5	2359			lsf Lge Air 21
☐	ZS-NVC	De Havilland DHC-2 Beaver I	665	N211LB	0053	0995	1 PW R-985	2313			Amphibian

FOSTER WEBB AIR CHARTER (Subs. of F.W.Hangers CC/Assoc.with Foster Webb Avn (Maint.) P/L, Foster Webb Sales & Foster Webb Constr.P/L)
Johannesburg-Lanseria

PO Box 464, Lanseria 1748, South Africa ☎ (11) 659 25 74 Tx: n/a Fax: (11) 701 32 15 SITA: n/a
F: 1982 ♦♦♦ 22 Head: Rodger A. Foster & Barrie Webb Net: n/a

	registration	type of aircraft	cn/fn	ex/ex*	mfd	del	powered by	mtow kg	configuration	selcal	name/fln/specialities/remarks
☐	ZS-MTA	Cessna 210M Centurion II	21062842	N6831B	0078		1 CO IO-520-L	1724			lsf Sentour CC
☐	ZS-JUH	Piper PA-34-200T Seneca II	34-7670190	N9178K	0076		2 CO TSIO-360-E	2073			lsf pvt
☐	ZS-JPM	Beech Baron 58	TH-639	N159D	0075		2 CO IO-520-C	2449			lsf Rio Charter CC
☐	ZS-MHI	Beech Baron 58	TH-821	N17805	0077		2 CO IO-520-C	2449			lsf Aircraft Hire CC
☐	ZS-NGV	Piper PA-31-350 Navajo Chieftain	31-7952071	N600JE	0079		2 LY TIO-540-J2BD	3175			
☐	ZS-NOW	Beech King Air B200	BB-1427	N8003U	0092	0798	2 PWC PT6A-42	5670			
☐	ZS-OFW	Learjet 31A	31A-031	N31HA	0091	1097	2 GA TFE731-2-3B	7484			lst AHA

HELIBIP, CC
Johannesburg-Grand Central

153 Cygnus Street, Waterkloof, Pretoria 0181, South Africa ☎ (12) 45 17 52 Tx: none Fax: (12) 45 17 52 SITA: n/a
F: 1995 ♦♦♦ 4 Head: Bernard Brandt Net: http://www.helibip.iafrica.co.2a Aircraft below MTOW 1361kg: Robinson R22

	registration	type of aircraft	cn/fn	ex/ex*	mfd	del	powered by	mtow kg	configuration	selcal	name/fln/specialities/remarks
☐	ZS-HVZ	Bell 206B JetRanger III	3825	N900JB	0084	0895	1 AN 250-C20J	1451			
☐	ZS-RHA	Eurocopter (Aerosp.) AS350B2 Ecureuil	2914		0095	0196	1 TU Arriel 1D1	2250			lsf B2 Partnership
☐	ZS-RJL	Bell 205A-1	30195	C-GVIK	0075	1297	1 LY T5313B	4309			

HELIQUIP, (Pty) Ltd
Johannesburg-Grand Central

PO Box 5526, Halfway House 1685, South Africa ☎ (11) 315 00 01 Tx: 7-21302 sa Fax: (11) 805 34 09 SITA: n/a
F: 1966 ♦♦♦ 35 Head: Peter Piggott Net: n/a

	registration	type of aircraft	cn/fn	ex/ex*	mfd	del	powered by	mtow kg	configuration	selcal	name/fln/specialities/remarks
☐	ZS-HIU	Eurocopter (Aerosp.) AS350B Ecureuil	1278		0080	0992	1 TU Arriel 1B	1950			
☐	ZS-HKJ	Eurocopter (Aerosp.) AS350B Ecureuil	1461		0082		1 TU Arriel 1B	1950	VIP		
☐	ZS-HVC	Eurocopter (Aerosp.) AS350B Ecureuil	1129		0080		1 TU Arriel 1B	1950			lsf Marlin Air P/L
☐	ZS-RGK	Eurocopter (Aerosp.) AS350B2 Ecureuil	2877		0095	0895	1 TU Arriel 1D1	2250			lsf Iscor Ltd

HEYNS HELICOPTERS, (Pty) Ltd
Nelspruit

PO Box 2113, Nelspruit 1200, South Africa ☎ (13) 741 45 29 Tx: none Fax: (13) 741 11 96 SITA: n/a
F: 1997 ♦♦♦ n/a Head: Nicolaas J. Heyns Net: http://www.heynsheli.co.za/

	registration	type of aircraft	cn/fn	ex/ex*	mfd	del	powered by	mtow kg	configuration	selcal	name/fln/specialities/remarks
☐	ZS-RIR	Mil Mi-8MTV-1 (Mi-17)	95957	RA-27130	0092	0097	2 IS TV3-117MT	13000			lsf TMN
☐	ZS-RIS	Mil Mi-8MTV-1 (Mi-17)	95958	RA-27131	0092	0097	2 IS TV3-117MT	13000			lsf TMN
☐	ZS-RIT	Mil Mi-8MTV-1 (Mi-17)	95964	RA-27113	0092	0097	2 IS TV3-117MT	13000			lsf TMN
☐	ZS-RIU	Mil Mi-8MTV-1 (Mi-17)	95955	RA-27128	0092	0097	2 IS TV3-117MT	13000			lsf TMN
☐	ZS-RIV	Mil Mi-8MTV-1 (Mi-17)	95965	RA-27114	0092	0097	2 IS TV3-117MT	13000			lsf TMN
☐	RA-22891	Mil Mi-8T	98417043	CCCP-22891	0084	0097	2 IS TV2-117A	12000			lsf TMN / opf UN
☐	RA-22925	Mil Mi-8T	98520442	CCCP-22925	0085	0097	2 IS TV2-117A	12000			lsf TMN
☐	RA-24171	Mil Mi-8T	98943075	CCCP-24171	0089	0097	2 IS TV2-117A	12000			lsf TMN
☐	RA-24248	Mil Mi-8T	98730937	CCCP-24248	0087	0097	2 IS TV2-117A	12000			lsf TMN
☐	RA-25139	Mil Mi-8T	99047492	CCCP-25139	0090	0097	2 IS TV2-117A	12000			lsf TMN
☐	RA-25165	Mil Mi-8T	99047964	CCCP-25165	0090	0097	2 IS TV2-117A	12000			lsf TMN
☐	RA-25934	Mil Mi-8T	5570	CCCP-25934	0075	0097	2 IS TV2-117A	12000			lsf TMN / opf UN
☐	RA-27129	Mil Mi-8MTV-1 (Mi-17)	95956	CCCP-27129	0092	0097	2 IS TV3-117MT	13000			lsf TMN

INTENSIVE AIR, (Pty) Ltd = IM / XRA
Johannesburg-Int'l & -Rand

PO Box 91212, Auckland Park 2006, South Africa ☎ (11) 788 76 59 Tx: none Fax: (11) 880 74 04 SITA: n/a
F: 1997 ♦♦♦ n/a Head: Jakobus W.K. Louw ICAO: INTENSIVE Net: n/a

	registration	type of aircraft	cn/fn	ex/ex*	mfd	del	powered by	mtow kg	configuration	selcal	name/fln/specialities/remarks
☐	ZS-XGE	BAe (HS) 748-351 Srs 2A	1770 / 252	G-BGPR*	0079	1097	2 RR Dart 535-2	20182	Y44		Pudding
☐	ZS-XGY	BAe (HS) 748-344 Srs 2A	1764 / 248	TN-AFI	0079	1097	2 RR Dart 534-2	20182	Y44		
☐	ZS-XGZ	BAe (HS) 748-286 Srs 2A (SCD)	1740 / 221	5H-WDL	0076	1097	2 RR Dart 535-2	21092	Y44 / Freighter		

INTER AIR = D6 / ILN (Inter Aviation Services (Pty) Ltd dba)
Johannesburg-Int'l

Private Bag 8, P.O. Johannesburg Int'l Airport 1627, South Africa ☎ (11) 390 25 55 Tx: none Fax: (11) 390 27 78 SITA: JNB00D6
F: 1993 ♦♦♦ 120 Head: David P. Tokoph IATA: 625 ICAO: INLINE Net: n/a

	registration	type of aircraft	cn/fn	ex/ex*	mfd	del	powered by	mtow kg	configuration	selcal	name/fln/specialities/remarks
☐	9J-AFW	Boeing 737-202C	19426 / 72	N801AL	0068	1097	2 PW JT8D-9A	49442	C12Y88		lsf RZL
☐	ZS-IJH	Boeing 727-116C	19813 / 594	N77AZ	0068	0299	3 PW JT8D-9A	76657	C12Y92		lsf Aviation Consultants
☐	ZS-IJI	Boeing 707-323C	19517 / 614	N29AZ	0067	0299	4 PW JT3D-3B (HK2/COM)	150850	C12Y144		lsf Grecoair

INTEROCEAN AIRWAYS, (Pty) Ltd (Flying Enterprise, Inc. dba)
Benoni-Brakpan

Operations office:, PO Box 4304, Dalpark 1543, South Africa ☎ (82) 550 14 31 Tx: none Fax: (82) 915 37 41 SITA: n/a
F: 1968 ♦♦♦ 30 Head: Andrew M. Smulian Net: n/a

	registration	type of aircraft	cn/fn	ex/ex*	mfd	del	powered by	mtow kg	configuration	selcal	name/fln/specialities/remarks
☐	3D-ATH	Boeing (Douglas) DC-3C (C-47A-25-DL)	9410	C9-ATH	0043	0788	2 PW R-1830	12202	Freighter		lst Uganda A.F.
☐	C9-ATE	De Havilland DHC-4A Caribou	221	63-9758	0065	0389	2 PW R-2000	12927	Freighter		std Benoni-Brakpan
☐	C9-ATV	De Havilland DHC-4A Caribou	78	N9012J	0063	0590	2 PW R-2000	12927	Freighter		std Beira
☐	N1016N	De Havilland DHC-4A Caribou	1	JW9011	0058		2 PW R-2000	12927	Freighter		

☐ N4365Y	De Havilland DHC-4A Caribou	172	63-9732	0064		2 PW R-2000	12927	Freighter		lsf Third World Hope Inc. / std BLZ
☐ 3D-ATF	Boeing (Douglas) DC-4 (C-54D-10-DC)	10811 / DC 542	C9-ATF	0045	0889	4 PW R-2000	33475	Freighter		
☐ EL-AWX	Boeing (Douglas) DC-4 (C-54D-15-DC)	22192 / DC 644	C9-ATS	0045	0391	4 PW R-2000	33475	Freighter		

JET AIR CHARTER, (Pty) Ltd (formerly Inter Air, (Pty) Ltd) — **Johannesburg-Lanseria**

PO Box 259, Lanseria 1748, South Africa ☎ (11) 659 15 74 Tx: 4-23559 sa Fax: (11) 659 24 98 SITA: n/a
F: 1979 ✱✱✱ 12 Head: Tom Robbins Net: http://www.jetair.co.za

☐ ZS-GLS	Beech Baron 58	TH-497	N7365R	0074		2 CO IO-520-C	2449			lsf NIC Nak Shoppe P/L
☐ ZS-RCC	Cessna 500 Citation	500-0106	N106CC	0073		2 PWC JT15D-1	5216			lsf Schwartz Diamonds P/L
☐ ZS-MTD	Learjet 25B	25B-160	3D-AEZ	0074		2 GE CJ610-6	6804			lsf Interjet Maintenance P/L / opf UN

KANGRA AVIATION (Kangra Group, Pty Ltd dba) — **Johannesburg-Lanseria**

PO Box 2465, Johannesburg 2000, South Africa ☎ (11) 643 73 71 Tx: none Fax: (11) 484 30 24 SITA: n/a
F: 1979 ✱✱✱ 3 Head: Capt. R.J.P. Johnson Net: n/a

☐ ZS-DGB	Canadair CL-604 (CL-600-2B16) Challen.	5390	N604KG	0998	0299	2 GE CF34-3B	21909	10 Pax		

KINDOC AIRWAYS, (Pty) Ltd (Member of Industrial Development Corporation of South Africa Limited) — **Johannesburg-Lanseria**

PO Box 784055, Sandton 2146, South Africa ☎ (11) 883 16 00 Tx: 4-27174 sa Fax: (11) 883 16 55 SITA: n/a
F: 1971 ✱✱✱ 2 Head: n/a Net: n/a

☐ ZS-OFM	Cessna 560 Citation V	560-0467	N5096S*	0098	0498	2 PWC JT15D-5A	7212			

LUFT AFRIQUE (Ibu Air (Pty) Ltd dba) — **Pretoria-Wonderboom**

PO Box 14806, Sinoville 0129, South Africa ☎ (12) 567 35 31 Tx: none Fax: (12) 567 35 86 SITA: n/a
F: 1997 ✱✱✱ n/a Head: n/a Net: n/a

☐ ZS-OEH	Fokker F27 Friendship 100 (F27 Mk100)	10152	C-1	0060	1297	2 RR Dart 514-7	18370	Y32		
☐ ZS-OEI	Fokker F27 Troopship 300M (F27 Mk300M)	10155	C-5	0060	1297	2 RR Dart 514-7	18370	Freighter		
☐ ZS-OEJ	Fokker F27 Troopship 300M (F27 Mk300M)	10154	C-4	0060	0798	2 RR Dart 514-7	18370	Frtr or Y32		
☐ ZS-OEK	Fokker F27 Troopship 300M (F27 Mk300M)	10161	C-11	0060	0798	2 RR Dart 514-7	18370	Freighter		

LUFTMEISTER AIR, (Pty) Ltd — **Johannesburg-Grand Central**

PO Box 74972, Lynnwood Ridge 7040, South Africa ☎ (12) 804 40 12 Tx: none Fax: (12) 804 40 16 SITA: n/a
F: 1998 ✱✱✱ n/a Head: Nick Palm Net: n/a

☐ ZS-OGE	CASA (IPTN) CN-235-10	C010	EC-EMK	0088	1288	2 GE CT7-7A	14400	Y40		
☐ ZS-OGF	CASA (IPTN) CN-235-10	C012	EC-EMN	0088	1298	2 GE CT7-7A	14400	Y40		
☐ ZS-OGG	CASA (IPTN) CN-235-10	C007	EC-EMJ	0088	1298	2 GE CT7-7A	14400	Y40		

MADIBA AIR, (Pty) Ltd — **Johannesburg-Lanseria**

PO Box 201, Lanseria 1748, South Africa ☎ (11) 701 32 14 Tx: none Fax: (11) 701 32 81 SITA: n/a
F: 1971 ✱✱✱ 20 Head: Gary Van Der Merwe Net: http://www.madiba-air.co.za Aircraft below MTOW 1361kg: Hiller FH1100, Hughes 269C (500C) & 369HS (500C)

☐ ZS-HXL	Bell 206B JetRanger III	4106	N7131N	0090		1 AN 250-C20J	1451			
☐ ZS-KJI	Beech Bonanza A36	E-1571	N6063X	0079	0898	1 CO IO-520-BB	1633			
☐ ZS-NHG	Beech Duke A60	P-259		0073	0498	2 LY TIO-541-E1B4	3073			
☐ ZS-HVR	Bell 222B	47152		0087	1297	2 LY LTS101-750C.1	3742			
☐ ZS-MLO	Beech King Air C90	LJ-526	N948K	0071	0498	2 PWC PT6A-20	4377			
☐ ZS-KGW	Beech King Air 200	BB-381	N4848M	0078		2 PWC PT6A-41	5670	12 Pax		
☐ ZS-NHW	GAC (Grumman) G-159 (F/SCD) Gulfstream I	141	N800PA	0064		2 RR Dart 529-8X	16329	19 Pax		cvtd G-159
☐ ZS-OCA	GAC (Grumman) G-159 Gulfstream I	042	ZS-MAS	0060	0797	2 RR Dart 529-8X	16329	19 Pax		

MAF South Africa – Mission Aviation Fellowship, SA — **Johannesburg-Rand**

PO Box 1688, Edenvale 1610, South Africa ☎ (11) 609 28 07 Tx: 747414 sa Fax: (11) 609 46 44 SITA: n/a
F: 1972 ✱✱✱ 9 Head: Tom de Waal Net: n/a Non-commercial multinational ecclesiastical consortium conducting flights for relief & development agencies & missions in remote areas of third world countries.

☐ ZS-FOM	Piper PA-32-300 Cherokee SIX	32-40156	9J-RFG	0067		1 LY IO-540-K1A5	1542			
☐ ZS-KNK	Cessna 210N Centurion II	21063536	N6492A	0079		1 CO IO-520-L	1724			
☐ ZS-KPD	Cessna 210N Centurion II	21063573	V5-KPD	0079	0397	1 CO IO-550-L	1724			Bonair modified incl Props

METAVIA AIRLINES, (Pty) Ltd (formerly Lima-Kilo) — **Johannesburg-Int'l**

PO Box 787106, Sandton 2146, South Africa ☎ (11) 883 00 72 Tx: 335234 sa Fax: (11) 883 00 78 SITA: n/a
F: 1984 ✱✱✱ 70 Head: Mrs. D. Ward Net: n/a

☐ ZS-NIJ	Let 410UVP-E20	922728	OK-XDM*	0092	0596	2 WA M-601E	6400	Y19		Gauteng / lsf Henric Exploration
☐ ZS-NIK	Let 410UVP-E20	922726	OK-XDN*	0092	0795	2 WA M-601E	6400	Y19		Mpumalanga / lsf Hernic Exploration P/L
☐ ZS-OBS	Let 410UVP-E20	972731	S9-TBA	0093	0597	2 WA M-601E	6600	Y19		lsf Hernic Explorations P/L

MILLIONAIR CHARTER, (Pty) Ltd — **Johannesburg-Lanseria**

PO Box 304, Lanseria 1748, South Africa ☎ (11) 659 26 83 Tx: none Fax: (11) 659 26 82 SITA: n/a
F: n/a ✱✱✱ n/a Head: n/a Net: n/a Beside aircraft listed, executive charters are operated with aircraft leased from other companies when required.

☐ ZS-IJE	Boeing 727-23	18443 / 111	N1987	0265	0798	3 PW JT8D-7B	72847	C10Y108		Joy
☐ ZS-IJF	Boeing 727-23	18444 / 114	N1988	0265	0898	3 PW JT8D-7B	72847	C10Y108		Faith
☐ ZS-NMX	Boeing 727-23	18426 / 15	N1970	0264	0396	3 PW JT8D-7B	72847	C10Y108	BH-DJ	
☐ ZS-NSA	Boeing 727-23	19130 / 213	N1901	1265	0297	3 PW JT8D-7B	72847	C10Y108	FJ-LM	std JNB

MRI Medical Rescue International, (Pty) Ltd — **Johannesburg-Rand & Cape Town-DF Malan**

PO Box 91622, Auckland Park 2006, South Africa ☎ (11) 403 70 80 Tx: none Fax: (11) 339 68 97 SITA: n/a
F: n/a ✱✱✱ n/a Head: n/a Net: n/a Conducting medical assistance & evacuation flights for subscripiton-members & also for outside contract partners.

☐ ZS-HVW	Bell 206L-3 LongRanger III	51081		0084		1 AN 250-C30P	1882	EMS		
☐ ZS-HWL	Bell 206L-3 LongRanger III	51101		0084		1 AN 250-C30P	1882	EMS		
☐ ZS-HXF	Bell 206L-3 LongRanger III	51186		0086		1 AN 250-C30P	1882	EMS		

NAC – National Airways = NTN (Division of National Airways Corp. (Pty) Ltd/Subsidiary of NAFCO Investments Ltd) — **Johannesburg-Lanseria & Durban**

PO Box 18016, Rand Airport 1419, South Africa ☎ (11) 827 93 33 Tx: 741025 nacav Fax: (11) 824 26 78 SITA: n/a
F: 1946 ✱✱✱ n/a Head: Nigel Forrester ICAO: NATCHAIR Net: http://www.natair.com

☐ ZS-ITP	Beech Baron B55 (95-B55)	TC-1511	ZS-YLR	0073		2 CO IO-470-L	2313			lsf Ruda Air CC
☐ ZS-MZA	Beech Baron 58	TH-1618		0090		2 CO IO-550-C	2495			lsf Merlin Aviation CC
☐ ZS-LXY	Cessna 402C II	402C0453	N402AS	0081		2 CO TSIO-520-VB	3107			lsf Surbiton 514
☐ ZS-LFU	Beech King Air B200	BB-1018		0082		2 PWC PT6A-42	5670			lsf LJ Investments CC
☐ ZS-NGI	Beech King Air 350 (B300)	FL-22		0091		2 PWC PT6A-60A	6804			lsf Lonmin Management Services P/L
☐ ZS-TOW	Learjet 35A	35A-475	3D-ADC	0082		2 GA TFE731-2-2B	8300			lsf Lonmin Management Services P/L

NAC HELICOPTERS = LFI (Division of National Airways Corp. (Helicopters) Ltd/Subsidiary of NAFCO Investments Ltd) — **Johannesburg-Rand & Nelspruit**

PO Box 18016, Rand Airport 1419, South Africa ☎ (11) 827 05 04 Tx: none Fax: (11) 827 51 64 SITA: n/a
F: n/a ✱✱✱ n/a Head: n/a ICAO: AEROMED Net: n/a Aircraft below MTOW 1361kg: Robinson R22

☐ ZS-HHC	Bell 206B JetRanger III	2257		0077		1 AN 250-C20B	1451			
☐ ZS-RDC	Bell 206L-3 LongRanger III	51589		0092		1 AN 250-C30P	1882			
☐ ZS-REC	Bell 206L-1 LongRanger II	45341	N1069Q	0079		1 AN 250-C28B	1882			

NATIONAL AIRLINES - NAL = YJ (Joint venture with NAC-National Airways & NAFCO Investments Group) — **Cape Town-Int'l**

P.O. Box 64, International Airport, Cape Town 7525, South Africa ☎ (21) 934 03 50 Tx: none Fax: (21) 934 33 73 SITA: n/a
F: 1982 ✱✱✱ 7 Head: Jean H. du Plessis Net: n/a

☐ ZS-NUC	Beech Catpass 250	BB-407	F-GFTT	0078	0296	2 PWC PT6A-41	5670	13 Pax		cvtd King Air 200

NATIONWIDE AIRLINES, (Pty) Ltd = CE / NTW (Nationwide Air Charter) — **Johannesburg-Int'l & Lanseria**

PO Box 422, Lanseria 1748, South Africa ☎ (11) 701 33 30 Tx: none Fax: (11) 701 32 43 SITA: n/a
F: 1991 ✱✱✱ n/a Head: Vernon Bricknell IATA: 567 ICAO: NATIONWIDE AIR Net: n/a Scheduled services (with BAe (BAC) One-Eleven & Boeing 727 aircraft are operated on a franchise agreement with SABENA, Belgium.
Most such aircraft are painted with both names. Charter flights are operated under the name NATIONWIDE AIR CHARTER (Pty) Ltd (a division) with same headquarter & fleet.

☐ ZS-NZI	Beech King Air 200	BB-593	N593	0080	0996	2 PWC PT6A-41	5670	Y9		
☐ ZS-NNM	BAe (BAC) One-Eleven 409AY (F)	108	G-BGTU	0067	0294	2 RR Spey 511-14W	39689	Freighter		
☐ ZS-NYZ	BAe (BAC) One-Eleven 416EK	132	G-AWBL	0068	0796	2 RR Spey 511-14DW	37999	Y74		std Lanseria
☐ ZS-OAF	BAe (BAC) One-Eleven 408EF	114	G-AVGP	0067	1296	2 RR Spey 511-14DW	37999	Y63		
☐ ZS-OAG	BAe (BAC) One-Eleven 401AK	066	G-BBME	0067	1296	2 RR Spey 511-14DW	37999	Y63		std Lanseria
☐ ZS-OAH	BAe (BAC) One-Eleven 408EF	115	G-BBMG	0068	0497	2 RR Spey 511-14DW	37999	Y63		
☐ ZS-NMS	BAe (BAC) One-Eleven 509EW	186	G-AWWZ	0469	1194	2 RR Spey 512-14DW	47400	F12Y82		
☐ ZS-NMT	BAe (BAC) One-Eleven 518FG	201	G-AXMG	1269	1194	2 RR Spey 512-14DW	47400	F12Y82		
☐ ZS-NUG	BAe (BAC) One-Eleven 531FS	237	G-AYWB	0571	0795	2 RR Spey 512-14DW	45000	F12Y82		
☐ ZS-NUH	BAe (BAC) One-Eleven 537GF	257	5B-DAG	0077	0795	2 RR Spey 512-14DW	45000	F12Y82		
☐ ZS-NUI	BAe (BAC) One-Eleven 537GF	258	5B-DAH	0078	0795	2 RR Spey 512-14DW	45000	F12Y82		The Right Whale/MTN Communications-cs
☐ ZS-NUJ	BAe (BAC) One-Eleven 537GF	261	5B-DAJ	0078	0795	2 RR Spey 512-14DW	45000	F12Y82		
☐ ZS-OIV	Boeing 737-230 (A)	22634 / 840	9A-CTE	1181	1298	2 PW JT8D-15	50890	Y110		lsf Aerotrans Ltd
☐ ZS-NYX	Boeing 727-116 (F)	19811 / 520	CC-CAG	0068	0696	3 PW JT8D-7B (Q)	77110	Freighter		cvtd -116
☐ ZS-NYY	Boeing 727-95	19251 / 315	CC-CHC	0066	0596	3 PW JT8D-7B (Q)	76885	F12Y82		
☐ ZS-ODO	Boeing 727-231 (A)	20843 / 1063	N54338	0074	0997	3 PW JT8D-9A	79818	F12Y134		

679 registration type of aircraft cn/fn ex/ex* mfd del powered by mtow kg configuration selcal name/fln/specialitites/remarks

NELAIR CHARTERS (Nelair, (Pty) Ltd dba / Associated with Nelair Engineering & Bonanza Hire) — **Nelspruit**

PO Box 2704, Nelspruit 1200, South Africa ☎ (1311) 42 012 Tx: 335342 sa Fax: (1311) 42 013 SITA: n/a
F: 1980 ⁂ 26 Head: Jacobus F. Pienaar Net: n/a Aircraft below MTOW 1361kg: Cessna 150.

☐	ZS-MWK	Cessna TR182 Turbo Skylane RG II	*R18200649*		*0079*	*0598*	*1 LY O-540-L3C5D*	*1406*			
☐	ZS-MSO	Piper PA-32-300 Cherokee SIX	*32-7540083*	*N33050*	*0075*		*1 LY IO-540-K1A5*	*1542*			
☐	ZS-EDG	Cessna U206 Super Skywagon	*U206-0382*	*N2182F*	*0065*	*0797*	*1 CO IO-520-A*	*1497*			
☐	ZS-KLG	Beech Bonanza F33A	*CE-900*	*N6723Y*	*0078*	*0598*	*1 CO IO-520-BA*	*1542*			
☐	ZS-JZX	Piper PA-34-200T Seneca II	*34-7770269*	*N5911V*	*0077*		*2 CO TSIO-360-E*	*2073*			
☐	ZS-MMY	Piper PA-34-200T Seneca II	*34-7670051*	*N4469X*	*0076*		*2 CO TSIO-360-E*	*2073*			
☐	ZS-JGW	Cessna 401B	*401B0106*	*N7966Q*	*0071*		*2 CO TSIO-520-VB*	*2858*			
☐	ZS-JTX	Piper PA-31-350 Navajo Chieftain	*31-7652059*	*N59800*	*0076*	*0293*	*2 LY TIO-540-J2BD*	*3175*			
☐	ZS-MHE	Piper PA-31-350 Navajo Chieftain	*31-7305096*		*0073*	*0598*	*2 LY TIO-540-J2BD*	*3175*			
☐	ZS-MGJ	Learjet 24B	*24B-207*	*N457JA*	*0069*		*2 GE CJ610-6*	*6123*			

NORSE AIR CHARTER (Metro D (Pty) Ltd dba) — **Johannesburg-Int'l & Pietersburg-Gateway Int'l**

PO Box 787106, Sandton 2146, South Africa ☎ (11) 883 00 72 Tx: none Fax: (11) 883 00 77 SITA: JNBTOGS
F: 1981 ⁂ 6 Head: Dietrie C. Ward Net: n/a Operates charter flights with aircraft leased from AIR PASS (3D-) when required.

NORTH ATLANTIC AIRWAYS, Pty Ltd – NAA — **Johannesburg-Int'l**

PO Box 7078, Midrand 1685, South Africa ☎ (11) 315 12 67 Tx: none Fax: (11) 315 12 69 SITA: n/a
F: 1998 ⁂ 53 Head: Bernard Stroiazzo-Mougin Net: n/a

☐	N710CK	Boeing 747-2B4B (SF)	*21097 / 262*	*OD-AGH*	*0075*	*1198*	*4 PW JT9D-7FW*	*362874*	*Freighter*		*lsf / opb CKS / cvtd -2B4B (M)*
☐	N713CK	Boeing 747-2B4B (SF)	*21099 / 264*	*N204AE*	*0075*	*1298*	*4 PW JT9D-7FW*	*362874*	*Freighter*		*lsf / opb CKS / cvtd -2B4B (M)*

ORION AIR CHARTER (Division of IDAS-Int'l Development & Aviation Services (Pty) Ltd) — **Johannesburg-Grand Central**

PO Box 50017, Randjesfontein 1683, South Africa ☎ (11) 805 60 68 Tx: none Fax: (11) 805 60 69 SITA: n/a
F: 1997 ⁂ 12 Head: J.J. Venter Net: n/a

☐	ZS-HKN	Eurocopter (Aerosp.) AS350B Ecureuil	*1483*		*0081*	*0097*	*1 TU Arriel 1B*	*1950*	*5 Pax*		
☐	ZS-RJV	Eurocopter (Aerosp.) AS350BA AStar	*9001*		*0098*	*0598*	*1 TU Arriel 1B*	*2100*	*5 Pax*		
☐	ZS-OAR	Cessna 208B Grand Caravan	*208B0441*		*0095*	*0097*	*1 PWC PT6A-114A*	*3969*	*13 Pax*		*lsf King Air Services Partnership*
☐	ZS-OED	Beech King Air B200	*BB-1149*	*N200HF*	*0083*	*0098*	*2 PWC PT6A-42*	*5670*	*10 Pax*		

ORSMOND AVIATION (Orsmond Aerial Spraying (Pty) Ltd dba) — **Bethlehem**

PO Box 144, Bethlehem 9700, South Africa ☎ (58) 303 52 61 Tx: none Fax: (58) 303 50 35 SITA: n/a
F: 1973 ⁂ n/a Head: Michael D. Williams Net: n/a

☐	ZS-CTU	Cessna 185A Skywagon	*185-0302*	*CR-AJF*	*0061*		*1 CO IO-520-D*	*1451*			
☐	ZS-LYN	Beech Baron 58	*TH-495*	*N59WC*	*0074*	*0597*	*2 CO IO-520-C*	*2449*			
☐	ZS-	Ayres LM200 Loadmaster					*1 AN CTP800-4T TwinPac*	*8618*	*Freighter*		*oo-delivery 0002*
☐	ZS-	Ayres LM200 Loadmaster					*1 AN CTP800-4T TwinPac*	*8618*	*Freighter*		*oo-delivery 0002*

PHOEBUS APOLLO AVIATION, CC — **Johannesburg-Rand**

PO Box 3211, Halfway House 1685, South Africa ☎ (11) 805 18 04 Tx: none Fax: (11) 805 29 99 SITA: n/a
F: 1997 ⁂ n/a Head: n/a Net: n/a

☐	ZS-MAR	Piper PA-31-310 Navajo	*31-352*	*ZS-FVI*	*0069*	*0798*	*2 LY TIO-540-A1A*	*2948*			
☐	ZS-NHZ	Piper PA-31-350 Navajo Chieftain	*31-7305082*		*0073*	*0898*	*2 LY TIO-540-J2BD*	*3175*			
☐	ZS-BAA	Boeing (Douglas) DC-3A-197	*1984*	*C9-ATG*	*0037*	*1197*	*2 PW R-1830*	*12202*	*Y28*		*being rebuild at Rand -mid 99*
☐	ZS-DIW	Boeing (Douglas) DC-3C (C-47A-1-DK)	*11991*	*SAAF6871*	*0042*	*0697*	*2 PW R-1830*	*12202*	*Y28 / Frtr*		
☐	ZS-PAI	Boeing (Douglas) DC-4 (C-54E-10-DO)	*27319 / DO 265*	*N4989K*	*0045*	*1296*	*4 PW R-2000*	*30241*	*Freighter*		

PROFESSIONAL AVIATION (Professional Aviation Services, (Pty) Ltd dba) — **Johannesburg-Lanseria**

PROFESSIONAL AVIATION

PO Box 515, Lanseria 1748, South Africa ☎ (11) 701 33 20 Tx: none Fax: (11) 659 13 36 SITA: n/a
F: 1979 ⁂ 5 Head: Robert C.H. & Christine T. Garbett Net: n/a

☐	ZS-LJI	Professional Aviation Jet Prop DC-3C	*34225*	*SAAF6871*	*0045*		*2 PWC PT6A-65AR*	*13041*	*Combi*		*Ruzizi / cvtd Douglas C-47B-45-DK*

RAPID AIR, (Pty) Ltd — **Pretoria**

PO Box 183, Bon Accord 0009, South Africa ☎ (12) 543 08 84 Tx: 321120 sa Fax: (12) 543 08 86 SITA: n/a
F: 1971 ⁂ 6 Head: C.G. Erasmus Net: n/a

☐	ZS-SWI	Piper PA-30-160 Twin Comanche C	*30-1808*	*ZS-FYE*	*0069*		*2 LY IO-320-B1A*	*1633*			*lsf C&D Aviation*
☐	ZS-MHG	Piper PA-34-200T Seneca II	*34-7770126*	*N1476H*	*0077*		*2 CO TSIO-360-E*	*2073*			
☐	ZS-NOT	Piper PA-31-350 Navajo Chieftain	*31-7405170*	*N66861*	*0074*		*2 LY TIO-540-J2BD*	*3175*			

ROSSAIR EXECUTIVE AIR CHARTER = RSS (Rossair, (Pty) Ltd dba / Affiliated with Absil Air Services, (Pty) Ltd) — **Johannesburg-Lanseria /-Grand Central &-Rand**

PO Box 428, Lanseria 1748, South Africa ☎ (11) 659 29 80 Tx: 421330 sa Fax: (11) 659 13 89 SITA: n/a
F: 1956 ⁂ n/a Head: Edi Absil ICAO: ROSS CHARTER Net: n/a

☐	ZS-OCH	Cessna U206G Stationair 6 II	*U20606344*	*TR-LAB*	*0081*	*0797*	*1 CO IO-520-F*	*1633*			
☐	ZS-OFX	Cessna 207A Stationair 8 II	*20700700*	*N9494M*	*0081*	*0198*	*1 CO IO-520-F*	*1724*			
☐	ZS-OFY	Cessna 207A Stationair 8 II	*20700732*	*N9801M*	*0081*	*0198*	*1 CO IO-520-F*	*1724*			
☐	ZS-KLK	Britten-Norman BN-2B-21 Islander	*862*	*SAAF-16*	*0078*	*0498*	*2 LY IO-540-K1B5*	*2994*			
☐	ZS-XGF	Britten-Norman BN-2A-21 Islander	*736*	*G-BCNF*	*0075*		*2 LY O-540-K1B5*	*2994*			
☐	ZS-TAS	Cessna 208B Grand Caravan	*208B0378*	*N208SA*	*0094*	*1096*	*1 PWC PT6A-114A*	*3969*			
☐	ZS-KMA	Beech King Air C90	*LJ-930*	*N3717J*	*0080*	*0792*	*2 PWC PT6A-21*	*4377*			
☐	ZS-OAM	Cessna 500 Citation	*500-0077*	*N869K*	*0073*	*0197*	*2 PWC JT15D-1*	*5375*			
☐	ZS-MES	Beech King Air 200	*BB-1038*	*N223MH*	*0082*		*2 PWC PT6A-42*	*5670*			
☐	ZS-MIN	Beech King Air 200	*BB-941*	*N36801*	*0081*		*2 PWC PT6A-41*	*5670*			
☐	ZS-MSK	Beech King Air 200	*BB-597*	*5Y-BJC*	*0080*		*2 PWC PT6A-41*	*5670*			
☐	ZS-NAX	Beech King Air 200C	*BL-8*	*5Y-NAX*	*0079*		*2 PWC PT6A-41*	*5670*			
☐	ZS-NUF	Beech King Air 200C	*BL-4*	*V5-AAL*	*0079*	*0895*	*2 PWC PT6A-41*	*5670*			
☐	ZS-MZB	De Havilland DHC-6 Twin Otter 300	*691*	*N230BV*	*0080*	*0391*	*2 PWC PT6A-27*	*5670*			
☐	ZS-NJK	De Havilland DHC-6 Twin Otter 300	*598*	*N403CA*	*0078*	*1193*	*2 PWC PT6A-27*	*5670*			
☐	ZS-OHS	De Havilland DHC-6 Twin Otter 300	*513*	*9Q-CBN*	*0076*	*0898*	*2 PWC PT6A-27*	*5670*			
☐	ZS-NPT	Beech 1900C-1 Airliner	*UC-113*	*5Y-HAC*	*0090*	*0295*	*2 PWC PT6A-65B*	*7530*			
☐	ZS-NXX	Beech 1900C Airliner	*UB-50*	*N812BE*	*0085*	*0896*	*2 PWC PT6A-65B*	*7530*			
☐	ZS-ODG	Beech 1900C-1 Airliner	*UC-158*	*N158YV*	*0591*	*0997*	*2 PWC PT6A-65B*	*7530*			
☐	ZS-OGZ	Beech 1900C-1 Airliner	*UC-65*	*5Y-ROS*	*0089*	*0795*	*2 PWC PT6A-65B*	*7530*			*lst Rossair Kenya as 5Y-ROS*
☐	ZS-OHE	Beech 1900C-1 Airliner	*UC-48*	*9J-AFJ*	*0088*	*0898*	*2 PWC PT6A-65B*	*7530*			
☐	ZS-SES	Learjet 35A	*35A-185*	*OE-GAV*	*0078*	*0598*	*2 GA TFE731-2-2B*	*8301*			
☐	ZS-OBU	AMI Turbo DC-3C	*27047*	*N376AS*	*0044*	*0497*	*2 PWC PT6A-65AR*	*12202*			*lst Rossair Kenya as 5Y-BNK/C-47B-20-DK*
☐	ZS-EDY	Fokker F27 Friendship 600 (F27 Mk600)	*10563*	*7P-LAJ*	*0077*	*1297*	*2 RR Dart 536-7R*	*20412*			

SAFAIR, (Pty) Ltd = FA / SFR (Subsidiary of Imperial Holdings (Pty) Ltd/formerly Safair Freighters, (Pty) Ltd) — **Johannesburg-Int'l**

PO Box 938, Kempton Park 1620, South Africa ☎ (11) 928 00 00 Tx: 7-42242 sa Fax: (11) 395 13 14 SITA: n/a
F: 1969 ⁂ 270 Head: Ralph Boettler IATA: 640 ICAO: SAFAIR Net: n/a

☐	ZS-MGI	Partenavia AP68TP-600 Viator	*9004*	*C9-ATQ*	*0088*	*0189*	*2 AN 250-B17C*	*2850*	*Surveyer*		*Kuswag VII / opf Pentowmarine/Dpt Envi.*
☐	ZS-OBF	Boeing (Douglas) MD-82 (DC-9-82)	*48019 / 1001*	*OE-LDU*	*0081*	*0597*	*2 PW JT8D-217C*	*67810*	*CY137*		*lst SSN / cvtd MD-81*
☐	ZS-OBG	Boeing (Douglas) MD-82 (DC-9-82)	*48020 / 1045*	*OE-LDV*	*1281*	*0497*	*2 PW JT8D-217C*	*67810*	*CY141*		*lst SSN / cvtd MD-81*
☐	ZS-OBH	Boeing (Douglas) MD-82 (DC-9-82)	*48059 / 1047*	*OE-LDW*	*0082*	*0597*	*2 PW JT8D-217C*	*67810*	*CY137*		*lst SSN / cvtd MD-81*
☐	ZS-OBI	Boeing (Douglas) MD-81 (DC-9-81)	*48016 / 941*	*OE-LDR*	*0080*	*0198*	*2 PW JT8D-217C*	*64410*	*CY137*		*lst SSN*
☐	ZS-OBJ	Boeing (Douglas) MD-81 (DC-9-81)	*48018 / 995*	*OE-LDT*	*0081*	*0198*	*2 PW JT8D-217C*	*64410*	*CY137*		*lst SSN*
☐	ZS-JIV	Lockheed L-382G (L-100-30) Hercules	*35C-4673*	*D2-THE*	*0076*	*0776*	*4 AN 501-D22A*	*70307*	*Freighter*		
☐	ZS-JIX	Lockheed L-382G (L-100-30) Hercules	*35C-4684*	*D2-THZ*	*0076*	*0876*	*4 AN 501-D22A*	*70307*	*Freighter*		
☐	ZS-JIY	Lockheed L-382G (L-100-30) Hercules	*35C-4691*	*9Q-CZS (1)*	*0076*	*0976*	*4 AN 501-D22A*	*70307*	*Freighter*		
☐	ZS-JIZ	Lockheed L-382G (L-100-30) Hercules	*35C-4695*	*F-GNMM*	*0076*	*1076*	*4 AN 501-D22A*	*70307*	*Freighter*		
☐	ZS-JVL	Lockheed L-382G (L-100-30) Hercules	*35C-4676*	*PH-RMH*	*0076*	*0776*	*4 AN 501-D22A*	*70307*	*Freighter*		
☐	ZS-RSC	Lockheed L-382G (L-100-30) Hercules	*28C-4475*	*S9-NAD*	*0072*	*1272*	*4 AN 501-D22A*	*70307*	*Freighter*		
☐	ZS-RSI	Lockheed L-382G (L-100-30) Hercules	*31C-4600*	*F-GIMV*	*0075*	*0675*	*4 AN 501-D22A*	*70307*	*Freighter*		*lst ABR*
☐	ZS-NPX	Boeing 727-23 (F)	*19131 / 218*	*N512FE*	*0066*	*0897*	*3 PW JT8D-7B*	*72575*	*Freighter*		*lst FLN / cvtd -23*
☐	ZS-NOU	Boeing 727-230 (A)	*21113 / 1176*	*TC-TCA*	*1175*	*1294*	*3 PW JT8D-15*	*86409*	*CY148*		*lst CAW*
☐	ZS-NOV	Boeing 727-230 (A)	*21114 / 1178*	*TC-TCB*	*1275*	*1294*	*3 PW JT8D-15*	*86409*	*CY148*		*lst CAW*
☐	ZS-NVR	Boeing 727-230 (A)	*20673 / 922*	*5N-NEC*	*0073*	*1195*	*3 PW JT8D-15*	*86409*	*CY146*		*lst SSN*
☐	ZS-NWA	Boeing 727-230 (A)	*20757 / 1002*	*5N-CMB*	*0074*	*1295*	*3 PW JT8D-15*	*86409*	*CY146*		*lst EZX*
☐	ZS-NZV	Boeing 727-230 (A)	*20792 / 1023*	*TC-RAC*	*0074*	*1196*	*3 PW JT8D-15*	*86409*	*CY148*		*lst CAW*
☐	ZS-OBN	Boeing 727-232 (F) (A)	*20637 / 920*	*N68782*	*0073*	*0798*	*3 PW JT8D-15 (HK3/FDX)*	*86409*	*Freighter*		*lsf Aircorp / sub-lst SAA / cvtd -232*
☐	ZS-OBO	Boeing 727-230 (A)	*21623 / 1433*	*OK-JGY*	*0079*	*0598*	*3 PW JT8D-15*	*86409*	*CY148*		*lst CAW*

SAPPHIRE EXECUTIVE AIR (Division of ESKOM-Electricity Supply Commission) — **Johannesburg-Grand Central**

PO Box 1439, Halfway House 1685, South Africa ☎ (11) 315 44 41 Tx: none Fax: (11) 805 24 18 SITA: n/a
F: 1961 ⁂ 18 Head: Claus Hildebrandt Net: n/a

☐	ZS-HKB	Bell 206B JetRanger III	*3338*		*0081*		*1 AN 250-C20B*	*1451*			
☐	ZS-RHL	MD Helicopters MD 600N (Hughes 600N)	*RN005*		*0097*	*0797*	*1 AN 250-C47M*	*1860*			
☐	ZS-HTZ	Bell 206L-3 LongRanger III	*51150*	*N51150*	*0085*		*1 AN 250-C30P*	*1882*			
☐	ZS-HUP	Bell 206L-3 LongRanger III	*51268*	*N7036L*	*0089*		*1 AN 250-C30P*	*1882*			
☐	ZS-RHK	Bell 407	*53034*		*0096*	*0896*	*1 AN 250-C47B*	*2268*			
☐	ZS-SEA	Dassault Falcon 10	*156*	*SE-DEK*	*0079*	*0897*	*2 GA TFE731-2-1C*	*8500*			

680 registration type of aircraft *cn/fn* *ex/ex** *mfd* *del* *powered by* *mtow kg* *configuration* *selcal* name/fln/specialitites/remarks

S.A. RED CROSS AIR AMBULANCE SERVICE (S.A. Red Cross Air Mercy Service dba/Div. of the South African Red Cross Society) — Cape Town-Int'l

PO Box 93, Cape Town International Airport 7525, South Africa ☎ (21) 934 09 16 Tx: none Fax: (21) 934 87 00 SITA: n/a
F: 1966 n/a Head: John Stone Net: n/a

☐ ZS-NYM	Pilatus PC-12/45	*147*	*HB-FRI**	*0096*	*0896*	*1 PWC PT6A-67B*	*4500*	*EMS*		
☐ ZS-OFN	Pilatus PC-12/45	*190*	*HB-FSY**	*0098*	*0598*	*1 PWC PT6A-67B*	*4500*	*EMS*		*lsf Swiss-Av P/L*
☐ ZS-RKV	Cessna 550 Citation II	*550-0051*	*N678CA*	*0079*	*0195*	*2 PWC JT15D-4*	*6033*	*EMS*		

SOUTH AFRICAN AIRLINK, (Pty) Ltd = 4Z / LNK (formerly Airlink Airlines, (Pty) Ltd) — Johannesburg-Int'l

PO Box 7529, Bonaero Park 1620, South Africa ☎ (11) 395 33 33 Tx: none Fax: (11) 395 13 11 SITA: n/a
F: 1978 250 Head: Richard Carter IATA: 749 ICAO: LINK Net: http://www.saairlink.co.za Some scheduled commuter flights are operated in conjuction with SAA as a SA CONNECTOR using SA flight numbers.

☐ ZS-NGW	Dornier 228-101	*7036*	*A2-ABA*	*0084*	*0493*	*2 GA TPE331-5-252D*	*5980*	*Y16*		*Bayonne / cvtd -100*
☐ ZS-NRN	Dornier 228-200	*8021*	*OY-CHK*	*0083*	*0295*	*2 GA TPE331-5-252D*	*5700*	*Y16*		
☐ ZS-NRE	BAe 4121 Jetstream 41	*41048*	*G-4-048**	*0095*	*0395*	*2 GA TPE331-14HR-805H*	*10886*	*Y28*		*lsf Midlands Aviation P/L*
☐ ZS-NRF	BAe 4121 Jetstream 41	*41050*	*G-4-050**	*0095*	*0495*	*2 GA TPE331-14HR-805H*	*10886*	*Y28*		*lsf Midlands Aviation P/L*
☐ ZS-NRG	BAe 4121 Jetstream 41	*41051*	*G-4-051**	*0095*	*0495*	*2 GA TPE331-14HR-805H*	*10886*	*Y28*		Pietermaritzburg / *lsf Midlands Avn*
☐ ZS-NRH	BAe 4121 Jetstream 41	*41054*	*G-4-054**	*0095*	*0495*	*2 GA TPE331-14HR-805H*	*10886*	*Y28*		Pietersburg / *lsf Midlands Aviation*
☐ ZS-NRI	BAe 4121 Jetstream 41	*41061*	*G-4-061**	*0095*	*0695*	*2 GA TPE331-14HR-805H*	*10886*	*Y28*		*lsf Midlands Aviation P/L*
☐ ZS-NRJ	BAe 4121 Jetstream 41	*41062*	*G-4-062**	*0095*	*0695*	*2 GA TPE331-14HR-805H*	*10886*	*Y28*		*lsf Midlands Aviation P/L*
☐ ZS-NRK	BAe 4121 Jetstream 41	*41065*	*G-4-065**	*0095*	*0795*	*2 GA TPE331-14HR-805H*	*10886*	*Y28*		*lsf Midlands Aviation P/L*
☐ ZS-NRL	BAe 4121 Jetstream 41	*41068*	*G-4-068**	*0095*	*0895*	*2 GA TPE331-14HR-805H*	*10886*	*Y28*		*lsf Midlands Aviation P/L*
☐ ZS-NRM	BAe 4121 Jetstream 41	*41069*	*G-4-069**	*0095*	*0995*	*2 GA TPE331-14HR-805H*	*10886*	*Y28*		Nelspruit / *lsf Midlands Aviation P/L*
☐ ZS-NUO	BAe 4121 Jetstream 41	*41044*	*VH-IMS*	*0094*	*0995*	*2 GA TPE331-14HR-805H*	*10886*	*Y28*		*lsf Midlands Aviation / modif. BAe 4107*
☐ ZS-NYK	BAe 4121 Jetstream 41	*41095*	*G-4-095**	*0096*	*1096*	*2 GA TPE331-14HR-805H*	*10886*	*Y28*		*opf Kwazulu-Natal Gvmt*
☐ ZS-OEX	BAe 4121 Jetstream 41	*41103*	*G-4-103**	*0098*	*0398*	*2 GA TPE331-14HR-805H*	*10886*	*Y28*		

SOUTH AFRICAN AIRWAYS - SAA = SA / SAA (Transnet Ltd dba) — Johannesburg-Int'l

South African Airways Towers, PO Box 7778, Johannesburg 2000, South Africa ☎ (11) 978 11 11 Tx: none Fax: (11) 970 43 87 SITA: n/a
F: 1934 10500 Head: T. Coleman Andrews IATA: 083 ICAO: SPRINGBOK Net: http://www.saa.co.za
SA CONNECTOR commuter flights are operated by SOUTH AFRICAN AIRLINK & SOUTH AFRICAN EXPRESS using SA flight numbers. For details – see under both companies.

☐ ZS-AFA	CASA 352L (Junkers Ju 52/3m)	*164*	*ZS-UYU*	*0051*		*3 PW R-1340-S1H1*	*10100*	*Y14*		Jan van Riebeeck / *Historic-Flight div.*
☐ ZS-BXF	Boeing (Douglas) DC-3C (C-47A-1-DK)	*12107*	*6888*	*0043*	*0791*	*2 PW R-1830*	*12202*	*Y28*		*Historic-Flight div.*
☐ ZS-BXJ	Boeing (Douglas) DC-3C (C-47A-10-DK)	*12413*	*6829*	*0043*	*1295*	*2 PW R-1830*	*12202*	*Y28*		*Historic-Flight div.*
☐ ZS-AUB	Boeing (Douglas) DC-4-1009	*42984 / D4 28*	*ZU-ILI*	*0046*	*1295*	*4 PW R-2000*	*33112*	*Y50*		*Historic-Flight div.*
☐ ZS-BMH	Boeing (Douglas) DC-4-1009	*43157 / D4 79*	*6904*	*0047*	*0393*	*4 PW R-2000*	*33112*	*Y50*		Lebombo / *Historic-Flight div.*
☐ ZS-SIA	Boeing 737-244 (A)	*22580 / 787*	*PP-SNW*	*0081*	*0881*	*2 PW JT8D-17A*	*53070*	*C25Y81*	*BK-DE*	Tugela
☐ ZS-SIB	Boeing 737-244 (A)	*22581 / 796*	*D6-CAJ*	*0081*	*0981*	*2 PW JT8D-17A*	*53070*	*C25Y81*	*BK-EH*	Limpopo
☐ ZS-SIC	Boeing 737-244 (A)	*22582 / 805*		*0081*	*1081*	*2 PW JT8D-17A*	*53070*	*C25Y81*	*BK-EJ*	Vaal
☐ ZS-SID	Boeing 737-244 (F) (A)	*22583 / 809*		*0081*	*1181*	*2 PW JT8D-17A*	*53070*	*Freighter*	*BK-EL*	Oranje / Orange / *cvtd -244*
☐ ZS-SIE	Boeing 737-244 (A)	*22584 / 821*		*0081*	*1281*	*2 PW JT8D-17A*	*53070*	*C25Y81*	*BK-EM*	Letaba
☐ ZS-SIF	Boeing 737-244 (F) (A)	*22585 / 828*		*0082*	*0182*	*2 PW JT8D-17A*	*53070*	*Freighter*	*BK-FG*	Komati / *cvtd -244*
☐ ZS-SIG	Boeing 737-244 (A)	*22586 / 829*		*0082*	*0182*	*2 PW JT8D-17A*	*53070*	*C25Y81*	*BK-FH*	Marico
☐ ZS-SIH	Boeing 737-244 (A)	*22587 / 835*		*0082*	*0582*	*2 PW JT8D-17A*	*53070*	*C25Y81*	*BK-FL*	Kei
☐ ZS-SII	Boeing 737-244 (A)	*22588 / 836*		*0082*	*0282*	*2 PW JT8D-17A*	*53070*	*C25Y81*	*BK-FM*	Berg
☐ ZS-SIJ	Boeing 737-244 (A)	*22589 / 843*	*CC-CHK*	*0082*	*0382*	*2 PW JT8D-17A*	*53070*	*C25Y81*	*FK-JL*	Caledon
☐ ZS-SIK	Boeing 737-244 (A)	*22590 / 854*		*0082*	*0482*	*2 PW JT8D-17A*	*53070*	*C25Y81*	*FK-JM*	Olifants
☐ ZS-SIL	Boeing 737-244 (A)	*22591 / 859*		*0082*	*0482*	*2 PW JT8D-17A*	*53070*	*C25Y81*	*FK-LM*	Wilge
☐ ZS-SIM	Boeing 737-244 (A)	*22828 / 881*		*0082*	*0682*	*2 PW JT8D-17A*	*53070*	*C25Y81*	*CD-JM*	Umgeni
☐ ZS-SHA	Airbus Industrie A320-231	*243*	*F-WWDL**	*0091*	*1191*	*2 IAE V2500-A1*	*73500*	*C35Y108*		Blue Crane
☐ ZS-SHB	Airbus Industrie A320-231	*249*	*F-WWDO**	*0091*	*1191*	*2 IAE V2500-A1*	*73500*	*C35Y108*		Bokmakierie
☐ ZS-SHC	Airbus Industrie A320-231	*250*	*F-WWBB**	*0091*	*1191*	*2 IAE V2500-A1*	*73500*	*C35Y108*		Hadida
☐ ZS-SHD	Airbus Industrie A320-231	*251*	*F-WWBC**	*0091*	*1191*	*2 IAE V2500-A1*	*73500*	*C35Y108*		Fish Eagle / Vis Arend
☐ ZS-SHE	Airbus Industrie A320-231	*334*	*F-WWBN**	*0092*	*0892*	*2 IAE V2500-A1*	*73500*	*C35Y108*		Bateleur / Berghaan
☐ ZS-SHF	Airbus Industrie A320-231	*335*	*F-WWBO**	*0092*	*0892*	*2 IAE V2500-A1*	*73500*	*C35Y108*		Loerie
☐ ZS-SHG	Airbus Industrie A320-231	*440*	*F-WWIQ**	*0093*	*0993*	*2 IAE V2500-A1*	*73500*	*C35Y108*		Korhaan
☐ ZS-OBN	Boeing 727-232 (F) (A)	*20637 / 920*	*N68782*	*0073*	*0798*	*3 PW JT8D-15 (HK3/FDX)*	*86409*	*Freighter*		*lsf SFR/jtlyopw Safron Courier/cvtd-232*
☐ ZS-SRA	Boeing 767-2B1 (ER)	*26471 / 511*		*0093*	*0893*	*2 PW PW4056*	*175540*	*C21Y168*	*ES-LQ*	Protea / *lsf LAM*
☐ ZS-SRB	Boeing 767-266 (ER)	*23179 / 98*	*N573SW*	*0084*	*1097*	*2 PW JT9D-7R4E*	*175540*	*C21Y168*		Syaya / *lsf UT Finance Corp./sublst AFJ*
☐ ZS-SRC	Boeing 767-266 (ER)	*23180 / 99*	*N575SW*	*0084*	*1297*	*2 PW JT9D-7R4E*	*175540*	*C21Y168*		Ngomeza / *lsf UT Finance Corp.*
☐ ZS-SDA	Airbus Industrie A300B2K-3C	*032*	*F-WLGA**	*0076*	*0176*	*2 GE CF6-50C2R*	*142000*	*C35Y247*	*DM-HJ*	Blesbok
☐ ZS-SDB	Airbus Industrie A300B2K-3C	*037*	*F-WUAU**	*0076*	*1276*	*2 GE CF6-50C2R*	*142000*	*C35Y247*	*DM-HK*	Gemsbok
☐ ZS-SDC	Airbus Industrie A300B2K-3C	*039*	*F-WLGB**	*0077*	*0177*	*2 GE CF6-50C2R*	*142000*	*C35Y247*	*DM-JK*	Waterbok
☐ ZS-SDD	Airbus Industrie A300B2K-3C	*040*	*F-WUAX**	*0077*	*0277*	*2 GE CF6-50C2R*	*142000*	*C35Y247*	*DM-KL*	Rooibok
☐ ZS-SDE	Airbus Industrie A300B4-203	*138*	*C-GIZJ*	*0081*	*0481*	*2 GE CF6-50C2*	*157500*	*C35Y247*		Springbok
☐ ZS-SDF	Airbus Industrie A300B4-203	*192*	*SU-DAN*	*0082*	*0682*	*2 GE CF6-50C2*	*157500*	*C35Y247*		Eland
☐ ZS-SDG	Airbus Industrie A300C4-203	*212*	*C-GIZN*	*0082*	*1082*	*2 GE CF6-50C2*	*165000*	*Freighter*	*FJ-AB*	Koedoe / Kudu
☐ ZS-SDH	Airbus Industrie A300B4-203	*222*	*RP-C3006*	*0082*	*0485*	*2 GE CF6-50C2*	*165000*	*C35Y247*		
☐ ZS-SPA	Boeing 747SP-44	*21132 / 280*	*3B-NAJ*	*0076*	*0376*	*4 PW JT9D-7FW*	*317967*	*F8C29Y206*	*AF-BD*	Matroosberg
☐ ZS-SPB	Boeing 747SP-44	*21133 / 282*	*LX-LGX*	*0076*	*0476*	*4 PW JT9D-7FW*	*317967*	*F8C28Y224*	*AF-BE*	Outeniqua
☐ ZS-SPC	Boeing 747SP-44	*21134 / 288*	*3B-NAG*	*0076*	*0676*	*4 PW JT9D-7FW*	*317967*	*F8C28Y224*	*AF-BG*	Maluti / *lst NMB*
☐ ZS-SPE	Boeing 747SP-44	*21254 / 298*	*V5-SPE*	*0076*	*1176*	*4 PW JT9D-7FW*	*317967*	*F8C28Y224*	*CK-EF*	Hantam
☐ ZS-SAL	Boeing 747-244B	*20237 / 154*	*N1795B**	*0071*	*0172*	*4 PW JT9D-7R4G2*	*369223*	*F16C47Y232*	*CD-AB*	Tafelberg
☐ ZS-SAM	Boeing 747-244B	*20238 / 158*	*PP-VNW*	*0071*	*1271*	*4 PW JT9D-7R4G2*	*369223*	*F16C47Y232*	*CD-AE*	Drakensberg
☐ ZS-SAN	Boeing 747-244B	*20239 / 160*		*0071*	*1071*	*4 PW JT9D-7R4G2*	*369223*	*F16C47Y232*	*CD-AF*	Lebombo
☐ ZS-SAO	Boeing 747-244B	*20556 / 194*		*0072*	*0872*	*4 PW JT9D-7R4G2*	*369223*	*F16C47Y232*	*FJ-CM*	Magaliesberg
☐ ZS-SAP	Boeing 747-244B	*20557 / 198*		*0072*	*0972*	*4 PW JT9D-7R4G2*	*369223*	*F16C47Y232*	*FJ-DE*	Swartberg
☐ ZS-SAR	Boeing 747-244B (SF)	*22170 / 486*	*3B-NAS*	*0080*	*1180*	*4 PW JT9D-7Q*	*369223*	*Freighter*	*FJ-EL*	Waterberg / *cvtd -244B (M)*
☐ ZS-SBJ	Boeing 747-212F (SCD)	*24177 / 710*	*N750SJ*	*0088*	*1198*	*4 PW JT9D-7R4G2*	*377842*	*Freighter 112t*		*lsf Finova Capital*
☐ ZS-SAC	Boeing 747-312	*23031 / 598*	*N120KF*	*0084*	*0695*	*4 PW JT9D-7R4G2*	*377842*	*F18C61Y255*	*CK-EM*	Shosholoza
☐ ZS-SAJ	Boeing 747-312	*23027 / 583*	*N116KB*	*0083*	*0196*	*4 PW JT9D-7R4G2*	*377842*	*F18C61Y255*	*AB-JL*	Ndizani / *special Olympic Team colors*
☐ ZS-SAT	Boeing 747-344	*22970 / 577*	*N8279V**	*0083*	*0583*	*4 PW JT9D-7R4G2*	*377842*	*F18C61Y258*	*FH-GJ*	Johannesburg
☐ ZS-SAU	Boeing 747-344	*22971 / 578*	*N8296V**	*0083*	*0483*	*4 PW JT9D-7R4G2*	*377842*	*F18C61Y258*	*FH-GM*	Cape Town / Kaapstad
☐ ZS-SAK	Boeing 747-444	*28468 / 1162*	*N60697**	*0098*	*0698*	*4 RR RB211-524G/H-T*	*394625*	*F18C66Y263*	*LS-FK*	Ebhayi
☐ ZS-SAV	Boeing 747-444	*24976 / 827*	*N6009F**	*0091*	*0191*	*4 RR RB211-524H*	*394625*	*F18C66Y263*	*FM-AQ*	Durban
☐ ZS-SAW	Boeing 747-444	*25152 / 861*	*N60668**	*0091*	*0691*	*4 RR RB211-524H*	*394625*	*F18C66Y263*	*FM-BQ*	Bloemfontein
☐ ZS-SAX	Boeing 747-444	*26637 / 943*		*0092*	*1092*	*4 RR RB211-524H*	*394625*	*F18C66Y263*	*CQ-AS*	Kempton Park
☐ ZS-SAY	Boeing 747-444	*26638 / 995*		*0093*	*1093*	*4 RR RB211-524H*	*394625*	*F18C66Y263*	*CQ-BR*	Vulindlela
☐ ZS-SAZ	Boeing 747-444	*29119 / 1187*		*1198*	*1198*	*4 RR RB211-524G/H-T*	*394625*	*F18C66Y263*		
☐ ZS-SBK	Boeing 747-4F6	*28959 / 1161*	*N1785B**	*0098*	*1298*	*4 GE CF6-80C2B1F*	*394625*	*F18C66Y263*		
☐ ZS-SBS	Boeing 747-4F6	*28960 / 1167*	*N60668**	*0098*	*1298*	*4 GE CF6-80C2B1F*	*394625*	*F18C66Y263*		

SOUTH AFRICAN EXPRESS Airways, (Pty) Ltd = YB / EXY (Subsidiary of Transnet, Ltd) — Johannesburg-Int'l

PO Box 101, Johannesburg-Int'l Airport 1627, South Africa ☎ (11) 978 55 77 Tx: none Fax: (11) 978 55 78 SITA: n/a
F: 1993 460 Head: Israel B. Skosana ICAO: EXPRESSWAYS Net: http://www.saexpress.co.za. Scheduled commuter flights are operated in conjunction with SAA as a SA CONNECTOR using SA flight numbers.

☐ ZS-NLW	De Havilland DHC-8-315 Dash 8	*338*	*C-GETI**	*0094*	*0394*	*2 PWC PW123B*	*19505*	*Y50*		301 / *cvtd -311*
☐ ZS-NLX	De Havilland DHC-8-315 Dash 8	*348*	*C-GDKL**	*0094*	*0794*	*2 PWC PW123B*	*19505*	*Y50*		302 / *cvtd -314*
☐ ZS-NLY	De Havilland DHC-8-315 Dash 8	*352*	*C-GFCF**	*0094*	*0494*	*2 PWC PW123B*	*19505*	*Y50*		303 / *cvtd -311*
☐ ZS-NLZ	De Havilland DHC-8-315 Dash 8	*354*	*C-GFRP**	*0094*	*0894*	*2 PWC PW123B*	*19505*	*Y50*	*JQ-MP*	304 / *cvtd -314*
☐ ZS-NMA	De Havilland DHC-8-315 Dash 8	*358*	*C-GDFT**	*0094*	*0794*	*2 PWC PW123B*	*19505*	*Y50*		305 / *cvtd -314*
☐ ZS-NMB	De Havilland DHC-8-315 Dash 8	*368*	*C-GDIU**	*0094*	*0694*	*2 PWC PW123B*	*19505*	*Y50*		306 / *cvtd -311*
☐ ZS-NMI	Canadair Regional Jet 200ER (CL-600-2B19)	*7153*	*C-FZAN**	*0097*	*0897*	*2 GE CF34-3B1*	*23133*	*Y50*		
☐ ZS-NMJ	Canadair Regional Jet 200ER (CL-600-2B19)	*7161*	*C-GAUG**	*0097*	*0997*	*2 GE CF34-3B1*	*23133*	*Y50*		
☐ ZS-NMK	Canadair Regional Jet 200ER (CL-600-2B19)	*7198*	*C-GBMF**	*0097*	*1197*	*2 GE CF34-3B1*	*23133*	*Y50*		
☐ ZS-NML	Canadair Regional Jet 200ER (CL-600-2B19)	*7201*	*C-GBLX**	*0097*	*1297*	*2 GE CF34-3B1*	*23133*	*Y50*		
☐ ZS-NMM	Canadair Regional Jet 200ER (CL-600-2B19)	*7234*		*0098*	*0498*	*2 GE CF34-3B1*	*23133*	*Y50*		
☐ ZS-NMN	Canadair Regional Jet 200ER (CL-600-2B19)	*7237*		*0098*	*0598*	*2 GE CF34-3B1*	*23133*	*Y50*	*JR-BP*	

SPEED AIR, (Pty) Ltd — Johannesburg-Lanseria

PO Box 310, Lanseria 1748, South Africa ☎ (11) 659 28 85 Tx: n/a Fax: (11) 659 17 75 SITA: n/a
F: n/a n/a Head: n/a Net: n/a Aircraft below MTOW 1361 kg: Cessna 172.

☐ ZS-IMO	Beech Baron B55 (95-B55)	*TC-1386*	*N9184Q*	*0071*		*2 CO IO-470-L*	*2313*			*lsf pvt*
☐ ZS-AMH	Cessna 421	*421-0096*	*ZS-MDC*	*0068*		*2 CO GTSIO-520-D*	*3084*			*lsf Speed Air Service Centre*
☐ ZS-FTI	Cessna 421	*421-0011*	*ZS-KMM*	*0068*		*2 CO GTSIO-520-D*	*3084*			*lsf Speed Air Service Centre*
☐ ZS-JRR	Cessna 421C Golden Eagle II	*421C0141*	*N3914C*	*0076*	*0498*	*2 CO GTSIO-520-L*	*3379*			
☐ ZS-KMB	Cessna 421B Golden Eagle	*421B0815*	*N103WE*	*0074*	*0898*	*2 CO GTSIO-520-H*	*3379*			

STREAMLINE AIR CHARTER = SLE (Streamline Aviation, CC dba) — Johannesburg-Rand

PO Box 18152, Rand Airport 1419, South Africa ☎ (11) 824 16 50 Tx: n/a Fax: (11) 824 17 57 SITA: n/a
F: n/a n/a Head: n/a ICAO: SLIPSTREAM Net: n/a

☐ ZS-NGY	Piper PA-31-350 Navajo Chieftain	*31-7852068*	*N51AD*	*0078*		*2 LY TIO-540-J2BD*	*3175*			*lsf Atev Aviation Partnership*
☐ ZS-NNK	Cessna 208B Grand Caravan	*208B0461*		*0095*		*1 PWC PT6A-114A*	*3969*			*lsf Karan Beef*

681 registration type of aircraft cn/fn ex/ex* mfd del powered by mtow kg configuration selcal name/fln/specialitites/remarks

SUN AIR = BV / SSN (Bop Air, (Pty) Ltd dba) — Mafikeng

Private Bag 145, PO International Airport, Johannesburg 1627, South Africa ☎ (11) 394 78 42 Tx: none Fax: (11) 397 10 08 SITA: n/a
F: 1979 ⁂ 240 Head: Johan Borstlap IATA: 928 ICAO: SUNSTREAM Net: n/a

☐ ZS-NNN	Boeing (Douglas) DC-9-32	47516 / 630	N1294L	0071	0394	2 PW JT8D-15	49895	CY98		
☐ ZS-NRA	Boeing (Douglas) DC-9-32	47430 / 609	G-BMAK	0070	1294	2 PW JT8D-11	49895	CY98		lsf The Sun Aircraft Trust
☐ ZS-NRB	Boeing (Douglas) DC-9-32	47468 / 611	G-BMAM	0071	1294	2 PW JT8D-11	49895	CY98		lsf The Sun Aircraft Trust
☐ ZS-NRC	Boeing (Douglas) DC-9-32	47090 / 190	N82702	1067	1195	2 PW JT8D-7B	49898	CY98		lsf The Sun Aircraft Trust
☐ ZS-NRD	Boeing (Douglas) DC-9-32	47037 / 121	N8270A	0667	0196	2 PW JT8D-7B	49898	CY98		lsf The Sun Aircraft Trust/sub-lst EZX
☐ ZS-OBF	Boeing (Douglas) MD-82 (DC-9-82)	48019 / 1001	OE-LDU	0081	0597	2 PW JT8D-217C	67810	CY137		lsf SFR / cvtd MD-81
☐ ZS-OBG	Boeing (Douglas) MD-82 (DC-9-82)	48020 / 1045	OE-LDV	1281	0597	2 PW JT8D-217C	67810	CY137		Maletsatsi / lsf SFR / cvtd MD-81
☐ ZS-OBH	Boeing (Douglas) MD-82 (DC-9-82)	48059 / 1047	OE-LDW	0082	0697	2 PW JT8D-217C	67810	CY137		lsf SFR / cvtd MD-81
☐ ZS-OBI	Boeing (Douglas) MD-81 (DC-9-81)	48016 / 941	OE-LDR	0080	0198	2 PW JT8D-217C	64410	CY137		lsf SFR
☐ ZS-OBJ	Boeing (Douglas) MD-81 (DC-9-81)	48018 / 995	OE-LDT	0081	0299	2 PW JT8D-217C	64410	CY137		lsf SFR
☐ ZS-NVR	Boeing 727-230 (A)	20673 / 922	5N-NEC	0073	0496	3 PW JT8D-15	86409	CY146	FJ-KL	lsf SFR

SUNRISE AVIATION, CC — Nelspruit

Box 3175, Nelspruit 1200, South Africa ☎ (13) 744 92 54 Tx: none Fax: (13) 744 92 51 SITA: n/a
F: 1998 ⁂ 2 Head: Mike Pingo Net: n/a

☐ ZS-HXM	Bell 206B JetRanger III	4105	N7131J	0090	0098	1 AN 250-C20J	1451			lsf Coppercraft P/L
☐ ZS-HSX	Bell 206L-3 LongRanger III	51097	N206JF	0084	0798	1 AN 250-C30P	1882			lsf David Cruse Helicopters P/L
☐ ZS-RGL	Bell 206L-3 LongRanger III	51489	N21HK	0091	0098	1 AN 250-C30P	1882			lsf Air Excellence P/L

SWIFTFLITE Charters, CC — Johannesburg-Lanseria

PO Box 300, Lanseria 1748, South Africa ☎ (11) 701 32 98 Tx: none Fax: (11) 701 35 29 SITA: n/a
F: 1990 ⁂ 6 Head: David James Net: n/a

☐ ZS-LAW	Beech King Air B200	BB-889	N3538K	0081		2 PWC PT6A-42	5670			lsf Rennies Shipping Holdings P/L
☐ ZS-NZK	Beech King Air B200	BB-1553	N10780	0096	0197	2 PWC PT6A-42	5670			lsf Reserve Air Charters P/L
☐ ZS-LHU	Cessna 550 Citation II	550-0165	3D-ACQ	0080		2 PWC JT15D-4	6033			lsf Ssangyong Motors

THE FLYING COMPANY (Associated with Skystream Air Charters) — Cape Town-Int'l

PO Box 5231, Cape Town 8000, South Africa ☎ (21) 934 60 85 Tx: none Fax: (21) 934 05 99 SITA: n/a
F: 1994 ⁂ 6 Head: Ms. Tanja Schürmann Net: n/a

☐ ZS-NHO	Cessna 550 Citation II	550-0237	3D-ACT	0080	0694	2 PWC JT15D-4	6033	8 Pax		lsf Commercial Air Services (OFS) P/L

WALKER FLYING SERVICE (Newton Walker dba) — Upington

PO Box 335, Upington 8800, South Africa ☎ (54) 332 36 85 Tx: none Fax: (54) 332 36 85 SITA: n/a
F: 1974 ⁂ 2 Head: Newton Walker Net: n/a

☐ ZS-KVD	Cessna 210N Centurion II	21063003	N6427N	0079	0498	1 CO IO-520-L	1724	6 Pax		
☐ ZS-LWV	Cessna 402B II	402B1223	N32LA	0077		2 CO TSIO-520-E	2858	8 Pax		

WESTLINE AVIATION, (Pty) Ltd (formerly Midwest Aviation) — Bloemfontein-New Tempe

PO Box 12794, Brandhof 9324, South Africa ☎ (51) 451 17 17 Tx: none Fax: (51) 451 16 41 SITA: n/a
F: 1990 ⁂ 6 Head: Les Daley Net: n/a Aircraft below MTOW 1361kg: Cessna 172 & Piper PA-28

☐ ZS-LPY	Cessna U206C Super Skywagon	U206-1042	9J-LPY	0068		1 CO IO-520-F	1633			lsf pvt
☐ ZS-JYM	Cessna 210M Centurion II	21061902		0077		1 CO IO-520-L	1724			lsf FGP Air Charters Vennootskap
☐ ZS-LXA	Piper PA-34-200T Seneca II	34-7970079	N2107J	0079		2 CO TSIO-360-EB	2073			lsf Resepkor Ltd

Z3 = MACEDONIA (Republic of Macedonia) (Republika Makedonija)

Capital: Skopje Official Language: Macedonian Population: 2,2 million Square Km: 25713 Dialling code: +389 Year established: 1991 Acting political head: Kiro Gligorov (President)

Government / Corporate / Executive / VIP Aircraft

☐ Z3-BAA	Learjet 25B	25B-205	YU-BKJ	0076		2 GE CJ610-6	6804	VIP		Gvmt
☐ Z3-BAB	Beech King Air 200	BB-652	YU-BMF	0080		2 PWC PT6A-41	5670	VIP		Gvmt

AVIOIMPEX = M4 / AXX (Division of Interimpex) — Skopje

PO Box 544, 11 Oktomvri K14, MK-91000 Skopje, Macedonia ☎ (91) 11 41 55 Tx: 51316 Fax: (91) 11 93 48 SITA: SKPTOM4
F: 1992 ⁂ 170 Head: Ilja Smilev IATA: 743 ICAO: AVIOIMPEX Net: http://www.avioimpex.nu Beside aircraft listed, additional aircraft (Tupolev 154M) are leased from VIA (LZ-) when required.

☐ Z3-ARA	Boeing (Douglas) DC-9-33F (RC)	47530 / 624	S5-ABG	0071	1294	2 PW JT8D-9A	51710	Y105	BD-JL	
☐ RA-42432	Yakovlev 42D	4520424410016	TC-ALY	1294	0897	3 LO D-36	56500	Y120		lsf SOV
☐ Z3-ARB	Boeing (Douglas) MD-81 (DC-9-81)	48046 / 977	N801VV	0081	0697	2 PW JT8D-217	63503	Y164		lsf McDonnell Dougl.Macedonia Lsng Inc.

BONIAIR = BOA — Kumanovo

Illidentska Road, MK-91300 Kumanovo, Macedonia ☎ (901) 41 40 35 Tx: none Fax: (901) 41 40 35 SITA: n/a
F: n/a ⁂ n/a Head: n/a ICAO: KUMANOVO Net: n/a

☐ Z3-BGJ	PZL Mielec (Antonov) An-2	1G166-04	LZ-1502	0075	1296	1 SH ASh-62IR	5500	Utility		
☐ Z3-BGK	PZL Mielec (Antonov) An-2	1G197-35	LZ-1504	0082	0097	1 SH ASh-62IR	5500	Utility		
☐ Z3-BGL	PZL Mielec (Antonov) An-2	1G201-19	LZ-1202	0083	0498	1 SH ASh-62IR	5500	Utility		

MACEDONIAN COMMERCIAL AVIATION (formerly Aviotransport) — Skopje-Stenkovec

Vilko Vakavic 24, MK-91000 Skopje, Macedonia ☎ (91) 66 61 24 Tx: none Fax: (91) 22 77 63 SITA: n/a
F: n/a ⁂ n/a Head: Dimitar Sekolov Net: n/a

☐ Z3-BGA	PZL Mielec (Antonov) An-2	1G167-01	YU-BJV	0075		1 SH ASh-62IR	5500	Utility		
☐ Z3-BGB	PZL Mielec (Antonov) An-2	1G160-15	YU-BLD	0075		1 SH ASh-62IR	5500	Utility		
☐ Z3-BGC	PZL Mielec (Antonov) An-2	1G167-03	YU-BJY	0075		1 SH ASh-62IR	5500	Utility		
☐ Z3-BGD	PZL Mielec (Antonov) An-2	1G111-15	YU-BGK	0069		1 SH ASh-62IR	5500	Utility		
☐ Z3-BGF	PZL Mielec (Antonov) An-2	1G231-55	YU-BPJ	0089		1 SH ASh-62IR	5500	Utility		
☐ Z3-BGG	PZL Mielec (Antonov) An-2	1G115-15	YU-BGZ	0069		1 SH ASh-62IR	5500	Utility		
☐ Z3-BGH	PZL Mielec (Antonov) An-2	1G111-12	YU-BGH	0069		1 SH ASh-62IR	5500	Utility		

MAT-MACEDONIAN AIRLINES = IN / MAK (Makedonskie Aviotransport) — Skopje

MAT Macedonian Airlines

Bulevar Partizanski Odredi 17a, MK-91000 Skopje, Macedonia ☎ (91) 13 44 56 Tx: none Fax: (91) 13 44 56 SITA: SKPTOIN
F: 1994 ⁂ 83 Head: Zlatko Petrovski ICAO: MAKAVIO Net: n/a

☐ Z3-ARD	Boeing (Douglas) DC-9-32	47568 / 689	YU-AJK	0073	0798	2 PW JT8D-9A	48988	Y107	GJ-HM	lsf JAT
☐ Z3-ARE	Boeing (Douglas) DC-9-32	47567 / 688	YU-AJJ	0373	0998	2 PW JT8D-9A (HK3/ABS)	48988	Y107	GJ-HL	lsf JAT
☐ Z3-ARF	Boeing 737-3H9	23716 / 1321	YU-ANL	0086	0697	2 CFMI CFM56-3B1	61235	Y137	KM-CF	lsf JAT

3A = MONACO (Principality of Monaco) (Principauté de Monaco)

Capital: Monaco-Ville Official Language: French Population: 0,1 million Square Km: 2 Dialling code: +377 Year established: 1489 Acting political head: Rainier III (Prince)

Government / Corporate / Executive / VIP Aircraft

☐ 3A-MGR	Dassault Falcon 20F	473	F-GEJR	0085		2 GE CF700-2D2	13000	VIP		Prince of Monaco

HELI AIR MONACO = YO / MCM — Monte Carlo-Heliport

HELI AIR MONACO

Héliport de Monaco, MC-98000 Monte Carlo, Monaco ☎ 92 05 00 50 Tx: 479343 eliair mc Fax: 92 05 76 17 SITA: MCMYOCR
F: 1976 ⁂ 110 Head: Jacques Crovetto IATA: 747 ICAO: HELI AIR Net: n/a

☐ 3A-MAC	Eurocopter (Aerosp.) AS350B Ecureuil	1673	HB-XBC	0083		1 TU Arriel 1B	1950			
☐ 3A-MMC	Eurocopter (Aerosp.) AS350BA Ecureuil	1709	F-WZFU	0084		1 TU Arriel 1B	2100			cvtd AS350B
☐ 3A-MTP	Eurocopter (Aerosp.) AS350B2 Ecureuil	1996	I-LOLO	0087	0898	1 TU Arriel 1D1	2250			cvtd AS350B1
☐ 3A-MTT	Eurocopter (Aerosp.) AS350B2 Ecureuil	1967	I-LUPJ	0086	0898	1 TU Arriel 1D1	2250			cvtd AS350B1
☐ 3A-MEC	Eurocopter (Aerosp.) AS355F1 Ecureuil 2	5271	I-LIEM	0083	0696	2 AN 250-C20F	2400			
☐ 3A-MJP	Eurocopter (Aerosp.) SA365C3 Dauphin 2	5015	N90049	0078	0991	2 TU Arriel 1C	3500			

MONACAIR, S.A.M. = MCR — Monte Carlo-Heliport

MONACAIR

Héliport de Monaco, MC-98000 Monte Carlo, Monaco ☎ 92 05 25 28 Tx: none Fax: 92 05 90 48 SITA: n/a
F: 1987 ⁂ 16 Head: Salim Zeghdar ICAO: MONACAIR Net: n/a

☐ 3A-MLD	Eurocopter (Aerosp.) AS350B Ecureuil	1357	F-GCQD	0080	0199	1 TU Arriel 1B	1950			
☐ 3A-MTV	Eurocopter (Aerosp.) SA365N Dauphin 2	6096	F-OHNZ	0083	0199	2 TU Arriel 1C	4000			

3B = MAURITIUS (Republic of Mauritius) (République d'Ile Maurice)

Capital: Port Louis Official Language: French, English Population: 1,2 million Square Km: 2040 Dialling code: +230 Year established: 1968 Acting political head: Dr Navinchandra Ramgoolam (Prime Minister)

AIR MAURITIUS, Ltd = MK / MAU — Mauritius

AIR MAURITIUS

Rogers House, 5 President John Kennedy Street, Port Louis, Mauritius ☎ 603 30 30 Tx: 4415 iw Fax: 208 83 31 SITA: MRUEZMK
F: 1967 ⁂ 1500 Head: Nashir Mallam-Hasham IATA: 239 ICAO: AIRMAURITIUS Net: http://www.air-mauritius.com

☐ 3B-NZD	Bell 206B JetRanger III	4464		0097	0797	1 AN 250-C20J	1451	Y4		
☐ 3B-NZE	Bell 206B JetRanger III	4465		0097	0797	1 AN 250-C20J	1451	Y4		

682 registration type of aircraft cn/fn ex/ex* mfd del powered by mtow kg configuration selcal name/fln/specialitites/remarks

☐ 3B-NZF	Bell 206B JetRanger III	4496		0098	1098	1 AN 250-C20J	1451	Y4		
☐ 3B-NAP	ATR 42-300	208	F-WWEV*	0090	0990	2 PWC PW120-B5	16700	Y48		Port Mathurin
☐ 3B-NBA	ATR 42-500	534	F-WWLF*	0097	0597	2 PWC PW127E	18600	Y48		Saint Brandon
☐ 3B-NBB	ATR 42-500	554	F-WWLL*	0097	0697	2 PWC PW127E	18600	Y48		Coin de Mire
☐ 3B-NAK	Boeing 767-23B (ER)	23973 / 208	N6046P*	0088	0488	2 GE CF6-80C2B4	172365	F12C18Y151	EG-FP	01 / City of Curepipe
☐ 3B-NAL	Boeing 767-23B (ER)	23974 / 214	N6018N*	0088	0488	2 GE CF6-80C2B4	172365	F12C18Y151	EG-HP	02 / City of Port Louis
☐ 3B-NAU	Airbus Industrie A340-312	076	F-WWJG*	0094	1094	4 CFMI CFM56-5C3	257000	F12C35Y254	GR-QS	Pink Pigeon
☐ 3B-NAV	Airbus Industrie A340-312	094	F-WWJF*	0095	0395	4 CFMI CFM56-5C3	257000	F12C35Y254	HQ-AF	Kestrel / lsf ILFC
☐ 3B-NAY	Airbus Industrie A340-313	152	F-WWJX*	0096	1196	4 CFMI CFM56-5C4	271000	F12C35Y254	JP-AR	Cardinal / lsf ILFC
☐ 3B-NBD	Airbus Industrie A340-313	194	F-WWJP*	0097	1097	4 CFMI CFM56-5C4	271000	F12C35Y254	MS-PR	Parakeet
☐ 3B-NBE	Airbus Industrie A340-313	268	F-WWJG*	0099	0499	4 CFMI CFM56-5C4	271000	F12C35Y254	DQ-JL	

XL AVIATION — Mauritius

Suite 701, Chancery House, Lislet Geoffroy Street, Port Louis, Mauritius ☎ 211 61 13 Tx: none Fax: 211 28 77 SITA: n/a
F: 1994 ⁂ n/a Head: Claude Jourda Net: n/a

☐ 3B-XLA	Dassault Falcon 900	7	TR-LCJ	0087	0498	3 GA TFE731-5BR-1C	21092			

3C = EQUATORIAL GUINEA (Republic of Equatorial Guinea) (Republica de Guinea Ecuatorial)

Capital: Malabo Official Language: Spanish Population: 0,4 million Square Km: 28051 Dialling code: +240 Year established: 1968 Acting political head: Colonel Teodoro Obiang Nguema Mbasogo (President)

Government / Corporate / Executive / VIP Aircraft

☐ 3C-5GE	Antonov 32	1609		0086		2 IV AI-20D	27000	VIP / Combi		Enrique Nvo Okene / Gvmt
☐ 3C-CGE	Yakovlev 40	9821557	3C-MNB	0078		3 IV AI-25	16000	VIP		Gvmt
☐ 3C-LKI	BAe (BAC) One-Eleven 414EG	158	HZ-KB1	0070	0399	2 RR Spey 511-14	40143	Executive		private / for sale

AIR CONSUL, S.A. = RCS — Malabo

Apartado 77, Malabo, Equatorial Guinea ☎ (9) 33 78 Tx: none Fax: (9) 32 91 SITA: n/a
F: 1995 ⁂ 11 Head: Ezequiel Rebordinos de las Vecillas ICAO: AEROCONSUL Net: n/a

☐ 3C-JJE	Piper PA-23-250 Aztec C	27-3180	EC-DTG	0065		2 LY IO-540-C4B5	2359			
☐ 3C-JJO	Piper PA-23-250 Aztec B	27-2136		0062		2 LY O-540-A1D5	2177			
☐ 3C-JJG	Piper PA-31-350 Navajo Chieftain	31-7552059	TR-LUQ	0075		2 LY TIO-540-J2BD	3175			
☐ EC-CIY	Piper PA-31-350 Navajo Chieftain	31-7405181	N66875	0074		2 LY TIO-540-J2BD	3175			lsf pvt

CESSAVIA = CSS — Malabo & Sharjah (UAE)

Operations Office:, c/o Transavia Travel Agency, PO Box 3962, Sharjah, United Arab Emirates ☎ (6) 52 28 33 Tx: none Fax: (6) 52 26 60 SITA: n/a
F: 1998 ⁂ n/a Head: Victor Butt ICAO: CESSAVIA Net: n/a

☐ 3C-KKM	Antonov 24T	1911803	3D-SBP	0071	0098	2 IV AI-24VT	22500	Combi		XX-vek
☐ 3C-KKO	Antonov 12BP	1901706	3D-SKN	0061	0098	4 IV AI-20M	61000	Freighter		Flying Cat
☐ 3C-KKJ	Ilyushin 18V	184006903	3D-SBC	1263	0098	4 IV AI-20M	64000	Combi		occ lst KAK
☐ 3C-KKK	Ilyushin 18D	186009202	3D-SBW	0666	0098	4 IV AI-20M	64000	Combi		

EGA – Ecuato Guineana de Aviacion = 8Y / EGA — Malabo

Apartado 665, Malabo, Equatorial Guinea ☎ (9) 44 97 Tx: none Fax: (9) 44 96 SITA: n/a
F: 1986 ⁂ 40 Head: n/a IATA: 112 Net: n/a Operates scheduled flights with Yakovlev 40 aircraft, leased from other companies when required.

GATS Guinea, S.A. = GTS (Assoc.with Gulf Aviation Technology & Services, U.A.E./formerly GATS, SA & GATS, Ltd) — Malabo & Abu Dhabi (UAE)

Operations Office:, PO Box 25298, Abu Dhabi, United Arab Emirates ☎ (2) 75 74 68 Tx: none Fax: (2) 75 74 78 SITA: AUHGT7X
F: 1992 ⁂ n/a Head: Vito G. Gomes ICAO: GATS AIR Net: n/a

☐ 3C-KKE	Ilyushin 76TD	1023411368	YN-CEX	0092	0096	4 SO D-30KP	190000	Freighter		
☐ 3C-KKF	Ilyushin 76TD	1023411384	YN-CEV	0092	0096	4 SO D-30KP	190000	Freighter		
☐ 3C-KKG	Ilyushin 76TD	1023410360	YN-CEW	0092	0096	4 SO D-30KP	190000	Freighter		

GEASA – Guinea Ecuatorial Airlines, S.A. = GEA — Malabo

Apartado 3, Malabo, Equatorial Guinea ☎ (9) 41 28 Tx: none Fax: none SITA: n/a
F: 1996 ⁂ n/a Head: n/a ICAO: GEASA Net: n/a

☐ RA-87587	Yakovlev 40	9221922	CCCP-87587	0072	0096	3 IV AI-25	16800	Y32		lsf Salyut Aviakompania/dmgd 200399Bata

J.A.M. AIR (Flight Dept. of Jesus Alive Ministries) — Johannesburg-Lanseria

South African Headquarters:, PO Box 1502, Johannesburg 2040, South Africa ☎ (11) 708 17 21 Tx: none Fax: (11) 708 19 90 SITA: n/a
F: n/a ⁂ n/a Head: Cass Watson Net: n/a Non-commercial non-profit missionary church organsiation conducting charity, relief & missionary support flights.

☐ 3C-JJX	BAe (HS) Andover C.1	6	EL-VDD	0066	0598	2 RR Dart 201	22680	Combi		

3D = SWAZILAND (Kingdom of Swaziland) (Umboso we Swatini)

Capital: Mbabane Official Language: English, Siswati Population: 1,1 million Square Km: 17364 Dialling code: +268 Year established: 1968 Acting political head: Mswati III (King)

AFRICAN INTERNATIONAL AIRWAYS, (Pty) Ltd – AIA = AIN (Associated with & managed by Intavia, Ltd) — Manzini-Matsapha Int'l

1 The Brunel Centre, Newton Road, Crawley, West Sussex RH10 2TU, England, Great Britain ☎ (1293) 54 47 06 Tx: 87130 inavia g Fax: (1293) 61 58 00 SITA: LGWIPXH
F: 1985 ⁂ 36 Head: Alan J. Stocks IATA: 648 ICAO: FLY CARGO Net: n/a

☐ 3D-ADV	Boeing (Douglas) DC-8-54F (JT)	46012 / 410	5N-AWZ	0068	0887	4 PW JT3D-3B (HK2/BAC)	149685	Freighter	BL-FM	
☐ 3D-AFR	Boeing (Douglas) DC-8-54F (JT)	45802 / 247	N46UA	0066	0590	4 PW JT3D-3B (HK2/QNC)	149685	Freighter	AK-JM	

INTERSTATE AIRWAYS, (Pty) Ltd — Johannesburg-Lanseria (South Africa)

Operations office:, PO Box 11719, Selcourt 1567, South Africa ☎ (11) 363 21 61 Tx: none Fax: (11) 363 21 61 SITA: n/a
F: 1998 ⁂ n/a Head: Johnny Pereira Net: n/a

☐ 3D-ADW	Boeing (Douglas) DC-4 (C-54A-15-DC)	10417 / DC 148	3D-NJN	0044	0298	4 PW R-2000	33112	Freighter		

ROYAL SWAZI NATIONAL AIRWAYS, Corp. = ZC / RSN — Manzini-Matsapha Int'l

PO Box 939, Manzini, Swaziland ☎ 84 444 Tx: 2064 wd Fax: 85 054 SITA: n/a
F: 1977 ⁂ 162 Head: Prince Gabheni Diamini IATA: 141 ICAO: SWAZI NATIONAL Net: n/a

☐ 3D-ALN	Fokker F28 Fellowship 3000 (F28 Mk3000)	11136	PH-ZBR*	0078	0778	2 RR Spey 555-15H	33112	F4Y55	DF-EM	Ijubantendele
☐ 3D-ALM	Fokker 100 (F28 Mk0100)	11335	PH-EZR*	0091	1293	2 RR Tay 650-15	44452	F12Y85		Ludvondvolo / lst LAM

SCAN AIR CHARTER, Ltd — Manzini-Matsapha Int'l

PO Box 1231, Manzini, Swaziland ☎ 84 474 Tx: none Fax: 86 340 SITA: n/a
F: 1976 ⁂ 6 Head: Felicity V. Hermansson Net: n/a

☐ 3D-AFF	Cessna 310R II	310R0624	C9-STC	0076	0091	2 CO IO-520-M	2495			lsf pvt
☐ 3D-JWR	Cessna 310Q II	310Q1094	ZS-JWR	0077		2 CO IO-470-VO	2495			
☐ 3D-JNC	Beech Baron 58	TH-568		0075		2 CO IO-520-C	2449			lsf Bambi Stewart (Pty) Ltd
☐ 3D-AFS	Cessna 402B	402B0033	OY-BSW	0070	1290	2 CO TSIO-520-E	2858			

SWAZI EXPRESS AIRWAYS = SWX (Steffen Air, Ltd dba) — Manzini-Matsapha Int'l

PO Box 1, Matata, Swaziland ☎ 363 65 31 Tx: none Fax: 363 65 31 SITA: n/a
F: 1998 ⁂ n/a Head: n/a ICAO: SWAZI EXPRESS Net: n/a

☐ ZS-NON	Cessna 208 Caravan I	20800036	5Y-NON	0085	0098	1 PWC PT6A-114	3629			Nisela / lsf Atin Air CC

3X = GUINEA (Republic of Guinea) (République de Guinée)

Capital: Conakry Official Language: French Population: 7,8 million Square Km: 245857 Dialling code: +224 Year established: 1958 Acting political head: Brig.-Gen. Lansana Conté (President)

AIR GUINEE = GIB — Conakry

BP 12, Conakry, Guinea ☎ 45 46 09 Tx: none Fax: 41 29 07 SITA: n/a
F: 1960 ⁂ 400 Head: Mamadou Aliou Sanoh ICAO: AIR GUINEE Net: n/a

☐ 3X-GCJ	De Havilland DHC-7-102 Dash 7	107	C-GEWQ*	0085	0785	4 PWC PT6A-50	19958	Y50		
☐ B-3499	Xian Yunshuji Y7-100	03702		0085	1097	2 WJ 5A-1	21800	Y52		lsf Xian Aircraft / cvtd Y7
☐ 3X-GCB	Boeing 737-2R6C (A)	22627 / 779		0081	0881	2 PW JT8D-17	54204	Y124	HL-BC	

GUINEE AIR SERVICE – GAS = GIS — Conakry

BP 1516, Conakry, Guinea ☎ 45 10 85 Tx: none Fax: 41 27 61 SITA: n/a
F: 1985 ⁂ n/a Head: Cdt Ibrahima Kouyate ICAO: GASS Net: n/a Operates passenger & cargo flights with Antonov 24/26 aircraft, leased from other companies when required.

GUINEE INTER AIR = GIE — Conakry

BP 2339, Conakry, Guinea ☎ 41 37 08 Tx: none Fax: 45 10 85 SITA: n/a
F: 1992 ⁂ n/a Head: n/a ICAO: GUINEE INTER Net: n/a

☐ EW-87419	Yakovlev 40	9421134	CCCP-87419	0574	0097	3 IV AI-25	16800	Y36		lsf MOG

683 registration type of aircraft cn/fn ex/ex* mfd del powered by mtow kg configuration selcal name/fln/specialitites/remarks

SOTAG – Société des Transports Aériens de Guinée, SàRL = GIT
Conakry

BP 2808, Conakry, Guinea ☎ 41 48 55 Tx: none Fax: 41 48 55 SITA: n/a
F: 1997 ⁂ n/a Head: n/a ICAO: SOTAG Net: n/a Operates charter flights with Tupolev 154 aircraft leased from Russian companies when required.

SUD AIR TRANSPORT, S.A. = GID
Conakry

BP 4586, Conakry, Guinée ☎ 41 25 69 Tx: none Fax: 46 39 93 SITA: n/a
F: 1992 ⁂ n/a Head: n/a ICAO: SUD TRANSPORT Net: n/a Operates charter flights with Antonov 24/26 leased from Russian companies (RA-) when required.

UTA – Union des Transports Africains de Guinée = GIH
Conakry

BP 751, Conakry, Guinea ☎ 45 38 03 Tx: none Fax: 45 38 02 SITA: n/a
F: 1997 ⁂ n/a Head: n/a ICAO: TRANSPORT AFRICAIN Net: n/a

☐ RA-47365	Antonov 24RV	77310802	CCCP-47365	0077	0997	2 IV AI-24VT	21800	Y48		lsf pvt

4K = AZERBAIJAN (Republic of Azerbaijan) (Azarbaycan Respublikasy)

Capital: Baku Official Language: Azeri Population: 7,5 million Square Km: 86600 Dialling code: +994 Year established: 1991 Acting political head: Geidar A. Aliyev (President)

Government / Corporate / Executive / VIP Aircraft

☐ AHY-78129	Ilyushin 76MD	0083489683	AHY-78001	0088		4 SO D-30KP	190000	Freighter		Ministry of Defence / AHY-titles
☐ RA-86810	Ilyushin 76M		CCCP-86810	0075		4 SO D-30KP	170000	Freighter		Ministry of Defence/to be 4K- reg.
☐ 4K-12425	Antonov 12	401103	CCCP-12425	0062		4 IV AI-20M	61000	Freighter		Ministry of Defence
☐ 4K-65496	Tupolev 134A-3	63468	4K-65985	0081		2 SO D-30-III	49000	VIP		Ministry of Defence / AHY-titles
☐ 4K-78130	Ilyushin 76MD	0043454611		0084		4 SO D-30KP	190000	Freighter		Ministry of Defence / occ opf AHY

AZERBAIJAN AIRLINES/AZAL Agro (Member of Azerbaijan Airlines Concern)
Yevlakh

Airport Yevlakh, 370036 Yevlakh, Azerbaijan ☎ (166) 66 622 Tx: none Fax: (12) 56 25 43 SITA: n/a
F: 1991 ⁂ n/a Head: N.I. Dzhumayev Net: n/a Some aircraft are still in Aeroflot colors but will be repainted in due course.

☐ 4K-07247	PZL Mielec (Antonov) An-2	1G147-38	CCCP-07247	0578	0091	1 SH ASh-62IR	5250	Sprayer / Frtr		
☐ 4K-07575	PZL Mielec (Antonov) An-2	1G156-15	CCCP-07575	0474	0091	1 SH ASh-62IR	5250	Sprayer / Frtr		
☐ 4K-07706	PZL Mielec (Antonov) An-2	1G158-26	CCCP-07706	0774	0091	1 SH ASh-62IR	5250	Sprayer / Frtr		
☐ 4K-07714	PZL Mielec (Antonov) An-2	1G158-34	CCCP-07714	0774	0091	1 SH ASh-62IR	5250	Sprayer / Frtr		
☐ 4K-07845	PZL Mielec (Antonov) An-2	1G169-60	CCCP-07845	0676	0091	1 SH ASh-62IR	5250	Sprayer / Frtr		
☐ 4K-16046	PZL Mielec (Antonov) An-2	1G163-54	CCCP-16046	0675	0091	1 SH ASh-62IR	5250	Sprayer / Frtr		
☐ 4K-16047	PZL Mielec (Antonov) An-2	1G163-55	CCCP-16047	0675	0091	1 SH ASh-62IR	5250	Sprayer / Frtr		
☐ 4K-17762	PZL Mielec (Antonov) An-2	1G203-23	CCCP-17762	0683	0091	1 SH ASh-62IR	5250	Sprayer / Frtr		
☐ 4K-17763	PZL Mielec (Antonov) An-2	1G203-24	CCCP-17763	0683	0091	1 SH ASh-62IR	5250	Sprayer / Frtr		
☐ 4K-17814	PZL Mielec (Antonov) An-2	1G204-15	CCCP-17814	0883	0091	1 SH ASh-62IR	5250	Sprayer / Frtr		
☐ 4K-17815	PZL Mielec (Antonov) An-2	1G204-16	CCCP-17815	0883	0091	1 SH ASh-62IR	5250	Sprayer / Frtr		
☐ 4K-17826	PZL Mielec (Antonov) An-2	1G204-27	CCCP-17826	0983	0091	1 SH ASh-62IR	5250	Sprayer / Frtr		
☐ 4K-17827	PZL Mielec (Antonov) An-2	1G204-28	CCCP-17827	0983	0091	1 SH ASh-62IR	5250	Sprayer / Frtr		
☐ 4K-19719	PZL Mielec (Antonov) An-2	1G165-33	CCCP-19719	0975	0091	1 SH ASh-62IR	5250	Sprayer / Frtr		
☐ 4K-31436	PZL Mielec (Antonov) An-2	1G197-59	CCCP-31436	0882	0091	1 SH ASh-62IR	5250	Sprayer / Frtr		
☐ 4K-31442	PZL Mielec (Antonov) An-2	1G198-07	CCCP-31442	0882	0091	1 SH ASh-62IR	5250	Sprayer / Frtr		
☐ 4K-31447	PZL Mielec (Antonov) An-2	1G198-12	CCCP-31447	0782	0091	1 SH ASh-62IR	5250	Sprayer / Frtr		
☐ 4K-31448	PZL Mielec (Antonov) An-2	1G198-13	CCCP-31448	0782	0091	1 SH ASh-62IR	5250	Sprayer / Frtr		
☐ 4K-31461	PZL Mielec (Antonov) An-2	1G198-26	CCCP-31461	0882	0091	1 SH ASh-62IR	5250	Sprayer / Frtr		
☐ 4K-32619	PZL Mielec (Antonov) An-2	1G219-18	CCCP-32619	0886	0091	1 SH ASh-62IR	5250	Sprayer / Frtr		
☐ 4K-32677	PZL Mielec (Antonov) An-2	1G211-36	CCCP-32677	0285	0091	1 SH ASh-62IR	5250	Sprayer / Frtr		
☐ 4K-33050	PZL Mielec (Antonov) An-2	1G218-37	CCCP-33050	0386	0091	1 SH ASh-62IR	5250	Sprayer / Frtr		
☐ 4K-33053	PZL Mielec (Antonov) An-2	1G218-40	CCCP-33053	0386	0091	1 SH ASh-62IR	5250	Sprayer / Frtr		
☐ 4K-33327	PZL Mielec (Antonov) An-2	1G225-46	CCCP-33327	0687	0091	1 SH ASh-62IR	5250	Sprayer / Frtr		
☐ 4K-33328	PZL Mielec (Antonov) An-2	1G225-47	CCCP-33328	0687	0091	1 SH ASh-62IR	5250	Sprayer / Frtr		
☐ 4K-33367	PZL Mielec (Antonov) An-2	1G226-26	CCCP-33367	0887	0091	1 SH ASh-62IR	5250	Sprayer / Frtr		
☐ 4K-33497	PZL Mielec (Antonov) An-2	1G228-49	CCCP-33497	0288	0091	1 SH ASh-62IR	5250	Sprayer / Frtr		
☐ 4K-33498	PZL Mielec (Antonov) An-2	1G228-50	CCCP-33498	0288	0091	1 SH ASh-62IR	5250	Sprayer / Frtr		
☐ 4K-33517	PZL Mielec (Antonov) An-2	1G229-09	CCCP-33517	0388	0091	1 SH ASh-62IR	5250	Sprayer / Frtr		
☐ 4K-33518	PZL Mielec (Antonov) An-2	1G229-10	CCCP-33518	0388	0091	1 SH ASh-62IR	5250	Sprayer / Frtr		
☐ 4K-33519	PZL Mielec (Antonov) An-2	1G229-11	CCCP-33519	0388	0091	1 SH ASh-62IR	5250	Sprayer / Frtr		
☐ 4K-40222	PZL Mielec (Antonov) An-2	1G220-12	CCCP-40222	0686	0091	1 SH ASh-62IR	5250	Sprayer / Frtr		
☐ 4K-40229	PZL Mielec (Antonov) An-2	1G220-19	CCCP-40229	0686	0091	1 SH ASh-62IR	5250	Sprayer / Frtr		
☐ 4K-40267	PZL Mielec (Antonov) An-2	1G220-57	CCCP-40267	0786	0091	1 SH ASh-62IR	5500	12 Pax		
☐ 4K-40414	PZL Mielec (Antonov) An-2	1G223-38	CCCP-40414	0287	0091	1 SH ASh-62IR	5250	Sprayer / Frtr		
☐ 4K-40474	PZL Mielec (Antonov) An-2	1G224-51	CCCP-40474	0487	0091	1 SH ASh-62IR	5250	Sprayer / Frtr		
☐ 4K-40475	PZL Mielec (Antonov) An-2	1G224-52	CCCP-40475	0487	0091	1 SH ASh-62IR	5250	Sprayer / Frtr		
☐ 4K-40638	PZL Mielec (Antonov) An-2	1G213-45	CCCP-40638	0585	0091	1 SH ASh-62IR	5250	Sprayer / Frtr		
☐ 4K-40639	PZL Mielec (Antonov) An-2	1G213-46	CCCP-40639	0585	0091	1 SH ASh-62IR	5250	Sprayer / Frtr		
☐ 4K-40703	PZL Mielec (Antonov) An-2	1G215-01	CCCP-40703	0885	0091	1 SH ASh-62IR	5250	Sprayer / Frtr		
☐ 4K-40704	PZL Mielec (Antonov) An-2	1G215-02	CCCP-40704	0885	0091	1 SH ASh-62IR	5250	Sprayer / Frtr		
☐ 4K-40750	PZL Mielec (Antonov) An-2	1G172-22	CCCP-40750	1176	0091	1 SH ASh-62IR	5250	Sprayer / Frtr		
☐ 4K-40754	PZL Mielec (Antonov) An-2	1G172-26	CCCP-40754	1276	0091	1 SH ASh-62IR	5250	Sprayer / Frtr		
☐ 4K-40756	PZL Mielec (Antonov) An-2	1G172-26	CCCP-40756	1176	0091	1 SH ASh-62IR	5250	Sprayer / Frtr		
☐ 4K-40759	PZL Mielec (Antonov) An-2	1G172-31	CCCP-40759	1176	0091	1 SH ASh-62IR	5250	Sprayer / Frtr		
☐ 4K-40761	PZL Mielec (Antonov) An-2	1G172-33	CCCP-40761	1176	0091	1 SH ASh-62IR	5250	Sprayer / Frtr		
☐ 4K-40803	PZL Mielec (Antonov) An-2	1G173-30	CCCP-40803	0277	0091	1 SH ASh-62IR	5250	Sprayer / Frtr		
☐ 4K-40805	PZL Mielec (Antonov) An-2	1G173-50	CCCP-40805	0277	0091	1 SH ASh-62IR	5250	Sprayer / Frtr		
☐ 4K-40823	PZL Mielec (Antonov) An-2	1G174-01	CCCP-40823	0377	0091	1 SH ASh-62IR	5250	Sprayer / Frtr		
☐ 4K-40866	PZL Mielec (Antonov) An-2	1G175-20	CCCP-40866	0577	0091	1 SH ASh-62IR	5250	Sprayer / Frtr		
☐ 4K-40868	PZL Mielec (Antonov) An-2	1G215-03	CCCP-40868	0885	0091	1 SH ASh-62IR	5250	Sprayer / Frtr		
☐ 4K-40936	PZL Mielec (Antonov) An-2	1G216-36	CCCP-40936	1085	0091	1 SH ASh-62IR	5250	Sprayer / Frtr		
☐ 4K-40937	PZL Mielec (Antonov) An-2	1G216-37	CCCP-40937	1085	0091	1 SH ASh-62IR	5250	Sprayer / Frtr		
☐ 4K-43958	PZL Mielec (Antonov) An-2	1G210-35	CCCP-43958	1084	0091	1 SH ASh-62IR	5250	Sprayer / Frtr		
☐ 4K-43959	PZL Mielec (Antonov) An-2	1G210-36	CCCP-43959	1184	0091	1 SH ASh-62IR	5250	Sprayer / Frtr		
☐ 4K-43961	PZL Mielec (Antonov) An-2	1G210-38	CCCP-43961	1184	0091	1 SH ASh-62IR	5250	Sprayer / Frtr		
☐ 4K-43962	PZL Mielec (Antonov) An-2	1G210-39	CCCP-43962	1184	0091	1 SH ASh-62IR	5250	Sprayer / Frtr		
☐ 4K-43963	PZL Mielec (Antonov) An-2	1G210-40	CCCP-43963	1184	0091	1 SH ASh-62IR	5250	Sprayer / Frtr		
☐ 4K-56358	PZL Mielec (Antonov) An-2	1G179-48	CCCP-56358	0478	0091	1 SH ASh-62IR	5250	Sprayer / Frtr		
☐ 4K-56359	PZL Mielec (Antonov) An-2	1G179-49	CCCP-56359	0578	0091	1 SH ASh-62IR	5250	Sprayer / Frtr		
☐ 4K-56361	PZL Mielec (Antonov) An-2	1G179-53	CCCP-56361	0578	0091	1 SH ASh-62IR	5250	Sprayer / Frtr		
☐ 4K-62499	PZL Mielec (Antonov) An-2	1G175-22	CCCP-62499	0577	0091	1 SH ASh-62IR	5250	Sprayer / Frtr		
☐ 4K-62508	PZL Mielec (Antonov) An-2	1G175-31	CCCP-62508	0577	0091	1 SH ASh-62IR	5250	Sprayer / Frtr		
☐ 4K-62522	PZL Mielec (Antonov) An-2	1G175-45	CCCP-62522	0677	0091	1 SH ASh-62IR	5250	Sprayer / Frtr		
☐ 4K-62540	PZL Mielec (Antonov) An-2	1G176-03	CCCP-62540	0777	0091	1 SH ASh-62IR	5250	Sprayer / Frtr		
☐ 4K-62551	PZL Mielec (Antonov) An-2	1G176-14	CCCP-62551	0777	0091	1 SH ASh-62IR	5250	Sprayer / Frtr		
☐ 4K-62666	PZL Mielec (Antonov) An-2	1G178-58	CCCP-62666	0378	0091	1 SH ASh-62IR	5250	Sprayer / Frtr		
☐ 4K-62672	PZL Mielec (Antonov) An-2	1G177-57	CCCP-62672	0378	0091	1 SH ASh-62IR	5250	Sprayer / Frtr		
☐ 4K-70760	PZL Mielec (Antonov) An-2	1G132-15	CCCP-70760	1071	0091	1 SH ASh-62IR	5500	12 Pax		
☐ 4K-81548	PZL Mielec (Antonov) An-2	1G208-52	CCCP-81548	0784	0091	1 SH ASh-62IR	5250	Sprayer / Frtr		
☐ 4K-81549	PZL Mielec (Antonov) An-2	1G208-53	CCCP-81549	0784	0091	1 SH ASh-62IR	5250	Sprayer / Frtr		
☐ 4K-82896	PZL Mielec (Antonov) An-2	1G169-13	CCCP-82896	0576	0091	1 SH ASh-62IR	5250	Sprayer / Frtr		
☐ 4K-82900	PZL Mielec (Antonov) An-2	1G169-17	CCCP-82900	0576	0091	1 SH ASh-62IR	5250	Sprayer / Frtr		
☐ 4K-82901	PZL Mielec (Antonov) An-2	1G169-18	CCCP-82901	0576	0091	1 SH ASh-62IR	5250	Sprayer / Frtr		
☐ 4K-92961	PZL Mielec (Antonov) An-2	1G171-18	CCCP-92961	0976	0091	1 SH ASh-62IR	5250	Sprayer / Frtr		
☐ 4K-92963	PZL Mielec (Antonov) An-2	1G171-20	CCCP-92963	0876	0091	1 SH ASh-62IR	5250	Sprayer / Frtr		

AZERBAIJAN AIRLINES/AZAL Avia = J2 / AHY (Member of Azerbaijan Airlines Concern)
Baku-Bina & Gyandzha

Bina Airport, 370109 Baku, Azerbaijan ☎ (12) 97 27 73 Tx: 142117 almaz Fax: (12) 97 25 36 SITA: BAKGWJ2
F: 1991 ⁂ n/a Head: Magarram A. Mukhtarov IATA: 771 ICAO: AZAL Net: n/a Beside aircraft listed, also leases Ilyushin 76 & Tupolev 154B from Gvmt/Ministry of Defence (4K-) & Belavia (EW-) when required.

☐ 4K-87218	Yakovlev 40	9441037	HA-LJC	1074	0094	3 IV AI-25	16800	C21		
☐ 4K-87257	Yakovlev 40	9311426	CCCP-87257	0173	0091	3 IV AI-25	16100	Y27		
☐ 4K-87278	Yakovlev 40	9311427	CCCP-87278	0373	0091	3 IV AI-25	16100	Y27		
☐ 4K-87415	Yakovlev 40	9420734	CCCP-87415	0574	0091	3 IV AI-25	16100	Y30		
☐ 4K-87478	Yakovlev 40	9440638	CCCP-87478	1274	0091	3 IV AI-25	16100	Y30		
☐ 4K-87812	Yakovlev 40	9230424	CCCP-87812	0972	0091	3 IV AI-25	16100	Y27		
☐ 4K-87817	Yakovlev 40	9230824	CCCP-87817	0972	0091	3 IV AI-25	16100	Y27		
☐ 4K-88174	Yakovlev 40	9621247	CCCP-88174	0576	0091	3 IV AI-25	16100	Y30		
☐ 4K-88211	Yakovlev 40K	9631749	CCCP-88211	0976	0091	3 IV AI-25	16100	Y30		
☐ 4K-65702	Tupolev 134B-3	63375	CCCP-65702	0880	0091	2 SO D-30-III	49000	Y76		
☐ 4K-65704	Tupolev 134B-3	63410	YL-LBJ	0080	0597	2 SO D-30-III	49000	Y76		
☐ 4K-65705	Tupolev 134B-3	63415	CCCP-65705	0980	0091	2 SO D-30-III	49000	Y76		
☐ 4K-65708	Tupolev 134B-3	63447	AL-65708	1080	0091	2 SO D-30-III	49000	Y76		
☐ 4K-65709	Tupolev 134B-3	63484	CCCP-65709	1280	0091	2 SO D-30-III	49000	Y76		

684 registration type of aircraft cn/fn ex/ex* mfd del powered by mtow kg configuration selcal name/fln/specialitites/remarks

☐ 4K-65710	Tupolev 134B-3	63490	AL-65710	1180	0091	2 SO D-30-III	49000	Y76		
☐ 4K-65711	Tupolev 134B-3	63498	AL-65711	1180	0091	2 SO D-30-III	49000	Y76		
☐ 4K-65712	Tupolev 134B-3	63515	YL-LBL	0081	0097	2 SO D-30-III	49000	Y76		
☐ 4K-65713	Tupolev 134B-3	63520	CCCP-65713	1280	0091	2 SO D-30-III	49000	Y76		
☐ 4K-65714	Tupolev 134B-3	63527	CCCP-65714	1280	0091	2 SO D-30-III	49000	Y76		
☐ 4K-AZ1	Boeing 727-235	19460 / 531	4K-4201	0268	1292	3 PW JT8D-7B (HK3/FDX)	78245	CY145		
☐ 4K-AZ8	Boeing 727-230	20525 / 870	OM-AHK	1171	1297	3 PW JT8D-15	79378	CY145		
☐ 4K-85192	Tupolev 154B-1	192	CCCP-85192	0177	0091	3 KU NK-8-2U	98000	Y164 or Combi		cvtd 154B
☐ 4K-85329	Tupolev 154B-2	329	CCCP-85329	0279	0091	3 KU NK-8-2U	98000	Y164		
☐ 4K-85364	Tupolev 154B-2	364	CCCP-85364	0879	0091	3 KU NK-8-2U	98000	Y164		
☐ 4K-85391	Tupolev 154B-2	391	CCCP-85391	0180	0091	3 KU NK-8-2U	98000	Y164		
☐ 4K-85548	Tupolev 154B-2	548	CCCP-85548	0782	0091	3 KU NK-8-2U	98000	Y164		
☐ 4K-85698	Tupolev 154M	871	CCCP-85698	0591	0091	3 SO D-30KU-154-II	100000	Y145		
☐ 4K-85729	Tupolev 154M	911	CCCP-85729	0492	0194	3 SO D-30KU-154-II	100000	VIP		
☐ 4K-85734	Tupolev 154M	916	CCCP-85734	0692	0092	3 SO D-30KU-154-II	100000	Y164		
☐ 4K-85738	Tupolev 154M	921	CCCP-85738	0092	0298	3 SO D-30KU-154-II	100000	Y164		
☐ 4K-AZ10	Tupolev 154M	1013		0098	0098	3 SO D-30KU-154-II	100000	VIP		
☐ 4K-	Boeing 757-200					2 RR RB211-535E4	115666			oo-delivery 0500
☐ 4K-	Boeing 757-200					2 RR RB211-535E4	115666			oo-delivery 0900

AZERBAIJAN AIRLINES/AZAL Avia Cargo = AHC (Member of Azerbaijan Airlines Concern / formerly an internal division of Azerbaijan Airlines/AZAL Avia) **Baku**

Bina Airport, 370109 Baku, Azerbaijan ☎ (12) 97 16 71 Tx: none Fax: (12) 97 16 71 SITA: n/a

F: 1997 n/a Head: Zair Okhundov ICAO: AZALAVIACARGO Net: n/a Also leases Antonov 12 & Ilyushin 76 from the Azerbaijan Ministry of Defence (4K-), ATI AIR COMPANY (UR-) & UZBEKISTAN AIRWAYS (UK-), when required.

☐ 4K-26584	Antonov 26B	13609	CCCP-26584	0684	0091	2 IV AI-24VT	24000	Freighter		
☐ 4K-26585	Antonov 26B	13802	CCCP-26585	0984	0091	2 IV AI-24VT	24000	Freighter		
☐ 4K-48136	Antonov 32B	3103	CCCP-48136	0592	0092	2 IV AI-20D	27000	Freighter		
☐ 4K-48137	Antonov 32B	3105	CCCP-48137	0592	0092	2 IV AI-20D	27000	Freighter		
☐ 4K-64452	Antonov 32B	2110	LZ-INL	1089	0093	2 IV AI-20D	27000	Freighter		opf ECT-East Convert Trade
☐ 4K-66752	Antonov 32B	2108	CCCP-66752	0989	0093	2 IV AI-20D	27000	Freighter		opf ECT-East Convert Trade
☐ 4K-66756	Antonov 32B	2109	CCCP-66756	1089	0093	2 IV AI-20D	27000	Freighter		opf ECT-East Convert Trade
☐ 4K-AZ11	Ilyushin 76TD	1013409280	RA-76354	0091	1198	4 SO D-30KP	190000	Freighter		
☐ UK-76447	Ilyushin 76TD	1023412389		0592	0098	4 SO D-30KP	190000	Freighter		lsf TWN
☐ UR-76700	Ilyushin 76MD	0063471134	CCCP-76700	0086	0098	4 SO D-30KP	190000	Freighter		lsf TII

AZERBAIJAN AIRLINES/AZAL Helikopter = AZK (Member of Azerbaijan Airlines Concern / formerly Azerbaijan Airlines/AZAL Aero) **Baku-Zabrat**

Airport Zabrat, 370036 Baku, Azerbaijan ☎ (12) 97 90 00 Tx: none Fax: (12) 98 85 34 SITA: n/a

F: 1991 n/a Head: Azer Yakubogly Aliev ICAO: AZALKOPTER Net: n/a Some aircraft are still in Aeroflot colors but will be repainted in due course.

☐ 4K-14071	PZL Swidnik (Mil) Mi-2	5210550048	CCCP-14071	0488	0091	2 IS GTD-350-4	3550	Sprayer / Frtr		
☐ 4K-14072	PZL Swidnik (Mil) Mi-2	5210616058	CCCP-14072	0688	0091	2 IS GTD-350-4	3550	Sprayer / Frtr		
☐ 4K-14073	PZL Swidnik (Mil) Mi-2	5210617058	CCCP-14073	0588	0091	2 IS GTD-350-4	3550	Sprayer / Frtr		
☐ 4K-14148	PZL Swidnik (Mil) Mi-2	5210406097	CCCP-14148	1087	0091	2 IS GTD-350-4	3550	Sprayer / Frtr		
☐ 4K-20366	PZL Swidnik (Mil) Mi-2	529813066	CCCP-20366	0686	0091	2 IS GTD-350-4	3550	Sprayer / Frtr		
☐ 4K-20367	PZL Swidnik (Mil) Mi-2	529814066	CCCP-20367	0686	0091	2 IS GTD-350-4	3550	Sprayer / Frtr		
☐ 4K-20368	PZL Swidnik (Mil) Mi-2	529815066	CCCP-20368	0686	0091	2 IS GTD-350-4	3550	Sprayer / Frtr		
☐ 4K-20874	PZL Swidnik (Mil) Mi-2	528235073	CCCP-20874	0783	0091	2 IS GTD-350-4	3550	Sprayer / Frtr		
☐ 4K-20876	PZL Swidnik (Mil) Mi-2	528237073	CCCP-20876	0783	0091	2 IS GTD-350-4	3550	Sprayer / Frtr		
☐ 4K-20930	PZL Swidnik (Mil) Mi-2	528612034	CCCP-20930	0484	0091	2 IS GTD-350-4	3550	Sprayer / Frtr		
☐ 4K-20985	PZL Swidnik (Mil) Mi-2	549720046	CCCP-20985	0486	0091	2 IS GTD-350-4	3550	Sprayer / Frtr		
☐ 4K-20986	PZL Swidnik (Mil) Mi-2	549721046	CCCP-20986	0486	0091	2 IS GTD-350-4	3550	Sprayer / Frtr		
☐ 4K-23253	PZL Swidnik (Mil) Mi-2	5210327087	CCCP-23253	0887	0091	2 IS GTD-350-4	3550	Sprayer / Frtr		
☐ 4K-23254	PZL Swidnik (Mil) Mi-2	5210328087	CCCP-23254	0887	0091	2 IS GTD-350-4	3550	Sprayer / Frtr		
☐ 4K-23255	PZL Swidnik (Mil) Mi-2	5210329087	CCCP-23255	0887	0091	2 IS GTD-350-4	3550	Sprayer / Frtr		
☐ 4K-22652	Mil Mi-8T	8099	CCCP-22652	1080	0091	2 IS TV2-117A	12000	24 Pax		
☐ 4K-24168	Mil Mi-8T	98941998	CCCP-24168	0489	0091	2 IS TV2-117A	12000	24 Pax		
☐ 4K-24173	Mil Mi-8P	98943127	CCCP-24173	0589	0091	2 IS TV2-117A	12000	24 Pax		
☐ 4K-24572	Mil Mi-8T	98839157	CCCP-24572	0288	0091	2 IS TV2-117A	12000	24 Pax		
☐ 4K-24573	Mil Mi-8T	98839212	CCCP-24573	0288	0091	2 IS TV2-117A	12000	24 Pax		
☐ 4K-24590	Mil Mi-8T	98839403	CCCP-24590	0488	0091	2 IS TV2-117A	12000	24 Pax		
☐ 4K-24596	Mil Mi-8T	98839439	CCCP-24596	0588	0091	2 IS TV2-117A	12000	24 Pax		
☐ 4K-25110	Mil Mi-8MTV-1	95726	CCCP-25110	0891	0091	2 IS TV3-117MT	13000	24 Pax		
☐ 4K-25115	Mil Mi-8MTV-1	95731	CCCP-25115	0891	0091	2 IS TV3-117MT	13000	24 Pax		
☐ 4K-25140	Mil Mi-8T	99047511	CCCP-25140	0790	0091	2 IS TV2-117A	12000	24 Pax		
☐ 4K-25152	Mil Mi-8T	99047749	CCCP-25152	0990	0091	2 IS TV2-117A	12000	24 Pax		
☐ 4K-25157	Mil Mi-8T	99047863	CCCP-25157	1090	0091	2 IS TV2-117A	12000	24 Pax		
☐ 4K-25193	Mil Mi-8T	98943859	CCCP-25193	1089	0091	2 IS TV2-117A	12000	24 Pax		
☐ 4K-25482	Mil Mi-8MTV-1	95627	CCCP-25482	0391	0091	2 IS TV3-117MT	13000	24 Pax		
☐ 4K-25494	Mil Mi-8MTV-1	95639	CCCP-25494	0391	0091	2 IS TV3-117MT	13000	24 Pax		
☐ 4K-25925	Mil Mi-8T	5560	CCCP-25925	0675	0091	2 IS TV2-117A	12000	24 Pax		
☐ 4K-27026	Mil Mi-8P	8699	CCCP-27026	0892	0092	2 IS TV2-117A	12000	VIP		
☐ 4K-27036	Mil Mi-8MTV-1	95870	CCCP-27036	0392	0092	2 IS TV3-117MT	13000	28 Pax		
☐ 4K-27037	Mil Mi-8MTV-1	95871	CCCP-27037	0392	0092	2 IS TV3-117MT	13000	28 Pax		
☐ 4K-27038	Mil Mi-8MTV-1	95872	CCCP-27038	0392	0092	2 IS TV3-117MT	13000	28 Pax		
☐ 4K-AZ6	Mil Mi-8MTV-1	96100		0393	0093	2 IS TV3-117MT	13000	24 Pax		
☐ 4K-AZ7	Mil Mi-8MTV-1	96122		0493	0093	2 IS TV3-117MT	13000	24 Pax		

IMAIR = IK / ITX (Division of Improtex) **Baku-Bina**

115 Hasi Aslanov Street, 370000 Baku, Azerbaijan ☎ (12) 93 41 71 Tx: none Fax: (12) 93 04 78 SITA: BAKIMIK

F: 1994 n/a Head: Zair Z. Shakhbazov IATA: 166 ICAO: IMPROTEX Net: n/a Beside aircraft listed, also leases Ilyushin 76MD from Veteran Airlines (UR-) & Tupolev 134B-3 from BALTIC Express Line (YL), when required.

☐ EW-65049	Tupolev 134A	49755	CCCP-65049	0076	0098	2 SO D-30-II	49000	Y76		lsf GOM
☐ 4K-85732	Tupolev 154M	914	CCCP-85732	0092	0094	3 SO D-30KU-154-II	100000	C8Y140		

TURAN AIR = 3T / URN (Azerbaijan-U.S. joint venture company) **Baku-Bina & Gyandzha**

Mardanov Brothers Street 102, 370022 Baku, Azerbaijan ☎ (12) 98 94 31 Tx: none Fax: (12) 98 94 34 SITA: BAKGAJ2

F: 1994 30 Head: Yusuf M. Akhverdiev IATA: 359 ICAO: TURAN Net: n/a

☐ 4K-325	Tupolev 154B-2	325	HA-LCM	0079	0097	3 KU NK-8-2U	98000	Y152		
☐ 4K-727	Tupolev 154M	727	SP-LCA	0086	0795	3 SO D-30KU-154-II	100000	Y152		
☐ 4K-733	Tupolev 154M	733	SP-LCB	0086	0895	3 SO D-30KU-154-II	100000	Y152		
☐ 4K-85524	Tupolev 154B-2	524	YL-LAG	0082	0097	3 KU NK-8-2U	100000	Y152		

4L = GEORGIA (Republic of Georgia) (Sakartvelos Respublikis)

Capital: Tbilisi Official Language: Georgian Population: 5,6 million Square Km: 69700 Dialling code: +995 Year established: 1990 Acting political head: Eduard Shevardnadze (President)

Government / Corporate / Executive / VIP Aircraft

☐ 4L-65993	Tupolev 134A	63860	RA-65993	0081	0097	2 SO D-30-II	48000	Y76		Ministry of Defence

ABAVIA = BVZ **Tbilisi-Int'l**

Ul. A. Kazbegi 12, 380060 Tbilisi, Georgia ☎ (32) 93 16 67 Tx: none Fax: (32) 98 96 39 SITA: n/a

F: n/a n/a Head: Georgi A. Patsatsia ICAO: ABAZIA Net: n/a

☐ 4L-65061	Tupolev 134A-3	49874	CCCP-65061	0977	0096	2 SO D-30-III	47000	Y80		
☐ 4L-65879	Tupolev 134A-3	31265	CCCP-65879	0675	0096	2 SO D-30-III	47000	Y80		

AIR GEORGIA = DA / GEO (Associated with Georgian Airlines) **Tbilisi-Int'l**

Chavchavadze Avenue 49A, 380062 Tbilisi, Georgia ☎ (32) 23 54 07 Tx: none Fax: (32) 23 34 23 SITA: TBSTO3P

F: 1992 n/a Head: Dvali Elgudzha IATA: 500 ICAO: AIR GEORGIA Net: n/a

☐ 4L-85547	Tupolev 154B-2	547	GR-85547	0782	0093	3 KU NK-8-2U	100000	F12C18Y102		
☐ 4L-85558	Tupolev 154B-2	558	YL-LAH	1082	0096	3 KU NK-8-2U	100000	F12C18Y102		

AIR ZENA Georgian Airlines = A9 / TGZ **Tbilisi-Int'l**

79 Airport Colony, 380058 Tbilisi, Georgia ☎ (32) 95 34 97 Tx: none Fax: (32) 99 07 98 SITA: n/a

F: 1994 n/a Head: Elberdi Nutsubidze IATA: 606 ICAO: TAMAZI Net: n/a

☐ 4L-85168	Tupolev 154B	168	CCCP-85168	0976	0097	3 KU NK-8-2U	98000	Y164		
☐ UK-86577	Ilyushin 62M	2748552	D-AOAL	0687	0097	4 SO D-30KU	167000	Y168		lsf UZB / opf Gvmt / fn 4805

AISI **Tbilisi-Int'l**

Tbilisi Airport, 380058 Tbilisi, Georgia ☎ (32) 94 77 74 Tx: none Fax: (32) 98 96 39 SITA: n/a

F: 1993 n/a Head: Tariel A. Guledani Net: n/a

☐ 4L-14065	PZL Swidnik (Mil) Mi-2	5410544038	CCCP-14065	0388		2 IS GTD-350-4	3500	Utility		
☐ 4L-14179	PZL Swidnik (Mil) Mi-2	5210520028	CCCP-14179	0288		2 IS GTD-350-4	3550	Utility		
☐ 4L-20290	PZL Swidnik (Mil) Mi-2	527425111	CCCP-20290	0182		2 IS GTD-350-4	3500	Utility		
☐ 4L-20372	PZL Swidnik (Mil) Mi-2	529819066	CCCP-20372	0686		2 IS GTD-350-4	3500	Utility		

685 registration type of aircraft cn/fn ex/ex* mfd del powered by mtow kg configuration selcal name/fln/specialitites/remarks

☐ 4L-20403	PZL Swidnik (Mil) Mi-2	529901086	CCCP-20403	0886		2 IS GTD-350-4	3500	Utility		
☐ 4L-20745	PZL Swidnik (Mil) Mi-2	527642052	CCCP-20745	0582		2 IS GTD-350-4	3500	Utility		
☐ 4L-20755	PZL Swidnik (Mil) Mi-2	547710062	CCCP-20755	1082		2 IS GTD-350-4	3500	Utility		
☐ 4L-20863	PZL Swidnik (Mil) Mi-2	528202053	CCCP-20863	0683		2 IS GTD-350-4	3500	Utility		
☐ 4L-20866	PZL Swidnik (Mil) Mi-2	528205053	CCCP-20866	0683		2 IS GTD-350-4	3500	Utility		
☐ 4L-20956	PZL Swidnik (Mil) Mi-2	528721054	CCCP-20956	0684		2 IS GTD-350-4	3500	Utility		
☐ 4L-23338	PZL Swidnik (Mil) Mi-2	549246065	CCCP-23338	0685		2 IS GTD-350-4	3500	Utility		
☐ 4L-23501	PZL Swidnik (Mil) Mi-2	526332109	CCCP-23501	1079		2 IS GTD-350-4	3500	Utility		
☐ 4L-24202	Mil Mi-8	98730117	CCCP-24202	0187		2 IS TV2-117A	12000	Utility		
☐ 4L-24204	Mil Mi-8	98730131	CCCP-24204	0187		2 IS TV2-117A	12000	Utility		
☐ 4L-24630	Mil Mi-8	8298	CCCP-24630	1281		2 IS TV2-117A	12000	Utility		
☐ 4L-24667	Mil Mi-8	9815727	CCCP-24667	0681		2 IS TV2-117A	12000	Utility		
☐ 4L-25174	Mil Mi-8MTV-1	95484	CCCP-25174	0890		2 IS TV3-117VM	13000	Utility		
☐ 4L-25176	Mil Mi-8MTV-1	95486	CCCP-25176	0990		2 IS TV3-117VM	13000	Utility		lst Saglam Air as TC-HIS
☐ 4L-25448	Mil Mi-8MTV-1	95587	CCCP-25448	0191		2 IS TV3-117VM	13000	Utility		
☐ 4L-25449	Mil Mi-8MTV-1	95588	CCCP-25449	0191		2 IS TV3-117VM	13000	Y24		lst Saglam Air as TC-HAG
☐ 4L-27012	Mil Mi-8	99254362	CCCP-27012	0392		2 IS TV2-117A	12000	Utility		

AVIAEXPRESSCRUISE = AEQ — Tbilisi-Int'l

Ul. Mardzhanishvili 31, 380012 Tbilisi, Georgia ☎ (32) 95 91 89 Tx: 212345 aeksu Fax: (32) 96 99 76 SITA: n/a
F: n/a ⁂ n/a Head: Palad I. Kadzanaya Net: n/a

☐ 4L-87358	Yakovlev 40	9340731	RA-87358	0073	0097	3 IV AI-25	17200	Y32		
☐ 4L-AAF	Tupolev 154M	890	RA-85714	0091	0398	3 SO D-30KU-154-II	100000	Y164		

BATUMI Adjarian Airlines = ADJ (formerly Adjarian Airlines-Adjal) — Batumi

Batumi Airport, 384513 Batumi, (Adzharia), Georgia ☎ (222) 76 626 Tx: n/a Fax: (222) 76 626 SITA: n/a
F: n/a ⁂ n/a Head: R. Diasamidze ICAO: ADJAL Net: n/a

☐ 4L-AAD	Tupolev 134B-3	63295	YL-LBF	0680	0097	2 SO D-30-III	48000	Y72		lsf Sukhumi Airlines

GACO = GAK (Gako Kavkasia) — Tbilisi-Int'l & Kutaisi

Tbilisi Airport, 380058 Tbilisi, Georgia ☎ (32) 94 70 77 Tx: none Fax: (32) 99 01 01 SITA: n/a
F: 1994 ⁂ n/a Head: Mrs Laura P. Gachava ICAO: LAURA Net: n/a

☐ 4L-65865	Tupolev 134A-3	28286	CCCP-65865	0375	0195	2 SO D-30-III	47000	Y80		std TBS
☐ ER-65071	Tupolev 134A-3	49915	CCCP-65071	0777	0097	2 SO D-30-III	47600	Y76		lsf MLD

GEORGIAN AIRLINES = 3P / GEG — Tbilisi-Int'l

Tbilisi Airport, 380058 Tbilisi, Georgia ☎ (32) 94 79 25 Tx: none Fax: (32) 94 04 63 SITA: TBSAP3P
F: 1997 ⁂ n/a Head: David Davitidze IATA: 684 ICAO: DEMURI Net: n/a

☐ 4L-87258	Yakovlev 40	9311526	CCCP-87258	0273	0097	3 IV AI-25	16800	VIP C15		
☐ 4L-87305	Yakovlev 40	9320129	CCCP-87305	0673	0097	3 IV AI-25	16800	Y27		
☐ 4L-87370	Yakovlev 40	9342031	CCCP-87370	0073	0097	3 IV AI-25	17200	Y34		
☐ 4L-87466	Yakovlev 40	9430537	CCCP-87466	0974	0097	3 IV AI-25	16800	Y32		
☐ 4L-88158	Yakovlev 40	9611246	CCCP-88158	0576	0097	3 IV AI-25	17200	Y32		
☐ 4L-65774	Tupolev 134A-3	62519	CCCP-65774	0479	0097	2 SO D-30-III	47000	C16Y56		
☐ 4L-65798	Tupolev 134A-3	63179	CCCP-65798	0380	0097	2 SO D-30-III	47000	C16Y56		
☐ 4L-85430	Tupolev 154B-2	430	CCCP-85430	0880	0097	3 KU NK-8-2U	98000	C18Y126		
☐ 4L-85496	Tupolev 154B-2	496	CCCP-85496	0681	0097	3 KU NK-8-2U	98000	C18Y126		
☐ 4L-85518	Tupolev 154B-2	518	CCCP-85518	1181	0097	3 KU NK-8-2U	100000	Combi Y62&Cargo		

GEORGIAN EXPRESS = GEX — Telavi

Telavi Airport, 380000 Telavi, Georgia ☎ (32) 98 33 10 Tx: none Fax: (32) 98 86 95 SITA: n/a
F: 1997 ⁂ n/a Head: n/a ICAO: TELAVI Net: n/a

☐ RA-11368	Antonov 12BP	8346006	75 RED	1068	0098	4 IV AI-20M	61000	Freighter		lsf TEY

LASARE AIR = LRE — Tbilisi-Int'l

Tbilisi Airport, 380058 Tbilisi, Georgia ☎ (32) 95 20 32 Tx: 212290 azon su Fax: (32) 95 32 97 SITA: n/a
F: 1995 ⁂ 5 Head: Dzhoni A. Lasareishvili ICAO: AERO LASARE Net: n/a

☐ 4L-11304	Antonov 12BP	0901304		0660	0095	4 IV AI-20M	61000	Freighter		

ORBI Air Company = NQ / DVU (Associated with Air Zena / formerly ORBI Georgian Airways) — Tbilisi-Int'l

Tbilisi Airport, 380058 Tbilisi, Georgia ☎ (32) 94 76 72 Tx: 212186 zena su Fax: (32) 99 07 98 SITA: n/a
F: 1991 ⁂ n/a Head: Vassili Jambazishvili IATA: 819 ICAO: ZENA Net: n/a

☐ 4L-AAE	Tupolev 134A	60282	OK-IFN	0078	1197	2 SO D-30-II	49000	C16Y56		

SUKHUMI AIRLINES = LOA (formerly Taifun) — Senaki & Moscow-Vnukovo (Russia)

Senaki Airport, 384640 Senaki, Georgia ☎ Moscow (095)4367129 Tx: none Fax: Moscow (095)4367395 SITA: n/a
F: n/a ⁂ n/a Head: Grigory S. Bechvaya ICAO: LOREKSI Net: n/a

☐ 4L-AAB	Tupolev 134B-3	63340	YL-LBH	0680	0096	2 SO D-30-III	48000	Y72		
☐ 4L-AAC	Tupolev 134B-3	63536	YL-LBM	0181	0096	2 SO D-30-III	48000	Y72		
☐ 4L-AAD	Tupolev 134B-3	63295	YL-LBF	0680	0096	2 SO D-30-III	48000	Y72		lst BATUMI Adjarian Airlines

TBILISI AGO = MCB (Tbilisskoe aviatsionnoe gosudarsvennoe ob'yedinenie) (Flying division of Tbilisi Aviation Prod. Association) — Tbilisi-Vali

Flying division / Letny otryad, Ul. Bogdana Khmelnitskogo 181, 380036 Tbilisi, Georgia ☎ (32) 70 84 12 Tx: 212134 Fax: (32) 98 25 51 SITA: n/a
F: 1983 ⁂ n/a Head: Pantiko Sh. Tordia ICAO: TSKHADAYA Net: n/a Operates non-commercial cargo & utility flights for itself only.

☐ 4L-26087	Antonov 26B	12601	GR-26087	0681	0083	2 IV AI-24VT	24000	Freighter		

4R = SRI LANKA (Democratic Socialist Republic of Sri Lanka) (Sri Lanka prjatantrika samajawadi janarajaya)

Capital: Colombo Official Language: Sinhala, Tamil, English Population: 19,0 million Square Km: 65610 Dialling code: +94 Year established: 1948 Acting political head: Mrs. Chandrika Kumaratunga (President)

Government / Corporate / Executive / VIP Aircraft

☐ CR842	Beech King Air B200T	BT-30	CR841	0083	0083	2 PWC PT6A-42	6350	VIP / miltrans		Sri Lanka Air Force/cvtd B200cn BB-1133

AIRLANKA, Ltd = UL / ALK (Associated with Emirates) — Colombo-Bandaranayike Int'l

AIRLANKA

37 Grindlays Bank Bldg, York Street, Colombo 1, Sri Lanka ☎ (1) 73 55 55 Tx: 21401 lankair ce Fax: (1) 73 51 22 SITA: CMBZZUL
F: 1979 ⁂ 4000 Head: Andrew Gray IATA: 603 ICAO: AIR LANKA Net: http://www.airlanka.com

☐ 4R-ABA	Airbus Industrie A320-231	374	F-WWDJ*	0092	1292	2 IAE V2500-A1	73500	F12Y138	EM-BD	Spirit of Saarc
☐ 4R-ABB	Airbus Industrie A320-231	406	F-WWDB*	0093	0493	2 IAE V2500-A1	73500	F12Y138	EM-CG	
☐ 4R-ULC	Lockheed L-1011-385-1-15 TriStar 100	193P-1053	4R-ALF	1173	0381	3 RR RB211-22B02	211374	F14C28Y234	AC-FM	City of Anuradhapura / cvtd TriStar 1
☐ 4R-ULE	Lockheed L-1011-385-1 TriStar 50	193P-1062	JA8503	0174	0383	3 RR RB211-22B02	204117	F12C28Y234	GJ-DE	City of Ratnapura / cvtd TriStar 1
☐ 4R-ULA	Lockheed L-1011-385-3 TriStar 500	293F-1235	G-BLUS	0782	0882	3 RR RB211-524B4	231332	F12C28Y204	AC-BJ	City of Sri Jayewardenepura
☐ 4R-ULB	Lockheed L-1011-385-3 TriStar 500	293F-1236	G-BLUT	0882	0982	3 RR RB211-524B4	231332	F12C28Y204	BF-JL	City of Kandy
☐ 4R-	Airbus Industrie A330-243	299				2 RR Trent 772B-60	230000	CY281		oo-delivery 0999
☐ 4R-	Airbus Industrie A330-243	306				2 RR Trent 772B-60	230000	CY281		oo-delivery 1199
☐ 4R-	Airbus Industrie A330-243	312				2 RR Trent 772B-60	230000	CY281		oo-delivery 1299
☐ 4R-	Airbus Industrie A330-243	314				2 RR Trent 772B-60	230000	CY281		oo-delivery 0100
☐ 4R-	Airbus Industrie A330-243	348				2 RR Trent 772B-60	230000	CY281		oo-delivery 0600
☐ 4R-	Airbus Industrie A330-243	353				2 RR Trent 772B-60	230000	CY281		oo-delivery 0800
☐ 4R-ADA	Airbus Industrie A340-311	032	F-WWJT*	0094	0994	4 CFMI CFM56-5C2	257000	F12C20Y260	EM-BD	
☐ 4R-ADB	Airbus Industrie A340-311	033	F-WWJU*	0094	1094	4 CFMI CFM56-5C2	257000	F12C20Y260	FK-AC	
☐ 4R-ADC	Airbus Industrie A340-311	034	F-WWJU*	0095	0395	4 CFMI CFM56-5C2	257000	F12C20Y260	AC-BK	

CEYLON AVIATION SERVICES, (Pvt) Ltd — Colombo-Ratmalana

Level 31, Unit 31-01 East Tower, World Trade Centre Bldg, Echelon Square, Colombo 1, Sri Lanka ☎ (1) 34 65 55 Tx: none Fax: (1) 34 65 57 SITA: n/a
F: 1997 ⁂ n/a Head: Gamani Jayasuriya Net: n/a

☐ 4R-CMY	Bell 206B JetRanger III	2446	4R-SRB	0078	0097	1 AN 250-C20B	1451			
☐ 4R-CMA	Bell 206L-1 LongRanger II	45177	4R-PUW	0078	0097	1 AN 250-C28B	1882			

EXPO AVIATION, (Pvt) Ltd = 8D / EXV — Colombo-Bandaranayike Int'l

466 Galle Road, Colombo 3, Sri Lanka ☎ (1) 57 60 43 Tx: none Fax: (1) 57 72 49 SITA: n/a
F: 1997 ⁂ n/a Head: Shafik Kassim ICAO: EXPOAVIA Net: n/a

☐ 4R-EXA	Antonov 8				0098	2 IV AI-20D	38000	Freighter		ex Santa Cruz-colors
☐ 4R-EXC	Antonov 12B				0098	4 IV AI-20M	64000	Freighter		ex Santa Cruz-colors

LANKAIR, (Pvt) Ltd (Joint venture of Ceylon Carriers Ltd, Sri Lanka & Transuniversal Corp., Russia) — Colombo-Ratmalana

104 Nawala Road, Narahenpita, Colombo 5, Sri Lanka ☎ (1) 58 99 60 Tx: none Fax: (1) 58 99 68 SITA: n/a
F: 1995 ⁂ n/a Head: Rohan Nanayakkara Net: n/a

☐ RA-24634	Mil Mi-8		CCCP-24634	0085	0095	2 IS TV2-117A	12000			lsf Transuniversal Corp.
☐ RA-25184	Mil Mi-8MTV-1		CCCP-25184	0090	0095	2 IS TV3-117MT	13000			lsf Transuniversal Corp.

686 registration type of aircraft cn/fn ex/ex* mfd del powered by mtow kg configuration selcal name/fln/specialitites/remarks

LIONAIR, (Pvt) Ltd = LNS

Colombo-Ratmalana

Asia Aviation Centre, Colombo Airport, Ratmalana, Sri Lanka ☎ (1) 62 26 22 Tx: none Fax: (1) 61 15 40 SITA: n/a
F: 1994 ☗ n/a Head: Palitha Wijesuriya ICAO: SRI-LION Aircraft below MTOW 1361kg: Cessna 152 & Jabiru ST-3 Also operates a flying school under the name ASIAN AEROSPACE COLLEGE (same headquarters).

☐ 4R-SRA	Bell 206B JetRanger III	2430	N5002G	0078	0096	1 AN 250-C20B	1451	Y4 / Trainer		
☐ 4R-ACE	Piper PA-34-200T Seneca II	34-7770102		0077	0095	2 CO TSIO-360-E	2073	Y5 / Trainer		
☐ EW-46483	Antonov 24RV	27308101	CCCP-46483	0972	0097	2 IV AI-24VT	21800	Y48		lsf GOM
☐ UN-26650	Antonov 26	7507	UR-26650	0079	0097	2 IV AI-24VT	24000	Freighter		lsf pvt

PARADISE AIR, (Pvt) Ltd = RI / RPI

Colombo-Bandaranayike Int'l

No. 265/2 Sri Saddharman Mawatha, Colombo 7, Sri Lanka ☎ (1) 69 21 66 Tx: none Fax: (1) 50 86 40 SITA: n/a
F: 1998 ☗ 20 Head: Roland Parolini ICAO: PARADISE AIR Net: n/a

☐ RA-87847	Yakovlev 40	9331630	CCCP-87847	0973	1198	3 IV AI-25	16800	Y30		lsf NVG

PEACEAIR, (Pvt) Ltd = PCA

Colombo-Bandaranayike Int'l

Peace Air Hotel, 1173 Maradana Road, Borella, Colombo 8, Sri Lanka ☎ (1) 68 90 20 Tx: none Fax: (1) 69 12 71 SITA: n/a
F: 1997 ☗ n/a Head: Gamini H. Wethasinghe ICAO: PEACEAIR Net: n/a Presently being set-up. Intends to start operations during 1999 with Boeing 747 aircraft.

SKY CABS, (Pvt) Ltd = 2E / SCB

Colombo-Bandaranayike Int'l

PO Box 683, 294 1/1, Union Place, Colombo 2, Sri Lanka ☎ (1) 63 33 32 Tx: none Fax: (1) 63 55 05 SITA: CMBSCCR
F: 1993 ☗ 30 Head: Ali Akber S. Jeevunjee IATA: 602 ICAO: SKY CABS Net: http://www.skycab.com Aircraft below MTOW 1361kg: Cessna 150 / 152 & 177

☐ 4R-SKI	Antonov 8	0D3420	RA-27215	0059	0397	2 IV AI-20D	38000	Freighter		
☐ 4R-SKJ	Antonov 8	0V3420	RA-79167	0059	0097	2 IV AI-20D	38000	Freighter		
☐ 4R-SKL	Antonov 12BP	3341505	RA-12174	0063	0598	4 IV AI-20M	61000	Freighter		

4X = ISRAEL (State of Israel) (Medinat Yisrael)

(including semi-autonomous Palestinian territories)
Capital: Jerusalem Official Language: Hebrew Population: 6,0 million Square Km: 20770 Dialling code: +972 Year established: 1948 Acting political head: Benyamin Netanyahu (Prime Minister)

PALESTINE
Capital: Gaza + Ramallah Official Language: Arabic, English Population: 1,0 million Square Km: - Dialling code: +972 Acting political head: Yassir Arafat (President)

Government / Corporate / Executive / VIP Aircraft

Israeli Air Force uses ICAO-code: IAF

☐ SU-YAF	Mil Mi-17M	202M08	4K-13208	0091	0096	2 IS TV3-117MT-3	13000	VIP		Palestinian Government
☐ SU-YAG	Mil Mi-17M	341M16	4K-15416	0093	0096	2 IS TV3-117MT-3	13000	VIP		Palestinian Government
☐ 242	Boeing 707-344C	20110 / 800	4X-BYQ	0069	0283	4 PW JT3D-7	151046	VIP / mil trans	AD-EH	4X-JYQ / Israeli Air Force
☐ 255	Boeing 707-3H7C	20629 / 863	4X-BYR	0072	0888	4 PW JT3D-3B	151046	VIP / mil trans		4X-JYR / Israeli Air Force
☐ 264	Boeing 707-3J6C	20721 / 875	B-2416	0174	1193	4 PW JT3D-7	151046	VIP / mil trans	GM-AE	4X-JYH / Israeli Air Force
☐ 4X-AOT	Boeing 737-297 (A)	21740 / 562	N70724	0079	0995	2 PW JT8D-9A	53070	Radar Testbed		Elta Electronics Ltd
☐ 4X-JYC	Boeing 707-328B	19291 / 536	N2090B	0067	0890	4 PW JT3D-3B	151046	VIP / mil trans		258 / Israeli Air Force
☐ 4X-JYN	Boeing 707-3J6B	20716 / 880	B-2406	0374	0793	4 PW JT3D-7	151046	VIP / mil trans	HK-BL	Israeli Air Force
☐ 4X-JYS	Boeing 707-344C	20230 / 819	4X-BYS	0069	0283	4 PW JT3D-7	151046	VIP / mil trans		244 / Israeli Air Force
☐ 4X-JYU	Boeing 707-331C	20429 / 846	N794TW	0070	0183	4 PW JT3D-3B	151046	VIP / mil trans		Israeli Air Force

AEROEL AIRWAYS, Ltd = ROL

Tel Aviv-Ben Gurion Int'l

PO Box 40, Ben Gurion Int'l Airport 70100, Israel ☎ (3) 536 25 80 Tx: none Fax: (3) 536 43 31 SITA: TLVRLXH
F: 1992 ☗ 30 Head: Michael Weinstein ICAO: AEROEL Net: http://www.aeroelairways.co.il

☐ 4X-ARH	GAC (Grumman) G-159 Gulfstream I	025	N725G	0059	0196	2 RR Dart 529-8X	16329	Y19		
☐ 4X-ARP	De Havilland DHC-8-311 Dash 8	266	C-GDBB	0091	0698	2 PWC PW123	18643	Y50		lsf GECA
☐ 4X-ARU	De Havilland DHC-8-311 Dash 8	267	C-GCEF	0091	0798	2 PWC PW123	18643	Y50		lsf GECA

ARKIA Israeli Airlines, Ltd = IZ / AIZ (Associated with Koor Industries, Ltd)

Tel Aviv-Ben Gurion Int'l & Sde Dov

PO Box 39301, Dov Airport, Tel Aviv 61392, Israel ☎ (3) 690 22 22 Tx: 341749 arkia il Fax: (3) 699 13 90 SITA: n/a
F: 1950 ☗ 1000 Head: Prof. Israel Borovich IATA: 238 ICAO: ARKIA Net: http://www.arkia.co.il/ Beside aircraft listed, also leases regularly 1-6 Boeing 757 (EL AL-colors, registrations varies) from EL AL when required.
ARKIA LEASING is the leasing division with Boeing 727-200, 737-200 & 747-100F which are leased to other airlines. Those aircraft are marked as such under the leasing carriers.

☐ 4X-CCD	Piper PA-31-350 Navajo Chieftain	31-7652166	N62919	0076		2 LY TIO-540-J2BD	3175	Y9		
☐ 4X-AYT	Britten-Norman BN-2A Islander	96	G-51-31*	0069		2 LY O-540-E4B5	2858	Y9		
☐ 4X-AHA	De Havilland DHC-7-102 Dash 7	060	C-GEWQ*	0081	0981	4 PWC PT6A-50	19958	Y54		Eilat
☐ 4X-AHC	De Havilland DHC-7-102 Dash 7	082	C-GFUM*	0082	0582	4 PWC PT6A-50	19958	Y54		Jerusalem
☐ 4X-AHD	De Havilland DHC-7-102 Dash 7	055	N8102N	0081	0689	4 PWC PT6A-50	19958	Y54		Upper-Gallile / tb Ist Empire Avn 0599
☐ 4X-AHE	De Havilland DHC-7-102 Dash 7	051	N929HA	0081	1292	4 PWC PT6A-50	19958	Y54		Kiryat-Shmona
☐ 4X-AHF	De Havilland DHC-7-102 Dash 7	077	G-BOAZ	0082	1193	4 PWC PT6A-50	19958	Y54		
☐ 4X-AHG	De Havilland DHC-7-102 Dash 7	033	N235SL	0080	0694	4 PWC PT6A-50	19958	Y54		Metulla
☐ 4X-AHH	De Havilland DHC-7-102 Dash 7	045	N7156J	0081	0294	4 PWC PT6A-50	19958	Y54		Arkia Special-white colors
☐ 4X-AHI	De Havilland DHC-7-103 Dash 7	008	C-GJSZ*	0083	0887	4 PWC PT6A-50	19958	Y54		Haifa / Visa credit card-cs
☐ 4X-AHJ	De Havilland DHC-7-102 Dash 7	050	G-BRYE	0081	0594	4 PWC PT6A-50	19958	Y54		
☐ 4X-AHL	De Havilland DHC-7-102 Dash 7	049	N340JK	0081	0696	4 PWC PT6A-50	19958	Y54		Hevel-Eilot / tb Ist Empire Avn 0599
☐ 4X-AHM	De Havilland DHC-7-102 Dash 7	073	N720AS	0082	0796	4 PWC PT6A-50	19958	Y54		
☐ 4X-AVU	ATR 72-500 (72-212A)	587	F-WWES*	0099	0399	2 PWC PW127F	22500	Y72		
☐ 4X-AVW	ATR 72-500 (72-212A)	583	F-WWER*	0099	0299	2 PWC PW127F	22500	Y72		
☐ 4X-AVZ	ATR 72-500 (72-212A)	577	F-WWEN*	0098	1298	2 PWC PW127F	22500	Y72		
☐ 4X-ABN	Boeing 737-258 (A)	22856 / 910	CC-CJK	0082	0189	2 PW JT8D-17A	57992	Y111	BH-GM	lsf/occ opf ELY in neutral-colors
☐ 4X-ABO	Boeing 737-258 (A)	22857 / 919	CC-CJM	0082	0189	2 PW JT8D-17A	57992	Y111	DE-LM	lsf/occ opf ELY in neutral-colors
☐ 4X-BAF	Boeing 737-281	20413 / 241	EI-BEE	0070	0593	2 PW JT8D-9A (HK3/AVA)	49000	Y117		
☐ 4X-BAG	Boeing 737-281	20276 / 231	N20727	0070	1196	2 PW JT8D-9A (HK3/AVA)	49000	Y117		
☐ 4X-BAZ	Boeing 757-236 (ER)	24121 / 183	TC-AHA	0088	0299	2 RR RB211-535E4	113400	Y231		
☐ 4X-	Boeing 757-300					2 RR RB211-535E4B	122470	Y265		oo-delivery 0100
☐ 4X-	Boeing 757-300					2 RR RB211-535E4B	122470	Y265		oo-delivery 0200

AYEET AVIATION, Ltd = AYT

Beer-Sheba

PO Box 5584, Beer-Sheba 84154, Israel ☎ (3) 699 01 85 Tx: n/a Fax: (3) 699 12 94 SITA: n/a
F: 1978 ☗ 15 Head: E. Peretz ICAO: AYEET Net: n/a Aircraft below MTOW 1361kg: Cessna 172 & Rallye 110.

☐ 4X-CIL	Piper PA-23-250 Aztec E	27-7405459	N541G	0074		2 LY IO-540-C4B5	2359			
☐ 4X-CAH	Britten-Norman BN-2A-26 Islander	150	G-PASW	0070	0093	2 LY O-540-E4C5	2994			
☐ 4X-AHP	De Havilland DHC-6 Twin Otter 100	75	C-FCSF	0067	1295	2 PWC PT6A-20	5252			lsf Lev-David Hotels Ltd

BARAK AVIATION SERVICES

Herzlia

26 Hahohit Street, Ramat Hasharon 47226, Israel ☎ (9) 958 65 52 Tx: n/a Fax: (9) 958 65 45 SITA: n/a
F: 1990 ☗ 5 Head: Amos Zamir Net: n/a Aircraft below MTOW 1361kg: Cessna 172.

☐ 4X-AYN	Britten-Norman BN-2A-7 Islander	616	SX-BBY	0070	1196	2 LY O-540-E4C5	2858			
☐ 4X-CCO	Britten-Norman BN-2A Islander	139	N139BT	0070	0991	2 LY O-540-E4C5	2858			std Herzlia
☐ 4X-CCR	Cessna 421B Golden Eagle	421B0207	N5964M	0072	0091	2 CO GTSIO-520-H	3379			

CAL Cargo Air Lines, Ltd = ICL (Cavei Avir Lemitanim)

Tel Aviv-Ben Gurion Int'l

11 Galgalei Haplada Street, Herzeliya 46722, Israel ☎ (9) 952 66 66 Tx: 35874 cal il Fax: (9) 951 32 32 SITA: n/a
F: 1976 ☗ 62 Head: Gilon Zohar IATA: 700 ICAO: CAL Net: n/a Operates cargo flights with Boeing 747 Freighter aircraft leased from EL AL as required.

CHIM-NIR Aviation Services & Airways, Ltd

Herzlia

PO Box 833, Kfar-Shmaryahu 46910, Israel ☎ (9) 950 40 95 Tx: 33882 chav il Fax: (9) 950 87 08 SITA: n/a
F: 1949 ☗ 135 Head: Baruch Rothmann Aircraft / Ag-aircraft below MTOW 1361 / 5000 kg: Bell 47G, Continental Tomcat 6B, Piper PA-18/28, Thrush Commander S2R & Turbo Trush Commander S2RT

☐ 4X-BJF	Bell 206B JetRanger	1778		0075		1 AN 250-C20	1451			
☐ 4X-BJH	Bell 206B JetRanger III	2224		0077		1 AN 250-C20B	1451			
☐ 4X-ANF	Piper PA-32-300C Cherokee SIX	32-40759	N8964N	0069		1 LY IO-540-K1A5	1542			
☐ 4X-ANR	Piper PA-32-300C Cherokee SIX	32-40901	N5209S	0070		1 LY IO-540-K1A5	1542			
☐ 4X-ANV	Piper PA-32-300C Cherokee SIX	32-40739	N5226S	0069		1 LY IO-540-K1A5	1542			
☐ 4X-BHG	Eurocopter (Aerosp.) SA341G Gazelle	1097	G-BLAO	0073		1 TU Astazou IIIA	1800			
☐ 4X-BHH	Eurocopter (Aerosp.) SA342L Gazelle	1747	IDFAF 904	0079		1 TU Astazou XIVH	1900			
☐ 4X-BJO	Bell 206L-1 LongRanger II	45361	C-FTOR	0080	0097	1 AN 250-C28B	1882			
☐ 4X-BJD	Bell 407	53053	N2087K	0096	0197	1 AN 250-C47B	2268			lsf ISCAR Blades Ltd
☐ 4X-BJA	Eurocopter (MBB) BO105CBS	S-600	N2913Y	0083	1095	2 AN 250-C20B	2400			
☐ 4X-BJV	Eurocopter (Aerosp.) AS355F2 Ecureuil 2	5464	N355FT	0091	0396	2 AN 250-C20F	2540			
☐ 4X-BJW	Eurocopter (Aerosp.) AS355F2 Ecureuil 2	5355	F-GKBD	0087	0794	2 AN 250-C20F	2540			
☐ 4X-ANU	Piper PA-31-310 Navajo	31-616	N6746L	0070		2 LY TIO-540-A1A	2948			
☐ 4X-DZT	Beech King Air C90	LJ-513	N913K	0071	1296	2 PWC PT6A-20	4377			
☐ 4X-BJN	Bell 212	30746	C-GZRC	0075	0097	2 PWC PT6T-3 TwinPac	5080			lsf SkyLink Aviation

687 registration type of aircraft cn/fn ex/ex* mfd del powered by mtow kg configuration selcal name/fln/specialitites/remarks

EL AL Israel Airlines, Ltd = LY / ELY
Tel Aviv-Ben Gurion Int'l

PO Box 41, Ben Gurion Int'l Airport 70100, Israel ☎ (3) 971 61 11 Tx: 381070 calbg il Fax: (3) 972 14 42 SITA: n/a
F: 1949 3400 Head: Joel Feldschuh IATA: 114 ICAO: ELAL Net: http://www.elal.co.il Beside aircraft listed, also uses a Boeing 747-200F lsf/opb ATLAS AIR (N) for all-cargo flights.

registration	type of aircraft	cn/fn	ex/ex*	mfd	del	powered by	mtow kg	configuration	selcal	name/fln/specialitites/remarks
☐ 4X-ABN	Boeing 737-258 (A)	22856 / 910	CC-CJK	0082	0982	2 PW JT8D-17A	57992	C16Y87 or Y111	BH-GM	301 / lst/opb AIZ in neutral-colors
☐ 4X-ABO	Boeing 737-258 (A)	22857 / 919	CC-CJM	0082	1182	2 PW JT8D-17A	57992	C16Y87 or Y111	DE-LM	302 / lst/opb AIZ in neutral-colors
☐ 4X-EKD	Boeing 737-758	29960				2 CFMI CFM56-7B24	69400			oo-delivery 1099
☐ 4X-EKE	Boeing 737-758	29961				2 CFMI CFM56-7B24	69400			oo-delivery 1199
☐ 4X-EKA	Boeing 737-858	29957 / 204	N1786B*	0099	0299	2 CFMI CFM56-7B26	79015	CY149	KQ-CG	Tiberias
☐ 4X-EKB	Boeing 737-858	29958 / 249		0099	0499	2 CFMI CFM56-7B26	79015	CY149		
☐ 4X-EKC	Boeing 737-858	29959				2 CFMI CFM56-7B26	79015	CY149		oo-delivery 0799
☐ 4X-EBF	Boeing 757-27B	24136 / 169	G-OAHF	0088	0596	2 RR RB211-535E4	108862	C24Y161 or Y197	BK-AG	532 / lsf INGL/op inall white-colors
☐ 4X-EBI	Boeing 757-258 (ER)	27622 / 745		0097	0397	2 RR RB211-535E4	113400	C24Y161 or Y197	QS-HL	lsf ILFC
☐ 4X-EBL	Boeing 757-258	23917 / 152		0087	1187	2 RR RB211-535E4	108862	C24Y161 or Y197	KL-DH	501
☐ 4X-EBM	Boeing 757-258	23918 / 156		0087	1287	2 RR RB211-535E4	108862	C24Y161 or Y197	KL-DJ	502
☐ 4X-EBR	Boeing 757-258	24254 / 185		0088	0788	2 RR RB211-535E4	108862	C24Y161 or Y197	JM-HL	503
☐ 4X-EBS	Boeing 757-258 (ER)	24884 / 325		0090	1190	2 RR RB211-535E4	113400	C24Y161 or Y197	JL-DM	504
☐ 4X-EBT	Boeing 757-258 (ER)	25036 / 356		0091	0491	2 RR RB211-535E4	113400	C24Y161 or Y197	AD-EH	505
☐ 4X-EBU	Boeing 757-258 (ER)	26053 / 529		0093	0393	2 RR RB211-535E4	113400	C24Y161 or Y197	CF-BK	506
☐ 4X-EBV	Boeing 757-258 (ER)	26054 / 547		0093	0593	2 RR RB211-535E4	113400	C24Y161 or Y197	GK-BH	507
☐ 4X-EAA	Boeing 767-258	22972 / 62	N6066Z*	0083	0783	2 PW JT9D-7R4D	140613	C24Y189	EJ-DM	601
☐ 4X-EAB	Boeing 767-258	22973 / 68	N6018N*	0083	0983	2 PW JT9D-7R4D	140613	C24Y189	DF-AE	602
☐ 4X-EAC	Boeing 767-258 (ER)	22974 / 86	N6018N*	0084	0384	2 PW JT9D-7R4D	163293	C24Y189	GK-EM	603
☐ 4X-EAD	Boeing 767-258 (ER)	22975 / 89	N6046P*	0084	0684	2 PW JT9D-7R4D	163293	C24Y189	DG-HK	604
☐ 4X-EAE	Boeing 767-27E (ER)	24832 / 316	F-GHGD	0790	0299	2 PW PW4060A	175540	C24Y181	AR-FG	605
☐ 4X-EAF	Boeing 767-27E (ER)	24854 / 326	F-GHGE	0990	0499	2 PW PW4060A	175540	C24Y181		606
☐ 4X-AXA	Boeing 747-258B	20135 / 140		0071	0571	4 PW JT9D-7J	362874	F10C51Y373	KL-JM	401 / std TLV
☐ 4X-AXB	Boeing 747-258B	20274 / 164		0071	1171	4 PW JT9D-7J	362874	F10C51Y373	KL-BD	402
☐ 4X-AXC	Boeing 747-258B	20704 / 212	N1799B*	0073	0473	4 PW JT9D-7J	369224	F10C51Y373	AG-FK	403
☐ 4X-AXD	Boeing 747-258C	21190 / 272		0075	1275	4 PW JT9D-7J	369224	F10C51Y373/Frtr	FJ-EK	404
☐ 4X-AXF	Boeing 747-258C	21594 / 327		0078	0678	4 PW JT9D-7J	369224	F10C51Y373/Frtr	BJ-EG	405
☐ 4X-AXH	Boeing 747-258B (M)	22254 / 418		0079	1279	4 PW JT9D-7J	369224	F10C51Y373/Frtr	BE-AM	407 / cvtd -258B
☐ 4X-AXK	Boeing 747-245F (SCD)	22151 / 478	9V-SQU	1080	0195	4 PW JT9D-7Q	377842	Freighter 112t	BE-AG	410
☐ 4X-AXL	Boeing 747-245F (SCD)	22150 / 476	9V-SQT	1080	0395	4 PW JT9D-7Q	377842	Freighter 112t	AD-FM	411
☐ 4X-AXQ	Boeing 747-238B	20841 / 233	VH-EBG	0074	0588	4 PW JT9D-7J	369224	F10C51Y373	AJ-FG	408
☐ 4X-ELA	Boeing 747-458	26055 / 1027		0094	0494	4 PW PW4056	394625	F12C42Y424	EK-CH	201
☐ 4X-ELB	Boeing 747-458	26056 / 1032	N60697*	0094	0594	4 PW PW4056	394625	F12C42Y424	EG-BH	202
☐ 4X-ELC	Boeing 747-458	27915 / 1062	N6009F*	0095	0595	4 PW PW4056	394625	F12C42Y424	HM-CK	203
☐ 4X-ELD	Boeing 747-458	29328		0099	0599	4 PW PW4056	394625	F12C42Y424		204

EL-ROM AIRLINES, Ltd = ELR (formerly Elrom Aviation and Development Services, Ltd)
Tel Aviv-Sde Dov

PO Box 48294, Tel Aviv 61480, Israel ☎ (3) 699 25 54 Tx: 5351 coc bs il Fax: (9) 957 46 41 SITA: n/a
F: 1969 17 Head: A. Porat Net: n/a

registration	type of aircraft	cn/fn	ex/ex*	mfd	del	powered by	mtow kg	configuration	selcal	name/fln/specialitites/remarks
☐ 4X-CAL	Piper PA-34-200 Seneca	34-7350101	D-GAHN	0073	0097	2 LY IO-360-C1E6	1905			
☐ 4X-CCF	Piper PA-31-350 Navajo Chieftain	31-7652169	N62921	0076		2 LY TIO-540-J2BD	3175			

GEVA AVIATION, Ltd
Tel Aviv-Ben Gurion Int'l & Herzyla

PO Box 8, Moshav Rantiya 73165, Israel ☎ (3) 933 50 05 Tx: none Fax: (3) 933 50 04 SITA: n/a
F: 1996 n/a Head: Mordehai Geva Net: n/a

registration	type of aircraft	cn/fn	ex/ex*	mfd	del	powered by	mtow kg	configuration	selcal	name/fln/specialitites/remarks
☐ 4X-CBT	Cessna 337G Super Skymaster	33701539	N72192	0073	1096	2 CO IO-360-G	2100			
☐ 4X-CBV	Cessna T337GP Press. Skymaster	P3370104	N574V	0073	1096	2 CO TSIO-360-C	2132			
☐ 4X-CBW	Cessna 337G Super Skymaster	33701615	N53424	0073	1096	2 CO IO-360-G	2100			
☐ 4X-CCP	Twin (Aero) Commander 500U	500U-1641-4	N27EH	0066	0096	2 LY IO-540-E1A5	3062			

GOLDEN WINGS AVIATION & TOURISM
Haifa

PO Box 6736, Haifa 31067, Israel ☎ (4) 872 50 55 Tx: 46400 bxhh il Fax: (4) 872 44 74 SITA: n/a
F: 1985 6 Head: S. Sharon Net: n/a Aircraft below MTOW 1361kg: Cessna 152 / 172 & Beech S-35.

registration	type of aircraft	cn/fn	ex/ex*	mfd	del	powered by	mtow kg	configuration	selcal	name/fln/specialitites/remarks
☐ 4X-ANS	Piper PA-32-260 Cherokee SIX	32-281	N321HF	0065	0391	1 LY O-540-E4B5	1542			
☐ 4X-AJN	Piper PA-23-250 Aztec D	27-4072	HB-LFB	0068		2 LY IO-540-C4B5	2359			

ISRAIR, Airlines & Tourism Ltd = 6H / ISR (formerly Kanfey-Ha'Emek Aviation dba Emek Wings)
Tel Aviv-Sde Dov & -Ben Gurion Int'l

6 Ohaliav Street, Ramat Gan 52522, Israel ☎ (3) 613 65 64 Tx: none Fax: (3) 751 94 30 SITA: n/a
F: 1989 50 Head: Ulli Harel IATA: 818 ICAO: ISRAIR Net: n/a

registration	type of aircraft	cn/fn	ex/ex*	mfd	del	powered by	mtow kg	configuration	selcal	name/fln/specialitites/remarks
☐ 4X-ATK	ATR 42-300	073	F-WQCX	0088	0796	2 PWC PW120	16700	Y46		
☐ 4X-ATL	ATR 42-300	089	F-WQCY	0088	0896	2 PWC PW120	16700	Y46		
☐ 4X-ATM	ATR 42-300	069	F-WQFS	0087	0497	2 PWC PW120	16700	Y46		
☐ 4X-ATN	ATR 42-300	053	F-WQGN	0087	0698	2 PWC PW120	16700	Y46		
☐ 4X-ATO	ATR 42-300	064	F-GPEC	0087	0798	2 PWC PW120	16700	Y46		
☐ 4X-ABJ	Boeing 737-73S	29079 / 194	N1786B*	0099	0299	2 CFMI CFM56-7B24	69400	Y148		lsf PEMB
☐ 4X-ABR	Boeing 737-73S	29081 / 215	N1786B*	0099	0499	2 CFMI CFM56-7B24	69400	Y148		lsf PEMB

JET LINK = JEK
Tel Aviv-Ben Gurion Int'l

13 Yehuda Moses Street, Tel Aviv 67442, Israel ☎ (3) 696 90 76 Tx: none Fax: (3) 696 90 72 SITA: n/a
F: 1996 10 Head: Capt Doron Yogev ICAO: JET OPS Net: n/a

registration	type of aircraft	cn/fn	ex/ex*	mfd	del	powered by	mtow kg	configuration	selcal	name/fln/specialitites/remarks
☐ 4X-CTE	IAI 1124A Westwind II	337	N900NW	0081	0294	2 GA TFE731-3-1G	10659	Executive		lsf Control Centers Ltd
☐ 4X-COV	Hawker 800XP	258283	N918H*	0096	0696	2 GA TFE731-5BR-1H	12701	Executive		lsf Iscar Blades Ltd
☐ 4X-CZM	Hawker 800XP	258279	G-BVZL*	0095	1295	2 GA TFE731-5BR-1H	12701	Executive		lsf Control Centers Ltd
☐ 4X-COE	Canadair CL-604 (CL-600-2B16) Challen.	5352	C-GBKE	0097	0398	2 GE CF34-3B	21591	Executive		lsf Iscar Blades Ltd

MEGIDDO AVIATION, Ltd
Megiddo

PO Box 2235, Afula 18323, Israel ☎ (6) 652 88 47 Tx: none Fax: (6) 659 37 11 SITA: n/a
F: 1996 n/a Head: Moshe Menahemi Net: n/a Aircraft below MTOW 1361kg: Cessna 150 & 172

registration	type of aircraft	cn/fn	ex/ex*	mfd	del	powered by	mtow kg	configuration	selcal	name/fln/specialitites/remarks
☐ 4X-CAB	Piper PA-34-200 Seneca	34-7350059	HB-LET	0073	0096	2 LY IO-360-C1E6	1905			
☐ 4X-AYY	Cessna 337C Super Skymaster	337-0776	N2476S	0067	1096	2 CO IO-360-C/D	1996			

MOONAIR AVIATION, Ltd
Tel Aviv-Sde Dov

PO Box 535, Raanana 43104, Israel ☎ (9) 958 72 80 Tx: none Fax: (9) 950 96 94 SITA: n/a
F: 1991 12 Head: Menahem Zur Net: n/a Aircraft below MTOW 1361kg: Cessna 152 & 172

registration	type of aircraft	cn/fn	ex/ex*	mfd	del	powered by	mtow kg	configuration	selcal	name/fln/specialitites/remarks
☐ 4X-AQH	Piper PA-32-300 Cherokee SIX	32-7740073	N5882V	0077		1 LY IO-540-K1G5	1542	5 Pax		
☐ 4X-AJM	Piper PA-23-250 Aztec C	27-3640	G-AYUU	0067		2 LY IO-540-C4B5	2359	5 Pax		
☐ 4X-CBY	Piper PA-23-250 Aztec E	27-7304990	N405PB	0073		2 LY IO-540-C4B5	2359	5 Pax		
☐ 4X-CBG	Cessna 340A II	340A0340	N340AP	0077		2 CO TSIO-520-N	2717	5 Pax		
☐ 4X-CCJ	Piper PA-31-350 Navajo Chieftain	31-7405140	G-FOEL	0074	0297	2 LY TIO-540-J2BD	3175	9 Pax		
☐ 4X-CIC	Piper PA-42 Cheyenne III	42-8001073	N321CF	0082	1197	2 PWC PT6A-41	5080	8 Pax		

NESHER AVIATION & TOURISM, Ltd
Herzlia & Tel Aviv-Sde Dov

PO Box 3117, Herzlia 46103, Israel ☎ (9) 950 50 54 Tx: none Fax: (9) 950 84 20 SITA: n/a
F: 1976 25 Head: Shay Hillel Net: n/a Aircraft below MTOW 1361 kg: Beechcraft 77, Cessna 152/172 & Mooney M20

registration	type of aircraft	cn/fn	ex/ex*	mfd	del	powered by	mtow kg	configuration	selcal	name/fln/specialitites/remarks
☐ 4X-CGU	Cessna 210L Centurion II	21060990	N99EM	0075	1292	1 CO IO-520-L	1724	5 Pax		
☐ 4X-CAC	Piper PA-23-250 Aztec D	27-4377	N6306Y	0069		2 LY IO-540-C4B5	2359	5 Pax		
☐ 4X-DZP	Cessna T310R II	310R0731	N816P	0076		2 CO TSIO-520-B	2495	5 Pax		
☐ 4X-AYH	Britten-Norman BN-2A-21 Islander	446	N93JA	0075		2 LY IO-540-K1B5	2994	9 Pax		
☐ 4X-CAY	Britten-Norman BN-2A-26 Islander	640	G-AYOC	0071		2 LY O-540-E4C5	2994	9 Pax		
☐ 4X-CBZ	Cessna 402B	402B0531	EC-CJE	0073	1298	2 CO TSIO-520-E	2858	9 Pax		

OFEK AERIAL PHOTOGRAPHY, Co.
Natania Helipad & Herzila

PO Box 8065, New Industrial, Natania 70145, Israel ☎ (9) 865 30 65 Tx: none Fax: (9) 865 00 86 SITA: n/a
F: 1987 80 Head: Gal Bracha Net: n/a

registration	type of aircraft	cn/fn	ex/ex*	mfd	del	powered by	mtow kg	configuration	selcal	name/fln/specialitites/remarks
☐ 4X-CAZ	Cessna TU206E Turbo Skywagon	U20601615	G-OFEK	0071		1 CO TSIO-520-C	1633			
☐ 4X-CAM	Piper PA-23-250 Aztec E	27-7554096	N54794	0075		2 LY IO-540-C4B5	2359			
☐ 4X-CSW	Cessna 401B	401B0205	N7986Q	0071		2 CO TSIO-520-E	2858			

PALESTINIAN AIRLINES = PF / PNW
Gaza

PO Box 4043, Gaza, Palestine, via Israel ☎ (7) 282 78 24 Tx: none Fax: (7) 282 13 09 SITA: AMMTOPF
F: 1996 n/a Head: Fayez Zaidan IATA: 400 ICAO: PALESTINIAN Net: n/a

registration	type of aircraft	cn/fn	ex/ex*	mfd	del	powered by	mtow kg	configuration	selcal	name/fln/specialitites/remarks
☐ SU-YAH	Fokker 50 (F27 Mk050)	20123	PH-FZJ	0088	0896	2 PWC PW125B	20820	Y48		
☐ SU-YAI	Fokker 50 (F27 Mk050)	20143	PH-FZI	0089	0896	2 PWC PW125B	20820	Y48		
☐ SU-YAK	Boeing 727-230 (A)	21621 / 1425	TC-AFR	0078	0598	3 PW JT8D-15	82782	Y170		lsf Kingdom 5-KR-80 Ltd

SHAHAF AIRLINES, Ltd (Affiliated with Shahaf Aviation Services, Ltd) — Herzlia & Tel Aviv-Sde Dov

PO Box 333, Herzlia 46103, Israel ☎ (9) 950 11 93 Tx: none Fax: (3) 947 90 97 SITA: n/a
F: 1971 ✝✝✝ 15 Head: Yossef Hadari Net: n/a Aircraft below MTOW 1361 kg: Cessna 152 & 172N.

☐ 4X-AYA	Britten-Norman BN-2A-6 Islander	171	G-AYCW	0071		2 LY O-540-E4C5	2858	9 Pax		
☐ 4X-AYS	Britten-Norman BN-2A-8 Islander	376	N88JA	0074		2 LY O-540-E4C5	2858	9 Pax		

SUN D'OR INTERNATIONAL AIRLINES, Ltd = ERO (Subsidiary of El Al Israel Airlines, Ltd) — Tel Aviv-Ben Gurion Int'l

PO Box 161, Ben Gurion Int'l Airport 70100, Israel ☎ (3) 971-6431 Tx: none Fax: (3) 972-1371 SITA: TLVEBLY
F: 1978 ✝✝✝ 15 Head: I. Meirovich ICAO: ECHO ROMEO Net: n/a Operates charter flights with aircraft leased from EL AL Israel Airlines when required.

WINGS OF JERUSALEM — Jerusalem

PO Box 27261, Jerusalem 91271, Israel ☎ (2) 583 14 44 Tx: none Fax: (2) 583 18 80 SITA: n/a
F: 1990 ✝✝✝ n/a Head: Haviv Matzliah Net: n/a Aircraft below MTOW 1361kg: Beech 24 & Cessna 152/172

☐ 4X-ANP	Piper PA-32-300C Cherokee SIX	32-40940	N5247S	0070		1 LY IO-540-K1A5	1542			
☐ 4X-AQM	Piper PA-32R-300 Lance	32R-7780257	N2654Q	0077	0596	1 LY IO-540-K1G5D	1633			
☐ 4X-CBE	Piper PA-23-250 Aztec F	27-7754020	N188DM	0077		2 LY IO-540-C4B5	2359			

5A = LIBYA (Socialist People's Libyan Arab Jamahiriya) (Libya, full name see below)

(al-Jamahiriya al-Arabiya al-Ishtirakiya al-Sha'abiya al-Libya)
Capital: Tripoli Official Language: Arabic Population: 6,0 million Square Km: 1759540 Dialling code: +218 Year established: 1951 Acting political head: Colonel Muammar al-Khaddafi (President)

Government / Corporate / Executive / VIP Aircraft

☐ 5A-DCA	De Havilland DHC-6 Twin Otter 300	599		0079		2 PWC PT6A-27	5670			Directorate of Civil Aviation
☐ 5A-DCO	Dassault Falcon 20C	190	5A-DAH	0070		2 GE CF700-2C	12000			Directorate of Civil Aviation

LIBYAN AIR AMBULANCE (Division of Ministry of Health) — Tripoli

c/o Ministry of Health, PO Box, Tripoli, Libya ☎ (21) 350 21 41 Tx: 20235 ly Fax: (21) 350 21 42 SITA: n/a
F: n/a ✝✝✝ n/a Head: n/a Net: n/a

☐ 5A-DHV	Eurocopter (Aerosp.) SA365C1 Dauphin 2	5065	F-BZCU	0081	0081	2 TU Arriel 1A1	3400	Ambulance		
☐ 5A-DHW	Eurocopter (Aerosp.) SA365C1 Dauphin 2	5067	F-BZCV	0081	0081	2 TU Arriel 1A1	3400	Ambulance		
☐ 5A-DHX	Eurocopter (Aerosp.) SA365C1 Dauphin 2	5069	F-WTNE*	0081	0081	2 TU Arriel 1A1	3400	Ambulance		
☐ 5A-DDT	Beech King Air 200C	BL-1	F-GBLT	0079	0079	2 PWC PT6A-41	5670	Ambulance		
☐ 5A-DDY	Beech King Air 200C	BL-6		0079	0079	2 PWC PT6A-41	5670	Ambulance		
☐ 5A-DCK	Aerospatiale SN601 Corvette	38	F-ODIF	0077	0678	2 PWC JT15D-4	7000	Ambulance		
☐ 5A-DAJ	Lockheed L-1329 JetStar 8	5136	LAAF001	0068	0177	4 PW JT12A-8	19005	Ambulance		

LIBYAN ARAB AIR CARGO = LCR (Division of Libyan Arab Airlines / formerly Jamahiriya Air Transport) — Tripoli

PO Box 2555, Tripoli, Libya ☎ (21) 60 68 37 Tx: 20193 libair ly Fax: (21) 60 20 85 SITA: n/a
F: 1979 ✝✝✝ n/a Head: n/a ICAO: LIBAC Net: n/a

☐ 5A-DOA	Antonov 26					2 IV AI-24VT	24000	Freighter		
☐ 5A-DOH	Antonov 26					2 IV AI-24VT	24000	Freighter		
☐ 5A-DJQ	Lockheed L-382G (L-100-30) Hercules	40C-4798	N501AK	0078	1279	4 AN 501-D22A	70307	Freighter		
☐ 5A-DOM	Lockheed L-382G (L-100-30) Hercules	62C-4992	N4268M*	0085	0685	4 AN 501-D22A	70307	Freighter		
☐ 5A-DHI	Lockheed L-382E (L-100-20) Hercules	19C-4355	5A-DHO	0069	0281	4 AN 501-D22A	70307	Freighter		
☐ 5A-DJR	Lockheed L-382E (L-100-20) Hercules	15C-4302	RP-C99	0076	0282	4 AN 501-D22A	70307	Freighter		
☐ 5A-DHL	Boeing 707-321C	18765 / 371	SU-BAG	0064	0880	4 PW JT3D-3B	151046	Freighter		std TIP
☐ 5A-DTF	Boeing 707-338C	19628 / 716	TF-IUD	0068	1287	4 PW JT3D-3B	151046	Freighter		std TIP
☐ 5A-DNA	Ilyushin 76TD	0023439140		0082	0082	4 SO D-30KP	190000	Freighter		std Moscow-Bykovo
☐ 5A-DNB	Ilyushin 76TD	0023437086		0082	0082	4 SO D-30KP	190000	Freighter		
☐ 5A-DNC	Ilyushin 76TD	0023437084		0082	0082	4 SO D-30KP	190000	Freighter		
☐ 5A-DND	Ilyushin 76TD	0033445299		0083	0083	4 SO D-30KP	190000	Freighter		
☐ 5A-DNE	Ilyushin 76T	0013432952		0081	0081	4 SO D-30KP	170000	Freighter		
☐ 5A-DNG	Ilyushin 76T	0013432961		0081	0081	4 SO D-30KP	170000	Freighter		
☐ 5A-DNH	Ilyushin 76TD	0033446356		0083	0083	4 SO D-30KP	190000	Freighter		
☐ 5A-DNI	Ilyushin 76T	0013430878		0081	0081	4 SO D-30KP	170000	Freighter		
☐ 5A-DNJ	Ilyushin 76T	0013430869		0081	0081	4 SO D-30KP	170000	Freighter		
☐ 5A-DNK	Ilyushin 76T	0013430882		0081	0081	4 SO D-30KP	170000	Freighter		
☐ 5A-DNO	Ilyushin 76TD	0043451509		0084	0084	4 SO D-30KP	190000	Freighter		
☐ 5A-DNP	Ilyushin 76TD	0043451516		0084	0084	4 SO D-30KP	190000	Freighter		
☐ 5A-DNQ	Ilyushin 76TD	0043454641		0084	0084	4 SO D-30KP	190000	Freighter		
☐ 5A-DNS	Ilyushin 76TD	0023439145		0083	0083	4 SO D-30KP	190000	Freighter		
☐ 5A-DNT	Ilyushin 76TD	0023439141		0082	0082	4 SO D-30KP	190000	Freighter		
☐ 5A-DNU	Ilyushin 76TD	0043454651		0085	0085	4 SO D-30KP	190000	Freighter		
☐ 5A-DNV	Ilyushin 76TD	0043454645		0085	0085	4 SO D-30KP	190000	Freighter		
☐ 5A-DRR	Ilyushin 76M	083415469		0079	0079	4 SO D-30KP	170000	Freighter		

LIBYAN ARAB AIRLINES = LN / LAA (Jamahiriya Libyan Arab Airlines dba / formerly Kingdom of Libya Airlines) — Tripoli

PO Box 2555, Tripoli, Libya ☎ (21) 60 88 60 Tx: 20333 libair ly Fax: (21) 60 20 85 SITA: TIPZKLN
F: 1964 ✝✝✝ 5100 Head: M. Ibsem IATA: 148 ICAO: LIBAIR Net: n/a

☐ 5A-DAG	Dassault Falcon 20C	143	F-WMKH*	0068	0568	2 GE CF700-2C	12000	VIP		
☐ 5A-DCM	Dassault Falcon 50	68	F-WZHQ*	0081	0981	3 GA TFE731-3-1C	17600	VIP		
☐ 5A-DBO	Fokker F27 Friendship 600 (F27 Mk600)	10513	PH-EXG*	0075	0775	2 RR Dart 532-7	19731	Y44		
☐ 5A-DBP	Fokker F27 Friendship 600 (F27 Mk600)	10515	PH-EXK*	0075	0775	2 RR Dart 532-7	19731	Y44		
☐ 5A-DBQ	Fokker F27 Friendship 400 (F27 Mk400)	10516	PH-EXU*	0075	0875	2 RR Dart 532-7	19731	Y44		
☐ 5A-DBS	Fokker F27 Friendship 600 (F27 Mk600)	10519	PH-EXA*	0075	1275	2 RR Dart 532-7	19731	Y44		
☐ 5A-DBT	Fokker F27 Friendship 600 (F27 Mk600)	10521	PH-EXB*	0075	1275	2 RR Dart 532-7	19731	Y44		
☐ 5A-DDU	Fokker F27 Friendship 600 (F27 Mk600)	10586	PH-EXA*	0079	0979	2 RR Dart 536-7	19731	Y44		
☐ 5A-DKD	Fokker F27 Friendship 600 (F27 Mk600)	10638	PH-EXF*	0082	0883	2 RR Dart 536-7	19731	Y44		
☐ 5A-DLK	Fokker F27 Friendship 600 (F27 Mk600)	10635	PH-EXD*	0082	0782	2 RR Dart 536-7	19731	Y44		
☐ 5A-DLM	Fokker F27 Friendship 600 (F27 Mk600)	10636	PH-EXB*	0082	0982	2 RR Dart 536-7	19731	Y44		
☐ 5A-DLN	Fokker F27 Friendship 600 (F27 Mk600)	10640	PH-EXH*	0082	1182	2 RR Dart 536-7	19731	Y44		
☐ 5A-DLO	Fokker F27 Friendship 600 (F27 Mk600)	10644	PH-EXM*	0082	0183	2 RR Dart 536-7	19731	Y44		
☐ 5A-DLQ	Fokker F27 Friendship 600 (F27 Mk600)	10646	PH-EXD*	0082	0483	2 RR Dart 536-7	19731	Y44		
☐ 5A-DLS	Fokker F27 Friendship 600 (F27 Mk600)	10648	TT-LAA	0083	0683	2 RR Dart 536-7	19731	Y44		
☐ 5A-DJE	Fokker F27 Friendship 500 (F27 Mk500)	10604	PH-FTZ*	0081	0981	2 RR Dart 536-7	20412	Y44		
☐ 5A-DJF	Fokker F27 Friendship 500 (F27 Mk500)	10611	PH-EXL*	0081	1081	2 RR Dart 536-7	20412	Y44		
☐ 5A-DDS	GAC (Grumman) G-1159 Gulfstream II	242		0079	0180	2 RR Spey 511-8	29393	VIP		
☐ 5A-DLU	Fokker F28 Fellowship 4000 (F28 Mk4000)	11197	PH-EXS*	0083	1183	2 RR Spey 555-15P	33112	Y85		
☐ 5A-DLV	Fokker F28 Fellowship 4000 (F28 Mk4000)	11200	PH-EXV*	0083	1183	2 RR Spey 555-15P	33112	Y85		
☐ 5A-DLW	Fokker F28 Fellowship 4000 (F28 Mk4000)	11194	PH-EXZ*	0083	0284	2 RR Spey 555-15P	33112	Y85		
☐ 5A-DAI	Boeing 727-224	20245 / 663	N1783B*	0069	0171	3 PW JT8D-9	78245	Y159	LM-AD	
☐ 5A-DIB	Boeing 727-2L5 (A)	21051 / 1109		0075	0275	3 PW JT8D-15	86409	Y159	LM-CJ	
☐ 5A-DIC	Boeing 727-2L5 (A)	21052 / 1110		0075	0375	3 PW JT8D-15	86409	Y159	LM-CK	
☐ 5A-DID	Boeing 727-2L5 (A)	21229 / 1213		0076	0776	3 PW JT8D-15	86409	Y159	LM-DF	
☐ 5A-DIE	Boeing 727-2L5 (A)	21230 / 1215		0076	0776	3 PW JT8D-15	86409	Y159	LM-DG	
☐ 5A-DIF	Boeing 727-2L5 (A)	21332 / 1257		0077	0477	3 PW JT8D-15	86409	Y159	KL-FM	
☐ 5A-DIG	Boeing 727-2L5 (A)	21333 / 1259		0077	0477	3 PW JT8D-15	86409	Y159	KL-GM	
☐ 5A-DIH	Boeing 727-2L5 (A)	21539 / 1371	N1253E*	0078	1178	3 PW JT8D-15	86409	Y159	KL-HM	
☐ 5A-DII	Boeing 727-2L5 (A)	21540 / 1386	N1261E*	0078	1178	3 PW JT8D-15	86409	Y159	KL-FJ	
☐ 5A-DAK	Boeing 707-3L5C	21228 / 911		0076	0776	4 PW JT3D-3B	151046	VIP	LM-AK	

LIGHT AIR TRANSPORT & TECHNICAL SERVICES = GLT — Tripoli

PO Box 84320, Tripoli, Libya ☎ (21) 333 00 60 Tx: 20441 libac ly Fax: (21) 333 30 48 SITA: n/a
F: 1990 ✝✝✝ 480 Head: Capt. Sabri Saad ICAO: LIGHT AIR Net: n/a

☐ 5A-DGC	Cessna 402C II	402C0045	N5800C	0078	0091	2 CO TSIO-520-VB	3107			
☐ 5A-DHG	Cessna 402C II	402C0464	N8737Q	0081	0091	2 CO TSIO-520-VB	3107			
☐ 5A-DHH	Cessna 402C II	402C0444	N6790F	0081	0091	2 CO TSIO-520-VB	3107			
☐ 5A-DHZ	Fairchild (Swearingen) SA226AT Merlin III	T-345	OO-HSC	0080	0091	2 GA TPE331-10U-501H	5670			
☐ 5A-DJB	Fairchild (Swearingen) SA226AT Merlin III	T-368	OO-XSC	0081	0091	2 GA TPE331-10U-501H	5670			
☐ 5A-DCT	De Havilland DHC-6 Twin Otter 300	627		0079	0091	2 PWC PT6A-27	5670			
☐ 5A-DCV	De Havilland DHC-6 Twin Otter 300	637		0079	0091	2 PWC PT6A-27	5670			
☐ 5A-DCX	De Havilland DHC-6 Twin Otter 300	641		0079	0091	2 PWC PT6A-27	5670			
☐ 5A-DCZ	De Havilland DHC-6 Twin Otter 300	645		0079	0091	2 PWC PT6A-27	5670			
☐ 5A-DDB	De Havilland DHC-6 Twin Otter 300	653		0079	0091	2 PWC PT6A-27	5670			
☐ 5A-DDC	De Havilland DHC-6 Twin Otter 300	670		0280	0091	2 PWC PT6A-27	5670			
☐ 5A-DDE	De Havilland DHC-6 Twin Otter 300	677		0080	0091	2 PWC PT6A-27	5670			
☐ 5A-DHN	De Havilland DHC-6 Twin Otter 300	712		0080	0091	2 PWC PT6A-27	5670			opf Agoco-Arabian Gulf Oil Co.
☐ 5A-DHY	De Havilland DHC-6 Twin Otter 300	661	C-GELZ*	0079	0091	2 PWC PT6A-27	5670			
☐ 5A-DJG	De Havilland DHC-6 Twin Otter 300	744	C-GFHQ*	0081	0091	2 PWC PT6A-27	5670			

689 registration type of aircraft cn/fn ex/ex* mfd del powered by mtow kg configuration selcal name/fln/specialitites/remarks

☐ 5A-DJH	De Havilland DHC-6 Twin Otter 300	747		0081	0091	2 PWC PT6A-27	5670			
☐ 5A-DJI	De Havilland DHC-6 Twin Otter 300	757		0081	0091	2 PWC PT6A-27	5670			
☐ 5A-DJJ	De Havilland DHC-6 Twin Otter 300	769		0081	0091	2 PWC PT6A-27	5670			
☐ 5A-DJK	De Havilland DHC-6 Twin Otter 300	775	C-GESR*	0081	0091	2 PWC PT6A-27	5670			

5B = CYPRUS (Republic of Cyprus) (Kypriaki Dimokratia)

(excluding Northern Cyprus)

Capital: Nicosia Official Language: Greek Population: 0,6 million Square Km: 5896 Dialling code: +357 Year established: 1960 Acting political head: Glafkos Kleridis (President)

AIMES – Flight Operations (Flight division of Aerospace International Management Engineering Services, Ltd) — Larnaca

PO Box 7677, Nicosia, Cyprus ☎ (2) 35 34 34 Tx: 4992 cy Fax: (2) 35 43 43 SITA: n/a

F: 1993 n/a Head: Andreas P. Panayides Net: n/a Private company conducting non-commercial executive flights for itself only.

☐ 5B-DBE	Boeing 727-30	18371 / 145	9M-SAS	0065	0595	3 PW JT8D-7 (HK3/FDX)	69173	Executive 20Pax	AG-CH	
☐ N60FM	Boeing 727-27	19535 / 456	N7294	0067	0196	3 PW JT8D-7B (HK3/FDX)	72802	Executive 20Pax	CE-BM	lsf Airfreight Services Inc.

ATHENIAN AIRLIFT, Co. Ltd — Athens

1 Costakis Pantelides Ave., Nicosia, Cyprus ☎ (2) 46 44 11 Tx: 2359 law Fax: (2) 47 33 88 SITA: n/a

F: 1982 1 Head: Lukas Papaphilippou Net: n/a

☐ 5B-CBE	Eurocopter (MBB) BO105CBS	S-579	D-HDQB*	0082		2 AN 250-C20B	2400			
☐ 5B-PBY	Consolidated PBY-5A Canso	CV-333	C-FPQF	0040	0894	2 PW R-1830-92S	13835			Amphibian

CAPITAL L AIRLINES, Ltd (Sister company of Louis Tourist Agency, Ltd) — Larnaca

c/o Louis Tours, PO Box 2301, CY-1096 Nicosia, Cyprus ☎ (2) 67 80 00 Tx: none Fax: (2) 67 85 61 SITA: n/a

F: 1999 n/a Head: Costas Loizou Net: n/a Presently being set-up. Intends to start charter operations in January 2000 with Airbus Industrie A320 or Boeing 737/757 aircraft.

CYPRUS AIRWAYS, Ltd = CY / CYP — Larnaca

PO Box 1903, Nicosia, Cyprus ☎ (2) 66 30 54 Tx: 2225 cyprusair Fax: (2) 66 31 67 SITA: NICDDCY

F: 1947 2000 Head: Takis G. Kyriakides IATA: 048 ICAO: CYPRUS Net: n/a

☐ 5B-DAT	Airbus Industrie A320-231	028	YU-AOB	0089	0589	2 IAE V2500-A1	73500	C27Y138	DH-EL	Praxandros
☐ 5B-DAU	Airbus Industrie A320-231	035	F-WWDX*	0089	0689	2 IAE V2500-A1	73500	C27Y138	HQ-GM	Evelthon
☐ 5B-DAV	Airbus Industrie A320-231	037	F-WWDN*	0089	0589	2 IAE V2500-A1	73500	C27Y138	DH-EG	Kinyras
☐ 5B-DAW	Airbus Industrie A320-231	038	F-WWDZ*	0089	0590	2 IAE V2500-A1	73500	C27Y138	DH-EJ	Agapinor
☐ 5B-DBA	Airbus Industrie A320-231	180	F-WWIT*	0091	0392	2 IAE V2500-A1	73500	C27Y138	AG-QR	Evagoras
☐ 5B-DBB	Airbus Industrie A320-231	256	F-WWBH*	0092	0392	2 IAE V2500-A1	74500	Y174	AG-QS	lst ECA
☐ 5B-DBC	Airbus Industrie A320-231	295	F-WWIE*	0092	0392	2 IAE V2500-A1	74500	Y174	CR-HJ	lst ECA
☐ 5B-DBD	Airbus Industrie A320-231	316	F-WWBC*	0092	0393	2 IAE V2500-A1	74500	Y174	CR-HK	lst ECA
☐ 5B-DAQ	Airbus Industrie A310-203	300	F-WZEG*	0084	0284	2 GE CF6-80A3	138600	C28Y213	DH-EK	Soli
☐ 5B-DAR	Airbus Industrie A310-203	309	F-WZEM*	0084	0384	2 GE CF6-80A3	138600	C28Y213	RS-AD	Aepia
☐ 5B-DAS	Airbus Industrie A310-203	352	F-WZEO*	0085	0385	2 GE CF6-80A3	138600	C28Y213	DH-FK	Salamis
☐ 5B-DAX	Airbus Industrie A310-204 (winglets)	486	F-WWBN*	0089	0289	2 GE CF6-80C2A2	138600	C28Y220	CP-JM	Engomi

EUROCYPRIA AIRLINES, Ltd = UI / ECA (Subsidiary of Cyprus Airways, Ltd) — Larnaca

PO Box 970, Larnaca, Cyprus ☎ (4) 65 80 00 Tx: 3889 eurcyp cy Fax: (4) 65 80 08 SITA: LCAOOUI

F: 1990 150 Head: Tanis Kyriakides ICAO: EUROCYPRIA Net: n/a

☐ 5B-DBB	Airbus Industrie A320-231	256	F-WWBH*	0092	0392	2 IAE V2500-A1	74500	Y174	AG-QS	Akamas / lsf CYP
☐ 5B-DBC	Airbus Industrie A320-231	295	F-WWIE*	0092	0392	2 IAE V2500-A1	74500	Y174	CR-HJ	Tefkros / lsf CYP
☐ 5B-DBD	Airbus Industrie A320-231	316	F-WWBC*	0092	0393	2 IAE V2500-A1	74500	Y174	CR-HK	Onosilos / lsf CYP

5H = TANZANIA (United Republic of Tanzania) (Jamhouri ya Mwungano wa Tanzania)

(including half-autonomous island of Zanzibar)

Capital: Dodoma+Dar-es-Salaam Official Language: Swahili, English Population: 30,0 million Square Km: 945087 Dialling code: +255 Year established: 1964 Acting political head: Ali Hassan Mwinyi (President)

Government / Corporate / Executive / VIP Aircraft

☐ 5H-CCM	Fokker F28 Fellowship 3000 (F28 Mk3000)	11137	PH-ZBS*	0078	1178	2 RR Spey 555-15H	33112	VIP		Uhuru na Umoja / Gvmt of Tanzania

AIR EXCEL, Ltd — Arusha

PO Box 12731, Arusha, Tanzania ☎ (57) 84 29 Tx: none Fax: (57) 84 29 SITA: n/a

F: 1998 10 Head: Mihail Kalaitzakis Net: n/a

☐ 5H-EMK	Cessna TU206G Turbo Stationair 6 II	U20604638	5H-SDA	0078	0098	1 CO TSIO-520-M	1633	5 Pax		
☐ 5H-SRT	Cessna T210N Turbo Centurion II	21063059	I-ALAS	0079	0098	1 CO TSIO-520-R	1814	5 Pax		
☐ 5H-AMK	Cessna 404 Titan II	404-0637	5H-PAV	0080	0098	2 CO GTSIO-520-M	3810	12 Pax		

AIR TANZANIA, Corp. = TC / ATC — Dar-es-Salaam

PO Box 543, Dar-es-Salaam, Tanzania ☎ (51) 11 02 73 Tx: 41077 atc tz Fax: (51) 11 31 14 SITA: DARDZTC

F: 1977 650 Head: Abbes Sykes IATA: 197 ICAO: TANZANIA Net: http://www.mwebmarketplace.co.za/airtan/

☐ 5H-MPU	Fokker F27 Friendship 600RF	10569	PH-FTE*	0077	1277	2 RR Dart 536-7R	20412	Y44 / Combi		Ruvuma
☐ 5H-MRM	Fokker F27 Friendship 600RF	10589	PH-FTP*	0079	0579	2 RR Dart 536-7R	20412	Y44 / Combi		Ruvu / std DAR
☐ 5H-ATC	Boeing 737-2R8C (A)	21710 / 546	N57001*	0078	1278	2 PW JT8D-17	53070	F12Y94 / Combi	BH-DJ	Kilimanjaro
☐ 5H-MRK	Boeing 737-2R8C (A)	21711 / 573		0079	0579	2 PW JT8D-17	53070	F12Y94 / Combi	BH-DK	Serengeti / lst NMB
☐ 5H-TCA	Boeing 737-33A	24790 / 1955	VT-JAA	0091	0299	2 CFMI CFM56-3C1	61235	F20Y100		lsf AWAS

AIR ZANZIBAR, Ltd = AZL — Zanzibar

PO Box 1784, Zanzibar, Tanzania ☎ (54) 33 767 Tx: 57380 airzan tz Fax: (54) 33 098 SITA: n/a

F: 1990 20 Head: Capt. Tim Hendriks ICAO: ZANZIBAR Net: http://www.zanzibar.net/airzan.html

☐ 5H-AZO	Partenavia P.68B	120	5H-ZAA	0077		2 LY IO-360-A1B6	1960			
☐ 5H-AZY	Partenavia P.68B	149	5Y-BCH	0078	0896	2 LY IO-360-A1B6	1960			
☐ 5H-AZN	Piper PA-31-350 Navajo Chieftain	31-7405220	N254BW	0074	0994	2 LY TIO-540-J2BD	3175			
☐ 5H-AZZ	Piper PA-31-310 Navajo B	31-823	5Y-WKC	0072	0896	2 LY TIO-540-A2C	2948			

ALLIANCE AIR = multinational state airline – see under 5X -markings

COASTAL TRAVELS, Ltd (Associated with Coastal Steel Industries) — Dar-es-Salaam

PO Box 3052, Dar-es-Salaam, Tanzania ☎ (51) 11 79 59 Tx: none Fax: (51) 11 86 47 SITA: n/a

F: 1987 31 Head: Anna Westh Net: n/a Aircraft below MTOW 1361kg: Cessna 172

☐ 5H-CTL	Cessna TU206F Turbo Stationair	U20601988		0073		1 CO TSIO-520-F	1633	5 Pax		
☐ 5H-JET	Piper PA-34-200T Seneca II	34-7870345		0078		2 CO TSIO-360-E	2073	5 Pax		
☐ 5H-JAY	Cessna 340	340-0226	5Y-ATC	0073		2 CO TSIO-520-K	2710	5 Pax		
☐ 5H-TOY	Cessna 404 Titan II	404-0668	5Y-MCK	0080	0497	2 CO GTSIO-520-M	3810	11 Pax		
☐ 5H-HOT	Cessna 208B Grand Caravan	208B0677	N1256N*	0098	1098	1 PWC PT6A-114A	3969	13 Pax		

FLEET AIR, Ltd — Arusha

PO Box 543, Arusha, Tanzania ☎ (57) 81 26 Tx: none Fax: (57) 81 26 SITA: n/a

F: 1990 15 Head: Kerstin D. Cameron Net: n/a Aircraft below MTOW 1361kg: Cessna 182.

☐ 5H-IJR	Cessna U206F Stationair II	U20603159		0076		1 CO IO-520-F	1633			lsf pvt
☐ 5H-MSV	Cessna U206G Stationair 6 II	U20604595		0078		1 CO IO-520-F	1633			lsf Wingest Indrose Safari Ltd
☐ 5H-RAY	Cessna 404 Titan II	404-0007		0076		2 CO GTSIO-520-M	3810			lsf Superior Aviation Enterprises, USA

MAF Tanzania – Missionary Aviation Fellowship (Huduma ya Ndege za Kikristo) (Branch of MAF Europe) — Dodoma

PO Box 491, Dodoma, Tanzania ☎ (61) 35 20 10 Tx: none Fax: (61) 35 46 35 SITA: n/a

F: 1977 34 Head: Chris Lukkien Net: n/a Non-commercial multinational ecclesiastical consortium conducting flights for relief & development agencies & missions in remote areas of third world countries.

☐ 5H-CBM	Cessna U206G Stationair 6 II Rob./STOL	U20604655	N732BV	0079		1 CO IO-520-F	1633			Flint Tip Tank
☐ 5H-MSM	Cessna U206G Stationair 6 II Horton/STOL	U20606535	N9507Z	0082		1 CO IO-550-F	1633			Flint Tip Tank
☐ 5H-MSN	Cessna U206G Stationair 6 II Horton/STOL	U20606349	N7139Z	0081		1 CO IO-520-F	1724			Flint Tip Tank
☐ 5H-MSO	Cessna U206G Stationair 6 II Horton/STOL	U20606096	N5336Z	0081		1 CO IO-520-F	1724			Flint Tip Tank
☐ 5H-MSP	Cessna U206G Stationair 6 II Horton/STOL	U20606061	N4979Z	0081		1 CO IO-550-F	1633			Flint Tip Tank
☐ 5H-MSY	Cessna U206G Stationair 6 II Horton/STOL	U20606027	N859P	0081		1 CO IO-550-F	1724			Flint Tip Tank
☐ 5H-MTJ	Cessna U206G Stationair 6 II Horton/STOL	U20606442	N9376Z	0082	1294	1 CO IO-520-F	1633			Flint Tip Tank
☐ 5H-PTL	Cessna U206G Stationair 6 II	U20606138	ZS-ODE	0081	1097	1 CO IO-550-F	1633			
☐ 5H-MSW	Cessna 210N Centurion II	21063789	N5548C	0080		1 CO IO-520-L	1724			
☐ 5H-ELC	Cessna 402C Businessliner III	402C0465	N4282L	0081	0492	2 CO TSIO-520-VB	3107			
☐ 5H-MAF	Cessna 402C Businessliner III	402C0490	N6841D	0081		2 CO TSIO-520-VB	3107			Flint Tip Tank

NAHALO AIR SAFARIS, Ltd (Member of Noble Azania) — Dar-es-Salaam

PO Box 20066, Dar-es-Salaam, Tanzania ☎ (51) 84 32 01 Tx: none Fax: (51) 11 67 11 SITA: n/a

F: n/a n/a Head: n/a Net: n/a

☐ 5H-SEA	Cessna U206F Stationair II	U20603319	LN-SAA	0076		1 CO IO-520-F	1633			
☐ 5H-BEC	Cessna 402B II	402B1227	I-CCRR	0077		2 CO TSIO-520-E	2858			

690 registration type of aircraft cn/fn ex/ex* mfd del powered by mtow kg configuration selcal name/fln/specialitites/remarks

NORTHERN AIR (Tanzania Game Tracker Safaris, Ltd dba) — Arusha

PO Box 2782, Arusha, Tanzania ☎ (57) 80 59 Tx: none Fax: (57) 80 59 SITA: n/a
F: 1985 ✝✝✝ 12 Head: Christopher Pereira Net: n/a

☐ 5H-TGT	Cessna U206G Stationair 6 II	U20605223	N777TG	0079		1 CO IO-520-F	1633	Y5		
☐ 5H-NAB	Beech Baron 58	TH-789	A2-ABE	0077		2 CO IO-520-C	2449	Y5		
☐ 5H-TGA	Cessna 402C II	402C0634	N6798Y	0082		2 CO TSIO-520-VB	3107	Y9		
☐ 5H-NAA	Cessna 208 Caravan I	20800109	N9628F	0086		1 PWC PT6A-114	3629	Y13		
☐ 5H-NAT	Cessna 404 Titan II	404-0805	N25GT	0081		2 CO GTSIO-520-M	3810	Y10		
☐ 5H-THF	Cessna 404 Titan II	404-0835	N6807T	0081		2 CO GTSIO-520-M	3810	Y10		

PRECISIONAIR Services, Ltd = PW / PRF — Arusha

PO Box 1636, Arusha, Tanzania ☎ (57) 69 03 Tx: none Fax: (57) 82 04 SITA: n/a
F: 1991 ✝✝✝ 85 Head: Mike N. Shirima ICAO: PRECISIONAIR Net: n/a

☐ 5H-MNT	Piper PA-23-250 Aztec C	27-3909	N6605Y	0068		2 LY IO-540-J4A5	2359	Y5		
☐ 5H-PAS	Cessna 404 Titan II	404-0410	N17AU	0079	0894	2 CO GTSIO-520-M	3810	Y11		
☐ 5H-PAB	Let 410UVP-E9	962715	OK-BDJ	0096	1098	2 WA M-601E	6400	Y17		
☐ 5H-PAC	Let 410UVP-E20D	922711	OK-XDI	0092	1098	2 WA M-601E	6400	Y19		
☐ 5H-PAD	Let 410UVP-E20	871811	OK-PAD	0087	1198	2 WA M-601E	6400	Y19		
☐ 5H-PAA	ATR 42-320	308	F-WQHB*	0092	0596	2 PWC PW121	16700	Y48		City of Arusha

REGIONAL AIR SERVICES, Ltd (Subsidiary of AirKenya) — Arusha

PO Box 14755, Arusha, Tanzania ☎ (57) 25 41 Tx: none Fax: (57) 41 64 SITA: n/a
F: 1997 ✝✝✝ 18 Head: Iris McCallum Net: n/a

☐ 5H-MUA	Cessna 208B Grand Caravan	208B0487	5Y-BLM	0095	0097	1 PWC PT6A-114A	3969	Y9		
☐ 5H-MTX	Piper PA-31T3-T1040	31T-8275011	5Y-BIG	0082	0597	2 PWC PT6A-11	4082	Y9		
☐ 5H-MUC	De Havilland DHC-6 Twin Otter 300	580	5Y-BIJ	0078	0098	2 PWC PT6A-27	5670	Y18		
☐ 5H-MUG	De Havilland DHC-6 Twin Otter 300	582	5Y-BIK	0078	0098	2 PWC PT6A-27	5670	Y18		

SKYAIR (Sky Tours, Ltd dba) — Dar-es-Salaam

PO Box 2161, Dar-es-Salaam, Tanzania ☎ (51) 84 30 49 Tx: none Fax: (51) 86 50 99 SITA: n/a
F: 1991 ✝✝✝ 13 Head: n/a Net: n/a

☐ 5H-SKX	Cessna 402B	402B0829	5Y-EAL	0074		2 CO TSIO-520-E	2858			
☐ 5H-SKT	Piper PA-31-350 Navajo Chieftain	31-8152058		0081		2 LY TIO-540-J2BD	3175			
☐ ZS-PAY	Pilatus PC-12/45	204		0098	0598	1 PWC PT6A-67B	4500			lsf Veranlise Air P/L

TANZANAIR – Tanzanian Air Services, Ltd — Dar-es-Salaam

PO Box 364, Dar-es-Salaam, Tanzania ☎ (51) 11 31 51 Tx: 41341 tanzanair Fax: (51) 11 29 46 SITA: n/a
F: 1969 ✝✝✝ 120 Head: Dinos J. Samaras Net: n/a

☐ 5H-TEA	Cessna U206F Stationair II	U20602699	5H-RHS	0075		1 CO IO-520-F	1633			
☐ 5H-TZJ	Beech Debonair B33 (35-B33)	CD-769	5H-MFL	0064		1 CO IO-470-K	1361			
☐ 5H-LDS	Cessna 310I	310I0029	5Y-AJN	0064		2 CO IO-470-U	2313			
☐ 5H-TZA	Cessna 310R II	310R1333	N6200C	0078		2 CO IO-520-M	2495			
☐ 5H-TZC	Reims/Cessna F406 Caravan II	F406-0028	N7037C	0088	0090	2 PWC PT6A-112	4468			
☐ 5H-TZE	Reims/Cessna F406 Caravan II	F406-0046	OY-PED	0089	0796	2 PWC PT6A-112	4468			lsf Nordic Aviation Contractor

TANZANIA POLICE AIRWING (Airwing division of Tanzania Police) — Dar-es-Salaam

PO Box 18006, Dar-es-Salaam, Tanzania ☎ (51) 84 42 47 Tx: none Fax: (51) 11 32 67 SITA: n/a
F: n/a ✝✝✝ n/a Head: Cmt Jua J. Goyayi Net: n/a

☐ 5H-MPD	Cessna 206 Super Skywagon	206-0295	5Y-AEW	0064	0075	1 CO IO-520-A	1497			
☐ 5H-PAW	Bell 206L-1 LongRanger II	45292		0079	1179	1 AN 250-C28B	1882			
☐ 5H-TPF	Bell 206L-1 LongRanger II	45306		0079	1179	1 AN 250-C28B	1882			

TWIN WINGS AIR, (Z), Ltd (Subsidiary of Avtech Aviation, Kenya / Associated with Ilyas Aviation, Zanzibar) — Zanzibar

PO Box 3379, Zanzibar, Tanzania ☎ (54) 30 747 Tx: none Fax: (54) 32 996 SITA: n/a
F: 1995 ✝✝✝ 6 Head: Capt. Amin M. Muhyidin Net: n/a

☐ 5H-AZT	Piper PA-34-200T Seneca II	34-7570151		0075		2 CO TSIO-360-EB	2073			
☐ 5H-WAY	Piper PA-31-310 Navajo	31-707	5Y-ANT	0070		2 LY TIO-540-A2C	2948			

ZANAIR, Ltd — Zanzibar

PO Box 2113, Zanzibar, Tanzania ☎ (54) 33 670 Tx: none Fax: (54) 33 670 SITA: n/a
F: 1992 ✝✝✝ 26 Head: Capt. Carl G. Salisbury Net: n/a

☐ 5H-ZAB	Piper PA-34-200T Seneca II	34-7870131	5Y-KLV	0078		2 CO TSIO-360-EB	2073			
☐ 5H-ZAK	Piper PA-34-200 Seneca	34-7250101	5H-MTN	0072		2 LY IO-360-C1E6	1905			
☐ 5H-ZAL	Cessna 402B	402B0640	TU-TJA	0074		2 CO TSIO-520-EB	2858			
☐ 5H-ZAZ	Cessna 402C II	402C0029	5Y-NNM	0079		2 CO TSIO-520-VB	3107			
☐ 5H-ZAY	Cessna 404 Titan II	404-0207	N798A	0078	0197	2 CO GTSIO-520-M	3810			

5N = NIGERIA (Federal Republic of Nigeria)

Capital: Abuja Official Language: English Population: 125,0 million Square Km: 923768 Dialling code: +234 Year established: 1960 Acting political head: Olusegun Obasanjo (President)

Government / Corporate / Executive / VIP Aircraft

☐ 5N-AGV	GAC (Grumman) G-1159 Gulfstream II	177	N17587	0076		2 RR Spey 511-8	29393	VIP		Federal Government
☐ 5N-AGZ	Hawker 800B (BAe 125-800B)	258143	5N-NPF	0089	0990	2 GA TFE731-5R-1H	12428	VIP		Federal Government
☐ 5N-AVH	Beech King Air 200	BB-538	N6724N	0079		2 PWC PT6A-41	5670	VIP / Liasion		Federal Civil Aviation Authority
☐ 5N-AVK	Hawker 700B (HS 125-700B)	257160	G-5-19*	0082		2 GA TFE731-3R-1H	11567	VIP / Liaison		Federal Civil Aviation Authority
☐ 5N-AVL	Cessna 501 Citation I/SP	501-0317	N2626Z	0082		2 PWC JT15D-1A	5375	VIP / Liaison		Federal Civil Aviation Authority
☐ 5N-AVM	Cessna 501 Citation I/SP	501-0233		0082		2 PWC JT15D-1A	5375	VIP / Liaison		Federal Civil Aviation Authority
☐ 5N-AYA	Cessna 550 Citation II	550-0632	N12570*	0090	0490	2 PWC JT15D-4	6033	VIP		Federal Government
☐ 5N-FGE	Dassault Falcon 900	96	5N-OIL	0090	1194	3 GA TFE731-5AR-1C	20638	VIP		Federal Government
☐ 5N-FGN	Boeing 727-2N6 (A)	22825 / 1805	5N-AGY	0082	0782	3 PW JT8D-15	89358	VIP	BH-DL	Federal Government
☐ 5N-FGO	Dassault Falcon 900	52	F-WWFC*	0088		3 GA TFE731-5A-1C	20638	VIP	GH-BE	Federal Government
☐ 5N-FGP	GAC G-IV Gulfstream IV	1126	N426GA*	0090	1190	2 RR Tay 611-8	33203	VIP	FG-PS	Federal Government
☐ 5N-FGR	Hawker 1000B (BAe 125-1000B)	259018	G-5-741*	0092	0992	2 PWC PW305	14061	VIP		Federal Government
☐ 5N-MPA	Beech 1900D Airliner	UE-149	N3217L*	0095	1095	2 PWC PT6A-67D	7688	Corporate		Mobil Producing Nigeria Ltd
☐ 5N-MPN	Beech 1900D Airliner	UE-77	N82936	0093	0194	2 PWC PT6A-67D	7688	Corporate		Mobil Producing Nigeria Ltd
☐ 5N-MPS	Dornier 228-201	8146	D-CALO*	0087	0093	2 GA TPE331-5-252D	6200	Corporate		NEPA-National Electric Power Authority

ADC AIRLINES = ADK (Aviation Development Company, Ltd dba) — Lagos

PMB 6392, Ikeja, Nigeria ☎ (1) 96 57 50 Tx: 27364 adcair ng Fax: (1) 96 26 57 SITA: n/a
F: 1984 ✝✝✝ 230 Head: Capt. A.I. Okon ICAO: ADCO Net: n/a

☐ 5N-BBF	Boeing 727-231	20049 / 693	N44316	0069	0695	3 PW JT8D-9A	78245		DM-EF	
☐ 5N-BBH	Boeing 727-231	20050 / 694	N74317	0069	1195	3 PW JT8D-9A	78245		DM-GH	
☐ 5N-BBD	Boeing 707-338C	19625 / 693	N862BX	0068	0494	4 PW JT3D-3B (HK2/COM)	151953	Freighter	JL-HM	std Manston

AEROCONTRACTORS Company of Nigeria, Ltd – ACN = NU / NIG (Associated with Schreiner Airways, Netherlands) — Lagos, Escravos, Warri, Port Harcourt & N'Djamena

PMB 21090, Ikeja, Nigeria ☎ (1) 497 53 46 Tx: none Fax: (1) 497 19 73 SITA: LOSMDNU
F: 1960 ✝✝✝ 300 Head: Ed van Dam ICAO: AEROLINE Net: n/a

☐ 5N-AOA	Eurocopter (Aerosp.) AS355F Ecureuil 2	5277	F-WZFB*	0083		2 AN 250-C20F	2300			opf NNPC
☐ 5N-AOB	Eurocopter (Aerosp.) AS355F Ecureuil 2	5278		0083		2 AN 250-C20F	2300			opf NNPC
☐ 5N-ALJ	Eurocopter (Aerosp.) SA365C2 Dauphin 2	5049	PH-SSI	0080		2 TU Arriel 1A2	3500			
☐ 5N-ALV	Eurocopter (Aerosp.) SA365C2 Dauphin 2	5050	PH-SSJ	0080		2 TU Arriel 1A2	3500			
☐ 5N-AQK	Eurocopter (Aerosp.) SA365N Dauphin 2	6108		0084		2 TU Arriel 1C	4000			opf NNPC
☐ 5N-AQL	Eurocopter (Aerosp.) SA365N Dauphin 2	6109		0084		2 TU Arriel 1C	4000			opf NNPC
☐ 5N-ARM	Eurocopter (Aerosp.) SA365N Dauphin 2	6062	PH-SSO	0083		2 TU Arriel 1C	4000			
☐ 5N-ATP	Eurocopter (Aerosp.) SA365N Dauphin 2	6087	PH-SSR	0084		2 TU Arriel 1C	4000			
☐ 5N-ATX	Eurocopter (Aerosp.) SA365N Dauphin 2	6074	PH-SSU	0083	0691	2 TU Arriel 1C	4000			
☐ 5N-BAF	Eurocopter (Aerosp.) AS365N2 Dauphin 2	6430	F-WYMC*	0091		2 TU Arriel 1C2	4250			opf NNPC
☐ 5N-ESO	Eurocopter (Aerosp.) SA365N Dauphin 2	6072	PH-SSP	0083	0798	2 TU Arriel 1C	4000			
☐ 5N-STO	Eurocopter (Aerosp.) SA365N Dauphin 2	6106	PH-SSV	0084	0898	2 TU Arriel 1C	4000			
☐ 5N-AKP	De Havilland DHC-6 Twin Otter 310	476	PH-STJ	0075	0176	2 PWC PT6A-27	5670			
☐ 5N-AKV	De Havilland DHC-6 Twin Otter 310	529		0077	0377	2 PWC PT6A-27	5670			
☐ 5N-AKY	De Havilland DHC-6 Twin Otter 310	572	PH-SAK	0077	0678	2 PWC PT6A-27	5670			
☐ 5N-AMO	De Havilland DHC-6 Twin Otter 310	233	CF-FTC*	0069	0097	2 PWC PT6A-27	5670			
☐ 5N-ASP	De Havilland DHC-6 Twin Otter 310	704	PH-SSF	0080	0681	2 PWC PT6A-27	5670			
☐ 5N-AVD	De Havilland DHC-6 Twin Otter 310	597		0078	0680	2 PWC PT6A-27	5670			
☐ 5N-AVG	De Havilland DHC-6 Twin Otter 310	634		0079	1179	2 PWC PT6A-27	5670			opf NNPC
☐ 5N-BAM	De Havilland DHC-6 Twin Otter 300	249	N23FL	0069	0395	2 PWC PT6A-27	5670			lsf Global Equipment Leasing Ltd
☐ 5N-BAN	De Havilland DHC-6 Twin Otter 300	372	N24RM	0073	0091	2 PWC PT6A-27	5670			lsf Global Equipment Leasing Ltd
☐ 5N-EVS	De Havilland DHC-6 Twin Otter 300	662	TT-EAH	0079	0097	2 PWC PT6A-27	5670			
☐ 5N-AYK	Hawker 600B (HS 125-600B)	256060	G-BFIC	0076		2 RR Viper 601	11567			

691 registration | type of aircraft | cn/fn | ex/ex* | mfd | del | powered by | mtow kg | configuration | selcal | name/fln/specialitites/remarks

☐ 5N-YFS	Hawker 600B (HS 125-600B)	256054	G-BCXF	0075		2 RR Viper 601	11567			
☐ 5N-NPC	Hawker 800B (BAe 125-800B)	258109	G-5-581*	0088		2 GA TFE731-5R-1H	12428			opf NNPC
☐ 5N-MGV	De Havilland DHC-8-102 Dash 8	024	C-GMOK	0086	1195	2 PWC PW120A	15649			cvtd -101
☐ 5N-EVD	De Havilland DHC-8-311 Dash 8	216	PH-SDI	0090	0497	2 PWC PW123	18640			

AIR ATLANTIC CARGO = ANI (Air Atlantic (Nig.), Ltd dba) — Lagos & Pula (Slovenia)

European HQ:, 29 London Road, Bromley, Kent BR1 1DG, Great Britain ☎ (181) 466 55 05 Tx: none Fax: (181) 313 36 33 SITA: n/a
F: 1994 n/a Head: Adrian Baulf ICAO: NIGALANTIC Net: n/a

☐ 5N-EEO	Boeing 707-321C	19270 / 572	N705FW	0067	0695	4 PW JT3D-3B (HK2/COM)	151500	Freighter	AK-EL	
☐ 5N-TNO	Boeing 707-369C	20085 / 760	N725FW	0068	0695	4 PW JT3D-3B (HK2/COM)	151500	Freighter	BM-EK	

AIR BORDER PATROL UNIT — Lagos

c/o Ministry for Internal Affairs, PMB 12600, Ikeja, Nigeria ☎ (1) 63 40 00 Tx: 21236 ng Fax: n/a SITA: n/a
F: n/a n/a Head: n/a Net: n/a Non-commercial government organisation conducting patrol and rescue flights.

☐ 5N-AUV	Dornier 228-101	7011	D-ICIP*	0083	0683	2 GA TPE331-5-252D	5980	Surveyer		
☐ 5N-AUW	Dornier 228-101	7018	D-IBLB*	0083	0484	2 GA TPE331-5-252D	5980	Surveyer		
☐ 5N-AUX	Dornier 228-101	7095	D-CAGE*	0086	1291	2 GA TPE331-5-252D	5980	Surveyer		
☐ 5N-AUY	Dornier 228-101	7116	D-CIMA*	0087	1189	2 GA TPE331-5-252D	5980	Surveyer		
☐ 5N-AUZ	Dornier 228-101	7167	D-CAFA*	0088	0192	2 GA TPE331-5-252D	5980	Surveyer		

BELLVIEW AIRLINES, Ltd = B3 / BLV — Lagos

PO Box 6571, Lagos, Nigeria ☎ (1) 497 00 61 Tx: n/a Fax: (1) 61 57 25 SITA: n/a
F: 1992 70 Head: Kayode Odukoya IATA: 208 ICAO: BELLVIEW AIRLINES Net: n/a

☐ 5N-BLV	Boeing (Douglas) DC-9-32	47276 / 373	9G-ADN	0868	0395	2 PW JT8D-7B	48988	C12Y86		lsf Boeing Capital Corp.
☐ 5N-KAY	Boeing (Douglas) DC-9-32	47259 / 409	5N-VWE	1168	1293	2 PW JT8D-7B	48988	C12Y86		lsf Boeing Capital Corp. / std NAP
☐ YU-AJH	Boeing (Douglas) DC-9-32	47562 / 685	N1345U*	0072	1298	2 PW JT8D-9A	48988	CY106	GJ-FM	Abuja Shuttle / lsf JAT
☐ 5N-BVU	Airbus Industrie A300-622R (A300B4-622R)	633	VH-BWF	0092	1197	2 PW PW4158	171700	C26Y237	EG-CP	lsf NORD

BRISTOW HELICOPTERS (Nigeria), Ltd = BHN — Lagos / Calabar / Eket / Port Harcourt & Warri

PO Box 11, Ikeja, Nigeria ☎ (1) 496 15 01 Tx: 26111 brstow ng Fax: (1) 496 15 01 SITA: n/a
F: 1969 300 Head: Capt. J.T. Black ICAO: BRISTOW HELICOPTERS Net: n/a

☐ 5N-AQJ	Agusta-Bell 206B JetRanger	8051	G-BLPL	0067		1 AN 250-C20	1451			cvtd 206A
☐ 5N-BAK	Eurocopter (Aerosp.) AS355F1 Ecureuil 2	5102	G-BUEH	0082	0592	2 AN 250-C20F	2400			
☐ 5N-BAL	Eurocopter (Aerosp.) AS355F1 Ecureuil 2	5112	G-BUFW	0082	0592	2 AN 250-C20F	2400			
☐ 5N-SKY	Sikorsky S-76A+	760084	G-BJVZ	0080	1092	2 TU Arriel 1S	4899			cvtd S-76A
☐ 5N-AJT	Bell 212	30636	G-BCLG	0074		2 PWC PT6T-3 TwinPac	5080			
☐ 5N-AJU	Bell 212	30632	G-BFDJ	0074		2 PWC PT6T-3 TwinPac	5080			
☐ 5N-AJV	Bell 212	30868	G-BGMK	0078		2 PWC PT6T-3 TwinPac	5080			
☐ 5N-AJW	Bell 212	30601	G-BGML	0073		2 PWC PT6T-3 TwinPac	5080			
☐ 5N-ALQ	Bell 212	30670	G-BGMF	0074		2 PWC PT6T-3 TwinPac	5080			
☐ 5N-ALS	Bell 212	31170	G-BJGU	0080		2 PWC PT6T-3 TwinPac	5080			
☐ 5N-ALT	Bell 212	31171	G-BJGV	0080		2 PWC PT6T-3 TwinPac	5080			
☐ 5N-ALU	Bell 212	31197	G-BJIT	0081		2 PWC PT6T-3 TwinPac	5080			
☐ 5N-AOF	Bell 212	31200	G-BJIU	0081		2 PWC PT6T-3 TwinPac	5080			
☐ 5N-AOV	Bell 212	30627	VR-BFA	0074		2 PWC PT6T-3 TwinPac	5080			
☐ 5N-AQV	Bell 212	30782	VR-BIJ	0076		2 PWC PT6T-3 TwinPac	5080			
☐ 5N-AXX	Bell 212	30787	G-BSOA	0076	0191	2 PWC PT6T-3 TwinPac	5080			
☐ 5N-AYX	Bell 212	30599	N212NK	0073	0491	2 PWC PT6T-3 TwinPac	5080			
☐ 5N-BEN	Bell 212	30681	G-BOEP	0075	1296	2 PWC PT6T-3 TwinPac	5080			
☐ 5N-BHE	Bell 212	30666	G-BMVF	0074	0196	2 PWC PT6T-3 TwinPac	5080			
☐ 5N-BHM	Bell 212	32134	G-BJJO	0080	1192	2 PWC PT6T-3 TwinPac	5080			
☐ 5N-BHN	Bell 212	32135	G-BJJP	0080	1192	2 PWC PT6T-3 TwinPac	5080			
☐ 5N-AJR	De Havilland DHC-6 Twin Otter 300	611	G-BFYX	0079	0379	2 PWC PT6A-27	5670			
☐ 5N-BFW	De Havilland DHC-6 Twin Otter 300	798	C-FTJD	0082	0695	2 PWC PT6A-27	5670			
☐ 5N-BFL	Beech King Air B200	BB-1213	N7234L	0085	1296	2 PWC PT6A-42	5670			
☐ 5N-BHL	Beech King Air 200	BB-387	G-BFOL	0078	1192	2 PWC PT6A-42	5670			
☐ 5N-BRI	Dornier 328-110	3104		0097	1298	2 PWC PW119B	13990			
☐ 5N-SPC	Dornier 328-110	3083	D-CDXO*	0097	0397	2 PWC PW119B	13990	Corporate		opf Shell Petroleum in Shell-colors
☐ 5N-SPD	Dornier 328-110	3086	D-CDXH*	0097	0497	2 PWC PW119B	13990	Corporate		opf Shell Petroleum in Shell-colors

CHANCHANGI AIRLINES (Nigeria), Ltd - CAL = NCH — Kaduna

PO Box 679, Kaduna, Nigeria ☎ (62) 23 17 78 Tx: none Fax: (62) 23 10 10 SITA: n/a
F: 1997 n/a Head: Trevor Worthington ICAO: CHANCHANGI Net: n/a

☐ YU-AKD	Boeing 727-2L8 (A)	21040 / 1142	OY-SBJ	0075	0898	3 PW JT8D-15	86409	Y178	KL-EF	lsf AGX
☐ YU-AKH	Boeing 727-2L8 (A)	21080 / 1146	OY-SBP	0075	1098	3 PW JT8D-15	86409	Y178		lsf AGX
☐ YU-AKM	Boeing 727-243 (A)	22702 / 1814	HK-3618X	0082	1298	3 PW JT8D-15	83007	Y178		lsf AGX

CITY-LINK AIRLINES, Ltd = CRG — Port Harcourt

Airport, Port Harcourt, Nigeria ☎ (90) 50 08 43 Tx: none Fax: (90) 23 02 38 SITA: n/a
F: 1988 28 Head: Capt. Theo U. Onu ICAO: COURAGE Net: n/a

☐ 5N-TRB	Embraer 110P1 Bandeirante (EMB-110P1)				0097	2 PWC PT6A-34	5670	Y19		occ lsf AFK

DANA - Dornier Aviation Nigeria AIEP, Ltd = DAV (formerly PMAS Regional Airline) — Kaduna

PO Box 2124, Kaduna, Nigeria ☎ (62) 23 88 43 Tx: 71327 ng Fax: (62) 23 73 25 SITA: n/a
F: 1979 350 Head: Klaus D. Gloege ICAO: DANA AIR Net: n/a

☐ 5N-ARF	Dornier 228-201	8047	D-CDWF*	0084	0885	2 GA TPE331-5-252D	5980	Y19		
☐ 5N-ARP	Dornier 228-201	8013	D-IDMI*	0083	0883	2 GA TPE331-5-252D	5980	Y19		
☐ 5N-AUN	Dornier 228-201	8076	D-CEPT*	0085	0386	2 GA TPE331-5-252D	5980	Y19		
☐ 5N-DOA	Dornier 228-202	8025	N228RP	0084	0795	2 GA TPE331-5-252D	6200	Y19		cvtd -201
☐ 5N-DOB	Dornier 228-202	8026	N232RP	0084	0795	2 GA TPE331-5-252D	6200	Y19		cvtd -201
☐ 5N-DOC	Dornier 228-202	8041	N234RP	0084	0795	2 GA TPE331-5-252D	6200	Y19		cvtd -201
☐ 5N-DOD	Dornier 228-202	8048	N235RP	0085	0795	2 GA TPE331-5-252D	6200	Y19		cvtd -201
☐ 5N-DOE	Dornier 228-202	8049	N236RP	0085	0795	2 GA TPE331-5-252D	6200	Y19		cvtd -201
☐ 5N-DOF	Dornier 228-202	8125	N245RP	0087	0795	2 GA TPE331-5-252D	6200	Y19		cvtd -201
☐ 5N-DOG	Dornier 228-202	8040	N233RP	0084	0795	2 GA TPE331-10	6200	Y19		cvtd -201
☐ 5N-DOH	Dornier 228-202	8134	N239RP	0087	0795	2 GA TPE331-5-252D	6200	Y19		
☐ 5N-DOI	Dornier 228-202	8137	N237RP	0087	0796	2 GA TPE331-5-252D	6200	Y19		
☐ 5N-DOJ	Dornier 228-202	8138	N238RP	0087	0795	2 GA TPE331-5-252D	6200	Y19		
☐ 5N-DOK	Dornier 228-202	8140	N240RP	0087	0396	2 GA TPE331-5-252D	6200	Y19		
☐ 5N-DOL	Dornier 228-202	8145	N241RP	0088	0996	2 GA TPE331-5-252D	6200	Y19		
☐ 5N-DOM	Dornier 228-202	8147	N242RP	0088	0696	2 GA TPE331-5-252D	6200	Y19		
☐ 5N-IEP	Dornier 328-110	3026	D-CDHL*	0094	0098	2 PWC PW119B	13990	Y33		
☐ 5N-SAG	Dornier 328-110	3016	D-CASU*	0095	0598	2 PWC PW119B	13990	Y33		cvtd -100

EAS AIRLINES = EXW (Executive Airline Services, Ltd dba) — Lagos

29 Adeniyi Jones Avenue, PO Box 2051, Ikeja-Lagos, Nigeria ☎ (1) 497 50 16 Tx: none Fax: (1) 496 57 36 SITA: LOSTO7G
F: 1985 100 Head: Capt. Idris I. Wada ICAO: ECHOLINE Net: n/a

☐ 5N-EAS	Hawker 403B (HS 125-403B)	25217	G-OLFR	0070	1193	2 RR Viper 522	10705	Y8		
☐ 5N-ESA	BAe (BAC) One-Eleven 501EX	174	G-AWYR	0069	1298	2 RR Spey 512-14DW(HK2)	41950	F20Y74		
☐ 5N-ESB	BAe (BAC) One-Eleven 501EX	175	G-AWYS	0069	1098	2 RR Spey 512-14DW(HK2)	41950	F20Y74		

EMPIRE AVIATION, Ltd (Associated with Arkia Israeli Airlines, Ltd & Koor Industries, Ltd) — Lagos

PO Box 340, Apapa-Lagos, Nigeria ☎ (1) 587 46 58 Tx: none Fax: (1) 587 40 21 SITA: n/a
F: 1999 n/a Head: Amatia Smir Net: n/a Presently being set-up. Intends to start operations 0599.

☐ 4X-AHD	De Havilland DHC-7-102 Dash 7	055	N8102N	0081		4 PWC PT6A-50	19958	Y54		to be lsf AIZ 0599
☐ 4X-AHL	De Havilland DHC-7-102 Dash 7	049	N340JK	0081		4 PWC PT6A-50	19958	Y54		to be lsf AIZ 0599

GAS AIR = NGS (General & Aviation Services, Ltd dba) — Lagos & Ostend

PMB 21231, Ikeja, Nigeria ☎ (1) 93 35 10 Tx: 27621 gasair ng Fax: (1) 96 28 41 SITA: n/a
F: 1973 150 Head: S.K.S. Olubadewo ICAO: GENAIR Net: n/a

☐ 5N-AXV	BAe (BAC) One-Eleven 424EU	159	YR-BCD	0069		2 RR Spey 511-14	39463	Y89		
☐ 5N-SKS	BAe (BAC) One-Eleven 481FW	243	7Q-YKF	0072	1192	2 RR Spey 512-14DW	41730	Y74		

HARKA AIR SERVICES (N), Ltd = HAK — Lagos

42 Allen Avenue, Ikeja, Nigeria ☎ (6) 221 21 39 Tx: none Fax: none SITA: n/a
F: 1992 n/a Head: Alhaji Rabiu Isyaku ICAO: HARKA SERVICES Net: n/a

☐ EW-87330	Yakovlev 40	9510139	CCCP-87330	0275	0097	3 IV AI-25	16800	Y36		lsf MOG

HOLD-TRADE AIR (Hold Trade Air Services, Ltd dba) — Kaduna

No. 6A Sokoto Road, Kaduna, Nigeria ☎ (62) 21 54 05 Tx: n/a Fax: (62) 23 53 68 SITA: n/a
F: 1991 230 Head: Zakari Hamura Net: n/a

☐ 5N-HTB	BAe (BAC) One-Eleven 208AL	052	EI-ANH	0065	0791	2 RR Spey 506-14	35834			
☐ 5N-HTC	BAe (BAC) One-Eleven 208AL	049	EI-ANE	0065	0991	2 RR Spey 506-14	35834			std SEN

692 registration type of aircraft cn/fn ex/ex* mfd del powered by mtow kg configuration selcal name/fln/specialitites/remarks

☐ 5N-HTD	BAe (BAC) One-Eleven 208AL	050	EI-ANF	0065	0392	2 RR Spey 506-14	35834			

IAT CARGO AIRLINES = VGO (International Air Tours dba)

Lagos

European HQ:, PO Box 48, B-8400 Ostend, Belgium ☎ (59) 55 15 84 Tx: none Fax: (59) 51 67 24 SITA: n/a
F: 1994 ⚲ n/a Head: Peter Barnes ICAO: VIRGO Net: n/a Suspended operations (with Boeing 707C aircraft) 1198 but intends to re-start in 1999.

KABO AIR = QNK (Kabo Air Travels dba / Subsidiary of Kabo Holdings, Ltd)

Kano

PO Box 3439, Kano, Nigeria ☎ (64) 64 95 91 Tx: 77277 kabotl ng Fax: (64) 64 93 30 SITA: KANDZKO
F: 1980 ⚲ 600 Head: Alhaji Dan Kabo ICAO: KABO Net: n/a

☐ 5N-CCC	BAe (BAC) One-Eleven 401AK	069	VR-CCS	0066	1196	2 RR Spey 511-14	40597	Executive		
☐ 5N-GGG	BAe (BAC) One-Eleven 423ET	154	G-BEJW	0069	0793	2 RR Spey 511-14W	39463	Y84		Muhammadu Sbubakar Rimi / std KAN
☐ 5N-HHH	BAe (BAC) One-Eleven 401AK	064	HZ-NB2	0066	0797	2 RR Spey 511-14	40597	Executive		
☐ 5N-KBE	BAe (BAC) One-Eleven 204AF	030	N1112J	0065	0291	2 RR Spey 506-14D	35834	Y84		
☐ 5N-KBM	BAe (BAC) One-Eleven 215AU	105	N1132J	0067	1091	2 RR Spey 506-14D	35834	Y84		Mahammadu Dikko
☐ 5N-KBW	BAe (BAC) One-Eleven 407AW	106	G-BSXV	0067	0292	2 RR Spey 511-14	39463	Y84		std KAN
☐ 5N-KKK	BAe (BAC) One-Eleven 414EG	160	G-BFMC	0070	0793	2 RR Spey 511-14W	38900	Y84		Malambarnabas
☐ 5N-VVV	BAe (BAC) One-Eleven 401AK	080	HZ-BL1	0066	0897	2 RR Spey 511-14 (HK)	40597	Executive		
☐ 5N-KBX	Boeing 727-225	20444 / 839	N8846E	0070	1192	3 PW JT8D-7B	78245	Y164	HM-EF	std KAN
☐ 5N-KBY	Boeing 727-225	20442 / 836	N8844E	0070	1192	3 PW JT8D-7B	78245	Y164	HM-DK	
☐ 5N-LLL	Boeing 727-224 (A)	20654 / 930	N32724	0073	1294	3 PW JT8D-9A	78245	Y164	FG-DH	
☐ 5N-MMM	Boeing 727-224 (A)	20656 / 938	N66726	0073	1194	3 PW JT8D-9A	78245	Y164	FG-EH	
☐ 5N-TTT	Boeing 727-224	20463 / 807	N32721	0072	1194	3 PW JT8D-9A	78245	Y164	DM-EH	cvtd -2F2
☐ 5N-AAA	Boeing 747-148	19745 / 108	EI-ASJ	0071	0297	4 PW JT9D-7A	322504	Y504	BL-CG	
☐ 5N-ZZZ	Boeing 747-148	19744 / 84	EI-ASI	0070	0297	4 PW JT9D-3A	322504	Y504	BL-CG	

KOLKOL AIRLINES = KKL

Lagos

Murtala Mohammed Airport, Domestic Terminal, Ikeja, Nigeria ☎ (1) 470 17 79 Tx: none Fax: none SITA: n/a
F: n/a ⚲ n/a Head: n/a ICAO: KOLKOL AIR Net: n/a

☐ ER-AFY	Antonov 24RV	47309809	YR-AMY	1074	0299	2 IV AI-24VT	21800	Y48		lsf RAN

NIGERIA AIRWAYS, Ltd = WT / NGA

Lagos

PMB 21024, Ikeja, Nigeria ☎ (1) 90 08 10 Tx: 22203 ng Fax: (1) 493 63 47 SITA: LOSCPWT
F: 1958 ⚲ 4300 Head: Grp. Capt. Peter N. Gana IATA: 087 ICAO: NIGERIA Net: n/a

☐ 5N-ANC	Boeing 737-2F9 (A)	20671 / 312		0072	0173	2 PW JT8D-15/-15A	52390	F12Y95	FH-DL	
☐ 5N-AND	Boeing 737-2F9 (A)	20672 / 313		0072	0173	2 PW JT8D-15/-15A	52390	Y123	FH-DM	
☐ 5N-ANW	Boeing 737-2F9 (A)	22771 / 866		0082	1082	2 PW JT8D-15/-15A	52390	Y129		
☐ 5N-ANY	Boeing 737-2F9 (A)	22773 / 893		0082	0283	2 PW JT8D-15/-15A	52390	Y129	AG-CH	
☐ 5N-AUB	Boeing 737-2F9 (A)	22986 / 925		0082	0283	2 PW JT8D-15/-15A	52390	Y129	AJ-FH	
☐ 5N-AUF	Airbus Industrie A310-222	285	F-WZEB*	0083	1284	2 PW JT9D-7R4E1	138600	F24Y195	EJ-DL	River Ethiope
☐ 5N-ANO	Boeing 707-3F9C	21428 / 929		0078	0178	4 PW JT3D-3B	151046	F16Y130	KL-DE	std DUB
☐ 5N-ANN	Boeing (Douglas) DC-10-30	46957 / 231		0076	1076	3 GE CF6-50C	251744	F32Y231	FK-CJ	Yankari

OKADA AIR, Ltd = OKJ

Benin City & Lagos

17B Sapele Road, Benin City, (Bendel), Nigeria ☎ (19) 24 15 04 Tx: n/a Fax: n/a SITA: n/a
F: 1983 ⚲ 2600 Head: Chief Gabriel Igbinedion ICAO: OKADA AIR Net: n/a

☐ 5N-AOM	BAe (BAC) One-Eleven 420EL	122	C-GQBP	0067	0286	2 RR Spey 511-14	39463			
☐ 5N-AOP	BAe (BAC) One-Eleven 320AZ	109	G-BKAV	0067	0983	2 RR Spey 511-14	40597			
☐ 5N-AOS	BAe (BAC) One-Eleven 420EL	123	C-GQBV	0067	1185	2 RR Spey 511-14	39463			
☐ 5N-AXQ	BAe (BAC) One-Eleven 432FD	157	G-AXMU	0068	1090	2 RR Spey 511-14	40597			
☐ 5N-AXT	BAe (BAC) One-Eleven 432FD	121	G-AXOX	0068	0690	2 RR Spey 511-14	40597			
☐ 5N-AYR	BAe (BAC) One-Eleven 409AY	162	G-AXBB	0069	1089	2 RR Spey 511-14	40597			
☐ 5N-AYS	BAe (BAC) One-Eleven 416EK	129	N390BA	0068	0987	2 RR Spey 511-14	40597			
☐ 5N-AYT	BAe (BAC) One-Eleven 416EK	131	N392BA	0068	0587	2 RR Spey 511-14	40597			
☐ 5N-AYU	BAe (BAC) One-Eleven 401AK	062	N800MC	0066	0587	2 RR Spey 511-14	40143			
☐ 5N-AYV	BAe (BAC) One-Eleven 408EF	128	G-NIII	0069	1186	2 RR Spey 511-14	39900			
☐ 5N-EHI	BAe (BAC) One-Eleven 401AK	074	G-BBMF	0066	0891	2 RR Spey 511-14	39900			
☐ 5N-MZE	BAe (BAC) One-Eleven 304AX	110	G-BPNX	0066	0591	2 RR Spey 511-14	40143			
☐ 5N-NRC	BAe (BAC) One-Eleven 217EA	124	5N-TOM	0067	1091	2 RR Spey 506-14	35834			
☐ 5N-OMO	BAe (BAC) One-Eleven 301AG	034	G-ATPK	0066	0591	2 RR Spey 511-14	40597			
☐ 5N-OVE	BAe (BAC) One-Eleven 304AX	112	G-WLAD	0066	0591	2 RR Spey 511-14	40143			
☐ 5N-SDP	BAe (BAC) One-Eleven 217EA	125	G-KROO	0068	0192	2 RR Spey 506-14	35834			
☐ 5N-BIN	BAe (BAC) One-Eleven 539GL	265	G-BGKG	0080	0791	2 RR Spey 512-14DW	44000			
☐ 5N-ORO	BAe (BAC) One-Eleven 539GL	264	G-BGKF	0080	0791	2 RR Spey 512-14DW	44000			
☐ 5N-USE	BAe (BAC) One-Eleven 524FF	235	7Q-YKK	0071	0792	2 RR Spey 512-14DW	47400			

ORIENTAL AIRLINES, Ltd = OAC

Lagos

PO Box 75543, Victoria Island, Lagos, Nigeria ☎ (1) 83 11 08 Tx: 27880 ng Fax: (1) 83 30 37 SITA: n/a
F: 1989 ⚲ n/a Head: Dr. Emanuel Iwanyanwu ICAO: ORIENTAL AIR Net: n/a

☐ 5N-ECI	BAe (BAC) One-Eleven 476FM	241	G-AZUK	0071	0596	2 RR Spey 512-14DW	44679	Executive		
☐ 5N-ENO	BAe (BAC) One-Eleven 515FB	208	G-OBWH	0070	0795	2 RR Spey 512-14DW	46948			
☐ 5N-EYI	BAe (BAC) One-Eleven 523FJ	211	EI-CCX	0270	1194	2 RR Spey 512-14DW	47400			
☐ 5N-OAL	BAe (BAC) One-Eleven 501EX	214	G-AXJM	0070	0993	2 RR Spey 512-14DW	41950			

PAN AFRICAN Airlines (Nigeria), Ltd

Lagos / Escravos

PMB 21054, Ikeja, Nigeria ☎ (1) 496 37 98 Tx: 26053 panafr ng Fax: (1) 496 39 72 SITA: n/a
F: 1961 ⚲ 94 Head: Chris Ogunbanjo Net: n/a

☐ 5N-APL	Bell 206B JetRanger	1527		0074		1 AN 250-C20	1451			
☐ 5N-AQO	Bell 206B JetRanger III	3765	N31800	0083		1 AN 250-C20J	1451			
☐ 5N-AVU	Bell 206B JetRanger III	2300	N30WA	0077	0289	1 AN 250-C20B	1451			
☐ 5N-BAG	Bell 206B JetRanger III	2728	N2760T	0079		1 AN 250-C20B	1451			
☐ 5N-BAJ	Bell 206B JetRanger III	2424	N5002D	0078		1 AN 250-C20B	1451			
☐ 5N-BAP	Bell 206B JetRanger III	3235	G-OCHL	0081	1293	1 AN 250-C20B	1451			
☐ 5N-AJC	Bell 206L LongRanger	45095		0077		1 AN 250-C20B	1814			
☐ 5N-AMQ	Bell 206L-1 LongRanger II	45746		0082		1 AN 250-C28B	1882			
☐ 5N-AQB	Bell 206L-1 LongRanger II	45506		0080		1 AN 250-C28B	1882			
☐ 5N-AQP	Bell 206L-1 LongRanger II	45604	N3907E	0081		1 AN 250-C28B	1882			
☐ 5N-BAS	Bell 206L-1 LongRanger II	45367	N1076K	0080		1 AN 250-C28B	1882			
☐ 5N-PAA	Bell 206L-1 LongRanger II	45659	N39118	0081		1 AN 250-C28B	1882			
☐ 5N-PAN	Cessna 208 Caravan I	20800200	N51558	0091	0193	1 PWC PT6A-114	3629			Amphibian
☐ 5N-WMB	Cessna 208 Caravan I	20800158	N705A	0089	0696	1 PWC PT6A-114	3629			Amphibian
☐ 5N-AMW	Cessna 425 Conquest I	425-0067	N6844V	0081		2 PWC PT6A-112	3719			
☐ 5N-WMA	Hawker 400B (HS 125-400B)	25178	G-OOSP	0069	0896	2 RR Viper 522	10569			

PREMIUM AIR SHUTTLE, Ltd - PAS = EMI

Lagos

Murtala Mohammed Airport, Domestic Terminal, Ikeja, Nigeria ☎ n/a Tx: none Fax: n/a SITA: n/a
F: 1996 ⚲ n/a Head: n/a ICAO: BLUE SHUTTLE Net: n/a

☐ 5N-BOS	Yakovlev 40	9341431	LZ-DOA	0073	0096	3 IV AI-25	16000	Executive		
☐ 5N-DAN	Yakovlev 40	9340632	LZ-DOD	1273	0096	3 IV AI-25	16000	Executive		
☐ 5N-MAR	Yakovlev 40		LZ-	0073	0096	3 IV AI-25	16000	Executive		

SKY POWER EXPRESS AIRWAYS = EAN (Express Airways Nigeria, Ltd dba / Associated with Nigeria Airways)

Lagos

PO Box 54110-Falomo, Lagos, Nigeria ☎ (1) 269 32 75 Tx: 22791 eal ng Fax: (1) 269 32 53 SITA: n/a
F: 1985 ⚲ 250 Head: Capt. Mohammed Joji ICAO: NIGERIA EXPRESS Net: n/a On order (letter of intent): 15 Embraer 145 Amazon.

☐ 5N-AXK	Embraer 110P1A Bandeirante (EMB-110P1A)	110449	PT-SHG*	0084	0586	2 PWC PT6A-34	5900			
☐ 5N-AXL	Embraer 110P1A Bandeirante (EMB-110P1A)	110455	PT-SHJ*	0084	1086	2 PWC PT6A-34	5900			
☐ 5N-AXM	Embraer 110P1A Bandeirante (EMB-110P1A)	110446	PT-SHD*	0084	0586	2 PWC PT6A-34	5900			
☐ 5N-AXR	Embraer 110P1A Bandeirante (EMB-110P1A)	110459	PT-SHM*	0085	0686	2 PWC PT6A-34	5900			

SMA AIRLINES (Nig.), Ltd = SMA

Lagos

Murtala Muhammed Airport, Cargo Terminal, Ikeja, Nigeria ☎ n/a Tx: none Fax: n/a SITA: n/a
F: 1997 ⚲ n/a Head: n/a ICAO: SESAME Net: n/a

☐ 5N-SMA	Boeing 727-23 (F)	19388 / 340	HC-BRF	0066	0598	3 PW JT8D-7B	76884	Freighter		lsf Natu Exports / cvtd -23

TRIAX AIRLINES, Ltd = TIX (Member of Triax Group of Companies)

Enugu

Airport, Enugu, Nigeria ☎ (42) 55 15 22 Tx: n/a Fax: (42) 25 30 00 SITA: n/a
F: 1992 ⚲ 200 Head: HRH Prince Arthur Eze ICAO: TRIAX Net: n/a

☐ 5N-TKE	Boeing 727-82	19406 / 430	C-GWGV	0067	1092	3 PW JT8D-7B	72724	F12Y98	JL-DM	Eze-Ukpo
☐ 5N-TKT	Boeing 727-22	18330 / 156	5N-ORI	0065	0296	3 PW JT8D-7B	72802	F12Y98		
☐ 5N-TTK	Boeing 727-264	20432 / 827	HK-3421X	0070	1193	3 PW JT8D-7B	83007	F12Y138		Chinweze / std LIS

693 registration type of aircraft cn/fn ex/ex* mfd del powered by mtow kg configuration selcal name/fln/specialitites/remarks

5R = MADAGASCAR (Democratic Republic of Madagascar) (République Démocratique de Madagascar)
Capital: Antananarivo Official Language: French, Malagasy Population: 15,0 million Square Km: 587041 Dialling code: +261 Year established: 1960 Acting political head: Didier Ratsiraka (President)

Government / Corporate / Executive / VIP Aircraft

registration	type of aircraft	cn/fn	ex/ex*	mfd	del	powered by	mtow kg	configuration	selcal	name/fln/specialitites/remarks
5R-MUA	Yakovlev 40	9840859		0078	1278	3 IV AI-25	16000	VIP		Armée de l'Air Malgache
5R-MUB	Yakovlev 40			0079		3 IV AI-25	16000	VIP		Armée de l'Air Malgache

AEROMARINE (Subsidiary of Société Industrielle et Commercial Barday Holding)   Antananarivo-Ivato
BP 3844, Antananarivo 101, Madagascar ☎ (2022) 46 831 Tx: none Fax: (2022) 46 832 SITA: n/a
F: 1991 ✦✦✦ 40 Head: Riaz Barday Net: n/a Aircraft below MTOW 1361kg: Maule MX7-180B

registration	type of aircraft	cn/fn	ex/ex*	mfd	del	powered by	mtow kg	configuration	selcal	name/fln/specialitites/remarks
5R-MLI	Cessna 207A Stationair 7 II	20700496	5R-MVR	0078		1 CO IO-520-F	1724			
5R-MIK	Piper PA-23-250 Aztec B	27-2191	TL-ABA	0062	0098	2 LY O-540-A1D5	2177			
5R-MIL	Piper PA-23-250 Aztec D	27-4178	TL-ACD	0069	0098	2 LY IO-540-C4B5	2359			
5R-MLK	Beech Baron C55 (95-C55)	TE-101	F-BOJG	0066	0998	2 CO IO-520-C	2404			
5R-MLJ	Cessna 310R II	310R1372	F-GBGB	0078	1097	2 CO IO-520-M	2495			
5R-MLT	Cessna 310R II	310R0328	F-BXLT	0075	1297	2 CO IO-520-M	2495			
5R-MBR	Aerospatiale SN601 Corvette	16	5R-MVN	0075	1098	2 PWC JT15D-4	7000			

AIR MADAGASCAR = MD / MDG (Sté Nat. Malgache de Transports Aériens dba)   Antananarivo-Ivato
BP 437, Antananarivo 101, Madagascar ☎ (2022) 44 222 Tx: 22232 madair tana Fax: (2022) 44 674 SITA: TNRDDMD
F: 1962 ✦✦✦ 1200 Head: Emmanuel Rakotovahiny IATA: 258 ICAO: AIR MADAGASCAR Net: n/a

registration	type of aircraft	cn/fn	ex/ex*	mfd	del	powered by	mtow kg	configuration	selcal	name/fln/specialitites/remarks
5R-MGC	De Havilland DHC-6 Twin Otter 300	328		0071	0771	2 PWC PT6A-27	5670	Y19		
5R-MGD	De Havilland DHC-6 Twin Otter 300	329		0071	0771	2 PWC PT6A-27	5670	Y19		
5R-MGE	De Havilland DHC-6 Twin Otter 300	330		0071	0771	2 PWC PT6A-27	5670	Y19		
5R-MGF	De Havilland DHC-6 Twin Otter 300	482		0076	0576	2 PWC PT6A-27	5670	Y19		
5R-MJC	ATR 42-300	132	5R-MVK	0089	0997	2 PWC PW120	16700	Y48		
5R-MJD	ATR 42-300	155	5R-MVX	0089	1097	2 PWC PW120	16700	Y48		
5R-MJA	BAe (HS) 748-360 Srs 2B (SCD)	1772 / 249		0079	0180	2 RR Dart 536-2	21092	Y44 / Combi		Kandreho
5R-MJB	BAe (HS) 748-360 Srs 2B (SCD)	1773 / 251		0080	1180	2 RR Dart 536-2	21092	Y44 / Combi		
5R-MFA	Boeing 737-2B2	20231 / 204		0069	0969	2 PW JT8D-9	49441	Y122	AC-DM	Boina
5R-MFB	Boeing 737-2B2 (A)	20680 / 314		0072	1272	2 PW JT8D-15	52390	Y125	AC-EF	Sambirano
5R-MFH	Boeing 737-3Q8	26305 / 2651		0094		2 CFMI CFM56-3C1	62142	Y140		Isf ILFC
5R-MVZ	Boeing 767-33A (ER)	25403 / 409	CC-CEU	0092	0498	2 PW PW4060	184612	F10C20Y185		Isf GECA
5R-MFT	Boeing 747-2B2B (M)	21614 / 353		0079	0179	4 PW JT9D-70A	362873	F16C24Y230 / Plt	AK-EF	Ankoay / for sale

MADAGASCAR FLYING SERVICE   Antananarivo-Ivato
BP 3947, Antananarivo 101, Madagascar ☎ (2022) 35 206 Tx: none Fax: (2022) 35 206 SITA: n/a
F: n/a ✦✦✦ n/a Head: n/a Net: n/a

registration	type of aircraft	cn/fn	ex/ex*	mfd	del	powered by	mtow kg	configuration	selcal	name/fln/specialitites/remarks
5R-MHR	Piper PA-31-350 Navajo Chieftain	31-7852082	OY-ATP	0078	0793	2 LY TIO-540-J2BD	3175			Isf pvt
5R-MVC	Cessna 402B	402B0014	F-BRSM	0070	0296	2 CO TSIO-520-E	2858			

MALAGASY AIRLINES = MLG (Subsidiary of ADF-Aerotours Développements Finance, S.A.)   Antananarivo-Ivato
BP 797, Antananarivo 101, Madagascar ☎ (2022) 44 137 Tx: none Fax: (2022) 44 330 SITA: n/a
F: 1996 ✦✦✦ n/a Head: Philippe Cazals&Laurent Razafimbahoaka Net: n/a

registration	type of aircraft	cn/fn	ex/ex*	mfd	del	powered by	mtow kg	configuration	selcal	name/fln/specialitites/remarks
5R-MVJ	Piper PA-23-250 Aztec A	27-409	HB-LCB	0060	0697	2 LY O-540-A1B5	2177			
5R-MVL	Cessna 208 Caravan I	20800001	HB-CLD	0084	0596	1 PWC PT6A-114	3629			Isf ADF, Paris

TAM – Transports & Travaux Aériens de Madagascar = OF / TML (Associated with Air Madagascar)   Antananarivo-Ivato, Majunga & Tulear
BP 876, Antananarivo 101, Madagascar ☎ (2022) 27 036 Tx: none Fax: (2022) 30 540 SITA: TNRWWMD
F: 1951 ✦✦✦ 135 Head: Aubry Redia IATA: 561 ICAO: TAM AIRLINE Net: http://www.madagascar-contacts.com/tam. Aircraft & Ag-aircraft below MTOW 1361/5000kg: Cessna 182, Piper PA-18, PA-25 & PA-36.

registration	type of aircraft	cn/fn	ex/ex*	mfd	del	powered by	mtow kg	configuration	selcal	name/fln/specialitites/remarks
5R-MCJ	Piper PA-23-250 Aztec C	27-3644	N6449Y	0067		2 LY IO-540-C4B5	2359	Y4		
5R-MCK	Piper PA-23-250 Aztec C	27-3652	N6441Y	0067		2 LY IO-540-C4B5	2359	Y4		
5R-MVT	ATR 42-320	044	F-WQAD*	0087	1294	2 PWC PW121	16700	Y48		Isf A.I.R. / cvtd -320

5T = MAURITANIA (Islamic Republic of Mauritania) (al-Jumhouriya al-Muslimiya al-Mauritaniya)
Capital: Nouakchott Official Language: Arabic Population: 2,5 million Square Km: 1025520 Dialling code: +222 Year established: 1960 Acting political head: Col. Maaouya Ould Sidi Ahmed Taya (President)

AIR AFRIQUE = multinational state carrier – see under TU- markings

AIR MAURITANIE = MR / MRT   Nouakchott
BP 41, Nouakchott 174, Mauritania ☎ (2) 52 721 Tx: 573 airrim Fax: (2) 52 721 SITA: n/a
F: 1962 ✦✦✦ 300 Head: Sidi Ould Zein IATA: 174 Net: n/a

registration	type of aircraft	cn/fn	ex/ex*	mfd	del	powered by	mtow kg	configuration	selcal	name/fln/specialitites/remarks
5T-TJY	Piper PA-31T Cheyenne II	31T-7920056	F-ODJS	0079		2 PWC PT6A-28	4082	Y5		
5T-CLG	Fokker F28 Fellowship 4000 (F28 Mk4000)	11093	PH-ZBL	0075	1283	2 RR Spey 555-15P	33112	Y79		cvtd -6000

5U = NIGER (Republic of Niger) (République de Niger)
Capital: Niamey Official Language: French Population: 9,0 million Square Km: 1267000 Dialling code: +227 Year established: 1960 Acting political head: General Ibrahim Barre Mainassara (President)

Government / Corporate / Executive / VIP Aircraft

registration	type of aircraft	cn/fn	ex/ex*	mfd	del	powered by	mtow kg	configuration	selcal	name/fln/specialitites/remarks
5U-BAG	Boeing 737-2N9C (A)	21499 / 513		0078	0478	2 PW JT8D-17	52390	VIP		Monts Baghezan / Gvmt

AIR AFRIQUE = multinational state carrier – see under TU- markings

AIR INTER NIGER = AWH   Niamey
BP 11090, Niamey, Niger ☎ 73 44 41 Tx: none Fax: 73 52 28 SITA: n/a
F: 1995 ✦✦✦ n/a Head: n/a ICAO: INTER NIGER Net: n/a Operates passenger flights with Embraer 110P2 Bandeirante aircraft, leased from AIR BURKINA (XT-) when required.

NIGER AIR SERVICE   Niamey
BP 10605, Niamey, Niger ☎ 72 31 87 Tx: n/a Fax: 72 40 54 SITA: n/a
F: 1995 ✦✦✦ n/a Head: Kabo Abdoulaye Net: n/a

registration	type of aircraft	cn/fn	ex/ex*	mfd	del	powered by	mtow kg	configuration	selcal	name/fln/specialitites/remarks
5U-AAP	Piper PA-31-350 Navajo Chieftain	31-7405406	N66876	0074		2 LY TIO-540-J2BD	3175			

NIGERAVIA (formerly Transniger Aviation, Sarl)   Niamey
PO Box 10454, Niamey, Niger ☎ 73 30 64 Tx: 5250 locavia ni Fax: 74 18 42 SITA: n/a
F: 1968 ✦✦✦ 30 Head: Jean Sylvestre Net: n/a Ag-Aircraft below MTOW 5000 kg: Cessna A188B AgTruck.

registration	type of aircraft	cn/fn	ex/ex*	mfd	del	powered by	mtow kg	configuration	selcal	name/fln/specialitites/remarks
5U-ARN	Piper PA-23-250 Aztec E	27-4830		0072		2 LY IO-540-C4B5	2360			
5U-ABZ	Britten-Norman BN-2A-8 Islander	702	OY-DZV	0074	0798	2 LY O-540-E4C5	2994			
5U-ABX	Beech King Air 200	BB-531	SE-LDM	0079	0297	2 PWC PT6A-41	5670			
5U-ABY	Beech King Air 200	BB-431	F-GILH	0078	0398	2 PWC PT6A-41	5670			

5V = TOGO (Togolese Republic) (République Togolaise)
Capital: Lomé Official Language: French Population: 4,5 million Square Km: 56785 Dialling code: +228 Year established: 1960 Acting political head: Etienne Gnassingbé Eyadéma (President)

Government / Corporate / Executive / VIP Aircraft

registration	type of aircraft	cn/fn	ex/ex*	mfd	del	powered by	mtow kg	configuration	selcal	name/fln/specialitites/remarks
5V-TAG	Boeing 707-312B	19739 / 765	N600CS	0068	0186	4 PW JT3D-3B (HK2)	146300	VIP	AB-HL	Gvmt
5V-TAI	Fokker F28 Fellowship 1000 (F28 Mk1000)	11079	5V-MAB	0074	0475	2 RR Spey 555-15	29480	VIP / Y65		Gvmt / occ lst/jtlyopw PCT

AFRICA WEST = 3L / WTA   Lome
BP 10019, Lomé, Togo ☎ 26 88 10 Tx: none Fax: 26 88 10 SITA: LFWAW8X
F: 1997 ✦✦✦ 19 Head: Yannick Erbs IATA: 360 ICAO: WEST TOGO Net: n/a Beside aircraft listed, also uses Antonov 12 & Boeing 707C aircraft, leased from other companies when required.

registration	type of aircraft	cn/fn	ex/ex*	mfd	del	powered by	mtow kg	configuration	selcal	name/fln/specialitites/remarks
ER-ADI	Antonov 32B	3205	RA-48140	0193	0098	2 IV AI-20D	27000	Freighter		Isf RAN

AIR AFRIQUE = multinational state carrier – see under TU- markings

PEACE AIR TOGO = PCT   Lome
BP 10187, Lomé, Togo ☎ 26 12 40 Tx: none Fax: 21 72 94 SITA: n/a
F: 1992 ✦✦✦ 30 Head: Djibom Tekoe Aristide ICAO: PEACEFUL Net: n/a

registration	type of aircraft	cn/fn	ex/ex*	mfd	del	powered by	mtow kg	configuration	selcal	name/fln/specialitites/remarks
5V-TAI	Fokker F28 Fellowship 1000 (F28 Mk1000)	11079	5V-MAB	0074		2 RR Spey 555-15	29480	Y65		occ lsf/jtly opw Gvmt

5W = SAMOA (Independent State of Western Samoa) (Malotuto'atasi o Samoa i Sisifo)
Capital: Apia Official Language: English, Samoan Population: 0,2 million Square Km: 2831 Dialling code: +685 Year established: 1962 Acting political head: Malietoa Tanufamili II (King)

PACIFIC HELICOPTERS   Apia-Fagali'I
PO Box 3016, Apia, Samoa ☎ 20 047 Tx: n/a Fax: 20 047 SITA: n/a
F: 1991 ✦✦✦ n/a Head: n/a Net: n/a

registration	type of aircraft	cn/fn	ex/ex*	mfd	del	powered by	mtow kg	configuration	selcal	name/fln/specialitites/remarks
5W-HWR	Bell 206B JetRanger	919	ZK-HWR	0072	1191	1 AN 250-C20	1451			

POLYNESIAN – Airline of Samoa = PH / PAO (Polynesian, Ltd dba) — Apia-Fagali'l & -Faleolo

PO Box 599, Apia, Samoa ☎ 21 261 Tx: 249 palapw sx Fax: 20 023 SITA: APWGZPH
F: 1959 ⁂ 300 Head: Hon Tuilaepa Sailele Malielegaoi IATA: 162 ICAO: POLYNESIAN Net: n/a

☐ 5W-FAV	Britten-Norman BN-2A-8 Islander	42	ZK-FMS	0066		2 LY O-540-E4C5	2858	Y9		Samoa Star
☐ 5W-FAY	De Havilland DHC-6 Twin Otter 320	690	VH-UQW	0080	0298	2 PWC PT6A-27	5670	Y19		
☐ 5W-PAH	De Havilland DHC-6 Twin Otter 320	516	VH-FNX	0076	1295	2 PWC PT6A-27	5670	Y19		
☐ 5W-ILF	Boeing 737-3Q8	26282 / 2355		0092	0992	2 CFMI CFM56-3B2	62142	CY126	FP-KR	To'oa

5X = UGANDA (Republic of Uganda) (Jamhouriya Uganda)

Capital: Kampala Official Language: Swahili, English Population: 22,0 million Square Km: 235880 Dialling code: +256 Year established: 1962 Acting political head: Lieutenant-General Yoweri Kaguta Museveni (President)

Government / Corporate / Executive / VIP Aircraft

☐ 5X-UOI	GAC G-1159A Gulfstream III	345	G-GIII	0082	1293	2 RR Spey 511-8	30935	VIP		Gvmt

DAS AIR CARGO = SE / DSR (Dairo Air Limited dba) — Entebbe

European office: 1st Floor, North Suite, Elm Park Court, Tilgate FBC, Brighton Road, Crawley, Sussex RH11 9BP, Great Britain ☎ (1293) 54 03 03 Tx: 878148 g Fax: (1293) 55 15 45 SITA: LGWCCSE
F: 1983 ⁂ 170 Head: Daisy & Capt. Joe Roy IATA: 761 ICAO: DASAIR Net: n/a

☐ 5X-JEF	Boeing 707-379C	19821 / 718	9G-WON	0068	0993	4 PW JT3D-3B (HK2/COM)	150955	Freighter	BD-EL	
☐ 5X-JET	Boeing 707-351C	19411 / 540	N740FW	0066	0294	4 PW JT3D-3B (HK2/COM)	150955	Freighter	EM-BJ	lsf Jet Com
☐ 5N-ARQ	Boeing 707-338C	18809 / 407	N4225J	0065	0184	4 PW JT3D-3B (HK2/COM)	150955	Freighter	AC-FG	
☐ 5X-JOE	Boeing (Douglas) DC-10-30F	47906 / 115	N116WA	0073	1095	3 GE CF6-50C2	256280	Freighter	CM-AK	cvtd (CF)
☐ N400JR	Boeing (Douglas) DC-10-30F	46976 / 254	N602DC	0078	1297	3 GE CF6-50C2	259455	Freighter	AM-EF	lsf GECA/cvtd -30/TFA Flower tail cs
☐ N800WR	Boeing (Douglas) DC-10-30F	46955 / 228	N301FV	0076	0599	3 GE CF6-50C2	259455	Freighter	EG-AD	lsf Finova Capital Corp. / cvtd -30

EAGLE UGANDA = EGU (Eagle Aviation (Uganda), Ltd dba) — Entebbe

PO Box 7392/312, Kampala, Uganda ☎ (41) 34 22 07 Tx: none Fax: (41) 34 45 01 SITA: n/a
F: 1996 ⁂ n/a Head: Capt. Tony Rubombara ICAO: AFRICAN EAGLE Net: n/a

☐ 5X-CNF	Let 410A	730208	OK-DKD	0073	0097	2 PWC PT6A-27	5700	Y17		
☐ 5X-GNF	Let 410UVP-E		RA-	0086	0097	2 WA M-601E	6400	Y19		
☐ 5X-JNF	Let 410UVP-E	861809	RA-67596	0086	0097	2 WA M-601E	6400	Y19		

FIKA SALAAMA AIRLINES, Ltd = HG / HGK — Entebbe & London-Gatwick

79 North Road, Three Bridges, Crawley, West Sussex RH10 1SB, Great Britain ☎ (171) 247 66 50 Tx: none Fax: (171) 377 50 90 SITA: n/a
F: 1994 ⁂ n/a Head: Sebeso Kabasobokwe ICAO: SALAAMA Net: n/a Operates cargo charter flights with Boeing 707C aircraft, currently leased when required.

MAF Uganda – Mission Aviation Fellowship (Branch of MAF Europe) — Entebbe

Box 1, Kampala, Uganda ☎ (41) 26 74 62 Tx: none Fax: (41) 26 74 33 SITA: n/a
F: n/a ⁂ n/a Head: n/a Net: n/a

☐ 5X-MAF	Cessna A185F Skywagon II	18503601	ET-AKH	0078	0098	1 CO IO-520-D	1520			Floats
☐ N1778R	Cessna A185F Skywagon	18502496	ET-AKQ	0074	0998	1 CO IO-520-D	1520			lsf Project Air Inc.
☐ N8248V	Cessna A185F Skywagon	18502722	ET-AKP	0075	0998	1 CO IO-520-D	1520			lsf Project Air Inc.
☐ N4942C	Cessna 210N Centurion II	21063681		0080		1 CO IO-520-L	1724			lsf Project Air Inc.
☐ N9792Y	Cessna 210N Centurion II	21064600		0082		1 CO IO-520-L	1724			lsf Project Air Inc.
☐ N9771F	Cessna 208 Caravan I	20800190	ET-AKL	0090	0998	1 PWC PT6A-114	3724			lsf Project Air Inc. / opf UN

SA ALLIANCE = Y2 / AFJ (African Joint Air Service dba/Joint venture between SAA-South African Airways & Governments of Uganda & Tanzania) — Entebbe

PO Box 2128, Kampala, Uganda ☎ (41) 34 40 11 Tx: none Fax: (41) 34 45 38 SITA: n/a
F: 1995 ⁂ 90 Head: John Murray IATA: 693 ICAO: JAMBO Net: http://www.imul.com/uganda/alliance.html Multinational airline of the following states: South Africa, Uganda & Tanzania.

☐ ZS-SRB	Boeing 767-266 (ER)	23179 / 98	N573SW	0084	0299	2 PW JT9D-7R4E	175540	C21Y168		lsf SAA

UGANDA AIR CARGO Corporation = UCC — Entebbe

PO Box 343, Entebbe, Uganda ☎ (42) 20 516 Tx: 61 166 dfce ug Fax: (42) 20 092 SITA: n/a
F: n/a ⁂ n/a Head: n/a ICAO: UGANDA CARGO Net: n/a

☐ 5X-UCF	Lockheed L-382G (L-100-30) Hercules	34C-4610	N108AK	0075	0875	4 AN 501-D22A	70307	Freighter	CH-DF	The Silver Lady

UGANDA AIRLINES, Corp. = QU / UGA — Entebbe

PO Box 5740, Kampala, Uganda ☎ (41) 23 29 90 Tx: 61239 goair kla Fax: (41) 25 72 79 SITA: n/a
F: 1977 ⁂ 350 Head: Benedict Motyaba IATA: 673 ICAO: UGANDA Net: n/a

☐ 5X-UWX	Fokker F27 Friendship 600 (F27 Mk600)	10571	5X-UAO	0078	0578	2 RR Dart 536-7	19731	Y43		
☐ 5X-USM	Boeing 737-53A	24785 / 1882	F-GGML	0090	0795	2 CFMI CFM56-3B1	59193	CY105	LQ-AG	lsf AWAS

5Y = KENYA (Republic of Kenya) (Jamhuri ya Kenya)

Capital: Nairobi Official Language: Swahili, English Population: 30,0 million Square Km: 582646 Dialling code: +254 Year established: 1963 Acting political head: Daniel Arap Moi (President)

Government / Corporate / Executive / VIP Aircraft

☐ KAF 304	De Havilland DHC-8-103 Dash 8	189	C-GLOT*	0089	0190	2 PWC PW121	15649	VIP / mil trans		Kenya Air Force
☐ KAF 305	De Havilland DHC-8-103 Dash 8	219	C-GFCF*	0090	0790	2 PWC PW121	15649	VIP / mil trans		Kenya Air Force
☐ KAF 306	De Havilland DHC-8-103 Dash 8	223	C-GFBW*	0090	0790	2 PWC PW121	15649	VIP / mil trans		Kenya Air Force
☐ KAF 308	Fokker 70 (F28 Mk0070)	11557	PH-MXM*	0095	1295	2 RR Tay 620-15	39915	VIP		Kenya Air Force / opf Gvmt

AD AVIATION (Aircharters), LTD — Nairobi-Wilson

PO Box 47906, Nairobi, Kenya ☎ (2) 50 05 02 Tx: none Fax: (2) 60 56 23 SITA: n/a
F: 1970 ⁂ 19 Head: Tony Abercromby-Dick Net: n/a

☐ 5Y-BKA	Beech King Air 200	BB-846	ZS-MIM	0081		2 PWC PT6A-41	5670			lsf Executive Aerospace
☐ 5Y-JMR	Beech King Air 200C	BL-17	F-GJMR	0080		2 PWC PT6A-41	5670			lsf Aerolite Investment Ltd

AFRICAN AIRLINES INTERNATIONAL, Ltd = AIK — Nairobi-Jomo Kenyatta Int'l

PO Box 19202, Nairobi, Kenya ☎ (2) 82 43 33 Tx: none Fax: (2) 82 39 99 SITA: n/a
F: 1990 ⁂ 167 Head: Capt. Musa Hassan Bulhan ICAO: AFRICAN AIRLINES Net: n/a

☐ 5Y-AXH	Fokker F28 Fellowship 1000 (F28 Mk1000)	11027	5V-TPO	0071	0499	2 RR Spey 555-15	29484	Y65		
☐ 5Y-AXB	Boeing 727-231	19565 / 603	5V-TPB	0068	0199	3 PW JT8D-7B	82327	F14Y136		
☐ 5Y-AXD	Boeing 727-243 (A)	22165 / 1635	5V-TPA	0080	0499	3 PW JT8D-9A	79605	F14Y136		
☐ 5Y-AXI	Boeing 707-330B	18927 / 454	Z-WKV	0065	0093	4 PW JT3D-7 (HK2/COM)	148778	Y164	FJ-CE	Isiolo / lsf Aviation Consultants
☐ 5Y-AXR	Boeing 707-351B	19634 / 695	5Y-BBI	0068	0595	4 PW JT3D-3B	151500	Y164	EL-AH	lsf Frontier Holdings Ltd / std NBO

AIM-AIR (Africa Inland Mission International Services dba) — Nairobi-Wilson

PO Box 21171, Nairobi, Kenya ☎ (2) 60 23 00 Tx: 25249 Fax: (2) 50 16 51 SITA: n/a
F: 1975 ⁂ 41 Head: Ron Shaw Net: n/a Non-commercial charity organisation conducting technical support flights.

☐ 5Y-BLD	Cessna U206F Stationair II	U20602962	N341EA	0075	1275	1 CO IO-520-F	1633			
☐ 5Y-BMD	Cessna U206G Stationair 6 II	U20605494	N348EA	0080	0582	1 CO IO-520-F	1724			
☐ N342EA	Cessna U206G Stationair 6 II	U20606197		0081	0586	1 CO IO-520-F	1633			
☐ N343EA	Cessna U206G Stationair 6	U20603699		0077	1282	1 CO IO-520-F	1633			
☐ N345EA	Cessna U206G Stationair 6 II	U20604764		0079	1080	1 CO IO-520-F	1633			
☐ N347EA	Cessna U206G Stationair 6 II	U20604797		0079	0881	1 CO IO-520-F	1633			
☐ 5Y-BLG	Cessna 210M Centurion II	21061898	N346EA	0077	0895	1 CO IO-520-L	1724			
☐ 5Y-SPK	Cessna 208B Caravan I Super Cargomaster	208B0243	N349EA	0090	1095	1 PWC PT6A-114	3969			lsf Samaritans Purse Inc.

AIR BATELEUR, Ltd (Associated with Aviation Assistance A/S, Denmark) — Nairobi-Wilson

PO Box 79373, Nairobi, Kenya ☎ (2) 56 49 23 Tx: none Fax: (2) 56 49 21 SITA: n/a
F: n/a ⁂ n/a Head: n/a Net: n/a

☐ 5Y-NBB	Beech King Air C90	LJ-528	N883AV	0071	0797	2 PWC PT6A-20	4377			
☐ 5Y-BMA	Beech King Air 200C	BB-155	OY-GEH	0076		2 PWC PT6A-41	5670			lsf Aviation Ass./opf ECHO/cvtd K.A.200
☐ 5Y-BMC	Beech King Air 200	BB-211	OY-BTR	0076		2 PWC PT6A-41	5670			lsf Aviation Assistance / opf ECHO
☐ 5Y-EKO	Beech King Air 200C	BL-2	OY-BVE	0079		2 PWC PT6A-41	5670			lsf Aviation Assistance / opf ECHO
☐ 5Y-ECO	Beech 1300 Airliner	BB-1343	OY-GER	0089	1098	2 PWC PT6A-42	5670			lsf Avn Assist./opf ECHO/cvtd K.A. B200
☐ 5Y-EOB	Beech 1300 Airliner	BB-1305	OY-GES	0089	0199	2 PWC PT6A-42	5670			lsf Avn Assist./opf ECHO/cvtd K.A. B200
☐ 5Y-BVI	Beech 1900C-1 Airliner	UC-55	OY-BVI	0089		2 PWC PT6A-65B	7530			lsf Aviation Assistance / opf ECHO

AIRCRAFT LEASING SERVICES, Ltd – ALS (Affiliated with Falcon Air Charters, Ltd) — Nairobi-Wilson

PO Box 41937, Nairobi, Kenya ☎ (2) 50 01 56 Tx: none Fax: (2) 50 45 63 SITA: n/a
F: n/a ⁂ n/a Head: Aslam Khan Net: n/a Aircraft below MTOW 1361kg: Cessna 150 & 182

☐ 5Y-BAF	Cessna 310R II	310R0633	N98890	0076		2 CO IO-520-M	2495			
☐ 5Y-HIN	Cessna 402B	402B0511		0073		2 CO TSIO-520-E	2858			
☐ 5Y-GSV	Cessna 208 Caravan I	20800024	N9358F	0085		1 PWC PT6A-114	3629			opf Ashraf/UNICEF
☐ 5Y-HAA	Cessna 208 Caravan I	20800021	N9349F	0085		1 PWC PT6A-114	3629			
☐ 5Y-MAK	Cessna 208 Caravan I	20800004	HB-CLI	0085		1 PWC PT6A-114	3629			lsf Falcon Air Chtrs/opf Ashraf/UNICEF
☐ 5Y-RAN	Cessna 208 Caravan I	20800037	HB-CKK	0085	0398	1 PWC PT6A-114	3629			
☐ 5Y-BLA	Beech King Air 200C	BL-10	C-FAMB	0080	0496	2 PWC PT6A-41	5670			

695 registration type of aircraft cn/fn ex/ex* mfd del powered by mtow kg configuration selcal name/fln/specialitites/remarks

AIRKENYA = QP (Air Kenya Aviation, Ltd dba)
Nairobi-Wilson

PO Box 30357, Nairobi, Kenya ☎ (2) 50 16 01 Tx: 22939 airkenya Fax: (2) 50 08 45 SITA: n/a
F: 1985 ✦✦✦ 160 Head: John Buckley IATA: 853 ICAO: AIRKENYA Net: n/a Aircraft below MTOW 1361 kg: Piper PA-28 & PA-38.

	registration	type of aircraft	cn/fn	ex/ex*	mfd	del	powered by	mtow kg	configuration	selcal	name/fln/specialitites/remarks
☐	5Y-BNA	Cessna 208B Grand Caravan	208B0606	N1127S*	0097	0198	1 PWC PT6A-114A	3969	Y12		
☐	5Y-BNN	Cessna 208B Grand Caravan	208B0683	N1126T*	0098	0998	1 PWC PT6A-114A	3969	Y12		
☐	5Y-BEK	De Havilland DHC-6 Twin Otter 200	181	5X-UVN	0068	0687	2 PWC PT6A-20	5252	Y18		
☐	5Y-BGH	De Havilland DHC-6 Twin Otter 300	574	N4226J	0078	0187	2 PWC PT6A-27	5670	Y18		
☐	5Y-BHR	De Havilland DHC-6 Twin Otter 300	424	N999AK	0074	0188	2 PWC PT6A-27	5670	Y18		
☐	5Y-BIO	De Havilland DHC-6 Twin Otter 300	579	5H-MRB	0078	0793	2 PWC PT6A-27	5670	Y18		
☐	5Y-BKP	Shorts 360-300 (SD3-60)	SH3750	G-BWMW	0089	0695	2 PWC PT6A-67R	12292	Y33		lsf Lynrise Air Lease
☐	5Y-BKW	Shorts 360-300 (SD3-60)	SH3717	G-BWMZ	0087	1295	2 PWC PT6A-67R	12292	Y33		
☐	5Y-BMJ	De Havilland DHC-7-102 Dash 7	083	N721AS	0082	0597	4 PWC PT6A-50	19958	Y48		
☐	5Y-BMP	De Havilland DHC-7-102 Dash 7	080	N780MG	0082	1097	4 PWC PT6A-50	19958	Y48		
☐	5Y-AAB	Fokker F27 Friendship 200 (F27 Mk200)	10211	VP-KSA	0062	0091	2 RR Dart 528-7E	19051	Y44		

AMREF – Flying Doctor Services (African Medical & Research Foundation dba)
Nairobi-Wilson

AMREF

PO Box 30125, Nairobi, Kenya ☎ (2) 50 65 21 Tx: 23254 amref Fax: (2) 50 92 84 SITA: n/a
F: 1957 ✦✦✦ 450 Head: Jim Heather-Hayes ICAO: FLYDOC Net: http://www.amref.org

☐	5Y-BCD	Cessna U206G Stationair 6 II	U20604308	N756RZ	0078		1 CO IO-520-F	1633	Ambulance		
☐	5Y-FDS	Cessna 210N Centurion II	21064755		0082		1 CO IO-520-L	1724	Ambulance		
☐	5Y-FBA	Cessna 402C II	402C0346	ZS-KYX	0080	0891	2 CO TSIO-520-VB	3107	Ambulance		
☐	5Y-DOC	Cessna 404 Titan II	404-0433		0079		2 CO GTSIO-520-M	3810	Ambulance		
☐	5Y-FDA	Cessna 208B Grand Caravan	208B0551		0096	0096	1 PWC PT6A-114A	3969	Ambulance		

ASA – African Safari Airways, Ltd = QSC
Mombasa & Basel-Mulhouse (Switzerland)

PO Box 81443, Mombasa, Kenya ☎ (11) 48 55 23 Tx: none Fax: (11) 48 50 32 SITA: MBAZSSK
F: 1967 ✦✦✦ 50 Head: Hanspeter Rüdin & Peter Reichert ICAO: ZEBRA Net: n/a

☐	5Y-MBA	Boeing (Douglas) DC-10-30	46952 / 185	PH-DTL	0075	1292	3 GE CF6-50C2	256280	F40C86Y148	AB-JM	

AUTAIR HELICOPTERS (Autair Helicopter (EA), Ltd dba)
Nairobi-Wilson

PO Box 41951, Nairobi, Kenya ☎ (2) 50 19 18 Tx: none Fax: (2) 50 33 62 SITA: n/a
F: 1966 ✦✦✦ n/a Head: Freddie Wilcox Net: n/a

☐	5Y-BLH	Bell 206B JetRanger III	3504	ZS-HAJ	0081		1 AN 250-C20B	1451			lsf Reef Helicopters Services
☐	5Y-TOR	Bell 206L-3 LongRanger III	51292	D-HHMU	0089		1 AN 250-C30P	1882			lsf Larkin Holdings

BLUE BIRD AVIATION, Ltd = BBZ
Nairobi-Wilson

PO Box 52382, Nairobi, Kenya ☎ (2) 50 60 04 Tx: none Fax: (2) 60 23 37 SITA: n/a
F: 1992 ✦✦✦ n/a Head: Hussein Ahmed Farah ICAO: COBRA Net: n/a

☐	5Y-HHE	Beech King Air 200	BB-547	ZS-NIP	0079	1097	2 PWC PT6A-41	5670	Y9		lsf Amazon Air Contracts Ltd
☐	5Y-BSA	Let 410UVP-E	892322	OK-UDC	0089	0398	2 WA M-601E	6400	Y19		
☐	5Y-HHB	Let 410AB	730209	OK-DDV	0073	0095	2 PWC PT6A-27	5700	Y17		lsf pvt
☐	5Y-HHC	Let 410A	730204	OK-DDU	0073	1295	2 PWC PT6A-27	5700	Y17		lsf pvt
☐	5Y-HHF	Let 410AB	710002	OK-ADR	0071	0398	2 PWC PT6A-27	5700	Y17		

CAPITAL AIRLINES, Ltd
Nairobi-Wilson

PO Box 49232, Nairobi, Kenya ☎ (2) 50 22 80 Tx: none Fax: (2) 50 41 48 SITA: n/a
F: 1993 ✦✦✦ n/a Head: Capt. Himat Vaghela Net: n/a

☐	5Y-JAI	Beech King Air 200	BB-557	OY-PAM	0079		2 PWC PT6A-41	5670			

COMMUTER AIR SERVICES, Ltd
Nairobi-Wilson

PO Box 46367, Nairobi, Kenya ☎ (2) 50 30 97 Tx: none Fax: (2) 60 26 04 SITA: n/a
F: 1994 ✦✦✦ 5 Head: Capt. Ramesh J. Peshavaria Net: n/a Aircraft below MTOW 1361kg: Cessna 172

☐	5Y-BJP	Cessna 310R II	310R0147		0075		2 CO IO-520-M	2495			lsf Skywest Ltd
☐	5Y-LEA	Cessna 404 Titan II	404-0614	5Y-EAG	0080	0098	2 CO GTSIO-520-M	3810			lst Western Airways

DAS AIR CARGO = DAZ (Subsidiary of DAS Air Cargo, Uganda)
Nairobi-Jomo Kenyatta Int'l

European office: 1st Floor, North Suite, Elm Park Court, Tilgate FBC, Brighton Road, Crawley, Sussex RH11 9BP, Great Britain ☎ (1293) 54 03 03 Tx: 878148 g Fax: (1293) 55 15 45 SITA: n/a
F: 1997 ✦✦✦ n/a Head: Daisy & Capt. Joe Roy ICAO: DASAIR Operates cargo flights with Boeing 707-320C & McDonnell Douglas DC-10-30F aircraft used from parent company DAS AIR CARGO, Uganda (5X-) when required.

DESERT LOCUST CONTROL – DESLOC (Organisation for Eastern Africa)
Nairobi-Wilson

PO Box 30023, Nairobi, Kenya ☎ (2) 50 17 94 Tx: 25510 desloc Fax: (2) 50 51 37 SITA: n/a
F: 1962 ✦✦✦ 120 Head: Dr. A.M.H.M. Karrar Net: n/a

☐	5Y-BCJ	De Havilland DHC-2 Beaver I	1572	KAF 106	0064		1 PW R-985	2313	Sprayer		
☐	5Y-BCK	De Havilland DHC-2 Beaver I	1579	KAF 108	0065		1 PW R-985	2313	Sprayer		
☐	5Y-BCL	De Havilland DHC-2 Beaver I	1552	KAF 102	0064		1 PW R-985	2313	Sprayer		
☐	5Y-KRD	De Havilland DHC-2 Beaver I	1439	VP-KRD	0061		1 PW R-985	2313	Sprayer		
☐	5Y-DLD	De Havilland DHC-2 Turbo Beaver III	1562TB3	C-FOEA	0064		1 PWC PT6A-15AG	2436	Sprayer		
☐	5Y-DLO	Beech Baron 58	TH-987	N4857M	0079		2 CO IO-520-CB	2449	5 Pax		
☐	5Y-DLA	Cessna 208 Caravan I	20800107	N9617F	0086	1297	1 PWC PT6A-114	3629	9 Pax		

DIRECTORATE OF CIVIL AVIATION KENYA – Flight Inspection Unit (Flight Inspection Unit of DCA-Directorate of Civil Aviation Kenya)
Nairobi-Jomo Kenyatta Int'l

PO Box 30163, Nairobi, Kenya ☎ (2) 82 29 50 Tx: none Fax: (2) 82 21 95 SITA: n/a
F: 1972 ✦✦✦ 8 Head: Walter N. Nambu Net: n/a Operates non-commercial calibration missions in Kenya & on commercial basis in neighbouring states.

☐	5Y-DCA	Aerospatiale (Nord) 262C-63	96	F-WNDA*	0072	0672	2 TU Bastan VIIC	10800	Calibrator		

EAGLE AVIATION, Ltd = Y4 / EQA
Mombasa

Eagle Aviation

PO Box 93926, Mombasa, Kenya ☎ (11) 43 45 02 Tx: none Fax: (11) 43 42 49 SITA: n/a
F: 1986 ✦✦✦ 115 Head: Capt. Kiran C. Patel IATA: 067 ICAO: MAGNUM Net: n/a

☐	5Y-ENT	Let 410A	730302	OK-DDY	0073	0095	2 PWC PT6A-27	5700	Y17		
☐	5Y-FNT	Let 410A	730210	OK-DDW	0073	0095	2 PWC PT6A-27	5700	Y17		
☐	5Y-GNT	Let 410A	730301	OK-DDX	0073	0094	2 PWC PT6A-27	5700	Y17		Good time
☐	5Y-HNT	Let 410A	720203	OK-CDS	0072	0095	2 PWC PT6A-27	5700	Y17		
☐	5Y-INT	ATR 42-320	041	F-ODUE	0087	0196	2 PWC PW121	16700	Y46		African Eagle, Ben Gillis / cvtd -300
☐	5Y-	ATR 42-320	205	N521JS	0090	0499	2 PWC PW121	16700	Y46		
☐	5Y-	ATR 42-320	240	N240JS	0091	0499	2 PWC PW121	16700	Y46		

EAST AFRICAN AIR CHARTERS, Ltd
Nairobi-Wilson

PO Box 42730, Nairobi, Kenya ☎ (2) 50 14 31 Tx: none Fax: (2) 50 23 58 SITA: n/a
F: 1992 ✦✦✦ 15 Head: Michael V. Seton Net: n/a Aircraft below MTOW 1361kg: Cessna 182.

☐	5Y-BCC	Cessna R182 Skylane RG II	R18200048	N7597T	0077		1 LY O-540-J3C5D	1406			lsf pvt
☐	5Y-ALY	Cessna U206F Stationair	U20602266	N1588U	0073		1 CO IO-520-F	1633			lsf pvt
☐	5Y-AOO	Cessna U206F Stationair	U20601710		0072		1 CO IO-520-F	1633			lsf pvt
☐	5Y-ART	Cessna 210L Centurion II	21059817		0073		1 CO IO-520-L	1724			lsf pvt
☐	5Y-BMH	Cessna 310R II	310R0501		0076		2 CO IO-520-M	2495			lsf pvt
☐	5Y-AHL	Cessna 401	401-0193	PH-MPS	0068		2 CO TSIO-520-E	2858			lsf pvt
☐	5Y-BLN	Cessna 208B Grand Caravan	208B0558	N50398	0096	0096	1 PWC PT6A-114A	3969			lsf pvt
☐	5Y-BIX	Reims/Cessna F406 Caravan II	F406-0055	N65912	0090	0194	2 PWC PT6A-112	4468			lsf pvt

EAST AFRICAN SAFARI AIR, Ltd = HSA (formerly CHS Aviation, Ltd)
Nairobi-Wilson

PO Box 28321, Nairobi, Kenya ☎ (2) 50 55 19 Tx: none Fax: (2) 50 01 69 SITA: n/a
F: 1989 ✦✦✦ 5 Head: Anthony A. Kegode Net: n/a Operates charter flights with Airbus A320 & Boeing 767-300 (ER) lsf/opb VOLARE AIRLINES (I-) & AIR EUROPE (I-), when required.

EVERETT AVIATION, Ltd
Nairobi-Wilson

PO Box 40813, Nairobi, Kenya ☎ (2) 60 16 38 Tx: none Fax: (2) 60 87 85 SITA: n/a
F: 1995 ✦✦✦ n/a Head: Simon Everett Net: n/a

☐	5Y-EXA	Eurocopter (Aerosp.) AS350B2 Squirrel	2906	ZS-RHT	0096	0097	1 TU Arriel 1D1	2250			
☐	5Y-EXB	Eurocopter (Aerosp.) AS350B2 Squirrel	3025		0097	0097	1 TU Arriel 1D1	2250			
☐	5Y-EXC	Eurocopter (Aerosp.) AS350B3 Squirrel					1 TU Arriel 2B	2250			oo-delivery 0099
☐	ZS-SRK	Pilatus PC-12/45	202		0097	1198	1 PWC PT6A-67B	4500			lsf Swiss Aviation

FAST AIRWAYS = TFS (Freight Air Service Transport, Ltd dba)
Nairobi-Jomo Kenyatta Int'l

PO Box 76020, Nairobi, Kenya ☎ (2) 82 44 77 Tx: none Fax: (2) 82 39 30 SITA: n/a
F: 1997 ✦✦✦ n/a Head: Raphael Nzomo ICAO: FAST TRANSPORT Net: n/a

☐	N482EV	Boeing 747-212B (SF)	20713 / 219	N729PA	0073	1098	4 PW JT9D-7J	362874	Freighter	FG-AH	lsf / opb EIA / cvtd -212B
☐	N485EV	Boeing 747-212B (SF)	20712 / 218	N728PA	0073	1098	4 PW JT9D-7J	362874	Freighter	AJ-GM	lsf / opb EIA / cvtd -212B

KENYA AIRWAYS, Ltd = KQ / KQA (Associated with Kenya Airfreight Handling, Ltd)
Nairobi-Jomo Kenyatta Int'l

Kenya Airways

PO Box 19002, Nairobi, Kenya ☎ (2) 82 34 56 Tx: 22771 kenair Fax: (2) 82 34 88 SITA: NBODDKQ
F: 1977 ✦✦✦ 2450 Head: Isaac O. Okero IATA: 706 ICAO: KENYA Net: n/a

☐	5Y-KQJ	Boeing 737-248 (A)	21714 / 565	N1714T	0079	0398	2 PW JT8D-9A	52000	F12Y91		lsf European Capital Corp.

☐ 5Y-KQK	Boeing 737-248 (A)	*21715 / 579*	*N1715Z*	*0079*	*0198*	*2 PW JT8D-9A*	*52000*	*F12Y91*		*lsf European Capital Corp.*
☐ 5Y-KQA	Boeing 737-3U8	*28746 / 2863*		*0097*	*0397*	*2 CFMI CFM56-3C1*	*62823*	*F16Y100*		*lsf Simba Finance Ltd*
☐ 5Y-KQB	Boeing 737-3U8	*28747 / 2884*		*0597*	*0597*	*2 CFMI CFM56-3C1*	*62823*	*F16Y100*		*lsf Simba Finance Ltd*
☐ 5Y-KQC	Boeing 737-3U8	*29088 / 3034*		*0098*	*0598*	*2 CFMI CFM56-3C1*	*62823*	*F16Y100*		*lsf Simba Finance Ltd*
☐ 5Y-KQD	Boeing 737-3U8	*29750 / 3095*	*N5573L**	*0099*	*0399*	*2 CFMI CFM56-3C1*	*62823*	*F16Y100*		
☐ 5Y-BEL	Airbus Industrie A310-304	*416*	*F-WWCK**	*0086*	*0586*	*2 GE CF6-80C2A2*	*153000*	*C18Y187*	*EF-BL*	Nyayo Star
☐ 5Y-BEN	Airbus Industrie A310-304	*426*	*F-WWCQ**	*0086*	*0986*	*2 GE CF6-80C2A2*	*153000*	*C18Y187*	*EF-DM*	Harambee Star
☐ 5Y-BFT	Airbus Industrie A310-304	*519*	*F-WWCG**	*0089*	*1189*	*2 GE CF6-80C2A2*	*153000*	*C18Y187*	*FG-LM*	Uhuru Star / *lsf ILFC*
☐ 5Y-KQL	Airbus Industrie A310-304	*485*	*D-AIDC*	*0088*	*0399*	*2 GE CF6-80C2A2*	*153000*	*C18Y187*		*lsf GOAL*

KENYA PIPELINE – Aviation Dept. (Aviation Dept. of Kenya Pipeline, Co. Ltd)

Nairobi-Wilson

PO Box 73442, Nairobi, Kenya ☎ (2) 50 15 80 Tx: none Fax: (2) 50 15 80 SITA: n/a
F: 1978 ⁂ n/a Head: Charles Wachita Net: n/a Beside non-commerical flights for itself also operates for outside customers when required.

☐ 5Y-BFL	Bell 206L-3 LongRanger III	*51237*		*0088*	*0088*	*1 AN 250-C30P*	*1882*			
☐ 5Y-BKR	Bell 206L-4 LongRanger IV	*52132*	*C-FVSU**	*0095*	*0895*	*1 AN 250-C30P*	*2018*			

KENYA POLICE AIRWING

Nairobi-Wilson

PO Box 30083, Nairobi, Kenya ☎ (2) 50 13 13 Tx: none Fax: (2) 50 13 13 SITA: n/a
F: n/a ⁂ n/a Head: Commander Maina Gaza Chege Net: n/a Aircraft below MTOW 1361kg: Bell 47G-3B-2 Non-commercial government organisation conducting aerial police & transport & EMS-flights.

☐ 5Y-BCF	Bell 206L-1 LongRanger II	*45161*		*0078*	*0078*	*1 AN 250-C28B*	*1882*			
☐ 5Y-KPA	Cessna 310R II	*310R2110*	*N6831E*	*0081*	*0081*	*2 CO IO-520-M*	*2495*			
☐ 5Y-PAW	Cessna 310R II	*310R0907*	*N3734G*	*0077*	*0777*	*2 CO IO-520-M*	*2495*			
☐ 5Y-PAX	Cessna 404 Titan II	*404-0104*	*N37094*	*0077*	*0777*	*2 CO GTSIO-520-M*	*3810*			

KENYA WILDLIFE SERVICES AIRWING

Nairobi-Wilson

PO Box 54582, Nairobi, Kenya ☎ (2) 60 94 51 Tx: none Fax: (2) 60 96 48 SITA: n/a
F: 1985 ⁂ n/a Head: n/a Net: n/a Aircraft below MTOW 1361kg: Cessna 180/182, Christen A-1 Husky & Hughes 369HS (500C) Non-commercial government organisation conducting transport, surveying & supervising flights.

☐ 5Y-KWF	Bell 206L-4 LongRanger IV	*52029*		*0093*	*0093*	*1 AN 250-C30P*	*2018*			
☐ 5Y-KWS	Cessna 402C II	*402C0450*		*0081*		*2 CO TSIO-520-VB*	*3107*			
☐ 5Y-KWT	Cessna 208B Grand Caravan	*208B0340*	*N1043N**	*0093*	*0093*	*1 PWC PT6A-114A*	*3969*			

MAF Kenya – Mission Aviation Fellowship (Branch of MAF Europe)

Nairobi-Wilson

PO Box 21123, Nairobi, Kenya ☎ (2) 50 12 67 Tx: none Fax: (2) 50 16 26 SITA: n/a
F: 1948 ⁂ 26 Head: Bill Harding Net: n/a Non-commercial multinational ecclesiastical consortium conducting flights for relief & development agencies & missions in remote areas of third world countries.

☐ 5Y-AUD	Cessna 210L Centurion II	*21060338*	*N93277*	*0074*		*1 CO IO-520-L*	*1724*			
☐ 5Y-BMU	Cessna 210N Centurion II	*21063739*	*5H-MRV*	*0080*	*0097*	*1 CO IO-520-L*	*1724*			
☐ 5Y-ZBZ	Cessna 208 Caravan I	*20800201*	*N9785F*	*0091*	*0095*	*1 PWC PT6A-114*	*3629*			
☐ 5Y-MAF	Pilatus PC-12/45	*243*	*HB-FRN**	*0099*	*0199*	*1 PWC PT6A-67B*	*4500*			

MOMBASA AIR SAFARI, Ltd – MAS

Mombasa

PO Box 93961, Mombasa, Kenya ☎ (11) 43 30 61 Tx: none Fax: (11) 43 42 64 SITA: n/a
F: n/a ⁂ n/a Head: n/a Net: n/a

☐ 5Y-LET	Let 410UVP-E9	*912620*	*OK-WDX*	*0091*	*0696*	*2 WA M-601E*	*6400*	*Y17*		*lsf Skoda Trading*
☐ 5Y-NIK	Let 410UVP-E9	*912619*	*OK-WDW*	*0091*	*0097*	*2 WA M-601E*	*6400*	*Y17*		*lsf Skoda Trading/sublst Comores Air S.*
☐ 5Y-UVP	Let 410UVP-E9	*912627*	*OK-WDY*	*0091*	*0796*	*2 WA M-601E*	*6400*	*Y17*		*lsf Skoda Trading*

PHOTOMAP, (K) Ltd

Nairobi-Wilson

PO Box 43805, Nairobi, Kenya ☎ (2) 72 60 27 Tx: none Fax: (2) 72 60 28 SITA: n/a
F: 1986 ⁂ 23 Head: Hedtjarn Wiklund Net: n/a

☐ 5Y-MAP	Piper PA-31-310 Navajo	*31-252*	*G-BBHB*	*0068*		*2 LY TIO-540-A2B*	*2948*	*Photo/Survey*		

QUEENSWAY AIR SERVICES (K), Ltd

Nairobi-Wilson

PO Box 42627, Nairobi, Kenya ☎ (2) 74 15 51 Tx: none Fax: (2) 74 31 19 SITA: n/a
F: 1997 ⁂ n/a Head: Irving Power Net: n/a

☐ 5Y-BKT	Beech King Air 200	*BB-256*	*ZS-NTM*	*0077*	*0097*	*2 PWC PT6A-41*	*5670*			*lsf Balmoral Central Contracts*

RIVER CROSS AIR SERVICES, Ltd

Nairobi-Wilson

PO Box 51948, Nairobi, Kenya ☎ (2) 60 56 78 Tx: none Fax: (2) 25 00 69 SITA: n/a
F: 1977 ⁂ 5 Head: D.N. Gachuche Net: n/a

☐ 5Y-ADK	Beech Baron C55 (95-C55)	*TE-170*		*0066*		*2 CO IO-520-C*	*2404*			

ROSSAIR KENYA, Ltd (Subsidiary of Rossair Pty Ltd, South Africa)

Nairobi-Wilson

PO Box 59174, Nairobi, Kenya ☎ (2) 60 18 74 Tx: none Fax: (2) 60 17 80 SITA: n/a
F: 1995 ⁂ n/a Head: Ian Brandt Net: n/a

☐ 5Y-ROS	Beech 1900C-1 Airliner	*UC-65*	*ZS-OGZ*	*0089*	*0795*	*2 PWC PT6A-65B*	*7530*			*lsf RSS*
☐ 5Y-BNK	AMI Turbo DC-3C	*27047*	*ZS-OBU*	*0044*	*0898*	*2 PWC PT6A-65AR*	*12202*			*lsf RSS / cvtd Douglas C-47B-20-DK*
☐ 5Y-RDS	AMI Turbo DC-3C	*27085*	*N146JR*	*0045*	*0097*	*2 PWC PT6A-65AR*	*12202*			*lsf Sembar Aviation AG/cvtd C-47B-20-DK*

SERENE AIR SERVICES, Ltd

Nairobi-Wilson

PO Box 74500, Nairobi, Kenya ☎ (2) 60 70 73 Tx: none Fax: (2) 22 10 01 SITA: n/a
F: 1997 ⁂ n/a Head: n/a Net: n/a

☐ 5Y-LAM	Cessna 402C II	*402C0463*	*OH-CIM*	*0081*	*0098*	*2 CO TSIO-520-VB*	*3107*			

SKYLINK Aeromanagement (K), Inc. (Associated with SkyLink Aviation, Inc., Canada)

Nairobi-Wilson

PO Box 61844, Nairobi, Kenya ☎ (2) 60 68 52 Tx: none Fax: (2) 60 65 08 SITA: n/a
F: n/a ⁂ 18 Head: John Okemwa Net: n/a

☐ 5Y-JAO	Cessna 208 Caravan I	*20800202*	*N208SN*	*0091*	*0793*	*1 PWC PT6A-114*	*3629*			*lsf Avex Inc., USA*
☐ 5Y-SEL	Beech King Air 200	*BB-99*	*C-FSKQ*	*0076*	*0197*	*2 PWC PT6A-41*	*5670*			*lsf SKK*

SKYMASTERS, Ltd

Nairobi-Wilson

PO Box 58771, Nairobi, Kenya ☎ (2) 50 15 93 Tx: 22973 ecta Fax: (2) 50 15 93 SITA: n/a
F: 1980 ⁂ n/a Head: Chandra K. Mehta Net: n/a

☐ 5Y-EAS	Cessna 402B	*402B0577*	*N141CE*	*0074*		*2 CO TSIO-520-E*	*2858*			*lsf KBM Ltd*

SKYTRAILS, Ltd (Affiliated with African Safari Club)

Mombasa

PO Box 81443, Mombasa, Kenya ☎ (11) 48 55 20 Tx: 21140 asa club Fax: (11) 48 59 09 SITA: n/a
F: 1982 ⁂ 45 Head: Roland Rüdin ICAO: SKYTRAILS Net: n/a

☐ 5Y-AFD	Cessna TU206B Super Skywagon	*U206-0724*	*N3424L*	*0066*		*1 CO TSIO-520-C*	*1633*	*5 Pax*		
☐ 5Y-EDH	Cessna 404 Titan II	*404-0241*	*N88728*	*0078*		*2 CO GTSIO-520-M*	*3810*	*12 Pax*		
☐ 5Y-SKA	De Havilland DHC-6 Twin Otter 300	*518*	*D-IDWT*	*0076*	*0586*	*2 PWC PT6A-27*	*5670*	*20 Pax*		
☐ 5Y-SKL	De Havilland DHC-6 Twin Otter 300	*715*	*N8489H*	*0080*	*0188*	*2 PWC PT6A-27*	*5670*	*20 Pax*		
☐ 5Y-SKS	De Havilland DHC-6 Twin Otter 300	*682*	*G-BGZP*	*0080*	*0390*	*2 PWC PT6A-27*	*5670*	*20 Pax*		
☐ 5Y-SKT	De Havilland DHC-6 Twin Otter 300	*503*	*PH-STC*	*0076*	*0885*	*2 PWC PT6A-27*	*5670*	*20 Pax*		

SKYWAYS KENYA, Ltd

Nairobi-Wilson

PO Box 60878, Nairobi, Kenya ☎ (2) 50 60 17 Tx: none Fax: (2) 50 60 18 SITA: n/a
F: 1996 ⁂ n/a Head: Capt. Patrick Ikena Net: n/a Beside aircraft listed, additional aircraft (Antonov 26/32) are leased from other companies when required.

☐ 5Y-BMB	Boeing (Douglas) DC-3C (C-47B-50-DK)	*34375*	*N2025A*	*0045*	*0996*	*2 PW R-1830*	*12202*	*Freighter*		*lsf Legion Express Inc.*

SUPERIOR AVIATION SERVICES, Ltd

Nairobi-Wilson

PO Box 42339, Nairobi, Kenya ☎ (2) 60 03 72 Tx: none Fax: (2) 50 34 16 SITA: n/a
F: 1977 ⁂ 25 Head: Kishore Patel Net: n/a Aircraft below MTOW 1361kg: Cessna 150 / 172 & 182.

☐ 5Y-ATH	Piper PA-23-250 Aztec E	*27-7305138*		*0073*		*2 LY TIO-540-C1A*	*2359*			
☐ 5Y-APO	Beech Baron E55	*TE-875*		*0072*		*2 CO IO-520-C*	*2404*			
☐ 5Y-ANE	Beech Baron 58	*TH-168*		*0071*		*2 CO IO-520-C*	*2449*			
☐ 5Y-PEA	Beech Baron 58	*TH-1087*	*N60664*	*0080*	*0594*	*2 CO IO-520-CB*	*2449*			
☐ 5Y-BGN	Cessna 404 Titan II	*404-0239*	*D-IEBB*	*0078*		*2 CO GTSIO-520-M*	*3810*			

TRACKMARK, Ltd

Nairobi-Wilson & Lokiochogio

PO Box 44007, Nairobi, Kenya ☎ (2) 50 01 53 Tx: none Fax: (2) 50 49 07 SITA: n/a
F: 1989 ⁂ n/a Head: Capt. Heather Stewart Net: n/a

☐ 5Y-NKG	Cessna 208 Caravan I	*20800178*	*ZS-NKG*	*0090*		*1 PWC PT6A-114*	*3629*			*lsf Kingair Services Partnership*
☐ 5Y-TMR	Cessna 404 Titan II	*404-0039*	*G-IFTD*	*0077*		*2 CO GTSIO-520-M*	*3810*			
☐ 5Y-NHB	Cessna 208B Grand Caravan	*208B0328*	*ZS-NHB*	*0093*		*1 PWC PT6A-114A*	*3969*			*lsf Kingair Services Partnership*
☐ 5Y-NIZ	Cessna 208B Grand Caravan	*208B0353*	*ZS-NIZ*	*0093*		*1 PWC PT6A-114A*	*3969*			*lsf Kingair Services Partnership*
☐ 5Y-NOM	Cessna 208B Grand Caravan	*208B0261*	*ZS-NOM*	*0091*		*1 PWC PT6A-114A*	*3969*			*lsf Kingair Services Partnership*
☐ 5Y-TAS	Cessna 208B Grand Caravan	*208B0381*	*N1119K**	*0094*	*0294*	*1 PWC PT6A-114A*	*3969*			*lsf INGL*
☐ 5Y-TLC	Cessna 208B Grand Caravan	*208B0472*	*N9147N**	*0095*		*1 PWC PT6A-114A*	*3969*			*lsf Kingair Services Partnership*
☐ 5Y-GAA	De Havilland DHC-5D Buffalo	*107A*	*C-FSKN*	*0082*	*0097*	*2 GE CT64-820-4*	*22317*	*Freighter*		*lsf Aero Support*

697 registration type of aircraft *cn/fn* *ex/ex** *mfd* *del* *powered by* *mtow kg* *configuration* *selcal* name/fln/specialitites/remarks

TRANSWORLD SAFARIS (K), Ltd — Nairobi-Wilson

PO Box 44690, Nairobi, Kenya ☎ (2) 60 43 15 Tx: none Fax: (2) 60 43 16 SITA: n/a
F: 1969 ✈ 116 Head: Bhaloo Patel Net: n/a Aircraft below MTOW 1361kg: Piper PA-28 & Hot Air Balloon Colts

registration	type of aircraft	cn/fn	ex/ex*	mfd	del	powered by	mtow kg	configuration	selcal	name/fln/remarks
☐ 5Y-ATJ	Piper PA-31-350 Navajo Chieftain	31-7305011	N7683L	0073		2 LY TIO-540-J2BD	3175			
☐ 5Y-ROH	Piper PA-31-350 Navajo Chieftain	31-8152038	N217JP	0081	0389	2 LY TIO-540-J2BD	3175			
☐ 5Y-TWG	Cessna 208B Grand Caravan	208B0674	N1286N*	0098	0698	1 PWC PT6A-114A	3969			lsf Aerolite Investments Ltd
☐ 5Y-TWA	Beech King Air 200	BB-803	G-WPLC	0081		2 PWC PT6A-41	5670			
☐ 5Y-TWB	Beech King Air 200	BB-696	N200GU	0080	0592	2 PWC PT6A-41	5670			
☐ 5Y-TWC	Beech King Air B200C	BL-37	G-IFTB	0081	0297	2 PWC PT6A-42	5670			lsf Aerolite Investments Ltd
☐ 5Y-TWE	Cessna 550 Citation II	550-0569	G-OSNB	0088	1197	2 PWC JT15D-4	6033			lst Aerolite Investments Ltd

TRIDENT ENTERPRISES, Ltd — Nairobi-Wilson & Lokichogio

PO Box 13501, Nairobi, Kenya ☎ (2) 72 74 45 Tx: none Fax: (2) 57 34 24 SITA: n/a
F: 1993 ✈ n/a Head: Emmanuel Anassas Net: n/a

registration	type of aircraft	cn/fn	ex/ex*	mfd	del	powered by	mtow kg	configuration	selcal	name/fln/remarks
☐ 5Y-OPL	De Havilland DHC-5D Buffalo	084A	A40-CD	0079	0098	2 GE CT64-820-4	22317	Freighter		
☐ 5Y-TAJ	De Havilland DHC-5E Buffalo	108	C-GDOB	0081	1293	2 GE CT64-820-4	22317			lsf AGES / opf UNDP / cvtd -5D

TRISTAR AVIATION, Ltd — Nairobi-Wilson

PO Box 26304, Nairobi, Kenya ☎ (2) 60 77 48 Tx: none Fax: (2) 60 77 49 SITA: n/a
F: 1997 ✈ n/a Head: Abdullah Seikh Ahamed Net: n/a

registration	type of aircraft	cn/fn	ex/ex*	mfd	del	powered by	mtow kg	configuration	selcal	name/fln/remarks
☐ 5Y-BIW	Beech King Air 200	BB-782	G-THUR	0080	0497	2 PWC PT6A-41	5670			lsf pvt

UNITED AIRLINES, Ltd — Nairobi-Wilson

PO Box 53521, Nairobi, Kenya ☎ (2) 50 62 66 Tx: none Fax: (2) 50 65 68 SITA: n/a
F: 1989 ✈ n/a Head: Capt. Elli Aluvale Net: n/a

registration	type of aircraft	cn/fn	ex/ex*	mfd	del	powered by	mtow kg	configuration	selcal	name/fln/remarks
☐ 5Y-LAV	Cessna 310R II	310R0882	N3644G	0077		2 CO IO-520-M	2495			
☐ 5Y-UAL	Piper PA-31T3-T1040	31T-8275002	N309SC	0082	0594	2 PWC PT6A-11	4082			
☐ 5Y-UAS	Let 410UVP-E9	841324	OK-ODF	0084	0398	2 WA M-601E	6400			lsf Omnipol Ltd

WESTERN AIRWAYS (Western Kenya Air Charter, Co. Ltd dba) — Nairobi-Wilson

PO Box S28409, Nairobi, Kenya ☎ (2) 50 37 42 Tx: 22303 lonrho Fax: (2) 50 37 42 SITA: n/a
F: 1966 ✈ 6 Head: Capt. Donald V. D'Sa Net: n/a

registration	type of aircraft	cn/fn	ex/ex*	mfd	del	powered by	mtow kg	configuration	selcal	name/fln/remarks
☐ 5Y-BIY	Cessna 404 Titan II	404-0061		0077		2 CO GTSIO-520-M	3810			
☐ 5Y-LEA	Cessna 404 Titan II	404-0614	5Y-EAG	0080		2 CO GTSIO-520-M	3810			lst Commuter Air Services

YELLOW WINGS AIR SERVICES, Ltd — Nairobi-Wilson

PO Box 19781, Nairobi, Kenya ☎ (2) 60 63 13 Tx: none Fax: (2) 60 57 25 SITA: n/a
F: 1997 ✈ 5 Head: Christian Strebel Net: n/a Aircraft below MTOW 1361kg: Cessna 182 & Piper PA-18

registration	type of aircraft	cn/fn	ex/ex*	mfd	del	powered by	mtow kg	configuration	selcal	name/fln/remarks
☐ 5Y-HVT	Cessna 206 Super Skywagon	206-0213		0064		1 CO IO-520-A	1497			

ZB AIR = ZBA (Z. Boskovic Air Charters, Ltd – Africair dba) — Nairobi-Wilson

PO Box 45646, Nairobi, Kenya ☎ (2) 50 12 19 Tx: 23061 bosky Fax: (2) 60 96 19 SITA: n/a
F: 1963 ✈ 60 Head: Capt. T.A.D. Watts ICAO: BOSKY Net: n/a Aircraft below MTOW 1361 kg: Cessna 150, 172 & 182.

registration	type of aircraft	cn/fn	ex/ex*	mfd	del	powered by	mtow kg	configuration	selcal	name/fln/remarks
☐ 5Y-AUN	Cessna U206F Stationair	U20602531	N1244V	0074		1 CO IO-520-F	1633			
☐ 5Y-AYB	Cessna 210L Centurion II	21060547	N94222	0074		1 CO IO-520-L	1724			
☐ 5Y-AIS	Beech Baron D55	TE-660		0069		2 CO IO-520-C	2404			
☐ 5Y-AYZ	Cessna 310R II	310R0121	N4940J	0075		2 CO IO-520-M	2495			
☐ 5Y-AZS	Cessna 310R II	310R0524	N87350	0076		2 CO IO-520-M	2495			
☐ 5Y-KPL	Cessna 310R II	310R1317		0073		2 CO IO-520-M	2495			
☐ 5Y-ZBC	Cessna T310R II	310R0322	N87252	0075		2 CO TSIO-520-B	2495			
☐ 5Y-HCN	Cessna 404 Titan II	404-0212	N88672	0078		2 CO GTSIO-520-M	3810			
☐ 5Y-SAB	Cessna 404 Titan II	404-0675	N6761X	0080		2 CO GTSIO-520-M	3810			
☐ 5Y-OPM	Cessna 208B Grand Caravan	208B0330	N1034S	0093		1 PWC PT6A-114A	3969			
☐ 5Y-ZBI	Cessna 208B Grand Caravan	208B0324	N1029P	0092	0193	1 PWC PT6A-114A	3969			
☐ 5Y-ZBL	Cessna 208B Grand Caravan	208B0338	N1042Y	0093	1093	1 PWC PT6A-114A	3969			
☐ 5Y-ZBR	Cessna 208B Grand Caravan	208B0446	N12922	0095		1 PWC PT6A-114A	3969			
☐ 5Y-ZBW	Cessna 208B Grand Caravan	208B0409	N1115W	0093	0295	1 PWC PT6A-114A	3969			

6O = SOMALIA (Somali Democratic Republic) (Jamhuuriyadda Dimugradiga Soomaaliya)

(including semi-independent slef-declared "Repuclic of Somaliland"; Capital: Hargeisa
Capital: Mogadishu Official Language: Somali, Arabic, Eglish, Italian Population: 9,5 million Square Km: 637657 Dialling code: +252 Acting political head: Ali Mahdi Mohmaed (President)

At present there is no Licenced commerical air operator in this country.

6V = SENEGAL (Republic of Senegal) (République du Sénégal)

Capital: Dakar Official Language: French, Wolof Population: 8,5 million Square Km: 196722 Dialling code: +221 Year established: 1960 Acting political head: Abdou Diouf (President)

Government / Corporate / Executive / VIP Aircraft

registration	type of aircraft	cn/fn	ex/ex*	mfd	del	powered by	mtow kg	configuration	selcal	name/fln/remarks
☐ 6V-AEF	Boeing 727-2M1 (A)	21091 / 1134	N40104*	0075	1176	3 PW JT8D-17	88360	VIP	EF-BM	Pointe de Sangomar / Gvmt
☐ 6V-AFF	De Havilland DHC-6 Twin Otter 300	788	C-GBOD*	0082	1282	2 PWC PT6A-27	6350	Surveyer		Gvmt-Sec. Etat Peche Martitime

AERO SERVICE ASF — Dakar-Yoff

BP 8080, Dakar, Senegal ☎ 820 63 11 Tx: none Fax: 821 67 77 SITA: n/a
F: 1997 ✈ n/a Head: Farba Se Net: n/a

registration	type of aircraft	cn/fn	ex/ex*	mfd	del	powered by	mtow kg	configuration	selcal	name/fln/remarks
☐ 6V-AHF	Cessna 208B Grand Caravan	208B0634	N12386*	0097	1197	1 PWC PT6A-114A	3969	Freighter		

AIR SENEGAL = DS / DSB (Sonatra – Société Nationale de Transport Aériens dba) — Dakar-Yoff

BP 8010, Dakar-Yoff, Senegal ☎ 20 09 13 Tx: none Fax: 20 00 33 SITA: n/a
F: 1971 ✈ 119 Head: Ibrahima Faye IATA: 223 ICAO: SONATRA-AIR SENEGAL Net: n/a

registration	type of aircraft	cn/fn	ex/ex*	mfd	del	powered by	mtow kg	configuration	selcal	name/fln/remarks
☐ 6V-ADD	De Havilland DHC-6 Twin Otter 300	380		0073	1073	2 PWC PT6A-27	5670	Y18		
☐ 6V-AHD	De Havilland DHC-8-102 Dash 8	121	C-FWZV	0088	0996	2 PWC PW120A	15650	Y37		lsf FSBU Trustee

ASECNA = XKX (Agence pour la Sécurité de la Navigation Aérienne en Afrique et à Madagascar dba) — Dakar-Yoff

BP 8163, Dakar-Yoff, Senegal ☎ 20 06 36 Tx: 31508 dmtu sg Fax: 20 12 27 SITA: n/a
F: 1960 ✈ 5900 Head: O.I. Oubandawaki Net: n/a Intergovernmental organisation conducting calibration flights for the 15 associated member states.

registration	type of aircraft	cn/fn	ex/ex*	mfd	del	powered by	mtow kg	configuration	selcal	name/fln/remarks
☐ 6V-AFW	ATR 42-300	117	F-WWEN*	0088	1288	2 PWC PW120	16700	Calibr./12 seats		

SAHELIENNE D'HELICOPTERE, S.A. — Dakar-Yoff

BP 8816, Dakar, Senegal ☎ 821 74 74 Tx: none Fax: 821 73 33 SITA: n/a
F: 1997 ✈ n/a Head: n/a Net: n/a

registration	type of aircraft	cn/fn	ex/ex*	mfd	del	powered by	mtow kg	configuration	selcal	name/fln/remarks
☐ F-GFEB	Eurocopter (Aerosp.) SA341G Gazelle	1491	N9002L	0077	0097	1 TU Astazou IIIA	1800			lsf Finloc
☐ 6V-AGO	Piper PA-31T Cheyenne II	31T-7620057	F-GDAL	0076	0097	2 PWC PT6A-28	4082			

SENEGALAIR = SGL — Dakar-Yoff

BP 8207, Dakar-Yoff, Senegal ☎ 20 00 20 Tx: none Fax: 25 32 56 SITA: n/a
F: 1985 ✈ 10 Head: Awa Diop ICAO: SENAIR Net: n/a Aircraft below MTOW 1361kg: Cessna 150/172 & Piper PA-28.

registration	type of aircraft	cn/fn	ex/ex*	mfd	del	powered by	mtow kg	configuration	selcal	name/fln/remarks
☐ 6V-AGS	Beech King Air 200	BB-28	F-GKPL	0074		2 PWC PT6A-41	5670			

6Y = JAMAICA

Capital: Kingston Official Language: English Population: 2,6 million Square Km: 10990 Dialling code: +1-876 Year established: 1962 Acting political head: James Percival Patterson (Prime Minister)

AIR JAMAICA, Ltd = JM / AJM — Kingston-Norman Manley

72-76 Harbour Street, Kingston, Jamaica ☎ (876) 922-3460 Tx: 2389 airjca Fax: (876) 922-0107 SITA: n/a
F: 1968 ✈ 1600 Head: Gordon Stewart IATA: 201 ICAO: JULIETT MIKE Net: http://www.airjamaica.com
Internal commuter flights are operated on behalf of Air Jamaica by AIR JAMAICA EXPRESS (with Dornier 228 & Shorts 360) usign JM-flight numbers. For details – see under that company.

registration	type of aircraft	cn/fn	ex/ex*	mfd	del	powered by	mtow kg	configuration	selcal	name/fln/remarks
☐ N191AJ	Boeing (Douglas) MD-83 (DC-9-83)	53191 / 2151	XA-THP	0096	1196	2 PW JT8D-219	72575	F12Y135		lsf AWAS
☐ N192AJ	Boeing (Douglas) MD-83 (DC-9-83)	53192 / 2155	XA-THQ	0096	1196	2 PW JT8D-219	72575	F12Y135		lsf AWAS
☐ 6Y-JMA	Airbus Industrie A320-212	528	TC-ONE	0095	1198	2 CFMI CFM56-5A3	77000	F12Y138		lsf ILFC
☐ 6Y-JMB	Airbus Industrie A320-212	422	G-OZBA	0094	0499	2 CFMI CFM56-5A3	77000	F12Y138	AE-HQ	lsf GECA
☐ N624AJ	Airbus Industrie A320-214	624	F-WWBV*	0096	1296	2 CFMI CFM56-5B4	77000	F12Y138	EQ-MR	Spirit of Caribbean / lsf WTC Trustee
☐ N626AJ	Airbus Industrie A320-214	626	F-WWBX*	0097	0297	2 CFMI CFM56-5B4	77000	F12Y138	EQ-MS	lsf WTC Trustee
☐ N628AJ	Airbus Industrie A320-214	628	F-WWBY*	0097	0797	2 CFMI CFM56-5B4	77000	F12Y138	ER-BQ	lsf Debis Aircraft Leasing IV B.V.
☐ N630AJ	Airbus Industrie A320-214	630	F-WWBZ*	0097	0797	2 CFMI CFM56-5B4	77000	F12Y138	ER-DM	lsf Debis Aircraft Leasing IV B.V.
☐ 6Y-JMD	Airbus Industrie A321-211	666	G-BXAW	0097	0199	2 CFMI CFM56-5B3/P	89000	F12Y175		lsf ILFC
☐ 6Y-JME	Airbus Industrie A321-211	775	G-BXNP	0098	0399	2 CFMI CFM56-5B3/P	89000	F12Y175		lsf ILFC
☐ N835AB	Airbus Industrie A310-325 (ET)	650	F-WWCI*	0092	0996	2 PW PW4156	164000	F18Y200	KS-DJ	lsf Airbus / cvtd -324
☐ N837AB	Airbus Industrie A310-325 (ET)	674	F-WWCH*	0093	0596	2 PW PW4156	164000	F18Y180	KS-DP	Spirit of Jamaica / lsf Airbus/cvtd-324
☐ N838AB	Airbus Industrie A310-324 (ET)	676	F-WWCP*	0093	0296	2 PW PW4152	157000	F18Y200	KS-DL	Spirit of Spanish Town / lsf Airbus

registration	type of aircraft	cn/fn	ex/ex*	mfd	del	powered by	mtow kg	configuration	selcal	name/fln/specialtites/remarks
☐ N839AD	Airbus Industrie A310-324 (ET)	678	F-WWCU*	0093	0196	2 PW PW4152	157000	F18Y200	KS-DH	Spirit of Negril / lsf Airbus
☐ N840AB	Airbus Industrie A310-324 (ET)	682	F-WWCN*	0093	1095	2 PW PW4152	157000	F18Y200	KS-DG	Spirit of Mandeville / lsf Airbus
☐ N841AB	Airbus Industrie A310-324 (ET)	686	F-WWCX*	0093	1096	2 PW PW4152	157000	F18Y200	KS-DM	Spirit of Morant Bay / lsf Airbus
☐ 6Y-JMC	Airbus Industrie A340-312	048	3B-NAT	0094	0599	4 CFMI CFM56-5C3	257000			lsf ILFC

AIR JAMAICA EXPRESS, Ltd = JQ / JMX (Subsidiary of Air Jamaica, Ltd)

Kingston-Tinson Pen

Kingston Tinson Pen Aerodrome, Kingston 11, Jamaica ☎ (876) 923-9498 Tx: none Fax: (876) 937-3807 SITA: KTPESJM
F: 1995 ♦♦♦ 84 Head: Gordon Stewart IATA: 100 ICAO: JAMAICA EXPRESS Net: www.airjaimaca.com Flights are operated on behalf of AIR JAMAICA using JM-flight numbers.

☐ 6Y-JQL	Dornier 228-202	8087	N254MC	0086	1095	2 GA TPE331-5-252D	6200	Y19		lsf Dornier Leasing / cvtd -201
☐ 6Y-JQN	Dornier 228-202	8118	N259MC	0087	1095	2 GA TPE331-5-252D	6200	Y19		lsf Dornier Leasing / cvtd -201
☐ 6Y-JMX	Shorts 360-300 (SD3-60)	SH3745	N261GA	0088	0498	2 PWC PT6A-67R	12292	Y36		lsf Lynrise Air Lease
☐ 6Y-JMY	Shorts 360-300 (SD3-60)	SH3729	N729PC	0087	0598	2 PWC PT6A-67R	12292	Y36		lsf Lynrise Air Lease

AIR NEGRIL = 5T (Runway Tours, Ltd dba / official carrier of SuperClubs Hotels)

Montego Bay

PO Box 477, P.O. 1, Montego Bay, Jamaica ☎ (876) 940-7747 Tx: none Fax: (876) 940-6491 SITA: n/a
F: 1993 ♦♦♦ 27 Head: Rugic Misir Net: http://www.AirNegril.com

☐ 6Y-JRD	Cessna U206G Stationair 6 II	U20604522	N9019M	0078	1297	1 CO IO-520-F	1633			
☐ 6Y-JRE	Cessna 208B Grand Caravan	208B0642	N1219N*	0097	0398	1 PWC PT6A-114A	3969			

AIRSPEED JAMAICA, Ltd

Kingston-Tinson Pen

Kingston Tinson Pen Aerodrome, Kingston 11, Jamaica ☎ (876) 923-0486 Tx: none Fax: (876) 923-0264 SITA: n/a
F: n/a ♦♦♦ n/a Head: Keith D. Charles Net: n/a

☐ 6Y-JJC	Cessna U206F Stationair II	U20602650	N33173	0075		1 CO IO-520-F	1633			
☐ 6Y-JKQ	Cessna 337H Super Skymaster II	33701939		0080	0797	2 CO IO-360-GB	2100			

DUSTAIR, Ltd

Boscobel-Oracabessa

Oracabessa PO, St. Mary, Jamaica ☎ (876) 975-3314 Tx: none Fax: (876) 975-3369 SITA: n/a
F: 1987 ♦♦♦ n/a Head: Dudley Beck Net: n/a Aircraft & Ag-aircraft below MTOW 1361/5000kg: Cessna 140 & Ayres S2R

☐ 6Y-JDB	Mitsubishi MU-2P (MU-2B-26A)	353SA	N738MA	0077	0297	2 GA TPE331-5-252M	4749			

HELITOURS JAMAICA, Ltd

Kingston-Tinson Pen

Reynolds Pier, Ocho Rios P.O., St. Ann, Jamaica ☎ (876) 974-0306 Tx: none Fax: (876) 974-0306 SITA: n/a
F: 1994 ♦♦♦ n/a Head: Francis Millwood Net: n/a Aircraft below MTOW 1361kg: Hughes 269C (300C)

☐ N32MV	Bell 206B JetRanger III	4255		0092	1194	1 AN 250-C20J	1451			lsf Rotorcraft Partnerships Ltd

JAMAICA AIR FREIGHTERS, Ltd – JAF

Miami-Int'l, FL (USA) & Kingston-Norman Manley

2600 NW 75th Avenue, Miami, FL 33122, USA ☎ (305) 470-8989 Tx: none Fax: (305) 526-3194 SITA: n/a
F: 1970 ♦♦♦ 18 Head: Ron Davis IATA: 605 Net: n/a Operates cargo charters with Boeing 727F & McDonnell Douglas DC-8F freighter aircraft, leased from ARROW AIR & KALITTA AMERICAN INT'L (N) when required.

JAMAICA AIRLINK (Rutair, Ltd dba)

Kingston-Tinson Pen

PO Box 1003, Kingston, Jamaica ☎ (876) 937-4807 Tx: none Fax: (876) 937-4453 SITA: n/a
F: 1996 ♦♦♦ n/a Head: Howard Levy Net: n/a Aircraft below MTOW 1361kg: Cessna 182

☐ 6Y-JEZ	Piper PA-32-260 Cherokee SIX	32-655	N3741W	0066	0096	1 LY O-540-E4B5	1542			
☐ 6Y-JQD	Cessna U206G Stationair 6 II	U20606547		0082	0096	1 CO IO-520-F	1633			
☐ 6Y-JQI	Cessna U206G Stationair 6 II	U20606469		0082	0096	1 CO IO-520-F	1633			
☐ 6Y-JLA	Britten-Norman BN-2A-9 Islander	341	N153A	0073	1098	2 LY O-540-E4C5	2858			lsf Premier Aviation Group Inc.

TIMAIR, Ltd

Montego Bay

PO Box 122, Montego Bay, Jamaica ☎ (876) 952-2516 Tx: none Fax: (876) 979-1113 SITA: n/a
F: 1993 ♦♦♦ n/a Head: Fraser O'Connell Net: n/a Aircraft below MTOW 1361kg: Cessna 182

☐ 6Y-JNA	Cessna U206G Stationair	U20603837		0077	0493	1 CO IO-520-F	1633			
☐ 6Y-JNB	Cessna U206G Stationair	U20603615	N7332N	0077	0593	1 CO IO-520-F	1633			
☐ 6Y-JNE	Cessna P206B Super Skylane	P206-0367	N4767F	0067	0893	1 CO IO-520-A	1633			
☐ 6Y-JNF	Cessna 337G Super Skymaster II	33701781	N53683	0077	1293	2 CO IO-360-G	2100			
☐ 6Y-JLU	Britten-Norman BN-2B-26 Islander	2170	6Y-JLG	0084	0496	2 LY O-540-E4C5	2994			

TROPICAL AIRLINES, Ltd = TOA

Kingston-Tinson Pen

2 Eastwood Avenue, Kingston 10, Jamaica ☎ (876) 926-4093 Tx: none Fax: (876) 926-4379 SITA: n/a
F: 1996 ♦♦♦ n/a Head: Donovan Grant ICAO: TROPICAL AIRLINES Net: n/a Suspended operations (with Beech 1900C-1 aircraft) 0199. Intends to restart.

WINGS JAMAICA, Ltd (formerly Wings, Ltd & Barnett Aviation)

Kingston-Tinson Pen

PO Box 380, Kingston 11, Jamaica ☎ (876) 923-5416 Tx: none Fax: (876) 923-5416 SITA: n/a
F: 1952 ♦♦♦ 10 Head: F. Carl Barnett Net: n/a Aircraft below MTOW 1361kg: Cessna 172 & 182

☐ 6Y-JIB	Beech Baron E55	TE-947		0073		2 CO IO-520-C	2404	Y5		

7O = YEMEN (Republic of Yemen) (al-Jumhouriya al-Yamania)

Capital: Sana'a Official Language: Arabic Population: 17,0 million Square Km: 527968 Dialling code: +967 Year established: 1918 Acting political head: Lieutenant-General Ali Abdallah Saleh (President)

Government / Corporate / Executive / VIP Aircraft   Additional Alyemda/Yemenia & Yemen Republic Aviation-titles are carried for marketing purposes.

Yemen Air Force Antonov 12/26 are occ. operated on the civil register using the same allocated registrations (7O-ABH/M/N/O, ACI/J) for different aircraft.

☐ 1190	Antonov 24RV					2 IV AI-24VT	21800	mil trans / VIP		Yemen AF/Yemen Republic Aviation-titles
☐ 611	Antonov 26	9503		0079		2 IV AI-24VT	24000	mil trans / VIP		Yemen A.F. / addit. Yemenia-titles
☐ 612	Antonov 26					2 IV AI-24VT	24000	mil trans / VIP		Yemen A.F. / addit. Yemenia-titles
☐ 615	Antonov 26					2 IV AI-24VT	24000	mil trans / VIP		Yemen A.F. / addit. Yemenia-titles
☐ 616	Antonov 26		YR-			2 IV AI-24VT	24000	mil trans / VIP		Yemen A.F. / addit. Yemenia-titles
☐ 617	Antonov 26B	12302		0082		2 IV AI-24VT	24000	mil trans / VIP		Yemen A.F. / addit. Yemenia-titles
☐ 618	Antonov 26		YR-			2 IV AI-24VT	24000	mil trans / VIP		Yemen A.F / addit. Yemenia-titles
☐ 622	Antonov 12					4 IV AI-20M	61000	mil trans / VIP		Yemen A.F / addit. Yemenia-titles
☐ 625	Antonov 12					4 IV AI-20M	61000	mil trans / VIP		Yemen A.F / addit. Yemenia-titles
☐ 626	Antonov 12					4 IV AI-20M	61000	mil trans / VIP		Yemen A.F / addit. Yemenia-titles
☐ 7O-ADG	Ilyushin 76TD	1023412402	RA-76405	0092	0095	4 SO D-30KP	190000	Freighter		Yemen Air Force

YEMENIA – Yemen Airways, Corp. = IY / IYE

Sana'a

PO Box 1183, Sana'a, Republic of Yemen ☎ (1) 23 23 80 Tx: 2204 yemair ye Fax: (1) 25 29 91 SITA: SAHCZIY
F: 1961 ♦♦♦ 2000 Head: Hassan Abdo Sobhi IATA: 635 ICAO: YEMENI Net: n/a

☐ 7O-ADH	De Havilland DHC-6 Twin Otter 310	764	G-GBAC	0081	1094	2 PWC PT6A-27	5670	Y19		lsf BACL / Yemenia joint venture div.
☐ 7O-ADI	De Havilland DHC-6 Twin Otter 300	664	HB-LRT	0080	0595	2 PWC PT6A-27	5670	Y19		Yemenia joint venture div.
☐ 7O-ACL	De Havilland DHC-7-103 Dash 7	023		0080	0596	4 PWC PT6A-50	19958	Y40		
☐ 7O-ACM	De Havilland DHC-7-103 Dash 7	031		0080	0596	4 PWC PT6A-50	19958	Y40		
☐ 7O-ACZ	De Havilland DHC-7-102 Dash 7	032	4W-ACK	0080	0979	4 PWC PT6A-50	19958	Y49		std ADE
☐ 7O-ADB	De Havilland DHC-7-102 Dash 7	035	4W-ACL	0080	1280	4 PWC PT6A-50	19958	Y49		
☐ 7O-ACQ	Boeing 737-2R4C (A)	23129 / 1034		0084	0596	2 PW JT8D-17A	58105	Y118	AH-DF	
☐ 7O-ACR	Boeing 737-2R4C (A)	23130 / 1040		0084	0596	2 PW JT8D-17A	58105	Freighter	AH-DJ	
☐ 7O-ACU	Boeing 737-2N8 (A)	21296 / 478	4W-ABZ	0076	1276	2 PW JT8D-15	53070	F11Y94	BF-JL	
☐ 7O-ADD	Lockheed L-382C (C-130H) Hercules	86D-4827	1160	0079	0492	4 AN T56-A-15	70307	Freighter		jtly opw Air Force
☐ 7O-ADE	Lockheed L-382C (C-130H) Hercules	86D-4825	1150	0079	0492	4 AN T56-A-15	70307	Freighter		jtly opw Air Force
☐ 7O-ACV	Boeing 727-2N8 (A)	21844 / 1518	4W-ACF	0079	0879	3 PW JT8D-17R	89358	F12Y137	BM-DJ	
☐ 7O-ACW	Boeing 727-2N8 (A)	21845 / 1529	4W-ACG	0079	1079	3 PW JT8D-17R	89358	F12Y137	BM-AF	
☐ 7O-ACX	Boeing 727-2N8 (A)	21846 / 1549	4W-ACH	0079	1179	3 PW JT8D-17R	89358	F12Y137	BM-AG	
☐ 7O-ACY	Boeing 727-2N8 (A)	21847 / 1557	4W-ACI	0079	1279	3 PW JT8D-17R	89358	F12Y137	BM-AJ	
☐ 7O-ADA	Boeing 727-2N8 (A)	21842 / 1512	4W-ACJ	0079	1180	3 PW JT8D-17R	89358	VIP	CE-JM	opf Gvmt
☐ F-OHPR	Airbus Industrie A310-325	702	F-WWCG*	0097	0397	2 PW PW4156A	164000	F12C21Y185		lsf Airbus Industrie Financial Services
☐ F-OHPS	Airbus Industrie A310-325	704	F-WWCL*	0097	0397	2 PW PW4156A	164000	F12C21Y185		lsf Airbus Industrie Financial Services

7P = LESOTHO (Kingdom of Lesotho) (Mmuso wa Lesotho)

Capital: Maseru Official Language: Sotho, English Population: 2,0 million Square Km: 30355 Dialling code: +266 Year established: 1966 Acting political head: Ntsu Mokhele (Prime Minister)

ANTONAIR INTERNATIONAL, (Pty) Ltd = ANP (Sister company of Aviation Company Pilot, Russia)

Maseru

PO Box 7475, Maseru 100, Lesotho ☎ Russia(2782)4142653 Tx: none Fax: Russia(2711)9552778 SITA: n/a
F: 1996 ♦♦♦ n/a Head: Vadim L. Lakhtin ICAO: ANTONAIR

☐ 7P-AND	PZL Mielec (Antonov) An-2	1G162-37	RA-07787	0075	0498	1 SH ASh-62IR	5500	Combi		lsf PIL
☐ 7P-ANA	Antonov 12BP	2340709	RA-11038	0062	0997	4 IV AI-20M	61000	Freighter		lsf PIL
☐ 7P-ANB	Antonov 12BP	4342404	RA-11760	0097	0997	4 IV AI-20M	64000	Freighter		lsf PIL
☐ 7P-ANC	Antonov 12BP	9346608	RA-11658	0069	0997	4 IV AI-20M	61000	Freighter		lsf PIL

MAF Lesotho – Mission Aviation Fellowship (Branch of MAF USA) — Maseru

PO Box 1459, Maseru, Lesotho ☎ 31 47 90 Tx: none Fax: 31 03 47 SITA: n/a
F: 1980 ✝✝✝ 10 Head: Fran Derocher Net: n/a Non-commercial multinational ecclesiastical consortium conducting flights for relief & development agencies & missions in remote areas of third world countries.

☐ 7P-AAK	Cessna TU206G Turbo Stationair 6 II	U20605635	ZS-KSB	0080	1281	1 CO TSIO-520-M	1633			
☐ 7P-AAL	Cessna TU206G Turbo Stationair 6 II	U20604718	N732TH	0079	0684	1 CO TSIO-520-M	1633			
☐ 7P-CMH	Cessna U206G Stationair 6 II	U20605411	9J-CMH	0080	0798	1 CO IO-520-F	1633			

7Q = MALAWI (Republic of Malawi) (Mfuko la Malawi)

Capital: Lilongwe Official Language: English, Chichewa Population: 12,0 million Square Km: 118484 Dialling code: +265 Year established: 1964 Acting political head: Bakili Muluzi (President)

Government / Corporate / Executive / VIP Aircraft

☐ MAAW-J1	Hawker 800B (BAe 125-800B)	258064		0086		2 GA TFE731-5R-1H	12428	VIP		Malawi Army Air Wing

AIR MALAWI = QM / AML — Blantyre

PO Box 84, Blantyre, Malawi ☎ 62 08 11 Tx: 44245 airmalawi btyr Fax: 62 00 42 SITA: BLZCDQM
F: 1964 ✝✝✝ 600 Head: V.T. Likaku IATA: 167 ICAO: MALAWI Net: n/a

☐ 7Q-YKR	Cessna 208B Grand Caravan	208B0668		0098	0498	1 PWC PT6A-114A	3969	Y9		
☐ 7Q-	Cessna 208B Grand Caravan	208B0679	N1239A*	0098	0998	1 PWC PT6A-114A	3969	Y9		
☐ 7Q-YKS	Dornier 228-212	8222	D-CLFA*	0093	1193	2 GA TPE331-5A-252D	6400	Y19		Nyika / std / for sale
☐ 7Q-YKQ	ATR 42-320	236	F-WWES*	0091	1291	2 PWC PW121	16700	Y46		Shire
☐ 7Q-YKP	Boeing 737-33A	25056 / 2045		0091	0591	2 CFMI CFM56-3C1	61235	C19Y112	AS-DE	Kwacha

LUSITANIA, Ltd — Blantyre

Box 996, Blantyre, Malawi ☎ 67 03 00 Tx: n/a Fax: n/a SITA: n/a
F: n/a ✝✝✝ n/a Head: n/a Net: n/a

☐ 7Q-YFZ	Partenavia P.68C-TC	277-19-TC	ZS-MJX	0083	0991	2 LY TIO-360-C1A6D	1990			

STANCOM AVIATION (Subsidiary of Stancom Tobacco) — Lilongwe

PO Box 30224, Lilongwe, Malawi ☎ 78 24 25 Tx: none Fax: 78 24 25 SITA: n/a
F: n/a ✝✝✝ n/a Head: Abel Pieterse Net: n/a

☐ 7Q-YST	Beech King Air 300	FA-139	ZS-MLL	0087	0292	2 PWC PT6A-60A	6350			

7T = ALGERIA (Democratic & Popular Republic of Algeria) (Algeria, full name see below)

(al-Jumhouriya al-Jaza'iriya dimuqratiya ash-sha'abiya)
Capital: Algiers Official Language: Arabic Population: 31,0 million Square Km: 2381741 Dialling code: +213 Year established: 1962 Acting political head: General Liamine Zeroual (President)

Government / Corporate / Executive / VIP Aircraft

☐ 7T-VCW	Hawker 700B (HS 125-700B)	257163	G-5-12*	0082		2 GA TFE731-3-1H	11567	VIP / Survey		Enesa
☐ 7T-VPA	Dassault Falcon 900	81		0090	0390	3 GA TFE731-5AR-1C	20638	VIP		Gvmt
☐ 7T-VPB	Dassault Falcon 900	82		0090	0590	3 GA TFE731-5AR-1C	20638	VIP		Gvmt
☐ 7T-VPR	GAC G-IV Gulfstream IV (SP)	1288	N403GA*	0096	1096	2 RR Tay 611-8	33838	VIP		Gvmt
☐ 7T-VPS	GAC G-IV Gulfstream IV (SP)	1291	N412GA*	0096	1196	2 RR Tay 611-8	33838	VIP		Gvmt
☐ 7T-VRN	Fokker F27 Friendship 600 (F27 Mk600)	10527	7T-WAN	0076	0476	2 RR Dart 536-7R	20412	VIP / liaison		Gvmt
☐ 7T-VRS	Beech King Air 200	BB-759	F-GCTC	0080		2 PWC PT6A-41	5670	VIP		Gvmt
☐ 7T-VRT	Beech King Air 200	BB-775	F-GCTD	0081		2 PWC PT6A-41	5670	VIP		Gvmt
☐ 7T-VRW	Fokker F27 Troopship 400M (F27 Mk400M)	10556	7T-WAV	0077	0777	2 RR Dart 536-7R	20412	VIP / liaison		Gvmt

AIR ALGERIE, SPA = AH / DAH — Algiers

Aéroport Houari Boumediène, DZ-16000 Algiers, Algeria ☎ (2) 50 93 92 Tx: 67145 algah dz Fax: (2) 50 93 89 SITA: n/a
F: 1953 ✝✝✝ 8900 Head: Belleili Chafik IATA: 124 ICAO: AIR ALGERIE Net: n/a Ag-Aircraft below MTOW 5000 kg: Grumman G-164A/B.
Beside aircraft listed, also uses De Havilland DHC-6 Twin Otter aircraft, jointly operated with BENAVIA (HB-) & TASSILI AIRLINES (7T-) on behalf of oil companies.

☐ 7T-WUA	Eurocopter (Aerosp.) SE3130 Alouette II	1061	F-OBCA	0057		1 TU Artouste IIC6	1500	Y4		
☐ 7T-WUE	Bell 206L-3 LongRanger III	51257	C-FDDI	0088	0789	1 AN 250-C30P	1882	Y5		
☐ 7T-WUF	Bell 206L-3 LongRanger III	51264		0088	0789	1 AN 250-C30P	1882	Y5		
☐ 7T-WUG	Bell 206L-3 LongRanger III	51269		0089	0789	1 AN 250-C30P	1882	Y5		
☐ 7T-WUK	Bell 206L-3 LongRanger III	51558	C-FTEX*	0092	1193	1 AN 250-C30P	1882	Y5		
☐ 7T-VIA	Beech Queen Air B80 (65-B80)	LD-505	N6775S	0075		2 LY IGSO-540-A1D	3992	Y7		
☐ 7T-VID	Beech Queen Air B80 (65-B80)	LD-462		0072		2 LY IGSO-540-A1D	3992	Y7		
☐ 7T-VIF	Beech Queen Air B80 (65-B80)	LD-464	N1761W	0073		2 LY IGSO-540-A1D	3992	Y7		
☐ 7T-VIH	Cessna 208B Grand Caravan	208B0384	N1120A*	0094	0395	1 PWC PT6A-114A	3969	Y9		
☐ 7T-VII	Cessna 208B Grand Caravan	208B0393	N1123G*	0094	0395	1 PWC PT6A-114A	3969	Y9		
☐ 7T-VIJ	Cessna 208B Grand Caravan	208B0552	N1132M*	0096	0696	1 PWC PT6A-114A	3969	Y9		
☐ 7T-VIK	Cessna 208B Grand Caravan	208B0573	N1009M*	0096	0197	1 PWC PT6A-114A	3969	Y9		
☐ 7T-VIL	Cessna 208B Grand Caravan	208B0601	N1247H*	0097	0497	1 PWC PT6A-114A	3969	Y9		
☐ 7T-VIM	Cessna 208B Grand Caravan	208B0602	N1247K*	0097	0497	1 PWC PT6A-114A	3969	Y9		
☐ 7T-VCV	Beech King Air A100	B-93	N9369Q	0071		2 PWC PT6A-28	5216	Y7		
☐ 7T-VRF	Beech King Air A100	B-147	N1828W	0072		2 PWC PT6A-28	5216	Y7		
☐ 7T-VHP	Lockheed L-1329 JetStar II	5233	YI-AKA	0079	0091	4 GA TFE731-3	20185	VIP		
☐ 7T-VRJ	Fokker F27 Troopship 400M (F27 Mk400M)	10547	7T-WAS	0076	0479	2 RR Dart 536-7R	20412	Y40		
☐ 7T-VRK	Fokker F27 Troopship 400M (F27 Mk400M)	10553	7T-WAT	0077	0479	2 RR Dart 536-7R	20412	Y38		
☐ 7T-VRL	Fokker F27 Troopship 400M (F27 Mk400M)	10495	7T-WAK	0073	0482	2 RR Dart 536-7R	20412	Y40		
☐ 7T-VRQ	Fokker F27 Troopship 400M (F27 Mk400M)	10526	7T-WAO	0076	0482	2 RR Dart 536-7R	20412	Y40		
☐ 7T-VRR	Fokker F27 Troopship 400M (F27 Mk400M)	10555	7T-WAU	0077	0683	2 RR Dart 536-7R	20412	Y40		
☐ 7T-VRU	Fokker F27 Troopship 400M (F27 Mk400M)	10494	7T-WAI	0073	0482	2 RR Dart 536-7R	20412	Y40		
☐ 7T-VRV	Fokker F27 Troopship 400M (F27 Mk400M)	10543	7T-WAQ	0076	0683	2 RR Dart 536-7R	20412	Y40		
☐ 7T-VEF	Boeing 737-2D6 (A)	20759 / 332		0073	1173	2 PW JT8D-15	52390	F12Y89	FH-DJ	Saoura
☐ 7T-VEG	Boeing 737-2D6 (A)	20884 / 361		0074	0574	2 PW JT8D-15	52390	F12Y89	FH-DE	Monts des Ouleds Neils
☐ 7T-VEJ	Boeing 737-2D6 (A)	21063 / 407		0075	0475	2 PW JT8D-15	52390	F12Y89	FK-AE	Chréa
☐ 7T-VEK	Boeing 737-2D6 (A)	21064 / 409		0075	0475	2 PW JT8D-15	52390	F12Y89	FK-AG	Edough
☐ 7T-VEL	Boeing 737-2D6 (A)	21065 / 416		0075	0675	2 PW JT8D-15	52390	F12Y89	FK-AH	Akfadou
☐ 7T-VEN	Boeing 737-2D6 (A)	21211 / 454		0076	0476	2 PW JT8D-15	52390	F12Y89	GM-EJ	La Soummam
☐ 7T-VEO	Boeing 737-2D6 (A)	21212 / 459		0076	0576	2 PW JT8D-15	52390	F12Y89	GM-EK	Le Titteri
☐ 7T-VEQ	Boeing 737-2D6 (A)	21285 / 473		0076	1076	2 PW JT8D-15	52390	F12Y89	GM-FH	Le Zaccar
☐ 7T-VER	Boeing 737-2D6 (A)	21286 / 482		0077	0177	2 PW JT8D-15	52390	F12Y89	GM-FK	Le Souf
☐ 7T-VES	Boeing 737-2D6C (A)	21287 / 486		0077	0477	2 PW JT8D-15	52390	F12Y89/Frtr	GM-FL	Le Tadmait
☐ 7T-VEY	Boeing 737-2D6 (A)	22766 / 853		0082	0382	2 PW JT8D-15	52390	F12Y89	GM-JL	Rhoufi
☐ 7T-VEZ	Boeing 737-2T4 (A)	22700 / 885	N4563H*	0082	1283	2 PW JT8D-17A	56472	F12Y89	BJ-CK	Monts du Daia
☐ 7T-VJB	Boeing 737-2T4 (A)	22801 / 900	N4558L*	0083	1283	2 PW JT8D-17A	56472	F12Y89	BJ-CM	Monts des Biban
☐ 7T-	Boeing 737-6D6					2 CFMI CFM56-7B20	65091			oo-delivery 0002
☐ 7T-	Boeing 737-6D6					2 CFMI CFM56-7B20	65091			oo-delivery 0002
☐ 7T-	Boeing 737-6D6					2 CFMI CFM56-7B20	65091			oo-delivery 0002
☐ 7T-VHG	Lockheed L-382G (L-100-30) Hercules	51C-4880	N4148M*	0081	0381	4 AN 501-D22A	70307	Freighter		
☐ 7T-VHL	Lockheed L-382G (L-100-30) Hercules	51D-4886	N4160M*	0081	0781	4 AN 501-D22A	70307	Freighter		
☐ 7T-	Boeing 737-8D6					2 CFMI CFM56-7B26	79015			oo-delivery 0300
☐ 7T-	Boeing 737-8D6					2 CFMI CFM56-7B26	79015			oo-delivery 0700
☐ 7T-	Boeing 737-8D6					2 CFMI CFM56-7B26	79015			oo-delivery 0101
☐ 7T-	Boeing 737-8D6					2 CFMI CFM56-7B26	79015			oo-delivery 0201
☐ 7T-	Boeing 737-8D6					2 CFMI CFM56-7B26	79015			oo-delivery 0501
☐ 7T-	Boeing 737-8D6					2 CFMI CFM56-7B26	79015			oo-delivery 0701
☐ 7T-	Boeing 737-8D6					2 CFMI CFM56-7B26	79015			oo-delivery 0901
☐ 7T-VEA	Boeing 727-2D6	20472 / 850		0071	0271	3 PW JT8D-9	78245	F18Y129	FH-EG	Tassili
☐ 7T-VEB	Boeing 727-2D6	20473 / 855		0071	0371	3 PW JT8D-9	78245	F18Y129	FH-EJ	Hoggar
☐ 7T-VEI	Boeing 727-2D6 (A)	21053 / 1111		0075	0375	3 PW JT8D-15	86409	F18Y129	FK-AD	Djebel Amour
☐ 7T-VEM	Boeing 727-2D6 (A)	21210 / 1204		0076	0576	3 PW JT8D-15	86409	F18Y129	GM-EH	Mont du Ksall
☐ 7T-VEP	Boeing 727-2D6 (A)	21284 / 1233		0076	1176	3 PW JT8D-15	86409	F18Y129	GM-EL	Mont du Tessala
☐ 7T-VET	Boeing 727-2D6 (A)	22372 / 1662		0080	0980	3 PW JT8D-15	86409	F18Y129	GM-DK	Georges du Rhumel
☐ 7T-VEU	Boeing 727-2D6 (A)	22373 / 1664		0080	0980	3 PW JT8D-15	86409	F18Y129	GM-DL	Djurdjura
☐ 7T-VEV	Boeing 727-2D6 (A)	22374 / 1711	N8292V*	0081	0381	3 PW JT8D-15	86409	F18Y129	GM-FJ	
☐ 7T-VEW	Boeing 727-2D6 (A)	22375 / 1723	N8295V*	0081	0381	3 PW JT8D-15	86409	F18Y129	GM-HJ	
☐ 7T-VEX	Boeing 727-2D6 (A)	22765 / 1801		0082	0582	3 PW JT8D-15	86409	F18Y129	GM-JK	Djemila
☐ 7T-VJC	Airbus Industrie A310-203	291	F-WZED*	0084	0884	2 GE CF6-80A3	138600	F18Y198	JK-BC	
☐ 7T-VJD	Airbus Industrie A310-203	293	F-WZEE*	0084	1284	2 GE CF6-80A3	138600	F18Y198	JK-CE	
☐ 7T-VJE	Airbus Industrie A310-203	295	5A-DLA	0083	0188	2 GE CF6-80A3	142000	F12Y195	DK-GH	Ist RJA
☐ 7T-VJF	Airbus Industrie A310-203	306	5A-DLB	0084	0188	2 GE CF6-80A3	142000	F12Y195	DK-GJ	Ist RJA
☐ 7T-VJG	Boeing 767-3D6	24766 / 310		0090	0690	2 GE CF6-80C2B2F	156489	F24Y229	HQ-LP	
☐ 7T-VJH	Boeing 767-3D6	24767 / 323		0090	0890	2 GE CF6-80C2B2F	156489	F24Y229	JQ-AB	
☐ 7T-VJI	Boeing 767-3D6	24768 / 332	N6009F*	0090	1090	2 GE CF6-80C2B2F	156489	F24Y229	JQ-AC	

700 registration type of aircraft cn/fn ex/ex* mfd del powered by mtow kg configuration selcal name/fln/specialitites/remarks

TASSILI AIRLINES, S.A. (Associated with BenAvia, Switzerland) — Hassi Messaoud

Blvd Mustapha ben Boulaid, DZ-301 Hassi Messaoud, Algeria ☎ (9) 73 84 25 Tx: none Fax: (9) 73 84 24 SITA: n/a
F: 1998 ⅄⅄⅄ 20 Head: Boubakeur Ben Senouçi Net: n/a Operates charter flights with De Havilland DHC-6 Twin Otter 300 aircraft, currently leased from BENAVIA (HB-) when required.

8P = BARBADOS

Capital: Bridgetown Official Language: English Population: 0,3 million Square Km: 430 Dialling code: +1-246 Year established: 1966 Acting political head: Owen Arthur (Prime Minister)

BAJAN HELICOPTERS, Ltd — Bridgetown Heliport

Bridgetown Heliport, The Wharf, Bridgetown, Barbados ☎ (246) 431-0069 Tx: n/a Fax: (246) 431-0086 SITA: n/a
F: 1989 ⅄⅄⅄ 9 Head: Carrol G. Morris Net: http://www.caribnet.net/copter/index.html

☐ 8P-BHB	Eurocopter (Aerosp.) AS350B Ecureuil	1874	N613LP	0085	0693	1 TU Arriel 1B	1950			
☐ 8P-BHC	Eurocopter (Aerosp.) AS350B Ecureuil	1566	N350DB	0082	0693	1 TU Arriel 1B	1950			
☐ 8P-BHM	Eurocopter (Aerosp.) SA365N Dauphin 2	6077	PH-SST	0084	0199	2 TU Arriel 1C	4000			

HELENAIR (Barbados), Ltd = HCB (Subsidiary of Helenair, St. Lucia) — Barbados-Grantley Adams Int'l

c/o Caribbean Aircraft Handling Ltd, Grantley Adams International Airport, Christ Church, Barbados ☎ (246) 420-7296 Tx: none Fax: (246) 420-7358 SITA: n/a
F: 1998 ⅄⅄⅄ n/a Head: Ms. Jackie Lewis ICAO: HELEN Net: n/a Operates passenger flights with Beech 1900C-1 Airliner aircraft used from parent company HELENAIR, St. Lucia (J6-), when required.

TRANS ISLAND AIR = TRD (Aero Services Barbados (1982), Ltd dba) — Barbados-Grantley Adams Int'l

South Ramp, Grantley Adams Int'l Airport, Christ Church, Barbados ☎ (246) 418-1651 Tx: 2583 aeroserv wb Fax: (246) 428-0916 SITA: n/a
F: 1982 ⅄⅄⅄ 50 Head: Senator Herbert Yearwood ICAO: TRANS ISLAND Net: n/a

☐ 8P-TAG	Britten-Norman BN-2B-20 Islander	2208	8P-SCA	0089	0295	2 LY IO-540-K1B5	2994	9 Pax		
☐ 8P-TAI	Britten-Norman BN-2B-20 Islander	2211	B-3905	0089	0094	2 LY IO-540-K1B5	2994	9 Pax		
☐ 8P-TAJ	Britten-Norman BN-2B-20 Islander	2210	8P-SCB	0089	0295	2 LY IO-540-K1B5	2994	9 Pax		
☐ 8P-TIB	De Havilland DHC-6 Vista Liner 300	772	N235SA	0081	0198	2 PWC PT6A-27	5670	18 Pax		cvtd Twin Otter 300
☐ 8P-TIA	Embraer 110P1 Bandeirante (EMB-110P1)	110311	G-DBAC	0081	0995	2 PWC PT6A-34	5670	19 Pax		

8Q = MALDIVES (Republic of Maldives) (Divehi Jumhouriya Maldanif)

Capital: Male Official Language: Maldivian, English Population: 0,3 million Square Km: 298 Dialling code: +960 Year established: 1965 Acting political head: Maumoon Abdul Gayoom (President)

AIR MALDIVES, Ltd = L6 / AMI (Associated with Malaysian Helicopter Services Berhad) — Male

PO Box 2049, Malé 20-05, Maldives ☎ 32 24 38 Tx: 77058 airmale mf Fax: 32 50 56 SITA: n/a
F: 1974 ⅄⅄⅄ 360 Head: Anbaree Abdul Sattar IATA: 900 ICAO: AIR MALDIVES Net: n/a

☐ 8Q-AMB	Dornier 228-212	8178	D-COLT*	0089	1289	2 GA TPE331-5A-252D	6400	Y19		
☐ 8Q-AMC	Dornier 228-212	8179	D-CISS*	0089	0690	2 GA TPE331-5A-252D	6400	Y19		
☐ 8Q-AMD	De Havilland DHC-8-202 Dash 8	429	C-GDKL*	0096	1196	2 PWC PW123D	16465	Y37		lsf Fulhangi Leasing
☐ F-OHPP	Airbus Industrie A310-222	331	F-WGYR	0084	0298	2 PW JT9D-7R4E1	142000	F20Y200	DL-EF	lsf Airbus Industrie Financial Services

HUMMINGBIRD ISLAND AIRWAYS, (Maldives) Pvt Ltd = HUM (formerly Hummingbird Helicopters, (Maldives) Pvt Ltd) — Male

PO Bag 6 GPO, Malé 20-06, Maldives ☎ 32 57 08 Tx: 66185 humbird mf Fax: 32 31 61 SITA: n/a
F: 1989 ⅄⅄⅄ 120 Head: Azad Shivdasani ICAO: HUM Net: n/a

☐ 8Q-HIC	Cessna 208 Caravan I	20800272	N5265B	0097	1297	1 PWC PT6A-114	3629	Y9		Amphibian
☐ 8Q-HID	Cessna 208 Caravan I	20800025	C-GBOP	0085	0498	1 PWC PT6A-114	3629	Y9		Amphibian
☐ 8Q-HIE	Cessna 208 Caravan I	20800288		0098	1098	1 PWC PT6A-114	3629	Y9		Amphibian
☐ 8Q-HIF	Cessna 208 Caravan I	20800289		0098	1098	1 PWC PT6A-114	3629	Y9		Amphibian
☐ 8Q-HIA	De Havilland DHC-6 Twin Otter 100	82	C-FSCF	0067	1297	2 PWC PT6A-20	5252	Y14		Floats
☐ 8Q-HIB	De Havilland DHC-6 Twin Otter 200	226	VH-ATK	0069	1297	2 PWC PT6A-20	5252	Y14		Floats
☐ 8Q-HIG	De Havilland DHC-6 Twin Otter 300	530	N530JM	0077	0998	2 PWC PT6A-27	5670	Y14		Amphibian

MALDIVIAN AIR TAXI, (Pte) Ltd — Male

PO Box 2023, Malé International Airport, Maldives ☎ 31 52 01 Tx: none Fax: 31 52 03 SITA: n/a
F: 1993 ⅄⅄⅄ 130 Head: Jesper Hougaard Net: http://www.mataxi.com

☐ 8Q-CSL	De Havilland DHC-6 Twin Otter 100	64	C-FCSL	0067	1294	2 PWC PT6A-20	5252	Y18		lsf KBA / Floats
☐ 8Q-MAA	De Havilland DHC-6 Twin Otter 300	693	C-GKBE	0080	1198	2 PWC PT6A-27	5670	Y18		lsf KBA / Floats
☐ 8Q-MAB	De Havilland DHC-6 Twin Otter 300	287	C-GKBV	0070	1198	2 PWC PT6A-27	5670	Y18		lsf KBA / Floats
☐ 8Q-MAC	De Havilland DHC-6 Twin Otter 100	60	C-GTKB	0067	1196	2 PWC PT6A-20	5252	Y18		lsf KBA / Floats
☐ 8Q-MAD	De Havilland DHC-6 Twin Otter 300	273	C-FIOK	0069	0197	2 PWC PT6A-27	5670	Y18		lsf KBA / Floats
☐ 8Q-MAE	De Havilland DHC-6 Twin Otter 300	464	C-FPOO	0075	0997	2 PWC PT6A-27	5670	Y18		lsf KBA / Floats
☐ 8Q-MAF	De Havilland DHC-6 Twin Otter 100	106	C-FGQH	0068	1097	2 PWC PT6A-20	5252	Y18		lsf KBA / Floats
☐ 8Q-MAG	De Havilland DHC-6 Twin Otter 200	224	C-GENT	0069	1197	2 PWC PT6A-20	5252	Y18		lsf KBA / Floats
☐ 8Q-MAH	De Havilland DHC-6 Twin Otter 300	374	C-FMYV	0073	1197	2 PWC PT6A-27	5670	Y18		lsf KBA / Floats
☐ 8Q-MAI	De Havilland DHC-6 Twin Otter 300	279	C-GKBM	0070	1297	2 PWC PT6A-27	5670	Y18		lsf KBA / Floats
☐ 8Q-MAJ	De Havilland DHC-6 Twin Otter 300	325	C-FTJJ	0072	0199	2 PWC PT6A-27	5670	Y18		lsf KBA / Floats
☐ 8Q-NTA	De Havilland DHC-6 Twin Otter 200	146	C-GNTA	0068	0296	2 PWC PT6A-20	5252	Y18		lsf KBA / Floats
☐ 8Q-OEQ	De Havilland DHC-6 Twin Otter 100	44	C-FOEQ	0067	1295	2 PWC PT6A-6	5252	Y18		lsf KBA / Floats
☐ 8Q-QBU	De Havilland DHC-6 Twin Otter 100	99	C-FQBU	0068	1195	2 PWC PT6A-20	5252	Y18		lsf KBA / Floats
☐ 8Q-QHC	De Havilland DHC-6 Twin Otter 100	21	C-FQHC	0067	1195	2 PWC PT6A-20	5252	Y18		lsf KBA / Floats

SUN EXPRESS Airlines Maldives (Pvt), Ltd (Member of The UB Group) — Male

2nd Floor, No. 35 Boduthakurufaanu Magu, Box 20104, Malé, Maldives ☎ 32 00 01 Tx: none Fax: 32 00 07 SITA: n/a
F: 1997 ⅄⅄⅄ 35 Head: Christopher H. Chambers Net: http://www.sunexpressair.com

☐ 8Q-SUN	De Havilland DHC-6 Twin Otter 300	272	C-GBEB	0069	0298	2 PWC PT6A-27	5670	Y19		lsf Beau del Leasing Inc. / Floats
☐ 8Q-	De Havilland DHC-6 Twin Otter 300	434	C-GCGW	0074	0499	2 PWC PT6A-27	5670	Y19		lsf Ashe Aircraft Enterprises / Floats

8R = GUYANA (Cooperative Republic of Guyana)

Capital: Georgetown Official Language: English Population: 1,1 million Square Km: 214969 Dialling code: +592 Year established: 1966 Acting political head: Mrs Janet Jagan (President)

AIR SERVICES, Ltd (formerly Express Air Service, Ltd & Air Services Guyana, Ltd) — Georgetown-Ogle

22A Wights Lane Street, Kingston, Georgetown, Guyana ☎ (2) 62 333 Tx: n/a Fax: (2) 66 046 SITA: n/a
F: n/a ⅄⅄⅄ n/a Head: Yacoob Ally Net: n/a Aircraft below MTOW 1361kg: Cessna 172 & 182.

☐ 8R-GFM	Cessna U206F Stationair	U20601731	N9531G	0072		1 CO IO-520-F	1633			
☐ 8R-GGE	Cessna U206F Stationair II	U20603358	N8501Q	0076	0488	1 CO IO-520-F	1633			Amphibian
☐ 8R-GYA	Cessna U206G Stationair (R/STOL)	U20603654	8R-GGF	0077		1 CO IO-550-F	1633			
☐ N1589U	Cessna U206F Stationair	U20602267		0073		1 CO IO-520-F	1633			lsf pvt
☐ 8R-GAA	Piper PA-34-200T Seneca II	34-7870451	8R-GGJ	0078		2 CO TSIO-360-E	2073			
☐ N5717M	Cessna 310P	310P0017		0068		2 CO IO-470-VO	2359			lsf pvt
☐ 8R-GFI	Britten-Norman BN-2A-9 Islander	677	G-AZGU	0072		2 LY O-540-E4C5	2858			

GUYANA AIRWAYS, Corp. = GY / GYA — Georgetown-Cheddi Jagan Int'l

32 Main Street, PO Box 10223, Georgetown, Guyana ☎ (2) 68 195 Tx: 2242 guyairco gy Fax: (2) 60 032 SITA: n/a
F: 1963 ⅄⅄⅄ 180 Head: R. Ramkarran IATA: 206 ICAO: GUYAIR Net: http://www.turq.com/guyana/guyanair.html

☐ 8R-GEI	De Havilland DHC-6 Twin Otter 300	432		0074	1274	2 PWC PT6A-27	5670	Y20		
☐ 8R-GHN	De Havilland DHC-6 Twin Otter 300	723	C-FWZA	0080	0496	2 PWC PT6A-27	5670	Y20		
☐ 8R-GGK	Shorts Skyvan 3 Variant 100 (SC-7)	SH1980	8P-ASG	0084	0096	2 GA TPE331-2-201A	5670	Y20		
☐ 8R-GRR	Shorts Skyvan 3 Variant 100 (SC-7)	SH1976	G-BJDA*	0081	0096	2 GA TPE331-2-201A	5670	Y20		
☐ N757GA	Boeing 757-28A	24260 / 204	C-GTSV	0088	1293	2 RR RB211-535E4	113398	Y231		lsf ILFC

GUYANA DEFENSE FORCE Air Corps — Georgetown-Cheddi Jagan Int'l

Camp Ayanganna, Thomas Lands, Georgetown, Guyana ☎ (2) 61 587 Tx: n/a Fax: (2) 66 049 SITA: n/a
F: 1975 ⅄⅄⅄ 70 Head: Major Derek Poole Net: n/a Non-profit state organisation conducting police transport/liaison missions and passenger & cargo operations.

☐ 8R-GFN	Britten-Norman BN-2A-2 Islander	289	N4249Y	0071		2 LY IO-540-K1B5	2858			
☐ 8R-GFP	Bell 412	33040		0081		2 PWC PT6T-3B TwinPac	5398			

GUYSUCO AIRCRAFT DEPARTMENT (Division of Guyana Sugar, Corp.) — Georgetown-Ogle

22 Church Street, Georgetown, Guyana ☎ (22) 24 09 Tx: n/a Fax: (2) 57 274 SITA: n/a
F: 1953 ⅄⅄⅄ 23 Head: Harcourt E. Browman Net: n/a Ag-Aircraft below MTOW 5000kg: Ayres S2R Trush Commander 600.

☐ 8R-GFH	Cessna A185F Skywagon II	18503995	N6094E	0080		1 CO IO-520-D	1520			

KAYMAN SANKAR AVIATION, Ltd – KSA (Member of the Kayman Sankar Group of Companies) — Georgetown-Ogle

Ogle Aerodrome, East Coast, Demerara, Guyana ☎ (22) 21 50 Tx: none Fax: (2) 59 65 SITA: n/a
F: 1985 ⅄⅄⅄ 85 Head: Ben Sankar Net: n/a Aircraft / Ag-Aircraft below MTOW 1361/5000kg: Ayres S2R-600 & Cessna 172

☐ 8R-GRS	Cessna U206G Stationair 6 II	U20606202	N206GX	0081		1 CO IO-520-F	1633			
☐ 8R-GGT	Britten-Norman BN-2A-26 Islander	635	VQ-TAG	0071	0989	2 LY O-540-E4C5	2994			
☐ 8R-GGY	Britten-Norman BN-2A-27 Islander	470	N81567	0075	1290	2 LY O-540-E4C5	2994			
☐ 8R-GHM	Britten-Norman BN-2A-27 Islander	216	PT-IAS	0070	0795	2 LY O-540-E4C5	2994			

701 registration type of aircraft cn/fn ex/ex* mfd del powered by mtow kg configuration selcal name/fln/specialitites/remarks

LAPARKAN AIRWAYS, Inc. = L8 — Georgetown-Cheddi Jagan Int'l

2-9 Lombard Street, Georgetown, Guyana ☎ (2) 50 837 Tx: none Fax: (2) 76 808 SITA: n/a
F: 1995 n/a Head: n/a IATA: 959 Net: n/a Operates cargo flights with Boeing 707/747 & McDonnell Douglas DC-8F, leased from other companies when required.

RORAIMA AIRWAYS, Inc. = ROR — Georgetown-Ogle

101 Cummings Street, Bourda, Georgetown, Guyana ☎ (2) 59 648 Tx: none Fax: (2) 59 646 SITA: n/a
F: 1991 28 Head: Capt. Gerald Gouveia ICAO: RORAIMA Net: n/a

☐ 8R-GRA	Britten-Norman BN-2A-26 Islander	3006	N42540	0084	0495	2 LY O-540-E4C5	3000			
☐ 8R-GRC	Britten-Norman BN-2B-27 Islander	2114	SX-DKA	0083	0197	2 LY O-540-E4C5	3000			
☐ 8R-GRB	Cessna 402B II	402B1320	8R-GGP	0078	0495	2 CO TSIO-520-E	2858			

TRANS GUYANA AIRWAYS, Ltd – TGA = TGY (Member of M.C. Correia Holdings, Ltd / formerly Trans Guyana Aviation, Ltd) — Georgetown-Ogle

158/159 Charlotte Street, Lacytown, Georgetown, Guyana ☎ (2) 73 188 Tx: none Fax: (2) 51 171 SITA: n/a
F: 1956 60 Head: M.O. Correia, Jnr. ICAO: TRANS GUYANA Net: n/a Aircraft below MTOW 1361kg: Cessna 172.

☐ 8R-GHF	Cessna A185F Skywagon II	18504134	N61257	0080	0993	1 CO IO-520-D	1520			Amphibian
☐ 8R-GGH	Cessna U206G Stationair 6 II	U20605338	N6133U	0079		1 CO IO-520-F	1633			
☐ 8R-GAC	Britten-Norman BN-2A-27 Islander	694	8R-GGN	0073		2 LY O-540-E4C5	2994			
☐ 8R-GHD	Britten-Norman BN-2A-27 Islander	622	C-GKES	0070		2 LY O-540-E4C5	2994			
☐ 8R-GTG	Cessna 208B Grand Caravan	208B0397	N397TA	0094	1096	1 PWC PT6A-114A	3969			
☐ 8R-GMC	Shorts Skyvan 3 Variant 100 (SC-7)	SH1959	OY-SUY	0078	0793	2 GA TPE331-2-201A	5670			

9A = CROATIA (Republic of Croatia) (Republika Hrvatska)

Capital: Zagreb Official Language: Croatian Population: 4,8 million Square Km: 56538 Dialling code: +385 Year established: 1991 Acting political head: Franjo Tudjman (President)

AVIO COMERCIO — Pula

Lino Mariani 5, HR-52000 Pula, Croatia ☎ (52) 21 09 81 Tx: none Fax: (52) 21 09 91 SITA: n/a
F: 1998 n/a Head: Denis Praget Net: n/a

☐ 9A-DAT	Piper PA-23-250 Aztec E	27-7554060	OY-BLK	0075	0698	2 LY IO-540-C4B5	2359			lsf Eudora Let d.o.o.

CROATIA AIRLINES, d.d. = OU / CTN (Hrvatska zrakoplovna tvrtka, d.d. dba / formerly ZAGAL - Zagreb Airlines) — Zagreb

Savska cesta 41, HR-10000 Zagreb, Croatia ☎ (1) 616 00 66 Tx: none Fax: (1) 617 68 45 SITA: ZAGDDOU
F: 1989 860 Head: Ivan Misetic IATA: 831 ICAO: CROATIA Net: http://www.ctn.tel.hr/ctn

☐ 9A-DFO	Cessna 310R II	310R1537	RC-DFO	0179	0991	2 CO IO-520-MB	2497	Executive		
☐ 9A-CTS	ATR 42-300 (QC)	312	F-WWEH*	0593	0693	2 PWC PW120	16700	Y48 / QC Frtr		Istra
☐ 9A-CTT	ATR 42-300 (QC)	317	F-WWEO*	0693	0693	2 PWC PW120	16700	Y48 / QC Frtr		Dalmacija
☐ 9A-CTU	ATR 42-300	394		0595	0595	2 PWC PW120	16700	Y48		Slavonija
☐ 9A-CTA	Boeing 737-230 (A)	22119 / 714	RC-CTA	0181	0492	2 PW JT8D-15	50890	CY110	KM-FH	Zagreb / for sale 0699
☐ 9A-CTB	Boeing 737-230 (A)	22116 / 701	RC-CTB	0181	0492	2 PW JT8D-15	50890	CY110	GM-DH	Dubrovnik
☐ 9A-CTC	Boeing 737-230 (A)	22118 / 704	RC-CTC	0181	0692	2 PW JT8D-15	50890	CY110	DJ-LM	Split
☐ 9A-CTD	Boeing 737-230 (A)	22140 / 793	D-ABHP	0981	0693	2 PW JT8D-15	50890	CY110	HJ-BD	Pula / lsf Lufthansa Leasing
☐ 9A-CTG	Airbus Industrie A319-112	767	D-AVYA*	0198	0198	2 CFMI CFM56-5B6/P	70000	CY132	GL-DH	Zadar
☐ 9A-CTH	Airbus Industrie A319-112	833	D-AVYJ*	0098	0698	2 CFMI CFM56-5B6/P	70000	CY132	DJ-EM	Zagreb
☐ 9A-CTI	Airbus Industrie A319-112	1043				2 CFMI CFM56-5B6/P	70000	CY132		oo-delivery 0699
☐ 9A-	Airbus Industrie A319-112					2 CFMI CFM56-5B6/P	70000	CY132		oo-delivery 0500
☐ 9A-	Airbus Industrie A319-112					2 CFMI CFM56-5B6/P	70000	CY132		oo-delivery 0800
☐ 9A-CTF	Airbus Industrie A320-211	258	F-OKAI	1091	0597	2 CFMI CFM56-5A1	73500	CY164	DJ-CE	Rijeka
☐ 9A-CTJ	Airbus Industrie A320-214	1009				2 CFMI CFM56-5B4/P	73500	CY164		oo-delivery 0699

GEODETSKI ZAVOD, d.d. Osijek — Osijek

L. Jägera 4, HR-31000 Osijek, Croatia ☎ (31) 21 10 44 Tx: none Fax: (31) 21 24 41 SITA: n/a
F: 1997 n/a Head: n/a Net: n/a

☐ 9A-DBD	Piper PA-31-325 Navajo C/R	31-7512008	D-INJA	0075	0997	2 LY TIO-540-F2BD	2948	Photo / Survey		
☐ 9A-DAE	Twin (Aero) Commander 560F	560F-1279-55	D-IACT	0063	0997	2 LY IGSO-540-B1A	3402	Photo / Survey		

IVAN-AIR, Ltd = IVN — Zagreb

PO Box 27, HR-10150 Zagreb-Airport, Croatia ☎ (1) 622 32 11 Tx: none Fax: (1) 622 25 11 SITA: n/a
F: 1996 n/a Head: John D. Barber ICAO: IVANAIR Net: n/a

☐ UR-26094	Antonov 26B	12706	CCCP-26094	0082	0097	2 IV AI-24VT	24000	Freighter		lsf ABA

LAUS AIR, Tourism & Air Transport Services Ltd = LSU — Zagreb

Ilica 153, HR-10000 Zagreb, Croatia ☎ (1) 377 88 36 Tx: none Fax: (1) 377 88 60 SITA: n/a
F: 1996 n/a Head: n/a ICAO: LAUS AIR Net: n/a

☐ HA-LAQ	Let 410UVP	841332	332	0084	0098	2 WA M-601D	6000	Freighter		lsf FAH
☐ HA-LAR	Let 410UVP-E	871923	923	0087	0098	2 WA M-601E	6400	Freighter		lsf FAH

NORTH ADRIA AVIATION = NAI — Vrsar

Airport, HR-52450 Vrsar, Croatia ☎ (52) 44 13 50 Tx: none Fax: (52) 44 13 50 SITA: n/a
F: 1993 9 Head: Rajko Tomasic ICAO: NORTH-ADRIA Net: n/a Aircraft below MTOW 1361kg: Cessna 150 & 177

☐ 9A-BPW	Piper PA-34-200 Seneca	34-7250191	RC-BPW	0072	0097	2 LY IO-360-C1E6	1905	Y5		
☐ 9A-BAA	PZL Mielec (Antonov) An-2	1G110-36	UR-35070	0069	0797	1 SH ASh-62IR	5500	Y12		
☐ 9A-BKK	PZL Mielec (Antonov) An-2	1G185-28	CCCP-54868	0079		1 SH ASh-62IR	5500	Y12		
☐ 9A-BAN	Let 410UVP	851407	UR-67503	0485	0797	2 WA M-601D	5800	Y17		
☐ 9A-BNA	Let 410UVP	851518	CCCP-67554	0085	0393	2 WA M-601D	5800	Y17		

REPUBLIC OF CROATIA – GOVERNMENT FLIGHT SERVICE (Flight division of Republic of Croatia Government/Vlada Republika Hrvatska) — Zagreb

PO Box 24, HR-10150 Zagreb Airport, Croatia ☎ (1) 626 57 40 Tx: none Fax: (1) 626 50 70 SITA: n/a
F: 1991 n/a Head: Amir Sehic Net: n/a Government agency conducting non-commercial VIP flights for the government.

☐ 9A-CRO	Canadair CL-604 (CL-600-2B16) Challen.	5322	N604CL	0096	0897	2 GE CF34-3B	21909	VIP	KM-FS	
☐ 9A-CRT	Canadair CL-601-3A (CL-600-2B16) Challen.	5067	9A-CRO	0090	0592	2 GE CF34-3A	19550	VIP	AB-MP	

TRADE AIR, d.o.o. = TDR — Zagreb

Josipa Stadlera 61, HR-10040 Zagreb, Croatia ☎ (1) 622 61 04 Tx: none Fax: (1) 622 61 05 SITA: n/a
F: 1994 6 Head: Michael Cvijin ICAO: TRADEAIR Net: n/a

☐ 9A-BTA	Let 410UVP-E19A	912538	OK-WDO	0091	0199	2 WA M-601E	6400	Y19		lsf SLD
☐ HA-LAV	Let 410UVP-E	892215	RA-67604	0089	0097	2 WA M-601E	6400	Y19		lsf BPS
☐ HA-YFD	Let 410UVP-E17	892324		1189	0097	2 WA M-601E	6400	Y19		lsf BPS

9G = GHANA (Republic of Ghana)

Capital: Accra Official Language: English Population: 18,0 million Square Km: 238537 Dialling code: +233 Year established: 1957 Acting political head: Flight Lt. Jerry Rawlings (President)

Government / Corporate / Executive / VIP Aircraft

☐ G525/F	Fokker F27 Troopship 400M (F27 Mk400M)	10520	G523/D	0075	1275	2 RR Dart 532-7	20412	VIP		Ghana Air Force
☐ G530	Fokker F28 Fellowship 3000 (F28 Mk3000)	11125	PH-ZBP*	0077	0978	2 RR Spey 555-15H	33112	VIP		Ghana Air Force
☐ 9G-AGF	Beech 1900D Airliner	UE-136	N3212K	0095	0395	2 PWC PT6A-67D	7688	Corporate		Ashanti Goldfields Company

AIR GHANA, Ltd = GHN — Accra

Kotaka Int'l Airport, PO Box 9892, Accra, Ghana ☎ (21) 77 52 28 Tx: none Fax: (21) 77 31 44 SITA: ACCAGXH
F: 1994 25 Head: Marwan Traboulsi ICAO: AIR GHANA Net: n/a Beside aircraft listed, also uses Boeing 747C/F & DC-8-62F aircraft, leased from other companies when required.

☐ 9G-AYO	Boeing 707-323C	19519 / 619	EL-RDS	0067	0198	4 PW JT3D-7 (HK2/COM)	146500	Freighter		lst/jtly opw Thai Flying

ANALINDA AIRLINES, Ltd — Accra & Libreville (Gabon)

c/o Phoenix Air Marketing Ltd, Phoenix House, High Steet, Henfield, West Sussex BN5 9DA, Great Britain ☎ (1273) 49 49 14 Tx: none Fax: (1273) 49 29 59 SITA: n/a
F: 1995 12 Head: Capt. Robert Sobek Net: n/a

☐ EL-AFY	BAe (HS) Andover C.1	19	9Q-CJR	0067	0597	2 RR Dart 201	22680	Freighter		based Libreville / op as Gabon Express
☐ EL-AIF	BAe (HS) 748-206 Srs 2A (Andover CC.2)	1565 / 50	XS793	0065	0697	2 RR Dart 534-2	21092	Y40		based Libreville / op as Gabon Express
☐ 9G-CDG	Boeing (Douglas) DC-8-55F (JT)	45821 / 255	9Q-CDG	0066	0598	4 PW JT3D-3B (HK2/QNC)	147418	Freighter		lst/jtly opw CCL
☐ 9G-ADS	Boeing 707-323C	19587 / 686	F-GHFT	0368	0296	4 PW JT3D-3B (HK2/COM)	151092	Freighter	DF-AM	lst/jtly opw CCL for RKA

CONTINENTAL CARGO AIRLINES = CCL (Continental Aviation, Ltd dba) — Accra

European HQ: c/o GM Airlines Ltd, 364-366 Kensington High Street, London W14 8NS, Great Britain ☎ (171) 602 70 55 Tx: none Fax: (171) 603 55 33 SITA: n/a
F: 1990 n/a Head: Dr. Charles L. Panagides ICAO: CONTICAL Net: n/a

☐ N359PA	Boeing 727-230 (A)	20789 / 1015	D-ABSI	0074	0394	3 PW JT8D-15	82781	Corporate	BK-EL	Nagham / lsf/jtly opw GM Airlines
☐ 9G-CDG	Boeing (Douglas) DC-8-55F (JT)	45821 / 255	9Q-CDG	0066	0598	4 PW JT3D-3B (HK2/QNC)	147418	Freighter		lsf/jtly opw Analinda Airlines
☐ 9G-ADM	Boeing 707-321C	19369 / 648	9G-ADL	1167	0690	4 PW JT3D-3B (HK2/COM)	151092	Freighter	KM-CF	Garissa / lsf/jtly opw GM Airlines
☐ 9G-ADS	Boeing 707-323C	19587 / 686	F-GHFT	0368	0296	4 PW JT3D-3B (HK2/COM)	151092	Freighter	DF-AM	lsf/jtly opw Analinda Airlines for RKA

FANAIR = FGH (Fan Airways, Ltd dba) — Accra

PO Box 13777, Accra, Ghana ☎ (21) 76 21 21 Tx: none Fax: (21) 77 54 00 SITA: n/a
F: 1997 57 Head: Prof. Frank A. Norvor ICAO: FANAIR Net: n/a

☐ 9G-FAN	Beech 1900C-1 Airliner	UC-137	N137YV	0090	0597	2 PWC PT6A-65B	7530	Y19		lsf Raytheon Aircraft Credit Corp.
☐ 9G-PFN	Beech 1900C-1 Airliner	UC-116	N55280	0090	0597	2 PWC PT6A-65B	7530	Y19		lsf Raytheon Aircraft Credit Corp.

702 registration type of aircraft cn/fn ex/ex* mfd del powered by mtow kg configuration selcal name/fln/specialitites/remarks

GHANA AIRWAYS, Corp. = GH / GHA (Ghana Airlink) Accra

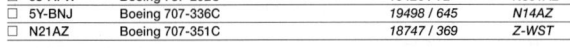

PO Box 1636, Accra, Ghana ☎ (21) 77 75 80 Tx: none Fax: (21) 77 76 75 SITA: ACCEZGH
F: 1958 ⁂ 1300 Head: Emmanuel L. Quartey, Jr. IATA: 237 ICAO: GHANA Net: http://www.iminet.com/SMS/Ghana/index.html
Domestic services are operated as GHANA AIRLINK (an internal division) with Fokker F27 aircraft in conjunction with GHANA AIR FORCE (in Air Force colors & titles).

☐ G524/E	Fokker F27 Friendship 600 (F27 Mk600)	10535	PH-EXX*	0076		2 RR Dart 532-7	20412	Y44		lsf / opb Ghana Air Force
☐ 9G-ADT	Boeing (Douglas) DC-9-51	47665 / 796	YV-90C	1075	0997	2 PW JT8D-17	54885	F12Y100		
☐ 9G-ADU	Boeing (Douglas) DC-9-51	47692 / 803	YV-80C	0075	1197	2 PW JT8D-17	54885	F12Y100		
☐ 9G-ANA	Boeing (Douglas) DC-10-30	48286 / 369		0083	0283	3 GE CF6-50C2	256280	C34Y238	DF-AJ	
☐ 9G-PHN	Boeing (Douglas) DC-10-30	46554 / 84	OO-PHN	0273	0596	3 GE CF6-50C	256280	C32Y238	JL-CH	lsf / opb SKJ in Ghana-colors

GOLDEN AIRWAYS, Ltd = GOG Accra & Kumasi

Box 4300, Accra, Ghana ☎ (21) 77 79 78 Tx: none Fax: (21) 77 65 10 SITA: n/a
F: 1996 ⁂ n/a Head: n/a ICAO: GOLDWAYS Net: n/a Suspended operations (with leased Mil Mi-8 & Antonov 24 aircraft) in 1998. Intends to restart.

IMPERIAL CARGO AIRLINES, Ltd = IMG Accra

PO Box 166, Accra, Ghana ☎ (21) 66 62 93 Tx: none Fax: (21) 66 62 91 SITA: n/a
F: n/a ⁂ n/a Head: n/a ICAO: IMPERIAL AIRLINES Net: n/a

☐ 9G-SGF	Boeing 707-321C	19372 / 655	9G-EBK	0067	0797	4 PW JT3D-3B (HK2/COM)	150000	Freighter		lsf Alpine Air

JOHNSONS AIR, Ltd = JON Accra

PO Box 9138, Accra, Ghana ☎ (21) 77 78 98 Tx: none Fax: (21) 77 78 98 SITA: n/a
F: 1995 ⁂ n/a Head: Mr. Johnson ICAO: JOHNSON AIR Net: n/a

☐ 9G-LCA	Canadair CL-44-0 Guppy	16	4K-GUP	0061	0798	4 RR Tyne 515-10	95254	Freighter		lsf/jtly opw FIA-First Int'l / cvtd -D4
☐ 9G-FIA	Boeing 707-331C	20069 / 815	P4-YYY	0769	0997	4 PW JT3D-3B (HK2/COM)	150850	Freighter		lsf / jtly opw FIA-First Int'l Airlines
☐ 9G-OLD	Boeing 707-324C	19350 / 537	YA-PAM	0066	1197	4 PW JT3D-3B (HK2/COM)	146500	Freighter	DJ-EF	lsf / jtly opw FIA-First Int'l Airlines
☐ 9G-OOD	Boeing 707-399C	19415 / 601	9G-ALD	0067	0998	4 PW JT3D-3B (HK2/COM)	146500	Freighter		lsf / jtly opw FIA-First Int'l Airlines

MK AIRLINES, Ltd = 7G / MKA (formerly MK Aircargo, Ltd) London-Gatwick

European office:, Landhurst, Hartfield, East Sussex TN7 4DL, Great Britain ☎ (1892) 77 00 11 Tx: n/a Fax: (1892) 77 00 22 SITA: n/a
F: 1990 ⁂ 100 Head: Capt. Michael C. Kruger IATA: 513 Net: n/a

☐ 9G-MKA	Boeing (Douglas) DC-8-55F (JT)	45804 / 254	N855BC	0066	1190	4 PW JT3D-3B (HK2/BAC)	147400	Freighter	DK-BG	
☐ 9G-MKC	Boeing (Douglas) DC-8-55F (JT)	45692 / 207	5V-TAF	0664	0193	4 PW JT3D-3B (HK2/BAC)	147400	Combi Y50/Cargo	JM-EK	
☐ 9G-MKE	Boeing (Douglas) DC-8-55F	45753 / 223	5N-MKE	0065	0395	4 PW JT3D-3B (HK2/QNC)	147400	Freighter	BF-DK	cvtd -55
☐ 9G-MKF	Boeing (Douglas) DC-8-55F (JT)	45820 / 246	C-FIWW	0065	0295	4 PW JT3D-3B (HK2/QNC)	147400	Freighter	GJ-AF	

MUK AIR (GH), Ltd = MUG (Subsidiary of Muk Air, Denmark) Accra

PMB, Accra Kotoka Airport, Accra, Ghana ☎ 77 88 99 Tx: none Fax: 22 40 11 SITA: n/a
F: 1997 ⁂ n/a Head: Knut Lindau ICAO: MUGGAN Net: n/a

☐	ATR 42-300					2 PWC PW120	16700	Y48		to be lsf ATR 0099

RACE CARGO AIRLINES, (Nig.) Ltd = RCN (formerly Rainbow Cargo Airlines) Accra, Ostend & Lagos

European HQ:, Unit 8, McKay Trading Estate, Blackthorne Road, Colnbrook, Berkshire SL3 0AH, Great Britain ☎ (1753) 68 24 23 Tx: 849641 rcauk g Fax: (1753) 68 14 34 SITA: n/a
F: 1986 ⁂ 29 Head: Des C. Ayto ICAO: SPEED CARGO Net: n/a Operates cargo flights, currently with aircraft (Boeing 707C & McDonnell Douglas DC-8-62F) leased from other companies when required.

9H = MALTA (Republic of Malta) (Repubblika ta'Malta)

Capital: Valletta Official Language: Maltese, English Population: 0,4 million Square Km: 316 Dialling code: +356 Year established: 1964 Acting political head: Edward Fenech Adami (Prime Minister)

AIR MALTA, Plc = KM / AMC Malta-Luqa

Head office, Luqa LQA 05, Malta ☎ 69 08 90 Tx: 1389 airmal mw Fax: 67 32 41 SITA: MLAPRKM
F: 1973 ⁂ 1770 Head: Louis Grech IATA: 643 ICAO: AIR MALTA Net: http://www.airmalta.com/
Scheduled helicopter flights between Malta-Luqa & Gozo are operated by subsidiary MALTA AIR CHARTER (with Mil Mi-8). For details – see under that company.

☐ 9H-ABE	Boeing 737-2Y5 (A)	23847 / 1414		0087	0787	2 PW JT8D-15A (HK3/NOR)	56472	CY129	JK-FM	Mellieha
☐ 9H-ABF	Boeing 737-2Y5 (A)	23848 / 1418		0087	0787	2 PW JT8D-15A	56472	CY129	JL-AH	Zurrieq
☐ 9H-ABR	Boeing 737-3Y5	25613 / 2446		0093	0393	2 CFMI CFM56-3C1	60555	CY138	CS-BK	Birkirkara
☐ 9H-ABS	Boeing 737-3Y5	25614 / 2467		0093	0493	2 CFMI CFM56-3C1	60555	CY138	CS-BL	Sliema
☐ 9H-ABT	Boeing 737-3Y5	25615 / 2478		0093	0593	2 CFMI CFM56-3C1	60555	CY138	CS-BM	Hamrun
☐ 9H-ADH	Boeing 737-33A	27459 / 3007	N1787B*	0098	0398	2 CFMI CFM56-3C1	60555	CY138	AS-HP	lsf AWAS
☐ 9H-ADI	Boeing 737-33A	27460 / 3021		0098	0498	2 CFMI CFM56-3C1	60555	CY138	BC-MP	lsf AWAS
☐ 9H-ADM	Boeing 737-382	24365 / 1695	CS-TIB	0089		2 CFMI CFM56-3B2	62822	CY138		to be lsf ILFC 0699 / ex TAP
☐ 9H-ADN	Boeing 737-382	25161 / 2226	CS-TIK	0092		2 CFMI CFM56-3B2	62822	CY138		to be lsf ILFC 0599 / ex TAP
☐ 9H-ADK	Boeing 737-4H6	27673 / 2852	9M-MQN	0097	0399	2 CFMI CFM56-3C1	62822	CY152		lsf MAS -1199
☐ 9H-ADL	Boeing 737-4H6	27674 / 2877	9M-MQO	0097	0399	2 CFMI CFM56-3C1	62822	CY152		lsf MAS -1199
☐ 9H-ABP	Airbus Industrie A320-211	112	F-WWIF*	0090	0890	2 CFMI CFM56-5A1	73500	CY168	JM-FQ	Rabat
☐ 9H-ABQ	Airbus Industrie A320-211	293	F-WWDZ*	0092	0392	2 CFMI CFM56-5A1	73500	CY168	JM-GQ	Zejtun

EUROJET, Ltd = JLN Malta-Luqa

Tumas Group, Triq il-Gifen, Bugibba SPB 03, Malta ☎ 44 42 34 Tx: none Fax: 44 07 38 SITA: n/a
F: 1994 ⁂ 4 Head: Capt. Lino Xuereb ICAO: JET LINE Net: n/a

☐ 9H-ACR	Cessna 550 Citation II	550-0025	N78PR	0078	1294	2 PWC JT15D-4	6577	Exec/Frtr/EMS		

EXECUTIVE FLIGHT SERVICES, Ltd = URF Malta-Luqa

Velbro House, Luqa Road, Qormi QRM 08, Malta ☎ 24 23 10 Tx: none Fax: 23 85 12 SITA: n/a
F: 1998 ⁂ 8 Head: Tyrone Dalea ICAO: EXECUTIVE EXPRESS Net: n/a

☐ 9H-ADD	Piper PA-42 Cheyenne III	42-8001101	N30MA	0080	0698	2 PWC PT6A-41	5080	7-8 Pax	AD-FQ	

MALTA AIR CHARTER, Company Ltd = R5 / MAC (Gozo Wings) (Subsidiary of Air Malta, Plc) Malta-Luqa

Head office – Air Malta Building, VJALL L-Aviazzioni, Luqa LQA 05, Malta ☎ 67 72 91 Tx: 1389 airmal mw Fax: 66 31 95 SITA: MLASHKM
F: 1975 ⁂ n/a Head: Charles T. Buttigieg ICAO: MALTA CHARTER Net: n/a Beside aircraft listed, also leases aircraft from AIR MALTA for charter flights as required.
GOZO WINGS is a marketing name used for the scheduled service Luqa-Gozo.

☐ LZ-CAE	Mil Mi-8P	10312		0075	0497	2 IS TV2-117A	12000	Y26		lsf HLR
☐ LZ-CAH	Mil Mi-8P	24024		0091	0497	2 IS TV2-117A	12000	Y26		lsf HLR
☐ LZ-CAZ	Mil Mi-8P	24023		0091	0098	2 IS TV2-117A	12000	Y26		lsf HLR

MED AVIA – Mediterranean Aviation, Company Ltd (Associated with Air Malta) Malta-Luqa

PO Box 48, M.I.A., Luqa LQA 05, Malta ☎ 68 98 43 Tx: 1975 medmte mw Fax: 64 01 69 SITA: n/a
F: 1978 ⁂ 53 Head: Dr. George Cassar Net: n/a

☐ 9H-AAP	CASA 212 Aviocar Srs 100	9	EC-CRV*	0078	0679	2 GA TPE331-5-251C	6500	19 Pax		
☐ 9H-AAQ	CASA 212 Aviocar Srs 100	119	ECT-105*	0078	0679	2 GA TPE331-5-251C	6500	19 Pax		
☐ 9H-AAR	CASA 212 Aviocar Srs 200	161		0080	0480	2 GA TPE331-10-511C	7700	26 Pax		
☐ 9H-AAS	CASA 212 Aviocar Srs 200	162		0080	0580	2 GA TPE331-10-511C	7700	26 Pax		

9J = ZAMBIA (Republic of Zambia)

Capital: Lusaka Official Language: English Population: 9,5 million Square Km: 752618 Dialling code: +260 Year established: 1964 Acting political head: Frederick Chiluba (President)

Government / Corporate / Executive / VIP Aircraft

☐ AF602	BAe (HS) 748-265 Srs 2A	1688 / 160		0070	0271	2 RR Dart 534-2	20183	VIP / mil trans		Zambia Air Force

AERO ZAMBIA, Ltd = Z9 / RZL Lusaka

Private Bag E717, Lusaka, Zambia ☎ (1) 22 61 47 Tx: none Fax: (1) 22 61 47 SITA: LUNTOZ9
F: 1994 ⁂ 250 Head: David P. Tokoph IATA: 509 ICAO: AERO ZAMBIA Net: n/a

☐ N63119	De Havilland DHC-6 Twin Otter 200	119		0068	1096	2 PWC PT6A-20	5252	Y19 / Freighter		lsf Grecoair
☐ 9J-AFU	Boeing 737-222	19075 / 97	N7383F	0068	0395	2 PW JT8D-9A	49442	C12Y88		lsf Aviation Consultants
☐ 9J-AFW	Boeing 737-202C	19426 / 72	N801AL	0068	0296	2 PW JT8D-9A	49442	C12Y88		lsf Aviation Consultants / sub-lst ILN
☐ 5Y-BNJ	Boeing 707-336C	19498 / 645	N14AZ	0067	0097	4 PW JT3D-3B (HK2/COM)	150850	Freighter		lsf Grecoair
☐ N21AZ	Boeing 707-351C	18747 / 369	Z-WST	0064	0298	4 PW JT3D-3B (HK2/COM)	150850	Freighter	AH-BG	lsf Grecoair

CHANI ENTERPRISES – Flight Operations (Flight division of Chani Enterprises, Ltd) Kitwe & Ndola

PO Box 20666, Kitwe, Zambia ☎ (2) 22 16 75 Tx: none Fax: (2) 20 666 SITA: n/a
F: n/a ⁂ n/a Head: n/a Net: n/a Operates non-commercial cargo flights for its parent, a mining company only.

☐ 9J-BTM	Lockheed L-182 (C-130A) Hercules	1A-3095	9J-AFV	0057	0795	4 AN T56-A-9D	56336	Freighter		

EAGLE AIR (Eagle Travel, Ltd dba) Lusaka

PO Box 34530, Lusaka, Zambia ☎ (1) 21 68 57 Tx: 40420 eagle za Fax: n/a SITA: n/a
F: n/a ⁂ n/a Head: n/a Net: n/a

☐ 9J-ABY	Beech Baron 58	TH-59	ZS-IHU	0070		2 CO IO-520-C	2449			

703 registration type of aircraft cn/fn ex/ex* mfd del powered by mtow kg configuration selcal name/fln/specialitites/remarks

EASTERN AIR, Ltd = EAZ
Lusaka

PO Box 32661, Lusaka, Zambia ☎ (1) 23 30 97 Tx: none Fax: (1) 28 65 08 SITA: n/a
F: 1995 ⁂ n/a Head: Yoosuf Zumla ICAO: EASAIR Net: n/a

☐ 9J-DCF	Beech King Air C90	LJ-575	N12RF	0073	0098	2 PWC PT6A-20	4377	Y8		
☐ 9J-YVZ	Beech King Air B90	LJ-338	ZS-LWZ	0068	0098	2 PWC PT6A-20	4377	Y8		
☐ 9J-EAZ	Let 410UVP-E8B	912539	OM-WDB	0091	0396	2 WA M-601E	6400	Y17		lsf OIR

LUPENGA AIR CHARTERS = LUP
Lusaka

PO Box 30131, Lusaka, Zambia ☎ (4) 22 12 80 Tx: 45790 za Fax: (4) 22 12 80 SITA: n/a
F: n/a ⁂ n/a Head: n/a ICAO: LUPENGA Net: n/a Operates cargo flights with Boeing 707C aircraft leased from other companies when required.

MISSION MEDIC AIR, Ltd
Luanshya

PO Box 509, Luanshya, Zambia ☎ (2) 51 19 57 Tx: n/a Fax: (2) 51 19 57 SITA: n/a
F: n/a ⁂ n/a Head: George Adams Net: n/a

☐ 9J-MMA	Cessna U206F Stationair II	U20602830	9J-AEA	0075		1 CO IO-520-F	1633			

PROFLIGHT AIR SERVICES, Ltd
Lusaka

PO Box 30536, Lusaka, Zambia ☎ (1) 26 36 87 Tx: none Fax: (1) 26 19 41 SITA: n/a
F: n/a ⁂ n/a Head: n/a Net: n/a

☐ 9J-KKN	Piper PA-31-350 Navajo Chieftain	31-8052113	ZS-KKN	0080	0097	2 LY TIO-540-J2BD	3175			

ROAN AIR = Q3 / MAZ (Mines Air Services, Ltd dba / formerly Jointair, Ltd)
Lusaka

PO Box 310277, Lusaka, Zambia ☎ (1) 27 10 66 Tx: 40410 Fax: (1) 27 10 54 SITA: n/a
F: 1988 ⁂ 40 Head: Musho Shandavu IATA: 391 ICAO: ROAN AIR Net: n/a

☐ 9J-MAS	Beech 1900D Airliner	UE-323	N23047*	0098	0898	2 PWC PT6A-67D	7688	Y18		
☐ 9J-MBO	Beech 1900D Airliner	UE-319	N23004*	0098	0798	2 PWC PT6A-67D	7688	Y18		Kaingo
☐ 9J-RON	Canadair CL-601-1A (CL-600-2A12) Challen.	3057	N19J	0086	0986	2 GE CF34-1A	19550	Y14		

SAFARI AFRICA Aviation, Ltd (Associated with Airvania, Ltd)
Lusaka

PO Box 35059, Lusaka, Zambia ☎ (1) 21 04 62 Tx: 40257 sasah za Fax: (1) 26 29 85 SITA: n/a
F: 1963 ⁂ 20 Head: Capt. R. McKay Net: n/a Aircraft below MTOW 1361 kg: Cessna 180. Also operated are 2 Flamboyan Free Balloon (Hot Air).

☐ 9J-MCK	Cessna 185A Skywagon	185-0240		0062		1 CO IO-470-F	1451			
☐ 9J-AFF	Cessna 337 Super Skymaster	337-0017	N2117X	0065		2 CO IO-360-C/D	1905			

SAFARI AIR SERVICES of Zambia, Ltd
Lusaka

PO Box CH46, Lusaka, Zambia ☎ (1) 21 34 44 Tx: 45140 sun air za Fax: n/a SITA: n/a
F: 1979 ⁂ 16 Head: Major A.J. Mumba Net: n/a Aircraft below MTOW 1361 kg: Bell 47G.

☐ 9J-REF	Beech Bonanza V35	D-8429		0067		1 CO IO-520-B	1542	4 Pax		
☐ 9J-AEF	Beech Baron 58	TH-610		0075		2 CO IO-520-C	2449	5 Pax		

STABO AIR, Ltd = SBO (formerly Stabo Freight, Ltd)
Lusaka

PO Box 32152, Lusaka, Zambia ☎ (1) 23 20 77 Tx: none Fax: (1) 23 34 81 SITA: n/a
F: 1989 ⁂ 7 Head: Christopher Mutale IATA: 380 ICAO: STABAIR Net: n/a

☐ 9J-EFI	Cessna 210N Centurion II	21064118	ZS-KOX	0080	1197	1 CO IO-520-L	1724			

TRAVEL INTERNATIONAL AIR CHARTER - TIAC = TIC
Chingola

PO Box 10724, Chingola, Zambia ☎ (2) 31 17 73 Tx: 54080 nae za Fax: (2) 31 35 21 SITA: n/a
F: 1976 ⁂ 14 Head: Ceiriog Hughes ICAO: TRAVEL INTERNATIONAL Net: n/a Aircraft below MTOW 1361 kg: Cessna 182 & Piper PA-28.

☐ 9J-AAG	Piper PA-23-250 Aztec D	27-4090	N6761Y	0069		2 LY IO-540-C4B5	2359			
☐ 9J-ACU	Piper PA-23-250 Aztec E	27-4646	N14034	0071		2 LY IO-540-C4B5	2359			
☐ 9J-LTA	Cessna 421A	421A0009	ZS-LTA	0069		2 CO GTSIO-520-D	3103			

ZAMBIA FLYING DOCTOR SERVICE
Ndola

PO Box 71856, Ndola, Zambia ☎ (26) 61 14 17 Tx: 33740 flydoc za Fax: (26) 61 40 54 SITA: n/a
F: 1965 ⁂ 350 Head: Dr. D.J. Kwendakwema Net: n/a

☐ 9J-ACB	Britten-Norman BN-2A-3 Islander	246	G-51-246*	0070		2 LY IO-540-K1B5	2858	EMS / 9 Pax		std / for sale
☐ 9J-ACC	Britten-Norman BN-2A-3 Islander	254	G-51-254*	0071		2 LY IO-540-K1B5	2858	EMS / 9 Pax		
☐ 9J-ACE	Britten-Norman BN-2A-3 Islander	260	G-51-260*	0071		2 LY IO-540-K1B5	2858	EMS / 9 Pax		
☐ 9J-ACG	Britten-Norman BN-2A-3 Islander	270	G-51-270*	0071		2 LY IO-540-K1B5	2858	EMS / 9 Pax		std / to be overhauled

9K = KUWAIT (State of Kuwait) (Dawlat al-Kuwait)

Capital: Kuwait Official Language: Arabic Population: 1,8 million Square Km: 17818 Dialling code: +965 Year established: 1961 Acting political head: Jab'r al-Ahmed al-Jab'r as-Sabah (Emir)

KUWAIT AIRWAYS, Corp. = KU / KAC (formerly Kuwait National Airways)
Kuwait

PO Box 394, Kuwait, State of Kuwait ☎ 431 02 47 Tx: n/a Fax: 431 67 13 SITA: KWIZZKU
F: 1954 ⁂ 5000 Head: Ahmad H. Al-Mishari IATA: 229 ICAO: KUWAITI Net: http://www.travelfirst.com/sub/kuwaitair.html
Beside aircraft listed, also uses a Boeing 707C for all-cargo services, lsf/opb TMA of Lebanon (OD-) when required.

☐ 9K-AJA	GAC G-IV Gulfstream IV	1157	N17581*	0091	1291	2 RR Tay 611-8	33203	Executive	DG-AR	
☐ 9K-AJB	GAC G-IV Gulfstream IV	1159	N17583*	0091	1291	2 RR Tay 611-8	33203	Executive	DG-AS	
☐ 9K-AJC	GAC G-IV Gulfstream IV	1169	N463GA*	0092	0192	2 RR Tay 611-8	33203	Executive	DG-BR	
☐ 9K-AGC	Boeing (Douglas) MD-83 (DC-9-83)	49809 / 1843	KAF26	0092	1097	2 PW JT8D-219	72575	VIP	AL-GH	opf State of Kuwait
☐ 9K-AKA	Airbus Industrie A320-212	181	F-WWIU*	0091	1092	2 CFMI CFM56-5A3	75500	F12Y119	DR-EP	Bubbyan / cvtd -211
☐ 9K-AKB	Airbus Industrie A320-212	182	F-WWIV*	0091	1292	2 CFMI CFM56-5A3	75500	F12Y119	DR-EQ	Kubber / cvtd -211
☐ 9K-AKC	Airbus Industrie A320-212	195	F-WWDP*	0091	1292	2 CFMI CFM56-5A3	75500	F12Y119	DR-ES	Qurtoba / cvtd -211
☐ 9K-AFA	Boeing 727-269 (A)	22359 / 1652	N8291V*	0080	0980	3 PW JT8D-17R	89358	VIP	DL-AB	opf State of Kuwait
☐ N181SK	Boeing (Douglas) DC-8-62F	45910 / 311	N803MG	0067	1298	4 PW JT3D-3B (HK3/BAC)	158757	Freighter	BC-KM	lsf/opb TCN in Kuwait Aw.-cs / cvtd -62
☐ 9K-ALA	Airbus Industrie A310-308	647	F-WWCQ*	0093	0593	2 GE CF6-80C2A8	157000	F18C21Y131	DR-FG	Al-Jahra
☐ 9K-ALB	Airbus Industrie A310-308	649	F-WWCV*	0093	0693	2 GE CF6-80C2A8	157000	F18C21Y131	DR-FH	Gharnada
☐ 9K-ALC	Airbus Industrie A310-308	663	F-WWCK*	0093	0693	2 GE CF6-80C2A8	157000	F18C21Y131	DR-FJ	Kadhma / lst RJA as JY-AGT
☐ 9K-ALD	Airbus Industrie A310-308	648	F-WWCR*	0093	1193	2 GE CF6-80C2A8	157000	VIP	ES-JM	Al-Salmiya / opf State of Kuwait
☐ 9K-AHI	Airbus Industrie A300C-620 (A300C4-620)	344	F-WZYK*	0084	0884	2 PW JT9D-7R4H1	165000	F22Y234 / Frtr	DG-EM	lst MNA as PK-MAY
☐ 9K-AMA	Airbus Industrie A300-605R (A300B4-605R)	673	F-WWAQ*	0093	0593	2 GE CF6-80C2A5	170500	F18C21Y196	DR-FK	Failaka
☐ 9K-AMB	Airbus Industrie A300-605R (A300B4-605R)	694	F-WWAV*	0093	0793	2 GE CF6-80C2A5	170500	F18C21Y196	DR-FL	Burghan
☐ 9K-AMC	Airbus Industrie A300-605R (A300B4-605R)	699	F-WWAM*	0093	0793	2 GE CF6-80C2A5	170500	F14C18Y228	DR-FM	Wafra
☐ 9K-AMD	Airbus Industrie A300-605R (A300B4-605R)	719	F-WWAB*	0093	0194	2 GE CF6-80C2A5	170500	F18C21Y196	DR-FP	Wara
☐ 9K-AME	Airbus Industrie A300-605R (A300B4-605R)	721	F-WWAG*	0093	0294	2 GE CF6-80C2A5	170500	F18C21Y196	DR-FQ	Al-Rawdhatain
☐ 9K-AOA	Boeing 777-269 (ER)	28743 / 125		0098	0398	2 GE GE90-92B	286897		DQ-GP	Al-Grain
☐ 9K-AOB	Boeing 777-269 (ER)	28744 / 145		0098	0698	2 GE GE90-92B	286897		DQ-HJ	
☐ 9K-ANA	Airbus Industrie A340-313	089	F-WWJX*	0095	0395	4 CFMI CFM56-5C4	257000	F18C24Y238	CF-HP	Warba
☐ 9K-ANB	Airbus Industrie A340-313	090	F-WWJZ*	0095	0495	4 CFMI CFM56-5C4	257000	F18C24Y238	CF-JP	Al-Sabahiya
☐ 9K-ANC	Airbus Industrie A340-313	101	F-WWJE*	0095	0595	4 CFMI CFM56-5C4	257000	F18C24Y238	CG-HP	Al-Mobarakia
☐ 9K-AND	Airbus Industrie A340-313	104	F-WWJJ*	0095	0795	4 CFMI CFM56-5C4	257000	F18C24Y238	CG-KP	Al-Riggah
☐ 9K-ADB	Boeing 747-269B (M)	21542 / 335		0078	0878	4 PW JT9D-7J	356070	F32C24Y322	DG-CJ	
☐ 9K-ADD	Boeing 747-269B (M)	22740 / 553		0082	0182	4 PW JT9D-7J	356070	F32C24Y322	DK-EH	
☐ 9K-ADE	Boeing 747-469 (M)	27338 / 1046		0094	1194	4 GE CF6-80C2B1F	394625	VIP or Combi	FJ-MR	Al-Jabariya / opf State of Kuwait

9L = SIERRA LEONE (Republic of Sierra Leone)

Capital: Freetown Official Language: English Population: 4,5 million Square Km: 71740 Dialling code: +232 Year established: 1961 Acting political head: Johnny Paul Koroma (President)

AFRIK AIR LINKS = AFK
Freetown

11 Charlotte Street, Freetown, Sierra Leone ☎ (22) 22 43 50 Tx: none Fax: (22) 22 58 80 SITA: n/a
F: 1991 ⁂ n/a Head: Alpa Ranu ICAO: AFRICA LINKS Net: n/a

☐ 5N-TRB	Embraer 110P1 Bandeirante (EMB-110P1)				0097	2 PWC PT6A-34	5670	Y19		occ lsf CRG
☐ RA-24574	Mil Mi-8		CCCP-24574	0088		2 IS TV2-117A	12000	Y24		lsf Petrozavodsk Air Enterprise

BELLVIEW AIRLINES (S/L), Ltd = BVU
Freetown

Lightfoot Boston Street, Freetown, Sierra Leone ☎ (22) 22 73 11 Tx: none Fax: (22) 22 82 47 SITA: n/a
F: n/a ⁂ n/a Head: n/a Net: n/a Operates passenger flights with McDonnell Douglas DC-9-32 aircraft, leased from Bellview Airlines, Nigeria (5N-) when required.

SIERRA NATIONAL AIRLINES = LJ / SLA (formerly Sierra Leone Airlines, Ltd)
Freetown

25 Pultney Street, PO Box 285, Freetown, Sierra Leone ☎ (22) 22 62 97 Tx: 3242 air leo sl Fax: (22) 22 20 26 SITA: n/a
F: 1990 ⁂ 200 Head: Stanley Palmer IATA: 690 ICAO: SELAIR Net: n/a Operates scheduled services with BAe (BAC) One-Eleven aircraft lsf/opb OKADA AIR (5N-) when required.

WEST COAST AIRWAYS, Ltd = WCA
Freetown

PO Box 366, Freetown, Sierra Leone ☎ (22) 22 75 61 Tx: none Fax: (22) 22 82 31 SITA: n/a
F: 1996 ⁂ n/a Head: Lakiss Khalil ICAO: WEST-LEONE Net: n/a

☐ 9L-LBJ	Let 410UVP	841202	RA-67438	0084	0096	2 WA M-601D	5800	Y15		lsf RYZ / opf Doren Air Africa
☐ 9L-LBM	Let 410UVP	841338	RA-67109	0084	0096	2 WA M-601D	5800	Y15		lsf RYZ / opf Doren Air Africa

704 registration type of aircraft cn/fn ex/ex* mfd del powered by mtow kg configuration selcal name/fln/specialitites/remarks

Government / Corporate / Executive / VIP Aircraft
ROYAL MALAYSIAN AIR FORCE – Tentera Udara Diraja Malaysia uses the ICAO code RMF and CALLSIGN: ANGKASA.

registration	type of aircraft	cn/fn	ex/ex*	mfd	del	powered by	mtow kg	configuration	selcal	name/fln/specialitites/remarks
M28-01	Fokker F28 Fellowship 1000 (F28 Mk1000)	11088	FM2101	0075	0575	2 RR Spey 555-15	29484	VIP		9M-EBE / Royal Malaysian Air Force
M37-01	Dassault Falcon 900	64	N446FJ*		0089	3 GA TFE731-5A-1C	20638	VIP		Royal Malaysian Air Force
M47-01	Canadair Regional Jet 100SE (CL-600-2B19)	7140	N260SE	0096	1197	2 GE CF34-3B1	24154	VIP		Royal Malaysian Air Force
M48-01	Bombardier BD-700-1A10 Global Express					2 BR BR710A2-20	42411	VIP		oo-delivery 0099 / Royal Malaysian A.F.
9M-BAB	Dassault Falcon 900B	121	N478FJ	0092	1292	3 GA TFE731-5BR-1C	21099	VIP		Gvmt of Sarawak
9M-CAL	Learjet 60	60-034	N5034Z*	0095	1295	2 PWC PW305A	10319	Calibr./Liaison		Dept of Civil Aviation
9M-FCL	Learjet 60	60-072	N5072L*	0095	0397	2 PWC PW305A	10319	Calibr./Liaison		Dept of Civil Aviation
9M-ISJ	GAC G-IV Gulfstream IV	1106	N17608*	0090	0090	2 RR Tay 611-8	33203	VIP		Gvmt of Johore
9M-JPD	Beech King Air 200T	BT-10	N6065D	0079		2 PWC PT6A-41	6350	EMS Medi-Air		DCA / cvtd Beech 200 cn BB-563

AIR ASIA, Sdn Bhd = AK / AXM (Joint venture between HICOM Holdings Berhad & Mofaz Air)
Kuala Lumpur-Sultan Abdul Aziz Shah

Level 6, Wisma Hicom, 2 Jalan U 1/8, 40000 Shah Alam, (Selangor Darul Ehsan), Malaysia ☎ (3) 202 79 99 Tx: none Fax: (3) 202 79 97 SITA: n/a
F: 1994 ✦✦✦ 108 Head: Y. Bhg. Dalo Tik Mustaffa IATA: 807 ICAO: ASIAN EXPRESS Net: n/a

| 9M-AAA | Boeing 737-3Y0 | 24907 / 2013 | UR-GAE | 0091 | 1196 | 2 CFMI CFM56-3C1 | 61235 | CY130 | | lsf GECA |
| 9M-AAB | Boeing 737-36N | 28555 / 2846 | | 0197 | 0297 | 2 CFMI CFM56-3C1 | 61235 | CY130 | | lsf GECA |

BERJAYA AIR, Sdn Bhd = J8 / BVT (Member of Berjaya Group/formerly Pacific Air Charter)
Kuala Lumpur-Sultan Abdul Aziz Shah

Lot 13, SP 2/2, Subang, 40150 Shah Alam (Selangor), Malaysia ☎ (3) 747 68 28 Tx: none Fax: (3) 747 62 28 SITA: KULRZJ8
F: 1989 ✦✦✦ 63 Head: Dato' Tengku Adnan Tengku Mansor IATA: 801 ICAO: BERJAYA Net: n/a

9M-TAF	Eurocopter (Aerosp.) SA365N Dauphin 2	6228		0089	0094	2 TU Arriel 1C	4000	Utility		
9M-TAK	De Havilland DHC-7-110 Dash 7	110	G-BOAW	0088	0595	4 PWC PT6A-50	19958	Y50		
9M-TAL	De Havilland DHC-7-110 Dash 7	112	G-BOAY	0088	1195	4 PWC PT6A-50	19958	Y50		

BORNEO AIRWAYS, Sdn Bhd = BOR (formerly Merpati Intan)
Miri

PO Box 46, 98007 Miri, (Sarawak), Malaysia ☎ (85) 42 42 42 Tx: none Fax: (85) 41 09 99 SITA: n/a
F: 1997 ✦✦✦ n/a Head: Johnson K.S. Liew IATA: 641 ICAO: BORNEO Net: n/a

| 9M-BOR | Dornier 228-212 | 8218 | 9M-MIB | 0092 | 0897 | 2 GA TPE331-5A-252D | 6400 | Y19 | | |

BOSKYM UDARA, Sdn Bhd (formerly Borneo Skyways (Miri), Sdn Bhd)
Miri

PO Box 682, 98007 Miri, (Sarawak), Malaysia ☎ (85) 34 242 Tx: 74344 borsky ma Fax: (85) 41 93 13 SITA: n/a
F: 1968 ✦✦✦ 25 Head: Jeffrey Lum Net: n/a

9M-BEE	Bell 206L-3 LongRanger III	51415	N6623B	0090	1290	1 AN 250-C30P	1882			
9M-BBD	Eurocopter (Aerosp.) AS350BA Ecureuil	2922		0096	0096	1 TU Arriel 1B	2100			
9M-BBE	Eurocopter (Aerosp.) AS350BA Ecureuil	2925		0096	0096	1 TU Arriel 1B	2100			
9M-BMM	De Havilland DHC-6 Twin Otter 310	626	9M-PEG	0079	0890	2 PWC PT6A-27	5670			
9M-AZT	Shorts Skyvan 3 Variant 100 (SC-7)	SH1968	OY-SUT	0079	0096	2 GA TPE331-2-201A	5670			for sale

F R AVIATION (Malaysia), Sdn Bhd (Subsidiary of F R Aviation Ltd, Gr. Brit.)
Kuala Lumpur-Sultan Abdul Aziz Shah

37-11-6 Serai Penaga, Jalan Medang, Serai Bukit, Bandar Raya, 59000 Kuala Lumpur, Malaysia ☎ (3) 253 56 81 Tx: none Fax: (3) 253 56 81 SITA: n/a
F: 1996 ✦✦✦ n/a Head: n/a Net: n/a

| 9M-BCR | Dassault Falcon 20C | 35 | N809P | 0066 | 0296 | 2 GE CF700-2D2 | 13000 | Executive | | |

HORNBILL SKYWAYS, Sdn Bhd
Kuching & Miri

PO Box 1387, 93728 Kuching, (Sarawak), Malaysia ☎ (82) 45 57 37 Tx: 70166 honbil ma Fax: (82) 45 57 36 SITA: n/a
F: 1977 ✦✦✦ 109 Head: Y.B. Tan Sri Datuk Amar Hj. Bujang Mohd Net: n/a

9M-AVL	Bell 206B JetRanger	1047			0073	1 AN 250-C20	1451			
9M-AVM	Bell 206B JetRanger II	2169			0077	1 AN 250-C20	1451			
9M-AVY	Bell 206B JetRanger III	2259			0077	1 AN 250-C20B	1451			
9M-AWE	Bell 206B JetRanger III	2363			0078	1 AN 250-C20B	1451			
9M-AYP	Bell 206B JetRanger III	3612	N2292Z		0082	1 AN 250-C20J	1451			
9M-AYQ	Bell 206B JetRanger III	3584	N2297L		0082	1 AN 250-C20J	1451			
9M-SGH	Bell 206B JetRanger III	4103	N7107Z	0090	0090	1 AN 250-C20J	1451			
9M-SGJ	Bell 206B JetRanger III	4059	N8129Y	0089	0090	1 AN 250-C20J	1451			
9M-SKJ	Bell 206B JetRanger III	4128	N7169S	0090	0090	1 AN 250-C20J	1451			
9M-HSM	Bell 222UT	47544	N222UT	0086		2 LY LTS101-750C.1	3742			
9M-AZZ	Hawker 800B (BAe 125-800B)	258219	G-5-740*	0092	0792	2 GA TFE731-5R-1H	12428			

LAYANG-LAYANG AEROSPACE, Sdn Bhd
Miri

Lot 3006, 1st Fl., Morsjaya Commercial Centre, Miri-Bintulu Road, PMM Box 206, 98000 Miri (Sarawak), Malaysia ☎ (85) 61 55 01 Tx: 426596 ma Fax: (85) 42 65 96 SITA: n/a
F: 1994 ✦✦✦ 25 Head: Albert K.C. Poong Net: n/a

| 9M-LLA | Shorts Skyvan 3 Variant 100 (SC-7) | SH1977 | ZS-LFG | 0081 | 1296 | 2 GA TPE331-2-201A | 5670 | Frtr/Pax/Para | | |

MAFIRA AIR CHARTER SERVICES, Sdn Bhd = 3A (Mafira Air Group, Sdn Bhd dba)
Kuala Lumpur-Sultan Abdul Aziz Shah

No. 7 Jalan PS 1/5, Bandar Pinggiran Subang, 40150 Shah Alam, Malaysia ☎ (3) 747 67 00 Tx: none Fax: (3) 747 67 70 SITA: n/a
F: 1997 ✦✦✦ 27 Head: Resdeen Hasnan Net: n/a

| 9M-AMZ | Fokker F28 Fellowship 4000 (F28 Mk4000) | 11168 | PH-ZCC | 0081 | 0997 | 2 RR Spey 555-15P | 33112 | C4Y62 | | |

MAJU AIR SERVICES, Sdn Bhd (Member of The Maju Group/formerly ASM Travel, Sdn. Bhd.)
Kuala Lumpur-Sungei Besi AFB

3 Jalan 3, Off Jalan Chan Sow Lin, Sungei Besi AFB, 55200 Kuala Lumpur, Malaysia ☎ (3) 718 81 44 Tx: none Fax: (3) 718 96 25 SITA: n/a
F: 1992 ✦✦✦ 10 Head: Maj. (r) Azhari Ghazali Net: n/a

| 9M-AZX | Bell 206L-3 LongRanger III | 51523 | N4289E | 0092 | | 1 AN 250-C30P | 1882 | 6 Pax | | |

MALAYSIA AIRLINES = MH / MAS (Malaysian Airline System Bhd dba)
Kuala Lumpur-Int'l, Kota Kinabalu & Kuching

Jalan Sultan Ismail, 33rd Floor, Bangunan MAS, 50250 Kuala Lumpur, (Selangor), Malaysia ☎ (3) 746 45 55 Tx: 37091 masap ma Fax: (3) 746 30 27 SITA: n/a
F: 1971 ✦✦✦ 16000 Head: Tan Sri Tajudin Ramli IATA: 232 ICAO: MALAYSIAN Net: http://www.malaysiaairlines.com.my
MASkargo is the marketing name used by the Cargo-division for its freighter flights (same headquarters).

9M-MDK	De Havilland DHC-6 Twin Otter 310	792	C-GESR*	0082	0382	2 PWC PT6A-27	5670	Y19		
9M-MDL	De Havilland DHC-6 Twin Otter 310	802	C-GDFT*	0083	0783	2 PWC PT6A-27	5670	Y19		
9M-MDM	De Havilland DHC-6 Twin Otter 310	804	C-GDKL*	0083	0783	2 PWC PT6A-27	5670	Y19		
9M-MDN	De Havilland DHC-6 Twin Otter 310	844	C-FDQL*	0089	1189	2 PWC PT6A-27	5670	Y19		
9M-MDO	De Havilland DHC-6 Twin Otter 310	629	ZK-KHA	0079	0592	2 PWC PT6A-27	5670	Y19		
9M-MGA	Fokker 50 (F27 Mk050)	20150	PH-EXM*	0089	0889	2 PWC PW125B	20820	Y50		
9M-MGB	Fokker 50 (F27 Mk050)	20156	PH-EXP*	0089	1089	2 PWC PW125B	20820	Y50		
9M-MGC	Fokker 50 (F27 Mk050)	20161	PH-EXK*	0089	1089	2 PWC PW125B	20820	Y50		
9M-MGD	Fokker 50 (F27 Mk050)	20164	PH-EXL*	0089	1289	2 PWC PW125B	20820	Y50		
9M-MGE	Fokker 50 (F27 Mk050)	20166	PH-EXN*	0089	1289	2 PWC PW125B	20820	Y50		
9M-MGF	Fokker 50 (F27 Mk050)	20167	PH-EXO*	0089	0190	2 PWC PW125B	20820	Y50		
9M-MGG	Fokker 50 (F27 Mk050)	20170	PH-EXS*	0089	0290	2 PWC PW125B	20820	Y50		
9M-MGI	Fokker 50 (F27 Mk050)	20175	PH-EXB*	0090	0490	2 PWC PW125B	20820	Y50		
9M-MGJ	Fokker 50 (F27 Mk050)	20204	PH-EXM*	0090	1290	2 PWC PW125B	20820	Y50		
9M-MGK	Fokker 50 (F27 Mk050)	20248	PH-EXR*	0092	0392	2 PWC PW125B	20820	Y50		
9M-MFC	Boeing 737-5H6	26448 / 2484		0093	0693	2 CFMI CFM56-3C1	52389	F16Y88	MQ-BF	lsf GECA
9M-MFD	Boeing 737-5H6	26450 / 2503		0093	0793	2 CFMI CFM56-3C1	52389	F16Y88	MQ-BG	
9M-MFE	Boeing 737-5H6	26454 / 2511		0093	0893	2 CFMI CFM56-3C1	52389	F16Y88	MQ-BH	lst NGE
9M-MFF	Boeing 737-5H6	26456 / 2527		0093	0993	2 CFMI CFM56-3C1	52389	F16Y88	MQ-BJ	
9M-MFG	Boeing 737-5H6	27354 / 2637		0094	0894	2 CFMI CFM56-3C1	52389	F16Y88	AD-QR	lsf GECA
9M-MFI	Boeing 737-5H6	27356 / 2654		0094	1094	2 CFMI CFM56-3C1	52389	F16Y88	AD-RS	lsf GECA
9M-MZA	Boeing 737-3H6 (F)	27125 / 2415		0092	0193	2 CFMI CFM56-3C1	59193	Freighter	AD-PS	cvtd -3H6 / MASkargo-division
9M-MZB	Boeing 737-3H6 (F)	27347 / 2615		0094	0594	2 CFMI CFM56-3C1	59193	Freighter	AD-QS	cvtd -3H6 / MASkargo-division
9M-	Boeing 737-7H6 (BBJ)					2 CFMI CFM56-7B26	77564	VIP		oo-delivery 1299
9M-MMA	Boeing 737-4H6	26443 / 2272		0092	0492	2 CFMI CFM56-3C1	62822	F16Y128	BC-ES	
9M-MMB	Boeing 737-4H6	26444 / 2308		0092	0692	2 CFMI CFM56-3C1	62822	F16Y128	BC-FR	
9M-MMC	Boeing 737-4H6	26453 / 2332		0092	0792	2 CFMI CFM56-3C1	62822	F16Y128	BC-FS	lst Royal Air Cambodge
9M-MMD	Boeing 737-4H6	26464 / 2340		0092	0892	2 CFMI CFM56-3C1	62822	F16Y128	BC-GR	
9M-MME	Boeing 737-4H6	26465 / 2362		0092	0992	2 CFMI CFM56-3C1	62822	F16Y128	BC-GS	
9M-MMF	Boeing 737-4H6	26466 / 2372		0092	1092	2 CFMI CFM56-3C1	62822	F16Y128	BC-HR	
9M-MMG	Boeing 737-4H6	26467 / 2388		0092	1092	2 CFMI CFM56-3C1	62822	F16Y128	BC-HS	
9M-MMH	Boeing 737-4H6	27084 / 2391		0092	1192	2 CFMI CFM56-3C1	62822	F16Y128	BC-LR	lst Myanmar Airways Int'l
9M-MMI	Boeing 737-4H6	27096 / 2395		0092	1192	2 CFMI CFM56-3C1	62822	F16Y128	BC-MR	
9M-MMJ	Boeing 737-4H6	27097 / 2399		0092	1292	2 CFMI CFM56-3C1	62822	F16Y128	BC-KR	
9M-MMK	Boeing 737-4H6	27083 / 2403		0092	1292	2 CFMI CFM56-3C1	62822	F16Y128	MQ-BL	
9M-MML	Boeing 737-4H6	27085 / 2407		0092	1292	2 CFMI CFM56-3C1	62822	F16Y128	MQ-BP	
9M-MMM	Boeing 737-4H6	27166 / 2410		0093	0193	2 CFMI CFM56-3C1	62822	F16Y128	MQ-CD	
9M-MMN	Boeing 737-4H6	27167 / 2419		0093	0193	2 CFMI CFM56-3C1	62822	F16Y128	MQ-CE	

☐	9M-MMQ	Boeing 737-4H6	27087 / 2441		0093	0393	2 CFMI CFM56-3C1	62822	F16Y128	MQ-CH	
☐	9M-MMR	Boeing 737-4H6	26468 / 2445		0093	0393	2 CFMI CFM56-3C1	62822	F16Y128	MQ-CJ	
☐	9M-MMS	Boeing 737-4H6	27169 / 2450		0093	0493	2 CFMI CFM56-3C1	62822	F16Y128	MQ-CK	
☐	9M-MMT	Boeing 737-4H6	27170 / 2462		0093	0493	2 CFMI CFM56-3C1	62822	F16Y128	MQ-BK	
☐	9M-MMU	Boeing 737-4H6	26447 / 2479		0093	0593	2 CFMI CFM56-3C1	62822	F16Y128	CL-KR	
☐	9M-MMV	Boeing 737-4H6	26449 / 2491		0093	0693	2 CFMI CFM56-3C1	62822	F16Y128	CL-KS	
☐	9M-MMW	Boeing 737-4H6	26451 / 2496		0093	0793	2 CFMI CFM56-3C1	62822	F16Y128	CL-MR	
☐	9M-MMX	Boeing 737-4H6	26452 / 2501		0093	0793	2 CFMI CFM56-3C1	62822	F16Y128	CL-MS	
☐	9M-MMY	Boeing 737-4H6	26455 / 2507		0093	0893	2 CFMI CFM56-3C1	62822	F16Y128	CL-PR	lst Myanmar Airways Int'l
☐	9M-MMZ	Boeing 737-4H6	26457 / 2521		0093	0993	2 CFMI CFM56-3C1	62822	F16Y128	CL-PS	
☐	9M-MQA	Boeing 737-4H6	26458 / 2525		0093	1093	2 CFMI CFM56-3C1	62822	F16Y128	CL-QR	
☐	9M-MQB	Boeing 737-4H6	26459 / 2530		0093	1093	2 CFMI CFM56-3C1	62822	F16Y128	CL-RS	
☐	9M-MQC	Boeing 737-4H6	26460 / 2533		0093	1093	2 CFMI CFM56-3C1	62822	F16Y128	CK-ER	
☐	9M-MQD	Boeing 737-4H6	26461 / 2536		0093	1193	2 CFMI CFM56-3C1	62822	F16Y128	CL-QS	
☐	9M-MQE	Boeing 737-4H6	26462 / 2542		0093	1293	2 CFMI CFM56-3C1	62822	F16Y128	CM-AR	lst GAP
☐	9M-MQF	Boeing 737-4H6	26463 / 2560		0093	0194	2 CFMI CFM56-3C1	62822	F16Y128	CM-AS	
☐	9M-MQG	Boeing 737-4H6	27190 / 2568		0094	0294	2 CFMI CFM56-3C1	62822	F16Y128	CM-BR	
☐	9M-MQH	Boeing 737-4H6	27352 / 2624		0094	0694	2 CFMI CFM56-3C1	62822	F16Y128	DK-ES	lsf GECA
☐	9M-MQI	Boeing 737-4H6	27353 / 2632	9H-ADJ	0094	0794	2 CFMI CFM56-3C1	62822	F16Y128	DK-FR	
☐	9M-MQJ	Boeing 737-4H6	27383 / 2657		0094	1194	2 CFMI CFM56-3C1	62822	F16Y128	DK-FS	lsf TOMB
☐	9M-MQK	Boeing 737-4H6	27384 / 2673		0094	1294	2 CFMI CFM56-3C1	62822	F16Y128	DK-GS	lst SAI
☐	9M-MQL	Boeing 737-4H6	27191 / 2676		0094	0195	2 CFMI CFM56-3C1	62822	F16Y128	DM-RS	lsf GECA
☐	9M-MQM	Boeing 737-4H6	27306 / 2685		0094	0195	2 CFMI CFM56-3C1	62822	F16Y128	DK-HR	lsf TOMB
☐	9M-MQN	Boeing 737-4H6	27673 / 2852	9H-ADK	0097	0397	2 CFMI CFM56-3C1	62822	F16Y128	DK-HS	lst AMC as 9H-ADK -1199
☐	9M-MQO	Boeing 737-4H6	27674 / 2877		0097	0497	2 CFMI CFM56-3C1	62822	F16Y128	DK-JR	lst AMC as 9H-ADL -1199
☐	9M-MKA	Airbus Industrie A330-322	067	F-WWKK*	0095	0395	2 PW PW4168	212000	F12C56Y213	ER-AM	
☐	9M-MKB	Airbus Industrie A330-322	068	F-WWKL*	0095	0295	2 PW PW4168	212000	F12C56Y213	ER-AP	
☐	9M-MKC	Airbus Industrie A330-322	069	F-WWKM*	0095	0295	2 PW PW4168	212000	F12C56Y213	ER-AQ	
☐	9M-MKD	Airbus Industrie A330-322	073	F-WWKN*	0095	0395	2 PW PW4168	212000	F12C56Y213	ER-AS	
☐	9M-MKE	Airbus Industrie A330-322	077	F-WWKO*	0095	0495	2 PW PW4168	212000	F12C56Y213	ER-BC	
☐	9M-MKF	Airbus Industrie A330-322	100	F-WWKZ*	0095	0695	2 PW PW4168	212000	F12C56Y213	ER-BD	
☐	9M-MKG	Airbus Industrie A330-322	107	F-WWKV*	0095	0895	2 PW PW4168	212000	F12C56Y213	ER-BF	
☐	9M-MKH	Airbus Industrie A330-322	110	F-WWKE*	0095	0895	2 PW PW4168	212000	F12C56Y213	ER-BG	
☐	9M-MKI	Airbus Industrie A330-322	116	F-WWKT*	0095	1195	2 PW PW4168	212000	F12C56Y213	ER-BH	
☐	9M-MKJ	Airbus Industrie A330-322	119	F-WWKJ*	0095	1295	2 PW PW4168	212000	F12C56Y213	ER-BJ	
☐	9M-MRA	Boeing 777-2H6 (ER)	28408 / 64	N5017V*	0097	0497	2 RR Trent 890	286897	F12C33Y233	QR-EF	
☐	9M-MRB	Boeing 777-2H6 (ER)	28409 / 74	N50217*	0597	0597	2 RR Trent 890	286897	F12C33Y233	QR-EG	
☐	9M-MRC	Boeing 777-2H6 (ER)	28410 / 78		0697	0697	2 RR Trent 890	286897	F12C33Y233	QR-EH	
☐	9M-MRD	Boeing 777-2H6 (ER)	28411 / 84		0797	0797	2 RR Trent 890	286897	F12C33Y233	QR-EJ	
☐	9M-MRE	Boeing 777-2H6 (ER)	28412 / 115		0198	0198	2 RR Trent 890	286897	F12C33Y233	QR-EK	
☐	9M-MRF	Boeing 777-2H6 (ER)	28413 / 128		0098	0398	2 RR Trent 890	286897	F12C33Y233	QR-EL	
☐	9M-MRG	Boeing 777-2H6 (ER)	28414 / 140		0098	0598	2 RR Trent 890	286897	F12C33Y233		
☐	9M-MRH	Boeing 777-2H6 (ER)	28415 / 151		0098	0798	2 RR Trent 890	286897	F12C33Y233		
☐	9M-MRI	Boeing 777-2H6 (ER)	28416 / 155		0098	1098	2 RR Trent 890	286897	F12C33Y233		
☐	9M-MRJ	Boeing 777-2H6 (ER)					2 RR Trent 890	286897	F12C33Y233		oo-delivery 0300
☐	9M-MRK	Boeing 777-2H6 (ER)					2 RR Trent 890	286897	F12C33Y233		oo-delivery 0400
☐	9M-MAV	Boeing (Douglas) DC-10-30	48283 / 350		0081	0281	3 GE CF6-50C2	251744	C30Y255		lsf WTC Trustee / std MZJ
☐	9M-MAW	Boeing (Douglas) DC-10-30	46959 / 234	OY-KDC	0077	1090	3 GE CF6-50C2	259455	Y380	AC-DG	lsf PKG Lease / sub-lst WOA
☐	9M-MAZ	Boeing (Douglas) DC-10-30	46933 / 159	N109WA	0074	0990	3 GE CF6-50C2	256280	Y380	AB-EL	lst WOA
☐	9M-MSA	Boeing 777-3H6					2 RR Trent 892	299371			oo-delivery 0003
☐	9M-MSB	Boeing 777-3H6					2 RR Trent 892	299371			oo-delivery 0003
☐	9M-MSC	Boeing 777-3H6					2 RR Trent 892	299371			oo-delivery 0003
☐	9M-MSD	Boeing 777-3H6					2 RR Trent 892	299371			oo-delivery 0003
☐	N275WA	Boeing (Douglas) MD-11F (CF)	48631 / 579		0095	0998	3 PW PW4462	280320	Freighter	GH-CR	lsf / opb WOA in MASkargo div.-colors
☐	9M-MHI	Boeing 747-236B (SF)	22304 / 502	G-BDXL ntu	0081	0382	4 RR RB211-524D4	377842	Freighter	CF-KL	Kuching / MASkargo-div./cvtd -236B
☐	9M-MHJ	Boeing 747-236B (SF)	22442 / 526	G-BDXN ntu	0081	0482	4 RR RB211-524D4	377842	Freighter	CF-KM	Johor Bahru / MASkargo-div./cvtd -236B
☐	9M-MHK	Boeing 747-3H6 (SF)	23600 / 650		0086	0786	4 PW JT9D-7R4G2	377842	Freighter	CF-LM	Kota Kinabalu / cvtd -3H6 (M)
☐	9M-MHL	Boeing 747-4H6 (M)	24315 / 738		0089	1189	4 GE CF6-80C2B1F	394625	F24C38Y227 / Plt	EP-GL	Kuala Lumpur
☐	9M-MHM	Boeing 747-4H6 (M)	24405 / 745		0089	1089	4 GE CF6-80C2B1F	394625	F24C38Y227 / Plt	EP-GM	Penang
☐	9M-MPA	Boeing 747-4H6	27042 / 932		0092	0892	4 PW PW4056	394625	F24C38Y363	MQ-AD	Ipoh
☐	9M-MPB	Boeing 747-4H6	25699 / 965		0093	0493	4 PW PW4056	394625	F24C60Y318	MQ-AE	Shah Alam
☐	9M-MPC	Boeing 747-4H6	25700 / 974		0093	0593	4 PW PW4056	394625	F24C60Y318	BJ-DS	Kuantan
☐	9M-MPD	Boeing 747-4H6	25701 / 997		0093	1093	4 PW PW4056	394625	F24C60Y318	BJ-ER	Seremban
☐	9M-MPE	Boeing 747-4H6	25702 / 999		0093	1193	4 PW PW4056	394625	F24C60Y318	BJ-ES	Kangar
☐	9M-MPF	Boeing 747-4H6	27043 / 1017		0094	0194	4 PW PW4056	394625	F24C60Y318	BJ-FR	Kota Bharu
☐	9M-MPG	Boeing 747-4H6	25703 / 1025		0094	0394	4 PW PW4056	394625	F24C60Y318	BJ-FS	Kuala Terengganu
☐	9M-MPH	Boeing 747-4H6	27044 / 1041	N60668*	0094	0994	4 PW PW4056	394625	F24C60Y318	BJ-GR	Langkawi
☐	9M-MPI	Boeing 747-4H6	27672 / 1091		0096	1096	4 PW PW4056	394625	F24C60Y318	BJ-GS	Tioman
☐	9M-MPJ	Boeing 747-4H6	28426 / 1130		1097	1097	4 PW PW4056	394625	F18C50Y318	QR-DE	Labuan
☐	9M-MPK	Boeing 747-4H6	28427 / 1147		0098	0398	4 PW PW4056	394625	F18C50Y318	QR-DF	
☐	9M-MPL	Boeing 747-4H6	28428 / 1150		0398	0398	4 PW PW4056	394625	F18C50Y318	QR-DG	
☐	9M-MPM	Boeing 747-4H6	28435 / 1152		0098	0498	4 PW PW4056	394625	F18C50Y318		
☐	9M-MPN	Boeing 747-4H6	28429				4 PW PW4056	394625	F18C50Y318	MQ-AB	oo-delivery 0599
☐	9M-MPO	Boeing 747-4H6	28430				4 PW PW4056	394625	F18C50Y318	MQ-AC	oo-delivery 0699
☐	9M-MPP	Boeing 747-4H6	28431				4 PW PW4056	394625	F18C50Y318		oo-delivery 1299
☐	9M-MPQ	Boeing 747-4H6					4 PW PW4056	394625	F18C50Y318		oo-delivery 0002
☐	9M-MPR	Boeing 747-4H6					4 PW PW4056	394625	F18C50Y318		oo-delivery 0003
☐	9M-MPS	Boeing 747-4H6					4 PW PW4056	394625	F18C50Y318		oo-delivery 0003

MHS AVIATION, Sendirian Berhad — Kerteh & Miri

12 Jalan Rahim Kajai, 14 Taman Tun Dr. Ismail, 60000 Kuala Lumpur, (Selangor), Malaysia ☎ (3) 719 11 76 Tx: 36430 mhsho ma Fax: (3) 719 56 26 SITA: n/a
F: 1981 540 Head: Masom Mahadi Net: n/a

☐	9M-SSV	Eurocopter (Aerosp.) AS355F2 Ecureuil 2	5476		0091	0091	2 AN 250-C20F	2540	5 Pax		
☐	9M-AXW	Sikorsky S-76A	760057	G-BHRT	0080		2 AN 250-C30	4672	12 Pax		
☐	9M-AYD	Sikorsky S-76A	760052	G-BJVW	0080		2 AN 250-C30	4672	12 Pax		
☐	9M-STA	Sikorsky S-76C	760383		0091	0991	2 TU Arriel 1S1	5307	12 Pax		
☐	9M-STB	Sikorsky S-76C	760384		0091	0991	2 TU Arriel 1S1	5307	12 Pax		
☐	9M-STC	Sikorsky S-76C	760392		0091	1291	2 TU Arriel 1S1	5307	12 Pax		
☐	9M-STD	Sikorsky S-76C	760397		0092	0592	2 TU Arriel 1S1	5307	12 Pax		
☐	9M-STE	Sikorsky S-76C	760398		0092	0592	2 TU Arriel 1S1	5307	12 Pax		
☐	9M-STF	Sikorsky S-76C	760400		0092	0992	2 TU Arriel 1S1	5307	12 Pax		
☐	9M-SSE	Eurocopter (Aerosp.) SA330J Puma	1557	G-BFTV	0078		2 TU Turmo IVC	7400	17 Pax		
☐	9M-STS	Eurocopter (Aerosp.) AS332L1 Super Puma	2387		0094	0194	2 TU Makila 1A1	8600	19 Pax		
☐	9M-STT	Eurocopter (Aerosp.) AS332L1 Super Puma	2405		0094	0294	2 TU Makila 1A1	8600	19 Pax		
☐	9M-STV	Eurocopter (Aerosp.) AS332L1 Super Puma	2408		0094	0594	2 TU Makila 1A1	8600	19 Pax		
☐	9M-AVO	Sikorsky S-61N	61766	G-BEKI	0077		2 GE CT58-140-1	9299	24 Pax		
☐	9M-AVP	Sikorsky S-61N	61768	G-BEKJ	0077		2 GE CT58-140-1	9299	24 Pax		
☐	9M-AVQ	Sikorsky S-61N	61736	G-BCLB	0075		2 GE CT58-140-1	9299	24 Pax		
☐	9M-AVT	Sikorsky S-61N	61735	9M-ELF	0075		2 GE CT58-140-1	9299	24 Pax		
☐	9M-AWN	Sikorsky S-61N	61714	G-BBHN	0073		2 GE CT58-140-1	9299	24 Pax		
☐	9M-PCM	Sikorsky S-61N	61720	G-BBVB	0074		2 GE CT58-140-1	9299	24 Pax		
☐	9M-SSR	Sikorsky S-61N	61719	LN-OSK	0074	0990	2 GE CT58-140-2	9299	24 Pax		
☐	9M-SSS	Sikorsky S-61N	61474	LN-OQL	0070	0291	2 GE CT58-140-2	9299	24 Pax		

MOFAZ AIR, Sdn Berhad = MFZ — Kuala Lumpur-Sultan Abdul Aziz Shah & Langkawi

36 Persiaran Zaaba, Taman Tun Dr. Ismail, 60000 Kuala Lumpur, (Selangor), Malaysia ☎ (3) 718 31 71 Tx: n/a Fax: (3) 717 89 52 SITA: n/a
F: 1992 n/a Head: Encik Shahareel bin Jaji Shafei ICAO: MOFAZ AIR Net: n/a Aircraft below MTOW 1361kg: Cessna 152/172 & Hughes 269C (300C).

☐	9M-FAM	Bell 206L-4 LongRanger IV	52011	N6162N*	0092	0293	1 AN 250-C30P	2018			
☐	9M-FAZ	Cessna 500 Citation	500-0245	N2019V	0075	0494	2 PWC JT15D-1A	5216			
☐	9M-FAT	Shorts Skyvan 3 Variant 400 (SC-7)	SH1964	OC-2	0079		2 GA TPE331-2-201A	5670			std Langkawi

NUSANTARA AIRLINES (Nusantara Sakti, Sdn Bhd dba) — Kuala Lumpur-Sultan Abdul Aziz Shah

Lot 10.1 Ground Floor, Fima Airtel Complex, Sultan Abdul Aziz Shah Airport, 47200 Subang (Selangor), Malaysia ☎ (3) 746 38 95 Tx: none Fax: (3) 746 38 91 SITA: n/a
F: 1991 22 Head: Mohammed Dalam Hashim Net: n/a

☐	9M-NSA	Cessna 550 Citation II	550-0610	9M-UEM	0089	0091	2 PWC JT15D-4	6033	Executive		

PAN-MALAYSIAN AIR TRANSPORT, Sdn Bhd = PMA — Kuala Lumpur-Sultan Abdul Aziz Shah

Hangar B, Sultan Abdul Aziz Shah Airport, 47200 Subang, (Selangor), Malaysia ☎ (3) 746 23 67 Tx: 37506 cgolux ma Fax: (3) 746 17 14 SITA: n/a
F: 1965 76 Head: Piaruddin bin Fathodin ICAO: PAN MALAYSIA Net: n/a Ag-Aircraft below MTOW 5000 kg: Transavia PL-12 (Sprayer).

☐	9M-PIH	Shorts Skyvan 3 Variant 400 (SC-7)	SH1962	G-BFUM	0078	0993	2 GA TPE331-2-201A	5670			

706 registration type of aircraft cn/fn ex/ex* mfd del powered by mtow kg configuration selcal name/fln/specialitites/remarks

PELANGI AIRWAYS, Sdn Bhd = 9P / PEG
Kuala Lumpur-Sultan Abdul Aziz Shah

18B, Level 2, Block 2, Worldwide Business Park, Jalan Tingu, 40675 Shah Alam (Selangor), Malaysia ☎ (3) 553 22 94 Tx: none Fax: (3) 553 22 92 SITA: HDQPGMH
F: 1987 ⅏ 340 Head: Zain Salahin IATA: 054 ICAO: PELANGI Net: http://www.asia123.com/pelangi/home.htm

☐ 9M-PEL	Dornier 228-202K	8174	D-CBCI*	0089	1189	2 GA TPE331-5-252D	6200	Y19	
☐ 9M-PEM	Dornier 228-202K	8175	D-CHIM*	0089	0690	2 GA TPE331-5-252D	6200	Y19	
☐ 9M-PEN	Dornier 228-202K	8172		0090	1090	2 GA TPE331-5-252D	6200	Y19	
☐ 9M-MEQ	Fokker 50 (F27 Mk050)	20225	PH-JXB*	0091	1091	2 PWC PW125B	20820	Y50	
☐ 9M-MER	Fokker 50 (F27 Mk050)	20245	PH-EXP*	0092	0392	2 PWC PW125B	20820	Y50	
☐ 9M-	Fokker F28 Fellowship 4000 (F28 Mk4000)	11138	PH-CHP	0078		2 RR Spey 555-15P	33100	Y79	to be lsf PEMB 0599
☐ 9M-	Fokker F28 Fellowship 4000 (F28 Mk4000)	11138	PH-CHP	0078		2 RR Spey 555-15P	33100	Y79	to be lsf PEMB 0599

POLIS DIRAJA MALAYSIA (Royal Malaysian Police Air Unit) (Air Unit div.of Royal Malaysian Police)
Kuala Lumpur-Sungei Besi AFB & Kota Kinabalu

Kommander Unit Badara, Jalan Lapangan Terbang Lama, 50460 Kuala Lumpur, Malaysia ☎ (3) 242 39 84 Tx: none Fax: (3) 248 08 57 SITA: n/a
F: 1979 ⅏ 270 Head: S. Husin Bin Syed Mohamad Net: n/a National force conducting non-commercial police search & survey, pollution control, transport, SAR and other duties-flights.

☐ 9M-PSA	Cessna U206G Stationair 6 II	U20605115	N4819U*	0079	1179	1 CO IO-520-F	1633		
☐ 9M-PSB	Cessna U206G Stationair 6 II	U20605006	N4621U*	0079	1179	1 CO IO-520-F	1633		
☐ 9M-PSD	Cessna U206G Stationair 6 II	U20605262	N5381U*	0079	0180	1 CO IO-520-F	1633		
☐ 9M-PSE	Pilatus PC-6/B2-H4 Turbo Porter	849	HB-FIT*	0086	0386	1 PWC PT6A-27	2800		cvtd PC-6/B2-H2
☐ 9M-PSG	Pilatus PC-6/B2-H4 Turbo Porter	851	HB-FIV*	0086	0586	1 PWC PT6A-27	2800		cvtd PC-6/B2-H2
☐ 9M-PSH	Pilatus PC-6/B2-H4 Turbo Porter	852	HB-FIW*	0086	0586	1 PWC PT6A-27	2800		cvtd PC-6/B2-H2
☐ 9M-PSI	Pilatus PC-6/B2-H4 Turbo Porter	853	HB-FIX*	0086	0686	1 PWC PT6A-27	2800		cvtd PC-6/B2-H2
☐ 9M-PSK	Pilatus PC-6/B2-H4 Turbo Porter	855	HB-FIZ*	0086	0686	1 PWC PT6A-27	2800		cvtd PC-6/B2-H2
☐ 9M-PHA	Eurocopter (Aerosp.) AS355F2 Ecureuil 2	5417		0089	0089	2 AN 250-C20F	2540		
☐ 9M-PHB	Eurocopter (Aerosp.) AS355F2 Ecureuil 2	5418		0089	0089	2 AN 250-C20F	2540		
☐ 9M-PHD	Eurocopter (Aerosp.) AS355N Ecureuil 2	5616		0096	0097	2 TU Arrius 1A	2540		
☐ 9M-PHE	Eurocopter (Aerosp.) AS355N Ecureuil 2	5617		0097	0097	2 TU Arrius 1A	2540		
☐ 9M-PHF	Eurocopter (Aerosp.) AS355N Ecureuil 2	5618	F-OHNV	0097	0097	2 TU Arrius 1A	2540		
☐ 9M-PHG	Eurocopter (Aerosp.) AS355N Ecureuil 2	5620	F-WQDR*	0097	0097	2 TU Arrius 1A	2540		
☐ 9M-PHH	Eurocopter (Aerosp.) AS355N Ecureuil 2	5624		0097	0097	2 TU Arrius 1A	2540		
☐ 9M-PHI	Eurocopter (Aerosp.) AS355N Ecureuil 2	5625		0097	0097	2 TU Arrius 1A	2540		
☐ 9M-PHJ	Eurocopter (Aerosp.) AS355N Ecureuil 2	5628		0098	0098	2 TU Arrius 1A	2540		
☐ 9M-PHK	Eurocopter (Aerosp.) AS355N Ecureuil 2	5629		0098	0098	2 TU Arrius 1A	2540		
☐ 9M-PSL	Cessna 208 Caravan I	20800229	N9826F*	0093	1093	1 PWC PT6A-114	3629		
☐ 9M-PSM	Cessna 208 Caravan I	20800230	N9829F*	0093	1093	1 PWC PT6A-114	3629		
☐ 9M-PSN	Cessna 208 Caravan I	20800231	N9833F*	0093	0194	1 PWC PT6A-114	3629		
☐ 9M-PSO	Cessna 208 Caravan I	20800232	N9834F*	0093	0394	1 PWC PT6A-114	3629		
☐ 9M-PSP	Cessna 208 Caravan I	20800233	N9835F*	0094	0494	1 PWC PT6A-114	3629		
☐ 9M-PSQ	Cessna 208 Caravan I	20800234	N9836F*	0094	0494	1 PWC PT6A-114	3629		

PROLINK HELICOPTERS (Prolink Development, Sdn Bhd dba)
Kuala Lumpur

15th Floor, Menara 2, Cebu Tower, Jalan Desa Bahagia Taman Besa, Off. JKL, 58100 Kuala Lumpur, Malaysia ☎ (3) 746 38 95 Tx: none Fax: (3) 746 38 91 SITA: n/a
F: n/a ⅏ n/a Head: Nusantara Sakti Net: n/a

☐ 9M-NSP	Eurocopter (Aerosp.) AS365N2 Dauphin 2	6480	F-OHNJ	0094	0995	2 TU Arriel 1C2	4250		

SABAH AIR - Penerbangan Sabah, Sdn Bhd = SAX
Kota Kinabalu

Locked Bag 113, 88999 Kota Kinabalu, (Sabah), Malaysia ☎ (88) 25 67 33 Tx: none Fax: (88) 23 51 95 SITA: n/a
F: 1975 ⅏ 113 Head: Tony Liew ICAO: SABAH AIR Net: http://www.borneo-online.com.my/sabahair

☐ 9M-AWB	Bell 206B JetRanger III	2330		0078		1 AN 250-C20B	1451		
☐ 9M-AWC	Bell 206B JetRanger III	2336		0078		1 AN 250-C20B	1451		
☐ 9M-AWD	Bell 206B JetRanger III	2351		0078		1 AN 250-C20B	1451		
☐ 9M-AXH	Bell 206B JetRanger III	2480		0078		1 AN 250-C20B	1451		
☐ 9M-AYN	Bell 206B JetRanger III	3022	N5738M	0080		1 AN 250-C20B	1451		
☐ 9M-SAC	Bell 206B JetRanger III	2510		0078		1 AN 250-C20B	1451		
☐ 9M-AZK	Bell 206L-3 LongRanger III	51484	N4196G*	0091	1191	1 AN 250-C30P	1882		
☐ 9M-TPS	Britten-Norman BN-2T-4S Turbine Islander	4009	G-BWPO	0097	1197	2 AN 250-B17F/1	3856		
☐ 9M-AUA	GAF N22B Nomad	N22B-7		0075	0875	2 AN 250-B17B	3856		
☐ 9M-ATC	Bell 212	30718		0075		2 PWC PT6T-3 TwinPac	5080		
☐ 9M-KNS	Beech King Air 200	BB-294	N18494	0077		2 PWC PT6A-41	5670		

TRANSMILE AIR SERVICES, (M) Sdn Bhd = TH / TSE (formerly Pelangi Mahjana (M) Sdn Bhd)
Kuala Lumpur-Sultan Abdul Aziz Shah

Mezzanine-2, Block B, Letter Box 20, Wisma Semantan, 12 Jalan Gelenggang, Bukit Damansara, 50490 Kuala Lumpur, Malaysia ☎ (3) 253 77 18 Tx: none Fax: (3) 253 77 19 SITA: n/a
F: 1993 ⅏ n/a Head: Tan Sri Zainol Mahmood IATA: 539 ICAO: TRANSMILE Net: n/a

☐ 9M-PMO	Cessna 208B Grand Caravan	208B0331	N1036C*	0093	0693	1 PWC PT6A-114A	3969	Freighter	
☐ 9M-PMT	Cessna 208B Grand Caravan	208B0475	N1220D*	0095	1195	1 PWC PT6A-114A	3969	Freighter	
☐ 9M-PMV	Cessna 208B Grand Caravan	208B0500		0096	0296	1 PWC PT6A-114A	3969	Freighter	
☐ 9M-PMM	Boeing 737-205C	20458 / 278	PK-GWR	0371	1193	2 PW JT8D-9A	53070	Freighter	lst Centennial Air
☐ 9M-PMP	Boeing 737-248C	20220 / 215	EI-ASE	0069	0394	2 PW JT8D-9A	50349	Freighter	opf Cen
☐ 9M-PMQ	Boeing 737-230C	20254 / 230	F-GFVJ	0070	0295	2 PW JT8D-9A	54204	Freighter	opf Poslaju Kurier National
☐ 9M-PMU	Boeing 737-2X6C (A)	23124 / 1046	N673MA	0084	0396	2 PW JT8D-17A	58060	Freighter	
☐ 9M-PMW	Boeing 737-209 (A)	24197 / 1581	B-1878	0788	1296	2 PW JT8D-9A	52390	Y123	lst RSO
☐ 9M-PMZ	Boeing 737-209 (A)	23796 / 1420	PK-RIV	0787	0197	2 PW JT8D-9A	52390	Y117	lst RSO

WIRAKRIS Udara, Sdn Bhd
Kuala Lumpur-Sultan Abdul Aziz Shah

Hangar C, Sultan Abdul Aziz Shah Airport, 47200 Subang (Selangor), Malaysia ☎ (3) 746 52 10 Tx: n/a Fax: (3) 746 52 12 SITA: n/a
F: n/a ⅏ n/a Head: Col. Mior Subir Net: n/a

☐ 9M-WKB	Shorts Skyvan 3 Variant 100 (SC-7)	SH1965	ZS-KMX	0079	0995	2 GA TPE331-2-201A	5670		

9N = NEPAL (Kingdom of Nepal) (Nepal Adhirajya)
Capital: Kathmandu Official Language: Nepali, English Population: 22,0 million Square Km: 140797 Dialling code: +977 Year established: 1768 Acting political head: Girija Prasad Koirala (Prime Minister)

ASIAN AIRLINES Helicopters, Pvt. Ltd
Kathmandu

Thamel PO Box 4695, Kathmandu, Nepal ☎ (1) 42 32 74 Tx: 2703 arniko np Fax: (1) 42 33 15 SITA: n/a
F: 1993 ⅏ 55 Head: RBA Tshering Sherpa Net: http://www.asian-trekking.com/heli.htm

☐ 9N-ACT	Mil Mi-17	96125		0093	0093	2 IS TV3-117VM-3	13000	Y24	
☐ 9N-ACU	Mil Mi-17	96120		0093	0093	2 IS TV3-117VM-3	13000	Y24	

BUDDHA AIR, Pvt. Ltd.
Kathmandu

Jawalakhal, Lalitpur, GPO Box 2167, Kathmandu, Nepal ☎ (1) 52 10 15 Tx: none Fax: (1) 53 77 26 SITA: n/a
F: 1997 ⅏ 160 Head: Birendra B. Basnet Net: http://www.buddhaair.com

☐ 9N-AEE	Beech 1900D Airliner	UE-286	N11194*	0097	0897	2 PWC PT6A-67D	7688	Y19	
☐ 9N-AEK	Beech 1900D Airliner	UE-295	N21540*	0097	1297	2 PWC PT6A-67D	7688	Y19	
☐ 9N-AEW	Beech 1900D Airliner	UE-328	N23179*	0098	1098	2 PWC PT6A-67D	7688	Y19	

COSMIC AIR, Ltd
Kathmandu

PO Box 3488, Kathmandu, Nepal ☎ (1) 42 71 50 Tx: none Fax: (1) 42 70 84 SITA: n/a
F: 1998 ⅏ n/a Head: n/a Net: n/a

☐ 9N-AEP	Dornier 228-201	8078	D-CBDC	0085	0098	2 GA TPE331-5-252D	5980	Y19	
☐ 9N-ADO	Mil Mi-8MTV-1 (Mi-17-1V)	95724	RA-25108	0091	0098	2 IS TV3-117VM	13000	Y24	std Pokhara
☐ 9N-ADP	Mil Mi-8MTV-1 (Mi-17-1V)	95898	RA-27062	0392	0098	2 IS TV3-117VM	13000	Y24	std Pokhara

DYNASTY HELICOPTERS (Division of Dynasty Aviation, Pvt Ltd./ Member of the Asia Pacific Helicopter Network)
Kathmandu

PO Box 10112, Kathmandu, Nepal ☎ (1) 41 19 12 Tx: none Fax: (1) 41 00 90 SITA: n/a
F: 1993 ⅏ 20 Head: Pokharel Navin Net: n/a

☐ 9N-ACR	Eurocopter (Aerosp.) AS350BA Ecureuil	1196	P2-PAC	0079		1 TU Arriel 1B	2100		lsf Pacific Helicopters / cvtd AS350B

FISHTAIL AIRLINES, Pvt Ltd
Kathmandu

Sinamangal Road, Int'l Airport, Kathmandu, Nepal ☎ (1) 48 51 86 Tx: none Fax: (1) 48 51 87 SITA: n/a
F: 1998 ⅏ n/a Head: n/a Net: n/a

☐ 9N-AEX	Eurocopter (Aerosp.) AS350B Ecureuil	1612	F-OHNX	0082	1198	1 TU Arriel 1B	1950		

GORKHA AIRLINES, Pvt. Ltd.
Kathmandu

PO Box 9451, Kathmandu, Nepal ☎ (1) 47 11 36 Tx: none Fax: (1) 41 41 02 SITA: n/a
F: 1996 ⅏ n/a Head: n/a Net: n/a

☐ 9N-ACV	Dornier 228-101	7024	SE-KTN	0084	0098	2 GA TPE331-5-252D	5980	Y16	cvtd -100 / std KTM
☐ 9N-AEO	Dornier 228-200	8010	SE-KTO	0083	0598	2 GA TPE331-5-252D	5700	Y16	
☐ 9N-ADS	Mil Mi-8MTV-1 (Mi-17-1V)	95603	RA-25459	0091	0096	2 IS TV3-117VM	13000	Y24	lsf Vladikavkaz Air Enterprise/std KTM
☐ 9N-ADT	Mil Mi-8MTV-1 (Mi-17-1V)	95604	RA-25460	0091	0096	2 IS TV3-117VM	13000	Y24	lsf Vladikavkaz Air Enterprise

707 registration type of aircraft cn/fn ex/ex* mfd del powered by mtow kg configuration selcal name/fln/specialitites/remarks

KARNALI AIR SERVICE, Pvt. Ltd.
Kathmandu

Sinamangal Road, International Airport, Kathmandu, Nepal ☎ (1) 47 31 41 Tx: none Fax: (1) 48 82 88 SITA: n/a
F: 1997 ⋔⋔⋔ Head: Lt-Col. Naran Singh Pun Net: n/a

	registration	type of aircraft	cn/fn	ex/ex*	mfd	del	powered by	mtow kg	configuration	selcal	name/fln/specialitites/remarks
☐	9N-AED	Eurocopter (Aerosp.) AS350B Ecureuil	1033	ZK-HXB	0078	0997	1 TU Arriel 1B	1950			
☐	9N-AEJ	Eurocopter (Aerosp.) AS350B Ecureuil	1269	ZK-HWB	0080	0298	1 TU Arriel 1B	1950			
☐	9N-AEL	Kawasaki (Eurocopter/MBB) BK117B-1	1045	ZK-HII	0090	0998	2 LY LTS101-750B.1	3200			
☐	9N-AER	Kawasaki (Eurocopter/MBB) BK117B-1	1046	ZK-HBK	0090	0798	2 LY LTS101-750B.1	3200			
☐	9N-AEY	Kawasaki (Eurocopter/MBB) BK117B-1	1058	ZK-HFK	0090	1298	2 LY LTS101-750B.1	3200			

LUMBINI AIRWAYS, Pvt. Ltd.
Kathmandu

PO Box 6215, Kathmandu, Nepal ☎ (1) 48 27 25 Tx: none Fax: (1) 48 33 80 SITA: n/a
F: 1996 ⋔⋔⋔ n/a Head: n/a Net: n/a

☐	9N-AEQ	De Havilland DHC-6 Twin Otter 300	708	C-GBQD	0080	0598	2 PWC PT6A-27	5670	Y19		

MANAKAMANA AIRWAYS, Pvt. Ltd.
Kathmandu

PO Box 12284, Kathmandu, Nepal ☎ (1) 48 21 87 Tx: none Fax: (1) 48 21 87 SITA: n/a
F: 1996 ⋔⋔⋔ n/a Head: Capt. Ravi Koarala Net: n/a

☐	9N-ADI	Eurocopter (Aerosp.) AS350B2 Ecureuil	2447	F-OHEU	0091	0097	1 TU Arriel 1D1	2250			

NECON AIR, Ltd = 3Z / NEC
Kathmandu

Necon Air

PO Box 10038, Kathmandu, Nepal ☎ (1) 47 38 60 Tx: 2739 necoa np Fax: (1) 47 14 59 SITA: n/a
F: 1992 ⋔⋔⋔ 480 Head: Deep Mani Rajbhandari IATA: 741 ICAO: NECON AIR Net: http://www.asian-trekking.com/neconair.htm

☐	9N-AEF	Cessna 208 Caravan I	20800270	N1115V*	0097	1097	1 PWC PT6A-114	3629	Y9		
☐	9N-ACP	BAe (HS) 748-256 Srs 2A	1667 / 159	G-BURJ	0069	0593	2 RR Dart 534-2	20182	Y44		
☐	9N-ADE	BAe (HS) 748-378 Srs 2B	1784 / 265	G-BOHY	0081	1094	2 RR Dart 536-2	21092	Y44		
☐	9N-AEG	BAe (HS) 748-501 Super 2B	1806 / 287	B-1771	0088	0097	2 RR Dart 536-2	21092	Y44		
☐	9N-AEH	BAe (HS) 748-501 Super 2B	1807 / 288	B-1773	0088	0097	2 RR Dart 536-2	21092	Y44		

ROYAL NEPAL AIRLINES, Corp. = RA / RNA
Kathmandu

PO Box 401, Kathmandu, Nepal ☎ (1) 22 22 68 Tx: 2212 sitanp np Fax: (1) 22 53 48 SITA: KTMADRA
F: 1958 ⋔⋔⋔ 2000 Head: Udaya Krishna Shrestha IATA: 285 ICAO: ROYAL NEPAL Net: http://www.asian-trekking.com/rnac.htm

☐	9N-ABB	De Havilland DHC-6 Twin Otter 300	302		0071	0671	2 PWC PT6A-27	5670	Y19		
☐	9N-ABM	De Havilland DHC-6 Twin Otter 300	455	N302EH	0075	0277	2 PWC PT6A-27	5670	Y19		
☐	9N-ABO	De Havilland DHC-6 Twin Otter 300	638		0079	0979	2 PWC PT6A-27	5670	Y19		
☐	9N-ABP	De Havilland DHC-6 Twin Otter 300	654		0079	1179	2 PWC PT6A-27	5670	Y19		
☐	9N-ABQ	De Havilland DHC-6 Twin Otter 300	655		0079	1279	2 PWC PT6A-27	5670	Y19		
☐	9N-ABT	De Havilland DHC-6 Twin Otter 300	812	C-GHHI	0084	1084	2 PWC PT6A-27	5670	Y19		
☐	9N-ABU	De Havilland DHC-6 Twin Otter 300	814	C-GHHY	0084	1084	2 PWC PT6A-27	5670	Y19		
☐	9N-ABX	De Havilland DHC-6 Twin Otter 300	830	C-GIQS	0085	1285	2 PWC PT6A-27	5670	Y19		
☐	9N-AAV	BAe (HS) 748-253 Srs 2A	1672 / 162	G-11*	0070	0370	2 RR Dart 534-2	20183	Y44		
☐	9N-ACA	Boeing 757-2F8	23850 / 142		0087	0987	2 RR RB211-535E4	108862	C16Y174	AP-EH	
☐	9N-ACB	Boeing 757-2F8 (M)	23863 / 182	N5573K*	0088	0988	2 RR RB211-535E4	108862	C16Y174 / Combi	AP-EJ	

V.V.I.P. FLIGHT
Kathmandu

PO Box 3267, Kathmandu, Nepal ☎ (1) 47 47 53 Tx: none Fax: (1) 47 27 35 SITA: n/a
F: 1975 ⋔⋔⋔ 70 Head: Brig. Gen. Puspa KC Net: n/a Government organisation conducting mainly VIP, transport, photography, rescue & charter flights.

☐	9N-RAI	Bell 206L-3 LongRanger III	51273	N8117J*	0089	0589	1 AN 250-C30P	1882	VIP		
☐	9N-RAL	Bell 206L-4 LongRanger IV	52021		0093	0793	1 AN 250-C30P	2018	VIP		
☐	9N-RAG	Eurocopter (Aerosp.) AS332L Super Puma	2148		0085	0085	2 TU Makila 1A	8600	VIP		
☐	9N-RAJ	Eurocopter (Aerosp.) AS332L1 Super Puma	2307		0090	0091	2 TU Makila 1A1	8600	VIP		

YETI AIRWAYS
Kathmandu

Lazipark, Kathmandu, Nepal ☎ (1) 49 39 01 Tx: none Fax: (1) 42 07 66 SITA: n/a
F: 1998 ⋔⋔⋔ n/a Head: Sarnam Sherpa Net: n/a

☐	9N-AET	De Havilland DHC-6 Twin Otter 300	619	C-GBQA	0079	0898	2 PWC PT6A-27	5670	Y19		
☐	9N-AEV	De Havilland DHC-6 Twin Otter 300	729	C-FWQF	0080	0898	2 PWC PT6A-27	5670	Y19		
☐	9N-AFF	Embraer 110P1 Bandeirante (EMB-110P1)	110400	C-GFKB	0082	0299	2 PWC PT6A-34	5670	Y19		

9Q = CONGO KINSHASA (Democratic Republic of Congo) (République Démocratique du Congo)
Capital: Kinshasa Official Language: French Population: 51,0 million Square Km: 2345409 Dialling code: +243 Year established: 1960 Acting political head: Laurent Désiré Kabila (President)

Government / Corporate / Executive / VIP Aircraft

☐	9Q-CDC	Boeing 727-30	18934 / 222	9Q-RDZ	0065	0786	3 PW JT8D-7	72802	VIP	AB-CL	Hewa Bora / Gvmt
☐	9Q-CDJ	Boeing 727-41	20424 / 817	PP-VLH	0070	0098	3 PW JT8D-9A	76884	Combi / VIP		Gvmt
☐	9Q-CZZ	Aerospatiale (Sud) SE210 Caravelle III	105	F-BJTI	0062	0098	2 RR Avon 527B	48000	Combi / VIP		Cmte Badibanga

AIR KASAI (formerly TAC-Transport Aérien Congo & TAZ-Transport Aérien Zairois)
Kinshasa-Ndolo

BP 4605, Kinshasa 2, Democratic Republic of Congo ☎ Sweden (8) 51177978 Tx: none Fax: Sweden (8) 51177978 SITA: n/a
F: 1983 ⋔⋔⋔ n/a Head: Anke Jansson Net: n/a Aircraft below MTOW 1361kg: Cessna 172.

☐	9Q-CFQ	Piper PA-23-250 Aztec C	27-2880	TN-ABH	0065		2 LY IO-540-C4B5	2359	Y5		
☐	9Q-CJA	Britten-Norman BN-2A-21 Islander	898	I-301	0080		2 LY IO-540-K1B5	2994	Y9		
☐	ES-CAM	PZL Mielec (Antonov) An-2	1G76-14	CCCP-09680	0066	0098	1 SH ASh-62IR	5500	Y11		
☐	SP-FAD	PZL Mielec (Antonov) An-2	1G52-20	PLW 5220	0065		1 SH ASh-62IR	5500	Y11		
☐	9Q-CTR	Boeing (Douglas) DC-3C (C-47A-30-DL)	9452	ZS-EDX	0043	0093	2 PW R-1830	12202	Y26		lsf Unibra Co.
☐	9Q-CUK	Boeing (Douglas) DC-3C (C-47B-35-DK)	33445	N99665	0045	0083	2 PW R-1830	12202	Y18		bsd Vallentuna,Swe./opf Aviatörförening
☐	9Q-CYC	Boeing (Douglas) DC-3C (C-47A-65-DL)	18977	N9984Q	0043		2 PW R-1830	12202	Y24		
☐	9Q-CYE	Boeing (Douglas) DC-3C (C-47A-80-DL)	19771	79004	0044	0484	2 PW R-1830	12202	Y26		
☐	9Q-CCD	Nord 2501TC Noratlas	135	F-GEXR	0061	0098	2 BR Hercules	21654	Freighter		std FIH
☐	9Q-CKO	Nord 2501TC Noratlas	169	F-WFYJ	0062	0098	2 BR Hercules	21654	Freighter		
☐	9Q-CNE	Nord 2501TC Noratlas	142	F-GEXS	0061	0098	2 BR Hercules	21654	Freighter		
☐	9Q-CUW	BAe (Vickers) Viscount 798D	391	XA-RJL	0058	0098	4 RR Dart 510	29257	Y44 / Combi		A la Grace de Dieu

AIR KATANGA
Kinshasa-Ndjili

European HQ: c/o A.J. Walter Aviation, Partridge Greet, West Sussex RH13 8RA, Great Britain ☎ (1403) 71 17 77 Tx: 87260 ajwuk g Fax: (1403) 71 09 36 SITA: LGWJWCR
F: 1998 ⋔⋔⋔ n/a Head: Ct. André Njambi Net: http://www.ajw-aviation.com

☐	9Q-CSJ	BAe (BAC) One-Eleven 201AC	013	EI-BWM	0064	0398	2 RR Spey 506-14	34015	Combi		

ATO – Air Transport Office
Kinshasa-Ndjili

Av. des Poids Lourds, Kigabwa, Kinshasa 1, Democratic Republic of Congo ☎ (88) 46 126 Tx: none Fax: (212) 372 36 55 SITA: n/a
F: 1991 ⋔⋔⋔ 250 Head: Patrick Latour & Herbert Skuvie Net: n/a

☐	9Q-CVK	BAe (HS) Andover E.3	17	P4-BLL	0066	1096	2 RR Dart 201	22680	Freighter		cvtd C.1
☐	EL-WCP	BAe (HS) Andover E.3	10	9Q-CVS	0066	1096	2 RR Dart 201	22680	Freighter		cvtd C.1 / std FIH

BAL – Blue Airlines = BUL
Kinshasa-Ndjili & -Ndolo

BP 1115, Kinshasa 1, Democratic Republic of Congo ☎ (12) 20 455 Tx: n/a Fax: n/a SITA: n/a
F: 1991 ⋔⋔⋔ n/a Head: Dr. T. Mayani ICAO: BLUE AIRLINES Net: n/a

☐	9Q-CZL	PZL Mielec (Antonov) An-28	1AJ006-01	RA-28793	0089	1294	2 GS TVD-10B	6500	Y17		
☐	9Q-CZN	PZL Mielec (Antonov) An-28	1AJ005-10	RA-28777	0089	1294	2 GS TVD-10B	6500	Y17		std FIH
☐	9Q-CZK	Antonov 26		RA-26230	0080	1194	2 IV AI-24VT	24000	Freighter		
☐	9Q-CDM	Boeing 727-81	18919 / 163	D-AHLM	0065	1191	3 PW JT8D-7A	73999	Y48 & Cargo	EM-AF	std Goma

BAZAIR
Kinshasa-Ndjili

BP 4564, Kinshasa 2, Democratic Republic of Congo ☎ n/a Tx: none Fax: none SITA: n/a
F: 1996 ⋔⋔⋔ n/a Head: n/a Net: n/a Suspended operations 1997. Intends to restart.

☐	9Q-CTU	BAe (Vickers) Viscount 757	277	CF-THQ	0058	0096	4 RR Dart 506	28576	Pax & Cargo		std FIH / to be made operational

BUSINESS AVIATION OF CONGO
Kinshasa-Ndolo

BP 435, Kinshasa 1, Democratic Republic of Congo ☎ (12) 21 505 Tx: none Fax: (12) 82 388 SITA: n/a
F: 1998 ⋔⋔⋔ n/a Head: n/a Net: n/a

☐	9Q-CMX	Cessna 404 Titan II	404-0415	N8801K	0079	0098	2 CO GTSIO-520-M	3810			
☐	9Q-CYM	Let 410UVP-E	902402	RA-67620	0090	0698	2 WA M-601E	6400			

CAL – Congo Airlines = EO / ALX (formerly Zaire Airlines, Zaire Express, Express City & Express City)
Kinshasa-Ndjili

BP 12847, Kinshasa 1, Democratic Republic of Congo ☎ (88) 46 947 Tx: none Fax: (12) 372 31 57 SITA: n/a
F: 1994 ⋔⋔⋔ 2000 Head: José Endundo-Bononge ICAO: ALLCONGO Net: n/a

☐	9Q-CPR	Hawker 403B (HS 125-403B)	25247	9Q-CSN	0071	0197	2 RR Viper 522	10569	VIP		
☐	9Q-CKY	BAe (BAC) One-Eleven 501EX	176	G-AWYT	0069	1094	2 RR Spey 512-14DWE	41950	Y99		Ville de M'bandaka
☐	9Q-CKZ	Boeing 737-293	19309 / 47	N464AC	0768	0495	2 PW JT8D-7A	46947	C10Y98		Ville de Lubumbashi / lsf Flightstar Av
☐	9Q-CRS	Boeing 727-214	19687 / 573	5H-ARS	0065	0197	3 PW JT8D-7B	78245	Y147		

708	registration	type of aircraft		cn/fn	ex/ex*	mfd	del	powered by		mtow kg	configuration	selcal	name/fln/specialitites/remarks

registration	type of aircraft	cn/fn	ex/ex*	mfd	del	powered by	mtow kg	configuration	selcal	name/fln/specialitites/remarks
☐ 9Q-CWA	Boeing 727-227 (A)	20775 / 998	N554PE	0073	0396	3 PW JT8D-9A	79651	Y163		Ville de Bukavu
☐ 9Q-CKB	Boeing 707-366C	20761 / 867	9Q-CKK	0073	0294	4 PW JT3D-7	151091	Freighter		Aisha / dmgd 280199 Mbuji Mayi
☐ 9Q-CKG	Boeing 707-366C	19844 / 744	9Q-CRA	0068	1195	4 PW JT3D-7 (HK2)	151091	Freighter		std Goma

CCA – Congo Commercial Airlines
Goma

Aéroport, Goma, (Kivu), Democratic Republic of Congo ☎ n/a Tx: none Fax: none SITA: n/a
F: 1997 ⋀⋀⋀ n/a Head: n/a Net: n/a

| ☐ 9Q-CGX | Let 410UVP | 851402 | 3D-NVD | 0085 | 1097 | 2 WA M-601D | 5800 | Y17 | | |

COMPAGNIE AFRICAINE D'AVIATION – CAA
Kinshasa-Ndolo

BP 2531, Kinshasa, Democratic Republic of Congo ☎ (88) 41 796 Tx: none Fax: (88) 41 048 SITA: n/a
F: 1992 ⋀⋀⋀ 60 Head: David Blattner Net: n/a

☐ 9Q-CBY	GAC (Grumman) G-159 Gulfstream I	033	N23AH	0060	1293	2 RR Dart 529-8X	16329	Y30		std FIH
☐ 9Q-CIB	Antonov 26	1701	YL-RAB	0074	1097	2 IV AI-24VT	24000	Freighter		
☐ 9Q-CEJ	Convair 580	79	C-GKFZ	0053	1193	2 AN 501-D13	26379	Y40 & Cargo		cvtd CV340-42

FILAIR, S.P.R.L.
Kinshasa-Ndjili **FILAIR**

Ave Tabora 1686, BP 14671, Kinshasa, Democratic Republic of Congo ☎ (12) 22 159 Tx: none Fax: Belgium (2) 6405847 SITA: n/a
F: 1987 ⋀⋀⋀ 185 Head: Cdt. Dany Philemotte Net: n/a

☐ 9Q-CEF	Antonov 26B			0082	0098	2 IV AI-24VT	24000	Freighter		
☐ 9Q-CZU	Boeing (Douglas) DC-6A (C-118A-DO)	44664 / 631	V5-NCC	0055	1296	4 PW R-2800	47083	Freighter		std FIH
☐ N869TA	Boeing (Douglas) DC-7CF	45188 / 837	N103LM	0057	0795	4 WR R-3350-93	58513	Freighter		lsf Trans-Air-Link/cvtd DC-7C/std FIH

ITAB – International Trans Air Business
Lubumbashi-Luano

BP 923, Lubumbashi, Democratic Republic of Congo ☎ (22) 24 74 Tx: n/a Fax: n/a SITA: n/a
F: n/a ⋀⋀⋀ n/a Head: José Demoura Net: n/a

☐ 9Q-CMB	Cessna U206G Stationair 6 II	U20604312		0078		1 CO IO-520-F	1633	Y5		
☐ 9Q-CFJ	Beech Baron C55 (95-C55)	TE-409		0067		2 CO IO-520-C	2404	Y5		
☐ 9Q-CYA	Britten-Norman BN-2A Islander	617	G-AYBB*	0070		2 LY O-540-E4C5	2722	Y9		
☐ 9Q-CAP	Aerospatiale (Nord) 262A-32	35	F-BPNT	0067	0094	2 TU Bastan VIC	10600	Y26		
☐ 9Q-CLL	BAe (HS) 748-206 Srs 2A (Andover CC.2)	1561 / 34	9L-LBF	0064	0698	2 RR Dart 534-2	21092	VIP		
☐ 9Q-COE	BAe (HS) Andover C.3A	28	VR-BOI	0067	1196	2 RR Dart 201	22680	Freighter		cvtd C.1
☐ 9Q-CVC	BAe (HS) Andover C.3	24	P4-TBL	0067	0097	2 RR Dart 201	22680	Freighter		cvtd C.1
☐ 9Q-CYB	BAe (HS) Andover C.1	22	NZ7628	0067	0497	2 RR Dart 201	22680	VIP		

KIVU AIR SERVICES
Bukavu

Aéroport, Bukavu, Democratic Republic of Congo ☎ n/a Tx: none Fax: none SITA: n/a
F: n/a ⋀⋀⋀ n/a Head: n/a Net: n/a

| ☐ 9Q-CVB | Partenavia P.68B | 177 | | 0078 | | 2 LY IO-360-A1B6 | 1960 | | | |
| ☐ 9Q-CSO | Piper PA-23-250 Aztec E | 27-7405369 | N8MK | 0074 | | 2 LY IO-540-C4B5 | 2359 | | | |

LAC – Lignes Aériennes Congolaises
Kinshasa-Ndjili

BP 8552, Kinshasa 1, Democratic Republic of Congo ☎ (12) 24 985 Tx: none Fax: (12) 24 658 SITA: n/a
F: 1997 ⋀⋀⋀ n/a Head: n/a Net: n/a

| ☐ 9Q-CNK | Boeing 737-298C (A) | 20795 / 348 | | 0074 | 0097 | 2 PW JT8D-15 | 52390 | F12Y110 | | dmgd 0199 Kilimanjaro |
| ☐ 9Q-CLV | Boeing (Douglas) DC-8-54F (FM) | 45610 / 122 | N803CK | 0061 | 0097 | 4 PW JT3D-3B (HK2/QNC) | 140523 | Freighter | FL-GK | cvtd DC-8-42 / std Goma |

MAF Congo – Mission Aviation Fellowship (Branch of MAF USA)
Kinshasa-Ndolo

BP 1898, Kinshasa 1, Democratic Republic of Congo ☎ (88) 50 850 Tx: 21435 maf zr Fax: (88) 46 544 SITA: n/a
F: 1961 ⋀⋀⋀ n/a Head: David Bloomberg Net: n/a Non-commercial multinational ecclesiastical consortium conducting flights for relief & development agencies & missions in remote areas of third world countries.

☐ 9Q-CCE	Cessna A185F Skywagon	18502110		0073		1 CO IO-520-D	1520			
☐ 9Q-CAR	Cessna TU206G Turbo Stationair 6 II	U20606585		0082		1 CO TSIO-520-M	1633			
☐ 9Q-CEI	Cessna TU206F Turbo Stationair II	U20602593	N1378V	0075		1 CO TSIO-520-C	1633			
☐ 9Q-CMA	Cessna U206G Stationair	U20603092	N756BP	0077		1 CO IO-520-F	1633			
☐ 9Q-CML	Cessna U206G Stationair 6 II	U20604973		0078		1 CO IO-520-F	1633			
☐ 9Q-CMO	Cessna U206F Stationair II	U20603292		0076		1 CO IO-520-F	1633			
☐ 9Q-CMR	Cessna U206F Stationair	U20602181	N7356Q	0073		1 CO IO-520-F	1633			
☐ 9Q-CMV	Cessna TU206G Turbo Stationair 6 II	U20604565	7P-AAM	0078		1 CO TSIO-520-M	1633			
☐ 9Q-CMY	Cessna U206G Stationair	U20603630	N7357N	0077		1 CO IO-520-F	1633			
☐ 9Q-CPA	Cessna U206G Stationair 6 II	U20604903	N735DW	0078		1 CO IO-520-F	1633			
☐ 9Q-CUI	Cessna U206G Stationair 6 II	U20606373		0081		1 CO IO-520-F	1633			
☐ N209KA	Cessna U206F Stationair	U20602338		0074		1 CO IO-520-F	1633			
☐ N9666R	Cessna U206G Stationair 6 II	U20606927		0086		1 CO IO-520-F	1633			
☐ 9Q-CAL	Cessna 207 Skywagon	20700320	N1720U	0076		1 CO IO-520-F	1724			
☐ 9Q-CLA	Cessna 210M Centurion II	21062378	N761NB	0078		1 CO IO-520-L	1724			
☐ 9Q-CAU	Cessna 208 Caravan I	20800010		0085		1 PWC PT6A-114	3311			

MALIFT AIR (formerly Malila Airlift)
Kinshasa-Ndjili

Aéroport Ndjili, Kinshasa, Democratic Republic of Congo ☎ n/a Tx: none Fax: none SITA: n/a
F: n/a ⋀⋀⋀ n/a Head: n/a Net: n/a

☐ 9Q-CPG	PZL Mielec (Antonov) An-28			0090	0098	2 GS TVD-10B	6500	Y17 / Freighter		
☐ EW-26127	Antonov 26B	12701	CCCP-26127	1282	0096	2 IV AI-24VT	24000	Freighter		lsf BRU
☐ 9Q-CMD	Antonov 32B				0098	2 IV AI-20D	27000	Freighter		Kevin

MALU AVIATION
Kinshasa-Ndolo

BP 7417, Kinshasa 1, Democratic Republic of Congo ☎ (12) 46 801 Tx: n/a Fax: +871 (1) 50 65 55 SITA: n/a
F: 1993 ⋀⋀⋀ 50 Head: Ngena Kasinoi Net: n/a

☐ 9Q-CDV	Partenavia P.68B Victor	207		0080		2 LY IO-360-A1B6	1960	Y5 / Frtr		
☐ 9Q-CRA	PZL Mielec (Antonov) An-28	1AJ008-08	RA-28922	0090	0098	2 GS TVD-10B	6500	Y17 / Freighter		
☐ 9Q-CSP	PZL Mielec (Antonov) An-28	1AJ008-09	RA-28923	0090	0098	2 GS TVD-10B	6500	Y17 / Freighter		

MIBA AVIATION (Aviation division of Société Minière de Bakwanga)
Mbuji Mayi

European office: 55 Blvd du Régent, B-1000 Brussels, Belgium ☎ (2) 511 08 10 Tx: n/a Fax: (2) 511 71 25 SITA: n/a
F: n/a ⋀⋀⋀ n/a Head: Mr. Mukamba Net: n/a

| ☐ 9Q-CPJ | Boeing 727-22 (F) | 19088 / 365 | N743EV | 0067 | 0494 | 3 PW JT8D-7A | 72756 | Freighter | | Dibindi / lsf Avnet Int'l Ltd/cvtd -22 |

SCIBE-AIRLIFT CONGO = SBZ (formerly Scibe-Airlift Zaire)
Kinshasa-Ndjili & Gbadolite

BP 614, Kinshasa 1, Democratic Republic of Congo ☎ (12) 26 237 Tx: 21003 scibe zr Fax: (212) 376 92 72 SITA: FIHDCZM
F: 1979 ⋀⋀⋀ n/a Head: Bemba Saolona IATA: 939 ICAO: SCIBE AIRLIFT Net: n/a

| ☐ 9Q-CBT | Boeing 727-89 | 19138 / 246 | D-AHLR | 0066 | 0583 | 3 PW JT8D-7 | 72802 | Y130 | | std FIH |
| ☐ 9Q-CBW | Boeing 707-329C | 20200 / 828 | 9Q-CBS | 0069 | 0185 | 4 PW JT3D-7 (HK2/COM) | 150900 | Freighter | CM-AB | std SEN |

SHUTTLE AIR CARGO
Ostend (Belgium)

European HQ: c/o MISCO, PO Box 156, B-1930 Zaventem, Belgium ☎ (2) 725 33 77 Tx: none Fax: (2) 725 38 05 SITA: n/a
F: 1996 ⋀⋀⋀ n/a Head: Thor Sandacker Net: n/a

| ☐ EL-ACP | Boeing 707-369C | 20547 / 861 | EL-ALG | 0072 | 0896 | 4 PW JT3D-3B (HK2/COM) | 151046 | Freighter | | opf ACS-Air Charter Service broker |

SWALA AIRLINES
Bukavu

BP 551, Bukavu, Democratic Republic of Congo ☎ (38) 25 94 19 Tx: none Fax: none SITA: n/a
F: n/a ⋀⋀⋀ n/a Head: n/a Net: n/a

| ☐ 9Q-CAD | Partenavia P.68B | 131 | 5Y-BBY | 0078 | | 2 LY IO-360-A1B6 | 1960 | | | |
| ☐ 9Q-CDA | Shorts Skyvan 3 Variant 100 (SC-7) | SH1903 | LN-NPG | 1072 | 0384 | 2 GA TPE331-2-201A | 5670 | | | |

TMK AIR COMMUTER (Société de Transports et Messageries au Kivu, Sprl. dba)
Goma **TMK AIR COMMUTER**

European office: c/o Mr. H.W. Esselen, 174 Av. Charles Michiels, Bte 36, B-1170 Bruxelles, Belgium ☎ (2) 672 48 55 Tx: none Fax: (2) 672 21 07 SITA: n/a
F: 1987 ⋀⋀⋀ 37 Head: Hubert W. Esselen Net: n/a

| ☐ 9Q-CBO | De Havilland DHC-6 Twin Otter 300 | 735 | N123SL | 1280 | 1189 | 2 PWC PT6A-27 | 5670 | Y19 | | Butembo |

VAC – Virunga Air Charter
Goma (Kivu)

BP 432, Goma, (Kivu), Democratic Republic of Congo ☎ (243) 888 50 85 Tx: 21692 zr Fax: (250) 40 718 SITA: n/a
F: 1978 ⋀⋀⋀ 55 Head: Ngezayo Kambale Net: n/a Aircraft below MTOW 1361 kg: Cessna 172.

☐ 9Q-CTL	Partenavia P.68B	145	5Y-BCG	0078		2 LY IO-360-A1B6	1960			
☐ 9Q-CTN	Partenavia P.68C-TC	238-04-TC	OO-TZT	0082		2 LY TIO-360-C1A6D	1960			
☐ 9Q-CDF	Cessna 402B	402B0510	5U-BAL	0073		2 CO TSIO-520-E	2858			
☐ 9Q-CDD	Dornier DO 28D-1 Skyservant	4025	D-IFAQ	0069		2 LY IGSO-540-A1E	3650			
☐ 9Q-CTX	Dornier 128-6 Turbo Skyservant		D-IDOO	0085		2 PWC PT6A-110	4350			
☐ 9Q-CAM	Boeing (Douglas) DC-3C (C-47B-50-DK)	34409	45-1139	0045		2 PW R-1830	12202			Simba Mzee

WALTAIR, S.P.R.L. — Kinshasa-Ndjili

European office:, c/o Mr. D. Devos, Kapucijnenstraat 35/12, B-8400 Ostend, Belgium ☎ (59) 70 44 09 Tx: none Fax: (59) 70 44 09 SITA: n/a
F: 1982 ⁂ 85 Head: Vincent Gillet Net: n/a

☐ 9Q-CPW	BAe (HS) Andover E.3	14	XS607	0066	0696	2 RR Dart 201	22680	Freighter		cvtd C.1
☐ 3D-AUG	Aerospatiale (Sud) SE210 Caravelle 11R	264	EL-AWY	0069	0098	2 PW JT8D-7	52000	Freighter		Ruth
☐ 9Q-CPI	Aerospatiale (Sud) SE210 Caravelle 10B3	169	9Q-CPY	0064	0796	2 PW JT8D-7B	56000	Freighter		std FIH

WETRAFA AIRLIFT — Mbuji-Mayi

BP 1358 Limete, Kinshasa, Democratic Republic of Congo ☎ (12) 23 369 Tx: 43765 zr Fax: none SITA: n/a
F: n/a ⁂ n/a Head: Kalambayi Mabika Faustin Net: n/a

☐ 9Q-CWT	Boeing 727-25	18291 / 204	N904TS	0065	0794	3 PW JT8D-7B	72802			

9U = BURUNDI (Republic of Burundi) (République du Burundi)

Capital: Bujumbura Official Language: French Population: 6,4 million Square Km: 27834 Dialling code: +257 Year established: 1962 Acting political head: Major Pierre Buyoya (President)

Government / Corporate / Executive / VIP Aircraft

☐ 9U-BTB	Dassault Falcon 50	66	N4413N	0081	0792	3 GA TFE731-3-1C	17600	VIP		Gvmt

AIR BURUNDI = PBU — Bujumbura

BP 2460, Bujumbura, Burundi ☎ 22 46 09 Tx: 5080 bdi Fax: 22 34 52 SITA: n/a
F: 1971 ⁂ 100 Head: Lieutenant Colonel Isaac Gafurero ICAO: AIR-BURUNDI Net: n/a

☐ 9U-BHA	De Havilland DHC-6 Twin Otter 300	552		0077	0977	2 PWC PT6A-27	5670	Y20		
☐ 9U-BHB	De Havilland DHC-6 Twin Otter 300	560		0077	1177	2 PWC PT6A-27	5670	Y19		
☐ 9U-BHD	Beech 1900C-1 Airliner	UC-147	N8207B	0091	0892	2 PWC PT6A-65B	7530	Y19		

AIR TANGANYIKA = TNY — Bujumbura & Charleroi (Belgium)

European office:, Section 7, Airport, B-6041 Charleroi, Belgium ☎ (71) 25 11 42 Tx: none Fax: (71) 25 11 45 SITA: n/a
F: 1997 ⁂ n/a Head: n/a ICAO: AIR TANGO Net: n/a Operates cargo flights with Boeing 707C aircraft, leased from SHUTTLE AIR CARGO (9Q-), when required.

TRANS LLOYD CARGO, Corp. — Bujumbura

Operations office:, PO Box 332, Lanseria Airport 1748, South Africa ☎ (11) 678 23 06 Tx: none Fax: (11) 678 23 06 SITA: n/a
F: 1996 ⁂ n/a Head: Michael Snow Net: n/a

☐ 9U-BIH	Canadair CL-44D4-2	25	EL-WLL	0061	0997	4 RR Tyne 515-10	95254	Freighter		

9V = SINGAPORE (Republic of Singapore)

Capital: Singapore Official Language: English Population: 4,0 million Square Km: 618 Dialling code: +65 Year established: 1965 Acting political head: Ong Teng Cheong (President)

AEROLIFT INTERNATIONAL, Pte Ltd = (LIFT) (Joint venture of Aeroflot Russian Int'l Airlines & Hevilift (PNG), Pty Ltd) — Singapore

11-05 Jit Poh Bldg., 19 Keppel Road, Singapore 0208, Republic of Singapore ☎ 225 78 71 Tx: none Fax: 225 76 87 SITA: n/a
F: n/a ⁂ n/a Head: Mike Bromley Net: n/a New & used helicopter leasing company.
Owner / lessor of following (main) helicopter types: Kamov Ka-32, Mil Mi-8 & Mi-26. Helicopters leased from Aerolift Int'l are listed & mentioned as lsf LIFT under the leasing carriers.

AEROSTAR LEASING, Pte Ltd = (STAR) (Sister company of Regionair, Pte Ltd) — Singapore

06-01 HPL House, 50 Cuscaden Road, Singapore 1024, Republic of Singapore ☎ 731 48 62 Tx: 20473 rs Fax: 732 03 47 SITA: n/a
F: 1995 ⁂ 5 Head: Seng Choon Kiat Net: n/a New and used aircraft leasing & financing company.
Owner / lessor of following (main) aircraft types: Airbus Industrie A320 Aircraft leased from STAR are listed and mentioned as such under the leasing carriers.

AIR MARK AVIATION (Singapore), Pte Ltd — Singapore-Selatar

Bldg 960A, West Wing, Selatar Airport, Singapore 797796, Republic of Singapore ☎ 482 48 64 Tx: none Fax: 484 28 92 SITA: n/a
F: n/a ⁂ n/a Head: Mohd Yunos Ishak Net: n/a

☐ LZ-SFH	Antonov 26	3904	RA-26570	0076	0097	2 IV AI-24VT	24000	Freighter		lsf SFB

GLOBAL AVIATION, Pte Ltd = GAZ (Associated with Air Castle & Hop-a-Jet (USA) / Member of The Winfair Aviation Alliance) — Singapore-Seletar

1072 West Camp Road, Seletar Airport, Singapore 797799, Republic of Singapore ☎ 481 95 22 Tx: none Fax: 481 99 97 SITA: n/a
F: 1988 ⁂ 11 Head: Capt. Fred Baudzus Net: http://www.globalaviation.com

☐ N950G	Learjet 36A	36A-032	HB-VLK	0077	0196	2 GA TFE731-2-2B	7711	Executive		lsf Air Castle

JAPAN FLEET SERVICE, (S) Pte Ltd = (JFSS) — Singapore & Tokyo

10 Shenton Way 11-08/09, MAS Building, Singapore 07-9117, Republic of Singapore ☎ 226 18 22 Tx: 21658 jfss rs Fax: 225 55 83 SITA: n/a
F: 1984 ⁂ 14 Head: Tim L. Watkins Net: n/a New and used aircraft & parts leasing & sales company.
Owner / lessor of following (main) aircraft types: Airbus A300-600R. Aircraft leased from JFSS are listed and mentioned as such under the leasing carriers.

PACIFIC FLIGHT SERVICES, Pte Ltd = PFA — Singapore-Seletar

Bldg 499, West Camp, Seletar Airport, Singapore 2879, Republic of Singapore ☎ 481 37 56 Tx: none Fax: 482 17 27 SITA: SINPFCR
F: 1991 ⁂ 9 Head: Richard Yong ICAO: PACIFIC SING Net: n/a

☐ VH-PFA	Learjet 35A	35A-661	N1268G	0090	0196	2 GA TFE731-2-2B	8301	EMS / Executive		lsf Unicorn Int'l, Australia

REGIONAIR, Pte Ltd = 7S / RGA — Singapore-Changi

Changi Airport PO Box 107, Singapore 918144, Republic of Singapore ☎ 542 46 33 Tx: 20473 rs Fax: 542 49 82 SITA: SINOD7S
F: 1988 ⁂ 40 Head: Gerard de Vaz ICAO: ORCHID Net: n/a

☐ S7-RGU	Boeing 767-324 (ER)	27568 / 593	EI-CMH	0095	0296	2 GE CF6-80C2B7F	186880	C25Y196	LS-CH	opf HVN
☐ S7-RGV	Boeing 767-324 (ER)	27392 / 568	EI-CMD	0095	0196	2 GE CF6-80C2B7F	186880	C25Y196	LS-CF	opf HVN
☐ S7-RGW	Boeing 767-324 (ER)	27393 / 571	EI-CME	0095	0296	2 GE CF6-80C2B7F	186880	C25Y196	LS-CG	opf HVN

SILKAIR = MI / SLK (Silkair (Singapore), Pte Ltd dba / Member of Singapore Airlines Group / formerly Tradewinds, (Pte) Ltd) — Singapore-Seletar & -Changi

Airmail Transit Centre, PO Box 501, Singapore 9181, Republic of Singapore ☎ 542 81 11 Tx: none Fax: 542 00 23 SITA: n/a
F: 1975 ⁂ 380 Head: Chew Choon Seng IATA: 629 ICAO: SILKAIR Net: http://www.pacific.net.sg/silkair/
Scheduled services to Tioman Island are operated in conjunction with PELANGI AIR (9M-) jointly using their Dornier 228 aircraft.

☐ 9V-SLK	Fokker 70 (F28 Mk0070)	11536	PH-EZH*	0095	0395	2 RR Tay 620-15	41730	Y79		
☐ 9V-SLL	Fokker 70 (F28 Mk0070)	11561	PH-EZR*	0095	1195	2 RR Tay 620-15	41730	Y79		
☐ 9V-TRA	Boeing 737-3Y0	24679 / 1897		0090	0790	2 CFMI CFM56-3B2	61235	C12Y106	FJ-GQ	lsf SALE
☐ 9V-TRC	Boeing 737-3L9	24570 / 1800	OY-MME	0090	1091	2 CFMI CFM56-3B2	63276	C12Y106	BR-AQ	
☐ 9V-TRD	Boeing 737-3M8	25017 / 2005	N760BE*	0091	0692	2 CFMI CFM56-3B2	61235	C12Y106	CS-ER	lsf GECA
☐ 9V-	Airbus Industrie A319-132	1074				2 IAE V2524-A5	70000	C12Y106		oo-delivery 0899
☐ 9V-	Airbus Industrie A319-132	1098				2 IAE V2524-A5	70000	C12Y106		oo-delivery 1099
☐ 9V-	Airbus Industrie A319-132					2 IAE V2524-A5	70000	C12Y106		oo-delivery 0300
☐ 9V-	Airbus Industrie A319-132					2 IAE V2524-A5	70000	C12Y106		oo-delivery 0601
☐ 9V-SLA	Airbus Industrie A320-232	872	F-WWBC*	0098	0998	2 IAE V2527-A5	77000	C16Y126		
☐ 9V-SLB	Airbus Industrie A320-232	899	F-WWDL*	0098	1198	2 IAE V2527-A5	77000	C16Y126		
☐ 9V-SLC	Airbus Industrie A320-232	969	F-WWBO*	0099	0399	2 IAE V2527-A5	77000	C16Y126		
☐ 9V-	Airbus Industrie A320-232					2 IAE V2527-A5	77000	C16Y126		oo-delivery 0999

SINGAPORE AIRCRAFT LEASING ENTERPRISE, Pte Ltd = (SALE) (Associated with Singapore Airlines Ltd) — Singapore

UIC Building, 5 Shenton Way 32-05, Singapore 068808, Republic of Singapore ☎ 323 55 59 Tx: none Fax: 323 69 62 SITA: n/a
F: 1993 ⁂ 20 Head: Robert J. Martin Net: n/a New & used aircraft leasing company.
Owner / lessor of following (main) aircraft types: Airbus Industrie A310-200/319/320/321, Boeing 737-300/747-400/767-300 (ER) & 777-200 (ER). Aircraft leased from SALE are listed & mentioned as such under the leasing carriers.

SINGAPORE AIRLINES, Ltd = SQ / SIA — Singapore-Changi

PO Box 501, Airmail Transit Centre, Singapore 918101, Republic of Singapore ☎ 542 33 33 Tx: 21241 siasin rs Fax: 545 50 34 SITA: n/a
F: 1972 ⁂ 28000 Head: Dr. Cheong Choong Kong IATA: 618 ICAO: SINGAPORE Net: http://www.singaporeair.com

☐ 9V-ATG	Learjet 45	45-029	N5013Y*	0099	0399	2 GA TFE731-20	9163	Trainer		
☐ 9V-ATH	Learjet 45	45-031	N5016V*	0099	0499	2 GA TFE731-20	9163	Trainer		
☐ 9V-ATI	Learjet 45	45-033	N5016Z*	0099	0499	2 GA TFE731-20	9163	Trainer		
☐ 9V-ATJ	Learjet 45	45-				2 GA TFE731-20	9163	Trainer		oo-delivery 0099
☐ 9V-STL	Airbus Industrie A310-222	363	F-WZEI*	0085	0385	2 PW JT9D-7R4E1	142000	F12C28Y140	JK-AE	
☐ 9V-STA	Airbus Industrie A310-324	665	F-WWCL*	0093	0393	2 PW PW4152	153000	F12C28Y143	CF-DP	
☐ 9V-STB	Airbus Industrie A310-324	669	F-WWCC*	0093	0493	2 PW PW4152	153000	F12C28Y143	CF-GR	
☐ 9V-STC	Airbus Industrie A310-324	680	F-WWCT*	0093	0993	2 PW PW4152	153000	F12C28Y143	EL-CS	
☐ 9V-STD	Airbus Industrie A310-324	684	F-WWCJ*	0093	1093	2 PW PW4152	153000	F12C28Y143	EL-DR	
☐ 9V-STE	Airbus Industrie A310-324	693	F-WWCI*	0094	0694	2 PW PW4152	153000	F12C28Y143	EM-PQ	
☐ 9V-STF	Airbus Industrie A310-324	697	F-WWCK*	0095	0395	2 PW PW4152	153000	F12C28Y143	GS-HR	
☐ 9V-STO	Airbus Industrie A310-324	433	F-WWCX*	0087	0787	2 PW PW4152	153000	F12C28Y143	FL-EH	
☐ 9V-STP	Airbus Industrie A310-324	443	F-WWCS*	0087	1287	2 PW PW4152	153000	F12C28Y143	FL-EJ	
☐ 9V-STQ	Airbus Industrie A310-324	493	F-WWCN*	0089	0389	2 PW PW4152	153000	F12C28Y143	AM-KL	
☐ 9V-STR	Airbus Industrie A310-324	500	F-WWCX*	0089	0889	2 PW PW4152	153000	F12C28Y143	DF-GL	
☐ 9V-STS	Airbus Industrie A310-324	501	F-WWCB*	0089	0989	2 PW PW4152	153000	F12C28Y143	DF-GM	
☐ 9V-STT	Airbus Industrie A310-324	534	F-WWCM*	0090	0290	2 PW PW4152	153000	F12C28Y143	DF-HK	
☐ 9V-STU	Airbus Industrie A310-324	548	F-WWCV*	0090	1090	2 PW PW4152	153000	F12C28Y143	AH-GJ	
☐ 9V-STV	Airbus Industrie A310-324	570	F-WWCF*	0091	0391	2 PW PW4152	153000	F12C28Y143	AH-GL	

710 registration type of aircraft cn/fn ex/ex* mfd del powered by mtow kg configuration selcal name/fln/specialitites/remarks

	registration	type of aircraft	cn/fn	ex/ex*	mfd	del	powered by	mtow kg	configuration	selcal	name/fln/specialitites/remarks
☐	9V-STW	Airbus Industrie A310-324	589	F-WWCO*	0091	0791	2 PW PW4152	153000	F12C28Y143	BF-ES	
☐	9V-STY	Airbus Industrie A310-324	634	F-WWCF*	0092	0292	2 PW PW4152	153000	F12C28Y143	BP-FR	
☐	9V-STZ	Airbus Industrie A310-324	654	F-WWCJ*	0092	0992	2 PW PW4152	153000	F12C28Y143	BP-FS	
☐	9V-SQA	Boeing 777-212 (ER)	28507 / 67		0097	0597	2 RR Trent 892	251744	F12C42Y234		
☐	9V-SQB	Boeing 777-212 (ER)	28508 / 83		0797	0797	2 RR Trent 892	251744	F12C42Y234		Jubilee
☐	9V-SQC	Boeing 777-212 (ER)	28509 / 86		0097	0897	2 RR Trent 892	251744	F12C42Y234		
☐	9V-SQD	Boeing 777-212 (ER)	28510 / 90		0097	0997	2 RR Trent 892	251744	F12C42Y234		
☐	9V-SQE	Boeing 777-212 (ER)	28511 / 122		0098	0298	2 RR Trent 892	251744	F12C42Y234		
☐	9V-SQF	Boeing 777-212 (ER)	28512 / 126		0098	0398	2 RR Trent 892	251744	F12C42Y234		
☐	9V-SRA	Boeing 777-212 (ER)	28513 / 144		0098	0698	2 RR Trent 892	251744	C30Y293		
☐	9V-SRB	Boeing 777-212 (ER)	28998 / 149		0698	0698	2 RR Trent 892	251744	C30Y293		
☐	9V-SRC	Boeing 777-212 (ER)	28999 / 150		0098	0798	2 RR Trent 892	251744	C30Y293		
☐	9V-SRD	Boeing 777-212 (ER)	28514 / 153		0098	0898	2 RR Trent 892	251744	C30Y293		
☐	9V-	Boeing 777-212 (ER)					2 RR Trent 892	286897			oo-delivery 0002
☐	9V-	Boeing 777-212 (ER)					2 RR Trent 892	286897			oo-delivery 0002
☐	9V-	Boeing 777-212 (ER)					2 RR Trent 892	286897			oo-delivery 0002
☐	9V-	Boeing 777-212 (ER)					2 RR Trent 892	286897			oo-delivery 0002
☐	9V-	Boeing 777-212 (ER)					2 RR Trent 892	286897			oo-delivery 0002
☐	9V-	Boeing 777-212 (ER)					2 RR Trent 892	286897			oo-delivery 0003
☐	9V-	Boeing 777-212 (ER)					2 RR Trent 892	286897			oo-delivery 0003
☐	9V-	Boeing 777-212 (ER)					2 RR Trent 892	286897			oo-delivery 0003
☐	9V-	Boeing 777-212 (ER)					2 RR Trent 892	286897			oo-delivery 0003
☐	9V-	Boeing 777-212 (ER)					2 RR Trent 892	286897			oo-delivery 0004
☐	9V-	Boeing 777-212 (ER)					2 RR Trent 892	286897			oo-delivery 0004
☐	9V-	Boeing 777-212 (ER)					2 RR Trent 892	286897			oo-delivery 0004
☐	9V-	Boeing 777-212 (ER)					2 RR Trent 892	286897			oo-delivery 0004
☐	9V-SYA	Boeing 777-312	28515 / 180		0098	1298	2 RR Trent 892	299371	F18C49Y265		
☐	9V-SYB	Boeing 777-312	28516 / 184		1298	1298	2 RR Trent 892	299371	F18C49Y265		
☐	9V-SYC	Boeing 777-312	28517 / 188		0199	0199	2 RR Trent 892	299371	F18C49Y265		
☐	9V-SYD	Boeing 777-312	28534 / 192		0199	0199	2 RR Trent 892	299371	F18C49Y265		
☐	9V-SYE	Boeing 777-312					2 RR Trent 892	299371	F18C49Y265		oo-delivery 0700
☐	9V-SYF	Boeing 777-312					2 RR Trent 892	299371	F18C49Y265		oo-delivery 1001
☐	9V-SYG	Boeing 777-312					2 RR Trent 892	299371	F18C49Y265		oo-delivery 1101
☐	9V-SJA	Airbus Industrie A340-313 (CELESTAR)	123	F-WWJK*	0096	0496	4 CFMI CFM56-5C4	275000	F10C30Y225	KQ-PS	
☐	9V-SJB	Airbus Industrie A340-313 (CELESTAR)	126	F-WWJL*	0096	0496	4 CFMI CFM56-5C4	275000	F10C30Y225	KR-AB	
☐	9V-SJC	Airbus Industrie A340-313 (CELESTAR)	128	F-WWJZ*	0096	0696	4 CFMI CFM56-5C4	275000	F10C30Y225	KR-AC	
☐	9V-SJD	Airbus Industrie A340-313 (CELESTAR)	139	F-WWJA*	0096	0696	4 CFMI CFM56-5C4	275000	F10C30Y225	KR-AD	
☐	9V-SJE	Airbus Industrie A340-313 (CELESTAR)	149	F-WWJJ*	0096	1096	4 CFMI CFM56-5C4	275000	F10C30Y225	KR-AE	
☐	9V-SJF	Airbus Industrie A340-313 (CELESTAR)	117	F-WWJM*	0096	1096	4 CFMI CFM56-5C4	275000	F10C30Y225	KR-AF	
☐	9V-SJG	Airbus Industrie A340-313 (CELESTAR)	163	F-WWJR*	0097	0397	4 CFMI CFM56-5C4	275000	F10C30Y225	FP-HQ	
☐	9V-SJH	Airbus Industrie A340-313 (CELESTAR)	166	F-WWJS*	0097	0397	4 CFMI CFM56-5C4	275000	F10C30Y225		
☐	9V-SJI	Airbus Industrie A340-313 (CELESTAR)	185	F-WWJK*	0097	0797	4 CFMI CFM56-5C4	275000	F10C30Y225	FJ-PS	
☐	9V-SJJ	Airbus Industrie A340-313 (CELESTAR)	190	F-WWJX*	0097	1097	4 CFMI CFM56-5C4	275000	F10C30Y225	FP-KQ	
☐	9V-SJK	Airbus Industrie A340-313 (CELESTAR)	202	F-WWJS*	0097	1297	4 CFMI CFM56-5C4	275000	F10C30Y225	FP-LQ	
☐	9V-SJL	Airbus Industrie A340-313 (CELESTAR)	212	F-WWJU*	0098	0498	4 CFMI CFM56-5C4	275000	F10C30Y225	FP-LR	
☐	9V-SJM	Airbus Industrie A340-313 (CELESTAR)	215	F-WWJV*	0098	0498	4 CFMI CFM56-5C4	275000	F10C30Y225	HL-ES	
☐	9V-SJN	Airbus Industrie A340-313 (CELESTAR)	236	F-WWJP*	0098	0998	4 CFMI CFM56-5C4	275000	F10C30Y225		
☐	9V-SJO	Airbus Industrie A340-313 (CELESTAR)	282	F-WWJX*			4 CFMI CFM56-5C4	275000	F10C30Y225		oo-delivery 0699
☐	9V-SJP	Airbus Industrie A340-313 (CELESTAR)	331				4 CFMI CFM56-5C4	275000	F10C30Y225		oo-delivery 0300
☐	9V-SJQ	Airbus Industrie A340-313 (CELESTAR)	363				4 CFMI CFM56-5C4	275000	F10C30Y225		oo-delivery 1000
☐	9V-	Airbus Industrie A340-541					4 RR Trent 553	365000			oo-delivery 0002
☐	9V-	Airbus Industrie A340-541					4 RR Trent 553	365000			oo-delivery 0003
☐	9V-	Airbus Industrie A340-541					4 RR Trent 553	365000			oo-delivery 0003
☐	9V-	Airbus Industrie A340-541					4 RR Trent 553	365000			oo-delivery 0003
☐	9V-	Airbus Industrie A340-541					4 RR Trent 553	365000			oo-delivery 0003
☐	9V-SKA	Boeing 747-312 (BIG TOP)	23026 / 580	N8279V*	0083	0483	4 PW JT9D-7R4G2	377842	F20C20Y340	KM-AG	lst AAA as VH-INH -0899
☐	9V-SKD	Boeing 747-312 (BIG TOP)	23029 / 590	N118KD	0083	1183	4 PW JT9D-7R4G2	377842	F20C20Y340	KM-BC	lst AAA as VH-INJ -0999
☐	9V-SKH	Boeing 747-312 (BIG TOP)	23033 / 609	N122KH	0085	0385	4 PW JT9D-7R4G2	377842	F20C20Y340	GL-DF	
☐	9V-SKJ	Boeing 747-312 (BIG TOP)	23243 / 612	N123KJ	0085	0485	4 PW JT9D-7R4G2	377842	F20C20Y340	JM-FK	std SIN / for sale
☐	9V-SKK	Boeing 747-312 (BIG TOP)	23244 / 621	N124KK	0085	0985	4 PW JT9D-7R4G2	377842	F20C20Y340	KL-AD	std SIN / for sale
☐	9V-SKL	Boeing 747-312 (BIG TOP)	23245 / 626	N125KL	0085	1285	4 PW JT9D-7R4G2	377842	F20C20Y340	KL-DE	std SIN / for sale
☐	9V-SKM	Boeing 747-312 (M) (BIG TOP)	23409 / 637	N6065Y*	0086	0386	4 PW JT9D-7R4G2	377842	F16C40Y248 / Plt	KL-DF	std SIN / for sale
☐	9V-SKP	Boeing 747-312 (M) (BIG TOP)	23769 / 666	N6005C*	0087	0387	4 PW JT9D-7R4G2	377842	F16C40Y248 / Plt	KL-DH	std SIN / for sale
☐	N117KC	Boeing 747-312 (BIG TOP)	23028 / 584	VH-INK	0083	0683	4 PW JT9D-7R4G2	377842	F20C20Y340	KM-AL	lsf WTC Trustee / std LAS / for sale
☐	9V-SFA	Boeing 747-412F (SCD) (MEGA ARK)	26563 / 1036	N60659*	0094	0894	4 PW PW4056	394625	Freighter	EL-BS	
☐	9V-SFB	Boeing 747-412F (SCD) (MEGA ARK)	26561 / 1042		0094	0994	4 PW PW4056	394625	Freighter	ES-MR	
☐	9V-SFC	Boeing 747-412F (SCD) (MEGA ARK)	26560 / 1052		0095	0295	4 PW PW4056	394625	Freighter	EQ-DR	
☐	9V-SFD	Boeing 747-412F (SCD) (MEGA ARK)	26553 / 1069		0095	0895	4 PW PW4056	394625	Freighter	GS-HQ	
☐	9V-SFE	Boeing 747-412F (SCD) (MEGA ARK)	28263 / 1094		0096	1196	4 PW PW4056	394625	Freighter	KS-FL	
☐	9V-SFF	Boeing 747-412F (SCD) (MEGA ARK)	28026 / 1105		0097	0397	4 PW PW4056	394625	Freighter	MS-CG	
☐	9V-SFG	Boeing 747-412F (SCD) (MEGA ARK)	26558 / 1173		0098	0998	4 PW PW4056	394625	Freighter		
☐	9V-SFH	Boeing 747-412F (SCD) (MEGA ARK)					4 PW PW4056	394625	Freighter		oo-delivery 0300
☐	9V-SMA	Boeing 747-412 (MEGATOP)	24061 / 717	N5573B*	0089	0389	4 PW PW4056	394625	F24C53Y316	AK-JL	
☐	9V-SMB	Boeing 747-412 (MEGATOP)	24062 / 722	N6005C*	0089	0389	4 PW PW4056	394625	F24C53Y316	AK-JM	to be lst AAA as VH-ANA, 0899
☐	9V-SMC	Boeing 747-412 (MEGATOP)	24063 / 736	3B-SMC	0089	0789	4 PW PW4056	394625	F24C53Y316	AK-LM	
☐	9V-SMD	Boeing 747-412 (MEGATOP)	24064 / 755		0089	1189	4 PW PW4056	394625	F24C53Y316	AL-BH	to be lst AAA as VH-ANB, 0999
☐	9V-SME	Boeing 747-412 (MEGATOP)	24065 / 761		0089	1289	4 PW PW4056	394625	F24C53Y316	AL-FM	
☐	9V-SMF	Boeing 747-412 (MEGATOP)	24066 / 791	N60668*	0090	0690	4 PW PW4056	394625	F24C53Y316	AL-FJ	
☐	9V-SMG	Boeing 747-412 (MEGATOP)	24226 / 809	N6005C*	0090	0990	4 PW PW4056	394625	F24C53Y316	AL-GH	
☐	9V-SMH	Boeing 747-412 (MEGATOP)	24227 / 831	N6009F*	0091	0191	4 PW PW4056	394625	F24C53Y316	AL-GJ	
☐	9V-SMI	Boeing 747-412 (MEGATOP)	24975 / 838		0091	0291	4 PW PW4056	394625	F24C53Y316	FM-BE	
☐	9V-SMJ	Boeing 747-412 (MEGATOP)	25068 / 852	N6005C*	0091	0591	4 PW PW4056	394625	F24C53Y316	FM-BG	
☐	9V-SMK	Boeing 747-412 (MEGATOP)	25127 / 859		0091	0691	4 PW PW4056	394625	F24C53Y316	FM-DE	
☐	9V-SML	Boeing 747-412 (MEGATOP)	25128 / 860		0091	0691	4 PW PW4056	394625	F24C53Y316	LM-AD	
☐	9V-SMM	Boeing 747-412 (MEGATOP)	26547 / 921	N6038E*	0092	0692	4 PW PW4056	394625	F24C53Y316	BP-GR	
☐	9V-SMN	Boeing 747-412 (MEGATOP)	26548 / 923		0092	0692	4 PW PW4056	394625	F24C53Y316	BP-GS	
☐	9V-SMO	Boeing 747-412 (MEGATOP)	27066 / 940		0092	1092	4 PW PW4056	394625	F24C53Y316	BP-HR	
☐	9V-SMP	Boeing 747-412 (MEGATOP)	27067 / 953		0092	1292	4 PW PW4056	394625	F24C53Y316	BP-HS	
☐	9V-SMQ	Boeing 747-412 (MEGATOP)	27132 / 955		0092	0193	4 PW PW4056	394625	F24C53Y316	BP-JR	
☐	9V-SMR	Boeing 747-412 (MEGATOP)	27133 / 962		0093	0293	4 PW PW4056	394625	F24C53Y316	BP-JS	
☐	9V-SMS	Boeing 747-412 (MEGATOP)	27134 / 981		0093	0693	4 PW PW4056	394625	F24C53Y316	BP-KR	
☐	9V-SMT	Boeing 747-412 (MEGATOP)	27137 / 990	N60697*	0093	0893	4 PW PW4056	394625	F24C53Y316	BP-KS	
☐	9V-SMU	Boeing 747-412 (MEGATOP)	27068 / 1000		0093	1093	4 PW PW4056	394625	F24C53Y316	AE-GS	
☐	9V-SMV	Boeing 747-412 (MEGATOP)	27069 / 1010		0093	1293	4 PW PW4056	394625	F24C53Y316	AE-HR	
☐	9V-SMW	Boeing 747-412 (MEGATOP)	27178 / 1015	N6018N*	0094	0194	4 PW PW4056	394625	F24C53Y316	DQ-AR	
☐	9V-SMY	Boeing 747-412 (MEGATOP)	27217 / 1023		0094	0394	4 PW PW4056	394625	F24C53Y316	DQ-AS	
☐	9V-SMZ	Boeing 747-412 (MEGATOP)	26549 / 1030	N6018N*	0094	0594	4 PW PW4056	394625	F24C53Y316	DQ-BR	
☐	9V-SPA	Boeing 747-412 (MEGATOP)	26550 / 1040		0094	0994	4 PW PW4056	394625	F24C53Y316	ER-AF	
☐	9V-SPB	Boeing 747-412 (MEGATOP)	26551 / 1045		0094	1094	4 PW PW4056	394625	F24C53Y316	ER-BM	
☐	9V-SPC	Boeing 747-412 (MEGATOP)	27070 / 1049		0094	1294	4 PW PW4056	396893	F24C53Y316	ES-MQ	
☐	9V-SPD	Boeing 747-412 (MEGATOP)	26552 / 1056	N6009F*	0095	0395	4 PW PW4056	394625	F24C53Y316	EQ-BR	
☐	9V-SPE	Boeing 747-412 (MEGATOP)	26554 / 1070		0095	1095	4 PW PW4056	396893	F16C65Y316	GS-JK	
☐	9V-SPF	Boeing 747-412 (MEGATOP)	27071 / 1072		0095	1295	4 PW PW4056	394625	F16C65Y316	GS-JL	
☐	9V-SPG	Boeing 747-412 (MEGATOP)	26562 / 1074		0296	0296	4 PW PW4056	396893	F16C65Y316	GS-JM	
☐	9V-SPH	Boeing 747-412 (MEGATOP)	26555 / 1075		0096	0396	4 PW PW4056	396893	F16C65Y316	JP-MS	
☐	9V-SPI	Boeing 747-412 (MEGATOP)	28022 / 1082		0096	0696	4 PW PW4056	396893	F16C65Y316	JS-LP	
☐	9V-SPJ	Boeing 747-412 (MEGATOP)	26556 / 1084		0096	0796	4 PW PW4056	396893	F16C65Y316	JS-LQ	
☐	9V-SPK	Boeing 747-412 (MEGATOP)	28023 / 1099		0097	0197	4 PW PW4056	396893	F12C56Y316	MS-CE	special Tropical Megatop-colors
☐	9V-SPL	Boeing 747-412 (MEGATOP)	26557 / 1101		0097	0197	4 PW PW4056	396893	F12C56Y316		special Tropical Megatop-colors
☐	9V-SPM	Boeing 747-412 (MEGATOP)	29950				4 PW PW4056	396893	F16C65Y316		oo-delivery 0599
☐	9V-SPN	Boeing 747-412 (MEGATOP)					4 PW PW4056	396893	F16C65Y316		oo-delivery 1099
☐	9V-SPO	Boeing 747-412 (MEGATOP)					4 PW PW4056	396893	F16C65Y316		oo-delivery 0300
☐	9V-SPP	Boeing 747-412 (MEGATOP)					4 PW PW4056	396893	F16C65Y316		oo-delivery 0500
☐	9V-SPQ	Boeing 747-412 (MEGATOP)					4 PW PW4056	396893	F16C65Y316		oo-delivery 0700
☐	9V-SPR	Boeing 747-412 (MEGATOP)					4 PW PW4056	396893	F16C65Y316		oo-delivery 1100
☐	9V-SPS	Boeing 747-412 (MEGATOP)					4 PW PW4056	396893	F16C65Y316		oo-delivery 0101
☐	9V-SPT	Boeing 747-412 (MEGATOP)					4 PW PW4056	396893	F16C65Y316		oo-delivery 0301

WENIC AIR SERVICES = WNC — **Singapore-Changi**

Airmail Transit Centre, PO Box 257, Singapore 9181, Republic of Singapore ☎ 241 30 02 Tx: n/a Fax: 448 28 09 SITA: n/a
F: n/a 👥 n/a Head: n/a ICAO: WENIC Net: n/a Operates charter flights with aircraft leased from other carriers when required.

9XR = RWANDA (Rwanda Republic) (République Rwandaise)

Capital: Kigali   Official Language: French   Population: 8,3 million   Square Km: 26338   Dialling code: +250   Year established: 1962   Acting political head: Pasteur Bizimungu (President)

ALLIANCE AIR EXPRESS = RWD (Air Rwanda dba / Associated with SA Alliance)   Kigali

BP 808, Kigali, Rwanda   ☎ 75 492   Tx: 554   Fax: 72 462   SITA: KGLDDRY
F: 1975   ⋔⋔⋔ 100   Head: J.M.V. Nyirimihigo   ICAO: AIR RWANDA   Net: n/a   Beside aircraft listed, also leases Boeing 707C & McDonnell Douglas DC-10F freighters from other companies when required.

	registration	type of aircraft	cn/fn	ex/ex*	mfd	del	powered by	mtow kg	configuration	selcal	name/fln/specialitites/remarks
☐	9XR-KD	De Havilland DHC-6 Twin Otter 300	827	C-GDFT*	0085	0985	2 PWC PT6A-27	5670	Y20		
☐	ZS-NWW	BAe (HS) 748-378 Srs 2B	1786 / 269	G-HDBC	0081	0998	2 RR Dart 536-2	19995	Y44		lsf EAS
☐	5H-TGF	Fokker 50 (F27 Mk050)	20231	PH-JXG*	0092	0498	2 PWC PW125B	20820	Y50		lsf Tanzanian Gvmt

RWANDA AIRLINES   Kigali

BP 3246, Kigali, Rwanda   ☎ 77 564   Tx: none   Fax: 77 669   SITA: n/a
F: 1998   ⋔⋔⋔ n/a   Head: Charles Ngarambe   Net: n/a

	registration	type of aircraft	cn/fn	ex/ex*	mfd	del	powered by	mtow kg	configuration	selcal	name/fln/specialitites/remarks
☐	9XR-RB	Let 410UVP-E				0098	2 WA M-601E	6400	Y19		
☐	9XR-RA	BAe (BAC) One-Eleven 201AC	011	YA-GAG	0064	0198	2 RR Spey 506-14A	35834	Y79		

9Y = TRINIDAD & TOBAGO (Republic of Trinidad & Tobago)

Capital: Port of Spain   Official Language: English   Population: 1,3 million   Square Km: 5130   Dialling code: +1-868   Year established: 1962   Acting political head: Arthur N.R. Robinson (President)

AIR CARIBBEAN, Ltd = C2 / CBB   Port of Spain

PO Box 1021, Port of Spain, Trinidad & Tobago   ☎ (868) 627-5109   Tx: none   Fax: (868) 627-4519   SITA: POSEDC2
F: 1993   ⋔⋔⋔ 180   Head: Leslie Lucky-Samaroo   IATA: 189   ICAO: IBIS   Net: http://www.sputnick.com/aircaribbean/

	registration	type of aircraft	cn/fn	ex/ex*	mfd	del	powered by	mtow kg	configuration	selcal	name/fln/specialitites/remarks
☐	9Y-THO	NAMC YS-11A-600	2169	N169RV	0071	0295	2 RR Dart 542-10J/K	25000	Freighter		std POS
☐	9Y-TIH	NAMC YS-11A-500	2064	N993CL	0073	0793	2 RR Dart 542-10J/K	24500	Y60		cvtd -202
☐	9Y-TII	NAMC YS-11A-500	2141	N992CL	0070	0793	2 RR Dart 542-10J/K	24500	Y60		cvtd -227
☐	9Y-TIK	NAMC YS-11A-500	2178	N4206V	0073	1093	2 RR Dart 542-10J/K	24500	Y60		cvtd -213 / std POS
☐	9Y-TIZ	NAMC YS-11A-500	2065	N990CL	0068	0996	2 RR Dart 542-10J/K	24500	Y60		cvtd -209
☐	9Y-TJB	NAMC YS-11A-500	2165	N996CL	0071	0298	2 RR Dart 542-10J/K	24500	Y60		cvtd -214
☐	9Y-TJC	Boeing 737-2H4 (A)	21339 / 495	N28SW	0677	0798	2 PW JT8D-9A	52390	Y122		
☐	9Y-TJG	Boeing 737-2Q8 (A)	21960 / 642	CC-CLD	0080	0399	2 PW JT8D-15A	54204	Y124		lsf GECA
☐	9Y-TJH	Boeing 737-2T5 (A)	22632 / 847	CC-CYP	0082	0399	2 PW JT8D-15	54204	Y124		lsf GECA

BRIKO AIR SERVICES, Ltd   Port of Spain

45 Southern Main Road, Chase Village, Carapichaima, Trinidad & Tobago   ☎ (868) 664-3915   Tx: none   Fax: (868) 679-4133   SITA: n/a
F: 1984   ⋔⋔⋔ 27   Head: Rooplal K. Dass   Net: n/a   Aircraft / Ag-aircraft below MTOW 1361 / 5000kg: Cessna 150, 152, 172 & A188B.

	registration	type of aircraft	cn/fn	ex/ex*	mfd	del	powered by	mtow kg	configuration	selcal	name/fln/specialitites/remarks
☐	9Y-TIS	Bell 206B JetRanger	1776	N298CA	0075	0295	1 AN 250-C20	1451			
☐	9Y-TIU	Bell 206L-1 LongRanger II	45682	N198DM	0081	0395	1 AN 250-C28B	1882			
☐	9Y-TGQ	Beech Baron B55 (95-B55)	TC-1858		0075		2 CO IO-470-L	2313			
☐	9Y-TIV	Eurocopter (Aerosp.) AS355F2 Ecureuil 2	5091	N5790B	0081	1295	2 AN 250-C20F	2540			
☐	9Y-TIX	Eurocopter (Aerosp.) AS355F2 Ecureuil 2	5105	N5785Y	0081	0196	2 AN 250-C20F	2540			
☐	N3146M	Cessna 402C II	402C0285		0080		2 CO TSIO-520-VB	3107			lsf pvt
☐	9Y-TJA	Beech King Air A100	B-208	N4475W	0074	0897	2 PWC PT6A-28	5216			

BRISTOW CARIBBEAN, Ltd (Associated with Bristow Helicopters, Ltd; U.K.)   Port of Spain

Bretton Hall, 16 Victoria Avenue, Port of Spain, Trinidad & Tobago   ☎ (868) 623-1241   Tx: none   Fax: (868) 623-1231   SITA: n/a
F: 1974   ⋔⋔⋔ 58   Head: H.D.E. Boyt   Net: n/a

	registration	type of aircraft	cn/fn	ex/ex*	mfd	del	powered by	mtow kg	configuration	selcal	name/fln/specialitites/remarks
☐	9Y-TEY	Bell 212	30640	VR-BFE	0074		2 PWC PT6T-3 TwinPac	5080			
☐	9Y-TFA	Bell 212	30687	G-BWBP	0076	1097	2 PWC PT6T-3 TwinPac	5080			
☐	9Y-THL	Bell 212	30639	HK-4103X	0074	0098	2 PWC PT6T-3 TwinPac	5080			
☐	9Y-TIF	Bell 212	30615	G-BTYA	0072	0692	2 PWC PT6T-3 TwinPac	5080			
☐	9Y-TIG	Bell 212	30544	G-BHDL	0072	0593	2 PWC PT6T-3 TwinPac	5080			

BWIA International Airways, Ltd = BW / BWA (BWee Express) (formerly Trinidad & Tobago (BWIA Int'l) Airways Corp.)   Port of Spain

Administration Bldg, Piarco Int'l Airport, Trinidad & Tobago   ☎ (868) 669-3000   Tx: 25523 wg   Fax: (868) 669-0453   SITA: POSDOBW
F: 1940   ⋔⋔⋔ 2380   Head: Conrad Aleong   IATA: 106   ICAO: WEST INDIAN   Net: http://www.bwia-international.com
DHC-8 regional flights are operated under the marketing name BWee Express, an internal division (same headquarters).

	registration	type of aircraft	cn/fn	ex/ex*	mfd	del	powered by	mtow kg	configuration	selcal	name/fln/specialitites/remarks
☐	9Y-WIL	De Havilland DHC-8-311 Dash 8Q	489	C-GFCW*	1098	0299	2 PWC PW123	19505	Y50		BWee Express-division
☐	9Y-WIN	De Havilland DHC-8-311 Dash 8Q	499	C-GDSG*	1098	0299	2 PWC PW123	19505	Y50		BWee Express-division
☐	9Y-	Boeing 737-7Q8	28209 / 14	HB-IIH	0398		2 CFMI CFM56-7B24	69400			to be lsf ILFC 0599
☐	9Y-THQ	Boeing (Douglas) MD-83 (DC-9-83)	49448 / 1313		0086	1086	2 PW JT8D-219	72575	F12Y108	JM-DF	Giselle La Ronde
☐	9Y-THR	Boeing (Douglas) MD-83 (DC-9-83)	49568 / 1380		0087	0687	2 PW JT8D-219	72575	F12Y108	JM-DG	Sunjet Jamaica / lsf PEGA
☐	9Y-THV	Boeing (Douglas) MD-83 (DC-9-83)	49632 / 1603		0089	0789	2 PW JT8D-219	72575	F12Y108	HM-DJ	Sunjet St. Vincent / lsf GECA
☐	9Y-THW	Boeing (Douglas) MD-83 (DC-9-83)	49786 / 1631		0089	0989	2 PW JT8D-219	72575	F12Y108	FG-BH	lsf GECA
☐	9Y-THX	Boeing (Douglas) MD-83 (DC-9-83)	49789 / 1642		0089	1089	2 PW JT8D-219	72575	F12Y108	FG-CE	Sunjet Anguilla / lsf GECA
☐	9Y-	Boeing 737-8Q8					2 CFMI CFM56-7B26	79016			to be lsf ILFC 1199
☐	9Y-	Boeing 737-8Q8					2 CFMI CFM56-7B26	79016			to be lsf ILFC 0000
☐	9Y-	Boeing 737-8Q8					2 CFMI CFM56-7B26	79016			to be lsf ILFC 0000
☐	9Y-	Boeing 737-8Q8					2 CFMI CFM56-7B26	79016			to be lsf ILFC 0000
☐	9Y-	Boeing 737-8Q8					2 CFMI CFM56-7B26	79016			to be lsf ILFC 0000
☐	9Y-	Boeing 737-8Q8					2 CFMI CFM56-7B26	79016			to be lsf ILFC 0000
☐	9Y-TGJ	Lockheed L-1011-385-3 TriStar 500	193G-1179		0079	0180	3 RR RB211-524B4	228611	F28Y210	FG-BC	595 / Sunjet Trinidad
☐	9Y-TGN	Lockheed L-1011-385-3 TriStar 500	193G-1191		0080	0880	3 RR RB211-524B4	228611	F28Y210	FG-AD	596 / Sunjet Barbados
☐	9Y-THA	Lockheed L-1011-385-3 TriStar 500	193G-1222		0081	1181	3 RR RB211-524B4	228611	F28Y210	HM-FJ	597 / Sunjet Antigua / lsf GATX
☐	N3140D	Lockheed L-1011-385-3 TriStar 500	193G-1233	9Y-THB ntu	0082	0782	3 RR RB211-524B4	228611	F28Y210	HM-FK	598/Sunjet Santa Lucia / lsf BancBoston

NATIONAL HELICOPTER SERVICES, Ltd – NHSL   Camden-NHSL Heliport

PO Bag 695, Couva, Trinidad & Tobago   ☎ (868) 679-2628   Tx: none   Fax: (868) 679-2345   SITA: n/a
F: 1990   ⋔⋔⋔ 46   Head: Nick Nothnagel   Net: n/a

	registration	type of aircraft	cn/fn	ex/ex*	mfd	del	powered by	mtow kg	configuration	selcal	name/fln/specialitites/remarks
☐	9Y-THP	Eurocopter (MBB) BO105CBS-4	S-758	N725MB	0086	0395	2 AN 250-C20B	2500			
☐	9Y-TIC	Eurocopter (MBB) BO105CBS-4	S-837	N7161N	0091		2 AN 250-C20B	2500			
☐	9Y-TIW	Eurocopter (MBB) BO105CBS-4	S-671	N4573S	0084	1296	2 AN 250-C20B	2500			
☐	9Y-TJE	Eurocopter (MBB) BO105CBS-4	S-559	N124EH	0082	1298	2 AN 250-C20B	2500			
☐	9Y-TJF	Eurocopter (MBB) BO105CBS-4	S-732	F-OHQZ	0086	0199	2 AN 250-C20B	2500			
☐	9Y-TGW	Sikorsky S-76A	760176		0081		2 AN 250-C30S	4672			
☐	9Y-TGX	Sikorsky S-76A	760185		0081		2 AN 250-C30S	4672			

SUN ISLANDS AVIATION, Ltd   Port of Spain

Skinner's Yard, Chaguaramas, Charanag, Trinidad & Tobago   ☎ (868) 634-4663   Tx: none   Fax: (868) 634-4179   SITA: n/a
F: n/a   ⋔⋔⋔ n/a   Head: n/a   Net: n/a   Aircraft below MTOW 1361kg: Cessna 152 & Piper PA-28

	registration	type of aircraft	cn/fn	ex/ex*	mfd	del	powered by	mtow kg	configuration	selcal	name/fln/specialitites/remarks
☐	9Y-TGG	Piper PA-34-200T Seneca II	34-7970043		0079		2 CO TSIO-360-EB	2073			

jp airline-fleets international 99/2000

Section 2

ALPHABETICAL AIRLINE PAGE NUMBER INDEX
ICAO three-letter-abbreviation index
IATA two-letter-abbreviation index
and
MISCELLANEOUS

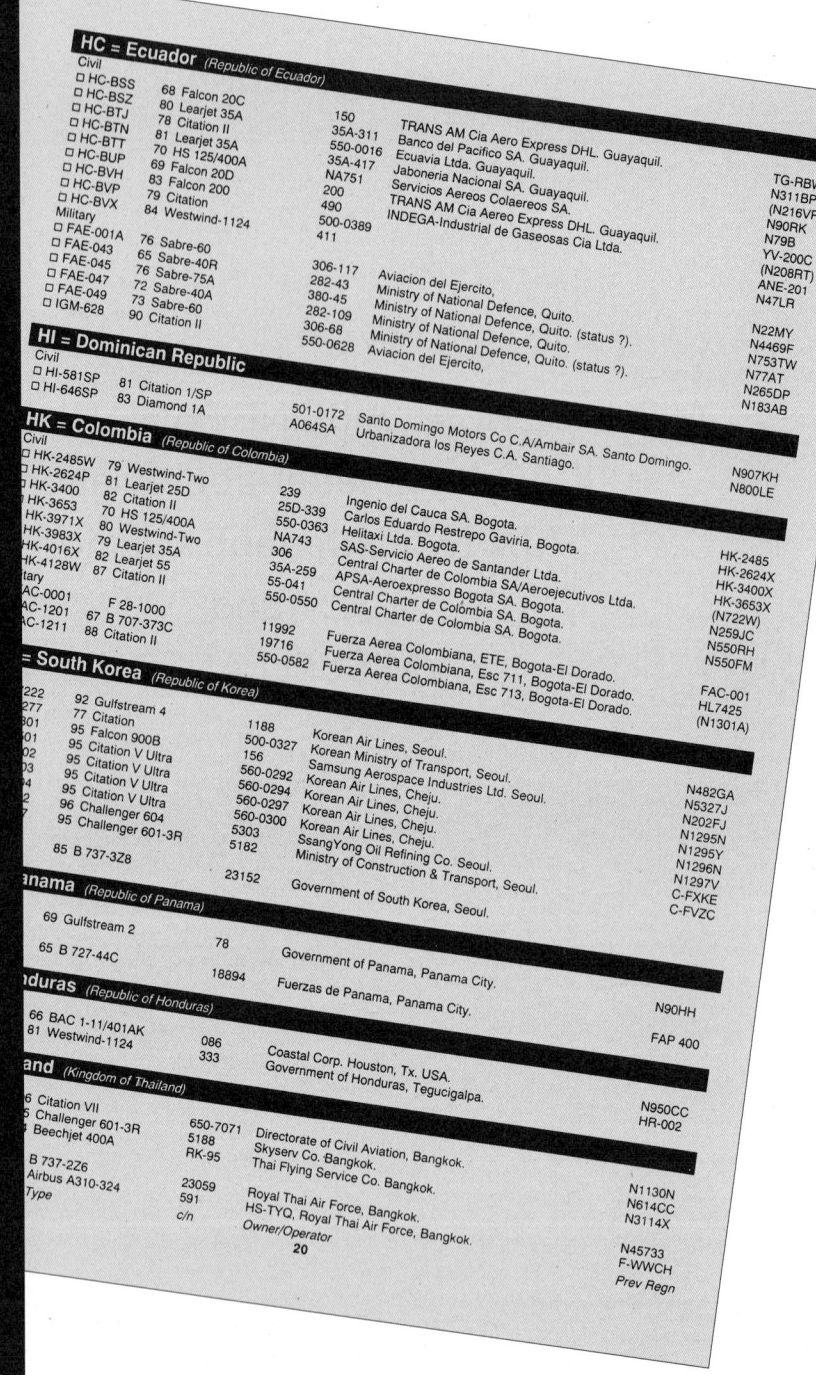
714

Index

The alphabetical airline page-number index will allow you to locate immediately the fleetlist of an airline, where you know only the name. The index is sorted first numerical and then alphabetical. This means, that AIR 500 is listed before AIR ABC.

Name	IATA	ICAO	LEASE	Page
BLADES AVIATION				39
BLAGOVESHCHENSKAVIA		BLD		530
BLASER AVIACION				236
BLOK AIR				39
BLUE BIRD AVIATION		BBZ		695
BLUE BIRD AVIATION, Co.				591
BLUE BIRD HELICOPTERS				288
BLUE CHIP JET, HB		VOL		582
BLUE DART AVIATION				646
BLUE HAWAIIAN HELICOPTERS				288
BLUE MOUNTAIN HELICOPTERS				288
BLUE PANORAMA AIRLINES, SpA	9S	BPA		212
BLUE SKY AVIATION				39
BLUE WATER AVIATION SERVICES				39
BLUEWATER AVIATION				624
BLUFFTON FLYING SERVICE, Co.				288
BMG Burgener Helikopter-Transporte				185
BMW FLUGDIENST		BMW		102
BOB SMITH HELICOPTER SERVICES				624
BODAIBO AIR ENTERPRISE				530
BOHAG Berner Oberländer Helikopter				185
BOHEMIA AIR SERVICE – BAS, s r.o.				480
BOHLKE INTERNATIONAL AIRWAYS – BIA				289
BOLTON LAKE AIR SERVICES				39
BOMA HELICOPTERS				676
BOMAS AIR Sti				597
BOMBARDIER – Amphibious Flight Operations				39
BOMBARDIER BUSINESS JET SOLUTIONS				289
BON AIR – Bonyad Airlines		IRJ		134
BON AIR Havacilik ve Tic. Lim. Sti.				597
BONANZA AIR				40
BOND HELICOPTERS		BND		164
BOND HELICOPTERS (Ireland)				131
BONIAIR		BOA		682
BONNEVILLE AIRCRAFT SERVICES				289
BONNYVILLE AIR SERVICES (1980)				40
BONSAI HELIKOPTER				185
BOOGIE PERFORMANCE, E.U.R.L.				150
BORDER CITY AVIATION				40
BORDER SECURITY FORCE – Flying Unit				646
BOREAL AVIACION, S.L.				124
BORINQUEN AIR – Air Puerto Rico				290
BORNEO AIRWAYS		BOR		704
BORONKAY HAVA Tasimaciligi, A.S.				597
BOSKYM UDARA				704
BOSTON-MAINE AIRWAYS				290
BOULLIOUN AVIATION SERVICES			BOUL	290
BOURAQ INDONESIA AIRLINES	BO	BOU		496
BOURNEMOUTH HELICOPTERS				164
BOWMAN AVIATION		BMN		290
BP EXPLORATION ALASKA				290
BPX Colombia		BPX		196
BRAATHEN LEASING, A/S			BRAL	231
BRAATHENS Malmö Aviation, AB	BU	SCW		582
BRAATHENS, ASA	BU	BRA		231
BRABO Taxi Aéreo				503
BRAINERD HELICOPTERS				290
BRAN AIR				290
BRANCH RIVER AIR SERVICE				290
BRANTFORD FLIGHT CENTRE				40
BRASSARD AIR SERVICE, Enr.				40
BRATA – BRASILIA Taxi Aéreo				503
BRATSK AVIA		BTK		530
BRAUNEGG LUFTTAXI				473
BRAVO HELICOPTERS & WING				290
BRENCORP HELI				624
BRIKO AIR SERVICES				711
BRILES WING & HELICOPTER				290
BRINDABELLA AIRLINES				624
BRISTOL BAY AIR SERVICE				290
BRISTOW CARIBBEAN				711
BRISTOW HELICOPTERS		BHL		164
BRISTOW HELICOPTERS (Australia)				624
BRISTOW HELICOPTERS (Nigeria)		BHN		691
BRIT AIR	DB	BZH		150
BRITANNIA AIRWAYS	BN	DBY		102
BRITANNIA AIRWAYS	BY	BAL		165
BRITANNIA AIRWAYS, AB	6B	BLX		582
BRITISH AEROSPACE ASSET – Turboprops			BAMT	290
BRITISH AEROSPACE ASSET MGMT – Jets			BAMJ	165
BRITISH AEROSPACE Corporate Flights		BAE		165
BRITISH AIRWAYS, Plc	BA	BAW		165
BRITISH ANTARCTIC SURVEY				644
BRITISH INTERNATIONAL	BS	BIH		168
BRITISH MEDITERRANEAN AIRWAYS	KJ	LAJ		168
BRITISH MIDLAND	BD	BMA		168
BRITISH MIDLAND COMMUTER		GNT		169
BRITISH REGIONAL AIRLINES	TH	BRT		169
BRITISH WORLD AIRLINES	VF	BWL		170
BROBY HELIKOPTER				582
BROCK AIR SERVICES		BRD		40
BROOK ARMSTRONG AVIATION SERVICES				624
BROOKS AIR TRANSPORT				290
BROOKS AVIATION				290
BROOKS FUEL Inc.				290
BROOKS RANGE AVIATION				291
BROOKS SEAPLANE SERVICE				291
BROOME AVIATION				624
BROUGHAM GEOQUEST				40
BRUCELANDAIR INTERNATIONAL				40
BRYANSK AIR ENTERPRISE				530
BRYMON AIRWAYS		BRY		170
BSF Hubschrauber-Dienste				103
BSF Luftbild & Vermessungen				103
BSP-SAV Flight Dept.				650
BUCKLEY AIR		BUK		670
BUDAPEST AIRCRAFT SERVICES		BPS		182
BUDDHA AIR, Pvt.				706
BUDVAIR, a.s.				480
BUFFALO AIRWAYS	J4	BFL		40
BUGURUSLAN FLYING SCHOOL				531
BULLDOG AIRLINES				291
BULLOCK CHARTER				291
BUNDESAMT EICH- & VERMESSUNG				473
BUNDESMINISTERIUM FUER INNERES				473
BURLINGTON AIR				291
BURMAN AVIATION (Charter)		BMM		170
BURUNDAIAVIA		IVR		610
BURYAT AVIA				532
BURYATIA AIRLINES				531
BUSH DRIFTERS				676
BUSH LAND AIRWAYS				40
BUSH PILOT				650
BUSINESS AIR		BEN		291
BUSINESS AIR CHARTER				103
BUSINESS AIR, Kft.		BHU		182
BUSINESS AVIATION				291
BUSINESS AVIATION OF CONGO				708
BUSINESS EXPRESS AIRLINES – BEX	HQ	GAA		291
BUSINESS FLIGHTS				40
BUSINESS HELICOPTERS				291
BUSINESS JET SOLUTIONS				291
BUSINESS JET SWEDEN, AB				583
BUSINESSWINGS Luftfahrtunternehmen				103
BUTLER AIR				292
BUTLER AIRCRAFT, Company				292
BUTTE AVIATION		PPS		292
BWIA International Airways	BW	BWA		711
BYERLY AVIATION				292
BYKOVO AVIA		BKU		532
C & D – Flight Dept.				292
C & M AIRCRAFT				292
C & M AIRWAYS				292
C.A.I. – Compagnia Aeronautica Italiana, SpA		KVY		212
C.A.T.E.X., S.A.		TEX		151
C.F. AVIATION				45
C.M. AERO SERVICES				580
CAAC Flying College				13
CAAC Special Services Division				13
CAB AIR		CVN		583
CABAIR Helicopters		CBR		170
CABI		CBI		615
CABO VERDE EXPRESS				121
CAC – Compagnie Aérienne de Centrafrique				604
CAE AVIATION, SàRL				239
CAF, Srl. – Consorzio Aeromobili Fiat		AFF		212
C-AIR				292
CAL – Congo Airlines	EO	ALX		708
CAL Cargo Air Lines		ICL		686
CALALASKA HELICOPTERS				292
CALEDONIAN AIRWAYS	KG	CKT		170
CALGARY POLICE SERVICE				40
CALM AIR	MO	CAV		40
CALSTAR				292
CAMAI AIR	R9	CAM		292
CAMBA Transportes Aéreos				91
CAMERON AIR SERVICE				41
CAMEROON AIRLINES	UY	UYC		604
CAMEROON HELICOPTERS – Camhel				604
CAMP AVIATION SERVICE				591
CAMPBELL HELICOPTERS				41
CANADA 3000 Airlines	2T	CMM		41
CANADA JET CHARTERS				41
CANADIAN – CANADIEN	CP	CDN		41
CANADIAN AIR-CRANE				41
CANADIAN AIRWAYS				41
CANADIAN HELICOPTERS		WSR		42
CANADIAN NORTH				43
CANADIAN REGIONAL AIRLINES (1998)	KI	CDR		43
CANADIAN TERRITORIAL HELICOPTERS				44
CANAGRAD SURVEYS				44
CANAIR Luftfahrtunternehmen				103
CANARIAS REGIONAL AIR, S.A.	FW	CNM		124
CANTERBURY AERO CLUB				670
CANTERBURY HELICOPTERS				670
CANUCK-AIR SERVICE				44
CAPE AIR	9K	KAP		292
CAPE FLYING SERVICES				677
CAPE SMYTHE AIR SERVICE	6C	CMY		293
CAPE YORK AIR	NS			624
CAPITAL AIR				677
CAPITAL AIRLINES		CAP		293
CAPITAL AIRLINES				695
CAPITAL AVIATION		EGL		170
CAPITAL CARGO INTERNATIONAL	PT	CCI		293
CAPITAL CITY AIR CARRIER				293
CAPITAL HELICOPTERS (1995)				44
CAPITAL L AIRLINES				689
CARAIBES AIR TRANSPORT				151
CARAJAS Taxi Aéreo				503
CARAVAN AVIATION				44
CARDINAL AIRLINES				293
CARD'S AIR SERVICES				579
CARDWELL AIR CHARTER				624
CARE FLIGHT AIR AMBULANCE				293
CAREFLIGHT				624
CAREFLIGHT QUEENSLAND				624
CAREFLITE				293
CARGAIR, Ltée				44
CARGO CARRIERS				677
CARGO EXPRESS CONGO				605
CARGO LION		TLX		239
CARGO THREE		CTW		203
CARGOLUX Airlines International, SA	CV	CLX		239
CARGOMASTER Corporation				293
CARIB AVIATION	K7	DEL		648
CARIB-AIR CARGO				293
CARIBAIR, SA				193
CARIBBEAN AVIATION				98
CARIBBEAN FLIGHTS		CIF		665
CARIBBEAN HELICOPTERS				151
CARIBBEAN HELICOPTERS				648
CARIBEE AIR SERVICE				649
CARIBJET		CBJ		648
CARIBOO CHILCOTIN HELICOPTERS				44
CARICARGA COLOMBIA – Cali Cargo				196
CARILL AVIATION				170
CARISCH HELICOPTERS				293
CAROLINA SHUTTLE				293
CAROLINA SKY SPORTS				294
CAROLINAS HISTORIC AVIATION				293
CAROLINE ISLAND AIR				650
CARRY AIR		EEC		151
CARSON AIR				44
CARSON HELICOPTERS				294
CARTER AIR SERVICES				45
CARTERS COUNTRY AVIATION				294
CASA AIR SERVICES				90
CASCADE HELICOPTERS				294
CASINO AIRLINES		CSO		294
CASINO EXPRESS	XP	CXP		294
CASPER AIR SERVICE		CSP		294
CASPIAN AIRLINES		CPN		134
CASSEL AERO, AB				583
CASSOVIA AIR, a.s.		CVI		482
CASTEL AIR, N.V.				484
CASTLE AIR				170
CASTLE AVIATION		CSJ		294
CAT AIR SERVICES				45
CAT AVIATION		CAZ		185
CAT ISLAND AIR				98
CATA Linea Aérea S.A.C.I.F.I.		CTZ		236
CATAIR Lineas Aéreas				124
CATALINA AIR				294
CATALINA FLYING BOATS		CBT		294
CATHAY PACIFIC	CX	CPA		21
CAUSEY AVIATION CHARTERS				294
CAVOK Taxi Aéreo				503
CAYMAN AIRWAYS	KX	CAY		644
CBM Taxi Aéreo				503
CCA – Congo Commercial Airlines				708
CCAIR	ED	CDL		294
CCF manager airline		CCF		103
CEBU PACIFIC AIR	5J	CPI		579
CEC FLIGHTEXEC		FEX		45
CECIL AIR		CIL		170
CEDTA				192
CEGA Aviation		CEG		170
CEGISA				124
CELTA Taxi Aéreo				97
CELTIC AIRWAYS				170
CELTIC HELICOPTERS				131
CENTAERO AVIATION				45
CENTAURUS Taxi Aéreo				503
CENTENNIAL AIR				580
CENTENNIAL FLIGHT Centre		CNS		45
CENTER FLIGHT, ApS				488
CENTER VOL, S.A. Helicopters				124
CENTER-SOUTH AIRLINES		CTS		532
CENTRAFRICAIN AIRLINES	GC	CET		604
CENTRAL AIR				624
CENTRAL AIR FLUGCHARTER				103
CENTRAL AIR SERVICE				295
CENTRAL AIR SERVICE				295
CENTRAL AIR SOUTHWEST		CTL		295
CENTRAL AMERICAN AIRWAYS				295
CENTRAL AVIATION				45
CENTRAL CHARTER de Colombia, S.A.		AJS		197
CENTRAL COPTERS				295
CENTRAL DISTRICTS AIRLINES		CDS		532
CENTRAL FLYING SERVICE				295
CENTRAL HELICOPTERS				625
CENTRAL HIGHLANDS AIR TRANSPORT				625
CENTRAL MOUNTAIN AIR	9M	GLR		45
CENTRELINE AIR CHARTER		CLF		171
CEP ATMOSPHAIR				45
CEPRISER				88
CERTEZA SURVEYING & AEROPHOTO				580
CESSAVIA		CSS		683
CETTA – Celso Tinoco Taxi Aéreo				503
CETTY Taxi Aéreo Nacional		CCT		655
CEYLON AVIATION SERVICES				685
CFC Canadian Flight Centre				45
CFF AIR SERVICE				45
CGA AUSTRALIA				625
CHAIKA Aircompany		CHJ		615
CHALAIR	M6	CLG		151
CHALK'S INTERNATIONAL AIRLINES	OP			295
CHALLENG'AIR			CHAL	151
CHALLENGE AIR CARGO – CAC	WE	CWC		296
CHALLENGE AIR Luftverkehrs				103
CHAMPAGNE AIRLINES		CPH		151
CHAMPION AIR	MG	CCP		296
CHAMPIONSHIP AIRWAYS				296
CHAMPLAIN AIR				296
CHAMPLAIN AIR SURVEYS				45
CHANCHANGI AIRLINES (Nigeria) – CAL		NCH		691
CHANI ENTERPRISES – Flight Operations				703
CHANNEL EXPRESS (Air Services)	LS	EXS		171
CHANNEL ISLANDS AIR SEARCH				171
CHANNEL ISLANDS AVIATION – CIA		CHN		296
CHANTILLY AIR				296
CHAPLEAU AIR SERVICES				45
CHARTAIR	TL			625
CHARTER AIR		CHW		473
CHARTER AMERICA				296
CHARTER SERVICE HETZLER				103
CHARTERFLUG FRUEHWALD				473
CHARTERFLUG STAHNKE				103
CHARTRIGHT AIR				45
CHAUFFAIR		CFR		171
CHAUTAUQUA AIRLINES	US	CHQ		296
CHEBOKSARY AIR ENTERPRISE		CBK		532
CHELAN AIRWAYS				296
CHELYABINSK AIR ENTERPRISE	H6	CHB		532
CHEM-AIR				297
CHEMTRAD AVIATION				580
CHEQAIR				171
CHERNOMOR-AVIA		CMK		533
CHERNOVTSY AVIATION ENTERPRISE				615
CHEROKEE AIR – Flight Service				98
CHEROKEE HELICOPTER SERVICE				297
CHERRY HELICOPTERS				297
CHERRY-AIR				297
CHESTER COUNTY AVIATION				297
CHEVRON AIRCRAFT OPERATIONS				297
CHICAGO EXPRESS AIRLINES	C8	WDY		297
CHIGNIK AIRWAYS				297
CHILD FLIGHT				625
CHILE INTER, S.A.		CLE		88
CHIM-NIR Aviation Services & Airways				686
CHIMO AIR SERVICE				45
CHINA AIRLINES	CI	CAL		22
CHINA CARGO AIRLINES, Co.				13
CHINA EASTERN AIRLINES, Co.	MU	CES		13
CHINA FLYING DRAGON AVIATION		CFA		14
CHINA NORTHERN AIRLINES	CJ	CBF		15
CHINA NORTHWEST AIRLINES – CNWA	WH	CNW		15
CHINA OCEAN HELICOPTER Corp. – COHC		CHC		16
CHINA POSTAL AIRLINES		CYZ		16
CHINA SOUTHERN AIRLINES, Co.	CZ	CSN		16
CHINA SOUTHWEST AIRLINES	SZ	CXN		16
CHINA UNITED AIRLINES		CUA		17
CHINA XINHUA AIRLINES		CXH		17
CHINA XINJIANG AIRLINES	XO	CXJ		17
CHINA YUNNAN AIRLINES	3Q	CYH		18
CHIPOLA AVIATION				297
CHITAAVIA	X7	CHF		533
CHKALOV NATIONAL AEROCLUB RUSSIA				533
CHOPPERLINE				625
CHRISTIAN AVIATION				671
CHRISTOPHORUS FLUGRETTUNGSVEREIN				473
CHRYSLER AVIATION				297
CHRYSLER PENTASTAR AVIATION		CYL		297
CHUKOTAVIA				533
CIACA – Centro Industrial Aeronautico, CA				665
CICADE Aerial Photo				484
CIELOS DEL PERU, S.A.		EXD		470
CIMARRON AIRE		CMN		298
CIMBER AIR, A/S	QI	CIM		488

	IATA	ICAO	LEASE	Page
EAGLE AIRWAYS				671
EAGLE AVIATION				133
EAGLE AVIATION				320
EAGLE AVIATION	Y4	EQA		695
EAGLE CANYON AIRLINES	FE	TLO		320
EAGLE EXECUTIVE CHARTER				320
EAGLE HELICOPTERS				172
EAGLE HELICOPTERS				320
EAGLE UGANDA		EGU		694
EAS AIRLINES		EXW		691
EAS Egle Air Service				105
EAS Executive-Air-Service Flug				105
EAST AFRICAN AIR CHARTERS				695
EAST AFRICAN SAFARI AIR		HSA		695
EAST ASIA AIRLINES				93
EAST COAST AIRWAYS		ECT		677
EAST HAMPTON AIRLINES				321
EAST LINE AIRLINES	P7	ESL		535
EAST MIDLANDS HELICOPTERS		CTK		172
EASTERN AIR		EAZ		703
EASTERN AIR CHARTER				321
EASTERN AIR EXECUTIVE		EAX		172
EASTERN AIRLINES		ERN		229
EASTERN AIRWAYS				646
EASTERN AIRWAYS (UK)		EZE		172
EASTERN AUSTRALIA AIRLINES		EAQ		626
EASTERN BAY/LAKELAND HELICOPTERS				671
EASTERN CHARTERS				677
EASTERN EXECUTIVE AIR CHARTER		GNS		172
EASTINDO				497
EASTLAND AIR – Moore's Air Charter	DK			626
EASTON AVIATION				321
EASTWAY AVIATION				321
EAST-WEST TRANSPORTATION				49
EASTWIND AIRLINES – The Bee Line	W9	BBE		321
EASYJET AIRLINE, Co.	U2	EZY		172
EASYJET SWITZERLAND	BH	EZS		186
EAT – European Air Transport, N.V.	QY	BCS		485
EAT Executive Air Transport		EXZ		186
ECLIPSE HELICOPTERS				49
ECO AIR Tours-Hawaii				321
ECOMEX AIR CARGO		ECX		121
ECUATORIANA de Aviacion, S.A.	EU	EEA		192
ECUAVIAa				192
EDELWEISS AIR		EDW		186
EDELWEISS AIR				321
EDINBURGH AIR CHARTER		EDC		173
ED'S FLYING SERVICE				321
ED'S FLYING SERVICE				321
EE AERONAUTIKA-KLUBI				138
EFOS FLIGHT-CHARTER				186
EFS Flug Service		FSD		105
EG HELISERVICE, N.V.				485
EG&G Special Projects				321
EGA – Ecuato Guineana de Aviacion	8Y	EGA		683
EGLI AIR HAUL				321
EGYPT AIR	MS	MSR		592
EIS Aircraft				106
EJA FRANCE		AEJ		152
EL AERO SERVICES				321
EL AL Israel Airlines	LY	ELY		687
EL DORADO Colombia		EDR		197
ELB FLYING SERVICES				677
ELBE HELICOPTER Rainer Zemke				106
ELBRUS-AVIA		NLK		536
ELDINDER AVIATION, Co.		DND		591
ELECTRA AVIATION – EAL			ELEC	173
ELF AIR		EFR		536
ELI FLY, SpA		EBS		213
ELIABRUZZO, Srl.				213
ELICAMPIGLIO, Srl.				213
ELIDOLOMITI, Srl		EDO		213
ELIFRIULIA, Srl.		EFG		213
ELIIP		EFE		536
ELILARIO, SpA		ELC		213
ELILIGURIA INTERNATIONAL, Srl.		HLL		213
ELILOMBARDA, Srl.				214
ELILOMBARDIA, SpA		ELB		214
ELIMEDITERRANEA, Srl.		MEE		214
ELINORD – Servizi Aerotrasporti Milano, Srl.				214
ELIOS, Srl		VUL		214
ELIOSSOLA, Srl.		EOS		214
ELIPIU', Srl.		IEP		214
ELISERVIZI ITALIANI, Srl.		ESI		214
ELISONDRIO, Srl				214
ELISUSA, Srl.		LDO		214
ELISYSTEM, SpA		EEI		214
ELITALIANA, SpA		ETI		214
ELITE HELICOPTERS				173
ELITELLINA, Srl.		FGS		214
ELITICINO, SA				186
ELITORINO, Srl		ELW		214
ELIVIT, Srl.				214
ELK AIRWAYS – Estonian Aviation Company	S8	ELK		138
ELLIOT LAKE AVIATION				49
ELLIOTT AVIATION		ELT		321
ELLIS AIR TAXI				322
ELLISON AIR				322
ELMHIRST VACATION AIR				49
EL-ROM AIRLINES		ELR		687
ELVEDEN INVESTMENT			ELVE	132
EMAIR				597
EMBRATAXI				504
EMENY Helicopter Services				671
EMERALD AIRWAYS	G3	JEM		173
EMERALD PACIFIC AIRLINES				23
EMERY WORLDWIDE Airlines	EB	EWW		322
EMIRATES	EK	UAE		10
EMPIRE AIRLINES	EM	CFS		322
EMPIRE AVIATION				691
EMPRESA AEREA HALCON, Srl.				236
EMPRESA BAIANA DE TAXI AEREO				504
EMU AIRWAYS				626
ENERGETIK-AVIA				536
ENGLAND JET				323
ENIMEX		ENI		138
ENKOR	5Z	ENK		536
ENTERPRISE AIR				49
ENTERPRISE FLYING				323
ENVIRONMENT CANADA – Flight Dept.				49
EPHESUS TWO TWENTY				49
EPPS AIR SERVICE		EPS		323
EQUAFLIGHT, S.A.	8H	EKA		605
EQUATOR LEASING			EQUA	323
EQUIP Taxi Aéreo				504
ERA – European Regions Airlines, S.A.	EA	EUA		124
ERA Aviation	7H	ERH		323

	IATA	ICAO	LEASE	Page
ERFOTO – Fotografia Aérea				93
ERICKSON AIR CRANE Company, Llc				324
ERIE AIRWAYS		ERE		325
ERIM International				325
ERIN AIR				325
ERSTER FFC HALLE e.V.				106
ESMA				152
ESPECIAL Taxi Aéreo				504
ESSOR-HELICOPTERES				49
ESTEIO Engenharia e Aerolevantamentos				504
ESTONIAN AIR	OV	ELL		138
ETA – Empresa de Taxi Aéreo				504
ETELEAIR Air Company		ETO		536
ETHIOPIAN AIRLINES Enterprise	ET	ETH		139
ETI 2000, Srl.		MJM		214
EUCATUR Taxi Aéreo				504
EURALAIR International	RN	EUL		152
EURASIA Air Company		EUS		537
EURAVIATION, Srl		EVN		214
EURECA, Srl. – European Regional Carrier	F4	URE		214
EURO CONTINENTAL AIR, S.L.		ECN		124
EURO EXEC EXPRESS		EXC		583
EURO EXECUTIVE JET				173
EURO FLUGDIENST Gerhard Spinker				106
EURO-ASIA AIR		EAK		610
EUROCYPRIA AIRLINES	UI	ECA		689
EUROFLUG FREIBURG Gerhard Frenzel				106
EUROFLY SERVICE, SpA		EEU		215
EUROFLY, SpA	GJ	EEZ		215
EUROHELI – Transportes Aéreos				93
EUROHELI Helicopterdienste				106
EUROJET		JLN		702
EUROJET AVIATION		GOJ		173
EUROJET ITALIA, Srl		ERJ		215
EUROLOT, S.A.		ELO		589
EUROPE ELITE	Y6	VIP		173
EUROPEAN AIRCHARTER – EAC		EAF		173
EUROPEAN FLIGHT CENTER, A/S				232
EUROPEAN HELICOPTER CENTER, AB				583
EUROSCOT AIRWAYS	MY	EUJ		173
EUROSENSE				106
EUROSENSE BELFOTOP, N.V.				485
EUROSENSE, B.V.				492
EUROWINGS	EW	EWG		106
EVA AIR	BR	EVA		23
EVERETT AVIATION				695
EVERGREEN HELICOPTERS				325
EVERGREEN INTERNATIONAL AIRLINES	EZ	EIA		325
EVERTS AIR FUEL				325
EVIN AIR		EVI		215
EXACT AIR				49
EXCEL AIR CHARTER, Llc				325
EXCEL AIR SERVICE – EXAS				221
EXCELSIOR AIR CHARTER				326
EXEC-AIR – Executive Air		AXE		667
EXECAIRE	MB	EXA		50
EXECUJET AIR CHARTER				677
EXECUJET SCANDINAVIA, A/S				489
EXECUTIVE AEROSPACE		EAS		677
EXECUTIVE AIR CHAR. OF NEW ORLEANS				326
EXECUTIVE AIR CHARTER				326
EXECUTIVE AIR CHARTER BOCA RATON				326
EXECUTIVE AIR LINK	C7			50
EXECUTIVE AIR TAXI				326
EXECUTIVE AIRLINES	YL	ORA		326
EXECUTIVE AIRLINES				326
EXECUTIVE AIRLINES				626
EXECUTIVE BEECHCRAFT				326
EXECUTIVE BEECHCRAFT STL				326
EXECUTIVE CHARTER				8
EXECUTIVE EDGE AIR CHARTER				50
EXECUTIVE FLIGHT SERVICES				326
EXECUTIVE FLIGHT SERVICES		URF		702
EXECUTIVE HELICOPTERS				50
EXECUTIVE JET AVIATION		EJA		326
EXECUTIVE JET INTERNATIONAL				329
EXECUTIVE JET MANAGEMENT		EJM		329
EXECUTIVE JET, S.A.				236
EXIN Co.		EXN		589
EXMOUTH AIR CHARTERS				626
EXPEDITAIR (1989)				50
EXPEDITION AIRWAYS (Pvt)	FO	XPD		667
EXPLOITS VALLEY AIR SERVICES				50
EXPO AVIATION	8D	EXV		686
EXPRESS		PSR		537
EXPRESS AIR SERVICES		FLN		678
EXPRESS AIRLINES I	9E	FLG		329
EXPRESS AIRWAYS		EPA		106
EXPRESS HELICOPTER SERVICE				594
EXPRESS ONE International	EO	LHN		330
EXPRESS POST, S.A.				236
EXPRESSAIR				50
EXTRAORDINAIR				330
EYETHU AIR CARGO				678
E-Z AIR				50
F AIR				481
F R AVIATION – FRA		FRA		174
F R AVIATION (Malaysia)				704
F.S. AIR SERVICE				341
F27 FRIENDSHIP FLIGHT ASSOCIATION				492
FAASA AVIACION		FAM		125
FAI AIRSERVICE		IFA		106
FALCON AIR				595
FALCON AIR EXPRESS	F2	FAO		330
FALCON AIR, AB	IH	FCN		583
FALCON AVIATION				330
FALCON EXPRESS CARGO AIRLINES	FC			11
FALCON JET CENTRE		FJC		173
FALCONAIR				678
FALWELL AVIATION		FAW		330
FANAIR		FGH		702
FAP – Força Aérea Portuguesa		AFP		93
FAR EASTERN AIR TRANSPORT – FAT	EF	FEA		23
FAR EASTERN CARGO AIRLINES		FEW		537
FAR WEST HELICOPTERS				50
FARAM HELICOPTERS				671
FARNAS AVIATION SERVICES		RAF		591
FARNER AIR TRANSPORT		FAT		186
FARNER AIR TRANSPORT Hungary, Kft.		FAH		183
FARNSWAY AIR CHARTER SERVICES				626
FARWEST AIRLINES, Llc				330
FAST AIR				50
FAST AIR CARRIER, S.A.		FST		88
FAST AIRWAYS		TFS		696
FAST HELICOPTERS		FHL		173
FATCA FLIGHT INSPECTION				663

	IATA	ICAO	LEASE	Page
FAUCETT PERU	CF	CFP		470
FAWNIE MOUNTAIN OUTFITTERS				50
FDZ Flugdienst Zwickau				106
FEDAIR		FDR		678
FEDERAL AIRLINES		FLL		591
FEDERAL AVIATION ADMINISTRATION – FAA		NHK		330
FEDERAL AVIATION, S.A.				236
FEDERICO HELICOPTERS		FDE		331
FEDERICO II AIRWAYS, SpA	2D	FDE		215
FEDEX – Federal Express Corporation	FX	FDX		331
FELTS FIELD AVIATION				337
FERMENA				93
FFA Air-Travel		FFA		186
FFD Franken Flug Dienst				106
FFH Flugdienst Freiburg Harter				107
FIA – First International Airlines				519
FIGAS – FALKLAND ISLANDS				644
FIKA SALAAMA AIRLINES	HG	HGK		694
FILAIR, S.P.R.L.				708
FILDER AIR SERVICE – FAS		NRX		107
FINE AIR	FB	FBF		337
FINIST' AIR		FTR		152
FINNAIR TRAINING CENTER				477
FINNAIR, Oyj	AY	FIN		477
FIORDLAND HELICOPTERS				671
FIRAT AVIATION				597
FIRDAFLY, A/S				232
FIREFLY AVIATION				337
FIREHAWK HELICOPTERS				337
FIREWEED HELICOPTERS				50
FIRFAX AIR CHARTER				174
FIRST AIR	7F	FAB		50
FIRST CITY AIR, Plc		MBL		174
FIRST INVEST, Oy				477
FISCHER AIR, s r.o.	8F	FFR		481
FISCHER-FLUG				107
FISHING and FLYING				337
FISHTAIL AIRLINES, Pvt				707
FISKEHAUK AIRWAYS				337
FISKFLYG, AB				583
FITZROY AVIATION QUEENSLAND				626
FIVE MILE LAKE LODGE & Air Service				51
FIVE STAR AVIATION				627
FIVESTAR AIRCRAFT			FACE	337
FJAELLFLYGARNA i ARJEPLOG, AB				583
FJELLANGER-WIDEROE, A/S				232
FJELLFLY				232
FJS-HELICOPTER LUFTTRANSPORT				107
FLAMINGO AIR		FMR		337
FLAMINGO AIR SERVICES				645
FLAMINGO FLIGHTS, CC				678
FLANAGAN ENTERPRISES				51
FLANDRE AIR	IX	FRS		153
FLEET AIR				689
FLEET HELICOPTERS				627
FLEXAIR				495
FLIGHT 2000				671
FLIGHT Air Company		FLV		537
FLIGHT CHARTER				627
FLIGHT Corporation		FCP		671
FLIGHT EXPRESS		EXR		338
FLIGHT INTERNATIONAL		IVJ		338
FLIGHT INTERNATIONAL AIR SERVICES				51
FLIGHT PRECISION		CLB		174
FLIGHT SERVICES GROUP – FSG				338
FLIGHT TRAILS HELICOPTERS				338
FLIGHT WEST AIRLINES	YC	FWQ		627
FLIGHTCRAFT		CSK		337
FLIGHTLINE		FLT		174
FLIGHTLINE, S.L.		FTL		125
FLIGT SERVICE				482
FLINDERS RANGES TOURIST SERVICES				627
FLINT AIR SERVICE		FAZ		339
FLITE vols touristiques				186
FLM AVIATION				107
FLN Frisia-Luftverkehr GmbH Norddeich				107
FLORIDA AIR CARGO				339
FLORIDA AIR TRANSPORT				339
FLORIDA JET SERVICE				339
FLORIDA WEST INTERNATIONAL AIRWAYS	RF	FWL		339
FLORIDA WINGS				339
FLOWERS AVIATION				51
FLUGBEREITSCHAFT				107
FLUGBEREITSCHAFT BADEN-BADEN				107
FLUG-CENTER WORMS				107
FLUGDIENST BAYREUTH				107
FLUGDIENST CARLOS DE PILAR				107
FLUGDIENST FEHLHABER		FFG		107
FLUGFELAG ISLANDS, h.f.	NY	FXI		601
FLUGFELAG VESTMANNAEYJA, h.f.				601
FLUGSCHULE EICHENBERGER – Airtaxi				186
FLUGSERVICE SOEMMERDA				107
FLUGTAXI GmbH Suben				474
FLY BVI				645
FLY DIRECT				627
FLY FTI		FTI		107
FLY JET, Srl.		FJT		215
FLY ONE, Llc				339
FLY, S.A. Linhas Aéreas		FLB		504
FLYGANDE VETERANER				583
FLYGTJAENST, AB				583
FLYING A FLIGHT SERVICE				339
FLYING COLOURS Airlines	MT	FCL		174
FLYING DEVIL, SA				187
FLYING DOLLAR AIR				339
FLYING ENTERPRISE, AB	F3	FLY		583
FLYING FIREMAN				339
FLYING MEDICAL SAMARITANS – FMS				580
FLYING MISSION				8
FLYING RANCH				187
FLYING SUPPORT, N.V.		IBS		485
FLYING TAXI AEREO				504
FLYMELL, S.A.				236
FLYSUL Aerotaxi				504
FLYWELL AIRLINES, Pvt		FEM		667
FM AVIATION SERVICES, Llc				339
FOLSOMS AIR SERVICE				339
FONNAFLY Sjö, A/S		NOF		232
FORCE AERIENNE DU BENIN				606
FORD HELICOPTERS				174
FORD MOTOR Company		FRD		339
FORDAIR		FOB		174
FORDE LAKE AIR SERVICES				51
FOREST HELICOPTERS				51
FOREST INDUSTRIES FLYING TANKERS				51
FOREST PROTECTION – FPL				51
FORESTRY COMMISSION OF NSW				627

Einer der Bestseller
von Bucher Publikationen:

Flugplan
Ankunft / Abflug

für
Besucher
des
Flughafens
Zürich

Intelligente Ausstattung:

✈ Der Besucher-Flugplan des Flughafens Zürich erscheint im Jahr zweimal (Sommer- und Winterflugplan).

✈ Er beinhaltet sämtliche Ankunfts- und Abflugszeiten aller Linienflüge sowie der regelmässigen Charterketten.

✈ Flüge, welche von Fluggesellschaften regelmässig zur Durchführung an andere Airlines delegiert werden, sind entsprechend vermerkt.

✈ Ankünfte und Abflüge sind getrennt chronologisch aufgeführt.

✈ Für optimale Ablesbarkeit ist jede zweite Linie grau unterlegt.

✈ Nach jeder Periode von 15 Minuten befindet sich eine weitere horizontale Linie. Damit ist leicht abschätzbar, wieviele Flüge Sie zu einer bestimmten Viertelstunde sehen.

✈ Im Mittelteil des Flugplans befinden sich diverse Abkürzungs-Aufschlüsselungen sowie weitere wichtige Informationen für Besucher (z.B. gute Foto-Standorte).

✈ Der Umschlag enthält zwei perforierte Postkarten, die abgetrennt werden können, ohne dass die Funktion des Flugplans beeinträchtigt wird.

Der Besucher-Flugplan wird im Auftrag der FDZ, Flughafendirektion Zürich, hergestellt.

Einzel-Verkaufs-Preis Fr. 2.50
plus Versandkosten

Der Besucher-Flugplan ist an über 20 Verkaufsstellen in und um den Flughafen Zürich erhältlich.

Abonnements nur bei

Bucher & Co., Publikationen, Postfach 2256, CH-8152 Glattbrugg / Schweiz

4 Ausgaben (2 Jahre) kosten inkl. Versand innerhalb der Schweiz Fr. 10.–.
Betrag bitte direkt einzahlen auf unser Postcheckkonto «Zürich 80-30353-6».

4 Ausgaben (2 Jahre) kosten inkl. Versand nach Deutschland DM 15.–.
Betrag bitte direkt einzahlen auf unser Postgirokonto in Frankfurt:
3010 21-604 (BLZ 500 100 60).

4 Ausgaben (2 Jahre) kosten inkl. Versand innerhalb des restlichen Europa SFr. 15.–.
Bitte senden Sie uns per Post einen Eurocheck im entsprechenden Betrag.

(Weitere Zahlungsmöglichkeiten siehe zweitletzte Seite dieses Jahrbuches).

727

	IATA	ICAO	LEASE	Page
LIB-AIR-T AVIATION (M.C.M.)				62
LIBERIA WORLD AIRLINES		LWA		134
LIBERTY AIR				391
LIBERTY HELICOPTERS				391
LIBYAN AIR AMBULANCE				688
LIBYAN ARAB AIR CARGO		LCR		688
LIBYAN ARAB AIRLINES	LN	LAA		688
LIDDLES AIR SERVICE, P/L				632
LIDER Taxi Aéreo, SA				506
LIFE FORCE AIR MEDICAL				391
LIFE LION Air Medical Program				391
LIFESTAR				391
LIGHT AIR TRANSPORT & TECHNICAL		GLT		688
LILLBAKA JETAIR, Oy		FPC		478
LINAIR-HUNGARIAN REGIONAL AIRLINES		LIN		183
LINDSAY AVIATION		LSY		391
LINEA AEREA COSTA NORTE, SA				89
LINEA AEREA MEXICANA DE CARGA		LMC		655
LINEAS AEREAS CANEDO – LAC				91
LINEAS AEREAS EJECUTIVAS de Durango				655
LINEAS AEREAS IXTLAN		IXT		655
LINEAS AEREAS MAYAS, S.A.				602
LINEAS AEREAS SURAMERICANAS		LAU		198
LINVIC FLYING CLUB				62
LIONAIR		LNS		686
LIONS AIR		LEU		188
LIP-AIR				632
LIP-AVIA		TTN		611
LIPETSK AIR ENTERPRISE		LIP		545
LIPS FLUGDIENST				111
LITHUANIAN AIRLINES – LAL	TE	LIL		240
LITTLE RED AIR SERVICE		LRA		62
LLOYD HELICOPTERS				632
LOCAVIA FRANCE				156
LOCAVIONS AERO SERVICES		PAU		156
LOCKHART AIR SERVICES				62
LOFOTFLY, A/S				233
LOGANAIR		LOG		177
LOKENFLY				233
LOMAKYLA INARIN LENTOPALVELU, Oy				478
LOMAS HELICOPTERS		LMS		177
LONDON EXECUTIVE AVIATION – LEA		LNX		177
LONG BEACH HELICOPTERS				62
LONG BEACH HELICOPTERS				391
LONG POINT AIRWAYS				62
LONGREACH AIR CHARTER				632
LOON HAUNT AIR SERVICE				62
LORAIR				391
LOST NATION AVIATION				391
LOT Polish Airlines	LO	LOT		589
LOTHIAN HELICOPTERS				177
LOTUS AIR		TAS		592
LOTUS AIRWAYS				134
LOUISIANA AIRCRAFT				392
LOVE AIR	4J	LOV		177
LOWA				392
LOYAL-AIR				62
LR AIRLINES		LRB		481
LRC Taxi Aéreo				507
LSC Letecké sportovni centrum				481
LTA – Linea Turistica Aereotuy, C.A.		TUY		665
LTE International Airways, S.A.	XO	LTE		128
LTO Lufttransport Osnabrück-Münster				111
LTU International Airways	LT	LTU		111
LUCKY AIR		BLF		241
LUFT AFRIQUE				679
LUFT-CHARTER-EMSLAND				111
LUFTHANSA	LH	DLH		112
LUFTHANSA Cargo	LH	GEC		114
LUFTHANSA CARGO INDIA, Pvt.	LF	LCI		647
LUFTHANSA CityLine	CL	CLH		114
LUFTHANSA Flight Training				115
LUFTHANSA Traditionsflug – LTG				115
LUFTMEISTER AIR				679
LUFTTAXI FLUG		LTF		115
LUFTTRANSPORT, A/S		LTR		233
LUG Taxi Aéreo				507
LUGANSK AVIATION ENTERPRISE		LHS		616
LUKIAVIATRANS				546
LUKOIL AVIA				546
LUMBINI AIRWAYS, Pvt				707
LUPENGA AIR CHARTERS		LUP		703
LUSITANIA				699
LUXAIR	LG	LGL		239
LUXAVIATION, S.A.		LXA		240
LUXEMBOURG AIR RESCUE, a.s.		LUV		240
LUXOR AIR		LXO		592
LVC HELICOPTERS, N.V.				485
LVD Luftfahrzeug-Vermietungs-Dienst				475
LVOV AIRLINES		UKW		616
LYNCH FLYING SERVICE		LCH		392
LYNDEN AIR CARGO, Llc	L2	LYC		392
LYNSTAR AVIATION				392
LYNTON AVIATION		LYN		177
LYNX AIR INTERNATIONAL				392
LYON AVIATION				392
M & N AVIATION	W4			393
MABUHAY AIRWAYS Philippines				580
MAC AIR Corporation				392
MAC AVIATION, S.L.		MAQ		128
MAC DAN AVIATION		MCN		392
MACAIR AIRLINES	CC			632
MACAIR JET, S.A.				238
MACAW HELICOPTERS				392
MACEDONIAN AIRLINES		MCS		594
MACEDONIAN COMMERCIAL AVIATION				682
MACH AIR				598
MACK AIR				8
MAD – Malaya Aviatsia Dona		MKK		546
MADAGASCAR FLYING SERVICE				693
MADIBA AIR				679
MADINA		MND		546
MADRI Taxi Aéreo				507
MAERSK AIR	VB	MSK		177
MAERSK AIR, A/S	DM	DAN		489
MAERSK HELICOPTERS				490
MAF Australia	FS			633
MAF Canada – Mission Aviation Fellowship				62
MAF Congo – Mission Aviation Fellowship				708
MAF Ethiopia – Mission Aviation Fellowship				139
MAF Indonesia – Mission Aviation Fellowship		MAF		498
MAF Kenya – Mission Aviation Fellowship				696
MAF Lesotho				699
MAF Papua New Guinea				517
MAF South Africa				679
MAF Suriname – Mission Aviation Fellowship				516

	IATA	ICAO	LEASE	Page
MAF Sweden – Mission Aviation Fellowship				584
MAF Tanzania				689
MAF Uganda – Mission Aviation Fellowship				694
MAF USA – Mission Aviation Fellowship				392
MAFIRA AIR CHARTER SERVICES	3A			704
MAGADAN 2nd Aviation Enterprise				546
MAGEC AVIATION		MGC		177
MAGHREB AERO SERVICE				90
MAGIC CARPET AVIATION				392
MAGNA AIR Luftfahrt		MGR		475
MAGNICHARTERS		GMT		655
MAGNITOGORSK AIR ENTERPRISE		MNG		546
MAHAN AIR		IRM		135
MAHFOOZ AVIATION (Gambia)	M2	MZS		97
MAINE AVIATION		MAT		392
MAINE FLIGHT				393
MAINE HELICOPTERS				393
MAINLAND AIR SERVICES				672
MAINTAERO				90
MAJESTIC AIR CARGO				393
MAJOR'S AIR SERVICES				98
MAJU AIR SERVICES				704
MAKANI KAI HELICOPTERS				393
MALAGA Taxi Aéreo				507
MALAGASY AIRLINES		MLG		693
MALAYSIA AIRLINES	MH	MAS		704
MALDIVIAN AIR TAXI, (Pte)				700
MALDONADO AIR				238
MALEV Hungarian Airlines, Plc	MA	MAH		183
MALI AIR Luftverkehr				475
MALIFT AIR				708
MALMILENTO, Oy				478
MALMO AIR TAXI, AB				585
MALTA AIR CHARTER, Company	R5	MAC		702
MALU AVIATION				708
MANACA Taxi Aéreo				507
MANAG'AIR		MRG		156
MANAKAMANA AIRWAYS, Pvt				707
MANDAIR				62
MANDALA AIRLINES		MDL		498
MANGYSTAUAVIA				611
MANHATTAN AIR		MHN		177
MANN AVIATION SERVICES				633
MANUNGGAL AIR				498
MANX AIRLINES	JE	MNX		178
MAPINDO PARAMA				498
MAPLAN AEROLEVANTAMENTOS, SA				507
MAPMAKERS				517
MAPS Geosystems				115
MAQUAYAN AIRWAYS				62
MARGIRIUS Taxi Aéreo, SA				507
MARICA Taxi Aéreo				507
MARINA AEROSERVICE, S.A.				128
MARINE HELICOPTERS				633
MARINE HELICOPTERS				673
MARINHA – Portuguese Navy		PON		94
MARIO'S AIR	M2			393
MARITIME AIR CHARTER				63
MARITIME HELICOPTERS				393
MARITIME SAFETY AGENCY – MSA				226
MARLBOROUGH HELICOPTERS (1981)				673
MARLIN AIR				393
MARLIN HELICOPTERS				63
MAROOMBA AIRLINES	KN			633
MARTHAKAL YOLNGU AIRLINE				633
MARTINAIR	MP	MPH		494
MARTINAIRE		MRA		393
MARYLAND AIRLINES				393
MARZ-AVIA				546
MAS AIR CARGO	MY	MAA		655
MASTER AVIATION, A/S		MSD		233
MAT-MACEDONIAN AIRLINES	IN	MAK		682
MATO GROSSO DO SUL Taxi Aéreo				507
MATT'S AIR SERVICE				63
MAUNA KEA HELICOPTERS				393
MAUS – Myachkovskie aviatsionnye uslugi		MKV		546
MAVERICK HELICOPTER				393
MAVIAL – Magadanskie avialinii	H5	MVL		547
MAXAIR				393
MAXAIR, AB	8M	MXL		585
MAXWELL AVIATION				63
MAY AIR X-PRESS		MXP		394
MAYA ISLAND AIR	MW	MYD		649
MAYAIR		MYI		656
MAYAN WORLD AIRLINES	EY	MYN		602
MAYFAIR Dove Aviation				178
MAYO AVIATION				394
MAYORAL		MYO		129
MBA	CG			517
MBD AIR				394
MCALISTER AIRWAYS				633
MCCALL & WILDERNESS AIR				394
MCCARTHY AIR				394
MCCAUSLAND AVIATION				394
MCGAVOCK LAKE AIR SERVICE				63
MCGEE AERIAL SERVICES				633
MCHS ROSSII		SUM		547
MCI TRANSCON – Flight Operations				394
MCIVER AVIATION				633
MCKINLEY AIR SERVICE				394
MCLEAN & MCLEAN AIR SERVICES				63
MCMAHAN AVIATION				394
MCMAHON HELICOPTERS				394
MCMURRAY AVIATION				63
MCNEELY CHARTER SERVICE				394
MDA AIRLINES	KR	MDD		547
MEA – Middle East Airlines	ME	MEA		471
MED AIRLINES, SpA	M8	MDS		216
MED AVIA – Mediterranean Aviation				702
MEDFORD AIR SERVICE				394
MEDIAIR				115
MEDIC AIR				394
MEDICAL AIR RESCUE				395
MEDICAL AIR RESCUE SERVICE				667
MEDICAL AIR SERVICES ASSOCIATION				395
MEDICAL AVIATION SERVICES – MAS		MCL		178
MEDICAL TRANSPORTATION				395
MEDICORP ARGENTINA				238
MEDIFLIGHT				673
MEDJET INTERNATIONAL		MEJ		395
MED-TRANS				395
MEGAPODE AIRLINES				647
MEGIDDO AVIATION				687
MEMPHIS JET SERVICE, L.P.				395
MENARD – Flight Dept.				395
MENASHA AIR				395
MENEKSE AIR				598

	IATA	ICAO	LEASE	Page
MERAVO Luftreederei Fluggesellschaft				115
MERCHANT CHARTERS				395
MERCY AIR				395
MERCY AIR AMBULANCE				395
MERCY FLIGHTS				395
MERCY MEDICAL AIRLIFT				395
MERCY WINGS				395
MERIDIAN AIR, Co.		MMM		547
MERIDIANA, SpA	IG	ISS		216
MERLIN EXPRESS		MEI		395
MERPATI	MZ	MNA		498
MESA AIRLINES	YV	ASH		396
MESABA AIRLINES	XJ	MES		397
MESCO AIRLINES				647
META – MESQUITA Transportes Aéreo		MSQ		507
METAVIA AIRLINES				679
METHOW AVIATION		MER		398
METRO AIR				598
METRO AVIATION				398
METRO Taxi Aéreo, SA				507
METROJET		MTJ		22
MEXICANA	MX	MXA		656
MEXICARGO	GJ	MXC		656
MFS Manager Flugservice				115
MG-AVIATION		MGM		156
MHS AVIATION, Sendirian Berhad				705
MHS HELICOPTER-FLUGSERVICE				115
MIAMI AIR	GL	BSK		398
MIAMI AIR LEASE				398
MIAMI CITY FLIGHTS				398
MIAMI VALLEY AVIATION – MVA				398
MIAT – Mongolian Airlines	OM	MGL		229
MI-AVIA		MIV		547
MIBA AVIATION				708
MICHAUDS AVIATION				399
MICHELIN AIR SERVICES				156
MICMAC AIR SERVICES				63
MID ATLANTIC AIR MUSEUM				399
MID COAST AIR SERVICES				63
MID EAST JET				206
MID VALLEY HELICOPTERS				399
MID-ATLANTIC FREIGHT		MDC		399
MID-COAST AIR CHARTER				399
MIDLAND AIR Oestersund, AB				585
MIDLANTIC JET CHARTERS				399
MIDLINE AIR FREIGHT				399
MID-OHIO AVIATION				399
MIDROC AVIATION				139
MIDT-FLY, A/S				233
MIDWAY AIRLINES	JI	MDW		399
MIDWEST AVIATION		MWT		399
MIDWEST CORPORATE AVIATION				400
MIDWEST EXPRESS AIRLINES	YX	MEP		400
MIDWEST FLYING SERVICE				400
MIDWEST HELICOPTER AIRWAYS				400
MIDWEST HELICOPTERES MEXICO		HTE		656
MIDWEST HELICOPTERS				63
MIKE DENIS AVIATION				63
MILFORD HELICOPTERS				673
MILLENNIUM EXECUTIVE AIR CHARTER				178
MILLER HELICOPTER SERVICES				673
MILLION AIR				647
MILLION AIR CHARTER TETERBORO				400
MILLION AIR DALLAS				400
MILLION AIR OKLAHOMA CITY				400
MILLION AIR OWENSBORO				400
MILLION AIR READING				400
MILLION AIR RICHMOND				400
MILLION AIR SALT LAKE CITY				401
MILLIONAIR CHARTER				679
MINAIR				604
MINDANAO EXPRESS				581
MINDEN AIR				401
MINERVA AIRLINES, SpA	Q2	MTC		216
MINILINER, Srl.		MNL		216
MINUTEMAN AVIATION – MAI				401
MIRABELLA YACHTS				401
MIRAGE AIR				633
MIRAVIA	N3	MRV		661
MISSION LODGE				401
MISSION MEDIC AIR				703
MISSIONAIR				401
MISTRAL AIR, Srl.		MSA		216
MISTY FJORD'S AIR & OUTFITTING				401
MITCHINSON FLYING SERVICE				63
MK AIRLINES	7G	MKA		702
MK AVIATION, S.A.			MKAV	203
MK FLUGFELAGID, e.h.f.		MKI		602
MNG CARGO AIRLINES	MB	MNB		598
MOBIL Global Aircraft Services				401
MOBIL OIL AVIATION		MBO		63
MOBLEY AVIATION				401
MODERN AIR				115
MOFAZ AIR, Sdn Berhad		MFZ		705
MOGILEVAVIA		MOG		140
MOLDAEROSERVICE		MLE		137
MOLDAVIAN AIRLINES	2M	MDV		137
MOLOKAI AIR SHUTTLE				401
MOMBASA AIR SAFARI – MAS				696
MONACAIR, S.A.M.		MCR		682
MONARCH AIRLINES	ZB	MON		178
MONTAIR AVIATION				63
MONT-BLANC HELICOPTERES				157
MONTENEGRO AIRLINES		MGX		663
MONTEX DRILLING – Aviation Dept.				401
MOONAIR AVIATION				687
MOORABBIN AIR CHARTER				633
MOREMI AIR SERVICES				8
MORGAN AIR SERVICES, Co.				63
MORIAN AVIATION				401
MORNINGSTAR AIR EXPRESS		MAL		63
MORRO VERMELHO Taxi Aéreo				507
MOSELEY AVIATION				401
MOTOR SICH Aviakompania		MSI		616
MOTORFLUGGRUPPE OBERENGADIN				189
MOUNT COOK AIRLINE	NM	NZM		673
MOUNT LAKE AIR SERVICES				395
MOUNTAIN AIR				673
MOUNTAIN AIR CARGO – MAC		MTN		401
MOUNTAIN EMPIRE FLYING SERVICE				402
MOUNTAIN FLYERS 80				189
MOUNTAIN HIGH AVIATION		MHA		402
MOUNTAIN VIEW HELICOPTERS				673
MOUNTAIN WEST HELICOPTERS, Llc				402
MOURAN Taxi Aéreo				507
MOYER AVIATION				402
MRI Medical Rescue International				679

	IATA	ICAO	LEASE	Page
SKYMASTER AVIATION				432
SKYMASTERS				696
SKYNET AIRWAYS				432
SKYPOL		PZL		590
SKYSERVICE		SSV		77
SKYSERVICE USA				432
SKY-SERVICE, B.V.B.A.		SKS		486
SKYTEAM		XST		118
SKYTECH CHARTERS				77
SKYTECH HELICOPTER SERVICE, SàRL				486
SKYTOUR Taxi Aéreo				509
SKYTRAILS				696
SKYTRAIN				432
SKYTRANS	NP			639
SKY-TREK AIRLINES		UKT		180
SKYWARD AVIATION	K9	SGK		77
SKYWAY AIRLINES	AL	SYX		432
SKYWAY Enterprises		SKZ		432
SKYWAYS				77
SKYWAYS AUSTRALIA				639
SKYWAYS KENYA				696
SKYWAYS, AB	JZ	SKX		588
SKYWEST AIRLINES	OO	SKW		432
SKYWEST AIRLINES	YT			639
SKYWORX AVIATION				640
SKYYWAY AVIATION				433
SLATE FALLS AIRWAYS (1987)		SYJ		78
SLAVE AIR (1988)				78
SLAVE LAKE HELICOPTERS				78
SLINGAIR				640
SLOANE HELICOPTERS		SLN		180
SLOV AIR, a.s.		OIR		482
SLOVACKY AEROKLUB				481
SLOVAK AIRLINES	6Q	SLL		482
SLOVAK GOVERNMENT FLYING SERVICE		SSG		482
SLS Sächsischer Luftfahrt-Service				118
SLV – Statens Luftfartsvaesen, Danmark				490
SMA AIRLINES (Nig.)		SMA		692
SMAELANDSFLYG, AB		SMF		588
SMART FLIGHTS				78
SMELT AIR				595
SMITHAIR		SMH		433
SMOLENSKAVIA				564
SNAKE FALLS AIRWAYS				78
SNAS AVIATION		RSE		208
SNOWY BUTTE HELICOPTERS				433
SOBELAIR, N.V.	Q7	SLR		486
SOCHISPETSAVIA		SOC		564
SOCIEDAD DE AVN PESQUERA – S.A.P.				89
SOCIEDADE DE TAXI AEREO WESTON				509
SOKOL ATSK		SOK		617
SOKOL Aviakompania				564
SOLID'AIR, S.A.				240
SOLINAIR Portoroz, d.o.o.		SOP		596
SOLLEY CONSTRUCTION, Co. Inc.				433
SOLOMONS – Solomon Airlines	IE	SOL		208
SONAIR – Helipetrol				121
SONMEZ AIRLINES		SMZ		599
SONTAIR				78
SOREM				217
SOS FLYGAMBULANS		SAG		588
SOS HELIKOPTERN GOTLAND, AB		MCG		588
SOTAG		GIT		684
SOTAN – SOCIEDADE DE T. A. NORDESTE				509
SOUND AVIATION				433
SOUND FLIGHT				433
SOUNDSAIR				674
SOURE Taxi Aéreo				510
SOUTH AERO				434
SOUTH AFRICAN AIRLINK	4Z	LNK		681
SOUTH AFRICAN AIRWAYS – SAA	SA	SAA		681
SOUTH AFRICAN EXPRESS Airways	YB	EXY		681
SOUTH COAST AIRWAYS		GAD		180
SOUTH COAST HELICOPTERS				434
SOUTH EAST AIR				674
SOUTH EAST REGIONAL POLICE				180
SOUTH MORESBY AIR CHARTERS				78
SOUTH NAHANNI AIRWAYS				78
SOUTH SEA HELICOPTERS				434
SOUTH WEST AIR SERVICE				640
SOUTHCENTRAL AIR	XE	SCA		434
SOUTHEAST AIR				434
SOUTHEAST AIR CHARTER				434
SOUTH-EAST AIR SERVICES				640
SOUTHEAST AIRMOTIVE		SPU		434
SOUTHEAST MISSISSIPPI AIR AMBULANCE				434
SOUTHEND CARGO AIRLINES		SYZ		667
SOUTHERN AIR		HSN		180
SOUTHERN AIR (1997)		RKU		674
SOUTHERN ALPS AIR				674
SOUTHERN AUSTRALIA AIRLINES				640
SOUTHERN AVIATION – SAL				78
SOUTHERN COMMANDER				640
SOUTHERN CROSS AIR				640
SOUTHERN CROSS AVIATION				667
SOUTHERN HELICOPTERS				434
SOUTHERN LAKES HELICOPTERS				674
SOUTHERN PRIDE – Flight Dept.				434
SOUTHERN SEAPLANE		SSC		434
SOUTHERN SKY AIRLINES				640
SOUTHERN WINDS, S.A.	A4	SWD		238
SOUTHLAND AIR CHARTER				674
SOUTHLAND FLOAT PLANE SERVICES				674
SOUTHSTAR AVIATION, Co. Inc.				581
SOUTHWEST AIR				518
SOUTHWEST AIRLINES, Company	WN	SWA		434
SOUTHWEST HELICOPTERS				438
SOUTH-WEST HELICOPTERS				674
SOUTHWEST SAFARIS				438
SOWIND AIR		SOW		78
SP AIRCRAFT				438
SP AVIATION – Superior Performance				438
SPAIR Air Transport Corporation		PAR		564
SPAN AIR, Pvt.				648
SPANAIR, S.A.	JK	JKK		129
SPASA – Servicios Politecnicos Aéreos, S.A.		SPS		129
SPECIAL AIR SERVICES, B.V. – SAS				494
SPECIAL AVIATION SYSTEMS				438
SPECIAL CARGO AIRLINES	C7	SCI		564
SPECIALIZED TRANSPORT INTL				438
SPECTRA AVIATION SERVICES				78
SPECTRUM AIRWAYS				78
SPEED AIR				681
SPEEDWINGS, SA		SPW		189
SPERNAK AIRWAYS				438
SPHAIR				159
SPIRIT AIRLINES	NK	NKS		438

	IATA	ICAO	LEASE	Page
SPORT HAWK INTERNATIONAL AIRLINES				78
SPORTSMAN'S LANDING				78
SPOTTED DOG AVIATION				438
SPRINGDALE AIR SERVICE		SPG		438
SPRINGDALE AVIATION				78
STABO AIR		SBO		703
STAC		FOC		189
STAERO		STB		565
STAF	FS	STU		238
STAGE AIR				78
STA-MALI		SBA		607
STAN REYNOLDS OUTFITTING & Airservice				79
STANCOM AVIATION				699
STANDARD Ag. Helicopter				79
STANLEY AIR TAXI				439
STANSON AIR, AB				588
STANTON AIRWAYS				79
STAP				92
STAR AIR CHARTER				640
STAR AIR, A/S		SRR		490
STAR AIRLINES	2R	SEU		159
STAR AVIATION				439
STAR CHARTER				640
STAR HELICOPTERS				79
STAR SERVICE INTERNATIONAL		SSD		159
STAR UP, S.A.				471
STAR WORK SKY, Sas – S.W.S.		SWP		217
STARFLITE				439
STARFLITE INTERNATIONAL				439
STARLING AIR				491
STARS AVIATION CANADA				79
STARSPEED		SSP		180
START Air Transport Company		STW		565
STARWEST AVIATION		FSR		79
STATE AVIATION GROUP				138
STATEWIDE AIR CHARTER – SWAC				640
STEARNS AIR ALASKA				439
STEIRISCHE MOTORFLUG-UNION & Airtaxi				475
STELA				565
STELLA MARIS AVIATION				98
STEPHENSON AVIATION				180
STERLING AIRWAYS				439
STERLING EUROPEAN AIRLINES – SEA		SNB		491
STERLING HELICOPTERS		GPH		180
STERLING HELICOPTERS				439
STERLING PACIFIC AIR				79
STERLITAMAK AIR ENTERPRISE				565
STEVENSON SKYWORK HELICOPTERS				674
STEWART AVIATION SERVICES		YBE		439
STORM FLYING SERVICE				439
STREAMLINE AIR CHARTER		SLE		681
STREAMLINE AVIATION		SSW		180
STREZHAVIA		STY		565
STREZHEVOI AIR ENTERPRISE				565
STUART JET CENTER				439
SUBIC INTERNATIONAL AIR CHARTER				581
SUBURBAN AIR FREIGHT		SUB		439
SUCKLING AIRWAYS	CB	SAY		180
SUD AEROCARGO		KSA		138
SUD AIR TRANSPORT, S.A.		GID		684
SUDAN AIRWAYS	SD	SUD		591
SUDBURY AVIATION				79
SUDHOLZ AIR CHARTER				640
SUDPACIFICO		SDP		657
SUGAR LAND JET CENTER				439
SUKHOI Aviakompania		SUH		565
SULESTE Taxi Aéreo				510
SULTAN'S FLIGHT				650
SUMMIT AIR CHARTERS				79
SUMMIT HELICOPTERS				439
SUN AIR	BV	SSN		682
SUN AIR, S.A.				595
SUN CARE AIR AMBULANCE				439
SUN COUNTRY AIRLINES	SY	SCX		440
SUN D'OR INTERNATIONAL AIRLINES		ERO		688
SUN EXPRESS Airlines Maldives (Pvt)				700
SUN ISLANDS AVIATION				711
SUN JET INTERNATIONAL AIRLINES	JX	SJI		440
SUN PACIFIC INTERNATIONAL		SNP		440
SUN QUEST EXECUTIVE AIR CHARTER				440
SUNAIR AVIATION				674
SUN-AIR of Scandinavia, A/S	EZ	SUS		491
SUNBIRD AIR SERVICES				439
SUNDANCE HELICOPTERS				440
SUNEXPRESS	XQ	SXS		599
SUNFLOWER AIRLINES, Limited	PI	SUF		120
SUNLOVER HELICOPTERS				640
SUNRISE AIRLINES	OQ			440
SUNRISE AVIATION				440
SUNRISE AVIATION, CC				682
SUNROCK AIRCRAFT			SUNR	132
SUNSHINE AERO INDUSTRIES				440
SUNSHINE AIRLINES		SON		440
SUNSHINE COAST AIR CHARTER				640
SUNSHINE COAST AIR SERVICES				79
SUNSHINE COAST HELICOPTER RESCUE				640
SUNSHINE EXPRESS	CQ			640
SUNSHINE HELICOPTERS				440
SUNSTATE AIRLINES (Qld)		SSQ		641
SUNWEST AVIATION		SWS		440
SUNWEST HELICOPTERS				79
SUNWEST INTERNATIONAL		CNK		79
SUNWORLD INTERNATIONAL AIRLINES	SM	SWI		440
SUOMEN LASKUVARJOKERHO, Ry				479
SUPER SHRIMP – Flight Dept.				519
SUPERIOR AIR CHARTER				441
SUPERIOR AVIATION	AB	HKA		441
SUPERIOR AVIATION SERVICES				696
SUPERIOR HELICOPTER, Llc				441
SUPERIOR HELICOPTERS Canada				79
SUPERJET Aerotaxi				510
SURINAM AIRWAYS	PY	SLM		516
SURVEILLANCE AUSTRALIA				641
SUSITNA AIR SERVICE				441
SUWEST AIRWAYS				441
SVB AOLOP Aviakompania				565
SVEA FLYG, AB	SI	SVB		588
SVEDIJOS PREKES				240
SVERDLOVSK 2nd Air Enterprise		UKU		565
SVG AIR		SVD		230
SWALA AIRLINES				708
SWAMP AIR CHARTERS				8
SWAN AERO				79
SWANN-AIR SERVICES				79
SWAZI EXPRESS AIRWAYS		SWX		683
SWEB HELICOPTER UNIT		ELE		181
SWEDEWAYS AIR LINES, AB	HJ	SWE		588

	IATA	ICAO	LEASE	Page
SWIFT AIR, S.A.		SWT		129
SWIFT COPTERS, S.A.				189
SWIFTAIR				582
SWIFTFLITE Charters, CC				682
SWISS AIR FORCE		SUI		191
SWISS AIR-AMBULANCE		SAZ		190
SWISS WORLD AIRWAYS, S.A. – SWA	SO	SWO		191
SWISSAIR	SR	SWR		190
SYDNEY AIR SCENICS				641
SYDNEY HARBOUR SEAPLANES				641
SYDNEY HELICOPTER SERVICE				641
SYDNEY HELI-SCENIC				641
SYLT FLUGCHARTER				118
SYMBOL, S.A. – Compania de Aviacion		SYB		130
SYR SUNKARY Aviakompania		SBM		611
SYRIANAIR – Syrian Arab Airlines	RB	SYR		659
SYSTEC 2000				441
SZER-BON, Rt.		HSB		183
T doble A – Transportes Aéreos Andahuaylas		TEA		471
T.D. AVIATION				442
T.I.A. – Travaux Internationaux Aériens, S.A.				487
TAA – Trans Asian Airlines	T7	SRT		611
TAAG Angola Airlines	DT	DTA		121
TA-AIR AIRLINE		IRF		136
TAAN – Transporte Aéreo Andino, SA		EAA		666
TAB HELICOPTERES				160
TABA – T. A. Regionais da Bacia Amazonica		TAB		510
TABLE ROCK HELICOPTERS				441
TAC – Air Centro, SA				95
TAC – Transportes Aéreos de Catamarca				238
TAC AIR				441
TACA – Transporte Aéreo Costa Atlantica				238
TACA International Airlines, SA	TA	TAI		662
TACSA – Taxi Aéreo Centroamericano, SA				603
TACSA – Transportes Aéreos de Coahuila				657
TACV – CABO VERDE AIRLINES	VR	TCV		121
TADAIR, S.A.		TDC		130
TAERCO				199
TAESA – Transportes Aéreos Ejecutivos	GD	TEJ		657
TAF HELICOPTERS, S.A.		HET		130
TAF Linhas Aéreas, SA		TSD		510
TAG – Transportes Aéreos Gerais				596
TAG – Transportes Aéreos Guatemaltecos		GUM		603
TAG AVIATION UKRAINE		AGK		617
TAG AVIATION, S.A.	FP	FPG		191
TAG Teuto Airways Germany		TEU		118
TAGISH AIR SERVICE				79
TAGUA Colombia				199
TAIGA AIR				79
TAIGA AIR SERVICES				80
TAIGA HELICOPTERS (1993)				80
TAIMYRTUR				566
TAINO AIR SERVICES				98
TAINO AIRLINES, SA		TIN		194
TAJIKISTAN AIRLINES	7J	TZK		141
TAKE FLIGHT ALASKA				441
TAL – Trade Airlines, S.A.				239
TAL AIR				441
TAL AIR CHARTERS				80
TAL Transair Luftreederei				118
TALKEETNA AIR TAXI				441
TALON HELICOPTERS				80
TAM – Transportes Aéreos Militares		AFP		95
TAM – Transports & Travaux Aériens	OF	TML		693
TAM Brasil	KK	TAM		510
TAM Express	JJ	BLC		511
TAM Jatos Executivos Marilia, S.A.				511
TAM Paraguay	PZ	LAP		676
TAMANDARE Taxi Aéreo				510
TAMARAC AIR SERVICE				80
TAMARACK AIR				441
TAME – T. A. Mercantiles Ecuator	EQ	TAE		192
TAMIG – TAXI AEREO MINAS GERAIS				511
TAMPA Colombia	QT	TPA		199
TAMPEREEN HELIKOPTERIKESKUS, Oy				479
TAMU – Transporte Aéreo Militar Uruguayo				97
TAN – Transportes Aéreos Neuquen, S.A.	T8	NQN		239
TANANA AIR SERVICE	4E	TNR		441
TANDEM-AERO, Srl.		TDM		138
TANS		ELV		471
TANSA – Transportes Aéreos de Nayarit, SA				657
TANTK		GMB		566
TANZANAIR – Tanzanian Air Services				690
TANZANIA POLICE AIRWING				690
TAO – Transportes Aéreos Orientales				192
TAP – Transportes Aéreos Presidente, S.A.		TPE		511
TAP AIR PORTUGAL	TP	TAP		95
TAPAJOS Taxi Aéreo				511
TAPO-AVIA	PQ	CTP		608
TAPSA – Transportes Aéreos Profesionales				603
TAPSA Aviacion		TPS		239
TAQUAN AIR SERVICE	K3	TQN		442
TAR AEROREGIONAL				471
TAR HEEL AVIATION		THC		442
TARA AIRLINES		IRR		136
TARARUA HELIWORK				674
TARAZ WINGS		TWC		611
TARKIM AIR				599
TARLTON HELICOPTERS				442
TARMAC AVIATION, SA				191
TAROM Romania	RO	ROT		661
TARSA – Transportes Angela Rosa, SA				239
TAS – Transportes Aéreos del Sur, S.A.		HSS		130
TASA – Trabajos Aéreos, S.A.		TGE		130
TASA – Transportes Aéreos San Antonioa				92
TASA – Transportes Aéreos, S.A.				471
TASAIR				641
TASAWI AIR SERVICES	9X	TWI		590
TASMAN AUSTRALIAN AIRLINES				641
TASMAN HELICOPTERS				80
TASSILI AIRLINES, S.A.				700
TASUL – TAXI AEREO SUL				512
TAT – Transportes Aéreos Terrestres, SA				658
TATARSTAN/BUGULMA AIR ENTERPRISE		BGM		566
TATARSTAN/KAZAN AIR ENTERPRISE		KAZ		566
TATARSTAN/NIZHNEKAMSK AIR		NKM		566
TATNEFTAERO		TNF		566
TATONDUK FLYING SERVICE	3K			442
TATRA AIR, a.s.	QS	TTR		483
TAUNUS AIR & Co		TAQ		118
TAUPO AIR SERVICES				674
TAUPO'S FLOATPLANE				674
TAUSA				471
TAVAJ – Transportes Aéreos Regulares, SA	4U	TVJ		512
TAVASA – Trabajos Aéreos Vascongados				130
TAVIA-Taganrog Aviation		TGR		566

734

The following airlines have been listed in the previous issue, but are no longer included in the **jp airline-fleets** international **98/99**.

ACE AIRTOURS, (Pvt) Ltd - suspended operations in 1997/not restarted
ACE HELICOPTERS, Ltd - renamed PREMIER HELICOPTERS, Ltd in 1998
ACS of Canada - renamed ICC Canada, 011298
ADI DOMESTIC AIRLINES, Inc. - suspended operations in 1998
ADVANTAGE HELICOPTERS, Ltd - suspended operations in 1998
ADVENTURE AIR SERVICE, Pty Ltd - suspended operations in 1998
AEN - renamed AGROAVIA in 1998
AERIAL SURVEYS AUSTRALIA - suspended operations in 1998
AERO AVENTURE KUEI, Inc. - suspended operations in 1998
AEROCANCUN - Aeronautica de Cancun - suspended ops in 1999
AEROCLUBUL ROMANIEI - now operates aircraft below MTOW 1361kg only
AERO COMORES - renamed COMORES AIR SERVICE, 010198
AEROCOPTER SERVICES, Ltd - suspended operations in 1998
AEROFACILIDADES, S.A. - suspended operations in 1998
AEROGAUCHO, S.A. - suspended operations in 1998
AEROLAT - suspended operations in 1998
AEROLEASING, SA - renamed TAG AVIATION, SA, 010199
AEROLEASING UKRAINE - renamed TAG AVIATION UKRAINE in 1998
AEROLINA, Inc. - suspended operations in 1998
AEROLINEAS ALPHA, SA - suspended operations in 1998
AEROLINEAS DEL OESTE - ALOSA - suspended operations in 1998
AEROLINEAS FIGUEROA y Cia Ltda - suspended operations in 1998
AEROLINEAS MITAD DEL MUNDO, S.A. - suspended operations in 1998
AEROLINEAS YASI, S.A. de C.V. - suspended own operations in 1998
AEROLINE INTERNATIONAL - correct/see under AEROLION INTERNATIONAL
AERO LOISIRS, Inc. - now operates aircraft below MTOW 1361kg only
AEROMANTA - suspended operations in 1998
AERONAVES DE COSTA RICA, SA - renamed AERONAVES DE AMERICA, SA in 1998
AERO NOLISE - renamed AERO 3000 in 1998
AERONOR - Aeronaves del Noroeste - renamed AIRNOR in 1998
AERO NORTH - suspended operations in 1998
AEROPOSTAL de México, SA de CV - ceased operations 0598
AERO SHELL Compania de Aviacion Ecuatoriana, Ltda - suspended ops in 1998
AEROSPACE FINANCE, Ltd - now a financing co. only
AEROTAXI ARACAJU, Ltda - suspended operations in 1998
AEROTRANS Flugcharter, GmbH - renamed BUSINESSWINGS, GmbH in 1998
AERO-2000 - suspended operations in 1998
AEROVIAS DEL NORTE, SA - suspended own operations in 1998
AEROVIAS, SA - suspended operations in 1998
AF AVIATION - suspended operations in 1998
AFRICAN CARGO SERVICES, Ltd - suspended operations in 1998
AIR ACTION - now operates helicopters below MTOW 1361kg only
AIR ADVENTURES 400 Parachute Centre, Inc. - suspended comm. ops in 1998
AIR AL-FARAJ - suspended operations in 1998
AIR ALLIANCE, Inc. - merged into AIR NOVA, Inc., 050499
AIR ALVIK, AB - suspended operations in 1998
AIR ANATOLIA - now dba/see under ANATOLIA - Anadolu Havacilik
AIR & ADVENTURE TOURS, Pty Ltd - suspended operations in 1998
AIR ATLANTIC - suspended operations 251098
AIR AVENTURE - suspended operations in 1998
AIR BAHIA - Aerotransporte Bahia - suspended operations in 1998
AIR CARAIBES - taken over by CARAIBES AIR TRANSPORT in 1998
AIR CENTRE - suspended operations in 1998
AIR CESS (Liberia), Inc. - suspended operations in 1998
AIR CHARTER - ceased operations 311098
AIR CHARTER, Inc. - suspended operations in 1998
AIRCHARTER Heinz Conzelmann - renamed AIRCHARTER Flugservice in 1998
AIR CLUB INTERNATIONAL, Inc. - suspended operations in 1998
AIR CONNECTION, Inc. - now operates aircraft below MTOW 1361kg only
AIRCRAFT FINANCING & TRADING, B.V. - taken over by PEMBROKE CAPITAL, 1298
AIR DABIA (Gambia), Ltd - suspended operations in 1998
AIR EASTERN AIR CHARTER SERVICES, Pty Ltd - suspended operations in 1998
AIR 4000, Inc. - operations not started
AIR FRANCE PARTNAIRS LEASING, N.V. - suspended own leasing in 1998
AIR-HI-O, Corp. - suspended operations in 1998
AIR LEMANIC, SA - suspended operations in 1998
AIRLEN - suspended operations in 1998
AIR LESOTHO, (Pty) Ltd - suspended operations 060299
AIRLIFT ALASKA - suspended operations in 1998
AIRLINE MANAGEMENT, Ltd - suspended contract operations in 1998
AIR LINK EXPRESS - renamed STARWEST AVIATION in 1998
AIRMED CANADA - merged into SAMARITAN AIR SERVICE Ltd, 011098
AIR NEVADA - taken over by EAGLE CANYON AIRLINES, Inc., 0298
AIR NIAGARA - suspended operations in 1998
AIR NICE - suspended own operations in 1998
AIRNORTH Central - renamed CHARTAIR in 1998
AIR ORLANDO HELICOPTERS, Inc. - suspended operations in 1998
AIR PARTNER International, GmbH - brokerage company only
AIR PASS, Pietersburg Aviation Services & Systems - suspended ops in 1998
AIR REUNION INTERNATIONAL - suspended operations in 1998
AIR SANDY, Inc. - suspended operations in 1998
AIR SERVICE LIEGE - now dba/see under ASL - A.S. Liège
AIR SERVICES COOPERATIVE, Inc. - suspended operations in 1998
AIR SERVICE Ukraine - suspended operations in 1998
AIR SILVER - now operates aircraft below MTOW 1361kg only
AIR STORD, A/S - suspended operations 190299
AIR SULTAN, Ltd - suspended own operations in 1998
AIR TIWI - suspended operations 0798
AIR TRACK, Lineas Aéreas - ceased operations 011197/not restarted
AIRTRAN AIRLINES, Inc. - merged into AIRTRAN AIRWAYS, Inc. in 1998
AIRTRANSIVOIRE - ATI - suspended operations in 1998
AIR TRANSPORT SUPPORT CENTRE - ATSC - aircraft lost 0898
AIRVANIA, Ltd - now operates aircraft below MTOW 1361kg only
AIR VIRGINIA, Inc. - suspended operations in 1998
AIRVITA Leasing Air Company - suspended operations in 1998
AIR WEST - suspended commercial operations in 1998
AIRWINGS, Oy - suspended operations 240998
AIRWORLD - intergrated into FLYING COLOURS AIRLINES Ltd, 011198
AIR ZORY, Ltd - suspended operations in 1998
AJ AIR SERVICES - suspended operations in 1998
ALAK, Joint-Stock Leasing Airline - suspended operations in 1998
ALC - Advance Leasing - now see under ADVANCE LEASING
ALC AIRLIFT Canada, Inc. - renamed STARS AVIATION CANADA, Inc. in 1998
ALFA 92 Aviakompania - suspended operations in 1998
ALLIANCE AIR - renamed dba SA ALLIANCE, 0299
ALLKAUF FLUGSERVICE, GmbH - renamed VIBRO AIR FLUGSERVICE, GmbH, 010199
ALM Antillean Airlines - renamed AIR ALM, 0898
ALMETA AIR Luftverkehrs, GmbH - suspended own operations in 1998
ALPHA AIRCRAFT CHARTER, Ltd - suspended commercial operations in 1998
A.L.T.A. - Asociados Latinoamericanos - suspended ops 0998
A.L.T.A. Lineas Aéreas, S.A. - suspended operations 0998
AL-WAHA AVIATION - suspended operations in 1998
ALWAYS AVIATION - suspended operations in 1998
AMERICAN INTERNATIONAL AIRWAYS, Inc. - renamed KITTY HAWK INT'L, 0399
AMERICA WEST EXPRESS/Mesa Airlines - now see under MESA AIRLINES, Inc.
AMIGOS AVIATION, Inc. - suspended operations in 1998
AMSAIR, Corp. - suspended operations in 1998
AMURTRANSAERO, Joint-Stock Company - ceased operations 0898
ANDES AIRLINES - susp. ops 1998
ANDESMAR LINEAS AEREAS, S.A. - ceased operations 0598
ANOKA AIR CHARTER, Inc. - now dba/see under AAC AIR CHARTER
ANT AIR TAXI - suspended operations in 1998
ANTARES AIR, Ltd - suspended operations in 1998
ANTONOV AIRTRACK - AAT - suspended operations in 1998
ANTONOV DESIGN BUREAU - now dba/see under ANTONOV AIRLINES
APARTE Taxi Aéreo, Ltda - suspended operations in 1998
APEL Colombia - susp. ops in 1998
APOLLO AIRLINES, S.A. - suspended operations in 1996/not restarted
ARAUCARIA Aerotaxi, Ltda - suspended operations in 1998
ARCO Aviation - suspended operations 1298
A.R.K. AVIATION, Ltd - renamed TAUPO'S FLOATPLANE, Ltd in 1998
ARNHEM AIR CHARTER, Pty Ltd - suspended operations 0698
ARO Colombia - susp. ops in 0098
ARRIVA AIR International, Inc. - own operations not started
ARROW EXPRESS - renamed JAMAICA AIRLINK, 010199
ASIA PACIFIC AIRWAYS, Ltd - operations not started
ASIA TENGGARA AVIATION SERVICES, Sdn Bhd - suspended operations in 1998
ATAIR Executive Jet Charter, (Pty) Ltd - suspended operations in 1998
ATASCO LEASING, Inc. - suspended operating leases in 1998
ATLANTIC AIRWAYS, Inc. - suspended operations in 1998
ATLANTIS TRANSPORTATION SERVICES, Inc. - suspended operations in 1998
ATMOSPHAIR - now dba/see under CEP ATHMOSPHAIR
ATR - Travessia Taxi - suspended operations in 1998
AUSSIE AIRWAYS, Pty Ltd - suspended operations in 1998
AVIAPLUS, Inc. - suspended operations in 1998
AVIAPRIMA Sochi Airlines - suspended operations in 1998
AVIATION NORTHWEST, Inc. - suspended operations in 1998
AVIATION PORTNEUF, Ltée - suspended operations in 1998
AVIATON - suspended operations in 1998
AVIA, Y. Petro's Airline, Ltd - suspended operations in 1998
AVILOND TAC - suspended operations in 1998
AVIOPACIFICO, SA - suspended operations in 1998
AVIOTRANSPORT - renamed MACEDONIAN COMMERCIAL AVIATION in 1998
AVISTAR (Cyprus), Ltd - suspended own operations in 1998
AVSAT, Ltd - Aviation San Antonio - suspended operations in 1998
AYAKS AIRLINES - suspended own operations in 1998
AYDIN LINYIT AIR - suspended operations in 1998
AZOVTRANSAVIA - suspended operations in 1998

BAKU EXPRESS - suspended operations in 1998
BAVARO SUN FLIGHT – suspended operations in 1998
BAYAIR Havacilik, A.S. – suspended operations in 1998
BELGIAN AIR SUPPORT, asbl/vzw – suspended operations in 1998
BERMUDA HELICOPTERS, Ltd – suspended operations in 1998
BFS Business Flugservice, GmbH – renamed SILVER CLOUD AIR, GmbH, 1298
BILLINGEN FLYG, AB – now operates aircraft below MTOW 1361kg only
BLANDING AIR AMBULANCE – now see under EAGLE AIR
BL AVIATION GROUP – now op. non-commercial aircraft below MTOW 5t only
BLEKINGEFLYG, AB – suspended operations in 1998
BLUE AIRLINES – now dba/see under BAL – Blue Airlines
BLUEBIRD AVIATION – suspended operations in 1998
BLUE SKY AIRWAYS, spol. s r.o. – suspended operations in 1998
BONAIRE AIRWAYS – operations not started
BP AIR, Inc. – suspended operations in 1998
BRAATHENS S.A.F.E. – renamed BRAATHENS, ASA, 0798
BRAATHENS SVERIGE – merged into BRAATHENS Malmö Aviation, 010299
BRATSK AIR ENTERPRISE – renamed BRATSK AVIA in 1998
BREMERHAVEN AIRLINE, GmbH – now see under BAL Bremerhaven Airline
BRIGHT AIR, B.V. – suspended operations in 1998
BRITISH SOUTH ATLANTIC – BSAA – operations not started
BSL AIRLINES – suspended operations in 1998
BUSINESSAIR, AG – suspended operations in 1998
BUSINESS AIR, Ltd – now dba/see under BRITISH MIDLAND COMMUTER
BUSINESS FLIGHT DALARNA, AB – suspended operations in 1998
BUSOL Aircompany – suspended operations in 1998

C-AIR – suspended operations 1298
CANADA WEST AIRLINES, Inc. – operations not started
CANADIAN HELI-LOG, Ltd – suspended operations in 1998
CARDINAL AIRLINES, Ltd – suspended operations in 1998
CARIBAIR – suspended operations in 1998
CARIBBEAN AIR – suspended operations in 1998
CARIBINTAIR, SA – suspended operations in 1998
CAROLINA AIR TRANSIT, Inc. – renamed CORPORATE AIR FLEET, Inc. in 1998
CAROLINE PACIFIC AIR – renamed CAROLINE ISLAND AIR during 1998
CASCADE AIR, Inc. – suspended operations in 1998
CASSOVIA AIR SERVICE, a.s. – renamed AIR SERVICE, a.s. in 1998
CAT AIR Foundation – suspended operations in 1998
CB AIR, Inc. – suspended operations in 1998
CEPAL – suspended own operations in 1998
CHALLENGAIR, S.A. – renamed BELGIAN WORLD AIRLINES, S.A., 0798
CHERNOMORSKIE AIRLINES – Cheral – renamed CHERNOMOR-AVIA in 1998
CHERNOMOR-SOYUZ Aviakompania – suspended operations in 1998
CHINA GENERAL AVIATION – CGAC – merged into CHINA EASTERN, 010198
CHS AVIATION, Ltd – renamed EAST AFRICAN SAFARI AIR, Ltd, 0198
CIRCLE AIR – suspended operations in 1998
CIRRUS Luftfahrt, GmbH – now dba/see under CIRRUS AIRLINES
CIVIL AIR Taxi Aéreo, Ltda – suspended operations in 1998
CLARENVILLE AVIATION, Ltd – suspended operations in 1998
CLASSIC AIRWAYS, Ltd – suspended operations 0898
CLOUDEX, Oy – suspended commercial operations 300998
COASTAL AIRWAYS, Pty Ltd – suspended operations in 1998
COASTAL AIRWAYS – suspended operations in 1998
COMAIR, Inc. – dba/see under COMAIR AIRLINES
COMECON AVIATION, Pvt Ltd – no own operations
COMMERCIAL AIR TRANSPORT, Inc. – suspended operations in 1998
CONGO AIR – suspended operations in 1998
CONGO COMMERICAL AIRLINES – dba/see under CCA
COPTRADE AIR TRANSPORT – now operates aircraft below MTOW 1361kg only
CORPORATE CHARTER SERVICE, Inc. – suspended operations in 1998
CORPORATE ONE – suspended operations in 1998
CPPAC – suspended comm. ops
CRASA Taxi Aéreo, Ltda – suspended operations in 1998
CREW CONCEPTS, Inc. – suspended operations in 1998
CYM Taxi Aéreo, Ltda – suspended operations in 1998
CZ AIRLINES, a.s. – operations not started
CZECH GOVERNMENT FLYING SERVICE – ceased operations 311298

DAC AIR, S.A. – suspended operations 0898
DAICOLO, Co. Ltd – suspended own operations in 1998
DANISH AIR TRANSPORT, A/S – dba/see under DAT
DAT Belgian Regional – now see under DAT – Delta Air Transport
D.B. AVIATION, Ltd – now dba/see under D.B. AIR
DEL RIO AVIATION, Inc. – suspended operations in 1998
DIGEX AERO CARGO – Di Gregorio Expresso – suspended ops in 1998
D.M. INTERNATIONAL AIRLINES, Co. Ltd – suspended operations in 1998
DONETSK AVIATION ENTERPRISE – taken over by DONBASS-EASTERN UKR. in 1998
DOWNEAST CHARTER FLIGHTS – suspended own operations in 1998
DROME Z HELICOPTERS, (Pty) Ltd – suspended operations in 1998
DUKE AIR, Pty Ltd – suspended operations in 1998

EAGLE JET CHARTER, Inc. – now dba/see under EAGLE AIR
EARLAIR, Ltd – suspended commercial operations in 1998
EARLTON AIRWAYS, Ltd – suspended commercial operations in 1998
EASTERN CONGO AIRLINES – suspended operations in 1998
EASTERN TRADE WINGS DENMARK, ApS – suspended operating leases in 1998
ECOCARRIER AVIATION, AG – suspended operations 1198
EDMONTON FLYING CLUB – suspended comm.photography&maintenance flt in 1998
EGLE AIR SERVICE GmbH & Co. KG – now see under EAS Egle Air Service
ELAN EXPRESS, Inc. – suspended operations in 1998
ELBEE AIRLINES – suspended operations in 1998
ELISTA AIR ENTERPRISE – suspended operations in 1998

EMBRAFOTO – susp.own flt in 1998
EQUATOR AIRLINES, Ltd – suspended operations in 1998
ERITREAN AIRLINES – now dba/see under RED SEA AIR
ERMOLINO FLYING TEST RESEARCH ENTERPRISE – now see under ELIIP
ERNIR AIRLINES Isafirdi – suspended own operations in 1998
ESAM AIRLINES – no own operations
ESPACE AVIATION SERVICES – suspended operations in 1998
ESTONIAN AVIATION COMPANY – see under ELK AIRWAYS
EURO-FLITE, Oy – taken over by JETFLITE, 280998
EUROPEAN AIR TAXI – suspended operations in 1998
EUROPEAN AIR TRANSPORT, N.V. – now see under EAT
EUROPEAN AIRWAYS, Ltd – suspended operations 0998
EUROPEAN REGIONS AIRLINES – now see under ERA-European Regions
EVEREST AIR, Ltd – suspended operations in 1998
EXECAIR – suspended operations in 1998
EXECUTIVE AIRCRAFT CHARTERS – suspended own operations in 1998
EXPORT AIR CARGO – renamed CIELOS DEL PERU in 1998
EXPRESS AIR, Inc. – now dba/see under SUNRISE AIRLINES
EXPRESS AIRWAYS, Inc. – suspended operations in 1998
EXTREMO SUL Taxi Aéreo, Ltda – suspended operations in 1998

F'AIRLINES, B.V. – taken over/integrated into KLM exel, 251098
FAIRLINES, S.A. – ceased operations 1198
FALCK AIR, A/S – integrated into NORTH FLYING, A/S, 0798
FALCON AIR CHARTER – suspended operations in 1998
FALCON AIR CHARTERS, Ltd – suspended own operations in 1998
FALCON AVIATION, AB – renamed FALCON AIR, AB, 0598
FAN AIRWAYS, Ltd – dba/see under FANAIR
FAR AIRLINES, SpA – suspended operations in 1998
FARNAIR EUROPE – see under MINILINER, Srl.
FARNAIR EUROPE – see under FARNER AIR TRANSPORT HUNGARY, Ltd
FARNAIR EUROPE – see under FARNER AIR TRANSPORT, AG
FASSEY AVIATION, Ltd – suspended operations in 1998
FAST DELIVERY SERVICE, Inc. – renamed DELIVERY SERVICE, Inc. in 1998
FASTWING AIR CHARTER – suspended operations in 1998
FINEMINSTER EUROPE – brokerage company only
FIVE STAR FLYERS, AB – suspended operations in 1998
FLAMENCO AIRWAYS, Inc. – suspended operations in 1998
FLIGHT CENTER – now operates aircraft below MTOW 1361kg only
FLIGHTLINE – suspended charter flights in 1998
FLM Flugschule Lufttaxi Mohrdieck – now dba/see under FLM AVIATION
FLUGFELAG AUSTURLANDS, h.f. – suspended own operations in 1998
FLUGTAK, e.h.f. – now a flying school only
FLYVENDE MUSEUMSFLY – now see under DANISH DAKOTA FRIENDS
FLY WRIGHT, Corp. – taken over by CLASSIC HELICOPTER Corp., 0698
FMD Flugdienst Magdeburg – now operates aircraft below MTOW 1361kg only
FOREST AVIATION (NZ), Ltd – suspended operations in 1998
FORREST AIR CHARTER, Inc. – suspended operations in 1998
FOUR WAY CHARTER – now dba/see SANDPIPER AIR
FRAMEAIR – suspended own operations in 1998
FRANCE DC-3 – renamed FRANCE DAKOTA in 1998
FRI FLY, SpA – suspended own operations in 1998
FROMHAGEN AVIATION, Inc. – suspended operations in 1998

GATEWAY NORTH AVIATION, Inc. – suspended operations in 1998
GATS, SA – renamed GATS Guinea, SA & moved to 3C-section in 1998
GATX-AIRLOG, Co. – now a Freighter conversion company only.
GATX CAPITAL Corp. – op. lease-management transf. to GATX Flightlease in 98
GAUTENG AIR CARGO, CC – suspended own operations in 1998
GENAVIA, Srl. – taken over by EUROJET ITALIA in 1998
GEYSERLAND AIRWAYS, Ltd – ceased operations 310399
GLASGOW AVIATION – suspended operations in 1998
GLENDON AVIATION – suspended operations in 1998
GLORIA AIR SERVICES – suspended operations in 1998
GOLDEN EAGLE AVIATION, Pty Ltd – now dba/see under GOLDEN EAGLE AIRLINES
GOLD EXECUTIVE AVIATION, GmbH – suspended operations in 1998
GOLEEAH AIR – Blackstone Aviation – suspended operations in 1998
GORDA AERO SERVICE, Inc. – suspended operations in 1998
GORIZONT – suspended operations in 1998
GOSNII GA – suspended commercial flights in 1998
GREAT CHINA AIRLINES, Ltd – merged into UNI AIR, 010798
GREAT LAKES CORPORATE AIR, Inc. – suspended operations in 1998
GRENADINES EXPRESS AIRLINES, Ltd – suspended operations in 1998
GTP Gesellschaft – susp. ops in 1998
GUILA-AIR – suspended operations in 1998
GULF AIR CHARTER, Pty Ltd – suspended operations in 1998

HALISA AIR – Les Ailes d'Haiti – suspended operations in 1998
HAN AIR – suspended operations in 1998
HARCO AIR SERVICES – suspended operations in 1998
HAWKAIR – merged into GOLD AIR INTERNATIONAL Ltd in 1998
H-E-H Heins, GmbH Energie-Helikopter – suspended operations in 1998
HELIALBA, S.A. – suspended operations in 1998
HELIARAGON – suspended operations in 1998
HELICOPTERE LA TUQUE, Inc. – renamed HELI-STAR Inc. in 1998
HELICOPTER EMERGENCY MEDICAL SERVICE – now see under VIRGIN HEMS
HELICOPTER-SERVICE HANNOVER – H-S-H – suspended operations in 1998
HELICOPTER SERVICE STAFFELSTEIN, GmbH – suspended operations in 1998
HELICOPTER WILDLIFE MANAGEMENT – suspended operations in 1998
HELIHIRE – suspended operations in 1998
HELILIFT, A/S – merged into AIRLIFT, A/S, 010199
HELIOPOLIS AIRLINE – ceased operations 0698
HELI-OUEST, SA – suspended operations in 1998
HELI-PROMOTION – suspended operations in 1998
HELI SIKA, Ltd – now operates helicopters below MTOW 1361kg only
HELI-TEAM HUNGARY – ceased operations in 1998
HELITOUR, S.L. – suspended operations in 1998
HELI TRANS Bedarfsflugunternehmen, GmbH – suspended operations in 1998
HELI-TRANSPORT, Inc. – see under HELICOPTER TRANSPORT SERVICES
HELIVIFRA – suspended operations in 1998
HELOG, S.A. – suspended operations in 1998
HFS – merged into HELIPORTUGAL, 1298
HILL AVIATION – suspended operations in 1998
HOLLIDAY AIRCRAFT SERVICES – suspended commerical operations in 1998
HUISSON AVIATION – renamed HELICOPTER TRANSPORT SERVICES, 010199
HUNTING CARGO AIRLINES (Ireland) Ltd – renamed AIR CONTRACTORS,290798
HUSTLER TOURS – suspended own operations in 1998

I.A.C. AIRLINES – suspended operations in 1998
IBIS AIR – suspended operations in 1998
IBIS AIR TRANSPORT, Ltd – suspendec own operations in 1998
IBIS AVIATION, Ltd – suspended operations in 1998
IBIS, N.V. – renamed FLYING SUPPORT, N.V. in 1998
I.D.G. TECHNOLOGY AIR – suspended operations 1197/not restarted
IFD – Inselflugdienst – suspended operations in 1998
IKAR Sakhalin Aircompany – suspended operations in 1998
IM-AIR, AB – suspended operations in 1998
IMPULSE-AERO – suspended operations in 1998
INDEPENDENT AIR FREIGHTERS, Pty Ltd – dba/see under IAF AIR FREIGHTERS
INTERAVIAS Havacilik, Ltd Sti – suspended operations in 1998
INTERCREDIT, Corp. – suspended operating leases in 1998
INTER FLIGHT, Ltd – suspended operations in 1998
INTERNATIONAL AVIATION, Pty Ltd – renamed HORIZON AIRLINES, P/L, 101298
INTERNATIONAL JET AVIATION, Inc. – operated/see under CHRYSLER AVIATION
ISLAND AIR, Ltd – suspended operations in 1998
ISLAND AIR CHARTER, Inc. – now dba ISLAND AIR

ITAPOAN Taxi Aéreo, Ltda – suspended operations in 1998
ITT Flight Operations, Inc. – now op. corporate aircr. below MTOW 35t only

JAKA AIR TRANSPORT, Corp. – correct/see under JAKA TRANSPORT, Corp.
JAPAN FLYING SERVICE, Co. Ltd – JFS – suspended operations in 1998
JET FLIGHT, Ltd – suspended own operations in 1998
JETSERV – suspended operations in 1998
JF SUPER AIR SERVICES – now operates aircraft below MTOW 1361kg only
JM Taxi Aéreo, Ltda – now operates aircraft below MTOW 1361kg only

KALININGRAD AIR Enterprise – renamed KALININGRADAVIA in 1998
KALITTA FLYING SERVICE, Inc. – now dba/see under KITTY HAWK CHARTERS
KALLAX FLYG, AB – suspended operations in 1998
KENSINGTON AVIATION, Ltd – suspended operations in 1998
KENTIALINK AUSTRALIA, Pty Ltd – renamed TASMAN AUSTRALIA AIRLINES, 010798
KEY-AVIA – suspended operations in 1998
KHABAROVSK AVIATION ENTERPRISE – renamed DALAVIA in 1998
KHARKOV AVIATION ENTERPRISE – taken over by AIR KHARKOV 0098
KHORTITSA-AIR – suspended operations in 1998
KIEV AIRCRAFT REPAIR PLANT No. 410 – suspended commercial flights in 1998
KIG AIR – suspended operations in 1998
KINGFISHER AVIATION – suspended operations in 1998
KING SOLOMON AIRWAYS – suspended operations in 1998
KIROVOGRAD AVIATION ENTERPRISE – taken over by AIR KIROVOGRAD in 1998
KOLYMAAVIA – ceased operations 1098
KOMAHAM LODGE AIR, Ltd – suspended own operations in 1998
KWATNA AIR SERVICE, Ltd – suspended operations in 1998
KWAZULU NATIONAL AIRWAYS, Corp. Ltd – suspended operations in 1998

LANDSEAAIR – suspended operations in 1998
LANGKAWI HELICOPTER SERVICES, Sdn Bhd – suspended operations in 1998
LA RONGE AVIATION SERVICES, Ltd – dba/see under AIR SASK
LEEDS CENTRAL HELICOPTERS, Ltd – suspended operations in 1998
LEE HELICOPTERS – suspended own operations in 1998
LEIGUFLUG Air Charter – renamed AIR CHARTER ICELAND in 1998
LEISURE INTERNATIONAL AIRWAYS, Ltd – integrated into AIR 2000, 011298
LENNOX AIRWAYS (Kenya), Ltd – suspended operations in 1998
LIGNES AERIENNES CONGOLAISES – now see under LAC
LIMBURG AIR PROMOTION, B.V.B.A. – suspended operations in 1998
LINA CONGO – suspended operations in 1998
LINDBERGH'S AIR SERVICE – suspended commerical operations in 1998
LONE STAR AIRLINES – suspended operations in 1998
LONG ISLAND WINGS – correct/see under ISLAND WINGS
L.O.S., Ltd – suspended operations 311298
LTHF AVIATION E.F. – now operates aircraft below MTOW 1361kg only
LTS LuftTaxiService – suspended operations in 1998
LUFTFAHRERSCHULE HANS LANGENBACH – renamed SFS Siebertz Flight in 1998
LUFTFAHRTUNTERNEHMEN MANFRED THONIUS – now dba/see under FFD Franken Flug
LUPINE AIR CHARTERS, Ltd – suspended operations in 1998
LYNTON JET – operated by Lynton Aviation Ltd

MAA Medical Air Assistance – now see under ANWB Medical Air Assistance
MACROASIA AIR – suspended commercial operations in 1998
MAF Zambia – aircraft transf. to Lesotho
MAGADANAEROGRUZ – suspended operations in 1998
MAHARANI AVIATION – no own operations
MALDINI AIR SERVICES, Ltd – renamed MOMBASA AIR SERVICES, Ltd, 010198
MALMO AVIATION – taken over by BRAATHENS Malmö 010299
MALS Air Company, Ltd – suspended operations in 1998
MANAGER FLUGSERVICE, GmbH – now see under MFG Manager Flugservice
MANOKOTAK AIR – now dba/see under STARFLITE, Inc.
MARIAVIA – suspended operations in 1998
MARIE GALANTE AVIATION – renamed MG-AVIATION in 1998
MARINE AIR SERVICES, Pty Ltd – suspended operations in 1998
MAROOMBA AIR SERVICE – renamed MAROOMBA AIRLINES in 1998
MARTINI AIRFREIGHT SERVICES, Ltd – renamed BENAIR, Ltd, 010199
MATTICE LAKE OUTFITTERS, Ltd – operated by/see under WABAKIMI AIR
MAURIA – suspended operations in 1998
MAURITANIENNE DE TRANSPORT AERIEN – suspended operations in 1998
MAVERICK AIRWAYS, Corp. – suspended operations in 1998
MAVEWA – susp. comm. ops in 1998
MECHTA AVIAKOMPANIA – suspended operations in 1998
MERCHANT EXPRESS AVIATION – suspended operations in 1998
MERCURY AIR – suspended operations in 1998
MERRITT ISLAND AIR SERVICE, Inc. – suspended operations in 1998
METRO JET, Oy – now dba NORDIC AIR AMBULANCE
MFG Milan-Flug, GmbH – integrated into SKYLINE FLIGHTS, GmbH, 010299
MIDGETTS FISHERIES & RESORTS, Ltd & Air Service – suspended ops in 1998
MIKMA, Ltd – renamed TIRAMAVIA in 1998
MILLER AVIATION, Inc. – merged into CORPORATE WINGS, 0898
MILLON AIR, Inc. – ceased operations 0598
MINISTIC AIR, Ltd – now see under KISTIGAN – Ministic Air, Ltd
MINSKAVIA – reintegrated into BELAVIA Belarusian Airlines
MONCTON FLIGHT CENTRE, Ltd – now a flying school only
MORESBY AVIATION, Pty Ltd – suspended own operations in 1998
MOSTAREZ AIR, spol. s r.o. – ceased operations in 1998
MOUNTAIN AIR EXPRESS – taken over by UNITED EXPRESS/Air Wisconsin, 0398
MOUNTAIN AVIATION, Inc. – taken over by HAINES AIRWAYS, Inc. in 1998
MOUNTAIN ROTORS, Inc. – taken over by HAWKINS & POWER AVIATION in 1998
MUKTI AIRWAYS, Pvt. Ltd – operations not started
MULTIAVIONICA, S.L. – renamed SKY SERVICES AVIATION in 1998

NALCHIK AIR ENTERPRISE – renamed ELBRUS-AVIA AIR ENTERPRISE in 1998
N&N CHARTERS – suspended own operations in 1998
NATIONAL AIRLINES (Chile), S.A. – integrated into AVANT AIRLINES, 010199
NATIONAL AIRLINES – suspended operations in 1998
NATIVE AMERICAN AIR SERVICES – see under NATIVE AMERICAN AIR AMBULANCE
NATRON AIR – suspended operations in 1998
NAVCOM AVIATION, Inc. – suspended operations in 1998
NCA EXECUTIVE EXPRESS – suspended commercial operations in 1998
NEFTEYUGANSK AIRLINES – suspended operations in 0399
NEPAL AIRWAYS, Pvt. Ltd. – suspended operations 1998
NEPAL AIRWAYS HELICOPTER SERVICES, Pvt. Ltd. – suspended operations 1998
NEPAL ROYAL V.V.I.P. FLIGHT – correct/see under V.V.I.P. FLIGHT
NEPC AIRLINES – suspended operations in 1998
NEWQUAY AIR, Ltd – suspended operations in 1998
NEW ZEALAND AIR CHARTER – now operates aircraft below MTOW 1361kg only
NICHOLSONS AIR SERVICE, Pty Ltd – suspended operations in 1998
NISTRANSAIR – suspended operations in 1998
NOMAD AVIATION, Ltd – now dba/see under BAY AIR AVIATION
NORDIC FLYING SERVICE – now operates aircraft below MTOW 1361kg only
NORTAVIA – now op. aircraft below MTOW 1361kg only
NORTH COUNTRY HELICOPTERS – suspended operations in 1998
NORTH-EAST AIRLINES, Ltd – suspended operations in 1998
NORTHERN AIRLINK, Ltd – suspended operations in 1998
NORTHERN AIR SERVICE – suspended operations in 1998
NORTHERN AIRWAYS, Inc. – suspended operations in 1998
NORTHERN WINGS AVIATION, Inc. – suspended operations in 1998
NORTHWEST AIRLINK-JET AIRLINK/Mesaba – now see under MESABA AIRLINES
NORTHWEST AIRLINK/Express Airlines I – now see under EXPRESS AIRLINES I
NORTH WIND AVIATION, Inc. – suspended operations in 1998
NORTH WRIGHT AIR, Ltd – renamed NORTH WRIGHT AIRWAYS, Ltd, 0198
NWT Air – merged into FIRST AIR, 240698

ODIN AIR – suspended operations in 1998
OLYMPIA AIR – suspended own operations in 1998

OMEGA AERO TRANSPORTES, SA – suspended operations in 1998
OMEGA – suspended operations in 1998
OURIVIO Taxi Aéreo, Ltda – suspended operations in 1998

PACIFIC AIR AVIATION, Inc. – suspended operations in 1998
PACIFIC AIR CHARTER, Inc. – suspended operations in 1998
PACIFICO SUR Taxi Aéreo – suspended operations in 1998
PACIFIC SOUTHWEST AIRLINES – PSA – suspended operations in 1998
PALMAIR FLIGHTLINE – see under FLIGHTLINE, Ltd
PALM BEACH AEROSPACE – Flight Dept. – suspended own ops in 1998
PAN AM AIR BRIDGE – renamed CHALK'S INTERNATIONAL AIRLINES, 0299
PANJNAD AVIATION, (Private) Ltd – suspended commercial operations in 1998
PARADISE AIRLINES – merged into GULFSTREAM INTERNATIONAL AIRLINES, 0499
PARA PORTER Flugbetriebs-Service – suspended operations in 1998
PARTNAIRS (NL), N.V. – suspended own leasing in 1998
PARTNER AIRLINES – suspended operations in 1998
PAUKN AIR – suspended operations 1098
PAX AIR SERVICES, (Pty) Ltd – suspended operations in 1998
PEACH AIR, Ltd – suspended operations 1198
PEREGRINE AIR SERVICE – suspended operations in 1998
PERMTRANSAVIA-PM – correct/see under PERMSKIE MOTORY Aviakompania
PHILLIP ISLAND AIR SERVICES – suspended operations in 1998
PIKANGIKUM AIR SERVICES, Ltd – suspended operations in 1998
PILOT – suspended operations in 1998
PILOT Aviakompania – suspended operations in 1998
PINE POINT AIR SERVICE – suspended operations in 1998
PINE RIDGE AIR SERVICES – suspended commercial operations in 1998
PINE STATE AIRLINES – now see under AROOSTOOK AVIATION, Inc.
P.L.N. – suspended own operations in 1998
POLISSYAAVIATRANS – suspended operations in 1998
POZEMNE STAVITELSTVO NITRA, a.s. – suspended commercial ops in 1998
PREMIER AIR, Ltd – suspended operations in 1998
PRIEWE AIR SERVICE, Inc. – now dba/see under COOK INLET AIR SERVICE
PRIMAIR Executive Charter, GmbH – suspended operations 0798
PRINCE AIR – suspended operations in 1998
PRINCESS VACATIONS – now see under L.B., Ltd
PROVINCIAL AIR TRANSPORT – suspended operations in 1998

Q.S. HELICOPTERS – now see under HELI SERVICE BELGIUM, N.V.

RATCLIFF AIRWAYS, Ltd – suspended operations in 1998
REAS Regional A.S. – now op. agricultural aircraft below MTOW 5000kg only
REED AVIATION, Ltd – no own operates/see under Emerald Airways
REGION AIR (Caribbean), Ltd – suspended operations in 1998
RICO Taxi Aéreo – renamed RICO Linhas Aéreas, S/A in 1998
RL-Trading, Oy – now operates aircraft below MTOW 1361kg only
ROTTNEST AIRLINES – suspended operations 0498
ROYALE HELICOPTER SERVICE, Inc. – suspended operations in 1998
RUGE AIR Luftfahrt, GmbH & Co. KG – suspended operations in 1998

SA AIRLINK – now dba/see under SOUTH AFRICAN AIRLINK
SACSA – suspended operations in 1998
SAEAGA AIRLINES, Sdn Bhd – suspended operations 0398
SAETA Colombia – susp.ops 1998
SAMANTA, SpA – renamed VULCAN AIR, SpA in 1998
SAMARITAN AIREVAC – renamed AIREVAC SERVICES, Inc., 010198
SANKURU AIR SERVICES – suspended operations in 1998
SAP – Servicios Aéreos Patagonicas – renamed SAPSA in 1998
SAWYER AVIATION, Inc. – suspended commercial operations in 1998
SCANDINAVIAN COMMUTER – now see under SCANDINAVIAN AIRLINES COMMUTER
SCANDINAVIAN SAS – now see under SCANDINAVIAN AIRLINES SAS
SCANJET SWEDEN, AB – suspended operations in 1998
SCAN TRANSPORTES AEREOS, SA – renamed UNIQUE AIR CHARTER, SA in 1998
SCHREINER NORTHSEA HELICOPTERS (UK) – integ. into SCHREINER, Netherlands
SCHWABENFLUG – now a flying school only
SEACOAST AIRLINES, Inc. – suspended operations in 1998
SEAPLANE TAXIS – suspended operations in 1998
SERVICIO AEREO VARGAS ESPANA – dba/see under SAVE
SERVICIOS AERONAUTICOS SIPESA, S.A. – now see under SIPESA
SFACT Opérations aériennes – renamed/see under SEFA
SHERWELL AVIATION, Pty Ltd – now dba/see under TWIN PIONAIR
SIMBA AIR CARGO, Ltd – suspended operations in 1998
SIMBIRSK-AERO – suspended operations in 1998
SINCEREWAYS KENYA, Ltd – suspended operations in 1998
SISAM – ceased ops 280199
SJOEFLYGARNA, AB – suspended operations in 1998
SK AIR, a.s. – suspended operations in 311298
SKYBUS AIRWAYS – now dba/see under KAL AVIATION, S.A.
SKY CHARTER, Inc. – suspended operations in 1998
SKYEJET AVIATION, Inc. – suspended operations in 1998
SKY FREIGHTERS, Ltd – suspended operations in 1998
SKY HARBOR AIR SERVICE, Inc. – suspended operations in 1998
SKYJET (Europe), S.A. – see under SKYJET, Inc. (V2-)
SKYLINE HELICOPTERS – suspended operations in 1998
SKYLINE INTERNATIONAL, Ltd – suspended operations in 1998
SKY RELIEF (Pvt), Ltd – suspended operations in 1998
SKYRIDERS, Inc. – suspended operations in 1998
SKYS UN-LIMITED AIR SERVICES, Ltd – suspended operations in 1998
SKYTEAM AIRLINES – operations not started
SKYTECH AVIATION, Ltd – now op in Antigua as CARIBBEAN HELICOPTERS
SKY TOURS, Ltd – now dba/see under SKYAIR
SKY TREK AIRWAYS – correct/see under SKY-TREK AIRLINES
SKYVEN Cielos de Venzuela, S.A. – operations not started
SOLOY HELICOPTERS, Inc. – suspended operations in 1998
SOUTHERN AIR TRANSPORT, Inc. – suspended operations 250998
SOUTHERN LAKES HELI.(Queenstown) Ltd – taken over by GLACIER HELICOPTERS
SOUTH EXPRESS – suspended operations in 1998
SOUTHFLIGHT AVIATION, Ltd – taken over by AIR ADVENTURES, 0798
SOUTH PACIFIC AIR, Pty Ltd – suspended own operations in 1998
SOUTH PACIFIC DC-3 AUSTRALIA – suspended own operations in 1998
SOUTH-WEST-AVIA – suspended operations in 1998
SOUTHWIND AIRLINES, Inc. – suspended operations in 1998
SPAERO JSP – suspended operations in 1998
SPAK Aviakompania – suspended operations in 1998
SPANAIR Maharashtra – suspended operations in 1998
SPECTRUM AVIATION Corporation – suspended operations in 1998
SPURWING AIR – suspended own operations in 1998
SS AVIATION, Inc. – renamed TC AVIATION, Inc., 010698
STAM – suspended operations in 1998
STARWELT TRANS LLOYD CARGO, Ltd – suspended operations in 1998

STATNA LETECKA INSPEKCIA – renamed LETECKY URAD SLOVENSKEJ in 1998
STRELETS – suspended operations in 1998
STREZHEVOI AIRLINES – see under STREZHAVIA
SUD OUEST AVIATION – renamed AQUITANIA AIRLINES & susp. operatins in 1998
SUDURFLUG, h.f. – now operates aircraft below MTOW 1361kg only
SULUIT AIR, A/S – suspended operations in 1998
SYNOT W, spol. s r.o. – suspended own operations in 1998

TACEZUL – TAXI AEREO CEU AZUL, Ltda – suspended operations in 1998
TACOL Colombia – suspended ops 1998
TAC – Transport Aérien Congo – renamed AIR KASAI in 1998
TAES – now op aircraft below MTOW 1361kg only
TAIPEI AIRLINES, Co. Ltd. – ceased operations 1298
TAIWAN AIRWAYS, Corp. – TAC – merged into UNI AIR, 010798
TAKE OFF AIR LIFT, GmbH – suspended operations in 1998
TAL Thuringia Airlines, GmbH – renamed TEMPELHOF EXPRESS, GmbH, 011198
TAMAIR, Pty Ltd – suspended operations 140898
T & G Aviation, Inc. – renamed INTERNATIONAL AIR RESPONSE, Inc., 0598
TASHKENT AIRCRAFT PRODUCTION CORPORATION – renamed TAPO-AVIA in 1999
TAWAKAL AIRLINES, Ltd – suspended operations in 1998
TAXAVIA – taken over by BUSINESS AVIATION OF CONGO in 1998
TAXI AEREO CIOATO, Ltda – suspended operations in 1998
TAXI AEREO GOIAS, Ltda – suspended operations in 1998
TAYFUNAIR – suspended own operations 100598
TEA SWITZERLAND – renamed EASYJET SWITZERLAND in 1998
THERON AIRWAYS, (Pty) Ltd – suspended operations in 1998
TIE AVIATION, Inc. – now dba/see under TRANS INTERNATIONAL EXPRESS
TIGER AIR – suspended operations in 1998
TIRAM AIR, Sdn Bhd – suspended operations in 1998
TOPAIR TTT, Ltd – suspended operations in 1998
TRANSAGO BORISPOL – renamed PRESTIGEAVIA in 1998
TRANSAIR, Ltd – suspended commerical operations in 1998
TRANSAIR CARGO – suspended operations in 1998
TRANS-ASIA – now see under TAA – Trans Asian Airlines
TRANS COTE, Inc. – suspended operations in 1998
TRANS HELICO CARAIBES – suspended operations in 1998
TRANSPERU – suspended ops in 1998
TRANSPORT AIR – renamed PATROUILLE AERIENNE DU QUEBEC, Inc., 010198
TRANSPORTES AEREOS BOLIVIANOS – suspended commerical ops in 1998
TRANS SERVICE AIRLIFT – suspended operations in 1998
TRAVELAIR Entreprises – suspended operations in 1998
TRITON ENERGY – suspended own operations in 1998
TUTCHONE AIR – now operates aircraft below MTOW 1361kg only
TWIN AVIATION, Inc. – suspended operations in 1998

UGLAND AIR, A/S – suspended operations in 1998
UIRAPURU Taxi Aéreo, Ltda – suspended operations in 1998
ULAN UDE AVIATION PLANT – now dba/see under BARGUZIN Aviakompania
ULTIMATE JET – suspended own operations in 1998
UNA Southern Independent Air Company – suspended operations in 1998
UNITED EXPRESS/Air Wisconsin – now see under AIR WISCONSIN AIRLINES
UNITED EXPRESS/Atlantic Coast Airlines – now see under ATLANTIC COAST
UNITED EXPRESS/Great Lakes Airlines – now see under GREAT LAKES AIRLINES
UNITED EXPRESS/Mesa Airlines – suspended operations 0598
UNITED EXPRESS/UFS – now see under UFS
UNITED EXPRESS/WestAir – suspended operations 0598
UNIVERSAL AVIA – suspended operations in 1998
UP AIR – renamed SGS AIRLINES in 1998
US AIRWAYS EXPRESS/Air Midwest – now see under AIR MIDWEST, Inc.
US AIRWAYS EXPRESS/ALLEGHENY AIRLINES – now see under ALLEGHENY AIRLINES
US AIRWAYS EXPRESS/CCAir – now see under CCAIR
US AIRWAYS EXPRESS/Chautauqua Airlines – now see under CHAUTAUQUA AIRL.
US AIRWAYS EXPRESS/Commutair – now see under COMMUTAIR
US AIRWAYS EXPRESS/Mesa Airlines – now see under MESA AIRLINES, Inc.
US AIRWAYS EXPRESS/Piedmont Airlines – now see under PIEDMONT AIRLINES
US AIRWAYS EXPRESS/PSA Airlines – now see under PSA AIRLINES
USL CAPITAL – suspended operating leases in 1998

VALLEY AVIATION, Inc. – suspended operations in 1998
VERKHNYAYA SALDA METALWORKS – suspended own flights in 1998
VIAMA – suspended operations in 1998
VIANA Colombia – suspended ops in 1998
VIARCO Colombia – suspended ops in 1998
VIP AIR i Lappland, AB – suspended operations in 1998
VIRGIN EXPRESS FRANCE, SA – suspended operations 0399
VIRGIN HELICOPTERS, Ltd – renamed SKYHOPPER, Ltd, 010199
VITAIR, Joint-Stock Company – suspended operations in 1998
VITORIA REGIA Taxi Aéreo, Ltda – suspended operations in 1998
VIVA AIR – ceased ops 0399
V. KELNER AIRWAYS, Ltd – suspended operations in 1998
VLIEGWERK HOLLAND, B.V. – now operates aircraft below MTOW 1361kg only
VOAR AIRLINES, Lda – suspended operations in 1998
VOLGA AIRLINES – renamed VOLGA AVIAEXPRESS, Joint-Stock Company in 1998

WALTAIR SERVICES – suspended operations in 1998
WANE AVIATION, Ltd – suspended operations in 1998
WAYCO AVIATION, Ltd – suspended operations in 1998
WEST COAST HELICOPTERS, Inc. – integrated into HELINET AVIATION, 0198
WESTERN EXPRESS AIR LINES, Inc. – dba/see under WESTEX AIRLINES
WESTERN KENYA AIR CHARTER, Co. Ltd – now dba/see under WESTERN AIRWAYS
WESTERN PACIFIC AIRLINE – suspended operations in 1998
WEST HELICOPTERS – suspended operations in 1998
WESTMINSTER AVIATION – suspended operations in 1998
WHITE AIR, Ltd – suspended operations in 1998
WHITE ISLAND AIRWAYS, Ltd – suspended operations in 1998
WILDERNESS AIRLINE (1975), Ltd – integrated into PACIFIC COASTAL, 010199
WILLIAMS AERO SERVICES – suspended operations in 1998
WING SAFARIS, Ltd – suspended operations in 1998
WINGS OF THE LAKELAND, Inc. – suspended operations in 1998
WINGZ NORTH AVIATION (Qld), Pty Ltd – taken over by LIP-AIR, 1298
WLD Welldone Flug, GmbH – suspended operations in 1998

YENISEISKY MERIDIAN – suspended operations 0499
YK AIR – suspended operations in 1998
YPFB Transportes Aéreos – renamed SAPSA in 1998

ZAMBIA GOVERNMENT COMMUNICATIONS FLIGHT – suspended own operations 1998
ZAMBIAN EXPRESS – suspended operations 050898
ZAPOROZHYE AVIATION ENTERPRISE – taken over by CONSTANTA Aviak. in 1998
ZULIANA DE AVIACION, C.A. – suspended operations in 1997/not restarted

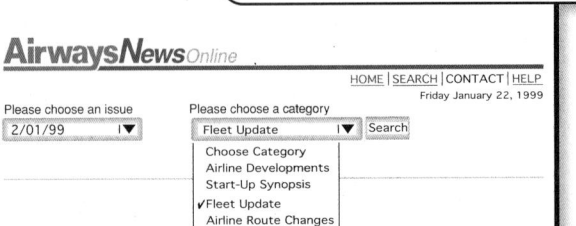
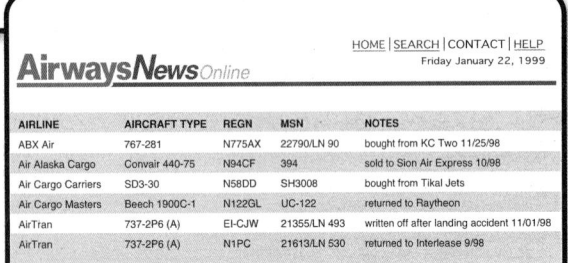

Decoding of the IATA-designators (two-character airline designator)

The designator is used to identify an airline for all commercial purposes. The two-character airline designator is assigned by IATA – International Air Transport Association in accordance with the provisions of Resolution 762. The two-character airline designators listed hereunder are for use in reservations, timetables, tickets, tariffs, air waybills, schedule publications and in airline interline telecommunications, as well as for other airline industry applications. IATA assigns three types of two-character airline designators: unique, numeric/alpha and controlled duplicate. Definition of a controlled duplicate designator is when two carriers have the same designator but operate different types of services.

In the **jp airline-fleets** international **99/2000** you will find the designator after the name of the airline, where applicable.

IATA		ICAO	Page
AA	= AMERICAN AIRLINES	AAL	263
AB	= AIR-BERLIN Luftverkehrs	BER	101
AB	= SUPERIOR AVIATION	HKA	441
AC	= AIR CANADA	ACA	28
AD	= AVIALEASING Aviation Company	TWN	607
AF	= AIR FRANCE	AFR	145
AG	= AIR CONTRACTORS (Ireland)	ABR	131
AG	= PROVINCIAL AIRLINES – PAL		73
AH	= AIR ALGERIE, SPA	DAH	699
AI	= AIR-INDIA	AIC	645
AJ	= AIR BELGIUM	ABB	483
AK	= AIR ASIA	AXM	704
AL	= SKYWAY AIRLINES	SYX	432
AL	= TRANS AVIA EXPORT Cargo Airlines	TXC	140
AM	= AEROMEXICO	AMX	653
AN	= ANSETT AIR FREIGHT	AAA	622
AN	= ANSETT AUSTRALIA	AAA	622
AO	= AVIACO – Aviacion y Comercio, S.A.	AYC	123
AP	= AIR ONE, SpA	ADH	209
AQ	= ALOHA AIRLINES	AAH	262
AR	= AEROLINEAS ARGENTINAS, SA	ARG	235
AS	= ALASKA AIRLINES	ASA	259
AT	= ROYAL AIR MAROC	RAM	90
AU	= AUSTRAL Lineas Aéreas	AUT	236
AV	= AVIANCA Colombia	AVA	196
AW	= DAS – P.T. Dirgantara Air Services	DIR	496
AW	= SCHREINER AIRWAYS, B.V.	SCH	494
AX	= AIR AURORA	AAI	247
AX	= BINTER MEDITERRANEO, S.A.	BIM	124
AY	= FINNAIR, Oyj	FIN	477
AZ	= ALITALIA – Linee Aeree Italiane, SpA	AZA	210
A4	= SOUTHERN WINDS, S.A.	SWD	238
A7	= ASTANAIR	STR	610
A8	= ARPA – Aerolineas Paraguayas	PAY	676
BA	= BRITISH AIRWAYS, Plc	BAW	165
BB	= BALAIR/CTA Leisure	BBB	185
BB	= SEABORNE AVIATION		429
BC	= SKYMARK AIRLINES, Co.	SKY	228
BD	= BRITISH MIDLAND	BMA	168
BF	= AERO SERVICE	RSR	604
BG	= BIMAN BANGLADESH AIRLINES	BBC	595
BH	= EASYJET SWITZERLAND	EZS	186
BH	= TRANSTATE AIRLINES		641
BI	= ROYAL BRUNEI AIRLINES	RBA	650
BJ	= NOUVELAIR TUNISIE	LBT	605
BJ	= SANTA BARBARA AIRLINES, C.A.	BBR	666
BL	= PACIFIC AIRLINES, Co	PIC	643
BM	= AIR SICILIA, SpA	SIC	209
BN	= BRITANNIA AIRWAYS	DBY	102
BO	= BOURAQ INDONESIA AIRLINES	BOU	496
BP	= AIR BOTSWANA	BOT	8
BQ	= AEROMAR AIRLINES	ROM	193
BR	= EVA AIR	EVA	23
BS	= BRITISH INTERNATIONAL	BIH	168
BT	= AIR BALTIC SIA	BTI	659
BU	= BRAATHENS Malmö Aviation, AB	SCW	582
BU	= BRAATHENS, ASA	BRA	231
BV	= SUN AIR	SSN	682
BW	= BWIA International Airways	BWA	711
BX	= COAST AIR, K/S	CST	231
BY	= BRITANNIA AIRWAYS	BAL	165
BZ	= KEYSTONE AIR SERVICE	KEE	60
B2	= BELAVIA Belarusian Airlines	BRU	139
B3	= BELLVIEW AIRLINES	BLV	691
B4	= BANKAIR	BKA	285
B4	= BHOJA AIRLINES	BHO	7
B8	= ITALAIR, SpA	DRG	216
CA	= AIR CHINA International	CCA	12
CB	= KITTY HAWK CHARTERS	KFS	388
CB	= KITTY HAWK INTERNATIONAL	CKS	389
CB	= SUCKLING AIRWAYS	SAY	180
CC	= AIR ATLANTA ICELAND	ABD	601
CC	= MACAIR AIRLINES		632
CD	= ALLIANCE AIR	LLR	646
CE	= NATIONWIDE AIRLINES	NTW	679
CF	= FAUCETT PERU	CFP	470
CG	= MBA		517
CH	= BEMIDJI AIRLINES	BMJ	287
CI	= CHINA AIRLINES	CAL	22
CJ	= CHINA NORTHERN AIRLINES	CBF	15
CL	= LUFTHANSA CityLine	CLH	114
CM	= COPA Panama	CMP	203
CN	= ISLANDS NATIONAIR		517
CO	= CONTINENTAL AIRLINES	COA	302
CO	= CONTINENTAL EXPRESS	BTA	306
CP	= CANADIAN – CANADIEN	CDN	41
CQ	= CONSTELLATION INTERNATIONAL	CIN	484
CQ	= SUNSHINE EXPRESS		640
CS	= CONTINENTAL MICRONESIA	CMI	308
CT	= AIR SOFIA	SFB	241
CU	= CUBANA de Aviacion, S.A.	CUB	96
CV	= AIR CHATHAMS	CVA	668
CV	= CARGOLUX Airlines International, SA	CLX	239
CW	= AIR MARSHALL ISLANDS – AMI	MRS	650
CX	= CATHAY PACIFIC	CPA	21
CY	= CYPRUS AIRWAYS	CYP	689
CZ	= CHINA SOUTHERN AIRLINES, Co.	CSN	16
C2	= AIR CARIBBEAN	CBB	711
C3	= ICAR AIRLINES – Independent Carrier	IPR	616
C4	= AIRLINES OF CARRIACOU	COU	230
C4	= ZIMEX AVIATION	IMX	191
C7	= EXECUTIVE AIR LINK		50
C7	= SPECIAL CARGO AIRLINES	SCI	564
C8	= CHICAGO EXPRESS AIRLINES	WDY	297
C9	= CIRRUS AIRLINES, Luftfahrt GmbH	RUS	103
C9	= CLA AIR TRANSPORT	CXX	580
DC	= GOLDEN AIR	GAO	583
DE	= CONDOR	CFG	103
DF	= AVIOSARDA AIRLINES	ADZ	212
DG	= CUSTOM AIR TRANSPORT	CTT	312
DG	= ISLAND AIRLINES		630
DH	= ATLANTIC COAST AIRLINES	BLR	281
DI	= DEUTSCHE BA Luftfahrt	BAG	104
DK	= EASTLAND AIR – Moore's Air Charter		626
DK	= PREMIAIR, A/S	VKG	490
DL	= DELTA AIR LINES	DAL	312
DM	= MAERSK AIR, A/S	DAN	489

IATA		ICAO	Page
DO	= AIR VALLEE, SpA	RVL	209
DP	= AIR 2000	AMM	162
DQ	= COASTAL AIR TRANSPORT	CXT	299
DR	= AIR LINK		621
DS	= AIR SENEGAL	DSB	697
DS	= DHL Aero Expreso, S.A.	DAE	203
DT	= TAAG Angola Airlines	DTA	121
DU	= HEMUS AIR – Bulgarian Aviation Company	HMS	241
DV	= DEUTSCHE RETTUNGSFLUGWACHT	AMB	104
DX	= DAT – Danish Air Transport, K/S	DTR	488
DY	= AIR DJIBOUTI – Red Sea Airlines	DJU	230
DZ	= TRANSCARAIBES AIR INTERNATIONAL	NOE	160
D3	= DAALLO AIRLINES	DAO	230
D4	= ALIDAUNIA, Srl.	LID	210
D6	= INTER AIR	ILN	678
D7	= DINAR Lineas Aéreas, S.A.	RDN	236
D9	= DONAVIA	DNV	535
DB	= BRIT AIR	BZH	150
EA	= ERA – European Regions Airlines, S.A.	EUA	124
EB	= EMERY WORLDWIDE Airlines	EWW	322
ED	= CCAIR	CDL	294
EF	= FAR EASTERN AIR TRANSPORT – FAT	FEA	23
EG	= JAPAN ASIA AIRWAYS, Co. – JAA	JAA	225
EH	= SAETA Air Ecuador	SET	192
EI	= AER LINGUS, Plc	EIN	131
EJ	= NEW ENGLAND AIRLINES	NEA	404
EK	= EMIRATES	UAE	10
EL	= AIR NIPPON, Co. – ANK Air Nippon, K.K.	ANK	219
EM	= EMPIRE AIRLINES	CFS	322
EM	= WESTERN AIRLINES		642
EN	= AIR DOLOMITI	DLA	209
EO	= CAL – Congo Airlines	ALX	708
EO	= EXPRESS ONE International	LHN	330
EQ	= TAME – T. A. Mercantiles Ecuator	TAE	192
ER	= DHL AIRWAYS	DHL	319
ES	= DHL AVIATION	DHX	12
ES	= TRANS AM AIRLINES		471
ET	= ETHIOPIAN AIRLINES Enterprise	ETH	139
EU	= ECUATORIANA de Aviacion, S.A.	EEA	192
EV	= ASA – Atlantic Southeast Airlines	ASE	279
EW	= EUROWINGS	EWG	106
EX	= AIR SANTO DOMINGO	SDO	193
EY	= MAYAN WORLD AIRLINES	MYN	602
EZ	= EVERGREEN INTERNATIONAL AIRLINES	EIA	325
EZ	= SUN-AIR of Scandinavia, A/S	SUS	491
E3	= DOMODEDOVO AIRLINES	DMO	535
E4	= AERO ASIA International	RSO	7
E5	= SAMARA AIRLINES	BRZ	560
E8	= ALPI EAGLES, SpA	ELG	212
E9	= AJT AIR INTERNATIONAL	TRJ	523
FA	= SAFAIR	SFR	680
FB	= FINE AIR	FBF	337
FB	= GUARD AIR, A/S	JAP	232
FC	= FALCON EXPRESS CARGO AIRLINES		11
FC	= TEMPELHOF EXPRESS – TEX	SBY	118
FD	= AIR FLORIDA Express		251
FD	= CITYFLYER EXPRESS	CFE	171
FE	= EAGLE CANYON AIRLINES	TLO	320
FF	= TOWER AIR	TOW	444
FG	= ARIANA AFGHAN AIRLINES	AFG	658
FH	= FUTURA International Airways	FUA	125
FI	= ICELANDAIR	ICE	601
FJ	= AIR PACIFIC	FJI	120
FL	= AIRTRAN AIRWAYS	TRS	257
FM	= SHANGHAI AIRLINES	CSH	19
FN	= REGIONAL AIR LINES	RGL	90
FO	= EXPEDITION AIRWAYS (Pvt)	XPD	667
FP	= PAR-AVION		635
FP	= TAG AVIATION, S.A.	FPG	191
FQ	= AIR ARUBA, N.V.	ARU	518
FR	= RYANAIR	RYR	132
FS	= MAF Australia		633
FS	= STAF	STU	238
FU	= AIR LITTORAL	LIT	148
FW	= CANARIAS REGIONAL AIR, S.A.	CNM	124
FX	= FEDEX – Federal Express Corporation	FDX	331
FZ	= AIR FACILITIES		620
F2	= FALCON AIR EXPRESS	FAO	330
F3	= FLYING ENTERPRISE, AB	FLY	583
F4	= EURECA, Srl. – European Regional Carrier	URE	214
F5	= ARCHANA AIRWAYS	ACY	646
F6	= CNAC-ZHEJIANG AIRLINES	CAG	18
F7	= VOLARE AVIATION ENTERPRISE	VRE	618
F8	= AIR MONTREAL	AMO	31
F9	= FRONTIER AIRLINES	FFT	340
GA	= GARUDA INDONESIA	GIA	497
GB	= AIRBORNE EXPRESS	ABX	247
GB	= AIR-GLACIERS, SA	AGV	184
GC	= CENTRAFRICAIN AIRLINES	CET	604
GD	= TAESA – Transportes Aéreos Ejecutivos	TEJ	657
GF	= GULF AIR Company, GSC	GFA	9
GG	= AIR HOLLAND	AHR	491
GH	= GHANA AIRWAYS	GHA	702
GJ	= EUROFLY, SpA	EEZ	215
GJ	= MEXICARGO	MXC	656
GK	= GO ONE AIR		175
GL	= GROENLANDSFLY, A/S	GRL	489
GL	= MIAMI AIR	BSK	398
GM	= AIR SLOVAKIA BWJ	SVK	482
GN	= AIR GABON	AGN	605
GP	= GESTAIR Executive Jet, S.A.	GES	125
GQ	= BIG SKY AIRLINES	BSY	288
GR	= AURIGNY AIR SERVICES	AUR	163
GR	= GEMINI AIR CARGO, Llc	GCO	341
GS	= AIRFOYLE	UPA	161
GS	= GRANT AVIATION		343
GT	= GB AIRWAYS	GBL	174
GU	= AVIATECA GUATEMALA	GUG	602
GV	= RIAIR – Riga Airlines	RIG	660
GW	= GOLDEN WEST AIRLINES		343
GW	= KUBAN AIRLINES	KIL	544
GX	= AIR ONTARIO	ONT	32
GX	= PACIFICAIR		581
GY	= GUYANA AIRWAYS	GYA	700
GZ	= AIR RAROTONGA		669
G3	= EMERALD AIRWAYS	JEM	173
G6	= VOLGA AVIAEXPRESS	VLA	575

IATA		ICAO	Page
G7	= GANDALF AIRLINES		215
G8	= GUJARAT AIRWAYS	GUJ	646
HA	= HAWAIIAN AIR	HAL	346
HB	= HARBOR AIRLINES	HAR	346
HC	= NASKE AIR	HCN	116
HD	= HOKKAIDO INTERNATIONAL	ADO	221
HE	= LGW Luftfahrtgesellschaft Walter, mbH	LGW	111
HF	= HAPAG-LLOYD Flug	HLF	109
HG	= FIKA SALAAMA AIRLINES	HGK	694
HH	= ISLANDSFLUG, h.f.	ICB	602
HI	= PAPILLON GRAND CANYON HELICOPTERS		413
HJ	= ASIAN EXPRESS AIRLINES	AXF	623
HJ	= SWEDEWAYS AIR LINES, AB	SWE	588
HK	= FOUR STAR AVIATION	FSC	340
HK	= YANGON AIRWAYS		658
HM	= AIR SEYCHELLES	SEY	596
HP	= AMERICA WEST AIRLINES	AWE	274
HQ	= BUSINESS EXPRESS AIRLINES – BEX	GAA	291
HR	= HAHN AIR BUSINESSLINE	HHN	108
HS	= HIGHLAND AIR, AB	HIL	584
HV	= TRANSAVIA AIRLINES, C.V.	TRA	495
HW	= NORTH WRIGHT AIRWAYS	NWL	67
HY	= UZBEKISTAN AIRWAYS	UZB	608
HZ	= SAT Airlines	SHU	561
H2	= CITY BIRD, S.A.	CTB	484
H3	= HARBOUR AIR SEAPLANES		54
H4	= HAINAN AIRLINES, Co.	CHH	18
H5	= MAVIAL – Magadanskie avialinii	MVL	547
H6	= CHELYABINSK AIR ENTERPRISE	CHB	532
H6	= HAGELAND AVIATION SERVICES		345
H7	= ALFA Hava Yollari, A.S.	LFA	596
H8	= DALAVIA	KHB	534
H9	= HELISUL Linhas Aéreas, S.A.	SUL	505
IA	= IRAQI AIRWAYS	IAW	659
IB	= IBERIA Lineas Aéreas de Espana, S.A.	IBE	126
IC	= INDIAN AIRLINES	IAC	646
ID	= AIR NORMANDIE	RNO	148
IE	= SOLOMONS – Solomon Airlines	SOL	208
IG	= MERIDIANA, SpA	ISS	216
IH	= FALCON AIR, AB	FCN	583
IJ	= AIR LIBERTE	LIB	147
IK	= IMAIR	ITX	685
IL	= ISTANBUL AIRLINES	IST	598
IM	= INTENSIVE AIR	XRA	678
IN	= MAT-MACEDONIAN AIRLINES	MAK	682
IQ	= AUGSBURG AIRWAYS	AUB	102
IR	= IRAN AIR	IRA	135
IS	= ISLAND AIRLINES	ISA	383
IU	= IBIS AIRLINES		630
IV	= FUJIAN AIRLINES	CFJ	18
IW	= AOM French Airlines	AOM	150
IX	= FLANDRE AIR	FRS	153
IY	= YEMENIA – Yemen Airways	IYE	698
IZ	= ARKIA Israeli Airlines	AIZ	686
JA	= AIR BOSNA	BON	607
JB	= HELIJET AIRWAYS	JBA	55
JC	= JAL Express, Co.	JEX	222
JD	= JAPAN AIR SYSTEM, Co. – JAS	JAS	224
JE	= MANX AIRLINES	MNX	178
JF	= LAB Flying Service	LAB	389
JG	= AIR GREECE – Aerodromisis, S.A.	AGJ	593
JH	= HARLEQUIN AIR	HLQ	221
JH	= NORDESTE Linhas Aéreas Regionais, SA	NES	507
JI	= MIDWAY AIRLINES	MDW	399
JJ	= TAM Express	BLC	511
JK	= SPANAIR, S.A.	JKK	129
JL	= JAPAN AIRLINES, Co. – JAL	JAL	222
JM	= AIR JAMAICA	AJM	697
JP	= ADRIA AIRWAYS Slovenija	ADR	595
JQ	= AIR JAMAICA EXPRESS	JMX	698
JR	= AEROCALIFORNIA, SA	SER	651
JS	= AIR KORYO	KOR	491
JU	= JAT Jugoslovenski Aerotransport	JAT	663
JV	= BEARSKIN AIRLINES	BLS	38
JW	= ARROW AIR	APW	279
JX	= NICE HELICOPTERES		157
JX	= SUN JET INTERNATIONAL AIRLINES	SJI	440
JY	= JERSEY EUROPEAN AIRWAYS – JEA	JEA	176
JZ	= JAPAN AIR CHARTER, Co. – JAZ	JAZ	222
JZ	= SKYWAYS, AB	SKX	588
J2	= AZERBAIJAN AIRLINES/AZAL Avia	AHY	684
J3	= NORTHWESTERN AIR	PLR	67
J4	= BUFFALO AIRWAYS	BFL	40
J6	= AVCOM – Aviation Commercial	AOC	526
J6	= LARRY'S FLYING SERVICE		390
J8	= BERJAYA AIR	BVT	704
KA	= DRAGONAIR Hong Kong	HDA	22
KD	= KENDELL AIRLINES (Australia)	KDA	631
KE	= KOREAN AIR	KAL	201
KF	= AIR BOTNIA	KFB	476
KG	= CALEDONIAN AIRWAYS	CKT	170
KG	= LAI – Linea Aérea I.A.A.C.A.		665
KI	= AIR ATLANTIQUE	APB	144
KI	= CANADIAN REGIONAL AIRLINES (1998)	CDR	43
KJ	= BRITISH MEDITERRANEAN AIRWAYS	LAJ	168
KK	= TAM Brasil	TAM	510
KL	= KLM – Royal Dutch Airlines	KLM	492
KM	= AIR MALTA, Plc	AMC	702
KN	= MAROOMBA AIRLINES		633
KN	= WINNPORT AIR CARGO	WNT	87
KO	= ALASKA CENTRAL EXPRESS	AER	260
KP	= KIWI INTERNATIONAL AIR LINES	KIA	389
KQ	= KENYA AIRWAYS	KQA	696
KR	= KITTY HAWK AIR CARGO	KHA	388
KR	= MDA AIRLINES	MDD	547
KS	= PENAIR	PEN	414
KT	= KAMPUCHEA AIRLINES	KMP	658
KU	= KUWAIT AIRWAYS	KAC	703
KV	= KMV – Kavkazskie Mineralnye Vody	MVD	540
KX	= CAYMAN AIRWAYS	CAY	644
KY	= AIR SAO TOME & PRINCIPE	EQL	596
KZ	= LASER	LER	665
KZ	= NIPPON CARGO AIRLINES, Co. – NCA	NCA	227
K2	= KYRGHYZSTAN AIRLINES	KGA	140
K3	= TAQUAN AIR SERVICE	TQN	442
K5	= WINGS OF ALASKA	WAK	467

IATA		ICAO	Page
W4	= AERO SERVICES EXECUTIVE, Sarl	BES	144
W4	= M & N AVIATION		393
W7	= SAYAKHAT	SAH	611
W9	= EASTWIND AIRLINES – The Bee Line	BBE	321
XC	= AIR CARIBBEAN	CLT	495
XC	= KD AIR Corporation	KDC	59
XE	= SOUTHCENTRAL AIR	SCA	434
XF	= VLADIVOSTOK AIR	VLK	574
XG	= NORTH AMERICAN AIRLINES	NAO	405
XJ	= MESABA AIRLINES	MES	397
XK	= COMPAGNIE CORSE MEDITERRANEE	CCM	151
XL	= COUNTRY CONNECTION AIRLINES	NSW	625
XM	= ALITALIA EXPRESS, SpA	SMX	211
XM	= AUSTRALIAN AIR EXPRESS	XME	623
XO	= CHINA XINJIANG AIRLINES	CXJ	17
XO	= LTE International Airways, S.A.	LTE	128
XP	= CASINO EXPRESS	CXP	294
XQ	= SUNEXPRESS	SXS	599
XV	= AIR EXPRESS i Norrköping, AB	GOT	582
X3	= BAIKAL AIRLINES	BKL	528
X5	= CRONUS AIRLINES	CUS	594
X7	= CHITAAVIA	CHF	533
X9	= KHORS Aircompany	KHO	616
X9	= OMNI AIR INTERNATIONAL – OAI	OAE	411
YB	= SOUTH AFRICAN EXPRESS Airways	EXY	681
YC	= FLIGHT WEST AIRLINES	FWQ	627
YD	= GOMELAVIA	GOM	139
YI	= AIR SUNSHINE	RSI	256
YJ	= NATIONAL AIRLINES – NAL		679
YK	= HORIZON AIRLINES		629
YL	= EXECUTIVE AIRLINES	ORA	326
YL	= YAMAL AIR TRANSPORT COMPANY		577
YN	= AIR CREEBEC	CRQ	29
YO	= HELI AIR MONACO	MCM	682
YP	= AERO LLOYD	AEF	100
YQ	= HELIKOPTERSERVICE Euro Air, AB	SCO	584
YR	= SCENIC AIRLINES	YRR	429
YS	= PROTEUS AIRLINES	PRB	157
YT	= SKYWEST AIRLINES		639
YU	= DOMINAIR	ADM	256
YV	= MESA AIRLINES	ASH	396
YW	= AIR NOSTRUM	ANS	123
YX	= MIDWEST EXPRESS AIRLINES	MEP	400
Y2	= SA ALLIANCE	AFJ	694
Y4	= EAGLE AVIATION	EQA	695
Y6	= EUROPE ELITE	VIP	173
Y8	= PASSAREDO Transportes Aéreos	PTB	508
ZA	= ACCESSAIR	CYD	243
ZB	= MONARCH AIRLINES	MON	178
ZC	= ROYAL SWAZI NATIONAL AIRWAYS	RSN	683
ZE	= COSMOS AIR Luftfahrtunternehmen	AZE	104
ZF	= AIRBORNE OF SWEDEN, AB	MIW	582
ZJ	= TEDDY AIR, A/S	TED	234
ZK	= GREAT LAKES AIRLINES	GLA	343
ZL	= AFFRETAIR, (Private)	AFM	666
ZL	= HAZELTON AIRLINES	HZL	628
ZN	= EAGLE AIRLINES Luftverkehrs	EAV	473
ZN	= AIR ST. THOMAS	STT	256
ZQ	= ANSETT NEW ZEALAND	AAA	670
ZR	= MUK AIR, A/S	MUK	490
ZS	= AZZURRAAIR, SpA	AZI	212
ZT	= VORONEZHAVIA	VRN	576
ZV	= AIR MIDWEST	AMW	254
ZW	= AIR WISCONSIN AIRLINES	AWI	258
ZX	= AIRBC	ABL	27
ZY	= ADA AIR Albania	ADE	667
Z3	= PRO MECH AIR		420
Z5	= GMG AIRLINES		595
Z6	= DNIPROAVIA	UDN	615
Z7	= ZIMBABWE EXPRESS AIRLINES	EZX	667
Z8	= DHL de Guatemala, SA	JOS	602
Z8	= PULKOVO AVIATION ENTERPRISE	PLK	555
Z9	= AERO ZAMBIA	RZL	702

IATA		ICAO	Page
2B	= ATA-AEROCONDOR – Transportes Aéreos	ARD	93
2D	= FEDERICO II AIRWAYS, SpA	FDE	215
2E	= SKY CABS	SCB	686
2F	= FRONTIER FLYING SERVICE	FTA	340
2G	= DEBONAIR AIRWAYS	DEB	172
2J	= AIR BURKINA	VBW	658
2M	= MOLDAVIAN AIRLINES	MDV	137
2P	= AIR PHILIPPINES	GAP	579
2Q	= RUSAIR, International Aviastransport	RMK	556
2R	= STAR AIRLINES	SEU	159
2S	= ISLAND EXPRESS	SDY	383
2T	= CANADA 3000 Airlines	CMM	41
2U	= KARAT	AKT	539
2Y	= HELENAIR	HCL	230
2Z	= AIR CHANGAN AIRLINES – ACA	CGN	12
2Z	= AIR PLUS COMET	MPD	123
3A	= MAFIRA AIR CHARTER SERVICES		704
3B	= AVIOR EXPRESS – Aviones de Oriente, C.A.	ROI	665
3C	= CORPORATE AIRLINES		309
3D	= DENIM AIR, B.V.	DNM	492
3D	= EAE European Air Express		105
3G	= ATLANT-SOYUZ AIRLINES	AYZ	525
3H	= AIR INUIT (1985)	AIE	30
3K	= AIR CARGO EXPRESS	FXG	249
3K	= TATONDUK FLYING SERVICE		442
3L	= AFRICA WEST	WTA	693
3L	= SCENIC AIR		429
3M	= GULFSTREAM INTERNATIONAL AIRLINES	GFT	345
3N	= AIR URGA	URG	614
3Q	= CHINA YUNNAN AIRLINES	CYH	18
3R	= AIR MOLDOVA INTERNATIONAL, SA	MLV	137
3S	= SHUSWAP AIR	SFC	76
3T	= TURAN AIR	URN	685
3U	= SICHUAN AIRLINES	CSC	20
3X	= JAPAN AIR COMMUTER, Co. – JAC	JAC	222
3Z	= NECON AIR	NEC	707
4A	= ARARAT AVIA, State Joint-Stock Company	ARK	133
4B	= OLSON AIR SERVICE		411
4C	= AIRES Colombia	ARE	195
4D	= AIR SINAI	ASD	592
4E	= TANANA AIR SERVICE	TNR	441
4G	= SHENZHEN AIRLINES	CSZ	20
4J	= LOVE AIR	LOV	177
4K	= KENN BOREK AIR	KBA	59
4N	= AIR NORTH	ANT	31
4Q	= AEROLYON	AEY	143
4R	= NT AIR	NTA	68
4U	= TAVAJ – Transportes Aéreos Regulares, SA	TVJ	512
4V	= VOYAGEUR AIRWAYS	VAL	84
4W	= WARBELOW'S AIR VENTURES	VNA	464
4X	= KLM exel	AXL	494
4Y	= YUTE AIR ALASKA	UYA	468
4Z	= SOUTH AFRICAN AIRLINK	LNK	681
5A	= ALPINE AIR	AIP	262
5B	= TRANS INTERNATIONAL EXPRESS – TIE		445
5E	= BASE Airlines	BRO	492
5G	= QUEEN AIR, Aeronaves Queen, S.A.	QNA	194
5H	= HELI-TRANS, A/S	HTA	233
5J	= CEBU PACIFIC AIR	CPI	579
5K	= ODESSA AIRLINES	ODS	617
5L	= AEROSUR		91
5M	= SIBAVIATRANS	SIB	562
5N	= AVL – Arkhangelskie vozdushnye linii	AUL	527
5P	= PENTA – Pena Transportes Aéreos, S.A.	PEP	508
5Q	= SKAERGARDSFLYG, Ab	LND	478
5R	= ROVER AIRWAYS INTERNATIONAL	ROV	426
5T	= AIR NEGRIL		698
5W	= ITAPEMIRIM Transportes Aéreos	ITM	506
5X	= UPS Airlines	UPS	456
5Y	= ATLAS AIR	GTI	282
5Y	= ISLES OF SCILLY SKY BUS	IOS	176
5Z	= ENKOR	ENK	536
6A	= AVIACSA – Consorcio Aviacsa	CHP	654

IATA		ICAO	Page
6B	= BAXTER AVIATION		38
6B	= BRITANNIA AIRWAYS, AB	BLX	582
6C	= CAPE SMYTHE AIR SERVICE	CMY	293
6F	= LAKER AIRWAYS	LKR	390
6G	= LAS VEGAS AIRLINES		391
6H	= ISRAIR, Airlines & Tourism	ISR	687
6L	= AKLAK AIR	AKK	34
6N	= AEROSUCRE, S.A.	KRE	195
6N	= TTA – Trans Travel Airlines, B.V.	TRQ	495
6Q	= SLOVAK AIRLINES	SLL	482
6T	= AIR MANDALAY, Limited		658
6U	= AIR UKRAINE	UKR	613
6V	= AIR VEGAS	VGA	258
6Y	= NICA Nicaraguenses de Aviacion, SA	NIS	660
7A	= HAINES AIRWAYS		345
7B	= KRAS AIR – Krasnoyarsk Airlines	KJC	543
7C	= COLUMBIA PACIFIC AIRLINES		299
7C	= COYNE AIRWAYS	COY	171
7D	= DONBASS-EASTERN UKRAINIAN AIRLINES	UDC	615
7E	= PANAGRA AIRWAYS		413
7F	= FIRST AIR	FAB	50
7G	= BELLAIR		286
7G	= MK AIRLINES	MKA	702
7H	= ERA Aviation	ERH	323
7J	= SKAGWAY AIR SERVICE	SGY	431
7J	= TAJIKISTAN AIRLINES	TZK	141
7K	= KOLAVIA	KGL	541
7L	= AB AIRLINES, Plc	AZX	160
7M	= TYUMEN AIRLINES	TYM	569
7P	= APA International Air, SA	APY	193
7Q	= SHOROUK AIR	SHK	593
7R	= RED SEA AIR	ERT	143
7S	= ARCTIC TRANSPORTATION SERVICES	RCT	278
7S	= REGIONAIR, Pte	RGA	709
7V	= AUSTIN EXPRESS	TXX	283
7W	= AIR SASK	ASK	32
7Z	= L.B. Limited	LBH	98
8C	= AIR TRANSPORT INTERNATIONAL	ATN	258
8C	= SHANXI AVIATION	CXI	20
8D	= EXPO AVIATION	EXV	686
8D	= VOLARE AIRLINES, SpA	VLE	217
8E	= BERING AIR	BRG	284
8F	= FISCHER AIR, s.r.o.	FFR	481
8G	= ANGEL AIRLINES, Co.	NGE	204
8H	= EQUAFLIGHT, S.A.	EKA	605
8K	= AIR OSTRAVA	VTR	479
8L	= GRANDAIR	GDI	585
8M	= MAXAIR, AB	MXL	585
8O	= WEST COAST AIR		85
8P	= PACIFIC COASTAL AIRLINES – PCA	PCO	69
8Q	= BAKER AVIATION	BAJ	284
8Q	= ONUR AIR Tasimacilik, A.S.	OHY	598
8R	= AVIA AIR, N.V.	ARB	518
8T	= AIR TINDI		34
8V	= WRIGHT AIR SERVICE		468
8W	= AIR TEAM, A/S	TTX	231
8W	= BAX GLOBAL		286
8Y	= EGA – Ecuato Guineana de Aviacion	EGA	683
9C	= GILL AIRWAYS	GIL	175
9E	= EXPRESS AIRLINES I	FLG	329
9J	= PACIFIC ISLAND AVIATION	PSA	412
9K	= CAPE AIR	KAP	292
9L	= COLGAN AIR		299
9M	= CENTRAL MOUNTAIN AIR	GLR	45
9N	= TRANS STATES AIRLINES	LOF	445
9P	= PELANGI AIRWAYS	PEG	706
9S	= BLUE PANORAMA AIRLINES, SpA	BPA	212
9T	= ATHABASKA AIRWAYS	ABS	36
9U	= AIR MOLDOVA	MLD	137
9V	= VIPAIR AIRLINES	VPA	612
9W	= JET AIRWAYS (India)	JAI	647
9X	= TASAWI AIR SERVICES	TWI	590
9Y	= AIR KAZAKSTAN	KZK	609

744

Decoding of the ICAO-designators (three-letter airline designator)

The ICAO – International Civil Aviation Organisation switched to three-letter designators on October 25th, 1987 due to the depletion of the ICAO two-letter designator system. The ICAO designators are used primarily for air traffic control communications and the aeronautical fixed telecommunications network (AFTN).
Three-letter designators are being assigned in cooperation with ICAO, FAA – Federal Aviation Administration of the United States and Transport Canada. When IATA converts to three-letter designators, the same designator assigned by ICAO will be assigned by IATA. List of ICAO designators are reflected in Section 6 and are also published in ICAO Document 8585.
In the **jp airline-fleets** international **98/99** you will find the designator after the name of the airline, where applicable.

ICAO		IATA	Page
AAA	= ANSETT AIR FREIGHT	AN	20
AAA	= ANSETT AUSTRALIA	AN	177
AAA	= ANSETT NEW ZEALAND	ZQ	59
AAB	= ABELAG Aviation, S.A.		31
AAF	= AIGLE AZUR		143
AAG	= ATLANTIC AIRLINES		68
AAH	= ALOHA AIRLINES	AQ	512
AAI	= AIR AURORA	AX	84
AAJ	= AIR ALMA		464
AAK	= ALASKA ISLAND AIR		494
AAL	= AMERICAN AIRLINES	AA	468
AAR	= ASIANA AIRLINES	OZ	681
AAS	= AIRTRANSSERVICE – ATS		262
AAT	= AUSTRIAN AIRTRANSPORT		445
ABA	= ARTEM-AVIA		492
ABB	= AIR BELGIUM	AJ	194
ABD	= AIR ATLANTA ICELAND	CC	233
ABF	= SCANWINGS, Oy		579
ABG	= ABAKAN-AVIA		617
ABJ	= ALA – Abaete Linhas Aéreas, SA		91
ABK	= ALBERTA CITYLINK		562
ABL	= AIRBC	ZX	527
ABO	= APSA Colombia		508
ABP	= ABA-AIR, a.s.		478
ABR	= AIR CONTRACTORS (Ireland)	AG	426
ABS	= ATHABASKA AIRWAYS	9T	698
ABX	= AIRBORNE EXPRESS	GB	506
ABY	= AIR BOURGOGNE EUROPE		456
ABZ	= AERO BELIZE		282
ACA	= AIR CANADA	AC	176
ACD	= ACADEMY Airlines		536
ACI	= AIRCALIN – Air Calédonie International	SB	654
ACL	= AIR CAVREL		38
ACO	= AIR COLUMBIA, Srl.		582
ACQ	= AERO CONTINENTE, SA	N6	293
ACX	= AIR CHARTERS		390
ACY	= ARCHANA AIRWAYS	F5	391
ADB	= ANTONOV AIRLINES		687
ADE	= ADA AIR Albania	ZY	34
ADH	= AIR ONE, SpA	AP	195
ADI	= AUDELI, S.A.		495
ADK	= ADC AIRLINES		482
ADM	= DOMINAIR	YU	658
ADN	= AERO-DIENST Executive Jet Service		613
ADO	= HOKKAIDO INTERNATIONAL	HD	258
ADR	= ADRIA AIRWAYS Slovenija	JP	660
ADS	= AVIONES DE SONORA, SA		345
ADU	= AIRDEAL, Oy		543
ADX	= ANDERSON AVIATION		299
ADZ	= AVIOSARDA AIRLINES	DF	171
AEA	= AIR EUROPA	UX	615
AED	= AERNORD, SpA		413
AEE	= AEGEAN AVIATION, S.A.		50
AEF	= AERO LLOYD	YP	286
AEJ	= EJA FRANCE		702
AEL	= AIR EUROPE, SpA	PE	323
AEN	= AIR ENTREPRISE		431
AER	= ALASKA CENTRAL EXPRESS	KO	141
AES	= ACES Colombia	VX	541
AEV	= AEROVENTAS, SA		160
AEW	= AEROSWEET AIRLINES	VV	569
AEY	= AEROLYON	4Q	193
AFD	= PANORAMA FLIGHT SERVICE – PFS		593
AFE	= AIRFAST Indonesia		143
AFF	= CAF, Srl. – Consorzio Aeromobili Fiat		278
AFG	= ARIANA AFGHAN AIRLINES	FG	709
AFJ	= SA ALLIANCE	Y2	283
AFK	= AFRIK AIR LINKS		32
AFL	= AEROFLOT Russian International Airlines	SU	98
AFM	= AFFRETAIR, (Private)	ZL	258
AFO	= AERO EMPRESA MEXICANA		20
AFP	= FAP – Força Aérea Portuguesa		686
AFP	= TAM – Transportes Aéreos Militares		217
AFR	= AIR FRANCE	AF	287
AGD	= AGDERFLY, A/S		481
AGJ	= AIR GREECE – Aerodromisis, S.A.	JG	204
AGK	= TAG AVIATION UKRAINE		605
AGL	= AIR ANGOULEME		479
AGN	= AIR GABON	GN	580
AGO	= ANGOLA AIR CHARTER – AAC		585
AGV	= AIR-GLACIERS, SA	GB	85
AGX	= AVIOGENEX		69
AGY	= AERO FLIGHT SERVICE		284
AGZ	= AGROLET		598
AHA	= AIR ALPHA, A/S		518
AHC	= AZERBAIJAN AIRLINES/AZAL Avia Cargo		34
AHE	= AIRPORT HELICOPTER BASEL, Müller		468
AHF	= ASPEN HELICOPTERS		231
AHG	= AEROCHAGO Airlines, SA		286
AHK	= AIRHONG KONG	LD	683
AHL	= AIR HANSON		175
AHN	= AIR HUNGARIA Air Transport, Co.		329
AHR	= AIR HOLLAND	GG	412
AHT	= HTA		292
AHY	= AZERBAIJAN AIRLINES/AZAL Avia	J2	299
AIA	= AVIES Air Company		45
AIC	= AIR-INDIA	AI	445
AID	= ALTI Air Company		706
AIE	= AIR INUIT (1985)	3H	30
AIG	= AIR INTER GABON, SA		212
AIH	= AIRTOURS INTERNATIONAL	VZ	36
AIJ	= AIR JET		137
AIK	= AFRICAN AIRLINES INTERNATIONAL		612
AIM	= AMBULANCIAS INSULARES, S.A.		647
AIN	= AFRICAN INTERNATIONAL AIRWAYS – AIA		590
AIO	= AVIS – Avia Service International		609
AIP	= ALPINE AIR	5A	238
AIX	= AIRCRUISING AUSTRALIA		610
AIZ	= ARKIA Israeli Airlines	IZ	676
AJI	= AMERISTAR JET CHARTER		263
AJM	= AIR JAMAICA	JM	101
AJO	= AEROEXO – Aeroejecutivo	SX	441
AJS	= CENTRAL CHARTER de Colombia, S.A.		28
AJT	= AMERIJET INTERNATIONAL	M6	607
AKA	= AIR KOREA, Co..		145
AKC	= ARCA Colombia – Aerovias Colombiana		131
AKH	= TURKMENISTAN/AKHAL Aircompany	T5	73
AKI	= IBK-PETRA AVIATION		699
AKK	= AKLAK AIR	6L	645

ICAO		IATA	Page
AKL	= AIR KILROE		483
AKN	= ALKAN-AIR		704
AKT	= KARAT	2U	539
AKY	= YAK SERVICE		432
AKZ	= AEROKUZNETSK		140
ALG	= AIR LOGISTICS, Llc		653
ALJ	= ALI CAPITOL, SpA		622
ALK	= AIRLANKA	UL	622
ALL	= ALISERIO, SpA		123
ALM	= AIR ALM	LM	209
ALO	= ALLEGHENY AIRLINES	US	262
ALP	= ALPLINER Rundflüge & Airtaxi		235
ALT	= SBS AIRCRAFT		259
ALX	= CAL – Congo Airlines	EO	90
ALZ	= ALTA FLIGHTS (Charters)		236
AMB	= DEUTSCHE RETTUNGSFLUGWACHT	DV	196
AMC	= AIR MALTA, Plc	KM	496
AMF	= AMERIFLIGHT		494
AMH	= ALAN MANN HELICOPTERS		247
AMI	= AIR MALDIVES	L6	124
AMK	= AMERER AIR		477
AML	= AIR MALAWI	QM	210
AMM	= AIR 2000	DP	139
AMO	= AIR MONTREAL	F8	691
AMP	= AERO TRANSPORTE, S.A. – ATSA		285
AMS	= AIR MUSKOKA		7
AMT	= AMERICAN TRANS AIR – ATA	TZ	216
AMU	= AIR MACAU, Co.	NX	165
AMV	= AMC AVIATION		185
AMW	= AIR MIDWEST	ZV	429
AMX	= AEROMEXICO	AM	228
ANA	= ALL NIPPON AIRWAYS – ANA	NH	168
ANG	= AIR NIUGINI	PX	604
ANI	= AIR ATLANTIC CARGO		595
ANK	= AIR NIPPON, Co. – ANK Air Nippon, K.K.	EL	186
ANL	= AIR NACOIA Exploraçao de Aeronaves		641
ANO	= AIRNORTH Regional	TL	650
ANP	= ANTONAIR INTERNATIONAL		605
ANS	= AIR NOSTRUM	YW	666
ANT	= AIR NORTH	4N	643
ANU	= AVIONAIR		209
ANZ	= AIR NEW ZEALAND	NZ	102
AOB	= AEROLION INTERNATIONAL, FZE		496
AOC	= AVCOM – Aviation Commercial	J6	8
AOD	= AERO VODOCHODY, a.s.		193
AOK	= AEROATLANTICO Colombia		23
AOM	= AOM French Airlines	IW	168
AOO	= AS Aviakompania		659
AOP	= AEROPILOTO		582
AOV	= AERO VISION		231
APB	= AIR ATLANTIQUE	KI	682
APC	= AIRPAC AIRLINES	LQ	711
APO	= AEROPRO		231
APP	= AEROPERLAS, S.A.	WL	165
APR	= AIR PROVENCE INTERNATIONAL		60
APT	= LAP Colombia		711
APW	= ARROW AIR	JW	616
APY	= APA International Air, SA	7P	230
APZ	= HYDRO-QUEBEC – Service Transport Aérien		191
AQE	= AQUELARRE – Linea Aérea Aquelarrea		50
AQT	= AVIOQUINTANA		564
ARB	= AVIA AIR, N.V.	8R	297
ARD	= ATA-AEROCONDOR – Transportes Aéreos	2B	93
ARE	= AIRES Colombia	4C	195
ARG	= AEROLINEAS ARGENTINAS, SA	AR	103
ARI	= AEROVICS		580
ARK	= ARARAT AVIA, State Joint-Stock Company	4A	133
ARL	= AIRLEC AIR ESPACE, S.A.		12
ARN	= AIR NOVA	QK	388
ARP	= L'AEROPOSTALE		389
ARU	= AIR ARUBA, N.V.	FQ	180
ARV	= ARAVCO		601
ARY	= ARGOSY AIRWAYS		632
ASA	= ALASKA AIRLINES	AS	646
ASB	= AIR SPRAY (1967)		679
ASD	= AIR SINAI	4D	592
ASE	= ASA – Atlantic Southeast Airlines	EV	470
ASF	= AIR SCHEFFERVILLE		517
ASH	= MESA AIRLINES	YV	287
ASJ	= AIR SATELLITE		22
ASK	= AIR SASK	7W	15
ASM	= AIR SAINT MARTIN	S6	114
ASO	= AERO SLOVAKIA, a.s.		203
ASQ	= ASIA SERVICE AIRLINES		517
ASW	= AIR SOUTHWEST		302
ASX	= AIR SPECIAL, a.s.		306
ASZ	= ASTRAKHAN Airlines		41
ATC	= AIR TANZANIA	TC	484
ATJ	= AIR TRAFFIC – Executive Jet Service		640
ATK	= AEROTACA Colombia		308
ATN	= AIR TRANSPORT INTERNATIONAL	8C	241
ATT	= AER TURAS Teoranta		96
ATV	= AVANTI-AIR Bedarfsflug		668
ATX	= AIR TAXIS		239
AUA	= AUSTRIAN AIRLINES	OS	650
AUB	= AUGSBURG AIRWAYS	IQ	21
AUF	= AUGUSTA AIR		689
AUH	= UNITED ARAB EMIRATES/Abu Dhabi	MO	16
AUI	= UKRAINE INTERNATIONAL AIRLINES	PS	230
AUL	= AVL – Arkhangelskie vozdushnye linii	5N	210
AUR	= AURIGNY AIR SERVICES	GR	678
AUS	= AUS-AIR	NO	236
AUT	= AUSTRAL Lineas Aéreas	AU	535
AUV	= ATRUVERA Air Transport Company		150
AVA	= AVIANCA Colombia	AV	583
AVB	= AVIATION BEAUPORT – A.B. AIR TAXI		103
AVC	= AEROVENCA		212
AVE	= AVENSA – Aerovias Venezolanas, S.A.	VE	312
AVH	= AVISER, S.A. – Aviacion Sanitaria		630
AVM	= AVEMEX – Aviacion Ejecutiva Mexicana		281
AVN	= AIR VANUATU	NF	104
AVS	= ARTAC AVIACION, S.L.		626
AVU	= AVIASUD Aérotaxi		490
AVW	= AVIATOR		312
AVX	= AP AIRLINES		489
AVZ	= AEROSERVICE KAZAKSTAN		209
AWC	= TITAN AIRWAYS		162
AWE	= AMERICA WEST AIRLINES	HP	299
AWH	= AIR INTER NIGER		621

ICAO		IATA	Page
AWI	= AIR WISCONSIN AIRLINES	ZW	697
AWR	= ARCTIC WINGS & ROTORS		203
AWS	= ARAB WINGS		121
AWS	= ROYAL WINGS		241
AWT	= AIR WEST		104
AWV	= AIRWAVE TRANSPORT		488
AXE	= EXEC-AIR – Executive Air		230
AXF	= ASIAN EXPRESS AIRLINES	HJ	160
AXL	= KLM exel	4X	535
AXM	= AIR ASIA	AK	7
AXQ	= ACTION AIRLINES		560
AXX	= AVIOIMPEX	M4	212
AYB	= BELGIAN ARMY – Light Aviation		523
AYC	= AVIACO – Aviacion y Comercio, S.A.	AO	124
AYM	= AIRMAN, S.A.		322
AYT	= AYEET AVIATION		294
AYZ	= ATLANT-SOYUZ AIRLINES	3G	525
AZA	= ALITALIA – Linee Aeree Italiane, SpA	AZ	23
AZB	= AZAMAT		225
AZE	= COSMOS AIR Luftfahrtunternehmen	ZE	192
AZF	= AIR ZERMATT		131
AZI	= AZZURRAAIR, SpA	ZS	404
AZK	= AZERBAIJAN AIRLINES/AZAL Helikopter		10
AZL	= AIR ZANZIBAR		219
AZM	= AEROCOZUMEL, SA		322
AZS	= AVIACON ZITOTRANS		642
AZT	= AZIMUT, S.A.		209
AZV	= AZOV-AVIA Aircompany		708
AZW	= AIR ZIMBABWE	UM	330
AZX	= AB AIRLINES, Plc	7L	192
AZZ	= AZZA TRANSPORT Company Limited		319
BAE	= BRITISH AEROSPACE Corporate Flights		12
BAF	= BELGIAN AIR FORCE – Transport Fleet		471
BAG	= DEUTSCHE BA Luftfahrt	DI	139
BAH	= BAHRAIN AMIRI FLIGHT		192
BAJ	= BAKER AVIATION	8Q	279
BAL	= BRITANNIA AIRWAYS	BY	106
BAW	= BRITISH AIRWAYS, Plc	BA	193
BAZ	= BARGUZIN Aviakompania		602
BBA	= BANNERT AIR Bedarfsflugunternehmen		325
BBB	= BALAIR/CTA Leisure	BB	491
BBC	= BIMAN BANGLADESH AIRLINES	BG	330
BBE	= EASTWIND AIRLINES – The Bee Line	W9	583
BBL	= IBM EUROFLIGHT		214
BBR	= SANTA BARBARA AIRLINES, C.A.	BJ	646
BBZ	= BLUE BIRD AVIATION		18
BCS	= EAT – European Air Transport, N.V.	QY	618
BCY	= CITYJET	WX	31
BDI	= AIR CENTER WEST		340
BEA	= BENAVIA, S.A.		680
BED	= BELGOROD AIR ENTERPRISE		337
BEI	= BENAIR, SpA		232
BEN	= BUSINESS AIR		11
BER	= AIR-BERLIN Luftverkehrs	AB	118
BES	= AERO SERVICES EXECUTIVE, Sarl	W4	251
BFB	= BF CARGO		171
BFC	= BASLER AIRLINES		320
BFF	= AIR NUNAVUT		444
BFL	= BUFFALO AIRWAYS	J4	658
BGA	= AIRBUS TRANSPORT INTERNATIONAL		125
BGM	= TATARSTAN/BUGULMA AIR ENTERPRISE		601
BHL	= BRISTOW HELICOPTERS		120
BHN	= BRISTOW HELICOPTERS (Nigeria)		257
BHO	= BHOJA AIRLINES	B4	19
BHR	= BIGHORN AIRWAYS		90
BHS	= BAHAMASAIR	UP	667
BHU	= BUSINESS AIR, Kft.		635
BIE	= AIR MEDITERRANEE		191
BIG	= BIG ISLAND AIR – BIA		518
BIH	= BRITISH INTERNATIONAL	BS	132
BIL	= BILLUND AIR CENTER, A/S		633
BIM	= BINTER MEDITERRANEO, S.A.	AX	238
BIO	= BIO Air Company		148
BIR	= BIRD AIR FLEET		124
BKA	= BANKAIR	B4	331
BKF	= BF-LENTO, Oy		620
BKJ	= BARKEN INTERNATIONAL		173
BKL	= BAIKAL AIRLINES	X3	575
BKN	= KHAKASIA AIRLINES		215
BKP	= BANGKOK AIR	PG	646
BKS	= AVIAEKSPRESSKRUIZ		497
BKU	= BYKOVO AVIA		247
BLA	= ALL CHARTER		184
BLC	= TAM Express	JJ	604
BLD	= BLAGOVESHCHENSKAVIA		657
BLF	= LUCKY AIR		9
BLI	= BELAIR Belarussian Airlines		491
BLK	= WEST COAST ENERGY – Flight Dept.		702
BLL	= BALTIC AIRLINES		215
BLN	= BALI AIR		656
BLR	= ATLANTIC COAST AIRLINES	DH	175
BLS	= BEARSKIN AIRLINES	JV	489
BLV	= BELLVIEW AIRLINES	B3	398
BLX	= BRITANNIA AIRWAYS, AB	6B	482
BLZ	= AERO BARLOZ		605
BMA	= BRITISH MIDLAND	BD	125
BMJ	= BEMIDJI AIRLINES	CH	288
BMM	= BURMAN AVIATION (Charter)		163
BMN	= BOWMAN AVIATION		341
BMW	= BMW FLUGDIENST		161
BND	= BOND HELICOPTERS		343
BNS	= BANC ONE SERVICES		174
BOA	= BONIAIR		602
BOB	= JET CLUB		660
BOI	= ABOITIZ AIR		343
BON	= AIR BOSNA	JA	544
BOR	= BORNEO AIRWAYS		32
BOT	= AIR BOTSWANA	BP	581
BOU	= BOURAQ INDONESIA AIRLINES	BO	700
BPA	= BLUE PANORAMA AIRLINES, SpA	9S	669
BPK	= BERKHUT Aviakompania		484
BPS	= BUDAPEST AIRCRAFT SERVICES		54
BPX	= BPX Colombia		18
BRA	= BRAATHENS, ASA	BU	547
BRD	= BROCK AIR SERVICES		532
BRG	= BERING AIR	8E	345
BRI	= AIR BOR		596
BRM	= AIR 500		534

ICAO		IATA	Page
KAW	KAZAIR WEST		523
KAZ	TATARSTAN/KAZAN AIR ENTERPRISE		523
KBA	KENN BOREK AIR	4K	245
KBV	KUSTBEVAKNING – Swedish Coast Guard		501
KCA	TRANS-KIEV		709
KDA	KENDELL AIRLINES (Australia)	KD	100
KDC	KD AIR Corporation	XC	652
KEA	KALAHARI EXPRESS AIRLINES		652
KEE	KEYSTONE AIR SERVICE	BZ	652
KEL	KBA Kieler Business Air		652
KFA	KELOWNA FLIGHTCRAFT Air Charter		619
KFB	AIR BOTNIA	KF	660
KFS	KITTY HAWK CHARTERS	CB	652
KGA	KYRGHYZSTAN AIRLINES	K2	194
KGL	KOLAVIA	7K	245
KHA	KITTY HAWK AIR CARGO	KR	245
KHB	DALAVIA	H8	693
KHO	KHORS Aircompany	X9	97
KHR	TURKMENISTAN/KHAZAR Aircompany		161
KHV	AIR KHARKOV		195
KHX	KNIGHTHAWK EXPRESS		88
KIA	KIWI INTERNATIONAL AIR LINES	KP	501
KIL	KUBAN AIRLINES	GW	235
KIS	CONTACT AIR Interregional		653
KJC	KRAS AIR – Krasnoyarsk Airlines	7B	92
KJI	KAIKEN Lineas Aéreas		246
KKL	KOLKOL AIRLINES		502
KLA	AIR LITHUANIA	TT	245
KLC	KLM cityhopper	WA	245
KLD	AIR KLAIPEDA		245
KLG	KARLOG AIR, A/S		603
KLM	KLM – Royal Dutch Airlines	KL	208
KLN	KALININGRADAVIA	K8	26
KLY	AIR CALYPSO		92
KMA	KOMIAVIATRANS		122
KMP	KAMPUCHEA AIRLINES	KT	246
KMV	KOMIINTERAVIA		26
KNM	KNAAPO		246
KNX	KNIGHTHAWK AIR EXPRESS		144
KOR	AIR KORYO	JS	619
KOT	SEVER Aviakompania		88
KPH	KVZ – Kazansky vertoletny zavod		92
KPR	KAPA AIR		619
KQA	KENYA AIRWAYS	KQ	653
KRE	AEROSUCRE, S.A.	6N	26
KRG	KRIMAVIAMONTAZH		100
KRI	KRYLO Aviakompania		653
KRL	KRYLA		653
KRM	CRIMEA UNIVERSAL AVIA		660
KRO	KROONK Air Agency		609
KRS	KORSAR Airlines		609
KRT	KOKSHETAU AIRLINES		609
KSA	SUD AEROCARGO		654
KSM	KOSMOS Aviakompania		664
KSP	SAEP – SERVICIOS AEREOS PETROLEROS		27
KTA	KIROV AIR ENTERPRISE		195
KTK	KATEKAVIA		612
KTR	HELIKOPTERTRANSPORT		709
KTS	KOTLASAVIA		502
KUS	KURSKAVIA		195
KVM	RUSAEROLEASING AIRLINE		654
KVS	KEVIS Air Company		27
KVY	C.A.I. – Compagnia Aeronautica Italiana, SpA		96
KYC	AVATLANTIC		195
KYN	KYRNAIR		502
KYV	KTHY – Kibris Türk Hava Yollari		469
KZH	ZHEZAIR		502
KZK	AIR KAZAKSTAN	9Y	502
LAA	LIBYAN ARAB AIRLINES	LN	654
LAB	LAB Flying Service	JF	100
LAE	LACOL Colombia		100
LAJ	BRITISH MEDITERRANEAN AIRWAYS	KJ	596
LAL	AIR LABRADOR – Wings of the North	WJ	502
LAM	LAM – Linhas Aéreas de Moçambique	TM	246
LAN	LAN Chile – Linea Aérea Nacional de Chile	LA	664
LAO	LAO AVIATION	QV	609
LAP	TAM Paraguay	PZ	654
LAU	LINEAS AEREAS SURAMERICANAS		182
LAV	AEROPOSTAL, Alas de Venezuela C.A.	VH	235
LAX	ALPAR, Flug- & Flugplatzgesellschaft AG		195
LAZ	BALKAN Bulgarian Airlines	LZ	664
LBC	ALBANIAN AIRLINES, M.A.K. S.H.P.K.	LV	208
LBH	L.B. Limited	7Z	654
LBT	NOUVELAIR TUNISIE	BJ	122
LCH	LYNCH FLYING SERVICE		654
LCI	LUFTHANSA CARGO INDIA, Pvt.	LF	88
LCO	LADECO Airlines	UC	654
LCR	LIBYAN ARAB AIR CARGO		654
LDA	LAUDA AIR Luftfahrt	NG	235
LDB	LADA AIR		195
LDE	LADE – Lineas Aéreas del Estado		235
LDF	IRS AERO		523
LDI	LAUDA AIR, SpA	L4	195
LDO	ELISUSA, Srl.		100
LEA	LEADAIR-UNIJET, SA		100
LEB	TURKMENISTAN/LEBAP Aircompany		247
LEO	LEOPAIR, SA		100
LER	LASER	KZ	654
LET	AEROLINEAS EJECUTIVAS		472
LEU	LIONS AIR		100
LFA	ALFA Hava Yollari, A.S.	H7	247
LFI	NAC HELICOPTERS		183
LGL	LUXAIR	LG	676
LGW	LGW Luftfahrtgesellschaft Walter, mbH	HE	694
LHN	EXPRESS ONE International	EO	683
LHS	LUGANSK AVIATION ENTERPRISE		703
LIA	LIAT – The Caribbean Airline	LI	606
LIB	AIR LIBERTE	IJ	100
LID	ALIDAUNIA, Srl.	D4	27
LII	GROMOV AIR		230
LIL	LITHUANIAN AIRLINES – LAL	TE	247
LIM	AIR LIMO		247
LIN	LINAIR-HUNGARIAN REGIONAL AIRLINES		100
LIO	AIR CHARTER ICELAND		619
LIP	LIPETSK AIR ENTERPRISE		92
LIT	AIR LITTORAL	FU	136
LIV	AIR LIVONIA		482
LJR	HELLAS WINGS		247
LKR	LAKER AIRWAYS	6F	502
LLB	LAB – Lloyd Aéreo Boliviano, S.A.M.	LB	27
LLR	ALLIANCE AIR	CD	247
LMC	LINEA AEREA MEXICANA DE CARGA		144
LMR	LEMANAIR, S.A.		694
LMS	LOMAS HELICOPTERS		689
LMX	LEMANAIR EXECUTIVE, S.A.		30
LND	SKAERGARDSFLYG, Ab	5Q	208
LNK	SOUTH AFRICAN AIRLINK	4Z	668
LNR	SKY LINERS, NV		604
LNS	LIONAIR		605
LNT	AEROLINEAS INTERNACIONALES	N2	247
LNX	LONDON EXECUTIVE AVIATION – LEA		101
LOF	TRANS STATES AIRLINES	9N	27
LOG	LOGANAIR		27
LOT	LOT Polish Airlines	LO	247
LOV	LOVE AIR	4J	487
LPN	LAOAG INTERNATIONAL AIRLINE	L7	487
LPR	LAPA – Lineas Aéreas Privadas	MJ	487
LRA	LITTLE RED AIR SERVICE		247
LRB	LR AIRLINES		247
LRC	LACSA Costa Rica	LR	144
LRO	ALROSA-AVIA		644
LRS	SANSA – Servicios Aéreos Nacionales, SA	RZ	144
LRT	AIRLINES OF SOUTH AUSTRALIA – ASA	RT	691
LSB	LENSIBAVIA		469
LSF	AIRAILES		619
LSK	AURELA, Co.		27
LSR	ALSAIR, SA		694
LSS	ASPEN MOUNTAIN AIR		27
LSU	LAUS AIR, Tourism & Air Transport Services		91
LSY	LINDSAY AVIATION		28
LTB	BALTIC Express Line		230
LTC	LAT CHARTER		144
LTE	LTE International Airways, S.A.	XO	691
LTF	LUFTTAXI FLUG		144
LTG	LATGALES AVIO		144
LTP	LATPASS AIRLINES	QJ	709
LTR	LUFTTRANSPORT, A/S		28
LTU	LTU International Airways	LT	161
LUP	LUPENGA AIR CHARTERS		620
LUV	LUXEMBOURG AIR RESCUE, a.s.		592
LVN	ALIVEN, Srl.		249
LWA	LIBERIA WORLD AIRLINES		145
LXA	LUXAVIATION, S.A.		249
LXO	LUXOR AIR		161
LXR	AIR LUXOR		620
LYC	LYNDEN AIR CARGO, Llc	L2	249
LYM	KEY LIME AIR		249
LYN	LYNTON AVIATION		249
MAA	MAS AIR CARGO	MY	249
MAC	MALTA AIR CHARTER, Company	R5	482
MAF	MAF Indonesia – Mission Aviation Fellowship		249
MAH	MALEV Hungarian Airlines, Plc	MA	250
MAK	MAT-MACEDONIAN AIRLINES	IN	161
MAL	MORNINGSTAR AIR EXPRESS		250
MAM	AERODROMO DE LA MANCHA, S.L.		487
MAQ	MAC AVIATION, S.L.		193
MAS	MALAYSIA AIRLINES	MH	620
MAT	MAINE AVIATION		676
MAU	AIR MAURITIUS	MK	250
MAW	MUSTIQUE AIRWAYS	Q4	250
MAZ	ROAN AIR	Q3	620
MBA	AUTOMOBILVERTRIEBS		250
MBL	FIRST CITY AIR, Plc		250
MBO	MOBIL OIL AVIATION		250
MCC	AEROCOM		601
MCD	AIR MED		668
MCG	SOS HELIKOPTERN GOTLAND, AB		250
MCL	MEDICAL AVIATION SERVICES – MAS		668
MCM	HELI AIR MONACO	YO	29
MCN	MAC DAN AVIATION		250
MCO	AEROLINEAS MARCOS		8
MCR	MONACAIR, S.A.M.		195
MCS	MACEDONIAN AIRLINES		209
MDC	MID-ATLANTIC FREIGHT		607
MDD	MDA AIRLINES	KR	161
MDG	AIR MADAGASCAR	MD	101
MDJ	JARO INTERNATIONAL, SA		29
MDL	MANDALA AIRLINES		683
MDR	COMPANIA MEXICANA DE AEROPLANOS		668
MDS	MED AIRLINES, SpA	M8	250
MDV	MOLDAVIAN AIRLINES	2M	137
MDW	MIDWAY AIRLINES	JI	483
MEA	MEA – Middle East Airlines	ME	193
MEE	ELIMEDITERRANEA, Srl.		250
MEI	MERLIN EXPRESS		251
MEJ	MEDJET INTERNATIONAL		30
MEP	MIDWEST EXPRESS AIRLINES	YX	251
MER	METHOW AVIATION		219
MES	MESABA AIRLINES	XJ	251
MFZ	MOFAZ AIR, Sdn Berhad		145
MGC	MAGEC AVIATION		122
MGD	NORTHERN-EAST CARGO AIRLINES		251
MGL	MIAT – Mongolian Airlines	OM	251
MGM	MG-AVIATION		101
MGR	MAGNA AIR Luftfahrt		101
MGX	MONTENEGRO AIRLINES		689
MHA	MOUNTAIN HIGH AVIATION		251
MHN	MANHATTAN AIR		251
MHS	AIR MEMPHIS		30
MIE	AEROPREMIER DE MEXICO		668
MIV	MI-AVIA		251
MIW	AIRBORNE OF SWEDEN, AB	ZF	30
MJM	ETI 2000, Srl.		620
MKA	MK AIRLINES	7G	668
MKI	MK FLUGFELAGID, e.h.f.		183
MKK	MAD – Malaya Aviatsia Dona		620
MKP	ADYGHEYA AVIA		147
MKS	PIMICHIKAMAC AIR		488
MKU	ISLAND AIR	WP	147
MKV	MAUS – Myachkovskie aviatsionnye uslugi		30
MLA	40-MILE AIR	Q5	251
MLD	AIR MOLDOVA	9U	701
MLE	MOLDAEROSERVICE		668
MLG	MALAGASY AIRLINES		92
MLI	AIR MALI, SA	L9	251
MLV	AIR MOLDOVA INTERNATIONAL, SA	3R	137
MMC	AERMARCHE, SpA.		251
MMD	AIR ALSIE, A/S		13
MMM	MERIDIAN AIR, Co.		209
MMP	AMP Air		184
MNA	MERPATI	MZ	683
MNB	MNG CARGO AIRLINES	MB	13
MND	MADINA		147
MNG	MAGNITOGORSK AIR ENTERPRISE		193
MNK	MURMANSK AIRLINES		161
MNL	MINILINER, Srl.		161
MNS	KISTIGAN – Ministic Air		30
MNX	MANX AIRLINES	JE	182
MOG	MOGILEVAVIA		605
MON	MONARCH AIRLINES	ZB	606
MOU	ANGLO AMERICAN AIRMOTIVE		693
MPD	AIR PLUS COMET	2Z	123
MPH	MARTINAIR	MP	593
MPX	AEROMEXPRESS	QO	30
MRA	MARTINAIRE		30
MRE	NCA – Namibia Commercial Aviation		147
MRG	MANAG'AIR		252
MRP	ABAS, spol. s r.o.		707
MRS	AIR MARSHALL ISLANDS – AMI	CW	120
MRT	AIR MAURITANIE	MR	707
MRV	MIRAVIA	N3	30
MSA	MISTRAL AIR, Srl.		252
MSD	MASTER AVIATION, A/S		612
MSG	AVIAMOST		30
MSI	MOTOR SICH Aviakompania		161
MSK	MAERSK AIR	VB	30
MSP	VIGILANCIA AEREA		607
MSQ	META – MESQUITA Transportes Aéreo		612
MSR	EGYPT AIR	MS	240
MSV	AERO-KAMOV		582
MTC	MINERVA AIRLINES, SpA	Q2	199
MTF	INTERJET, Srl.		483
MTJ	METROJET		31
MTL	RAF-AVIA		579
MTM	MTM Aviation		138
MTN	MOUNTAIN AIR CARGO – MAC		101
MUA	MURRAY AVIATION		253
MUG	MUK AIR (GH)		252
MUI	TRANS AIR	P6	92
MUK	MUK AIR, A/S	ZR	209
MVD	KMV – Kavkazskie Mineralnye Vody	KV	253
MVK	HELICOPTER TRAINING & HIRE		122
MVL	MAVIAL – Magadanskie avialinii	H5	253
MWR	RASLAN AIR SERVICE		593
MWT	MIDWEST AVIATION		516
MXA	MEXICANA	MX	621
MXC	MEXICARGO	GJ	709
MXL	MAXAIR, AB	8M	668
MXP	MAY AIR X-PRESS		148
MYA	MYFLUG, h.f.		253
MYD	MAYA ISLAND AIR	MW	240
MYI	MAYAIR		161
MYN	MAYAN WORLD AIRLINES	EY	253
MYO	MAYORAL		148
MZL	AEROVIAS MONTES AZULES		148
MZS	MAHFOOZ AVIATION (Gambia)	M2	31
NAA	NOAA Aircraft Operations		592
NAC	NORTHERN AIR CARGO	NC	253
NAE	NATIONS AIR	N5	31
NAG	NORTHERN AIR CHARTER, ApS & Co		31
NAI	NORTH ADRIA AVIATION		148
NAL	NORTHWAY AVIATION		621
NAO	NORTH AMERICAN AIRLINES	XG	31
NAP	DOTHAN AIR CHARTER		120
NAW	NEWAIR Airservice		668
NAX	NORWEGIAN AIR SHUTTLE, A/S		668
NAY	NAYSA Aerotaxis		668
NBA	NEBA – North East Bolivian Airwaysa		255
NCA	NIPPON CARGO AIRLINES, Co. – NCA	KZ	668
NCB	NORTH CARIBOO AIR		31
NCH	CHANCHANGI AIRLINES (Nigeria) – CAL		31
NDS	NORDSTRESS (Australia)		621
NEA	NEW ENGLAND AIRLINES	EJ	31
NEC	NECON AIR	3Z	707
NEE	NORTHEAST AIRLINES		31
NEF	NORDFLYG, AB		161
NES	NORDESTE Linhas Aéreas Regionais, SA	JH	32
NEX	NORTHERN EXECUTIVE AVIATION	NV	219
NFA	NORTH FLYING, A/S		255
NFT	NEFTEYUGANSK AIR ENTERPRISE		149
NGA	NIGERIA AIRWAYS	WT	255
NGE	ANGEL AIRLINES, Co.	8G	32
NGL	NIZHEGORODSKIE AVIALINII		255
NGS	GAS AIR		595
NHK	FEDERAL AVIATION ADMINISTRATION – FAA		195
NIA	NORDAVIA Flug		149
NIG	AEROCONTRACTORS	NU	669
NII	NIIIS ATP		149
NIR	NORSK FLYTJENESTE, A/S		32
NIS	NICA Nicaraguenses de Aviacion, SA	6Y	255
NJS	NATIONAL JET SYSTEMS	NC	32
NKM	TATARSTAN/NIZHNEKAMSK AIR		255
NKS	SPIRIT AIRLINES	NK	483
NLB	NOVOSIBIRSK AIRLINES	L8	255
NLK	ELBRUS-AVIA		255
NLS	NATIONALE LUCHTVAART SCHOOL – NLS		255
NLT	NALAIR		32
NMB	AIR NAMIBIA	SW	669
NMD	BAY AIR AVIATION		669
NMI	PACIFIC WINGS	LW	32
NOE	TRANSCARAIBES AIR INTERNATIONAL	DZ	32
NOF	FONNAFLY Sjö, A/S		256
NOL	NATIONAL OVERSEAS AIRLINE – N.O.A.		256
NOO	NOR AVIATION, A/S		33
NOR	NORSK HELIKOPTER, A/S		256
NOT	SEVERAERO		161
NPO	NAPO-Aviatrans		33
NPP	NPP MIR Aviakompania		33
NPR	AIR NAPIER		149
NQN	TAN – Transportes Aéreos Neuquen, S.A.	T8	209
NRD	NORD AIR		480
NRE	AVIONES ARE		605
NRG	ROSS AVIATION		182
NRL	NOVOROSSISK AIRLINES		149
NRO	AERO RENT		101
NRS	ARCO Flight Operations		482
NRT	NOREST AIR, S.L.		235
NRV	NORTH VANCOUVER AIRLINES	VL	149
NRX	FILDER AIR SERVICE – FAS		256
NSA	NILE SAFARIS AVIATON		700
NSE	SATENA		33
NSW	COUNTRY CONNECTION AIRLINES	XL	480
NTA	NT AIR	4R	33
NTC	HEARTLAND AVIATION		649
NTL	ANATOLIA – Anadolu Havacilik, A.S.	TD	256
NTM	NORTH AMERICAN AIRLINES		33
NTN	NAC – National Airways		621
NTR	TNT International Aviation Services		256
NTS	CIRRUSAIR		709
NTW	NATIONWIDE AIRLINES	CE	235
NVC	NAV CANADA		669
NVG	NOVGOROD AIR ENTERPRISE		621
NVL	HUNTING AVIATION		488
NVR	NOVAIR		33
NWA	NORTHWEST AIRLINES	NW	193
NWL	NORTH WRIGHT AIRWAYS	HW	161
NYB	BELGIAN NAVY – Heliflight		606
NZM	MOUNT COOK AIRLINE	NM	256

ICAO		IATA	Page
OAC	ORIENTAL AIRLINES		33
OAE	OMNI AIR INTERNATIONAL – OAI	X9	101
OAF	AERZTEFLUGAMBULANZ		256
OAL	OLYMPIC AIRWAYS, S.A.	OA	208
OAO	ARKHANGELSK 2nd Aviation Enterprise		257
OAV	OMNI – Aviaçao & Tecnologia		257
OBA	AEROBANANA		482
OBM	AVIAOBSHCHEMASH Aviakompania		258
OCA	ASERCA AIRLINES	R7	523
OCE	HELICOCEAN		149
OCM	O'CONNOR – Mount Gambier's Airline	UQ	34
OCT	OCCIDENTAL AIRLINES		258
ODS	ODESSA AIRLINES	5K	664
OEA	ORIENT THAI AIRLINES, Co.	OX	476
OEG	ORIENT EAGLE AIRWAYS		610
OGN	ORIGIN PACIFIC AIRWAYS	QO	120
OHY	ONUR AIR Tasimacilik, A.S.	8Q	209
OIR	SLOV AIR, a.s.		669
OJF	OCCITANIA JET FLEET		34
OKJ	OKADA AIR		34
OLT	OLT Ostfriesische Lufttransport	OL	34
OLX	OLIMEX, spol. s r.o.		258
OLY	OLYMPIC AVIATION, S.A.		591
OMA	OMAN AIR	WY	621
OMG	AEROMEGA HELICOPTERS		480
OMS	OMSKAVIA		662
OND	CONDOMETT, Srl.		689
ONT	AIR ONTARIO	GX	184
OPE	AEROPE 3S AVIATION		144
OPN	AIR OPEN SKY, S.A.		247
ORA	EXECUTIVE AIRLINES	YL	247
ORB	ORENBURG AIRLINES	R2	248
ORF	OMAN ROYAL FLIGHT	RS	249
ORK	ORCAAIR		12
ORM	OREL AIR ENTERPRISE		620
ORO	CLIPPER NATIONAL AIR, S.A.		620
ORS	ACTION AIR, Srl.		28
ORZ	ZOREX AIR TRANSPORT		249
OSA	AEROASTRA, SA		144
OST	ALANIA, Leasing Airline		249
OTX	AEROTEX		101
OVA	AERONOVA, S.L.		29
OWN	OWENSAIR		250
OWR	CROWN AIR, s r.o.		231
OXE	OXAERO		620
OZB	ZONA BLAVA, S.L.		250
PAA	PAN AM		695
PAC	POLAR AIR CARGO	PO	479
PAG	PERIMETER AVIATION		7
PAJ	ALIPARMA, Srl.		250
PAL	PHILIPPINES – Philippine Airlines	PR	250
PAM	PHOENIX AIR		620
PAO	POLYNESIAN – Airline of Samoa	PH	30
PAQ	PACIFIC AIR EXPRESS (Solomon Islands)		476
PAR	SPAIR Air Transport Corporation		476
PAS	PELITA AIR		620
PAU	LOCAVIONS AERO SERVICES		251
PAV	VIP AVIA		251
PAX	PAN AIR		496
PAY	ARPA – Aerolineas Paraguayas	A8	620
PBA	PB AIR		161
PBU	AIR BURUNDI		147
PCA	PEACEAIR		620
PCM	WEST AIR		582
PCO	PACIFIC COASTAL AIRLINES – PCA	8P	231
PCT	PEACE AIR TOGO		184
PDG	PDG HELICOPTERS		252
PDT	PIEDMONT AIRLINES	US	252
PEA	PAN EUROPEENNE AIR SERVICE		620
PEC	PACIFIC EAST ASIA CARGO Airlines		131
PEG	PELANGI AIRWAYS	9P	472
PEL	AEROPELICAN Air Services		161
PEM	PEM-AIR	PD	235
PEN	PENAIR	KS	254
PEP	PENTA – Pena Transportes Aéreos, S.A.	5P	254
PER	PRINCESS AIRLINES, S.A.		122
PFA	PACIFIC FLIGHT SERVICES, Pte		255
PFC	PACIFIC INTERNATIONAL AIRLINES		184
PGA	PGA PORTUGALIA AIRLINES	NI	184
PGE	PRESTIGEAVIA		255
PGP	PERM AIRLINES		256
PGT	PEGASUS AIRLINES		596
PGX	PARAGON AIR EXPRESS		256
PHA	PHOENIX AIR		101
PHD	DUNCAN AVIATION		579
PHE	PAWAN HANS HELICOPTERS		33
PHM	PETROLEUM HELICOPTERS – PHI		256
PHR	PHARAOH AIRLINES, S.A.E.		33
PIA	PIA – Pakistan International Airlines	PK	698
PIC	PACIFIC AIRLINES, Co	BL	523
PIT	PANAIR Compagnia Aerea Mediterranea		149
PJS	JET AVIATION BUSINESS JETS	PP	256
PKR	PAKKER AVIO		472
PKW	SIERRA WEST AIRLINES		472
PLA	POLYNESIAN AIRWAYS		256
PLB	POLYUS-Centre for Parachute		621
PLC	POLICE AVIATION SERVICES		480
PLI	AEROPERU	PL	523
PLK	PULKOVO AVIATION ENTERPRISE	Z8	209
PLR	NORTHWESTERN AIR	J3	483
PLS	PALIO AIR SERVICE, SpA		93
PMA	PAN-MALAYSIAN AIR TRANSPORT		34
PMC	PRIMAC AIR		621
PMI	AIR EUROPA EXPRESS		258
PMS	PLANEMASTERS		258
PMT	PERMSKIE MOTORY Aviakompania		210
PND	POND AIR EXPRESS		258
PNL	AERO PERSONAL		149
PNM	PANORAMA		669
PNR	PAN AIR Lineas Aéreas, S.A.	PV	669
PNS	PENAS		621
PNW	PALESTINIAN AIRLINES	PF	676
PNZ	PENZA AIR ENTERPRISE		258
PON	MARINHA – Portuguese Navy		259
POT	POLET Aviakompania		610
PPK	RAMP 66		35
PPS	BUTTE AVIATION		502
PRB	PROTEUS AIRLINES	YS	259
PRF	PRECISIONAIR Services	PW	120
PRG	ASPAR – Aeroservicio Parraguea		259
PRH	PRO AIR	P9	259
PRN	PETRONORD-AVIA		162
PRO	PROPAIR		523
PSA	PACIFIC ISLAND AVIATION	9J	191
PSD	PRESIDENT AIRLINES	TO	469

ICAO		IATA	Page
PSR	EXPRESS		235
PST	AIR POST		259
PSW	PSKOVAVIA		260
PTB	PASSAREDO Transportes Aéreos	Y8	260
PTI	PRIVATAIR, SA		260
PTK	PETROPAVLOVSK-KAMCHATSKY		260
PTN	PANTANAL Linhas Aéreas Sul-Matogrossenses	P8	260
PTO	NORTH WEST GEOMATICS		260
PTR	PROVINCE OF NOVA-SCOTIA		260
PUA	PLUNA	PU	260
PVV	CONTINENTAL AIRWAYS	PC	260
PXX	AROOSTOOK AVIATION		260
PYR	PYRAMID AIRLINES		260
PZL	SKYPOL		260
PZR	SKY TREK INTERNATIONAL AIRLINES		260
QAC	QATAR AIR CARGO		210
QAF	QATAR AMIRI FLIGHT		101
QAH	QUICK AIRWAYS HOLLAND		184
QAJ	QUICK AIR JET CHARTER		34
QAT	AEROTAXI		34
QFA	QANTAS Airways	QF	472
QKC	AERO TAXI		195
QLA	AVIATION QUEBEC LABRADOR, Ltée		261
QNA	QUEEN AIR, Aeronaves Queen, S.A.	5G	133
QNK	KABO AIR		261
QSC	ASA – African Safari Airways		676
QTR	QATAR AIRWAYS, (W.L.L.)	QR	261
QUE	GOUVERNEMENT DU QUEBEC		34
QWA	PEL-AIR	QD	88
QXE	HORIZON AIR	QX	480
RAD	ALADA – Empresa de Transportes Aéreos		595
RAF	FARNAS AVIATION SERVICES		34
RAG	REGIO-AIR – Mecklenburger Flugdienst		210
RAK	RIGA AEROCLUB		195
RAM	ROYAL AIR MAROC	AT	621
RAN	RENAN		195
RAS	RAS		210
RAX	ROYAL AIR FREIGHT		210
RAZ	RAS – Rijnmond Air Services, B.V.		261
RBA	ROYAL BRUNEI AIRLINES	BI	210
RBB	RABBIT-AIR		210
RBN	RED BARON AVIATION		212
RBV	AIR ROBERVAL, Ltée		35
RCA	RICHLAND AVIATION		162
RCC	ACE AIR CHARTERS		35
RCN	RACE CARGO AIRLINES, (Nig.)		162
RCS	AIR CONSUL, S.A.		221
RCT	ARCTIC TRANSPORTATION SERVICES	7S	262
RCU	AIR ATLANTIC, S.L.	QD	261
RCX	AIR SERVICE CENTER, Srl. – A.S.C.		35
RDK	AER ATLANTIC		261
RDN	DINAR Lineas Aéreas, S.A.	D7	261
RDS	RHOADES INTERNATIONAL		711
REA	AER ARANN	RE	261
REF	REGULJAIR i SKELLEFTEA, AB	R8	261
REN	AERORENT		261
REU	AIR AUSTRAL	UU	261
REX	RAM AIR FREIGHT		622
REY	AERO-REY		262
RFS	ROSSAIR CHARTER		35
RGA	REGIONAIR, Pte	7S	262
RGI	REGIONAL AIRLINES, S.A.	VM	162
RGL	REGIONAL AIR LINES	FN	524
RGM	AIR COMMUTER		35
RGN	CYGNUS AIR, S.A.		184
RGS	RENOWN AVIATION		35
RHC	REDHILL CHARTERS		472
RHL	AIR ARCHIPELS		35
RHO	RHONAIR EXECUTIVE		101
RIG	RIAIR – Riga Airlines	GV	262
RIT	ASIAN SPIRIT		262
RIV	AIR VIP		262
RJA	ROYAL JORDANIAN	RJ	101
RKA	AIR AFRIQUE	RK	262
RKU	SOUTHERN AIR (1997)		262
RLB	HIGHLAND AIRWAYS		35
RLC	AVIAL Aviation Company		184
RLD	RAS Flug	RW	35
RLE	RICO Linhas Aéreas, S.A.		262
RLK	AIR NELSON		262
RLN	RUSLAN Aviakompania		35
RLT	RELIANT AIRLINES		184
RMA	ROCKY MOUNTAIN HELICOPTERS – RMH		524
RME	ARMENIAN AIRLINES	R3	150
RMK	RUSAIR, International Aviastransport	2Q	556
RMN	RM AVIATION		589
RMO	RYBINSK MOTORS		35
RMV	ROMAVIA, R.A.	WQ	150
RMX	AIR MAX		524
RMY	RAM AIR		610
RNA	ROYAL NEPAL AIRLINES	RA	262
RNO	AIR NORMANDIE	ID	262
RNT	RENTAVION, CA		496
ROA	RENO AIR	QQ	101
ROI	AVIOR EXPRESS – Aviones de Oriente, C.A.	3B	665
ROL	AEROEL AIRWAYS		221
ROM	AEROMAR AIRLINES	BQ	669
RON	AIR NAURU	ON	502
ROP	ROYAL OMAN POLICE – Flight Operations		469
ROR	RORAIMA AIRWAYS		502
ROS	ATS – Aviation Transport Services		262
ROT	TAROM Romania	RO	263
ROV	ROVER AIRWAYS INTERNATIONAL	5R	263
ROY	ROYAL AVIATION	QN	123
RPA	PROVENCE AERO SERVICE – PAS		592
RPB	AEROREPUBLICA, S.A.	P5	263
RPI	PARADISE AIR	RI	472
RPX	BAC EXPRESS AIRLINES		263
RQX	AIR ENGIADINA	RQ	270
RRM	ACVILA AIR Romanian Carrier	WZ	269
RRR	ROYAL AIR FORCE – Air Transport	RR	270
RSE	SNAS AVIATION		273
RSI	AIR SUNSHINE	YI	235
RSL	RIO-SUL Serviços Aéreos Regionais SA	SL	273
RSN	ROYAL SWAZI NATIONAL AIRWAYS	ZC	273
RSO	AERO ASIA International	E4	273
RSR	AERO SERVICE	BF	273
RSS	ROSSAIR EXECUTIVE AIR CHARTER		235
RSZ	AIR SERVICE HUNGARY		273
RTE	AERONORTE – Transportes Aereos		274
RTL	RHEINTALFLUG	WE	275
RTM	TRANS AM Cia Aero Express DHL		275
RTS	RELIEF TRANSPORT SERVICES		277
RUC	RUTACA – Rutas Aéreas, CA		277
RUS	CIRRUS AIRLINES, Luftfahrt GmbH	C9	695

ICAO		IATA	Page
RUZ	ROSTVERTOL		525
RVC	RICHARDS AVIATION		670
RVE	AIRVENTURE, B.V.B.A.		277
RVL	AIR VALLEE, SpA	DO	277
RVP	AIRVIP		596
RVR	RAVENAIR		701
RVV	REEVE ALEUTIAN AIRWAYS – RAA	RV	597
RWD	ALLIANCE AIR EXPRESS		36
RWG	REDWING AIRWAYS	RX	36
RWL	RWL-Luftfahrtgesellschaft, mbH		277
RXM	REMEX		277
RXP	ROYAL EXPRESS		670
RXR	ARAX AIRWAYS		582
RYN	RYAN INTERNATIONAL AIRLINES		502
RYR	RYANAIR	FR	277
RYZ	RYAZANAVIATRANS		36
RZL	AERO ZAMBIA	Z9	277
RZO	SATA International	S4	162
RZV	RZHEVKA AIR ENTERPRISE		121
SAA	SOUTH AFRICAN AIRWAYS – SAA	SA	277
SAB	SABENA, S.A.	SN	36
SAC	SASCO AIR LINES		622
SAG	SOS FLYGAMBULANS		36
SAH	SAYAKHAT	W7	202
SAI	SHAHEEN AIR INTERNATIONAL	NL	670
SAM	SAM Colombia	MM	622
SAN	SAN – Servicios Aéreos Nacionales, S.A.	WB	162
SAP	SARDAIRLINE, So. Coop. Arl.		277
SAS	SCANDINAVIAN AIRLINES SAS	SK	525
SAT	SATA Air Açores	SP	699
SAV	SANAIR		614
SAX	SABAH AIR – Penerbangan Sabah		483
SAY	SUCKLING AIRWAYS	CB	491
SAZ	SWISS AIR-AMBULANCE		676
SBA	STA-MALI		240
SBD	SIBIA Aviakompania		36
SBE	SABRE AIRWAYS		277
SBF	SEVEN BAR FLYING SERVICE		196
SBI	SIBIR AIRLINES	S7	470
SBK	AIR SRPSKA	R6	623
SBM	SYR SUNKARY Aviakompania		670
SBO	STABO AIR		88
SBR	SABER CARGO AIRLINES		277
SBX	NORTH STAR AIR CARGO		502
SBY	TEMPELHOF EXPRESS – TEX	FC	229
SBZ	SCIBE-AIRLIFT CONGO		205
SCA	SOUTHCENTRAL AIR	XE	196
SCB	SKY CABS	2E	686
SCH	SCHREINER AIRWAYS, B.V.	AW	162
SCI	SPECIAL CARGO AIRLINES	C7	277
SCO	HELIKOPTERSERVICE Euro Air, AB	YQ	133
SCP	SCORPIO AVIATION		196
SCR	SI-CHANG FLYING SERVICE, Co		278
SCS	AIR MARLBOROUGH		150
SCT	SAAB AIR, AB		278
SCW	BRAATHENS Malmö Aviation, AB	BU	36
SCX	SUN COUNTRY AIRLINES	SY	278
SCY	AIR SCANDIC International Aviation, Oy		278
SDK	SADELCA Colombia		278
SDM	RUSSIA State Transport Company	R4	231
SDO	AIR SANTO DOMINGO	EX	582
SDP	SUDPACIFICO		278
SDV	SELVA Colombia		36
SDY	ISLAND EXPRESS	2S	383
SEE	SHAHEEN AIR CARGO (Private)		36
SEN	SENAIR CHARTER		278
SER	AEROCALIFORNIA, SA	JR	278
SET	SAETA Air Ecuador	EH	36
SEU	STAR AIRLINES	2R	159
SEY	AIR SEYCHELLES	HM	102
SEZ	SEC Colombia		278
SFB	AIR SOFIA	CT	670
SFC	SHUSWAP AIR	3S	76
SFD	SKYFIELD AIRLINES		36
SFF	SAFEWING AVIATION, Co. Inc.		525
SFN	SAFIRAN AIRLINES		278
SFR	SAFAIR	FA	278
SGK	SKYWARD AVIATION	K9	480
SGL	SENEGALAIR		36
SGS	PROVINCE OF SASKATCHEWAN		236
SGV	AEROSEGOVIA, S.A.		278
SGY	SKAGWAY AIR SERVICE	7J	278
SHC	SKY HARBOR AIR SERVICE		279
SHE	SHELL AIRCRAFT		279
SHI	SEOUL AIR INTERNATIONAL – SAI		279
SHJ	UNITED ARAB EMIRATES/Sharjah		623
SHK	SHOROUK AIR	7Q	525
SHP	SAF HELICOPTERES, S.A.		582
SHU	SAT Airlines	HZ	279
SHX	SAGAWA HELICOPTER EXPRESS		236
SIA	SINGAPORE AIRLINES	SQ	593
SIB	SIBAVIATRANS	5M	279
SIC	AIR SICILIA, SpA	BM	279
SIK	ARMADORA, S.A.		279
SIN	SINAIR		36
SIO	SIRIO, SpA		279
SIR	AIR ALASKA CARGO		36
SJI	SUN JET INTERNATIONAL AIRLINES	JX	123
SKC	SKYMASTER AIRLINES		614
SKI	SKYKING AIRLINES	RU	614
SKJ	SKYJET		695
SKK	SKYLINK AVIATION		280
SKL	SKYCHARTER		184
SKS	SKY-SERVICE, B.V.B.A.		697
SKT	SKY SERVICES AVIATION, S.L.		654
SKW	SKYWEST AIRLINES	OO	525
SKX	SKYWAYS, AB	JZ	36
SKY	SKYMARK AIRLINES, Co.	BC	670
SKZ	SKYWAY Enterprises		280
SLA	SIERRA NATIONAL AIRLINES	LJ	221
SLD	SILVER AIR, spol. s r.o.		22
SLE	STREAMLINE AIR CHARTER		610
SLF	SKYLINE FLIGHTS		706
SLH	SILVERHAWK AVIATION		579
SLI	AEROLITORAL		623
SLK	SILKAIR	MI	483
SLL	SLOVAK AIRLINES	6Q	143
SLM	SURINAM AIRWAYS	PY	88
SLN	SLOANE HELICOPTERS		280
SLP	SALPA AVIATION, Co.		280
SLR	SOBELAIR, N.V.	Q7	281
SMA	SMA AIRLINES (Nig.)		281
SMC	S.M.A.C – P.T. Sabang Merauke Raya Air Charter		281
SMF	SMAELANDSFLYG, AB		623
SMH	SMITHAIR		670
SMK	SEMEIAVIA		525

ICAO			IATA	Page
SMX	=	ALITALIA EXPRESS, SpA	XM	281
SMZ	=	SONMEZ AIRLINES		196
SNA	=	SENATOR AVIATION Charter		502
SNB	=	STERLING EUROPEAN AIRLINES – SEA		36
SNC	=	AIR CARGO CARRIERS		212
SND	=	SAN Air Company	S3	488
SNP	=	SUN PACIFIC INTERNATIONAL		196
SNZ	=	SANTA CRUZ IMPERIAL AIRLINES – SCI		102
SOC	=	SOCHISPETSAVIA		102
SOK	=	SOKOL ATSK		689
SOL	=	SOLOMONS – Solomon Airlines	IE	281
SON	=	SUNSHINE AIRLINES		614
SOP	=	SOLINAIR Portoroz, d.o.o.		37
SOV	=	SARAVIA – Saratovskie avialinii		281
SOW	=	SOWIND AIR		163
SOY	=	A. SORIANO AVIATION		503
SPA	=	SIERRA PACIFIC AIRLINES	SI	281
SPD	=	AIRSPEED AVIATION		281
SPG	=	SPRINGDALE AIR SERVICE		281
SPK	=	DIAMOND AVIATION		162
SPM	=	AIR SAINT-PIERRE, SA	PJ	281
SPN	=	SCORPION AIR		649
SPS	=	SPASA – Servicios Politecnicos Aéreos, S.A.		37
SPU	=	SOUTHEAST AIRMOTIVE		503
SPW	=	SPEEDWINGS, SA		150
SPZ	=	AIRWORLD		150
SQL	=	SERVICIOS DE ALQUILER AEREO		134
SRA	=	SAIR AVIATION		102
SRB	=	SERB AIR		707
SRC	=	SEARCA		503
SRI	=	AIR SAFARIS & SERVICES, (NZ)		37
SRK	=	SKY WORK		526
SRL	=	V-AIR	T9	660
SRR	=	STAR AIR, A/S		654
SRS	=	SELKIRK REMOTE SENSING		610
SRT	=	TAA – Trans Asian Airlines	T7	282
SSB	=	SASAIR – Service Aérien du Saint-Laurent		282
SSC	=	SOUTHERN SEAPLANE		670
SSD	=	STAR SERVICE INTERNATIONAL		123
SSG	=	SLOVAK GOVERNMENT FLYING SERVICE		102
SSN	=	SUN AIR	BV	282
SSP	=	STARSPEED		240
SSQ	=	SUNSTATE AIRLINES (Qld)		623
SSR	=	SEMPATI AIR	SG	623
SSS	=	SAESA – Servicios Aéreos Espanoles, S.A.		623
SSV	=	SKYSERVICE		623
SSW	=	STREAMLINE AVIATION		623
STB	=	STAERO		623
STF	=	SFT SUDANESE FLIGHT		623
STK	=	AEROPAK		623
STQ	=	SIBIRINTERAVIA		623
STR	=	ASTANAIR	A7	623
STT	=	AIR ST. THOMAS	ZP	473
STU	=	STAF	FS	191
STW	=	START Air Transport Company		473
STY	=	STREZHAVIA		695
STZ	=	SATAIR	SP	283
SUB	=	SUBURBAN AIR FREIGHT		473
SUD	=	SUDAN AIRWAYS	SD	283
SUF	=	SUNFLOWER AIRLINES, Limited	PI	102
SUH	=	SUKHOI Aviakompania		473
SUI	=	SWISS AIR FORCE		283
SUL	=	HELISUL Linhas Aéreas, S.A.	H9	283
SUM	=	MCHS ROSSII		283
SUS	=	SUN-AIR of Scandinavia, A/S	EZ	602
SUY	=	AERIAL SURVEYS		184
SUZ	=	PREMIAIR CHARTER		150
SVA	=	SAUDI ARABIAN Airlines	SV	654
SVB	=	SVEA FLYG, AB	SI	283
SVD	=	SVG AIR		240
SVI	=	SETRA – Servicios de Transporte Aéreo		283
SVK	=	AIR SLOVAKIA BWJ	GM	163
SVL	=	SAAK, Stavropol Joint-Stock Airline		470
SVM	=	AEROSERVICIOS MONTERREY		526
SVN	=	SAVANAIR		526
SVP	=	SAZ – Saratovskiy aviatsionny zavod		526
SVR	=	URAL AIRLINES	U6	526
SVT	=	SAKHAVIATRANS		614
SVV	=	SERVIVENSA – Servicios Avensa, S.A.	VC	526
SVX	=	SECURITY AVIATION		526
SVY	=	COOPER AERIAL SURVEYS		150
SWA	=	SOUTHWEST AIRLINES, Company	WN	123
SWD	=	SOUTHERN WINDS, S.A.	A4	527
SWE	=	SWEDEWAYS AIR LINES, AB	HJ	614
SWI	=	SUNWORLD INTERNATIONAL AIRLINES	SM	527
SWL	=	SAE Swe Aviation Europe, AB		196
SWN	=	WEST AIR SWEDEN, AB		527
SWO	=	SWISS WORLD AIRWAYS, S.A. – SWA	SO	527
SWP	=	STAR WORK SKY, Sas – S.W.S.		150
SWR	=	SWISSAIR	SR	483
SWS	=	SUNWEST AVIATION		470
SWT	=	SWIFT AIR, S.A.		527
SWX	=	SWAZI EXPRESS AIRWAYS		660
SWZ	=	SERVAIR		488
SXS	=	SUNEXPRESS	XQ	37
SYB	=	SYMBOL, S.A. – Compania de Aviacion		163
SYJ	=	SLATE FALLS AIRWAYS (1987)		37
SYL	=	SAYANY AIRLINES		623
SYR	=	SYRIANAIR – Syrian Arab Airlines	RB	283
SYX	=	SKYWAY AIRLINES	AL	283
SYZ	=	SOUTHEND CARGO AIRLINES		283
TAB	=	TABA – T. A. Regionais da Bacia Amazonica		37
TAE	=	TAME – T. A. Mercantiles Ecuator	EQ	527
TAH	=	AIR MOOREA		283
TAI	=	TACA International Airlines, SA	TA	37
TAJ	=	TUNISAVIA		163
TAM	=	TAM Brasil	KK	283
TAO	=	AEROMAR AIRLINES	VW	37
TAP	=	TAP AIR PORTUGAL	TP	283
TAQ	=	TAUNUS AIR & Co		37
TAR	=	TUNISAIR	TU	37
TAS	=	LOTUS AIR		283
TAW	=	SKYAIR CARGO		37
TAX	=	TRAVEL AIR Flug		284
TAZ	=	TRANSAMAZONICA Colombia		483
TBA	=	TRANSBRASIL	TR	150
TCF	=	SHUTTLE AMERICA	S5	284
TCH	=	TRANS-CHARTER Airlines		120
TCI	=	TURKS & CAICOS AIRWAYS	QW	284
TCJ	=	TRANSPORTES CHARTER DO BRASIL		37
TCL	=	COASTAL AIR TRANSPORT		593
TCN	=	TRANS CONTINENTAL AIRLINES		610
TCO	=	ATC Colombia		202
TCR	=	TRANS COSTA RICA		133
TCT	=	TRANSCONTINENTAL SUR, Srl.		150
TCV	=	TACV – CABO VERDE AIRLINES	VR	196

ICAO			IATA	Page
TDB	=	WELCH AVIATION		138
TDC	=	TADAIR, S.A.		284
TDM	=	TANDEM-AERO, Srl.		503
TDR	=	TRADE AIR, d.o.o.		184
TDX	=	TRADEWINDS AIRLINES	WI	701
TEA	=	T doble A – Transportes Aéreos Andahuaylas		212
TED	=	TEDDY AIR, A/S	ZJ	663
TEG	=	TEA – Trans European Airlines, S.A.		37
TEJ	=	TAESA – Transportes Aéreos Ejecutivos	GD	655
TEL	=	TELFORD AVIATION		655
TEP	=	TRANSEUROPEAN AIRLINES	UE	603
TEU	=	TAG Teuto Airways Germany		655
TEX	=	C.A.T.E.X., S.A.		593
TEY	=	ANTEY		655
TFA	=	TRANS FLORIDA AIRLINES		284
TFH	=	THAI FLYING HELICOPTER SERVICE		212
TFS	=	FAST AIRWAYS		614
TGC	=	TG AVIATION		614
TGE	=	TASA – Trabajos Aéreos, S.A.		123
TGO	=	TRANSPORT CANADA		185
TGR	=	TAVIA-Taganrog Aviation		527
TGT	=	NYGE AERO, AB		284
TGY	=	TRANS GUYANA AIRWAYS – TGA		284
THA	=	THAI AIRWAYS INTERNATIONAL	TG	37
THC	=	TAR HEEL AVIATION		163
THD	=	JETPORT		38
THK	=	THK – Türk Hava Kurumu/Hava Taksi Isletmesi		163
THT	=	AIR TAHITI NUI	TN	579
THU	=	THUNDER AIRLINES		686
THY	=	TURKISH AIRLINES	TK	610
THZ	=	THS HELICOPTERES		684
TIC	=	TRAVEL INTERNATIONAL AIR CHARTER		685
TIH	=	ION TIRIAC AIR, S.A.		685
TII	=	ATI Aircompany		124
TIN	=	TAINO AIRLINES, SA		614
TIS	=	TESIS	UZ	591
TIT	=	TITAN CARGO		
TIX	=	TRIAX AIRLINES		285
TJN	=	TIEN-SHAN		38
TKA	=	AIR TROIKA		473
TKO	=	TRETYAKOVO Air Transport company		284
TLA	=	TRANSAER International Airlines		284
TLB	=	ATLANTIQUE AIR ASSISTANCE – AAA		284
TLE	=	AIR TOULOUSE INTERNATIONAL	SH	38
TLO	=	EAGLE CANYON AIRLINES	FE	163
TLP	=	TULIP AIR, B.V.		163
TLT	=	TURTLE AIRWAYS		670
TLX	=	CARGO LION		102
TLY	=	TOP FLY, S.L.		102
TMA	=	TMA OF LEBANON	TL	12
TML	=	TAM – Transports & Travaux Aériens	OF	528
TMM	=	TMC AIRLINES		38
TMN	=	TYUMENAVIATRANS	P2	236
TMO	=	TOMSKNEFT		284
TMS	=	TEMSCO HELICOPTERS		700
TNF	=	TATNEFTAERO		38
TNI	=	TRANSAIR INTERNATIONAL Linhas Aéreas		707
TNR	=	TANANA AIR SERVICE	4E	441
TNT	=	TRANS NORTH AIR		102
TNY	=	AIR TANGANYIKA		528
TNZ	=	ANSETT NEW ZEALAND REGIONAL		284
TOA	=	TROPICAL AIRLINES		38
TOL	=	TOLAIR Services	TI	496
TON	=	AEROTONALA		284
TOO	=	ALIEUROPE, Srl.		284
TOP	=	TOP AIR Havacilik Sanayi ve Ticaret, A.S.		529
TOR	=	TORONTAIR		659
TOS	=	TROPIC AIR	PM	284
TOW	=	TOWER AIR	FF	284
TPA	=	TAMPA Colombia	QT	503
TPC	=	AIR CALEDONIE	TY	473
TPE	=	TAP – Transportes Aéreos Presidente, S.A.		285
TPG	=	PEGASO – Transportes Aéreos Pegaso		38
TPS	=	TAPSA Aviacion		686
TQN	=	TAQUAN AIR SERVICE	K3	530
TRA	=	TRANSAVIA AIRLINES, C.V.	HV	285
TRD	=	TRANS ISLAND AIR		285
TRI	=	PROVINCE OF ONTARIO		624
TRJ	=	AJT AIR INTERNATIONAL	E9	139
TRL	=	TRANSEAST AIRLINES	T4	124
TRQ	=	TTA – Trans Travel Airlines, B.V.	6N	503
TRR	=	TRAMSON AIRLINES		285
TRS	=	AIRTRAN AIRWAYS	FL	286
TRT	=	TRANS ARABIAN AIR TRANSPORT		624
TRZ	=	TRANSMERIDIAN AIRLINES	T9	503
TSC	=	AIR TRANSAT	TS	38
TSD	=	TAF Linhas Aéreas, SA		624
TSE	=	TRANSMILE AIR SERVICES, (M) Sdn Bhd	TH	38
TSG	=	TRANS AIR CONGO – TAC		286
TSI	=	TRANSPORT AIR		286
TSK	=	TOMSK AIR ENTERPRISE		286
TSL	=	TRANS AERO-SAMARA Aviakompania		286
TSO	=	TRANSAERO AIRLINES	UN	102
TSP	=	INTER – Transportes Aéreos Inter, S.A.		286
TSU	=	CONTRACT AIR CARGO		649
TSY	=	TRISTAR AIR		670
TTA	=	TTA		286
TTF	=	224th FLIGHT UNIT, State Airlines		597
TTL	=	TOTAL Linhas Aéreas, SA		707
TTN	=	LIP-AVIA		185
TTR	=	TATRA AIR, a.s.	QS	163
TTX	=	AIR TEAM, A/S	8W	624
TUI	=	TUNINTER	UG	286
TUL	=	TULPAR Aviation Company		286
TUM	=	AERIANTUR-M AIRLINES		582
TUP	=	TUPOLEV-AEROTRANS		286
TUQ	=	AIR TURQUOISE		38
TUS	=	ABSA CARGO	M3	38
TUV	=	TURAVIA Air Transport & Travel		286
TUY	=	LTA – Linea Turistica Aereotuy, C.A.		670
TVI	=	TIRAMAVIA		286
TVJ	=	TAVAJ – Transportes Aéreos Regulares, SA	4U	624
TVL	=	AVIATA		150
TVM	=	TAVRIA-MAK		139
TVR	=	TAVRIA Aviakompania	T6	483
TVS	=	TRAVEL SERVICE AIRLINES		483
TVT	=	TRANSAVIATION, S.A.		484
TWA	=	TRANS WORLD AIRLINES	TW	484
TWC	=	TARAZ WINGS		484
TWG	=	TRANS WING, A/S		484
TWI	=	TASAWI AIR SERVICES	9X	484
TWN	=	AVIALEASING Aviation Company	AD	530
TWW	=	TRANS AIR WELWITCHIA		597
TXC	=	TRANS AVIA EXPORT Cargo Airlines	AL	286
TXE	=	TRANSAERO-EXPRESS		39
TXI	=	ATSA – Aero Taxis		624
TXM	=	TAXI AEREO DE MEXICO, SA		286

ICAO			IATA	Page
TXO	=	AEROTAX MONSE		704
TXT	=	TEXAS AIR CHARTERS		670
TXX	=	AUSTIN EXPRESS	7V	185
TYG	=	TRYGG-FLYG Erik Trygg, AB		287
TYJ	=	TYROLEAN JET SERVICE		480
TYM	=	TYUMEN AIRLINES	7M	163
TYR	=	TYROLEAN AIRWAYS, Tiroler Luftfahrt AG	VO	212
TZK	=	TAJIKISTAN AIRLINES	7J	185
UAC	=	UNITED AIR SERVICES		646
UAE	=	EMIRATES	EK	530
UAK	=	AVIANT – Kiev Aviation Plant		610
UAL	=	UNITED AIRLINES	UA	530
UAR	=	AEROSTAR		287
UBA	=	MYANMA AIRWAYS Corp.	UB	39
UBA	=	MYANMAR AIRWAYS INTERNATIONAL	UB	287
UCA	=	COMMUTAIR		503
UCC	=	UGANDA AIR CARGO Corporation		212
UCR	=	AERO-CHARTER UKRAINE		236
UDC	=	DONBASS-EASTERN UKRAINIAN AIRLINES	7D	503
UDD	=	DONBASS AIR LINES		287
UDN	=	DNIPROAVIA	Z6	102
UES	=	UES-AVIA		676
UFA	=	UKRAINE FLIGHT STATE ACADEMY		287
UFI	=	UMBRIA FLY, Srl.		287
UFS	=	UFS	U2	241
UGA	=	UGANDA AIRLINES	QU	476
UGP	=	SHAR INK		646
UHS	=	ULYANOVSK HIGHER CIVIL AVIATION		287
UKA	=	KLM uk	UK	39
UKL	=	UKRAINE AIR ALLIANCE		39
UKN	=	UKRAINA Aviapredpriatie		39
UKR	=	AIR UKRAINE	6U	288
UKS	=	UKRAINIAN CARGO AIRWAYS – UCA		163
UKT	=	SKY-TREK AIRLINES		287
UKU	=	SVERDLOVSK 2nd Air Enterprise		39
UKW	=	LVOV AIRLINES		288
ULB	=	ULBA Aviakompania		143
UMB	=	AIRUMBRIA, Srl.		288
UMK	=	YUZHMASHAVIA		288
UNF	=	UNION FLIGHTS		488
UNR	=	ROVNO UNIVERSAL AVIA		488
UNS	=	UPS Uensped Paket Servisi		102
UNX	=	UNEX AIRLINES		597
UPA	=	AIRFOYLE	GS	607
UPD	=	AIRFOYLE CHARTER AIRLINES		530
UPL	=	UKRAINIAN PILOT SCHOOL		39
UPS	=	UPS Airlines	5X	288
URE	=	EURECA, Srl. – European Regional Carrier	F4	288
URF	=	EXECUTIVE FLIGHT SERVICES		288
URG	=	AIR URGA	3N	614
URN	=	TURAN AIR	3T	685
URT	=	AVIA-URARTU		288
URV	=	URAIAVIA		102
USA	=	US AIRWAYS	US	163
USC	=	AIRNET SYSTEMS		39
USS	=	US AIRWAYS SHUTTLE	TB	39
UTL	=	AVIATIA UTILITARA, SA – AV.U		39
UYA	=	YUTE AIR ALASKA	4Y	164
UYC	=	CAMEROON AIRLINES	UY	39
UZA	=	CONSTANTA Airlines		530
UZB	=	UZBEKISTAN AIRWAYS	HY	236
UZH	=	YUZHNOE		39
VAL	=	VOYAGEUR AIRWAYS	4V	695
VAR	=	VALET AIR SERVICES		591
VAS	=	ATRAN – Aviatrans Cargo Airlines	V8	288
VAT	=	AVANT AIRLINES Chile	OT	582
VBR	=	VIABRASIL – Air Club Transportes Aéreos		646
VBW	=	AIR BURKINA	2J	658
VCA	=	VICA AIRLINES		288
VCN	=	AVCON		288
VDA	=	VOLGA-DNEPR AIRLINES	VI	39
VEC	=	VENESCAR INTERNACIONAL		39
VEE	=	VICTOR ECHO, S.A.		624
VEG	=	VEG AIR, Srl.		288
VEI	=	VIRGIN EXPRESS (Ireland)	VK	185
VEJ	=	AEROEJECUTIVOS, CA		102
VES	=	VIEQUES AIR LINK	VI	624
VET	=	AEROVENTO, S.A.		530
VEX	=	VIRGIN EXPRESS, S.A.	TV	185
VGA	=	AIR VEGAS	6V	480
VGD	=	VANGUARD AIRLINES	NJ	289
VGE	=	AIR SERVICE VOSGES		39
VGO	=	IAT CARGO AIRLINES		676
VGS	=	WINGS		597
VGV	=	VOLOGDA AIR ENTERPRISE		39
VID	=	AVIAPRAD		289
VIH	=	VICHI		134
VIM	=	VIA – Air VIA Bulgarian Airways	VL	597
VIN	=	VINAIR – Aeroserviços, S.A.		40
VIO	=	AVIONIC AIR SERVICES		164
VIP	=	EUROPE ELITE	Y6	131
VIR	=	VIRGIN ATLANTIC	VS	682
VJG	=	AVIORIPRESE JET EXECUTIVE, SpA		289
VKG	=	PREMIAIR, A/S	DK	40
VKO	=	VNUKOVO AIRLINES	V5	185
VLA	=	VOLGA AVIAEXPRESS	G6	150
VLE	=	VOLARE AIRLINES, SpA	8D	40
VLF	=	VALDRESFLY, A/S		646
VLK	=	VLADIVOSTOK AIR	XF	124
VLM	=	VLM Vlaamse Luchttransportmaatschappij	VG	290
VLN	=	VALAN International Cargo Charter		704
VNA	=	WARBELOW'S AIR VENTURES	4W	597
VOG	=	AEROVOLGA		704
VOL	=	BLUE CHIP JET, HB		290
VPA	=	VIPAIR AIRLINES	9V	290
VPB	=	VETERAN AIRLINES		164
VPI	=	VIP-AIR Flug		290
VRA	=	SALVIRAJ		290
VRE	=	VOLARE AVIATION ENTERPRISE	F7	196
VRG	=	VARIG Brasil	RG	231
VRI	=	AEROTAXI VILLA RICA		503
VRN	=	VORONEZHAVIA	ZT	290
VSA	=	VOSTSIBAERO		290
VSO	=	VASO		290
VSP	=	VASP	VP	40
VTA	=	AIR TAHITI	VT	40
VTI	=	AVIRCITI		503
VTK	=	VOSTOK Airlines		530
VTR	=	AIR OSTRAVA	8K	473
VUL	=	ELIOS, Srl		290
VUN	=	AIR IVOIRE	VU	624
VZA	=	AIR VENEZUELA		711
VZL	=	VZLET		290
VZR	=	AVIAZUR		624

Decoding of the Leasing-Company-designators (four-letter leasing-company designator)

We, Bucher & Co., Publications, have decided to assign four-letter designators to the leasing companies. Due to the fact, that the «remarks»column in most of the cases is not wide enough to print the full names of the leasing companies and in order to easy identify if an aircraft is leased from another carrier or from a leasing company, we created the four-letter designators.
In the jp airline-fleets international 99/2000 you will find the designator after the name of the airline, where applicable.

LEASE			Page
AARL	=	AAR FINANCIAL SERVICES, Corp. - Leasing Operations	243
AERO	=	AEROLEASE International, Inc.	245
AFGR	=	AFG AIR FINANCE, Inc.	247
AGES	=	AGES AIRCRAFT SALES & LEASING, A Limited Partnership	247
AIRG	=	AIRCONTACTGRUPPEN, A/S	231
ALGI	=	AVIATION LEASING GROUP, Inc.	283
ALMA	=	ALM Aircraft Leasing & Management	162
ANAU	=	AERONAUTICS LEASING, Inc.	245
ARON	=	AERON AVIATION, Corp.	246
ATEC	=	AEROTEC International, Lda	596
AVEG	=	AVENGAIR, Inc.	283
AVII	=	AVIATION INVESTORS INTERNATIONAL, Inc.	283
AVIS	=	AVIATION INVESTOR SERVICES, Ltd	163
AVLI	=	AVLINE LEASING, Corp.	284
AWAS	=	ANSETT WORLDWIDE Aviation Services	622
BACL	=	BAC LEASING, Ltd	163
BALG	=	BA LEASING & Capital, Corp.	284
BAMJ	=	BRITISH AEROSPACE ASSET MANAGEMENT – Jets	165
BAMT	=	BRITISH AEROSPACE ASSET MANAGEMENT, Inc. – Turboprops	290
BATL	=	BELL ATLANTIC TRICON LEASING, Inc.	286
BAVA	=	BAVARIA International Aircraft Leasing, GmbH & Co. KG	102
BBAM	=	BABCOCK & BROWN AIRCRAFT MANAGEMENT, Inc.	284
BOUL	=	BOULLIOUN AVIATION SERVICES, Inc.	290
BRAL	=	BRAATHEN LEASING, A/S	231

LEASE			Page
CHAL	=	CHALLENG'AIR	151
CISA	=	CIS AIR, Corp.	298
CITG	=	CIT GROUP – Capital Equipment Financing	298
CSAV	=	C-S AVIATION SERVICES, Inc.	311
ELEC	=	ELECTRA AVIATION, Ltd - EAL	173
ELVE	=	ELVEDEN INVESTMENT, Ltd	132
EQUA	=	EQUATOR LEASING, Inc.	323
FACE	=	FIVESTAR AIRCRAFT	337
GATX	=	GATX Flightlease Management, GmbH	187
GOAL	=	GERMAN OPERATING AIRCRAFT LEASING GmbH & Co. KG	108
IALI	=	INTERNATIONAL AIR LEASES, Inc.	382
IASG	=	INTERNATIONAL AIRLINE SUPPORT GROUP, Inc.	382
ILFC	=	INTERNATIONAL LEASE FINANCE, Corp.	383
INGL	=	ING LEASE INTERNATIONAL EQUIPMENT MANAGEMENT, B.V.	492
INGO	=	INDIGO AVIATION, AB	584
INTL	=	INTERLEASE AVIATION Corporation	382
IPID	=	INTREPID AVIATION PARTNERS, Llc	383
ITOH	=	ITOCHU AirLease, Inc.	384
JETZ	=	JETZ	385
JFSS	=	JAPAN FLEET SERVICE, (S) Pte Ltd	709
KAWA	=	KAWASAKI LEASING International	226
LIFT	=	AEROLIFT INTERNATIONAL, Pte Ltd	709

LEASE			Page
MKAV	=	MK AVIATION, S.A.	203
OASL	=	ONTARIO AIRCRAFT SALES & LEASING, Inc.	68
OMEG	=	OMEGA AIR, Ltd	132
ORIX	=	ORIX Aviation Systems, Ltd	132
PACA	=	PACIFIC AVIATION Holding Company	412
PACE	=	PACE - Pinnacle Air Cargo Enterprises, Inc.	412
PEGA	=	PEGASUS CAPITAL, Corp.	414
PEMB	=	PEMBROKE CAPITAL, Ltd	132
PLMI	=	PLM Transportation Equipment, Corp.	418
POLA	=	POLARIS AIRCRAFT LEASING, Corp.	419
POTO	=	POTOMAC Capital Investment, Corp.	419
SALA	=	SALENIA AVIATION, AB	586
SALE	=	SINGAPORE AIRCRAFT LEASING ENTERPRISE, Pte Ltd	709
SIRO	=	SIROCCO AEROSPACE INTERNATIONAL (U.K.), Ltd	180
SNNL	=	SHANNONAIR LEASING, Ltd	132
STAR	=	AEROSTAR LEASING, Pte Ltd	709
SUNR	=	SUNROCK AIRCRAFT, Corp. Ltd	132
TOMB	=	TOMBO AVIATION Inc.	444
TRIN	=	TRINITY AVIATION, Ltd	22
TRIT	=	TRITON AVIATION SERVICES, Inc.	449
TWIN	=	TWIN OTTER INTERNATIONAL, Ltd	83
USAL	=	US AIRWAYS LEASING & SALES, Inc.	462

Configuration

In section 1 we incorporate the exact configuration of each aircraft. Since we have to rely on the cooperation of the airlines, this column is not yet complete. All aircraft which are not used for transportation of passengers are already marked with their effective use. The following list shows you the possibilities of exemptions:

– Ambulance (equipped with stretchers)
– Calibrator (used by aviation authorities to calibrate airways and airport landing aids)
– Charter (aircraft used exclusively for charter flights)
– Corporate (used for corporates only)
– Convertible (quickly changeable from passenger aircraft into freighter)
– EMS (Emergency Medical Service)
– Executive (luxurious interior for corporates)
– Flt insp. (Flight inspection)
– Freighter (Cargo plane)
– Frtr/Pax (Freighter or passenger use)
– Photo (equipped with camera, used for mapping)
– Photo/Survey (combination of use of camera and surveying)
– Sprayer (used to spray chemicals against insects or oil polluted sea)
– Surveyer (surveying of traffic, smuggling areas, forest-fires etc)
– Tanker (used to spray water against forest-fires)
– Trainer (used for training flights mostly)
– Variable (passenger seating configuration may be changed very quickly)
– VIP (very important person – state official)

We are still working on the introduction of the exact passenger seating arrangements and hope to be able to finish this expansion programme in one of the subsequent issues of jp airline-fleets international.

The following list indicates the meaning of the internationally used abbreviations:

C	=	Business Class	F	=	First Class	Y	=	Economy/Coach Class
		Business Class Discounted			First Class Discounted			Economy/Coach Class Discounted
		Business Class Premium			First Class Premium			Economy/Coach Class Premium
					Supersonic Class			Air Shuttle (no reservation)

The use of «Plt» after a slash indicates pallets (if possible with number) used for transportation of freight on the same aircraft (Combi).

Call Sign Alphabet

A	= Alpha	E	= Echo	I	= India	M	= Mike	Q	= Quebec	U	= Uniform	Y	= Yankee
B	= Bravo	F	= Foxtrott	J	= Juliette	N	= November	R	= Romeo	V	= Victor	Z	= Zulu
C	= Charlie	G	= Golf	K	= Kilo	O	= Oscar	S	= Sierra	W	= Whiskey		
D	= Delta	H	= Hotel	L	= Lima	P	= Papa	T	= Tango	X	= Xray		

The Russian Alphabet – Русский алфавит

А а	= A	Е е	= JE	Й й	= short I	О о	= O	У у	= U	Ш ш	= SCH
Б б	= B	Ё ё	= JO	К к	= K	П п	= P	Ф ф	= F	Щ щ	= SCHTSCH
В в	= W	Ж ж	= J	Л л	= L	Р р	= R	Х х	= CH	Э э	= Ä
Г г	= G	З з	= S	М м	= M	С с	= ß	Ц ц	= Z	Ю ю	= JU
Д д	= D	И и	= I	Н н	= N	Т т	= T	Ч ч	= TSCH	Я я	= JA

Books, m@g@zines, models, postc@rds – @nd much more:

@ll @v@il@ble for shopping in our E-SHOP

No Problem!

We are always

near you,

no matter
what time,

no matter

what weather!

We are
the experts
in your region!

Living **too far** away

to visit the

BUCHairSHOPS

regularly?

Raining or snowing,
you do not want
to leave your home
for shopping?

Address: http://www.buchairnet.com/

BUCHairNET

Our e-mail-address: **jp@buchair.ch**

BUCHair E-SHOP

buch+air+club

colorBirds

1999

jp airline-fleets international

BUCHairNET
About BUCHair

www.buchairnet.com

Please visit our E-SHOP. We are updating it daily for your easy shopping from your comfortable office or home.

BUCH*air*SHOP *by Bucher & Co., Publikationen*

Auch in Zürich-Flughafen, Besucher-Terrasse, Terminal B

Also at Zurich-Airport, Spectators Terrace, Terminal B

Alles für den Flughafen-Besucher!

Visit us!

BUCH*air*SHOP
Besucher-Terrasse, Terminal B
CH-8058 Zürich-Flughafen / Schweiz

Phone: +41 (01) 8741 747
Fax: +41 (01) 8741 757

E-mail: jp@buchair.ch
Internet: http://www.buchairnet.com

Öffnungszeiten:
Dienstag bis Sonntag sowie Feiertage
je von ca. 10 Uhr bis ca. 17 Uhr

Geschlossen:
«Normale» Montage sowie
Mitte Dezember bis Mitte Januar

- Bücher
- Verzeichnisse
- Zeitschriften
- Plastikmodell-Baukasten
- Flugfunkempfänger
- Besucher-Flugplan
- Postkarten
- Batterien
- Kalender
- Schirme
- Modelle
- T-Shirts
- Jacken
- Tassen
- Videos
- Filme

jp airline-fleets Back Issues – Lieferbare Ausgaben / Available Issues

	Pick-up BUCHairSHOP Glattbrugg & Flughafen SFr.	Schweiz Switzerland SFr.	Europa, ohne D & G Europe, excl. D & G SFr.	Übersee, ohne N Overseas, excl. N SFr.	Grossbritannien Great Britain UK £	USA US $
BUCHairREPRINT 1966 (First reprint in standard size)	18.--	21.--	23.25	30.--		
jp airline-fleets 1978 (Small size book: 12 x 17,5 cms)	15.--	20.--	25.50	40.--		
jp airline-fleets international 1982	35.--	41.--	55.25	85.--		
jp airline-fleets international 1985	40.--	46.--	56.50	90.--		
jp airline-fleets international 1986	42.50	48.50	59.75	92.50		
jp airline-fleets international 1991 / 92	54.--	60.--	74.25	105.--		
jp airline-fleets international 1992 / 93	56.--	62.--	75.--	106.--		
jp airline-fleets international 1993 / 94	60.--	66.--	76.--	111.--		
jp airline-fleets international 1994 / 95	60.--	67.50	80.--	115.--		
jp airline-fleets international 1995 / 96	65.--	72.50	90.--	125.--		
jp airline-fleets international 1997 / 98	65.--	75.--	90.--	120.--		
jp airline-fleets international 1998 / 99	69.90	75.--	90.--	120.--		
jp airline-fleets international 99 / 2000	64.50	72.50	85.--	110.--		

Great Britain / USA columns: **Please ask:**

Great Britain

BUCHair (U.K.) Ltd
Ronald P. Harman
P.O. Box 89
Reigate, Surrey RH2 7FG
Great Britain

Phone: (01737) 224 747
Fax: (01737) 226 777
E-mail: buchair_uk@compuserve.com
Internet: http://www.buchair.rotor.com

USA

BUCHair (USA) Inc.
Kivanc N. Hurturk
P.O. Box 750515
Forest Hills, NY
USA 11375-0515

Phone: (718) 263-8748
Fax: (718) 275-6190
E-mail: buchair@mail.idt.net
Internet: http://www.buchair.com

Konto / Account Nr. Postcheck postal giro 80-30353-6

Credit cards AMEXCO / DINERS / VISA / EURO

Bestellen mit gleichzeitiger Zahlung / Pay with your order

Worldwide, except Great Britain and USA:

Bucher & Co., Publikationen
P.O. Box 44
CH-8058 Zurich-Airport / Switzerland

Telefon / Phone: +41 (01) 8741 747
Telefax / Fax: +41 (01) 8741 757
E-mail: jp@buchair.ch
Internet / E-Shop: http://www.buchairnet.com

Postcheck postal giro ZRH 80-30353-6
AMEXCO / DINERS / VISA / EURO
SFr. cheques any Swiss bank
AMEXCO / DINERS / VISA / EURO

Fragen Sie uns nach dem von Ihnen benötigten Jahrgang; wir verfügen noch über einzelne Exemplare!

Ask us about back-issues not listed, we hold some single copies dated back to 1966!

Contents – Int'l Civil Aircraft Markings

Contents – Countries listed alphabetical